Internal Revenue Code

Income, Estate, Gift,
Employment and Excise
Taxes § 861-End

As of May 31, 2024

Volume 2

Wolters Kluwer Editorial Staff Publication

This publication is designed to provide accurate and authoritative information in regard to the subject matter covered. It is sold with the understanding that the publisher is not engaged in rendering legal, accounting or other professional service. If legal advice or other expert assistance is required, the services of a competent professional person should be sought.

ISBN: 978-0-8080-6031-4 (2-Volume Set)

©2024 CCH Incorporated and its affiliates. All rights reserved.

2700 Lake Cook Road
Riverwoods, IL 60015
800 344 3734
ShopTax.WoltersKluwer.com/en

No claim is made to original government works; however, within this publication, the following are subject to CCH Incorporated's copyright: (1) the gathering, compilation, and arrangement of such government materials; (2) the magnetic translation and digital conversion of data, if applicable; (3) the historical, statutory and other notes and references; and (4) the commentary and other materials.

Printed in Canada

Table of Contents

Page

VOLUME ONE

Tax Rate Tables
- Income Tax ... vii
- Corporation Income Taxes ... viii
- Estate and Gift Taxes ... ix
- Other Taxes ... x
- Excise Taxes ... xi

Code Text
- Contents of Code ... 1
- Income Taxes (§§ 1–860G) ... 51

Topical Index ... 2001
Public Laws Amending the Internal Revenue Code ... 2041

VOLUME TWO

Code Text
- Contents of Code ... 2501
- Income Taxes (§§ 861–1563) ... 2551
- Estate and Gift Taxes (§§ 2001–2801) ... 3301
- Employment Taxes (§§ 3101–3512) ... 3501
- Miscellaneous Excise Taxes (§§ 4041–5000C) ... 3701
- Alcohol, Tobacco, and Certain Other Excise Taxes (§§ 5001–5891) ... 4101
- Procedure and Administration (§§ 6001–7874) ... 4301
- The Joint Committee on Taxation (§§ 8001–8023) ... 5201
- Financing of Presidential Election Campaigns (§§ 9001–9042) ... 5301
- Trust Fund Code (§§ 9500–9602) ... 5401
- Coal Industry Health Benefits (§§ 9701–9722) ... 5501
- Group Health Plan Requirements (§§ 9801–9834) ... 5601

Topical Index ... 5701
Public Laws Amending the Internal Revenue Code ... 5741

TABLE OF CONTENTS

UNITED STATES CODE
TITLE 26—INTERNAL REVENUE CODE
SUBTITLE A—INCOME TAXES
Chapter 1—Normal Taxes and Surtaxes
SUBCHAPTER A. DETERMINATION OF TAX LIABILITY
PART I—TAX ON INDIVIDUALS

Sec. 1.	Tax imposed
Sec. 2.	Definitions and special rules
Sec. 3.	Tax tables for individuals
Sec. 5.	Cross references relating to tax on individuals

PART II—TAX ON CORPORATIONS

Sec. 11.	Tax imposed
Sec. 12.	Cross references relating to tax on corporations

PART III—CHANGES IN RATES DURING A TAXABLE YEAR

Sec. 15.	Effect of changes

PART IV—CREDITS AGAINST TAX
Subpart A—Nonrefundable Personal Credits

Sec. 21.	Expenses for household and dependent care services necessary for gainful employment
Sec. 22.	Credit for the elderly and the permanently and totally disabled
Sec. 23.	Adoption expenses
Sec. 24.	Child tax credit
Sec. 25.	Interest on certain home mortgages
Sec. 25A.	American Opportunity and Lifetime Learning credits
Sec. 25B.	Elective deferrals and IRA contributions by certain individuals
Sec. 25C.	Energy efficient home improvement credit
Sec. 25D.	Residential clean energy credit
Sec. 25E.	Previously-owned clean vehicles
Sec. 26.	Limitation based on tax liability; definition of tax liability

Subpart B—Other Credits

Sec. 27.	Taxes of foreign countries and possessions of the United States
Sec. 30B.	Alternative motor vehicle credit
Sec. 30C.	Alternative fuel vehicle refueling property credit
Sec. 30D.	Clean vehicle credit

Subpart C—Refundable Credits

Sec. 31.	Tax withheld on wages
Sec. 32.	Earned income
Sec. 33.	Tax withheld at source on nonresident aliens and foreign corporations
Sec. 34.	Certain uses of gasoline and special fuels
Sec. 35.	Health insurance costs of eligible individuals
Sec. 36.	First-time homebuyer credit
Sec. 36B.	Refundable credit for coverage under a qualified health plan
Sec. 37.	Overpayments of tax

Subpart D—Business Related Credits

Sec. 38.	General business credit
Sec. 39.	Carryback and carryforward of unused credits
Sec. 40.	Alcohol, etc., used as fuel
Sec. 40A.	Biodiesel and renewable diesel used as fuel
Sec. 40B.	Sustainable aviation fuel credit
Sec. 41.	Credit for increasing research activities
Sec. 42.	Low-income housing credit
Sec. 43.	Enhanced oil recovery credit
Sec. 44.	Expenditures to provide access to disabled individuals
Sec. 45.	Electricity produced from certain renewable resources, etc.
Sec. 45A.	Indian employment credit
Sec. 45B.	Credit for portion of employer social security taxes paid with respect to employee cash tips
Sec. 45C.	Clinical testing expenses for certain drugs for rare diseases or conditions
Sec. 45D.	New markets tax credit
Sec. 45E.	Small employer pension plan startup costs
Sec. 45F.	Employer-provided child care credit
Sec. 45G.	Railroad track maintenance credit
Sec. 45H.	Credit for production of low sulfur diesel fuel
Sec. 45I.	Credit for producing oil and gas from marginal wells
Sec. 45J.	Credit for production from advanced nuclear power facilities

Internal Revenue Code

CODE—TABLE OF CONTENTS

Sec. 45K.	Credit for producing fuel from a nonconventional source
Sec. 45L.	New energy efficient home credit
Sec. 45N.	Mine rescue team training credit
Sec. 45O.	Agricultural chemicals security credit
Sec. 45P.	Employer wage credit for employees who are active duty members of the uniformed services
Sec. 45Q.	Credit for carbon oxide sequestration
Sec. 45R.	Employee health insurance expenses of small employers
Sec. 45S.	Employer credit for paid family and medical leave
Sec. 45T.	Auto-enrollment option for retirement savings options provided by small employers
Sec. 45U.	Zero-emission nuclear power production credit
Sec. 45V.	Credit for production of clean hydrogen
Sec. 45W.	Credit for qualified commercial clean vehicles
Sec. 45X.	Advanced manufacturing production credit
Sec. 45Y.	Clean electricity production credit
Sec. 45Z.	Clean fuel production credit
Sec. 45AA.	Military spouse retirement plan eligibility credit for small employers

Subpart E—Rules for Computing Investment Credit

Sec. 46.	Amount of credit
Sec. 47.	Rehabilitation credit
Sec. 48.	Energy credit
Sec. 48A.	Qualifying advanced coal project credit
Sec. 48B.	Qualifying gasification project credit
Sec. 48C.	Qualifying advanced energy project credit
Sec. 48D.	Advanced manufacturing investment credit
Sec. 48E.	Clean electricity investment credit
Sec. 49.	At-risk rules
Sec. 50.	Other special rules

Subpart F—Rules for Computing Work Opportunity Credit

Sec. 51.	Amount of credit
Sec. 52.	Special rules

Subpart G—Credit Against Regular Tax for Prior Year Minimum Tax Liability

Sec. 53.	Credit for prior year minimum tax liability

PART V—TAX SURCHARGE—[REPEALED]

PART VI—ALTERNATIVE MINIMUM TAX

Sec. 55.	Alternative minimum tax imposed
Sec. 56.	Adjustments in computing alternative minimum taxable income
Sec. 56A.	Adjusted financial statement income
Sec. 57.	Items of tax preference
Sec. 58.	Denial of certain losses
Sec. 59.	Other definitions and special rules

PART VII—BASE EROSION AND ANTI-ABUSE TAX

Sec. 59A.	Tax on base erosion payments of taxpayers with substantial gross receipts

PART VII—ENVIRONMENTAL TAX—[STRICKEN]

PART VIII—SUPPLEMENTAL MEDICARE PREMIUM—[REPEALED]

SUBCHAPTER B. COMPUTATION OF TAXABLE INCOME

PART I—DEFINITION OF GROSS INCOME, ADJUSTED GROSS INCOME, TAXABLE INCOME, ETC.

Sec. 61.	Gross income defined
Sec. 62.	Adjusted gross income defined
Sec. 63.	Taxable income defined
Sec. 64.	Ordinary income defined
Sec. 65.	Ordinary loss defined
Sec. 66.	Treatment of community income
Sec. 67.	2-percent floor on miscellaneous itemized deductions
Sec. 68.	Overall limitation on itemized deductions

PART II—ITEMS SPECIFICALLY INCLUDED IN GROSS INCOME

Sec. 71.	Alimony and separate maintenance payments
Sec. 72.	Annuities; certain proceeds of endowment and life insurance contracts
Sec. 73.	Services of child
Sec. 74.	Prizes and awards
Sec. 75.	Dealers in tax-exempt securities
Sec. 77.	Commodity credit loans
Sec. 78.	Dividends received from certain foreign corporations by domestic corporations choosing foreign tax credit
Sec. 79.	Group-term life insurance purchased for employees
Sec. 80.	Restoration of value of certain securities
Sec. 82.	Reimbursement for expenses of moving
Sec. 83.	Property transferred in connection with performance of services
Sec. 84.	Transfer of appreciated property to political organization
Sec. 85.	Unemployment compensation

CODE—TABLE OF CONTENTS

Sec. 86.	Social security and tier 1 railroad retirement benefits
Sec. 87.	Alcohol and biodiesel fuels credits
Sec. 88.	Certain amounts with respect to nuclear decommissioning costs
Sec. 90.	Illegal federal irrigation subsidies
Sec. 91.	Certain foreign branch losses transferred to specified 10-percent owned foreign corporations

Part III—Items Specifically Excluded From Gross Income

Sec. 101.	Certain death benefits
Sec. 102.	Gifts and inheritances
Sec. 103.	Interest on state and local bonds
Sec. 104.	Compensation for injuries or sickness
Sec. 105.	Amounts received under accident and health plans
Sec. 106.	Contributions by employer to accident and health plans
Sec. 107.	Rental value of parsonages
Sec. 108.	Income from discharge of indebtedness
Sec. 109.	Improvements by lessee on lessor's property
Sec. 110.	Qualified lessee construction allowances for short-term leases
Sec. 111.	Recovery of tax benefit items
Sec. 112.	Certain combat zone compensation of members of the Armed Forces
Sec. 115.	Income of States, municipalities, etc.
Sec. 117.	Qualified scholarships
Sec. 118.	Contributions to the capital of a corporation
Sec. 119.	Meals or lodging furnished for the convenience of the employer
Sec. 121.	Exclusion of gain from sale of principal residence
Sec. 122.	Certain reduced uniformed services retirement pay
Sec. 123.	Amounts received under insurance contracts for certain living expenses
Sec. 125.	Cafeteria plans
Sec. 126.	Certain cost-sharing payments
Sec. 127.	Educational assistance programs
Sec. 129.	Dependent care assistance programs
Sec. 130.	Certain personal injury liability assignments
Sec. 131.	Certain foster care payments
Sec. 132.	Certain fringe benefits
Sec. 134.	Certain military benefits
Sec. 135.	Income from United States savings bonds used to pay higher education tuition and fees
Sec. 136.	Energy conservation subsidies provided by public utilities
Sec. 137.	Adoption assistance programs
Sec. 138.	Medicare Advantage MSA
Sec. 139.	Disaster relief payments
Sec. 139A.	Federal subsidies for prescription drug plans
Sec. 139B.	Benefits provided to volunteer firefighters and emergency medical responders
Sec. 139C.	Certain disability-related first responder retirement payments
Sec. 139D.	Indian health care benefits
Sec. 139E.	Certain disability-related first responder retirement payments
Sec. 139F.	Certain amounts received by wrongfully incarcerated individuals
Sec. 139G.	Assignments to Alaska Native Settlement Trusts
Sec. 139H.	Interest received in action to recover property seized by the Internal Revenue Service based on structuring transaction
Sec. 139I.	Continuation coverage premium assistance
Sec. 140.	Cross references to other Acts

Part IV—Tax Exemption Requirements for State and Local Bonds

Subpart A—Private Activity Bonds

Sec. 141.	Private activity bond; qualified bond
Sec. 142.	Exempt facility bond
Sec. 143.	Mortgage revenue bonds; qualified mortgage bond and qualified veterans' mortgage bond
Sec. 144.	Qualified small issue bond; qualified student loan bond; qualified redevelopment bond
Sec. 145.	Qualified 501(c)(3) bond
Sec. 146.	Volume cap
Sec. 147.	Other requirements applicable to certain private activity bonds

Subpart B—Requirements Applicable to All State and Local Bonds

Sec. 148.	Arbitrage
Sec. 149.	Bonds must be registered to be tax exempt; other requirements

Subpart C—Definitions and Special Rules

Sec. 150.	Definitions and special rules

Part V—Deductions for Personal Exemptions

Sec. 151.	Allowance of deductions for personal exemptions
Sec. 152.	Dependent defined
Sec. 153.	Cross references

Part VI—Itemized Deductions for Individuals and Corporations

Sec. 161.	Allowance of deductions
Sec. 162.	Trade or business expenses
Sec. 163.	Interest

Internal Revenue Code

Sec. 164.	Taxes
Sec. 165.	Losses
Sec. 166.	Bad debts
Sec. 167.	Depreciation
Sec. 168.	Accelerated cost recovery system
Sec. 169.	Amortization of pollution control facilities
Sec. 170.	Charitable, etc., contributions and gifts
Sec. 171.	Amortizable bond premium
Sec. 172.	Net operating loss deduction
Sec. 173.	Circulation expenditures
Sec. 174.	Amortization of research and experimental expenditures
Sec. 175.	Soil and water conservation expenditures; endangered species recovery expenditures
Sec. 176.	Payments with respect to employees of certain foreign corporations
Sec. 178.	Amortization of cost of acquiring a lease
Sec. 179.	Election to expense certain depreciable business assets
Sec. 179B.	Deduction for capital costs incurred in complying with Environmental Protection Agency sulfur regulations
Sec. 179C.	Election to expense certain refineries
Sec. 179D.	Energy efficient commercial buildings deduction
Sec. 179E.	Election to expense advanced mine safety equipment
Sec. 180.	Expenditures by farmers for fertilizer, etc.
Sec. 181.	Treatment of certain qualified film and television and live theatrical productions
Sec. 183.	Activities not engaged in for profit
Sec. 186.	Recoveries of damages for antitrust violations, etc.
Sec. 190.	Expenditures to remove architectural and transportation barriers to the handicapped and elderly
Sec. 192.	Contributions to black lung benefit trust
Sec. 193.	Tertiary injectants
Sec. 194.	Treatment of reforestation expenditures
Sec. 194A.	Contributions to employer liability trusts
Sec. 195.	Start-up expenditures
Sec. 196.	Deduction for certain unused business credits
Sec. 197.	Amortization of goodwill and certain other intangibles
Sec. 198.	Expensing of environmental remediation costs
Sec. 199A.	Qualified business income

Part VII—Additional Itemized Deductions for Individuals

Sec. 211.	Allowance of deductions
Sec. 212.	Expenses for production of income
Sec. 213.	Medical, dental, etc., expenses
Sec. 215.	Alimony, etc., payments
Sec. 216.	Deduction of taxes, interest, and business depreciation by cooperative housing corporation tenant-stockholder
Sec. 217.	Moving expenses
Sec. 219.	Retirement savings
Sec. 220.	Archer MSAs
Sec. 221.	Interest on education loans
Sec. 222.	Qualified tuition and related expenses
Sec. 223.	Health savings accounts
Sec. 224.	Cross reference

Part VIII—Special Deductions for Corporations

Sec. 241.	Allowance of special deductions
Sec. 243.	Dividends received by corporations
Sec. 245.	Dividends received from certain foreign corporations
Sec. 245A.	Deduction for foreign source-portion of dividends received by domestic corporations from specified 10-percent owned foreign corporations
Sec. 246.	Rules applying to deductions for dividends received
Sec. 246A.	Dividends received deduction reduced where portfolio stock is debt financed
Sec. 247.	Contributions to Alaska Native Settlement Trusts
Sec. 248.	Organizational expenditures
Sec. 249.	Limitation on deduction of bond premium on repurchase
Sec. 250.	Foreign-derived intangible income and global intangible low-taxed income

Part IX—Items Not Deductible

Sec. 261.	General rule for disallowance of deductions
Sec. 262.	Personal, living, and family expenses
Sec. 263.	Capital expenditures
Sec. 263A.	Capitalization and inclusion in inventory costs of certain expenses
Sec. 264.	Certain amounts paid in connection with insurance contracts
Sec. 265.	Expenses and interest relating to tax-exempt income
Sec. 266.	Carrying charges
Sec. 267.	Losses, expenses, and interest with respect to transactions between related taxpayers
Sec. 267A.	Certain related party amounts paid or accrued in hybrid transactions or with hybrid entities
Sec. 268.	Sale of land with unharvested crop
Sec. 269.	Acquisitions made to evade or avoid income tax
Sec. 269A.	Personal service corporations formed or availed of to avoid or evade income tax
Sec. 269B.	Stapled entities

CODE—TABLE OF CONTENTS

Sec. 271.	Debts owed by political parties, etc.
Sec. 272.	Disposal of coal or domestic iron ore
Sec. 273.	Holders of life or terminable interest
Sec. 274.	Disallowance of certain entertainment, etc., expenses
Sec. 275.	Certain taxes
Sec. 276.	Certain indirect contributions to political parties
Sec. 277.	Deductions incurred by certain membership organizations in transactions with members
Sec. 279.	Interest on indebtedness incurred by corporation to acquire stock or assets of another corporation
Sec. 280A.	Disallowance of certain expenses in connection with business use of home, rental of vacation homes, etc.
Sec. 280B.	Demolition of structures
Sec. 280C.	Certain expenses for which credits are allowable
Sec. 280E.	Expenditures in connection with the illegal sale of drugs
Sec. 280F.	Limitation on depreciation for luxury automobiles; limitation where certain property used for personal purposes
Sec. 280G.	Golden parachute payments
Sec. 280H.	Limitation on certain amounts paid to employee-owners by personal service corporations electing alternative taxable years

Part X—Terminal Railroad Corporations and Their Shareholders

Sec. 281.	Terminal railroad corporations and their shareholders

Part XI—Special Rules Relating to Corporate Preference Items

Sec. 291.	Special rules relating to corporate preference items

SUBCHAPTER C. CORPORATE DISTRIBUTIONS AND ADJUSTMENTS

Part I—Distributions by Corporations

Subpart A—Effects on Recipients

Sec. 301.	Distributions of property
Sec. 302.	Distributions in redemption of stock
Sec. 303.	Distributions in redemption of stock to pay death taxes
Sec. 304.	Redemption through use of related corporations
Sec. 305.	Distributions of stock and stock rights
Sec. 306.	Dispositions of certain stock
Sec. 307.	Basis of stock and stock rights acquired in distributions

Subpart B—Effects on Corporation

Sec. 311.	Taxability of corporation on distribution
Sec. 312.	Effect on earnings and profits

Subpart C—Definitions; Constructive Ownership of Stock

Sec. 316.	Dividend defined
Sec. 317.	Other definitions
Sec. 318.	Constructive ownership of stock

Part II—Corporate Liquidations

Subpart A—Effects on Recipients

Sec. 331.	Gain or loss to shareholders in corporate liquidations
Sec. 332.	Complete liquidations of subsidiaries
Sec. 334.	Basis of property received in liquidations

Subpart B—Effects on Corporation

Sec. 336.	Gain or loss recognized on property distributed in complete liquidation
Sec. 337.	Nonrecognition for property distributed to parent in complete liquidation of subsidiary
Sec. 338.	Certain stock purchases treated as asset acquisitions

Subpart C—Collapsible Corporations—[Repealed]

Subpart D—Definition and Special Rule

Sec. 346.	Definition and special rule

Part III—Corporate Organizations and Reorganizations

Subpart A—Corporate Organizations

Sec. 351.	Transfer to corporation controlled by transferor

Subpart B—Effects on Shareholders and Security Holders

Sec. 354.	Exchanges of stock and securities in certain reorganizations
Sec. 355.	Distribution of stock and securities of a controlled corporation
Sec. 356.	Receipt of additional consideration
Sec. 357.	Assumption of liability
Sec. 358.	Basis to distributees

Subpart C—Effects on Corporations

Sec. 361.	Nonrecognition of gain or loss to corporations; treatment of distributions
Sec. 362.	Basis to corporations

Subpart D—Special Rule; Definitions

Sec. 367.	Foreign corporations
Sec. 368.	Definitions relating to corporate reorganizations

Internal Revenue Code

CODE—TABLE OF CONTENTS

Part IV—Insolvency Reorganizations—[Repealed]

Part V—Carryovers

Sec. 381.	Carryovers in certain corporate acquisitions
Sec. 382.	Limitation on net operating loss carryforwards and certain built-in losses following ownership change
Sec. 383.	Special limitations on certain excess credits, etc.
Sec. 384.	Limitation on use of preacquisition losses to offset built-in gains

Part VI—Treatment of Certain Corporate Interests as Stock or Indebtedness

Sec. 385.	Treatment of certain interests in corporations as stock or indebtedness

Part VII—Miscellaneous Corporate Provisions—[Repealed]

SUBCHAPTER D. DEFERRED COMPENSATION, ETC.

Part I—Pension, Profit-Sharing, Stock Bonus Plans, Etc.

Subpart A—General Rule

Sec. 401.	Qualified pension, profit-sharing, and stock bonus plans
Sec. 402.	Taxability of beneficiary of employees' trust
Sec. 402A.	Optional treatment of elective deferrals as Roth contributions
Sec. 403.	Taxation of employee annuities
Sec. 404.	Deduction for contributions of an employer to an employees' trust or annuity plan and compensation under a deferred-payment plan
Sec. 404A.	Deduction for certain foreign deferred compensation plans
Sec. 406.	Employees of foreign affiliates covered by section 3121(l) agreements
Sec. 407.	Certain employees of domestic subsidiaries engaged in business outside the United States
Sec. 408.	Individual retirement accounts
Sec. 408A.	Roth IRAs
Sec. 409.	Qualifications for tax credit employee stock ownership plans
Sec. 409A.	Inclusion in gross income of deferred compensation under nonqualified deferred compensation plans

Subpart B—Special Rules

Sec. 410.	Minimum participation standards
Sec. 411.	Minimum vesting standards
Sec. 412.	Minimum funding standards
Sec. 413.	Collectively bargained plans, etc.
Sec. 414.	Definitions and special rules
Sec. 414A.	Requirements related to automatic enrollment
Sec. 415.	Limitations on benefits and contributions under qualified plans
Sec. 416.	Special rules for top-heavy plans
Sec. 417.	Definitions and special rules for purposes of minimum survivor annuity requirements

Subpart C—Insolvent Plans

Sec. 418E.	Insolvent plans

Subpart D—Treatment of Welfare Benefit Funds

Sec. 419.	Treatment of funded welfare benefit plans
Sec. 419A.	Qualified asset account; limitation on additions to account

Subpart E—Treatment of Transfers to Retiree Health Accounts

Sec. 420.	Transfers of excess pension assets to retiree health accounts

Part II—Certain Stock Options

Sec. 421.	General rules
Sec. 422.	Incentive stock options
Sec. 423.	Employee stock purchase plans
Sec. 424.	Definitions and special rules

Part III—Rules Relating to Minimum Funding Standards and Benefit Limitations

Subpart A—Minimum Funding Standards for Pension Plans

Sec. 430.	Minimum funding standards for single-employer defined benefit pension plans
Sec. 431.	Minimum funding standards for multiemployer plans
Sec. 432.	Additional funding rules for multiemployer plans in endangered status or critical status
Sec. 433.	Minimum funding standards for CSEC plans

Subpart B—Benefit Limitations Under Single-Employer Plans

Sec. 436.	Funding-based limits on benefits and benefit accruals under single-employer plans

SUBCHAPTER E. ACCOUNTING PERIODS AND METHODS OF ACCOUNTING

Part I—Accounting Periods

Sec. 441.	Period for computation of taxable income
Sec. 442.	Change of annual accounting period
Sec. 443.	Returns for a period of less than 12 months
Sec. 444.	Election of taxable year other than required taxable year

Part II—Methods of Accounting

Subpart A—Methods of Accounting in General

Sec. 446.	General rule for methods of accounting
Sec. 447.	Method of accounting for corporations engaged in farming

CODE—TABLE OF CONTENTS

Sec. 448. Limitation on use of cash method of accounting

Subpart B—Taxable Year for Which Items of Gross Income Included

Sec. 451. General rule for taxable year of inclusion
Sec. 453. Installment method
Sec. 453A. Special rules for nondealers
Sec. 453B. Gain or loss on disposition of installment obligations
Sec. 454. Obligations issued at discount
Sec. 455. Prepaid subscription income
Sec. 456. Prepaid dues income of certain membership organizations
Sec. 457. Deferred compensation plans of State and local governments and tax-exempt organizations
Sec. 457A. Nonqualified deferred compensation from certain tax indifferent parties
Sec. 458. Magazines, paperbacks, and records returned after the close of the taxable year
Sec. 460. Special rules for long-term contracts

Subpart C—Taxable Year for Which Deductions Taken

Sec. 461. General rule for taxable year of deduction
Sec. 464. Limitations on deductions for certain farming [expenses]
Sec. 465. Deductions limited to amount at risk
Sec. 467. Certain payments for the use of property or services
Sec. 468. Special rules for mining and solid waste reclamation and closing costs
Sec. 468A. Special rules for nuclear decommissioning costs
Sec. 468B. Special rules for designated settlement funds
Sec. 469. Passive activity losses and credits limited
Sec. 470. Limitation on deductions allocable to property used by governments or other tax-exempt entities

Subpart D—Inventories

Sec. 471. General rule for inventories
Sec. 472. Last-in, first-out inventories
Sec. 473. Qualified liquidations of LIFO inventories
Sec. 474. Simplified dollar-value LIFO method for certain small businesses
Sec. 475. Mark to market accounting method for dealers in securities

PART III—ADJUSTMENTS

Sec. 481. Adjustments required by changes in method of accounting
Sec. 482. Allocation of income and deductions among taxpayers
Sec. 483. Interest on certain deferred payments

SUBCHAPTER F. EXEMPT ORGANIZATIONS

PART I—GENERAL RULE

Sec. 501. Exemption from tax on corporations, certain trusts, etc.
Sec. 502. Feeder organizations
Sec. 503. Requirements for exemption
Sec. 504. Status after organization ceases to qualify for exemption under section 501(c)(3) because of substantial lobbying or because of political activities
Sec. 505. Additional requirements for organizations described in paragraph (9) or (17) of section 501(c)
Sec. 506. Organizations required to notify secretary of intent to operate under 501(c)(4)

PART II—PRIVATE FOUNDATIONS

Sec. 507. Termination of private foundation status
Sec. 508. Special rules with respect to section 501(c)(3) organizations
Sec. 509. Private foundation defined

PART III—TAXATION OF BUSINESS INCOME OF CERTAIN EXEMPT ORGANIZATIONS

Sec. 511. Imposition of tax on unrelated business income of charitable, etc., organizations
Sec. 512. Unrelated business taxable income
Sec. 513. Unrelated trade or business
Sec. 514. Unrelated debt-financed income
Sec. 515. Taxes of foreign countries and possessions of the United States

PART IV—FARMERS' COOPERATIVES

Sec. 521. Exemption of farmers' cooperatives from tax

PART V—SHIPOWNERS' PROTECTION AND INDEMNITY ASSOCIATIONS

Sec. 526. Shipowners' protection and indemnity associations

PART VI—POLITICAL ORGANIZATIONS

Sec. 527. Political organizations

PART VII—CERTAIN HOMEOWNERS ASSOCIATIONS

Sec. 528. Certain homeowners associations

PART VIII—CERTAIN SAVINGS ENTITIES

Sec. 529. Qualified tuition programs
Sec. 529A. Qualified able programs
Sec. 530. Coverdell education savings accounts

SUBCHAPTER G. CORPORATIONS USED TO AVOID INCOME TAX ON SHAREHOLDERS

PART I—CORPORATIONS IMPROPERLY ACCUMULATING SURPLUS

Sec. 531. Imposition of accumulated earnings tax

Internal Revenue Code

Sec. 532.	Corporations subject to accumulated earnings tax
Sec. 533.	Evidence of purpose to avoid income tax
Sec. 534.	Burden of proof
Sec. 535.	Accumulated taxable income
Sec. 536.	Income not placed on annual basis
Sec. 537.	Reasonable needs of the business

PART II—PERSONAL HOLDING COMPANIES

Sec. 541.	Imposition of personal holding company tax
Sec. 542.	Definition of personal holding company
Sec. 543.	Personal holding company income
Sec. 544.	Rules for determining stock ownership
Sec. 545.	Undistributed personal holding company income
Sec. 546.	Income not placed on annual basis
Sec. 547.	Deduction for deficiency dividends

PART III—FOREIGN PERSONAL HOLDING COMPANIES—[REPEALED]

PART IV—DEDUCTION FOR DIVIDENDS PAID

Sec. 561.	Definition of deduction for dividends paid
Sec. 562.	Rules applicable in determining dividends eligible for dividends paid deduction
Sec. 563.	Rules relating to dividends paid after close of taxable year
Sec. 564.	Dividend carryover
Sec. 565.	Consent dividends

SUBCHAPTER H. BANKING INSTITUTIONS

PART I—RULES OF GENERAL APPLICATION TO BANKING INSTITUTIONS

Sec. 581.	Definition of bank
Sec. 582.	Bad debts, losses, and gains with respect to securities held by financial institutions
Sec. 584.	Common trust funds
Sec. 585.	Reserves for losses on loans of banks

PART II—MUTUAL SAVINGS BANKS, ETC.

Sec. 591.	Deduction for dividends paid on deposits
Sec. 593.	Reserves for losses on loans
Sec. 594.	Alternative tax for mutual savings banks conducting life insurance business
Sec. 597.	Treatment of transactions in which federal financial assistance provided

SUBCHAPTER I. NATURAL RESOURCES

PART I—DEDUCTIONS

Sec. 611.	Allowance of deduction for depletion
Sec. 612.	Basis for cost depletion
Sec. 613.	Percentage depletion
Sec. 613A.	Limitations on percentage depletion in case of oil and gas wells
Sec. 614.	Definition of property
Sec. 616.	Development expenditures
Sec. 617.	Deduction and recapture of certain mining exploration expenditures

PART II—EXCLUSIONS FROM GROSS INCOME—[REPEALED]

PART III—SALES AND EXCHANGES

Sec. 631.	Gain or loss in the case of timber, coal, or domestic iron ore

PART IV—MINERAL PRODUCTION PAYMENTS

Sec. 636.	Income tax treatment of mineral production payments

PART V—CONTINENTAL SHELF AREAS

Sec. 638.	Continental shelf areas

SUBCHAPTER J. ESTATES, TRUSTS, BENEFICIARIES, AND DECEDENTS

PART I—ESTATES, TRUSTS, AND BENEFICIARIES

Subpart A—General Rules for Taxation of Estates and Trusts

Sec. 641.	Imposition of tax
Sec. 642.	Special rules for credits and deductions
Sec. 643.	Definitions applicable to subparts A, B, C, and D
Sec. 644.	Taxable year of trusts
Sec. 645.	Certain revocable trusts treated as part of estate
Sec. 646.	Tax treatment of electing Alaska Native Settlement Trusts

Subpart B—Trusts Which Distribute Current Income Only

Sec. 651.	Deduction for trusts distributing current income only
Sec. 652.	Inclusion of amounts in gross income of beneficiaries of trusts distributing current income only

Subpart C—Estates and Trusts Which May Accumulate Income or Which Distribute Corpus

Sec. 661.	Deduction for estates and trusts accumulating income or distributing corpus
Sec. 662.	Inclusion of amounts in gross income of beneficiaries of estates and trusts accumulating income or distributing corpus
Sec. 663.	Special rules applicable to sections 661 and 662
Sec. 664.	Charitable remainder trusts

CODE—TABLE OF CONTENTS

Subpart D—Treatment of Excess Distributions by Trusts

Sec. 665.	Definitions applicable to subpart D
Sec. 666.	Accumulation distribution allocated to preceding years
Sec. 667.	Treatment of amounts deemed distributed by trust in preceding years
Sec. 668.	Interest charge on accumulation distributions from foreign trusts

Subpart E—Grantors and Others Treated as Substantial Owners

Sec. 671.	Trust income, deductions, and credits attributable to grantors and others as substantial owners
Sec. 672.	Definitions and rules
Sec. 673.	Reversionary interests
Sec. 674.	Power to control beneficial enjoyment
Sec. 675.	Administrative powers
Sec. 676.	Power to revoke
Sec. 677.	Income for benefit of grantor
Sec. 678.	Person other than grantor treated as substantial owner
Sec. 679.	Foreign trusts having one or more United States beneficiaries

Subpart F—Miscellaneous

Sec. 681.	Limitation on charitable deduction
Sec. 682.	Income of an estate or trust in case of divorce, etc.
Sec. 683.	Use of trust as an exchange fund
Sec. 684.	Recognition of gain on certain transfers to certain foreign trusts and estates
Sec. 685.	Treatment of funeral trusts

Part II—Income in Respect of Decedents

Sec. 691.	Recipients of income in respect of decedents
Sec. 692.	Income taxes of members of Armed Forces, astronauts, and victims of certain terrorist attacks on death

SUBCHAPTER K. PARTNERS AND PARTNERSHIPS

Part I—Determination of Tax Liability

Sec. 701.	Partners, not partnership, subject to tax
Sec. 702.	Income and credits of partner
Sec. 703.	Partnership computations
Sec. 704.	Partner's distributive share
Sec. 705.	Determination of basis of partner's interest
Sec. 706.	Taxable years of partner and partnership
Sec. 707.	Transactions between partner and partnership
Sec. 708.	Continuation of partnership
Sec. 709.	Treatment of organization and syndication fees

Part II—Contributions, Distributions, and Transfers

Subpart A—Contributions to a Partnership

Sec. 721.	Nonrecognition of gain or loss on contribution
Sec. 722.	Basis of contributing partner's interest
Sec. 723.	Basis of property contributed to partnership
Sec. 724.	Character of gain or loss on contributed unrealized receivables, inventory items, and capital loss property

Subpart B—Distributions by a Partnership

Sec. 731.	Extent of recognition of gain or loss on distribution
Sec. 732.	Basis of distributed property other than money
Sec. 733.	Basis of distributee partner's interest
Sec. 734.	Adjustment to basis of undistributed partnership property where section 754 election or substantial basis reduction
Sec. 735.	Character of gain or loss on disposition of distributed property
Sec. 736.	Payments to a retiring partner or a deceased partner's successor in interest
Sec. 737.	Recognition of precontribution gain in case of certain distributions to contributing partner

Subpart C—Transfers of Interests in a Partnership

Sec. 741.	Recognition and character of gain or loss on sale or exchange
Sec. 742.	Basis of transferee partner's interest
Sec. 743.	Special rules where section 754 election or substantial built-in loss

Subpart D—Provisions Common to Other Subparts

Sec. 751.	Unrealized receivables and inventory items
Sec. 752.	Treatment of certain liabilities
Sec. 753.	Partner receiving income in respect of decedent
Sec. 754.	Manner of electing optional adjustment to basis of partnership property
Sec. 755.	Rules for allocation of basis

Part III—Definitions

Sec. 761.	Terms defined

Part IV—Special Rules for Electing Large Partnerships

Sec. 771.	Application of subchapter to electing large partnerships
Sec. 772.	Simplified flow-through
Sec. 773.	Computations at partnership level
Sec. 774.	Other modifications
Sec. 775.	Electing large partnership defined
Sec. 776.	Special rules for partnership holding oil and gas properties

Internal Revenue Code

CODE—TABLE OF CONTENTS

Sec. 777. Regulations

SUBCHAPTER L. INSURANCE COMPANIES

PART I—LIFE INSURANCE COMPANIES

Subpart A—Tax Imposed

Sec. 801. Tax imposed

Subpart B—Life Insurance Gross Income

Sec. 803. Life insurance gross income

Subpart C—Life Insurance Deductions

Sec. 804. Life insurance deductions
Sec. 805. General deductions
Sec. 807. Rules for certain reserves
Sec. 808. Policyholder dividends deduction

Subpart D—Accounting, Allocation, and Foreign Provisions

Sec. 811. Accounting provisions
Sec. 812. Definition of company's share and policyholders' share
Sec. 814. Contiguous country branches of domestic life insurance companies

Subpart E—Definitions and Special Rules

Sec. 816. Life insurance company defined
Sec. 817. Treatment of variable contracts
Sec. 817A. Special rules for modified guaranteed contracts
Sec. 818. Other definitions and special rules

PART II—OTHER INSURANCE COMPANIES

Sec. 831. Tax on insurance companies other than life insurance companies
Sec. 832. Insurance company taxable income
Sec. 833. Treatment of Blue Cross and Blue Shield organizations, etc.
Sec. 834. Determination of taxable investment income
Sec. 835. Election by reciprocal

PART III—PROVISIONS OF GENERAL APPLICATION

Sec. 841. Credit for foreign taxes
Sec. 842. Foreign companies carrying on insurance business
Sec. 843. Annual accounting period
Sec. 845. Certain reinsurance agreements
Sec. 846. Discounted unpaid losses defined
Sec. 848. Capitalization of certain policy acquisition expenses

SUBCHAPTER M. REGULATED INVESTMENT COMPANIES AND REAL ESTATE INVESTMENT TRUSTS

PART I—REGULATED INVESTMENT COMPANIES

Sec. 851. Definition of regulated investment company
Sec. 852. Taxation of regulated investment companies and their shareholders
Sec. 853. Foreign tax credit allowed to shareholders
Sec. 853A. Credits from tax credit bonds allowed to shareholders
Sec. 854. Limitations applicable to dividends received from regulated investment company
Sec. 855. Dividends paid by regulated investment company after close of taxable year

PART II—REAL ESTATE INVESTMENT TRUSTS

Sec. 856. Definition of real estate investment trust
Sec. 857. Taxation of real estate investment trusts and their beneficiaries
Sec. 858. Dividends paid by real estate investment trust after close of taxable year
Sec. 859. Adoption of annual accounting period

PART III—PROVISIONS WHICH APPLY TO BOTH REGULATED INVESTMENT COMPANIES AND REAL ESTATE INVESTMENT TRUSTS

Sec. 860. Deduction for deficiency dividends

PART IV—REAL ESTATE MORTGAGE INVESTMENT CONDUITS

Sec. 860A. Taxation of REMIC's
Sec. 860B. Taxation of holders of regular interests
Sec. 860C. Taxation of residual interests
Sec. 860D. REMIC defined
Sec. 860E. Treatment of income in excess of daily accruals on residual interests
Sec. 860F. Other rules
Sec. 860G. Other definitions and special rules

PART V—FINANCIAL ASSET SECURITIZATION INVESTMENT TRUSTS—[REPEALED]

SUBCHAPTER N. TAX BASED ON INCOME FROM SOURCES WITHIN OR WITHOUT THE UNITED STATES

PART I—SOURCE RULES AND OTHER GENERAL RULES RELATING TO FOREIGN INCOME

Sec. 861. Income from sources within the United States
Sec. 862. Income from sources without the United States
Sec. 863. Special rules for determining source
Sec. 864. Definitions and special rules
Sec. 865. Source rules for personal property sales

CODE—TABLE OF CONTENTS

PART II—NONRESIDENT ALIENS AND FOREIGN CORPORATIONS

Subpart A—Nonresident Alien Individuals

Sec. 871.	Tax on nonresident alien individuals
Sec. 872.	Gross income
Sec. 873.	Deductions
Sec. 874.	Allowance of deductions and credits
Sec. 875.	Partnerships; beneficiaries of estates and trusts
Sec. 876.	Alien residents of Puerto Rico, Guam, American Samoa, or the Northern Mariana Islands
Sec. 877.	Expatriation to avoid tax
Sec. 877A.	Tax responsibilities of expatriation
Sec. 878.	Foreign educational, charitable, and certain other exempt organizations
Sec. 879.	Tax treatment of certain community income in the case of nonresident alien individuals

Subpart B—Foreign Corporations

Sec. 881.	Tax on income of foreign corporations not connected with United States business
Sec. 882.	Tax on income of foreign corporations connected with United States business
Sec. 883.	Exclusions from gross income
Sec. 884.	Branch profits tax
Sec. 885.	Cross references

Subpart C—Tax on Gross Transportation Income

Sec. 887.	Imposition of tax on gross transportation income of nonresident aliens and foreign corporations

Subpart D—Miscellaneous Provisions

Sec. 891.	Doubling of rates of tax on citizens and corporations of certain foreign countries
Sec. 892.	Income of foreign governments and of international organizations
Sec. 893.	Compensation of employees of foreign governments or international organizations
Sec. 894.	Income affected by treaty
Sec. 895.	Income derived by a foreign central bank of issue from obligations of the United States or from bank deposits
Sec. 896.	Adjustment of tax on nationals, residents, and corporations of certain foreign countries
Sec. 897.	Disposition of investment in United States real property
Sec. 898.	Taxable year of certain foreign corporations

PART III—INCOME FROM SOURCES WITHOUT THE UNITED STATES

Subpart A—Foreign Tax Credit

Sec. 901.	Taxes of foreign countries and of possessions of United States
Sec. 903.	Credit for taxes in lieu of income, etc., taxes
Sec. 904.	Limitation on credit
Sec. 905.	Applicable rules
Sec. 906.	Nonresident alien individuals and foreign corporations
Sec. 907.	Special rules in case of foreign oil and gas income
Sec. 908.	Reduction of credit for participation in or cooperation with an international boycott
Sec. 909.	Suspension of taxes and credits until related income taken into account

Subpart B—Earned Income of Citizens or Residents of United States

Sec. 911.	Citizens or residents of the United States living abroad
Sec. 912.	Exemption for certain allowances

Subpart C—Taxation of Foreign Sales Corporations—[Repealed]

Subpart D—Possessions of the United States

Sec. 931.	Income from sources within Guam, American Samoa, or the Northern Mariana Islands
Sec. 932.	Coordination of United States and Virgin Islands income taxes
Sec. 933.	Income from sources within Puerto Rico
Sec. 934.	Limitation on reduction in income tax liability incurred to the Virgin Islands
Sec. 935.	Coordination of United States and Guam individual income taxes
Sec. 937.	Residence and source rules involving possessions

Subpart E—Qualifying Foreign Trade Income—[Repealed]

Subpart F—Controlled Foreign Corporations

Sec. 951.	Amounts included in gross income of United States shareholders
Sec. 951A.	Global intangible low-taxed income included in gross income of United States shareholders
Sec. 952.	Subpart F income defined
Sec. 953.	Insurance income
Sec. 954.	Foreign base company income
Sec. 956.	Investment of earnings in United States property
Sec. 957.	Controlled foreign corporations; United States persons
Sec. 958.	Rules for determining stock ownership
Sec. 959.	Exclusion from gross income of previously taxed earnings and profits
Sec. 960.	Deemed paid credit for subpart F inclusions
Sec. 961.	Adjustments to basis of stock in controlled foreign corporations and of other property
Sec. 962.	Election by individuals to be subject to tax at corporate rates
Sec. 964.	Miscellaneous provisions
Sec. 965.	Treatment of deferred foreign income upon transition to participation exemption system of taxation

Subpart G—Export Trade Corporations

Sec. 970.	Reduction of subpart F income of export trade corporations

Internal Revenue Code

Sec. 971. Definitions

Subpart H—Income of Certain Nonresident United States Citizens Subject to Foreign Community Property Laws—[Repealed]

Subpart I—Admissibility of Documentation Maintained in Foreign Countries

Sec. 982. Admissibility of documentation maintained in foreign countries

Subpart J—Foreign Currency Transactions

Sec. 985. Functional currency
Sec. 986. Determination of foreign taxes and foreign corporation's earnings and profits
Sec. 987. Branch transactions
Sec. 988. Treatment of certain foreign currency transactions
Sec. 989. Other definitions and special rules

PART IV—DOMESTIC INTERNATIONAL SALES CORPORATIONS

Subpart A—Treatment of Qualifying Corporations

Sec. 991. Taxation of a domestic international sales corporation
Sec. 992. Requirements of a domestic international sales corporation
Sec. 993. Definitions
Sec. 994. Inter-company pricing rules

Subpart B—Treatment of Distributions to Shareholders

Sec. 995. Taxation of DISC income to shareholders
Sec. 996. Rules for allocation in the case of distributions and losses
Sec. 997. Special subchapter C rules

PART V—INTERNATIONAL BOYCOTT DETERMINATIONS

Sec. 999. Reports by taxpayers; determinations

SUBCHAPTER O. GAIN OR LOSS ON DISPOSITION OF PROPERTY

PART I—DETERMINATION OF AMOUNT OF AND RECOGNITION OF GAIN OR LOSS

Sec. 1001. Determination of amount of and recognition of gain or loss

PART II—BASIS RULES OF GENERAL APPLICATION

Sec. 1011. Adjusted basis for determining gain or loss
Sec. 1012. Basis of property—cost
Sec. 1013. Basis of property included in inventory
Sec. 1014. Basis of property acquired from a decedent
Sec. 1015. Basis of property acquired by gifts and transfers in trust
Sec. 1016. Adjustments to basis
Sec. 1017. Discharge of indebtedness
Sec. 1019. Property on which lessee has made improvements
Sec. 1021. Sale of annuities
Sec. 1023. Cross references

PART III—COMMON NONTAXABLE EXCHANGES

Sec. 1031. Exchange of real property held for productive use or investment
Sec. 1032. Exchange of stock for property
Sec. 1033. Involuntary conversions
Sec. 1035. Certain exchanges of insurance policies
Sec. 1036. Stock for stock of same corporation
Sec. 1037. Certain exchanges of United States obligations
Sec. 1038. Certain reacquisitions of real property
Sec. 1040. Transfer of certain farm, etc., real property
Sec. 1041. Transfers of property between spouses or incident to divorce
Sec. 1042. Sales of stock to employee stock ownership plans or certain cooperatives
Sec. 1043. Sale of property to comply with conflict-of-interest requirements
Sec. 1045. Rollover of gain from qualified small business stock to another qualified small business stock

PART IV—SPECIAL RULES

Sec. 1052. Basis established by the Revenue Act of 1932 or 1934 or by the Internal Revenue Code of 1939
Sec. 1053. Property acquired before March 1, 1913
Sec. 1054. Certain stock of Federal National Mortgage Association
Sec. 1055. Redeemable ground rents
Sec. 1058. Transfer of securities under certain agreements
Sec. 1059. Corporate shareholder's basis in stock reduced by nontaxed portion of extraordinary dividends
Sec. 1059A. Limitation on taxpayer's basis or inventory cost in property imported from related persons
Sec. 1060. Special allocation rules for certain asset acquisitions
Sec. 1061. Partnership interests held in connection with performance of services
Sec. 1062. Cross references

PART V—CHANGES TO EFFECTUATE F.C.C. POLICY—[STRICKEN]

PART VI—EXCHANGES IN OBEDIENCE TO S.E.C. ORDERS—[REPEALED]

PART VII—WASH SALES; STRADDLES

Sec. 1091. Loss from wash sales of stock or securities
Sec. 1092. Straddles

CODE—TABLE OF CONTENTS

PART VIII—DISTRIBUTIONS PURSUANT TO BANK HOLDING COMPANY ACT—[REPEALED]

SUBCHAPTER P. CAPITAL GAINS AND LOSSES

PART I—TREATMENT OF CAPITAL GAINS

Sec. 1202.	Partial exclusion for gain from certain small business stock

PART II—TREATMENT OF CAPITAL LOSSES

Sec. 1211.	Limitation on capital losses
Sec. 1212.	Capital loss carrybacks and carryovers

PART III—GENERAL RULES FOR DETERMINING CAPITAL GAINS AND LOSSES

Sec. 1221.	Capital asset defined
Sec. 1222.	Other terms relating to capital gains and losses
Sec. 1223.	Holding period of property

PART IV—SPECIAL RULES FOR DETERMINING CAPITAL GAINS AND LOSSES

Sec. 1231.	Property used in the trade or business and involuntary conversions
Sec. 1233.	Gains and losses from short sales
Sec. 1234.	Options to buy or sell
Sec. 1234A.	Gains or losses from certain terminations
Sec. 1234B.	Gains or losses from securities futures contracts
Sec. 1235.	Sale or exchange of patents
Sec. 1236.	Dealers in securities
Sec. 1237.	Real property subdivided for sale
Sec. 1239.	Gain from sale of depreciable property between certain related taxpayers
Sec. 1241.	Cancellation of lease or distributor's agreement
Sec. 1242.	Losses on small business investment company stock
Sec. 1243.	Loss of small business investment company
Sec. 1244.	Losses on small business stock
Sec. 1245.	Gain from dispositions of certain depreciable property
Sec. 1248.	Gain from certain sales or exchanges of stock in certain foreign corporations
Sec. 1249.	Gain from certain sales or exchanges of patents, etc., to foreign corporations
Sec. 1250.	Gain from dispositions of certain depreciable realty
Sec. 1252.	Gain from disposition of farm land
Sec. 1253.	Transfers of franchises, trademarks, and trade names
Sec. 1254.	Gain from disposition of interest in oil, gas, geothermal, or other mineral properties
Sec. 1255.	Gain from disposition of section 126 property
Sec. 1256.	Section 1256 contracts marked to market
Sec. 1257.	Disposition of converted wetlands or highly erodible croplands
Sec. 1258.	Recharacterization of gain from certain financial transactions
Sec. 1259.	Constructive sales treatment for appreciated financial positions
Sec. 1260.	Gains from constructive ownership transactions

PART V—SPECIAL RULES FOR BONDS AND OTHER DEBT INSTRUMENTS

Subpart A—Original Issue Discount

Sec. 1271.	Treatment of amounts received on retirement or sale or exchange of debt instruments
Sec. 1272.	Current inclusion in income of original issue discount
Sec. 1273.	Determination of amount of original issue discount
Sec. 1274.	Determination of issue price in the case of certain debt instruments issued for property
Sec. 1274A.	Special rules for certain transactions where stated principal amount does not exceed $2,800,000
Sec. 1275.	Other definitions and special rules

Subpart B—Market Discount on Bonds

Sec. 1276.	Disposition gain representing accrued market discount treated as ordinary income
Sec. 1277.	Deferral of interest deduction allocable to accrued market discount
Sec. 1278.	Definitions and special rules

Subpart C—Discount on Short-Term Obligations

Sec. 1281.	Current inclusion in income of discount on certain short-term obligations
Sec. 1282.	Deferral of interest deduction allocable to accrued discount
Sec. 1283.	Definitions and special rules

Subpart D—Miscellaneous Provisions

Sec. 1286.	Tax treatment of stripped bonds
Sec. 1287.	Denial of capital gain treatment for gains on certain obligations not in registered form
Sec. 1288.	Treatment of original issue discount on tax-exempt obligations

PART VI—TREATMENT OF CERTAIN PASSIVE FOREIGN INVESTMENT COMPANIES

Subpart A—Interest on Tax Deferral

Sec. 1291.	Interest on tax deferral

Subpart B—Treatment of Qualified Electing Funds

Sec. 1293.	Current taxation of income from qualified electing funds
Sec. 1294.	Election to extend time for payment of tax on undistributed earnings
Sec. 1295.	Qualified electing fund

Subpart C—Election of Mark to Market for Marketable Stock

Sec. 1296.	Election of mark to market for marketable stock

Subpart D—General Provisions

Sec. 1297.	Passive foreign investment company
Sec. 1298.	Special rules

SUBCHAPTER Q. READJUSTMENT OF TAX BETWEEN YEARS AND SPECIAL LIMITATIONS

PART I—INCOME AVERAGING

Sec. 1301.	Averaging of farm income

PART II—MITIGATION OF EFFECT OF LIMITATIONS AND OTHER PROVISIONS

Sec. 1311.	Correction of error
Sec. 1312.	Circumstances of adjustment
Sec. 1313.	Definitions
Sec. 1314.	Amount and method of adjustment

PART III—INVOLUNTARY LIQUIDATION AND REPLACEMENT OF LIFO INVENTORIES—[REPEALED]

PART IV—WAR LOSS RECOVERIES—[REPEALED]

PART V—CLAIM OF RIGHT

Sec. 1341.	Computation of tax where taxpayer restores substantial amount held under claim of right

PART VI—MAXIMUM RATE ON PERSONAL SERVICE INCOME—[REPEALED]

PART VII—RECOVERIES OF FOREIGN EXPROPRIATION LOSSES

Sec. 1351.	Treatment of recoveries of foreign expropriation losses

SUBCHAPTER R. ELECTION TO DETERMINE CORPORATE TAX ON CERTAIN INTERNATIONAL SHIPPING ACTIVITIES USING PER TON RATE

Sec. 1352.	Alternative tax on qualifying shipping activities
Sec. 1353.	Notional shipping income
Sec. 1354.	Alternative tax election; revocation; termination
Sec. 1355.	Definitions and special rules
Sec. 1356.	Qualifying shipping activities
Sec. 1357.	Items not subject to regular tax; depreciation; interest
Sec. 1358.	Allocation of credits, income, and deductions
Sec. 1359.	Disposition of qualifying vessels

SUBCHAPTER S. TAX TREATMENT OF S CORPORATIONS AND THEIR SHAREHOLDERS

PART I—IN GENERAL

Sec. 1361.	S corporation defined
Sec. 1362.	Election; revocation; termination
Sec. 1363.	Effect of election on corporation

PART II—TAX TREATMENT OF SHAREHOLDERS

Sec. 1366.	Pass-thru of items to shareholders
Sec. 1367.	Adjustments to basis of stock of shareholders, etc.
Sec. 1368.	Distributions

PART III—SPECIAL RULES

Sec. 1371.	Coordination with subchapter C
Sec. 1372.	Partnership rules to apply for fringe benefit purposes
Sec. 1373.	Foreign income
Sec. 1374.	Tax imposed on certain built-in gains
Sec. 1375.	Tax imposed when passive investment income of corporation having accumulated earnings and profits exceeds 25 percent of gross receipts

PART IV—DEFINITIONS; MISCELLANEOUS

Sec. 1377.	Definitions and special rule
Sec. 1378.	Taxable year of S corporation
Sec. 1379.	Transitional rules on enactment

SUBCHAPTER T. COOPERATIVES AND THEIR PATRONS

PART I—TAX TREATMENT OF COOPERATIVES

Sec. 1381.	Organizations to which part applies
Sec. 1382.	Taxable income of cooperatives
Sec. 1383.	Computation of tax where cooperative redeems nonqualified written notices of allocation or nonqualified per-unit retain certificates

PART II—TAX TREATMENT BY PATRONS OF PATRONAGE DIVIDENDS AND PER-UNIT RETAIN ALLOCATIONS

Sec. 1385.	Amounts includible in patron's gross income

PART III—DEFINITIONS; SPECIAL RULES

Sec. 1388.	Definitions; special rules

SUBCHAPTER U. DESIGNATION AND TREATMENT OF EMPOWERMENT ZONES, ENTERPRISE COMMUNITIES, AND RURAL DEVELOPMENT INVESTMENT AREAS

PART I—DESIGNATION

Sec. 1391.	Designation procedure
Sec. 1392.	Eligibility criteria
Sec. 1393.	Definitions and special rules

CODE—TABLE OF CONTENTS

PART II—TAX-EXEMPT FACILITY BONDS FOR EMPOWERMENT ZONES AND ENTERPRISE COMMUNITIES

Sec. 1394.	Tax-exempt enterprise zone facility bonds

PART III—ADDITIONAL INCENTIVES FOR EMPOWERMENT ZONES

Subpart A—Empowerment Zone Employment Credit

Sec. 1396.	Empowerment zone employment credit
Sec. 1397.	Other definitions and special rules

Subpart B—Additional Expensing

Sec. 1397A.	Increase in expensing under section 179

Subpart C—Nonrecognition of Gain on Rollover of Empowerment Zone Investments

Sec. 1397B.	Nonrecognition of gain on rollover of empowerment zone investments

Subpart D—General Provisions

Sec. 1397C.	Enterprise zone business defined
Sec. 1397D.	Qualified zone property defined

PART IV—INCENTIVES FOR EDUCATION ZONES—[STRICKEN]

PART V—REGULATIONS

Sec. 1397F.	Regulations

SUBCHAPTER U. GENERAL STOCK OWNERSHIP CORPORATIONS—[REPEALED]

SUBCHAPTER V. TITLE 11 CASES

Sec. 1398.	Rules relating to individuals' title 11 cases
Sec. 1399.	No separate taxable entities for partnerships, corporations, etc.

SUBCHAPTER W. DISTRICT OF COLUMBIA ENTERPRISE ZONE—[STRICKEN]

SUBCHAPTER X. RENEWAL COMMUNITIES—[STRICKEN]

SUBCHAPTER Y. SHORT-TERM REGIONAL BENEFITS—[STRICKEN]

SUBCHAPTER Z. OPPORTUNITY ZONES

Sec. 1400Z-1.	Designation
Sec. 1400Z-2.	Special rules for capital gains invested in opportunity zones

Chapter 2—Tax on Self-Employment Income

Sec. 1401.	Rate of tax
Sec. 1402.	Definitions
Sec. 1403.	Miscellaneous provisions

Chapter 2A—Unearned Income Medicare Contribution

Sec. 1411.	Imposition of tax

Chapter 3—Withholding of Tax on Nonresident Aliens and Foreign Corporations

SUBCHAPTER A. NONRESIDENT ALIENS AND FOREIGN CORPORATIONS

Sec. 1441.	Withholding of tax on nonresident aliens
Sec. 1442.	Withholding of tax on foreign corporations
Sec. 1443.	Foreign tax-exempt organizations
Sec. 1444.	Withholding on Virgin Islands source income
Sec. 1445.	Withholding of tax on dispositions of United States real property interests
Sec. 1446.	Withholding tax on foreign partners' share of effectively connected income

SUBCHAPTER B. APPLICATION OF WITHHOLDING PROVISIONS

Sec. 1461.	Liability for withheld tax
Sec. 1462.	Withheld tax as credit to recipient of income
Sec. 1463.	Tax paid by recipient of income
Sec. 1464.	Refunds and credits with respect to withheld tax

Chapter 4—Taxes To Enforce Reporting on Certain Foreign Accounts

Sec. 1471.	Withholdable payments to foreign financial institutions
Sec. 1472.	Withholdable payments to other foreign entities
Sec. 1473.	Definitions
Sec. 1474.	Special rules

Chapter 4—Rules Applicable to Recovery of Excessive Profits on Government Contracts—[Repealed]

Chapter 5—Tax on Transfers to Avoid Income Tax—[Repealed]

Chapter 6—Consolidated Returns

SUBCHAPTER A. RETURNS AND PAYMENT OF TAX

Sec. 1501.	Privilege to file consolidated returns
Sec. 1502.	Regulations
Sec. 1503.	Computation and payment of tax
Sec. 1504.	Definitions
Sec. 1505.	Cross references

Internal Revenue Code

CODE—TABLE OF CONTENTS

SUBCHAPTER B. RELATED RULES

PART I—IN GENERAL

Sec. 1552.	Earnings and profits

PART II—CERTAIN CONTROLLED CORPORATIONS

Sec. 1561.	Limitation on accumulated earnings credit in the case of certain controlled corporations
Sec. 1563.	Definitions and special rules

SUBTITLE B—ESTATE AND GIFT TAXES

Chapter 11—Estate Tax

SUBCHAPTER A. ESTATES OF CITIZENS OR RESIDENTS

PART I—TAX IMPOSED

Sec. 2001.	Imposition and rate of tax
Sec. 2002.	Liability for payment

PART II—CREDITS AGAINST TAX

Sec. 2010.	Unified credit against estate tax
Sec. 2012.	Credit for gift tax
Sec. 2013.	Credit for tax on prior transfers
Sec. 2014.	Credit for foreign death taxes
Sec. 2015.	Credit for death taxes on remainders
Sec. 2016.	Recovery of taxes claimed as credit

PART III—GROSS ESTATE

Sec. 2031.	Definition of gross estate
Sec. 2032.	Alternate valuation
Sec. 2032A.	Valuation of certain farm, etc., real property
Sec. 2033.	Property in which the decedent had an interest
Sec. 2034.	Dower or curtesy interests
Sec. 2035.	Adjustments for certain gifts made within 3 years of decedent's death
Sec. 2036.	Transfers with retained life estate
Sec. 2037.	Transfers taking effect at death
Sec. 2038.	Revocable transfers
Sec. 2039.	Annuities
Sec. 2040.	Joint interests
Sec. 2041.	Powers of appointment
Sec. 2042.	Proceeds of life insurance
Sec. 2043.	Transfers for insufficient consideration
Sec. 2044.	Certain property for which marital deduction was previously allowed
Sec. 2045.	Prior interests
Sec. 2046.	Disclaimers

PART IV—TAXABLE ESTATE

Sec. 2051.	Definition of taxable estate
Sec. 2053.	Expenses, indebtedness, and taxes
Sec. 2054.	Losses
Sec. 2055.	Transfers for public, charitable, and religious uses
Sec. 2056.	Bequests, etc., to surviving spouse
Sec. 2056A.	Qualified domestic trust
Sec. 2058.	State death taxes

SUBCHAPTER B. ESTATES OF NONRESIDENTS NOT CITIZENS

Sec. 2101.	Tax imposed
Sec. 2102.	Credits against tax
Sec. 2103.	Definition of gross estate
Sec. 2104.	Property within the United States
Sec. 2105.	Property without the United States
Sec. 2106.	Taxable estate
Sec. 2107.	Expatriation to avoid tax
Sec. 2108.	Application of pre-1967 estate tax provisions

SUBCHAPTER C. MISCELLANEOUS

Sec. 2201.	Combat zone-related deaths of members of the Armed Forces, deaths of astronauts, and deaths of victims of certain terrorist attacks
Sec. 2203.	Definition of executor
Sec. 2204.	Discharge of fiduciary from personal liability
Sec. 2205.	Reimbursement out of estate
Sec. 2206.	Liability of life insurance beneficiaries
Sec. 2207.	Liability of recipient of property over which decedent had power of appointment
Sec. 2207A.	Right of recovery in the case of certain marital deduction property
Sec. 2207B.	Right of recovery where decedent retained interest
Sec. 2208.	Certain residents of possessions considered citizens of the United States
Sec. 2209.	Certain residents of possessions considered nonresidents not citizens of the United States
Sec. 2210.	Termination

Chapter 12—Gift Tax

SUBCHAPTER A. DETERMINATION OF TAX LIABILITY

Sec. 2501.	Imposition of tax
Sec. 2502.	Rate of tax
Sec. 2503.	Taxable gifts
Sec. 2504.	Taxable gifts for preceding calendar periods
Sec. 2505.	Unified credit against gift tax

SUBCHAPTER B. TRANSFERS

Sec. 2511.	Transfers in general
Sec. 2512.	Valuation of gifts
Sec. 2513.	Gift by husband or wife to third party
Sec. 2514.	Powers of appointment
Sec. 2515.	Treatment of generation-skipping transfer tax
Sec. 2516.	Certain property settlements
Sec. 2518.	Disclaimers
Sec. 2519.	Dispositions of certain life estates

SUBCHAPTER C. DEDUCTIONS

Sec. 2522.	Charitable and similar gifts
Sec. 2523.	Gift to spouse
Sec. 2524.	Extent of deductions

Chapter 13—Tax on Generation-Skipping Transfers

SUBCHAPTER A. TAX IMPOSED

Sec. 2601.	Tax imposed
Sec. 2602.	Amount of tax
Sec. 2603.	Liability for tax

SUBCHAPTER B. GENERATION-SKIPPING TRANSFERS

Sec. 2611.	Generation-skipping transfer defined
Sec. 2612.	Taxable termination; taxable distribution; direct skip
Sec. 2613.	Skip person and non-skip person defined

SUBCHAPTER C. TAXABLE AMOUNT

Sec. 2621.	Taxable amount in case of taxable distribution
Sec. 2622.	Taxable amount in case of taxable termination
Sec. 2623.	Taxable amount in case of direct skip
Sec. 2624.	Valuation

SUBCHAPTER D. GST EXEMPTION

Sec. 2631.	GST exemption
Sec. 2632.	Special rules for allocation of GST exemption

SUBCHAPTER E. APPLICABLE RATE; INCLUSION RATIO

Sec. 2641.	Applicable rate
Sec. 2642.	Inclusion ratio

SUBCHAPTER F. OTHER DEFINITIONS AND SPECIAL RULES

Sec. 2651.	Generation assignment
Sec. 2652.	Other definitions
Sec. 2653.	Taxation of multiple skips
Sec. 2654.	Special rules

SUBCHAPTER G. ADMINISTRATION

Sec. 2661.	Administration
Sec. 2662.	Return requirements
Sec. 2663.	Regulations
Sec. 2664.	Termination

Chapter 14—Special Valuation Rules

Sec. 2701.	Special valuation rules in case of transfers of certain interests in corporations or partnerships
Sec. 2702.	Special valuation rules in case of transfers of interests in trusts
Sec. 2703.	Certain rights and restrictions disregarded
Sec. 2704.	Treatment of certain lapsing rights and restrictions

Chapter 15—Gifts and Bequests From Expatriates

Sec. 2801.	Imposition of tax

SUBTITLE C—EMPLOYMENT TAXES

Chapter 21—Federal Insurance Contributions Act

SUBCHAPTER A. TAX ON EMPLOYEES

Sec. 3101.	Rate of tax
Sec. 3102.	Deduction of tax from wages

SUBCHAPTER B. TAX ON EMPLOYERS

Sec. 3111.	Rate of tax

Sec. 3112. Instrumentalities of the United States

SUBCHAPTER C. GENERAL PROVISIONS

Sec. 3121. Definitions
Sec. 3122. Federal service
Sec. 3123. Deductions as constructive payments
Sec. 3124. Estimate of revenue reduction
Sec. 3125. Returns in the case of governmental employees in States, Guam, American Samoa, and the District of Columbia
Sec. 3126. Return and payment by governmental employer
Sec. 3127. Exemption for employers and their employees where both are members of religious faiths opposed to participation in social security act programs
Sec. 3128. Short title

SUBCHAPTER D. CREDITS

Sec. 3131. Credit for paid sick leave
Sec. 3132. Payroll credit for paid family leave
Sec. 3133. Special rule related to tax on employers
Sec. 3134. Employee retention credit for employers subject to closure due to COVID-19

Chapter 22—Railroad Retirement Tax Act

SUBCHAPTER A. TAX ON EMPLOYEES

Sec. 3201. Rate of tax
Sec. 3202. Deduction of tax from compensation

SUBCHAPTER B. TAX ON EMPLOYEE REPRESENTATIVES

Sec. 3211. Rate of tax
Sec. 3212. Determination of compensation

SUBCHAPTER C. TAX ON EMPLOYERS

Sec. 3221. Rate of tax

SUBCHAPTER D. GENERAL PROVISIONS

Sec. 3231. Definitions
Sec. 3232. Court jurisdiction
Sec. 3233. Short title

SUBCHAPTER E. TIER 2 TAX RATE DETERMINATION

Sec. 3241. Determination of tier 2 tax rate based on average account benefits ratio

Chapter 23—Federal Unemployment Tax Act

Sec. 3301. Rate of tax
Sec. 3302. Credits against tax
Sec. 3303. Conditions of additional credit allowance
Sec. 3304. Approval of State laws
Sec. 3305. Applicability of State law
Sec. 3306. Definitions
Sec. 3307. Deductions as constructive payments
Sec. 3308. Instrumentalities of the United States
Sec. 3309. State law coverage of services performed for nonprofit organizations or governmental entities
Sec. 3310. Judicial review
Sec. 3311. Short title

Chapter 23A—Railroad Unemployment Repayment Tax

Sec. 3321. Imposition of tax
Sec. 3322. Definitions

Chapter 24—Collection of Income Tax at Source on Wages

SUBCHAPTER A. WITHHOLDING FROM WAGES

Sec. 3401. Definitions
Sec. 3402. Income tax collected at source
Sec. 3403. Liability for tax
Sec. 3404. Return and payment by governmental employer
Sec. 3405. Special rules for pensions, annuities, and certain other deferred income
Sec. 3406. Backup withholding

SUBCHAPTER B. WITHHOLDING FROM INTEREST AND DIVIDENDS—[REPEALED]

Chapter 25—General Provisions Relating to Employment Taxes

Sec. 3501. Collection and payment of taxes
Sec. 3502. Nondeductibility of taxes in computing taxable income
Sec. 3503. Erroneous payments
Sec. 3504. Acts to be performed by agents
Sec. 3505. Liability of third parties paying or providing for wages
Sec. 3506. Individuals providing companion sitting placement services
Sec. 3508. Treatment of real estate agents and direct sellers
Sec. 3509. Determination of employer's liability for certain employment taxes
Sec. 3510. Coordination of collection of domestic service employment taxes with collection of income taxes
Sec. 3511. Certified professional employer organizations

CODE—TABLE OF CONTENTS

Sec. 3512.   Treatment of certain persons as employers with respect to motion picture projects

SUBTITLE D—MISCELLANEOUS EXCISE TAXES

Chapter 31—Retail Excise Taxes

SUBCHAPTER A—LUXURY PASSENGER AUTOMOBILES—[Stricken]

SUBCHAPTER B—SPECIAL FUELS

Sec. 4041.	Imposition of tax
Sec. 4042.	Tax on fuel used in commercial transportation on inland waterways
Sec. 4043.	Surtax on fuel used in aircraft part of a fractional ownership program

SUBCHAPTER C—HEAVY TRUCKS AND TRAILERS

Sec. 4051.	Imposition of tax on heavy trucks and trailers sold at retail
Sec. 4052.	Definitions and special rules
Sec. 4053.	Exemptions

Chapter 32—Manufacturers Excise Taxes

SUBCHAPTER A. AUTOMOTIVE AND RELATED ITEMS

PART I—GAS GUZZLERS

Sec. 4064.	Gas guzzler[s] tax

PART II—TIRES

Sec. 4071.	Imposition of tax
Sec. 4072.	Definitions
Sec. 4073.	Exemptions

PART III—PETROLEUM PRODUCTS

Subpart A—Motor and Aviation Fuels

Sec. 4081.	Imposition of tax
Sec. 4082.	Exemptions for diesel fuel and kerosene
Sec. 4083.	Definitions; special rule; administrative authority
Sec. 4084.	Cross references

Subpart B— Special Provisions Applicable to Fuels Tax

Sec. 4101.	Registration and bond
Sec. 4102.	Inspection of records by local officers
Sec. 4103.	Certain additional persons liable for tax where willful failure to pay
Sec. 4104.	Information reporting for persons claiming certain tax benefits
Sec. 4105.	Two-party exchanges

SUBCHAPTER B. COAL

Sec. 4121.	Imposition of tax

SUBCHAPTER C. CERTAIN VACCINES

Sec. 4131.	Imposition of tax
Sec. 4132.	Definitions and special rules

SUBCHAPTER D. RECREATIONAL EQUIPMENT

PART I—SPORTING GOODS

Sec. 4161.	Imposition of tax
Sec. 4162.	Definitions; treatment of certain resales

PART II—PHOTOGRAPHIC EQUIPMENT—[REPEALED]

PART III—FIREARMS

Sec. 4181.	Imposition of tax
Sec. 4182.	Exemptions

SUBCHAPTER E. MEDICAL DEVICES—[STRICKEN]

SUBCHAPTER E. OTHER ITEMS—[REPEALED]

SUBCHAPTER F. SPECIAL PROVISIONS APPLICABLE TO MANUFACTURERS TAX

Sec. 4216.	Definition of price
Sec. 4217.	Leases
Sec. 4218.	Use by manufacturer or importer considered sale
Sec. 4219.	Application of tax in case of sales by other than manufacturer or importer

SUBCHAPTER G. EXEMPTIONS, REGISTRATION, ETC.

Sec. 4221.	Certain tax-free sales
Sec. 4222.	Registration
Sec. 4223.	Special rules relating to further manufacture
Sec. 4225.	Exemption of articles manufactured or produced by Indians
Sec. 4227.	Cross references

Internal Revenue Code

CODE—TABLE OF CONTENTS

Chapter 33—Facilities and Services

SUBCHAPTER A. ADMISSIONS AND DUES—[REPEALED]

SUBCHAPTER B. COMMUNICATIONS

Sec. 4251.	Imposition of tax
Sec. 4252.	Definitions
Sec. 4253.	Exemptions
Sec. 4254.	Computation of tax

SUBCHAPTER C. TRANSPORTATION BY AIR

PART I—PERSONS

Sec. 4261.	Imposition of tax
Sec. 4262.	Definition of taxable transportation
Sec. 4263.	Special rules

PART II—PROPERTY

Sec. 4271.	Imposition of tax
Sec. 4272.	Definition of taxable transportation, etc.

PART III—SPECIAL PROVISIONS APPLICABLE TO TAXES ON TRANSPORTATION BY AIR

Sec. 4281.	Small aircraft on nonestablished lines
Sec. 4282.	Transportation by air for other members of affiliated group

SUBCHAPTER D. SAFE DEPOSIT BOXES—[REPEALED]

SUBCHAPTER E. SPECIAL PROVISIONS APPLICABLE TO SERVICES AND FACILITIES TAXES

Sec. 4291.	Cases where persons receiving payment must collect tax
Sec. 4293.	Exemption for United States and possessions

Chapter 34—Taxes on certain insurance policies

SUBCHAPTER A. POLICIES ISSUED BY FOREIGN INSURERS

Sec. 4371.	Imposition of tax
Sec. 4372.	Definitions
Sec. 4373.	Exemptions
Sec. 4374.	Liability for tax

SUBCHAPTER B. INSURED AND SELF-INSURED HEALTH PLANS

Sec. 4375.	Health insurance
Sec. 4376.	Self-insured health plans
Sec. 4377.	Definitions and special rules

Chapter 35—Taxes on Wagering

SUBCHAPTER A. TAX ON WAGERS

Sec. 4401.	Imposition of tax
Sec. 4402.	Exemptions
Sec. 4403.	Record requirements
Sec. 4404.	Territorial extent
Sec. 4405.	Cross references

SUBCHAPTER B. OCCUPATIONAL TAX

Sec. 4411.	Imposition of tax
Sec. 4412.	Registration
Sec. 4413.	Certain provisions made applicable
Sec. 4414.	Cross references

SUBCHAPTER C. MISCELLANEOUS PROVISIONS

Sec. 4421.	Definitions
Sec. 4422.	Applicability of federal and state laws
Sec. 4423.	Inspection of books
Sec. 4424.	Disclosure of wagering tax information

Chapter 36—Certain Other Excise Taxes

SUBCHAPTER A. HARBOR MAINTENANCE TAX

Sec. 4461.	Imposition of tax
Sec. 4462.	Definitions and special rules

SUBCHAPTER B. TRANSPORTATION BY WATER

Sec. 4471.	Imposition of tax
Sec. 4472.	Definitions

SUBCHAPTER C. OCCUPATIONAL TAX ON BOWLING ALLEYS, BILLIARD AND POOL TABLES—[REPEALED]

SUBCHAPTER D. TAX ON USE OF CERTAIN VEHICLES

Sec. 4481.	Imposition of tax
Sec. 4482.	Definitions
Sec. 4483.	Exemptions
Sec. 4484.	Cross references

CODE—TABLE OF CONTENTS

SUBCHAPTER E. TAX ON USE OF CIVIL AIRCRAFT—[REPEALED]
SUBCHAPTER F. TAX ON REMOVAL OF HARD MINERAL RESOURCES FROM DEEP SEABED—[REPEALED]

Chapter 37—Repurchase of Corporate Stock

Sec. 4501.	Repurchase of corporate stock

Chapter 37—Sugar—[Repealed]

Chapter 38—Environmental Taxes

SUBCHAPTER A. TAX ON PETROLEUM

Sec. 4611.	Imposition of tax
Sec. 4612.	Definitions and special rules

SUBCHAPTER B. TAX ON CERTAIN CHEMICALS

Sec. 4661.	Imposition of tax
Sec. 4662.	Definitions and special rules

SUBCHAPTER C. TAX ON CERTAIN IMPORTED SUBSTANCES

Sec. 4671.	Imposition of tax
Sec. 4672.	Definitions and special rules

SUBCHAPTER D. OZONE DEPLETING CHEMICALS, ETC.

Sec. 4681.	Imposition of tax
Sec. 4682.	Definitions and special rules

Chapter 39—Registration-Required Obligations

Sec. 4701.	Tax on issuer of registration-required obligation not in registered form

Chapter 40—General Provisions Relating to Occupational Taxes

Sec. 4901.	Payment of tax
Sec. 4902.	Liability of partners
Sec. 4903.	Liability in case of business in more than one location
Sec. 4904.	Liability in case of different businesses of same ownership and location
Sec. 4905.	Liability in case of death or change of location
Sec. 4906.	Application of state laws
Sec. 4907.	Federal agencies or instrumentalities

Chapter 41—Public Charities

Sec. 4911.	Tax on excess expenditures to influence legislation
Sec. 4912.	Tax on disqualifying lobbying expenditures of certain organizations

Chapter 42—Private Foundations and Certain Other Tax-Exempt Organizations

SUBCHAPTER A. PRIVATE FOUNDATIONS

Sec. 4940.	Excise tax based on investment income
Sec. 4941.	Taxes on self-dealing
Sec. 4942.	Taxes on failure to distribute income
Sec. 4943.	Taxes on excess business holdings
Sec. 4944.	Taxes on investments which jeopardize charitable purpose
Sec. 4945.	Taxes on taxable expenditures
Sec. 4946.	Definitions and special rules
Sec. 4947.	Application of taxes to certain nonexempt trusts
Sec. 4948.	Application of taxes and denial of exemption with respect to certain foreign organizations

SUBCHAPTER B. BLACK LUNG BENEFIT TRUSTS

Sec. 4951.	Taxes on self-dealing
Sec. 4952.	Taxes on taxable expenditures
Sec. 4953.	Tax on excess contributions to black lung benefit trusts

SUBCHAPTER C. POLITICAL EXPENDITURES OF SECTION 501(c)(3) ORGANIZATIONS

Sec. 4955.	Taxes on political expenditures of section 501(c)(3) organizations

SUBCHAPTER D. FAILURE BY CERTAIN CHARITABLE ORGANIZATIONS TO MEET CERTAIN QUALIFICATION REQUIREMENTS

Sec. 4958.	Taxes on excess benefit transactions
Sec. 4959.	Taxes on failures by hospital organizations
Sec. 4960.	Tax on excess tax-exempt organization executive compensation

SUBCHAPTER E. ABATEMENT OF FIRST AND SECOND TIER TAXES IN CERTAIN CASES

Sec. 4961.	Abatement of second tier taxes where there is correction
Sec. 4962.	Abatement of first tier taxes in certain cases
Sec. 4963.	Definitions

SUBCHAPTER F. TAX SHELTER TRANSACTIONS

Sec. 4965.	Excise tax on certain tax-exempt entities entering into prohibited tax shelter transactions

SUBCHAPTER G. DONOR ADVISED FUNDS

Sec. 4966.	Taxes on taxable distributions
Sec. 4967.	Taxes on prohibited benefits

SUBCHAPTER H. EXCISE TAX BASED ON INVESTMENT INCOME OF PRIVATE COLLEGES AND UNIVERSITIES

Sec. 4968.	Excise tax based on investment income of private colleges and universities

Internal Revenue Code

CODE—TABLE OF CONTENTS

Chapter 43—Qualified Pension, Etc., Plans

Sec. 4971.	Taxes on failure to meet minimum funding standards
Sec. 4972.	Tax on nondeductible contributions to qualified employer plans
Sec. 4973.	Tax on excess contributions to certain tax-favored accounts and annuities
Sec. 4974.	Excise tax on certain accumulations in qualified retirement plans
Sec. 4975.	Tax on prohibited transactions
Sec. 4976.	Taxes with respect to funded welfare benefit plans
Sec. 4977.	Tax on certain fringe benefits provided by an employer
Sec. 4978.	Tax on certain dispositions by employee stock ownership plans and certain cooperatives
Sec. 4979.	Tax on certain excess contributions
Sec. 4979A.	Tax on certain prohibited allocations of qualified securities
Sec. 4980.	Tax on reversion of qualified plan assets to employer
Sec. 4980B.	Failure to satisfy continuation coverage requirements of group health plans
Sec. 4980C.	Requirements for issuers of qualified long-term care insurance contracts
Sec. 4980D.	Failure to meet certain group health plan requirements
Sec. 4980E.	Failure of employer to make comparable Archer MSA contributions
Sec. 4980F.	Failure of applicable plans reducing benefit accruals to satisfy notice requirements
Sec. 4980G.	Failure of employer to make comparable health savings account contributions
Sec. 4980H.	Shared responsibility for employers regarding health coverage

Chapter 44—Qualified Investment Entities

Sec. 4981.	Excise tax on undistributed income of real estate investment trusts
Sec. 4982.	Excise tax on undistributed income of regulated investment companies

Chapter 45—Provisions Relating to Expatriated Entities

Sec. 4985.	Stock compensation of insiders in expatriated corporations

Chapter 46—Golden Parachute Payments

Sec. 4999.	Golden parachute payments

Chapter 47—Certain Group Health Plans

Sec. 5000.	Certain group health plans

Chapter 48—Maintenance of Minimum Essential Coverage

Sec. 5000A.	Requirement to maintain minimum essential coverage

Chapter 49—Cosmetic Services

Sec. 5000B.	Imposition of tax on indoor tanning services

Chapter 50—Foreign Procurement

Sec. 5000C.	Imposition of tax on certain foreign procurement

Chapter 50A—Designated Drugs

Sec. 5000D.	Designated drugs during noncompliance periods

SUBTITLE E—ALCOHOL, TOBACCO, AND CERTAIN OTHER EXCISE TAXES

Chapter 51—Distilled Spirits, Wines, and Beer

SUBCHAPTER A. GALLONAGE AND OCCUPATIONAL TAXES

Part I—Gallonage Taxes

Subpart A—Distilled Spirits

Sec. 5001.	Imposition, rate, and attachment of tax
Sec. 5002.	Definitions
Sec. 5003.	Cross references to exemptions, etc.
Sec. 5004.	Lien for tax
Sec. 5005.	Persons liable for tax
Sec. 5006.	Determination of tax
Sec. 5007.	Collection of tax on distilled spirits
Sec. 5008.	Abatement, remission, refund, and allowance for loss or destruction of distilled spirits
Sec. 5010.	Credit for wine content and for flavors content
Sec. 5011.	Income tax credit for average cost of carrying excise tax

Subpart B—Rectification—[Repealed]

Subpart C—Wines

Sec. 5041.	Imposition and rate of tax
Sec. 5042.	Exemption from tax
Sec. 5043.	Collection of taxes on wines
Sec. 5044.	Refund of tax on wine
Sec. 5045.	Cross references

Subpart D—Beer

Sec. 5051.	Imposition and rate of tax
Sec. 5052.	Definitions
Sec. 5053.	Exemptions
Sec. 5054.	Determination and collection of tax on beer
Sec. 5055.	Drawback of tax

CODE—TABLE OF CONTENTS

Sec. 5056. Refund and credit of tax, or relief from liability

Subpart E—General Provisions

Sec. 5061. Method of collecting tax
Sec. 5062. Refund and drawback in case of exportation
Sec. 5064. Losses resulting from disaster, vandalism, or malicious mischief
Sec. 5065. Territorial extent of law
Sec. 5066. Distilled spirits for use of foreign embassies, legations, etc.
Sec. 5067. Reduced rates not allowed for smuggled or illegally produced beer, wine, or spirits
Sec. 5068. Cross reference

PART II—MISCELLANEOUS PROVISIONS

Subpart A—Manufacturers of Stills

Sec. 5101. Notice of manufacture of still; notice of set up of still
Sec. 5102. Definition of manufacturer of stills

Subpart B—Nonbeverage Domestic Drawback Claimants

Sec. 5111. Eligibility
Sec. 5112. Registration and regulation
Sec. 5113. Investigation of claims
Sec. 5114. Drawback

Subpart C—Recordkeeping and Registration by Dealers

Sec. 5121. Recordkeeping by wholesale dealers
Sec. 5122. Recordkeeping by retail dealers
Sec. 5123. Preservation and inspection of records, and entry of premises for inspection
Sec. 5124. Registration by dealers

Subpart D—Other Provisions

Sec. 5131. Packaging distilled spirits for industrial uses
Sec. 5132. Prohibited purchases by dealers

SUBCHAPTER B. QUALIFICATION REQUIREMENTS FOR DISTILLED SPIRITS PLANTS

Sec. 5171. Establishment
Sec. 5172. Application
Sec. 5173. Bonds
Sec. 5175. Export bonds
Sec. 5176. New or renewed bonds
Sec. 5177. Other provisions relating to bonds
Sec. 5178. Premises of distilled spirits plants
Sec. 5179. Registration of stills
Sec. 5180. Signs
Sec. 5181. Distilled spirits for fuel use
Sec. 5182. Cross references

SUBCHAPTER C. OPERATION OF DISTILLED SPIRITS PLANTS

PART I—GENERAL PROVISIONS

Sec. 5201. Regulation of operations
Sec. 5202. Supervision of operations
Sec. 5203. Entry and examination of premises
Sec. 5204. Gauging
Sec. 5206. Containers
Sec. 5207. Records and reports

PART II—OPERATIONS ON BONDED PREMISES

Subpart A—General

Sec. 5211. Production and entry of distilled spirits
Sec. 5212. Transfer of distilled spirits between bonded premises
Sec. 5213. Withdrawal of distilled spirits from bonded premises on determination of tax
Sec. 5214. Withdrawal of distilled spirits from bonded premises free of tax or without payment of tax
Sec. 5215. Return of tax determined distilled spirits to bonded premises
Sec. 5216. Regulation of operations

Subpart B—Production

Sec. 5221. Commencement, suspension, and resumption of operations
Sec. 5222. Production, receipt, removal, and use of distilling materials
Sec. 5223. Redistillation of spirits, articles, and residues

Subpart C—Storage

Sec. 5231. Entry for deposit
Sec. 5232. Imported distilled spirits
Sec. 5235. Bottling of alcohol for industrial purposes
Sec. 5236. Discontinuance of storage facilities and transfer of distilled spirits

Subpart D—Denaturation

Sec. 5241. Authority to denature
Sec. 5242. Denaturing materials
Sec. 5243. Sale of abandoned spirits for denaturation without collection of tax

Internal Revenue Code

| Sec. 5244. | Cross references |

PART III—OPERATIONS ON BOTTLING PREMISES—[REPEALED]

SUBCHAPTER D. INDUSTRIAL USE OF DISTILLED SPIRITS

Sec. 5271.	Permits
Sec. 5272.	Bonds
Sec. 5273.	Sale, use, and recovery of denatured distilled spirits
Sec. 5274.	Applicability of other laws
Sec. 5275.	Records and reports

SUBCHAPTER E. GENERAL PROVISIONS RELATING TO DISTILLED SPIRITS

PART I—RETURN OF MATERIALS USED IN THE MANUFACTURE OR RECOVERY OF DISTILLED SPIRITS

| Sec. 5291. | General |

PART II—REGULATION OF TRAFFIC IN CONTAINERS OF DISTILLED SPIRITS

| Sec. 5301. | General |

PART III—MISCELLANEOUS PROVISIONS

Sec. 5311.	Detention of containers
Sec. 5312.	Production and use of distilled spirits for experimental research
Sec. 5313.	Withdrawal of distilled spirits from customs custody free of tax for use of the United States
Sec. 5314.	Special applicability of certain provisions

SUBCHAPTER F. BONDED AND TAXPAID WINE PREMISES

PART I—ESTABLISHMENT

Sec. 5351.	Bonded wine cellar
Sec. 5352.	Taxpaid wine bottling house
Sec. 5353.	Bonded wine warehouse
Sec. 5354.	Bond
Sec. 5355.	General provisions relating to bonds
Sec. 5356.	Application
Sec. 5357.	Premises

PART II—OPERATIONS

Sec. 5361.	Bonded wine cellar operations
Sec. 5362.	Removals of wine from bonded wine cellars
Sec. 5363.	Taxpaid wine bottling house operations
Sec. 5364.	Wine imported in bulk
Sec. 5365.	Segregation of operations
Sec. 5366.	Supervision
Sec. 5367.	Records
Sec. 5368.	Gauging and marking
Sec. 5369.	Inventories
Sec. 5370.	Losses
Sec. 5371.	Insurance coverage, etc.
Sec. 5372.	Sampling
Sec. 5373.	Wine spirits

PART III—CELLAR TREATMENT AND CLASSIFICATION OF WINE

Sec. 5381.	Natural wine
Sec. 5382.	Cellar treatment of natural wine
Sec. 5383.	Amelioration and sweetening limitations for natural grape wines
Sec. 5384.	Amelioration and sweetening limitations for natural fruit and berry wines
Sec. 5385.	Specially sweetened natural wines
Sec. 5386.	Special natural wines
Sec. 5387.	Agricultural wines
Sec. 5388.	Designation of wines

PART IV—GENERAL

| Sec. 5391. | Exemption from distilled spirits taxes |
| Sec. 5392. | Definitions |

SUBCHAPTER G. BREWERIES

PART I—ESTABLISHMENT

Sec. 5401.	Qualifying documents
Sec. 5402.	Definitions
Sec. 5403.	Cross references

PART II—OPERATIONS

Sec. 5411.	Use of brewery
Sec. 5412.	Removal of beer in containers or by pipeline
Sec. 5413.	Brewers procuring beer from other brewers
Sec. 5414.	Removals from one brewery to another belonging to the same brewer
Sec. 5415.	Records and returns
Sec. 5416.	Definitions of package and packaging
Sec. 5417.	Pilot brewing plants
Sec. 5418.	Beer imported in bulk

CODE—TABLE OF CONTENTS

SUBCHAPTER H. MISCELLANEOUS PLANTS AND WAREHOUSES

PART I—VINEGAR PLANTS

Sec. 5501.	Establishment
Sec. 5502.	Qualification
Sec. 5503.	Construction and equipment
Sec. 5504.	Operation
Sec. 5505.	Applicability of provisions of this chapter

PART II—VOLATILE FRUIT-FLAVOR CONCENTRATE PLANTS

Sec. 5511.	Establishment and operation
Sec. 5512.	Control of products after manufacture

PART III—MANUFACTURING BONDED WAREHOUSES—[REPEALED]

SUBCHAPTER I. MISCELLANEOUS GENERAL PROVISIONS

Sec. 5551.	General provisions relating to bonds
Sec. 5552.	Installation of meters, tanks, and other apparatus
Sec. 5553.	Supervision of premises and operations
Sec. 5554.	Pilot operations
Sec. 5555.	Records, statements, and returns
Sec. 5556.	Regulations
Sec. 5557.	Officers and agents authorized to investigate, issue search warrants, and prosecute for violations
Sec. 5558.	Authority of enforcement officers
Sec. 5559.	Determinations
Sec. 5560.	Other provisions applicable
Sec. 5561.	Exemptions to meet the requirements of the national defense
Sec. 5562.	Exemptions from certain requirements in cases of disaster

SUBCHAPTER J. PENALTIES, SEIZURES, AND FORFEITURES RELATING TO LIQUORS

PART I—PENALTY, SEIZURE, AND FORFEITURE PROVISIONS APPLICABLE TO DISTILLING, RECTIFYING, AND DISTILLED AND RECTIFIED PRODUCTS

Sec. 5601.	Criminal penalties
Sec. 5602.	Penalty for tax fraud by distiller
Sec. 5603.	Penalty relating to records, returns, and reports
Sec. 5604.	Penalties relating to marks, brands, and containers
Sec. 5605.	Penalty relating to return of materials used in the manufacture of distilled spirits, or from which distilled spirits may be recovered
Sec. 5606.	Penalty relating to containers of distilled spirits
Sec. 5607.	Penalty and forfeiture for unlawful use, recovery, or concealment of denatured distilled spirits, or articles
Sec. 5608.	Penalty and forfeiture for fraudulent claims for export drawback or unlawful relanding
Sec. 5609.	Destruction of unregistered stills, distilling apparatus, equipment, and materials
Sec. 5610.	Disposal of forfeited equipment and material for distilling
Sec. 5611.	Release of distillery before judgment
Sec. 5612.	Forfeiture of taxpaid distilled spirits remaining on bonded premises
Sec. 5613.	Forfeiture of distilled spirits not closed, marked, or branded as required by law
Sec. 5614.	Burden of proof in cases of seizure of spirits
Sec. 5615.	Property subject to forfeiture

PART II—PENALTY AND FORFEITURE PROVISIONS APPLICABLE TO WINE AND WINE PRODUCTION

Sec. 5661.	Penalty and forfeiture for violation of laws and regulations relating to wine
Sec. 5662.	Penalty for alteration of wine labels
Sec. 5663.	Cross reference

PART III—PENALTY, SEIZURE, AND FORFEITURE PROVISIONS APPLICABLE TO BEER AND BREWING

Sec. 5671.	Penalty and forfeiture for evasion of beer tax and fraudulent noncompliance with requirements
Sec. 5672.	Penalty for failure of brewer to comply with requirements and to keep records and file returns
Sec. 5673.	Forfeiture for flagrant and willful removal of beer without tax payment
Sec. 5674.	Penalty for unlawful production or removal of beer
Sec. 5675.	Penalty for intentional removal or defacement of brewer's marks and brands

PART IV—PENALTY, SEIZURE, AND FORFEITURE PROVISIONS COMMON TO LIQUORS

Sec. 5681.	Penalty relating to signs
Sec. 5682.	Penalty for breaking locks or gaining access
Sec. 5683.	Penalty and forfeiture for removal of liquors under improper brands
Sec. 5684.	Penalties relating to the payment and collection of liquor taxes
Sec. 5685.	Penalty and forfeiture relating to possession of devices for emitting gas, smoke, etc., explosives and firearms, when violating liquor laws
Sec. 5686.	Penalty for having, possessing, or using liquor or property intended to be used in violating provisions of this chapter
Sec. 5687.	Penalty for offenses not specifically covered
Sec. 5688.	Disposition and release of seized property
Sec. 5690.	Definition of the term "person"

PART V—PENALTIES APPLICABLE TO OCCUPATIONAL TAXES—[REPEALED]

Chapter 52—Tobacco Products and Cigarette Papers and Tubes

SUBCHAPTER A. DEFINITIONS; RATE AND PAYMENT OF TAX; EXEMPTION FROM TAX; AND REFUND AND DRAWBACK OF TAX

Sec. 5701.	Rate of tax
Sec. 5702.	Definitions

Sec. 5703.	Liability for tax and method of payment
Sec. 5704.	Exemption from tax
Sec. 5705.	Credit, refund, or allowance of tax
Sec. 5706.	Drawback of tax
Sec. 5708.	Losses caused by disaster

SUBCHAPTER B. QUALIFICATION REQUIREMENTS FOR MANUFACTURERS AND IMPORTERS OF TOBACCO PRODUCTS AND CIGARETTE PAPERS AND TUBES, AND EXPORT WAREHOUSE PROPRIETORS

Sec. 5711.	Bond
Sec. 5712.	Application for permit
Sec. 5713.	Permit

SUBCHAPTER C. OPERATIONS BY MANUFACTURERS AND IMPORTERS OF TOBACCO PRODUCTS AND CIGARETTE PAPERS AND TUBES AND EXPORT WAREHOUSE PROPRIETORS

Sec. 5721.	Inventories
Sec. 5722.	Reports
Sec. 5723.	Packages, marks, labels, and notices

SUBCHAPTER D. OCCUPATIONAL TAX

Sec. 5731.	Imposition and rate of tax
Sec. 5732.	Payment of tax
Sec. 5733.	Provisions relating to liability for occupational taxes
Sec. 5734.	Application of State laws

SUBCHAPTER E. RECORDS OF MANUFACTURERS AND IMPORTERS OF TOBACCO PRODUCTS AND CIGARETTE PAPERS AND TUBES, AND EXPORT WAREHOUSE PROPRIETORS

| Sec. 5741. | Records to be maintained |

SUBCHAPTER F. GENERAL PROVISIONS

Sec. 5751.	Purchase, receipt, possession, or sale of tobacco products and cigarette papers and tubes, after removal
Sec. 5752.	Restrictions relating to marks, labels, notices, and packages
Sec. 5753.	Disposal of forfeited, condemned, and abandoned tobacco products, and cigarette papers and tubes
Sec. 5754.	Restriction on importation of previously exported tobacco products

SUBCHAPTER G. PENALTIES AND FORFEITURES

Sec. 5761.	Civil penalties
Sec. 5762.	Criminal penalties
Sec. 5763.	Forfeitures

Chapter 53—Machine Guns, Destructive Devices, and Certain Other Firearms

SUBCHAPTER A. TAXES

Part I—Special (Occupational) Taxes

| Sec. 5801. | Imposition of tax |
| Sec. 5802. | Registration of importers, manufacturers, and dealers |

Part II—Tax on Transferring Firearms

| Sec. 5811. | Transfer tax |
| Sec. 5812. | Transfers |

Part III—Tax on Making Firearms

| Sec. 5821. | Making tax |
| Sec. 5822. | Making |

SUBCHAPTER B. GENERAL PROVISIONS AND EXEMPTIONS

Part I—General Provisions

Sec. 5841.	Registration of firearms
Sec. 5842.	Identification of firearms
Sec. 5843.	Records and returns
Sec. 5844.	Importation
Sec. 5845.	Definitions
Sec. 5846.	Other laws applicable
Sec. 5847.	Effect on other laws
Sec. 5848.	Restrictive use of information
Sec. 5849.	Citation of chapter

Part II—Exemptions

Sec. 5851.	Special (occupational) tax exemption
Sec. 5852.	General transfer and making tax exemption
Sec. 5853.	Transfer and making tax exemption available to certain governmental entities
Sec. 5854.	Exportation of firearms exempt from transfer tax

SUBCHAPTER C. PROHIBITED ACTS

| Sec. 5861. | Prohibited acts |

SUBCHAPTER D. PENALTIES AND FORFEITURES

| Sec. 5871. | Penalties |
| Sec. 5872. | Forfeitures |

CODE—TABLE OF CONTENTS

Chapter 54—Greenmail

Sec. 5881.	Greenmail

Chapter 55—Structured Settlement Factoring Transactions

Sec. 5891.	Structured settlement factoring transactions

SUBTITLE F—PROCEDURE AND ADMINISTRATION

Chapter 61—Information and Returns

SUBCHAPTER A. RETURNS AND RECORDS

PART I—RECORDS, STATEMENTS, AND SPECIAL RETURNS

Sec. 6001.	Notice or regulations requiring records, statements, and special returns

PART II—TAX RETURNS OR STATEMENTS

Subpart A—General Requirement

Sec. 6011.	General requirement of return, statement, or list

Subpart B—Income Tax Returns

Sec. 6012.	Persons required to make returns of income
Sec. 6013.	Joint returns of income tax by husband and wife
Sec. 6014.	Income tax return—tax not computed by taxpayer
Sec. 6015.	Relief from joint and several liability on joint return
Sec. 6017.	Self-employment tax returns

Subpart C—Estate and Gift Tax Returns

Sec. 6018.	Estate tax returns
Sec. 6019.	Gift tax returns

Subpart D—Miscellaneous Provisions

Sec. 6020.	Returns prepared for or executed by Secretary
Sec. 6021.	Listing by Secretary of taxable objects owned by nonresidents of internal revenue districts

PART III—INFORMATION RETURNS

Subpart A—Information Concerning Persons Subject to Special Provisions

Sec. 6031.	Return of partnership income
Sec. 6032.	Returns of banks with respect to common trust funds
Sec. 6033.	Returns by exempt organizations
Sec. 6034.	Returns by certain trusts
Sec. 6034A.	Information to beneficiaries of estates and trusts
Sec. 6035.	Basis information to persons acquiring property from decedent
Sec. 6036.	Notice of qualification as executor or receiver
Sec. 6037.	Return of S corporation
Sec. 6038.	Information reporting with respect to certain foreign corporations and partnerships
Sec. 6038A.	Information with respect to certain foreign-owned corporations
Sec. 6038B.	Notice of certain transfers to foreign persons
Sec. 6038C.	Information with respect to foreign corporations engaged in U.S. business
Sec. 6038D.	Information with respect to foreign financial assets
Sec. 6038E.	Information with respect to assignment of lower rates or refunds by foreign producers of beer, wine, and distilled spirits
Sec. 6039.	Returns required in connection with certain options
Sec. 6039C.	Returns with respect to foreign persons holding direct investments in United States real property interests
Sec. 6039D.	Returns and records with respect to certain fringe benefit plans
Sec. 6039E.	Information concerning resident status
Sec. 6039F.	Notice of large gifts received from foreign persons
Sec. 6039G.	Information on individuals losing United States citizenship
Sec. 6039H.	Information with respect to Alaska Native Settlement Trusts and Native Corporations
Sec. 6039I.	Returns and records with respect to employer-owned life insurance contracts
Sec. 6039J.	Information reporting with respect to commodity credit corporation transactions
Sec. 6040.	Cross references

Subpart B—Information Concerning Transactions With Other Persons

Sec. 6041.	Information at source
Sec. 6041A.	Returns regarding payments of remuneration for services and direct sales
Sec. 6042.	Returns regarding payments of dividends and corporate earnings and profits
Sec. 6043.	Liquidating, etc., transactions
Sec. 6043A.	Returns relating to taxable mergers and acquisitions
Sec. 6044.	Returns regarding payments of patronage dividends
Sec. 6045.	Returns of brokers
Sec. 6045A.	Information required in connection with transfers of covered securities to brokers
Sec. 6045B.	Returns relating to actions affecting basis of specified securities
Sec. 6046.	Returns as to organization or reorganization of foreign corporations and as to acquisitions of their stock
Sec. 6046A.	Returns as to interests in foreign partnerships
Sec. 6047.	Information relating to certain trusts and annuity plans
Sec. 6048.	Information with respect to certain foreign trusts
Sec. 6049.	Returns regarding payments of interest
Sec. 6050A.	Reporting requirements of certain fishing boat operators

Internal Revenue Code

Sec. 6050B.	Returns relating to unemployment compensation
Sec. 6050D.	Returns relating to energy grants and financing
Sec. 6050E.	State and local income tax refunds
Sec. 6050F.	Returns relating to social security benefits
Sec. 6050G.	Returns relating to certain railroad retirement benefits
Sec. 6050H.	Returns relating to mortgage interest received in trade or business from individuals
Sec. 6050I.	Returns relating to cash received in trade or business, etc.
Sec. 6050J.	Returns relating to foreclosures and abandonments of security
Sec. 6050K.	Returns relating to exchanges of certain partnership interests
Sec. 6050L.	Returns relating to certain donated property
Sec. 6050M.	Returns relating to persons receiving contracts from Federal executive agencies
Sec. 6050N.	Returns regarding payments of royalties
Sec. 6050P.	Returns relating to the cancellation of indebtedness by certain entities
Sec. 6050Q.	Certain long-term care benefits
Sec. 6050R.	Returns relating to certain purchases of fish
Sec. 6050S.	Returns relating to higher education tuition and related expenses
Sec. 6050T.	Returns relating to credit for health insurance costs of eligible individuals
Sec. 6050U.	Charges or payments for qualified long-term care insurance contracts under combined arrangements
Sec. 6050V.	Returns relating to applicable insurance contracts in which certain exempt organizations hold interests
Sec. 6050W.	Returns relating to payments made in settlement of payment card and third party network transactions
Sec. 6050X.	Information with respect to certain fines, penalties, and other amounts
Sec. 6050Y.	Returns relating to certain life insurance contract transactions
Sec. 6050Z.	Reports relating to long-term care premium statements

Subpart C—Information Regarding Wages Paid Employees

Sec. 6051.	Receipts for employees
Sec. 6052.	Returns regarding payment of wages in the form of group-term life insurance
Sec. 6053.	Reporting of tips

Subpart D—Information Regarding Health Insurance Coverage

Sec. 6055.	Reporting of health insurance coverage
Sec. 6056.	Certain employers required to report on health insurance coverage

Subpart D—Information Concerning Private Foundations—[Repealed]

Subpart E—Registration of and Information Concerning Pension, Etc., Plans

Sec. 6057.	Annual registration, etc.
Sec. 6058.	Information required in connection with certain plans of deferred compensation
Sec. 6059.	Periodic report of actuary

Subpart F—Information Concerning Tax Return Preparers

Sec. 6060.	Information returns of tax return preparers

PART IV—SIGNING AND VERIFYING OF RETURNS AND OTHER DOCUMENTS

Sec. 6061.	Signing of returns and other documents
Sec. 6062.	Signing of corporation returns
Sec. 6063.	Signing of partnership returns
Sec. 6064.	Signature presumed authentic
Sec. 6065.	Verification of returns

PART V—TIME FOR FILING RETURNS AND OTHER DOCUMENTS

Sec. 6071.	Time for filing returns and other documents
Sec. 6072.	Time for filing income tax returns
Sec. 6075.	Time for filing estate and gift tax returns

PART VI—EXTENSION OF TIME FOR FILING RETURNS

Sec. 6081.	Extension of time for filing returns

PART VII—PLACE FOR FILING RETURNS OR OTHER DOCUMENTS

Sec. 6091.	Place for filing returns or other documents

PART VIII—DESIGNATION OF INCOME TAX PAYMENTS TO PRESIDENTIAL ELECTION CAMPAIGN FUND

Sec. 6096.	Designation by individuals

SUBCHAPTER B. MISCELLANEOUS PROVISIONS

Sec. 6101.	Period covered by returns or other documents
Sec. 6102.	Computations on returns or other documents
Sec. 6103.	Confidentiality and disclosure of returns and return information
Sec. 6104.	Publicity of information required from certain exempt organizations and certain trusts
Sec. 6105.	Confidentiality of information arising under treaty obligations
Sec. 6107.	Tax return preparer must furnish copy of return to taxpayer and must retain a copy or list
Sec. 6108.	Statistical publications and studies
Sec. 6109.	Identifying numbers
Sec. 6110.	Public inspection of written determinations
Sec. 6111.	Disclosure of reportable transactions
Sec. 6112.	Material advisors of reportable transactions must keep lists of advisees, etc.
Sec. 6113.	Disclosure of nondeductibility of contributions
Sec. 6114.	Treaty-based return positions
Sec. 6115.	Disclosure related to quid pro quo contributions
Sec. 6116.	Requirement for prisons located in United States to provide information for tax administration

CODE—TABLE OF CONTENTS

Sec. 6117. Cross reference

Chapter 62—Time and Place for Paying Tax

SUBCHAPTER A. PLACE AND DUE DATE FOR PAYMENT OF TAX

Sec. 6151. Time and place for paying tax shown on returns
Sec. 6155. Payment on notice and demand
Sec. 6157. Payment of Federal unemployment tax on quarterly or other time period basis
Sec. 6159. Agreements for payment of tax liability in installments

SUBCHAPTER B. EXTENSIONS OF TIME FOR PAYMENT

Sec. 6161. Extension of time for paying tax
Sec. 6163. Extension of time for payment of estate tax on value of reversionary or remainder interest in property
Sec. 6164. Extension of time for payment of taxes by corporations expecting carrybacks
Sec. 6165. Bonds where time to pay tax or deficiency has been extended
Sec. 6166. Extension of time for payment of estate tax where estate consists largely of interest in closely held business
Sec. 6167. Extension of time for payment of tax attributable to recovery of foreign expropriation losses

Chapter 63—Assessment

SUBCHAPTER A. IN GENERAL

Sec. 6201. Assessment authority
Sec. 6202. Establishment by regulations of mode or time of assessment
Sec. 6203. Method of assessment
Sec. 6204. Supplemental assessments
Sec. 6205. Special rules applicable to certain employment taxes
Sec. 6206. Special rules applicable to excessive claims under certain sections
Sec. 6207. Cross references

SUBCHAPTER B. DEFICIENCY PROCEDURES IN THE CASE OF INCOME, ESTATE, GIFT, AND CERTAIN EXCISE TAXES

Sec. 6211. Definition of a deficiency
Sec. 6212. Notice of deficiency
Sec. 6213. Restrictions applicable to deficiencies; petition to Tax Court
Sec. 6214. Determinations by Tax Court
Sec. 6215. Assessment of deficiency found by Tax Court
Sec. 6216. Cross references

SUBCHAPTER C. TREATMENT OF PARTNERSHIPS

Part I—In General

Sec. 6221. Determination at partnership level
Sec. 6222. Partner's return must be consistent with partnership return
Sec. 6223. Designation of partnership representative [sic]

Part II—Partnership Adjustments

Sec. 6225. Partnership adjustment by Secretary
Sec. 6226. Alternative to payment of imputed underpayment by partnership
Sec. 6227. Administrative adjustment request by partnership

Part III—Procedure

Sec. 6231. Notice of proceedings and adjustment
Sec. 6232. Assessment, collection, and payment
Sec. 6233. Interest and penalties
Sec. 6234. Judicial review of partnership adjustment
Sec. 6235. Period of limitations on making adjustments

Part IV—Definitions and Special Rules

Sec. 6241. Definitions and special rules

SUBCHAPTER C. TAX TREATMENT OF PARTNERSHIP ITEMS

Sec. 6221. Tax treatment determined at partnership level
Sec. 6222. Partner's return must be consistent with partnership return or Secretary notified of inconsistency
Sec. 6223. Notice to partners of proceedings
Sec. 6224. Participation in administrative proceedings; waivers; agreements
Sec. 6225. Assessments made only after partnership level proceedings are completed
Sec. 6226. Judicial review of final partnership administrative adjustments
Sec. 6227. Administrative adjustment requests
Sec. 6228. Judicial review where administrative adjustment request is not allowed in full
Sec. 6229. Period of limitations for making assessments
Sec. 6230. Additional administrative provisions
Sec. 6231. Definitions and special rules
Sec. 6233. Extension to entities filing partnership returns, etc.
Sec. 6234. Declaratory judgment relating to treatment of items other than partnership items with respect to an oversheltered return

SUBCHAPTER D. TREATMENT OF ELECTING LARGE PARTNERSHIPS

Part I—Treatment of Partnership Items and Adjustments

Sec. 6240. Application of subchapter
Sec. 6241. Partner's return must be consistent with partnership return
Sec. 6242. Procedure for taking partnership adjustments into account

CODE—TABLE OF CONTENTS

PART II—PARTNERSHIP LEVEL ADJUSTMENTS

Subpart A—Adjustments by Secretary

Sec. 6245. Secretarial authority
Sec. 6246. Restrictions on partnership adjustments
Sec. 6247. Judicial review of partnership adjustment
Sec. 6248. Period of limitations for making adjustments

Subpart B—Claims for Adjustments by Partnership

Sec. 6251. Administrative adjustment requests
Sec. 6252. Judicial review where administrative adjustment request is not allowed in full

PART III—DEFINITIONS AND SPECIAL RULES

Sec. 6255. Definitions and special rules

Chapter 64—Collection

SUBCHAPTER A. GENERAL PROVISIONS

Sec. 6301. Collection authority
Sec. 6302. Mode or time of collection
Sec. 6303. Notice and demand for tax
Sec. 6304. Fair tax collection practices
Sec. 6305. Collection of certain liability
Sec. 6306. Qualified tax collection contracts
Sec. 6307. Special compliance personnel program account

SUBCHAPTER B. RECEIPT OF PAYMENT

Sec. 6311. Payment of tax by commercially acceptable means
Sec. 6313. Fractional parts of a cent
Sec. 6314. Receipt for taxes
Sec. 6315. Payments of estimated income tax
Sec. 6316. Payment by foreign currency
Sec. 6317. Payments of Federal unemployment tax for calendar quarter

SUBCHAPTER C. LIEN FOR TAXES

PART I—DUE PROCESS FOR LIENS

Sec. 6320. Notice and opportunity for hearing upon filing of notice of lien

PART II—LIENS

Sec. 6321. Lien for taxes
Sec. 6322. Period of lien
Sec. 6323. Validity and priority against certain persons
Sec. 6324. Special liens for estate and gift taxes
Sec. 6324A. Special lien for estate tax deferred under section 6166
Sec. 6324B. Special lien for additional estate tax attributable to farm, etc., valuation
Sec. 6325. Release of lien or discharge of property
Sec. 6326. Administrative appeal of liens
Sec. 6327. Cross references

SUBCHAPTER D. SEIZURE OF PROPERTY FOR COLLECTION OF TAXES

PART I—DUE PROCESS FOR COLLECTIONS

Sec. 6330. Notice and opportunity for hearing before levy

PART II—LEVY

Sec. 6331. Levy and distraint
Sec. 6332. Surrender of property subject to levy
Sec. 6333. Production of books
Sec. 6334. Property exempt from levy
Sec. 6335. Sale of seized property
Sec. 6336. Sale of perishable goods
Sec. 6337. Redemption of property
Sec. 6338. Certificate of sale; deed of real property
Sec. 6339. Legal effect of certificate of sale of personal property and deed of real property
Sec. 6340. Records of sale
Sec. 6341. Expense of levy and sale
Sec. 6342. Application of proceeds of levy
Sec. 6343. Authority to release levy and return property
Sec. 6344. Cross references

SUBCHAPTER E. COLLECTION OF STATE INDIVIDUAL INCOME TAXES—[REPEALED]

Chapter 65—Abatements, Credits, and Refunds

SUBCHAPTER A. PROCEDURE IN GENERAL

Sec. 6401. Amounts treated as overpayments
Sec. 6402. Authority to make credits or refunds
Sec. 6403. Overpayment of installment
Sec. 6404. Abatements
Sec. 6405. Reports of refunds and credits

CODE—TABLE OF CONTENTS

Sec. 6406.	Prohibition of administrative review of decisions
Sec. 6407.	Date of allowance of refund or credit
Sec. 6408.	State escheat laws not to apply
Sec. 6409.	Refunds disregarded in the administration of federal programs and federally assisted programs

SUBCHAPTER B. RULES OF SPECIAL APPLICATION

Sec. 6411.	Tentative carryback and refund adjustments
Sec. 6412.	Floor stocks refunds
Sec. 6413.	Special rules applicable to certain employment taxes
Sec. 6414.	Income tax withheld
Sec. 6415.	Credits or refunds to persons who collected certain taxes
Sec. 6416.	Certain taxes on sales and services
Sec. 6417.	Elective payment of applicable credits
Sec. 6418.	Transfer of certain credits
Sec. 6419.	Excise tax on wagering
Sec. 6420.	Gasoline used on farms
Sec. 6421.	Gasoline used for certain nonhighway purposes, used by local transit systems, or sold for certain exempt purposes
Sec. 6422.	Cross references
Sec. 6423.	Conditions to allowance in the case of alcohol and tobacco taxes
Sec. 6425.	Adjustment of overpayment of estimated income tax by corporation
Sec. 6426.	Credit for alcohol fuel, biodiesel, and alternative fuel mixtures
Sec. 6427.	Fuels not used for taxable purposes
Sec. 6428.	2020 Recovery rebates for individuals
Sec. 6428A.	Additional 2020 recovery rebates for individuals
Sec. 6428B.	2021 Recovery rebates to individuals
Sec. 6430.	Treatment of tax imposed at Leaking Underground Storage Tank Trust Fund financing rate
Sec. 6432.	Continuation coverage premium assistance
Sec. 6433.	Saver's match

Chapter 66—Limitations

SUBCHAPTER A. LIMITATIONS ON ASSESSMENT AND COLLECTION

Sec. 6501.	Limitations on assessment and collection
Sec. 6502.	Collection after assessment
Sec. 6503.	Suspension of running of period of limitation
Sec. 6504.	Cross references

SUBCHAPTER B. LIMITATIONS ON CREDIT OR REFUND

Sec. 6511.	Limitations on credit or refund
Sec. 6512.	Limitations in case of petition to Tax Court
Sec. 6513.	Time return deemed filed and tax considered paid
Sec. 6514.	Credits or refunds after period of limitation
Sec. 6515.	Cross references

SUBCHAPTER C. MITIGATION OF EFFECT OF PERIOD OF LIMITATIONS

Sec. 6521.	Mitigation of effect of limitation in case of related taxes under different chapters

SUBCHAPTER D. PERIODS OF LIMITATION IN JUDICIAL PROCEEDINGS

Sec. 6531.	Periods of limitation on criminal prosecutions
Sec. 6532.	Periods of limitation on suits
Sec. 6533.	Cross references

Chapter 67—Interest

SUBCHAPTER A. INTEREST ON UNDERPAYMENTS

Sec. 6601.	Interest on underpayment, nonpayment, or extensions of time for payment, of tax
Sec. 6602.	Interest on erroneous refund recoverable by suit
Sec. 6603.	Deposits made to suspend running of interest on potential underpayments, etc.

SUBCHAPTER B. INTEREST ON OVERPAYMENTS

Sec. 6611.	Interest on overpayments
Sec. 6612.	Cross references

SUBCHAPTER C. DETERMINATION OF INTEREST RATE; COMPOUNDING OF INTEREST

Sec. 6621.	Determination of rate of interest
Sec. 6622.	Interest compounded daily

SUBCHAPTER D. NOTICE REQUIREMENTS

Sec. 6631.	Notice requirements

Chapter 68—Additions to the Tax, Additional Amounts, and Assessable Penalties

SUBCHAPTER A. ADDITIONS TO THE TAX AND ADDITIONAL AMOUNTS

PART I—GENERAL PROVISIONS

Sec. 6651.	Failure to file tax return or to pay tax
Sec. 6652.	Failure to file certain information returns, registration statements, etc.
Sec. 6653.	Failure to pay stamp tax
Sec. 6654.	Failure by individual to pay estimated income tax
Sec. 6655.	Failure by corporation to pay estimated income tax
Sec. 6656.	Failure to make deposit of taxes

Internal Revenue Code

Sec. 6657.	Bad checks
Sec. 6658.	Coordination with title 11

Part II—Accuracy-Related and Fraud Penalties

Sec. 6662.	Imposition of accuracy-related penalty on underpayments
Sec. 6662A.	Imposition of accuracy-related penalty on understatements with respect to reportable transactions
Sec. 6663.	Imposition of fraud penalty
Sec. 6664.	Definitions and special rules

Part III—Applicable Rules

Sec. 6665.	Applicable rules

SUBCHAPTER B. ASSESSABLE PENALTIES

Part I—General Provisions

Sec. 6671.	Rules for application of assessable penalties
Sec. 6672.	Failure to collect and pay over tax, or attempt to evade or defeat tax
Sec. 6673.	Sanctions and costs awarded by courts
Sec. 6674.	Fraudulent statement or failure to furnish statement to employee
Sec. 6675.	Excessive claims with respect to the use of certain fuels
Sec. 6676.	Erroneous claim for refund or credit
Sec. 6677.	Failure to file information with respect to certain foreign trusts
Sec. 6679.	Failure to file returns, etc., with respect to foreign corporations or foreign partnerships
Sec. 6682.	False information with respect to withholding
Sec. 6684.	Assessable penalties with respect to liability for tax under chapter 42
Sec. 6685.	Assessable penalty with respect to public inspection requirements for certain tax-exempt organizations
Sec. 6686.	Failure to file returns or supply information by DISC or former FSC
Sec. 6688.	Assessable penalties with respect to information required to be furnished under section 7654
Sec. 6689.	Failure to file notice of redetermination of foreign tax
Sec. 6690.	Fraudulent statement or failure to furnish statement to plan participant
Sec. 6692.	Failure to file actuarial report
Sec. 6693.	Failure to provide reports on certain tax-favored accounts or annuities; penalties relating to designated nondeductible contributions
Sec. 6694.	Understatement of taxpayer's liability by tax return preparer
Sec. 6695.	Other assessable penalties with respect to the preparation of tax returns for other persons
Sec. 6695A.	Substantial and gross valuation misstatements attributable to incorrect appraisals
Sec. 6696.	Rules applicable with respect to sections 6694, 6695, and 6695A
Sec. 6698.	Failure to file partnership return
Sec. 6699.	Failure to file S corporation return
Sec. 6700.	Promoting abusive tax shelters, etc.
Sec. 6701.	Penalties for aiding and abetting understatement of tax liability
Sec. 6702.	Frivolous tax submissions
Sec. 6703.	Rules applicable to penalties under sections 6700, 6701, and 6702
Sec. 6704.	Failure to keep records necessary to meet reporting requirements under section 6047(d)
Sec. 6705.	Failure by broker to provide notice to payors
Sec. 6706.	Original issue discount information requirements
Sec. 6707.	Failure to furnish information regarding reportable transactions
Sec. 6707A.	Penalty for failure to include reportable transaction information with return
Sec. 6708.	Failure to maintain lists of advisees with respect to reportable transactions
Sec. 6709.	Penalties with respect to mortgage credit certificates
Sec. 6710.	Failure to disclose that contributions are nondeductible
Sec. 6711.	Failure by tax-exempt organization to disclose that certain information or service available from Federal Government
Sec. 6712.	Failure to disclose treaty-based return positions
Sec. 6713.	Disclosure or use of information by preparers of returns
Sec. 6714.	Failure to meet disclosure requirements applicable to quid pro quo contributions
Sec. 6715.	Dyed fuel sold for use or used in taxable use, etc.
Sec. 6715A.	Tampering with or failing to maintain security requirements for mechanical dye injection systems
Sec. 6717.	Refusal of entry
Sec. 6718.	Failure to display tax registration on vessels
Sec. 6719.	Failure to register or reregister
Sec. 6720.	Fraudulent acknowledgments with respect to donations of motor vehicles, boats, and airplanes
Sec. 6720A.	Penalty with respect to certain adulterated fuels
Sec. 6720B.	Fraudulent identification of exempt use property
Sec. 6720C.	Penalty for failure to notify health plan of cessation of eligibility for continuation coverage premium assistance

Part II—Failure to Comply with Certain Information Reporting Requirements

Sec. 6721.	Failure to file correct information returns
Sec. 6722.	Failure to furnish correct payee statements
Sec. 6723.	Failure to comply with other information reporting requirements
Sec. 6724.	Waiver; definitions and special rules
Sec. 6725.	Failure to report information under section 4101

SUBCHAPTER C. PROCEDURAL REQUIREMENTS

Sec. 6751.	Procedural requirements

Chapter 69—General Provisions Relating to Stamps

Sec. 6801.	Authority for establishment, alteration, and distribution
Sec. 6802.	Supply and distribution

CODE—TABLE OF CONTENTS

Sec. 6803.	Accounting and safeguarding
Sec. 6804.	Attachment and cancellation
Sec. 6805.	Redemption of stamps
Sec. 6806.	Occupational tax stamps
Sec. 6807.	Stamping, marking, and branding seized goods
Sec. 6808.	Special provisions relating to stamps

Chapter 70—Jeopardy, Receiverships, Etc.

SUBCHAPTER A. JEOPARDY

PART I—TERMINATION OF TAXABLE YEAR

Sec. 6851.	Termination assessments of income tax
Sec. 6852.	Termination assessments in case of flagrant political expenditures of section 501(c)(3) organizations

PART II—JEOPARDY ASSESSMENTS

Sec. 6861.	Jeopardy assessments of income, estate, gift, and certain excise taxes
Sec. 6862.	Jeopardy assessment of taxes other than income, estate, gift, and certain excise taxes
Sec. 6863.	Stay of collection of jeopardy assessments
Sec. 6864.	Termination of extended period for payment in case of carryback

PART III—SPECIAL RULES WITH RESPECT TO CERTAIN CASH

Sec. 6867.	Presumptions where owner of large amount of cash is not identified

SUBCHAPTER B. RECEIVERSHIPS, ETC.

Sec. 6871.	Claims for income, estate, gift, and certain excise taxes in receivership proceedings, etc.
Sec. 6872.	Suspension of period on assessment
Sec. 6873.	Unpaid claims

Chapter 71—Transferees and Fiduciaries

Sec. 6901.	Transferred assets
Sec. 6902.	Provisions of special application to transferees
Sec. 6903.	Notice of fiduciary relationship
Sec. 6904.	Prohibition of injunctions
Sec. 6905.	Discharge of executor from personal liability for decedent's income and gift taxes

Chapter 72—Licensing and Registration

SUBCHAPTER A. LICENSING

Sec. 7001.	Collection of foreign items

SUBCHAPTER B. REGISTRATION

Sec. 7011.	Registration—persons paying a special tax
Sec. 7012.	Cross references

Chapter 73—Bonds

Sec. 7101.	Form of bonds
Sec. 7102.	Single bond in lieu of multiple bonds
Sec. 7103.	Cross references—other provisions for bonds

Chapter 74—Closing Agreements and Compromises

Sec. 7121.	Closing agreements
Sec. 7122.	Compromises
Sec. 7123.	Appeals dispute resolution procedures
Sec. 7124.	Cross references

Chapter 75—Crimes, Other Offenses, and Forfeitures

SUBCHAPTER A. CRIMES

PART I—GENERAL PROVISIONS

Sec. 7201.	Attempt to evade or defeat tax
Sec. 7202.	Willful failure to collect or pay over tax
Sec. 7203.	Willful failure to file return, supply information, or pay tax
Sec. 7204.	Fraudulent statement or failure to make statement to employees
Sec. 7205.	Fraudulent withholding exemption certificate or failure to supply information
Sec. 7206.	Fraud and false statements
Sec. 7207.	Fraudulent returns, statements, or other documents
Sec. 7208.	Offenses relating to stamps
Sec. 7209.	Unauthorized use or sale of stamps
Sec. 7210.	Failure to obey summons
Sec. 7211.	False statements to purchasers or lessees relating to tax
Sec. 7212.	Attempts to interfere with administration of internal revenue laws
Sec. 7213.	Unauthorized disclosure of information
Sec. 7213A.	Unauthorized inspection of returns or return information
Sec. 7214.	Offenses by officers and employees of the United States
Sec. 7215.	Offenses with respect to collected taxes
Sec. 7216.	Disclosure or use of information by preparers of returns
Sec. 7217.	Prohibition on executive branch influence over taxpayer audits and other investigations

Internal Revenue Code

PART II—PENALTIES APPLICABLE TO CERTAIN TAXES

Sec. 7231.	Failure to obtain license for collection of foreign items
Sec. 7232.	Failure to register or reregister under section 4101, false representations of registration status, etc.

SUBCHAPTER B. OTHER OFFENSES

Sec. 7261.	Representation that retailers' excise tax is excluded from price of article
Sec. 7262.	Violation of occupational tax laws relating to wagering—failure to pay special tax
Sec. 7268.	Possession with intent to sell in fraud of law or to evade tax
Sec. 7269.	Failure to produce records
Sec. 7270.	Insurance policies
Sec. 7271.	Penalties for offenses relating to stamps
Sec. 7272.	Penalty for failure to register or reregister
Sec. 7273.	Penalties for offenses relating to special taxes
Sec. 7275.	Penalty for offenses relating to certain airline tickets and advertising

SUBCHAPTER C. FORFEITURES

PART I—PROPERTY SUBJECT TO FORFEITURE

Sec. 7301.	Property subject to tax
Sec. 7302.	Property used in violation of internal revenue laws
Sec. 7303.	Other property subject to forfeiture
Sec. 7304.	Penalty for fraudulently claiming drawback

PART II—PROVISIONS COMMON TO FORFEITURES

Sec. 7321.	Authority to seize property subject to forfeiture
Sec. 7322.	Delivery of seized personal property to United States marshal
Sec. 7323.	Judicial action to enforce forfeiture
Sec. 7324.	Special disposition of perishable goods
Sec. 7325.	Personal property valued at $100,000 or less
Sec. 7327.	Customs laws applicable
Sec. 7328.	Cross references

SUBCHAPTER D. MISCELLANEOUS PENALTY AND FORFEITURE PROVISIONS

Sec. 7341.	Penalty for sales to evade tax
Sec. 7342.	Penalty for refusal to permit entry or examination
Sec. 7343.	Definition of term "person"
Sec. 7344.	Extended application of penalties relating to officers of the Treasury Department
Sec. 7345.	Revocation or denial of passport in case of certain tax delinquencies

Chapter 76—Judicial Proceedings

SUBCHAPTER A. CIVIL ACTIONS BY THE UNITED STATES

Sec. 7401.	Authorization
Sec. 7402.	Jurisdiction of district courts
Sec. 7403.	Action to enforce lien or to subject property to payment of tax
Sec. 7404.	Authority to bring civil action for estate taxes
Sec. 7405.	Action for recovery of erroneous refunds
Sec. 7406.	Disposition of judgments and moneys recovered
Sec. 7407.	Action to enjoin tax return preparers
Sec. 7408.	Actions to enjoin specified conduct related to tax shelters and reportable transactions
Sec. 7409.	Action to enjoin flagrant political expenditures of section 501(c)(3) organizations
Sec. 7410.	Cross references

SUBCHAPTER B. PROCEEDINGS BY TAXPAYERS AND THIRD PARTIES

Sec. 7421.	Prohibition of suits to restrain assessment or collection
Sec. 7422.	Civil actions for refund
Sec. 7423.	Repayments to officers or employees
Sec. 7424.	Intervention
Sec. 7425.	Discharge of liens
Sec. 7426.	Civil actions by persons other than taxpayers
Sec. 7427.	Tax return preparers
Sec. 7428.	Declaratory judgments relating to status and classification of organizations under section 501(c)(3), etc.
Sec. 7429.	Review of jeopardy levy or assessment procedures
Sec. 7430.	Awarding of costs and certain fees
Sec. 7431.	Civil damages for unauthorized inspection or disclosure of returns and return information
Sec. 7432.	Civil damages for failure to release lien
Sec. 7433.	Civil damages for certain unauthorized collection actions
Sec. 7433A.	Civil damages for certain unauthorized collection actions by persons performing services under qualified tax collection contracts
Sec. 7434.	Civil damages for fraudulent filing of information returns
Sec. 7435.	Civil damages for unauthorized enticement of information disclosure
Sec. 7436.	Proceedings for determination of employment status
Sec. 7437.	Cross references

SUBCHAPTER C. THE TAX COURT

PART I—ORGANIZATION AND JURISDICTION

Sec. 7441.	Status
Sec. 7442.	Jurisdiction

CODE—TABLE OF CONTENTS

Sec. 7443.	Membership
Sec. 7443A.	Special trial judges
Sec. 7444.	Organization
Sec. 7445.	Offices
Sec. 7446.	Times and places of sessions
Sec. 7447.	Retirement
Sec. 7447A.	Retirement for special trial judges
Sec. 7448.	Annuities to surviving spouses and dependent children of judges and special trial judges

PART II—PROCEDURE

Sec. 7451.	Petition
Sec. 7452.	Representation of parties
Sec. 7453.	Rules of practice, procedure, and evidence
Sec. 7454.	Burden of proof in fraud, foundation manager, and transferee cases
Sec. 7455.	Service of process
Sec. 7456.	Administration of oaths and procurement of testimony
Sec. 7457.	Witness fees
Sec. 7458.	Hearings
Sec. 7459.	Reports and decisions
Sec. 7460.	Provisions of special application to divisions
Sec. 7461.	Publicity of proceedings
Sec. 7462.	Publication of reports
Sec. 7463.	Disputes involving $50,000 or less
Sec. 7464.	Intervention by trustee of debtor's estate
Sec. 7465.	Provisions of special application to transferees
Sec. 7466.	Judicial conduct and disability procedures

PART III—MISCELLANEOUS PROVISIONS

Sec. 7470.	Administration
Sec. 7470A.	Judicial conference
Sec. 7471.	Employees
Sec. 7472.	Expenditures
Sec. 7473.	Disposition of fees
Sec. 7474.	Fee for transcript of record
Sec. 7475.	Practice fee

PART IV—DECLARATORY JUDGMENTS

Sec. 7476.	Declaratory judgments relating to qualification of certain retirement plans
Sec. 7477.	Declaratory judgments relating to value of certain gifts
Sec. 7478.	Declaratory judgments relating to status of certain governmental obligations
Sec. 7479.	Declaratory judgments relating to eligibility of estate with respect to installment payments under section 6166

SUBCHAPTER D. COURT REVIEW OF TAX COURT DECISIONS

Sec. 7481.	Date when Tax Court decision becomes final
Sec. 7482.	Courts of review
Sec. 7483.	Notice of appeal
Sec. 7484.	Change of incumbent in office
Sec. 7485.	Bond to stay assessment and collection
Sec. 7486.	Refund, credit, or abatement of amounts disallowed
Sec. 7487.	Cross references

SUBCHAPTER E. BURDEN OF PROOF

Sec. 7491.	Burden of proof

Chapter 77—Miscellaneous Provisions

Sec. 7501.	Liability for taxes withheld or collected
Sec. 7502.	Timely mailing treated as timely filing and paying
Sec. 7503.	Time for performance of acts where last day falls on Saturday, Sunday, or legal holiday
Sec. 7504.	Fractional parts of a dollar
Sec. 7505.	Sale of personal property acquired by the United States
Sec. 7506.	Administration of real estate acquired by the United States
Sec. 7507.	Exemption of insolvent banks from tax
Sec. 7508.	Time for performing certain acts postponed by reason of service in combat zone or contingency operation
Sec. 7508A.	Authority to postpone certain deadlines by reason of Federally declared disaster, significant fire, or terroristic or military actions
Sec. 7509.	Expenditures incurred by the United States Postal Service
Sec. 7510.	Exemption from tax of domestic goods purchased for the United States
Sec. 7512.	Separate accounting for certain collected taxes, etc.
Sec. 7513.	Reproduction of returns and other documents
Sec. 7514.	Authority to prescribe or modify seals
Sec. 7516.	Supplying training and training aids on request
Sec. 7517.	Furnishing on request of statement explaining estate or gift evaluation
Sec. 7518.	Tax incentives relating to merchant marine capital construction funds
Sec. 7519.	Required payments for entities electing not to have required taxable year
Sec. 7520.	Valuation tables
Sec. 7521.	Procedures involving taxpayer interviews
Sec. 7522.	Content of tax due, deficiency, and other notices
Sec. 7523.	Graphic presentation of major categories of Federal outlays and income

Sec. 7524.	Annual notice of tax delinquency
Sec. 7525.	Confidentiality privileges relating to taxpayer communications
Sec. 7526.	Low income taxpayer clinics
Sec. 7526A.	Return preparation programs for applicable taxpayers
Sec. 7527.	Advance payment of credit for health insurance costs of eligible individuals
Sec. 7527A.	Advance payment of child tax credit
Sec. 7528.	Internal Revenue Service user fees
Sec. 7529.	Notification of suspected identity theft
Sec. 7530.	Application of earned income tax credit to possessions of the United States

Chapter 78—Discovery of Liability and Enforcement of Title

SUBCHAPTER A. EXAMINATION AND INSPECTION

Sec. 7601.	Canvass of districts for taxable persons and objects
Sec. 7602.	Examination of books and witnesses
Sec. 7603.	Service of summons
Sec. 7604.	Enforcement of summons
Sec. 7605.	Time and place of examination
Sec. 7606.	Entry of premises for examination of taxable objects
Sec. 7608.	Authority of internal revenue enforcement officers
Sec. 7609.	Special procedures for third-party summonses
Sec. 7610.	Fees and costs for witnesses
Sec. 7611.	Restrictions on church tax inquiries and examinations
Sec. 7612.	Special procedures for summonses for computer software
Sec. 7613.	Cross references

SUBCHAPTER B. GENERAL POWERS AND DUTIES

Sec. 7621.	Internal revenue districts
Sec. 7622.	Authority to administer oaths and certify
Sec. 7623.	Expenses of detection of underpayments and fraud, etc.
Sec. 7624.	Reimbursement to state and local law enforcement agencies

SUBCHAPTER C. SUPERVISION OF OPERATIONS OF CERTAIN MANUFACTURERS—[REPEALED]

SUBCHAPTER D. POSSESSIONS

Sec. 7651.	Administration and collection of taxes in possessions
Sec. 7652.	Shipments to the United States
Sec. 7653.	Shipments from the United States
Sec. 7654.	Coordination of United States and certain possession individual income taxes
Sec. 7655.	Cross references

Chapter 79—Definitions

Sec. 7701.	Definitions
Sec. 7702.	Life insurance contract defined
Sec. 7702A.	Modified endowment contract defined
Sec. 7702B.	Treatment of qualified long-term care insurance
Sec. 7703.	Determination of marital status
Sec. 7704.	Certain publicly traded partnerships treated as corporations
Sec. 7705.	Certified professional employer organizations.

Chapter 80—General Rules

SUBCHAPTER A. APPLICATION OF INTERNAL REVENUE LAWS

Sec. 7801.	Authority of the Department of the Treasury
Sec. 7802.	Internal Revenue Service Oversight Board
Sec. 7803.	Commissioner of Internal Revenue; other officials
Sec. 7804.	Other personnel
Sec. 7805.	Rules and regulations
Sec. 7806.	Construction of title
Sec. 7807.	Rules in effect upon enactment of this title
Sec. 7808.	Depositaries for collections
Sec. 7809.	Deposit of collections
Sec. 7810.	Revolving fund for redemption of real property
Sec. 7811.	Taxpayer assistance orders
Sec. 7812.	Streamlined critical pay authority for information technology positions

SUBCHAPTER B. EFFECTIVE DATE AND RELATED PROVISIONS

Sec. 7851.	Applicability of revenue laws
Sec. 7852.	Other applicable rules

SUBCHAPTER C. PROVISIONS AFFECTING MORE THAN ONE SUBTITLE

Sec. 7871.	Indian tribal governments treated as States for certain purposes
Sec. 7872.	Treatment of loans with below-market interest rates
Sec. 7873.	Federal tax treatment of income derived by Indians from exercise of fishing rights secured by treaty, etc.
Sec. 7874.	Rules relating to expatriated entities and their foreign parents

CODE—TABLE OF CONTENTS

SUBTITLE G—THE JOINT COMMITTEE ON TAXATION

Chapter 91—Organization and Membership of the Joint Committee

Sec. 8001.	Authorization
Sec. 8002.	Membership
Sec. 8003.	Election of chairman and vice chairman
Sec. 8004.	Appointment and compensation of staff
Sec. 8005.	Payment of expenses

Chapter 92—Powers and Duties of the Joint Committee

Sec. 8021.	Powers
Sec. 8022.	Duties
Sec. 8023.	Additional powers to obtain data

SUBTITLE H—FINANCING OF PRESIDENTIAL ELECTION CAMPAIGNS

Chapter 95—Presidential Election Campaign Fund

Sec. 9001.	Short title
Sec. 9002.	Definitions
Sec. 9003.	Condition for eligibility for payments
Sec. 9004.	Entitlement of eligible candidates to payments
Sec. 9005.	Certification by Commission
Sec. 9006.	Payments to eligible candidates
Sec. 9007.	Examinations and audits; repayments
Sec. 9008.	Payments for presidential nominating conventions
Sec. 9009.	Reports to Congress; regulations
Sec. 9010.	Participation by Commission in judicial proceedings
Sec. 9011.	Judicial review
Sec. 9012.	Criminal penalties

Chapter 96—Presidential Primary Matching Payment Account

Sec. 9031.	Short title
Sec. 9032.	Definitions
Sec. 9033.	Eligibility for payments
Sec. 9034.	Entitlement of eligible candidates to payments
Sec. 9035.	Qualified campaign expense limitations
Sec. 9036.	Certification by Commission
Sec. 9037.	Payments to eligible candidates
Sec. 9038.	Examinations and audits; repayments
Sec. 9039.	Reports to Congress; regulations
Sec. 9040.	Participation by Commission in judicial proceedings
Sec. 9041.	Judicial review
Sec. 9042.	Criminal penalties

SUBTITLE I—TRUST FUND CODE

Chapter 98—Trust Fund Code

SUBCHAPTER A. ESTABLISHMENT OF TRUST FUNDS

Sec. 9501.	Black Lung Disability Trust Fund
Sec. 9502.	Airport and Airway Trust Fund
Sec. 9503.	Highway Trust Fund
Sec. 9504.	Sport Fish Restoration and Boating Trust Fund
Sec. 9505.	Harbor Maintenance Trust Fund
Sec. 9506.	Inland Waterways Trust Fund
Sec. 9507.	Hazardous Substance Superfund
Sec. 9508.	Leaking Underground Storage Tank Trust Fund
Sec. 9509.	Oil Spill Liability Trust Fund
Sec. 9510.	Vaccine Injury Compensation Trust Fund
Sec. 9511.	Patient-centered outcomes research trust fund

SUBCHAPTER B. GENERAL PROVISIONS

Sec. 9601.	Transfer of amounts
Sec. 9602.	Management of trust funds

SUBTITLE J—COAL INDUSTRY HEALTH BENEFITS

Chapter 99—Coal Industry Health Benefits

SUBCHAPTER A. DEFINITIONS OF GENERAL APPLICABILITY

Sec. 9701.	Definitions of general applicability

SUBCHAPTER B. COMBINED BENEFIT FUND

Part I—Establishment and Benefits

Sec. 9702.	Establishment of the United Mine Workers of America Combined Benefit Fund
Sec. 9703.	Plan benefits

Internal Revenue Code

PART II—Financing

Sec. 9704. Liability of assigned operators
Sec. 9705. Transfers
Sec. 9706. Assignment of eligible beneficiaries

PART III—Enforcement

Sec. 9707. Failure to pay premium

PART IV—Other Provisions

Sec. 9708. Effect on pending claims or obligations

SUBCHAPTER C. HEALTH BENEFITS OF CERTAIN MINERS

PART I—Individual Employer Plans

Sec. 9711. Continued obligations of individual employer plans

PART II—1992 UMWA Benefit Plan

Sec. 9712. Establishment and coverage of 1992 UMWA Benefit Plan

SUBCHAPTER D. OTHER PROVISIONS

Sec. 9721. Civil enforcement
Sec. 9722. Sham transactions

SUBTITLE K—GROUP HEALTH PLAN REQUIREMENTS

Chapter 100—Group Health Plan Requirements

SUBCHAPTER A. REQUIREMENTS RELATING TO PORTABILITY, ACCESS, AND RENEWABILITY

Sec. 9801. Increased portability through limitation on preexisting condition exclusions
Sec. 9802. Prohibiting discrimination against individual participants and beneficiaries based on health status
Sec. 9803. Guaranteed renewability in multiemployer plans and certain multiple employer welfare arrangements

SUBCHAPTER B. OTHER REQUIREMENTS

Sec. 9811. Standards relating to benefits for mothers and newborns
Sec. 9812. Parity in mental health and substance use disorder benefits
Sec. 9813. Coverage of dependent students on medically necessary leave of absence
Sec. 9815. Additional market reforms
Sec. 9816. Preventing surprise medical bills
Sec. 9817. Ending surprise air ambulance bills
Sec. 9818. Continuity of care
Sec. 9819. Maintenance of price comparison tool
Sec. 9820. Protecting patients and improving the accuracy of provider directory information
Sec. 9822. Other patient protections
Sec. 9823. Air ambulance report requirements
Sec. 9824. Increasing transparency by removing gag clauses on price and quality information
Sec. 9825. Reporting on pharmacy benefits and drug costs

SUBCHAPTER C. GENERAL PROVISIONS

Sec. 9831. General exceptions
Sec. 9832. Definitions
Sec. 9833. Regulations
Sec. 9834. Enforcement

[The next page is 2551.]

Subchapter N—Tax Based on Income From Sources Within or Without the United States

Part I. Source rules and other general rules relating to foreign income.
Part II. Nonresident aliens and foreign corporations.
Part III. Income from sources without the United States.
Part IV. Domestic international sales corporations.
Part V. International boycott determinations.

PART I—SOURCE RULES AND OTHER GENERAL RULES RELATING TO FOREIGN INCOME

Sec. 861. Income from sources within the United States.
Sec. 862. Income from sources without the United States.
Sec. 863. Special rules for determining source.
Sec. 864. Definitions and special rules.
Sec. 865. Source rules for personal property sales.

[Sec. 861]

SEC. 861. INCOME FROM SOURCES WITHIN THE UNITED STATES.

[Sec. 861(a)]

(a) GROSS INCOME FROM SOURCES WITHIN UNITED STATES.—The following items of gross income shall be treated as income from sources within the United States:

(1) INTEREST.—Interest from the United States or the District of Columbia, and interest on bonds, notes, or other interest-bearing obligations of noncorporate residents or domestic corporations, not including—

(A) interest—

(i) on deposits with a foreign branch of a domestic corporation or a domestic partnership if such branch is engaged in the commercial banking business, and

(ii) on amounts satisfying the requirements of subparagraph (B) of section 871(i)(3) which are paid by a foreign branch of a domestic corporation or a domestic partnership, and

(B) in the case of a foreign partnership, which is predominantly engaged in the active conduct of a trade or business outside the United States, any interest not paid by a trade or business engaged in by the partnership in the United States and not allocable to income which is effectively connected (or treated as effectively connected) with the conduct of a trade or business in the United States.

(2) DIVIDENDS.—The amount received as dividends—

(A) from a domestic corporation, or

(B) from a foreign corporation unless less than 25 percent of the gross income from all sources of such foreign corporation for the 3-year period ending with the close of its taxable year preceding the declaration of such dividends (or for such part of such period as the corporation has been in existence) was effectively connected (or treated as effectively connected other than income described in section 884(d)(2)) with the conduct of a trade or business within the United States; but only in an amount which bears the same ratio to such dividends as the gross income of the corporation for such period which was effectively connected (or treated as effectively connected other than income described in section 884(d)(2)) with the conduct of a trade or business within the United States bears to its gross income from all sources; but dividends (other than dividends for which a deduction is allowable under section 245(b)) from a foreign corporation shall, for purposes of subpart A of part III (relating to foreign tax credit), be treated as income from sources without the United States to the extent (and only to the extent) exceeding the amount which is 100/50th of the amount of the deduction allowable under section 245 in respect of such dividends, or

(C) from a foreign corporation to the extent that such amount is required by section 243(e) (relating to certain dividends from foreign corporations) to be treated as dividends from a domestic corporation which is subject to taxation under this chapter, and to such extent subparagraph (B) shall not apply to such amount, or

(D) from a DISC or former DISC (as defined in section 992(a)) except to the extent attributable (as determined under regulations prescribed by the Secretary) to qualified export receipts described in section 993(a)(1) (other than interest and gains described in section 995(b)(1)).

In the case of any dividend from a 20-percent owned corporation (as defined in section 243(c)(2)), subparagraph (B) shall be applied by substituting "100/65th" for "100/50th".

(3) PERSONAL SERVICES.—Compensation for labor or personal services performed in the United States; except that compensation for labor or services performed in the United States shall not be deemed to be income from sources within the United States if—

(A) the labor or services are performed by a nonresident alien individual temporarily present in the United States for a period or periods not exceeding a total of 90 days during the taxable year,

(B) such compensation does not exceed $3,000 in the aggregate, and

(C) the compensation is for labor or services performed as an employee of or under a contract with—

(i) a nonresident alien, foreign partnership, or foreign corporation, not engaged in trade or business within the United States, or

(ii) an individual who is a citizen or resident of the United States, a domestic partnership, or a domestic corporation, if such labor or services are performed for an office or place of business maintained in a foreign country or in a possession of the United States by such individual, partnership, or corporation.

In addition, compensation for labor or services performed in the United States shall not be deemed to be income from sources within the United States if the labor or services are performed by a nonresident alien individual in connection with the individual's temporary presence in the United States as a regular member of the crew of a foreign vessel engaged in transportation between the United States and a foreign country or a possession of the United States.

(4) RENTALS AND ROYALTIES.—Rentals or royalties from property located in the United States or from any interest in such property, including rentals or royalties for the use of or for the privilege of using in the United States patents, copyrights, secret processes and formulas, good will, trade-marks, trade brands, franchises, and other like property.

(5) DISPOSITION OF UNITED STATES REAL PROPERTY INTEREST.—Gains, profits, and income from the disposition of a United States real property interest (as defined in section 897(c)).

(6) SALE OR EXCHANGE OF INVENTORY PROPERTY.—Gains, profits, and income derived from the purchase of inventory property (within the meaning of section 865(i)(1)) without the United States (other than within a possession of the United States) and its sale or exchange within the United States.

(7) Amounts received as underwriting income (as defined in section 832(b)(3)) derived from the issuing (or reinsuring) of any insurance or annuity contract—

INCOME TAX—SOURCES OF INCOME

(A) in connection with property in, liability arising out of an activity in, or in connection with the lives or health of residents of, the United States, or

(B) in connection with risks not described in subparagraph (A) as a result of any arrangement whereby another corporation receives a substantially equal amount of premiums or other consideration in respect to issuing (or reinsuring) any insurance or annuity contract in connection with property in, liability arising out of activity in, or in connection with the lives or health of residents of, the United States.

(8) SOCIAL SECURITY BENEFITS.—Any social security benefit (as defined in section 86(d)).

(9) GUARANTEES.—Amounts received, directly or indirectly, from—

(A) a noncorporate resident or domestic corporation for the provision of a guarantee of any indebtedness of such resident or corporation, or

(B) any foreign person for the provision of a guarantee of any indebtedness of such person, if such amount is connected with income which is effectively connected (or treated as effectively connected) with the conduct of a trade or business in the United States.

Amendments

• **2018, Tax Technical Corrections Act of 2018 (P.L. 115-141)**

P.L. 115-141, §401(d)(1)(D)(ix), Div. U:

Amended Code Sec. 861(a)(2)(A) by striking "other than a corporation which has an election in effect under section 936" following "from a domestic corporation". **Effective** 3-23-2018. For a special rule, see Act Sec. 401(e), Div. U, below.

P.L. 115-141, §401(e), Div. U, provides:

(e) GENERAL SAVINGS PROVISION WITH RESPECT TO DEADWOOD PROVISIONS.—If—

(1) any provision amended or repealed by the amendments made by subsection (b) or (d) applied to—

(A) any transaction occurring before the date of the enactment of this Act,

(B) any property acquired before such date of enactment, or

(C) any item of income, loss, deduction, or credit taken into account before such date of enactment, and

(2) the treatment of such transaction, property, or item under such provision would (without regard to the amendments or repeals made by such subsection) affect the liability for tax for periods ending after such date of enactment,

nothing in the amendments or repeals made by this section shall be construed to affect the treatment of such transaction, property, or item for purposes of determining liability for tax for periods ending after such date of enactment.

• **2017, Tax Cuts and Jobs Act (P.L. 115-97)**

P.L. 115-97, §13002(e)(1)-(2):

Amended Code Sec. 861(a)(2) by striking "100/70th" and inserting "100/50th" in subparagraph (B), and in the flush sentence at the end by striking "100/80th" and inserting "100/65th", and by striking "100/70th" and inserting "100/50th". **Effective** for tax years beginning after 12-31-2017.

• **2010, Creating Small Business Jobs Act of 2010 (P.L. 111-240)**

P.L. 111-240, §2122(a):

Amended Code Sec. 861(a) by adding at the end a new paragraph (9). **Effective** for guarantees issued after 9-27-2010.

• **2010, (P.L. 111-226)**

P.L. 111-226, §217(a):

Amended Code Sec. 861(a)(1) by striking subparagraph (A) and by redesignating subparagraphs (B) and (C) as subparagraphs (A) and (B), respectively. **Effective** generally for tax years beginning after 12-31-2010. For a grandfather rule, see Act Sec. 217(d)(2), below. Prior to being stricken, Code Sec. 861(a)(1)(A), read as follows:

(A) interest from a resident alien individual or domestic corporation, if such individual or corporation meets the 80-percent foreign business requirements of subsection (c)(1),

P.L. 111-226, §217(d)(2), provides:

(2) GRANDFATHER RULE FOR OUTSTANDING DEBT OBLIGATIONS.—

(A) IN GENERAL.—The amendments made by this section shall not apply to payments of interest on obligations issued before the date of the enactment of this Act.

(B) EXCEPTION FOR RELATED PARTY DEBT.—Subparagraph (A) shall not apply to any interest which is payable to a related person (determined under rules similar to the rules of section 954(d)(3)).

(C) SIGNIFICANT MODIFICATIONS TREATED AS NEW ISSUES.—For purposes of subparagraph (A), a significant modification of the terms of any obligation (including any extension of the term of such obligation) shall be treated as a new issue.

• **2006, Pension Protection Act of 2006 (P.L. 109-280)**

P.L. 109-280, §811, provides:

SEC. 811. PENSIONS AND INDIVIDUAL RETIREMENT ARRANGEMENT PROVISIONS OF ECONOMIC GROWTH AND TAX RELIEF RECONCILIATION ACT OF 2001 MADE PERMANENT.

Title IX of the Economic Growth and Tax Relief Reconciliation Act of 2001 [P.L. 107-16] shall not apply to the provisions of, and amendments made by, subtitles A through F of title VI [§§601-666]of such Act (relating to pension and individual retirement arrangement provisions).

• **2004, American Jobs Creation Act of 2004 (P.L. 108-357)**

P.L. 108-357, §410(a):

Amended Code Sec. 861(a)(1) by striking "and" at the end of subparagraph (A), by striking the period at the end of subparagraph (B) and inserting ", and", and by adding at the end a new subparagraph (C). **Effective** for tax years beginning after 12-31-2003.

• **2001, Economic Growth and Tax Relief Reconciliation Act of 2001 (P.L. 107-16)**

P.L. 107-16, §621(a):

Amended the second sentence of Code Sec. 861(a)(3) by striking "except for purposes of sections 79 and 105 and subchapter D," after "In addition,". **Effective** for remuneration for services performed in plan years beginning after 12-31-2001.

P.L. 107-16, §901(a)-(b), provides [but see P.L. 109-280, §811, above]:

SEC. 901. SUNSET OF PROVISIONS OF ACT.

(a) IN GENERAL.—All provisions of, and amendments made by, this Act shall not apply—

(1) to taxable, plan, or limitation years beginning after December 31, 2010, or

(2) in the case of title V, to estates of decedents dying, gifts made, or generation skipping transfers, after December 31, 2010.

(b) APPLICATION OF CERTAIN LAWS.—The Internal Revenue Code of 1986 and the Employee Retirement Income Security Act of 1974 shall be applied and administered to years, estates, gifts, and transfers described in subsection (a) as if the provisions and amendments described in subsection (a) had never been enacted.

• **1997, Taxpayer Relief Act of 1997 (P.L. 105-34)**

P.L. 105-34, §1174(a)(1):

Amended Code Sec. 861(a)(3) by adding at the end a new flush sentence. **Effective** for remuneration for services performed in tax years beginning after 12-31-97.

• **1990, Omnibus Budget Reconciliation Act of 1990 (P.L. 101-508)**

P.L. 101-508, §11801(a)(29):

Repealed Code Sec. 861(a)(1)(C) and (D). **Effective** 11-5-90. Prior to repeal, Code Sec. 861(a)(1)(C) and (D) read as follows:

(C) interest on a debt obligation which was part of an issue with respect to which an election has been made under subsection (c) of section 4912 (as in effect before July 1, 1974) and which, when issued (or treated as issued under subsection (c)(2) of such section), had a maturity not exceeding 15 years and, when issued, was purchased by one or more underwriters with a view to distribution through resale, but only with respect to interest attributable to periods after the date of such election, and

(D) interest on a debt obligation which was part of an issue which—

(i) was part of an issue outstanding on April 1, 1971,

(ii) was guaranteed by a United States person,

(iii) was treated under chapter 41 as a debt obligation of a foreign obligor,

(iv) as of June 30, 1974, had a maturity of not more than 15 years, and

(v) when issued, was purchased by one or more underwriters for the purpose of distribution through resale.

P.L. 101-508, §11801(c)(14):

Amended Code Sec. 861(a)(1) by inserting "and" at the end of subparagraph (A) and by striking the comma at the end of subparagraph (B) and inserting a period. **Effective** 11-5-90.

P.L. 101-508, §11821(b), provides:

(b) SAVINGS PROVISION.—If—

(1) any provision amended or repealed by this part applied to—

(A) any transaction occurring before the date of the enactment of this Act,

(B) any property acquired before such date of enactment, or

(C) any item of income, loss, deduction, or credit taken into account before such date of enactment, and

(2) the treatment of such transaction, property, or item under such provision would (without regard to the amendments made by this part) affect liability for tax for periods ending after such date of enactment,

nothing in the amendments made by this part shall be construed to affect the treatment of such transaction, property, or item for purposes of determining liability for tax for periods ending after such date of enactment.

• **1989, Omnibus Budget Reconciliation Act of 1989 (P.L. 101-239)**

P.L. 101-239, §7811(i)(2):

Amended Code Sec. 861(a)(6) by striking "865(h)(1)" and inserting "865(i)(1)". **Effective** as if included in the provision of P.L. 100-647 to which it relates.

P.L. 100-647, §1012(g)(1), provides:

(1)(A) Paragraph (1) of section 1214(d) of the Reform Act is amended to read as follows:

"(1) IN GENERAL.—The amendments made by this section shall apply to payments made in a taxable year of the payor beginning after December 31, 1986."

INCOME TAX—SOURCES OF INCOME

(B) A taxpayer may elect not to have the amendment made by subparagraph (A) apply and to have section 1214(d)(1) of the Reform Act apply as in effect before such amendment. Such election shall be made at such time and in such manner as the Secretary of the Treasury or his delegate may prescribe.

P.L. 100-647, §1012(i)(10):

Amended Code Sec. 861(a)(7). **Effective** as if included in the provision of P.L. 99-514 to which it relates. Prior to amendment, Code Sec. 861(a)(7) read as follows:

(7) Amounts received as underwriting income (as defined in section 832(b)(3)) derived from the insurance of United States risks (as defined in section 953(a)).

P.L. 100-647, §1012(q)(7):

Amended Code Sec. 861(a)(2)(B) by striking out "other than under section 884(d)(2)" each place it appears and inserting in lieu thereof "other than income described in section 884(d)(2)". **Effective** as if included in the provision of P.L. 99-514 to which it relates.

P.L. 100-647, §1012(q)(15):

Amended Code Sec. 861(a)(2)(C) by striking out "section 243(d)" and inserting in lieu thereof "section 243(e)". **Effective** as if included in the provision of P.L. 99-514 to which it relates.

P.L. 100-647, §1018(u)(39):

Amended Code Sec. 861(a)(6) by striking out "personal property" and inserting in lieu thereof "inventory property" in the paragraph heading. **Effective** as if included in the provision of P.L. 99-514 to which it relates. For a special rule, see Act Sec. 1006(b)(1)(B), below.

P.L. 100-647, §1006, provides:

(b) AMENDMENTS RELATED TO SECTIONS 611 AND 612 OF THE REFORM ACT.—

(1) In the case of dividends received or accrued during 1987—

* * *

(B) subparagraph (B) of section 861(a)(2) of the 1986 Code shall be applied by substituting "100/80ths" for the fraction specified therein.

P.L. 100-647, §4009, provides:

SEC. 1009. ALLOCATION OF RESEARCH AND EXPERIMENTAL EXPENDITURES.

(a) GENERAL RULE.—For purposes of sections 861(b), 862(b), and 863(b) of the 1986 Code, qualified research and experimental expenditures shall be allocated and apportioned as follows:

(1) Any qualified research and experimental expenditures expended solely to meet legal requirements imposed by a political entity with respect to the improvement or marketing of specific products or processes for purposes not reasonably expected to generate gross income (beyond de minimis amounts) outside the jurisdiction of the political entity shall be allocated only to gross income from sources within such jurisdiction.

(2) In the case of any qualified research and experimental expenditures (not allocated under paragraph (1)) to the extent—

(A) that such expenditures are attributable to activities conducted in the United States, 64 percent of such expenditures shall be allocated and apportioned to income from sources within the United States and deducted from such income in determining the amount of taxable income from sources within the United States, and

(B) that such expenditures are attributable to activities conducted outside the United States, 64 percent of such expenditures shall be allocated and apportioned to income from sources outside the United States and deducted from such income in determining the amount of taxable income from sources outside the United States.

(3) The remaining portion of qualified research and experimental expenditures (not allocated under paragraphs (1) and (2)) shall be apportioned, at the annual election of the taxpayer, on the basis of gross sales or gross income, except that, if the taxpayer elects to apportion on the basis of gross income, the amount apportioned to income from sources outside the United States shall be at least 30 percent of the amount which would be so apportioned on the basis of gross sales.

(b) QUALIFIED RESEARCH AND EXPERIMENTAL EXPENDITURES.—For purposes of this section, the term "qualified research and experimental expenditures" means amounts which are research and experimental expenditures within the meaning of section 174 of the 1986 Code. For purposes of this subsection, rules similar to the rules of subsection (c) of section 174 of the 1986 Code shall apply.

(c) SPECIAL RULES FOR EXPENDITURES ATTRIBUTABLE TO ACTIVITIES CONDUCTED IN SPACE, ETC.—

(1) IN GENERAL.—Any qualified research and experimental expenditures described in paragraph (2)—

(A) if incurred by a United States person, shall be allocated and apportioned under this section in the same manner as if they were attributable to activities conducted in the United States, and

(B) if incurred by a person other than a United States person, shall be allocated and apportioned under this section in the same manner as if they were attributable to activities conducted outside the United States.

(2) DESCRIPTION OF EXPENDITURES.—For purposes of paragraph (1), qualified research and experimental expenditures are described in this paragraph if such expenditures are attributable to activities conducted—

(A) in space,

(B) on or under water not within the jurisdiction (as recognized by the United States) of a foreign country, possession of the United States, or the United States, or

(C) in Antarctica.

(d) AFFILIATED GROUP.—

(1) Except as provided in paragraph (2), the allocation and apportionment required by subsection (a) shall be determined as if all members of the affiliated group (as defined in subsection (e)(5) of section 864 of the 1986 Code) were a single corporation.

(2) For purposes of the allocation and apportionment required by subsection (a)—

(A) sales and gross income from products produced in whole or in part in a possession by an electing corporation (within the meaning of section 936(h)(5)(E) of the 1986 Code); and

(B) dividends from an electing corporation,

shall not be taken into account, except that this paragraph shall not apply to sales of (and gross income and dividends attributable to sales of) products with respect to which an election under section 936(h)(5)(F) of the 1986 Code is not in effect.

(3) The qualified research and experimental expenditures taken into account for purposes of subsection (a) shall be adjusted to reflect the amount of such expenditures included in computing the cost-sharing amount (determined under section 936(h)(5)(C)(i)(I) of the 1986 Code).

(4) The Secretary of the Treasury or his delegate may prescribe such regulations as may be necessary to carry out the purposes of this subsection, including regulations providing for the source of gross income and the allocation and apportionment of deductions to take into account the adjustments required by paragraph (3).

(5) Paragraph (6) of section 864(e) of the 1986 Code shall not apply to qualified research and experimental expenditures.

(e) YEARS TO WHICH SECTION APPLIES.—

(1) IN GENERAL.—Except as provided in this subsection, this section shall apply to the taxpayer's 1st taxable year beginning after August 1, 1987.

(2) REDUCTION IN AMOUNTS TO WHICH SECTION APPLIES.—Notwithstanding paragraph (1), this section shall only apply to that portion of the qualified research and experimental expenditures for the taxable year referred to in paragraph (1) which bears the same ratio to the total amount of such expenditures as—

(A) the lesser of 4 months or the number of months in the taxable year, bears to

(B) the number of months in the taxable year.

• **1987, Revenue Act of 1987 (P.L. 100-203)**

P.L. 100-203, §10221(d)(4)(A)-(B):

Amended Code Sec. 861(a)(2) by striking out "100/85th" and inserting in lieu thereof "100/70th", and by adding at the end thereof a new sentence. **Effective** for dividends received or accrued after 12-31-87, in tax years ending after such date.

• **1986, Tax Reform Act of 1986 (P.L. 99-514)**

P.L. 99-514, §1211(b)(1)(B):

Amended Code Sec. 861(a)(6) by striking out "personal property" and inserting in lieu thereof "inventory property (within the meaning of section 865(h)(1))". **Effective** for tax years beginning after 12-31-86 [see also P.L. 100-647, §1012(g)(1), above]. For a special rule, see Act Sec. 1211(c)(2), below.

P.L. 99-514, §1211(c)(2), provides:

(2) SPECIAL RULE FOR FOREIGN PERSONS.—In the case of any foreign person other than any controlled foreign corporations (within the meaning of section 957(a) of the Internal Revenue Code of 1954), the amendments made by this section shall apply to transactions entered into after March 18, 1986.

P.L. 99-514, §1214(a)(1):

Amended Code Sec. 861(a)(1)(B). **Effective**, generally, for payments after 12-31-86. For special and transitional rules, see Act Sec. 1214(d)(2)-(4) following Code Sec. 861(d). Prior to amendment, Code Sec. 861(a)(1)(B) read as follows:

(B) interest received from a resident alien individual or a domestic corporation, when it is shown to the satisfaction of the Secretary that less than 20 percent of the gross income from all sources of such individual or such corporation has been derived from sources within the United States, as determined under the provisions of this part, for the 3-year period ending with the close of the taxable year of such individual or such corporation preceding the payment of such interest, or for such part of such period as may be applicable,

P.L. 99-514, §1214(b):

Amended Code Sec. 861(a)(2)(A). **Effective**, generally, for payments after 12-31-86 [see also P.L. 100-647, §1012(g)(1), above]. For special and transitional rules, see Act Sec. 1214(d)(2)-(4) following Code Sec. 861(d). Prior to amendment, Code Sec. 861(a)(2)(A) read as follows:

(A) from a domestic corporation other than a corporation which has an election in effect under section 936, and other than a corporation less than 20 percent of whose gross income is shown to the satisfaction of the Secretary to have been derived from sources within the United States, as determined under the provisions of this part, for the 3-year period ending with the close of the taxable year of such corporation preceding the declaration of such dividends (or for such part of such period as the corporation has been in existence), or

P.L. 99-514, §1214(c)(5)(A):

Amended Code Sec. 861(a)(1) by striking out subparagraphs (A) and (E) and by redesignating subparagraphs (B), (C), (D), (F), (G), and (H) as subparagraphs (A), (B), (C), (D), (E), and (F), respectively. **Effective**, generally, for payments after 12-31-86 [see also P.L. 100-647, §1012(g)(1), above]. For special and transitional rules, see Act Sec. 1214(d)(2)-(4) following Code Sec. 861(d). Prior to amendment, subparagraphs (A) and (E) read as follows:

(A) interest on amounts described in subsection (c) received by a nonresident alien individual or a foreign corporation, if such interest is not effectively connected with the conduct of a trade or business within the United States,

(E) income derived by a foreign central bank of issue from bankers' acceptances,

P.L. 99-514, §1214(c)(5)(B):

Amended Code Sec. 861(a)(1)(D) by striking out "paragraph (2) or subsection (c)" and inserting in lieu thereof "subparagraph (B) of section 871(i)(3)",. **Effective**, generally, for payments after 12-31-86. For special and transitional rules, see Act Sec. 1214(d)(2)-(4) following Code Sec. 861(d).

INCOME TAX—SOURCES OF INCOME

P.L. 99-514, § 1241(b)(1)(A):

Amended Code Sec. 861(a)(1) by striking out "residents, corporate or otherwise," in the matter preceding subparagraph (A) and inserting in lieu thereof "noncorporate residents or domestic corporations". **Effective** for tax years beginning after 12-31-86.

P.L. 99-514, § 1241(b)(1)(B):

Amended Code Sec. 861(a)(1) by striking out subparagraphs (B) and (C) and by redesignating subparagraphs (D), (E), and (F) as subparagraphs (B), (C), and (D), respectively. **Effective** for tax years beginning after 12-31-86. Prior to amendment, Code Sec. 861(a)(1)(B) and (C) read as follows:

(B) interest received from a foreign corporation (other than interest paid or credited by a domestic branch of a foreign corporation, if such branch is engaged in the commercial banking business), when it is shown to the satisfaction of the Secretary that less than 50 percent of the gross income from all sources of such foreign corporation for the 3-year period ending with the close of its taxable year preceding the payment of such interest (or for such part of such period as the corporation has been in existence) was effectively connected with the conduct of a trade or business within the United States,

(C) in the case of interest received from a foreign corporation (other than interest paid or credited by a domestic branch of a foreign corporation, if such branch is engaged in the commercial banking business), 50 percent or more of the gross income of which from all sources for the 3-year period ending with the close of its taxable year preceding the payment of such interest (or for such part of such period as the corporation has been in existence) was effectively connected with the conduct of a trade or business within the United States, an amount of such interest which bears the same ratio to such interest as the gross income of such foreign corporation for such period which was not effectively connected with the conduct of a trade or business within the United States bears to its gross income from all sources,

P.L. 99-514, § 1241(b)(2)(A):

Amended Code Sec. 861(a)(2)(B) by striking out "50 percent" and inserting in lieu thereof "25 percent". **Effective** for tax years beginning after 12-31-86.

P.L. 99-514, § 1241(b)(2)(B):

Amended Code Sec. 861(a)(2)(B) by striking out "effectively connected" each place it appears and inserting in lieu thereof "effectively connected (or treated as effectively connected other than under section 884(a)(2))". **Effective** for tax years beginning after 12-31-86.

- **1983, Social Security Amendments of 1983 (P.L. 98-21)**

P.L. 98-21, § 121(d):

Added Code Sec. 861(a)(8). **Effective** for benefits received after 1983 in tax years ending after 1983.

- **1980, Omnibus Reconciliation Act of 1980 (P.L. 96-499)**

P.L. 96-499, § 1124:

Amended Code Sec. 861(a)(5). For the **effective** date, see the historical comment under Code Sec. 897(i). Prior to amendment, Code Sec. 861(a)(5) read as follows:

(5) SALE OR EXCHANGE OF REAL PROPERTY.—Gains, profits, and income from the sale or exchange of real property located in the United States.

- **1978, Revenue Act of 1978 (P.L. 95-600)**

P.L. 95-600, § 540(a):

Amended Code Sec. 861(a)(1)(F). **Effective** for tax years beginning after 11-6-78. Prior to amendment, Code Sec. 861(a)(1)(F) read as follows:

(F) interest on deposits with a foreign branch of a domestic corporation or a domestic partnership, if such branch is engaged in the commercial banking business,

- **1976, Tax Reform Act of 1976 (P.L. 94-455)**

P.L. 94-455, § 1036(a):

Added a new paragraph (7). **Effective** for tax years beginning after 12-31-76.

P.L. 94-455, § 1051(h)(3):

Substituted "other than a corporation which has an election in effect under section 936," for "other than a corporation entitled to the benefits of section 931," in Code Sec. 861(a)(2)(A). For the **effective** date, see Act Sec. 1051(i), below.

P.L. 94-455, § 1051(i), provides:

(1) Except as provided by paragraph (2), the amendments made by this section shall apply to taxable years beginning after December 31, 1975, except that "qualified possession source investment income" as defined in section 936(d)(2) of the Internal Revenue Code of 1954 shall include income from any source outside the United States if the taxpayer establishes to the satisfaction of the Secretary of the Treasury or his delegate that the income from such sources was earned before October 1, 1976.

P.L. 94-455, § 1901(b)(26)(A):

Added "or exchange" after "sale" wherever it appeared in paragraphs (5) and (6). **Effective** for tax years beginning after 12-31-76.

P.L. 94-455, § 1901(c)(7):

Struck out ", any Territory, any political subdivision of a Territory," after "United States" in Code Sec. 861(a)(1). **Effective** for tax years beginning after 12-31-76.

P.L. 94-455, § 1904(b)(10):

Substituted "subsection (c) of section 4912 (as in effect before July 1, 1974)" for "section 4912(c)" and substituted "subsection (c)(2) of such section" for "section 4912(c)(2)" in subparagraph (1)(G). **Effective** 2-1-77.

P.L. 94-455, § 1906(b)(13)(A):

Amended 1954 Code by substituting "Secretary" for "Secretary or his delegate" each place it appeared. **Effective** 2-1-77.

Sec. 861(a)(9)(B)

- **1975 (P.L. 93-625)**

P.L. 93-625, § 9(a):

Amended Code Sec. 861(a) by deleting "and" at the end of subparagraph (F), by adding ", and" at the end of subparagraph (G), and by adding new subparagraph (H). **Effective** for interest paid after 1-3-75.

- **1971, Revenue Act of 1971 (P.L. 92-178)**

P.L. 92-178, § 503:

Amended Code Sec. 861(a)(2) by adding subparagraph (D). **Effective** date is governed by the effective date of Code Sec. 992.

- **1971, Interest Equalization Tax Extension Act of 1971 (P.L. 92-9)**

P.L. 92-9, § 3(a)(2):

Amended Code Sec. 861(a)(1) by deleting "and" at the end of subparagraph (E), and by adding ", and" at the end of subparagraph (F), and new subparagraph (G). **Effective** 4-1-71.

- **1969, Tax Reform Act of 1969 (P.L. 91-172)**

P.L. 91-172, § 435(a)(1):

Amended Code Secs. 861(a)(1)(C) and 861(a)(1)(D) by deleting "after December 31, 1972". **Effective** with respect to amounts paid or credited after 12-31-69. Prior to amendment, Code Secs. 861(a)(1)(C) and 861(a)(1)(D) read as follows:

(C) interest received from a foreign corporation (other than interest paid or credited after December 31, 1972, by a domestic branch of a foreign corporation, if such branch is engaged in the commercial banking business), when it is shown to the satisfaction of the Secretary or his delegate that less than 50 percent of the gross income from all sources of such foreign corporation for the 3-year period ending with the close of its taxable year preceding the payment of such interest (or for such part of such period as the corporation has been in existence) was effectively connected with the conduct of a trade or business within the United States,

(D) in the case of interest received from a foreign corporation (other than interest paid or credited after December 31, 1972, by a domestic branch of a foreign corporation, if such branch is engaged in the commercial banking business), 50 percent or more of the gross income of which from all sources for the 3-year period ending with the close of its taxable year preceding the payment of such interest (or for such part of such period as the corporation has been in existence) was effectively connected with the conduct of a trade or business within the United States, an amount of such interest which bears the same ratio to such interest as the gross income of such foreign corporation for such period which was not effectively connected with the conduct of a trade or business within the United States bears to its gross income from all sources,

- **1966, Foreign Investors Tax Act of 1966 (P.L. 89-809)**

P.L. 89-809, § 102(a)(1):

Amended Code Sec. 861(a)(1)(A). Prior to amendment, Sec. 861(a)(1)(A) read as follows:

(A) interest on deposits with persons carrying on the banking business paid to persons not engaged in business within the United States,

P.L. 89-809, § 102(a)(2):

Amended Code Sec. 861(a)(1) by striking out subparagraphs (B) and (C) and inserting new subparagraphs (B)-(F). **Effective** 1-1-67. Prior to amendment, subparagraphs (B) and (C) read as follows:

(B) interest received from a resident alien individual, a resident foreign corporation, or a domestic corporation, when it is shown to the satisfaction of the Secretary or his delegate that less than 20 percent of the gross income of such resident payor or domestic corporation has been derived from sources within the United States, as determined under the provisions of this part, for the 3-year period ending with the close of the taxable year of such payor preceding the payment of such interest, or for such part of such period as may be applicable, and

(C) income derived by a foreign central bank of issue from bankers' acceptances.

P.L. 89-809, § 102(b):

Amended Code Sec. 861(a)(2)(B). **Effective** with respect to amounts received after 12-31-66. Prior to amendment, Sec. 861(a)(2)(B) read as follows:

"(B) from a foreign corporation unless less than 50 percent of the gross income of such foreign corporation for the 3-year period ending with the close of its taxable year preceding the declaration of such dividends (or for such part of such period as the corporation has been in existence) was derived from sources within the United States as determined under the provisions of this part; but only in an amount which bears the same ratio to such dividends as the gross income of the corporation for such period derived from sources within the United States bears to its gross income from all sources; but dividends from a foreign corporation shall, for purposes of subpart A of part III (relating to foreign tax credit), be treated as income from sources without the United States to the extent exceeding the amount which is 100/85th of the amount of the deduction allowable under section 245 in respect of such dividends, or"

P.L. 89-809, § 102(c):

Amended Code Sec. 861(a)(3)(C)(ii). Prior to amendment, Sec. 861(a)(3)(C)(ii) read as follows:

"(ii) a domestic corporation, if such labor or services are performed for an office or place of business maintained in a foreign country or in a possession of the United States by such corporation."

INCOME TAX—SOURCES OF INCOME

• **1962, Revenue Act of 1962 (P.L. 87-834)**

P.L. 87-834, §9(c):

Amended Code Sec. 861(a)(2)(B) by substituting "to the extent exceeding the amount which is 100/85ths of the amount of the deduction allowable under section 245 in respect of such dividends" for "to the extent exceeding the amount of the deduction allowable under section 245 in respect of such dividends". **Effective** with respect to distributions received by domestic corporations after 12-31-64, and for distributions received by domestic corporations before 1-1-65, in a tax year of such corporation beginning after 12-31-62, but only to the extent that such distribution is made out of accumulated profits of a foreign corporation for a taxable year beginning after 12-31-62.

• **1960 (P.L. 86-779)**

P.L. 86-779, §3(b):

Amended Code Sec. 861(a)(2) by striking out the period at the end of subparagraph (B) and substituting ", or", and by adding after subparagraph (B) a new paragraph (C). **Effective** for dividends received after 1959 in tax years ending after 1959.

[Sec. 861(b)]

(b) TAXABLE INCOME FROM SOURCES WITHIN UNITED STATES.—From the items of gross income specified in subsection (a) as being income from sources within the United States there shall be deducted the expenses, losses, and other deductions properly apportioned or allocated thereto and a ratable part of any expenses, losses, or other deductions which cannot definitely be allocated to some item or class of gross income. The remainder, if any, shall be included in full as taxable income from sources within the United States. In the case of an individual who does not itemize deductions, an amount equal to the standard deduction shall be considered a deduction which cannot definitely be allocated to some item or class of gross income.

Amendments

• **1986, Tax Reform Act of 1986 (P.L. 99-514)**

P.L. 99-514, §104(b)(11):

Amended Code Sec. 861(b) by striking out "the zero bracket amount" and inserting in lieu thereof "the standard deduction". **Effective** for tax years beginning after 12-31-86.

• **1984, Deficit Reduction Act of 1984 (P.L. 98-369)**

P.L. 98-369, §126, provides:

SEC. 126. ALLOCATION UNDER SECTION 861 OF RESEARCH AND EXPERIMENTAL EXPENDITURES.

(a) IN GENERAL.—For purposes of section 861(b), section 862(b), and section 863(b) of the Internal Revenue Code of 1954, all amounts allowable as a deduction for qualified research and experimental expenditures shall be allocated to income from sources within the United States and deducted from such income in determining the amount of taxable income from sources within the United States.

(b) QUALIFIED RESEARCH AND EXPERIMENTAL EXPENDITURES.—For purposes of this section—

(1) IN GENERAL.—The term "qualified research and experimental expenditures" means amounts—

(A) which are research and experimental expenditures within the meaning of section 174 of such Code, and

(B) which are attributable to activities conducted in the United States.

(2) TREATMENT OF DEPRECIATION, ETC.—Rules similar to the rules of subsection (c) of section 174 of such Code shall apply.

(c) EFFECTIVE DATES.—

(1) IN GENERAL.—This section shall apply to taxable years beginning after August 13, 1983, and on or before August 1, 1985.

(2) SPECIAL RULE.—If the taxpayer's 3rd taxable year beginning after August 13, 1981, is not described in paragraph (1), this section shall apply also to such 3rd taxable year.

• **1977, Tax Reduction and Simplification Act of 1977 (P.L. 95-30)**

P.L. 95-30, §102(b)(9):

Amended Code Sec. 861(b) by adding the last sentence. **Effective** for tax years beginning after 12-31-76.

[Sec. 861(c)—Stricken]

Amendments

• **2010, (P.L. 111-226)**

P.L. 111-226, §217(c)(1):

Amended Code Sec. 861 by striking subsection (c) and by redesignating subsections (d), (e), and (f) as subsections (c), (d), and (e), respectively. **Effective** generally for tax years beginning after 12-31-2010. For a grandfather rule, see Act Sec. 217(d)(2), below. Prior to being stricken, Code Sec. 861(c) read as follows:

(c) FOREIGN BUSINESS REQUIREMENTS.—

(1) FOREIGN BUSINESS REQUIREMENTS.—

(A) IN GENERAL.—An individual or corporation meets the 80-percent foreign business requirements of this paragraph if it is shown to the satisfaction of the Secretary that at least 80 percent of the gross income from all sources of such individual or corporation for the testing period is active foreign business income.

(B) ACTIVE FOREIGN BUSINESS INCOME.—For purposes of subparagraph (A), the term "active foreign business income" means gross income which—

(i) is derived from sources outside the United States (as determined under this subchapter) or, in the case of a corporation, is attributable to income so derived by a subsidiary of such corporation, and

(ii) is attributable to the active conduct of a trade or business in a foreign country or possession of the United States by the individual or corporation (or by a subsidiary).

For purposes of this subparagraph, the term "subsidiary" means any corporation in which the corporation referred to in this subparagraph owns (directly or indirectly) stock meeting the requirements of section 1504(a)(2) (determined by substituting "50 percent" for "80 percent" each place it appears).

(C) TESTING PERIOD.—For purposes of this subsection, the term "testing period" means the 3-year period ending with the close of the taxable year of the individual or corporation preceding the payment (or such part of such period as may be applicable). If the individual or corporation has no gross income for such 3-year period (or part thereof), the testing period shall be the taxable year in which the payment is made.

(2) LOOK-THRU WHERE RELATED PERSON RECEIVES INTEREST.—

(A) IN GENERAL.—In the case of interest received by a related person from a resident alien individual or domestic corporation meeting the 80-percent foreign business requirements of paragraph (1), subsection (a)(1)(A) shall apply only to a percentage of such interest equal to the percentage which—

(i) the gross income of such individual or corporation for the testing period from sources outside the United States (as determined under this subchapter), is of

(ii) the total gross income of such individual or corporation for the testing period.

(B) RELATED PERSON.—For purposes of this paragraph, the term "related person" has the meaning given such term by section 954(d)(3), except that—

(i) such section shall be applied by substituting "the individual or corporation making the payment" for "controlled foreign corporation" each place it appears, and

(ii) such section shall be applied by substituting "10 percent or more" for "more than 50 percent" each place it appears.

P.L. 111-226, §217(d)(2), provides:

(2) GRANDFATHER RULE FOR OUTSTANDING DEBT OBLIGATIONS.—

(A) IN GENERAL.—The amendments made by this section shall not apply to payments of interest on obligations issued before the date of the enactment of this Act.

(B) EXCEPTION FOR RELATED PARTY DEBT.—Subparagraph (A) shall not apply to any interest which is payable to a related person (determined under rules similar to the rules of section 954(d)(3)).

(C) SIGNIFICANT MODIFICATIONS TREATED AS NEW ISSUES.—For purposes of subparagraph (A), a significant modification of the terms of any obligation (including any extension of the term of such obligation) shall be treated as a new issue.

• **1988, Technical and Miscellaneous Revenue Act of 1988 (P.L. 100-647)**

P.L. 100-647, §1012(g)(3)(A)-(C):

Amended Code Sec. 861(c)(1)(B) by striking out "subchapter" in clause (i) and inserting in lieu thereof "subchapter) or, in the case of a corporation, is attributable to income so derived by a subsidiary of such corporation" after "subsidiary", by striking out "or chain of subsidiaries of such corporation" in clause (ii), and by adding at the end thereof a new sentence. **Effective** as if included in the provision of P.L. 99-514 to which it relates.

P.L. 100-647, §1012(i)(14)(B):

Amended Code Sec. 861(c)(2)(B)(ii). **Effective** as if included in the provision of P.L. 99-514 to which it relates. Prior to amendment, Code Sec. 861(c)(2)(B)(ii) read as follows:

(ii) such section shall be applied by substituting "10 percent" for "50 percent" each place it appears.

• **1986, Tax Reform Act of 1986 (P.L. 99-514)**

P.L. 99-514, §1214(a)(2):

Amended Code Sec. 861(c). **Effective**, generally, for payments after 12-31-86 [see also P.L. 100-647, §1012(g)(1) following Code Sec. 861(d), below]. However, for special and transitional rules, see Act Sec. 1214(d)(2)-(4) following Code Sec. 861(d). Prior to amendment, Code Sec. 861(c) read as follows:

(c) INTEREST ON DEPOSITS, ETC.—For purposes of subsection (a)(1)(A), the amounts described in this subsection are—

(1) deposits with persons carrying on the banking business,

(2) deposits or withdrawable accounts with savings institutions chartered and supervised as savings and loan or similar associations under Federal or State law, but only to the extent that amounts paid or credited on such deposits or accounts are deductible under section 591 (determined without regard to section 265) in computing the taxable income of such institutions, and

(3) amounts held by an insurance company under an agreement to pay interest thereon.

• **1976, Tax Reform Act of 1976 (P.L. 94-455)**

P.L. 94-455, §1041:

Deleted the last sentence of Code Sec. 861(c). **Effective** 10-4-76. Prior to repeal, the last sentence read as follows:

Effective with respect to amounts paid or credited after December 31, 1976, subsection (a)(1)(A) and this subsection shall cease to apply.

• **1975 (P.L. 93-625)**

P.L. 93-625, §8:

Amended Code Sec. 861(c) by substituting "December 31, 1976" for "December 31, 1975" in the last sentence. **Effective** 1-3-75.

INCOME TAX—SOURCES OF INCOME

- **1969, Tax Reform Act of 1969 (P.L. 91-172)**

P.L. 91-172, § 435(a)(2):

Amended the last sentence of Sec. 861(c) by inserting "1975" in lieu of "1972".

- **1966, Foreign Investors Tax Act of 1966 (P.L. 89-809)**

P.L. 89-809, § 102(a)(1):

Added Code Sec. 861(c). **Effective** 1-1-67.

[Sec. 861(c)]

(c) SPECIAL RULE FOR APPLICATION OF SUBSECTION (a)(2)(B).—For purposes of subsection (a)(2)(B), if the foreign corporation has no gross income from any source for the 3-year period (or part thereof) specified, the requirements of such subsection shall be applied with respect to the taxable year of such corporation in which the payment of the dividend is made.

Amendments

- **2010, (P.L. 111-226)**

P.L. 111-226, § 217(c)(1):

Amended Code Sec. 861 by redesignating subsection (d) as subsection (c). **Effective** generally for tax years beginning after 12-31-2010. For a grandfather rule, see Act Sec. 217(d)(2), below.

P.L. 111-226, § 217(d)(2), provides:

(2) GRANDFATHER RULE FOR OUTSTANDING DEBT OBLIGATIONS.—

(A) IN GENERAL.—The amendments made by this section shall not apply to payments of interest on obligations issued before the date of the enactment of this Act.

(B) EXCEPTION FOR RELATED PARTY DEBT.—Subparagraph (A) shall not apply to any interest which is payable to a related person (determined under rules similar to the rules of section 954(d)(3)).

(C) SIGNIFICANT MODIFICATIONS TREATED AS NEW ISSUES.—For purposes of subparagraph (A), a significant modification of the terms of any obligation (including any extension of the term of such obligation) shall be treated as a new issue.

- **1988, Technical and Miscellaneous Revenue Act of 1988 (P.L. 100-647)**

P.L. 100-647, § 1012(g)(1), provides:

(1)(A) Paragraph (1) of section 1214(d) of the Reform Act is amended to read as follows:

"(1) IN GENERAL.—The amendments made by this section shall apply to payments made in a taxable year of the payor beginning after December 31, 1986."

(B) A taxpayer may elect not to have the amendment made by subparagraph (A) apply and to have section 1214(d)(1) of the Reform Act apply as in effect before such amendment. Such election shall be made at such time and in such manner as the Secretary of the Treasury or his delegate may prescribe.

- **1986, Tax Reform Act of 1986 (P.L. 99-514)**

P.L. 99-514, § 1214(c)(5)(C):

Amended Code Sec. 861(d). **Effective**, generally, for payments after 12-31-86 [but see P.L. 100-647, § 1012(g)(1), above]. For special and transitional rules, see Act Sec. 1214(d)(2)-(4), below. Prior to amendment, Code Sec. 861(d) read as follows:

(d) SPECIAL RULES FOR APPLICATION OF PARAGRAPHS (1)(B), (1)(C), (1)(D), AND (2)(B) OF SUBSECTION (a).—

(1) NEW ENTITIES.—For purposes of paragraphs (1)(B), (1)(C), (1)(D), and (2)(B) of subsection (a), if the resident alien individual, domestic corporation, or foreign corporation, as the case may be, has no gross income from any source for the 3-year period (or part thereof) specified, the 20 percent test or the 50 percent test, as the case may be, shall be applied with respect to the taxable year of the payor in which payment of the interest or dividends, as the case may be, is made.

(2) TRANSITION RULE.—For purposes of paragraphs (1)(C), (1)(D), and (2)(B) of subsection (a), the gross income of the foreign corporation for any period before the first taxable year beginning after December 31, 1966, which is effectively connected with the conduct of a trade or business within the United States is an amount equal to the gross income for such period from sources within the United States.

P.L. 99-514, § 1214(d)(2)-(4), as amended by P.L. 100-647, § 1012(g)(2), provides:

(2) TREATMENT OF CERTAIN INTEREST.—

(A) IN GENERAL.—The amendments made by this section shall not apply to any interest paid or accrued on any obligation outstanding on December 31, 1985. The preceding sentence shall not apply to any interest paid pursuant to any extension or renewal of such an obligation agreed to after December 31, 1985.

(B) SPECIAL RULE FOR RELATED PAYEE.—If the payee of any interest to which subparagraph (A) applies is related (within the meaning of section 904(d)(2)(H) of the Internal Revenue Code of 1986) to the payor, such interest shall be treated for purposes of section 904 of such Code as if the payor were a controlled foreign corporation (within the meaning of section 957(a) of such Code).

(3) TRANSITIONAL RULE.—

(A) YEARS BEFORE 1988.—In applying the amendments made by this section to any payment made by a corporation in a taxable year of such corporation beginning before January 1, 1988, the requirements of clause (ii) of section 861(c)(1)(B) of the Internal Revenue Code of 1986 (relating to active business requirements), as amended by this section, shall not apply to gross income of such corporation for taxable years beginning before January 1, 1987.

(B) YEARS AFTER 1987.—In applying the amendments made by this section to any payment made by a corporation in a taxable year of such corporation beginning after December 31, 1987, the testing period for purposes of section 861(c) of such Code (as so amended) shall not include any taxable year beginning before January 1, 1987.

(4) CERTAIN DIVIDENDS.—

(A) IN GENERAL.—The amendments made by this section shall not apply to any dividend paid before January 1, 1991, by a qualified corporation with respect to stock which was outstanding on May 31, 1985.

(B) QUALIFIED CORPORATION.—For purposes of subparagraph (A), the term "qualified corporation" means any business systems corporation which—

(i) was incorporated in Delaware in February, 1979,

(ii) is headquartered in Garden City, New York, and

(iii) the parent corporation of which is a resident of Sweden.

P.L. 99-514, § 1216, provides:

SEC. 1216. 1-YEAR MODIFICATION IN REGULATIONS PROVIDING FOR ALLOCATION OF RESEARCH AND EXPERIMENTAL EXPENDITURES.

(a) GENERAL RULE.—For purposes of section 861(b), section 862(b), and section 863(b) of the Internal Revenue Code of 1954, notwithstanding section 864(e) of such Code—

(1) 50 percent of all amounts allowable as a deduction for qualified research and experimental expenditures shall be apportioned to income from sources within the United States and deducted from such income in determining the amount of taxable income from sources within the United States, and

(2) the remaining portion of such amounts shall be apportioned on the basis of gross sales or gross income.

The preceding sentence shall not apply to any expenditures described in section 1.861-8(e)(3)(i)(B) of the Income Tax Regulations.

(b) QUALIFIED RESEARCH AND EXPERIMENTAL EXPENDITURES.—For purposes of this section—

(1) IN GENERAL.—The term "qualified research and experimental expenditures" means amounts—

(A) which are research and experimental expenditures within the meaning of section 174 of such Code, and

(B) which are attributable to activities conducted in the United States.

(2) TREATMENT OF DEPRECIATION, ETC.—Rules similar to the rules of section 174(c) of such Code shall apply.

(c) EFFECTIVE DATE.—This section shall apply to taxable years beginning after August 1, 1986, and on or before August 1, 1987.

- **1966, Foreign Investors Tax Act of 1966 (P.L. 89-809)**

P.L. 89-809, § 102(a)(3):

Added Code Sec. 861(d). **Effective** 1-1-67.

[Sec. 861(e)—Stricken]

Amendments

- **1986, Tax Reform Act of 1986 (P.L. 99-514)**

P.L. 99-514, § 1212(d):

Amended Code Sec. 861 by striking out subsection (e) and by redesignating subsection (f) as subsection (e). **Effective**, generally, for tax years beginning after 12-31-86. For special rules, see Act Sec. 1212(f)(2) and (3), below. Prior to being stricken, Code Sec. 861(e) read as follows:

(e) INCOME FROM CERTAIN LEASED AIRCRAFT, VESSELS, AND SPACECRAFT TREATED AS INCOME FROM SOURCES WITHIN THE UNITED STATES.—

(1) IN GENERAL.—For purposes of subsection (a) and section 862(a), if—

(A) a taxpayer owning a craft which is section 38 property (or would be section 38 property but for section 48(a)(5)) leases such craft to a United States person, other than a member of the same controlled group of corporations (as defined in section 1563) as the taxpayer, and

(B) such craft is manufactured or constructed in the United States,

then all amounts includible in gross income by the taxpayer with respect to such craft for any taxable year ending after the commencement of such lease (whether during or after the period of such lease), including gain from sale, exchange, or other disposition of such craft, shall be treated as income from sources within the United States.

(2) CERTAIN TRANSFERS INVOLVING CARRYOVER BASIS.—If the taxpayer transfers or distributes a craft to which paragraph (1) applied and the basis of such craft in the hands of the transferee or distributee is determined by reference to its basis in the hands of the transferor or distributor, paragraph (1) shall continue to apply to such craft in the hands of the transferee or distributee.

(3) CRAFT DEFINED.—For purposes of this subsection, the term "craft" means a vessel, aircraft, or spacecraft.

P.L. 99-514, § 1212(f)(2)-(3), provides:

(2) SPECIAL RULE FOR CERTAIN LEASED PROPERTY.—The amendments made by subsections (a) and (d) shall not apply to any income attributable to property held by the taxpayer on January 1, 1986, if such property was first leased by the taxpayer before January 1, 1986, in a lease to which section 863(c)(2)(B) or 861(e) of the Internal Revenue Code of 1954 (as in effect on the day before the date of the enactment of this Act) applied.

(3) SPECIAL RULE OF CERTAIN SHIPS LEASED BY THE UNITED STATES NAVY.—

(A) IN GENERAL.—In the case of any property described in subparagraph (B), paragraph (2) shall be applied by substituting "1987" for "1986" each place it appears.

(B) PROPERTY TO WHICH PARAGRAPH APPLIES.—Property described in this subparagraph consists of 4 ships which are to be leased by the United States Navy and which

INCOME TAX—SOURCES OF INCOME

are the subject of Internal Revenue Service rulings bearing the following dates and which involved the following amount of financing, respectively:

March 5, 1986	$176,844,000
February 5, 1986	64,567,000
April 22, 1986	64,598,000
May 22, 1986	175,300,000

● **1980, Miscellaneous Revenue Act of 1980 (P.L. 96-605)**

P.L. 96-605, § 104(a):

Amended Code Sec. 861(e). **Effective** with respect to property first leased after 12-28-80. Prior to amendment, Code Sec. 861(e) read as follows:

(e) ELECTION TO TREAT INCOME FROM CERTAIN AIRCRAFT AND VESSELS AS INCOME FROM SOURCES WITHIN THE UNITED STATES.—

(1) IN GENERAL.—For purposes of subsection (a) and section 862(a), if a taxpayer owning an aircraft or vessel which is section 38 property (or would be section 38 property but for section 48(a)(5)) leases such aircraft or vessel to a United States person, other than a member of the same controlled group of corporations (as defined in section 1563) as the taxpayer, and if such aircraft or vessel is manufactured or constructed in the United States, the taxpayer may elect, for any taxable year ending after the commencement of such lease, to treat all amounts includible in gross income with respect to such aircraft or vessel (whether during or after the period of any such lease), including gain from sale, exchange, or other disposition of such aircraft or vessel, as income from sources within the United States.

(2) EFFECT OF ELECTION.—An election under paragraph (1) made with respect to any aircraft or vessel shall apply to the taxable year for which made and to all subsequent taxable years. Such election may not be revoked except with the consent of the Secretary.

(3) MANNER AND TIME OF ELECTION AND REVOCATION.—An election under paragraph (1), and any revocation of such election, shall be made in such manner and at such time as the Secretary or his delegate prescribes by regulations.

(4) CERTAIN TRANSFERS INVOLVING CARRYOVER BASIS.—If the taxpayer transfers or distributes an aircraft or vessel which is subject to an election under paragraph (1) and the basis of such aircraft or vessel in the hands of the transferee or distributee is determined by reference to its basis in the hands of the transferor or distributor, the transferee or distributee shall, for purposes of paragraph (1), be treated as having made an election with respect to such aircraft or vessel.

● **1976, Tax Reform Act of 1976 (P.L. 94-455)**

P.L. 94-455, § 1901(b)(26):

Substituted "sale, exchange, or other disposition" for "sale or other disposition" in paragraph (1). **Effective** for tax years beginning after 12-31-76.

P.L. 94-455, § 1906(b)(13)(A):

Amended 1954 Code by substituting "Secretary" for "Secretary or his delegate" each place it appeared. **Effective** 2-1-77.

● **1971, Revenue Act of 1971 (P.L. 92-178)**

P.L. 92-178, § 314(a):

Added Code Sec. 861(e). **Effective** for tax years ending after 8-15-71, but only with respect to leases entered into after such date.

[Sec. 861(d)]

(d) INCOME FROM CERTAIN RAILROAD ROLLING STOCK TREATED AS INCOME FROM SOURCES WITHIN THE UNITED STATES.—

(1) GENERAL RULE.—For purposes of subsection (a) and section 862(a), if—

(A) a taxpayer leases railroad rolling stock which is section 1245 property (as defined in section 1245(a)(3)) to a domestic common carrier by railroad or a corporation which is controlled, directly or indirectly, by one or more such common carriers, and

(B) the use under such lease is expected to be use[d] within the United States,

all amounts includible in gross income by the taxpayer with respect to such railroad rolling stock (including gain from sale or other disposition of such railroad rolling stock) shall be treated as income from sources within the United States. The requirements of subparagraph (B) of the preceding sentence shall be treated as satisfied if the only expected use outside the United States is use by a person (whether or not a United States person) in Canada or Mexico on a temporary basis which is not expected to exceed a total of 90 days in any taxable year.

(2) PARAGRAPH (1) NOT TO APPLY WHERE LESSOR IS A MEMBER OF CONTROLLED GROUP WHICH INCLUDES A RAILROAD.—Paragraph (1) shall not apply to a lease between two members of the same controlled group of corporations (as defined in section 1563) if any member of such group is a domestic common carrier by railroad or a switching or terminal company all of whose stock is owned by one or more domestic common carriers by railroad.

(3) DENIAL OF FOREIGN TAX CREDIT.—No credit shall be allowed under section 901 for any payments to foreign countries with respect to any amount received by the taxpayer with respect to railroad rolling stock which is subject to paragraph (1).

Amendments

● **2010, (P.L. 111-226)**

P.L. 111-226, § 217(c)(1):

Amended Code Sec. 861 by redesignating subsection (e) as subsection (d). **Effective** generally for tax years beginning after 12-31-2010. For a grandfather rule, see Act Sec. 217(d)(2), below.

P.L. 111-226, § 217(d)(2), provides:

(2) GRANDFATHER RULE FOR OUTSTANDING DEBT OBLIGATIONS.—

(A) IN GENERAL.—The amendments made by this section shall not apply to payments of interest on obligations issued before the date of the enactment of this Act.

(B) EXCEPTION FOR RELATED PARTY DEBT.—Subparagraph (A) shall not apply to any interest which is payable to a related person (determined under rules similar to the rules of section 954(d)(3)).

(C) SIGNIFICANT MODIFICATIONS TREATED AS NEW ISSUES.—For purposes of subparagraph (A), a significant modification of the terms of any obligation (including any extension of the term of such obligation) shall be treated as a new issue.

● **1990, Omnibus Budget Reconciliation Act of 1990 (P.L. 101-508)**

P.L. 101-508, § 11801(c)(6)(C):

Amended Code Sec. 861(e)(2) by striking "referred to in subparagraph (B) of section 184(d)(1)" and inserting "all of whose stock is owned by one or more domestic common carriers by railroad". **Effective** 11-5-90.

P.L. 101-508, § 11821(b), provides:

(b) SAVINGS PROVISION.—If—

(1) any provision amended or repealed by this part applied to—

(A) any transaction occurring before the date of the enactment of this Act,

(B) any property acquired before such date of enactment, or

(C) any item of income, loss, deduction, or credit taken into account before such date of enactment, and

(2) the treatment of such transaction, property, or item under such provision would (without regard to the amendments made by this part) affect liability for tax for periods ending after such date of enactment,

nothing in the amendments made by this part shall be construed to affect the treatment of such transaction, property, or item for purposes of determining liability for tax for periods ending after such date of enactment.

P.L. 101-508, § 11813(b)(17) (as amended by P.L. 104-188, § 1702(h)(9)):

Amended Code Sec. 861(e)(1)(A) by striking "which is section 38 property (or would be section 38 property but for section 48(a)(5))" and inserting "which is section 1245 property (as defined in section 1245(a)(3))". **Effective**, generally, for property placed in service after 12-31-90. For exceptions, see Act Sec. 11813(c)(2), below.

P.L. 101-508, § 11813(c)(2), provides:

(2) EXCEPTIONS.—The amendments made by this section shall not apply to—

(A) any transition property (as defined in section 49(e) of the Internal Revenue Code of 1986 (as in effect on the date before the date of the enactment of this Act),

(B) any property with respect to which qualified progress expenditures were previously taken into account under section 46(d) of such Code (as so in effect), and

(C) any property described in section 46(b)(2)(C) of such Code (as so in effect).

● **1989, Omnibus Budget Reconciliation Act of 1989 (P.L. 101-239)**

P.L. 101-239, § 7841(d)(9):

Amended Code Sec. 861(e)(1) by striking "section 826(a)" and inserting "section 862(a)". **Effective** 12-19-89.

● **1986, Tax Reform Act of 1986 (P.L. 99-514)**

P.L. 99-514, § 1212(d):

Amended Code Sec. 861 by striking out subsection (e) and by redesignating subsection (f) as subsection (e). **Effective**, generally, for tax years beginning after 12-31-86. For special rules, see Act Sec. 1212(f)(2)-(3), following repealed Code Sec. 861(e).

● **1981, Economic Recovery Tax Act of 1981 (P.L. 97-34)**

P.L. 97-34, § 223, provides:

SEC. 223. SUSPENSIONS OF REGULATIONS RELATING TO ALLOCATION UNDER SECTION 861 OF RESEARCH AND EXPERIMENTAL EXPENDITURES.

(a) 2-YEAR SUSPENSION.—In the case of the taxpayer's first 2 taxable years beginning within 2 years after the date of the enactment of this Act, all research and experimental expenditures (within the meaning of section 174 of the Internal Revenue Code of 1954) which are paid or incurred in such year for research activities conducted in the United States shall be allocated or apportioned to sources within the United States.

(b) STUDY.—

(1) IN GENERAL.—The Secretary of the Treasury shall conduct a study with respect to the impact which section 1.861-8 of the Internal Revenue Service Regulations would have (A) on research and experimental activities conducted in the United States and (B) on the availability of the foreign tax credit.

(2) REPORT.—Not later than the date 6 months after the date of the enactment of this Act, the Secretary of the Treasury shall submit to the Committee on Ways and Means of the House of Representatives and the Committee on Finance of the Senate a report

INCOME TAX—SOURCES OF INCOME

on the study conducted under paragraph (1) (together with such recommendations as he may deem advisable).

- **1978, Revenue Act of 1978 (P.L. 95-600)**

P.L. 95-600, §370(a):

Added Code Sec. 861(f). For the **effective** date, see Act Sec. 370(b), below.

P.L. 95-600, §370(b), provides:

(b) EFFECTIVE DATES.—

(1) IN GENERAL.—The amendment made by subsection (a) shall apply to all railroad rolling stock placed in service with respect to the taxpayer after the date of the enactment of this Act.

(2) ELECTION TO EXTEND SECTION 861(f) TO RAILROAD ROLLING STOCK PLACED IN SERVICE BEFORE DATE OF ENACTMENT.

(A) IN GENERAL.—At the election of the taxpayer, the amendment made by subsection (a) shall also apply, for taxable years beginning after the date of the enactment of this Act, to all railroad rolling stock placed in service with respect to the taxpayer on or before such date of enactment. Such an election may not be revoked except with the consent of the Secretary of the Treasury or his delegate.

(B) MANNER AND TIME OF ELECTION AND REVOCATION.—An election under subparagraph (A), and any revocation of such an election, shall be made in such manner and at such time as the Secretary of the Treasury or his delegate may by regulations prescribe.

[Sec. 861(e)]

(e) CROSS REFERENCE.—

For treatment of interest paid by the branch of a foreign corporation, see section 884(f).

Amendments

- **2010, (P.L. 111-226)**

P.L. 111-226, §217(c)(1):

Amended Code Sec. 861 by redesignating subsection (f) as subsection (e). **Effective** generally for tax years beginning after 12-31-2010. For a grandfather rule, see Act Sec. 217(d)(2), below.

P.L. 111-226, §217(d)(2), provides:

(2) GRANDFATHER RULE FOR OUTSTANDING DEBT OBLIGATIONS.—

(A) IN GENERAL.—The amendments made by this section shall not apply to payments of interest on obligations issued before the date of the enactment of this Act.

(B) EXCEPTION FOR RELATED PARTY DEBT.—Subparagraph (A) shall not apply to any interest which is payable to a related person (determined under rules similar to the rules of section 954(d)(3)).

(C) SIGNIFICANT MODIFICATIONS TREATED AS NEW ISSUES.—For purposes of subparagraph (A), a significant modification of the terms of any obligation (including any extension of the term of such obligation) shall be treated as a new issue.

- **1988, Technical and Miscellaneous Revenue Act of 1988 (P.L. 100-647)**

P.L. 100-647, §1012(q)(9):

Amended Code Sec. 861 by adding at the end thereof new subsection (f). **Effective** as if included in the provision of P.L. 99-514 to which it relates.

[Sec. 862]

SEC. 862. INCOME FROM SOURCES WITHOUT THE UNITED STATES.

[Sec. 862(a)]

(a) GROSS INCOME FROM SOURCES WITHOUT UNITED STATES.—The following items of gross income shall be treated as income from sources without the United States:

(1) interest other than that derived from sources within the United States as provided in section 861(a)(1);

(2) dividends other than those derived from sources within the United States as provided in section 861(a)(2);

(3) compensation for labor or personal services performed without the United States;

(4) rentals or royalties from property located without the United States or from any interest in such property, including rentals or royalties for the use of or for the privilege of using without the United States patents, copyrights, secret processes and formulas, good will, trade-marks, trade brands, franchises, and other like properties;

(5) gains, profits, and income from the sale or exchange of real property located without the United States;

(6) gains, profits, and income derived from the purchase of inventory property (within the meaning of section 865(i)(1)) within the United States and its sale or exchange without the United States;

(7) underwriting income other than that derived from sources within the United States as provided in section 861(a)(7);

(8) gains, profits, and income from the disposition of a United States real property interest (as defined in section 897(c)) when the real property is located in the Virgin Islands; and

(9) amounts received, directly or indirectly, from a foreign person for the provision of a guarantee of indebtedness of such person other than amounts which are derived from sources within the United States as provided in section 861(a)(9).

Amendments

- **2010, Creating Small Business Jobs Act of 2010 (P.L. 111-240)**

P.L. 111-240, §2122(b):

Amended Code Sec. 862(a) by striking "and" at the end of paragraph (7), by striking the period at the end of paragraph (8) and inserting "; and", and by adding at the end a new paragraph (9). **Effective** for guarantees issued after 9-27-2010.

- **1989, Omnibus Budget Reconciliation Act of 1989 (P.L. 101-239)**

P.L. 101-239, §7811(i)(2):

Amended Code Sec. 862(a)(6) by striking "865(h)(1)" and inserting "865(i)(1)". **Effective** as if included in the provision of P.L. 100-647 to which it relates.

- **1986, Tax Reform Act of 1986 (P.L. 99-514)**

P.L. 99-514, §1211(b)(1)(C):

Amended Code Sec. 862(a)(6) by striking out "personal property" and inserting in lieu thereof "inventory property (within the meaning of section 865(h)(1))". **Effective** for tax years beginning after 12-31-86. For a special rule, see Act Sec. 1211(c)(2), below.

P.L. 99-514, §1211(c)(2), provides:

(2) SPECIAL RULE FOR FOREIGN PERSONS.—In the case of any foreign person other than any controlled foreign corporations (within the meaning of section 957(a) of the Internal Revenue Code of 1954), the amendments made by this section shall apply to transactions entered into after March 18, 1986.

For general rules, see Act Sec. 1216 following Code Sec. 861.

- **1981, Economic Recovery Tax Act of 1981 (P.L. 97-34)**

P.L. 97-34, §831(a)(2):

Amended Code Sec. 862(a) by striking out "and" at the end of paragraph (5), by striking out the period at the end of paragraph (6) and inserting a semicolon, by striking out "Underwriting" in paragraph (7) and inserting "underwriting", by striking out the period at the end of paragraph (7) and inserting "; and", and by adding paragraph (8). **Effective** for dispositions after 6-18-80, in tax years ending after that date.

- **1976, Tax Reform Act of 1976 (P.L. 94-455)**

P.L. 94-455, §1036(b):

Added a new paragraph (7). **Effective** for tax years beginning after 12-31-76.

P.L. 94-455, §1901(b)(26):

Substituted "sale or exchange" for "sale" in paragraphs (5) and (6). **Effective** for tax years beginning after 12-31-76.

[Sec. 862(b)]

(b) TAXABLE INCOME FROM SOURCES WITHOUT UNITED STATES.—From the items of gross income specified in subsection (a) there shall be deducted the expenses, losses, and other deductions properly apportioned or allocated thereto, and a ratable part of any expenses, losses, or other deductions which cannot definitely be allocated to some item or class of gross income. The remainder, if any, shall be treated in full as taxable income from sources without the United States. In the case of an individual who does not itemize deductions, an amount equal to the standard deduction shall be considered a deduction which cannot definitely be allocated to some item or class of gross income.

Amendments

- **1986, Tax Reform Act of 1986 (P.L. 99-514)**

P.L. 99-514, §104(b)(12):

Amended Code Sec. 862(b) by striking out "the zero bracket amount" and inserting in lieu thereof "the standard deduction". **Effective** for tax years beginning after 12-31-86.

- **1977, Tax Reduction and Simplification Act of 1977 (P.L. 95-30)**

P.L. 95-30, §102(b)(10):

Amended Code Sec. 862(b) by adding the last sentence. **Effective** for tax years beginning after 12-31-76. For special rules regarding allocation of R & E expenditures under Code Sec. 861, see P.L. 98-369, §126, following Code Sec. 861(b).

INCOME TAX—SOURCES OF INCOME

[Sec. 862(c)—Repealed]

Amendments

• **1988, Technical and Miscellaneous Revenue Act of 1988 (P.L. 100-647)**

P.L. 100-647, § 1012(e)(4):

Repealed Code Sec. 862(c). **Effective** as if included in the provision of P.L. 99-514 to which it relates. For a special rule, see Act Sec. 4009 in the amendment notes following Code Sec. 861(a). Prior to repeal, Code Sec. 862(c) read as follows:

(c) CROSS REFERENCE.—

For source of amounts attributable to certain aircraft and vessels, see section 861(e).

• **1971, Revenue Act of 1971 (P.L. 92-178)**

P.L. 92-178, § 314(b):

Added Code Sec. 862(c).

[Sec. 863]

SEC. 863. SPECIAL RULES FOR DETERMINING SOURCE.

[Sec. 863(a)]

(a) ALLOCATION UNDER REGULATIONS.—Items of gross income, expenses, losses, and deductions, other than those specified in sections 861(a) and 862(a), shall be allocated or apportioned to sources within or without the United States, under regulations prescribed by the Secretary. Where items of gross income are separately allocated to sources within the United States, there shall be deducted (for the purpose of computing the taxable income therefrom) the expenses, losses, and other deductions properly apportioned or allocated thereto and a ratable part of other expenses, losses, or other deductions which cannot definitely be allocated to some item or class of gross income. The remainder, if any, shall be included in full as taxable income from sources within the United States.

Amendments

• **1988, Technical and Miscellaneous Revenue Act of 1988 (P.L. 100-647)**

P.L. 100-647, § 1012(e)(3)(A):

Amended the heading of Code Sec. 863. **Effective** as if included in the provision of P.L. 99-514 to which it relates. Prior to amendment, the heading of Code Sec. 863 read as follows:

SEC. 863. ITEMS NOT SPECIFIED IN SECTION 861 OR 862.

• **1976, Tax Reform Act of 1976 (P.L. 94-455)**

P.L. 94-455, § 1906(b)(13)(A):

Amended 1954 Code by substituting "Secretary" for "Secretary or his delegate" each place it appeared. **Effective** 2-1-77.

[Sec. 863(b)]

(b) INCOME PARTLY FROM WITHIN AND PARTLY FROM WITHOUT THE UNITED STATES.—In the case of gross income derived from sources partly within and partly without the United States, the taxable income may first be computed by deducting the expenses, losses, or other deductions apportioned or allocated thereto and a ratable part of any expenses, losses, or other deductions which cannot definitely be allocated to some item or class of gross income; and the portion of such taxable income attributable to sources within the United States may be determined by processes or formulas of general apportionment prescribed by the Secretary. Gains, profits, and income—

   (1) from services rendered partly within and partly without the United States,

   (2) from the sale or exchange of inventory property (within the meaning of section 865(i)(1)) produced (in whole or in part) by the taxpayer within and sold or exchanged without the United States, or produced (in whole or in part) by the taxpayer without and sold or exchanged within the United States, or

   (3) derived from the purchase of inventory property (within the meaning of section 865(i)(1)) within a possession of the United States and its sale or exchange within the United States,

shall be treated as derived partly from sources within and partly from sources without the United States. Gains, profits, and income from the sale or exchange of inventory property described in paragraph (2) shall be allocated and apportioned between sources within and without the United States solely on the basis of the production activities with respect to the property.

Amendments

• **2017, Tax Cuts and Jobs Act (P.L. 115-97)**

P.L. 115-97, § 14303(a):

Amended Code Sec. 863(b) by adding at the end a new sentence. **Effective** for tax years beginning after 12-31-2017.

• **1989, Omnibus Budget Reconciliation Act of 1989 (P.L. 101-239)**

P.L. 101-239, § 7811(i)(2):

Amended Code Sec. 863(b)(2) by striking "865(h)(1)" and inserting "865(i)(1)". **Effective** as if included in the provision of P.L. 100-647 to which it relates.

P.L. 101-239, § 7811(i)(2):

Amended Code Sec. 863(b)(3) by striking "865(h)(1)" and inserting "865(i)(1)". **Effective** as if included in the provision of P.L. 100-647 to which it relates.

• **1986, Tax Reform Act of 1986 (P.L. 99-514)**

P.L. 99-514, § 1211(b)(1)(A):

Amended Code Sec. 863(b)(2) and (3) by striking out "personal property" and inserting in lieu thereof "inventory property (within the meaning of section 856(g)(1)". **Effective** for tax years beginning after 12-31-86. For a special rule, see Act Sec. 1211(c)(2), below.

P.L. 99-514, § 1211(c)(2), provides:

(2) SPECIAL RULE FOR FOREIGN PERSONS.—In the case of any foreign person other than any controlled foreign corporations (within the meaning of section 957(a) of the Internal Revenue Code of 1954), the amendments made by this section shall apply to transactions entered into after March 18, 1986.

P.L. 99-514, § 1212(e):

Amended Code Sec. 863(b)(1) by striking out "transportation or other services" and inserting in lieu thereof "services". **Effective**, generally, for tax years beginning after 12-31-86. For special rules, see Act Sec. 1212(f)(2)-(3) following Code Sec. 861. For special rules regarding allocation of R & E expenditures under Code Sec. 861, see P.L. 98-369, § 126, following Code Sec. 861(b).

• **1976, Tax Reform Act of 1976 (P.L. 94-455)**

P.L. 94-455, § 1906(b)(13)(A):

Amended 1954 Code by substituting "Secretary" for "Secretary or his delegate" each place it appeared. **Effective** 2-1-77.

P.L. 94-455, § 1901(b)(26):

Substituted "sale or exchange" for "sale" and "sold or exchanged" for "sold" in paragraph (2). **Effective** for tax years beginning after 12-31-76.

[Sec. 863(c)]

(c) SOURCE RULE FOR CERTAIN TRANSPORTATION INCOME.—

   (1) TRANSPORTATION BEGINNING AND ENDING IN THE UNITED STATES.—All transportation income attributable to transportation which begins and ends in the United States shall be treated as derived from sources within the United States.

   (2) OTHER TRANSPORTATION HAVING UNITED STATES CONNECTION.—

      (A) IN GENERAL.—50 percent of all transportation income attributable to transportation which—

         (i) is not described in paragraph (1), and

         (ii) begins or ends in the United States,

      shall be treated as from sources in the United States.

      (B) SPECIAL RULE FOR PERSONAL SERVICE INCOME.—Subparagraph (A) shall not apply to any transportation income which is income derived from personal services performed by the taxpayer, unless such income is attributable to transportation which—

         (i) begins in the United States and ends in a possession of the United States, or

         (ii) begins in a possession of the United States and ends in the United States.

   In the case of transportation income derived from, or in connection with, a vessel, this subparagraph shall only apply if the taxpayer is a citizen or resident alien.

   (3) TRANSPORTATION INCOME.—For purposes of this subsection, the term "transportation income" means any income derived from, or in connection with—

      (A) the use (or hiring or leasing for use) of a vessel or aircraft, or

INCOME TAX—SOURCES OF INCOME

(B) the performance of services directly related to the use of a vessel or aircraft.

For purposes of the preceding sentence, the term "vessel or aircraft" includes any container used in connection with a vessel or aircraft.

Amendments

• **1997, Taxpayer Relief Act of 1997 (P.L. 105-34)**

P.L. 105-34, § 1174(a)(2):

Amended Code Sec. 863(c)(2)(B) by adding at the end a new flush sentence. **Effective** for remuneration for services performed in tax years beginning after 12-31-97.

• **1986, Tax Reform Act of 1986 (P.L. 99-514)**

P.L. 99-514, § 1212(a):

Amended Code Sec. 863(c)(2). **Effective**, generally, for tax years beginning after 12-31-86. For special rules, see Act Sec. 1212(f)(2)-(3) following Code Sec. 861. Prior to amendment, Code Sec. 863(c)(2) read as follows:

(2) TRANSPORTATION BETWEEN UNITED STATES AND ANY POSSESSION.—

(A) IN GENERAL.—50 percent of all transportation income attributable to transportation which

(i) begins in the United States and ends in a possession of the United States, or

(ii) begins in a possession of the United States and ends in the United States,

shall be treated as derived from sources within the United States.

(B) SPECIAL RULE FOR CERTAIN LESSORS OF AIRCRAFT.—If—

(i) the taxpayer owns an aircraft which is section 38 property and leases such aircraft to a United States person (other than a member of the same controlled group of corporations (as defined in section 1563) as the taxpayer), and

(ii) such United States person is a regularly scheduled air carrier,

subparagraph (A) shall be applied by substituting "100 percent" for "50 percent".

• **1984, Deficit Reduction Act of 1984 (P.L. 98-369)**

P.L. 98-369, § 124(a):

Added Code Sec. 863(c). **Effective** for transporation beginning after 7-18-84 in tax years ending after such date. Special rules appear in P.L. 98-369, § 126, following Code Sec. 861(b).

[Sec. 863(d)]

(d) SOURCE RULES FOR SPACE AND CERTAIN OCEAN ACTIVITIES.—

(1) IN GENERAL.—Except as provided in regulations, any income derived from a space or ocean activity—

(A) if derived by a United States person, shall be sourced in the United States, and

(B) if derived by a person other than a United States person, shall be sourced outside the United States.

(2) SPACE OR OCEAN ACTIVITY.—For purposes of paragraph (1)—

(A) IN GENERAL.—The term "space or ocean activity" means—

(i) any activity conducted in space, and

(ii) any activity conducted on or under water not within the jurisdiction (as recognized by the United States) of a foreign country, possession of the United States, or the United States.

Such term includes any activity conducted in Antarctica.

(B) EXCEPTION FOR CERTAIN ACTIVITIES.—The term "space or ocean activity" shall not include—

(i) any activity giving rise to transportation income (as defined in section 863(c)),

(ii) any activity giving rise to international communications income (as defined in subsection (e)(2)), and

(iii) any activity with respect to mines, oil and gas wells, or other natural deposits to the extent within the United States or any foreign country or possession of the United States (as defined in section 638).

For purposes of applying section 638, the jurisdiction of any foreign country shall not include any jurisdiction not recognized by the United States.

Amendments

• **1986, Tax Reform Act of 1986 (P.L. 99-514)**

P.L. 99-514, § 1213(a):

Amended Code Sec. 863 by adding at the end thereof new subsection (d). **Effective** for tax years beginning after 12-31-86. For general rules, see Act Sec. 1216 following Code Sec. 861.

[Sec. 863(e)]

(e) INTERNATIONAL COMMUNICATIONS INCOME.—

(1) SOURCE RULES.—

(A) UNITED STATES PERSONS.—In the case of any United States person, 50 percent of any international communications income shall be sourced in the United States and 50 percent of such income shall be sourced outside the United States.

(B) FOREIGN PERSONS.—

(i) IN GENERAL.—Except as provided in regulations or clause (ii), in the case of any person other than a United States person, any international communications income shall be sourced outside the United States.

(ii) SPECIAL RULE FOR INCOME ATTRIBUTABLE TO OFFICE OR FIXED PLACE OF BUSINESS IN THE UNITED STATES.—In the case of any person (other than a United States person) who maintains an office or other fixed place of business in the United States, any international communications income attributable to such office or other fixed place of business shall be sourced in the United States.

(2) DEFINITION.—For purposes of this section, the term "international communications income" includes all income derived from the transmission of communications or data from the United States to any foreign country (or possession of the United States) or from any foreign country (or possession of the United States) to the United States.

Amendments

• **1988, Technical and Miscellaneous Revenue Act of 1988 (P.L. 100-647)**

P.L. 100-647, § 1012(f):

Amended Code Sec. 863(e)(2) by striking out "foreign country" each place it appears and inserting in lieu thereof "foreign country (or possession of the United States)". **Effective** as if included in the provision of P.L. 99-514 to which it relates. For a special rule, see Act Sec. 4009 in the amendment notes following Code Sec. 861(a).

• **1986, Tax Reform Act of 1986 (P.L. 99-514)**

P.L. 99-514, § 1213(a):

Amended Code Sec. 863 by adding at the end thereof new subsection (e). **Effective** for tax years beginning after 12-31-86. For general rules, see Act Sec. 1216 following Code Sec. 861.

[Sec. 864]

SEC. 864. DEFINITIONS AND SPECIAL RULES.

[Sec. 864(a)]

(a) PRODUCED.—For purposes of this part, the term "produced" includes created, fabricated, manufactured, extracted, processed, cured, or aged.

Amendments

• **1986, Tax Reform Act of 1986 (P.L. 99-514)**

P.L. 99-514, § 1215(b)(1):

Amended the section heading for Code Sec. 864. **Effective**, generally, for tax years beginning after 12-31-86. For special and transitional rules, see Act Sec. 1215(c)(2)-(6), below. Prior to amendment, the section heading for Code Sec. 864 read as follows:

SEC. 864. DEFINITIONS.

P.L. 99-514, § 1215(c)(2)-(6), as amended by P.L. 100-647, § 1012(h)(7) and P.L. 104-191, § 521(a), provides:

(2) TRANSITIONAL RULES.—

(A) GENERAL PHASE-IN.—

INCOME TAX—SOURCES OF INCOME

(i) IN GENERAL.—In the case of the 1st 3 taxable years of the taxpayer beginning after December 31, 1986, the amendments made by this section shall not apply to interest expenses paid or accrued by the taxpayer during the taxable year with respect to an aggregate amount of indebtedness which does not exceed the general phase-in amount.

(ii) GENERAL PHASE-IN AMOUNT.—Except as provided in clause (iii), the general phase-in amount for purposes of clause (i) is the applicable percentage (determined under the following table) of the aggregate amount of indebtedness of the taxpayer outstanding on November 16, 1985:

In the case of the:	The applicable percentage is:
1st taxable year	75
2nd taxable year	50
3rd taxable year	25

(iii) LOWER LIMIT WHERE TAXPAYER REDUCES INDEBTEDNESS.—For purposes of applying this subparagraph to interest expenses attributable to any month, the general phase-in amount shall in no event exceed the lowest amount of indebtedness of the taxpayer outstanding as of the close of any preceding month beginning after November 16, 1985. To the extent provided in regulations, the average amount of indebtedness outstanding during any month shall be used (in lieu of the amount outstanding as of the close of such month) for purposes of the preceding sentence.

(B) CONSOLIDATION RULE NOT TO APPLY TO CERTAIN INTEREST.—

(i) IN GENERAL.—In the case of the 1st 5 taxable years of the taxpayer beginning after December 31, 1986—

(I) subparagraph (A) shall not apply for purposes of paragraph (1) of section 864(e) of the Internal Revenue Code of 1986 (as added by this section), but

(II) such paragraph (1) shall not apply to interest expenses paid or accrued by the taxpayer during the taxable year with respect to an aggregate amount of indebtedness which does not exceed the special phase-in amount.

(ii) SPECIAL PHASE-IN AMOUNT.—The special phase-in amount for purposes of clause (i) is the sum of—

(I) the general phase-in amount as determined for purposes of subparagraph (A),

(II) the 5-year phase-in amount, and

(III) the 4-year phase-in amount.

For purposes of applying this subparagraph to interest expense attributable to any month, the special phase-in amount shall in no event exceed the limitation determined under subparagraph (A)(iii).

(iii) 5-YEAR PHASE-IN AMOUNT.—The 5-year phase-in amount is the lesser of—

(I) the applicable percentage (determined under the following table for purposes of this subclause) of the 5-year debt amount, or

(II) the applicable percentage (determined under the following table for purposes of this subclause) of the 5-year debt amount reduced by paydowns:

In the case of the:	The applicable percentage for purposes of subclause (I) is:	The applicable percentage for purposes of subclause (II) is:
1st taxable year	$8^{1}/_{2}$	10
2nd taxable year	$16^{2}/_{3}$	25
3rd taxable year	25	50
4th taxable year	$33^{1}/_{3}$	100
5th taxable year	$16^{2}/_{3}$	100

(iv) 4-YEAR PHASE-IN AMOUNT.—The 4-year phase-in amount is the lesser of—

(I) the applicable percentage (determined under the following table for purposes of this subclause) of the 4-year debt amount, or

(II) the applicable percentage (determined under the following table for purposes of this subclause) of the 4-year debt amount reduced by paydowns to the extent such paydowns exceed the 5-year debt amount:

In the case of the:	The applicable percentage for purposes of subclause (I) is:	The applicable percentage for purposes of subclause (II) is:
1st taxable year	5	$6^{1}/_{4}$
2nd taxable year	10	$16^{2}/_{3}$
3rd taxable year	15	$37^{1}/_{2}$
4th taxable year	20	100
5th taxable year	0	0

(v) 5-YEAR DEBT AMOUNT.—The term "5-year debt amount" means the excess (if any) of—

(I) the amount of the outstanding indebtedness of the taxpayer on May 29, 1985, over

(II) the amount of the outstanding indebtedness of the taxpayer as of the close of December 31, 1983.

The 5-year debt amount shall not exceed the aggregate amount of indebtedness of the taxpayer outstanding on November 16, 1985.

(vi) 4-YEAR DEBT AMOUNT.—The term "4-year debt amount" means the excess (if any) of—

(I) the amount referred to in clause (v)(II), over

(II) the amount of the outstanding indebtedness of the taxpayer as of the close of December 31, 1982.

The 4-year debt amount shall not exceed the aggregate amount of indebtedness of the taxpayer outstanding on November 16, 1985, reduced by the 5-year debt amount.

(vii) PAYDOWNS.—For purposes of applying this subparagraph to interest expenses attributable to any month, the term "paydowns" means the excess (if any) of—

(I) the aggregate amount of indebtedness of the taxpayer outstanding on November 16, 1985, over

(II) the lowest amount of indebtedness of the taxpayer outstanding as of the close of any preceding month beginning after November 16, 1985 (or, to the extent provided in regulations under subparagraph (A)(iii), the average amount of indebtedness outstanding during any such month).

(C) COORDINATION OF SUBPARAGRAPHS (A) AND (B).—In applying subparagraph (B), there shall first be taken into account indebtedness to which subparagraph (A) applies.

(D) SPECIAL RULES.—

(i) In the case of the 1st 9 taxable years of the taxpayer beginning after December 31, 1986, the amendments made by this section shall not apply to interest expenses paid or accrued by the taxpayer during the taxable year with respect to an aggregate amount of indebtedness which does not exceed the applicable percentage (determined under the following table) of the indebtedness described in clause (iii) or (iv):

In the case of the:	The applicable percentage is:
1st taxable year	90
2nd taxable year	80
3rd taxable year	70
4th taxable year	60
5th taxable year	50
6th taxable year	40
7th taxable year	30
8th taxable year	20
9th taxable year	10

(ii) The provisions of this subparagraph shall apply in lieu of the provisions of subparagraphs (A) and (B).

(iii) INDEBTEDNESS OUTSTANDING ON MAY 29, 1985.—Indebtedness is described in this clause if it is indebtedness (which was outstanding on May 29, 1985) of a corporation incorporated on June 13, 1917, which has its principal place of business in Bartlesville, Oklahoma.

(iv) INDEBTEDNESS OUTSTANDING ON MAY 29, 1985.—Indebtedness is described in this clause if it is indebtedness (which was outstanding on May 29, 1985) of a member of an affiliated group (as defined in section 1504(a)), the common parent of which was incorporated on August 26, 1926, and has its principal place of business in Harrison, New York.

(E) TREATMENT OF AFFILIATED GROUP.—For purposes of this paragraph, all members of the same affiliated group of corporations (as defined in section 864(e)(5)(A) of the Internal Revenue Code of 1986, as added by this section) shall be treated as 1 taxpayer whether or not such members filed a consolidated return.

(F) ELECTION TO HAVE PARAGRAPH NOT APPLY.—A taxpayer may elect (at such time and in such manner as the Secretary of the Treasury or his delegate may prescribe) to have this paragraph not apply. In the case of members of the same affiliated group (as so defined), such an election may be made only if each member consents to such election.

(3) SPECIAL RULE.—

(A) IN GENERAL.—In the case of a qualified corporation, in lieu of applying paragraph (2), the amendments made by this section shall not apply to interest expenses allocable to any indebtedness to the extent such indebtedness does not exceed $500,000,000 if—

(i) the indebtedness was incurred to develop or improve existing property that is owned by the taxpayer on November 16, 1985, and was acquired with the intent to develop or improve the property,

(ii) the loan agreement with respect to the indebtedness provides that the funds are to be utilized for purposes of developing or improving the above property, and

(iii) the debt to equity ratio of the companies that join in the filing of the consolidated return is less than 15 percent.

(B) QUALIFIED CORPORATION.—For purposes of subparagraph (A), the term "qualified corporation" means a corporation—

(i) which was incorporated in Delaware on June 29, 1964,

(ii) the principal subsidiary of which is a resident of Arkansas, and

(iii) which is a member of an affiliated group the average daily United States production of oil of which is less than 50,000 barrels and the average daily United States refining of which is less than 150,000 barrels.

(4) SPECIAL RULES FOR SUBSIDIARY.—The amendments made by this section shall not apply to interest on up to the applicable dollar amount of indebtedness of a subsidiary incorporated on February 11, 1975, the indebtedness of which on May 6, 1986, included—

(A) $100,000,000 face amount of $11^{3}/_{4}$ percent notes due in 1990,

(B) $100,000,000 of $8^{3}/_{4}$ percent notes due in 1989,

(C) $6^{3}/_{4}$ percent Japanese yen notes due in 1991, and

(D) $5^{3}/_{8}$ percent Swiss franc bonds due in 1994.

For purposes of this paragraph, the term "applicable dollar amount" means $600,000,000 in the case of taxable years beginning in 1987 through 1991, $500,000,000 in the case of the taxable year beginning in 1992, $400,000,000 in the case of the taxable year beginning in 1993, $300,000,000 in the case of the taxable year beginning in 1994, $200,000,000 in the case of the taxable year beginning in 1995, $100,000,000 in

INCOME TAX—SOURCES OF INCOME

the case of the taxable year beginning in 1996, and zero in the case of taxable years beginning after 1996.

(5) [Repealed.]

(6) SPECIAL RULES FOR ALLOCATING GENERAL AND ADMINISTRATIVE EXPENSES.—

(A) IN GENERAL.—In the case of an affiliated group of domestic corporations the common parent of which has its principal office in New Brunswick, New Jersey, and has a certificate of organization which was filed with the Secretary of the State of New Jersey on November 10, 1887, the amendments made by this section shall not apply to the phase-in percentage of general and administrative expenses paid or incurred in its 1st 3 taxable years beginning after December 31, 1986.

(B) PHASE-IN PERCENTAGE.—For purposes of subparagraph (A):

In the case of taxable years beginning in:	The phase-in percentage is:
1987	75
1988	50
1989	25

- **1996, Health Insurance Portability and Accountability Act of 1996 (P.L. 104-191)**

P.L. 104-191, § 521(a):

Repealed Act Sec. 1215(c)(5) of P.L. 99-514. **Effective**, generally, for tax years beginning after 12-31-95. For a special rule, see Act Sec. 521(b), below. Prior to repeal, Act Sec. 1215(c)(5) read as follows:

(5) SPECIAL RULE FOR FINANCIAL CORPORATION.—For purposes of section 864(e)(5) of the Internal Revenue Code of 1986 (as added by this section), a corporation shall be treated as described in subparagraph (C) of such section for any taxable year if—

(A) such corporation is a Delaware corporation unincorporated on August 20, 1959, and

(B) such corporation was primarily engaged in the financing of dealer inventory or consumer purchases on May 29, 1985, and at all times thereafter before the close of the taxable year.

P.L. 104-191, § 521(b), provides:

(2) SPECIAL RULE.—In the case of the first taxable year beginning after December 31, 1995, the pre-effective date portion of the interest expense of the corporation referred to in such paragraph (5) of such section 1215(c) for such taxable year shall be allocated and apportioned without regard to such amendment. For purposes of the preceding sentence, the pre-effective date portion is the amount which bears the same ratio to the interest expense for such taxable year as the number of days during such taxable year before the date of the enactment of this Act bears to 366.

- **1976, Tax Reform Act of 1976 (P.L. 94-455)**

P.L. 94-455, § 1901(a)(113):

Amended Code Sec. 864(a). **Effective** for tax years beginning after 12-31-76. Prior to amendment, Code Sec. 864(a) read as follows:

(a) SALE, ETC.—For purposes of this part, the word "sale" includes "exchange"; the word "sold" includes "exchanged"; and the word "produced" includes "created", "fabricated", "manufactured", "extracted", "processed", "cured", or "aged".

[Sec. 864(b)]

(b) TRADE OR BUSINESS WITHIN THE UNITED STATES.—For purposes of this part, part II, and chapter 3, the term "trade or business within the United States" includes the performance of personal services within the United States at any time within the taxable year, but does not include—

(1) PERFORMANCE OF PERSONAL SERVICES FOR FOREIGN EMPLOYER.—The performance of personal services—

(A) for a nonresident alien individual, foreign partnership, or foreign corporation, not engaged in trade or business within the United States, or

(B) for an office or place of business maintained in a foreign country or in a possession of the United States by an individual who is a citizen or resident of the United States or by a domestic partnership or a domestic corporation,

by a nonresident alien individual temporarily present in the United States for a period or periods not exceeding a total of 90 days during the taxable year and whose compensation for such services does not exceed in the aggregate $3,000.

(2) TRADING IN SECURITIES OR COMMODITIES.—

(A) STOCKS AND SECURITIES.—

(i) IN GENERAL.—Trading in stocks or securities through a resident broker, commission agent, custodian, or other independent agent.

(ii) TRADING FOR TAXPAYER'S OWN ACCOUNT.—Trading in stocks or securities for the taxpayer's own account, whether by the taxpayer or his employees or through a resident broker, commission agent, custodian, or other agent, and whether or not any such employee or agent has discretionary authority to make decisions in effecting the transactions. This clause shall not apply in the case of a dealer in stocks or securities.

(B) COMMODITIES.—

(i) IN GENERAL.—Trading in commodities through a resident broker, commission agent, custodian, or other independent agent.

(ii) TRADING FOR TAXPAYER'S OWN ACCOUNT.—Trading in commodities for the taxpayer's own account, whether by the taxpayer or his employees or through a resident broker, commission agent, custodian, or other agent, and whether or not any such employee or agent has discretionary authority to make decisions in effecting the transactions. This clause shall not apply in the case of a dealer in commodities.

(iii) LIMITATION.—Clauses (i) and (ii) shall apply only if the commodities are of a kind customarily dealt in on an organized commodity exchange and if the transaction is of a kind customarily consummated at such place.

(C) LIMITATION.—Subparagraphs (A)(i) and (B)(i) shall apply only if, at no time during the taxable year, the taxpayer has an office or other fixed place of business in the United States through which or by the direction of which the transactions in stocks or securities, or in commodities, as the case may be, are effected.

Amendments

- **1997, Taxpayer Relief Act of 1997 (P.L. 105-34)**

P.L. 105-34, § 1162(a):

Amended Code Sec. 864(b)(2)(A)(ii) by striking ", or in the case of a corporation" and all that follows in the last sentence and inserting a period. **Effective** for tax years beginning after 12-31-97. Prior to amendment, the last sentence of Code Sec. 864(b)(2)(A)(ii) read as follows:

This clause shall not apply in the case of a dealer in stocks or securities, or in the case of a corporation (other than a corporation which is, or but for section 542(c)(7), 542(c)(10), or 543(b)(1)(C) would be, a personal holding company) the principal business of which is trading in stocks or securities for its own account, if its principal office is in the United States.

- **1988, Technical and Miscellaneous Revenue Act of 1988 (P.L. 100-647)**

P.L. 100-647, § 1012(p)(30):

Amended Code Sec. 864(b)(2)(A)(ii) by striking out "section 542(c)(7)" and inserting in lieu thereof "section 542(c)(7), 542(c)(10),". **Effective** as if included in the provision of P.L. 99-514 to which it relates.

[Sec. 864(c)]

(c) EFFECTIVELY CONNECTED INCOME, ETC.—

(1) GENERAL RULE.—For purposes of this title—

(A) In the case of a nonresident alien individual or a foreign corporation engaged in trade or business within the United States during the taxable year, the rules set forth in paragraphs (2), (3), (4), (6), (7), and (8) shall apply in determining the income, gain, or loss which shall be treated as effectively connected with the conduct of a trade or business within the United States.

(B) Except as provided in paragraph (6)[,] (7), or (8) or in section 871(d) or sections 882(d) and (e), in the case of a nonresident alien individual or a foreign corporation not engaged in trade or business within the United States during the taxable year, no income, gain, or loss shall be treated as effectively connected with the conduct of a trade or business within the United States.

(2) PERIODICAL, ETC., INCOME FROM SOURCES WITHIN UNITED STATES—FACTORS.—In determining whether income from sources within the United States of the types described in section 871(a)(1), section 871(h), section 881(a), or section 881(c), or whether gain or loss from sources within the United States from the sale or exchange of capital assets, is effectively connected with the conduct of a trade or business within the United States, the factors taken into account shall include whether—

(A) the income, gain, or loss is derived from assets used in or held for use in the conduct of such trade or business, or

INCOME TAX—SOURCES OF INCOME

(B) the activities of such trade or business were a material factor in the realization of the income, gain, or loss.

In determining whether an asset is used in or held for use in the conduct of such trade or business or whether the activities of such trade or business were a material factor in realizing an item of income, gain, or loss, due regard shall be given to whether or not such asset or such income, gain, or loss was accounted for through such trade or business.

(3) OTHER INCOME FROM SOURCES WITHIN UNITED STATES.—All income, gain, or loss from sources within the United States (other than income, gain, or loss to which paragraph (2) applies) shall be treated as effectively connected with the conduct of a trade or business within the United States.

(4) INCOME FROM SOURCES WITHOUT UNITED STATES.—

(A) Except as provided in subparagraphs (B) and (C), no income, gain, or loss from sources without the United States shall be treated as effectively connected with the conduct of a trade or business within the United States.

(B) Income, gain, or loss from sources without the United States shall be treated as effectively connected with the conduct of a trade or business within the United States by a nonresident alien individual or a foreign corporation if such person has an office or other fixed place of business within the United States to which such income, gain, or loss is attributable and such income, gain, or loss—

(i) consists of rents or royalties for the use of or for the privilege of using intangible property described in section 862(a)(4) derived in the active conduct of such trade or business;

(ii) consists of dividends, interest, or amounts received for the provision of guarantees of indebtedness, and either is derived in the active conduct of a banking, financing, or similar business within the United States or is received by a corporation the principal business of which is trading in stocks or securities for its own account; or

(iii) is derived from the sale or exchange (outside the United States) through such office or other fixed place of business of personal property described in section 1221(a)(1), except that this clause shall not apply if the property is sold or exchanged for use, consumption, or disposition outside the United States and an office or other fixed place of business of the taxpayer in a foreign country participated materially in such sale.

Any income or gain which is equivalent to any item of income or gain described in clause (i), (ii), or (iii) shall be treated in the same manner as such item for purposes of this subparagraph.

(C) In the case of a foreign corporation taxable under part I or part II of subchapter L, any income from sources without the United States which is attributable to its United States business shall be treated as effectively connected with the conduct of a trade or business within the United States.

(D) No income from sources without the United States shall be treated as effectively connected with the conduct of a trade or business within the United States if it either—

(i) consists of dividends, interest, or royalties paid by a foreign corporation in which the taxpayer owns (within the meaning of section 958(a)), or is considered as owning (by applying the ownership rules of section 958(b)), more than 50 percent of the total combined voting power of all classes of stock entitled to vote, or

(ii) is subpart F income within the meaning of section 952(a).

(5) RULES FOR APPLICATION OF PARAGRAPH (4)(B).—For purposes of subparagraph (B) of paragraph (4)—

(A) in determining whether a nonresident alien individual or a foreign corporation has an office or other fixed place of business, an office or other fixed place of business of an agent shall be disregarded unless such agent (i) has the authority to negotiate and conclude contracts in the name of the nonresident alien individual or foreign corporation and regularly exercises that authority or has a stock of merchandise from which he regularly fills orders on behalf of such individual or foreign corporation, and (ii) is not a general commission agent, broker, or other agent of independent status acting in the ordinary course of his business,

(B) income, gain, or loss shall not be considered as attributable to an office or other fixed place of business within the United States unless such office or fixed place of business is a material factor in the production of such income, gain, or loss and such office or fixed place of business regularly carries on activities of the type from which such income, gain, or loss is derived, and

(C) the income, gain, or loss which shall be attributable to an office or other fixed place of business within the United States shall be the income, gain, or loss properly allocable thereto, but, in the case of a sale or exchange described in clause (iii) of such subparagraph, the income which shall be treated as attributable to an office or other fixed place of business within the United States shall not exceed the income which would be derived from sources within the United States if the sale or exchange were made in the United States.

(6) TREATMENT OF CERTAIN DEFERRED PAYMENTS, ETC.—For purposes of this title, in the case of any income or gain of a nonresident alien individual or a foreign corporation which—

(A) is taken into account for any taxable year, but

(B) is attributable to a sale or exchange of property or the performance of services (or any other transaction) in any other taxable year,

the determination of whether such income or gain is taxable under section 871(b) or 882 (as the case may be) shall be made as if such income or gain were taken into account in such other taxable year and without regard to the requirement that the taxpayer be engaged in a trade or business within the United States during the taxable year referred to in subparagraph (A).

(7) TREATMENT OF CERTAIN PROPERTY TRANSACTIONS.—For purposes of this title, if—

(A) any property ceases to be used or held for use in connection with the conduct of a trade or business within the United States, and

(B) such property is disposed of within 10 years after such cessation,

the determination of whether any income or gain attributable to such disposition is taxable under section 871(b) or 882 (as the case may be) shall be made as if such sale or exchange occurred immediately before such cessation and without regard to the requirement that the taxpayer be engaged in a trade or business within the United States during the taxable year for which such income or gain is taken into account.

(8) GAIN OR LOSS OF FOREIGN PERSONS FROM SALE OR EXCHANGE OF CERTAIN PARTNERSHIP INTERESTS.—

(A) IN GENERAL.—Notwithstanding any other provision of this subtitle, if a nonresident alien individual or foreign corporation owns, directly or indirectly, an interest in a partnership which is engaged in any trade or business within the United States, gain or loss on the

INCOME TAX—SOURCES OF INCOME

sale or exchange of all (or any portion of) such interest shall be treated as effectively connected with the conduct of such trade or business to the extent such gain or loss does not exceed the amount determined under subparagraph (B).

(B) AMOUNT TREATED AS EFFECTIVELY CONNECTED.—The amount determined under this subparagraph with respect to any partnership interest sold or exchanged—

(i) in the case of any gain on the sale or exchange of the partnership interest, is—

(I) the portion of the partner's distributive share of the amount of gain which would have been effectively connected with the conduct of a trade or business within the United States if the partnership had sold all of its assets at their fair market value as of the date of the sale or exchange of such interest, or

(II) zero if no gain on such deemed sale would have been so effectively connected, and

(ii) in the case of any loss on the sale or exchange of the partnership interest, is—

(I) the portion of the partner's distributive share of the amount of loss on the deemed sale described in clause (i)(I) which would have been so effectively connected, or

(II) zero if no loss on such deemed sale would be [sic] have been so effectively connected.

For purposes of this subparagraph, a partner's distributive share of gain or loss on the deemed sale shall be determined in the same manner as such partner's distributive share of the non-separately stated taxable income or loss of such partnership.

(C) COORDINATION WITH UNITED STATES REAL PROPERTY INTERESTS.—If a partnership described in subparagraph (A) holds any United States real property interest (as defined in section 897(c)) at the time of the sale or exchange of the partnership interest, then the gain or loss treated as effectively connected income under subparagraph (A) shall be reduced by the amount so treated with respect to such United States real property interest under section 897.

(D) SALE OR EXCHANGE.—For purposes of this paragraph, the term "sale or exchange" means any sale, exchange, or other disposition.

(E) SECRETARIAL AUTHORITY.—The Secretary shall prescribe such regulations or other guidance as the Secretary determines appropriate for the application of this paragraph, including with respect to exchanges described in section 332, 351, 354, 355, 356, or 361.

Amendments

• **2017, Tax Cuts and Jobs Act (P.L. 115-97)**

P.L. 115-97, § 13501(a)(1):

Amended Code Sec. 864(c) by adding at the end a new paragraph (8). **Effective** for sales, exchanges, and dispositions on or after 11-27-2017.

P.L. 115-97, § 13501(a)(2)(A)-(B):

Amended Code Sec. 864(c)(1) by striking "and (7)" in subparagraph (A), and inserting "(7), and (8)", and by striking "or (7)" in subparagraph (B), and inserting "(7), or (8)". **Effective** for sales, exchanges, and dispositions on or after 11-27-2017.

• **2010, Creating Small Business Jobs Act of 2010 (P.L. 111-240)**

P.L. 111-240, § 2122(c):

Amended Code Sec. 864(c)(4)(B)(ii) by striking "dividends or interest" and inserting "dividends, interest, or amounts received for the provision of guarantees of indebtedness". **Effective** for guarantees issued after 9-27-2010.

• **2004, American Jobs Creation Act of 2004 (P.L. 108-357)**

P.L. 108-357, § 894(a):

Amended Code Sec. 864(c)(4)(B) by adding at the end a new flush sentence. **Effective** for tax years beginning after 10-22-2004.

• **1999, Tax Relief Extension Act of 1999 (P.L. 106-170)**

P.L. 106-170, § 532(c)(2)(N):

Amended Code Sec. 864(c)(4)(B)(iii) by striking "section 1221(1)" and inserting "section 1221(a)(1)". **Effective** for any instrument held, acquired, or entered into, any transaction entered into, and supplies held or acquired on or after 12-17-99.

• **1988, Technical and Miscellaneous Revenue Act of 1988 (P.L. 100-647)**

P.L. 100-647, § 1012(d)(7):

Amended Code Sec. 864(c)(4)(B) by striking out "or" at the end of clause (i), by striking out the period at the end of clause (ii) and inserting in lieu thereof "; or" and by adding at the end thereof new clause (iii). **Effective** as if included in the provision of P.L. 99-514 to which it relates.

P.L. 100-647, § 1012(d)(10)(A)-(B):

Amended Code Sec. 864(c)(4)(B) by striking out "(including any gain or loss realized on the sale or exchange of such property)" after "section 862(a)(4)" in clause (i), and by striking out ", or gain or loss from the sale or exchange of stock or notes, bonds, or other evidences of indebtedness" after "interest" in clause (ii). **Effective** as if included in the provision of P.L. 99-514 to which it relates.

P.L. 100-647, § 1012(g)(5):

Amended Code Sec. 864(c)(2) by striking out the last sentence. **Effective** as if included in the provision of P.L. 99-514 to which it relates. Prior to amendment, the last sentence of Code Sec. 864(c)(2) read as follows:

In applying this paragraph and paragraph (4), interest referred to in section 861(a)(1)(A) shall be considered income from sources within the United States.

P.L. 100-647, § 1012(r)(1):

Amended Code Sec. 864(c)(7). **Effective** as if included in the provision of P.L. 99-514 to which it relates. Prior to amendment, Code Sec. 864(c)(7) read as follows:

(7) TREATMENT OF CERTAIN PROPERTY TRANSACTIONS.—For purposes of this title, if any property ceases to be used or held for use in connection with the conduct of a trade or business within the United States, the determination of whether any income or gain attributable to a sale or exchange of such property occurring within 10 years after such cessation is effectively connected with the conduct of a trade or business within the United States shall be made as if such sale or exchange occurred immediately before such cessation.

P.L. 100-647, § 1012(r)(2):

Amended Code Sec. 864(c)(6). **Effective** as if included in the provision of P.L. 99-514 to which it relates. Prior to amendment, Code Sec. 864(c)(6) read as follows:

(6) TREATMENT OF CERTAIN DEFERRED PAYMENTS, ETC.—For purposes of this title, any income or gain of a nonresident alien individual or a foreign corporation for any taxable year which is attributable to a sale or exchange of property or the performance of services (or any other transaction) in any other taxable year shall be treated as effectively connected with the conduct of a trade or business within the United States if it would have been so treated if such income or gain were taken into account in such other taxable year.

• **1987, Revenue Act of 1987 (P.L. 100-203)**

P.L. 100-203, § 10242(b):

Amended Code Sec. 864(c)(4)(C) by inserting "or part II" after "part I". **Effective** for tax years beginning after 12-31-87.

• **1986, Tax Reform Act of 1986 (P.L. 99-514)**

P.L. 99-514, § 1211(b)(2):

Amended Code Sec. 864(c)(4)(B)(i)-(iii) by adding "or" at the end of clause (i), by striking out "; or" at the end of clause (ii) and inserting in lieu thereof a period, and by striking out clause (iii). **Effective** for tax years beginning after 12-31-86. However, see the special rule provided in Act Sec. 1211(c)(2) in the amendment notes following Code Sec. 863. Prior to amendment, Code Sec. 864(c)(4)(B)(iii) read as follows:

(iii) is derived from the sale or exchange (without the United States) through such office or other fixed place of business of personal property described in section 1221(1), except that this clause shall not apply if the property is sold or exchanged for use, consumption, or disposition outside the United States and an office or other fixed place of business of the taxpayer outside the United States participated materially in such sale.

P.L. 99-514, § 1242(a):

Amended Code Sec. 864(c) by adding at the end thereof new paragraphs (6) and (7). **Effective** for tax years beginning after 12-31-86.

P.L. 99-514, § 1242(b)(1)-(2):

Amended Code Sec. 864(c)(1)(A)-(B) by striking out "and (4)" in subparagraph (A) and inserting in lieu thereof "(4), (6), and (7)", and by striking out "as provided in" subparagraph (B) an inserting in lieu thereof "as provided in paragraph (6) or (7) or in". **Effective** for tax years beginning after 12-31-86.

P.L. 99-514, § 1899A(21):

Amended Code Sec. 864(c)(2) by striking out "section 871(h) section 881(a)" and inserting in lieu thereof "section 871(h), section 881(a)". **Effective** as of 10-22-86.

• **1984, Deficit Reduction Act of 1984 (P.L. 98-369)**

P.L. 98-369, § 127(c):

Amended Code Sec. 864(c)(2) by striking out "section 871(a)(1) or section 881(a)" and inserting in lieu thereof "section 871(a)(1), section 871(h), section 881(a), or section 881(c)". **Effective** for interest received after 7-18-84, with respect to obligations issued after such date, in tax years ending after such date. However, see Act Sec. 127(g)(2) under Code Sec. 881 for special rules regarding obligations of certain U.S. affiliates.

• **1976, Tax Reform Act of 1976 (P.L. 94-455)**

P.L. 94-455, § 1901(a)(113):

Substituted "sale or exchange" for "sale" and "sold or exchanged" for "sold" everywhere they appear in clauses (4)(B)(i) and (iii) and subparagraph (5)(C). **Effective** for tax years beginning after 12-31-76.

• **1966, Foreign Investors Tax Act of 1966 (P.L. 89-809)**

P.L. 89-809, § 102(d):

Amended Code Sec. 864 by inserting "(a) Sale, Etc.—" immediately before "For purposes of this part," and by adding new subsections (b) and (c). **Effective** for tax years beginning after 12-31-66, except that in applying Sec. 864(c)(4)(B)(iii) with respect to a binding contract entered into on or before 2-24-66, activities in the United States on or before such date in negotiating or carrying out such contract shall not be taken into account.

INCOME TAX—SOURCES OF INCOME

[Sec. 864(d)]

(d) TREATMENT OF RELATED PERSON FACTORING INCOME.—

(1) IN GENERAL.—For purposes of the provisions set forth in paragraph (2), if any person acquires (directly or indirectly) a trade or service receivable from a related person, any income of such person from the trade or service receivable so acquired shall be treated as if it were interest on a loan to the obligor under the receivable.

(2) PROVISIONS TO WHICH PARAGRAPH (1) APPLIES.—The provisions set forth in this paragraph are as follows:

(A) Section 904 (relating to limitation on foreign tax credit).

(B) Subpart F of part III of this subchapter (relating to controlled foreign corporations).

(3) TRADE OR SERVICE RECEIVABLE.—For purposes of this subsection, the term "trade or service receivable" means any account receivable or evidence of indebtedness arising out of—

(A) the disposition by a related person of property described in section 1221(a)(1), or

(B) the performance of services by a related person.

(4) RELATED PERSON.—For purposes of this subsection, the term "related person" means—

(A) any person who is a related person (within the meaning of section 267(b)), and

(B) any United States shareholder (as defined in section 951(b)) and any person who is a related person (within the meaning of section 267(b)) to such a shareholder.

(5) CERTAIN PROVISIONS NOT TO APPLY.—The following provisions shall not apply to any amount treated as interest under paragraph (1) or (6):

(A) Section 904(d)(2)(B)(iii)(I) (relating to exceptions for export financing interest).

(B) Subparagraph (A) of section 954(b)(3) (relating to exception where foreign base company income is less than 5 percent or $1,000,000).

(C) Subparagraph (B) of section 954(c)(2) (relating to certain export financing).

(D) Clause (i) of section 954(c)(3)(A) (relating to certain income received from related persons).

(6) SPECIAL RULE FOR CERTAIN INCOME FROM LOANS OF A CONTROLLED FOREIGN CORPORATION.—Any income of a controlled foreign corporation (within the meaning of section 957(a)) from a loan to a person for the purpose of financing—

(A) the purchase of property described in section 1221(a)(1) of a related person, or

(B) the payment for the performance of services by a related person,

shall be treated as interest described in paragraph (1).

(7) EXCEPTION FOR CERTAIN RELATED PERSONS DOING BUSINESS IN SAME FOREIGN COUNTRY.—Paragraph (1) shall not apply to any trade or service receivable acquired by any person from a related person if—

(A) the person acquiring such receivable and such related person are created or organized under the laws of the same foreign country and such related person has a substantial part of its assets used in its trade or business located in such same foreign country, and

(B) such related person would not have derived any foreign base company income (as defined in section 954(a), determined without regard to section 954(b)(3)(A)), or any income effectively connected with the conduct of a trade or business within the United States, from such receivable if it had been collected by such related person.

(8) REGULATIONS.—The Secretary shall prescribe such regulations as may be necessary to prevent the avoidance of the provisions of this subsection or section 956(c)(3).

Amendments

• **2018, Tax Technical Corrections Act of 2018 (P.L. 115-141)**

P.L. 115-141, §401(a)(152), Div. U:

Amended Code Sec. 864(d)(8) by striking "section 956(b)(3)" and inserting "section 956(c)(3)". **Effective** 3-23-2018.

P.L. 115-141, §401(d)(1)(D)(x), Div. U:

Amended Code Sec. 864(d)(5). **Effective** 3-23-2018. For a special rule, see Act Sec. 401(e), Div. U, below. Prior to amendment, Code Sec. 864(d)(5) read as follows:

(5) CERTAIN PROVISIONS NOT TO APPLY.—

(A) CERTAIN EXCEPTIONS.—The following provisions shall not apply to any amount treated as interest under paragraph (1) or (6):

(i) Subparagraph (A)(iii)(II), (B)(ii), and (C)(iii)(II) of section 904(d)(2) (relating to exceptions for export financing interest).

(ii) Subparagraph (A) of section 954(b)(3) (relating to exception where foreign base company income is less than 5 percent or $1,000,000).

(iii) Subparagraph (B) of section 954(c)(2) (relating to certain export financing).

(iv) Clause (i) of section 954(c)(3)(A) (relating to certain income received from related persons).

(B) SPECIAL RULES FOR POSSESSIONS.—An amount treated as interest under paragraph (1) shall not be treated as income described in subparagraph (A) or (B) of section 936(a)(1) unless such amount is from sources within a possession of the United States (determined after the application of paragraph (1)).

P.L. 115-141, §401(e), Div. U, provides:

(e) GENERAL SAVINGS PROVISION WITH RESPECT TO DEADWOOD PROVISIONS.—If—

(1) any provision amended or repealed by the amendments made by subsection (b) or (d) applied to—

(A) any transaction occurring before the date of the enactment of this Act,

(B) any property acquired before such date of enactment, or

(C) any item of income, loss, deduction, or credit taken into account before such date of enactment, and

(2) the treatment of such transaction, property, or item under such provision would (without regard to the amendments or repeals made by such subsection) affect the liability for tax for periods ending after such date of enactment,

nothing in the amendments or repeals made by this section shall be construed to affect the treatment of such transaction, property, or item for purposes of determining liability for tax for periods ending after such date of enactment.

• **2004, American Jobs Creation Act of 2004 (P.L. 108-357)**

P.L. 108-357, §403(b)(6):

Amended Code Sec. 864(d)(5)(A)(i) by striking "(C)(iii)(III)" and inserting "(C)(iii)(II)". **Effective** for tax years beginning after 12-31-2002.

P.L. 108-357, §413(c)(12):

Amended Code Sec. 864(d)(2) by striking subparagraph (A) and by redesignating subparagraphs (B) and (C) as subparagraphs (A) and (B), respectively. **Effective** for tax years of foreign corporations beginning after 12-31-2004, and for tax years of United States shareholders with or within which such tax years of foreign corporations end. Prior to being stricken, Code Sec. 864(d)(2)(A) read as follows:

(A) Part III of subchapter G of this chapter (relating to foreign personal holding companies).

• **1999, Tax Relief Extension Act of 1999 (P.L. 106-170)**

P.L. 106-170, §532(c)(2)(O):

Amended Code Sec. 864(d)(3)(A) by striking "section 1221(1)" and inserting "section 1221(a)(1)". **Effective** for any instrument held, acquired, or entered into, any transaction entered into, and supplies held or acquired on or after 12-17-99.

P.L. 106-170, §532(c)(2)(P):

Amended Code Sec. 864(d)(6)(A) by striking "section 1221(1)" and inserting "section 1221(a)(1)". **Effective** for any instrument held, acquired, or entered into, any transaction entered into, and supplies held or acquired on or after 12-17-99.

• **1988, Technical and Miscellaneous Revenue Act of 1988 (P.L. 100-647)**

P.L. 100-647, §1012(a)(1)(B):

Amended Code Sec. 864(d)(5)(A)(i) by striking out "(C)(iii)" and inserting in lieu thereof "(C)(iii)(III)". **Effective** as if included in the provision of P.L. 99-514 to which it relates.

• **1986, Tax Reform Act of 1986 (P.L. 99-514)**

P.L. 99-514, §1201(d)(4):

Amended Code Sec. 864(d)(5)(A)(i). **Effective**, generally, for tax years beginning after 12-31-86. For special rules, see Act Sec. 1201(e)(2)-(3) in the amendment notes following Code Sec. 904. Prior to amendment, Code Sec. 864(d)(5)(A)(i) read as follows:

INCOME TAX—SOURCES OF INCOME

(i) Subparagraphs (A), (B), (C), and (D) of section 904(d)(2) (relating to interest income to which separate limitation applies and subparagraph (J) of section 904(d)(3) (relating to interest from members of same affiliated group).

P.L. 99-514, § 1221(a)(2):

Amended Code Sec. 864(d)(5)(A)(iii) and (iv) by striking out clauses (iii) and (iv) and inserting in lieu thereof clauses (iii) and (iv). **Effective**, generally, for tax years of foreign corporations beginning after 12-31-86. For special rules, see Act Sec. 1221(g)(2)-(3) in the amendment notes following Code Sec. 954. Prior to amendment, Code Sec. 864(d)(5)(A)(iii) and (iv) read as follows:

(iii) Subparagraph (B) of section 954(c)(3) (relating to certain income derived in active conduct of trade or business).

(iv) Subparagraphs (A) and (B) of section 954(c)(4) (relating to exception for certain income received from related persons).

P.L. 99-514, § 1223(b)(1):

Amended Code Sec. 864(d)(5)(A)(ii) by striking out "less than 10 percent" and inserting in lieu thereof "less than 5 percent or $1,000,000". **Effective** for tax years beginning after 12-31-86.

P.L. 99-514, § 1275(c)(7):

Amended Code Sec. 864(d)(5)(B). **Effective**, generally, for tax years beginning after 12-31-86. For special rules, see Act Sec. 1277(b)-(e) in the amendment notes following Code Sec. 48. Prior to amendment, Code Sec. 864(d)(5)(B) read as follows:

(B) SPECIAL RULES FOR POSSESSIONS.—

(i) PUERTO RICO AND POSSESSIONS TAX CREDIT.—Any amount treated as interest under paragraph (1) shall not be treated as income described in subparagraph (A) or (B) of section 936(a)(1) unless such amount is from sources within a possession of the United States (determined after the application of paragraph (1)).

(ii) VIRGIN ISLANDS CORPORATIONS.—Subsection (b) of section 934 shall not apply to any amount treated as interest under paragraph (1) unless such amount is from sources within the Virgin Islands (determined after the application of paragraph (1)).

P.L. 99-514, § 1810(c)(2):

Amended Code Sec. 864(d) by redesignating paragraph (7) as paragraph (8) and by inserting after paragraph (6) new paragraph (7). **Effective** as if included in the provision of P.L. 98-369 to which it relates.

P.L. 99-514, § 1810(c)(3):

Amended Code Sec. 864(d)(5)(A)(i) by inserting before the period at the end thereof "and subparagraph (J) of section 904(d)(3) (relating to interest from members of same affiliated group)". **Effective** as if included in the provision of P.L. 98-369 to which it relates.

• **1984, Deficit Reduction Act of 1984 (P.L. 98-369)**

P.L. 98-369, § 123(a):

Amended Code Sec. 864 by adding subsection (d). **Effective** for accounts receivable and evidences of indebtedness transferred after 3-1-84, in tax years ending after such date. For transitional rules, see Act Sec. 123(c)(2), below.

P.L. 98-369, § 123(c)(2), provides:

(2) Transitional Rule.—The amendments made by this section shall not apply to accounts receivable and evidences of indebtedness acquired after March 1, 1984, and before March 1, 1994, by a Belgian corporation in existence on March 1, 1984, in any taxable year ending after such date, but only to the extent that the amount includible in gross income by reason of section 956 of the Internal Revenue Code of 1954 with respect to such corporation for all such taxable years is not reduced by reason of this paragraph by more than the lesser of—

(A) $15,000,000 or

(B) the amount of the Belgian corporation's adjusted basis on March 1, 1984, in stock of a foreign corporation formed to issue bonds outside the United States to the public.

[Sec. 864(e)]

(e) RULES FOR ALLOCATING INTEREST, ETC.—For purposes of this subchapter—

(1) TREATMENT OF AFFILIATED GROUPS.—The taxable income of each member of an affiliated group shall be determined by allocating and apportioning interest expense of each member as if all members of such group were a single corporation.

(2) GROSS INCOME AND FAIR MARKET VALUE METHODS MAY NOT BE USED FOR INTEREST.—All allocations and apportionments of interest expense shall be determined using the adjusted bases of assets rather than on the basis of the fair market value of the assets or gross income.

(3) TAX-EXEMPT ASSETS NOT TAKEN INTO ACCOUNT.—For purposes of allocating and apportioning any deductible expense, any tax-exempt asset (and any income from such an asset) shall not be taken into account. A similar rule shall apply in the case of the portion of any dividend (other than a qualifying dividend as defined in section 243(b)) equal to the deduction allowable under section 243 or 245(a) with respect to such dividend and in the case of a like portion of any stock the dividends on which would be so deductible and would not be qualifying dividends (as so defined).

(4) BASIS OF STOCK IN NONAFFILIATED 10-PERCENT OWNED CORPORATIONS ADJUSTED FOR EARNINGS AND PROFITS CHANGES.—

(A) IN GENERAL.—For purposes of allocating and apportioning expenses on the basis of assets, the adjusted basis of any stock in a nonaffiliated 10-percent owned corporation shall be—

(i) increased by the amount of the earnings and profits of such corporation attributable to such stock and accumulated during the period the taxpayer held such stock, or

(ii) reduced (but not below zero) by any deficit in earnings and profits of such corporation attributable to such stock for such period.

(B) NONAFFILIATED 10-PERCENT OWNED CORPORATION.—For purposes of this paragraph, the term "nonaffiliated 10-percent owned corporation" means any corporation if—

(i) such corporation is not included in the taxpayer's affiliated group, and

(ii) members of such affiliated group own 10 percent or more of the total combined voting power of all classes of stock of such corporation entitled to vote.

(C) EARNINGS AND PROFITS OF LOWER TIER CORPORATIONS TAKEN INTO ACCOUNT.—

(i) IN GENERAL.—If, by reason of holding stock in a nonaffiliated 10-percent owned corporation, the taxpayer is treated under clause (iii) as owning stock in another corporation with respect to which the stock ownership requirements of clause (ii) are met, the adjustment under subparagraph (A) shall include an adjustment for the amount of the earnings and profits (or deficit therein) of such other corporation which are attributable to the stock the taxpayer is so treated as owning and to the period during which the taxpayer is treated as owning such stock.

(ii) STOCK OWNERSHIP REQUIREMENTS.—The stock ownership requirements of this clause are met with respect to any corporation if members of the taxpayer's affiliated group own (directly or through the application of clause (iii)) 10 percent or more of the total combined voting power of all classes of stock of such corporation entitled to vote.

(iii) STOCK OWNED THROUGH ENTITIES.—For purposes of this subparagraph, stock owned (directly or indirectly) by a corporation, partnership, or trust shall be treated as being owned proportionately by its shareholders, partners, or beneficiaries. Stock considered to be owned by a person by reason of the application of the preceding sentence, shall, for purposes of applying such sentence, be treated as actually owned by such person.

(D) COORDINATION WITH SUBPART F, ETC.—For purposes of this paragraph, proper adjustment shall be made to the earnings and profits of any corporation to take into account any earnings and profits included in gross income under section 951 or under any other provision of this title and reflected in the adjusted basis of the stock.

(5) AFFILIATED GROUP.—For purposes of this subsection—

(A) IN GENERAL.—Except as provided in subparagraph (B), the term "affiliated group" has the meaning given such term by section 1504. Notwithstanding the preceding sentence, a foreign corporation shall be treated as a member of the affiliated group if—

(i) more than 50 percent of the gross income of such foreign corporation for the taxable year is effectively connected with the conduct of a trade or business within the United States, and

(ii) at least 80 percent of either the vote or value of all outstanding stock of such foreign corporation is owned directly or indirectly by members of the affiliated group (determined with regard to this sentence).

INCOME TAX—SOURCES OF INCOME

(B) TREATMENT OF CERTAIN FINANCIAL INSTITUTIONS.—For purposes of subparagraph (A), any corporation described in subparagraph (C) shall be treated as an includible corporation for purposes of section 1504 only for purposes of applying such section separately to corporations so described. This subparagraph shall not apply for purposes of paragraph (6).

(C) DESCRIPTION.—A corporation is described in this subparagraph if—

(i) such corporation is a financial institution described in section 581 or 591,

(ii) the business of such financial institution is predominantly with persons other than related persons (within the meaning of subsection (d)(4)) or their customers, and

(iii) such financial institution is required by State or Federal law to be operated separately from any other entity which is not such an institution.

(D) TREATMENT OF BANK HOLDING COMPANIES.—To the extent provided in regulations—

(i) a bank holding company (within the meaning of section 2(a) of the Bank Holding Company Act of 1956), and

(ii) any subsidiary of a financial institution described in section 581 or 591 or of any bank holding company if such subsidiary is predominantly engaged (directly or indirectly) in the active conduct of a banking, financing, or similar business,

shall be treated as a corporation described in subparagraph (C).

(6) ALLOCATION AND APPORTIONMENT OF OTHER EXPENSES.—Expenses other than interest which are not directly allocable or apportioned to any specific income producing activity shall be allocated and apportioned as if all members of the affiliated group were a single corporation.

(7) REGULATIONS.—The Secretary shall prescribe such regulations as may be necessary or appropriate to carry out the purposes of this section, including regulations providing—

(A) for the resourcing of income of any member of an affiliated group or modifications to the consolidated return regulations to the extent such resourcing or modification is necessary to carry out the purposes of this section,

(B) for direct allocation of interest expense incurred to carry out an integrated financial transaction to any interest (or interest-type income) derived from such transaction and in other circumstances where such allocation would be appropriate to carry out the purposes of this subsection,

(C) for the apportionment of expenses allocated to foreign source income among the members of the affiliated group and various categories of income described in section 904(d)(1),

(D) for direct allocation of interest expense in the case of indebtedness resulting in a disallowance under section 246A,

(E) for appropriate adjustments in the application of paragraph (3) in the case of an insurance company,

(F) preventing assets or interest expense from being taken into account more than once, and

(G) that this subsection shall not apply for purposes of any provision of this subchapter to the extent the Secretary determines that the application of this subsection for such purposes would not be appropriate.

Amendments

- **2018, Tax Technical Corrections Act of 2018 (P.L. 115-141)**

P.L. 115-141, §401(d)(1)(D)(xvii)(IV), Div. U:

Amended Code Sec. 864(e)(5)(A) by striking "(determined without regard to paragraph (4) of section 1504(b))" following "such term by section 1504". **Effective** 3-23-2018. For a special rule, see Act Sec. 401(e), Div. U, below.

P.L. 115-141, §401(e), Div. U, provides:

(e) GENERAL SAVINGS PROVISION WITH RESPECT TO DEADWOOD PROVISIONS.—If—

(1) any provision amended or repealed by the amendments made by subsection (b) or (d) applied to—

(A) any transaction occurring before the date of the enactment of this Act,

(B) any property acquired before such date of enactment, or

(C) any item of income, loss, deduction, or credit taken into account before such date of enactment, and

(2) the treatment of such transaction, property, or item under such provision would (without regard to the amendments or repeals made by such subsection) affect the liability for tax for periods ending after such date of enactment,

nothing in the amendments or repeals made by this section shall be construed to affect the treatment of such transaction, property, or item for purposes of determining liability for tax for periods ending after such date of enactment.

- **2017, Tax Cuts and Jobs Act (P.L. 115-97)**

P.L. 115-97, §14502(a):

Amended Code Sec. 864(e)(2). **Effective** for tax years beginning after 12-31-2017. Prior to amendment, Code Sec. 864(e)(2) read as follows:

(2) GROSS INCOME METHOD MAY NOT BE USED FOR INTEREST.—All allocations and apportionments of interest expense shall be made on the basis of assets rather than gross income.

- **2010, (P.L. 111-226)**

P.L. 111-226, §216(a):

Amended Code Sec. 864(e)(5)(A) by adding at the end "Notwithstanding the preceding sentence, a foreign corporation shall be treated as a member of the affiliated group if—" and new clauses (i)-(ii). **Effective** for tax years beginning after 8-10-2010.

- **2004, American Jobs Creation Act of 2004 (P.L. 108-357)**

P.L. 108-357, §101(b)(6)(A)-(B):

Amended Code Sec. 864(e)(3) by striking "(3) TAX-EXEMPT ASSETS NOT TAKEN INTO ACCOUNT.—(A) IN GENERAL.—For purposes of" and inserting "(3) TAX-EXEMPT ASSETS NOT TAKEN INTO ACCOUNT.—For purposes of", and by striking subparagraph (B). **Effective** for transactions after 12-31-2004. For transitional and special rules, see Act Secs. 101(d)-(f), below. Prior to being stricken, Code Sec. 864(e)(3)(B) read as follows:

(B) ASSETS PRODUCING EXEMPT EXTRATERRITORIAL INCOME.—For purposes of allocating and apportioning any interest expense, there shall not be taken into account any qualifying foreign trade property (as defined in section 943(a)) which is held by the taxpayer for lease or rental in the ordinary course of trade or business for use by the lessee outside the United States (as defined in section 943(b)(2)).

P.L. 108-357, §101(d)-(f) (as amended by P.L. 113-295, §219(a), Division A), provides:

(d) TRANSITIONAL RULE FOR 2005 AND 2006.—

(1) IN GENERAL.—In the case of transactions during 2005 or 2006, the amount includible in gross income by reason of the amendments made by this section shall not exceed the applicable percentage of the amount which would have been so included but for this subsection.

(2) APPLICABLE PERCENTAGE.—For purposes of paragraph (1), the applicable percentage shall be as follows:

(A) For 2005, the applicable percentage shall be 20 percent.

(B) For 2006, the applicable percentage shall be 40 percent.

(3) COORDINATION WITH SECTION 199.—This subsection shall be applied without regard to any deduction allowable under section 199.

(e) REVOCATION OF ELECTION TO BE TREATED AS DOMESTIC CORPORATION.—If, during the 1-year period beginning on the date of the enactment of this Act, a corporation for which an election is in effect under section 943(e) of the Internal Revenue Code of 1986 revokes such election, no gain or loss shall be recognized with respect to property treated as transferred under clause (ii) of section 943(e)(4)(B) of such Code to the extent such property—

(1) was treated as transferred under clause (i) thereof, or

(2) was acquired during a taxable year to which such election applies and before May 1, 2003, in the ordinary course of its trade or business.

The Secretary of the Treasury (or such Secretary's delegate) may prescribe such regulations as may be necessary to prevent the abuse of the purposes of this subsection.

[Note: Act Sec. 101(f) of P.L. 108-357, below, was stricken by P.L. 109-222, §513(b), applicable to tax years beginning after 5-17-2006.—CCH.]

(f) BINDING CONTRACTS.—The amendments made by this section shall not apply to any transaction in the ordinary course of a trade or business which occurs pursuant to a binding contract—

(1) which is between the taxpayer and a person who is not a related person (as defined in section 943(b)(3) of such Code, as in effect on the day before the date of the enactment of this Act), and

(2) which is in effect on September 17, 2003, and at all times thereafter.

For purposes of this subsection, a binding contract shall include a purchase option, renewal option, or replacement option which is included in such contract and which is enforceable against the seller or lessor.

P.L. 108-357, §401(b)(1)-(2):

Amended Code Sec. 864(e)(7) by inserting before the comma at the end of subparagraph (B) "and in other circumstances where such allocation would be appropriate to carry out the purposes of this subsection", and by striking "and" at the end of subparagraph (E), by redesignating subparagraph (F) as subparagraph (G), and by inserting after subparagraph (E) a new subparagraph (F). **Effective** for tax years beginning after 12-31-2008.

Internal Revenue Code   Sec. 864(e)(7)(G)

INCOME TAX—SOURCES OF INCOME

- **2000, FSC Repeal and Extraterritorial Income Exclusion Act of 2000 (P.L. 106-519)**

P.L. 106-519, §4(3)(A)-(B):

Amended Code Sec. 864(e)(3) by striking "For purposes of" and inserting "(A) IN GENERAL.—For purposes of"; and by adding at the end a new subparagraph (B). **Effective**, generally, for transactions after 9-30-2000. For special rules, see Act Sec. 5(b)-(d) in the amendment notes following Code Sec. 921.

- **1988, Technical and Miscellaneous Revenue Act of 1988 (P.L. 100-647)**

P.L. 100-647, §1012(h)(1):

Amended Code Sec. 864(e)(4). **Effective** as if included in the provision of P.L. 99-514 to which it relates. Prior to amendment, Code Sec. 864(e)(4) read as follows:

(4) BASIS OF STOCK IN CERTAIN CORPORATIONS ADJUSTED FOR EARNINGS AND PROFITS CHANGES.—For purposes of allocating and apportioning expenses on the basis of assets, the adjusted basis of any asset which is stock in a corporation which is not included in the affiliated group and in which members of the affiliated group own 10 percent or more of the total combined voting power of all classes of stock entitled to vote in such corporation shall be—

(A) increased by the amount of the earnings and profits of such corporation attributable to such stock and accumulated during the period the taxpayers held such stock, or

(B) reduced (but not below zero) by any deficit in earnings and profits of such corporation attributable to such stock for such period.

P.L. 100-647, §1012(h)(2)(A):

Amended Code Sec. 864(e)(1) by striking out "from sources outside the United States" after "affiliated group". **Effective** as if included in the provision of P.L. 99-514 to which it relates.

P.L. 100-647, §1012(h)(3):

Amended Code Sec. 864(e)(3) by striking out the last sentence and inserting in lieu thereof a new sentence. **Effective** as if included in the provision of P.L. 99-514 to which it relates. Prior to amendment, the last sentence of Code Sec. 864(e)(3) read as follows:

A similar rule shall apply in the case of any dividend (other than a qualifying dividend as defined in section 243(b)) for which a deduction is allowable under section 243 or 245(a) and any stock the dividends on which would be so deductible and would not be qualifying dividends (as so defined).

P.L. 100-647, §1012(h)(4)(A):

Amended Code Sec. 864(e)(5) by adding at the end thereof new subparagraph (D). **Effective** as if included in the provision of P.L. 99-514 to which it relates.

P.L. 100-647, §1012(h)(4)(B):

Amended Code Sec. 864(e)(5)(B) by adding at the end thereof a new sentence. **Effective** as if included in the provision of P.L. 99-514 to which it relates.

P.L. 100-647, §1012(h)(5):

Amended Code Sec. 864(e)(6) by striking out "directly allocable and apportioned" and inserting in lieu thereof "directly allocable or apportioned". **Effective** as if included in the provision of P.L. 99-514 to which it relates.

P.L. 100-647, §1012(h)(6)(A):

Amended Code Sec. 864(e)(7) by striking out "and" at the end of subparagraph (B), by striking out the period at the end of subparagraph (C) and inserting in lieu thereof a comma, and by adding at the end thereof new subparagraphs (D)-(F). **Effective** as if included in the provision of P.L. 99-514 to which it relates.

P.L. 100-647, §1012(h)(6)(B):

Amended Code Sec. 864(e) by striking out "(except as provided in regulations)" after "subchapter" in the material preceding paragraph (1). **Effective** as if included in the provision of P.L. 99-514 to which it relates.

- **1986, Tax Reform Act of 1986 (P.L. 99-514)**

P.L. 99-514, §1215(a):

Amended Code Sec. 864 by adding at the end thereof new subsection (e). **Effective**, generally, for tax years beginning after 12-31-86. For special and transitional rules, see Act Sec. 1215(c)(2)-(6), following Code Sec. 864(a).

[Sec. 864(f)—Stricken]

Amendments

- **2021, American Rescue Plan Act of 2021 (P.L. 117-2)**

P.L. 117-2, §9671(a):

Amended Code Sec. 864 by striking subsection (f). **Effective** for tax years beginning after 12-31-2020. Prior to being stricken, Code Sec. 864(f) read as follows:

(f) ELECTION TO ALLOCATE INTEREST, ETC. ON WORLDWIDE BASIS.—For purposes of this subchapter, at the election of the worldwide affiliated group—

(1) ALLOCATION AND APPORTIONMENT OF INTEREST EXPENSE.—

(A) IN GENERAL.—The taxable income of each domestic corporation which is a member of a worldwide affiliated group shall be determined by allocating and apportioning interest expense of each member as if all members of such group were a single corporation.

(B) TREATMENT OF WORLDWIDE AFFILIATED GROUP.—The taxable income of the domestic members of a worldwide affiliated group from sources outside the United States shall be determined by allocating and apportioning the interest expense of such domestic members to such income in an amount equal to the excess (if any) of—

(i) the total interest expense of the worldwide affiliated group multiplied by the ratio which the foreign assets of the worldwide affiliated group bears to all the assets of the worldwide affiliated group, over

(ii) the interest expense of all foreign corporations which are members of the worldwide affiliated group to the extent such interest expense of such foreign corporations would have been allocated and apportioned to foreign source income if this subsection were applied to a group consisting of all the foreign corporations in such worldwide affiliated group.

(C) WORLDWIDE AFFILIATED GROUP.—For purposes of this paragraph, the term "worldwide affiliated group" means a group consisting of—

(i) the includible members of an affiliated group (as defined in section 1504(a), determined without regard to paragraph (2) of section 1504(b)), and

(ii) all controlled foreign corporations in which such members in the aggregate meet the ownership requirements of section 1504(a)(2) either directly or indirectly through applying paragraph (2) of section 958(a) or through applying rules similar to the rules of such paragraph to stock owned directly or indirectly by domestic partnerships, trusts, or estates.

(2) ALLOCATION AND APPORTIONMENT OF OTHER EXPENSES.—Expenses other than interest which are not directly allocable or apportioned to any specific income producing activity shall be allocated and apportioned as if all members of the affiliated group were a single corporation. For purposes of the preceding sentence, the term "affiliated group" has the meaning given such term by section 1504 (determined without regard to paragraph (4) of section 1504(b)).

(3) TREATMENT OF TAX-EXEMPT ASSETS; BASIS OF STOCK IN NONAFFILIATED 10-PERCENT OWNED CORPORATIONS.—The rules of paragraphs (3) and (4) of subsection (e) shall apply for purposes of this subsection, except that paragraph (4) shall be applied on a worldwide affiliated group basis.

(4) TREATMENT OF CERTAIN FINANCIAL INSTITUTIONS.—

(A) IN GENERAL.—For purposes of paragraph (1), any corporation described in subparagraph (B) shall be treated as an includible corporation for purposes of section 1504 only for purposes of applying this subsection separately to corporations so described.

(B) DESCRIPTION.—A corporation is described in this subparagraph if—

(i) such corporation is a financial institution described in section 581 or 591,

(ii) the business of such financial institution is predominantly with persons other than related persons (within the meaning of subsection (d)(4)) or their customers, and

(iii) such financial institution is required by State or Federal law to be operated separately from any other entity which is not such an institution.

(C) TREATMENT OF BANK AND FINANCIAL HOLDING COMPANIES.—To the extent provided in regulations—

(i) a bank holding company (within the meaning of section 2(a) of the Bank Holding Company Act of 1956 (12 U.S.C. 1841(a)),

(ii) a financial holding company (within the meaning of section 2(p) of the Bank Holding Company Act of 1956 (12 U.S.C. 1841(p)), and

(iii) any subsidiary of a financial institution described in section 581 or 591, or of any such bank or financial holding company, if such subsidiary is predominantly engaged (directly or indirectly) in the active conduct of a banking, financing, or similar business,

shall be treated as a corporation described in subparagraph (B).

(5) ELECTION TO EXPAND FINANCIAL INSTITUTION GROUP OF WORLDWIDE GROUP.—

(A) IN GENERAL.—If a worldwide affiliated group elects the application of this subsection, all financial corporations which—

(i) are members of such worldwide affiliated group, but

(ii) are not corporations described in paragraph (4)(B),

shall be treated as described in paragraph (4)(B) for purposes of applying paragraph (4)(A). This subsection (other than this paragraph) shall apply to any such group in the same manner as this subsection (other than this paragraph) applies to the pre-election worldwide affiliated group of which such group is a part.

(B) FINANCIAL CORPORATION.—For purposes of this paragraph, the term "financial corporation" means any corporation if at least 80 percent of its gross income is income described in section 904(d)(2)(D)(ii) and the regulations thereunder which is derived from transactions with persons who are not related (within the meaning of section 267(b) or 707(b)(1)) to the corporation. For purposes of the preceding sentence, there shall be disregarded any item of income or gain from a transaction or series of transactions a principal purpose of which is the qualification of any corporation as a financial corporation.

(C) ANTI-ABUSE RULES.—In the case of a corporation which is a member of an electing financial institution group, to the extent that such corporation—

(i) distributes dividends or makes other distributions with respect to its stock after the date of the enactment of this paragraph to any member of the pre-election worldwide affiliated group (other than to a member of the electing financial institution group) in excess of the greater of—

(I) its average annual dividend (expressed as a percentage of current earnings and profits) during the 5-taxable-year period ending with the taxable year preceding the taxable year, or

(II) 25 percent of its average annual earnings and profits for such 5-taxable-year period, or

(ii) deals with any person in any manner not clearly reflecting the income of the corporation (as determined under principles similar to the principles of section 482),

an amount of indebtedness of the electing financial institution group equal to the excess distribution or the understatement or overstatement of income, as the case may be, shall be recharacterized (for the taxable year and subsequent taxable years) for purposes of this paragraph as indebtedness of the worldwide affiliated group (excluding the electing financial institution group). If a corporation has not been in existence for 5 taxable years, this subparagraph shall be applied with respect to the period it was in existence.

(D) ELECTION.—An election under this paragraph with respect to any financial institution group may be made only by the common parent of the pre-election worldwide affiliated group and may be made only for the first taxable year beginning after December 31, 2020, in which such affiliated group includes 1 or more financial corporations. Such an election, once made, shall apply to all financial corporations which are members of the electing financial institution group for such taxable year and all subsequent years unless revoked with the consent of the Secretary.

(E) DEFINITIONS RELATING TO GROUPS.—For purposes of this paragraph—

(i) PRE-ELECTION WORLDWIDE AFFILIATED GROUP.—The term "pre-election worldwide affiliated group" means, with respect to a corporation, the worldwide affiliated group of which such corporation would (but for an election under this paragraph) be a member for purposes of applying paragraph (1).

(ii) ELECTING FINANCIAL INSTITUTION GROUP.—The term "electing financial institution group" means the group of corporations to which this subsection applies separately by reason of the application of paragraph (4)(A) and which includes financial corporations by reason of an election under subparagraph (A).

(F) REGULATIONS.—The Secretary shall prescribe such regulations as may be appropriate to carry out this subsection, including regulations—

(i) providing for the direct allocation of interest expense in other circumstances where such allocation would be appropriate to carry out the purposes of this subsection,

(ii) preventing assets or interest expense from being taken into account more than once, and

(iii) dealing with changes in members of any group (through acquisitions or otherwise) treated under this paragraph as an affiliated group for purposes of this subsection.

(6) ELECTION.—An election to have this subsection apply with respect to any worldwide affiliated group may be made only by the common parent of the domestic affiliated group referred to in paragraph (1)(C) and may be made only for the first taxable year beginning after December 31, 2020, in which a worldwide affiliated group exists which includes such affiliated group and at least 1 foreign corporation. Such an election, once made, shall apply to such common parent and all other corporations which are members of such worldwide affiliated group for such taxable year and all subsequent years unless revoked with the consent of the Secretary.

• **2018, Tax Technical Corrections Act of 2018 (P.L. 115-141)**

P.L. 115-141, § 401(d)(1)(D)(xvii)(V), Div. U:

Amended Code Sec. 864(f)(1)(C)(i) and (2) by striking "paragraphs (2) and (4)" and inserting "paragraph (2)". [Note: The text "paragraphs (2) and (4)" does not appear in Code Sec. 964(f)(2) and so cannot be stricken.—CCH] **Effective** 3-23-2018. For a special rule, see Act Sec. 401(e), Div. U, below.

P.L. 115-141, § 401(e), Div. U, provides:

(e) GENERAL SAVINGS PROVISION WITH RESPECT TO DEADWOOD PROVISIONS.—If—

(1) any provision amended or repealed by the amendments made by subsection (b) or (d) applied to—

(A) any transaction occurring before the date of the enactment of this Act,

(B) any property acquired before such date of enactment, or

(C) any item of income, loss, deduction, or credit taken into account before such date of enactment, and

(2) the treatment of such transaction, property, or item under such provision would (without regard to the amendments or repeals made by such subsection) affect the liability for tax for periods ending after such date of enactment,

nothing in the amendments or repeals made by this section shall be construed to affect the treatment of such transaction, property, or item for purposes of determining liability for tax for periods ending after such date of enactment.

• **2010, Hiring Incentives to Restore Employment Act (P.L. 111-147)**

P.L. 111-147, § 551(a):

Amended Code Sec. 864(f)(5)(D) and (6) by striking "December 31, 2017" and inserting "December 31, 2020". **Effective** 3-18-2010.

• **2009, Worker, Homeownership, and Business Assistance Act of 2009 (P.L. 111-92)**

P.L. 111-92, § 15(a):

Amended Code Sec. 864(f)(5)(D) and (6) by striking "December 31, 2010" and inserting "December 31, 2017". **Effective** for tax years beginning after 12-31-2010.

P.L. 111-92, § 15(b):

Amended Code Sec. 864(f) by striking paragraph (7). **Effective** for tax years beginning after 12-31-2010. Prior to being stricken, Code Sec. 864(f)(7) read as follows:

(7) TRANSITION.—In the case of the first taxable year to which this subsection applies, the increase (if any) in the amount of the interest expense allocable to sources within the United States by reason of the application of this subsection shall be 30 percent of the amount of such increase determined without regard to this paragraph.

• **2008, Housing Assistance Tax Act of 2008 (P.L. 110-289)**

P.L. 110-289, § 3093(a):

Amended Code Sec. 864(f)(5)(D) and (6) by striking "December 31, 2008" and inserting "December 31, 2010". **Effective** for tax years beginning after 12-31-2008.

P.L. 110-289, § 3093(b):

Amended Code Sec. 864(f) by adding at the end a new paragraph (7). **Effective** for tax years beginning after 12-31-2008.

• **2004, American Jobs Creation Act of 2004 (P.L. 108-357)**

P.L. 108-357, § 401(a):

Amended Code Sec. 864 by redesignating subsection (f) as subsection (g) and by inserting after subsection (e) a new subsection (f). **Effective** for tax years beginning after 12-31-2008.

[Sec. 864(g)]

(g) ALLOCATION OF RESEARCH AND EXPERIMENTAL EXPENDITURES.—

(1) IN GENERAL.—For purposes of sections 861(b), 862(b), and 863(b), qualified research and experimental expenditures shall be allocated and apportioned as follows:

(A) Any qualified research and experimental expenditures expended solely to meet legal requirements imposed by a political entity with respect to the improvement or marketing of specific products or processes for purposes not reasonably expected to generate gross income (beyond de minimis amounts) outside the jurisdiction of the political entity shall be allocated only to gross income from sources within such jurisdiction.

(B) In the case of any qualified research and experimental expenditures (not allocated under subparagraph (A)) to the extent—

(i) that such expenditures are attributable to activities conducted in the United States, 50 percent of such expenditures shall be allocated and apportioned to income from sources within the United States and deducted from such income in determining the amount of taxable income from sources within the United States, and

(ii) that such expenditures are attributable to activities conducted outside the United States, 50 percent of such expenditures shall be allocated and apportioned to income from sources outside the United States and deducted from such income in determining the amount of taxable income from sources outside the United States.

(C) The remaining portion of qualified research and experimental expenditures (not allocated under subparagraphs (A) and (B)) shall be apportioned, at the annual election of the taxpayer, on the basis of gross sales or gross income, except that, if the taxpayer elects to apportion on the basis of gross income, the amount apportioned to income from sources outside the United States shall at least be 30 percent of the amount which would be so apportioned on the basis of gross sales.

(2) QUALIFIED RESEARCH AND EXPERIMENTAL EXPENDITURES.—For purposes of this section, the term "qualified research and experimental expenditures" means amounts which are research and experimental expenditures within the meaning of section 174. For purposes of this paragraph, rules similar to the rules of subsection (c) of section 174 shall apply. Any qualified research and experimental expenditures treated as deferred expenses under subsection (b) of section 174 shall be taken into account under this subsection for the taxable year for which such expenditures are allowed as a deduction under such subsection.

(3) SPECIAL RULES FOR EXPENDITURES ATTRIBUTABLE TO ACTIVITIES CONDUCTED IN SPACE, ETC.—

(A) IN GENERAL.—Any qualified research and experimental expenditures described in subparagraph (B)—

(i) if incurred by a United States person, shall be allocated and apportioned under this section in the same manner as if they were attributable to activities conducted in the United States, and

(ii) if incurred by a person other than a United States person, shall be allocated and apportioned under this section in the same manner as if they were attributable to activities conducted outside the United States.

(B) DESCRIPTION OF EXPENDITURES.—For purposes of subparagraph (A), qualified research and experimental expenditures are described in this subparagraph if such expenditures are attributable to activities conducted—

(i) in space,

(ii) on or under water not within the jurisdiction (as recognized by the United States) of a foreign country, possession of the United States, or the United States, or

(iii) in Antarctica.

INCOME TAX—SOURCES OF INCOME

(4) AFFILIATED GROUP.—

(A) Except as provided in subparagraph (B), the allocation and apportionment required by paragraph (1) shall be determined as if all members of the affiliated group (as defined in subsection (e)(5)) were a single corporation.

(B) For purposes of the allocation and apportionment required by paragraph (1)—

(i) sales and gross income from products produced in whole or in part in a possession by an electing corporation (within the meaning of section 936(h)(5)(E)), and

(ii) dividends from an electing corporation,

shall not be taken into account, except that this subparagraph shall not apply to sales of (and gross income and dividends attributable to sales of) products with respect to which an election under section 936(h)(5)(F) is not in effect.

(C) The qualified research and experimental expenditures taken into account for purposes of paragraph (1) shall be adjusted to reflect the amount of such expenditures included in computing the cost-sharing amount (determined under section 936(h)(5)(C)(i)(I)).

(D) The Secretary may prescribe such regulations as may be necessary to carry out the purposes of this paragraph, including regulations providing for the source of gross income and the allocation and apportionment of deductions to take into account the adjustments required by subparagraph (B) or (C).

(E) Paragraph (6) of subsection (e) shall not apply to qualified research and experimental expenditures.

(5) REGULATIONS.—The Secretary shall prescribe such regulations as may be appropriate to carry out the purposes of this subsection, including regulations relating to the determination of whether any expenses are attributable to activities conducted in the United States or outside the United States and regulations providing such adjustments to the provisions of this subsection as may be appropriate in the case of cost-sharing arrangements and contract research.

(6) APPLICABILITY.—This subsection shall apply to the taxpayer's first taxable year (beginning on or before August 1, 1994) following the taxpayer's last taxable year to which Revenue Procedure 92-56 applies or would apply if the taxpayer elected the benefits of such Revenue Procedure.

Amendments

• **2004, American Jobs Creation Act of 2004 (P.L. 108-357)**

P.L. 108-357, § 401(a):

Amended Code Sec. 864 by redesignating subsection (f) as subsection (g). **Effective** for tax years beginning after 12-31-2008.

• **1993, Omnibus Budget Reconciliation Act of 1993 (P.L. 103-66)**

P.L. 103-66, § 13234(a):

Amended Code Sec. 864(f)(1)(B) by striking "64 percent" each place it appeared and inserting "50 percent". **Effective** 8-10-93.

P.L. 103-66, § 13234(b)(1):

Amended Code Sec. 864(f) by striking paragraph (5) and inserting new paragraphs (5) and (6). **Effective** 8-10-93. Prior to amendment, Code Sec. 864(f)(5) read as follows:

(5) YEARS TO WHICH RULE APPLIES.—

(A) IN GENERAL.—This subsection shall apply to the taxpayer's first 3 taxable years beginning after August 1, 1989, and on or before August 1, 1992.

(B) REDUCTION.—Notwithstanding subparagraph (A), in the case of the taxpayer's first taxable year beginning after August 1, 1991, this subsection shall only apply to qualified research and experimental expenditures incurred during the first 6 months of such taxable year.

P.L. 103-66, § 13234(b)(2):

Amended Code Sec. 864(f)(4)(D) by striking "subparagraph (C)" and inserting "subparagraph (B) or (C)". **Effective** 8-10-93.

• **1991, Tax Extension Act of 1991 (P.L. 102-227)**

P.L. 102-227, § 101(a):

Amended Code Sec. 864(f)(5). **Effective** for tax years beginning after 8-1-89. Prior to amendment, Code Sec. 864(f)(5) read as follows:

(5) YEARS TO WHICH RULE APPLIES.—This subsection shall apply to the taxpayer's first 2 taxable years beginning after August 1, 1989, and on or before August 1, 1991.

• **1990, Omnibus Budget Reconciliation Act of 1990 (P.L. 101-508)**

P.L. 101-508, § 11401(a):

Amended Code Sec. 864(f)(5). **Effective** for tax years beginning after 8-1-89. Prior to amendment, Code Sec. 864(f)(5) read as follows:

(5) YEAR TO WHICH RULE APPLIES.—

(A) IN GENERAL.—Except as provided in this paragraph, this subsection shall apply to the taxpayer's first taxable year beginning after August 1, 1989, and before August 2, 1990.

(B) REDUCTION.—Notwithstanding subparagraph (A), this subsection shall only apply to that portion of the qualified research and experimental expenditures for the taxable year referred to in subparagraph (A) which bears the same ratio to the total amount of such expenditures as—

(i) the lesser of 9 months or the number of months in the taxable year, bears to

(ii) the number of months in the taxable year.

• **1989, Omnibus Budget Reconciliation Act of 1989 (P.L. 101-239)**

P.L. 101-239, § 7111:

Amended Code Sec. 864 by adding at the end thereof a new subsection (f). **Effective** 12-19-89.

[Sec. 865]

SEC. 865. SOURCE RULES FOR PERSONAL PROPERTY SALES.

[Sec. 865(a)]

(a) GENERAL RULE.—Except as otherwise provided in this section, income from the sale of personal property—

(1) by a United States resident shall be sourced in the United States, or

(2) by a nonresident shall be sourced outside the United States.

[Sec. 865(b)]

(b) EXCEPTION FOR INVENTORY PROPERTY.—In the case of income derived from the sale of inventory property—

(1) this section shall not apply, and

(2) such income shall be sourced under the rules of sections 861(a)(6), 862(a)(6), and 863.

Notwithstanding the preceding sentence, any income from the sale of any unprocessed timber which is a softwood and was cut from an area in the United States shall be sourced in the United States and the rules of sections 862(a)(6) and 863(b) shall not apply to any such income. For purposes of the preceding sentence, the term "unprocessed timber" means any log, cant, or similar form of timber.

Amendments

• **1996, Small Business Job Protection Act of 1996 (P.L. 104-188)**

P.L. 104-188, § 1704(f)(4)(A):

Amended Code Sec. 865(b)(2) by striking "863(b)" and inserting "863". **Effective** as if included in the amendments made by section 1211 of P.L. 99-514.

• **1993, Omnibus Budget Reconciliation Act of 1993 (P.L. 103-66)**

P.L. 103-66, § 13239(c):

Amended Code Sec. 865(b) by adding two new sentences at the end thereof. **Effective** for sales, exchanges, or other dispositions after 8-10-93.

[Sec. 865(c)]

(c) EXCEPTION FOR DEPRECIABLE PERSONAL PROPERTY.—

(1) IN GENERAL.—Gain (not in excess of the depreciation adjustments) from the sale of depreciable personal property shall be allocated between sources in the United States and sources outside the United States—

(A) by treating the same proportion of such gain as sourced in the United States as the United States depreciation adjustments with respect to such property bear to the total depreciation adjustments, and

(B) by treating the remaining portion of such gain as sourced outside the United States.

Sec. 864(g)(4)

INCOME TAX—SOURCES OF INCOME

(2) GAIN IN EXCESS OF DEPRECIATION.—Gain (in excess of the depreciation adjustments) from the sale of depreciable personal property shall be sourced as if such property were inventory property.

(3) UNITED STATES DEPRECIATION ADJUSTMENTS.—For purposes of this subsection—

(A) IN GENERAL.—The term "United States depreciation adjustments" means the portion of the depreciation adjustments to the adjusted basis of the property which are attributable to the depreciation deductions allowable in computing taxable income from sources in the United States.

(B) SPECIAL RULE FOR CERTAIN PROPERTY.—Except in the case of property of a kind described in section 168(g)(4), if, for any taxable year—

(i) such property is used predominantly in the United States, or

(ii) such property is used predominantly outside the United States,

all of the depreciation deductions allowable for such year shall be treated as having been allocated to income from sources in the United States (or, where clause (ii) applies, from sources outside the United States).

(4) OTHER DEFINITIONS.—For purposes of this subsection—

(A) DEPRECIABLE PERSONAL PROPERTY.—The term "depreciable personal property" means any personal property if the adjusted basis of such property includes depreciation adjustments.

(B) DEPRECIATION ADJUSTMENTS.—The term "depreciation adjustments" means adjustments reflected in the adjusted basis of any property on account of depreciation deductions (whether allowed with respect to such property or other property and whether allowed to the taxpayer or to any other person).

(C) DEPRECIATION DEDUCTIONS.—The term "depreciation deductions" means any deductions for depreciation or amortization or any other deduction allowable under any provision of this chapter which treats an otherwise capital expenditure as a deductible expense.

Amendments

- **1990, Omnibus Budget Reconciliation Act of 1990 (P.L. 101-508)**

P.L. 101-508, §11813(b)(18):

Amended Code Sec. 865(c)(3)(B) by striking "section 48(a)(2)(B)" and inserting "section 168(g)(4)". **Effective**, generally, for property placed in service after 12-31-90. For exceptions, see Act Sec. 11813(c)(2) below.

P.L. 101-508, §11813(c)(2), provides:

(2) EXCEPTIONS.—The amendments made by this section shall not apply to—

(A) any transition property (as defined in section 49(e) of the Internal Revenue Code of 1986 (as in effect on the day before the date of the enactment of this Act),

(B) any property with respect to which qualified progress expenditures were previously taken into account under section 46(d) of such Code (as so in effect), and

(C) any property described in section 46(b)(2)(C) of such Code (as so in effect).

[Sec. 865(d)]

(d) EXCEPTION FOR INTANGIBLES.—

(1) IN GENERAL.—In the case of any sale of an intangible—

(A) this section shall apply only to the extent the payments in consideration of such sale are not contingent on the productivity, use, or disposition of the intangible, and

(B) to the extent such payments are so contingent, the source of such payments shall be determined under this part in the same manner as if such payments were royalties.

(2) INTANGIBLE.—For purposes of paragraph (1), the term "intangible" means any patent, copyright, secret process or formula, goodwill, trademark, trade brand, franchise, or other like property.

(3) SPECIAL RULE IN THE CASE OF GOODWILL.—To the extent this section applies to the sale of goodwill, payments in consideration of such sale shall be treated as from sources in the country in which such goodwill was generated.

(4) COORDINATION WITH SUBSECTION (c).—

(A) GAIN NOT IN EXCESS OF DEPRECIATION ADJUSTMENTS SOURCED UNDER SUBSECTION (c).—Notwithstanding paragraph (1), any gain from the sale of an intangible shall be sourced under subsection (c) to the extent such gain does not exceed the depreciation adjustments with respect to such intangible.

(B) SUBSECTION (c)(2) NOT TO APPLY TO INTANGIBLES.—Paragraph (2) of subsection (c) shall not apply to any gain from the sale of an intangible.

Amendments

- **1988, Technical and Miscellaneous Revenue Act of 1988 (P.L. 100-647)**

P.L. 100-647, §1012(d)(1):

Amended Code Sec. 865(d) by adding at the end thereof new paragraph (4). **Effective** as if included in the provision of P.L. 99-514 to which it relates.

P.L. 100-647, §1012(d)(12):

Amended Code Sec. 865(d) by inserting "franchise," after "trade brand,". **Effective** as if included in the provision of P.L. 99-514 to which it relates.

[Sec. 865(e)]

(e) SPECIAL RULES FOR SALES THROUGH OFFICES OR FIXED PLACES OF BUSINESS.—

(1) SALES BY RESIDENTS.—

(A) IN GENERAL.—In the case of income not sourced under subsection (b), (c), (d)(1)(B) or (3), or (f), if a United States resident maintains an office or other fixed place of business in a foreign country, income from sales of personal property attributable to such office or other fixed place of business shall be sourced outside the United States.

(B) TAX MUST BE IMPOSED.—Subparagraph (A) shall not apply unless an income tax equal to at least 10 percent of the income from the sale is actually paid to a foreign country with respect to such income.

(2) SALES BY NONRESIDENTS.—

(A) IN GENERAL.—Notwithstanding any other provisions of this part, if a nonresident maintains an office or other fixed place of business in the United States, income from any sale of personal property (including inventory property) attributable to such office or other fixed place of business shall be sourced in the United States. The preceding sentence shall not apply for purposes of section 971 (defining export trade corporation).

(B) EXCEPTION.—Subparagraph (A) shall not apply to any sale of inventory property which is sold for use, disposition, or consumption outside the United States if an office or other fixed place of business of the taxpayer in a foreign country materially participated in the sale.

(3) SALES ATTRIBUTABLE TO AN OFFICE OR OTHER FIXED PLACE OF BUSINESS.—The principles of section 864(c)(5) shall apply in determining whether a taxpayer has an office or other fixed place of business and whether a sale is attributable to such an office or other fixed place of business.

INCOME TAX—SOURCES OF INCOME

Amendments
• **1988, Technical and Miscellaneous Revenue Act of 1988 (P.L. 100-647)**

P.L. 100-647, § 1012(d)(2):

Amended Code Sec. 865(e)(1)(A) by striking out "(d), or (f)" and inserting in lieu thereof "(d)(1)(B) or (3), or (f)". **Effective** as if included in the provision of P.L. 99-514 to which it relates.

P.L. 100-647, § 1012(d)(5):

Amended Code Sec. 865(e)(2)(B). **Effective** with respect to tax years beginning after 12-31-87. Prior to amendment, Code Sec. 865(e)(2)(B) read as follows:

(B) EXCEPTION.—Subparagraph (A) shall not apply to—

(i) any sale of inventory property which is sold for use, disposition, or consumption outside the United States if an office or other fixed place of business of the taxpayer outside the United States materially participated in the sale, or

(ii) any amount included in gross income under section 951(a)(1)(A).

P.L. 100-647, § 1012(d)(9):

Amended Code Sec. 865(e)(1)(A) by striking out "outside the United States" the first place it appears and inserting in lieu thereof "in a foreign country". **Effective** as if included in the provision of P.L. 99-514 to which it relates.

[Sec. 865(f)]

(f) STOCK OF AFFILIATES.—If—

(1) a United States resident sells stock in an affiliate which is a foreign corporation,

(2) such sale occurs in a foreign country in which such affiliate is engaged in the active conduct of a trade or business, and

(3) more than 50 percent of the gross income of such affiliate for the 3-year period ending with the close of such affiliate's taxable year immediately preceding the year in which the sale occurred was derived from the active conduct of a trade or business in such foreign country,

any gain from such sale shall be sourced outside the United States. For purposes of paragraphs (2) and (3), the United States resident may elect to treat an affiliate and all other corporations which are wholly owned (directly or indirectly) by the affiliate as one corporation.

Amendments
• **1988, Technical and Miscellaneous Revenue Act of 1988 (P.L. 100-647)**

P.L. 100-647, § 1012(d)(4):

Amended Code Sec. 865(f). **Effective** as if included in the provision of P.L. 99-514 to which it relates. Prior to amendment, Code Sec. 865(f) read as follows:

(f) STOCK OF AFFILIATES.—If—

(1) a United States resident sells stock in an affiliate which is a foreign corporation,

(2) such affiliate is engaged in the active conduct of a trade or business, and

(3) such sale occurs in the foreign country in which the affiliate derived more than 50 percent of its gross income for the 3-year period ending with the close of the affiliate's taxable year immediately preceding the year during which such sale occurred,

any gain from such sale shall be sourced outside the United States.

[Sec. 865(g)]

(g) UNITED STATES RESIDENT; NONRESIDENT.—For purposes of this section—

(1) IN GENERAL.—Except as otherwise provided in this subsection—

(A) UNITED STATES RESIDENT.—The term "United States resident" means—

(i) any individual who—

(I) is a United States citizen or a resident alien and does not have a tax home (as defined in section 911(d)(3)) in a foreign country, or

(II) is a nonresident alien and has a tax home (as so defined) in the United States, and

(ii) any corporation, trust, or estate which is a United States person (as defined in section 7701(a)(30)).

(B) NONRESIDENT.—The term "nonresident" means any person other than a United States resident.

(2) SPECIAL RULES FOR UNITED STATES CITIZENS AND RESIDENT ALIENS.—For purposes of this section, a United States citizen or resident alien shall not be treated as a nonresident with respect to any sale of personal property unless an income tax equal to a least 10 percent of the gain derived from such sale is actually paid to a foreign country with respect to that gain.

(3) SPECIAL RULE FOR CERTAIN STOCK SALES BY RESIDENTS OF PUERTO RICO.—Paragraph (2) shall not apply to the sale by an individual who was a bona fide resident of Puerto Rico during the entire taxable year of stock in a corporation if—

(A) such corporation is engaged in the active conduct of a trade or business in Puerto Rico, and

(B) more than 50 percent of its gross income for the 3-year period ending with the close of such corporation's taxable year immediately preceding the year in which such sale occurred was derived from the active conduct of a trade or business in Puerto Rico.

For purposes of the preceding sentence, the taxpayer may elect to treat a corporation and all other corporations which are wholly owned (directly or indirectly) by such corporation as one corporation.

Amendments
• **1988, Technical and Miscellaneous Revenue Act of 1988 (P.L. 100-647)**

P.L. 100-647, § 1012(d)(3)(A):

Amended Code Sec. 865(g)(1)(A)(ii) by striking out "partnership," after "corporation". **Effective** as if included in the provision of P.L. 99-514 to which it relates.

P.L. 100-647, § 1012(d)(6)(A):

Amended Code Sec. 865(g) by adding at the end thereof new paragraph (3). **Effective** as if included in the provision of P.L. 99-514 to which it relates.

P.L. 100-647, § 1012(d)(11):

Amended Code Sec. 865(g)(1)(A)(i). **Effective** as if included in the provision of P.L. 99-514 to which it relates. Prior to amendment, Code Sec. 865(g)(1)(A)(i) read as follows:

(i) any individual who has a tax home (as defined in section 911(d)(3)) in the United States, and

[Sec. 865(h)]

(h) TREATMENT OF GAINS FROM SALE OF CERTAIN STOCK OR INTANGIBLES AND FROM CERTAIN LIQUIDATIONS.—

(1) IN GENERAL.—In the case of gain to which this subsection applies—

(A) such gain shall be sourced outside the United States, but

(B) subsections (a), (b), and (c) of section 904 and sections 907 and 960 shall be applied separately with respect to such gain.

(2) GAIN TO WHICH SUBSECTION APPLIES.—This subsection shall apply to—

(A) GAIN FROM SALE OF CERTAIN STOCK OR INTANGIBLES.—Any gain—

(i) which is from the sale of stock in a foreign corporation or an intangible (as defined in subsection (d)(2)) and which would otherwise be sourced in the United States under this section,

(ii) which, under a treaty obligation of the United States (applied without regard to this section), would be sourced outside the United States, and

(iii) with respect to which the taxpayer chooses the benefits of this subsection.

(B) GAIN FROM LIQUIDATION IN POSSESSION.—Any gain which is derived from the receipt of any distribution in liquidation of a corporation—

(i) which is organized in a possession of the United States, and

(ii) more than 50 percent of the gross income of which during the 3-taxable year period ending with the close of the taxable year immediately preceding the taxable year in which the distribution is received from the active conduct of a trade or business in such possession.

INCOME TAX—SOURCES OF INCOME

Amendments

• **2017, Tax Cuts and Jobs Act (P.L. 115-97)**

P.L. 115-97, §14301(c)(6):

Amended Code Sec. 865(h)(1)(B) by striking "902, 907," and inserting "907". **Effective** for tax years of foreign corporations beginning after 12-31-2017, and to tax years of United States shareholders in which or with which such tax years of foreign corporations end.

• **1988, Technical and Miscellaneous Revenue Act of 1988 (P.L. 100-647)**

P.L. 100-647, §1012(d)(8):

Amended Code Sec. 865 by redesignating subsections (h), (i), and (j) as subsections (i), (j), and (k), respectively, and by inserting after subsection (g) new subsection (h). **Effective** as if included in the provision of P.L. 99-514 to which it relates.

[Sec. 865(i)]

(i) OTHER DEFINITIONS.—For purposes of this section—

(1) INVENTORY PROPERTY.—The term "inventory property" means personal property described in paragraph (1) of section 1221(a).

(2) SALE INCLUDES EXCHANGE.—The term "sale" includes an exchange or any other disposition.

(3) TREATMENT OF POSSESSIONS.—Any possession of the United States shall be treated as a foreign country.

(4) AFFILIATE.—The term "affiliate" means a member of the same affiliated group (within the meaning of section 1504(a) without regard to section 1504(b)).

(5) TREATMENT OF PARTNERSHIPS.—In the case of a partnership, except as provided in regulations, this section shall be applied at the partner level.

Amendments

• **1999, Tax Relief Extension Act of 1999 (P.L. 106-170)**

P.L. 106-170, §532(c)(1)(E):

Amended Code Sec. 865(i)(1) by striking "section 1221" and inserting "section 1221(a)". **Effective** for any instrument held, acquired, or entered into, any transaction entered into, and supplies held or acquired on or after 12-17-99.

• **1988, Technical and Miscellaneous Revenue Act of 1988 (P.L. 100-647)**

P.L. 100-647, §1012(d)(3)(B):

Amended Code Sec. 865(h) by adding at the end thereof new paragraph (5). **Effective** as if included in the provision of P.L. 99-514 to which it relates.

P.L. 100-647, §1012(d)(8):

Amended Code Sec. 865 by redesignating subsection (h) as subsection (i). **Effective** as if included in the provision of P.L. 99-514 to which it relates.

[Sec. 865(j)]

(j) REGULATIONS.—The Secretary shall prescribe such regulations as may be necessary or appropriate to carry out the purpose of this section, including regulations—

(1) relating to the treatment of losses from sales of personal property,

(2) applying the rules of this section to income derived from trading in futures contracts, forward contracts, options contracts, and other instruments, and

(3) providing that, subject to such conditions (which may include provisions comparable to section 877) as may be provided in such regulations, subsections (e)(1)(B) and (g)(2) shall not apply for purposes of sections 931 and 933.

Amendments

• **2018, Tax Technical Corrections Act of 2018 (P.L. 115-141)**

P.L. 115-141, §401(d)(1)(D)(xi), Div. U:

Amended Code Sec. 865(j)(3) by striking ", 933, and 936" and inserting "and 933". **Effective** 3-23-2018. For a special rule, see Act Sec. 401(e), Div. U, below.

P.L. 115-141, §401(e), Div. U, provides:

(e) GENERAL SAVINGS PROVISION WITH RESPECT TO DEADWOOD PROVISIONS.—If—

(1) any provision amended or repealed by the amendments made by subsection (b) or (d) applied to—

(A) any transaction occurring before the date of the enactment of this Act,

(B) any property acquired before such date of enactment, or

(C) any item of income, loss, deduction, or credit taken into account before such date of enactment, and

(2) the treatment of such transaction, property, or item under such provision would (without regard to the amendments or repeals made by such subsection) affect the liability for tax for periods ending after such date of enactment,

nothing in the amendments or repeals made by this section shall be construed to affect the treatment of such transaction, property, or item for purposes of determining liability for tax for periods ending after such date of enactment.

• **1988, Technical and Miscellaneous Revenue Act of 1988 (P.L. 100-647)**

P.L. 100-647, §1012(d)(6)(B):

Amended Code Sec. 865(i) by striking out "and" at the end of paragraph (1), by striking out the period at the end of paragraph (2) and inserting in lieu thereof ", and" and by adding at the end thereof a new paragraph (3). **Effective** as if included in the provision of P.L. 99-514 to which it relates.

P.L. 100-647, §1012(d)(8):

Amended Code Sec. 865 by redesignating subsection (i) as subsection (j). **Effective** as if included in the provision of P.L. 99-514 to which it relates.

[Sec. 865(k)]

(k) CROSS REFERENCES.—

(1) For provisions relating to the characterization as dividends for source purposes of gains from the sale of stock in certain foreign corporations, see section 1248.

(2) For sourcing of income from certain foreign currency transactions, see section 988.

Amendments

• **1988, Technical and Miscellaneous Revenue Act of 1988 (P.L. 100-647)**

P.L. 100-647, §1012(d)(8):

Amended Code Sec. 865 by redesignating subsection (j) as subsection (k). **Effective** as if included in the provision of P.L. 99-514 to which it relates.

• **1986, Tax Reform Act of 1986 (P.L. 99-514)**

P.L. 99-514, §1211(a):

Added new Code Sec. 865. **Effective**, generally, for tax years beginning after 12-31-86. However, see the special rule provided in Act Sec. 1211(c)(2), below.

P.L. 99-514, §1211(c)(2), provides:

(2) SPECIAL RULE FOR FOREIGN PERSONS.—In the case of any foreign person other than any controlled foreign corporations (within the meaning of section 957(a) of the Internal Revenue Code of 1954), the amendments made by this section shall apply to transactions entered into after March 18, 1986.

PART II—NONRESIDENT ALIENS AND FOREIGN CORPORATIONS

Subpart A.	Nonresident alien individuals.
Subpart B.	Foreign corporations.
Subpart C.	Tax on gross transportation income.
Subpart D.	Miscellaneous provisions.

Subpart A—Nonresident Alien Individuals

Sec. 871.	Tax on nonresident alien individuals.
Sec. 872.	Gross income.

INCOME TAX—NONRESIDENT ALIENS

Sec. 873.	Deductions.
Sec. 874.	Allowance of deductions and credits.
Sec. 875.	Partnerships; beneficiaries of estates and trusts.
Sec. 876.	Alien residents of Puerto Rico, Guam, American Samoa, or the Northern Mariana Islands.
Sec. 877.	Expatriation to avoid tax.
Sec. 877A.	Tax responsibilities of expatriation.
Sec. 878.	Foreign educational, charitable, and certain other exempt organizations.
Sec. 879.	Tax treatment of certain community income in the case of nonresident alien individuals.

[Sec. 871]

SEC. 871. TAX ON NONRESIDENT ALIEN INDIVIDUALS.

[Sec. 871(a)]

(a) INCOME NOT CONNECTED WITH UNITED STATES BUSINESS—30 PERCENT TAX.—

(1) INCOME OTHER THAN CAPITAL GAINS.—Except as provided in subsection (h), there is hereby imposed for each taxable year a tax of 30 percent of the amount received from sources within the United States by a nonresident alien individual as—

(A) interest (other than original issue discount as defined in section 1273), dividends, rents, salaries, wages, premiums, annuities, compensations, remunerations, emoluments, and other fixed or determinable annual or periodical gains, profits, and income,

(B) gains described in subsection (b) or (c) of section 631,

(C) in the case of—

(i) a sale or exchange of an original issue discount obligation, the amount of the original issue discount accruing while such obligation was held by the nonresident alien individual (to the extent such discount was not theretofore taken into account under clause (ii)), and

(ii) a payment on an original issue discount obligation, an amount equal to the original issue discount accruing while such obligation was held by the nonresident alien individual (except that such original issue discount shall be taken into account under this clause only to the extent such discount was not theretofore taken into account under this clause and only to the extent that the tax thereon does not exceed the payment less the tax imposed by subparagraph (A) thereon), and

(D) gains from the sale or exchange after October 4, 1966, of patents, copyrights, secret processes and formulas, good will, trademarks, trade brands, franchises, and other like property, or of any interest in any such property, to the extent such gains are from payments which are contingent on the productivity, use, or disposition of the property or interest sold or exchanged,

but only to the extent the amount so received is not effectively connected with the conduct of a trade or business within the United States.

(2) CAPITAL GAINS OF ALIENS PRESENT IN THE UNITED STATES 183 DAYS OR MORE.—In the case of a nonresident alien individual present in the United States for a period or periods aggregating 183 days or more during the taxable year, there is hereby imposed for such year a tax of 30 percent of the amount by which his gains, derived from sources within the United States, from the sale or exchange at any time during such year of capital assets exceed his losses, allocable to sources within the United States, from the sale or exchange at any time during such year of capital assets. For purposes of this paragraph, gains and losses shall be taken into account only if, and to the extent that, they would be recognized and taken into account if such gains and losses were effectively connected with the conduct of a trade or business within the United States, except that such gains and losses shall be determined without regard to section 1202 and such losses shall be determined without the benefits of the capital loss carryover provided in section 1212. Any gain or loss which is taken into account in determining the tax under paragraph (1) or subsection (b) shall not be taken into account in determining the tax under this paragraph. For purposes of the 183-day requirement of this paragraph, a nonresident alien individual not engaged in trade or business within the United States who has not established a taxable year for any prior period shall be treated as having a taxable year which is the calendar year.

(3) TAXATION OF SOCIAL SECURITY BENEFITS.—For purposes of this section and section 1441—

(A) 85 percent of any social security benefit (as defined in section 86(d)) shall be included in gross income (notwithstanding section 207 of the Social Security Act), and

(B) section 86 shall not apply.

Amendments

• **2018, Tax Technical Corrections Act of 2018 (P.L. 115-141)**

P.L. 115-141, §401(b)(29), Div. U:

Amended Code Sec. 871(a)(3) by striking the last sentence thereof. **Effective** 3-23-2018. For a special rule, see Act Sec. 401(e), Div. U, below. Prior to being stricken, the last sentence of Code Sec. 871(a)(3) read as follows:

For treatment of certain citizens of possessions of the United States, see section 932(c).

P.L. 115-141, §401(e), Div. U, provides:

(e) GENERAL SAVINGS PROVISION WITH RESPECT TO DEADWOOD PROVISIONS.—If—

(1) any provision amended or repealed by the amendments made by subsection (b) or (d) applied to—

(A) any transaction occurring before the date of the enactment of this Act,

(B) any property acquired before such date of enactment, or

(C) any item of income, loss, deduction, or credit taken into account before such date of enactment, and

(2) the treatment of such transaction, property, or item under such provision would (without regard to the amendments or repeals made by such subsection) affect the liability for tax for periods ending after such date of enactment,

nothing in the amendments or repeals made by this section shall be construed to affect the treatment of such transaction, property, or item for purposes of determining liability for tax for periods ending after such date of enactment.

• **2014, Tax Technical Corrections Act of 2014 (P.L. 113-295)**

P.L. 113-295, §221(a)(71), Division A:

Amended Code Sec. 871(a)(1)(B). **Effective** generally 12-19-2014. For a special rule, see Act Sec. 221(b)(2), Division A, below. Prior to amendment, Code Sec. 871(a)(1)(B) read as follows:

(B) gains described in section 631(b) or (c), and gains on transfers described in section 1235 made on or before October 4, 1966,

P.L. 113-295, §221(b)(2), Division A, provides:

(2) SAVINGS PROVISION.—If—

(A) any provision amended or repealed by the amendments made by this section applied to—

(i) any transaction occurring before the date of the enactment of this Act,

(ii) any property acquired before such date of enactment, or

(iii) any item of income, loss, deduction, or credit taken into account before such date of enactment, and

(B) the treatment of such transaction, property, or item under such provision would (without regard to the amendments or repeals made by this section) affect the liability for tax for periods ending after date of enactment, nothing in the amendments or repeals made by this section shall be construed to affect the treatment of such transaction, property, or item for purposes of determining liability for tax for periods ending after such date of enactment.

• **1994, Uruguay Round Agreements Act (P.L. 103-465)**

P.L. 103-465, §733(a):

Amended Code Sec. 871(a)(3)(A) by striking "one-half" and inserting "85 percent". **Effective** for benefits paid after 12-31-94, in tax years ending after such date.

• **1993, Omnibus Budget Reconciliation Act of 1993 (P.L. 103-66)**

P.L. 103-66, §13113(d)(5):

Amended Code Sec. 871(a)(2) by inserting "such gains and losses shall be determined without regard to section 1202 and" after "except that" in the second sentence. **Effective** for stock issued after 8-10-93.

INCOME TAX—NONRESIDENT ALIENS

• **1992, Unemployment Compensation Amendments of 1992 (P.L. 102-318)**

P.L. 102-318, §521(b)(28):

Amended Code Sec. 871(a)(1)(B) by striking "402(a)(2), 403(a)(2), or" following "described in section". **Effective** for distributions after 12-31-92.

• **1986, Tax Reform Act of 1986 (P.L. 99-514)**

P.L. 99-514, §301(b)(9):

Amended Code Sec. 871(a)(2) by striking out "such gains and losses shall be determined without regard to section 1202 (relating to deduction for capital gains) and". **Effective** for tax years beginning after 12-31-86. Prior to amendment, Code Sec. 871(a)(2) read as follows:

(2) CAPITAL GAINS OF ALIENS PRESENT IN THE UNITED STATES 183 DAYS OR MORE.—In the case of a nonresident alien individual present in the United States for a period or periods aggregating 183 days or more during the taxable year, there is hereby imposed for such year a tax of 30 percent of the amount by which his gains, derived from sources within the United States, from the sale or exchange at any time during such year of capital assets exceed his losses, allocable to sources within the United States, from the sale or exchange at any time during such year of capital assets. For purposes of this paragraph, gains and losses shall be taken into account only if, and to the extent that, they would be recognized and taken into account if such gains and losses were effectively connected with the conduct of a trade or business within the United States, except that such gains and losses shall be determined without regard to section 1202 (relating to deduction for capital gains) and such losses shall be determined without the benefits of the capital loss carryover provided in section 1212. Any gain or loss which is taken into account in determining the tax under paragraph (1) or subsection (b) shall not be taken into account in determining the tax under this paragraph. For purposes of the 183-day requirement of this paragraph, a nonresident alien individual not engaged in trade or business within the United States who has not established a taxable year for any prior period shall be treated as having a taxable year which is the calendar year.

P.L. 99-514, §1211(b)(4):

Amended Code Sec. 871(a)(1)(D) by striking out "or from payments which are treated as being so contingent under subsection (e),". **Effective** for tax years beginning after 12-31-86. However, for a special rule, see Act Sec. 1211(c)(2) following Code Sec. 871(e). Prior to amendment, Code Sec. 871(a)(1)(D) read as follows:

(D) gains from the sale or exchange after October 4, 1966, of patents, copyrights, secret processes and formulas, good will, trademarks, trade brands, franchises, and other like property, or of any interest in any such property, to the extent such gains are from payments which are contingent on the productivity, use, or disposition of the property or interest sold or exchanged, or from payments which are treated as being so contingent under subsection (e).

P.L. 99-514, §1810(d)(3)(A):

Amended Code Sec. 871(a)(1) by striking out "provided in subsection (i)" in the matter preceding subparagraph (A), and inserting in lieu thereof "provided in subsection (h)". **Effective** as if included in the provision of P.L. 98-369 to which it relates.

P.L. 99-514, §1810(e)(2)(A):

Amended Code Sec. 871(a)(1)(C). **Effective** as if included in the provision of P.L. 98-369 to which it relates. Prior to amendment, Code Sec. 871(a)(1)(C) read as follows:

(C) in the case of—

(i) a sale or exchange of an original issue discount obligation, the amount of any gain not in excess of the original issue discount accruing while such obligation was held by the nonresident alien individual (to the extent such discount was not theretofore taken into account under clause (ii)), and

(ii) the payment of interest on an original issue discount obligation, an amount equal to the original issue discount accrued on such obligation since the last payment of interest thereon (except that such original issue discount shall be taken into account under this clause only to the extent that the tax thereon does not exceed the interest payment less the tax imposed by subparagraph (A) thereon), and

• **1986, Consolidated Omnibus Budget Reconciliation Act of 1985 (P.L. 99-272)**

P.L. 99-272, §12103(b):

Amended Code Sec. 871(a)(3) by adding the new sentence at the end thereof (after and below subparagraph (B)). **Effective** for benefits received after 12-31-83, in tax years ending after such date.

• **1984, Deficit Reduction Act of 1984 (P.L. 98-369)**

P.L. 98-369, §42(a)(9):

Amended Code Sec. 871(a)(1)(A) by striking out "section 1232(b)" and inserting in lieu thereof "section 1273". **Effective** for tax years ending after 7-18-84.

P.L. 98-369, §127(a)(2):

Amended Code Sec. 871(a)(1) by striking out "There" and inserting in lieu thereof "Except as provided in subsection (i), there". **Effective** for interest received after 7-18-84, with respect to obligations issued after such date in tax years ending after such date.

P.L. 98-369, §128(a)(1):

Amended Code Sec. 871(a)(1)(C). **Effective** for payments made on or after 9-16-84, with respect to obligations issued after 3-31-72. Prior to amendment, it read as follows:

(C) in the case of—

(i) bonds or other evidences of indebtedness issued after September 28, 1965, and before April 1, 1972, amounts which under section 1232(a)(2)(B) are considered as ordinary income, and, in the case of corporate obligations issued after May 27, 1969, and before April 1, 1972, amounts which would be so considered but for the fact the obligations were issued after May 27, 1969.

(ii) bonds or other evidences of indebtedness issued after March 31, 1972, and payable more than 6 months from the date of original issue (without regard to the period held by the taxpayer), amounts which under section 1232(a)(2)(B) would be considered as ordinary income but for the fact such obligations were issued after May 27, 1969, and

(iii) the payment of interest on an obligation described in clause (ii), an amount equal to the original issue discount (but not in excess of such interest less the tax imposed by subparagraph (A) thereon) accrued on such obligation since the last payment of interest thereon, and

• **1983, Social Security Amendments of 1983 (P.L. 98-21)**

P.L. 98-21, §121(c)(1):

Added Code Sec. 871(a)(3). **Effective**, generally, for benefits received after 1983 in tax years ending after 1983.

P.L. 98-21, §335(b)(2)(B):

Amended Code Sec. 871(a)(3)(A) (as added by Act Sec. 121(c)(1)) by inserting "(notwithstanding section 207 of the Social Security Act)" after "income". **Effective** 4-20-83, with respect to benefits received after 1983 in tax years ending after 1983.

• **1976, Tax Reform Act of 1976 (P.L. 94-455)**

P.L. 94-455, §1901(b)(3)(I):

Substituted "ordinary income" for "gain from the sale or exchange of property which is not a capital asset" in clauses (1)(C)(i) and (ii). **Effective** for tax years beginning after 12-31-76.

• **1971, Revenue Act of 1971 (P.L. 92-178)**

P.L. 92-178, §313(a):

Added "(other than original issue discount as defined in section 1232(b))" after "interest" in Code Sec. 871(a)(1)(A). **Effective** for tax years beginning after 12-31-66.

P.L. 92-178, §313(b):

Amended Code Sec. 871(a)(1)(C). **Effective** for tax years ending after 12-31-66. Prior to amendment, Code Sec. 871(a)(1)(C) read as follows:

(C) in the case of bonds or other evidences of indebtedness issued after September 28, 1965, amounts which under section 1232 are considered as gains from the sale or exchange of property which is not a capital asset, and.

• **1966, Foreign Investors Tax Act of 1966 (P.L. 89-809)**

P.L. 89-809, §103(a)(1):

Amended Code Sec. 871(a). Prior to amendment, Code Sec. 871(a) read as follows:

(a) No United States Business—30 Percent Tax.—

(1) Imposition of tax.—Except as otherwise provided in subsection (b) there is hereby imposed for each taxable year, in lieu of the tax imposed by section 1, on the amount received, by every nonresident alien individual not engaged in trade or business within the United States, from sources within the United States, as interest (except interest on deposits with persons carrying on the banking business), dividends, rents, salaries, wages, premiums, annuities, compensations, remunerations, emoluments, or other fixed or determinable annual or periodical gains, profits, and income (including amounts described in section 402(a)(2), section 403(a)(2), section 631(b) and (c), and section 1235, which are considered to be gains from the sale or exchange of capital assets), a tax of 30 percent of such amount.

(2) Capital gains of aliens temporarily present in the United States.—In the case of a nonresident alien individual not engaged in trade or business in the United States, there is hereby imposed for each taxable year, in addition to the tax imposed by paragraph (1)—

(A) if he is present in the United States for a period or periods aggregating less than 90 days during such taxable year—a tax of 30 percent of the amount by which his gains, derived from sources within the United States, from sales or exchanges of capital assets effected during his presence in the United States exceed his losses, allocable to sources within the United States, from such sales or exchanges effected during such presence; or

(B) if he is present in the United States for a period or periods aggregating 90 days or more during such taxable year—a tax of 30 percent of the amount by which his gains, derived from sources within the United States, from sales or exchanges of capital assets effected at any time during such year exceed his losses, allocable to sources within the United States, from such sales or exchanges effected at any time during such year.

For purposes of this paragraph, gains and losses shall be taken into account only if, and to the extent that, they would be recognized and taken into account if such individual were engaged in trade or business in the United States, except that such gains and losses shall be computed without regard to section 1202 (relating to deduction for capital gains) and such losses shall be determined without the benefits of the capital loss carryover provided in section 1212.

• **1964, Revenue Act of 1964 (P.L. 88-272)**

P.L. 88-272, §113(b):

Amended heading of subsection (a). **Effective** for tax years beginning after 12-31-63. Prior to amendment the heading read as follows:

(a) No United States Business and Gross Income of Not More than $15,400.

• **1958, Technical Amendments Act of 1958 (P.L. 85-866)**

P.L. 85-866, §40(a):

Amended Code Sec. 871(a)(1) by adding the phrase "section 403(a)(2)," after the phrase "section 402(a)(2),". **Effective** for tax years ending after 9-2-58.

INCOME TAX—NONRESIDENT ALIENS

[Sec. 871(b)]

(b) INCOME CONNECTED WITH UNITED STATES BUSINESS—GRADUATED RATE OF TAX.—

(1) IMPOSITION OF TAX.—A nonresident alien individual engaged in trade or business within the United States during the taxable year shall be taxable as provided in section 1 or 55 on his taxable income which is effectively connected with the conduct of a trade or business within the United States.

(2) DETERMINATION OF TAXABLE INCOME.—In determining taxable income for purposes of paragraph (1), gross income includes only gross income which is effectively connected with the conduct of a trade or business within the United States.

Amendments

• **1996, Small Business Job Protection Act of 1996 (P.L. 104-188)**

P.L. 104-188, §1401(b)(10):

Amended Code Sec. 871(b)(1) by striking "section 1, 55, or 402(d)(1)" and inserting "section 1 or 55". **Effective**, generally, for tax years beginning after 12-31-99. For a special transitional rule, see Act Sec. 1401(c)(2) in the amendment notes following Code Sec. 402(d).

• **1992, Unemployment Compensation Amendments of 1992 (P.L. 102-318)**

P.L. 102-318, §521(b)(29):

Amended Code Sec. 871(b)(1) by striking "402(e)(1)" and inserting "402(d)(1)". **Effective** for distributions after 12-31-92.

• **1980, Technical Corrections Act of 1979 (P.L. 96-222)**

P.L. 96-222, §104(a)(4)(H)(v):

Amended Code Sec. 871(b)(1) by changing "section 55" to "55". **Effective** for tax years beginning after 12-31-78.

• **1978, Revenue Act of 1978 (P.L. 95-600)**

P.L. 95-600, §401(b)(3):

Amended Code Sec. 871(b)(1) by striking out "section 1, 402(e)(1), or 1201(b)" and inserting in lieu thereof "section 1 or 402(e)(1)". **Effective** for tax years beginning after 12-31-78.

P.L. 95-600, §421(e)(4):

Amended Code Sec. 871(b)(1) by inserting ", section 55" after "section 1". **Effective** for tax years beginning after 12-31-78.

• **1974, Employee Retirement Income Security Act of 1974 (P.L. 93-406)**

P.L. 93-406, §2005(c)(8):

Amended Code Sec. 871(b)(1) by adding ", 402(e)(1)," after "section 1". **Effective** for distributions and payments made after 12-31-73, in tax years beginning after such date.

• **1966, Foreign Investors Tax Act of 1966 (P.L. 89-809)**

P.L. 89-809, §103(a)(1):

Amended and consolidated Code Sec. 871(b) and (c). Prior to amendment, Code Sec. 871(b) and (c) read as follows:

(b) NO UNITED STATES BUSINESS—REGULAR TAX.—A nonresident alien individual not engaged in trade or business within the United States shall be taxable without regard to subsection (a) if during the taxable year the sum of the aggregate amount received from the sources specified in subsection (a)(1), plus the amount by which gains from sales or exchanges of capital assets exceed losses from such sales or exchanges (determined in accordance with subsection (a)(2)) is more than $19,000 in the case of a taxable year beginning in 1964 or more than $21,200 in the case of a taxable year beginning after 1964, except that—

(1) the gross income shall include only income from the sources specified in subsection (a)(1) plus any gain (to the extent provided in subchapter P; sec. 1201 and following, relating to capital gains and losses) from a sale or exchange of a capital asset if such gain would be taken into account were the tax being determined under subsection (a)(2);

(2) the deductions (other than the deduction for charitable contributions and gifts provided in section 873(c)) shall be allowed only if and to the extent that they are properly allocable to the gross income from the sources specified in subsection (a), except that any loss from the sale or exchange of a capital asset shall be allowed (to the extent provided in subchapter P without the benefit of the capital loss carryover provided in section 1212) if such loss would be taken into account were the tax being determined under subsection (a)(2).

If (without regard to this sentence) the amount of the taxes imposed in the case of such an individual under section 1 or under section 1201(b), minus the credit under section 35, is an amount which is less than 30 percent of the sum of—

(A) the aggregate amount received from the sources specified in subsection (a)(1), plus

(B) the amount, determined under subsection (a)(2), by which gains from sales or exchanges of capital assets exceed losses from such sales or exchanges,

then this subsection shall not apply and subsection (a) shall apply. For purposes of this subsection, the term "aggregate amount received from the sources specified in subsection (a)(1)" shall be applied without any exclusion under section 116.

(c) UNITED STATES BUSINESS.—A nonresident alien individual engaged in trade or business within the United States shall be taxable without regard to subsection (a). For purposes of part I, this section, sections 881 and 882, and chapter 3, the term "engaged in trade or business within the United States" includes the performance of personal services within the United States at any time within the taxable year, but does not include the performance of personal services—

(1) for a nonresident alien individual, foreign partnership, or foreign corporation, not engaged in trade or business within the United States, or

(2) for an office or place of business maintained by a domestic corporation in a foreign country or in a possession of the United States,

by a nonresident alien individual temporarily present in the United States for a period or periods not exceeding a total of 90 days during the taxable year and whose compensation for such services does not exceed in the aggregate $3,000. Such term does not include the effecting, through a resident broker, commission agent, or custodian, of transactions in the United States in stocks or securities, or in commodities (if of a kind customarily dealt in on an organized commodity exchange, if the transaction is of the kind customarily consummated at such place, and if the alien, partnership, or corporation has no office or place of business in the United States at any time during the taxable year through which or by the direction of which such transactions in commodities are effected).

• **1964, Revenue Act of 1964 (P.L. 88-272)**

P.L. 88-272, §113(b)(1):

Amended that portion of subsection (b) which precedes paragraph (1). **Effective** for tax years beginning after 12-31-63. Prior to amendment, the first portion of subsection (b) read:

(b) NO UNITED STATES BUSINESS AND GROSS INCOME OF MORE THAN $15,400.—A nonresident alien individual not engaged in trade or business within the United States shall be taxable without regard to subsection (a) if during the taxable year the sum of the aggregate amount received from the sources specified in subsection (a)(1), plus the amount by which gains from sales or exchanges of capital assets exceed losses from such sales or exchanges (determined in accordance with subsection (a)(2)) is more than $15,400, except that—

• **1964, Revenue Act of 1964 (P.L. 88-272)**

P.L. 88-272, §201(d)(12):

Amended Code Sec. 871(b) by inserting "the credit under section 35" in lieu of "the sum of the credits under sections 34 and 35". **Effective** with respect to dividends received after 12-31-64, in tax years ending after such date.

• **1958, Technical Amendments Act of 1958 (P.L. 85-866)**

P.L. 85-866, §41(a)(1):

Inserted a period in lieu of the semicolon at the end of Code Sec. 871(b)(2). **Effective** for tax years ending after 12-31-57.

P.L. 85-866, §41(a)(2):

Struck out paragraph (3) of Code Sec. 871(b). **Effective** for tax years ending after 12-31-57. Prior to amendment, paragraph (3) read as follows:

(3) the taxes imposed by this subtitle (under section 1, or under section 1201(b)) shall, in no case, be less than 30 percent of the sum of—

(A) the aggregate amount received from the sources specified in subsection (a)(1), plus

(B) the amount, determined under subsection (a)(2), by which gains from sales or exchanges of capital assets exceed losses from such sales or exchanges.

P.L. 85-866, §41(a)(3):

Added the last sentence in Code Sec. 871(b). **Effective** for tax years ending after 12-31-57.

[Sec. 871(c)]

(c) PARTICIPANTS IN CERTAIN EXCHANGE OR TRAINING PROGRAMS.—For purposes of this section, a nonresident alien individual who (without regard to this subsection) is not engaged in trade or business within the United States and who is temporarily present in the United States as a nonimmigrant under subparagraph (F), (J), (M), or (Q) of section 101(a)(15) of the Immigration and Nationality Act, as amended (8 U.S.C. 1101(a)(15)(F), (J), (M), or (Q)), shall be treated as a nonresident alien individual engaged in trade or business within the United States, and any income described in the second sentence of section 1441(b) which is received by such individual shall, to the extent derived from sources within the United States, be treated as effectively connected with the conduct of a trade or business within the United States.

Amendments

• **1994, Social Security Independence and Program Improvements Act of 1994 (P.L. 103-296)**

P.L. 103-296, §320(a)(1)(A):

Amended Code Sec. 871(c) by striking "(J), or (M)" each place it appears and inserting "(J), (M), or (Q)". **Effective** with the calendar quarter following 8-15-94.

• **1988, Technical and Miscellaneous Revenue Act of 1988 (P.L. 100-647)**

P.L. 100-647, §1001(d)(2)(B)(i)-(ii):

Amended Code Sec. 871(c) by striking out "section 1441(b)(1) or (2)" and inserting in lieu thereof "the second sentence of section 1441(b)"; and by striking out "(F) or (J)" each place it appears and inserting in lieu thereof "(F), (J), or (M)". **Effective** as if included in the provision of P.L. 99-514 to which it relates.

INCOME TAX—NONRESIDENT ALIENS

• **1966, Foreign Investors Tax Act of 1966 (P.L. 89-809)**

P.L. 89-809, §103(a)(1):

Redesignated former Code Sec. 871(c) as consolidated Code Sec. 871(b), redesignated former Code Sec. 871(d) as Code Sec. 871(c) and amended new Code Sec. 871(c). Prior to amendment, former Code Sec. 871(d) read as follows:

(d) PARTICIPANTS IN CERTAIN EXCHANGE OR TRAINING PROGRAMS.—For purposes of this section, a nonresident alien individual who (without regard to this subsection) is not engaged in trade or business within the United States and who is temporarily present in the United States as a nonimmigrant under subparagraph (F) or (J) of section 101(a)(15) of the Immigration and Nationality Act, as amended, shall be treated as a nonresident alien individual engaged in trade or business within the United States.

[Sec. 871(d)]

(d) ELECTION TO TREAT REAL PROPERTY INCOME AS INCOME CONNECTED WITH UNITED STATES BUSINESS.—

(1) IN GENERAL.—A nonresident alien individual who during the taxable year derives any income—

(A) from real property held for the production of income and located in the United States, or from any interest in such real property, including (i) gains from the sale or exchange of such real property or an interest therein, (ii) rents or royalties from mines, wells, or other natural deposits, and (iii) gains described in section 631(b) or (c), and

(B) which, but for this subsection, would not be treated as income which is effectively connected with the conduct of a trade or business within the United States,

may elect for such taxable year to treat all such income as income which is effectively connected with the conduct of a trade or business within the United States. In such case, such income shall be taxable as provided in subsection (b)(1) whether or not such individual is engaged in trade or business within the United States during the taxable year. An election under this paragraph for any taxable year shall remain in effect for all subsequent taxable years, except that it may be revoked with the consent of the Secretary with respect to any taxable year.

(2) ELECTION AFTER REVOCATION.—If an election has been made under paragraph (1) and such election has been revoked, a new election may not be made under such paragraph for any taxable year before the 5th taxable year which begins after the first taxable year for which such revocation is effective, unless the Secretary consents to such new election.

(3) FORM AND TIME OF ELECTION AND REVOCATION.—An election under paragraph (1), and any revocation of such an election, may be made only in such manner and at such time as the Secretary may by regulations prescribe.

Amendments

• **1976, Tax Reform Act of 1976 (P.L. 94-455)**

P.L. 94-455, §1906(b)(13)(A):

Amended 1954 Code by substituting "Secretary" for "Secretary or his delegate" each place it appeared. **Effective** 2-1-77.

• **1966, Foreign Investors Tax Act of 1966 (P.L. 89-809)**

P.L. 89-809, §103(a)(1):

Redesignated former Code Sec. 871(d) as Code Sec. 871(c) and added a new Code Sec. 871(d).

• **1961, Mutual Educational and Cultural Exchange Act of 1961 (P.L. 87-256)**

P.L. 87-256, §110(b):

Redesignated former Code Sec. 871(d) as Code Sec. 871(e), and added a new Code Sec. 871(d). **Effective** for tax years beginning after 1961.

• **1960 (P.L. 86-437)**

P.L. 86-437, §2(b):

Amended Code Sec. 871(d). **Effective** for tax years beginning after 12-31-59. Prior to amendment, Code Sec. 871(d) read as follows:

(d) DOUBLING OF TAX.—

For doubling of tax on citizens of certain foreign countries, see section 891.

[Sec. 871(e)—Repealed]

Amendments

• **1986, Tax Reform Act of 1986 (P.L. 99-514)**

P.L. 99-514, §1211(b)(5):

Repealed Code Sec. 871(e). **Effective** for tax years beginning after 12-31-86. However, for a special rule, see Act Sec. 1211(c)(2), below. Prior to repeal, Code Sec. 871(e) read as follows:

(e) GAINS FROM SALE OR EXCHANGE OF CERTAIN INTANGIBLE PROPERTY.—For purposes of subsection (a)(1)(D), and for purposes of sections 881(a)(4), 1441(b), and 1442(a)—

(1) PAYMENTS TREATED AS CONTINGENT ON USE, ETC.—If more than 50 percent of the gain for any taxable year from the sale or exchange of any patent, copyright, secret process or formula, good will, trademark, trade brand, franchise, or other like property, or of any interest in any such property, is from payments which are contingent on the productivity, use, or disposition of such property or interest, all of the gain for the taxable year from the sale or exchange of such property or interest shall be treated as being from payments which are contingent on the productivity, use, or disposition of such property or interest.

(2) SOURCE RULE.—In determining whether gains described in subsection (a)(1)(D) and section 881(a)(4) are received from sources within the United States, such gains shall be treated as rentals or royalties for the use of, or privilege of using, property or an interest in property.

P.L. 99-514, §1211(c)(2), provides:

(2) SPECIAL RULE FOR FOREIGN PERSONS.—In the case of any foreign person other than any controlled foreign corporations (within the meaning of section 957(a) of the Internal Revenue Code of 1954), the amendments made by this section shall apply to transactions entered into after March 18, 1986.

• **1966, Foreign Investors Tax Act of 1966 (P.L. 89-809)**

P.L. 89-809, §103(a)(1):

Redesignated Code Sec. 871(e) as Code Sec. 871(g) and added a new Code Sec. 871(g).

• **1961, Mutual Educational and Cultural Exchange Act of 1961 (P.L. 87-256)**

P.L. 87-256, §110(b):

Redesignated former Code Sec. 871(d) as Code Sec. 871(e). **Effective** for tax years beginning after 1961.

[Sec. 871(f)]

(f) CERTAIN ANNUITIES RECEIVED UNDER QUALIFIED PLANS.—

(1) IN GENERAL.—For purposes of this section, gross income does not include any amount received as an annuity under a qualified annuity plan described in section 403(a)(1), or from a qualified trust described in section 401(a) which is exempt from tax under section 501(a), if—

(A) all of the personal services by reason of which the annuity is payable were either—

(i) personal services performed outside the United States by an individual who, at the time of performance of such personal services, was a nonresident alien, or

(ii) personal services described in section 864(b)(1) performed within the United States by such individual, and

(B) at the time the first amount is paid as an annuity under the annuity plan or by the trust, 90 percent or more of the employees for whom contributions or benefits are provided under such annuity plan, or under the plan or plans of which the trust is a part, are citizens or residents of the United States.

(2) EXCLUSION.—Income received during the taxable year which would be excluded from gross income under this subsection but for the requirement of paragraph (1)(B) shall not be included in gross income if—

(A) the recipient's country of residence grants a substantially equivalent exclusion to residents and citizens of the United States; or

(B) the recipient's country of residence is a beneficiary developing country under title V of the Trade Act of 1974 (19 U.S.C. 2461 et seq.).

Amendments

• **2000, Community Renewal Tax Relief Act of 2000 (P.L. 106-554)**

P.L. 106-554, §319(11):

Amended Code Sec. 871(f)(2)(B) by striking "19 U.S.C." and inserting "(19 U.S.C.". **Effective** 12-21-2000.

• **1998, IRS Restructuring and Reform Act of 1998 (P.L. 105-206)**

P.L. 105-206, §6023(10):

Amended Code Sec. 871(f)(2)(B) by striking "(19 U.S.C. 2462)" and inserting "19 U.S.C. 2461 et seq.)". **Effective** 7-22-98.

INCOME TAX—NONRESIDENT ALIENS

• **1996, Small Business Job Protection Act of 1996 (P.L. 104-188)**

P.L. 104-188, § 1954(b)(1):

Amended Code Sec. 871(f)(2)(B) by striking "within the meaning of section 502" and inserting "under title V". **Effective** 8-20-96.

• **1980, Miscellaneous Revenue Act of 1980 (P.L. 96-605)**

P.L. 96-605, § 227(a):

Amended Code Sec. 871(f). **Effective** with respect to amounts received after 7-1-79. Prior to amendment, Code Sec. 871(f) read as follows:

(f) CERTAIN ANNUITIES RECEIVED UNDER QUALIFIED PLANS.—For purposes of this section, gross income does not include any amount received as an annuity under a qualified annuity plan described in section 403(a)(1), or from a qualified trust described in section 401(a) which is exempt from tax under section 501(a), if—

(1) all of the personal services by reason of which such annuity is payable were either (A) personal services performed outside the United States by an individual who, at the time of performance of such personal services, was a nonresident alien, or (B) personal services described in section 864(b)(1) performed within the United States by such individual, and

(2) at the time the first amount is paid as such annuity under such annuity plan, or by such trust, 90 percent or more of the employees for whom contributions or benefits are provided under such annuity plan, or under the plan or plans of which such trust is a part, are citizens or residents of the United States.

• **1966, Foreign Investors Tax Act of 1966 (P.L. 89-809)**

P.L. 89-809:

Added Code Sec. 871(f).

[Sec. 871(g)]

(g) SPECIAL RULES FOR ORIGINAL ISSUE DISCOUNT.—For purposes of this section and section 881—

(1) ORIGINAL ISSUE DISCOUNT OBLIGATION.—

(A) IN GENERAL.—Except as provided in subparagraph (B), the term "original issue discount obligation" means any bond or other evidence of indebtedness having original issue discount (within the meaning of section 1273).

(B) EXCEPTIONS.—The term "original issue discount obligation" shall not include—

(i) CERTAIN SHORT-TERM OBLIGATIONS.— Any obligation payable 183 days or less from the date of original issue (without regard to the period held by the taxpayer).

(ii) TAX-EXEMPT OBLIGATIONS.—Any obligation the interest on which is exempt from tax under section 103 or under any other provision of law without regard to the identity of the holder.

(2) DETERMINATION OF PORTION OF ORIGINAL ISSUE DISCOUNT ACCRUING DURING ANY PERIOD.—The determination of the amount of the original issue discount which accrues during any period shall be made under the rules of section 1272 (or the corresponding provisions of prior law) without regard to any exception for short-term obligations.

(3) SOURCE OF ORIGINAL ISSUE DISCOUNT.—Except to the extent provided in regulations prescribed by the Secretary, the determination of whether any amount described in subsection (a)(1)(C) is from sources within the United States shall be made at the time of the payment (or sale or exchange) as if such payment (or sale or exchange) involved the payment of interest.

(4) STRIPPED BONDS.—The provisions of section 1286 (relating to the treatment of stripped bonds and stripped coupons as obligations with original issue discount) shall apply for purposes of this section.

Amendments

• **1984, Deficit Reduction Act of 1984 (P.L. 98-369)**

P.L. 98-369, § 128(a)(2):

Amended Code Sec. 871 by redesignating subsection (g) as subsection (h) and by inserting after subsection (f) new subsection (g). **Effective** for payments made on or after 9-16-84, with respect to obligations issued after 3-31-72.

[Sec. 871(h)]

(h) REPEAL OF TAX ON INTEREST OF NONRESIDENT ALIEN INDIVIDUALS RECEIVED FROM CERTAIN PORTFOLIO DEBT INVESTMENTS.—

(1) IN GENERAL.—In the case of any portfolio interest received by a nonresident individual from sources within the United States, no tax shall be imposed under paragraph (1)(A) or (1)(C) of subsection (a).

(2) PORTFOLIO INTEREST.—For purposes of this subsection, the term "portfolio interest" means any interest (including original issue discount) which—

(A) would be subject to tax under subsection (a) but for this subsection, and

(B) is paid on an obligation—

(i) which is in registered form, and

(ii) with respect to which—

(I) the United States person who would otherwise be required to deduct and withhold tax from such interest under section 1441(a) receives a statement (which meets the requirements of paragraph (5)) that the beneficial owner of the obligation is not a United States person, or

(II) the Secretary has determined that such a statement is not required in order to carry out the purposes of this subsection.

(3) PORTFOLIO INTEREST NOT TO INCLUDE INTEREST RECEIVED BY 10-PERCENT SHAREHOLDERS.—For purposes of this subsection—

(A) IN GENERAL.—The term "portfolio interest" shall not include any interest described in paragraph (2) which is received by a 10-percent shareholder.

(B) 10-PERCENT SHAREHOLDER.—The term "10-percent shareholder" means—

(i) in the case of an obligation issued by a corporation, any person who owns 10 percent or more of the total combined voting power of all classes of stock of such corporation entitled to vote, or

(ii) in the case of an obligation issued by a partnership, any person who owns 10 percent or more of the capital or profits interest in such partnership.

(C) ATTRIBUTION RULES.—For purposes of determining ownership of stock under subparagraph (B)(i) the rules of section 318(a) shall apply, except that—

(i) section 318(a)(2)(C) shall be applied without regard to the 50-percent limitation therein,

(ii) section 318(a)(3)(C) shall be applied—

(I) without regard to the 50-percent limitation therein; and

(II) in any case where such section would not apply but for subclause (I), by considering a corporation as owning the stock (other than stock in such corporation) which is owned by or for any shareholder of such corporation in that proportion which the value of the stock which such shareholder owns in such corporation bears to the value of all stock in such corporation, and

(iii) any stock which a person is treated as owning after application of section 318(a)(4) shall not, for purposes of applying paragraphs (2) and (3) of section 318(a), be treated as actually owned by such person.

Under regulations prescribed by the Secretary, rules similar to the rules of the preceding sentence shall be applied in determining the ownership of the capital or profits interest in a partnership for purposes of subparagraph (B)(ii).

(4) PORTFOLIO INTEREST NOT TO INCLUDE CERTAIN CONTINGENT INTEREST.—For purposes of this subsection—

INCOME TAX—NONRESIDENT ALIENS

(A) IN GENERAL.—Except as otherwise provided in this paragraph, the term "portfolio interest" shall not include—

(i) any interest if the amount of such interest is determined by reference to—

(I) any receipts, sales or other cash flow of the debtor or a related person,

(II) any income or profits of the debtor or a related person,

(III) any change in value of any property of the debtor or a related person, or

(IV) any dividend, partnership distributions, or similar payments made by the debtor or a related person, or

(ii) any other type of contingent interest that is identified by the Secretary by regulation, where a denial of the portfolio interest exemption is necessary or appropriate to prevent avoidance of Federal income tax.

(B) RELATED PERSON.—The term "related person" means any person who is related to the debtor within the meaning of section 267(b) or 707(b)(1), or who is a party to any arrangement undertaken for a purpose of avoiding the application of this paragraph.

(C) EXCEPTIONS.—Subparagraph (A)(i) shall not apply to—

(i) any amount of interest solely by reason of the fact that the timing of any interest or principal payment is subject to a contingency,

(ii) any amount of interest solely by reason of the fact that the interest is paid with respect to nonrecourse or limited recourse indebtedness,

(iii) any amount of interest all or substantially all of which is determined by reference to any other amount of interest not described in subparagraph (A) (or by reference to the principal amount of indebtedness on which such other interest is paid),

(iv) any amount of interest solely by reason of the fact that the debtor or a related person enters into a hedging transaction to manage the risk of interest rate or currency fluctuations with respect to such interest,

(v) any amount of interest determined by reference to—

(I) changes in the value of property (including stock) that is actively traded (within the meaning of section 1092(d)) other than property described in section 897(c)(1) or (g),

(II) the yield on property described in subclause (I), other than a debt instrument that pays interest described in subparagraph (A), or stock or other property that represents a beneficial interest in the debtor or a related person, or

(III) changes in any index of the value of property described in subclause (I) or of the yield on property described in subclause (II), and

(vi) any other type of interest identified by the Secretary by regulation.

(D) EXCEPTION FOR CERTAIN EXISTING INDEBTEDNESS.—Subparagraph (A) shall not apply to any interest paid or accrued with respect to any indebtedness with a fixed term—

(i) which was issued on or before April 7, 1993, or

(ii) which was issued after such date pursuant to a written binding contract in effect on such date and at all times thereafter before such indebtedness was issued.

(5) CERTAIN STATEMENTS.—A statement with respect to any obligation meets the requirements of this paragraph if such statement is made by—

(A) the beneficial owner of such obligation, or

(B) a securities clearing organization, a bank, or other financial institution that holds customers' securities in the ordinary course of its trade or business.

The preceding sentence shall not apply to any statement with respect to payment of interest on any obligation by any person if, at least one month before such payment, the Secretary has published a determination that any statement from such person (or any class including such person) does not meet the requirements of this paragraph.

(6) SECRETARY MAY PROVIDE SUBSECTION NOT TO APPLY IN CASES OF INADEQUATE INFORMATION EXCHANGE.—

(A) IN GENERAL.—If the Secretary determines that the exchange of information between the United States and a foreign country is inadequate to prevent evasion of the United States income tax by United States persons, the Secretary may provide in writing (and publish a statement) that the provisions of this subsection shall not apply to payments of interest to any person within such foreign country (or payments addressed to, or for the account of, persons within such foreign country) during the period—

(i) beginning on the date specified by the Secretary, and

(ii) ending on the date that the Secretary determines that the exchange of information between the United States and the foreign country is adequate to prevent the evasion of United States income tax by United States persons.

(B) EXCEPTION FOR CERTAIN OBLIGATIONS.—Subparagraph (A) shall not apply to the payment of interest on any obligation which is issued on or before the date of the publication of the Secretary's determination under such subparagraph.

(7) REGISTERED FORM.—For purposes of this subsection, the term "registered form" has the same meaning given such term by section 163(f).

Amendments

- **2010, Hiring Incentives to Restore Employment Act (P.L. 111-147)**

P.L. 111-147, § 502(b)(1):

Amended Code Sec. 871(h)(2). **Effective** for obligations issued after the date which is 2 years after 3-18-2010. Prior to amendment, Code Sec. 871(h)(2) read as follows:

(2) PORTFOLIO INTEREST.—For purposes of this subsection, the term "portfolio interest" means any interest (including original issue discount) which would be subject to tax under subsection (a) but for this subsection and which is described in any of the following subparagraphs:

(A) CERTAIN OBLIGATIONS WHICH ARE NOT REGISTERED.—Interest which is paid on any obligation which—

(i) is not in registered form, and

(ii) is described in section 163(f)(2)(B).

(B) CERTAIN REGISTERED OBLIGATIONS.—Interest which is paid on an obligation—

(i) which is in registered form, and

(ii) with respect to which the United States person who would otherwise be required to deduct and withhold tax from such interest under section 1441(a) receives a statement (which meets the requirements of paragraph (5)) that the beneficial owner of the obligation is not a United States person.

P.L. 111-147, § 502(b)(2)(A):

Amended Code Sec. 871(h)(3)(A) by striking "subparagraph (A) or (B) of" following "any interest described in". **Effective** for obligations issued after the date which is 2 years after 3-18-2010.

- **1999, Tax Relief Extension Act of 1999 (P.L. 106-170)**

P.L. 106-170, § 532(b)(2):

Amended Code Sec. 871(h)(4)(C)(iv) by striking "to reduce" and inserting "to manage". **Effective** for any instrument held, acquired, or entered into, any transaction entered into, and supplies held or acquired on or after 12-17-99.

- **1993, Omnibus Budget Reconciliation Act of 1993 (P.L. 103-66)**

P.L. 103-66, § 13237(a)(1):

Amended Code Sec. 871(h) by redesignating paragraphs (4), (5), and (6) as paragraphs (5), (6), and (7), respectively, and by inserting after paragraph (3) new paragraph (4). **Effective** for interest received after 12-31-93.

P.L. 103-66, § 13237(c)(1):

Amended Code Sec. 871(h)(2)(B)(ii) by striking "paragraph (4)" and inserting "paragraph (5)". **Effective** for interest received after 12-31-93.

- **1986, Tax Reform Act of 1986 (P.L. 99-514)**

P.L. 99-514, § 1810(d)(1)(A):

Amended Code Sec. 871(h)(2) by striking out "which is described in" in the matter preceding subparagraph (A) and inserting in lieu thereof "which would be subject to tax under subsection (a) but for this subsection and which is described in". **Effective** as if included in the provision of P.L. 98-369 to which it relates.

INCOME TAX—NONRESIDENT ALIENS

P.L. 99-514, § 1810(d)(2):

Amended Code Sec. 871(h)(3)(C)(i)-(iii) by striking out "and" at the end of clause (i), by redesignating clause (ii) as clause (iii), and by inserting after clause (i) new clause (ii). **Effective** as if included in the provision of P.L. 98-369 to which it relates.

P.L. 99-514, § 1810(d)(3)(B):

Amended Code Sec. 871(h)(2)(B)(ii) by striking out "has received" and inserting in lieu thereof "receives". **Effective**, generally, for tax years beginning after 12-31-86. However, for special and transitional rules, see Act Sec. 1214(d)(2)-(4) following Code Sec. 861.

- **1984, Deficit Reduction Act of 1984 (P.L. 98-369)**

P.L. 98-369, § 127(a)(1):

Amended Code Sec. 871, as amended by this Act, by redesignating subsection (h) as subsection (i) and by adding at the end thereof new subsection (h). **Effective** for interest received after 7-18-84, (with respect to obligations issued after 7-18-84) in tax years ending after such date. See also the notes for P.L. 98-369 following Code Sec. 881(a) for a special rule.

[Sec. 871(i)]

(i) TAX NOT TO APPLY TO CERTAIN INTEREST AND DIVIDENDS.—

(1) IN GENERAL.—No tax shall be imposed under paragraph (1)(A) or (1)(C) of subsection (a) on any amount described in paragraph (2).

(2) AMOUNTS TO WHICH PARAGRAPH (1) APPLIES.—The amounts described in this paragraph are as follows:

(A) Interest on deposits, if such interest is not effectively connected with the conduct of a trade or business within the United States.

(B) The active foreign business percentage of—

(i) any dividend paid by an existing 80/20 company, and

(ii) any interest paid by an existing 80/20 company.

(C) Income derived by a foreign central bank of issue from bankers' acceptances.

(D) Dividends paid by a foreign corporation which are treated under section 861(a)(2)(B) as income from sources within the United States.

(3) DEPOSITS.—For purposes of paragraph (2), the term "deposit" means amounts which are—

(A) deposits with persons carrying on the banking business,

(B) deposits or withdrawable accounts with savings institutions chartered and supervised as savings and loan or similar associations under Federal or State law, but only to the extent that amounts paid or credited on such deposits or accounts are deductible under section 591 (determined without regard to sections 265 and 291) in computing the taxable income of such institutions, and

(C) amounts held by an insurance company under an agreement to pay interest thereon.

Amendments

- **2010, (P.L. 111-226)**

P.L. 111-226, § 217(b)(1):

Amended Code Sec. 871(i)(2)(B). **Effective** generally for tax years beginning after 12-31-2010. For a grandfather rule, see Act Sec. 217(d)(2), below. Prior to amendment, Code Sec. 871(i)(2)(B) read as follows:

(B) A percentage of any dividend paid by a domestic corporation meeting the 80-percent foreign business requirements of section 861(c)(1) equal to the percentage determined for purposes of section 861(c)(2)(A).

P.L. 111-226, § 217(d)(2), provides:

(2) GRANDFATHER RULE FOR OUTSTANDING DEBT OBLIGATIONS.—

(A) IN GENERAL.—The amendments made by this section shall not apply to payments of interest on obligations issued before the date of the enactment of this Act.

(B) EXCEPTION FOR RELATED PARTY DEBT.—Subparagraph (A) shall not apply to any interest which is payable to a related person (determined under rules similar to the rules of section 954(d)(3)).

(C) SIGNIFICANT MODIFICATIONS TREATED AS NEW ISSUES.—For purposes of subparagraph (A), a significant modification of the terms of any obligation (including any extension of the term of such obligation) shall be treated as a new issue.

- **2004, American Jobs Creation Act of 2004 (P.L. 108-357)**

P.L. 108-357, § 409(a):

Amended Code Sec. 871(i)(2) by adding at the end a new subparagraph (D). **Effective** for payments made after 12-31-2004.

- **1986, Tax Reform Act of 1986 (P.L. 99-514)**

P.L. 99-514, § 1214(c)(1):

Amended Code Sec. 871 by redesignating subsection (i) as subsection (j) and by inserting after subsection (h) new subsection (i). **Effective**, generally, for tax years beginning after 12-31-86. For special and transitional rules, see Act Sec. 1214(d)(2)-(4) following Code Sec. 861.

[Sec. 871(j)]

(j) EXEMPTION FOR CERTAIN GAMBLING WINNINGS.—No tax shall be imposed under paragraph (1)(A) of subsection (a) on the proceeds from a wager placed in any of the following games: blackjack, baccarat, craps, roulette, or big-6 wheel. The preceding sentence shall not apply in any case where the Secretary determines by regulation that the collection of the tax is administratively feasible.

Amendments

- **1988, Technical and Miscellaneous Revenue Act of 1988 (P.L. 100-647)**

P.L. 100-647, § 6134(a)(1):

Amended Code Sec. 871 by redesignating subsection (j) as subsection (k) and by inserting after subsection (i) new subsection (j). **Effective** 11-10-88.

[Sec. 871(k)]

(k) EXEMPTION FOR CERTAIN DIVIDENDS OF REGULATED INVESTMENT COMPANIES.—

(1) INTEREST-RELATED DIVIDENDS.—

(A) IN GENERAL.—Except as provided in subparagraph (B), no tax shall be imposed under paragraph (1)(A) of subsection (a) on any interest-related dividend received from a regulated investment company which meets the requirements of section 852(a) for the taxable year with respect to which the dividend is paid.

(B) EXCEPTIONS.—Subparagraph (A) shall not apply—

(i) to any interest-related dividend received from a regulated investment company by a person to the extent such dividend is attributable to interest (other than interest described in subparagraph (E) (i) or (iii)) received by such company on indebtedness issued by such person or by any corporation or partnership with respect to which such person is a 10-percent shareholder,

(ii) to any interest-related dividend with respect to stock of a regulated investment company unless the person who would otherwise be required to deduct and withhold tax from such dividend under chapter 3 receives a statement (which meets requirements similar to the requirements of subsection (h)(5)) that the beneficial owner of such stock is not a United States person, and

(iii) to any interest-related dividend paid to any person within a foreign country (or any interest-related dividend payment addressed to, or for the account of, persons within such foreign country) during any period described in subsection (h)(6) with respect to such country.

Clause (iii) shall not apply to any dividend with respect to any stock which was acquired on or before the date of the publication of the Secretary's determination under subsection (h)(6).

(C) INTEREST-RELATED DIVIDEND.—For purposes of this paragraph—

(i) IN GENERAL.—Except as provided in clause (ii), an interest related dividend is any dividend, or part thereof, which is reported by the company as an interest related dividend in written statements furnished to its shareholders.

INCOME TAX—NONRESIDENT ALIENS

(ii) EXCESS REPORTED AMOUNTS.—If the aggregate reported amount with respect to the company for any taxable year exceeds the qualified net interest income of the company for such taxable year, an interest related dividend is the excess of—

(I) the reported interest related dividend amount, over

(II) the excess reported amount which is allocable to such reported interest related dividend amount.

(iii) ALLOCATION OF EXCESS REPORTED AMOUNT.—

(I) IN GENERAL.—Except as provided in subclause (II), the excess reported amount (if any) which is allocable to the reported interest related dividend amount is that portion of the excess reported amount which bears the same ratio to the excess reported amount as the reported interest related dividend amount bears to the aggregate reported amount.

(II) SPECIAL RULE FOR NONCALENDAR YEAR TAXPAYERS.—In the case of any taxable year which does not begin and end in the same calendar year, if the post-December reported amount equals or exceeds the excess reported amount for such taxable year, subclause (I) shall be applied by substituting "post-December reported amount" for "aggregate reported amount" and no excess reported amount shall be allocated to any dividend paid on or before December 31 of such taxable year.

(iv) DEFINITIONS.—For purposes of this subparagraph—

(I) REPORTED INTEREST RELATED DIVIDEND AMOUNT.—The term "reported interest related dividend amount" means the amount reported to its shareholders under clause (i) as an interest related dividend.

(II) EXCESS REPORTED AMOUNT.—The term "excess reported amount" means the excess of the aggregate reported amount over the qualified net interest income of the company for the taxable year.

(III) AGGREGATE REPORTED AMOUNT.—The term "aggregate reported amount" means the aggregate amount of dividends reported by the company under clause (i) as interest related dividends for the taxable year (including interest related dividends paid after the close of the taxable year described in section 855).

(IV) POST-DECEMBER REPORTED AMOUNT.—The term "post-December reported amount" means the aggregate reported amount determined by taking into account only dividends paid after December 31 of the taxable year.

(D) QUALIFIED NET INTEREST INCOME.—For purposes of subparagraph (C), the term "qualified net interest income" means the qualified interest income of the regulated investment company reduced by the deductions properly allocable to such income.

(E) QUALIFIED INTEREST INCOME.—For purposes of subparagraph (D), the term "qualified interest income" means the sum of the following amounts derived by the regulated investment company from sources within the United States:

(i) Any amount includible in gross income as original issue discount (within the meaning of section 1273) on an obligation payable 183 days or less from the date of original issue (without regard to the period held by the company).

(ii) Any interest includible in gross income (including amounts recognized as ordinary income in respect of original issue discount or market discount or acquisition discount under part V of subchapter P and such other amounts as regulations may provide) on an obligation which is in registered form; except that this clause shall not apply to—

(I) any interest on an obligation issued by a corporation or partnership if the regulated investment company is a 10-percent shareholder in such corporation or partnership, and

(II) any interest which is treated as not being portfolio interest under the rules of subsection (h)(4).

(iii) Any interest referred to in subsection (i)(2)(A) (without regard to the trade or business of the regulated investment company).

(iv) Any interest-related dividend includable in gross income with respect to stock of another regulated investment company.

(F) 10-PERCENT SHAREHOLDER.—For purposes of this paragraph, the term "10-percent shareholder" has the meaning given such term by subsection (h)(3)(B).

(2) SHORT-TERM CAPITAL GAIN DIVIDENDS.—

(A) IN GENERAL.—Except as provided in subparagraph (B), no tax shall be imposed under paragraph (1)(A) of subsection (a) on any short-term capital gain dividend received from a regulated investment company which meets the requirements of section 852(a) for the taxable year with respect to which the dividend is paid.

(B) EXCEPTION FOR ALIENS TAXABLE UNDER SUBSECTION (a)(2).—Subparagraph (A) shall not apply in the case of any nonresident alien individual subject to tax under subsection (a)(2).

(C) SHORT-TERM CAPITAL GAIN DIVIDEND.—For purposes of this paragraph—

(i) IN GENERAL.—Except as provided in clause (ii), the term "short-term capital gain dividend" means any dividend, or part thereof, which is reported by the company as a short-term capital gain dividend in written statements furnished to its shareholders.

(ii) EXCESS REPORTED AMOUNTS.—If the aggregate reported amount with respect to the company for any taxable year exceeds the qualified short-term gain of the company for such taxable year, the term "short-term capital gain dividend" means the excess of—

(I) the reported short-term capital gain dividend amount, over

(II) the excess reported amount which is allocable to such reported short-term capital gain dividend amount.

(iii) ALLOCATION OF EXCESS REPORTED AMOUNT.—(I) IN GENERAL.—Except as provided in subclause (II), the excess reported amount (if any) which is allocable to the reported short-term capital gain dividend amount is that portion of the excess reported amount which bears the same ratio to the excess reported amount as the reported short-term capital gain dividend amount bears to the aggregate reported amount.

(II) SPECIAL RULE FOR NONCALENDAR YEAR TAXPAYERS.—In the case of any taxable year which does not begin and end in the same calendar year, if the post-December reported amount equals or exceeds the excess reported amount for such taxable year, subclause (I) shall be applied by substituting "post-December reported amount" for "aggregate reported amount" and no excess reported amount shall be allocated to any dividend paid on or before December 31 of such taxable year.

(iv) DEFINITIONS.—For purposes of this subparagraph—

(I) REPORTED SHORT-TERM CAPITAL GAIN DIVIDEND AMOUNT.—The term "reported short-term capital gain dividend amount" means the amount reported to its shareholders under clause (i) as a short-term capital gain dividend.

(II) EXCESS REPORTED AMOUNT.—The term "excess reported amount" means the excess of the aggregate reported amount over the qualified short-term gain of the company for the taxable year.

(III) AGGREGATE REPORTED AMOUNT.—The term "aggregate reported amount" means the aggregate amount of dividends reported by the company under clause (i) as short-term capital gain dividends for the taxable year (including short-term capital gain dividends paid after the close of the taxable year described in section 855).

(IV) POST-DECEMBER REPORTED AMOUNT.—The term "post-December reported amount" means the aggregate reported amount determined by taking into account only dividends paid after December 31 of the taxable year.

INCOME TAX—NONRESIDENT ALIENS

(D) QUALIFIED SHORT-TERM GAIN.—For purposes of subparagraph (C), the term "qualified short-term gain" means the excess of the net short-term capital gain of the regulated investment company for the taxable year over the net long-term capital loss (if any) of such company for such taxable year. For purposes of this subparagraph, the net short-term capital gain of the regulated investment company shall be computed by treating any short-term capital gain dividend includible in gross income with respect to stock of another regulated investment company as a short-term capital gain.

(E) CERTAIN DISTRIBUTIONS.—In the case of a distribution to which section 897 does not apply by reason of the second sentence of section 897(h)(1), the amount which would be treated as a short-term capital gain dividend to the shareholder (without regard to this subparagraph)—

(i) shall not be treated as a short-term capital gain dividend, and

(ii) shall be included in such shareholder's gross income as a dividend from the regulated investment company.

Amendments

• **2015, Protecting Americans from Tax Hikes Act of 2015 (P.L. 114-113)**

P.L. 114-113, §125(a), Div. Q:

Amended Code Sec. 871(k) by striking clause (1)(C)(v) and (2)(C)(v). **Effective** for tax years beginning after 12-31-2014. Prior to being stricken, Code Sec. 871(k)(1)(C)(v) and (2)(C)(v) read as follows:

(v) TERMINATION.—The term "interest related dividend" shall not include any dividend with respect to any taxable year of the company beginning after December 31, 2014.

* * *

(v) TERMINATION.—The term "short-term capital gain dividend" shall not include any dividend with respect to any taxable year of the company beginning after December 31, 2014.

• **2014, Tax Increase Prevention Act of 2014 (P.L. 113-295)**

P.L. 113-295, §132(a), Division A:

Amended Code Sec. 871(k)(1)(C)(v) and (2)(C)(v) by striking "December 31, 2013" and inserting "December 31, 2014". **Effective** for tax years beginning after 12-31-2013.

• **2013, American Taxpayer Relief Act of 2012 (P.L. 112-240)**

P.L. 112-240, §320(a):

Amended Code Sec. 871(k)(1)(C)(v) and (2)(C)(v) by striking "December 31, 2011" and inserting "December 31, 2013". **Effective** for tax years beginning after 12-31-2011.

• **2010, Tax Relief, Unemployment Insurance Reauthorization, and Job Creation Act of 2010 (P.L. 111-312)**

P.L. 111-312, §748(a):

Amended Code Sec. 871(k)(1)(C)[(v)] and (2)(C)[(v)] by striking "December 31, 2009" and inserting "December 31, 2011". **Effective** for tax years beginning after 12-31-2009.

• **2010, Regulated Investment Company Modernization Act of 2010 (P.L. 111-325)**

P.L. 111-325, §301(f)(1):

Amended Code Sec. 871(k)(1)(C) by striking all that precedes "any taxable year of the company beginning" and inserting text. **Effective** for tax years beginning after 12-22-2010. Prior to amendment, Code Sec. 871(k)(1)(C) read as follows:

(C) INTEREST-RELATED DIVIDEND.—For purposes of this paragraph, the term "interest-related dividend" means any dividend (or part thereof) which is designated by the regulated investment company as an interest-related dividend in a written notice mailed to its shareholders not later than 60 days after the close of its taxable year. If the aggregate amount so designated with respect to a taxable year of the company (including amounts so designated with respect to dividends paid after the close of the taxable year described in section 855) is greater than the qualified net interest income of the company for such taxable year, the portion of each distribution which shall be an interest-related dividend shall be only that portion of the amounts so designated which such qualified net interest income bears to the aggregate amount so designated. Such term shall not include any dividend with respect to any taxable year of the company beginning after December 31, 2009.

P.L. 111-325, §301(f)(2):

Amended Code Sec. 871(k)(2)(C) by striking all that precedes "any taxable year of the company beginning" and inserting new text. **Effective** for tax years beginning after 12-22-2010. Prior to the amendment, Code Sec. 871(k)(2)(C) read as follows:

(C) SHORT-TERM CAPITAL GAIN DIVIDEND.—For purposes of this paragraph, the term "short-term capital gain dividend" means any dividend (or part thereof) which is designated by the regulated investment company as a short-term capital gain dividend in a written notice mailed to its shareholders not later than 60 days after the close of its taxable year. If the aggregate amount so designated with respect to a taxable year of the company (including amounts so designated with respect to dividends paid after the close of the taxable year described in section 855) is greater than the qualified short-term gain of the company for such taxable year, the portion of each distribution which shall be a short-term capital gain dividend shall be only that portion of the amounts so designated which such qualified short-term gain bears to the aggregate amount so designated. Such term shall not include any dividend with respect to any taxable year of the company beginning December 31, 2009.

P.L. 111-325, §302(b)(2):

Amended Code Sec. 871(k)(1)(A) and 871(k)(2)(A) by inserting "which meets the requirements of section 852(a) for the taxable year with respect to which the dividend is paid" before the period at the end. **Effective** for tax years beginning after 12-22-2010.

P.L. 111-325, §308(b)(3):

Amended Code Sec. 871(k)(2)(D) by striking the last two sentences and inserting a new sentence. **Effective** for tax years beginning after 12-22-2010. Prior to amendment, Code Sec. 871(k)(2)(D) read as follows:

(D) QUALIFIED SHORT-TERM GAIN.—For purposes of subparagraph (C), the term "qualified short-term gain" means the excess of the net short-term capital gain of the regulated investment company for the taxable year over the net long-term capital loss (if any) of such company for such taxable year. For purposes of this subparagraph—

(i) the net short-term capital gain of the regulated investment company shall be computed by treating any short-term capital gain dividend includible in gross income with respect to stock of another regulated investment company as a short-term capital gain, and

(ii) the excess of the net short-term capital gain for a taxable year over the net long-term capital loss for a taxable year (to which an election under section 4982(e)(4) does not apply) shall be determined without regard to any net capital loss or net short-term capital loss attributable to transactions after October 31 of such year, and any such net capital loss or net short-term capital loss shall be treated as arising on the 1st day of the next taxable year.

To the extent provided in regulations, clause (ii) shall apply also for purposes of computing the taxable income of the regulated investment company.

• **2008, Tax Extenders and Alternative Minimum Tax Relief Act of 2008 (P.L. 110-343)**

P.L. 110-343, Division C, §206(a):

Amended Code Sec. 871(k)(1)(C) by striking "December 31, 2007" and inserting "December 31, 2009". **Effective** for dividends with respect to tax years of regulated investment companies beginning after 12-31-2007.

P.L. 110-343, Division C, §206(b):

Amended Code Sec. 871(k)(2)(C) by striking "December 31, 2007" and inserting "December 31, 2009". **Effective** for dividends with respect to tax years of regulated investment companies beginning after 12-31-2007.

• **2006, Tax Increase Prevention and Reconciliation Act of 2005 (P.L. 109-222)**

P.L. 109-222, §505(c)(2):

Amended Code Sec. 871(k)(2) by adding at the end a new subparagraph (E). **Effective** for tax years of qualified investment entities beginning after 12-31-2005, except that no amount shall be required to be withheld under Code Sec. 1441, 1442, or 1445 with respect to any distribution before 5-17-2006 if such amount was not otherwise required to be withheld under any such section as in effect before such amendments.

• **2004, American Jobs Creation Act of 2004 (P.L. 108-357)**

P.L. 108-357, §411(a)(1):

Amended Code Sec. 871 by redesignating subsection (k) as subsection (l) and by inserting after subsection (j) a new subsection (k). **Effective** for dividends with respect to tax years of regulated investment companies beginning after 12-31-2004.

[Sec. 871(l)]

(l) RULES RELATING TO EXISTING 80/20 COMPANIES.—For purposes of this subsection and subsection (i)(2)(B)—

(1) EXISTING 80/20 COMPANY.—

(A) IN GENERAL.—The term "existing 80/20 company" means any corporation if—

(i) such corporation met the 80-percent foreign business requirements of section 861(c)(1) (as in effect before the date of the enactment of this subsection) for such corporation's last taxable year beginning before January 1, 2011,

(ii) such corporation meets the 80-percent foreign business requirements of subparagraph (B) with respect to each taxable year after the taxable year referred to in clause (i), and

(iii) there has not been an addition of a substantial line of business with respect to such corporation after the date of the enactment of this subsection.

INCOME TAX—NONRESIDENT ALIENS

(B) FOREIGN BUSINESS REQUIREMENTS.—

(i) IN GENERAL.—Except as provided in clause (iv), a corporation meets the 80-percent foreign business requirements of this subparagraph if it is shown to the satisfaction of the Secretary that at least 80 percent of the gross income from all sources of such corporation for the testing period is active foreign business income.

(ii) ACTIVE FOREIGN BUSINESS INCOME.—For purposes of clause (i), the term "active foreign business income" means gross income which—

(I) is derived from sources outside the United States (as determined under this subchapter), and

(II) is attributable to the active conduct of a trade or business in a foreign country or possession of the United States.

(iii) TESTING PERIOD.—For purposes of this subsection, the term "testing period" means the 3-year period ending with the close of the taxable year of the corporation preceding the payment (or such part of such period as may be applicable). If the corporation has no gross income for such 3-year period (or part thereof), the testing period shall be the taxable year in which the payment is made.

(iv) TRANSITION RULE.—In the case of a taxable year for which the testing period includes 1 or more taxable years beginning before January 1, 2011—

(I) a corporation meets the 80-percent foreign business requirements of this subparagraph if and only if the weighted average of—

(aa) the percentage of the corporation's gross income from all sources that is active foreign business income (as defined in subparagraph (B) of section 861(c)(1) (as in effect before the date of the enactment of this subsection)) for the portion of the testing period that includes taxable years beginning before January 1, 2011, and

(bb) the percentage of the corporation's gross income from all sources that is active foreign business income (as defined in clause (ii) of this subparagraph) for the portion of the testing period, if any, that includes taxable years beginning on or after January 1, 2011,

is at least 80 percent, and

(II) the active foreign business percentage for such taxable year shall equal the weighted average percentage determined under subclause (I).

(2) ACTIVE FOREIGN BUSINESS PERCENTAGE.—Except as provided in paragraph (1)(B)(iv), the term "active foreign business percentage" means, with respect to any existing 80/20 company, the percentage which—

(A) the active foreign business income of such company for the testing period, is of

(B) the gross income of such company for the testing period from all sources.

(3) AGGREGATION RULES.—For purposes of applying paragraph (1) (other than subparagraphs (A)(i) and (B)(iv) thereof) and paragraph (2)—

(A) IN GENERAL.—The corporation referred to in paragraph (1)(A) and all of such corporation's subsidiaries shall be treated as one corporation.

(B) SUBSIDIARIES.—For purposes of subparagraph (A), the term "subsidiary" means any corporation in which the corporation referred to in subparagraph (A) owns (directly or indirectly) stock meeting the requirements of section 1504(a)(2) (determined by substituting "50 percent" for "80 percent" each place it appears and without regard to section 1504(b)(3)).

(4) REGULATIONS.—The Secretary may issue such regulations or other guidance as is necessary or appropriate to carry out the purposes of this section, including regulations or other guidance which provide for the proper application of the aggregation rules described in paragraph (3).

Amendments

- 2010, (P.L. 111-226)

P.L. 111-226, § 217(b)(2):

Amended Code Sec. 871 by redesignating subsections (l) and (m) as subsections (m) and (n), respectively, and by inserting after subsection (k) a new subsection (l). **Effective** generally for tax years beginning after 12-31-2010. For a grandfather rule, see Act Sec. 217(d)(2), below.

P.L. 111-226, § 217(d)(2), provides:

(2) GRANDFATHER RULE FOR OUTSTANDING DEBT OBLIGATIONS.—

(A) IN GENERAL.—The amendments made by this section shall not apply to payments of interest on obligations issued before the date of the enactment of this Act.

(B) EXCEPTION FOR RELATED PARTY DEBT.—Subparagraph (A) shall not apply to any interest which is payable to a related person (determined under rules similar to the rules of section 954(d)(3)).

(C) SIGNIFICANT MODIFICATIONS TREATED AS NEW ISSUES.—For purposes of subparagraph (A), a significant modification of the terms of any obligation (including any extension of the term of such obligation) shall be treated as a new issue.

[Sec. 871(m)]

(m) TREATMENT OF DIVIDEND EQUIVALENT PAYMENTS.—

(1) IN GENERAL.—For purposes of subsection (a), sections 881 and 4948(a), and chapters 3 and 4, a dividend equivalent shall be treated as a dividend from sources within the United States.

(2) DIVIDEND EQUIVALENT.—For purposes of this subsection, the term "dividend equivalent" means—

(A) any substitute dividend made pursuant to a securities lending or a sale-repurchase transaction that (directly or indirectly) is contingent upon, or determined by reference to, the payment of a dividend from sources within the United States,

(B) any payment made pursuant to a specified notional principal contract that (directly or indirectly) is contingent upon, or determined by reference to, the payment of a dividend from sources within the United States, and

(C) any other payment determined by the Secretary to be substantially similar to a payment described in subparagraph (A) or (B).

(3) SPECIFIED NOTIONAL PRINCIPAL CONTRACT.—For purposes of this subsection, the term "specified notional principal contract" means—

(A) any notional principal contract if—

(i) in connection with entering into such contract, any long party to the contract transfers the underlying security to any short party to the contract,

(ii) in connection with the termination of such contract, any short party to the contract transfers the underlying security to any long party to the contract,

(iii) the underlying security is not readily tradable on an established securities market,

(iv) in connection with entering into such contract, the underlying security is posted as collateral by any short party to the contract with any long party to the contract, or

(v) such contract is identified by the Secretary as a specified notional principal contract,

(B) in the case of payments made after the date which is 2 years after the date of the enactment of this subsection, any notional principal contract unless the Secretary determines that such contract is of a type which does not have the potential for tax avoidance.

(4) DEFINITIONS.—For purposes of paragraph (3)(A)—

INCOME TAX—NONRESIDENT ALIENS

(A) LONG PARTY.—The term "long party" means, with respect to any underlying security of any notional principal contract, any party to the contract which is entitled to receive any payment pursuant to such contract which is contingent upon, or determined by reference to, the payment of a dividend from sources within the United States with respect to such underlying security.

(B) SHORT PARTY.—The term "short party" means, with respect to any underlying security of any notional principal contract, any party to the contract which is not a long party with respect to such underlying security.

(C) UNDERLYING SECURITY.—The term "underlying security" means, with respect to any notional principal contract, the security with respect to which the dividend referred to in paragraph (2)(B) is paid. For purposes of this paragraph, any index or fixed basket of securities shall be treated as a single security.

(5) PAYMENTS DETERMINED ON GROSS BASIS.—For purposes of this subsection, the term "payment" includes any gross amount which is used in computing any net amount which is transferred to or from the taxpayer.

(6) PREVENTION OF OVER-WITHHOLDING.—In the case of any chain of dividend equivalents one or more of which is subject to tax under subsection (a) or section 881, the Secretary may reduce such tax, but only to the extent that the taxpayer can establish that such tax has been paid with respect to another dividend equivalent in such chain, or is not otherwise due, or as the Secretary determines is appropriate to address the role of financial intermediaries in such chain. For purposes of this paragraph, a dividend shall be treated as a dividend equivalent.

(7) COORDINATION WITH CHAPTERS 3 AND 4.—For purposes of chapters 3 and 4, each person that is a party to any contract or other arrangement that provides for the payment of a dividend equivalent shall be treated as having control of such payment.

Amendments

- 2010, (P.L. 111-226)

P.L. 111-226, §217(b)(2):

Amended Code Sec. 871 by redesignating subsection (l) as subsection (m). **Effective** generally for tax years beginning after 12-31-2010. For a grandfather rule, see Act Sec. 217(d)(2), below.

P.L. 111-226, §217(d)(2), provides:

(2) GRANDFATHER RULE FOR OUTSTANDING DEBT OBLIGATIONS.—

(A) IN GENERAL.—The amendments made by this section shall not apply to payments of interest on obligations issued before the date of the enactment of this Act.

(B) EXCEPTION FOR RELATED PARTY DEBT.—Subparagraph (A) shall not apply to any interest which is payable to a related person (determined under rules similar to the rules of section 954(d)(3)).

(C) SIGNIFICANT MODIFICATIONS TREATED AS NEW ISSUES.—For purposes of subparagraph (A), a significant modification of the terms of any obligation (including any extension of the term of such obligation) shall be treated as a new issue.

- 2010, Hiring Incentives to Restore Employment Act (P.L. 111-147)

P.L. 111-147, §541(a):

Amended Code Sec. 871 by redesignating subsection (l) as subsection (m) and by inserting after subsection (k) a new subsection (l). **Effective** for payments made on or after the date that is 180 days after 3-18-2010.

[Sec. 871(n)]

(n) CROSS REFERENCES.—

(1) For tax treatment of certain amounts distributed by the United States to nonresident alien individuals, see section 402(e)(2).

(2) For taxation of nonresident alien individuals who are expatriate United States citizens, see section 877.

(3) For doubling of tax on citizens of certain foreign countries, see section 891.

(4) For adjustment of tax in case of nationals or residents of certain foreign countries, see section 896.

(5) For withholding of tax at source on nonresident alien individuals, see section 1441.

(6) For election to treat married nonresident alien individual as resident of United States in certain cases, see subsections (g) and (h) of section 6013.

(7) For special tax treatment of gain or loss from the disposition by a nonresident alien individual of a United States real property interest, see section 897.

Amendments

- 2010, (P.L. 111-226)

P.L. 111-226, §217(b)(2):

Amended Code Sec. 871 by redesignating subsection (m) as subsection (n). **Effective** generally for tax years beginning after 12-31-2010. For a grandfather rule, see Act Sec. 217(d)(2), below.

P.L. 111-226, §217(d)(2), provides:

(2) GRANDFATHER RULE FOR OUTSTANDING DEBT OBLIGATIONS.—

(A) IN GENERAL.—The amendments made by this section shall not apply to payments of interest on obligations issued before the date of the enactment of this Act.

(B) EXCEPTION FOR RELATED PARTY DEBT.—Subparagraph (A) shall not apply to any interest which is payable to a related person (determined under rules similar to the rules of section 954(d)(3)).

(C) SIGNIFICANT MODIFICATIONS TREATED AS NEW ISSUES.—For purposes of subparagraph (A), a significant modification of the terms of any obligation (including any extension of the term of such obligation) shall be treated as a new issue.

- 2010, Hiring Incentives to Restore Employment Act (P.L. 111-147)

P.L. 111-147, §541(a):

Amended Code Sec. 871 by redesignating subsection (l) as subsection (m). **Effective** for payments made on or after the date that is 180 days after 3-18-2010.

- 2004, American Jobs Creation Act of 2004 (P.L. 108-357)

P.L. 108-357, §411(a)(1):

Amended Code Sec. 871 by redesignating subsection (k) as subsection (l). **Effective** for dividends with respect to tax years of regulated investment companies beginning after 12-31-2004.

- 1992, Unemployment Compensation Amendments of 1992 (P.L. 102-318)

P.L. 102-318, §521(b)(30):

Amended Code Sec. 871(k)(1) by striking "section 402(a)(4)" and inserting "section 402(e)(2)". **Effective** for distributions after 12-31-92.

- 1988, Technical and Miscellaneous Revenue Act of 1988 (P.L. 100-647)

P.L. 100-647, §6134(a)(1):

Amended Code Sec. 871 by redesignating subsection (j) as subsection (k). **Effective** 11-10-88.

- 1986, Tax Reform Act of 1986 (P.L. 99-514)

P.L. 99-514, §1214(c)(1):

Amended Code Sec. 871 by redesignating subsection (i) as subsection (j) and by inserting after subsection (h) new subsection (i). **Effective**, generally, for tax years beginning after 12-31-86 [see also P.L. 100-647, §1012(g)(1) following Code Sec. 861(d)]. However, for special and transitional rules, see Act Sec. 1214(d)(2)-(4) following Code Sec. 861.

- 1984, Deficit Reduction Act of 1984 (P.L. 98-369)

P.L. 98-369, §127(a)(1):

Amended Code Sec. 871 by redesignating subsection (h) as subsection (i) and by adding at the end thereof new subsection (h). **Effective** for interest received after 7-18-84, in tax years ending after such date.

P.L. 98-369, §128(a)(2):

Amended Code Sec. 871 by redesignating subsection (g) as subsection (h) and by inserting after subsection (f) new subsection (g). **Effective** for payments made on or after 9-16-84, with respect to obligations issued after 3-31-72.

P.L. 98-369, §412(b)(1):

Amended Code Sec. 871(g) (redesignated (h) and (i) by Act Secs. 128(a)(2) and 127(a)(1)) by striking out paragraph (6) and by redesignating paragraphs (7) and (8) as paragraphs (6) and (7), respectively. **Effective** with respect to tax years beginning after 12-31-84. Prior to amendment, Code Sec. 871(g)(6) read as follows:

(6) For the requirement of making a declaration of estimated tax by certain nonresident alien individuals, see section 6015(j).

- 1981, Economic Recovery Tax Act of 1981 (P.L. 97-34)

P.L. 97-34, §725(c)(1):

Amended Code Sec. 871(g)(6) by striking out "6015(i)" and inserting "6015(j)". **Effective** 1-1-81.

- 1980, Omnibus Reconciliation Act of 1980 (P.L. 96-499)

P.L. 96-499, §1122(c)(1):

Added Code Sec. 871(g)(8). For the **effective** date, see the historical comment under Code Sec. 897(i).

- 1976, Tax Reform Act of 1976 (P.L. 94-455)

P.L. 94-455, §1012(a):

Added subparagraph (7). **Effective** for tax years ending on or after 12-31-75.

Sec. 871(m)(4)(A)

INCOME TAX—NONRESIDENT ALIENS

• **1966, Foreign Investors Tax Act of 1966 (P.L. 89-809)**

P.L. 89-809:

Redesignated former Code Sec. 871(e) as Code Sec. 871(g) and added paragraphs (2), (4), (5), and (6) and redesignated former paragraphs (1) and (2) as (3) and (1), respectively.

[Sec. 872]

SEC. 872. GROSS INCOME.

[Sec. 872(a)]

(a) GENERAL RULE.—In the case of a nonresident alien individual, except where the context clearly indicates otherwise, gross income includes only—

(1) gross income which is derived from sources within the United States and which is not effectively connected with the conduct of a trade or business within the United States, and

(2) gross income which is effectively connected with the conduct of a trade or business within the United States.

Amendments

• **1988, Technical and Miscellaneous Revenue Act of 1988 (P.L. 100-647)**

P.L. 100-647, §1012(s)(2)(A):

Amended Code Sec. 872(a) by striking out "the case of a nonresident alien individual" and inserting in lieu thereof "the case of a nonresident alien individual, except where the context clearly indicates otherwise". **Effective** as if included in the provision of P.L. 99-514 to which it relates.

• **1966, Foreign Investors Tax Act of 1966 (P.L. 89-809)**

P.L. 89-809, §103(b)(1):

Amended Code Sec. 872(a). **Effective** 1-1-67. Prior to amendment, Sec. 872(a) read as follows:

(a) General Rule.—In the case of a nonresident alien individual gross income includes only the gross income from sources within the United States.

[Sec. 872(b)]

(b) EXCLUSIONS.—The following items shall not be included in gross income of a nonresident alien individual, and shall be exempt from taxation under this subtitle:

(1) SHIPS OPERATED BY CERTAIN NONRESIDENTS.—Gross income derived by an individual resident of a foreign country from the international operation of a ship or ships if such foreign country grants an equivalent exemption to individual residents of the United States.

(2) AIRCRAFT OPERATION BY CERTAIN NONRESIDENTS.—Gross income derived by an individual resident of a foreign country from the international operation of aircraft if such foreign country grants an equivalent exemption to individual residents of the United States.

(3) COMPENSATION OF PARTICIPANTS IN CERTAIN EXCHANGE OR TRAINING PROGRAMS.—Compensation paid by a foreign employer to a nonresident alien individual for the period he is temporarily present in the United States as a nonimmigrant under subparagraph (F), (J), or (Q) of section 101(a)(15) of the Immigration and Nationality Act, as amended. For purposes of this paragraph, the term "foreign employer" means—

(A) a nonresident alien individual, foreign partnership, or foreign corporation, or

(B) an office or place of business maintained in a foreign country or in a possession of the United States by a domestic corporation, a domestic partnership, or an individual who is a citizen or resident of the United States.

(4) CERTAIN BOND INCOME OF RESIDENTS OF THE RYUKYU ISLANDS OR THE TRUST TERRITORY OF THE PACIFIC ISLANDS.—Income derived by a nonresident alien individual from a series E or series H United States savings bond, if such individual acquired such bond while a resident of the Ryukyu Islands or the Trust Territory of the Pacific Islands.

(5) INCOME DERIVED FROM WAGERING TRANSACTIONS IN CERTAIN PARIMUTUEL POOLS.—Gross income derived by a nonresident alien individual from a legal wagering transaction initiated outside the United States in a parimutuel pool with respect to a live horse race or dog race in the United States.

(6) CERTAIN RENTAL INCOME.—Income to which paragraphs (1) and (2) apply shall include income which is derived from the rental on a full or bareboat basis of a ship or ships or aircraft, as the case may be.

(7) APPLICATION TO DIFFERENT TYPES OF TRANSPORTATION.—The Secretary may provide that this subsection be applied separately with respect to income from different types of transportation.

(8) TREATMENT OF POSSESSIONS.—To the extent provided in regulations, a possession of the United States shall be treated as a foreign country for purposes of this subsection.

Amendments

• **2004, American Jobs Creation Act of 2004 (P.L. 108-357)**

P.L. 108-357, §419(a):

Amended Code Sec. 872(b) by redesignating paragraphs (5), (6), and (7) as paragraphs (6), (7), and (8), respectively, and inserting after paragraph (4) a new paragraph (5). **Effective** for wagers made after 10-22-2004.

• **1994, Social Security Independence and Program Improvements Act of 1994 (P.L. 103-296)**

P.L. 103-296, §320(a)(2):

Amended Code Sec. 872(b)(3) by striking "(F) or (J)" and inserting "(F), (J), or (Q)". **Effective** with the calendar quarter following 8-15-94.

• **1989, Omnibus Budget Reconciliation Act of 1989 (P.L. 101-239)**

P.L. 101-239, §7811(i)(8)(C):

Amended Code Sec. 872(b) by adding at the end thereof a new paragraph (7). **Effective** as if included in the provision of P.L. 100-647 to which it relates.

• **1988, Technical and Miscellaneous Revenue Act of 1988 (P.L. 100-647)**

P.L. 100-647, §1012(e)(2)(B):

Amended Code Sec. 872(b)(1) and (2) by striking out "to citizens of the United States and to corporations organized in the United States" and inserting in lieu thereof "to individual residents of the United States". **Effective** as if included in the provision of P.L. 99-514 to which it relates.

P.L. 100-647, §1012(e)(5):

Amended Code Sec. 872(b)(1) and (2) by striking out "operation" and inserting in lieu thereof "international operation". **Effective** as if included in the provision of P.L. 99-514 to which it relates.

• **1986, Tax Reform Act of 1986 (P.L. 99-514)**

P.L. 99-514, §1212(c)(1):

Amended Code Sec. 872(b) by striking out paragraphs (1) and (2) and inserting in lieu thereof new paragraphs (1) and (2). **Effective** for tax years beginning after 12-31-86. Prior to amendment, Code Sec. 872(b)(1) and (2) read as follows:

(1) SHIPS UNDER FOREIGN FLAG.—Earnings derived from the operation of a ship or ships documented under the laws of a foreign country which grants an equivalent exemption to citizens of the United States and to corporations organized in the United States.

(2) AIRCRAFT OF FOREIGN REGISTRY.—Earnings derived from the operation of aircraft registered under the laws of a foreign country which grants an equivalent exemption to citizens of the United States and to corporations organized in the United States.

P.L. 99-514, §1212(c)(2):

Amended Code Sec. 872(b) by adding at the end thereof new paragraphs (5) and (6). **Effective** for tax years beginning after 12-31-86.

• **1966, Foreign Investors Tax Act of 1966 (P.L. 89-809)**

P.L. 89-809, §103(b)(2):

Amended Code Sec. 872(b)(3)(B) by substituting "by a domestic corporation, a domestic partnership, or an individual who is a citizen or resident of the United States" for "by a domestic corporation". **Effective** 1-1-67.

P.L. 89-809, §103(b)(3):

Added Code Sec. 872(b)(4). **Effective** 1-1-67.

• **1961, Mutual Educational and Cultural Exchange Act of 1961 (P.L. 87-256)**

P.L. 87-256, §110(c):

Added paragraph (3). **Effective** for tax years beginning after 1961.

INCOME TAX—NONRESIDENT ALIENS

[Sec. 873]

SEC. 873. DEDUCTIONS.

[Sec. 873(a)]

(a) GENERAL RULE.—In the case of a nonresident alien individual, the deductions shall be allowed only for purposes of section 871(b) and (except as provided by subsection (b)) only if and to the extent that they are connected with income which is effectively connected with the conduct of a trade or business within the United States; and the proper apportionment and allocation of the deductions for this purpose shall be determined as provided in regulations prescribed by the Secretary.

Amendments

• **1976, Tax Reform Act of 1976 (P.L. 94-455)**

P.L. 94-455, §1906(b)(13)(A):

Amended 1954 Code by substituting "Secretary" for "Secretary or his delegate" each place it appeared. **Effective** 2-1-77.

[Sec. 873(b)]

(b) EXCEPTIONS.—The following deductions shall be allowed whether or not they are connected with income which is effectively connected with the conduct of a trade or business within the United States:

(1) LOSSES.—The deduction allowed by section 165 for casualty or theft losses described in paragraph (2) or (3) of section 165(c), but only if the loss is of property located within the United States.

(2) CHARITABLE CONTRIBUTIONS.—The deduction for charitable contributions and gifts allowed by section 170.

(3) PERSONAL EXEMPTION.—The deduction for personal exemptions allowed by section 151, except that only one exemption shall be allowed under section 151 unless the taxpayer is a resident of a contiguous country or is a national of the United States.

Amendments

• **1998, Tax and Trade Relief Extension Act of 1998 (P.L. 105-277)**

P.L. 105-277, §4004(b)(3):

Amended Code Sec. 873(b)(1). **Effective** for tax years beginning after 12-31-83. Prior to amendment, Code Sec. 873(b)(1) read as follows:

(1) LOSSES.—The deduction for losses allowed by section 165(c)(3), but only if the loss is of property located within the United States.

• **1984, Deficit Reduction Act of 1984 (P.L. 98-369)**

P.L. 98-369, §711(c)(2)(A)(iv):

Amended Code Sec. 873(b)(1) by striking out ", for losses of property not connected with the trade or business if arising from certain casualties or theft," and inserting in lieu thereof "for losses". **Effective** for tax years beginning after 12-31-83. For a transitional rule, see Act Sec. 711(c)(2)(B) below.

P.L. 98-369, §711(c)(2)(B), provides:

(B) Transitional Rule.—In the case of taxable years beginning before January 1, 1984—

(i) For purposes of paragraph (1)(B) of section 165(h) of the Internal Revenue Code of 1954, adjusted gross income shall be determined without regard to the application of section 1231 of such Code to any gain or loss from an involuntary conversion of property described in subsection (c)(3) of section 165 of such Code arising from fire, storm, shipwreck, or other casualty or from theft.

(ii) Section 1231 of such Code shall be applied after the application of paragraph (1) of section 165(h) of such Code.

[Sec. 873(c)]

(c) CROSS REFERENCES.—

For rule that certain foreign taxes are not to be taken into account in determining deduction or credit, see section 906(b)(1).

Amendments

• **1977, Tax Reduction and Simplification Act of 1977 (P.L. 95-30)**

P.L. 95-30, §101(d)(11):

Amended Code Sec. 873(c). **Effective** for tax years beginning after 12-31-76. Prior to amendment, Code Sec. 873(c) read as follows:

(c) CROSS REFERENCES.—

(1) For disallowance of standard deduction, see section 142(b)(1).

(2) For rule that certain foreign taxes are not to be taken into account in determining deduction or credit, see section 906(b)(1).

• **1972 (P.L. 92-580)**

P.L. 92-580, §1(b):

Amended Code Sec. 873(b)(3). **Effective** for tax years beginning after 12-31-71. Prior to amendment, Code Sec. 873(b)(3) read as follows:

(3) Personal exemption.—The deduction for personal exemptions allowed by section 151, except that in the case of a nonresident alien individual who is not a resident of a contiguous country only one exemption shall be allowed under section 151.

• **1966, Foreign Investors Tax Act of 1966 (P.L. 89-809)**

P.L. 89-809, §103(c)(1):

Amended Code Sec. 873. **Effective** 1-1-67. Prior to amendment, Code Sec. 873 read as follows:

SEC. 873. DEDUCTIONS.

(a) General Rule.—In the case of a nonresident alien individual the deductions shall be allowed only if and to the extent that they are connected with income from sources within the United States; and the proper apportionment and allocation of the deductions with respect to sources of income within and without the United States shall be determined as provided in part I, under regulations prescribed by the Secretary or his delegate.

(b) Losses.—

(1) The deduction, for losses not connected with the trade or business if incurred in transactions entered into for profit, allowed by section 165(c)(2) (relating to losses) shall be allowed whether or not connected with income from sources within the United States, but only if the profit, if such transaction had resulted in a profit, would be taxable under this subtitle.

(2) The deduction for losses of property not connected with the trade or business if arising from certain casualties or theft, allowed by section 165(c)(3), shall be allowed whether or not connected with income from sources within the United States, but only if the loss is of property within the United States.

(c) Charitable Contributions.—The deduction for charitable contributions and gifts provided by section 170 shall be allowed whether or not connected with income from sources within the United States, but only as to contributions or gifts made to domestic corporations, or to community chests, funds, or foundations, created in the United States.

(d) Personal Exemption.—In the case of a nonresident alien individual who is not a resident of a contiguous country, only one exemption under section 151 shall be allowed as a deduction.

(e) Standard Deduction.—

For disallowance of standard deduction, see section 142(b)(1).

[Sec. 874]

SEC. 874. ALLOWANCE OF DEDUCTIONS AND CREDITS.

[Sec. 874(a)]

(a) RETURN PREREQUISITE TO ALLOWANCE.—A nonresident alien individual shall receive the benefit of the deductions and credits allowed to him in this subtitle only by filing or causing to be filed with the Secretary a true and accurate return, in the manner prescribed in subtitle F (sec. 6001 and following, relating to procedure and administration), including therein all the information which the Secretary may deem necessary for the calculation of such deductions and credits. This subsection shall not be construed to deny the credits provided by sections 31 and 33 for tax withheld at source or the credit provided by section 34 for certain uses of gasoline and special fuels.

Amendments

• **1984, Deficit Reduction Act of 1984 (P.L. 98-369)**

P.L. 98-369, §474(r)(19):

Amended Code Sec. 874(a) by striking out "32" and inserting in lieu thereof "33", and by striking out "section 39" and inserting in lieu thereof "section 34". **Effective** for tax years beginning after 12-31-83, and to carrybacks from such years.

• **1983, Surface Transportation Act of 1982 (P.L. 97-424)**

P.L. 97-424, §515(b)(6)(E):

Amended Code Sec. 874(a) by striking out "special fuels, and lubricating oil" and inserting in lieu thereof "and special fuels". **Effective** with respect to articles sold after 1-6-83.

INCOME TAX—NONRESIDENT ALIENS

- **1976, Tax Reform Act of 1976 (P.L. 94-455)**

P.L. 94-455, §1906(b)(13)(A):

Amended 1954 Code by substituting "Secretary" for "Secretary or his delegate" each place it appeared. **Effective** 2-1-77.

- **1970 (P.L. 91-258)**

P.L. 91-258, §207(d)(1):

Added ", special fuels," in the last sentence of Code Sec. 874(a). **Effective** 7-1-70.

- **1966, Foreign Investors Tax Act of 1966 (P.L. 89-809)**

P.L. 89-809, §103(d):

Amended Code Sec. 874(a). **Effective** 1-1-67. Prior to amendment, Sec. 874(a) read as follows:

"(a) Return Prerequisite to Allowance.—A nonresident alien individual shall receive the benefit of the deductions and credits allowed to him in this subtitle only by filing or causing to be filed a true and accurate return of his total income received from all sources in the United States, in the manner prescribed in subtitle F (sec. 6001 and following, relating to procedure and administration), including therein all the information which the Secretary or his delegate may deem necessary for the calculation of such deductions and credits. This subsection shall not be construed to deny the credits provided by sections 31 and 32 for tax withheld at the source or the credit provided by section 39 for certain uses of gasoline and lubricating oil."

- **1965, Excise Tax Reduction Act of 1965 (P.L. 89-44)**

P.L. 89-44, §809(d)(3):

Amended Sec. 874(a) by adding the phrase: "or the credit provided by section 39 for certain uses of gasoline and lubricating oil" in the last sentence. **Effective** 7-1-65.

[Sec. 874(b)]

(b) TAX WITHHELD AT SOURCE.—The benefit of the deduction for exemptions under section 151 may, in the discretion of the Secretary, and under regulations prescribed by the Secretary, be received by a nonresident alien individual entitled thereto, by filing a claim therefor with the withholding agent.

Amendments

- **1976, Tax Reform Act of 1976 (P.L. 94-455)**

P.L. 94-455, §1906(b)(13)(A):

Amended 1954 Code by substituting "Secretary" for "Secretary or his delegate" each place it appeared. **Effective** 2-1-77.

[Sec. 874(c)]

(c) FOREIGN TAX CREDIT.—Except as provided in section 906, a nonresident alien individual shall not be allowed the credits against the tax for taxes of foreign countries and possessions of the United States allowed by section 901.

Amendments

- **1966, Foreign Investors Tax Act of 1966 (P.L. 89-809)**

P.L. 89-809, §106(a)(3):

Amended Code Sec. 874(c) by substituting "(c) Foreign Tax Credit.—Except as provided in section 906, a nonresident" for "(c) Foreign Tax Credit Not Allowed.—A nonresident". **Effective** 1-1-67.

[Sec. 875]

SEC. 875. PARTNERSHIPS; BENEFICIARIES OF ESTATES AND TRUSTS.

For purposes of this subtitle—

(1) a nonresident alien individual or foreign corporation shall be considered as being engaged in a trade or business within the United States if the partnership of which such individual or corporation is a member is so engaged, and

(2) a nonresident alien individual or foreign corporation which is a beneficiary of an estate or trust which is engaged in any trade or business within the United States shall be treated as being engaged in such trade or business within the United States.

Amendments

- **1966, Foreign Investors Tax Act of 1966 (P.L. 89-809)**

P.L. 89-809, §103(e)(1):

Amended Code Sec. 875. **Effective** 1-1-67. Prior to amendment, Code Sec. 875 read as follows:

SEC. 875. PARTNERSHIPS.

For purposes of this subtitle, a nonresident alien individual shall be considered as being engaged in a trade or business within the United States if the partnership of which he is a member is so engaged.

[Sec. 876]

SEC. 876. ALIEN RESIDENTS OF PUERTO RICO, GUAM, AMERICAN SAMOA, OR THE NORTHERN MARIANA ISLANDS.

[Sec. 876(a)]

(a) GENERAL RULE.—This subpart shall not apply to any alien individual who is a bona fide resident of Puerto Rico, Guam, American Samoa, or the Northern Mariana Islands during the entire taxable year and such alien shall be subject to the tax imposed by section 1.

[Sec. 876(b)]

(b) CROSS REFERENCES.—For exclusion from gross income of income derived from sources within—

(1) Guam, American Samoa, and the Northern Mariana Islands, see section 931, and

(2) Puerto Rico, see section 933.

Amendments

- **1986, Tax Reform Act of 1986 (P.L. 99-514)**

P.L. 99-514, §1272(b):

Amended Code Sec. 876. For the **effective** date, as well as special rules, see Act Sec. 1277, as amended by P.L. 100-647, §1012(z)(1)-(2), below. Prior to amendment, Code Sec. 876 read as follows:

SEC. 876. ALIEN RESIDENTS OF PUERTO RICO.

(a) NO APPLICATION TO CERTAIN ALIEN RESIDENTS OF PUERTO RICO.—This subpart shall not apply to an alien individual who is a bona fide resident of Puerto Rico during the entire taxable year, and such alien shall be subject to the tax imposed by section 1.

(b) CROSS REFERENCE.—

For exclusion from gross income of income derived from sources within Puerto Rico, see section 933.

P.L. 99-514, §1277, as amended by P.L. 100-647, §1012(z)(1)-(2), provides:

SEC. 1277. EFFECTIVE DATE.

(a) IN GENERAL.—Except as otherwise provided in this section, the amendments made by this subtitle shall apply to taxable years beginning after December 31, 1986.

(b) SPECIAL RULE FOR GUAM, AMERICAN SAMOA, AND THE NORTHERN MARIANA ISLANDS.—The amendments made by this subtitle shall apply with respect to Guam, American Samoa, or the Northern Mariana Islands (and to residents thereof and corporations created or organized therein) only if (and so long as) an implementing agreement under section 1271 is in effect between the United States and such possession.

(c) SPECIAL RULES FOR THE VIRGIN ISLANDS.—

(1) IN GENERAL.—The amendments made by section 1275(c) shall apply with respect to the Virgin Islands (and residents thereof and corporations created or organized therein) only if (and so long as) an implementing agreement is in effect between the United States and the Virgin Islands with respect to the establishment of rules under which the evasion or avoidance of United States income tax shall not be permitted or facilitated by such possession. Any such implementing agreement shall be executed on behalf of the United States by the Secretary of the Treasury, after consultation with the Secretary of the Interior.

(2) SECTION 1275(b).—

(A) IN GENERAL.—The amendment made by section 1275(b) shall apply with respect to—

(i) any taxable year beginning after December 31, 1986, and

(ii) any pre-1987 open year.

(B) SPECIAL RULES.—In the case of any pre-1987 open year—

(i) the amendment made by section 1275(b) shall not apply to income from sources in the Virgin Islands or income effectively connected with the conduct of a trade or business in the Virgin Islands, and

(ii) the taxpayer shall be allowed a credit—

INCOME TAX—NONRESIDENT ALIENS

(I) against any additional tax imposed by subtitle A of the Internal Revenue Code of 1954 (by reason of the amendment made by section 1275(b)) on income not described in clause (i) and from sources in the United States.

(II) for any tax paid to the Virgin Islands before the date of the enactment of this Act and attributable to such income.

For purposes of clause (ii)(II), any tax paid before January 1, 1987, pursuant to a process in effect before August 16, 1986, shall be treated as paid before the date of the enactment of this Act.

(C) PRE-1987 OPEN YEAR.—For purposes of this paragraph, the term "pre-1987 open year" means any taxable year beginning before January 1, 1987, if on the date of the enactment of this Act the assessment of a deficiency of income tax for such taxable year is not barred by any law or rule of law.

(D) EXCEPTION.—In the case of any pre-1987 open year, the amendment made by section 1275(b) shall not apply to any domestic corporation if—

(i) during the fiscal year which ended May 31, 1986, such corporation was actively engaged directly or through a subsidiary in the conduct of a trade or business in the Virgin Islands and such trade or business consists of business related to marine activities, and

(ii) such corporation was incorporated on March 31, 1983, in Delaware.

(E) EXCEPTION FOR CERTAIN TRANSACTIONS.—

(i) IN GENERAL.—In the case of any pre-1987 open year, the amendment made by section 1275(b) shall not apply to any income derived from transactions described in clause (ii) by 1 or more corporations which were formed in Delaware on or about March 6, 1981, and which have owned 1 or more office buildings in St. Thomas, United States Virgin Islands, for at least 5 years before the date of the enactment of this Act.

(ii) DESCRIPTION OF TRANSACTIONS.—The transactions described in this clause are—

(I) the redemptions of limited partnership interests for cash and property described in an agreement (as amended) dated March 12, 1981,

(II) the subsequent disposition of the properties distributed in such redemptions, and

(III) interest earned before January 1, 1987, on bank deposits of proceeds received from such redemptions to the extent such deposits are located in the United States Virgin Islands.

(iii) LIMITATION.—The aggregate reduction in tax by reason of this subparagraph shall not exceed $8,312,000. If the taxes which would be payable as the result of the application of the amendment made by section 1275(b) to pre-1987 open years exceeds the limitation of the preceding sentence, such excess shall be treated as attributable to income received in taxable years in reverse chronological order.

(d) REPORT ON IMPLEMENTING AGREEMENTS.—If, during the 1-year period beginning on the date of the enactment of this Act, any implementing agreement described in subsection (b) or (c) is not executed, the Secretary of the Treasury or his delegate shall report to the Committee on Finance of the United States Senate, the Committee on Ways and Means, and the Committee on Interior and Insular Affairs of the House of Representatives with respect to—

(1) the status of such negotiations, and

(2) the reason why such agreement has not been executed.

(e) TREATMENT OF CERTAIN UNITED STATES PERSONS.—Except as otherwise provided in regulations prescribed by the Secretary of the Treasury or his delegate, if a United States person becomes a resident of Guam, American Samoa, or the Northern Mariana Islands, the rules of section 877(c) of the Internal Revenue Code of 1954 shall apply to such person during the 10-year period beginning when such person became such a resident. Notwithstanding subsection (b), the preceding sentence shall apply to dispositions after December 31, 1985, in taxable years ending after such date.

(f) EXEMPTION FROM WITHHOLDING.—Notwithstanding subsection (b), the modification of section 884 of the Internal Revenue Code of 1986 by reason of the amendment to section 881 of such Code by section 1273(b)(1) of this Act shall apply to taxable years beginning after December 31, 1986.

[Sec. 877]

SEC. 877. EXPATRIATION TO AVOID TAX.

[Sec. 877(a)]

(a) TREATMENT OF EXPATRIATES.—

(1) IN GENERAL.—Every nonresident alien individual to whom this section applies and who, within the 10-year period immediately preceding the close of the taxable year, lost United States citizenship shall be taxable for such taxable year in the manner provided in subsection (b) if the tax imposed pursuant to such subsection (after any reduction in such tax under the last sentence of such subsection) exceeds the tax which, without regard to this section, is imposed pursuant to section 871.

(2) INDIVIDUALS SUBJECT TO THIS SECTION.—This section shall apply to any individual if—

(A) the average annual net income tax (as defined in section 38(c)(1)) of such individual for the period of 5 taxable years ending before the date of the loss of United States citizenship is greater than $124,000,

(B) the net worth of the individual as of such date is $2,000,000 or more, or

(C) such individual fails to certify under penalty of perjury that he has met the requirements of this title for the 5 preceding taxable years or fails to submit such evidence of such compliance as the Secretary may require.

In the case of the loss of United States citizenship in any calendar year after 2004, such $124,000 amount shall be increased by an amount equal to such dollar amount multiplied by the cost-of-living adjustment determined under section 1(f)(3)for such calendar year by substituting "2003" for "1992" in subparagraph (B) thereof. Any increase under the preceding sentence shall be rounded to the nearest multiple of $1,000.

Amendments

• **2004, American Jobs Creation Act of 2004 (P.L. 108-357)**

P.L. 108-357, § 804(a)(1):

Amended Code Sec. 877(a). **Effective** for individuals who expatriate after 6-3-2004. Prior to amendment, Code Sec. 877(a) read as follows:

(a) TREATMENT OF EXPATRIATES.—

(1) IN GENERAL.—Every nonresident alien individual who, within the 10-year period immediately preceding the close of the taxable year, lost United States citizenship, unless such loss did not have for one of its principal purposes the avoidance of taxes under this subtitle or subtitle B, shall be taxable for such taxable year in the manner provided in subsection (b) if the tax imposed pursuant to such subsection (after any reduction in such tax under the last sentence of such subsection) exceeds the tax which, without regard to this section, is imposed pursuant to section 871.

(2) CERTAIN INDIVIDUALS TREATED AS HAVING TAX AVOIDANCE PURPOSE.—For purposes of paragraph (1), an individual shall be treated as having a principal purpose to avoid such taxes if—

(A) the average annual net income tax (as defined in section 38(c)(1)) of such individual for the period of 5 taxable years ending before the date of the loss of United States citizenship is greater than $100,000, or

(B) the net worth of the individual as of such date is $500,000 or more.

In the case of the loss of United States citizenship in any calendar year after 1996, such $100,000 and $500,000 amounts shall be increased by an amount equal to such dollar amount multiplied by the cost-of-living adjustment determined under section 1(f)(3) for such calendar year by substituting "1994" for "1992" in subparagraph (B) thereof. Any increase under the preceding sentence shall be rounded to the nearest multiple of $1,000.

• **1996, Health Insurance Portability and Accountability Act of 1996 (P.L. 104-191)**

P.L. 104-191, § 511(a):

Amended Code Sec. 877(a). For the **effective** date, see Act Sec. 511(g), below. Prior to amendment, Code Sec. 877(a) read as follows:

(a) IN GENERAL.—Every nonresident alien individual who at any time after March 8, 1965, and within the 10-year period immediately preceding the close of the taxable year lost United States citizenship, unless such loss did not have for one of its principal purposes the avoidance of taxes under this subtitle or subtitle B, shall be taxable for such taxable year in the manner provided in subsection (b) if the tax imposed pursuant to such subsection exceeds the tax which, without regard to this section, is imposed pursuant to section 871.

P.L. 104-191, § 511(d)(2):

Amended Code Sec. 877(a)[1], as amended by Act Sec. 511(a), by inserting "(after any reduction in such tax under the last sentence of such subsection)" after "such subsection". For the **effective** date, see Act Sec. 511(g), below.

P.L. 104-191, § 511(g), provides:

(g) EFFECTIVE DATE.—

(1) IN GENERAL.—The amendments made by this section shall apply to—

(A) individuals losing United States citizenship (within the meaning of section 877 of the Internal Revenue Code of 1986) on or after February 6, 1995, and

(B) long-term residents of the United States with respect to whom an event described in subparagraph (A) or (B) of section 877(e)(1) of such Code occurs on or after February 6, 1995.

(2) RULING REQUESTS.—In no event shall the 1-year period referred to in section 877(c)(1)(B) of such Code, as amended by this section, expire before the date which is 90 days after the date of the enactment of this Act.

(3) SPECIAL RULE.—

(A) IN GENERAL.—In the case of an individual who performed an act of expatriation specified in paragraph (1), (2), (3), or (4) of section 349(a) of the Immigration and Nationality Act (8 U.S.C. 1481(a)(1)-(4)) before February 6, 1995, but who did not, on or before such date, furnish to the United States Department of State a signed statement of voluntary relinquishment of United States nationality confirming the performance of such act, the amendments made by this section and section 512 shall apply to such individual except that the 10-year period described in section 877(a) of such Code shall not expire before the end of the 10-year period beginning on the date such statement is so furnished.

(B) EXCEPTION.—Subparagraph (A) shall not apply if the individual establishes to the satisfaction of the Secretary of the Treasury that such loss of United States citizenship occurred before February 6, 1994.

INCOME TAX—NONRESIDENT ALIENS

[Sec. 877(b)]

(b) ALTERNATIVE TAX.—A nonresident alien individual described in subsection (a) shall be taxable for the taxable year as provided in section 1 or 55, except that—

(1) the gross income shall include only the gross income described in section 872(a) (as modified by subsection (d) of this section), and

(2) the deductions shall be allowed if and to the extent that they are connected with the gross income included under this section, except that the capital loss carryover provided by section 1212(b) shall not be allowed; and the proper allocation and apportionment of the deductions for this purpose shall be determined as provided under regulations prescribed by the Secretary.

For purposes of paragraph (2), the deductions allowed by section 873(b) shall be allowed; and the deduction (for losses not connected with the trade or business if incurred in transactions entered into for profit) allowed by section 165(c)(2) shall be allowed, but only if the profit, if such transaction had resulted in a profit, would be included in gross income under this section. The tax imposed solely by reason of this section shall be reduced (but not below zero) by the amount of any income, war profits, and excess profits taxes (within the meaning of section 903) paid to any foreign country or possession of the United States on any income of the taxpayer on which tax is imposed solely by reason of this section.

Amendments

• **1996, Health Insurance Portability and Accountability Act of 1996 (P.L. 104-191)**

P.L. 104-191, §511(b)(2):

Amended Code Sec. 877(b)(1) by striking "subsection (c)" and inserting "subsection (d)". For the **effective** date, see Act Sec. 511(g), in the amendment notes following Code Sec. 877(a).

P.L. 104-191, §511(d)(1):

Amended Code Sec. 877(b) by adding at the end a new sentence. For the **effective** date, see Act Sec. 511(g), in the amendment notes following Code Sec. 877(a).

• **1996, Small Business Job Protection Act of 1996 (P.L. 104-188)**

P.L. 104-188, §1401(b)(11):

Amended Code Sec. 877(b) by striking "section 1, 55, or 402(d)(1)" and inserting "section 1 or 55". **Effective**, generally, for tax years beginning after 12-31-99. For a special transitional rule, see Act Sec. 1401(c)(2) in the amendment notes following Code Sec. 402(d).

• **1992, Unemployment Compensation Amendments of 1992 (P.L. 102-318)**

P.L. 102-318, §521(b)(31):

Amended Code Sec. 877(b) by striking "402(e)(1)" and inserting "402(d)(1)". **Effective** for distributions after 12-31-92.

• **1980, Technical Corrections Act of 1979 (P.L. 96-222)**

P.L. 96-222, §104(a)(1):

Amended Code Sec. 877(b) by changing "402(e)(1), or section 1201(b)" to "or 402(e)(1)". **Effective** for tax years beginning after 12-31-78.

P.L. 96-222, §104(a)(4)(H)(v):

Amended Code Sec. 877(b) by changing "section 55" to "55". **Effective** for tax years beginning after 12-31-79.

• **1978, Revenue Act of 1978 (P.L. 95-600)**

P.L. 95-600, §421(e)(5):

Amended Code Sec. 877(b) by inserting ", section 55," after "section 1". **Effective** for tax years beginning after 12-31-78.

• **1974, Employee Retirement Income Security Act of 1974 (P.L. 93-406)**

P.L. 93-406, §2005(c)(8):

Amended Code Sec. 877(b) by adding ", 402(e)(1)," after "section 1". **Effective** for distributions and payments made after 12-31-73, in tax years beginning after such date.

[Sec. 877(c)]

(c) EXCEPTIONS.—

(1) IN GENERAL.—Subparagraphs (A) and (B) of subsection (a)(2) shall not apply to an individual described in paragraph (2) or (3).

(2) DUAL CITIZENS.—

(A) IN GENERAL.—An individual is described in this paragraph if—

(i) the individual became at birth a citizen of the United States and a citizen of another country and continues to be a citizen of such other country, and

(ii) the individual has had no substantial contacts with the United States.

(B) SUBSTANTIAL CONTACTS.—An individual shall be treated as having no substantial contacts with the United States only if the individual—

(i) was never a resident of the United States (as defined in section 7701(b)),

(ii) has never held a United States passport, and

(iii) was not present in the United States for more than 30 days during any calendar year which is 1 of the 10 calendar years preceding the individual's loss of United States citizenship.

(3) CERTAIN MINORS.—An individual is described in this paragraph if—

(A) the individual became at birth a citizen of the United States,

(B) neither parent of such individual was a citizen of the United States at the time of such birth,

(C) the individual's loss of United States citizenship occurs before such individual attains age $18^1/_2$, and

(D) the individual was not present in the United States for more than 30 days during any calendar year which is 1 of the 10 calendar years preceding the individual's loss of United States citizenship.

Amendments

• **2004, American Jobs Creation Act of 2004 (P.L. 108-357)**

P.L. 108-357, §804(a)(2):

Amended Code Sec. 877(c). **Effective** for individuals who expatriate after 6-3-2004. Prior to amendment, Code Sec. 877(c) read as follows:

(c) TAX AVOIDANCE NOT PRESUMED IN CERTAIN CASES.—

(1) IN GENERAL.—Subsection (a)(2) shall not apply to an individual if—

(A) such individual is described in a subparagraph of paragraph (2) of this subsection, and

(B) within the 1-year period beginning on the date of the loss of United States citizenship, such individual submits a ruling request for the Secretary's determination as to whether such loss has for one of its principal purposes the avoidance of taxes under this subtitle or subtitle B.

(2) INDIVIDUALS DESCRIBED.—

(A) DUAL CITIZENSHIP, ETC.—An individual is described in this subparagraph if—

(i) the individual became at birth a citizen of the United States and a citizen of another country and continues to be a citizen of such other country, or

(ii) the individual becomes (not later than the close of a reasonable period after loss of United States citizenship) a citizen of the country in which—

(I) such individual was born,

(II) if such individual is married, such individual's spouse was born, or

(III) either of such individual's parents were born.

(B) LONG-TERM FOREIGN RESIDENTS.—An individual is described in this subparagraph if, for each year in the 10-year period ending on the date of loss of United States citizenship, the individual was present in the United States for 30 days or less. The rule of section 7701(b)(3)(D)(ii) shall apply for purposes of this subparagraph.

(C) RENUNCIATION UPON REACHING AGE OF MAJORITY.—An individual is described in this subparagraph if the individual's loss of United States citizenship occurs before such individual attains age $18^1/_2$.

(D) INDIVIDUALS SPECIFIED IN REGULATIONS.—An individual is described in this subparagraph if the individual is described in a category of individuals prescribed by regulation by the Secretary.

• **1996, Health Insurance Portability and Accountability Act of 1996 (P.L. 104-191)**

P.L. 104-191, §511(b)(1):

Amended Code Sec. 877 by striking subsection (d), by redesignating subsection (c) as subsection (d) and by inserting after subsection (b) a new subsection (c). For the **effective** date, see Act Sec. 511(g) in the amendment notes following Code Sec. 877(a). Prior to amendment, Code Sec. 877(d) read as follows:

(d) EXCEPTION FOR LOSS OF CITIZENSHIP FOR CERTAIN CAUSES.—Subsection (a) shall not apply to a nonresident alien individual whose loss of United States citizenship resulted from the application of section 301(b), 350, or 355 of the Immigration and Nationality Act, as amended (8 U.S.C. 1401(b), 1482, or 1487).

INCOME TAX—NONRESIDENT ALIENS

[Sec. 877(d)]

(d) SPECIAL RULES FOR SOURCE, ETC.—For purposes of subsection (b)—

(1) SOURCE RULES.—The following items of gross income shall be treated as income from sources within the United States:

(A) SALE OF PROPERTY.—Gains on the sale or exchange of property (other than stock or debt obligations) located in the United States.

(B) STOCK OR DEBT OBLIGATIONS.—Gains on the sale or exchange of stock issued by a domestic corporation or debt obligations of United States persons or of the United States, a State or political subdivision thereof, or the District of Columbia.

(C) INCOME OR GAIN DERIVED FROM CONTROLLED FOREIGN CORPORATION.—Any income or gain derived from stock in a foreign corporation but only—

(i) if the individual losing United States citizenship owned (within the meaning of section 958(a)), or is considered as owning (by applying the ownership rules of section 958(b)), at any time during the 2-year period ending on the date of the loss of United States citizenship, more than 50 percent of—

(I) the total combined voting power of all classes of stock entitled to vote of such corporation, or

(II) the total value of the stock of such corporation, and

(ii) to the extent such income or gain does not exceed the earnings and profits attributable to such stock which were earned or accumulated before the loss of citizenship and during periods that the ownership requirements of clause (i) are met.

(2) GAIN RECOGNITION ON CERTAIN EXCHANGES.—

(A) IN GENERAL.—In the case of any exchange of property to which this paragraph applies, notwithstanding any other provision of this title, such property shall be treated as sold for its fair market value on the date of such exchange, and any gain shall be recognized for the taxable year which includes such date.

(B) EXCHANGES TO WHICH PARAGRAPH APPLIES.—This paragraph shall apply to any exchange during the 10-year period beginning on the date the individual loses United States citizenship if—

(i) gain would not (but for this paragraph) be recognized on such exchange in whole or in part for purposes of this subtitle,

(ii) income derived from such property was from sources within the United States (or, if no income was so derived, would have been from such sources), and

(iii) income derived from the property acquired in the exchange would be from sources outside the United States.

(C) EXCEPTION.—Subparagraph (A) shall not apply if the individual enters into an agreement with the Secretary which specifies that any income or gain derived from the property acquired in the exchange (or any other property which has a basis determined in whole or part by reference to such property) during such 10-year period shall be treated as from sources within the United States. If the property transferred in the exchange is disposed of by the person acquiring such property, such agreement shall terminate and any gain which was not recognized by reason of such agreement shall be recognized as of the date of such disposition.

(D) SECRETARY MAY EXTEND PERIOD.—To the extent provided in regulations prescribed by the Secretary, subparagraph (B) shall be applied by substituting the 15-year period beginning 5 years before the loss of United States citizenship for the 10-year period referred to therein. In the case of any exchange occurring during such 5 years, any gain recognized under this subparagraph shall be recognized immediately after such loss of citizenship.

(E) SECRETARY MAY REQUIRE RECOGNITION OF GAIN IN CERTAIN CASES.—To the extent provided in regulations prescribed by the Secretary—

(i) the removal of appreciated tangible personal property from the United States, and

(ii) any other occurrence which (without recognition of gain) results in a change in the source of the income or gain from property from sources within the United States to sources outside the United States,

shall be treated as an exchange to which this paragraph applies.

(3) SUBSTANTIAL DIMINISHING OF RISKS OF OWNERSHIP.—For purposes of determining whether this section applies to any gain on the sale or exchange of any property, the running of the 10-year period described in subsection (a) and the period applicable under paragraph (2) shall be suspended for any period during which the individual's risk of loss with respect to the property is substantially diminished by—

(A) the holding of a put with respect to such property (or similar property),

(B) the holding by another person of a right to acquire the property, or

(C) a short sale or any other transaction.

(4) TREATMENT OF PROPERTY CONTRIBUTED TO CONTROLLED FOREIGN CORPORATIONS.—

(A) IN GENERAL.—If—

(i) an individual losing United States citizenship contributes property during the 10-year period beginning on the date the individual loses United States citizenship to any corporation which, at the time of the contribution, is described in subparagraph (B), and

(ii) income derived from such property immediately before such contribution was from sources within the United States (or, if no income was so derived, would have been from such sources),

any income or gain on such property (or any other property which has a basis determined in whole or part by reference to such property) received or accrued by the corporation shall be treated as received or accrued directly by such individual and not by such corporation. The preceding sentence shall not apply to the extent the property has been treated under subparagraph (C) as having been sold by such corporation.

(B) CORPORATION DESCRIBED.—A corporation is described in this subparagraph with respect to an individual if, were such individual a United States citizen—

(i) such corporation would be a controlled foreign corporation (as defined in section 957), and

(ii) such individual would be a United States shareholder (as defined in section 951(b)) with respect to such corporation.

(C) DISPOSITION OF STOCK IN CORPORATION.—If stock in the corporation referred to in subparagraph (A) (or any other stock which has a basis determined in whole or part by reference to such stock) is disposed of during the 10-year period referred to in subsection (a) and while the property referred to in subparagraph (A) is held by such corporation, a pro rata share of such property (determined on the basis of the value of such stock) shall be treated as sold by the corporation immediately before such disposition.

(D) ANTI-ABUSE RULES.—The Secretary shall prescribe such regulations as may be necessary to prevent the avoidance of the purposes of this paragraph, including where—

(i) the property is sold to the corporation, and

(ii) the property taken into account under subparagraph (A) is sold by the corporation.

(E) INFORMATION REPORTING.—The Secretary shall require such information reporting as is necessary to carry out the purposes of this paragraph.

INCOME TAX—NONRESIDENT ALIENS

Amendments

• **2018, Tax Technical Corrections Act of 2018 (P.L. 115-141)**

P.L. 115-141, §401(a)(153), Div. U:

Amended Code Sec. 877(d)(4)(B)(i) by striking "in 957" and inserting "in section 957". **Effective** 3-23-2018.

• **1997, Taxpayer Relief Act of 1997 (P.L. 105-34)**

P.L. 105-34, §1602(g)(1):

Amended Code Sec. 877(d)(2)(B) by striking "the 10-year period described in subsection (a)" and inserting "the 10-year period beginning on the date the individual loses United States citizenship". **Effective** as if included in the provision of P.L. 104-191 to which it relates [generally **effective** for individuals losing U.S. citizenship on or after 2-6-95, and long-term U.S. residents who end U.S. residency or begin foreign residency on or after 2-6-95.—CCH].

P.L. 105-34, §1602(g)(2):

Amended Code Sec. 877(d)(2)(D) by adding at the end a new sentence. **Effective** as if included in the provision of P.L. 104-191 to which it relates [generally **effective** for individuals losing U.S. citizenship on or after 2-6-95, and long-term U.S. residents who end U.S. residency or begin foreign residency on or after 2-6-95.—CCH].

P.L. 105-34, §1602(g)(3):

Amended Code Sec. 877(d)(3) by inserting "and the period applicable under paragraph (2)" after "subsection (a)". **Effective** as if included in the provision of P.L. 104-191 to which it relates [generally **effective** for individuals losing U.S. citizenship on or after 2-6-95, and long-term U.S. residents who end U.S. residency or begin foreign residency on or after 2-6-95.—CCH].

P.L. 105-34, §1602(g)(4)(A)-(C):

Amended Code Sec. 877(d)(4)(A) by inserting "during the 10-year period beginning on the date the individual loses United States citizenship" after "contributes property" in clause (i), by inserting "immediately before such contribution" after "from such property", and by striking "during the 10-year period referred to in subsection (a)," at the beginning of the flush left material. **Effective** as if included in the provision of P.L. 104-191 to which it relates [generally **effective** for individuals losing U.S. citizenship on or after 2-6-95, and long-term U.S. residents who end U.S. residency or begin foreign residency on or after 2-6-95.—CCH].

• **1996, Health Insurance Portability and Accountability Act of 1996 (P.L. 104-191)**

P.L. 104-191, §511(b)(1):

Amended Code Sec. 877 by striking subsection (d) and by redesignating subsection (c) as subsection (d). For the **effective** date, see Act Sec. 511(g), in the amendment notes following Code Sec. 877(a).

P.L. 104-191, §511(c):

Amended Code Sec. 877(d), as redesignated by Act Sec. 511(b)(1). For the **effective** date, see Act Sec. 511(g), in the amendment notes following Code Sec. 877(a). Prior to amendment, Code Sec. 877(d) read as follows:

(d) SPECIAL RULES OF SOURCE.—For purposes of subsection (b), the following items of gross income shall be treated as income from sources within the United States:

(1) SALE OF PROPERTY.—Gains on the sale or exchange of property (other than stock or debt obligations) located in the United States.

(2) STOCK OR DEBT OBLIGATIONS.—Gains on the sale or exchange of stock issued by a domestic corporation or debt obligations of United States persons or of the United States, a State or political subdivision thereof, or the District of Columbia.

For purposes of this section, gain on the sale or exchange of property which has a basis determined in whole or in part by reference to property described in paragraph (1) or (2) shall be treated as gain described in paragraph (1) or (2).

• **1986, Tax Reform Act of 1986 (P.L. 99-514)**

P.L. 99-514, §1243(a):

Amended Code Sec. 877(c) by adding at the end thereof a new sentence. **Effective** for sales or exchanges of property received in exchange after 9-25-85.

[Sec. 877(e)]

(e) COMPARABLE TREATMENT OF LAWFUL PERMANENT RESIDENTS WHO CEASE TO BE TAXED AS RESIDENTS.—

(1) IN GENERAL.—Any long-term resident of the United States who ceases to be a lawful permanent resident of the United States (within the meaning of section 7701(b)(6)) shall be treated for purposes of this section and sections 2107, 2501, and 6039G in the same manner as if such resident were a citizen of the United States who lost United States citizenship on the date of such cessation or commencement.

(2) LONG-TERM RESIDENT.—For purposes of this subsection, the term "long-term resident" means any individual (other than a citizen of the United States) who is a lawful permanent resident of the United States in at least 8 taxable years during the period of 15 taxable years ending with the taxable year during which the event described in paragraph (1) occurs. For purposes of the preceding sentence, an individual shall not be treated as a lawful permanent resident for any taxable year if such individual is treated as a resident of a foreign country for the taxable year under the provisions of a tax treaty between the United States and the foreign country and does not waive the benefits of such treaty applicable to residents of the foreign country.

(3) SPECIAL RULES.—

(A) EXCEPTIONS NOT TO APPLY.—Subsection (c) shall not apply to an individual who is treated as provided in paragraph (1).

(B) STEP-UP IN BASIS.—Solely for purposes of determining any tax imposed by reason of this subsection, property which was held by the long-term resident on the date the individual first became a resident of the United States shall be treated as having a basis on such date of not less than the fair market value of such property on such date. The preceding sentence shall not apply if the individual elects not to have such sentence apply. Such an election, once made, shall be irrevocable.

(4) AUTHORITY TO EXEMPT INDIVIDUALS.—This subsection shall not apply to an individual who is described in a category of individuals prescribed by regulation by the Secretary.

(5) REGULATIONS.—The Secretary shall prescribe such regulations as may be appropriate to carry out this subsection, including regulations providing for the application of this subsection in cases where an alien individual becomes a resident of the United States during the 10-year period after being treated as provided in paragraph (1).

Amendments

• **2014, Tax Technical Corrections Act of 2014 (P.L. 113-295)**

P.L. 113-295, §213(c)(2), Division A:

Amended Code Sec. 877(e)(2) by striking "subparagraph (A) or (B) of" before "paragraph (1)". **Effective** as if included in the provision of the Heroes Earnings Assistance and Relief Tax Act of 2008 (P.L. 110-245) to which it relates [**effective** for any individual whose expatriation date (as so defined) is on or after 6-17-2008.—CCH].

• **2008, Heroes Earnings Assistance and Relief Tax Act of 2008 (P.L. 110-245)**

P.L. 110-245, §301(c)(2)(A):

Amended Code Sec. 877(e)(1). **Effective** for any individual whose expatriation date (as so defined) is on or after 6-17-2008. Prior to amendment, Code Sec. 877(e)(1) read as follows:

(1) IN GENERAL.—Any long-term resident of the United States who—

(A) ceases to be a lawful permanent resident of the United States (within the meaning of section 7701(b)(6)), or

(B) commences to be treated as a resident of a foreign country under the provisions of a tax treaty between the United States and the foreign country and who does not waive the benefits of such treaty applicable to residents of the foreign country,

shall be treated for purposes of this section and sections 2107, 2501, and 6039G in the same manner as if such resident were a citizen of the United States who lost United States citizenship on the date of such cessation or commencement.

• **1997, Taxpayer Relief Act of 1997 (P.L. 105-34)**

P.L. 105-34, §1602(h)(3):

Amended Code Sec. 877(e)(1) by striking "6039F" and inserting "6039G". **Effective** as if included in the provision of P.L. 104-191 to which it relates [generally **effective** for individuals losing U.S. citizenship on or after 2-6-95, and long-term U.S. residents who end U.S. residency or begin foreign residency on or after 2-6-95.—CCH].

• **1996, Health Insurance Portability and Accountability Act of 1996 (P.L. 104-191)**

P.L. 104-191, §511(f)(1):

Amended Code Sec. 877 by redesignating subsection (e) as subsection (f) and by inserting after subsection (d) a new subsection (e). For the **effective** date, see Act Sec. 511(g), in the amendment notes following Code Sec. 877(a).

[Sec. 877(f)]

(f) BURDEN OF PROOF.—If the Secretary establishes that it is reasonable to believe that an individual's loss of United States citizenship would, but for this section, result in a substantial reduction for the taxable year in the taxes on his probable income for such year, the burden of proving for such taxable year that such loss of citizenship did not have for one of its principal purposes the avoidance of taxes under this subtitle or subtitle B shall be on such individual.

Internal Revenue Code   Sec. 877(f)

INCOME TAX—NONRESIDENT ALIENS

Amendments

• **1996, Health Insurance Portability and Accountability Act of 1996 (P.L. 104-191)**

P.L. 104-191, § 511(f)(1):

Amended Code Sec. 877 by redesignating subsection (e) as subsection (f). For the **effective** date, see Act Sec. 511(g), in the amendment notes following Code Sec. 877(a).

• **1976, Tax Reform Act of 1976 (P.L. 94-455)**

P.L. 94-455, § 1906(b)(13)(A):

Amended 1954 Code by substituting "Secretary" for "Secretary or his delegate" each place it appeared. **Effective** 2-1-77.

• **1966, Foreign Investors Tax Act of 1966 (P.L. 89-809)**

P.L. 89-809, § 103(f)(1):

Redesignated former Code Sec. 877 as Sec. 878 and added new Code Sec. 877. **Effective** 1-1-67.

[Sec. 877(g)]

(g) PHYSICAL PRESENCE.—

(1) IN GENERAL.—This section shall not apply to any individual to whom this section would otherwise apply for any taxable year during the 10-year period referred to in subsection (a) in which such individual is physically present in the United States at any time on more than 30 days in the calendar year ending in such taxable year, and such individual shall be treated for purposes of this title as a citizen or resident of the United States, as the case may be, for such taxable year.

(2) EXCEPTION.—

(A) IN GENERAL.—In the case of an individual described in any of the following subparagraphs of this paragraph, a day of physical presence in the United States shall be disregarded if the individual is performing services in the United States on such day for an employer. The preceding sentence shall not apply if—

(i) such employer is related (within the meaning of section 267 and 707) to such individual, or

(ii) such employer fails to meet such requirements as the Secretary may prescribe by regulations to prevent the avoidance of the purposes of this paragraph.

Not more than 30 days during any calendar year may be disregarded under this subparagraph.

(B) INDIVIDUALS WITH TIES TO OTHER COUNTRIES.—An individual is described in this subparagraph if—

(i) the individual becomes (not later than the close of a reasonable period after loss of United States citizenship or termination of residency) a citizen or resident of the country in which—

(I) such individual was born,

(II) if such individual is married, such individual's spouse was born, or

(III) either of such individual's parents were born, and

(ii) the individual becomes fully liable for income tax in such country.

(C) MINIMAL PRIOR PHYSICAL PRESENCE IN THE UNITED STATES.—An individual is described in this subparagraph if, for each year in the 10-year period ending on the date of loss of United States citizenship or termination of residency, the individual was physically present in the United States for 30 days or less. The rule of section 7701(b)(3)(D) shall apply for purposes of this subparagraph.

Amendments

• **2005, Gulf Opportunity Zone Act of 2005 (P.L. 109-135)**

P.L. 109-135, § 403(v)(1):

Amended Code Sec. 877(g)(2)(C) by striking "section 7701(b)(3)(D)(ii)" and inserting "section 7701(b)(3)(D)". **Effective** as if included in the provision of the American Jobs Creation Act of 2004 (P.L. 108-357) to which it relates [**effective** for individuals who expatriate after 6-3-2004.—CCH].

• **2004, American Jobs Creation Act of 2004 (P.L. 108-357)**

P.L. 108-357, § 804(c):

Amended Code Sec. 877 by adding at the end a new subsection (g). **Effective** for individuals who expatriate after 6-3-2004.

[Sec. 877(h)]

(h) TERMINATION.—This section shall not apply to any individual whose expatriation date (as defined in section 877A(g)(3)) is on or after the date of the enactment of this subsection.

Amendments

• **2008, Heroes Earnings Assistance and Relief Tax Act of 2008 (P.L. 110-245)**

P.L. 110-245, § 301(d):

Amended Code Sec. 877 by adding at the end a new subsection (h). **Effective** for any individual whose expatriation date (as so defined) is on or after 6-17-2008.

[Sec. 877A]

SEC. 877A. TAX RESPONSIBILITIES OF EXPATRIATION.

[Sec. 877A(a)]

(a) GENERAL RULES.—For purposes of this subtitle—

(1) MARK TO MARKET.—All property of a covered expatriate shall be treated as sold on the day before the expatriation date for its fair market value.

(2) RECOGNITION OF GAIN OR LOSS.—In the case of any sale under paragraph (1)—

(A) notwithstanding any other provision of this title, any gain arising from such sale shall be taken into account for the taxable year of the sale, and

(B) any loss arising from such sale shall be taken into account for the taxable year of the sale to the extent otherwise provided by this title, except that section 1091 shall not apply to any such loss.

Proper adjustment shall be made in the amount of any gain or loss subsequently realized for gain or loss taken into account under the preceding sentence, determined without regard to paragraph (3).

(3) EXCLUSION FOR CERTAIN GAIN.—

(A) IN GENERAL.—The amount which would (but for this paragraph) be includible in the gross income of any individual by reason of paragraph (1) shall be reduced (but not below zero) by $600,000.

(B) ADJUSTMENT FOR INFLATION.—

(i) IN GENERAL.—In the case of any taxable year beginning in a calendar year after 2008, the dollar amount in subparagraph (A) shall be increased by an amount equal to—

INCOME TAX—NONRESIDENT ALIENS

(I) such dollar amount, multiplied by

(II) the cost-of-living adjustment determined under section 1(f)(3) for the calendar year in which the taxable year begins, by substituting "calendar year 2007" for "calendar year 2016" in subparagraph (A)(ii) thereof.

(ii) ROUNDING.—If any amount as adjusted under clause (i) is not a multiple of $1,000, such amount shall be rounded to the nearest multiple of $1,000.

Amendments

• **2017, Tax Cuts and Jobs Act (P.L. 115-97)**

P.L. 115-97, §11002(d)(1)(BB):

Amended Code Sec. 877A(a)(3)(B)(i)(II) by striking "for 'calendar year 1992' in subparagraph (B)" and inserting "for 'calendar year 2016' in subparagraph (A)(ii)". **Effective** for tax years beginning after 12-31-2017.

[Sec. 877A(b)]

(b) ELECTION TO DEFER TAX.—

(1) IN GENERAL.—If the taxpayer elects the application of this subsection with respect to any property treated as sold by reason of subsection (a), the time for payment of the additional tax attributable to such property shall be extended until the due date of the return for the taxable year in which such property is disposed of (or, in the case of property disposed of in a transaction in which gain is not recognized in whole or in part, until such other date as the Secretary may prescribe).

(2) DETERMINATION OF TAX WITH RESPECT TO PROPERTY.—For purposes of paragraph (1), the additional tax attributable to any property is an amount which bears the same ratio to the additional tax imposed by this chapter for the taxable year solely by reason of subsection (a) as the gain taken into account under subsection (a) with respect to such property bears to the total gain taken into account under subsection (a) with respect to all property to which subsection (a) applies.

(3) TERMINATION OF EXTENSION.—The due date for payment of tax may not be extended under this subsection later than the due date for the return of tax imposed by this chapter for the taxable year which includes the date of death of the expatriate (or, if earlier, the time that the security provided with respect to the property fails to meet the requirements of paragraph (4), unless the taxpayer corrects such failure within the time specified by the Secretary).

(4) SECURITY.—

(A) IN GENERAL.—No election may be made under paragraph (1) with respect to any property unless adequate security is provided with respect to such property.

(B) ADEQUATE SECURITY.—For purposes of subparagraph (A), security with respect to any property shall be treated as adequate security if—

(i) it is a bond which is furnished to, and accepted by, the Secretary, which is conditioned on the payment of tax (and interest thereon), and which meets the requirements of section 6325, or

(ii) it is another form of security for such payment (including letters of credit) that meets such requirements as the Secretary may prescribe.

(5) WAIVER OF CERTAIN RIGHTS.—No election may be made under paragraph (1) unless the taxpayer makes an irrevocable waiver of any right under any treaty of the United States which would preclude assessment or collection of any tax imposed by reason of this section.

(6) ELECTIONS.—An election under paragraph (1) shall only apply to property described in the election and, once made, is irrevocable.

(7) INTEREST.—For purposes of section 6601, the last date for the payment of tax shall be determined without regard to the election under this subsection.

[Sec. 877A(c)]

(c) EXCEPTION FOR CERTAIN PROPERTY.—Subsection (a) shall not apply to—

(1) any deferred compensation item (as defined in subsection (d)(4)),

(2) any specified tax deferred account (as defined in subsection (e)(2)), and

(3) any interest in a nongrantor trust (as defined in subsection (f)(3)).

[Sec. 877A(d)]

(d) TREATMENT OF DEFERRED COMPENSATION ITEMS.—

(1) WITHHOLDING ON ELIGIBLE DEFERRED COMPENSATION ITEMS.—

(A) IN GENERAL.—In the case of any eligible deferred compensation item, the payor shall deduct and withhold from any taxable payment to a covered expatriate with respect to such item a tax equal to 30 percent thereof.

(B) TAXABLE PAYMENT.—For purposes of subparagraph (A), the term "taxable payment" means with respect to a covered expatriate any payment to the extent it would be includible in the gross income of the covered expatriate if such expatriate continued to be subject to tax as a citizen or resident of the United States. A deferred compensation item shall be taken into account as a payment under the preceding sentence when such item would be so includible.

(2) OTHER DEFERRED COMPENSATION ITEMS.—In the case of any deferred compensation item which is not an eligible deferred compensation item—

(A)(i) with respect to any deferred compensation item to which clause (ii) does not apply, an amount equal to the present value of the covered expatriate's accrued benefit shall be treated as having been received by such individual on the day before the expatriation date as a distribution under the plan, and

(ii) with respect to any deferred compensation item referred to in paragraph (4)(D), the rights of the covered expatriate to such item shall be treated as becoming transferable and not subject to a substantial risk of forfeiture on the day before the expatriation date,

(B) no early distribution tax shall apply by reason of such treatment, and

(C) appropriate adjustments shall be made to subsequent distributions from the plan to reflect such treatment.

(3) ELIGIBLE DEFERRED COMPENSATION ITEMS.—For purposes of this subsection, the term "eligible deferred compensation item" means any deferred compensation item with respect to which—

(A) the payor of such item is—

(i) a United States person, or

(ii) a person who is not a United States person but who elects to be treated as a United States person for purposes of paragraph (1) and meets such requirements as the Secretary may provide to ensure that the payor will meet the requirements of paragraph (1), and

(B) the covered expatriate—

INCOME TAX—NONRESIDENT ALIENS

(i) notifies the payor of his status as a covered expatriate, and

(ii) makes an irrevocable waiver of any right to claim any reduction under any treaty with the United States in withholding on such item.

(4) DEFERRED COMPENSATION ITEM.—For purposes of this subsection, the term "deferred compensation item" means—

(A) any interest in a plan or arrangement described in section 219(g)(5),

(B) any interest in a foreign pension plan or similar retirement arrangement or program,

(C) any item of deferred compensation, and

(D) any property, or right to property, which the individual is entitled to receive in connection with the performance of services to the extent not previously taken into account under section 83 or in accordance with section 83.

(5) EXCEPTION.—Paragraphs (1) and (2) shall not apply to any deferred compensation item to the extent attributable to services performed outside the United States while the covered expatriate was not a citizen or resident of the United States.

(6) SPECIAL RULES.—

(A) APPLICATION OF WITHHOLDING RULES.—Rules similar to the rules of subchapter B of chapter 3 shall apply for purposes of this subsection.

(B) APPLICATION OF TAX.—Any item subject to the withholding tax imposed under paragraph (1) shall be subject to tax under section 871.

(C) COORDINATION WITH OTHER WITHHOLDING REQUIREMENTS.—Any item subject to withholding under paragraph (1) shall not be subject to withholding under section 1441 or chapter 24.

[Sec. 877A(e)]

(e) TREATMENT OF SPECIFIED TAX DEFERRED ACCOUNTS.—

(1) ACCOUNT TREATED AS DISTRIBUTED.—In the case of any interest in a specified tax deferred account held by a covered expatriate on the day before the expatriation date—

(A) the covered expatriate shall be treated as receiving a distribution of his entire interest in such account on the day before the expatriation date,

(B) no early distribution tax shall apply by reason of such treatment, and

(C) appropriate adjustments shall be made to subsequent distributions from the account to reflect such treatment.

(2) SPECIFIED TAX DEFERRED ACCOUNT.—For purposes of paragraph (1), the term "specified tax deferred account" means an individual retirement plan (as defined in section 7701(a)(37)) other than any arrangement described in subsection (k) or (p) of section 408, a qualified tuition program (as defined in section 529), a qualified ABLE program (as defined in section 529A), a Coverdell education savings account (as defined in section 530), a health savings account (as defined in section 223), and an Archer MSA (as defined in section 220).

Amendments

• 2014, Stephen Beck, Jr., Achieving a Better Life Experience Act of 2014 (P.L. 113-295)

P.L. 113-295, § 102(e)(2)(A), Division B:

Amended Code Sec. 877A(e)(2) by inserting "a qualified ABLE program (as defined in section 529A)," after "529),". **Effective** for tax years beginning after 12-31-2014.

[Sec. 877A(f)]

(f) SPECIAL RULES FOR NONGRANTOR TRUSTS.—

(1) IN GENERAL.—In the case of a distribution (directly or indirectly) of any property from a nongrantor trust to a covered expatriate—

(A) the trustee shall deduct and withhold from such distribution an amount equal to 30 percent of the taxable portion of the distribution, and

(B) if the fair market value of such property exceeds its adjusted basis in the hands of the trust, gain shall be recognized to the trust as if such property were sold to the expatriate at its fair market value.

(2) TAXABLE PORTION.—For purposes of this subsection, the term "taxable portion" means, with respect to any distribution, that portion of the distribution which would be includible in the gross income of the covered expatriate if such expatriate continued to be subject to tax as a citizen or resident of the United States.

(3) NONGRANTOR TRUST.—For purposes of this subsection, the term "nongrantor trust" means the portion of any trust that the individual is not considered the owner of under subpart E of part I of subchapter J. The determination under the preceding sentence shall be made immediately before the expatriation date.

(4) SPECIAL RULES RELATING TO WITHHOLDING.—For purposes of this subsection—

(A) rules similar to the rules of subsection (d)(6) shall apply, and

(B) the covered expatriate shall be treated as having waived any right to claim any reduction under any treaty with the United States in withholding on any distribution to which paragraph (1)(A) applies unless the covered expatriate agrees to such other treatment as the Secretary determines appropriate.

(5) APPLICATION.—This subsection shall apply to a nongrantor trust only if the covered expatriate was a beneficiary of the trust on the day before the expatriation date.

[Sec. 877A(g)]

(g) DEFINITIONS AND SPECIAL RULES RELATING TO EXPATRIATION.—For purposes of this section—

(1) COVERED EXPATRIATE.—

(A) IN GENERAL.—The term "covered expatriate" means an expatriate who meets the requirements of subparagraph (A), (B), or (C) of section 877(a)(2).

(B) EXCEPTIONS.—An individual shall not be treated as meeting the requirements of subparagraph (A) or (B) of section 877(a)(2) if—

(i) the individual—

(I) became at birth a citizen of the United States and a citizen of another country and, as of the expatriation date, continues to be a citizen of, and is taxed as a resident of, such other country, and

(II) has been a resident of the United States (as defined in section 7701(b)(1)(A)(ii)) for not more than 10 taxable years during the 15-taxable year period ending with the taxable year during which the expatriation date occurs, or

(ii)(I) the individual's relinquishment of United States citizenship occurs before such individual attains age $18^{1}/_{2}$, and

INCOME TAX—NONRESIDENT ALIENS

(II) the individual has been a resident of the United States (as so defined) for not more than 10 taxable years before the date of relinquishment.

(C) COVERED EXPATRIATES ALSO SUBJECT TO TAX AS CITIZENS OR RESIDENTS.—In the case of any covered expatriate who is subject to tax as a citizen or resident of the United States for any period beginning after the expatriation date, such individual shall not be treated as a covered expatriate during such period for purposes of subsections (d)(1) and (f) and section 2801.

(2) EXPATRIATE.—The term "expatriate" means—

(A) any United States citizen who relinquishes his citizenship, and

(B) any long-term resident of the United States who ceases to be a lawful permanent resident of the United States (within the meaning of section 7701(b)(6)).

(3) EXPATRIATION DATE.—The term "expatriation date" means—

(A) the date an individual relinquishes United States citizenship, or

(B) in the case of a long-term resident of the United States, the date on which the individual ceases to be a lawful permanent resident of the United States (within the meaning of section 7701(b)(6)).

(4) RELINQUISHMENT OF CITIZENSHIP.—A citizen shall be treated as relinquishing his United States citizenship on the earliest of—

(A) the date the individual renounces his United States nationality before a diplomatic or consular officer of the United States pursuant to paragraph (5) of section 349(a) of the Immigration and Nationality Act (8 U.S.C. 1481(a)(5)),

(B) the date the individual furnishes to the United States Department of State a signed statement of voluntary relinquishment of United States nationality confirming the performance of an act of expatriation specified in paragraph (1), (2), (3), or (4) of section 349(a) of the Immigration and Nationality Act (8 U.S.C. 1481(a)(1)-(4)),

(C) the date the United States Department of State issues to the individual a certificate of loss of nationality, or

(D) the date a court of the United States cancels a naturalized citizen's certificate of naturalization.

Subparagraph (A) or (B) shall not apply to any individual unless the renunciation or voluntary relinquishment is subsequently approved by the issuance to the individual of a certificate of loss of nationality by the United States Department of State.

(5) LONG-TERM RESIDENT.—The term "long-term resident" has the meaning given to such term by section 877(e)(2).

(6) EARLY DISTRIBUTION TAX.—The term "early distribution tax" means any increase in tax imposed under section 72(t), 220(f)(4), 223(f)(4), 409A(a)(1)(B), 529(c)(6), 529A(c)(3), or 530(d)(4).

Amendments

• 2018, Tax Technical Corrections Act of 2018 (P.L. 115-141)

P.L. 115-141, §401(a)(154), Div. U:
Amended Code Sec. 877A(g)(6) by striking "220(e)(4)" and inserting "220(f)(4)". **Effective** 3-23-2018.

• 2014, Stephen Beck, Jr., Achieving a Better Life Experience Act of 2014 (P.L. 113-295)

P.L. 113-295, §102(e)(2)(B), Division B:
Amended Code Sec. 877A(g)(6) by inserting "529A(c)(3)," after "529(c)(6),". **Effective** for tax years beginning after 12-31-2014.

[Sec. 877A(h)]

(h) OTHER RULES.—

(1) TERMINATION OF DEFERRALS, ETC.—In the case of any covered expatriate, notwithstanding any other provision of this title—

(A) any time period for acquiring property which would result in the reduction in the amount of gain recognized with respect to property disposed of by the taxpayer shall terminate on the day before the expatriation date, and

(B) any extension of time for payment of tax shall cease to apply on the day before the expatriation date and the unpaid portion of such tax shall be due and payable at the time and in the manner prescribed by the Secretary.

(2) STEP-UP IN BASIS.—Solely for purposes of determining any tax imposed by reason of subsection (a), property which was held by an individual on the date the individual first became a resident of the United States (within the meaning of section 7701(b)) shall be treated as having a basis on such date of not less than the fair market value of such property on such date. The preceding sentence shall not apply if the individual elects not to have such sentence apply. Such an election, once made, shall be irrevocable.

(3) COORDINATION WITH SECTION 684.—If the expatriation of any individual would result in the recognition of gain under section 684, this section shall be applied after the application of section 684.

[Sec. 877A(i)]

(i) REGULATIONS.—The Secretary shall prescribe such regulations as may be necessary or appropriate to carry out the purposes of this section.

Amendments

• 2008, Heroes Earnings Assistance and Relief Tax Act of 2008 (P.L. 110-245)

P.L. 110-245, §301(a):
Amended subpart A of part II of subchapter N of chapter 1 by inserting after Code Sec. 877 a new Code Sec. 877A. **Effective** for any individual whose expatriation date (as so defined) is on or after 6-17-2008.

[Sec. 878]

SEC. 878. FOREIGN EDUCATIONAL, CHARITABLE, AND CERTAIN OTHER EXEMPT ORGANIZATIONS.

For special provisions relating to foreign educational, charitable, and other exempt organizations, see sections 512(a) and 4948.

Amendments

• 1969, Tax Reform Act of 1969 (P.L. 91-172)

P.L. 91-172, §101(j)(20):
Amended Code Sec. 878. **Effective** for tax years beginning after 12-31-69. Prior to amendment, Code Sec. 878 read as follows:
For special provisions relating to unrelated business income of foreign educational, charitable, and other exempt trusts, see section 512(a).

• 1966, Foreign Investors Tax Act of 1966 (P.L. 89-809)

P.L. 89-809, §103(f)(1):
Redesignated former Code Sec. 877 as Sec. 878. **Effective** 1-1-67.

[Sec. 879]

SEC. 879. TAX TREATMENT OF CERTAIN COMMUNITY INCOME IN THE CASE OF NONRESIDENT ALIEN INDIVIDUALS.

[Sec. 879(a)]

(a) GENERAL RULE.—In the case of a married couple 1 or both of whom are nonresident alien individuals and who have community income for the taxable year, such community income shall be treated as follows:

(1) Earned income (within the meaning of section 911(d)(2)), other than trade or business income and a partner's distributive share of partnership income, shall be treated as the income of the spouse who rendered the personal services,

INCOME TAX—FOREIGN CORPORATIONS

(2) Trade or business income, and a partner's distributive share of partnership income, shall be treated as provided in section 1402(a)(5),

(3) Community income not described in paragraph (1) or (2) which is derived from the separate property (as determined under the applicable community property law) of one spouse shall be treated as the income of such spouse, and

(4) All other such community income shall be treated as provided in the applicable community property law.

Amendments

• **1984, Deficit Reduction Act of 1984 (P.L. 98-369)**

P.L. 98-369, §139(a):

Amended the language preceding Code Sec. 879(a)(1). **Effective** for tax years beginning after 12-31-84. Prior to amendment, it read as follows:

(a) GENERAL RULE.—In the case of a citizen or resident of the United States who is married to a nonresident alien individual and who has community income for the taxable year, such community income shall be treated as follows:

P.L. 98-369, §139(b)(1):

Amended the heading of Code Sec. 879. **Effective** for tax years beginning after 12-31-84. Prior to amendment, it read as follows:

Sec. 879. Tax Treatment of Certain Community Income in the Case of a Resident or Citizen of the United States Who Is Married to a Nonresident Alien Individual.

• **1981, Economic Recovery Tax Act of 1981 (P.L. 97-34)**

P.L. 97-34, §111(b)(4):

Amended Code Sec. 879(a)(1) by striking out "section 911(b)" and inserting in lieu thereof "section 911(d)(2)". **Effective** with respect to tax years beginning after 12-31-81.

• **1976, Tax Reform Act of 1976 (P.L. 94-455)**

P.L. 94-455, §1012(b)(1):

Added Code Sec. 879(a). **Effective** for tax years beginning after 12-31-76.

[Sec. 879(b)]

(b) EXCEPTION WHERE ELECTION UNDER SECTION 6013(g) IS IN EFFECT.—Subsection (a) shall not apply for any taxable year for which an election under subsection (g) or (h) of section 6013 (relating to election to treat nonresident alien individual as resident of the United States) is in effect.

Amendments

• **1976, Tax Reform Act of 1976 (P.L. 94-455)**

P.L. 94-455, §1012(b)(1):

Added Code Sec. 879(b). **Effective** for tax years beginning after 12-31-76.

[Sec. 879(c)]

(c) DEFINITIONS AND SPECIAL RULES.—For purposes of this section—

(1) COMMUNITY INCOME.—The term "community income" means income which, under applicable community property laws, is treated as community income.

(2) COMMUNITY PROPERTY LAWS.—The term "community property laws" means the community property laws of a State, a foreign country, or a possession of the United States.

(3) DETERMINATION OF MARITAL STATUS.—The determination of marital status shall be made under section 7703(a).

Amendments

• **1986, Tax Reform Act of 1986 (P.L. 99-514)**

P.L. 99-514, §1301(j)(9):

Amended Code Sec. 879(c)(3) by striking out "143(a)" and inserting in lieu thereof "7703(a)". **Effective** for bonds issued after 8-15-86. For transitional rules, see Act Secs. 1312-1318, reproduced under the amendment notes for Code Sec. 103.

• **1976, Tax Reform Act of 1976 (P.L. 94-455)**

P.L. 94-455, §1012(b)(1):

Added Code Sec. 879(c). **Effective** for tax years beginning after 12-31-76.

Subpart B—Foreign Corporations

Sec. 881.	Tax on income of foreign corporations not connected with United States business.
Sec. 882.	Tax on income of foreign corporations connected with United States business.
Sec. 883.	Exclusions from gross income.
Sec. 884.	Branch profits tax.
Sec. 885.	Cross references.

[Sec. 881]

SEC. 881. TAX ON INCOME OF FOREIGN CORPORATIONS NOT CONNECTED WITH UNITED STATES BUSINESS.

[Sec. 881(a)]

(a) IMPOSITION OF TAX.—Except as provided in subsection (c), there is hereby imposed for each taxable year a tax of 30 percent of the amount received from sources within the United States by a foreign corporation as—

(1) interest (other than original issue discount as defined in section 1273), dividends, rents, salaries, wages, premiums, annuities, compensations, remunerations, emoluments, and other fixed or determinable annual or periodical gains, profits, and income,

(2) gains described in section 631(b) or (c),

(3) in the case of—

(A) a sale or exchange of an original issue discount obligation, the amount of the original issue discount accruing while such obligation was held by the foreign corporation (to the extent such discount was not theretofore taken into account under subparagraph (B)), and

(B) a payment on an original issue discount obligation, an amount equal to the original issue discount accruing while such obligation was held by the foreign corporation (except that such original issue discount shall be taken into account under this subparagraph only to the extent such discount was not theretofore taken into account under this subparagraph and only to the extent that the tax thereon does not exceed the payment less the tax imposed by paragraph (1) thereon), and

(4) gains from the sale or exchange after October 4, 1966, of patents, copyrights, secret processes and formulas, good will, trademarks, trade brands, franchises, and other like property, or of any interest in any such property, to the extent such gains are from payments which are contingent on the productivity, use, or disposition of the property or interest sold or exchanged,

but only to the extent the amount so received is not effectively connected with the conduct of a trade or business within the United States.

Amendments

• **1986, Tax Reform Act of 1986 (P.L. 99-514)**

P.L. 99-514, §1211(b)(6):

Amended Code Sec. 881(a) by striking out the phrase "or from payments which are treated as being so contingent under section 871(e)," from the end of the paragraph. **Effective**, generally, for tax years beginning after 12-31-86. However, see Act Sec. 1211(c)(2), below, for special rule.

P.L. 99-514, §1211(c)(2), provides:

(2) SPECIAL RULE FOR FOREIGN PERSONS.—In the case of any foreign person other than any controlled foreign corporations (within the meaning of section 957(a) of the Internal Revenue Code of 1954), the amendments made by this section shall apply to transactions entered into after March 18, 1986.

INCOME TAX—FOREIGN CORPORATIONS

P.L. 99-514, §1810(e)(2)(B):

Amended Code Sec. 881(a)(3). **Effective** as if included in the provision of P.L. 98-369 to which it relates. Prior to amendment, Code Sec. 881(a)(3) read as follows:

(3) in the case of—

(A) a sale or exchange of an original issue discount obligation, the amount of any gain not in excess of the original issue discount accruing while such obligation was held by the foreign corporation (to the extent such discount was not therefore taken into account under subparagraph (B)), and

(B) the payment of interest on an original issue discount obligation, an amount equal to the original issue discount accrued on such obligation since the last payment of interest thereon (except that such original issue discount shall be taken into account under this subparagraph only to the extent that the tax thereon does not exceed the interest payment less the tax imposed by paragraph (1) thereon), and

- **1984, Deficit Reduction Act of 1984 (P.L. 98-369)**

P.L. 98-369, §42(a)(10):

Amended Code Sec. 881(a)(1) by striking out "section 1232(b)" and inserting in lieu thereof "section 1273". **Effective** for tax years ending after 7-18-84.

P.L. 98-369, §127(b)(2):

Amended Code Sec. 881(a) by striking out "There" and inserting in lieu thereof "Except as provided in subsection (c), there". **Effective** for interest received after 7-18-84, in tax years ending after such date. However, see Act Sec. 127(g), below, for special rules.

P.L. 98-369, §127(g), as amended by P.L. 100-647, §6128(a), provides:

(3) Special Rule for Certain United States Affiliate Obligations.—

(A) In General.—For purposes of the Internal Revenue Code of 1954, payments of interest on a United States affiliate obligation to an applicable CFC in existence on or before June 22, 1984, shall be treated as payments to a resident of the country in which the applicable CFC is incorporated.

(B) Exception.—Subparagraph (A) shall not apply to any applicable CFC which did not meet requirements which are based on the principles set forth in Revenue Rulings 69-501, 69-377, 70-645, and 73-110 as such principles are applied in Revenue Ruling 86-6, except that the maximum debt-to-equity ratio described in such Revenue Rulings shall be increased from 5-to-1 to 25-to-1.

(C) Definitions.—

(i) The term "applicable CFC" has the meaning given such term by section 121(b)(2)(D) of this Act, except that such section shall be applied by substituting "the date of interest payment" for "March 31, 1984," in clause (i) thereof.

(ii) The term "United States affiliate obligation" means an obligation described in section 121(b)(2)(F) of this Act which was issued before June 22, 1984.

P.L. 98-369, §128(b)(1):

Amended Code Sec. 881(a)(3). **Effective** for payments made on or after 9-16-84, with respect to obligations issued after 3-31-72. Prior to amendment, it read as follows:

(3) in the case of—

(A) bonds or other evidences of indebtedness issued after September 28, 1965, and before April 1, 1972, amounts which under section 1232(a)(2)(B) are considered as ordinary income, and, in the case of corporate obligations issued after May 27, 1969, and before April 1, 1972, amounts which would be so considered but for the fact the obligations were issued after May 27, 1969,

(B) bonds or other evidences of indebtedness issued after March 31, 1972, and payable more than 6 months from the date of original issue (without regard to the period held by the taxpayer), amounts which under section 1232(a)(2)(B) would be considered as ordinary income but for the fact such obligations were issued after May 27, 1969, and

(C) the payment of interest on an obligation described in subparagraph (B), an amount equal to the original issue discount (but not in excess of such interest less the tax imposed by paragraph (1) thereon) accrued on such obligation since the last payment of interest thereon, and

- **1976, Tax Reform Act of 1976 (P.L. 94-455)**

P.L. 94-455, §1901(b)(3)(I):

Substituted "ordinary income" for "gain from the sale or exchange of property which is not a capital asset" in Code Sec. 881(a)(3)(A) and (B). **Effective** for tax years beginning after 12-31-76.

- **1971, Revenue Act of 1971 (P.L. 92-178)**

P.L. 92-178, §313(a):

Added "(other than original issue discount as defined in section 1232(b))" after "interest" in Code Sec. 881(a)(1). **Effective** for tax years beginning after 12-31-66.

P.L. 92-178, §313(c):

Amended Code Sec. 881(a)(3). **Effective** for tax years ending after 12-31-66. Prior to amendment, Code Sec. 881(a)(3) read as follows:

(3) in the case of bonds or other evidences of indebtedness issued after September 28, 1965, amounts which under section 1232 are considered as gains from the sale or exchange of property which is not a capital asset, and

- **1966, Foreign Investors Tax Act of 1966 (P.L. 89-809)**

P.L. 89-809, §104(a):

Amended Code Sec. 881(a). Prior to amendment, Code Sec. 881(a) read as follows:

SEC. 881. TAX ON FOREIGN CORPORATIONS NOT ENGAGED IN BUSINESS IN UNITED STATES.

(a) Imposition of Tax.—In the case of every foreign corporation not engaged in trade or business within the United States, there is hereby imposed for each taxable year, in lieu of the taxes imposed by section 11, a tax of 30 percent of the amount received from sources within the United States as interest (except interest on deposits with persons carrying on the banking business), dividends, rents, salaries, wages, premiums, annuities, compensations, remunerations, emoluments, or other fixed or determinable annual or periodical gains, profits, and income (including amounts described in section 631(b) and (c) which are considered to be gains from the sale or exchange of capital assets).

[Sec. 881(b)]

(b) EXCEPTION FOR CERTAIN POSSESSIONS.—

(1) GUAM, AMERICAN SAMOA, THE NORTHERN MARIANA ISLANDS, AND THE VIRGIN ISLANDS.—For purposes of this section and section 884, a corporation created or organized in Guam, American Samoa, the Northern Mariana Islands, or the Virgin Islands or under the law of any such possession shall not be treated as a foreign corporation for any taxable year if—

(A) at all times during such taxable year less than 25 percent in value of the stock of such corporation is beneficially owned (directly or indirectly) by foreign persons,

(B) at least 65 percent of the gross income of such corporation is shown to the satisfaction of the Secretary to be effectively connected with the conduct of a trade or business in such a possession or the United States for the 3-year period ending with the close of the taxable year of such corporation (or for such part of such period as the corporation or any predecessor had been in existence), and

(C) no substantial part of the income of such corporation is used (directly or indirectly) to satisfy obligations to persons who are not bona fide residents of such a possession or the United States.

(2) COMMONWEALTH OF PUERTO RICO.—

(A) IN GENERAL.—If dividends are received during a taxable year by a corporation—

(i) created or organized in, or under the law of, the Commonwealth of Puerto Rico, and

(ii) with respect to which the requirements of subparagraphs (A), (B), and (C) of paragraph (1) are met for the taxable year,

subsection (a) shall be applied for such taxable year by substituting "10 percent" for "30 percent".

(B) APPLICABILITY.—If, on or after the date of the enactment of this paragraph, an increase in the rate of the Commonwealth of Puerto Rico's withholding tax which is generally applicable to dividends paid to United States corporations not engaged in a trade or business in the Commonwealth to a rate greater than 10 percent takes effect, this paragraph shall not apply to dividends received on or after the effective date of the increase.

(3) DEFINITIONS.—

(A) FOREIGN PERSON.—For purposes of paragraph (1), the term "foreign person" means any person other than—

(i) a United States person, or

(ii) a person who would be a United States person if references to the United States in section 7701 included references to a possession of the United States.

(B) INDIRECT OWNERSHIP RULES.—For purposes of paragraph (1), the rules of section 318(a)(2) shall apply except that "5 percent" shall be substituted for "50 percent" in subparagraph (C) thereof.

Amendments

- **2004, American Jobs Creation Act of 2004 (P.L. 108-357)**

P.L. 108-357, §420(a):

Amended Code Sec. 881(b) by redesignating paragraph (2) as paragraph (3) and by inserting after paragraph (1) a new paragraph (2). **Effective** for dividends paid after 10-22-2004.

P.L. 108-357, §420(c)(1):

Amended the heading of Code Sec. 881(b) by striking "GUAM AND VIRGIN ISLANDS CORPORATIONS" and inserting "POSSESSIONS". **Effective** for dividends paid after 10-22-2004.

INCOME TAX—FOREIGN CORPORATIONS

P.L. 108-357, § 420(c)(2):

Amended the heading of Code Sec. 881(b)(1) by striking "IN GENERAL" and inserting "GUAM, AMERICAN SAMOA, THE NORTHERN MARIANA ISLANDS, AND THE VIRGIN ISLANDS". **Effective** for dividends paid after 10-22-2004.

• **1986, Tax Reform Act of 1986 (P.L. 99-514)**

P.L. 99-514, § 1273(b)(1):

Amended Code Sec. 881(b) by striking out paragraphs (1) and (2) and inserting in lieu thereof paragraph (1). **Effective**, generally, for tax years beginning after 12-31-86. For special rules, see Act Sec. 1276(b)-(e), under the amendment notes at Code Sec. 48. Prior to amendment, Code Sec. 881(b)(1) and (2) read as follows:

(1) IN GENERAL.—For purposes of this section a corporation created or organized in Guam or the Virgin Islands or under the law of Guam or the Virgin Islands shall not be treated as a foreign corporation for any taxable year if—

(A) at all times during such taxable year less than 25 percent in value of the stock of such corporation is owned (directly or indirectly) by foreign persons, and

(B) at least 20 percent of the gross income of such corporation is shown to the satisfaction of the Secretary to have been derived from sources within Guam or the Virgin Islands (as the case may be) for the 3-year period ending with the close of the preceding taxable year of such corporaton (or for such part of such period as the corporation has been in existence).

(2) PARAGRAPH (1) NOT TO APPLY TO TAX IMPOSED IN GUAM.—For purposes of applying this subsection with respect to income tax liability incurred to Guam—

(A) paragraph (1) shall not apply, and

(B) for purposes of this section, the term "foreign corporation" does not include a corporation created or organized in Guam or under the law of Guam.

P.L. 99-514, § 1273(b)(2)(A):

Amended Code Sec. 881(b) by redesignating paragraph (3) as paragraph (2) and by striking out paragraph (4). **Effective**, generally, for tax years beginning after 12-31-86. For special rules, see Act Sec. 1276(b)-(e) under the amendment notes at Code Sec. 48. Prior to amendment, Code Sec. 881(b)(4) read as follows:

(4) CROSS REFERENCE.—

For tax imposed in the Virgin Islands, see sections 934 and 934A.

P.L. 99-514, § 1899A(22):

Amended Code Sec. 881(b)(2)(A) by striking out "Paragraph" and inserting in lieu thereof "paragraph". **Effective** 10-22-86.

• **1984, Deficit Reduction Act of 1984 (P.L. 98-369)**

P.L. 98-369, § 130(a):

Amended Code Sec. 881(b). **Effective** for payments made after 3-1-84, in tax years ending after such date. Prior to amendment, it read as follows:

(b) Exception for Guam Corporations.—For purposes of this section, the term "foreign corporation" does not include a corporation created or organized in Guam or under the law of Guam.

• **1972 (P.L. 92-606)**

P.L. 92-606, § 1(e)(1):

Redesignated former Code Sec. 881(b) as Code Sec. 881(c) and added new Code Sec. 881(b). **Effective** for tax years beginning after 12-31-71.

[Sec. 881(c)]

(c) REPEAL OF TAX ON INTEREST OF FOREIGN CORPORATIONS RECEIVED FROM CERTAIN PORTFOLIO DEBT INVESTMENTS.—

(1) IN GENERAL.—In the case of any portfolio interest received by a foreign corporation from sources within the United States, no tax shall be imposed under paragraph (1) or (3) of subsection (a).

(2) PORTFOLIO INTEREST.—For purposes of this subsection, the term "portfolio interest" means any interest (including original issue discount) which—

(A) would be subject to tax under subsection (a) but for this subsection, and

(B) is paid on an obligation—

(i) which is in registered form, and

(ii) with respect to which—

(I) the person who would otherwise be required to deduct and withhold tax from such interest under section 1442(a) receives a statement which meets the requirements of section 871(h)(5) that the beneficial owner of the obligation is not a United States person, or

(II) the Secretary has determined that such a statement is not required in order to carry out the purposes of this subsection.

(3) PORTFOLIO INTEREST SHALL NOT INCLUDE INTEREST RECEIVED BY CERTAIN PERSONS.—For purposes of this subsection, the term "portfolio interest" shall not include any portfolio interest which—

(A) except in the case of interest paid on an obligation of the United States, is received by a bank on an extension of credit made pursuant to a loan agreement entered into in the ordinary course of its trade or business,

(B) is received by a 10-percent shareholder (within the meaning of section 871(h)(3)(B)), or

(C) is received by a controlled foreign corporation from a related person (within the meaning of section 864(d)(4)).

(4) PORTFOLIO INTEREST NOT TO INCLUDE CERTAIN CONTINGENT INTEREST.—For purposes of this subsection, the term "portfolio interest" shall not include any interest which is treated as not being portfolio interest under the rules of section 871(h)(4).

(5) SPECIAL RULES FOR CONTROLLED FOREIGN CORPORATIONS.—

(A) IN GENERAL.—In the case of any portfolio interest received by a controlled foreign corporation, the following provisions shall not apply:

(i) Subparagraph (A) of section 954(b)(3) (relating to exception where foreign base company income is less than 5 percent or $1,000,000).

(ii) Paragraph (4) of section 954(b) (relating to exception for certain income subject to high foreign taxes).

(iii) Clause (i) of section 954(c)(3)(A) (relating to certain income received from related persons).

(B) CONTROLLED FOREIGN CORPORATION.—For purposes of this subsection, the term "controlled foreign corporation" has the meaning given to such term by section 957(a).

(6) SECRETARY MAY CEASE APPLICATION OF THIS SUBSECTION.—Under rules similar to the rules of section 871(h)(6), the Secretary may provide that this subsection shall not apply to payments of interest described in section 871(h)(6).

(7) REGISTERED FORM.—For purposes of this subsection, the term "registered form" has the meaning give such term by section 163(f).

Amendments

• **2010, Hiring Incentives to Restore Employment Act (P.L. 111-147)**

P.L. 111-147, § 502(b)(2)(B):

Amended Code Sec. 881(c)(2). **Effective** for obligations issued after the date which is 2 years after 3-18-2010. Prior to amendment, Code Sec. 881(c)(2) read as follows:

(2) PORTFOLIO INTEREST.—For purposes of this subsection, the term "portfolio interest" means any interest (including original issue discount) which would be subject to tax under subsection (a) but for this subsection and which is described in any of the following subparagraphs:

(A) CERTAIN OBLIGATIONS WHICH ARE NOT REGISTERED.—Interest which is paid on any obligation which is described in section 871(h)(2)(A).

(B) CERTAIN REGISTERED OBLIGATIONS.—Interest which is paid on an obligation—

(i) which is in registered form, and

(ii) with respect to which the person who would otherwise be required to deduct and withhold tax from such interest under section 1442(a) receives a statement which meets the requirements of section 871(h)(5) that the beneficial owner of the obligation is not a United States person.

• **1993, Omnibus Budget Reconciliation Act of 1993 (P.L. 103-66)**

P.L. 103-66, § 13237(a)(2):

Amended Code Sec. 881(c) by redesignating paragraphs (4), (5), and (6) as paragraphs (5), (6), and (7), respectively, and by inserting after paragraph (3) a new paragraph (4). **Effective** for interest received after 12-31-93.

P.L. 103-66, § 13237(c)(2):

Amended Code Sec. 881(c)(2)(B)(ii) by striking "section 871(h)(4)" and inserting "section 871(h)(5)". **Effective** for interest received after 12-31-93.

P.L. 103-66, § 13237(c)(3):

Amended Code Sec. 881(c)(6), as redesignated by Act Sec. 13237(a)(2), by striking "section 871(h)(5)" each place it appears and inserting "section 871(h)(6)". **Effective** for interest received after 12-31-93.

INCOME TAX—FOREIGN CORPORATIONS

• **1988, Technical and Miscellaneous Revenue Act of 1988 (P.L. 100-647)**

P.L. 100-647, §1012(i)(17):

Amended Code Sec. 881(c)(4)(A) by striking out clauses (ii), (iii), (iv), and (v) and inserting in lieu thereof new clauses (ii)-(iii). **Effective** as if included in the provision of P.L. 99-514 to which it relates. Prior to amendment, Code Sec. 881(c)(4)(A)(ii)-(v) read as follows:

(ii) Paragraph (4) of section 954(b) (relating to corporations not formed or availed of to avoid tax).

(iii) Subparagraph (B) of section 954(c)(3) (relating to certain income derived in active conduct of trade or business).

(iv) Subparagraph (C) of section 954(c)(3) (relating to certain income derived by an insurance company).

• **1986, Tax Reform Act of 1986 (P.L. 99-514)**

P.L. 99-514, §1223(b)(2):

Amended Code Sec. 881(c)(4)(A)(i) by striking out "less than 10 percent" and inserting in lieu thereof "less than 5 percent or $1,000,000". **Effective** for tax years beginning after 12-31-86.

P.L. 99-514, §1810(d)(1)(B):

Amended Code Sec. 881(c)(2) by striking out "which is described in" in the matter preceding subparagraph (1) and inserting in lieu thereof "which would be subject to tax under subsection (a) but for this subsection and which is described in". **Effective** as if included in the provision of P.L. 98-369 to which it relates.

P.L. 99-514, §1810(d)(3)(C):

Amended Code Sec. 881(c)(2)(B)(ii) by striking out "has received" and inserting in lieu thereof "receives". **Effective** as if included in the provision of P.L. 98-369 to which it relates.

P.L. 99-514, §1899A(23):

Amended Code Sec. 881(c)(3)(C) by striking out "section 864(d)(4)." and inserting in lieu thereof "section 864(d)(4))." **Effective** 10-22-86.

• **1984, Deficit Reduction Act of 1984 (P.L. 98-369)**

P.L. 98-369, §127(b)(1):

Amended Code Sec. 881, as amended by this Act, by redesignating subsection (c) as subsection (d) and by adding after subsection (b) new subsection (c). **Effective** for interest received after 7-18-84, with respect to obligations issued after such date, in tax years ending after such date. However, see Act Sec. 127(g) following Code Sec. 881(a) for special rules.

[Sec. 881(d)]

(d) TAX NOT TO APPLY TO CERTAIN INTEREST AND DIVIDENDS.—No tax shall be imposed under paragraph (1) or (3) of subsection (a) on any amount described in section 871(i)(2).

Amendments

• **1986, Tax Reform Act of 1986 (P.L. 99-514)**

P.L. 99-514, §1214(c)(2):

Amended Code Sec. 881 by redesignating subsection (d) as subsection (e) and by inserting after subsection (c) new subsection (d). **Effective**, generally, for payments after 12-31-86. For special rules, see Act Sec. 1214(c)(2)-(4) under the amendment notes for Code Sec. 861.

[Sec. 881(e)]

(e) TAX NOT TO APPLY TO CERTAIN DIVIDENDS OF REGULATED INVESTMENT COMPANIES.—

(1) INTEREST-RELATED DIVIDENDS.—

(A) IN GENERAL.—Except as provided in subparagraph (B), no tax shall be imposed under paragraph (1) of subsection (a) on any interest-related dividend (as defined in section 871(k)(1)) received from a regulated investment company.

(B) EXCEPTION.—Subparagraph (A) shall not apply—

(i) to any dividend referred to in section 871(k)(1)(B), and

(ii) to any interest-related dividend received by a controlled foreign corporation (within the meaning of section 957(a)) to the extent such dividend is attributable to interest received by the regulated investment company from a person who is a related person (within the meaning of section 864(d)(4)) with respect to such controlled foreign corporation.

(C) TREATMENT OF DIVIDENDS RECEIVED BY CONTROLLED FOREIGN CORPORATIONS.—The rules of subsection (c)(5)(A) shall apply to any interest-related dividend received by a controlled foreign corporation (within the meaning of section 957(a)) to the extent such dividend is attributable to interest received by the regulated investment company which is described in clause (ii) of section 871(k)(1)(E) (and not described in clause (i) or (iii) of such section).

(2) SHORT-TERM CAPITAL GAIN DIVIDENDS.—No tax shall be imposed under paragraph (1) of subsection (a) on any short-term capital gain dividend (as defined in section 871(k)(2)) received from a regulated investment company.

Amendments

• **2005, Gulf Opportunity Zone Act of 2005 (P.L. 109-135)**

P.L. 109-135, §412(jj):

Amended Code Sec. 881(e)(1)(C) by inserting "interest-related dividend received by a controlled foreign corporation" after "shall apply to any". **Effective** 12-21-2005.

• **2004, American Jobs Creation Act of 2004 (P.L. 108-357)**

P.L. 108-357, §411(a)(2):

Amended Code Sec. 881 by redesignating subsection (e) as subsection (f) and by inserting after subsection (d) a new subsection (e). **Effective** for dividends with respect to tax years of regulated investment companies beginning after 12-31-2004.

[Sec. 881(f)]

(f) CROSS REFERENCE.—

For doubling of tax on corporations of certain foreign countries, see section 891.

For special rules for original issue discount, see section 871(g).

Amendments

• **2004, American Jobs Creation Act of 2004 (P.L. 108-357)**

P.L. 108-357, §411(a)(2):

Amended Code Sec. 881 by redesignating subsection (e) as subsection (f). **Effective** for dividends with respect to tax years of regulated investment companies beginning after 12-31-2004.

• **1986, Tax Reform Act of 1986 (P.L. 99-514)**

P.L. 99-514, §1214(c)(2):

Amended Code Sec. 881 by redesignating subsection (d) as subsection (e) and by inserting after subsection (c) new subsection (d). **Effective**, generally, for payments after 12-31-86 [see also P.L. 100-647, §1012(g)(1) following Code Sec. 861(d)]. However, see Act Sec. 1214(c)(2)-(4) under the amendment notes for Code Sec. 861 for special rules.

• **1984, Deficit Reduction Act of 1984 (P.L. 98-369)**

P.L. 98-369, §127(b)(1):

Amended Code Sec. 881, as amended by this Act, by redesignating subsection (c) as subsection (d). For the **effective** date, see the notes for P.L. 98-369 following Code Sec. 881(c).

P.L. 98-369, §128(b)(2):

Amended Code Sec. 881(c) (redesignated as (d) by Act Sec. 127(b)(1)). **Effective** for payments made on or after 9-16-84, with respect to obligations issued after 3-31-72. Prior to amendment, it read as follows:

(c) Doubling of Tax.—

For doubling of tax on corporations of certain foreign countries, see section 891.

• **1972 (P.L. 92-606)**

P.L. 92-606, §1(e)(1):

Redesignated former Code Sec. 881(b) as Code Sec. 881(c). **Effective** for tax years beginning after 12-31-71.

INCOME TAX—FOREIGN CORPORATIONS

[Sec. 882]

SEC. 882. TAX ON INCOME OF FOREIGN CORPORATIONS CONNECTED WITH UNITED STATES BUSINESS.

[Sec. 882(a)]

(a) IMPOSITION OF TAX.—

(1) IN GENERAL.—A foreign corporation engaged in trade or business within the United States during the taxable year shall be taxable as provided in section 11, 55, or 59A, on its taxable income which is effectively connected with the conduct of a trade or business within the United States.

(2) DETERMINATION OF TAXABLE INCOME.—In determining taxable income for purposes of paragraph (1), gross income includes only gross income which is effectively connected with the conduct of a trade or business within the United States.

(3) [CROSS-REFERENCE.—]

For special tax treatment of gain or loss from the disposition by a foreign corporation of a United States real property interest, see section 897.

Amendments

• **2022, Inflation Reduction Act of 2022 (P.L. 117-169)**

P.L. 117-169, §10101(a)(4)(E):

Amended Code Sec. 882(a)(1) by inserting ", 55," after "section 11". **Effective** for tax years beginning after 12-31-2022.

• **2017, Tax Cuts and Jobs Act (P.L. 115-97)**

P.L. 115-97, §12001(b)(14):

Amended Code Sec. 882(a)(1) by striking ", 55," following "section 11". **Effective** for tax years beginning after 12-31-2017.

P.L. 115-97, §13001(b)(2)(L):

Amended Code Sec. 882(a)(1), as amended by Act Sec. 12001, by striking "or 1201(a)" following "section 11". **Effective** for tax years beginning after 12-31-2017.

P.L. 115-97, §14401(d)(2):

Amended Code Sec. 882(a)(1), as amended by this Act, by inserting "or 59A," after "section 11,"[sic]. **Effective** for base erosion payments (as defined in Code Sec. 59A(d), as added by Act. Sec. 14401) paid or accrued in tax years beginning after 12-31-2017.

• **2014, Tax Technical Corrections Act of 2014 (P.L. 113-295)**

P.L. 113-295, §221(a)(12)(F), Division A:

Amended Code Sec. 882(a)(1) by striking ", 59A" following "section 11, 55". **Effective** generally 12-19-2014. For a special rule, see Act Sec. 221(b)(2), Division A, below.

P.L. 113-295, §221(b)(2), Division A, provides:

(2) SAVINGS PROVISION.—If—

(A) any provision amended or repealed by the amendments made by this section applied to—

(i) any transaction occurring before the date of the enactment of this Act,

(ii) any property acquired before such date of enactment, or

(iii) any item of income, loss, deduction, or credit taken into account before such date of enactment, and

(B) the treatment of such transaction, property, or item under such provision would (without regard to the amendments or repeals made by this section) affect the liability for tax for periods ending after date of enactment, nothing in the amendments or repeals made by this section shall be construed to affect the treatment of such transaction, property, or item for purposes of determining liability for tax for periods ending after such date of enactment.

• **1988, Technical and Miscellaneous Revenue Act of 1988 (P.L. 100-647)**

P.L. 100-647, §2001(c)(2):

Amended Code Sec. 882(a)(1) by inserting "59A," after "55,". **Effective** as if included in the provision of P.L. 99-499 to which it relates.

• **1986, Tax Reform Act of 1986 (P.L. 99-514)**

P.L. 99-514, §701(e)(4)(F):

Amended Code Sec. 882(a)(1) by striking out "or 1201(a)" and inserting in lieu thereof ", 55, or 1201(a)". **Effective**, generally, for tax years beginning after 12-31-86. However, see Act Sec. 701(f)(2)-(7) under the amendment notes for Code Sec. 56 for special rules.

• **1980, Omnibus Reconciliation Act of 1980 (P.L. 96-499)**

P.L. 96-499, §1122(c)(2):

Added Code Sec. 882(a)(3). For the **effective** date of this paragraph, see the historical comment under Code Sec. 897(i).

• **1978, Revenue Act of 1978 (P.L. 95-600)**

P.L. 95-600, §301(b)(13):

Amended the headings for subsection (a) and for paragraph (1). **Effective** for tax years beginning after 12-31-78. Prior to amendment, those headings read as follows:

(a) NORMAL TAX AND SURTAX.—

(1) IMPOSITION OF TAX.—

• **1966, Foreign Investors Tax Act of 1966 (P.L. 89-809)**

P.L. 89-809, §104(b)(1):

Amended Code Sec. 882(a). **Effective** 1-1-67. Prior to amendment, Code Sec. 882(a) read as follows:

SEC. 882. TAX ON RESIDENT FOREIGN CORPORATIONS.

(a) Imposition of Tax.—A foreign corporation engaged in trade or business within the United States shall be taxable as provided in section 11.

[Sec. 882(b)]

(b) GROSS INCOME.—In the case of a foreign corporation, except where the context clearly indicates otherwise, gross income includes only—

(1) gross income which is derived from sources within the United States and which is not effectively connected with the conduct of a trade or business within the United States, and

(2) gross income which is effectively connected with the conduct of a trade or business within the United States.

Amendments

• **1988, Technical and Miscellaneous Revenue Act of 1988 (P.L. 100-647)**

P.L. 100-647, §1012(s)(2)(B):

Amended Code Sec. 882(b) by striking out "the case of a foreign corporation" and inserting in lieu thereof "the case of a foreign corporation, except where the context clearly indicates otherwise". **Effective** as if included in the provision of P.L. 99-514 to which it relates.

• **1966, Foreign Investors Tax Act of 1966 (P.L. 89-809)**

P.L. 89-809, §104(b)(1):

Amended Code Sec. 882(b). **Effective** 1-1-67. Prior to amendment, Code Sec. 882(b) read as follows:

(b) Gross Income.—In the case of a foreign corporation, gross income includes only the gross income from sources within the United States.

[Sec. 882(c)]

(c) ALLOWANCE OF DEDUCTIONS AND CREDITS.—

(1) ALLOCATION OF DEDUCTIONS.—

(A) GENERAL RULE.—In the case of a foreign corporation, the deductions shall be allowed only for purposes of subsection (a) and (except as provided by subparagraph (B)) only if and to the extent that they are connected with income which is effectively connected with the conduct of a trade or business within the United States; and the proper apportionment and allocation of the deductions for this purpose shall be determined as provided in regulations prescribed by the Secretary.

(B) CHARITABLE CONTRIBUTIONS.—The deduction for charitable contributions and gifts provided by section 170 shall be allowed whether or not connected with income which is effectively connected with the conduct of a trade or business within the United States.

(2) DEDUCTIONS AND CREDITS ALLOWED ONLY IF RETURN FILED.—A foreign corporation shall receive the benefit of the deductions and credits allowed to it in this subtitle only by filing or causing to be filed with the Secretary a true and accurate return, in the manner prescribed in subtitle F, including therein all the information which the Secretary may deem necessary for the calculation of such deductions and credits. The preceding sentence shall not apply for purposes of the tax imposed by section 541 (relating to personal holding company tax), and shall not be construed to deny the credit provided by section 33 for tax withheld at source or the credit provided by section 34 for certain uses of gasoline.

(3) FOREIGN TAX CREDIT.—Except as provided by section 906, foreign corporations shall not be allowed the credit against the tax for taxes of foreign countries and possessions of the United States allowed by section 901.

INCOME TAX—FOREIGN CORPORATIONS

(4) CROSS REFERENCE.—

For rule that certain foreign taxes are not to be taken into account in determining deduction or credit, see section 906(b)(1).

Amendments

• **1984, Deficit Reduction Act of 1984 (P.L. 98-369)**

P.L. 98-369, § 474(r)(19):

Amended Code Sec. 882(c)(2) by striking out "32" and inserting in lieu thereof "33", and by striking out "section 39" and inserting in lieu thereof "section 34". **Effective** for tax years beginning after 12-31-83, and to carrybacks from such years.

• **1983, Surface Transportation Act of 1982 (P.L. 97-424)**

P.L. 97-424, § 515(b)(6)(F):

Amended Code Sec. 882(c)(2) by striking out "and lubricating oil" after "certain uses of gasoline". **Effective** with respect to articles sold after 1-6-83.

• **1976, Tax Reform Act of 1976 (P.L. 94-455)**

P.L. 94-455, § 1906(b)(13)(A):

Amended 1954 Code by substituting "Secretary" for "Secretary or his delegate" each place it appeared. **Effective** 2-1-77.

• **1966, Foreign Investors Tax Act of 1966 (P.L. 89-809)**

P.L. 89-809, § 104(b)(1):

Amended Code Sec. 882(c). **Effective** 1-1-67. Prior to amendment, Code Sec. 882(c) read as follows:

(c) ALLOWANCE OF DEDUCTIONS AND CREDITS.—

(1) DEDUCTIONS ALLOWED ONLY IF RETURN FILED.—A foreign corporation shall receive the benefit of the deductions allowed to it in this subtitle only by filing or causing to be filed with the Secretary or his delegate a true and accurate return of its total income received from all sources in the United States, in the manner prescribed in subtitle F. including therein all the information which the Secretary or his delegate may deem necessary for the calculation of such deductions.

(2) ALLOCATION OF DEDUCTIONS.—In the case of a foreign corporation the deductions shall be allowed only if and to the extent that they are connected with income from sources within the United States; and the proper apportionment and allocation of the deductions with respect to sources within and without the United States shall be determined as provided in part I, under regulations prescribed by the Secretary or his delegate.

(3) CHARITABLE CONTRIBUTIONS.—The deduction for charitable contributions and gifts provided by section 170 shall be allowed whether or not connected with income from sources within the United States.

(4) FOREIGN TAX CREDIT.—Foreign corporations shall not be allowed the credits against the tax for taxes of foreign countries and possessions of the United States allowed by section 901.

[Sec. 882(d)]

(d) ELECTION TO TREAT REAL PROPERTY INCOME AS INCOME CONNECTED WITH UNITED STATES BUSINESS.—

(1) IN GENERAL.—A foreign corporation which during the taxable year derives any income—

(A) from real property located in the United States, or from any interest in such real property, including (i) gains from the sale or exchange of real property or an interest therein, (ii) rents or royalties from mines, wells, or other natural deposits, and (iii) gains described in section 631(b) or (c), and

(B) which, but for this subsection, would not be treated as income effectively connected with the conduct of a trade or business within the United States,

may elect for such taxable year to treat all such income as income which is effectively connected with the conduct of a trade or business within the United States. In such case, such income shall be taxable as provided in subsection (a)(1) whether or not such corporation is engaged in trade or business within the United States during the taxable year. An election under this paragraph for any taxable year shall remain in effect for all subsequent taxable years, except that it may be revoked with the consent of the Secretary with respect to any taxable year.

(2) ELECTION AFTER REVOCATION, ETC.—Paragraphs (2) and (3) of section 871(d) shall apply in respect of elections under this subsection in the same manner and to the same extent as they apply in respect of elections under section 871(d).

Amendments

• **1976, Tax Reform Act of 1976 (P.L. 94-455)**

P.L. 94-455, § 1906(b)(13)(A):

Amended 1954 Code by substituting "Secretary" for "Secretary or his delegate" each place it appeared. **Effective** 2-1-77.

• **1966, Foreign Investors Tax Act of 1966 (P.L. 89-809)**

P.L. 89-809, § 104(b)(1):

Amended Code Sec. 882(d). **Effective** 1-1-67. Prior to amendment, Code Sec. 882(d) read as follows:

(d) Returns of Tax by Agent.—If any foreign corporation has no office or place of business in the United States but has an agent in the United States, the return required under section 6012 shall be made by the agent.

[Sec. 882(e)]

(e) INTEREST ON UNITED STATES OBLIGATIONS RECEIVED BY BANKS ORGANIZED IN POSSESSIONS.—In the case of a corporation created or organized in, or under the law of, a possession of the United States which is carrying on the banking business in a possession of the United States, interest on obligations of the United States which is not portfolio interest (as defined in section 881(c)(2)) shall—

(1) for purposes of this subpart, be treated as income which is effectively connected with the conduct of a trade or business within the United States, and

(2) shall be taxable as provided in subsection (a)(1) whether or not such corporation is engaged in trade or business within the United States during the taxable year.

Amendments

• **1988, Technical and Miscellaneous Revenue Act of 1988 (P.L. 100-647)**

P.L. 100-647, § 6133(a)(1)-(2):

Amended Code Sec. 882(e) by inserting "which is not portfolio interest (as defined in section 881(c)(2))" before "shall" and by striking out the last sentence thereof. **Effective** for tax years beginning after 12-31-88. Prior to amendment, the last sentence of Code Sec. 882(e) read as follows:

The preceding sentence shall not apply to any Guam corporation which is treated as not being a foreign corporation by section 881(b)(1) for the taxable year.

• **1986, Tax Reform Act of 1986 (P.L. 99-514)**

P.L. 99-514, § 1236(a):

Amended Code Sec. 882(e) by adding at the end thereof a new sentence. **Effective** for tax years beginning after 11-16-85.

• **1966, Foreign Investors Tax Act of 1966 (P.L. 89-809)**

P.L. 89-809, § 104(b)(1):

Added Code Sec. 882(e). **Effective** 1-1-67.

[Sec. 882(f)]

(f) RETURNS OF TAX BY AGENT.—If any foreign corporation has no office or place of business in the United States but has an agent in the United States, the return required under section 6012 shall be made by the agent.

Amendments

• **1966, Foreign Investors Tax Act of 1966 (P.L. 89-809)**

P.L. 89-809, § 104(b)(1):

Redesignated former Code Sec. 882(d) as Code Sec. 882(f). **Effective** 1-1-67.

[Sec. 883]

SEC. 883. EXCLUSIONS FROM GROSS INCOME.

[Sec. 883(a)]

(a) INCOME OF FOREIGN CORPORATIONS FROM SHIPS AND AIRCRAFT.—The following items shall not be included in gross income of a foreign corporation, and shall be exempt from taxation under this subtitle:

INCOME TAX—FOREIGN CORPORATIONS

(1) SHIPS OPERATED BY CERTAIN FOREIGN CORPORATIONS.—Gross income derived by a corporation organized in a foreign country from the international operation of a ship or ships if such foreign country grants an equivalent exemption to corporations organized in the United States.

(2) AIRCRAFT OPERATED BY CERTAIN FOREIGN CORPORATIONS.—Gross income derived by a corporation organized in a foreign country from the international operation of aircraft if such foreign country grants an equivalent exemption to corporations organized in the United States.

(3) RAILROAD ROLLING STOCK OF FOREIGN CORPORATIONS.—Earnings derived from payments by a common carrier for the use on a temporary basis (not expected to exceed a total of 90 days in any taxable year) of railroad rolling stock owned by a corporation of a foreign country which grants an equivalent exemption to corporations organized in the United States.

(4) SPECIAL RULES.—The rules of paragraphs (6), (7), and (8) of section 872(b) shall apply for purposes of this subsection.

(5) SPECIAL RULE FOR COUNTRIES WHICH TAX ON RESIDENCE BASIS.—For purposes of this subsection, there shall not be taken into account any failure of a foreign country to grant an exemption to a corporation organized in the United States if such corporation is subject to tax by such foreign country on a residence basis pursuant to provisions of foreign law which meets such standards (if any) as the Secretary may prescribe.

Amendments

• **2004, American Jobs Creation Act of 2004 (P.L. 108-357)**

P.L. 108-357, §419(b):

Amended Code Sec. 883(a)(4) by striking "(5), (6), and (7)" and inserting "(6), (7), and (8)". **Effective** for wagers made after 10-22-2004.

P.L. 108-357, §423, provides:

SEC. 423. DELAY IN EFFECTIVE DATE OF FINAL REGULATIONS GOVERNING EXCLUSION OF INCOME FROM INTERNATIONAL OPERATION OF SHIPS OR AIRCRAFT.

Notwithstanding the provisions of Treasury regulation §1.883-5, the final regulations issued by the Secretary of the Treasury relating to income derived by foreign corporations from the international operation of ships or aircraft (Treasury regulations §1.883-1 through §1.883-5) shall apply to taxable years of a foreign corporation seeking qualified foreign corporation status beginning after September 24, 2004.

• **1989, Omnibus Budget Reconciliation Act of 1989 (P.L. 101-239)**

P.L. 101-239, §7811(i)(8)(D):

Amended Code Sec. 883(a)(4) by striking "(5) and (6)" and inserting "(5), (6), and (7)". **Effective** as if included in the provision of P.L. 100-647 to which it relates.

P.L. 101-239, §7811(i)(10):

Amended Code Sec. 883(a) by adding at the end thereof a new paragraph (5). **Effective** as if included in the provision of P.L. 100-647 to which it relates.

• **1988, Technical and Miscellaneous Revenue Act of 1988 (P.L. 100-647)**

P.L. 100-647, §1012(e)(2)(A):

Amended Code Sec. 883(a)(1) and (2) by striking out "to citizens of the United States and" after "exemption". **Effective** as if included in the provision of P.L. 99-514 to which it relates.

P.L. 100-647, §1012(e)(5):

Amended Code Sec. 883(a)(1) and (2) by striking out "operation" and inserting in lieu thereof "international operation". **Effective** as if included in the provision of P.L. 99-514 to which it relates.

• **1986, Tax Reform Act of 1986 (P.L. 99-514)**

P.L. 99-514, §1212(c)(2):

Amended Code Sec. 883(a) by striking out paragraphs (1) and (2) and inserting in lieu thereof new paragraphs (1)-(2). **Effective** for tax years beginning after 12-31-86. Prior to amendment, Code Sec. 883(a)(1) and (2) read as follows:

(1) SHIPS UNDER FOREIGN FLAG.—Earnings derived from the operation of a ship or ships documented under the laws of a foreign country which grants an equivalent exemption to citizens of the United States and to corporations organized in the United States.

(2) AIRCRAFT OF FOREIGN REGISTRY.—Earnings derived from the operation of aircraft registered under the laws of a foreign country which grants an equivalent exemption to citizens of the United States and to corporations organized in the United States.

P.L. 99-514, §1212(c)(4):

Amended Code Sec. 883(a) by adding at the end thereof new paragraph (4). **Effective** for tax years beginning after 12-31-86.

• **1975, Revenue Adjustment Act of 1975 (P.L. 94-164)**

P.L. 94-164, §6(a):

Amended Code Sec. 883 by adding subsection (a)(3). **Effective** for payments made after 11-18-74.

• **1968 (P.L. 90-622)**

P.L. 90-622:

Amended Code Sec. 883 by adding "(a) INCOME OF FOREIGN CORPORATIONS FROM SHIPS AND AIRCRAFT" at the beginning of the section and by adding subsection (b). **Effective** with respect to tax years beginning after 12-31-66.

[Sec. 883(b)]

(b) EARNINGS DERIVED FROM COMMUNICATIONS SATELLITE SYSTEM.—The earnings derived from the ownership or operation of a communications satellite system by a foreign entity designated by a foreign government to participate in such ownership or operation shall be exempt from taxation under this subtitle, if the United States, through its designated entity, participates in such system pursuant to the Communications Satellite Act of 1962 (47 U.S.C. 701 and following).

[Sec. 883(c)]

(c) TREATMENT OF CERTAIN FOREIGN CORPORATIONS.—

(1) IN GENERAL.—Paragraphs (1) or (2) of subsection (a) (as the case may be) shall not apply to any foreign corporation if 50 percent or more of the value of the stock of such corporation is owned by individuals who are not residents of such foreign country or another foreign country meeting the requirements of such paragraph.

(2) TREATMENT OF CONTROLLED FOREIGN CORPORATIONS.—Paragraph (1) shall not apply to any foreign corporation which is a controlled foreign corporation (as defined in section 957(a)).

(3) SPECIAL RULES FOR PUBLICLY TRADED CORPORATIONS.—

(A) EXCEPTION.—Paragraph (1) shall not apply to any corporation which is organized in a foreign country meeting the requirements of paragraph (1) or (2) of subsection (a) (as the case may be) and the stock of which is primarily and regularly traded on an established securities market in such foreign country, another foreign country meeting the requirements of such paragraph, or the United States.

(B) TREATMENT OF STOCK OWNED BY PUBLICLY TRADED CORPORATION.—Any stock in another corporation which is owned (directly or indirectly) by a corporation meeting the requirements of subparagraph (A) shall be treated as owned by individuals who are residents of the foreign country in which the corporation meeting the requirements of subparagraph (A) is organized.

(4) STOCK OWNERSHIP THROUGH ENTITIES.—For purposes of paragraph (1), stock owned (directly or indirectly) by or for a corporation, partnership, trust, or estate shall be treated as being owned proportionately by its shareholders, partners, or beneficiaries. Stock considered to be owned by a person by reason of the application of the preceding sentence shall, for purposes of applying such sentence, be treated as actually owned by such person.

Amendments

• **1988, Technical and Miscellaneous Revenue Act of 1988 (P.L. 100-647)**

P.L. 100-647, §1012(e)(1)(A):

Amended Code Sec. 883(c)(3). **Effective** as if included in the provision of P.L. 99-514 to which it relates. Prior to amendment, Code Sec. 883(c)(3) read as follows:

(3) EXCEPTION FOR PUBLICLY TRADED CORPORATIONS.—Paragraph (1) shall not apply to any foreign corporation—

(A) the stock of which is primarily and regularly traded on an established securities market in the foreign country in which such corporation is organized, or

(B) which is wholly owned (either directly or indirectly) by another corporation meeting the requirements of subparagraph (A) and is organized in the same foreign country as such other corporation.

P.L. 100-647, §1012(e)(1)(B)(i)-(ii):

Amended Code Sec. 883(c)(1) by striking out "Paragraphs (1) and (2) of subsection (a)" and inserting in lieu thereof "Paragraph (1) or (2) of subsection (a) (as the case may be)", and by striking out "such paragraphs (1) and (2)" and inserting in lieu thereof "such paragraph". **Effective** as if included in the provision of P.L. 99-514 to which it relates.

INCOME TAX—FOREIGN CORPORATIONS

• **1986, Tax Reform Act of 1986 (P.L. 99-514)**
P.L. 99-514, §1212(c)(5):
Amended Code Sec. 883 by adding at the end thereof new subsection (c). **Effective** for tax years beginning after 12-31-86.

[Sec. 884]

SEC. 884. BRANCH PROFITS TAX.

[Sec. 884(a)]

(a) IMPOSITION OF TAX.—In addition to the tax imposed by section 882 for any taxable year, there is hereby imposed on any foreign corporation a tax equal to 30 percent of the dividend equivalent amount for the taxable year.

[Sec. 884(b)]

(b) DIVIDEND EQUIVALENT AMOUNT.—For purposes of subsection (a), the term "dividend equivalent amount" means the foreign corporation's effectively connected earnings and profits for the taxable year adjusted as provided in this subsection:

(1) REDUCTION FOR INCREASE IN U.S. NET EQUITY.—If—

(A) the U.S. net equity of the foreign corporation as of the close of the taxable year, exceeds

(B) the U.S. net equity of the foreign corporation as of the close of the preceding taxable year,

the effectively connected earnings and profits for the taxable year shall be reduced (but not below zero) by the amount of such excess.

(2) INCREASE FOR DECREASE IN NET EQUITY.—

(A) IN GENERAL.—If—

(i) the U.S. net equity of the foreign corporation as of the close of the preceding taxable year, exceeds

(ii) the U.S. net equity of the foreign corporation as of the close of the taxable year,

the effectively connected earnings and profits for the taxable year shall be increased by the amount of such excess.

(B) LIMITATION.—

(i) IN GENERAL.—The increase under subparagraph (A) for any taxable year shall not exceed the accumulated effectively connected earnings and profits as of the close of the preceding taxable year.

(ii) ACCUMULATED EFFECTIVELY CONNECTED EARNINGS AND PROFITS.—For purposes of clause (i), the term "accumulated effectively connected earnings and profits" means the excess of—

(I) the aggregate effectively connected earnings and profits for preceding taxable years beginning after December 31, 1986, over

(II) the aggregate dividend equivalent amounts determined for such preceding taxable years.

Amendments

• **1988, Technical and Miscellaneous Revenue Act of 1988 (P.L. 100-647)**
P.L. 100-647, §1012(q)(1)(A):
Amended Code Sec. 884(b)(2)(B). **Effective** as if included in the provision of P.L. 99-514 to which it relates. Prior to amendment, Code Sec. 884(b)(2)(B) read as follows:

(B) LIMITATION.—The increase under subparagraph (A) for any taxable year shall not exceed the aggregate reductions under paragraph (1) for prior taxable years to the extent not previously taken into account under subparagraph (A).

[Sec. 884(c)]

(c) U.S. NET EQUITY.—For purposes of this section—

(1) IN GENERAL.—The term "U.S. net equity" means—

(A) U.S. assets, reduced (including below zero) by

(B) U.S. liabilities.

(2) U.S. ASSETS AND U.S. LIABILITIES.—For purposes of paragraph (1)—

(A) U.S. ASSETS.—The term "U.S. assets" means the money and aggregate adjusted bases of property of the foreign corporation treated as connected with the conduct of a trade or business in the United States under regulations prescribed by the Secretary. For purposes of the preceding sentence, the adjusted basis of any property shall be its adjusted basis for purposes of computing earnings and profits.

(B) U.S. LIABILITIES.—The term "U.S. liabilities" means the liabilities of the foreign corporation treated as connected with the conduct of a trade or business in the United States under regulations prescribed by the Secretary.

(C) REGULATIONS TO BE CONSISTENT WITH ALLOCATION OF DEDUCTIONS.—The regulations prescribed under subparagraphs (A) and (B) shall be consistent with the allocation of deductions under section 882(c)(1).

[Sec. 884(d)]

(d) EFFECTIVELY CONNECTED EARNINGS AND PROFITS.—For purposes of this section—

(1) IN GENERAL.—The term "effectively connected earnings and profits" means earnings and profits (without diminution by reason of any distributions made during the taxable year) which are attributable to income which is effectively connected (or treated as effectively connected) with the conduct of a trade or business within the United States.

(2) EXCEPTION FOR CERTAIN INCOME.—The term "effectively connected earnings and profits" shall not include any earnings and profits attributable to—

(A) income not includible in gross income under paragraph (1) or (2) of section 883(a),

(B) income treated as effectively connected with the conduct of a trade or business within the United States under section 921(d) or 926(b) (as in effect before their repeal by the FSC Repeal and Extraterritorial Income Exclusion Act of 2000),

(C) gain on the disposition of a United States real property interest described in section 897(c)(1)(A)(ii),

(D) income treated as effectively connected with the conduct of a trade or business within the United States under section 953(c)(3)(C), or

(E) income treated as effectively connected with the conduct of a trade or business within the United States under section 882(e).

Property and liabilities of the foreign corporation treated as connected with such income under regulations prescribed by the Secretary shall not be taken into account in determining the U.S. assets or U.S. liabilities of the foreign corporation.

INCOME TAX—FOREIGN CORPORATIONS

Amendments

• **2007, Tax Technical Corrections Act of 2007 (P.L. 110-172)**

P.L. 110-172, §11(g)(8):

Amended Code Sec. 884(d)(2)(B) by inserting "(as in effect before their repeal by the FSC Repeal and Extraterritorial Income Exclusion Act of 2000)" before the comma. **Effective** 12-29-2007.

• **1988, Technical and Miscellaneous Revenue Act of 1988 (P.L. 100-647)**

P.L. 100-647, §6133(b):

Amended Code Sec. 884(d)(2) by striking out "or" at the end of subparagraph (C), by striking out the period at the end of subparagraph (D) and inserting in lieu thereof ", or" and by inserting after subparagraph (D) a new subparagraph (E). **Effective** for tax years beginning after 12-31-88.

[Sec. 884(e)]

(e) COORDINATION WITH INCOME TAX TREATIES; ETC.—

(1) LIMITATION ON TREATY EXEMPTION.—No treaty between the United States and a foreign country shall exempt any foreign corporation from the tax imposed by subsection (a) (or reduce the amount thereof) unless—

(A) such treaty is an income tax treaty, and

(B) such foreign corporation is a qualified resident of such foreign country.

(2) TREATY MODIFICATIONS.—If a foreign corporation is a qualified resident of a foreign country with which the United States has an income tax treaty—

(A) the rate of tax under subsection (a) shall be the rate of tax specified in such treaty—

(i) on branch profits if so specified, or

(ii) if not so specified, on dividends paid by a domestic corporation to a corporation resident in such country which wholly owns such domestic corporation, and

(B) any other limitations under such treaty on the tax imposed by subsection (a) shall apply.

(3) COORDINATION WITH WITHHOLDING TAX.—

(A) IN GENERAL.—If a foreign corporation is subject to the tax imposed by subsection (a) for any taxable year (determined after the application of any treaty), no tax shall be imposed by section 871(a), 881(a), 1441, or 1442 on any dividends paid by such corporation out of its earnings and profits for such taxable year.

(B) LIMITATION ON CERTAIN TREATY BENEFITS.—If—

(i) any dividend described in section 861(a)(2)(B) is received by a foreign corporation, and

(ii) subparagraph (A) does not apply to such dividend,

rules similar to the rules of subparagraphs (A) and (B) of subsection (f)(3) shall apply to such dividend.

(4) QUALIFIED RESIDENT.—For purposes of this subsection—

(A) IN GENERAL.—Except as otherwise provided in this paragraph, the term "qualified resident" means, with respect to any foreign country, any foreign corporation which is a resident of such foreign country unless—

(i) 50 percent or more (by value) of the stock of such foreign corporation is owned (within the meaning of section 883(c)(4)) by individuals who are not residents of such foreign country and who are not United States citizens or resident aliens, or

(ii) 50 percent or more of its income is used (directly or indirectly) to meet liabilities to persons who are not residents of such foreign country or citizens or residents of the United States.

(B) SPECIAL RULE FOR PUBLICLY TRADED CORPORATIONS.—A foreign corporation which is a resident of a foreign country shall be treated as a qualified resident of such foreign country if—

(i) the stock of such corporation is primarily and regularly traded on an established securities market in such foreign country, or

(ii) such corporation is wholly owned (either directly or indirectly) by another foreign corporation which is organized in such foreign country and the stock of which is so traded.

(C) CORPORATIONS OWNED BY PUBLICLY TRADED DOMESTIC CORPORATIONS.—A foreign corporation which is a resident of a foreign country shall be treated as a qualified resident of such foreign country if—

(i) such corporation is wholly owned (directly or indirectly) by a domestic corporation, and

(ii) the stock of such domestic corporation is primarily and regularly traded on an established securities market in the United States.

(D) SECRETARIAL AUTHORITY.—The Secretary may, in his sole discretion, treat a foreign corporation as being a qualified resident of a foreign country if such corporation establishes to the satisfaction of the Secretary that such corporation meets such requirements as the Secretary may establish to ensure that individuals who are not residents of such foreign country do not use the treaty between such foreign country and the United States in a manner inconsistent with the purposes of this subsection.

(5) EXCEPTION FOR INTERNATIONAL ORGANIZATIONS.—This section shall not apply to an international organization (as defined in section 7701(a)(18)).

Amendments

• **1988, Technical and Miscellaneous Revenue Act of 1988 (P.L. 100-647)**

P.L. 100-647, §1012(q)(2)(A):

Amended Code Sec. 884(e)(1). **Effective** as if included in the provision of P.L. 99-514 to which it relates. Prior to amendment, Code Sec. 884(e)(1) read as follows:

(1) LIMITATION ON TREATY EXEMPTION.—No income tax treaty between the United States and a foreign country shall exempt any foreign corporation from the tax imposed by subsection (a) (or reduce the amount thereof) unless—

(A) such foreign corporation is a qualified resident of such foreign country, or

(B) such foreign corporation is not a qualified resident of such foreign country but such income tax treaty permits a withholding tax on dividends described in section 861(a)(2)(B) which are paid by such foreign corporation.

P.L. 100-647, §1012(q)(2)(B):

Amended Code Sec. 884(e)(3). **Effective** as if included in the provision of P.L. 99-514 to which it relates. Prior to amendment, Code Sec. 884(e)(3) read as follows:

(3) COORDINATION WITH 2ND TIER WITHHOLDING TAX.—

(A) IN GENERAL.—If a foreign corporation is not exempt for any taxable year from the tax imposed by subsection (a) by reason of a treaty, no tax shall be imposed by section 871(a), 881(a), 1441, or 1442 on any dividends paid by such corporation during the taxable year.

(B) LIMITATION ON CERTAIN TREATY BENEFITS.—No foreign corporation which is not a qualified resident of a foreign country shall be entitled to claim benefits under any income tax treaty between the United States and such foreign country with respect to dividends—

(i) which are paid by such foreign corporation and with respect to which such foreign corporation is otherwise required to deduct and withhold tax under section 1441 or 1442, or

(ii) which are received by such foreign corporation and are described in section 861(a)(2)(B).

P.L. 100-647, §1012(q)(4):

Amended Code Sec. 884(e)(4) by redesignating subparagraph (C) as subparagraph (D) and by inserting after subparagraph (B) new subparagraph (C). **Effective** as if included in the provision of P.L. 99-514 to which it relates.

P.L. 100-647, §1012(q)(5)(A)-(B):

Amended Code Sec. 884(e)(4)(A) by striking out "more than 50 percent" in clause (i) and inserting in lieu thereof "50 percent or more", and by striking out "or the United States" in clause (ii) and inserting in lieu thereof "or citizens or residents of the United States". **Effective** as if included in the provision of P.L. 99-514 to which it relates.

P.L. 100-647, §1012(q)(6):

Amended Code Sec. 884(e) by adding at the end thereof new paragraph (5). **Effective** as if included in the provision of P.L. 99-514 to which it relates.

INCOME TAX—FOREIGN CORPORATIONS

[Sec. 884(f)]

(f) TREATMENT OF INTEREST ALLOCABLE TO EFFECTIVELY CONNECTED INCOME.—

(1) IN GENERAL.—In the case of a foreign corporation engaged in a trade or business in the United States (or having gross income treated as effectively connected with the conduct of a trade or business in the United States), for purposes of this subtitle—

(A) any interest paid by such trade or business in the United States shall be treated as if it were paid by a domestic corporation, and

(B) to the extent that the allocable interest exceeds the interest described in subparagraph (A), such foreign corporation shall be liable for tax under section 881(a) in the same manner as if such excess were interest paid to such foreign corporation by a wholly owned domestic corporation on the last day of such foreign corporation's taxable year.

To the extent provided in regulations, subparagraph (A) shall not apply to interest in excess of the amounts reasonably expected to be allocable interest.

(2) ALLOCABLE INTEREST.—For purposes of this subsection, the term "allocable interest" means any interest which is allocable to income which is effectively connected (or treated as effectively connected) with the conduct of a trade or business in the United States.

(3) COORDINATION WITH TREATIES.—

(A) PAYOR MUST BE QUALIFIED RESIDENT.—In the case of any interest described in paragraph (1) which is paid or accrued by a foreign corporation, no benefit under any treaty between the United States and the foreign country of which such corporation is a resident shall apply unless—

(i) such treaty is an income tax treaty, and

(ii) such foreign corporation is a qualified resident of such foreign country.

(B) RECIPIENT MUST BE QUALIFIED RESIDENT.—In the case of any interest described in paragraph (1) which is received or accrued by any corporation, no benefit under any treaty between the United States and the foreign country of which such corporation is a resident shall apply unless—

(i) such treaty is an income treaty, and

(ii) such foreign corporation is a qualified resident of such foreign country.

Amendments

• 1996, Small Business Job Protection Act of 1996 (P.L. 104-188)

P.L. 104-188, §1704(f)(3)(A)(i):

Amended Code Sec. 884(f)(1)(B) by striking "to the extent" and all that follows down through "subparagraph (A)" and inserting "to the extent that the allocable interest exceeds the interest described in subparagraph (A)". **Effective** as if included in the amendments made by section 1241(a) of P.L. 99-514. Prior to amendment, Code Sec. 884(f)(1)(B) read as follows:

(B) to the extent the amount of interest allowable as a deduction under section 882 in computing the effectively connected taxable income of such foreign corporation exceeds the interest described in subparagraph (A), such foreign corporation shall be liable for tax under section 881(a) in the same manner as if such excess were interest paid to such foreign corporation by a wholly owned domestic corporation on the last day of such foreign corporation's taxable year.

P.L. 104-188, §1704(f)(3)(A)(ii):

Amended Code Sec. 884(f)(1) by striking "reasonably expected" and all that follows down through the period at the end of the second sentence and inserting "reasonably expected to be allocable interest.". **Effective** as if included in the amendments made by section 1241(a) of P.L. 99-514. Prior to amendment, the last sentence of Code Sec. 884(f) read as follows:

To the extent provided in regulations, subparagraph (A) shall not apply to interest in excess of the amounts reasonably expected to be deductible under section 882 in computing the effectively connected taxable income of such foreign corporation.

P.L. 104-188, §1704(f)(3)(A)(iii):

Amended Code Sec. 884(f)(2). **Effective** as if included in the amendments made by section 1241(a) of P.L. 99-514. Prior to amendment, Code Sec. 884(f)(2) read as follows:

(2) EFFECTIVELY CONNECTED TAXABLE INCOME.—For purposes of this subsection, the term "effectively connected taxable income" means taxable income which is effectively connected (or treated as effectively connected) with the conduct of a trade or business within the United States.

• 1988, Technical and Miscellaneous Revenue Act of 1988 (P.L. 100-647)

P.L. 100-647, §1012(q)(2)(C)(i)-(ii):

Amended Code Sec. 884(f) by striking out the 2nd sentence of paragraph (1), and by adding at the end thereof new paragraph (3). **Effective** as if included in the provision of P.L. 99-514 to which it relates. For a special rule, see Act Sec. 1012(q)(1)(B), below. Prior to amendment, the 2nd sentence of Code Sec. 884(f)(1) read as follows:

Rules similar to the rules of subsection (e)(3)(B) shall apply to interest described in the preceding sentence.

P.L. 100-647, §1012(q)(3)(A)-(B):

Amended Code Sec. 884(f)(1) by striking out "sections 871, 881, 1441, and 1442" and inserting in lieu thereof "this subtitle", and by adding at the end thereof a new sentence. **Effective** as if included in the provision of P.L. 99-514 to which it relates. For a special rule, see Act Sec. 1012(q)(1)(B), below.

P.L. 100-647, §1012(q)(14):

Amended Code Sec. 884(f)(1) by inserting "(or having gross income treated as effectively connected with the conduct of a trade or business in the United States)" after "United States" in the material preceding subparagraph (A) thereof. **Effective** as if included in the provision of P.L. 99-514 to which it relates. For a special rule, see Act Sec. 1012(q)(1)(B), below.

P.L. 100-647, §1012(q)(1)(B), as amended by P.L. 101-239, §7811(i)(5)(A)-(B), provides:

(B) For purposes of applying section 884 of the 1986 Code, the earnings and profits of any corporation shall be determined without regard to any increase in earnings and profits under sections 1023(e)(3)(C) and 1021(c)(2)(C) of the Reform Act or arising from section 832(b)(4)(C) of the 1986 Code.

[Sec. 884(g)]

(g) REGULATIONS.—The Secretary shall prescribe such regulations as may be necessary or appropriate to carry out the purposes of this section, including regulations providing for appropriate adjustments in the determination of the dividend equivalent amount in connection with the distribution to shareholders or transfer to a controlled corporation of the taxpayer's U.S. assets and other adjustments in such determination as are necessary or appropriate to carry out the purposes of this section.

Amendments

• 1986, Tax Reform Act of 1986 (P.L. 99-514)

P.L. 99-514, §1241(a):

Amended subpart B of part II of subchapter N of chapter 1 by redesignating Code Sec. 884 as Code Sec. 885 and by inserting after Code Sec. 883 new Code Sec. 884. **Effective** for tax years beginning after 12-31-86.

[Sec. 885]

SEC. 885. CROSS REFERENCES.

(1) For special provisions relating to foreign corporations carrying on an insurance business within the United States, see section 842.

(2) For rules applicable in determining whether any foreign corporation is engaged in trade or business within the United States, see section 864(b).

(3) For adjustment of tax in case of corporations of certain foreign countries, see section 896.

(4) For allowance of credit against the tax in case of a foreign corporation having income effectively connected with the conduct of a trade or business within the United States, see section 906.

(5) For withholding at source of tax on income of foreign corporations, see section 1442.

INCOME TAX—GROSS TRANSPORTATION INCOME

Amendments

• **1986, Tax Reform Act of 1986 (P.L. 99-514)**

P.L. 99-514, §1241(a):

Amended subpart B of part II of subchapter N of chapter 1 by redesignating Code Sec. 884 as Code Sec. 885. **Effective** for tax years beginning after 12-31-86.

• **1969, Tax Reform Act of 1969 (P.L. 91-172)**

P.L. 91-172, §101(j)(21):

Deleted former paragraph (1) in Code Sec. 884 and renumbered the subsequent paragraphs. **Effective** for tax years beginning after 12-31-69. Prior to deletion, paragraph (1) read as follows:

"(1) For special provisions relating to unrelated business income of foreign educational, charitable, and certain other exempt organizations, see section 512(a)."

• **1966, Foreign Investors Tax Act of 1966 (P.L. 89-809)**

P.L. 89-809, §104(m)(1):

Amended Code Sec. 884. **Effective** 1-1-67. Prior to amendment, Sec. 884 read as follows:

SEC. 884. CROSS REFERENCES.

(1) For withholding at source of tax on income of foreign corporations, see section 1442.

(2) For rules applicable in determining whether any foreign corporation is engaged in trade or business within the United States, see section 871(c).

(3) For special provisions relating to foreign insurance companies, see subchapter L (sec. 801 and following).

(4) For special provisions relating to unrelated business income of foreign educational, charitable, and certain other exempt organizations, see section 512(a).

Subpart C—Tax on Gross Transportation Income

Sec. 887. Imposition of tax on gross transportation income of nonresident aliens and foreign corporations.

[Sec. 887]

SEC. 887. IMPOSITION OF TAX ON GROSS TRANSPORTATION INCOME OF NONRESIDENT ALIENS AND FOREIGN CORPORATIONS.

[Sec. 887(a)]

(a) IMPOSITION OF TAX.—In the case of any nonresident alien individual or foreign corporation, there is hereby imposed for each taxable year a tax equal to 4 percent of such individual's or corporation's United States source gross transportation income for such taxable year.

[Sec. 887(b)]

(b) UNITED STATES SOURCE GROSS TRANSPORTATION INCOME.—

(1) IN GENERAL.—Except as provided in paragraphs (2) and (3), the term "United States source gross transportation income" means any gross income which is transportation income (as defined in section 863(c)(3)) to the extent such income is treated as from sources in the United States under section 863(c)(2). To the extent provided in regulations, such term does not include any income of a kind to which an exemption under paragraph (1) or (2) of section 883(a) would not apply.

(2) EXCEPTION FOR CERTAIN INCOME EFFECTIVELY CONNECTED WITH BUSINESS IN THE UNITED STATES.—The term "United States source gross transportation income" shall not include any income taxable under section 871(b) or 882.

(3) EXCEPTION FOR CERTAIN INCOME TAXABLE IN POSSESSIONS.—The term "United States source gross transportation income" does not include any income taxable in a possession of the United States under the provisions of this title as made applicable in such possession.

(4) DETERMINATION OF EFFECTIVELY CONNECTED INCOME.—For purposes of this chapter, United States source gross transportation income of any taxpayer shall not be treated as effectively connected with the conduct of a trade or business in the United States unless—

(A) the taxpayer has a fixed place of business in the United States involved in the earning of United States source gross transportation income, and

(B) substantially all of the United States source gross transportation income (determined without regard to paragraph (2)) of the taxpayer is attributable to regularly scheduled transportation (or, in the case of income from the leasing of a vessel or aircraft, is attributable to a fixed place of business in the United States).

Amendments

• **1989, Omnibus Budget Reconciliation Act of 1989 (P.L. 101-239)**

P.L. 101-239, §7811(i)(8)(A):

Amended Code Sec. 887(b) by redesignating paragraph (3) as paragraph (4) and by inserting after paragraph (2) a new paragraph (3). **Effective** as if included in the provision of P.L. 100-647 to which it relates.

P.L. 101-239, §7811(i)(8)(B):

Amended Code Sec. 887(b)(1) by striking "paragraph (2)" and inserting "paragraphs (2) and (3)". **Effective** as if included in the provision of P.L. 100-647 to which it relates.

P.L. 101-239, §7811(i)(9):

Amended Code Sec. 887(b)(4), as redesignated by paragraph (8), by striking "transportation income" the first two places it appears and inserting "United States source gross transportation income". **Effective** as if included in the provision of P.L. 100-647 to which it relates.

• **1988, Technical and Miscellaneous Revenue Act of 1988 (P.L. 100-647)**

P.L. 100-647, §1012(e)(6)(A)-(B):

Amended Code Sec. 887(b)(1) by striking out "under section 863(c)" and inserting in lieu thereof "under section 863(c)(2)", and by adding at the end thereof a new sentence. **Effective** as if included in the provision of P.L. 99-514 to which it relates.

[Sec. 887(c)]

(c) COORDINATION WITH OTHER PROVISIONS.—Any income taxable under this section shall not be taxable under section 871, 881, or 882.

Amendments

• **1986, Tax Reform Act of 1986 (P.L. 99-514)**

P.L. 99-514, §1212(b)(1):

Amended part II of subchapter N of chapter 1 by redesignating subpart C as subpart D and inserting after subpart B new subpart C, which contains Code Sec. 887. **Effective** for tax years beginning after 12-31-86.

Subpart D—Miscellaneous Provisions

Sec. 891.	Doubling of rates of tax on citizens and corporations of certain foreign countries.
Sec. 892.	Income of foreign governments and of international organizations.
Sec. 893.	Compensation of employees of foreign governments or international organizations.
Sec. 894.	Income affected by treaty.
Sec. 895.	Income derived by a foreign central bank of issue from obligations of the United States or from bank deposits.
Sec. 896.	Adjustment of tax on nationals, residents, and corporations of certain foreign countries.
Sec. 897.	Disposition of investment in United States real property.
Sec. 898.	Taxable year of certain foreign corporations.

INCOME TAX—MISCELLANEOUS PROVISIONS

[Sec. 891]

SEC. 891. DOUBLING OF RATES OF TAX ON CITIZENS AND CORPORATIONS OF CERTAIN FOREIGN COUNTRIES.

Whenever the President finds that, under the laws of any foreign country, citizens or corporations of the United States are being subjected to discriminatory or extraterritorial taxes, the President shall so proclaim and the rates of tax imposed by sections 1, 3, 11, 801, 831, 852, 871, and 881 shall, for the taxable year during which such proclamation is made and for each taxable year thereafter, be doubled in the case of each citizen and corporation of such foreign country; but the tax at such doubled rate shall be considered as imposed by such sections as the case may be. In no case shall this section operate to increase the taxes imposed by such sections (computed without regard to this section) to an amount in excess of 80 percent of the taxable income of the taxpayer (computed without regard to the deductions allowable under section 151 and under part VIII of subchapter B). Whenever the President finds that the laws of any foreign country with respect to which the President has made a proclamation under the preceding provisions of this section have been modified so that discriminatory and extraterritorial taxes applicable to citizens and corporations of the United States have been removed, he shall so proclaim, and the provisions of this section providing for doubled rates of tax shall not apply to any citizen or corporation of such foreign country with respect to any taxable year beginning after such proclamation is made.

Amendments

• **1986, Tax Reform Act of 1986 (P.L. 99-514)**

P.L. 99-514, § 1024(c)(13):

Amended Code Sec. 891 by striking out "821" in the first sentence of that section after "801". **Effective** for tax years beginning after 12-31-86.

• **1984, Deficit Reduction Act of 1984 (P.L. 98-369)**

P.L. 98-369, § 211(b)(12):

Amended Code Sec. 891 by striking out "802" and inserting in lieu thereof "801". **Effective** for tax years beginning after 12-31-83.

• **1959, Life Insurance Company Income Tax Act of 1959 (P.L. 86-69)**

P.L. 86-69, § 3(f)(1):

Amended Code Sec. 891 by striking out "811," where it appeared following "802,". **Effective** for tax years beginning after 12-31-57.

• **1956, Life Insurance Company Tax Act for 1955 (P.L. 429, 84th Cong.)**

P.L. 429, 84th Cong., § 5(6):

Amended Sec. 891 by inserting "811," after "802,". **Effective** 1-1-55.

[Sec. 892]

SEC. 892. INCOME OF FOREIGN GOVERNMENTS AND OF INTERNATIONAL ORGANIZATIONS.

[Sec. 892(a)]

(a) FOREIGN GOVERNMENTS.—

  (1) IN GENERAL.—The income of foreign governments received from—

    (A) investments in the United States in—

      (i) stock, bonds, or other domestic securities owned by such foreign governments, or

      (ii) financial instruments held in the execution of governmental financial or monetary policy, or

    (B) interest on deposits in banks in the United States of moneys belonging to such foreign governments,

shall not be included in gross income and shall be exempt from taxation under this subtitle.

  (2) INCOME RECEIVED DIRECTLY OR INDIRECTLY FROM COMMERCIAL ACTIVITIES.—

    (A) IN GENERAL.—Paragraph (1) shall not apply to any income—

      (i) derived from the conduct of any commercial activity (whether within or outside the United States),

      (ii) received by a controlled commercial entity or received (directly or indirectly) from a controlled commercial entity, or

      (iii) derived from the disposition of any interest in a controlled commercial entity.

    (B) CONTROLLED COMMERCIAL ENTITY.—For purposes of subparagraph (A), the term "controlled commercial entity" means any entity engaged in commercial activities (whether within or outside the United States) if the government—

      (i) holds (directly or indirectly) any interest in such entity which (by value or voting interest) is 50 percent or more of the total of such interests in such entity, or

      (ii) holds (directly or indirectly) any other interest in such entity which provides the foreign government with effective control of such entity.

For purposes of the preceding sentence, a central bank of issue shall be treated as a controlled commercial entity only if engaged in commercial activities within the United States.

  (3) TREATMENT AS RESIDENT.—For purposes of this title, a foreign government shall be treated as a corporate resident of its country. A foreign government shall be so treated for purposes of any income tax treaty obligation of the United States if such government grants equivalent treatment to the Government of the United States.

Amendments

• **1988, Technical and Miscellaneous Revenue Act of 1988 (P.L. 100-647)**

P.L. 100-647, § 1012(t)(1):

Amended Code Sec. 892(a)(2)(A) by striking out "or" at the end of clause (i), by striking out the period at the end of clause (ii) and inserting in lieu thereof ", or", and by adding at the end thereof new clause (iii). **Effective** as if included in the provision of P.L. 99-514 to which it relates.

P.L. 100-647, § 1012(t)(2):

Amended Code Sec. 892(a)(2)(A)(ii). **Effective** as if included in the provision of P.L. 99-514 to which it relates. Prior to amendment, Code Sec. 892(a)(2)(A)(ii) read as follows:

(ii) received from or by a controlled commercial entity.

P.L. 100-647, § 1012(t)(3):

Amended Code Sec. 892(a) by adding at the end thereof new paragraph (3). **Effective** as if included in the provision of P.L. 99-514 to which it relates.

[Sec. 892(b)]

(b) INTERNATIONAL ORGANIZATIONS.—The income of international organizations received from investments in the United States in stocks, bonds, or other domestic securities owned by such international organizations, or from interest on deposits in banks in the United States of moneys belonging to such international organizations, or from any other source within the United States, shall not be included in gross income and shall be exempt from taxation under this subtitle.

[Sec. 892(c)]

(c) REGULATIONS.—The Secretary shall prescribe such regulations as may be necessary or appropriate to carry out the purposes of this section.

Amendments

• **1986, Tax Reform Act of 1986 (P.L. 99-514)**

P.L. 99-514, § 1247(a):

Amended Code Sec. 892. For the **effective** date, see Act Sec. 633 following Code Sec. 26. Prior to amendment, Code Sec. 892 read as follows:

SEC. 892. INCOME OF FOREIGN GOVERNMENTS AND OF INTERNATIONAL ORGANIZATIONS.

The income of foreign governments or international organizations received from investments in the United States in stocks, bonds, or other domestic securities, owned by such foreign governments or by international organizations, or from interest on deposits in banks in the United States of moneys belonging to such foreign governments or international organizations, or from any other source within the United States, shall not be included in gross income and shall be exempt from taxation under this subtitle.

Internal Revenue Code

INCOME TAX—MISCELLANEOUS PROVISIONS

P.L. 99-514, § 1228, provides:

SEC. 1228. SPECIAL RULE FOR APPLYING SECTION 897.

(A) IN GENERAL.—For purposes of section 897 of the Internal Revenue Code of 1986, gain shall not be recognized on the transfer, sale, exchange, or other disposition, of shares of stock of a United States real property holding company, if—

(1) such United States real property holding company is a Delaware corporation incorporated on January 17, 1984,

(2) the transfer, sale, exchange, or other disposition is to any member of a qualified ownership group,

(3) the recipient of the share of stock elects, for purposes of such section 897, a carryover basis in the transferred shares, and

(4) an election under this section applies to such transfer, sale, exchange, or other disposition.

(b) MEMBER OF A QUALIFIED OWNERSHIP GROUP.—For purposes of this section, the term "member of a qualified ownership group" means a corporation incorporated on June 16, 1890, under the laws of the Netherlands or a corporation incorporated on October 18, 1897, under the laws of the United Kingdom or any corporation owned directly or indirectly by either or both such corporations.

(c) ELECTION.—An election under this section shall be made at such time and in such manner as the Secretary of the Treasury or his delegate may prescribe, and an election under this section may only be made with respect to 1 transfer, sale, exchange, or other disposition.

(d) EFFECTIVE DATE.—The provisions of this section shall take effect on the date of the enactment of this section.

[Sec. 893]

SEC. 893. COMPENSATION OF EMPLOYEES OF FOREIGN GOVERNMENTS OR INTERNATIONAL ORGANIZATIONS.

[Sec. 893(a)]

(a) RULE FOR EXCLUSION.—Wages, fees, or salary of any employee of a foreign government or of an international organization (including a consular or other officer, or a nondiplomatic representative), received as compensation for official services to such government or international organization shall not be included in gross income and shall be exempt from taxation under this subtitle if—

(1) such employee is not a citizen of the United States, or is a citizen of the Republic of the Philippines (whether or not a citizen of the United States); and

(2) in the case of an employee of a foreign government, the services are of a character similar to those performed by employees of the Government of the United States in foreign countries; and

(3) in the case of an employee of a foreign government, the foreign government grants an equivalent exemption to employees of the Government of the United States performing similar services in such foreign country.

[Sec. 893(b)]

(b) CERTIFICATE BY SECRETARY OF STATE.—The Secretary of State shall certify to the Secretary of the Treasury the names of the foreign countries which grant an equivalent exemption to the employees of the Government of the United States performing services in such foreign countries, and the character of the services performed by employees of the Government of the United States in foreign countries.

[Sec. 893(c)]

(c) LIMITATION ON EXCLUSION.—Subsection (a) shall not apply to—

(1) any employee of a controlled commercial entity (as defined in section 892(a)(2)(B)), or

(2) any employee of a foreign government whose services are primarily in connection with a commercial activity (whether within or outside the United States) of the foreign government.

Amendments

• **1988, Technical and Miscellaneous Revenue Act of 1988 (P.L. 100-647)**

P.L. 100-647, § 1012(t)(4):

Amended Code Sec. 893 by adding at the end thereof new subsection (c). **Effective** as if included in the provision of P.L. 99-514 to which it relates.

[Sec. 894]

SEC. 894. INCOME AFFECTED BY TREATY.

[Sec. 894(a)]

(a) TREATY PROVISIONS.—

(1) IN GENERAL.—The provisions of this title shall be applied to any taxpayer with due regard to any treaty obligation of the United States which applies to such taxpayer.

(2) CROSS REFERENCE.—

For relationship between treaties and this title, see section 7852(d).

Amendments

• **1988, Technical and Miscellaneous Revenue Act of 1988 (P.L. 100-647)**

P.L. 100-647, § 1012(aa)(6):

Amended Code Sec. 894(a). **Effective** as if included in the provision of P.L. 99-514 to which it relates. Prior to amendment, Code Sec. 894(a) read as follows:

(a) INCOME EXEMPT UNDER TREATY.—Income of any kind, to the extent required by any treaty obligation of the United States, shall not be included in gross income and shall be exempt from taxation under this subtitle.

• **1966, Foreign Investors Tax Act of 1966 (P.L. 89-809)**

P.L. 89-809, § 105(a):

Amended the heading and added the subsection (a) designation to former Code Sec. 894. **Effective** 1-1-67. Prior to amendment, Code Sec. 894 read as follows:

SEC. 894. INCOME EXEMPT UNDER TREATY.

Income of any kind, to the extent required by any treaty obligation of the United States, shall not be included in gross income and shall be exempt from taxation under this subtitle.

[Sec. 894(b)]

(b) PERMANENT ESTABLISHMENT IN UNITED STATES.—For purposes of applying any exemption from, or reduction of, any tax provided by any treaty to which the United States is a party with respect to income which is not effectively connected with the conduct of a trade or business within the United States, a nonresident alien individual or a foreign corporation shall be deemed not to have a permanent establishment in the United States at any time during the taxable year. This subsection shall not apply in respect of the tax computed under section 877(b).

Amendments

• **1966, Foreign Investors Tax Act of 1966 (P.L. 89-809)**

P.L. 89-809, § 105(a):

Added Code Sec. 894(b). **Effective** 1-1-67.

[Sec. 894(c)]

(c) DENIAL OF TREATY BENEFITS FOR CERTAIN PAYMENTS THROUGH HYBRID ENTITIES.—

(1) APPLICATION TO CERTAIN PAYMENTS.—A foreign person shall not be entitled under any income tax treaty of the United States with a foreign country to any reduced rate of any withholding tax imposed by this title on an item of income derived through an entity which is treated as a partnership (or is otherwise treated as fiscally transparent) for purposes of this title if—

(A) such item is not treated for purposes of the taxation laws of such foreign country as an item of income of such person,

INCOME TAX—MISCELLANEOUS PROVISIONS

(B) the treaty does not contain a provision addressing the applicability of the treaty in the case of an item of income derived through a partnership, and

(C) the foreign country does not impose tax on a distribution of such item of income from such entity to such person.

(2) REGULATIONS.—The Secretary shall prescribe such regulations as may be necessary or appropriate to determine the extent to which a taxpayer to which paragraph (1) does not apply shall not be entitled to benefits under any income tax treaty of the United States with respect to any payment received by, or income attributable to any activities of, an entity organized in any jurisdiction (including the United States) that is treated as a partnership or is otherwise treated as fiscally transparent for purposes of this title (including a common investment trust under section 584, a grantor trust, or an entity that is disregarded for purposes of this title) and is treated as fiscally nontransparent for purposes of the tax laws of the jurisdiction of residence of the taxpayer.

Amendments

- **1997, Taxpayer Relief Act of 1997 (P.L. 105-34)**

P.L. 105-34, §1054(a):

Amended Code Sec. 894 by inserting after subsection (b) a new subsection (c).
Effective 8-5-97.

[Sec. 895]

SEC. 895. INCOME DERIVED BY A FOREIGN CENTRAL BANK OF ISSUE FROM OBLIGATIONS OF THE UNITED STATES OR FROM BANK DEPOSITS.

Income derived by a foreign central bank of issue from obligations of the United States or of any agency or instrumentality thereof (including beneficial interests, participations, and other instruments issued under section 302(c) of the Federal National Mortgage Association Charter Act (12 U. S. C. 1717)) which are owned by such foreign central bank of issue, or derived from interest on deposits with persons carrying on the banking business, shall not be included in gross income and shall be exempt from taxation under this subtitle unless such obligations or deposits are held for, or used in connection with, the conduct of commercial banking functions or other commercial activities. For purposes of the preceding sentence the Bank for International Settlements shall be treated as a foreign central bank of issue.

Amendments

- **1966, Foreign Investors Tax Act of 1966 (P.L. 89-809)**

P.L. 89-809, §102(a)(4):

Amended Code Sec. 895. Effective 1-1-67. Prior to amendment, Sec. 895 read as follows:

SEC. 895. INCOME DERIVED BY A FOREIGN CENTRAL BANK OF ISSUE FROM OBLIGATIONS OF THE UNITED STATES.

Income derived by a foreign central bank of issue from obligations of the United States owned by such foreign central bank of issue shall not be included in gross income and shall be exempt from taxation under this subtitle unless such obligations are held for, or used in connection with, the conduct of commercial banking functions or other commercial activities.

- **1961 (P.L. 87-29)**

P.L. 87-29, §[1]:

Added Code Sec. 895. Effective for income received in tax years beginning after 12-31-60.

[Sec. 896]

SEC. 896. ADJUSTMENT OF TAX ON NATIONALS, RESIDENTS, AND CORPORATIONS OF CERTAIN FOREIGN COUNTRIES.

[Sec. 896(a)]

(a) IMPOSITION OF MORE BURDENSOME TAXES BY FOREIGN COUNTRY.—Whenever the President finds that—

(1) under the laws of any foreign country, considering the tax system of such foreign country, citizens of the United States not residents of such foreign country or domestic corporations are being subjected to more burdensome taxes, on any item of income received by such citizens or corporations from sources within such foreign country, than taxes imposed by the provisions of this subtitle on similar income derived from sources within the United States by residents or corporations of such foreign country,

(2) such foreign country, when requested by the United States to do so, has not acted to revise or reduce such taxes so that they are no more burdensome than taxes imposed by the provisions of this subtitle on similar income derived from sources within the United States by residents or corporations of such foreign country, and

(3) it is in the public interest to apply pre-1967 tax provisions in accordance with the provisions of this subsection to residents or corporations of such foreign country,

the President shall proclaim that the tax on such similar income derived from sources within the United States by residents or corporations of such foreign country shall, for taxable years beginning after such proclamation, be determined under this subtitle without regard to amendments made to this subchapter and chapter 3 on or after the date of enactment of this section.

[Sec. 896(b)]

(b) IMPOSITION OF DISCRIMINATORY TAXES BY FOREIGN COUNTRY.—Whenever the President finds that—

(1) under the laws of any foreign country, citizens of the United States or domestic corporations (or any class of such citizens or corporations) are, with respect to any item of income, being subjected to a higher effective rate of tax than are nationals, residents, or corporations of such foreign country (or a similar class of such nationals, residents, or corporations) under similar circumstances;

(2) such foreign country, when requested by the United States to do so, has not acted to eliminate such higher effective rate of tax; and

(3) it is in the public interest to adjust, in accordance with the provisions of this subsection, the effective rate of tax imposed by this subtitle on similar income of nationals, residents, or corporations of such foreign country (or such similar class of such nationals, residents, or corporations),

the President shall proclaim that the tax on similar income of nationals, residents, or corporations of such foreign country (or such similar class of such nationals, residents, or corporations) shall, for taxable years beginning after such proclamation, be adjusted so as to cause the effective rate of tax imposed by this subtitle on such similar income to be substantially equal to the effective rate of tax imposed by such foreign country on such item of income of citizens of the United States or domestic corporations (or such class of citizens or corporations). In implementing a proclamation made under this subsection, the effective rate of tax imposed by this subtitle on an item of income may be adjusted by the disallowance, in whole or in part, of any deduction, credit, or exemption which would otherwise be allowed with respect to that item of income or by increasing the rate of tax otherwise applicable to that item of income.

[Sec. 896(c)]

(c) ALLEVIATION OF MORE BURDENSOME OR DISCRIMINATORY TAXES.—Whenever the President finds that—

(1) the laws of any foreign country with respect to which the President has made a proclamation under subsection (a) have been modified so that citizens of the United States not residents of such foreign country or domestic corporations are no longer subject to more burdensome taxes on the item of income derived by such citizens or corporations from sources within such foreign country, or

(2) the laws of any foreign country with respect to which the President has made a proclamation under subsection (b) have been modified so that citizens of the United States or domestic corporations (or any class of such citizens or corporations) are no longer subject to a higher effective rate of tax on the item of income,

INCOME TAX—MISCELLANEOUS PROVISIONS

he shall proclaim that the tax imposed by this subtitle on the similar income of nationals, residents, or corporations of such foreign country shall, for any taxable year beginning after such proclamation, be determined under this subtitle without regard to such subsection.

[Sec. 896(d)]

(d) NOTIFICATION OF CONGRESS REQUIRED.—No proclamation shall be issued by the President pursuant to this section unless, at least 30 days prior to such proclamation, he has notified the Senate and the House of Representatives of his intention to issue such proclamation.

[Sec. 896(e)]

(e) IMPLEMENTATION BY REGULATIONS.—The Secretary shall prescribe such regulations as he deems necessary or appropriate to implement this section.

Amendments

- **1976, Tax Reform Act of 1976 (P.L. 94-455)**

P.L. 94-455, §1906(b)(13)(A):

Amended 1954 Code by substituting "Secretary" for "Secretary or his delegate" each place it appeared. **Effective** 2-1-77.

- **1966, Foreign Investors Tax Act of 1966 (P.L. 89-809)**

P.L. 89-809, §105(b):

Added new Code Sec. 896. **Effective** 1-1-67.

[Sec. 897]

SEC. 897. DISPOSITION OF INVESTMENT IN UNITED STATES REAL PROPERTY.

[Sec. 897(a)]

(a) GENERAL RULE.—

(1) TREATMENT AS EFFECTIVELY CONNECTED WITH UNITED STATES TRADE OR BUSINESS.—For purposes of this title, gain or loss of a nonresident alien individual or a foreign corporation from the disposition of a United States real property interest shall be taken into account—

(A) in the case of a nonresident alien individual, under section 871(b)(1), or

(B) in the case of a foreign corporation, under section 882(a)(1),

as if the taxpayer were engaged in a trade or business within the United States during the taxable year and as if such gain or loss were effectively connected with such trade or business.

(2) MINIMUM TAX ON NONRESIDENT ALIEN INDIVIDUALS.—

(A) IN GENERAL.—In the case of any nonresident alien individual, the taxable excess for purposes of section 55(b)(1) shall not be less than the lesser of—

(i) the individual's alternative minimum taxable income (as defined in section 55(b)(1)(D)) for the taxable year, or

(ii) the individual's net United States real property gain for the taxable year.

(B) NET UNITED STATES REAL PROPERTY GAIN.—For purposes of subparagraph (A), the term "net United States real property gain" means the excess of—

(i) the aggregate of the gains for the taxable year from dispositions of United States real property interests, over

(ii) the aggregate of the losses for the taxable year from dispositions of such interests.

Amendments

- **2022, Inflation Reduction Act of 2022 (P.L. 117-169)**

P.L. 117-169, §10101(a)(4)(B)(iii):

Amended Code Sec. 897(a)(2)(A)(i) by striking "55(b)(2)" and inserting "55(b)(1)(D)". **Effective** for tax years beginning after 12-31-2022.

- **2018, Tax Technical Corrections Act of 2018 (P.L. 115-141)**

P.L. 115-141, §401(a)(155), Div. U:

Amended Code Sec. 897(a)(1)(A) by striking "section 871(B)(1)" and inserting "section 871(b)(1)". **Effective** 3-23-2018.

- **2017, Tax Cuts and Jobs Act (P.L. 115-97)**

P.L. 115-97, §12001(b)(3)(D):

Amended Code Sec. 897(a)(2)(A) by striking "section 55(b)(1)(A)" and inserting "section 55(b)(1)". **Effective** for tax years beginning after 12-31-2017.

- **1993, Omnibus Budget Reconciliation Act of 1993 (P.L. 103-66)**

P.L. 103-66, §13203(c)(2)(A):

Amended Code Sec. 897(a)(2)(A) by striking "the amount determined under section 55(b)(1)(A) shall not be less than 21 percent of" and inserting "the taxable excess for purposes of section 55(b)(1)(A) shall not be less than". **Effective** for tax years beginning after 12-31-92.

P.L. 103-66, §13203(c)(2)(B):

Amended Code Sec. 897(a)(2) by striking "21-PERCENT" in the heading before "MINIMUM". **Effective** for tax years beginning after 12-31-92.

- **1986, Tax Reform Act of 1986 (P.L. 99-514)**

P.L. 99-514, §701(e)(4)(G):

Amended so much of Code Sec. 897(a)(2) as precedes subparagraph (B). **Effective**, generally, for tax years beginning after 12-31-86. However, for special rules see Act Sec. 701(f)(2)-(7) following Code Sec. 56. Prior to amendment, so much of Code Sec. 897(a)(2) as precedes subparagraph (B) read as follows:

(2) 20-PERCENT MINIMUM TAX ON NONRESIDENT ALIEN INDIVIDUALS.—

(A) IN GENERAL.—In the case of any nonresident alien individual, the amount determined under section 55(a)(1) for the taxable year shall not be less than 20 percent of the lesser of—

(i) the individual's alternative minimum taxable income (as defined in section 55(b)) for the taxable year, or

(ii) the individual's net United States real property gain for the taxable year.

- **1983, Technical Corrections Act of 1982 (P.L. 97-448)**

P.L. 97-448, §306(a)(1)(A):

Amended P.L. 97-248, §201, by redesignating the second subsection (c) as subsection (d).

- **1982, Tax Equity and Fiscal Responsibility Act of 1982 (P.L. 97-248)**

P.L. 97-248, §201(d)(6):

Amended Code Sec. 897(a)(2)(A). **Effective** for tax years beginning after 12-31-82. Prior to amendment, it read as follows:

"(A) In general.—In the case of any nonresident alien individual, the amount determined under section 55(a)(1)(A) for the taxable year shall not be less than 20 percent of whichever of the following is the least:

(i) the individual's alternative minimum taxable income (as defined in section 55(b)(1)) for the taxable year,

(ii) the individual's net United States real property gain for the taxable year, or

(iii) $60,000."

[Sec. 897(b)]

(b) LIMITATION ON LOSSES OF INDIVIDUALS.—In the case of an individual, a loss shall be taken into account under subsection (a) only to the extent such loss would be taken into account under section 165(c) (determined without regard to subsection (a) of this section).

[Sec. 897(c)]

(c) UNITED STATES REAL PROPERTY INTEREST.—For purposes of this section—

(1) UNITED STATES REAL PROPERTY INTEREST.—

(A) IN GENERAL.—Except as provided in subparagraph (B) or subsection (k), the term "United States real property interest" means—

(i) an interest in real property (including an interest in a mine, well, or other natural deposit) located in the United States or the Virgin Islands, and

(ii) any interest (other than an interest solely as a creditor) in any domestic corporation unless the taxpayer establishes (at such time and in such manner as the Secretary by regulations prescribes) that such corporation was at no time a United States real property holding corporation during the shorter of—

(I) the period after June 18, 1980, during which the taxpayer held such interest, or

(II) the 5-year period ending on the date of the disposition of such interest.

(B) EXCLUSION FOR INTEREST IN CERTAIN CORPORATIONS.—The term "United States real property interest" does not include any interest in a corporation if—

(i) as of the date of the disposition of such interest, such corporation did not hold any United States real property interests,

(ii) all of the United States real property interests held by such corporation at any time during the shorter of the periods described in subparagraph (A)(ii)—

(I) were disposed of in transactions in which the full amount of the gain (if any) was recognized, or

(II) ceased to be United States real property interests by reason of the application of this subparagraph to 1 or more other corporations, and

(iii) neither such corporation nor any predecessor of such corporation was a regulated investment company or a real estate investment trust at any time during the shorter of the periods described in subparagraph (A)(ii).

(2) UNITED STATES REAL PROPERTY HOLDING CORPORATION.—The term "United States real property holding corporation" means any corporation if—

(A) the fair market value of its United States real property interests equals or exceeds 50 percent of

(B) the fair market value of—

(i) its United States real property interests,

(ii) its interests in real property located outside the United States, plus

(iii) any other of its assets which are used or held for use in a trade or business.

(3) EXCEPTION FOR STOCK REGULARLY TRADED ON ESTABLISHED SECURITIES MARKETS.—If any class of stock of a corporation is regularly traded on an established securities market, stock of such class shall be treated as a United States real property interest only in the case of a person who, at some time during the shorter of the periods described in paragraph (1)(A)(ii), held more than 5 percent of such class of stock.

(4) INTERESTS HELD BY FOREIGN CORPORATIONS AND BY PARTNERSHIPS, TRUSTS, AND ESTATES.—For purpose of determining whether any corporation is a United States real property holding corporation—

(A) FOREIGN CORPORATIONS.—Paragraph (1)(A)(ii) shall be applied by substituting "any corporation (whether foreign or domestic)" for "any domestic corporation".

(B) ASSETS HELD BY PARTNERSHIPS, ETC.—Under regulations prescribed by the Secretary, assets held by a partnership, trust, or estate shall be treated as held proportionately by its partners or beneficiaries. Any asset treated as held by a partner or beneficiary by reason of this subparagraph which is used or held for use by the partnership, trust, or estate in a trade or business shall be treated as so used or held by the partner or beneficiary. Any asset treated as held by a partner or beneficiary by reason of this subparagraph shall be so treated for purposes of applying this subparagraph successively to partnerships, trusts, or estates which are above the first partnership, trust, or estate in a chain thereof.

(5) TREATMENT OF CONTROLLING INTERESTS.—

(A) IN GENERAL.—Under regulations, for purposes of determining whether any corporation is a United States real property holding corporation, if any corporation (hereinafter in this paragraph referred to as the "first corporation") holds a controlling interest in a second corporation—

(i) the stock which the first corporation holds in the second corporation shall not be taken into account,

(ii) the first corporation shall be treated as holding a portion of each asset of the second corporation equal to the percentage of the fair market value of the stock of the second corporation represented by the stock held by the first corporation, and

(iii) any asset treated as held by the first corporation by reason of clause (ii) which is used or held for use by the second corporation in a trade or business shall be treated as so used or held by the first corporation.

Any asset treated as held by the first corporation by reason of the preceding sentence shall be so treated for purposes of applying the preceding sentence successively to corporations which are above the first corporation in a chain of corporations.

(B) CONTROLLING INTEREST.—For purposes of subparagraph (A), the term "controlling interest" means 50 percent or more of the fair market value of all classes of stock of a corporation.

(6) OTHER SPECIAL RULES.—

(A) INTEREST IN REAL PROPERTY.—The term "interest in real property" includes fee ownership and co-ownership of land or improvements thereon, leaseholds of land or improvements thereon, options to acquire land or improvements thereon, and options to acquire leaseholds of land or improvements thereon.

(B) REAL PROPERTY INCLUDES ASSOCIATED PERSONAL PROPERTY.—The term "real property" includes movable walls, furnishings, and other personal property associated with the use of the real property.

(C) CONSTRUCTIVE OWNERSHIP RULES.—For purposes of determining under paragraph (3) whether any person holds more than 5 percent of any class of stock and of determining under paragraph (5) whether a person holds a controlling interest in any corporation, section 318(a) shall apply (except that paragraphs (2)(C) and (3)(C) of section 318(a) shall be applied by substituting "5 percent" for "50 percent").

Amendments

- **2015, Protecting Americans from Tax Hikes Act of 2015 (P.L. 114-113)**

P.L. 114-113, §322(a)(2)(A), Div. Q:

Amended Code Sec. 897(c)(1)(A) by inserting "or subsection (k)" after "subparagraph (B)" in the matter preceding clause (i). For the **effective** date, see Act Sec. 322(c)(1), below.

P.L. 114-113, §322(c)(1), Div. Q, provides:

(1) IN GENERAL.—The amendments made by subsection (a) shall take effect on the date of enactment and shall apply to—

(A) any disposition on and after the date of the enactment of this Act, and

(B) any distribution by a real estate investment trust on or after the date of the enactment of this Act which is treated as a deduction for a taxable year of such trust ending after such date.

P.L. 114-113, §325(a), Div. Q:

Amended Code Sec. 897(c)(1)(B) by striking "and" at the end of clause (i), by striking the period at the end of clause (ii)(II) and inserting ", and", and by adding at the end a new clause (iii). **Effective** for dispositions on or after 12-18-2015.

- **1981, Economic Recovery Tax Act of 1981 (P.L. 97-34)**

P.L. 97-34, §831(a)(1):

Amended Code Sec. 897(c)(1)(A)(i) by adding after "United States" the phrase "or the Virgin Islands". **Effective** for dispositions after 6-18-80, in tax years ending after that date.

P.L. 97-34, §831(b):

Amended Code Sec. 897(c)(4)(B). **Effective** for dispositions after 6-18-80, in tax years ending after that date. Prior to amendment, Code Sec. 897(c)(4)(B) read as follows:

(B) INTERESTS HELD BY PARTNERSHIPS, ETC.—United States real property interests held by a partnership, trust, or estate shall be treated as owned proportionately by its partners or beneficiaries.

INCOME TAX—MISCELLANEOUS PROVISIONS

[Sec. 897(d)]

(d) TREATMENT OF DISTRIBUTIONS BY FOREIGN CORPORATIONS.—

(1) IN GENERAL.—Except to the extent otherwise provided in regulations, notwithstanding any other provision of this chapter, gain shall be recognized by a foreign corporation on the distribution (including a distribution in liquidation or redemption) of a United States real property interest in an amount equal to the excess of the fair market value of such interest (as of the time of the distribution) over its adjusted basis.

(2) EXCEPTIONS.—Gain shall not be recognized under paragraph (1)—

(A) if—

(i) at the time of the receipt of the distributed property, the distributee would be subject to taxation under this chapter on a subsequent disposition of the distributed property, and

(ii) the basis of the distributed property in the hands of the distributee is no greater than the adjusted basis of such property before the distribution, increased by the amount of gain (if any) recognized by the distributing corporation, or

(B) if such nonrecognition is provided in regulations prescribed by the Secretary under subsection (e)(2).

Amendments

• **1986, Tax Reform Act of 1986 (P.L. 99-514)**

P.L. 99-514, §631(e)(12):

Amended Code Sec. 897(d) by striking out paragraph (2), striking out "(1) Distributions", striking out "subparagraph (A)" in paragraph (2) (as so redesignated) and inserting in lieu thereof "paragraph (1)", striking out ", Etc.," and by appropriately redesignating each subparagraph, clause, and subclause of paragraph (1) as a paragraph or clause, as the case may be. For the **effective** dates, see Act Sec. 633 following Code Sec. 26.

P.L. 99-514, §1228, as amended by P.L. 100-647, §1012(m), provides:

SEC. 1228. SPECIAL RULE FOR APPLYING SECTION 897.

(a) IN GENERAL.—For purposes of section 897 of the Internal Revenue Code of 1986, gain shall not be recognized on the transfer, sale, exchange, or other disposition of shares of stock of a United States real property holding company, if—

(1) such United States real property holding company is a Delaware corporation incorporated on January 17, 1984,

(2) the transfer, sale, exchange, or other disposition is to any member of a qualified ownership group,

(3) the recipient of the share of stock elects, for purposes of such section 897, a carryover basis in the transferred shares,

(4) the transfer, sale, exchange, or other disposition is part of a single integrated plan, whereby the stock of the corporation described in paragraph (1) becomes owned directly by the 2 corporations specifically referred to in subsection (b) or by such 2 corporations and by 1 or both of their jointly owned direct subsidiaries.

(5) within 20 days after each transfer, sale, exchange, or other disposition, the person making such transfer, sale, exchange, or other disposition notifies the Internal Revenue Service of the transaction, the date of the transaction, the basis of the stock involved, the holding period for such stock, and such other information as the Internal Revenue Service may require, and

(6) the integrated plan is completed before the date 4 years after the date of the enactment of the Technical and Miscellaneous Revenue Act of 1988.

In the case of any underpayment attributable to a failure to meet any requirement of this subsection, the period during which such underpayment may be assessed shall in no event expire before the date 5 years after the date of enactment of the Technical and Miscellaneous Revenue Act of 1988.

(b) MEMBER OF A QUALIFIED OWNERSHIP GROUP.—For purposes of this section, the term "member of a qualified ownership group" means a corporation incorporated on June 16, 1890, under the laws of the Netherlands or a corporation incorporated on October 18, 1897, under the laws of the United Kingdom or any corporation owned directly or indirectly by either or both such corporations.

(c) [Repealed.]

(d) EFFECTIVE DATE.—The provisions of this section shall take effect on the date of the enactment of this section.

• **1981, Economic Recovery Tax Act of 1981 (P.L. 97-34)**

P.L. 97-34, §831(c):

Amended Code Sec. 897(d)(1)(B). **Effective** for dispositions after 6-18-80, in tax years ending after that date. Prior to amendment, Code Sec. 897(d)(1)(B) read as follows:

(B) EXCEPTION WHERE THERE IS A CARRYOVER BASIS.—Subparagraph (A) shall not apply if the basis of the distributed property in the hands of the distributee is the same as the adjusted basis of such property before the distribution increased by the amount of any gain recognized by the distributing corporation.

[Sec. 897(e)]

(e) COORDINATION WITH NONRECOGNITION PROVISIONS.—

(1) IN GENERAL.—Except to the extent otherwise provided in subsection (d) and paragraph (2) of this subsection, any nonrecognition provision shall apply for purposes of this section to a transaction only in the case of an exchange of a United States real property interest for an interest the sale of which would be subject to taxation under this chapter.

(2) REGULATIONS.—The Secretary shall prescribe regulations (which are necessary or appropriate to prevent the avoidance of Federal income taxes) providing—

(A) the extent to which nonrecognition provisions shall, and shall not, apply for purposes of this section, and

(B) the extent to which—

(i) transfers of property in reorganization, and

(ii) changes in interests in, or distributions from, a partnership, trust, or estate,

shall be treated as sales of property at fair market value.

(3) NONRECOGNITION PROVISION DEFINED.—For purposes of this subsection, the term "nonrecognition provision" means any provision of this title for not recognizing gain or loss.

[Sec. 897(f)—Stricken]

Amendments

• **1996, Small Business Job Protection Act of 1996 (P.L. 104-188)**

P.L. 104-188, §1702(g)(2):

Amended Code Sec. 897 by striking subsection (f). **Effective** as if included in the provision of P.L. 101-508 to which it relates. Prior to being stricken, Code Sec. 897(f) read as follows:

(f) DISTRIBUTIONS BY DOMESTIC CORPORATIONS TO FOREIGN SHAREHOLDERS.—If a domestic corporation distributes a United States real property interest to a nonresident alien individual or a foreign corporation in a distribution to which section 301 applies, notwithstanding any other provision of this chapter, the basis of such United States real property interest in the hands of such non-resident alien individual or foreign corporation shall not exceed—

(1) the adjusted basis of such property before the distribution, increased by

(2) the sum of—

(A) any gain recognized by the distributing corporation on the distribution, and

(B) any tax paid under this chapter by the distributee on such distribution.

[Sec. 897(g)]

(g) SPECIAL RULE FOR SALES OF INTEREST IN PARTNERSHIPS, TRUSTS, AND ESTATES.—Under regulations prescribed by the Secretary, the amount of any money, and the fair market value of any property, received by a nonresident alien individual or foreign corporation in exchange for all or part of its interest in a partnership, trust, or estate shall, to the extent attributable to United States real property interests, be considered as an amount received from the sale or exchange in the United States of such property.

[Sec. 897(h)]

(h) SPECIAL RULES FOR CERTAIN INVESTMENT ENTITIES.—For purposes of this section—

(1) LOOK-THROUGH OF DISTRIBUTIONS.—Any distribution by a qualified investment entity to a nonresident alien individual, a foreign corporation, or other qualified investment entity shall, to the extent attributable to gain from sales or exchanges by the qualified investment entity of United States real property interests, be treated as gain recognized by such nonresident alien individual, foreign corporation, or other qualified investment entity from the sale or exchange of a United States real property interest. Notwithstanding the preceding sentence, any distribution by a qualified investment entity to a nonresident alien individual or a foreign corporation with respect to any class of stock which is regularly traded on an established securities market located in the United States shall not be treated as gain recognized from the sale or

exchange of a United States real property interest if such individual or corporation did not own more than 5 percent of such class of stock at any time during the 1-year period ending on the date of such distribution.

(2) SALE OF STOCK IN DOMESTICALLY CONTROLLED ENTITY NOT TAXED.—The term "United States real property interest" does not include any interest in a domestically controlled qualified investment entity.

(3) DISTRIBUTIONS BY DOMESTICALLY CONTROLLED QUALIFIED INVESTMENT ENTITIES.—In the case of a domestically controlled qualified investment entity, rules similar to the rules of subsection (d) shall apply to the foreign ownership percentage of any gain.

(4) DEFINITIONS AND SPECIAL RULES.—

(A) QUALIFIED INVESTMENT ENTITY.—The term "qualified investment entity" means—

(i) any real estate investment trust, and

(ii) any regulated investment company which is a United States real property holding corporation or which would be a United States real property holding corporation if the exceptions provided in subsections (c)(3) and (h)(2) did not apply to interests in any real estate investment trust or regulated investment company.

(B) DOMESTICALLY CONTROLLED.—The term "domestically controlled qualified investment entity" means any qualified investment entity in which at all times during the testing period less than 50 percent in value of the stock was held directly or indirectly by foreign persons.

(C) FOREIGN OWNERSHIP PERCENTAGE.—The term "foreign ownership percentage" means that percentage of the stock of the qualified investment entity which was held (directly or indirectly) by foreign persons at the time during the testing period during which the direct and indirect ownership of stock by foreign persons was greatest.

(D) TESTING PERIOD.—The term "testing period" means whichever of the following periods is the shortest:

(i) the period beginning on June 19, 1980, and ending on the date of the disposition or of the distribution, as the case may be,

(ii) the 5-year period ending on the date of the disposition or of the distribution, as the case may be, or

(iii) the period during which the qualified investment entity was in existence.

(E) SPECIAL OWNERSHIP RULES.—For purposes of determining the holder of stock under subparagraphs (B) and (C)—

(i) in the case of any class of stock of the qualified investment entity which is regularly traded on an established securities market in the United States, a person holding less than 5 percent of such class of stock at all times during the testing period shall be treated as a United States person unless the qualified investment entity has actual knowledge that such person is not a United States person,

(ii) any stock in the qualified investment entity held by another qualified investment entity—

(I) any class of stock of which is regularly traded on an established securities market, or

(II) which is a regulated investment company which issues redeemable securities (within the meaning of section 2 of the Investment Company Act of 1940),

shall be treated as held by a foreign person, except that if such other qualified investment entity is domestically controlled (determined after application of this subparagraph), such stock shall be treated as held by a United States person, and

(iii) any stock in the qualified investment entity held by any other qualified investment entity not described in subclause (I) or (II) of clause (ii) shall only be treated as held by a United States person in proportion to the stock of such other qualified investment entity which is (or is treated under clause (ii) or (iii) as) held by a United States person.

(5) TREATMENT OF CERTAIN WASH SALE TRANSACTIONS.—

(A) IN GENERAL.—If an interest in a domestically controlled qualified investment entity is disposed of in an applicable wash sale transaction, the taxpayer shall, for purposes of this section, be treated as having gain from the sale or exchange of a United States real property interest in an amount equal to the portion of the distribution described in subparagraph (B) with respect to such interest which, but for the disposition, would have been treated by the taxpayer as gain from the sale or exchange of a United States real property interest under paragraph (1).

(B) APPLICABLE WASH SALES TRANSACTION.—For purposes of this paragraph—

(i) IN GENERAL.—The term "applicable wash sales transaction" means any transaction (or series of transactions) under which a nonresident alien individual, foreign corporation, or qualified investment entity—

(I) disposes of an interest in a domestically controlled qualified investment entity during the 30-day period preceding the ex-dividend date of a distribution which is to be made with respect to the interest and any portion of which, but for the disposition, would have been treated by the taxpayer as gain from the sale or exchange of a United States real property interest under paragraph (1), and

(II) acquires, or enters into a contract or option to acquire, a substantially identical interest in such entity during the 61-day period beginning with the 1st day of the 30-day period described in subclause (I).

For purposes of subclause (II), a nonresident alien individual, foreign corporation, or qualified investment entity shall be treated as having acquired any interest acquired by a person related (within the meaning of section 267(b) or 707(b)(1)) to the individual, corporation, or entity, and any interest which such person has entered into any contract or option to acquire.

(ii) APPLICATION TO SUBSTITUTE DIVIDEND AND SIMILAR PAYMENTS.—Subparagraph (A) shall apply to—

(I) any substitute dividend payment (within the meaning of section 861), or

(II) any other similar payment specified in regulations which the Secretary determines necessary to prevent avoidance of the purposes of this paragraph.

The portion of any such payment treated by the taxpayer as gain from the sale or exchange of a United States real property interest under subparagraph (A) by reason of this clause shall be equal to the portion of the distribution such payment is in lieu of which would have been so treated but for the transaction giving rise to such payment.

(iii) EXCEPTION WHERE DISTRIBUTION ACTUALLY RECEIVED.—A transaction shall not be treated as an applicable wash sales transaction if the nonresident alien individual, foreign corporation, or qualified investment entity receives the distribution described in clause (i)(I) with respect to either the interest which was disposed of, or acquired, in the transaction.

(iv) EXCEPTION FOR CERTAIN PUBLICLY TRADED STOCK.—A transaction shall not be treated as an applicable wash sales transaction if it involves the disposition of any class of stock in a qualified investment entity which is regularly traded on an established securities market within the United States but only if the nonresident alien individual, foreign corporation, or qualified investment entity did not own more than 5 percent of such class of stock at any time during the 1-year period ending on the date of the distribution described in clause (i)(I).

INCOME TAX—MISCELLANEOUS PROVISIONS

Amendments

- **2018, Tax Technical Corrections Act of 2018 (P.L. 115-141)**

P.L. 115-141, §101(p)(6), Div. U, provides:

(6) Section 322 of the Protecting Americans from Tax Hikes Act of 2015 is amended by striking subsections (b)(2) and (c)(3), and the Internal Revenue Code of 1986 shall be applied as if such subsections, and amendments made thereby, had never been enacted.

- **2015, Protecting Americans from Tax Hikes Act of 2015 (P.L. 114-113)**

P.L. 114-113, §133(a)(1)-(2), Div. Q:

Amended Code Sec. 897(h)(4)(A) by striking clause (ii), and by striking all that precedes "regulated investment company which" and inserting:

"(A) QUALIFIED INVESTMENT ENTITY.—The term 'qualified investment' entity means—

"(i) any real estate investment trust, and

"(ii) any". For the **effective** date, see Act Sec. 133(b), below. Prior to amendment, Code Sec. 897(h)(4)(A) read as follows:

(A) QUALIFIED INVESTMENT ENTITY.—

(i) IN GENERAL.—The term "qualified investment entity" means—

(I) any real estate investment trust, and

(II) any regulated investment company which is a United States real property holding corporation or which would be a United States real property holding corporation if the exceptions provided in subsections (c)(3) and (h)(2) did not apply to interests in any real estate investment trust or regulated investment company.

(ii) TERMINATION.—Clause (i)(II) shall not apply after December 31, 2014. Notwithstanding the preceding sentence, an entity described in clause (i)(II) shall be treated as a qualified investment entity for purposes of applying paragraphs (1) and (5) and section 1445 with respect to any distribution by the entity to a nonresident alien individual or a foreign corporation which is attributable directly or indirectly to a distribution to the entity from a real estate investment trust.

P.L. 114-113, §133(b), Div. Q, provides:

(b) EFFECTIVE DATE.—

(1) IN GENERAL.—The amendments made by this section shall take effect on January 1, 2015. Notwithstanding the preceding sentence, such amendments shall not apply with respect to the withholding requirement under section 1445 of the Internal Revenue Code of 1986 for any payment made before the date of the enactment of this Act.

(2) AMOUNTS WITHHELD ON OR BEFORE DATE OF ENACTMENT.—In the case of a regulated investment company—

(A) which makes a distribution after December 31, 2014, and before the date of the enactment of this Act, and

(B) which would (but for the second sentence of paragraph (1)) have been required to withhold with respect to such distribution under section 1445 of such Code,

such investment company shall not be liable to any person to whom such distribution was made for any amount so withheld and paid over to the Secretary of the Treasury.

P.L. 114-113, §322(b)(1)(A), Div. Q:

Amended Code Sec. 897(h)(4) by adding at the end a new subparagraph (E). **Effective** with respect to testing periods (as defined in Code Sec. 897(h)(4)(D)) ending on or after 12-18-2015 [effective date changed by P.L. 115-141, §101(p)(7), Div. U.—CCH].

P.L. 114-113, §322(b)(1)(B), Div. Q:

Amended the heading of Code Sec. 897(h)(4) by inserting "AND SPECIAL RULES" after "DEFINITIONS". **Effective** with respect to testing periods (as defined in Code Sec. 897(h)(4)(D)) ending on or after 12-18-2015 [effective date changed by P.L. 115-141, §101(p)(7), Div. U.—CCH].

P.L. 114-113, §322(b)(2), Div. Q [but see P.L. 115-141, §101(p)(6), Div. U, above]:

Amended Code Sec. 897(h)(4)(A)(ii) by inserting "and for purposes of determining whether a real estate investment trust is a domestically controlled qualified investment entity under this subsection" after "real estate investment trust". **Effective** 1-1-2015.

- **2014, Tax Increase Prevention Act of 2014 (P.L. 113-295)**

P.L. 113-295, §133(a), Division A:

Amended Code Sec. 897(h)(4)(A)(ii) by striking "December 31, 2013" and inserting "December 31, 2014". **Effective** generally on 1-1-2014. Notwithstanding the preceding sentence, such amendment shall not apply with respect to the withholding requirement under section 1445 of the Internal Revenue Code of 1986 for any payment made before 12-19-2014. For a special rule, see Act Sec. 133(b)(2), Division A, below.

P.L. 113-295, §133(b)(2), Division A, provides:

(2) AMOUNTS WITHHELD ON OR BEFORE DATE OF ENACTMENT.—In the case of a regulated investment company—

(A) which makes a distribution after December 31, 2013, and before the date of the enactment of this Act, and

(B) which would (but for the second sentence of paragraph (1)) have been required to withhold with respect to such distribution under section 1445 of such Code,

such investment company shall not be liable to any person to whom such distribution was made for any amount so withheld and paid over to the Secretary of the Treasury.

- **2013, American Taxpayer Relief Act of 2012 (P.L. 112-240)**

P.L. 112-240, §321(a):

Amended Code Sec. 897(h)(4)(A)(ii) by striking "December 31, 2011" and inserting "December 31, 2013". For the **effective** date, see Act Sec. 321(b)(1)-(2), below.

P.L. 112-240, §321(b)(1)-(2), provides:

(b) EFFECTIVE DATE.—

(1) IN GENERAL.—The amendment made by subsection (a) shall take effect on January 1, 2012. Notwithstanding the preceding sentence, such amendment shall not apply with respect to the withholding requirement under section 1445 of the Internal Revenue Code of 1986 for any payment made before the date of the enactment of this Act.

(2) AMOUNTS WITHHELD ON OR BEFORE DATE OF ENACTMENT.—In the case of a regulated investment company—

(A) which makes a distribution after December 31, 2011, and before the date of the enactment of this Act; and

(B) which would (but for the second sentence of paragraph (1)) have been required to withhold with respect to such distribution under section 1445 of such Code,

such investment company shall not be liable to any person to whom such distribution was made for any amount so withheld and paid over to the Secretary of the Treasury.

- **2010, Tax Relief, Unemployment Insurance Reauthorization, and Job Creation Act of 2010 (P.L. 111-312)**

P.L. 111-312, §749(a):

Amended Code Sec. 897(h)(4)(A)(ii) by striking "December 31, 2009" and inserting "December 31, 2011". For the **effective** date, see Act Sec. 749(b), below.

P.L. 111-312, §749(b), provides:

(b) EFFECTIVE DATE.—

(1) IN GENERAL.—The amendment made by subsection (a) shall take effect on January 1, 2010. Notwithstanding the preceding sentence, such amendment shall not apply with respect to the withholding requirement under section 1445 of the Internal Revenue Code of 1986 for any payment made before the date of the enactment of this Act.

(2) AMOUNTS WITHHELD ON OR BEFORE DATE OF ENACTMENT.—In the case of a regulated investment company—

(A) which makes a distribution after December 31, 2009, and before the date of the enactment of this Act; and

(B) which would (but for the second sentence of paragraph (1)) have been required to withhold with respect to such distribution under section 1445 of such Code,

such investment company shall not be liable to any person to whom such distribution was made for any amount so withheld and paid over to the Secretary of the Treasury.

- **2008, Tax Extenders and Alternative Minimum Tax Relief Act of 2008 (P.L. 110-343)**

P.L. 110-343, Division C, §208(a):

Amended Code Sec. 897(h)(4)(A)(ii) by striking "December 31, 2007" and inserting "December 31, 2009". For the **effective** date, see Act Sec. 208(b)(1)-(2), below.

P.L. 110-343, Division C, §208(b) (as amended by P.L. 113-295, §211(a), Division A), provides:

(b) EFFECTIVE DATE.—

(1) IN GENERAL.—The amendment made by subsection (a) shall take effect on January 1, 2008. Notwithstanding the preceding sentence, such amendment shall not apply with respect to the withholding requirement under section 1445 of the Internal Revenue Code of 1986 for any payment made before October 4, 2008.

(2) AMOUNTS WITHHELD ON OR BEFORE DATE OF ENACTMENT.— In the case of a regulated investment company—

(A) which makes a distribution after December 31, 2007, and before October 4, 2008, and

(B) which would (but for the second sentence of paragraph (1)) have been required to withhold with respect to such distribution under section 1445 of such Code,

such investment company shall not be liable to any person to whom such distribution was made for any amount so withheld and paid over to the Secretary of the Treasury.

- **2006, Tax Increase Prevention and Reconciliation Act of 2005 (P.L. 109-222)**

P.L. 109-222, §504(a):

Amended Code Sec. 897(h)(4)(A)(i)(II) by inserting "which is a United States real property holding corporation or which would be a United States real property holding corporation if the exceptions provided in subsections (c)(3) and (h)(2) did not apply to interests in any real estate investment trust or regulated investment company" after "regulated investment company". **Effective** as if included in the provisions of section 411 of the American Jobs Creation Act of 2004 (P.L. 108-357) to which it relates [effective after 12-31-2004.—CCH].

P.L. 109-222, §505(a)(1)(A)-(C):

Amended Code Sec. 897(h)(1) by striking "a nonresident alien individual or a foreign corporation" in the first sentence and inserting "a nonresident alien individual, a foreign corporation, or other qualified investment entity", by striking "such nonresident alien individual or foreign corporation" in the first sentence and inserting "such nonresident alien individual, foreign corporation, or other qualified investment entity", and by striking the second sentence and inserting a new sentence. **Effective** for tax years of qualified investment entities beginning after 12-31-2005, except that no amount shall be required to be withheld under Code Sec. 1441, 1442, or 1445 with respect to any distribution before 5-17-2006 if such amount was not otherwise required to be withheld under any such section as in effect before such amendments. Prior to being stricken, the second sentence of Code Sec. 897(h)(1) read as follows:

Notwithstanding the preceding sentence, any distribution by a real estate investment trust with respect to any class of stock which is regularly traded on an established

INCOME TAX—MISCELLANEOUS PROVISIONS

securities market located in the United States shall not be treated as gain recognized from the sale or exchange of a United States real property interest if the shareholder did not own more than 5 percent of such class of stock at any time during the 1-year period ending on the date of the distribution.

P.L. 109-222, §505(a)(2):

Amended Code Sec. 897(h)(4)(A)(ii) by adding at the end a new sentence. **Effective** for tax years of qualified investment entities beginning after 12-31-2005, except that no amount shall be required to be withheld under Code Sec. 1441, 1442, or 1445 with respect to any distribution before 5-17-2006 if such amount was not otherwise required to be withheld under any such section as in effect before such amendments.

P.L. 109-222, §506(a):

Amended Code Sec. 897(h) by adding at the end a new paragraph (5). **Effective** for tax years beginning after 12-31-2005, except that such amendment shall not apply to any distribution, or substitute dividend payment, occurring before the date that is 30 days after 5-17-2006.

- **2005, Gulf Opportunity Zone Act of 2005 (P.L. 109-135)**

P.L. 109-135, §403(p)(1)(A)-(B):

Amended the second sentence of Code Sec. 897(h)(1) by striking "any distribution" and all that follows through "any class of stock" and inserting "any distribution by a real estate investment trust with respect to any class of stock", and by striking "the taxable year" and inserting "the 1-year period ending on the date of the distribution". **Effective** as if included in the provision of the American Jobs Creation Act of 2004 (P.L. 108-357) to which it relates [**effective** for any distribution by a real estate investment trust which is treated as a deduction for a tax year of such trust beginning after 10-22-2004, and for any distribution by a real estate investment trust made after such date which is treated as a deduction under Code Sec. 860 for a tax year of such trust beginning on or before such date.—CCH]. Prior to amendment, the second sentence of Code Sec. 897(h)(1) read as follows:

Notwithstanding the preceding sentence, any distribution by a REIT with respect to any class of stock which is regularly traded on an established securities market located in the United States shall not be treated as gain recognized from the sale or exchange of a United States real property interest if the shareholder did not own more than 5 percent of such class of stock at any time during the taxable year.

- **2004, American Jobs Creation Act of 2004 (P.L. 108-357)**

P.L. 108-357, §411(c)(1):

Amended Code Sec. 897(h)(1) by striking "REIT" each place it appears and inserting "qualified investment entity". **Effective** for dividends with respect to tax years of regulated investment companies beginning after 12-31-2004.

P.L. 108-357, §411(c)(2):

Amended Code Sec. 897(h)(2) and (3). **Effective** after 12-31-2004. Prior to amendment, Code Sec. 897(h)(2) and (3) read as follows:

(2) SALE OF STOCK IN DOMESTICALLY-CONTROLLED REIT NOT TAXED.—The term "United States real property interest" does not include any interest in a domestically-controlled REIT.

(3) DISTRIBUTIONS BY DOMESTICALLY-CONTROLLED REITS.—In the case of a domestically-controlled REIT, rules similar to the rules of subsection (d) shall apply to the foreign ownership percentage of any gain.

P.L. 108-357, §411(c)(3):

Amended Code Sec. 897(h)(4)(A) and (B). **Effective** after 12-31-2004. Prior to amendment, Code Sec. 897(h)(4)(A) and (B) read as follows:

(A) REIT.—The term "REIT" means a real estate investment trust.

(B) DOMESTICALLY-CONTROLLED REIT.—The term "domestically-controlled REIT" means a REIT in which at all times during the testing period less than 50 percent in value of the stock was held directly or indirectly by foreign persons.

P.L. 108-357, §411(c)(4):

Amended Code Sec. 897(h)(4)(C) and (D) by striking "REIT" and inserting "qualified investment entity". **Effective** after 12-31-2004.

P.L. 108-357, §411(c)(5):

Amended the heading for Code Sec. 897(h) by striking "REITS" and inserting "CERTAIN INVESTMENT ENTITIES". **Effective** after 12-31-2004.

P.L. 108-357, §418(a):

Amended Code Sec. 897(h)(1) by adding at the end a new sentence. For the **effective** date, see Act Sec. 418(c), below.

P.L. 108-357, §418(c), as amended by P.L. 109-135, §403(p)(2), provides:

(c) EFFECTIVE DATE.—The amendments made by this section shall apply to—

(1) any distribution by a real estate investment trust which is treated as a deduction for a taxable year of such trust beginning after the date of the enactment of this Act, and

(2) any distribution by a real estate investment trust made after such date which is treated as a deduction under section 860 for a taxable year of such trust beginning on or before such date.

[Sec. 897(i)]

(i) ELECTION BY FOREIGN CORPORATION TO BE TREATED AS DOMESTIC CORPORATION.—

(1) IN GENERAL.—If—

(A) a foreign corporation holds a United States real property interest, and

(B) under any treaty obligation of the United States the foreign corporation is entitled to nondiscriminatory treatment with respect to that interest,

then such foreign corporation may make an election to be treated as a domestic corporation for purposes of this section, section 1445, and section 6039C.

(2) REVOCATION ONLY WITH CONSENT.—Any election under paragraph (1), once made, may be revoked only with the consent of the Secretary.

(3) MAKING OF ELECTION.—An election under paragraph (1) may be made only—

(A) if all of the owners of all classes of interests (other than interests solely as a creditor) in the foreign corporation at the time of the election consent to the making of the election and agree that gain, if any, from the disposition of such interest after June 18, 1980, which would be taken into account under subsection (a) shall be taxable notwithstanding any provision to the contrary in a treaty to which the United States is a party, and

(B) subject to such other conditions as the Secretary may prescribe by regulations with respect to the corporation or its shareholders.

In the case of a class of interest (other than an interest solely as a creditor) which is regularly traded on an established securities market, the consent described in subparagraph (A) need only be made by any person if such person held more than 5 percent of such class of interest at some time during the shorter of the periods described in subsection (c)(1)(A)(ii). The constructive ownership rules of subsection (c)(6)(C) shall apply in determining whether a person held more than 5 percent of a class of interest.

(4) EXCLUSIVE METHOD OF CLAIMING NONDISCRIMINATION.—The election provided by paragraph (1) shall be the exclusive remedy for any person claiming discriminatory treatment with respect to this section, section 1445, and section 6039C.

Amendments

- **1986, Tax Reform Act of 1986 (P.L. 99-514)**

P.L. 99-514, §1810(f)(1)(A):

Amended Code Sec. 897(i)(1) by striking out "and section 6039C" and inserting in lieu thereof ", section 1445, and section 6039C". **Effective** as if included in the provision of P.L. 98-369 to which it relates.

P.L. 99-514, §1810(f)(1)(B):

Amended Code Sec. 897(i)(4) by striking out "this section and section 6039C" and inserting in lieu thereof "this section, section 1445, and section 6039C". **Effective** as if included in the provision of P.L. 98-369 to which it relates.

- **1981, Economic Recovery Tax Act of 1981 (P.L. 97-34)**

P.L. 97-34, §831(d):

Amended Code Sec. 897(i). **Effective** for dispositions after 6-18-80, in tax years ending after that date. Prior to amendment, Code Sec. 897(i) read:

(i) ELECTION BY FOREIGN CORPORATION TO BE TREATED AS DOMESTIC CORPORATION.—

(1) IN GENERAL.—If—

(A) a foreign corporation has a permanent establishment in the United States, and

(B) under any treaty, such permanent establishment may not be treated less favorably than domestic corporations carrying on the same activities,

then such foreign corporation may make an election to be treated as a domestic corporation for purposes of this section and section 6039C.

(2) REVOCATION ONLY WITH CONSENT.—Any election under paragraph (1), once made, may be revoked only with the consent of the Secretary.

(3) MAKING OF ELECTION.—An election under paragraph (1) may be made only subject to such conditions as may be prescribed by the Secretary.

- **1980, Omnibus Reconciliation Act of 1980 (P.L. 96-499)**

P.L. 96-499, §1122(a):

Added Code Sec. 897. For the **effective** date, see Act Sec. 1125, below.

P.L. 96-499, §1125, as amended by P.L. 97-34, §831(h), provides:

SEC. 1125. EFFECTIVE DATE.

(a) IN GENERAL.—Except as provided in subsection (b) [relating to reporting requirements], the amendments made by this subtitle shall apply to dispositions after June 18, 1980.

* * *

(c) SPECIAL RULE FOR TREATIES.—

(1) IN GENERAL.—Except as provided in paragraph (2), after December 31, 1984, nothing in section 894(a) or 7852(d) of the Internal Revenue Code of 1954 or in any other provision of law shall be treated as requiring, by reason of any treaty obligation

INCOME TAX—MISCELLANEOUS PROVISIONS

of the United States, an exemption from (or reduction of) any tax imposed by section 871 or 882 of such Code on a gain described in section 897 of such Code.

(2) Special rule for treaties renegotiated before 1985.—If—

(A) any treaty (hereinafter in this paragraph referred to as the "old treaty") is renegotiated to resolve conflicts between such treaty and the provisions of section 897 of the Internal Revenue Code of 1954, and

(B) the new treaty is signed on or after January 1, 1981, and before January 1, 1985, then paragraph (1) shall be applied with respect to obligations under the old treaty by substituting for "December 31, 1984" the date (not later than 2 years after the new treaty was signed) specified in the new treaty (or accompanying exchange of notes).

(d) ADJUSTMENT IN BASIS FOR CERTAIN TRANSACTIONS BETWEEN RELATED PERSONS.—

(1) IN GENERAL.—In the case of any disposition after December 31, 1979, of a United States real property interest (as defined in section 897(c) of the Internal Revenue Code of 1954) to a related person (within the meaning of section 453(f)(1) of such Code), the basis of the interest in the hands of the person acquiring it shall be reduced by the amount of any nontaxed gain.

(2) NONTAXED GAIN.—For purposes of paragraph (1), the term "nontaxed gain" means any gain which is not subject to tax under section 871(b)(1) or 882(a)(1) of such Code—

(A) because the disposition occurred before June 19, 1980, or

(B) because of any treaty obligation of the United States.".

[Sec. 897(j)]

(j) CERTAIN CONTRIBUTIONS TO CAPITAL.—Except to the extent otherwise provided in regulations, gain shall be recognized by a nonresident alien individual or foreign corporation on the transfer of a United States real property interest to a foreign corporation if the transfer is made as paid in surplus or as a contribution to capital, in the amount of the excess of—

(1) the fair market value of such property transferred, over

(2) the sum of—

(A) the adjusted basis of such property in the hands of the transferor, plus

(B) the amount of gain, if any, recognized to the transferor under any other provision at the time of the transfer.

Amendments

• **1981, Economic Recovery Tax Act of 1981 (P.L. 97-34)**

P.L. 97-34, §831(f):

Added Code Sec. 897(j). **Effective** for disposition after 6-18-80, in tax years ending after that date. Also, see the amendment note following Code Sec. 897(i), for special rule with respect to treaties.

[Sec. 897(k)]—Repealed]

Amendments

• **1990, Omnibus Budget Reconciliation Act of 1990 (P.L. 101-508)**

P.L. 101-508, §11801(a)(30):

Repealed Code Sec. 897(k). **Effective** 11-5-90. Prior to repeal, Code Sec. 897(k) read as follows:

(k) FOREIGN CORPORATIONS ACQUIRED BEFORE ENACTMENT.—If—

(1) a foreign corporation adopts, or has adopted, a plan of liquidation described in section 334(b)(2)(A), and

(2) the 12-month period described in section 334(b)(2)(B) for the acquisition by purchase of the stock of the foreign corporation, began after December 31, 1979, and before November 26, 1980,

then such foreign corporation may make an election to be treated, for the period following June 18, 1980, as a domestic corporation pursuant to section 897(i)(1). Notwithstanding an election under the preceding sentence, any selling shareholder of such corporation shall be considered to have sold the stock of a foreign corporation.

P.L. 101-508, §11821(b), provides:

(b) SAVINGS PROVISION.—If—

(1) any provision amended or repealed by this part applied to—

(A) any transaction occurring before the date of the enactment of this Act,

(B) any property acquired before such date of enactment, or

(C) any item of income, loss, deduction, or credit taken into account before such date of enactment, and

(2) the treatment of such transaction, property, or item under such provision would (without regard to the amendments made by this part) affect liability for tax for periods ending after such date of enactment,

nothing in the amendments made by this part shall be construed to affect the treatment of such transaction, property, or item for purposes of determining liability for tax for periods ending after such date of enactment.

• **1981, Economic Recovery Tax Act of 1981 (P.L. 97-34)**

P.L. 97-34, §831(g):

Added Code Sec. 897(k). **Effective** for disposition after 6-18-80, in tax years ending after that date. Also, see the amendment note following Code Sec. 897(i) for the special rule with respect to treaties.

[Sec. 897(k)]

(k) SPECIAL RULES RELATING TO REAL ESTATE INVESTMENT TRUSTS.—

(1) INCREASE IN PERCENTAGE OWNERSHIP FOR EXCEPTIONS FOR PERSONS HOLDING PUBLICLY TRADED STOCK.—

(A) DISPOSITIONS.—In the case of any disposition of stock in a real estate investment trust, paragraphs (3) and (6)(C) of subsection (c) shall each be applied by substituting "more than 10 percent" for "more than 5 percent".

(B) DISTRIBUTIONS.—In the case of any distribution from a real estate investment trust, subsection (h)(1) shall be applied by substituting "10 percent" for "5 percent".

(2) STOCK HELD BY QUALIFIED SHAREHOLDERS NOT TREATED AS UNITED STATES REAL PROPERTY INTEREST.—

(A) IN GENERAL.—Except as provided in subparagraph (B)—

(i) stock of a real estate investment trust which is held directly (or indirectly through 1 or more partnerships) by a qualified shareholder shall not be treated as a United States real property interest, and

(ii) notwithstanding subsection (h)(1), any distribution to a qualified shareholder shall not be treated as gain recognized from the sale or exchange of a United States real property interest to the extent the stock of the real estate investment trust held by such qualified shareholder is not treated as a United States real property interest under clause (i).

(B) EXCEPTION.—In the case of a qualified shareholder with one or more applicable investors—

(i) subparagraph (A)(i) shall not apply to the applicable percentage of the stock of the real estate investment trust held by the qualified shareholder, and

(ii) the applicable percentage of the amounts realized by the qualified shareholder with respect to any disposition of stock in the real estate investment trust or with respect to any distribution from the real estate investment trust attributable to gain from sales or exchanges of a United States real property interest shall be treated as amounts realized from the disposition of United States real property interests.

(C) SPECIAL RULE FOR CERTAIN DISTRIBUTIONS TREATED AS SALE OR EXCHANGE.—If a distribution by a real estate investment trust is treated as a sale or exchange of stock under section 301(c)(3), 302, or 331 with respect to a qualified shareholder—

(i) in the case of an applicable investor, subparagraph (B) shall apply with respect to such distribution, and

(ii) in the case of any other person, such distribution shall be treated under section 857(b)(3)(F) as a dividend from a real estate investment trust notwithstanding any other provision of this title.

(D) APPLICABLE INVESTOR.—For purposes of this subsection, the term "applicable investor" means, with respect to any qualified shareholder holding stock in a real estate investment trust, a person (other than a qualified shareholder) which—

(i) holds an interest (other than an interest solely as a creditor) in such qualified shareholder, and

(ii) holds more than 10 percent of the stock of such real estate investment trust (whether or not by reason of the person's ownership interest in the qualified shareholder).

INCOME TAX—MISCELLANEOUS PROVISIONS

(E) CONSTRUCTIVE OWNERSHIP RULES.—For purposes of subparagraphs (B)(i) and (D), the constructive ownership rules under subsection (c)(6)(C) shall apply.

(F) APPLICABLE PERCENTAGE.—For purposes of subparagraph (B), the term "applicable percentage" means the percentage of the value of the interests (other than interests held solely as a creditor) in the qualified shareholder held by applicable investors.

(3) QUALIFIED SHAREHOLDER.—For purposes of this subsection—

(A) IN GENERAL.—The term "qualified shareholder" means a foreign person which—

(i)(I) is eligible for benefits of a comprehensive income tax treaty with the United States which includes an exchange of information program and the principal class of interests of which is listed and regularly traded on 1 or more recognized stock exchanges (as defined in such comprehensive income tax treaty), or

(II) is a foreign partnership that is created or organized under foreign law as a limited partnership in a jurisdiction that has an agreement for the exchange of information with respect to taxes with the United States and has a class of limited partnership units which is regularly traded on the New York Stock Exchange or Nasdaq Stock Market and such class of limited partnership units value is greater than 50 percent of the value of all the partnership units,

(ii) is a qualified collective investment vehicle, and

(iii) maintains records on the identity of each person who, at any time during the foreign person's taxable year, holds directly 5 percent or more of the class of interest described in subclause (I) or (II) of clause (i), as the case may be.

(B) QUALIFIED COLLECTIVE INVESTMENT VEHICLE.—For purposes of this subsection, the term "qualified collective investment vehicle" means a foreign person—

(i) which—

(I) is eligible for benefits under the comprehensive income tax treaty described in subparagraph (A)(i)(I), but only if the dividends article of such treaty imposes conditions on the benefits allowable in the case of dividends paid by a real estate investment trust, and

(II) is eligible under such treaty for a reduced rate of withholding with respect to ordinary dividends paid by a real estate investment trust even if such person holds more than 10 percent of the stock of such real estate investment trust,

(ii) which—

(I) is a publicly traded partnership (as defined in section 7704(b)) to which subsection (a) of section 7704 does not apply,

(II) is a withholding foreign partnership for purposes of chapters 3, 4, and 61, and

(III) if such foreign partnership were a domestic corporation, would be a United States real property holding corporation (determined without regard to paragraph (1)) at any time during the 5-year period ending on the date of disposition of, or distribution with respect to, such partnership's interests in a real estate investment trust, or

(iii) which is designated as a qualified collective investment vehicle by the Secretary and is either—

(I) fiscally transparent within the meaning of section 894, or

(II) required to include dividends in its gross income, but entitled to a deduction for distributions to persons holding interests (other than interests solely as a creditor) in such foreign person.

(4) PARTNERSHIP ALLOCATIONS.—

(A) IN GENERAL.—For the purposes of this subsection, in the case of an applicable investor who is a nonresident alien individual or a foreign corporation and is a partner in a partnership that is a qualified shareholder, if such partner's proportionate share of USRPI gain for the taxable year exceeds such partner's distributive share of USRPI gain for the taxable year, then

(i) such partner's distributive share of the amount of gain taken into account under subsection (a)(1) by the partner for the taxable year (determined without regard to this paragraph) shall be increased by the amount of such excess, and

(ii) such partner's distributive share of items of income or gain for the taxable year that are not treated as gain taken into account under subsection (a)(1) (determined without regard to this paragraph) shall be decreased (but not below zero) by the amount of such excess.

(B) USRPI GAIN.—For the purposes of this paragraph, the term "USRPI gain" means the excess (if any) of—

(i) the sum of—

(I) any gain recognized from the disposition of a United States real property interest, and

(II) any distribution by a real estate investment trust that is treated as gain recognized from the sale or exchange of a United States real property interest, over

(ii) any loss recognized from the disposition of a United States real property interest.

(C) PROPORTIONATE SHARE OF USRPI GAIN.—For purposes of this paragraph, an applicable investor's proportionate share of USRPI gain shall be determined on the basis of such investor's share of partnership items of income or gain (excluding gain allocated under section 704(c)), whichever results in the largest proportionate share. If the investor's share of partnership items of income or gain (excluding gain allocated under section 704(c)) may vary during the period such investor is a partner in the partnership, such share shall be the highest share such investor may receive.

Amendments

- **2018, Tax Technical Corrections Act of 2018 (P.L. 115-141)**

P.L. 115-141, §101(p)(1)(A)-(B), Div. U:

Amended Code Sec. 897(k)(2) by striking so much of subparagraph (B) as precedes "amounts realized by the qualified shareholder" and inserting a new subparagraph (B), and by adding at the end a new subparagraph (F). **Effective** as if included in the provision of the Protecting Americans from Tax Hikes Act of 2015 to which it relates [**effective** 12-18-2015 and applicable to any disposition on or after such date, and any distribution by a REIT on or after such date which is treated as a deduction for a tax year of such trust ending after such date.—CCH]. Prior to being amended, Code Sec. 897(k)(2)(B) read as follows:

(B) EXCEPTION.—In the case of a qualified shareholder with 1 or more applicable investors—

(i) subparagraph (A)(i) shall not apply to so much of the stock of a real estate investment trust held by a qualified shareholder as bears the same ratio to the value of the interests (other than interests held solely as a creditor) held by such applicable investors in the qualified shareholder bears to value of all interests (other than interests held solely as a creditor) in the qualified shareholder, and

(ii) a percentage equal to the ratio determined under clause (i) of the amounts realized by the qualified shareholder with respect to any disposition of stock in the real estate investment trust or with respect to any distribution from the real estate investment trust attributable to gain from sales or exchanges of a United States real property interest shall be treated as amounts realized from the disposition of United States real property interests.

P.L. 115-141, §101(p)(2), Div. U:

Amended Code Sec. 897(k)(2)(D) by striking "paragraph" and inserting "subsection". **Effective** as if included in the provision of the Protecting Americans from Tax Hikes Act of 2015 to which it relates [**effective** 12-18-2015 and applicable to any disposition on or after such date, and any distribution by a REIT on or after such date which is treated as a deduction for a tax year of such trust ending after such date.—CCH].

P.L. 115-141, §101(p)(3), Div. U:

Amended Code Sec. 897(k)(2)(E) by striking "and (C) and paragraph (4)" and inserting "and (D)". **Effective** as if included in the provision of the Protecting Americans from Tax Hikes Act of 2015 to which it relates [**effective** 12-18-2015 and applicable to any disposition on or after such date, and any distribution by a REIT on or after such date which is treated as a deduction for a tax year of such trust ending after such date.—CCH].

P.L. 115-141, §101(p)(4), Div. U:

Amended Code Sec. 897(k)(3)(B)(i) by striking so much as precedes "for a reduced rate of withholding" and inserting a new clause (i). **Effective** as if included in the

INCOME TAX—MISCELLANEOUS PROVISIONS

provision of the Protecting Americans from Tax Hikes Act of 2015 to which it relates [**effective** 12-18-2015 and applicable to any disposition on or after such date, and any distribution by a REIT on or after such date which is treated as a deduction for a tax year of such trust ending after such date.—CCH]. Prior to being amended, Code Sec. 897(k)(3)(B)(i) read as follows:

(i) which, under the comprehensive income tax treaty described in subparagraph (A)(i), is eligible for a reduced rate of withholding with respect to ordinary dividends paid by a real estate investment trust even if such person holds more than 10 percent of the stock of such real estate investment trust,

P.L. 115-141, §101(p)(5)(A)-(B), Div. U:

Amended Code Sec. 897(k)(3)(B)(ii) by adding "and" at the end of subclause (II), and by striking "United States corporation" in subclause (III) and inserting "domestic corporation". **Effective** as if included in the provision of the Protecting Americans from Tax Hikes Act of 2015 to which it relates [**effective** 12-18-2015 and applicable to any disposition on or after such date, and any distribution by a REIT on or after such date which is treated as a deduction for a tax year of such trust ending after such date.—CCH].

Amendments

• **1988, Technical and Miscellaneous Revenue Act of 1988 (P.L. 100-647)**

P.L. 100-647, §1006(e)(19):

Repealed Code Sec. 897(l). **Effective** as if included in the provision of P.L. 99-514 to which it relates. Prior to repeal, Code Sec. 897(l) read as follows:

(l) SPECIAL RULE FOR CERTAIN UNITED STATES SHAREHOLDERS OF LIQUIDATING FOREIGN CORPORATIONS.—If a corporation adopts a plan of complete liquidation and if, solely by reason of section 897(d), section 337(a) does not apply to sales or exchanges, or section 336 does not apply to distributions, of United States real property interests by such corporation, then, in the case of any shareholder who is a United States citizen or resident and who has held stock in such corporation continuously since June 18, 1980, for the first taxable year of such shareholder in which he receives a distribution in complete liquidation with respect to such stock—

(1) the amount realized by such shareholder on the distribution shall be increased by his proportionate share of the amount by which the tax imposed by this subtitle of

P.L. 115-141, §401(a)(156), Div. U:

Amended the heading of Code Sec. 897(k)(2) by striking "USRPI" and inserting "UNITED STATES REAL PROPERTY INTEREST". **Effective** 3-23-2018.

• **2015, Protecting Americans from Tax Hikes Act of 2015 (P.L. 114-113)**

P.L. 114-113, §322(a)(1), Div. Q:

Amended Code Sec. 897 by adding at the end a new subsection (k). For the **effective** date, see Act Sec. 322(c)(1), below.

P.L. 114-113, §322(c)(1), Div. Q, provides:

(1) IN GENERAL.—The amendments made by subsection (a) shall take effect on the date of enactment and shall apply to—

(A) any disposition on and after the date of the enactment of this Act, and

(B) any distribution by a real estate investment trust on or after the date of the enactment of this Act which is treated as a deduction for a taxable year of such trust ending after such date.

[Sec. 897(l)—Repealed]

such corporation would have been reduced if section 897(d) had not been applicable, and

(2) for purposes of this title, such shareholder shall be deemed to have paid, on the last day prescribed by law for the payment of the tax imposed by this subtitle on such shareholder for such taxable year, an amount of tax equal to the amount of the increase described in paragraph (1).

• **1981, Economic Recovery Tax Act of 1981 (P.L. 97-34)**

P.L. 97-34, §831(g):

Added Code Sec. 897(l). **Effective** for dispositions after 6-18-80, in tax years ending after that date. Also, see the amendment note following Code Sec. 897(i) for the special rule with respect to treaties.

[Sec. 897(l)]

(l) EXCEPTION FOR QUALIFIED FOREIGN PENSION FUNDS.—

(1) IN GENERAL.—For purposes of this section, a qualified foreign pension fund shall not be treated as a nonresident alien individual or a foreign corporation. For purposes of the preceding sentence, an entity all the interests of which are held by a qualified foreign pension fund shall be treated as such a fund.

(2) QUALIFIED FOREIGN PENSION FUND.—For purposes of this subsection, the term "qualified foreign pension fund" means any trust, corporation, or other organization or arrangement—

(A) which is created or organized under the law of a country other than the United States,

(B) which is established—

(i) by such country (or one or more political subdivisions thereof) to provide retirement or pension benefits to participants or beneficiaries that are current or former employees (including self-employed individuals) or persons designated by such employees, as a result of services rendered by such employees to their employers, or

(ii) by one or more employers to provide retirement or pension benefits to participants or beneficiaries that are current or former employees (including self-employed individuals) or persons designated by such employees in consideration for services rendered by such employees to such employers,

(C) which does not have a single participant or beneficiary with a right to more than five percent of its assets or income,

(D) which is subject to government regulation and with respect to which annual information about its beneficiaries is provided, or is otherwise available, to the relevant tax authorities in the country in which it is established or operates, and

(E) with respect to which, under the laws of the country in which it is established or operates—

(i) contributions to such trust, corporation, organization, or arrangement which would otherwise be subject to tax under such laws are deductible or excluded from the gross income of such entity or arrangement or taxed at a reduced rate, or

(ii) taxation of any investment income of such trust, corporation, organization or arrangement is deferred, or such income is excluded from the gross income of such entity or arrangement or is taxed at a reduced rate.

(3) REGULATIONS.—The Secretary shall prescribe such regulations as may be necessary or appropriate to carry out the purposes of this subsection.

Amendments

• **2018, Tax Technical Corrections Act of 2018 (P.L. 115-141)**

P.L. 115-141, §101(q)(1), Div. U:

Amended so much of Code Sec. 897(l) as precedes paragraph (2) thereof. **Effective** as if included in the provision of the Protecting Americans from Tax Hikes Act of 2015 to which it relates [**effective** for dispositions and distributions after 12-18-2015.—CCH]. Prior to being amended, so much of Code Sec. 897(l) as precedes paragraph (2) thereof read as follows:

(l) EXCEPTION FOR INTERESTS HELD BY FOREIGN PENSION FUNDS.—

(1) IN GENERAL.—This section shall not apply to any United States real property interest held directly (or indirectly through 1 or more partnerships) by, or to any distribution received from a real estate investment trust by—

(A) a qualified foreign pension fund, or

(B) any entity all of the interests of which are held by a qualified foreign pension fund.

P.L. 115-141, §101(q)(2), Div. U:

Amended Code Sec. 897(l)(2)(B). **Effective** as if included in the provision of the Protecting Americans from Tax Hikes Act of 2015 to which it relates [**effective** for dispositions and distributions after 12-18-2015.—CCH]. Prior to amendment, Code Sec. 897(l)(2)(B) read as follows:

(B) which is established to provide retirement or pension benefits to participants or beneficiaries that are current or former employees (or persons designated by such employees) of one or more employers in consideration for services rendered,

P.L. 115-141, §101(q)(3), Div. U:

Amended Code Sec. 897(l)(2)(D) by striking "provides annual information reporting about its beneficiaries to the relevant tax authorities" and inserting "with respect to which annual information about its beneficiaries is provided, or is otherwise available, to the relevant tax authorities". **Effective** as if included in the provision of the Protecting Americans from Tax Hikes Act of 2015 to which it relates [**effective** for dispositions and distributions after 12-18-2015.—CCH].

P.L. 115-141, §101(q)(4)(A)-(B), Div. U:

Amended Code Sec. 897(l)(2)(E) by striking "such entity" in clause (i) and inserting "such entity or arrangement", and by striking "or such income is taxed at a reduced rate" in clause (ii) and inserting ", or such income is excluded from the gross income of such entity or arrangement or is taxed at a reduced rate". **Effective** as if included in the provision of the Protecting Americans from Tax Hikes Act of 2015 to which it relates [**effective** for dispositions and distributions after 12-18-2015.—CCH].

• **2015, Protecting Americans from Tax Hikes Act of 2015 (P.L. 114-113)**

P.L. 114-113, §323(a), Div. Q:

Amended Code Sec. 897, as amended by this Act, by adding at the end a new subsection (l). **Effective** for dispositions and distributions after 12-18-2015.

Sec. 897(l)—Repealed

INCOME TAX—MISCELLANEOUS PROVISIONS

[Sec. 898]
SEC. 898. TAXABLE YEAR OF CERTAIN FOREIGN CORPORATIONS.

[Sec. 898(a)]
(a) GENERAL RULE.—For purposes of this title, the taxable year of any specified foreign corporation shall be the required year determined under subsection (c).

[Sec. 898(b)]
(b) SPECIFIED FOREIGN CORPORATION.—For purposes of this section—

(1) IN GENERAL.—The term "specified foreign corporation" means any foreign corporation—

(A) which is treated as a controlled foreign corporation for any purpose under subpart F of part III of this subchapter, and

(B) with respect to which the ownership requirements of paragraph (2) are met.

(2) OWNERSHIP REQUIREMENTS.—

(A) IN GENERAL.—The ownership requirements of this paragraph are met with respect to any foreign corporation if a United States shareholder owns, on each testing day, more than 50 percent of—

(i) the total voting power of all classes of stock of such corporation entitled to vote, or

(ii) the total value of all classes of stock of such corporation.

(B) OWNERSHIP.—For purposes of subparagraph (A), the rules of subsections (a) and (b) of section 958 shall apply in determining ownership.

(3) UNITED STATES SHAREHOLDER.—The term "United States shareholder" has the meaning given to such term by section 951(b), except that, in the case of a foreign corporation having related person insurance income (as defined in section 953(c)(2)), the Secretary may treat any person as a United States shareholder for purposes of this section if such person is treated as a United States shareholder under section 953(c)(1).

Amendments

• **2004, American Jobs Creation Act of 2004 (P.L. 108-357)**

P.L. 108-357, §413(c)(13)(A):

Amended Code Sec. 898(b)(1)(A). **Effective** for tax years of foreign corporations beginning after 12-31-2004, and for tax years of United States shareholders with or within which such tax years of foreign corporations end. Prior to amendment, Code Sec. 898(b)(1)(A) read as follows:

(A) which is—

(i) treated as a controlled foreign corporation for any purpose under subpart F of part III of this subchapter, or

(ii) a foreign personal holding company (as defined in section 552), and

P.L. 108-357, §413(c)(13)(B):

Amended Code Sec. 898(b)(2)(B) by striking "and sections 551(f) and 554, whichever are applicable," immediately following "section 958". **Effective** for tax years of foreign corporations beginning after 12-31-2004, and for tax years of United States shareholders with or within which such tax years of foreign corporations end.

P.L. 108-357, §413(c)(13)(C):

Amended Code Sec. 898(b)(3). **Effective** for tax years of foreign corporations beginning after 12-31-2004, and for tax years of United States shareholders with or within which such tax years of foreign corporations end. Prior to amendment, Code Sec. 898(b)(3) read as follows:

(3) UNITED STATES SHAREHOLDER.—

(A) IN GENERAL.—The term "United States shareholder" has the meaning given to such term by section 951(b), except that, in the case of a foreign corporation having related person insurance income (as defined in section 953(c)(2)), the Secretary may treat any person as a United States shareholder for purposes of this section if such person is treated as a United States shareholder under section 953(c)(1).

(B) FOREIGN PERSONAL HOLDING COMPANIES.—In the case of any foreign personal holding company (as defined in section 552) which is not a specified foreign corporation by reason of paragraph (1)(A)(i), the term "United States shareholder" means any person who is treated as a United States shareholder under section 551.

[Sec. 898(c)]
(c) DETERMINATION OF REQUIRED YEAR.—

(1) IN GENERAL.—The required year is—

(A) the majority U.S. shareholder year, or

(B) if there is no majority U.S. shareholder year, the taxable year prescribed under regulations.

(2) 1-MONTH DEFERRAL ALLOWED.—A specified foreign corporation may elect, in lieu of the taxable year under paragraph (1)(A), a taxable year beginning 1 month earlier than the majority U.S. shareholder year.

(3) MAJORITY U.S. SHAREHOLDER YEAR.—

(A) IN GENERAL.—For purposes of this subsection, the term "majority U.S. shareholder year" means the taxable year (if any) which, on each testing day, constituted the taxable year of—

(i) each United States shareholder described in subsection (b)(2)(A), and

(ii) each United States shareholder not described in clause (i) whose stock was treated as owned under subsection (b)(2)(B) by any shareholder described in such clause.

(B) TESTING DAY.—The testing days shall be—

(i) the first day of the corporation's taxable year (determined without regard to this section), or

(ii) the days during such representative period as the Secretary may prescribe.

Amendments

• **2004, American Jobs Creation Act of 2004 (P.L. 108-357)**

P.L. 108-357, §413(c)(13)(D):

Amended Code Sec. 898(c). **Effective** for tax years of foreign corporations beginning after 12-31-2004, and for tax years of United States shareholders with or within which such tax years of foreign corporations end. Prior to amendment, Code Sec. 898(c) read as follows:

(c) DETERMINATION OF REQUIRED YEAR.—

(1) CONTROLLED FOREIGN CORPORATIONS.—

(A) IN GENERAL.—In the case of a specified foreign corporation described in subsection (b)(1)(A)(i), the required year is—

(i) the majority U.S. shareholder year, or

(ii) if there is no majority U.S. shareholder year, the taxable year prescribed under regulations.

(B) 1-MONTH DEFERRAL ALLOWED.—A specified foreign corporation may elect, in lieu of the taxable year under subparagraph (A)(i), a taxable year beginning 1 month earlier than the majority U.S. shareholder year.

(C) MAJORITY U.S. SHAREHOLDER YEAR.—

(i) IN GENERAL.—For purposes of this subsection, the term "majority U.S. shareholder year" means the taxable year (if any) which, on each testing day, constituted the taxable year of—

(I) each United States shareholder described in subsection (b)(2)(A), and

(II) each United States shareholder not described in subclause (I) whose stock was treated as owned under subsection (b)(2)(B) by any shareholder described in such subclause.

(ii) TESTING DAY.—The testing days shall be—

(I) the first day of the corporation's taxable year (determined without regard to this section), or

(II) the days during such representative period as the Secretary may prescribe.

(2) FOREIGN PERSONAL HOLDING COMPANIES.—In the case of a foreign personal holding company described in subsection (b)(3)(B), the required year shall be determined under paragraph (1), except that subparagraph (B) of paragraph (1) shall not apply.

• **1989, Omnibus Budget Reconciliation Act of 1989 (P.L. 101-239)**

P.L. 101-239, §7401(a):

Amended subpart D of part II of subchapter N of chapter 1 by adding at the end thereof a new section 898. **Effective** for tax years of foreign corporations beginning after 7-10-89. For special rules, see Act Sec. 7401(d)(2), below.

P.L. 101-239, §7401(d)(2), provides:

(2) SPECIAL RULES.—If any foreign corporation is required by the amendments made by this section to change its taxable year for its first taxable year beginning after July 10, 1989—

Internal Revenue Code   **Sec. 898(c)(3)(B)(ii)**

INCOME TAX—FOREIGN TAX CREDIT

(A) such change shall be treated as initiated by the taxpayer,

(B) such change shall be treated as having been made with the consent of the Secretary of the Treasury or his delegate, and

(C) if, by reason of such change, any United States person is required to include in gross income for 1 taxable year amounts attributable to 2 taxable years of such foreign corporation, the amount which would otherwise be required to be included in gross income for such 1 taxable year by reason of the short taxable year of the foreign corporation resulting from such change shall be included in gross income ratably over the 4-taxable-year period beginning with such 1 taxable year.

PART III—INCOME FROM SOURCES WITHOUT THE UNITED STATES

Subpart A.	Foreign tax credit.
Subpart B.	Earned income of citizens or residents of United States.
Subpart C.	[Repealed.]
Subpart D.	Possessions of the United States.
Subpart E.	[Repealed.]
Subpart F.	Controlled foreign corporations.
Subpart G.	Export trade corporations.
Subpart H.	[Repealed.]
Subpart I.	Admissibility of documentation maintained in foreign countries.
Subpart J.	Foreign currency transactions.

Subpart A—Foreign Tax Credit

Sec. 901.	Taxes of foreign countries and of possessions of United States.
Sec. 903.	Credit for taxes in lieu of income, etc., taxes.
Sec. 904.	Limitation on credit.
Sec. 905.	Applicable rules.
Sec. 906.	Nonresident alien individuals and foreign corporations.
Sec. 907.	Special rules in case of foreign oil and gas income.
Sec. 908.	Reduction of credit for participation in or cooperation with an international boycott.
Sec. 909.	Suspension of taxes and credits until related income taken into account.

[Sec. 901]

SEC. 901. TAXES OF FOREIGN COUNTRIES AND OF POSSESSIONS OF UNITED STATES.

[Sec. 901(a)]

(a) ALLOWANCE OF CREDIT.—If the taxpayer chooses to have the benefits of this subpart, the tax imposed by this chapter shall, subject to the limitation of section 904, be credited with the amounts provided in the applicable paragraph of subsection (b) plus, in the case of a corporation, the taxes deemed to have been paid under section 960. Such choice for any taxable year may be made or changed at any time before the expiration of the period prescribed for making a claim for credit or refund of the tax imposed by this chapter for such taxable year. The credit shall not be allowed against any tax treated as a tax not imposed by this chapter under section 26(b).

Amendments

• **2017, Tax Cuts and Jobs Act (P.L. 115-97)**

P.L. 115-97, §14301(c)(7):

Amended Code Sec. 901(a) by striking "sections 902 and 960" and inserting "section 960". **Effective** for tax years of foreign corporations beginning after 12-31-2017, and to tax years of United States shareholders in which or with which such tax years of foreign corporations end.

• **1984, Deficit Reduction Act of 1984 (P.L. 98-369)**

P.L. 98-369, §474(r)(20):

Amended Code Sec. 901(a) by striking out the last sentence and inserting in lieu thereof a new sentence. **Effective** for tax years beginning after 12-31-83, and to carrybacks from such years. Prior to amendment, but after the amendment made by Act Sec. 713(c)(1)(C), Code Sec. 901(a) read as follows:

(a) Allowance of Credit.—If the taxpayer chooses to have the benefits of this subpart, the tax imposed by this chapter shall, subject to the limitation of section 904, be credited with the amounts provided in the applicable paragraph of subsection (b) plus, in the case of a corporation, the taxes deemed to have been paid under sections 902 and 960. Such choice for any taxable year may be made or changed at any time before the expiration of the period prescribed for making a claim for credit or refund of the tax imposed by this chapter for such taxable year. The credit shall not be allowed against the tax imposed by section 56 (relating to corporate minimum tax), against the tax imposed for the taxable year under section 72(m)(5)(B) (relating to 10 percent tax on premature distributions to *key* employees), section 72(q)(1) (relating to 5-percent tax on premature distributions under annuity contracts), against the tax imposed by section 402(e) (relating to tax on lump sum distributions), against the tax imposed for the taxable year by section 408(f) (relating to additional tax on income from certain retirement accounts), against the tax imposed by section 531 (relating to the tax on accumulated earnings), against the additional tax imposed for the taxable year under section 1351 (relating to recoveries of foreign expropriation losses), or against the personal holding company tax imposed by section 541.

• **1984, Deficit Reduction Act of 1984 (P.L. 98-369)**

P.L. 98-369, §612(e)(1):

Amended Code Sec. 901(a) (as amended by this Act) by striking out "section 25(b)" and inserting in lieu thereof "section 26(b)". **Effective** for interest paid or accrued after 12-31-84, on indebtedness incurred after 12-31-84.

P.L. 98-369, §713(c)(1)(C):

Amended Code Sec. 901(a) by striking out "tax on premature distributions to owner-employees" and inserting in lieu thereof "tax on premature distributions to key employees". **Effective** as if included in the provision of P.L. 97-248 to which it relates.

• **1983, Technical Corrections Act of 1982 (P.L. 97-448)**

P.L. 97-448, §306(a)(1)(A):

Amended P.L. 97-248, §201, by redesignating the second subsection (c) as subsection (d).

• **1982, Tax Equity and Fiscal Responsibility Act of 1982 (P.L. 97-248)**

P.L. 97-248, §201(d)(8)(A):

Amended Code Sec. 901(a) by striking out "(relating to minimum tax for tax preferences)" and inserting in lieu thereof "(relating to corporate minimum tax)". **Effective** for tax years beginning after 12-31-82.

P.L. 97-248, §265(b)(2)(A)(iv):

Amended Code Sec. 901(a) by inserting "section 72(q)(1) (relating to 5-percent tax on premature distributions under annuity contracts)," after "owner-employees),". **Effective** for distributions after 12-31-82.

• **1976, Tax Reform Act of 1976 (P.L. 94-455)**

P.L. 94-455, §1031(b)(1):

Substituted "limitation" for "applicable limitation" in Code Sec. 901(a). **Effective** as noted in Act Sec. 1031(c), below.

P.L. 94-455, §1031(c), provides:

(c) EFFECTIVE DATES.

(1) IN GENERAL.—Except as provided in paragraphs (2) and (3), the amendments made by this section shall apply to taxable years beginning after December 31, 1975.

(2) EXCEPTION FOR CERTAIN MINING OPERATIONS.—In the case of a domestic corporation or includible corporation in an affiliated group (as defined in section 1504 of the Internal Revenue Code of 1954) which has as of October 1, 1975—

(A) been engaged in the active conduct of the trade or business of the extraction of minerals (of a character with respect to which a deduction for depletion is allowable under section 613 of such Code) outside the United States or its possessions for less than 5 years preceding the date of enactment of this Act,

(B) had deductions properly apportioned or allocated to its gross income from such trade or business in excess of such gross income in at least 2 taxable years,

(C) 80 percent of its gross receipts are from the sale of such minerals, and

(D) made commitments for substantial expansion of such mineral extraction activities,

Sec. 901

the amendments made by this section shall apply to taxable years beginning after December 31, 1978. In the case of losses sustained in taxable years beginning before January 1, 1979, by any corporation to which this paragraph applies, the provisions of section 904(f) of such Code shall be applied with respect to such losses under the principles of section 904(a)(1) of such Code as in effect before the enactment of this Act.

(3) EXCEPTION FOR INCOME FROM POSSESSIONS.—In the case of gross income from sources within a possession of the United States (and the deductions properly apportioned or allocated thereto), the amendments made by this section shall apply to taxable years beginning after December 31, 1978. In the case of losses sustained in a possession of the United States in taxable years beginning before January 1, 1979, the provisions of section 904(f) of such Code shall be applied with respect to such losses under the principles of section 904(a)(1) of such Code as in effect before the enactment of this Act.

(4) CARRYBACKS AND CARRYOVERS IN THE CASE OF MINING OPERATIONS AND INCOME FROM A POSSESSION.—In the case of a taxpayer to whom paragraph (2) or (3) of this subsection applies, section 904(e) of such Code shall apply except that "January 1, 1979" shall be substituted for "January 1, 1976" each place it appears therein. If such a taxpayer elects the overall limitation for a taxable year beginning before January 1, 1979, such section 904(e) shall be applied by substituting "the January 1, of the last year for which such taxpayer is on the per-country limitation" for "January 1, 1976" each place it appears therein.

P.L. 94-455, §1901(b)(37)(A):

Struck out "under section 1333 (relating to war loss recoveries) or" before "under section 1351" in the third sentence of Code Sec. 901(a). **Effective** for tax years beginning after 12-31-76.

- **1974, Employee Retirement Income Security Act of 1974 (P.L. 93-406)**

P.L. 93-406, §§2001(g)(2), 2002(g)(3), 2005(c)(5):

Amended Code Sec. 901(a). For the **effective** dates, see the amendment notes for Code Secs. 72(m)(5)(B), 402(e) and 408(f). Prior to amendment, Code Sec. 901(a) read as follows:

(a) ALLOWANCE OF CREDIT.—If the taxpayer chooses to have the benefits of this subpart, the tax imposed by this chapter shall, subject to the applicable limitation of section 904, be credited with the amounts provided in the applicable paragraph of subsection (b) plus, in the case of a corporation, the taxes deemed to have been paid under sections 902 and 960. Such choice for any taxable year may be made or changed at any time before the expiration of the period prescribed for making a claim for credit or refund of the tax imposed by this chapter for such taxable year. The credit shall not be allowed against the tax imposed by section 56 (relating to minimum tax for tax preferences), against the tax imposed by section 531 (relating to the tax on accumulated earnings), against the additional tax imposed for the taxable year under section 1333 (relating to war loss recoveries) or under section 1351 (relating to recoveries of foreign expropriation losses), or against the personal holding company tax imposed by section 541.

- **1969, Tax Reform Act of 1969 (P.L. 91-172)**

P.L. 91-172, §301(b)(9):

Amended Code Sec. 901(a) by adding the phrase "against the tax imposed by section 56 (relating to minimum tax for tax preferences),". **Effective** 1-1-70.

- **1966 (P.L. 89-834)**

P.L. 89-384, §1(c):

Amended Code Sec. 901(a) by inserting "or under section 1351 (relating to recoveries of foreign expropriation losses)" immediately after "section 1333 (relating to war loss recoveries)" in the last sentence. **Effective** for amounts received after 12-31-64, in respect of foreign expropriation losses sustained after 12-31-58.

- **1962, Revenue Act of 1962 (P.L. 87-834)**

P.L. 87-834, §12(b)(1):

Amended Code Sec. 901(a) by substituting "sections 902 and 960" for "section 902" in the first sentence. **Effective** 10-17-62.

- **1960 (P.L. 86-780)**

P.L. 86-780, §3(a):

Amended Code Sec. 901(a) by inserting the word "applicable" immediately preceding the word "limitation" in the first sentence. **Effective** for tax years beginning after 12-31-60.

P.L. 86-780, §3(b):

Amended the second sentence of Code Sec. 901(a). **Effective** for tax years beginning after 12-31-53 and ending after 8-16-54. Prior to amendment, that sentence read as follows:

"Such choice may be made or changed at any time prior to the expiration of the period prescribed for making a claim for credit or refund of the tax against which the credit is allowable."

[Sec. 901(b)]

(b) AMOUNT ALLOWED.—Subject to the limitation of section 904, the following amounts shall be allowed as the credit under subsection (a):

(1) CITIZENS AND DOMESTIC CORPORATIONS.—In the case of a citizen of the United States and of a domestic corporation, the amount of any income, war profits, and excess profits taxes paid or accrued during the taxable year to any foreign country or to any possession of the United States; and

(2) RESIDENT OF THE UNITED STATES OR PUERTO RICO.—In the case of a resident of the United States and in the case of an individual who is a bona fide resident of Puerto Rico during the entire taxable year, the amount of any such taxes paid or accrued during the taxable year to any possession of the United States; and

(3) ALIEN RESIDENT OF THE UNITED STATES OR PUERTO RICO.—In the case of an alien resident of the United States and in the case of an alien individual who is a bona fide resident of Puerto Rico during the entire taxable year, the amount of any such taxes paid or accrued during the taxable year to any foreign country; and

(4) NONRESIDENT ALIEN INDIVIDUALS AND FOREIGN CORPORATIONS.—In the case of any nonresident alien individual not described in section 876 and in the case of any foreign corporation, the amount determined pursuant to section 906; and

(5) PARTNERSHIPS AND ESTATES.—In the case of any person described in paragraph (1), (2), (3), or (4), who is a member of a partnership or a beneficiary of an estate or trust, the amount of his proportionate share of the taxes (described in such paragraph) of the partnership or the estate or trust paid or accrued during the taxable year to a foreign country or to any possession of the United States, as the case may be. Under rules or regulations prescribed by the Secretary, in the case of any foreign trust of which the settlor or another person would be treated as owner of any portion of the trust under subpart E but for section 672(f), [the term "taxes imposed on the trust" includes] the allocable amount of any income, war profits, and excess profits taxes imposed by any foreign country or possession of the United States on the settlor or such other person in respect of trust income.

Amendments

- **2004, American Jobs Creation Act of 2004 (P.L. 108-357)**

P.L. 108-357, §405(b):

Amended Code Sec. 901(b)(5) by striking "any individual" and inserting "any person". **Effective** for taxes of foreign corporations for tax years of such corporations beginning after 10-22-2004.

- **1996, Small Business Job Protection Act of 1996 (P.L. 104-188)**

P.L. 104-188, §1904(b)(2):

Amended Code Sec. 901(b)(5) by adding at the end a new sentence. **Effective** 8-20-96. For special and transitional rules, see Act Sec. 1904(d)(2) and (e), below.

P.L. 104-188, §1904(d)(2) and (e), provide:

(2) EXCEPTION FOR CERTAIN TRUSTS.—The amendments made by this section shall not apply to any trust—

(A) which is treated as owned by the grantor under section 676 or 677 (other than subsection (a)(3) thereof) of the Internal Revenue Code of 1986, and

(B) which is in existence on September 19, 1995.

The preceding sentence shall not apply to the portion of any such trust attributable to any transfer to such trust after September 19, 1995.

(e) TRANSITIONAL RULE.—If—

(1) by reason of the amendments made by this section, any person other than a United States person ceases to be treated as the owner of a portion of a domestic trust, and

(2) before January 1, 1997, such trust becomes a foreign trust, or the assets of such trust are transferred to a foreign trust,

no tax shall be imposed by section 1491 of the Internal Revenue Code of 1986 by reason of such trust becoming a foreign trust or the assets of such trust being transferred to a foreign trust.

- **1976, Tax Reform Act of 1976 (P.L. 94-455)**

P.L. 94-455, §1031(b)(1):

Substituted "limitation" for "applicable limitation" in Code Sec. 901(b). For **effective** date information, see amendment note for P.L. 94-455, Act Sec. 1031(b)(1), following Code Sec. 901(a).

- **1966, Foreign Investors Tax Act of 1966 (P.L. 89-809)**

P.L. 89-809, §106(a)(4):

Redesignated Code Sec. 901(b)(4) as Sec. 901(b)(5) and added new Code Sec. 901(b)(4). **Effective** 1-1-67.

P.L. 89-809, §106(a)(5):

Amended Code Sec. 901(b)(5) (as redesignated) by substituting "(3), or (4)," for "or (3),". **Effective** 1-1-67.

P.L. 89-809, §106(b)(1):

Amended Code Sec. 901(b)(3) by striking out ", if the foreign country of which such alien resident is a citizen or subject, in imposing such taxes, allows a similar credit to citizens of the United States residing in such country". **Effective** 1-1-67.

INCOME TAX—FOREIGN TAX CREDIT

[Sec. 901(c)]

(c) SIMILAR CREDIT REQUIRED FOR CERTAIN ALIEN RESIDENTS.—Whenever the President finds that—

(1) a foreign country, in imposing income, war profits, and excess profits taxes, does not allow to citizens of the United States residing in such foreign country a credit for any such taxes paid or accrued to the United States or any foreign country, as the case may be, similar to the credit allowed under subsection (b)(3),

(2) such foreign country, when requested by the United States to do so, has not acted to provide such a similar credit to citizens of the United States residing in such foreign country, and

(3) it is in the public interest to allow the credit under subsection (b)(3) to citizens or subjects of such foreign country only if it allows such a similar credit to citizens of the United States residing in such foreign country,

the President shall proclaim that, for taxable years beginning while the proclamation remains in effect, the credit under subsection (b)(3) shall be allowed to citizens or subjects of such foreign country only if such foreign country, in imposing income, war profits, and excess profits taxes, allows to citizens of the United States residing in such foreign country such a similar credit.

Amendments

• **1966, Foreign Investors Tax Act of 1966 (P.L. 89-809)**

P.L. 89-809, §106(b)(2):

Redesignated Code Secs. 901(c) and (d) as Secs. 901(d) and (e) and added new Code Sec. 901(c).

[Sec. 901(d)]

(d) TREATMENT OF DIVIDENDS FROM A DISC OR FORMER DISC.—For purposes of this subpart, dividends from a DISC or former DISC (as defined in section 992(a)) shall be treated as dividends from a foreign corporation to the extent such dividends are treated under part I as income from sources without the United States.

Amendments

• **1976, Tax Reform Act of 1976 (P.L. 94-455)**

P.L. 94-455, §1051(d)(1):

Amended Code Sec. 901(d). **Effective** for tax years beginning after 12-31-75. Prior to amendment, Code Sec. 901(d) read as follows:

(d) CORPORATIONS TREATED AS FOREIGN.—For purposes of this subpart, the following corporations shall be treated as foreign corporations:

(1) a corporation entitled to the benefits of section 931, by reason of receiving a large percentage of its gross income from sources within a possession of the United States; and

(2) a corporation organized under the China Trade Act, 1922 (15 U. S. C., chapter 4), and entitled to the deduction provided in section 941.

For purposes of this subpart, dividends from a DISC or former DISC (as defined in section 992(a)) shall be treated as dividends from a foreign corporation to the extent such dividends are treated under part I as income from sources without the United States.

• **1971, Revenue Act of 1971 (P.L. 92-178)**

P.L. 92-178, §502(b)(1):

Amended Code Sec. 901(d) by adding the last sentence therein. **Effective** date is governed by the effective date for Code Sec. 992.

• **1966, Foreign Investors Tax Act of 1966 (P.L. 89-809)**

P.L. 89-809, §106(b)(2):

Redesignated former Code Sec. 901(c) as Sec. 901(d). **Effective** 1-1-67.

[Sec. 901(e)]

(e) FOREIGN TAXES ON MINERAL INCOME.—

(1) REDUCTION IN AMOUNT ALLOWED.—Notwithstanding subsection (b), the amount of any income, war profits, and excess profits taxes paid or accrued during the taxable year to any foreign country or possession of the United States with respect to foreign mineral income from sources within such country or possession which would (but for this paragraph) be allowed under such subsection shall be reduced by the amount (if any) by which—

(A) the amount of such taxes (or, if smaller, the amount of the tax which would be computed under this chapter with respect to such income determined without the deduction allowed under section 613), exceeds

(B) the amount of the tax computed under this chapter with respect to such income.

(2) FOREIGN MINERAL INCOME DEFINED.—For purposes of paragraph (1), the term "foreign mineral income" means income derived from the extraction of minerals from mines, wells, or other natural deposits, the processing of such minerals into their primary products, and the transportation, distribution, or sale of such minerals or primary products. Such term includes, but is not limited to that portion of the taxpayer's distributive share of the income of partnerships attributable to foreign mineral income.

Amendments

• **2017, Tax Cuts and Jobs Act (P.L. 115-97)**

P.L. 115-97, §14301(c)(8):

Amended Code Sec. 901(e)(2) by striking "but is not limited to—"and all that follows through "that portion" and inserting "but is not limited to that portion". **Effective** for tax years of foreign corporations beginning after 12-31-2017, and to tax years of United States shareholders in which or with which such tax years of foreign corporations end. Prior to being stricken, "but is not limited to—"and all that follows through "that portion" in Code Sec. 901(e)(2) read as follows:

but is not limited to—

(A) dividends received from a foreign corporation in respect of which taxes are deemed paid by the taxpayer under section 902, to the extent such dividends are attributable to foreign mineral income, and

(B) that portion of the taxpayer's distributive share of the income of partnerships attributable to foreign mineral income.

• **1969, Tax Reform Act of 1969 (P.L. 91-172)**

P.L. 91-172, §506(a)(2):

Added new subsection (e). **Effective** for tax years beginning after 12-31-69.

[Sec. 901(f)]

(f) CERTAIN PAYMENTS FOR OIL OR GAS NOT CONSIDERED AS TAXES.—Notwithstanding subsection (b) and section 960, the amount of any income, or profits, and excess profits taxes paid or accrued during the taxable year to any foreign country in connection with the purchase and sale of oil or gas extracted in such country is not to be considered as tax for purposes of section 275(a) and this section if—

(1) the taxpayer has no economic interest in the oil or gas to which section 611(a) applies, and

(2) either such purchase or sale is at a price which differs from the fair market value for such oil or gas at the time of such purchase or sale.

Amendments

• **2017, Tax Cuts and Jobs Act (P.L. 115-97)**

P.L. 115-97, §14301(c)(9):

Amended Code Sec. 901(f) by striking "sections 902 and 960" and inserting "section 960". **Effective** for tax years of foreign corporations beginning after 12-31-2017, and to tax years of United States shareholders in which or with which such tax years of foreign corporations end.

• **1975, Tax Reduction Act of 1975 (P.L. 94-12)**

P.L. 94-12, §601(b):

Redesignated Sec. 901(f) as (g) and added new Sec. 901(f). **Effective** for tax years ending after 12-31-74.

INCOME TAX—FOREIGN TAX CREDIT

[Sec. 901(g)]

(g) CERTAIN TAXES PAID WITH RESPECT TO DISTRIBUTIONS FROM POSSESSIONS CORPORATIONS.—

(1) IN GENERAL.—For purposes of this chapter, any tax of a foreign country or possession of the United States which is paid or accrued with respect to any distribution from a corporation—

(A) to the extent that such distribution is attributable to periods during which such corporation is a possessions corporation, and

(B) (i) if a dividends received deduction is allowable with respect to such distribution under part VIII of subchapter B, or

(ii) to the extent that such distribution is received in connection with a liquidation or other transaction with respect to which gain or loss is not recognized,

shall not be treated as income, war profits, or excess profits taxes paid or accrued to a foreign country or possession of the United States, and no deduction shall be allowed under this title with respect to any amount so paid or accrued.

(2) POSSESSIONS CORPORATION.—For purposes of paragraph (1), a corporation shall be treated as a possessions corporation for any period during which an election under section 936 (as in effect on the day before the date of the enactment of the Tax Technical Corrections Act of 2018) applied to such corporation, during which section 931 (as in effect on the day before the date of the enactment of the Tax Reform Act of 1976) applied to such corporation, or during which section 957(c) (as in effect on the day before the date of the enactment of the Tax Reform Act of 1986) applied to such corporation.

Amendments

• **2018, Tax Technical Corrections Act of 2018 (P.L. 115-141)**

P.L. 115-141, §401(d)(1)(D)(xii), Div. U:

Amended Code Sec. 901(g)(2) by inserting "(as in effect on the day before the date of the enactment of the Tax Technical Corrections Act of 2018)" after "section 936". **Effective** 3-23-2018. For a special rule, see Act Sec. 401(e), Div. U, below.

P.L. 115-141, §401(e), Div. U, provides:

(e) GENERAL SAVINGS PROVISION WITH RESPECT TO DEADWOOD PROVISIONS.—If—

(1) any provision amended or repealed by the amendments made by subsection (b) or (d) applied to—

(A) any transaction occurring before the date of the enactment of this Act,

(B) any property acquired before such date of enactment, or

(C) any item of income, loss, deduction, or credit taken into account before such date of enactment, and

(2) the treatment of such transaction, property, or item under such provision would (without regard to the amendments or repeals made by such subsection) affect the liability for tax for periods ending after such date of enactment,

nothing in the amendments or repeals made by this section shall be construed to affect the treatment of such transaction, property, or item for purposes of determining liability for tax for periods ending after such date of enactment.

• **1988, Technical and Miscellaneous Revenue Act of 1988 (P.L. 100-647)**

P.L. 100-647, §1012(j):

Amended Code Sec. 901(g)(2) by striking out "section 957(c)" and inserting in lieu thereof "section 957(c) (as in effect on the day before the date of the enactment of the Tax Reform Act of 1986)". **Effective** as if included in the provision of P.L. 99-514 to which it relates.

Amendments

• **2007, Tax Technical Corrections Act of 2007 (P.L. 110-172)**

P.L. 110-172, §11(g)(9):

Amended Code Sec. 901 by striking subsection (h). **Effective** 12-29-2007. Prior to being stricken, Code Sec. 901(h) read as follows:

(h) TAXES PAID WITH RESPECT TO FOREIGN TRADE INCOME.—No credit shall be allowed under this section for any income, war profits, and excess profits taxes paid or accrued with respect to the foreign trade income (within the meaning of section 923(b)) of a FSC, other than section 923(a)(2) non-exempt income (within the meaning of section 927(d)(6)).

• **1978, Revenue Act of 1978 (P.L. 95-600)**

P.L. 95-600, §701(u)(1)(A):

Amended Code Sec. 901(g)(1). **Effective** as set forth in P.L. 94-455, §1051(d)(2). Prior to amendment, Code Sec. 901(g)(1) read as follows:

(1) IN GENERAL.—For purposes of this chapter, any tax of a foreign country or possession of the United States which is paid or accrued with respect to any distribution from a corporation, to the extent that such distribution is attributable to periods during which such corporation is a possessions corporation, shall not be treated as income, war profits, or excess profits taxes paid or accrued to a foreign country or possession of the United States, and no deduction shall be allowed under this title with respect to any amount so paid or accrued.

P.L. 95-600, §701(u)(1)(B):

Amended Code Sec. 901(g)(2). **Effective** for distributions made after 11-6-78, in tax years ending after such date. Prior to amendment, Code Sec. 901(g)(2) read as follows:

(2) POSSESSIONS CORPORATION.—For purposes of paragraph (1), a corporation shall be treated as a possessions corporation for any period during which an election under section 936 applied to such corporation or during which section 931 (as in effect on the day before the date of the enactment of the Tax Reform Act of 1976) applied to such corporation.

• **1976, Tax Reform Act of 1976 (P.L. 94-455)**

P.L. 94-455, §1051(d)(2):

Redesignated former Code Sec. 901(g) as Code Sec. 901(h) and added Code Sec. 901(g). **Effective** for tax years beginning after 12-31-75. The amendment shall not apply, however, to any tax imposed by a possession of the United States with respect to the complete liquidation of a corporation before 1-1-79, to the extent that the tax is attributable to earnings and profits accumulated by the corporation during periods ending before 1-1-76.

[Sec. 901(h)—Stricken]

• **1986, Tax Reform Act of 1986 (P.L. 99-514)**

P.L. 99-514, §1876(p)(2):

Amended Code Sec. 901(h) by striking out "section 927(d)(6)" and inserting in lieu thereof "section 927(d)(6)". **Effective** as if included in the provision of P.L. 98-369 to which it relates.

• **1984, Deficit Reduction Act of 1984 (P.L. 98-369)**

P.L. 98-369, §801(d)(1):

Amended Code Sec. 901 by redesignating subsection (h) as subsection (i) and inserting after subsection (g) new subsection (h). **Effective** for transactions after 12-31-84, in tax years ending after such date.

[Sec. 901(i)]

(i) TAXES USED TO PROVIDE SUBSIDIES.—Any income, war profits, or excess profits tax shall not be treated as a tax for purposes of this title to the extent—

(1) the amount of such tax is used (directly or indirectly) by the country imposing such tax to provide a subsidy by any means to the taxpayer, a related person (within the meaning of section 482), or any party to the transaction or to a related transaction, and

(2) such subsidy is determined (directly or indirectly) by reference to the amount of such tax, or the base used to compute the amount of such tax.

Amendments

• **1986, Tax Reform Act of 1986 (P.L. 99-514)**

P.L. 99-514, §1204(a):

Amended Code Sec. 901 by redesignating subsection (i) as subsection (j) and inserting after subsection (h) new subsection (i). **Effective** for foreign taxes paid or accrued in tax years beginning after 12-31-86.

[Sec. 901(j)]

(j) DENIAL OF FOREIGN TAX CREDIT, ETC., WITH RESPECT TO CERTAIN FOREIGN COUNTRIES.—

(1) IN GENERAL.—Notwithstanding any other provision of this part—

(A) no credit shall be allowed under subsection (a) for any income, war profits, or excess profits taxes paid or accrued (or deemed paid under section 960) to any country if such taxes are with respect to income attributable to a period during which this subsection applies to such country, and

(B) subsections (a), (b), and (c) of section 904 and section 960 shall be applied separately with respect to income attributable to such a period from sources within such country.

INCOME TAX—FOREIGN TAX CREDIT

(2) COUNTRIES TO WHICH SUBSECTION APPLIES.—

(A) IN GENERAL.—This subsection shall apply to any foreign country—

(i) the government of which the United States does not recognize, unless such government is otherwise eligible to purchase defense articles or services under the Arms Export Control Act,

(ii) with respect to which the United States has severed diplomatic relations,

(iii) with respect to which the United States has not severed diplomatic relations but does not conduct such relations, or

(iv) which the Secretary of State has, pursuant to section 6(j) of the Export Administration Act of 1979, as amended, designated as a foreign country which repeatedly provides support for acts of international terrorisms.

(B) PERIOD FOR WHICH SUBSECTION APPLIES.—This subsection shall apply to any foreign country described in subparagraph (A) during the period—

(i) beginning on the later of—

(I) January 1, 1987, or

(II) 6 months after such country becomes a country described in subparagraph (A), and

(ii) ending on the date the Secretary of State certifies to the Secretary of the Treasury that such country is no longer described in subparagraph (A).

(3) TAXES ALLOWED AS A DEDUCTION, ETC.—Sections 275 and 78 shall not apply to any tax which is not allowable as a credit under subsection (a) by reason of this subsection.

(4) REGULATIONS.—The Secretary shall prescribe such regulations as may be necessary or appropriate to carry out the purposes of this subsection, including regulations which treat income paid through 1 or more entities as derived from a foreign country to which this subsection applies if such income was, without regard to such entities, derived from such country.

(5) WAIVER OF DENIAL.—

(A) IN GENERAL.—Paragraph (1) shall not apply with respect to taxes paid or accrued to a country if the President—

(i) determines that a waiver of the application of such paragraph is in the national interest of the United States and will expand trade and investment opportunities for United States companies in such country; and

(ii) reports such waiver under subparagraph (B).

(B) REPORT.—Not less than 30 days before the date on which a waiver is granted under this paragraph, the President shall report to Congress—

(i) the intention to grant such waiver; and

(ii) the reason for the determination under subparagraph (A)(i).

Amendments

• **2017, Tax Cuts and Jobs Act (P.L. 115-97)**

P.L. 115-97, §14301(c)(10):

Amended Code Sec. 901(j)(1)(A) by striking "902 or" following "paid under section". **Effective** for tax years of foreign corporations beginning after 12-31-2017, and to tax years of United States shareholders in which or with which such tax years of foreign corporations end.

P.L. 115-97, §14301(c)(11):

Amended Code Sec. 901(j)(1)(B) by striking "sections 902 and 960" and inserting "section 960". **Effective** for tax years of foreign corporations beginning after 12-31-2017, and to tax years of United States shareholders in which or with which such tax years of foreign corporations end.

• **2000, Trade and Development Act of 2000 (P.L. 106-200)**

P.L. 106-200, §601(a):

Amended Code Sec. 901(j) by adding at the end new paragraph (5). **Effective** on or after 2-1-2001.

• **1993, South African Democratic Transition Support Act of 1993 (P.L. 103-149)**

P.L. 103-149, §4(b)(8)(A):

Repealed Code Sec. 901(j)(2)(C). **Effective** 11-23-93. Prior to repeal, Code Sec. 901(j)(2)(C) read as follows:

(C) SPECIAL RULE FOR SOUTH AFRICA.—

(i) IN GENERAL.—In addition to any period during which this subsection would otherwise apply to South Africa, this subsection shall apply to South Africa during the period—

(I) beginning on January 1, 1988, and

(II) ending on the date the Secretary of State certifies to the Secretary of the Treasury that South Africa meets the requirements of section 311(a) of the Comprehensive Anti-Apartheid Act of 1986 (as in effect on the date of the enactment of this subparagraph).

(ii) SOUTH AFRICA DEFINED.—For purposes of clause (i) the term "South Africa" has the meaning given to such term by paragraph (6) of section (3) of the Comprehensive Anti-Apartheid Act of 1986 (as so in effect).

P.L. 103-149, §4(b)(8)(B), provides:

(B) Subparagraph (A) shall not be construed as affecting any of the transitional rules contained in Revenue Ruling 92-62 which apply by reason of the termination of the period for which section 901(j) of the Internal Revenue Code of 1986 was applicable to South Africa.

• **1988, Technical and Miscellaneous Revenue Act of 1988 (P.L. 100-647)**

P.L. 100-647, §2003(c)(1)(A)-(B):

Amended Code Sec. 901(j)(3) by striking out "Section 275" and inserting in lieu thereof "Sections 275 and 78", and by inserting ", ETC." after "DEDUCTION" in the paragraph heading. **Effective** 1-1-87.

• **1987, Revenue Act of 1987 (P.L. 100-203)**

P.L. 100-203, §10231(a):

Amended Code Sec. 901(j)(2) by adding at the end thereof new subparagraph (C). **Effective** for tax years beginning after 12-31-87.

P.L. 100-203, §10231(b)(1)-(2):

Amended Code Sec. 901(j)(1) by striking out "to which" in subparagraph (A) and inserting in lieu thereof "during which", and by striking out "any country so identified" and inserting in lieu thereof "such country". **Effective** for tax years beginning after 12-31-87.

• **1986, Omnibus Budget Reconciliation Act of 1986 (P.L. 99-509)**

P.L. 99-509, §8041(a):

Amended Code Sec. 901, as amended by the Tax Reform Act of 1986, by redesignating subsection (j) as subsection (k) and by inserting after subsection (i) new subsection (j). **Effective** 1-1-87.

[Sec. 901(k)]

(k) MINIMUM HOLDING PERIOD FOR CERTAIN TAXES ON DIVIDENDS.—

(1) WITHHOLDING TAXES.—

(A) IN GENERAL.—In no event shall a credit be allowed under subsection (a) for any withholding tax on a dividend with respect to stock in a corporation if—

(i) such stock is held by the recipient of the dividend for 15 days or less during the 31-day period beginning on the date which is 15 days before the date on which such share becomes ex-dividend with respect to such dividend, or

(ii) to the extent that the recipient of the dividend is under an obligation (whether pursuant to a short sale or otherwise) to make related payments with respect to positions in substantially similar or related property.

(B) WITHHOLDING TAX.—For purposes of this paragraph, the term "withholding tax" includes any tax determined on a gross basis; but does not include any tax which is in the nature of a prepayment of a tax imposed on a net basis.

(2) DEEMED PAID TAXES.—In the case of income, war profits, or excess profits taxes deemed paid under section 853 or 960 through a chain of ownership of stock in 1 or more corporations, no credit shall be allowed under subsection (a) for such taxes if—

INCOME TAX—FOREIGN TAX CREDIT

(A) any stock of any corporation in such chain (the ownership of which is required to obtain credit under subsection (a) for such taxes) is held for less than the period described in paragraph (1)(A)(i), or

(B) the corporation holding the stock is under an obligation referred to in paragraph (1)(A)(ii).

(3) 45-DAY RULE IN THE CASE OF CERTAIN PREFERENCE DIVIDENDS.—In the case of stock having preference in dividends and dividends with respect to such stock which are attributable to a period or periods aggregating in excess of 366 days, paragraph (1)(A)(i) shall be applied—

(A) by substituting "45 days" for "15 days" each place it appears, and

(B) by substituting "91-day period" for "31-day period".

(4) EXCEPTION FOR CERTAIN TAXES PAID BY SECURITIES DEALERS.—

(A) IN GENERAL.—Paragraphs (1) and (2) shall not apply to any qualified tax with respect to any security held in the active conduct in a foreign country of a business as a securities dealer of any person—

(i) who is registered as a securities broker or dealer under section 15(a) of the Securities Exchange Act of 1934,

(ii) who is registered as a Government securities broker or dealer under section 15C(a) of such Act, or

(iii) who is licensed or authorized in such foreign country to conduct securities activities in such country and is subject to bona fide regulation by a securities regulating authority of such country.

(B) QUALIFIED TAX.—For purposes of subparagraph (A), the term "qualified tax" means a tax paid to a foreign country (other than the foreign country referred to in subparagraph (A)) if—

(i) the dividend to which such tax is attributable is subject to taxation on a net basis by the country referred to in subparagraph (A), and

(ii) such country allows a credit against its net basis tax for the full amount of the tax paid to such other foreign country.

(C) REGULATIONS.—The Secretary may prescribe such regulations as may be appropriate to carry out this paragraph, including regulations to prevent the abuse of the exception provided by this paragraph and to treat other taxes as qualified taxes.

(5) CERTAIN RULES TO APPLY.—For purposes of this subsection, the rules of paragraphs (3) and (4) of section 246(c) shall apply.

(6) TREATMENT OF BONA FIDE SALES.—If a person's holding period is reduced by reason of the application of the rules of section 246(c)(4) to any contract for the bona fide sale of stock, the determination of whether such person's holding period meets the requirements of paragraph (2) with respect to taxes deemed paid under section 960 shall be made as of the date such contract is entered into.

(7) TAXES ALLOWED AS DEDUCTION, ETC.—Sections 275 and 78 shall not apply to any tax which is not allowable as a credit under subsection (a) by reason of this subsection.

Amendments

- **2017, Tax Cuts and Jobs Act (P.L. 115-97)**

P.L. 115-97, §14301(c)(12):

Amended Code Sec. 901(k)(2) by striking ", 902," following "section 853". **Effective** for tax years of foreign corporations beginning after 12-31-2017, and to tax years of United States shareholders in which or with which such tax years of foreign corporations end.

P.L. 115-97, §14301(c)(13):

Amended Code Sec. 901(k)(6) by striking "902 or" following "paid under section". **Effective** for tax years of foreign corporations beginning after 12-31-2017, and to tax years of United States shareholders in which or with which such tax years of foreign corporations end.

- **2004, American Jobs Creation Act of 2004 (P.L. 108-357)**

P.L. 108-357, §832(b):

Amended the heading of Code Sec. 901(k) by inserting "ON DIVIDENDS" after "TAXES". **Effective** for amounts paid or accrued more than 30 days after 10-22-2004.

- **2004, Working Families Tax Relief Act of 2004 (P.L. 108-311)**

P.L. 108-311, §406(g)(1):

Amended Code Sec. 901(k)(1)(A)(i) by striking "30-day period" and inserting "31-day period". **Effective** as if included in the provision of the Taxpayer Relief Act of 1997 (P.L. 105-34) to which it relates [**effective** for dividends paid or accrued after 9-4-97.—CCH].

P.L. 108-311, §406(g)(2)(A)-(B):

Amended Code Sec. 901(k)(3)(B) by striking "90-day period" and inserting "91-day period" and by striking "30-day period" and inserting "31-day period". **Effective** as if included in the provision of the Taxpayer Relief Act of 1997 (P.L. 105-34) to which it relates [**effective** for dividends paid or accrued after 9-4-97.—CCH].

- **1998, IRS Restructuring and Reform Act of 1998 (P.L. 105-206)**

P.L. 105-206, §6010(k)(3):

Amended Code Sec. 901(k)(4)(A) by striking "securities business" and inserting "business as a securities dealer". **Effective** as if included in the provision of P.L. 105-34 to which it relates [**effective** for dividends paid or accrued after 9-4-97.—CCH].

- **1997, Taxpayer Relief Act of 1997 (P.L. 105-34)**

P.L. 105-34, §1053(a):

Amended Code Sec. 901 by redesignating subsection (k) as subsection (l) and by inserting after subsection (j) a new subsection (k). **Effective** for dividends paid or accrued more than 30 days after 8-5-97.

[Sec. 901(l)]

(l) MINIMUM HOLDING PERIOD FOR WITHHOLDING TAXES ON GAIN AND INCOME OTHER THAN DIVIDENDS ETC.—

(1) IN GENERAL.—In no event shall a credit be allowed under subsection (a) for any withholding tax (as defined in subsection (k)) on any item of income or gain with respect to any property if—

(A) such property is held by the recipient of the item for 15 days or less during the 31-day period beginning on the date which is 15 days before the date on which the right to receive payment of such item arises, or

(B) to the extent that the recipient of the item is under an obligation (whether pursuant to a short sale or otherwise) to make related payments with respect to positions in substantially similar or related property.

This paragraph shall not apply to any dividend to which subsection (k) applies.

(2) EXCEPTION FOR TAXES PAID BY DEALERS.—

(A) IN GENERAL.—Paragraph (1) shall not apply to any qualified tax with respect to any property held in the active conduct in a foreign country of a business as a dealer in such property.

(B) QUALIFIED TAX.—For purposes of subparagraph (A), the term "qualified tax" means a tax paid to a foreign country (other than the foreign country referred to in subparagraph (A)) if—

(i) the item to which such tax is attributable is subject to taxation on a net basis by the country referred to in subparagraph (A), and

(ii) such country allows a credit against its net basis tax for the full amount of the tax paid to such other foreign country.

(C) DEALER.—For purposes of subparagraph (A), the term "dealer" means—

(i) with respect to a security, any person to whom paragraphs (1) and (2) of subsection (k) would not apply by reason of paragraph (4) thereof, and

(ii) with respect to any other property, any person with respect to whom such property is described in section 1221(a)(1).

(D) REGULATIONS.—The Secretary may prescribe such regulations as may be appropriate to carry out this paragraph, including regulations to prevent the abuse of the exception provided by this paragraph and to treat other taxes as qualified taxes.

INCOME TAX—FOREIGN TAX CREDIT

(3) EXCEPTIONS.—The Secretary may by regulation provide that paragraph (1) shall not apply to property where the Secretary determines that the application of paragraph (1) to such property is not necessary to carry out the purposes of this subsection.

(4) CERTAIN RULES TO APPLY.—Rules similar to the rules of paragraphs (5), (6), and (7) of subsection (k) shall apply for purposes of this subsection.

(5) DETERMINATION OF HOLDING PERIOD.—Holding periods shall be determined for purposes of this subsection without regard to section 1235 or any similar rule.

Amendments

• 2005, Gulf Opportunity Zone Act of 2005 (P.L. 109-135)

P.L. 109-135, §403(aa)(2):

Amended Code Sec. 901(l)(2)(C)(i) by striking "if such security were stock" after "thereof". **Effective** as if included in the provision of the American Jobs Creation Act of 2004 (P.L. 108-357) to which it relates [effective for amounts paid or accrued more than 30 days after 10-22-2004.—CCH].

• 2004, American Jobs Creation Act of 2004 (P.L. 108-357)

P.L. 108-357, §832(a):

Amended Code Sec. 901 by redesignating subsection (l) as subsection (m) and by inserting after subsection (k) a new subsection (l). **Effective** for amounts paid or accrued more than 30 days after 10-22-2004.

[Sec. 901(m)]

(m) DENIAL OF FOREIGN TAX CREDIT WITH RESPECT TO FOREIGN INCOME NOT SUBJECT TO UNITED STATES TAXATION BY REASON OF COVERED ASSET ACQUISITIONS.—

(1) IN GENERAL.—In the case of a covered asset acquisition, the disqualified portion of any foreign income tax determined with respect to the income or gain attributable to the relevant foreign assets—

(A) shall not be taken into account in determining the credit allowed under subsection (a), and

(B) in the case of a foreign income tax paid by a foreign corporation, shall not be taken into account for purposes of section 960.

(2) COVERED ASSET ACQUISITION.—For purposes of this section, the term "covered asset acquisition" means—

(A) a qualified stock purchase (as defined in section 338(d)(3)) to which section 338(a) applies,

(B) any transaction which—

(i) is treated as an acquisition of assets for purposes of this chapter, and

(ii) is treated as the acquisition of stock of a corporation (or is disregarded) for purposes of the foreign income taxes of the relevant jurisdiction,

(C) any acquisition of an interest in a partnership which has an election in effect under section 754, and

(D) to the extent provided by the Secretary, any other similar transaction.

(3) DISQUALIFIED PORTION.—For purposes of this section—

(A) IN GENERAL.—The term "disqualified portion" means, with respect to any covered asset acquisition, for any taxable year, the ratio (expressed as a percentage) of—

(i) the aggregate basis differences (but not below zero) allocable to such taxable year under subparagraph (B) with respect to all relevant foreign assets, divided by

(ii) the income on which the foreign income tax referred to in paragraph (1) is determined (or, if the taxpayer fails to substantiate such income to the satisfaction of the Secretary, such income shall be determined by dividing the amount of such foreign income tax by the highest marginal tax rate applicable to such income in the relevant jurisdiction).

(B) ALLOCATION OF BASIS DIFFERENCE.—For purposes of subparagraph (A)(i)—

(i) IN GENERAL.—The basis difference with respect to any relevant foreign asset shall be allocated to taxable years using the applicable cost recovery method under this chapter.

(ii) SPECIAL RULE FOR DISPOSITION OF ASSETS.—Except as otherwise provided by the Secretary, in the case of the disposition of any relevant foreign asset—

(I) the basis difference allocated to the taxable year which includes the date of such disposition shall be the excess of the basis difference with respect to such asset over the aggregate basis difference with respect to such asset which has been allocated under clause (i) to all prior taxable years, and

(II) no basis difference with respect to such asset shall be allocated under clause (i) to any taxable year thereafter.

(C) BASIS DIFFERENCE.—

(i) IN GENERAL.—The term "basis difference" means, with respect to any relevant foreign asset, the excess of—

(I) the adjusted basis of such asset immediately after the covered asset acquisition, over

(II) the adjusted basis of such asset immediately before the covered asset acquisition.

(ii) BUILT-IN LOSS ASSETS.—In the case of a relevant foreign asset with respect to which the amount described in clause (i)(II) exceeds the amount described in clause (i)(I), such excess shall be taken into account under this subsection as a basis difference of a negative amount.

(iii) SPECIAL RULE FOR SECTION 338 ELECTIONS.—In the case of a covered asset acquisition described in paragraph (2)(A), the covered asset acquisition shall be treated for purposes of this subparagraph as occurring at the close of the acquisition date (as defined in section 338(h)(2)).

(4) RELEVANT FOREIGN ASSETS.—For purposes of this section, the term "relevant foreign asset" means, with respect to any covered asset acquisition, any asset (including any goodwill, going concern value, or other intangible) with respect to such acquisition if income, deduction, gain, or loss attributable to such asset is taken into account in determining the foreign income tax referred to in paragraph (1).

(5) FOREIGN INCOME TAX.—For purposes of this section, the term "foreign income tax" means any income, war profits, or excess profits tax paid or accrued to any foreign country or to any possession of the United States.

(6) TAXES ALLOWED AS A DEDUCTION, ETC.— Sections 275 and 78 shall not apply to any tax which is not allowable as a credit under subsection (a) by reason of this subsection.

(7) REGULATIONS.—The Secretary may issue such regulations or other guidance as is necessary or appropriate to carry out the purposes of this subsection, including to exempt from the application of this subsection certain covered asset acquisitions, and relevant foreign assets with respect to which the basis difference is de minimis.

Amendments

• 2017, Tax Cuts and Jobs Act (P.L. 115-97)

P.L. 115-97, §14301(c)(14):

Amended Code Sec. 901(m)(1)(B). **Effective** for tax years of foreign corporations beginning after 12-31-2017, and to tax years of United States shareholders in which or with which such tax years of foreign corporations end. Prior to amendment, Code Sec. 901(m)(1)(B) read as follows:

(B) in the case of a foreign income tax paid by a section 902 corporation (as defined in section 909(d)(5)), shall not be taken into account for purposes of section 902 or 960.

INCOME TAX—FOREIGN TAX CREDIT

- 2010, (P.L. 111-226)

P.L. 111-226, §212(a):

Amended Code Sec. 901 by redesignating subsection (m) as subsection (n) and by inserting after subsection (l) a new subsection (m). For the **effective** date, see Act Sec. 212(b)(1)-(3), below.

P.L. 111-226, §212(b)(1)-(3), provides:

(b) EFFECTIVE DATE.—

(1) IN GENERAL.—Except as provided in paragraph (2), the amendments made by this section shall apply to covered asset acquisitions (as defined in section 901(m)(2) of the Internal Revenue Code of 1986, as added by this section) after December 31, 2010.

(2) TRANSITION RULE.—The amendments made by this section shall not apply to any covered asset acquisition (as so defined) with respect to which the transferor and the transferee are not related if such acquisition is—

(A) made pursuant to a written agreement which was binding on January 1, 2011, and at all times thereafter,

(B) described in a ruling request submitted to the Internal Revenue Service on or before July 29, 2010, or

(C) described on or before January 1, 2011, in a public announcement or in a filing with the Securities and Exchange Commission.

(3) RELATED PERSONS.—For purposes of this subsection, a person shall be treated as related to another person if the relationship between such persons is described in section 267 or 707(b) of the Internal Revenue Code of 1986.

[Sec. 901(n)]

(n) CROSS REFERENCE.—

(1) For deductions of income, war profits, and excess profits taxes paid to a foreign country or a possession of the United States, see sections 164 and 275.

(2) For right of each partner to make election under this section, see section 703(b).

(3) For right of estate or trust to the credit for taxes imposed by foreign countries and possessions of the United States under this section, see section 642(a).

(4) For reduction of credit for failure of a United States person to furnish certain information with respect to a foreign corporation or partnership controlled by him, see section 6038.

Amendments

- 2010, (P.L. 111-226)

P.L. 111-226, §212(a):

Amended Code Sec. 901 by redesignating subsection (m) as subsection (n). For the **effective** date, see Act Sec. 212(b)(1)-(3), below.

P.L. 111-226, §212(b)(1)-(3), provides:

(b) EFFECTIVE DATE.—

(1) IN GENERAL.—Except as provided in paragraph (2), the amendments made by this section shall apply to covered asset acquisitions (as defined in section 901(m)(2) of the Internal Revenue Code of 1986, as added by this section) after December 31, 2010.

(2) TRANSITION RULE.—The amendments made by this section shall not apply to any covered asset acquisition (as so defined) with respect to which the transferor and the transferee are not related if such acquisition is—

(A) made pursuant to a written agreement which was binding on January 1, 2011, and at all times thereafter,

(B) described in a ruling request submitted to the Internal Revenue Service on or before July 29, 2010, or

(C) described on or before January 1, 2011, in a public announcement or in a filing with the Securities and Exchange Commission.

(3) RELATED PERSONS.—For purposes of this subsection, a person shall be treated as related to another person if the relationship between such persons is described in section 267 or 707(b) of the Internal Revenue Code of 1986.

- 2004, American Jobs Creation Act of 2004 (P.L. 108-357)

P.L. 108-357, §832(a):

Amended Code Sec. 901 by redesignating subsection (l) as subsection (m). **Effective** for amounts paid or accrued more than 30 days after 10-22-2004.

- 1997, Taxpayer Relief Act of 1997 (P.L. 105-34)

P.L. 105-34, §1053(a):

Amended Code Sec. 901 by redesignating subsection (k) as subsection (l). **Effective** for dividends paid or accrued more than 30 days after 8-5-97.

P.L. 105-34, §1142(e)(4):

Amended Code Sec. 901(k)[(l)](4) by striking "foreign corporation" and inserting "foreign corporation or partnership". **Effective** for annual accounting periods beginning after 8-5-97.

- 1986, Tax Reform Act of 1986 (P.L. 99-514)

P.L. 99-514, §112(b)(3):

Amended Code Sec. 901(i)(3) by striking out "section 642(a)(1)" and inserting in lieu thereof "section 642(a)". **Effective** for tax years beginning after 12-31-86.

P.L. 99-514, §1204(a):

Redesignated subsection (i) as subsection (j). **Effective** for foreign taxes paid or accrued in tax years beginning after 12-31-86.

- 1986, Omnibus Budget Reconciliation Act of 1986 (P.L. 99-509)

P.L. 99-509, §8041(a):

Redesignated subsection (j) as subsection (k). **Effective** 1-1-87.

- 1984, Deficit Reduction Act of 1984 (P.L. 98-369)

P.L. 98-369, §801(d)(1):

Amended Code Sec. 901 by redesignating subsection (h) as subsection (i). **Effective** for transactions after 12-31-84, in tax years ending after such date.

- 1976, Tax Reform Act of 1976 (P.L. 94-455)

P.L. 94-455, §1051(d)(2):

Redesignated former Code Sec. 901(g) as Code Sec. 901(h). **Effective** for tax years beginning after 12-31-75. The amendment shall not apply, however, to any tax imposed by a possession of the United States with respect to the complete liquidation of a corporation before 1-1-79, to the extent that the tax is attributable to earnings and profits accumulated by the corporation during periods ending before 1-1-76.

P.L. 94-455, §1901(b)(1)(H)(iii):

Substituted "section 642(a)(1)" for "section 642(a)(2)" in Code Sec. 901(g)(3) (redesignated as Code Sec. 901(h)(3)). **Effective** for tax years beginning after 12-31-76.

- 1975, Tax Reduction Act of 1975 (P.L. 94-12)

P.L. 94-12, §601(b):

Redesignated former Code Sec. 901(f) as Code Sec. 901(g).

- 1969, Tax Reform Act of 1969 (P.L. 91-172)

P.L. 91-172, §506(a)(1):

Redesignated subsection (e) as (f).

- 1966, Foreign Investors Tax Act of 1966 (P.L. 89-809)

P.L. 89-809, §106(b)(2):

Redesignated former Code Sec. 901(d) as Sec. 901(e). **Effective** 1-1-67.

- 1964, Revenue Act of 1964 (P.L. 88-272)

P.L. 88-272, §207(b)(7):

Amended paragraph (1) of section (d) by inserting the words "sections 164 and 275" in lieu of "section 164". **Effective** 1-1-64.

- 1962, Revenue Act of 1962 (P.L. 87-834)

P.L. 87-834, §9(d)(3):

Amended Code Sec. 901(d) by adding paragraph (4). **Effective** 10-17-62.

[Sec. 902—Stricken]

Amendments

- 2017, Tax Cuts and Jobs Act (P.L. 115-97)

P.L. 115-97, §14301(a):

Amended subpart A of part III of subchapter N of chapter 1 by striking Code Sec. 902. **Effective** for tax years of foreign corporations beginning after 12-31-2017, and to tax years of United States shareholders in which or with which such tax years of foreign corporations end. Prior to being stricken, Code Sec. 902 read as follows:

SEC. 902. DEEMED PAID CREDIT WHERE DOMESTIC CORPORATION OWNS 10 PERCENT OR MORE OF VOTING STOCK OF FOREIGN CORPORATION.

[Sec. 902(a)]

(a) TAXES PAID BY FOREIGN CORPORATION TREATED AS PAID BY DOMESTIC CORPORATION.—For purposes of this subpart, a domestic corporation which owns 10 percent or more of the voting stock of a foreign corporation from which it receives dividends in any taxable year shall be deemed to have paid the same proportion of such foreign corporation's post-1986 foreign income taxes as—

(1) the amount of such dividends (determined without regard to section 78), bears to

(2) such foreign corporation's post-1986 undistributed earnings.

[Sec. 902(b)]

(b) DEEMED TAXES INCREASED IN CASE OF CERTAIN LOWER TIER CORPORATIONS.—

(1) IN GENERAL.—If—

(A) any foreign corporation is a member of a qualified group, and

(B) such foreign corporation owns 10 percent or more of the voting stock of another member of such group from which it receives dividends in any taxable year,

such foreign corporation shall be deemed to have paid the same proportion of such other member's post-1986 foreign income taxes as would be determined under subsection (a) if such foreign corporation were a domestic corporation.

(2) QUALIFIED GROUP.—For purposes of paragraph (1), the term "qualified group" means—

INCOME TAX—FOREIGN TAX CREDIT

(A) the foreign corporation described in subsection (a), and

(B) any other foreign corporation if—

(i) the domestic corporation owns at least 5 percent of the voting stock of such other foreign corporation indirectly through a chain of foreign corporations connected through stock ownership of at least 10 percent of their voting stock,

(ii) the foreign corporation described in subsection (a) is the first tier corporation in such chain, and

(iii) such other corporation is not below the sixth tier in such chain.

The term "qualified group" shall not include any foreign corporation below the third tier in the chain referred to in clause (i) unless such foreign corporation is a controlled foreign corporation (as defined in section 957) and the domestic corporation is a United States shareholder (as defined in section 951(b)) in such foreign corporation. Paragraph (1) shall apply to those taxes paid by a member of the qualified group below the third tier only with respect to periods during which it was a controlled foreign corporation.

Amendments

- **1997, Taxpayer Relief Act of 1997 (P.L. 105-34)**

P.L. 105-34, § 1113(a)(1):

Amended Code Sec. 902(b). **Effective**, generally, for taxes of foreign corporations for tax years of such corporations beginning after 8-5-97. For a special rule, see Act Sec. 1113(c)(2), below. Prior to amendment, Code Sec. 902(b) read as follows:

(b) DEEMED TAXES INCREASED IN CASE OF CERTAIN 2ND AND 3RD TIER FOREIGN CORPORATIONS.—

(1) 2ND TIER.—If the foreign corporation described in subsection (a) (hereinafter in this section referred to as the "1st tier corporation") owns 10 percent or more of the voting stock of a 2nd foreign corporation from which it receives dividends in any taxable year, the 1st tier corporation shall be deemed to have paid the same proportion of such 2nd foreign corporation's post-1986 foreign income taxes as would be determined under subsection (a) if such 1st tier corporation were a domestic corporation.

(2) 3RD TIER.—If such 1st tier corporation owns 10 percent or more of the voting stock of a 2nd foreign corporation which, in turn, owns 10 percent or more of the voting stock of a 3rd foreign corporation from which the 2nd corporation receives dividends in any taxable year, such 2nd foreign corporation shall be deemed to have paid the same proportion of such 3rd foreign corporation's post-1986 foreign income taxes as would be determined under subsection (a) if such 2nd foreign corporation were a domestic corporation.

(3) 5 PERCENT STOCK REQUIREMENT.—For purposes of this subpart—

(A) FOR 2ND TIER.—Paragraph (1) shall not apply unless the percentage of voting stock owned by the domestic corporation in the 1st tier corporation and the percentage of voting stock owned by the 1st tier corporation in the 2nd foreign corporation when multiplied together equal at least 5 percent.

(B) FOR 3RD TIER.—Paragraph (2) shall not apply unless the percentage arrived at for purposes of applying paragraph (1) when multiplied by the percentage of voting stock owned by the 2nd foreign corporation in the 3rd foreign corporation is equal to at least 5 percent.

P.L. 105-34, § 1113(c)(2), provides:

(2) SPECIAL RULE.—In the case of any chain of foreign corporations described in clauses (i) and (ii) of section 902(b)(2)(B) of the Internal Revenue Code of 1986 (as amended by this section), no liquidation, reorganization, or similar transaction in a taxable year beginning after the date of the enactment of this Act shall have the effect of permitting taxes to be taken into account under section 902 of the Internal Revenue Code of 1986 which could not have been taken into account under such section but for such transaction.

[Sec. 902(c)]

(c) DEFINITIONS AND SPECIAL RULES.—For purposes of this section—

(1) POST-1986 UNDISTRIBUTED EARNINGS.—The term "post-1986 undistributed earnings" means the amount of the earnings and profits of the foreign corporation (computed in accordance with sections 964(a) and 986) accumulated in taxable years beginning after December 31, 1986—

(A) as of the close of the taxable year of the foreign corporation in which the dividend is distributed, and

(B) without diminution by reason of dividends distributed during such taxable year.

(2) POST-1986 FOREIGN INCOME TAXES.—The term "post-1986 foreign income taxes" means the sum of—

(A) the foreign income taxes with respect to the taxable year of the foreign corporation in which the dividend is distributed, and

(B) the foreign income taxes with respect to prior taxable years beginning after December 31, 1986, to the extent such foreign taxes were not attributable to dividends distributed by the foreign corporation in prior taxable years.

(3) SPECIAL RULE WHERE FOREIGN CORPORATION FIRST QUALIFIES AFTER DECEMBER 31, 1986.—

(A) IN GENERAL.—If the 1st day on which the requirements of subparagraph (B) are met with respect to any foreign corporation is in a taxable year of such corporation beginning after December 31, 1986, the post-1986 undistributed earnings and the post-1986 foreign income taxes of such foreign corporation shall be determined by taking into account only periods beginning on and after the 1st day of the 1st taxable year in which such requirements are met.

(B) REQUIREMENTS.—The requirements of this subparagraph are met with respect to any foreign corporation if—

(i) 10 percent of more of the voting stock of such foreign corporation is owned by a domestic corporation, or

(ii) the requirements of subsection (b)(2) are met with respect to such foreign corporation.

(4) FOREIGN INCOME TAXES.—

(A) IN GENERAL.—The term "foreign income taxes" means any income, war profits, or excess profits taxes paid by the foreign corporation to any foreign country or possession of the United States.

(B) TREATMENT OF DEEMED TAXES.—Except for purposes of determining the amount of the post-1986 foreign income taxes of a sixth tier foreign corporation referred to in subsection (b)(2), the term "foreign income taxes" includes any such taxes deemed to be paid by the foreign corporation under this section.

(5) ACCOUNTING PERIODS.—In the case of a foreign corporation the income, war profits, and excess profits taxes of which are determined on the basis of an accounting period of less than 1 year, the word "year" as used in this subsection shall be construed to mean such accounting period.

(6) TREATMENT OF DISTRIBUTIONS FROM EARNINGS BEFORE 1987.—

(A) IN GENERAL.—In the case of any dividend paid by a foreign corporation out of accumulated profits (as defined in this section as in effect on the day before the date of the enactment of the Tax Reform Act of 1986) for taxable years beginning before the 1st taxable year taken into account in determining the post-1986 undistributed earnings of such corporation—

(i) this section (as amended by the Tax Reform Act of 1986) shall not apply, but

(ii) this section (as in effect on the day before the date of the enactment of such Act) shall apply.

(B) DIVIDENDS PAID FIRST OUT OF POST-1986 EARNINGS.—Any dividend in a taxable year beginning after December 31, 1986, shall be treated as made out of post-1986 undistributed earnings to the extent thereof.

(7) CONSTRUCTIVE OWNERSHIP THROUGH PARTNERSHIPS.—Stock owned, directly or indirectly, by or for a partnership shall be considered as being owned proportionately by its partners. Stock considered to be owned by a person by reason of the preceding sentence shall, for purposes of applying such sentence, be treated as actually owned by such person. The Secretary may prescribe such regulations as may be necessary to carry out the purposes of this paragraph, including rules to account for special partnership allocations of dividends, credits, and other incidents of ownership of stock in determining proportionate ownership.

(8) REGULATIONS.—The Secretary shall provide such regulations as may be necessary or appropriate to carry out the provisions of this section and section 960, including provisions which provide for the separate application of this section and section 960 to reflect the separate application of section 904 to separate types of income and loss.

Amendments

- **2004, American Jobs Creation Act of 2004 (P.L. 108-357)**

P.L. 108-357, § 405(a):

Amended Code Sec. 902(c) by redesignating paragraph (7) as paragraph (8) and by inserting after paragraph (6) a new paragraph (7). **Effective** for taxes of foreign corporations for tax years of such corporations beginning after 10-22-2004.

- **1997, Taxpayer Relief Act of 1997 (P.L. 105-34)**

P.L. 105-34, § 1113(a)(2)(A):

Amended Code Sec. 902(c)(3)(B) by adding "or" at the end of clause (i) and by striking clauses (ii) and (iii) and inserting a new clause (ii). **Effective**, generally, for taxes of foreign corporations for tax years of such corporations beginning after 8-5-97. For a special rule, see Act Sec. 1113(c)(2), below. Prior to amendment, Code Sec. 902(c)(3)(B)(ii)-(iii) read as follows:

(ii) the requirements of subsection (b)(3)(A) are met with respect to such foreign corporation and 10 percent or more of the voting stock of such foreign corporation is owned by another foreign corporation described in clause (i), or

(iii) the requirements of subsection (b)(3)(B) are met with respect to such foreign corporation and 10 percent or more of the voting stock of such foreign corporation is owned by another foreign corporation described in clause (ii).

P.L. 105-34, § 1113(a)(2)(B):

Amended Code Sec. 902(c)(4)(B) by striking "3rd foreign corporation" and inserting "sixth tier foreign corporation". **Effective**, generally, for taxes of foreign corporations for tax years of such corporations beginning after 8-5-97. For a special rule, see Act Sec. 1113(c)(2), below.

P.L. 105-34, § 1113(a)(2)(C):

Amended Code Sec. 902(c)(3) by striking "WHERE DOMESTIC CORPORATION ACQUIRES 10 PERCENT OF FOREIGN CORPORATION" in the heading and inserting "WHERE FOREIGN CORPORATION FIRST QUALIFIES". **Effective**, generally, for taxes of foreign corporations for tax years of such corporations beginning after 8-5-97. For a special rule, see Act Sec. 1113(c)(2), below.

P.L. 105-34, § 1113(a)(2)(D):

Amended Code Sec. 902(c)(3) by striking "ownership" each place it appears. **Effective**, generally, for taxes of foreign corporations for tax years of such corporations beginning after 8-5-97. For a special rule, see Act Sec. 1113(c)(2), below. Prior to amendment, Code Sec. 902(c)(3) read as follows:

(3) SPECIAL RULE WHERE DOMESTIC CORPORATION ACQUIRES 10 PERCENT OF FOREIGN CORPORATION AFTER DECEMBER 31, 1986.—

(A) IN GENERAL.—If the 1st day on which the ownership requirements of subparagraph (B) are met with respect to any foreign corporation is in a taxable year of such corporation beginning after December 31, 1986, the post-1986 undistributed earnings and the post-1986 foreign income taxes of such foreign corporation shall be determined by taking into account only periods beginning on and after the 1st day of the 1st taxable year in which such ownership requirements are met.

(B) OWNERSHIP REQUIREMENTS.—The ownership requirements of this subparagraph are met with respect to any foreign corporation if—

(i) 10 percent of more of the voting stock of such foreign corporation is owned by a domestic corporation,

(ii) the requirements of subsection (b)(3)(A) are met with respect to such foreign corporation and 10 percent or more of the voting stock of such foreign corporation is owned by another foreign corporation described in clause (i), or

(iii) the requirements of subsection (b)(3)(B) are met with respect to such foreign corporation and 10 percent or more of the voting stock of such foreign corporation is owned by another foreign corporation described in clause (ii).

P.L. 105-34, §1113(c)(2), provides:

(2) SPECIAL RULE.—In the case of any chain of foreign corporations described in clauses (i) and (ii) of section 902(b)(2)(B) of the Internal Revenue Code of 1986 (as amended by this section), no liquidation, reorganization, or similar transaction in a taxable year beginning after the date of the enactment of this Act shall have the effect of permitting taxes to be taken into account under section 902 of the Internal Revenue Code of 1986 which could not have been taken into account under such section but for such transaction.

P.L. 105-34, §1163(a):

Amended Code Sec. 902(c)(2)(B) by striking "deemed paid with respect to" and inserting "attributable to". **Effective** 8-5-97.

- **1988, Technical and Miscellaneous Revenue Act of 1988 (P.L. 100-647)**

P.L. 100-647, §1012(b)(1)(A)-(B):

Amended Code Sec. 902(c)(7) by striking out "section 960" and inserting in lieu thereof "section 960", and by striking out "this section" the second place it appears and inserting in lieu thereof "this section and section 960". **Effective** as if included in the provision of P.L. 99-514 to which it relates. For a special rule, see Act Sec. 1012(b)(3), below.

P.L. 100-647, §1012(b)(2):

Amended Code Sec. 902(c)(1) by striking out "sections 964 and 986" and inserting in lieu thereof "sections 964(a) and 986". **Effective** as if included in the provision of P.L. 99-514 to which it relates. For a special rule, see Act Sec. 1012(b)(3), below.

P.L. 100-647, §1012(b)(3), provides:

(3) For purposes of sections 902 and 960 of the 1986 Code, the increase in earnings and profits of any foreign corporation under section 1023(e)(3)(C) of the Reform Act shall be taken into account ratably over the 10-year period beginning with the corporation's first taxable year beginning after December 31, 1986.

[Sec. 902(d)]

(d) CROSS REFERENCES.—

(1) For inclusion in gross income of an amount equal to taxes deemed paid under subsection (a), see section 78.

(2) For application of subsections (a) and (b) with respect to taxes deemed paid in a prior taxable year by a United States shareholder with respect to a controlled foreign corporation, see section 960.

(3) For reduction of credit with respect to dividends paid out of post-1986 undistributed earnings for years for which certain information is not furnished, see section 6038.

Amendments
- **1986, Tax Reform Act of 1986 (P.L. 99-514)**

P.L. 99-514, §1202(a):

Amended Code Sec. 902. **Effective** for distributions by foreign corporations out of, and to inclusions under section 951(a) of the Internal Revenue Code of 1986 attributable to, earnings and profits for tax years beginning after 12-31-86. Prior to amendment, Code Sec. 902 read as follows:

SEC. 902. CREDIT FOR CORPORATE STOCKHOLDER IN FOREIGN CORPORATION.

[Sec. 902(a)]

(a) TREATMENT OF TAXES PAID BY FOREIGN CORPORATION.—For purposes of this subpart, a domestic corporation which owns at least 10 percent of the voting stock of a foreign corporation from which it receives dividends in any taxable year shall be deemed to have paid the same proportion of any income, war profits, or excess profits taxes paid or deemed to be paid by such foreign corporation to any foreign country or to any possession of the United States, on or with respect to the accumulated profits of such foreign corporation from which such dividends were paid, which the amount of such dividends (determined without regard to section 78) bears to the amount of such accumulated profits in excess of such income, war profits, and excess profits taxes (other than those deemed paid).

Amendments
- **1976, Tax Reform Act of 1976 (P.L. 94-455)**

P.L. 94-455, §1033(a):

Amended Code Sec. 902(a). **Effective** as provided in §1033(c), below. Prior to amendment, Code Sec. 902(a) read as follows:

(a) TREATMENT OF TAXES PAID BY FOREIGN CORPORATION.—For purposes of this subpart, a domestic corporation which owns at least 10 percent of the voting stock of a foreign corporation from which it receives dividends in any taxable year shall—

(1) to the extent such dividends are paid by such foreign corporation out of accumulated profits (as defined in subsection (c)(1)(A)) of a year for which such foreign corporation is not a less developed country corporation, be deemed to have paid the same proportion of any income, war profits, or excess profits taxes paid or deemed to be paid by such foreign corporation to any foreign country or to any possession of the United States on or with respect to such accumulated profits, which the amount of such dividends (determined without regard to section 78) bears to the amount of such accumulated profits in excess of such income, war profits, and excess profits taxes (other than those deemed paid); and

(2) to the extent such dividends are paid by such foreign corporation out of accumulated profits (as defined in subsection (c)(1)(B)) of a year for which such foreign corporation is a less developed country corporation, be deemed to have paid the same proportion of any income, war profits, or excess profits taxes paid or deemed to be paid by such foreign corporation to any foreign country or to any possession of the United States on or with respect to such accumulated profits, which the amount of such dividends bears to the amount of such accumulated profits.

P.L. 94-455, §1033(c), provides:

(c) EFFECTIVE DATES.—The amendments made by this section shall apply—

(1) in respect of any distribution received by a domestic corporation after December 31, 1977, and

(2) in respect of any distribution received by a domestic corporation before January 1, 1978, in a taxable year of such corporation beginning after December 31, 1975, but only to the extent that such distribution is made out of the accumulated profits of a foreign corporation for a taxable year (of such foreign corporation) beginning after December 31, 1975.

For purposes of paragraph (2), a distribution made by a foreign corporation out of its profits which are attributable to a distribution received from a foreign corporation to which section 902(b) of the Internal Revenue Code of 1954 applies shall be treated as made out of the accumulated profits of a foreign corporation for a taxable year beginning before January 1, 1976, to the extent that such distribution was paid out of the accumulated profits of such foreign corporation for a taxable year beginning before January 1, 1976.

[Sec. 902(b)]

(b) FOREIGN SUBSIDIARY OF FIRST AND SECOND FOREIGN CORPORATION.—

(1) ONE TIER.—If the foreign corporation described in subsection (a) (hereinafter in this subsection referred to as the "first foreign corporation") owns 10 percent or more of the voting stock of a second foreign corporation from which it receives dividends in any taxable year, it shall be deemed to have paid the same proportion of any income, war profits, or excess profits taxes paid or deemed to be paid by such second foreign corporation to any foreign country or to any possession of the United States, on or with respect to the accumulated profits of such second foreign corporation from which such dividends were paid, which the amount of such dividends bears to the amount of such accumulated profits in excess of such income, war profits, and excess profits taxes (other than those deemed paid).

(2) TWO TIERS.—If such first foreign corporation owns 10 percent or more of the voting stock of a second foreign corporation which, in turn, owns 10 percent or more of the voting stock of a third foreign corporation from which the second foreign corporation receives dividends in any taxable year, the second foreign corporation shall be deemed to have paid the same proportion of any income, war profits, or excess profits taxes paid by such third foreign corporation to any foreign country or to any possession of the United States, on or with respect to the accumulated profits of such third foreign corporation from which such dividends were paid, which the amount of such dividends bears to the amount of such accumulated profits in excess of such income, war profits, and excess profits taxes.

(3) VOTING STOCK REQUIREMENT.—For purposes of this subpart—

(A) paragraph (1) shall not apply unless the percentage of voting stock owned by the domestic corporation in the first foreign corporation and the percentage of voting stock owned by the first foreign corporation in the second foreign corporation when multiplied together equal at least 5 percent, and

(B) paragraph (2) shall not apply unless the percentage arrived at for purposes of applying paragraph (1) when multiplied by the percentage of voting stock owned by the second foreign corporation in the third foreign corporation is equal to at least 5 percent.

Amendments
- **1976, Tax Reform Act of 1976 (P.L. 94-455)**

P.L. 94-455, §1033(a):

Amended Code Sec. 902(b). See amendatory note for P.L. 94-455, §1033(a) following Code Sec. 902(a) for **effective** date information. Prior to amendment, Code Sec. 902(b) read as follows:

(b) FOREIGN SUBSIDIARY OF FIRST AND SECOND FOREIGN CORPORATION.—

(1) If the foreign corporation described in subsection (a) (hereinafter in this subsection referred to as the "first foreign corporation") owns 10 percent or more of the voting stock of a second foreign corporation from which it receives dividends in any taxable year, it shall be deemed to have paid the same proportion of any income, war profits, or excess profits taxes paid or deemed to be paid by such second foreign corporation to any foreign country or to any possession of the United States on or with respect to the accumulated profits of the corporation from which such dividends were paid which—

(A) for purposes of applying subsection (a)(1), the amount of such dividends bears to the amount of the accumulated profits (as defined in subsection (c)(1)(A)) of such second foreign corporation from which such dividends were paid in excess of such income, war profits, and excess profits taxes, or

(B) for purposes of applying subsection (a)(2), the amount of such dividends bears to the amount of the accumulated profits (as defined in subsection (c)(1)(B)) of such second foreign corporation from which such dividends were paid.

(2) If such first foreign corporation owns 10 percent or more of the voting stock of a second foreign corporation which, in turn, owns 10 percent or more of the voting stock of a third foreign corporation from which the second foreign corporation receives dividends in any taxable year, the second foreign corporation shall be deemed to have paid the same proportion of any income, war profits, or excess profits taxes paid by such third foreign corporation to any foreign country or to any possession of the United States on or with respect to the accumulated profits of the corporation from which such dividends were paid which—

(A) for purposes of applying subsection (a)(1), the amount of such dividends bears to the amount of the accumulated profits (as defined in subsection (c)(1)(A)) of such third foreign corporation from which such dividends were paid in excess of such income, war profits, and excess profits taxes, or

(B) for purposes of applying subsection (a)(2), the amount of such dividends bears to the amount of the accumulated profits (as defined in subsection (c)(1)(B)) of such third foreign corporation from which such dividends were paid.

(3) For purposes of this subpart, subsection (b)(1) shall not apply unless the percentage of voting stock owned by the domestic corporation in the first foreign corporation and the percentage of voting stock owned by the first foreign corporation

INCOME TAX—FOREIGN TAX CREDIT

in the second foreign corporation when multiplied together equal at least 5 percent, and for purposes of this subpart, subsection (b)(2) shall not apply unless the percentage arrived at for purposes of applying subsection (b)(1) when multiplied by the percentage of voting stock owned by the second foreign corporation in the third foreign corporation is equal to at least 5 percent.

- **1971 (P.L. 91-684)**

P.L. 91-684, § 1:

Amended Code Sec. 902(b). **Effective** for tax years of domestic corporations ending after 1-12-71, but only in respect of dividends paid by one corporation to another corporation after that date. Prior to amendment, Code Sec. 902(b) read as follows:

(b) Foreign Subsidiary of Foreign Corporation.—If such foreign corporation owns 50 percent or more of the voting stock of another foreign corporation from which it receives dividends in any taxable year, it shall be deemed to have paid the same proportion of any income, war profits, or excess profits taxes paid by such other foreign corporation to any foreign country or to any possession of the United States, on or with respect to the accumulated profits of the corporation from which such dividends were paid which—

(1) for purposes of applying subsection (a)(1), the amount of such dividends bears to the amount of the accumulated profits (as defined in subsection (c)(1)(A)) of such other foreign corporation from which such dividends were paid in excess of such income, war profits, and excess profits taxes, or

(2) for purposes of applying subsection (a)(2), the amount of such dividends bears to the amount of the accumulated profits (as defined in subsection (c)(1)(B)) of such other foreign corporation from which such dividends were paid.

[Sec. 902(c)]

(c) APPLICABLE RULES.—

(1) ACCUMULATED PROFITS DEFINED.—For purposes of this section, the term "accumulated profits" means, with respect to any foreign corporation, the amount of its gains, profits, or income computed without reduction by the amount of the income, war profits, and excess profits taxes imposed on or with respect to such profits or income by any foreign country or by any possession of the United States. The Secretary shall have full power to determine from the accumulated profits of what year or years such dividends were paid, treating dividends paid in the first 60 days of any year as having been paid from the accumulated profits of the preceding year or years (unless to his satisfaction shown otherwise), and in other respects treating dividends as having been paid from the most recently accumulated gains, profits, or earnings.

(2) ACCOUNTING PERIODS.—In the case of a foreign corporation the income, war profits, and excess profits taxes of which are determined on the basis of an accounting period of less than 1 year, the word "year" as used in this subsection shall be construed to mean such accounting period.

Amendments

- **1976, Tax Reform Act of 1976 (P.L. 94-455)**

P.L. 94-455, § 1033(a):

Amended Code Sec. 902(c). For **effective** date information, see amendatory note for P.L. 94-455, § 1033(a) following Code Sec. 902(a). Prior to amendment, Code Sec. 902(c) read as follows:

(c) APPLICABLE RULES.—

(1) ACCUMULATED PROFITS DEFINED.—For purposes of this section, the term "accumulated profits" means with respect to any foreign corporation—

(A) for purposes of subsections (a)(1), (b)(1)(A), and (b)(2)(A), the amount of its gains, profits, or income computed without reduction by the amount of the income, war profits, and excess profits taxes imposed on or with respect to such profits or income by any foreign country or any possession of the United States; and

(B) for purposes of subsections (a)(2), (b)(1)(B), and (b)(2)(B), the amount of its gains, profits, or income in excess of the income, war profits, and excess profits taxes imposed on or with respect to such profits or income.

The Secretary or his delegate shall have full power to determine from the accumulated profits of what year or years such dividends were paid, treating dividends paid in the first 60 days of any year as having been paid from the accumulated profits of the preceding year or years (unless to his satisfaction shown otherwise), and in other respects treating dividends as having been paid from the most recently accumulated gains, profits, or earnings.

(2) ACCOUNTING PERIODS.—In the case of a foreign corporation, the income, war profits, and excess profits taxes of which are determined on the basis of an accounting period of less than 1 year, the word "year" as used in this subsection shall be construed to mean such accounting period.

- **1971 (P.L. 91-684)**

P.L. 91-684, § 2:

Substituted "(a)(1), (b)(1)(A), and (b)(2)(A)" for "(a)(2) and (b)(2)" in Code Sec. 902(c)(1)(A). Substituted "(a)(2), (b)(1)(B), and (b)(2)(B)" for "(a)(2) and (b)(2)" in Code Sec. 902(c)(1)(B). **Effective** for all tax years of domestic corporations ending after 1-12-71, but only with respect to dividends paid by one corporation to another corporation after that date.

[Sec. 902(d)]

(d) CROSS REFERENCES.—

(1) For inclusion in gross income of an amount equal to taxes deemed paid under subsection (a), see section 78.

(2) For application of subsections (a) and (b) with respect to taxes deemed paid in a prior taxable year by a United States shareholder with respect to a controlled foreign corporation, see section 960.

(3) For reduction of credit with respect to dividends paid out of accumulated profits for years for which certain information is not furnished, see section 6038.

Amendments

- **1976, Tax Reform Act of 1976 (P.L. 94-455)**

P.L. 94-455, § 1033(a):

Amended Code Sec. 902(d). See amendatory note for P.L. 94-455, § 1033(a) following Code Sec. 902(a) for **effective** date information. Amended Code Sec. 902(d)

corresponds to former Code Sec. 902(e). Prior to amendment of Code Sec. 902, Code Secs. 902(d) and 902(e) read as follows:

(d) LESS DEVELOPED COUNTRY CORPORATION DEFINED.—For purposes of this section, the term "less developed country corporation" means—

(1) a foreign corporation which, for its taxable year, is a less developed country corporation within the meaning of paragraph (3) or (4), and

(2) a foreign corporation which owns 10 percent or more of the total combined voting power of all classes of stock entitled to vote of a foreign corporation which is a less developed country corporation within the meaning of paragraph (3), and—

(A) 80 percent or more of the gross income of which for its taxable year meets the requirement of paragraph (3)(A), and

(B) 80 percent or more in value of the assets of which on each day of such year consists of property described in paragraph (3)(B).

A foreign corporation which is a less developed country corporation for its first taxable year beginning after December 31, 1962, shall, for purposes of this section, be treated as having been a less developed country corporation for each of its taxable years beginning before January 1, 1963.

(3) The term "less developed country corporation" means a foreign corporation which during the taxable year is engaged in the active conduct of one or more trades or businesses and—

(A) 80 percent or more of the gross income of which for the taxable year is derived from sources within less developed countries; and

(B) 80 percent or more in value of the assets of which on each day of the taxable year consists of—

(i) property used in such trades or businesses and located in less developed countries,

(ii) money, and deposits with persons carrying on the banking business,

(iii) stock, and obligations which, at the time of their acquisition, have a maturity of one year or more, of any other less developed country corporation,

(iv) an obligation of a less developed country,

(v) an investment which is required because of restrictions imposed by a less developed country, and

(vi) property described in section 956(b)(2).

For purposes of subparagraph (A), the determination as to whether income is derived from sources within less developed countries shall be made under regulations prescribed by the Secretary or his delegate.

(4) The term "less developed country corporation" also means a foreign corporation—

(A) 80 percent or more of the gross income of which for the taxable year consists of—

(i) gross income derived from, or in connection with, the using (or hiring or leasing for use) in foreign commerce of aircraft or vessels registered under the laws of a less developed country, or from, or in connection with, the performance of services directly related to use of such aircraft or vessels, or from the sale or exchange of such aircraft or vessels, and

(ii) dividends and interest received from foreign corporations which are less developed country corporations within the meaning of this paragraph and 10 percent or more of the total combined voting power of all classes of stock of which are owned by the foreign corporation, and gain from the sale or exchange of stock or obligations of foreign corporations which are such less developed country corporations, and

(B) 80 percent or more of the assets of which on each day of the taxable year consists of (i) assets used, or held for use, for or in connection with the production of income described in subparagraph (A), and (ii) property described in section 956(b)(2).

(5) The term "less developed country" means (in respect to any foreign corporation) any foreign country (other than an area within the SinoSoviet bloc) or any possession of the United States with respect to which, on the first day of the taxable year, there is in effect an Executive order by the President of the United States designating such country or possession as an economically less developed country for purposes of this section. For purposes of the preceding sentence, an overseas territory, department, province, or possession may be treated as a separate country. No designation shall be made under this paragraph with respect to—

Australia	Luxembourg
Austria	Monaco
Belgium	Netherlands
Canada	New Zealand
Denmark	Norway
France	Union of South Africa
Germany (Federal Republic)	San Marino
Hong Kong	Sweden
Italy	Switzerland
Japan	United Kingdom
Liechtenstein	

After the President has designated any foreign country or any possession of the United States as an economically less developed country for purposes of this section, he shall not terminate such designation (either by issuing an Executive order for that purpose or by issuing an Executive order under the first sentence of this paragraph which has the effect of terminating such designation) unless, at least 30 days prior to such termination, he has notified the Senate and the House of Representatives of his intention to terminate such designation. Any designation in effect on March 26, 1975, under section 955(c)(3) (as in effect before the enactment of the Tax Reduction Act of 1975) shall be treated as made under this paragraph.

(e) CROSS REFERENCES.—

Sec. 902—Stricken

INCOME TAX—FOREIGN TAX CREDIT

(1) For inclusion in gross income of an amount equal to taxes deemed paid under subsection (a)(1), see section 78.

(2) For application of Subsections (a) and (b) with respect to taxes deemed paid in a prior taxable year by a United States shareholder with respect to a controlled foreign corporation, see section 960.

(3) For reduction of credit with respect to dividends paid out of accumulated profits for years for which certain information is not furnished, see section 6038.

- **1975, Tax Reduction Act of 1975 (P.L. 94-12)**

P.L. 94-12, §602(c)(6):

Amended Code Sec. 902(d). **Effective** for tax years of foreign corporations beginning after 1975 and to tax years of U. S. shareholders within which or with which such tax years of such foreign corporations end. Prior to amendment, the section read as follows:

"(d) Less Developed Country Corporation Defined.—For purposes of this section, the term 'less developed country corporation' means—

"(1) a foreign corporation which, for its taxable year, is a less developed country corporation within the meaning of section 955(c)(1) or (2), and

"(2) a foreign corporation which owns 10 percent or more of the total combined voting power of all classes of stock entitled to vote of a foreign corporation which is a less developed country corporation within the meaning of section 955(c)(1), and—

"(A) 80 percent or more of the gross income of which for its taxable year meets the requirement of section 955(c)(1)(A); and

"(B) 80 percent or more in value of the assets of which on each day of such year consists of property described in section 955(c)(1)(B).

A foreign corporation which is a less developed country corporation for its first taxable year beginning after December 31, 1962, shall, for purposes of this section, be treated as having been a less developed country corporation for each of its taxable years beginning before January 1, 1963."

- **1962, Revenue Act of 1962 (P.L. 87-834)**

P.L. 87-834, §9(a):

Amended Code Sec. 902. **Effective** (1) in respect of any distribution received by a domestic corporation after 12-31-64, and (2) in respect of any distribution received by a domestic corporation before 1-1-65, in a tax year of such corporation beginning after 12-31-62, but only to the extent that such distribution is made out of the accumulated profits of a foreign corporation for a tax year (of such foreign corporation) beginning after 12-31-62. For purposes of (2), a distribution made by a foreign corporation out of its profits which are attributable to a distribution received from a foreign subsidiary to which section 902(b) applies shall be treated as made out of the accumulated profits of a foreign corporation for a tax year beginning before 1-1-63, to the extent that such distribution was paid out of the accumulated profits of such foreign subsidiary for a tax year beginning before 1-1-63. Prior to amendment, Code Sec. 902 read as follows:

SEC. 902. CREDIT FOR CORPORATE STOCKHOLDER IN FOREIGN CORPORATION.

(a) Treatment of Taxes Paid by Foreign Corporation.—For purposes of this subpart, a domestic corporation which owns at least 10 percent of the voting stock of a foreign corporation from which it receives dividends in any taxable year shall be deemed to have paid the same proportion of any income, war profits, or excess profits taxes paid or deemed to be paid by such foreign corporation to any foreign country or to any possession of the United States, on or with respect to the accumulated profits of such foreign corporation from which such dividends were paid, which the amount of such dividends bears to the amount of such accumulated profits.

(b) Foreign Subsidiary of Foreign Corporation.—If such foreign corporation owns 50 percent or more of the voting stock of another foreign corporation from which it receives dividends in any taxable year, it shall be deemed to have paid the same proportion of any income, war profits, or excess profits taxes paid by such other foreign corporation to any foreign country or to any possession of the United States, on or with respect to the accumulated profits of the corporation from which such dividends were paid, which the amount of such dividends bears to the amount of such accumulated profits.

(c) Applicable Rules.—

(1) The term "accumulated profits", when used in this section in reference to a foreign corporation, means the amount of its gains, profits, or income in excess of the income, war profits, and excess profits taxes imposed on or with respect to such profits or income; and the Secretary or his delegate shall have full power to determine from the accumulated profits of what year or years such dividends were paid, treating dividends paid in the first 60 days of any year as having been paid from the accumulated profits of the preceding year or years (unless to his satisfaction shown otherwise), and in other respects treating dividends as having been paid from the most recently accumulated gains, profits, or earnings.

(2) In the case of a foreign corporation, the income, war profits, and excess profits taxes of which are determined on the basis of an accounting period of less than 1 year, the word "year" as used in this subsection shall be construed to mean such accounting period.

(d) Special Rules for Certain Wholly-Owned Foreign Corporations.—For purposes of this subtitle, if—

(1) a domestic corporation owns, directly or indirectly, 100 percent of all classes of outstanding stock of a foreign corporation engaged in manufacturing, production, or mining,

(2) such domestic corporation receives property in the form of a royalty or compensation from such foreign corporation pursuant to any form of contractual arrangement under which the domestic corporation agrees to furnish services or property in consideration for the property so received, and

(3) such contractual arrangement provides that the property so received by such domestic corporation shall be accepted by such domestic corporation in lieu of dividends and that such foreign corporation shall neither declare nor pay any dividends of any kind in any calendar year in which such property is paid to such domestic corporation by such foreign corporation.

then the excess of the fair market value of such property so received by such domestic corporation over the cost to such domestic corporation of the property and services so furnished by such domestic corporation shall be treated as a distribution by such foreign corporation to such domestic corporation, and for purposes of section 301, the amount of such distribution shall be such excess, in lieu of any amount otherwise determined under section 301 without regard to this subsection; and the basis of such property so received by such domestic corporation shall be the fair market value of such property, in lieu of the basis otherwise determined under section 301(d) without regard to this subsection.

[Sec. 902(e)]

(e) Cross Reference.—

For reduction of credit with respect to dividends paid out of accumulated profits for years for which certain information is not furnished, see section 6038.

- **1960 (P.L. 86-780)**

P.L. 86-780, §6(b)(2):

Added subsection (e). **Effective** 1-1-61.

[Sec. 903]

SEC. 903. CREDIT FOR TAXES IN LIEU OF INCOME, ETC., TAXES.

For purposes of this part and of sections 164(a) and 275(a), the term "income, war profits, and excess profits taxes" shall include a tax paid in lieu of a tax on income, war profits, or excess profits otherwise generally imposed by any foreign country or by any possession of the United States.

Amendments

- **2004, American Jobs Creation Act of 2004 (P.L. 108-357)**

P.L. 108-357, §101(b)(7):

Amended Code Sec. 903 by striking "114, 164(a)," and inserting "164(a)". **Effective** for transactions after 12-31-2004. For transitional and special rules, see Act Secs. 101(d)-(f), below.

P.L. 108-357, §101(d)-(f) (as amended by P.L. 113-295, §219(a), Division A), provides:

(d) TRANSITIONAL RULE FOR 2005 AND 2006.—

(1) IN GENERAL.—In the case of transactions during 2005 or 2006, the amount includible in gross income by reason of the amendments made by this section shall not exceed the applicable percentage of the amount which would have been so included but for this subsection.

(2) APPLICABLE PERCENTAGE.—For purposes of paragraph (1), the applicable percentage shall be as follows:

(A) For 2005, the applicable percentage shall be 20 percent.

(B) For 2006, the applicable percentage shall be 40 percent.

(3) COORDINATION WITH SECTION 199.—This subsection shall be applied without regard to any deduction allowable under section 199.

(e) REVOCATION OF ELECTION TO BE TREATED AS DOMESTIC CORPORATION.—If, during the 1-year period beginning on the date of the enactment of this Act, a corporation for which an election is in effect under section 943(e) of the Internal Revenue Code of 1986 revokes such election, no gain or loss shall be recognized with respect to property treated as transferred under clause (ii) of section 943(e)(4)(B) of such Code to the extent such property—

(1) was treated as transferred under clause (i) thereof, or

(2) was acquired during a taxable year to which such election applies and before May 1, 2003, in the ordinary course of its trade or business.

The Secretary of the Treasury (or such Secretary's delegate) may prescribe such regulations as may be necessary to prevent the abuse of the purposes of this subsection.

[**Note:** Act Sec. 101(f) of P.L. 108-357, below, was stricken by P.L. 109-222, §513(b), applicable to tax years beginning after 5-17-2006.—CCH.]

(f) BINDING CONTRACTS.—The amendments made by this section shall not apply to any transaction in the ordinary course of a trade or business which occurs pursuant to a binding contract—

(1) which is between the taxpayer and a person who is not a related person (as defined in section 943(b)(3) of such Code, as in effect on the day before the date of the enactment of this Act), and

(2) which is in effect on September 17, 2003, and at all times thereafter.

For purposes of this subsection, a binding contract shall include a purchase option, renewal option, or replacement option which is included in such contract and which is enforceable against the seller or lessor.

INCOME TAX—FOREIGN TAX CREDIT

- **2000, FSC Repeal and Extraterritorial Income Exclusion Act of 2000 (P.L. 106-519)**

P.L. 106-519, §4(4):

Amended Code Sec. 903 by striking "164(a)" and inserting "114, 164(a),". **Effective**, generally, for transactions after 9-30-2000. For special rules, see Act Sec. 5(b)-(d) in the amendment notes following Code Sec. 921.

- **1988, Technical and Miscellaneous Revenue Act of 1988 (P.L. 100-647)**

P.L. 100-647, §1012(v)(9):

Amended Code Sec. 903 by striking out "this subpart" and inserting in lieu thereof "this part". **Effective** as if included in the provision of P.L. 99-514 to which it relates.

- **1964, Revenue Act of 1964 (P.L. 88-272)**

P.L. 88-272, §207(b)(8):

Amended section 903 by inserting the words "sections 164(a) and 275(a)" in lieu of "section 164(b)". **Effective** 1-1-64.

[Sec. 904]

SEC. 904. LIMITATION ON CREDIT.

[Sec. 904(a)]

(a) LIMITATION.—The total amount of the credit taken under section 901(a) shall not exceed the same proportion of the tax against which such credit is taken which the taxpayer's taxable income from sources without the United States (but not in excess of the taxpayer's entire taxable income) bears to his entire taxable income for the same taxable year.

Amendments

- **1986, Tax Reform Act of 1986 (P.L. 99-514)**

P.L. 99-514, §104(b)(13):

Amended Code Sec. 904(a) by striking out the last sentence. **Effective** for tax years beginning after 12-31-86. Prior to amendment, the last sentence read as follows:

For purposes of the preceding sentence in the case of an individual the entire taxable income shall be reduced by an amount equal to the zero bracket amount.

- **1977, Tax Reduction and Simplification Act of 1977 (P.L. 95-30)**

P.L. 95-30, §102(b)(11):

Amended Code Sec. 904(a) by adding the last sentence. **Effective** for tax years beginning after 12-31-76.

- **1976, Tax Reform Act of 1976 (P.L. 94-455)**

P.L. 94-455, §1031(a):

Amended Code Sec. 904(a). For **effective** dates, see §1031(c), below. Prior to amendment, Code Sec. 904(a) read as follows:

(a) ALTERNATIVE LIMITATIONS.—

(1) PER-COUNTRY LIMITATION.—In the case of any taxpayer who does not elect the limitation provided by paragraph (2), the amount of the credit in respect of the tax paid or accrued to any foreign country or possession of the United States shall not exceed the same proportion of the tax against which such credit is taken which the taxpayer's taxable income from sources within such country or possession (but not in excess of the taxpayer's entire taxable income) bears to his entire taxable income for the same taxable year.

(2) OVERALL LIMITATION.—In the case of any taxpayer who elects the limitation provided by this paragraph, the total amount of the credit in respect of taxes paid or accrued to all foreign countries and possessions of the United States shall not exceed the same proportion of the tax against which such credit is taken which the taxpayer's taxable income from sources without the United States (but not in excess of the taxpayer's entire taxable income) bears to his entire taxable income for the same taxable year.

P.L. 94-455, §1031(c), as amended by P.L. 95-600, §§701(u)(6) and 701(u)(7)(B)(ii), provides:

(c) EFFECTIVE DATES.—

(1) IN GENERAL.—Except as provided in paragraphs (2) and (3), the amendments made by this section shall apply to taxable years beginning after December 31, 1975.

(2) EXCEPTION FOR CERTAIN MINING OPERATIONS.—In the case of a domestic corporation or includible corporation in an affiliated group (as defined in section 1504 of the Internal Revenue Code of 1954) which has as of October 1, 1975—

(A) been engaged in the active conduct of the trade or business of the extraction of minerals (of a character with respect to which a deduction for depletion is allowable under section 613 of such Code) outside the United States or its possessions for less than 5 years preceding the date of enactment of this Act,

(B) had deductions properly apportioned or allocated to its gross income from such trade or business in excess of such gross income in at least 2 taxable years,

(C) 80 percent of its gross receipts are from the sale of such minerals, and

(D) made commitments for substantial expansion of such mineral extraction activities,

the amendments made by this section shall apply to taxable years beginning after December 31, 1978. In the case of a loss sustained in a taxable year beginning before January 1, 1979, by any corporation to which this paragraph applies, if section 904(a)(1) of such Code (as in effect before the enactment of this Act) applies with respect to such taxable year, the provisions of section 904(f) of such Code shall be applied with respect to such loss under the principles of section 904(a)(1).

(3) EXCEPTION FOR INCOME FROM POSSESSIONS.—In the case of gross income from sources within a possession of the United States (and the deductions properly apportioned or allocated thereto), the amendments made by this section shall apply to taxable years beginning after December 31, 1978.

(4) CARRYBACKS AND CARRYOVERS IN THE CASE OF MINING OPERATIONS AND INCOME FROM A POSSESSION.—In the case of a taxpayer to whom paragraph (2) or (3) of this subsection applies, section 904(e) of such Code shall apply except that "January 1, 1979" shall be substituted for "January 1, 1976" each place it appears therein. If such a taxpayer elects the overall limitation for a taxable year beginning before January 1, 1979, such section 904(e) shall be applied by substituting "the January 1, of the last year for which such taxpayer is on the per-country limitation" for "January 1, 1976" each place it appears therein.

- **1960 (P.L. 86-780)**

P.L. 86-780, §[1](a):

Amended Code Sec. 904(a). **Effective** for tax years beginning after 12-31-60. Prior to amendment, Code Sec. 904(a) read as follows:

"(a) Limitation.—The amount of the credit in respect of the tax paid or accrued to any country shall not exceed the same proportion of the tax against which such credit is taken which the taxpayer's taxable income from sources within such country (but not in excess of the taxpayer's entire taxable income) bears to his entire taxable income for the same taxable year."

[Sec. 904(b)]

(b) TAXABLE INCOME FOR PURPOSE OF COMPUTING LIMITATION.—

(1) PERSONAL EXEMPTIONS.—For purposes of subsection (a), the taxable income in the case of an individual, estate, or trust shall be computed without any deduction for personal exemptions under section 151 or 642(b).

(2) CAPITAL GAINS.—For purposes of this section—

(A) IN GENERAL.—Taxable income from sources outside the United States shall include gain from the sale or exchange of capital assets only to the extent of foreign source capital gain net income.

(B) SPECIAL RULES WHERE CAPITAL GAIN RATE DIFFERENTIAL.—In the case of any taxable year for which there is a capital gain rate differential—

(i) in lieu of applying subparagraph (A), the taxable income from sources outside the United States shall include gain from the sale or exchange of capital assets only in an amount equal to foreign source capital gain net income reduced by the rate differential portion of foreign source net capital gain,

(ii) the entire taxable income shall include gain from the sale or exchange of capital assets only in an amount equal to capital gain net income reduced by the rate differential portion of net capital gain, and

(iii) for purposes of determining taxable income from sources outside the United States, any net capital loss (and any amount which is a short-term capital loss under section 1212(a)) from sources outside the United States to the extent taken into account in determining capital gain net income for the taxable year shall be reduced by an amount equal to the rate differential portion of the excess of the net capital gain from sources within the United States over net capital gain.

(C) COORDINATION WITH CAPITAL GAINS RATES.—The Secretary may by regulations modify the application of this paragraph and paragraph (3) to the extent necessary to properly reflect any capital gain rate differential under section 1(h) and the computation of net capital gain.

(3) DEFINITIONS.—For purposes of this subsection—

(A) FOREIGN SOURCE CAPITAL GAIN NET INCOME.—The term "foreign source capital gain net income" means the lesser of—

(i) capital gain net income from sources without the United States, or

(ii) capital gain net income.

(B) FOREIGN SOURCE NET CAPITAL GAIN.—The term "foreign source net capital gain" means the lesser of—

(i) net capital gain from sources without the United States, or

(ii) net capital gain.

(C) SECTION 1231 GAINS.—The term "gain from the sale or exchange of capital assets" includes any gain so treated under section 1231.

(D) CAPITAL GAIN RATE DIFFERENTIAL.—There is a capital gain rate differential for any year if subsection (h) of section 1 applies to such taxable year.

(E) RATE DIFFERENTIAL PORTION.—The rate differential portion of foreign source net capital gain, net capital gain, or the excess of net capital gain from sources within the United States over net capital gain, as the case may be, is the same proportion of such amount as—

(i) the excess of—

(I) the highest rate of tax set forth in subsection (a), (b), (c), (d), or (e) of section 1 (whichever applies), over

(II) the alternative rate of tax determined under section 1(h), bears to

(ii) that rate referred to in subclause (I).

(4) TREATMENT OF DIVIDENDS FOR WHICH DEDUCTION IS ALLOWED UNDER SECTION 245A.—For purposes of subsection (a), in the case of a domestic corporation which is a United States shareholder with respect to a specified 10-percent owned foreign corporation, such shareholder's taxable income from sources without the United States (and entire taxable income) shall be determined without regard to—

(A) the foreign-source portion of any dividend received from such foreign corporation, and

(B) any deductions properly allocable or apportioned to—

(i) income (other than amounts includible under section 951(a)(1) or 951A(a)) with respect to stock of such specified 10-percent owned foreign corporation, or

(ii) such stock to the extent income with respect to such stock is other than amounts includible under section 951(a)(1) or 951A(a).

Any term which is used in section 245A and in this paragraph shall have the same meaning for purposes of this paragraph as when used in such section.

Amendments

• **2018, Tax Technical Corrections Act of 2018 (P.L. 115-141)**

P.L. 115-141, § 401(d)(1)(D)(xiii), Div. U:

Amended Code Sec. 904(b) by striking paragraph (4) and by redesignating paragraph (5) as paragraph (4). **Effective** 3-23-2018. For a special rule, see Act Sec. 401(e), Div. U, below. Prior to being stricken, Code Sec. 904(b)(4) read as follows:

(4) COORDINATION WITH SECTION 936.—For purposes of subsection (a), in the case of a corporation, the taxable income shall not include any portion thereof taken into account for purposes of the credit (if any) allowed by section 936 (without regard to subsections (a)(4) and (i) thereof).

P.L. 115-141, § 401(e), Div. U, provides:

(e) GENERAL SAVINGS PROVISION WITH RESPECT TO DEADWOOD PROVISIONS.—If—

(1) any provision amended or repealed by the amendments made by subsection (b) or (d) applied to—

(A) any transaction occurring before the date of the enactment of this Act,

(B) any property acquired before such date of enactment, or

(C) any item of income, loss, deduction, or credit taken into account before such date of enactment, and

(2) the treatment of such transaction, property, or item under such provision would (without regard to the amendments or repeals made by such subsection) affect the liability for tax for periods ending after such date of enactment,

nothing in the amendments or repeals made by this section shall be construed to affect the treatment of such transaction, property, or item for purposes of determining liability for tax for periods ending after such date of enactment.

• **2017, Tax Cuts and Jobs Act (P.L. 115-97)**

P.L. 115-97, § 13001(b)(2)(M)(i)-(iii):

Amended Code Sec. 904(b) by striking "or 1201(a)" in paragraph (2)(C) following "under section 1(h)", by striking paragraph (3)(D) and inserting a new paragraph (3)(D), and by striking paragraph (3)(E) and inserting a new paragraph (3)(E). **Effective** for tax years beginning after 12-31-2017. Prior to being stricken, Code Sec. 904(b)(3)(D) and (E) read as follows:

(D) CAPITAL GAIN RATE DIFFERENTIAL.—There is a capital gain rate differential for any taxable year if—

(i) in the case of a taxpayer other than a corporation, subsection (h) of section 1 applies to such taxable year, or

(ii) in the case of a corporation, any rate of tax imposed by section 11, 511, or 831(a) or (b) (whichever applies) exceeds the alternative rate of tax under section 1201(a) (determined without regard to the last sentence of section 11(b)(1)).

(E) RATE DIFFERENTIAL PORTION.—

(i) IN GENERAL.—The rate differential portion of foreign source net capital gain, net capital gain, or the excess of net capital gain from sources within the United States over net capital gain, as the case may be, is the same proportion of such amount as—

(I) the excess of the highest applicable tax rate over the alternative tax rate, bears to

(II) the highest applicable tax rate.

(ii) HIGHEST APPLICABLE TAX RATE.—For purposes of clause (i), the term "highest applicable tax rate" means—

(I) in the case of a taxpayer other than a corporation, the highest rate of tax set forth in subsection (a), (b), (c), (d), or (e) of section 1 (whichever applies), or

(II) in the case of a corporation, the highest rate of tax specified in section 11(b).

(iii) ALTERNATIVE TAX RATE.—For purposes of clause (i), the term "alternative tax rate" means—

(I) in the case of a taxpayer other than a corporation, the alternative rate of tax determined under section 1(h), or

(II) in the case of a corporation, the alternative rate of tax under section 1201(a).

P.L. 115-97, § 14101(d):

Amended Code Sec. 904(b) by adding at the end a new paragraph (5). **Effective** for distributions made after, and deductions with respect to tax years ending after, 12-31-2017.

• **1997, Taxpayer Relief Act of 1997 (P.L. 105-34)**

P.L. 105-34, § 311(c)(3):

Amended Code Sec. 904(b)(2) by adding at the end a new subparagraph (C). **Effective** for tax years ending after 5-6-97.

• **1993, Omnibus Budget Reconciliation Act of 1993 (P.L. 103-66)**

P.L. 103-66, § 13227(d):

Amended Code Sec. 904(b)(4) by inserting before the period at the end thereof "(without regard to subsections (a)(4) and (i) thereof)". **Effective** for tax years beginning after 12-31-93.

• **1990, Omnibus Budget Reconciliation Act of 1990 (P.L. 101-508)**

P.L. 101-508, § 11101(d)(5)(A):

Amended Code Sec. 904(b)(3)(D)(i) by striking "subsection (j)" and inserting "subsection (h)". **Effective** for tax years beginning after 12-31-90.

P.L. 101-508, § 11101(d)(5)(B):

Amended Code Sec. 904(b)(3)(E)(iii)(I) by striking "section 1(j)" and inserting "section 1(h)". **Effective** for tax years beginning after 12-31-90.

• **1988, Technical and Miscellaneous Revenue Act of 1988 (P.L. 100-647)**

P.L. 100-647, § 1003(b)(2)(A):

Amended Code Sec. 904(b)(2). **Effective** as if included in the provision of P.L. 99-514 to which it relates. Prior to amendment, Code Sec. 904(b)(2) read as follows:

(2) CAPITAL GAINS.—For purposes of this section—

(A) CORPORATIONS.—In the case of a corporation—

(i) the taxable income of such corporation from sources without the United States shall include gain from the sale or exchange of capital assets only in an amount equal to foreign source capital gain net income reduced by the rate differential portion of foreign source net capital gain,

(ii) the entire taxable income of such corporation shall include gain from the sale or exchange of capital assets only in an amount equal to capital gain net income reduced by the rate differential portion of net capital gain, and

(iii) for purposes of determining taxable income from sources without the United States, any net capital loss (and any amount which is a short-term capital loss under section 1212(a)) from sources without the United States to the extent taken into account in determining capital gain net income for the taxable year shall be reduced by an amount equal to the rate differential portion of the excess of net capital gain from sources within the United States over net capital gain.

(B) OTHER TAXPAYERS.—In the case of a taxpayer other than a taxpayer described in subparagraph (A), taxable income from sources without the United States shall include gain from the sale or exchange of capital assets only to the extent of foreign source capital gain net income.

P.L. 100-647, § 1003(b)(2)(B):

Amended Code Sec. 904(b)(3) by striking out subparagraph (D) and inserting in lieu thereof new subparagraphs (D)-(E). **Effective** as if included in the provision of P.L. 99-514 to which it relates. Prior to amendment, Code Sec. 904(b)(3)(D) read as follows:

(D) RATE DIFFERENTIAL PORTION.—The "rate differential portion" of foreign source net capital gain, net capital gain, or the excess of net capital gain from sources within the United States over net capital gain, as the case may be, is the same proportion of such amount as the excess of the highest rate of tax specified in section 11(b) over the

INCOME TAX—FOREIGN TAX CREDIT

alternative rate of tax under section 1201(a) bears to the highest rate of tax specified in section 11(b).

P.L. 100-647, § 2004(l):

Amended Code Sec. 904(b)(3)(D)(ii), as amended, by striking out "section 11(b)" and inserting in lieu thereof "section 11(b)(1)". **Effective** as if included in the provision of P.L. 100-203 to which it relates.

- **1986, Tax Reform Act of 1986 (P.L. 99-514)**

P.L. 99-514, § 1211(b)(3):

Amended Code Sec. 904(b)(3) by striking out subparagraphs (C) and (D) and redesignating subparagraphs (E) and (F) as subparagraphs (C) and (D), respectively. **Effective** for tax years beginning after 12-31-86. However, for a special rule, see Act Sec. 1211(c)(2), below. Prior to amendment, Code Sec. 904(b)(3)(C) and (D) read as follows:

(C) EXCEPTION FOR GAIN FROM THE SALE OF CERTAIN PERSONAL PROPERTY.—There shall be included as gain from sources within the United States any gain from sources without the United States from the sale or exchange of a capital asset which is personal property which—

(i) in the case of an individual is sold or exchanged outside of the country (or possession) of the individual's residence,

(ii) in the case of a corporation, is stock in a second corporation sold or exchanged other than in a country (or possession) in which such second corporation derived more than 50 percent of its gross income for the 3-year period ending with the close of such second corporation's taxable year immediately preceding the year during which the sale or exchange occurred, or

(iii) in the case of any taxpayer, is personal property (other than stock in a corporation) sold or exchanged other than in a country (or possession) in which such property is used in a trade or business of the taxpayer or in which such taxpayer derived more than 50 percent of its gross income for the 3-year period ending with the close of its taxable year immediately preceding the year during which the sale or exchange occurred,

unless such gain is subject to an income, war profits, or excess profits tax of a foreign country or possession of the United States, and the rate of tax applicable to such gain is 10 percent or more of the gain from the sale or exchange (computed under this chapter).

(D) GAIN FROM LIQUIDATION OF CERTAIN FOREIGN CORPORATIONS.—Subparagraph (C) shall not apply with respect to a distribution in liquidation of a foreign corporation to which part II of subchapter C applies if such corporation derived less than 50 percent of its gross income from sources within the United States for the 3-year period ending with the close of such corporation's taxable year immediately preceding the year during which the distribution occurred.

P.L. 99-514, § 1211(c)(2), provides:

(2) SPECIAL RULE FOR FOREIGN PERSONS.—In the case of any foreign person other than any controlled foreign corporations (within the meaning of section 957(a) of the Internal Revenue Code of 1954), the amendments made by this section shall apply to transactions entered into after March 18, 1986.

- **1980, Technical Corrections Act of 1979 (P.L. 96-222)**

P.L. 96-222, § 104(a)(3)(D)(i):

Amended Code Sec. 904(b)(3) by redesignating paragraph (E) as paragraph (F). **Effective** 11-6-78.

- **1978, Revenue Act of 1978 (P.L. 95-600)**

P.L. 95-600, § 403(c)(4):

Amended Code Sec. 904(b) by striking out "three-eighths" wherever it appeared and inserting in lieu thereof "the rate differential portion", and by striking out the period at the end of Code Sec. 904(b)(3)(D), inserting a comma in lieu thereof, and by adding a new subparagraph (E). **Effective** 11-6-78.

P.L. 95-600, § 701(u)(2)(A):

Amended Code Sec. 904(b)(2) by striking out "For purposes of subsection (a)—" and inserting in lieu thereof "For purposes of this section—". **Effective** for tax years beginning after 12-31-75.

P.L. 95-600, § 701(u)(2)(B):

Amended Code Sec. 904(b)(3)(C) by striking out "For purposes of this paragraph, there" and inserting in lieu thereof "There". **Effective** for tax years beginning after 12-31-75.

P.L. 95-600, § 701(u)(2)(C):

Amended Code Sec. 904(b)(3) by redesignating subparagraph (D) as subparagraph (E) and by adding a new subparagraph (D). **Effective** for tax years beginning after 12-31-75.

P.L. 95-600, 701(u)(3)(A):

Amended Code Sec. 904(b)(2)(iii). **Effective** for tax years beginning after 1975. Prior to amendment, clause (iii) of Code Sec. 904(b)(2) read as follows:

(iii) any net capital loss from sources without the United States to the extent taken into account in determining capital gain net income for the taxable year shall be reduced by an amount equal to three eighths of the excess of net capital gain from sources within the United States over net capital gain.

- **1976, Tax Reform Act of 1976 (P.L. 94-455)**

P.L. 94-455, § 1031(a):

Amended Code Sec. 904(b). For **effective** date information, see amendment note for P.L. 94-455, Act Sec. 1031(a), following Code Sec. 904(a). Prior to amendment, Code Sec. 904(b) read as follows:

(b) ELECTION OF OVERALL LIMITATION.—

(1) IN GENERAL.—A taxpayer may elect the limitation provided by subsection (a)(2) for any taxable year beginning after December 31, 1960. An election under this paragraph for any taxable year shall remain in effect for all subsequent taxable years, except that it may be revoked (A) with the consent of the Secretary or his delegate with respect to any taxable year or (B) for the taxpayer's first taxable year beginning after December 31, 1969.

(2) ELECTION AFTER REVOCATION.—Except in a case to which paragraph (1)(B) applies, if the taxpayer has made an election under paragraph (1) and such election has been revoked, such taxpayer shall not be eligible to make a new election under paragraph (1) for any taxable year, unless the Secretary or his delegate consents to such new election.

(3) FORM AND TIME OF ELECTION AND REVOCATION.—An election under paragraph (1), and any revocation of such an election, may be made only in such manner as the Secretary or his delegate may by regulations prescribe. Such an election or revocation with respect to any taxable year may be made or changed at any time before the expiration of the period prescribed for making a claim for credit or refund of the tax imposed by this chapter for such taxable year.

P.L. 94-455, § 1034(a):

Amended Code Sec. 904(b). **Effective** for tax years beginning after 12-31-75. The provisions of Code Sec. 904(b)(3)(C), however, shall apply only to sales or exchanges made after 11-12-75.

P.L. 94-455, § 1051(e):

Added Code Sec. 904(b)(4). **Effective** for tax years beginning after 12-31-75.

- **1969, Tax Reform Act of 1969 (P.L. 91-172)**

P.L. 91-172, § 506(b):

Amended paragraph (b)(1) by inserting "(A) with the consent of the Secretary or his delegate with respect to any taxable year or (B) for the taxpayer's first taxable year beginning after December 31, 1969" in lieu of "with the consent of the Secretary or his delegate with respect to any taxable year" at the end of the last sentence, and by inserting "Except in a case to which paragraph (1)(B) applies, if the taxpayer" in lieu of "If a taxpayer" in paragraph (b)(2). **Effective** for tax years beginning after 12-31-69.

- **1960 (P.L. 86-780)**

P.L. 86-780, § [1](a):

Added subsection (b) to Code Sec. 904. **Effective** for tax years beginning after 12-31-60.

[Sec. 904(c)]

(c) CARRYBACK AND CARRYOVER OF EXCESS TAX PAID.—Any amount by which all taxes paid or accrued to foreign countries or possessions of the United States for any taxable year for which the taxpayer chooses to have the benefits of this subpart exceed the limitation under subsection (a) shall be deemed taxes paid or accrued to foreign countries or possessions of the United States in the first preceding taxable year, and in any of the first 10 succeeding taxable years, in that order and to the extent not deemed taxes paid or accrued in a prior taxable year, in the amount by which the limitation under subsection (a) for such preceding or succeeding taxable year exceeds the sum of the taxes paid or accrued to foreign countries or possessions of the United States for such preceding or succeeding taxable year and the amount of the taxes for any taxable year earlier than the current taxable year which shall be deemed to have been paid or accrued in such preceding or subsequent taxable year (whether or not the taxpayer chooses to have the benefits of this subpart with respect to such earlier taxable year). Such amount deemed paid or accrued in any year may be availed of only as a tax credit and not as a deduction and only if the taxpayer for such year chooses to have the benefits of this subpart as to taxes paid or accrued for that year to foreign countries or possessions of the United States. This subsection shall not apply to taxes paid or accrued with respect to amounts described in subsection (d)(1)(A).

Amendments

- **2017, Tax Cuts and Jobs Act (P.L. 115-97)**

P.L. 115-97, § 14201(b)(2)(C):

Amended Code Sec. 904(c) by adding at the end a new sentence. **Effective** for tax years of foreign corporations beginning after 12-31-2017, and to tax years of United States shareholders in which or with which such tax years of foreign corporations end.

- **2004, American Jobs Creation Act of 2004 (P.L. 108-357)**

P.L. 108-357, § 417(a)(1):

Amended Code Sec. 904(c) by striking "in the second preceding taxable year," immediately preceding "in the first preceding taxable year". **Effective** for excess foreign taxes arising in tax years beginning after 10-22-2004.

INCOME TAX—FOREIGN TAX CREDIT

P.L. 108-357, § 417(a)(2):

Amended Code Sec. 904(c) by striking ", and in the first, second, third, fourth, or fifth" and inserting "and in any of the first 10". **Effective** for excess foreign taxes which (without regard to the amendments made by Act Sec. 417) may be carried to any tax year ending after 10-22-2004.

• **1976, Tax Reform Act of 1976 (P.L. 94-455)**

P.L. 94-455, § 1031(a):

Amended Code Sec. 904(c). See amendment note for P.L. 94-455, Act Sec. 1031(a), following Code Sec. 904(a) for **effective** date information. Prior to amendment, Code Sec. 904(c) read as follows:

(c) TAXABLE INCOME FOR PURPOSE OF COMPUTING LIMITATION.—For purposes of computing the applicable limitation under subsection (a), the taxable income in the case of an individual, estate, or trust shall be computed without any deduction for personal exemptions under section 151 or 642(b).

• **1960 (P.L. 86-780)**

P.L. 86-780, §[1](b):

Redesignated subsection (b) of Code Sec. 904 as subsection (c) and amended it by inserting the word "applicable" immediately preceding the word "limitation". **Effective** for tax years beginning after 12-31-60.

[Sec. 904(d)]

(d) SEPARATE APPLICATION OF SECTION WITH RESPECT TO CERTAIN CATEGORIES OF INCOME.—

(1) IN GENERAL.—The provisions of subsections (a), (b), and (c) and sections 902, 907, and 960 shall be applied separately with respect to—

(A) any amount includible in gross income under section 951A (other than passive category income),

(B) foreign branch income,

(C) passive category income, and

(D) general category income.

(2) DEFINITIONS AND SPECIAL RULES.—For purposes of this subsection—

(A) CATEGORIES.—

(i) PASSIVE CATEGORY INCOME.—The term "passive category income" means passive income and specified passive category income.

(ii) GENERAL CATEGORY INCOME.—The term "general category income" means income other than income described in paragraph (1)(A), foreign branch income, and passive category income.

(B) PASSIVE INCOME.—

(i) IN GENERAL.—Except as otherwise provided in this subparagraph, the term "passive income" means any income received or accrued by any person which is of a kind which would be foreign personal holding company income (as defined in section 954(c)).

(ii) CERTAIN AMOUNTS INCLUDED.—Except as provided in clause (iii), subparagraph (E)(ii), or paragraph (3)(H), the term "passive income" includes any amount includible in gross income under section 1293 (relating to certain passive foreign investment companies).

(iii) EXCEPTIONS.—The term "passive income" shall not include—

(I) any export financing interest, and

(II) any high-taxed income.

(iv) CLARIFICATION OF APPLICATION OF SECTION 864(d)(6).—In determining whether any income is of a kind which would be foreign personal holding company income, the rules of section 864(d)(6) shall apply only in the case of income of a controlled foreign corporation.

(v) SPECIFIED PASSIVE CATEGORY INCOME.—The term "specified passive category income" means—

(I) dividends from a DISC or former DISC (as defined in section 992(a)) to the extent such dividends are treated as income from sources without the United States, and

(II) distributions from a former FSC (as defined in section 922) out of earnings and profits attributable to foreign trade income (within the meaning of section 923(b)) or interest or carrying charges (as defined in section 927(d)(1)) derived from a transaction which results in foreign trade income (as defined in section 923(b)).

Any reference in subclause (II) to section 922, 923, or 927 shall be treated as a reference to such section as in effect before its repeal by the FSC Repeal and Extraterritorial Income Exclusion Act of 2000.

(C) TREATMENT OF FINANCIAL SERVICES INCOME AND COMPANIES.—

(i) IN GENERAL.—Financial services income shall be treated as general category income in the case of—

(I) a member of a financial services group,

(II) any other person if such person is predominantly engaged in the active conduct of a banking, insurance, financing, or similar business.

(ii) FINANCIAL SERVICES GROUP.—The term "financial services group" means any affiliated group (as defined in section 1504(a) without regard to paragraphs (2) and (3) of section 1504(b)) which is predominantly engaged in the active conduct of a banking, insurance, financing, or similar business. In determining whether such a group is so engaged, there shall be taken into account only the income of members of the group that are—

(I) United States corporations, or

(II) controlled foreign corporations in which such United States corporations own, directly or indirectly, at least 80 percent of the total voting power and value of the stock.

(iii) PASS-THRU ENTITIES.—The Secretary shall by regulation specify for purposes of this subparagraph the treatment of financial services income received or accrued by partnerships and by other pass-thru entities which are not members of a financial services group.

(D) FINANCIAL SERVICES INCOME.—

(i) IN GENERAL.—Except as otherwise provided in this subparagraph, the term "financial services income" means any income which is received or accrued by any person predominantly engaged in the active conduct of a banking, insurance, financing, or similar business, and which is—

(I) described in clause (ii), or

(II) passive income (determined without regard to subparagraph (B)(iii)(II)).

(ii) GENERAL DESCRIPTION OF FINANCIAL SERVICES INCOME.—Income is described in this clause if such income is—

(I) derived in the active conduct of a banking, financing, or similar business,

(II) derived from the investment by an insurance company of its unearned premiums or reserves ordinary and necessary for the proper conduct of its insurance business, or

(III) of a kind which would be insurance income as defined in section 953(a) determined without regard to those provisions of paragraph (1)(A) of such section which limit insurance income to income from countries other than the country in which the corporation was created or organized.

INCOME TAX—FOREIGN TAX CREDIT

(E) NONCONTROLLED SECTION 902 CORPORATION.—

(i) NONCONTROLLED 10-PERCENT OWNED FOREIGN CORPORATION.—The term "noncontrolled 10-percent owned foreign corporation" means any foreign corporation which is—

(I) a specified 10-percent owned foreign corporation (as defined in section 245A(b)), or

(II) a passive foreign investment company (as defined in section 1297(a)) with respect to which the taxpayer meets the stock ownership requirements of section 902(a) (or, for purposes of applying paragraphs (3) and (4), the requirements of section 902(b)).

A controlled foreign corporation shall not be treated as a noncontrolled 10-percent owned foreign corporation with respect to any distribution out of its earnings and profits for periods during which it was a controlled foreign corporation. Any reference to section 902 in this clause shall be treated as a reference to such section as in effect before its repeal.

(ii) TREATMENT OF INCLUSIONS UNDER SECTION 1293.—If any foreign corporation is a noncontrolled 10-percent owned foreign corporation with respect to the taxpayer, any inclusion under section 1293 with respect to such corporation shall be treated as a dividend from such corporation.

(F) HIGH-TAXED INCOME.—The term "high-taxed income" means any income which (but for this subparagraph) would be passive income if the sum of—

(i) the foreign income taxes paid or accrued by the taxpayer with respect to such income, and

(ii) the foreign income taxes deemed paid by the taxpayer with respect to such income under section 902 or 960,

exceeds the highest rate of tax specified in section 1 or 11 (whichever applies) multiplied by the amount of such income (determined with regard to section 78). For purposes of the preceding sentence, the term "foreign income taxes" means any income, war profits, or excess profits tax imposed by any foreign country or possession of the United States.

(G) EXPORT FINANCING INTEREST.—For purposes of this paragraph, the term "export financing interest" means any interest derived from financing the sale (or other disposition) for use or consumption outside the United States of any property—

(i) which is manufactured, produced, grown, or extracted in the United States by the taxpayer or a related person, and

(ii) not more than 50 percent of the fair market value of which is attributable to products imported into the United States.

For purposes of clause (ii), the fair market value of any property imported into the United States shall be its appraised value, as determined by the Secretary under section 402 of the Tariff Act of 1930 (19 U.S.C. 1401a) in connection with its importation.

(H) TREATMENT OF INCOME TAX BASE DIFFERENCES.—

(i) IN GENERAL.—In the case of taxable years beginning after December 31, 2006, tax imposed under the law of a foreign country or possession of the United States on an amount which does not constitute income under United States tax principles shall be treated as imposed on income described in paragraph (1)(B) [(1)(D)].

(ii) SPECIAL RULE FOR YEARS BEFORE 2007.—

(I) IN GENERAL.—In the case of taxes paid or accrued in taxable years beginning after December 31, 2004, and before January 1, 2007, a taxpayer may elect to treat tax imposed under the law of a foreign country or possession of the United States on an amount which does not constitute income under United States tax principles as tax imposed on income described in subparagraph (C) or (I) of paragraph (1).

(II) ELECTION IRREVOCABLE.—Any such election shall apply to the taxable year for which made and all subsequent taxable years described in subclause (I) unless revoked with the consent of the Secretary.

(I) RELATED PERSON.—For purposes of this paragraph, the term "related person" has the meaning given such term by section 954(d)(3), except that such section shall be applied by substituting "the person with respect to whom the determination is being made" for "controlled foreign corporation" each place it appears.

(J) FOREIGN BRANCH INCOME.—

(i) IN GENERAL.—The term "foreign branch income" means the business profits of such United States person which are attributable to 1 or more qualified business units (as defined in section 989(a)) in 1 or more foreign countries. For purposes of the preceding sentence, the amount of business profits attributable to a qualified business unit shall be determined under rules established by the Secretary.

(ii) EXCEPTION.—Such term shall not include any income which is passive category income.

(K) TRANSITIONAL RULES FOR 2007 CHANGES.—For purposes of paragraph (1)—

(i) taxes carried from any taxable year beginning before January 1, 2007, to any taxable year beginning on or after such date, with respect to any item of income, shall be treated as described in the subparagraph of paragraph (1) in which such income would be described were such taxes paid or accrued in a taxable year beginning on or after such date, and

(ii) the Secretary may by regulations provide for the allocation of any carryback of taxes with respect to income from a taxable year beginning on or after January 1, 2007, to a taxable year beginning before such date for purposes of allocating such income among the separate categories in effect for the taxable year to which carried.

(3) LOOK-THRU IN CASE OF CONTROLLED FOREIGN CORPORATIONS.—

(A) IN GENERAL.—Except as otherwise provided in this paragraph, dividends, interest, rents, and royalties received or accrued by the taxpayer from a controlled foreign corporation in which the taxpayer is a United States shareholder shall not be treated as passive category income.

(B) SUBPART F INCLUSIONS.—Any amount included in gross income under section 951(a)(1)(A) shall be treated as passive category income to the extent the amount so included is attributable to passive category income.

(C) INTEREST, RENTS, AND ROYALTIES.—Any interest, rent, or royalty which is received or accrued from a controlled foreign corporation in which the taxpayer is a United States shareholder shall be treated as passive category income to the extent it is properly allocable (under regulations prescribed by the Secretary) to passive category income of the controlled foreign corporation.

(D) DIVIDENDS.—Any dividend paid out of the earnings and profits of any controlled foreign corporation in which the taxpayer is a United States shareholder shall be treated as passive category income in proportion to the ratio of—

(i) the portion of the earnings and profits attributable to passive category income, to

(ii) the total amount of earnings and profits.

(E) LOOK-THRU APPLIES ONLY WHERE SUBPART F APPLIES.—If a controlled foreign corporation meets the requirements of section 954(b)(3)(A) (relating to de minimis rule) for any taxable year, for purposes of this paragraph, none of its foreign base company income (as defined in section 954(a) without regard to section 954(b)(5)) and none of its gross insurance income (as defined in section 954(b)(3)(C)) for such taxable year shall be treated as passive category income, except that this sentence shall not apply to any income which (without regard to this sentence) would be treated as financial services income. Solely for purposes of applying subparagraph (D), passive income of a controlled foreign corporation shall not be treated as passive category income if the requirements of section 954(b)(4) are met with respect to such income.

(F) COORDINATION WITH HIGH-TAXED INCOME PROVISIONS.—

(i) In determining whether any income of a controlled foreign corporation is passive category income, subclause (II) of paragraph (2)(B)(iii) shall not apply.

(ii) Any income of the taxpayer which is treated as passive category income under this paragraph shall be so treated notwithstanding any provision of paragraph (2); except that the determination of whether any amount is high-taxed income shall be made after the application of this paragraph.

(G) DIVIDEND.—For purposes of this paragraph, the term "dividend" includes any amount included in gross income in section 951(a)(1)(B). Any amount included in gross income under section 78 to the extent attributable to amounts included in gross income in section 951(a)(1)(A) shall not be treated as a dividend but shall be treated as included in gross income under section 951(a)(1)(A).

(H) LOOK-THRU APPLIES TO PASSIVE FOREIGN INVESTMENT COMPANY INCLUSION.—If—

(i) a passive foreign investment company is a controlled foreign corporation, and

(ii) the taxpayer is a United States shareholder in such controlled foreign corporation,

any amount included in gross income under section 1293 shall be treated as income in a separate category to the extent such amount is attributable to income in such category.

(4) LOOK-THRU APPLIES TO DIVIDENDS FROM NONCONTROLLED 10-PERCENT OWNED FOREIGN CORPORATIONS.—

(A) IN GENERAL.—For purposes of this subsection, any dividend from a noncontrolled 10-percent owned foreign corporation with respect to the taxpayer shall be treated as income described in a subparagraph of paragraph (1) in proportion to the ratio of—

(i) the portion of earnings and profits attributable to income described in such subparagraph, to

(ii) the total amount of earnings and profits.

(B) EARNINGS AND PROFITS OF CONTROLLED FOREIGN CORPORATIONS.—In the case of any distribution from a controlled foreign corporation to a United States shareholder, rules similar to the rules of subparagraph (A) shall apply in determining the extent to which earnings and profits of the controlled foreign corporation which are attributable to dividends received from a noncontrolled 10-percent owned foreign corporation may be treated as income in a separate category.

(C) SPECIAL RULES.—For purposes of this paragraph—

(i) EARNINGS AND PROFITS.—

(I) IN GENERAL.—The rules of section 316 shall apply.

(II) REGULATIONS.—The Secretary may prescribe regulations regarding the treatment of distributions out of earnings and profits for periods before the taxpayer's acquisition of the stock to which the distributions relate.

(ii) INADEQUATE SUBSTANTIATION.—If the Secretary determines that the proper subparagraph of paragraph (1) in which a dividend is described has not been substantiated, such dividend shall be treated as income described in paragraph (1)(A).

(iii) COORDINATION WITH HIGH-TAXED INCOME PROVISIONS.—Rules similar to the rules of paragraph (3)(F) shall apply for purposes of this paragraph.

(iv) LOOK-THRU WITH RESPECT TO CARRYOVER OF CREDIT.—Rules similar to subparagraph (A) also shall apply to any carryforward under subsection (c) from a taxable year beginning before January 1, 2003, of tax allocable to a dividend from a noncontrolled 10-percent owned foreign corporation with respect to the taxpayer. The Secretary may by regulations provide for the allocation of any carryback of tax allocable to a dividend from a noncontrolled 10-percent owned foreign corporation from a taxable year beginning on or after January 1, 2003, to a taxable year beginning before such date for purposes of allocating such dividend among the separate categories in effect for the taxable year to which carried.

(5) CONTROLLED FOREIGN CORPORATION; UNITED STATES SHAREHOLDER.—For purposes of this subsection—

(A) CONTROLLED FOREIGN CORPORATION.—The term "controlled foreign corporation" has the meaning given such term by section 957 (taking into account section 953(c)).

(B) UNITED STATES SHAREHOLDER.—The term "United States shareholder" has the meaning given such term by section 951(b) (taking into account section 953(c)).

(6) SEPARATE APPLICATION TO ITEMS RESOURCED UNDER TREATIES.—

(A) IN GENERAL.—If—

(i) without regard to any treaty obligation of the United States, any item of income would be treated as derived from sources within the United States,

(ii) under a treaty obligation of the United States, such item would be treated as arising from sources outside the United States, and

(iii) the taxpayer chooses the benefits of such treaty obligation,

subsections (a), (b), and (c) of this section and sections 907 and 960 shall be applied separately with respect to each such item.

(B) COORDINATION WITH OTHER PROVISIONS.—This paragraph shall not apply to any item of income to which subsection (h)(10) or section 865(h) applies.

(C) REGULATIONS.—The Secretary may issue such regulations or other guidance as is necessary or appropriate to carry out the purposes of this paragraph, including regulations or other guidance which provides that related items of income may be aggregated for purposes of this paragraph.

(7) REGULATIONS.—The Secretary shall prescribe such regulations as may be necessary or appropriate for the purposes of this subsection, including regulations—

(A) for the application of paragraph (3) and subsection (f)(5) in the case of income paid (or loans made) through 1 or more entities or between 2 or more chains of entities,

(B) preventing the manipulation of the character of income the effect of which is to avoid the purposes of this subsection, and

(C) providing that rules similar to the rules of paragraph (3)(C) shall apply to interest, rents, and royalties received or accrued from entities which would be controlled foreign corporations if they were foreign corporations.

Amendments

- **2018, Tax Technical Corrections Act of 2018 (P.L. 115-141)**

P.L. 115-141, § 401(a)(157)(A)-(B), Div. U:

Amended Code Sec. 904(d)(2)(B)(ii) by striking ", except as provided in subparagraph (E)(iii) or paragraph (3)(I)," before "any amount includible", and by inserting "subparagraph (E)(ii), or paragraph (3)(H)," after "Except as provided in clause (iii),". **Effective** 3-23-2018. Prior to amendment, Code Sec. 904(d)(2)(B)(ii) read as follows:

(ii) CERTAIN AMOUNTS INCLUDED.—Except as provided in clause (iii), the term "passive income" includes, except as provided in subparagraph (E)(iii) or paragraph (3)(I), any amount includible in gross income under section 1293 (relating to certain passive foreign investment companies).

INCOME TAX—FOREIGN TAX CREDIT

- **2017, Tax Cuts and Jobs Act (P.L. 115-97)**

P.L. 115-97, §14201(b)(2)(A):

Amended Code Sec. 904(d)(1) by redesignating subparagraphs (A) and (B) as subparagraphs (B) and (C), respectively, and by inserting before subparagraph (B) (as so redesignated) a new subparagraph (A). **Effective** for tax years of foreign corporations beginning after 12-31-2017, and to tax years of United States shareholders in which or with which such tax years of foreign corporations end.

P.L. 115-97, §14201(b)(2)(B):

Amended Code Sec. 904(d)(2)(A)(ii) by inserting "income described in paragraph (1)(A) and" before "passive category income". **Effective** for tax years of foreign corporations beginning after 12-31-2017, and to tax years of United States shareholders in which or with which such tax years of foreign corporations end.

P.L. 115-97, §14301(c)(15)(A)-(B):

Amended Code Sec. 904(d)(2)(E) by amending clause (i), and by striking "noncontrolled section 902 corporation" in clause (ii) and inserting "noncontrolled 10-percent owned foreign corporation". **Effective** for tax years of foreign corporations beginning after 12-31-2017, and to tax years of United States shareholders in which or with which such tax years of foreign corporations end. Prior to amendment, Code Sec. 904(d)(2)(E)(i) read as follows:

(i) IN GENERAL.—The term "noncontrolled section 902 corporation" means any foreign corporation with respect to which the taxpayer meets the stock ownership requirements of section 902(a) (or, for purposes of applying paragraph (3) or (4), the requirements of section 902(b)). A controlled foreign corporation shall not be treated as a noncontrolled section 902 corporation with respect to any distribution out of its earnings and profits for periods during which it was a controlled foreign corporation.

P.L. 115-97, §14301(c)(16)(A)-(B):

Amended Code Sec. 904(d)(4) by striking "noncontrolled section 902 corporation" each place it appears and inserting "noncontrolled 10-percent owned foreign corporation", and by striking "NONCONTROLLED SECTION 902 CORPORATIONS" in the heading thereof and inserting "NONCONTROLLED 10-PERCENT OWNED FOREIGN CORPORATIONS". **Effective** for tax years of foreign corporations beginning after 12-31-2017, and to tax years of United States shareholders in which or with which such tax years of foreign corporations end.

P.L. 115-97, §14301(c)(17):

Amended Code Sec. 904(d)(6)(A) by striking "902, 907," and inserting "907". **Effective** for tax years of foreign corporations beginning after 12-31-2017, and to tax years of United States shareholders in which or with which such tax years of foreign corporations end.

P.L. 115-97, §14302(a):

Amended Code Sec. 904(d)(1), as amended by Act Sec. 14201, by redesignating subparagraphs (B) and (C) as subparagraphs (C) and (D), respectively, and by inserting after subparagraph (A) a new subparagraph (B). **Effective** for tax years beginning after 12-31-2017.

P.L. 115-97, §14302(b)(1):

Amended Code Sec. 904(d)(2) by inserting after subparagraph (I) a new subparagraph (J). **Effective** for tax years beginning after 12-31-2017.

P.L. 115-97, §14302(b)(2):

Amended Code Sec. 904(d)(2)(A)(ii), as amended by Act Sec. 14201, by striking "income described in paragraph (1)(A) and" and inserting "income described in paragraph (1)(A), foreign branch income, and". **Effective** for tax years beginning after 12-31-2017.

- **2014, Tax Technical Corrections Act of 2014 (P.L. 113-295)**

P.L. 113-295, §221(a)(72), Division A:

Amended Code Sec. 904(d)(2) by striking subparagraph (J). **Effective** generally 12-19-2014. For a special rule, see Act Sec. 221(b)(2), Division A, below. Prior to being stricken, Code Sec. 904(d)(2)(J) read as follows:

(J) TRANSITIONAL RULE.—For purposes of paragraph (1)—

(i) taxes paid or accrued in a taxable year beginning before January 1, 1987, with respect to income which was described in subparagraph (A) of paragraph (1) (as in effect on the day before the date of the enactment of the Tax Reform Act of 1986) shall be treated as taxes paid or accrued with respect to income described in subparagraph (A) of paragraph (1) (as in effect after such date),

(ii) taxes paid or accrued in a taxable year beginning before January 1, 1987, with respect to income which was described in subparagraph (E) of paragraph (1) (as in effect on the day before the date of the enactment of the Tax Reform Act of 1986) shall be treated as taxes paid or accrued with respect to income described in subparagraph (I) of paragraph (1) (as in effect after such date) except that

(I) such taxes shall be treated as paid or accrued with respect to shipping income to the extent the taxpayer establishes to the satisfaction of the Secretary that such taxes were paid or accrued with respect to such income,

(II) in the case of a person described in subparagraph (C)(i), such taxes shall be treated as paid or accrued with respect to financial services income to the extent the taxpayer establishes to the satisfaction of the Secretary that such taxes were paid or accrued with respect to such income, and

(III) such taxes shall be treated as paid or accrued with respect to high withholding tax interest to the extent the taxpayer establishes to the satisfaction of the Secretary that such taxes were paid or accrued with respect to such income, and

(iii) taxes paid or accrued in a taxable year beginning before January 1, 1987, with respect to income described in any other subparagraph of paragraph (1) (as so in effect before such date) shall be treated as taxes paid or accrued with respect to income described in the corresponding subparagraph of paragraph (1) (as so in effect after such date).

P.L. 113-295, §221(b)(2), Division A, provides:

(2) SAVINGS PROVISION.—If—

(A) any provision amended or repealed by the amendments made by this section applied to—

(i) any transaction occurring before the date of the enactment of this Act,

(ii) any property acquired before such date of enactment, or

(iii) any item of income, loss, deduction, or credit taken into account before such date of enactment, and

(B) the treatment of such transaction, property, or item under such provision would (without regard to the amendments or repeals made by this section) affect the liability for tax for periods ending after date of enactment, nothing in the amendments or repeals made by this section shall be construed to affect the treatment of such transaction, property, or item for purposes of determining liability for tax for periods ending after such date of enactment.

- **2010, (P.L. 111-226)**

P.L. 111-226, §213(a):

Amended Code Sec. 904(d) by redesignating paragraph (6) as paragraph (7) and by inserting after paragraph (5) a new paragraph (6). **Effective** for tax years beginning after 8-10-2010.

- **2007, Tax Technical Corrections Act of 2007 (P.L. 110-172)**

P.L. 110-172, §11(g)(10)(A)-(C):

Amended Code Sec. 904(d)(2)(B)(v) by inserting "and" at the end of subclause (I), by striking subclause (II), and by redesignating subclause (III) as subclause (II), by striking "a FSC (or a former FSC)" in subclause (II) (as so redesignated) and inserting "a former FSC (as defined in section 922)", and by adding at the end a new flush sentence. **Effective** 12-29-2007. Prior to being stricken, Code Sec. 904(d)(2)(B)(v)(II) read as follows:

(II) taxable income attributable to foreign trade income (within the meaning of section 923(b)), and

- **2005, Gulf Opportunity Zone Act of 2005 (P.L. 109-135)**

P.L. 109-135, §403(o):

Amended Code Sec. 904(d)(2)(D) by inserting "as in effect before its repeal" after "section 954(f)". **Effective** as if included in the provision of the American Jobs Creation Act of 2004 (P.L. 108-357) to which it relates [effective for tax years of foreign corporations beginning after 12-31-2004, and for tax years of United States shareholders with or within which such tax years of foreign corporations end.—CCH].

- **2004, American Jobs Creation Act of 2004 (P.L. 108-357)**

P.L. 108-357, §403(a):

Amended Code Sec. 904(d)(4). **Effective** for tax years beginning after 12-31-2002. For a transition rule, see Act Sec. 403(d), below. Prior to amendment, Code Sec. 904(d)(4) read as follows:

(4) LOOK-THRU APPLIES TO DIVIDENDS FROM NONCONTROLLED SECTION 902 CORPORATIONS.—

(A) IN GENERAL.—For purposes of this subsection, any applicable dividend shall be treated as income in a separate category in proportion to the ratio of—

(i) the portion of the earnings and profits described in subparagraph (B)(ii) attributable to income in such category, to

(ii) the total amount of such earnings and profits.

(B) APPLICABLE DIVIDEND.—For purposes of subparagraph (A), the term "applicable dividend" means any dividend—

(i) from a noncontrolled section 902 corporation with respect to the taxpayer, and

(ii) paid out of earnings and profits accumulated in taxable years beginning after December 31, 2002.

(C) SPECIAL RULES.—

(i) IN GENERAL.—Rules similar to the rules of paragraph (3)(F) shall apply for purposes of this paragraph.

(ii) EARNINGS AND PROFITS.—For purposes of this paragraph and paragraph (1)(E)—

(I) IN GENERAL.—The rules of section 316 shall apply.

(II) REGULATIONS.—The Secretary may prescribe regulations regarding the treatment of distributions out of earnings and profits for periods prior to the taxpayer's acquisition of such stock.

P.L. 108-357, §403(b)(1):

Repealed Code Sec. 904(d)(1)(E). **Effective** for tax years beginning after 12-31-2002. For a transition rule, see Act Sec. 403(d), below. Prior to repeal, Code Sec. 904(d)(1)(E) read as follows:

(E) in the case of a corporation, dividends from noncontrolled section 902 corporations out of earnings and profits accumulated in taxable years beginning before January 1, 2003,

P.L. 108-357, §403(b)(2):

Amended Code Sec. 904(d)(2)(C)(iii) by adding "and" at the end of subclause (I), by striking subclause (II), and by redesignating subclause (III) as subclause (II). **Effective** for tax years beginning after 12-31-2002. For a transition rule, see Act Sec. 403(d), below. Prior to being stricken, Code Sec. 904(d)(2)(C)(iii)(II) read as follows:

(II) any dividend from a noncontrolled section 902 corporation out of earnings and profits accumulated in taxable years beginning before January 1, 2003, and

P.L. 108-357, §403(b)(3):

Amended the last sentence of Code Sec. 904(d)(2)(D). **Effective** for tax years beginning after 12-31-2002. For a transition rule, see Act Sec. 403(d), below. Prior to amendment, the last sentence of Code Sec. 904(d)(2)(D) read as follows:

Such term does not include any dividend from a noncontrolled section 902 corporation out of earnings and profits accumulated in taxable years beginning before January 1, 2003 and does not include any financial services income.

P.L. 108-357, §403(b)(4)(A)-(B):

Amended Code Sec. 904(d)(2)(E) by inserting "or (4)" after "paragraph (3)" in clause (i), and by striking clauses (ii) and (iv), and by redesignating clause (iii) as clause (ii). **Effective** for tax years beginning after 12-31-2002. For a transition rule, see Act Sec. 403(d), below. Prior to being stricken, Code Sec. 904(d)(2)(E)(ii) and (iv) read as follows:

(ii) SPECIAL RULE FOR TAXES ON HIGH-WITHHOLDING TAX INTEREST.—If a foreign corporation is a noncontrolled section 902 corporation with respect to the taxpayer, taxes on high withholding tax interest (to the extent imposed at a rate in excess of 5 percent) shall not be treated as foreign taxes for purposes of determining the amount of foreign taxes deemed paid by the taxpayer under section 902.

* * *

(iv) ALL NON-PFICS TREATED AS ONE.—All noncontrolled section 902 corporations which are not passive foreign investment companies (as defined in section 1297) shall be treated as one noncontrolled section 902 corporation for purposes of paragraph (1).

P.L. 108-357, §403(b)(5):

Amended Code Sec. 904(d)(3)(F) by striking "(D), or (E)" and inserting "or (D)". **Effective** for tax years beginning after 12-31-2002. For a transition rule, see Act Sec. 403(d), below.

P.L. 108-357, §403(d), as added by P.L. 109-135, §403(l), provides:

(d) TRANSITION RULE.—If the taxpayer elects (at such time and in such form and manner as the Secretary of the Treasury may prescribe) to have the rules of this subsection apply—

(1) the amendments made by this section shall not apply to taxable years beginning after December 31, 2002, and before January 1, 2005, and

(2) in the case of taxable years beginning after December 31, 2004, clause (iv) of section 904(d)(4)(C) of the Internal Revenue Code of 1986 (as amended by this section) shall be applied by substituting "January 1, 2005" for "January 1, 2003" both places it appears.

P.L. 108-357, §404(a):

Amended Code Sec. 904(d)(1). **Effective** for tax years beginning after 12-31-2006. Prior to amendment, but as amended by Act Sec. 403(b)(1), Code Sec. 904(d)(1) read as follows:

(1) IN GENERAL.—The provisions of subsections (a), (b), and (c) and sections 902, 907, and 960 shall be applied separately with respect to each of the following items of income:

(A) passive income,

(B) high withholding tax interest,

(C) financial services income,

(D) shipping income,

(E) [Repealed]

(F) dividends from a DISC or former DISC (as defined in section 992(a)) to the extent such dividends are treated as income from sources without the United States,

(G) taxable income attributable to foreign trade income (within the meaning of section 923(b)),

(H) distributions from a FSC (or former FSC) out of earnings and profits attributable to foreign trade income (within the meaning of section 923(b) or interest or carrying charges (as defined in section 927(d)(1)) derived from a transaction which results in foreign trade income (as defined in section 923(b)), and

(I) income other than income described in any of the preceding subparagraphs.

P.L. 108-357, §404(b):

Amended Code Sec. 904(d)(2) by striking subparagraph (B), by redesignating subparagraph (A) as subparagraph (B), and by inserting before subparagraph (B) (as so redesignated) a new subparagraph (A). **Effective** for tax years beginning after 12-31-2006. Prior to being stricken, Code Sec. 904(d)(2)(B) read as follows:

(B) HIGH WITHHOLDING TAX INTEREST.—

(i) IN GENERAL.—Except as otherwise provided in this subparagraph, the term "high withholding tax interest" means any interest if—

(I) such interest is subject to a withholding tax of a foreign country or possession of the United States (or other tax determined on a gross basis), and

(II) the rate of such tax applicable to such interest is at least 5 percent.

(ii) EXCEPTION FOR EXPORT FINANCING.—The term "high withholding tax interest" shall not include any export financing interest.

(iii) REGULATIONS.—The Secretary may by regulations provide that—

(I) amounts (not otherwise high withholding tax interest) shall be treated as high withholding tax interest where necessary to prevent avoidance of the purposes of this subparagraph, and

(II) a tax shall not be treated as a withholding tax or other tax imposed on a gross basis if such tax is in the nature of a prepayment of a tax imposed on a net basis.

P.L. 108-357, §404(c):

Amended Code Sec. 904(d)(2)(B), as so redesignated, by adding at the end a new clause (v). **Effective** for tax years beginning after 12-31-2006.

P.L. 108-357, §404(d):

Amended Code Sec. 904(d)(2), as amended by Act Sec. 403(b)(3), by striking subparagraph (D), by redesignating subparagraph (C) as subparagraph (D), and by inserting before subparagraph (D) (as so redesignated) a new subparagraph (C). **Effective** for tax years beginning after 12-31-2006. Prior to being stricken, but as amended by Act Sec. 403(b)(3), Code Sec. 904(d)(2)(D) read as follows:

(D) SHIPPING INCOME.—The term "shipping income" means any income received or accrued by any person which is of a kind which would be foreign base company shipping income (as defined in section 954(f) as in effect before its repeal). Such term does not include any financial services income.

P.L. 108-357, §404(e):

Amended Code Sec. 904(d)(2) by redesignating subparagraphs (H) and (I) as subparagraphs (I) and (J), respectively, and by inserting after subparagraph (G) a new subparagraph (H). **Effective** generally for tax years beginning after 12-31-2006. For a transitional rule, see Act Sec. 404(g)(2), below.

P.L. 108-357, §404(f)(1):

Amended Code Sec. 904(d)(2)(B)(iii), as so redesignated, by striking subclause (I) and by redesignating subclauses (II) and (III) as subclauses (I) and (II), respectively. **Effective** for tax years beginning after 12-31-2006. Prior to being stricken, but as redesignated by Act Sec. 404(b), Code Sec. 904(d)(2)(B)(iii)(I) read as follows:

(I) any income described in a subparagraph of paragraph (1) other than subparagraph (A),

P.L. 108-357, §404(f)(2):

Amended Code Sec. 904(d)(2)(D)(i), as so redesignated, by adding "or" at the end of subclause (I) and by striking subclauses (II) and (III) and inserting a new subclause (II). **Effective** for tax years beginning after 12-31-2006. Prior to being stricken, but as redesignated by Act Sec. 404(d), Code Sec. 904(d)(2)(D)(i)(II) and (III) read as follows:

(II) passive income (determined without regard to subclauses (I) and (III) of subparagraph (A)(iii)), or

(III) export financing interest which (but for subparagraph (B)(ii)) would be high withholding tax interest.

P.L. 108-357, §404(f)(3):

Amended Code Sec. 904(d)(2)(D), as so redesignated and amended by Act Sec. 403(b)(3)[403(b)(2)], by striking clause (iii). **Effective** for tax years beginning after 12-31-2006. Prior to being stricken, but as amended by Act Sec. 403(b)(2) and redesignated by Act Sec. 404(d), Code Sec. 904(d)(2)(D)(iii) read as follows:

(iii) EXCEPTIONS.—The term "financial services income" does not include—

(I) any high withholding tax interest, and

(II) any export financing interest not described in clause (i)(III).

P.L. 108-357, §404(f)(4):

Amended Code Sec. 904(d)(3). **Effective** for tax years beginning after 12-31-2006. Prior to amendment, Code Sec. 904(d)(3) read as follows:

(3) LOOK-THRU IN CASE OF CONTROLLED FOREIGN CORPORATIONS.—

(A) IN GENERAL.—Except as otherwise provided in this paragraph, dividends, interest, rents, and royalties received or accrued by the taxpayer from a controlled foreign corporation in which the taxpayer is a United States shareholder shall not be treated as income in a separate category.

(B) SUBPART F INCLUSIONS.—Any amount included in gross income under section 951(a)(1)(A) shall be treated as income in a separate category to the extent the amount so included is attributable to income in such category.

(C) INTEREST, RENTS, AND ROYALTIES.—Any interest, rent, or royalty which is received or accrued from a controlled foreign corporation in which the taxpayer is a United States shareholder shall be treated as income in a separate category to the extent it is properly allocable (under regulations prescribed by the Secretary) to income of the controlled foreign corporation in such category.

(D) DIVIDENDS.—Any dividend paid out of the earnings and profits of any controlled foreign corporation in which the taxpayer is a United States shareholder shall be treated as income in a separate category in proportion to the ratio of—

(i) the portion of the earnings and profits attributable to income in such category, to

(ii) the total amount of earnings and profits.

(E) LOOK-THRU APPLIES ONLY WHERE SUBPART F APPLIES.—If a controlled foreign corporation meets the requirements of section 954(b)(3)(A) (relating to de minimis rule) for any taxable year, for purposes of this paragraph, none of its foreign base company income (as defined in section 954(a) without regard to section 954(b)(5)) and none of its gross insurance income (as defined in section 954(b)(3)(C)) for such taxable year shall be treated as income in a separate category, except that this sentence shall not apply to any income which (without regard to this sentence) would be treated as financial services income. Solely for purposes of applying subparagraph (D), passive income of a controlled foreign corporation shall not be treated as income in a separate category if the requirements of section 954(b)(4) are met with respect to such income.

(F) SEPARATE CATEGORY.—For purposes of this paragraph—

(i) IN GENERAL.—Except as provided in clause (ii), the term "separate category" means any category of income described in subparagraph (A), (B), (C), or (D) of paragraph (1).

(ii) COORDINATION WITH HIGH-TAXED INCOME PROVISIONS.—

(I) In determining whether any income of a controlled foreign corporation is in a separate category, subclause (III) of paragraph (2)(A)(iii) shall not apply.

(II) Any income of the taxpayer which is treated as income in a separate category under this paragraph shall be so treated notwithstanding any provision of paragraph (2); except that the determination of whether any amount is high-taxed income shall be made after the application of this paragraph.

(G) DIVIDEND.—For purposes of this paragraph, the term "dividend" includes any amount included in gross income in section 951(a)(1)(B). Any amount included in gross income under section 78 to the extent attributable to amounts included in gross income in section 951(a)(1)(A) shall not be treated as a dividend but shall be treated as included in gross income under section 951(a)(1)(A).

(H) EXCEPTION FOR CERTAIN HIGH WITHHOLDING TAX INTEREST.—This paragraph shall not apply to any amount which—

(i) without regard to this paragraph, is high withholding tax interest (including any amount treated as high withholding tax interest under paragraph (2)(B)(iii)), and

(ii) would (but for this subparagraph) be treated as financial services income under this paragraph.

The amount to which this paragraph does not apply by reason of the preceding sentence shall not exceed the interest or equivalent income of the controlled foreign corporation taken into account in determining financial services income without regard to this subparagraph.

(I) LOOK-THRU APPLIES TO PASSIVE FOREIGN INVESTMENT COMPANY INCLUSION.—If—

(i) a passive foreign investment company is a controlled foreign corporation, and

(ii) the taxpayer is a United States shareholder in such controlled foreign corporation,

INCOME TAX—FOREIGN TAX CREDIT

any amount included in gross income under section 1293 shall be treated as income in a separate category to the extent such amount is attributable to income in such category.

P.L. 108-357, § 404(f)(5):

Amended Code Sec. 904(d)(2) by adding at the end a new subparagraph (K). **Effective** for tax years beginning after 12-31-2006.

P.L. 108-357, § 404(g)(2), provides:

(2) TRANSITIONAL RULE RELATING TO INCOME TAX BASE DIFFERENCE.—Section 904(d)(2)(H)(ii) of the Internal Revenue Code of 1986, as added by subsection (e), shall apply to taxable years beginning after December 31, 2004.

P.L. 108-357, § 413(c)(14):

Amended Code Sec. 904(d)(2)(A)(ii), prior to redesignation by Act Sec. 404(b). **Effective** for tax years of foreign corporations beginning after 12-31-2004, and for tax years of United States shareholders with or within which such tax years of foreign corporations end. Prior to amendment and redesignation, Code Sec. 904(d)(2)(A)(ii) read as follows:

(ii) CERTAIN AMOUNTS INCLUDED.—Except as provided in clause (iii), the term "passive income" includes any amount includible in gross income under section 551 or, except as provided in subparagraph (E)(iii) or paragraph (3)(I), section 1293 (relating to certain passive foreign investment companies).

- **1997, Taxpayer Relief Act of 1997 (P.L. 105-34)**

P.L. 105-34, § 1105(a)(1):

Amended Code Sec. 904(d)(1)(E). **Effective** for tax years beginning after 12-31-2002. Prior to amendment, Code Sec. 904(d)(1)(E) read as follows:

(E) in a case of a corporation, dividends from each noncontrolled section 902 corporation,

P.L. 105-34, § 1105(a)(2):

Amended Code Sec. 904(d)(2)(E) by adding at the end a new clause (iv). **Effective** for tax years beginning after 12-31-2002.

P.L. 105-34, § 1105(a)(3):

Amended Code Sec. 904(d)(2)(C)(iii)(II) and (D) by inserting "out of earnings and profits accumulated in taxable years beginning before January 1, 2003" after "corporation". **Effective** for tax years beginning after 12-31-2002.

P.L. 105-34, § 1105(b):

Amended Code Sec. 904(d) by redesignating paragraphs (4) and (5) as paragraphs (5) and (6), respectively, and by inserting after paragraph (3) a new paragraph (4). **Effective** for tax years beginning after 12-31-2002.

P.L. 105-34, § 1111(b):

Amended Code Sec. 904(d)(2)(E)(i) by striking "and except as provided in regulations, the taxpayer was a United States shareholder in such corporation" before the period in the second sentence. **Effective** for distributions after 8-5-97.

P.L. 105-34, § 1163(b):

Amended Code Sec. 904(d)(2)(C)(i)(II) by striking "subclause (I)" and inserting "subclauses (I) and (III)". **Effective** 8-5-97.

- **1996, Small Business Job Protection Act of 1996 (P.L. 104-188)**

P.L. 104-188, § 1501(b)(1):

Amended Code Sec. 904(d)(3)(G), as amended by Act Sec. 1703(i)(1), by striking "subparagraph (B) or (C) of section 951(a)(1)" and inserting "section 951(a)(1)(B)". **Effective** for tax years of foreign corporations beginning after 12-31-96, and to tax years of United States shareholders within which or with which such tax years of foreign corporations end.

P.L. 104-188, § 1501(b)(12):

Amended Code Sec. 904(d)(3)(G) by striking "subparagraph (B) or (C) of section 951(a)(1)" and inserting "section 951(a)(1)(B)". [Note: This amendment is identical to the one made by Act Sec. 1501(b)(1).—CCH.] **Effective** for tax years of foreign corporations beginning after 12-31-96, and to tax years of United States shareholders within which or with which such tax years of foreign corporations end.

P.L. 104-188, § 1703(i)(1):

Amended Code Sec. 904(d)(3)(G) by striking "section 951(a)(1)(B)" and inserting "subparagraph (B) or (C) of section 951(a)(1)". **Effective** as if included in the provisions of P.L. 103-66 to which it relates.

- **1993, Omnibus Budget Reconciliation Act of 1993 (P.L. 103-66)**

P.L. 103-66, § 13235(a)(2):

Amended Code Sec. 904(d)(2)(A)(iii) by inserting "and" at the end of subclause (II), by striking ", and" at the end of subclause (III) and inserting a period, and by striking subclause (IV). **Effective** for tax years beginning after 12-31-92. Prior to amendment subclause (IV) read as follows:

(IV) any foreign oil and gas extraction income (as defined in section 907(c)).

- **1989, Omnibus Budget Reconciliation Act of 1989 (P.L. 101-239)**

P.L. 101-239, § 7811(i)(1):

Amended Code Sec. 904(d)(1)(H) by striking "qualified interest and carrying charges (as defined in section 245(c))" and inserting "interest or carrying charges (as defined in section 927(d)(1)) derived from a transaction which results in foreign trade income (as defined in section 923(b))". **Effective** as if included in the provision of P.L. 100-647 to which it relates.

- **1988, Technical and Miscellaneous Revenue Act of 1988 (P.L. 100-647)**

P.L. 100-647, § 1012(a)(1)(A):

Amended Code Sec. 904(d)(2)(C). **Effective** as if included in the provision of P.L. 99-514 to which it relates. Prior to amendment, Code Sec. 904(d)(2)(C) read as follows:

(C) FINANCIAL SERVICES INCOME.—

(i) IN GENERAL.—Except as otherwise provided in this subparagraph, the term "financial services income" means income received or accrued by any person which is not passive income (determined without regard to subparagraph (A)(iii)(I)) and which—

(I) is derived in the active conduct of a banking, financing, or similar business, or derived from the investment by an insurance company of its unearned premiums or reserves ordinary and necessary for the proper conduct of its insurance business,

(II) is of a kind which would be insurance income as defined in section 953(a) determined without regard to those provisions of paragraph (1)(A) of such section which limit insurance income to income from countries other than the country in which the corporation was created or organized.

(ii) SPECIAL RULE IF ENTITY PREDOMINANTLY ENGAGED IN BANKING, ETC., BUSINESS.—If, for any taxable year, an entity is predominantly engaged in the active conduct of a banking, insurance, financing, or similar business, the term "financial services income" includes any passive income (determined without regard to subparagraph (A)(iii)(I)) of such corporation for such taxable year. In the case of any entity described in the preceding sentence, the term "shipping income" shall not include any income treated as financial services income under the preceding sentence.

(iii) EXCEPTION FOR EXPORT FINANCING.—The term "financial services income" does not include any export financing interest.

(iv) HIGH WITHHOLDING TAX INTEREST.—The term "financial services income" does not include any high withholding tax interest.

P.L. 100-647, § 1012(a)(2):

Amended Code Sec. 904(d)(2)(D) by adding at the end thereof a new sentence. **Effective** as if included in the provision of P.L. 99-514 to which it relates.

P.L. 100-647, § 1012(a)(3):

Amended Code Sec. 904(d)(3) by adding at the end thereof new subparagraph (H). **Effective** as if included in the provision of P.L. 99-514 to which it relates.

P.L. 100-647, § 1012(a)(4)(A)-(B):

Amended Code Sec. 904(d)(3)(E) by striking out the first sentence and inserting a new first sentence, and by striking out "income (other than high withholding tax interest and dividends from a noncontrolled section 902 corporation)" and inserting in lieu thereof "passive income". **Effective** as if included in the provision of P.L. 99-514 to which it relates. Prior to amendment, the first sentence of Code Sec. 904(d)(3)(E) read as follows:

If a controlled foreign corporation meets the requirements of section 954(b)(3)(A) (relating to de minimis rule) for any taxable year, for purposes of this paragraph, none of its income for such taxable year shall be treated as income in a separate category.

P.L. 100-647, § 1012(a)(6)(A)-(B):

Amended Code Sec. 904(d)(2)(A) by striking out "The term" in clause (ii) and inserting in lieu thereof "Except as provided in clause (iii), the term", and by adding at the end thereof new clause (iv). **Effective** as if included in the provision of P.L. 99-514 to which it relates.

P.L. 100-647, § 1012(a)(7):

Amended Code Sec. 904(d)(3)(F). **Effective** as if included in the provision of P.L. 99-514 to which it relates. Prior to amendment, Code Sec. 904(d)(3)(F) read as follows:

(F) SEPARATE CATEGORY.—For purposes of this paragraph, the term "separate category" means any category of income described in subparagraph (A), (B), (C), (D), or (E) of paragraph (1).

P.L. 100-647, § 1012(a)(8):

Amended Code Sec. 904(d)(2)(B)(iii). **Effective** as if included in the provision of P.L. 99-514 to which it relates. Prior to amendment, Code Sec. 904(d)(2)(B)(iii) read as follows:

(iii) REGULATIONS.—The Secretary may by regulations provide that amounts (not otherwise high withholding tax interest) shall be treated as high withholding tax interest where necessary to prevent avoidance of the purposes of this subparagraph.

P.L. 100-647, § 1012(a)(9):

Amended Code Sec. 904(d)(2)(I)(ii) by striking out "except to the extent that" and all that follows down through "and" at the end thereof and inserting the new material. **Effective** as if included in the provision of P.L. 99-514 to which it relates. Prior to amendment, Code Sec. 904(d)(2)(I)(ii) read as follows:

(ii) taxes paid or accrued in a taxable year beginning before January 1, 1987, with respect to income which was described in subparagraph (E) of paragraph (1) (as in effect on the day before the date of enactment of the Tax Reform Act of 1986) shall be treated as taxes paid or accrued with respect to income decribed in subparagraph (I) of paragraph (1) (as in effect after such date) except to the extent that—

(I) the taxpayer establishes to the satisfaction of the Secretary that such taxes were paid or accrued with respect to shipping income, or

(II) in the case of an entity meeting the requirements of subparagraph (C)(ii), the taxpayer establishes to the satisfaction of the Secretary that such taxes were paid or accrued with respect to financial services income, and

P.L. 100-647, § 1012(a)(10):

Amended Code Sec. 904(d)(2)(E)(i) by striking out "during which it was a controlled foreign corporation" and inserting in lieu thereof "during which it was a controlled foreign corporation and except as provided in regulations, the taxpayer was a United States shareholder in such corporation." **Effective** as if included in the provision of P.L. 99-514 to which it relates.

P.L. 100-647, § 1012(a)(11):

Amended Code Sec. 904(d)(1)(E) by striking out "dividends" and inserting in lieu thereof "in the case of a corporation, dividends". **Effective** as if included in the provision of P.L. 99-514 to which it relates.

P.L. 100-647, § 1012(p)(11):

Amended Code Sec. 904(d)(3) by adding at the end thereof new subparagraph (I). **Effective** as if included in the provision of P.L. 99-514 to which it relates.

Sec. 904(d)(7)(C)

P.L. 100-647, §1012(p)(29)(A):

Amended Code Sec. 904(d)(2)(A)(ii) by striking out "or section 1293" and inserting in lieu thereof "or, except as provided in subparagraph (E)(iii) or paragraph (3)(I), section 1293". **Effective** as if included in the provision of P.L. 99-514 to which it relates.

P.L. 100-647, §1012(p)(29)(B):

Amended Code Sec. 904(d)(2)(E) by adding at the end thereof a new clause (iii). **Effective** as if included in the provision of P.L. 99-514 to which it relates.

• **1986, Tax Reform Act of 1986 (P.L. 99-514)**

P.L. 99-514, §1201(a):

Amended Code Sec. 904(d)(1) by striking out subparagraph (A), by redesignating subparagraphs (B), (C), (D), and (E) as subparagraphs (F), (G), (H), and (I), respectively, and inserting before subparagraph (F) (as so redesignated) new subparagraphs (A), (B), (C), (D) and (E). **Effective**, generally, for tax years beginning after 12-31-86. However, for special rules, see Act Sec. 1201(e)(2)-(3), below. Prior to amendment, Code Sec. 904(d)(1)(A) read as follows:

(A) the interest income described in paragraph (2),

P.L. 99-514, §1201(b):

Amended Code Sec. 904(d) by striking out paragraphs (2) and (3) and inserting in lieu thereof new paragraphs (2)-(5). **Effective**, generally, for tax years beginning after 12-31-86. However, for special rules, see Act Sec. 1201(e)(2)-(3), below. Prior to amendment, Code Sec. 904(d)(2) and (3) read as follows:

(2) INTEREST INCOME TO WHICH APPLICABLE.—For purposes of this subsection, the interest income described in this paragraph is interest other than interest—

(A) derived from any transaction which is directly related to the active conduct by the taxpayer of a trade or business in a foreign country or a possession of the United States,

(B) derived in the conduct by the taxpayer of a banking, financing, or similar business,

(C) received from a corporation in which the taxpayer (or one or more includible corporations in an affiliated group, as defined in section 1504, of which the taxpayer is a member) owns, directly or indirectly, at least 10 percent of the voting stock, or

(D) received on obligations acquired as a result of the disposition of a trade or business actively conducted by the taxpayer in a foreign country or possession of the United States or as a result of the disposition of stock or obligations of a corporation in which the taxpayer owned at least 10 percent of the voting stock.

For purposes of subparagraph (C), stock owned, directly or indirectly, by or for a foreign corporation, shall be considered as being proportionately owned by its shareholders. For purposes of this subsection, interest (after the operation of section 904(d)(3)) received from a designated payor corporation described in section 904(d)(3)(E)(iii) by a taxpayer which owns directly or indirectly less than 10 percent of the voting stock of such designated payor corporation shall be treated as interest described in subparagraph (A) to the extent such interest would have been so treated had such taxpayer received it from other than a designated payor corporation.

(3) CERTAIN AMOUNTS ATTRIBUTABLE TO UNITED STATES-OWNED FOREIGN CORPORATIONS, ETC., TREATED AS INTEREST.—

(A) IN GENERAL.—For purposes of this subsection, dividends and interest—

(i) paid or accrued by a designated payor corporation, and

(ii) attributable to any taxable year of such corporation,

shall be treated as interest income described in paragraph (2) to the extent that the aggregate amount of such dividends and interest does not exceed the separate limitation interest of the designated payor corporation for such taxable year.

(B) SEPARATE LIMITATION INTEREST.—For purposes of this subsection, the term "separate limitation interest" means, with respect to any taxable year—

(i) the aggregate amount of the interest income described in paragraph (2) (including amounts treated as so described by reason of this paragraph) which is received or accrued by the designated payor corporation during the taxable year, reduced by

(ii) the deductions properly allocable (under regulations prescribed by the Secretary) to such income.

(C) EXCEPTION WHERE DESIGNATED CORPORATION HAS SMALL AMOUNT OF SEPARATE LIMITATION INTEREST.—Subparagraph (A) shall not apply to any amount attributable to the taxable year of a designated payor corporation, if—

(i) such corporation has earnings and profits for such taxable year, and

(ii) less than 10 percent of such earnings and profits is attributable to separate limitation interest.

The preceding sentence shall not apply to any amount includible in gross income under section 551 or 951.

(D) TREATMENT OF CERTAIN INTEREST.—For purposes of this paragraph, the amount of the separate limitation interest and the earnings and profits of any designated payor corporation shall be determined without any reduction for interest paid or accrued to a United States shareholder (as defined in section 951(b)) or a related person (within the meaning of section 267(b)) to such a shareholder.

(E) DESIGNATED PAYOR CORPORATION.—For purposes of this paragraph, the term "designated payor corporation" means—

(i) any United States-owned foreign corporation (within the meaning of subsection (g)(6)),

(ii) any other foreign corporation in which a United States person is a United States shareholder (as defined in section 951(b)) at any time during the taxable year of such foreign corporation,

(iii) any regulated investment company, and

(iv) any other corporation formed or availed of for purposes of avoiding the provisions of this paragraph.

(F) DETERMINATION OF YEAR TO WHICH AMOUNT IS ATTRIBUTABLE.—For purposes of determining whether an amount is attributable to a taxable year of a designated payor corporation—

(i) any amount includible in gross income under section 551 or 951 in respect of such taxable year,

(ii) any interest paid or accrued by such corporation during such taxable year, and

(iii) any dividend paid out of the earnings and profits of such corporation for such taxable year,

shall be treated as attributable to such taxable year.

(G) ORDERING RULES.—Subparagraph (A) shall be applied to amounts described therein in the order in which such amounts are described in subparagraph (F).

(H) DIVIDEND.—For purposes of this paragraph, the term "dividend" includes—

(i) any amount includible in gross income under section 551 or 951, and

(ii) any gain treated as ordinary income under section 1246 or as a dividend under section 1248.

(I) INTEREST AND DIVIDENDS FROM MEMBERS OF SAME AFFILIATED GROUP.—For purposes of this paragraph, dividends and interest received or accrued by the designated payor corporation from another member of the same affiliated group (determined under section 1504 without regard to subsection (b)(3) thereof) shall be treated as separate limitation interest if (and only if) such amounts are attributable (directly or indirectly) to separate limitation interest of any other member of such group.

(J) DISTRIBUTIONS THROUGH OTHER ENTITIES.—The Secretary shall prescribe such regulations as may be necessary to carry out the purposes of this paragraph in the case of distributions or payments through 1 or more entities.

P.L. 99-514, §1201(c)(3):

Amended Code Sec. 904(d)(1) by inserting "and sections 902 and 960" after "subsections (a), (b), and (c)". **Effective**, generally, for tax years beginning after 12-31-86. However, for special rules, see Act Sec. 1201(e)(2)-(3), below.

P.L. 99-514, §1201(d)(1):

Amended the subsection heading of Code Sec. 904(d). **Effective**, generally, for tax years beginning after 12-31-86. However, for special rules, see Act Sec. 1201(e)(2)-(3), below. Prior to amendment, it read as follows:

(d) SEPARATE APPLICATION OF SECTION WITH RESPECT TO CERTAIN INTEREST INCOME AND INCOME FROM DISC, FORMER DISC, FSC, OR FORMER FSC.—

P.L. 99-514, §1201(d)(2):

Amended Code Sec. 904(d)(1)(I) (as redesignated by Act Sec. 901(a)) by striking out "in subparagraph (A), (B), (C), or (D)" and inserting in lieu thereof "in any of the preceding subparagraphs". **Effective**, generally, for tax years beginning after 12-31-86. However, for special rules, see Act Sec. 1201(e)(2)-(3), below.

P.L. 99-514, §1201(e)(2)-(3), as amended by P.L. 100-647, §1012(a)(5), and P.L. 101-239, §7404(a), provides:

(e) EFFECTIVE DATES.—

(1) IN GENERAL.—Except as provided in this subsection, the amendments made by this section apply to taxable years beginning after December 31, 1986.

[Note: Act Sec. 1201(e)(2), below, was repealed by P.L. 101-239, §7404(a), applicable for tax years beginning after December 31, 1989.]

(2) QUALIFIED LOANS.—

(A) IN GENERAL.—The following shall not be treated as high withholding tax interest for purposes of applying section 904(d) of the Internal Revenue Code of 1986 (as amended by this section):

(i) Any interest received or accrued by any taxpayer during any taxable year beginning after December 31, 1986, and before January 1, 1990, on any pre-1990 qualified loan, and

(ii) The phase-out percentage of any interest received or accrued by any taxpayer during any taxable year beginning after December 31, 1989 on any post-1989 qualified loan.

(B) PHASE-OUT PERCENTAGE.—For purposes of subparagraph (A) the phase-out percentage is—

In the case of the following taxable years beginning after 12/31/89:	The phase out percentage is:
1st	80
2nd	60
3rd	40
4th	20
5th or succeeding	0

(C) PRE-1990 QUALIFIED LOAN.—For purposes of subparagraph (A), the term "pre-1990 qualified loan" means with respect to any taxable year beginning before January 1, 1990, any qualified loan outstanding at any time during such taxable year to the extent that the total amount of foreign taxes which would be creditable (without regard to the limitation of section 904 of the Internal Revenue Code of 1986) with respect to all qualified loans outstanding at any time during such taxable year does not exceed the applicable credit limit for such taxable year.

(D) POST-1989 QUALIFIED LOANS.—For purposes of subparagraph (A), the term "post-1989 qualified loan" means any qualified loan outstanding as of the close of the 1st taxable year of the taxpayer beginning after December 31, 1988, to the extent that the total amount of foreign taxes which would be creditable (without regard to the limitation of section 904 of the Internal Revenue Code of 1986) with respect to all qualified loans outstanding as of the close of such taxable year does not exceed the applicable credit limit for post-1989 qualified loans.

(E) CLASSIFICATION OF QUALIFIED LOANS.—For purposes of this paragraph, if the foreign taxes creditable for any taxable year beginning before January 1, 1990, with respect to any qualified loan, when added to the aggregate amount of foreign taxes creditable for such taxable year with respect to qualified loans entered into by the taxpayer before the date on which such qualified loan was entered into, exceed the applicable credit limit, then that portion of a qualified loan which causes the taxpayer to exceed the applicable credit limit shall not be treated as a pre-1990 or post-1989 qualified loan, as the case may be.

(F) APPLICABLE CREDIT LIMIT.—

INCOME TAX—FOREIGN TAX CREDIT

(i) IN GENERAL.—The applicable credit limit shall be equal to—

(I) except as provided in subclause (II), 110 percent of the base credit amount multiplied by the applicable interest rate adjustment for the taxable year, and

(II) in the case of post-1989 qualified loans, the amount determined under subclause (I) (without regard to the interest rate adjustment) multiplied by the interest rate adjustment for post-1989 qualified loans.

(ii) BASE CREDIT AMOUNT.—The base credit amount of a taxpayer shall be an amount equal to the principal amount of qualified loans held by such taxpayer on November 16, 1985, multiplied by the product of—

(I) the interest rate applicable to such loan on November 16, 1985, and

(II) the foreign withholding tax rate applicable to interest payable with respect to such loan on November 16, 1985.

(G) INTEREST RATE ADJUSTMENT.—

(i) IN GENERAL.—Except as provided in clause (ii), the applicable interest rate adjustment shall equal the ratio of the weighted average 6-month London Interbank Offered Rate (LIBOR) for the taxable year in question to LIBOR on November 15, 1985.

(ii) POST-1989 QUALIFIED LOANS.—The applicable interest rate adjustment for post-1989 qualified loans shall be equal to the ratio of LIBOR on the last day of the taxpayer's 1st taxable year beginning after December 31, 1988 to LIBOR on November 15, 1985.

(H) QUALIFIED LOAN.—For purposes of this subsection, the term "qualified loan" means any loan made by the taxpayer to any of the following countries or any resident thereof for use in such country:

(i) Argentina.
(ii) Bolivia.
(iii) Brazil.
(iv) Chile.
(v) Colombia.
(vi) Costa Rica.
(vii) The Dominican Republic.
(viii) Ecuador.
(ix) Guyana.
(x) Honduras.
(xi) The Ivory Coast.
(xii) Jamaica.
(xiii) Liberia.
(xiv) Madagascar.
(xv) Malawi.
(xvi) Mexico.
(xvii) Morocco.
(xviii) Mozambique.
(xix) Niger.
(xx) Nigeria.
(xxi) Panama.
(xxii) Peru.
(xxiii) The Philippines.
(xxiv) Romania.
(xxv) Senegal.
(xxvi) Sierra Leone.
(xxvii) The Sudan.
(xviii) Togo.
(xxix) Uruguay.
(xxx) Venezuela.
(xxxi) Yugoslavia.
(xxxii) Zaire.
(xxxiii) Zambia.

(I) NO BENEFIT FOR INCREASED WITHHOLDING TAXES.—No benefit shall be allowable by reason of this paragraph for any foreign withholding tax imposed on interest payable with respect to any qualified loan to the extent the rate of such tax exceeds the foreign withholding tax rate applicable to interest payable with respect to such loan on November 16, 1985.

(J) TREATMENT OF AFFILIATED GROUP FILING CONSOLIDATED RETURN.—For purposes of this paragraph, all members of an affiliated group of corporations filing a consolidated return shall be treated as 1 corporation.

(3) SPECIAL RULE FOR TAXPAYER WITH OVERALL FOREIGN LOSS.—

(A) IN GENERAL.—If a taxpayer incorporated on June 20, 1928, the principal headquarters of which is in Minneapolis, Minnesota, sustained an overall foreign loss (as defined in section 904(f)(2) of the Internal Revenue Code of 1954) in taxable years beginning before January 1, 1986, in connection with 2 separate trades or business which the taxpayer had, during 1985, substantially disposed of in tax-free transactions pursuant to section 355 of such Code, then an amount, not to exceed $40,000,000 of foreign source income, which, but for this paragraph, would not be treated as overall limitation income, shall be so treated.

(B) SUBSTANTIAL DISPOSITION.—For purposes of this paragraph, a taxpayer shall be treated as having substantially disposed of a trade or business if the retained portion of such business had sales of less than 10 percent of the annual sales of such business for taxable years ending in 1985.

P.L. 99-514, §1810(b)(1):

Amended Code Sec. 904(d)(3)(C) by adding at the end thereof a new sentence. **Effective** as if included in the provision of P.L. 98-369 to which it relates.

P.L. 99-514, §1810(b)(2):

Amended Code Sec. 904(d)(3) by striking out subparagraph (J), by redesignating subparagraph (I) as subparagraph (J), and by inserting after subparagraph (H) new subparagraph (I). **Effective** as if included in the provision of P.L. 98-369 to which it relates. Prior to amendment, Code Sec. 904(d)(3)(J) read as follows:

(J) INTEREST FROM MEMBERS OF SAME AFFILIATED GROUP.—For purposes of this paragraph, interest received or accrued by the designated payor corporation from another member of the same affiliated group (determined under section 1504 without regard to subsection (b)(3) thereof) shall not be treated as separate limitation interest, unless such interest is attributable directly or indirectly to separate limitation interest of such other member.

P.L. 99-514, §1810(b)(3):

Amended Code Sec. 904(d)(2) by inserting at the end a new sentence. **Effective** as if included in the provision of P.L. 98-369 to which it relates.

P.L. 99-514, §1810(b)(4)(A):

Amended Code Sec. 904(d)(3)(E) by striking out "and" at the end of clause (ii), by striking out the period at the end of clause (iii) and inserting in lieu thereof ", and", and by adding at the end thereof new clause. For the **effective** date, see Act Sec. 1810(b)(4)(B), below.

P.L. 99-514, §1810(b)(4)(B), provides:

(B) EFFECTIVE DATES.—

(i) The amendment made by subparagraph (A) insofar as it adds the last sentence to subparagraph (E) of section 905(d)(3) shall take effect on March 28, 1985. In the case of any taxable year ending after such date of any corporation treated as a designated payor corporation by reason of the amendment made by subparagraph (A)—

(I) only income received or accrued by such corporation after such date shall be taken into account under section 904(d)(3) of the Internal Revenue Code of 1954; except that

(II) subparagraph (C) of such section 904(d)(3) shall be applied by taking into account all income received or accrued by such corporation during such taxable year.

(ii) The amendment made by subparagraph (A) insofar as it adds clause (iv) to subparagraph (E) of section 904(d)(3) shall take effect on December 31, 1985. For purposes of such amendment, the rule of the second sentence of clause (i) shall be applied by taking into account December 31, 1985, in lieu of March 28, 1985.

P.L. 99-514, §1876(d)(2):

Amended Code Sec. 904(d)(1)(D). **Effective** as if included in the provision of P.L. 98-369 to which it relates. Prior to amendment, Code Sec. 904(d)(1)(D) read as follows:

(D) distributions from a FSC (or former FSC) out of earnings and profits attributable to foreign trade income (within the meaning of section 923(b)), and

P.L. 99-514, §1899A(24):

Amended Code Sec. 904(d)(1) by amending the heading of paragraph (1). **Effective** 10-22-86. Prior to amendment, Code Sec. 904(d)(1) read as follows:

(1) IN GENERAL.—The provisions of subsections (a), (b), and (c) shall be applied separately with respect to each of the following items of income:

• **1984, Deficit Reduction Act of 1984 (P.L. 98-369)**

P.L. 98-369, §122(a):

Amended Code Sec. 904(d) by adding at the end thereof new paragraph (3). **Effective** 7-18-84; however, see Act Sec. 122(b)(2)-(3) below.

P.L. 98-369, §122(b)(2)-(3), provides:

(2) Special Rules for Interest Income.—

(A) In General.—Interest income received or accrued by a designated payor corporation shall be taken into account for purposes of the amendment made by subsection (a) only in taxable years beginning after the date of the enactment of this Act.

(B) Exception For Investment After June 22, 1984.—Notwithstanding subparagraph (A), the amendment made by subsection (a) shall apply to interest income received or accrued by a designated payor corporation after the date of enactment of this Act if it is attributable to investment in the designated payor corporation after June 22, 1984.

(3) Term Obligations of Designated Payor Corporation Which Is Not Applicable CFC.—In the case of any designated payor corporation which is not an applicable CFC (as defined in section 121(b)(2)(D)), any interest received or accrued by such corporation on a term obligation held by such corporation on March 7, 1984, shall not be taken into account.

P.L. 98-369, §801(d)(2)(A):

Amended Code Sec. 904(d)(1) by striking out "and" at the end of subparagraph (B). **Effective** for transactions after 12-31-84, in tax years ending after such date.

P.L. 98-369, §801(d)(2)(B):

Amended Code Sec. 904(d)(1) by striking out subparagraph (C) and inserting in lieu thereof subparagraphs (C), (D) and (E). **Effective** for transactions after 12-31-84, in tax years ending after such date. Prior to amendment, subparagraph (C) read as follows:

(C) income other than the interest income described in paragraph (2) and dividends described in subparagraph (B).

P.L. 98-369, §801(d)(2)(C):

Amended the heading of Code Sec. 904(d). **Effective** for transactions after 12-31-84, in tax years ending after such date. Prior to amendment, the heading for Code sec. 904(d) read as follows:

(d) Application of Section in Case of Certain Interest Income and Dividends from a DISC or Former DISC.—

• **1976, Tax Reform Act of 1976 (P.L. 94-455)**

P.L. 94-455, §1031(a):

Amended Code Sec. 904(d). See amendment note for P.L. 94-455, Act Sec. 1031(a), following Code Sec. 904(a) for **effective** date. As amended, Code Sec. 904(d) is similar to former Code Sec. 904(f). Prior to amendment, Code Sec. 904(d) read as follows:

INCOME TAX—FOREIGN TAX CREDIT

(d) CARRYBACK AND CARRYOVER OF EXCESS TAX PAID.—Any amount by which any such tax paid or accrued to any foreign country or possession of the United States for any taxable year beginning after December 31, 1957, for which the taxpayer chooses to have the benefits of this subpart exceeds the applicable limitation under subsection (a) shall be deemed tax paid or accrued to such foreign country or possession of the United States in the second preceding taxable year, in the first preceding taxable year, and in the first, second, third, fourth, or fifth succeeding taxable years, in that order and to the extent not deemed tax paid or accrued in a prior taxable year, in the amount by which the applicable limitation under subsection (a) for such preceding or succeeding taxable year exceeds the sum of the tax paid or accrued to such foreign country or possession for such preceding or succeeding taxable year and the amount of the tax for any taxable year earlier than the current taxable year which shall be deemed to have been paid or accrued in such preceding or subsequent taxable year (whether or not the taxpayer chooses to have the benefits of this subpart with respect to such earlier taxable year). Such amount deemed paid or accrued in any year may be availed of only as a tax credit and not as a deduction and only if taxpayer for such year chooses to have the benefits of this subpart as to taxes paid or accrued for that year to foreign countries or possessions. For purposes of this subsection, the terms "second preceding taxable year" and "first preceding taxable year" do not include any taxable year beginning before January 1, 1958.

• **1960 (P.L. 86-780)**

P.L. 86-780, §[1](c):

Redesignated subsection (c) of Code Sec. 904 as subsection (d) and amended it by inserting the word "applicable" before the word "limitation" each place it appears. **Effective** for tax years beginning after 12-31-60.

• **1958, Technical Amendments Act of 1958 (P.L. 85-866)**

P.L. 85-866, §42(a):

Added new subsection (c) (redesignated as (d)) to Sec. 904. **Effective** for tax years beginning after 12-31-57.

[Sec. 904(e)—Repealed]

Amendments

• **1990, Omnibus Budget Reconciliation Act of 1990 (P.L. 101-508)**

P.L. 101-508, §11801(a)(31):

Repealed Code Sec. 904(e). **Effective** 11-5-90. Prior to repeal, Code Sec. 904(e) read as follows:

(e) TRANSITIONAL RULES FOR CARRYBACKS AND CARRYOVERS FOR TAXPAYERS ON THE PER-COUNTRY LIMITATION.—

(1) APPLICATION OF SUBSECTION.—This subsection shall apply only to a taxpayer who is on the per-country limitation for his last taxable year beginning before January 1, 1976.

(2) CARRYOVERS TO YEARS BEGINNING AFTER DECEMBER 31, 1975.—In the case of any taxpayer to whom this subsection applies, any carryover from a taxable year beginning before January 1, 1976, may be used in taxable years beginning after December 31, 1975, to the extent provided in subsection (c), but only to the extent such carryover could have been used in such succeeding taxable years if the per-country limitation continued to apply to all taxable years beginning after December 31, 1975.

(3) CARRYBACKS TO YEARS BEGINNING BEFORE JANUARY 1, 1976.—In the case of any taxpayer to whom this subsection applies, any carryback from a taxable year beginning after December 31, 1975, may be used in taxable years beginning before January 1, 1976, to the extent provided in subsection (c), but only to the extent such carryback could have been used in such preceding taxable year if the per-country limitation continued to apply to all taxable years beginning after December 31, 1975.

(4) APPLICATION OF LIMITATIONS.—For purposes of this subsection—

(A) the overall limitation shall be applied before the per-country limitation, and

(B) where the amount of any carryback or carryover is reduced by the overall limitation, the reduction shall be allocated to the amounts carried from each country or possession in proportion to the taxes paid or accrued to such country or possession in the taxable year from which such amount is being carried.

P.L. 101-508, §11821(b), provides:

(b) SAVINGS PROVISION.—If—

(1) any provision amended or repealed by this part applied to—

(A) any transaction occurring before the date of the enactment of this Act,

(B) any property acquired before such date of enactment, or

(C) any item of income, loss, deduction, or credit taken into account before such date of enactment, and

(2) the treatment of such transaction, property, or item under such provision would (without regard to the amendments made by this part) affect liability for tax for periods ending after such date of enactment,

nothing in the amendments made by this part shall be construed to affect the treatment of such transaction, property, or item for purposes of determining liability for tax for periods ending after such date of enactment.

• **1976, Tax Reform Act of 1976 (P.L. 94-455)**

P.L. 94-455, §1031(a):

Amended Code Sec. 904(e). See amendment note for P.L. 94-455, Act Sec. 1031(a), following Code Sec. 904(a) for **effective** date. Prior to amendment, Code Sec. 904(e) read as follows:

(e) CARRYBACKS AND CARRYOVERS WHERE OVERALL LIMITATION IS ELECTED.—

(1) FOREIGN TAXES TO BE AGGREGATED FOR PURPOSES OF SUBSECTION (d).—With respect to each taxable year of the taxpayer to which the limitation provided by subsection (a)(2) applies, the taxes referred to in the first sentence of subsection (d) shall, for purposes of applying such first sentence, be aggregated on an overall basis (rather than taken into account on a per-country basis).

(2) FOREIGN TAXES MAY NOT BE CARRIED FROM PERCOUNTRY YEAR TO OVERALL YEAR OR FROM OVERALL YEAR TO PER-COUNTRY YEAR.—No amount paid or accrued for any taxable year to which the limitation provided by subsection (a)(1) applies shall (except for purposes of determining the number of taxable years which have elapsed) be deemed paid or accrued under subsection (d) in any taxable year to which the limitation provided by subsection (a)(2) applies. No amount paid or accrued for any taxable year to which the limitation provided by subsection (a)(2) applies shall (except for purposes of determining the number of taxable years which have elapsed) be deemed paid or accrued under subsection (d) in any taxable year to which the limitation provided by subsection (a)(1) applies.

• **1960 (P.L. 86-780)**

P.L. 86-780, §[1](d):

Added subsection (e). **Effective** for tax years beginning after 12-31-60.

[Sec. 904(f)]

(f) RECAPTURE OF OVERALL FOREIGN LOSS.—

(1) GENERAL RULE.—For purposes of this subpart, in the case of any taxpayer who sustains an overall foreign loss for any taxable year, that portion of the taxpayer's taxable income from sources without the United States for each succeeding taxable year which is equal to the lesser of—

(A) the amount of such loss (to the extent not used under this paragraph in prior taxable years), or

(B) 50 percent (or such larger percent as the taxpayer may choose) of the taxpayer's taxable income from sources without the United States for such succeeding taxable year,

shall be treated as income from sources within the United States (and not as income from sources without the United States).

(2) OVERALL FOREIGN LOSS DEFINED.—For purposes of this subsection, the term "overall foreign loss" means the amount by which the gross income for the taxable year from sources without the United States (whether or not the taxpayer chooses the benefits of this subpart for such taxable year) for such year is exceeded by the sum of the deductions properly apportioned or allocated thereto, except that there shall not be taken into account—

(A) any net operating loss deduction allowable for such year under section 172(a), and

(B) any—

(i) foreign expropriation loss for such year, as defined in section 172(h) (as in effect on the day before the date of the enactment of the Revenue Reconciliation Act of 1990), or

(ii) loss for such year which arises from fire, storm, shipwreck, or other casualty, or from theft,

to the extent such loss is not compensated for by insurance or otherwise.

(3) DISPOSITIONS.—

(A) IN GENERAL.—For purposes of this chapter, if property which has been used predominantly without the United States in a trade or business is disposed of during any taxable year—

(i) the taxpayer, notwithstanding any other provision of this chapter (other than paragraph (1)), shall be deemed to have received and recognized taxable income from sources without the United States in the taxable year of the disposition, by reason of such disposition, in an amount equal to the lesser of the excess of the fair market value of such property over the taxpayer's adjusted basis in such property or the remaining amount of the overall foreign losses which were not used under paragraph (1) for such taxable year or any prior taxable year, and

(ii) paragraph (1) shall be applied with respect to such income by substituting "100 percent" for "50 percent".

INCOME TAX—FOREIGN TAX CREDIT

In determining for purposes of this subparagraph whether the predominant use of any property has been without the United States, there shall be taken into account use during the 3-year period ending on the date of the disposition (or, if shorter, the period during which the property has been used in the trade or business).

(B) DISPOSITION DEFINED AND SPECIAL RULES.—

(i) For purposes of this subsection, the term "disposition" includes a sale, exchange, distribution, or gift of property whether or not gain or loss is recognized on the transfer.

(ii) Any taxable income recognized solely by reason of subparagraph (A) shall have the same characterization it would have had if the taxpayer had sold or exchanged the property.

(iii) The Secretary shall prescribe such regulations as he may deem necessary to provide for adjustments to the basis of property to reflect taxable income recognized solely by reason of subparagraph (A).

(C) EXCEPTIONS.—Notwithstanding subparagraph (B), the term "disposition" does not include—

(i) a disposition of property which is not a material factor in the realization of income by the taxpayer, or

(ii) a disposition of property to a domestic corporation in a distribution or transfer described in section 381(a).

(D) APPLICATION TO CERTAIN DISPOSITIONS OF STOCK IN CONTROLLED FOREIGN CORPORATION.—

(i) IN GENERAL.—This paragraph shall apply to an applicable disposition in the same manner as if it were a disposition of property described in subparagraph (A), except that the exception contained in subparagraph (C)(i) shall not apply.

(ii) APPLICABLE DISPOSITION.—For purposes of clause (i), the term "applicable disposition" means any disposition of any share of stock in a controlled foreign corporation in a transaction or series of transactions if, immediately before such transaction or series of transactions, the taxpayer owned more than 50 percent (by vote or value) of the stock of the controlled foreign corporation. Such term shall not include a disposition described in clause (iii) or (iv), except that clause (i) shall apply to any gain recognized on any such disposition.

(iii) EXCEPTION FOR CERTAIN EXCHANGES WHERE OWNERSHIP PERCENTAGE RETAINED.—A disposition shall not be treated as an applicable disposition under clause (ii) if it is part of a transaction or series of transactions—

(I) to which section 351 or 721 applies, or under which the transferor receives stock in a foreign corporation in exchange for the stock in the controlled foreign corporation and the stock received is exchanged basis property (as defined in section 7701(a)(44)), and

(II) immediately after which, the transferor owns (by vote or value) at least the same percentage of stock in the controlled foreign corporation (or, if the controlled foreign corporation is not in existence after such transaction or series of transactions, in another foreign corporation stock in which was received by the transferor in exchange for stock in the controlled foreign corporation) as the percentage of stock in the controlled foreign corporation which the taxpayer owned immediately before such transaction or series of transactions.

(iv) EXCEPTION FOR CERTAIN ASSET ACQUISITIONS.—A disposition shall not be treated as an applicable disposition under clause (ii) if it is part of a transaction or series of transactions in which the taxpayer (or any member of an affiliated group of corporations filing a consolidated return under section 1501 which includes the taxpayer) acquires the assets of a controlled foreign corporation in exchange for the shares of the controlled foreign corporation in a liquidation described in section 332 or a reorganization described in section 368(a)(1).

(v) CONTROLLED FOREIGN CORPORATION.—For purposes of this subparagraph, the term "controlled foreign corporation" has the meaning given such term by section 957.

(vi) STOCK OWNERSHIP.—For purposes of this subparagraph, ownership of stock shall be determined under the rules of subsections (a) and (b) of section 958.

(4) ACCUMULATION DISTRIBUTIONS OF FOREIGN TRUST.—For purposes of this chapter, in the case of amounts of income from sources without the United States which are treated under section 666 (without regard to subsections (b) and (c) thereof if the taxpayer chose to take a deduction with respect to the amounts described in such subsections under section 667(d)(1)(B)) as having been distributed by a foreign trust in a preceding taxable year, that portion of such amounts equal to the amount of any overall foreign loss sustained by the beneficiary in a year prior to the taxable year of the beneficiary in which such distribution is received from the trust shall be treated as income from sources within the United States (and not income from sources without the United States) to the extent that such loss was not used under this subsection in prior taxable years, or in the current taxable year, against other income of the beneficiary.

(5) TREATMENT OF SEPARATE LIMITATION LOSSES.—

(A) IN GENERAL.—The amount of the separate limitation losses for any taxable year shall reduce income from sources within the United States for such taxable year only to the extent the aggregate amount of such losses exceeds the aggregate amount of the separate limitation incomes for such taxable year.

(B) ALLOCATION OF LOSSES.—The separate limitation losses for any taxable year (to the extent such losses do not exceed the separate limitation incomes for such year) shall be allocated among (and operate to reduce) such incomes on a proportionate basis.

(C) RECHARACTERIZATION OF SUBSEQUENT INCOME.—If—

(i) a separate limitation loss from any income category (hereinafter in this subparagraph referred to as "the loss category") was allocated to income from any other category under subparagraph (B), and

(ii) the loss category has income for a subsequent taxable year,

such income (to the extent it does not exceed the aggregate separate limitation losses from the loss category not previously recharacterized under this subparagraph) shall be recharacterized as income from such other category in proportion to the prior reductions under subparagraph (B) in such other category not previously taken into account under this subparagraph. Nothing in the preceding sentence shall be construed as recharacterizing any tax.

(D) SPECIAL RULES FOR LOSSES FROM SOURCES IN THE UNITED STATES.—Any loss from sources in the United States for any taxable year (to the extent such loss does not exceed the separate limitation incomes from such year) shall be allocated among (and operate to reduce) such incomes on a proportionate basis. This subparagraph shall be applied after subparagraph (B).

(E) DEFINITIONS.—For purposes of this paragraph—

(i) INCOME CATEGORY.—The term "income category" means each separate category of income described in subsection (d)(1).

(ii) SEPARATE LIMITATION INCOME.—The term "separate limitation income" means, with respect to any income category, the taxable income from sources outside the United States, separately computed for such category.

(iii) SEPARATE LIMITATION LOSS.—The term "separate limitation loss" means, with respect to any income category, the loss from such category determined under the principles of section 907(c)(4)(B).

(F) DISPOSITIONS.—If any separate limitation loss for any taxable year is allocated against any separate limitation income for such taxable year, except to the extent provided in regulations, rules similar to the rules of paragraph (3) shall apply to any disposition of property if gain from such disposition would be in the income category with respect to which there was such separate limitation loss.

Amendments

- **2018, Tax Technical Corrections Act of 2018 (P.L. 115-141)**

P.L. 115-141, §401(d)(1)(D)(xiv), Div. U:

Amended Code Sec. 904(f)(1) by striking "and section 936" following "For purposes of this subpart". **Effective** 3-23-2018. For a special rule, see Act Sec. 401(e), Div. U, below.

P.L. 115-141, §401(e), Div. U, provides:

(e) GENERAL SAVINGS PROVISION WITH RESPECT TO DEADWOOD PROVISIONS.—If—

(1) any provision amended or repealed by the amendments made by subsection (b) or (d) applied to—

(A) any transaction occurring before the date of the enactment of this Act,

(B) any property acquired before such date of enactment, or

(C) any item of income, loss, deduction, or credit taken into account before such date of enactment, and

(2) the treatment of such transaction, property, or item under such provision would (without regard to the amendments or repeals made by such subsection) affect the liability for tax for periods ending after such date of enactment,

nothing in the amendments or repeals made by this section shall be construed to affect the treatment of such transaction, property, or item for purposes of determining liability for tax for periods ending after such date of enactment.

- **2007, Tax Technical Corrections Act of 2007 (P.L. 110-172)**

P.L. 110-172, §11(f)(3):

Amended Code Sec. 904(f)(3)(D)(iv) by striking "a controlled group" and inserting "an affiliated group". **Effective** as if included in the provision of the American Jobs Creation Act of 2004 (P.L. 108-357) to which it relates [**effective** for dispositions after 10-22-2004.—CCH].

- **2004, American Jobs Creation Act of 2004 (P.L. 108-357)**

P.L. 108-357, §895(a):

Amended Code Sec. 904(f)(3) by adding at the end new subparagraph (D). **Effective** for dispositions after 10-22-2004.

- **1996, Small Business Job Protection Act of 1996 (P.L. 104-188)**

P.L. 104-188, §1704(t)(36):

Amended Code Sec. 904(f)(2)(B)(i) by inserting "(as in effect on the day before the date of the enactment of the Revenue Reconciliation Act of 1990)" after "section 172(h)". **Effective** 8-20-96.

- **1988, Technical and Miscellaneous Revenue Act of 1988 (P.L. 100-647)**

P.L. 100-647, §1012(c):

Amended Code Sec. 904(f)(5) by adding at the end thereof new subparagraph (F). **Effective** as if included in the provision of P.L. 99-514 to which it relates.

- **1986, Tax Reform Act of 1986 (P.L. 99-514)**

P.L. 99-514, §1203(a):

Amended Code Sec. 904(f) by adding at the end thereof new paragraph (5). **Effective** for losses incurred in tax years beginning after 12-31-86.

P.L. 99-514, §1205 provides:

SEC. 1205. LIMITATION ON CARRYBACK OF FOREIGN TAX CREDITS TO TAXABLE YEARS BEGINNING BEFORE 1987.

(a) DETERMINATION OF EXCESS CREDITS.—

(1) IN GENERAL.—Any taxes paid or accrued in a taxable year beginning after 1986 may be treated under section 904(c) of the Internal Revenue Code of 1954 as paid or accrued in a taxable year beginning before 1987 only to the extent such taxes would be so treated if the tax imposed by chapter 1 of such Code for the taxable year beginning after 1986 were determined by applying section 1 or 11 of such Code (as the case may be) as in effect on the day before the date of the enactment of this Act.

(2) ADJUSTMENTS.—Under regulations prescribed by the Secretary of the Treasury or his delegate proper adjustments shall be made in the application of paragraph (1) to take into account—

(A) the repeal of the zero bracket amount, and

(B) the changes in the treatment of capital gains.

(b) COORDINATION WITH SEPARATE BASKETS.—Any taxes paid or accrued in a taxable year beginning after 1986 which (after the application of subsection (a)) are treated as paid or accrued in a taxable year beginning before 1987 shall be treated as imposed on income described in section 904(d)(1)(E) of the Internal Revenue Code of 1954 (as in effect on the day before the date of the enactment of this Act). No taxes paid or accrued in a taxable year beginning after 1986 with respect to high withholding tax interest (as defined in section 904(d)(2)(B) of the Internal Revenue Code of 1986 as amended by this Act) may be treated as paid or accrued in a taxable year beginning before 1987.

- **1982, Tax Equity and Fiscal Responsibility Act of 1982 (P.L. 97-248)**

P.L. 97-248, §211(c)(2):

Amended Code Sec. 904(f) by striking out paragraph (4) and redesignating paragraphs (5) and (6) [Note: There is no subparagraph (6)] as paragraph (4) and (5) [sic]. **Effective** for tax years beginning after 12-31-82. Prior to amendment, paragraph (4) read as follows:

(4) Determination of foreign oil related loss where section 907 applies.—In making the separate computation under this subsection with respect to foreign oil related income which is required by section 907(b) the foreign oil related loss shall be the amount by which the gross income for the taxable year from sources without the United States and its possessions (whether or not the taxpayer chooses the benefits of this subpart for such taxable year) taken into account in determining the foreign oil related income for such year is exceeded by the sum of the deductions properly apportioned or allocated thereto, except that there shall not be taken into account—

(A) any net operating loss deduction allowable for such year under section 172(a) and

(B) any—

(i) foreign expropriation loss for such year, as defined in section 172(h), or

(ii) loss for such year which arises from fire, storm, shipwreck, or other casualty, or from theft,

to the extent such loss is not compensated for by insurance or otherwise.

P.L. 97-248, §211(e)(2), as amended by P.L. 97-448, §306(a)(5), and P.L. 98-369, §712(e), provides:

"(2) Retention of old sections 907(b) and 904(f)(4) where taxpayer had separate basket foreign loss.—

"(A) IN GENERAL.—If, after applying old sections 907(b) and 904(f)(4) to a taxable year beginning before January 1, 1983, the taxpayer had a separate basket foreign loss, such loss shall not be recaptured from income of a kind not taken into account in computing the amount of such separate basket foreign loss more rapidly than ratably over the 8-year period (or such shorter period as the taxpayer may select) beginning with the first taxable year beginning after December 31, 1982.

"(B) DEFINITIONS.—For purposes of this paragraph—

"(i) The term 'separate basket foreign loss' means any foreign loss attributable to activities taken into account (or not taken into account) in determining foreign oil related income (as defined in old section 907(c)(2)).

"(ii) An 'old' section is such section as in effect on the day before the date of the enactment of this Act."

- **1978, Revenue Act of 1978 (P.L. 95-600)**

P.L. 95-600, §701(q)(2):

Amended Code Sec. 904(f) by adding a new subparagraph (5). **Effective** as set forth in P.L. 94-455, Act Sec. 1032(a).

P.L. 95-600, §701(u)(4):

Amended Code Sec. 904(f)(2)(A) and 904(f)(4)(A) by striking out "or any capital loss carrybacks and carryovers to such year under section 1212" after "section 172(a)". **Effective** for overall foreign losses sustained in tax years beginning after 12-31-75, and for foreign oil related losses sustained in tax years ending after 12-31-75.

P.L. 95-600, §701(u)(8)(C):

Amended Code Sec. 904(f)(4) by striking out "In the case of a corporation to which section 907(b)(1) applies" and inserting in lieu thereof "In making the separate computation under this subsection with respect to foreign oil related income which is required by section 907(b)". **Effective** for tax years ending after 12-31-76.

- **1976, Tax Reform Act of 1976 (P.L. 94-455)**

P.L. 94-455, §1031(a):

Amended Code Sec. 904(f). See amendment note for P.L. 94-455, Act Sec. 1031(a), following Code Sec. 904(a) for **effective** date. Prior to amendment, Code Sec. 904(f) read as follows:

(f) APPLICATION OF SECTION IN CASE OF CERTAIN INTEREST INCOME AND DIVIDENDS FROM A DISC OR FORMER DISC.—

(1) IN GENERAL.—The provisions of subsections (a), (c), (d), and (e) of this section shall be applied separately with respect to each of the following items of income—

(A) the interest income described in paragraph (2),

(B) dividends from a DISC or former DISC (as defined in section 992(a)) to the extent such dividends are treated as income from sources without the United States, and

(C) income other than the interest income described in paragraph (2) and dividends described in subparagraph (B).

(2) INTEREST INCOME TO WHICH APPLICABLE.—For purposes of this subsection, the interest income described in this paragraph is interest other than interest—

(A) derived from any transaction which is directly related to the active conduct of a trade or business in a foreign country or a possession of the United States,

(B) derived in the conduct of a banking, financing, or similar business,

(C) received from a corporation in which the taxpayer (or one or more includible corporations in an affiliated group, as defined in section 1504, of which the taxpayer is a member) owns, directly or indirectly, at least 10 percent of the voting stock,

(D) received on obligations acquired as a result of the disposition of a trade or business actively conducted by the taxpayer in a foreign country or possession of the United States or as a result of the disposition of stock or obligations of a corporation in which the taxpayer owned at least 10 percent of the voting stock.

For purposes of subparagraph (C), stock owned, directly or indirectly, by or for a foreign corporation shall be considered as being proportionately owned by its shareholders.

(3) OVERALL LIMITATION NOT TO APPLY.—The limitation provided by subsection (a)(2) shall not apply with respect to the interest income described in paragraph (2) or to dividends described in paragraph (1)(B). The Secretary or his delegate shall by regulations prescribe the manner of application of subsection (e) with respect to cases in which the limitation provided by subsection (a)(2) applies with respect to income described in paragraph (1)(B) and (C).

(4) TRANSITIONAL RULES FOR CARRYBACKS AND CARRYOVERS.—

(A) CARRYBACKS TO YEARS PRIOR TO REVENUE ACT OF 1962.—Where, under the provisions of subsection (d), taxes (i) paid or accrued to any foreign country or possession of the United States in any taxable year beginning after the date of the enactment of

INCOME TAX—FOREIGN TAX CREDIT

the Revenue Act of 1962 are deemed (ii) paid or accrued in one or more taxable years beginning on or before the date of enactment of the Revenue Act of 1962, the amount of such taxes deemed paid or accrued shall be determined without regard to the provisions of this subsection. To the extent the taxes paid or accrued to a foreign country or possession of the United States in any taxable year described in clause (i) are not, with the application of the preceding sentence, deemed paid or accrued in any taxable year described in clause (ii), such taxes shall, for purposes of applying subsection (d), be deemed paid or accrued in a taxable year beginning after the date of the enactment of the Revenue Act of 1962, with respect to interest income described in paragraph (2), and with respect to income other than interest income described in paragraph (2), in the same ratios as the amount of such taxes paid or accrued with respect to interest income described in paragraph (2), and the amount of such taxes paid or accrued with respect to income other than interest income described in paragraph (2), respectively, bear to the total amount of such taxes paid or accrued to such foreign country or possession of the United States.

(B) CARRYOVERS TO YEARS AFTER REVENUE ACT OF 1962.—Where, under the provisions of subsection (d), taxes (i) paid or accrued to any foreign country or possession of the United States in any taxable year beginning on or before the date of the enactment of the Revenue Act of 1962 are deemed (ii) paid or accrued in one or more taxable years beginning after the date of the enactment of the Revenue Act of 1962, the amount of such taxes deemed paid or accrued in any year described in clause (ii) shall, with respect to interest income described in paragraph (2), be an amount which bears the same ratio to the amount of such taxes deemed paid or accrued as the amount of the taxes paid or accrued to such foreign country or possession for such year with respect to interest income described in paragraph (2) bears to the total amount of the taxes paid or accrued to such foreign country or possession for such year; and the amount of such taxes deemed paid or accrued in any year described in clause (ii) with respect to income other than interest income described in paragraph (2) shall be an amount which bears the same ratio to the amount of such taxes deemed paid or accrued for such year as the amount of taxes paid or accrued to such foreign country or possession for such year with respect to income other than interest income described in paragraph (2) bears to the total amount of the taxes paid or accrued to such foreign country or possession for such year.

(5) DISC DIVIDENDS AGGREGATED FOR PURPOSES OF PERCOUNTRY LIMITATION.—In the case of a taxpayer who for the taxable year has dividends described in paragraph (1)(B) from more than one corporation, the limitation provided by subsection (a)(1) shall be applied with respect to the aggregate of such dividends.

P.L. 94-455, § 1032(a):

Redesignated former Code Sec. 904(f), as amended by P.L. 94-455, § 1031(a), as Code Sec. 904(g) and added new Code Sec. 904(f).

P.L. 94-455, § 1032(c), as amended by P.L. 95-600, §§ 701(u)(5)(A), (B) and 701(u)(7)(A), (B), provides:

(c) EFFECTIVE DATES.—

(1) IN GENERAL.—Except as provided in paragraphs (2), (3), and (5) the amendment made by subsection (a) shall apply to losses sustained in taxable years beginning after December 31, 1975. The amendment made by subsection (b)(1) shall apply to taxable years beginning after December 31, 1975. The amendment made by subsection (b)(2) shall apply to losses sustained in taxable years ending after December 31, 1975.

(2) OBLIGATIONS OF FOREIGN GOVERNMENTS.—The amendments made by subsection (a) shall not apply to losses on the sale, exchange, or other disposition of bonds, notes, or other evidences of indebtedness issued before May 14, 1976, by a foreign government or instrumentality thereof for the acquisition of property located in that country or stock of a corporation (created or organized in or under the laws of that foreign country) or indebtedness of such corporation.

(3) SUBSTANTIAL WORTHLESSNESS BEFORE ENACTMENT.—The amendments made by subsection (a) shall not apply to losses incurred on the loss from stock or indebtedness of a corporation in which the taxpayer owned at least 10 percent of the voting stock and which has sustained losses in 3 out of the last 5 taxable years beginning before January 1, 1976, which has sustained an overall loss for those 5 years, and with respect to which the taxpayer has terminated or will terminate all operations by reason of sale, liquidation, or other disposition before January 1, 1977, of such corporation or its assets.

(4) LIMITATION BASED ON DEFICIT IN EARNINGS AND PROFITS.—If paragraph (3) would apply to a taxpayer but for the fact that the loss is sustained after December 31, 1976, and if the loss is sustained in a taxable year beginning before January 1, 1979, the amendments made by subsection (a) shall not apply to such loss to the extent that there was on December 31, 1975, a deficit in earnings and profits in the corporation from which the loss arose. For purposes of the preceding sentence, there shall be taken into account only earnings and profits of the corporation which (A) were accumulated in taxable years of the corporation beginning after December 31, 1962, and during the period in which the stock of such corporation from which the loss arose was held by the taxpayer and (B) are attributable to such stock.

(5) FOREIGN OIL RELATED LOSSES.—The amendment made by subsection (a) shall apply to foreign oil related losses sustained in taxable years ending after December 31, 1975.

(6) RECAPTURE OF POSSESSION LOSSES DURING TRANSITIONAL PERIOD WHERE TAXPAYER IS ON A PER-COUNTRY BASIS.—

(A) APPLICATION OF PARAGRAPH.—This paragraph shall apply if—

(i) the taxpayer sustained a loss in a possession of the United States in a taxable year beginning after December 31, 1975, and before January 1, 1979,

(ii) such loss is attributable to a trade or business engaged in by the taxpayer in such possession on January 1, 1976, and

(iii) the taxpayer chooses to have the benefits of subpart A of part III of subchapter N apply for such taxable year and section 904(a)(1) of the Internal Revenue Code of 1954 (as in effect before the enactment of this Act) applies with respect to such taxable year.

(B) NO RECAPTURE DURING TRANSITION PERIOD.—In any case to which this paragraph applies, for purposes of determining the liability for tax of the taxpayer for taxable years beginning before January 1, 1979, section 904(f) of the Internal Revenue Code of 1954 shall not apply with respect to the loss described in subparagraph (A)(i).

(C) RECAPTURE OF LOSS AFTER THE TRANSITION PERIOD.—In any case to which this paragraph applies—

(i) for purposes of determining the liability for tax of the taxpayer for taxable years beginning after December 31, 1978, section 904(f) of the Internal Revenue Code of 1954 shall be applied with respect to the loss described in subparagraph (A)(i) under the principles of section 904(a)(1) of such Code (as in effect before the enactment of this Act); but

(ii) in the case of any taxpayer and any possession, the aggregate amount to which such section 904(f) applies by reason of clause (i) shall not exceed the sum of the net incomes of all affiliated corporations from such possession for taxable years of such affiliated corporations beginning after December 31, 1975, and before January 1, 1979.

(D) TAXPAYERS NOT ENGAGED IN TRADE OR BUSINESS ON JANUARY 1, 1976.—In any case to which this paragraph applies but for the fact that the taxpayer was not engaged in a trade or business in such possession on January 1, 1976, for purposes of determining the liability for tax of the taxpayer for taxable years beginning before January 1, 1979; if section 904(a)(1) of such Code (as in effect before the enactment of this Act) applies with respect to such taxable year, the provisions of section 904(f) of such Code shall be applied with respect to the loss described in subparagraph (A)(i) under the principles of such section 904(a)(1).

(E) AFFILIATED CORPORATION DEFINED.—For purposes of subparagraph (C)(ii), the term "affiliated corporation" means a corporation which, for the taxable year for which the net income is being determined, was not a member of the same affiliated group (within the meaning of section 1504 of the Internal Revenue Code of 1954) as the taxpayer but would have been a member of such group but for the application of subsection (b) of such section 1504.

P.L. 94-455, § 1901(b)(10)(B):

Substituted "section 172(h)" for "section 172(k)(1)" in Code Sec. 904(f)(2)(B)(i) and in Code Sec. 904(f)(4)(B)(i). **Effective** for tax years beginning after 12-31-76.

• **1971, Revenue Act of 1971 (P.L. 92-178)**

P.L. 92-178, § 502(b)(2)-(4):

Amended Code Sec. 904(f). **Effective** as noted under Code Sec. 992, as follows:

The heading of Code Sec. 904(f) and paragraph (1) was amended. Prior to amendment, these read as follows:

"(f) Application of Section in Case of Certain Interest Income.—

"(1) In general.—The provisions of subsections (a), (c), (d), and (e) of this section shall be applied separately with respect to—

"(A) the interest income described in paragraph (2), and

"(B) income other than the interest income described in paragraph (2)."

Paragraph (3) of Code Sec. 904(f) was amended. Prior to amendment, paragraph (3) read as follows:

"(3) Overall limitation not to apply.—The limitation provided by subsection (a)(2) shall not apply with respect to the interest income described in paragraph (2). The Secretary or his delegate shall by regulations prescribe the manner of application of subsection (e) with respect to cases in which the limitation provided by subsection (a)(2) applies with respect to income other than the interest income described in paragraph (2)."

Paragraph (5) was added to Code Sec. 904(f).

• **1966, Foreign Investors Tax Act of 1966 (P.L. 89-809)**

P.L. 89-809, § 106(c)(1):

Amended Code Sec. 904(f)(2)(C) and amended Code Sec. 904(f)(2) by adding the last sentence. **Effective** with respect to interest received after 12-31-65, in tax years ending after that date. Prior to amendment, Sec. 904(f)(2)(C) read as follows:

"(C) received from a corporation in which the taxpayer owns at least 10 percent of the voting stock, or".

• **1962, Revenue Act of 1962 (P.L. 87-834)**

P.L. 87-834, § 10(a):

Amended Code Sec. 904 by adding subsection (f). **Effective** for tax years beginning after 10-16-62, but only with respect to interest resulting from transactions consummated after 4-2-62.

[Sec. 904(g)]

(g) RECHARACTERIZATION OF OVERALL DOMESTIC LOSS.—

(1) GENERAL RULE.—For purposes of this subpart and section 936, in the case of any taxpayer who sustains an overall domestic loss for any taxable year beginning after December 31, 2006, that portion of the taxpayer's taxable income from sources within the United States for each succeeding taxable year which is equal to the lesser of—

(A) the amount of such loss (to the extent not used under this paragraph in prior taxable years), or

(B) 50 percent of the taxpayer's taxable income from sources within the United States for such succeeding taxable year,

shall be treated as income from sources without the United States (and not as income from sources within the United States).

(2) OVERALL DOMESTIC LOSS.—For purposes of this subsection—

(A) IN GENERAL.—The term "overall domestic loss" means—

(i) with respect to any qualified taxable year, the domestic loss for such taxable year to the extent such loss offsets taxable income from sources without the United States for the taxable year or for any preceding qualified taxable year by reason of a carryback, and

(ii) with respect to any other taxable year, the domestic loss for such taxable year to the extent such loss offsets taxable income from sources without the United States for any preceding qualified taxable year by reason of a carryback.

(B) DOMESTIC LOSS.—For purposes of subparagraph (A), the term "domestic loss" means the amount by which the gross income for the taxable year from sources within the United States is exceeded by the sum of the deductions properly apportioned or allocated thereto (determined without regard to any carryback from a subsequent taxable year).

(C) QUALIFIED TAXABLE YEAR.—For purposes of subparagraph (A), the term "qualified taxable year" means any taxable year for which the taxpayer chose the benefits of this subpart.

(3) CHARACTERIZATION OF SUBSEQUENT INCOME.—

(A) IN GENERAL.—Any income from sources within the United States that is treated as income from sources without the United States under paragraph (1) shall be allocated among and increase the income categories in proportion to the loss from sources within the United States previously allocated to those income categories.

(B) INCOME CATEGORY.—For purposes of this paragraph, the term "income category" has the meaning given such term by subsection (f)(5)(E)(i).

(4) COORDINATION WITH SUBSECTION (f).—The Secretary shall prescribe such regulations as may be necessary to coordinate the provisions of this subsection with the provisions of subsection (f).

(5) ELECTION TO INCREASE PERCENTAGE OF TAXABLE INCOME TREATED AS FOREIGN SOURCE.—

(A) IN GENERAL.—If any pre-2018 unused overall domestic loss is taken into account under paragraph (1) for any applicable taxable year, the taxpayer may elect to have such paragraph applied to such loss by substituting a percentage greater than 50 percent (but not greater than 100 percent) for 50 percent in subparagraph (B) thereof.

(B) PRE-2018 UNUSED OVERALL DOMESTIC LOSS.—For purposes of this paragraph, the term "pre-2018 unused overall domestic loss" means any overall domestic loss which—

(i) arises in a qualified taxable year beginning before January 1, 2018, and

(ii) has not been used under paragraph (1) for any taxable year beginning before such date.

(C) APPLICABLE TAXABLE YEAR.—For purposes of this paragraph, the term "applicable taxable year" means any taxable year of the taxpayer beginning after December 31, 2017, and before January 1, 2028.

Amendments

- **2017, Tax Cuts and Jobs Act (P.L. 115-97)**

P.L. 115-97, §14304(a):

Amended Code Sec. 904(g) by adding at the end a new paragraph (5). **Effective** for tax years beginning after 12-31-2017.

- **2005, Gulf Opportunity Zone Act of 2005 (P.L. 109-135)**

P.L. 109-135, §403(k):

Amended Code Sec. 904(g)(2). **Effective** as if included in the provision of the American Jobs Creation Act of 2004 (P.L. 108-357) to which it relates [**effective** for losses for tax years beginning after 12-31-2006.—CCH]. Prior to amendment, Code Sec. 904(g)(2) read as follows:

(2) OVERALL DOMESTIC LOSS DEFINED.—For purposes of this subsection—

(A) IN GENERAL.—The term "overall domestic loss" means any domestic loss to the extent such loss offsets taxable income from sources without the United States for the taxable year or for any preceding taxable year by reason of a carryback. For purposes of the preceding sentence, the term "domestic loss" means the amount by which the gross income for the taxable year from sources within the United States is exceeded by the sum of the deductions properly apportioned or allocated thereto (determined without regard to any carryback from a subsequent taxable year).

(B) TAXPAYER MUST HAVE ELECTED FOREIGN TAX CREDIT FOR YEAR OF LOSS.—The term "overall domestic loss" shall not include any loss for any taxable year unless the taxpayer chose the benefits of this subpart for such taxable year.

- **2004, American Jobs Creation Act of 2004 (P.L. 108-357)**

P.L. 108-357, §402(a):

Amended Code Sec. 904 by redesignating subsections (g), (h), (i), (j), and (k) as subsections (h), (i), (j), (k), and (l) respectively, and by inserting after subsection (f) a new subsection (g). **Effective** for losses for tax years beginning after 12-31-2006.

[Sec. 904(h)]

(h) SOURCE RULES IN CASE OF UNITED STATES-OWNED FOREIGN CORPORATIONS.—

(1) IN GENERAL.—The following amounts which are derived from a United States-owned foreign corporation and which would be treated as derived from sources outside the United States without regard to this subsection shall, for purposes of this section, be treated as derived from sources within the United States to the extent provided in this subsection:

(A) Any amount included in gross income under—

(i) section 951(a) (relating to amounts included in gross income of United States shareholders), or

(ii) section 1293 (relating to current taxation of income from qualified funds).

(B) Interest.

(C) Dividends.

(2) SUBPART F AND PASSIVE FOREIGN INVESTMENT COMPANY INCLUSIONS.—Any amount described in subparagraph (A) of paragraph (1) shall be treated as derived from sources within the United States to the extent such amount is attributable to income of the United States-owned foreign corporation from sources within the United States.

(3) CERTAIN INTEREST ALLOCABLE TO UNITED STATES SOURCE INCOME.—Any interest which—

(A) is paid or accrued by a United States-owned foreign corporation during any taxable year,

(B) is paid or accrued to a United States shareholder (as defined in section 951(b)) or a related person (within the meaning of section 267(b)) to such a shareholder, and

(C) is properly allocable (under regulations prescribed by the Secretary) to income of such foreign corporation for the taxable year from sources within the United States,

shall be treated as derived from sources within the United States.

(4) DIVIDENDS.—

(A) IN GENERAL.—The United States source ratio of any dividend paid or accrued by a United States-owned foreign corporation shall be treated as derived from sources within the United States.

(B) UNITED STATES SOURCE RATIO.—For purposes of subparagraph (A), the term "United States source ratio" means, with respect to any dividend paid out of the earnings and profits for any taxable year, a fraction—

(i) the numerator of which is the portion of the earnings and profits for such taxable year from sources within the United States, and

(ii) the denominator of which is the total amount of earnings and profits for such taxable year.

INCOME TAX—FOREIGN TAX CREDIT

(5) EXCEPTION WHERE UNITED STATES-OWNED FOREIGN CORPORATION HAS SMALL AMOUNT OF UNITED STATES SOURCE INCOME.—Paragraph (3) shall not apply to interest paid or accrued during any taxable year (and paragraph (4) shall not apply to any dividends paid out of the earnings and profits for such taxable year) if—

(A) the United States-owned foreign corporation has earnings and profits for such taxable year, and

(B) less than 10 percent of such earnings and profits is attributable to sources within the United States.

For purposes of the preceding sentence, earnings and profits shall be determined without any reduction for interest described in paragraph (3) (determined without regard to subparagraph (C) thereof).

(6) UNITED STATES-OWNED FOREIGN CORPORATION.—For purposes of this subsection, the term "United States-owned foreign corporation" means any foreign corporation if 50 percent or more of—

(A) the total combined voting power of all classes of stock of such corporation entitled to vote, or

(B) the total value of the stock of such corporation,

is held directly (or indirectly through applying paragraphs (2) and (3) of section 958(a) and paragraph (4) of section 318(a)) by United States persons (as defined in section 7701(a)(30)).

(7) DIVIDEND.—For purposes of this subsection, the term "dividend" includes any gain treated as a dividend under section 1248.

(8) COORDINATION WITH SUBSECTION (f).—This subsection shall be applied before subsection (f).

(9) TREATMENT OF CERTAIN DOMESTIC CORPORATIONS.—In the case of any dividend treated as not from sources within the United States under section 861(a)(2)(A), the corporation paying such dividend shall be treated for purposes of this subsection as a United States-owned foreign corporation.

(10) COORDINATION WITH TREATIES.—

(A) IN GENERAL.—If—

(i) any amount derived from a United States-owned foreign corporation would be treated as derived from sources within the United States under this subsection by reason of an item of income of such United States-owned foreign corporation,

(ii) under a treaty obligation of the United States (applied without regard to this subsection and by treating any amount included in gross income under section 951(a)(1) as a dividend), such amount would be treated as arising from sources outside the United States, and

(iii) the taxpayer chooses the benefits of this paragraph,

this subsection shall not apply to such amount to the extent attributable to such item of income (but subsections (a), (b), and (c) of this section and sections 907 and 960 shall be applied separately with respect to such amount to the extent so attributable).

(B) SPECIAL RULE.—Amounts included in gross income under section 951(a)(1) shall be treated as a dividend under subparagraph (A)(ii) only if dividends paid by each corporation (the stock in which is taken into account in determining whether the shareholder is a United States shareholder in the United States-owned foreign corporation), if paid to the United States shareholder, would be treated under a treaty obligation of the United States as arising from sources outside the United States (applied without regard to this subsection).

(11) REGULATIONS.—The Secretary shall prescribe such regulations as may be necessary or appropriate for purposes of this subsection, including—

(A) regulations for the application of this subsection in the case of interest or dividend payments through 1 or more entities, and

(B) regulations providing that this subsection shall apply to interest paid or accrued to any person (whether or not a United States shareholder).

Amendments

- **2017, Tax Cuts and Jobs Act (P.L. 115-97)**

P.L. 115-97, §14301(c)(18):

Amended Code Sec. 904(h)(10)(A) by striking "sections 902, 907, and 960" and inserting "sections 907 and 960". **Effective** for tax years of foreign corporations beginning after 12-31-2017, and to tax years of United States shareholders in which or with which such tax years of foreign corporations end.

- **2014, Tax Technical Corrections Act of 2014 (P.L. 113-295)**

P.L. 113-295, §219(c), Division A:

Amended Code Sec. 904(h)(7) by striking "as ordinary income under section 1246 or" following "any gain treated". **Effective** as if included in the provision of the American Jobs Creation Act of 2004 (P.L. 108-357) to which it relates [effective for tax years of foreign corporations beginning after 12-31-2004, and to tax years of United States shareholders with or within which such tax years of foreign corporations end.—CCH].

- **2010, (P.L. 111-226)**

P.L. 111-226, §217(c)(2):

Amended Code Sec. 904(h)(9). **Effective** generally for tax years beginning after 12-31-2010. For a grandfather rule, see Act Sec. 217(d)(2), below. Prior to amendment, Code Sec. 904(h)(9) read as follows:

(9) TREATMENT OF CERTAIN DOMESTIC CORPORATIONS.—For purposes of this subsection—

(A) in the case of interest treated as not from sources within the United States under section 861(a)(1)(A), the corporation paying such interest shall be treated as a United States-owned foreign corporation, and

(B) in the case of any dividend treated as not from sources within the United States under section 861(a)(2)(A), the corporation paying such dividend shall be treated as a United States-owned foreign corporation.

P.L. 111-226, §217(d)(2), provides:

(2) GRANDFATHER RULE FOR OUTSTANDING DEBT OBLIGATIONS.—

(A) IN GENERAL.—The amendments made by this section shall not apply to payments of interest on obligations issued before the date of the enactment of this Act.

(B) EXCEPTION FOR RELATED PARTY DEBT.—Subparagraph (A) shall not apply to any interest which is payable to a related person (determined under rules similar to the rules of section 954(d)(3)).

(C) SIGNIFICANT MODIFICATIONS TREATED AS NEW ISSUES.—For purposes of subparagraph (A), a significant modification of the terms of any obligation (including any extension of the term of such obligation) shall be treated as a new issue.

- **2004, American Jobs Creation Act of 2004 (P.L. 108-357)**

P.L. 108-357, §402(a):

Amended Code Sec. 904 by redesignating subsection (g) as subsection (h). **Effective** for losses for tax years beginning after 12-31-2006.

P.L. 108-357, §413(c)(15)(A):

Amended Code Sec. 904(h)(1)(A), as redesignated by Act Sec. 402(a), by adding "or" at the end of clause (i), by striking clause (ii), and by redesignating clause (iii) as clause (ii). **Effective** for tax years of foreign corporations beginning after 12-31-2004, and for tax years of United States shareholders with or within which such tax years of foreign corporations end. Prior to being stricken, Code Sec. 904(h)(1)(A)(ii) read as follows:

(ii) section 551 (relating to foreign personal holding company income taxed to United States shareholders), or

P.L. 108-357, §413(c)(15)(B):

Amended the heading of Code Sec. 904(h)(2), as redesignated by Act Sec. 402(a), by striking "FOREIGN PERSONAL HOLDING OR" immediately preceding "PASSIVE FOREIGN INVESTMENT". **Effective** for tax years of foreign corporations beginning after 12-31-2004, and for tax years of United States shareholders with or within which such tax years of foreign corporations end.

- **1988, Technical and Miscellaneous Revenue Act of 1988 (P.L. 100-647)**

P.L. 100-647, §1012(q)(12):

Amended Code Sec. 904(g)(9)(A) by striking out "861(a)(1)(B)" and inserting in lieu thereof "861(a)(1)(A)". **Effective** as if included in the provision of P.L. 99-514 to which it relates.

P.L. 100-647, §1012(bb)(4)(A):

Amended Code Sec. 904(g) by redesignating paragraph (10) as paragraph (11) and by inserting after paragraph (9) new paragraph (10). **Effective** as if included in the amendment made by section 121 of P.L. 98-369.

- **1986, Tax Reform Act of 1986 (P.L. 99-514)**

P.L. 99-514, §1235(f)(4)(A):

Amended Code Sec. 904(g)(1)(A) by striking out "or" at the end of clause (i), by striking out the period at the end of clause (ii) and inserting in lieu thereof ", or", and by adding at the end thereof new clause (iii). **Effective** for tax years of foreign corporations beginning after 12-31-86.

P.L. 99-514, §1235(f)(4)(B):

Amended the paragraph heading of Code Sec. 904(g)(2) by striking out "HOLDING COMPANY" and inserting in lieu thereof "HOLDING OR PASSIVE FOREIGN

INVESTMENT COMPANY". **Effective** for tax years of foreign corporations beginning after 12-31-86.

P.L. 99-514, §1810(a)(1)(A):

Amended Code Sec. 904(g) by redesignating paragraph (9) as paragraph (10), and by inserting after paragraph (8) new paragraph (9). For the **effective** date, see Act Sec. 1810(a)(1)(B) and (a)(5), below.

P.L. 99-514, §1810(a)(1)(B), (a)(4) and (a)(5), as amended by P.L. 100-647, §1018(g)(1), provides:

(B) EFFECTIVE DATE.—The amendment made by subparagraph (A) shall take effect on March 28, 1985. In the case of any taxable year ending after such date of any corporation treated as a United States-owned foreign corporation by reason of the amendment made by subparagraph (A)—

(i) only income received or accrued by such corporation after such date shall be taken into account under section 904(g) of the Internal Revenue Code of 1954; except that

(ii) paragraph (5) of such section 904(g) shall be applied by taking into account all income received or accrued by such corporation during such taxable year.

* * *

(4) COORDINATION WITH TREATY OBLIGATIONS.—Section 904(g) of the Internal Revenue Code of 1954 shall apply notwithstanding any treaty obligation of the United States to the contrary (whether entered into on, before, or after the date of the enactment of this Act) unless (in the case of a treaty entered into after the date of the enactment of this Act) such treaty by specific reference to such section 904(g) clearly expresses the intent to override the provisions of such section.

(5) TRANSITIONAL RULE RELATED TO SECTION 121(b)(5) OF THE ACT.—For purposes of section 121(b)(5) of the Tax Reform Act of 1984 (relating to separate application of section 904 in case of income covered by transitional rules), any carryover under section 904(c) of the Internal Revenue Code of 1954 allowed to a taxpayer which was incorporated on August 31, 1962, attributable to taxes paid or accrued in taxable years beginning in 1981, 1982, 1983, or 1984, with respect to amounts included in gross income under section 951 of such Code in respect of a controlled foreign corporation which was incorporated on May 27, 1977, shall be treated as taxes paid or accrued on income separately treated under such section 121(b)(5).

• **1984, Deficit Reduction Act of 1984 (P.L. 98-369)**

P.L. 98-369, §121(a):

Amended Code Sec. 904 by redesignating subsections (g) and (h) as subsections (h) and (i) and by inserting after subsection (f) new subsection (g). **Effective** as noted in Act Sec. 121(b), below:

P.L. 98-369, §121(b), as amended by P.L. 99-514, §1810(a), provides:

(b) Effective Date.—

(1) In General.—Except as otherwise provided in this subsection, the amendment made by subsection (a) shall take effect on the date of the enactment of this Act. In the case of any taxable year of any United States-owned foreign corporation ending after the date of the enactment of this Act—

(A) only income received or accrued by such foreign corporation after such date of enactment shall be taken into account under section 904(g) of the Internal Revenue Code of 1954 (as added by subsection (a)); except that

(B) paragraph (5) of such section 904(g) (relating to exception where small amount of United States source income) shall be applied by taking into account all income received or accrued by such foreign corporation during such taxable year.

(2) Special Rule for Applicable CFC.—

(A) In General.—In the case of qualified interest received or accrued by an applicable CFC before January 1, 1992—

(i) such interest shall not be taken into account under section 904(g) of the Internal Revenue Code of 1954 (as added by subsection (a)), except that

(ii) such interest shall be taken into account for purposes of applying paragraph (5) of such section 904(g) (relating to exception where small amount of United States source income).

(B) Qualified Interest.—For purposes of subparagraph (A), the term "qualified interest" means—

(i) the aggregate amount of interest received or accrued during any taxable year by an applicable CFC on United States affiliate obligations held by such applicable CFC, multiplied by,

(ii) a fraction (not in excess of 1)—

(I) the numerator of which is the sum of the aggregate principal amount of United States affiliate obligations held by the applicable CFC on March 31, 1984, but not in excess of the applicable limit, and

(II) the denominator of which is the average daily principal amount of United States affiliate obligations held by such applicable CFC during the taxable year.

Proper adjustments shall be made to the numerator described in clause (ii)(I) for original issue discount accruing after March 31, 1984, on CFC obligations and United States affiliate obligations.

(C) Adjustment for Retirement of CFC Obligations.—The amount described in subparagraph (B)(ii)(I) for any taxable year shall be reduced by the sum of—

(i) the excess of (I) the aggregate principal amount of CFC obligations which are outstanding on March 31, 1984, but only with respect to obligations issued before March 8, 1984, or issued after March 7, 1984, by the applicable CFC pursuant to a binding commitment in effect on March 7, 1984, over (II) the average daily outstanding principal amount during the taxable year of the CFC obligations described in subclause (I), and

(ii) the portion of the equity of such applicable CFC allocable to the excess described in clause (i) (determined on the basis of the debt-equity ratio of such applicable CFC on March 31, 1984).

(D) Applicable CFC.—For purposes of this paragraph, the term "applicable CFC" means any controlled foreign corporation (within the meaning of section 957)—

(i) which was in existence on March 31, 1984, and

(ii) the principal purpose of which on such date consisted of the issuing of CFC obligations (or short-term borrowings from nonaffiliated persons) and lending the proceeds of such obligations (or such borrowings) to affiliates.

(E) Affiliates: United States Affiliates.—For purposes of this paragraph—

(i) Affiliate.—The term "affiliate" means any person who is a related person (within the meaning of section 482 of the Internal Revenue Code of 1954) to the applicable CFC.

(ii) United States Affiliate.—The term "United States affiliate" means any United States person which is an affiliate of the applicable CFC.

(iii) Treatment of Certain Foreign Corporations Engaged in Business in United States.—For purposes of clause (ii), a foreign corporation shall be treated as a United States person with respect to any interest payment made by such corporation if—

(I) at least 50 percent of the gross income from all sources of such corporation for the 3-year period ending with the close of its last taxable year ending on or before March 31, 1984, was effectively connected with the conduct of a trade or business within the United States, and

(II) at least 50 percent of the gross income from all sources of such corporation for the 3-year period ending with the close of its taxable year preceding the payment of such interest was effectively connected with the conduct of a trade or business within the United States.

(F) United States Affiliate Obligations.—For purposes of this paragraph, the term "United States affiliate obligations" means any obligation of (and payable by) a United States affiliate.

(G) CFC Obligation.—For purposes of this paragraph, the term "CFC obligation" means any obligation of (and issued by) a CFC if—

(i) the requirements of clause (i) of section 163(f)(2)(B) of the Internal Revenue Code of 1954 are met with respect to such obligation, and

(ii) in the case of an obligation issued after December 31, 1982, the requirements of clause (ii) of such section 163(f)(2)(B) are met with respect to such obligation.

(H) Treatment of Obligations with Original Issue Discount.—For purposes of this paragraph, in the case of any obligation with original issue discount, the principal amount of such obligation as of any day shall be treated as equal to the revised issue price as of such day (as defined in section 1278(a)(4) of the Internal Revenue Code of 1954).

(I) Applicable Limit.—For purposes of subparagraph (B)(ii)(I), the term "applicable limit" means the sum of—

(i) the equity of the applicable CFC on March 31, 1984, and

(ii) the aggregate principal amount of CFC obligations outstanding on March 31, 1984, which were issued by an applicable CFC—

(I) before March 8, 1984, or

(II) after March 7, 1984, pursuant to a binding commitment in effect on March 7, 1984.

(3) Exception for Certain Term Obligations.—The amendments made by subsection (a) shall not apply to interest on any term obligations held by a foreign corporation on March 7, 1984. The preceding sentence shall not apply to any United States affiliate obligation (as defined in paragraph (2)(F)) held by an applicable CFC (as defined in paragraph (2)(D)).

(4) Definitions.—Any term used in this subsection which is also used in section 904(g) of the Internal Revenue Code of 1954 (as added by subsection (a)) shall have the meaning given such term by such section 904(g).

(5) Separate Application of Section 904 in Case of Income Covered by Transitional Rules.—Subsections (a), (b), and (c) of section 904 of the Internal Revenue Code of 1954 shall be applied separately to any amount not treated as income derived from sources within the United States but which (but for the provisions of paragraph (2) or (3) of this subsection) would be so treated under the amendments made by subsection (a). Any such separate application shall be made before any separate application required under section 904(d) of such Code.

(6) Application of Paragraph (5) Delayed in Certain Cases.—In the case of a foreign corporation—

(A) which is a subsidiary of a domestic corporation which has been engaged in manufacturing for more than 50 years, and

(B) which issued certificates with respect to obligations on—

(i) September 24, 1979, denominated in French francs,

(ii) September 10, 1981, denominated in Swiss francs,

(iii) July 14, 1982, denominated in Swiss francs, and

(iv) December 1, 1982, denominated in United States dollars,

with a total principal amount of less than 200,000,000 United States dollars,

then paragraph (5) shall not apply to the proceeds from relending such obligations or related capital before January 1, 1986.

[Sec. 904(i)—Stricken]

Amendments

• **2013, American Taxpayer Relief Act of 2012 (P.L. 112-240)**

P.L. 112-240, §101(a)(1) and (3), provides:

SEC. 101. PERMANENT EXTENSION AND MODIFICATION OF 2001 TAX RELIEF.

(a) PERMANENT EXTENSION.—

(1) IN GENERAL.—The Economic Growth and Tax Relief Reconciliation Act of 2001 is amended by striking title IX.

* * *

(3) EFFECTIVE DATE.—The amendments made by this subsection shall apply to taxable, plan, or limitation years beginning after December 31, 2012, and estates of

INCOME TAX—FOREIGN TAX CREDIT

decedents dying, gifts made, or generation skipping transfers after December 31, 2012.

P.L. 112-240, §104(c)(2)(K):

Amended Code Sec. 904 by striking subsection (i) and by redesignating subsections (j), (k), and (l) as subsections (i), (j), and (k), respectively. **Effective** for tax years beginning after 12-31-2011. Prior to being stricken, Code Sec. 904(i) read as follows:

(i) COORDINATION WITH NONREFUNDABLE PERSONAL CREDITS.—In the case of any taxable year of an individual to which section 26(a)(2) does not apply, for purposes of subsection (a), the tax against which the credit is taken is such tax reduced by the sum of the credits allowable under subpart A of part IV of subchapter A of this chapter (other than sections 23, 24, 25A(i), 25B, 30, 30B, and 30D).

- **2010, Tax Relief, Unemployment Insurance Reauthorization, and Job Creation Act of 2010 (P.L. 111-312)**

P.L. 111-312, §101(b)(1):

Amended Code Sec. 904(i) to read as such provision would read if section 10909 of the Patient Protection and Affordable Care Act (P.L. 111-148) had never been enacted. **Effective** for tax years beginning after 12-31-2011.

- **2010, Patient Protection and Affordable Care Act (P.L. 111-148)**

P.L. 111-148, §10909(b)(2)(K):

Amended Code Sec. 904(i) by striking "23," before "24". **Effective** for tax years beginning after 12-31-2009.

P.L. 111-148, §10909(c), as amended by P.L. 111-312, §101(b)(1), provides:

(c) SUNSET PROVISION.—Each provision of law amended by this section is amended to read as such provision would read if this section had never been enacted. The amendments made by the preceding sentence shall apply to taxable years beginning after December 31, 2011.

- **2009, American Recovery and Reinvestment Tax Act of 2009 (P.L. 111-5)**

P.L. 111-5, §1004(b)(5):

Amended Code Sec. 904(i) by inserting "25A(i)," after "24,". **Effective** for tax years beginning after 12-31-2008.

P.L. 111-5, §1142(b)(1)(E):

Amended Code Sec. 904(i) by striking "and 25B" and inserting "25B, 30, and 30D". **Effective** for vehicles acquired after 2-17-2009. For a transitional rule, see Act Sec. 1142(d) in the amendment notes for Code Sec. 30.

P.L. 111-5, §1144(b)(1)(E):

Amended Code Sec. 904(i), as amended by this Act, by inserting "30B," after "30". **Effective** for tax years beginning after 12-31-2008.

- **2006, Pension Protection Act of 2006 (P.L. 109-280)**

P.L. 109-280, §811, provides:

SEC. 811. PENSIONS AND INDIVIDUAL RETIREMENT ARRANGEMENT PROVISIONS OF ECONOMIC GROWTH AND TAX RELIEF RECONCILIATION ACT OF 2001 MADE PERMANENT.

Title IX of the Economic Growth and Tax Relief Reconciliation Act of 2001 [P.L. 107-16] shall not apply to the provisions of, and amendments made by, subtitles A through F of title VI [§§601-666]of such Act (relating to pension and individual retirement arrangement provisions).

- **2005, Gulf Opportunity Zone Act of 2005 (P.L. 109-135)**

P.L. 109-135, §402(i)(3)(G):

Amended Code Sec. 904(i). **Effective** for tax years beginning after 12-31-2005. Prior to amendment, Code Sec. 904(i) read as follows:

(i) COORDINATION WITH NONREFUNDABLE PERSONAL CREDITS.—In the case of an individual, for purposes of subsection (a), the tax against which the credit is taken is such tax reduced by the sum of the credits allowable under subpart A of part IV of subchapter A of this chapter (other than sections 23, 24, and 25B). This subsection shall not apply to taxable years beginning during 2000, 2001, 2002, 2003, 2004, or 2005.

P.L. 109-135, §402(i)(3)(H), provides:

(H) APPLICATION OF EGTRRA SUNSET.—The amendments made by this paragraph (and each part thereof) shall be subject to title IX of the Economic Growth and Tax Relief Reconciliation Act of 2001 in the same manner as the provisions of such Act to which such amendment (or part thereof) relates.

- **2004, American Jobs Creation Act of 2004 (P.L. 108-357)**

P.L. 108-357, §402(a):

Amended Code Sec. 904 by redesignating subsection (h) as subsection (i). **Effective** for losses for tax years beginning after 12-31-2006.

- **2004, Working Families Tax Relief Act of 2004 (P.L. 108-311)**

P.L. 108-311, §312(b)(1):

Amended Code Sec. 904(h) by striking "or 2003" and inserting "2003, 2004, or 2005". **Effective** for tax years beginning after 12-31-2003.

P.L. 108-311, §312(b)(2), provides:

(2) The amendments made by sections 201(b), 202(f), and 618(b) of the Economic Growth and Tax Relief Reconciliation Act of 2001 shall not apply to taxable years beginning during 2004 or 2005.

- **2002, Job Creation and Worker Assistance Act of 2002 (P.L. 107-147)**

P.L. 107-147, §601(b)(1):

Amended Code Sec. 904(h) by striking "during 2000 or 2001" and inserting "during 2000, 2001, 2002, or 2003". **Effective** for to tax years beginning after 12-31-2001.

P.L. 107-147, §601(b)(2), provides:

(2) The amendments made by sections 201(b), 202(f), and 618(b) of the Economic Growth and Tax Relief Reconciliation Act of 2001 shall not apply to taxable years beginning during 2002 and 2003.

- **2001, Economic Growth and Tax Relief Reconciliation Act of 2001 (P.L. 107-16)**

P.L. 107-16, §201(b)(2)(G):

Amended Code Sec. 904(h) by inserting "(other than section 24)" after "chapter". **Effective** for tax years beginning after 12-31-2001. [But, see P.L. 107-147, §601(b)(2), and P.L. 108-311, §312(b)(2), above.—CCH.]

P.L. 107-16, §202(f)(2)(C):

Amended Code Sec. 904(h), as amended by Act Sec. 201(b), by striking "section 24" and inserting "sections 23 and 24". **Effective** for tax years beginning after 12-31-2001. [But, see P.L. 107-147, §601(b)(2), and P.L. 108-311, §312(b)(2), above.—CCH.]

P.L. 107-16, §618(b)(2)(D) (as amended by P.L. 107-147, §417(23)(B)):

Amended Code Sec. 904(h), as amended by Act Secs. 201(b) and 202(f), by striking "and 24" and inserting ", 24, and 25B". **Effective** for tax years beginning after 12-31-2001. [But, see P.L. 107-147, §601(b)(2), and P.L. 108-311, §312(b)(2), above.—CCH.]

P.L. 107-16, §901(a)-(b), as amended by P.L. 111-312, §101(a)(1), provides [but see P.L. 109-280, §811, P.L. 111-148, §10909(c), and P.L. 112-240, §101(a)(1) and (3) above]:

SEC. 901. SUNSET OF PROVISIONS OF ACT.

(a) IN GENERAL.—All provisions of, and amendments made by, this Act shall not apply—

(1) to taxable, plan, or limitation years beginning after December 31, 2012, or

(2) in the case of title V, to estates of decedents dying, gifts made, or generation skipping transfers, after December 31, 2012.

(b) APPLICATION OF CERTAIN LAWS.—The Internal Revenue Code of 1986 and the Employee Retirement Income Security Act of 1974 shall be applied and administered to years, estates, gifts, and transfers described in subsection (a) as if the provisions and amendments described in subsection (a) had never been enacted. **Effective** for tax years beginning after 12-31-2001. [But, see P.L. 107-147, §601(b)(2), above.—CCH.]

- **1999, Tax Relief Extension Act of 1999 (P.L. 106-170)**

P.L. 106-170, §501(b)(2):

Amended Code Sec. 904(h) by adding at the end the following: "This subsection shall not apply to taxable years beginning during 2000 or 2001.". **Effective** for tax years beginning after 12-31-98.

- **1984, Deficit Reduction Act of 1984 (P.L. 98-369)**

P.L. 98-369, §121(a):

Amended Code Sec. 904 by redesignating subsection (g) as subsection (h). **Effective** as noted in Act Sec. 121(b) following Code Sec. 904(g).

P.L. 98-369, §474(r)(21):

Amended Code Sec. 904(g), redesignated as (h) by Act Sec. 121. **Effective** for tax years beginning after 12-31-83, and to carrybacks from such years. Prior to amendment, Code Sec. 904(g) read as follows:

(g) Coordination With Credit for the Elderly.—In the case of an individual, for purposes of subsection (a) the tax against which the credit is taken is such tax reduced by the amount of the credit (if any) for the taxable year allowable under section 37 (relating to credit for the elderly and the permanently and totally disabled).

- **1983, Social Security Amendments of 1983 (P.L. 98-21)**

P.L. 98-21, §122(c)(1):

Amended Code Sec. 904(g) by striking out "relating to credit for the elderly" and inserting in place thereof "relating to credit for the elderly and the permanently and totally disabled". **Effective**, generally, for tax years beginning after 1983.

- **1976, Tax Reform Act of 1976 (P.L. 94-455)**

P.L. 94-455, §503(b)(1):

Redesignated Code Sec. 904(g) as Code Sec. 904(h) and added a new Code Sec. 904(g). **Effective** for tax years beginning after 12-31-75.

P.L. 94-455, §1032(a):

Redesignated former Code Sec. 904(f) as Code Sec. 904(g). See amendment note for P.L. 94-455, §1032(a), following Code Sec. 904(f) for **effective** date. Prior to amendment, Code Sec. 904(g) read as follows:

(g) CROSS REFERENCE.—

(1) For increase of applicable limitation under subsection (a) for taxes paid with respect to amounts received which were included in the gross income of the taxpayer for a prior taxable year as a United States shareholder with respect to a controlled foreign corporation, see section 960(b).

(2) For special rule relating to the application of the credit provided by section 901 in the case of affiliated groups which include Western Hemisphere trade corporations for years in which the limitation provided by subsection (a)(2) applies, see section 1503(b).

- **1964, Revenue Act of 1964 (P.L. 88-272)**

P.L. 88-272, §234(b)(6):

Amended Code Sec. 904(g)(2) to change "1503(d)" to "1503(b)". **Effective** for tax years beginning after 12-31-63.

Sec. 904(i)—Stricken

INCOME TAX—FOREIGN TAX CREDIT

• **1962, Revenue Act of 1962 (P.L. 87-834)**

P.L. 87-834, §10(a):

Redesignated Code Sec. 904(f) as 904(g). **Effective** 10-17-62.

P.L. 87-834, §12(b)(2):

Amended Code Sec. 904(g). **Effective** 10-17-62. Prior to amendment, Sec. 904(g) read as follows:

For special rule relating to the application of the credit provided by section 901 in the case of affiliated groups which include Western Hemisphere trade corporations

for years in which the limitation provided by subsection (a)(2) applies, see section 1503(d).

• **1960 (P.L. 86-780)**

P.L. 86-780, §[1](d):

Added subsection (f). **Effective** for tax years beginning after 12-31-60.

[Sec. 904(i)]

(i) LIMITATION ON USE OF DECONSOLIDATION TO AVOID FOREIGN TAX CREDIT LIMITATIONS.—If 2 or more domestic corporations would be members of the same affiliated group if—

(1) section 1504(b) were applied without regard to the exceptions contained therein, and

(2) the constructive ownership rules of section 1563(e) applied for purposes of section 1504(a),

the Secretary may by regulations provide for resourcing the income of any of such corporations or for modifications to the consolidated return regulations to the extent that such resourcing or modifications are necessary to prevent the avoidance of the provisions of this subpart.

Amendments

• **2013, American Taxpayer Relief Act of 2012 (P.L. 112-240)**

P.L. 112-240, §104(c)(2)(K):

Amended Code Sec. 904 by redesignating subsection (j) as subsection (i). **Effective** for tax years beginning after 12-31-2011.

• **2004, American Jobs Creation Act of 2004 (P.L. 108-357)**

P.L. 108-357, §402(a):

Amended Code Sec. 904 by redesignating subsection (i) as subsection (j). **Effective** for losses for tax years beginning after 12-31-2006.

• **1989, Omnibus Budget Reconciliation Act of 1989 (P.L. 101-239)**

P.L. 101-239, §7402(a):

Amended Code Sec. 904 by redesignating subsection (i) as subsection (j) and by inserting after subsection (h) a new subsection (i). **Effective** for tax years beginning after 7-10-89.

[Sec. 904(j)]

(j) CERTAIN INDIVIDUALS EXEMPT.—

(1) IN GENERAL.—In the case of an individual to whom this subsection applies for any taxable year—

(A) the limitation of subsection (a) shall not apply,

(B) no taxes paid or accrued by the individual during such taxable year may be deemed paid or accrued under subsection (c) in any other taxable year, and

(C) no taxes paid or accrued by the individual during any other taxable year may be deemed paid or accrued under subsection (c) in such taxable year.

(2) INDIVIDUALS TO WHOM SUBSECTION APPLIES.—This subsection shall apply to an individual for any taxable year if—

(A) the entire amount of such individual's gross income for the taxable year from sources without the United States consists of qualified passive income,

(B) the amount of the creditable foreign taxes paid or accrued by the individual during the taxable year does not exceed $300 ($600 in the case of a joint return), and

(C) such individual elects to have this subsection apply for the taxable year.

(3) DEFINITIONS.—For purposes of this subsection—

(A) QUALIFIED PASSIVE INCOME.—The term "qualified passive income" means any item of gross income if—

(i) such item of income is passive income (as defined in subsection (d)(2)(B) without regard to clause (iii) thereof), and

(ii) such item of income is shown on a payee statement furnished to the individual.

(B) CREDITABLE FOREIGN TAXES.—The term "creditable foreign taxes" means any taxes for which a credit is allowable under section 901; except that such term shall not include any tax unless such tax is shown on a payee statement furnished to such individual.

(C) PAYEE STATEMENT.—The term "payee statement" has the meaning given to such term by section 6724(d)(2).

(D) ESTATES AND TRUSTS NOT ELIGIBLE.—This subsection shall not apply to any estate or trust.

Amendments

• **2013, American Taxpayer Relief Act of 2012 (P.L. 112-240)**

P.L. 112-240, §104(c)(2)(K):

Amended Code Sec. 904 by redesignating subsection (k) as subsection (j). **Effective** for tax years beginning after 12-31-2011.

• **2004, American Jobs Creation Act of 2004 (P.L. 108-357)**

P.L. 108-357, §402(a):

Amended Code Sec. 904 by redesignating subsection (j) as subsection (k). **Effective** for losses for tax years beginning after 12-31-2006.

P.L. 108-357, §404(f)(6):

Amended Code Sec. 904(j)(3)(A)(i) [prior to redesignation by §402(a)]by striking "subsection (d)(2)(A)" and inserting "subsection (d)(2)(B)". **Effective** generally for tax years beginning after 12-31-2006.

• **1997, Taxpayer Relief Act of 1997 (P.L. 105-34)**

P.L. 105-34, §1101(a):

Amended Code Sec. 904 by redesignating subsection (j) as subsection (k) and by inserting after subsection (i) a new subsection (j). **Effective** for tax years beginning after 12-31-97.

[Sec. 904(k)]

(k) CROSS REFERENCES.—For increase of limitation under subsection (a) for taxes paid with respect to amounts received which were included in the gross income of the taxpayer for a prior taxable year as a United States shareholder with respect to a controlled foreign corporation, see section 960(c).

Amendments

• **2017, Tax Cuts and Jobs Act (P.L. 115-97)**

P.L. 115-97, §14301(c)(19):

Amended Code Sec. 904(k). **Effective** for tax years of foreign corporations beginning after 12-31-2017, and to tax years of United States shareholders in which or with which such tax years of foreign corporations end. Prior to amendment, Code Sec. 904(k) read as follows:

(k) CROSS REFERENCES.—

(1) For increase of limitation under subsection (a) for taxes paid with respect to amounts received which were included in the gross income of the taxpayer for a prior taxable year as a United States shareholder with respect to a controlled foreign corporation, see section 960(b).

(2) For modification of limitation under subsection (a) for purposes of determining the amount of credit which can be taken against the alternative minimum tax, see section 59(a).

• **2013, American Taxpayer Relief Act of 2012 (P.L. 112-240)**

P.L. 112-240, §104(c)(2)(K):

Amended Code Sec. 904 by redesignating subsection (l) as subsection (k). **Effective** for tax years beginning after 12-31-2011.

INCOME TAX—FOREIGN TAX CREDIT

• **2004, American Jobs Creation Act of 2004 (P.L. 108-357)**

P.L. 108-357, § 402(a):

Amended Code Sec. 904 by redesignating subsection (k) as subsection (l). **Effective** for losses for tax years beginning after 12-31-2006.

• **1997, Taxpayer Relief Act of 1997 (P.L. 105-34)**

P.L. 105-34, § 1101(a):

Amended Code Sec. 904 by redesignating subsection (j) as subsection (k). **Effective** for tax years beginning after 12-31-97.

• **1989, Omnibus Budget Reconciliation Act of 1989 (P.L. 101-239)**

P.L. 101-239, § 7402(a):

Amended Code Sec. 904 by redesignating subsection (i) as subsection (j). **Effective** for tax years beginning after 7-10-89.

• **1986, Tax Reform Act of 1986 (P.L. 99-514)**

P.L. 99-514, § 701(e)(4)(H):

Amended Code Sec. 904(i)(2) by striking out "by an individual" and all that follows and inserting in lieu thereof "against the alternative minimum tax, see section 59(a)." **Effective**, generally, for tax years beginning after 12-31-86. However, for special rules, see Act Sec. 701(f)(2)-(7) reproduced under Code Sec. 56. Prior to amendment, Code Sec. 904(i)(2) read as follows:

(2) For modification of limitation under subsection (a) for purposes of determining the amount of credit which can be taken by an individual against the alternative minimum tax, see section 55(c).

• **1984, Deficit Reduction Act of 1984 (P.L. 98-369)**

P.L. 98-369, § 121(a):

Amended Code Sec. 904 by redesignating subsection (h) as subsection (i). **Effective** as noted in Act Sec. 121(b) following Code Sec. 904(g).

• **1978, Revenue Act of 1978 (P.L. 95-600)**

P.L. 95-600, § 421(e)(6):

Amended Code Sec. 904(h). **Effective** for tax years beginning after 12-31-78. Prior to amendment, Code Sec. 904(h) read as follows:

(h) CROSS REFERENCE.—

For increase of limitation under subsection (a) for taxes paid with respect to amounts received which were included in the gross income of the taxpayer for a prior taxable year as a United States shareholder with respect to a controlled foreign corporation, see section 960(b).

• **1976, Tax Reform Act of 1976 (P.L. 94-455)**

P.L. 94-455, § 503(b)(1):

Redesignated former Code Sec. 904(g) as Code Sec. 904(h). **Effective** for tax years beginning after 12-31-75.

P.L. 94-455, § 1031(a):

Amended Code Sec. 904(f). See amendatory note for P.L. 94-455, § 1031(a), following Code Sec. 904(a), for **effective** date. See amendment note for P.L. 94-455, § 1031(a), following Code Sec. 904(f), for prior text of Code Sec. 904(f).

P.L. 94-455, § 1032(a):

Redesignated former Code Sec. 904(f) as Code Sec. 904(g). See amendment note for P.L. 94-455, § 1032(a), following Code Sec. 904(f), for **effective** date.

[Sec. 905]

SEC. 905. APPLICABLE RULES.

[Sec. 905(a)]

(a) YEAR IN WHICH CREDIT TAKEN.—The credits provided in this subpart may, at the option of the taxpayer and irrespective of the method of accounting employed in keeping his books, be taken in the year in which the taxes of the foreign country or the possession of the United States accrued, subject, however, to the conditions prescribed in subsection (c). If the taxpayer elects to take such credits in the year in which the taxes of the foreign country or the possession of the United States accrued, the credits for all subsequent years shall be taken on the same basis, and no portion of any such taxes shall be allowed as a deduction in the same or any succeeding year.

[Sec. 905(b)]

(b) PROOF OF CREDITS.—The credits provided in this subpart shall be allowed only if the taxpayer establishes to the satisfaction of the Secretary—

(1) the total amount of income derived from sources without the United States, determined as provided in part I,

(2) the amount of income derived from each country, the tax paid or accrued to which is claimed as a credit under this subpart, such amount to be determined under regulations prescribed by the Secretary, and

(3) all other information necessary for the verification and computation of such credits.

Amendments

• **1976, Tax Reform Act of 1976 (P.L. 94-455)**

P.L. 94-455, § 1901(a)(114):

Struck out the last sentence of Code Sec. 905(b). **Effective** for tax years beginning after 12-31-76. Prior to being stricken, the last sentence of Code Sec. 905(b) read as follows:

For purposes of this subpart, the recipient of a royalty or other amount paid or accrued as consideration for the use of, or for the privilege of using, copyrights, patents, designs, secret processes and formulas, trademarks, and other like property, and derived from sources within the United Kingdom of Great Britain and Northern Ireland, shall be deemed to have paid or accrued any income, warprofits and excessprofits taxes paid or accrued to the United Kingdom with respect to such royalty or other amount (including the amount by which the payor's United Kingdom tax was increased by inability to deduct such royalty or other amount) if such recipient elects to include in its gross income the amount of such United Kingdom tax.

P.L. 94-455, § 1906(b)(13)(A):

Amended 1954 Code by substituting "Secretary" for "Secretary or his delegate" each place it appeared. **Effective** 2-1-77.

• **1958, Technical Amendments Act of 1958 (P.L. 85-866)**

P.L. 85-866, § 103(b):

Amended Code Sec. 905(b) by adding the last sentence as deleted by P.L. 94-455. **Effective** 1-1-54.

[Sec. 905(c)]

(c) ADJUSTMENTS TO ACCRUED TAXES.—

(1) IN GENERAL.—If—

(A) accrued taxes when paid differ from the amounts claimed as credits by the taxpayer,

(B) accrued taxes are not paid before the date 2 years after the close of the taxable year to which such taxes relate, or

(C) any tax paid is refunded in whole or in part,

the taxpayer shall notify the Secretary, who shall redetermine the amount of the tax for the year or years affected.

(2) SPECIAL RULE FOR TAXES NOT PAID WITHIN 2 YEARS.—

(A) IN GENERAL.—Except as provided in subparagraph (B), in making the redetermination under paragraph (1), no credit shall be allowed for accrued taxes not paid before the date referred to in subparagraph (B) of paragraph (1).

(B) TAXES SUBSEQUENTLY PAID.—Any such taxes if subsequently paid—

(i) shall be taken into account for the taxable year to which such taxes relate, and

(ii) shall be translated as provided in section 986(a)(2)(A).

(3) ADJUSTMENTS.—The amount of tax (if any) due on any redetermination under paragraph (1) shall be paid by the taxpayer on notice and demand by the Secretary, and the amount of tax overpaid (if any) shall be credited or refunded to the taxpayer in accordance with subchapter B of chapter 66 (section 6511 et seq.).

(4) BOND REQUIREMENTS.—In the case of any tax accrued but not paid, the Secretary, as a condition precedent to the allowance of the credit provided in this subpart, may require the taxpayer to give a bond, with sureties satisfactory to and approved by the Secretary, in such sum as the Secretary may require, conditioned on the payment by the taxpayer of any amount of tax found due on any such redetermination. Any such bond shall contain such further conditions as the Secretary may require.

INCOME TAX—FOREIGN TAX CREDIT

(5) OTHER SPECIAL RULES.—In any redetermination under paragraph (1) by the Secretary of the amount of tax due from the taxpayer for the year or years affected by a refund, the amount of the taxes refunded for which credit has been allowed under this section shall be reduced by the amount of any tax described in section 901 imposed by the foreign country or possession of the United States with respect to such refund; but no credit under this subpart, or deduction under section 164, shall be allowed for any taxable year with respect to any such tax imposed on the refund. No interest shall be assessed or collected on any amount of tax due on any redetermination by the Secretary, resulting from a refund to the taxpayer, for any period before the receipt of such refund, except to the extent interest was paid by the foreign country or possession of the United States on such refund for such period.

Amendments

• **2017, Tax Cuts and Jobs Act (P.L. 115-97)**

P.L. 115-97, §14301(c)(20):

Amended Code Sec. 905(c)(1) by striking the last sentence. **Effective** for tax years of foreign corporations beginning after 12-31-2017, and to tax years of United States shareholders in which or with which such tax years of foreign corporations end. Prior to being stricken, the last sentence of Code Sec. 905(c)(1) read as follows:

The Secretary may prescribe adjustments to the pools of post-1986 foreign income taxes and the pools of post-1986 undistributed earnings under sections 902 and 960 in lieu of the redetermination under the preceding sentence.

P.L. 115-97, §14301(c)(21):

Amended Code Sec. 905(c)(2)(B)(i). **Effective** for tax years of foreign corporations beginning after 12-31-2017, and to tax years of United States shareholders in which or with which such tax years of foreign corporations end. Prior to being amended, Code Sec. 905(c)(2)(B)(i) read as follows:

(i) shall be taken into account—

(I) in the case of taxes deemed paid under section 902 or section 960, for the taxable year in which paid (and no redetermination shall be made under this section by reason of such payment), and

(II) in any other case, for the taxable year to which such taxes relate, and

• **1997, Taxpayer Relief Act of 1997 (P.L. 105-34)**

P.L. 105-34, §1102(a)(2):

Amended Code Sec. 905(c). **Effective** for taxes which relate to tax years beginning after 12-31-97. Prior to amendment, Code Sec. 905(c) read as follows:

(c) ADJUSTMENTS ON PAYMENT OF ACCRUED TAXES.—If accrued taxes when paid differ from the amounts claimed as credits by the taxpayer, or if any tax paid is refunded in whole or in part, the taxpayer shall notify the Secretary, who shall redetermine the amount of the tax for the year or years affected. The amount of tax due on such redetermination, if any, shall be paid by the taxpayer on notice and demand by the Secretary, or the amount of tax overpaid, if any, shall be credited or refunded to the taxpayer in accordance with subchapter B of chapter 66 (sec. 6511 and following). In the case of such a tax accrued but not paid, the Secretary, as a condition precedent to the allowance of this credit, may require the taxpayer to give a bond, with sureties satisfactory to and to be approved by the Secretary, in such sum as the Secretary may require, conditioned on the payment by the taxpayer of any amount of tax found due on any such redetermination; and the bond herein prescribed shall contain such further conditions as the Secretary may require. In such redetermination by the Secretary of the amount of tax due from the taxpayer for the year or years affected by a refund, the amount of the taxes refunded for which credit has been allowed under this section shall be reduced by the amount of any tax described in section 901 imposed by the foreign country or possession of the United States with respect to such refund; but no credit under this subpart, and no deduction under section 164 (relating to deduction for taxes) shall be allowed for any taxable year with respect to such tax imposed on the refund. No interest shall be assessed or collected on any amount of tax due on any redetermination by the Secretary, resulting from a refund to the taxpayer, for any period before the receipt of such refund, except to the extent interest was paid by the foreign country or possession of the United States on such refund for such period.

• **1982, Tax Equity and Fiscal Responsibility Act of 1982 (P.L. 97-248)**

P.L. 97-248, §343(a):

Amended Code Sec. 905(c) by striking out the last sentence. **Effective** as if the last sentence of Code Sec. 905(e) had never been enacted. Prior to amendment, the last sentence read as follows: "The preceding sentence shall not apply (with respect to any period after the refund or adjustment in the foreign taxes) if the taxpayer fails to notify the Secretary (on or before the date prescribed by regulations for giving such notice) unless it is shown that such failure is due to reasonable cause and not due to willful neglect."

• **1980 (P.L. 96-603)**

P.L. 96-603, §2(c)(1):

Amended Code Sec. 905(c) by adding a new last sentence. **Effective** with respect to employer contributions or accruals for taxable years beginning after 1979. However, see the historical comment for P.L. 96-603 under Code Sec. 404A(h) for details of elections permitting retroactive application of this amendment with respect to foreign subsidiaries and permitting allowance of prior deductions in case of certain funded branch plans.

• **1976, Tax Reform Act of 1976 (P.L. 94-455)**

P.L. 94-455, §1906(b)(13)(A):

Amended 1954 Code by substituting "Secretary" for "Secretary or his delegate" each place it appeared. **Effective** 2-1-77.

[Sec. 906]

SEC. 906. NONRESIDENT ALIEN INDIVIDUALS AND FOREIGN CORPORATIONS.

[Sec. 906(a)]

(a) ALLOWANCE OF CREDIT.—A nonresident alien individual or a foreign corporation engaged in trade or business within the United States during the taxable year shall be allowed a credit under section 901 for the amount of any income, war profits, and excess profits taxes paid or accrued during the taxable year to any foreign country or possession of the United States with respect to income effectively connected with the conduct of a trade or business within the United States.

Amendments

• **2017, Tax Cuts and Jobs Act (P.L. 115-97)**

P.L. 115-97, §14301(c)(22):

Amended Code Sec. 906(a) by striking "(or deemed, under section 902, paid or accrued during the taxable year)" following "accrued during the taxable year". **Effective** for tax years of foreign corporations beginning after 12-31-2017, and to tax years of United States shareholders in which or with which such tax years of foreign corporations end.

[Sec. 906(b)]

(b) SPECIAL RULES.—

(1) For purposes of subsection (a) and for purposes of determining the deductions allowable under sections 873(a) and 882(c), in determining the amount of any tax paid or accrued to any foreign country or possession there shall not be taken into account any amount of tax to the extent the tax so paid or accrued is imposed with respect to income from sources within the United States which would not be taxed by such foreign country or possession but for the fact that—

(A) in the case of a nonresident alien individual, such individual is a citizen or resident of such foreign country or possession, or

(B) in the case of a foreign corporation, such corporation was created or organized under the law of such foreign country or possession or is domiciled for tax purposes in such country or possession.

(2) For purposes of subsection (a), in applying section 904 the taxpayer's taxable income shall be treated as consisting only of the taxable income effectively connected with the taxpayer's conduct of a trade or business within the United States.

(3) The credit allowed pursuant to subsection (a) shall not be allowed against any tax imposed by section 871(a) (relating to income of nonresident alien individual not connected with United States business) or 881 (relating to income of foreign corporations not connected with United States business).

(4) [Stricken.]

(5) [Stricken.]

(6) No credit shall be allowed under this section against the tax imposed by section 884.

Amendments

• **2017, Tax Cuts and Jobs Act (P.L. 115-97)**

P.L. 115-97, §14301(c)(23):

Amended Code Sec. 906(b) by striking paragraphs (4) and (5). **Effective** for tax years of foreign corporations beginning after 12-31-2017, and to tax years of United States shareholders in which or with which such tax years of foreign corporations end. Prior to being stricken, Code Sec. 906(b)(4)-(5) read as follows:

(4) For purposes of sections 902(a) and 78, a foreign corporation choosing the benefits of this subpart which receives dividends shall, with respect to such dividends, be treated as a domestic corporation.

INCOME TAX—FOREIGN TAX CREDIT

(5) For purposes of section 902, any income, war profits, and excess profits taxes paid or accrued (or deemed paid or accrued) to any foreign country or possession of the United States with respect to income effectively connected with the conduct of a trade or business within the United States shall not be taken into account, and any accumulated profits attributable to such income shall not be taken into account.

• **2007, Tax Technical Corrections Act of 2007 (P.L. 110-172)**

P.L. 110-172, §11(g)(11):

Amended Code Sec. 906(b) by striking paragraph (5) and redesignating paragraphs (6) and (7) as paragraphs (5) and (6), respectively. **Effective** 12-29-2007. Prior to being stricken, Code Sec. 906(b)(5) read as follows:

(5) No credit shall be allowed under this section for any income, war profits, and excess profits taxes paid or accrued with respect to the foreign trade income (within the meaning of section 923(b)) of a FSC.

• **1988, Technical and Miscellaneous Revenue Act of 1988 (P.L. 100-647)**

P.L. 100-647, §1012(q)(10):

Amended Code Sec. 906(b) by redesignating paragraph (6), which was added by P.L. 99-514, §1241(c), as paragraph (7). **Effective** as if included in the provision of P.L. 99-514 to which it relates.

• **1986, Tax Reform Act of 1986 (P.L. 99-514)**

P.L. 99-514, §1241(c):

Amended Code Sec. 906(b) by adding at the end thereof paragraph (6). **Effective** for tax years beginning after 12-31-86.

P.L. 99-514, §1876(d)(3):

Amended Code Sec. 906(b) by adding at the end thereof new paragraph (6). **Effective** as if included in the provision of P.L. 98-369 to which it relates.

• **1984, Deficit Reduction Act of 1984 (P.L. 98-369)**

P.L. 98-369, §801(d)(3):

Amended Code Sec. 906(b) by adding new paragraph (5). **Effective** for transactions after 12-31-84, in tax years ending after such date.

• **1966, Foreign Investors Tax Act of 1966 (P.L. 89-809)**

P.L. 89-809, §106(a)(1):

Added new Code Sec. 906. **Effective** for tax years beginning after 12-31-66. In applying Code Sec. 904 with respect to Code Sec. 906, no amount may be carried from or to any tax year beginning before 1-1-67, and no such year shall be taken into account.

[Sec. 907]

SEC. 907. SPECIAL RULES IN CASE OF FOREIGN OIL AND GAS INCOME.

[Sec. 907(a)]

(a) REDUCTION IN AMOUNT ALLOWED AS FOREIGN TAX UNDER SECTION 901.—In applying section 901, the amount of any foreign oil and gas taxes paid or accrued (or deemed to have been paid) during the taxable year which would (but for this subsection) be taken into account for purposes of section 901 shall be reduced by the amount (if any) by which the amount of such taxes exceeds the product of—

(1) the amount of the combined foreign oil and gas income for the taxable year,

(2) multiplied by—

(A) in the case of a corporation, the percentage which is equal to the highest rate of tax specified under section 11(b), or

(B) in the case of an individual, a fraction the numerator of which is the tax against which the credit under section 901(a) is taken and the denominator of which is the taxpayer's entire taxable income.

Amendments

• **2008, Energy Improvement and Extension Act of 2008 (P.L. 110-343)**

P.L. 110-343, Division B, §402(a):

Amended Code Sec. 907(a). **Effective** for tax years beginning after 12-31-2008. Prior to amendment, Code Sec. 907(a) read as follows:

(a) REDUCTION IN AMOUNT ALLOWED AS FOREIGN TAX UNDER SECTION 901.—In applying section 901, the amount of any oil and gas extraction taxes paid or accrued (or deemed to have been paid) during the taxable year which would (but for this subsection) be taken into account for purposes of section 901 shall be reduced by the amount (if any) by which the amount of such taxes exceeds the product of—

(1) the amount of the foreign oil and gas extraction income for the taxable year,

(2) multiplied by—

(A) in the case of a corporation, the percentage which is equal to the highest rate of tax specified under section 11(b), or

(B) in the case of an individual, a fraction the numerator of which is the tax against which the credit under section 901(a) is taken and the denominator of which is the taxpayer's entire taxable income.

• **1978, Revenue Act of 1978 (P.L. 95-600)**

P.L. 95-600, §301(b)(14):

Amended Code Sec. 907(a)(2) to read "(2) the percentage which is equal to the highest rate of tax specified in section 11(b).". **Effective** for tax years beginning after 12-31-78. [This amendment apparently duplicates the amendment to Code Sec. 907(a) made by P.L. 95-600, §701(u)(8)(A)—CCH.]

P.L. 95-600, §701(u)(8)(A):

Amended Code Sec. 907(a). **Effective** as set forth in P.L. 95-600, §701(u)(8)(D), below. Prior to amendment, Code Sec. 907(a) read as follows:

(a) REDUCTION IN AMOUNT ALLOWED AS FOREIGN TAX UNDER SECTION 901.—In applying section 901, the amount of any oil and gas extraction taxes paid or accrued (or deemed to have been paid) during the taxable year which would (but for this subsection) be taken into account for purposes of section 901 shall be reduced by the amount (if any) by which the amount of such taxes exceeds the product of—

(1) the amount of the foreign oil and gas extraction income for the taxable year, multiplied by

(2) the percentage which is the sum of the normal tax rate and the surtax rate for the taxable year specified in section 11.

P.L. 95-600, §701(u)(8)(D), provides:

(D) Effective dates.—

(i) The amendments made by this paragraph shall apply, in the case of individuals, to taxable years ending after December 31, 1974, and, in the case of corporations, to taxable years ending after December 31, 1976.

(ii) In the case of any taxable year ending after December 31, 1975, with respect to foreign oil related income (within the meaning of section 907(c) of the Internal Revenue Code of 1954), the overall limitation provided by section 904(a)(2) of such Code shall apply and the per-country limitation provided by section 904(a)(1) of such Code shall not apply.

• **1976, Tax Reform Act of 1976 (P.L. 94-455)**

P.L. 94-455, §1035(a):

Amended Code Sec. 907(a). **Effective** for tax years ending after 12-31-76. Prior to amendment, Code Sec. 907(a) read as follows:

(a) REDUCTION IN AMOUNT ALLOWED AS FOREIGN TAX UNDER SECTION 901.—In applying section 901, the amount of any income, war profits, and excess profits taxes paid or accrued (or deemed to have been paid) during the taxable year with respect to foreign oil and gas extraction income which would (but for this subsection) be taken into account for purposes of section 901 shall be reduced by the amount (if any) by which the amount of such taxes exceeds the product of—

(1) the amount of the foreign oil and gas extraction income for the taxable year, multiplied by

(2) the percentage which is—

(A) in taxable years ending in 1975, 110 percent of,

(B) in taxable years ending in 1976, 105 percent of, and

(C) in taxable years ending after 1976, 2 percentage points above,

the sum of the normal tax rate and the surtax rate for the taxable year specified in section 11.

P.L. 94-455, §1035(c) (as amended by P.L. 95-600, §701(u)(9) and §703(h)(1)), provides:

(c) TAX CREDIT FOR PRODUCTION-SHARING CONTRACTS.

(1) For purposes of section 901 of the Internal Revenue Code of 1954, there shall be treated as income, war profits, and excess profits taxes to be taken into account under section 907(a) of such Code amounts designated as income taxes of a foreign government by such government (which otherwise would not be treated as taxes for purposes of section 901 of such Code) with respect to production-sharing contracts for the extraction of foreign oil or gas.

(2) The amounts specified in paragraph (1) shall not exceed the lesser of—

(A) the product of the foreign oil and gas extraction income (as defined in section 907(c) of such Code) with respect to all such production-sharing contracts multiplied by the sum of the normal tax rate and the surtax rate for the taxable year specified in section 11 of such Code, or

(B) the excess of the total amount of foreign oil and gas extraction income (as so defined) for the taxable year multiplied by the sum of the normal tax rate and the surtax rate for the taxable year specified in section 11 of such Code over the amount of any income, war profits, and excess profits taxes paid or accrued (or deemed to have been paid) without regard to paragraph (1) during the taxable year with respect to foreign oil and gas extraction income.

(3) The production-sharing contracts taken into account for purposes of paragraph (1) shall be those contracts which were entered into before April 8, 1976, for the sharing of foreign oil and gas production with a foreign government (or an entity owned by such government) with respect to which amounts claimed as taxes paid or accrued to such foreign government for taxable years beginning before June 30, 1976, will not be disallowed as taxes. A contract described in the preceding sentence shall be taken into account under paragraph (1) only with respect to amounts (A) paid or accrued to the foreign government before January 1, 1978, and (B) attributable to income earned before such date.

[Sec. 907(b)]

(b) COMBINED FOREIGN OIL AND GAS INCOME; FOREIGN OIL AND GAS TAXES.—For purposes of this section—

(1) COMBINED FOREIGN OIL AND GAS INCOME.—The term "combined foreign oil and gas income" means, with respect to any taxable year, the sum of—

(A) foreign oil and gas extraction income, and

(B) foreign oil related income.

(2) FOREIGN OIL AND GAS TAXES.—The term "foreign oil and gas taxes" means, with respect to any taxable year, the sum of—

(A) oil and gas extraction taxes, and

(B) any income, war profits, and excess profits taxes paid or accrued (or deemed to have been paid or accrued under section 960) during the taxable year with respect to foreign oil related income (determined without regard to subsection (c)(4)) or loss which would be taken into account for purposes of section 901 without regard to this section.

Amendments

- **2017, Tax Cuts and Jobs Act (P.L. 115-97)**

P.L. 115-97, §14301(c)(24):

Amended Code Sec. 907(b)(2)(B) by striking "902 or" following "accrued under section". **Effective** for tax years of foreign corporations beginning after 12-31-2017, and to tax years of United States shareholders in which or with which such tax years of foreign corporations end.

- **2008, Energy Improvement and Extension Act of 2008 (P.L. 110-343)**

P.L. 110-343, Division B, §402(a):

Amended Code Sec. 907(b). **Effective** for tax years beginning after 12-31-2008. Prior to amendment, Code Sec. 907(b) read as follows:

(b) FOREIGN TAXES ON FOREIGN OIL RELATED INCOME.—For purposes of this subtitle, in the case of taxes paid or accrued to any foreign country with respect to foreign oil related income, the term "income, war profits, and excess profits taxes" shall not include any amount paid or accrued after December 31, 1982, to the extent that the Secretary determines that the foreign law imposing such amount of tax is structured, or in fact operates, so that the amount of tax imposed with respect to foreign oil related income will generally be materially greater, over a reasonable period of time, than the amount generally imposed on income that is neither foreign oil related income nor foreign oil and gas extraction income. In computing the amount not treated as tax under this subsection, such amount shall be treated as a deduction under the foreign law.

- **1982, Tax Equity and Fiscal Responsibility Act of 1982 (P.L. 97-248)**

P.L. 97-248, §211(c)(1):

Amended Code Sec. 907(b). **Effective** for tax years beginning after 12-31-82. Prior to amendment, Code Sec. 907(b) read as follows:

"(b) Application of Section 904 Limitation.—The provisions of section 904 shall be applied separately with respect to—

(1) foreign oil related income, and

(2) other taxable income."

P.L. 97-248, §211(e)(2), as amended by P.L. 97-448, §306(a)(5) and P.L. 98-369, §712(e), provides:

"(2) Retention of old sections 907(b) and 904(f)(4) where taxpayer had separate basket foreign loss.—

"(A) IN GENERAL.—If, after applying old sections 907(b) and 904(f)(4) to a taxable year beginning before January 1, 1983, the taxpayer had a separate basket foreign loss, such loss shall not be recaptured from income of a kind not taken into account in computing the amount of such separate basket foreign loss more rapidly than ratably over the 8-year period (or such shorter period as the taxpayer may select) beginning with the first taxable year beginning after December 31, 1982.

"(B) DEFINITIONS.—For purposes of this paragraph—

"(i) The term 'separate basket foreign loss' means any foreign loss attributable to activities taken into account (or not taken into account) in determining foreign oil related income (as defined in old section 907(c)(2)).

"(ii) An 'old' section is such section as in effect on the day before the date of the enactment of this Act."

- **1978, Revenue Act of 1978 (P.L. 95-600)**

P.L. 95-600, §701(u)(8)(B):

Amended Code Sec. 907(b). **Effective** as set forth in §701(u)(8)(D). See historical comment on P.L. 95-600, §701(u)(8)(D) under Code Sec. 907(a). Prior to amendment, Code Sec. 907(b) read as follows:

"(b) APPLICATION OF SECTION 904 LIMITATION.—

(1) CORPORATIONS.—In the case of a corporation, the provisions of section 904 shall be applied separately with respect to—

(A) foreign oil related income, and

(B) other taxable income.

(2) OTHER TAXPAYERS.—In the case of a taxpayer other than a corporation, the provisions of subsection (a) shall not apply and the provisions of section 904 shall be applied separately with respect to—

(A) foreign oil and gas extraction income, and

(B) other taxable income (including other foreign oil related income)."

- **1976, Tax Reform Act of 1976 (P.L. 94-455)**

P.L. 94-455, §1032(b)(1):

Struck out "In the case of a corporation, with respect to foreign oil-related income, and in the case of a taxpayer other than a corporation, with respect to foreign oil and gas extraction income, the overall limitation provided by section 904(a)(2) shall apply and the per-country limitation provided by subsection (a)(1) shall not apply." at the end of Code Sec. 907(b). **Effective** for tax years beginning after 12-31-75.

P.L. 94-455, §1035(b):

Amended Code Sec. 907(b). **Effective** for tax years ending after 12-31-74, except that the last sentence (deleted by P.L. 94-455, §1032(b)(1)) of Code Sec. 907(b) shall apply only to tax years ending after 12-31-75. Prior to amendment, Code Sec. 907(b) read as follows:

(b) APPLICATION OF SECTION 904 LIMITATION.—The provisions of section 904 shall be applied separately with respect to—

(1) foreign oil related income, and

(2) other taxable income.

With respect to foreign oil related income, the overall limitation provided by section 904(a)(2) shall apply and the percountry limitation provided by section 904(a)(1) shall not apply.

[Sec. 907(c)]

(c) FOREIGN INCOME DEFINITIONS AND SPECIAL RULES.—For purposes of this section—

(1) FOREIGN OIL AND GAS EXTRACTION INCOME.—The term "foreign oil and gas extraction income" means the taxable income derived from sources without the United States and its possessions from—

(A) the extraction (by the taxpayer or any other person) of minerals from oil or gas wells, or

(B) the sale or exchange of assets used by the taxpayer in the trade or business described in subparagraph (A).

Such term does not include any dividend or interest income which is passive income (as defined in section 904(d)(2)(A)).

(2) FOREIGN OIL RELATED INCOME.—The term "foreign oil related income" means the taxable income derived from sources outside the United States and its possessions from—

(A) the processing of minerals extracted (by the taxpayer or by any other person) from oil or gas wells into their primary products,

(B) the transportation of such minerals or primary products,

(C) the distribution or sale of such minerals or primary products,

(D) the disposition of assets used by the taxpayer in the trade or business described in subparagraph (A), (B), or (C), or

(E) the performance of any other related service.

Such term does not include any dividend or interest income which is passive income (as defined in section 904(d)(2)(A)).

(3) DIVIDENDS, INTEREST, PARTNERSHIP DISTRIBUTION, ETC.—The term "foreign oil and gas extraction income" and the term "foreign oil related income" include—

(A) interest, to the extent the category of income of such interest is determined under section 904(d)(3),

(B) amounts with respect to which taxes are deemed paid under section 960, and

(C) the taxpayer's distributive share of the income of partnerships,

to the extent such dividends, interest, amounts, or distributive share is attributable to foreign oil and gas extraction income, or to foreign oil related income, as the case may be; except that interest described in subparagraph (A) shall not be taken into account in computing foreign oil and gas extraction income but shall be taken into account in computing foreign oil-related income.

(4) RECAPTURE OF FOREIGN OIL AND GAS LOSSES BY RECHARACTERIZING LATER COMBINED FOREIGN OIL AND GAS INCOME.—

(A) IN GENERAL.—The combined foreign oil and gas income of a taxpayer for a taxable year (determined without regard to this paragraph) shall be reduced—

(i) first by the amount determined under subparagraph (B), and

INCOME TAX—FOREIGN TAX CREDIT

(ii) then by the amount determined under subparagraph (C).

The aggregate amount of such reductions shall be treated as income (from sources without the United States) which is not combined foreign oil and gas income.

(B) REDUCTION FOR PRE-2009 FOREIGN OIL EXTRACTION LOSSES.—The reduction under this paragraph shall be equal to the lesser of—

(i) the foreign oil and gas extraction income of the taxpayer for the taxable year (determined without regard to this paragraph), or

(ii) the excess of—

(I) the aggregate amount of foreign oil extraction losses for preceding taxable years beginning after December 31, 1982, and before January 1, 2009, over

(II) so much of such aggregate amount as was recharacterized under this paragraph (as in effect before and after the date of the enactment of the Energy Improvement and Extension Act of 2008) for preceding taxable years beginning after December 31, 1982.

(C) REDUCTION FOR POST-2008 FOREIGN OIL AND GAS LOSSES.—The reduction under this paragraph shall be equal to the lesser of—

(i) the combined foreign oil and gas income of the taxpayer for the taxable year (determined without regard to this paragraph), reduced by an amount equal to the reduction under subparagraph (A) for the taxable year, or

(ii) the excess of—

(I) the aggregate amount of foreign oil and gas losses for preceding taxable years beginning after December 31, 2008, over

(II) so much of such aggregate amount as was recharacterized under this paragraph for preceding taxable years beginning after December 31, 2008.

(D) FOREIGN OIL AND GAS LOSS DEFINED.—

(i) IN GENERAL.—For purposes of this paragraph, the term "foreign oil and gas loss" means the amount by which—

(I) the gross income for the taxable year from sources without the United States and its possessions (whether or not the taxpayer chooses the benefits of this subpart for such taxable year) taken into account in determining the combined foreign oil and gas income for such year, is exceeded by

(II) the sum of the deductions properly apportioned or allocated thereto.

(ii) NET OPERATING LOSS DEDUCTION NOT TAKEN INTO ACCOUNT.—For purposes of clause (i), the net operating loss deduction allowable for the taxable year under section 172(a) shall not be taken into account.

(iii) EXPROPRIATION AND CASUALTY LOSSES NOT TAKEN INTO ACCOUNT.—For purposes of clause (i), there shall not be taken into account—

(I) any foreign expropriation loss (as defined in section 172(h) (as in effect on the day before the date of the enactment of the Revenue Reconciliation Act of 1990)) for the taxable year, or

(II) any loss for the taxable year which arises from fire, storm, shipwreck, or other casualty, or from theft,

to the extent such loss is not compensated for by insurance or otherwise.

(iv) FOREIGN OIL EXTRACTION LOSS.—For purposes of subparagraph (B)(ii)(I), foreign oil extraction losses shall be determined under this paragraph as in effect on the day before the date of the enactment of the Energy Improvement and Extension Act of 2008.

(5) OIL AND GAS EXTRACTION TAXES.—The term "oil and gas extraction taxes" means any income, war profits, and excess profits tax paid or accrued (or deemed to have been paid under section 960) during the taxable year with respect to foreign oil and gas extraction income (determined without regard to paragraph (4)) or loss which would be taken into account for purposes of section 901 without regard to this section.

Amendments

• **2018, Tax Technical Corrections Act of 2018 (P.L. 115-141)**

P.L. 115-141, §401(a)(158), Div. U:

Amended Code Sec. 907(c)(3)(C) by striking the period after "partnerships" and inserting a comma. **Effective** 3-23-2018.

• **2017, Tax Cuts and Jobs Act (P.L. 115-97)**

P.L. 115-97, §14301(c)(25)(A)-(B):

Amended Code Sec. 907(c)(3)(A) [sic] by striking subparagraph (A) and inserting a new subpargraph (A), and by striking "section 960(a)" in subparagraph (B) and inserting "section 960". **Effective** for tax years of foreign corporations beginning after 12-31-2017, and to tax years of United States shareholders in which or with which such tax years of foreign corporations end. Prior to being stricken, Code Sec. 907(c)(3)(A) read as follows:

(A) dividends and interest from a foreign corporation in respect of which taxes are deemed paid by the taxpayer under section 902,

P.L. 115-97, §14301(c)(26):

Amended Code Sec. 907(c)(5) by striking "902 or" following "paid under section". **Effective** for tax years of foreign corporations beginning after 12-31-2017, and to tax years of United States shareholders in which or with which such tax years of foreign corporations end.

• **2008, Energy Improvement and Extension Act of 2008 (P.L. 110-343)**

P.L. 110-343, Division B, §402(b):

Amended Code Sec. 907(c)(4). **Effective** for tax years beginning after 12-31-2008. Prior to amendment, Code Sec. 907(c)(4) read as follows:

(4) RECAPTURE OF FOREIGN OIL AND GAS EXTRACTION LOSSES BY RECHARACTERIZING LATER EXTRACTION INCOME.—

(A) IN GENERAL.—That portion of the income of the taxpayer for the taxable year which (but for this paragraph) would be treated as foreign oil and gas extraction income shall be treated as income (from sources without the United States) which is not foreign oil and gas extraction income to the extent of the excess of—

(i) the aggregate amount of foreign oil extraction losses for preceding taxable years beginning after December 31, 1982, over

(ii) so much of such aggregate amount as was recharacterized under this subparagraph for preceding taxable years beginning after December 31, 1982.

(B) FOREIGN OIL EXTRACTION LOSS DEFINED.—

(i) IN GENERAL.—For purposes of this paragraph, the term "foreign oil extraction loss" means the amount by which—

(I) the gross income for the taxable year from sources without the United States and its possessions (whether or not the taxpayer chooses the benefits of this subpart for such taxable year) taken into account in determining the foreign oil and gas extraction income for such year, is exceeded by

(II) the sum of the deductions properly apportioned or allocated thereto.

(ii) NET OPERATING LOSS DEDUCTION NOT TAKEN INTO ACCOUNT.—For purposes of clause (i), the net operating loss deduction allowable for the taxable year under section 172(a) shall not be taken into account.

(iii) EXPROPRIATION AND CASUALTY LOSSES NOT TAKEN INTO ACCOUNT.—For purposes of clause (i), there shall not be taken into account—

(I) any foreign expropriation loss (as defined in section 172(h) (as in effect on the day before the date of the enactment of the Revenue Reconciliation Act of 1990)) for the taxable year, or

(II) any loss for the taxable year which arises from fire, storm, shipwreck, or other casualty, or from theft,

to the extent such loss is not compensated for by insurance or otherwise.

• **1996, Small Business Job Protection Act of 1996 (P.L. 104-188)**

P.L. 104-188, §1704(t)(36):

Amended Code Sec. 907(c)(4)(B)(iii)(I) by inserting "(as in effect on the day before the date of the enactment of the Revenue Reconciliation Act of 1990)" after "section 172(h)". **Effective** 8-20-96.

• **1993, Omnibus Budget Reconciliation Act of 1993 (P.L. 103-66)**

P.L. 103-66, §13235(a)(1)(A):

Amended Code Sec. 907(c)(1) by adding at the end thereof a new flush sentence. **Effective** for tax years beginning after 12-31-92.

P.L. 103-66, §13235(a)(1)(B):

Amended Code Sec. 907(c)(2) by adding at the end thereof a new flush sentence. **Effective** for tax years beginning after 12-31-92.

• **1988, Technical and Miscellaneous Revenue Act of 1988 (P.L. 100-647)**

P.L. 100-647, §1012(g)(6)(A)-(B):

Amended Code Sec. 907(c)(3) by striking out subparagraph (B) and redesignating subparagraphs (C) and (D) as subparagraphs (B) and (C), respectively, and by striking out "and dividends described in subparagraph (B)" after "subparagraph (A)". **Effective** as if included in the provision of P.L. 99-514 to which it relates. Prior to amendment, Code Sec. 907(c)(3)(B) read as follows:

Sec. 907(c)(4)(A)(ii)

INCOME TAX—FOREIGN TAX CREDIT

(B) dividends from a domestic corporation which are treated under section 861(a)(2)(A) as income from sources without the United States,

• **1982, Tax Equity and Fiscal Responsibility Act of 1982 (P.L. 97-248)**

P.L. 97-248, §211(a):

Amended Code Sec. 907(c)(4). **Effective** for tax years beginning after 12-31-82. See the amendment notes for P.L. 97-248 following Code Sec. 907(b) for a special rule. Prior to amendment, it read as follows:

"(4) Certain losses.—If for any foreign country for any taxble year the taxpayer would have a net operating loss if only items from sources within such country (including deductions properly apportioned or allocated thereto) which relate to the extraction of minerals from oil or gas wells were taken into account, such items—

(A) shall not be taken into account in computing foreign oil and gas extraction income for such year, but

(B) shall be taken into account in computing foreign oil related income for such year."

P.L. 97-248, §211(b):

Amended Code Sec. 907(c)(2). **Effective** for tax years beginning after 12-31-82. See also the amendment notes for P.L. 97-248 following Code Sec. 907(b) for a special rule. Prior to amendment, Code Sec. 907(c)(2) read as follows:

"(2) Foreign oil related income.—The term `foreign oil related income' means the taxable income derived from sources outside the United States and its possessions from—

(A) the extraction (by the taxpayer or any other person) of minerals from oil or gas wells,

(B) the processing of such minerals into their primary products,

(C) the transportation of such minerals or primary products,

(D) the distribution or sale of such minerals or primary products, or

(E) the sale or exchange of assets used by the taxpayer in the trade or business described in subparagraph (A), (B), (C), or (D)."

• **1976, Tax Reform Act of 1976 (P.L. 94-455)**

P.L. 94-455, §1035(d)(2):

Added Code Sec. 907(c)(5). **Effective** for taxes paid or accrued during tax years ending after 10-4-76.

[Sec. 907(d)]

(d) DISREGARD OF CERTAIN POSTED PRICES, ETC.—For purposes of this chapter, in determining the amount of taxable income in the case of foreign oil and gas extraction income, if the oil or gas is disposed of, or is acquired other than from the government of a foreign country, at a posted price (or other pricing arrangement) which differs from the fair market value for such oil or gas, such fair market value shall be used in lieu of such posted price (or other pricing arrangement).

[Sec. 907(e)—Repealed]

Amendments

• **1990, Omnibus Budget Reconciliation Act of 1990 (P.L. 101-508)**

P.L. 101-508, §11801(a)(32):

Repealed Code Sec. 907(e). **Effective** 11-5-90. Prior to repeal, Code Sec. 907(e) read as follows:

(e) TRANSITIONAL RULES.—

(1) CREDITS ARISING IN TAXABLE YEARS BEGINNING BEFORE JANUARY 1, 1983.—The amount of taxes paid or accrued in any taxable year beginning before January 1, 1983 (hereinafter in this paragraph referred to as the "excess credit year") which under section 904(c) or 907(f) may be deemed paid or accrued in a taxable year beginning after December 31, 1982, shall not exceed the amount which could have been deemed paid or accrued if sections 907(b), 907(f), 907(f)(4) (as in effect on the day before the date of the enactment of the Tax Equity and Fiscal Responsibility Act of 1982) remained in effect for taxable years beginning after December 31, 1982.

(2) CARRYBACK OF CREDITS ARISING IN TAXABLE YEARS BEGINNING AFTER DECEMBER 31, 1982.—The amount of the taxes paid or accrued in a taxable year beginning after December 31, 1982, which may be deemed paid or accrued under section 904(c) or 907(f) in a taxable year beginning before January 1, 1983, shall not exceed the amount which could have been deemed paid or accrued if sections 907(b), 907(f), and 904(f)(4) (as in effect on the day before the date of the enactment of the Tax Equity and Fiscal Responsibility Act of 1982) remained in effect for taxable years beginning after December 31, 1982.

P.L. 101-508, §11821(b), provides:

(b) SAVINGS PROVISION.—If—

(1) any provision amended or repealed by this part) applied to—

(A) any transaction occurring before the date of the enactment of this Act,

(B) any property acquired before such date of enactment, or

(C) any item of income, loss, deduction, or credit taken into account before such date of enactment, and

(2) the treatment of such transaction, property, or item under such provision would (without regard to the amendments made by this part) affect liability for tax for period ending after such date of enactment,

nothing in the amendments made by this part shall be construed to affect the treatment of such transaction, property, or item for purposes of determining liability for tax for periods ending after such date of enactment.

• **1982, Tax Equity and Fiscal Responsibility Act of 1982 (P.L. 97-248)**

P.L. 97-248, §211(d)(1):

Amended Code Sec. 907(e). **Effective** for tax years beginning after 12-31-82. See also the amendment notes for P.L. 97-248 following Code Sec. 907(b) for a special rule. Prior to amendment, it read as follows:

"(e) Transitional Rules.—

(1) Taxable years ending after December 31, 1974.—In applying subsections (d) and (e) of section 904 (as in effect on the day before the date of enactment of the Tax Reform Act of 1976) for purposes of determining the amount which may be carried over from a taxable year ending before January 1, 1975, to any taxable year ending after December 31, 1974—

(A) subsection (a) of this section shall be deemed to have been in effect for such prior taxable year and for all taxable years thereafter, and

(B) the carryover from such prior year shall be divided (effective as of the first day of the first taxable year ending after December 31, 1974) into—

(i) a foreign oil related carryover, and

(ii) another carryover,

on the basis of the proportionate share of the foreign oil related income, or the other taxable income, as the case may be, of the total taxable income taken into account in computing the amount of such carryover.

(2) Taxable years ending after December 31, 1975.—In applying subsections (d) and (e) of section 904 (as in effect on the day before the date of enactment of the Tax Reform Act of 1976) for purposes of determining the amount which may be carried over from a taxable year ending before January 1, 1976, to any taxable year ending after December 31, 1975, if the per-country limitation provided by section 904(a)(1) (as so in effect) applied to such prior taxable year and to the taxpayer's last taxable year ending before January 1, 1976, then in the case of any foreign oil related carryover—

(A) the first sentence of section 904(e)(2) (as so in effect) shall not apply, but

(B) such amount may not exceed the amount which could have been used in such succeeding taxable year if the per-country limitation continued to apply."

• **1976, Tax Reform Act of 1976 (P.L. 94-455)**

P.L. 94-455, §1031(b)(6):

Substituted "(d) and (e) of section 904 (as in effect on the day before the date of enactment of the Tax Reform Act of 1976)" for "(d) and (e) of section 904" in Code Secs. 907(e)(1) and 907(e)(2), substituted "section 904(a)(1) (as so in effect)" for "section 904(a)(1)" in Code Sec. 907(e)(2), and substituted "section 904(e)(2) (as so in effect)" for "section 904(e)(2)" in Code Sec. 907(e)(2)(A). **Effective** as noted in Act Sec. 1031(c), below.

P.L. 94-455, §1031(c), as amended by P.L. 95-600, §§701(u)(6) and 701(u)(7)(B)(ii), provides as follows:

(c) EFFECTIVE DATES.—

(1) IN GENERAL.—Except as provided in paragraphs (2) and (3), the amendments made by this section shall apply to taxable years beginning after December 31, 1975.

(2) EXCEPTION FOR CERTAIN MINING OPERATIONS.—In the case of a domestic corporation or includible corporation in an affiliated group (as defined in section 1504 of the Internal Revenue Code of 1954) which has as of October 1, 1975—

(A) been engaged in the active conduct of the trade or business of the extraction of minerals (of a character with respect to which a deduction for depletion is allowable under section 613 of such Code) outside the United States or its possessions for less than 5 years preceding the date of enactment of this Act,

(B) had deductions properly apportioned or allocated to its gross income from such trade or business in excess of such gross income in at least 2 taxable years,

(C) 80 percent of its gross receipts are from the sale of such minerals, and

(D) made commitments for substantial expansion of such mineral extraction activities

the amendments made by this section shall apply to taxable years beginning after December 31, 1978. In the case of a loss sustained in a taxable year beginning before January 1, 1979, by any corporation to which this paragraph applies, if section 904(a)(1) of such Code (as in effect before the enactment of this Act) applies with respect to such taxable year, the provisions of section 904(f) of such Code shall be applied with respect to such loss under the principles of such section 904(a)(1).

(3) EXCEPTION FOR INCOME FROM POSSESSIONS.—In the case of gross income from sources within a possession of the United States (and the deductions properly apportioned or allocated thereto), the amendments made by this section shall apply to taxable years beginning after December 31, 1978.

(4) CARRYBACKS AND CARRYOVERS IN THE CASE OF MINING OPERATIONS AND INCOME FROM A POSSESSION.—In the case of a taxpayer to whom paragraph (2) or (3) of this subsection applies, section 904(e) of such Code shall apply except that "January 1, 1979" shall be substituted for "January 1, 1976" each place it appears therein. If such a taxpayer elects the overall limitation for a taxable year beginning before January 1, 1979, such section 904(e) shall be applied by substituting "the January 1, of the last year for which such taxpayer is on the per-country limitation" for "January 1, 1976" each place it appears therein.

INCOME TAX—FOREIGN TAX CREDIT

[Sec. 907(f)]

(f) CARRYBACK AND CARRYOVER OF DISALLOWED CREDITS.—

(1) IN GENERAL.—If the amount of the foreign oil and gas taxes paid or accrued during any taxable year exceeds the limitation provided by subsection (a) for such taxable year (hereinafter in this subsection referred to as the "unused credit year"), such excess shall be deemed to be foreign oil and gas taxes paid or accrued in the first preceding taxable year and in any of the first 10 succeeding taxable years, in that order and to the extent not deemed tax paid or accrued in a prior taxable year by reason of the limitation imposed by paragraph (2). Such amount deemed paid or accrued in any taxable year may be availed of only as a tax credit and not as a deduction and only if the taxpayer for such year chooses to have the benefits of this subpart as to taxes paid or accrued for that year to foreign countries or possessions.

(2) LIMITATION.—The amount of the unused foreign oil and gas taxes which under paragraph (1) may be deemed paid or accrued in any preceding or succeeding taxable year shall not exceed the lesser of—

(A) the amount by which the limitation provided by subsection (a) for such taxable year exceeds the sum of—

(i) the foreign oil and gas taxes paid or accrued during such taxable year, plus

(ii) the amounts of the foreign oil and gas taxes which by reason of this subsection are deemed paid or accrued in such taxable year and are attributable to taxable years preceding the unused credit year; or

(B) the amount by which the limitation provided by section 904 for such taxable year exceeds the sum of—

(i) the taxes paid or accrued (or deemed to have been paid under section 960) to all foreign countries and possessions of the United States during such taxable year,

(ii) the amount of such taxes which were deemed paid or accrued in such taxable year under section 904(c) and which are attributable to taxable years preceding the unused credit year, plus

(iii) the amount of the foreign oil and gas taxes which by reason of this subsection are deemed paid or accrued in such taxable year and are attributable to taxable years preceding the unused credit year.

(3) SPECIAL RULES.—

(A) In the case of any taxable year which is an unused credit year under this subsection and which is an unused credit year under section 904(c), the provisions of this subsection shall be applied before section 904(c).

(B) For purposes of determining the amount of taxes paid or accrued in any taxable year which may be deemed paid or accrued in a preceding or succeeding taxable year under section 904(c), any tax deemed paid or accrued in such preceding or succeeding taxable year under this subsection shall be considered to be tax paid or accrued in such preceding or succeeding taxable year.

(4) TRANSITION RULES FOR PRE-2009 AND 2009 DISALLOWED CREDITS.—

(A) PRE-2009 CREDITS.—In the case of any unused credit year beginning before January 1, 2009, this subsection, as in effect on the day before the date of the enactment of the Energy Improvement and Extension Act of 2008, shall apply to unused oil and gas extraction taxes carried from such unused credit year to a taxable year beginning after December 31, 2008.

(B) 2009 CREDITS.—In the case of any unused credit year beginning in 2009, the amendments made to this subsection by the Energy Improvement and Extension Act of 2008 shall be treated as being in effect for any preceding year beginning before January 1, 2009, solely for purposes of determining how much of the unused foreign oil and gas taxes for such unused credit year may be deemed paid or accrued in such preceding year.

Amendments

• **2018, Tax Technical Corrections Act of 2018 (P.L. 115-141)**

P.L. 115-141, §401(a)(159), Div. U:

Amended Code Sec. 907(f)(1) by striking "year," and inserting "years,". **Effective** 3-23-2018.

• **2017, Tax Cuts and Jobs Act (P.L. 115-97)**

P.L. 115-97, §14301(c)(27):

Amended Code Sec. 907(f)(2)(B)(i) by striking "902 or" following "paid under section". **Effective** for tax years of foreign corporations beginning after 12-31-2017, and to tax years of United States shareholders in which or with which such tax years of foreign corporations end.

• **2014, Tax Technical Corrections Act of 2014 (P.L. 113-295)**

P.L. 113-295, §210(e), Division A:

Amended Code Sec. 907(f)(4)(A) by striking "this subsection shall be applied" and all that follows through the period at the end and inserting "this subsection, as in effect on the day before the date of the enactment of the Energy Improvement and Extension Act of 2008, shall apply to unused oil and gas extraction taxes carried from such unused credit year to a taxable year beginning after December 31, 2008.". **Effective** as if included in the provision of the Energy Improvement and Extension Act of 2008 (P.L. 110-343) to which it relates [**effective** for tax years beginning after 12-31-2008.—CCH]. Prior to amendment, Code Sec. 907(f)(4)(A) read as follows:

(A) PRE-2009 CREDITS.—In the case of any unused credit year beginning before January 1, 2009, this subsection shall be applied to any unused oil and gas extraction taxes carried from such unused credit year to a year beginning after December 31, 2008—

(i) by substituting "oil and gas extraction taxes" for "foreign oil and gas taxes" each place it appears in paragraphs (1), (2), and (3), and

(ii) by computing, for purposes of paragraph (2)(A), the limitation under subparagraph (A) for the year to which such taxes are carried by substituting "foreign oil and gas extraction income" for "foreign oil and gas income" in subsection (a).

• **2008, Energy Improvement and Extension Act of 2008 (P.L. 110-343)**

P.L. 110-343, Division B, §402(c)(1)-(2):

Amended Code Sec. 907(f) by striking "oil and gas extraction taxes" each places it appears and inserting "foreign oil and gas taxes", and by adding at the end a new paragraph (4). **Effective** for tax years beginning after 12-31-2008.

• **2004, American Jobs Creation Act of 2004 (P.L. 108-357)**

P.L. 108-357, §417(b)(1):

Amended Code Sec. 907(f)(1) by striking "in the second preceding taxable year," immediately preceding "in the first preceding taxable year". **Effective** for excess foreign taxes arising in tax years beginning after 10-22-2004.

P.L. 108-357, §417(b)(2):

Amended Code Sec. 907(f)(1) by striking ", and in the first, second, third, fourth, or fifth" and inserting "and in any of the first 10". **Effective** for excess foreign taxes which (without regard to the amendments made by this section) may be carried to any tax year ending after 10-22-2004.

P.L. 108-357, §417(b)(3):

Amended Code Sec. 907(f)(1) by striking the last sentence. **Effective** after 10-22-2004. Prior to amendment, the last sentence of Code Sec. 907(f)(1) read as follows:

For purposes of this subsection, the terms "second preceding taxable year", and "first preceding taxable year" do not include any taxable year ending before January 1, 1975.

• **1990, Omnibus Budget Reconciliation Act of 1990 (P.L. 101-508)**

P.L. 101-508, §11801(a)(32):

Repealed Code Sec. 907(f)(3)(C). **Effective** 11-5-90. Prior to repeal, Code Sec. 907(f)(3)(C) read as follows:

(C) For purposes of determining the amount of the unused oil and gas extraction taxes which under paragraph (1) may be deemed paid or accrued in any taxable year ending before January 1, 1977, subparagraph (A) of paragraph (2) shall be applied as if the amendment made by section 1035(a) of the Tax Reform Act of 1976 applied to such taxable year.

P.L. 101-508, §11821(b), provides:

(b) SAVINGS PROVISION.—If—

(1) any provision amended or repealed by this part applied to—

(A) any transaction occurring before the date of the enactment of this Act,

(B) any property acquired before such date of enactment, or

(C) any item of income, loss, deduction, or credit taken into account before such date of enactment, and

(2) the treatment of such transaction, property, or item under such provision would (without regard to the amendments made by this part) affect liability for tax for periods ending after such date of enactment,

nothing in the amendments made by this part shall be construed to affect the treatment of such transaction, property, or item for purposes of determining liability for tax for periods ending after such date of enactment.

• **1982, Tax Equity and Fiscal Responsibility Act of 1982 (P.L. 97-248)**

P.L. 97-248, §211(d)(2)(A):

Amended paragraph (1) of Code Sec. 907(f) by striking out "so much of such excess as does not exceed 2 percent of foreign oil and gas extraction income for such taxable year" and inserting in lieu thereof "such excess" and by striking out the last sentence thereof. **Effective** for tax years beginning after 12-31-82. See, also, amendment notes for P.L. 97-248 following Code. Sec. 907(b) for a special rule. Prior to amendment, the last sentence read as follows:

"For purposes of determining the amount of such taxes which may be deemed paid or accrued in any taxable year ending in 1975, 1976, or 1977, the first sentence of this paragraph shall be applied by substituting 'such excess' for 'so much of such excess as does not exceed 2 percent of the foreign oil and gas extraction income for such taxable year'."

P.L. 97-248, §211(d)(2)(B):

Amended paragraph (2)(B) of Code Sec. 907(f) by striking out "on taxes paid or accrued with respect to foreign oil related income" following "section 904" and by striking out "with respect to such income" in clause (i) following "United States"; and amended paragraph (3) of Code Sec. 907(f) by striking out "with respect to oil-related income" preceding "the provisions" and by striking out "oil-related" preceding "taxes paid". **Effective** for tax years beginning after 12-31-82. See, also, the amendment notes following Code Sec. 907(b) for a special rule. Prior to amendment by Act Sec. 211(d)(2), Code Sec. 907(f) read as follows:

(f) Carryback and Carryover of Disallowed Credits.—

(1) In General.—If the amount of the oil and gas extraction taxes paid or accrued during any taxable year exceeds the limitation provided by subsection (a) for such taxable year (hereinafter in this subsection referred to as the 'unused credit year'), so much of such excess as does not exceed 2 percent of foreign oil and gas extraction income for such taxable year shall be deemed to be oil and gas extraction taxes paid or accrued in the second preceding taxable year, in the first preceding taxable year, and in the first, second, third, fourth, or fifth succeeding taxable year, in that order and to the extent not deemed tax paid or accrued in a prior taxable year by reason of the limitation imposed by paragraph (2). Such amount deemed paid or accrued in any taxable year may be availed of only as a tax credit and not as a deduction and only if the taxpayer for such year chooses to have the benefits of this subpart as to taxes paid or accrued for that year to foreign countries or possessions. For purposes of this subsection, the terms 'second preceding taxable year', and 'first preceding taxable year' do not include any taxable year ending before January 1, 1975. For purposes of determining the amount of such taxes which may be deemed paid or accrued in any taxable year ending in 1975, 1976, or 1977, the first sentence of this paragraph shall be applied by substituting 'such excess' for 'so much of such excess as does not exceed 2 percent of the foreign oil and gas extraction income for such taxable year'.

(2) Limitation.—The amount of the unused oil and gas extraction taxes which under paragraph (1) may be deemed paid or accrued in any preceding or succeeding taxable year shall not exceed the lesser of—

(A) the amount by which the limitation provided by subsection (a) for such taxable year exceeds the sum of—

(i) the oil and gas extraction taxes paid or accrued during such taxable year, plus

(ii) the amounts of the oil and gas extraction taxes which by reason of this subsection are deemed paid or accrued in such taxable year and are attributable to taxable years preceding the unused credit year; or

(B) the amount by which the limitation provided by section 904 on taxes paid or accrued with respect to foreign oil-related income for such taxable year exceeds the sum of—

(i) the taxes paid or accrued (or deemed to have been paid under section 902 or 960) to all foreign countries and possessions of the United States with respect to such income during such taxable year,

(ii) the amount of such taxes which were deemed paid or accrued in such taxable year under section 904(c) and which are attributable to taxable years preceding the unused credit year, plus

(iii) the amount of the oil and gas extraction taxes which by reason of this subsection are deemed paid or accrued in such taxable year and are attributable to taxable years preceding the unused credit year.

(3) Special rules.—

(A) In the case of any taxable year which is an unused credit year under this subsection and which is an unused credit year under section 904(c) with respect to oil-related income, the provisions of this subsection shall be applied before section 904(c).

(B) For purposes of determining the amount of oil-related taxes paid or accrued in any taxable year which may be deemed paid or accrued in a preceding or succeeding taxable year under section 904(c), any tax deemed paid or accrued in such preceding or succeeding taxable year under this subsection shall be considered to be tax paid or accrued in such preceding or succeeding taxable year.

(C) For purposes of determining the amount of the unused oil and gas extraction taxes which under paragraph (1) may be deemed paid or accrued in any taxable year ending before January 1, 1977, subparagraph (A) of paragraph (2) shall be applied as if the amendment made by section 1035(a) of the Tax Reform Act of 1976 applied to such taxable year.

[Sec. 907(g)—Repealed]

Amendments

• **1976, Tax Reform Act of 1976 (P.L. 94-455)**

P.L. 94-455, §1052(c)(4):

Repealed Code Sec. 907(g). **Effective** for tax years beginning after 12-31-79. Prior to repeal, Code Sec. 907(g) read as follows:

(g) WESTERN HEMISPHERE TRADE CORPORATIONS WHICH ARE MEMBERS OF AN AFFILIATED GROUP.—If a Western Hemisphere trade corporation is a member of an affiliated group for the taxable year, then in applying section 901, the amount of any income, war profits, and excess profits taxes paid or accrued (or deemed to have been paid)

• **1976, Tax Reform Act of 1976 (P.L. 94-455)**

P.L. 94-455, §1032(b)(2):

Struck out former Code Sec. 907(f) and redesignated Code Sec. 907(g) as Code Sec. 907(f). **Effective** for losses sustained in tax years beginning after 12-31-75. Prior to being stricken, Code Sec. 907(f) read as follows:

(f) RECAPTURE OF FOREIGN OIL RELATED LOSS.—

(1) GENERAL RULE.—For purposes of this subpart, in the case of any taxpayer who sustains a foreign oil related loss for any taxable year—

(A) that portion of the foreign oil related income for each succeeding taxable year which is equal to the lesser of—

(i) the amount of such loss (to the extent not used under this paragraph in prior years), or

(ii) 50 percent of the foreign oil related income for such succeeding taxable year,

shall be treated as income from sources within the United States (and not as income from sources without the United States), and

(B) the amount of the income, war profits, and excess profits taxes paid or accrued (or deemed to have been paid) to a foreign country for such succeeding taxable year with respect to foreign oil related income shall be reduced by an amount which bears the same proportion to the total amount of such foreign taxes as the amount treated as income from sources within the United States under subparagraph (A) bears to the total foreign oil related income for such succeeding taxable year.

For purposes of this chapter, the amount of any foreign taxes for which credit is denied under subparagraph (B) of the preceding sentence shall not be allowed as a deduction for any taxable year. For purposes of this subsection, foreign oil related income shall be determined without regard to this subsection.

(2) FOREIGN OIL RELATED LOSS DEFINED.—For purposes of this subsection, the term "foreign oil related loss" means the amount by which the gross income for the taxable year from sources without the United States and its possessions (whether or not the taxpayer chooses the benefits of this subpart for such taxable year) taken into account in determining the foreign oil related income for such year is exceeded by the sum of the deductions properly apportioned or allocated thereto, except that there shall not be taken into account—

(A) any net operating loss deduction allowable for such year under section 172(a) or any capital loss carrybacks and carryovers to such year under section 1212, and

(B) any—

(i) foreign expropriation loss for such year, as defined in section 172(k)(1), or

(ii) loss for such year which arises from fire, storm, shipwreck, or other casualty, or from theft,

to the extent such loss is not compensated for by insurance or otherwise.

(3) DISPOSITIONS.—

(A) IN GENERAL.—For purposes of this chapter, if property used in a trade or business described in subparagraph (A), (B), (C), or (D) of subsection (c)(2) is disposed of during any taxable year—

(i) the taxpayer notwithstanding any other provision of this chapter (other than paragraph (1)) shall be deemed to have received and recognized foreign oil related income in the taxable year of the disposition, by reason of such disposition, in an amount equal to the lesser of the excess of the fair market value of such property over the taxpayer's adjusted basis in such property or the remaining amount of the foreign oil related losses which were not used under paragraph (1) for such taxable year or any prior taxable year, and

(ii) paragraph (1) shall be applied with respect to such income by substituting "100 percent" for "50 percent".

(B) DISPOSITION DEFINED.—For purposes of this subsection, the term "disposition" includes a sale, exchange, distribution, or gift of property, whether or not gain or loss is recognized on the transfer.

(C) EXCEPTIONS.—Notwithstanding subparagraph (B), the term "disposition" does not include—

(i) a disposition of property which is not a material factor in the realization of income by the taxpayer, or

(ii) a disposition of property to a domestic corporation in a distribution or transfer described in section 381(a).

P.L. 94-455, §1035(d)(1):

Redesignated Code Sec. 907(f) as Code Sec. 907(g) and added a new Code Sec. 907(f). **Effective** for taxes paid or accrued during tax years ending after 10-4-76.

• **1975, Tax Reduction Act of 1975 (P.L. 94-12)**

P.L. 94-12, §601(a):

Added Code Sec. 907. **Effective** for tax years ending after 12-31-74, except that Sec. 907(f) applies to losses sustained in tax years ending after 12-31-75.

during the taxable year with respect to foreign oil and gas extraction income which would (but for this section and section 1503(b)) be taken into account for purposes of section 901 shall be reduced by the greater of—

(1) the reduction with respect to such taxes provided by subsection (a) of this section, or

(2) the reduction determined under section 1503(b) by applying section 1503(b) separately with respect to such taxes,

but not by both such reductions.

INCOME TAX—FOREIGN TAX CREDIT

[Sec. 908]

SEC. 908. REDUCTION OF CREDIT FOR PARTICIPATION IN OR COOPERATION WITH AN INTERNATIONAL BOYCOTT.

[Sec. 908(a)]

(a) IN GENERAL.—If a person, or a member of a controlled group (within the meaning of section 993(a)(3)) which includes such person, participates in or cooperates with an international boycott during the taxable year (within the meaning of section 999(b)), the amount of the credit allowable under section 901 to such person, or under section 960 to United States shareholders of such person, for foreign taxes paid during the taxable year shall be reduced by an amount equal to the product of—

(1) the amount of the credit which, but for this section, would be allowed under section 901 for the taxable year, multiplied by

(2) the international boycott factor (determined under section 999).

Amendments

- **2017, Tax Cuts and Jobs Act (P.L. 115-97)**

P.L. 115-97, § 14301(c)(28):

Amended Code Sec. 908(a) by striking "902 or" following "or under section". **Effective** for tax years of foreign corporations beginning after 12-31-2017, and to tax years of United States shareholders in which or with which such tax years of foreign corporations end.

[Sec. 908(b)]

(b) APPLICATION WITH SECTIONS 275(a)(4) AND 78.—Section 275(a)(4) and section 78 shall not apply to any amount of taxes denied credit under subsection (a).

Amendments

- **1976, Tax Reform Act of 1976 (P.L. 94-455)**

P.L. 94-455, § 1061(a):

Added Code Sec. 908. **Effective** for participation in or cooperation with an international boycott more than 30 days after 10-4-76. In the case of operations which constitute participation in or cooperation with an international boycott and which are carried out in accordance with the terms of a binding contract entered into before 9-2-76, Code Sec. 908(b) applies to such participation or cooperation after 12-31-77.

[Sec. 909]

SEC. 909. SUSPENSION OF TAXES AND CREDITS UNTIL RELATED INCOME TAKEN INTO ACCOUNT.

[Sec. 909(a)]

(a) IN GENERAL.—If there is a foreign tax credit splitting event with respect to a foreign income tax paid or accrued by the taxpayer, such tax shall not be taken into account for purposes of this title before the taxable year in which the related income is taken into account under this chapter by the taxpayer.

[Sec. 909(b)]

(b) SPECIAL RULES WITH RESPECT TO SPECIFIED 10-PERCENT OWNED FOREIGN CORPORATIONS.—If there is a foreign tax credit splitting event with respect to a foreign income tax paid or accrued by a specified 10-percent owned foreign corporation (as defined in section 245A(b) without regard to paragraph (2) thereof), such tax shall not be taken into account—

(1) for purposes of section 960, or

(2) for purposes of determining earnings and profits under section 964(a),

before the taxable year in which the related income is taken into account under this chapter by such specified 10-percent owned foreign corporation or a domestic corporation which is a United States shareholder with respect to such specified 10-percent owned foreign corporation.

Amendments

- **2017, Tax Cuts and Jobs Act (P.L. 115-97)**

P.L. 115-97, § 14301(c)(29)(A)-(D):

Amended Code Sec. 909(b) by striking "section 902 corporation" in the matter preceding paragraph (1) and inserting "specified 10-percent owned foreign corporation (as defined in section 245A(b) without regard to paragraph (2) thereof)", by striking "902 or" in paragraph (1) following "for purposes of section", by striking "by such section 902 corporation" and all that follows in the matter following paragraph (2) and inserting "by such specified 10-percent owned foreign corporation or a domestic corporation which is a United States shareholder with respect to such specified 10-percent owned foreign corporation.", and by striking "SECTION 902 CORPORATIONS" in the heading thereof and inserting "SPECIFIED 10-PERCENT OWNED FOREIGN CORPORATIONS". **Effective** for tax years of foreign corporations beginning after 12-31-2017, and to tax years of United States shareholders in which or with which such tax years of foreign corporations end. Prior to being stricken, "by such section 902 corporation" and all that follows in the matter following Code Sec. 909(b)(2) read as follows:

by such section 902 corporation or a domestic corporation which meets the ownership requirements of subsection (a) or (b) of section 902 with respect to such section 902 corporation.

[Sec. 909(c)]

(c) SPECIAL RULES.—For purposes of this section—

(1) APPLICATION TO PARTNERSHIPS, ETC.—In the case of a partnership, subsections (a) and (b) shall be applied at the partner level. Except as otherwise provided by the Secretary, a rule similar to the rule of the preceding sentence shall apply in the case of any S corporation or trust.

(2) TREATMENT OF FOREIGN TAXES AFTER SUSPENSION.—In the case of any foreign income tax not taken into account by reason of subsection (a) or (b), except as otherwise provided by the Secretary, such tax shall be so taken into account in the taxable year referred to in such subsection (other than for purposes of section 986(a)) as a foreign income tax paid or accrued in such taxable year.

[Sec. 909(d)]

(d) DEFINITIONS.—For purposes of this section—

(1) FOREIGN TAX CREDIT SPLITTING EVENT.—There is a foreign tax credit splitting event with respect to a foreign income tax if the related income is (or will be) taken into account under this chapter by a covered person.

(2) FOREIGN INCOME TAX.—The term "foreign income tax" means any income, war profits, or excess profits tax paid or accrued to any foreign country or to any possession of the United States.

(3) RELATED INCOME.—The term "related income" means, with respect to any portion of any foreign income tax, the income (or, as appropriate, earnings and profits) to which such portion of foreign income tax relates.

(4) COVERED PERSON.—The term "covered person" means, with respect to any person who pays or accrues a foreign income tax (hereafter in this paragraph referred to as the "payor")—

(A) any entity in which the payor holds, directly or indirectly, at least a 10 percent ownership interest (determined by vote or value),

(B) any person which holds, directly or indirectly, at least a 10 percent ownership interest (determined by vote or value) in the payor,

(C) any person which bears a relationship to the payor described in section 267(b) or 707(b), and

(D) any other person specified by the Secretary for purposes of this paragraph.

INCOME TAX—EARNED INCOME OF U.S. CITIZENS

Amendments

• **2017, Tax Cuts and Jobs Act (P.L. 115-97)**

P.L. 115-97, §14301(c)(30):

Amended Code Sec. 909(d) by striking paragraph (5). **Effective** for tax years of foreign corporations beginning after 12-31-2017, and to tax years of United States shareholders in which or with which such tax years of foreign corporations end. Prior to being stricken, Code Sec. 909(d)(5) read as follows:

(5) SECTION 902 CORPORATION.—The term "section 902 corporation" means any foreign corporation with respect to which one or more domestic corporations meets the ownership requirements of subsection (a) or (b) of section 902.

[Sec. 909(e)]

(e) REGULATIONS.—The Secretary may issue such regulations or other guidance as is necessary or appropriate to carry out the purposes of this section, including regulations or other guidance which provides—

(1) appropriate exceptions from the provisions of this section, and

(2) for the proper application of this section with respect to hybrid instruments.

• **2010, (P.L. 111-226)**

P.L. 111-226, §211(a):

Amended subpart A of part III of subchapter N of chapter 1 by adding at the end a new Code Sec. 909. For the **effective** date, see Act Sec. 211(c), below.

P.L. 111-226, §211(c), provides:

(c) EFFECTIVE DATE.—The amendments made by this section shall apply to—

(1) foreign income taxes (as defined in section 909(d) of the Internal Revenue Code of 1986, as added by this section) paid or accrued in taxable years beginning after December 31, 2010; and

(2) foreign income taxes (as so defined) paid or accrued by a section 902 corporation (as so defined) in taxable years beginning on or before such date (and not deemed paid under section 902(a) or 960 of such Code on or before such date), but only for purposes of applying sections 902 and 960 with respect to periods after such date.

Section 909(b)(2) of the Internal Revenue Code of 1986, as added by this section, shall not apply to foreign income taxes described in paragraph (2).

Subpart B—Earned Income of Citizens or Residents of United States

Sec. 911. Citizens or residents of the United States living abroad.
Sec. 912. Exemption for certain allowances.

[Sec. 911]

SEC. 911. CITIZENS OR RESIDENTS OF THE UNITED STATES LIVING ABROAD.

[Sec. 911(a)]

(a) EXCLUSION FROM GROSS INCOME.—At the election of a qualified individual (made separately with respect to paragraphs (1) and (2)), there shall be excluded from the gross income of such individual, and exempt from taxation under this subtitle, for any taxable year—

(1) the foreign earned income of such individual, and

(2) the housing cost amount of such individual.

Amendments

• **1981, Economic Recovery Tax Act of 1981 (P.L. 97-34)**

P.L. 97-34, §111(a):

Amended Code Sec. 911(a). **Effective** for tax years beginning after 12-31-81. Prior to amendment, Code Sec. 911(a) read as follows:

SEC. 911. INCOME EARNED BY INDIVIDUALS IN CERTAIN CAMPS OR FROM CHARITABLE SERVICES.

(a) GENERAL RULE.—In the case of an individual described in section 913(a) who, because of his employment, resides in a camp located in a hardship area, or who performs qualified charitable services in a lesser developed country, the following items shall not be included in gross income and shall be exempt from taxation under this subtitle:

(1) BONA FIDE RESIDENT OF FOREIGN COUNTRY.—If such individual is described in section 913(a)(1), amounts received from sources within a foreign country or countries (except amounts paid by the United States or any agency thereof) which constitute earned income attributable to services performed during the period of bona fide residence. The amount excluded under this paragraph for any taxable year shall be computed by applying the special rules contained in subsection (c).

(2) PRESENCE IN FOREIGN COUNTRY FOR 17 MONTHS.—If such individual is described in section 913(a)(2), amounts received from sources within a foreign country or countries (except amounts paid by the United States or any agency thereof) which constitute earned income attributable to services performed during the 18-month period. The amount excluded under this paragraph for any taxable year shall be computed by applying the special rules contained in subsection (c).

An individual shall not be allowed as a deduction from his gross income any deduction or as a credit against the tax imposed by this chapter any credit for the amount of taxes paid or accrued to a foreign country or possession of the United States, to the extent that such deduction or credit is properly allocable to or chargeable against amounts excluded from gross income under this subsection, other than the deduction allowed by section 217 (relating to moving expenses).

• **1980 (P.L. 96-595)**

P.L. 96-595, §4(a):

Amended Code Sec. 911(a) by inserting "or who performs qualified charitable services in a lesser developed country," after "hardship area,". **Effective** for tax years beginning after 1978.

• **1980, Technical Corrections Act of 1979 (P.L. 96-222)**

P.L. 96-222, §107(a)(1)(B):

Amended the effective date provided in P.L. 95-600, §701(u)(10) for the amendment of Code Sec. 911(a) to read as follows:

"(B) EFFECTIVE DATE.—The amendment made by subparagraph (A) shall apply to taxable years beginning in calendar year 1978 but only in the case of taxpayers who make an election under section 209(c) of the Foreign Earned Income Act of 1978."

P.L. 96-222, §108(a)(1)(C):

Amended Code Sec. 911(a)(2) by changing "qualified foreign" to "a foreign country or". **Effective** as set forth in P.L. 95-615, §209.

P.L. 96-222, §108(a)(1)(D):

Amended Code Sec. 911(a) by adding "any deduction" after "his gross income" and by changing "deductions allowed by sections 217" to "deduction allowed by section 217". **Effective** as set forth in P.L. 95-615, §209.

• **1978, Tax Treatment Extension Act of 1978 (P.L. 95-615)**

P.L. 95-615, §202(a), (f)(1):

Amended Code Sec. 911(a). **Effective** as set forth in P.L. 95-615, §209. Prior to amendment, Code Sec. 911(a) read as follows:

SEC. 911. EARNED INCOME FROM SOURCES WITHOUT THE UNITED STATES.

(a) GENERAL RULE.—The following items shall not be included in gross income and shall be exempt from taxation under this subtitle:

(1) BONA FIDE RESIDENT OF FOREIGN COUNTRY.—In the case of an individual citizen of the United States who establishes to the satisfaction of the Secretary that he has been a bona fide resident of a foreign country or countries for an uninterrupted period which includes an entire taxable year, amounts received from sources without the United States (except amounts paid by the United States or any agency thereof) which constitute earned income attributable to services performed during such uninterrupted period. The amount excluded under this paragraph for any taxable year shall be computed by applying the special rules contained in subsection (c).

(2) PRESENCE IN FOREIGN COUNTRY FOR 17 MONTHS.—In the case of an individual citizen of the United States who during any period of 18 consecutive months is present in a foreign country or countries during at least 510 full days in such period, amounts received from sources without the United States (except amounts paid by the United States or any agency thereof) which constitute earned income attributable to services performed during such 18-month period. The amount excluded under this paragraph for any taxable year shall be computed by applying the special rules contained in subsection (c).

An individual shall not be allowed as a deduction from his gross income any deductions (other than those allowed by section 151, relating to personal exemptions), to the extent that such deductions are properly allocable to or chargeable against amounts excluded from gross income under this subsection. For purposes of this title, the amount of the income, war profits, and excess profits taxes paid or accrued by any individual to a foreign country or possession of the United States for any taxable year shall be reduced by an amount determined by multiplying the amount of such taxes by a fraction—

(A) the numerator of which is the tax determined under subsection (d)(1)(B), and

(B) the denominator of which is the sum of the amount referred to in subparagraph (A), plus the limitation imposed for the taxable year by section 904(a).

P.L. 95-615, §209 provides:

SEC. 209. EFFECTIVE DATES.

(a) GENERAL RULE.—Except as provided in subsections (b) and (c) the amendments made by this title shall apply to taxable years beginning after December 31, 1977.

* * *

(c) ELECTION OF PRIOR LAW.—

INCOME TAX—EARNED INCOME OF U.S. CITIZENS

(1) A taxpayer may elect not to have the amendments made by this title apply with respect to any taxable year beginning after December 31, 1977, and before January 1, 1979.

(2) An election under this subsection shall be filed with a taxpayer's timely filed return for the first taxable year beginning after December 31, 1977.

• **1978, Revenue Act of 1978 (P.L. 95-600)**

P.L. 95-600, § 701(u)(10):

Amended the last sentence of Code Sec. 911(a). **Effective** for tax years beginning after 12-31-76 [but, see P.L. 96-222, § 107(a)(1)(B), above]. Prior to amendment, the last sentence of Code Sec. 911(a) read as follows:

"An individual shall not be allowed as a deduction from his gross income any deductions (other than those allowed by section 151, relating to personal exemptions), or as a credit against the tax imposed by this chapter any credit for the amount of taxes paid or accrued to a foreign country or possession of the United States, to the extent that such deductions or credit is properly allocable to or chargeable against amounts excluded from gross income under this subsection."

• **1976, Tax Reform Act of 1976 (P.L. 94-455)**

P.L. 94-455, § 1011(b)(1), as amended by P.L. 95-30, § 302:

Amended the last sentence of Code Sec. 911(a). **Effective** for tax years beginning after 12-31-75. However, P.L. 95-30, § 302 changed the effective date to tax years beginning after 12-31-76. Prior to amendment, the last sentence of Code Sec. 911(a) read as follows:

An individual shall not be allowed, as a deduction from his gross income, any deductions (other than those allowed by section 151, relating to personal exemptions), properly allocable to or chargeable against amounts excluded from gross income under this subsection.

P.L. 94-455, § 1906(b)(13)(A):

Amended 1954 Code by substituting "Secretary" for "Secretary or his delegate" each place it appeared. **Effective** 2-1-77.

• **1962, Revenue Act of 1962 (P.L. 87-834)**

P.L. 87-834, § 11(a):

Amended Code Sec. 911(a). **Effective** for tax years ending after 9-4-62, but only with respect to amounts received after 3-12-62 attributable to services performed after 12-31-62, or amounts received after 12-31-62 attributable to services performed on or before 12-31-62, unless on 3-12-62 there existed a right (whether forfeitable or nonforfeitable) to receive such amounts. Prior to amendment, Sec. 911(a) read as follows:

"(a) General Rule.—The following items shall not be included in gross income and shall be exempt from taxation under this subtitle:

"(1) Bona fide resident of foreign country.—In the case of an individual citizen of the United States, who establishes to the satisfaction of the Secretary or his delegate that he has been a bona fide resident of a foreign country or countries for an uninterrupted period which includes an entire taxable year, amounts received from sources without the United States (except amounts paid by the United States or any agency thereof) if such amounts constitute earned income (as defined in subsection (b)) attributable to such period; but such individual shall not be allowed as a deduction from his gross income any deductions (other than those allowed by section 151, relating to personal exemptions) properly allocable to or chargeable against amounts excluded from gross income under this paragraph.

"(2) Presence in foreign country for 17 months.—In the case of an individual citizen of the United States, who during any period of 18 consecutive months is present in a foreign country or countries during at least 510 full days in such period, amounts received from sources without the United States (except amounts paid by the United States or an agency thereof) if such amounts constitute earned income (as defined in subsection (b)) attributable to such period; but such individual shall not be allowed as a deduction from his gross income any deductions (other than those allowed by section 151, relating to personal exemptions) properly allocable to or chargeable against amounts excluded from gross income under this paragraph. If the 18-month period includes the entire taxable year, the amount excluded under this paragraph for such taxable year shall not exceed $20,000. If the 18-month period does not include the entire taxable year, the amount excluded under this paragraph for such taxable year shall not exceed an amount which bears the same ratio to $20,000 as the number of days in the part of the taxable year within the 18-month period bears to the total number of days in such year."

[Sec. 911(b)]

(b) FOREIGN EARNED INCOME.—

(1) DEFINITION.—For purposes of this section—

(A) IN GENERAL.—The term "foreign earned income" with respect to any individual means the amount received by such individual from sources within a foreign country or countries which constitute earned income attributable to services performed by such individual during the period described in subparagraph (A) or (B) of subsection (d)(1), whichever is applicable.

(B) CERTAIN AMOUNTS NOT INCLUDED IN FOREIGN EARNED INCOME.—The foreign earned income for an individual shall not include amounts—

(i) received as a pension or annuity,

(ii) paid by the United States or an agency thereof to an employee of the United States or an agency thereof,

(iii) included in gross income by reason of section 402(b) (relating to taxability of beneficiary of nonexempt trust) or section 403(c) (relating to taxability of beneficiary under a nonqualified annuity), or

(iv) received after the close of the taxable year following the taxable year in which the services to which the amounts are attributable are performed.

(2) LIMITATION ON FOREIGN EARNED INCOME.—

(A) IN GENERAL.—The foreign earned income of an individual which may be excluded under subsection (a)(1) for any taxable year shall not exceed the amount of foreign earned income computed on a daily basis at an annual rate equal to the exclusion amount for the calendar year in which such taxable year begins.

(B) ATTRIBUTION TO YEAR IN WHICH SERVICES ARE PERFORMED.—For purposes of applying subparagraph (A), amounts received shall be considered received in the taxable year in which the services to which the amounts are attributable are performed.

(C) TREATMENT OF COMMUNITY INCOME.—In applying subparagraph (A) with respect to amounts received from services performed by a husband or wife which are community income under community property laws applicable to such income, the aggregate amount which may be excludable from the gross income of such husband and wife under subsection (a)(1) for any taxable year shall equal the amount which would be so excludable if such amounts did not constitute community income.

(D) EXCLUSION AMOUNT.—

(i) IN GENERAL.—The exclusion amount for any calendar year is $80,000.

(ii) INFLATION ADJUSTMENT.—In the case of any taxable year beginning in a calendar year after 2005, the $80,000 amount in clause (i) shall be increased by an amount equal to the product of—

(I) such dollar amount, and

(II) the cost-of-living adjustment determined under section 1(f)(3) for the calendar year in which the taxable year begins, determined by substituting "2004" for "2016" in subparagraph (A)(ii) thereof.

If any increase determined under the preceding sentence is not a multiple of $100, such increase shall be rounded to the next lowest multiple of $100.

Amendments

• **2017, Tax Cuts and Jobs Act (P.L. 115-97)**

P.L. 115-97, § 11002(d)(9):

Amended Code Sec. 911(b)(2)(D)(ii)(II) by striking "for '1992' in subparagraph (B)" and inserting "for '2016' in subparagraph (A)(ii)". **Effective** for tax years beginning after 12-31-2017.

• **2014, Tax Technical Corrections Act of 2014 (P.L. 113-295)**

P.L. 113-295, § 221(a)(73), Division A:

Amended Code Sec. 911(b)(2)(D)(i). **Effective** generally 12-19-2014. For a special rule, see Act Sec. 221(b)(2), Division A, below. Prior to amendment, Code Sec. 911(b)(2)(D)(i) read as follows:

(i) IN GENERAL.—The exclusion amount for any calendar year is the exclusion amount determined in accordance with the following table (as adjusted by clause (ii)):

For calendar year—	The exclusion amount is—
1998	$72,000
1999	74,000
2000	76,000

INCOME TAX—EARNED INCOME OF U.S. CITIZENS

Year	Amount
2001	78,000
2002 and thereafter	80,000

P.L. 113-295, §221(b)(2), Division A, provides:

(2) SAVINGS PROVISION.—If—

(A) any provision amended or repealed by the amendments made by this section applied to—

(i) any transaction occurring before the date of the enactment of this Act,

(ii) any property acquired before such date of enactment, or

(iii) any item of income, loss, deduction, or credit taken into account before such date of enactment, and

(B) the treatment of such transaction, property, or item under such provision would (without regard to the amendments or repeals made by this section) affect the liability for tax for periods ending after date of enactment, nothing in the amendments or repeals made by this section shall be construed to affect the treatment of such transaction, property, or item for purposes of determining liability for tax for periods ending after such date of enactment.

• **2006, Tax Increase Prevention and Reconciliation Act of 2005 (P.L. 109-222)**

P.L. 109-222, §515(a)(1)-(2):

Amended Code Sec. 911(b)(2)(D)(ii) by striking "2007" and inserting "2005", and by striking "2006" in subclause (II) and inserting "2004". **Effective** for tax years beginning after 12-31-2005.

• **1997, Taxpayer Relief Act of 1997 (P.L. 105-34)**

P.L. 105-34, §1172(a)(1)-(2):

Amended Code Sec. 911(b)(2) by striking "of $70,000" in subparagraph (A) and inserting "equal to the exclusion amount for the calendar year in which such taxable year begins", and by adding at the end a new subparagraph (D). **Effective** for tax years beginning after 12-31-97.

• **1986, Tax Reform Act of 1986 (P.L. 99-514)**

P.L. 99-514, §1233(a):

Amended Code Sec. 911(b)(2)(A). **Effective** for tax years beginning after 12-31-86. Prior to amendment, Code Sec. 911(b)(2)(A) read as follows:

(A) IN GENERAL.—The foreign earned income of an individual which may be excluded under subsection (a)(1) for any taxable year shall not exceed the amount of foreign earned income computed on a daily basis at the annual rate set forth in the following table for each day of the taxable year within the applicable period described in subparagraph (A) or (B) of subsection (d)(1):

In the case of taxable years beginning in:	The annual rate is:
1983, 1984, 1985, 1986, or 1987	$80,000

Year	Amount
1988	85,000
1989	90,000
1990 and thereafter	95,000

• **1984, Deficit Reduction Act of 1984 (P.L. 98-369)**

P.L. 98-369, §17:

Amended Code Sec. 911(b)(2)(A) by striking out the table contained therein and inserting in lieu thereof another table. **Effective** for tax years ending after 12-31-83. Prior to amendment, it read as follows:

In the case of taxable years beginning in:	The annual rate is:
1982	$75,000
1983	80,000
1984	85,000
1985	90,000
1986 and thereafter	95,000

• **1981, Economic Recovery Tax Act of 1981 (P.L. 97-34)**

P.L. 97-34, §111(a):

Amended Code Sec. 911(b). **Effective** with respect to tax years beginning after 12-31-81. Prior to amendment, Code Sec. 911(b) read as follows:

(b) DEFINITION OF EARNED INCOME.—For purposes of this section, the term "earned income" means wages, salaries, or professional fees, and other amounts received as compensation for personal services actually rendered, but does not include that part of the compensation derived by the taxpayer for personal services rendered by him to a corporation which represents a distribution of earnings or profits rather than a reasonable allowance as compensation for the personal services actually rendered. In the case of a taxpayer engaged in a trade or business in which both personal services and capital are material income-producing factors, under regulations prescribed by the Secretary, a reasonable allowance as compensation for the personal services rendered by the taxpayer, not in excess of 30 percent of his share of the net profits of such trade or business, shall be considered as earned income.

• **1976, Tax Reform Act of 1976 (P.L. 94-455)**

P.L. 94-455, §1906(b)(13)(A):

Amended 1954 Code by substituting "Secretary" for "Secretary or his delegate" each place it appeared. **Effective** 2-1-77.

[Sec. 911(c)]

(c) HOUSING COST AMOUNT.—For purposes of this section—

(1) IN GENERAL.—The term "housing cost amount" means an amount equal to the excess of—

(A) the housing expenses of an individual for the taxable year to the extent such expenses do not exceed the amount determined under paragraph (2), over

(B) an amount equal to the product of—

(i) 16 percent of the amount (computed on a daily basis) in effect under subsection (b)(2)(D) for the calendar year in which such taxable year begins, multiplied by

(ii) the number of days of such taxable year within the applicable period described in subparagraph (A) or (B) of subsection (d)(1).

(2) LIMITATION.—

(A) IN GENERAL.—The amount determined under this paragraph is an amount equal to the product of—

(i) 30 percent (adjusted as may be provided under subparagraph (B)) of the amount (computed on a daily basis) in effect under subsection (b)(2)(D) for the calendar year in which the taxable year of the individual begins, multiplied by

(ii) the number of days of such taxable year within the applicable period described in subparagraph (A) or (B) of subsection (d)(1).

(B) REGULATIONS.—The Secretary may issue regulations or other guidance providing for the adjustment of the percentage under subparagraph (A)(i) on the basis of geographic differences in housing costs relative to housing costs in the United States.

(3) HOUSING EXPENSES.—

(A) IN GENERAL.—The term "housing expenses" means the reasonable expenses paid or incurred during the taxable year by or on behalf of an individual for housing for the individual (and, if they reside with him, for his spouse and dependents) in a foreign country. The term—

(i) includes expenses attributable to the housing (such as utilities and insurance), but

(ii) does not include interest and taxes of the kind deductible under section 163 or 164 or any amount allowable as a deduction under section 216(a).

Housing expenses shall not be treated as reasonable to the extent such expenses are lavish or extravagant under the circumstances.

(B) SECOND FOREIGN HOUSEHOLD.—

(i) IN GENERAL.—Except as provided in clause (ii), only housing expenses incurred with respect to that abode which bears the closest relationship to the tax home of the individual shall be taken into account under paragraph (1).

(ii) SEPARATE HOUSEHOLD FOR SPOUSE AND DEPENDENTS.—If an individual maintains a separate abode outside the United States for his spouse and dependents and they do not reside with him because of living conditions which are dangerous, unhealthful, or otherwise adverse, then—

INCOME TAX—EARNED INCOME OF U.S. CITIZENS

(I) the words "if they reside with him" in subparagraph (A) shall be disregarded, and

(II) the housing expenses incurred with respect to such abode shall be taken into account under paragraph (1).

(4) SPECIAL RULES WHERE HOUSING EXPENSES NOT PROVIDED BY EMPLOYER.—

(A) IN GENERAL.—To the extent the housing cost amount of any individual for any taxable year is not attributable to employer provided amounts, such amount shall be treated as a deduction allowable in computing adjusted gross income to the extent of the limitation of subparagraph (B).

(B) LIMITATION.—For purposes of subparagraph (A), the limitation of this subparagraph is the excess of—

(i) the foreign earned income of the individual for the taxable year, over

(ii) the amount of such income excluded from gross income under subsection (a) for the taxable year.

(C) 1-YEAR CARRYOVER OF HOUSING AMOUNTS NOT ALLOWED BY REASON OF SUBPARAGRAPH (B).—

(i) IN GENERAL.—The amount not allowable as a deduction for any taxable year under subparagraph (A) by reason of the limitation of subparagraph (B) shall be treated as a deduction allowable in computing adjusted gross income for the succeeding taxable year (and only for the succeeding taxable year) to the extent of the limitation of clause (ii) for such succeeding taxable year.

(ii) LIMITATION.—For purposes of clause (i), the limitation of this clause for any taxable year is the excess of—

(I) the limitation of subparagraph (B) for such taxable year, over

(II) amounts treated as a deduction under subparagraph (A) for such taxable year.

(D) EMPLOYER PROVIDED AMOUNTS.—For purposes of this paragraph, the term "employer provided amounts" means any amount paid or incurred on behalf of the individual by the individual's employer which is foreign earned income included in the individual's gross income for the taxable year (without regard to this section).

(E) FOREIGN EARNED INCOME.—For purposes of this paragraph, an individual's foreign earned income for any taxable year shall be determined without regard to the limitation of subparagraph (A) of subsection (b)(2).

Amendments

- **2006, Tax Increase Prevention and Reconciliation Act of 2005 (P.L. 109-222)**

P.L. 109-222, §515(b)(1):

Amended Code Sec. 911(c)(1)(B)(i). **Effective** for tax years beginning after 12-31-2005. Prior to amendment, Code Sec. 911(c)(1)(B)(i) read as follows:

(i) 16 percent of the salary (computed on a daily basis) of an employee of the United States who is compensated at a rate equal to the annual rate paid for step 1 of grade GS-14, multiplied by

P.L. 109-222, §515(b)(2)(A):

Amended Code Sec. 911(c)(1)(A) by inserting "to the extent such expenses do not exceed the amount determined under paragraph (2)" after "the taxable year". **Effective** for tax years beginning after 12-31-2005.

P.L. 109-222, §515(b)(2)(B):

Amended Code Sec. 911(c) by redesignating paragraphs (2) and (3) as paragraphs (3) and (4), respectively, and by inserting after paragraph (1) a new paragraph (2). **Effective** for tax years beginning after 12-31-2005.

- **1983, Technical Corrections Act of 1982 (P.L. 97-448)**

P.L. 97-448, §101(c)(2):

Amended Code Sec. 911(c)(3)(B)(ii) by striking out "subsection (a)(1)" and inserting in lieu thereof "subsection (a)". **Effective** as if included in the provision of P.L. 97-34 to which it relates.

- **1981, Economic Recovery Tax Act of 1981 (P.L. 97-34)**

P.L. 97-34, §111(a):

Amended Code Sec. 911(c). **Effective** with respect to tax years beginning after 12-31-81. Prior to amendment, Code Sec. 911(c) read as follows:

(c) SPECIAL RULES.—For purposes of computing the amount excludable under subsection (a), the following rules shall apply:

(1) LIMITATIONS ON AMOUNT OF EXCLUSION.

(A) DOLLAR LIMITATIONS.—

(i) CAMP RESIDENTS.—In the case of an individual who resides in a camp located in a hardship area, the amount excluded from the gross income of the individual under subsection (a) for any taxable year shall not exceed an amount which shall be computed on a daily basis at an annual rate of $20,000 for days during which he resides in a camp.

(ii) EMPLOYEES OF CHARITABLE ORGANIZATIONS.—If any individual performs qualified charitable services in a lesser developed country during any taxable year, the amount of the earned income attributable to such services excluded from the gross income of the individual under subsection (a) for the taxable year shall not exceed an amount which shall be computed on a daily basis at an annual rate of $20,000.

(iii) SPECIAL RULE.—If any individual performs qualified charitable services in a lesser developed country and performs other services while residing in a camp located in a hardship area during any taxable year, the amount of the earned income attributable to such other services excluded from the gross income of the individual under subsection (a) for the taxable year shall not (after the application of clause (i) with respect to such earned income) exceed $20,000 reduced by the amount of the earned income attributable to qualified charitable services excluded from gross income under subsection (a) for the taxable year.

(B) CAMP.—For purposes of this section, an individual shall not be considered to reside in a camp because of his employment unless the camp constitutes substandard lodging which is—

(i) provided by or on behalf of the employer for the convenience of the employer because the place at which such individual renders services is in a remote area where satisfactory housing is not available on the open market,

(ii) located, as near as practicable, in the vicinity of the place at which such individual renders services, and

(iii) furnished in a common area (or enclave) which is not available to the public and which normally accommodates 10 or more employees.

(C) HARDSHIP AREA.—For purposes of this section, the term "hardship area" has the same meaning as in section 913(h).

(D) QUALIFIED CHARITABLE SERVICES.—For purposes of this subsection, the term "qualified charitable services" means services performed by an employee for an employer which—

(i) meets the requirements of section 501(c)(3), and

(ii) is not a private foundation (within the meaning of section 509(a)).

(E) LESSER DEVELOPED COUNTRY.—The term "lesser developed country" means any foreign country other than—

(i) a country listed in the first sentence of section 502(b) of the Trade Act of 1974 (19 U.S.C. 2462), or

(ii) a country designated by the President as not being a lesser developed country.

(2) ATTRIBUTION TO YEAR IN WHICH SERVICES ARE PERFORMED.—For purposes of applying paragraph (1), amounts received shall be considered received in the taxable year in which the services to which the amounts are attributable are performed.

(3) TREATMENT OF COMMUNITY INCOME.—In applying paragraph (1) with respect to amounts received for services performed by a husband or wife which are community income under community property laws applicable to such income, the aggregate amount excludable under subsection (a) from the gross income of such husband and wife shall equal the amount which would be excludable if such amounts did not constitute such community income.

(4) REQUIREMENT AS TO TIME OF RECEIPT.—No amount received after the close of the taxable year following the taxable year in which the services to which the amounts are attributable are performed may be excluded under subsection (a).

(5) CERTAIN AMOUNTS NOT EXCLUDABLE.—No amount—

(A) received as a pension or annuity, or

(B) included in gross income by reason of section 402(b) (relating to taxability of beneficiary of nonexempt trust), section 403(c) (relating to taxability of beneficiary under a nonqualified annuity), or section 403(d) (relating to taxability of beneficiary under certain forfeitable contracts purchased by exempt organization),

may be excluded under subsection (a).

(6) TEST OF BONA FIDE RESIDENCE.—A statement by an individual who has earned income from sources within a foreign country to the authorities of that country that he is not a resident of that country, if he is held not subject as a resident of that country to the income tax of that country by its authorities with respect to such earnings, shall be conclusive evidence with respect to such earnings that he is not a bona fide resident of that country for purposes of subsection (a)(1).

(7) BUSINESS PREMISES OF THE EMPLOYER.—In the case of an individual residing in a camp who elects the exclusion provided in this section for a taxable year, the camp shall be considered to be part of the business premises of the employer for purposes of section 119 for such taxable year.

- **1980 (P.L. 96-595)**

P.L. 96-595, §4(b):

Amended Code Sec. 911(c)(1)(A) and added new subparagraphs (D) and (E). **Effective** for tax years ending after 1978. Prior to amendment, Code Sec. 911(c)(1)(A) provided:

"(A) IN GENERAL.—The amount excluded from the gross income of an individual under subsection (a) for any taxable year shall not exceed an amount which shall be computed on a daily basis at an annual rate of $20,000 for days during which he resides in a camp."

- **1978, Tax Treatment Extension Act of 1978 (P.L. 95-615)**

P.L. 95-615, §202(b):

Amended Code Sec. 911(c)(1). **Effective** as set forth in P.L. 95-615, §209. See historical comment on P.L. 95-615, §209 under Code Sec. 911(a). Prior to amendment, Code Sec. 911(c)(1) read as follows:

(1) LIMITATIONS ON AMOUNT OF EXCLUSION.—

(A) IN GENERAL.—Except as provided in subparagraphs (B) and (C), the amount excluded from the gross income of an individual under subsection (a) for any taxable year shall not exceed an amount which shall be computed on a daily basis at an annual rate of $15,000.

(B) EMPLOYEES OF CHARITABLE ORGANIZATIONS.—If any individual performs qualified charitable services during any taxable year, the amount of the earned income attributable to such services excluded from the gross income of the individual under subsection (a) for the taxable year shall not exceed an amount which shall be computed on a daily basis at an annual rate of $20,000.

(C) SPECIAL RULE.—If any individual performs qualified charitable services and other services during any taxable year, the amount of the earned income attributable to such other services excluded from the gross income of the individual under subsection (a) for the taxable year shall not (after the application of subparagraph (A) with respect to such earned income) exceed $15,000 reduced by the amount of the earned income attributable to qualified charitable services excluded from gross income under subsection (a) for the taxable year.

(D) QUALIFIED CHARITABLE SERVICES.—For purposes of this subsection, the term "qualified charitable services" means services performed by an employee for an employer created or organized in the United States, or under the law of the United States, any State, or the District of Columbia, which meets the requirements of section 501(c)(3).

P.L. 95-600, §202(c):

Added a new Code Sec. 911(c)(7). **Effective** as set forth in P.L. 95-615, §209. See historical comment on P.L. 95-615, §209 under Code Sec. 911(a).

P.L. 95-615, §202(e):

Repealed Code Sec. 911(c)(8). **Effective** as set forth in P.L. 95-615, §209. See historical comment on P.L. 95-615, §209 under Code Sec. 911(a). Prior to repeal, Code Sec. 911(c)(8) read as follows:

"(8) REQUIREMENT AS TO PLACE OF RECEIPT.—No amount received by an individual during the taxable year which constitutes earned income (entitled to the exclusion under subsection (a)) attributable to services performed in a foreign country or countries shall be excluded under subsection (a) if such amount is received by such individual outside of the foreign country or countries where such services were performed and if one of the purposes is the avoidance of any tax imposed by such foreign country or countries on such amount."

• **1978, Revenue Act of 1978 (P.L. 95-600)**

P.L. 95-600, §703(e):

Redesignated Code Sec. 911(c)(8) as 911(c)(7). **Effective** 10-4-76. [Note: This amendment conflicts with the amendment to Code Sec. 911(c) made by P.L. 95-615, §202(c) and (e).—CCH.]

• **1976, Tax Reform Act of 1976 (P.L. 94-455)**

P.L. 94-455, §1011(a), as amended by P.L. 95-30, §302:

Amended Code Sec. 911(c)(1). **Effective** for tax years beginning after 12-31-75. However, P.L. 95-30, §302, changed this effective date to tax years beginning after 12-31-76. Prior to amendment, Code Sec. 911(c)(1) read as follows:

(1) LIMITATIONS ON AMOUNT OF EXCLUSION.—The amount excluded from the gross income of an individual under subsection (a) for any taxable year shall not exceed an amount which shall be computed on a daily basis at an annual rate of—

(A) except as provided in subparagraph (B), $20,000, in the case of an individual who qualifies under subsection (a), or

(B) $25,000 in the case of an individual who qualifies under subsection (a)(1), but only with respect to that portion of such taxable year occurring after such individual has been a bona fide resident of a foreign country or countries for an uninterrupted period of 3 consecutive years.

P.L. 94-455, §1011(b)(2), as amended by P.L. 95-30, §302:

Added Code Sec. 911(c)(8). **Effective** for tax years beginning after 12-31-75. However, P.L. 95-30, §302, changed this effective date to tax years beginning after 12-31-76.

P.L. 94-455, §1901(a)(115):

Struck out Code Sec. 911(c)(7), but did not renumber (8). **Effective** for tax years beginning after 12-31-76. Prior to striking, Code Sec. 911(c)(7) read as follows:

(7) CERTAIN NONCASH REMUNERATION.—If an individual who qualifies under subsection (a)(1) receives compensation from sources without the United States (except from the United States or any agency thereof) in the form of the right to use property or facilities, the limitation under paragraph (1) applicable with respect to such individual—

(A) for a taxable year ending in 1963, shall be increased by an amount equal to the amount of such compensation so received during such taxable year;

(B) for a taxable year ending in 1964, shall be increased by an amount equal to two-thirds of such compensation so received during such taxable year; and

(C) for a taxable year ending in 1965, shall be increased by an amount equal to one-third of such compensation so received during such taxable year.

• **1964, Revenue Act of 1964 (P.L. 88-272)**

P.L. 88-272, §237(a):

Amended subsection (c)(1) by inserting in subparagraph (B) "$25,000" in lieu of "$35,000". **Effective** with respect to tax years beginning after 12-31-64. Consequently, for tax years beginning before 1-1-65 the limitation under Code Sec. 911(c)(1)(B) on the exclusion is $35,000.

• **1962, Revenue Act of 1962 (P.L. 87-834)**

P.L. 87-834, §11(a):

Redesignated Code Sec. 911(c) as Sec. 911(d) and added new Sec. 911(c). For **effective** date, see amendment note following Code Sec. 911(a).

[Sec. 911(d)]

(d) DEFINITIONS AND SPECIAL RULES.—For purposes of this section—

(1) QUALIFIED INDIVIDUAL.—The term "qualified individual" means an individual whose tax home is in a foreign country and who is—

(A) a citizen of the United States and establishes to the satisfaction of the Secretary that he has been a bona fide resident of a foreign country or countries for an uninterrupted period which includes an entire taxable year, or

(B) a citizen or resident of the United States and who, during any period of 12 consecutive months, is present in a foreign country or countries during at least 330 full days in such period.

(2) EARNED INCOME.—

(A) IN GENERAL.—The term "earned income" means wages, salaries, or professional fees, and other amounts received as compensation for personal services actually rendered, but does not include that part of the compensation derived by the taxpayer for personal services rendered by him to a corporation which represents a distribution of earnings or profits rather than a reasonable allowance as compensation for the personal services actually rendered.

(B) TAXPAYER ENGAGED IN TRADE OR BUSINESS.—In the case of a taxpayer engaged in a trade or business in which both personal services and capital are material income-producing factors, under regulations prescribed by the Secretary, a reasonable allowance as compensation for the personal services rendered by the taxpayer, not in excess of 30 percent of his share of the net profits of such trade or business, shall be considered as earned income.

(3) TAX HOME.—The term "tax home" means, with respect to any individual, such individual's home for purposes of section 162(a)(2) (relating to traveling expenses while away from home). An individual shall not be treated as having a tax home in a foreign country for any period for which his abode is within the United States, unless such individual is serving in an area designated by the President of the United States by Executive order as a combat zone for purposes of section 112 in support of the Armed Forces of the United States.

(4) WAIVER OF PERIOD OF STAY IN FOREIGN COUNTRY.—Notwithstanding paragraph (1), an individual who—

(A) is a bona fide resident of, or is present in, a foreign country for any period,

(B) leaves such foreign country after August 31, 1978—

(i) during any period during which the Secretary determines, after consultation with the Secretary of State or his delegate, that individuals were required to leave such foreign country because of war, civil unrest, or similar adverse conditions in such foreign country which precluded the normal conduct of business by such individuals, and

(ii) before meeting the requirements of such paragraph (1), and

(C) establishes to the satisfaction of the Secretary that such individual could reasonably have been expected to have met such requirements but for the conditions referred to in clause (i) of subparagraph (B),

shall be treated as a qualified individual with respect to the period described in subparagraph (A) during which he was a bona fide resident of, or was present in, the foreign country, and in applying subsections (b)(2)(A), (c)(1)(B)(ii), and (c)(2)(A)(ii) with respect to such individual, only the days within such period shall be taken into account.

(5) TEST OF BONA FIDE RESIDENCE.—If—

(A) an individual who has earned income from sources within a foreign country submits a statement to the authorities of that country that he is not a resident of that country, and

INCOME TAX—EARNED INCOME OF U.S. CITIZENS

(B) such individual is held not subject as a resident of that country to the income tax of that country by its authorities with respect to such earnings,

then such individual shall not be considered a bona fide resident of that country for purposes of paragraph (1)(A).

(6) DENIAL OF DOUBLE BENEFITS.—No deduction or exclusion from gross income under this subtitle or credit against the tax imposed by this chapter (including any credit or deduction for the amount of taxes paid or accrued to a foreign country or possession of the United States) shall be allowed to the extent such deduction, exclusion, or credit is properly allocable to or chargeable against amounts excluded from gross income under subsection (a).

(7) AGGREGATE BENEFIT CANNOT EXCEED FOREIGN EARNED INCOME.—The sum of the amount excluded under subsection (a) and the amount deducted under subsection (c)(4)(A) for the taxable year shall not exceed the individual's foreign earned income for such year.

(8) LIMITATION ON INCOME EARNED IN RESTRICTED COUNTRY.—

(A) IN GENERAL.—If travel (or any transaction in connection with such travel) with respect to any foreign country is subject to the regulations described in subparagraph (B) during any period—

(i) the term "foreign earned income" shall not include any income from sources within such country attributable to services performed during such period,

(ii) the term "housing expenses" shall not include any expenses allocable to such period for housing in such country or for housing of the spouse or dependents of the taxpayer in another country while the taxpayer is present in such country, and

(iii) an individual shall not be treated as a bona fide resident of, or as present in, a foreign country for any day during which such individual was present in such country during such period.

(B) REGULATIONS.—For purposes of this paragraph, regulations are described in this subparagraph if such regulations—

(i) have been adopted pursuant to the Trading With the Enemy Act (50 U.S.C. 4301 et seq.), or the International Emergency Economic Powers Act (50 U.S.C. 1701 et seq.), and

(ii) include provisions generally prohibiting citizens and residents of the United States from engaging in transactions related to travel to, from, or within a foreign country.

(C) EXCEPTION.—Subparagraph (A) shall not apply to any individual during any period in which such individual's activities are not in violation of the regulations described in subparagraph (B).

(9) REGULATIONS.—The Secretary shall prescribe such regulations as may be necessary or appropriate to carry out the purposes of this section, including regulations providing rules—

(A) for cases where a husband and wife each have earned income from sources outside the United States, and

(B) for married individuals filing separate returns.

Amendments

• **2018, Tax Technical Corrections Act of 2018 (P.L. 115-141)**

P.L. 115-141, §401(a)(160), Div. U:

Amended Code Sec. 911(d)(8)(B)(i) by striking "(50 U.S.C. App. 1 et seq.)" and inserting "(50 U.S.C. 4301 et seq.)". **Effective** 3-23-2018.

• **2018, Bipartisan Budget Act of 2018 (P.L. 115-123)**

P.L. 115-123, §41116(a), Div. D:

Amended Code Sec. 911(d)(3) by inserting before the period at the end of the second sentence the following: ", unless such individual is serving in an area designated by the President of the United States by Executive order as a combat zone for purposes of section 112 in support of the Armed Forces of the United States". **Effective** for tax years beginning after 12-31-2017.

• **2006, Tax Increase Prevention and Reconciliation Act of 2005 (P.L. 109-222)**

P.L. 109-222, §515(b)(2)(C)(i):

Amended Code Sec. 911(d)(4) by striking "and (c)(1)(B)(ii)" and inserting ", (c)(1)(B)(ii), and (c)(2)(A)(ii)". **Effective** for tax years beginning after 12-31-2005.

P.L. 109-222, §515(b)(2)(C)(ii):

Amended Code Sec. 911(d)(7) by striking "subsection (c)(3)" and inserting "subsection (c)(4)". **Effective** for tax years beginning after 12-31-2005.

• **1986, Tax Reform Act of 1986 (P.L. 99-514)**

P.L. 99-514, §1233(b):

Amended Code Sec. 911(d) by redesignating paragraph (8) as paragraph (9) and by inserting after paragraph (7) new paragraph (8). **Effective** for tax years beginning after 12-31-86.

• **1983, Technical Corrections Act of 1982 (P.L. 97-448)**

P.L. 97-448, §101(c)(1):

Amended Code Sec. 911(d) by redesignating paragraph (7) as paragraph (8) and by inserting after paragraph (6) new paragraph (7). **Effective** as if included in the provision of P.L. 97-34 to which it relates.

• **1981, Economic Recovery Tax Act of 1981 (P.L. 97-34)**

P.L. 97-34, §111(a):

Amended Code Sec. 911(d). **Effective** with respect to tax years beginning after 12-31-81. Prior to amendment, Code Sec. 911(d) read:

(d) SECTION NOT TO APPLY.—An individual entitled to the benefits of this section for a taxable year may elect, in such manner and at such time as shall be prescribed by the Secretary, not to have the provisions of this section apply for the taxable year.

• **1978, Tax Treatment Extension Act of 1978 (P.L. 95-615)**

P.L. 95-615, §202(d)(1):

Amended Code Sec. 911(d). **Effective** as set forth in P.L. 95-615, §209. See historical comment on P.L. 95-615, §209 under Code Sec. 911(a). Prior to amendment, Code Sec. 911(d) read as follows:

(d) AMOUNT EXCLUDED UNDER SUBSECTION (a) INCLUDED IN COMPUTATION OF TAX.—

(1) COMPUTATION OF TAX.—If for any taxable year an individual has earned income which is excluded from gross income under subsection (a), the tax imposed by section 1 or section 1201 shall be the excess of—

(A) the tax imposed by section 1 or section 1201 (whichever is applicable) on the amount of net taxable income, over

(B) the tax imposed by section 1 or section 1201 (whichever is applicable) on the sum of—

(i) the amount of net excluded earned income, and

(ii) the zero bracket amount.

(2) DEFINITIONS.—For purposes of this subsection—

(A) the term "net taxable income" means an amount equal to the sum of the amount of taxable income for the taxable year plus the amount of net excluded earned income of such individual for such taxable year; and

(B) the term "net excluded earned income" means the excess of the amount of earned income excluded under subsection (a) for the taxable year over the amount of the deductions disallowed with respect to such excluded earned income for such taxable year under subsection (a).

• **1978, Revenue Act of 1978 (P.L. 95-600)**

P.L. 95-600, §401(b)(4):

Amended Code Sec. 911(d) (before amendment by P.L. 95-615, §202(d)(1)) by striking out "section 1 or section 1201" each place it appears and inserting in lieu thereof "section 1", and by striking out "(whichever is applicable)" each place it appeared. **Effective** for tax years beginning after 12-31-78. This amendment conflicts with the amendment made by P.L. 95-615, §202(d)(1).

• **1977, Tax Reduction and Simplification Act of 1977 (P.L. 95-30)**

P.L. 95-30, §102(b)(12):

Amended subparagraph (B) of Code Sec. 911(d)(1). **Effective** for tax years beginning after 12-31-76. Prior to amendment, subparagraph (B) of Code Sec. 911(d)(1) read as follows:

"(B) the tax imposed by section 1 or section 1201 (whichever is applicable) on the amount of net excluded earned income."

• **1976, Tax Reform Act of 1976 (P.L. 94-455)**

P.L. 94-455, §1011(b)(3), as amended by P.L. 95-30, §302:

Redesignated former Code Sec. 911(d) as Code Sec. 911(f) and added new Code Sec. 911(d). **Effective** for tax years beginning after 12-31-75. However, P.L. 95-30, §302, changed this effective date to tax years beginning after 12-31-76.

[Sec. 911(e)]

(e) ELECTION.—

(1) IN GENERAL.—An election under subsection (a) shall apply to the taxable year for which made and to all subsequent taxable years unless revoked under paragraph (2).

(2) REVOCATION.—A taxpayer may revoke an election made under paragraph (1) for any taxable year after the taxable year for which such election was made. Except with the consent of the Secretary, any taxpayer who makes such a revocation for any taxable year may not make another election under this section for any subsequent taxable year before the 6th taxable year after the taxable year for which such revocation was made.

Amendments

- **1981, Economic Recovery Tax Act of 1981 (P.L. 97-34)**

P.L. 97-34, § 111(a):

Amended Code Sec. 911(e). **Effective** with respect to tax years beginning after 12-31-81. Prior to amendment, Code Sec. 911(e) read as follows:

(e) CROSS REFERENCES.—

(1) For administrative and penal provisions relating to the exclusion provided for in this section, see sections 6001, 6011, 6012(c), and the other provisions of subtitle F.

(2) For elections as to treatment of income subject to foreign community property laws, see section 981.

- **1978, Tax Treatment Extension Act of 1978 (P.L. 95-615)**

P.L. 95-615, § 202(d)(1), (2):

Repealed Code Sec. 911(e), and redesignated the former Code Sec. 911(f) as 911(d). **Effective** for tax years beginning after 12-31-77, as set forth in P.L. 95-615, § 209. See historical comment on P.L. 95-615, § 209 under Code Sec. 911(a). Prior to repeal, Code Sec. 911(e) read as follows:

(e) SECTION NOT TO APPLY.—

(1) IN GENERAL.—An individual entitled to the benefits of this section for a taxable year may elect, in such manner and at such time as shall be prescribed by the Secretary, not to have the provisions of this section apply.

(2) EFFECT OF ELECTION.—An election under paragraph (1) shall apply to the taxable year for which made and to all subsequent taxable years. Such election may not be revoked except with the consent of the Secretary.

- **1976, Tax Reform Act of 1976 (P.L. 94-455)**

P.L. 94-455, § 1011(b)(3), as amended by P.L. 95-30, § 302:

Redesignated former Code Sec. 911(d) as Code Sec. 911(f), and added Code Sec. 911(e). **Effective** for tax years beginning after 12-31-75. However, P.L. 95-30, § 302, changed this effective date to tax years beginning after 12-31-76.

- **1966, Foreign Investors Tax Act of 1966 (P.L. 89-809)**

P.L. 89-809, § 105(e):

Amended Code Sec. 911(d) by inserting "(1)" before "For administrative" and by adding new paragraph (2). **Effective** 11-13-66.

- **1962, Revenue Act of 1962 (P.L. 87-834)**

P.L. 87-834, § 11(a):

Redesignated Code Sec. 911(c) as Sec. 911(d).

- **1958, Technical Amendments Act of 1958 (P.L. 85-866)**

P.L. 85-866, § 72(b):

Added Sec. 911(c). **Effective** for tax years beginning after 12-31-57.

[Sec. 911(f)]

(f) DETERMINATION OF TAX LIABILITY.—

(1) IN GENERAL.—If, for any taxable year, any amount is excluded from gross income of a taxpayer under subsection (a), then, notwithstanding sections 1 and 55—

(A) if such taxpayer has taxable income for such taxable year, the tax imposed by section 1 for such taxable year shall be equal to the excess (if any) of—

(i) the tax which would be imposed by section 1 for such taxable year if the taxpayer's taxable income were increased by the amount excluded under subsection (a) for such taxable year, over

(ii) the tax which would be imposed by section 1 for such taxable year if the taxpayer's taxable income were equal to the amount excluded under subsection (a) for such taxable year, and

(B) if such taxpayer has a taxable excess (as defined in section 55(b)(1)(B)) for such taxable year, the amount determined under the first sentence of section 55(b)(1)(A) for such taxable year shall be equal to the excess (if any) of—

(i) the amount which would be determined under such sentence for such taxable year (subject to the limitation of section 55(b)(3)) if the taxpayer's taxable excess (as so defined) were increased by the amount excluded under subsection (a) for such taxable year, over

(ii) the amount which would be determined under such sentence for such taxable year if the taxpayer's taxable excess (as so defined) were equal to the amount excluded under subsection (a) for such taxable year.

For purposes of this paragraph, the amount excluded under subsection (a) shall be reduced by the aggregate amount of any deductions or exclusions disallowed under subsection (d)(6) with respect to such excluded amount.

(2) SPECIAL RULES.—

(A) REGULAR TAX.—In applying section 1(h) for purposes of determining the tax under paragraph (1)(A)(i) for any taxable year in which, without regard to this subsection, the taxpayer's net capital gain exceeds taxable income (hereafter in this subparagraph referred to as the capital gain excess)—

(i) the taxpayer's net capital gain (determined without regard to section 1(h)(11)) shall be reduced (but not below zero) by such capital gain excess,

(ii) the taxpayer's qualified dividend income shall be reduced by so much of such capital gain excess as exceeds the taxpayer's net capital gain (determined without regard to section 1(h)(11) and the reduction under clause (i)), and

(iii) adjusted net capital gain, unrecaptured section 1250 gain, and 28-percent rate gain shall each be determined after increasing the amount described in section 1(h)(4)(B) by such capital gain excess.

(B) ALTERNATIVE MINIMUM TAX.—In applying section 55(b)(3) for purposes of determining the tax under paragraph (1)(B)(i) for any taxable year in which, without regard to this subsection, the taxpayer's net capital gain exceeds the taxable excess (as defined in section 55(b)(1)(B))—

(i) the rules of subparagraph (A) shall apply, except that such subparagraph shall be applied by substituting "the taxable excess (as defined in section 55(b)(1)(B))" for "taxable income", and

(ii) the reference in section 55(b)(3)(B) to the excess described in section 1(h)(1)(B), and the reference in section 55(b)(3)(C)(ii) to the excess described in section 1(h)(1)(C)(ii), shall each be treated as a reference to each such excess as determined under the rules of subparagraph (A) for purposes of determining the tax under paragraph (1)(A)(i).

(C) DEFINITIONS.—Terms used in this paragraph which are also used in section 1(h) shall have the respective meanings given such terms by section 1(h), except that in applying subparagraph (B) the adjustments under part VI of subchapter A shall be taken into account.

Amendments

- **2017, Tax Cuts and Jobs Act (P.L. 115-97)**

P.L. 115-97, § 12001(b)(3)(E)(i)-(ii):

Amended Code Sec. 911(f) in paragraph (1)(B), by striking "section 55(b)(1)(A)(ii)" and inserting "section 55(b)(1)(B)" and by striking "section 55(b)(1)(A)(i)" and inserting "section 55(b)(1)(A)", and in paragraph (2)(B), by striking "section 55(b)(1)(A)(ii)" each place it appears and inserting "section 55(b)(1)(B)". **Effective** for tax years beginning after 12-31-2017.

- **2014, Tax Technical Corrections Act of 2014 (P.L. 113-295)**

P.L. 113-295, § 202(b), Division A:

Amended Code Sec. 911(f)(2)(B)(ii) by striking "described in section 1(h)(1)(B) shall be treated as a reference to such excess as determined" and inserting "described in section 1(h)(1)(B), and the reference in section 55(b)(3)(C)(ii) to the excess described in section 1(h)(1)(C)(ii), shall each be treated as a reference to each such excess as determined". **Effective** as if included in the provision of the American Taxpayer

INCOME TAX—EARNED INCOME OF U.S. CITIZENS

Relief Act of 2012 (P.L. 112-240) to which it relates [**effective** for tax years beginning after 12-31-2012.—CCH].

P.L. 113-295, § 215(a), Division A:

Amended Code Sec. 911(f)(1) by adding at the end a new flush sentence. **Effective** as if included in the provision of the Tax Technical Corrections Act of 2007 (P.L. 110-172) to which it relates [effective for tax years beginning after 12-31-2006.—CCH].

- **2007, Tax Technical Corrections Act of 2007 (P.L. 110-172)**

P.L. 110-172, § 4(c):

Amended Code Sec. 911(f). **Effective** for tax years beginning after 12-31-2006. Prior to amendment, Code Sec. 911(f) read as follows:

(f) DETERMINATION OF TAX LIABILITY ON NONEXCLUDED AMOUNTS.—For purposes of this chapter, if any amount is excluded from the gross income of a taxpayer under subsection (a) for any taxable year, then, notwithstanding section 1 or 55—

(1) the tax imposed by section 1 on the taxpayer for such taxable year shall be equal to the excess (if any) of—

(A) the tax which would be imposed by section 1 for the taxable year if the taxpayer's taxable income were increased by the amount excluded under subsection (a) for the taxable year, over

(B) the tax which would be imposed by section 1 for the taxable year if the taxpayer's taxable income were equal to the amount excluded under subsection (a) for the taxable year, and

(2) the tentative minimum tax under section 55 for such taxable year shall be equal to the excess (if any) of—

(A) the amount which would be such tentative minimum tax for the taxable year if the taxpayer's taxable excess were increased by the amount excluded under subsection (a) for the taxable year, over

(B) the amount which would be such tentative minimum tax for the taxable year if the taxpayer's taxable excess were equal to the amount excluded under subsection (a) for the taxable year.

For purposes of this subsection, the amount excluded under subsection (a) shall be reduced by the aggregate amount of any deductions or exclusions disallowed under subsection (d)(6) with respect to such excluded amount.

- **2006, Tax Increase Prevention and Reconciliation Act of 2005 (P.L. 109-222)**

P.L. 109-222, § 515(c):

Amended Code Sec. 911 by redesignating subsection (f) as subsection (g) and by inserting after subsection (e) a new subsection (f). **Effective** for tax years beginning after 12-31-2005.

[Sec. 911(g)]

(g) CROSS REFERENCES.—

For administrative and penal provisions relating to the exclusions provided for in this section, see sections 6001, 6011, 6012(c), and the other provisions of subtitle F.

Amendments

- **2006, Tax Increase Prevention and Reconciliation Act of 2005 (P.L. 109-222)**

P.L. 109-222, § 515(c):

Amended Code Sec. 911 by redesignating subsection (f) as subsection (g). **Effective** for tax years beginning after 12-31-2005.

- **1981, Economic Recovery Tax Act of 1981 (P.L. 97-34)**

P.L. 97-34, § 111(a):

Added Code Sec. 911(f). **Effective** with respect to tax years beginning after 12-31-81.

P.L. 97-34, § 114, provides:

SEC. 114. REPORTS BY SECRETARY.

Section 208 of the Foreign Earned Income Act of 1978 is amended to read as follows:

"SEC. 208. REPORTS BY SECRETARY.

"(a) GENERAL RULE.—As soon as practicable after the date of the enactment of the Economic Recovery Tax Act of 1981, and as soon as practicable after the close of each fourth calendar year thereafter, the Secretary of the Treasury shall transmit a report to the Committee on Ways and Means of the House of Representatives and to the Committee on Finance of the Senate on the operation and effects of sections 911 and 912 of the Internal Revenue Code of 1954.

"(b) INFORMATION FROM FEDERAL AGENCIES.—Each agency of the Federal Government which pays allowances excludable from gross income under section 912 of such Code shall furnish to the Secretary of the Treasury such information as he determines to be necessary to carry out his responsibility under subsection (a)."

[Sec. 912]

SEC. 912. EXEMPTION FOR CERTAIN ALLOWANCES.

The following items shall not be included in gross income, and shall be exempt from taxation under this subtitle:

(1) FOREIGN AREAS ALLOWANCES.—In the case of civilian officers and employees of the Government of the United States, amounts received as allowances or otherwise (but not amounts received as post differentials) under—

(A) chapter 9 of title I of the Foreign Service Act of 1980,

(B) section 4 of the Central Intelligence Agency Act of 1949, as amended (50 U.S.C. 3505),

(C) title II of the Overseas Differentials and Allowances Act, or

(D) subsection (e) or (f) of the first section of the Administrative Expenses Act of 1946, as amended, or section 22 of such Act.

(2) COST-OF-LIVING ALLOWANCES.—In the case of civilian officers or employees of the Government of the United States stationed outside the continental United States (other than Alaska), amounts (other than amounts received under title II of the Overseas Differentials and Allowances Act) received as cost-of-living allowances in accordance with regulations approved by the President (or in the case of judicial officers or employees of the United States, in accordance with rules similar to such regulations).

(3) PEACE CORPS ALLOWANCES.—In the case of an individual who is a volunteer or volunteer leader within the meaning of the Peace Corps Act and members of his family, amounts received as allowances under section 5 or 6 of the Peace Corps Act other than amounts received as—

(A) termination payments under section 5(c) or section 6(1) of such Act,

(B) leave allowances,

(C) if such individual is a volunteer leader training in the United States, allowances to members of his family, and

(D) such portion of living allowances as the President may determine under the Peace Corps Act as constituting basic compensation.

Amendments

- **2018, Tax Technical Corrections Act of 2018 (P.L. 115-141)**

P.L. 115-141, § 401(a)(161), Div. U:

Amended Code Sec. 912(1)(B) by striking "(50 U.S.C., sec. 403e)" and inserting "(50 U.S.C. 3505)". **Effective** 3-23-2018.

- **2006 (P.L. 109-234)**

P.L. 109-234, § 1603(a) and (c), provide:

(a) IN GENERAL.—During fiscal years 2006, 2007, and 2008, the head of an agency may, in the agency head's discretion, provide to an individual employed by, or assigned or detailed to, such agency allowances, benefits, and gratuities comparable to those provided by the Secretary of State to members of the Foreign Service under section 413 and chapter 9 of title I of the Foreign Service Act of 1980 (22 U.S.C. 3973; 4081 et seq.), if such individual is on official duty in Iraq or Afghanistan.

* * *

(c) APPLICABILITY OF CERTAIN AUTHORITIES.—Section 912(a) [sic] of the Internal Revenue Code of 1986 shall apply with respect to amounts received as allowances or otherwise under this section in the same manner as section 912 of the Internal Revenue Code of 1986 applies with respect to amounts received by members of the Foreign Service as allowances or otherwise under chapter 9 of title I of the Foreign Service Act of 1980.

- **1988, Technical and Miscellaneous Revenue Act of 1988 (P.L. 100-647)**

P.L. 100-647, § 6137(a):

Amended Code Sec. 912(2) by inserting "(or in the case of judicial officers or employees of the United States, in accordance with rules similar to such regulations)" after "President". **Effective** for allowances received after 10-12-87, in tax years ending after such date.

- **1981, Economic Recovery Tax Act of 1981 (P.L. 97-34)**

P.L. 97-34, § 114, provides:

SEC. 114. REPORTS BY SECRETARY.

Section 208 of the Foreign Earned Income Act of 1978 is amended to read as follows:

SEC. 208. REPORTS BY SECRETARY.

(a) GENERAL RULE.—As soon as practicable after the date of the enactment of the Economic Recovery Tax Act of 1981, and as soon as practicable after the close of each fourth calendar year thereafter, the Secretary of the Treasury shall transmit a report to the Committee on Ways and Means of the House of Representatives and to the Committee on Finance of the Senate on the operation and effects of sections 911 and 912 of the Internal Revenue Code of 1954.

(b) INFORMATION FROM FEDERAL AGENCIES.—Each agency of the Federal Government which pays allowances excludable from gross income under section 912 of such Code shall furnish to the Secretary of the Treasury such information as he determines to be necessary to carry out his responsibility under subsection (a).

• 1980, Foreign Service Act of 1980 (P.L. 96-465)

P.L. 96-465, § 2206(e)(3):

Amended Code Sec. 912(1)(A) by striking out "(A) title IX of the Foreign Service Act of 1946, as amended (22 U. S. C., sec. 1131 and following)," and inserting in lieu thereof "(A) chapter 9 of title I of the Foreign Service Act of 1980,". **Effective** 2-15-81.

• 1961, Peace Corps Act (P.L. 87-293)

P.L. 87-293, § 201(a):

Added Code Sec. 921(3). **Effective** for tax years ending after 3-1-61.

Amendments

• 1981, Economic Recovery Tax Act of 1981 (P.L. 97-34)

P.L. 97-34, § 112(a):

Repealed Code Sec. 913. **Effective** with respect to tax years beginning after 12-31-81. Prior to repeal, Code Sec. 913 read as follows:

SEC. 913. DEDUCTION FOR CERTAIN EXPENSES OF LIVING ABROAD.

(a) ALLOWANCE OF DEDUCTION.—In the case of an individual who is—

(1) BONA FIDE RESIDENT OF FOREIGN COUNTRY.—A citizen of the United States and who establishes to the satisfaction of the Secretary that he has been a bona fide resident of a foreign country or countries for an uninterrupted period which includes an entire taxable year, or

(2) PRESENCE IN FOREIGN COUNTRY FOR 17 MONTHS.—A citizen or resident of the United States and who during any period of 18 consecutive months is present in a foreign country or countries during at least 510 full days in such period,

there shall be allowed as a deduction for such taxable year or for any taxable year which contains part of such period, the sum of the amounts set forth in subsection (b).

(b) AMOUNTS.—The amounts referred to in this subsection are:

(1) The qualified cost-of-living differential.
(2) The qualified housing expenses.
(3) The qualified schooling expenses.
(4) The qualified home leave travel expenses.
(5) The qualified hardship area deduction.

(c) DEDUCTION NOT TO EXCEED NET FOREIGN SOURCE EARNED INCOME.—

(1) IN GENERAL.—The deduction allowed by subsection (a) to any individual for the taxable year shall not exceed—

(A) such individual's earned income from sources outside the United States for the portion of the taxable year in which such individual's tax home is in a foreign country, reduced by

(B) the sum of—

(i) any earned income referred to in subparagraph (A) which is excluded from gross income under section 119, and

(ii) the allocable deductions.

(2) ALLOCABLE DEDUCTIONS DEFINED.—For purposes of paragraph (1)(B)(ii), the term "allocable deductions" means the deductions properly allocable to or chargeable against the earned income referred to in paragraph (1)(A), other than the deduction allowed by this section.

(d) QUALIFIED COST-OF-LIVING DIFFERENTIAL.—

(1) IN GENERAL.—For purposes of this section, the term "qualified cost-of-living differential" means a reasonable amount determined under tables (or under another method) prescribed by the Secretary establishing the amount (if any) by which the general cost of living in the foreign place in which the individual's tax home is located exceeds the general cost of living for the metropolitan area in the continental United States (excluding Alaska) having the highest general cost of living. The tables (or other methods) so prescribed shall be revised at least once during each calendar year.

(2) SPECIAL RULES.—For purposes of paragraph (1)—

(A) COMPUTATION ON DAILY BASIS.—The differential shall be computed on a daily basis for the period during which the individual's tax home is in a foreign country.

(B) DIFFERENTIAL TO BE BASED ON DAILY LIVING EXPENSES.—An individual's cost-of-living differential shall be determined by reference to reasonable daily living expenses (excluding housing and schooling expenses).

(C) BASIS OF COMPARISON.—The differential prescribed for any foreign place—

(i) shall vary depending on the composition of the family (spouse and dependents) residing with the individual (or at a qualified second household), and

(ii) shall reflect the costs of living of a family whose income is equal to the salary of an employee of the United States who is compensated at a rate equal to the annual rate paid for step 1 of grade GS-14.

(D) STATE DEPARTMENT'S INDEX MAY BE TAKEN INTO ACCOUNT.—The Secretary, in determining the qualified cost-of-living differential for any foreign place, may take into account the Department of State's Local Index of Living Costs Abroad as it relates to such place.

(E) NO DIFFERENTIAL FOR PERIODS DURING WHICH INDIVIDUAL IS ELIGIBLE UNDER SECTION 119.—Except as provided in subsection (i)(1)(A)(ii) an individual shall not be entitled to any qualified cost-of-living differential for any period for which such individual's meals and lodging are excluded from gross income under section 119.

(e) QUALIFIED HOUSING EXPENSES.—

• 1960, Overseas Differentials and Allowances Act (P.L. 86-707)

P.L. 86-707, § 523(a):

Amended paragraphs (1) and (2) of Code Sec. 912. **Effective** for amounts received on or after 9-6-60 in tax years ending on or after that date. Prior to amendment, they read as follows:

(1) COST-OF LIVING ALLOWANCES.—In the case of civilian officers or employees of the Government of the United States stationed outside continental United States, amounts received as cost-of-living allowances in accordance with regulations approved by the President.

(2) FOREIGN SERVICE ALLOWANCES.—In the case of an officer or employee of the Foreign Service of the United States, amounts received by such officer or employee as allowances or otherwise under the terms of title IX of the Foreign Service Act of 1946 (22 U. S. C. 1131-1158).

[Sec. 913—Repealed]

(1) IN GENERAL.—For purposes of this section, the term "qualified housing expenses" means the excess of—

(A) the individual's housing expenses, over

(B) the individual's base housing amount.

(2) HOUSING EXPENSES.—

(A) IN GENERAL.—For purposes of paragraph (1), the term "housing expenses" means the reasonable expenses paid or incurred during the taxable year by or on behalf of the individual for housing for the individual (and, if they reside with him, for his spouse and dependents), in a foreign country. Such term—

(i) except as provided in clause (ii), includes expenses attributable to the housing (such as utilities and insurance), and

(ii) does not include interest and taxes of the kind deductible under section 163 or 164 or any amount allowable as a deduction under section 216(a).

(B) PORTION WHICH IS LAVISH OR EXTRAVAGANT NOT ALLOWED.—For purposes of subparagraph (A), housing expenses shall not be treated as reasonable to the extent such expenses are lavish or extravagant under the circumstances.

(3) BASE HOUSING AMOUNT.—For purposes of paragraph (1)—

(A) IN GENERAL.—The term "base housing amount" means 20 percent of the excess of—

(i) the individual's housing income (reduced by the deductions properly allocable to or chargeable against such housing income (other than the deduction allowed by this section)), over

(ii) the sum of—

(I) the housing expenses taken into account under paragraph (1)(A) of this subsection,

(II) the qualified cost-of-living differential,

(III) the qualified school expenses,

(IV) the qualified home leave travel expenses, and

(V) the qualified hardship area deduction.

(B) BASE HOUSING AMOUNT TO BE ZERO IN CERTAIN CASES.—If, because of adverse living conditions, the individual maintains a household for his spouse and dependents at a foreign place other than his tax home which is in addition to the household he maintains as his tax home, and if his tax home is in a hardship area as defined in subsection (h), the base housing amount for the household maintained at his tax home shall be zero.

(4) PERIODS TAKEN INTO ACCOUNT.—

(A) IN GENERAL.—The expenses taken into account under this subsection shall be only those which are attributable to housing during periods for which—

(i) the individual's tax home is in a foreign country, and

(ii) except as provided in subsection (i)(1)(B)(iii), the value of the individual's housing is not excluded under section 119.

(B) DETERMINATION OF BASE HOUSING AMOUNT.—The base housing amount shall be determined for the periods referred to in subparagraph (A) (as modified by subsection (i)(1)(B)(iii)).

(5) ONLY ONE HOUSE PER PERIOD.—If, but for this paragraph, housing expenses for any individual would be taken into account under paragraph (2) of subsection (b) with respect to more than one abode for any period, only housing expenses with respect to that abode which bears the closest relationship to the individual's tax home shall be taken into account under such paragraph (2) for such period.

(6) HOUSING INCOME.—For purposes of this subsection, the term "housing income" has the meaning given to the term "earned income" by section 911(b) (determined with the rule set forth in paragraph (3) of section 911(c)).

(7) RECAPTURE OF EXCESS HOUSING DEDUCTIONS ATTRIBUTABLE TO TREATMENT OF AFTER-RECEIVED COMPENSATION.—

(A) IN GENERAL.—There shall be included in the gross income of the individual for the taxable year in which any after-received compensation is received an amount equal to any excess housing deduction determined for such year.

(B) EXCESS HOUSING DEDUCTION.—For purposes of subparagraph (A), the excess housing deduction determined for any taxable year is the excess (if any) of—

(i) the aggregate amount which has been allowed as a housing deduction (for such taxable year and all prior taxable years), over

(ii) the aggregate amount which would have been allowable as a housing deduction (for such taxable year and all prior taxable years for which a housing deduction has been allowed), by taking after-received compensation into account under this subsection as if it had been received in the taxable year in which the services were performed.

INCOME TAX—EARNED INCOME OF U.S. CITIZENS

In applying the preceding sentence to any taxable year, proper adjustment shall be made for the effect of applying such sentence for purposes of all prior taxable years.

(C) TREATMENT OF AMOUNT INCLUDED IN INCOME.—Any amount included in gross income under subparagraph (A) shall not be treated as income for purposes of applying subsection (c) of this section.

(D) DEFINITIONS.—For purposes of this paragraph—

(i) HOUSING DEDUCTION.—The term "housing deduction" means that portion of the deduction allowable under subsection (a) for any taxable year which is attributable to qualified housing expenses. For such purpose, qualified housing expenses shall be taken into account after all other amounts described in subsection (b).

(ii) AFTER-RECEIVED COMPENSATION.—The term "after-received compensation" means compensation received by an individual in a taxable year which is attributable to services performed by such individual in the third preceding, second preceding, or first preceding taxable year.

(f) QUALIFIED SCHOOLING EXPENSES.—

(1) IN GENERAL.—For purposes of this section, the term "qualified schooling expenses" means the reasonable schooling expenses paid or incurred by or on behalf of the individual during the taxable year for the education of each dependent of the individual at the elementary or secondary level. For purposes of the preceding sentence, the elementary or secondary level means education which is the equivalent of education from the kindergarten through the 12th grade in a United States-type school.

(2) EXPENSES INCLUDED.—For purposes of paragraph (1), the term "schooling expenses" means the cost of tuition, fees, books, and local transportation and of other expenses required by the school. Except as provided in paragraph (3), such term does not include expenses of room and board or expenses of transportation other than local transportation.

(3) ROOM, BOARD, AND TRAVEL ALLOWED IN CERTAIN CASES.—If an adequate United States-type school is not available within a reasonable commuting distance of the individual's tax home, the expenses of room and board of the dependent and the expenses of the transportation of the dependent each school year between such tax home and the location of the school shall be treated as schooling expenses.

(4) DETERMINATION OF REASONABLE EXPENSES.—If—

(A) there is an adequate United States-type school available within a reasonable commuting distance of the individual's tax home, and

(B) the dependent attends a school other than the school referred to in subparagraph (A),

then the amount taken into account under paragraph (2) shall not exceed the aggregate amount which would be charged for the period by the school referred to in subparagraph (A).

(5) PERIOD TAKEN INTO ACCOUNT.—An amount shall be taken into account as a qualified schooling expense only if it is attributable to education for a period during which the individual's tax home is in a foreign country.

(g) QUALIFIED HOME LEAVE TRAVEL EXPENSES.—

(1) IN GENERAL.—For purposes of this section, the term "qualified home leave travel expenses" means the reasonable amounts paid or incurred by or on behalf of an individual for the transportation of such individual, his spouse, and each dependent—

(A) from a point outside the United States to the individual's principal domestic residence, and

(B) from the individual's principal domestic residence to a point outside the United States.

(2) LIMITATION TO COST BETWEEN TAX HOME AND PLACE OF RESIDENCE.—The amount taken into account under subparagraph (A) or (B) of paragraph (1) with respect to any transportation shall not exceed the reasonable amount for transportation between the location of the individual's tax home outside the United States and the individual's principal domestic residence.

(3) SUBSTITUTION OF NEAREST PORT OF ENTRY IN CERTAIN CASES.—With respect to any person whose travel in the United States is not travel to and from the individual's principal domestic residence, paragraphs (1) and (2) shall be applied by substituting the nearest port of entry in the United States for the individual's principal domestic residence.

(4) NEAREST PORT OF ENTRY.—For purposes of paragraph (3), the nearest port of entry in the United States shall not include a nearest port of entry located in Alaska or Hawaii unless the individual elects to have such port of entry taken into account.

(5) PRINCIPAL DOMESTIC RESIDENCE DEFINED.—For purposes of this subsection, an individual's principal domestic residence is the location of such individual's present (or, if none, most recent) principal residence in the United States.

(6) 1 ROUND TRIP PER 12-MONTH PERIOD ABROAD.—Amounts may be taken into account under paragraph (4) of subsection (b) only with respect to 1 trip to the United States, and 1 trip from the United States, per person for each continuous period of 12 months for which the individual's tax home is in a foreign country.

(h) QUALIFIED HARDSHIP AREA DEDUCTION.—

(1) IN GENERAL.—For purposes of this section, the term "qualified hardship area deduction" means an amount computed on a daily basis at an annual rate of $5,000 for days during which the individual's tax home is in a hardship area.

(2) HARDSHIP AREA DEFINED.—For purposes of this section, the term "hardship area" means any foreign place designated by the Secretary of State as a hardship post where extraordinarily difficult living conditions, notably unhealthful conditions, or excessive physical hardships exist and for which a post differential of 15 percent or more—

(A) is provided under section 5925 of title 5, United States Code, or

(B) would be so provided if officers and employees of the Government of the United States were present at that place.

(i) SPECIAL RULES WHERE INDIVIDUAL MAINTAINS SEPARATE HOUSEHOLD FOR SPOUSE AND DEPENDENTS BECAUSE OF ADVERSE LIVING CONDITIONS AT TAX HOME.—

(1) IN GENERAL.—For any period during which an individual maintains a qualified second household—

(A) QUALIFIED COST-OF-LIVING DIFFERENTIAL.—

(i) ALLOWANCE DETERMINED BY REFERENCE TO LOCATION OF QUALIFIED SECOND HOUSEHOLD.—Paragraph (1) of subsection (d) shall be applied by substituting "the qualified second household" for "the individual's tax home".

(ii) DISREGARD OF SECTION 119 RULE.—Subparagraph (E) of subsection (d)(2) shall not apply with respect to the spouse and dependents.

(B) QUALIFIED HOUSING EXPENSES.—

(i) EXPENSES WITH RESPECT TO QUALIFIED SECOND HOUSEHOLD TAKEN INTO ACCOUNT.—For purposes of subsection (e), the expenses for housing of an individual's spouse and dependents at the qualified second household shall be treated as housing expenses if they would meet the requirements of subsection (e)(2) if the individual resided at such household.

(ii) SEPARATE APPLICATION OF SUBSECTION (e).—Subsection (e) shall be applied separately with respect to the housing expenses for the qualified second household; except that, in determining the base housing amount, the housing expenses (if any) of the individual for housing at his tax home shall also be taken into account under subsection (e)(3)(A)(ii).

(iii) CERTAIN RULES NOT TO APPLY.—Paragraphs (4)(A)(ii) and (5) of subsection (e) shall not apply with respect to housing expenses for the qualified second household.

(C) REQUIREMENT THAT SPOUSE AND DEPENDENTS RESIDE WITH INDIVIDUAL FOR PURPOSES OF SCHOOLING AND HOME LEAVE.—

(i) IN GENERAL.—The requirement of subsection (j)(3) that the dependent or spouse of the individual (as the case may be) reside with the individual at his tax home shall be treated as met if such spouse or dependent resides at the qualified second household.

(ii) SUBSTITUTION OF HOUSEHOLD FOR TAX HOME.—In any case where clause (i) applies, paragraphs (3) and (4) of subsection (f), and subsection (g), shall be applied with respect to amounts paid or incurred for the spouse or dependent by substituting the location of the qualified second household for the individual's tax home.

(2) DEFINITION OF QUALIFIED SECOND HOUSEHOLD.—For purposes of this section, the term "qualified second household" means any household maintained in a foreign country by an individual for the spouse and dependents of such individual at a place other than the tax home of such individual because of adverse living conditions at the individual's tax home.

(j) OTHER DEFINITIONS AND SPECIAL RULES.—

(1) DEFINITIONS.—For purposes of this section—

(A) EARNED INCOME.—The term "earned income" has the meaning given to such term by section 911(b) (determined with the rules set forth in paragraphs (2), (3), (4), and (5) of section 911(c)), except that such term does not include amounts paid by the United States or any agency thereof.

(B) TAX HOME.—The term "tax home" means, with respect to any individual, such individual's home for purposes of section 162(a)(2) (relating to traveling expenses while away from home). An individual shall not be treated as having a tax home in a foreign country for any period for which his abode is within the United States.

(C) RESIDENCE AT TAX HOME.—A household or residence shall be treated as at the tax home of an individual if such household or residence is within a reasonable commuting distance of such tax home.

(D) ADVERSE LIVING CONDITIONS.—The term "adverse living conditions" means living conditions which are dangerous, unhealthful, or otherwise adverse.

(E) UNITED STATES.—The term "United States", when used in a geographical sense, includes the possessions of the United States and the areas set forth in paragraph (1) of section 638 and so much of paragraph (2) of section 638 as relates to the possessions of the United States.

(2) LIMITATION TO COACH OR ECONOMY FARE.—The amount taken into account under this section for any transportation by air shall not exceed the lowest coach or economy rate at the time of such transportation charged by a commercial airline for such transportation during the calendar month in which such transportation is furnished. If there is no such coach or economy rate or if the individual is required to use first-class transportation because of a physical impairment, the preceding sentence shall be applied by substituting "first-class" for "coach or economy".

(3) REQUIREMENT THAT SPOUSE AND DEPENDENTS RESIDE WITH INDIVIDUAL FOR PURPOSES OF SCHOOLING AND HOME LEAVE.—Except as provided in subsection (i)(1)(C)(i), amounts may be taken into account under subsection (f) with respect to any dependent of the individual, and under subsection (g) with respect to the individual's spouse or any dependent of the individual, only for the period that such spouse or dependent (as the case may be) resides with the individual at his tax home.

(4) WAIVER OF PERIOD OF STAY IN FOREIGN COUNTRY.—For purposes of paragraphs (1) and (2) of subsection (a), an individual who—

(A) for any period is a bona fide resident of or is present in a foreign country,

(B) leaves such foreign country after August 31, 1978—

(i) during any period during which the Secretary determines, after consultation with the Secretary of State or his delegate, that individuals were required to leave such foreign country because of war, civil unrest, or similar adverse conditions in such foreign country which precluded the normal conduct of business by such individuals, and

(ii) before meeting the requirements of such paragraphs (1) and (2), and

(C) establishes to the satisfaction of the Secretary that he could reasonably have been expected to have met such requirements but for the conditions referred to in clause (i) of subparagraph (B),

shall be treated as having met such requirements with respect to the period described in subparagraph (A) during which he was a bona fide resident or was present in the foreign country.

(k) CERTAIN DOUBLE BENEFITS DISALLOWED.—An individual shall not be allowed—

(1) as a deduction (other than the deduction under section 151),

(2) as an exclusion, or

(3) as a credit under section 44A (relating to household and dependent care services),

any amount to the extent that such amount is taken into account under subsection (d), (e), (f), or (g).

Sec. 913—Repealed

INCOME TAX—FOREIGN SALES CORPORATIONS

(l) APPLICATION WITH SECTION 911.—An individual shall not be allowed the deduction allowed by subsection (a) for any taxable year with respect to which he elects the exclusion provided in section 911.

(m) REGULATIONS.—The Secretary shall prescribe such regulations as may be necessary or appropriate to carry out the purposes of this section, including regulations providing rules—

(1) for cases where a husband and wife each have earned income from sources outside the United States, and

(2) for married individuals filing separate returns.

Amendments

• **1980 (P.L. 96-608)**

P.L. 96-608, §1(a):

Amended Code Sec. 913(j) by adding paragraph (4). **Effective** with respect to tax years beginning after 12-31-77. However, in the case of an individual who leaves the foreign country after 8-31-78, rules similar to the rules of Code Sec. 913(j)(4), as added by this Act shall apply for purposes of applying Code Sec. 911 for tax years beginning in 1977 or 1978.

• **1980, Technical Corrections Act of 1979 (P.L. 96-222)**

P.L. 96-222, §108(a)(1)(B)(i):

Amended Code Sec. 913(e)(3)(A)(i) by changing "earned income" to "housing income" each place it appeared. **Effective** as set forth in P.L. 95-615, §209.

P.L. 96-222, §108(a)(1)(B)(ii):

Amended Code Sec. 913(e) by adding paragraphs (6) and (7). **Effective** as set forth in P.L. 95-615, §209.

P.L. 96-222, §108(a)(1)(F)(i):

Amended Code Sec. 913(g). **Effective** as set forth in P.L. 95-615, §209. Prior to amendment Code Sec. 913(g) read as follows:

(g) QUALIFIED HOME LEAVE TRAVEL EXPENSES.—

(1) IN GENERAL.—For purposes of this section, the term "qualified home leave travel expenses" means the reasonable amounts paid or incurred by or on behalf of an individual for the transportation of such individual, his spouse, and each dependent from the location of the individual's tax home outside the United States to—

(A) the individual's present (or, if none, most recent) principal residence in the United States, or

(B) if subparagraph (A) does not apply to the individual, the nearest port of entry in the continental United States (excluding Alaska)

and return

(2) ONE TRIP PER 12-MONTH PERIOD ABROAD.—Amounts may be taken into account under paragraph (4) of subsection (b) only with respect to one round trip per person for each continuous period of 12 months for which the individual's tax home is in a foreign country.

P.L. 96-222, §108(a)(1)(F)(ii):

Amended Code Sec. 913(i)(1)(C)(ii) by changing "and paragraph (1) of subsection (g)" to "and subsection (g)". **Effective** as set forth in P.L. 95-615, §209.

• **1978, Tax Treatment Extension Act of 1978 (P.L. 95-615)**

P.L. 95-615, §203(a):

Added Code Sec. 913. **Effective** as set forth in Act Sec. 209, below.

P.L. 95-615, §209(a), (c), provides:

(a) GENERAL RULE.—Except as provided in subsections (b) and (c) the amendments made by this title shall apply to taxable years beginning after December 31, 1977.

* * *

(c) ELECTION OF PRIOR LAW.—

(1) A taxpayer may elect not to have the amendments made by this title apply with respect to any taxable year beginning after December 31, 1977, and before January 1, 1979.

(2) An election under this subsection shall be filed with a taxpayer's timely filed return for the first taxable year beginning after December 31, 1977.

Subpart C—Taxation of Foreign Sales Corporations—[Repealed]

[Sec. 921—Repealed]

Amendments

• **2000, FSC Repeal and Extraterritorial Income Exclusion Act of 2000 (P.L. 106-519)**

P.L. 106-519, §2:

Repealed subpart C of part III of subchapter N of chapter 1 (Code Secs. 921-927). **Effective** generally for transactions after 9-30-2000. For special rules, see Act Sec. 5(b)-(d), below. The text of repealed Code Sec. 921 appears after Act Sec. 5(b)-(d).

P.L. 106-519, §5(b)-(d), as amended by P.L. 109-222, §513(a), provides:

(b) NO NEW FSCs; TERMINATION OF INACTIVE FSCs.—

(1) NO NEW FSCs.—No corporation may elect after September 30, 2000, to be a FSC (as defined in section 922 of the Internal Revenue Code of 1986, as in effect before the amendments made by this Act).

(2) TERMINATION OF INACTIVE FSCs.—If a FSC has no foreign trade income (as defined in section 923(b) of such Code, as so in effect) for any period of 5 consecutive taxable years beginning after December 31, 2001, such FSC shall cease to be treated as a FSC for purposes of such Code for any taxable year beginning after such period.

(c) TRANSITION PERIOD FOR EXISTING FOREIGN SALES CORPORATIONS.—

(1) IN GENERAL.—In the case of a FSC (as so defined) in existence on September 30, 2000, and at all times thereafter, the amendments made by this Act shall not apply to any transaction in the ordinary course of trade or business involving a FSC which occurs before January 1, 2002.

(2) ELECTION TO HAVE AMENDMENTS APPLY EARLIER.—A taxpayer may elect to have the amendments made by this Act apply to any transaction by a FSC or any related person to which such amendments would apply but for the application of paragraph (1). Such election shall be effective for the taxable year for which made and all subsequent taxable years, and, once made, may be revoked only with the consent of the Secretary of the Treasury.

(3) EXCEPTION FOR OLD EARNINGS AND PROFITS OF CERTAIN CORPORATIONS.—

(A) IN GENERAL.—In the case of a foreign corporation to which this paragraph applies—

(i) earnings and profits of such corporation accumulated in taxable years ending before October 1, 2000, shall not be included in the gross income of the persons holding stock in such corporation by reason of section 943(e)(4)(B)(i); and

(ii) rules similar to the rules of clauses (ii), (iii), and (iv) of section 953(d)(4)(B) shall apply with respect to such earnings and profits.

The preceding sentence shall not apply to earnings and profits acquired in a transaction after September 30, 2000, to which section 381 applies unless the distributor or transferor corporation was immediately before the transaction a foreign corporation to which this paragraph applies.

(B) EXISTING FSCs.—This paragraph shall apply to any controlled foreign corporation (as defined in section 957) if—

(i) such corporation is a FSC (as so defined) in existence on September 30, 2000;

(ii) such corporation is eligible to make the election under section 943(e) by reason of being described in paragraph (2)(B) of such section; and

(iii) such corporation makes such election not later than for its first taxable year beginning after December 31, 2001.

(C) OTHER CORPORATIONS.—This paragraph shall apply to any controlled foreign corporation (as defined in section 957), and such corporation shall (notwithstanding any provision of section 943(e)) be treated as an applicable foreign corporation for purposes of section 943(e), if—

(i) such corporation is in existence on September 30, 2000;

(ii) as of such date, such corporation is wholly owned (directly or indirectly) by a domestic corporation (determined without regard to any election under section 943(e));

(iii) for each of the 3 taxable years preceding the first taxable year to which the election under section 943(e) by such controlled foreign corporation applies—

(I) all of the gross income of such corporation is subpart F income (as defined in section 952), including by reason of section 954(b)(3)(B); and

(II) in the ordinary course of such corporation's trade or business, such corporation regularly sold (or paid commissions) to a FSC which on September 30, 2000, was a related person to such corporation;

(iv) such corporation has never made an election under section 922(a)(2) (as in effect before the date of the enactment of this paragraph) to be treated as a FSC; and

(v) such corporation makes the election under section 943(e) not later than for its first taxable year beginning after December 31, 2001.

The preceding sentence shall cease to apply as of the date that the domestic corporation referred to in clause (ii) ceases to wholly own (directly or indirectly) such controlled foreign corporation.

(4) RELATED PERSON.—For purposes of this subsection, the term "related person" has the meaning given to such term by section 943(b)(3).

(5) SECTION REFERENCES.—Except as otherwise expressly provided, any reference in this subsection to a section or other provision shall be considered to be a reference to a section or other provision of the Internal Revenue Code of 1986, as amended by this Act.

(d) SPECIAL RULES RELATING TO LEASING TRANSACTIONS.—

(1) SALES INCOME.—If foreign trade income in connection with the lease or rental of property described in section 927(a)(1)(B) of such Code (as in effect before the amendments made by this Act) is treated as exempt foreign trade income for purposes of section 921(a) of such Code (as so in effect), such property shall be treated as property described in section 941(c)(1)(B) of such Code (as added by this Act) for purposes of applying section 941(c)(2) of such Code (as so added) to any subsequent transaction involving such property to which the amendments made by this Act apply.

(2) LIMITATION ON USE OF GROSS RECEIPTS METHOD.—If any person computed its foreign trade income from any transaction with respect to any property on the basis of a transfer price determined under the method described in section 925(a)(1) of such Code (as in effect before the amendments made by this Act), then the qualifying foreign trade income (as defined in section 941(a) of such Code, as in effect after such amendment) of such person (or any related person) with respect to any other transaction involving such property (and to which the amendments made by this Act apply) shall be zero.

Prior to repeal, Code Sec. 921 read as follows:

SEC. 921. EXEMPT FOREIGN TRADE INCOME EXCLUDED FROM GROSS INCOME.

[Sec. 921(a)]

(a) EXCLUSION.—Exempt foreign trade income of a FSC shall be treated as foreign source income which is not effectively connected with the conduct of a trade or business within the United States.

[Sec. 921(b)]

(b) PROPORTIONATE ALLOCATION OF DEDUCTIONS TO EXEMPT FOREIGN TRADE INCOME.—Any deductions of the FSC properly apportioned and allocated to the foreign trade income derived by a FSC from any transaction shall be allocated between—

(1) the exempt foreign trade income derived from such transaction, and

INCOME TAX—FOREIGN SALES CORPORATIONS

(2) the foreign trade income (other than exempt foreign trade income) derived from such transaction, on a proportionate basis.

[Sec. 921(c)]

(c) DENIAL OF CREDITS.—Notwithstanding any other provision of this chapter, no credit (other than a credit allowable under section 27(a), 33, or 34) shall be allowed under this chapter to any FSC.

[Sec. 921(d)]

(d) FOREIGN TRADE INCOME, INVESTMENT INCOME, AND CARRYING CHARGES TREATED AS EFFECTIVELY CONNECTED WITH UNITED STATES BUSINESS.—For purposes of this chapter—

(1) all foreign trade income of a FSC other than—

(A) exempt foreign trade income, and

(B) section 923(a)(2) non-exempt income,

(2) all interest, dividends, royalties, and other investment income received or accrued by a FSC, and

(3) all carrying charges received or accrued by a FSC,

shall be treated as income effectively connected with a trade or business conducted through a permanent establishment of such corporation within the United States. Income described in paragraph (1) shall be treated as derived from sources within the United States.

Amendments

- **1984, Deficit Reduction Act of 1984 (P.L. 98-369)**

P.L. 98-369, §801(a):

Amended Part III of subchapter N of chapter 1 by inserting new subpart C, consisting of Code Secs. 921-927. **Effective** for transactions after 12-31-84, in tax years ending after such date. Prior to amendment, former Code Sec. 921 read as follows:

SEC. 921. DEFINITION OF WESTERN HEMISPHERE TRADE CORPORATIONS.

For purposes of this subtitle, the term "Western Hemisphere trade corporation" means a domestic corporation all of whose business (other than incidental purchases) is done in any country or countries in North, Central, or South America, or in the West Indies, and which satisfies the following conditions:

(1) if 95 percent or more of the gross income of such domestic corporation for the 3-year period immediately preceding the close of the taxable year (or for such part of such period during which the corporation was in existence) was derived from sources without the United States; and

(2) if 90 percent or more of its gross income for such period or such part thereof was derived from the active conduct of a trade or business.

- **1976, Tax Reform Act of 1976 (P.L. 94-455)**

P.L. 94-455, §1052(b):

Repealed Code Sec. 921. **Effective** for tax years beginning after 12-31-79.

P.L. 94-455, §1901(a)(116):

Struck out the last sentence of Code Sec. 921. **Effective** for tax years beginning after 12-31-76. Prior to striking, the last sentence of Code Sec. 921 read as follows:

For any taxable year beginning prior to January 1, 1954, the determination as to whether any corporation meets the requirements of section 109 of the Internal Revenue Code of 1939 shall be made as if this section had not been enacted and without inferences drawn from the fact that this section is not expressly made applicable with respect to taxable years beginning prior to January 1, 1954.

- **1971, Revenue Act of 1971 (P.L. 92-178)**

P.L. 92-178, §307, provides:

For purposes of applying the income tax laws of the United States with respect to the Virgin Islands under the Act of July 12, 1921 (42 Stat. 123; 48 U. S. C. 1397), subpart C of part III of subchapter N of chapter 1 of the Internal Revenue Code of 1954 (relating to Western Hemisphere Trade Corporations) shall be treated as having been repealed effective with respect to taxable years beginning after the date of the enactment [December 10, 1971] of this Act.

[Sec. 922—Repealed]

Amendments

- **2000, FSC Repeal and Extraterritorial Income Exclusion Act of 2000 (P.L. 106-519)**

P.L. 106-519, §2:

Repealed subpart C of part III of subchapter N of chapter 1 (Code Secs. 921-927). **Effective**, generally, to transactions after 9-30-2000. For special rules, see Act Sec. 5(b)-(d) in the amendment notes following repealed Code Sec. 921. Prior to repeal, Code Sec. 922 read as follows:

SEC. 922. FSC DEFINED.

[Sec. 922(a)]

(a) FSC DEFINED.—For purposes of this title, the term "FSC" means any corporation—

(1) which—

(A) was created or organized—

(i) under the laws of any foreign country which meets the requirements of section 927(e)(3), or

(ii) under the laws applicable to any possession of the United States,

(B) has no more than 25 shareholders at any time during the taxable year,

(C) does not have any preferred stock outstanding at any time during the taxable year,

(D) during the taxable year—

(i) maintains an office located outside the United States in a foreign country which meets the requirements of section 927(e)(3) or in any possession of the United States,

(ii) maintains a set of the permanent books of account (including invoices) of such corporation at such office, and

(iii) maintains at a location within the United States the records which such corporation is required to keep under section 6001,

(E) at all times during the taxable year, has a board of directors which includes at least one individual who is not a resident of the United States, and

(F) is not a member, at any time during the taxable year, of any controlled group of corporations of which a DISC is a member, and

(2) which has made an election (at the time and in the manner provided in section 927(f)(1)) which is in effect for the taxable year to be treated as a FSC.

[Sec. 922(b)]

(b) SMALL FSC DEFINED.—For purposes of this title, a FSC is a small FSC with respect to any taxable year if—

(1) such corporation has made an elecion (at the time and in the manner provided in section 927(f)(1)) which is in effect for the taxable year to be treated as a small FSC, and

(2) such corporation is not a member, at any time during the taxable year, of controlled group of corporations which includes a FSC unless such other FSC has also made an election under paragraph (1) which is in effect for such year.

Amendments

- **1984, Deficit Reduction Act of 1984 (P.L. 98-369)**

P.L. 98-369, §801(a):

Amended Part III of Subchapter 1 by adding new subpart C, consisting of Code Secs. 921-927. **Effective** for transactions after 12-31-84, in tax years ending after such date. Prior to amendment, former Code Sec. 922 read as follows:

SEC. 922. SPECIAL DEDUCTION.

[Sec. 922(a)]

(a) GENERAL RULE.—In the case of a Western Hemisphere trade corporation there shall be allowed as a deduction in computing taxable income an amount computed as follows—

(1) First determine the taxable income of such corporation computed without regard to this section.

(2) Then multiply the amount determined under paragraph (1) by the fraction—

(A) the numerator of which is 14 percent, and

(B) the denominator of which is that percentage which equals the highest rate of tax specified in section 11(b).

No deduction shall be allowed under this section to a corporation for a taxable year for which it is a DISC or in which it owns at any time stock in a DISC or former DISC (as defined in section 992(a)).

Amendments

- **1978, Revenue Act of 1978 (P.L. 95-600)**

P.L. 95-600, §301(b)(15):

Amended Code Sec. 922(a)(2)(B) by striking out "the sum of the normal tax rate and the surtax rate for the taxable year prescribed by section 11" and inserting in lieu thereof "the highest rate of tax specified in section 11(b)". **Effective** for tax years beginning after 12-31-78.

- **1976, Tax Reform Act of 1976 (P.L. 94-455)**

P.L. 94-455, §1052(b):

Repealed Code Sec. 922. **Effective** for tax years beginning after 12-31-79.

P.L. 94-455, §1052(c)(1):

Substituted "(a) GENERAL RULE.—In the case of" for "In the case of" in the first sentence of Code Sec. 922. **Effective** for tax years beginning after 12-31-75.

- **1971, Revenue Act of 1971 (P.L. 92-178)**

P.L. 92-178, §307:

For the amendment, see the amendatory note under Code Sec. 921.

P.L. 92-178, §502(c):

Added the last sentence in Code Sec. 922.

[Sec. 922(b)]

(b) PHASEOUT OF DEDUCTION.—In the case of a taxable year beginning after December 31, 1975, and before January 1, 1980, the percent specified in subsection (a)(2)(A) shall be (in lieu of 14 percent) the percent specified in the following table:

For a taxable year beginning in—	The percentage shall be—
1976	11
1977	8
1978	5
1979	2

Amendments:

- **1976, Tax Reform Act of 1976 (P.L. 94-455)**

P.L. 94-455, §1052(a):

Added Code Sec. 922(b). **Effective** for tax years beginning after 12-31-75.

P.L. 94-455, §1052(b):

Repealed Code Sec. 922. **Effective** for tax years beginning after 12-31-79.

INCOME TAX—FOREIGN SALES CORPORATIONS

[Sec. 923—Repealed]

Amendments

• **2000, FSC Repeal and Extraterritorial Income Exclusion Act of 2000 (P.L. 106-519)**

P.L. 106-519, § 2:

Repealed subpart C of part III of subchapter N of chapter 1 (Code Secs. 921-927). **Effective**, generally, to transactions after 9-30-2000. For special rules, see Act Sec. 5(b)-(d) in the amendment notes following repealed Code Sec. 921. Prior to repeal, Code Sec. 923 read as follows:

SEC. 923. EXEMPT FOREIGN TRADE INCOME.

[Sec. 923(a)]

(a) EXEMPT FOREIGN TRADE INCOME.—For purposes of this subpart—

(1) IN GENERAL.—The term "exempt foreign trade income" means the aggregate amount of all foreign trade income of a FSC for the taxable year which is described in paragraph (2) or (3).

(2) INCOME DETERMINED WITHOUT REGARD TO ADMINISTRATIVE PRICING RULES.—In the case of any transaction to which paragraph (3) does not apply, 32 percent of the foreign trade income derived from such transaction shall be treated as described in this paragraph. For purposes of the preceding sentence, foreign trade income shall not include any income properly allocable to excluded property described in subparagraph (B) of section 927(a)(2) (relating to intangibles).

(3) INCOME DETERMINED WITH REGARD TO ADMINISTRATIVE PRICING RULES.—In the case of any transaction with respect to which paragraph (1) or (2) of section 925(a) (or the corresponding provisions of the regulations prescribed under section 925(b)) applies, 16/23 of the foreign trade income derived from such transaction shall be treated as described in this paragraph.

(4) SPECIAL RULE FOR FOREIGN TRADE INCOME ALLOCABLE TO A COOPERATIVE.—

(A) IN GENERAL.—In any case in which a qualified cooperative is a shareholder of a FSC, paragraph (3) shall be applied with respect to that portion of the foreign trade income of such FSC for any taxable year which is properly allocable to the marketing of agricultural or horticultural products (or the providing of related services) by such cooperative by substituting "100 percent" for "16/23".

(B) PARAGRAPH ONLY TO APPLY TO AMOUNTS FSC DISTRIBUTES.—Subparagraph (A) shall not apply for any taxable year unless the FSC distributes to the qualified cooperative the amount which (but for such subparagraph) would not be treated as exempt foreign trade income. Any distribution under this subparagraph for any taxable year—

(i) shall be made before the due date for filing the return of tax for such taxable year, but

(ii) shall be treated as made on the last day of such taxable year.

(5) SPECIAL RULE FOR MILITARY PROPERTY.—Under regulations prescribed by the Secretary, that portion of the foreign trading gross receipts of the FSC for the taxable year attributable to the disposition of, or services relating to, military property (within the meaning of section 995(b)(3)(B)) which may be treated as exempt foreign trade income shall equal 50 percent of the amount which (but for this paragraph) would be treated as exempt foreign trade income.

(6) CROSS REFERENCE.—For reduction in amount of exempt foreign trade income, see section 291(a)(4).

[Sec. 923(b)]

(b) FOREIGN TRADE INCOME DEFINED.—For purposes of this subpart, the term "foreign trade income" means the gross income of a FSC attributable to foreign trading gross receipts.

Amendments

• **1986, Tax Reform Act of 1986 (P.L. 99-514)**

P.L. 99-514, § 1876(b)(3):

Amended Code Sec. 923(a) by adding at the end thereof new paragraph (6). **Effective** as if included in the provision of P.L. 98-369 to which it relates.

• **1984, Deficit Reduction Act of 1984 (P.L. 98-369)**

P.L. 98-369, § 801(a):

Added Code Sec. 923, as part of new subpart C. **Effective** for transactions after 12-31-84, in tax years ending after such date.

[Sec. 924—Repealed]

Amendments

• **2000, FSC Repeal and Extraterritorial Income Exclusion Act of 2000 (P.L. 106-519)**

P.L. 106-519, § 2:

Repealed subpart C of part III of subchapter N of chapter 1 (Code Secs. 921-927). **Effective**, generally, to transactions after 9-30-2000. For special rules, see Act Sec. 5(b)-(d) in the amendment notes following repealed Code Sec. 921. Prior to repeal, Code Sec. 924 read as follows:

SEC. 924. FOREIGN TRADING GROSS RECEIPTS.

[Sec. 924(a)]

(a) IN GENERAL.—Except as otherwise provided in this section, for purposes of this subpart, the term "foreign trading gross receipts" means the gross receipts of any FSC which are—

(1) from the sale, exchange, or other disposition of export property,

(2) from the lease or rental of export property for use by the lessee outside the United States,

(3) for services which are related and subsidiary to—

(A) any sale, exchange, or other disposition of export property by such corporation, or

(B) any lease or rental of export property described in paragraph (2) by such corporation,

(4) for engineering or architectural services for construction projects located (or proposed for location) outside the United States, or

(5) for the performance of managerial services for an unrelated FSC or DISC in furtherance of the production of foreign trading gross receipts described in paragraph (1), (2), or (3).

Paragraph (5) shall not apply to a FSC for any taxable year unless at least 50 percent of its gross receipts for such taxable year is derived from activities described in paragraph (1), (2), or (3).

[Sec. 924(b)]

(b) FOREIGN MANAGEMENT AND FOREIGN ECONOMIC PROCESS REQUIREMENTS.—

(1) IN GENERAL.—Except as provided in paragraph (2)—

(A) a FSC shall be treated as having foreign trading gross receipts for the taxable year only if the management of such corporation during such taxable year takes place outside the United States as required by subsection (c), and

(B) a FSC has foreign trading gross receipts from any transaction only if economic processes with respect to such transaction take place outside the United States as required by subsection (d).

(2) EXCEPTION FOR SMALL FSC.—

(A) IN GENERAL.—Paragraph (1) shall not apply with respect to any small FSC.

(B) LIMITATION ON AMOUNT OF FOREIGN TRADING GROSS RECEIPTS OF SMALL FSC TAKEN INTO ACCOUNT.—

(i) IN GENERAL.—Any foreign trading gross receipts of a small FSC for the taxable year which exceed $5,000,000 shall not be taken into account in determining the exempt foreign trade income of such corporation and shall not be taken into account under any other provision of this subpart.

(ii) ALLOCATION OF LIMITATION.—If the foreign trading gross receipts of a small FSC exceed the limitation of clause (i), the corporation may allocate such limitation among such gross receipts in such manner as it may select (at such time and in such manner as may be prescribed in regulations).

(iii) RECEIPTS OF CONTROLLED GROUP AGGREGATED.—For purposes of applying clauses (i) and (ii), all small FSC's which are members of the same controlled group of corporations shall be treated as a single corporation.

(iv) ALLOCATION OF LIMITATION AMONG MEMBERS OF CONTROLLED GROUP.—The limitation under clause (i) shall be allocated among the foreign trading gross receipts of small FSC's which are members of the same controlled group of corporations in a manner provided in regulations prescribed by the Secretary.

[Sec. 924(c)]

(c) REQUIREMENT THAT FSC BE MANAGED OUTSIDE THE UNITED STATES.—The management of a FSC meets the requirements of this subsection for the taxable year if—

(1) all meetings of the board of directors of the corporation, and all meetings of the shareholders of the corporation, are outside the United States,

(2) the principal bank account of the corporation is maintained in a foreign country which meets the requirements of section 927(e)(3) or in a possession of the United States at all times during the taxable year, and

(3) all dividends, legal and accounting fees, and salaries of officers and members of the board of directors of the corporation disbursed during the taxable year are disbursed out of bank accounts of the corporation maintained outside the United States.

Amendments

• **1986, Tax Reform Act of 1986 (P.L. 99-514)**

P.L. 99-514, § 1876(e)(2):

Amended Code Sec. 924(c)(2). **Effective** for periods after 3-28-85. Prior to amendment, Code Sec. 924(c)(2) read as follows:

(2) the principal bank account of the corporation is maintained outside the United States at all times during the taxable year, and

[Sec. 924(d)]

(d) REQUIREMENT THAT ECONOMIC PROCESSES TAKE PLACE OUTSIDE THE UNITED STATES.—

(1) IN GENERAL.—The requirements of this subsection are met with respect to the gross receipts of a FSC derived from any transaction if—

(A) such corporation (or any person acting under a contract with such corporation) has participated outside the United States in the solicitation (other than advertising), the negotiation, or the making of the contract relating to such transaction, and

(B) the foreign direct costs incurred by the FSC attributable to the transaction equal or exceed 50 percent of the total direct costs attributable to the transaction.

(2) ALTERNATIVE 85-PERCENT TEST.—A corporation shall be treated as satisfying the requirements of paragraph (1)(B) with respect to any transaction if, with respect to each of at least 2 paragraphs of subsection (e), the foreign direct costs incurred by such corporation attributable to activities described in such paragraph equal or exceed 85 percent of the total direct costs attributable to activities described in such paragraph.

(3) DEFINITIONS.—For purposes of this subsection—

(A) TOTAL DIRECT COSTS.—The term "total direct costs" means, with respect to any transaction, the total direct costs incurred by the FSC attributable to activities described in subsection (e) performed at any location by the FSC or any person acting under a contract with such FSC.

(B) FOREIGN DIRECT COSTS.—The term "foreign direct costs" means, with respect to any transaction, the portion of the total direct costs which are attributable to activities performed outside the United States.

INCOME TAX—FOREIGN SALES CORPORATIONS

(4) RULES FOR COMMISSIONS, ETC.—The Secretary shall prescribe such regulations as may be necessary to carry out the purposes of this subsection and subsection (e) in the case of commissions, rentals, and furnishing of services.

[Sec. 924(e)]

(e) ACTIVITIES RELATING TO DISPOSITION OF EXPORT PROPERTY.—The activities referred to in subsection (d) are—

(1) advertising and sales promotion,

(2) the processing of customer orders and the arranging for delivery of the export property,

(3) transportation from the time of acquisition by the FSC (or, in the case of a commission relationship, from the beginning of such relationship for such transaction) to the delivery to the customer,

(4) the determination and transmittal of a final invoice or statement of account and the receipt of payment, and

(5) the assumption of credit risk.

[Sec. 924(f)]

(f) CERTAIN RECEIPTS NOT INCLUDED IN FOREIGN TRADING GROSS RECEIPTS.—

(1) CERTAIN RECEIPTS EXCLUDED ON BASIS OF USE; SUBSIDIZED RECEIPTS AND RECEIPTS FROM RELATED PARTIES EXCLUDED.—The term "foreign trading gross receipts" shall not include receipts of a FSC from a transaction if—

(A) the export property or services—

(i) are for ultimate use in the United States, or

(ii) are for use by the United States or any instrumentality thereof and such use of export property or services is required by law or regulation,

(B) such transaction is accomplished by a subsidy granted by the United States or any instrumentality thereof, or

(C) such receipts are from another FSC which is a member of the same controlled group of corporations of which such corporation is a member.

In the case of gross receipts of a FSC from a transaction involving any property, subparagraph (C) shall not apply if such FSC (and all other FSC's which are members of the same controlled group and which receive gross receipts from a transaction involving such property) do not use the pricing rules under paragraph (1) of section 925(a) (or the corresponding provisions of the regulations prescribed under section 925(b))with respect to any transaction involving such property.

(2) INVESTMENT INCOME; CARRYING CHARGES.—The term "foreign trading gross receipts" shall not include any investment income or carrying charges.

Amendments

• **1986, Tax Reform Act of 1986 (P.L. 99-514)**

P.L. 99-514, §1876(l):

Amended Code Sec. 924(f)(1) by adding at the end thereof a new sentence. **Effective** as if included in the provision of P.L. 98-369 to which it relates.

• **1984, Deficit Reduction Act of 1984 (P.L. 98-369)**

P.L. 98-369, §801(a):

Added Code Sec. 924, as part of new subpart C. **Effective** for transactions after 12-31-84, in tax years ending after such date. Special rules appear below in Act Sec. 805(a)(2), below.

P.L. 98-369, §805(a)(2), as amended by P.L. 99-514, §1876(o), provides:

(2) SPECIAL RULE FOR CERTAIN CONTRACTS.—To the extent provided in regulations prescribed by the Secretary of the Treasury or his delegate, any event or activity required to occur or required to be performed, before January 1, 1985, by section 924(c) or (d) or 925(c) of the Internal Revenue Code of 1954 shall be treated as meeting the requirements of such section if such event or activity is with respect to—

(A) any lease of more than 3 years duration which was entered into before January 1, 1985,

(B) any contract with respect to which the taxpayer uses the completed contract method of accounting which was entered into before January 1, 1985, or

(C) in the case of any contract other than a lease or contract described in subparagraph (A) or (B), any contract which was entered into before January 1, 1985; except that this subparagraph shall only apply to the first 3 taxable years of the FSC ending after January 1, 1985, or such later taxable years as the Secretary of the Treasury or his delegate may prescribe.

[Sec. 925—Repealed]

Amendments

• **2000, FSC Repeal and Extraterritorial Income Exclusion Act of 2000 (P.L. 106-519)**

P.L. 106-519, §2:

Repealed subpart C of part III of subchapter N of chapter 1 (Code Secs. 921-927). **Effective**, generally, to transactions after 9-30-2000. For special rules, see Act Sec. 5(b)-(d) in the amendment notes following repealed Code Sec. 921. Prior to repeal, Code Sec. 925 read as follows:

SEC. 925. TRANSFER PRICING RULES.

(a) IN GENERAL.—In the case of a sale of export property to a FSC by a person described in section 482, the taxable income of such FSC and such person shall be based upon a transfer price which would allow such FSC to derive taxable income attributable to such sale (regardless of the sales price actually charged) in an amount which does not exceed the greatest of—

(1) 1.83 percent of the foreign trading gross receipts derived from the sale of such property by such FSC,

(2) 23 percent of the combined taxable income of such FSC and such person which is attributable to the foreign trading gross receipts derived from the sale of such property by such FSC, or

(3) taxable income based upon the sale price actually charged (but subject to the rules provided in section 482).

Paragraphs (1) and (2) shall apply only if the FSC meets the requirements of subsection (c) with respect to the sale.

(b) RULES FOR COMMISSIONS, RENTALS, AND MARGINAL COSTING.—The Secretary shall prescribe regulations setting forth—

(1) rules which are consistent with the rules set forth in subsection (a) for the application of this section in the case of commissions, rentals, and other income, and

(2) rules for the allocation of expenditures in computing combined taxable income under subsection (a)(2) in those cases where a FSC is seeking to establish or maintain a market for export property.

(c) REQUIREMENTS FOR USE OF ADMINISTRATIVE PRICING RULES.—A sale by a FSC meets the requirements of this subsection if—

(1) all of the activities described in section 924(e) attributable to such sale, and

(2) all of the activities relating to the solicitation (other than advertising), negotiation, and making of the contract for such sale,

have been performed by such FSC (or by another person acting under a contract with such FSC).

(d) LIMITATION ON GROSS RECEIPTS PRICING RULE.—The amount determined under subsection (a)(1) with respect to any transaction shall not exceed 2 times the amount which would be determined under subsection (a)(2) with respect to such transaction.

(e) TAXABLE INCOME.—For purposes of this section, the taxable income of a FSC shall be determined without regard to section 921.

(f) SPECIAL RULE FOR COOPERATIVES.—In any case in which a qualified cooperative sells export property to a FSC, in computing the combined taxable income of such FSC and such organization for purposes of subsection (a)(2), there shall not be taken into account any deduction allowable under subsection (b) or (c) of section 1382 (relating to patronage dividends, per-unit retain allocations, and nonpatronage distributions).

• **1984, Deficit Reduction Act of 1984 (P.L. 98-369)**

P.L. 98-369, §801(a):

Added Code Sec. 925, as part of new subpart C. **Effective** for transactions after 12-31-84, in tax years ending after such date.

[Sec. 926—Repealed]

Amendments

• **2000, FSC Repeal and Extraterritorial Income Exclusion Act of 2000 (P.L. 106-519)**

P.L. 106-519, §2:

Repealed subpart C of part III of subchapter N of chapter 1 (Code Secs. 921-927). **Effective**, generally, to transactions after 9-30-2000. For special rules, see Act Sec. 5(b)-(d) in the amendment notes following repealed Code Sec. 921. Prior to repeal, Code Sec. 926 read as follows:

SEC. 926. DISTRIBUTIONS TO SHAREHOLDERS.

(a) DISTRIBUTIONS MADE FIRST OUT OF FOREIGN TRADE INCOME.—For purposes of this title, any distribution to a shareholder of a FSC by such FSC which is made out of earnings and profits shall be treated as made—

(1) first, out of earnings and profits attributable to foreign trade income, to the extent thereof, and

(2) then, out of any other earnings and profits.

(b) DISTRIBUTIONS BY FSC TO NONRESIDENT ALIENS AND FOREIGN CORPORATIONS TREATED AS UNITED STATES CONNECTED.—For purposes of this title, any distribution by a FSC which is made out of earnings and profits attributable to foreign trade income to any shareholder of such corporation which is a foreign corporation or a nonresident alien individual shall be treated as a distribution—

(1) which is effectively connected with the conduct of a trade or business conducted through a permanent establishment of such shareholder within the United States, and

(2) of income which is derived from sources within the United States.

(c) FSC INCLUDES FORMER FSC.—For purposes of this section, the term "FSC" includes a former FSC.

• **1984, Deficit Reduction Act of 1984 (P.L. 98-369)**

P.L. 98-369, §801(a):

Added Code Sec. 926, as part of new subpart C. **Effective** for transactions after 12-31-84, in tax years ending after such date. For special and transitional rules, see the amendment notes following repealed Code Sec. 924.

INCOME TAX—FOREIGN SALES CORPORATIONS

[Sec. 927—Repealed]

Amendments

• **2000, FSC Repeal and Extraterritorial Income Exclusion Act of 2000 (P.L. 106-519)**

P.L. 106-519, § 2:

Repealed subpart C of part III of subchapter N of chapter 1 (Code Secs. 921-927). **Effective**, generally, to transactions after 9-30-2000. For special rules, see Act Sec. 5(b)-(d) in the amendment notes following repealed Code Sec. 921. Prior to repeal, Code Sec. 927 read as follows:

SEC. 927. OTHER DEFINITIONS AND SPECIAL RULES.

[Sec. 927(a)]

(a) EXPORT PROPERTY.—For purposes of this subpart—

(1) IN GENERAL.—The term "export property" means property—

(A) manufactured, produced, grown, or extracted in the United States by a person other than a FSC,

(B) held primarily for sale, lease, or rental, in the ordinary course of trade or business, by, or to, a FSC, for direct use, consumption, or disposition outside the United States, and

(C) not more than 50 percent of the fair market value of which is attributable to articles imported into the United States.

For purposes of subparagraph (C), the fair market value of any article imported into the United States shall be its appraised value, as determined by the Secretary under section 402 of the Tariff Act of 1930 (19 U.S.C. 1401a) in connection with its importation.

(2) EXCLUDED PROPERTY.—The term "export property" shall not include—

(A) property leased or rented by a FSC for use by any member of a controlled group of corporations of which such FSC is a member,

(B) patents, inventions, models, designs, formulas, or processes whether or not patented, copyrights (other than films, tapes, records, or similar reproductions, and other than computer software (whether or not patented), for commercial or home use), good will, trademarks, trade brands, franchises, or other like property,

(C) oil or gas (or any primary product thereof),

(D) products the export of which is prohibited or curtailed to effectuate the policy set forth in paragraph (2)(C) of section 3 of the Export Administration Act of 1979 (relating to the protection of the domestic economy), or

(E) any unprocessed timber which is a softwood.

For purposes of subparagraph (E), the term "unprocessed timber" means any log, cant, or similar form of timber.

(3) PROPERTY IN SHORT SUPPLY.—If the President determines that the supply of any property described in paragraph (1) is insufficient to meet the requirements of the domestic economy, he may by Executive order designate the property as in short supply. Any property so designated shall not be treated as export property during the period beginning with the date specified in the Executive order and ending with the date specified in an Executive order setting forth the President's determination that the property is no longer in short supply.

(4) QUALIFIED COOPERATIVE.—The term "qualified cooperative" means any organization to which part I of subchapter T applies which is engaged in the marketing of agricultural or horticultural products.

Amendments

• **1997, Taxpayer Relief Act of 1997 (P.L. 105-34)**

P.L. 105-34, § 1171(a):

Amended Code Sec. 927(a)(2)(B) by inserting ", and other than computer software (whether or not patented)" before ", for commercial or home use". **Effective** for gross receipts attributable to periods after 12-31-97, in tax years ending after such date.

• **1993, Omnibus Budget Reconciliation Act of 1993 (P.L. 103-66)**

P.L. 103-66, § 13239(a):

Amended Code Sec. 927(a)(2) by striking "or" at the end of subparagraph (C), by striking the period at the end of subparagraph (D), and inserting ", or" and by adding at the end thereof a new subparagraph (E) and a new flush sentence. **Effective** for sales, exchanges, or other dispositions after 8-10-93.

[Sec. 927(b)]

(b) GROSS RECEIPTS.—

(1) IN GENERAL.—For purposes of this subpart, the term "gross receipts" means—

(A) the total receipts from the sale, lease, or rental of property held primarily for sale, lease, or rental in the ordinary course of trade or business, and

(B) gross income from all other sources.

(2) GROSS RECEIPTS TAKEN INTO ACCOUNT IN CASE OF COMMISSIONS.—In the case of commissions on the sale, lease, or rental of property, the amount taken into account for purposes of this subpart as gross receipts shall be the gross receipts on the sale, lease, or rental of the property on which such commissions arose.

[Sec. 927(c)]

(c) INVESTMENT INCOME.—For purposes of this subpart, the term "investment income" means—

(1) dividends,

(2) interest,

(3) royalties,

(4) annuities,

(5) rents (other than rents from the lease or rental of export property for use by the lessee outside of the United States),

(6) gains from the sale or exchange of stock or securities,

(7) gains from futures transactions in any commodity on, or subject to the rules of, a board of trade or commodity exchange (other than gains which arise out of a bona fide hedging transaction reasonably necessary to conduct the business of the FSC in the manner in which such business is customarily conducted by others),

(8) amounts includible in computing the taxable income of the corporation under part I of subchapter J, and

(9) gains from the sale or other disposition of any interest in an estate or trust.

[Sec. 927(d)]

(d) OTHER DEFINITIONS.—For purposes of this subpart—

(1) CARRYING CHARGES.—The term "carrying charges" means—

(A) carrying charges, and

(B) under regulations prescribed by the Secretary, any amount in excess of the price for an immediate cash sale and any other unstated interest.

(2) TRANSACTION.—

(A) IN GENERAL.—The term "transaction" means—

(i) any sale, exchange, or other disposition,

(ii) any lease or rental, and

(iii) any furnishing of services.

(B) GROUPING OF TRANSACTIONS.—To the extent provided in regulations, any provision of this subpart which, but for this subparagraph, would be applied on a transaction-by-transaction basis may be applied by the taxpayer on the basis of groups of transactions based on product lines or recognized industry or trade usage. Such regulations may permit different groupings for different purposes.

(3) UNITED STATES DEFINED.—The term "United States" includes the Commonwealth of Puerto Rico.

(4) CONTROLLED GROUP OF CORPORATIONS.—The term "controlled group of corporations" has the meaning given to such term by section 1563(a), except that—

(A) "more than 50 percent" shall be substituted for "at least 80 percent" each place it appears therein, and

(B) section 1563(b) shall not apply.

(5) POSSESSIONS.—The term "possession of the United States" means Guam, American Samoa, the Commonwealth of the Northern Mariana Islands, and the Virgin Islands of the United States.

(6) SECTION 923(a)(2) NON-EXEMPT INCOME.—The term "section 923(a)(2) non-exempt income" means any foreign trade income from a transaction with respect to which paragraph (1) or (2) of section 925(a) does not apply and which is not exempt foreign trade income. Such term shall not include any income which is effectively connected with the conduct of a trade or business within the United States (determined without regard to this subpart).

Amendments

• **1986, Tax Reform Act of 1986 (P.L. 99-514)**

P.L. 99-514, § 1876(a)(1):

Amended Code Sec. 927(d)(6) by adding at the end thereof a new sentence. **Effective** as if included in the provision of P.L. 98-369 to which it relates.

[Sec. 927(e)]

(e) SPECIAL RULES.—

(1) SOURCE RULES FOR RELATED PERSONS.—Under regulations, the income of a person described in section 482 from a transaction giving rise to foreign trading gross receipts of a FSC which is treated as from sources outside the United States shall not exceed the amount which would be treated as foreign source income earned by such person if the pricing rule under section 994 which corresponds to the rule used under section 925 with respect to such transaction applied to such transaction.

(2) PARTICIPATION IN INTERNATIONAL BOYCOTTS, ETC.—Under regulations prescribed by the Secretary, the exempt foreign trade income of a FSC for any taxable year shall be limited under rules similar to the rules of clauses (ii) and (iii) of section 995(b)(1)(F).

(3) EXCHANGE OF INFORMATION REQUIREMENTS.—For purposes of this title, the term "FSC" shall not include any corporation which was created or organized under the laws of any foreign country unless there is in effect between such country and the United States—

(A) a bilateral or multilateral agreement described in section 274(h)(6)(C) (determined by treating any reference to a beneficiary country as being a reference to any foreign country and by applying such section without regard to clause (ii) thereof), or

(B) an income tax treaty which contains an exchange of information program—

(i) which the Secretary certifies (and has not revoked such certification) is satisfactory in practice for purposes of this title, and

(ii) to which the FSC is subject.

(4) DISALLOWANCE OF TREATY BENEFITS.—Any corporation electing to be treated as a FSC under subsection (f)(1) may not claim any benefits under any income tax treaty between the United States and any foreign country.

(5) COORDINATION WITH POSSESSIONS TAXATION.—

(A) EXEMPTION.—No tax shall be imposed by any possession of the United States on any foreign trade income derived before January 1, 1987. The preceding sentence shall not apply to any income attributable to the sale of property or the performance of services for ultimate use, consumption, or disposition within the possession.

(B) CLARIFICATION THAT POSSESSION MAY EXEMPT CERTAIN INCOME FROM TAX.—Nothing in any provision of law shall be construed as prohibiting any possession of the United States from exempting from tax any foreign trade income of a FSC or any other income of a FSC described in paragraph (2) or (3) of section 921(d).

(C) NO COVER OVER OF TAXES IMPOSED ON FSC.—Nothing in any provision of law shall be construed as requiring any tax imposed by this title on a FSC to be covered over (or otherwise transferred) to any possession of the United States.

Amendments

• **1986, Tax Reform Act of 1986 (P.L. 99-514)**

P.L. 99-514, § 1876(e)(1)(A)-(C):

Amended Code Sec. 927(e)(3) by striking out "unless, at the same time such corporation was created or organized, there was" and inserting in lieu thereof "unless there is", by striking out "section 274(h)(6)(C)" in subparagraph (A) and inserting in lieu thereof "section 274(h)(6)(C) (determined by treating any reference to

INCOME TAX—U.S. POSSESSIONS

a beneficiary country as being a reference to any foreign country and by applying such section without regard to clause (ii) thereof)", and by amending subparagraph (B). **Effective** as if included in the provision of P.L. 98-369 to which it relates. Prior to amendment, Code Sec. 927(e)(3)(B) read as follows:

(B) an income tax treaty with respect to which the Secretary certifies that the exchange of information program with such country under such treaty carries out the purposes of this paragraph.

P.L. 99-514, § 1876(f)(1):

Amended Code Sec. 927(e)(5). **Effective** as if included in the provision of P.L. 98-369 to which it relates. Prior to amendment, Code Sec. 927(e)(5) read as follows:

(5) EXEMPTION FROM CERTAIN OTHER TAXES.—No tax shall be imposed by any jurisdiction described in subsection (d)(5) on any foreign trade income derived before January 1, 1987.

P.L. 99-514, § 1876(p)(5):

Amended Code Sec. 927(e)(2) by striking out "clauses (i) and (ii)" and inserting in lieu thereof "clauses (ii) and (iii)". **Effective** as if included in the provision of P.L. 98-369 to which it relates.

[Sec. 927(f)]

(f) ELECTION OF STATUS AS FSC (AND AS SMALL FSC).—

(1) ELECTION.—

(A) TIME FOR MAKING.—An election by a corporation under section 922(a)(2) to be treated as a FSC, and an election under section 922(b)(1) to be a small FSC, shall be made by such corporation for a taxable year at any time during the 90-day period immediately preceding the beginning of the taxable year, except that the Secretary may give his consent to the making of an election at such other times as he may designate.

(B) MANNER OF ELECTION.—An election under subparagraph (A) shall be made in such manner as the Secretary shall prescribe and shall be valid only if all persons who are shareholders in such corporation on the first day of the first taxable year for which such election is effective consent to such election.

(2) EFFECT OF ELECTION.—If a corporation makes an election under paragraph (1), then the provisions of this subpart shall apply to such corporation for the taxable year of the corporation for which made and for all succeeding taxable years.

(3) TERMINATION OF ELECTION.—

(A) REVOCATION.—An election under this subsection made by any corporation may be terminated by revocation of such election for any taxable year of the corporation after the first taxable year of the corporation for which the election is effective. A termination under this paragraph shall be effective with respect to such election—

(i) for the taxable year in which made, if made at any time during the first 90 days of such taxable year, or

(ii) for the taxable year following the taxable year in which made, if made after the close of such 90 days, and

for all succeeding taxable years of the corporation. Such termination shall be made in such manner as the Secretary shall prescribe by regulations.

(B) CONTINUED FAILURE TO BE A FSC.—If a corporation is not a FSC for each of any 5 consecutive taxable years of the corporation for which an election under this subsection is effective, the election to be a FSC shall be terminated and not be in effect for any taxable year of the corporation after such 5th year.

Amendments

• **1984, Deficit Reduction Act of 1984 (P.L. 98-369)**

P.L. 98-369, § 801(a):

Added Code Sec. 927, as part of new subpart C. **Effective** for transactions after 12-31-84, in tax years ending after such date.

[Sec. 927(g)]

(g) TREATMENT OF SHARED FSC'S.—

(1) IN GENERAL.—Except as provided in paragraph (2), each separate account referred to in paragraph (3) maintained by a shared FSC shall be treated as a separate corporation for purposes of this subpart.

(2) CERTAIN REQUIREMENTS APPLIED AT SHARED FSC LEVEL.— Paragraph (1) shall not apply—

(A) for purposes of—

(i) subparagraphs (A), (B), (D), and (E) of section 922(a)(1),

(ii) paragraph (2) of section 922(a),

(iii) subsections (b), (c), and (e) of section 924, and

(iv) subsection (f) of this section, and

(B) for such other purposes as the Secretary may by regulations prescribe.

(3) SHARED FSC.—For purposes of this subsection, the term "shared FSC" means any corporation if—

(A) such corporation maintains a separate account for transactions with each shareholder (and persons related to such shareholder),

(B) distributions to each shareholder are based on the amounts in the separate account maintained with respect to such shareholder, and

(C) such corporation meets such other requirements as the Secretary may by regulations prescribe.

Amendments

• **1990, Omnibus Budget Reconciliation Act of 1990 (P.L. 101-508)**

P.L. 101-508, § 11704(a)(10):

Amended Code Sec. 927(g)(2)(B) by striking "prescribed" and inserting "prescribe". **Effective** 11-5-90.

• **1988, Technical and Miscellaneous Revenue Act of 1988 (P.L. 100-647)**

P.L. 100-647, § 1012(bb)(8)(A):

Amended Code Sec. 927 by adding at the end thereof a new subsection (g). **Effective** as if included in the provision of P.L. 98-369 to which it relates.

Subpart D—Possessions of the United States

Sec. 931.	Income from sources within Guam, American Samoa, or the Northern Mariana Islands.
Sec. 932.	Coordination of United States and Virgin Islands income taxes.
Sec. 933.	Income from sources within Puerto Rico.
Sec. 934.	Limitation on reduction in income tax liability incurred to the Virgin Islands.
Sec. 937.	Residence and source rules involving possessions.

[Sec. 931]

SEC. 931. INCOME FROM SOURCES WITHIN GUAM, AMERICAN SAMOA, OR THE NORTHERN MARIANA ISLANDS.

[Sec. 931(a)]

(a) GENERAL RULE.—In the case of an individual who is a bona fide resident of a specified possession during the entire taxable year, gross income shall not include—

(1) income derived from sources within any specified possession, and

(2) income effectively connected with the conduct of a trade or business by such individual within any specified possession.

Amendments

• **2021, American Rescue Plan Act of 2021 (P.L. 117-2)**

P.L. 117-2, § 9601(b) and (c)(2), provides:

SEC. 9601. 2021 RECOVERY REBATES TO INDIVIDUALS.

* * *

(b) TREATMENT OF CERTAIN POSSESSIONS.—

(1) PAYMENTS TO POSSESSIONS WITH MIRROR CODE TAX SYSTEMS.—The Secretary of the Treasury shall pay to each possession of the United States which has a mirror code tax system amounts equal to the loss (if any) to that possession by reason of the amendments made by this section. Such amounts shall be determined by the Secretary of the Treasury based on information provided by the government of the respective possession.

(2) PAYMENTS TO OTHER POSSESSIONS.—The Secretary of the Treasury shall pay to each possession of the United States which does not have a mirror code tax system amounts estimated by the Secretary of the Treasury as being equal to the aggregate benefits (if any) that would have been provided to residents of such possession by reason of the amendments made by this section if a mirror code tax system had been in effect in such possession. The preceding sentence shall not apply unless the respective possession has a plan, which has been approved by the Secretary of the Treasury, under which such possession will promptly distribute such payments to its residents.

(3) INCLUSION OF ADMINISTRATIVE EXPENSES.—The Secretary of the Treasury shall pay to each possession of the United States to which the Secretary makes a payment under paragraph (1) or (2) an amount equal to the lesser of—

(A) the increase (if any) of the administrative expenses of such possession—

(i) in the case of a possession described in paragraph (1), by reason of the amendments made by this section, and

(ii) in the case of a possession described in paragraph (2), by reason of carrying out the plan described in such paragraph, or

(B) $500,000 ($10,000,000 in the case of Puerto Rico).

The amount described in subparagraph (A) shall be determined by the Secretary of the Treasury based on information provided by the government of the respective possession.

(4) COORDINATION WITH CREDIT ALLOWED AGAINST UNITED STATES INCOME TAXES.—No credit shall be allowed against United States income taxes under section 6428B of the Internal Revenue Code of 1986 (as added by this section), nor shall any credit or refund be made or allowed under subsection (g) of such section, to any person—

(A) to whom a credit is allowed against taxes imposed by the possession by reason of the amendments made by this section, or

(B) who is eligible for a payment under a plan described in paragraph (2).

(5) MIRROR CODE TAX SYSTEM.—For purposes of this subsection, the term "mirror code tax system" means, with respect to any possession of the United States, the

income tax system of such possession if the income tax liability of the residents of such possession under such system is determined by reference to the income tax laws of the United States as if such possession were the United States.

(6) TREATMENT OF PAYMENTS.—For purposes of section 1324 of title 31, United States Code, the payments under this subsection shall be treated in the same manner as a refund due from a credit provision referred to in subsection (b)(2) of such section.

(c) ADMINISTRATIVE PROVISIONS.—

* * *

(2) EXCEPTION FROM REDUCTION OR OFFSET.—Any refund payable by reason of section 6428B(g) of the Internal Revenue Code of 1986 (as added by this section), or any such refund payable by reason of subsection (b) of this section, shall not be—

(A) subject to reduction or offset pursuant to subsection (c), (d), (e), or (f) of section 6402 of the Internal Revenue Code of 1986 or any similar authority permitting offset, or

(B) reduced or offset by other assessed Federal taxes that would otherwise be subject to levy or collection.

* * *

P.L. 117-2, § 9626(d), provides:
SEC. 9626. TEMPORARY SPECIAL RULE FOR DETERMINING EARNED INCOME FOR PURPOSES OF EARNED INCOME TAX CREDIT.

* * *

(d) TREATMENT OF CERTAIN POSSESSIONS.—

(1) PAYMENTS TO POSSESSIONS WITH MIRROR CODE TAX SYSTEMS.—The Secretary of the Treasury shall pay to each possession of the United States which has a mirror code tax system amounts equal to the loss (if any) to that possession by reason of the application of the provisions of this section (other than this subsection) with respect to section 32 of the Internal Revenue Code of 1986. Such amounts shall be determined by the Secretary of the Treasury based on information provided by the government of the respective possession.

(2) PAYMENTS TO OTHER POSSESSIONS.—The Secretary of the Treasury shall pay to each possession of the United States which does not have a mirror code tax system amounts estimated by the Secretary of the Treasury as being equal to the aggregate benefits (if any) that would have been provided to residents of such possession by reason of the provisions of this section (other than this subsection) with respect to section 32 of the Internal Revenue Code of 1986 if a mirror code tax system had been in effect in such possession. The preceding sentence shall not apply unless the respective possession has a plan, which has been approved by the Secretary of the Treasury, under which such possession will promptly distribute such payments to its residents.

(3) MIRROR CODE TAX SYSTEM.—For purposes of this section, the term "mirror code tax system" means, with respect to any possession of the United States, the income tax system of such possession if the income tax liability of the residents of such possession under such system is determined by reference to the income tax laws of the United States as if such possession were the United States.

(4) TREATMENT OF PAYMENTS.—For purposes of section 1324 of title 31, United States Code, the payments under this section shall be treated in the same manner as a refund due from a credit provision referred to in subsection (b)(2) of such section.

P.L. 117-2, § 9642(g)-(h), provides:
SEC. 9642. CREDIT FOR SICK LEAVE FOR CERTAIN SELF-EMPLOYED INDIVIDUALS.

* * *

(g) APPLICATION OF CREDIT IN CERTAIN POSSESSIONS.—

(1) PAYMENTS TO POSSESSIONS WITH MIRROR CODE TAX SYSTEMS.—The Secretary shall pay to each possession of the United States which has a mirror code tax system amounts equal to the loss (if any) to that possession by reason of the application of the provisions of this section. Such amounts shall be determined by the Secretary based on information provided by the government of the respective possession.

(2) PAYMENTS TO OTHER POSSESSIONS.—The Secretary shall pay to each possession of the United States which does not have a mirror code tax system amounts estimated by the Secretary as being equal to the aggregate benefits (if any) that would have been provided to residents of such possession by reason of the provisions of this section if a mirror code tax system had been in effect in such possession. The preceding sentence shall not apply unless the respective possession has a plan, which has been approved by the Secretary, under which such possession will promptly distribute such payments to its residents.

(3) MIRROR CODE TAX SYSTEM.—For purposes of this section, the term "mirror code tax system" means, with respect to any possession of the United States, the income tax system of such possession if the income tax liability of the residents of such possession under such system is determined by reference to the income tax laws of the United States as if such possession were the United States.

(4) TREATMENT OF PAYMENTS.—For purposes of section 1324 of title 31, United States Code, the payments under this subsection shall be treated in the same manner as a refund due from a credit provision referred to in subsection (b)(2) of such section.

(h) REGULATIONS.—The Secretary shall prescribe such regulations or other guidance as may be necessary to carry out the purposes of this section, including—

(1) regulations or other guidance to effectuate the purposes of this section, and

(2) regulations or other guidance to minimize compliance and record-keeping burdens under this section.

P.L. 117-2, § 9643(g)-(h), provides:
SEC. 9643. CREDIT FOR FAMILY LEAVE FOR CERTAIN SELF-EMPLOYED INDIVIDUALS.

* * *

(g) APPLICATION OF CREDIT IN CERTAIN POSSESSIONS.—

(1) PAYMENTS TO POSSESSIONS WITH MIRROR CODE TAX SYSTEMS.—The Secretary shall pay to each possession of the United States which has a mirror code tax system amounts equal to the loss (if any) to that possession by reason of the application of the provisions of this section. Such amounts shall be determined by the Secretary based on information provided by the government of the respective possession.

(2) PAYMENTS TO OTHER POSSESSIONS.—The Secretary shall pay to each possession of the United States which does not have a mirror code tax system amounts estimated by the Secretary as being equal to the aggregate benefits (if any) that would have been provided to residents of such possession by reason of the provisions of this section if a mirror code tax system had been in effect in such possession. The preceding sentence shall not apply unless the respective possession has a plan, which has been approved by the Secretary, under which such possession will promptly distribute such payments to its residents.

(3) MIRROR CODE TAX SYSTEM.—For purposes of this section, the term "mirror code tax system" means, with respect to any possession of the United States, the income tax system of such possession if the income tax liability of the residents of such possession under such system is determined by reference to the income tax laws of the United States as if such possession were the United States.

(4) TREATMENT OF PAYMENTS.—For purposes of section 1324 of title 31, United States Code, the payments under this subsection shall be treated in the same manner as a refund due from a credit provision referred to in subsection (b)(2) of such section.

(h) REGULATIONS.—The Secretary shall prescribe such regulations or other guidance as may be necessary to carry out the purposes of this section, including—

(1) regulations or other guidance to prevent the avoidance of the purposes of this section, and

(2) regulations or other guidance to minimize compliance and record-keeping burdens under this section.

• 2020, COVID-related Tax Relief Act of 2020 (P.L. 116-260)

P.L. 116-260, § 272(c)-(d), Div. N, provides:
SEC. 272. ADDITIONAL 2020 RECOVERY REBATES FOR INDIVIDUALS.

* * *

(c) TREATMENT OF POSSESSIONS.—

(1) PAYMENTS TO POSSESSIONS.—

(A) MIRROR CODE POSSESSION.—The Secretary of the Treasury shall pay to each possession of the United States which has a mirror code tax system amounts equal to the loss (if any) to that possession by reason of the amendments made by this section. Such amounts shall be determined by the Secretary of the Treasury based on information provided by the government of the respective possession.

(B) OTHER POSSESSIONS.—The Secretary of the Treasury shall pay to each possession of the United States which does not have a mirror code tax system amounts estimated by the Secretary of the Treasury as being equal to the aggregate benefits (if any) that would have been provided to residents of such possession by reason of the amendments made by this section if a mirror code tax system had been in effect in such possession. The preceding sentence shall not apply unless the respective possession has a plan, which has been approved by the Secretary of the Treasury, under which such possession will promptly distribute such payments to its residents.

(2) COORDINATION WITH CREDIT ALLOWED AGAINST UNITED STATES INCOME TAXES.—No credit shall be allowed against United States income taxes under section 6428A of the Internal Revenue Code of 1986 (as added by this section) to any person—

(A) to whom a credit is allowed against taxes imposed by the possession by reason of the amendments made by this section, or

(B) who is eligible for a payment under a plan described in paragraph (1)(B).

(3) DEFINITIONS AND SPECIAL RULES.—

(A) POSSESSION OF THE UNITED STATES.—For purposes of this subsection, the term "possession of the United States" includes the Commonwealth of Puerto Rico and the Commonwealth of the Northern Mariana Islands.

(B) MIRROR CODE TAX SYSTEM.—For purposes of this subsection, the term "mirror code tax system" means, with respect to any possession of the United States, the income tax system of such possession if the income tax liability of the residents of such possession under such system is determined by reference to the income tax laws of the United States as if such possession were the United States.

(C) TREATMENT OF PAYMENTS.—For purposes of section 1324 of title 31, United States Code, the payments under this subsection shall be treated in the same manner as a refund due from a credit provision referred to in subsection (b)(2) of such section.

(d) ADMINISTRATIVE PROVISIONS.—

(1) EXCEPTION FROM REDUCTION OR OFFSET.—Any refund payable by reason of section 6428A(f) of the Internal Revenue Code of 1986 (as added by this section), or any such refund payable by reason of subsection (c) of this section, shall not be—

(A) subject to reduction or offset pursuant to section 3716 or 3720A of title 31, United States Code,

(B) subject to reduction or offset pursuant to subsection (c), (d), (e), or (f) of section 6402 of the Internal Revenue Code of 1986, or

(C) reduced or offset by other assessed Federal taxes that would otherwise be subject to levy or collection.

(2) ASSIGNMENT OF BENEFITS.—

(A) IN GENERAL.—The right of any person to any applicable payment shall not be transferable or assignable, at law or in equity, and no applicable payment shall be subject to, execution, levy, attachment, garnishment, or other legal process, or the operation of any bankruptcy or insolvency law.

* * *

(D) NO RECLAMATION RIGHTS.—This paragraph shall not alter the status of applicable payments as tax refunds or other nonbenefit payments for purpose of any reclamation rights of the Department of the Treasury or the Internal Revenue Service as per part 210 of title 31, Code of Federal Regulations.

(E) DEFINITIONS.—For purposes of this paragraph—

(i) ACCOUNT HOLDER.—The term "account holder" means a natural person whose name appears in a financial institution's records as the direct or beneficial owner of an account.

INCOME TAX—U.S. POSSESSIONS

(ii) ACCOUNT REVIEW.—The term "account review" means the process of examining deposits in an account to determine if an applicable payment has been deposited into the account during the lookback period. The financial institution shall perform the account review following the procedures outlined in section 212.5 of title 31, Code of Federal Regulations and in accordance with the requirements of section 212.6 of title 31, Code of Federal Regulations.

(iii) APPLICABLE PAYMENT.—The term "applicable payment" means—

(I) any advance refund amount paid pursuant to section 6428A(f) of Internal Revenue Code of 1986 (as added by this section),

(II) any payment made by a possession of the United States with a mirror code tax system (as defined in subsection (c) of this section) pursuant to such subsection which corresponds to a payment described in subclause (I), and

(III) any payment made by a possession of the United States without a mirror code tax system (as so defined) pursuant to subsection (c) of this section.

(iv) GARNISHMENT.—The term "garnishment" means execution, levy, attachment, garnishment, or other legal process.

(v) GARNISHMENT ORDER.—The term "garnishment order" means a writ, order, notice, summons, judgment, levy, or similar written instruction issued by a court, a State or State agency, a municipality or municipal corporation, or a State child support enforcement agency, including a lien arising by operation of law for overdue child support or an order to freeze the assets in an account, to effect a garnishment against a debtor.

(vi) LOOKBACK PERIOD.—The term "lookback period" means the two month period that begins on the date preceding the date of account review and ends on the corresponding date of the month two months earlier, or on the last date of the month two months earlier if the corresponding date does not exist.

(3) AGENCY INFORMATION SHARING AND ASSISTANCE.—

(A) IN GENERAL.—The Commissioner of Social Security, the Railroad Retirement Board, and the Secretary of Veterans Affairs shall each provide the Secretary of the Treasury (or the Secretary's delegate) such information and assistance as the Secretary of the Treasury (or the Secretary's delegate) may require for purposes of—

(i) making payments under section 6428A(f) of the Internal Revenue Code of 1986 to individuals described in paragraph (5)(A) thereof, or

(ii) providing administrative assistance to a possession of the United States (as defined in subsection (c)(3)(A)) to allow such possession to promptly distribute payments under subsection (c) to its residents.

(B) EXCHANGE OF INFORMATION WITH POSSESSIONS.—Any information provided to the Secretary of the Treasury (or the Secretary's delegate) pursuant to subparagraph (A)(ii) may be exchanged with a possession of the United States in accordance with the applicable tax coordination agreement for information exchange and administrative assistance that the Internal Revenue Service has agreed to with such possession.

* * *

• **2020, Taxpayer Certainty and Disaster Tax Relief Act of 2020 (P.L. 116-260)**

P.L. 116-260, §306(a)-(c), Div. EE, provides:

SEC. 306. TREATMENT OF CERTAIN POSSESSIONS.

(a) PAYMENTS TO POSSESSIONS WITH MIRROR CODE TAX SYSTEMS.—The Secretary of the Treasury shall pay to each possession of the United States which has a mirror code tax system amounts equal to the loss (if any) to that possession by reason of the application of the provisions of this title. Such amounts shall be determined by the Secretary of the Treasury based on information provided by the government of the respective possession.

(b) PAYMENTS TO OTHER POSSESSIONS.—The Secretary of the Treasury shall pay to each possession of the United States which does not have a mirror code tax system amounts estimated by the Secretary of the Treasury as being equal to the aggregate benefits (if any) that would have been provided to residents of such possession by reason of the provisions of this title if a mirror code tax system had been in effect in such possession. The preceding sentence shall not apply unless the respective possession has a plan, which has been approved by the Secretary of the Treasury, under which such possession will promptly distribute such payments to its residents.

(c) MIRROR CODE TAX SYSTEM.—For purposes of this section, the term "mirror code tax system" means, with respect to any possession of the United States, the income tax system of such possession if the income tax liability of the residents of such possession under such system is determined by reference to the income tax laws of the United States as if such possession were the United States.

* * *

• **2020, Coronavirus Aid, Relief, and Economic Security (CARES) Act (P.L. 116-136)**

P.L. 116-136, §2201(c)-(d) (as amended by P.L. 116-260, §273(b)(1), Div. N), provides:

SEC. 2201. 2020 RECOVERY REBATES FOR INDIVIDUALS.

* * *

(c) TREATMENT OF POSSESSIONS.—

(1) PAYMENTS TO POSSESSIONS.—

(A) MIRROR CODE POSSESSION.—The Secretary of the Treasury shall pay to each possession of the United States which has a mirror code tax system amounts equal to the loss (if any) to that possession by reason of the amendments made by this section. Such amounts shall be determined by the Secretary of the Treasury based on information provided by the government of the respective possession.

(B) OTHER POSSESSIONS.—The Secretary of the Treasury shall pay to each possession of the United States which does not have a mirror code tax system amounts estimated by the Secretary of the Treasury as being equal to the aggregate benefits (if any) that would have been provided to residents of such possession by reason of the amendments made by this section if a mirror code tax system had been in effect in such possession. The preceding sentence shall not apply unless the respective possession has a plan, which has been approved by the Secretary of the Treasury, under which such possession will promptly distribute such payments to its residents.

(2) COORDINATION WITH CREDIT ALLOWED AGAINST UNITED STATES INCOME TAXES.—No credit shall be allowed against United States income taxes under section 6428 of the Internal Revenue Code of 1986 (as added by this section) to any person—

(A) to whom a credit is allowed against taxes imposed by the possession by reason of the amendments made by this section, or

(B) who is eligible for a payment under a plan described in paragraph (1)(B).

(3) DEFINITIONS AND SPECIAL RULES.—

(A) POSSESSION OF THE UNITED STATES.— For purposes of this subsection, the term "possession of the United States" includes the Commonwealth of Puerto Rico and the Commonwealth of the Northern Mariana Islands.

(B) MIRROR CODE TAX SYSTEM.—For purposes of this subsection, the term "mirror code tax system" means, with respect to any possession of the United States, the income tax system of such possession if the income tax liability of the residents of such possession under such system is determined by reference to the income tax laws of the United States as if such possession were the United States.

(C) TREATMENT OF PAYMENTS.—For purposes of section 1324 of title 31, United States Code, the payments under this subsection shall be treated in the same manner as a refund due from a credit provision referred to in subsection (b)(2) of such section.

(d) EXCEPTION FROM REDUCTION OR OFFSET.—Any refund payable by reason of section 6428(f) of the Internal Revenue Code of 1986 (as added by this section), or any such refund payable by reason of subsection (c) of this section, shall not be—

(1) subject to reduction or offset pursuant to section 3716 or 3720A of title 31, United States Code,

(2) subject to reduction or offset pursuant to subsection (d), (e), or (f) of section 6402 of the Internal Revenue Code of 1986, or

(3) reduced or offset by other assessed Federal taxes that would otherwise be subject to levy or collection.

* * *

• **2020, Families First Coronavirus Response Act (P.L. 116-127)**

P.L. 116-127, §7002(f), provides:

SEC. 7002. CREDIT FOR SICK LEAVE FOR CERTAIN SELF-EMPLOYED INDIVIDUALS.

* * *

(f) APPLICATION OF CREDIT IN CERTAIN POSSESSIONS.—

(1) PAYMENTS TO POSSESSIONS WITH MIRROR CODE TAX SYSTEMS.—The Secretary of the Treasury (or the Secretary's delegate) shall pay to each possession of the United States which has a mirror code tax system amounts equal to the loss (if any) to that possession by reason of the application of the provisions of this section. Such amounts shall be determined by the Secretary of the Treasury (or the Secretary's delegate) based on information provided by the government of the respective possession.

(2) PAYMENTS TO OTHER POSSESSIONS.—The Secretary of the Treasury (or the Secretary's delegate) shall pay to each possession of the United States which does not have a mirror code tax system amounts estimated by the Secretary of the Treasury (or the Secretary's delegate) as being equal to the aggregate benefits (if any) that would have been provided to residents of such possession by reason of the provisions of this section if a mirror code tax system had been in effect in such possession. The preceding sentence shall not apply unless the respective possession has a plan, which has been approved by the Secretary of the Treasury (or the Secretary's delegate), under which such possession will promptly distribute such payments to its residents.

(3) MIRROR CODE TAX SYSTEM.—For purposes of this section, the term "mirror code tax system" means, with respect to any possession of the United States, the income tax system of such possession if the income tax liability of the residents of such possession under such system is determined by reference to the income tax laws of the United States as if such possession were the United States.

(4) TREATMENT OF PAYMENTS.—For purposes of section 1324 of title 31, United States Code, the payments under this section shall be treated in the same manner as a refund due from a credit provision referred to in subsection (b)(2) of such section.

* * *

P.L. 116-127, §7004(f), provides:

SEC. 7004. CREDIT FOR FAMILY LEAVE FOR CERTAIN SELF-EMPLOYED INDIVIDUALS.

* * *

(f) APPLICATION OF CREDIT IN CERTAIN POSSESSIONS.—

(1) PAYMENTS TO POSSESSIONS WITH MIRROR CODE TAX SYSTEMS.—The Secretary of the Treasury (or the Secretary's delegate) shall pay to each possession of the United States which has a mirror code tax system amounts equal to the loss (if any) to that possession by reason of the application of the provisions of this section. Such amounts shall be determined by the Secretary of the Treasury (or the Secretary's delegate) based on information provided by the government of the respective possession.

(2) PAYMENTS TO OTHER POSSESSIONS.—The Secretary of the Treasury (or the Secretary's delegate) shall pay to each possession of the United States which does not have a mirror code tax system amounts estimated by the Secretary of the Treasury (or the Secretary's delegate) as being equal to the aggregate benefits (if any) that would have been provided to residents of such possession by reason of the provisions of this section if a mirror code tax system had been in effect in such possession. The preceding sentence shall not apply unless the respective possession has a plan, which has been approved by the Secretary of the Treasury (or the Secretary's delegate), under which such possession will promptly distribute such payments to its residents.

(3) MIRROR CODE TAX SYSTEM.—For purposes of this section, the term "mirror code tax system" means, with respect to any possession of the United States, the income tax system of such possession if the income tax liability of the residents of such possession under such system is determined by reference to the income tax laws of the United States as if such possession were the United States.

INCOME TAX—U.S. POSSESSIONS

(4) TREATMENT OF PAYMENTS.—For purposes of section 1324 of title 31, United States Code, the payments under this section shall be treated in the same manner as a refund due from a credit provision referred to in subsection (b)(2) of such section.

* * *

- **2019, Taxpayer Certainty and Disaster Tax Relief Act of 2019 (P.L. 116-94)**

P.L. 116-94, §208, Div. Q, provides:
SEC. 208. TREATMENT OF CERTAIN POSSESSIONS.

(a) PAYMENTS TO POSSESSIONS WITH MIRROR CODE TAX SYSTEMS.—The Secretary of the Treasury shall pay to each possession of the United States which has a mirror code tax system amounts equal to the loss (if any) to that possession by reason of the application of the provisions of this title. Such amounts shall be determined by the Secretary of the Treasury based on information provided by the government of the respective possession.

(b) PAYMENTS TO OTHER POSSESSIONS.—The Secretary of the Treasury shall pay to each possession of the United States which does not have a mirror code tax system amounts estimated by the Secretary of the Treasury as being equal to the aggregate benefits (if any) that would have been provided to residents of such possession by reason of the provisions of this title if a mirror code tax system had been in effect in such possession. The preceding sentence shall not apply unless the respective possession has a plan, which has been approved by the Secretary of the Treasury, under which such possession will promptly distribute such payments to its residents.

(c) MIRROR CODE TAX SYSTEM.—For purposes of this section, the term "mirror code tax system" means, with respect to any possession of the United States, the income tax system of such possession if the income tax liability of the residents of such possession under such system is determined by reference to the income tax laws of the United States as if such possession were the United States.

(d) TREATMENT OF PAYMENTS.—For purposes of section 1324 of title 31, United States Code, the payments under this section shall be treated in the same manner as a refund due from a credit provision referred to in subsection (b)(2) of such section.

[Sec. 931(b)]

(b) DEDUCTIONS, ETC. ALLOCABLE TO EXCLUDED AMOUNTS NOT ALLOWABLE.—An individual shall not be allowed—

(1) as a deduction from gross income any deductions (other than the deduction under section 151, relating to personal exemptions), or

(2) any credit,

properly allocable or chargeable against amounts excluded from gross income under this section.

[Sec. 931(c)]

(c) SPECIFIED POSSESSION.—For purposes of this section, the term "specified possession" means Guam, American Samoa, and the Northern Mariana Islands.

[Sec. 931(d)]

(d) EMPLOYEES OF THE UNITED STATES.—Amounts paid for services performed as an employee of the United States (or any agency thereof) shall be treated as not described in paragraph (1) or (2) of subsection (a).

Amendments

- **2004, American Jobs Creation Act of 2004 (P.L. 108-357)**

P.L. 108-357, §908(c)(1):

Amended Code Sec. 931(d). **Effective** for tax years ending after 10-22-2004. Prior to amendment, Code. Sec. 931(d) read as follows:

(d) SPECIAL RULES.—For purposes of this section—

(1) EMPLOYEES OF THE UNITED STATES.—Amounts paid for services performed as an employee of the United States (or any agency thereof) shall be treated as not described in paragraph (1) or (2) of subsection (a).

(2) DETERMINATION OF SOURCE, ETC.—The determination as to whether income is described in paragraph (1) or (2) of subsection (a) shall be made under regulations prescribed by the Secretary.

(3) DETERMINATION OF RESIDENCY.—For purposes of this section and section 876, the determination of whether an individual is a bona fide resident of Guam, American Samoa, or the Northern Marina Islands shall be made under regulations prescribed by the Secretary.

- **1986, Tax Reform Act of 1986 (P.L. 99-514)**

P.L. 99-514, §1272(a):

Amended Code Sec. 931. **Effective**, generally, for tax years beginning after 12-31-86. However, see Act Sec. 1277(b)-(e) under the amendment notes for Code Sec. 48 for special rules. Prior to amendment, Code Sec. 931 read as follows:

SEC. 931. INCOME FROM SOURCES WITHIN POSSESSIONS OF THE UNITED STATES.

[Sec. 931(a)]

(a) GENERAL RULE.—In the case of individual citizens of the United States, gross income means only gross income from sources within the United States if the conditions of both paragraph (1) and paragraph (2) are satisfied:

(1) 3-YEAR PERIOD.—If 80 percent or more of the gross income of such citizen (computed without the benefit of this section) for the 3-year period immediately preceding the close of the taxable year (or for such part of such period immediately preceding the close of such taxable year as may be applicable) was derived from sources within a possession of the United States; and

(2) TRADE OR BUSINESS.—If 50 percent or more of his gross income (computed without the benefit of this section) for such period or such part thereof was derived from the active conduct of a trade or business within a possession of the United States either on his own account or as an employee or agent of another.

Amendments

- **1976, Tax Reform Act of 1976 (P.L. 94-455)**

P.L. 94-455, §1051(c)(1):

Amended Code Sec. 931(a). **Effective** for tax years beginning after 12-31-75. Prior to amendment, Code Sec. 931(a) read as follows:

(a) GENERAL RULE.—In the case of citizens of the United States or domestic corporations, gross income means only gross income from sources within the United States if the conditions of both paragraph (1) and paragraph (2) are satisfied:

(1) THREE-YEAR PERIOD.—If 80 percent or more of the gross income of such citizen or domestic corporation (computed without the benefit of this section) for the 3-year period immediately preceding the close of the taxable year (or for such part of such period immediately preceding the close of such taxable year as may be applicable) was derived from sources within a possession of the United States; and

(2) TRADE OR BUSINESS.—If—

(A) in the case of such corporation, 50 percent or more of its gross income (computed without the benefit of this section) for such period or such part thereof was derived from the active conduct of a trade or business within a possession of the United States; or

(B) in the case of such citizen, 50 percent or more of his gross income (computed without the benefit of this section) for such period or such part thereof was derived from the active conduct of a trade or business within a possession of the United States either on his own account or as an employee or agent of another.

This section shall not apply in the case of a corporation for a taxable year for which it is a DISC or in which it owns at any time stock in a DISC or former DISC (as defined in section 992(a)).

- **1971, Revenue Act of 1971 (P.L. 92-178)**

P.L. 92-178, §502(d):

Added the last sentence in Code Sec. 931(a). **Effective** 12-10-71.

[Sec. 931(b)]

(b) AMOUNTS RECEIVED IN UNITED STATES.—Notwithstanding subsection (a), there shall be included in gross income all amounts received by such citizens or corporations within the United States, whether derived from sources within or without the United States.

[Sec. 931(c)]

(c) DEFINITION.—For purposes of this section, the term "possession of the United States" does not include the Commonwealth of Puerto Rico, the Virgin Islands of the United States, or Guam.

- **1976, Tax Reform Act of 1976 (P.L. 94-455)**

P.L. 94-455, §1051(c)(2):

Amended Code Sec. 931(c). **Effective** for tax years beginning after 12-31-75. Prior to amendment, Code Sec. 931(c) read as follows:

(c) DEFINITION.—For purposes of this section, the term "possession of the United States" does not include the Virgin Islands of the United States, and such term when used with respect to citizens of the United States does not include Puerto Rico or Guam.

- **1972 (P.L. 92-606)**

P.L. 92-606, §1(f)(1):

Added "or Guam" at the end of Code Sec. 931(c). **Effective** for tax years beginning after 12-31-72.

[Sec. 931(d)]

(d) DEDUCTIONS.—

(1) GENERAL RULE.—Except as otherwise provided in this subsection and subsection (e), in the case of a citizen of the United States entitled to the benefits of this section the deductions shall be allowed only if and to the extent that they are connected with income from sources within the United States; and the proper apportionment and allocation of the deductions with respect to sources of income within and without the United States shall be determined as provided in part I, under regulations prescribed by the Secretary.

(2) EXCEPTIONS.—The following deductions shall be allowed whether or not they are connected with income from sources within the United States:

(A) The deduction, for losses not connected with the trade or business if incurred in transactions entered into for profit, allowed by section 165(c)(2), but only if the profit, if such transaction had resulted in a profit, would be taxable under this subtitle.

(B) The deduction, for losses allowed by section 165(c)(3), but only if the loss is of property within the United States.

(C) The deduction for charitable contributions and gifts allowed by section 170.

INCOME TAX—U.S. POSSESSIONS

Amendments

• **1984, Deficit Reduction Act of 1984 (P.L. 98-369)**

P.L. 98-369, § 711(c)(2)(A)(iv):

Amended Code Sec. 931(d)(2)(B) by striking out ", for losses of property not connected with the trade or business if arising from certain casualties or theft," and inserting in lieu thereof "for losses". **Effective** for tax years beginning after 12-31-83.

• **1977, Tax Reduction and Simplification Act of 1977 (P.L. 95-30)**

P.L. 95-30, § 101(d)(12):

Amended Code Sec. 931(d) by repealing paragraph (3). **Effective** for tax years beginning after 12-31-76. Prior to amendment, paragraph (3) of Code Sec. 931(d) read as follows:

(3) DEDUCTION DISALLOWED.—

For disallowance of standard deduction, see section 142(b)(2).

• **1976, Tax Reform Act of 1976 (P.L. 94-455)**

P.L. 94-455, § 1051(c)(2):

Substituted "a citizen of the United States" for "persons" in Code Sec. 931(d). **Effective** for tax years beginning after 12-31-75.

P.L. 94-455, § 1906(b)(13)(A):

Amended 1954 Code by substituting "Secretary" for "Secretary or his delegate" each place it appeared. **Effective** 2-1-77.

• **1966, Foreign Investors Tax Act of 1966 (P.L. 89-809)**

P.L. 89-809, § 107(a):

Amended Code Sec. 931(d). **Effective** 1-1-67. Prior to amendment, Sec. 931(d) read as follows:

"(d) Deductions.—

"(1) Citizens of the United States entitled to the benefits of this section shall have the same deductions as are allowed by section 873 in the case of a nonresident alien individual engaged in trade or business within the United States.

"(2) Domestic corporations entitled to the benefits of this section shall have the same deductions as are allowed by section 882(c) in the case of a foreign corporation engaged in trade or business within the United States."

[Sec. 931(e)]

(e) DEDUCTION FOR PERSONAL EXEMPTION.—A citizen of the United States entitled to the benefits of this section shall be allowed a deduction for only one exemption under section 151.

[Sec. 931(f)]

(f) ALLOWANCE OF DEDUCTIONS AND CREDITS.—A citizen of the United States entitled to the benefits of this section shall receive the benefit of the deductions and credits allowed to them in this subtitle only by filing or causing to be filed with the Secretary a true and accurate return of their total income received from all sources in the United States, in the manner prescribed in subtitle F, including therein all the information which the Secretary may deem necessary for the calculation of such deductions and credits.

Amendments

• **1976, Tax Reform Act of 1976 (P.L. 94-455)**

P.L. 94-455, § 1051(c)(3):

Substitutes "A citizen of the United States" for "Persons" in Code Sec. 931(f). **Effective** for tax years beginning after 12-31-75.

P.L. 94-455, § 1906(b)(13)(A):

Amended 1954 Code by substituting "Secretary" for "Secretary or his delegate" each place it appeared. **Effective** 2-1-77.

[Sec. 931(g)]

(g) FOREIGN TAX CREDIT.—Persons entitled to the benefits of this section shall not be allowed the credits against the tax for taxes of foreign countries and possessions of the United States allowed by section 901.

[Sec. 931(h)]

(h) EMPLOYEES OF THE UNITED STATES.—For purposes of this section, amounts paid for services performed by a citizen of the United States as an employee of the United States or any agency thereof shall be deemed to be derived from sources within the United States.

Amendments

• **1976, Tax Reform Act of 1976 (P.L. 94-455)**

P.L. 94-455, § 1901(a)(117):

Repealed Code Sec. 931(h) and redesignated Code Sec. 931(i) as Code Sec. 931(h). **Effective** for tax years beginning after 12-31-76. Prior to repeal, Code Sec. 931(h) read as follows:

(h) INTERNEES.—In the case of a citizen of the United States interned by the enemy while serving as an employee within a possession of the United States—

(1) if such citizen was confined in any place not within a possession of the United States, such place of confinement shall, for purposes of this section, be considered as within a possession of the United States; and

(2) subsection (b) shall not apply to any compensation received within the United States by such citizen attributable to the period of time during which such citizen was interned by the enemy.

[Sec. 932]

SEC. 932. COORDINATION OF UNITED STATES AND VIRGIN ISLANDS INCOME TAXES.

[Sec. 932(a)]

(a) TREATMENT OF UNITED STATES RESIDENTS.—

(1) APPLICATION OF SUBSECTION.—This subsection shall apply to an individual for the taxable year if—

(A) such individual—

(i) is a citizen or resident of the United States (other than a bona fide resident of the Virgin Islands during the entire taxable year), and

(ii) has income derived from sources within the Virgin Islands, or effectively connected with the conduct of a trade or business within such possession, for the taxable year, or

(B) such individual files a joint return for the taxable year with an individual described in subparagraph (A).

(2) FILING REQUIREMENT.—Each individual to whom this subsection applies for the taxable year shall file his income tax return for the taxable year with both the United States and the Virgin Islands.

(3) EXTENT OF INCOME TAX LIABILITY.—In the case of an individual to whom this subsection applies in a taxable year for purposes of so much of this title (other than this section and section 7654) as relates to the taxes imposed by this chapter, the United States shall be treated as including the Virgin Islands.

Amendments

• **2021, American Rescue Plan Act of 2021 (P.L. 117-2)**

P.L. 117-2, § 9601(b) and (c)(2), provides:

SEC. 9601. 2021 RECOVERY REBATES TO INDIVIDUALS.

* * *

(b) TREATMENT OF CERTAIN POSSESSIONS.—

(1) PAYMENTS TO POSSESSIONS WITH MIRROR CODE TAX SYSTEMS.—The Secretary of the Treasury shall pay to each possession of the United States which has a mirror code tax system amounts equal to the loss (if any) to that possession by reason of the amendments made by this section. Such amounts shall be determined by the Secretary of the Treasury based on information provided by the government of the respective possession.

(2) PAYMENTS TO OTHER POSSESSIONS.—The Secretary of the Treasury shall pay to each possession of the United States which does not have a mirror code tax system amounts estimated by the Secretary of the Treasury as being equal to the aggregate benefits (if any) that would have been provided to residents of such possession by reason of the amendments made by this section if a mirror code tax system had been in effect in such possession. The preceding sentence shall not apply unless the respective possession has a plan, which has been approved by the Secretary of the Treasury, under which such possession will promptly distribute such payments to its residents.

(3) INCLUSION OF ADMINISTRATIVE EXPENSES.—The Secretary of the Treasury shall pay to each possession of the United States to which the Secretary makes a payment under paragraph (1) or (2) an amount equal to the lesser of—

(A) the increase (if any) of the administrative expenses of such possession—

(i) in the case of a possession described in paragraph (1), by reason of the amendments made by this section, and

(ii) in the case of a possession described in paragraph (2), by reason of carrying out the plan described in such paragraph, or

(B) $500,000 ($10,000,000 in the case of Puerto Rico).

The amount described in subparagraph (A) shall be determined by the Secretary of the Treasury based on information provided by the government of the respective possession.

(4) COORDINATION WITH CREDIT ALLOWED AGAINST UNITED STATES INCOME TAXES.—No credit shall be allowed against United States income taxes under section 6428B of the Internal Revenue Code of 1986 (as added by this section), nor shall any credit or refund be made or allowed under subsection (g) of such section, to any person—

(A) to whom a credit is allowed against taxes imposed by the possession by reason of the amendments made by this section, or

(B) who is eligible for a payment under a plan described in paragraph (2).

(5) MIRROR CODE TAX SYSTEM.—For purposes of this subsection, the term "mirror code tax system" means, with respect to any possession of the United States, the income tax system of such possession if the income tax liability of the residents of such possession under such system is determined by reference to the income tax laws of the United States as if such possession were the United States.

(6) TREATMENT OF PAYMENTS.—For purposes of section 1324 of title 31, United States Code, the payments under this subsection shall be treated in the same manner as a refund due from a credit provision referred to in subsection (b)(2) of such section.

INCOME TAX—U.S. POSSESSIONS

(c) ADMINISTRATIVE PROVISIONS.—

***

(2) EXCEPTION FROM REDUCTION OR OFFSET.—Any refund payable by reason of section 6428B(g) of the Internal Revenue Code of 1986 (as added by this section), or any such refund payable by reason of subsection (b) of this section, shall not be—

(A) subject to reduction or offset pursuant to subsection (c), (d), (e), or (f) of section 6402 of the Internal Revenue Code of 1986 or any similar authority permitting offset, or

(B) reduced or offset by other assessed Federal taxes that would otherwise be subject to levy or collection.

***

P.L. 117-2, §9626(d), provides:

SEC. 9626. TEMPORARY SPECIAL RULE FOR DETERMINING EARNED INCOME FOR PURPOSES OF EARNED INCOME TAX CREDIT.

***

(d) TREATMENT OF CERTAIN POSSESSIONS.—

(1) PAYMENTS TO POSSESSIONS WITH MIRROR CODE TAX SYSTEMS.—The Secretary of the Treasury shall pay to each possession of the United States which has a mirror code tax system amounts equal to the loss (if any) to that possession by reason of the application of the provisions of this section (other than this subsection) with respect to section 32 of the Internal Revenue Code of 1986. Such amounts shall be determined by the Secretary of the Treasury based on information provided by the government of the respective possession.

(2) PAYMENTS TO OTHER POSSESSIONS.—The Secretary of the Treasury shall pay to each possession of the United States which does not have a mirror code tax system amounts estimated by the Secretary of the Treasury as being equal to the aggregate benefits (if any) that would have been provided to residents of such possession by reason of the provisions of this section (other than this subsection) with respect to section 32 of the Internal Revenue Code of 1986 if a mirror code tax system had been in effect in such possession. The preceding sentence shall not apply unless the respective possession has a plan, which has been approved by the Secretary of the Treasury, under which such possession will promptly distribute such payments to its residents.

(3) MIRROR CODE TAX SYSTEM.—For purposes of this section, the term "mirror code tax system" means, with respect to any possession of the United States, the income tax system of such possession if the income tax liability of the residents of such possession under such system is determined by reference to the income tax laws of the United States as if such possession were the United States.

(4) TREATMENT OF PAYMENTS.—For purposes of section 1324 of title 31, United States Code, the payments under this section shall be treated in the same manner as a refund due from a credit provision referred to in subsection (b)(2) of such section.

P.L. 117-2, §9642(g)-(h), provides:

SEC. 9642. CREDIT FOR SICK LEAVE FOR CERTAIN SELF-EMPLOYED INDIVIDUALS.

***

(g) APPLICATION OF CREDIT IN CERTAIN POSSESSIONS.—

(1) PAYMENTS TO POSSESSIONS WITH MIRROR CODE TAX SYSTEMS.—The Secretary shall pay to each possession of the United States which has a mirror code tax system amounts equal to the loss (if any) to that possession by reason of the application of the provisions of this section. Such amounts shall be determined by the Secretary based on information provided by the government of the respective possession.

(2) PAYMENTS TO OTHER POSSESSIONS.—The Secretary shall pay to each possession of the United States which does not have a mirror code tax system amounts estimated by the Secretary as being equal to the aggregate benefits (if any) that would have been provided to residents of such possession by reason of the provisions of this section if a mirror code tax system had been in effect in such possession. The preceding sentence shall not apply unless the respective possession has a plan, which has been approved by the Secretary, under which such possession will promptly distribute such payments to its residents.

(3) MIRROR CODE TAX SYSTEM.—For purposes of this section, the term "mirror code tax system" means, with respect to any possession of the United States, the income tax system of such possession if the income tax liability of the residents of such possession under such system is determined by reference to the income tax laws of the United States as if such possession were the United States.

(4) TREATMENT OF PAYMENTS.—For purposes of section 1324 of title 31, United States Code, the payments under this subsection shall be treated in the same manner as a refund due from a credit provision referred to in subsection (b)(2) of such section.

(h) REGULATIONS.—The Secretary shall prescribe such regulations or other guidance as may be necessary to carry out the purposes of this section, including—

(1) regulations or other guidance to effectuate the purposes of this section, and

(2) regulations or other guidance to minimize compliance and record-keeping burdens under this section.

P.L. 117-2, §9643(g)-(h), provides:

SEC. 9643. CREDIT FOR FAMILY LEAVE FOR CERTAIN SELF-EMPLOYED INDIVIDUALS.

***

(g) APPLICATION OF CREDIT IN CERTAIN POSSESSIONS.—

(1) PAYMENTS TO POSSESSIONS WITH MIRROR CODE TAX SYSTEMS.—The Secretary shall pay to each possession of the United States which has a mirror code tax system amounts equal to the loss (if any) to that possession by reason of the application of the provisions of this section. Such amounts shall be determined by the Secretary based on information provided by the government of the respective possession.

(2) PAYMENTS TO OTHER POSSESSIONS.—The Secretary shall pay to each possession of the United States which does not have a mirror code tax system amounts estimated by the Secretary as being equal to the aggregate benefits (if any) that would have been provided to residents of such possession by reason of the provisions of this section if a mirror code tax system had been in effect in such possession. The preceding sentence shall not apply unless the respective possession has a plan, which has been approved by the Secretary, under which such possession will promptly distribute such payments to its residents.

(3) MIRROR CODE TAX SYSTEM.—For purposes of this section, the term "mirror code tax system" means, with respect to any possession of the United States, the income tax system of such possession if the income tax liability of the residents of such possession under such system is determined by reference to the income tax laws of the United States as if such possession were the United States.

(4) TREATMENT OF PAYMENTS.—For purposes of section 1324 of title 31, United States Code, the payments under this subsection shall be treated in the same manner as a refund due from a credit provision referred to in subsection (b)(2) of such section.

(h) REGULATIONS.—The Secretary shall prescribe such regulations or other guidance as may be necessary to carry out the purposes of this section, including—

(1) regulations or other guidance to prevent the avoidance of the purposes of this section, and

(2) regulations or other guidance to minimize compliance and record-keeping burdens under this section.

• **2020, COVID-related Tax Relief Act of 2020 (P.L. 116-260)**

P.L. 116-260, §272(c)-(d), Div. N, provides:

SEC. 272. ADDITIONAL 2020 RECOVERY REBATES FOR INDIVIDUALS.

***

(c) TREATMENT OF POSSESSIONS.—

(1) PAYMENTS TO POSSESSIONS.—

(A) MIRROR CODE POSSESSION.—The Secretary of the Treasury shall pay to each possession of the United States which has a mirror code tax system amounts equal to the loss (if any) to that possession by reason of the amendments made by this section. Such amounts shall be determined by the Secretary of the Treasury based on information provided by the government of the respective possession.

(B) OTHER POSSESSIONS.—The Secretary of the Treasury shall pay to each possession of the United States which does not have a mirror code tax system amounts estimated by the Secretary of the Treasury as being equal to the aggregate benefits (if any) that would have been provided to residents of such possession by reason of the amendments made by this section if a mirror code tax system had been in effect in such possession. The preceding sentence shall not apply unless the respective possession has a plan, which has been approved by the Secretary of the Treasury, under which such possession will promptly distribute such payments to its residents.

(2) COORDINATION WITH CREDIT ALLOWED AGAINST UNITED STATES INCOME TAXES.—No credit shall be allowed against United States income taxes under section 6428A of the Internal Revenue Code of 1986 (as added by this section) to any person—

(A) to whom a credit is allowed against taxes imposed by the possession by reason of the amendments made by this section, or

(B) who is eligible for a payment under a plan described in paragraph (1)(B).

(3) DEFINITIONS AND SPECIAL RULES.—

(A) POSSESSION OF THE UNITED STATES.—For purposes of this subsection, the term "possession of the United States" includes the Commonwealth of Puerto Rico and the Commonwealth of the Northern Mariana Islands.

(B) MIRROR CODE TAX SYSTEM.—For purposes of this subsection, the term "mirror code tax system" means, with respect to any possession of the United States, the income tax system of such possession if the income tax liability of the residents of such possession under such system is determined by reference to the income tax laws of the United States as if such possession were the United States.

(C) TREATMENT OF PAYMENTS.—For purposes of section 1324 of title 31, United States Code, the payments under this subsection shall be treated in the same manner as a refund due from a credit provision referred to in subsection (b)(2) of such section.

(d) ADMINISTRATIVE PROVISIONS.—

(1) EXCEPTION FROM REDUCTION OR OFFSET.—Any refund payable by reason of section 6428A(f) of the Internal Revenue Code of 1986 (as added by this section), or any such refund payable by reason of subsection (c) of this section, shall not be—

(A) subject to reduction or offset pursuant to section 3716 or 3720A of title 31, United States Code,

(B) subject to reduction or offset pursuant to subsection (c), (d), (e), or (f) of section 6402 of the Internal Revenue Code of 1986, or

(C) reduced or offset by other assessed Federal taxes that would otherwise be subject to levy or collection.

(2) ASSIGNMENT OF BENEFITS.—

(A) IN GENERAL.—The right of any person to any applicable payment shall not be transferable or assignable, at law or in equity, and no applicable payment shall be subject to, execution, levy, attachment, garnishment, or other legal process, or the operation of any bankruptcy or insolvency law.

***

(D) NO RECLAMATION RIGHTS.—This paragraph shall not alter the status of applicable payments as tax refunds or other nonbenefit payments for purpose of any reclamation rights of the Department of the Treasury or the Internal Revenue Service as per part 210 of title 31, Code of Federal Regulations.

(E) DEFINITIONS.—For purposes of this paragraph—

(i) ACCOUNT HOLDER.—The term "account holder" means a natural person whose name appears in a financial institution's records as the direct or beneficial owner of an account.

(ii) ACCOUNT REVIEW.—The term "account review" means the process of examining deposits in an account to determine if an applicable payment has been deposited into the account during the lookback period. The financial institution shall perform the account review following the procedures outlined in section 212.5 of title 31, Code of Federal Regulations and in accordance with the requirements of section 212.6 of title 31, Code of Federal Regulations.

(iii) APPLICABLE PAYMENT.—The term "applicable payment" means—

INCOME TAX—U.S. POSSESSIONS

(I) any advance refund amount paid pursuant to section 6428A(f) of Internal Revenue Code of 1986 (as added by this section),

(II) any payment made by a possession of the United States with a mirror code tax system (as defined in subsection (c) of this section) pursuant to such subsection which corresponds to a payment described in subclause (I), and

(III) any payment made by a possession of the United States without a mirror code tax system (as so defined) pursuant to subsection (c) of this section.

(iv) GARNISHMENT.—The term "garnishment" means execution, levy, attachment, garnishment, or other legal process.

(v) GARNISHMENT ORDER.—The term "garnishment order" means a writ, order, notice, summons, judgment, levy, or similar written instruction issued by a court, a State or State agency, a municipality or municipal corporation, or a State child support enforcement agency, including a lien arising by operation of law for overdue child support or an order to freeze the assets in an account, to effect a garnishment against a debtor.

(vi) LOOKBACK PERIOD.—The term "lookback period" means the two month period that begins on the date preceding the date of account review and ends on the corresponding date of the month two months earlier, or on the last date of the month two months earlier if the corresponding date does not exist.

(3) AGENCY INFORMATION SHARING AND ASSISTANCE.—

(A) IN GENERAL.—The Commissioner of Social Security, the Railroad Retirement Board, and the Secretary of Veterans Affairs shall each provide the Secretary of the Treasury (or the Secretary's delegate) such information and assistance as the Secretary of the Treasury (or the Secretary's delegate) may require for purposes of—

(i) making payments under section 6428A(f) of the Internal Revenue Code of 1986 to individuals described in paragraph (5)(A) thereof, or

(ii) providing administrative assistance to a possession of the United States (as defined in subsection (c)(3)(A)) to allow such possession to promptly distribute payments under subsection (c) to its residents.

(B) EXCHANGE OF INFORMATION WITH POSSESSIONS.—Any information provided to the Secretary of the Treasury (or the Secretary's delegate) pursuant to subparagraph (A)(ii) may be exchanged with a possession of the United States in accordance with the applicable tax coordination agreement for information exchange and administrative assistance that the Internal Revenue Service has agreed to with such possession.

* * *

- **2020, Taxpayer Certainty and Disaster Tax Relief Act of 2020 (P.L. 116-260)**

P.L. 116-260, § 306(a)-(c), Div. EE, provides:

SEC. 306. TREATMENT OF CERTAIN POSSESSIONS.

(a) PAYMENTS TO POSSESSIONS WITH MIRROR CODE TAX SYSTEMS.—The Secretary of the Treasury shall pay to each possession of the United States which has a mirror code tax system amounts equal to the loss (if any) to that possession by reason of the application of the provisions of this title. Such amounts shall be determined by the Secretary of the Treasury based on information provided by the government of the respective possession.

(b) PAYMENTS TO OTHER POSSESSIONS.—The Secretary of the Treasury shall pay to each possession of the United States which does not have a mirror code tax system amounts estimated by the Secretary of the Treasury as being equal to the aggregate benefits (if any) that would have been provided to residents of such possession by reason of the provisions of this title if a mirror code tax system had been in effect in such possession. The preceding sentence shall not apply unless the respective possession has a plan, which has been approved by the Secretary of the Treasury, under which such possession will promptly distribute such payments to its residents.

(c) MIRROR CODE TAX SYSTEM.—For purposes of this section, the term "mirror code tax system" means, with respect to any possession of the United States, the income tax system of such possession if the income tax liability of the residents of such possession under such system is determined by reference to the income tax laws of the United States as if such possession were the United States.

* * *

- **2020, Coronavirus Aid, Relief, and Economic Security (CARES) Act (P.L. 116-136)**

P.L. 116-136, § 2201(c)-(d) (as amended by P.L. 116-260, § 273(b)(1), Div. N), provides:

SEC. 2201. 2020 RECOVERY REBATES FOR INDIVIDUALS.

* * *

(c) TREATMENT OF POSSESSIONS.—

(1) PAYMENTS TO POSSESSIONS.—

(A) MIRROR CODE POSSESSION.—The Secretary of the Treasury shall pay to each possession of the United States which has a mirror code tax system amounts equal to the loss (if any) to that possession by reason of the amendments made by this section. Such amounts shall be determined by the Secretary of the Treasury based on information provided by the government of the respective possession.

(B) OTHER POSSESSIONS.—The Secretary of the Treasury shall pay to each possession of the United States which does not have a mirror code tax system amounts estimated by the Secretary of the Treasury as being equal to the aggregate benefits (if any) that would have been provided to residents of such possession by reason of the amendments made by this section if a mirror code tax system had been in effect in such possession. The preceding sentence shall not apply unless the respective possession has a plan, which has been approved by the Secretary of the Treasury, under which such possession will promptly distribute such payments to its residents.

(2) COORDINATION WITH CREDIT ALLOWED AGAINST UNITED STATES INCOME TAXES.—No credit shall be allowed against United States income taxes under section 6428 of the Internal Revenue Code of 1986 (as added by this section) to any person—

(A) to whom a credit is allowed against taxes imposed by the possession by reason of the amendments made by this section, or

(B) who is eligible for a payment under a plan described in paragraph (1)(B).

Sec. 932(a)(3)

(3) DEFINITIONS AND SPECIAL RULES.—

(A) POSSESSION OF THE UNITED STATES.— For purposes of this subsection, the term "possession of the United States" includes the Commonwealth of Puerto Rico and the Commonwealth of the Northern Mariana Islands.

(B) MIRROR CODE TAX SYSTEM.—For purposes of this subsection, the term "mirror code tax system" means, with respect to any possession of the United States, the income tax system of such possession if the income tax liability of the residents of such possession under such system is determined by reference to the income tax laws of the United States as if such possession were the United States.

(C) TREATMENT OF PAYMENTS.—For purposes of section 1324 of title 31, United States Code, the payments under this subsection shall be treated in the same manner as a refund due from a credit provision referred to in subsection (b)(2) of such section.

(d) EXCEPTION FROM REDUCTION OR OFFSET.—Any refund payable by reason of section 6428(f) of the Internal Revenue Code of 1986 (as added by this section), or any such refund payable by reason of subsection (c) of this section, shall not be—

(1) subject to reduction or offset pursuant to section 3716 or 3720A of title 31, United States Code,

(2) subject to reduction or offset pursuant to subsection (d), (e), or (f) of section 6402 of the Internal Revenue Code of 1986, or

(3) reduced or offset by other assessed Federal taxes that would otherwise be subject to levy or collection.

* * *

- **2020, Families First Coronavirus Response Act (P.L. 116-127)**

P.L. 116-127, § 7002(f), provides:

SEC. 7002. CREDIT FOR SICK LEAVE FOR CERTAIN SELF-EMPLOYED INDIVIDUALS.

* * *

(f) APPLICATION OF CREDIT IN CERTAIN POSSESSIONS.—

(1) PAYMENTS TO POSSESSIONS WITH MIRROR CODE TAX SYSTEMS.—The Secretary of the Treasury (or the Secretary's delegate) shall pay to each possession of the United States which has a mirror code tax system amounts equal to the loss (if any) to that possession by reason of the application of the provisions of this section. Such amounts shall be determined by the Secretary of the Treasury (or the Secretary's delegate) based on information provided by the government of the respective possession.

(2) PAYMENTS TO OTHER POSSESSIONS.—The Secretary of the Treasury (or the Secretary's delegate) shall pay to each possession of the United States which does not have a mirror code tax system amounts estimated by the Secretary of the Treasury (or the Secretary's delegate) as being equal to the aggregate benefits (if any) that would have been provided to residents of such possession by reason of the provisions of this section if a mirror code tax system had been in effect in such possession. The preceding sentence shall not apply unless the respective possession has a plan, which has been approved by the Secretary of the Treasury (or the Secretary's delegate), under which such possession will promptly distribute such payments to its residents.

(3) MIRROR CODE TAX SYSTEM.—For purposes of this section, the term "mirror code tax system" means, with respect to any possession of the United States, the income tax system of such possession if the income tax liability of the residents of such possession under such system is determined by reference to the income tax laws of the United States as if such possession were the United States.

(4) TREATMENT OF PAYMENTS.—For purposes of section 1324 of title 31, United States Code, the payments under this section shall be treated in the same manner as a refund due from a credit provision referred to in subsection (b)(2) of such section.

* * *

P.L. 116-127, § 7004(f), provides:

SEC. 7004. CREDIT FOR FAMILY LEAVE FOR CERTAIN SELF-EMPLOYED INDIVIDUALS.

* * *

(f) APPLICATION OF CREDIT IN CERTAIN POSSESSIONS.—

(1) PAYMENTS TO POSSESSIONS WITH MIRROR CODE TAX SYSTEMS.—The Secretary of the Treasury (or the Secretary's delegate) shall pay to each possession of the United States which has a mirror code tax system amounts equal to the loss (if any) to that possession by reason of the application of the provisions of this section. Such amounts shall be determined by the Secretary of the Treasury (or the Secretary's delegate) based on information provided by the government of the respective possession.

(2) PAYMENTS TO OTHER POSSESSIONS.—The Secretary of the Treasury (or the Secretary's delegate) shall pay to each possession of the United States which does not have a mirror code tax system amounts estimated by the Secretary of the Treasury (or the Secretary's delegate) as being equal to the aggregate benefits (if any) that would have been provided to residents of such possession by reason of the provisions of this section if a mirror code tax system had been in effect in such possession. The preceding sentence shall not apply unless the respective possession has a plan, which has been approved by the Secretary of the Treasury (or the Secretary's delegate), under which such possession will promptly distribute such payments to its residents.

(3) MIRROR CODE TAX SYSTEM.—For purposes of this section, the term "mirror code tax system" means, with respect to any possession of the United States, the income tax system of such possession if the income tax liability of the residents of such possession under such system is determined by reference to the income tax laws of the United States as if such possession were the United States.

(4) TREATMENT OF PAYMENTS.—For purposes of section 1324 of title 31, United States Code, the payments under this section shall be treated in the same manner as a refund due from a credit provision referred to in subsection (b)(2) of such section.

* * *

INCOME TAX—U.S. POSSESSIONS

• **2019, Taxpayer Certainty and Disaster Tax Relief Act of 2019 (P.L. 116-94)**

P.L. 116-94, § 208, Div. Q, provides:

SEC. 208. TREATMENT OF CERTAIN POSSESSIONS.

(a) PAYMENTS TO POSSESSIONS WITH MIRROR CODE TAX SYSTEMS.—The Secretary of the Treasury shall pay to each possession of the United States which has a mirror code tax system amounts equal to the loss (if any) to that possession by reason of the application of the provisions of this title. Such amounts shall be determined by the Secretary of the Treasury based on information provided by the government of the respective possession.

(b) PAYMENTS TO OTHER POSSESSIONS.—The Secretary of the Treasury shall pay to each possession of the United States which does not have a mirror code tax system amounts estimated by the Secretary of the Treasury as being equal to the aggregate benefits (if any) that would have been provided to residents of such possession by reason of the provisions of this title if a mirror code tax system had been in effect in such possession. The preceding sentence shall not apply unless the respective possession has a plan, which has been approved by the Secretary of the Treasury, under which such possession will promptly distribute such payments to its residents.

(c) MIRROR CODE TAX SYSTEM.—For purposes of this section, the term "mirror code tax system" means, with respect to any possession of the United States, the income tax system of such possession if the income tax liability of the residents of such possession under such system is determined by reference to the income tax laws of the United States as if such possession were the United States.

(d) TREATMENT OF PAYMENTS.—For purposes of section 1324 of title 31, United States Code, the payments under this section shall be treated in the same manner as a refund due from a credit provision referred to in subsection (b)(2) of such section.

• **2004, American Jobs Creation Act of 2004 (P.L. 108-357)**

P.L. 108-357, § 908(c)(2):

Amended Code Sec. 932 by striking "at the close of the taxable year" and inserting "during the entire taxable year" each place it appears. **Effective** for tax years ending after 10-22-2004.

[Sec. 932(b)]

(b) PORTION OF UNITED STATES TAX LIABILITY PAYABLE TO THE VIRGIN ISLANDS.—

(1) IN GENERAL.—Each individual to whom subsection (a) applies for the taxable year shall pay the applicable percentage of the taxes imposed by this chapter for such taxable year (determined without regard to paragraph (3)) to the Virgin Islands.

(2) APPLICABLE PERCENTAGE.—

(A) IN GENERAL.—For purposes of paragraph (1), the term "applicable percentage" means the percentage which Virgin Islands adjusted gross income bears to adjusted gross income.

(B) VIRGIN ISLANDS ADJUSTED GROSS INCOME.—For purposes of subparagraph (A), the term "Virgin Islands adjusted gross income" means adjusted gross income determined by taking into account only income derived from sources within the Virgin Islands and deductions properly apportioned or allocable thereto.

(3) AMOUNTS PAID ALLOWED AS CREDIT.—There shall be allowed as a credit against the tax imposed by this chapter for the taxable year an amount equal to the taxes required to be paid to the Virgin Islands under paragraph (1) which are so paid.

[Sec. 932(c)]

(c) TREATMENT OF VIRGIN ISLANDS RESIDENTS.—

(1) APPLICATION OF SUBSECTION.—This subsection shall apply to an individual for the taxable year if—

(A) such individual is a bona fide resident of the Virgin Islands during the entire taxable year, or

(B) such individual files a joint return for the taxable year with an individual described in subparagraph (A).

(2) FILING REQUIREMENT.—Each individual to whom this subsection applies for the taxable year shall file an income tax return for the taxable year with the Virgin Islands.

(3) EXTENT OF INCOME TAX LIABILITY.—In the case of an individual to whom this subsection applies in a taxable year for purposes of so much of this title (other than this section and section 7654) as relates to the taxes imposed by this chapter, the Virgin Islands shall be treated as including the United States.

(4) RESIDENTS OF THE VIRGIN ISLANDS.—In the case of an individual—

(A) who is a bona fide resident of the Virgin Islands during the entire taxable year,

(B) who, on his return of income tax to the Virgin Islands, reports income from all sources and identifies the source of each item shown on such return, and

(C) who fully pays his tax liability referred to in section 934(a) to the Virgin Islands with respect to such income,

for purposes of calculating income tax liability to the United States, gross income shall not include any amount included in gross income on such return, and allocable deductions and credits shall not be taken into account.

Amendments

• **2004, American Jobs Creation Act of 2004 (P.L. 108-357)**

P.L. 108-357, § 908(c)(2):

Amended Code Sec. 932 by striking "at the close of the taxable year" and inserting "during the entire taxable year" each place it appears. **Effective** for tax years ending after 10-22-2004.

• **1988, Technical and Miscellaneous Revenue Act of 1988 (P.L. 100-647)**

P.L. 100-647, § 1012(w)(2):

Amended Code Sec. 932(c)(4). **Effective** as if included in the provision of P.L. 99-514 to which it relates. Prior to amendment, Code Sec. 932(c)(4) read as follows:

(4) RESIDENTS OF THE VIRGIN ISLANDS.—In the case of an individual who is a bona fide resident of the Virgin Islands at the close of the taxable year and who, on his return of income tax to the Virgin Islands, reports income from all sources and identifies the source of each item shown on such return, for purposes of calculating income tax liability to the United States gross income shall not include any amount included in gross income on such return.

P.L. 100-647, § 1012(w)(3):

Amended Code Sec. 932(c)(2) by striking out "his income tax return" and inserting in lieu thereof "an income tax return". **Effective** as if included in the provision of P.L. 99-514 to which it relates.

[Sec. 932(d)]

(d) SPECIAL RULE FOR JOINT RETURNS.—In the case of a joint return, this section shall be applied on the basis of the residence of the spouse who has the greater adjusted gross income (determined without regard to community property laws) for the taxable year.

[Sec. 932(e)]

(e) SPECIAL RULE FOR APPLYING SECTION TO TAX IMPOSED IN VIRGIN ISLANDS.—In applying this section for purposes of determining income tax liability incurred to the Virgin Islands, the provisions of this section shall not be affected by the provisions of Federal law referred to in section 934(a).

• **1988, Technical and Miscellaneous Revenue Act of 1988 (P.L. 100-647)**

P.L. 100-647, § 1012(w)(1):

Amended Code Sec. 932(e). **Effective** as if included in the provision of P.L. 99-514 to which it relates. Prior to amendment, Code Sec. 932(e) read as follows:

(e) SECTION NOT TO APPLY TO TAX IMPOSED IN VIRGIN ISLANDS.—This section shall not apply for purposes of determining income tax liability incurred to the Virgin Islands.

• **1986, Tax Reform Act of 1986 (P.L. 99-514)**

P.L. 99-514, § 1274(a):

Amended subpart D of part III of subchapter N of chapter 1 by adding new Code Sec. 932. **Effective**, generally, for tax years beginning after 12-31-86. However, see Act Sec. 1277(b)-(e) under the amendment notes for Code Sec. 48 for special rules.

Internal Revenue Code — Sec. 932(e)

INCOME TAX—U.S. POSSESSIONS

[Sec. 932—Repealed]

Amendments

• **1986, Tax Reform Act of 1986 (P.L. 99-514)**

P.L. 99-514, § 1272(d)(1):

Repealed Code Sec. 932. **Effective**, generally, for tax years beginning after 12-31-86. However, see Act Sec. 1277(b)-(e) under the amendment notes for Code Sec. 48. Prior to repeal, Code Sec. 932 read as follows:

SEC. 932. CITIZENS OF POSSESSIONS OF THE UNITED STATES.

[Sec. 932(a)]

(a) GENERAL RULE.—Any individual who is a citizen of any possession of the United States (but not otherwise a citizen of the United States) and who is not a resident of the United States shall be subject to taxation under this subtitle in the same manner and subject to the same conditions as in the case of a nonresident alien individual. This section shall have no application in the case of a citizen of Puerto Rico or Guam.

Amendments

• **1972 (P.L. 92-606)**

P.L. 92-606, § 1(f)(2):

Added "or Guam" at the end of Code Sec. 932(a). **Effective** with respect to tax years beginning after 12-31-72.

• **1966, Foreign Investors Tax Act of 1966 (P.L. 89-809)**

P.L. 89-809, § 103(m):

Amended the first sentence of Code Sec. 932(a). **Effective** 1-1-67. Prior to amendment, the first sentence of such Sec. read as follows:

"(a) General Rule.—Any individual who is a citizen of any possession of the United States (but not otherwise a citizen of the United States) and who is not a resident of the United States shall be subject to taxation under this subtitle only as to income derived from sources within the United States, and in such case the tax shall be computed and paid in the same manner and subject to the same conditions as in the case of other persons who are taxable only as to income derived from such sources."

[Sec. 932(b)]

(b) VIRGIN ISLANDS.—Nothing in this section shall be construed to alter or amend the Act entitled "An Act making appropriations for the naval service for the fiscal year ending June 30, 1922, and for other purposes", approved July 12, 1921 (48 U. S. C. 1397), relating to the imposition of income taxes in the Virgin Islands of the United States.

[Sec. 932(c)]

(c) TAXATION OF SOCIAL SECURITY BENEFITS.—If, for purposes of an income tax imposed in the possession, any social security benefit (as defined in section 86(d)) received by an individual described in subsection (a) is treated in a manner equivalent to that provided by section 86, then—

(1) such benefit shall be exempt from the tax imposed by section 871, and

(2) no amount shall be deducted and withheld from such benefit under section 1441.

Any income tax imposed in a possession which treats social security benefits (as defined in section 86(d)) in a manner equivalent to section 86, and which first becomes effective within 15 months after the date of the enactment of this subsection, shall, for purposes of this section, be deemed to have been in effect as of January 1, 1984.

Amendments

• **1986, Consolidated Omnibus Budget Reconciliation Act of 1985 (P.L. 99-272)**

P.L. 99-272, § 12103(a):

Amended Code Sec. 932 by redesignating subsection (c) as subsection (d) and by inserting after subsection (b) new subsection (c). **Effective** for benefits received after 12-31-83, in tax years ending after such date.

[Sec. 932(d)]

(d) GUAM.—

For provisions relating to the individual income tax in the case of Guam, see sections 935 and 7654; see also sections 30 and 31 of the Act of August 1, 1950 (48 U. S. C., secs. 1421h and 1421i).

Amendments

• **1986, Consolidated Omnibus Budget Reconciliation Act of 1985 (P.L. 99-272)**

P.L. 99-272, § 12103(a):

Redesignated Code Sec. 932(c) as Code Sec. 932(d). **Effective** for benefits received after 12-31-83, in tax years ending after such date.

• **1972 (P.L. 92-606)**

P.L. 92-606, § 1(f)(3):

Amended Code Sec. 932(c). **Effective** for tax years beginning after 12-31-72. Prior to amendment, the section read as follows:

"For applicability of United States income tax laws in Guam, see section 31 of the Act of August 1, 1950 (48 U. S. C. 1421 i); for disposition of the proceeds of such taxes, see section 30 of such Act (48 U. S. C. 1421h)."

[Sec. 933]

SEC. 933. INCOME FROM SOURCES WITHIN PUERTO RICO.

The following items shall not be included in gross income and shall be exempt from taxation under this subtitle:

(1) RESIDENT OF PUERTO RICO FOR ENTIRE TAXABLE YEAR.—In the case of an individual who is a bona fide resident of Puerto Rico during the entire taxable year, income derived from sources within Puerto Rico (except amounts received for services performed as an employee of the United States or any agency thereof); but such individual shall not be allowed as a deduction from his gross income any deductions (other than the deduction under section 151, relating to personal exemptions), or any credit, properly allocable to or chargeable against amounts excluded from gross income under this paragraph.

(2) TAXABLE YEAR OF CHANGE OF RESIDENCE FROM PUERTO RICO.—In the case of an individual citizen of the United States who has been a bona fide resident of Puerto Rico for a period of at least 2 years before the date on which he changes his residence from Puerto Rico, income derived from sources therein (except amounts received for services performed as an employee of the United States or any agency thereof) which is attributable to that part of such period of Puerto Rican residence before such date; but such individual shall not be allowed as a deduction from his gross income any deductions (other than the deduction for personal exemptions under section 151), or any credit, properly allocable to or chargeable against amounts excluded from gross income under this paragraph.

Amendments

• **2021, American Rescue Plan Act of 2021 (P.L. 117-2)**

P.L. 117-2, § 9601(b) and (c)(2), provides:

SEC. 9601. 2021 RECOVERY REBATES TO INDIVIDUALS.

* * *

(b) TREATMENT OF CERTAIN POSSESSIONS.—

(1) PAYMENTS TO POSSESSIONS WITH MIRROR CODE TAX SYSTEMS.—The Secretary of the Treasury shall pay to each possession of the United States which has a mirror code tax system amounts equal to the loss (if any) to that possession by reason of the amendments made by this section. Such amounts shall be determined by the Secretary of the Treasury based on information provided by the government of the respective possession.

(2) PAYMENTS TO OTHER POSSESSIONS.—The Secretary of the Treasury shall pay to each possession of the United States which does not have a mirror code tax system amounts estimated by the Secretary of the Treasury as being equal to the aggregate benefits (if any) that would have been provided to residents of such possession by reason of the amendments made by this section if a mirror code tax system had been in effect in such possession. The preceding sentence shall not apply unless the respective possession has a plan, which has been approved by the Secretary of the Treasury, under which such possession will promptly distribute such payments to its residents.

(3) INCLUSION OF ADMINISTRATIVE EXPENSES.—The Secretary of the Treasury shall pay to each possession of the United States to which the Secretary makes a payment under paragraph (1) or (2) an amount equal to the lesser of—

(A) the increase (if any) of the administrative expenses of such possession—

(i) in the case of a possession described in paragraph (1), by reason of the amendments made by this section, and

(ii) in the case of a possession described in paragraph (2), by reason of carrying out the plan described in such paragraph, or

(B) $500,000 ($10,000,000 in the case of Puerto Rico).

The amount described in subparagraph (A) shall be determined by the Secretary of the Treasury based on information provided by the government of the respective possession.

(4) COORDINATION WITH CREDIT ALLOWED AGAINST UNITED STATES INCOME TAXES.—No credit shall be allowed against United States income taxes under section 6428B of the Internal Revenue Code of 1986 (as added by this section), nor shall any credit or refund be made or allowed under subsection (g) of such section, to any person—

(A) to whom a credit is allowed against taxes imposed by the possession by reason of the amendments made by this section, or

(B) who is eligible for a payment under a plan described in paragraph (2).

(5) MIRROR CODE TAX SYSTEM.—For purposes of this subsection, the term "mirror code tax system" means, with respect to any possession of the United States, the income tax system of such possession if the income tax liability of the residents of such possession under such system is determined by reference to the income tax laws of the United States as if such possession were the United States.

(6) TREATMENT OF PAYMENTS.—For purposes of section 1324 of title 31, United States Code, the payments under this subsection shall be treated in the same manner as a refund due from a credit provision referred to in subsection (b)(2) of such section.

(c) ADMINISTRATIVE PROVISIONS.—

* * *

(2) EXCEPTION FROM REDUCTION OR OFFSET.—Any refund payable by reason of section 6428B(g) of the Internal Revenue Code of 1986 (as added by this section), or any such refund payable by reason of subsection (b) of this section, shall not be—

(A) subject to reduction or offset pursuant to subsection (c), (d), (e), or (f) of section 6402 of the Internal Revenue Code of 1986 or any similar authority permitting offset, or

(B) reduced or offset by other assessed Federal taxes that would otherwise be subject to levy or collection.

* * *

P.L. 117-2, § 9626(d), provides:
SEC. 9626. TEMPORARY SPECIAL RULE FOR DETERMINING EARNED INCOME FOR PURPOSES OF EARNED INCOME TAX CREDIT.

* * *

(d) TREATMENT OF CERTAIN POSSESSIONS.—

(1) PAYMENTS TO POSSESSIONS WITH MIRROR CODE TAX SYSTEMS.—The Secretary of the Treasury shall pay to each possession of the United States which has a mirror code tax system amounts equal to the loss (if any) to that possession by reason of the application of the provisions of this section (other than this subsection) with respect to section 32 of the Internal Revenue Code of 1986. Such amounts shall be determined by the Secretary of the Treasury based on information provided by the government of the respective possession.

(2) PAYMENTS TO OTHER POSSESSIONS.—The Secretary of the Treasury shall pay to each possession of the United States which does not have a mirror code tax system amounts estimated by the Secretary of the Treasury as being equal to the aggregate benefits (if any) that would have been provided to residents of such possession by reason of the provisions of this section (other than this subsection) with respect to section 32 of the Internal Revenue Code of 1986 if a mirror code tax system had been in effect in such possession. The preceding sentence shall not apply unless the respective possession has a plan, which has been approved by the Secretary of the Treasury, under which such possession will promptly distribute such payments to its residents.

(3) MIRROR CODE TAX SYSTEM.—For purposes of this section, the term "mirror code tax system" means, with respect to any possession of the United States, the income tax system of such possession if the income tax liability of the residents of such possession under such system is determined by reference to the income tax laws of the United States as if such possession were the United States.

(4) TREATMENT OF PAYMENTS.—For purposes of section 1324 of title 31, United States Code, the payments under this section shall be treated in the same manner as a refund due from a credit provision referred to in subsection (b)(2) of such section.

P.L. 117-2, § 9642(g)-(h), provides:
SEC. 9642. CREDIT FOR SICK LEAVE FOR CERTAIN SELF-EMPLOYED INDIVIDUALS.

* * *

(g) APPLICATION OF CREDIT IN CERTAIN POSSESSIONS.—

(1) PAYMENTS TO POSSESSIONS WITH MIRROR CODE TAX SYSTEMS.—The Secretary shall pay to each possession of the United States which has a mirror code tax system amounts equal to the loss (if any) to that possession by reason of the application of the provisions of this section. Such amounts shall be determined by the Secretary based on information provided by the government of the respective possession.

(2) PAYMENTS TO OTHER POSSESSIONS.—The Secretary shall pay to each possession of the United States which does not have a mirror code tax system amounts estimated by the Secretary as being equal to the aggregate benefits (if any) that would have been provided to residents of such possession by reason of the provisions of this section if a mirror code tax system had been in effect in such possession. The preceding sentence shall not apply unless the respective possession has a plan, which has been approved by the Secretary, under which such possession will promptly distribute such payments to its residents.

(3) MIRROR CODE TAX SYSTEM.—For purposes of this section, the term "mirror code tax system" means, with respect to any possession of the United States, the income tax system of such possession if the income tax liability of the residents of such possession under such system is determined by reference to the income tax laws of the United States as if such possession were the United States.

(4) TREATMENT OF PAYMENTS.—For purposes of section 1324 of title 31, United States Code, the payments under this subsection shall be treated in the same manner as a refund due from a credit provision referred to in subsection (b)(2) of such section.

(h) REGULATIONS.—The Secretary shall prescribe such regulations or other guidance as may be necessary to carry out the purposes of this section, including—

(1) regulations or other guidance to effectuate the purposes of this section, and

(2) regulations or other guidance to minimize compliance and record-keeping burdens under this section.

P.L. 117-2, § 9643(g)-(h), provides:
SEC. 9643. CREDIT FOR FAMILY LEAVE FOR CERTAIN SELF-EMPLOYED INDIVIDUALS.

* * *

(g) APPLICATION OF CREDIT IN CERTAIN POSSESSIONS.—

(1) PAYMENTS TO POSSESSIONS WITH MIRROR CODE TAX SYSTEMS.—The Secretary shall pay to each possession of the United States which has a mirror code tax system amounts equal to the loss (if any) to that possession by reason of the application of the provisions of this section. Such amounts shall be determined by the Secretary based on information provided by the government of the respective possession.

(2) PAYMENTS TO OTHER POSSESSIONS.—The Secretary shall pay to each possession of the United States which does not have a mirror code tax system amounts estimated by the Secretary as being equal to the aggregate benefits (if any) that would have been provided to residents of such possession by reason of the provisions of this section if a mirror code tax system had been in effect in such possession. The preceding sentence shall not apply unless the respective possession has a plan, which has been approved by the Secretary, under which such possession will promptly distribute such payments to its residents.

(3) MIRROR CODE TAX SYSTEM.—For purposes of this section, the term "mirror code tax system" means, with respect to any possession of the United States, the income tax system of such possession if the income tax liability of the residents of such possession under such system is determined by reference to the income tax laws of the United States as if such possession were the United States.

(4) TREATMENT OF PAYMENTS.—For purposes of section 1324 of title 31, United States Code, the payments under this subsection shall be treated in the same manner as a refund due from a credit provision referred to in subsection (b)(2) of such section.

(h) REGULATIONS.—The Secretary shall prescribe such regulations or other guidance as may be necessary to carry out the purposes of this section, including—

(1) regulations or other guidance to prevent the avoidance of the purposes of this section, and

(2) regulations or other guidance to minimize compliance and record-keeping burdens under this section.

• 2020, COVID-related Tax Relief Act of 2020 (P.L. 116-260)
P.L. 116-260, § 272(c)-(d), Div. N, provides:
SEC. 272. ADDITIONAL 2020 RECOVERY REBATES FOR INDIVIDUALS.

* * *

(c) TREATMENT OF POSSESSIONS.—

(1) PAYMENTS TO POSSESSIONS.—

(A) MIRROR CODE POSSESSION.—The Secretary of the Treasury shall pay to each possession of the United States which has a mirror code tax system amounts equal to the loss (if any) to that possession by reason of the amendments made by this section. Such amounts shall be determined by the Secretary of the Treasury based on information provided by the government of the respective possession.

(B) OTHER POSSESSIONS.—The Secretary of the Treasury shall pay to each possession of the United States which does not have a mirror code tax system amounts estimated by the Secretary of the Treasury as being equal to the aggregate benefits (if any) that would have been provided to residents of such possession by reason of the amendments made by this section if a mirror code tax system had been in effect in such possession. The preceding sentence shall not apply unless the respective possession has a plan, which has been approved by the Secretary of the Treasury, under which such possession will promptly distribute such payments to its residents.

(2) COORDINATION WITH CREDIT ALLOWED AGAINST UNITED STATES INCOME TAXES.—No credit shall be allowed against United States income taxes under section 6428A of the Internal Revenue Code of 1986 (as added by this section) to any person—

(A) to whom a credit is allowed against taxes imposed by the possession by reason of the amendments made by this section; or

(B) who is eligible for a payment under a plan described in paragraph (1)(B).

(3) DEFINITIONS AND SPECIAL RULES.—

(A) POSSESSION OF THE UNITED STATES.—For purposes of this subsection, the term "possession of the United States" includes the Commonwealth of Puerto Rico and the Commonwealth of the Northern Mariana Islands.

(B) MIRROR CODE TAX SYSTEM.—For purposes of this subsection, the term "mirror code tax system" means, with respect to any possession of the United States, the income tax system of such possession if the income tax liability of the residents of such possession under such system is determined by reference to the income tax laws of the United States as if such possession were the United States.

(C) TREATMENT OF PAYMENTS.—For purposes of section 1324 of title 31, United States Code, the payments under this subsection shall be treated in the same manner as a refund due from a credit provision referred to in subsection (b)(2) of such section.

(d) ADMINISTRATIVE PROVISIONS.—

(1) EXCEPTION FROM REDUCTION OR OFFSET.—Any refund payable by reason of section 6428A(f) of the Internal Revenue Code of 1986 (as added by this section), or any such refund payable by reason of subsection (c) of this section, shall not be—

(A) subject to reduction or offset pursuant to section 3716 or 3720A of title 31, United States Code,

(B) subject to reduction or offset pursuant to subsection (c), (d), (e), or (f) of section 6402 of the Internal Revenue Code of 1986, or

(C) reduced or offset by other assessed Federal taxes that would otherwise be subject to levy or collection.

(2) ASSIGNMENT OF BENEFITS.—

(A) IN GENERAL.—The right of any person to any applicable payment shall not be transferable or assignable, at law or in equity, and no applicable payment shall be subject to, execution, levy, attachment, garnishment, or other legal process, or the operation of any bankruptcy or insolvency law.

* * *

(D) NO RECLAMATION RIGHTS.—This paragraph shall not alter the status of applicable payments as tax refunds or other nonbenefit payments for purpose of any reclamation rights of the Department of the Treasury or the Internal Revenue Service as per part 210 of title 31, Code of Federal Regulations.

(E) DEFINITIONS.—For purposes of this paragraph—

(i) ACCOUNT HOLDER.—The term "account holder" means a natural person whose name appears in a financial institution's records as the direct or beneficial owner of an account.

(ii) ACCOUNT REVIEW.—The term "account review" means the process of examining deposits in an account to determine if an applicable payment has been deposited into the account during the lookback period. The financial institution shall perform the account review following the procedures outlined in section 212.5 of title 31, Code of Federal Regulations and in accordance with the requirements of section 212.6 of title 31, Code of Federal Regulations.

(iii) APPLICABLE PAYMENT.—The term "applicable payment" means—

(I) any advance refund amount paid pursuant to section 6428A(f) of Internal Revenue Code of 1986 (as added by this section),

(II) any payment made by a possession of the United States with a mirror code tax system (as defined in subsection (c) of this section) pursuant to such subsection which corresponds to a payment described in subclause (I), and

(III) any payment made by a possession of the United States without a mirror code tax system (as so defined) pursuant to subsection (c) of this section.

INCOME TAX—U.S. POSSESSIONS

(iv) GARNISHMENT.—The term "garnishment" means execution, levy, attachment, garnishment, or other legal process.

(v) GARNISHMENT ORDER.—The term "garnishment order" means a writ, order, notice, summons, judgment, levy, or similar written instruction issued by a court, a State or State agency, a municipality or municipal corporation, or a State child support enforcement agency, including a lien arising by operation of law for overdue child support or an order to freeze the assets in an account, to effect a garnishment against a debtor.

(vi) LOOKBACK PERIOD.—The term "lookback period" means the two month period that begins on the date preceding the date of account review and ends on the corresponding date of the month two months earlier, or on the last date of the month two months earlier if the corresponding date does not exist.

(3) AGENCY INFORMATION SHARING AND ASSISTANCE.—

(A) IN GENERAL.—The Commissioner of Social Security, the Railroad Retirement Board, and the Secretary of Veterans Affairs shall each provide the Secretary of the Treasury (or the Secretary's delegate) such information and assistance as the Secretary of the Treasury (or the Secretary's delegate) may require for purposes of—

(i) making payments under section 6428A(f) of the Internal Revenue Code of 1986 to individuals described in paragraph (5)(A) thereof, or

(ii) providing administrative assistance to a possession of the United States (as defined in subsection (c)(3)(A)) to allow such possession to promptly distribute payments under subsection (c) to its residents.

(B) EXCHANGE OF INFORMATION WITH POSSESSIONS.—Any information provided to the Secretary of the Treasury (or the Secretary's delegate) pursuant to subparagraph (A)(ii) may be exchanged with a possession of the United States in accordance with the applicable tax coordination agreement for information exchange and administrative assistance that the Internal Revenue Service has agreed to with such possession.

* * *

• 2020, Taxpayer Certainty and Disaster Tax Relief Act of 2020 (P.L. 116-260)

P.L. 116-260, §306(a)-(c), Div. EE, provides:

SEC. 306. TREATMENT OF CERTAIN POSSESSIONS.

(a) PAYMENTS TO POSSESSIONS WITH MIRROR CODE TAX SYSTEMS.—The Secretary of the Treasury shall pay to each possession of the United States which has a mirror code tax system amounts equal to the loss (if any) to that possession by reason of the application of the provisions of this title. Such amounts shall be determined by the Secretary of the Treasury based on information provided by the government of the respective possession.

(b) PAYMENTS TO OTHER POSSESSIONS.—The Secretary of the Treasury shall pay to each possession of the United States which does not have a mirror code tax system amounts estimated by the Secretary of the Treasury as being equal to the aggregate benefits (if any) that would have been provided to residents of such possession by reason of the provisions of this title if a mirror code tax system had been in effect in such possession. The preceding sentence shall not apply unless the respective possession has a plan, which has been approved by the Secretary of the Treasury, under which such possession will promptly distribute such payments to its residents.

(c) MIRROR CODE TAX SYSTEM.—For purposes of this section, the term "mirror code tax system" means, with respect to any possession of the United States, the income tax system of such possession if the income tax liability of the residents of such possession under such system is determined by reference to the income tax laws of the United States as if such possession were the United States.

* * *

• 2020, Coronavirus Aid, Relief, and Economic Security (CARES) Act (P.L. 116-136)

P.L. 116-136, §2201(c)-(d) (as amended by P.L. 116-260, §273(b)(1), Div. N), provides:

SEC. 2201. 2020 RECOVERY REBATES FOR INDIVIDUALS.

* * *

(c) TREATMENT OF POSSESSIONS.—

(1) PAYMENTS TO POSSESSIONS.—

(A) MIRROR CODE POSSESSION.—The Secretary of the Treasury shall pay to each possession of the United States which has a mirror code tax system amounts equal to the loss (if any) to that possession by reason of the amendments made by this section. Such amounts shall be determined by the Secretary of the Treasury based on information provided by the government of the respective possession.

(B) OTHER POSSESSIONS.—The Secretary of the Treasury shall pay to each possession of the United States which does not have a mirror code tax system amounts estimated by the Secretary of the Treasury as being equal to the aggregate benefits (if any) that would have been provided to residents of such possession by reason of the amendments made by this section if a mirror code tax system had been in effect in such possession. The preceding sentence shall not apply unless the respective possession has a plan, which has been approved by the Secretary of the Treasury, under which such possession will promptly distribute such payments to its residents.

(2) COORDINATION WITH CREDIT ALLOWED AGAINST UNITED STATES INCOME TAXES.—No credit shall be allowed against United States income taxes under section 6428 of the Internal Revenue Code of 1986 (as added by this section) to any person—

(A) to whom a credit is allowed against taxes imposed by the possession by reason of the amendments made by this section, or

(B) who is eligible for a payment under a plan described in paragraph (1)(B).

(3) DEFINITIONS AND SPECIAL RULES.—

(A) POSSESSION OF THE UNITED STATES.— For purposes of this subsection, the term "possession of the United States" includes the Commonwealth of Puerto Rico and the Commonwealth of the Northern Mariana Islands.

(B) MIRROR CODE TAX SYSTEM.—For purposes of this subsection, the term "mirror code tax system" means, with respect to any possession of the United States, the income tax system of such possession if the income tax liability of the residents of such possession under such system is determined by reference to the income tax laws of the United States as if such possession were the United States.

(C) TREATMENT OF PAYMENTS.—For purposes of section 1324 of title 31, United States Code, the payments under this subsection shall be treated in the same manner as a refund due from a credit provision referred to in subsection (b)(2) of such section.

(d) EXCEPTION FROM REDUCTION OR OFFSET.—Any refund payable by reason of section 6428(f) of the Internal Revenue Code of 1986 (as added by this section), or any such refund payable by reason of subsection (c) of this section, shall not be—

(1) subject to reduction or offset pursuant to section 3716 or 3720A of title 31, United States Code,

(2) subject to reduction or offset pursuant to subsection (d), (e), or (f) of section 6402 of the Internal Revenue Code of 1986, or

(3) reduced or offset by other assessed Federal taxes that would otherwise be subject to levy or collection.

* * *

• 2020, Families First Coronavirus Response Act (P.L. 116-127)

P.L. 116-127, §7002(f), provides:

SEC. 7002. CREDIT FOR SICK LEAVE FOR CERTAIN SELF-EMPLOYED INDIVIDUALS.

* * *

(f) APPLICATION OF CREDIT IN CERTAIN POSSESSIONS.—

(1) PAYMENTS TO POSSESSIONS WITH MIRROR CODE TAX SYSTEMS.—The Secretary of the Treasury (or the Secretary's delegate) shall pay to each possession of the United States which has a mirror code tax system amounts equal to the loss (if any) to that possession by reason of the application of the provisions of this section. Such amounts shall be determined by the Secretary of the Treasury (or the Secretary's delegate) based on information provided by the government of the respective possession.

(2) PAYMENTS TO OTHER POSSESSIONS.—The Secretary of the Treasury (or the Secretary's delegate) shall pay to each possession of the United States which does not have a mirror code tax system amounts estimated by the Secretary of the Treasury (or the Secretary's delegate) as being equal to the aggregate benefits (if any) that would have been provided to residents of such possession by reason of the provisions of this section if a mirror code tax system had been in effect in such possession. The preceding sentence shall not apply unless the respective possession has a plan, which has been approved by the Secretary of the Treasury (or the Secretary's delegate), under which such possession will promptly distribute such payments to its residents.

(3) MIRROR CODE TAX SYSTEM.—For purposes of this section, the term "mirror code tax system" means, with respect to any possession of the United States, the income tax system of such possession if the income tax liability of the residents of such possession under such system is determined by reference to the income tax laws of the United States as if such possession were the United States.

(4) TREATMENT OF PAYMENTS.—For purposes of section 1324 of title 31, United States Code, the payments under this section shall be treated in the same manner as a refund due from a credit provision referred to in subsection (b)(2) of such section.

* * *

P.L. 116-127, §7004(f), provides:

SEC. 7004. CREDIT FOR FAMILY LEAVE FOR CERTAIN SELF-EMPLOYED INDIVIDUALS.

* * *

(f) APPLICATION OF CREDIT IN CERTAIN POSSESSIONS.—

(1) PAYMENTS TO POSSESSIONS WITH MIRROR CODE TAX SYSTEMS.—The Secretary of the Treasury (or the Secretary's delegate) shall pay to each possession of the United States which has a mirror code tax system amounts equal to the loss (if any) to that possession by reason of the application of the provisions of this section. Such amounts shall be determined by the Secretary of the Treasury (or the Secretary's delegate) based on information provided by the government of the respective possession.

(2) PAYMENTS TO OTHER POSSESSIONS.—The Secretary of the Treasury (or the Secretary's delegate) shall pay to each possession of the United States which does not have a mirror code tax system amounts estimated by the Secretary of the Treasury (or the Secretary's delegate) as being equal to the aggregate benefits (if any) that would have been provided to residents of such possession by reason of the provisions of this section if a mirror code tax system had been in effect in such possession. The preceding sentence shall not apply unless the respective possession has a plan, which has been approved by the Secretary of the Treasury (or the Secretary's delegate), under which such possession will promptly distribute such payments to its residents.

(3) MIRROR CODE TAX SYSTEM.—For purposes of this section, the term "mirror code tax system" means, with respect to any possession of the United States, the income tax system of such possession if the income tax liability of the residents of such possession under such system is determined by reference to the income tax laws of the United States as if such possession were the United States.

(4) TREATMENT OF PAYMENTS.—For purposes of section 1324 of title 31, United States Code, the payments under this section shall be treated in the same manner as a refund due from a credit provision referred to in subsection (b)(2) of such section.

* * *

• 2019, Taxpayer Certainty and Disaster Tax Relief Act of 2019 (P.L. 116-94)

P.L. 116-94, §208, Div. Q, provides:

SEC. 208. TREATMENT OF CERTAIN POSSESSIONS.

(a) PAYMENTS TO POSSESSIONS WITH MIRROR CODE TAX SYSTEMS.—The Secretary of the Treasury shall pay to each possession of the United States which has a mirror code tax system amounts equal to the loss (if any) to that possession by reason of the application of the provisions of this title. Such amounts shall be determined by the Secretary of the Treasury based on information provided by the government of the respective possession.

INCOME TAX—U.S. POSSESSIONS

(b) PAYMENTS TO OTHER POSSESSIONS.—The Secretary of the Treasury shall pay to each possession of the United States which does not have a mirror code tax system amounts estimated by the Secretary of the Treasury as being equal to the aggregate benefits (if any) that would have been provided to residents of such possession by reason of the provisions of this title if a mirror code tax system had been in effect in such possession. The preceding sentence shall not apply unless the respective possession has a plan, which has been approved by the Secretary of the Treasury, under which such possession will promptly distribute such payments to its residents.

(c) MIRROR CODE TAX SYSTEM.—For purposes of this section, the term "mirror code tax system" means, with respect to any possession of the United States, the income tax system of such possession if the income tax liability of the residents of such possession under such system is determined by reference to the income tax laws of the United States as if such possession were the United States.

(d) TREATMENT OF PAYMENTS.—For purposes of section 1324 of title 31, United States Code, the payments under this section shall be treated in the same manner as a refund due from a credit provision referred to in subsection (b)(2) of such section.

• 1986, Tax Reform Act of 1986 (P.L. 99-514)

P.L. 99-514, §1272(d)(3):

Amended Code Sec. 933(1) and (2) by inserting ", or any credit," before "properly". **Effective**, generally, for tax years beginning after 12-31-86. However, see Act Sec. 1277(b)-(e) under the amendment notes for Code Sec. 48 for special rules.

[Sec. 934]

SEC. 934. LIMITATION ON REDUCTION IN INCOME TAX LIABILITY INCURRED TO THE VIRGIN ISLANDS.

[Sec. 934(a)]

(a) GENERAL RULE.—Tax liability incurred to the Virgin Islands pursuant to this subtitle, as made applicable in the Virgin Islands by the Act entitled "An Act making appropriations for the naval service for the fiscal year ending June 30, 1922, and for other purposes", approved July 12, 1921 (48 U. S. C. 1397), or pursuant to section 28(a) of the Revised Organic Act of the Virgin Islands, approved July 22, 1954 (48 U. S. C. 1642), shall not be reduced or remitted in any way, directly or indirectly, whether by grant, subsidy, or other similar payment, by any law enacted in the Virgin Islands, except to the extent provided in subsection (b).

Amendments

• 1986, Tax Reform Act of 1986 (P.L. 99-514)

P.L. 99-514, §1275(c)(2)(A):

Amended Code Sec. 934(a) by striking out "or (c) or in section 934A" after "subsection (b)". **Effective**, generally, for tax years beginning after 12-31-86. However, see Act Sec. 1277(b)-(e) under the amendment notes for Code Sec. 48 for special rules.

• 1983 (P.L. 97-455)

P.L. 97-455, §1(c):

Amended Code Sec. 934(a) by inserting before the period at the end thereof "or in section 934A". **Effective** for amounts received after 1-12-83, in tax years ending after such date.

• 1960 (P.L. 86-779)

P.L. 86-779, §4(a):

Added Code Sec. 934(a). **Effective** for tax years beginning on or after 1-1-60.

[Sec. 934(b)]

(b) REDUCTIONS PERMITTED WITH RESPECT TO CERTAIN INCOME.—

(1) IN GENERAL.—Except as provided in paragraph (2), subsection (a) shall not apply with respect to so much of the tax liability referred to in subsection (a) as is attributable to income derived from sources within the Virgin Islands or income effectively connected with the conduct of a trade or business within the Virgin Islands.

(2) EXCEPTION FOR LIABILITY PAID BY CITIZENS OR RESIDENTS OF THE UNITED STATES.—Paragraph (1) shall not apply to any liability payable to the Virgin Islands under section 932(b).

(3) SPECIAL RULE FOR NON-UNITED STATES INCOME OF CERTAIN FOREIGN CORPORATIONS.—

(A) IN GENERAL.—In the case of a qualified foreign corporation, subsection (a) shall not apply with respect to so much of the tax liability referred to in subsection (a) as is attributable to income which is derived from sources outside the United States and which is not effectively connected with the conduct of a trade or business within the United States.

(B) QUALIFIED FOREIGN CORPORATION.—For purposes of subparagraph (A), the term "qualified foreign corporation" means any foreign corporation if less than 10 percent of—

(i) the total voting power of the stock of such corporation, and

(ii) the total value of the stock of such corporation,

is owned or treated as owned (within the meaning of section 958) by 1 or more United States persons.

(4) DETERMINATION OF INCOME SOURCE, ETC.—The determination as to whether income is derived from sources within the United States or is effectively connected with the conduct of a trade or business within the United States shall be made under regulations prescribed by the Secretary.

Amendments

• 2004, American Jobs Creation Act of 2004 (P.L. 108-357)

P.L. 108-357, §908(c)(3):

Amended Code Sec. 934(b)(4) by striking "the Virgin Islands or" each place it appears after "within". **Effective** for tax years ending after 10-22-2004.

• 1986, Tax Reform Act of 1986 (P.L. 99-514)

P.L. 99-514, §1275(c)(1):

Amended Code Sec. 934 by striking out subsection (b). **Effective**, generally, for tax years beginning after 12-31-86. However, see Act Sec. 1277(b)-(e) under the amendment notes for Code Sec. 48 for special rules. Prior to amendment, Code Sec. 934(b) read as follows:

(b) EXCEPTION FOR CERTAIN DOMESTIC AND VIRGIN ISLANDS CORPORATIONS.—In the case of a domestic corporation or a Virgin Islands corporation, subsection (a) shall not apply (if the information required by subsection (d) is supplied) to the extent such corporation derived its income from sources without the United States if the conditions of both paragraph (1) and paragraph (2) are satisfied:

(1) THREE-YEAR PERIOD.—If 80 percent or more of the gross income of such corporation for the 3-year period immediately preceding the close of the taxable year (or for such part of such period immediately preceding the close of such taxable year as may be applicable) was derived from sources within the Virgin Islands; and

(2) TRADE OR BUSINESS.—If 65 percent or more of the gross income of such corporation for such period or such part thereof was derived from the active conduct of a trade or business within the Virgin Islands.

For purposes of the preceding sentence, the gross income of a Virgin Islands corporation, and the sources from which the income of such corporation is derived, shall be determined as if such corporation were a domestic corporation.

P.L. 99-514, §1275(c)(2)(B):

Amended Code Sec. 934 by inserting subsection (b) following subsection (a). **Effective**, generally, for tax years beginning after 12-31-86. However, see Act Sec. 1277(b)-(e) under the amendment notes for Code Sec. 48 for special rules.

• 1982, Tax Equity and Fiscal Responsibility Act of 1982 (P.L. 97-248)

P.L. 97-248, §213(b):

Amended Code Sec. 934(b)(2) by striking out "50 percent" and inserting in lieu thereof "65 percent". **Effective** for tax years beginning after 12-31-82.

• 1976, Tax Reform Act of 1976 (P.L. 94-455)

P.L. 94-455, §1901(a)(118):

Struck out the last sentence of Code Sec. 934(b). **Effective** for tax years beginning after 12-31-76. Prior to striking, the last sentence of Code Sec. 934(b) read as follows:

For the purposes of this subsection, all amounts received by such corporation within the United States, whether derived from sources within or without the United States, shall be considered as being derived from sources within the United States.

• 1960 (P.L. 86-779)

P.L. 86-779, §4(a):

Added Code Sec. 934(b). **Effective** for tax years beginning on or after 1-1-60.

INCOME TAX—U.S. POSSESSIONS

[Sec. 934(c)—Stricken]

Amendments

• **1986, Tax Reform Act of 1986 (P.L. 99-514)**

P.L. 99-514, § 1275(c)(1):

Amended Code Sec. 934 by striking out subsection (c). **Effective**, generally, for tax years beginning after 12-31-86. However, see Act Sec. 1277(b)-(e) under the amendment notes for Code Sec. 48 for special rules. Prior to amendment, Code Sec. 934(c) read as follows:

(c) EXCEPTION FOR CERTAIN RESIDENTS OF THE VIRGIN ISLANDS.—Subsection (a) shall not apply in the case of an individual citizen of the United States who is a bona fide resident of the Virgin Islands during the entire taxable year (if the information required by subsection (d) is supplied), to the extent his income is derived from sources within the Virgin Islands (except that subsection (a) shall apply in the case of amounts received for services performed as an employee of the United States or any agency thereof). For purposes of the preceding sentence, gain or loss from the sale or exchange of any security (as defined in section 165(g)(2)) shall not be treated as derived from sources within the Virgin Islands.

• **1960 (P.L. 86-779)**

P.L. 86-779, § 4(a):

Added Code Sec. 934(c). **Effective** for tax years beginning on or after 1-1-60.

[Sec. 934(d)—Stricken]

Amendments

• **1986, Tax Reform Act of 1986 (P.L. 99-514)**

P.L. 99-514, § 1275(c)(1):

Amended Code Sec. 934 by striking out subsection (d). **Effective**, generally, for tax years beginning after 12-31-86. However, see Act Sec. 1277(b)-(e) under the amendment notes for Code Sec. 48 for special rules. Prior to amendment, Code Sec. 934(d) read as follows:

(d) REQUIREMENT TO SUPPLY INFORMATION.—Subsections (b) and (c) shall apply only in the case of persons who supply (at such time and in such manner as the Secretary may by regulations prescribe) such information as the Secretary may by regulations prescribe for purposes of determining the applicability of such subsections.

• **1976, Tax Reform Act of 1976 (P.L. 94-455)**

P.L. 94-455, § 1906(b)(13)(A):

Amended 1954 Code by substituting "Secretary" for "Secretary or his delegate" each place it appeared. **Effective** 2-1-77.

• **1960 (P.L. 86-779)**

P.L. 86-779, § 4(a):

Added Code Sec. 934(d). **Effective** for tax years beginning on or after 1-1-60.

[Sec. 934(e)—Stricken]

Amendments

• **1986, Tax Reform Act of 1986 (P.L. 99-514)**

P.L. 99-514, § 1275(a)(2)(A):

Amended Code Sec. 934 by striking out subsection (e). **Effective**, generally, for tax years beginning after 12-31-86. However, see Act Sec. 1277(b)-(e) under the amendment notes for Code Sec. 48 for special rules. Prior to amendment, Code Sec. 934(e) read as follows:

(e) TAX TREATMENT OF INTANGIBLE PROPERTY INCOME OF CERTAIN DOMESTIC CORPORATIONS.—

(1) IN GENERAL.—

(A) INCOME ATTRIBUTABLE TO SHAREHOLDER.—The intangible property income (within the meaning of section 936(h)(3)) for any taxable year of any domestic corporation which is described in subsection (b) and which is an inhabitant of the Virgin Islands (within the meaning of section 28(a) of the Revised Organic Act of the Virgin Islands (48 U.S.C. 1642)), shall be included on a pro rata basis in the gross income of all shareholders of such corporation at the close of the taxable year of such corporation as income from sources within the United States for the taxable year of such shareholder in which or with which the taxable year of such corporation ends.

(B) EXCLUSION FROM THE INCOME OF THE CORPORATION.—Any intangible property income of a corporation described in subparagraph (A) which is included in the gross income of a shareholder of such corporation by reason of subparagraph (A) shall be excluded from the gross income of such corporation.

(2) FOREIGN SHAREHOLDERS; SHAREHOLDERS NOT SUBJECT TO TAX; INHABITANTS OF THE VIRGIN ISLANDS.—

(A) IN GENERAL.—Paragraph (1)(A) shall not apply with respect to any shareholder—

(i) who is not a United States person,

(ii) who is not subject to tax under this title on intangible property income which would be allocated to such shareholder (but for this subparagraph), or

(iii) who is an inhabitant of the Virgin Islands.

(B) TREATMENT OF NONALLOCATED INTANGIBLE PROPERTY INCOME.—For purposes of this subtitle, intangible property income of a corporation described in paragraph (1)(A) which is not included in the gross income of a shareholder of such corporation by reason of subparagraph (A)—

(i) shall be treated as income from sources within the United States, and

(ii) shall not be taken into account for purposes of determining whether the conditions specified in paragraph (1) or (2) of subsection (b) are satisfied.

(3) DISTRIBUTION TO MEET QUALIFICATION REQUIREMENTS.—

(A) IN GENERAL.—If the Secretary determines that a corporation does not satisfy a condition specified in paragraph (1) or (2) of subsection (b) for any taxable year by reason of the exclusion from gross income under paragraph (1)(B), such corporation shall nevertheless be treated as satisfying such condition for such year if it makes a pro rata distribution of property after the close of such taxable year to its shareholders (designated at the time of such distribution as a distribution to meet qualification requirements) with respect to their stock in an amount which is equal to—

(i) if the condition of subsection (b)(1) is not satisfied, that portion of the gross income for the period described in subsection (b)(1)—

(I) which was not derived from sources within the Virgin Islands, and

(II) which exceeds the amount of such income for such period which would enable such corporation to satisfy the condition of subsection (b)(1),

(ii) if the condition of subsection (b)(2) is not satisfied, that portion of the aggregate gross income for such period—

(I) which was not derived from the active conduct of a trade or business within the Virgin Islands, and

(II) which exceeds the amount of such income for such period which would enable such corporation to satisfy the conditions of subsection (b)(2), or

(iii) if neither of such conditions is satisfied, that portion of the gross income which exceeds the amount of gross income for such period which would enable such corporation to satisfy the conditions of paragraphs (1) and (2) of subsection (b).

(B) EFFECTIVELY CONNECTED INCOME.—In the case of a shareholder who is a nonresident alien individual, an inhabitant of the Virgin Islands, or a foreign corporation, trust, or estate, any distribution described in subparagraph (A) shall be treated as income which is effectively connected with the conduct of a trade or business conducted through a permanent establishment of such shareholder within the United States.

(C) DISTRIBUTION DENIED IN CASE OF FRAUD OR WILLFUL NEGLECT.—Subparagraph (A) shall not apply to a corporation if the determination of the Secretary described in subparagraph (A) contains a finding that the failure of such corporation to satisfy the conditions in subsection (b) was due in whole or in part to fraud with intent to evade tax or willful neglect on the part of such corporation.

(4) CERTAIN PROVISIONS OF SECTION 936 TO APPLY.—

(A) IN GENERAL.—The rules contained in paragraphs (5), (6), and (7) of section 936(h) shall apply to a domestic corporation described in paragraph (1)(A) of this subsection.

(B) CERTAIN MODIFICATIONS.—For purposes of subparagraph (A), section 936(h) shall be applied by substituting wherever appropriate—

(i) "Virgin Islands" for "possession", and

(ii) qualification under paragraphs (1) and (2) of subsection (b) for qualification under section 936(a)(2).

• **1982, Tax Equity and Fiscal Responsibility Act of 1982 (P.L. 97-248)**

P.L. 97-248, § 213(b):

Added subsection (e). **Effective** for tax years beginning after 12-31-82.

[Sec. 934(f)—Stricken]

Amendments

• **1986, Tax Reform Act of 1986 (P.L. 99-514)**

P.L. 99-514, § 1275(a)(2)(A):

Amended Code Sec. 934 by striking out subsection (f). **Effective**, generally, for tax years beginning after 12-31-86. However, see Act Sec. 1277(b)-(e) under the amendment notes for Code Sec. 48 for special rules. Prior to amendment, Code Sec. 934(f) read as follows:

(f) TRANSITIONAL RULE.—In applying subsection (b)(2) with respect to taxable years beginning after December 31, 1982, and before January 1, 1985, the following percentage shall be substituted for "65 percent":

For taxable years beginning in calendar year:	The percentage is:
1983	55
1984	60

• **1982, Tax Equity and Fiscal Responsibility Act of 1982 (P.L. 97-248)**

P.L. 97-248, § 213(b):

Added subsection (f). **Effective** for tax years beginning after 12-31-82.

INCOME TAX—U.S. POSSESSIONS

[Sec. 934(f)[(g)]—Stricken]

Amendments

• **1986, Tax Reform Act of 1986 (P.L. 99-514)**

P.L. 99-514, § 1876(f)(2):

Amended Code Sec. 934 by striking out subsection (f)[g]. **Effective** as if included in the provision of P.L. 98-369 to which it relates. Prior to amendment, Code Sec. 934(f)[g] read as follows:

(f)[g] FSC.—Subsection (a) shall not apply in the case of a Virgin Islands corporation which is a FSC.

• **1984, Deficit Reduction Act of 1984 (P.L. 98-369)**

P.L. 98-369, § 801(d)(7):

Amended Code Sec. 934 by adding new subsection (f)[g]. **Effective** for transactions after 12-31-84, in tax years ending after such date.

[Sec. 934A—Repealed]

Amendments

• **1986, Tax Reform Act of 1986 (P.L. 99-514)**

P.L. 99-514, § 1275(c)(3):

Repealed Code Sec. 934A. **Effective**, generally, for tax years beginning after 12-31-86. However, see Act Sec. 1277(b)-(e) under the amendment notes for Code Sec. 48 for special rules. Prior to repeal, Code Sec. 934A read as follows:

SEC. 934A. INCOME TAX RATE ON VIRGIN ISLANDS SOURCE INCOME.

(a) GENERAL RULE.—For purposes of determining the tax liability incurred by citizens and resident alien individuals of the United States, and corporations organized in the United States, to the Virgin Islands pursuant to this title with respect to amounts received from sources within the Virgin Islands—

(1) the taxes imposed by sections 871(a)(1) and 881 (as made applicable to the Virgin Islands) shall apply except that "10 percent" shall be substituted for "30 percent", and

(2) subsection (a) of section 934 shall not apply to such taxes.

(b) SUBSECTION (a) RATES NOT TO APPLY TO PRE-EFFECTIVE DATE EARNINGS.—

(1) IN GENERAL.—Any change under subsection (a)(1), and any reduction under section 934 pursuant to subsection (a)(2), in a rate of tax imposed by section 871(a)(1) or 881 shall not apply to dividends paid out of earnings and profits accumulated for taxable years beginning before the effective date of the change or reduction.

(2) ORDERING RULE.—For purposes of paragraph (1), dividends shall be treated as first being paid out of earnings and profits accumulated for taxable years beginning before the effective date of the change or reduction (to the extent thereof).

• **1983 (P.L. 97-455)**

P.L. 97-455, § 1(a):

Added Code Sec. 934A. **Effective** for amounts received after 1-12-83, in tax years ending after such date.

⟫→ *Caution: Code Sec. 935, below, was repealed by P.L. 99-514 but remains effective until an implementing agreement between the U.S. and Guam is entered into.*

[Sec. 935]

SEC. 935. COORDINATION OF UNITED STATES AND GUAM INDIVIDUAL INCOME TAXES.

[Sec. 935(a)]

(a) APPLICATION OF SECTION.—This section shall apply to any individual who, during the entire taxable year—

(1) is a bona fide resident of Guam,

(2) is a citizen of Guam but not otherwise a citizen of the United States,

(3) has income derived from Guam for the taxable year and is a citizen or resident of the United States, or

(4) files a joint return for the taxable year with an individual who satisfies paragraph (1), (2), or (3) for the taxable year.

Amendments

• **2021, American Rescue Plan Act of 2021 (P.L. 117-2)**

P.L. 117-2, § 9601(b) and (c)(2), provides:

SEC. 9601. 2021 RECOVERY REBATES TO INDIVIDUALS.

* * *

(b) TREATMENT OF CERTAIN POSSESSIONS.—

(1) PAYMENTS TO POSSESSIONS WITH MIRROR CODE TAX SYSTEMS.—The Secretary of the Treasury shall pay to each possession of the United States which has a mirror code tax system amounts equal to the loss (if any) to that possession by reason of the amendments made by this section. Such amounts shall be determined by the Secretary of the Treasury based on information provided by the government of the respective possession.

(2) PAYMENTS TO OTHER POSSESSIONS.—The Secretary of the Treasury shall pay to each possession of the United States which does not have a mirror code tax system amounts estimated by the Secretary of the Treasury as being equal to the aggregate benefits (if any) that would have been provided to residents of such possession by reason of the amendments made by this section if a mirror code tax system had been in effect in such possession. The preceding sentence shall not apply unless the respective possession has a plan, which has been approved by the Secretary of the Treasury, under which such possession will promptly distribute such payments to its residents.

(3) INCLUSION OF ADMINISTRATIVE EXPENSES.—The Secretary of the Treasury shall pay to each possession of the United States to which the Secretary makes a payment under paragraph (1) or (2) an amount equal to the lesser of—

(A) the increase (if any) of the administrative expenses of such possession—

(i) in the case of a possession described in paragraph (1), by reason of the amendments made by this section, and

(ii) in the case of a possession described in paragraph (2), by reason of carrying out the plan described in such paragraph, or

(B) $500,000 ($10,000,000 in the case of Puerto Rico).

The amount described in subparagraph (A) shall be determined by the Secretary of the Treasury based on information provided by the government of the respective possession.

(4) COORDINATION WITH CREDIT ALLOWED AGAINST UNITED STATES INCOME TAXES.—No credit shall be allowed against United States income taxes under section 6428B of the Internal Revenue Code of 1986 (as added by this section), nor shall any credit or refund be made or allowed under subsection (g) of such section, to any person—

(A) to whom a credit is allowed against taxes imposed by the possession by reason of the amendments made by this section, or

(B) who is eligible for a payment under a plan described in paragraph (2).

(5) MIRROR CODE TAX SYSTEM.—For purposes of this subsection, the term "mirror code tax system" means, with respect to any possession of the United States, the income tax system of such possession if the income tax liability of the residents of such possession under such system is determined by reference to the income tax laws of the United States as if such possession were the United States.

(6) TREATMENT OF PAYMENTS.—For purposes of section 1324 of title 31, United States Code, the payments under this subsection shall be treated in the same manner as a refund due from a credit provision referred to in subsection (b)(2) of such section.

(c) ADMINISTRATIVE PROVISIONS.—

* * *

(2) EXCEPTION FROM REDUCTION OR OFFSET.—Any refund payable by reason of section 6428B(g) of the Internal Revenue Code of 1986 (as added by this section), or any such refund payable by reason of subsection (b) of this section, shall not be—

(A) subject to reduction or offset pursuant to subsection (c), (d), (e), or (f) of section 6402 of the Internal Revenue Code of 1986 or any similar authority permitting offset, or

(B) reduced or offset by other assessed Federal taxes that would otherwise be subject to levy or collection.

* * *

P.L. 117-2, § 9626(d), provides:

SEC. 9626. TEMPORARY SPECIAL RULE FOR DETERMINING EARNED INCOME FOR PURPOSES OF EARNED INCOME TAX CREDIT.

* * *

(d) TREATMENT OF CERTAIN POSSESSIONS.—

(1) PAYMENTS TO POSSESSIONS WITH MIRROR CODE TAX SYSTEMS.—The Secretary of the Treasury shall pay to each possession of the United States which has a mirror code tax system amounts equal to the loss (if any) to that possession by reason of the application of the provisions of this section (other than this subsection) with respect to section 32 of the Internal Revenue Code of 1986. Such amounts shall be determined by the Secretary of the Treasury based on information provided by the government of the respective possession.

(2) PAYMENTS TO OTHER POSSESSIONS.—The Secretary of the Treasury shall pay to each possession of the United States which does not have a mirror code tax system amounts estimated by the Secretary of the Treasury as being equal to the aggregate benefits (if any) that would have been provided to residents of such possession by reason of the provisions of this section (other than this subsection) with respect to section 32 of the Internal Revenue Code of 1986 if a mirror code tax system had been in effect in such possession. The preceding sentence shall not apply unless the respective possession has a plan, which has been approved by the Secretary of the Treasury, under which such possession will promptly distribute such payments to its residents.

(3) MIRROR CODE TAX SYSTEM.—For purposes of this section, the term "mirror code tax system" means, with respect to any possession of the United States, the income tax system of such possession if the income tax liability of the residents of such possession under such system is determined by reference to the income tax laws of the United States as if such possession were the United States.

(4) TREATMENT OF PAYMENTS.—For purposes of section 1324 of title 31, United States Code, the payments under this section shall be treated in the same manner as a refund due from a credit provision referred to in subsection (b)(2) of such section.

INCOME TAX—U.S. POSSESSIONS

P.L. 117-2, § 9642(g)-(h), provides:

SEC. 9642. CREDIT FOR SICK LEAVE FOR CERTAIN SELF-EMPLOYED INDIVIDUALS.

* * *

(g) APPLICATION OF CREDIT IN CERTAIN POSSESSIONS.—

(1) PAYMENTS TO POSSESSIONS WITH MIRROR CODE TAX SYSTEMS.—The Secretary shall pay to each possession of the United States which has a mirror code tax system amounts equal to the loss (if any) to that possession by reason of the application of the provisions of this section. Such amounts shall be determined by the Secretary based on information provided by the government of the respective possession.

(2) PAYMENTS TO OTHER POSSESSIONS.—The Secretary shall pay to each possession of the United States which does not have a mirror code tax system amounts estimated by the Secretary as being equal to the aggregate benefits (if any) that would have been provided to residents of such possession by reason of the provisions of this section if a mirror code tax system had been in effect in such possession. The preceding sentence shall not apply unless the respective possession has a plan, which has been approved by the Secretary, under which such possession will promptly distribute such payments to its residents.

(3) MIRROR CODE TAX SYSTEM.—For purposes of this section, the term "mirror code tax system" means, with respect to any possession of the United States, the income tax system of such possession if the income tax liability of the residents of such possession under such system is determined by reference to the income tax laws of the United States as if such possession were the United States.

(4) TREATMENT OF PAYMENTS.—For purposes of section 1324 of title 31, United States Code, the payments under this subsection shall be treated in the same manner as a refund due from a credit provision referred to in subsection (b)(2) of such section.

(h) REGULATIONS.—The Secretary shall prescribe such regulations or other guidance as may be necessary to carry out the purposes of this section, including—

(1) regulations or other guidance to effectuate the purposes of this section, and

(2) regulations or other guidance to minimize compliance and record-keeping burdens under this section.

P.L. 117-2, § 9643(g)-(h), provides:

SEC. 9643. CREDIT FOR FAMILY LEAVE FOR CERTAIN SELF-EMPLOYED INDIVIDUALS.

* * *

(g) APPLICATION OF CREDIT IN CERTAIN POSSESSIONS.—

(1) PAYMENTS TO POSSESSIONS WITH MIRROR CODE TAX SYSTEMS.—The Secretary shall pay to each possession of the United States which has a mirror code tax system amounts equal to the loss (if any) to that possession by reason of the application of the provisions of this section. Such amounts shall be determined by the Secretary based on information provided by the government of the respective possession.

(2) PAYMENTS TO OTHER POSSESSIONS.—The Secretary shall pay to each possession of the United States which does not have a mirror code tax system amounts estimated by the Secretary as being equal to the aggregate benefits (if any) that would have been provided to residents of such possession by reason of the provisions of this section if a mirror code tax system had been in effect in such possession. The preceding sentence shall not apply unless the respective possession has a plan, which has been approved by the Secretary, under which such possession will promptly distribute such payments to its residents.

(3) MIRROR CODE TAX SYSTEM.—For purposes of this section, the term "mirror code tax system" means, with respect to any possession of the United States, the income tax system of such possession if the income tax liability of the residents of such possession under such system is determined by reference to the income tax laws of the United States as if such possession were the United States.

(4) TREATMENT OF PAYMENTS.—For purposes of section 1324 of title 31, United States Code, the payments under this subsection shall be treated in the same manner as a refund due from a credit provision referred to in subsection (b)(2) of such section.

(h) REGULATIONS.—The Secretary shall prescribe such regulations or other guidance as may be necessary to carry out the purposes of this section, including—

(1) regulations or other guidance to prevent the avoidance of the purposes of this section, and

(2) regulations or other guidance to minimize compliance and record-keeping burdens under this section.

• **2020, COVID-related Tax Relief Act of 2020 (P.L. 116-260)**

P.L. 116-260, § 272(c)-(d), Div. N, provides:

SEC. 272. ADDITIONAL 2020 RECOVERY REBATES FOR INDIVIDUALS.

* * *

(c) TREATMENT OF POSSESSIONS.—

(1) PAYMENTS TO POSSESSIONS.—

(A) MIRROR CODE POSSESSION.—The Secretary of the Treasury shall pay to each possession of the United States which has a mirror code tax system amounts equal to the loss (if any) to that possession by reason of the amendments made by this section. Such amounts shall be determined by the Secretary of the Treasury based on information provided by the government of the respective possession.

(B) OTHER POSSESSIONS.—The Secretary of the Treasury shall pay to each possession of the United States which does not have a mirror code tax system amounts estimated by the Secretary of the Treasury as being equal to the aggregate benefits (if any) that would have been provided to residents of such possession by reason of the amendments made by this section if a mirror code tax system had been in effect in such possession. The preceding sentence shall not apply unless the respective possession has a plan, which has been approved by the Secretary of the Treasury, under which such possession will promptly distribute such payments to its residents.

(2) COORDINATION WITH CREDIT ALLOWED AGAINST UNITED STATES INCOME TAXES.—No credit shall be allowed against United States income taxes under section 6428A of the Internal Revenue Code of 1986 (as added by this section) to any person—

(A) to whom a credit is allowed against taxes imposed by the possession by reason of the amendments made by this section, or

(B) who is eligible for a payment under a plan described in paragraph (1)(B).

(3) DEFINITIONS AND SPECIAL RULES.—

(A) POSSESSION OF THE UNITED STATES.—For purposes of this subsection, the term "possession of the United States" includes the Commonwealth of Puerto Rico and the Commonwealth of the Northern Mariana Islands.

(B) MIRROR CODE TAX SYSTEM.—For purposes of this subsection, the term "mirror code tax system" means, with respect to any possession of the United States, the income tax system of such possession if the income tax liability of the residents of such possession under such system is determined by reference to the income tax laws of the United States as if such possession were the United States.

(C) TREATMENT OF PAYMENTS.—For purposes of section 1324 of title 31, United States Code, the payments under this subsection shall be treated in the same manner as a refund due from a credit provision referred to in subsection (b)(2) of such section.

(d) ADMINISTRATIVE PROVISIONS.—

(1) EXCEPTION FROM REDUCTION OR OFFSET.—Any refund payable by reason of section 6428A(f) of the Internal Revenue Code of 1986 (as added by this section), or any such refund payable by reason of subsection (c) of this section, shall not be—

(A) subject to reduction or offset pursuant to section 3716 or 3720A of title 31, United States Code,

(B) subject to reduction or offset pursuant to subsection (c), (d), (e), or (f) of section 6402 of the Internal Revenue Code of 1986, or

(C) reduced or offset by other assessed Federal taxes that would otherwise be subject to levy or collection.

(2) ASSIGNMENT OF BENEFITS.—

(A) IN GENERAL.—The right of any person to any applicable payment shall not be transferable or assignable, at law or in equity, and no applicable payment shall be subject to, execution, levy, attachment, garnishment, or other legal process, or the operation of any bankruptcy or insolvency law.

* * *

(D) NO RECLAMATION RIGHTS.—This paragraph shall not alter the status of applicable payments as tax refunds or other nonbenefit payments for purpose of any reclamation rights of the Department of the Treasury or the Internal Revenue Service as per part 210 of title 31, Code of Federal Regulations.

(E) DEFINITIONS.—For purposes of this paragraph—

(i) ACCOUNT HOLDER.—The term "account holder" means a natural person whose name appears in a financial institution's records as the direct or beneficial owner of an account.

(ii) ACCOUNT REVIEW.—The term "account review" means the process of examining deposits in an account to determine if an applicable payment has been deposited into the account during the lookback period. The financial institution shall perform the account review following the procedures outlined in section 212.5 of title 31, Code of Federal Regulations and in accordance with the requirements of section 212.6 of title 31, Code of Federal Regulations.

(iii) APPLICABLE PAYMENT.—The term "applicable payment" means—

(I) any advance refund amount paid pursuant to section 6428A(f) of Internal Revenue Code of 1986 (as added by this section),

(II) any payment made by a possession of the United States with a mirror code tax system (as defined in subsection (c) of this section) pursuant to such subsection which corresponds to a payment described in subclause (I), and

(III) any payment made by a possession of the United States without a mirror code tax system (as so defined) pursuant to subsection (c) of this section.

(iv) GARNISHMENT.—The term "garnishment" means execution, levy, attachment, garnishment, or other legal process.

(v) GARNISHMENT ORDER.—The term "garnishment order" means a writ, order, notice, summons, judgment, levy, or similar written instruction issued by a court, a State or State agency, a municipality or municipal corporation, or a State child support enforcement agency, including a lien arising by operation of law for overdue child support or an order to freeze the assets in an account, to effect a garnishment against a debtor.

(vi) LOOKBACK PERIOD.—The term "lookback period" means the two month period that begins on the date preceding the date of account review and ends on the corresponding date of the month two months earlier, or on the last date of the month two months earlier if the corresponding date does not exist.

(3) AGENCY INFORMATION SHARING AND ASSISTANCE.—

(A) IN GENERAL.—The Commissioner of Social Security, the Railroad Retirement Board, and the Secretary of Veterans Affairs shall each provide the Secretary of the Treasury (or the Secretary's delegate) such information and assistance as the Secretary of the Treasury (or the Secretary's delegate) may require for purposes of—

(i) making payments under section 6428A(f) of the Internal Revenue Code of 1986 to individuals described in paragraph (5)(A) thereof, or

(ii) providing administrative assistance to a possession of the United States (as defined in subsection (c)(3)(A)) to allow such possession to promptly distribute payments under subsection (c) to its residents.

(B) EXCHANGE OF INFORMATION WITH POSSESSIONS.—Any information provided to the Secretary of the Treasury (or the Secretary's delegate) pursuant to subparagraph (A)(ii) may be exchanged with a possession of the United States in accordance with the applicable tax coordination agreement for information exchange and administrative assistance that the Internal Revenue Service has agreed to with such possession.

* * *

• **2020, Taxpayer Certainty and Disaster Tax Relief Act of 2020 (P.L. 116-260)**

P.L. 116-260, § 306(a)-(c), Div. EE, provides:

SEC. 306. TREATMENT OF CERTAIN POSSESSIONS.

(a) PAYMENTS TO POSSESSIONS WITH MIRROR CODE TAX SYSTEMS.—The Secretary of the Treasury shall pay to each possession of the United States which has a mirror code tax system amounts equal to the loss (if any) to that possession by reason of the application of the provisions of this title. Such amounts shall be determined by the

Secretary of the Treasury based on information provided by the government of the respective possession.

(b) PAYMENTS TO OTHER POSSESSIONS.—The Secretary of the Treasury shall pay to each possession of the United States which does not have a mirror code tax system amounts estimated by the Secretary of the Treasury as being equal to the aggregate benefits (if any) that would have been provided to residents of such possession by reason of the provisions of this title if a mirror code tax system had been in effect in such possession. The preceding sentence shall not apply unless the respective possession has a plan, which has been approved by the Secretary of the Treasury, under which such possession will promptly distribute such payments to its residents.

(c) MIRROR CODE TAX SYSTEM.—For purposes of this section, the term "mirror code tax system" means, with respect to any possession of the United States, the income tax system of such possession if the income tax liability of the residents of such possession under such system is determined by reference to the income tax laws of the United States as if such possession were the United States.

* * *

• 2020, Coronavirus Aid, Relief, and Economic Security (CARES) Act (P.L. 116-136)

P.L. 116-136, §2201(c)-(d) (as amended by P.L. 116-260, §273(b)(1), Div. N), provides:

SEC. 2201. 2020 RECOVERY REBATES FOR INDIVIDUALS.

* * *

(c) TREATMENT OF POSSESSIONS.—

(1) PAYMENTS TO POSSESSIONS.—

(A) MIRROR CODE POSSESSION.—The Secretary of the Treasury shall pay to each possession of the United States which has a mirror code tax system amounts equal to the loss (if any) to that possession by reason of the amendments made by this section. Such amounts shall be determined by the Secretary of the Treasury based on information provided by the government of the respective possession.

(B) OTHER POSSESSIONS.—The Secretary of the Treasury shall pay to each possession of the United States which does not have a mirror code tax system amounts estimated by the Secretary of the Treasury as being equal to the aggregate benefits (if any) that would have been provided to residents of such possession by reason of the amendments made by this section if a mirror code tax system had been in effect in such possession. The preceding sentence shall not apply unless the respective possession has a plan, which has been approved by the Secretary of the Treasury, under which such possession will promptly distribute such payments to its residents.

(2) COORDINATION WITH CREDIT ALLOWED AGAINST UNITED STATES INCOME TAXES.—No credit shall be allowed against United States income taxes under section 6428 of the Internal Revenue Code of 1986 (as added by this section) to any person—

(A) to whom a credit is allowed against taxes imposed by the possession by reason of the amendments made by this section, or

(B) who is eligible for a payment under a plan described in paragraph (1)(B).

(3) DEFINITIONS AND SPECIAL RULES.—

(A) POSSESSION OF THE UNITED STATES.— For purposes of this subsection, the term "possession of the United States" includes the Commonwealth of Puerto Rico and the Commonwealth of the Northern Mariana Islands.

(B) MIRROR CODE TAX SYSTEM.—For purposes of this subsection, the term "mirror code tax system" means, with respect to any possession of the United States, the income tax system of such possession if the income tax liability of the residents of such possession under such system is determined by reference to the income tax laws of the United States as if such possession were the United States.

(C) TREATMENT OF PAYMENTS.—For purposes of section 1324 of title 31, United States Code, the payments under this subsection shall be treated in the same manner as a refund due from a credit provision referred to in subsection (b)(2) of such section.

(d) EXCEPTION FROM REDUCTION OR OFFSET.—Any refund payable by reason of section 6428(f) of the Internal Revenue Code of 1986 (as added by this section), or any such refund payable by reason of subsection (c) of this section, shall not be—

(1) subject to reduction or offset pursuant to section 3716 or 3720A of title 31, United States Code,

(2) subject to reduction or offset pursuant to subsection (d), (e), or (f) of section 6402 of the Internal Revenue Code of 1986, or

(3) reduced or offset by other assessed Federal taxes that would otherwise be subject to levy or collection.

* * *

• 2020, Families First Coronavirus Response Act (P.L. 116-127)

P.L. 116-127, §7002(f), provides:

SEC. 7002. CREDIT FOR SICK LEAVE FOR CERTAIN SELF-EMPLOYED INDIVIDUALS.

* * *

(f) APPLICATION OF CREDIT IN CERTAIN POSSESSIONS.—

(1) PAYMENTS TO POSSESSIONS WITH MIRROR CODE TAX SYSTEMS.—The Secretary of the Treasury (or the Secretary's delegate) shall pay to each possession of the United States which has a mirror code tax system amounts equal to the loss (if any) to that possession by reason of the application of the provisions of this section. Such amounts shall be determined by the Secretary of the Treasury (or the Secretary's delegate) based on information provided by the government of the respective possession.

(2) PAYMENTS TO OTHER POSSESSIONS.—The Secretary of the Treasury (or the Secretary's delegate) shall pay to each possession of the United States which does not have a mirror code tax system amounts estimated by the Secretary of the Treasury (or the Secretary's delegate) as being equal to the aggregate benefits (if any) that would have been provided to residents of such possession by reason of the provisions of this section if a mirror code tax system had been in effect in such possession. The preceding sentence shall not apply unless the respective possession has a plan, which has been approved by the Secretary of the Treasury (or the Secretary's delegate), under which such possession will promptly distribute such payments to its residents.

(3) MIRROR CODE TAX SYSTEM.—For purposes of this section, the term "mirror code tax system" means, with respect to any possession of the United States, the income tax system of such possession if the income tax liability of the residents of such possession under such system is determined by reference to the income tax laws of the United States as if such possession were the United States.

(4) TREATMENT OF PAYMENTS.—For purposes of section 1324 of title 31, United States Code, the payments under this section shall be treated in the same manner as a refund due from a credit provision referred to in subsection (b)(2) of such section.

* * *

P.L. 116-127, §7004(f), provides:

SEC. 7004. CREDIT FOR FAMILY LEAVE FOR CERTAIN SELF-EMPLOYED INDIVIDUALS.

* * *

(f) APPLICATION OF CREDIT IN CERTAIN POSSESSIONS.—

(1) PAYMENTS TO POSSESSIONS WITH MIRROR CODE TAX SYSTEMS.—The Secretary of the Treasury (or the Secretary's delegate) shall pay to each possession of the United States which has a mirror code tax system amounts equal to the loss (if any) to that possession by reason of the application of the provisions of this section. Such amounts shall be determined by the Secretary of the Treasury (or the Secretary's delegate) based on information provided by the government of the respective possession.

(2) PAYMENTS TO OTHER POSSESSIONS.—The Secretary of the Treasury (or the Secretary's delegate) shall pay to each possession of the United States which does not have a mirror code tax system amounts estimated by the Secretary of the Treasury (or the Secretary's delegate) as being equal to the aggregate benefits (if any) that would have been provided to residents of such possession by reason of the provisions of this section if a mirror code tax system had been in effect in such possession. The preceding sentence shall not apply unless the respective possession has a plan, which has been approved by the Secretary of the Treasury (or the Secretary's delegate), under which such possession will promptly distribute such payments to its residents.

(3) MIRROR CODE TAX SYSTEM.—For purposes of this section, the term "mirror code tax system" means, with respect to any possession of the United States, the income tax system of such possession if the income tax liability of the residents of such possession under such system is determined by reference to the income tax laws of the United States as if such possession were the United States.

(4) TREATMENT OF PAYMENTS.—For purposes of section 1324 of title 31, United States Code, the payments under this section shall be treated in the same manner as a refund due from a credit provision referred to in subsection (b)(2) of such section.

* * *

• 2019, Taxpayer Certainty and Disaster Tax Relief Act of 2019 (P.L. 116-94)

P.L. 116-94, §208, Div. Q, provides:

SEC. 208. TREATMENT OF CERTAIN POSSESSIONS.

(a) PAYMENTS TO POSSESSIONS WITH MIRROR CODE TAX SYSTEMS.—The Secretary of the Treasury shall pay to each possession of the United States which has a mirror code tax system amounts equal to the loss (if any) to that possession by reason of the application of the provisions of this title. Such amounts shall be determined by the Secretary of the Treasury based on information provided by the government of the respective possession.

(b) PAYMENTS TO OTHER POSSESSIONS.—The Secretary of the Treasury shall pay to each possession of the United States which does not have a mirror code tax system amounts estimated by the Secretary of the Treasury as being equal to the aggregate benefits (if any) that would have been provided to residents of such possession by reason of the provisions of this title if a mirror code tax system had been in effect in such possession. The preceding sentence shall not apply unless the respective possession has a plan, which has been approved by the Secretary of the Treasury, under which such possession will promptly distribute such payments to its residents.

(c) MIRROR CODE TAX SYSTEM.—For purposes of this section, the term "mirror code tax system" means, with respect to any possession of the United States, the income tax system of such possession if the income tax liability of the residents of such possession under such system is determined by reference to the income tax laws of the United States as if such possession were the United States.

(d) TREATMENT OF PAYMENTS.—For purposes of section 1324 of title 31, United States Code, the payments under this section shall be treated in the same manner as a refund due from a credit provision referred to in subsection (b)(2) of such section.

• 2004, American Jobs Creation Act of 2004 (P.L. 108-357)

P.L. 108-357, §908(c)(4)(A)-(B):

Amended Code Sec. 935, as in effect before the effective date of its repeal, by striking "for the taxable year who" in subsection (a) and inserting "who, during the entire taxable year", and by inserting "bona fide" before "resident" in subsection (a)(1). **Effective** for tax years ending after 10-22-2004.

[Sec. 935(b)]

(b) FILING REQUIREMENT.—

(1) IN GENERAL.—Each individual to whom this section applies for the taxable year shall file his income tax return for the taxable year—

INCOME TAX—U.S. POSSESSIONS

(A) with the United States (other than a bona fide resident of Guam during the entire taxable year), if he is a resident of the United States,

(B) with Guam, if he is a bona fide resident of Guam, and

(C) if neither subparagraph (A) nor subparagraph (B) applies—

(i) with Guam, if he is a citizen of Guam but not otherwise a citizen of the United States, or

(ii) with the United States, if clause (i) does not apply.

(2) DETERMINATION DATE.—For purposes of this section, determinations of citizenship for the taxable year shall be made as of the close of the taxable year.

(3) SPECIAL RULE FOR JOINT RETURNS.—In the case of a joint return, this subsection shall be applied on the basis of the residence and citizenship of the spouse who has the greater adjusted gross income (determined without regard to community property laws) for the taxable year.

Amendments

• **2004, American Jobs Creation Act of 2004 (P.L. 108-357)**

P.L. 108-357, § 908(c)(4)(C)(i)-(ii):

Amended Code Sec. 935(b)(1), as in effect before the effective date of its repeal, by inserting "(other a bona fide resident of Guam during the entire taxable year)" after "United States" in subparagraph (A), and by inserting "bona fide" before "resident" in subparagraph (B). **Effective** for tax years ending after 10-22-2004.

P.L. 108-357, § 908(c)(4)(D):

Amended Code Sec. 935(b)(2), as in effect before the effective date of its repeal, by striking "residence and" before "citizenship". **Effective** for tax years ending after 10-22-2004.

[Sec. 935(c)]

(c) EXTENT OF INCOME TAX LIABILITY.—In the case of any individual to whom this section applies for the taxable year—

(1) for purposes of so much of this title (other than this section and section 7654) as relates to the taxes imposed by this chapter, the United States shall be treated as including Guam,

(2) for purposes of the Guam territorial income tax, Guam shall be treated as including the United States, and

(3) such individual is hereby relieved of liability for income tax for such year to the jurisdiction (the United States or Guam) other than the jurisdiction with which he is required to file under subsection (b).

[Sec. 935(d)]

(d) SPECIAL RULES FOR ESTIMATED INCOME TAX.—If there is reason to believe that this section will apply to an individual for the taxable year, then—

(1) he shall file any declaration of estimated income tax (and all amendments thereto) with the jurisdiction with which he would be required to file a return for such year under subsection (b) if his taxable year closed on the date he is required to file such declaration,

(2) he is hereby relieved of any liability to file a declaration of estimated income tax (and amendments thereto) for such taxable year to the other jurisdiction, and

(3) his liability for underpayments of estimated income tax shall be to the jurisdiction with which he is required to file his return for the taxable year (determined under subsection (b)).

Amendments

• **1986, Tax Reform Act of 1986 (P.L. 99-514)**

P.L. 99-514, § 1272(d)(2):

Repealed Code Sec. 935. **Effective**, generally, for tax years beginning after 12-31-86. However, see Act Sec. 1277(b)-(e) under the amendment notes for Code Sec. 48 for special rules. Prior to repeal, and as amended by P.L. 108-357, § 908(c)(4)(A)-(D), Code Sec. 935 read as follows:

SEC. 935. COORDINATION OF UNITED STATES AND GUAM INDIVIDUAL INCOME TAXES.

[Sec. 935(a)]

(a) APPLICATION OF SECTION.—This section shall apply to any individual who, during the entire taxable year—

(1) is a bona fide resident of Guam,

(2) is a citizen of Guam but not otherwise a citizen of the United States,

(3) has income derived from Guam for the taxable year and is a citizen or resident of the United States, or

(4) files a joint return for the taxable year with an individual who satisfies paragraph (1), (2), or (3) for the taxable year.

Amendments

• **2004, American Jobs Creation Act of 2004 (P.L. 108-357)**

P.L. 108-357, § 908(c)(4)(A)-(B):

Amended Code Sec. 935, as in effect before the effective date of its repeal, by striking "for the taxable year who" in subsection (a) and inserting "who, during the entire taxable year", and by inserting "bona fide" before "resident" in subsection (a)(1). **Effective** for tax years ending after 10-22-2004.

[Sec. 935(b)]

(b) FILING REQUIREMENT.—

(1) IN GENERAL.—Each individual to whom this section applies for the taxable year shall file his income tax return for the taxable year—

(A) with the United States (other than a bona fide resident of Guam during the entire taxable year), if he is a resident of the United States,

(B) with Guam, if he is a bona fide resident of Guam, and

(C) if neither subparagraph (A) nor subparagraph (B) applies—

(i) with Guam, if he is a citizen of Guam but not otherwise a citizen of the United States, or

(ii) with the United States, if clause (i) does not apply.

(2) DETERMINATION DATE.—For purposes of this section, determinations of citizenship for the taxable year shall be made as of the close of the taxable year.

(3) SPECIAL RULE FOR JOINT RETURNS.—In the case of a joint return, this subsection shall be applied on the basis of the residence and citizenship of the spouse who has the greater adjusted gross income (determined without regard to community property laws) for the taxable year.

Amendments

• **2004, American Jobs Creation Act of 2004 (P.L. 108-357)**

P.L. 108-357, § 908(c)(4)(C)(i)-(ii):

Amended Code Sec. 935(b)(1), as in effect before the effective date of its repeal, by inserting "(other a bona fide resident of Guam during the entire taxable year)" after "United States" in subparagraph (A), and by inserting "bona fide" before "resident" in subparagraph (B). **Effective** for tax years ending after 10-22-2004.

P.L. 108-357, § 908(c)(4)(D):

Amended Code Sec. 935(b)(2), as in effect before the effective date of its repeal, by striking "residence and" before "citizenship". **Effective** for tax years ending after 10-22-2004.

[Sec. 935(c)]

(c) EXTENT OF INCOME TAX LIABILITY.—In the case of any individual to whom this section applies for the taxable year—

(1) for purposes of so much of this title (other than this section and section 7654) as relates to the taxes imposed by this chapter, the United States shall be treated as including Guam,

(2) for purposes of the Guam territorial income tax, Guam shall be treated as including the United States, and

(3) such individual is hereby relieved of liability for income tax for such year to the jurisdiction (the United States or Guam) other than the jurisdiction with which he is required to file under subsection (b).

[Sec. 935(d)]

(d) SPECIAL RULES FOR ESTIMATED INCOME TAX.—If there is reason to believe that this section will apply to an individual for the taxable year, then—

(1) he shall file any declaration of estimated income tax (and all amendments thereto) with the jurisdiction with which he would be required to file a return for such year under subsection (b) if his taxable year closed on the date he is required to file such declaration,

(2) he is hereby relieved of any liability to file a declaration of estimated income tax (and amendments thereto) for such taxable year to the other jurisdiction, and

(3) his liability for underpayments of estimated income tax shall be to the jurisdiction with which he is required to file his return for the taxable year (determined under subsection (b)).

• **1972 (P.L. 92-606)**

P.L. 92-606, § 1(a):

Added Code Sec. 935. **Effective** for tax years beginning after 12-31-72.

INCOME TAX—U.S. POSSESSIONS

[Sec. 936—Stricken]

Amendments

• **2018, Tax Technical Corrections Act of 2018 (P.L. 115-141)**

P.L. 115-141, §401(d)(1)(C), Div. U:

Amended subpart C of part III of subchapter N of chapter 1 by striking Code Sec. 936. **Effective** 3-23-2018. For a special rule, see Act Sec. 401(e), Div. U, below. Prior to being stricken, Code Sec. 936 read as follows:

SEC. 936. PUERTO RICO AND POSSESSION TAX CREDIT.

[Sec. 936(a)]

(a) ALLOWANCE OF CREDIT.—

(1) IN GENERAL.—Except as otherwise provided in this section, if a domestic corporation elects the application of this section and if the conditions of both subparagraph (A) and subparagraph (B) of paragraph (2) are satisfied, there shall be allowed as a credit against the tax imposed by this chapter an amount equal to the portion of the tax which is attributable to the sum of—

(A) the taxable income, from sources without the United States, from—

(i) the active conduct of a trade or business within a possession of the United States, or

(ii) the sale or exchange of substantially all of the assets used by the taxpayer in the active conduct of such trade or business, and

(B) the qualified possession source investment income.

(2) CONDITIONS WHICH MUST BE SATISFIED.—The conditions referred to in paragraph (1) are:

(A) 3-YEAR PERIOD.—If 80 percent or more of the gross income of such domestic corporation for the 3-year period immediately preceding the close of the taxable year (or for such part of such period immediately preceding the close of such taxable year as may be applicable) was derived from sources within a possession of the United States (determined without regard to subsections (f) and (g) of section 904); and

(B) TRADE OR BUSINESS.—If 75 percent or more of the gross income of such domestic corporation for such period or such part thereof was derived from the active conduct of a trade or business within a possession of the United States.

(3) CREDIT NOT ALLOWED AGAINST CERTAIN TAXES.—The credit provided by paragraph (1) shall not be allowed against the tax imposed by—

(A) section 531 (relating to the tax on accumulated earnings),

(B) section 541 (relating to personal holding company tax), or

(C) section 1351 (relating to recoveries of foreign expropriation losses).

(4) LIMITATIONS ON CREDIT FOR ACTIVE BUSINESS INCOME.—

(A) IN GENERAL.—The amount of the credit determined under paragraph (1) for any taxable year with respect to income referred to in subparagraph (A) thereof shall not exceed the sum of the following amounts:

(i) 60 percent of the sum of—

(I) the aggregate amount of the possession corporation's qualified possession wages for such taxable year, plus

(II) the allocable employee fringe benefit expenses of the possession corporation for the taxable year.

(ii) The sum of—

(I) 15 percent of the depreciation allowances for the taxable year with respect to short-life qualified tangible property;

(II) 40 percent of the depreciation allowances for the taxable year with respect to medium-life qualified tangible property, and

(III) 65 percent of the depreciation allowances for the taxable year with respect to long-life qualified tangible property.

(iii) If the possession corporation does not have an election to use the method described in subsection (h)(5)(C)(ii) (relating to profit split) in effect for the taxable year, the amount of qualified possession income taxes for the taxable year allocable to nonsheltered income.

(B) ELECTION TO TAKE REDUCED CREDIT.—

(i) IN GENERAL.—If an election under this subparagraph applies to a possession corporation for any taxable year—

(I) subparagraph (A), and the provisions of subsection (i), shall not apply to such possession corporation for such taxable year, and

(II) the credit determined under paragraph (1) for such taxable year with respect to income referred to in subparagraph (A) thereof shall be the applicable percentage of the credit which would otherwise have been determined under such paragraph with respect to such income.

Notwithstanding subclause (I), a possession corporation to which an election under this subparagraph applies shall be entitled to the benefits of subsection (i)(3)(B) for taxes allocable (on a pro rata basis) to taxable income the tax on which is not offset by reason of this subparagraph.

(ii) APPLICABLE PERCENTAGE.—The term "applicable percentage" means the percentage determined in accordance with the following table:

In the case of taxable years beginning in:	The percentage is:
1994	60
1995	55
1996	50
1997	45
1998 and thereafter	40

(iii) ELECTION.—

(I) IN GENERAL.—An election under this subparagraph by any possession corporation may be made only for the corporation's first taxable year beginning after December 31, 1993, for which it is a possession corporation.

(II) PERIOD OF ELECTION.—An election under this subparagraph shall apply to the taxable year for which made and all subsequent taxable years unless revoked.

(III) AFFILIATED GROUPS.—If, for any taxable year, an election is not in effect for any possession corporation which is a member of an affiliated group, any election under this subparagraph for any other member of such group is revoked for such taxable year and all subsequent taxable years. For purposes of this subclause, members of an affiliated group shall be determined without regard to the exceptions contained in section 1504(b) and as if the constructive ownership rules of section 1563(e) applied for purposes of section 1504(a). The Secretary may prescribe regulations to prevent the avoidance of this subclause through deconsolidation or otherwise.

(C) CROSS REFERENCE.—

For definitions and special rules applicable to this paragraph, see subsection (i).

Amendments

• **2014, Tax Technical Corrections Act of 2014 (P.L. 113-295)**

P.L. 113-295, §221(a)(12)(G), Div. A:

Amended Code Sec. 936(a)(3) by striking subparagraph (A) and by redesignating subparagraphs (B), (C), and (D) as subparagraphs (A), (B), and (C), respectively. **Effective** generally 12-19-2014. For a special rule, see Act Sec. 221(b)(2), Div. A, below. Prior to being stricken, Code Sec. 936(a)(3)(A) read as follows:

(A) section 59A (relating to environmental tax),

P.L. 113-295, §221(b)(2), Div. A, provides:

(2) SAVINGS PROVISION.—If—

(A) any provision amended or repealed by the amendments made by this section applied to—

(i) any transaction occurring before the date of the enactment of this Act,

(ii) any property acquired before such date of enactment, or

(iii) any item of income, loss, deduction, or credit taken into account before such date of enactment, and

(B) the treatment of such transaction, property, or item under such provision would (without regard to the amendments or repeals made by this section) affect the liability for tax for periods ending after date of enactment, nothing in the amendments or repeals made by this section shall be construed to affect the treatment of such transaction, property, or item for purposes of determining liability for tax for periods ending after such date of enactment.

• **2004, American Jobs Creation Act of 2004 (P.L. 108-357)**

P.L. 108-357, §402(b)(2):

Amended Code Sec. 936(a)(2)(A) by striking "section 904(f)" and inserting "subsections (f) and (g) of section 904". **Effective** for losses for tax years beginning after 12-31-2006.

• **1996, Small Business Job Protection Act of 1996 (P.L. 104-188)**

P.L. 104-188, §1704(t)(80):

Amended Code Sec. 936(a)(4)(A)(ii)(I) by striking "deprecation" and inserting "depreciation". **Effective** 8-20-96.

• **1993, Omnibus Budget Reconciliation Act of 1993 (P.L. 103-66)**

P.L. 103-66, §13227(a)(1)-(2):

Amended Code Sec. 936(a) by striking "as provided in paragraph (3)" in paragraph (1) and inserting "as otherwise provided in this section", and by adding at the end thereof new paragraph (4). **Effective** for tax years beginning after 12-31-93.

• **1986, Tax Reform Act of 1986 (P.L. 99-514)**

P.L. 99-514, §701(e)(4)(I):

Amended Code Sec. 936(a)(3) by striking out subparagraph (A) and by redesignating subparagraphs (B), (C), and (E) as subparagraphs (A), (B), and (C), respectively. **Effective**, generally, for tax years beginning after 12-31-86. However, for special rules and exceptions, see Act Sec. 701(f)(2)-(7) following Code Sec. 56. Prior to amendment, Code Sec. 936(a)(3)(A) read as follows:

(A) section 56 (relating to corporate minimum tax),

P.L. 99-514, §1231(d)(1):

Amended Code Sec. 936(a)(2)(B) by striking out "65 percent" and inserting in lieu thereof "75 percent". **Effective**, generally, for tax years beginning after 12-31-86. However, see Act Sec. 1231(g)(4), below.

P.L. 99-514, §1231(d)(2):

Amended Code Sec. 936(a)(2)(C) by striking out subparagraph (C). **Effective**, generally, for tax years beginning after 12-31-86. However, see Act Sec. 1231(g)(4), below. Prior to amendment, Code Sec. 936(a)(2)(C) read as follows:

(C) TRANSITIONAL RULE.—In applying subparagraph (B) with respect to taxable years beginning after December 31, 1982, and before January 1, 1985, the following percentage shall be substituted for "65 percent":

For taxable years beginning in calendar year:	The percentage is:
1983	55
1984	60

P.L. 99-514, §1231(g)(4), provides:

(4) TRANSITIONAL RULE.—In the case of a corporation—

(A) with respect to which an election under section 936 of the Internal Revenue Code of 1986 (relating to possessions tax credit) is in effect,

(B) which produced an end-product form in Puerto Rico on or before September 3, 1982,

INCOME TAX—U.S. POSSESSIONS

(C) which began manufacturing a component of such product in Puerto Rico in its taxable year beginning in 1983, and

(D) with respect to which a Puerto Rican tax exemption was granted on June 27, 1983,

such corporation shall treat such component as a separate product for such taxable year for purposes of determining whether such corporation had a significant business presence in Puerto Rico with respect to such product and its income with respect to such product.

- **1986, Superfund Amendments and Reauthorization Act of 1986 (P.L. 99-499)**

P.L. 99-499, § 516(b)(1)(B):

Amended Code Sec. 936(a)(3), as amended by P.L. 99-514, by redesignating subparagraphs (A), (B), and (C) as subparagraphs (B), (C), and (D), respectively, and by inserting before subparagraph (B) (as so redesignated) new subparagraph (A). **Effective** for tax years beginning after 12-31-86.

- **1984, Deficit Reduction Act of 1984 (P.L. 98-369)**

P.L. 98-369, § 712(g):

Amended the table contained in Code Sec. 936(a)(2)(C) by striking out "The percentage tax is" and inserting in lieu thereof "The percentage is". **Effective** as if included in the provision of P.L. 97-248 to which it relates.

- **1983, Technical Corrections Act of 1982 (P.L. 97-448)**

P.L. 97-448, § 306(a)(1)(A):

Amended P.L. 97-248, § 201 by redesignating the second subsection (c) as subsection (d).

- **1982, Tax Equity and Fiscal Responsibility Act of 1982 (P.L. 97-248)**

P.L. 97-248, § 201(d)(8)(B):

Amended Code Sec. 936(a)(3)(A) by striking out "(relating to minimum tax)" and inserting in lieu thereof "(relating to corporate minimum tax)". **Effective** for tax years beginning after 12-31-82.

P.L. 97-248, § 213(a)(1):

Amended Code Sec. 936(a)(2) by striking out "50 percent" in subparagraph (B) and inserting "65 percent", and by adding at the end new subparagraph (C). **Effective** for tax years beginning after 12-31-82.

- **1978, Revenue Act of 1978 (P.L. 95-600)**

P.L. 95-600, § 701(u)(11)(A):

Redesignated Code Sec. 936(a)(2) as 936(a)(3), amended the first paragraph of Code Sec. 936(a)(1), and added so much of paragraph (2) as precedes subparagraph (A). **Effective** for tax years beginning after 12-31-75. Prior to amendment, Code Sec. 936(a) read as follows:

(a) ALLOWANCE OF CREDIT.—

(1) IN GENERAL.—Except as provided in paragraph (2), in the case of a domestic corporation which elects the application of this section, there shall be allowed as a credit against the tax imposed by this chapter an amount equal to the portion of the tax which is attributable to taxable income, from sources without the United States, from the active conduct of a trade or business within a possession of the United States, and from qualified possession source investment income, if the conditions of both subparagraph (A) and subparagraph (B) are satisfied:

(A) 3-YEAR PERIOD.—If 80 percent or more of the gross income of such domestic corporation for the 3-year period immediately preceding the close of the taxable year (or for such part of such period immediately preceding the close of such taxable year as may be applicable) was derived from sources within a possession of the United States (determined without regard to section 904(f)); and

(B) TRADE OR BUSINESS.—If 50 percent or more of the gross income of such domestic corporation for such period or such part thereof was derived from the active conduct of a trade or business within a possession of the United States.

(2) CREDIT NOT ALLOWED AGAINST CERTAIN TAXES.—The credit provided by paragraph (1) shall not be allowed against the tax imposed by—

(A) section 56 (relating to minimum tax),

(B) section 531 (relating to the tax on accumulated earnings),

(C) section 541 (relating to personal holding company tax), or

(E)[D] section 1351 (relating to recoveries of foreign expropriation losses).

- **1976, Tax Reform Act of 1976 (P.L. 94-455)**

P.L. 94-455, § 1901(b)(37)(B)(i):

Inserted "or" at the end of Code Sec. 936(a)(2)(C). **Effective** for tax years beginning after 12-31-76.

P.L. 94-455, § 1901(b)(37)(B)(ii):

Struck out Code Sec. 936(a)(2)(D) [but did not renumber (E)]. **Effective** for tax years beginning after 12-31-76. Prior to striking, Code Sec. 936(a)(2)(D) read as follows:

(D) section 1333 (relating to war loss recoveries), or

[Sec. 936(b)]

(b) AMOUNTS RECEIVED IN UNITED STATES.—In determining taxable income for purposes of subsection (a), there shall not be taken into account as income from sources without the United States any gross income which was received by such domestic corporation within the United States, whether derived from sources within or without the United States. This subsection shall not apply to any amount described in subsection (a)(1)(A)(i) received from a person who is not a related person (within the meaning of subsection (h)(3) but without regard to subparagraphs (D)(ii) and (E)(i) thereof) with respect to the domestic corporation.

Sec. 936—Stricken

Amendments

- **1996, Small Business Job Protection Act of 1996 (P.L. 104-188)**

P.L. 104-188, § 1704(t)(37):

Amended Code Sec. 936(b) by striking "subparagraphs (D)(ii)(I)" and inserting "subparagraphs (D)(ii)". **Effective** 8-20-96.

- **1986, Tax Reform Act of 1986 (P.L. 99-514)**

P.L. 99-514, § 1231(b):

Amended Code Sec. 936(b) by adding at the end thereof a new sentence. **Effective**, generally, for tax years beginning after 12-31-86. However, see Act Sec. 1231(g)(4) following Code Sec. 936 for a transitional rule.

[Sec. 936(c)]

(c) TREATMENT OF CERTAIN FOREIGN TAXES.—For purposes of this title, any tax of a foreign country or a possession of the United States which is paid or accrued with respect to taxable income which is taken into account in computing the credit under subsection (a) shall not be treated as income, war profits, or excess profits taxes paid or accrued to a foreign country or possession of the United States, and no deduction shall be allowed under this title with respect to any amounts so paid or accrued.

[Sec. 936(d)]

(d) DEFINITIONS AND SPECIAL RULES.—For purposes of this section—

(1) POSSESSION.—The term "possession of the United States" includes the Commonwealth of Puerto Rico, and the Virgin Islands.

(2) QUALIFIED POSSESSION SOURCE INVESTMENT INCOME.—The term "qualified possession source investment income" means gross income which—

(A) is from sources within a possession of the United States in which a trade or business is actively conducted, and

(B) the taxpayer establishes to the satisfaction of the Secretary is attributable to the investment in such possession (for use therein) of funds derived from the active conduct of a trade or business in such possession, or from such investment,

less the deductions properly apportioned or allocated thereto.

(3) CARRYOVER BASIS PROPERTY.

(A) IN GENERAL.—Income from the sale or exchange of any asset the basis of which is determined in whole or in part by reference to its basis in the hands of another person shall not be treated as income described in subparagraph (A) or (B) of subsection (a)(1).

(B) EXCEPTION FOR POSSESSIONS CORPORATIONS, ETC.—For purposes of subparagraph (A), the holding of any asset by another person shall not be taken into account if throughout the period for which such asset was held by such person section 931, this section, or section 957(c) (as in effect on the day before the date of the enactment of the Tax Reform Act of 1986) applied to such person.

(4) INVESTMENT IN QUALIFIED CARIBBEAN BASIN COUNTRIES.—

(A) IN GENERAL.—For purposes of paragraph (2)(B), an investment in a financial institution shall, subject to such conditions as the Secretary may prescribe by regulations, be treated as for use in Puerto Rico to the extent used by such financial institution (or by the Government Development Bank for Puerto Rico or the Puerto Rico Economic Development Bank)—

(i) for investment, consistent with the goals and purposes of the Caribbean Basin Economic Recovery Act, in—

(I) active business assets in a qualified Caribbean Basin country, or

(II) development projects in a qualified Caribbean Basin country, and

(ii) in accordance with a specific authorization granted by the Commissioner of Financial Institutions of Puerto Rico pursuant to regulations issued by such Commissioner.

A similar rule shall apply in the case of a direct investment in the Government Development Bank for Puerto Rico or the Puerto Rico Economic Development Bank.

(B) QUALIFIED CARIBBEAN BASIN COUNTRY.—For purposes of this subsection, the term "qualified Caribbean Basin country" means any beneficiary country (within the meaning of section 212(a)(1)(A) of the Caribbean Basin Economic Recovery Act) which meets the requirements of clauses (i) and (ii) of section 274(h)(6)(A) and the Virgin Islands.

(C) ADDITIONAL REQUIREMENTS.—Subparagraph (A) shall not apply to any investment made by a financial institution (or by the Government Development Bank for Puerto Rico or the Puerto Rico Economic Development Bank) unless—

(i) the person in whose trade or business such investment is made (or such other recipient of the investment) and the financial institution or such Bank certify to the Secretary and the Commissioner of Financial Institutions of Puerto Rico that the proceeds of the loan will be promptly used to acquire active business assets or to make other authorized expenditures, and

(ii) the financial institution (or the Government Development Bank for Puerto Rico or the Puerto Rico Economic Development Bank) and the recipient of the investment funds agree to permit the Secretary and the Commissioner of Financial Institutions of Puerto Rico to examine such of their books and records as may be necessary to ensure that the requirements of this paragraph are met.

(D) REQUIREMENT FOR INVESTMENT IN CARIBBEAN BASIN COUNTRIES.—

(i) IN GENERAL.—For each calendar year, the government of Puerto Rico shall take such steps as may be necessary to ensure that at least $100,000,000 of qualified Caribbean Basin country investments are made during such calendar year.

(ii) QUALIFIED CARIBBEAN BASIN COUNTRY INVESTMENT.—For purposes of clause (i), the term "qualified Caribbean Basin country investment" means any investment if—

(I) the income from such investment is treated as qualified possession source investment income by reason of subparagraph (A), and

INCOME TAX—U.S. POSSESSIONS

(II) such investment is not (directly or indirectly) a refinancing of a prior investment (whether or not such prior investment was a qualified Caribbean Basin country investment).

Amendments

• **1990, Customs and Trade Act of 1990 (P.L. 101-382)**

P.L. 101-382, §227(a):

Amended Code Sec. 936(d)(4) by adding at the end thereof a new subparagraph (D). **Effective** for calendar years after 1989.

• **1988, Technical and Miscellaneous Revenue Act of 1988 (P.L. 100-647)**

P.L. 100-647, §1012(j):

Amended Code Sec. 936(d)(3)(B) by striking out "section 957(c)" and inserting in lieu thereof "section 957(c) (as in effect on the day before the date of the enactment of the Tax Reform Act of 1986)". **Effective** as if included in the provision of P.L. 99-514 to which it relates.

P.L. 100-647, §1012(n)(5)(A):

Amended Code Sec. 936(d)(4)(A)(ii). **Effective** as if included in the provision of P.L. 99-514 to which it relates. Prior to amendment, Code Sec. 936(d)(4)(A)(ii) read as follows:

(ii) in accordance with a specific authorization granted by the Government Development Bank for Puerto Rico pursuant to regulations issued by the Secretary of the Treasury of Puerto Rico.

P.L. 100-647, §1012(n)(5)(B):

Amended Code Sec. 936(d)(4)(C)(i) and (ii) by striking out "the Secretary of the Treasury of Puerto Rico" and inserting in lieu thereof "the Commissioner of Financial Institutions of Puerto Rico". **Effective** as if included in the provision of P.L. 99-514 to which it relates.

P.L. 100-647, §6132(a):

Amended Code Sec. 936(d)(4)(B) by inserting "and the Virgin Islands" after "section 274(h)(6)(A)". **Effective** for investments made after 11-10-88.

• **1986, Tax Reform Act of 1986 (P.L. 99-514)**

P.L. 99-514, §1231(c):

Amended Code Sec. 936(d) by adding at the end thereof new paragraph (4). **Effective**, generally, for tax years beginning after 12-31-86. However, see Act Sec. 1231(g)(4) following Code Sec. 936(a) for a transitional rule.

P.L. 99-514, §1275(a)(1):

Amended Code Sec. 936(d)(1) by striking out ", but does not include the Virgin Islands of the United States" and inserting in lieu thereof "and the Virgin Islands". **Effective**, generally, for tax years beginning after 12-31-86. However, for special rules and exceptions, see Act Sec. 1277(b)-(e) following Code Sec. 48.

• **1978, Revenue Act of 1978 (P.L. 95-600)**

P.L. 95-600, §701(u)(11)(B)(i):

Added Code Sec. 936(d)(3). **Effective** for tax years beginning after 12-31-75.

P.L. 95-600, §701(u)(11)(B)(ii):

Amended the heading of Code Sec. 936(d) by striking out "(d) Definitions.—" and, inserting in lieu thereof "(d) Definitions and Special Rules.—". **Effective** for tax years beginning after 12-31-75.

• **1976, Tax Reform Act of 1976 (P.L. 94-455)**

P.L. 94-455, §1051(b):

Added Code Sec. 936(d). **Effective** for tax years beginning after 12-31-75, except that "qualified possession source investment income" as defined in Code Sec. 936(d)(2) shall include income from any source outside the United States if the taxpayer establishes to the satisfaction of the Secretary of the Treasury or his delegate that the income from such sources was earned before 10-1-76.

[Sec. 936(e)]

(e) ELECTION.—

(1) PERIOD OF ELECTION.—The election provided in subsection (a) shall be made at such time and in such manner as the Secretary may by regulations prescribe. Any such election shall apply to the first taxable year for which such election was made and for which the domestic corporation satisfied the conditions of subparagraphs (A) and (B) of subsection (a)(2) and for each taxable year thereafter until such election is revoked by the domestic corporation under paragraph (2). If any such election is revoked by the domestic corporation under paragraph (2), such domestic corporation may make a subsequent election under subsection (a) for any taxable year thereafter for which such domestic corporation satisfies the conditions of subparagraphs (A) and (B) of subsection (a)(2) and any such subsequent election shall remain in effect until revoked by such domestic corporation under paragraph (2).

(2) REVOCATION.—An election under subsection (a)—

(A) may be revoked for any taxable year beginning before the expiration of the 9th taxable year following the taxable year for which such election first applies only with the consent of the Secretary; and

(B) may be revoked for any taxable year beginning after the expiration of such 9th taxable year without the consent of the Secretary.

Amendments

• **1990, Omnibus Budget Reconciliation Act of 1990 (P.L. 101-508)**

P.L. 101-508, §11704(a)(11):

Amended Code Sec. 936(e)(1) by striking "subsection (a)(1)" each place it appears and inserting "subsection (a)(2)". **Effective** 11-5-90.

[Sec. 936(f)]

(f) LIMITATION ON CREDIT FOR DISC'S AND FSC'S.—No credit shall be allowed under this section to a corporation for any taxable year—

(1) for which it is a DISC or former DISC, or

(2) in which it owns at any time stock in a—

(A) DISC or former DISC, or

(B) former FSC.

Amendments

• **2007, Tax Technical Corrections Act of 2007 (P.L. 110-172)**

P.L. 110-172, §11(g)(12):

Amended Code Sec. 936(f)(2)(B) by striking "FSC or" before "former FSC". **Effective** 12-29-2007.

• **1984, Deficit Reduction Act of 1984 (P.L. 98-369)**

P.L. 98-369, §801(d)(11):

Amended Code Sec. 936(f). **Effective** for transactions after 12-31-84, in tax years ending after such date. Prior to amendment, Act Sec. 936(f) read as follows:

(f) DISC or Former DISC Corporation Ineligible for Creidt.—No credit shall be allowed under this section to a corporation for a taxable year for which it is a DISC or former DISC (as defined in section 992(a)) or in which it owns at any time stock in a DISC or former DISC.

[Sec. 936(g)]

(g) EXCEPTION TO ACCUMULATED EARNINGS TAX.—

(1) For purposes of section 535, the term "accumulated taxable income" shall not include taxable income entitled to the credit under subsection (a).

(2) For purposes of section 537, the term "reasonable needs of the business" includes assets which produce income eligible for the credit under subsection (a).

Amendments

• **1976, Tax Reform Act of 1976 (P.L. 94-455)**

P.L. 94-455, §1051(b):

Added Code Sec. 936. **Effective** for tax years beginning after 12-31-75.

[Sec. 936(h)]

(h) TAX TREATMENT OF INTANGIBLE PROPERTY INCOME.—

(1) IN GENERAL.—

(A) INCOME ATTRIBUTABLE TO SHAREHOLDERS.—The intangible property income of a corporation electing the application of this section for any taxable year shall be included on a pro rata basis in the gross income of all shareholders of such electing corporation at the close of the taxable year of such electing corporation as income from sources within the United States for the taxable year of such shareholder in which or with which the taxable year of such electing corporation ends.

(B) EXCLUSION FROM THE INCOME OF AN ELECTING CORPORATION.—Any intangible property income of a corporation electing the application of this section which is included in the gross income of a shareholder of such corporation by reason of subparagraph (A) shall be excluded from the gross income of such corporation.

(2) FOREIGN SHAREHOLDERS; SHAREHOLDERS NOT SUBJECT TO TAX.—

(A) IN GENERAL.—Paragraph (1)(A) shall not apply with respect to any shareholder—

(i) who is not a United States person, or

(ii) who is not subject to tax under this title on intangible property income which would be allocated to such shareholder (but for this subparagraph).

(B) TREATMENT OF NONALLOCATED INTANGIBLE PROPERTY INCOME.—For purposes of this subtitle, intangible property income of a corporation electing the application of this section which is not included in the gross income of a shareholder of such corporation by reason of subparagraph (A)—

(i) shall be treated as income from sources within the United States, and

(ii) shall not be taken into account under subsection (a)(2).

(3) INTANGIBLE PROPERTY INCOME.—For purposes of this subsection—

(A) IN GENERAL.—The term "intangible property income" means the gross income of a corporation attributable to any intangible property other than intangible property which has been licensed to such corporation since prior to 1948 and is in use by such corporation on the date of the enactment of this subparagraph.

(B) INTANGIBLE PROPERTY.—The term "intangible property" means any—

(i) patent, invention, formula, process, design, pattern, or knowhow;

(ii) copyright, literary, musical, or artistic composition;

(iii) trademark, trade name, or brand name;

(iv) franchise, license, or contract;

(v) method, program, system, procedure, campaign, survey, study, forecast, estimate, customer list, or technical data;

(vi) any goodwill, going concern value, or workforce in place (including its composition and terms and conditions (contractual or otherwise) of its employment); or

(vii) any other item the value or potential value of which is not attributable to tangible property or the services of any individual.

(C) EXCLUSION OF REASONABLE PROFIT.—The term "intangible property income" shall not include any portion of the income from the sale, exchange or other disposition of any product, or from the rendering of services, by a corporation electing the application of this section which is determined by the Secretary to be a reasonable profit on the direct and indirect costs incurred by such electing corporation which are attributable to such income.

(D) RELATED PERSON.—

(i) IN GENERAL.—A person (hereinafter referred to as the "related person") is related to any person if—

(I) the related person bears a relationship to such person specified in section 267(b) or section 707(b)(1), or

(II) the related person and such person are members of the same controlled group of corporations.

INCOME TAX—U.S. POSSESSIONS

(ii) SPECIAL RULE.—For purposes of clause (i), section 267(b) and section 707(b)(1) shall be applied by substituting "10 percent" for "50 percent".

(E) CONTROLLED GROUP OF CORPORATIONS.—The term "controlled group of corporations" has the meaning given to such term by section 1563(a), except that—

(i) "more than 10 percent" shall be substituted for "at least 80 percent" and "more than 50 percent" each place either appears in section 1563(a), and

(ii) the determination shall be made without regard to subsections (a)(4), (b)(2), and (e)(3)(C) of section 1563.

(4) DISTRIBUTIONS TO MEET QUALIFICATION REQUIREMENTS.—

(A) IN GENERAL.—If the Secretary determines that a corporation does not satisfy a condition specified in subparagraph (A) or (B) of subsection (a)(2) for any taxable year by reason of the exclusion from gross income under paragraph (1)(B), such corporation shall nevertheless be treated as satisfying such condition for such year if it makes a pro rata distribution of property after the close of such taxable year to its shareholders (designated at the time of such distribution as a distribution to meet qualification requirements) with respect to their stock in an amount which is equal to—

(i) if the condition of subsection (a)(2)(A) is not satisfied, that portion of the gross income for the period described in subsection (a)(2)(A)—

(I) which was not derived from sources within a possession, and

(II) which exceeds the amount of such income for such period which would enable such corporation to satisfy the condition of subsection (a)(2)(A),

(ii) if the condition of subsection (a)(2)(B) is not satisfied, that portion of the gross income for such period—

(I) which was not derived from the active conduct of a trade or business within a possession, and

(II) which exceeds the amount of such income for such period which would enable such corporation to satisfy the conditions of subsection (a)(2)(B), or

(iii) if neither of such conditions is satisfied, that portion of the gross income which exceeds the amount of gross income for such period which would enable such corporation to satisfy the conditions of subparagraphs (A) and (B) of subsection (a)(2).

(B) EFFECTIVELY CONNECTED INCOME.—In the case of a shareholder who is a nonresident alien individual or a foreign corporation, trust, or estate, any distribution described in subparagraph (A) shall be treated as income which is effectively connected with the conduct of a trade or business conducted through a permanent establishment of such shareholder within the United States.

(C) DISTRIBUTION DENIED IN CASE OF FRAUD OR WILLFUL NEGLECT.—Subparagraph (A) shall not apply to a corporation if the determination of the Secretary described in subparagraph (A) contains a finding that the failure of such corporation to satisfy the conditions in subsection (a)(2) was due in whole or in part to fraud with intent to evade tax or willful neglect on the part of such corporation.

(5) ELECTION OUT.—

(A) IN GENERAL.—The rules contained in paragraphs (1) through (4) do not apply for any taxable year if an election pursuant to subparagraph (F) is in effect to use one of the methods specified in subparagraph (C).

(B) ELIGIBILITY.—

(i) REQUIREMENT OF SIGNIFICANT BUSINESS PRESENCE.—An election may be made to use one of the methods specified in subparagraph (C) with respect to a product or type of service only if an electing corporation has a significant business presence in a possession with respect to such product or type of service. An election may remain in effect with respect to such product or type of service for any subsequent taxable year only if such electing corporation maintains a significant business presence in a possession with respect to such product or type of service in such subsequent taxable year. If an election is not in effect for a taxable year because of the preceding sentence, the electing corporation shall be deemed to have revoked the election on the first day of such taxable year.

(ii) DEFINITION.—For purposes of this subparagraph, an electing corporation has a "significant business presence" in a possession for a taxable year with respect to a product or type of service if:

(I) the total production costs (other than direct material costs and other than interest excluded by regulations prescribed by the Secretary) incurred by the electing corporation in the possession in producing units of that product sold or otherwise disposed of during the taxable year by the affiliated group to persons who are not members of the affiliated group are not less than 25 percent of the difference between (a) the gross receipts from sales or other dispositions during the taxable year by the affiliated group to persons who are not members of the affiliated group of such units of the product produced, in whole or in part, by the electing corporation in the possession, and (b) the direct material costs of the purchase of materials for such units of that product by all members of the affiliated group from persons who are not members of the affiliated group; or

(II) no less than 65 percent of the direct labor costs of the affiliated group for units of the product produced during the taxable year in whole or in part by the electing corporation or for the type of service rendered by the electing corporation during the taxable year, is incurred by the electing corporation and is compensation for services performed in the possession; or

(III) with respect to purchases and sales by an electing corporation of all goods not produced in whole or in part by any member of the affiliated group and sold by the electing corporation to persons other than members of the affiliated group, no less than 65 percent of the total direct labor costs of the affiliated group in connection with all purchases and sales of such goods sold during the taxable year by such electing corporation is incurred by such electing corporation and is compensation for services performed in the possession.

Notwithstanding satisfaction of one of the foregoing tests, an electing corporation shall not be treated as having a significant business presence in a possession with respect to a product produced in whole or in part by the electing corporation in the possession, for purposes of an election to use the method specified in subparagraph (C)(ii), unless such product is manufactured or produced in the possession by the electing corporation within the meaning of subsection (d)(1)(A) of section 954.

(iii) SPECIAL RULES.—

(I) An electing corporation which produces a product or renders a type of service in a possession on the date of the enactment of this clause is not required to meet the significant business presence test in a possession with respect to such product or type of service for its taxable years beginning before January 1, 1986.

(II) For purposes of this subparagraph, the costs incurred by an electing corporation or any other member f the affiliated group in connection with contract manufacturing by a person other than a member of the affiliated group, or in connection with a similar arrangement thereto, shall be treated as direct labor costs of the affiliated group and shall not be treated as production costs incurred by the electing corporation in the possession or as direct material costs or as compensation for services performed in the possession, except to the extent as may be otherwise provided in regulations prescribed by the Secretary.

(iv) REGULATIONS.—The Secretary may prescribe regulations setting forth:

(I) an appropriate transitional (but not in excess of three taxable years) significant business presence test for commencement in a possession of operations with respect to products or types of service after the date of the enactment of this clause and not described in subparagraph (B)(iii)(I),

(II) a significant business presence test for other appropriate cases, consistent with the tests specified in subparagraph (B)(ii),

(III) rules for the definition of a product or type of service, and

(IV) rules for treating components produced in whole or in part by a related person as materials, and the costs (including direct labor costs) related thereto as a cost of materials, where there is an independent resale price for such components or where otherwise consistent with the intent of the substantial business presence tests.

(C) METHODS OF COMPUTATION OF TAXABLE INCOME.—If an election of one of the following methods is in effect pursuant to subparagraph (F) with respect to a product or type of service, an electing corporation shall compute its income derived from the active conduct of a trade or business in a possession with respect to such product or type of service in accordance with the method which is elected.

(i) COST SHARING.—

(I) PAYMENT OF COST SHARING.—If an election of this method is in effect, the electing corporation must make a payment for its share of the cost (if any) of product area research which is paid or accrued by the affiliated group during that taxable year. Such share shall not be less than the same proportion of 110 percent of the cost of such product area research which the amount of "possession sales" bears to the amount of "total sales" of the affiliated group. The cost of product area research paid or accrued solely by the electing corporation in a taxable year (excluding amounts paid directly or indirectly to or on behalf of related persons and excluding amounts paid under any cost sharing agreements with related persons) will reduce (but not below zero) the amount of the electing corporation's cost sharing payment under this method for that year. In the case of intangible property described in subsection (h)(3)(B)(i) which the electing corporation is treated as owning under subclause (II), in no event shall the payment required under this subclause be less than the inclusion or payment which would be required under section 367(d)(2)(A)(ii) or section 482 if the electing corporation were a foreign corporation.

(a) PRODUCT AREA RESEARCH.—For purposes of this section, the term "product area research" includes (notwithstanding any provision to the contrary) the research, development and experimental costs, losses, expenses and other related deductions—including amounts paid or accrued for the performance of research or similar activities by another person; qualified research expenses within the meaning of section 41(b); amounts paid or accrued for the use of, or the right to use, research or any of the items specified in subsection (h)(3)(B)(i); and a proper allowance for amounts incurred for the acquisition of any of the items specified in subsection (h)(3)(B)(i)—which are properly apportioned or allocated to the same product area as that in which the electing corporation conducts its activities, and a ratable part of any such costs, losses, expenses and other deductions which cannot definitely be allocated to a particular product area.

(b) AFFILIATED GROUP.—For purposes of this subsection, the term "affiliated group" shall mean the electing corporation and all other organizations, trades or businesses (whether or not incorporated, whether or not organized in the United States, and whether or not affiliated) owned or controlled directly or indirectly by the same interests, within the meaning of section 482.

(c) POSSESSION SALES.—For purposes of this section, the term "possession sales" means the aggregate sales or other dispositions for the taxable year to persons who are not members of the affiliated group by members of the affiliated group of products produced, in whole or in part, by the electing corporation in the possession which are in the same product area as is used for determining the amount of product area research, and of services rendered, in whole or in part, in the possession in such product area to persons who are not members of the affiliated group.

(d) TOTAL SALES.—For purposes of this section, the term "total sales" means the aggregate sales or other dispositions for the taxable year to persons who are not members of the affiliated group by members of the affiliated group of all products in the same product area as is used for determining the amount of product area research, and of services rendered in such product area to persons who are not members of the affiliated group.

(e) PRODUCT AREA.—For purposes of this section, the term "product area" shall be defined by reference to the three-digit classification of the Standard Industrial Classification code. The Secretary may provide for the aggregation of two or more three-digit classifications where appropriate, and for a classification system other than the Standard Industrial Classification code in appropriate cases.

(II) EFFECT OF ELECTION.—For purposes of determining the amount of its gross income derived from the active conduct of a trade or business in a possession with respect to a product produced by, or type of service rendered by, the electing corporation for a taxable year, if an election of this method is in effect, the electing corporation shall be treated as the owner (for purposes of obtaining a return thereon) of intangible property described in subsection (h)(3)(B)(i) which is related to the units of the product produced, or type of service rendered, by the electing corporation. Such electing corporation shall not be treated as the owner (for purposes of obtaining a return thereon) of any intangible property described in subsection (h)(3)(B)(ii)

Sec. 936—Stricken

through (v) (to the extent not described in subsection (h)(3)(B)(i)) or of any other nonmanufacturing intangible. Notwithstanding the preceding sentence, an electing corporation shall be treated as the owner (for purposes of obtaining a return thereon) of (a) intangible property which was developed solely by such corporation in a possession and is owned by such corporation, (b) intangible property described in subsection (h)(3)(B)(i) acquired by such corporation from a person who was not related to such corporation (or to any person related to such corporation) at the time of, or in connection with, such acquisition, and (c) any intangible property described in subsection (h)(3)(B)(ii) through (v) (to the extent not described in subsection (h)(3)(B)(i)) and other nonmanufacturing intangibles which relate to sales of units of products, or services rendered, to unrelated persons for ultimate consumption or use in the possession in which the electing corporation conducts its trade or business.

(III) PAYMENT PROVISIONS.—

(a) The cost sharing payment determined under subparagraph (C)(i)(I) for any taxable year shall be made to the person or persons specified in subparagraph (C)(i)(IV)(a) not later than the time prescribed by law for filing the electing corporation's return for such taxable year (including any extensions thereof). If all or part of such payment is not timely made, the amount of the cost sharing payment required to be paid shall be increased by the amount of interest that would have been due under section 6601(a) had the portion of the cost sharing payment that is not timely made been an amount of tax imposed by this title and had the last date prescribed for payment been the due date of the electing corporations return (determined without regard to any extension thereof). The amount by which a cost sharing payment determined under subparagraph (C)(i)(I) is increased by reason of the preceding sentence shall not be treated as a cost sharing payment or as interest. If failure to make timely payment is due in whole or in part to fraud or willful neglect, the electing corporation shall be deemed to have revoked the election made under subparagraph (A) on the first day of the taxable year for which the cost sharing payment was required.

(b) For purposes of this title, any tax of a foreign country or possession of the United States which is paid or accrued with respect to the payment or receipt of a cost sharing payment determined under subparagraph (C)(i)(I) or of an amount of increase referred to in subparagraph (C)(i)(III)(a) shall not be treated as income, war profits, or excess profits taxes paid or accrued to a foreign country or possession of the United States, and no deduction shall be allowed under this title with respect to any amounts of such tax so paid or accrued.

(IV) SPECIAL RULES.—

(a) The amount of the cost sharing payment determined under subparagraph (C)(i)(I), and any increase in the amount thereof in accordance with subparagraph (C)(i)(III)(a), shall not be treated as income of the recipient, but shall reduce the amount of the deductions (and the amount of reductions in earnings and profits) otherwise allowable to the appropriate domestic member or members (other than an electing corporation) of the affiliated group, or, if there is no such domestic member, to the foreign member or members of such affiliated group as the Secretary may provide under regulations.

(b) If an election of this method is in effect, the electing corporation shall determine its intercompany pricing under the appropriate section 482 method, provided, however, that an electing corporation shall not be denied use of the resale price method for purposes of such intercompany pricing merely because the reseller adds more than an insubstantial amount to the value of the product by the use of intangible property.

(c) The amount of qualified research expenses, within the meaning of section 41, of any member of the controlled group of corporations (as defined in section 41(f)) of which the electing corporation is a member shall not be affected by the cost sharing payment required under this method.

(ii) PROFIT SPLIT.—

(I) GENERAL RULE.—If an election of this method is in effect, the electing corporation's taxable income derived from the active conduct of a trade or business in a possession with respect to units of a product produced or type of service rendered, in whole or in part, by the electing corporation shall be equal to 50 percent of the combined taxable income of the affiliated group (other than foreign affiliates) derived from covered sales of units of the product produced or type of service rendered, in whole or in part, by the electing corporation in a possession.

(II) COMPUTATION OF COMBINED TAXABLE INCOME.—Combined taxable income shall be computed separately for each product produced or type of service rendered, in whole or in part, by the electing corporation in a possession. Combined taxable income shall be computed (notwithstanding any provision to the contrary) for each such product or type of service rendered by deducting from the gross income of the affiliated group (other than foreign affiliates) derived from covered sales of such product or type of service all expenses, losses, and other deductions properly apportioned or allocated to gross income from such sales or services, and a ratable part of all expenses, losses, or other deductions which cannot definitely be allocated to some item or class of gross income, which are incurred by the affiliated group (other than foreign affiliates). Notwithstanding any other provision to the contrary, in computing the combined taxable income for each such product or type of service rendered, the research, development, and experimental costs, expenses and related deductions for the taxable year which would otherwise be apportioned or allocated to the gross income of the affiliated group (other than foreign affiliates) derived from covered sales of such product produced or type of service rendered, in whole or in part, by the electing corporation in a possession, shall not be less than the same proportion of the amount of the share of product area research determined under subparagraph (C)(i)(I) (without regard to the third and fourth sentences thereof, by substituting "120 percent" for "110 percent" in the second sentence thereof) in the product area which includes such product or type of service, that such gross income from the product or type of service bears to such gross income from all products and types of services, within such product area, produced or rendered, in whole or part, by the electing corporation in a possession.

(III) DIVISION OF COMBINED TAXABLE INCOME.—50 percent of the combined taxable income computed as provided in subparagraph (C)(ii)(II) shall be allocated to the electing corporation. Combined taxable income, computed without regard to the last sentence of subparagraph (C)(ii)(II), less the amount allocated to the electing corporation, under the preceding sentence, shall be allocated to the appropriate domestic member or members (other than any electing corporation) of the affiliated group and shall be treated as income from sources within the United States, or, if there is no such domestic member, to a foreign member or members of such affiliated group as the Secretary may provide under regulations.

(IV) COVERED SALES.—For purposes of this paragraph, the term "covered sales" means sales by members of the affiliated group (other than foreign affiliates) to persons who are not members of the affiliated group or to foreign affiliates.

(D) UNRELATED PERSON.—For purposes of this paragraph, the term "unrelated person" means any person other than a person related within the meaning of paragraph (3)(D) to the electing corporation.

(E) ELECTING CORPORATION.—For purposes of this subsection, the term "electing corporation" means a domestic corporation for which an election under this section is in effect.

(F) TIME AND MANNER OF ELECTION; REVOCATION.—

(i) IN GENERAL.—An election under subparagraph (A) to use one of the methods under subparagraph (C) shall be made only on or before the due date prescribed by law (including extensions) for filing the tax return of the electing corporation for its first taxable year beginning after December 31, 1982. If an election of one of such methods is made, such election shall be binding on the electing corporation and such method must be used for each taxable year thereafter until such election is revoked by the electing corporation under subparagraph (F)(iii). If any such election is revoked by the electing corporation under subparagraph (F)(iii), such electing corporation may make a subsequent election under subparagraph (A) only with the consent of the Secretary.

(ii) MANNER OF MAKING ELECTION.—An election under subparagraph (A) to use one of the methods under subparagraph (C) shall be made by filing a statement to such effect with the return referred to in subparagraph (F)(i) or in such other manner as the Secretary may prescribe by regulations.

(iii) REVOCATION.—

(I) Except as provided in subparagraph (F)(iii)(II), an election may be revoked for any taxable year only with the consent of the Secretary.

(II) An election shall be deemed revoked for the year in which the electing corporation is deemed to have revoked such election under subparagraph (B)(i) or (C) (i)(III)(a).

(iv) AGGREGATION.—

(I) Where more than one electing corporation in the affiliated group produces any product or renders any services in the same product area, all such electing corporations must elect to compute their taxable income under the same method under subparagraph (C).

(II) All electing corporations in the same affiliated group that produce any products or render any services in the same product area may elect, subject to such terms and conditions as the Secretary may prescribe by regulations, to compute their taxable income from export sales under a different method from that used for all other sales and services. For this purpose, export sales means all sales by the electing corporation of products to foreign persons for use or consumption outside the United States and its possessions, provided such products are manufactured or produced in the possession within the meaning of subsection (d)(1)(A) of section 954, and further provided (except to the extent otherwise provided by regulations) the income derived by such foreign person on resale of such products (in the same state or in an altered state) is not included in foreign base company income for purposes of section 954(a).

(III) All members of an affiliated group must consent to an election under this subsection at such time and in such manner as shall be prescribed by the Secretary by regulations.

(6) TREATMENT OF CERTAIN SALES MADE AFTER JULY 1, 1982.—

(A) IN GENERAL.—For purposes of this section, in the case of a disposition of intangible property made by a corporation after July 1, 1982, any gain or loss from such disposition shall be treated as gain or loss from sources within the United States to which paragraph (5) does not apply.

(B) EXCEPTION.—Subparagraph (A) shall not apply to any disposition by a corporation of intangible property if such disposition is to a person who is not a related person to such corporation.

(C) PARAGRAPH DOES NOT AFFECT ELIGIBILITY.—This paragraph shall not apply for purposes of determining whether the corporation meets the requirements of subsection (a)(2).

(7) SECTION 864(e)(1) NOT TO APPLY.—This subsection shall be applied as if section 864(e)(1) (relating to treatment of affiliated groups) had not been enacted.

(8) REGULATIONS.—The Secretary shall prescribe such regulations as may be necessary or appropriate to carry out the purposes of this subsection, including rules for the application of this subsection to income from leasing of products to unrelated persons.

Amendments

• **2017, Tax Cuts and Jobs Act (P.L. 115-97)**

P.L. 115-97, § 14221(a)(1)-(3):

Amended Code Sec. 936(h)(3)(B) by striking "or" at the end of clause (v), by striking clause (vi) and inserting new clauses (vi) and (vii), and by striking the flush language after clause (vii), as added by Act Sec. 14221(a)(2). **Effective** generally for transfers in tax years beginning after 12-31-2017. For a special rule, see Act Sec. 14221(c)(2), below. Prior to being stricken, Code Sec. 936(h)(3)(B)(vi) and the flush language after new Code Sec. 936(h)(3)(B)(vii) read as follows:

(vi) any similar item,

which has substantial value independent of the services of any individual.

P.L. 115-97, § 14221(c)(2), provides:

(2) NO INFERENCE.—Nothing in the amendment made by subsection (a) shall be construed to create any inference with respect to the application of section 936(h)(3) of the Internal Revenue Code of 1986, or the authority of the Secretary of the Treasury to provide regulations for such application, with respect to taxable years beginning before January 1, 2018.

INCOME TAX—U.S. POSSESSIONS

• **1988, Technical and Miscellaneous Revenue Act of 1988 (P.L. 100-647)**

P.L. 100-647, §1002(h)(3)(A)-(B):

Amended Code Sec. 936(h)(5)(C)(i)(IV)(c) by striking out "section 30" and inserting in lieu thereof "section 41", and by striking out "section 30(f)" and inserting in lieu thereof "section 41(f)". **Effective** as if included in the provision of P.L. 99-514 to which it relates.

P.L. 100-647, §1012(h)(2)(B):

Amended Code Sec. 936(h) by redesignating paragraph (7) as paragraph (8) and by inserting after paragraph (6) new paragraph (7). **Effective** as if included in the provision of P.L. 99-514 to which it relates.

• **1986, Tax Reform Act of 1986 (P.L. 99-514)**

P.L. 99-514, §231(d)(3)(G):

Amended Code Sec. 936(h)(5)(C)(i)(I)(a) by striking out "section 30(b)" and inserting in lieu thereof "section 41(b)". **Effective** for tax years beginning after 12-31-85.

P.L. 99-514, §1231(a)(1)(A)-(B):

Amended Code Sec. 936(h)(5)(C)(i)(I) by striking out "the same proportion of the cost" and inserting in lieu thereof "the same proportion of 110 percent of the cost", and by adding at the end thereof the above new sentence. **Effective**, generally, for tax years beginning after 12-31-86. However, see Act Sec. 1231(g)(4) following Code Sec. 936(a), for a special rule.

P.L. 99-514, §1231(a)(2):

Amended Code Sec. 936(h)(5)(C)(ii)(II) by striking out "the third sentence thereof" and inserting in lieu thereof "the third and fourth sentences thereof, by substituting `120 percent' for `110 percent' in the second sentence thereof)". **Effective**, generally, for tax years beginning after 12-31-86. However, see Act Sec. 1231(g)(4) following Code Sec. 936(a), for a special rule.

P.L. 99-514, §1231(f):

Amended Code Sec. 936(h)(5)(C)(ii)(II) by striking out "all products produced and types of service rendered" and inserting in lieu thereof "all products and types of services, within such product area, produced or rendered". **Effective** for tax years beginning after 12-31-82.

P.L. 99-514, §1812(c)(4)(C):

Amended Code Sec. 936(h)(3)(D)(ii). **Effective** as if included in the provision of P.L. 96-369 to which it relates. Prior to amendment, Code Sec. 936(h)(3)(D)(ii) read as follows:

(ii) SPECIAL RULES.—For purposes of clause (i)—

(I) section 267(b) and section 707(b)(1) shall be applied by substituting "10 percent" for "50 percent", and

(II) section 267(b)(3) shall be applied without regard to whether a person was a personal holding company or a foreign personal holding company.

• **1984, Deficit Reduction Act of 1984 (P.L. 98-369)**

P.L. 98-369, §474(r)(22)(A)-(B):

Amended Code Sec. 936(h)(5)(C)(i)(I)(a) by striking out "section 44F(b)" and inserting in lieu thereof "section 30(b)", and amended Code Sec. 936(h)(5)(C)(i)(IV)(c) by striking out "section 44F" and inserting in lieu thereof "section 30", and by striking out "section 44F(f)" and inserting in lieu thereof "section 30(f)". **Effective** for tax years beginning after 12-31-83, and to carrybacks from such years.

• **1982, Tax Equity and Fiscal Responsibility Act of 1982 (P.L. 97-248)**

P.L. 97-248, §213(a)(2):

Amended Code Sec. 936 by adding at the end thereof new subsection (h). **Effective** for tax years beginning after 12-31-82. Paragraph (6) of section 936(h) of the Internal Revenue Code of 1954, and so much of section 934 to which such paragraph applies by reason of section 934(e)(4) of such Code, shall apply to tax years ending after 7-1-82.

[Sec. 936(i)]

(i) DEFINITIONS AND SPECIAL RULES RELATING TO LIMITATIONS OF SUBSECTION (a)(4).—

(1) QUALIFIED POSSESSION WAGES.—For purposes of this section—

(A) IN GENERAL.—The term "qualified possession wages" paid or incurred by the possession corporation during the taxable year in connection with the active conduct of a trade or business within a possession of the United States to any employee for services performed in such possession, but only if such services are performed while the principal place of employment of such employee is within such possession.

(B) LIMITATION ON AMOUNT OF WAGES TAKEN INTO ACCOUNT.—

(i) IN GENERAL.—The amount of wages which may be taken into account under subparagraph (A) with respect to any employee for any taxable year shall not exceed 85 percent of the contribution and benefit base determined under section 230 of the Social Security Act for the calendar year in which such taxable year begins.

(ii) TREATMENT OF PART-TIME EMPLOYEES, ETC.—If—

(I) any employee is not employed by the possession corporation on a substantially full-time basis at all times during the taxable year, or

(II) the principal place of employment of any employee with the possession corporation is not within a possession at all times during the taxable year,

the limitation applicable under clause (i) with respect to such employee shall be the appropriate portion (as determined by the Secretary) of the limitation which would otherwise be in effect under clause (i).

(C) TREATMENT OF CERTAIN EMPLOYEES.—The term "qualified possession wages" shall not include any wages paid to employees who are assigned by the employer to perform services for another person, unless the principal trade or business of the employer is to make employees available for temporary periods to other persons in return for compensation. All possession corporations treated as 1 corporation under paragraph (5) shall be treated as 1 employer for purposes of the preceding sentence.

Sec. 936—Stricken

(D) WAGES.—

(i) IN GENERAL.—Except as provided in clause (ii), the term "wages" has the meaning given to such term by subsection (b) of section 3306 (determined without regard to any dollar limitation contained in such section). For purposes of the preceding sentence, such subsection (b) shall be applied as if the term "United States" included all possessions of the United States.

(ii) SPECIAL RULE FOR AGRICULTURAL LABOR AND RAILWAY LABOR.—In any case to which subparagraph (A) or (B) of paragraph (1) of section 51(h) applies, the term "wages" has the meaning given to such term by section 51(h)(2).

(2) ALLOCABLE EMPLOYEE FRINGE BENEFIT EXPENSES.—

(A) IN GENERAL.—The allocable employee fringe benefit expenses of any possession corporation for any taxable year is an amount which bears the same ratio to the amount determined under subparagraph (B) for such taxable year as—

(i) the aggregate amount of the possession corporation's qualified possession wages for such taxable year, bears to

(ii) the aggregate amount of the wages paid or incurred by such possession corporation during such taxable year.

In no event shall the amount determined under the preceding sentence exceed 15 percent of the amount referred to in clause (i).

(B) EXPENSES TAKEN INTO ACCOUNT.—For purposes of subparagraph (A), the amount determined under this subparagraph for any taxable year is the aggregate amount allowable as a deduction under this chapter to the possession corporation for such taxable year with respect to—

(i) employer contributions under a stock bonus, pension, profit-sharing, or annuity plan,

(ii) employer-provided coverage under any accident or health plan for employees, and

(iii) the cost of life or disability insurance provided to employees.

Any amount treated as wages under paragraph (1)(D) shall not be taken into account under this subparagraph.

(3) TREATMENT OF POSSESSION TAXES.—

(A) AMOUNT OF CREDIT FOR POSSESSION CORPORATIONS NOT USING PROFIT SPLIT.—

(i) IN GENERAL.—For purposes of subsection (a)(4)(A)(iii), the amount of the qualified possession income taxes for any taxable year allocable to nonsheltered income shall be an amount which bears the same ratio to the possession income taxes for such taxable year as—

(I) the increase in the tax liability of the possession corporation under this chapter for the taxable year by reason of subsection (a)(4)(A) (without regard to clause (iii) thereof), bears to

(II) the tax liability of the possession corporation under this chapter for the taxable year determined without regard to the credit allowable under this section.

(ii) LIMITATION ON AMOUNT OF TAXES TAKEN INTO ACCOUNT.—Possession income taxes shall not be taken into account under clause (i) for any taxable year to the extent that the amount of such taxes exceeds 9 percent of the amount of the taxable income for such taxable year.

(B) DEDUCTION FOR POSSESSION CORPORATIONS USING PROFIT SPLIT.—Notwithstanding subsection (c), if a possession corporation is not described in subsection (a)(4)(A)(iii) for the taxable year, such possession corporation shall be allowed a deduction for such taxable year in an amount which bears the same ration to the possession income taxes for such taxable year as—

(i) the increase in the tax liability of the possession corporation under this chapter for the taxable year by reason of subsection (a)(4)(A), bears to

(ii) the tax liability of the possession corporation under this chapter for the taxable year determined without regard to the credit allowable under this section.

In determining the credit under subsection (a) and in applying the preceding sentence, taxable income shall be determined without regard to the preceding sentence.

(C) POSSESSION INCOME TAXES.—For purposes of this paragraph, the term "possession income taxes" means any taxes of a possession of the United States which are treated as not being income, war profits, or excess profits taxes paid or accrued to a possession of the United States by reason of subsection (c).

(4) DEPRECIATION RULES.—For purposes of this section—

(A) DEPRECIATION ALLOWANCES.—The term "depreciation allowances" means the depreciation deductions allowable under section 167 to the possession corporation.

(B) CATEGORIES OF PROPERTY.—

(i) QUALIFIED TANGIBLE PROPERTY.—The term "qualified tangible property" means any tangible property used by the possession corporation in a possession of the United States in the active conduct of a trade or business within such possession.

(ii) SHORT-LIFE QUALIFIED TANGIBLE PROPERTY.—The term "short-life qualified tangible property" means any qualified tangible property to which section 168 applies and which is 3-year property or 5-year property for purposes of such section.

(iii) MEDIUM-LIFE QUALIFIED TANGIBLE PROPERTY.—The term "medium-life qualified tangible property" means any qualified tangible property to which section 168 applies and which is 7-year property or 10-year property for purposes of such section.

(iv) LONG-LIFE QUALIFIED TANGIBLE PROPERTY.—The term "long-life qualified tangible property" means any qualified tangible property to which section 168 applies and which is not described in clause (ii) or (iii).

(v) TRANSITIONAL RULE.—In the case of any qualified tangible property to which section 168 (as in effect on the day before the date of the enactment of the Tax Reform Act of 1986) applies, any reference in this paragraph to section 168 shall be treated as a reference to such section as so in effect.

(5) ELECTION TO COMPUTE CREDIT ON CONSOLIDATED BASIS.—

(A) IN GENERAL.—Any affiliated group may elect to treat all possession corporations which would be members of such group but for section 1504(b)(3) or (4) as 1 corporation for purposes of this section. The credit determined under this section

INCOME TAX—U.S. POSSESSIONS

with respect to such 1 corporation shall be allocated among such possession corporations in such manner as the Secretary may prescribe.

(B) ELECTION.—An election under subparagraph (A) shall apply to the taxable year for which made and all succeeding taxable years unless revoked with the consent of the Secretary.

(6) POSSESSION CORPORATION.—The term "possession corporation" means a domestic corporation for which the election provided in subsection (a) is in effect.

Amendments

• **1993, Omnibus Budget Reconciliation Act of 1993 (P.L. 103-66)**

P.L. 103-66, §13227(b):

Amended Code Sec. 936 by adding at the end thereof a new subsection (j). **Effective** for tax years beginning after 12-31-93.

[Sec. 936(j)]

(j) TERMINATION.—

(1) IN GENERAL.—Except as otherwise provided in this subsection, this section shall not apply to any taxable year beginning after December 31, 1995.

(2) TRANSITION RULES FOR ACTIVE BUSINESS INCOME CREDIT.—Except as provided in paragraph (3)—

(A) ECONOMIC ACTIVITY CREDIT.—In the case of an existing credit claimant—

(i) with respect to a possession other than Puerto Rico, and

(ii) to which subsection (a)(4)(B) does not apply,

the credit determined under subsection (a)(1)(A) shall be allowed for taxable years beginning after December 31, 1995, and before January 1, 2002.

(B) SPECIAL RULE FOR REDUCED CREDIT.—

(i) IN GENERAL.—In the case of an existing credit claimant to which subsection (a)(4)(B) applies, the credit determined under subsection (a)(1)(A) shall be allowed for taxable years beginning after December 31, 1995, and before January 1, 1998.

(ii) ELECTION IRREVOCABLE AFTER 1997.—An election under subsection (a)(4)(B)(iii) which is in effect for the taxpayer's last taxable year beginning before 1997 may not be revoked unless it is revoked for the taxpayer's first taxable year beginning in 1997 and all subsequent taxable years.

(C) ECONOMIC ACTIVITY CREDIT FOR PUERTO RICO.—For economic activity credit for Puerto Rico, see section 30A.

(3) ADDITIONAL RESTRICTED CREDIT.—

(A) IN GENERAL.—In the case of an existing credit claimant—

(i) the credit under subsection (a)(1)(A) shall be allowed for the period beginning with the first taxable year after the last taxable year to which subparagraph (A) or (B) of paragraph (2), whichever is appropriate, applied and ending with the last taxable year beginning before January 1, 2006, except that

(ii) the aggregate amount of taxable income taken into account under subsection (a)(1)(A) for any such taxable year shall not exceed the adjusted base period income of such claimant.

(B) COORDINATION WITH SUBSECTION (a)(4).—The amount of income described in subsection (a)(1)(A) which is taken into account in applying subsection (a)(4) shall be such income as reduced under this paragraph.

(4) ADJUSTED BASE PERIOD INCOME.—For purposes of paragraph (3)—

(A) IN GENERAL.—The term "adjusted base period income" means the average of the inflation-adjusted possession incomes of the corporation for each base period year.

(B) INFLATION-ADJUSTED POSSESSION INCOME.—For purposes of subparagraph (A), the inflation-adjusted possession income of any corporation for any base period year shall be an amount equal to the sum of—

(i) the possession income of such corporation for such base period year, plus

(ii) such possession income multiplied by the inflation adjustment percentage for such base period year.

(C) INFLATION ADJUSTMENT PERCENTAGE.—For purposes of subparagraph (B), the inflation adjustment percentage for any base period year means the percentage (if any) by which—

(i) the CPI for 1995, exceeds

(ii) the CPI for the calendar year in which the base period year for which the determination is being made ends.

For purposes of the preceding sentence, the CPI for any calendar year is the CPI (as defined in section 1(f)(5)) for such year under section 1(f)(4).

(D) INCREASE IN INFLATION ADJUSTMENT PERCENTAGE FOR GROWTH DURING BASE YEARS.—The inflation adjustment percentage (determined under subparagraph (C) without regard to this subparagraph) for each of the 5 taxable years referred to in paragraph (5)(A) shall be increased by—

(i) 5 percentage points in the case of a taxable year ending during the 1-year period ending on October 13, 1995;

(ii) 10.25 percentage points in the case of a taxable year ending during the 1-year period ending on October 13, 1994;

(iii) 15.76 percentage points in the case of a taxable year ending during the 1-year period ending on October 13, 1993;

(iv) 21.55 percentage points in the case of a taxable year ending during the 1-year period ending on October 13, 1992; and

(v) 27.63 percentage points in the case of a taxable year ending during the 1-year period ending on October 13, 1991.

(5) BASE PERIOD YEAR.—For purposes of this subsection—

(A) IN GENERAL.—The term "base period year" means each of 3 taxable years which are among the 5 most recent taxable years of the corporation ending before October 14, 1995, determined by disregarding—

(i) one taxable year for which the corporation had the largest inflation-adjusted possession income, and

(ii) one taxable year for which the corporation had the smallest inflation-adjusted possession income.

(B) CORPORATIONS NOT HAVING SIGNIFICANT POSSESSION INCOME THROUGHOUT 5-YEAR PERIOD.—

(i) IN GENERAL.—If a corporation does not have significant possession income for each of the most recent 5 taxable years ending before October 14, 1995, then, in lieu of applying subparagraph (A), the term "base period year" means only those taxable years (of such 5 taxable years) for which the corporation has significant possession income; except that, if such corporation has significant possession income for 4 of such 5 taxable years, the rule of subparagraph (A)(ii) shall apply.

(ii) SPECIAL RULE.—If there is no year (of such 5 taxable years) for which a corporation has significant possession income—

(I) the term "base period year" means the first taxable year ending on or after October 14, 1995, but

(II) the amount of possession income for such year which is taken into account under paragraph (4) shall be the amount which would be determined if such year were a short taxable year ending on September 30, 1995.

(iii) SIGNIFICANT POSSESSION INCOME.—For purposes of this subparagraph, the term "significant possession income" means possession income which exceeds 2 percent of the possession income of the taxpayer for the taxable year (of the period of 6 taxable years ending with the first taxable year ending on or after October 14, 1995) having the greatest possession income.

(C) ELECTION TO USE ONE BASE PERIOD YEAR.—

(i) IN GENERAL.—At the election of the taxpayer, the term "base period year" means—

(I) only the last taxable year of the corporation ending in calendar year 1992, or

(II) a deemed taxable year which includes the first ten months of calendar year 1995.

(ii) BASE PERIOD INCOME FOR 1995.—In determining the adjusted base period income of the corporation for the deemed taxable year under clause (i)(II), the possession income shall be annualized and shall be determined without regard to any extraordinary item.

(iii) ELECTION.—An election under this subparagraph by any possession corporation may be made only for the corporation's first taxable year beginning after December 31, 1995, for which it is a possession corporation. The rules of subclauses (II) and (III) of subsection (a)(4)(B)(iii) shall apply to the election under this subparagraph.

(D) ACQUISITIONS AND DISPOSITIONS.—Rules similar to the rules of subparagraphs (A) and (B) of section 41(f)(3) shall apply for purposes of this subsection.

(6) POSSESSION INCOME.—For purposes of this subsection, the term "possession income" means, with respect to any possession, the income referred to in subsection (a)(1)(A) determined with respect to that possession. In no event shall possession income be treated as being less than zero.

(7) SHORT YEARS.—If the current year or a base period year is a short taxable year, the application of this subsection shall be made with such annualizations as the Secretary shall prescribe.

(8) SPECIAL RULES FOR CERTAIN POSSESSIONS.—

(A) IN GENERAL.—In the case of an existing credit claimant with respect to an applicable possession, this section (other than the preceding paragraphs of this subsection) shall apply to such claimant with respect to such applicable possession for taxable years beginning after December 31, 1995, and before January 1, 2006.

(B) APPLICABLE POSSESSION.—For purposes of this paragraph, the term "applicable possession" means Guam, American Samoa, and the Commonwealth of the Northern Mariana Islands.

(9) EXISTING CREDIT CLAIMANT.—For purposes of this subsection—

(A) IN GENERAL.—The term "existing credit claimant" means a corporation—

(i)(I) which was actively conducting a trade or business in a possession on October 13, 1995, and

(II) with respect to which an election under this section is in effect for the corporation's taxable year which includes October 13, 1995, or

(ii) which acquired all of the assets of a trade or business of a corporation which—

(I) satisfied the requirements of subclause (I) of clause (i) with respect to such trade or business, and

(II) satisfied the requirements of subclause (II) of clause (i).

(B) NEW LINES OF BUSINESS PROHIBITED.—If, after October 13, 1995, a corporation which would (but for this subparagraph) be an existing credit claimant adds a substantial new line of business (other than in an acquisition described in subparagraph (A)(ii)), such corporation shall cease to be treated as an existing credit claimant as of the close of the taxable year ending before the date of such addition.

(C) BINDING CONTRACT EXCEPTION.—If, on October 13, 1995, and at all times thereafter, there is in effect with respect to a corporation a binding contract for the acquisition of assets to be used in, or for the sale of assets to be produced from, a trade or business, the corporation shall be treated for purposes of this paragraph as actively conducting such trade or business on October 13, 1995. The preceding sentence shall not apply if such trade or business is not actively conducted before January 1, 1996.

(10) SEPARATE APPLICATION TO EACH POSSESSION.—For purposes of determining—

(A) whether a taxpayer is an existing credit claimant, and

(B) the amount of the credit allowed under this section,

this subsection (and so much of this section as relates to this subsection) shall be applied separately with respect to each possession.

Amendments

• **2006, Tax Relief and Health Care Act of 2006 (P.L. 109-432)**

P.L. 109-432, Div. A, §119 (as amended by P.L. 110-343, Div. C, §309(a)(1)-(2), P.L. 111-312, §756(a)(1)-(2), P.L. 112-240, §330, P.L. 113-295, §141(a), Div. A, P.L. 114-113, §173(a), Div. Q, P.L. 115-123, §40312(a)(1)-(2), Div. D, P.L. 116-94, §119(a)-(b), Div. Q, and P.L. 116-260, §139, Div. EE) provides:

SEC. 119. AMERICAN SAMOA ECONOMIC DEVELOPMENT CREDIT.

INCOME TAX—U.S. POSSESSIONS

(a) IN GENERAL.—For purposes of section 30A of the Internal Revenue Code of 1986, a domestic corporation shall be treated as a qualified domestic corporation to which such section applies if—

(1) in the case of a taxable year beginning before January 1, 2012, such corporation—

(A) is an existing credit claimant with respect to American Samoa, and

(B) elected the application of section 936 of the Internal Revenue Code of 1986 for its last taxable year beginning before January 1, 2006, and

(2) in the case of a taxable year beginning after December 31, 2011, such corporation meets the requirements of subsection (e).

(b) SPECIAL RULES FOR APPLICATION OF SECTION.—The following rules shall apply in applying section 30A of the Internal Revenue Code of 1986 for purposes of this section:

(1) AMOUNT OF CREDIT.—Notwithstanding section 30A(a)(1) of such Code, the amount of the credit determined under section 30A(a)(1) of such Code for any taxable year shall be the amount determined under section 30A(d) of such Code, except that section 30A(d) shall be applied without regard to paragraph (3) thereof.

(2) SEPARATE APPLICATION.—In applying section 30A(a)(3) of such Code in the case of a corporation treated as a qualified domestic corporation by reason of this section, section 30A of such Code (and so much of section 936 of such Code as relates to such section 30A) shall be applied separately with respect to American Samoa.

(3) FOREIGN TAX CREDIT ALLOWED.—Notwithstanding section 30A(e) of such Code, the provisions of section 936(c) of such Code shall not apply with respect to the credit allowed by reason of this section.

(c) DEFINITIONS.—For purposes of this section, any term which is used in this section which is also used in section 30A or 936 of such Code shall have the same meaning given such term by such section 30A or 936.

(d) APPLICATION OF SECTION.—Notwithstanding section 30A(h) or section 936(j) of such Code, this section (and so much of section 30A and section 936 of such Code as relates to this section) shall apply—

(1) in the case of a corporation that meets the requirements of subparagraphs (A) and (B) of subsection (a)(1), to the first 16 taxable years of such corporation which begin after December 31, 2006, and before January 1, 2022, and

(2) in the case of a corporation that does not meet the requirements of subparagraphs (A) and (B) of subsection (a)(1), to the first 10 taxable years of such corporation which begin after December 31, 2011, and before January 1, 2022.

In the case of a corporation described in subsection (a)(2), the Internal Revenue Code of 1986 shall be applied and administered without regard to the amendments made by section 401(d)(1) of the Tax Technical Corrections Act of 2018.

(e) QUALIFIED PRODUCTION ACTIVITIES INCOME REQUIREMENT.—A corporation meets the requirement of this subsection if such corporation has qualified production activities income, as defined in subsection (c) of section 199 of the Internal Revenue Code of 1986 (as in effect before its repeal), determined by substituting "American Samoa" for "the United States" each place it appears in paragraphs (3), (4), and (6) of such subsection (c), for the taxable year. References in this subsection to section 199 of the Internal Revenue Code of 1986 (as in effect before its repeal) shall be treated as references to such section in effect before its repeal.

• **1996, Small Business Job Protection Act of 1996 (P.L. 104-188)**

P.L. 104-188, § 1601(a):

Amended Code Sec. 936 by adding at the end a new subsection (j). **Effective** for tax years beginning after 12-31-95. For special rules, see Act Sec. 1601(c)(2)-(3), below.

P.L. 104-188, § 1601(c)(2)-(3), provides:

(2) SPECIAL RULE FOR QUALIFIED POSSESSION SOURCE INVESTMENT INCOME.—The amendments made by this section shall not apply to qualified possession source investment income received or accrued before July 1, 1996, without regard to the taxable year in which received or accrued.

(3) SPECIAL TRANSITION RULE FOR PAYMENT OF ESTIMATED TAX INSTALLMENT.—In determining the amount of any installment due under section 6655 of the Internal Revenue Code of 1986 after the date of the enactment of this Act and before October 1, 1996, only 1/2 of any increase in tax (for the taxable year for which such installment is made) by reason of the amendments made by subsections (a) and (b) shall be taken into account. Any reduction in such installment by reason of the preceding sentence shall be recaptured by increasing the next required installment for such year by the amount of such reduction.

P.L. 115-141, § 401(e), Div. U, provides:

(e) GENERAL SAVINGS PROVISION WITH RESPECT TO DEADWOOD PROVISIONS.—If—

(1) any provision amended or repealed by the amendments made by subsection (b) or (d) applied to—

(A) any transaction occurring before the date of the enactment of this Act,

(B) any property acquired before such date of enactment, or

(C) any item of income, loss, deduction, or credit taken into account before such date of enactment, and

(2) the treatment of such transaction, property, or item under such provision would (without regard to the amendments or repeals made by such subsection) affect the liability for tax for periods ending after such date of enactment,

nothing in the amendments or repeals made by this section shall be construed to affect the treatment of such transaction, property, or item for purposes of determining liability for tax for periods ending after such date of enactment.

[Sec. 937]

SEC. 937. RESIDENCE AND SOURCE RULES INVOLVING POSSESSIONS.

[Sec. 937(a)]

(a) BONA FIDE RESIDENT.—For purposes of this subpart, section 865(g)(3), section 876, section 881(b), paragraphs (2) and (3) of section 901(b), section 957(c), section 3401(a)(8)(C), and section 7654(a), except as provided in regulations, the term "bona fide resident" means a person—

(1) who is present for at least 183 days during the taxable year in Guam, American Samoa, the Northern Mariana Islands, Puerto Rico, or the Virgin Islands, as the case may be, and

(2) who does not have a tax home (determined under the principles of section 911(d)(3) without regard to the second sentence thereof) outside such specified possession during the taxable year and does not have a closer connection (determined under the principles of section 7701(b)(3)(B)(ii)) to the United States or a foreign country than to such specified possession.

For purposes of paragraph (1), the determination as to whether a person is present for any day shall be made under the principles of section 7701(b).

[Sec. 937(b)]

(b) SOURCE RULES.—Except as provided in regulations, for purposes of this title—

(1) except as provided in paragraph (2), rules similar to the rules for determining whether income is income from sources within the United States or is effectively connected with the conduct of a trade or business within the United States shall apply for purposes of determining whether income is from sources within a possession specified in subsection (a)(1) or effectively connected with the conduct of a trade or business within any such possession, and

(2) any income treated as income from sources within the United States or as effectively connected with the conduct of a trade or business within the United States shall not be treated as income from sources within any such possession or as effectively connected with the conduct of a trade or business within any such possession.

[Sec. 937(c)]

(c) REPORTING REQUIREMENT.—

(1) IN GENERAL.—If, for any taxable year, an individual takes the position for United States income tax reporting purposes that the individual became, or ceases to be, a bona fide resident of a possession specified in subsection (a)(1), such individual shall file with the Secretary, at such time and in such manner as the Secretary may prescribe, notice of such position.

(2) TRANSITION RULE.—If, for any of an individual's 3 taxable years ending before the individual's first taxable year ending after the date of the enactment of this subsection, the individual took a position described in paragraph (1), the individual shall file with the Secretary, at such time and in such manner as the Secretary may prescribe, notice of such position.

Amendments

• **2004, American Jobs Creation Act of 2004 (P.L. 108-357)**

P.L. 108-357, § 908(a):

Amended subpart D of part III of subchapter N of chapter 1 by adding at the end new Code Sec. 937. **Effective** generally for tax years ending after 10-22-2004. For special rules, see Act Sec. 908(d)(2)-(3), below.

P.L. 108-357, § 908(d)(2)-(3), provides:

(2) 183-DAY RULE.—Section 937(a)(1) of the Internal Revenue Code of 1986 (as added by this section) shall apply to taxable years beginning after 10-22-2004.

(3) SOURCING.—Section 937(b)(2) of such Code (as so added) shall apply to income earned after 10-22-2004.

INCOME TAX—FOREIGN TRADE INCOME

Subpart E—Qualifying Foreign Trade Income—[Repealed]

[Sec. 941—Repealed]

Amendments

- **2004, American Jobs Creation Act of 2004 (P.L. 108-357)**

P.L. 108-357, §101(b)(1):

Repealed subpart E of part III of subchapter N of chapter 1 (Code Secs. 941-943). **Effective** for transactions after 12-31-2004. For transitional and special rules, see Act Sec. 101(d)-(f), below.

P.L. 108-357, §101(d)-(f) (as amended by P.L. 113-295, §219(a), Division A), provides:

(d) TRANSITIONAL RULE FOR 2005 AND 2006.—

(1) IN GENERAL.—In the case of transactions during 2005 or 2006, the amount includible in gross income by reason of the amendments made by this section shall not exceed the applicable percentage of the amount which would have been so included but for this subsection.

(2) APPLICABLE PERCENTAGE.—For purposes of paragraph (1), the applicable percentage shall be as follows:

(A) For 2005, the applicable percentage shall be 20 percent.

(B) For 2006, the applicable percentage shall be 40 percent.

(3) COORDINATION WITH SECTION 199.—This subsection shall be applied without regard to any deduction allowable under section 199.

(e) REVOCATION OF ELECTION TO BE TREATED AS DOMESTIC CORPORATION.—If, during the 1-year period beginning on the date of the enactment of this Act, a corporation for which an election is in effect under section 943(e) of the Internal Revenue Code of 1986 revokes such election, no gain or loss shall be recognized with respect to property treated as transferred under clause (ii) of section 943(e)(4)(B) of such Code to the extent such property—

(1) was treated as transferred under clause (i) thereof, or

(2) was acquired during a taxable year to which such election applies and before May 1, 2003, in the ordinary course of its trade or business.

The Secretary of the Treasury (or such Secretary's delegate) may prescribe such regulations as may be necessary to prevent the abuse of the purposes of this subsection.

[Note: Act Sec. 101(f) of P.L. 108-357, below, was stricken by P.L. 109-222, §513(b), applicable to tax years beginning after 5-17-2006.—CCH.]

(f) BINDING CONTRACTS.—The amendments made by this section shall not apply to any transaction in the ordinary course of a trade or business which occurs pursuant to a binding contract—

(1) which is between the taxpayer and a person who is not a related person (as defined in section 943(b)(3) of such Code, as in effect on the day before the date of the enactment of this Act), and

(2) which is in effect on September 17, 2003, and at all times thereafter.

For purposes of this subsection, a binding contract shall include a purchase option, renewal option, or replacement option which is included in such contract and which is enforceable against the seller or lessor.

Prior to repeal, Code Sec. 941 read as follows:

SEC. 941. QUALIFYING FOREIGN TRADE INCOME.

[Sec. 941(a)]

(a) QUALIFYING FOREIGN TRADE INCOME.—For purposes of this subpart and section 114—

(1) IN GENERAL.—The term "qualifying foreign trade income" means, with respect to any transaction, the amount of gross income which, if excluded, will result in a reduction of the taxable income of the taxpayer from such transaction equal to the greatest of—

(A) 30 percent of the foreign sale and leasing income derived by the taxpayer from such transaction,

(B) 1.2 percent of the foreign trading gross receipts derived by the taxpayer from the transaction, or

(C) 15 percent of the foreign trade income derived by the taxpayer from the transaction.

In no event shall the amount determined under subparagraph (B) exceed 200 percent of the amount determined under subparagraph (C).

(2) ALTERNATIVE COMPUTATION.—A taxpayer may compute its qualifying foreign trade income under a subparagraph of paragraph (1) other than the subparagraph which results in the greatest amount of such income.

(3) LIMITATION ON USE OF FOREIGN TRADING GROSS RECEIPTS METHOD.—If any person computes its qualifying foreign trade income from any transaction with respect to any property under paragraph (1)(B), the qualifying foreign trade income of such person (or any related person) with respect to any other transaction involving such property shall be zero.

(4) RULES FOR MARGINAL COSTING.—The Secretary shall prescribe regulations setting forth rules for the allocation of expenditures in computing foreign trade income under paragraph (1)(C) in those cases where a taxpayer is seeking to establish or maintain a market for qualifying foreign trade property.

(5) PARTICIPATION IN INTERNATIONAL BOYCOTTS, ETC.—Under regulations prescribed by the Secretary, the qualifying foreign trade income of a taxpayer for any taxable year shall be reduced (but not below zero) by the sum of—

(A) an amount equal to such income multiplied by the international boycott factor determined under section 999, and

(B) any illegal bribe, kickback, or other payment (within the meaning of section 162(c)) paid by or on behalf of the taxpayer directly or indirectly to an official, employee, or agent in fact of a government.

[Sec. 941(b)]

(b) FOREIGN TRADE INCOME.—For purposes of this subpart—

(1) IN GENERAL.—The term "foreign trade income" means the taxable income of the taxpayer attributable to foreign trading gross receipts of the taxpayer.

(2) SPECIAL RULE FOR COOPERATIVES.—In any case in which an organization to which part I of subchapter T applies which is engaged in the marketing of agricultural or horticultural products sells qualifying foreign trade property, in computing the taxable income of such cooperative, there shall not be taken into account any deduction allowable under subsection (b) or (c) of section 1382 (relating to patronage dividends, per-unit retain allocations, and nonpatronage distributions).

[Sec. 941(c)]

(c) FOREIGN SALE AND LEASING INCOME.—For purposes of this section—

(1) IN GENERAL.—The term "foreign sale and leasing income" means, with respect to any transaction—

(A) foreign trade income properly allocable to activities which—

(i) are described in paragraph (2)(A)(i) or (3) of section 942(b), and

(ii) are performed by the taxpayer (or any person acting under a contract with such taxpayer) outside the United States, or

(B) foreign trade income derived by the taxpayer in connection with the lease or rental of qualifying foreign trade property for use by the lessee outside the United States.

(2) SPECIAL RULES FOR LEASED PROPERTY.—

(A) SALES INCOME.—The term "foreign sale and leasing income" includes any foreign trade income derived by the taxpayer from the sale of property described in paragraph (1)(B).

(B) LIMITATION IN CERTAIN CASES.—Except as provided in regulations, in the case of property which—

(i) was manufactured, produced, grown, or extracted by the taxpayer, or

(ii) was acquired by the taxpayer from a related person for a price which was not determined in accordance with the rules of section 482,

the amount of foreign trade income which may be treated as foreign sale and leasing income under paragraph (1)(B) or subparagraph (A) of this paragraph with respect to any transaction involving such property shall not exceed the amount which would have been determined if the taxpayer had acquired such property for the price determined in accordance with the rules of section 482.

(3) SPECIAL RULES.—

(A) EXCLUDED PROPERTY.—Foreign sale and leasing income shall not include any income properly allocable to excluded property described in subparagraph (B) of section 943(a)(3) (relating to intangibles).

(B) ONLY DIRECT EXPENSES TAKEN INTO ACCOUNT.—For purposes of this subsection, any expense other than a directly allocable expense shall not be taken into account in computing foreign trade income.

Amendments

- **2000, FSC Repeal and Extraterritorial Income Exclusion Act of 2000 (P.L. 106-519)**

P.L. 106-519, §3(b):

Amended part III of subchapter N of chapter 1 by inserting after subpart D a new subpart E (Code Secs. 941-943). **Effective** generally for transactions after 9-30-2000. For special rules, see Act Sec. 5(b)-(d) in the amendment notes following Code Sec. 921.

[Sec. 941—Repealed]

Amendments

- **1976, Tax Reform Act of 1971 (P.L. 94-455)**

P.L. 94-455, §1053(c):

Repealed Code Sec. 941. **Effective** for tax years beginning after 12-31-77. Prior to repeal, Code Sec. 941 read as follows:

SEC. 941. SPECIAL DEDUCTION FOR CHINA TRADE ACT CORPORATIONS.

[Sec. 941(a)]

(a) ALLOWANCE OF DEDUCTION.—For purposes only of the taxes imposed by section 11, there shall be allowed, in the case of a corporation organized under the China Trade Act, 1922 (15 U.S.C. ch. 4, sec. 141 and following), in addition to the deductions from taxable income otherwise allowed such corporation, a special deduction, in computing the taxable income, of an amount equal to the proportion of the taxable income derived from sources within Formosa and Hong Kong (determined without regard to this section and determined in a similar manner to that provided in part I) which the par value of the shares of stock of the corporation owned on the last day of the taxable year by—

(1) persons resident in Formosa, Hong Kong, the United States, or possessions of the United States, and

(2) individual citizens of the United States wherever resident,

bears to the par value of the whole number of shares of stock of the corporation outstanding on such date. In no case shall the diminution, by reason of such special deduction, of the taxes imposed by section 11 (computed without regard to this section) exceed the amount of the special dividend certified under subsection (b) of this section.

[Sec. 941(b)]

(b) SPECIAL DIVIDEND.—The special deduction provided in subsection (a) shall not be allowed unless the Secretary of Commerce has certified to the Secretary of the Treasury—

INCOME TAX—FOREIGN TRADE INCOME

(1) the amount which, during the year ending on the date fixed by law for filing the return, the corporation has distributed as a special dividend to or for the benefit of such persons as on the last day of the taxable year were resident in Formosa, Hong Kong, the United States, or possessions of the United States, or were individual citizens of the United States, and owned shares of stock of the corporation;

(2) that such special dividend was in addition to all other amounts, payable or to be payable to such persons or for their benefit, by reason of their interest in the corporation; and

(3) that such distribution has been made to or for the benefit of such persons in proportion to the par value of the shares of stock of the corporation owned by each; except that if the corporation has more than one class of stock, the certificates shall contain a statement that the articles of incorporation provide a method for the apportionment of such special dividend among such persons, and that the amount certified has been distributed in accordance with the method so provided.

Amendments

• **1976, Tax Reform Act of 1976 (P.L. 94-455)**

P.L. 94-455, §1906(b)(13)(A):

Amended 1954 Code by substituting "Secretary" for "Secretary or his delegate" each place it appeared. **Effective** 2-1-77.

[Sec. 941(c)]

(c) OWNERSHIP OF STOCK.—For purposes of this section, shares of stock of a corporation shall be considered to be owned by the person in whom the equitable right to the income from such shares is in good faith vested.

[Sec. 941(d)]

(d) PHASEOUT OF DEDUCTION.—In the case of a taxable year beginning after December 31, 1975, and before January 1, 1978, the amount of the special deduction under subsection (a) (determined without regard to this subsection) shall be reduced by the percentage reduction specified in the following table:

For a taxable year beginning in:	The percentage reduction shall be—
1976	$33^{1}/_{3}$
1977	$66^{2}/_{3}$

Amendments

• **1976, Tax Reform Act of 1976 (P.L. 94-455)**

P.L. 94-455, §1053(a):

Added Code Sec. 941(d). **Effective** for tax years beginning after 12-31-75.

[Sec. 942—Repealed]

Amendments

• **2004, American Jobs Creation Act of 2004 (P.L. 108-357)**

P.L. 108-357, §101(b)(1):

Repealed subpart E of part III of subchapter N of chapter 1 (Code Secs. 941-943). **Effective** for transactions after 12-31-2004. For transitional and special rules, see Act Sec. 101(d)-(f), below.

P.L. 108-357, §101(d)-(f) (as amended by P.L. 113-295, §219(a), Division A), provides:

(d) TRANSITIONAL RULE FOR 2005 AND 2006.—

(1) IN GENERAL.—In the case of transactions during 2005 or 2006, the amount includible in gross income by reason of the amendments made by this section shall not exceed the applicable percentage of the amount which would have been so included but for this subsection.

(2) APPLICABLE PERCENTAGE.—For purposes of paragraph (1), the applicable percentage shall be as follows:

(A) For 2005, the applicable percentage shall be 20 percent.

(B) For 2006, the applicable percentage shall be 40 percent.

(3) COORDINATION WITH SECTION 199.—This subsection shall be applied without regard to any deduction allowable under section 199.

(e) REVOCATION OF ELECTION TO BE TREATED AS DOMESTIC CORPORATION.—If, during the 1-year period beginning on the date of the enactment of this Act, a corporation for which an election is in effect under section 943(e) of the Internal Revenue Code of 1986 revokes such election, no gain or loss shall be recognized with respect to property treated as transferred under clause (ii) of section 943(e)(4)(B) of such Code to the extent such property—

(1) was treated as transferred under clause (i) thereof, or

(2) was acquired during a taxable year to which such election applies and before May 1, 2003, in the ordinary course of its trade or business.

The Secretary of the Treasury (or such Secretary's delegate) may prescribe such regulations as may be necessary to prevent the abuse of the purposes of this subsection.

[**Note:** Act Sec. 101(f) of P.L. 108-357, below, was stricken by P.L. 109-222, §513(b), applicable to tax years beginning after 5-17-2006.—CCH.]

(f) BINDING CONTRACTS.—The amendments made by this section shall not apply to any transaction in the ordinary course of a trade or business which occurs pursuant to a binding contract—

(1) which is between the taxpayer and a person who is not a related person (as defined in section 943(b)(3) of such Code, as in effect on the day before the date of the enactment of this Act), and

(2) which is in effect on September 17, 2003, and at all times thereafter.

For purposes of this subsection, a binding contract shall include a purchase option, renewal option, or replacement option which is included in such contract and which is enforceable against the seller or lessor.

Prior to repeal, Code Sec. 942 read as follows:

SEC. 942. FOREIGN TRADING GROSS RECEIPTS.

[Sec. 942(a)]

(a) FOREIGN TRADING GROSS RECEIPTS.—

(1) IN GENERAL.—Except as otherwise provided in this section, for purposes of this subpart, the term "foreign trading gross receipts" means the gross receipts of the taxpayer which are—

(A) from the sale, exchange, or other disposition of qualifying foreign trade property,

(B) from the lease or rental of qualifying foreign trade property for use by the lessee outside the United States,

(C) for services which are related and subsidiary to—

(i) any sale, exchange, or other disposition of qualifying foreign trade property by such taxpayer, or

(ii) any lease or rental of qualifying foreign trade property described in subparagraph (B) by such taxpayer,

(D) for engineering or architectural services for construction projects located (or proposed for location) outside the United States, or

(E) for the performance of managerial services for a person other than a related person in furtherance of the production of foreign trading gross receipts described in subparagraph (A), (B), or (C).

Subparagraph (E) shall not apply to a taxpayer for any taxable year unless at least 50 percent of its foreign trading gross receipts (determined without regard to this sentence) for such taxable year is derived from activities described in subparagraph (A), (B), or (C).

(2) CERTAIN RECEIPTS EXCLUDED ON BASIS OF USE; SUBSIDIZED RECEIPTS EXCLUDED.—The term "foreign trading gross receipts" shall not include receipts of a taxpayer from a transaction if—

(A) the qualifying foreign trade property or services—

(i) are for ultimate use in the United States, or

(ii) are for use by the United States or any instrumentality thereof and such use of qualifying foreign trade property or services is required by law or regulation, or

(B) such transaction is accomplished by a subsidy granted by the government (or any instrumentality thereof) of the country or possession in which the property is manufactured, produced, grown, or extracted.

(3) ELECTION TO EXCLUDE CERTAIN RECEIPTS.—The term "foreign trading gross receipts" shall not include gross receipts of a taxpayer from a transaction if the taxpayer elects not to have such receipts taken into account for purposes of this subpart.

[Sec. 942(b)]

(b) FOREIGN ECONOMIC PROCESS REQUIREMENTS.—

(1) IN GENERAL.—Except as provided in subsection (c), a taxpayer shall be treated as having foreign trading gross receipts from any transaction only if economic processes with respect to such transaction take place outside the United States as required by paragraph (2).

(2) REQUIREMENT.—

(A) IN GENERAL.—The requirements of this paragraph are met with respect to the gross receipts of a taxpayer derived from any transaction if—

(i) such taxpayer (or any person acting under a contract with such taxpayer) has participated outside the United States in the solicitation (other than advertising), the negotiation, or the making of the contract relating to such transaction, and

(ii) the foreign direct costs incurred by the taxpayer attributable to the transaction equal or exceed 50 percent of the total direct costs attributable to the transaction.

(B) ALTERNATIVE 85-PERCENT TEST.—A taxpayer shall be treated as satisfying the requirements of subparagraph (A)(ii) with respect to any transaction if, with respect to each of at least 2 subparagraphs of paragraph (3), the foreign direct costs incurred by such taxpayer attributable to activities described in such subparagraph equal or exceed 85 percent of the total direct costs attributable to activities described in such subparagraph.

(C) DEFINITIONS.—For purposes of this paragraph—

(i) TOTAL DIRECT COSTS.—The term "total direct costs" means, with respect to any transaction, the total direct costs incurred by the taxpayer attributable to activities described in paragraph (3) performed at any location by the taxpayer or any person acting under a contract with such taxpayer.

(ii) FOREIGN DIRECT COSTS.—The term "foreign direct costs" means, with respect to any transaction, the portion of the total direct costs which are attributable to activities performed outside the United States.

(3) ACTIVITIES RELATING TO QUALIFYING FOREIGN TRADE PROPERTY.—The activities described in this paragraph are any of the following with respect to qualifying foreign trade property—

(A) advertising and sales promotion,

(B) the processing of customer orders and the arranging for delivery,

(C) transportation outside the United States in connection with delivery to the customer,

(D) the determination and transmittal of a final invoice or statement of account or the receipt of payment, and

(E) the assumption of credit risk.

INCOME TAX—FOREIGN TRADE INCOME

(4) ECONOMIC PROCESSES PERFORMED BY RELATED PERSONS.—A taxpayer shall be treated as meeting the requirements of this subsection with respect to any sales transaction involving any property if any related person has met such requirements in such transaction or any other sales transaction involving such property.

[Sec. 942(c)]

(c) EXCEPTION FROM FOREIGN ECONOMIC PROCESS REQUIREMENT.—

(1) IN GENERAL.—The requirements of subsection (b) shall be treated as met for any taxable year if the foreign trading gross receipts of the taxpayer for such year do not exceed $5,000,000.

(2) RECEIPTS OF RELATED PERSONS AGGREGATED.—All related persons shall be treated as one person for purposes of paragraph (1), and the limitation under paragraph (1) shall be allocated among such persons in a manner provided in regulations prescribed by the Secretary.

Amendments

• 1976, Tax Reform Act of 1976 (P.L. 94-455)

P.L. 94-455, §1053(c):

Repealed Code Sec. 942. **Effective** for tax years beginning after 12-31-77. Prior to repeal, Code Sec. 942 read as follows:

Amendments

• 2004, American Jobs Creation Act of 2004 (P.L. 108-357)

P.L. 108-357, §101(b)(1):

Repealed subpart E of part III of subchapter N of chapter 1 (Code Secs. 941-943). **Effective** for transactions after 12-31-2004. For transitional and special rules, see Act Sec. 101(d)-(f), below.

P.L. 108-357, §101(d)-(f) (as amended by P.L. 113-295, §219(a), Division A), provides:

(d) TRANSITIONAL RULE FOR 2005 AND 2006.—

(1) IN GENERAL.—In the case of transactions during 2005 or 2006, the amount includible in gross income by reason of the amendments made by this section shall not exceed the applicable percentage of the amount which would have been so included but for this subsection.

(2) APPLICABLE PERCENTAGE.—For purposes of paragraph (1), the applicable percentage shall be as follows:

(A) For 2005, the applicable percentage shall be 20 percent.

(B) For 2006, the applicable percentage shall be 40 percent.

(3) COORDINATION WITH SECTION 199.—This subsection shall be applied without regard to any deduction allowable under section 199.

(e) REVOCATION OF ELECTION TO BE TREATED AS DOMESTIC CORPORATION.—If, during the 1-year period beginning on the date of the enactment of this Act, a corporation for which an election is in effect under section 943(e) of the Internal Revenue Code of 1986 revokes such election, no gain or loss shall be recognized with respect to property treated as transferred under clause (ii) of section 943(e)(4)(B) of such Code to the extent such property—

(1) was treated as transferred under clause (i) thereof, or

(2) was acquired during a taxable year to which such election applies and before May 1, 2003, in the ordinary course of its trade or business.

The Secretary of the Treasury (or such Secretary's delegate) may prescribe such regulations as may be necessary to prevent the abuse of the purposes of this subsection.

[Note: Act Sec. 101(f) of P.L. 108-357, below, was stricken by P.L. 109-222, §513(b), applicable to tax years beginning after 5-17-2006.—CCH.]

(f) BINDING CONTRACTS.—The amendments made by this section shall not apply to any transaction in the ordinary course of a trade or business which occurs pursuant to a binding contract—

(1) which is between the taxpayer and a person who is not a related person (as defined in section 943(b)(3) of such Code, as in effect on the day before the date of the enactment of this Act), and

(2) which is in effect on September 17, 2003, and at all times thereafter.

For purposes of this subsection, a binding contract shall include a purchase option, renewal option, or replacement option which is included in such contract and which is enforceable against the seller or lessor.

Prior to repeal, Code Sec. 943 read as follows:

SEC. 943. OTHER DEFINITIONS AND SPECIAL RULES.

[Sec. 943(a)]

(a) QUALIFYING FOREIGN TRADE PROPERTY.—For purposes of this subpart—

(1) IN GENERAL.—The term "qualifying foreign trade property" means property—

(A) manufactured, produced, grown, or extracted within or outside the United States,

(B) held primarily for sale, lease, or rental, in the ordinary course of trade or business for direct use, consumption, or disposition outside the United States, and

(C) not more than 50 percent of the fair market value of which is attributable to—

(i) articles manufactured, produced, grown, or extracted outside the United States, and

(ii) direct costs for labor (determined under the principles of section 263A) performed outside the United States.

For purposes of subparagraph (C), the fair market value of any article imported into the United States shall be its appraised value, as determined by the Secretary under section 402 of the Tariff Act of 1930 (19 U.S.C. 1401a) in connection with its importation, and the direct costs for labor under clause (ii) do not include costs that would be treated under the principles of section 263A as direct labor costs attributable to articles described in clause (i).

(3) SPECIAL RULE FOR PASS-THRU ENTITIES.—In the case of a partnership, S corporation, or other pass-thru entity, the limitation under paragraph (1) shall apply with respect to the partnership, S corporation, or entity and with respect to each partner, shareholder, or other owner.

Amendments

• 2000, FSC Repeal and Extraterritorial Income Exclusion Act of 2000 (P.L. 106-519)

P.L. 106-519, §3(b):

Amended part III of subchapter N of chapter 1 by inserting after subpart D a new subpart E (Code Secs. 941-943). **Effective** generally for transactions after 9-30-2000. For special rules, see Act Sec. 5(b)-(d) in the amendment notes following Code Sec. 921.

[Sec. 942—Repealed]

SEC. 942. DISALLOWANCE OF FOREIGN TAX CREDIT.

A corporation organized under the China Trade Act, 1922, shall not be allowed the credits against the tax for taxes of foreign countries and possessions of the United States allowed by section 901.

[Sec. 943—Repealed]

(2) U.S. TAXATION TO ENSURE CONSISTENT TREATMENT.—Property which (without regard to this paragraph) is qualifying foreign trade property and which is manufactured, produced, grown, or extracted outside the United States shall be treated as qualifying foreign trade property only if it is manufactured, produced, grown, or extracted by—

(A) a domestic corporation,

(B) an individual who is a citizen or resident of the United States,

(C) a foreign corporation with respect to which an election under subsection (e) (relating to foreign corporations electing to be subject to United States taxation) is in effect, or

(D) a partnership or other pass-thru entity all of the partners or owners of which are described in subparagraph (A), (B), or (C).

Except as otherwise provided by the Secretary, tiered partnerships or pass-thru entities shall be treated as described in subparagraph (D) if each of the partnerships or entities is directly or indirectly wholly owned by persons described in subparagraph (A), (B), or (C).

(3) EXCLUDED PROPERTY.—The term "qualifying foreign trade property" shall not include—

(A) property leased or rented by the taxpayer for use by any related person,

(B) patents, inventions, models, designs, formulas, or processes whether or not patented, copyrights (other than films, tapes, records, or similar reproductions, and other than computer software (whether or not patented), for commercial or home use), goodwill, trademarks, trade brands, franchises, or other like property,

(C) oil or gas (or any primary product thereof),

(D) products the transfer of which is prohibited or curtailed to effectuate the policy set forth in paragraph (2)(C) of section 3 of Public Law 96-72, or

(E) any unprocessed timber which is a softwood.

For purposes of subparagraph (E), the term "unprocessed timber" means any log, cant, or similar form of timber.

(4) PROPERTY IN SHORT SUPPLY.—If the President determines that the supply of any property described in paragraph (1) is insufficient to meet the requirements of the domestic economy, the President may by Executive order designate the property as in short supply. Any property so designated shall not be treated as qualifying foreign trade property during the period beginning with the date specified in the Executive order and ending with the date specified in an Executive order setting forth the President's determination that the property is no longer in short supply.

[Sec. 943(b)]

(b) OTHER DEFINITIONS AND RULES.—For purposes of this subpart—

(1) TRANSACTION.—

(A) IN GENERAL.—The term "transaction" means—

(i) any sale, exchange, or other disposition,

(ii) any lease or rental, and

(iii) any furnishing of services.

(B) GROUPING OF TRANSACTIONS.—To the extent provided in regulations, any provision of this subpart which, but for this subparagraph, would be applied on a transaction-by-transaction basis may be applied by the taxpayer on the basis of groups of transactions based on product lines or recognized industry or trade usage. Such regulations may permit different groupings for different purposes.

(2) UNITED STATES DEFINED.—The term "United States" includes the Commonwealth of Puerto Rico. The preceding sentence shall not apply for purposes of determining whether a corporation is a domestic corporation.

(3) RELATED PERSON.—A person shall be related to another person if such persons are treated as a single employer under subsection (a) or (b) of section 52 or subsection (m) or (o) of section 414, except that determinations under subsections (a) and (b) of section 52 shall be made without regard to section 1563(b).

(4) GROSS AND TAXABLE INCOME.—Section 114 shall not be taken into account in determining the amount of gross income or foreign trade income from any transaction.

[Sec. 943(c)]

(c) SOURCE RULE.—Under regulations, in the case of qualifying foreign trade property manufactured, produced, grown, or extracted within the United States, the amount of income of a taxpayer from any sales transaction with respect to such property which is treated as from sources without the United States shall not exceed—

INCOME TAX—FOREIGN TRADE INCOME

(1) in the case of a taxpayer computing its qualifying foreign trade income under section 941(a)(1)(B), the amount of the taxpayer's foreign trade income which would (but for this subsection) be treated as from sources without the United States if the foreign trade income were reduced by an amount equal to 4 percent of the foreign trading gross receipts with respect to the transaction, and

(2) in the case of a taxpayer computing its qualifying foreign trade income under section 941(a)(1)(C), 50 percent of the amount of the taxpayer's foreign trade income which would (but for this subsection) be treated as from sources without the United States.

[Sec. 943(d)]

(d) TREATMENT OF WITHHOLDING TAXES.—

(1) IN GENERAL.—For purposes of section 114(d), any withholding tax shall not be treated as paid or accrued with respect to extraterritorial income which is excluded from gross income under section 114(a). For purposes of this paragraph, the term "withholding tax" means any tax which is imposed on a basis other than residence and for which credit is allowable under section 901 or 903.

(2) EXCEPTION.—Paragraph (1) shall not apply to any taxpayer with respect to extraterritorial income from any transaction if the taxpayer computes its qualifying foreign trade income with respect to the transaction under section 941(a)(1)(A).

[Sec. 943(e)]

(e) ELECTION TO BE TREATED AS DOMESTIC CORPORATION.—

(1) IN GENERAL.—An applicable foreign corporation may elect to be treated as a domestic corporation for all purposes of this title if such corporation waives all benefits to such corporation granted by the United States under any treaty. No election under section 1362(a) may be made with respect to such corporation.

(2) APPLICABLE FOREIGN CORPORATION.—For purposes of paragraph (1), the term "applicable foreign corporation" means any foreign corporation if—

(A) such corporation manufactures, produces, grows, or extracts property in the ordinary course of such corporation's trade or business, or

(B) substantially all of the gross receipts of such corporation are foreign trading gross receipts.

(3) PERIOD OF ELECTION.—

(A) IN GENERAL.—Except as otherwise provided in this paragraph, an election under paragraph (1) shall apply to the taxable year for which made and all subsequent taxable years unless revoked by the taxpayer. Any revocation of such election shall apply to taxable years beginning after such revocation.

(B) TERMINATION.—If a corporation which made an election under paragraph (1) for any taxable year fails to meet the requirements of subparagraph (A) or (B) of paragraph (2) for any subsequent taxable year, such election shall not apply to any taxable year beginning after such subsequent taxable year.

(C) EEFFECT OF REVOCATION OR TERMINATION.—If a corporation which made an election under paragraph (1) revokes such election or such election is terminated under subparagraph (B), such corporation (and any successor corporation) may not make such election for any of the 5 taxable years beginning with the first taxable year for which such election is not in effect as a result of such revocation or termination.

(4) SPECIAL RULES.—

(A) REQUIREMENTS.—This subsection shall not apply to an applicable foreign corporation if such corporation fails to meet the requirements (if any) which the Secretary may prescribe to ensure that the taxes imposed by this chapter on such corporation are paid.

(B) EFFECT OF ELECTION, REVOCATION, AND TERMINATION.—

(i) ELECTION.—For purposes of section 367, a foreign corporation making an election under this subsection shall be treated as transferring (as of the first day of the first taxable year to which the election applies) all of its assets to a domestic corporation in connection with an exchange to which section 354 applies.

(ii) REVOCATION AND TERMINATION.—For purposes of section 367, if—

(I) an election is made by a corporation under paragraph (1) for any taxable year, and

(II) such election ceases to apply for any subsequent taxable year,

such corporation shall be treated as a domestic corporation transferring (as of the 1st day of the first such subsequent taxable year to which such election ceases to apply) all of its property to a foreign corporation in connection with an exchange to which section 354 applies.

(C) ELIGIBILITY FOR ELECTION.—The Secretary may by regulation designate one or more classes of corporations which may not make the election under this subsection.

Amendments

• 2002, Job Creation and Worker Assistance Act of 2002 (P.L. 107-147)

P.L. 107-147, § 417(14):

Amended Code Sec. 943(e)(4)(B) by aligning the left margin of the flush language with subparagraph (A). **Effective** 3-9-2002.

[Sec. 943(f)]

(f) RULES RELATING TO ALLOCATIONS OF QUALIFYING FOREIGN TRADE INCOME FROM SHARED PARTNERSHIPS.—

(1) IN GENERAL.—If—

(A) a partnership maintains a separate account for transactions (to which this subpart applies) with each partner,

(B) distributions to each partner with respect to such transactions are based on the amounts in the separate account maintained with respect to such partner, and

(C) such partnership meets such other requirements as the Secretary may by regulations prescribe,

then such partnership shall allocate to each partner items of income, gain, loss, and deduction (including qualifying foreign trade income) from any transaction to which this subpart applies on the basis of such separate account.

(2) SPECIAL RULES.—For purposes of this subpart, in the case of a partnership to which paragraph (1) applies—

(A) any partner's interest in the partnership shall not be taken into account in determining whether such partner is a related person with respect to any other partner, and

(B) the election under section 942(a)(3) shall be made separately by each partner with respect to any transaction for which the partnership maintains separate accounts for each partner.

[Sec. 943(g)]

(g) EXCLUSION FOR PATRONS OF AGRICULTURAL AND HORTICULTURAL COOPERATIVES.—Any amount described in paragraph (1) or (3) of section 1385(a)—

(1) which is received by a person from an organization to which part I of subchapter T applies which is engaged in the marketing of agricultural or horticultural products, and

(2) which is allocable to qualifying foreign trade income and designated as such by the organization in a written notice mailed to its patrons during the payment period described in section 1382(d),

shall be treated as qualifying foreign trade income of such person for purposes of section 114. The taxable income of the organization shall not be reduced under section 1382 by reason of any amount to which the preceding sentence applies.

[Sec. 943(h)]

(h) SPECIAL RULE FOR DISCs.—Section 114 shall not apply to any taxpayer for any taxable year if, at any time during the taxable year, the taxpayer is a member of any controlled group of corporations (as defined in section 927(d)(4), as in effect before the date of the enactment of this subsection) of which a DISC is a member.

Amendments

• 2000, FSC Repeal and Extraterritorial Income Exclusion Act of 2000 (P.L. 106-519)

P.L. 106-519, § 3(b):

Amended part III of subchapter N of chapter 1 by inserting after subpart D a new subpart E (Code Secs. 941-943). **Effective** generally for transactions after 9-30-2000. For special rules, see Act Sec. 5(b)-(d) in the amendment notes following Code Sec. 921.

[Sec. 943—Repealed]

Amendments

• 1976, Tax Reform Act of 1976 (P.L. 94-455)

P.L. 94-455, § 1053(c):

Repealed Code Sec. 943. **Effective** for tax years beginning after 12-31-77. Prior to repeal, Code Sec. 943 read as follows:

SEC. 943. EXCLUSION OF DIVIDENDS TO RESIDENTS OF FORMOSA OR HONG KONG.

Amounts distributed as dividends to or for the benefit of any person by a corporation organized under the China Trade Act, 1922, shall not be included in gross income and shall be exempt from taxation under this subtitle if, at the time of such distribution, such person is a resident of Formosa or Hong Kong, and the equitable right to the income of the shares of stock of the corporation is in good faith vested in him. In the case of a taxable year beginning after December 31, 1975, and before January 1, 1978, the amount of the distributions which are excludable from gross income under this section (determined without regard to this sentence) shall be reduced by the percentage reduction specified in the following table:

For a taxable year beginning in—	The percentage reduction shall be—
1976	33 1/3
1977	66 2/3

P.L. 94-455, § 1053(b):

Added the last sentence of Code Sec. 943. **Effective** for tax years beginning after 12-31-75.

Subpart F—Controlled Foreign Corporations

Sec. 951.	Amounts included in gross income of United States shareholders.
Sec. 951A.	Global intangible low-taxed income included in gross income of united states shareholders.
Sec. 952.	Subpart F income defined.
Sec. 953.	Insurance income.
Sec. 954.	Foreign base company income.
Sec. 956.	Investment of earnings in United States property.

INCOME TAX—CONTROLLED FOREIGN CORPORATIONS

Sec. 957. Controlled foreign corporations; United States persons.
Sec. 958. Rules for determining stock ownership.
Sec. 959. Exclusion from gross income of previously taxed earnings and profits.
Sec. 960. Special rules for foreign tax credit.
Sec. 961. Adjustments to basis of stock in controlled foreign corporations and of other property.
Sec. 962. Election by individuals to be subject to tax at corporate rates.
Sec. 964. Miscellaneous provisions.
Sec. 965. Treatment of deferred foreign income upon transition to participation exemption system of taxation.

[Sec. 951]

SEC. 951. AMOUNTS INCLUDED IN GROSS INCOME OF UNITED STATES SHAREHOLDERS.

[Sec. 951(a)]

(a) AMOUNTS INCLUDED.—

(1) IN GENERAL.—If a foreign corporation is a controlled foreign corporation at any time during any taxable year, every person who is a United States shareholder (as defined in subsection (b)) of such corporation and who owns (within the meaning of section 958(a)) stock in such corporation on the last day, in such year, on which such corporation is a controlled foreign corporation shall include in his gross income, for his taxable year in which or with which such taxable year of the corporation ends—

(A) his pro rata share (determined under paragraph (2)) of the corporation's subpart F income for such year, and

(B) the amount determined under section 956 with respect to such shareholder for such year (but only to the extent not excluded from gross income under section 959(a)(2)).

(2) PRO RATA SHARE OF SUBPART F INCOME.—The pro rata share referred to in paragraph (1)(A)(i) [sic] in the case of any United States shareholder is the amount—

(A) which would have been distributed with respect to the stock which such shareholder owns (within the meaning of section 958(a)) in such corporation if on the last day, in its taxable year, on which the corporation is a controlled foreign corporation it had distributed pro rata to its shareholders an amount (i) which bears the same ratio to its subpart F income for the taxable year, as (ii) the part of such year during which the corporation is a controlled foreign corporation bears to the entire year, reduced by

(B) the amount of distributions received by any other person during such year as a dividend with respect to such stock, but only to the extent of the dividend which would have been received if the distribution by the corporation had been the amount (i) which bears the same ratio to the subpart F income of such corporation for the taxable year, as (ii) the part of such year during which such shareholder did not own (within the meaning of section 958(a)) such stock bears to the entire year. For purposes of subparagraph (B), any gain included in the gross income of any person as a dividend under section 1248 shall be treated as a distribution received by such person with respect to the stock involved.

Amendments

• **2017, Tax Cuts and Jobs Act (P.L. 115-97)**

P.L. 115-97, §14212(b)(1)(A):

Amended Code Sec. 951(a)(1)(A). **Effective** for tax years of foreign corporations beginning after 12-31-2017, and to tax years of United States shareholders in which or with which such tax years of foreign corporations end. Prior to amendment, Code Sec. 951(a)(1)(A) read as follows:

(A) the sum of—

(i) his pro rata share (determined under paragraph (2)) of the corporation's subpart F income for such year,

(ii) his pro rata share (determined under section 955(a)(3) as in effect before the enactment of the Tax Reduction Act of 1975) of the corporation's previously excluded subpart F income withdrawn from investment in less developed countries for such year, and

(iii) his pro rata share (determined under section 955(a)(3)) of the corporation's previously excluded subpart F income withdrawn from foreign base company shipping operations for such year; and

P.L. 115-97, §14212(b)(2):

Amended Code Sec. 951(a) by striking paragraph (3). **Effective** for tax years of foreign corporations beginning after 12-31-2017, and to tax years of United States shareholders in which or with which such tax years of foreign corporations end. Prior to being stricken, Code Sec. 951(a)(3) read as follows:

(3) LIMITATION ON PRO RATA SHARE OF PREVIOUSLY EXCLUDED SUBPART F INCOME WITHDRAWN FROM INVESTMENT.—For purposes of paragraph (1)(A)(iii), the pro rata share of any United States shareholder of the previously excluded subpart F income of a controlled foreign corporation withdrawn from investment in foreign base company shipping operations shall not exceed an amount—

(A) which bears the same ratio to his pro rata share of such income withdrawn (as determined under section 955(a)(3)) for the taxable year, as

(B) the part of such year during which the corporation is a controlled foreign corporation bears to the entire year.

P.L. 115-97, §14215(a):

Amended Code Sec. 951(a)(1) by striking "for an uninterrupted period of 30 days or more" and inserting "at any time". **Effective** for tax years of foreign corporations beginning after 12-31-2017, and to tax years of United States shareholders with or within which such tax years of foreign corporations end.

• **1997, Taxpayer Relief Act of 1997 (P.L. 105-34)**

P.L. 105-34, §1112(a)(1):

Amended Code Sec. 951(a)(2) by adding at the end thereof a new sentence. **Effective** for dispositions after 8-5-97.

• **1996, Small Business Job Protection Act of 1996 (P.L. 104-188)**

P.L. 104-188, §1501(a)(1):

Amended Code Sec. 951(a)(1) by striking subparagraph (C), striking "; and" at the end of subparagraph (B) and inserting a period, and adding "and" at the end of subparagraph (A). **Effective** for tax years of foreign corporations beginning after 12-31-96, and to tax years of United States shareholders within which or with which such tax years of foreign corporations end. Prior to being stricken, Code Sec. 951(a)(1)(C) read as follows:

(C) the amount determined under section 956A with respect to such shareholder for such year (but only to the extent not excluded from gross income under section 959(a)(3)).

• **1993, Omnibus Budget Reconciliation Act of 1993 (P.L. 103-66)**

P.L. 103-66, §13231(a):

Amended Code Sec. 951(a)(1) by striking "and" at the end of subparagraph (A), by striking the period at the end of subparagraph (B) and inserting "; and", and by adding at the end thereof a new subparagraph (C). **Effective** for tax years of foreign corporations beginning after 9-30-93, and tax years of United States shareholders in which or with which such tax years of foreign corporations end.

P.L. 103-66, §13232(c)(1):

Amended Code Sec. 951(a)(1)(B). **Effective** for tax years of controlled foreign corporations beginning after 9-30-93, and to tax years of United States shareholders in which or with which such tax years of controlled foreign corporations end. Prior to amendment, Code Sec 951(a)(1)(B) read as follows:

(B) his pro rata share (determined under section 956(a)(2)) of the corporation's increase in earnings invested in United States property for such year (but only to the extent not excluded from gross income under section 959(a)(2)); and

P.L. 103-66, §13232(c)(2):

Amended Code Sec. 951(a) by striking paragraph (4). **Effective** for tax years of controlled foreign corporations beginning after 9-30-93, and to tax years of United States shareholders in which or with which such tax years of controlled foreign corporations end. Prior to amendment, Code Sec. 951(a)(4) read as follows:

(4) LIMITATION ON PRO RATA SHARE OF INVESTMENT IN UNITED STATES PROPERTY.—For purposes of paragraph (1)(B), the pro rata share of any United States shareholder in the increase of the earnings of a controlled foreign corporation invested in United States property shall not exceed an amount (A) which bears the same ratio to his pro rata share of such increase (as determined under section 956(a)(2)) for the taxable year, as (B) the part of such year during which the corporation is a controlled foreign corporation bears to the entire year.

• **1976, Tax Reform Act of 1976 (P.L. 94-455)**

P.L. 94-455, §1901(a)(119):

Struck out "beginning after December 31, 1962" after "during any taxable year" in Code Sec. 951(a)(1). **Effective** for tax years beginning after 12-31-76.

• **1975, Tax Reduction Act of 1975 (P.L. 94-12)**

P.L. 94-12, §602(a)(3)(B):

Amended Code Sec. 951(a)(1)(A)(i). **Effective** for tax years of foreign corporations beginning after 12-31-75, and to tax years of U. S. shareholders within which or with which such tax years of such foreign corporations end. Prior to amendment, this section read as follows:

INCOME TAX—CONTROLLED FOREIGN CORPORATIONS

"(A) the sum of—

(1) except as provided in section 963, his pro rata share (determined under paragraph (2)) of the corporation's subpart F income for such year, and".

P.L. 94-12, § 602(c)(3):

Amended Code Sec. 951(a)(1)(A)(ii) by substituting "(determined under section 955(a)(3) as in effect before enactment of the Tax Reduction Act of 1975)" for "determined under section 955(a)(3)." **Effective** for tax years of foreign corporations beginning after 12-31-75, and to tax years of U. S. shareholders within which or with which such tax years of such foreign corporations end.

P.L. 94-12, §§ 602(c)(4) and 602(d)(2)(B):

Amended Code Sec. 951(a)(3). **Effective** for tax years of foreign corporations beginning after 12-31-75, and to tax years of U. S. shareholders within which or with which such tax years of such foreign corporations end. Prior to amendment, this section read as follows:

"(3) Limitation on pro rata share of previously excluded subpart F income withdrawn from investment.—For purposes of paragraph (1)(A)(ii), the pro rata share of any United States shareholder of the previously excluded subpart F income of a controlled foreign corporation withdrawn from investment in less developed countries shall not exceed an amount (A) which bears the same ratio to his pro rata share of such income withdrawn (as determined under section 955(a)(3)) for the taxable year, as (B) the part of such year during which the corporation is a controlled foreign corporation bears to the entire year."

P.L. 94-12, § 602(d)(2)(A):

Amended Code Sec. 951(a)(1)(A) by adding new clause (iii). **Effective** for tax years of foreign corporations beginning after 12-31-75, and to tax years of U. S. shareholders within which or with which such tax years of such foreign corporations end.

• **1962, Revenue Act of 1962 (P.L. 87-834)**

P.L. 87-834, § 12(a):

Amended Part III of subchapter N of chapter 1 by adding subpart F, which includes Code Sec. 951. **Effective** for tax years of foreign corporations beginning after 12-31-62, and for tax years of United States shareholders within which or with which such tax years of such foreign corporations end.

[Sec. 951(b)]

(b) UNITED STATES SHAREHOLDER DEFINED.—For purposes of this title, the term "United States shareholder" means, with respect to any foreign corporation, a United States person (as defined in section 957(c)) who owns (within the meaning of section 958(a)), or is considered as owning by applying the rules of ownership of section 958(b), 10 percent or more of the total combined voting power of all classes of stock entitled to vote of such foreign corporation, or 10 percent or more of the total value of shares of all classes of stock of such foreign corporation.

Amendments

• **2017, Tax Cuts and Jobs Act (P.L. 115-97)**

P.L. 115-97, § 14101(e)(1):

Amended Code Sec. 951(b) by striking "subpart" and inserting "title". **Effective** for distributions made after 12-31-2017.

P.L. 115-97, § 14214(a):

Amended Code Sec. 951(b) by inserting ", or 10 percent or more of the total value of shares of all classes of stock of such foreign corporation" after "such foreign corporation". **Effective** for tax years of foreign corporations beginning after 12-31-2017, and to tax years of United States shareholders with or within which such tax years of foreign corporations end.

• **1988, Technical and Miscellaneous Revenue Act of 1988 (P.L. 100-647)**

P.L. 100-647, § 1012(i)(15):

Amended Code Sec. 951(b) by striking out "section 957(d)" and inserting in lieu thereof "section 957(c)". **Effective** as if included in the provision of P.L. 99-514 to which it relates.

[Sec. 951(c)—Stricken]

(c) COORDINATION WITH ELECTION OF A FOREIGN INVESTMENT COMPANY TO DISTRIBUTE INCOME.—A United States shareholder who, for his taxable year, is a qualified shareholder (within the meaning of section 1247(c)) of a foreign investment company with respect to which an election under section 1247 is in effect shall not be required to include in gross income, for such taxable year, any amount under subsection (a) with respect to such company.

Amendments

• **2004, American Jobs Creation Act of 2004 (P.L. 108-357)**

P.L. 108-357, § 413(c)(16):

Amended Code Sec. 951 by striking subsections (c) and (d) and by redesignating subsections (e) and (f) as subsections (c) and (d), respectively. **Effective** for tax years of foreign corporations beginning after 12-31-2004, and for tax years of United States shareholders with or within which such tax years of foreign corporations end. Prior to being stricken, Code Sec. 951(c) read as follows:

[Sec. 951(d)—Stricken]

Amendments

• **2004, American Jobs Creation Act of 2004 (P.L. 108-357)**

P.L. 108-357, § 413(c)(16):

Amended Code Sec. 951 by striking subsection (d). **Effective** for tax years of foreign corporations beginning after 12-31-2004, and for tax years of United States shareholders with or within which such tax years of foreign corporations end. Prior to being stricken, Code Sec. 951(d) read as follows:

(d) COORDINATION WITH FOREIGN PERSONAL HOLDING COMPANY PROVISIONS.—If, but for this subsection, an amount would be included in the gross income of a United States shareholder for any taxable year both under subsection (a)(1)(A)(i) and under section 551(b) (relating to foreign personal holding company income included in gross income of United States shareholder), such amount shall be included in the gross income of such shareholder only under subsection (a)(1)(A).

[Sec. 951(c)—Stricken]

Amendments

• **2007, Tax Technical Corrections Act of 2007 (P.L. 110-172)**

P.L. 110-172, § 11(g)(13):

Amended Code Sec. 951 by striking subsection (c) and by redesignating subsection (d) as subsection (c). **Effective** 12-29-2007. Prior to being stricken, Code Sec. 951(c) read as follows:

(c) FOREIGN TRADE INCOME NOT TAKEN INTO ACCOUNT.—

(1) IN GENERAL.—The foreign trade income of a FSC and any deductions which are apportioned or allocated to such income shall not be taken into account under this subpart.

(2) FOREIGN TRADE INCOME.—For purposes of this subsection, the term "foreign trade income" has the meaning given such term by section 923(b), but does not include section 923(a)(2) non-exempt income (within the meaning of section 927(d)(6)).

• **2004, American Jobs Creation Act of 2004 (P.L. 108-357)**

P.L. 108-357, § 413(c)(16):

Amended Code Sec. 951 by redesignating subsection (e) as subsection (c). **Effective** for tax years of foreign corporations beginning after 12-31-2004, and for tax years of United States shareholders with or within which such tax years of foreign corporations end.

• **1986, Tax Reform Act of 1986 (P.L. 99-514)**

P.L. 99-514, § 1876(c)(2):

Amended Code Sec. 951(e)(1) by striking out the last sentence. **Effective** as if included in the provision of P.L. 98-369 to which it relates. Prior to amendment, the last sentence read as follows:

For purposes of the preceding sentence, income described in paragraph (2) or (3) of section 921(d) shall be treated as derived from sources within the United States.

• **1984, Deficit Reduction Act of 1984 (P.L. 98-369)**

P.L. 98-369, § 801(d)(4):

Amended Code Sec. 951 by adding new subsection (e). **Effective** for transactions after 12-31-84, in tax years ending after such date.

[Sec. 951(c)]

(c) COORDINATION WITH PASSIVE FOREIGN INVESTMENT COMPANY PROVISIONS.—If, but for this subsection, an amount would be included in the gross income of a United States shareholder for any taxable year both under subsection (a)(1)(A)(i) and under section 1293 (relating to current taxation of income from certain passive foreign investment companies), such amount shall be included in the gross income of such shareholder only under subsection (a)(1)(A).

Sec. 951(b)

INCOME TAX—CONTROLLED FOREIGN CORPORATIONS

Amendments

• **2007, Tax Technical Corrections Act of 2007 (P.L. 110-172)**

P.L. 110-172, §11(g)(13):

Amended Code Sec. 951 by redesignating subsection (d) as subsection (c). **Effective** 12-29-2007.

• **2004, American Jobs Creation Act of 2004 (P.L. 108-357)**

P.L. 108-357, §413(c)(16):

Amended Code Sec. 951 by redesignating subsection (f) as subsection (d). **Effective** for tax years of foreign corporations beginning after 12-31-2004, and for tax years of United States shareholders with or within which such tax years of foreign corporations end.

• **1986, Tax Reform Act of 1986 (P.L. 99-514)**

P.L. 99-514, §1235(c):

Added new Code Sec. 951(f). **Effective** for tax years of foreign corporations beginning after 12-31-86.

[Sec. 951A]

SEC. 951A. GLOBAL INTANGIBLE LOW-TAXED INCOME INCLUDED IN GROSS INCOME OF UNITED STATES SHAREHOLDERS.

[Sec. 951A(a)]

(a) IN GENERAL.—Each person who is a United States shareholder of any controlled foreign corporation for any taxable year of such United States shareholder shall include in gross income such shareholder's global intangible low-taxed income for such taxable year.

[Sec. 951A(b)]

(b) GLOBAL INTANGIBLE LOW-TAXED INCOME.—For purposes of this section—

(1) IN GENERAL.—The term "global intangible low-taxed income" means, with respect to any United States shareholder for any taxable year of such United States shareholder, the excess (if any) of—

(A) such shareholder's net CFC tested income for such taxable year, over

(B) such shareholder's net deemed tangible income return for such taxable year.

(2) NET DEEMED TANGIBLE INCOME RETURN.—The term "net deemed tangible income return" means, with respect to any United States shareholder for any taxable year, the excess of—

(A) 10 percent of the aggregate of such shareholder's pro rata share of the qualified business asset investment of each controlled foreign corporation with respect to which such shareholder is a United States shareholder for such taxable year (determined for each taxable year of each such controlled foreign corporation which ends in or with such taxable year of such United States shareholder), over

(B) the amount of interest expense taken into account under subsection (c)(2)(A)(ii) in determining the shareholder's net CFC tested income for the taxable year to the extent the interest income attributable to such expense is not taken into account in determining such shareholder's net CFC tested income.

[Sec. 951A(c)]

(c) NET CFC TESTED INCOME.—For purposes of this section—

(1) IN GENERAL.—The term "net CFC tested income" means, with respect to any United States shareholder for any taxable year of such United States shareholder, the excess (if any) of—

(A) the aggregate of such shareholder's pro rata share of the tested income of each controlled foreign corporation with respect to which such shareholder is a United States shareholder for such taxable year of such United States shareholder (determined for each taxable year of such controlled foreign corporation which ends in or with such taxable year of such United States shareholder), over

(B) the aggregate of such shareholder's pro rata share of the tested loss of each controlled foreign corporation with respect to which such shareholder is a United States shareholder for such taxable year of such United States shareholder (determined for each taxable year of such controlled foreign corporation which ends in or with such taxable year of such United States shareholder).

(2) TESTED INCOME; TESTED LOSS.—For purposes of this section—

(A) TESTED INCOME.—The term "tested income" means, with respect to any controlled foreign corporation for any taxable year of such controlled foreign corporation, the excess (if any) of—

(i) the gross income of such corporation determined without regard to—

(I) any item of income described in section 952(b),

(II) any gross income taken into account in determining the subpart F income of such corporation,

(III) any gross income excluded from the foreign base company income (as defined in section 954) and the insurance income (as defined in section 953) of such corporation by reason of section 954(b)(4),

(IV) any dividend received from a related person (as defined in section 954(d)(3)), and

(V) any foreign oil and gas extraction income (as defined in section 907(c)(1)) of such corporation, over

(ii) the deductions (including taxes) properly allocable to such gross income under rules similar to the rules of section 954(b)(5) (or to which such deductions would be allocable if there were such gross income).

(B) TESTED LOSS.—

(i) IN GENERAL.—The term "tested loss" means, with respect to any controlled foreign corporation for any taxable year of such controlled foreign corporation, the excess (if any) of the amount described in subparagraph (A)(ii) over the amount described in subparagraph (A)(i).

(ii) COORDINATION WITH SUBPART F TO DENY DOUBLE BENEFIT OF LOSSES.—Section 952(c)(1)(A) shall be applied by increasing the earnings and profits of the controlled foreign corporation by the tested loss of such corporation.

[Sec. 951A(d)]

(d) QUALIFIED BUSINESS ASSET INVESTMENT.—For purposes of this section—

(1) IN GENERAL.—The term "qualified business asset investment" means, with respect to any controlled foreign corporation for any taxable year, the average of such corporation's aggregate adjusted bases as of the close of each quarter of such taxable year in specified tangible property—

(A) used in a trade or business of the corporation, and

(B) of a type with respect to which a deduction is allowable under section 167.

(2) SPECIFIED TANGIBLE PROPERTY.—

(A) IN GENERAL.—The term "specified tangible property" means, except as provided in subparagraph (B), any tangible property used in the production of tested income.

INCOME TAX—CONTROLLED FOREIGN CORPORATIONS

(B) DUAL USE PROPERTY.—In the case of property used both in the production of tested income and income which is not tested income, such property shall be treated as specified tangible property in the same proportion that the gross income described in subsection (c)(1)(A) produced with respect to such property bears to the total gross income produced with respect to such property.

(3) DETERMINATION OF ADJUSTED BASIS.—For purposes of this subsection, notwithstanding any provision of this title (or any other provision of law) which is enacted after the date of the enactment of this section, the adjusted basis in any property shall be determined—

(A) by using the alternative depreciation system under section 168(g), and

(B) by allocating the depreciation deduction with respect to such property ratably to each day during the period in the taxable year to which such depreciation relates.

(3) [sic] PARTNERSHIP PROPERTY.—For purposes of this subsection, if a controlled foreign corporation holds an interest in a partnership at the close of such taxable year of the controlled foreign corporation, such controlled foreign corporation shall take into account under paragraph (1) the controlled foreign corporation's distributive share of the aggregate of the partnership's adjusted bases (determined as of such date in the hands of the partnership) in tangible property held by such partnership to the extent such property—

(A) is used in the trade or business of the partnership,

(B) is of a type with respect to which a deduction is allowable under section 167, and

(C) is used in the production of tested income (determined with respect to such controlled foreign corporation's distributive share of income with respect to such property).

For purposes of this paragraph, the controlled foreign corporation's distributive share of the adjusted basis of any property shall be the controlled foreign corporation's distributive share of income with respect to such property.

(4) REGULATIONS.—The Secretary shall issue such regulations or other guidance as the Secretary determines appropriate to prevent the avoidance of the purposes of this subsection, including regulations or other guidance which provide for the treatment of property if—

(A) such property is transferred, or held, temporarily, or

(B) the avoidance of the purposes of this paragraph is a factor in the transfer or holding of such property.

[Sec. 951A(e)]

(e) DETERMINATION OF PRO RATA SHARE, ETC.—For purposes of this section—

(1) IN GENERAL.—The pro rata shares referred to in subsections (b), (c)(1)(A), and (c)(1)(B), respectively, shall be determined under the rules of section 951(a)(2) in the same manner as such section applies to subpart F income and shall be taken into account in the taxable year of the United States shareholder in which or with which the taxable year of the controlled foreign corporation ends.

(2) TREATMENT AS UNITED STATES SHAREHOLDER.—A person shall be treated as a United States shareholder of a controlled foreign corporation for any taxable year of such person only if such person owns (within the meaning of section 958(a)) stock in such foreign corporation on the last day in the taxable year of such foreign corporation on which such foreign corporation is a controlled foreign corporation.

(3) TREATMENT AS CONTROLLED FOREIGN CORPORATION.—A foreign corporation shall be treated as a controlled foreign corporation for any taxable year if such foreign corporation is a controlled foreign corporation at any time during such taxable year.

[Sec. 951A(f)]

(f) TREATMENT AS SUBPART F INCOME FOR CERTAIN PURPOSES.—

(1) IN GENERAL.—

(A) APPLICATION.—Except as provided in subparagraph (B), any global intangible low-taxed income included in gross income under subsection (a) shall be treated in the same manner as an amount included under section 951(a)(1)(A) for purposes of applying sections 168(h)(2)(B), 535(b)(10), 851(b), 904(h)(1), 959, 961, 962, 993(a)(1)(E), 996(f)(1), 1248(b)(1), 1248(d)(1), 6501(e)(1)(C), 6654(d)(2)(D), and 6655(e)(4).

(B) EXCEPTION.—The Secretary shall provide rules for the application of subparagraph (A) to other provisions of this title in any case in which the determination of subpart F income is required to be made at the level of the controlled foreign corporation.

(2) ALLOCATION OF GLOBAL INTANGIBLE LOW-TAXED INCOME TO CONTROLLED FOREIGN CORPORATIONS.—For purposes of the sections referred to in paragraph (1), with respect to any controlled foreign corporation any pro rata amount from which is taken into account in determining the global intangible low-taxed income included in gross income of a United States shareholder under subsection (a), the portion of such global intangible low-taxed income which is treated as being with respect to such controlled foreign corporation is—

(A) in the case of a controlled foreign corporation with no tested income, zero, and

(B) in the case of a controlled foreign corporation with tested income, the portion of such global intangible low-taxed income which bears the same ratio to such global intangible low-taxed income as—

(i) such United States shareholder's pro rata amount of the tested income of such controlled foreign corporation, bears to

(ii) the aggregate amount described in subsection (c)(1)(A) with respect to such United States shareholder.

Amendments

- 2017, Tax Cuts and Jobs Act (P.L. 115-97)

P.L. 115-97, §14201(a):

Amended subpart F of part III of subchapter N of chapter 1 by inserting after Code Sec. 951 a new Code Sec. 951A. **Effective** for tax years of foreign corporations beginning after 12-31-2017, and to tax years of United States shareholders in which or with which such tax years of foreign corporations end.

[Sec. 952]

SEC. 952. SUBPART F INCOME DEFINED.

[Sec. 952(a)]

(a) IN GENERAL.—For purposes of this subpart, the term "subpart F income" means, in the case of any controlled foreign corporation, the sum of—

(1) insurance income (as defined under section 953),

(2) the foreign base company income (as determined under section 954),

(3) an amount equal to the product of—

(A) the income of such corporation other than income which—

(i) is attributable to earnings and profits of the foreign corporation included in the gross income of a United States person under section 951 (other than by reason of this paragraph), or

(ii) is described in subsection (b),

multiplied by

(B) the international boycott factor (as determined under section 999),

Sec. 951A(d)(2)(B)

INCOME TAX—CONTROLLED FOREIGN CORPORATIONS

(4) the sum of the amounts of any illegal bribes, kickbacks, or other payments (within the meaning of section 162(c)) paid by or on behalf of the corporation during the taxable year of the corporation directly or indirectly to an official, employee, or agent in fact of a government, and

(5) the income of such corporation derived from any foreign country during any period during which section 901(j) applies to such foreign country.

The payments referred to in paragraph (4) are payments which would be unlawful under the Foreign Corrupt Practices Act of 1977 if the payor were a United States person. For purposes of paragraph (5), the income described therein shall be reduced, under regulations prescribed by the Secretary, so as to take into account deductions (including taxes) properly allocable to such income.

Amendments

• **1986, Tax Reform Act of 1986 (P.L. 99-514)**

P.L. 99-514, § 1221(b)(3)(A):

Amended Code Sec. 952(a)(1). **Effective**, generally, for tax years of foreign corporations beginning after 12-31-86. However, for special rules and exceptions, see Act Sec. 1221(g)(2)-(3) following Code Sec. 954. Prior to amendment, Code Sec. 952(a)(1) read as follows:

(1) the income derived from the insurance of United States risks (as determined under section 953),

• **1986, Omnibus Budget Reconciliation Act of 1986 (P.L. 99-509)**

P.L. 99-509, § 8041(b)(1)(A)-(B):

Amended Code Sec. 952(a) by striking out "and" at the end of paragraph (3), by striking out the period at the end of paragraph (4) and inserting in lieu thereof ", and", and by inserting immediately after paragraph (4) new paragraph (5), and by adding at the end of Code Sec. 952(a) a new sentence. **Effective** 1-1-87.

• **1982, Tax Equity and Fiscal Responsibility Act of 1982 (P.L. 97-248)**

P.L. 97-248, § 288(b)(1):

Amended Code Sec. 952(a) by adding a sentence at the end. **Effective** for payments made after 9-3-82.

• **1976, Tax Reform Act of 1976 (P.L. 94-455)**

P.L. 94-455, § 1062(a):

Struck out "and" at the end of Code Sec. 952(a)(1), substituted ", and" for the period at the end of Code Sec. 952(a)(2), and added a new Code Sec. 952(a)(3). **Effective** for participation in or cooperation with an international boycott more than 30 days after 10-4-76. In the case of operations which constitute participation in or cooperation with an international boycott and which are carried out in accordance with the terms of a binding contract entered into before 9-2-76, Code Sec. 952(a)(3) applies to such participation or cooperation after 12-31-77.

P.L. 94-455, § 1065(a)(1):

Struck out "and" at the end of Code Sec. 952(a)(2), substituted, "and" for the period at the end of Code Sec. 952(a)(3), and added Code Sec. 952(a)(4). **Effective** for payments described in Code Sec.162(c) made more than 30 days after 10-4-76.

[Sec. 952(b)]

(b) EXCLUSION OF UNITED STATES INCOME.—In the case of a controlled foreign corporation, subpart F income does not include any item of income from sources within the United States which is effectively connected with the conduct by such corporation of a trade or business within the United States unless such item is exempt from taxation (or is subject to a reduced rate of tax) pursuant to a treaty obligation of the United States. For purposes of this subsection, any exemption (or reduction) with respect to the tax imposed by section 884 shall not be taken into account.

Amendments

• **2007, Tax Technical Corrections Act of 2007 (P.L. 110-172)**

P.L. 110-172, § 11(g)(14):

Amended Code Sec. 952(b) by striking the second sentence. **Effective** 12-29-2007. Prior to being stricken, the second sentence of Code Sec. 952(b) read as follows:

For purposes of the preceding sentence, income described in paragraph (2) or (3) of section 921(d) shall be treated as derived from sources within the United States.

• **1997, Taxpayer Relief Act of 1997 (P.L. 105-34)**

P.L. 105-34, § 1112(c)(1):

Amended Code Sec. 952(b) by adding at the end thereof a new sentence. **Effective** for tax years beginning after 12-31-86.

• **1986, Tax Reform Act of 1986 (P.L. 99-514)**

P.L. 99-514, § 1876(c)(1):

Amended Code Sec. 952(b) by adding at the end thereof a new sentence. **Effective** as if included in the provision of P.L. 98-369 to which it relates.

• **1966, Foreign Investors Tax Act of 1966 (P.L. 89-809)**

P.L. 89-809, § 104(j):

Amended Code Sec. 952(b). **Effective** 1-1-67. Prior to amendment, Sec. 952(b) read as follows:

"(b) Exclusion of United States Income.—Subpart F income does not include any item includible in gross income under this chapter (other than this subpart) as income derived from sources within the United States of a foreign corporation engaged in trade or business in the United States."

[Sec. 952(c)]

(c) LIMITATION.—

(1) IN GENERAL.—

(A) SUBPART F INCOME LIMITED TO CURRENT EARNINGS AND PROFITS.—For purposes of subsection (a), the subpart F income of any controlled foreign corporation for any taxable year shall not exceed the earnings and profits of such corporation for such taxable year.

(B) CERTAIN PRIOR YEAR DEFICITS MAY BE TAKEN INTO ACCOUNT.—

(i) IN GENERAL.—The amount included in the gross income of any United States shareholder under section 951(a)(1)(A) for any taxable year and attributable to a qualified activity shall be reduced by the amount of such shareholder's pro rata share of any qualified deficit.

(ii) QUALIFIED DEFICIT.—The term "qualified deficit" means any deficit in earnings and profits of the controlled foreign corporation for any prior taxable year which began after December 31, 1986, and for which the controlled foreign corporation was a controlled foreign corporation; but only to the extent such deficit—

(I) is attributable to the same qualified activity as the activity giving rise to the income being offset, and

(II) has not previously been taken into account under this subparagraph.

In determining the deficit attributable to qualified activities described in subclause (II) or (III) of clause (iii), deficits in earnings and profits (to the extent not previously taken into account under this section) for taxable years beginning after 1962 and before 1987 also shall be taken into account. In the case of the qualified activity described in clause (iii)(I), the rule of the preceding sentence shall apply, except that "1982" shall be substituted for "1962".

(iii) QUALIFIED ACTIVITY.—For purposes of this paragraph, the term "qualified activity" means any activity giving rise to—

(I) foreign base company sales income,

(II) foreign base company services income,

(III) in the case of a qualified insurance company, insurance income or foreign personal holding company income, or

(IV) in the case of a qualified financial institution, foreign personal holding company income.

(iv) PRO RATA SHARE.—For purposes of this paragraph, the shareholder's pro rata share of any deficit for any prior taxable year shall be determined under rules similar to rules under section 951(a)(2) for whichever of the following yields the smaller share:

(I) the close of the taxable year, or

(II) the close of the taxable year in which the deficit arose.

(v) QUALIFIED INSURANCE COMPANY.—For purposes of this subparagraph, the term "qualified insurance company" means any controlled foreign corporation predominantly engaged in the active conduct of an insurance business in the taxable year and in the prior taxable years in which the deficit arose.

INCOME TAX—CONTROLLED FOREIGN CORPORATIONS

(vi) QUALIFIED FINANCIAL INSTITUTION.—For purposes of this paragraph, the term "qualified financial institution" means any controlled foreign corporation predominantly engaged in the active conduct of a banking, financing, or similar business in the taxable year and in the prior taxable year in which the deficit arose.

(vii) SPECIAL RULES FOR INSURANCE INCOME.—

(I) IN GENERAL.—An election may be made under this clause to have section 953(a) applied for purposes of this title without regard to the same country exception under paragraph (1)(A) thereof. Such election, once made, may be revoked only with the consent of the Secretary.

(II) SPECIAL RULES FOR AFFILIATED GROUPS.—In the case of an affiliated group of corporations (within the meaning of section 1504 but without regard to section 1504(b)(3) and by substituting "more than 50 percent" for "at least 80 percent" each place it appears), no election may be made under subclause (I) for any controlled foreign corporation unless such election is made for all other controlled foreign corporations who are members of such group and who were created or organized under the laws of the same country as such controlled foreign corporation. For purposes of clause (v), in determining whether any controlled corporation described in the preceding sentence is a qualified insurance company, all such corporations shall be treated as 1 corporation.

(C) CERTAIN DEFICITS OF MEMBER OF THE SAME CHAIN OF CORPORATIONS MAY BE TAKEN INTO ACCOUNT.—

(i) IN GENERAL.—A controlled foreign corporation may elect to reduce the amount of its subpart F income for any taxable year which is attributable to any qualified activity by the amount of any deficit in earnings and profits of a qualified chain member for a taxable year ending with (or within) the taxable year of such controlled foreign corporation to the extent such deficit is attributable to such activity. To the extent any deficit reduces subpart F income under the preceding sentence, such deficit shall not be taken into account under subparagraph (B).

(ii) QUALIFIED CHAIN MEMBER.—For purposes of this subparagraph, the term "qualified chain member" means, with respect to any controlled foreign corporation, any other corporation which is created or organized under the laws of the same foreign country as the controlled foreign corporation but only if—

(I) all the stock of such other corporation (other than directors' qualifying shares) is owned at all times during the taxable year in which the deficit arose (directly or through 1 or more corporations other than the common parent) by such controlled foreign corporation, or

(II) all the stock of such controlled foreign corporation (other than directors' qualifying shares) is owned at all times during the taxable year in which the deficit arose (directly or through 1 or more corporations other than the common parent) by such other corporation.

(iii) COORDINATION.—This subparagraph shall be applied after subparagraphs (A) and (B).

(2) RECHARACTERIZATION IN SUBSEQUENT TAXABLE YEARS.—If the subpart F income of any controlled foreign corporation for any taxable year was reduced by reason of paragraph (1)(A), any excess of the earnings and profits of such corporation for any subsequent taxable year over the subpart F income of such foreign corporation for such taxable year shall be recharacterized as subpart F income under rules similar to the rules applicable under section 904(f)(5).

(3) SPECIAL RULE FOR DETERMINING EARNINGS AND PROFITS.—For purposes of this subsection, earnings and profits of any controlled foreign corporation shall be determined without regard to paragraphs (4), (5), and (6) of section 312(n). Under regulations, the preceding sentence shall not apply to the extent it would increase earnings and profits by an amount which was previously distributed by the controlled foreign corporation.

Amendments

- **2017, Tax Cuts and Jobs Act (P.L. 115-97)**

P.L. 115-97, §14211(b)(1):

Amended Code Sec. 952(c)(1)(B)(iii) by striking subclause (I) and redesignating subclauses (II) through (V) as subclauses (I) through (IV), respectively. **Effective** for tax years of foreign corporations beginning after 12-31-2017, and to tax years of United States shareholders with or within which such tax years of foreign corporations end. Prior to being stricken, Code Sec. 952(c)(1)(B)(iii)(I) read as follows:

(I) foreign base company oil related income,

P.L. 115-97, §14212(b)(1)(C):

Amended Code Sec. 952(c)(1)(B)(i) by striking "section 951(a)(1)(A)(i)" and inserting "section 951(a)(1)(A)". **Effective** for tax years of foreign corporations beginning after 12-31-2017, and to tax years of United States shareholders in which or with which such tax years of foreign corporations end.

- **2005, Gulf Opportunity Zone Act of 2005 (P.L. 109-135)**

P.L. 109-135, §412(kk)(1)-(2):

Amended Code Sec. 952(c)(1)(B)(ii) by striking "clause (iii)(III) or (IV)" and inserting "subclause (II) or (III) of clause (iii)", and by striking "clause (iii)(II) and inserting "clause (iii)(I)". **Effective** 12-21-2005.

- **2004, American Jobs Creation Act of 2004 (P.L. 108-357)**

P.L. 108-357, §415(c)(1):

Amended Code Sec. 952(c)(1)(B)(iii) by striking subclause (I) and redesignating subclauses (II) through (VI) as subclauses (I) through (V), respectively. **Effective** for tax years of foreign corporations beginning after 12-31-2004, and for tax years of United States shareholders with or within which such tax years of foreign corporations end. Prior to being stricken, Code Sec. 952(c)(1)(B)(iii)(I) read as follows:

(I) foreign base company shipping income,

- **1988, Technical and Miscellaneous Revenue Act of 1988 (P.L. 100-647)**

P.L. 100-647, §1012(i)(16):

Amended Code Sec. 952(c) by adding at the end thereof new paragraph (3). **Effective** as if included in the provision of P.L. 99-514 to which it relates.

P.L. 100-647, §1012(i)(22):

Amended Code Sec. 952(c)(1)(B)(iii)(III) by striking out "insurance income" and inserting in lieu thereof "insurance income or foreign personal holding company income,". **Effective** as if included in the provision of P.L. 99-514 to which it relates.

P.L. 100-647, §1012(i)(23):

Amended Code Sec. 952(c)(1)(B)(iii) by redesignating subclauses (III) and (IV) as subclauses (V) and (VI), respectively, and by inserting after subclause (II) new subclauses (III)-(IV). **Effective** as if included in the provision of P.L. 99-514 to which it relates.

P.L. 100-647, §1012(i)(24):

Amended Code Sec. 952(c)(1)(B)(ii) by adding at the end thereof a new sentence. **Effective** as if included in the provision of P.L. 99-514 to which it relates.

P.L. 100-647, §1012(i)(25)(A):

Amended Code Sec. 952(c)(1) by adding at the end thereof a new subparagraph (C). **Effective** as if included in the provision of P.L. 99-514 to which it relates.

P.L. 100-647, §1012(i)(6), provides:

(6) For purposes of applying section 952(c)(1)(A) of the 1986 Code, the earnings and profits of any corporation shall be determined without regard to any increase in earnings and profits under section 1023(e)(3)(C) of the Reform Act.

P.L. 100-647, §6131(a):

Amended Code Sec. 952(c)(1)(B) by adding at the end thereof new clause (vii). **Effective** as if included in the amendments made by section 1221(f) of P.L. 99-514.

- **1986, Tax Reform Act of 1986 (P.L. 99-514)**

P.L. 99-514, §1221(f):

Amended Code Sec. 952 by striking out subsections (c) and (d) and inserting in lieu thereof new subsection (c). **Effective**, generally, for tax years of foreign corporations beginning after 12-31-86. However, for special rules and exceptions, see Act Sec. 1221(g)(2)-(3) following Code Sec. 954. Prior to amendment Code Sec. 952(c) read as follows:

(c) LIMITATION.—For purposes of subsection (a), the subpart F income of any controlled foreign corporation for any taxable year shall not exceed the earnings and profits of such corporation for such year reduced by the amount (if any) by which—

(1) an amount equal to—

(A) the sum of the deficits in earnings and profits for prior taxable years beginning after December 31, 1962, plus

(B) the sum of the deficits in earnings and profits for taxable years beginning after December 31, 1959, and before January 1, 1963 (reduced by the sum of the earnings and profits for such taxable years); exceeds

(2) an amount equal to the sum of the earnings and profits for prior taxable years beginning after December 31, 1962, allocated to other earnings and profits under section 959(c)(3).

For purposes of the preceding sentence, any deficit in earnings and profits for any prior taxable year shall be taken into account under paragraph (1) for any taxable year only to the extent it has not been taken into account under such paragraph for any preceding taxable year to reduce earnings and profits of such preceding year.

INCOME TAX—CONTROLLED FOREIGN CORPORATIONS

[Sec. 952(d)]

(d) INCOME DERIVED FROM FOREIGN COUNTRY.—The Secretary shall prescribe such regulations as may be necessary or appropriate to carry out the purposes of subsection (a)(5), including regulations which treat income paid through 1 or more entities as derived from a foreign country to which section 901(j) applies if such income was, without regard to such entities, derived from such country.

Amendments

• **1986, Omnibus Budget Reconciliation Act of 1986 (P.L. 99-509)**

P.L. 99-509, §8041(b)(2):

Amended Code Sec. 952, as amended by P.L. 99-514, by adding at the end thereof new subsection (d). **Effective** 1-1-87.

[Sec. 952(d)—Stricken]

Amendments

• **1986, Tax Reform Act of 1986 (P.L. 99-514)**

P.L. 99-514, §1221(f):

Amended Code Sec. 952 by striking out (d). **Effective** for tax years of foreign corporations beginning after 12-31-86. However, for special rules and exceptions, see Act Sec. 1221(g)(2)-(3) following Code Sec. 954. Prior to amendment Code Sec. 952(d) read as follows:

(d) SPECIAL RULE IN CASE OF INDIRECT OWNERSHIP.—For purposes of subsection (c), if—

(1) a United States shareholder owns (within the meaning of section 958(a)) stock of a foreign corporation, and by reason of such ownership owns (within the meaning of such section) stock of any other foreign corporation, and

(2) any of such foreign corporations has a deficit in earnings and profits for the taxable year,

then the earnings and profits for the taxable year of each such foreign corporation which is a controlled foreign corporation shall, with respect to such United States shareholder, be properly reduced to take into account any deficit described in paragraph (2) in such manner as the Secretary shall prescribe by regulations.

• **1976, Tax Reform Act of 1976 (P.L. 94-455)**

P.L. 94-455, §1906(b)(13)(A):

Amended 1954 Code by substituting "Secretary" for "Secretary or his delegate" each place it appeared. **Effective** 2-1-77.

[Sec. 953]

SEC. 953. INSURANCE INCOME.

[Sec. 953(a)]

(a) INSURANCE INCOME.—

(1) IN GENERAL.—For purposes of section 952(a)(1), the term "insurance income" means any income which—

(A) is attributable to the issuing (or reinsuring) of an insurance or annuity contract, and

(B) would (subject to the modifications provided by subsection (b)) be taxed under subchapter L of this chapter if such income were the income of a domestic insurance company.

(2) EXCEPTION.—Such term shall not include any exempt insurance income (as defined in subsection (e)).

Amendments

• **1998, Tax and Trade Relief Extension Act of 1998 (P.L. 105-277)**

P.L. 105-277, §1005(b)(1)(A):

Amended Code Sec. 953(a). **Effective** 10-21-98. Prior to amendment, Code Sec. 953(a) read as follows:

(a) GENERAL RULE.—For purposes of section 952(a)(1), the term "insurance income" means any income which—

(1) is attributable to the issuing (or reinsuring) of any insurance or annuity contract—

(A) in connection with property in, liability arising out of activity in, or in connection with the lives or health of residents of, a country other than the country under the laws of which the controlled foreign corporation is created or organized, or

(B) in connection with risks not described in subparagraph (A) as the result of any arrangement whereby another corporation receives a substantially equal amount of premiums or other consideration in respect of issuing (or reinsuring) a contract described in subparagraph (A), and

(2) would (subject to the modifications provided by paragraphs (1) and (2) of subsection (b)) be taxed under subchapter L of this chapter if such income were the income of a domestic insurance company.

• **1986, Tax Reform Act of 1986 (P.L. 99-514)**

P.L. 99-514, §1221(b)(1):

Amended Code Sec. 953(a). **Effective**, generally, for tax years of foreign corporations beginning after 12-31-86. However, for special rules and exceptions, see Act Sec. 1221(g)(2)-(3) following Code Sec. 954. Prior to amendment, Code Sec. 953(a) read as follows:

(a) GENERAL RULE.—For purposes of section 952(a)(1), the term "income derived from the insurance of United States risks" means that income which—

(1) is attributable to the reinsurance or the issuing of any insurance or annuity contract—

(A) in connection with property in, or liability arising out of activity in, or in connection with the lives or health of residents of, the United States, or

(B) in connection with risks not included in subparagraph (A) as the result of any arrangement whereby another corporation receives a substantially equal amount of premiums or other consideration in respect to any reinsurance or the issuing of any insurance or annuity contract in connection with property in, or liability arising out of activity in, or in connection with the lives or health of residents of, the United States, and

(2) would (subject to the modifications provided by paragraphs (1) and (2) of subsection (b)) be taxed under subchapter L of this chapter if such income were the income of a domestic insurance corporation.

This section shall apply only in the case of a controlled foreign corporation which receives, during any taxable year, premiums or other consideration in respect of the reinsurance, and the issuing, of insurance and annuity contracts described in paragraph (1) in excess of 5 percent of the total of premiums and other consideration received during such taxable year in respect of all reinsurance and issuing of insurance and annuity contracts.

P.L. 99-514, §1221(b)(1), (3)(D):

Amended Code Sec. 953 by changing the section heading. **Effective**, generally, for tax years of foreign corporations beginning after 12-31-86. However, for special rules and exceptions, see Act Sec. 1221(g)(2)-(3) following Code Sec. 954. Prior to amendment, the section heading to Code Sec. 953 read as follows:

SEC. 953. INCOME FROM INSURANCE OF UNITED STATES RISKS.

• **1984, Deficit Reduction Act of 1984 (P.L. 98-369)**

P.L. 98-369, §211(b)(13)(D):

Amended Code Sec. 953(a)(2) by striking out ", (2), and (3)" and inserting in lieu thereof "and (2)". **Effective** for tax years beginning after 12-31-83.

[Sec. 953(b)]

(b) SPECIAL RULES.—For purposes of subsection (a)—

(1) The following provisions of subchapter L shall not apply:

(A) So much of section 805(a)(8) as relates to the deduction allowed under section 172.

(B) Section 832(c)(5) (relating to certain capital losses).

(2) The items referred to in—

(A) section 803(a)(1) (relating to gross amount of premiums and other considerations),

(B) section 803(a)(2) (relating to net decrease in reserves),

(C) section 805(a)(2) (relating to net increase [in] reserves), and

(D) section 832(b)(4) (relating to premiums earned on insurance contracts),

shall be taken into account only to the extent they are in respect of any reinsurance or the issuing of any insurance or annuity contract described in subsection (a)(1).

(3) Reserves for any insurance or annuity contract shall be determined in the same manner as under section 954(i).

INCOME TAX—CONTROLLED FOREIGN CORPORATIONS

(4) All items of income, expenses, losses, and deductions shall be properly allocated or apportioned under regulations prescribed by the Secretary.

Amendments

• **2017, Tax Cuts and Jobs Act (P.L. 115-97)**

P.L. 115-97, §13511(b)(7):

Amended Code Sec. 953(b)(1)(B). **Effective** for losses arising in tax years beginning after 12-31-2017. Prior to amendment, Code Sec. 953(b)(1)(B) read as follows:

(B) Section 805(a)(5) (relating to operations loss deduction).

P.L. 115-97, §13512(b)(8):

Amended Code Sec. 953(b)(1), as amended by Act Sec. 13511, by striking subparagraph (A) and by redesignating subparagraphs (B) and (C) as subparagraphs (A) and (B), respectively. **Effective** for tax years beginning after 12-31-2017. Prior to being stricken, Code Sec. 953(b)(1)(A) read as follows:

(A) The small life insurance company deduction.

• **1998, Tax and Trade Relief Extension Act of 1998 (P.L. 105-277)**

P.L. 105-277, §1005(b)(3):

Amended Code Sec. 953(b) by redesignating paragraph (3) as paragraph (4) and by inserting after paragraph (2) a new paragraph (3). **Effective** 10-21-98.

• **1988, Technical and Miscellaneous Revenue Act of 1988 (P.L. 100-647)**

P.L. 100-647, §1012(i)(7)(A)-(C):

Amended Code Sec. 953(b) by striking out paragraph (1) and redesignating paragraphs (2), (3), and (4) as paragraphs (1), (2), and (3), respectively, by striking out subparagraph (A) of paragraph (1) (as so redesignated) and inserting in lieu thereof new subparagraph (A), and by striking out "(other than those taken into account under paragraph (3))" after "deductions" in paragraph (3) (as so redesignated). **Effective** as if included in the provision of P.L. 99-514 to which it relates. Prior to amendment, Code Sec. 953(b)(1) and (b)(2)(A) read as follows:

(1) A corporation which would, if it were a domestic insurance corporation, be taxable under part II of subchapter L shall apply subsection (a) as if it were taxable under part III of subchapter L.

(2) The following provisions of subchapter L shall not apply:

(A) The special life insurance company deduction and the small life insurance company deduction.

• **1984, Deficit Reduction Act of 1984 (P.L. 98-369)**

P.L. 98-369, §211(b)(13)(A):

Amended Code Sec. 953(b) by striking out paragraph (1) and by redesignating paragraphs (2), (3), (4), and (5) as paragraphs (1), (2), (3), and (4), respectively. **Effective** for tax years beginning after 12-31-83. Prior to amendment, paragraph (1) read as follows:

(1) In the application of part I of subchapter L, life insurance company taxable income is the gain from operations as defined in section 809(b).

P.L. 98-369, §211(b)(13)(B):

Amended Code Sec. 953(b)(2), as redesignated. **Effective** for tax years beginning after 12-31-83. Prior to amendment, Code Sec. 953(b)(2) (formerly (3)) read as follows:

(3) The following provisions of subchapter L shall not apply:

(A) Section 809(d)(4) (operations loss deduction).

(B) Section 809(d)(5) (certain nonparticipating contracts).

(C) Section 809(d)(6) (group life, accident, and health insurance).

(D) Section 809(d)(10) (small business deduction).

(E) Section 817(b) (gain on property held on December 31, 1958, and certain substituted property acquired after 1958).

(F) Section 832(c)(5) (certain capital losses).

P.L. 98-369, §211(b)(13)(C):

Amended Code Sec. 953(b)(3), as redesignated, by striking out "section 809(c)(1)" and inserting in lieu thereof "section 803(a)(1)", and by striking out "section 809(c)(2)" and inserting in lieu thereof "section 803(a)(2)" and by striking out "section 809(d)(2)" and inserting in lieu thereof "section 805(a)(2)". **Effective** for tax years beginning after 12-31-83.

P.L. 98-369, §211(b)(13)(E):

Amended Code Sec. 953(b)(4), as redesignated, by striking out "paragraph (4)" and inserting in lieu thereof "paragraph (3)". **Effective** for tax years beginning after 12-31-83.

• **1976, Tax Reform Act of 1976 (P.L. 94-455)**

P.L. 94-455, §1906(b)(13)(A):

Amended 1954 Code by substituting "Secretary" for "Secretary or his delegate" each place it appeared. **Effective** 2-1-77.

• **1966, Foreign Investors Tax Act of 1966 (P.L. 89-809)**

P.L. 89-809, §104(m)(2):

Amended Code Sec. 953(b)(3)(F) by substituting "832(c)(5)" for "832(b)(5)". **Effective** 1-1-67.

[Sec. 953(c)]

(c) SPECIAL RULE FOR CERTAIN CAPTIVE INSURANCE COMPANIES.—

(1) IN GENERAL.—For purposes only of taking into account related person insurance income—

(A) the term "United States shareholder" means, with respect to any foreign corporation, a United States person (as defined in section 957(c)) who owns (within the meaning of section 958(a)) any stock of the foreign corporation,

(B) the term "controlled foreign corporation" has the meaning given to such term by section 957(a) determined by substituting "25 percent or more" for "more than 50 percent", and

(C) the pro rata share referred to in section 951(a)(1)(A) shall be determined under paragraph (5) of this subsection.

(2) RELATED PERSON INSURANCE INCOME.—For purposes of this subsection, the term "related person insurance income" means any insurance income (within the meaning of subsection (a)) attributable to a policy of insurance or reinsurance with respect to which the person (directly or indirectly) insured is a United States shareholder in the foreign corporation or a related person to such a shareholder.

(3) EXCEPTIONS.—

(A) CORPORATIONS NOT HELD BY INSUREDS.—Paragraph (1) shall not apply to any foreign corporation if at all times during the taxable year of such foreign corporation—

(i) less than 20 percent of the total combined voting power of all classes of stock of such corporation entitled to vote, and

(ii) less than 20 percent of the total value of such corporation,

is owned (directly or indirectly under the principles of section 883(c)(4)) by persons who are (directly or indirectly) insured under any policy of insurance or reinsurance issued by such corporation or who are related persons to any such person.

(B) DE MINIMIS EXCEPTION.—Paragraph (1) shall not apply to any foreign corporation for a taxable year of such corporation if the related person insurance income (determined on a gross basis) of such corporation for such taxable year is less than 20 percent of its insurance income (as so determined) for such taxable year determined without regard to those provisions of subsection (a)(1) which limit insurance income to income from countries other than the country in which the corporation was created or organized.

(C) ELECTION TO TREAT INCOME AS EFFECTIVELY CONNECTED.—Paragraph (1) shall not apply to any foreign corporation for any taxable year if—

(i) such corporation elects (at such time and in such manner as the Secretary may prescribe)—

(I) to treat its related person insurance income for such taxable year as income effectively connected with the conduct of a trade or business in the United States, and

(II) to waive all benefits (other than with respect to section 884) with respect to related person insurance income granted by the United States under any treaty between the United States and any foreign country, and

(ii) such corporation meets such requirements as the Secretary shall prescribe to ensure that the tax imposed by this chapter on such income is paid.

An election under this subparagraph made for any taxable year shall not be effective if the corporation (or any predecessor thereof) was a disqualified corporation for the taxable year for which the election was made or for any prior taxable year beginning after 1986.

(D) SPECIAL RULES FOR SUBPARAGRAPH (C).—

(i) PERIOD DURING WHICH ELECTION IN EFFECT.—

(I) IN GENERAL.—Except as provided in subclause (II), any election under subparagraph (C) shall apply to the taxable year for which made and all subsequent taxable years unless revoked with the consent of the Secretary.

INCOME TAX—CONTROLLED FOREIGN CORPORATIONS

(II) TERMINATION.—If a foreign corporation which made an election under subparagraph (C) for any taxable year is a disqualified corporation for any subsequent taxable year, such election shall not apply to any taxable year beginning after such subsequent taxable year.

(ii) EXEMPTION FROM TAX IMPOSED BY SECTION 4371.—The tax imposed by section 4371 shall not apply with respect to any related person insurance income treated as effectively connected with the conduct of a trade or business within the United States under subparagraph (C).

(E) DISQUALIFIED CORPORATION.—For purposes of this paragraph the term "disqualified corporation" means, with respect to any taxable year, any foreign corporation which is a controlled foreign corporation for an uninterrupted period of 30 days or more during such taxable year (determined without regard to this subsection) but only if a United States shareholder (determined without regard to this subsection) owns (within the meaning of section 958(a)) stock in such corporation at some time during such taxable year.

(4) TREATMENT OF MUTUAL INSURANCE COMPANIES.—In the case of a mutual insurance company—

(A) this subsection shall apply,

(B) policyholders of such company shall be treated as shareholders, and

(C) appropriate adjustments in the application of this subpart shall be made under regulations prescribed by the Secretary.

(5) DETERMINATION OF PRO RATA SHARE.—

(A) IN GENERAL.—The pro rata share determined under this paragraph for any United States shareholder is the lesser of—

(i) the amount which would be determined under paragraph (2) of section 951(a) if—

(I) only related person insurance income were taken into account,

(II) stock owned (within the meaning of section 958(a)) by United States shareholders on the last day of the taxable year were the only stock in the foreign corporation, and

(III) only distributions received by United States shareholders were taken into account under subparagraph (B) of such paragraph (2), or

(ii) the amount which would be determined under paragraph (2) of section 951(a) if the entire earnings and profits of the foreign corporation for the taxable year were subpart F income.

(B) COORDINATION WITH OTHER PROVISIONS.—The Secretary shall prescribe regulations providing for such modifications to the provisions of this subpart as may be necessary or appropriate by reason of subparagraph (A).

(6) RELATED PERSON.—For purposes of this subsection—

(A) IN GENERAL.—Except as provided in subparagraph (B), the term "related person" has the meaning given such term by section 954(d)(3).

(B) TREATMENT OF CERTAIN LIABILITY INSURANCE POLICIES.—In the case of any policy of insurance covering liability arising from services performed as a director, officer, or employee of a corporation or as a partner or employee of a partnership, the person performing such services and the entity for which such services are performed shall be treated as related persons.

(7) COORDINATION WITH SECTION 1248.—For purposes of section 1248, if any person is (or would be but for paragraph (3)) treated under paragraph (1) as a United States shareholder with respect to any foreign corporation which would be taxed under subchapter L if it were a domestic corporation and which is (or would be but for paragraph (3)) treated under paragraph (1) as a controlled foreign corporation—

(A) such person shall be treated as meeting the stock ownership requirements of section 1248(a)(2) with respect to such foreign corporation, and

(B) such foreign corporation shall be treated as a controlled foreign corporation.

(8) REGULATIONS.—The Secretary shall prescribe such regulations as may be necessary to carry out the purposes of this subsection, including—

(A) regulations preventing the avoidance of this subsection through cross insurance arrangements or otherwise, and

(B) regulations which may provide that a person will not be treated as a United States shareholder under paragraph (1) with respect to any foreign corporation if neither such person (nor any related person to such person) is (directly or indirectly) insured under any policy of insurance or reinsurance issued by such foreign corporation.

Amendments

- **2017, Tax Cuts and Jobs Act (P.L. 115-97)**

P.L. 115-97, §14212(b)(1)(D):

Amended Code Sec. 953(c)(1)(C) by striking "section 951(a)(1)(A)(i)" and inserting "section 951(a)(1)(A)". **Effective** for tax years of foreign corporations beginning after 12-31-2017, and to tax years of United States shareholders in which or with which such tax years of foreign corporations end.

- **1988, Technical and Miscellaneous Revenue Act of 1988 (P.L. 100-647)**

P.L. 100-647, §1012(i)(1)(A):

Amended Code Sec. 953(c)(3)(C) by adding at the end thereof a new sentence. **Effective** as if included in the provision of P.L. 99-514 to which it relates.

P.L. 100-647, §1012(i)(1)(B):

Amended Code Sec. 953(c)(3)(D)(i). **Effective** as if included in the provision of P.L. 99-514 to which it relates. Prior to amendment, Code Sec. 953(c)(3)(D)(i) read as follows:

(i) ELECTION IRREVOCABLE.—Any election under subparagraph (C) shall apply to the taxable year for which made and all subsequent taxable years unless revoked with the consent of the Secretary.

P.L. 100-647, §1012(i)(1)(C):

Amended Code Sec. 953(c)(3) by adding at the end thereof a new subparagraph (E). **Effective** as if included in the provision of P.L. 99-514 to which it relates.

P.L. 100-647, §1012(i)(2)(A):

Amended Code Sec. 953(c)(1) by striking out "and" at the end of subparagraph (A), by striking out the period at the end of subparagraph (B) and inserting in lieu thereof ", and", and by adding at the end thereof new subparagraph (C). **Effective** as if included in the provision of P.L. 99-514 to which it relates.

P.L. 100-647, §1012(i)(2)(B):

Amended Code Sec. 953(c) by redesignating paragraph (5) as paragraph (6) and inserting after paragraph (4) new paragraph (5). **Effective** as if included in the provision of P.L. 99-514 to which it relates.

P.L. 100-647, §1012(i)(3)(A):

Amended Code Sec. 953(c)(2) by striking out "with respect to which the primary insured is" and inserting in lieu thereof "with respect to which the person (directly or indirectly) insured is". **Effective** for tax years beginning after 12-31-87, to the extent it adds the phrase "(directly or indirectly)".

P.L. 100-647, §1012(i)(3)(B)(i)-(ii):

Amended Code Sec. 953(c)(3)(A) by striking out "persons who are the primary insured" and inserting in lieu thereof "persons who are (directly or indirectly) insured", and by striking out "to any such primary insured" and inserting in lieu thereof "to any such person". **Effective** for tax years beginning after 12-31-87, to the extent it adds the phrase "(directly or indirectly)".

P.L. 100-647, §1012(i)(4)(A):

Amended Code Sec. 953(c) by redesignating paragraph (6) as paragraph (7) and by inserting after paragraph (5) new paragraph (6). **Effective** as if included in the provision of P.L. 99-514 to which it relates.

P.L. 100-647, §1012(i)(4)(B):

Amended Code Sec. 953(c)(2) and (3)(A) by striking out "(within the meaning of section 954(d)(3))" after "related person". **Effective** as if included in the provision of P.L. 99-514 to which it relates.

P.L. 100-647, §1012(i)(5):

Amended Code Sec. 953(c)(2) by striking out "insurance income attributable" and inserting in lieu therof "insurance income (within the meaning of subsection (a)) attributable". **Effective** as if included in the provision of P.L. 99-514 to which it relates.

P.L. 100-647, §1012(i)(8)(A)-(B):

Amended Code Sec. 953(c)(3)(B) by striking out "related person insurance income" and inserting in lieu thereof "related person insurance income (determined on a gross basis)", and by striking out "its insurance income" and inserting in lieu thereof "its insurance income (as so determined)". **Effective** as if included in the provision of P.L. 99-514 to which it relates.

INCOME TAX—CONTROLLED FOREIGN CORPORATIONS

P.L. 100-647, § 1012(i)(9)(A)-(B):

Amended Code Sec. 953(c)(3)(C)(i)(II) by striking out "all benefits" and inserting in lieu thereof "all benefits (other than with respect to section 884)", and by striking out "under any income tax treaty" and inserting in lieu thereof "granted by the United States under any treaty". **Effective** as if included in the provision of P.L. 99-514 to which it relates.

P.L. 100-647, § 1012(i)(21):

Amended Code Sec. 953(c) by striking out paragraph (7) and inserting in lieu thereof new paragraphs (7)-(8). **Effective** as if included in the provision of P.L. 99-514 to which it relates. Prior to amendment, Code Sec. 953(c)(7) read as follows:

(7) REGULATIONS.—The Secretary shall prescribe such regulations as may be necessary to carry out the purposes of this subsection, including regulations preventing the avoidance of this subsection through cross insurance arrangements or otherwise.

• **1986, Tax Reform Act of 1986 (P.L. 99-514)**

P.L. 99-514, § 1221(b)(2):

Added new Code Sec. 953(c). **Effective**, generally, for tax years of foreign corporations beginning after 12-31-86. However, for special rules and exceptions, see Act Sec. 1221(g)(2)-(3) following Code Sec. 954(a).

[Sec. 953(d)]

(d) ELECTION BY FOREIGN INSURANCE COMPANY TO BE TREATED AS DOMESTIC CORPORATION.—

(1) IN GENERAL.—If—

(A) a foreign corporation is a controlled foreign corporation (as defined in section 957(a) by substituting "25 percent or more" for "more than 50 percent" and by using the definition of United States shareholder under 953(c)(1)(A)),

(B) such foreign corporation would qualify under part I or II of subchapter L for the taxable year if it were a domestic corporation,

(C) such foreign corporation meets such requirements as the Secretary shall prescribe to ensure that the taxes imposed by this chapter on such foreign corporation are paid, and

(D) such foreign corporation makes an election to have this paragraph apply and waives all benefits to such corporation granted by the United States under any treaty,

for purposes of this title, such corporation shall be treated as a domestic corporation.

(2) PERIOD DURING WHICH ELECTION IS IN EFFECT.—

(A) IN GENERAL.—Except as provided in subparagraph (B), an election under paragraph (1) shall apply to the taxable year for which made and all subsequent taxable years unless revoked with the consent of the Secretary.

(B) TERMINATION.—If a corporation which made an election under paragraph (1) for any taxable year fails to meet the requirements of subparagraphs (A), (B), and (C), of paragraph (1) for any subsequent taxable year, such election shall not apply to any taxable year beginning after such subsequent taxable year.

(3) TREATMENT OF LOSSES.—If any corporation treated as a domestic corporation under this subsection is treated as a member of an affiliated group for purposes of chapter 6 (relating to consolidated returns), any loss of such corporation shall be treated as a dual consolidated loss for purposes of section 1503(d) without regard to paragraph (2)(B) thereof.

(4) EFFECT OF ELECTION.—

(A) IN GENERAL.—For purposes of section 367, any foreign corporation making an election under paragraph (1) shall be treated as transferring (as of the 1st day of the 1st taxable year to which such election applies) all of its assets to a domestic corporation in connection with an exchange to which section 354 applies.

(B) EXCEPTION FOR PRE-1988 EARNINGS AND PROFIT.—

(i) IN GENERAL.—Earnings and profits of the foreign corporation accumulated in taxable years beginning before January 1, 1988, shall not be included in the gross income of the persons holding stock in such corporation by reason of subparagraph (A).

(ii) TREATMENT OF DISTRIBUTIONS.—For purposes of this title, any distribution made by a corporation to which an election under paragraph (1) applies out of earnings and profits accumulated in taxable years beginning before January 1, 1988, shall be treated as a distribution made by a foreign corporation.

(iii) CERTAIN RULES TO CONTINUE TO APPLY TO PRE-1988 EARNINGS.—The provisions specified in clause (iv) shall be applied without regard to paragraph (1), except that, in the case of a corporation to which an election under paragraph (1) applies, only earnings and profits accumulated in taxable years beginning before January 1, 1988, shall be taken into account.

(iv) SPECIFIED PROVISIONS.—The provisions specified in this clause are:

(I) Section 1248 (relating to gain from certain sales or exchanges of stock in certain foreign corporations).

(II) Subpart F of part III of subchapter N to the extent such subpart relates to earnings invested in United States property.

(III) Section 884 to the extent the foreign corporation reinvested 1987 earnings and profits in United States assets.

(5) EFFECT OF TERMINATION.—For purposes of section 367, if—

(A) an election is made by a corporation under paragraph (1) for any taxable year, and

(B) such election ceases to apply for any subsequent taxable year,

such corporation shall be treated as a domestic corporation transferring (as of the 1st day of such subsequent taxable year) all of its property to a foreign corporation in connection with an exchange to which section 354 applies.

(6) ADDITIONAL TAX ON CORPORATION MAKING ELECTION.—

(A) IN GENERAL.—If a corporation makes an election under paragraph (1), the amount of tax imposed by this chapter for the 1st taxable year to which such election applies shall be increased by the amount determined under subparagraph (B).

(B) AMOUNT OF TAX.—The amount of tax determined under this paragraph shall be equal to the lesser of—

(i) $3/4$ of 1 percent of the aggregate amount of capital and accumulated surplus of the corporation as of December 31, 1987, or

(ii) $1,500,000.

Amendments

• **2017, Tax Cuts and Jobs Act (P.L. 115-97)**

P.L. 115-97, § 14212(b)(3):

Amended Code Sec. 953(d)(4)(B)(iv)(II) by striking "or amounts referred to in clause (ii) or (iii) of section 951(a)(1)(A)" following "in United States property". **Effective** for tax years of foreign corporations beginning after 12-31-2017, and to tax years of United States shareholders in which or with which such tax years of foreign corporations end.

• **1989, Omnibus Budget Reconciliation Act of 1989 (P.L. 101-239)**

P.L. 101-239, § 7816(p):

Amended Code Sec. 953(d)(3) by striking "(as defined in section 1503(d))" and inserting "for purposes of section 1503(d) without regard to paragraph (2)(B) thereof". **Effective** as if included in the provision of P.L. 100-647 to which it relates.

• **1988, Technical and Miscellaneous Revenue Act of 1988 (P.L. 100-647)**

P.L. 100-647, § 6135(a):

Amended Code Sec. 953 by adding at the end thereof new subsection (d). **Effective** for tax years beginning after 12-31-87.

[Sec. 953(e)]

(e) EXEMPT INSURANCE INCOME.—For purposes of this section—

(1) EXEMPT INSURANCE INCOME DEFINED.—

(A) IN GENERAL.—The term "exempt insurance income" means income derived by a qualifying insurance company which—

(i) is attributable to the issuing (or reinsuring) of an exempt contract by such company or a qualifying insurance company branch of such company, and

(ii) is treated as earned by such company or branch in its home country for purposes of such country's tax laws.

(B) EXCEPTION FOR CERTAIN ARRANGEMENTS.—Such term shall not include income attributable to the issuing (or reinsuring) of an exempt contract as the result of any arrangement whereby another corporation receives a substantially equal amount of premiums or other consideration in respect of issuing (or reinsuring) a contract which is not an exempt contract.

(C) DETERMINATIONS MADE SEPARATELY.—For purposes of this subsection and section 954(i), the exempt insurance income and exempt contracts of a qualifying insurance company or any qualifying insurance company branch of such company shall be determined separately for such company and each such branch by taking into account—

(i) in the case of the qualifying insurance company, only items of income, deduction, gain, or loss, and activities of such company not properly allocable or attributable to any qualifying insurance company branch of such company, and

(ii) in the case of a qualifying insurance company branch, only items of income, deduction, gain, or loss and activities properly allocable or attributable to such branch.

(2) EXEMPT CONTRACT.—

(A) IN GENERAL.—The term "exempt contract" means an insurance or annuity contract issued or reinsured by a qualifying insurance company or qualifying insurance company branch in connection with property in, liability arising out of activity in, or the lives or health of residents of, a country other than the United States.

(B) MINIMUM HOME COUNTRY INCOME REQUIRED.—

(i) IN GENERAL.—No contract of a qualifying insurance company or of a qualifying insurance company branch shall be treated as an exempt contract unless such company or branch derives more than 30 percent of its net written premiums from exempt contracts (determined without regard to this subparagraph)—

(I) which cover applicable home country risks, and

(II) with respect to which no policyholder, insured, annuitant, or beneficiary is a related person (as defined in section 954(d)(3)).

(ii) APPLICABLE HOME COUNTRY RISKS.—The term "applicable home country risks" means risks in connection with property in, liability arising out of activity in, or the lives or health of residents of, the home country of the qualifying insurance company or qualifying insurance company branch, as the case may be, issuing or reinsuring the contract covering the risks.

(C) SUBSTANTIAL ACTIVITY REQUIREMENTS FOR CROSS BORDER RISKS.—A contract issued by a qualifying insurance company or qualifying insurance company branch which covers risks other than applicable home country risks (as defined in subparagraph (B)(ii)) shall not be treated as an exempt contract unless such company or branch, as the case may be—

(i) conducts substantial activity with respect to an insurance business in its home country, and

(ii) performs in its home country substantially all of the activities necessary to give rise to the income generated by such contract.

(3) QUALIFYING INSURANCE COMPANY.—The term "qualifying insurance company" means any controlled foreign corporation which—

(A) is subject to regulation as an insurance (or reinsurance) company by its home country, and is licensed, authorized, or regulated by the applicable insurance regulatory body for its home country to sell insurance, reinsurance, or annuity contracts to persons other than related persons (within the meaning of section 954(d)(3)) in such home country,

(B) derives more than 50 percent of its aggregate net written premiums from the issuance or reinsurance by such controlled foreign corporation and each of its qualifying insurance company branches of contracts—

(i) covering applicable home country risks (as defined in paragraph (2)) of such corporation or branch, as the case may be, and

(ii) with respect to which no policyholder, insured, annuitant, or beneficiary is a related person (as defined in section 954(d)(3)),

except that in the case of a branch, such premiums shall only be taken into account to the extent such premiums are treated as earned by such branch in its home country for purposes of such country's tax laws, and

(C) is engaged in the insurance business and would be subject to tax under subchapter L if it were a domestic corporation.

(4) QUALIFYING INSURANCE COMPANY BRANCH.—The term "qualifying insurance company branch" means a qualified business unit (within the meaning of section 989(a)) of a controlled foreign corporation if—

(A) such unit is licensed, authorized, or regulated by the applicable insurance regulatory body for its home country to sell insurance, reinsurance, or annuity contracts to persons other than related persons (within the meaning of section 954(d)(3)) in such home country, and

(B) such controlled foreign corporation is a qualifying insurance company, determined under paragraph (3) as if such unit were a qualifying insurance company branch.

(5) LIFE INSURANCE OR ANNUITY CONTRACT.—For purposes of this section and section 954, the determination of whether a contract issued by a controlled foreign corporation or a qualified business unit (within the meaning of section 989(a)) is a life insurance contract or an annuity contract shall be made without regard to sections 72(s), 101(f), 817(h), and 7702 if—

(A) such contract is regulated as a life insurance or annuity contract by the corporation's or unit's home country, and

(B) no policyholder, insured, annuitant, or beneficiary with respect to the contract is a United States person.

(6) HOME COUNTRY.—For purposes of this subsection, except as provided in regulations—

(A) CONTROLLED FOREIGN CORPORATION.—The term "home country" means, with respect to a controlled foreign corporation, the country in which such corporation is created or organized.

(B) QUALIFIED BUSINESS UNIT.—The term "home country" means, with respect to a qualified business unit (as defined in section 989(a)), the country in which the principal office of such unit is located and in which such unit is licensed, authorized, or regulated by the applicable insurance regulatory body to sell insurance, reinsurance, or annuity contracts to persons other than related persons (as defined in section 954(d)(3)) in such country.

(7) ANTI-ABUSE RULES.—For purposes of applying this subsection and section 954(i)—

(A) the rules of section 954(h)(7) (other than subparagraph (B) thereof) shall apply,

(B) there shall be disregarded any item of income, gain, loss, or deduction of, or derived from, an entity which is not engaged in regular and continuous transactions with persons which are not related persons,

(C) there shall be disregarded any change in the method of computing reserves a principal purpose of which is the acceleration or deferral of any item in order to claim the benefits of this subsection or section 954(i),

(D) a contract of insurance or reinsurance shall not be treated as an exempt contract (and premiums from such contract shall not be taken into account for purposes of paragraph (2)(B) or (3)) if—

INCOME TAX—CONTROLLED FOREIGN CORPORATIONS

(i) any policyholder, insured, annuitant, or beneficiary is a resident of the United States and such contract was marketed to such resident and was written to cover a risk outside the United States, or

(ii) the contract covers risks located within and without the United States and the qualifying insurance company or qualifying insurance company branch does not maintain such contemporaneous records, and file such reports, with respect to such contract as the Secretary may require,

(E) the Secretary may prescribe rules for the allocation of contracts (and income from contracts) among 2 or more qualifying insurance company branches of a qualifying insurance company in order to clearly reflect the income of such branches, and

(F) premiums from a contract shall not be taken into account for purposes of paragraph (2)(B) or (3) if such contract reinsures a contract issued or reinsured by a related person (as defined in section 954(d)(3)).

For purposes of subparagraph (D), the determination of where risks are located shall be made under the principles of section 953.

(8) COORDINATION WITH SUBSECTION (c).—In determining insurance income for purposes of subsection (c), exempt insurance income shall not include income derived from exempt contracts which cover risks other than applicable home country risks.

(9) REGULATIONS.—The Secretary shall prescribe such regulations as may be necessary or appropriate to carry out the purposes of this subsection and section 954(i).

(10) CROSS REFERENCE.—

For income exempt from foreign personal holding company income, see section 954(i).

Amendments

• **2015, Protecting Americans from Tax Hikes Act of 2015 (P.L. 114-113)**

P.L. 114-113, §128(a), Div. Q:

Amended Code Sec. 953(e) by striking paragraph (10) and by redesignating paragraph (11) as paragraph (10). **Effective** for tax years of foreign corporations beginning after 12-31-2014, and to tax years of United States shareholders with or within which any such tax year of such foreign corporation ends. Prior to being stricken, Code Sec. 953(e)(10) read as follows:

(10) APPLICATION.—This subsection and section 954(i) shall apply only to taxable years of a foreign corporation beginning after December 31, 1998, and before January 1, 2015, and to taxable years of United States shareholders with or within which any such taxable year of such foreign corporation ends. If this subsection does not apply to a taxable year of a foreign corporation beginning after December 31, 2014 (and taxable years of United States shareholders ending with or within such taxable year), then, notwithstanding the preceding sentence, subsection (a) shall be applied to such taxable years in the same manner as it would if the taxable year of the foreign corporation began in 1998.

• **2014, Tax Increase Prevention Act of 2014 (P.L. 113-295)**

P.L. 113-295, §134(a)(1)-(2), Division A:

Amended Code Sec. 953(e)(10) by striking "January 1, 2014" and inserting "January 1, 2015", and by striking "December 31, 2013" and inserting "December 31, 2014". **Effective** for tax years of foreign corporations beginning after 12-31-2013, and to tax years of United States shareholders with or within which any such tax year of such foreign corporation ends.

• **2013, American Taxpayer Relief Act of 2012 (P.L. 112-240)**

P.L. 112-240, §322(a)(1)-(2):

Amended Code Sec. 953(e)(10) by striking "January 1, 2012" and inserting "January 1, 2014", and by striking "December 31, 2011" and inserting "December 31, 2013". **Effective** for tax years of foreign corporations beginning after 12-31-2011, and to tax years of United States shareholders with or within which any such tax year of such foreign corporation ends.

• **2010, Tax Relief, Unemployment Insurance Reauthorization, and Job Creation Act of 2010 (P.L. 111-312)**

P.L. 111-312, §750(a):

Amended Code Sec. 953(e)(10) by striking "January 1, 2010" and inserting "January 1, 2012". **Effective** for tax years of foreign corporations beginning after 12-31-2009, and to tax years of United States shareholders with or within which any such tax year of such foreign corporation ends.

P.L. 111-312, §750(b):

Amended Code Sec. 953(e)(10) by striking "December 31, 2009" and inserting "December 31, 2011". **Effective** for tax years of foreign corporations beginning after 12-31-2009, and to tax years of United States shareholders with or within which any such tax year of such foreign corporation ends.

• **2008, Tax Extenders and Alternative Minimum Tax Relief Act of 2008 (P.L. 110-343)**

P.L. 110-343, Division C, §303(a)(1)-(2):

Amended Code Sec. 953(e)(10) by striking "January 1, 2009" and inserting "January 1, 2010", and by striking "December 31, 2008" and inserting "December 31, 2009". **Effective** 10-3-2008.

• **2006, Tax Increase Prevention and Reconciliation Act of 2005 (P.L. 109-222)**

P.L. 109-222, §103(a)(1)(A)-(B):

Amended Code Sec. 953(e)(10) by striking "January 1, 2007" and inserting "January 1, 2009", and by striking "December 31, 2006" and inserting "December 31, 2008". **Effective** 5-17-2006.

• **2002, Job Creation and Worker Assistance Act of 2002 (P.L. 107-147)**

P.L. 107-147, §614(a)(1)(A)-(B):

Amended Code Sec. 953(e)(10) by striking "January 1, 2002" and inserting "January 1, 2007", and by striking "December 31, 2001" and inserting "December 31, 2006". **Effective** for tax years beginning after 12-31-2001.

• **1999, Tax Relief Extension Act of 1999 (P.L. 106-170)**

P.L. 106-170, §503(a)(1)-(3):

Amended Code Sec. 953(e)(10) by striking "the first taxable year" and inserting "taxable years", by striking "January 1, 2000" and inserting "January 1, 2002", and by striking "within which such" and inserting "within which any such". **Effective** for tax years beginning after 12-31-99.

P.L. 106-170, §503(b):

Amended Code Sec. 953(e)(10) by adding at the end a new sentence. **Effective** for tax years beginning after 12-31-99.

• **1998, Tax and Trade Relief Extension Act of 1998 (P.L. 105-277)**

P.L. 105-277, §1005(b)(1)(B):

Amended Code Sec. 953 by adding at the end a new subsection (e). **Effective** 10-21-98.

[Sec. 954]

SEC. 954. FOREIGN BASE COMPANY INCOME.

[Sec. 954(a)]

(a) FOREIGN BASE COMPANY INCOME.—For purposes of section 952(a)(2), the term "foreign base company income" means for any taxable year the sum of—

(1) the foreign personal holding company income for the taxable year (determined under subsection (c) and reduced as provided in subsection (b)(5)),

(2) the foreign base company sales income for the taxable year (determined under subsection (d) and reduced as provided in subsection (b)(5)), and

(3) the foreign base company services income for the taxable year (determined under subsection (e) and reduced as provided in subsection (b)(5)).

Amendments

• **2017, Tax Cuts and Jobs Act (P.L. 115-97)**

P.L. 115-97, §14211(a)(1)-(3):

Amended Code Sec. 954(a) by inserting "and" at the end of paragraph (2), by striking the comma at the end of paragraph (3) and inserting a period, and by striking paragraph (5). **Effective** for tax years of foreign corporations beginning after 12-31-2017, and to tax years of United States shareholders with or within which such tax years of foreign corporations end. Prior to being stricken, Code Sec. 954(a)(5) read as follows:

(5) the foreign base company oil related income for the taxable year (determined under subsection (g) and reduced as provided in subsection (b)(5)).

• **2004, American Jobs Creation Act of 2004 (P.L. 108-357)**

P.L. 108-357, §415(a)(1):

Amended Code Sec. 954(a) by striking paragraph (4). **Effective** for tax years of foreign corporations beginning after 12-31-2004 and for tax years of United States shareholders with or within which such tax years of foreign corporations end. Prior to being stricken, Code Sec. 954(a)(4) read as follows:

(4) the foreign base company shipping income for the taxable year (determined under subsection (f) and reduced as provided in subsection (b)(5)), and

INCOME TAX—CONTROLLED FOREIGN CORPORATIONS

• **1986, Tax Reform Act of 1986 (P.L. 99-514)**

P.L. 99-514, §1221(c)(3)(A)(ii):

Amended Code Sec. 954(a)(5) by striking out "determined under subsection (h)" and inserting in lieu thereof "determined under subsection (g)". **Effective**, generally, for tax years of foreign corporations beginning after 12-31-86. However, for special rules and exceptions, see Act Sec. 1221(g)(2)-(3) below.

P.L. 99-514, §1221(g)(2)-(3), as amended by P.L. 100-647, §1012(i)(13), provides:

(2) SPECIAL RULE FOR REPEAL OF EXCLUSION FOR REINVESTMENT SHIPPING INCOME.—

(A) IN GENERAL.—In the case of any qualified controlled foreign corporation—

(i) the amendments made by subsection (c) shall apply to taxable years ending on or after January 1, 1992, and

(ii) sections 955(a)(1)(A) and 955(a)(2)(A) of the Internal Revenue Code of 1986 (as amended by subsection (c)(3)) shall be applied by substituting "ending before 1992" for "beginning before 1987".

(B) QUALIFIED CONTROLLED FOREIGN CORPORATION.—For purposes of subparagraph (A), the term "qualified controlled foreign corporation" means any controlled foreign corporation (as defined in section 957 of such Code)—

(i) if the United States agent of such corporation is a domestic corporation incorporated on March 13, 1951, and

(ii) if—

(I) the certificate of incorporation of such corporation is dated July 23, 1963, and

(II) such corporation has a wholly owned subsidiary and its certificate of incorporation is dated November 2, 1965.

(3) EXCEPTION FOR CERTAIN REINSURANCE CONTRACTS.—

(A) IN GENERAL.—In the case of the 1st 3 taxable years of a qualified controlled foreign insurer beginning after December 31, 1986, the amendments made by this section shall not apply to the phase-in percentage of any qualified reinsurance income.

(B) PHASE-IN PERCENTAGE.—For purposes of subparagraph (A):

In the case of taxable years beginning in:	The phase-in percentage is:
1987	75
1988	50
1989	25

(C) QUALIFIED CONTROLLED FOREIGN INSURER.—For purposes of this paragraph, the term "qualified controlled foreign insurer" means—

(i) any controlled foreign corporation which on August 16, 1986, was a member of an affiliated group (as defined in section 1504(a) of the Internal Revenue Code of 1986 without regard to subsection (b)(3) thereof) which had as its common parent a corporation incorporated in Delaware on June 9, 1967, with executive offices in New York, New York, or

(ii) any controlled foreign corporation which on August 16, 1986, was a member of an affiliated group (as so defined) which had as its common parent a corporation incorporated in Delaware on November 3, 1981, with executive offices in Philadelphia, Pennsylvania.

(D) QUALIFIED REINSURANCE INCOME.—For purposes of this paragraph, the term "qualified reinsurance income" means any insurance income attributable to risks (other than risks described in section 953(a) or 954(e) of such Code as in effect on the day before the date of the enactment of this Act) assumed under a reinsurance contract. For purposes of this subparagraph, insurance income shall mean the underwriting income (as defined in section 832(b)(3) of such Code) and investment income derived from an amount of assets (to be segregated and separately identified) equivalent to the ordinary and necessary insurance reserves and necessary surplus equal to $1/3$ of earned premium attributable to such contracts. For purposes of this paragraph, the amount of qualified reinsurance income shall not exceed the amount of insurance income from reinsurance contracts for calendar year 1985. In the case of controlled foreign corporations described in subparagraph (C)(ii), the preceding sentence shall not apply and the qualified reinsurance income of any such corporation shall not exceed such corporation's proportionate share of $27,000,000 (determined on the basis of respective amounts of qualified reinsurance income determined without regard to this subparagraph).

• **1982, Tax Equity and Fiscal Responsibility Act of 1982 (P.L. 97-248)**

P.L. 97-248, §212(a):

Amended Code Sec. 954(a) by adding paragraph (5). **Effective** for tax years of foreign corporations beginning after 12-31-82, and to tax years of United States shareholders in which, or with which, such tax years of foreign corporations end.

P.L. 97-248, §212(e):

Amended Code Sec. 954(a) by striking out "and" at the end of paragraph (3) and by striking out the period at the end of paragraph (4) and inserting in lieu thereof ", and." **Effective** for tax years of foreign corporations beginning after 12-31-82, and to tax years of United States shareholders in which or with which such tax years of foreign corporations end.

• **1975, Tax Reduction Act of 1975 (P.L. 94-12)**

P.L. 94-12, §602(d)(1)(A):

Amended Code Sec. 954(a) by adding new paragraph (4).

[Sec. 954(b)]

(b) EXCLUSIONS AND SPECIAL RULES.—

(1) [Repealed.]

(2) [Repealed.]

(3) DE MINIMIS, ETC., RULES.—For purposes of subsection (a) and section 953—

(A) DE MINIMIS RULE.—If the sum of foreign base company income (determined without regard to paragraph (5)) and the gross insurance income for the taxable year is less than the lesser of—

(i) 5 percent of gross income, or

(ii) $1,000,000,

no part of the gross income for the taxable year shall be treated as foreign base company income or insurance income.

(B) FOREIGN BASE COMPANY INCOME AND INSURANCE INCOME IN EXCESS OF 70 PERCENT OF GROSS INCOME.—If the sum of the foreign base company income (determined without regard to paragraph (5)) and the gross insurance income for the taxable year exceeds 70 percent of gross income, the entire gross income for the taxable year shall, subject to the provisions of paragraphs (4) and (5), be treated as foreign base company income or insurance income (whichever is appropriate).

(C) GROSS INSURANCE INCOME.—For purposes of subparagraphs (A) and (B), the term "gross insurance income" means any item of gross income taken into account in determining insurance income under section 953.

(4) EXCEPTION FOR CERTAIN INCOME SUBJECT TO HIGH FOREIGN TAXES.—For purposes of subsection (a) and section 953, foreign base company income and insurance income shall not include any item of income received by a controlled foreign corporation if the taxpayer establishes to the satisfaction of the Secretary that such income was subject to an effective rate of income tax imposed by a foreign country greater than 90 percent of the maximum rate of tax specified in section 11.

(5) DEDUCTIONS TO BE TAKEN INTO ACCOUNT.—For purposes of subsection (a), the foreign personal holding company income, the foreign base company sales income, and the foreign base company services income shall be reduced, under regulations prescribed by the Secretary, so as to take into account deductions (including taxes) properly allocable to such income. Except to the extent provided in regulations prescribed by the Secretary, any interest which is paid or accrued by the controlled foreign corporation to any United States shareholder in such corporation (or any controlled foreign corporation related to such a shareholder) shall be allocated first to foreign personal holding company income which is passive income (within the meaning of section 904(d)(2)) of such corporation to the extent thereof. The Secretary may, by regulations, provide that the preceding sentence shall apply also to interest paid or accrued to other persons.

***

(6) FOREIGN BASE COMPANY OIL RELATED INCOME NOT TREATED AS ANOTHER KIND OF BASE COMPANY INCOME.—Income of a corporation which is foreign base company oil related income shall not be considered foreign base company income of such corporation under paragraph (2), or (3) of subsection (a).

Amendments

• **2017, Tax Cuts and Jobs Act (P.L. 115-97)**

P.L. 115-97, §14211(b)(2)(A)-(C):

Amended Code Sec. 954(b) by striking the second sentence of paragraph (4), by striking "the foreign base company services income, and the foreign base company oil related income" in paragraph (5) and inserting "and the foreign base company services income", and by striking paragraph (6). **Effective** for tax years of foreign corporations beginning after 12-31-2017, and to tax years of United States shareholders with or within which such tax years of foreign corporations end. Prior to being stricken, the second sentence of Code Sec. 954(b)(4) and Code Sec. 954(b)(6) read as follows:

The preceding sentence shall not apply to foreign base company oil-related income described in subsection (a)(5).

• **2004, American Jobs Creation Act of 2004 (P.L. 108-357)**

P.L. 108-357, §415(c)(2)(A):

Amended Code Sec. 954(b)(5) by striking "the foreign base company shipping income," immediately following "the foreign base company services income,". **Effective** for tax years of foreign corporations beginning after 12-31-2004 and for tax years of United States shareholders with or within which such tax years of foreign corporations end.

INCOME TAX—CONTROLLED FOREIGN CORPORATIONS

P.L. 108-357, § 415(c)(2)(B)-(C):

Amended Code Sec. 954(b) by striking paragraphs (6) and (7) and by redesignating paragraph (8) as paragraph (6). **Effective** for tax years of foreign corporations beginning after 12-31-2004 and for tax years of United States shareholders with or within which such tax years of foreign corporations end. Prior to being stricken, Code Sec. 954(b)(6)-(7) read as follows:

(6) SPECIAL RULES FOR FOREIGN BASE COMPANY SHIPPING INCOME.—Income of a corporation which is foreign base company shipping income under paragraph (4) of subsection (a)—

(A) shall not be considered foreign base company income of such corporation under any other paragraph of subsection (a) and

(B) if distributed through a chain of ownership described under section 958(a), shall not be included in foreign base company income of another controlled foreign corporation in such chain.

(7) SPECIAL EXCLUSION FOR FOREIGN BASE COMPANY SHIPPING INCOME.—Income of a corporation which is foreign base company shipping income under paragraph (4) of subsection (a) shall be excluded from foreign base company income if derived by a controlled foreign corporation from, or in connection with, the use (or hiring or leasing for use) of an aircraft or vessel in foreign commerce between two points within the foreign country in which such corporation is created or organized and such aircraft or vessel is registered.

- **1993, Omnibus Budget Reconciliation Act of 1993 (P.L. 103-66)**

P.L. 103-66, § 13235(a)(3)(B):

Amended Code Sec. 954(b)(8) by striking "(1)," after "paragraph". **Effective** for tax years beginning after 12-31-92.

- **1988, Technical and Miscellaneous Revenue Act of 1988 (P.L. 100-647)**

P.L. 100-647, § 1012(i)(12):

Amended Code Sec. 954(b)(6) and (7) by striking out "(determined without regard to the exclusion under paragraph (2) of this subsection)" after "subsection (a)". **Effective** as if included in the provision of P.L. 99-514 to which it relates.

- **1986, Tax Reform Act of 1986 (P.L. 99-514)**

P.L. 99-514, § 1201(c):

Amended Code Sec. 954(b)(5) by adding a new sentence at the end. **Effective**, generally, for tax years beginning after 12-31-86. However, for special rules, see Act Sec. 1201(e) following Code Sec. 904.

P.L. 99-514, § 1221(c)(1):

Repealed Code Sec. 954(b)(2). **Effective**, generally, for tax years of foreign corporations beginning after 12-31-86. However, for special rules and exceptions, see Act Sec. 1221(g)(2)-(3) in the amendment note to Code Sec. 954(a). Prior to repeal, Code Sec. 954(b)(2) read as follows:

(2) EXCLUSION FOR REINVESTED SHIPPING INCOME.—For purposes of subsection (a), foreign base company income does not include foreign base company shipping income to the extent that the amount of such income does not exceed the increase for the taxable year in qualified investments in foreign base company shipping operations of the controlled foreign corporation (as determined under subsection (g)).

P.L. 99-514, § 1221(d):

Amended Code Sec. 954(b)(4). **Effective**, generally, for tax years of foreign corporations beginning after 12-31-86. However, for special rules and exceptions, see Act Sec. 1221(g)(2)-(3) in the amendment note to Code Sec. 954(a). Prior to amendment, Code Sec. 954(b)(4) read as follows:

(4) EXCEPTION FOR FOREIGN CORPORATIONS NOT AVAILED OF TO REDUCE TAXES.—For purposes of subsection (a), foreign base company income does not include any item of income received by a controlled foreign corporation if it is established to the satisfaction of the Secretary that neither—

(A) the creation or organization of such controlled foreign corporation under the laws of the foreign country in which it is incorporated (or, in the case of a controlled foreign corporation which is an acquired corporation, the acquisition of such corporation created or organized under the laws of the foreign country in which it is incorporated), nor

(B) the effecting of the transaction giving rise to such income through the controlled foreign corporation,

has as one of its significant purposes a substantial reduction of income, war profits, or excess profits or similar taxes. The preceding sentence shall not apply to foreign base company oil related income described in subsection (a)(5).

P.L. 99-514, § 1223(a):

Amended Code Sec. 954(b)(3). **Effective** for tax years beginning after 12-31-86. For a special rule, see Act Sec. 1227, below. Prior to amendment, Code Sec. 954(b)(3) read as follows:

(3) SPECIAL RULE WHERE FOREIGN BASE COMPANY INCOME IS LESS THAN 10 PERCENT OR MORE THAN 70 PERCENT OF GROSS INCOME.—For purposes of subsection (a)—

(A) If the foreign base company income (determined without regard to paragraphs (2) and (5)) is less than 10 percent of gross income, no part of the gross income of the taxable year shall be treated as foreign base company income.

(B) If the foreign base company income (determined without regard to paragraphs (2) and (5)) exceeds 70 percent of gross income, the entire gross income of the taxable year shall, subject to the provisions of paragraphs (2), (4), and (5), be treated as foreign base company income.

P.L. 99-514, § 1227, provides:

SEC. 1227. SPECIAL RULE FOR APPLICATION OF SECTION 954 TO CERTAIN DIVIDENDS.

(a) IN GENERAL.—For purposes of section 954(c)(3)(A) of the Internal Revenue Code of 1986, any dividends received by a qualified controlled foreign corporation (within the meaning of section 951 of such Code) during any of its 1st 5 taxable years beginning after December 31, 1986, with respect to its 32.7 percent interest in a Brazilian corporation shall be treated as if such Brazilian corporation were a related person to the qualified controlled foreign corporation to the extent the Brazilian corporation's income is attributable to its interest in the trade or business of mining in Brazil.

(b) QUALIFIED CONTROLLED FOREIGN CORPORATION.—For purposes of this section, a qualified controlled foreign corporation is a corporation the greater than 99 percent shareholder of which is a company originally imcorporated in Montana on July 9, 1951 (the name of which was changed on August 10, 1966).

(c) EFFECTIVE DATE.—The amendment made by this section shall apply to dividends received after December 31, 1986.

- **1982, Tax Equity and Fiscal Responsibility Act of 1982 (P.L. 97-248)**

P.L. 97-248, § 212(b)(1):

Amended Code Sec. 954(b)(5) by striking out "and the foreign base company shipping income" and inserting in lieu thereof ", the foreign base company shipping income, and the foreign base company oil related income." **Effective** for tax years of foreign corporations beginning after 12-31-82, and to tax years of United States shareholders in which or with which such tax years of foreign corporations end.

P.L. 97-248, § 212(b)(2):

Amended Code Sec. 954(b) by adding paragraph (8). **Effective** for tax years of foreign corporations beginning after 12-31-82, and to tax years of United States shareholders in which or with which such tax years of foreign corporations end.

P.L. 97-248, § 212(d):

Amended Code Sec. 954(b)(4) by adding the last sentence. **Effective** for tax years of foreign corporations beginning after 12-31-82, and to tax years of United States shareholders in which or with which such tax years of foreign corporations end.

- **1976, Tax Reform Act of 1976 (P.L. 94-455)**

P.L. 94-455, § 1024(a):

Added Code Sec. 954(b)(7). **Effective** for tax years of foreign corporations beginning after 12-31-75, and to tax years of United States shareholders (within the meaning of Code Sec. 951(b)) within which or with which such tax years of such foreign corporations end.

- **1976, Tax Reform Act of 1976 (P.L. 94-455)**

P.L. 94-455, § 1906(b)(13)(A):

Amended 1954 Code by substituting "Secretary" for "Secretary or his delegate" each place it appeared. **Effective** 2-1-77.

- **1975, Tax Reduction Act of 1975 (P.L. 94-12)**

P.L. 94-12, § 602(c):

Repealed Code Sec. 954(b)(1). **Effective** for tax years of foreign corporations beginning after 12-31-75, and for tax years of U. S. shareholders within which or with which such tax years of such foreign corporations end.

P.L. 94-12, § 602(d)(1)(B):

Amended Code Sec. 954(b)(2). **Effective** for tax years of foreign corporations beginning after 12-31-75, and for tax years of U. S. shareholders within which or with which such tax years of such foreign corporations end. Prior to amendment it read as follows:

"(2) Exclusion of certain shipping income.—For purposes of subsection (a), foreign base company income does not include income derived from, or in connection with, the use (or hiring or leasing for use) of any aircraft or vessel in foreign commerce, or the performance of services directly related to the use of any such aircraft or vessel."

P.L. 94-12, § 602(d)(1)(C):

Amended Code Sec. 954(b)(3)(A) and (B) by substituting paragraphs "(2) and (5)" for paragraphs "(1) and (5)" and amended subparagraph (B) by substituting "(2)" for "(1), (2)". **Effective** for tax years of foreign corporations beginning after 12-31-75, and for tax years of U. S. shareholders within which or with which such tax years of such foreign corporations end.

P.L. 94-12, § 602(d)(E):

Amended Code Sec. 954(b)(5) by substituting "the foreign base company services income, and the foreign base company shipping income" for "the foreign base company services income." **Effective** for tax years of foreign corporations beginning after 12-31-75, and for tax years of U. S. shareholders within which or with which such tax years of such foreign corporations end.

P.L. 94-12, § 602(d)(1)(F):

Amended Code Sec. 954(b) by adding new paragraph (6). **Effective** for tax years of foreign corporations beginning after 12-31-75, and for tax years of U. S. shareholders within which or with which such tax years of such foreign corporations end.

P.L. 94-12, § 602(e):

Amended Code Sec. 954(b)(3) by substituting "10 percent" for "30 percent." **Effective** for tax years of foreign corporations beginning after 12-31-75, and for tax years of U. S. shareholders within which or with which such tax years of such foreign corporations end.

- **1969, Tax Reform Act of 1969 (P.L. 91-172)**

P.L. 91-172, § 909(a):

Amended Code Sec. 954(b)(4). **Effective** for tax years ending after 10-9-69. Prior to amendment Sec. 954(b)(4) read as follows:

"(4) Exception for foreign corporations not availed of to reduce taxes.—For purposes of subsection (a), foreign base company income does not include any item of income received by a controlled foreign corporation if it is established to the satisfaction of the Secretary or his delegate with respect to such item that the creation or organization of the controlled foreign corporation receiving such item under the laws of the foreign country in which it is incorporated does not have the effect of substantial reduction of income, war profits, or excess profits taxes or similar taxes."

Sec. 954(b)(5)

INCOME TAX—CONTROLLED FOREIGN CORPORATIONS

[Sec. 954(c)]

(c) FOREIGN PERSONAL HOLDING COMPANY INCOME.—

(1) IN GENERAL.—For purposes of subsection (a)(1), the term "foreign personal holding company income" means the portion of the gross income which consists of:

(A) DIVIDENDS, ETC.—Dividends, interest, royalties, rents, and annuities.

(B) CERTAIN PROPERTY TRANSACTIONS.—The excess of gains over losses from the sale or exchange of property—

(i) which gives rise to income described in subparagraph (A) (after application of paragraph (2)(A)) other than property which gives rise to income not treated as foreign personal holding company income by reason of subsection (h) or (i) for the taxable year,

(ii) which is an interest in a trust, partnership, or REMIC, or

(iii) which does not give rise to any income.

Gains and losses from the sale or exchange of any property which, in the hands of the controlled foreign corporation, is properly described in section 1221(a)(1) shall not be taken into account under this subparagraph.

(C) COMMODITIES TRANSACTIONS.—The excess of gains over losses from transactions (including futures, forward, and similar transactions) in any commodities. This subparagraph shall not apply to gains or losses which—

(i) arise out of commodity hedging transactions (as defined in paragraph (5)(A)),

(ii) are active business gains or losses from the sale of commodities, but only if substantially all of the controlled foreign corporation's commodities are property described in paragraph (1), (2), or (8) of section 1221(a), or

(iii) are foreign currency gains or losses (as defined in section 988(b)) attributable to any section 988 transactions.

(D) FOREIGN CURRENCY GAINS.—The excess of foreign currency gains over foreign currency losses (as defined in section 988(b)) attributable to any section 988 transactions. This subparagraph shall not apply in the case of any transaction directly related to the business needs of the controlled foreign corporation.

(E) INCOME EQUIVALENT TO INTEREST.—Any income equivalent to interest, including income from commitment fees (or similar amounts) for loans actually made.

(F) INCOME FROM NOTIONAL PRINCIPAL CONTRACTS.—

(i) IN GENERAL.—Net income from notional principal contracts.

(ii) COORDINATION WITH OTHER CATEGORIES OF FOREIGN PERSONAL HOLDING COMPANY INCOME.—Any item of income, gain, deduction, or loss from a notional principal contract entered into for purposes of hedging any item described in any preceding subparagraph shall not be taken into account for purposes of this subparagraph but shall be taken into account under such other subparagraph.

(G) PAYMENTS IN LIEU OF DIVIDENDS.—Payments in lieu of dividends which are made pursuant to an agreement to which section 1058 applies.

(H) PERSONAL SERVICE CONTRACTS.—

(i) Amounts received under a contract under which the corporation is to furnish personal services if—

(I) some person other than the corporation has the right to designate (by name or by description) the individual who is to perform the services, or

(II) the individual who is to perform the services is designated (by name or by description) in the contract, and

(ii) amounts received from the sale or other disposition of such a contract.

This subparagraph shall apply with respect to amounts received for services under a particular contract only if at some time during the taxable year 25 percent or more in value of the outstanding stock of the corporation is owned, directly or indirectly, by or for the individual who has performed, is to perform, or may be designated (by name or by description) as the one to perform, such services.

(2) EXCEPTION FOR CERTAIN AMOUNTS.—

(A) RENTS AND ROYALTIES DERIVED IN ACTIVE BUSINESS.—Foreign personal holding company income shall not include rents and royalties which are derived in the active conduct of a trade or business and which are received from a person other than a related person (within the meaning of subsection (d)(3)). For purposes of the preceding sentence, rents derived from leasing an aircraft or vessel in foreign commerce shall not fail to be treated as derived in the active conduct of a trade or business if, as determined under regulations prescribed by the Secretary, the active leasing expenses are not less than 10 percent of the profit on the lease.

(B) CERTAIN EXPORT FINANCING.—Foreign personal holding company income shall not include any interest which is derived in the conduct of a banking business and which is export financing interest (as defined in section 904(d)(2)(G)).

(C) EXCEPTION FOR DEALERS.—Except as provided by regulations, in the case of a regular dealer in property which is property described in paragraph (1)(B), forward contracts, option contracts, or similar financial instruments (including notional principal contracts and all instruments referenced to commodities), there shall not be taken into account in computing foreign personal holding company income—

(i) any item of income, gain, deduction, or loss (other than any item described in subparagraph (A), (E), or (G) of paragraph (1)) from any transaction (including hedging transactions and transactions involving physical settlement) entered into in the ordinary course of such dealer's trade or business as such a dealer, and

(ii) if such dealer is a dealer in securities (within the meaning of section 475), any interest or dividend or equivalent amount described in subparagraph (E) or (G) of paragraph (1) from any transaction (including any hedging transaction or transaction described in section 956(c)(2)(I)) entered into in the ordinary course of such dealer's trade or business as such a dealer in securities, but only if the income from the transaction is attributable to activities of the dealer in the country under the laws of which the dealer is created or organized (or in the case of a qualified business unit described in section 989(a), is attributable to activities of the unit in the country in which the unit both maintains its principal office and conducts substantial business activity).

(3) CERTAIN INCOME RECEIVED FROM RELATED PERSONS.—

(A) IN GENERAL.—Except as provided in subparagraph (B), the term "foreign personal holding company income" does not include—

(i) dividends and interest received from a related person which (I) is a corporation created or organized under the laws of the same foreign country under the laws of which the controlled foreign corporation is created or organized, and (II) has a substantial part of its assets used in its trade or business located in such same foreign country, and

(ii) rents and royalties received from a corporation which is a related person for the use of, or the privilege of using, property within the country under the laws of which the controlled foreign corporation is created or organized.

To the extent provided in regulations, payments made by a partnership with 1 or more corporate partners shall be treated as made by such corporate partners in proportion to their respective interests in the partnership.

(B) EXCEPTION NOT TO APPLY TO ITEMS WHICH REDUCE SUBPART F INCOME.—Subparagraph (A) shall not apply in the case of any interest, rent, or royalty to the extent such interest, rent, or royalty reduces the payor's subpart F income or creates (or increases) a deficit which under section 952(c) may reduce the subpart F income of the payor or another controlled foreign corporation.

INCOME TAX—CONTROLLED FOREIGN CORPORATIONS

(C) EXCEPTION FOR CERTAIN DIVIDENDS.—Subparagraph (A)(i) shall not apply to any dividend with respect to any stock which is attributable to earnings and profits of the distributing corporation accumulated during any period during which the person receiving such dividend did not hold such stock either directly, or indirectly through a chain of one or more subsidiaries each of which meets the requirements of subparagraph (A)(i).

(4) LOOK-THRU RULE FOR CERTAIN PARTNERSHIP SALES.—

(A) IN GENERAL.—In the case of any sale by a controlled foreign corporation of an interest in a partnership with respect to which such corporation is a 25-percent owner, such corporation shall be treated for purposes of this subsection as selling the proportionate share of the assets of the partnership attributable to such interest. The Secretary shall prescribe such regulations as may be appropriate to prevent abuse of the purposes of this paragraph, including regulations providing for coordination of this paragraph with the provisions of subchapter K.

(B) 25-PERCENT OWNER.—For purposes of this paragraph, the term "25-percent owner" means a controlled foreign corporation which owns directly 25 percent or more of the capital or profits interest in a partnership. For purposes of the preceding sentence, if a controlled foreign corporation is a shareholder or partner of a corporation or partnership, the controlled foreign corporation shall be treated as owning directly its proportionate share of any such capital or profits interest held directly or indirectly by such corporation or partnership. If a controlled foreign corporation is treated as owning a capital or profits interest in a partnership under constructive ownership rules similar to the rules of section 958(b), the controlled foreign corporation shall be treated as owning such interest directly for purposes of this subparagraph.

(5) DEFINITION AND SPECIAL RULES RELATING TO COMMODITY TRANSACTIONS.—

(A) COMMODITY HEDGING TRANSACTIONS.—For purposes of paragraph (1)(C)(i), the term "commodity hedging transaction" means any transaction with respect to a commodity if such transaction—

(i) is a hedging transaction as defined in section 1221(b)(2), determined—

(I) without regard to subparagraph (A)(ii) thereof,

(II) by applying subparagraph (A)(i) thereof by substituting "ordinary property or property described in section 1231(b)" for "ordinary property", and

(III) by substituting "controlled foreign corporation" for "taxpayer" each place it appears, and

(ii) is clearly identified as such in accordance with section 1221(a)(7).

(B) TREATMENT OF DEALER ACTIVITIES UNDER PARAGRAPH (1)(C).—Commodities with respect to which gains and losses are not taken into account under paragraph (2)(C) in computing a controlled foreign corporation's foreign personal holding company income shall not be taken into account in applying the substantially all test under paragraph (1)(C)(ii) to such corporation.

(C) REGULATIONS.—The Secretary shall prescribe such regulations as are appropriate to carry out the purposes of paragraph (1)(C) in the case of transactions involving related parties.

(6) LOOK-THRU RULE FOR RELATED CONTROLLED FOREIGN CORPORATIONS.—

(A) IN GENERAL.—For purposes of this subsection, dividends, interest, rents, and royalties received or accrued from a controlled foreign corporation which is a related person shall not be treated as foreign personal holding company income to the extent attributable or properly allocable (determined under rules similar to the rules of subparagraphs (C) and (D) of section 904(d)(3)) to income of the related person which is neither subpart F income nor income treated as effectively connected with the conduct of a trade or business in the United States. For purposes of this subparagraph, interest shall include factoring income which is treated as income equivalent to interest for purposes of paragraph (1)(E). The Secretary shall prescribe such regulations as may be necessary or appropriate to carry out this paragraph, including such regulations as may be necessary or appropriate to prevent the abuse of the purposes of this paragraph.

(B) EXCEPTION.—Subparagraph (A) shall not apply in the case of any interest, rent, or royalty to the extent such interest, rent, or royalty creates (or increases) a deficit which under section 952(c) may reduce the subpart F income of the payor or another controlled foreign corporation.

(C) APPLICATION.—Subparagraph (A) shall apply to taxable years of foreign corporations beginning after December 31, 2005, and before January 1, 2026, and to taxable years of United States shareholders with or within which such taxable years of foreign corporations end.

Amendments

• **2020, Taxpayer Certainty and Disaster Tax Relief Act of 2020 (P.L. 116-260)**

P.L. 116-260, §111(a), Div. EE:

Amended Code Sec. 954(c)(6)(C) by striking "January 1, 2021" and inserting "January 1, 2026". **Effective** for tax years of foreign corporations beginning after 12-31-2020, and to tax years of United States shareholders with or within which such tax years of foreign corporations end.

• **2019, Taxpayer Certainty and Disaster Tax Relief Act of 2019 (P.L. 116-94)**

P.L. 116-94, §145(a), Div. Q:

Amended Code Sec. 954(c)(6)(C) by striking "January 1, 2020" and inserting "January 1, 2021". **Effective** for tax years of foreign corporations beginning after 12-31-2019, and to tax years of United States shareholders with or within which such tax years of foreign corporations end.

• **2015, Protecting Americans from Tax Hikes Act of 2015 (P.L. 114-113)**

P.L. 114-113, §144(a), Div. Q:

Amended Code Sec. 954(c)(6)(C) by striking "January 1, 2015" and inserting "January 1, 2020". **Effective** for tax years of foreign corporations beginning after 12-31-2014, and to tax years of United States shareholders with or within which such tax years of foreign corporations end.

• **2014, Tax Increase Prevention Act of 2014 (P.L. 113-295)**

P.L. 113-295, §135(a), Division A:

Amended Code Sec. 954(c)(6)(C) by striking "January 1, 2014" and inserting "January 1, 2015". **Effective** for tax years of foreign corporations beginning after 12-31-2013, and to tax years of United States shareholders with or within which such tax years of foreign corporations end.

• **2013, American Taxpayer Relief Act of 2012 (P.L. 112-240)**

P.L. 112-240, §323(a):

Amended Code Sec. 954(c)(6)(C) by striking "January 1, 2012" and inserting "January 1, 2014". **Effective** for tax years of foreign corporations beginning after 12-31-2011, and to tax years of United States shareholders with or within which such tax years of foreign corporations end.

• **2010, Tax Relief, Unemployment Insurance Reauthorization, and Job Creation Act of 2010 (P.L. 111-312)**

P.L. 111-312, §751(a):

Amended Code Sec. 954(c)(6)(C) by striking "January 1, 2010" and inserting "January 1, 2012". **Effective** for tax years of foreign corporations beginning after 12-31-2009, and to tax years of United States shareholders with or within which any such tax year of such foreign corporation ends.

• **2008, Tax Extenders and Alternative Minimum Tax Relief Act of 2008 (P.L. 110-343)**

P.L. 110-343, Division C, §304(a):

Amended Code Sec. 954(c)(6)(C) by striking "January 1, 2009" and inserting "January 1, 2010". **Effective** for tax years of foreign corporations beginning after 12-31-2007, and to tax years of United States shareholders with or within which such tax years of foreign corporations end.

• **2007, Tax Technical Corrections Act of 2007 (P.L. 110-172)**

P.L. 110-172, §4(a):

Amended Code Sec. 954(c)(6) by redesignating subparagraph (B) as subparagraph (C) and inserting after subparagraph (A) a new subparagraph (B). **Effective** as if included in the provision of the Tax Increase Prevention and Reconciliation Act of 2005 (P.L. 109-222) to which it relates [**effective** for tax years of foreign corporations

INCOME TAX—CONTROLLED FOREIGN CORPORATIONS

beginning after 12-31-2005, and to tax years of United States shareholders with or within which such tax years of foreign corporations end.—CCH].

P.L. 110-172, §11(a)(19):

Amended Code Sec. 954(c)(1)(F). **Effective** 12-29-2007. Prior to amendment, Code Sec. 954(c)(1)(F) read as follows:

(F) INCOME FROM NOTIONAL PRINCIPAL CONTRACTS.—Any item of income, gain, deduction, or loss from a notional principal contract entered into for purposes of hedging any item described in any preceding subparagraph shall not be taken into account for purposes of this subparagraph but shall be taken into account under such other subparagraph.

P.L. 110-172, §11(a)(20):

Amended Code Sec. 954(c)(1) by redesignating subparagraph (I) as subparagraph (H). **Effective** 12-29-2007.

P.L. 110-172, §11(g)(15)(B):

Amended Code Sec. 954(c)(2)(C)(ii) by striking "section 956(c)(2)(J)" and inserting "section 956(c)(2)(I)". **Effective** 12-29-2007.

- **2006, Tax Relief and Health Care Act of 2006 (P.L. 109-432)**

P.L. 109-432, Division A, §426(a)(1)(A):

Amended the first sentence of Code Sec. 954(c)(6)(A) by striking "which is not subpart F income" and inserting "which is neither subpart F income nor income treated as effectively connected with the conduct of a trade or business in the United States". **Effective** as if included in section 103(b) of the Tax Increase Prevention and Reconciliation Act of 2005 (P.L. 109-222) [**effective** for tax years of foreign corporations beginning after 12-31-2005, and to tax years of United States shareholders with or within which such tax years of foreign corporations end.—CCH].

P.L. 109-432, Division A, §426(a)(1)(B):

Amended Code Sec. 954(c)(6)(A) by striking the last sentence and inserting a new sentence. **Effective** as if included in section 103(b) of the Tax Increase Prevention and Reconciliation Act of 2005 (P.L. 109-222) [**effective** for tax years of foreign corporations beginning after 12-31-2005, and to tax years of United States shareholders with or within which such tax years of foreign corporations end.—CCH]. Prior to being stricken, the last sentence of Code Sec. 954(c)(6)(A) read as follows:

The Secretary shall prescribe such regulations as may be appropriate to prevent the abuse of the purposes of this paragraph.

- **2006, Tax Increase Prevention and Reconciliation Act of 2005 (P.L. 109-222)**

P.L. 109-222, §103(b)(1):

Amended Code Sec. 954(c) by adding at the end a new paragraph (6). **Effective** for tax years of foreign corporations beginning after 12-31-2005, and to tax years of United States shareholders with or within which such tax years of foreign corporations end.

- **2005, Gulf Opportunity Zone Act of 2005 (P.L. 109-135)**

P.L. 109-135, §403(m):

Amended Code Sec. 954(c)(4)(B) by adding at the end a new sentence. **Effective** as if included in the provision of the American Jobs Creation Act of 2004 (P.L. 108-357) to which it relates [**effective** for tax years of foreign corporations beginning after 12-31-2004, and to tax years of United States shareholders with or within which such tax years of foreign corporations end.—CCH].

P.L. 109-135, §412(ll):

Amended Code Sec. 954(c)(1)(C)(i) by striking "paragraph (4)(A)" and inserting "paragraph (5)(A)". **Effective** 12-21-2005.

P.L. 109-135, §412(mm):

Amended Code Sec. 954(c)(1)(F) by striking "Net income from notional principal contracts." after "Income from notional principal contracts.—". **Effective** 12-21-2005.

- **2004, American Jobs Creation Act of 2004 (P.L. 108-357)**

P.L. 108-357, §412(a):

Amended Code Sec. 954(c) by adding after paragraph (3) a new paragraph (4). **Effective** for tax years of foreign corporations beginning after 12-31-2004, and for tax years of United States shareholders with or within which such tax years of foreign corporations end.

P.L. 108-357, §413(b)(2):

Amended Code Sec. 954(c)(1) by adding at the end a new subparagraph (I)[H]. **Effective** for tax years of foreign corporations beginning after 12-31-2004, and for tax years of United States shareholders with or within which such tax years of foreign corporations end.

P.L. 108-357, §414(a):

Amended Code Sec. 954(c)(1)(C)(i)-(ii). **Effective** for transactions entered into after 12-31-2004. Prior to amendment, Code Sec. 954(c)(1)(C)(i)-(ii) read as follows:

(i) arise out of bona fide hedging transactions reasonably necessary to the conduct of any business by a producer, processor, merchant, or handler of a commodity in the manner in which such business is customarily and usually conducted by others, or

(ii) are active business gains or losses from the sale of commodities, but only if substantially all of the controlled foreign corporation's business is as an active producer, processor, merchant, or handler of commodities, or

P.L. 108-357, §414(b):

Amended Code Sec. 954(c) by adding after paragraph (4), as amended by this Act, a new paragraph (5). **Effective** for transactions entered into after 12-31-2004.

P.L. 108-357, §414(c):

Amended Code Sec. 954(c)(2)(C)(i) by inserting "and transactions involving physical settlement" after "(including hedging transactions)". **Effective** for transactions entered into after 12-31-2004.

P.L. 108-357, §415(b):

Amended Code Sec. 954(c)(2)(A) by adding at the end a new sentence. **Effective** for tax years of foreign corporations beginning after 12-31-2004 and for tax years of United States shareholders with or within which such tax years of foreign corporations end.

- **1999, Tax Relief Extension Act of 1999 (P.L. 106-170)**

P.L. 106-170, §532(c)(2)(Q), as amended by P.L. 107-147, §417(24)(B)(ii):

Amended Code Sec. 954(c)(1)(B) by striking "section 1221(1)" and inserting "section 1221(a)(1)". **Effective** for any instrument held, acquired, or entered into, any transaction entered into, and supplies held or acquired on or after 12-17-99.

- **1998, Tax and Trade Relief Extension Act of 1998 (P.L. 105-277)**

P.L. 105-277, §1005(c):

Amended Code Sec. 954(c)(2)(C). **Effective** 10-21-98. Prior to amendment, Code Sec. 954(c)(2)(C) read as follows:

(C) EXCEPTION FOR DEALERS.—Except as provided in subparagraph (A), (E), or (G) of paragraph (1) or by regulations, in the case of a regular dealer in property (within the meaning of paragraph (1)(B)), forward contracts, option contracts, or similar financial instruments (including notional principal contracts and all instruments referenced to commodities), there shall not be taken into account in computing foreign personal holding income any item of income, gain, deduction, or loss from any transaction (including hedging transactions) entered into in the ordinary course of such dealer's trade or business as such a dealer.

P.L. 105-277, §1005(e):

Amended Code Sec. 954(c)(1)(B)(i) by inserting "other than property which gives rise to income not treated as foreign personal holding company income by reason of subsection (h) or (i) for the taxable year" before the comma at the end. **Effective** 10-21-98.

- **1997, Taxpayer Relief Act of 1997 (P.L. 105-34)**

P.L. 105-34, §1051(a)(1):

Amended Code Sec. 954(c)(1) by adding at the end new subparagraphs (F) and (G). **Effective** for tax years beginning after 8-5-97.

P.L. 105-34, §1051(a)(2)(A)-(B):

Amended Code Sec. 954(c)(1)(B) by striking the second sentence and by striking "also" after "1221(1)" in the last sentence. **Effective** for tax years beginning after 8-5-97. Prior to being stricken, the second sentence of Code Sec. 954(c)(1)(B) read as follows:

In the case of any regular dealer in property, gains and losses from the sale or exchange of any such property or arising out of bona fide hedging transactions reasonably necessary to the conduct of the business of being a dealer in such property shall not be taken into account under this subparagraph.

P.L. 105-34, §1051(b):

Amended Code Sec. 954(c)(2) by adding at the end a new subparagraph (C). **Effective** for tax years beginning after 8-5-97.

- **1993, Omnibus Budget Reconciliation Act of 1993 (P.L. 103-66)**

P.L. 103-66, §13233(a)(1):

Amended Code Sec. 954(c)(3) by adding at the end thereof a new subparagraph (C). **Effective** for tax years of controlled foreign corporations beginning after 9-30-93, and to tax years of United States shareholders in which or with which such tax years of controlled foreign corporations end.

- **1989, Omnibus Budget Reconciliation Act of 1989 (P.L. 101-239)**

P.L. 101-239, §7811(i)(3)(A)-(C) (as amended by P.L. 104-188, §1704(t)(25)):

Amended Code Sec. 954(c)(3)(A) by striking "is created" the first place it appears in clause (i) and inserting "is a corporation created", and by striking "from a related person" in clause (ii), inserting "from a corporation which is a related person" and by adding at the end a new sentence. **Effective** as if included in the provision of P.L. 100-647 to which it relates.

- **1988, Technical and Miscellaneous Revenue Act of 1988 (P.L. 100-647)**

P.L. 100-647, §1012(i)(18):

Amended Code Sec. 954(c)(1)(B) by striking out "or" at the end of clause (i), by redesignating clause (ii) as clause (iii), and by inserting after clause (i) a new clause (ii). **Effective** as if included in the provision of P.L. 99-514 to which it relates.

P.L. 100-647, §1012(i)(20):

Amended Code Sec. 954(c)(1)(B) by striking out the last sentence and inserting in lieu thereof a new sentence. **Effective** as if included in the provision of P.L. 99-514 to which it relates. Prior to amendment, the last sentence of Code Sec. 954(c)(1)(B) read as follows:

This subparagraph shall not apply to gain from the sale or exchange of any property which, in the hands of the taxpayer, is property described in section 1221(1) or to gain from the sale or exchange of any property by a regular dealer in such property.

P.L. 100-647, §1012(i)(25)(B):

Amended Code Sec. 954(c)(3)(B) by inserting before the period "or creates (or increases) a deficit which under section 952(c) may reduce the subpart F income of the payor or another controlled foreign corporation". **Effective** as if included in the provision of P.L. 99-514 to which it relates.

- **1986, Tax Reform Act of 1986 (P.L. 99-514)**

P.L. 99-514, §1221(a)(1):

Amended Code Sec. 954(c). **Effective** for tax years of foreign corporations beginning after 12-31-86. However, for special rules and exceptions, see Act Sec. 1221(g)(2)-(3) in the amendment note to Code Sec. 954(a). Prior to amendment, Code Sec. 954(c) read as follows:

INCOME TAX—CONTROLLED FOREIGN CORPORATIONS

(c) FOREIGN PERSONAL HOLDING COMPANY INCOME.—

(1) IN GENERAL.—For purposes of subsection (a)(1), the term "foreign personal holding company income" means the foreign personal holding company income (as defined in section 553), modified and adjusted as provided in paragraphs (2), (3), and (4).

(2) RENTS INCLUDED WITHOUT REGARD TO 50 PERCENT LIMITATION.—For purposes of paragraph (1), all rents shall be included in foreign personal holding company income without regard to whether or not such rents constitute 50 percent or more of gross income.

(3) CERTAIN INCOME DERIVED IN ACTIVE CONDUCT OF TRADE OR BUSINESS.—For purposes of paragraph (1), foreign personal holding company income does not include—

(A) rents and royalties which are derived in the active conduct of a trade or business and which are received from a person other than a related person (within the meaning of subsection (d)(3));

(B) dividends, interest, and gains from the sale or exchange of stock or securities derived in the conduct of a banking, financing, or similar business, or derived from the investments made by an insurance company of its unearned premiums or reserves ordinary and necessary for the proper conduct of its insurance business, and which are received from a person other than a related person (within the meaning of subsection (d)(3)), or

(C) dividends, interest, and gains from the sale or exchange of stock or securities received from a person other than a related person (within the meaning of subsection (d)(3)) derived from investments made by an insurance company of an amount of its assets equal to one-third of its premiums earned on insurance contracts (other than life insurance and annuity contracts) during the taxable year (as defined in section 832(b)(4)) which are not directly or indirectly attributable to the insurance or reinsurance of risks of persons who are related persons (within the meaning of subsection (d)(3)).

(4) CERTAIN INCOME RECEIVED FROM RELATED PERSONS.—For purposes of paragraph (1), foreign personal holding company income does not include—

(A) dividends and interest received from a related person which (i) is created or organized under the laws of the same foreign country under the laws of which the controlled foreign corporation is created or organized, and (ii) has a substantial part of its assets used in its trade or business located in such same foreign country;

(B) interest received in the conduct of a banking, financing, or similar business from a related person engaged in the conduct of a banking, financing, or similar business if the businesses of the recipient and the payor are predominantly with persons other than related persons; and

(C) rents, royalties, and similar amounts received from a related person for the use of, or the privilege of using, property within the country under the laws of which the controlled foreign corporation is created or organized.

• **1976, Tax Reform Act of 1976 (P.L. 94-455)**

P.L. 94-455, § 1023(a):

Struck out "or" at the end of Code Sec. 954(c)(3)(A), substituted ", or" for the period at the end of Code Sec. 954(c)(3)(B), and added Code Sec. 954 (c)(3)(C). **Effective** for tax years of foreign corporations beginning after 12-31-75, and to tax years of United States shareholders (within the meaning of Code Sec. 951(b)) within which or with which such tax years of such foreign corporations end.

[Sec. 954(d)]

(d) FOREIGN BASE COMPANY SALES INCOME.—

(1) IN GENERAL.—For purposes of subsection (a)(2), the term "foreign base company sales income" means income (whether in the form of profits, commissions, fees, or otherwise) derived in connection with the purchase of personal property from a related person and its sale to any person, the sale of personal property to any person on behalf of a related person, the purchase of personal property from any person and its sale to a related person, or the purchase of personal property from any person on behalf of a related person where—

(A) the property which is purchased (or in the case of property sold on behalf of a related person, the property which is sold) is manufactured, produced, grown, or extracted outside the country under the laws of which the controlled foreign corporation is created or organized, and

(B) the property is sold for use, consumption, or disposition outside such foreign country, or, in the case of property purchased on behalf of a related person, is purchased for use, consumption, or disposition outside such foreign country.

For purposes of this subsection, personal property does not include agricultural commodities which are not grown in the United States in commercially marketable quantities.

(2) CERTAIN BRANCH INCOME.—For purposes of determining foreign base company sales income in situations in which the carrying on of activities by a controlled foreign corporation through a branch or similar establishment outside the country of incorporation of the controlled foreign corporation has substantially the same effect as if such branch or similar establishment were a wholly owned subsidiary corporation deriving such income, under regulations prescribed by the Secretary the income attributable to the carrying on of such activities of such branch or similar establishment shall be treated as income derived by a wholly owned subsidiary of the controlled foreign corporation and shall constitute foreign base company sales income of the controlled foreign corporation.

(3) RELATED PERSON DEFINED.—For purposes of this section, a person is a related person with respect to a controlled foreign corporation, if—

(A) such person is an individual, corporation, partnership, trust, or estate which controls, or is controlled by, the controlled foreign corporation, or

(B) such person is a corporation, partnership, trust, or estate which is controlled by the same person or persons which control the controlled foreign corporation.

For purposes of the preceding sentence, control means, with respect to a corporation, the ownership, directly or indirectly, of stock possessing more than 50 percent of the total voting power of all classes of stock entitled to vote or of the total value of stock of such corporation. In the case of a partnership, trust, or estate, control means the ownership, directly or indirectly, more than 50 percent (by value) of the beneficial interests in such partnership, trust, or estate. For purposes of this paragraph, rules similar to the rules of section 958 shall apply.

(4) SPECIAL RULE FOR CERTAIN TIMBER PRODUCTS.—For purposes of subsection (a)(2), the term "foreign base company sales income" includes any income (whether in the form of profits, commissions, fees, or otherwise) derived in connection with—

(A) the sale of any unprocessed timber referred to in section 865(b), or

(B) the milling of any such timber outside the United States.

Subpart G shall not apply to any amount treated as subpart F income by reason of this paragraph.

Amendments

• **1993, Omnibus Budget Reconciliation Act of 1993 (P.L. 103-66)**

P.L. 103-66, § 13239(d):

Amended Code Sec. 954(d) by adding at the end thereof a new paragraph (4). **Effective** for sales, exchanges, or other dispositions after 8-10-93.

• **1988, Technical and Miscellaneous Revenue Act of 1988 (P.L. 100-647)**

P.L. 100-647, § 1012(i)(14)(A):

Amended Code Sec. 954(d)(3) by striking out "50 percent or more" each place it appears and inserting in lieu thereof "more than 50 percent". **Effective** as if included in the provision of P.L. 99-514 to which it relates.

• **1986, Tax Reform Act of 1986 (P.L. 99-514)**

P.L. 99-514, § 1221(e)(1):

Amended Code Sec. 954(d)(3)(A)-(C) by striking out subparagraphs (A), (B), and (C) and inserting in lieu thereof subparagraphs (A) and (B). **Effective** for tax years of foreign corporations beginning after 12-31-86.

P.L. 99-514, § 1221(e)(2):

Amended Code Sec. 954(d)(3) by striking out the last two sentences and inserting in lieu thereof new sentences. **Effective** for tax years of foreign corporations beginning after 12-31-86. However, for special rules and exceptions, see Act Sec. 1221(g)(2)-(3) in the amendment note to Code Sec. 954(a). Prior to amendment, Code Sec. 954(d)(3) read as follows:

(3) RELATED PERSON DEFINED.—For purposes of this section, a person is a related person with respect to a controlled foreign corporation, if—

(A) such person is an individual, partnership, trust, or estate which controls the controlled foreign corporation;

(B) such person is a corporation which controls, or is controlled by, the controlled foreign corporation; or

(C) such person is a corporation which is controlled by the same person or persons which control the controlled foreign corporation.

For purposes of the preceding sentence, control means the ownership, directly or indirectly, of stock possessing more than 50 percent of the total combined voting power of all classes of stock entitled to vote. For purposes of this paragraph, the rules for determining ownership of stock prescribed by section 958 shall apply.

• **1976, Tax Reform Act of 1976 (P.L. 94-455)**

P.L. 94-455, § 1906(b)(13)(A):

Amended 1954 Code by substituting "Secretary" for "Secretary or his delegate" each place it appeared. **Effective** 2-1-77.

INCOME TAX—CONTROLLED FOREIGN CORPORATIONS

- **1975, Tax Reduction Act of 1975 (P.L. 94-12)**

P.L. 94-12, § 602(b):

Amended Sec. 954(d)(1) by adding at the end thereof the new sentence. **Effective** for tax years of foreign corporations beginning after 12-31-75, and to tax years of U. S. shareholders within which or with which such tax years of such foreign corporations end.

[Sec. 954(e)]

(e) FOREIGN BASE COMPANY SERVICES INCOME.—

(1) IN GENERAL.—For purposes of subsection (a)(3), the term "foreign base company services income" means income (whether in the form of compensation, commissions, fees, or otherwise) derived in connection with the performance of technical, managerial, engineering, architectural, scientific, skilled, industrial, commercial, or like services which—

(A) are performed for or on behalf of any related person (within the meaning of subsection (d)(3)), and

(B) are performed outside the country under the laws of which the controlled foreign corporation is created or organized.

(2) EXCEPTION.—Paragraph (1) shall not apply to income derived in connection with the performance of services which are directly related to—

(A) the sale or exchange by the controlled foreign corporation of property manufactured, produced, grown, or extracted by it and which are performed before the time of the sale or exchange, or

(B) an offer or effort to sell or exchange such property.

Paragraph (1) shall also not apply to income which is exempt insurance income (as defined in section 953(e)) or which is not treated as foreign personal holding income by reason of subsection (c)(2)(C)(ii), (h), or (i).

Amendments

- **1998, Tax and Trade Relief Extension Act of 1998 (P.L. 105-277)**

P.L. 105-277, § 1005(d):

Amended Code Sec. 954(e)(2) by inserting "or" at the end of subparagraph (A), by striking ", or" at the end of subparagraph (B) and inserting a period, by striking subparagraph (C), and by adding at the end a new flush sentence. **Effective** 10-21-98. Prior to being stricken, Code Sec. 954(e)(2)(C), as amended by Act Sec. 4003(j), read as follows:

(C) in the case of taxable years described in subsection (h)(9), the active conduct by a controlled foreign corporation of a banking, financing, insurance, or similar business, but only if the corporation is predominantly engaged in the active conduct of such business (within the meaning of subsection (h)(3)) or is a qualifying insurance company.

P.L. 105-277, § 4003(j):

Amended Code Sec. 954(e)(2)(C) by striking "subsection (h)(8)" and inserting "subsection (h)(9)". **Effective** as if included in the provision of P.L. 105-34 to which it relates [**effective** for the first full tax year of a foreign corporation beginning after 12-31-97, and before 1-1-99, and to tax years of U.S. shareholders with or within which such tax year of such foreign corporation ends.—CCH].

- **1997, Taxpayer Relief Act of 1997 (P.L. 105-34)**

P.L. 105-34, § 1175(b):

Amended Code Sec. 954(e)(2) by striking "or" at the end of subparagraph (A), by striking the period at the end of subparagraph (B) and inserting ", or", and by adding at the end a new subparagraph (C). **Effective** for the first full tax year of a foreign corporation beginning after 12-31-97, and before 1-1-99, and to tax years of United States shareholders with or within which such tax year of such foreign corporation ends.

- **1986, Tax Reform Act of 1986 (P.L. 99-514)**

P.L. 99-514, § 1221(b)(3)(B):

Amended Code Sec. 954(e) [as amended by Act Sec. 1810(k)] by striking out the last sentence. **Effective**, generally, for tax years of foreign corporations beginning after 12-31-86. However, for special rules and exceptions, see Act Sec. 1221(g)(2)-(3) in the amendment notes to Code Sec. 954(a). Prior to amendment, the last sentence of Code Sec. 954(e) read as follows:

(3) TREATMENT OF CERTAIN INSURANCE CONTRACTS.—For purposes of paragraph (1), in the case of any services performed with respect to any policy of insurance or reinsurance with respect to which the primary insured is a related person (within the meaning of section 864(d)(4))—

(A) such primary insured shall be treated as a related person for purposes of paragraph (1)(A) (whether or not the requirements of subsection (d)(3) are met),

(B) such services shall be treated as performed in the country within which the insured hazards, risks, losses, or liabilities occur, and

(C) except as otherwise provided in regulations by the Secretary, rules similar to the rules of section 953(b) shall be applied in determining the income from such services.

P.L. 99-514, § 1810(k):

Amended Code Sec. 954(e). **Effective** as if included in the provision of P.L. 98-369 to which it relates. Prior to amendment, Code Sec. 954(e) read as follows:

(e) FOREIGN BASE COMPANY SERVICES INCOME.—For purposes of subsection (a)(3), the term "foreign base company services income" means income (whether in the form of compensation, commissions, fees, or otherwise) derived in connection with the performance of technical, managerial, engineering, architectural, scientific, skilled, industrial, commercial, or like services which—

(1) are performed for or on behalf of any related person (within the meaning of subsection (d)(3)), and

(2) are performed outside the country under the laws of which the controlled foreign corporation is created or organized.

The preceding sentence shall not apply to income derived in connection with the performance of services which are directly related to the sale or exchange by the controlled foreign corporation of property manufactured, produced, grown, or extracted by it and which are performed prior to the time of the sale or exchange, or of services directly related to an offer or effort to sell or exchange such property. For purposes of paragraph (2), any services performed with respect to any policy of insurance or reinsurance with respect to which the primary insured is a related person (within the meaning of section 864(d)(4)) shall be treated as having been performed in the country within which the insured hazards, risks, losses, or liabilities occur, and except as provided in regulations prescribed by the Secretary, rules similar to the rules of section 953(b) shall be applied in determining the income from such services.

- **1984, Deficit Reduction Act of 1984 (P.L. 98-369)**

P.L. 98-369, § 137(a):

Amended Code Sec. 954(e) by adding the sentence at the end thereof. **Effective** for tax years of controlled foreign corporations beginning after 7-18-84.

[Sec. 954(f)—Stricken]

Amendments

- **2004, American Jobs Creation Act of 2004 (P.L. 108-357)**

P.L. 108-357, § 415(a)(2):

Amended Code Sec. 954 by striking subsection (f). **Effective** for tax years of foreign corporations beginning after 12-31-2004 and for tax years of United States shareholders with or within which such tax years of foreign corporations end. Prior to being stricken, Code Sec. 954(f) read as follows:

(f) FOREIGN BASE COMPANY SHIPPING INCOME.—For purposes of subsection (a)(4), the term "foreign base company shipping income" means income derived from, or in connection with, the use (or hiring or leasing for use) of any aircraft or vessel in foreign commerce, or from, or in connection with, the performance of services directly related to the use of any such aircraft, or vessel, or from the sale, exchange, or other disposition of any such aircraft or vessel. Such term includes, but is not limited to—

(1) dividends and interest received from a foreign corporation in respect of which taxes are deemed paid under section 902, and gain from the sale, exchange, or other disposition of stock or obligations of such a foreign corporation to the extent that such dividends, interest, and gains are attributable to foreign base company shipping income, and

(2) that portion of the distributive share of the income of a partnership attributable to foreign base company shipping income.

Such term includes any income derived from a space or ocean activity (as defined in section 863(d)(2)). Except as provided in paragraph (1), such term shall not include any dividend or interest income which is foreign personal holding company income (as defined in subsection (c)).

- **1993, Omnibus Budget Reconciliation Act of 1993 (P.L. 103-66)**

P.L. 103-66, § 13235(b):

Amended Code Sec. 954(f) by adding at the end thereof a new sentence. **Effective** for tax years beginning after 12-31-92.

- **1986, Tax Reform Act of 1986 (P.L. 99-514)**

P.L. 99-514, § 1221(c)(2):

Amended Code Sec. 954(f) by adding at the end thereof a new sentence. **Effective**, generally, for tax years of foreign corporations beginning after 12-31-86. However, for special rules and exceptions, see Act Sec. 1221(g)(2)-(3) in the amendment note to Code Sec. 954(a).

- **1975, Tax Reduction Act of 1975 (P.L. 94-12)**

P.L. 94-12, § 602(c)(2):

Repealed Sec. 954(f). **Effective** for tax years of foreign corporations beginning after 12-31-75, and for tax years of U.S. shareholders within which or with which such tax years of such foreign corporations end. Prior to repeal Code Sec. 954(f) read as follows:

"(f) Increase in Qualified Investments in Less Developed Countries.—For purposes of subsection (b)(1), the increase for any taxable year in qualified investments in less developed countries of any controlled foreign corporation is the amount by which—

"(1) the qualified investments in less developed countries (as defined in section 955(b)) of the controlled foreign corporation at the close of the taxable year, exceeds

INCOME TAX—CONTROLLED FOREIGN CORPORATIONS

"(2) the qualified investments in less developed countries (as so defined) of the controlled foreign corporation at the close of the preceding taxable year."

P.L. 94-12, §602(d)(1)(G):

Enacted new Code Sec. 954(f). **Effective** for tax years of foreign corporations beginning after 12-31-75, and for tax years of U.S. shareholders within which or with which such tax years of such foreign corporations end.

Amendments

- **2017, Tax Cuts and Jobs Act (P.L. 115-97)**

P.L. 115-97, §14211(b)(3):

Amended Code Sec. 954 by striking subsection (g). **Effective** for tax years of foreign corporations beginning after 12-31-2017, and to tax years of United States shareholders with or within which such tax years of foreign corporations end. Prior to being stricken, Code Sec. 954(g) read as follows:

(g) FOREIGN BASE COMPANY OIL RELATED INCOME.—For purposes of this section—

(1) IN GENERAL.—Except as otherwise provided in this subsection, the term "foreign base company oil related income" means foreign oil related income (within the meaning of paragraphs (2) and (3) of section 907(c)) other than income derived from a source within a foreign country in connection with—

(A) oil or gas which was extracted from an oil or gas well located in such foreign country, or

(B) oil, gas, or a primary product of oil or gas which is sold by the foreign corporation or a related person for use or consumption within such country or is loaded in such country on a vessel or aircraft as fuel for such vessel or aircraft.

Such term shall not include any foreign personal holding company income (as defined in subsection (c)).

(2) PARAGRAPH (1) APPLIES ONLY WHERE CORPORATION HAS PRODUCED 1,000 BARRELS PER DAY OR MORE.—

(A) IN GENERAL.—The term "foreign base company oil related income" shall not include any income of a foreign corporation if such corporation is not a large oil producer for the taxable year.

(B) LARGE OIL PRODUCER.—For purposes of subparagraph (A), the term "large oil producer" means any corporation if, for the taxable year or for the preceding taxable year, the average daily production of foreign crude oil and natural gas of the related group which includes such corporation equaled or exceeded 1,000 barrels.

(C) RELATED GROUP.—The term "related group" means a group consisting of the foreign corporation and any other person who is a related person with respect to such corporation.

(D) AVERAGE DAILY PRODUCTION OF FOREIGN CRUDE OIL AND NATURAL GAS.—For purposes of this paragraph, the average daily production of foreign crude oil or natural gas of any related group for any taxable year (and the conversion of cubic feet of natural gas into barrels) shall be determined under rules similar to the rules of section 613A except that only crude oil or natural gas from a well located outside the United States shall be taken into account.

- **1993, Omnibus Budget Reconciliation Act of 1993 (P.L. 103-66)**

P.L. 103-66, §13235(a)(3)(A):

Amended Code Sec. 954(g)(1) by adding at the end thereof a new flush sentence. **Effective** for tax years beginning after 12-31-92.

- **1962, Revenue Act of 1962 (P.L. 87-834)**

P.L. 87-834, §12(a):

Added Code Sec. 954. **Effective** for tax years of foreign corporations beginning after 12-31-62, and for tax years of United States shareholders within which or with which such tax years of such foreign corporations end.

[Sec. 954(g)—Stricken]

- **1986, Tax Reform Act of 1986 (P.L. 99-514)**

P.L. 99-514, §1221(c)(3)(A)(i):

Amended Code Sec. 954(g)-(h) by striking out subsection (g) and by redesignating subsection (h) as subsection (g). **Effective**, generally, for tax years of foreign corporations beginning after 12-31-86. However, for special rules and exceptions, see Act Sec. 1221(g)(2)-(3) in the amendment notes to Code Sec. 954(a). Prior to amendment, Code Sec. 954(g) read as follows:

(g) INCREASE IN QUALIFIED INVESTMENTS IN FOREIGN BASE COMPANY SHIPPING OPERATIONS.—For purposes of subsection (b)(2), the increase for any taxable year in qualified investments in foreign base company shipping operations of any controlled foreign corporation is the amount by which—

(1) the qualified investments in foreign base company shipping operations (as defined in section 955(b)) of the controlled foreign corporation at the close of the taxable year, exceed

(2) the qualified investments in foreign base company shipping operations (as so defined) of the controlled foreign corporation at the close of the preceding taxable year.

- **1984, Deficit Reduction Act of 1984 (P.L. 98-369)**

P.L. 98-369, §712(f):

Amended Code Sec. 954(h)(1) by striking out "section 907(c)(2)" and inserting in lieu thereof "paragraphs (2) and (3) of section 907(c)". **Effective** as if included in the provision of P.L. 97-248 to which it relates.

- **1982, Tax Equity and Fiscal Responsibility Act of 1982 (P.L. 97-248)**

P.L. 97-248, §212(c):

Amended Code Sec. 954 by adding at the end thereof subsection (h). **Effective** for tax years of foreign corporations beginning after 12-31-82, and to tax years of United States shareholders in which, or with which, such tax years of foreign corporations end.

- **1975, Tax Reduction Act of 1975 (P.L. 94-12)**

P.L. 94-12, §602(d):

Added Code Sec. 954(g). **Effective** for tax years of foreign corporations beginning after 12-31-75, and for tax years of U.S. shareholders within which or with which such tax years of such foreign corporations end.

[Sec. 954(h)]

(h) SPECIAL RULE FOR INCOME DERIVED IN THE ACTIVE CONDUCT OF BANKING, FINANCING, OR SIMILAR BUSINESSES.—

(1) IN GENERAL.—For purposes of subsection (c)(1), foreign personal holding company income shall not include qualified banking or financing income of an eligible controlled foreign corporation.

(2) ELIGIBLE CONTROLLED FOREIGN CORPORATION.—For purposes of this subsection—

(A) IN GENERAL.—The term "eligible controlled foreign corporation" means a controlled foreign corporation which—

(i) is predominantly engaged in the active conduct of a banking, financing, or similar business, and

(ii) conducts substantial activity with respect to such business.

(B) PREDOMINANTLY ENGAGED.—A controlled foreign corporation shall be treated as predominantly engaged in the active conduct of a banking, financing, or similar business if—

(i) more than 70 percent of the gross income of the controlled foreign corporation is derived directly from the active and regular conduct of a lending or finance business from transactions with customers which are not related persons,

(ii) it is engaged in the active conduct of a banking business and is an institution licensed to do business as a bank in the United States (or is any other corporation not so licensed which is specified by the Secretary in regulations), or

(iii) it is engaged in the active conduct of a securities business and is registered as a securities broker or dealer under section 15(a) of the Securities Exchange Act of 1934 or is registered as a Government securities broker or dealer under section 15C(a) of such Act (or is any other corporation not so registered which is specified by the Secretary in regulations).

(3) QUALIFIED BANKING OR FINANCING INCOME.—For purposes of this subsection—

(A) IN GENERAL.—The term "qualified banking or financing income" means income of an eligible controlled foreign corporation which—

(i) is derived in the active conduct of a banking, financing, or similar business by—

(I) such eligible controlled foreign corporation, or

(II) a qualified business unit of such eligible controlled foreign corporation,

(ii) is derived from one or more transactions—

(I) with customers located in a country other than the United States, and

(II) substantially all of the activities in connection with which are conducted directly by the corporation or unit in its home country, and

(iii) is treated as earned by such corporation or unit in its home country for purposes of such country's tax laws.

Sec. 954(g)—Stricken

INCOME TAX—CONTROLLED FOREIGN CORPORATIONS

(B) LIMITATION ON NONBANKING AND NONSECURITIES BUSINESSES.—No income of an eligible controlled foreign corporation not described in clause (ii) or (iii) of paragraph (2)(B) (or of a qualified business unit of such corporation) shall be treated as qualified banking or financing income unless more than 30 percent of such corporation's or unit's gross income is derived directly from the active and regular conduct of a lending or finance business from transactions with customers which are not related persons and which are located within such corporation's or unit's home country.

(C) SUBSTANTIAL ACTIVITY REQUIREMENT FOR CROSS BORDER INCOME.—The term "qualified banking or financing income" shall not include income derived from 1 or more transactions with customers located in a country other than the home country of the eligible controlled foreign corporation or a qualified business unit of such corporation unless such corporation or unit conducts substantial activity with respect to a banking, financing, or similar business in its home country.

(D) DETERMINATIONS MADE SEPARATELY.—For purposes of this paragraph, the qualified banking or financing income of an eligible controlled foreign corporation and each qualified business unit of such corporation shall be determined separately for such corporation and each such unit by taking into account—

(i) in the case of the eligible controlled foreign corporation, only items of income, deduction, gain, or loss and activities of such corporation not properly allocable or attributable to any qualified business unit of such corporation, and

(ii) in the case of a qualified business unit, only items of income, deduction, gain, or loss and activities properly allocable or attributable to such unit.

(E) DIRECT CONDUCT OF ACTIVITIES.—For purposes of subparagraph (A)(ii)(II), an activity shall be treated as conducted directly by an eligible controlled foreign corporation or qualified business unit in its home country if the activity is performed by employees of a related person and—

(i) the related person is an eligible controlled foreign corporation the home country of which is the same as the home country of the corporation or unit to which subparagraph (A)(ii)(II) is being applied,

(ii) the activity is performed in the home country of the related person, and

(iii) the related person is compensated on an arm's-length basis for the performance of the activity by its employees and such compensation is treated as earned by such person in its home country for purposes of the home country's tax laws.

(4) LENDING OR FINANCE BUSINESS.—For purposes of this subsection, the term "lending or finance business" means the business of—

(A) making loans,

(B) purchasing or discounting accounts receivable, notes, or installment obligations,

(C) engaging in leasing (including entering into leases and purchasing, servicing, and disposing of leases and leased assets),

(D) issuing letters of credit or providing guarantees,

(E) providing charge and credit card services, or

(F) rendering services or making facilities available in connection with activities described in subparagraphs (A) through (E) carried on by—

(i) the corporation (or qualified business unit) rendering services or making facilities available, or

(ii) another corporation (or qualified business unit of a corporation) which is a member of the same affiliated group (as defined in section 1504, but determined without regard to section 1504(b)(3)).

(5) OTHER DEFINITIONS.—For purposes of this subsection—

(A) CUSTOMER.—The term "customer" means, with respect to any controlled foreign corporation or qualified business unit, any person which has a customer relationship with such corporation or unit and which is acting in its capacity as such.

(B) HOME COUNTRY.—Except as provided in regulations—

(i) CONTROLLED FOREIGN CORPORATION.—The term "home country" means, with respect to any controlled foreign corporation, the country under the laws of which the corporation was created or organized.

(ii) QUALIFIED BUSINESS UNIT.—The term "home country" means, with respect to any qualified business unit, the country in which such unit maintains its principal office.

(C) LOCATED.—The determination of where a customer is located shall be made under rules prescribed by the Secretary.

(D) QUALIFIED BUSINESS UNIT.—The term "qualified business unit" has the meaning given such term by section 989(a).

(E) RELATED PERSON.—The term "related person" has the meaning given such term by subsection (d)(3).

(6) COORDINATION WITH EXCEPTION FOR DEALERS.—Paragraph (1) shall not apply to income described in subsection (c)(2)(C)(ii) of a dealer in securities (within the meaning of section 475) which is an eligible controlled foreign corporation described in paragraph (2)(B)(iii).

(7) ANTI-ABUSE RULES.—For purposes of applying this subsection and subsection (c)(2)(C)(ii)—

(A) there shall be disregarded any item of income, gain, loss, or deduction with respect to any transaction or series of transactions one of the principal purposes of which is qualifying income or gain for the exclusion under this section, including any transaction or series of transactions a principal purpose of which is the acceleration or deferral of any item in order to claim the benefits of such exclusion through the application of this subsection,

(B) there shall be disregarded any item of income, gain, loss, or deduction of an entity which is not engaged in regular and continuous transactions with customers which are not related persons,

(C) there shall be disregarded any item of income, gain, loss, or deduction with respect to any transaction or series of transactions utilizing, or doing business with—

(i) one or more entities in order to satisfy any home country requirement under this subsection, or

(ii) a special purpose entity or arrangement, including a securitization, financing, or similar entity or arrangement,

if one of the principal purposes of such transaction or series of transactions is qualifying income or gain for the exclusion under this subsection, and

(D) a related person, an officer, a director, or an employee with respect to any controlled foreign corporation (or qualified business unit) which would otherwise be treated as a customer of such corporation or unit with respect to any transaction shall not be so treated if a principal purpose of such transaction is to satisfy any requirement of this subsection.

(8) REGULATIONS.—The Secretary shall prescribe such regulations as may be necessary or appropriate to carry out the purposes of this subsection, subsection (c)(1)(B)(i), subsection (c)(2)(C)(ii), and the last sentence of subsection (e)(2).

Amendments

• **2015, Protecting Americans from Tax Hikes Act of 2015 (P.L. 114-113)**

P.L. 114-113, §128(b), Div. Q:

Amended Code Sec. 954(h) by striking paragraph (9). **Effective** for tax years of foreign corporations beginning after 12-31-2014, and to tax years of United States shareholders with or within which any such tax year of such foreign corporation ends. Prior to being stricken, Code Sec. 954(h)(9) read as follows:

(9) APPLICATION.—This subsection, subsection (c)(2)(C)(ii), and the last sentence of subsection (e)(2) shall apply only to taxable years of a foreign corporation beginning after December 31, 1998, and before January 1, 2015, and to taxable years of United

INCOME TAX—CONTROLLED FOREIGN CORPORATIONS

States shareholders with or within which any such taxable year of such foreign corporation ends.

- **2014, Tax Increase Prevention Act of 2014 (P.L. 113-295)**

P.L. 113-295, §134(b), Division A:

Amended Code Sec. 954(h)(9) by striking "January 1, 2014" and inserting "January 1, 2015". **Effective** for tax years of foreign corporations beginning after 12-31-2013, and to tax years of United States shareholders with or within which any such tax year of such foreign corporation ends.

- **2013, American Taxpayer Relief Act of 2012 (P.L. 112-240)**

P.L. 112-240, §322(b):

Amended Code Sec. 954(h)(9) by striking "January 1, 2012" and inserting "January 1, 2014". **Effective** for tax years of foreign corporations beginning after 12-31-2011, and to tax years of United States shareholders with or within which any such tax year of such foreign corporation ends.

- **2010, Tax Relief, Unemployment Insurance Reauthorization, and Job Creation Act of 2010 (P.L. 111-312)**

P.L. 111-312, §750(a):

Amended Code Sec. 954(h)(9) by striking "January 1, 2010" and inserting "January 1, 2012". **Effective** for tax years of foreign corporations beginning after 12-31-2009, and to tax years of United States shareholders with or within which any such tax year of such foreign corporation ends.

- **2008, Tax Extenders and Alternative Minimum Tax Relief Act of 2008 (P.L. 110-343)**

P.L. 110-343, Division C, §303(b):

Amended Code Sec. 954(h)(9) by striking "January 1, 2009" and inserting "January 1, 2010". **Effective** 10-3-2008.

- **2006, Tax Increase Prevention and Reconciliation Act of 2005 (P.L. 109-222)**

P.L. 109-222, §103(a)(2):

Amended Code Sec. 954(h)(9) by striking "January 1, 2007" and inserting "January 1, 2009". **Effective** 5-17-2006.

- **2004, American Jobs Creation Act of 2004 (P.L. 108-357)**

P.L. 108-357, §416(a):

Amended Code Sec. 954(h)(3) by adding at the end a new paragraph (E). **Effective** for tax years of such foreign corporations beginning after 12-31-2004 and for tax years of United States shareholders with or within which such tax years of such foreign corporations end.

- **2002, Job Creation and Worker Assistance Act of 2002 (P.L. 107-147)**

P.L. 107-147, §614(a)(2):

Amended Code Sec. 954(h)(9) by striking "January 1, 2002" and inserting "January 1, 2007". **Effective** for tax years beginning after 12-31-2001.

- **1999, Tax Relief Extension Act of 1999 (P.L. 106-170)**

P.L. 106-170, §503(a)(1)-(3):

Amended Code Sec. 954(h)(9) by striking "the first taxable year" and inserting "taxable years", by striking "January 1, 2000" and inserting "January 1, 2002", and by striking "within which such" and inserting "within which any such". **Effective** for tax years beginning after 12-31-99.

- **1998, Tax and Trade Relief Extension Act of 1998 (P.L. 105-277)**

P.L. 105-277, §1005(a):

Amended Code Sec. 954(h). **Effective** 10-21-98. Prior to amendment, Code Sec. 954(h) read as follows:

(h) SPECIAL RULE FOR INCOME DERIVED IN THE ACTIVE CONDUCT OF BANKING, FINANCING, OR SIMILAR BUSINESSES.—

(1) IN GENERAL.—For purposes of subsection (c)(1), foreign personal holding company income shall not include income which is—

(A) derived in the active conduct by a controlled foreign corporation of a banking, financing, or similar business, but only if the corporation is predominantly engaged in the active conduct of such business,

(B) received from a person other than a related person (within the meaning of subsection (d)(3)) and derived from the investments made by a qualifying insurance company of its reserves or of 80 percent of its unearned premiums (as both are determined in the manner prescribed under paragraph (4)), or

(C) received from a person other than a related person (within the meaning of subsection (d)(3)) and derived from investments made by a qualifying insurance company of an amount of its assets equal to—

(i) in the case of contracts regulated in the country in which sold as property, casualty, or health insurance contracts, one-third of its premiums earned on such insurance contracts during the taxable year (as defined in section 832(b)(4)), and

(ii) in the case of contracts regulated in the country in which sold as life insurance or annuity contracts, the greater of—

(I) 10 percent of the reserves described in subparagraph (B) for such contracts, or

(II) in the case of a qualifying insurance company which is a start-up company, $10,000,000.

(2) PRINCIPLES FOR DETERMINING APPLICABLE INCOME.—

(A) BANKING AND FINANCING INCOME.—The determination as to whether income is described in paragraph (1)(A) shall be made—

(i) except as provided in clause (ii), in accordance with the applicable principles of section 904(d)(2)(C)(ii), except that such income shall include income from all leases entered into in the ordinary course of the active conduct of a banking, financing, or similar business, and

(ii) in the case of a corporation described in paragraph (3)(B), in accordance with the applicable principles of section 1296(b) (as in effect on the day before the enactment of the Taxpayer Relief Act of 1997) for determining what is not passive income.

(B) INSURANCE INCOME.—Under rules prescribed by the Secretary, for purposes of paragraphs (1) (B) and (C)—

(i) in the case of contracts which are separate account-type contracts (including variable contracts not meeting the requirements of section 817), only income specifically allocable to such contracts shall be taken into account, and

(ii) in the case of other contracts, income not allocable under clause (i) shall be allocated ratably among such contracts.

(C) LOOK-THRU RULES.—The Secretary shall prescribe regulations consistent with the principles of section 904(d)(3) which provide that dividends, interest, income equivalent to interest, rents, or royalties received or accrued from a related person (within the meaning of subsection (d)(3)) shall be subject to look-thru treatment for purposes of this subsection.

(3) PREDOMINANTLY ENGAGED.—For purposes of paragraph (1)(A), a corporation shall be deemed predominantly engaged in the active conduct of a banking, financing, or similar business only if—

(A) more than 70 percent of its gross income is derived from such business from transactions with persons which are not related persons (as defined in subsection (d)(3)) and which are located within the country under the laws of which the controlled foreign corporation is created or organized, or

(B) the corporation is—

(i) engaged in the active conduct of a banking or securities business (within the meaning of section 1296(b), as in effect before the enactment of the Taxpayer Relief Act of 1997), or

(ii) a qualified bank affiliate or a qualified securities affiliate (within the meaning of the proposed regulations under such section 1296(b)).

(4) METHODS FOR DETERMINING UNEARNED PREMIUMS AND RESERVES.—For purposes of paragraph (1)(B)—

(A) PROPERTY AND CASUALTY CONTRACTS.—The unearned premiums and reserves of a qualifying insurance company with respect to property, casualty, or health insurance contracts shall be determined using the same methods and interest rates which would be used if such company were subject to tax under subchapter L.

(B) LIFE INSURANCE AND ANNUITY CONTRACTS.—The reserves of a qualifying insurance company with respect to life insurance or annuity contracts shall be determined under the method described in paragraph (5) which such company elects to apply for purposes of this paragraph. Such election shall be made at such time and in such manner as the Secretary may prescribe and, once made, shall be irrevocable without the consent of the Secretary.

(C) LIMITATION ON RESERVES.—In no event shall the reserve determined under this paragraph for any contract as of any time exceed the amount which would be taken into account with respect to such contract as of such time in determining foreign annual statement reserves (less any catastrophe or deficiency reserves).

(5) METHODS.—The methods described in this paragraph are as follows:

(A) U.S. METHOD.—The method which would apply if the qualifying insurance company were subject to tax under subchapter L, except that the interest rate used shall be an interest rate determined for the foreign country in which such company is created or organized and which is calculated in the same manner as the Federal mid-term rate under section 1274(d).

(B) FOREIGN METHOD.—A preliminary term method, except that the interest rate used shall be the interest rate determined for the foreign country in which such company is created or organized and which is calculated in the same manner as the Federal mid-term rate under section 1274(d). If a qualifying insurance company uses such a preliminary term method with respect to contracts insuring risks located in such foreign country, such method shall apply if such company elects the method under this clause.

(C) CASH SURRENDER VALUE.—A method under which reserves are equal to the net surrender value (as defined in section 807(e)(1)(A)) of the contract.

(6) DEFINITIONS.—For purposes of this subsection—

(A) TERMS RELATING TO INSURANCE COMPANIES.—

(i) QUALIFYING INSURANCE COMPANY.—The term "qualifying insurance company" means any entity which—

(I) is subject to regulation as an insurance company under the laws of its country of incorporation,

(II) realizes at least 50 percent of its net written premiums from the insurance or reinsurance of risks located within the country in which such entity is created or organized, and

(III) is engaged in the active conduct of an insurance business and would be subject to tax under subchapter L if it were a domestic corporation.

(ii) START-UP COMPANY.—A qualifying insurance company shall be treated as a start-up company if such company (and any predecessor) has not been engaged in the active conduct of an insurance business for more than 5 years as of the beginning of the taxable year of such company.

(B) LOCATED.—For purposes of paragraph (3)(A)—

(i) IN GENERAL.—A person shall be treated as located—

(I) except as provided in subclause (II), within the country in which it maintains an office or other fixed place of business through which it engages in a trade or business and by which the transaction is effected, or

(II) in the case of a natural person, within the country in which such person is physically located when such person enters into a transaction.

(ii) SPECIAL RULE FOR QUALIFIED BUSINESS UNITS.—Gross income derived by a corporation's qualified business unit (within the meaning of section 989(a)) from transactions with persons which are not related persons (as defined in subsection (d)(3)) and which are located in the country in which the qualified business unit both maintains its principal office and conducts substantial business activity shall be treated as derived from transactions with persons which are not related persons (as defined in

INCOME TAX—CONTROLLED FOREIGN CORPORATIONS

subsection (d)(3)) and which are located within the country under the laws of which the controlled foreign corporation is created or organized.

(7) ANTI-ABUSE RULES.—For purposes of applying this subsection, there shall be disregarded any item of income, gain, loss, or deduction with respect to any transaction or series of transactions one of the principal purposes of which is qualifying income or gain for the exclusion under this section, including any change in the method of computing reserves or any other transaction or series of transactions a principal purpose of which is the acceleration or deferral of any item in order to claim the benefits of such exclusion through the application of this subsection.

(8) COORDINATION WITH SECTION 953.—This subsection shall not apply to investment income allocable to contracts that insure related party risks or risks located in a foreign country other than the country in which the qualifying insurance comapny is created or organized.

(9) APPLICATION.—This subsection shall apply to the first full taxable year of a foreign corporation beginning after December 31, 1997, and before January 1, 1999, and to taxable years of United States shareholders with or within which such taxable year of such foreign corporation ends.

• **1997, Taxpayer Relief Act of 1997 (P.L. 105-34)**

P.L. 105-34, §1175(a):

Amended Code Sec. 954 by adding at the end a new subsection (h). **Effective** for the first full tax year of a foreign corporation beginning after 12-31-97, and before 1-1-99, and to tax years of United States shareholders with or within which such tax year of such foreign corporation ends.

[Sec. 954(i)]

(i) SPECIAL RULE FOR INCOME DERIVED IN THE ACTIVE CONDUCT OF INSURANCE BUSINESS.—

(1) IN GENERAL.—For purposes of subsection (c)(1), foreign personal holding company income shall not include qualified insurance income of a qualifying insurance company.

(2) QUALIFIED INSURANCE INCOME.—The term "qualified insurance income" means income of a qualifying insurance company which is—

(A) received from a person other than a related person (within the meaning of subsection (d)(3)) and derived from the investments made by a qualifying insurance company or a qualifying insurance company branch of its reserves allocable to exempt contracts or of 80 percent of its unearned premiums from exempt contracts (as both are determined in the manner prescribed under paragraph (4)), or

(B) received from a person other than a related person (within the meaning of subsection (d)(3)) and derived from investments made by a qualifying insurance company or a qualifying insurance company branch of an amount of its assets allocable to exempt contracts equal to—

(i) in the case of property, casualty, or health insurance contracts, one-third of its premiums earned on such insurance contracts during the taxable year (as defined in section 832(b)(4)), and

(ii) in the case of life insurance or annuity contracts, 10 percent of the reserves described in subparagraph (A) for such contracts.

(3) PRINCIPLES FOR DETERMINING INSURANCE INCOME.—Except as provided by the Secretary, for purposes of subparagraphs (A) and (B) of paragraph (2)—

(A) in the case of any contract which is a separate account-type contract (including any variable contract not meeting the requirements of section 817), income credited under such contract shall be allocable only to such contract, and

(B) income not allocable under subparagraph (A) shall be allocated ratably among contracts not described in subparagraph (A).

(4) METHODS FOR DETERMINING UNEARNED PREMIUMS AND RESERVES.—For purposes of paragraph (2)(A)—

(A) PROPERTY AND CASUALTY CONTRACTS.—The unearned premiums and reserves of a qualifying insurance company or a qualifying insurance company branch with respect to property, casualty, or health insurance contracts shall be determined using the same methods and interest rates which would be used if such company or branch were subject to tax under subchapter L, except that—

(i) the interest rate determined for the functional currency of the company or branch, and which, except as provided by the Secretary, is calculated in the same manner as the Federal mid-term rate under section 1274(d), shall be substituted for the applicable Federal interest rate, and

(ii) such company or branch shall use the appropriate foreign loss payment pattern.

(B) LIFE INSURANCE AND ANNUITY CONTRACTS.—

(i) IN GENERAL.—Except as provided in clause (ii), the amount of the reserve of a qualifying insurance company or qualifying insurance company branch for any life insurance or annuity contract shall be equal to the greater of—

(I) the net surrender value of such contract (as defined in section 807(e)(1)(A)), or

(II) the reserve determined under paragraph (5).

(ii) RULING REQUEST, ETC.—The amount of the reserve under clause (i) shall be the foreign statement reserve for the contract (less any catastrophe, deficiency, equalization, or similar reserves), if, pursuant to a ruling request submitted by the taxpayer or as provided in published guidance, the Secretary determines that the factors taken into account in determining the foreign statement reserve provide an appropriate means of measuring income.

(C) LIMITATION ON RESERVES.—In no event shall the reserve determined under this paragraph for any contract as of any time exceed the amount which would be taken into account with respect to such contract as of such time in determining foreign statement reserves (less any catastrophe, deficiency, equalization, or similar reserves).

(5) AMOUNT OF RESERVE.—The amount of the reserve determined under this paragraph with respect to any contract shall be determined in the same manner as it would be determined if the qualifying insurance company or qualifying insurance company branch were subject to tax under subchapter L, except that in applying such subchapter—

(A) the interest rate determined for the functional currency of the company or branch, and which, except as provided by the Secretary, is calculated in the same manner as the Federal mid-term rate under section 1274(d), shall be substituted for the applicable Federal interest rate,

(B) the highest assumed interest rate permitted to be used in determining foreign statement reserves shall apply, and

(C) tables for mortality and morbidity which reasonably reflect the current mortality and morbidity risks in the company's or branch's home country shall be substituted for the mortality and morbidity tables otherwise used for such subchapter.

The Secretary may provide that the interest rate and mortality and morbidity tables of a qualifying insurance company may be used for 1 or more of its qualifying insurance company branches when appropriate.

(6) DEFINITIONS.—For purposes of this subsection, any term used in this subsection which is also used in section 953(e) shall have the meaning given such term by section 953.

Amendments

• **2017, Tax Cuts and Jobs Act (P.L. 115-97)**

P.L. 115-97, §13517(b)(5):

Amended Code Sec. 954(i)(5)(B) by striking "shall be substituted for the prevailing State assumed interest rate," and inserting "shall apply,". **Effective** generally for tax years beginning after 12-31-2017. For a transition rule, see Act Sec. 13517(c)(2), below.

P.L. 115-97, §13517(c)(2), provides:

(2) TRANSITION RULE.—For the first taxable year beginning after December 31, 2017, the reserve with respect to any contract (as determined under section 807(d) of the Internal Revenue Code of 1986) at the end of the preceding taxable year shall be determined as if the amendments made by this section had applied to such reserve in such preceding taxable year.

• **2002, Job Creation and Worker Assistance Act of 2002 (P.L. 107-147)**

P.L. 107-147, §614(b)(1):

Amended Code Sec. 954(i)(4)(B). **Effective** for tax years beginning after 12-31-2001. Prior to amendment, Code Sec. 954(i)(4)(B) read as follows:

(B) LIFE INSURANCE AND ANNUITY CONTRACTS.—The amount of the reserve of a qualifying insurance company or qualifying insurance company branch for any life insurance or annuity contract shall be equal to the greater of—

INCOME TAX—CONTROLLED FOREIGN CORPORATIONS

(i) the net surrender value of such contract (as defined in section 807(e)(1)(A)), or

(ii) the reserve determined under paragraph (5).

• **1998, Tax and Trade Relief Extension Act of 1998 (P.L. 105-277)**

P.L. 105-277, § 1005(b)(2):

Amended Code Sec. 954 by adding at the end a new subsection (i). **Effective** 10-21-98.

[Sec. 955—Stricken]

Amendments

• **2017, Tax Cuts and Jobs Act (P.L. 115-97)**

P.L. 115-97, § 14212(a):

Amended subpart F of part III of subchapter N of chapter 1 by striking Code Sec. 955. **Effective** for tax years of foreign corporations beginning after 12-31-2017, and to tax years of United States shareholders in which or with which such tax years of foreign corporations end. Prior to being stricken, Code Sec. 955 read as follows:

SEC. 955. WITHDRAWAL OF PREVIOUSLY EXCLUDED SUBPART F INCOME FROM QUALIFIED INVESTMENT.

[Sec. 955(a)]

(a) GENERAL RULES.—

(1) AMOUNT WITHDRAWN.—For purposes of this subpart, the amount of previously excluded subpart F income of any controlled foreign corporation withdrawn from investment in foreign base company shipping operations for any taxable year is an amount equal to the decrease in the amount of qualified investments in foreign base company shipping operations of the controlled foreign corporation for such year, but only to the extent that the amount of such decrease does not exceed an amount equal to—

(A) the sum of the amounts excluded under section 954(b)(2) from the foreign base company income of such corporation for all prior taxable years beginning before 1987, reduced by

(B) the sum of the amounts of previously excluded subpart F income withdrawn from investment in foreign base company shipping operations of such corporation determined under this subsection for all prior taxable years.

(2) DECREASE IN QUALIFIED INVESTMENTS.—For purposes of paragraph (1), the amount of the decrease in qualified investments in foreign base company shipping operations of any controlled foreign corporation for any taxable year is the amount by which—

(A) the amount of qualified investments in foreign base company shipping operations of the controlled foreign corporation as of the close of the last taxable year beginning before 1987 (to the extent such amounts exceed the sum of the decreases in qualified investments determined under this paragraph for prior taxable years beginning after 1986), exceeds

(B) the amount of qualified investments in foreign base company shipping operations of the controlled foreign corporation at the close of the taxable year,

to the extent that the amount of such decrease does not exceed the sum of the earnings and profits for the taxable year and the earnings and profits accumulated for prior taxable years beginning after December 31, 1975, and the amount of previously excluded subpart F income invested in less developed country corporations described in section 955(c)(2) (as in effect before the enactment of the Tax Reduction Act of 1975) to the extent attributable to earnings and profits accumulated for taxable years beginning after December 31, 1962. For purposes of this paragraph, if qualified investments in foreign base company shipping operations are disposed of by the controlled foreign corporation during the taxable year, the amount of the decrease in qualified investments in foreign base company shipping operations of such controlled foreign corporation for such year shall be reduced by an amount equal to the amount (if any) by which the losses on such dispositions during such year exceed the gains on such dispositions during such year.

(3) PRO RATA SHARE OF AMOUNT WITHDRAWN.—In the case of any United States shareholder, the pro rata share of the amount of previously excluded subpart F income of any controlled foreign corporation withdrawn from investment in foreign base company shipping operations for any taxable year is his pro rata share of the amount determined under paragraph (1).

Amendments

• **1988, Technical and Miscellaneous Revenue Act of 1988 (P.L. 100-647)**

P.L. 100-647, § 1012(i)(11):

Amended Code Sec. 955(a)(2)(A) by striking out "beginning before 1987" and inserting in lieu thereof "beginning before 1987 (to the extent such amount exceeds the sum of the decreases in qualified investments determined under this paragraph for prior taxable years beginning after 1986)". **Effective** as if included in the provision of P.L. 99-514 to which it relates.

[Sec. 955(b)]

(b) QUALIFIED INVESTMENTS IN FOREIGN BASE COMPANY SHIPPING OPERATIONS.—

(1) IN GENERAL.—For purposes of this subpart, the term "qualified investments in foreign base company shipping operations" means investments in—

(A) any aircraft or vessel used in foreign commerce, and

(B) other assets which are used in connection with the performance of services directly related to the use of any such aircraft or vessel.

Such term includes, but is not limited to, investments by a controlled foreign corporation in stock or obligations of another controlled foreign corporation which is a related person (within the meaning of section 954(d)(3)) and which holds assets described in the preceding sentence, but only to the extent that such assets are so used.

(2) QUALIFIED INVESTMENTS BY RELATED PERSONS.—For purposes of determining the amount of qualified investments in foreign base company shipping operations, an investment (or a decrease in investment) in such operations by one or more controlled foreign corporations may, under regulations prescribed by the Secretary, be treated as an investment (or a decrease in investment) by another corporation which is a controlled foreign corporation and is a related person (as defined in section 954(d)(3)) with respect to the corporation actually making or withdrawing the investment.

(3) SPECIAL RULE.—For purposes of this subpart, a United States shareholder of a controlled foreign corporation may, under regulations prescribed by the Secretary, elect to make the determinations under subsection (a)(2) of this section and under subsection (g) of section 954 as of the close of the years following the years referred to in such subsections, or as of the close of such longer period of time as such regulations may permit, in lieu of on the last day of such years. Any election under this paragraph made with respect to any taxable year shall apply to such year and to all succeeding taxable years unless the Secretary consents to the revocation of such election.

(4) AMOUNT ATTRIBUTABLE TO PROPERTY.—The amount taken into account under this subpart with respect to any property described in paragraph (1) shall be its adjusted basis, reduced by any liability to which such property is subject.

(5) INCOME EXCLUDED UNDER PRIOR LAW.—Amounts invested in less developed country corporations described in section 955(c)(2) (as in effect before the enactment of the Tax Reduction Act of 1975) shall be treated as qualified investments in foreign base company shipping operations and shall not be treated as investments in less developed countries for purposes of section 951(a)(1)(A)(ii).

Amendments

• **1986, Tax Reform Act of 1986 (P.L. 99-514)**

P.L. 99-514, § 1221(c)(3)(B):

Amended Code Sec. 955(a)(1)(A) by striking out "all prior taxable years" and inserting in lieu thereof "all prior taxable years beginning before 1987". **Effective**, generally, for tax years of foreign corporations beginning after 12-31-86. However, for special rules, see the amendment notes for Act Sec. 1221(g)(2)-(3) following Code Sec. 954.

P.L. 99-514, § 1221(c)(3)(C):

Amended Code Sec. 955(a)(2)(A) by striking out "at the close of the preceding taxable year" and inserting in lieu thereof "as of the close of the last taxable year beginning before 1987". **Effective**, generally, for tax years of foreign corporations beginning after 12-31-86. However, for special rules, see the amendment notes for Act Sec. 1221(g)(2)-(3) following Code Sec. 954.

• **1976, Tax Reform Act of 1976 (P.L. 94-455)**

P.L. 94-455, § 1906(b)(13)(A):

Amended 1954 Code by substituting "Secretary" for "Secretary or his delegate" each place it appeared. **Effective** 2-1-77.

• **1975, Tax Reduction Act of 1975 (P.L. 94-12)**

P.L. 94-12, § 602(c)(5):

Repealed Code Sec. 955. **Effective** for tax years of foreign corporations beginning after 12-31-75, and for tax years of U. S. shareholders within which or with which such tax years of such foreign corporations end. Prior to repeal, Code Sec. 955 read as follows:

"(a) General Rules.—

"(1) Amount withdrawn.—For purposes of this subpart, the amount of previously excluded subpart F income of any controlled foreign corporation withdrawn from investment in less developed countries for any taxable year is an amount equal to the decrease in the amount of qualified investments in less developed countries of the controlled foreign corporation for such year, but only to the extent that the amount of such decrease does not exceed an amount equal to—

"(A) the sum of the amounts excluded under section 954(b)(1) from the foreign base company income of such corporation for all prior taxable years, reduced by

"(B) the sum of the amounts previously excluded subpart F income withdrawn from investment in less developed countries of such corporation determined under this subsection for all prior taxable years.

"(2) Decrease in qualified investments.—For purposes of paragraph (1), the amount of the decrease in qualified investments in less developed countries of any controlled foreign corporation for any taxable year is the amount by which—

"(A) the amount of qualified investments in less developed countries of the controlled foreign corporation at the close of the preceding taxable year, exceeds

"(B) the amount of qualified investments in less developed countries of the controlled foreign corporation at the close of the taxable year,

to the extent the amount of such decrease does not exceed the sum of the earnings and profits for the taxable year and the earnings and profits accumulated for prior taxable years beginning after December 31, 1962. For purposes of this paragraph, if qualified investments in less developed countries are disposed of by the controlled foreign corporation during the taxable year, the amount of the decrease in qualified investments in less developed countries of such controlled foreign corporation for such year shall be reduced by an amount equal to the amount (if any) by which the losses on such dispositions during such year exceed the gains on such dispositions during such year.

"(3) Pro rata share of amount withdrawn.—In the case of any United States shareholder, the pro rata share of the amount of previously excluded subpart F income of any controlled foreign corporation withdrawn from investment in less developed countries for any taxable year is his pro rata share of the amount determined under paragraph (1).

"(b) Qualified Investments in Less Developed Countries.—

INCOME TAX—CONTROLLED FOREIGN CORPORATIONS

"(1) In general.—For purposes of this subpart, the term 'qualified investments in less developed countries' means property which is—

"(A) stock of a less developed country corporation held by the controlled foreign corporation, but only if the controlled foreign corporation owns 10 percent or more of the total combined voting power of all classes of stock of such less developed country corporation;

"(B) an obligation of a less developed country corporation held by the controlled foreign corporation, which, at the time of its acquisition by the controlled foreign corporation, has a maturity of one year or more, but only if the controlled foreign corporation owns 10 percent or more of the total combined voting power of all classes of stock of such less developed country corporation; or

"(C) an obligation of a less developed country.

"(2) Country ceases to be less developed country.—For purposes of this subpart, property which would be a qualified investment in less developed countries, but for the fact that a foreign country has, after the acquisition of such property by the controlled foreign corporation, ceased to be a less developed country, shall be treated as a qualified investment in less developed countries.

"(3) Special rule.—For purposes of this subpart, a United States shareholder of a controlled foreign corporation may, under regulations prescribed by the Secretary or his delegate, make the determinations under subsection (a)(2) of this section and under subsection (f) of section 954 as of the close of the years following the years referred to in such subsections, or as of the close of such longer period of time as such regulations may permit, in lieu of on the last day of such years. Any election under this paragraph made with respect to any taxable year shall apply to such year and to all succeeding taxable years unless the Secretary or his delegate consents to the revocation of such election.

"(4) Exception.—For purposes of this subpart, property shall not constitute qualified investments in less developed countries if such property is disposed of within 6 months after the date of its acquisition.

"(5) Amount attributable to property.—The amount taken into account under this subpart with respect to any property described in paragraph (1) or (2) shall be its adjusted basis, reduced by any liability to which such property is subject.

"(c) Less Developed Country Corporations.—

"(1) In general.—For purposes of this subpart, the term 'less developed country corporation' means a foreign corporation which during the taxable year is engaged in the active conduct of one or more trades or businesses and—

"(A) 80 percent or more of the gross income of which for the taxable year is derived from sources within less developed countries; and

"(B) 80 percent or more in value of the assets of which on each day of the taxable year consists of—

"(i) property used in such trades or businesses and located in less developed countries,

"(ii) money, and deposits with persons carrying on the banking business,

"(iii) stock, and obligations which, at the time of their acquisition, have a maturity of one year or more, of any other less developed country corporation,

"(iv) an obligation of a less developed country,

"(v) an investment which is required because of restrictions imposed by a less developed country, and

"(vi) property described in section 956(b)(2).

For purposes of subparagraph (A), the determination as to whether income is derived from sources within less developed countries shall be made under regulations prescribed by the Secretary or his delegate.

"(2) Shipping companies.—For purposes of this subpart, the term 'less developed country corporation' also means a foreign corporation—

"(A) 80 percent or more of the gross income of which for the taxable year consists of—

"(i) gross income derived from, or in connection with, the using (or hiring or leasing for use) in foreign commerce of aircraft or vessels registered under the laws of a less developed country, or from, or in connection with, the performance of services directly related to use of such aircraft or vessels, or from the sale or exchange of such aircraft or vessels, and

"(ii) dividends and interest received from foreign corporations which are less developed country corporations within the meaning of this paragraph and 10 percent or more of the total combined voting power of all classes of stock of which are owned by the foreign corporation, and gain from the sale or exchange of stock or obligations of foreign corporations which are such less developed country corporations, and

"(B) 80 percent or more of the assets of which on each day of the taxable year consists of (i) assets used, or held for use, for or in connection with the production of income described in subparagraph (A), and (ii) property described in section 956(b)(2).

"(3) Less developed country defined.—For purposes of this subpart, the term 'less developed country' means (in respect of any foreign corporation) any foreign country (other than an area within the Sino-Soviet bloc) or any possession of the United States with respect to which, on the first day of the taxable year, there is in effect an Executive order by the President of the United States designating such country or possession as an economically less developed country for purposes of this subpart. For purposes of the preceding sentence, an overseas territory, department, province, or possession may be treated as a separate country. No designation shall be made under this paragraph with respect to—

Australia	Liechtenstein
Austria	Luxembourg
Belgium	Monaco
Canada	Netherlands
Denmark	New Zealand
France	Norway
Germany (Federal Republic)	Union of South Africa
	San Marino
Hong Kong	Sweden
Italy	Switzerland
Japan	United Kingdom

After the President has designated any foreign country or any possession of the United States as an economically less developed country for purposes of this subpart, he shall not terminate such designation (either by issuing an Executive order for that purpose or by issuing an Executive order under the first sentence of this paragraph which has the effect of terminating such designation) unless, at least 30 days prior to such termination, he has notified the Senate and the House of Representatives of his intention to terminate such designation."

P.L. 94-12, § 602(d)(3)(A):

Added Code Sec. 955. **Effective** for tax years of foreign corporations beginning after 12-31-75, and for tax years of U.S. shareholders within which or with which such tax years of such foreign corporations end.

• **1962, Revenue Act of 1962 (P.L. 87-834)**

P.L. 87-834, § 12(a):

Amended Part III of subchapter N of chapter 1 by adding subpart F, which includes Code Sec. 955. **Effective** for tax years of foreign corporations beginning after 12-31-62, and for tax years of United States shareholders within which or with which such tax years of such foreign corporations end.

[Sec. 956]
SEC. 956. INVESTMENT OF EARNINGS IN UNITED STATES PROPERTY.

[Sec. 956(a)]

(a) GENERAL RULE.—In the case of any controlled foreign corporation, the amount determined under this section with respect to any United States shareholder for any taxable year is the lesser of—

(1) the excess (if any) of—

(A) such shareholder's pro rata share of the average of the amounts of United States property held (directly or indirectly) by the controlled foreign corporation as of the close of each quarter of such taxable year, over

(B) the amount of earnings and profits described in section 959(c)(1)(A) with respect to such shareholder, or

(2) such shareholder's pro rata share of the applicable earnings of such controlled foreign corporation.

The amount taken into account under paragraph (1) with respect to any property shall be its adjusted basis as determined for purposes of computing earnings and profits, reduced by any liability to which the property is subject.

Amendments

• **1993, Omnibus Budget Reconciliation Act of 1993 (P.L. 103-66)**

P.L. 103-66, § 13232(a)(1)-(2):

Amended Code Sec. 956 by redesignating subsections (b) and (c) as subsections (c) and (d), respectively, and by striking subsection (a) and inserting new subsections (a) and (b). **Effective** for tax years of controlled foreign corporations beginning after 9-30-93, and to tax years of United States shareholders in which or with which such tax years of controlled foreign corporations end. Prior to amendment, subsection (a) read as follows:

(a) GENERAL RULES.—For purposes of this subpart—

(1) AMOUNT OF INVESTMENT.—The amount of earnings of a controlled foreign corporation invested in United States property at the close of any taxable year is the aggregate amount of such property held, directly or indirectly, by the controlled foreign corporation at the close of the taxable year, to the extent such amount would have constituted a dividend (determined after the application of section 955(a)) if it had been distributed.

(2) PRO RATA SHARE OF INCREASE FOR YEAR.—In the case of any United States shareholder, the pro rata share of the increase for any taxable year in the earnings of a controlled foreign corporation invested in United States property is the amount determined by subtracting his pro rata share of—

(A) the amount determined under paragraph (1) for the close of the preceding taxable year, reduced by amounts paid during such preceding taxable year to which section 959(c)(1) applies, from

(B) the amount determined under paragraph (1) for the close of the taxable year.

The determinations under subparagraphs (A) and (B) shall be made on the basis of stock owned (within the meaning of section 958(a)) by such United States share-

INCOME TAX—CONTROLLED FOREIGN CORPORATIONS

holder on the last day during the taxable year on which the foreign corporation is a controlled foreign corporation.

(3) AMOUNT ATTRIBUTABLE TO PROPERTY.—The amount taken into account under paragraph (1) or (2) with respect to any property shall be its adjusted basis, reduced by any liability to which the property is subject.

[Sec. 956(b)]

(b) SPECIAL RULES.—

(1) APPLICABLE EARNINGS.—For purposes of this section, the term "applicable earnings" means, with respect to any controlled foreign corporation, the sum of—

(A) the amount (not including a deficit) referred to in section 316(a)(1) to the extent such amount was accumulated in prior taxable years, and

(B) the amount referred to in section 316(a)(2),

but reduced by distributions made during the taxable year and by earnings and profits described in section 959(c)(1).

(2) SPECIAL RULE FOR U.S. PROPERTY ACQUIRED BEFORE CORPORATION IS A CONTROLLED FOREIGN CORPORATION.—In applying subsection (a) to any taxable year, there shall be disregarded any item of United States property which was acquired by the controlled foreign corporation before the first day on which such corporation was treated as a controlled foreign corporation. The aggregate amount of property disregarded under the preceding sentence shall not exceed the portion of the applicable earnings of such controlled foreign corporation which were accumulated during periods before such first day.

(3) SPECIAL RULE WHERE CORPORATION CEASES TO BE CONTROLLED FOREIGN CORPORATION.—If any foreign corporation ceases to be a controlled foreign corporation during any taxable year—

(A) the determination of any United States shareholder's pro rata share shall be made on the basis of stock owned (within the meaning of section 958(a)) by such shareholder on the last day during the taxable year on which the foreign corporation is a controlled foreign corporation,

(B) the average referred to in subsection (a)(1)(A) for such taxable year shall be determined by only taking into account quarters ending on or before such last day, and

(C) in determining applicable earnings, the amount taken into account by reason of being described in paragraph (2) of section 316(a) shall be the portion of the amount so described which is allocable (on a pro rata basis) to the part of such year during which the corporation is a controlled foreign corporation.

Amendments

• **1997, Taxpayer Relief Act of 1997 (P.L. 105-34)**

P.L. 105-34, §1601(e):

Amended Code Sec. 956(b)(1)(A) by inserting "to the extent such amount was accumulated in prior taxable years" after "section 316(a)(1)". **Effective** as if included in the provision of P.L. 104-188 to which it relates [**effective** for tax years of foreign corporations beginning after 12-31-96, and tax years of U.S. shareholders within which or with which such tax years of foreign corporations end.—CCH].

• **1996, Small Business Job Protection Act of 1996 (P.L. 104-188)**

P.L. 104-188, §1501(b)(2):

Amended Code Sec. 956(b)(1). **Effective** for tax years of foreign corporations beginning after 12-31-96, and to tax years of United States shareholders within which or with which such tax years of foreign corporations end. Prior to amendment, Code Sec. 956(b)(1) read as follows:

(1) APPLICABLE EARNINGS.—For purposes of this section, the term "applicable earnings" has the meaning given to such term by section 956A(b), except that the provisions of such section excluding earnings and profits accumulated in taxable years beginning before October 1, 1993, shall be disregarded.

P.L. 104-188, §1501(b)(3):

Amended Code Sec. 956(b)(3). **Effective** for tax years of foreign corporations beginning after 12-31-96, and to tax years of United States shareholders within which or with which such tax years of foreign corporations end. Prior to amendment, Code Sec. 956(b)(3) read as follows:

(3) SPECIAL RULE WHERE CORPORATION CEASES TO BE CONTROLLED FOREIGN CORPORATION.—Rules similar to the rules of section 956A(e) shall apply for purposes of this section.

• **1993, Omnibus Budget Reconciliation Act of 1993 (P.L. 103-66)**

P.L. 103-66, §13232(a)(1)-(2):

Amended Code Sec. 956 by redesignating subsections (b) and (c) as subsections (c) and (d), respectively, and by striking subsection (a) and inserting new subsections (a) and (b). **Effective** for tax years of controlled foreign corporations beginning after 9-30-93, and to tax years of United States shareholders in which or with which such tax years of controlled foreign corporations end.

[Sec. 956(c)]

(c) UNITED STATES PROPERTY DEFINED.—

(1) IN GENERAL.—For purposes of subsection (a), the term "United States property" means any property acquired after December 31, 1962, which is—

(A) tangible property located in the United States;

(B) stock of a domestic corporation;

(C) an obligation of a United States person; or

(D) any right to the use in the United States of—

(i) a patent or copyright,

(ii) an invention, model, or design (whether or not patented),

(iii) a secret formula or process, or

(iv) any other similar property right,

which is acquired or developed by the controlled foreign corporation for use in the United States.

(2) EXCEPTIONS.—For purposes of subsection (a), the term "United States property" does not include—

(A) obligations of the United States, money, or deposits with—

(i) any bank (as defined by section 2(c) of the Bank Holding Company Act of 1956 (12 U.S.C. 1841(c)), without regard to subparagraphs (C) and (G) of paragraph (2) of such section), or

(ii) any corporation not described in clause (i) with respect to which a bank holding company (as defined by section 2(a) of such Act) or financial holding company (as defined by section 2(p) of such Act) owns directly or indirectly more than 80 percent by vote or value of the stock of such corporation;

(B) property located in the United States which is purchased in the United States for export to, or use in, foreign countries;

(C) any obligation of a United States person arising in connection with the sale or processing of property if the amount of such obligation outstanding at no time during the taxable year exceeds the amount which would be ordinary and necessary to carry on the trade or business of both the other party to the sale or processing transaction and the United States person had the sale or processing transaction been made between unrelated persons;

(D) any aircraft, railroad rolling stock, vessel, motor vehicle, or container used in the transportation of persons or property in foreign commerce and used predominantly outside the United States;

(E) an amount of assets of an insurance company equivalent to the unearned premiums or reserves ordinary and necessary for the proper conduct of its insurance business attributable to contracts which are contracts described in section 953(e)(2);

INCOME TAX—CONTROLLED FOREIGN CORPORATIONS

(F) the stock or obligations of a domestic corporation which is neither a United States shareholder (as defined in section 951(b)) of the controlled foreign corporation, nor a domestic corporation, 25 percent or more of the total combined voting power of which, immediately after the acquisition of any stock in such domestic corporation by the controlled foreign corporation, is owned, or is considered as being owned, by such United States shareholders in the aggregate;

(G) any movable property (other than a vessel or aircraft) which is used for the purpose of exploring for, developing, removing, or transporting resources from ocean waters or under such waters when used on the Continental Shelf of the United States;

(H) an amount of assets of the controlled foreign corporation equal to the earnings and profits accumulated after December 31, 1962, and excluded from subpart F income under section 952(b);

(I) deposits of cash or securities made or received on commercial terms in the ordinary course of a United States or foreign person's business as a dealer in securities or in commodities, but only to the extent such deposits are made or received as collateral or margin for (i) a securities loan, notional principal contract, options contract, forward contract, or futures contract, or (ii) any other financial transaction in which the Secretary determines that it is customary to post collateral or margin;

(J) an obligation of a United States person to the extent the principal amount of the obligation does not exceed the fair market value of readily marketable securities sold or purchased pursuant to a sale and repurchase agreement or otherwise posted or received as collateral for the obligation in the ordinary course of its business by a United States or foreign person which is a dealer in securities or commodities;

(K) securities acquired and held by a controlled foreign corporation in the ordinary course of its business as a dealer in securities if—

(i) the dealer accounts for the securities as securities held primarily for sale to customers in the ordinary course of business, and

(ii) the dealer disposes of the securities (or such securities mature while held by the dealer) within a period consistent with the holding of securities for sale to customers in the ordinary course of business; and

(L) an obligation of a United States person which—

(i) is not a domestic corporation, and

(ii) is not—

(I) a United States shareholder (as defined in section 951(b)) of the controlled foreign corporation, or

(II) a partnership, estate, or trust in which the controlled foreign corporation, or any related person (as defined in section 954(d)(3)), is a partner, beneficiary, or trustee immediately after the acquisition of any obligation of such partnership, estate, or trust by the controlled foreign corporation.

For purposes of subparagraphs (I), (J), and (K), the term "dealer in securities" has the meaning given such term by section 475(c)(1), and the term "dealer in commodities" has the meaning given such term by section 475(e), except that such term shall include a futures commission merchant.

(3) CERTAIN TRADE OR SERVICE RECEIVABLES ACQUIRED FROM RELATED UNITED STATES PERSONS.—

(A) IN GENERAL.—Notwithstanding paragraph (2) (other than subparagraph (H) thereof), the term "United States property" includes any trade or service receivable if—

(i) such trade or service receivable is acquired (directly or indirectly) from a related person who is a United States person, and

(ii) the obligor under such receivable is a United States person.

(B) DEFINITIONS.—For purposes of this paragraph, the term "trade or service receivable" and "related person" have the respective meanings given to such terms by section 864(d).

Amendments

• **2018, Tax Technical Corrections Act of 2018 (P.L. 115-141)**

P.L. 115-141, §401(a)(162), Div. U:

Amended Code Sec. 956(c)(2)(E) by striking "which are not contracts described in section 953(a)(1)" and inserting "which are contracts described in section 953(e)(2)". **Effective** 3-23-2018.

• **2007, Tax Technical Corrections Act of 2007 (P.L. 110-172)**

P.L. 110-172, §11(g)(15)(A)(i)-(ii):

Amended Code Sec. 956(c)(2) by striking subparagraph (I) and by redesignating subparagraphs (J) through (M) as subparagraphs (I) through (L), respectively, and by striking "subparagraphs (J), (K), and (L)" in the flush sentence at the end and inserting "subparagraphs (I), (J), and (K)". **Effective** 12-29-2007. Prior to being stricken, Code Sec. 956(c)(2)(I) read as follows:

(I) to the extent provided in regulations prescribed by the Secretary, property which is otherwise United States property which is held by a FSC and which is related to the export activities of such FSC;

• **2004, American Jobs Creation Act of 2004 (P.L. 108-357)**

P.L. 108-357, §407(a):

Amended Code Sec. 956(c)(2) by striking "and" at the end of subparagraph (J), by striking the period at the end of subparagraph (K) and inserting a semicolon, and by adding at the end new subparagraphs (L) and (M). **Effective** for tax years of foreign corporations beginning after 12-31-2004, and for tax years of United States shareholders with or within which such tax years of foreign corporations end.

P.L. 108-357, §407(b):

Amended Code Sec. 956(c)(2) by striking "and (K)" in the last sentence and inserting ", (K), and (L)". **Effective** for tax years of foreign corporations beginning after 12-31-2004, and for tax years of United States shareholders with or within which such tax years of foreign corporations end.

P.L. 108-357, §837(a):

Amended Code Sec. 956(c)(2)(A). **Effective** on 10-22-2004. Prior to amendment, Code Sec. 956(c)(2)(A) read as follows:

(A) obligations of the United States, money, or deposits with persons carrying on the banking business;

• **1997, Taxpayer Relief Act of 1997 (P.L. 105-34)**

P.L. 105-34, §1173(a):

Amended Code Sec. 956(c)(2) by striking "and" at the end of subparagraph (H), by striking the period at the end of subparagraph (I) and inserting a semicolon, and by adding at the end new subparagraphs (J) and (K) and a new flush sentence. **Effective** for tax years of foreign corporations beginning after 12-31-97, and to tax years of United States shareholders with or within which such tax years of foreign corporations end.

• **1993, Omnibus Budget Reconciliation Act of 1993 (P.L. 103-66)**

P.L. 103-66, §13232(a)(1)-(2):

Redesignated Code Sec. 956(b) as Code Sec. 956(c). **Effective** for tax years of controlled foreign corporations beginning after 9-30-93, and to tax years of United States shareholders in which or with which such tax years of controlled foreign corporations end.

• **1986, Tax Reform Act of 1986 (P.L. 99-514)**

P.L. 99-514, §1810(c)(1):

Amended Code Sec. 956(b)(3)(A) by striking out "paragraph (2)" and inserting in lieu thereof "paragraph (2) (other than subparagraph (H) thereof)". **Effective** as if included in the provision of P.L. 98-369 to which it relates.

• **1984, Deficit Reduction Act of 1984 (P.L. 98-369)**

P.L. 98-369, §123(b):

Amended Code Sec. 956(b) by adding new paragraph (3). **Effective** for accounts receivable and evidences of indebtedness transferred after 3-1-84, in tax years ending after such date. A special rule appears in Act Sec. 123(c)(2), below.

P.L. 98-369, §123(c)(2), provides:

(2) Transitional Rule.—The amendments made by this section shall not apply to accounts receivable and evidences of indebtedness acquired after March 1, 1984, and before March 1, 1984, by a Belgian corporation in existence on March 1, 1994, in any taxable year ending after such date, but only to the extent that the amount includible in gross income by reason so section 956 of the Internal Revenue Code of 1954 with respect to such corporation for all such taxable years is not reduced by reason of this paragraph by more than the lesser of—

(A) $15,000,000 or

(B) the amount of the Belgian corporation's adjusted basis on March 1, 1984 in stock of a foreign corporation formed to issue bonds outside the United States to the public.

P.L. 98-369, §801(d)(8):

Amended Code Sec. 956(b)(2) by striking out "and" at the end of subparagraph (G), by striking out the period at the end of subparagraph (H) and inserting in lieu thereof a semicolon and "and", and by adding new subparagraph (I). **Effective** for transactions after 12-31-84, in tax years ending after such date.

INCOME TAX—CONTROLLED FOREIGN CORPORATIONS

• **1976, Tax Reform Act of 1976 (P.L. 94-455)**

P.L. 94-455, § 1021(a):

Struck out "and" at the end of Code Sec. 956(b)(2)(E), redesignated former Code Sec. 956(b)(2)(F) as Code Sec. 956(b)(2)(H), and added Code Secs. 956(b)(2)(F) and 956(b)(2)(G). For the **effective** date, see Act Sec. 1021(c), below.

P.L. 94-455, § 1021(c), provides:

(c) EFFECTIVE DATE.—The amendments made by this section shall apply to taxable years of foreign corporations beginning after December 31, 1975, and to taxable years of United States shareholders (within the meaning of section 951(b) of the Internal Revenue Code of 1954) within which or with which such taxable years of such foreign corporations end. In determining for purposes of any taxable year referred to in the preceding sentence the amount referred to in section 956(a)(2)(A) of the Internal Revenue Code of 1954 for the last taxable year of a corporation beginning before January 1, 1976, the amendments made by this section shall be deemed also to apply to such last taxable year.

[Sec. 956(d)]

(d) PLEDGES AND GUARANTEES.—For purposes of subsection (a), a controlled foreign corporation shall, under regulations prescribed by the Secretary, be considered as holding an obligation of a United States person if such controlled foreign corporation is a pledgor or guarantor of such obligation.

Amendments

• **1993, Omnibus Budget Reconciliation Act of 1993 (P.L. 103-66)**

P.L. 103-66, § 13232(a)(1)-(2):

Redesignated Code Sec. 956(c) as Code Sec. 956(d). **Effective** for tax years of controlled foreign corporations beginning after 9-30-93, and to tax years of United States shareholders in which or with which such tax years of controlled foreign corporations end.

• **1976, Tax Reform Act of 1976 (P.L. 94-455)**

P.L. 94-455, § 1906(b)(13)(A):

Amended 1954 Code by substituting "Secretary" for "Secretary or his delegate" each place it appeared. **Effective** 2-1-77.

[Sec. 956(e)]

(e) REGULATIONS.—The Secretary shall prescribe such regulations as may be necessary to carry out the purposes of this section, including regulations to prevent the avoidance of the provisions of this section through reorganizations or otherwise.

Amendments

• **2018, Tax Technical Corrections Act of 2018 (P.L. 115-141)**

P.L. 115-141, § 401(a)(163), Div. U:

Amended Code Sec. 956(e) by striking "provisons" and inserting "provisions". **Effective** 3-23-2018.

• **1993, Omnibus Budget Reconciliation Act of 1993 (P.L. 103-66)**

P.L. 103-66, § 13232(b):

Amended Code Sec. 956 by adding at the end thereof new subsection (e). **Effective** for tax years of controlled foreign corporations beginning after 9-30-93, and to tax years of United States shareholders in which or with which such tax years of controlled foreign corporations end.

[Sec. 956A—Repealed]

Amendments

• **1996, Small Business Job Protection Act of 1996 (P.L. 104-188)**

P.L. 104-188, § 1501(a)(2):

Repealed Code Sec. 956A. **Effective** for tax years of foreign corporations beginning after 12-31-96, and to tax years of United States shareholders within which or with which such tax years of foreign corporations end. Prior to repeal, Code Sec. 956A read as follows:

SEC. 956A. EARNINGS INVESTED IN EXCESS PASSIVE ASSETS.

(a) GENERAL RULE.—In the case of any controlled foreign corporation, the amount determined under this section with respect to any United States shareholder for any taxable year is the lesser of—

(1) the excess (if any) of—

(A) such shareholder's pro rata share of the amount of the controlled foreign corporation's excess passive assets for such taxable year, over

(B) the amount of earnings and profits described in section 959(c)(1)(B) with respect to such shareholder, or

(2) such shareholder's pro rata share of the applicable earnings of such controlled foreign corporation determined after the application of section 951(a)(1)(B).

(b) APPLICABLE EARNINGS.—For purposes of this section, the term "applicable earnings" means, with respect to any controlled foreign corporation, the sum of—

(1) the amount (not including a deficit) referred to in section 316(a)(1) to the extent such amount was accumulated in prior taxable years beginning after September 30, 1993, and

(2) the amount referred to in section 316(a)(2),

but reduced by distributions made during the taxable year and reduced by the earnings and profits described in section 959(c)(1) to the extent that the earnings and profits so described were accumulated in taxable years beginning after September 30, 1993.

(c) EXCESS PASSIVE ASSETS.—For purposes of this section—

(1) IN GENERAL.—The excess passive assets of any controlled foreign corporation for any taxable year is the excess (if any) of—

(A) the average of the amounts of passive assets held by such corporation as of the close of each quarter of such taxable year, over

(B) 25 percent of the average of the amounts of total assets held by such corporation as of the close of each quarter of such taxable year.

For purposes of the preceding sentence, the amount taken into account with respect to any asset shall be its adjusted basis as determined for purposes of computing earnings and profits.

(2) PASSIVE ASSET.—

(A) IN GENERAL.—Except as otherwise provided in this section, the term "passive asset" means any asset held by the controlled foreign corporation which produces passive income (as defined in section 1296(b)) or is held for the production of such income.

(B) COORDINATION WITH SECTION 956.—The term "passive asset" shall not include any United States property (as defined in section 956).

(3) CERTAIN RULES TO APPLY.—For purposes of this subsection, the rules of the following provisions shall apply:

(A) Section 1296(c) (relating to look-thru rules).

(B) Section 1297(d) (relating to leasing rules).

(C) Section 1297(e) (relating to intangible property).

(d) TREATMENT OF CERTAIN GROUPS OF CONTROLLED FOREIGN CORPORATIONS.—

(1) IN GENERAL.—For purposes of applying subsection (c)—

(A) all controlled foreign corporations which are members of the same CFC group shall be treated as 1 controlled foreign corporation, and

(B) the amount of the excess passive assets determined with respect to such 1 corporation shall be allocated among the controlled foreign corporations which are members of such group in proportion to their respective amounts of applicable earnings.

(2) CFC GROUP.—For purposes of paragraph (1), the term "CFC group" means 1 or more chains of controlled foreign corporations connected through stock ownership with a top tier corporation which is a controlled foreign corporation, but only if—

(A) the top tier corporation owns directly more than 50 percent (by vote or value) of the stock of at least 1 of the other controlled foreign corporations, and

(B) more than 50 percent (by vote or value) of the stock of each of the controlled foreign corporations (other than the top tier corporation) is owned (directly or indirectly) by one or more other members of the group.

(e) SPECIAL RULE WHERE CORPORATION CEASES TO BE CONTROLLED FOREIGN CORPORATION DURING TAXABLE YEAR.—If any foreign corporation ceases to be a controlled foreign corporation during any taxable year—

(1) the determination of any United States shareholder's pro rata share shall be made on the basis of stock owned (within the meaning of section 958(a)) by such shareholder on the last day during the taxable year on which the foreign corporation is a controlled foreign corporation, and

(2) the amount of such corporation's excess passive assets for such taxable year shall be determined by only taking into account quarters ending on or before such last day, and

(3) in determining applicable earnings, the amount taken into account by reason of being described in paragraph (2) of section 316(a) shall be the portion of the amount so described which is allocable (on a pro rata basis) to the part of such year during which the corporation is a controlled foreign corporation.

(f) REGULATIONS.—The Secretary shall prescribe such regulations as may be necessary to carry out the purposes of this section, including regulations to prevent the avoidance of the provisions of this section through reorganizations or otherwise and regulations coordinating the provisions of subsections (c)(3)(A) and (d).

P.L. 104-188, § 1703(i)(2):

Amended Code Sec. 956A(b)(1). **Effective** as if included in the provision of P.L. 103-66 to which it relates. Prior to amendment, Code Sec. 956A(b)(1) read as follows:

(1) the amount referred to in section 316(a)(1) to the extent such amount was accumulated in taxable years beginning after September 30, 1993, and

P.L. 104-188, § 1703(i)(3):

Amended Code Sec. 956A(f) by inserting before the period at the end thereof "and regulations coordinating the provisions of subsections (c)(3)(A) and (d)". **Effective** as if included in the provision of P.L. 103-66 to which it relates.

• **1993, Omnibus Budget Reconciliation Act of 1993 (P.L. 103-66)**

P.L. 103-66, § 13231(b):

Amended subpart F of part III of subchapter N of chapter 1 by inserting after section 956 a new section 956A. **Effective** for tax years of foreign corporations beginning after 9-30-93, and to tax years of United States shareholders in which or with which such tax years of foreign corporations end.

INCOME TAX—CONTROLLED FOREIGN CORPORATIONS

[Sec. 957]

SEC. 957. CONTROLLED FOREIGN CORPORATIONS; UNITED STATES PERSONS.

[Sec. 957(a)]

(a) GENERAL RULE.—For purposes of this title, the term "controlled foreign corporation" means any foreign corporation if more than 50 percent of—

(1) the total combined voting power of all classes of stock of such corporation entitled to vote, or

(2) the total value of the stock of such corporation,

is owned (within the meaning of section 958(a)), or is considered as owned by applying the rules of ownership of section 958(b), by United States shareholders on any day during the taxable year of such foreign corporation.

Amendments

• **2017, Tax Cuts and Jobs Act (P.L. 115-97)**

P.L. 115-97, §14101(e)(2):

Amended Code Sec. 957(a) by striking "subpart" in the matter preceding paragraph (1) and inserting "title". **Effective** for distributions made after 12-31-2017.

Amendments

• **1986, Tax Reform Act of 1986 (P.L. 99-514)**

P.L. 99-514, §1222(a)(1):

Amended Code Sec. 957(a). **Effective**, generally, for tax years of foreign corporations beginning after 12-31-86; except that for purposes of applying sections 951(a)(1)(B) and 956 of the Internal Revenue Code of 1986, it shall take effect on 8-16-86. However, for a transitional rule, see Act Sec. 1222(c)(2)-(3), below. Prior to amendment, Code Sec. 957(a) read as follows:

(a) GENERAL RULE.—For purposes of this subpart, the term "controlled foreign corporation" means any foreign corporation of which more than 50 percent of the total combined voting power of all classes of stock entitled to vote is owned (within the meaning of section 958(a)), or is considered as owned by applying the rules of ownership of section 958(b), by United States shareholders on any day during the taxable year of such foreign corporation.

P.L. 99-514, §1222(c)(2)-(3), provides:

(2) TRANSITIONAL RULE.—In the case of any corporation treated as a controlled foreign corporation by reason of the amendments made by this section, property acquired before August 16, 1986, shall not be taken into account under section 956(b) of the Internal Revenue Code of 1986.

(3) SPECIAL RULE FOR BENEFICIARY OF TRUST.—In the case of an individual—

(A) who is a beneficiary of a trust which was established on December 7, 1979, under the laws of a foreign jurisdiction, and

(B) who was not a citizen or resident of the United States on the date the trust was established,

amounts which are included in the gross income of such beneficiary under section 951(a) of the Internal Revenue Code of 1986 with respect to stock held by the trust (and treated as distributed to the trust) shall be treated as the first amounts which are distributed by the trust to such beneficiary and as amounts to which section 959(a) of such Code applies.

[Sec. 957(b)]

(b) SPECIAL RULE FOR INSURANCE.—For purposes only of taking into account income described in section 953(a) (relating to insurance income), the term "controlled foreign corporation" includes not only a foreign corporation as defined by subsection (a) but also one of which more than 25 percent of the total combined voting power of all classes of stock (or more than 25 percent of the total value of the stock) is owned (within the meaning of section 958(a)), or is considered as owned by applying the rules of ownership of section 958(b), by United States shareholders on any day during the taxable year of such corporation, if the gross amount of premiums or other consideration in respect of the reinsurance or the issuing of insurance or annuity contracts not described in section 953(e)(2) exceeds 75 percent of the gross amount of all premiums or other consideration in respect of all risks.

Amendments

• **2018, Tax Technical Corrections Act of 2018 (P.L. 115-141)**

P.L. 115-141, §401(a)(164), Div. U:

Amended Code Sec. 957(b) by striking "contracts described in section 953(a)(1)" and inserting "contracts not described in section 953(e)(2)". **Effective** 3-23-2018.

• **1986, Tax Reform Act of 1986 (P.L. 99-514)**

P.L. 99-514, §1221(b)(3)(C):

Amended Code Sec. 957(b) by striking out "income derived from insurance of United States risks" and inserting in lieu thereof "insurance income". **Effective** for tax years of foreign corporations beginning after 12-31-86. However, for special rules and exceptions, see Act Sec. 1221(g)(2)-(3) under the amendment notes to Code Sec. 954.

P.L. 99-514, §1222(a)(2):

Amended Code Sec. 957(b) by striking out "all classes of stock" and inserting in lieu thereof "all classes of stock (or more than 25 percent of the total value of the stock)". **Effective**, generally, for tax years of foreign corporations beginning after 12-31-86; except that for purposes of applying sections 951(a)(1)(B) and 956 of the Internal Revenue Code of 1986, such amendments shall take effect on 8-16-86. However, for a transitional rule, see Act Sec. 1222(c)(2)-(3) under the amendment note to Code Sec. 957(a).

[Sec. 957(c)]

(c) UNITED STATES PERSON.—For purposes of this subpart, the term "United States person" has the meaning assigned to it by section 7701(a)(30) except that—

(1) with respect to a corporation organized under the laws of the Commonwealth of Puerto Rico, such term does not include an individual who is a bona fide resident of Puerto Rico, if a dividend received by such individual during the taxable year from such corporation would, for purposes of section 933(1), be treated as income derived from sources within Puerto Rico, and

(2) with respect to a corporation organized under the laws of Guam, American Samoa, or the Northern Mariana Islands—

(A) 80 percent or more of the gross income of which for the 3-year period ending at the close of the taxable year (or for such part of such period as such corporation or any predecessor has been in existence) was derived from sources within such a possession or was effectively connected with the conduct of a trade or business in such a possession, and

(B) 50 percent or more of the gross income of which for such period (or part) was derived from the active conduct of a trade or business within such a possession,

such term does not include an individual who is a bona fide resident of Guam, American Samoa, or the Northern Mariana Islands.

For purposes of subparagraph (A) and (B) of paragraph (2), the determination as to whether income was derived from the active conduct of a trade or business within a possession shall be made under regulations prescribed by the Secretary.

Amendments

• **2004, American Jobs Creation Act of 2004 (P.L. 108-357)**

P.L. 108-357, §908(c)(5)(A)-(B):

Amended Code Sec. 957(c) by striking "conduct of an active" in paragraph (2)(B) and inserting "active conduct of a", and by striking "derived from sources within a possession, was effectively connected with the conduct of a trade or business within a possession, or" after "whether income was" in the last sentence. **Effective** for tax years ending after 10-22-2004.

• **1986, Tax Reform Act of 1986 (P.L. 99-514)**

P.L. 99-514, §1224(a):

Amended Code Sec. 957 by striking out subsection (c) and by redesignating subsection (d) as subsection (c). **Effective**, generally, for tax years of foreign corporations beginning after 12-31-86; except that for purposes of applying sections 951(a)(1)(B) and 956 of the Internal Revenue Code of 1986, such amendments shall take effect on 8-16-86. For a transitional rule see Act Sec. 1224(b)(2), below. Prior to deletion, Code Sec. 957(c) read as follows:

(c) CORPORATIONS ORGANIZED IN UNITED STATES POSSESSIONS.—For purposes of this subpart, the term "controlled foreign corporation" does not include any corporation created or organized in the Commonwealth of Puerto Rico or a possession of the United States or under the laws of the Commonwealth of Puerto Rico or a possession of the United States if—

(1) 80 percent or more of the gross income of such corporation for the 3-year period immediately preceding the close of the taxable year (or for such part of such period immediately preceding the close of such taxable year as may be applicable) was derived from sources within the Commonwealth of Puerto Rico or a possession of the United States; and

(2) 50 percent or more of the gross income of such corporation for such period, or for such part thereof, was derived from the active conduct within the Commonwealth of Puerto Rico or a possession of the United States of any trades or businesses constituting the manufacture or processing of goods, wares, merchandise, or other tangible personal property; the processing of agricultural or horticultural products or commodities (including but not limited to livestock, poultry, or fur-bearing animals); the catching or taking of any kind of fish or the mining or extraction of natural

INCOME TAX—CONTROLLED FOREIGN CORPORATIONS

resources, or any manufacturing or processing of any products or commodities obtain[ed] from such activities; or the ownership or operation of hotels.

For purposes of paragraphs (1) and (2), the determination as to whether income was derived from sources within the Commonwealth of Puerto Rico or a possession of the United States and was derived from the active conduct of a described trade or business within the Commonwealth of Puerto Rico or a possession of the United States shall be made under regulations prescribed by the Secretary.

P.L. 99-514, §1224(b)(2), provides:

(2) TRANSITIONAL RULE.—In the case of any corporation treated as a controlled foreign corporation by reason of the amendment made by subsection (a), property acquired before August 16, 1986, shall not be taken into account under section 956(b) of the Internal Revenue Code of 1986.

P.L. 99-514, §1273(a):

Amended Code Sec. 957(c)(1)-(3), as amended by Act Sec. 924, by adding "and" at the end of paragraph (1) and by striking out paragraphs (2) and (3) and inserting in lieu thereof new paragraph (2). For the **effective** date as well as special rules, see Act Sec. 1277 following Code Sec. 48. Prior to amendment, Code Sec. 957(c)(2) and (3) read as follows:

(2) with respect to a corporation organized under the laws of the Virgin Islands, such term does not include an individual who is a bona fide resident of the Virgin Islands and whose income tax obligation under this subtitle for the taxable year is satisfied pursuant to section 28(a) of the Revised Organic Act of the Virgin Islands, approved July 22, 1954 (48 U.S.C. 1642), by paying tax on income derived from all sources both within and outside the Virgin Islands into the treasury of the Virgin Islands, and

(3) with respect to a corporation organized under the laws of any other possession of the United States, such term does not include an individual who is a bona fide resident of any such other possession and whose income derived from sources within possessions of the United States is not, be [by] reason of section 931(a), includible in gross income under this subtitle for the taxable year.

• **1976, Tax Reform Act of 1976 (P.L. 94-455)**

P.L. 94-455, §1906(b)(13)(A):

Amended 1954 Code by substituting "Secretary" for "Secretary or his delegate" each place it appeared. **Effective** 2-1-77.

[Sec. 958]

SEC. 958. RULES FOR DETERMINING STOCK OWNERSHIP.

[Sec. 958(a)]

(a) DIRECT AND INDIRECT OWNERSHIP.—

(1) GENERAL RULE.—For purposes of this subpart (other than section 960), stock owned means—

(A) stock owned directly, and

(B) stock owned with the application of paragraph (2).

(2) STOCK OWNERSHIP THROUGH FOREIGN ENTITIES.—For purposes of subparagraph (B) of paragraph (1), stock owned, directly or indirectly, by or for a foreign corporation, foreign partnership, or foreign trust or foreign estate (within the meaning of section 7701(a)(31)) shall be considered as being owned proportionately by its shareholders, partners, or beneficiaries. Stock considered to be owned by a person by reason of the application of the preceding sentence shall, for purposes of applying such sentence, be treated as actually owned by such person.

(3) SPECIAL RULE FOR MUTUAL INSURANCE COMPANIES.—For purposes of applying paragraph (1) in the case of a foreign mutual insurance company, the term "stock" shall include any certificate entitling the holder to voting power in the corporation.

Amendments

• **2017, Tax Cuts and Jobs Act (P.L. 115-97)**

P.L. 115-97, §14301(c)(31):

Amended Code Sec. 958(a)(1) by striking "960(a)(1)" and inserting "960". **Effective** for tax years of foreign corporations beginning after 12-31-2017, and to tax years of United States shareholders in which or with which such tax years of foreign corporations end.

• **1996, Small Business Job Protection Act of 1996 (P.L. 104-188)**

P.L. 104-188, §1704(t)(7):

Amended Code Sec. 958(a)(1) by striking "sections 955(b)(1)(A) and (B), 955(c)(2)(A)(ii), and 960(a)(1)" and inserting "section 960(a)(1)". **Effective** 8-20-96.

[Sec. 958(b)]

(b) CONSTRUCTIVE OWNERSHIP.—For purposes of sections 951(b), 954(d)(3), 956(c)(2), and 957, section 318(a) (relating to constructive ownership of stock) shall apply to the extent that the effect is to treat any United States person as a United States shareholder within the meaning of section 951(b), to treat a person as a related person within the meaning of section 954(d)(3), to treat the stock of a domestic corporation as owned by a United States shareholder of the controlled foreign corporation for purposes of section 956(c)(2), or to treat a foreign corporation as a controlled foreign corporation under section 957, except that—

(1) In applying paragraph (1)(A) of section 318(a), stock owned by a nonresident alien individual (other than a foreign trust or foreign estate) shall not be considered as owned by a citizen or by a resident alien individual.

(2) In applying subparagraphs (A), (B), and (C) of section 318(a)(2), if a partnership, estate, trust, or corporation owns, directly or indirectly, more than 50 percent of the total combined voting power of all classes of stock entitled to vote of a corporation, it shall be considered as owning all the stock entitled to vote.

(3) In applying subparagraph (C) of section 318(a)(2), the phrase "10 percent" shall be substituted for the phrase "50 percent" used in subparagraph (C).

Paragraph (1) shall not apply for purposes of section 956(c)(2) to treat stock of a domestic corporation as not owned by a United States shareholder.

Amendments

• **2017, Tax Cuts and Jobs Act (P.L. 115-97)**

P.L. 115-97, §14213(a)(1)-(2):

Amended Code Sec. 958(b) by striking paragraph (4), and by striking "Paragraphs (1) and (4)" in the last sentence and inserting "Paragraph (1)". **Effective** for the last tax year of foreign corporations beginning before 1-1-2018, and each subsequent tax year of such foreign corporations, and tax years of United States shareholders in which or with which such tax years of foreign corporations end. Prior to being stricken, Code Sec. 958(b)(4) read as follows:

(4) Subparagraphs (A), (B), and (C) of section 318(a)(3) shall not be applied so as to consider a United States person as owning stock which is owned by a person who is not a United States person.

• **1996, Small Business Job Protection Act of 1996 (P.L. 104-188)**

P.L. 104-188, §1703(i)(4):

Amended Code Sec. 958(b) by striking "956(b)(2)" each place it appears and inserting "956(c)(2)". **Effective** as if included in the provision of P.L. 103-66 to which it relates.

• **1976, Tax Reform Act of 1976 (P.L. 94-455)**

P.L. 94-455, §1021(b):

Substituted "954(d)(3), 956(b)(2)," for "954(d)(3)," the first place it appeared in Code Sec. 958(b), substituted "954(d)(3), to treat the stock of a domestic corporation as owned by a United States shareholder of the controlled foreign corporation for purposes of section 956(b)(2)," for "954(d)(3)," the second place it appeared in Code Sec. 958(b), and added the final sentence of Code Sec. 958(b). **Effective** for tax years of foreign corporations beginning after 12-31-75, and to tax years of United States shareholders (within the meaning of Code Sec. 951(b)) within which or with which such tax years of such foreign corporations end.

• **1964 (P.L. 88-554)**

P.L. 88-554, §5(b)(5):

Amended Code Sec. 958(b) by substituting "subparagraphs (A), (B), and (C)" for "the first sentence of subparagraphs (A) and (B), and in applying clause (i) of subparagraph (C)" in paragraph (2), by deleting paragraph (3), by substituting "(3) In applying subparagraph (C)" for "(4) In applying clause (i) of subparagraph (C)", and by substituting "(4) Subparagraphs (A), (B), and (C) of section 318(a)(3)" for "(5) The second sentence of subparagraphs (A) and (B), and clause (ii) of subparagraph (C), of section 318(a)(2)". **Effective** 8-31-64.

[Sec. 959]

SEC. 959. EXCLUSION FROM GROSS INCOME OF PREVIOUSLY TAXED EARNINGS AND PROFITS.

[Sec. 959(a)]

(a) EXCLUSION FROM GROSS INCOME OF UNITED STATES PERSONS.—For purposes of this chapter, the earnings and profits of a foreign corporation attributable to amounts which are, or have been, included in the gross income of a United States shareholder under section 951(a) shall not, when—

INCOME TAX—CONTROLLED FOREIGN CORPORATIONS

(1) such amounts are distributed to, or

(2) such amounts would, but for this subsection, be included under section 951(a)(1)(B) in the gross income of,

such shareholder (or any other United States person who acquires from any person any portion of the interest of such United States shareholder in such foreign corporation, but only to the extent of such portion, and subject to such proof of the identity of such interest as the Secretary may by regulations prescribe) directly or indirectly through a chain of ownership described under section 958(a), be again included in the gross income of such United States shareholder (or of such other United States person). The rules of subsection (c) shall apply for purposes of paragraph (1) of this subsection and the rules of subsection (f) shall apply for purposes of paragraph (2) of this subsection.

Amendments

• **1996, Small Business Job Protection Act of 1996 (P.L. 104-188)**

P.L. 104-188, §1501(b)(4):

Amended Code Sec. 959(a) by adding "or" at the end of paragraph (1), by striking "or" at the end of paragraph (2), and by striking paragraph (3). **Effective** for tax years of foreign corporations beginning after 12-31-96, and to tax years of United States shareholders within which or with which such tax years of foreign corporations end. Prior to being stricken, Code Sec. 959(a)(3) read as follows:

(3) such amounts would, but for this subsection, be included under section 951(a)(1)(C) in the gross income of,

P.L. 104-188, §1501(b)(5):

Amended Code Sec. 959(a) by striking "paragraphs (2) and (3)" in the last sentence and inserting "paragraph (2)". **Effective** for tax years of foreign corporations beginning after 12-31-96, and to tax years of United States shareholders within which or with which such tax years of foreign corporations end.

• **1993, Omnibus Budget Reconciliation Act of 1993 (P.L. 103-66)**

P.L. 103-66, §13231(c)(1):

Amended Code Sec. 959(a) by striking "or" at the end of paragraph (1), by adding "or" at the end of paragraph (2), and by inserting after paragraph (2) a new paragraph (3). **Effective** for tax years of foreign corporations beginning after 9-30-93, and to tax years of United States shareholders in which or with which such tax years of foreign corporations end.

P.L. 103-66, §13231(c)(2)(A):

Amended Code Sec. 959(a) by adding at the end thereof the new sentence. **Effective** for tax years of foreign corporations beginning after 9-30-93, and to tax years of United States shareholders in which or with which such tax years of foreign corporations end.

P.L. 103-66, §13231(c)(4)(A):

Amended Code Sec. 959(a) by striking "earnings and profits for a taxable year" and inserting "earnings and profits". **Effective** for tax years of foreign corporations beginning after 9-30-93, and to tax years of United States shareholders in which or with which such tax years of foreign corporations end.

• **1976, Tax Reform Act of 1976 (P.L. 94-455)**

P.L. 94-455, §1906(b)(13)(A):

Amended 1954 Code by substituting "Secretary" for "Secretary or his delegate" each place it appeared. **Effective** 2-1-77.

[Sec. 959(b)]

(b) EXCLUSION FROM GROSS INCOME OF CERTAIN FOREIGN SUBSIDIARIES.—For purposes of section 951(a), the earnings and profits of a controlled foreign corporation attributable to amounts which are, or have been, included in the gross income of a United States shareholder under section 951(a), shall not, when distributed through a chain of ownership described under section 958(a), be also included in the gross income of another controlled foreign corporation in such chain for purposes of the application of section 951(a) to such other controlled foreign corporation with respect to such United States shareholder (or to any other United States shareholder who acquires from any person any portion of the interest of such United States shareholder in the controlled foreign corporation, but only to the extent of such portion, and subject to such proof of identity of such interest as the Secretary may prescribe by regulations).

Amendments

• **1993, Omnibus Budget Reconciliation Act of 1993 (P.L. 103-66)**

P.L. 103-66, §13231(c)(4)(A):

Amended Code Sec. 959(b) by striking "earnings and profits for a taxable year" and inserting "earnings and profits". **Effective** for tax years of foreign corporations beginning after 9-30-93, and to tax years of United States shareholders in which or with which such tax years of foreign corporations end.

• **1976, Tax Reform Act of 1976 (P.L. 94-455)**

P.L. 94-455, §1906(b)(13)(A):

Amended 1954 Code by substituting "Secretary" for "Secretary or his delegate" each place it appeared. **Effective** 2-1-77.

[Sec. 959(c)]

(c) ALLOCATION OF DISTRIBUTIONS.—For purposes of subsections (a) and (b), section 316(a) shall be applied by applying paragraph (2) thereof, and then paragraph (1) thereof—

(1) first to the aggregate of—

(A) earnings and profits attributable to amounts included in gross income under section 951(a)(1)(B) (or which would have been included except for subsection (a)(2) of this section), and

(B) earnings and profits attributable to amounts included in gross income under section 951(a)(1)(C) (or which would have been included except for subsection (a)(3) of this section),

with any distribution being allocated between earnings and profits described in subparagraph (A) and earnings and profits described in subparagraph (B) proportionately on the basis of the respective amounts of such earnings and profits,

(2) then to earnings and profits attributable to amounts included in gross income under section 951(a)(1)(A) (but reduced by amounts not included under subparagraph (B) or (C) of section 951(a)(1) because of the exclusions in paragraphs (2) and (3) of subsection (a) of this section), and

(3) then to other earnings and profits.

References in this subsection to section 951(a)(1)(C) and subsection (a)(3) shall be treated as references to such provisions as in effect on the day before the date of the enactment of the Small Business Job Protection Act of 1996.

Amendments

• **1996, Small Business Job Protection Act of 1996 (P.L. 104-188)**

P.L. 104-188, §1501(b)(6):

Amended Code Sec. 959(c) by adding at the end a new flush sentence. **Effective** for tax years of foreign corporations beginning after 12-31-96, and to tax years of United States shareholders within which or with which such tax years of foreign corporations end.

• **1993, Omnibus Budget Reconciliation Act of 1993 (P.L. 103-66)**

P.L. 103-66, §13231(c)(2)(C):

Amended Code Sec. 959(c)(1). **Effective** for tax years of foreign corporations beginning after 9-30-93, and to tax years of United States shareholders in which or with which such tax years of foreign corporations end. Prior to amendment, Code Sec. 959(c)(1) read as follows:

(1) first to earnings and profits attributable to amounts included in gross income under section 951(a)(1)(B) (or which would have been included except for subsection (a)(2) of this section),

P.L. 103-66, §13231(c)(4)(B):

Amended Code Sec. 959(c)(2). **Effective** for tax years of foreign corporations beginning after 9-30-93, and to tax years of United States shareholders in which or with which such tax years of foreign corporations end. Prior to amendment, Code Sec. 959(c)(2) read as follows:

(2) then to earnings and profits attributable to amounts included in gross income under section 951(a)(1)(A) (but reduced by amounts not included under section 951(a)(1)(B) because of the exclusion in subsection (a)(2) of this section), and

[Sec. 959(d)]

(d) DISTRIBUTIONS EXCLUDED FROM GROSS INCOME NOT TO BE TREATED AS DIVIDENDS.—Any distribution excluded from gross income under subsection (a) shall be treated, for purposes of this chapter, as a distribution which is not a dividend; except that such distributions shall immediately reduce earnings and profits.

INCOME TAX—CONTROLLED FOREIGN CORPORATIONS

Amendments

• **2017, Tax Cuts and Jobs Act (P.L. 115-97)**

P.L. 115-97, § 14301(c)(32):

Amended Code Sec. 959(d) by striking "Except as provided in section 960(a)(3), any" and inserting "Any". **Effective** for tax years of foreign corporations beginning after 12-31-2017, and to tax years of United States shareholders in which or with which such tax years of foreign corporations end.

• **1986, Tax Reform Act of 1986 (P.L. 99-514)**

P.L. 99-514, § 1226(b):

Amended Code Sec. 959(d) by striking out the period at the end thereof and inserting in lieu thereof "; except that such distributions shall immediately reduce earnings and profits." **Effective** for distributions after 10-22-86.

[Sec. 959(e)]

(e) COORDINATION WITH AMOUNTS PREVIOUSLY TAXED UNDER SECTION 1248.—For purposes of this section and section 960(c), any amount included in the gross income of any person as a dividend by reason of subsection (a) or (f) of section 1248 shall be treated as an amount included in the gross income of such person (or, in any case to which section 1248(e) applies, of the domestic corporation referred to in section 1248(e)(2)) under section 951(a)(1)(A).

Amendments

• **2017, Tax Cuts and Jobs Act (P.L. 115-97)**

P.L. 115-97, § 14301(c)(33):

Amended Code Sec. 959(e) by striking "section 960(b)" and inserting "section 960(c)". **Effective** for tax years of foreign corporations beginning after 12-31-2017, and to tax years of United States shareholders in which or with which such tax years of foreign corporations end.

• **1988, Technical and Miscellaneous Revenue Act of 1988 (P.L. 100-647)**

P.L. 100-647, § 1012(bb)(7)(A):

Amended Code Sec. 959(e) by striking out "such person under" and inserting in lieu thereof "such person (or, in any case to which section 1248(e) applies, of the domestic corporation referred to in section 1248(e)(2)) under". **Effective** in the case of transactions to which section 1248(e) of the 1986 Code applies and which occur after 12-31-86.

• **1984, Deficit Reduction Act of 1984 (P.L. 98-369)**

P.L. 98-369, § 133(b):

Amended Code Sec. 959 by adding at the end thereof a new subsection (e). **Effective** with respect to transactions to which subsection (a) or (f) of section 1248 of the Internal Revenue Code of 1954 applies occurring after 7-18-84. For a special election, see Act Sec. 133(d)(3), below.

P.L. 98-369, § 133(d)(3), as amended by P.L. 99-514, § 1810(i) and P.L. 100-647, § 1018(g)(2), provides:

(3) Election of Earlier Date for Certain Transactions.—

(A) In General.—If the appropriate election is made under subparagraph (B), the amendments made by subsection (b) shall apply with respect to transactions to which subsection (a) or (f) of section 1248 of such Code applies occurring after October 9, 1975.

(B) Election.—

(i) Subparagraph (A) shall apply with respect to transactions to which subsection (a) of section 1248 of such Code applies if the foreign corporation described in such subsection (or its successor in interest) so elects.

(ii) Subparagraph (A) shall apply with respect to transactions to which subsection (f) of section 1248 of such Code applies if the domestic corporation described in section 1248(f)(1) of such Code (or its successor) so elects.

(iii) Any election under clause (i) or (ii) shall be made not later than the date which is 1 year after the date of the enactment of the Tax Reform Act of 1986, and shall be made in such manner as the Secretary of the Treasury or his delegate shall prescribe.

[Sec. 959(f)]

(f) ALLOCATION RULES FOR CERTAIN INCLUSIONS.—

(1) IN GENERAL.—For purposes of this section, amounts that would be included under subparagraph (B) of section 951(a)(1) (determined without regard to this section) shall be treated as attributable first to earnings described in subsection (c)(2), and then to earnings described in subsection (c)(3).

(2) TREATMENT OF DISTRIBUTIONS.—In applying this section, actual distributions shall be taken into account before amounts that would be included under section 951(a)(1)(B) (determined without regard to this section).

Amendments

• **1996, Small Business Job Protection Act of 1996 (P.L. 104-188)**

P.L. 104-188, § 1501(b)(7):

Amended Code Sec. 959(f)(1). **Effective** for tax years of foreign corporations beginning after 12-31-96, and to tax years of United States shareholders within which or with which such tax years of foreign corporations end. Prior to amendment, Code Sec. 959(f)(1) read as follows:

(1) IN GENERAL.—For purposes of this section—

(A) amounts that would be included under subparagraph (B) of section 951(a)(1) (determined without regard to this section) shall be treated as attributable first to earnings described in subsection (c)(2), and then to earnings described in subsection (c)(3), and

(B) amounts that would be included under subparagraph (C) of section 951(a)(1) (determined without regard to this section) shall be treated as attributable first to earnings described in subsection (c)(2) to the extent the earnings so described were accumulated in taxable years beginning after September 30, 1993, and then to earnings described in subsection (c)(3).

P.L. 104-188, § 1501(b)(8):

Amended Code Sec. 959(f)(2) by striking "subparagraphs (B) and (C) of section 951(a)(1)" and inserting "section 951(a)(1)(B)". **Effective** for tax years of foreign corporations beginning after 12-31-96, and to tax years of United States shareholders within which or with which such tax years of foreign corporations end.

• **1993, Omnibus Budget Reconciliation Act of 1993 (P.L. 103-66)**

P.L. 103-66, § 13231(c)(2)(B):

Amended Code Sec. 959 by adding subsection (f) at the end thereof. **Effective** for tax years of foreign corporations beginning after 9-30-93, and to tax years of United States shareholders in which or with which such tax years of foreign corporations end.

[Sec. 960]

SEC. 960. DEEMED PAID CREDIT FOR SUBPART F INCLUSIONS.

[Sec. 960(a)]

(a) IN GENERAL.—For purposes of subpart A of this part, if there is included in the gross income of a domestic corporation any item of income under section 951(a)(1) with respect to any controlled foreign corporation with respect to which such domestic corporation is a United States shareholder, such domestic corporation shall be deemed to have paid so much of such foreign corporation's foreign income taxes as are properly attributable to such item of income.

Amendments

• **2017, Tax Cuts and Jobs Act (P.L. 115-97)**

P.L. 115-97, § 14301(b)(1):

Amended Code Sec. 960, as amended by Act Sec. 14201, by striking subsection (c), by redesignating subsection (b) as subsection (c), by striking all that precedes subsection (c) (as so redesignated) and inserting a new section heading and new subsections (a) and (b). **Effective** for tax years of foreign corporations beginning after 12-31-2017, and to tax years of United States shareholders in which or with which such tax years of foreign corporations end. Prior to being stricken, the section heading for Code Sec. 960 read as follows:

SEC. 960. SPECIAL RULES FOR FOREIGN TAX CREDIT.

[Sec. 960(a)—Stricken]

(a) TAXES PAID BY A FOREIGN CORPORATION.—

(1) DEEMED PAID CREDIT.—For purposes of subpart A of this part, if there is included under section 951(a) in the gross income of a domestic corporation any amount attributable to earnings and profits of a foreign corporation which is a member of a qualified group (as defined in section 902(b)) with respect to the domestic corporation, then, except to the extent provided in regulations, section 902 shall be applied as if the amount so included were a dividend paid by such foreign corporation (determined by applying section 902(c) in accordance with section 904(d)(3)(B)).

Amendments

• **2017, Tax Cuts and Jobs Act (P.L. 115-97)**

P.L. 115-97, § 14301(b)(1):

Amended Code Sec. 960, as amended by Act Sec. 14201, by striking subsection (c), and by redesignating subsection (b) as subsection (c), by striking all that precedes subsection (c) (as so redesignated). **Effective** for tax years of foreign corporations beginning after 12-31-2017, and to tax years of United States shareholders in which or with which such tax years of foreign corporations end. Prior to being stricken, Code Sec. 960(a) read as follows:

(2) TAXES PREVIOUSLY DEEMED PAID BY DOMESTIC CORPORATION.—If a domestic corporation receives a distribution from a foreign corporation, any portion of which is excluded from gross income under section 959, the income, war profits, and excess profits taxes paid or deemed paid by such foreign corporation to any foreign country or to any possession of the United States in connection with the earnings and profits of such foreign corporation from which such distribution is made shall not be taken into account for purposes of section 902, to the extent such taxes were deemed paid by a domestic corporation under paragraph (1) for any prior taxable year.

(3) TAXES PAID BY FOREIGN CORPORATION AND NOT PREVIOUSLY DEEMED PAID BY DOMESTIC CORPORATION.—Any portion of a distribution from a foreign corporation received by a domestic corporation which is excluded from gross income under section 959(a) shall be treated by the domestic corporation as a dividend, solely for purposes of taking into account under section 902 any income, war profits, or excess profits taxes paid to any foreign country or to any possession of the United States, on or with respect to the accumulated profits of such foreign corporation from which such distribution is made, which were not deemed paid by the domestic corporation under paragraph (1) for any prior taxable year.

- **1997, Taxpayer Relief Act of 1997 (P.L. 105-34)**

P.L. 105-34, § 1113(b):

Amended Code Sec. 960(a)(1). **Effective**, generally, for taxes of foreign corporations for tax years of such corporations beginning after 8-5-97. For a special rule, see Act Sec. 1113(c)(2), below. Prior to amendment, Code Sec. 960(a)(1) read as follows:

(1) GENERAL RULE.—For purposes of subpart A of this part, if there is included, under section 951(a), in the gross income of a domestic corporation any amount attributable to earnings and profits—

(A) of a foreign corporation (hereafter in this subsection referred to as the "first foreign corporation") at least 10 percent of the voting stock of which is owned by such domestic corporation, or

(B) of a second foreign corporation (hereinafter in this subsection referred to as the "second foreign corporation") at least 10 percent of the voting stock of which is owned by the first foreign corporation, or

(C) of a third foreign corporation (hereinafter in this subsection referred to as the "third foreign corporation") at least 10 percent of the voting stock of which is owned by the second foreign corporation,

then, except to the extent provided in regulations, such domestic corporation shall be deemed to have paid a portion of such foreign corporation's post-1986 foreign income taxes determined under section 902 in the same manner as if the amount so included were a dividend paid by such foreign corporation (determined by applying section 902(c) in accordance with section 904(d)(3)(B)). This paragraph shall not apply with respect to any amount included in the gross income of such domestic corporation attributable to earnings and profits of the second foreign corporation or of the third foreign corporation unless, in the case of the second foreign corporation, the percentage-of-voting-stock requirement of section 902(b)(3)(A) is satisfied, and in the case of the third foreign corporation, the percentage-of-voting-stock requirement of section 902(b)(3)(B) is satisfied.

P.L. 105-34, § 1113(c)(2), provides:

(2) SPECIAL RULE.—In the case of any chain of foreign corporations described in clauses (i) and (ii) of section 902(b)(2)(B) of the Internal Revenue Code of 1986 (as amended by this section), no liquidation, reorganization, or similar transaction in a taxable year beginning after the date of the enactment of this Act shall have the effect of permitting taxes to be taken into account under section 902 of the Internal Revenue Code of 1986 which could not have been taken into account under such section but for such transaction.

- **1986, Tax Reform Act of 1986 (P.L. 99-514)**

P.L. 99-514, § 1202(b):

Amended Code Sec. 960(a)(1) by striking out "then" and all that follows down through the period at the end thereof in the first sentence and inserting the new material. **Effective** for distributions by foreign corporations out of, and to inclusions under section 951(a) of the Internal Revenue Code of 1954 attributable to, earnings and profits for tax years beginning after 12-31-86. Prior to amendment, that part of the first sentence read as follows:

then, under regulations prescribed by the Secretary, such domestic corporation shall be deemed to have paid the same proportion of the total income, war profits, and excess profits taxes paid (or deemed paid) by such foreign corporation to a foreign country or possession of the United States for the taxable year on or with respect to the earnings and profits of such foreign corporation which the amount of earnings and profits of such foreign corporation so included in gross income of the domestic corporation bears to the entire amount of the earnings and profits of such foreign corporation for such taxable year.

- **1976, Tax Reform Act of 1976 (P.L. 94-455)**

P.L. 94-455, § 1033(b)(2):

Substituted "bears to the entire amount of earnings and profits of such foreign corporation for such taxable year." for "bears to—" and all the text that followed in Code Sec. 960(a)(1). For the **effective** date, see Act Sec. 1033(c), below.

P.L. 94-455, § 1033(c), provides:

(c) EFFECTIVE DATES.—The amendments made by this section shall apply—

(1) in respect of any distribution received by a domestic corporation after December 31, 1977, and

(2) in respect of any distribution received by a domestic corporation before January 1, 1978, in a taxable year of such corporation beginning after December 31, 1975, but only to the extent that such distribution is made out of the accumulated profits of a foreign corporation for a taxable year (of such foreign corporation) beginning after December 31, 1975.

For purposes of paragraph (2), a distribution made by a foreign corporation out of its profits which are attributable to a distribution received from a foreign corporation to which section 902(b) of the Internal Revenue Code of 1954 applies shall be treated as made out of the accumulated profits of a foreign corporation for a taxable year beginning before January 1, 1976, to the extent that such distribution was paid out of the accumulated profits of such foreign corporation for a taxable year beginning before January 1, 1976.

Prior to amendment, Code Sec. 960(a)(1) read as follows:

(1) GENERAL RULE.—For purposes of subpart A of this part, if there is included, under section 951(a), in the gross income of a domestic corporation any amount attributable to earnings and profits—

(A) of a foreign corporation at least 10 percent of the voting stock of which is owned by such domestic corporation, or

(B) of a foreign corporation at least 50 percent of the voting stock of which is owned by a foreign corporation at least 10 percent of the voting stock of which is in turn owned by such domestic corporation,

then, under regulations prescribed by the Secretary or his delegate, such domestic corporation shall be deemed to have paid the same proportion of the total income, war profits, and excess profits taxes paid (or deemed paid) by such foreign corporation to a foreign country or possession of the United States for the taxable year on or with respect to the earnings and profits of such foreign corporation which the amount of earnings and profits of such foreign corporation so included in gross income of the domestic corporation bears to—

(C) if the foreign corporation at least 10 percent of the voting stock of which is owned by such domestic corporation referred to in subparagraph (A) or (B) is not a less developed country corporation (as defined in section 902(d)) for such taxable year, the entire amount of the earnings and profits of such foreign corporation for such taxable year, or

(D) if the foreign corporation at least 10 percent of the voting stock of which is owned by such domestic corporation referred to in subparagraph (A) or (B) is a less developed country corporation (as defined in section 902(d)) for such taxable year, the sum of the entire amount of the earnings and profits of such foreign corporation for such taxable year and the total income, war profits and excess profits taxes paid by such foreign corporation to foreign countries or possessions of the United States for such taxable year.

P.L. 94-455, § 1037(a):

Amended Code Sec. 960(a)(1), as amended by P.L. 94-455, § 1033(b)(2). **Effective** with respect to earnings and profits of a foreign corporation included (under Code Sec. 951(a)) in the gross income of a domestic corporation in tax years beginning after 12-31-76.

[Sec. 960(b)]

(b) SPECIAL RULES FOR DISTRIBUTIONS FROM PREVIOUSLY TAXED EARNINGS AND PROFITS.—For purposes of subpart A of this part—

(1) IN GENERAL.—If any portion of a distribution from a controlled foreign corporation to a domestic corporation which is a United States shareholder with respect to such controlled foreign corporation is excluded from gross income under section 959(a), such domestic corporation shall be deemed to have paid so much of such foreign corporation's foreign income taxes as—

(A) are properly attributable to such portion, and

(B) have not been deemed to have to [sic] been paid by such domestic corporation under this section for the taxable year or any prior taxable year.

(2) TIERED CONTROLLED FOREIGN CORPORATIONS.—If section 959(b) applies to any portion of a distribution from a controlled foreign corporation to another controlled foreign corporation, such controlled foreign corporation shall be deemed to have paid so much of such other controlled foreign corporation's foreign income taxes as—

(A) are properly attributable to such portion, and

(B) have not been deemed to have been paid by a domestic corporation under this section for the taxable year or any prior taxable year.

Amendments

- **2017, Tax Cuts and Jobs Act (P.L. 115-97)**

P.L. 115-97, § 14301(b)(1):

Amended Code Sec. 960, as amended by Act Sec. 14201, by striking subsection (c), by redesignating subsection (b) as subsection (c), by striking all that precedes subsection (c) (as so redesignated) and inserting a new section heading and subsections (a) and (b). **Effective** for tax years of foreign corporations beginning after 12-31-2017, and to tax years of United States shareholders in which or with which such tax years of foreign corporations end.

INCOME TAX—CONTROLLED FOREIGN CORPORATIONS

[Sec. 960(c)]

(c) Special Rules for Foreign Tax Credit in Year of Receipt of Previously Taxed Earnings and Profits.—

(1) Increase in section 904 limitation.—In the case of any taxpayer who—

(A) either (i) chose to have the benefits of subpart A of this part for a taxable year beginning after September 30, 1993, in which he was required under section 951(a) to include any amount in his gross income, or (ii) did not pay or accrue for such taxable year any income, war profits, or excess profits taxes to any foreign country or to any possession of the United States,

(B) chooses to have the benefits of subpart A of this part for any taxable year in which he receives 1 or more distributions or amounts which are excludable from gross income under section 959(a) and which are attributable to amounts included in his gross income for taxable years referred to in subparagraph (A), and

(C) for the taxable year in which such distributions or amounts are received, pays, or is deemed to have paid, or accrues income, war profits, or excess profits taxes to a foreign country or to any possession of the United States with respect to such distributions or amounts,

the limitation under section 904 for the taxable year in which such distributions or amounts are received shall be increased by the lesser of the amount of such taxes paid, or deemed paid, or accrued with respect to such distributions or amounts or the amount in the excess limitation account as of the beginning of such taxable year.

(2) Excess limitation account.—

(A) Establishment of account.—Each taxpayer meeting the requirements of paragraph (1)(A) shall establish an excess limitation account. The opening balance of such account shall be zero.

(B) Increases in account.—For each taxable year beginning after September 30, 1993, the taxpayer shall increase the amount in the excess limitation account by the excess (if any) of—

(i) the amount by which the limitation under section 904(a) for such taxable year was increased by reason of the total amount of the inclusions in gross income under section 951(a) for such taxable year, over

(ii) the amount of any income, war profits, and excess profits taxes paid, or deemed paid, or accrued to any foreign country or possession of the United States which were allowable as a credit under section 901 for such taxable year and which would not have been allowable but for the inclusions in gross income described in clause (i).

Proper reductions in the amount added to the account under the preceding sentence for any taxable year shall be made for any increase in the credit allowable under section 901 for such taxable year by reason of a carryback if such increase would not have been allowable but for the inclusions in gross income described in clause (i).

(C) Decreases in account.—For each taxable year beginning after September 30, 1993, for which the limitation under section 904 was increased under paragraph (1), the taxpayer shall reduce the amount in the excess limitation account by the amount of such increase.

(3) Distributions of income previously taxed in years beginning before October 1, 1993.—If the taxpayer receives a distribution or amount in a taxable year beginning after September 30, 1993, which is excluded from gross income under section 959(a) and is attributable to any amount included in gross income under section 951(a) for a taxable year beginning before October 1, 1993, the limitation under section 904 for the taxable year in which such amount or distribution is received shall be increased by the amount determined under this subsection as in effect on the day before the date of the enactment of the Revenue Reconciliation Act of 1993.

(4) Cases in which taxes not to be allowed as deduction.—In the case of any taxpayer who—

(A) chose to have the benefits of subpart A of this part for a taxable year in which he was required under section 951(a) to include in his gross income an amount in respect of a controlled foreign corporation, and

(B) does not choose to have the benefits of subpart A of this part for the taxable year in which he receives a distribution or amount which is excluded from gross income under section 959(a) and which is attributable to earnings and profits of the controlled foreign corporation which was included in his gross income for the taxable year referred to in subparagraph (A),

no deduction shall be allowed under section 164 for the taxable year in which such distribution or amount is received for any income, war profits, or excess profits taxes paid or accrued to any foreign country or to any possession of the United States on or with respect to such distribution or amount.

(5) Insufficient taxable income.—If an increase in the limitation under this subsection exceeds the tax imposed by this chapter for such year, the amount of such excess shall be deemed an overpayment of tax for such year.

Amendments

- **2017, Tax Cuts and Jobs Act (P.L. 115-97)**

P.L. 115-97, §14301(b)(1):

Amended Code Sec. 960, as amended by Act Sec. 14201, by striking subsection (c), and by redesignating subsection (b) as subsection (c). **Effective** for tax years of foreign corporations beginning after 12-31-2017, and to tax years of United States shareholders in which or with which such tax years of foreign corporations end.

- **1993, Omnibus Budget Reconciliation Act of 1993 (P.L. 103-66)**

P.L. 103-66, §13233(b)(1)(A)-(B):

Amended Code Sec. 960(c) by redesignating paragraphs (3) and (4) as paragraphs (4) and (5), respectively, and by striking paragraphs (1) and (2) and inserting new paragraphs (1), (2) and (3). **Effective** for tax years beginning after 9-30-93. Prior to amendment, paragraphs (1) and (2) read as follows:

(1) Increase in section 904 limitation.—In the case of any taxpayer who—

(A) either (i) chose to have the benefits of subpart A of this part for a taxable year in which he was required under section 951(a) to include in his gross income an amount in respect of a controlled foreign corporation, or (ii) did not pay or accrue for such taxable year any income, war profits, or excess profits taxes to any foreign country or to any possession of the United States, and

(B) chooses to have the benefits of subpart A of this part for the taxable year in which he receives a distribution or amount which is excluded from gross income under section 959(a) and which is attributable to earnings and profits of the controlled foreign corporation which was included in his gross income for the taxable year referred to in subparagraph (A), and

(C) for the taxable year in which such distribution or amount is received, pays, or is deemed to have paid, or accrues income, war profits, or excess profits taxes to a foreign country or to any possession of the United States with respect to such distribution or amount,

the limitation under section 904 for the taxable year in which such distribution or amount is received shall be increased as provided in paragraph (2), but such increase shall not exceed the amount of such taxes paid, or deemed paid, or accrued with respect to such distribution or amount.

(2) Amount of increase.—The amount of increase of the limitation under section 904(a) for the taxable year in which the distribution or amount referred to in paragraph (1)(B) is received shall be an amount equal to—

(A) the amount by which the limitation under section 904(a) for the taxable year referred to in paragraph (1)(A) was increased by reason of the inclusion in gross income under section 951(a) of the amount in respect of the controlled foreign corporation, reduced by

(B) the amount of any income, war profits, and excess profits taxes paid, or deemed paid, or accrued to any foreign country or possession of the United States which were allowable as a credit under section 901 for the taxable year referred to in paragraph (1)(A) and which would not have been allowable but for the inclusion in gross income of the amount described in subparagraph (A).

- **1976, Tax Reform Act of 1976 (P.L. 94-455)**

P.L. 94-455, §1031(b)(1):

Substituted "limitation" for "applicable limitation" each place it appeared in Code Sec. 960(c). **Effective** as noted in Act Sec. 1031(c), below.

P.L. 94-455, §1031(c), provides:

(c) Effective Dates.—

(1) In general.—Except as provided in paragraphs (2) and (3), the amendments made by this section shall apply to taxable years beginning after December 31, 1975.

(2) Exception for certain mining operations.—In the case of a domestic corporation or includible corporation in an affiliated group (as defined in section 1504 of the Internal Revenue Code of 1954) which has as of October 1, 1975—

(A) been engaged in the active conduct of the trade or business of the extraction of minerals (of a character with respect to which a deduction for depletion is allowable under section 613 of such Code) outside the United States or its possessions for less than 5 years preceding the date of enactment of this Act,

(B) had deductions properly apportioned or allocated to its gross income from such trade or business in excess of such gross income in at least 2 taxable years,

(C) 80 percent of its gross receipts are from the sale of such minerals, and

(D) made commitments for substantial expansion of such mineral extraction activities,

the amendments made by this section shall apply to taxable years beginning after December 31, 1978. In the case of losses sustained in taxable years beginning before January 1, 1979, by any corporation to which this paragraph applies, the provisions of section 904(f) of such Code shall be applied with respect to such losses under the principles of section 904(a)(1) of such Code as in effect before the enactment of this Act.

(3) EXCEPTION FOR INCOME FROM POSSESSIONS.—In the case of gross income from sources within a possession of the United States (and the deductions properly apportioned or allocated thereto), the amendments made by this section shall apply to taxable years beginning after December 31, 1978. In the case of losses sustained in a possession of the United States in taxable years beginning before January 1, 1979, the provisions of section 904(f) of such Code shall be applied with respect to such losses under the principles of section 904(a)(1) of such Code as in effect before the enactment of this Act.

(4) CARRYBACKS AND CARRYOVERS IN THE CASE OF MINING OPERATIONS AND INCOME FROM A POSSESSION.—In the case of a taxpayer to whom paragraph (2) or (3) of this subsection applies, section 904(e) of such Code shall apply except that "January 1, 1979" shall be substituted for "January 1, 1976" each place it appears therein. If such a taxpayer elects the overall limitation for a taxable year beginning before January 1, 1979, such section 904(e) shall be applied by substituting "the January 1, of the last year for which such taxpayer is on the per-country limitation" for "January 1, 1976" each place it appears therein.

[Sec. 960(c)—Stricken]

Amendments

• **2017, Tax Cuts and Jobs Act (P.L. 115-97)**

P.L. 115-97, §14301(b)(1):

Amended Code Sec. 960, as amended by Act. Sec. 14201, by striking subsection (c). **Effective** for tax years of foreign corporations beginning after 12-31-2017, and to tax years of United States shareholders in which or with which such tax years of foreign corporations end. Prior to being stricken, Code Sec. 960(c) read as follows:

(c) LIMITATION WITH RESPECT TO SECTION 956 INCLUSIONS.—

(1) IN GENERAL.—If there is included under section 951(a)(1)(B) in the gross income of a domestic corporation any amount attributable to the earnings and profits of a foreign corporation which is a member of a qualified group (as defined in section 902(b)) with respect to the domestic corporation, the amount of any foreign income taxes deemed to have been paid during the taxable year by such domestic corporation under section 902 by reason of subsection (a) with respect to such inclusion in gross income shall not exceed the amount of the foreign income taxes which would have been deemed to have been paid during the taxable year by such domestic corporation if cash in an amount equal to the amount of such inclusion in gross income were distributed as a series of distributions (determined without regard to any foreign taxes which would be imposed on an actual distribution) through the chain of ownership which begins with such foreign corporation and ends with such domestic corporation.

(2) AUTHORITY TO PREVENT ABUSE.—The Secretary shall issue such regulations or other guidance as is necessary or appropriate to carry out the purposes of this subsection, including regulations or other guidance which prevent the inappropriate use of the foreign corporation's foreign income taxes not deemed paid by reason of paragraph (1).

• **2010, (P.L. 111-226)**

P.L. 111-226, §214(a):

Amended Code Sec. 960 by adding at the end a new subsection (c). **Effective** for acquisitions of United States property (as defined in Code Sec. 956(c)) after 12-31-2010.

[Sec. 960(d)]

(d) DEEMED PAID CREDIT FOR TAXES PROPERLY ATTRIBUTABLE TO TESTED INCOME.—

(1) IN GENERAL.—For purposes of subpart A of this part, if any amount is includible in the gross income of a domestic corporation under section 951A, such domestic corporation shall be deemed to have paid foreign income taxes equal to 80 percent of the product of—

(A) such domestic corporation's inclusion percentage, multiplied by

(B) the aggregate tested foreign income taxes paid or accrued by controlled foreign corporations.

(2) INCLUSION PERCENTAGE.—For purposes of paragraph (1), the term "inclusion percentage" means, with respect to any domestic corporation, the ratio (expressed as a percentage) of—

(A) such corporation's global intangible low-taxed income (as defined in section 951A(b)), divided by

(B) the aggregate amount described in section 951A(c)(1)(A) with respect to such corporation.

(3) TESTED FOREIGN INCOME TAXES.—For purposes of paragraph (1), the term "tested foreign income taxes" means, with respect to any domestic corporation which is a United States shareholder of a controlled foreign corporation, the foreign income taxes paid or accrued by such foreign corporation which are properly attributable to the tested income of such foreign corporation taken into account by such domestic corporation under section 951A.

Amendments

• **2017, Tax Cuts and Jobs Act (P.L. 115-97)**

P.L. 115-97, §14201(b)(1):

Amended Code Sec. 960 by adding at the end a new subsection (d). **Effective** for tax years of foreign corporations beginning after 12-31-2017, and to tax years of United States shareholders in which or with which such tax years of foreign corporations end.

[Sec. 960(e)]

(e) FOREIGN INCOME TAXES.—The term "foreign income taxes" means any income, war profits, or excess profits taxes paid or accrued to any foreign country or possession of the United States.

• **2017, Tax Cuts and Jobs Act (P.L. 115-97)**

P.L. 115-97, §14301(b)(2):

Amended Code Sec. 960 by adding after subsection (d) (as added by Act Sec. 14201) new subsections (e) and (f). **Effective** for tax years of foreign corporations beginning after 12-31-2017, and to tax years of United States shareholders in which or with which such tax years of foreign corporations end.

[Sec. 960(f)]

(f) REGULATIONS.—The Secretary shall prescribe such regulations or other guidance as may be necessary or appropriate to carry out the provisions of this section.

• **2017, Tax Cuts and Jobs Act (P.L. 115-97)**

P.L. 115-97, §14301(b)(2):

Amended Code Sec. 960 by adding after subsection (d) (as added by Act Sec. 14201) new subsections (e) and (f). **Effective** for tax years of foreign corporations beginning after 12-31-2017, and to tax years of United States shareholders in which or with which such tax years of foreign corporations end.

[Sec. 961]

SEC. 961. ADJUSTMENTS TO BASIS OF STOCK IN CONTROLLED FOREIGN CORPORATIONS AND OF OTHER PROPERTY.

[Sec. 961(a)]

(a) INCREASE IN BASIS.—Under regulations prescribed by the Secretary, the basis of a United States shareholder's stock in a controlled foreign corporation, and the basis of property of a United States shareholder by reason of which he is considered under section 958(a)(2) as owning stock of a controlled foreign corporation, shall be increased by the amount required to be included in his gross income under section 951(a) with respect to such stock or with respect to such property, as the case may be, but only to the extent to which such amount was included in the gross income of such United States shareholder. In the case of a United States shareholder who has made an election under section 962 for the taxable year, the increase in basis provided by this subsection shall not exceed an amount equal to the amount of tax paid under this chapter with respect to the amounts required to be included in his gross income under section 951(a).

INCOME TAX—CONTROLLED FOREIGN CORPORATIONS

Amendments

• 1976, Tax Reform Act of 1976 (P.L. 94-455)

P.L. 94-455, §1906(b)(13)(A):

Amended 1954 Code by substituting "Secretary" for "Secretary or his delegate" each place it appeared. **Effective** 2-1-77.

[Sec. 961(b)]

(b) REDUCTION IN BASIS.—

(1) IN GENERAL.—Under regulations prescribed by the Secretary, the adjusted basis of stock or other property with respect to which a United States shareholder or a United States person receives an amount which is excluded from gross income under section 959(a) shall be reduced by the amount so excluded. In the case of a United States shareholder who has made an election under section 962 for any prior taxable year, the reduction in basis provided by this paragraph shall not exceed an amount equal to the amount received which is excluded from gross income under section 959(a) after the application of section 962(d).

(2) AMOUNT IN EXCESS OF BASIS.—To the extent that an amount excluded from gross income under section 959(a) exceeds the adjusted basis of the stock or other property with respect to which it is received, the amount shall be treated as gain from the sale or exchange of property.

Amendments

• 1976, Tax Reform Act of 1976 (P.L. 94-455)

P.L. 94-455, §1906(b)(13)(A):

Amended 1954 Code by substituting "Secretary" for "Secretary or his delegate" each place it appeared. **Effective** 2-1-77.

[Sec. 961(c)]

(c) BASIS ADJUSTMENTS IN STOCK HELD BY FOREIGN CORPORATIONS.—Under regulations prescribed by the Secretary, if a United States shareholder is treated under section 958(a)(2) as owning stock in a controlled foreign corporation which is owned by another controlled foreign corporation, then adjustments similar to the adjustments provided by subsections (a) and (b) shall be made to—

(1) the basis of such stock, and

(2) the basis of stock in any other controlled foreign corporation by reason of which the United States shareholder is considered under section 958(a)(2) as owning the stock described in paragraph (1),

but only for the purposes of determining the amount included under section 951 in the gross income of such United States shareholder (or any other United States shareholder who acquires from any person any portion of the interest of such United States shareholder by reason of which such shareholder was treated as owning such stock, but only to the extent of such portion, and subject to such proof of identity of such interest as the Secretary may prescribe by regulations). The preceding sentence shall not apply with respect to any stock to which a basis adjustment applies under subsection (a) or (b).

Amendments

• 2005, Gulf Opportunity Zone Act of 2005 (P.L. 109-135)

P.L. 109-135, §409(b):

Amended Code Sec. 961(c). **Effective** as if included in the provision of the Taxpayer Relief Act of 1997 (P.L. 105-34) to which it relates [**effective** for purposes of determining inclusions for tax years of United States shareholders beginning after 12-31-97.—CCH]. Prior to amendment, Code Sec. 961(c) read as follows:

(c) BASIS ADJUSTMENTS IN STOCK HELD BY FOREIGN CORPORATION.—Under regulations prescribed by the Secretary, if a United States shareholder is treated under section 958(a)(2) as owning any stock in a controlled foreign corporation which is actually owned by another controlled foreign corporation, adjustments similar to the adjustments provided by subsections (a) and (b) shall be made to the basis of such stock in the hands of such other controlled foreign corporation, but only for the purposes of determining the amount included under section 951 in the gross income of such United States shareholder (or any other United States shareholder who acquires from any person any portion of the interest of such United States shareholder by reason of which such shareholder was treated as owning such stock, but only to the extent of such portion, and subject to such proof of identity of such interest as the Secretary may prescribe by regulations).

• 1997, Taxpayer Relief Act of 1997 (P.L. 105-34)

P.L. 105-34, §1112(b)(1):

Amended Code Sec. 961 by adding at the end a new subsection (c). **Effective** for purposes of determining inclusions for tax years of United States shareholders beginning after 12-31-97.

[Sec. 961(d)]

(d) BASIS IN SPECIFIED 10-PERCENT OWNED FOREIGN CORPORATION REDUCED BY NONTAXED PORTION OF DIVIDEND FOR PURPOSES OF DETERMINING LOSS.—If a domestic corporation received a dividend from a specified 10-percent owned foreign corporation (as defined in section 245A) in any taxable year, solely for purposes of determining loss on any disposition of stock of such foreign corporation in such taxable year or any subsequent taxable year, the basis of such domestic corporation in such stock shall be reduced (but not below zero) by the amount of any deduction allowable to such domestic corporation under section 245A with respect to such stock except to the extent such basis was reduced under section 1059 by reason of a dividend for which such a deduction was allowable.

Amendments

• 2017, Tax Cuts and Jobs Act (P.L. 115-97)

P.L. 115-97, §14102(b)(1):

Amended Code Sec. 961 by adding at the end a new subsection (d). **Effective** for distributions made after 12-31-2017.

[Sec. 962]

SEC. 962. ELECTION BY INDIVIDUALS TO BE SUBJECT TO TAX AT CORPORATE RATES.

[Sec. 962(a)]

(a) GENERAL RULE.—Under regulations prescribed by the Secretary, in the case of a United States shareholder who is an individual and who elects to have the provisions of this section apply for the taxable year—

(1) the tax imposed under this chapter on amounts which are included in his gross income under section 951(a) shall (in lieu of the tax determined under sections 1 and 55) be an amount equal to the tax which would be imposed under section 11 if such amounts were received by a domestic corporation, and

(2) for purposes of applying the provisions of section 960 (relating to foreign tax credit) such amounts shall be treated as if they were received by a domestic corporation.

Amendments

• 2017, Tax Cuts and Jobs Act (P.L. 115-97)

P.L. 115-97, §12001(b)(15):

Amended Code Sec. 962(a)(1) by striking "sections 11 and 55" and inserting "section 11". **Effective** for tax years beginning after 12-31-2017.

• 1988, Technical and Miscellaneous Revenue Act of 1988 (P.L. 100-647)

P.L. 100-647, §1007(g)(11)(A)-(B):

Amended Code Sec. 962(a)(1) by striking out "section 1" and inserting in lieu thereof "sections 1 and 55", and by striking out "section 11" and inserting in lieu

INCOME TAX—CONTROLLED FOREIGN CORPORATIONS

thereof "sections 11 and 55". **Effective** as if included in the provision of P.L. 99-514 to which it relates.

- **1976, Tax Reform Act of 1976 (P.L. 94-455)**

P.L. 94-455, §1906(b)(13)(A):

Amended 1954 Code by substituting "Secretary" for "Secretary or his delegate" each place it appeared. **Effective** 2-1-77.

[Sec. 962(b)]

(b) ELECTION.—An election to have the provisions of this section apply for any taxable year shall be made by a United States shareholder at such time and in such manner as the Secretary shall prescribe by regulations. An election made for any taxable year may not be revoked except with the consent of the Secretary.

Amendments

- **1976, Tax Reform Act of 1976 (P.L. 94-455)**

P.L. 94-455, §1906(b)(13)(A):

Amended 1954 Code by substituting "Secretary" for "Secretary or his delegate" each place it appeared. **Effective** 2-1-77.

[Sec. 962(c)]

(c) PRO RATION OF EACH SECTION 11 BRACKET AMOUNT.—For purposes of applying subsection (a)(1), the amount in each taxable income bracket in the tax table in section 11(b) shall not exceed an amount which bears the same ratio to such bracket amount as the amount included in the gross income of the United States shareholder under section 951(a) for the taxable year bears to such shareholder's pro rata share of the earnings and profits for the taxable year of all controlled foreign corporations with respect to which such shareholder includes any amount in gross income under section 951(a).

Amendments

- **1978, Revenue Act of 1978 (P.L. 95-600)**

P.L. 95-600, §301(b)(16):

Amended Code Sec. 962(c). **Effective** for tax years beginning after 12-31-78. Prior to amendment, Code Sec. 962(c) read as follows:

"(c) SURTAX EXEMPTION.—For purposes of applying subsection (a)(1), the surtax exemption provided by section 11(c) shall not exceed, in the case of any United States shareholder, an amount which bears the same ratio to the surtax exemption as the amount included in his gross income under section 951(a) for the taxable year bears to his pro rata share of the earnings and profits for the taxable year of all controlled foreign corporations with respect to which such United States shareholder includes any amount in gross income under section 951(a)."

- **1975, Revenue Adjustment Act of 1975 (P.L. 94-164)**

P.L. 94-164, §4(d):

Amended Sec. 962(c) by substituting "the surtax exemption" for "$50,000". **Effective** as it affects tax years ending after 12-31-75.

- **1975, Tax Reduction Act of 1975 (P.L. 94-12)**

P.L. 94-12, §303(c):

Amended Sec. 962(c) by substituting "$50,000" for "$25,000." **Effective** for tax years ending after 12-31-75.

[Sec. 962(d)]

(d) SPECIAL RULE FOR ACTUAL DISTRIBUTIONS.—The earnings and profits of a foreign corporation attributable to amounts which were included in the gross income of a United States shareholder under section 951(a) and with respect to which an election under this section applied shall, when such earnings and profits are distributed, notwithstanding the provisions of section 959(a)(1), be included in gross income to the extent that such earnings and profits so distributed exceed the amount of tax paid under this chapter on the amounts to which such election applied.

Amendments

- **1962, Revenue Act of 1962 (P.L. 87-834)**

P.L. 87-834, §12(a):

Amended Part III of subchapter N of chapter 1 by adding subpart F, which includes Code Secs. 951-964. **Effective** for tax years of foreign corporations beginning after 12-31-62, and for tax years of United States shareholders within which or with which such tax years of such foreign corporations end.

[Sec. 963—Repealed]

Amendments

- **1975, Tax Reduction Act of 1975 (P.L. 94-12)**

P.L. 94-12, §602(a):

Repealed Code Sec. 963. **Effective** for tax years of foreign corporations beginning after 12-31-75, and for tax years of U.S. shareholders within which or with which such tax years of such foreign corporations end. Prior to repeal, Code Sec. 963 read as follows:

SEC. 963. RECEIPT OF MINIMUM DISTRIBUTIONS BY DOMESTIC CORPORATIONS.

[Sec. 963(a)]

(a) GENERAL RULE.—In the case of a United States shareholder which is a domestic corporation and which consents to all the regulations prescribed by the Secretary or his delegate under this section prior to the last day prescribed by law for filing its return of the tax imposed by this chapter for the taxable year, no amount shall be included in gross income under section 951(a)(1)(A)(i) for the taxable year with respect to the subpart F income of a controlled foreign corporation, if—

(1) in the case of a controlled foreign corporation described in subsection (c)(1), the United States shareholder receives a minimum distribution of the earnings and profits for the taxable year of such controlled foreign corporation;

(2) in the case of controlled foreign corporations described in subsection (c)(2), the United States shareholder receives a minimum distribution with respect to the consolidated earnings and profits for the taxable year of all such controlled foreign corporations; or

(3) in the case of controlled foreign corporations described in subsection (c)(3), the United States shareholder receives a minimum distribution of the consolidated earnings and profits for the taxable year of all such controlled foreign corporations.

[Sec. 963(b)]

(b) MINIMUM DISTRIBUTION.—For purposes of this section, a minimum distribution with respect to the earnings and profits for the taxable year of any controlled foreign corporation or corporations shall, in the case of any United States shareholder, be its pro rata share of an amount determined in accordance with whichever of the following tables applies to the taxable year:

(1) TAXABLE YEARS BEGINNING IN 1963 AND TAXABLE YEARS ENTIRELY WITHIN THE SURCHARGE PERIOD ENDING BEFORE JANUARY 1, 1970.—

If the effective foreign tax rate is (percentage)—	The required minimum distribution of earnings and profits is (percentage)—
Under 10	90
10 or over but less than 20	86
20 or over but less than 28	82
28 or over but less than 34	75
34 or over but less than 39	68
39 or over but less than 42	55
42 or over but less than 44	40
44 or over but less than 46	27
46 or over but less than 47	14
47 or over	0

(2) TAXABLE YEARS BEGINNING IN 1964 AND TAXABLE YEARS BEGINNING IN 1969 AND ENDING IN 1970 TO THE EXTENT SUBPARAGRAPH (B) APPLIES.—

If the effective foreign tax rate is (percentage)—	The required minimum distribution of earnings and profits is (percentage)—
Under 10	87
10 or over but less than 19	83
19 or over but less than 27	79

INCOME TAX—CONTROLLED FOREIGN CORPORATIONS

27 or over but less than 33	72
33 or over but less than 37	65
37 or over but less than 40	53
40 or over but less than 42	38
42 or over but less than 44	26
44 or over but less than 45	13
45 or over	0

(3) TAXABLE YEARS BEGINNING AFTER 1964 (EXCEPT TAXABLE YEARS WHICH INCLUDE ANY PART OF THE SURCHARGE PERIOD).—

If the effective foreign tax rate is (percentage)—	The required minimum distribution of earnings and profits is (percentage)—
Under 9	83
9 or over but less than 18	79
18 or over but less than 26	76
26 or over but less than 32	69
32 or over but less than 36	63
36 or over but less than 39	51
39 or over but less than 41	37
41 or over but less than 42	25
42 or over but less than 43	13
43 or over	0

In the case of a taxable year beginning before the surcharge period and ending within the surcharge period, or beginning within the surcharge period and ending after the surcharge period, or beginning before January 1, 1970, and ending after December 31, 1969, the required minimum distribution shall be equal to the sum of—

(A) that portion of the minimum distribution which would be required if the provisions of paragraph (1) were applicable to the taxable year, which the number of days in such taxable year which are within the surcharge period and before January 1, 1970, bears to the total number of days in such taxable year,

(B) that portion of the minimum distribution which would be required if the provisions of paragraph (2) were applicable to such taxable year, which the number of days in such taxable year which are within the surcharge period and after December 31, 1969, bears to the total number of days in such taxable year, and

(C) that portion of the minimum distribution which would be required if the provisions of paragraph (3) were applicable to such taxable year, which the number of days in such taxable year which are not within the surcharge period bears to the total number of days in such taxable year.

As used in this subsection, the term "surcharge period" means the period beginning January 1, 1968, and ending June 30, 1970.

Amendments

- **1969, Tax Reform Act of 1969 (P.L. 91-172)**

P.L. 91-172, § 701(b):

Amended the heading of Code Sec. 963(b)(1) by adding "ending before January 1, 1970". Amended the heading of Code Sec. 963(b)(2) by adding "and taxable years beginning in 1969 and ending in 1970 to the extent subparagraph (B) applies." Amended the last two sentences of Code Sec. 963(b). **Effective** for tax years ending after 12-31-69 and beginning before 7-1-70. Prior to amendment, the last two sentences of Code Sec. 963(b) read as follows:

In the case of a taxable year beginning before the surcharge period and ending within the surcharge period, or beginning within the surcharge period and ending after the surcharge period, the required minimum distribution shall be an amount equal to the sum of—

(A) that portion of the minimum distribution which would be required if the provisions of paragraph (1) were applicable to the taxable year, which the number of days in such taxable year which are within the surcharge period bears to the total number of days in such taxable year, plus

(B) that portion of the minimum distribution which would be required if the provisions of paragraph (3) were applicable to such taxable year, which the number of days in such taxable year which are not within the surcharge period bears to the total number of days in such taxable year.

As used in this subsection, the term "surcharge period" means the period beginning January 1, 1968, and ending December 31, 1969.

- **1969 (P.L. 91-53)**

P.L. 91-53, § 5(b):

Amended Code Sec. 963(b) by substituting "December 31, 1969" for "June 30, 1969" in the last sentence. **Effective** for tax years ending after 6-30-69, and beginning before 1-1-70.

- **1968, Revenue and Expenditure Control Act of 1968 (P.L. 90-364)**

P.L. 90-364, § 102(b):

Substituted headings in paragraphs (1) and (3) for the following: "(1) TAXABLE YEARS BEGINNING IN 1963.—" and "(3) TAXABLE YEARS BEGINNING AFTER DECEMBER 31, 1964.—", and added the material following the table in paragraph (3). **Effective** with respect to tax years ending after 12-31-67, and beginning before 7-1-69.

- **1964, Revenue Act of 1964 (P.L. 88-272)**

P.L. 88-272, § 123(b):

Amended subsection (b). **Effective** with respect to tax years beginning after 12-31-63. Prior to amendment, subsection (b) read as follows:

"(b) Minimum Distributions.—For purposes of this section, a minimum distribution with respect to the earnings and profits for the taxable year of any controlled foreign corporation or corporations shall, in the case of any United States shareholder, be its pro rata share of an amount determined in accordance with the following table:

If the effective foreign tax rate is (percentage)—	The required minimum distribution of earnings and profits is (percentage)—
Under 10	90
10 or over but less than 20	86
20 or over but less than 28	82
28 or over but less than 34	75
34 or over but less than 39	68
39 or over but less than 42	55
42 or over but less than 44	40
44 or over but less than 46	27
46 or over but less than 47	14
47 or over	0"

[Sec. 963(c)]

(c) AMOUNTS TO WHICH SECTION APPLIES.—

(1) FOREIGN SUBSIDIARIES.—Subsection (a)(1) shall apply to amounts which (but for the provisions of this section) would be included in the gross income of the United States shareholder under section 951(a)(1)(A)(i) by reason of its ownership, within the meaning of section 958(a)(1)(A), of stock of a controlled foreign corporation.

(2) CHAIN OF CONTROLLED FOREIGN CORPORATIONS.—Subsection (a)(2) shall apply to amounts which (but for the provisions of this section) would be included in the gross income of the United States shareholder under section 951(a)(1)(A)(i)—

(A) by reason of its ownership, within the meaning of section 958(a)(1)(A), of stock of a controlled foreign corporation, and

(B) to the extent that the United States shareholder so elects, by reason of its ownership, within the meaning of section 958(a)(2), of stock of any other controlled foreign corporation (on account of its ownership of the stock described in subparagraph (A) or of stock described in this subparagraph), but only if there is taken into account the earnings and profits of each foreign corporation, whether or not a controlled foreign corporation, by reason of which the United States shareholder owns, within the meaning of section 958(a)(2), stock of such controlled foreign corporation.

(3) ALL CONTROLLED FOREIGN CORPORATIONS.—Except as provided in paragraph (4), subsection (a)(3) shall apply to amounts which (but for the provisions of this section) would be included in the gross income of the United States shareholder under section 951(a)(1)(A)(i)—

(A) by reason of its ownership, within the meaning of section 958(a)(1)(A), of stock of all controlled foreign corporations in which its owns stock within the meaning of such section, and

(B) by reason of its ownership, within the meaning of section 958(a)(2), of stock of all controlled foreign corporations in which it owns stock within the meaning of such section, but only if there is taken into account the earnings and profits of each foreign corporation, whether or not a controlled foreign corporation, by reason of which the United States shareholder owns, within the meaning of section 958(a), stock of any of such controlled foreign corporations.

(4) EXCEPTIONS AND SPECIAL RULES.—

(A) LESS DEVELOPED COUNTRY CORPORATIONS.—If the United States shareholder so elects, subsection (a)(3) and paragraph (3) of this subsection shall not apply to amounts which would be included in the gross income of such shareholder under section 951(a)(1)(A)(i) by reason of its ownership, within the meaning of section 958(a), of stock of controlled foreign corporations which are less developed country corporations (as defined in section 955(c)). This subparagraph shall not apply with respect to a less developed country corporation if, by reason of the ownership of the stock of such corporation, the United States shareholder owns, within the meaning of section 958(a)(2), stock of any other controlled foreign corporation which is not a less developed country corporation. Except as provided in the preceding sentence, an election under this subparagraph may be made only with respect to all controlled foreign corporations which are less developed country corporations and with respect to which the domestic corporation making the election is a United States shareholder.

(B) FOREIGN BRANCHES.—In applying subsection (a)(3) and paragraph (3) of this subsection, if a United States shareholder so elects, all branches maintained by such shareholder in foreign countries, the Commonwealth of Puerto Rico, or possessions of the United States shall, under regulations prescribed by the Secretary or his delegate, be treated as wholly owned subsidiary corporations of such shareholder organized under the laws of such foreign countries, the Commonwealth of Puerto Rico, or possessions of the United States, as the case may be. Each branch so treated shall, for purposes of this section, be considered to have distributed to the United States shareholder all of its earnings and profits for the taxable year. This subparagraph shall not apply to a branch maintained by a United States shareholder in the Commonwealth of Puerto Rico or a possession of the United States unless—

(i) such branch would be a controlled foreign corporation (as defined in section 957) if it were incorporated under the laws of the Commonwealth of Puerto Rico or the possession of the United States, as the case may be, and

Sec. 963—Repealed

INCOME TAX—CONTROLLED FOREIGN CORPORATIONS

(ii) the gross income of the United States shareholder for the taxable year includes income derived from sources within the Commonwealth of Puerto Rico and possessions of the United States.

(C) BLOCKED FOREIGN INCOME.—If a United States shareholder so elects, the provisions of subsection (a)(3) and of paragraph (3) of this subsection shall not apply with respect to any foreign corporation, if it is established to the satisfaction of the Secretary or his delegate that the earnings and profits of such foreign corporation could not have been distributed to United States shareholders who own (within the meaning of section 958(a)) stock of such foreign corporation because of currency or other restrictions or limitations imposed under the laws of any foreign country.

[Sec. 963(d)]

(d) EFFECTIVE FOREIGN TAX RATE.—For purposes of this section, the term "effective foreign tax rate" means—

(1) with respect to a single controlled foreign corporation, the percentage which—

(A) the income, war profits, or excess profits taxes paid or accrued to foreign countries or possessions of the United States by the controlled foreign corporation for the taxable year on or with respect to its earnings and profits for the taxable year, is of

(B) the sum of (i) the earnings and profits of the controlled foreign corporation described in subparagraph (A) and (ii) the taxes described in subparagraph (A); and

(2) with respect to two or more foreign corporations, the percentage which—

(A) the total income, war profits, or excess profits taxes paid or accrued to foreign countries or possessions of the United States by such foreign corporations for the taxable year on or with respect to the consolidated earnings and profits of such foreign corporations for the taxable year, is of

(B) the sum of (i) the consolidated earnings and profits of such foreign corporations described in subparagraph (A) and (ii) the taxes described in subparagraph (A).

For purposes of the preceding sentence, in the case of any United States shareholder, the computation of the effective foreign tax rate applicable with respect to any controlled foreign corporation or corporations shall be made without regard to distributions made by such controlled foreign corporation or corporations to such United States shareholder.

[Sec. 963(e)]

(e) SPECIAL RULES.—

(1) YEAR FROM WHICH DISTRIBUTIONS ARE MADE.—For purposes of this section, the second sentence of section 902(c)(1) shall apply in determining from the earnings and profits of what year distributions are made by any foreign corporation, except that the Secretary or his delegate may by regulations provide a period in excess of 60 days in lieu of the 60-day period prescribed in such section.

(2) INSUFFICIENT DISTRIBUTIONS.—If—

(A) a United States shareholder, in making its return of the tax imposed by this chapter for any taxable year, applies the provisions of this section with respect to any controlled foreign corporation,

(B) it is subsequently determined that this section did not apply with respect to such controlled foreign corporation for such taxable year due to the failure of the United States shareholder to receive a minimum distribution with respect to such controlled foreign corporation, and

(C) such failure is due to reasonable cause,

then a subsequent distribution made with respect to such controlled foreign corporation may, if made at a time and in a manner prescribed by the Secretary or his delegate by regulations, be treated, for purposes of this chapter, as having been made for, and received in, the taxable year of the United States shareholder for which such shareholder applied the provisions of this section.

(3) AFFILIATED GROUPS OF CORPORATIONS.—An affiliated group of corporations which makes a consolidated return under section 1501 for the taxable year, may, if it so elects, be treated as a single United States shareholder for purposes of applying this section for the taxable year.

[Sec. 963(f)]

(f) REGULATIONS.—The Secretary or his delegate shall prescribe such regulations as he may deem necessary to carry out the provisions of this section, including regulations for the determination of the amount of foreign tax credit in the case of distributions with respect to the earnings and profits of two or more foreign corporations.

[Sec. 964]

SEC. 964. MISCELLANEOUS PROVISIONS.

[Sec. 964(a)]

(a) EARNINGS AND PROFITS.—Except as provided in section 312(k)(4), for purposes of this subpart, the earnings and profits of any foreign corporation, and the deficit in earnings and profits of any foreign corporation, for any taxable year shall be determined according to rules substantially similar to those applicable to domestic corporations, under regulations prescribed by the Secretary. In determining such earnings and profits, or the deficit in such earnings and profits, the amount of any illegal bribe, kickback, or other payment (within the meaning of section 162(c)) shall not be taken into account to decrease such earnings and profits or to increase such deficit. The payments referred to in the preceding sentence are payments which would be unlawful under the Foreign Corrupt Practices Act of 1977 if the payor were a United States person.

Amendments

- **1982, Tax Equity and Fiscal Responsibility Act of 1982 (P.L. 97-248)**

P.L. 97-248, §288(b)(2):

Added the last sentence to subsection (a). **Effective** for payments made after 9-3-82.

- **1981, Economic Recovery Tax Act of 1981 (P.L. 97-34)**

P.L. 97-34, §206(c):

Amended Code Sec. 964(a) by striking out "section 312(k)(3)" and inserting in lieu thereof "section 312(k)(4)". **Effective** for property placed in service after 12-31-80, in tax years ending after such date.

- **1976, Tax Reform Act of 1976 (P.L. 94-455)**

P.L. 94-455, §1065(b):

Added the last sentence of Code Sec. 964(a). **Effective** for payments described in Code Sec. 162(c) made more than 30 days after 10-4-76.

P.L. 94-455, §1901(b)(32)(B)(iii):

Substituted "312(k)(3)" for "312(m)(3)" in Code Sec. 964(a). **Effective** for tax years beginning after 12-31-76.

P.L. 94-455, §1906(b)(13)(A):

Amended 1954 Code by substituting "Secretary" for "Secretary or his delegate" each place it appeared. **Effective** 2-1-77.

- **1969, Tax Reform Act of 1969 (P.L. 91-172)**

P.L. 91-172, §442(b)(1):

Amended subsection (a) by inserting "Except as provided in section 312(m)(3), for purposes of this subpart" in lieu of "For purposes of this subpart,". **Effective** for tax years beginning after 6-30-72.

[Sec. 964(b)]

(b) BLOCKED FOREIGN INCOME.—Under regulations prescribed by the Secretary, no part of the earnings and profits of a controlled foreign corporation for any taxable year shall be included in earnings and profits for purposes of sections 952 and 956, if it is established to the satisfaction of the Secretary that such part could not have been distributed by the controlled foreign corporation to United States shareholders who own (within the meaning of section 958(a)) stock of such controlled foreign corporation because of currency or other restrictions or limitations imposed under the laws of any foreign country.

Amendments

- **2017, Tax Cuts and Jobs Act (P.L. 115-97)**

P.L. 115-97, §14212(b)(4):

Amended Code Sec. 964(b) by striking ", 955," following "sections 952". **Effective** for tax years of foreign corporations beginning after 12-31-2017, and to tax years of United States shareholders in which or with which such tax years of foreign corporations end.

- **1976, Tax Reform Act of 1976 (P.L. 94-455)**

P.L. 94-455, §1906(b)(13)(A):

Amended 1954 Code by substituting "Secretary" for "Secretary or his delegate" each place it appeared. **Effective** 2-1-77.

[Sec. 964(c)]

(c) RECORDS AND ACCOUNTS OF UNITED STATES SHAREHOLDERS.—

(1) RECORDS AND ACCOUNTS TO BE MAINTAINED.—The Secretary may by regulations require each person who is, or has been, a United States shareholder of a controlled foreign corporation to maintain such records and accounts as may be prescribed by such regulations as necessary to carry out the provisions of this subpart and subpart G.

(2) TWO OR MORE PERSONS REQUIRED TO MAINTAIN OR FURNISH THE SAME RECORDS AND ACCOUNTS WITH RESPECT TO THE SAME FOREIGN CORPORATION.—Where, but for this paragraph, two or more United States persons would be required to maintain or furnish the same records and accounts as may by regulations be required under paragraph (1) with respect to the same controlled foreign corporation for the same period, the Secretary

INCOME TAX—CONTROLLED FOREIGN CORPORATIONS

may by regulations provide that the maintenance or furnishing of such records and accounts by only one such person shall satisfy the requirements of paragraph (1) for such other persons.

Amendments

• **1976, Tax Reform Act of 1976 (P.L. 94-455)**

P.L. 94-455, § 1906(b)(13)(A):

Amended 1954 Code by substituting "Secretary" for "Secretary or his delegate" each place it appeared. **Effective** 2-1-77.

• **1962, Revenue Act of 1962 (P.L. 87-834)**

P.L. 87-834, § 12(a):

Amended Part III of subchapter N of chapter 1 by adding subpart F, which includes Code Secs. 951-964. **Effective** for tax years of foreign corporations beginning after 12-31-62, and for tax years of United States shareholders within which or with which such tax years of such foreign corporations end.

[Sec. 964(d)]

(d) TREATMENT OF CERTAIN BRANCHES.—

(1) IN GENERAL.—For purposes of this chapter, section 6038, section 6046, and such other provisions as may be specified in regulations—

(A) a qualified insurance branch of a controlled foreign corporation shall be treated as a separate foreign corporation created under the laws of the foreign country with respect to which such branch qualifies under paragraph (2), and

(B) except as provided in regulations, any amount directly or indirectly transferred or credited from such branch to one or more other accounts of such controlled foreign corporation shall be treated as a dividend paid to such controlled foreign corporation.

(2) QUALIFIED INSURANCE BRANCH.—For purposes of paragraph (1), the term "qualified insurance branch" means any branch of a controlled foreign corporation which is licensed and predominantly engaged on a permanent basis in the active conduct of an insurance business in a foreign country if—

(A) separate books and accounts are maintained for such branch,

(B) the principal place of business of such branch is in such foreign country,

(C) such branch would be taxable under subchapter L if it were a separate domestic corporation, and

(D) an election under this paragraph applies to such branch.

An election under this paragraph shall apply to the taxable year for which made and all subsequent taxable years unless revoked with the consent of the Secretary.

(3) REGULATIONS.—The Secretary shall prescribe such regulations as may be necessary or appropriate to carry out the purposes of this subsection.

Amendments

• **1988, Technical and Miscellaneous Revenue Act of 1988 (P.L. 100-647)**

P.L. 100-647, § 6129(a):

Amended Code Sec. 964 by adding new subsection (d). **Effective** for tax years of foreign corporations beginning after 12-31-88.

[Sec. 964(e)]

(e) GAIN ON CERTAIN STOCK SALES BY CONTROLLED FOREIGN CORPORATIONS TREATED AS DIVIDENDS.—

(1) IN GENERAL.—If a controlled foreign corporation sells or exchanges stock in any other foreign corporation, gain recognized on such sale or exchange shall be included in the gross income of such controlled foreign corporation as a dividend to the same extent that it would have been so included under section 1248(a) if such controlled foreign corporation were a United States person. For purposes of determining the amount which would have been so includible, the determination of whether such other foreign corporation was a controlled foreign corporation shall be made without regard to the preceding sentence.

(2) SAME COUNTRY EXCEPTION NOT APPLICABLE.—Clause (i) of section 954(c)(3)(A) shall not apply to any amount treated as a dividend by reason of paragraph (1).

(3) CLARIFICATION OF DEEMED SALES.—For purposes of this subsection, a controlled foreign corporation shall be treated as having sold or exchanged any stock if, under any provision of this subtitle, such controlled foreign corporation is treated as having gain from the sale or exchange of such stock.

(4) COORDINATION WITH DIVIDENDS RECEIVED DEDUCTION.—

(A) IN GENERAL.—If, for any taxable year of a controlled foreign corporation beginning after December 31, 2017, any amount is treated as a dividend under paragraph (1) by reason of a sale or exchange by the controlled foreign corporation of stock in another foreign corporation held for 1 year or more, then, notwithstanding any other provision of this title—

(i) the foreign-source portion of such dividend shall be treated for purposes of section 951(a)(1)(A) as subpart F income of the selling controlled foreign corporation for such taxable year,

(ii) a United States shareholder with respect to the selling controlled foreign corporation shall include in gross income for the taxable year of the shareholder with or within which such taxable year of the controlled foreign corporation ends an amount equal to the shareholder's pro rata share (determined in the same manner as under section 951(a)(2)) of the amount treated as subpart F income under clause (i), and

(iii) the deduction under section 245A(a) shall be allowable to the United States shareholder with respect to the subpart F income included in gross income under clause (ii) in the same manner as if such subpart F income were a dividend received by the shareholder from the selling controlled foreign corporation.

(B) APPLICATION OF BASIS OR SIMILAR ADJUSTMENT.—For purposes of this title, in the case of a sale or exchange by a controlled foreign corporation of stock in another foreign corporation in a taxable year of the selling controlled foreign corporation beginning after December 31, 2017, rules similar to the rules of section 961(d) shall apply.

(C) FOREIGN-SOURCE PORTION.—For purposes of this paragraph, the foreign-source portion of any amount treated as a dividend under paragraph (1) shall be determined in the same manner as under section 245A(c).

Amendments

• **2017, Tax Cuts and Jobs Act (P.L. 115-97)**

P.L. 115-97, § 14102(c):

Amended Code Sec. 964(e) by adding at the end a new paragraph (4). **Effective** for sales or exchanges after 12-31-2017.

• **1997, Taxpayer Relief Act of 1997 (P.L. 105-34)**

P.L. 105-34, § 1111(a):

Amended Code Sec. 964 by adding at the end a new subsection (e). **Effective** for gain recognized on transactions occurring after 8-5-97.

INCOME TAX—CONTROLLED FOREIGN CORPORATIONS

[Sec. 965]

SEC. 965. TREATMENT OF DEFERRED FOREIGN INCOME UPON TRANSITION TO PARTICIPATION EXEMPTION SYSTEM OF TAXATION.

[Sec. 965(a)]

(a) TREATMENT OF DEFERRED FOREIGN INCOME AS SUBPART F INCOME.—In the case of the last taxable year of a deferred foreign income corporation which begins before January 1, 2018, the subpart F income of such foreign corporation (as otherwise determined for such taxable year under section 952) shall be increased by the greater of—

(1) the accumulated post-1986 deferred foreign income of such corporation determined as of November 2, 2017, or

(2) the accumulated post-1986 deferred foreign income of such corporation determined as of December 31, 2017.

[Sec. 965(b)]

(b) REDUCTION IN AMOUNTS INCLUDED IN GROSS INCOME OF UNITED STATES SHAREHOLDERS OF SPECIFIED FOREIGN CORPORATIONS WITH DEFICITS IN EARNINGS AND PROFITS.—

(1) IN GENERAL.—In the case of a taxpayer which is a United States shareholder with respect to at least one deferred foreign income corporation and at least one E&P deficit foreign corporation, the amount which would (but for this subsection) be taken into account under section 951(a)(1) by reason of subsection (a) as such United States shareholder's pro rata share of the subpart F income of each deferred foreign income corporation shall be reduced by the amount of such United States shareholder's aggregate foreign E&P deficit which is allocated under paragraph (2) to such deferred foreign income corporation.

(2) ALLOCATION OF AGGREGATE FOREIGN E&P DEFICIT.—The aggregate foreign E&P deficit of any United States shareholder shall be allocated among the deferred foreign income corporations of such United States shareholder in an amount which bears the same proportion to such aggregate as—

(A) such United States shareholder's pro rata share of the accumulated post-1986 deferred foreign income of each such deferred foreign income corporation, bears to

(B) the aggregate of such United States shareholder's pro rata share of the accumulated post-1986 deferred foreign income of all deferred foreign income corporations of such United States shareholder.

(3) DEFINITIONS RELATED TO E&P DEFICITS.—For purposes of this subsection—

(A) AGGREGATE FOREIGN E&P DEFICIT.—

(i) IN GENERAL.—The term "aggregate foreign E&P deficit" means, with respect to any United States shareholder, the lesser of—

(I) the aggregate of such shareholder's pro rata shares of the specified E&P deficits of the E&P deficit foreign corporations of such shareholder, or

(II) the amount determined under paragraph (2)(B).

(ii) ALLOCATION OF DEFICIT.—If the amount described in clause (i)(II) is less than the amount described in clause (i)(I), then the shareholder shall designate, in such form and manner as the Secretary determines—

(I) the amount of the specified E&P deficit which is to be taken into account for each E&P deficit corporation with respect to the taxpayer, and

(II) in the case of an E&P deficit corporation which has a qualified deficit (as defined in section 952), the portion (if any) of the deficit taken into account under subclause (I) which is attributable to a qualified deficit, including the qualified activities to which such portion is attributable.

(B) E&P DEFICIT FOREIGN CORPORATION.—The term "E&P deficit foreign corporation" means, with respect to any taxpayer, any specified foreign corporation with respect to which such taxpayer is a United States shareholder, if, as of November 2, 2017—

(i) such specified foreign corporation has a deficit in post-1986 earnings and profits,

(ii) such corporation was a specified foreign corporation, and

(iii) such taxpayer was a United States shareholder of such corporation.

(C) SPECIFIED E&P DEFICIT.—The term "specified E&P deficit" means, with respect to any E&P deficit foreign corporation, the amount of the deficit referred to in subparagraph (B).

(4) TREATMENT OF EARNINGS AND PROFITS IN FUTURE YEARS.—

(A) REDUCED EARNINGS AND PROFITS TREATED AS PREVIOUSLY TAXED INCOME WHEN DISTRIBUTED.—For purposes of applying section 959 in any taxable year beginning with the taxable year described in subsection (a), with respect to any United States shareholder of a deferred foreign income corporation, an amount equal to such shareholder's reduction under paragraph (1) which is allocated to such deferred foreign income corporation under this subsection shall be treated as an amount which was included in the gross income of such United States shareholder under section 951(a).

(B) E&P DEFICITS.—For purposes of this title, with respect to any taxable year beginning with the taxable year described in subsection (a), a United States shareholder's pro rata share of the earnings and profits of any E&P deficit foreign corporation under this subsection shall be increased by the amount of the specified E&P deficit of such corporation taken into account by such shareholder under paragraph (1), and, for purposes of section 952, such increase shall be attributable to the same activity to which the deficit so taken into account was attributable.

(5) NETTING AMONG UNITED STATES SHAREHOLDERS IN SAME AFFILIATED GROUP.—

(A) IN GENERAL.—In the case of any affiliated group which includes at least one E&P net surplus shareholder and one E&P net deficit shareholder, the amount which would (but for this paragraph) be taken into account under section 951(a)(1) by reason of subsection (a) by each such E&P net surplus shareholder shall be reduced (but not below zero) by such shareholder's applicable share of the affiliated group's aggregate unused E&P deficit.

(B) E&P NET SURPLUS SHAREHOLDER.—For purposes of this paragraph, the term "E&P net surplus shareholder" means any United States shareholder which would (determined without regard to this paragraph) take into account an amount greater than zero under section 951(a)(1) by reason of subsection (a).

(C) E&P NET DEFICIT SHAREHOLDER.—For purposes of this paragraph, the term "E&P net deficit shareholder" means any United States shareholder if—

(i) the aggregate foreign E&P deficit with respect to such shareholder (as defined in paragraph (3)(A) without regard to clause (i)(II) thereof), exceeds

(ii) the amount which would (but for this subsection) be taken into account by such shareholder under section 951(a)(1) by reason of subsection (a).

(D) AGGREGATE UNUSED E&P DEFICIT.—For purposes of this paragraph—

INCOME TAX—CONTROLLED FOREIGN CORPORATIONS

(i) IN GENERAL.—The term "aggregate unused E&P deficit" means, with respect to any affiliated group, the lesser of—

(I) the sum of the excesses described in subparagraph (C), determined with respect to each E&P net deficit shareholder in such group, or

(II) the amount determined under subparagraph (E)(ii).

(ii) REDUCTION WITH RESPECT TO E&P NET DEFICIT SHAREHOLDERS WHICH ARE NOT WHOLLY OWNED BY THE AFFILIATED GROUP.—If the group ownership percentage of any E&P net deficit shareholder is less than 100 percent, the amount of the excess described in subparagraph (C) which is taken into account under clause (i)(I) with respect to such E&P net deficit shareholder shall be such group ownership percentage of such amount.

(E) APPLICABLE SHARE.—For purposes of this paragraph, the term "applicable share" means, with respect to any E&P net surplus shareholder in any affiliated group, the amount which bears the same proportion to such group's aggregate unused E&P deficit as—

(i) the product of—

(I) such shareholder's group ownership percentage, multiplied by

(II) the amount which would (but for this paragraph) be taken into account under section 951(a)(1) by reason of subsection (a) by such shareholder, bears to

(ii) the aggregate amount determined under clause (i) with respect to all E&P net surplus shareholders in such group.

(F) GROUP OWNERSHIP PERCENTAGE.—For purposes of this paragraph, the term "group ownership percentage" means, with respect to any United States shareholder in any affiliated group, the percentage of the value of the stock of such United States shareholder which is held by other includible corporations in such affiliated group. Notwithstanding the preceding sentence, the group ownership percentage of the common parent of the affiliated group is 100 percent. Any term used in this subparagraph which is also used in section 1504 shall have the same meaning as when used in such section.

[Sec. 965(c)]

(c) APPLICATION OF PARTICIPATION EXEMPTION TO INCLUDED INCOME.—

(1) IN GENERAL.—In the case of a United States shareholder of a deferred foreign income corporation, there shall be allowed as a deduction for the taxable year in which an amount is included in the gross income of such United States shareholder under section 951(a)(1) by reason of this section an amount equal to the sum of—

(A) the United States shareholder's 8 percent rate equivalent percentage of the excess (if any) of—

(i) the amount so included as gross income, over

(ii) the amount of such United States shareholder's aggregate foreign cash position, plus

(B) the United States shareholder's 15.5 percent rate equivalent percentage of so much of the amount described in subparagraph (A)(ii) as does not exceed the amount described in subparagraph (A)(i).

(2) 8 AND 15.5 PERCENT RATE EQUIVALENT PERCENTAGES.—For purposes of this subsection—

(A) 8 PERCENT RATE EQUIVALENT PERCENTAGE.—The term "8 percent rate equivalent percentage" means, with respect to any United States shareholder for any taxable year, the percentage which would result in the amount to which such percentage applies being subject to a 8 percent rate of tax determined by only taking into account a deduction equal to such percentage of such amount and the highest rate of tax specified in section 11 for such taxable year. In the case of any taxable year of a United States shareholder to which section 15 applies, the highest rate of tax under section 11 before the effective date of the change in rates and the highest rate of tax under section 11 after the effective date of such change shall each be taken into account under the preceding sentence in the same proportions as the portion of such taxable year which is before and after such effective date, respectively.

(B) 15.5 PERCENT RATE EQUIVALENT PERCENTAGE.—The term "15.5 percent rate equivalent percentage" means, with respect to any United States shareholder for any taxable year, the percentage determined under subparagraph (A) applied by substituting "15.5 percent rate of tax" for "8 percent rate of tax".

(3) AGGREGATE FOREIGN CASH POSITION.—For purposes of this subsection—

(A) IN GENERAL.—The term "aggregate foreign cash position" means, with respect to any United States shareholder, the greater of—

(i) the aggregate of such United States shareholder's pro rata share of the cash position of each specified foreign corporation of such United States shareholder determined as of the close of the last taxable year of such specified foreign corporation which begins before January 1, 2018, or

(ii) one half of the sum of—

(I) the aggregate described in clause (i) determined as of the close of the last taxable year of each such specified foreign corporation which ends before November 2, 2017, plus

(II) the aggregate described in clause (i) determined as of the close of the taxable year of each such specified foreign corporation which precedes the taxable year referred to in subclause (I).

(B) CASH POSITION.—For purposes of this paragraph, the cash position of any specified foreign corporation is the sum of—

(i) cash held by such foreign corporation,

(ii) the net accounts receivable of such foreign corporation, plus

(iii) the fair market value of the following assets held by such corporation:

(I) Personal property which is of a type that is actively traded and for which there is an established financial market.

(II) Commercial paper, certificates of deposit, the securities of the Federal government and of any State or foreign government.

(III) Any foreign currency.

(IV) Any obligation with a term of less than one year.

(V) Any asset which the Secretary identifies as being economically equivalent to any asset described in this subparagraph.

(C) NET ACCOUNTS RECEIVABLE.—For purposes of this paragraph, the term "net accounts receivable" means, with respect to any specified foreign corporation, the excess (if any) of—

(i) such corporation's accounts receivable, over

(ii) such corporation's accounts payable (determined consistent with the rules of section 461).

(D) PREVENTION OF DOUBLE COUNTING.—Cash positions of a specified foreign corporation described in clause (ii), (iii)(I), or (iii)(IV) of subparagraph (B) shall not be taken into account by a United States shareholder under subparagraph (A) to the extent that such United States shareholder demonstrates to the satisfaction of the Secretary that such amount is so taken into account by such United States shareholder with respect to another specified foreign corporation.

INCOME TAX—CONTROLLED FOREIGN CORPORATIONS

(E) CASH POSITIONS OF CERTAIN NON-CORPORATE ENTITIES TAKEN INTO ACCOUNT.—An entity (other than a corporation) shall be treated as a specified foreign corporation of a United States shareholder for purposes of determining such United States shareholder's aggregate foreign cash position if any interest in such entity is held by a specified foreign corporation of such United States shareholder (determined after application of this subparagraph) and such entity would be a specified foreign corporation of such United States shareholder if such entity were a foreign corporation.

(F) ANTI-ABUSE.—If the Secretary determines that a principal purpose of any transaction was to reduce the aggregate foreign cash position taken into account under this subsection, such transaction shall be disregarded for purposes of this subsection.

[Sec. 965(d)]

(d) DEFERRED FOREIGN INCOME CORPORATION; ACCUMULATED POST-1986 DEFERRED FOREIGN INCOME.—For purposes of this section—

(1) DEFERRED FOREIGN INCOME CORPORATION.—The term "deferred foreign income corporation" means, with respect to any United States shareholder, any specified foreign corporation of such United States shareholder which has accumulated post-1986 deferred foreign income (as of the date referred to in paragraph (1) or (2) of subsection (a)) greater than zero.

(2) ACCUMULATED POST-1986 DEFERRED FOREIGN INCOME.—The term "accumulated post-1986 deferred foreign income" means the post-1986 earnings and profits except to the extent such earnings—

(A) are attributable to income of the specified foreign corporation which is effectively connected with the conduct of a trade or business within the United States and subject to tax under this chapter, or

(B) in the case of a controlled foreign corporation, if distributed, would be excluded from the gross income of a United States shareholder under section 959.

To the extent provided in regulations or other guidance prescribed by the Secretary, in the case of any controlled foreign corporation which has shareholders which are not United States shareholders, accumulated post-1986 deferred foreign income shall be appropriately reduced by amounts which would be described in subparagraph (B) if such shareholders were United States shareholders.

(3) POST-1986 EARNINGS AND PROFITS.—The term "post-1986 earnings and profits" means the earnings and profits of the foreign corporation (computed in accordance with sections 964(a) and 986, and by only taking into account periods when the foreign corporation was a specified foreign corporation) accumulated in taxable years beginning after December 31, 1986, and determined—

(A) as of the date referred to in paragraph (1) or (2) of subsection (a), whichever is applicable with respect to such foreign corporation, and

(B) without diminution by reason of dividends distributed during the taxable year described in subsection (a) other than dividends distributed to another specified foreign corporation.

[Sec. 965(e)]

(e) SPECIFIED FOREIGN CORPORATION.—

(1) IN GENERAL.—For purposes of this section, the term "specified foreign corporation" means—

(A) any controlled foreign corporation, and

(B) any foreign corporation with respect to which one or more domestic corporations is a United States shareholder.

(2) APPLICATION TO CERTAIN FOREIGN CORPORATIONS.—For purposes of sections 951 and 961, a foreign corporation described in paragraph (1)(B) shall be treated as a controlled foreign corporation solely for purposes of taking into account the subpart F income of such corporation under subsection (a) (and for purposes of applying subsection (f)).

(3) EXCLUSION OF PASSIVE FOREIGN INVESTMENT COMPANIES.—Such term shall not include any corporation which is a passive foreign investment company (as defined in section 1297) with respect to the shareholder and which is not a controlled foreign corporation.

[Sec. 965(f)]

(f) DETERMINATIONS OF PRO RATA SHARE.—

(1) IN GENERAL.—For purposes of this section, the determination of any United States shareholder's pro rata share of any amount with respect to any specified foreign corporation shall be determined under rules similar to the rules of section 951(a)(2) by treating such amount in the same manner as subpart F income (and by treating such specified foreign corporation as a controlled foreign corporation).

(2) SPECIAL RULES.—The portion which is included in the income of a United States shareholder under section 951(a)(1) by reason of subsection (a) which is equal to the deduction allowed under subsection (c) by reason of such inclusion—

(A) shall be treated as income exempt from tax for purposes of sections 705(a)(1)(B) and 1367(a)(1)(A), and

(B) shall not be treated as income exempt from tax for purposes of determining whether an adjustment shall be made to an accumulated adjustment account under section 1368(e)(1)(A).

[Sec. 965(g)]

(g) DISALLOWANCE OF FOREIGN TAX CREDIT, ETC.—

(1) IN GENERAL.—No credit shall be allowed under section 901 for the applicable percentage of any taxes paid or accrued (or treated as paid or accrued) with respect to any amount for which a deduction is allowed under this section.

(2) APPLICABLE PERCENTAGE.—For purposes of this subsection, the term "applicable percentage" means the amount (expressed as a percentage) equal to the sum of—

(A) 0.771 multiplied by the ratio of—

(i) the excess to which subsection (c)(1)(A) applies, divided by

(ii) the sum of such excess plus the amount to which subsection (c)(1)(B) applies, plus

(B) 0.557 multiplied by the ratio of—

(i) the amount to which subsection (c)(1)(B) applies, divided by

(ii) the sum described in subparagraph (A)(ii).

(3) DENIAL OF DEDUCTION.—No deduction shall be allowed under this chapter for any tax for which credit is not allowable under section 901 by reason of paragraph (1) (determined by treating the taxpayer as having elected the benefits of subpart A of part III of subchapter N).

(4) COORDINATION WITH SECTION 78.—With respect to the taxes treated as paid or accrued by a domestic corporation with respect to amounts which are includible in gross income of such domestic corporation by reason of this section, section 78 shall apply only to so much of such taxes as bears the same proportion to the amount of such taxes as—

(A) the excess of—

(i) the amounts which are includible in gross income of such domestic corporation by reason of this section, over

(ii) the deduction allowable under subsection (c) with respect to such amounts, bears to

INCOME TAX—CONTROLLED FOREIGN CORPORATIONS

(B) such amounts.

[Sec. 965(h)]

(h) ELECTION TO PAY LIABILITY IN INSTALLMENTS.—

(1) IN GENERAL.—In the case of a United States shareholder of a deferred foreign income corporation, such United States shareholder may elect to pay the net tax liability under this section in 8 installments of the following amounts:

(A) 8 percent of the net tax liability in the case of each of the first 5 of such installments,

(B) 15 percent of the net tax liability in the case of the 6th such installment,

(C) 20 percent of the net tax liability in the case of the 7th such installment, and

(D) 25 percent of the net tax liability in the case of the 8th such installment.

(2) DATE FOR PAYMENT OF INSTALLMENTS.—If an election is made under paragraph (1), the first installment shall be paid on the due date (determined without regard to any extension of time for filing the return) for the return of tax for the taxable year described in subsection (a) and each succeeding installment shall be paid on the due date (as so determined) for the return of tax for the taxable year following the taxable year with respect to which the preceding installment was made.

(3) ACCELERATION OF PAYMENT.—If there is an addition to tax for failure to timely pay any installment required under this subsection, a liquidation or sale of substantially all the assets of the taxpayer (including in a title 11 or similar case), a cessation of business by the taxpayer, or any similar circumstance, then the unpaid portion of all remaining installments shall be due on the date of such event (or in the case of a title 11 or similar case, the day before the petition is filed). The preceding sentence shall not apply to the sale of substantially all the assets of a taxpayer to a buyer if such buyer enters into an agreement with the Secretary under which such buyer is liable for the remaining installments due under this subsection in the same manner as if such buyer were the taxpayer.

(4) PRORATION OF DEFICIENCY TO INSTALLMENTS.—If an election is made under paragraph (1) to pay the net tax liability under this section in installments and a deficiency has been assessed with respect to such net tax liability, the deficiency shall be prorated to the installments payable under paragraph (1). The part of the deficiency so prorated to any installment the date for payment of which has not arrived shall be collected at the same time as, and as a part of, such installment. The part of the deficiency so prorated to any installment the date for payment of which has arrived shall be paid upon notice and demand from the Secretary. This subsection shall not apply if the deficiency is due to negligence, to intentional disregard of rules and regulations, or to fraud with intent to evade tax.

(5) ELECTION.—Any election under paragraph (1) shall be made not later than the due date for the return of tax for the taxable year described in subsection (a) and shall be made in such manner as the Secretary shall provide.

(6) NET TAX LIABILITY UNDER THIS SECTION.—For purposes of this subsection—

(A) IN GENERAL.—The net tax liability under this section with respect to any United States shareholder is the excess (if any) of—

(i) such taxpayer's net income tax for the taxable year in which an amount is included in the gross income of such United States shareholder under section 951(a)(1) by reason of this section, over

(ii) such taxpayer's net income tax for such taxable year determined—

(I) without regard to this section, and

(II) without regard to any income or deduction properly attributable to a dividend received by such United States shareholder from any deferred foreign income corporation.

(B) NET INCOME TAX.—The term "net income tax" means the regular tax liability reduced by the credits allowed under subparts A, B, and D of part IV of subchapter A.

[Sec. 965(i)]

(i) SPECIAL RULES FOR S CORPORATION SHAREHOLDERS.—

(1) IN GENERAL.—In the case of any S corporation which is a United States shareholder of a deferred foreign income corporation, each shareholder of such S corporation may elect to defer payment of such shareholder's net tax liability under this section with respect to such S corporation until the shareholder's taxable year which includes the triggering event with respect to such liability. Any net tax liability payment of which is deferred under the preceding sentence shall be assessed on the return of tax as an addition to tax in the shareholder's taxable year which includes such triggering event.

(2) TRIGGERING EVENT.—

(A) IN GENERAL.—In the case of any shareholder's net tax liability under this section with respect to any S corporation, the triggering event with respect to such liability is whichever of the following occurs first:

(i) Such corporation ceases to be an S corporation (determined as of the first day of the first taxable year that such corporation is not an S corporation).

(ii) A liquidation or sale of substantially all the assets of such S corporation (including in a title 11 or similar case), a cessation of business by such S corporation, such S corporation ceases to exist, or any similar circumstance.

(iii) A transfer of any share of stock in such S corporation by the taxpayer (including by reason of death, or otherwise).

(B) PARTIAL TRANSFERS OF STOCK.—In the case of a transfer of less than all of the taxpayer's shares of stock in the S corporation, such transfer shall only be a triggering event with respect to so much of the taxpayer's net tax liability under this section with respect to such S corporation as is properly allocable to such stock.

(C) TRANSFER OF LIABILITY.—A transfer described in clause (iii) of subparagraph (A) shall not be treated as a triggering event if the transferee enters into an agreement with the Secretary under which such transferee is liable for net tax liability with respect to such stock in the same manner as if such transferee were the taxpayer.

(3) NET TAX LIABILITY.—A shareholder's net tax liability under this section with respect to any S corporation is the net tax liability under this section which would be determined under subsection (h)(6) if the only subpart F income taken into account by such shareholder by reason of this section were allocations from such S corporation.

(4) ELECTION TO PAY DEFERRED LIABILITY IN INSTALLMENTS.—In the case of a taxpayer which elects to defer payment under paragraph (1)—

(A) subsection (h) shall be applied separately with respect to the liability to which such election applies,

(B) an election under subsection (h) with respect to such liability shall be treated as timely made if made not later than the due date for the return of tax for the taxable year in which the triggering event with respect to such liability occurs,

(C) the first installment under subsection (h) with respect to such liability shall be paid not later than such due date (but determined without regard to any extension of time for filing the return), and

(D) if the triggering event with respect to any net tax liability is described in paragraph (2)(A)(ii), an election under subsection (h) with respect to such liability may be made only with the consent of the Secretary.

INCOME TAX—CONTROLLED FOREIGN CORPORATIONS

(5) JOINT AND SEVERAL LIABILITY OF S CORPORATION.—If any shareholder of an S corporation elects to defer payment under paragraph (1), such S corporation shall be jointly and severally liable for such payment and any penalty, addition to tax, or additional amount attributable thereto.

(6) EXTENSION OF LIMITATION ON COLLECTION.—Any limitation on the time period for the collection of a liability deferred under this subsection shall not be treated as beginning before the date of the triggering event with respect to such liability.

(7) ANNUAL REPORTING OF NET TAX LIABILITY.—

(A) IN GENERAL.—Any shareholder of an S corporation which makes an election under paragraph (1) shall report the amount of such shareholder's deferred net tax liability on such shareholder's return of tax for the taxable year for which such election is made and on the return of tax for each taxable year thereafter until such amount has been fully assessed on such returns.

(B) DEFERRED NET TAX LIABILITY.—For purposes of this paragraph, the term "deferred net tax liability" means, with respect to any taxable year, the amount of net tax liability payment of which has been deferred under paragraph (1) and which has not been assessed on a return of tax for any prior taxable year.

(C) FAILURE TO REPORT.—In the case of any failure to report any amount required to be reported under subparagraph (A) with respect to any taxable year before the due date for the return of tax for such taxable year, there shall be assessed on such return as an addition to tax 5 percent of such amount.

(8) ELECTION.—Any election under paragraph (1)—

(A) shall be made by the shareholder of the S corporation not later than the due date for such shareholder's return of tax for the taxable year which includes the close of the taxable year of such S corporation in which the amount described in subsection (a) is taken into account, and

(B) shall be made in such manner as the Secretary shall provide.

[Sec. 965(j)]

(j) REPORTING BY S CORPORATION.—Each S corporation which is a United States shareholder of a specified foreign corporation shall report in its return of tax under section 6037(a) the amount includible in its gross income for such taxable year by reason of this section and the amount of the deduction allowable by subsection (c). Any copy provided to a shareholder under section 6037(b) shall include a statement of such shareholder's pro rata share of such amounts.

[Sec. 965(k)]

(k) EXTENSION OF LIMITATION ON ASSESSMENT.—Notwithstanding section 6501, the limitation on the time period for the assessment of the net tax liability under this section (as defined in subsection (h)(6)) shall not expire before the date that is 6 years after the return for the taxable year described in such subsection was filed.

[Sec. 965(l)]

(l) RECAPTURE FOR EXPATRIATED ENTITIES.—

(1) IN GENERAL.—If a deduction is allowed under subsection (c) to a United States shareholder and such shareholder first becomes an expatriated entity at any time during the 10-year period beginning on the date of the enactment of the Tax Cuts and Jobs Act (with respect to a surrogate foreign corporation which first becomes a surrogate foreign corporation during such period), then—

(A) the tax imposed by this chapter shall be increased for the first taxable year in which such taxpayer becomes an expatriated entity by an amount equal to 35 percent of the amount of the deduction allowed under subsection (c), and

(B) no credits shall be allowed against the increase in tax under subparagraph (A).

(2) EXPATRIATED ENTITY.—For purposes of this subsection, the term "expatriated entity" has the same meaning given such term under section 7874(a)(2), except that such term shall not include an entity if the surrogate foreign corporation with respect to the entity is treated as a domestic corporation under section 7874(b).

(3) SURROGATE FOREIGN CORPORATION.—For purposes of this subsection, the term "surrogate foreign corporation" has the meaning given such term in section 7874(a)(2)(B).

[Sec. 965(m)]

(m) SPECIAL RULES FOR UNITED STATES SHAREHOLDERS WHICH ARE REAL ESTATE INVESTMENT TRUSTS.—

(1) IN GENERAL.—If a real estate investment trust is a United States shareholder in 1 or more deferred foreign income corporations—

(A) any amount required to be taken into account under section 951(a)(1) by reason of this section shall not be taken into account as gross income of the real estate investment trust for purposes of applying paragraphs (2) and (3) of section 856(c) to any taxable year for which such amount is taken into account under section 951(a)(1), and

(B) if the real estate investment trust elects the application of this subparagraph, notwithstanding subsection (a), any amount required to be taken into account under section 951(a)(1) by reason of this section shall, in lieu of the taxable year in which it would otherwise be included in gross income (for purposes of the computation of real estate investment trust taxable income under section 857(b)), be included in gross income as follows:

(i) 8 percent of such amount in the case of each of the taxable years in the 5-taxable year period beginning with the taxable year in which such amount would otherwise be included.

(ii) 15 percent of such amount in the case of the 1st taxable year following such period.

(iii) 20 percent of such amount in the case of the 2nd taxable year following such period.

(iv) 25 percent of such amount in the case of the 3rd taxable year following such period.

(2) RULES FOR TRUSTS ELECTING DEFERRED INCLUSION.—

(A) ELECTION.—Any election under paragraph (1)(B) shall be made not later than the due date for the first taxable year in the 5-taxable year period described in clause (i) of paragraph (1)(B) and shall be made in such manner as the Secretary shall provide.

(B) SPECIAL RULES.—If an election under paragraph (1)(B) is in effect with respect to any real estate investment trust, the following rules shall apply:

(i) APPLICATION OF PARTICIPATION EXEMPTION.—For purposes of subsection (c)(1)—

(I) the aggregate amount to which subparagraph (A) or (B) of subsection (c)(1) applies shall be determined without regard to the election,

(II) each such aggregate amount shall be allocated to each taxable year described in paragraph (1)(B) in the same proportion as the amount included in the gross income of such United States shareholder under section 951(a)(1) by reason of this section is allocated to each such taxable year.

(III) NO INSTALLMENT PAYMENTS.—The real estate investment trust may not make an election under subsection (g) for any taxable year described in paragraph (1)(B).

INCOME TAX—CONTROLLED FOREIGN CORPORATIONS

(ii) ACCELERATION OF INCLUSION.—If there is a liquidation or sale of substantially all the assets of the real estate investment trust (including in a title 11 or similar case), a cessation of business by such trust, or any similar circumstance, then any amount not yet included in gross income under paragraph (1)(B) shall be included in gross income as of the day before the date of the event and the unpaid portion of any tax liability with respect to such inclusion shall be due on the date of such event (or in the case of a title 11 or similar case, the day before the petition is filed).

[Sec. 965(n)]

(n) ELECTION NOT TO APPLY NET OPERATING LOSS DEDUCTION.—

(1) IN GENERAL.—If a United States shareholder of a deferred foreign income corporation elects the application of this subsection for the taxable year described in subsection (a), then the amount described in paragraph (2) shall not be taken into account—

(A) in determining the amount of the net operating loss deduction under section 172 of such shareholder for such taxable year, or

(B) in determining the amount of taxable income for such taxable year which may be reduced by net operating loss carryovers or carrybacks to such taxable year under section 172.

(2) AMOUNT DESCRIBED.—The amount described in this paragraph is the sum of—

(A) the amount required to be taken into account under section 951(a)(1) by reason of this section (determined after the application of subsection (c)), plus

(B) in the case of a domestic corporation which chooses to have the benefits of subpart A of part III of subchapter N for the taxable year, the taxes deemed to be paid by such corporation under subsections (a) and (b) of section 960 for such taxable year with respect to the amount described in subparagraph (A) which are treated as a dividends [sic] under section 78.

(3) ELECTION.—Any election under this subsection shall be made not later than the due date (including extensions) for filing the return of tax for the taxable year and shall be made in such manner as the Secretary shall prescribe.

[Sec. 965(o)]

(o) REGULATIONS.—The Secretary shall prescribe such regulations or other guidance as may be necessary or appropriate to carry out the provisions of this section, including—

(1) regulations or other guidance to provide appropriate basis adjustments, and

(2) regulations or other guidance to prevent the avoidance of the purposes of this section, including through a reduction in earnings and profits, through changes in entity classification or accounting methods, or otherwise.

Amendments

• **2017, Tax Cuts and Jobs Act (P.L. 115-97)**

P.L. 115-97, §14103(a):

Amended Code Sec. 965. **Effective** 12-22-2017. Prior to amendment, Code Sec. 965 read as follows:

SEC. 965. TEMPORARY DIVIDENDS RECEIVED DEDUCTION.

[Sec. 965(a)]

(a) DEDUCTION.—

(1) IN GENERAL.—In the case of a corporation which is a United States shareholder and for which the election under this section is in effect for the taxable year, there shall be allowed as a deduction an amount equal to 85 percent of the cash dividends which are received during such taxable year by such shareholder from controlled foreign corporations.

(2) DIVIDENDS PAID INDIRECTLY FROM CONTROLLED FOREIGN CORPORATIONS.—If, within the taxable year for which the election under this section is in effect, a United States shareholder receives a cash distribution from a controlled foreign corporation which is excluded from gross income under section 959(a), such distribution shall be treated for purposes of this section as a cash dividend to the extent of any amount included in income by such United States shareholder under section 951(a)(1)(A) as a result of any cash dividend during such taxable year to—

(A) such controlled foreign corporation from another controlled foreign corporation that is in a chain of ownership described in section 958(a), or

(B) any other controlled foreign corporation in such chain of ownership from another controlled foreign corporation in such chain of ownership, but only to the extent of cash distributions described in section 959(b) which are made during such taxable year to the controlled foreign corporation from which such United States shareholder received such distribution.

Amendments

• **2005, Gulf Opportunity Zone Act of 2005 (P.L. 109-135)**

P.L. 109-135, §403(q)(1):

Amended Code Sec. 965(a)(2)(B) by inserting "from another controlled foreign corporation in such chain of ownership" before ", but only to the extent". **Effective** as if included in the provision of the American Jobs Creation Act of 2004 (P.L. 108-357) to which it relates [**effective** for tax years ending on or after 10-22-2004.—CCH].

[Sec. 965(b)]

(b) LIMITATIONS.—

(1) IN GENERAL.—The amount of dividends taken into account under subsection (a) shall not exceed the greater of—

(A) $500,000,000,

(B) the amount shown on the applicable financial statement as earnings permanently reinvested outside the United States, or

(C) in the case of an applicable financial statement which fails to show a specific amount of earnings permanently reinvested outside the United States and which shows a specific amount of tax liability attributable to such earnings, the amount equal to the amount of such liability divided by 0.35.

The amounts described in subparagraphs (B) and (C) shall be treated as being zero if there is no such statement or such statement fails to show a specific amount of such earnings or liability, as the case may be.

(2) DIVIDENDS MUST BE EXTRAORDINARY.—The amount of dividends taken into account under subsection (a) shall not exceed the excess (if any) of—

(A) the cash dividends received during the taxable year by such shareholder from controlled foreign corporations, over

(B) the annual average for the base period years of—

(i) the dividends received during each base period year by such shareholder from controlled foreign corporations,

(ii) the amounts includible in such shareholder's gross income for each base period year under section 951(a)(1)(B) with respect to controlled foreign corporations, and

(iii) the amounts that would have been included for each base period year but for section 959(a) with respect to controlled foreign corporations.

The amount taken into account under clause (iii) for any base period year shall not include any amount which is not includible in gross income by reason of an amount described in clause (ii) with respect to a prior taxable year. Amounts described in subparagraph (B) for any base period year shall be such amounts as shown on the most recent return filed for such year; except that amended returns filed after June 30, 2003, shall not be taken into account.

(3) REDUCTION OF BENEFIT IF INCREASE IN RELATED PARTY INDEBTEDNESS.—The amount of dividends which would (but for this paragraph) be taken into account under subsection (a) shall be reduced by the excess (if any) of—

(A) the amount of indebtedness of the controlled foreign corporation to any related person (as defined in section 954(d)(3)) as of the close of the taxable year for which the election under this section is in effect, over

(B) the amount of indebtedness of the controlled foreign corporation to any related person (as so defined) as of the close of October 3, 2004.

All controlled foreign corporations with respect to which the taxpayer is a United States shareholder shall be treated as 1 controlled foreign corporation for purposes of this paragraph. The Secretary may prescribe such regulations as may be necessary or appropriate to prevent the avoidance of the purposes of this paragraph, including regulations which provide that cash dividends shall not be taken into account under subsection (a) to the extent such dividends are attributable to the direct or indirect transfer (including through the use of intervening entities or capital contributions) of cash or other property from a related person (as so defined) to a controlled foreign corporation.

(4) REQUIREMENT TO INVEST IN UNITED STATES.—Subsection (a) shall not apply to any dividend received by a United States shareholder unless the amount of the dividend is invested in the United States pursuant to a domestic reinvestment plan which—

(A) is approved by the taxpayer's president, chief executive officer, or comparable official before the payment of such dividend and subsequently approved by the taxpayer's board of directors, management committee, executive committee, or similar body, and

(B) provides for the reinvestment of such dividend in the United States (other than as payment for executive compensation), including as a source for the funding of worker hiring and training, infrastructure, research and development, capital investments, or the financial stabilization of the corporation for the purposes of job retention or creation.

Amendments

• **2005, Gulf Opportunity Zone Act of 2005 (P.L. 109-135)**

P.L. 109-135, §403(q)(2):

Amended Code Sec. 965(b)(2)(A) by inserting "cash" before "dividends". **Effective** as if included in the provision of the American Jobs Creation Act of 2004 (P.L. 108-357) to which it relates [**effective** for tax years ending on or after 10-22-2004.—CCH].

INCOME TAX—CONTROLLED FOREIGN CORPORATIONS

P.L. 109-135, § 403(q)(3):

Amended Code Sec. 965(b)(3) by adding at the end a new sentence. **Effective** as if included in the provision of the American Jobs Creation Act of 2004 (P.L. 108-357) to which it relates [**effective** for tax years ending on or after 10-22-2004.—CCH].

[Sec. 965(c)]

(c) DEFINITIONS AND SPECIAL RULES.—For purposes of this section—

(1) APPLICABLE FINANCIAL STATEMENT.—The term "applicable financial statement" means—

(A) with respect to a United States shareholder which is required to file a financial statement with the Securities and Exchange Commission (or which is included in such a statement so filed by another person), the most recent audited annual financial statement (including the notes which form an integral part of such statement) of such shareholder (or which includes such shareholder)—

(i) which was so filed on or before June 30, 2003, and

(ii) which was certified on or before June 30, 2003, as being prepared in accordance with generally accepted accounting principles, and

(B) with respect to any other United States shareholder, the most recent audited financial statement (including the notes which form an integral part of such statement) of such shareholder (or which includes such shareholder)—

(i) which was certified on or before June 30, 2003, as being prepared in accordance with generally accepted accounting principles, and

(ii) which is used for the purposes of a statement or report—

(I) to creditors,

(II) to shareholders, or

(III) for any other substantial nontax purpose.

(2) BASE PERIOD YEARS.—

(A) IN GENERAL.—The base period years are the 3 taxable years—

(i) which are among the 5 most recent taxable years ending on or before June 30, 2003, and

(ii) which are determined by disregarding—

(I) 1 taxable year for which the sum of the amounts described in clauses (i), (ii), and (iii) of subsection (b)(2)(B) is the largest, and

(II) 1 taxable year for which such sum is the smallest.

(B) SHORTER PERIOD.—If the taxpayer has fewer than 5 taxable years ending on or before June 30, 2003, then in lieu of applying subparagraph (A), the base period years shall include all the taxable years of the taxpayer ending on or before June 30, 2003.

(C) MERGERS, ACQUISITIONS, ETC.—

(i) IN GENERAL.—Rules similar to the rules of subparagraphs (A) and (B) of section 41(f)(3) shall apply for purposes of this paragraph.

(ii) SPIN-OFFS, ETC.—If there is a distribution to which section 355 (or so much of section 356 as relates to section 355) applies during the 5-year period referred to in subparagraph (A)(i) and the controlled corporation (within the meaning of section 355) is a United States shareholder—

(I) the controlled corporation shall be treated as being in existence during the period that the distributing corporation (within the meaning of section 355) is in existence, and

(II) for purposes of applying subsection (b)(2) to the controlled corporation and the distributing corporation, amounts described in subsection (b)(2)(B) which are received or includible by the distributing corporation or controlled corporation (as the case may be) before the distribution referred to in subclause (I) from a controlled foreign corporation shall be allocated between such corporations in proportion to their respective interests as United States shareholders of such controlled foreign corporation immediately after such distribution.

Subclause (II) shall not apply if neither the controlled corporation nor the distributing corporation is a United States shareholder of such controlled foreign corporation immediately after such distribution.

(3) DIVIDEND.—The term "dividend" shall not include amounts includible in gross income as a dividend under section 78, 367, or 1248. In the case of a liquidation under section 332 to which section 367(b) applies, the preceding sentence shall not apply to the extent the United States shareholder actually receives cash as part of the liquidation.

(4) COORDINATION WITH DIVIDENDS RECEIVED DEDUCTION.—No deduction shall be allowed under section 243 or 245 for any dividend for which a deduction is allowed under this section.

(5) CONTROLLED GROUPS.—

(A) IN GENERAL.—All United States shareholders which are members of an affiliated group filing a consolidated return under section 1501 shall be treated as one United States shareholder.

(B) APPLICATION OF $500,000,000 LIMIT.—All corporations which are treated as a single employer under section 52(a) shall be limited to one $500,000,000 amount in subsection (b)(1)(A), and such amount shall be divided among such corporations under regulations prescribed by the Secretary.

(C) PERMANENTLY REINVESTED EARNINGS.—If a financial statement is an applicable financial statement for more than 1 United States shareholder, the amount applicable under subparagraph (B) or (C) of subsection (b)(1) shall be divided among such shareholders under regulations prescribed by the Secretary.

Amendments

• **2005, Gulf Opportunity Zone Act of 2005 (P.L. 109-135)**

P.L. 109-135, § 403(q)(4):

Amended Code Sec. 965(c)(1). **Effective** as if included in the provision of the American Jobs Creation Act of 2004 (P.L. 108-357) to which it relates [**effective** for tax years ending on or after 10-22-2004.—CCH]. Prior to amendment, Code Sec. 965(c)(1) read as follows:

(1) APPLICABLE FINANCIAL STATEMENT.—The term "applicable financial statement" means, with respect to a United States shareholder, the most recently audited financial statement (including notes and other documents which accompany such statement) which includes such shareholder—

(A) which is certified on or before June 30, 2003, as being prepared in accordance with generally accepted accounting principles, and

(B) which is used for the purposes of a statement or report—

(i) to creditors,

(ii) to shareholders, or

(iii) for any other substantial nontax purpose.

In the case of a corporation required to file a financial statement with the Securities and Exchange Commission, such term means the most recent such statement filed on or before June 30, 2003.

[Sec. 965(d)]

(d) DENIAL OF FOREIGN TAX CREDIT; DENIAL OF CERTAIN EXPENSES.—

(1) FOREIGN TAX CREDIT.—No credit shall be allowed under section 901 for any taxes paid or accrued (or treated as paid or accrued) with respect to the deductible portion of—

(A) any dividend, or

(B) any amount described in subsection (a)(2) which is included in income under section 951(a)(1)(A).

No deduction shall be allowed under this chapter for any tax for which credit is not allowable by reason of the preceding sentence.

(2) EXPENSES.—No deduction shall be allowed for expenses directly allocable to the deductible portion described in paragraph (1).

(3) DEDUCTIBLE PORTION.—For purposes of paragraph (1), unless the taxpayer otherwise specifies, the deductible portion of any dividend or other amount is the amount which bears the same ratio to the amount of such dividend or other amount as the amount allowed as a deduction under subsection (a) for the taxable year bears to the amount described in subsection (b)(2)(A) for such year.

(4) COORDINATION WITH SECTION 78.—Section 78 shall not apply to any tax which is not allowable as a credit under section 901 by reason of this subsection.

Amendments

• **2005, Gulf Opportunity Zone Act of 2005 (P.L. 109-135)**

P.L. 109-135, § 403(q)(5):

Amended Code Sec. 965(d)(2) by striking "properly allocated and apportioned" and inserting "directly allocable". **Effective** as if included in the provision of the American Jobs Creation Act of 2004 (P.L. 108-357) to which it relates [**effective** for tax years ending on or after 10-22-2004.—CCH].

P.L. 109-135, § 403(q)(6):

Amended Code Sec. 965(d) by adding at the end a new paragraph (4). **Effective** as if included in the provision of the American Jobs Creation Act of 2004 (P.L. 108-357) to which it relates [**effective** for tax years ending on or after 10-22-2004.—CCH].

[Sec. 965(e)]

(e) INCREASE IN TAX ON INCLUDED AMOUNTS NOT REDUCED BY CREDITS, ETC.—

(1) IN GENERAL.—Any tax under this chapter by reason of nondeductible CFC dividends shall not be treated as tax imposed by this chapter for purposes of determining—

(A) the amount of any credit allowable under this chapter, or

(B) the amount of the tax imposed by section 55.

Subparagraph (A) shall not apply to the credit under section 53 or to the credit under section 27(a) with respect to taxes which are imposed by foreign countries and possessions of the United States and are attributable to such dividends.

(2) LIMITATION ON REDUCTION IN TAXABLE INCOME, ETC.—

(A) IN GENERAL.—The taxable income of any United States shareholder for any taxable year shall in no event be less than the amount of nondeductible CFC dividends received during such year.

(B) COORDINATION WITH SECTION 172.—The nondeductible CFC dividends for any taxable year shall not be taken into account—

(i) in determining under section 172 the amount of any net operating loss for such taxable year, and

(ii) in determining taxable income for such taxable year for purposes of the 2nd sentence of section 172(b)(2).

(3) NONDEDUCTIBLE CFC DIVIDENDS.—For purposes of this subsection, the term "nondeductible CFC dividends" means the excess of the amount of dividends taken into account under subsection (a) over the deduction allowed under subsection (a) for such dividends.

Amendments

• **2005, Gulf Opportunity Zone Act of 2005 (P.L. 109-135)**

P.L. 109-135, § 403(q)(7):

Amended the last sentence of Code Sec. 965(e)(1) by inserting "which are imposed by foreign countries and possessions of the United States and are" after "taxes". **Effective** as if included in the provision of the American Jobs Creation Act of 2004 (P.L. 108-357) to which it relates [**effective** for tax years ending on or after 10-22-2004.—CCH].

[Sec. 965(f)]

(f) ELECTION.—The taxpayer may elect to apply this section to—

(1) the taxpayer's last taxable year which begins before the date of the enactment of this section, or

(2) the taxpayer's first taxable year which begins during the 1-year period beginning on such date.

Such election may be made for a taxable year only if made on or before the due date (including extensions) for filing the return of tax for such taxable year.

INCOME TAX—EXPORT TRADE CORPORATIONS

Amendments
- **2005, Gulf Opportunity Zone Act of 2005 (P.L. 109-135)**

P.L. 109-135, §403(q)(8):

Amended Code Sec. 965(f) by inserting "on or" before "before the due date". **Effective** as if included in the provision of the American Jobs Creation Act of 2004 (P.L. 108-357) to which it relates [**effective** for tax years ending on or after 10-22-2004.—CCH].

- **2004, American Jobs Creation Act of 2004 (P.L. 108-357)**

P.L. 108-357, §422(a):

Amended subpart F of part III of subchapter N of chapter 1 by adding at the end a new Code Sec. 965. **Effective** for tax years ending on or after 10-22-2004.

Subpart G—Export Trade Corporations

Sec. 970.   Reduction of subpart F income of export trade corporations.
Sec. 971.   Definitions.

[Sec. 970]

SEC. 970. REDUCTION OF SUBPART F INCOME OF EXPORT TRADE CORPORATIONS.

[Sec. 970(a)]

(a) EXPORT TRADE INCOME CONSTITUTING FOREIGN BASE COMPANY INCOME.—

(1) IN GENERAL.—In the case of a controlled foreign corporation (as defined in section 957) which for the taxable year is an export trade corporation, the subpart F income (determined without regard to this subpart) of such corporation for such year shall be reduced by an amount equal to so much of the export trade income (as defined in section 971(b)) of such corporation for such year as constitutes foreign base company income (as defined in section 954), but only to the extent that such amount does not exceed whichever of the following amounts is the lesser:

(A) an amount equal to $1^1/_2$ times so much of the export promotion expenses (as defined in section 971(d)) of such corporation for such year as is properly allocable to the export trade income which constitutes foreign base company income of such corporation for such year, or

(B) an amount equal to 10 percent of so much of the gross receipts for such year (or, in the case of gross receipts arising from commissions, fees, or other compensation for its services, so much of the gross amount upon the basis of which such commissions, fees, or other compensation is computed) accruing to such export trade corporation from the sale, installation, operation, maintenance, or use of property in respect of which such corporation derives export trade income as is properly allocable to the export trade income which constitutes foreign base company income of such corporation for such year.

The allocations with respect to export trade income which constitutes foreign base company income under subparagraphs (A) and (B) shall be made under regulations prescribed by the Secretary.

(2) OVERALL LIMITATION.—The reduction under paragraph (1) for any taxable year shall not exceed an amount which bears the same ratio to the increase in the investments in export trade assets (as defined in section 971(c)) of such corporation for such year as the export trade income which constitutes foreign base company income of such corporation for such year bears to the entire export trade income of such corporation for such year.

Amendments
- **1976, Tax Reform Act of 1976 (P.L. 94-455)**

P.L. 94-455, §1906(b)(13)(A):

Amended 1954 Code by substituting "Secretary" for "Secretary or his delegate" each place it appeared. **Effective** 2-1-77.

[Sec. 970(b)—Stricken]

Amendments
- **2017, Tax Cuts and Jobs Act (P.L. 115-97)**

P.L. 115-97, §14212(b)(5):

Amended Code Sec. 970 by striking subsection (b). **Effective** for tax years of foreign corporations beginning after 12-31-2017, and to tax years of United States shareholders in which or with which such tax years of foreign corporations end. Prior to being stricken, Code Sec. 970(b) read as follows:

(b) INCLUSION OF CERTAIN PREVIOUSLY EXCLUDED AMOUNTS.—Each United States shareholder of a controlled foreign corporation which for any prior taxable year was an export trade corporation shall include in his gross income under section 951(a)(1)(A)(ii), as an amount to which section 955 (relating to withdrawal of previously excluded subpart F income from qualified investment) applies, his pro rata share of the amount of decrease in the investments in export trade assets of such corporation for such year, but only to the extent that his pro rata share of such amount does not exceed an amount equal to—

(1) his pro rata share of the sum of (A) the amounts by which the subpart F income of such corporation was reduced for all prior taxable years under subsection (a), and (B) the amounts not included in subpart F income (determined without regard to this subpart) for all prior taxable years by reason of the treatment (under section 972 as in effect before the date of the enactment of the Tax Reform Act of 1976) of two or more controlled foreign corporations which are export trade corporations as a single controlled foreign corporation, reduced by

(2) the sum of the amounts which were included in his gross income under section 951(a)(1)(A)(ii) under the provisions of this subsection for all prior taxable years.

- **1976, Tax Reform Act of 1976 (P.L. 94-455)**

P.L. 94-455, §1901(b)(27)(A):

Substituted "treatment (under section 972 as in effect before the date of the enactment of the Tax Reform Act of 1976) of two or more controlled foreign corporations which are export trade corporations as a single controlled foreign corporation" for "application of section 972" in Code Sec. 970(b)(1). **Effective** for tax years beginning after 12-31-76.

[Sec. 970(c)]

(c) INVESTMENTS IN EXPORT TRADE ASSETS.—

(1) AMOUNT OF INVESTMENTS.—For purposes of this section, the amount taken into account with respect to any export trade asset shall be its adjusted basis, reduced by any liability to which the asset is subject.

(2) INCREASE IN INVESTMENTS IN EXPORT TRADE ASSETS.—For purposes of subsection (a), the amount of increase in investments in export trade assets of any controlled foreign corporation for any taxable year is the amount by which—

(A) the amount of such investments at the close of the taxable year, exceeds

(B) the amount of such investments at the close of the preceding taxable year.

(3) DECREASE IN INVESTMENTS IN EXPORT TRADE ASSETS.—For purposes of subsection (b), the amount of decrease in investments in export trade assets of any controlled foreign corporation for any taxable year is the amount by which—

(A) the amount of such investments at the close of the preceding taxable year (reduced by an amount equal to the amount of net loss sustained during the taxable year with respect to export trade assets), exceeds

(B) the amount of such investments at the close of the taxable year.

(4) SPECIAL RULE.—A United States shareholder of an export trade corporation may, under regulations prescribed by the Secretary, make the determinations under paragraphs (2) and (3) as of the close of the 75th day after the close of the years referred to in such paragraphs in lieu of on the last day of such years. A United States shareholder of an export trade corporation may, under regulations prescribed by the Secretary, make the determinations under paragraphs (2) and (3) with respect to export trade assets described in section 971(c)(3) as of the close of the

INCOME TAX—EXPORT TRADE CORPORATIONS

years following the years referred to in such paragraphs, or as of the close of such longer period of time as such regulations may permit, in lieu of on the last day of such years and in lieu of on the day prescribed in the preceding sentence. Any election under this paragraph made with respect to any taxable year shall apply to such year and to all succeeding taxable years unless the Secretary consents to the revocation of such election.

Amendments

• **1976, Tax Reform Act of 1976 (P.L. 94-455)**

P.L. 94-455, §1906(b)(13)(A):

Amended 1954 Code by substituting "Secretary" for "Secretary or his delegate" each place it appeared. **Effective** 2-1-77.

[Sec. 971]

SEC. 971. DEFINITIONS.

[Sec. 971(a)]

(a) EXPORT TRADE CORPORATIONS.—For purposes of this subpart, the term "export trade corporation" means—

(1) IN GENERAL.—A controlled foreign corporation (as defined in section 957) which satisfies the following conditions:

(A) 90 percent or more of the gross income of such corporation for the 3-year period immediately preceding the close of the taxable year (or such part of such period subsequent to the effective date of this subpart during which the corporation was in existence) was derived from sources without the United States, and

(B) 75 percent or more of the gross income of such corporation for such period constituted gross income in respect of which such corporation derived export trade income.

(2) SPECIAL RULE.—If 50 percent or more of the gross income of a controlled foreign corporation in the period specified in subsection (a)(1)(A) is gross income in respect of which such corporation derived export trade income in respect of agricultural products grown in the United States, it may qualify as an export trade corporation although it does not meet the requirements of subsection (a)(1)(B).

(3) LIMITATION.—No controlled foreign corporation may qualify as an export trade corporation for any taxable year beginning after October 31, 1971, unless it qualified as an export trade corporation for any taxable year beginning before such date. If a corporation fails to qualify as an export trade corporation for a period of any 3 consecutive taxable years beginning after such date, it may not qualify as an export trade corporation for any taxable year beginning after such period.

Amendments

• **1971, Revenue Act of 1971 (P.L. 92-178)**

P. L. 92-178, §505:

Amended Code Sec. 971(a) by adding paragraph (3). **Effective** as noted in Code Sec. 971(a)(3).

P.L. 92-178, §505(a)-(b), provides:

"(a) Use of Terms—Except as otherwise expressly provided, whenever in this section a reference is made to a section, chapter, or other provision, the reference shall be considered to be made to a section, chapter, or other provision of the Internal Revenue Code of 1954, and terms used in this section shall have the same meaning as when used in such Code.

"(b) Transfer to a DISC of Assets of Export Trade Corporation.—

"(1) In general.—If a corporation (hereinafter in this section called "parent") owns all of the outstanding stock of an export trade corporation (as defined in section 971), and the export trade corporation, during a taxable year beginning before January 1, 1976, transfers property, without receiving consideration, to a DISC (as defined in section 992(a)) all of whose outstanding stock is owned by the parent, and if the amount transferred by the export trade corporation is not less than the amount of its untaxed subpart F income (as defined in paragraph (2) of this subsection) at the time of such transfer, then—

"(A) notwithstanding section 367 or any other provision of chapter 1, no gain or loss to the export trade corporation, the parent, or the DISC shall be recognized by reason of such transfer;

"(B) the earnings and profits of the DISC shall be increased by the amount transferred to it by the export trade corporation and such amount shall be included in accumulated DISC income, and for purposes of section 861(a)(2)(D) shall be considered to be qualified export receipts;

"(C) the adjusted basis of the assets transferred to the DISC shall be the same in the hands of the DISC as in the hands of the export trade corporation;

"(D) the earnings and profits of the export trade corporation shall be reduced by the amount transferred to the DISC, to the extent thereof, with the reduction being applied first to the untaxed subpart F income and then to the other earnings and profits in the order in which they were most recently accumulated;

"(E) the basis of the parent's stock in the export trade corporation shall be decreased by the amount obtained by multiplying its basis in such stock by a fraction the numerator of which is the amount transferred to the DISC and the denominator of which is the aggregate adjusted basis of all the assets of the export trade corporation immediately before such transfer;

"(F) the basis of the parent's stock in the DISC shall be increased by the amount of the reduction under subparagraph (E) of its basis in the stock of the export trade corporation;

"(G) the property transferred to the DISC shall not be considered to reduce the investments of the export trade corporation in export trade assets for purposes of applying section 970(b); and

"(H) any foreign income taxes which would have been deemed under section 902 to have been paid by the parent if the transfer had been made to the parent shall be treated as foreign income taxes paid by the DISC.

For purposes of this section, the amount transferred by the export trade corporation to the DISC shall be the aggregate of the adjusted basis of the properties transferred, with proper adjustment for any indebtedness secured by such property or assumed by the DISC in connection with the transfer. For purposes of this section, a foreign corporation which qualified as an export trade corporation for any 3 taxable years beginning before November 1, 1971, shall be treated as an export trade corporation.

"(2) Definition of untaxed subpart F income.—For purposes of this section, the term 'untaxed subpart F income' means with respect to an export trade corporation the amount by which—

"(A) the sum of the amounts by which the subpart F income of such corporation was reduced for the taxable year and all prior taxable years under section 970(a) and the amounts not included in subpart F income (determined without regard to subpart G of subchapter N of chapter 1) for all prior taxable years by reason of the application of section 972, exceeds

"(B) the sum of the amounts which were included in the gross income of the shareholders of such corporation under section 951(a)(1)(A)(ii) and under the provision of section 970(b) for all prior taxable years, determined without regard to the transfer of property described in paragraph (1) of this subsection.

"(3) Special cases.—If the provisions of paragraph (1) of this subsection are not applicable solely because the export trade corporation or the DISC, or both, are not owned in the manner prescribed in such paragraph, the provisions shall nevertheless be applicable in such cases to the extent, and in accordance with such rules, as may be prescribed by the Secretary or his delegate.

"(4) Treatment of export trade assets.—If the provisions of this subsection are applicable, accounts receivable held by an export trade corporation and transferred to a DISC, to the extent such receivables were export trade assets in the hands of the export trade corporation, shall be treated as qualified export assets for purposes of section 993(b)."

[Sec. 971(b)]

(b) EXPORT TRADE INCOME.—For the purposes of this subpart the term "export trade income" means net income from—

(1) the sale to an unrelated person for use, consumption, or disposition outside the United States of export property (as defined in subsection (e)), or from commissions, fees, compensation, or other income from the performance of commercial, industrial, financial, technical, scientific, managerial, engineering, architectural, skilled, or other services in respect of such sales or in respect of the installation or maintenance of such export property;

(2) commissions, fees, compensation, or other income from commercial, industrial, financial, technical, scientific, managerial, engineering, architectural, skilled, or other services performed in connection with the use by an unrelated person outside the United States of patents, copyrights, secret processes and formulas, goodwill, trademarks, trade brands, franchises, and other like property acquired or developed and owned by the manufacturer, producer, grower, or extractor of export property in respect of which the export trade corporation earns export trade income under paragraph (1);

(3) commissions, fees, rentals, or other compensation or income attributable to the use of export property by an unrelated person or attributable to the use of export property in the rendition of technical, scientific, or engineering services to an unrelated person; and

(4) interest from export trade assets described in subsection (c)(4).

INCOME TAX—EXPORT TRADE CORPORATIONS

For purposes of paragraph (3), if a controlled foreign corporation receives income from an unrelated person attributable to the use of export property in the rendition of services to such unrelated person together with income attributable to the rendition of other services to such unrelated person, including personal services, the amount of such aggregate income which shall be considered to be attributable to the use of the export property shall (if such amount cannot be established by reference to transactions between unrelated persons) be that part of such aggregate income which the cost of the export property consumed in the rendition of such services (including a reasonable allowance for depreciation) bears to the total costs and expenses attributable to such aggregate income.

[Sec. 971(c)]

(c) EXPORT TRADE ASSETS.—For purposes of this subpart, the term "export trade assets" means—

(1) working capital reasonably necessary for the production of export trade income,

(2) inventory of export property held for use, consumption, or disposition outside the United States,

(3) facilities located outside the United States for the storage, handling, transportation, packaging, or servicing of export property, and

(4) evidences of indebtedness executed by persons, other than related persons, in connection with payment for purchases of export property for use, consumption, or disposition outside the United States, or in connection with the payment for services described in subsections (b)(2) and (3).

[Sec. 971(d)]

(d) EXPORT PROMOTION EXPENSES.—For purposes of this subpart, the term "export promotion expenses" means the following expenses paid or incurred in the receipt or production of export trade income—

(1) a reasonable allowance for salaries or other compensation for personal services actually rendered for such purpose,

(2) rentals or other payments for the use of property actually used for such purpose,

(3) a reasonable allowance for the exhaustion, wear and tear, or obsolescence of property actually used for such purpose, and

(4) any other ordinary and necessary expenses of the corporation to the extent reasonably allocable to the receipt or production of export trade income.

No expense incurred within the United States shall be treated as an export promotion expense within the meaning of the preceding sentence, unless at least 90 percent of each category of expenses described in such sentence is incurred outside the United States.

[Sec. 971(e)]

(e) EXPORT PROPERTY.—For purposes of this subpart, the term "export property" means any property or any interest in property manufactured, produced, grown, or extracted in the United States.

[Sec. 971(f)]

(f) UNRELATED PERSON.—For purposes of this subpart, the term "unrelated person" means a person other than a related person as defined in section 954(d)(3).

Subpart H—Income of Certain Nonresident United States Citizens Subject to Foreign Community Property Law—[Repealed]

[Sec. 981—Repealed]

Amendments

- 1976, Tax Reform Act of 1976 (P.L. 94-455)

P.L. 94-455, § 1012(b)(3):

Repealed Code Sec. 981. **Effective** for tax years beginning after 1976. Prior to repeal, Code Sec. 981 read:

SEC. 981. ELECTION AS TO TREATMENT OF INCOME SUBJECT TO FOREIGN COMMUNITY PROPERTY LAWS.

(a) GENERAL RULE.—In the case of any taxable year beginning after December 31, 1966, if—

(1) an individual is (A) a citizen of the United States, (B) a bona fide resident of a foreign country or countries during the entire taxable year, and (C) married at the close of the taxable year to a spouse who is a nonresident alien during the entire taxable year, and

(2) such individual and his spouse elect to have subsection (b) apply to their community income under foreign community property laws,

then subsection (b) shall apply to such income of such individual and such spouse for the taxable year and for all subsequent taxable years for which the requirements of paragraph (1) are met, unless the Secretary or his delegate consents to a termination of the election.

(b) TREATMENT OF COMMUNITY INCOME.—For any taxable year to which an election made under subsection (a) applies, the community income under foreign community property laws of the husband and wife making the election shall be treated as follows:

(1) Earned income (within the meaning of the first sentence of section 911(b)), other than trade or business income and a partner's distributive share of partnership income, shall be treated as the income of the spouse who rendered the personal services.

(2) Trade or business income, and a partner's distributive share of partnership income, shall be treated as provided in section 1402(a)(5).

(3) Community income not described in paragraph (1) or (2) which is derived from the separate property (as determined under the applicable foreign community property law) of one spouse shall be treated as the income of such spouse.

(4) All other such community income shall be treated as provided in the applicable foreign community property law.

(c) ELECTION FOR PRE-1967 YEARS.—

(1) ELECTION.—If an individual meets the requirements of subsections (a)(1)(A) and (C) for any taxable year beginning before January 1, 1967, and if such individual and the spouse referred to in subsection (a)(1)(C) elect under this subsection, then paragraph (2) of this subsection shall apply to their community income under foreign community property laws for all open taxable years beginning before January 1, 1967 (whether under this chapter, the corresponding provisions of the Internal Revenue Code of 1939, or the corresponding provisions of prior revenue laws), for which the requirements of subsection (a)(1)(A) and (C) are met.

(2) EFFECT OF ELECTION.—For any taxable year to which an election made under this subsection applies, the community income under foreign community property laws of the husband and wife making the election shall be treated as provided by subsection (b), except that the other community income described in paragraph (4) of subsection (b) shall be treated as the income of the spouse who, for such taxable year, had gross income under paragraphs (1), (2), and (3) of subsection (b), plus separate gross income, greater than that of the other spouse.

(d) TIME FOR MAKING ELECTIONS; PERIOD OF LIMITATIONS; ETC.

(1) TIME.—An election under subsection (a) or (c) for a taxable year may be made at any time while such year is still open, and shall be made in such manner as the Secretary or his delegate shall by regulations prescribe.

(2) EXTENSION OF PERIOD FOR ASSESSING DEFICIENCIES AND MAKING REFUNDS.—If any taxable year to which an election under subsection (a) or (c) applies is open at the time such election is made, the period for assessing a deficiency against, and the period for filing claim for credit or refund of any overpayment by, the husband and wife for such taxable year, to the extent such deficiency or overpayment is attributable to such an election, shall not expire before 1 year after the date of such election.

(3) ALIEN SPOUSE NEED NOT JOIN IN SUBSECTION (c) ELECTION IN CERTAIN CASES.—If the Secretary or his delegate determines—

(A) that an election under subsection (c) would not affect the liability for Federal income tax of the spouse referred to in subsection (a)(1)(C) for any taxable year, or

(B) that the effect on such liability for tax cannot be ascertained and that to deny the election to the citizen of the United States would be inequitable and cause undue hardship,

such spouse shall not be required to join in such election, and paragraph (2) of this subsection shall not apply with respect to such spouse.

(4) INTEREST.—To the extent that any overpayment or deficiency for a taxable year is attributable to an election made under this section, no interest shall be allowed or paid for any period before the day which is 1 year after the date of such election.

(e) DEFINITIONS AND SPECIAL RULES.—For purposes of this section—

(1) DEDUCTIONS.—Deductions shall be treated in a manner consistent with the manner provided by this section for the income to which they relate.

(2) OPEN YEARS.—A taxable year of a citizen of the United States and his spouse shall be treated as "open" if the period for assessing a deficiency against such citizen for such year has not expired before the date of the election under subsection (a) or (c), as the case may be.

(3) ELECTIONS IN CASE OF DECEDENTS.—If a husband or wife is deceased his election under this section may be made by his executor, administrator, or other person charged with his property.

(4) DEATH OF SPOUSE DURING TAXABLE YEAR.—In applying subsection (a)(1)(C), and in determining under subsection (c)(2) which spouse has the greater income for a taxable year, if a husband or wife dies the taxable year of the surviving spouse shall be treated as ending on the date of such death.

INCOME TAX—FOREIGN-BASED DOCUMENTATION

• 1966, Foreign Investors Tax Act of 1966 (P.L. 89-809)

P.L. 89-809, §105(e):

Added Code Sec. 981. **Effective** 11-13-66.

Subpart I—Admissibility of Documentation Maintained in Foreign Countries

Sec. 982.   Admissibility of documentation maintained in foreign countries.

[Sec. 982]

SEC. 982. ADMISSIBILITY OF DOCUMENTATION MAINTAINED IN FOREIGN COUNTRIES.

[Sec. 982(a)]

(a) GENERAL RULE.—If the taxpayer fails to substantially comply with any formal document request arising out of the examination of the tax treatment of any item (hereinafter in this section referred to as the "examined item") before the 90th day after the date of the mailing of such request on motion by the Secretary, any court having jurisdiction of a civil proceeding in which the tax treatment of the examined item is an issue shall prohibit the introduction by the taxpayer of any foreign-based documentation covered by such request.

[Sec. 982(b)]

(b) REASONABLE CAUSE EXCEPTION.—

(1) IN GENERAL.—Subsection (a) shall not apply with respect to any documentation if the taxpayer establishes that the failure to provide the documentation as requested by the Secretary is due to reasonable cause.

(2) FOREIGN NONDISCLOSURE LAW NOT REASONABLE CAUSE.—For purposes of paragraph (1), the fact that a foreign jurisdiction would impose a civil or criminal penalty on the taxpayer (or any other person) for disclosing the requested documentation is not reasonable cause.

[Sec. 982(c)]

(c) FORMAL DOCUMENT REQUEST.—For purposes of this section—

(1) FORMAL DOCUMENT REQUEST.—The term "formal document request" means any request (made after the normal request procedures have failed to produce the requested documentation) for the production of foreign-based documentation which is mailed by registered or certified mail to the taxpayer at his last known address and which sets forth—

(A) the time and place for the production of the documentation,

(B) a statement of the reason the documentation previously produced (if any) is not sufficient,

(C) a description of the documentation being sought, and

(D) the consequences to the taxpayer of the failure to produce the documentation described in subparagraph (C).

(2) PROCEEDING TO QUASH.—

(A) IN GENERAL.—Notwithstanding any other law or rule of law, any person to whom a formal document request is mailed shall have the right to begin a proceeding to quash such request not later than the 90th day after the day such request was mailed. In any such proceeding, the Secretary may seek to compel compliance with such request.

(B) JURISDICTION.—The United States district court for the district in which the person (to whom the formal document request is mailed) resides or is found shall have jurisdiction to hear any proceeding brought under subparagraph (A). An order denying the petition shall be deemed a final order which may be appealed.

(C) SUSPENSION OF 90-DAY PERIOD.—The running of the 90-day period referred to in subsection (a) shall be suspended during any period during which a proceeding brought under subparagraph (A) is pending.

[Sec. 982(d)]

(d) DEFINITIONS AND SPECIAL RULES.—For purposes of this section—

(1) FOREIGN-BASED DOCUMENTATION.—The term "foreign-based documentation" means any documentation which is outside the United States and which may be relevent or material to the tax treatment of the examined item.

(2) DOCUMENTATION.—The term "documentation" includes books and records.

(3) AUTHORITY TO EXTEND 90-DAY PERIOD.—The Secretary, and any court having jurisdiction over a proceeding under subsection (c)(2), may extend the 90-day period referred to in subsection (a).

Amendments

• 1984, Deficit Reduction Act of 1984 (P.L. 98-369)

P.L. 98-369, §714(k):

Amended Code Sec. 982(d) by striking out paragraph (3) and by redesignating paragraph (4) as paragraph (3). **Effective** as if included in the provision of P.L. 97-248 to which it relates. Prior to amendment, paragraph (3) read as follows:

(3) Foreign-Connected.—An item shall be treated as foreign connected if—

(A) such item is directly or indirectly from a source outside the United States, or

(B) such item (in whole or in part)—

(i) purports to arise outside the United States, or

(ii) is otherwise dependent on transactions occurring outside the United States.

[Sec. 982(e)]

(e) SUSPENSION OF STATUTE OF LIMITATIONS.—If any person takes any action as provided in subsection (c)(2), the running of any period of limitations under section 6501 (relating to the assessment and collection of tax) or under section 6531 (relating to criminal prosecutions) with respect to such person shall be suspended for the period during which the proceeding under such subsection, and appeals therein, are pending.

Amendments

• 1982, Tax Equity and Fiscal Responsibility Act of 1982 (P.L. 97-248)

P.L. 97-248, §337(a):

Added subpart I. **Effective** with respect to formal document requests (as defined in Code Sec. 982(c)(1)) mailed after 9-3-82.

Subpart J—Foreign Currency Transactions

Sec. 985.   Functional currency.
Sec. 986.   Determination of foreign taxes and foreign corporation's earnings and profits.
Sec. 987.   Branch transactions.
Sec. 988.   Treatment of certain foreign currency transactions.
Sec. 989.   Other definitions and special rules.

INCOME TAX—FOREIGN CURRENCY TRANSACTIONS

[Sec. 985]

SEC. 985. FUNCTIONAL CURRENCY.

[Sec. 985(a)]

(a) IN GENERAL.—Unless otherwise provided in regulations, all determinations under this subtitle shall be made in the taxpayer's functional currency.

[Sec. 985(b)]

(b) FUNCTIONAL CURRENCY.—

(1) IN GENERAL.—For purposes of this subtitle, the term "functional currency" means—

(A) except as provided in subparagraph (B), the dollar, or

(B) in the case of a qualified business unit, the currency of the economic environment in which a significant part of such unit's activities are conducted and which is used by such unit in keeping its books and records.

(2) FUNCTIONAL CURRENCY WHERE ACTIVITIES PRIMARILY CONDUCTED IN DOLLARS.—The functional currency of any qualified business unit shall be the dollar if activities of such unit are primarily conducted in dollars.

(3) ELECTION.—To the extent provided in regulations, the taxpayer may elect to use the dollar as the functional currency for any qualified business unit if—

(A) such unit keeps its books and records in dollars, or

(B) the taxpayer uses a method of accounting that approximates a separate transactions method.

Any such election shall apply to the taxable year for which made and all subsequent taxable years unless revoked with the consent of the Secretary.

(4) CHANGE IN FUNCTIONAL CURRENCY TREATED AS A CHANGE IN METHOD OF ACCOUNTING.—Any change in the functional currency shall be treated as a change in the taxpayer's method of accounting for purposes of section 481 under procedures to be established by the Secretary.

Amendments

• **1986, Tax Reform Act of 1986 (P.L. 99-514)**

P.L. 99-514, §1261(a):

Added new Code Sec. 985. **Effective** for tax years beginning after 12-31-86. However, see Act Sec. 1261(e)(2), below, for special rules.

P.L. 99-514, §1261(e)(2), provides:

(2) SPECIAL RULES FOR PURPOSES OF SECTIONS 902 AND 960.—For purposes of applying sections 902 and 960 of the Internal Revenue Code of 1986, the amendments made by this section shall apply to—

(A) earnings and profits of the foreign corporation for taxable years beginning after December 31, 1986, and

(B) foreign taxes paid or accrued by the foreign corporation with respect to such earnings and profits.

[Sec. 986]

SEC. 986. DETERMINATION OF FOREIGN TAXES AND FOREIGN CORPORATION'S EARNINGS AND PROFITS.

[Sec. 986(a)]

(a) FOREIGN INCOME TAXES.—

(1) TRANSLATION OF ACCRUED TAXES.—

(A) IN GENERAL.—For purposes of determining the amount of the foreign tax credit, in the case of a taxpayer who takes foreign income taxes into account when accrued, the amount of any foreign income taxes (and any adjustment thereto) shall be translated into dollars by using the average exchange rate for the taxable year to which such taxes relate.

(B) EXCEPTION FOR CERTAIN TAXES.—Subparagraph (A) shall not apply to any foreign income taxes—

(i) paid after the date 2 years after the close of the taxable year to which such taxes relate, or

(ii) paid before the beginning of the taxable year to which such taxes relate.

(C) EXCEPTION FOR INFLATIONARY CURRENCIES.—Subparagraph (A) shall not apply to any foreign income taxes the liability for which is denominated in any inflationary currency (as determined under regulations).

(D) ELECTIVE EXCEPTION FOR TAXES PAID OTHER THAN IN FUNCTIONAL CURRENCY.—

(i) IN GENERAL.—At the election of the taxpayer, subparagraph (A) shall not apply to any foreign income taxes the liability for which is denominated in any currency other than in the taxpayer's functional currency.

(ii) APPLICATION TO QUALIFIED BUSINESS UNITS.—An election under this subparagraph may apply to foreign income taxes attributable to a qualified business unit in accordance with regulations prescribed by the Secretary.

(iii) ELECTION.—Any such election shall apply to the taxable year for which made and all subsequent taxable years unless revoked with the consent of the Secretary.

(E) SPECIAL RULE FOR REGULATED INVESTMENT COMPANIES.—In the case of a regulated investment company which takes into account income on an accrual basis, subparagraphs (A) through (D) shall not apply and foreign income taxes paid or accrued with respect to such income shall be translated into dollars using the exchange rate as of the date the income accrues.

(F) CROSS REFERENCE.—

For adjustments where tax is not paid within 2 years, see section 905(c).

(2) TRANSLATION OF TAXES TO WHICH PARAGRAPH (1) DOES NOT APPLY.—For purposes of determining the amount of the foreign tax credit, in the case of any foreign income taxes to which subparagraph (A) or (E) of paragraph (1) does not apply—

(A) such taxes shall be translated into dollars using the exchange rates as of the time such taxes were paid to the foreign country or possession of the United States, and

(B) any adjustment to the amount of such taxes shall be translated into dollars using—

(i) except as provided in clause (ii), the exchange rate as of the time when such adjustment is paid to the foreign country or possession, or

(ii) in the case of any refund or credit of foreign income taxes, using the exchange rate as of the time of the original payment of such foreign income taxes.

(3) AUTHORITY TO PERMIT USE OF AVERAGE RATES.—To the extent prescribed in regulations, the average exchange rate for the period (specified in such regulations) during which the taxes or adjustment is paid may be used instead of the exchange rate as of the time of such payment.

(4) FOREIGN INCOME TAXES.—For purposes of this subsection, the term "foreign income taxes" means any income, war profits, or excess profits taxes paid or accrued to any foreign country or to any possession of the United States.

INCOME TAX—FOREIGN CURRENCY TRANSACTIONS

(a) FOREIGN TAXES.—

(1) IN GENERAL.—For purposes of determining the amount of the foreign tax credit—

(A) any foreign income taxes shall be translated into dollars using the exchange rates as of the time such taxes were paid to the foreign country or possession of the United States, and

(B) any adjustment to the amount of foreign income taxes shall be translated into dollars using—

(i) except as provided in clause (ii), the exchange rate as of the time when such adjustment is paid to the foreign country or possession, or

(ii) in the case of any refund or credit of foreign income taxes, using the exchange rate as of the time of original payment of such foreign income taxes.

(2) FOREIGN INCOME TAXES.—For purposes of paragraph (1), "foreign income taxes" means any income, war profits, or excess profits taxes paid to any foreign country or to any possession of the United States.

Amendments

• **2004, American Jobs Creation Act of 2004 (P.L. 108-357)**

P.L. 108-357, § 408(a):

Amended Code Sec. 986(a)(1) by redesignating subparagraph (D) as subparagraph (E) and by inserting after subparagraph (C) a new subparagraph (D). **Effective** for tax years beginning after 12-31-2004.

P.L. 108-357, § 408(b)(1):

Amended Code Sec. 986(a)(1), as amended by Act Sec. 408(a), by redesignating subparagraph (E) as subparagraph (F) and by inserting after subparagraph (D) a new subparagraph (E). **Effective** for tax years beginning after 12-31-2004.

P.L. 108-357, § 408(b)(2):

Amended Code Sec. 986(a)(2) by inserting "or (E)" after "subparagraph (A)". **Effective** for tax years beginning after 12-31-2004.

• **1997, Taxpayer Relief Act of 1997 (P.L. 105-34)**

P.L. 105-34, § 1102(a)(1):

Amended Code Sec. 986(a). **Effective** for taxes paid or accrued in tax years beginning after 12-31-97. Prior to amendment, Code Sec. 986(a) read as follows:

P.L. 105-34, § 1102(b)(1):

Amended Code Sec. 986(a) (as amended by Act Sec. 1102(a)) by redesignating paragraph (3) as paragraph (4) and inserting after paragraph (2) a new paragraph (3). **Effective** for taxes paid or accrued in tax years beginning after 12-31-97.

[Sec. 986(b)]

(b) EARNINGS AND PROFITS AND DISTRIBUTIONS.—For purposes of determining the tax under this subtitle—

(1) of any shareholder of any foreign corporation, the earnings and profits of such corporation shall be determined in the corporation's functional currency, and

(2) in the case of any United States person, the earnings and profits determined under paragraph (1) (when distributed, deemed distributed, or otherwise taken into account under this subtitle) shall (if necessary) be translated into dollars using the appropriate exchange rate.

Amendments

• **1988, Technical and Miscellaneous Revenue Act of 1988 (P.L. 100-647)**

P.L. 100-647, § 1012(v)(1)(A):

Amended so much of Code Sec. 986 as precedes subsection (c). **Effective** as if included in the provision of P.L. 99-514 to which it relates. Prior to amendment, so much of Code Sec. 986 as precedes subsection (c) read as follows:

SEC. 986. DETERMINATION OF FOREIGN CORPORATION'S EARNINGS AND PROFITS AND FOREIGN TAXES.

(a) EARNINGS AND PROFITS AND DISTRIBUTIONS.—For purposes of determining the tax under this subtitle—

(1) of any shareholder of any foreign corporation, the earnings and profits of such corporation shall be determined in the corporation's functional currency, and

(2) in the case of any United States person, the earnings and profits determined under paragraph (1) (when distributed, deemed distributed, or otherwise taken into account under this subtitle) shall (if necessary) be translated into dollars using the appropriate exchange rate.

(b) FOREIGN TAXES.—

(1) IN GENERAL.—In determining the amount of foreign taxes deemed paid under section 902 or 960—

(A) any foreign income taxes paid by a foreign corporation shall be translated into dollars using the exchange rates as of the time of payment, and

(B) any adjustment to the amount of foreign income taxes paid by a foreign corporation shall be translated into dollars using—

(i) except as provided in clause (ii), the appropriate exchange rate as of when such adjustment is made, and

(ii) in the case of any refund or credit of foreign taxes, using the exchange rate as of the time of original payment of such foreign income taxes.

(2) FOREIGN INCOME TAXES.—For purposes of paragraph (1), "foreign income taxes" means any income, war profits, or excess profits taxes paid to any foreign country or to any possession of the United States.

[Sec. 986(c)]

(c) PREVIOUSLY TAXED EARNINGS AND PROFITS.—

(1) IN GENERAL.—Foreign currency gain or loss with respect to distributions of previously taxed earnings and profits (as described in section 959 or 1293(c)) attributable to movements in exchange rates between the times of deemed and actual distribution shall be recognized and treated as ordinary income or loss from the same source as the associated income inclusion.

(2) DISTRIBUTIONS THROUGH TIERS.—The Secretary shall prescribe regulations with respect to the treatment of distributions of previously taxed earnings and profits through tiers of foreign corporations.

Amendments

• **1986, Tax Reform Act of 1986 (P.L. 99-514)**

P.L. 99-514, § 1261(a):

Added new Code Sec. 986. **Effective** for tax years beginning after 12-31-86. However, see Act Sec. 1261(e)(2) under the amendment note to Code Sec. 985 for special rules.

[Sec. 987]

SEC. 987. BRANCH TRANSACTIONS.

In the case of any taxpayer having 1 or more qualified business units with a functional currency other than the dollar, taxable income of such taxpayer shall be determined—

(1) by computing the taxable income or loss separately for each such unit in its functional currency,

(2) by translating the income or loss separately computed under paragraph (1) at the appropriate exchange rate, and

(3) by making proper adjustments (as prescribed by the Secretary) for transfers of property between qualified business units of the taxpayer having different functional currencies, including—

(A) treating post-1986 remittances from each such unit as made on a pro rata basis out of post-1986 accumulated earnings, and

(B) treating gain or loss determined under this paragraph as ordinary income or loss, respectively, and sourcing such gain or loss by reference to the source of the income giving rise to post-1986 accumulated earnings.

Amendments

• **1988, Technical and Miscellaneous Revenue Act of 1988 (P.L. 100-647)**

P.L. 100-647, § 1012(v)(1)(B):

Amended Code Sec. 987 by inserting "and" at the end of paragraph (2), by striking out ", and" at the end of paragraph (3) and inserting in lieu thereof a period, and by striking out paragraph (4). **Effective** as if included in the provision of P.L. 99-514 to which it relates. Prior to amendment, Code Sec. 987(4) read as follows:

(4) by translating foreign income taxes paid by each qualified business unit of the taxpayer in the same manner as provided under section 986(b).

• **1986, Tax Reform Act of 1986 (P.L. 99-514)**

P.L. 99-514, § 1261(a):

Added new Code Sec. 987. **Effective** for tax years beginning after 12-31-86. However, see Act Sec. 1261(e)(2), under the amendment note to Code Sec. 985, for special rules.

INCOME TAX—FOREIGN CURRENCY TRANSACTIONS

[Sec. 988]

SEC. 988. TREATMENT OF CERTAIN FOREIGN CURRENCY TRANSACTIONS.

[Sec. 988(a)]

(a) GENERAL RULE.—Notwithstanding any other provisions of this chapter—

(1) TREATMENT AS ORDINARY INCOME OR LOSS.—

(A) IN GENERAL.—Except as otherwise provided in this section, any foreign currency gain or loss attributable to a section 988 transaction shall be computed separately and treated as ordinary income or loss (as the case may be).

(B) SPECIAL RULE FOR FORWARD CONTRACTS, ETC.—Except as provided in regulations, a taxpayer may elect to treat any foreign currency gain or loss attributable to a forward contract, a futures contract, or option described in subsection (c)(1)(B)(iii) which is a capital asset in the hands of the taxpayer and which is not a part of a straddle (within the meaning of section 1092(c), without regard to paragraph (4) thereof) as capital gain or loss (as the case may be) if the taxpayer makes such election and identifies such transaction before the close of the day on which such transaction is entered into (or such earlier time as the Secretary may prescribe).

(2) GAIN OR LOSS TREATED AS INTEREST FOR CERTAIN PURPOSES.—To the extent provided in regulations, any amount treated as ordinary income or loss under paragraph (1) shall be treated as interest income or expense (as the case may be).

(3) SOURCE.—

(A) IN GENERAL.—Except as otherwise provided in regulations, in the case of any amount treated as ordinary income or loss under paragraph (1) (without regard to paragraph (1)(B)), the source of such amount shall be determined by reference to the residence of the taxpayer or the qualified business unit of the taxpayer on whose books the asset, liability, or item of income or expense is properly reflected.

(B) RESIDENCE.—For purposes of this subpart—

(i) IN GENERAL.—The residence of any person shall be—

(I) in the case of an individual, the country in which such individual's tax home (as defined in section 911(d)(3)) is located,

(II) in the case of any corporation, partnership, trust, or estate which is a United States person (as defined in section 7701(a)(30)), the United States, and

(III) in the case of any corporation, partnership, trust, or estate which is not a United States person, a country other than the United States.

If an individual does not have a tax home (as so defined), the residence of such individual shall be the United States if such individual is a United States citizen or a resident alien and shall be a country other than the United States if such individual is not a United States citizen or a resident alien.

(ii) EXCEPTION.—In the case of a qualified business unit of any taxpayer (including an individual), the residence of such unit shall be the country in which the principal place of business of such qualified business unit is located.

(iii) SPECIAL RULE FOR PARTNERSHIPS.—To the extent provided in regulations, in the case of a partnership, the determination of residence shall be made at the partner level.

(C) SPECIAL RULE FOR CERTAIN RELATED PARTY LOANS.—Except to the extent provided in regulations, in the case of a loan by a United States person or a related person to a 10-percent owned foreign corporation which is denominated in a currency other than the dollar and bears interest at a rate at least 10 percentage points higher than the Federal mid-term rate (determined under section 1274(d)) at the time such loan is entered into, the following rules shall apply:

(i) For purposes of section 904 only, such loan shall be marked to market on an annual basis.

(ii) Any interest income earned with respect to such loan for the taxable year shall be treated as income from sources within the United States to the extent of any loss attributable to clause (i).

For purposes of this subparagraph, the term "related person" has the meaning given such term by section 954(d)(3), except that such section shall be applied by substituting "United States person" for "controlled foreign corporation" each place such term appears.

(D) 10-PERCENT OWNED FOREIGN CORPORATION.—The term "10-percent owned foreign corporation" means any foreign corporation in which the United States person owns directly or indirectly at least 10 percent of the voting stock.

Amendments

• **1989, Omnibus Budget Reconciliation Act of 1989 (P.L. 101-239)**

P.L. 101-239, § 7811(i)(7):

Amended Code Sec. 988(a) by inserting "Notwithstanding any other provisions of this chapter—" after the subsection heading. **Effective** as if included in the provision of P.L. 100-647 to which it relates.

• **1988, Technical and Miscellaneous Revenue Act of 1988 (P.L. 100-647)**

P.L. 100-647, § 1012(v)(7):

Amended Code Sec. 988(a)(3)(B) by adding at the end thereof a new clause (iii). **Effective** as if included in the provision of P.L. 99-514 to which it relates.

P.L. 100-647, § 1012(v)(8):

Amended Code Sec. 988(a)(3)(B)(i) by adding at the end thereof a new sentence. **Effective** as if included in the provision of P.L. 99-514 to which it relates.

[Sec. 988(b)]

(b) FOREIGN CURRENCY GAIN OR LOSS.—For purposes of this section—

(1) FOREIGN CURRENCY GAIN.—The term "foreign currency gain" means any gain from a section 988 transaction to the extent such gain does not exceed gain realized by reason of changes in exchange rates on or after the booking date and before the payment date.

(2) FOREIGN CURRENCY LOSS.—The term "foreign currency loss" means any loss from a section 988 transaction to the extent such loss does not exceed the loss realized by reason of changes in exchange rates on or after the booking date and before the payment date.

(3) SPECIAL RULE FOR CERTAIN CONTRACTS, ETC.—In the case of any section 988 transaction described in subsection (c)(1)(B)(iii), any gain or loss from such transaction shall be treated as foreign currency gain or loss (as the case may be).

Amendments

• **1988, Technical and Miscellaneous Revenue Act of 1988 (P.L. 100-647)**

P.L. 100-647, § 1012(v)(3)(A):

Amended Code Sec. 988(b) by adding at the end thereof new paragraph (3). **Effective** as if included in the provision of P.L. 99-514 to which it relates.

[Sec. 988(c)]

(c) OTHER DEFINITIONS.—For purposes of this section—

(1) SECTION 988 TRANSACTION.—

(A) IN GENERAL.—The term "section 988 transaction" means any transaction described in subparagraph (B) if the amount which the taxpayer is entitled to receive (or is required to pay) by reason of such transaction—

(i) is denominated in terms of a nonfunctional currency, or

INCOME TAX—FOREIGN CURRENCY TRANSACTIONS

(ii) is determined by reference to the value of 1 or more nonfunctional currencies.

(B) DESCRIPTION OF TRANSACTIONS.—For purposes of subparagraph (A), the following transactions are described in this subparagraph:

(i) The acquisition of a debt instrument or becoming the obligor under a debt instrument.

(ii) Accruing (or otherwise taking into account) for purposes of this subtitle any item of expense or gross income or receipts which is to be paid or received after the date on which so accrued or taken into account.

(iii) Entering into or acquiring any forward contract, futures contract, option, or similar financial instrument.

The Secretary may prescribe regulations excluding from the application of clause (ii) any class of items the taking into account of which is not necessary to carry out the purposes of this section by reason of the small amounts or short periods involved, or otherwise.

(C) SPECIAL RULES FOR DISPOSITION OF NONFUNCTIONAL CURRENCY.—

(i) IN GENERAL.—In the case of any disposition of any nonfunctional currency—

(I) such disposition shall be treated as a section 988 transaction, and

(II) any gain or loss from such transaction shall be treated as foreign currency gain or loss (as the case may be).

(ii) NONFUNCTIONAL CURRENCY.—For purposes of this section, the term "nonfunctional currency" includes coin or currency, and nonfunctional currency denominated demand or time deposits or similar instruments issued by a bank or other financial institution.

(D) EXCEPTION FOR CERTAIN INSTRUMENTS MARKED TO MARKET.—

(i) IN GENERAL.—Clause (iii) of subparagraph (B) shall not apply to any regulated futures contract or nonequity option which would be marked to market under section 1256 if held on the last day of the taxable year.

(ii) ELECTION OUT.—

(I) IN GENERAL.—The taxpayer may elect to have clause (i) not apply to such taxpayer. Such an election shall apply to contracts held at any time during the taxable year for which such election is made or any succeeding taxable year unless such election is revoked with the consent of the Secretary.

(II) TIME FOR MAKING ELECTION.—Except as provided in regulations, an election under subclause (I) for any taxable year shall be made on or before the 1st day of such taxable year (or, if later, on or before the 1st day during such year on which the taxpayer holds a contract described in clause (i)).

(III) SPECIAL RULE FOR PARTNERSHIPS, ETC.—In the case of a partnership, an election under subclause (I) shall be made by each partner separately. A similar rule shall apply in the case of an S corporation.

(iii) TREATMENT OF CERTAIN PARTNERSHIPS.—This subparagraph shall not apply to any income or loss of a partnership for any taxable year if such partnership made an election under subparagraph (E)(iii)(V) for such year or any preceding year.

(E) SPECIAL RULES FOR CERTAIN FUNDS.—

(i) IN GENERAL.—In the case of a qualified fund, clause (iii) of subparagraph (B) shall not apply to any instrument which would be marked to market under section 1256 if held on the last day of the taxable year (determined after the application of clause (iv)).

(ii) SPECIAL RULE WHERE ELECTING PARTNERSHIP DOES NOT QUALIFY.—If any partnership made an election under clause (iii)(V) for any taxable year and such partnership has a net loss for such year or any succeeding year from instruments referred to in clause (i), the rules of clauses (i) and (iv) shall apply to any such loss year whether or not such partnership is a qualified fund for such year.

(iii) QUALIFIED FUND DEFINED.—For purposes of this subparagraph, the term "qualified fund" means any partnership if—

(I) at all times during the taxable year (and during each preceding taxable year to which an election under subclause (V) applied), such partnership has at least 20 partners and no single partner owns more than 20 percent of the interests in the capital or profits of the partnership,

(II) the principal activity of such partnership for such taxable year (and each such preceding taxable year) consists of buying and selling options, futures, or forwards with respect to commodities,

(III) at least 90 percent of the gross income of the partnership for the taxable year (and for each such preceding taxable year) consisted of income or gains described in subparagraph (A), (B), or (G) of section 7704(d)(1) or gain from the sale or disposition of capital assets held for the production of interest or dividends,

(IV) no more than a de minimis amount of the gross income of the partnership for the taxable year (and each such preceding taxable year) was derived from buying and selling commodities, and

(V) an election under this subclause applies to the taxable year.

An election under subclause (V) for any taxable year shall be made on or before the 1st day of such taxable year (or, if later, on or before the 1st day during such year on which the partnership holds an instrument referred to in clause (i)). Any such election shall apply to the taxable year for which made and all succeeding taxable years unless revoked with the consent of the Secretary.

(iv) TREATMENT OF CERTAIN CURRENCY CONTRACTS.—

(I) IN GENERAL.—Except as provided in regulations, in the case of a qualified fund, any bank forward contract, any foreign currency futures contract traded on a foreign exchange, or to the extent provided in regulations any similar instrument, which is not otherwise a section 1256 contract shall be treated as a section 1256 contract for purposes of section 1256.

(II) GAINS AND LOSSES TREATED AS SHORT-TERM.—In the case of any instrument treated as a section 1256 contract under subclause (I), subparagraph (A) of section 1256(a)(3) shall be applied by substituting "100 percent" for "40 percent" (and subparagraph (B) of such section shall not apply).

(v) SPECIAL RULES FOR CLAUSE (iii)(I).—

(I) CERTAIN GENERAL PARTNERS.—The interest of a general partner in the partnership shall not be treated as failing to meet the 20-percent ownership requirements of clause (iii)(I) for any taxable year of the partnership if, for the taxable year of the partner in which such partnership taxable year ends, such partner (and each corporation filing a consolidated return with such partner) had no ordinary income or loss from a section 988 transaction which is foreign currency gain or loss (as the case may be).

(II) TREATMENT OF INCENTIVE COMPENSATION.—For purposes of clause (iii)(I), any income allocable to a general partner as incentive compensation based on profits rather than capital shall not be taken into account in determining such partner's interest in the profits of the partnership.

(III) TREATMENT OF TAX-EXEMPT PARTNERS.—Except as provided in regulations, the interest of a partner in the partnership shall not be treated as failing to meet the 20-percent ownership requirements of clause (iii)(I) if none of the income of such partner from such partnership is subject to tax under this chapter (whether directly or through 1 or more pass-thru entities).

(IV) LOOK-THRU RULE.—In determining whether the requirements of clause (iii)(I) are met with respect to any partnership, except to the extent provided in regulations, any interest in such partnership held by another partnership shall be treated as held proportionately by the partners in such other partnership.

(vi) OTHER SPECIAL RULES.—For purposes of this subparagraph—

INCOME TAX—FOREIGN CURRENCY TRANSACTIONS

(I) RELATED PERSONS.—Interest in the partnership held by persons related to each other (within the meaning of sections 267(b) and 707(b)) shall be treated as held by 1 person.

(II) PREDECESSORS.—References to any partnership shall include a reference to any predecessor thereof.

(III) INADVERTENT TERMINATIONS.—Rules similar to the rules of section 7704(e) shall apply.

(IV) TREATMENT OF CERTAIN DEBT INSTRUMENTS.—For purposes of clause (iii)(IV), any debt instrument which is a section 988 transaction shall be treated as a commodity.

(2) BOOKING DATE.—The term "booking date" means—

(A) in the case of a transaction described in paragraph (1)(B)(i), the date of acquisition or on which the taxpayer becomes the obligor, or

(B) in the case of a transaction described in paragraph (1)(B)(ii), the date on which accrued or otherwise taken into account.

(3) PAYMENT DATE.—The term "payment date" means the date on which the payment is made or received.

(4) DEBT INSTRUMENT.—The term "debt instrument" means a bond, debenture, note, or certificate or other evidence of indebtedness. To the extent provided in regulations, such term shall include preferred stock.

(5) SPECIAL RULES WHERE TAXPAYER TAKES OR MAKES DELIVERY.—If the taxpayer takes or makes delivery in connection with any section 988 transaction described in paragraph (1)(B)(iii), any gain or loss (determined as if the taxpayer sold the contract, option, or instrument on the date on which he took or made delivery for its fair market value on such date) shall be recognized in the same manner as if such contract, option, or instrument were so sold.

Amendments

• **1988, Technical and Miscellaneous Revenue Act of 1988 (P.L. 100-647)**

P.L. 100-647, § 1012(v)(2)(A):

Amended Code Sec. 988(c) by adding at the end thereof new paragraph (5). Not **effective** in any case in which the taxpayer takes or makes delivery before 6-11-87.

P.L. 100-647, § 1012(v)(3)(B):

Amended Code Sec. 988(c)(1)(C)(i)(II). **Effective** as if included in the provision of P.L. 99-514 to which it relates. Prior to amendment, Code Sec. 988(c)(1)(C)(i)(II) read as follows:

(II) for purposes of determining the foreign currency gain or loss from such transaction, paragraphs (1) and (2) of subsection (b) shall be applied by substituting "acquisition date" for "booking date" and "disposition" for "payment date".

P.L. 100-647, § 1012(v)(3)(C):

Amended Code Sec. 988(c)(2) by inserting "or" at the end of subparagraph (A), by striking out ", or" at the end of subparagraph (B) and inserting in lieu thereof a period, and by striking out subparagraph (C). **Effective** as if included in the provision of P.L. 99-514 to which it relates. Prior to amendment, Code Sec. 988(c)(2)(C) read as follows:

(C) in the case of a transaction described in paragraph (1)(B)(iii), the date on which the position is entered into or acquired.

P.L. 100-647, § 1012(v)(3)(D):

Amended Code Sec. 988(c)(3). **Effective** as if included in the provision of P.L. 99-514 to which it relates. Prior to amendment, Code Sec. 988(c)(3) read as follows:

(3) PAYMENT DATE.—The term "payment date" means—

(A) in the case of a transaction described in paragraph (1)(B)(i) or (ii), the date on which payment is made or received, or

(B) in the case of a transaction described in paragraph (1)(B)(iii), the date payment is made or received or the date the taxpayer's rights with respect to the position are terminated.

P.L. 100-647, § 1012(v)(6):

Amended Code Sec. 988(c)(1)(B)(iii). **Effective** as if included in the provision of P.L. 99-514 to which it relates. Prior to amendment, Code Sec. 988(c)(1)(B)(iii) read as follows:

(iii) Entering into or acquiring any forward contract, futures contract, option, or similar financial instrument if such instrument is not marked to market at the close of the taxable year under section 1256.

P.L. 100-647, § 6130(a):

Amended Code Sec. 988(c)(1)(B)(iii), as amended by title I, by striking out "unless such instrument would be marked to market under section 1256 if held on the last day of the taxable year" before the period at the end thereof. For the **effective** date and special transitional rules, see Act Sec. 6130(d), below.

P.L. 100-647, § 6130(b):

Amended Code Sec. 988(c)(1) by adding at the end thereof new subparagraphs (D) and (E). For the **effective** date and special transitional rules, see Act Sec. 6130(d), below.

P.L. 100-647, § 6130(d), provides:

(d) EFFECTIVE DATE.—

(1) IN GENERAL.—The amendments made by this section shall apply with respect to forward contracts, future contracts, options, and similar instruments entered into or acquired after October 21, 1988.

(2) TIME FOR MAKING ELECTION.—The time for making any election under subparagraph (D) or (E) of section 988(c)(1) of the 1986 Code shall not expire before the date 30 days after the date of the enactment of this Act.

(3) TRANSITIONAL RULES.—

(A) The requirements of subclause (IV) of section 988(c)(1)(E)(iii) of the 1986 Code (as added by subsection (b)) shall not apply to periods before the date of the enactment of this Act.

(B) In the case of any partner in an existing partnership, the 20-percent ownership requirements of subclause (I) of such section 988(c)(1)(E)(iii) shall be treated as met during any period during which such partner does not own a percentage interest in the capital or profits of such partnership greater than $33^{1}/_{3}$ percent (or, if lower, the lowest such percentage interest of such partner during any prior period after October 21, 1988, during which such partnership is in existence). For purposes of the preceding sentence, the term "existing partnership" means any partnership if—

(i) such partnership was in existence on October 21, 1988, and principally engaged on such date in buying and selling options, futures, or forwards with respect to commodities, or

(ii) a registration statement was filed with respect to such partnership with the Securities and Exchange Commission on or before such date and such registration statement indicated that the principal activity of such partnership will consist of buying and selling instruments referred to in clause (i).

[Sec. 988(d)]

(d) TREATMENT OF 988 HEDGING TRANSACTIONS.—

(1) IN GENERAL.—To the extent provided in regulations, if any section 988 transaction is part of a 988 hedging transaction, all transactions which are part of such 988 hedging transaction shall be integrated and treated as a single transaction or otherwise treated consistently for purposes of this subtitle. For purposes of the preceding sentence, the determination of whether any transaction is a section 988 transaction shall be determined without regard to whether such transaction would otherwise be marked-to-market under Section 475 or 1256 and such term shall not include any transaction with respect to which an election is made under subsection (a)(1)(B). Sections 475, 1092, and 1256 shall not apply to a transaction covered by this subsection.

(2) 988 HEDGING TRANSACTION.—For purposes of paragraph (1), the term "988 hedging transaction" means any transaction—

(A) entered into by the taxpayer primarily—

(i) to manage risk of currency fluctuations with respect to property which is held or to be held by the taxpayer, or

(ii) to manage risk of currency fluctuations with respect to borrowings made or to be made, or obligations incurred or to be incurred, by the taxpayer, and

(B) identified by the Secretary or the taxpayer as being a 988 hedging transaction.

Amendments

• **1999, Tax Relief Extension Act of 1999 (P.L. 106-170)**

P.L. 106-170, § 532(b)(3):

Amended Code Sec. 988(d)(2)(A)(i) and (ii) by striking "to reduce" and inserting "to manage". **Effective** for any instrument held, acquired, or entered into, any transaction entered into, and supplies held or acquired on or after 12-17-99.

• **1993, Omnibus Budget Reconciliation Act of 1993 (P.L. 103-66)**

P.L. 103-66, § 13223(b)(1)(A)-(B):

Amended Code Sec. 988(d)(1) by striking "section 1256" and inserting "section 475 or 1256", and by striking "1092 and 1256" and inserting "475, 1092, and 1256". **Effective** for tax years ending on or after 12-31-93.

INCOME TAX—OTHER DEFINITIONS AND SPECIAL RULES

• **1988, Technical and Miscellaneous Revenue Act of 1988 (P.L. 100-647)**

P.L. 100-647, § 1012(v)(4):

Amended Code Sec. 988(d)(1) by striking out "this section" in the first sentence and inserting in lieu thereof "this subtitle". **Effective** as if included in the provision of P.L. 99-514 to which it relates.

[Sec. 988(e)]

(e) APPLICATION TO INDIVIDUALS.—

(1) IN GENERAL.—The preceding provisions of this section shall not apply to any section 988 transaction entered into by an individual which is a personal transaction.

(2) EXCLUSION FOR CERTAIN PERSONAL TRANSACTIONS.—If—

(A) nonfunctional currency is disposed of by an individual in any transaction, and

(B) such transaction is a personal transaction,

no gain shall be recognized for purposes of this subtitle by reason of changes in exchange rates after such currency was acquired by such individual and before such disposition. The preceding sentence shall not apply if the gain which would otherwise be recognized on the transaction exceeds $200.

(3) PERSONAL TRANSACTIONS.—For purposes of this subsection, the term "personal transaction" means any transaction entered into by an individual, except that such term shall not include any transaction to the extent that expenses properly allocable to such transaction meet the requirements of—

(A) section 162 (other than traveling expenses described in subsection (a)(2) thereof), or

(B) section 212 (other than that part of section 212 dealing with expenses incurred in connection with taxes).

Amendments

• **1997, Taxpayer Relief Act of 1997 (P.L. 105-34)**

P.L. 105-34, § 1104(a):

Amended Code Sec. 988(e). **Effective** for tax years beginning after 12-31-97. Prior to amendment, Code Sec. 988(e) read as follows:

(e) APPLICATION TO INDIVIDUALS.—This section shall apply to section 988 transactions entered into by an individual only to the extent expenses properly allocable to such transactions meet the requirements of section 162 or 212 (other than that part of section 212 dealing with expenses incurred in connection with taxes).

• **1986, Tax Reform Act of 1986 (P.L. 99-514)**

P.L. 99-514, § 1261(a):

Added new Code Sec. 988. **Effective** for tax years beginning after 12-31-86. However, see Act Sec. 1261(e)(2), under the amendment note to Code Sec. 985, for special rules.

SEC. 989. OTHER DEFINITIONS AND SPECIAL RULES.

[Sec. 989(a)]

(a) QUALIFIED BUSINESS UNIT.—For purposes of this subpart, the term "qualified business unit" means any separate and clearly identified unit of a trade or business of a taxpayer which maintains separate books and records.

[Sec. 989(b)]

(b) APPROPRIATE EXCHANGE RATE.—Except as provided in regulations, for purposes of this subpart, the term "appropriate exchange rate" means—

(1) in the case of an actual distribution of earnings and profits, the spot rate on the date such distribution is included in income,

(2) in the case of an actual or deemed sale or exchange of stock in a foreign corporation treated as a dividend under section 1248, the spot rate on the date the deemed dividend is included in income,

(3) in the case of any amounts included in income under section 951(a)(1)(A) or 1293(a), the averaged exchange rate for the taxable year of the foreign corporation, or

(4) in the case of any other qualified business unit of a taxpayer, the average exchange rate for the taxable year of such qualified business unit.

For purposes of the preceding sentence, any amount included in income under section 951(a)(1)(B) shall be treated as an actual distribution made on the last day of the taxable year for which such amount was so included.

Amendments

• **2004, American Jobs Creation Act of 2004 (P.L. 108-357)**

P.L. 108-357, § 413(c)(17):

Amended Code Sec. 989(b)(3) by striking ", 551(a)," immediately preceding "or 1293(a)". **Effective** for tax years of foreign corporations beginning after 12-31-2004, and for tax years of United States shareholders with or within which such tax years of foreign corporations end.

• **1997, Taxpayer Relief Act of 1997 (P.L. 105-34)**

P.L. 105-34, § 1102(b)(3):

Amended Code Sec. 989(b) by striking "weighted" each place it appears. **Effective** for taxes paid or accrued in tax years beginning after 12-31-97. Prior to amendment, Code Sec. 989(b) read as follows:

(b) APPROPRIATE EXCHANGE RATE.—Except as provided in regulations, for purposes of this subpart, the term "appropriate exchange rate" means—

(1) in the case of an actual distribution of earnings and profits, the spot rate on the date such distribution is included in income,

(2) in the case of an actual or deemed sale or exchange of stock in a foreign corporation treated as a dividend under section 1248, the spot rate on the date the deemed dividend is included in income,

(3) in the case of any amounts included in income under section 951(a)(1)(A), 551(a), or 1293(a), the weighted averaged exchange rate for the taxable year of the foreign corporation, or

(4) in the case of any other qualified business unit of a taxpayer, the weighted average exchange rate for the taxable year of such qualified business unit.

For purposes of the preceding sentence, any amount included in income under section 951(a)(1)(B) shall be treated as an actual distribution made on the last day of the taxable year for which such amount was so included.

• **1996, Small Business Job Protection Act of 1996 (P.L. 104-188)**

P.L. 104-188, § 1501(b)(9):

Amended Code Sec. 989(b) by striking "subparagraph (B) or (C) of section 951(a)(1)" and inserting "section 951(a)(1)(B)". **Effective** for tax years of foreign corporations beginning after 12-31-96, and to tax years of United States shareholders within which or with which such tax years of foreign corporations end.

• **1993, Omnibus Budget Reconciliation Act of 1993 (P.L. 103-66)**

P.L. 103-66, § 13231(c)(4)(C):

Amended Code Sec. 989(b) by striking "section 951(a)(1)(B)" and inserting "subparagraph (B) or (C) of section 951(a)(1)". **Effective** for tax years of foreign corporations beginning after 9-30-93, and to tax years of United States shareholders in which or with which such tax years of foreign corporations end.

• **1988, Technical and Miscellaneous Revenue Act of 1988 (P.L. 100-647)**

P.L. 100-647, § 1012(v)(5)(A)-(B):

Amended Code Sec. 989(b) by striking out "951(a)" in paragraph (3) and inserting in lieu thereof "951(a)(1)(A)", and by adding at the end thereof a new sentence. **Effective** as if included in the provision of P.L. 99-514 to which it relates.

[Sec. 989(c)]

(c) REGULATIONS.—The Secretary shall prescribe such regulations as may be necessary or appropriate to carry out the purposes of this subpart, including regulations—

INCOME TAX—DOM. INT'L SALES CORPS.

(1) setting forth procedures to be followed by taxpayers with qualified business units using a net worth method of accounting before the enactment of this subpart,

(2) limiting the recognition of foreign currency loss on certain remittances from qualified business units,

(3) providing for the recharacterization of interest and principal payments with respect to obligations denominated in certain hyperinflationary currencies,

(4) providing for alternative adjustments to the application of section 905(c),

(5) providing for the appropriate treatment of related party transactions (including transactions between qualified business units of the same taxpayer), and

(6) setting forth procedures for determining the average exchange rate for any period.

Amendments

• **1997, Taxpayer Relief Act of 1997 (P.L. 105-34)**

P.L. 105-34, §1102(b)(2):

Amended Code Sec. 989(c) by striking "and" at the end of paragraph (4), by striking the period at the end of paragraph (5) and inserting ", and", and by adding at the end thereof a new paragraph (6). **Effective** for taxes paid or accrued in tax years beginning after 12-31-97.

• **1986, Tax Reform Act of 1986 (P.L. 99-514)**

P.L. 99-514, §1261(a):

Added new Code Sec. 989. **Effective** for tax years beginning after 12-31-86. However, see Act Sec. 1261(e)(2), under the amendment note to Code Sec. 985, for special rules.

PART IV—DOMESTIC INTERNATIONAL SALES CORPORATIONS

Subpart A. Treatment of qualifying corporations.
Subpart B. Treatment of distributions to shareholders.

Subpart A—Treatment of Qualifying Corporations

Sec. 991. Taxation of a domestic international sales corporation.
Sec. 992. Requirements of a domestic international sales corporation.
Sec. 993. Definitions.
Sec. 994. Inter-company pricing rules.

[Sec. 991]

SEC. 991. TAXATION OF A DOMESTIC INTERNATIONAL SALES CORPORATION.

For purposes of the taxes imposed by this subtitle upon a DISC (as defined in section 992(a)), a DISC shall not be subject to the taxes imposed by this subtitle.

Amendments

• **1998, IRS Restructuring and Reform Act of 1998 (P.L. 105-206)**

P.L. 105-206, §6011(e)(1):

Amended Code Sec. 991 by striking "except for the tax imposed by chapter 5" before the period. **Effective** as if included in the provision of P.L. 105-34 to which it relates [effective 8-5-97.—CCH].

• **1971, Revenue Act of 1971 (P.L. 92-178)**

P. L. 92-178, §501:

Added Code Sec. 991. **Effective** for tax years ending after 12-31-71, except that a corporation may not be a DISC (as defined in Code Sec. 992(a)) for any tax year beginning before 1-1-72.

[Sec. 992]

SEC. 992. REQUIREMENTS OF A DOMESTIC INTERNATIONAL SALES CORPORATION.

[Sec. 992(a)]

(a) DEFINITION OF "DISC" AND "FORMER DISC".—

(1) DISC.—For purposes of this title, the term "DISC" means, with respect to any taxable year, a corporation which is incorporated under the laws of any State and satisfies the following conditions for the taxable year:

(A) 95 percent or more of the gross receipts (as defined in section 993(f)) of such corporation consist of qualified export receipts (as defined in section 993(a)),

(B) the adjusted basis of the qualified export assets (as defined in section 993(b)) of the corporation at the close of the taxable year equals or exceeds 95 percent of the sum of the adjusted basis of all assets of the corporation at the close of the taxable year,

(C) such corporation does not have more than one class of stock and the par or stated value of its outstanding stock is at least $2,500 on each day of the taxable year, and

(D) the corporation has made an election pursuant to subsection (b) to be treated as a DISC and such election is in effect for the taxable year.

(2) STATUS AS DISC AFTER HAVING FILED A RETURN AS A DISC.—The Secretary shall prescribe regulations setting forth the conditions under and the extent to which a corporation which has filed a return as a DISC for a taxable year shall be treated as a DISC for such taxable year for all purposes of this title, notwithstanding the fact that the corporation has failed to satisfy the conditions of paragraph (1).

(3) "FORMER DISC".—For purposes of this title, the term "former DISC" means, with respect to any taxable year, a corporation which is not a DISC for such year but was a DISC in a preceding taxable year and at the beginning of the taxable year has undistributed previously taxed income or accumulated DISC income.

Amendments

• **2007, Tax Technical Corrections Act of 2007 (P.L. 110-172)**

P.L. 110-172, §11(g)(16):

Amended Code Sec. 992(a)(1) by striking subparagraph (E), by inserting "and" at the end of subparagraph (C), and by striking ", and" at the end of subparagraph (D) and inserting a period. **Effective** 12-29-2007. Prior to being stricken, Code Sec. 992(a)(1)(E) read as follows:

(E) such corporation is not a member of any controlled group of which a FSC is a member.

• **1984, Deficit Reduction Act of 1984 (P.L. 98-369)**

P.L. 98-369, §802(c)(1):

Amended Code Sec. 992(a)(1) by striking out "and" at the end of subparagraph (C), by striking out the period at the end of subparagraph (D) and inserting in lieu thereof ", and", and by adding at the end thereof new subparagraph (E). **Effective** for transactions after 12-31-84, in tax years ending after such date.

• **1976, Tax Reform Act of 1976 (P.L. 94-455)**

P.L. 94-455, §1906(b)(13)(A):

Amended 1954 Code by substituting "Secretary" for "Secretary or his delegate" each place it appeared. **Effective** 2-1-77.

Sec. 989(c)(1)

INCOME TAX—DOM. INT'L SALES CORPS.

[Sec. 992(b)]

(b) ELECTION.—

(1) ELECTION.—

(A) An election by a corporation to be treated as a DISC shall be made by such corporation for a taxable year at any time during the 90-day period immediately preceding the beginning of the taxable year, except that the Secretary may give his consent to the making of an election at such other times as he may designate.

(B) Such election shall be made in such manner as the Secretary shall prescribe and shall be valid only if all persons who are shareholders in such corporation on the first day of the first taxable year for which such election is effective consent to such election.

(2) EFFECT OF ELECTION.—If a corporation makes an election under paragraph (1), then the provisions of this part shall apply to such corporation for the taxable year of the corporation for which made and for all succeeding taxable years and shall apply to each person who at any time is a shareholder of such corporation for all periods on or after the first day of the first taxable year of the corporation for which the election is effective.

(3) TERMINATION OF ELECTION.—

(A) REVOCATION.—An election under this subsection made by any corporation may be terminated by revocation of such election for any taxable year of the corporation after the first taxable year of the corporation for which the election is effective. A termination under this paragraph shall be effective with respect to such election—

(i) for the taxable year in which made, if made at any time during the first 90 days of such taxable year, or

(ii) for the taxable year following the taxable year in which made, if made after the close of such 90 days,

and for all succeeding taxable years of the corporation. Such termination shall be made in such manner as the Secretary shall prescribe by regulations.

(B) CONTINUED FAILURE TO BE DISC.—If a corporation is not a DISC for each of any 5 consecutive taxable years of the corporation for which an election under this subsection is effective, the election shall be terminated and not be in effect for any taxable year of the corporation after such 5th year.

Amendments

- **1976, Tax Reform Act of 1976 (P.L. 94-455)**

P.L. 94-455, § 1906(b)(13)(A):

Amended 1954 Code by substituting "Secretary" for "Secretary or his delegate" each place it appeared. **Effective** 2-1-77.

[Sec. 992(c)]

(c) DISTRIBUTIONS TO MEET QUALIFICATION REQUIREMENTS.—

(1) IN GENERAL.—Subject to the conditions provided by paragraph (2), a corporation which for a taxable year does not satisfy a condition specified in paragraph (1)(A) (relating to gross receipts) or (1)(B) (relating to assets) of subsection (a) shall nevertheless be deemed to satisfy such condition for such year if it makes a pro rata distribution of property after the close of the taxable year to its shareholders (designated at the time of such distribution as a distribution to meet qualification requirements) with respect to their stock in an amount which is equal to—

(A) if the condition of subsection (a)(1)(A) is not satisfied, the portion of such corporation's taxable income attributable to its gross receipts which are not qualified export receipts for such year,

(B) if the condition of subsection (a)(1)(B) is not satisfied, the fair market value of those assets which are not qualified export assets on the last day of such taxable year, or

(C) if neither of such conditions is satisfied, the sum of the amounts required by subparagraphs (A) and (B).

(2) REASONABLE CAUSE FOR FAILURE.—The conditions under paragraph (1) shall be deemed satisfied in the case of a distribution made under such paragraph—

(A) if the failure to meet the requirements of subsection (a)(1)(A) or (B), and the failure to make such distribution prior to the date on which made, are due to reasonable cause; and

(B) the corporation pays, within the 30-day period beginning with the day on which such distribution is made, to the Secretary, if such corporation makes such distribution after the 15th day of the 9th month after the close of the taxable year, an amount determined by multiplying (i) the amount equal to $4^{1}/_{2}$ percent of such distribution, by (ii) the number of its taxable years which begin after the taxable year with respect to which such distribution is made and before such distribution is made. For purposes of this title, any payment made pursuant to this paragraph shall be treated as interest.

(3) CERTAIN DISTRIBUTIONS MADE WITHIN $8^{1}/_{2}$ MONTHS AFTER CLOSE OF TAXABLE YEAR DEEMED FOR REASONABLE CAUSE.—A distribution made on or before the 15th day of the 9th month after the close of the taxable year shall be deemed for reasonable cause for purposes of paragraph 2(A) if—

(A) at least 70 percent of the gross receipts of such corporation for such taxable year consist of qualified export receipts, and

(B) the adjusted basis of the qualified export assets held by the corporation on the last day of each month of the taxable year equals or exceeds 70 percent of the sum of the adjusted basis of all assets held by the corporation on such day.

Amendments

- **1976, Tax Reform Act of 1976 (P.L. 94-455)**

P.L. 94-455, § 1906(b)(13)(A):

Amended 1954 Code by substituting "Secretary" for "Secretary or his delegate" each place it appeared. **Effective** 2-1-77.

[Sec. 992(d)]

(d) INELIGIBLE CORPORATIONS.—The following corporations shall not be eligible to be treated as a DISC—

(1) a corporation exempt from tax by reason of section 501,

(2) a personal holding company (as defined in section 542),

(3) a financial institution to which section 581 applies,

(4) an insurance company subject to the tax imposed by subchapter L,

(5) a regulated investment company (as defined in section 851(a)), or

(6) an S corporation.

INCOME TAX—DOM. INT'L SALES CORPS.

Amendments

• **2018, Tax Technical Corrections Act of 2018 (P.L. 115-141)**

P.L. 115-141, § 401(b)(30), Div. U:

Amended Code Sec. 992(d) by striking paragraph (6), by inserting "or" at the end of paragraph (5), and by redesignating paragraph (7) as paragraph (6). **Effective** 3-23-2018. For a special rule, see Act Sec. 401(e), Div. U, below. Prior to being stricken, Code Sec. 992(d)(6) read as follows:

(6) a China Trade Act corporation receiving the special deduction provided in section 941(a), or

P.L. 115-141, § 401(e), Div. U, provides:

(e) GENERAL SAVINGS PROVISION WITH RESPECT TO DEADWOOD PROVISIONS.—If—

(1) any provision amended or repealed by the amendments made by subsection (b) or (d) applied to—

(A) any transaction occurring before the date of the enactment of this Act,

(B) any property acquired before such date of enactment, or

(C) any item of income, loss, deduction, or credit taken into account before such date of enactment, and

(2) the treatment of such transaction, property, or item under such provision would (without regard to the amendments or repeals made by such subsection) affect the liability for tax for periods ending after such date of enactment,

nothing in the amendments or repeals made by this section shall be construed to affect the treatment of such transaction, property, or item for purposes of determining liability for tax for periods ending after such date of enactment.

• **1996, Small Business Job Protection Act of 1996 (P.L. 104-188)**

P.L. 104-188, § 1616(b)(11):

Amended Code Sec. 992(d)(3) by striking "or 593" after "581". **Effective** for tax years beginning after 12-31-95.

• **1982, Subchapter S Revision Act of 1982 (P.L. 97-354)**

P.L. 97-354, § 5(a)(32):

Amended Code Sec. 992(d)(7). **Effective** for tax years beginning after 12-31-82. Prior to amendment, it read as follows:

"(7) an electing small business corporation (as defined in section 1371(b))."

[Sec. 992(e)]

(e) COORDINATION WITH PERSONAL HOLDING COMPANY PROVISIONS IN CASE OF CERTAIN PRODUCED FILM RENTS.—If—

(1) a corporation (hereinafter in this subsection referred to as "subsidiary") was established to take advantage of the provisions of this part, and

(2) a second corporation (hereinafter in this subsection referred to as "parent") throughout the taxable year owns directly at least 80 percent of the stock of the subsidiary,

then, for purposes of applying subsection (d)(2) and section 541 (relating to personal holding company tax) to the subsidiary for the taxable year, there shall be taken into account under section 543(a)(5) (relating to produced film rents) any interest in a film acquired by the parent and transferred to the subsidiary as if such interest were acquired by the subsidiary at the time it was acquired by the parent.

Amendments

• **1971, Revenue Act of 1971 (P.L. 92-178)**

P. L. 92-178, § 501:

Added Code Sec. 992. **Effective** for tax years ending after 12-31-71, except that a corporation may not be a DISC (as defined in Code Sec. 992(a)) for any tax year beginning before 1-1-72.

[Sec. 993]

SEC. 993. DEFINITIONS AND SPECIAL RULES.

[Sec. 993(a)]

(a) QUALIFIED EXPORT RECEIPTS.—

(1) GENERAL RULE.—For purposes of this part, except as provided by regulations under paragraph (2), the qualified export receipts of a corporation are—

(A) gross receipts from the sale, exchange, or other disposition of export property,

(B) gross receipts from the lease or rental of export property, which is used by the lessee of such property outside the United States,

(C) gross receipts for services which are related and subsidiary to any qualified sale, exchange, lease, rental, or other disposition of export property by such corporation,

(D) gross receipts from the sale, exchange, or other disposition of qualified export assets (other than export property),

(E) dividends (or amounts includible in gross income under section 951) with respect to stock of a related foreign export corporation (as defined in subsection (e)),

(F) interest on any obligation which is a qualified export asset,

(G) gross receipts for engineering or architectural services for construction projects located (or proposed for location) outside the United States, and

(H) gross receipts for the performance of managerial services in furtherance of the production of other qualified export receipts of a DISC.

(2) EXCLUDED RECEIPTS.—The Secretary may under regulations designate receipts from the sale, exchange, lease, rental, or other disposition of export property, and from services, as not being receipts described in paragraph (1) if he determines that such sale, exchange, lease, rental, or other disposition, or furnishing of services—

(A) is for ultimate use in the United States;

(B) is accomplished by a subsidy granted by the United States or any instrumentality thereof;

(C) is for use by the United States or any instrumentality thereof where the use of such export property or services is required by law or regulation.

For purposes of this part, the term "qualified export receipts" does not include receipts from a corporation which is a DISC for its taxable year in which the receipts arise and which is a member of a controlled group (as defined in paragraph (3)) which includes the recipient corporation.

(3) DEFINITION OF CONTROLLED GROUP.—For purposes of this part, the term "controlled group" has the meaning assigned to the term "controlled group of corporations" by section 1563(a), except that the phrase "more than 50 percent" shall be substituted for the phrase "at least 80 percent" each place it appears therein, and section 1563(b) shall not apply.

Amendments

• **2018, Tax Technical Corrections Act of 2018 (P.L. 115-141)**

P.L. 115-141, § 401(a)(165), Div. U:

Amended the heading of Code Sec. 993 by inserting "AND SPECIAL RULES" after "DEFINITIONS". **Effective** 3-23-2018.

• **1984, Deficit Reduction Act of 1984 (P.L. 98-369)**

P.L. 98-369, § 802(c)(2):

Amended Code Sec. 993(a)(3) by striking out "such term by" and inserting in lieu thereof "the term `controlled group of corporations' by". **Effective** for transactions after 12-31-84, in tax years ending after such date.

• **1976, Tax Reform Act of 1976 (P.L. 94-455)**

P.L. 94-455, § 1906(b)(13)(A):

Amended 1954 Code by substituting "Secretary" for "Secretary or his delegate" each place it appeared. **Effective** 2-1-77.

INCOME TAX—DOM. INT'L SALES CORPS.

[Sec. 993(b)]

(b) QUALIFIED EXPORT ASSETS.—For purposes of this part, the qualified export assets of a corporation are—

(1) export property (as defined in subsection (c));

(2) assets used primarily in connection with the sale, lease, rental, storage, handling, transportation, packaging, assembly, or servicing of export property, or the performance of engineering or architectural services described in subparagraph (G) of subsection (a)(1) or managerial services in furtherance of the production of qualified export receipts described in subparagraphs (A), (B), (C), and (G) of subsection (a)(1);

(3) accounts receivable and evidences of indebtedness which arise by reason of transactions of such corporation or of another corporation which is a DISC and which is a member of a controlled group which includes such corporation described in subparagraph (A), (B), (C), (D), (G), or (H), of subsection (a)(1);

(4) money, bank deposits, and other similar temporary investments, which are reasonably necessary to meet the working capital requirements of such corporation;

(5) obligations arising in connection with a producer's loan (as defined in subsection (d));

(6) stock or securities of a related foreign export corporation (as defined in subsection (e));

(7) obligations issued, guaranteed, or insured, in whole or in part, by the Export-Import Bank of the United States or the Foreign Credit Insurance Association in those cases where such obligations are acquired from such Bank or Association or from the seller or purchaser of the goods or services with respect to which such obligations arose;

(8) obligations issued by a domestic corporation organized solely for the purpose of financing sales of export property pursuant to an agreement with the Export-Import Bank of the United States under which such corporation makes export loans guaranteed by such bank; and

(9) amounts (other than reasonable working capital) on deposit in the United States that are utilized during the period provided for in, and otherwise in accordance with, regulations prescribed by the Secretary to acquire other qualified export assets.

Amendments

• **1976, Tax Reform Act of 1976 (P.L. 94-455)**

P.L. 94-455, §1906(b)(13)(A):

Amended 1954 Code by substituting "Secretary" for "Secretary or his delegate" each place it appeared. **Effective** 2-1-77.

• **1974 (P.L. 93-482)**

P.L. 93-482, §3:

Amended Code Sec. 993(b)(3). **Effective** for tax years beginning after 12-31-73 and, at the election of the taxpayer made within 90 days after 10-26-74, effective for any tax year beginning after 12-31-71, and before 1-1-74. Prior to amendment, Code Sec. 993(b)(3) read as follows:

"(3) accounts receivable and evidences of indebtedness which arise by reason of transactions of such corporation described in subparagraph (A), (B), (C), (D), (G), or (H), of subsection (a)(1)."

[Sec. 993(c)]

(c) EXPORT PROPERTY.—

(1) IN GENERAL.—For purposes of this part, the term "export property" means property—

(A) manufactured, produced, grown, or extracted in the United States by a person other than a DISC,

(B) held primarily for sale, lease, or rental, in the ordinary course of trade or business, by, or to, a DISC, for direct use, consumption, or disposition outside the United States, and

(C) not more than 50 percent of the fair market value of which is attributable to articles imported into the United States.

In applying subparagraph (C), the fair market value of any article imported into the United States shall be its appraised value, as determined by the Secretary under section 402 of the Tariff Act of 1930 (19 U.S.C. 1401(a) in connection with its importation.

(2) EXCLUDED PROPERTY.—For purposes of this part, the term "export property" does not include—

(A) property leased or rented by a DISC for use by any member of a controlled group (as defined in subsection (a)(3)) which includes the DISC,

(B) patents, inventions, models, designs, formulas, or processes, whether or not patented, copyrights (other than films, tapes, records, or similar reproductions, for commercial or home use), good will, trademarks, trade brands, franchises, or other like property,

(C) products of a character with respect to which a deduction for depletion is allowable (including oil, gas, coal, or uranium products) under section 613 or 613A,

(D) products the export of which is prohibited or curtailed under section 7(a) of the Export Administration Act of 1979 to effectuate the policy set forth in paragraph (2)(C) of section 3 of such Act (relating to the protection of the domestic economy), or

(E) any unprocessed timber which is a softwood.

Subparagraph (C) shall not apply to any commodity or product at least 50 percent of the fair market value of which is attributable to manufacturing or processing, except that subparagraph (C) shall apply to any primary product from oil, gas, coal, or uranium. For purposes of the preceding sentence, the term "processing" does not include extracting or handling, packing, packaging, grading, storing, or transporting. For purposes of subparagraph (E), the term "unprocessed timber" means any log, cant, or similar form of timber.

(3) PROPERTY IN SHORT SUPPLY.—If the President determines that the supply of any property described in paragraph (1) is insufficient to meet the requirements of the domestic economy, he may by Executive order designate the property as in short supply. Any property so designated shall be treated as property not described in paragraph (1) during the period beginning with the date specified in the Executive order and ending with the date specified in an Executive order setting forth the President's determination that the property is no longer in short supply.

Amendments

• **1993, Omnibus Budget Reconciliation Act of 1993 (P.L. 103-66)**

P.L. 103-66, §13239(b)(1)-(2):

Amended Code Sec. 993(c)(2) by striking "or" at the end of subparagraph (C), by striking the period at the end of subparagraph (D) and inserting ", or", by adding after subparagraph (D) new subparagraph (E), and by adding at the end a new sentence. **Effective** for sales, exchanges, or other dispositions after 8-10-93.

• **1979, Export Administration Act of 1979 (P.L. 96-72)**

P.L. 96-72, §22(c):

Amended Code Sec. 993(c)(2)(D) by striking out "4(b) of the Export Administration Act of 1969 (50 U.S.C. App. 2403(b))" and inserting "7(a) of the Export Administration Act of 1979"; and by striking out "(A)" and inserting "(C)". **Effective** 10-1-79.

• **1979, Trade Agreements Act of 1979 (P.L. 96-39)**

P.L. 96-39, §202(c)(2):

Amended Code Sec. 993(c)(1) by changing "or 402a of the Tariff Act of 1930 (19 U.S.C., sec. 1401a or 1402)" to "of the Tariff Act of 1930 (19 U.S.C. 1401a)". **Effective** 1-1-81.

• **1976, Tax Reform Act of 1976 (P.L. 94-455)**

P.L. 94-455, §1101(b):

Struck out "or" at the end of Code Sec. 993(c)(2)(B), and substituted "under section 613 or 613A" for "under section 611" in Code Sec. 993(c)(2)(C). **Effective** for sales, exchanges and other dispositions made after 3-18-75, in tax years ending after such date.

P.L. 94-455, §1906(b)(13)(A):

Amended 1954 Code by substituting "Secretary" for "Secretary or his delegate" each place it appeared. **Effective** 2-1-77.

• **1975, Tax Reduction Act of 1975 (P.L. 94-12)**

P.L. 94-12, §603(a):

Amended Code Sec. 993(c)(2) by adding new subparagraphs (C) and (D) and adding the last paragraph. **Effective** for sales, exchanges, and other dispositions made after 3-18-75, in tax years ending after such date. For special rules, see Act Sec. 603(b), below.

P.L. 94-12, 603(b), as amended by P.L. 94-455, §1101(f), provides:

(b) EFFECTIVE DATES.—

INCOME TAX—DOM. INT'L SALES CORPS.

(1) IN GENERAL.—Except as provided in paragraph (2), the amendments made by subsection (a) shall apply to sales, exchanges, and other dispostions made after March 18, 1975, in taxable years ending after such date.

(2) BINDING CONTRACT.—The amendments made by subsection (a) shall not apply to sales, exchanges, and other dispositions made after March 18, 1975, but before March 19, 1980, if such sales, exchanges, and other dispositions are made pursuant to a fixed contract. The term "fixed contract" means a contract which was, on March 18, 1975, and is at all times thereafter binding on the DISC or a taxpayer which was a member of the same controlled group (within the meaning of section 993(a)(3) of the Internal Revenue Code of 1954) as the DISC, which was entered into after the date on which the DISC qualified as a DISC and the DISC and the taxpayer became members of the same controlled group, and under which the price and quantity of the products sold, exchanged, or otherwise disposed of cannot be increased.

[Sec. 993(d)]

(d) PRODUCER'S LOANS.—

(1) IN GENERAL.—An obligation, subject to the rules provided in paragraphs (2) and (3), shall be treated as arising out of a producer's loan if—

(A) the loan, when added to the unpaid balance of all other producer's loans made by the DISC, does not exceed the accumulated DISC income at the beginning of the month in which the loan is made;

(B) the obligation is evidenced by a note (or other evidence of indebtedness) with a stated maturity date not more than 5 years from the date of the loan;

(C) the loan is made to a person engaged in the United States in the manufacturing, production, growing, or extraction of export property determined without regard to subparagraph (C) or (D) of subsection (c)(2), (referred to hereinafter as the "borrower"); and

(D) at the time of such loan it is designated as a producer's loan.

(2) LIMITATION.—An obligation shall be treated as arising out of a producer's loan only to the extent that such loan, when added to the unpaid balance of all other producer's loans to the borrower outstanding at the time such loan is made, does not exceed an amount determined by multiplying the sum of—

(A) the amount of the borrower's adjusted basis determined at the beginning of the borrower's taxable year in which the loan is made, in plant, machinery, and equipment, and supporting production facilities in the United States;

(B) the amount of the borrower's property held primarily for sale, lease, or rental, to customers in the ordinary course of trade or business, at the beginning of such taxable year; and

(C) the aggregate amount of the borrower's research and experimental expenditures (within the meaning of section 174) in the United States during all preceding taxable years beginning after December 31, 1971,

by the percentage which the borrower's receipts, during the 3 taxable years immediately preceding the taxable year (but not including any taxable year commencing prior to 1972) in which the loan is made, from the sale, lease, or rental outside the United States of property which would be export property (determined without regard to subparagraph (C) or (D) of subsection (c)(2)) if held by a DISC is of the gross receipts during such 3 taxable years from the sale, lease, or rental of property held by such borrower primarily for sale, lease, or rental to customers in the ordinary course of the trade or business of such borrower.

(3) INCREASED INVESTMENT REQUIREMENT.—An obligation shall be treated as arising out of a producer's loan in a taxable year only to the extent that such loan, when added to the unpaid balance of all other producer's loans to the borrower made during such taxable year, does not exceed an amount equal to—

(A) the amount by which the sum of the adjusted basis of assets described in paragraph (2)(A) and (B) on the last day of the taxable year in which the loan is made exceeds the sum of the adjusted basis of such assets on the first day of such taxable year; plus

(B) the aggregate amount of the borrower's research and experimental expenditures (within the meaning of section 174) in the United States during such taxable year.

(4) SPECIAL LIMITATION IN THE CASE OF DOMESTIC FILM MAKER.—

(A) IN GENERAL.—In the case of a borrower who is a domestic film maker and who incurs an obligation to a DISC for the making of a film, and such DISC is engaged in the trade or business of selling, leasing, or renting films which are export property, the limitation described in paragraph (2) may be determined (to the extent provided under regulations prescribed by the Secretary) on the basis of—

(i) the sum of the amounts described in subparagraphs (A), (B), and (C) thereof plus reasonable estimates of all such amounts to be incurred at any time by the borrower with respect to films which are commenced within the taxable year in which the loan is made, and

(ii) the percentage which, based on the experience of producers of similar films, the annual receipts of such producers from the sale, lease, or rental of such films outside the United States is of the annual gross receipts of such producers from the sale, lease, or rental of such films.

(B) DOMESTIC FILM MAKER.—For purposes of this paragraph, a borrower is a domestic film maker with respect to a film if—

(i) such borrower is a United States person within the meaning of section 7701(a)(30), except that with respect to a partnership, all of the partners must be United States persons, and with respect to a corporation, all of its officers and at least a majority of its directors must be United States persons;

(ii) such borrower is engaged in the trade or business of making the film with respect to which the loan is made;

(iii) the studio, if any, used or to be used for the taking of photographs and the recording of sound incorporated into such film is located in the United States;

(iv) the aggregate playing time of portions of such film photographed outside the United States does not or will not exceed 20 percent of the playing time of such film; and

(v) not less than 80 percent of the total amount paid or to be paid for services performed in the making of such film is paid or to be paid to persons who are United States persons at the time such services are performed or consists of amounts which are fully taxable by the United States.

(C) SPECIAL RULES FOR APPLICATION OF SUBPARAGRAPH (B)(v).—For purposes of clause (v) of subparagraph (B)—

(i) there shall not be taken into account any amount which is contingent upon receipts or profits of the film and which is fully taxable by the United States (within the meaning of clause (ii)); and

(ii) any amount paid or to be paid to a United States person, to a non-resident alien individual, or to a corporation which furnishes the services of an officer or employee to the borrower with respect to the making of a film, shall be treated as fully taxable by the United States only if the total amount received by such person, individual, officer, or employee for services performed in the making of such films is fully included in gross income for purposes of this chapter.

Amendments

- **1976, Tax Reform Act of 1976 (P.L. 94-455)**

P.L. 94-455, §1101(c):

Added "determined without regard to subparagraph (C) or (D) of subsection (c)(2)," immediately after "export property" in Code Sec. 993(d)(1)(C), and added "(determined without regard to subparagraph (C) or (D) of subsection (c)(2))" immediately after "of property which would be export property" in Code Sec. 993(d)(2). **Effective** for tax years ending after 3-18-75.

P.L. 94-455, §1906(b)(13)(A):

Amended 1954 Code by substituting "Secretary" for "Secretary or his delegate" each place it appeared. **Effective** 2-1-77.

INCOME TAX—DOM. INT'L SALES CORPS.

[Sec. 993(e)]

(e) RELATED FOREIGN EXPORT CORPORATION.—In determining whether a corporation (hereinafter in this subsection referred to as "the domestic corporation") is a DISC—

(1) FOREIGN INTERNATIONAL SALES CORPORATION.—A foreign corporation is a related foreign export corporation if—

(A) stock possessing more than 50 percent of the total combined voting power of all classes of stock entitled to vote is owned directly by the domestic corporation,

(B) 95 percent or more of such foreign corporation's gross receipts for its taxable year ending with or within the taxable year of the domestic corporation consists of qualified export receipts described in subparagraphs (A), (B), (C), and (D) of subsection (a)(1) and interest on any obligation described in paragraphs (3) and (4) of subsection (b), and

(C) the adjusted basis of the qualified export assets (described in paragraphs (1), (2), (3), and (4) of subsection (b)) held by such foreign corporation at the close of such taxable year equals or exceeds 95 percent of the sum of the adjusted basis of all assets held by it at the close of such taxable year.

(2) REAL PROPERTY HOLDING COMPANY.—A foreign corporation is a related foreign export corporation if—

(A) stock possessing more than 50 percent of the total combined voting power of all classes of stock entitled to vote is owned directly by the domestic corporation, and

(B) its exclusive function is to hold real property for the exclusive use (under a lease or otherwise) of the domestic corporation.

(3) ASSOCIATED FOREIGN CORPORATION.—A foreign corporation is a related foreign export corporation if—

(A) less than 10 percent of the total combined voting power of all classes of stock entitled to vote of such foreign corporation is owned (within the meaning of section 1563(d) and (e)) by the domestic corporation or by a controlled group of corporations (within the meaning of section 1563) of which the domestic corporation is a member, and

(B) the ownership of stock or securities in such foreign corporation by the domestic corporation is determined (under regulations prescribed by the Secretary) to be reasonably in furtherance of a transaction or transactions giving rise to qualified export receipts of the domestic corporation.

Amendments

• **1976, Tax Reform Act of 1976 (P.L. 94-455)**

P.L. 94-455, § 1906(b)(13)(A):

Amended 1954 Code by substituting "Secretary" for "Secretary or his delegate" each place it appeared. **Effective** 2-1-77.

[Sec. 993(f)]

(f) GROSS RECEIPTS.—For purposes of this part, the term "gross receipts" means the total receipts from the sale, lease, or rental of property held primarily for sale, lease, or rental in the ordinary course of trade or business, and gross income from all other sources. In the case of commissions on the sale, lease, or rental of property, the amount taken into account for purposes of this part as gross receipts shall be the gross receipts on the sale, lease, or rental of the property on which such commissions arose.

[Sec. 993(g)]

(g) UNITED STATES DEFINED.—For purposes of this part, the term "United States" includes the Commonwealth of Puerto Rico and the possessions of the United States.

Amendments

• **1971, Revenue Act of 1971 (P.L. 92-178)**

P.L. 92-178, § 501:

Added Code Sec. 993. **Effective** for tax years ending after 12-31-71, except that a corporation may not be a DISC (as defined in Code Sec. 992(a)) for any tax year beginning before 1-1-72.

[Sec. 994]

SEC. 994. INTER-COMPANY PRICING RULES.

[Sec. 994(a)]

(a) IN GENERAL.—In the case of a sale of export property to a DISC by a person described in section 482, the taxable income of such DISC and such person shall be based upon a transfer price which would allow such DISC to derive taxable income attributable to such sale (regardless of the sales price actually charged) in an amount which does not exceed the greatest of—

(1) 4 percent of the qualified export receipts on the sale of such property by the DISC plus 10 percent of the export promotion expenses of such DISC attributable to such receipts,

(2) 50 percent of the combined taxable income of such DISC and such person which is attributable to the qualified export receipts on such property derived as the result of a sale by the DISC plus 10 percent of the export promotion expenses of such DISC attributable to such receipts, or

(3) taxable income based upon the sale price actually charged (but subject to the rules provided in section 482).

[Sec. 994(b)]

(b) RULES FOR COMMISSIONS, RENTALS, AND MARGINAL COSTING.—The Secretary shall prescribe regulations setting forth—

(1) rules which are consistent with the rules set forth in subsection (a) for the application of this section in the case of commissions, rentals, and other income, and

(2) rules for the allocation of expenditures in computing combined taxable income under subsection (a)(2) in those cases where a DISC is seeking to establish or maintain a market for export property.

Amendments

• **1976, Tax Reform Act of 1976 (P.L. 94-455)**

P.L. 94-455, § 1906(b)(13)(A):

Amended 1954 Code by substituting "Secretary" for "Secretary or his delegate" each place it appeared. **Effective** 2-1-77.

[Sec. 994(c)]

(c) EXPORT PROMOTION EXPENSES.—For purposes of this section, the term "export promotion expenses" means those expenses incurred to advance the distribution or sale of export property for use, consumption, or distribution outside of the United States, but does not include income taxes. Such expenses shall also include freight expenses to the extent of 50 percent of the cost of shipping export property aboard airplanes owned

INCOME TAX—DOM. INT'L SALES CORPS.

and operated by United States persons or ships documented under the laws of the United States in those cases where law or regulations does not require that such property be shipped aboard such airplanes or ships.

Amendments

• 1971, Revenue Act of 1971 (P.L. 92-178)

P.L. 92-178, § 501:

Added Code Sec. 994. **Effective** for tax years ending after 12-31-71, except that a corporation may not be a DISC (as defined in Code Sec. 992(a)) for any tax year beginning before 1-1-72.

Subpart B—Treatment of Distributions to Shareholders

Sec. 995.	Taxation of DISC income to shareholders.
Sec. 996.	Rules for allocation in the case of distributions and losses.
Sec. 997.	Special subchapter C rules.

[Sec. 995]

SEC. 995. TAXATION OF DISC INCOME TO SHAREHOLDERS.

[Sec. 995(a)]

(a) GENERAL RULE.—A shareholder of a DISC or former DISC shall be subject to taxation on the earnings and profits of a DISC as provided in this chapter, but subject to the modifications of this subpart.

[Sec. 995(b)]

(b) DEEMED DISTRIBUTIONS.—

(1) DISTRIBUTIONS IN QUALIFIED YEARS.—A shareholder of a DISC shall be treated as having received a distribution taxable as a dividend with respect to his stock in an amount which is equal to his pro rata share of the sum (or, if smaller, the earnings and profits for the taxable year) of—

(A) the gross interest derived during the taxable year from producer's loans,

(B) the gain recognized by the DISC during the taxable year on the sale or exchange of property, other than property which in the hands of the DISC is a qualified export asset, previously transferred to it in a transaction in which gain was not recognized in whole or in part, but only to the extent that the transferor's gain on the previous transfer was not recognized,

(C) the gain (other than the gain described in subparagraph (B)) recognized by the DISC during the taxable year on the sale or exchange of property (other than property which in the hands of the DISC is stock in trade or other property described in section 1221(a)(1)) previously transferred to it in a transaction in which gain was not recognized in whole or in part, but only to the extent that the transferor's gain on the previous transfer was not recognized and would have been treated as ordinary income if the property had been sold or exchanged rather than transferred to the DISC,

(D) 50 percent of the taxable income of the DISC for the taxable year attributable to military property.[,]

(E) the taxable income of the DISC attributable to qualified export receipts of the DISC for the taxable year which exceed $10,000,000,

(F) the sum of—

(i) in the case of a shareholder which is a C corporation, one-seventeenth of the excess of the taxable income of the DISC for the taxable year, before reduction for any distributions during the year, over the sum of the amounts deemed distributed for the taxable year under subparagraphs (A), (B), (C), (D), and (E),

(ii) an amount equal to $^{16}/_{17}$ of the excess referred to in clause (i) multiplied by the international boycott factor determined under section 999, and

(iii) any illegal bribe, kickback, or other payment (within the meaning of section 162(c)) paid by or on behalf of the DISC directly or indirectly to an official, employee, or agent in fact of a government, and

(G) the amount of foreign investment attributable to producer's loans (as defined in subsection (d)) of a DISC for the taxable year.

Distributions described in this paragraph shall be deemed to be received on the last day of the taxable year of the DISC in which the income was derived. In the case of a distribution described in subparagraph (G), earnings and profits for the taxable year shall include accumulated earnings and profits.

(2) DISTRIBUTIONS UPON DISQUALIFICATION.—

(A) A shareholder of a corporation which revoked its election to be treated as a DISC or failed to satisfy the conditions of section 992(a)(1) for a taxable year shall be deemed to have received (at the time specified in subparagraph (B)) a distribution taxable as a dividend equal to his pro rata share of the DISC income of such corporation accumulated during the immediately preceding consecutive taxable years for which the corporation was a DISC.

(B) Distributions described in subparagraph (A) shall be deemed to be received in equal installments on the last day of each of the 10 taxable years of the corporation following the year of the termination or disqualification described in subparagraph (A) (but in no case over more than twice the number of immediately preceding consecutive taxable years during which the corporation was a DISC).

(3) TAXABLE INCOME ATTRIBUTABLE TO MILITARY PROPERTY.—

(A) IN GENERAL.—For purposes of paragraph (1)(D), taxable income of a DISC for the taxable year attributable to military property shall be determined by only taking into account—

(i) the gross income of the DISC for the taxable year which is attributable to military property, and

(ii) the deductions which are properly apportioned or allocated to such income.

(B) MILITARY PROPERTY.—For purposes of subparagraph (A), the term "military property" means any property which is an arm, ammunition, or implement of war designated in the munitions list published pursuant to section 38 of the Arms Export Control Act (22 U.S.C. 2778).

(4) AGGREGATION OF QUALIFIED EXPORT RECEIPTS.—

(A) IN GENERAL.—For purposes of applying paragraph (1)(E), all DISC's which are members of the same controlled group shall be treated as a single corporation.

(B) ALLOCATION.—The dollar amount under paragraph (1)(E) shall be allocated among the DISC's which are members of the same controlled group in a manner provided in regulations prescribed by the Secretary.

INCOME TAX—DOM. INT'L SALES CORPS.

Amendments

• **2002, Job Creation and Worker Assistance Act of 2002 (P.L. 107-147)**

P.L. 107-147, §417(15):

Amended Code Sec. 995(b)(3)(B) by striking "International Security Assistance and Arms Export Control Act of 1976" and inserting "Arms Export Control Act". **Effective** 3-9-2002.

• **2000, Community Renewal Tax Relief Act of 2000 (P.L. 106-554)**

P.L. 106-554, §319(12):

Amended Code Sec. 995(b)(3)(B) by striking "the Military Security Act of 1954 (22 U.S.C. 1934)" and inserting "section 38 of the International Security Assistance and Arms Export Control Act of 1976 (22 U.S.C. 2778)". **Effective** 12-21-2000.

• **1999, Tax Relief Extension Act of 1999 (P.L. 106-170)**

P.L. 106-170, §532(c)(2)(R):

Amended Code Sec. 995(b)(1)(C) by striking "section 1221(1)" and inserting "section 1221(a)(1)". **Effective** for any instrument held, acquired, or entered into, any transaction entered into, and supplies held or acquired on or after 12-17-99.

• **1986, Tax Reform Act of 1986 (P.L. 99-514)**

P.L. 99-514, §1876(b)(2)(A)-(B):

Amended Code Sec. 995(b)(1)(F) by inserting "in the case of a shareholder which is a C corporation," before "one-seventeenth" in clause (i), and by striking out "the amount determined under clause (i)" in clause (ii) and inserting in lieu thereof "$^{16}/_{17}$ of the excess referred to in clause (i),". **Effective** as if included in the provision of P.L. 98-369 to which it relates.

• **1984, Deficit Reduction Act of 1984 (P.L. 98-369)**

P.L. 98-369, §68(d):

Amended Code Sec. 995(b)(1)(F)(i) by striking out "one-half" and inserting in lieu thereof "one-seventeenth". **Effective** for tax years beginning after 12-31-84.

P.L. 98-369, §802(b)(1):

Amended Code Sec. 995(b)(1)(E). **Effective** for transactions after 12-31-84, in tax years ending after such date. Special rules appear in Act Sec. 805(b)-(c) following Code Sec. 995(f). Prior to amendment, Code Sec. 995(b)(1)(E) read as follows:

(E) the taxable income for the taxable year attributable to base period export gross receipts (as defined in subsection (e)),

P.L. 98-369, §802(b)(2):

Amended Code Sec. 995(b) by adding new paragraph (4). **Effective** for transactions after 12-31-84, in tax years ending after such date. Special rules appear in Act Sec. 805(b)-(c) following Code Sec. 995(f).

• **1978, Revenue Act of 1978 (P.L. 95-600)**

P.L. 95-600, §703(i)(1)(A)-(B):

Amended the last two sentences of Code Sec. 995(b)(1). **Effective** 10-4-76. Prior to amendment, such sentences read:

"Distributions described in this paragraph shall be deemed to be received on the last day of the taxable year of the DISC in which the gross income (taxable income in the case of subparagraph (D)) was derived. In the case of a distribution described in subparagraph (E), earnings and profits for the taxable year shall include accumulated earnings and profits."

P.L. 95-600, §703(i)(2):

Amended Code Sec. 995(b)(1)(G) by striking out "subsection (D)" and inserting in place thereof "subsection (d)". **Effective** 10-4-76.

• **1976, Tax Reform Act of 1976 (P.L. 94-455)**

P.L. 94-455, §1063(a):

Amended Code Sec. 995(b)(1)(D) (redesignated as Code Sec. 995(b)(1)(F)) to read as prior to the amendment made by P.L. 94-455, §1065(a)(2). **Effective** for participation in or cooperation with an international boycott more than 30 days after 10-4-76. In the case of operations which constitute participation in or cooperation with an international boycott and which are carried out in accordance with the terms of a binding contract entered into before 9-2-76, the amendment applies to such participation or cooperation after 12-31-77.

P.L. 94-455, §1065(a)(2):

Amended Code Sec. 995(b)(1)(D), redesignated as Code Sec. 995(b)(1)(F), by striking out "and" at the end of clause (i) and by adding clause (iii). **Effective** for payments described in Code Sec. 162(c) made more than 30 days after 10-4-76.

P.L. 94-455, §1101(a)(1)-(3):

Redesignated Code Sec. 995(b)(1)(D) as Code Sec. 995(b)(1)(F); redesignated Code Sec. 995(b)(1)(E) as Code Sec. 995(b)(1)(G); substituted "(C), (D), and (E)" for "and (C)" in Code Sec. 995(b)(1)(F) as redesignated; added new Code Secs. 995(b)(1)(D) and 995(b)(1)(E), substituted "more than twice the number" for "more than the number" in Code Sec. 995(b)(2)(B); and added Code Sec. 995(b)(3). **Effective** for tax years beginning after 12-31-75.

P.L. 94-455, §1901(b)(3)(K):

Substituted "ordinary income" for "gain from the sale or exchange of property which is neither a capital asset nor property described in section 1231" in Code Sec. 995(b)(1)(C). **Effective** for tax years beginning after 12-31-76.

[Sec. 995(c)]

(c) GAIN ON DISPOSITION OF STOCK IN A DISC.—

(1) IN GENERAL.—If—

(A) a shareholder disposes of stock in a DISC or former DISC any gain recognized on such disposition shall be included in gross income as a dividend to the extent provided in paragraph (2), or

(B) stock of a DISC or former DISC is disposed of in a transaction in which the separate corporate existence of the DISC or former DISC is terminated other than by a mere change in place of organization, however effected, any gain realized on the disposition of such stock in the transaction shall be recognized notwithstanding any other provision of this title to the extent provided in paragraph (2) and to the extent so recognized shall be included in gross income as a dividend.

(2) AMOUNT INCLUDED.—The amounts described in paragraph (1) shall be included in gross income as a dividend to the extent of the accumulated DISC income of the DISC or former DISC which is attributable to the stock disposed of and which was accumulated in taxable years of such corporation during the period or periods the stock disposed of was held by the shareholder which disposed of such stock.

Amendments

• **1988, Technical and Miscellaneous Revenue Act of 1988 (P.L. 100-647)**

P.L. 100-647, §1006(e)(15):

Amended Code Sec. 995(c)(1) by inserting "or" at the end of subparagraph (A), by striking out ", or" at the end of subparagraph (B) and inserting in lieu thereof a period, and by striking out subparagraph (C) and the sentence following subparagraph (C). **Effective** as if included in the provision of P.L. 99-514 to which it relates. Prior to amendment, Code Sec. 995(c)(1)(C) and the sentence following subparagraph (C) read as follows:

(C) a shareholder distributes, sells, or exchanges stock in a DISC or former DISC in a transaction to which section 311, 336, or 337 applies, then an amount equal to the excess of the fair market value of such stock over its adjusted basis in the hands of the shareholder shall, notwithstanding any provision of this title, be included in gross income of the shareholder as a dividend to the extent provided in paragraph (2). Subparagraph (C) shall not apply if the person receiving the stock in the disposition has a holding period for the stock which includes the period for which the stock was held by the shareholder disposing of such stock.

• **1978, Revenue Act of 1978 (P.L. 95-600)**

P.L. 95-600, §701(u)(12)(B), (C):

Amended Code Sec. 995(c)(1). **Effective** for dispositions made after 12-31-76, in tax years ending after such date, by adding the last sentence.

• **1976, Tax Reform Act of 1976 (P.L. 94-455)**

P.L. 94-455, §1101(d)(1):

Amended Code Sec. 995(c) as amended by P.L. 95-600, §701(u)(12)(A). **Effective** for sales, exchanges, or other dispositions made after 12-31-76, in tax years ending after such date. Prior to amendment, Code Sec. 995(c) read as follows:

(c) GAIN ON DISPOSITION OF STOCK IN A DISC.—If a shareholder disposes of stock in a DISC or former DISC, any gain recognized on such disposition shall be included in gross income as a dividend to the extent of the accumulated DISC income of such DISC or former DISC which is attributable to such stock and which was accumulated in taxable years of such corporation during the period or periods the stock disposed of was held by such shareholder. If stock of the DISC or former DISC is disposed of in a transaction in which the separate corporate existence of the DISC or former DISC is terminated other than by a mere change in place of organization, however effected, any gain realized on the disposition of such stock in the transaction shall be recognized notwithstanding any other provision of this title to the extent of the accumulated DISC income of such DISC or former DISC which is attributable to such stock and which was accumulated in taxable years of such corporation during the period or periods the stock disposed of was held by the stockholder which disposed of such stock, and such gain shall be included in gross income as a dividend.

[Sec. 995(d)]

(d) FOREIGN INVESTMENT ATTRIBUTABLE TO DISC EARNINGS.—For the purposes of this part—

(1) IN GENERAL.—The amount of foreign investment attributable to producer's loans of a DISC for a taxable year shall be the smallest of—

(A) the net increase in foreign assets by members of the controlled group (as defined in section 993(a)(3)) which includes the DISC,

(B) the actual foreign investment by domestic members of such group, or

(C) the amount of outstanding producer's loans by such DISC to members of such controlled group.

Internal Revenue Code   **Sec. 995(d)(1)(C)**

INCOME TAX—DOM. INT'L SALES CORPS.

(2) NET INCREASE IN FOREIGN ASSETS.—The term "net increase in foreign assets" of a controlled group means the excess of—

(A) the amount incurred by such group to acquire assets (described in section 1231(b)) located outside the United States over,

(B) the sum of—

(i) the depreciation with respect to assets of such group located outside the United States;

(ii) the outstanding amount of stock or debt obligations of such group issued after December 31, 1971, to persons other than the United States persons or any member of such group;

(iii) one-half the earnings and profits of foreign members of such group and foreign branches of domestic members of such group;

(iv) one-half the royalties and fees paid by foreign members of such group to domestic members of such group; and

(v) the uncommitted transitional funds of the group as determined under paragraph (4).

For purposes of this paragraph, assets which are qualified export assets of a DISC (or would be qualified export assets if owned by a DISC) shall not be taken into account. Amounts described in this paragraph (other than in subparagraphs (B)(ii) and (v)) shall be taken into account only to the extent they are attributable to taxable years beginning after December 31, 1971.

(3) ACTUAL FOREIGN INVESTMENT.—The term "actual foreign investment" by domestic members of a controlled group means the sum of—

(A) contributions to capital of foreign members of the group by domestic members of the group after December 31, 1971,

(B) the outstanding amount of stock or debt obligations of foreign members of such group (other than normal trade indebtedness) issued after December 31, 1971, to domestic members of such group,

(C) amounts transferred by domestic members of the group after December 31, 1971, to foreign branches of such members, and

(D) one-half the earnings and profits of foreign members of such group and foreign branches of domestic members of such group for taxable years beginning after December 31, 1971.

As used in this subsection, the term "domestic member" means a domestic corporation which is a member of a controlled group (as defined in section 993(a)(3)), and the term "foreign member" means a foreign corporation which is a member of such a controlled group.

(4) UNCOMMITTED TRANSITIONAL FUNDS.—The uncommitted transitional funds of the group shall be an amount equal to the sum of—

(A) the excess of—

(i) the amount of stock or debt obligations of domestic members of such group outstanding on December 31, 1971, and issued on or after January 1, 1968, to persons other than United States persons or any members of such group, but only to the extent the taxpayer establishes that such amount constitutes a long-term borrowing for purposes of the foreign direct investment program, over

(ii) the net amount of actual foreign investment by domestic members of such group during the period that such stock or debt obligations have been outstanding; and

(B) the amount of liquid assets to the extent not included in subparagraph (A) held by foreign members of such group and foreign branches of domestic members of such group on October 31, 1971, in excess of their reasonable working capital needs on such date.

For purposes of this paragraph, the term "liquid assets" means money, bank deposits (not including time deposits), and indebtedness of 2 years or less to maturity on the date of acquisition; and the actual foreign investment shall be determined under paragraph (3) without regard to the date in subparagraph (A) of such paragraph and without regard to subparagraph (D) of such paragraph.

(5) SPECIAL RULE.—Under regulations prescribed by the Secretary the determinations under this subsection shall be made on a cumulative basis with proper adjustments for amounts previously taken into account.

Amendments

• **1976, Tax Reform Act of 1976 (P.L. 94-455)**

P.L. 94-455, § 1906(b)(13)(A):

Amended 1954 Code by substituting "Secretary" for "Secretary or his delegate" each place it appeared. **Effective** 2-1-77.

• **1971, Revenue Act of 1971 (P.L. 92-178)**

P.L. 92-178, § 501:

Added Code Sec. 995. **Effective** for tax years ending after 12-31-71, except that a corporation may not be a DISC (as defined in Code Sec. 992(a)) for any year beginning before 1-1-72.

[Sec. 995(e)]

(e) CERTAIN TRANSFERS OF DISC ASSETS.—If—

(1) a corporation owns, directly or indirectly, all of the stock of a subsidiary and a DISC,

(2) the subsidiary has been engaged in the active conduct of a trade or business (within the meaning of section 355(b)) throughout the 5-year period ending on the date of the transfer and continues to be so engaged thereafter, and

(3) during the taxable year of the subsidiary in which its stock is transferred and its preceding taxable year, such trade or business gives rise to qualified export receipts of the subsidiary and the DISC,

then, under such terms and conditions as the Secretary by regulations shall prescribe, transfers of assets, stock, or both, will be deemed to be a reorganization within the meaning of section 368, a transaction to which section 355 applies, an exchange of stock to which section 351 applies, or a combination thereof. The preceding sentence shall apply only to the extent that the transfer or transfers involved are for the purpose of preventing the separation of the ownership of the stock in the DISC from the ownership of the trade or business which (during the base period) produced the export gross receipts of the DISC.

Amendments

• **1984, Deficit Reduction Act of 1984 (P.L. 98-369)**

P.L. 98-369, § 802(a):

Amended Code Sec. 995 by striking out subsection (e) and by redesignating subsection (g) as subsection (e). **Effective** for transactions after 12-31-84, in tax years ending after such date. Special rules appear in Act Sec. 805(b)-(c) following Code Sec. 995(f). Prior to being stricken, Code Sec. 995(e) read as follows:

(e) DEFINITIONS AND SPECIAL RULES RELATING TO COMPUTATION OF TAXABLE INCOME ATTRIBUTABLE TO BASE PERIOD EXPORT GROSS RECEIPTS.—

(1) TAXABLE INCOME ATTRIBUTABLE TO BASE PERIOD EXPORT GROSS RECEIPTS.—For purposes of this section, the taxable income attributable to base period export gross receipts shall be an amount equal to that portion of the adjusted taxable income of a DISC which—

(A) the amount of the adjusted base period export gross receipts, bears to

INCOME TAX—DOM. INT'L SALES CORPS.

(B) the amount of the export gross receipts of the DISC for the taxable year.

(2) ADJUSTED TAXABLE INCOME.—For purposes of this section, the term "adjusted taxable income" means the income of a DISC for the taxable year, reduced by the amounts described in subparagraphs (A), (B), (C), and (D) of paragraph (1) of subsection (b).

(3) ADJUSTED BASE PERIOD EXPORT GROSS RECEIPTS.—For purposes of this section, the term "adjusted base period export gross receipts" means 67 percent of the average of the export gross receipts of the DISC for taxable years during the base period (as defined in paragraph (5)). For purposes of the preceding sentence, if any property would not qualify during the taxable year as export property by reason of section 993(c)(2), gross receipts from such property shall be excluded from export gross receipts during the taxable years in the base period.

(4) EXPORT GROSS RECEIPTS.—For purposes of this section, the term "export gross receipts" means—

(A) qualified export receipts described in subparagraphs (A), (B), (C), (G), and (H) of section 993(a)(1), reduced by

(B) 50 percent of such qualified export receipts which are attributable to military property (as defined in subsection (b)(3)(B)).

(5) BASE PERIOD.—For purposes of paragraph (3)—

(A) for any taxable year beginning before 1980, the base period shall be the taxable years beginning in 1972, 1973, 1974, and 1975, and

(B) for any taxable year beginning in any calendar year after 1979, the base period shall be the taxable years beginning in the fourth, fifth, sixth, and seventh calendar years preceding such calendar year.

(6) NO BASE PERIOD YEAR.—If a DISC did not have a taxable year beginning in a calendar year specified in paragraph (5), then, for purposes of computing the adjusted base period export gross receipts, such DISC is deemed to have a taxable year and export gross receipts of zero for that year.

(7) SHORT TAXABLE YEAR.—The Secretary shall prescribe such regulations as he deems necessary with respect to a short taxable year for purposes of computing base period export gross receipts of a DISC, or a short taxable year in which deemed distributions (as described in subsection (b)) are made, including the circumstances under which the short taxable year shall be annualized, and the proper method of annualization.

(8) CONTROLLED GROUP.—If more than one member of a controlled group (as defined in section 993(a)(3)) for the taxable year qualifies as a DISC, then subsection (b)(1)(E), this subsection, and subsection (f) shall each be applied in a manner provided by regulations prescribed by the Secretary by aggregating the export gross receipts and taxable income of such DISCs for the taxable year and by aggregating the export gross receipts of such DISCs for each taxable year in the base period.

(9) SPECIAL RULE WHERE THE OWNERSHIP OF DISC STOCK AND THE TRADE OR BUSINESS GIVING RISE TO EXPORT GROSS RECEIPTS OF THE DISC ARE SEPARATED.—

(A) IN GENERAL.—If, at any time after the beginning of the base period, there has been a separation of the ownership of the stock in the DISC from the ownership of the trade or business which (during the base period) produced the export gross receipts of the DISC, then the persons who own the trade or business during the taxable year shall be treated as having had additional export gross receipts during the base period attributable to such trade or business.

(B) EXCEPTIONS.—Subparagraph (A) shall not apply—

(i) where the stock in the DISC and the trade or business are owned throughout the taxable year by members of the same controlled group, and

(ii) to the extent that the taxpayer's ownership of the stock in the DISC for the taxable year is proportionate to his ownership during the taxable year of the trade or business.

(10) DISC BASE PERIOD ATTRIBUTED THROUGH SHAREHOLDERS IN CERTAIN CASES.—

(A) IN GENERAL.—If—

(i) any person owns 5 percent or more of the stock of a DISC (hereinafter in this paragraph referred to as "first DISC"), and

(ii) such person at any time during the base period of the first DISC owned 5 percent or more of the stock of a second DISC,

then, to the extent provided in such regulations as the Secretary may prescribe to prevent circumvention of the application of subsection (b)(1)(E), an amount equal to such shareholder's share of the base period export gross receipts of the second DISC shall be added to the base period export gross receipts of the first DISC.

(B) OWNERSHIP OF STOCK.—For purposes of subparagraph (A), the ownership of stock shall be determined under section 318.

• 1976, Tax Reform Act of 1976 (P.L. 94-455)

P.L. 94-455, §1101(a)(4):

Added Code Sec. 995(g), to read as prior to redesignation as (e) by P.L. 98-369. **Effective** for tax years beginning after 12-31-75.

P.L. 94-455, §1101(a)(4):

Added Code Sec. 995(e). **Effective** for tax years beginning after 12-31-75.

P.L. 94-455, §1101(g)(5), as amended by P.L. 95-600, §703(i)(4), (r), provides:

(5) PRORATION OF BASE PERIOD IN CASE OF FIXED CONTRACTS.—For purposes of determining adjusted base period export gross receipts (under section 995(e)(3) of the Internal Revenue Code of 1954, as amended by this section), if any DISC has export gross receipts from export property by reason of paragraph (2) of section 603(b) of the Tax Reduction Act of 1975, then the export gross receipts of such DISC for the taxable years of the base period shall be increased by an amount equal to the amount of gross receipts which were excluded from export gross receipts during each taxable year of the base period by reason of the last sentence of section 995(e)(3) of such Code multiplied by a fraction, the numerator of which is the amount of the gross receipts in the taxable year which are export gross receipts by reason of paragraph (2) of section 603(b) of the Tax Reduction Act of 1975 and the denominator of which is the amount of total gross receipts which are excluded from export gross receipts in the taxable year by reason of subparagraph (C) or (D) of paragraph (2) of section 993(c) (determined without regard to paragraph (2) of section 603(b) of the Tax Reduction Act of 1975).

[Sec. 995(f)]

(f) INTEREST ON DISC-RELATED DEFERRED TAX LIABILITY.—

(1) IN GENERAL.—A shareholder of a DISC shall pay for each taxable year interest in an amount equal to the product of—

(A) the shareholder's DISC-related deferred tax liability for such year, and

(B) the base period T-bill rate.

(2) SHAREHOLDER'S DISC-RELATED DEFERRED TAX LIABILITY.—For purposes of this subsection—

(A) IN GENERAL.—The term "shareholder's DISC-related deferred tax liability" means, with respect to any taxable year of a shareholder of a DISC, the excess of—

(i) the amount which would be the tax liability of the shareholder for the taxable year if the deferred DISC income of such shareholder for such taxable year were included in gross income as ordinary income, over

(ii) the actual amount of the tax liability of such shareholder for such taxable year.

Determinations under the preceding sentence shall be made without regard to carrybacks to such taxable year.

(B) ADJUSTMENTS FOR LOSSES, CREDITS, AND OTHER ITEMS.—The Secretary shall prescribe regulations which provide such adjustments—

(i) to the accounts of the DISC, and

(ii) to the amount of any carryover or carryback of the shareholder,

as may be necessary or appropriate in the case of net operating losses, credits, and carryovers, and carrybacks of losses and credits.

(C) TAX LIABILITY.—The term "tax liability" means the amount of the tax imposed by this chapter for the taxable year reduced by credits allowable against such tax (other than credits allowable under sections 31, 32, and 34).

(3) DEFERRED DISC INCOME.—For purposes of this subsection—

(A) IN GENERAL.—The term "deferred DISC income" means, with respect to any taxable year of a shareholder, the excess of—

(i) the shareholder's pro rata share of accumulated DISC income (for periods after 1984) of the DISC as of the close of the computation year, over

(ii) the amount of the distributions-in-excess-of-income for the taxable year of the DISC following the computation year.

(B) COMPUTATION YEAR.—For purposes of applying subparagraph (A) with respect to any taxable year of a shareholder, the computation year is the taxable year of the DISC which ends with (or within) the taxable year of the shareholder which precedes the taxable year of the shareholder for which the amount of deferred DISC income is being determined.

(C) DISTRIBUTIONS-IN-EXCESS-OF-INCOME.—For purposes of subparagraph (A), the term "distributions-in-excess-of-income" means, with respect to any taxable year of a DISC, the excess (if any) of—

(i) the amount of actual distributions to the shareholder out of accumulated DISC income, over

(ii) the shareholder's pro rata share of the DISC income for such taxable year.

(4) BASE PERIOD T-BILL RATE.—For purposes of this subsection, the term "base period T-bill rate" means the annual rate of interest determined by the Secretary to be equivalent to the average of the 1-year constant maturity Treasury yields, as published by the Board of Governors of the Federal Reserve System, for the 1-year period ending on September 30 of the calendar year ending with (or of the most recent calendar year ending before) the close of the taxable year of the shareholder.

(5) SHORT YEARS.—The Secretary shall prescribe such regulations as may be necessary for the application of this subsection to short years of the DISC, the shareholder, or both.

(6) PAYMENT AND ASSESSMENT AND COLLECTION OF INTEREST.—The interest accrued during any taxable year which a shareholder is required to pay under paragraph (1) shall be treated, for purposes of this title, as interest payable under section 6601 and shall be paid by the shareholder at the time the tax imposed by this chapter for such taxable year is required to be paid.

(7) DISC INCLUDES FORMER DISC.—For purposes of this subsection, the term "DISC" includes a former DISC.

Amendments

- **2000, Community Renewal Tax Relief Act of 2000 (P.L. 106-554)**

P.L. 106-554, §307(c):

Amended Code Sec. 995(f)(4) by striking "the average investment yield of United States Treasury bills with maturities of 52 weeks which were auctioned during the 1-year period" and inserting "the average of the 1-year constant maturity Treasury yields, as published by the Board of Governors of the Federal Reserve System, for the 1-year period". **Effective** 12-21-2000.

- **1986, Tax Reform Act of 1986 (P.L. 99-514)**

P.L. 99-514, §1876(g):

Amended Code Sec. 995(f) by adding at the end thereof new paragraph (7). **Effective** as if included in the provision of P.L. 98-369 to which it relates.

P.L. 99-514, §1876(p)(1):

Amended Code Sec. 995(f) by redesignating the paragraphs following paragraph (3) as paragraphs (4), (5), and (6). **Effective** as if included in the provision of P.L. 98-369 to which it relates.

- **1984, Deficit Reduction Act of 1984 (P.L. 98-369)**

P.L. 98-369, §802(a):

Amended Code Sec. 995 by striking out subsection (f) and by adding new subsection (f). **Effective** for transactions after 12-31-84, in tax years ending after such date. Special rules appear in Act Sec. 805(b)-(c), below. Prior to amendment, Code Sec. 995(f) read as follows:

(f) SMALL DISCs.—

(1) ADJUSTED TAXABLE INCOME OF $100,000 OR LESS.—If a DISC has adjusted taxable income of $100,000 or less for a taxable year, subsection (b)(1)(E) shall not apply with respect to such year.

(2) SPECIAL RULE.—If a DISC has adjusted taxable income of more than $100,000 for a taxable year, then the amount taken into account under subsection (b)(1)(E) shall be deemed to be an amount equal to the excess (if any) of—

(A) the amount which would (but for this paragraph) be taken into account under subsection (b)(1)(E), over

(B) twice the excess (if any) of $150,000 over the adjusted taxable income.

P.L. 98-369, §805(b)-(c), as amended by P.L. 99-514, §1876, provide:

(b) Transition Rules for DISC's.—

(1) Close of 1984 Taxable Years of DISC's.—

(A) In General.—For purposes of applying the Internal Revenue Code of 1954, the taxable year of each DISC which begins before January 1, 1985, and which (but for this paragraph) would include January 1, 1985, shall close on December 31, 1984. For purposes of such Code, the requirements of section 992(a)(1)(B) of such Code (relating to percentage of qualified export assets on last day of the taxable year) shall not apply to any taxable year ending on December 31, 1984.

(B) Underpayments of Estimated Tax.—To the extent provided in regulations prescribed by the Secretary of the Treasury or his delegate, no addition to tax shall be made under section 6654 or 6655 of such Code with respect to any underpayment of any installment required to be paid before April 13, 1985, to the extent the underpayment was created or increased by reason of subparagraph (A).

(2) Exemption of Accumulated DISC Income from Tax.—

(A) In General.—For purposes of applying the Internal Revenue Code of 1954 with respect to actual distributions made after December 31, 1984, by a DISC or former DISC which was a DISC on December 31, 1984, any accumulated DISC income of a DISC or former DISC (within the meaning of section 996(f)(1) of such Code) which is derived before January 1, 1985, shall be treated as previously taxed income (within the meaning of section 996(f)(2) of such Code) with respect to which there had previously been a deemed distribution to which section 996(e)(1) of such Code applied. For purposes of the preceding sentence, the term "actual distribution" includes a distribution in liquidation, and the earnings and profits of any corporation receiving a distribution not included in gross income by reason of the preceding sentence shall be increased by the amount of such distribution.

(B) Exception for Distribution of Amounts Previously Disqualified—Subparagraph (A) shall not apply to the distribution of any accumulated DISC income of a DISC or former DISC to which section 995(b)(2) of such Code applied by reason of any revocation or disqualification (other than a revocation which under regulations prescribed by the Secretary results solely from the provisions of this title).

(C) Treatment of Distribution of Accumulated DISC Income Received by Cooperatives.—In the case of any actual distribution received by an organization described in section 1381 of such Code and excluded from the gross income of such corporation by reason of subparagraph (A)—

(i) such amount shall not be included in gross income of any member of such organization when distributed in the form of a patronage dividend or otherwise, and

(ii) no deduction shall be allowed to such organization by reason of any such distribution.

(3) Installment Treatment of Certain Deemed Distributions of Shareholders.—

(A) In General.—Notwithstanding section 995(b) of such Code, if a shareholder of a DISC elects the application of this paragraph, any qualified distribution shall be treated, for purposes of such Code, as received by such shareholder in 10 equal installments on the last day of each of the 10 taxable years of such shareholder which begins after the first taxable year of such shareholder beginning in 1984. The preceding sentence shall apply without regard to whether the DISC exists after December 31, 1984.

(B) Qualified Distribution.—The term "qualified distribution" means any distribution which a shareholder is deemed to have received by reason of section 995(b) of such Code with respect to income derived by the DISC in the first taxable year of the DISC beginning—

(i) in 1984, and

(ii) after the date in 1984 on which the taxable year of such shareholder begins.

(C) Shorter Period for Installments.—The Secretary of the Treasury or his delegate may by regulations provide for the election by any shareholder to be treated as receiving a qualified distribution over such shorter period as the taxpayer may elect.

(D) Elections.—Any election under this paragraph shall be made at such time and in such manner as the Secretary of the Treasury or his delegate may prescribe.

(4) Treatment of Transfers from DISC to FSC.—Except to the extent provided in regulations, section 367 of such Code shall not apply to transfers made before January 1, 1986 (or, if later, the date 1 year after the date on which the corporation ceases to be a DISC), to a FSC of qualified export assets (as defined in section 993(b)

of such Code) held on August 4, 1983, by a DISC in a transaction described in section 351 or 368(a)(i) of such Code.

(5) Deemed Termination of a DISC.—Under regulations prescribed by the Secretary, if any controlled group of corporations of which a DISC is a member establishes a FSC, then any DISC which is a member of such group shall be treated as having terminated its DISC status.

(6) Definitions.—For purposes of this subsection, the terms "DISC" and "former DISC" have the respective meanings given to such terms by section 992 of such Code.

(c) Special Rule for Export Trade Corporations.—

(1) In General.—If, before January 1, 1985, any export trade corporation—

(A) makes an election under section 927(f)(1) of the Internal Revenue Code of 1954 to be treated as a FSC, or

(B) elects not to be treated as an export trade corporation with respect to taxable years beginning after December 31, 1984,

rules similar to the rules of paragraphs (2) and (4) of subsection (b) shall apply to such export trade corporation.

(2) Treatment of Transfers to FSC.—In the case of any export trade corporation which—

(A) makes an election described in paragraph (1), and

(B) transfers before January 1, 1986, any portion of its property to a FSC in a transaction described in section 351 or 368(a)(1), then, subject to such rules as the Secretary of the Treasury or his delegate may prescribe based on principles similar to the principles of section 505(a) and (b) of the Revenue Act of 1971, no income, gain, or loss shall be recognized on such transfer or on the distribution of any stock of the FSC received (or treated as received) in connection with such transfer.

(3) Export Trade Corporation.—For purposes of this subsection, the term "export trade corporation" has the meaning given such term by section 971 of the Internal Revenue Code of 1954.

P.L. 94-455, § 1101(a)(4):

Added Code Sec. 995(f). **Effective** for tax years beginning after 12-31-75.

[Sec. 995(g)]

(g) Treatment of Tax-Exempt Shareholders.—If any organization described in subsection (a)(2) or (b)(2) of section 511 (or any other person otherwise subject to tax under section 511) is a shareholder in a DISC—

(1) any amount deemed distributed to such shareholder under subsection (b),

(2) any actual distribution to such shareholder which under section 996 is treated as out of accumulated DISC income, and

(3) any gain which is treated as a dividend under subsection (c),

shall be treated as derived from the conduct of an unrelated trade or business (and the modifications of section 512(b) shall not apply). The rules of the preceding sentence shall apply also for purposes of determining any such shareholder's DISC-related deferred tax liability under subsection (f).

Amendments

• **1989, Omnibus Budget Reconciliation Act of 1989 (P.L. 101-239)**

P.L. 101-239, § 7811(i)(12):

Amended Code Sec. 995(g) by striking "section 511" and inserting "section 511 (or any other person otherwise subject to tax under section 511)". **Effective** as if included in the provision of P.L. 100-647 to which it relates.

• **1988, Technical and Miscellaneous Revenue Act of 1988 (P.L. 100-647)**

P.L. 100-647, § 1012(bb)(6)(A):

Amended Code Sec. 995 by adding at the end thereof a new subsection (g). **Effective** for tax years beginning after 12-31-87.

[Sec. 996]

SEC. 996. RULES FOR ALLOCATION IN THE CASE OF DISTRIBUTIONS AND LOSSES.

[Sec. 996(a)]

(a) Rules for Actual Distributions and Certain Deemed Distributions.—

(1) In general.—Any actual distribution (other than a distribution described in paragraph (2) or to which section 995(c) applies) to a shareholder by a DISC (or former DISC) which is made out of earnings and profits shall be treated as made—

(A) first, out of previously taxed income, to the extent thereof,

(B) second, out of accumulated DISC income, to the extent thereof, and

(C) finally, out of other earnings and profits.

(2) Qualifying distributions.—Any actual distribution made pursuant to section 992(c) (relating to distributions to meet qualification requirements), and any deemed distribution pursuant to section 995(b)(1)(G) (relating to foreign investment attributable to producer's loans), shall be treated as made—

(A) first, out of accumulated DISC income, to the extent thereof,

(B) second, out of the earnings and profits described in paragraph (1)(C), to the extent thereof, and

(C) finally, out of previously taxed income.

In the case of any amount of any actual distribution to a C corporation made pursuant to section 992(c) which is required to satisfy the condition of section 992(a)(1)(A), the preceding sentence shall apply to $^{16}/_{17}$ths of such amount, and paragraph (1) shall apply to the remaining $^{1}/_{17}$th of such amount.

(3) Exclusion from gross income.—Amounts distributed out of previously taxed income shall be excluded by the distributee from gross income except for gains described in subsection (e)(2), and shall reduce the amount of the previously taxed income.

Amendments

• **1986, Tax Reform Act of 1986 (P.L. 99-514)**

P.L. 99-514, § 1876(k):

Amended Code Sec. 996(a)(2) by striking out the last sentence and inserting in lieu thereof "In the case of any amount of any actual distribution to a C corporation made pursuant to section 992(c) which is required to satisfy the condition of section 992(a)(1)(A), the preceding sentence shall apply to $^{16}/_{17}$ths of such amount and paragraph (1) shall apply to the remaining $^{1}/_{17}$th of such amount." **Effective** as if included in the provision of P.L. 98-369 to which it relates. Prior to amendment, the last sentence read as follows:

In the case of any amount of any actual distribution made pursuant to section 992(c) which is required to satisfy the condition of section 992(a)(1)(A), the preceding sentence shall apply to one-half of such amount, and paragraph (1) shall apply to the remaining one-half of such amount.

• **1978, Revenue Act of 1978 (P.L. 95-600)**

P.L. 95-600, § 703(i)(3), (r):

Amended Code Sec. 996(a)(2) by striking out "section 995(b)(1)(E)" and inserting in place thereof "section 995(b)(1)(G)". **Effective** 10-4-76.

• **1976, Tax Reform Act of 1976 (P.L. 94-455)**

P.L. 94-455, § 1101(e):

Added the last sentence of Code Sec. 996(a)(2). **Effective** for tax years beginning after 12-31-75.

INCOME TAX—DOM. INT'L SALES CORPS.

[Sec. 996(b)]

(b) ORDERING RULES FOR LOSSES.—If for any taxable year a DISC, or a former DISC, incurs a deficit in earnings and profits, such deficit shall be chargeable—

   (1) first, to earnings and profits described in subsection (a)(1)(C), to the extent thereof,

   (2) second, to accumulated DISC income, to the extent thereof, and

   (3) finally, to previously taxed income, except that a deficit in earnings and profits shall not be applied against accumulated DISC income which has been determined is to be deemed distributed to the shareholders (pursuant to section 995(b)(2)(A)) as a result of a revocation of election or other disqualification.

[Sec. 996(c)]

(c) PRIORITY OF DISTRIBUTIONS.—Any actual distribution made during a taxable year shall be treated as being made subsequent to any deemed distribution made during such year. Any actual distribution made pursuant to section 992(c) (relating to distributions to meet qualification requirements) shall be treated as being made before any other actual distributions during the taxable year.

[Sec. 996(d)]

(d) SUBSEQUENT EFFECT OF PREVIOUS DISPOSITION OF DISC STOCK.—

   (1) SHAREHOLDER PREVIOUSLY TAXED INCOME ADJUSTMENT.—If—

      (A) gain with respect to a share of stock of a DISC or former DISC is treated under section 995(c) as a dividend or as ordinary income, and

      (B) any person subsequently receives an actual distribution made out of accumulated DISC income, or a deemed distribution made pursuant to section 995(b)(2), with respect to such share,

such person shall treat such distribution in the same manner as a distribution from previously taxed income to the extent that (i) the gain referred to in subparagraph (A), exceeds (ii) any other amounts with respect to such share which were treated under this paragraph as made from previously taxed income. In applying this paragraph with respect to a share of stock in a DISC or former DISC, gain on the acquisition of such share by the DISC or former DISC or gain on a transaction prior to such acquisition shall not be considered gain referred to in subparagraph (A).

   (2) CORPORATE ADJUSTMENT UPON REDEMPTION.—If section 995(c) applies to a redemption of stock in a DISC or former DISC, the accumulated DISC income shall be reduced by an amount equal to the gain described in section 995(c) with respect to such stock which is (or has been) treated as ordinary income, except to the extent distributions with respect to such stock have been treated under paragraph (1).

Amendments

- **1976, Tax Reform Act of 1976 (P.L. 94-455)**

P.L. 94-455, § 1901(b)(3)(I):

Substituted "ordinary income" for "gain from the sale or exchange of property which is not a capital asset" in Code Sec. 996(d)(1)(A) and (2). **Effective** for tax years beginning after 12-31-76.

[Sec. 996(e)]

(e) ADJUSTMENT TO BASIS.—

   (1) ADDITIONS TO BASIS.—Amounts representing deemed distributions as provided in section 995(b) shall increase the basis of the stock with respect to which the distribution is made.

   (2) REDUCTIONS OF BASIS.—The portion of an actual distribution made out of previously taxed income shall reduce the basis of the stock with respect to which it is made, and to the extent that it exceeds the adjusted basis of such stock, shall be treated as gain from the sale or exchange of property. In the case of stock includible in the gross estate of a decedent for which an election is made under section 2032 (relating to alternate valuation), this paragraph shall not apply to any distribution made after the date of the decedent's death and before the alternate valuation date provided by section 2032.

[Sec. 996(f)]

(f) DEFINITIONS OF DIVISIONS OF EARNINGS AND PROFITS.—For purposes of this part:

   (1) DISC INCOME.—The earnings and profits derived by a corporation during a taxable year in which such corporation is a DISC, before reduction for any distributions during the year, but reduced by amounts deemed distributed under section 995(b)(1), shall constitute the DISC income for such year. The earnings and profits of a DISC for a taxable year include any amounts includible in such DISC's gross income pursuant to section 951(a) for such year. Accumulated DISC income shall be reduced by deemed distributions under section 995(b)(2).

   (2) PREVIOUSLY TAXED INCOME.—Earnings and profits deemed distributed under section 995(b) for a taxable year shall constitute previously taxed income for such year.

   (3) OTHER EARNINGS AND PROFITS.—The earnings and profits for a taxable year which are described in neither paragraph (1) nor (2) shall constitute the other earnings and profits for such year.

[Sec. 996(g)]

(g) EFFECTIVELY CONNECTED INCOME.—In the case of a shareholder who is a nonresident alien individual or a foreign corporation, trust, or estate, gains referred to in section 995(c) and all distributions out of accumulated DISC income including deemed distributions shall be treated as gains and distributions which are effectively connected with the conduct of a trade or business conducted through a permanent establishment of such shareholder within the United States and which are derived from sources within the United States.

INCOME TAX—INT'L BOYCOTT DETERMINATIONS

Amendments

• **1984, Deficit Reduction Act of 1984 (P.L. 98-369)**

P.L. 98-369, § 801(d)(10):

Amended Code Sec. 996(g) by inserting "and which are derived from sources within the United States" after "United States". **Effective** for distributions on or after 6-22-84.

• **1971, Revenue Act of 1971 (P.L. 92-178)**

P.L. 92-178, § 501:

Added Code Sec. 996. **Effective** for tax years ending after 12-31-71, except that a corporation may not be a DISC (as defined in Code Sec. 992(a)) for any tax year beginning before 1-1-72.

[Sec. 997]

SEC. 997. SPECIAL SUBCHAPTER C RULES.

For purposes of applying the provisions of subchapter C of chapter 1, any distribution in property to a corporation by a DISC or former DISC which is made out of previously taxed income or accumulated DISC income shall—

(1) be treated as a distribution in the same amount as if such distribution of property were made to an individual, and

(2) have a basis, in the hands of the recipient corporation, equal to the amount determined under paragraph (1).

Amendments

• **1971, Revenue Act of 1971 (P.L. 92-178)**

P.L. 92-178, § 501:

Added Code Sec. 997. **Effective** for tax years ending after 12-31-71, except that a corporation may not be a DISC (as defined in Code Sec. 992(a)) for any tax year beginning before 1-1-72.

PART V—INTERNATIONAL BOYCOTT DETERMINATIONS

Sec. 999.   Reports by taxpayers; determinations.

[Sec. 999]

SEC. 999. REPORTS BY TAXPAYERS; DETERMINATIONS.

[Sec. 999(a)]

(a) INTERNATIONAL BOYCOTT REPORTS BY TAXPAYERS.—

(1) REPORT REQUIRED.—If any person, or a member of a controlled group (within the meaning of section 993(a)(3)) which includes that person, has operations in, or related to—

(A) a country (or with the government, a company, or a national of a country) which is on the list maintained by the Secretary under paragraph (3), or

(B) any other country (or with the government, a company, or a national of that country) in which such person or such member had operations during the taxable year if such person (or, if such person is a foreign corporation, any United States shareholder of that corporation) knows or has reason to know that participation in or cooperation with an international boycott is required as a condition of doing business within such country or with such government, company, or national,

that person or shareholder (within the meaning of section 951(b)) shall report such operations to the Secretary at such time and in such manner as the Secretary prescribes, except that in the case of a foreign corporation such report shall be required only of a United States shareholder (within the meaning of such section) of such corporation.

(2) PARTICIPATION AND COOPERATION; REQUEST THEREFOR.—A taxpayer shall report whether he, a foreign corporation of which he is a United States shareholder, or any member of a controlled group which includes the taxpayer or such foreign corporation has participated in or cooperated with an international boycott at any time during the taxable year, or has been requested to participate in or cooperate with such a boycott, and, if so, the nature of any operation in connection with which there was participation in or cooperation with such boycott (or there was a request to participate or cooperate).

(3) LIST TO BE MAINTAINED.—The Secretary shall maintain and publish not less frequently than quarterly a current list of countries which require or may require participation in or cooperation with an international boycott (within the meaning of subsection (b)(3)).

[Sec. 999(b)]

(b) PARTICIPATION IN OR COOPERATION WITH AN INTERNATIONAL BOYCOTT.—

(1) GENERAL RULE.—If the person or a member of a controlled group (within the meaning of section 993(a)(3)) which includes the person participates in or cooperates with an international boycott in the taxable year, all operations of the taxpayer or such group in that country and in any other country which requires participation in or cooperation with the boycott as a condition of doing business within that country, or with the government, a company, or a national of that country, shall be treated as operations in connection with which such participation or cooperation occurred, except to the extent that the person can clearly demonstrate that a particular operation is a clearly separate and identifiable operation in connection with which there was no participation in or cooperation with an international boycott.

(2) SPECIAL RULE.—

(A) NONBOYCOTT OPERATIONS.—A clearly separate and identifiable operation of a person, or of a member of the controlled group (within the meaning of section 993(a)(3)) which includes that person, in or related to any country within the group of countries referred to in paragraph (1) shall not be treated as an operation in or related to a group of countries associated in carrying out an international boycott if the person can clearly demonstrate that he, or that such member, did not participate in or cooperate with the international boycott in connection with that operation.

INCOME TAX—INT'L BOYCOTT DETERMINATIONS

(B) SEPARATE AND IDENTIFIABLE OPERATIONS.—A taxpayer may show that different operations within the same country, or operations in different countries, are clearly separate and identifiable operations.

(3) DEFINITION OF BOYCOTT PARTICIPATION AND COOPERATION.—For purposes of this section, a person participates in or cooperates with an international boycott if he agrees—

(A) as a condition of doing business directly or indirectly within a country or with the government, a company, or a national of a country—

(i) to refrain from doing business with or in a country which is the object of the boycott or with the government, companies, or nationals of that country;

(ii) to refrain from doing business with any United States person engaged in trade in a country which is the object of the boycott or with the government, companies, or nationals of that country;

(iii) to refrain from doing business with any company whose ownership or management is made up, all or in part, of individuals of a particular nationality, race, or religion, or to remove (or refrain from selecting) corporate directors who are individuals of a particular nationality, race, or religion; or

(iv) to refrain from employing individuals of a particular nationality, race, or religion; or

(B) as a condition of the sale of a product to the government, a company, or a national of a country, to refrain from shipping or insuring that product on a carrier owned, leased, or operated by a person who does not participate in or cooperate with an international boycott (within the meaning of subparagraph (A)).

(4) COMPLIANCE WITH CERTAIN LAWS.—This section shall not apply to any agreement by a person (or such member)—

(A) to meet requirements imposed by a foreign country with respect to an international boycott if United States law or regulations, or an Executive Order, sanctions participation in, or cooperation with, that international boycott,

(B) to comply with a prohibition on the importation of goods produced in whole or in part in any country which is the object of an international boycott, or

(C) to comply with a prohibition imposed by a country on the exportation of products obtained in such country to any country which is the object of an international boycott.

[Sec. 999(c)]

(c) INTERNATIONAL BOYCOTT FACTOR.—

(1) INTERNATIONAL BOYCOTT FACTOR.—For purposes of sections 908(a), 952(a)(3), and 995(b)(1)(F)(ii), the international boycott factor is a fraction, determined under regulations prescribed by the Secretary, the numerator of which reflects the world-wide operations of a person (or, in the case of a controlled group (within the meaning of section 993(a)(3)) which includes that person, of the group) which are operations in or related to a group of countries associated in carrying out an international boycott in or with which that person or a member of that controlled group has participated or cooperated in the taxable year, and the denominator of which reflects the world-wide operations of that person or group.

(2) SPECIFICALLY ATTRIBUTABLE TAXES AND INCOME.—If the taxpayer clearly demonstrates that the foreign taxes paid and income earned for the taxable year are attributable to specific operations, then, in lieu of applying the international boycott factor for such taxable year, the amount of the credit disallowed under section 908(a), the addition to subpart F income under section 952(a)(3), and the amount of deemed distribution under section 995(b)(1)(F)(ii) for the taxable year, if any, shall be the amount specifically attributable to the operations in which there was participation in or cooperation with an international boycott under section 999(b)(1).

(3) WORLD-WIDE OPERATIONS.—For purposes of this subsection, the term "world-wide operations" means operations in or related to countries other than the United States.

Amendments

• **2004, American Jobs Creation Act of 2004 (P.L. 108-357)**

P.L. 108-357, § 101(b)(8):

Amended Code Sec. 999(c)(1) by striking "941(a)(5)," immediately following "908(a),". **Effective** for transactions after 12-31-2004. For transitional and special rules, see Act Sec. 101(d)-(f), below.

P.L. 108-357, § 101(d)-(f) (as amended by P.L. 113-295, § 219(a), Division A), provides:

(d) TRANSITIONAL RULE FOR 2005 AND 2006.—

(1) IN GENERAL.—In the case of transactions during 2005 or 2006, the amount includible in gross income by reason of the amendments made by this section shall not exceed the applicable percentage of the amount which would have been so included but for this subsection.

(2) APPLICABLE PERCENTAGE.—For purposes of paragraph (1), the applicable percentage shall be as follows:

(A) For 2005, the applicable percentage shall be 20 percent.

(B) For 2006, the applicable percentage shall be 40 percent.

(3) COORDINATION WITH SECTION 199.—This subsection shall be applied without regard to any deduction allowable under section 199.

(e) REVOCATION OF ELECTION TO BE TREATED AS DOMESTIC CORPORATION.—If, during the 1-year period beginning on the date of the enactment of this Act, a corporation for which an election is in effect under section 943(e) of the Internal Revenue Code of 1986 revokes such election, no gain or loss shall be recognized with respect to property treated as transferred under clause (ii) of section 943(e)(4)(B) of such Code to the extent such property—

(1) was treated as transferred under clause (i) thereof, or

(2) was acquired during a taxable year to which such election applies and before May 1, 2003, in the ordinary course of its trade or business.

The Secretary of the Treasury (or such Secretary's delegate) may prescribe such regulations as may be necessary to prevent the abuse of the purposes of this subsection.

[Note: Act Sec. 101(f) of P.L. 108-357, below, was stricken by P.L. 109-222, § 513(b), applicable to tax years beginning after 5-17-2006.—CCH.]

(f) BINDING CONTRACTS.—The amendments made by this section shall not apply to any transaction in the ordinary course of a trade or business which occurs pursuant to a binding contract—

(1) which is between the taxpayer and a person who is not a related person (as defined in section 943(b)(3) of such Code, as in effect on the day before the date of the enactment of this Act), and

(2) which is in effect on September 17, 2003, and at all times thereafter.

For purposes of this subsection, a binding contract shall include a purchase option, renewal option, or replacement option which is included in such contract and which is enforceable against the seller or lessor.

INCOME TAX—INT'L BOYCOTT DETERMINATIONS

• 2000, FSC Repeal and Extraterritorial Income Exclusion Act of 2000 (P.L. 106-519)

P.L. 106-519, §4(5):

Amended Code Sec. 999(c)(1) by inserting "941(a)(5)," after "908(a),". **Effective**, generally, to transactions after 9-30-2000. For special rules, see Act Sec. 5(b)-(d) in the amendment notes following Code Sec. 921.

• 1986, Tax Reform Act of 1986 (P.L. 99-514)

P.L. 99-514, §1876(p)(3):

Repealed P.L. 98-369, §802(c)(3). **Effective** as if included in the provision of P.L. 98-369 to which it relates.

• 1984, Deficit Reduction Act of 1984 (P.L. 98-369)

P.L. 98-369, §802(c)(3):

Amended Code Sec. 999(c) by striking out "995(b)(1)(F)(ii)" and inserting in lieu thereof "995(b)(1)(F)(i)" each place it appeared. **Effective** for transactions after 12-31-84, in tax years ending after such date.

• 1978, Revenue Act of 1978 (P.L. 95-600)

P.L. 95-600, §703(h)(2), (r):

Amended Code Sec. 999(c)(1) by striking out "995(b)(3)" and inserting in place thereof "995(b)(1)(F)(ii)". **Effective** 10-4-76.

P.L. 95-600, §703(h)(3), (r):

Amended Code Sec. 999(c)(2) by striking out "995(b)(1)(D)(ii)" and inserting in place thereof "995(b)(1)(F)(ii)". **Effective** 10-4-76.

[Sec. 999(d)]

(d) DETERMINATIONS WITH RESPECT TO PARTICULAR OPERATIONS.—Upon a request made by the taxpayer, the Secretary shall issue a determination with respect to whether a particular operation of a person, or of a member of a controlled group which includes that person, constitutes participation in or cooperation with an international boycott. The Secretary may issue such a determination in advance of such operation in cases which are of such a nature that an advance determination is possible and appropriate under the circumstances. If the request is made before the operation is commenced, or before the end of a taxable year in which the operation is carried out, the Secretary may decline to issue such a determination before the close of the taxable year.

[Sec. 999(e)]

(e) PARTICIPATION OR COOPERATION BY RELATED PERSONS.—If a person controls (within the meaning of section 304(c)) a corporation—

(1) participation in or cooperation with an international boycott by such corporation shall be presumed to be such participation or cooperation by such person, and

(2) participation in or cooperation with such a boycott by such person shall be presumed to be such participation or cooperation by such corporation.

[Sec. 999(f)]

(f) WILLFUL FAILURE TO REPORT.—Any person (within the meaning of section 6671(b)) required to report under this section who willfully fails to make such report shall, in addition to other penalties provided by law, be fined not more than $25,000, imprisoned for not more than one year, or both.

Amendments

• 1976, Tax Reform Act of 1976 (P.L. 94-455)

P.L. 94-455, §1064(a):

Added a new part V to subchapter N of chapter 1. The new part V included Code Sec. 999. **Effective** for participation in or cooperation with an international boycott more than 30 days after 10-4-76. In the case of operations which constitute participation in or cooperation with an international boycott and which are carried out in accordance with the terms of a binding contract entered into before 9-2-76, Code Sec. 999(f) shall apply to such participation or cooperation after 12-31-77.

P.L. 94-455, §1067(a)-(b), provides:

(a) REPORTS TO THE CONGRESS.—As soon after the close of each calendar year as the data become available, the Secretary shall transmit a report to the Committee on Ways and Means of the House of Representatives and to the Committee on Finance of the Senate setting forth, for that calendar year—

(1) the number of reports filed under section 999(a) of the Internal Revenue Code of 1954 for taxable years ending with or within such taxable year,

(2) the number of such reports on which the taxpayer indicated international boycott participation or cooperation (within the meaning of section 999(b)(3) of such Code), and

(3) a detailed description of the manner in which the provisions of such Code relating to international boycott activity have been administered during such calendar year.

(b) INITIAL LIST.—The Secretary of the Treasury shall publish an initial list of those countries which may require participation in or cooperation with an international boycott as a condition of doing business within such country, or with the government, a company, or a national of such country (within the meaning of section 999(b) of the Internal Revenue Code of 1954) within 30 days after the enactment of this Act.

Subchapter O—Gain or Loss on Disposition of Property

Part I.	Determination of amount of and recognition of gain or loss.
Part II.	Basis rules of general application.
Part III.	Common nontaxable exchanges.
Part IV.	Special rules.
Part V.	[Stricken.]
Part VI.	Exchanges in obedience to S.E.C. orders [repealed].
Part VII.	Wash sales; straddles.
Part VIII.	[Repealed.]

PART I—DETERMINATION OF AMOUNT OF AND RECOGNITION OF GAIN OR LOSS

Sec. 1001.   Determination of amount of and recognition of gain or loss.

INCOME TAX—GAIN OR LOSS

[Sec. 1001]

SEC. 1001. DETERMINATION OF AMOUNT OF AND RECOGNITION OF GAIN OR LOSS.

[Sec. 1001(a)]

(a) COMPUTATION OF GAIN OR LOSS.—The gain from the sale or other disposition of property shall be the excess of the amount realized therefrom over the adjusted basis provided in section 1011 for determining gain, and the loss shall be the excess of the adjusted basis provided in such section for determining loss over the amount realized.

[Sec. 1001(b)]

(b) AMOUNT REALIZED.—The amount realized from the sale or other disposition of property shall be the sum of any money received plus the fair market value of the property (other than money) received. In determining the amount realized—

(1) there shall not be taken into account any amount received as reimbursement for real property taxes which are treated under section 164(d) as imposed on the purchaser, and

(2) there shall be taken into account amounts representing real property taxes which are treated under section 164(d) as imposed on the taxpayer if such taxes are to be paid by the purchaser.

[Sec. 1001(c)]

(c) RECOGNITION OF GAIN OR LOSS.—Except as otherwise provided in this subtitle, the entire amount of the gain or loss, determined under this section, on the sale or exchange of property shall be recognized.

Amendments

• **1976, Tax Reform Act of 1976 (P.L. 94-455)**

P.L. 94-455, § 1901(a)(121):

Amended Code Sec. 1001(c). **Effective** for tax years beginning after 12-31-76. Prior to amendment, Code Sec. 1001(c) read as follows:

(c) RECOGNITION OF GAIN OR LOSS.—In the case of a sale or exchange of property, the extent to which the gain or loss determined under this section shall be recognized for purposes of this subtitle shall be determined under section 1002.

[Sec. 1001(d)]

(d) INSTALLMENT SALES.—Nothing in this section shall be construed to prevent (in the case of property sold under contract providing for payment in installments) the taxation of that portion of any installment payment representing gain or profit in the year in which such payment is received.

[Sec. 1001(e)]

(e) CERTAIN TERM INTERESTS.—

(1) IN GENERAL.—In determining gain or loss from the sale or other disposition of a term interest in property, that portion of the adjusted basis of such interest which is determined pursuant to section 1014, 1015, or 1041 (to the extent that such adjusted basis is a portion of the entire adjusted basis of the property) shall be disregarded.

(2) TERM INTEREST IN PROPERTY DEFINED.—For purposes of paragraph (1), the term "term interest in property" means—

(A) a life interest in property,

(B) an interest in property for a term of years, or

(C) an income interest in a trust.

(3) EXCEPTION.—Paragraph (1) shall not apply to a sale or other disposition which is a part of a transaction in which the entire interest in property is transferred to any person or persons.

Amendments

• **1984, Deficit Reduction Act of 1984 (P.L. 98-369)**

P.L. 98-369, § 421(b)(4):

Amended Code Sec. 1001(e)(1) by striking out "section 1014 or 1015" and inserting in lieu thereof "section 1014, 1015, or 1041". **Effective** for transfers after 7-18-84, in tax years ending after such date.

• **1980, Crude Oil Windfall Profit Tax Act of 1980 (P.L. 96-223)**

P.L. 96-223, § 401(a):

Repealed Code Sec. 1001(e)(1) as amended by P.L. 95-600, Act Sec. 702(c)(9). **Effective** with respect to decedents dying after 12-31-76. However, see the amendment note for P.L. 96-223, § 401(a), that follows Code Sec. 1014(d) for the text of Act Sec. 401(d) that authorizes the election of the carryover basis rules in the case of a decedent dying after 12-31-76 and before 11-7-78. Prior to repeal, Code Sec. 1001(e)(1) read as follows:

(1) IN GENERAL.—In determining gain or loss from the sale or other disposition of a term interest in property, that portion of the adjusted basis of such interest which is determined pursuant to section 1014, 1015, or 1023 (to the extent that such adjusted basis is a portion of the entire adjusted basis of the property) shall be disregarded.

P.L. 96-223, § 401(b):

Revived Code Sec. 1001(e)(1) before its amendment by P.L. 96-600, Act Sec. 702(c)(9). **Effective** with respect to decedents dying after 12-31-76. However, see the amendment note for Act Sec. 401(a).

• **1978, Revenue Act of 1978 (P.L. 95-600)**

P.L. 95-600, § 702(c)(9), (10):

Amended Code Sec. 1001(e)(1) by striking out "section 1014 or 1015" and inserting in place thereof "section 1014, 1015, or 1023". **Effective** as if included in amendments made by P.L. 94-455 [Sec. 2005(f)(1), applicable to estates of decedents dying after 12-31-79, as amended by P.L. 95-600, § 515(6)].

• **1969, Tax Reform Act of 1969 (P.L. 91-172)**

P.L. 91-172, § 516(a):

Amended Code Sec. 1001 by adding section 1001(e). **Effective** for sales or other dispositions after 10-9-69.

INCOME TAX—BASIS RULES

[Sec. 1001(f)—Stricken]

Amendments

• **1993, Omnibus Budget Reconciliation Act of 1993 (P.L. 103-66)**

P.L. 103-66, §13213(a)(2)(E):

Amended Code Sec. 1001 by striking subsection (f). **Effective** for expenses incurred after 12-31-93. Prior to amendment, subsection (f) read as follows:

(f) CROSS REFERENCE.—For treatment of certain expenses incident to the sale of a residence which were deducted as moving expenses by the taxpayer or his spouse under section 217(a), see section 217(e).

• **1969, Tax Reform Act of 1969 (P.L. 91-172)**

P.L. 91-172, §231(c)(2):

Added subsection 1001(f). **Effective** for tax years beginning after 12-31-69.

[Sec. 1002—Repealed]

SEC. 1002. RECOGNITION OF GAIN OR LOSS.

Amendments

• **1976, Tax Reform Act of 1976 (P.L. 94-455)**

P.L. 94-455, §1901(b)(28)(B)(i):

Repealed Code Sec. 1002. **Effective** for tax years beginning after 1976. Prior to repeal, Code Sec. 1002 read as follows:

Except as otherwise provided in this subtitle, on the sale or exchange of property the entire amount of the gain or loss, determined under section 1001, shall be recognized.

PART II—BASIS RULES OF GENERAL APPLICATION

Sec. 1011.	Adjusted basis for determining gain or loss.
Sec. 1012.	Basis of property—cost.
Sec. 1013.	Basis of property included in inventory.
Sec. 1014.	Basis of property acquired from a decedent.
Sec. 1015.	Basis of property acquired by gifts and transfers in trust.
Sec. 1016.	Adjustments to basis.
Sec. 1017.	Discharge of indebtedness.
Sec. 1019.	Property on which lessee has made improvements.
Sec. 1021.	Sale of annuities.
Sec. 1022.	Treatment of property acquired from a decedent dying after December 31, 2009.
Sec. 1023.	Cross references.

[Sec. 1011]

SEC. 1011. ADJUSTED BASIS FOR DETERMINING GAIN OR LOSS.

[Sec. 1011(a)]

(a) GENERAL RULE.—The adjusted basis for determining the gain or loss from the sale or other disposition of property, whenever acquired, shall be the basis (determined under section 1012 or other applicable sections of this subchapter and subchapters C (relating to corporate distributions and adjustments), K (relating to partners and partnerships), and P (relating to capital gains and losses)), adjusted as provided in section 1016.

[Sec. 1011(b)]

(b) BARGAIN SALE TO A CHARITABLE ORGANIZATION.—If a deduction is allowable under section 170 (relating to charitable contributions) by reason of a sale, then the adjusted basis for determining the gain from such sale shall be that portion of the adjusted basis which bears the same ratio to the adjusted basis as the amount realized bears to the fair market value of the property.

Amendments

• **1969, Tax Reform Act of 1969 (P.L. 91-172)**

P.L. 91-172, §201(f):

Amended Code Sec. 1011. **Effective** with respect to sales made after 12-19-69. Prior to amendment, Code Sec. 1011 read as follows:

"The adjusted basis for determining the gain or loss from the sale or other disposition of property, whenever acquired, shall be the basis (determined under section 1012 or other applicable sections of this subchapter and subchapters C (relating to corporate distributions and adjustments), K (relating to partners and partnerships), and P (relating to capital gains and losses)), adjusted as provided in section 1016."

[Sec. 1012]

SEC. 1012. BASIS OF PROPERTY—COST.

[Sec. 1012(a)]

(a) IN GENERAL.—The basis of property shall be the cost of such property, except as otherwise provided in this subchapter and subchapters C (relating to corporate distributions and adjustments), K (relating to partners and partnerships), and P (relating to capital gains and losses).

[Sec. 1012(b)]

(b) SPECIAL RULE FOR APPORTIONED REAL ESTATE TAXES.—The cost of real property shall not include any amount in respect of real property taxes which are treated under section 164(d) as imposed on the taxpayer.

INCOME TAX—BASIS RULES

[Sec. 1012(c)]

(c) DETERMINATIONS BY ACCOUNT.—

(1) IN GENERAL.—In the case of the sale, exchange, or other disposition of a specified security on or after the applicable date, the conventions prescribed by regulations under this section shall be applied on an account by account basis.

(2) APPLICATION TO CERTAIN REGULATED INVESTMENT COMPANIES.—

(A) IN GENERAL.—Except as provided in subparagraph (B), any stock for which an average basis method is permissible under this section which is acquired before January 1, 2012, shall be treated as a separate account from any such stock acquired on or after such date.

(B) ELECTION FOR TREATMENT AS SINGLE ACCOUNT.—If a regulated investment company described in subparagraph (A) elects to have this subparagraph apply with respect to one or more of its stockholders—

(i) subparagraph (A) shall not apply with respect to any stock in such regulated investment company held by such stockholders, and

(ii) all stock in such regulated investment company which is held by such stockholders shall be treated as covered securities described in section 6045(g)(3) without regard to the date of the acquisition of such stock.

A rule similar to the rule of the preceding sentence shall apply with respect to a broker holding such stock as a nominee.

(3) DEFINITIONS.—For purposes of this section, the terms "specified security" and "applicable date" shall have the meaning given such terms in section 6045(g).

Amendments

• **2014, Tax Technical Corrections Act of 2014 (P.L. 113-295)**

P.L. 113-295, §210(f)(1)(A)-(C), Division A:

Amended Code Sec. 1012(c)(2) by striking "FUNDS" in the heading and inserting "REGULATED INVESTMENT COMPANIES", by striking "FUND" following "ELECTION" in the heading for subparagraph (B), and by striking "fund" each place it appears in paragraph (2) and inserting "regulated investment company". **Effective** as if included in the provision of the Energy Improvement and Extension Act of 2008 (P.L. 110-343) to which it relates [effective 1-1-2011.—CCH]. Prior to amendment, Code Sec. 1012(c)(2) read as follows:

(2) APPLICATION TO CERTAIN FUNDS.—

(A) IN GENERAL.—Except as provided in subparagraph (B), any stock for which an average basis method is permissible under section 1012 which is acquired before January 1, 2012, shall be treated as a separate account from any such stock acquired on or after such date.

(B) ELECTION FUND FOR TREATMENT AS SINGLE ACCOUNT.—If a fund described in subparagraph (A) elects to have this subparagraph apply with respect to one or more of its stockholders—

(i) subparagraph (A) shall not apply with respect to any stock in such fund held by such stockholders, and

(ii) all stock in such fund which is held by such stockholders shall be treated as covered securities described in section 6045(g)(3) without regard to the date of the acquisition of such stock.

A rule similar to the rule of the preceding sentence shall apply with respect to a broker holding such stock as a nominee.

P.L. 113-295, §220(n), Division A:

Amended Code Sec. 1012(c)(2)(A) by striking "section 1012" and inserting "this section". **Effective** 12-19-2014.

[Sec. 1012(d)]

(d) AVERAGE BASIS FOR STOCK ACQUIRED PURSUANT TO A DIVIDEND REINVESTMENT PLAN.—

(1) IN GENERAL.—In the case of any stock acquired after December 31, 2011, in connection with a dividend reinvestment plan, the basis of such stock while held as part of such plan shall be determined using one of the methods which may be used for determining the basis of stock in a regulated investment company.

(2) TREATMENT AFTER TRANSFER.—In the case of the transfer to another account of stock to which paragraph (1) applies, such stock shall have a cost basis in such other account equal to its basis in the dividend reinvestment plan immediately before such transfer (properly adjusted for any fees or other charges taken into account in connection with such transfer).

(3) SEPARATE ACCOUNTS; ELECTION FOR TREATMENT AS SINGLE ACCOUNT.—

(A) IN GENERAL.—Rules similar to the rules of subsection (c)(2) shall apply for purposes of this subsection.

(B) AVERAGE BASIS METHOD.—Notwithstanding paragraph (1), in the case of an election under rules similar to the rules of subsection (c)(2)(B) with respect to stock held in connection with a dividend reinvestment plan, the average basis method is permissible with respect to all such stock without regard to the date of the acquisition of such stock.

(4) DIVIDEND REINVESTMENT PLAN.—For purposes of this subsection—

(A) IN GENERAL.—The term "dividend reinvestment plan" means any arrangement under which dividends on any stock are reinvested in stock identical to the stock with respect to which the dividends are paid.

(B) INITIAL STOCK ACQUISITION TREATED AS ACQUIRED IN CONNECTION WITH PLAN.—Stock shall be treated as acquired in connection with a dividend reinvestment plan if such stock is acquired pursuant to such plan or if the dividends paid on such stock are subject to such plan.

Amendments

• **2014, Tax Technical Corrections Act of 2014 (P.L. 113-295)**

P.L. 113-295, §210(f)(2)(A)-(B), Division A:

Amended Code Sec. 1012(d)(1) by striking "December 31, 2010" and inserting "December 31, 2011", and by striking "an open-end fund" and inserting "a regulated investment company". **Effective** as if included in the provision of the Energy Improvement and Extension Act of 2008 (P.L. 110-343) to which it relates [effective 1-1-2011.—CCH].

P.L. 113-295, §210(f)(3), Division A:

Amended Code Sec. 1012(d)(3). **Effective** as if included in the provision of the Energy Improvement and Extension Act of 2008 (P.L. 110-343) to which it relates [effective 1-1-2011.—CCH]. Prior to amendment, Code Sec. 1012(d)(3) read as follows:

(3) SEPARATE ACCOUNTS; ELECTION FOR TREATMENT AS SINGLE ACCOUNT.—Rules similar to the rules of subsection (c)(2) shall apply for purposes of this subsection.

• **2008, Energy Improvement and Extension Act of 2008 (P.L. 110-343)**

P.L. 110-343, Division B, §403(b)(1)-(3):

Amended Code Sec. 1012 by striking "The basis of property" and inserting "(a) IN GENERAL.—The basis of property", by striking "The cost of real property", and inserting "(b) SPECIAL RULE FOR APPORTIONED REAL ESTATE TAXES.—The cost of real property", and by adding at the end new subsections (c)-(d). **Effective** 1-1-2011. Prior to amendment, Code Sec. 1012 read as follows:

SEC. 1012. BASIS OF PROPERTY—COST.

The basis of property shall be the cost of such property, except as otherwise provided in this subchapter and subchapters C (relating to corporate distributions

INCOME TAX—BASIS RULES

and adjustments), K (relating to partners and partnerships), and P (relating to capital gains and losses). The cost of real property shall not include any amount in respect of real property taxes which are treated under section 164(d) as imposed on the taxpayer.

[Sec. 1013]
SEC. 1013. BASIS OF PROPERTY INCLUDED IN INVENTORY.

If the property should have been included in the last inventory, the basis shall be the last inventory value thereof.

[Sec. 1014]
SEC. 1014. BASIS OF PROPERTY ACQUIRED FROM A DECEDENT.

[Sec. 1014(a)]

(a) IN GENERAL.—Except as otherwise provided in this section, the basis of property in the hands of a person acquiring the property from a decedent or to whom the property passed from a decedent shall, if not sold, exchanged, or otherwise disposed of before the decedent's death by such person, be—

(1) the fair market value of the property at the date of the decedent's death,

(2) in the case of an election under section 2032, its value at the applicable valuation date prescribed by such section,

(3) in the case of an election under section 2032A, its value determined under such section, or

(4) to the extent of the applicability of the exclusion described in section 2031(c), the basis in the hands of the decedent.

Amendments

• **2014, Tax Technical Corrections Act of 2014 (P.L. 113-295)**

P.L. 113-295, § 221(a)(74)(A), Division A:

Amended Code Sec. 1014(a)(2). **Effective** generally 12-19-2014. For a special rule, see Act Sec. 221(b)(2), Division A, below. Prior to amendment, Code Sec. 1014(a)(2) read as follows:

(2) in the case of an election under either section 2032 or section 811(j) of the Internal Revenue Code of 1939 where the decedent died after October 21, 1942, its value at the applicable valuation date prescribed by those sections,

P.L. 113-295, § 221(b)(2), Division A, provides:

(2) SAVINGS PROVISION.—If—

(A) any provision amended or repealed by the amendments made by this section applied to—

(i) any transaction occurring before the date of the enactment of this Act,

(ii) any property acquired before such date of enactment, or

(iii) any item of income, loss, deduction, or credit taken into account before such date of enactment, and

(B) the treatment of such transaction, property, or item under such provision would (without regard to the amendments or repeals made by this section) affect the liability for tax for periods ending after date of enactment, nothing in the amendments or repeals made by this section shall be construed to affect the treatment of such transaction, property, or item for purposes of determining liability for tax for periods ending after such date of enactment.

• **1997, Taxpayer Relief Act of 1997 (P.L. 105-34)**

P.L. 105-34, § 508(b):

Amended Code Sec. 1014(a) by striking "or" at the end of paragraphs (1) and (2), by striking the period at the end of paragraph (3) and inserting ", or" and by adding at the end a new paragraph (4). **Effective** for estates of decedents dying after 12-31-97.

• **1980, Technical Corrections Act of 1979 (P.L. 96-222)**

P.L. 96-222, § 107(a)(2)(A):

Amended Code Sec. 1014(a)(3) by changing "section 2032.1" to "section 2032A". **Effective** for estates of decedents dying after 12-31-76.

• **1978, Revenue Act of 1978 (P.L. 95-600)**

P.L. 95-600, § 702(c)(1)(A), (c)(10):

Amended Code Sec. 1014(a). **Effective** as if included in amendments made by P.L. 94-455 [Sec. 2003(e), applicable to estates of decedents dying after 12-31-76]. Prior to amendment, such section read:

"(a) IN GENERAL.—Except as otherwise provided in this section, the basis of property in the hands of a person acquiring the property from a decedent or to whom the property passed from a decedent shall, if not sold, exchanged, or otherwise disposed of before the decedent's death by such person, be the fair market value of the property at the date of the decedent's death, or, in the case of an election under either section 2032 or section 811(j) of the Internal Revenue Code of 1939 where the decedent died after October 21, 1942, its value at the applicable valuation date prescribed by those sections."

[Sec. 1014(b)]

(b) PROPERTY ACQUIRED FROM THE DECEDENT.—For purposes of subsection (a), the following property shall be considered to have been acquired from or to have passed from the decedent:

(1) Property acquired by bequest, devise, or inheritance, or by the decedent's estate from the decedent;

(2) Property transferred by the decedent during his lifetime in trust to pay the income for life to or on the order or direction of the decedent, with the right reserved to the decedent at all times before his death to revoke the trust;

(3) In the case of decedents dying after December 31, 1951, property transferred by the decedent during his lifetime in trust to pay the income for life to or on the order or direction of the decedent with the right reserved to the decedent at all times before his death to make any change in the enjoyment thereof through the exercise of a power to alter, amend, or terminate the trust;

(4) Property passing without full and adequate consideration under a general power of appointment exercised by the decedent by will;

(5) In the case of decedents dying after August 26, 1937, and before January 1, 2005, property acquired by bequest, devise, or inheritance or by the decedent's estate from the decedent, if the property consists of stock or securities of a foreign corporation, which with respect to its taxable year next preceding the date of the decedent's death was, under the law applicable to such year, a foreign personal holding company. In such case, the basis shall be the fair market value of such property at the date of the decedent's death or the basis in the hands of the decedent, whichever is lower;

(6) In the case of decedents dying after December 31, 1947, property which represents the surviving spouse's one-half share of community property held by the decedent and the surviving spouse under the community property laws of any State, or possession of the United States or any foreign country, if at least one-half of the whole of the community interest in such property was includible in determining the value of the decedent's gross estate under chapter 11 of subtitle B (section 2001 and following, relating to estate tax) or section 811 of the Internal Revenue Code of 1939;

(7) [Stricken.]

(8) [Stricken.]

INCOME TAX—BASIS RULES

(9) In the case of decedents dying after December 31, 1953, property acquired from the decedent by reason of death, form of ownership, or other conditions (including property acquired through the exercise or non-exercise of a power of appointment), if by reason thereof the property is required to be included in determining the value of the decedent's gross estate under chapter 11 of subtitle B or under the Internal Revenue Code of 1939. In such case, if the property is acquired before the death of the decedent, the basis shall be the amount determined under subsection (a) reduced by the amount allowed to the taxpayer as deductions in computing taxable income under this subtitle or prior income tax laws for exhaustion, wear and tear, obsolescence, amortization, and depletion on such property before the death of the decedent. Such basis shall be applicable to the property commencing on the death of the decedent. This paragraph shall not apply to—

(A) annuities described in section 72;

(B) property to which paragraph (5) would apply if the property had been acquired by bequest; and

(C) property described in any other paragraph of this subsection.

(10) Property includible in the gross estate of the decedent under section 2044 (relating to certain property for which marital deduction was previously allowed). In any such case, the last 3 sentences of paragraph (9) shall apply as if such property were described in the first sentence of paragraph (9).

Amendments

• **2014, Tax Technical Corrections Act of 2014 (P.L. 113-295)**

P.L. 113-295, § 221(a)(74)(B), Division A:

Amended Code Sec. 1014(b) by striking paragraphs (7) and (8). **Effective** generally 12-19-2014. For a special rule, see Act Sec. 221(b)(2), Division A, below. Prior to being stricken, Code Sec. 1014(b)(7)-(8) read as follows:

(7) In the case of decedents dying after October 21, 1942, and on or before December 31, 1947, such part of any property, representing the surviving spouse's one-half share of property held by a decedent and the surviving spouse under the community property laws of any State, or possession of the United States or any foreign country, as was included in determining the value of the gross estate of the decedent, if a tax under chapter 3 of the Internal Revenue Code of 1939 was payable on the transfer of the net estate of the decedent. In such case, nothing in this paragraph shall reduce the basis below that which would exist if the Revenue Act of 1948 had not been enacted;

(8) In the case of decedents dying after December 31, 1950, and before January 1, 1954, property which represents the survivor's interest in a joint and survivor's annuity if the value of any part of such interest was required to be included in determining the value of decedent's gross estate under section 811 of the Internal Revenue Code of 1939;

P.L. 113-295, § 221(b)(2), Division A, provides:

(2) SAVINGS PROVISION.—If—

(A) any provision amended or repealed by the amendments made by this section applied to—

(i) any transaction occurring before the date of the enactment of this Act,

(ii) any property acquired before such date of enactment, or

(iii) any item of income, loss, deduction, or credit taken into account before such date of enactment, and

(B) the treatment of such transaction, property, or item under such provision would (without regard to the amendments or repeals made by this section) affect the liability for tax for periods ending after date of enactment, nothing in the amendments or repeals made by this section shall be construed to affect the treatment of such transaction, property, or item for purposes of determining liability for tax for periods ending after such date of enactment.

• **2004, American Jobs Creation Act of 2004 (P.L. 108-357)**

P.L. 108-357, § 413(c)(18):

Amended Code Sec. 1014(b)(5) by inserting "and before January 1, 2005," after "August 26, 1937,". **Effective** for tax years of foreign corporations beginning after 12-31-2004, and for tax years of United States shareholders with or within which such tax years of foreign corporations end.

• **1983, Technical Corrections Act of 1982 (P.L. 97-448)**

P.L. 97-448, § 104(a)(1)(A):

Added Code Sec. 1014(b)(10). **Effective** as if included in the provision of P.L. 97-34 to which it relates.

• **1976, Tax Reform Act of 1976 (P.L. 94-455)**

P.L. 94-455, § 1901(c)(8):

Struck out "Territory," following "State," in Code Secs. 1014(b)(6) and 1014(b)(7). **Effective** for tax years beginning after 12-31-76.

[Sec. 1014(c)]

(c) PROPERTY REPRESENTING INCOME IN RESPECT OF A DECEDENT.—This section shall not apply to property which constitutes a right to receive an item of income in respect of a decedent under section 691.

[Sec. 1014(d)]

(d) SPECIAL RULE WITH RESPECT TO DISC STOCK.—If stock owned by a decedent in a DISC or former DISC (as defined in section 992(a)) acquires a new basis under subsection (a), such basis (determined before the application of this subsection) shall be reduced by the amount (if any) which would have been included in gross income under section 995(c) as a dividend if the decedent had lived and sold the stock at its fair market value on the estate tax valuation date. In computing the gain the decedent would have had if he had lived and sold the stock, his basis shall be determined without regard to the last sentence of section 996(e)(2) (relating to reductions of basis of DISC stock). For purposes of this subsection, the estate tax valuation date is the date of the decedent's death or, in the case of an election under section 2032, the applicable valuation date prescribed by that section.

Amendments

• **1980, Crude Oil Windfall Profit Tax Act of 1980 (P.L. 96-223)**

P.L. 96-223, § 401(a):

Repealed Code Sec. 1014(d) as amended by P.L. 94-455, Act Sec. 2005(a)(1). **Effective** in respect of decedents dying after 12-31-76. However, in the case of a decedent dying after 12-31-76 and before 11-7-78, the executor of an estate may make a special election of the carryover basis rules. The text of Act Sec. 401(d) which authorizes such an election is reproduced below. Prior to repeal, Code Sec. 1014(d) read as follows:

(d) DECEDENTS DYING AFTER DECEMBER 31, 1979.—In the case of a decedent dying after December 31, 1979, this section shall not apply to any property for which a carryover basis is provided by section 1023.

P.L. 96-223, § 401(b):

Revived Code Sec. 1014(d) before its amendment by P.L. 94-455 and P.L. 95-600. **Effective** in respect of decedents dying after 12-31-76.

P.L. 96-223, § 401(d), provides:

(d) ELECTION OF CARRYOVER BASIS RULES BY CERTAIN ESTATES.—Notwithstanding any other provision of law, in the case of a decedent dying after December 31, 1976, and before November 7, 1978, the executor (within the meaning of section 2203 of the Internal Revenue Code of 1954) of such decedent's estate may irrevocably elect, within 120 days following the date of enactment of this Act and in such manner as the Secretary of the Treasury or his delegate shall prescribe, to have the basis of all property acquired from or passing from the decedent (within the meaning of section 1014(b) of the Internal Revenue Code of 1954) determined for all purposes under such Code as though the provisions of section 2005 of the Tax Reform Act of 1976 (as amended by the provisions of section 702(c) of the Revenue Act of 1978) applied to such property acquired or passing from such decedent.

INCOME TAX—BASIS RULES

• **1978, Revenue Act of 1978 (P.L. 95-600)**

P.L. 95-600, § 515(1):

Amended Code Sec. 1014(d) by striking out "December 31, 1976" and inserting in place thereof "December 31, 1979" in the caption and text of such section. **Effective** 11-7-78.

• **1976, Tax Reform Act of 1976 (P.L. 94-455)**

P.L. 94-455, § 2005(a)(1), (f)(1):

Amended Code Sec. 1014(d). **Effective** in respect of decedents dying after 12-31-79, as amended by P.L. 95-600, § 515(6). Prior to amendment, Code Sec. 1014(d) read as follows:

(d) SPECIAL RULE WITH RESPECT TO DISC STOCK.—If stock owned by a decedent in a DISC or former DISC (as defined in section 992(a)) acquires a new basis under subsection (a), such basis (determined before the application of this subsection) shall be reduced by the amount (if any) which would have been included in gross income under section 995(c) as a dividend if the decedent had lived and sold the stock at its fair market value on the estate tax valuation date. In computing the gain the decedent would have had if he had lived and sold the stock, his basis shall be determined without regard to the last sentence of section 996(e)(2) (relating to reductions of basis of DISC stock). For purposes of this subsection, the estate tax valuation date is the date of the decedent's death or, in the case of an election under section 2032, the applicable valuation date prescribed by that section.

• **1971, Revenue Act of 1971 (P.L. 92-178)**

P.L. 92-178, § 502(f):

Added Code Sec. 1014(d). **Effective** date is governed by the effective date for Code Sec. 992.

• **1958 (P.L. 85-320)**

P.L. 85-320, § 2:

Repealed 1954 Code Sec. 1014(d). **Effective** with respect to tax years ending after 12-31-56, but only in the case of employees dying after such date. Prior to repeal, Sec. 1014(d) read:

"(d) Employee Stock Options.—This section shall not apply to restricted stock options described in section 421 which the employee has not exercised at death."

[Sec. 1014(e)]

(e) APPRECIATED PROPERTY ACQUIRED BY DECEDENT BY GIFT WITHIN 1 YEAR OF DEATH.—

(1) IN GENERAL.—In the case of a decedent dying after December 31, 1981, if—

(A) appreciated property was acquired by the decedent by gift during the 1-year period ending on the date of the decedent's death, and

(B) such property is acquired from the decedent by (or passes from the decedent to) the donor of such property (or the spouse of such donor),

the basis of such property in the hands of such donor (or spouse) shall be the adjusted basis of such property in the hands of the decedent immediately before the death of the decedent.

(2) DEFINITIONS.—For purposes of paragraph (1)—

(A) APPRECIATED PROPERTY.—The term "appreciated property" means any property if the fair market value of such property on the day it was transferred to the decedent by gift exceeds its adjusted basis.

(B) TREATMENT OF CERTAIN PROPERTY SOLD BY ESTATE.—In the case of any appreciated property described in subparagraph (A) of paragraph (1) sold by the estate of the decedent or by a trust of which the decedent was the grantor, rules similar to the rules of paragraph (1) shall apply to the extent the donor of such property (or the spouse of such donor) is entitled to the proceeds from such sale.

Amendments

• **1981, Economic Recovery Tax Act of 1981 (P.L. 97-34)**

P.L. 97-34, § 425(a):

Added Code Sec. 1014(e). **Effective** for property acquired after 8-13-81 by decedents dying after 12-31-81.

[Sec. 1014(f)]

(f) BASIS MUST BE CONSISTENT WITH ESTATE TAX RETURN.—For purposes of this section—

(1) IN GENERAL.—The basis of any property to which subsection (a) applies shall not exceed—

(A) in the case of property the final value of which has been determined for purposes of the tax imposed by chapter 11 on the estate of such decedent, such value, and

(B) in the case of property not described in subparagraph (A) and with respect to which a statement has been furnished under section 6035(a) identifying the value of such property, such value.

(2) EXCEPTION.—Paragraph (1) shall only apply to any property whose inclusion in the decedent's estate increased the liability for the tax imposed by chapter 11 (reduced by credits allowable against such tax) on such estate.

(3) DETERMINATION.—For purposes of paragraph (1), the basis of property has been determined for purposes of the tax imposed by chapter 11 if—

(A) the value of such property is shown on a return under section 6018 and such value is not contested by the Secretary before the expiration of the time for assessing a tax under chapter 11,

(B) in a case not described in subparagraph (A), the value is specified by the Secretary and such value is not timely contested by the executor of the estate, or

(C) the value is determined by a court or pursuant to a settlement agreement with the Secretary.

(4) REGULATIONS.—The Secretary may by regulations provide exceptions to the application of this subsection.

Amendments

• **2015, Surface Transportation and Veterans Health Care Choice Improvement Act of 2015 (P.L. 114-41)**

P.L. 114-41, § 2004(a):

Amended Code Sec. 1014 by adding at the end a new subsection (f). **Effective** for property with respect to which an estate tax return is filed after 7-31-2015.

INCOME TAX—BASIS RULES

[Sec. 1014(f)—Repealed]

Amendments

• **2013, American Taxpayer Relief Act of 2012 (P.L. 112-240)**

P.L. 112-240, §101(a)(1)-(3), provides:

SEC. 101. PERMANENT EXTENSION AND MODIFICATION OF 2001 TAX RELIEF.

(a) PERMANENT EXTENSION.—

(1) IN GENERAL.—The Economic Growth and Tax Relief Reconciliation Act of 2001 is amended by striking title IX.

(2) CONFORMING AMENDMENT.—The Tax Relief, Unemployment Insurance Reauthorization, and Job Creation Act of 2010 is amended by striking section 304.

(3) EFFECTIVE DATE.—The amendments made by this subsection shall apply to taxable, plan, or limitation years beginning after December 31, 2012, and estates of decedents dying, gifts made, or generation skipping transfers after December 31, 2012.

• **2010, Tax Relief, Unemployment Insurance Reauthorization, and Job Creation Act of 2010 (P.L. 111-312)**

P.L. 111-312, §301(a):

Amended Code Sec. 1014(f) to read as such provision would read if subtitle E of title V of the Economic Growth and Tax Relief Reconciliation Act of 2001 (P.L. 107-16) had never been enacted. [P.L. 107-16, §541, amended Code Sec. 1014 by adding a new subsection (f). Therefore, P.L. 111-312, §301(a), effectively repealed Code Sec. 1014(f).—CCH] **Effective** for estates of decedents dying, and transfers made, after 12-31-2009. For a special rule, see Act Sec. 301(c), below. Prior to amendment by P.L. 111-312, Code Sec. 1014(f) read as follows:

(f) TERMINATION.—This section shall not apply with respect to decedents dying after December 31, 2009.

P.L. 111-312, §301(c), provides:

(c) SPECIAL ELECTION WITH RESPECT TO ESTATES OF DECEDENTS DYING IN 2010.—Notwithstanding subsection (a), in the case of an estate of a decedent dying after December 31, 2009, and before January 1, 2011, the executor (within the meaning of section 2203 of the Internal Revenue Code of 1986) may elect to apply such Code as though the amendments made by subsection (a) do not apply with respect to chapter 11 of such Code and with respect to property acquired or passing from such decedent (within the meaning of section 1014(b) of such Code). Such election shall be made at such time and in such manner as the Secretary of the Treasury or the Secretary's delegate shall provide. Such an election once made shall be revocable only with the consent of the Secretary of the Treasury or the Secretary's delegate. For purposes of section 2652(a)(1) of such Code, the determination of whether any property is subject to the tax imposed by such chapter 11 shall be made without regard to any election made under this subsection.

P.L. 111-312, §304, provides [but see P.L. 112-240, §101(a)(2)-(3), above]:

SEC. 304. APPLICATION OF EGTRRA SUNSET TO THIS TITLE.

Section 901 of the Economic Growth and Tax Relief Reconciliation Act of 2001 shall apply to the amendments made by this title.

• **2001, Economic Growth and Tax Relief Reconciliation Act of 2001 (P.L. 107-16)**

P.L. 107-16, §541:

Amended Code Sec. 1014 by adding at the end a new subsection (f). **Effective** 6-7-2001.

P.L. 107-16, §901(a)-(b), as amended by P.L. 111-312, §101(a)(1), provides [but see P.L. 112-240, §101(a)(1) and (3), above]:

SEC. 901. SUNSET OF PROVISIONS OF ACT.

(a) IN GENERAL.—All provisions of, and amendments made by, this Act shall not apply—

(1) to taxable, plan, or limitation years beginning after December 31, 2012, or

(2) in the case of title V, to estates of decedents dying, gifts made, or generation skipping transfers, after December 31, 2012.

(b) APPLICATION OF CERTAIN LAWS.—The Internal Revenue Code of 1986 and the Employee Retirement Income Security Act of 1974 shall be applied and administered to years, estates, gifts, and transfers described in subsection (a) as if the provisions and amendments described in subsection (a) had never been enacted.

[Sec. 1015]

SEC. 1015. BASIS OF PROPERTY ACQUIRED BY GIFTS AND TRANSFERS IN TRUST.

[Sec. 1015(a)]

(a) GIFTS AFTER DECEMBER 31, 1920.—If the property was acquired by gift after December 31, 1920, the basis shall be the same as it would be in the hands of the donor or the last preceding owner by whom it was not acquired by gift, except that if such basis (adjusted for the period before the date of the gift as provided in section 1016) is greater than the fair market value of the property at the time of the gift, then for the purpose of determining loss the basis shall be such fair market value. If the facts necessary to determine the basis in the hands of the donor or the last preceding owner are unknown to the donee, the Secretary shall, if possible, obtain such facts from such donor or last preceding owner, or any other person cognizant thereof. If the Secretary finds it impossible to obtain such facts, the basis in the hands of such donor or last preceding owner shall be the fair market value of such property as found by the Secretary as of the date or approximate date at which, according to the best information that the Secretary is able to obtain, such property was acquired by such donor or last preceding owner.

Amendments

• **1976, Tax Reform Act of 1976 (P.L. 94-455)**

P.L. 94-455, §1906(b)(13)(A):

Amended 1954 Code by substituting "Secretary" for "Secretary or his delegate" each place it appeared. **Effective** 2-1-77.

[Sec. 1015(b)]

(b) TRANSFER IN TRUST AFTER DECEMBER 31, 1920.—If the property was acquired after December 31, 1920, by a transfer in trust (other than by a transfer in trust by a gift, bequest, or devise), the basis shall be the same as it would be in the hands of the grantor increased in the amount of gain or decreased in the amount of loss recognized to the grantor on such transfer under the law applicable to the year in which the transfer was made.

[Sec. 1015(c)]

(c) GIFT OR TRANSFER IN TRUST BEFORE JANUARY 1, 1921.—If the property was acquired by gift or transfer in trust on or before December 31, 1920, the basis shall be the fair market value of such property at the time of such acquisition.

[Sec. 1015(d)]

(d) INCREASED BASIS FOR GIFT TAX PAID.—

(1) IN GENERAL.—If—

(A) the property is acquired by gift on or after September 2, 1958, the basis shall be the basis determined under subsection (a), increased (but not above the fair market value of the property at the time of the gift) by the amount of gift tax paid with respect to such gift, or

Sec. 1014(f)—Repealed

INCOME TAX—BASIS RULES

(B) the property was acquired by gift before September 2, 1958, and has not been sold, exchanged, or otherwise disposed of before such date, the basis of the property shall be increased on such date by the amount of gift tax paid with respect to such gift, but such increase shall not exceed an amount equal to the amount by which the fair market value of the property at the time of the gift exceeded the basis of the property in the hands of the donor at the time of the gift.

(2) AMOUNT OF TAX PAID WITH RESPECT TO GIFT.—For purposes of paragraph (1), the amount of gift tax paid with respect to any gift is an amount which bears the same ratio to the amount of gift tax paid under chapter 12 with respect to all gifts made by the donor for the calendar year (or preceding calendar period) in which such gift is made as the amount of such gift bears to the taxable gifts (as defined in section 2503(a) but computed without the deduction allowed by section 2521) made by the donor during such calendar year or period. For purposes of the preceding sentence, the amount of any gift shall be the amount included with respect to such gift in determining (for the purposes of section 2503(a)) the total amount of gifts made during the calendar year or period, reduced by the amount of any deduction allowed with respect to such gift under section 2522 (relating to charitable deduction) or under section 2523 (relating to marital deduction).

(3) GIFTS TREATED AS MADE ONE-HALF BY EACH SPOUSE.—For purposes of paragraph (1), where the donor and his spouse elected, under section 2513 to have the gift considered as made one-half by each, the amount of gift tax paid with respect to such gift under chapter 12 shall be the sum of the amounts of tax paid with respect to each half of such gift (computed in the manner provided in paragraph (2)).

(4) TREATMENT AS ADJUSTMENT TO BASIS.—For purposes of section 1016(b), an increase in basis under paragraph (1) shall be treated as an adjustment under section 1016(a).

(5) APPLICATION TO GIFTS BEFORE 1955.—With respect to any property acquired by gift before 1955, references in this subsection to any provision of this title shall be deemed to refer to the corresponding provision of the Internal Revenue Code of 1939 or prior revenue laws which was effective for the year in which such gift was made.

(6) SPECIAL RULE FOR GIFTS MADE AFTER DECEMBER 31, 1976.—

(A) IN GENERAL.—In the case of any gift made after December 31, 1976, the increase in basis provided by this subsection with respect to any gift for the gift tax paid under chapter 12 shall be an amount (not in excess of the amount of tax so paid) which bears the same ratio to the amount of tax so paid as—

(i) the net appreciation in value of the gift, bears to

(ii) the amount of the gift.

(B) NET APPRECIATION.—For purposes of paragraph (1), the net appreciation in value of any gift is the amount by which the fair market value of the gift exceeds the donor's adjusted basis immediately before the gift.

Amendments

• **1981, Economic Recovery Tax Act of 1981 (P.L. 97-34)**

P.L. 97-34, §442(d)(1):

Amended Code Sec. 1015(d)(2), by striking out "calendar quarter (or calendar year if the gift was made before January 1, 1971)" and inserting "calendar year (or preceding calendar period)", and by striking out "calendar quarter or year" each place it appears and inserting "calendar year or period". **Effective** with respect to estates of decedents dying after 12-31-81.

• **1976, Tax Reform Act of 1976 (P.L. 94-455)**

P.L. 94-455, §1901(a)(122):

Substituted "September 2, 1958" for "the date of the enactment of the Technical Amendments Act of 1958" in Code Sec. 1015(d)(1)(A) and (B). **Effective** for tax years beginning after 12-31-76.

P.L. 94-455, §2005(c):

Added Code Sec. 1015(d)(6). **Effective** for gifts made after 12-31-76.

• **1970, Excise, Estate, and Gift Tax Adjustment Act of 1970 (P.L. 91-164)**

P.L. 91-614, §102(d)(1):

Amended Code Sec. 1015(d)(2) by substituting "calendar quarter (or calendar year if the gift was made before January 1, 1971)" for "calendar year" in the first sentence and by substituting "calendar quarter or year" for "calendar year" at the end of such sentence. In the second sentence, "calendar quarter or year" was substituted for "calendar year." **Effective** for gifts made after 12-31-70.

• **1958, Technical Amendments Act of 1958 (P.L. 85-866)**

P.L. 85-866, §43(a);

Added new subsection (d) to Sec. 1015 to read as prior to amendment by P.L. 91-614 and P.L. 94-455. **Effective** 1-1-54.

[Sec. 1015(e)]

(e) GIFTS BETWEEN SPOUSES.—In the case of any property acquired by gift in a transfer described in section 1041(a), the basis of such property in the hands of the transferee shall be determined under section 1041(b)(2) and not this section.

Amendments

• **1984, Deficit Reduction Act of 1984 (P.L. 98-369)**

P.L. 98-369, §421(b)(5):

Amended Code Sec. 1015 by adding at the end thereof a new subsection (e). **Effective** for transfers after 7-18-84, in tax years ending after such date. Special rules appear in Act Sec. 421(d)(2)-(4) following Code Sec. 1041.

[Sec. 1016]

SEC. 1016. ADJUSTMENTS TO BASIS.

[Sec. 1016(a)]

(a) GENERAL RULE.—Proper adjustment in respect of the property shall in all cases be made—

(1) for expenditures, receipts, losses, or other items, properly chargeable to capital account, but no such adjustment shall be made—

(A) for—

(i) taxes or other carrying charges described in section 266; or

(ii) expenditures described in section 173 (relating to circulation expenditures),

for which deductions have been taken by the taxpayer in determining taxable income for the taxable year or prior taxable years; or

(B) for mortality, expense, or other reasonable charges incurred under an annuity or life insurance contract;

INCOME TAX—BASIS RULES

(2) in respect of any period since February 28, 1913, for exhaustion, wear and tear, obsolescence, amortization, and depletion, to the extent of the amount—

(A) allowed as deductions in computing taxable income under this subtitle or prior income tax laws, and

(B) resulting (by reason of the deductions so allowed) in a reduction for any taxable year of the taxpayer's taxes under this subtitle (other than chapter 2, relating to tax on self-employment income), or prior income, war-profits, or excess-profits tax laws,

but not less than the amount allowable under this subtitle or prior income tax laws. Where no method has been adopted under section 167 (relating to depreciation deduction), the amount allowable shall be determined under the straight line method. Subparagraph (B) of this paragraph shall not apply in respect of any period since February 28, 1913, and before January 1, 1952, unless an election has been made under section 1020 (as in effect before the date of the enactment of the Tax Reform Act of 1976). Where for any taxable year before the taxable year 1932 the depletion allowance was based on discovery value or a percentage of income, then the adjustment for depletion for such year shall be based on the depletion which would have been allowable for such year if computed without reference to discovery value or a percentage of income;

(3) in respect of any period—

(A) before March 1, 1913,

(B) since February 28, 1913, during which such property was held by a person or an organization not subject to income taxation under this chapter or prior income tax laws,

(C) since February 28, 1913, and before January 1, 1958, during which such property was held by a person subject to tax under part I of subchapter L (or the corresponding provisions of prior income tax laws), to the extent that paragraph (2) does not apply, and

(D) since February 28, 1913, during which such property was held by a person subject to tax under part II of subchapter L as in effect prior to its repeal by the Tax Reform Act of 1986 (or the corresponding provisions of prior income tax laws), to the extent that paragraph (2) does not apply,

for exhaustion, wear and tear, obsolescence, amortization, and depletion, to the extent sustained;

(4) in the case of stock (to the extent not provided for in the foregoing paragraphs) for the amount of distributions previously made which, under the law applicable to the year in which the distribution was made, either were tax-free or were applicable in reduction of basis (not including distributions made by a corporation which was classified as a personal service corporation under the provisions of the Revenue Act of 1918 (40 Stat. 1057), or the Revenue Act of 1921 (42 Stat. 227), out of its earnings or profits which were taxable in accordance with the provisions of section 218 of the Revenue Act of 1918 or 1921);

(5) in the case of any bond (as defined in section 171(d)) the interest on which is wholly exempt from the tax imposed by this subtitle, to the extent of the amortizable bond premium disallowable as a deduction pursuant to section 171(a)(2), and in the case of any other bond (as defined in section 171(d)) to the extent of the deductions allowable pursuant to section 171(a)(1) (or the amount applied to reduce interest payments under section 171(e)(2)) with respect thereto;

(6) in the case of any municipal bond (as defined in section 75(b)), to the extent provided in section 75(a)(2);

(7) in the case of a residence the acquisition of which resulted, under section 1034 (as in effect on the day before the date of the enactment of the Taxpayer Relief Act of 1997), in the nonrecognition of any part of the gain realized on the sale, exchange, or involuntary conversion of another residence, to the extent provided in section 1034(e) (as so in effect);

(8) in the case of property pledged to the Commodity Credit Corporation, to the extent of the amount received as a loan from the Commodity Credit Corporation and treated by the taxpayer as income for the year in which received pursuant to section 77, and to the extent of any deficiency on such loan with respect to which the taxpayer has been relieved from liability;

(9) for amounts allowed as deductions as deferred expenses under section 616(b) (relating to certain expenditures in the development of mines) and resulting in a reduction of the taxpayer's taxes under this subtitle, but not less than the amounts allowable under such section for the taxable year and prior years;

(10) [Stricken.]

(11) for deductions to the extent disallowed under section 268 (relating to sale of land with unharvested crops), notwithstanding the provisions of any other paragraph of this subsection;

(12) [Stricken.]

(13) [Stricken.]

(14) for amounts allowed as deductions as deferred expenses under section 174(b)(1) (relating to research and experimental expenditures) and resulting in a reduction of the taxpayers' taxes under this subtitle, but not less than the amounts allowable under such section for the taxable year and prior years;

(15) for deductions to the extent disallowed under section 272 (relating to disposal of coal or domestic iron ore), notwithstanding the provisions of any other paragraph of this subsection;

(16) in the case of any evidence of indebtedness referred to in section 811(b) (relating to amortization of premium and accrual of discount in the case of life insurance companies), to the extent of the adjustments required under section 811(b) (or the corresponding provisions of prior income tax laws) for the taxable year and all prior taxable years;

(17) to the extent provided in section 1367 in the case of stock of, and indebtedness owed to, shareholders of an S corporation;

(18) to the extent provided in section 961 in the case of stock in controlled foreign corporations (or foreign corporations which were controlled foreign corporations) and of property by reason of which a person is considered as owning such stock;

(19) to the extent provided in section 50(c), in the case of expenditures with respect to which a credit has been allowed under section 38;

(20) for amounts allowed as deductions under section 59(e) (relating to optional 10-year writeoff of certain tax preferences);

(21) to the extent provided in section 1059 (relating to reduction in basis for extraordinary dividends);

(22) in the case of qualified replacement property the acquisition of which resulted under section 1042 in the nonrecognition of any part of the gain realized on the sale or exchange of any property, to the extent provided in section 1042(d),

Sec. 1016(a)(2)

INCOME TAX—BASIS RULES

(23) in the case of property the acquisition of which resulted under section 1043, 1045, or 1397B in the nonrecognition of any part of the gain realized on the sale of other property, to the extent provided in section 1043(c), 1045(b)(3), or 1397B(b)(4), as the case may be,

(24) [Stricken.]

(25) [Stricken.]

(26) to the extent provided in sections 23(g) and 137(e),

(27) [Stricken.]

(28) in the case of a facility with respect to which a credit was allowed under section 45F, to the extent provided in section 45F(f)(1),

(29) in the case of railroad track with respect to which a credit was allowed under section 45G, to the extent provided in section 45G(e)(3),

(30) to the extent provided in section 179B(c),

(31) to the extent provided in section 179D(e),

(32) to the extent provided in section 45L(e), in the case of amounts with respect to which a credit has been allowed under section 45L,

(33) to the extent provided in section 25C(g), in the case of amounts with respect to which a credit has been allowed under section 25C,

(34) to the extent provided in section 25D(f), in the case of amounts with respect to which a credit has been allowed under section 25D,

(35) to the extent provided in section 30B(h)(4),

(36) to the extent provided in section 30C(e)(1),

(37) to the extent provided in section 30D(f)(1), and

(38) to the extent provided in subsections (b)(2) and (c) of section 1400Z–2.

Amendments

• **2022, Inflation Reduction Act of 2022 (P.L. 117-169)**

P.L. 117-169, §13301(f)(3)(B):

Amended Code Sec. 1016(a)(33) by striking "section 25C(f)" and inserting "section 25C(g)". **Effective** for property placed in service after 12-31-2022.

• **2018, Tax Technical Corrections Act of 2018 (P.L. 115-141)**

P.L. 115-141, §401(a)(166), Div. U:

Amended Code Sec. 1016(a)(3)(D) by inserting "as in effect prior to its repeal by the Tax Reform Act of 1986" before "(or the corresponding provisions of prior income tax laws)". **Effective** 3-23-2018.

P.L. 115-141, §401(d)(4)(B)(iv), Div. U:

Amended Code Sec. 1016(a) by striking paragraph (27). **Effective** 3-23-2018. For a special rule, see Act Sec. 401(e), Div. U, below. Prior to being stricken, Code Sec. 1016(a)(27) read as follows:

(27) in the case of a residence with respect to which a credit was allowed under section 1400C, to the extent provided in section 1400C(h),

P.L. 115-141, §401(e), Div. U, provides:

(e) GENERAL SAVINGS PROVISION WITH RESPECT TO DEADWOOD PROVISIONS.—If—

(1) any provision amended or repealed by the amendments made by subsection (b) or (d) applied to—

(A) any transaction occurring before the date of the enactment of this Act,

(B) any property acquired before such date of enactment, or

(C) any item of income, loss, deduction, or credit taken into account before such date of enactment, and

(2) the treatment of such transaction, property, or item under such provision would (without regard to the amendments or repeals made by such subsection) affect the liability for tax for periods ending after such date of enactment,

nothing in the amendments or repeals made by this section shall be construed to affect the treatment of such transaction, property, or item for purposes of determining liability for tax for periods ending after such date of enactment.

• **2017, Tax Cuts and Jobs Act (P.L. 115-97)**

P.L. 115-97, §13313(b)(1)-(2):

Amended Code Sec. 1016(a)(23) by striking "1044," following "under section 1043,", and by striking "1044(d)," following "in section 1043(c),". **Effective** for sales after 12-31-2017.

P.L. 115-97, §13521(a):

Amended Code Sec. 1016(a)(1) by striking subparagraph (A) and all that follows and inserting new subparagraphs (A) and (B). **Effective** for transactions entered into after 8-25-2009. Prior to being stricken, subparagraph (A) and all that follows in Code Sec. 1016(a)(1) read as follows:

(A) for taxes or other carrying charges described in section 266, or

(B) for expenditures described in section 173 (relating to circulation expenditures),

for which deductions have been taken by the taxpayer in determining taxable income for the taxable year or prior taxable years;

P.L. 115-97, §13823(b):

Amended Code Sec. 1016(a) by striking "and" at the end of paragraph (36), by striking the period at the end of paragraph (37) and inserting ", and", and by inserting after paragraph (37) a new paragraph (38). **Effective** 12-22-2017.

• **2014, Tax Technical Corrections Act of 2014 (P.L. 113-295)**

P.L. 113-295, §209(j)(2), Division A:

Amended Code Sec. 1016(a)(37) by striking "section 30D(e)(4)" and inserting "section 30D(f)(1)". **Effective** as if included in the provision of the American Recovery and Reinvestment Tax Act of 2009 (P.L. 111-5) to which it relates [**effective** for vehicles acquired after 12-31-2009.—CCH.].

P.L. 113-295, §221(a)(2)(D), Division A:

Amended Code Sec. 1016(a) by striking paragraph (25). **Effective** generally 12-19-2014. For a special rule, see Act Sec. 221(b)(2), Division A, below. Prior to being stricken, Code Sec. 1016(a)(25) read as follows:

(25) to the extent provided in section 30(e)(1),

P.L. 113-295, §221(a)(34)(G), Division A:

Amended Code Sec. 1016(a) by striking paragraph (24). **Effective** generally 12-19-2014. For a special rule, see Act Sec. 221(b)(2), Division A, below. Prior to being stricken, Code Sec. 1016(a)(24) read as follows:

(24) to the extent provided in section 179A(e)(6)(A),

P.L. 113-295, §221(a)(75), Division A:

Amended Code Sec. 1016(a) by striking paragraph (12). **Effective** generally 12-19-2014. For a special rule, see Act Sec. 221(b)(2), Division A, below. Prior to being stricken, Code Sec. 1016(a)(12) read as follows:

(12) to the extent provided in section 28(h) of the Internal Revenue Code of 1939 in the case of amounts specified in a shareholder's consent made under section 28 of such code;

P.L. 113-295, §221(b)(2), Division A, provides:

(2) SAVINGS PROVISION.—If—

(A) any provision amended or repealed by the amendments made by this section applied to—

(i) any transaction occurring before the date of the enactment of this Act,

(ii) any property acquired before such date of enactment, or

(iii) any item of income, loss, deduction, or credit taken into account before such date of enactment, and

(B) the treatment of such transaction, property, or item under such provision would (without regard to the amendments or repeals made by this section) affect the liability for tax for periods ending after date of enactment, nothing in the amendments or repeals made by this section shall be construed to affect the treatment of such transaction, property, or item for purposes of determining liability for tax for periods ending after such date of enactment.

INCOME TAX—BASIS RULES

- **2013, American Taxpayer Relief Act of 2012 (P.L. 112-240)**

P.L. 112-240, §101(a)(1) and (3), provides:

SEC. 101. PERMANENT EXTENSION AND MODIFICATION OF 2001 TAX RELIEF.

(a) PERMANENT EXTENSION.—

(1) IN GENERAL.—The Economic Growth and Tax Relief Reconciliation Act of 2001 is amended by striking title IX.

* * *

(3) EFFECTIVE DATE.—The amendments made by this subsection shall apply to taxable, plan, or limitation years beginning after December 31, 2012, and estates of decedents dying, gifts made, or generation skipping transfers after December 31, 2012.

- **2010, Tax Relief, Unemployment Insurance Reauthorization, and Job Creation Act of 2010 (P.L. 111-312)**

P.L. 111-312, §101(b)(1):

Amended Code Sec. 1016(a)(26) to read as such provision would read if section 10909 of the Patient Protection and Affordable Care Act (P.L. 111-148) had never been enacted. **Effective** for tax years beginning after 12-31-2011.

- **2010, Patient Protection and Affordable Care Act (P.L. 111-148)**

P.L. 111-148, §10909(b)(2)(L):

Amended Code Sec. 1016(a)(26) by striking "23(g)" and inserting "36C(g)". **Effective** for tax years beginning after 12-31-2009.

P.L. 111-148, §10909(c), as amended by P.L. 111-312, §101(b)(1), provides:

(c) SUNSET PROVISION.—Each provision of law amended by this section is amended to read as such provision would read if this section had never been enacted. The amendments made by the preceding sentence shall apply to taxable years beginning after December 31, 2011.

- **2009, American Recovery and Reinvestment Tax Act of 2009 (P.L. 111-5)**

P.L. 111-5, §1141(b)(3):

Amended Code Sec. 1016(a)(25) by striking "section 30D(e)(4)" and inserting "section 30D(f)(1)". [The text "section 30D(e)(4)" does not exist. Therefore, this amendment cannot be made.—CCH] **Effective** for vehicles acquired after 12-31-2009.

P.L. 111-5, §1142(b)(6):

Amended Code Sec. 1016(a)(25) by striking "section 30(d)(1)" and inserting "section 30(e)(1)". **Effective** for vehicles acquired after 2-17-2009. For a transitional rule, see Act Sec. 1142(d) in the amendment notes for Code Sec. 30.

- **2008, Energy Improvement and Extension Act of 2008 (P.L. 110-343)**

P.L. 110-343, Division B, §205(d)(2):

Amended Code Sec. 1016(a) by striking "and" at the end of paragraph (35), by striking the period at the end of paragraph (36) and inserting ", and", and by adding at the end a new paragraph (37). **Effective** for tax years beginning after 12-31-2008.

- **2007, Tax Technical Corrections Act of 2007 (P.L. 110-172)**

P.L. 110-172, §7(a)(1)(C):

Amended Code Sec. 1016(a) by striking paragraph (31) and by redesignating paragraphs (32) through (37) as paragraphs (31) through (36), respectively. **Effective** as if included in the provision of the American Jobs Creation Act of 2004 (P.L. 108-357) to which it relates [**effective** for expenses paid or incurred after 12-31-2002, in tax years ending after such date.—CCH]. Prior to being stricken, Code Sec. 1016(a)(31) read as follows:

(31) in the case of a facility with respect to which a credit was allowed under section 45H, to the extent provided in section 45H(d),

P.L. 110-172, §11(a)(21):

Amended Code Sec. 1016(a)(33), as redesignated by Act Sec. 7(a)(1)(C), by striking "section 25C(e)" and inserting "section 25C(f)". **Effective** 12-29-2007.

P.L. 110-172, §11(a)(22):

Amended Code Sec. 1016(a)(36), as redesignated by Act Sec. 7(a)(1)(C), by striking "section 30C(f)" and inserting "section 30C(e)(1)". **Effective** 12-29-2007.

- **2005, Gulf Opportunity Zone Act of 2005 (P.L. 109-135)**

P.L. 109-135, §412(nn):

Amended Code Sec. 1016(a)(23) by striking "1045(b)(4)" and inserting "1045(b)(3)". **Effective** 12-21-2005.

- **2005, Energy Tax Incentives Act of 2005 (P.L. 109-58)**

P.L. 109-58, §1331(b)(1):

Amended Code Sec. 1016(a) by striking "and" at the end of paragraph (30), by striking the period at the end of paragraph (31) and inserting ", and", and by adding at the end a new paragraph (32). **Effective** for property placed in service after 12-31-2005.

P.L. 109-58, §1332(c):

Amended Code Sec. 1016(a), as amended by this Act, by striking "and" at the end of paragraph (31), by striking the period at the end of paragraph (32) and inserting ", and", and by adding at the end a new paragraph (33). **Effective** for qualified new energy efficient homes acquired after 12-31-2005, in tax years ending after such date.

P.L. 109-58, §1333(b)(1):

Amended Code Sec. 1016(a), as amended by this Act, by striking "and" at the end of paragraph (32), by striking the period at the end of paragraph (33) and inserting ", and", and by adding at the end a new paragraph (34). **Effective** for property placed in service after 12-31-2005.

P.L. 109-58, §1335(b)(4):

Amended Code Sec. 1016(a), as amended by this Act, by striking "and" at the end of paragraph (33), by striking the period at the end of paragraph (34) and inserting ", and", and by adding at the end a new paragraph (35). **Effective** for property placed in service after 12-31-2005, in tax years ending after such date.

P.L. 109-58, §1341(b)(2):

Amended Code Sec. 1016(a), as amended by this Act, by striking "and" at the end of paragraph (34), by striking the period at the end of paragraph (35) and inserting ", and", and by adding at the end a new paragraph (36). **Effective** for property placed in service after 12-31-2005, in tax years ending after such date.

P.L. 109-58, §1342(b)(2):

Amended Code Sec. 1016(a), as amended by this Act, by striking "and" at the end of paragraph (35), by striking the period at the end of paragraph (36) and inserting ", and", and by adding at the end a new paragraph (37). **Effective** for property placed in service after 12-31-2005, in tax years ending after such date.

- **2004, American Jobs Creation Act of 2004 (P.L. 108-357)**

P.L. 108-357, §245(c)(2):

Amended Code Sec. 1016(a) by striking "and" at the end of paragraph (27), by striking the period at the end of paragraph (28) and inserting ", and", and by inserting after paragraph (28) a new paragraph (29). **Effective** for tax years beginning after 12-31-2004.

P.L. 108-357, §338(b)(4):

Amended Code Sec. 1016(a) by striking "and" at the end of paragraph (28), by striking the period at the end of paragraph (29) and inserting ", and", and by inserting after paragraph (29) a new paragraph (30). **Effective** for expenses paid or incurred after 12-31-2002, in tax years ending after such date.

P.L. 108-357, §339(d):

Amended Code Sec. 1016(a), as amended by this Act, by striking "and" at the end of paragraph (29), by striking the period at the end of paragraph (30) and inserting ", and", and by inserting after paragraph (30) a new paragraph (31). **Effective** for expenses paid or incurred after 12-31-2002, in tax years ending after such date.

P.L. 108-357, §413(c)(19):

Amended Code Sec. 1016(a) by striking paragraph (13). **Effective** for tax years of foreign corporations beginning after 12-31-2004, and for tax years of United States shareholders with or within which such tax years of foreign corporations end. Prior to being stricken, Code Sec. 1016(a)(13) read as follows:

(13) to the extent provided in section 551(e) in the case of the stock of United States shareholders in a foreign personal holding company;

- **2001, Economic Growth and Tax Relief Reconciliation Act of 2001 (P.L. 107-16)**

P.L. 107-16, §205(b)(3):

Amended Code Sec. 1016(a) by striking "and" at the end of paragraph (26), by striking the period at the end of paragraph (27) and inserting ", and", and by adding at the end a new subparagraph (28). **Effective** for tax years beginning after 12-31-2001.

P.L. 107-16, §901(a)-(b), as amended by P.L. 111-312, §101(a)(1), provides [but see P.L. 111-148, §10909(c), and P.L. 112-240, §101(a)(1) and (3), above]:

SEC. 901. SUNSET OF PROVISIONS OF ACT.

(a) IN GENERAL.—All provisions of, and amendments made by, this Act shall not apply—

INCOME TAX—BASIS RULES

(1) to taxable, plan, or limitation years beginning after December 31, 2012, or

(2) in the case of title V, to estates of decedents dying, gifts made, or generation skipping transfers, after December 31, 2012.

(b) APPLICATION OF CERTAIN LAWS.—The Internal Revenue Code of 1986 and the Employee Retirement Income Security Act of 1974 shall be applied and administered to years, estates, gifts, and transfers described in subsection (a) as if the provisions and amendments described in subsection (a) had never been enacted.

• **2000, Community Renewal Tax Relief Act of 2000 (P.L. 106-554)**

P.L. 106-554, §116(b)(1)(A)-(B):

Amended Code Sec. 1016(a)(23) by striking "or 1045" and inserting "1045, or 1397B", and by striking "or 1045(b)(4)" and inserting "1045(b)(4), or 1397B(b)(4)". **Effective** for qualified empowerment zone assets acquired after 12-21-2000.

• **1997, Taxpayer Relief Act of 1997 (P.L. 105-34)**

P.L. 105-34, §312(d)(6):

Amended Code Sec. 1016(a)(7) by inserting "(as in effect on the day before the date of the enactment of the Taxpayer Relief Act of 1997)" after "1034" and by inserting "(as so in effect)" after "1034(e)". **Effective**, generally, for sales and exchanges after 5-6-97.

P.L. 105-34, §313(b)(1)(A)-(B):

Amended Code Sec. 1016(a)(23) by striking "or 1044" and inserting ", 1044, or 1045", and by striking "or 1044(d)" and inserting ", 1044(d), or 1045(b)(4)". **Effective** for sales after 8-5-97.

P.L. 105-34, §701(b)(2):

Amended Code Sec. 1016(a) by striking "and" at the end of paragraph (25), by striking the period at the end of paragraph (26) and inserting ", and", and by adding at the end a new paragraph (27). **Effective** 8-5-97.

• **1996, Small Business Job Protection Act of 1996 (P.L. 104-188)**

P.L. 104-188, §1807(c)(5):

Amended Code Sec. 1016(a) by striking "and" at the end of paragraph (24), by striking the period at the end of paragraph (25) and inserting ", and ", and by adding at the end a new paragraph (26). **Effective** for tax years beginning after 12-31-96.

• **1993, Omnibus Budget Reconciliation Act of 1993 (P.L. 103-66)**

P.L. 103-66, §13114(b)(1)-(2):

Amended Code Sec. 1016(a)(24) by striking "section 1043" and inserting "section 1043 or 1044", and by striking "section 1043(c)" and inserting "section 1043(c) or 1044(d), as the case may be". **Effective** for sales on and after 8-10-93, in tax years ending on and after such date.

P.L. 103-66, §13261(f)(3):

Amended Code Sec. 1016(a) by striking paragraph (19) and by redesignating paragraphs (20)-(26) as paragraphs (19)-(25). **Effective** with respect to property acquired after 8-10-93, except as provided in Act Sec. 13261(g)(2)-(3), below. Prior to amendment, paragraph (19) read as follows:

(19) for amounts allowed as deductions for payments made on account of transfers of franchises, trademarks, or trade names under section 1253(d)(2);

P.L. 103-66, §13261(g)(2)-(3), provides:

(2) ELECTION TO HAVE AMENDMENTS APPLY TO PROPERTY ACQUIRED AFTER JULY 25, 1991.—

(A) IN GENERAL.—If an election under this paragraph applies to the taxpayer—

(i) the amendments made by this section shall apply to property acquired by the taxpayer after July 25, 1991,

(ii) subsection (c)(1)(A) of section 197 of the Internal Revenue Code of 1986 (as added by this section) (and so much of subsection (f)(9)(A) of such section 197 as precedes clause (i) thereof) shall be applied with respect to the taxpayer by treating July 25, 1991, as the date of the enactment of such section, and

(iii) in applying subsection (f)(9) of such section, with respect to any property acquired by the taxpayer on or before the date of the enactment of this Act, only holding or use on July 25, 1991, shall be taken into account.

(B) ELECTION.—An election under this paragraph shall be made at such time and in such manner as the Secretary of the Treasury or his delegate may prescribe. Such an election by any taxpayer, once made—

(i) may be revoked only with the consent of the Secretary, and

(ii) shall apply to the taxpayer making such election and any other taxpayer under common control with the taxpayer (within the meaning of subparagraphs (A) and (B) of section 41(f)(1) of such Code) at any time after August 2, 1993, and on or before the date on which such election is made.

(3) ELECTIVE BINDING CONTRACT EXCEPTION.—

(A) IN GENERAL.—The amendments made by this section shall not apply to any acquisition of property by the taxpayer if—

(i) such acquisition is pursuant to a written binding contract in effect on the date of the enactment of this Act and at all times thereafter before such acquisition,

(ii) an election under paragraph (2) does not apply to taxpayer, and

(iii) The taxpayer makes an election under this paragraph with respect to such contract.

(B) ELECTION.—An election under this paragraph shall be made at such time and in such manner as the Secretary of the Treasury or his delegate shall prescribe. Such an election, once made—

(i) may be revoked only with the consent of the Secretary, and

(ii) shall apply to all property acquired pursuant to the contract with respect to which such election was made.

• **1992, Energy Policy Act of 1992 (P.L. 102-486)**

P.L. 102-486, §1913(a)(3)(A):

Amended Code Sec. 1016(a) by striking "and" at the end of paragraph (23), by striking the period at the end of paragraph (24) and inserting ", and", and by adding at the end thereof new paragraph (25). **Effective** for property placed in service after 6-30-93.

P.L. 102-486, §1913(b)(2)(B):

Amended Code Sec. 1016(a) (as amended) by striking "and" at the end of paragraph (24), by striking the period at the end of paragraph (25) and inserting ", and", and by adding at the end thereof new paragraph (26). **Effective** for property placed in service after 6-30-93.

• **1990, Omnibus Budget Reconciliation Act of 1990 (P.L. 101-508)**

P.L. 101-508, §11801(c)(1):

Amended Code Sec. 1016(a) by striking paragraph (20) and by redesignating paragraphs (21) through (25) as paragraphs (20) through (24). **Effective** 11-5-90. Prior to repeal, Code Sec. 1016(a)(20) read as follows:

(20) to the extent provided in section 23(e), in the case of property with respect to which a credit has been allowed under section 23;

P.L. 101-508, §11821(b)(1)-(2), provides:

(b) SAVINGS PROVISION.—If—

(1) any provision amended or repealed by this part applied to—

(A) any transaction occurring before the date of the enactment of this Act,

(B) any property acquired before such date of enactment, or

(C) any item of income, loss, deduction, or credit taken into account before such date of enactment, and

(2) the treatment of such transaction, property, or item under such provision would (without regard to the amendments made by this part) affect liability for tax for periods ending after such date of enactment,

nothing in the amendments made by this part shall be construed to affect the treatment of such transaction, property, or item for purposes of determining liability for tax for periods ending after such date of enactment.

P.L. 101-508, §11812(b)(10):

Amended Code Sec. 1016(a)(2) by striking "under section 167(b)(1)" and inserting "under the straight line method". **Effective**, generally, for property placed in service after 11-5-90. However, for exceptions, see Act Sec. 11812(c)(2)-(3), below.

P.L. 101-508, §11812(c)(2)-(3), provides:

(2) EXCEPTION.—The amendments made by this section shall not apply to any property to which section 168 of the Internal Revenue Code of 1986 does not apply by reason of subsection (f)(5) thereof.

(3) EXCEPTION FOR PREVIOUSLY GRANDFATHER EXPENDITURES.—The amendments made by this section shall not apply to rehabilitation expenditures described in section 252(f)(5) of the Tax Reform Act of 1986 (as added by section 1002(l)(31) of the Technical and Miscellaneous Revenue Act of 1988).

P.L. 101-508, §11813(b)(19) (as amended by P.L. 104-188, §1704(t)(56)):

Amended Code Sec. 1016(a)(20), as redesignated by section 11801, by striking "section 48(q)" and inserting "section 50(c)". **Effective** for property placed in service after 12-31-90.

• **1989, Ethics Reform Act (P.L. 101-194)**

P.L. 101-194, §502(b)(2):

Amended Code Sec. 1016(a) by striking "and" at the end of paragraph (23), by striking the period at the end of paragraph (24) and inserting ", and", and by adding at the end thereof a new paragraph (25). **Effective** for sales after 11-30-89.

• **1988, Technical and Miscellaneous Revenue Act of 1988 (P.L. 100-647)**

P.L. 100-647, §1006(j)(1)(B):

Amended Code Sec. 1016(a)(5) by striking out "allowable pursuant to section 171(a)(1)" and inserting in lieu thereof "allowable pursuant to section 171(a)(1) (or the amount applied to reduce interest payments under section 171(e)(2))". **Effective** in the case of obligations acquired after 12-31-87; except that the taxpayer may elect to have such amendment apply to obligations acquired after 10-22-86.

INCOME TAX—BASIS RULES

P.L. 100-647, §1018(u)(22):

Amended Code Sec. 1016(a) by striking out all that follows paragraph (20) and inserting new paragraphs (21)-(24). **Effective** as if included in the provision of P.L. 99-514 to which it relates. Prior to amendment, all that followed paragraph (20) in Code Sec. 1016(a) read as follows:

(21) to the extent provided in section 1023, relating to carryover basis for certain property acquired from a decedent dying after December 31, 1979;

(22) to the extent provided in section 48(q), in the case of expenditures with respect to which a credit has been allowed under section 38;

(23) for amounts allowed as deductions under section 59(d) (relating to optional 10-year writeoff of certain tax preferences);

(24) to the extent provided in section 1059 (relating to reduction in basis for extraordinary dividends), and

(25) in the case of qualified replacement property, the acquisition of which resulted under section 1042 in the nonrecognition of any part of the gain realized on the sale or exchange of any property, to the extent provided in section 1042(c).

• **1986, Tax Reform Act of 1986 (P.L. 99-514)**

P.L. 99-514, §241(b)(2):

Amended Code Sec. 1016(a) by striking out paragraph (16) and by redesignating paragraphs (17) through (27) as paragraphs (16) through (26), respectively. **Effective** for expenditures paid or incurred after 12-31-86. For a transitional rule see Act Sec. 241(c)(2), below. Prior to amendment, Code Sec. 1016(a)(16) read as follows:

(16) for amounts allowed as deductions for expenditures treated as deferred expenses under section 177 (relating to trademark and trade name expenditures) and resulting in a reduction of the taxpayer's taxes under this subtitle, but not less than the amounts allowable under such section for the taxable year and prior years;

P.L. 99-514, §241(c)(2), provides:

(2) TRANSITIONAL RULE.—The amendments made by this section shall not apply to any expenditure incurred—

(A) pursuant to a binding contract entered into before March 2, 1986, or

(B) with respect to the development, protection, expansion, registration, or defense of a trademark or trade name commenced before March 2, 1986, but only if not less than the lesser of $1,000,000 or 5 percent of the aggregate cost of such development, protection, expansion, registration, or defense has been incurred or committed before such date. The preceding sentence shall not apply to any expenditure with respect to a trademark or trade name placed in service after December 31, 1987.

P.L. 99-514, §701(e)(4)(D):

Amended Code Sec. 1016(a)(24), as redesignated by Act Sec. 241(b)(2), by striking out "section 58(i)" and inserting in lieu thereof "section 59(d)". **Effective,** generally, for tax years beginning after 12-31-86. However, see Act Sec. 701(f)(2)-(7), at Code Sec. 56, for special rules.

P.L. 99-514, §1303(b)(3):

Amended Code Sec. 1016(a) by striking out paragraph (21), as redesignated by Act Sec. 241(b)(2), and by redesignating paragraphs (22) through (26) as paragraphs (21) through (25), respectively. For the **effective** dates, as well as exceptions and special rules, see Act Sec. 1311 following Code Sec. 103. Prior to amendment, Code Sec. 1016(a)(21) read as follows:

(21) to the extent provided in section 1395 in the case of stock of shareholders of a general stock ownership corporation (as defined in section 1391) which makes the election provided by section 1392;

P.L. 99-514, §1899A(25):

Amended Code Sec. 1016(a)(23)-(26) by striking out the comma at the end thereof and inserting in lieu thereof a semicolon. **Effective** as if included in the provision of P.L. 98-369 to which it relates.

• **1984, Deficit Reduction Act of 1984 (P.L. 98-369)**

P.L. 98-369, §53(d)(3):

Amended Code Sec. 1016(a) by striking out "and" at the end of paragraph (24), by striking out the period at the end of paragraph (25) and inserting in lieu thereof ", and" and by adding at the end thereof a new paragraph (26). **Effective** for distributions after 3-1-84, in tax years ending after such date.

P.L. 98-369, §211(b)(14):

Amended Code Sec. 1016(a)(17) by striking out "section 818(b)" each place it appeared and inserting in lieu thereof "section 811(b)". **Effective** for tax years beginning after 12-31-83.

P.L. 98-369, §474(r)(23):

Amended Code Sec. 1016(a)(21) by striking out "section 44C(e)" and inserting in lieu thereof "section 23(e)", and by striking out "section 44C" and inserting in lieu thereof "section 23". **Effective** for tax years beginning after 12-31-83, and to carrybacks from such years.

P.L. 98-369, §541(b)(2):

Amended Code Sec. 1016(a), as amended by this Act, by striking out the period at the end of paragraph (26) and inserting in lieu thereof ", and", and by adding at the end thereof new paragraph (27). **Effective** for sales of securities in tax years beginning after 7-18-84.

• **1982, Subchapter S Revision Act of 1982 (P.L. 97-354)**

P.L. 97-354, §5(a)(33):

Amended Code Sec. 1016(a)(18). **Effective** for tax years beginning after 12-31-82. Prior to amendment, it read as follows:

"(18) to the extent provided in section 1376 in the case of stock of, and indebtedness owing, shareholders of an electing small business corporation (as defined in section 1371(b));"

• **1982, Tax Equity and Fiscal Responsibility Act of 1982 (P.L. 97-248)**

P.L. 97-248, §201(c)(2):

Amended Code Sec. 1016(a) by striking out "and" at the end of paragraph (23), by striking out the period at the end of paragraph (24) and inserting in lieu thereof ", and" and by adding paragraph (25). **Effective** for tax years beginning after 12-31-82.

P.L. 97-248, §205(a)(5)(B):

Amended Code Sec. 1016(a)(24) by striking out "section 48(g)(5)" and inserting in lieu thereof "section 48(q)". **Effective** for periods after 12-31-82, under rules similar to those of Code Sec. 48(m). See amendment notes for P.L. 97-248 following Code Sec. 48 for an exemption.

• **1981, Economic Recovery Tax Act of 1981 (P.L. 97-34)**

P.L. 97-34, §212(d)(2)(G):

Amended Code Sec. 1016(a) by striking out "and" at the end of paragraph (22); by striking out the period at the end of paragraph (23) and inserting in lieu thereof ", and"; and by adding at the end thereof new paragraph (24). **Effective** for expenditures incurred after 12-31-81, in tax years ending after such date.

P.L. 97-34, §212(e)(2), as amended by P.L. 97-448, §102(f)(1), provides:

(2) TRANSITIONAL RULE.—The amendments made by this section shall not apply with respect to any rehabilitation of a building if—

(A) the physical work on such rehabilitation began before January 1, 1982, and

(B) such building does not meet the requirements of paragraph (1) of section 48(g) of the Internal Revenue Code of 1954 (as amended by this Act).

• **1980, Crude Oil Windfall Profit Tax Act of 1980 (P.L. 96-223)**

P.L. 96-223, §401(a):

Repealed Code Sec. 1016(a)(23) as added by P.L. 94-455, Act Sec. 2005(a)(3). **Effective** in respect of decedents dying after 12-31-76. However, see the amendment note for P.L. 96-223, §401(a), that follows Code Sec. 1014(d) for the text of Act Sec. 401(d) that authorizes the election of the carryover basis rules in the case of a decedent dying after 12-31-76 and before 11-7-78.

• **1980, Technical Corrections Act of 1979 (P.L. 96-222)**

P.L. 96-222, §106(a)(2):

Redesignated Code Sec. 1016(a)(21) as added by P.L. 95-600, §601(b)(3), as Code Sec. 1016(a)(22). **Effective** with respect to corporations chartered after 12-31-78, and before 1-1-84.

• **1978, Energy Tax Act of 1978 (P.L. 95-618)**

P.L. 95-618, §101(b)(3):

Added Code Sec. 1016(a)(21). **Effective** for tax years ending on or after 4-20-77.

• **1978, Revenue Act of 1978 (P.L. 95-600)**

P.L. 95-600, §515(2):

Amended Code Sec. 1016(a)(23) by striking out "December 31, 1976" and inserting in lieu thereof "December 31, 1979". **Effective** 11-7-78.

P.L. 95-600, §601(b)(3):

Added Code Sec. 1016(a)(21) [22], and redesignated Code Sec. 1016(a)(23) as 1016(a)(22). **Effective** with respect to corporations chartered after 12-31-78, and before 1-1-84.

P.L. 95-600, §702(r)(3):

Redesignated Code Sec. 1016(a)(23) as 1016(a)(21). **Effective** for estates of decedents dying after 12-31-76. This redesignation conflicts with amendments made to Code Sec. 1016(a) by P.L. 95-600, §601(b)(3).

INCOME TAX—BASIS RULES

• **1976, Tax Reform Act of 1976 (P.L. 94-455)**

P.L. 94-455, §1901(a)(123):

Struck out Code Sec. 1016(a)(19). **Effective** for tax years beginning after 12-31-76. Prior to being stricken, Code Sec. 1016(a)(19) read as follows:

(19) to the extent provided in section 48(g) and in section 203(a)(2) of the Revenue Act of 1964, in the case of property which is or has been section 38 property (as defined in section 48(a));

P.L. 94-455, §1901(b)(1)(F)(ii):

Substituted "section 551(e)" for "section 551(f)" in Code Sec. 1016(a)(13). **Effective** for tax years beginning after 12-31-76.

P.L. 94-455, §1901(b)(21)(G):

Struck out Code Sec. 1016(a)(10) (but did not renumber other paragraphs). **Effective** for tax years beginning after 12-31-76. Prior to being stricken, Code Sec. 1016(a)(10) read as follows:

(10) for amounts allowed as deductions as deferred expenses under section 615(b) (relating to certain pre-1970 exploration expenditures) and resulting in a reduction of the taxpayer's taxes under this subtitle but not less than the amounts allowable under such section for the taxable year and prior years;

P.L. 94-455, §1901(b)(29)(A):

Substituted "under section 1020 (as in effect before the date of the enactment of the Tax Reform Act of 1976)" for "under section 1020" in the third sentence of Code Sec. 1016(a). **Effective** for tax years beginning after 12-31-76.

P.L. 94-455, §1901(b)(30)(A)(i):

Struck out Code Sec. 1016(a)(21). **Effective** with respect to stock or securities acquired from a decedent dying after 10-4-76. Prior to striking, Code Sec. 1016(a)(21) read as follows:

(21) to the extent provided in section 1022, relating to increase in basis for certain foreign personal holding company stock or securities;

P.L. 94-455, §1901(b)(30)(A)(ii):

Redesignated Code Secs. 1016(a)(20) and 1016(a)(22) as Code Secs. 1016(a)(19) and 1016(a)(20), respectively. **Effective** for tax years beginning after 12-31-76.

P.L. 94-455, §2005(a)(3):

Added Code Sec. 1016(a)(23). **Effective** in respect of decedents dying after 12-31-79, as amended by P.L. 95-600, §515(6). (This, with the renumbering noted above, left no paragraph (21) or (22).)

• **1969, Tax Reform Act of 1969 (P.L. 91-172)**

P.L. 91-172, §504(c)(4):

Amended paragraph 1016(a)(10) by inserting "pre-1970" in the parenthetical language. **Effective** with respect to exploration expenditures paid or incurred after 12-31-69.

P.L. 91-172, §516(c)(2)(B), (f)(1):

Amended Code Sec. 1016(a) by adding new paragraph (22). **Effective** for transfers after 12-31-69, except that section 1253(d)(1) of the Internal Revenue Code of 1954 (as added by subsection (c)) shall, at the election of the taxpayer (made at such time and in such manner as the Secretary or his delegate may by regulations prescribe), apply to transfers before 1-1-70, but only with respect to payments made in tax years ending after 12-31-69, and beginning before 1-1-80.

• **1964, Revenue Act of 1964 (P.L. 88-272)**

P.L. 88-272, §203(a)(3):

Amended paragraph (19). **Effective** 1-1-64. Prior to amendment, paragraph (19) read as follows:

"(19) to the extent provided in section 48(g) in the case of property which is or has been section 38 property (as defined in section 48(a));".

P.L. 88-272, §225(j)(2):

Added paragraph (21). **Effective** in respect to decedents dying after 12-31-63.

P.L. 88-272, §227(b)(5):

Amended paragraph (15) of subsection (a) by adding "or domestic iron ore" after the word "coal". **Effective** 1-1-64.

• **1962, Revenue Act of 1962 (P.L. 87-834)**

P.L. 87-834, §2:

Amended Code Sec. 1016(a) by inserting a semicolon in lieu of the period at the end of paragraph (18) and by adding after paragraph (18) a new paragraph (19). **Effective** for tax years ending after 12-31-61.

P.L. 87-834, §8:

Amended Code Sec. 1016(a)(3) by striking out "and" at the end of subparagraph (B), by inserting "and" at the end of subparagraph (C), and by inserting after subparagraph (C) a new subparagraph (D). **Effective** for tax years beginning after 12-31-62.

P.L. 87-834, §12(b)(4):

Amended Code Sec. 1016(a) by substituting a semicolon for the period at the end of paragraph (19) and by adding a new paragraph (20). **Effective** for tax years of foreign corporations beginning after 12-31-62 and for tax years of United States shareholders within which or with which such tax years of such foreign corporations end.

• **1959, Life Insurance Company Income Tax Act of 1959 (P.L. 86-69)**

P.L. 86-69, §3(d):

Amended Code Sec. 1016(a)(3) by striking out "and" where it appeared at the end of subparagraph (A), by inserting "and" at the end of subparagraph (B), and by adding a new subparagraph (C). Amended Code Sec. 1016(a) by adding a new paragraph (17). **Effective** for tax years beginning after 12-31-57.

• **1958, Technical Amendments Act of 1958 (P.L. 85-866)**

P.L. 85-866, §2(b):

Amended Sec. 1016(a)(6) by striking out "short term" where it appeared immediately preceding "municipal bond". **Effective** only for obligations acquired after 12-31-57.

P.L. 85-866, §64(d):

Amended Sec. 1016(a) by adding paragraph (18).

• **1956 (P.L. 629, 84th Cong.)**

P.L. 629, 84th Cong., §4(c):

Amended Sec. 1016(a) by striking the period at the end of paragraph (15) and substituting a semicolon (;), and by adding a new paragraph (16). **Effective** 1-1-56.

[Sec. 1016(b)]

(b) SUBSTITUTED BASIS.—Whenever it appears that the basis of property in the hands of the taxpayer is a substituted basis, then the adjustments provided in subsection (a) shall be made after first making in respect of such substituted basis proper adjustments of a similar nature in respect of the period during which the property was held by the transferor, donor, or grantor, or during which the other property was held by the person for whom the basis is to be determined. A similar rule shall be applied in the case of a series of substituted bases.

Amendments

• **1984, Deficit Reduction Act of 1984 (P.L. 98-369)**

P.L. 98-369, §43(a)(2):

Amended Code Sec. 1016(b) by striking out the last sentence. **Effective** for tax years ending after 7-18-84. Prior to amendment, the sentence read as follows:

The term "substituted basis" as used in this section means a basis determined under any provision of this subchapter and subchapters C (relating to corporate distributions and adjustments), K (relating to partners and partnerships), and P (relating to capital gains and losses), or under any corresponding provision of a prior income tax law, providing that the basis shall be determined—

(1) by reference to the basis in the hands of a transferor, donor, or grantor, or

(2) by reference to other property held at any time by the person for whom the basis is to be determined.

[Sec. 1016(c)]

(c) INCREASE IN BASIS OF PROPERTY ON WHICH ADDITIONAL ESTATE TAX IS IMPOSED.—

(1) TAX IMPOSED WITH RESPECT TO ENTIRE INTEREST.—If an additional estate tax is imposed under section 2032A(c)(1) with respect to any interest in property and the qualified heir makes an election under this subsection with respect to the imposition of such tax, the adjusted basis of such interest shall be increased by an amount equal to the excess of—

(A) the fair market value of such interest on the date of the decedent's death (or the alternate valuation date under section 2032, if the executor of the decedent's estate elected the application of such section), over

INCOME TAX—BASIS RULES

(B) the value of such interest determined under section 2032A(a).

(2) PARTIAL DISPOSITIONS.—

(A) IN GENERAL.—In the case of any partial disposition for which an election under this subsection is made, the increase in basis under paragraph (1) shall be an amount—

(i) which bears the same ratio to the increase which would be determined under paragraph (1) (without regard to this paragraph) with respect to the entire interest, as

(ii) the amount of the tax imposed under section 2032A(c)(1) with respect to such disposition bears to the adjusted tax difference attributable to the entire interest (as determined under section 2032A(c)(2)(B)).

(B) PARTIAL DISPOSITION.—For purposes of subparagraph (A), the term "partial disposition" means any disposition or cessation to which subsection (c)(2)(D), (h)(1)(B), or (i)(1)(B) of section 2032A applies.

(3) TIME ADJUSTMENT MADE.—Any increase in basis under this subsection shall be deemed to have occurred immediately before the disposition or cessation resulting in the imposition of the tax under section 2032A(c)(1).

(4) SPECIAL RULE IN THE CASE OF SUBSTITUTED PROPERTY.—If the tax under section 2032A(c)(1) is imposed with respect to qualified replacement property (as defined in section 2032A(h)(3)(B)) or qualified exchange property (as defined in section 2032A(i)(3)), the increase in basis under paragraph (1) shall be made by reference to the property involuntarily converted or exchanged (as the case may be).

(5) ELECTION.—

(A) IN GENERAL.—An election under this subsection shall be made at such time and in such manner as the Secretary shall by regulations prescribe. Such an election, once made, shall be irrevocable.

(B) INTEREST ON RECAPTURED AMOUNT.—If an election is made under this subsection with respect to any additional estate tax imposed under section 2032A(c)(1), for purposes of section 6601 (relating to interest on underpayments), the last date prescribed for payment of such tax shall be deemed to be the last date prescribed for payment of the tax imposed by section 2001 with respect to the estate of the decedent (as determined for purposes of section 6601).

Amendments

• **1981, Economic Recovery Tax Act of 1981 (P.L. 97-34)**

P.L. 97-34, § 421(g):

Amended Code Sec. 1016(c). **Effective** with respect to decedents dying after 12-31-81. Prior to amendment, Code Sec. 1016(c) read as follows:

(c) INCREASE IN BASIS IN THE CASE OF CERTAIN INVOLUNTARY CONVERSIONS.—

(1) IN GENERAL.—If—

(A) there is a compulsory or involuntary conversion (within the meaning of section 1033) of any property, and

(B) an additional estate tax is imposed on such conversion under section 2032A(c), then the adjusted basis of such property shall be increased by the amount of such tax.

(2) TIME ADJUSTMENT MADE.—Any adjustment under paragraph (1) shall be deemed to have occurred immediately before the compulsory or involuntary conversion.

• **1980, Crude Oil Windfall Profit Tax Act of 1980 (P.L. 96-223)**

P.L. 96-223, § 401(c)(1):

Amended Code Sec. 1016(c). **Effective** with respect to decedents dying after 12-31-76. See the amendment note for P.L. 96-223, § 401(a), that follows Code Sec. 1014(d) for the text of Act Sec. 401(d) that authorizes the election of the carryover basis rules in the case of a decedent dying after 12-31-76 and before 11-7-78. Prior to amendment, Code Sec. 1016(c) read:

(c) INCREASE IN BASIS IN THE CASE OF CERTAIN INVOLUNTARY CONVERSIONS.—

(1) IN GENERAL.—If there is a compulsory or involuntary conversion (within the meaning of section 1033) of any property the basis of which is determined under section 1023 and an additional estate tax is imposed on such conversion under section 2032A(c), then the adjusted basis of such property shall be increased by an amount which bears the same ratio to such tax with respect to the conversion of that property as—

(A) the net appreciation in value of such property, bears to

(B) the excess of—

(i) the value of such property for purposes of chapter 11 as determined with respect to the estate of the decedent without regard to section 2032A; over

(ii) the value of such property for purposes of chapter 11 as determined with respect to the estate of the decedent with regard to section 2032A.

(2) NET APPRECIATION IN VALUE.—For purposes of this subsection, the net appreciation in value of any property shall be determined in accordance with section 1023(f)(2) except that—

(A) the adjusted basis taken into account shall be increased by any adjustment under section 1023,

(B) the fair market value of such property shall be determined without regard to section 2032A, and

(C) any net appreciation in value in excess of the amount determined under paragraph (1)(B) shall be disregarded.

(3) TIME ADJUSTMENT MADE.—Any adjustment under paragraph (1) shall be deemed to have occurred immediately before the compulsory or involuntary conversion.

• **1978 (P.L. 95-472)**

P.L. 95-472, § 4(b), (d):

Added Code Sec. 1016(c). **Effective** for involuntary conversions after 1976.

[Sec. 1016(d)]

(d) REDUCTION IN BASIS OF AUTOMOBILE ON WHICH GAS GUZZLER TAX WAS IMPOSED.—If—

(1) the taxpayer acquires any automobile with respect to which a tax was imposed by section 4064, and

(2) the use of such automobile by the taxpayer begins not more than 1 year after the date of the first sale for ultimate use of such automobile,

the basis of such automobile shall be reduced by the amount of the tax imposed by section 4064 with respect to such automobile. In the case of importation, if the date of entry or withdrawal from warehouse for consumption is later than the date of the first sale for ultimate use, such later date shall be substituted for the date of such first sale in the preceding sentence.

Amendments

• **1978, Energy Tax Act of 1978 (P.L. 95-618)**

P.L. 95-618, § 201(b):

Added Code Sec. 1016(d), and redesignated the former Code Sec. 1016(d) as 1016(e). **Effective** with respect to 1980 and later model year automobiles (as defined in Code Sec. 4064(b)).

[Sec. 1016(e)]

(e) CROSS REFERENCE.—

For treatment of separate mineral interests as one property, see section 614.

INCOME TAX—BASIS RULES

Amendments

• **1993, Omnibus Budget Reconciliation Act of 1993 (P.L. 103-66)**

P.L. 103-66, §13213(a)(2)(F):

Amended Code Sec. 1016(e). **Effective** for expenses incurred after 12-31-93. Prior to amendment, subsection (e) read as follows:

(e) CROSS REFERENCES.—

(1) For treatment of certain expenses incident to the purchase of a residence which were deducted as moving expenses by the taxpayer or his spouse under section 217(a), see section 217(e).

(2) For treatment of separate mineral interests as one property, see section 614.

• **1978, Energy Tax Act of 1978 (P.L. 95-618)**

P.L. 95-618, §201(b):

Redesignated Code Sec. 1016(d) as Code Sec. 1016(e). **Effective** with respect to 1980 and later model year automobiles.

• **1978 (P.L. 95-472)**

P.L. 95-472, §4(b), (d):

Redesignated subsection (c) as subsection (d). **Effective** for involuntary conversions after 1976.

• **1969, Tax Reform Act of 1969 (P.L. 91-172)**

P.L. 91-172, §231(c)(3):

Amended Sec. 1016(c). **Effective** for tax years beginning after 12-31-69. Prior to amendment, Sec. 1016(c) read as follows:

(c) SEPARATE MINERAL INTERESTS TREATED AS ONE PROPERTY.—For treatment of separate mineral interests as one property, see section 614.

[Sec. 1017]

SEC. 1017. DISCHARGE OF INDEBTEDNESS.

[Sec. 1017(a)]

(a) GENERAL RULE.—If—

(1) an amount is excluded from gross income under subsection (a) of section 108 (relating to discharge of indebtedness), and

(2) under subsection (b)(2)(E), (b)(5), or (c)(1) of section 108, any portion of such amount is to be applied to reduce basis,

then such portion shall be applied in reduction of the basis of any property held by the taxpayer at the beginning of the taxable year following the taxable year in which the discharge occurs.

Amendments

• **1998, IRS Restructuring and Reform Act of 1998 (P.L. 105-206)**

P.L. 105-206, §6023(11):

Amended Code Sec. 1017(a)(2) by striking "(b)(2)(D)" and inserting "(b)(2)(E)". **Effective** 7-22-98.

• **1993, Omnibus Budget Reconciliation Act of 1993 (P.L. 103-66)**

P.L. 103-66, §13150(c)(6):

Amended Code Sec. 1017(a)(2) by striking "or (b)(5)" and inserting ", (b)(5), or (c)(1)". **Effective** for discharges after 12-31-92, in tax years ending after such date.

• **1986, Tax Reform Act of 1986 (P.L. 99-514)**

P.L. 99-514, §822(b)(4):

Amended Code Sec. 1017(a)(2) by striking out ", (b)(5), or (c)(1)(A)" and inserting in lieu thereof "or (b)(5)". **Effective** for discharges after 12-31-86.

• **1980, Bankruptcy Tax Act of 1980 (P.L. 96-589)**

P.L. 96-589, §2(b):

Divided Code Sec. 1017 into four subsections, (a) through (d). For the text of Code Sec. 1017 prior to amendment and the **effective** date of Code Sec. 1017(a), see the historical comment for P.L. 96-589 under Code Sec. 1017(d).

[Sec. 1017(b)]

(b) AMOUNT AND PROPERTIES DETERMINED UNDER REGULATIONS.—

(1) IN GENERAL.—The amount of reduction to be applied under subsection (a) (not in excess of the portion referred to in subsection (a)), and the particular properties the bases of which are to be reduced, shall be determined under regulations prescribed by the Secretary.

(2) LIMITATION IN TITLE 11 CASE OR INSOLVENCY.—In the case of a discharge to which subparagraph (A) or (B) of section 108(a)(1) applies, the reduction in basis under subsection (a) of this section shall not exceed the excess of—

(A) the aggregate of the bases of the property held by the taxpayer immediately after the discharge, over

(B) the aggregate of the liabilities of the taxpayer immediately after the discharge.

The preceding sentence shall not apply to any reduction in basis by reason of an election under section 108(b)(5).

(3) CERTAIN REDUCTIONS MAY ONLY BE MADE IN THE BASIS OF DEPRECIABLE PROPERTY.—

(A) IN GENERAL.—Any amount which under subsection (b)(5) or (c)(1) of section 108 is to be applied to reduce basis shall be applied only to reduce the basis of depreciable property held by the taxpayer.

(B) DEPRECIABLE PROPERTY.—For purposes of this section, the term "depreciable property" means any property of a character subject to the allowance for depreciation, but only if a basis reduction under subsection (a) will reduce the amount of depreciation or amortization which otherwise would be allowable for the period immediately following such reduction.

(C) SPECIAL RULE FOR PARTNERSHIP INTERESTS.—For purposes of this section, any interest of a partner in a partnership shall be treated as depreciable property to the extent of such partner's proportionate interest in the depreciable property held by such partnership. The preceding sentence shall apply only if there is a corresponding reduction in the partnership's basis in depreciable property with respect to such partner.

(D) SPECIAL RULE IN CASE OF AFFILIATED GROUP.—For purposes of this section, if—

(i) a corporation holds stock in another corporation (hereinafter in this subparagraph referred to as the "subsidiary"), and

(ii) such corporations are members of the same affiliated group which file a consolidated return under section 1501 for the taxable year in which the discharge occurs,

then such stock shall be treated as depreciable property to the extent that such subsidiary consents to a corresponding reduction in the basis of its depreciable property.

(E) ELECTION TO TREAT CERTAIN INVENTORY AS DEPRECIABLE PROPERTY.—

(i) IN GENERAL.—At the election of the taxpayer, for purposes of this section, the term "depreciable property" includes any real property which is described in section 1221(a)(1).

INCOME TAX—BASIS RULES

(ii) ELECTION.—An election under clause (i) shall be made on the taxpayer's return for the taxable year in which the discharge occurs or at such other time as may be permitted in regulations prescribed by the Secretary. Such an election, once made, may be revoked only with the consent of the Secretary.

(F) SPECIAL RULES FOR QUALIFIED REAL PROPERTY BUSINESS INDEBTEDNESS.—In the case of any amount which under section 108(c)(1) is to be applied to reduce basis—

(i) depreciable property shall only include depreciable real property for purposes of subparagraphs (A) and (C),

(ii) subparagraph (E) shall not apply, and

(iii) in the case of property taken into account under section 108(c)(2)(B), the reduction with respect to such property shall be made as of the time immediately before disposition if earlier than the time under subsection (a).

(4) SPECIAL RULES FOR QUALIFIED FARM INDEBTEDNESS.—

(A) IN GENERAL.—Any amount which under subsection (b)(2)(E) of section 108 is to be applied to reduce basis and which is attributable to an amount excluded under subsection (a)(1)(C) of section 108—

(i) shall be applied only to reduce the basis of qualified property held by the taxpayer, and

(ii) shall be applied to reduce the basis of qualified property in the following order:

(I) First the basis of qualified property which is depreciable property.

(II) Second the basis of qualified property which is land used or held for use in the trade or business of farming.

(III) Then the basis of other qualified property.

(B) QUALIFIED PROPERTY.—For purposes of this paragraph, the term "qualified property" has the meaning given to such term by section 108(g)(3)(C).

(C) CERTAIN RULES MADE APPLICABLE.—Rules similar to the rules of subparagraphs (C), (D), and (E) of paragraph (3) shall apply for purposes of this paragraph and section 108(g).

Amendments

• **1999, Tax Relief Extension Act of 1999 (P.L. 106-170)**

P.L. 106-170, § 532(c)(2)(S):

Amended Code Sec. 1017(b)(3)(E)(i) by striking "section 1221(1)" and inserting "section 1221(a)(1)". **Effective** for any instrument held, acquired, or entered into, any transaction entered into, and supplies held or acquired on or after 12-17-99.

• **1996, Small Business Job Protection Act of 1996 (P.L. 104-188)**

P.L. 104-188, § 1703(n)(5):

Amended Code Sec. 1017(b)(4)(A) by striking "subsection (b)(2)(D)" and inserting "subsection (b)(2)(E)". **Effective** as if included in the provision of P.L. 103-66 to which it relates.

• **1993, Omnibus Budget Reconciliation Act of 1993 (P.L. 103-66)**

P.L. 103-66, § 13150(c)(7):

Amended Code Sec. 1017(b)(3)(A) by inserting "or (c)(1)" after "subsection (b)(5)". **Effective** for discharges after 12-31-92, in tax years ending after such date.

P.L. 103-66, § 13150(c)(8):

Amended Code Sec. 1017(b)(3) by adding at the end new paragraph (F). **Effective** for discharges after 12-31-92, in tax years ending after such date.

• **1990, Omnibus Budget Reconciliation Act of 1990 (P.L. 101-508)**

P.L. 101-508, § 11704(a)(12):

Amended Code Sec. 1017(b)(4)(C) by striking "subparagraph" and inserting "subparagraphs". **Effective** 11-5-90.

• **1988, Technical and Miscellaneous Revenue Act of 1988 (P.L. 100-647)**

P.L. 100-647, § 1004(a)(5):

Amended Code Sec. 1017(b)(4). **Effective** as if included in the provision of P.L. 99-514 to which it relates. Prior to amendment, Code Sec. 1017(b)(4) read as follows:

(4) ORDERING RULE IN THE CASE OF QUALIFIED FARM INDEBTEDNESS.—Any amount which is excluded from gross income under section 108(a) by reason of the discharge of qualified farm indebtedness (within the meaning of section 108(g)(2)) and which under subsection (b) of section 108 is to be applied to reduce basis shall be applied—

(A) first to reduce the tax attributes described in section 108(b)(2) (other than subparagraph (D) thereof),

(B) then to reduce basis of property other than property described in subparagraph (C), and

(C) then to reduce the basis of land used or held for use in the trade or business of farming.

• **1986, Tax Reform Act of 1986 (P.L. 99-514)**

P.L. 99-514, § 405(b):

Amended Code Sec. 1017(b) by adding at the end thereof new paragraph (4). **Effective** for discharges of indebtedness occurring after 4-9-86, in tax years ending after that date.

P.L. 99-514, § 822(b)(5):

Amended Code Sec. 1017(b)(3)(A) by striking out "or (c)(1)(A)". **Effective** for discharges after 12-31-86.

• **1980, Bankruptcy Tax Act of 1980 (P.L. 96-589)**

P.L. 96-589, § 2(b):

Divided Code Sec. 1017 into four subsections, (a) through (d). For the text of Code Sec. 1017 prior to amendment and the **effective** date of Code Sec. 1017(b), see the historical comment for P.L. 96-589 under Code Sec. 1017(d).

[Sec. 1017(c)]

(c) SPECIAL RULES.—

(1) REDUCTION NOT TO BE MADE IN EXEMPT PROPERTY.—In the case of an amount excluded from gross income under section 108(a)(1)(A), no reduction in basis shall be made under this section in the basis of property which the debtor treats as exempt property under section 522 of title 11 of the United States Code.

(2) REDUCTIONS IN BASIS NOT TREATED AS DISPOSITIONS.—For purposes of this title, a reduction in basis under this section shall not be treated as a disposition.

Amendments

• **1980, Bankruptcy Tax Act of 1980 (P.L. 96-589)**

P.L. 96-589, § 2(b):

Divided Code Sec. 1017 into four subsections, (a) through (d). For the text of Code Sec. 1017 prior to amendment and the **effective** date of Code Sec. 1017(c), see the historical comment for P.L. 96-589 under Code Sec. 1017(d).

INCOME TAX—BASIS RULES

[Sec. 1017(d)]

(d) RECAPTURE OF REDUCTIONS.—

(1) IN GENERAL.—For purposes of sections 1245 and 1250—

(A) any property the basis of which is reduced under this section and which is neither section 1245 property nor section 1250 property shall be treated as section 1245 property, and

(B) any reduction under this section shall be treated as a deduction allowed for depreciation.

(2) SPECIAL RULE FOR SECTION 1250 .—For purposes of section 1250(b), the determination of what would have been the depreciation adjustments under the straight line method shall be made as if there had been no reduction under this section.

Amendments

• 1980, Bankruptcy Tax Act of 1980 (P.L. 96-589)

P.L. 96-589, §2(b):

Divided Code Sec. 1017 into four subsections, (a) through (d). **Effective** as noted in Act Sec. 7, below. Prior to amendment, Code Sec. 1017 read as follows:

Where any amount is excluded from gross income under section 108 (relating to income from discharge of indebtedness) on account of the discharge of indebtedness the whole or a part of the amount so excluded from gross income shall be applied in reduction of the basis of any property held (whether before or after the time of the discharge) by the taxpayer during any portion of the taxable year in which such discharge occurred. The amount to be so applied (not in excess of the amount so excluded from gross income, reduced by the amount of any deduction disallowed under section 108) and the particular properties to which the reduction shall be allocated, shall be determined under regulations (prescribed by the Secretary) in effect at the time of the filing of the consent by the taxpayer referred to in section 108. The reduction shall be made as of the first day of the taxable year in which the discharge occurred, except in the case of property not held by the taxpayer on such first day, in which case it shall take effect as of the time the holding of the taxpayer began.

P.L. 96-589, §7, provides:

(a) For section 2 (Relating to Tax Treatment of Discharge of Indebtedness).—

(1) IN GENERAL.—Except as provided in paragraph (2), the amendments made by section 2 shall apply to any transaction which occurs after December 31, 1980, other than a transaction which occurs in a proceeding in a bankruptcy case or similar judicial proceeding (or in a proceeding under the Bankruptcy Act) commencing on or before December 31, 1980.

(2) TRANSITIONAL RULE.—In the case of any discharge of indebtedness to which subparagraph (A) or (B) of section 108(a)(1) of the Internal Revenue Code of 1954 (relating to exclusion from gross income), as amended by section 2, applies and which occurs before January 1, 1982, or which occurs in a proceeding in a bankruptcy case or similar judicial proceedings commencing before January 1, 1982, then—

(A) section 108(b)(2) of such Code (relating to reduction of tax attributes), as so amended, shall be applied without regard to subparagraphs (A), (B), (C), and (E) thereof, and

(B) the basis of any property shall not be reduced under section 1017 of such Code (relating to reduction in basis in connection with discharges of indebtedness), as so amended, below the fair market value of such property on the date the debt is discharged.

* * *

(f) ELECTION TO SUBSTITUTE SEPTEMBER 30, 1979, FOR DECEMBER 31, 1980.—

(1) IN GENERAL.—The debtor (or debtors) in a bankruptcy case or similar judicial proceeding may (with the approval of the court) elect to apply subsections (a), (c), and (d) by substituting "September 30, 1979" for "December 31, 1980" each place it appears in such subsections.

(2) EFFECT OF ELECTION.—Any election made under paragraph (1) with respect to any proceeding shall apply to all parties to the proceeding.

(3) REVOCATION ONLY WITH CONSENT.—Any election under this subsection may be revoked only with the consent of the Secretary of the Treasury or his delegate.

(4) TIME AND MANNER OF ELECTION.—Any election under this subsection shall be made at such time, and in such manner, as the Secretary of the Treasury or his delegate may by regulations prescribe.

(g) DEFINITIONS.—For purposes of this section—

(1) BANKRUPTCY CASE.—The term "bankruptcy case" means any case under title 11 of the United States Code (as recodified by Public Law 95-598).

(2) SIMILAR JUDICIAL PROCEEDING.—The term "similar judicial proceeding" means a receivership, foreclosure, or similar proceeding in a Federal or State court (as modified by section 368(a)(3)(D) of the Internal Revenue Code of 1954).

• 1976, Tax Reform Act of 1976 (P.L. 94-455)

P.L. 94-455, §1906(b)(13)(A):

Amended 1954 Code by substituting "Secretary" for "Secretary or his delegate" each place it appeared. **Effective** 2-1-77.

P.L. 94-455, §1951(c)(1):

Substituted "section 108" for "section 108(a)" each time it appeared in Code Sec. 1017. **Effective** for tax years beginning after 12-31-76.

[Sec. 1018—Repealed]

Amendments

• 1980, Bankruptcy Tax Act of 1980 (P.L. 96-589)

P.L. 96-589, §6(h)(1):

Repealed Code Sec. 1018. **Effective** 10-1-79. However, such repeal is inapplicable to any proceeding under the Bankruptcy Act commenced before 10-1-79. Prior to repeal, Code Sec. 1018 read as follows:

SEC. 1018. ADJUSTMENT OF CAPITAL STRUCTURE BEFORE SEPTEMBER 22, 1938.

Where a plan of reorganization of a corporation, approved by the court in a proceeding under section 77B of the National Bankruptcy Act, as amended (48 Stat. 912), is consummated by adjustment of the capital or debt structure of such corporation without the transfer of its assets to another corporation, and a final judgment or decree in such proceeding has been entered before September 22, 1938, then the provisions of section 270 of the Bankruptcy Act, as amended (11 U. S. C. 670), shall not apply in respect of the property of such corporation. For purposes of this section, the term "reorganization" shall not be limited by the definition of such term in section 112 (g) of the Internal Revenue Code of 1939.

• 1976, Tax Reform Act of 1976 (P.L. 94-455)

P.L. 94-455, §1901(a)(124):

Struck out "54 Stat. 709;" before "11 U.S.C. 670" in Code Sec. 1018. **Effective** for tax years beginning after 12-31-76.

[Sec. 1019]

SEC. 1019. PROPERTY ON WHICH LESSEE HAS MADE IMPROVEMENTS.

Neither the basis nor the adjusted basis of any portion of real property shall, in the case of the lessor of such property, be increased or diminished on account of income derived by the lessor in respect of such property and excludable from gross income under section 109 (relating to improvements by lessee on lessor's property).

Amendments

• 2014, Tax Technical Corrections Act of 2014 (P.L. 113-295)

P.L. 113-295, §221(a)(76), Division A:

Amended Code Sec. 1019 by striking the last sentence. **Effective** generally 12-19-2014. For a special rule, see Act Sec. 221(b)(2), Division A, below. Prior to amendment, the last sentence of Code Sec. 1019 read as follows:

If an amount representing any part of the value of real property attributable to buildings erected or other improvements made by a lessee in respect of such property was included in gross income of the lessor for any taxable year beginning before January 1, 1942, the basis of each portion of such property shall be properly adjusted for the amount so included in gross income.

P.L. 113-295, §221(b)(2), Division A, provides:

(2) SAVINGS PROVISION.—If—

(A) any provision amended or repealed by the amendments made by this section applied to—

(i) any transaction occurring before the date of the enactment of this Act,

(ii) any property acquired before such date of enactment, or

(iii) any item of income, loss, deduction, or credit taken into account before such date of enactment, and

(B) the treatment of such transaction, property, or item under such provision would (without regard to the amendments or repeals made by this section) affect the

INCOME TAX—BASIS RULES

liability for tax for periods ending after date of enactment, nothing in the amendments or repeals made by this section shall be construed to affect the treatment of such transaction, property, or item for purposes of determining liability for tax for periods ending after such date of enactment.

[Sec. 1021]

SEC. 1021. SALE OF ANNUITIES.

In case of the sale of an annuity contract, the adjusted basis shall in no case be less than zero.

[Sec. 1022—Repealed]

Amendments

- **2013, American Taxpayer Relief Act of 2012 (P.L. 112-240)**

P.L. 112-240, §101(a)(1)-(3), provides:

SEC. 101. PERMANENT EXTENSION AND MODIFICATION OF 2001 TAX RELIEF.

(a) PERMANENT EXTENSION.—

(1) IN GENERAL.—The Economic Growth and Tax Relief Reconciliation Act of 2001 is amended by striking title IX.

(2) CONFORMING AMENDMENT.—The Tax Relief, Unemployment Insurance Reauthorization, and Job Creation Act of 2010 is amended by striking section 304.

(3) EFFECTIVE DATE.—The amendments made by this subsection shall apply to taxable, plan, or limitation years beginning after December 31, 2012, and estates of decedents dying, gifts made, or generation skipping transfers after December 31, 2012.

- **2010, Tax Relief, Unemployment Insurance Reauthorization, and Job Creation Act of 2010 (P.L. 111-312)**

P.L. 111-312, §301(a):

Amended Code Sec. 1022 to read as such provision would read if subtitle E of title V of the Economic Growth and Tax Relief Reconciliation Act of 2001 (P.L. 107-16) had never been enacted. [P.L. 107-16, §542(a), added a new Code Sec. 1022. Therefore, P.L. 111-312, §301(a), effectively repealed Code Sec. 1022.—CCH] **Effective** for estates of decedents dying, and transfers made, after 12-31-2009. For a special rule, see Act Sec. 301(c), below. Prior to amendment by P.L. 111-312, Code Sec. 1022 read as follows:

SEC. 1022. TREATMENT OF PROPERTY ACQUIRED FROM A DECEDENT DYING AFTER DECEMBER 31, 2009.

[Sec. 1022(a)]

(a) IN GENERAL.—Except as otherwise provided in this section—

(1) property acquired from a decedent dying after December 31, 2009, shall be treated for purposes of this subtitle as transferred by gift, and

(2) the basis of the person acquiring property from such a decedent shall be the lesser of—

(A) the adjusted basis of the decedent, or

(B) the fair market value of the property at the date of the decedent's death.

[Sec. 1022(b)]

(b) BASIS INCREASE FOR CERTAIN PROPERTY.—

(1) IN GENERAL.—In the case of property to which this subsection applies, the basis of such property under subsection (a) shall be increased by its basis increase under this subsection.

(2) BASIS INCREASE.—For purposes of this subsection—

(A) IN GENERAL.—The basis increase under this subsection for any property is the portion of the aggregate basis increase which is allocated to the property pursuant to this section.

(B) AGGREGATE BASIS INCREASE.—In the case of any estate, the aggregate basis increase under this subsection is $1,300,000.

(C) LIMIT INCREASED BY UNUSED BUILT-IN LOSSES AND LOSS CARRYOVERS.—The limitation under subparagraph (B) shall be increased by—

(i) the sum of the amount of any capital loss carryover under section 1212(b), and the amount of any net operating loss carryover under section 172, which would (but for the decedent's death) be carried from the decedent's last taxable year to a later taxable year of the decedent, plus

(ii) the sum of the amount of any losses that would have been allowable under section 165 if the property acquired from the decedent had been sold at fair market value immediately before the decedent's death.

(3) DECEDENT NONRESIDENTS WHO ARE NOT CITIZENS OF THE UNITED STATES.—In the case of a decedent nonresident not a citizen of the United States—

(A) paragraph (2)(B) shall be applied by substituting "$60,000" for "$1,300,000", and

(B) paragraph (2)(C) shall not apply.

[Sec. 1022(c)]

(c) ADDITIONAL BASIS INCREASE FOR PROPERTY ACQUIRED BY SURVIVING SPOUSE.—

(1) IN GENERAL.—In the case of property to which this subsection applies and which is qualified spousal property, the basis of such property under subsection (a) (as increased under subsection (b)) shall be increased by its spousal property basis increase.

(2) SPOUSAL PROPERTY BASIS INCREASE.—For purposes of this subsection—

(A) IN GENERAL.—The spousal property basis increase for property referred to in paragraph (1) is the portion of the aggregate spousal property basis increase which is allocated to the property pursuant to this section.

(B) AGGREGATE SPOUSAL PROPERTY BASIS INCREASE.—In the case of any estate, the aggregate spousal property basis increase is $3,000,000.

(3) QUALIFIED SPOUSAL PROPERTY.—For purposes of this subsection, the term "qualified spousal property" means—

(A) outright transfer property, and

(B) qualified terminable interest property.

(4) OUTRIGHT TRANSFER PROPERTY.—For purposes of this subsection—

(A) IN GENERAL.—The term "outright transfer property" means any interest in property acquired from the decedent by the decedent's surviving spouse.

(B) EXCEPTION.—Subparagraph (A) shall not apply where, on the lapse of time, on the occurrence of an event or contingency, or on the failure of an event or contingency to occur, an interest passing to the surviving spouse will terminate or fail—

(i) (I) if an interest in such property passes or has passed (for less than an adequate and full consideration in money or money's worth) from the decedent to any person other than such surviving spouse (or the estate of such spouse), and

(II) if by reason of such passing such person (or his heirs or assigns) may possess or enjoy any part of such property after such termination or failure of the interest so passing to the surviving spouse, or

(ii) if such interest is to be acquired for the surviving spouse, pursuant to directions of the decedent, by his executor or by the trustee of a trust.

For purposes of this subparagraph, an interest shall not be considered as an interest which will terminate or fail merely because it is the ownership of a bond, note, or similar contractual obligation, the discharge of which would not have the effect of an annuity for life or for a term.

(C) INTEREST OF SPOUSE CONDITIONAL ON SURVIVAL FOR LIMITED PERIOD.—For purposes of this paragraph, an interest passing to the surviving spouse shall not be considered as an interest which will terminate or fail on the death of such spouse if—

(i) such death will cause a termination or failure of such interest only if it occurs within a period not exceeding 6 months after the decedent's death, or only if it occurs as a result of a common disaster resulting in the death of the decedent and the surviving spouse, or only if it occurs in the case of either such event, and

(ii) such termination or failure does not in fact occur.

(5) QUALIFIED TERMINABLE INTEREST PROPERTY.—For purposes of this subsection—

(A) IN GENERAL.—The term "qualified terminable interest property" means property—

(i) which passes from the decedent, and

(ii) in which the surviving spouse has a qualifying income interest for life.

(B) QUALIFYING INCOME INTEREST FOR LIFE.—The surviving spouse has a qualifying income interest for life if—

(i) the surviving spouse is entitled to all the income from the property, payable annually or at more frequent intervals, or has a usufruct interest for life in the property, and

(ii) no person has a power to appoint any part of the property to any person other than the surviving spouse.

Clause (ii) shall not apply to a power exercisable only at or after the death of the surviving spouse. To the extent provided in regulations, an annuity shall be treated in a manner similar to an income interest in property (regardless of whether the property from which the annuity is payable can be separately identified).

(C) PROPERTY INCLUDES INTEREST THEREIN.—The term "property" includes an interest in property.

(D) SPECIFIC PORTION TREATED AS SEPARATE PROPERTY.—A specific portion of property shall be treated as separate property. For purposes of the preceding sentence, the

INCOME TAX—BASIS RULES

term "specific portion" only includes a portion determined on a fractional or percentage basis.

[Sec. 1022(d)]

(d) DEFINITIONS AND SPECIAL RULES FOR APPLICATION OF SUBSECTIONS (b) AND (c).—

(1) PROPERTY TO WHICH SUBSECTIONS (b) AND (c) APPLY.—

(A) IN GENERAL.—The basis of property acquired from a decedent may be increased under subsection (b) or (c) only if the property was owned by the decedent at the time of death.

(B) RULES RELATING TO OWNERSHIP.—

(i) JOINTLY HELD PROPERTY.—In the case of property which was owned by the decedent and another person as joint tenants with right of survivorship or tenants by the entirety—

(I) if the only such other person is the surviving spouse, the decedent shall be treated as the owner of only 50 percent of the property,

(II) in any case (to which subclause (I) does not apply) in which the decedent furnished consideration for the acquisition of the property, the decedent shall be treated as the owner to the extent of the portion of the property which is proportionate to such consideration, and

(III) in any case (to which subclause (I) does not apply) in which the property has been acquired by gift, bequest, devise, or inheritance by the decedent and any other person as joint tenants with right of survivorship and their interests are not otherwise specified or fixed by law, the decedent shall be treated as the owner to the extent of the value of a fractional part to be determined by dividing the value of the property by the number of joint tenants with right of survivorship.

(ii) REVOCABLE TRUSTS.—The decedent shall be treated as owning property transferred by the decedent during life to a qualified revocable trust (as defined in section 645(b)(1)).

(iii) POWERS OF APPOINTMENT.—The decedent shall not be treated as owning any property by reason of holding a power of appointment with respect to such property.

(iv) COMMUNITY PROPERTY.—Property which represents the surviving spouse's one-half share of community property held by the decedent and the surviving spouse under the community property laws of any State or possession of the United States or any foreign country shall be treated for purposes of this section as owned by, and acquired from, the decedent if at least one-half of the whole of the community interest in such property is treated as owned by, and acquired from, the decedent without regard to this clause.

(C) PROPERTY ACQUIRED BY DECEDENT BY GIFT WITHIN 3 YEARS OF DEATH.—

(i) IN GENERAL.—Subsections (b) and (c) shall not apply to property acquired by the decedent by gift or by inter vivos transfer for less than adequate and full consideration in money or money's worth during the 3-year period ending on the date of the decedent's death.

(ii) EXCEPTION FOR CERTAIN GIFTS FROM SPOUSE.—Clause (i) shall not apply to property acquired by the decedent from the decedent's spouse unless, during such 3-year period, such spouse acquired the property in whole or in part by gift or by inter vivos transfer for less than adequate and full consideration in money or money's worth.

(D) STOCK OF CERTAIN ENTITIES.—Subsections (b) and (c) shall not apply to—

(i) stock or securities of a foreign personal holding company,

(ii) stock of a DISC or former DISC,

(iii) stock of a foreign investment company, or

(iv) stock of a passive foreign investment company unless such company is a qualified electing fund (as defined in section 1295) with respect to the decedent.

(2) FAIR MARKET VALUE LIMITATION.—The adjustments under subsections (b) and (c) shall not increase the basis of any interest in property acquired from the decedent above its fair market value in the hands of the decedent as of the date of the decedent's death.

(3) ALLOCATION RULES.—

(A) IN GENERAL.—The executor shall allocate the adjustments under subsections (b) and (c) on the return required by section 6018.

(B) CHANGES IN ALLOCATION.—Any allocation made pursuant to subparagraph (A) may be changed only as provided by the Secretary.

(4) INFLATION ADJUSTMENT OF BASIS ADJUSTMENT AMOUNTS.—

(A) IN GENERAL.—In the case of decedents dying in a calendar year after 2010, the $1,300,000, $60,000, and $3,000,000 dollar amounts in subsections (b) and (c)(2)(B) shall each be increased by an amount equal to the product of—

(i) such dollar amount, and

(ii) the cost-of-living adjustment determined under section 1(f)(3) for such calendar year, determined by substituting "2009" for "1992" in subparagraph (B) thereof.

(B) ROUNDING.—If any increase determined under subparagraph (A) is not a multiple of—

(i) $100,000 in the case of the $1,300,000 amount,

(ii) $5,000 in the case of the $60,000 amount, and

(iii) $250,000 in the case of the $3,000,000 amount,

such increase shall be rounded to the next lowest multiple thereof.

[Sec. 1022(e)]

(e) PROPERTY ACQUIRED FROM THE DECEDENT.—For purposes of this section, the following property shall be considered to have been acquired from the decedent:

(1) Property acquired by bequest, devise, or inheritance, or by the decedent's estate from the decedent.

(2) Property transferred by the decedent during his lifetime—

(A) to a qualified revocable trust (as defined in section 645(b)(1)), or

(B) to any other trust with respect to which the decedent reserved the right to make any change in the enjoyment thereof through the exercise of a power to alter, amend, or terminate the trust.

(3) Any other property passing from the decedent by reason of death to the extent that such property passed without consideration.

[Sec. 1022(f)]

(f) COORDINATION WITH SECTION 691.—This section shall not apply to property which constitutes a right to receive an item of income in respect of a decedent under section 691.

[Sec. 1022(g)]

(g) CERTAIN LIABILITIES DISREGARDED.—

(1) IN GENERAL.—In determining whether gain is recognized on the acquisition of property—

(A) from a decedent by a decedent's estate or any beneficiary other than a tax-exempt beneficiary, and

(B) from the decedent's estate by any beneficiary other than a tax-exempt beneficiary,

and in determining the adjusted basis of such property, liabilities in excess of basis shall be disregarded.

(2) TAX-EXEMPT BENEFICIARY.—For purposes of paragraph (1), the term "tax-exempt beneficiary" means—

(A) the United States, any State or political subdivision thereof, any possession of the United States, any Indian tribal government (within the meaning of section 7871), or any agency or instrumentality of any of the foregoing,

(B) an organization (other than a cooperative described in section 521) which is exempt from tax imposed by chapter 1,

(C) any foreign person or entity (within the meaning of section 168(h)(2)), and

(D) to the extent provided in regulations, any person to whom property is transferred for the principal purpose of tax avoidance.

[Sec. 1022(h)]

(h) REGULATIONS.—The Secretary shall prescribe such regulations as may be necessary to carry out the purposes of this section.

P.L. 111-312, § 301(c), provides:

(c) SPECIAL ELECTION WITH RESPECT TO ESTATES OF DECEDENTS DYING IN 2010.—Notwithstanding subsection (a), in the case of an estate of a decedent dying after December 31, 2009, and before January 1, 2011, the executor (within the meaning of section 2203 of the Internal Revenue Code of 1986) may elect to apply such Code as though the amendments made by subsection (a) do not apply with respect to chapter 11 of such Code and with respect to property acquired or passing from such decedent (within the meaning of section 1014(b) of such Code). Such election shall be made at such time and in such manner as the Secretary of the Treasury or the Secretary's delegate shall provide. Such an election once made shall be revocable only with the consent of the Secretary of the Treasury or the Secretary's delegate. For purposes of section 2652(a)(1) of such Code, the determination of whether any property is subject to the tax imposed by such chapter 11 shall be made without regard to any election made under this subsection.

P.L. 111-312, § 304, provides [but see P.L. 112-240, § 101(a)(2)-(3), above]:

SEC. 304. APPLICATION OF EGTRRA SUNSET TO THIS TITLE.

Section 901 of the Economic Growth and Tax Relief Reconciliation Act of 2001 shall apply to the amendments made by this title.

Amendments

• **2001, Economic Growth and Tax Relief Reconciliation Act of 2001 (P.L. 107-16)**

P.L. 107-16, § 542(a):

Amended part II of subchapter O of chapter 1 by inserting after Code Sec. 1021 a new Code Sec. 1022. **Effective** for estates of decedents dying after 12-31-2009.

P.L. 107-16, § 901(a)-(b), as amended by P.L. 111-312, § 101(a)(1), provides [but see P.L. 112-240, § 101(a)(1) and (3), above]:

SEC. 901. SUNSET OF PROVISIONS OF ACT.

(a) IN GENERAL.—All provisions of, and amendments made by, this Act shall not apply—

INCOME TAX—BASIS RULES

(1) to taxable, plan, or limitation years beginning after December 31, 2012, or

(2) in the case of title V, to estates of decedents dying, gifts made, or generation skipping transfers, after December 31, 2012.

(b) APPLICATION OF CERTAIN LAWS.—The Internal Revenue Code of 1986 and the Employee Retirement Income Security Act of 1974 shall be applied and administered to years, estates, gifts, and transfers described in subsection (a) as if the provisions and amendments described in subsection (a) had never been enacted.

Amendments

• **1976, Tax Reform Act of 1976 (P.L. 94-455)**

P.L. 94-455, §1901(a)(126):

Repealed Code Sec. 1022. **Effective** with respect to stock or securities acquired from a decedent dying after 10-4-76. Prior to repeal, Sec. 1022 read as follows:

SEC. 1022. INCREASE IN BASIS WITH RESPECT TO CERTAIN FOREIGN PERSONAL HOLDING COMPANY STOCK OR SECURITIES.

(a) GENERAL RULE.—The basis (determined under section 1014(b)(5), relating to basis of stock or securities in a foreign personal holding company) of a share of stock or a security, acquired from a decedent dying after December 31, 1963, of a corporation which was a foreign personal holding company for its most recent taxable year ending before the date of the decedent's death shall be increased by its proportionate share of any Federal estate tax attributable to the net appreciation in value of all such shares and securities determined as provided in this section.

(b) PROPORTIONATE SHARE.—For purposes of subsection (a), the proportionate share of a share of stock or of a security is that amount which bears the same ratio to the aggregate increase determined under subsection (c)(2) as the appreciation in value of such share or security bears to the aggregate appreciation in value of all such shares and securities having appreciation in value.

[Sec. 1022—Repealed]

(c) SPECIAL RULES AND DEFINITIONS.—For purposes of this section—

(1) FEDERAL ESTATE TAX.—The term "Federal estate tax" means only the tax imposed by section 2001 or 2101, reduced by any credit allowable with respect to a tax on prior transfers by section 2013 or 2102.

(2) FEDERAL ESTATE TAX ATTRIBUTABLE TO NET APPRECIATION IN VALUE.—The Federal estate tax attributable to the net appreciation in value of all shares of stock and securities to which subsection (a) applies is that amount which bears the same ratio to the Federal estate tax as the net appreciation in value of all of such shares and securities bears to the value of the gross estate as determined under chapter 11 (including section 2032, relating to alternate valuation).

(3) NET APPRECIATION.—The net appreciation in value of all shares and securities to which subsection (a) applies is the amount by which the fair market value of all such shares and securities exceeds the adjusted basis of such property in the hands of the decedent.

(4) FAIR MARKET VALUE.—For purposes of this section, the term "fair market value" means fair market value determined under chapter 11 (including section 2032, relating to alternate valuation).

(d) LIMITATIONS.—This section shall not apply to any foreign personal holding company referred to in section 342(a)(2).

[Sec. 1023]

SEC. 1023. CROSS REFERENCES.

(1) For certain distributions by a corporation which are applied in reduction of basis of stock, see section 301(c)(2).

(2) For basis in case of construction of new vessels, see chapter 533 of title 46, United States Code.

Amendments

• **2006 (P.L. 109-304)**

P.L. 109-304, §17(e)(4):

Amended Code Sec. 1023(2) by striking "section 511 of the Merchant Marine Act, 1936, as amended (46 U.S.C. 1161)" and substituting "chapter 533 of title 46, United States Code". **Effective** 10-6-2006.

• **1980, Bankruptcy Tax Act of 1980 (P.L. 96-589)**

P.L. 96-589, §6(i)(4):

Amended Code Sec. 1023 by striking out paragraph (2) and by redesignating paragraph (3) as paragraph (2). **Effective** 10-1-79, but inapplicable to any proceeding under the Bankruptcy Act commenced before that date. Former Code Sec. 1023(2) provided:

"(2) For basis of property in case of certain reorganizations and arrangements under the Bankruptcy Act, see sections 270, 396, and 522 of that Act, as amended (11 U.S.C. 670, 796, 922)."

• **1980, Crude Oil Windfall Profit Tax Act of 1980 (P.L. 96-223)**

P.L. 96-223, §401(a):

Repealed the redesignation of Code Sec. 1023 as Code Sec. 1024 by P.L. 94-455, §2005(a)(2). **Effective** for tax years beginning after 12-31-76.

• **1976, Tax Reform Act of 1976 (P.L. 94-455)**

P.L. 94-455, §1901(a)(127):

Struck out Code Sec. 1024(4) as redesignated by P.L. 94-455, §2005(a)(2). **Effective** for tax years beginning after 12-31-76. Prior to striking, Code Sec. 1024(4) read as follows:

(4) For rules applicable in case of payments in violation of Defense Production Act of 1950, as amended, see section 405 of that Act.

P.L. 94-455, §2005(a)(2), (f)(1)

Redesignated former Code Sec. 1023 as Code Sec. 1024. **Effective** for decedents dying after 12-31-79, as amended by P.L. 95-600, Sec. 515(6).

• **1964, Revenue Act of 1964 (P.L. 88-272)**

P.L. 88-272, §225(j)(1):

The section above was renumbered from 1022 to 1023.

[Sec. 1023—Repealed]

Amendments

• **1980, Crude Oil Windfall Profit Tax Act of 1980 (P.L. 96-223)**

P.L. 96-223, §401(a):

Repealed the addition of Code Sec. 1023 by P.L. 94-455, §2005(a)(2). **Effective** in respect of decedents dying after 12-31-76. However, see the amendment note for P.L. 96-223, §401(a), that follows Code Sec. 1014(d) for the text of Act Sec. 401(d) that authorizes the election of the carryover basis rules in the case of a decedent dying after 12-31-76 and before 11-7-78. Prior to repeal, Code Sec. 1023 read as follows:

SEC. 1023. CARRYOVER BASIS FOR CERTAIN PROPERTY ACQUIRED FROM A DECEDENT DYING AFTER DECEMBER 31, 1979.

[Sec. 1023(a)]

(a) GENERAL RULE.—

(1) CARRYOVER BASIS.—Except as otherwise provided in this section, the basis of carryover basis property acquired from a decedent dying after December 31, 1979, in the hands of the person so acquiring it shall be the adjusted basis of the property immediately before the death of the decedent, further adjusted as provided in this section.

(2) LOSS ON PERSONAL AND HOUSEHOLD EFFECTS.—In the case of any carryover basis property which, in the hands of the decedent, was a personal or household effect, for purposes of determining loss, the basis of such property in the hands of the person acquiring such property from the decedent shall not exceed its fair market value.

Amendments

• **1978, Revenue Act of 1978 (P.L. 95-600)**

P.L. 95-600, §515(3), (4):

Amended the heading of Code Sec. 1023 and Code Sec. 1023(a)(1) by striking out "December 31, 1976" and inserting in place thereof "December 31, 1979". **Effective** 11-7-78.

[Sec. 1023(b)]

(b) CARRYOVER BASIS PROPERTY DEFINED.—

(1) IN GENERAL.—For purposes of this section, the term "carryover basis property" means any property which is acquired from or passed from a decedent (within the meaning of section 1014(b)) and which is not excluded pursuant to paragraph (2) or (3).

(2) CERTAIN PROPERTY NOT CARRYOVER BASIS PROPERTY.—The term "carryover basis property" does not include—

(A) any item of gross income in respect of a decedent described in section 691;

INCOME TAX—BASIS RULES

(B) property described in section 2042 (relating to proceeds of life insurance);

(C) a joint and survivor annuity under which the surviving annuitant is taxable under section 72, and payments and distributions under a deferred compensation plan described in part I of subchapter D of chapter 1 to the extent such payments and distributions are taxable to the decedent's beneficiary under chapter 1;

(D) property included in the decedent's gross estate by reason of section 2035, 2038, or 2041 which has been disposed of before the decedent's death in a transaction in which gain or loss is recognizable for purposes of chapter 1;

(E) stock or a stock option passing from the decedent to the extent income in respect of such stock or stock option is includible in gross income under section 422(c)(1), 423(c), or 424(c)(1); and

(F) property described in section 1014(b)(5).

(3) $10,000 EXCLUSION FOR CERTAIN ASSETS.—

(A) EXCLUSION.—The term "carryover basis property" does not include any asset—

(i) which, in the hands of the decedent, was a personal or household effect, and

(ii) with respect to which the executor has made an election under this paragraph.

(B) LIMITATION.—The fair market value of all assets designated under this subsection with respect to any decedent shall not exceed $10,000.

(C) ELECTION.—An election under this paragraph with respect to any asset shall be made by the executor not later than the date prescribed by section 6075(a) for filing the return of the tax imposed by section 2001 or 2101 (including extensions thereof), and shall be made in such manner as the Secretary shall by regulations prescribe.

[Sec. 1023(c)]

(c) INCREASE IN BASIS FOR FEDERAL AND STATE ESTATE TAXES ATTRIBUTABLE TO APPRECIATION.—

(1) FEDERAL ESTATE TAXES.—The basis of appreciated carryover basis property (determined after any adjustment under subsection (h)) which is subject to the tax imposed by section 2001 or 2101 in the hands of the person acquiring it from the decedent shall be increased by an amount which bears the same ratio to the Federal estate taxes as—

(A) the net appreciation in value of such property, bears to

(B) the fair market value of all property which is subject to the tax imposed by section 2001 or 2101.

(2) STATE ESTATE TAXES.—The basis of appreciated carryover basis property (determined after any adjustment under subsection (h)) which is subject to State estate taxes in the hands of the person acquiring it from the decedent shall be increased by an amount which bears the same ratio to the State estate taxes as—

(A) the net appreciation in value of such property, bears to

(B) the fair market value of all property which is subject to the State estate taxes.

Amendments

• **1978, Revenue Act of 1978 (P.L. 95-600)**

P.L. 95-600, §702(c)(6)(A), (c)(10):

Amended Code Sec. 1023(c). **Effective** as if included in the amendments made by P.L. 94-455 [Sec. 2005(f)(1) (effective date), as amended by P.L. 95-600, Sec 515(b), effective for decedents dying after 12-31-1979]. Prior to amendment, such section read:

"(c) INCREASE IN BASIS FOR FEDERAL AND STATE ESTATE TAXES ATTRIBUTABLE TO APPRECIATION.—The basis of appreciated carryover basis property (determined after any adjustment under subsection (h)) which is subject to the tax imposed by section 2001 or 2101 in the hands of the person acquiring it from the decedent shall be increased by an amount which bears the same ratio to the Federal and State estate taxes as—

(1) the net appreciation in value of such property, bears to

(2) the fair market value of all property which is subject to the tax imposed by section 2001 or 2101."

[Sec. 1023(d)]

(d) $60,000 MINIMUM FOR BASES OF CARRYOVER BASIS PROPERTIES.—

(1) IN GENERAL.—If $60,000 exceeds the aggregate bases (as determined after any adjustment under subsection (h) or (c)) of all carryover basis property, the basis of each appreciated carryover basis property (after any adjustment under subsection (h) or (c)) shall be increased by an amount which bears the same ratio to the amount of such excess as—

(A) the net appreciation in value of such property, bears to

(B) the net appreciation in value of all such property.

(2) SPECIAL RULE FOR PERSONAL OR HOUSEHOLD EFFECT.—For purposes of paragraph (1), the basis of any property which is a personal or household effect shall be treated as not greater than the fair market value of such property.

(3) NONRESIDENT NOT CITIZEN.—This subsection shall not apply to any carryover basis property acquired from any decedent who was (at the time of his death) a nonresident not a citizen of the United States.

[Sec. 1023(e)]

(e) FURTHER INCREASE IN BASIS FOR CERTAIN STATE SUCCESSION TAX PAID BY TRANSFEREE OF PROPERTY.—If—

(1) any person acquires appreciated carryover basis property from a decedent, and

(2) such person actually pays an amount of estate, inheritance, legacy, or succession taxes with respect to such property to any State or the District of Columbia,

then the basis of such property (after any adjustment under subsection (h), (c) or (d)) shall be increased by an amount which bears the same ratio to the aggregate amount of all such taxes paid by such person as—

(A) the net appreciation in value of such property, bears to

(B) the fair market value of all property acquired by such person which is subject to such taxes.

Amendments

• **1978, Revenue Act of 1978 (P.L. 95-600)**

P.L. 95-600, §702(c)(7), (10):

Amended Code Sec. 1023(e)(2) by striking out "for which the estate is not liable" after "District of Columbia". **Effective** as if included in amendments made by P.L. 94-455 [Sec. 2005(f)(1) (effective date), as amended by P.L. 95-600, Sec. 515(b), effective for decedents dying after 12-31-79].

[Sec. 1023(f)]

(f) SPECIAL RULES AND DEFINITIONS FOR APPLICATION OF SUBSECTIONS (c), (d), AND (e).—

(1) FAIR MARKET VALUE LIMITATION.—The adjustments under subsections (c), (d), and (e) shall not increase the basis of property above its fair market value.

(2) NET APPRECIATION.—For purposes of this section, the net appreciation in value of any property is the amount by which the fair market value of such property exceeds the adjusted basis of such property immediately before the death of the decedent (as determined after any adjustment under subsection (h)). For purposes of paragraph (2) of subsection (c), such adjusted basis shall be increased by the amount of any adjustment under paragraph (1) of subsection (c), for purposes of subsection (d), such adjusted basis shall be increased by the amount of any adjustment under subsection (c), and, for purposes of subsection (e), such adjusted basis shall be increased by the amount of any adjustment under subsection (c) or (d).

(3) FEDERAL AND STATE ESTATE TAXES.—For purposes of subsection (c)—

(A) FEDERAL ESTATE TAXES.—The term "Federal estate taxes" means the tax imposed by section 2001 or 2101, reduced by the credits against such tax.

(B) STATE ESTATE TAXES.—The term "State estate taxes" means any estate, inheritance, legacy, or succession taxes, for which the estate is liable, actually paid by the estate to any State or the District of Columbia.

(4) CERTAIN MARITAL AND CHARITABLE DEDUCTION PROPERTY TREATED AS NOT SUBJECT TO TAX.—For purposes of subsections (c) and (e), property shall be treated as not subject to a tax—

(A) with respect to the tax imposed by section 2001 or 2101, to the extent that a deduction is allowable with respect to such property under section 2055 or 2056 or under section 2106(a)(2), and

(B) with respect to State estate taxes and with respect to the State taxes referred to in subsection (e)(2), to the extent that such property is not subject to such taxes.

(5) APPRECIATED CARRYOVER BASIS PROPERTY.—For purposes of this section, the term "appreciated carryover basis property" means any carryover basis property if the fair market value of such property exceeds the adjusted basis of such property immediately before the death of the decedent.

Amendments

• **1978, Revenue Act of 1978 (P.L. 95-600)**

P.L. 95-600, §702(c)(6)(B), (c)(10):

Amended Code Sec. 1023(f)(2). **Effective** as if included in amendments made by P.L. 94-455 [Sec. 2005(f)(1) (effective date), as amended by P.L. 95-600, Sec. 515(b), effective for decedents dying after 12-31-79]. Prior to amendment, such section read:

"(2) NET APPRECIATION.—For purposes of this section, the net appreciation in value of any property is the amount by which the fair market value of such property exceeds the adjusted basis of such property immediately before the death of the decedent (as determined after any adjustment under subsection (h)). For purposes of subsection (d), such adjusted basis shall be increased by the amount of any adjustment under subsection (c), and, for purposes of subsection (e), such adjusted basis shall be increased by the amount of any adjustment under subsection (c) or (d)."

P.L. 95-600, §702(c)(6)(C), (c)(10):

Amended Code Sec. 1023(f)(3). **Effective** as if included in amendments made by P.L. 94-455 [Sec. 2005(f)(1) (effective date), as amended by P.L. 95-600, Sec. 515(b), effective for decedents dying after 12-31-79]. Prior to amendment such section read:

"(3) FEDERAL AND STATE ESTATE TAXES.—For purposes of subsection (c), the term "Federal and State estate taxes" means—

(A) the tax imposed by section 2001 or 2101, reduced by the credits against such tax, and

(B) any estate, inheritance, legacy, or succession taxes, for which the estate is liable, actually paid by the estate to any State or the District of Columbia."

[Sec. 1023(g)]

(g) OTHER SPECIAL RULES AND DEFINITIONS.—

(1) FAIR MARKET VALUE.—For purposes of this section, when not otherwise distinctly expressed, the term "fair market value" means value as determined under chapter 11 (without regard to whether there is a mortgage on, or indebtedness in respect of, the property).

INCOME TAX—BASIS RULES

(2) PROPERTY PASSING FROM THE DECEDENT.—For purposes of this section, property passing from the decedent shall be treated as property acquired from the decedent.

(3) DECEDENT'S BASIS UNKNOWN.—If the facts necessary to determine the basis (unadjusted) of carryover basis property immediately before the death of the decedent are unknown and cannot be reasonably ascertained, such basis shall be treated as being the fair market value of such property as of the date (or approximate date) at which such property was acquired by the decedent or by the last preceding owner in whose hands it did not have a basis determined in whole or in part by reference to its basis in the hands of a prior holder.

Amendments

• **1978, Revenue Act of 1978 (P.L. 95-600)**

P.L. 95-600, §702(c)(3)(A), (c)(10):

Amended Code Sec. 1023(g)(1) by inserting "(without regard to whether there is a mortgage on, or indebtedness in respect of, the property)" after "chapter 11". **Effective** as if included in amendments made by P.L. 94-455 [Sec. 2005(f)(1) (effective date), as amended by P.L. 95-600, Sec. 515(b), effective for decedents dying after 12-31-79].

P.L. 95-600, §702(c)(2)(B), (c)(10):

Amended Code Sec. 1023(g)(3). **Effective** as if included in amendments made by P.L. 94-455 [Sec. 2005(f)(1) (effective date), as amended by P.L. 95-600, Sec. 515(b), effective for decedents dying after 12-31-79]. Prior to amendment, such section read:

(3) DECEDENT'S BASIS UNKNOWN.—If the facts necessary to determine the basis (unadjusted) of carryover basis property immediately before the death of the decedent are unknown to the person acquiring such property from the decedent, such basis shall be treated as being the fair market value of such property as of the date (or approximate date) at which such property was acquired by the decedent or by the last preceding owner in whose hands it did not have a basis determined in whole or in part by reference to its basis in the hands of a prior holder.

P.L. 95-600, §702(c)(3)(B), (c)(10):

Repealed Code Sec. 1023(g)(4). **Effective** as if included in amendments made by P.L. 94-455 [Sec. 2005(f)(1) (effective date), as amended by P.L. 95-600, Sec. 515(b), effective for decedents dying after 12-31-79]. Prior to repeal, such section read:

"(4) CERTAIN MORTGAGES.—For purposes of subsections (c), (d), and (e), if—

(A) there is an unpaid mortgage on, or indebtedness in respect of, property,

(B) such mortgage or indebtedness does not constitute a liability of the estate, and

(C) such property is included in the gross estate undiminished by such mortgage or indebtedness,

then the fair market value of such property to be treated as included in the gross estate shall be the fair market value of such property, diminished by such mortgage or indebtedness."

[Sec. 1023(h)]

(h) ADJUSTMENT TO BASIS FOR DECEMBER 31, 1976, FAIR MARKET VALUE.—

(1) MARKETABLE BONDS AND SECURITIES.—If the adjusted basis immediately before the death of the decedent of any property which is carryover basis property reflects the adjusted basis of any marketable bond or security on December 31, 1976, and if the fair market value of such bond or security on December 31, 1976, exceeded its adjusted basis on such date, then, for purposes of determining gain and applying this section, the adjusted basis of such property shall be increased by the amount of such excess.

(2) PROPERTY OTHER THAN MARKETABLE BONDS AND SECURITIES.—

(A) IN GENERAL.—If—

(i) the adjusted basis immediately before the death of the decedent of any property which is carryover basis property reflects the adjusted basis on December 31, 1976, of any property other than a marketable bond or security, and

(ii) the value of such carryover basis property (as determined with respect to the estate of the decedent without regard to section 2032) exceeds the adjusted basis of such property immediately before the death of the decedent (determined without regard to this subsection),

then, for purposes of determining gain and applying this section, the adjusted basis of such property immediately before the death of the decedent (determined without regard to this subsection) shall be increased by the amount determined under subparagraph (B).

(B) AMOUNT OF INCREASE.—The amount of the increase under this subparagraph for any property is the sum of—

(i) the excess referred to in subparagraph (A)(ii), reduced by an amount equal to all adjustments for depreciation, amortization, or depletion for the holding period of such property, and then multiplied by the applicable fraction determined under subparagraph (C), and

(ii) the adjustments to basis for depreciation, amortization, or depletion which are attributable to that portion of the holding period for such property which occurs before January 1, 1977.

(C) APPLICABLE FRACTION.—For purposes of subparagraph (B)(i), the term "applicable fraction" means, with respect to any property, a fraction—

(i) the numerator of which is the number of days in the holding period with respect to such property which occurs before January 1, 1977, and

(ii) the denominator of which is the total number of days in such holding period.

(D) SUBSTANTIAL IMPROVEMENTS.—Under regulations prescribed by the Secretary, if there is a substantial improvement of any property, such substantial improvement shall be treated as a separate property for purposes of this paragraph.

(E) DEFINITIONS.—For purposes of this paragraph—

(i) The term "marketable bond or security" means any security for which, as of December 1976, there was a market on a stock exchange, in an over-the-counter market, or otherwise.

(ii) The term "holding period" means, with respect to any carryover basis property, the period during which the decedent (or, if any other person held such property immediately before the death of the decedent, such other person) held such property as determined under section 1223; except that such period shall end on the date of the decedent's death.

(3) MINIMUM BASIS FOR TANGIBLE PERSONAL PROPERTY.—

(A) IN GENERAL.—If the holding period for any carryover basis property which is tangible personal property includes December 31, 1976, then, for purposes of determining gain and applying this section, the adjusted basis of such property immediately before the death of the decedent shall be treated as being not less than the amount determined under subparagraph (B).

(B) AMOUNT.—The amount determined under this subparagraph for any property is—

(i) the value of such property (as determined with respect to the estate of the decedent without regard to section 2032) divided by

(ii) 1.0066 to the nth power where n equals the number of full calendar months which have elapsed between December 31, 1976, and the date of the decedent's death.

(4) ONLY ONE FRESH START.—There shall be no increase in basis under this subsection by reason of the death of any decedent if the adjusted basis of the property in the hands of such decedent reflects the adjusted basis of property which was carryover basis property with respect to a prior decedent.

Amendments

• **1978, Revenue Act of 1978 (P.L. 95-600)**

P.L. 95-600, §702(c)(8), (c)(10):

Amended Code Sec. 1023(h)(1) and (2)(A) by striking out "for purposes of determining gain" and inserting in place thereof "for purposes of determining gain and applying this section". **Effective** as if included in amendments made by P.L. 94-455 [Sec. 2005(f)(1) (effective date), as amended by P.L. 95-600, Sec. 515(b), effective for decedents dying after 12-31-79].

P.L. 95-600, §702(c)(2)(A), (c)(10):

Added Code Sec. 1023(h)(3). **Effective** as if included in amendments made by P.L. 94-455 [Sec. 2005(f)(1) (effective date), as amended by P.L. 95-600, Sec. 515(b), effective for decedents dying after 12-31-79].

P.L. 95-600, §702(c)(4), (c)(10):

Added Code Sec. 1023(h)(4). **Effective** as if included in amendments made by P.L. 94-455 [Sec. 2005(f)(1) (effective date), as amended by P.L. 95-600, Sec. 515(b), effective for decedents dying after 12-31-79].

[Sec. 1023(i)]

(i) REGULATIONS.—The Secretary shall prescribe such regulations as may be necessary to carry out the purposes of this section.

Amendments

• **1976, Tax Reform Act of 1976 (P.L. 94-455)**

P.L. 94-455, §2005(a)(2), (f)(1):

Redesignated former Code Sec. 1023 as Code Sec. 1024 and added new Code Sec. 1023. **Effective** in respect of decedents dying after 12-31-79, as amended by P.L. 95-600, §515(6).

PART III—COMMON NONTAXABLE EXCHANGES

Sec. 1031.	Exchange of real property held for productive use or investment.
Sec. 1032.	Exchange of stock for property.
Sec. 1033.	Involuntary conversions.
Sec. 1035.	Certain exchanges of insurance policies.
Sec. 1036.	Stock for stock of same corporation.
Sec. 1037.	Certain exchanges of United States obligations.
Sec. 1038.	Certain reacquisitions of real property.
Sec. 1040.	Transfer of certain farm, etc., real property
Sec. 1041.	Transfers of property between spouses or incident to divorce.
Sec. 1042.	Sales of stock to employee stock ownership plans or certain cooperatives.
Sec. 1043.	Sale of property to comply with conflict-of-interest requirements.
Sec. 1045.	Rollover of gain from qualified small business stock to another qualified small business stock.

Sec. 1023—Repealed

INCOME TAX—NONTAXABLE EXCHANGES

[Sec. 1031]

SEC. 1031. EXCHANGE OF REAL PROPERTY HELD FOR PRODUCTIVE USE OR INVESTMENT.

[Sec. 1031(a)]

(a) NONRECOGNITION OF GAIN OR LOSS FROM EXCHANGES SOLELY IN KIND.—

(1) IN GENERAL.—No gain or loss shall be recognized on the exchange of real property held for productive use in a trade or business or for investment if such real property is exchanged solely for real property of like kind which is to be held either for productive use in a trade or business or for investment.

(2) EXCEPTION FOR REAL PROPERTY HELD FOR SALE.—This subsection shall not apply to any exchange of real property held primarily for sale.

(3) REQUIREMENT THAT PROPERTY BE IDENTIFIED AND THAT EXCHANGE BE COMPLETED NOT MORE THAN 180 DAYS AFTER TRANSFER OF EXCHANGED PROPERTY.—For purposes of this subsection, any property received by the taxpayer shall be treated as property which is not like-kind property if—

(A) such property is not identified as property to be received in the exchange on or before the day which is 45 days after the date on which the taxpayer transfers the property relinquished in the exchange, or

(B) such property is received after the earlier of—

(i) the day which is 180 days after the date on which the taxpayer transfers the property relinquished in the exchange, or

(ii) the due date (determined with regard to extension) for the transferor's return of the tax imposed by this chapter for the taxable year in which the transfer of the relinquished property occurs.

Amendments

• **2017, Tax Cuts and Jobs Act (P.L. 115-97)**

P.L. 115-97, §13303(a):

Amended Code Sec. 1031(a)(1) by striking "property" each place it appears and inserting "real property". **Effective** generally for exchanges completed after 12-31-2017. For a transition rule, see Act Sec. 13303(c)(2), below.

P.L. 115-97, §13303(b)(1)(A):

Amended Code Sec. 1031(a)(2). **Effective** generally for exchanges completed after 12-31-2017. For a transition rule, see Act Sec. 13303(c)(2), below. Prior to amendment, Code Sec. 1031(a)(2) read as follows:

(2) EXCEPTION.—This subsection shall not apply to any exchange of—

(A) stock in trade or other property held primarily for sale,

(B) stocks, bonds, or notes,

(C) other securities or evidences of indebtedness or interest,

(D) interests in a partnership,

(E) certificates of trust or beneficial interests, or

(F) choses in action.

For purposes of this section, an interest in a partnership which has in effect a valid election under section 761(a) to be excluded from the application of all of subchapter K shall be treated as an interest in each of the assets of such partnership and not as an interest in a partnership.

P.L. 115-97, §13303(b)(5):

Amended the heading of Code Sec. 1031 by striking "**PROPERTY**" and inserting "**REAL PROPERTY**". **Effective** generally for exchanges completed after 12-31-2017. For a transition rule, see Act Sec. 13303(c)(2), below.

P.L. 115-97, §13303(c)(2), provides:

(2) TRANSITION RULE.—The amendments made by this section shall not apply to any exchange if—

(A) the property disposed of by the taxpayer in the exchange is disposed of on or before December 31, 2017, or

(B) the property received by the taxpayer in the exchange is received on or before December 31, 2017.

• **1990, Omnibus Budget Reconciliation Act of 1990 (P.L. 101-508)**

P.L. 101-508, §11703(d)(1):

Amended Code Sec. 1031(a)(2) by adding at the end thereof a new sentence. **Effective** for transfers after 7-18-84.

• **1986, Tax Reform Act of 1986 (P.L. 99-514)**

P.L. 99-514, §1805(d):

Amended Code Sec. 1031(a)(3)(A) by striking out "before the day" and inserting in lieu thereof "on or before the day". **Effective** as if included in the provision of P.L. 98-369 to which such amendment relates.

• **1984, Deficit Reduction Act of 1984 (P.L. 98-369)**

P.L. 98-369, §77(a):

Amended Code Sec. 1031(a). **Effective** for transfers made after 7-18-84, in tax years ending after such date. Special rules appear in Act Sec. 77(b)(2)-(5), below. Prior to amendment, Code Sec. 1031(a) read as follows:

(a) Nonrecognition of Gain or Loss From Exchanges Solely in Kind.—No gain or loss shall be recognized if property held for productive use in trade or business or for investment (not including stock in trade or other property held primarily for sale, no stocks, bonds, notes, choses in action, certificates of trust or beneficial interest, or other securities or evidences of indebtedness or interest) is exchanged solely for property of a like kind to be held either for productive use in trade or business or for investment.

P.L. 98-369, §77(b)(2)-(5), provides:

(2) Binding Contract Exception for Transfer of Partnership Interests.—Paragraph (2)(D) of section 1031(a) of the Internal Revenue Code of 1954 (as amended by subsection (a)) shall not apply in the case of any exchange pursuant to a binding contract in effect on March 1, 1984, and at all times thereafter before the exchange.

(3) Requirement That Property Be Identified Within 45 Days and That Exchange Be Completed Within 180 Days.—Paragraph (3) of section 1031(a) of the Internal Revenue Code of 1954 (as amended by subsection (a)) shall apply—

(A) to transfers after the date of the enactment of this Act, and

(B) to transfers on or before such date of enactment if the property to be received in the exchange is not received before January 1, 1987.

In the case of any transfer on or before the date of the enactment of this Act which the taxpayer treated as part of a like-kind exchange, the period for assessing any deficiency of tax attributable to the amendment made by subsection (a) shall not expire before January 1, 1988.

(4) Special Rule Where Property Identified in Binding Contract.—If the property to be received in the exchange is identified in a binding contract in effect on June 13, 1984, and at all times thereafter before the transfer, paragraph (3) shall be applied—

(A) by substituting "January 1, 1989" for "January 1, 1987", and

(B) by substituting "January 1, 1990" for "January 1, 1988".

(5) Special Rule for Like-Kind Exchange of Partnership Interests.—Paragraph (2)(D) of section 1031(a) of the Internal Revenue Code of 1954 (as amended by subsection (a)) shall not apply to any exchange of an interest as general partner pursuant to a plan of reorganization of ownership interest under a contract which took effect on March 29, 1984, and which was executed on or before March 31, 1984, but only if all the exchanges contemplated by the reorganization plan are completed on or before December 31, 1984.

[Sec. 1031(b)]

(b) GAIN FROM EXCHANGES NOT SOLELY IN KIND.—If an exchange would be within the provisions of subsection (a), of section 1035(a), of section 1036(a), or of section 1037(a), if it were not for the fact that the property received in exchange consists not only of property permitted by such provisions to be received without the recognition of gain, but also of other property or money, then the gain, if any, to the recipient shall be recognized, but in an amount not in excess of the sum of such money and the fair market value of such other property.

Amendments

• **1959 (P.L. 86-346)**

P.L. 86-346, §102(c):

Amended Code Sec. 1031(b) by striking out "the provisions of subsection (a), of section 1035(a), or of section 1036(a)," and by substituting "the provisions of subsection (a), of section 1035(a), of section 1036(a), or of section 1037(a),". **Effective** for tax years ending after 9-22-59.

[Sec. 1031(c)]

(c) LOSS FROM EXCHANGES NOT SOLELY IN KIND.—If an exchange would be within the provisions of subsection (a), of section 1035(a), of section 1036(a), or of section 1037(a), if it were not for the fact that the property received in exchange consists not only of property permitted by such provisions to be received without the recognition of gain or loss, but also of other property or money, then no loss from the exchange shall be recognized.

INCOME TAX—NONTAXABLE EXCHANGES

Amendments

• 1959 (P.L. 86-346)

P.L. 86-346, §102(d):

Amended Code Sec. 1031(c) by striking out "the provisions of subsection (a), of section 1035(a), or of section 1036(a)," and by substituting "the provisions of subsection (a), of section 1035(a), of section 1036(a), or of section 1037(a),". **Effective** for tax years ending after 9-22-59.

[Sec. 1031(d)]

(d) BASIS.—If property was acquired on an exchange described in this section, section 1035(a), section 1036(a), or section 1037(a), then the basis shall be the same as that of the property exchanged, decreased in the amount of any money received by the taxpayer and increased in the amount of gain or decreased in the amount of loss to the taxpayer that was recognized on such exchange. If the property so acquired consisted in part of the type of property permitted by this section, section 1035(a), section 1036(a), or section 1037(a), to be received without the recognition of gain or loss, and in part of other property, the basis provided in this subsection shall be allocated between the properties (other than money) received, and for the purpose of the allocation there shall be assigned to such other property an amount equivalent to its fair market value at the date of the exchange. For purposes of this section, section 1035(a), and section 1036(a), where as part of the consideration to the taxpayer another party to the exchange assumed (as determined under section 357(d)) a liability of the taxpayer, such assumption shall be considered as money received by the taxpayer on the exchange.

Amendments

• 1999, Miscellaneous Trade and Technical Corrections Act of 1999 (P.L. 106-36)

P.L. 106-36, §3001(c)(2)(A)-(B):

Amended the last sentence of Code Sec. 1031(d) by striking "assumed a liability of the taxpayer or acquired from the taxpayer property subject to a liability" and inserting "assumed (as determined under section 357(d)) a liability of the taxpayer", and by striking "or acquisition (in the amount of the liability)" following "such assumption". **Effective** for transfers after 10-18-98.

• 1959 (P.L. 86-346)

P.L. 86-346, §102(e):

Amended the first and second sentences of Code Sec. 1031(d) by striking out "this section, section 1035(a), or section 1036(a)," and by substituting "this section, section 1035(a), section 1036(a), or section 1037(a),". **Effective** for tax years ending after 9-22-59.

• 1958, Technical Amendments Act of 1958 (P.L. 85-866)

P.L. 85-866, §44(a):

Amended the first sentence of subsection (d) of Sec. 1031 and amended the second sentence of subsection (d) of Sec. 1031 by striking out the word "paragraph" where it appeared preceding the phrase "shall be allocated" and substituted the word "subsection". **Effective** 1-1-54. Prior to amendment, the first sentence of subsection (d) read as follows: "If property was acquired on an exchange described in this section, section 1035 (a), or section 1036 (a), then the basis shall be the same as that of the property exchanged decreased in the amount of any money received by the taxpayer and increased in the amount of gain to the taxpayer that was recognized on such exchange."

[Sec. 1031(e)]

(e) APPLICATION TO CERTAIN PARTNERSHIPS.—For purposes of this section, an interest in a partnership which has in effect a valid election under section 761(a) to be excluded from the application of all of subchapter K shall be treated as an interest in each of the assets of such partnership and not as an interest in a partnership.

Amendments

• 2017, Tax Cuts and Jobs Act (P.L. 115-97)

P.L. 115-97, §13303(b)(3):

Amended Code Sec. 1031, as amended by Act Sec. 13303(b)(2), by inserting after subsection (d) a new subsection (e). **Effective** generally for exchanges completed after 12-31-2017. For a transition rule, see Act Sec. 13303(c)(2), below.

Amendments

• 2017, Tax Cuts and Jobs Act (P.L. 115-97)

P.L. 115-97, §13303(b)(2):

Amended Code Sec. 1031 by striking subsection (e). **Effective** generally for exchanges completed after 12-31-2017. For a transition rule, see Act Sec. 13303(c)(2), below. Prior to being stricken, Code Sec. 1031(e) read as follows:

(e) EXCHANGES OF LIVESTOCK OF DIFFERENT SEXES.—For purposes of this section, livestock of different sexes are not property of a like kind.

P.L. 115-97, §13303(c)(2), provides:

(2) TRANSITION RULE.—The amendments made by this section shall not apply to any exchange if—

P.L. 115-97, §13303(c)(2), provides:

(2) TRANSITION RULE.—The amendments made by this section shall not apply to any exchange if—

(A) the property disposed of by the taxpayer in the exchange is disposed of on or before December 31, 2017, or

(B) the property received by the taxpayer in the exchange is received on or before December 31, 2017.

[Sec. 1031(e)—Stricken]

(A) the property disposed of by the taxpayer in the exchange is disposed of on or before December 31, 2017, or

(B) the property received by the taxpayer in the exchange is received on or before December 31, 2017.

• 1969, Tax Reform Act of 1969 (P.L. 91-172)

P.L. 91-172, §212(c):

Amended Code Sec. 1031 by adding subsection (e). **Effective** for tax years to which the 1954 Code applies.

[Sec. 1031(f)]

(f) SPECIAL RULES FOR EXCHANGES BETWEEN RELATED PERSONS.—

(1) IN GENERAL.—If—

(A) a taxpayer exchanges property with a related person,

(B) there is nonrecognition of gain or loss to the taxpayer under this section with respect to the exchange of such property (determined without regard to this subsection), and

(C) before the date 2 years after the date of the last transfer which was part of such exchange—

(i) the related person disposes of such property, or

(ii) the taxpayer disposes of the property received in the exchange from the related person which was of like kind to the property transferred by the taxpayer,

there shall be no nonrecognition of gain or loss under this section to the taxpayer with respect to such exchange; except that any gain or loss recognized by the taxpayer by reason of this subsection shall be taken into account as of the date on which the disposition referred to in subparagraph (C) occurs.

(2) CERTAIN DISPOSITIONS NOT TAKEN INTO ACCOUNT.—For purposes of paragraph (1)(C), there shall not be taken into account any disposition—

(A) after the earlier of the death of the taxpayer or the death of the related person,

(B) in a compulsory or involuntary conversion (within the meaning of section 1033) if the exchange occurred before the threat or imminence of such conversion, or

(C) with respect to which it is established to the satisfaction of the Secretary that neither the exchange nor such disposition had as one of its principal purposes the avoidance of Federal income tax.

(3) RELATED PERSON.—For purposes of this subsection, the term "related person" means any person bearing a relationship to the taxpayer described in section 267(b) or 707(b)(1).

INCOME TAX—NONTAXABLE EXCHANGES

(4) TREATMENT OF CERTAIN TRANSACTIONS.—This section shall not apply to any exchange which is part of a transaction (or series of transactions) structured to avoid the purposes of this subsection.

Amendments

• **1990, Omnibus Budget Reconciliation Act of 1990 (P.L. 101-508)**

P.L. 101-508, §11701(h):

Amended Code Sec. 1031(f)(3) by striking "section 267(b)", and inserting "section 267(b) or 707(b)(1)". **Effective** with respect to transfers after 8-3-90.

• **1989, Omnibus Budget Reconciliation Act of 1989 (P.L. 101-239)**

P.L. 101-239, §7601(a):

Amended Code Sec. 1031 by adding at the end thereof new subsection (f). **Effective** for transfers after 7-10-89, in tax years ending after such date, except as provided in Act Sec. 7601(b)(2), below.

P.L. 101-239, §7601(b)(2), provides:

(2) BINDING CONTRACT.—The amendments made by this section shall not apply to any transfer pursuant to a written binding contract in effect on July 10, 1989, and at all times thereafter before the transfer.

[Sec. 1031(g)]

(g) SPECIAL RULE WHERE SUBSTANTIAL DIMINUTION OF RISK.—

(1) IN GENERAL.—If paragraph (2) applies to any property for any period, the running of the period set forth in subsection (f)(1)(C) with respect to such property shall be suspended during such period.

(2) PROPERTY TO WHICH SUBSECTION APPLIES.—This paragraph shall apply to any property for any period during which the holder's risk of loss with respect to the property is substantially diminished by—

    (A) the holding of a put with respect to such property,

    (B) the holding by another person of a right to acquire such property, or

    (C) a short sale or any other transaction.

Amendments

• **1989, Omnibus Budget Reconciliation Act of 1989 (P.L. 101-239)**

P.L. 101-239, §7601(a):

Amended Code Sec. 1031 by adding at the end thereof a new subsection (g). **Effective** for transfers after 7-10-89, in tax years ending after such date, except as provided in Act Sec. 7601(b)(2), below.

P.L. 101-239, §7601(b)(2), provides:

(2) BINDING CONTRACT.—The amendments made by this section shall not apply to any transfer pursuant to a written binding contract in effect on July 10, 1989, and at all times thereafter before the transfer.

[Sec. 1031(h)]

(h) SPECIAL RULES FOR FOREIGN REAL PROPERTY.—Real property located in the United States and real property located outside the United States are not property of a like kind.

Amendments

• **2017, Tax Cuts and Jobs Act (P.L. 115-97)**

P.L. 115-97, §13303(b)(4):

Amended Code Sec. 1031(h). **Effective** generally for exchanges completed after 12-31-2017. For a transition rule, see Act Sec. 13303(c)(2), below. Prior to amendment, Code Sec. 1031(h) read as follows:

(h) SPECIAL RULES FOR FOREIGN REAL AND PERSONAL PROPERTY.—For purposes of this section—

(1) REAL PROPERTY.—Real property located in the United States and real property located outside the United States are not property of a like kind.

(2) PERSONAL PROPERTY.—

(A) IN GENERAL.—Personal property used predominantly within the United States and personal property used predominantly outside the United States are not property of a like kind.

(B) PREDOMINANT USE.—Except as provided in subparagraphs (C) and (D), the predominant use of any property shall be determined based on—

(i) in the case of the property relinquished in the exchange, the 2-year period ending on the date of such relinquishment, and

(ii) in the case of the property acquired in the exchange, the 2-year period beginning on the date of such acquisition.

(C) PROPERTY HELD FOR LESS THAN 2 YEARS.—Except in the case of an exchange which is part of a transaction (or series of transactions) structured to avoid the purposes of this subsection—

(i) only the periods the property was held by the person relinquishing the property (or any related person) shall be taken into account under subparagraph (B)(i), and

(ii) only the periods the property was held by the person acquiring the property (or any related person) shall be taken into account under subparagraph (B)(ii).

(D) SPECIAL RULE FOR CERTAIN PROPERTY.—Property described in any subparagraph of section 168(g)(4) shall be treated as used predominantly in the United States.

P.L. 115-97, §13303(c)(2), provides:

(2) TRANSITION RULE.—The amendments made by this section shall not apply to any exchange if—

(A) the property disposed of by the taxpayer in the exchange is disposed of on or before December 31, 2017, or

(B) the property received by the taxpayer in the exchange is received on or before December 31, 2017.

• **2005, Gulf Opportunity Zone Act of 2005 (P.L. 109-135)**

P.L. 109-135, §412(pp):

Amended the matter preceding Code Sec. 1031(h)(2)(B)(i) by striking "subparagraph" and inserting "subparagraphs". **Effective** 12-21-2005.

• **1997, Taxpayer Relief Act of 1997 (P.L. 105-34)**

P.L. 105-34, §1052(a):

Amended Code Sec. 1031(h). **Effective**, generally, for transfers after 6-8-97, in tax years ending after such date. For a special rule, see Act Sec. 1052(b)(2), below. Prior to amendment, Code Sec. 1031(h) read as follows:

(h) SPECIAL RULE FOR FOREIGN REAL PROPERTY.—For purposes of this section, real property located in the United States and real property located outside the United States are not property of a like kind.

P.L. 105-34, §1052(b)(2), provides:

(2) BINDING CONTRACTS.—The amendment made by this section shall not apply to any transfer pursuant to a written binding contract in effect on June 8, 1997, and at all times thereafter before the disposition of property. A contract shall not fail to meet the requirements of the preceding sentence solely because—

(A) it provides for a sale in lieu of an exchange, or

(B) the property to be acquired as replacement property was not identified under such contract before June 9, 1997.

• **1989, Omnibus Budget Reconciliation Act of 1989 (P.L. 101-239)**

P.L. 101-239, §7601(a):

Amended Code Sec. 1031 by adding at the end thereof a new subsection (h). **Effective** for transfers after 7-10-89, in tax years ending after such date, except as provided in Act Sec. 7601(b)(2), below.

P.L. 101-239, §7601(b)(2), provides:

(2) BINDING CONTRACT.—The amendments made by this section shall not apply to any transfer pursuant to a written binding contract in effect on July 10, 1989, and at all times thereafter before the transfer.

[Sec. 1031(i)—Stricken]

Amendments

• **2017, Tax Cuts and Jobs Act (P.L. 115-97)**

P.L. 115-97, §13303(b)(1)(B):

Amended Code Sec. 1031 by striking subsection (i). **Effective** generally for exchanges completed after 12-31-2017. For a transition rule, see Act Sec. 13303(c)(2), below. Prior to being stricken, Code Sec. 1031(i) read as follows:

(i) SPECIAL RULES FOR MUTUAL DITCH, RESERVOIR, OR IRRIGATION COMPANY STOCK .—For purposes of subsection (a)(2)(B), the term "stocks" shall not include shares in a mutual ditch, reservoir, or irrigation company if at the time of the exchange—

(1) the mutual ditch, reservoir, or irrigation company is an organization described in section 501(c)(12)(A) (determined without regard to the percentage of its income that is collected from its members for the purpose of meeting losses and expenses), and

(2) the shares in such company have been recognized by the highest court of the State in which such company was organized or by applicable State statute as constituting or representing real property or an interest in real property.

P.L. 115-97, §13303(c)(2), provides:

(2) TRANSITION RULE.—The amendments made by this section shall not apply to any exchange if—

(A) the property disposed of by the taxpayer in the exchange is disposed of on or before December 31, 2017, or

(B) the property received by the taxpayer in the exchange is received on or before December 31, 2017.

INCOME TAX—NONTAXABLE EXCHANGES

• **2008, Heartland, Habitat, Harvest, and Horticulture Act of 2008 (P.L. 110-246)**

P.L. 110-246, §15342(a):

Amended Code Sec. 1031 by adding at the end a new subsection (i). **Effective** for exchanges completed after 5-22-2008.

[Sec. 1032]

SEC. 1032. EXCHANGE OF STOCK FOR PROPERTY.

[Sec. 1032(a)]

(a) NONRECOGNITION OF GAIN OR LOSS.—No gain or loss shall be recognized to a corporation on the receipt of money or other property in exchange for stock (including treasury stock) of such corporation. No gain or loss shall be recognized by a corporation with respect to any lapse or acquisition of an option, or with respect to a securities futures contract (as defined in section 1234B), to buy or sell its stock (including treasury stock).

Amendments

• **2000, Community Renewal Tax Relief Act of 2000 (P.L. 106-554)**

P.L. 106-554, §401(c):

Amended the second sentence of Code Sec. 1032(a) by inserting ", or with respect to a securities futures contract (as defined in section 1234B)," after "an option". **Effective** 12-21-2000.

• **1984, Deficit Reduction Act of 1984 (P.L. 98-369)**

P.L. 98-369, §57(a):

Amended Code Sec. 1032(a) by adding at the end thereof a new sentence. **Effective** for options acquired or lapsed after 7-18-84, in tax years ending after such date.

[Sec. 1032(b)]

(b) BASIS.—For basis of property acquired by a corporation in certain exchanges for its stock, see section 362.

[Sec. 1033]

SEC. 1033. INVOLUNTARY CONVERSIONS.

[Sec. 1033(a)]

(a) GENERAL RULE.—If property (as a result of its destruction in whole or in part, theft, seizure, or requisition or condemnation or threat or imminence thereof) is compulsorily or involuntarily converted—

(1) CONVERSION INTO SIMILAR PROPERTY.—Into property similar or related in service or use to the property so converted, no gain shall be recognized.

(2) CONVERSION INTO MONEY.—Into money or into property not similar or related in service or use to the converted property, the gain (if any) shall be recognized except to the extent hereinafter provided in this paragraph:

(A) NONRECOGNITION OF GAIN.—If the taxpayer during the period specified in subparagraph (B), for the purpose of replacing the property so converted, purchases other property similar or related in service or use to the property so converted, or purchases stock in the acquisition of control of a corporation owning such other property, at the election of the taxpayer the gain shall be recognized only to the extent that the amount realized upon such conversion (regardless of whether such amount is received in one or more taxable years) exceeds the cost of such other property or such stock. Such election shall be made at such time and in such manner as the Secretary may by regulations prescribe. For purposes of this paragraph—

(i) no property or stock acquired before the disposition of the converted property shall be considered to have been acquired for the purpose of replacing such converted property unless held by the taxpayer on the date of such disposition; and

(ii) the taxpayer shall be considered to have purchased property or stock only if, but for the provisions of subsection (b) of this section, the unadjusted basis of such property or stock would be its cost within the meaning of section 1012.

(B) PERIOD WITHIN WHICH PROPERTY MUST BE REPLACED.—The period referred to in subparagraph (A) shall be the period beginning with the date of the disposition of the converted property, or the earliest date of the threat or imminence of requisition or condemnation of the converted property, whichever is the earlier, and ending—

(i) 2 years after the close of the first taxable year in which any part of the gain upon the conversion is realized, or

(ii) subject to such terms and conditions as may be specified by the Secretary, at the close of such later date as the Secretary may designate on application by the taxpayer. Such application shall be made at such time and in such manner as the Secretary may by regulations prescribe.

(C) TIME FOR ASSESSMENT OF DEFICIENCY ATTRIBUTABLE TO GAIN UPON CONVERSION.—If a taxpayer has made the election provided in subparagraph (A), then—

(i) the statutory period for the assessment of any deficiency, for any taxable year in which any part of the gain on such conversion is realized, attributable to such gain shall not expire prior to the expiration of 3 years from the date the Secretary is notified by the taxpayer (in such manner as the Secretary may by regulations prescribe) of the replacement of the converted property or of an intention not to replace, and

(ii) such deficiency may be assessed before the expiration of such 3-year period notwithstanding the provisions of section 6212(c) or the provisions of any other law or rule of law which would otherwise prevent such assessment.

(D) TIME FOR ASSESSMENT OF OTHER DEFICIENCIES ATTRIBUTABLE TO ELECTION.—If the election provided in subparagraph (A) is made by the taxpayer and such other property or such stock was purchased before the beginning of the last taxable year in which any part of the gain upon such conversion is realized, any deficiency, to the extent resulting from such election, for any taxable year ending before such last taxable year may be assessed (notwithstanding the provisions] of section 6212(c) or 6501 or the provisions of any other law or rule of law which would otherwise prevent such assessment) at any time before the expiration of the period within which a deficiency for such last taxable year may be assessed.

(E) DEFINITIONS.—For purposes of this paragraph—

(i) CONTROL.—The term "control" means the ownership of stock possessing at least 80 percent of the total combined voting power of all classes of stock entitled to vote and at least 80 percent of the total number of shares of all other classes of stock of the corporation.

(ii) DISPOSITION OF THE CONVERTED PROPERTY.—The term "disposition of the converted property" means the destruction, theft, seizure, requisition, or condemnation of the converted property, or the sale or exchange of such property under threat or imminence of requisition or condemnation.

INCOME TAX—NONTAXABLE EXCHANGES

Amendments

• **2005, Katrina Emergency Tax Relief Act of 2005 (P.L. 109-73)**

P.L. 109-73, §405 [but see P.L. 110-246, §15345, in the amendment notes for Code Sec. 1400N(d), and P.L. 110-343, Division C, §702, in the amendment notes for Code Sec. 1400N(a)], provides:

SEC. 405. EXTENSION OF REPLACEMENT PERIOD FOR NONRECOGNITION OF GAIN FOR PROPERTY LOCATED IN HURRICANE KATRINA DISASTER AREA.

Clause (j) of section 1033(a)(2)(B) of the Internal Revenue Code of 1986 shall be applied by substituting "5 years" for "2 years" with respect to property in the Hurricane Katrina disaster area which is compulsorily or involuntarily converted on or after August 25, 2005, by reason of Hurricane Katrina, but only if substantially all of the use of the replacement property is in such area.

• **1978, Revenue Act of 1978 (P.L. 95-600)**

P.L. 95-600, §703(j)(5), (r):

Amended Code Sec. 1033(a)(2)(A)(ii) by striking out "subsection (c)" and inserting in place thereof "subsection (b)". **Effective** 10-4-76.

• **1976, Tax Reform Act of 1976 (P.L. 94-455)**

P.L. 94-455, §1901(a)(128)(A):

Struck out Code Sec. 1033(a)(2) and redesignated Code Sec. 1033(a)(3) as Code Sec. 1033(a)(2). **Effective** for tax years beginning after 12-31-76. Prior to striking, Code Sec. 1033(a)(2) read as follows:

(2) CONVERSION INTO MONEY WHERE DISPOSITION OCCURRED PRIOR TO 1951.—Into money, and the disposition of the converted property occurred before January 1, 1951, no gain shall be recognized if such money is forthwith in good faith, under regulations prescribed by the Secretary or his delegate, expended in the acquisition of other property similar or related in service or use to the property so converted, or in the acquisition of control of a corporation owning such other property, or in the establishment of a replacement fund. If any part of the money is not so expended, the gain shall be recognized to the extent of the money which is not so expended (regardless of whether such money is received in one or more taxable years and regardless of whether or not the money which is not so expended constitutes gain). For purposes of this paragraph and paragraph (3), the term "disposition of the converted property" means the destruction, theft, seizure, requisition, or condemnation of the converted property, or the sale or exchange of such property under threat or imminence of requisition or condemnation. For purposes of this paragraph and paragraph (3), the term "control" means the ownership of stock possessing at least 80 percent of the total combined voting power of all classes of stock entitled to vote and at least 80 percent of the total number of shares of all other classes of stock of the corporation.

P.L. 94-455, §1901(a)(128)(B):

Struck out "WHERE DISPOSITION OCCURRED AFTER 1950" in the heading of redesignated Code Sec. 1033(a)(2), struck out "and the disposition of the converted property (as defined in paragraph (2)) occurred after December 31, 1950," following "use to the converted property," in the first sentence of redesignated Code Sec. 1033(a)(2), and added Code Sec. 1033(a)(2)(E). **Effective** for tax years beginning after 12-31-76.

P.L. 94-455, §1906(b)(13)(A):

Amended 1954 Code by substituting "Secretary" for "Secretary or his delegate" each place it appeared. **Effective** 2-1-77.

• **1969, Tax Reform Act of 1969 (P.L. 91-172)**

P.L. 91-172, §915(a):

Amended subdivision (a)(3)(B)(i) by inserting "2 years" in lieu of "one year". **Effective** only if the disposition of the converted property within the meaning of section 1033(a)(2) of the Internal Revenue Code of 1954 occurs after 12-30-69.

• **1958, Technical Amendments Act of 1958 (P.L. 85-866)**

P.L. 85-866, §45:

Added the last sentence in Sec. 1033(a)(2). **Effective** 1-1-54.

[Sec. 1033(b)]

(b) BASIS OF PROPERTY ACQUIRED THROUGH INVOLUNTARY CONVERSION.—

(1) CONVERSIONS DESCRIBED IN SUBSECTION (a)(1).—If the property was acquired as the result of a compulsory or involuntary conversion described in subsection (a)(1), the basis shall be the same as in the case of the property so converted—

(A) decreased in the amount of any money received by the taxpayer which was not expended in accordance with the provisions of law (applicable to the year in which such conversion was made) determining the taxable status of the gain or loss upon such conversion, and

(B) increased in the amount of gain or decreased in the amount of loss to the taxpayer recognized upon such conversion under the law applicable to the year in which such conversion was made.

(2) CONVERSIONS DESCRIBED IN SUBSECTION (a)(2).—In the case of property purchased by the taxpayer in a transaction described in subsection (a)(2) which resulted in the nonrecognition of any part of the gain realized as the result of a compulsory or involuntary conversion, the basis shall be the cost of such property decreased in the amount of the gain not so recognized; and if the property purchased consists of more than 1 piece of property, the basis determined under this sentence shall be allocated to the purchased properties in proportion to their respective costs.

(3) PROPERTY HELD BY CORPORATION THE STOCK OF WHICH IS REPLACEMENT PROPERTY.—

(A) IN GENERAL.—If the basis of stock in a corporation is decreased under paragraph (2), an amount equal to such decrease shall also be applied to reduce the basis of property held by the corporation at the time the taxpayer acquired control (as defined in subsection (a)(2)(E)) of such corporation.

(B) LIMITATION.—Subparagraph (A) shall not apply to the extent that it would (but for this subparagraph) require a reduction in the aggregate adjusted bases of the property of the corporation below the taxpayer's adjusted basis of the stock in the corporation (determined immediately after such basis is decreased under paragraph (2)).

(C) ALLOCATION OF BASIS REDUCTION.—The decrease required under subparagraph (A) shall be allocated—

(i) first to property which is similar or related in service or use to the converted property,

(ii) second to depreciable property (as defined in section 1017(b)(3)(B)) not described in clause (i), and

(iii) then to other property.

(D) SPECIAL RULES.—

(i) REDUCTION NOT TO EXCEED ADJUSTED BASIS OF PROPERTY.—No reduction in the basis of any property under this paragraph shall exceed the adjusted basis of such property (determined without regard to such reduction).

(ii) ALLOCATION OF REDUCTION AMONG PROPERTIES.—If more than 1 property is described in a clause of subparagraph (C), the reduction under this paragraph shall be allocated among such property in proportion to the adjusted bases of such property (as so determined).

Amendments

• **1996, Small Business Job Protection Act of 1996 (P.L. 104-188)**

P.L. 104-188, §1610(a):

Amended Code Sec. 1033(b). **Effective** for involuntary conversions occurring after 8-20-96. Prior to amendment, Code Sec. 1033(b) read as follows:

(b) BASIS OF PROPERTY ACQUIRED THROUGH INVOLUNTARY CONVERSION.—If the property was acquired, after February 28, 1913, as the result of a compulsory or involuntary conversion described in subsection (a)(1) or section 112(f)(2) of the Internal Revenue Code of 1939, the basis shall be the same as in the case of the property so converted, decreased in the amount of any money received by the taxpayer which was not expended in accordance with the provisions of law (applicable to the year in which such conversion was made) determining the taxable status of the gain or loss upon such conversion, and increased in the amount of gain or decreased in the amount of loss to the taxpayer recognized upon such conversion under the law applicable to the year in which such conversion was made. This subsection shall not apply in respect of property acquired as a result of a compulsory or involuntary conversion of property used by the taxpayer as his principal residence if the destruction, theft, seizure, requisition, or condemnation of such residence, or the sale or exchange of such residence under threat or imminence thereof, occurred after December 31, 1950, and before January 1, 1954. In the case of property purchased by the taxpayer in a transaction described in subsection (a) [(2)which resulted in the nonrecognition of any part of the gain realized as the result of a compulsory or involuntary conversion, the basis shall be the cost of such property decreased in the amount of the gain not so recognized; and if the property purchased consists of more than one piece of property, the basis determined under this sentence shall be allocated to the purchased properties in proportion to their respective costs.

• **1976, Tax Reform Act of 1976 (P.L. 94-455)**

P.L. 94-455, §1901(a)(128)(C):

Struck out Code Sec. 1033(b) and redesignated Code Sec. 1033(c) as Code Sec. 1033(b). **Effective** for tax years beginning after 12-31-76. Prior to striking, Code Sec. 1033(b) read as follows:

(b) RESIDENCE OF TAXPAYER.—Subsection (a) shall not apply, in the case of property used by the taxpayer as his principal residence, if the destruction, theft, seizure, requisition, or condemnation of the residence, or the sale or exchange of such

INCOME TAX—NONTAXABLE EXCHANGES

residence under threat or imminence thereof, occurred after December 31, 1950, and before January 1, 1954.

P.L. 94-455, § 1901(a)(128)(D):

Substituted "or section 112(f)(2) of the Internal Revenue Code of 1939" for "or (2)" in the first sentence of redesignated Code Sec. 1033(b). **Effective** for tax years beginning after 12-31-76.

[Sec. 1033(c)]

(c) PROPERTY SOLD PURSUANT TO RECLAMATION LAWS.—For purposes of this subtitle, if property lying within an irrigation project is sold or otherwise disposed of in order to conform to the acreage limitation provisions of Federal reclamation laws, such sale or disposition shall be treated as an involuntary conversion to which this section applies.

Amendments

• **1976, Tax Reform Act of 1976 (P.L. 94-455)**

P.L. 94-455, § 1901(a)(128)(C):

Redesignated former Code Sec. 1033(d) as Code Sec. 1033(c). **Effective** for tax years beginning after 12-31-76.

[Sec. 1033(d)]

(d) LIVESTOCK DESTROYED BY DISEASE.—For purposes of this subtitle, if livestock are destroyed by or on account of disease, or are sold or exchanged because of disease, such destruction or such sale or exchange shall be treated as an involuntary conversion to which this section applies.

Amendments

• **1976, Tax Reform Act of 1976 (P.L. 94-455)**

P.L. 94-455, § 1901(a)(128)(C):

Redesignated former Code Sec. 1033(e) as Code Sec. 1033(d). **Effective** for tax years beginning after 12-31-76.

[Sec. 1033(e)]

(e) LIVESTOCK SOLD ON ACCOUNT OF DROUGHT, FLOOD, OR OTHER WEATHER-RELATED CONDITIONS.—

(1) IN GENERAL.—For purposes of this subtitle, the sale or exchange of livestock (other than poultry) held by a taxpayer for draft, breeding, or dairy purposes in excess of the number the taxpayer would sell if he followed his usual business practices shall be treated as an involuntary conversion to which this section applies if such livestock are sold or exchanged by the taxpayer solely on account of drought, flood, or other weather-related conditions.

(2) EXTENSION OF REPLACEMENT PERIOD.—

(A) IN GENERAL.—In the case of drought, flood, or other weather-related conditions described in paragraph (1) which result in the area being designated as eligible for assistance by the Federal Government, subsection (a)(2)(B) shall be applied with respect to any converted property by substituting "4 years" for "2 years".

(B) FURTHER EXTENSION BY SECRETARY.—The Secretary may extend on a regional basis the period for replacement under this section (after the application of subparagraph (A)) for such additional time as the Secretary determines appropriate if the weather-related conditions which resulted in such application continue for more than 3 years.

Amendments

• **2004, American Jobs Creation Act of 2004 (P.L. 108-357)**

P.L. 108-357, § 311(b)(1)-(2):

Amended Code Sec. 1033(e) by striking "CONDITIONS.—For purposes" and inserting "CONDITIONS.—" followed by "(1) IN GENERAL.—For purposes", and by adding at the end a new paragraph (2). **Effective** for any tax year with respect to which the due date (without regard to extensions) for the return is after 12-31-2002.

• **1997, Taxpayer Relief Act of 1997 (P.L. 105-34)**

P.L. 105-34, § 913(b)(1)-(2):

Amended Code Sec. 1033(e) by inserting ", flood, or other weather-related conditions" before the period at the end thereof and by inserting ", FLOOD, OR OTHER WEATHER-RELATED CONDITIONS" after "DROUGHT" in the heading. **Effective** for sales and exchanges after 12-31-96.

• **1976, Tax Reform Act of 1976 (P.L. 94-455)**

P.L. 94-455, § 1901(a)(128)(C):

Redesignated former Code Sec. 1033(f) as Code Sec. 1033(e). **Effective** for tax years beginning after 12-31-76.

• **1956 (P.L. 629, 84th Cong.)**

P.L. 629, 84th Cong., § 5:

Amended Sec. 1033 by adding a new subsection (f). **Effective** for tax years ending after 1955, but only in the case of sales and exchanges of livestock after 1955.

[Sec. 1033(f)]

(f) REPLACEMENT OF LIVESTOCK WITH OTHER FARM PROPERTY IN CERTAIN CASES.—For purposes of subsection (a), if, because of drought, flood, or other weather-related conditions, or soil contamination or other environmental contamination, it is not feasible for the taxpayer to reinvest the proceeds from compulsorily or involuntarily converted livestock in property similar or related in use to the livestock so converted, other property (including real property in the case of soil contamination or other environmental contamination) used for farming purposes shall be treated as property similar or related in service or use to the livestock so converted.

Amendments

• **2004, American Jobs Creation Act of 2004 (P.L. 108-357)**

P.L. 108-357, § 311(a)(1)-(3):

Amended Code Sec. 1033(f) by inserting "drought, flood, or other weather-related conditions, or" after "because of", by inserting "in the case of soil contamination or other environmental contamination" after "including real property", and by striking "WHERE THERE HAS BEEN ENVIRONMENTAL CONTAMINATION" in the heading and inserting "IN CERTAIN CASES". **Effective** for any tax year with respect to which the due date (without regard to extensions) for the return is after 12-31-2002.

• **1978, Revenue Act of 1978 (P.L. 95-600)**

P.L. 95-600, § 542(a), (b):

Redesignated former Code Sec. 1033(f) as Code Sec. 1033(g) and added a new subsection (f). **Effective** for tax years beginning after 12-31-74.

[Sec. 1033(g)]

(g) CONDEMNATION OF REAL PROPERTY HELD FOR PRODUCTIVE USE IN TRADE OR BUSINESS OR FOR INVESTMENT.—

(1) SPECIAL RULE.—For purposes of subsection (a), if real property (not including stock in trade or other property held primarily for sale) held for productive use in trade or business or for investment is (as the result of its seizure, requisition, or condemnation, or threat or imminence thereof) compulsorily or involuntarily converted, property of a like kind to be held either for productive use in trade or business or for investment shall be treated as property similar or related in service or use to the property so converted.

(2) LIMITATION.—Paragraph (1) shall not apply to the purchase of stock in the acquisition of control of a corporation described in subsection (a)(2)(A).

(3) ELECTION TO TREAT OUTDOOR ADVERTISING DISPLAYS AS REAL PROPERTY.—

(A) IN GENERAL.—A taxpayer may elect, at such time and in such manner as the Secretary may prescribe, to treat property which constitutes an outdoor advertising display as real property for purposes of this chapter. The election provided by this subparagraph may not be made with respect to any property with respect to which an election under section 179(a) (relating to election to expense certain depreciable business assets) is in effect.

(B) ELECTION.—An election made under subparagraph (A) may not be revoked without the consent of the Secretary.

(C) OUTDOOR ADVERTISING DISPLAY.—For purposes of this paragraph, the term "outdoor advertising display" means a rigidly assembled sign, display, or device permanently affixed to the ground or permanently attached to a building or other inherently permanent structure constituting, or used for the display of, a commercial or other advertisement to the public.

(D) CHARACTER OF REPLACEMENT PROPERTY.—For purposes of this subsection, an interest in real property purchased as replacement property for a compulsorily or involuntarily converted outdoor advertising display defined in subparagraph (C) (and treated by the taxpayer as real property) shall be considered property of a like kind as the property converted without regard to whether the taxpayer's interest in the replacement property is the same kind of interest the taxpayer held in the converted property.

(4) SPECIAL RULE.—In the case of a compulsory or involuntary conversion described in paragraph (1), subsection (a)(2)(B)(i) shall be applied by substituting "3 years" for "2 years".

Amendments

• **1990, Omnibus Budget Reconciliation Act of 1990 (P.L. 101-508)**

P.L. 101-508, §11813(b)(20):

Amended Code Sec. 1033(g)(3)(A) by striking "with respect to which the investment credit determined under section 46(a) is or has been claimed or" after "to any property". **Effective**, generally, for property placed in service after 12-31-90. However, for exceptions, see Act Sec. 11813(c)(2), below.

P.L. 101-508, §11813(c)(2), provides:

(2) EXCEPTIONS.—The amendments made by this section shall not apply to—

(A) any transition property (as defined in section 49(e) of the Internal Revenue Code of 1986 (as in effect on the day before the date of the enactment of this Act),

(B) any property with respect to which qualified progress expenditures were previously taken into account under section 46(d) of such Code (as so in effect), and

(C) any property described in section 46(b)(2)(C) of such Code (as so in effect).

• **1984, Deficit Reduction Act of 1984 (P.L. 98-369)**

P.L. 98-369, §474(r)(24):

Amended Code Sec. 1033(g)(3)(A) by striking out "the credit allowed by section 38 (relating to investment in certain depreciable property)" and inserting in lieu thereof "the investment credit determined under section 46(a)". **Effective** for tax years beginning after 12-31-83, and to carrybacks from such years. Prior to amendment, subparagraph (A) read as follows:

(A) IN GENERAL.—A taxpayer may elect, at such time and in such manner as the Secretary may prescribe, to treat property which constitutes an outdoor advertising display as real property for purposes of this chapter. The election provided by this subparagraph may not be made with respect to any property with respect to which the credit allowed by section 38 (relating to investment in certain depreciable property) is or has been claimed or with respect to which an election under section 179(a) (relating to election to expense certain depreciable business assets) is in effect.

• **1981, Economic Recovery Tax Act of 1981 (P.L. 97-34)**

P.L. 97-34, §202(d)(2):

Amended Code Sec. 1033(g)(3)(A) by striking out "(relating to additional first-year depreciation allowance for small business)" and inserting in lieu thereof "(relating to election to expense certain depreciable business assets).". **Effective** for property placed in service after 12-31-80, in tax years ending after such date.

• **1978, Revenue Act of 1978 (P.L. 95-600)**

P.L. 95-600, §542(a), (b):

Redesignated former Code Sec. 1033(f) as subsection (g). **Effective** for tax years beginning after 12-31-74.

• **1976, Tax Reform Act of 1976 (P.L. 94-455)**

P.L. 94-455, §1901(a)(128)(C):

Redesignated former Code Sec. 1033(g) as Code Sec. 1033(f). **Effective** for tax years beginning after 12-31-76.

P.L. 94-455, §1901(a)(128)(E):

Amended Code Sec. 1033(f)(2). **Effective** for tax years beginning after 12-31-76. Prior to amendment, Code Sec. 1033(f)(2) read as follows:

(2) LIMITATIONS.—

(A) PURCHASE OF STOCK.—Paragraph (1) shall not apply to the purchase of stock in the acquisition of control of a corporation described in subsection (a)(3)(A).

(B) CONVERSIONS BEFORE JANUARY 1, 1958.—Paragraph (1) shall apply with respect to the compulsory or involuntary conversion of any real property only if the disposition of the converted property (within the meaning of subsection (a)(2)) occurs after December 31, 1957.

P.L. 94-455, §1901(a)(128)(F):

Substituted "(a)(2)(B)(i)" for "(a)(3)(B)(i)" in Code Sec. 1033(g)(4) (redesignated as Code Sec. 1033(f)(4)). **Effective** with respect to tax years beginning after 12-31-76.

P.L. 94-455, §2127(a):

Added Code Sec. 1033(g)(3) (redesignated as Code Sec. 1033(f)(3)). **Effective** for tax years beginning after 12-31-70.

P.L. 94-455, §2140(a):

Added Code Sec. 1033(g)(4) (redesignated asto be Code Sec. 1033(f)(4)) to read as before amendment by P.L. 94-455, §1901(a)(128)(F). **Effective** with respect to any disposition of converted property after 12-31-74, unless a condemnation proceeding with respect to such property began before 10-4-76.

• **1958, Technical Amendments Act of 1958 (P.L. 85-866)**

P.L. 85-866, §46(a):

Added new subsection (g) to Sec. 1033. **Effective** 1-1-54.

[Sec. 1033(h)]

(h) SPECIAL RULES FOR PROPERTY DAMAGED BY FEDERALLY DECLARED DISASTERS.—

(1) PRINCIPAL RESIDENCES.—If the taxpayer's principal residence or any of its contents is located in a disaster area and is compulsorily or involuntarily converted as a result of a federally declared disaster—

(A) TREATMENT OF INSURANCE PROCEEDS.—

(i) EXCLUSION FOR UNSCHEDULED PERSONAL PROPERTY.—No gain shall be recognized by reason of the receipt of any insurance proceeds for personal property which was part of such contents and which was not scheduled property for purposes of such insurance.

(ii) OTHER PROCEEDS TREATED AS COMMON FUND.—In the case of any insurance proceeds (not described in clause (i)) for such residence or contents—

(I) such proceeds shall be treated as received for the conversion of a single item of property, and

(II) any property which is similar or related in service or use to the residence so converted (or contents thereof) shall be treated for purposes of subsection (a)(2) as property similar or related in service or use to such single item of property.

(B) EXTENSION OF REPLACEMENT PERIOD.—Subsection (a)(2)(B) shall be applied with respect to any property so converted by substituting "4 years" for "2 years".

(2) TRADE OR BUSINESS AND INVESTMENT PROPERTY.—If a taxpayer's property held for productive use in a trade or business or for investment is located in a disaster area and is compulsorily or involuntarily converted as a result of a federally declared disaster, tangible property of a type held for productive use in a trade or business shall be treated for purposes of subsection (a) as property similar or related in service or use to the property so converted.

(3) FEDERALLY DECLARED DISASTER; DISASTER AREA.—The terms "federally declared disaster" and "disaster area" shall have the respective meaning given such terms by section 165(i)(5).

(4) PRINCIPAL RESIDENCE.—For purposes of this subsection, the term "principal residence" has the same meaning as when used in section 121, except that such term shall include a residence not treated as a principal residence solely because the taxpayer does not own the residence.

Amendments

• **2018, Tax Technical Corrections Act of 2018 (P.L. 115-141)**

P.L. 115-141, §401(a)(167), Div. U:

Amended Code Sec. 1033(h)(2) by inserting "is" before "located". **Effective** 3-23-2018.

• **2014, Tax Technical Corrections Act of 2014 (P.L. 113-295)**

P.L. 113-295, §211(c)(1)(A), Division A:

Amended Code Sec. 1033(h)(2) by inserting "is" before "compulsorily". **Effective** generally 12-19-2014. For a special rule, see Act Sec. 221(b)(2), Division A, below.

INCOME TAX—NONTAXABLE EXCHANGES

P.L. 113-295, §221(a)(27)(D), Division A:

Amended Code Sec. 1033(h)(3) by striking "section 165(h)(3)(C)" and inserting "section 165(i)(5)". **Effective** generally 12-19-2014. For a special rule, see Act Sec. 221(b)(2), Division A, below.

P.L. 113-295, §221(b)(2), Division A, provides:

(2) SAVINGS PROVISION.—If—

(A) any provision amended or repealed by the amendments made by this section applied to—

(i) any transaction occurring before the date of the enactment of this Act,

(ii) any property acquired before such date of enactment, or

(iii) any item of income, loss, deduction, or credit taken into account before such date of enactment, and

(B) the treatment of such transaction, property, or item under such provision would (without regard to the amendments or repeals made by this section) affect the liability for tax for periods ending after date of enactment, nothing in the amendments or repeals made by this section shall be construed to affect the treatment of such transaction, property, or item for purposes of determining liability for tax for periods ending after such date of enactment.

- **2008, Tax Extenders and Alternative Minimum Tax Relief Act of 2008 (P.L. 110-343)**

P.L. 110-343, Division C, §706(a)(2)(D)(i):

Amended so much of Code Sec. 1033(h) as precedes subparagraph (1)(A). **Effective** for disasters declared in tax years beginning after 12-31-2007. Prior to amendment, so much of Code Sec. 1033(h) as precedes subparagraph (1)(A) read as follows:

(h) SPECIAL RULES FOR PROPERTY DAMAGED BY PRESIDENTIALLY DECLARED DISASTERS.—

(1) PRINCIPAL RESIDENCES.—If the taxpayer's principal residence or any of its contents is compulsorily or involuntarily converted as a result of a Presidentially declared disaster—

P.L. 110-343, Division C, §706(a)(2)(D)(ii):

Amended Code Sec. 1033(h)(2) by striking "investment" and all that follows through "disaster" and inserting "investment [is] located in a disaster area and [is] compulsorily or involuntarily converted as a result of a federally declared disaster". **Effective** for disasters declared in tax years beginning after 12-31-2007. Prior to being stricken, "investment" and all that follows through "disaster" read as follows:

investment is compulsorily or involuntarily converted as a result of a Presidentially declared disaster

P.L. 110-343, Division C, §706(a)(2)(D)(iii):

Amended Code Sec. 1033(h)(3). **Effective** for disasters declared in tax years beginning after 12-31-2007. Prior to amendment, Code Sec. 1033(h)(3) read as follows:

(3) PRESIDENTIALLY DECLARED DISASTER.—For purposes of this subsection, the term "Presidentially declared disaster" means any disaster which, with respect to the area in which the property is located, resulted in a subsequent determination by the President that such area warrants assistance by the Federal Government under the Robert T. Stafford Disaster Relief and Emergency Assistance Act.

- **2004, Working Families Tax Relief Act of 2004 (P.L. 108-311)**

P.L. 108-311, §408(a)(7)(C):

Amended Code Sec. 1033(h)(3) by inserting "Robert T. Stafford" before "Disaster Relief and Emergency Assistance Act". **Effective** 10-4-2004.

- **1997, Taxpayer Relief Act of 1997 (P.L. 105-34)**

P.L. 105-34, §312(d)(1):

Amended Code Sec. 1033(h)(4) by striking "section 1034" and inserting "section 121". **Effective** for sales and exchanges after 5-6-97.

- **1996, Small Business Job Protection Act of 1996 (P.L. 104-188)**

P.L. 104-188, §1119(a):

Amended Code Sec. 1033(h) by redesignating paragraphs (2) and (3) as paragraphs (3) and (4), respectively, and by inserting after paragraph (1) a new paragraph (2). **Effective** for disasters declared after 12-31-94, in tax years ending after such date.

P.L. 104-188, §1119(b)(1)-(3):

Amended Code Sec. 1033(h) by striking "residence" in paragraph (3), as redesignated by Act Sec. 1119(a), and inserting "property", by striking "PRINCIPAL RESIDENCES" in the heading and inserting "PROPERTY", and by striking "(1) IN GENERAL.—" and inserting "(1) PRINCIPAL RESIDENCES.—". **Effective** for disasters declared after 12-31-94, in tax years ending after such date.

- **1993, Omnibus Budget Reconciliation Act of 1993 (P.L. 103-66)**

P.L. 103-66, §13431(a):

Amended Code Sec. 1033 by redesignating subsection (h) as subsection (i) and by inserting after subsection (g) a new subsection (h). **Effective** for property compulsorily or involuntarily converted as a result of disasters for which the determination referred to in Code Sec. 1033(h)(2) is made on or after 9-1-91, and to tax years ending on or after such date.

[Sec. 1033(i)]

(i) REPLACEMENT PROPERTY MUST BE ACQUIRED FROM UNRELATED PERSON IN CERTAIN CASES.—

(1) IN GENERAL.—If the property which is involuntarily converted is held by a taxpayer to which this subsection applies, subsection (a) shall not apply if the replacement property or stock is acquired from a related person. The preceding sentence shall not apply to the extent that the related person acquired the replacement property or stock from an unrelated person during the period applicable under subsection (a)(2)(B).

(2) TAXPAYERS TO WHICH SUBSECTION APPLIES.—This subsection shall apply to—

(A) a C corporation,

(B) a partnership in which 1 or more C corporations own, directly or indirectly (determined in accordance with section 707(b)(3)), more than 50 percent of the capital interest, or profits interest, in such partnership at the time of the involuntary conversion, and

(C) any other taxpayer if, with respect to property which is involuntarily converted during the taxable year, the aggregate of the amount of realized gain on such property on which there is realized gain exceeds $100,000.

In the case of a partnership, subparagraph (C) shall apply with respect to the partnership and with respect to each partner. A similar rule shall apply in the case of an S corporation and its shareholders.

(3) RELATED PERSON.—For purposes of this subsection, a person is related to another person if the person bears a relationship to the other person described in section 267(b) or 707(b)(1).

Amendments

- **1997, Taxpayer Relief Act of 1997 (P.L. 105-34)**

P.L. 105-34, §1087(a):

Amended Code Sec. 1033(i). **Effective** for involuntary conversions occurring after 6-8-97. Prior to amendment, Code Sec. 1033(i) read as follows:

(i) NONRECOGNITION NOT TO APPLY IF CORPORATION ACQUIRES REPLACEMENT PROPERTY FROM RELATED PERSON.—

(1) IN GENERAL.—In the case of—

(A) a C corporation, or

(B) a partnership in which 1 or more C corporations own, directly or indirectly (determined in accordance with section 707(b)(3)), more than 50 percent of the capital interest, or profits interest, in such partnership at the time of the involuntary conversion,

subsection (a) shall not apply if the replacement property or stock is acquired from a related person. The preceding sentence shall not apply to the extent that the related person acquired the replacement property or stock from an unrelated person during the period described in subsection (a)(2)(B).

(2) RELATED PERSON.—For purposes of this subsection, a person is related to another person if the person bears a relationship to the other person described in section 267(b) or 707(b)(1).

- **1995, Self-Employed Health Insurance Act (P.L. 104-7)**

P.L. 104-7, §3(a)(1):

Amended Code Sec. 1033 by redesignating subsection (i) as subsection (j) and by inserting after subsection (h) a new subsection (i). **Effective** for involuntary conversions occurring on or after 2-6-95.

[Sec. 1033(j)—Stricken]

certified by the Federal Communications Commission as having been made by a taxpayer in connection with the relocation of the taxpayer from the 1850-1990MHz spectrum by reason of the Federal Communications Commission's reallocation of that spectrum for use for personal communications services. The Commission shall transmit copies of certifications under this paragraph to the Secretary.

P.L. 113-295, §221(b)(2), Division A, provides:

(2) SAVINGS PROVISION.—If—

(A) any provision amended or repealed by the amendments made by this section applied to—

(i) any transaction occurring before the date of the enactment of this Act,

(ii) any property acquired before such date of enactment, or

(iii) any item of income, loss, deduction, or credit taken into account before such date of enactment, and

Amendments

- **2014, Tax Technical Corrections Act of 2014 (P.L. 113-295)**

P.L. 113-295, §221(a)(77), Division A:

Amended Code Sec. 1033 by striking subsection (j) and by redesignating subsections (k) and (l) as subsections (j) and (k), respectively. **Effective** generally 12-19-2014. For a special rule, see Act Sec. 221(b)(2), Division A, below. Prior to being stricken, Code Sec. 1033(j) read as follows:

(j) SALES OR EXCHANGES TO IMPLEMENT MICROWAVE RELOCATION POLICY.—

(1) IN GENERAL.—For purposes of this subtitle, if a taxpayer elects the application of this subsection to a qualified sale or exchange, such sale or exchange shall be treated as an involuntary conversion to which this section applies.

(2) QUALIFIED SALE OR EXCHANGE.—For purposes of paragraph (1), the term "qualified sale or exchange" means a sale or exchange before January 1, 2000, which is

INCOME TAX—NONTAXABLE EXCHANGES

(B) the treatment of such transaction, property, or item under such provision would (without regard to the amendments or repeals made by this section) affect the liability for tax for periods ending after date of enactment, nothing in the amendments or repeals made by this section shall be construed to affect the treatment of such transaction, property, or item for purposes of determining liability for tax for periods ending after such date of enactment.

[Sec. 1033(j)]

(j) SALES OR EXCHANGES UNDER CERTAIN HAZARD MITIGATION PROGRAMS.—For purposes of this subtitle, if property is sold or otherwise transferred to the Federal Government, a State or local government, or an Indian tribal government to implement hazard mitigation under the Robert T. Stafford Disaster Relief and Emergency Assistance Act (as in effect on the date of the enactment of this subsection) or the National Flood Insurance Act (as in effect on such date), such sale or transfer shall be treated as an involuntary conversion to which this section applies.

Amendments

• **2014, Tax Technical Corrections Act of 2014 (P.L. 113-295)**

P.L. 113-295, §221(a)(77), Division A:

Amended Code Sec. 1033 by redesignating subsection (k) as subsection (j). **Effective** generally 12-19-2014. For a special rule, see Act Sec. 221(b)(2), Division A, below.

P.L. 113-295, §221(b)(2), Division A, provides:

(2) SAVINGS PROVISION.—If—

(A) any provision amended or repealed by the amendments made by this section applied to—

(i) any transaction occurring before the date of the enactment of this Act,

(ii) any property acquired before such date of enactment, or

(iii) any item of income, loss, deduction, or credit taken into account before such date of enactment, and

(B) the treatment of such transaction, property, or item under such provision would (without regard to the amendments or repeals made by this section) affect the liability for tax for periods ending after date of enactment, nothing in the amendments or repeals made by this section shall be construed to affect the treatment of such transaction, property, or item for purposes of determining liability for tax for periods ending after such date of enactment.

• **2005 (P.L. 109-7)**

P.L. 109-7, §1(b):

Amended Code Sec. 1033 by redesignating subsection (k) as subsection (l) and by inserting after subsection (j) a new subsection (k). **Effective** for sales or other dispositions before, on, or after 4-15-2005.

[Sec. 1033(k)]

(k) CROSS REFERENCES.—

(1) For determination of the period for which the taxpayer has held property involuntarily converted, see section 1223.

(2) For treatment of gains from involuntary conversions as capital gains in certain cases, see section 1231(a).

(3) For exclusion from gross income of gain from involuntary conversion of principal residence, see section 121.

Amendments

• **2014, Tax Technical Corrections Act of 2014 (P.L. 113-295)**

P.L. 113-295, §221(a)(77), Division A:

Amended Code Sec. 1033 by redesignating subsection (l) as subsection (k). **Effective** generally 12-19-2014. For a special rule, see Act Sec. 221(b)(2), Division A, below.

P.L. 113-295, §221(b)(2), Division A, provides:

(2) SAVINGS PROVISION.—If—

(A) any provision amended or repealed by the amendments made by this section applied to—

(i) any transaction occurring before the date of the enactment of this Act,

(ii) any property acquired before such date of enactment, or

(iii) any item of income, loss, deduction, or credit taken into account before such date of enactment, and

(B) the treatment of such transaction, property, or item under such provision would (without regard to the amendments or repeals made by this section) affect the liability for tax for periods ending after date of enactment, nothing in the amendments or repeals made by this section shall be construed to affect the treatment of such transaction, property, or item for purposes of determining liability for tax for periods ending after such date of enactment.

• **2005 (P.L. 109-7)**

P.L. 109-7, §1(b):

Amended Code Sec. 1033 by redesignating subsection (k) as subsection (l). **Effective** for sales or other dispositions before, on, or after 4-15-2005.

• **1997, Taxpayer Relief Act of 1997 (P.L. 105-34)**

P.L. 105-34, §312(d)(7):

Amended Code Sec. 1033(k)(3). **Effective** for sales and exchanges after 5-6-97. Prior to amendment, Code Sec. 1033(k)(3) read as follows:

(3) For one-time exclusion from gross income of gain from involuntary conversion of principal residence by individual who has attained age 55, see section 121.

• **1995, Self-Employed Health Insurance Act (P.L. 104-7)**

P.L. 104-7, §3(a)(1):

Amended Code Sec. 1033 by redesignating subsection (i) as subsection (j). **Effective** for involuntary conversions occurring on or after 2-6-95.

• **1995, Self-Employed Health Insurance Act (P.L. 104-7)**

P.L. 104-7, §3(b)(1):

Amended Code Sec. 1033, as amended by Act. Sec. 3(a)(1), by redesignating subsection (j) as subsection (k) and by inserting after subsection (i) a new subsection (j). **Effective** for sales or exchanges after 3-14-95.

P.L. 104-7, §3(b)(1):

Amended Code Sec. 1033, as amended by Act. Sec. 3(a), by redesignating subsection (j) as subsection (k). **Effective** for sales or exchanges after 3-14-95.

• **1993, Omnibus Budget Reconciliation Act of 1993 (P.L. 103-66)**

P.L. 103-66, §13431(a):

Amended Code Sec. 1033 by redesignating subsection (h) as subsection (i). **Effective** for property compulsorily or involuntarily converted as a result of disasters for which the determination referred to in Code Sec. 1033(h)(2) is made on or after 9-1-91, and to tax years ending on or after such date.

• **1978, Revenue Act of 1978 (P.L. 95-600)**

P.L. 95-600, §404(c)(4), (d)(1):

Amended Code Sec. 1033(g)(3). **Effective** for sales and exchanges after 7-26-78, in tax years ending after such date. Before amendment, such section read:

(3) For exclusion from gross income of certain gain from involuntary conversion of residence of taxpayer who has attained age 65, see section 121.

P.L. 95-600, §542(a), (b):

Redesignated former Code Sec. 1033(g) as subsection (h). **Effective** for tax years beginning after 12-31-74.

• **1976, Tax Reform Act of 1976 (P.L. 94-455)**

P.L. 94-455, §1901(a)(128)(C):

Redesignated subsection (h) as (g). **Effective** for tax years beginning after 12-31-76.

• **1964, Revenue Act of 1964 (P.L. 88-272)**

P.L. 88-272, §206(b)(3):

Amended subsection (h) by adding paragraph (3) thereto. **Effective** 1-1-64.

• **1958, Technical Amendments Act of 1958 (P.L. 85-866)**

P.L. 85-866, §46(a):

Redesignated subsection (g) of Sec. 1033 as subsection (h). **Effective** 1-1-54.

• **1956 (P.L. 629, 84th Cong.)**

P.L. 629, 84th Cong., §5:

Amended Sec. 1033 by redesignating subsection (f) as subsection (g).

[Sec. 1034—Repealed]

Amendments

• **1997, Taxpayer Relief Act of 1997 (P.L. 105-34)**

P.L. 105-34, §312(b):

Repealed Code Sec. 1034. **Effective**, generally, for sales and exchanges after 5-6-97. For special rules, see Act Sec. 312(d)[(e)](2)-(4), below.

P.L. 105-34, §312(d)[(e)](2)-(4) (as amended by P.L. 105-206, §6005(e)(3)), provides:

(2) SALES ON OR BEFORE DATE OF ENACTMENT.—At the election of the taxpayer, the amendments made by this section shall not apply to any sale or exchange on or before the date of the enactment of this Act.

(3) CERTAIN SALES WITHIN 2 YEARS AFTER DATE OF ENACTMENT.—Section 121 of the Internal Revenue Code of 1986 (as amended by this section) shall be applied without regard to subsection (c)(2)(B) thereof in the case of any sale or exchange of property during the 2-year period beginning on the date of the enactment of this Act if the taxpayer held such property on the date of the enactment of this Act and fails to meet the ownership and use requirements of subsection (a) thereof with respect to such property.

(4) BINDING CONTRACTS.—At the election of the taxpayer, the amendments made by this section shall not apply to a sale or exchange after the date of the enactment of this Act, if—

(A) such sale or exchange is pursuant to a contract which was binding on such date, or

(B) without regard to such amendments, gain would not be recognized under section 1034 of the Internal Revenue Code of 1986 (as in effect on the day before the date of the enactment of this Act) on such sale or exchange by reason of a new residence acquired on or before such date or with respect to the acquisition of which by the taxpayer a binding contract was in effect on such date.

INCOME TAX—NONTAXABLE EXCHANGES

This paragraph shall not apply to any sale or exchange by an individual if the treatment provided by section 877(a)(1) of the Internal Revenue Code of 1986 applies to such individual.

Prior to repeal, Code Sec. 1034 read as follows:

SEC. 1034. ROLLOVER OF GAIN ON SALE OF PRINCIPAL RESIDENCE.

[Sec. 1034(a)]

(a) NONRECOGNITION OF GAIN.—If property (in this section called "old residence") used by the taxpayer as his principal residence is sold by him and, within a period beginning 2 years before the date of such sale and ending 2 years after such date, property (in this section called "new residence") is purchased and used by the taxpayer as his principal residence, gain (if any) from such sale shall be recognized only to the extent that the taxpayer's adjusted sales price (as defined in subsection (b)) of the old residence exceeds the taxpayer's cost of purchasing the new residence.

Amendments

- **1981, Economic Recovery Tax Act of 1981 (P.L. 97-34)**

P.L. 97-34, § 122(a):

Amended Code Sec. 1034(a) by striking out "18 months" and inserting in lieu thereof "2 years". **Effective** with respect to old residences (within the meaning of Code Sec. 1034) sold or exchanged after 7-20-81, or on or before 7-20-81, if the former 18-month rollover expires on or after such date. However, P.L. 97-448, § 101(d) provides that the taxpayer may elect to have the amendments made by this section not apply to any old residence sold or exchanged on or before 8-13-81. Such an election shall be made at such time and in such manner as the Secretary of the Treasury or his delegate shall by regulations prescribe.

- **1978, Revenue Act of 1978 (P.L. 95-600)**

P.L. 95-600, § 405(c)(1), (d):

Amended the section heading of Code Sec. 1034. **Effective** for sales and exchanges of residences after 7-26-78, in tax years ending after such date. Before amendment, such heading read:

SEC. 1034. SALE OR EXCHANGE OF RESIDENCE.

- **1976, Tax Reform Act of 1976 (P.L. 94-455)**

P.L. 94-455, § 1901(a)(129)(A):

Struck out "after December 31, 1953," following "is sold by him" in Code Sec. 1034(a). **Effective** for tax years beginning after 12-31-76.

- **1975, Tax Reduction Act of 1975 (P.L. 94-12)**

P.L. 94-12, § 207(a):

Amended Code Sec. 1034(a) by substituting "18 months" for "1 year". **Effective** for residences sold or exchanged after 12-31-74, in tax years ending after such date.

[Sec. 1034(b)]

(b) ADJUSTED SALES PRICE DEFINED.—

(1) IN GENERAL.—For purposes of this section, the term "adjusted sales price" means the amount realized, reduced by the aggregate of the expenses for work performed on the old residence in order to assist in its sale.

(2) LIMITATIONS.—The reduction provided in paragraph (1) applies only to expenses—

(A) for work performed during the 90-day period ending on the day on which the contract to sell the old residence is entered into;

(B) which are paid on or before the 30th day after the date of the sale of the old residence; and

(C) which are—

(i) not allowable as deductions in computing taxable income under section 63 (defining taxable income), and

(ii) not taken into account in computing the amount realized from the sale of the old residence.

Amendments

- **1977, Tax Reduction and Simplification Act of 1977 (P.L. 95-30)**

P.L. 95-30, § 102(b)(13):

Amended clause (i) of Code Sec. 1034(b)(2)(C) by striking out "section 63(a)" and inserting in lieu thereof "section 63". **Effective** for tax years beginning after 12-31-76.

- **1976, Tax Reform Act of 1976 (P.L. 94-455)**

P.L. 94-455, § 1901(a)(129)(B):

Struck out Code Sec. 1034(b)(3). **Effective** for tax years beginning after 12-31-76. Prior to being stricken, Code Sec. 1034(b)(3) read as follows:

(3) EFFECTIVE DATE.—The reduction provided in paragraph (1) applies to expenses for work performed in any taxable year (whether beginning before, on, or after January 1, 1954), but only in the case of a sale or exchange of an old residence which occurs after December 31, 1953.

[Sec. 1034(c)]

(c) RULES FOR APPLICATION OF SECTION.—For purposes of this section:

(1) An exchange by the taxpayer of his residence for other property shall be treated as a sale of such residence, and the acquisition of a residence on the exchange of property shall be treated as a purchase of such residence.

(2) A residence any part of which was constructed or reconstructed by the taxpayer shall be treated as purchased by the taxpayer. In determining the taxpayer's cost of purchasing a residence, there shall be included only so much of his cost as is attributable to the acquisition, construction, reconstruction, and improvements made which are properly chargeable to capital account, during the period specified in subsection (a).

(3) If a residence is purchased by the taxpayer before the date of his sale of the old residence, the purchased residence shall not be treated as his new residence if sold or otherwise disposed of by him before the date of the sale of the old residence.

(4) If the taxpayer, during the period described in subsection (a), purchases more than one residence which is used by him as his principal residence at some time within 2 years after the date of the sale of the old residence, only the last of such residences so used by him after the date of such sale shall constitute the new residence. If a principal residence is sold in a sale to which subsection (d)(2) applies within 2 years after the sale of the old residence, for purposes of applying the preceding sentence with respect to the old residence, the principal residence so sold shall be treated as the last residence used during such 2-year period.

Amendments

- **1981, Economic Recovery Tax Act of 1981 (P.L. 97-34)**

P.L. 97-34, § 122(a):

Amended Code Sec. 1034(c) by striking out "18 months" and inserting in lieu thereof "2 years". **Effective** with respect to old residences (within the meaning of Code Sec. 1034) sold or exchanged after 7-20-81, or on or before 7-20-81, if the former 18-month rollover expires on or after such date. See, however, the amendment note for P.L. 97-34 under Code Sec. 1034(a) for a special rule.

P.L. 97-34, § 122(b):

Amended Code Sec. 1034(c)(4) by striking out "18-month" and inserting in lieu thereof "2-year" and repealed Code Sec. 1034(c)(5). **Effective** with respect to old residences (within the meaning of Code Sec. 1034) sold or exchanged after 7-20-81, or on or before 7-20-81, if the former 18-month rollover expires on or after such date. See, however, the amendment note for P.L. 97-34 under Code Sec. 1034(a) for a special rule. Prior to repeal, Code Sec. 1034(c)(5) read as follows:

(5) In the case of a new residence the construction of which was commenced by the taxpayer before the expiration of 18 months after the date of the sale of the old residence, the period specified in subsection (a), and the 18 months referred to in paragraph (4) of this subsection, shall be treated as including a period of 2 years beginning with the date of the sale of the old residence.

- **1978, Revenue Act of 1978 (P.L. 95-600)**

P.L. 95-600, § 405(b), (d):

Amended Code Sec. 1034(c)(4). **Effective** for sales and exchanges of residences after 7-26-78, in tax years ending after such date, by adding the last sentence.

- **1975, Tax Reduction Act of 1975 (P.L. 94-12)**

P.L. 94-12, § 207(a) and (b):

Amended Code Sec. 1034(c)(4) and (5) by substituting "18 months" for "1 year" and amended Code Sec. 1034(c)(5) by substituting "2 years" for "18 months". **Effective** for residences sold or exchanged after 12-31-74, in tax years ending after such date.

[Sec. 1034(d)]

(d) LIMITATION.—

(1) IN GENERAL.—Subsection (a) shall not apply with respect to the sale of the taxpayer's residence if within 2 years before the date of such sale the taxpayer sold at a gain other property used by him as his principal residence, and any part of such gain was not recognized by reason of subsection (a).

(2) SUBSEQUENT SALE CONNECTED WITH COMMENCING WORK AT NEW PLACE.—Paragraph (1) shall not apply with respect to the sale of the taxpayer's residence if—

(A) such sale was in connection with the commencement of work by the taxpayer as an employee or as a self-employed individual at a new principal place of work, and

(B) if the residence so sold is treated as the former residence for purposes of section 217 (relating to moving expenses), the taxpayer would satisfy the conditions of subsection (c) of section 217 (as modified by the other subsections of such section).

Amendments

- **1981, Economic Recovery Tax Act of 1981 (P.L. 97-34)**

P.L. 97-34, § 122(a):

Amended Code Sec. 1034(d) by striking out "18 months" and inserting in lieu thereof "2 years". **Effective** with respect to old residences (within the meaning of Code Sec. 1034) sold or exchanged after 7-20-81, or on or before 7-20-81, if the former 18-month rollover expires on or after such date. See, however, the amendment note for P.L. 97-34 under Code Sec. 1034(a) for a special rule.

- **1978, Revenue Act of 1978 (P.L. 95-600)**

P.L. 95-600, § 405(a), (d):

Amended Code Sec. 1034(d). **Effective** for sales and exchanges of residences after 7-26-78, in tax years ending after such date. Before amendment, such subsection read:

"(d) LIMITATION.—Subsection (a) shall not apply with respect to the sale of the taxpayer's residence if within 18 months before the date of such sale the taxpayer sold at a gain other property used by him as his principal residence, and any part of such gain was not recognized by reason of subsection (a)."

- **1976, Tax Reform Act of 1976 (P.L. 94-455)**

P.L. 94-455, § 1901(a)(129)(C):

Struck out "or section 112(n) of the Internal Revenue Code of 1939" following "subsection (a)" at the end of Code Sec. 1034(d). **Effective** for tax years beginning after 12-31-76.

- **1975, Tax Reduction Act of 1975 (P.L. 94-12)**

P.L. 94-12, § 207(d):

Amended Code Sec. 1034(d) by substituting "18 months" for "1 year". **Effective** for residences sold or exchanged after 12-31-74, in tax years ending after such date.

[Sec. 1034(e)]

(e) BASIS OF NEW RESIDENCE.—Where the purchase of a new residence results, under subsection (a) or under section 112(n)) of the Internal Revenue Code of 1939, in the nonrecognition of gain on the sale of an old residence, in determining the adjusted basis of the new residence as of any time following the sale of the old residence, the adjustments to basis shall include a reduction by an amount equal to the amount of the gain not so recognized on the sale of the old residence. For this purpose, the amount of the gain not so recognized on the sale of the old residence includes only so much of such gain as is not recognized by reason of the cost, up to such time, of purchasing the new residence.

[Sec. 1034(f)]

(f) TENANT-STOCKHOLDER IN A COOPERATIVE HOUSING CORPORATION.—For purposes of this section, section 1016 (relating to adjustments to basis), and section 1223 (relating to holding period), references to property used by the taxpayer as his principal residence, and references to the residence of a taxpayer, shall include stock held by a tenant-stockholder (as defined in section 216, relating to deduction for amounts representing taxes and interest paid to a cooperative housing corporation) in a cooperative housing corporation (as defined in such section) if—

(1) in the case of stock sold, the house or apartment which the taxpayer was entitled to occupy as such stockholder was used by him as his principal residence, and

(2) in the case of stock purchased, the taxpayer used as his principal residence the house or apartment which he was entitled to occupy as such stockholder.

[Sec. 1034(g)]

(g) HUSBAND AND WIFE.—If the taxpayer and his spouse, in accordance with regulations which shall be prescribed by the Secretary pursuant to this subsection, consent to the application of paragraph (2) of this subsection, then—

(1) for purposes of this section—

(A) the taxpayer's adjusted sales price of the old residence is the adjusted sales price (of the taxpayer, or of the taxpayer and his spouse) of the old residence, and

(B) the taxpayer's cost of purchasing the new residence is the cost (to the taxpayer, his spouse, or both) of purchasing the new residence (whether held by the taxpayer, his spouse, or the taxpayer and his spouse); and

(2) so much of the gain on the sale of the old residence as is not recognized solely by reason of this subsection, and so much of the adjustment under subsection (e) to the basis of the new residence as results solely from this subsection shall be allocated between the taxpayer and his spouse as provided in such regulations.

This subsection shall apply only if the old residence and the new residence are each used by the taxpayer and his spouse as their principal residence. In case the taxpayer and his spouse do not consent to the application of paragraph (2) of this subsection then the recognition of gain on the sale of the old residence shall be determined under this section without regard to the rules provided in this subsection. For purposes of this subsection, except to the extent provided in regulations, in the case of an individual who dies after the date of the sale of the old residence and is married on the date of death, consent to the application of paragraph (2) by such individual's spouse and use of the new residence as the principal residence of such spouse shall be treated as consent and use by such individual.

Amendments

• **1988, Technical and Miscellaneous Revenue Act of 1988 (P.L. 100-647)**

P.L. 100-647, §6002(a):

Amended Code Sec. 1034(g) by adding at the end thereof a new sentence. **Effective** for sales and exchanges of old residences (within the meaning of Code Sec. 1034) after 12-31-84, in tax years ending after that date.

• **1976, Tax Reform Act of 1976 (P.L. 94-455)**

P.L. 94-455, §1906(b)(13)(A):

Amended 1954 Code by substituting "Secretary" for "Secretary or his delegate" each place it appeared. **Effective** 2-1-77.

[Sec. 1034(h)]

(h) MEMBERS OF ARMED FORCES.—

(1) IN GENERAL.—The running of any period of time specified in subsection (a) or (c) (other than the 2 years referred to in subsection (c)(4)) shall be suspended during any time that the taxpayer (or his spouse if the old residence and the new residence are each used by the taxpayer and his spouse as their principal residence) serves on extended active duty with the Armed Forces of the United States after the date of the sale of the old residence, except that any such period of time as so suspended shall not extend beyond the date 4 years after the date of the sale of the old residence.

(2) MEMBERS STATIONED OUTSIDE THE UNITED STATES OR REQUIRED TO RESIDE IN GOVERNMENT QUARTERS.—In the case of any taxpayer who, during any period of time the running of which is suspended by paragraph (1)—

(A) is stationed outside of the United States, or

(B) after returning from a tour of duty outside of the United States and pursuant to a determination by the Secretary of Defense that adequate off-base housing is not available at a remote base site, is required to reside in on-base Government quarters,

any such period of time as so suspended shall not expire before the day which is 1 year after the last day described in subparagraph (A) or (B), as the case may be, except that any such period of time as so suspended shall not extend beyond the date which is 8 years after the date of the sale of the old residence.

(3) EXTENDED ACTIVE DUTY DEFINED.—For purposes of this subsection, the term "extended active duty" means any period of active duty pursuant to a call or order to such duty for a period in excess of 90 days or for an indefinite period.

Amendments

• **1986, Tax Reform Act of 1986 (P.L. 99-514)**

P.L. 99-514, §1878(g):

Amended Code Sec. 1034(h)(2) by striking out "before the last day described" and inserting in lieu thereof "before the day which is 1 year after the last day described". **Effective** as if included in the provision of P.L. 98-369 to which it relates.

Internal Revenue Code

INCOME TAX—NONTAXABLE EXCHANGES

• **1984, Deficit Reduction Act of 1984 (P.L. 98-369)**

P.L. 98-369, §1053(a):

Amended Code Sec. 1034(h). **Effective** for sales of old residences (within the meaning of section 1034 of the Internal Revenue Code of 1954) after 7-18-84. Prior to amendment subsection (h) read as follows:

(h) Members of Armed Forces.—The running of any period of time specified in subsection (a) or (c) (other than the 2 years referred to in subsection (c)(4)) shall be suspended during any time that the taxpayer (or his spouse if the old residence and the new residence are each used by the taxpayer and his spouse as their principal residence) serves on extended active duty with the Armed Forces of the United States after the date of the sale of the old residence except that any such period of time as so suspended shall not extend beyond the date 4 years after the date of the sale of the old residence. For purposes of this subsection, the term "extended active duty" means any period of active duty pursuant to a call or order to such duty for a period in excess of 90 days or for an indefinite period.

• **1981, Economic Recovery Tax Act of 1981 (P.L. 97-34)**

P.L. 97-34, §122(a):

Amended Code Sec. 1034(h) by striking out "18 months" and inserting in lieu thereof "2 years". **Effective** with respect to old residences (within the meaning of Code Sec. 1034) sold or exchanged after 7-20-81, or on or before 7-20-81, if the former 18-month rollover expires on or after such date. See, however, the amendment note for P.L. 97-34 under Code Sec. 1034(a) for a special rule.

• **1975, Tax Reduction Act of 1975 (P.L. 94-12)**

P.L. 94-12, §207(a):

Amended Code Sec. 1034(h) by substituting "18 months" for the "1 year". **Effective** for residences sold or exchanged after 12-31-74, in tax years ending after such date.

• **1975 (P.L. 93-597)**

P.L. 93-597, §6(a):

Amended Code Sec. 1034(h) by deleting "and during an induction period (as defined in section 112(c)(5))" that formerly appeared after "old residence". **Effective** 7-1-73.

[Sec. 1034(i)]

(i) SPECIAL RULE FOR CONDEMNATION.—In the case of the seizure, requisition, or condemnation of a residence, or the sale or exchange of a residence under threat or imminence thereof, the provisions of this section, in lieu of section 1033 (relating to involuntary conversions), shall be applicable if the taxpayer so elects. If such election is made, such seizure, requisition, or condemnation shall be treated as the sale of the residence. Such election shall be made at such time and in such manner as the Secretary shall prescribe by regulations.

Amendments

• **1976, Tax Reform Act of 1976 (P.L. 94-455)**

P.L. 94-455, §1901(a)(129)(D):

Amended Code Sec. 1034(i). **Effective** for tax years beginning after 12-31-76. Prior to amendment, Code Sec. 1034(i) read as follows:

(i) SPECIAL RULE FOR INVOLUNTARY CONVERSIONS.—

(1) IN GENERAL.—For purposes of this section, the destruction, theft, seizure, requisition, or condemnation of property, or the sale or exchange of property under threat or imminence thereof—

(A) if occurring after December 31, 1950, and before January 1, 1954, shall be treated as the sale of such property; and

(B) if occurring after December 31, 1953, shall not be treated as the sale of such property.

(2) CONDEMNATIONS AFTER DECEMBER 31, 1957.—For purposes of this section, the seizure, requisition, or condemnation of property, or the sale or exchange of property under threat or imminence thereof, if occurring after December 31, 1957, shall, at the election of the taxpayer, be treated as the sale of such property. Such election shall be made at such time and in such manner as the Secretary or his delegate shall prescribe by regulations.

(3) CROSS REFERENCE.—

For treatment of residences involuntarily converted after December 31, 1953, see section 1033 (relating to involuntary conversions).

• **1958, Technical Amendments Act of 1958 (P.L. 85-866)**

P.L. 85-866, §46(b):

Redesignated paragraph (2) of Sec. 1034(i) as paragraph (3) and added a new paragraph (2) to read as prior to amendment by P.L. 94-455. **Effective** 1-1-54.

[Sec. 1034(j)]

(j) STATUTE OF LIMITATIONS.—If the taxpayer during a taxable year sells at a gain property used by him as his principal residence, then—

(1) the statutory period for the assessment of any deficiency attributable to any part of such gain shall not expire before the expiration of 3 years from the date the Secretary is notified by the taxpayer (in such manner as the Secretary may by regulations prescribe) of—

(A) the taxpayer's cost of purchasing the new residence which the taxpayer claims results in nonrecognition of any part of such gain,

(B) the taxpayer's intention not to purchase a new residence within the period specified in subsection (a), or

(C) a failure to make such purchase within such period; and

Sec. 1034—Repealed

INCOME TAX—NONTAXABLE EXCHANGES

(2) such deficiency may be assessed before the expiration of such 3-year period notwithstanding the provisions of any other law or rule of law which would otherwise prevent such assessment.

Amendments

• **1976, Tax Reform Act of 1976 (P.L. 94-455)**

P.L. 94-455, §1901(a)(129)(E):

Struck out "after December 31, 1950," following "If" in Code Sec. 1034(j). **Effective** for tax years beginning after 12-31-76.

P.L. 94-455, §1906(b)(13)(A):

Amended 1954 Code by substituting "Secretary" for "Secretary or his delegate" each place it appeared. **Effective** 2-1-77.

[Sec. 1034(k)]

(k) INDIVIDUAL WHOSE TAX HOME IS OUTSIDE THE UNITED STATES.—The running of any period of time specified in subsection (a) or (c) (other than the 2 years referred to in subsection (c)(4)) shall be suspended during any time that the taxpayer (or his spouse if the old residence and the new residence are each used by the taxpayer and his spouse as their principal residence) has a tax home (as defined in section 911(d)(3) outside the United States after the date of the sale of the old residence; except that any such period of time as so suspended shall not extend beyond the date 4 years after the date of the sale of the old residence.

Amendments

• **1981, Economic Recovery Tax Act of 1981 (P.L. 97-34)**

P.L. 97-34, §112(b)(4):

Amended Code Sec. 1034(k) by striking out "section 913(j)(1)(B)" and inserting in lieu thereof "section 911(d)(3)". **Effective** with respect to tax years beginning after 12-31-81.

P.L. 97-34, §122(a):

Amended Code Sec. 1034(k) by striking out "18 months" and inserting in lieu thereof "2 years". **Effective** with respect to old residences (within the meaning of Code Sec. 1034) sold or exchanged after 7-20-81, or on or before 7-20-81, if the former 18-month rollover expires on or after such date. See, however, the amendment note for P.L. 97-34 under Code Sec. 1034(a) for a special rule.

• **1978, Tax Treatment Extension Act of 1978 (P.L. 95-615)**

P.L. 95-615, §206, 209:

Redesignated former Code Sec. 1034(k) as subsection (l), and added a new subsection (k). **Effective** as provided in Act Sec. 209, below.

P.L. 95-615, §209, provides:

(a) GENERAL RULE.—Except as provided in subsections (b) and (c) the amendments made by this title shall apply to taxable years beginning after December 31, 1977.

* * *

(c) ELECTION OF PRIOR LAW.—

(1) A taxpayer may elect not to have the amendments made by this title apply with respect to any taxable year beginning after December 31, 1977, and before January 1, 1979.

(2) An election under this subsection shall be filed with a taxpayer's timely filed return for the first taxable year beginning after December 31, 1977.

[Sec. 1034(l)]

(l) CROSS REFERENCE.—

For one-time exclusion from gross income of gain from sale of principal residence by individual who has attained age 55, see section 121.

Amendments

• **1978, Tax Treatment Extension Act of 1978 (P.L. 95-615)**

P.L. 95-615, §206:

Redesignated former Code Sec. 1034(k) as subsection (l), effective as provided in Act Sec. 209 (see the amendment note following former Code Sec. 1034(k), above).

• **1978, Revenue Act of 1978 (P.L. 95-600)**

P.L. 95-600, §404(c)(5), (d):

Amended Code Sec. 1034(k). **Effective** for sales or exchanges made after 7-26-78, in tax years ending after such date. Before amendment, such section read:

"(k) CROSS REFERENCE.—

For exclusion from gross income of certain gain from sale or exchange of residence of taxpayer who has attained age 65, see section 121."

• **1964, Revenue Act of 1964 (P.L. 88-272)**

P.L. 88-272, §206(b)(4):

Amended section 1034 to add subsection (k). **Effective** 1-1-64.

[Sec. 1035]

SEC. 1035. CERTAIN EXCHANGES OF INSURANCE POLICIES.

[Sec. 1035(a)]

(a) GENERAL RULES.—No gain or loss shall be recognized on the exchange of—

(1) a contract of life insurance for another contract of life insurance or for an endowment or annuity contract or for a qualified long-term care insurance contract;

(2) a contract of endowment insurance (A) for another contract of endowment insurance which provides for regular payments beginning at a date not later than the date payments would have begun under the contract exchanged, or (B) for an annuity contract, or (C) for a qualified long-term care insurance contract;

(3) an annuity contract for an annuity contract or for a qualified long-term care insurance contract; or

(4) a qualified long-term care insurance contract for a qualified long-term care insurance contract.

Amendments

• **2018, Tax Technical Corrections Act of 2018 (P.L. 115-141)**

P.L. 115-141, §401(a)(168), Div. U:

Amended Code Sec. 1035(a)(1) by striking "; or" and inserting a semicolon. **Effective** 3-23-2018.

• **2006, Pension Protection Act of 2006 (P.L. 109-280)**

P.L. 109-280, §844(b)(3)(A)-(C):

Amended Code Sec. 1035(a) by inserting "or for a qualified long-term care insurance contract" before the semicolon at the end of paragraph (1), by inserting ", or (C) for a qualified long-term care insurance contract" before the semicolon at the end of paragraph (2), and by inserting "or for a qualified long-term care insurance contract" before the period at the end of paragraph (3). **Effective** with respect to exchanges occurring after 12-31-2009.

P.L. 109-280, §844(b)(4):

Amended Code Sec. 1035(a) by striking "or" at the end the end of paragraph (2), by striking the period at the end of paragraph (3) and inserting "; or", and by inserting after paragraph (3) a new paragraph (4). **Effective** with respect to exchanges occurring after 12-31-2009.

[Sec. 1035(b)]

(b) DEFINITIONS.—For the purpose of this section—

(1) ENDOWMENT CONTRACT.—A contract of endowment insurance is a contract with an insurance company which depends in part on the life expectancy of the insured, but which may be payable in full in a single payment during his life.

(2) ANNUITY CONTRACT.—An annuity contract is a contract to which paragraph (1) applies but which may be payable during the life of the annuitant only in installments. For purposes of the preceding sentence, a contract shall not fail to be treated as an annuity contract solely because a qualified long-term care insurance contract is a part of or a rider on such contract.

(3) LIFE INSURANCE CONTRACT.—A contract of life insurance is a contract to which paragraph (1) applies but which is not ordinarily payable in full during the life of the insured. For purposes of the preceding sentence, a contract shall not fail to be treated as a life insurance contract solely because a qualified long-term care insurance contract is a part of or a rider on such contract.

Amendments

• **2006, Pension Protection Act of 2006 (P.L. 109-280)**

P.L. 109-280, §844(b)(1):

Amended Code Sec. 1035(b)(2) by adding at the end a new sentence. **Effective** with respect to exchanges occurring after 12-31-2009.

P.L. 109-280, §844(b)(2):

Amended Code Sec. 1035(b)(3) by adding at the end a new sentence. **Effective** with respect to exchanges occurring after 12-31-2009.

• **1986, Tax Reform Act of 1986 (P.L. 99-514)**

P.L. 99-514, §1828:

Amended Code Sec. 1035(b)(1) by striking out "subject to tax under subchapter L". **Effective** as if included in the provision of P.L. 98-369 to which it relates.

INCOME TAX—NONTAXABLE EXCHANGES

• **1984, Deficit Reduction Act of 1984 (P.L. 98-369)**

P.L. 98-369, §211(b)(15):
Amended Code Sec. 1035(b)(1) by striking out "section 801" and inserting in lieu thereof "section 816". **Effective** for tax years beginning after 12-31-83.

P.L. 98-369, §224(a):
Amended Code Sec. 1035(b)(1) by striking out "a life insurance company as defined in section 801" and inserting in lieu thereof "an insurance company subject to tax under subchapter L". **Effective** for all exchanges whether before, on, or after 7-18-84.

[Sec. 1035(c)]

(c) EXCHANGES INVOLVING FOREIGN PERSONS.—To the extent provided in regulations, subsection (a) shall not apply to any exchange having the effect of transferring property to any person other than a United States person.

Amendments

• **1997, Taxpayer Relief Act of 1997 (P.L. 105-34)**

P.L. 105-34, §1131(b)[(c)](1):
Amended Code Sec. 1035 by redesignating subsection (c) as subsection (d) and inserting after subsection (b) a new subsection (c). **Effective** 8-5-97.

[Sec. 1035(d)]

(d) CROSS REFERENCES.—

(1) For rules relating to recognition of gain or loss where an exchange is not solely in kind, see subsections (b) and (c) of section 1031.

(2) For rules relating to the basis of property acquired in an exchange described in subsection (a), see subsection (d) of section 1031.

Amendments

• **1997, Taxpayer Relief Act of 1997 (P.L. 105-34)**

P.L. 105-34, §1131(b)[(c)](1):
Amended Code Sec. 1035 by redesignating subsection (c) as subsection (d). **Effective** 8-5-97.

[Sec. 1036]

SEC. 1036. STOCK FOR STOCK OF SAME CORPORATION.

[Sec. 1036(a)]

(a) GENERAL RULE.—No gain or loss shall be recognized if common stock in a corporation is exchanged solely for common stock in the same corporation, or if preferred stock in a corporation is exchanged solely for preferred stock in the same corporation.

[Sec. 1036(b)]

(b) NONQUALIFIED PREFERRED STOCK NOT TREATED AS STOCK.—For purposes of this section, nonqualified preferred stock (as defined in section 351(g)(2)) shall be treated as property other than stock.

Amendments

• **1997, Taxpayer Relief Act of 1997 (P.L. 105-34)**

P.L. 105-34, §1014(e)(3):
Amended Code Sec. 1036 by redesignating subsection (b) as subsection (c) and by inserting after subsection (a) a new subsection (b). **Effective**, generally, for transactions after 7-8-97. For a transition rule, see Act Sec. 1014(f)(2), below.

P.L. 105-34, §1014(f)(2), provides:
(2) TRANSITION RULE.—The amendments made by this section shall not apply to any transaction after June 8, 1997, if such transaction is—

(A) made pursuant to a written agreement which was binding on such date and at all times thereafter,

(B) described in a ruling request submitted to the Internal Revenue Service on or before such date, or

(C) described on or before such date in a public announcement or in a filing with the Securities and Exchange Commission required solely by reason of the transaction.

[Sec. 1036(c)]

(c) CROSS REFERENCES.—

(1) For rules relating to recognition of gain or loss where an exchange is not solely in kind, see subsections (b) and (c) of section 1031.

(2) For rules relating to the basis of property acquired in an exchange described in subsection (a), see subsection (d) of section 1031.

Amendments

• **1997, Taxpayer Relief Act of 1997 (P.L. 105-34)**

P.L. 105-34, §1014(e)(3):
Amended Code Sec. 1036 by redesignating subsection (b) as subsection (c). **Effective** for transactions after 6-8-97. For a transition rule, see Act Sec. 1014(f)(2) in the amendment notes following Code Sec. 1036(b).

[Sec. 1037]

SEC. 1037. CERTAIN EXCHANGES OF UNITED STATES OBLIGATIONS.

[Sec. 1037(a)]

(a) GENERAL RULE.—When so provided by regulations promulgated by the Secretary in connection with the issue of obligations of the United States, no gain or loss shall be recognized on the surrender to the United States of obligations of the United States issued under chapter 31 of title 31 in exchange solely for other obligations issued under such chapter.

Amendments

• **1983 (P.L. 97-452)**

P.L. 97-452, §2(c)(3):
Amended Code Sec. 1037(a) by striking out "the Second Liberty Bond Act" and "Act" and substituting "chapter 31 of title 31" and "chapter", respectively.

[Sec. 1037(b)]

(b) APPLICATION OF ORIGINAL ISSUE DISCOUNT RULES.—

(1) EXCHANGES INVOLVING OBLIGATIONS ISSUED AT A DISCOUNT.—In any case in which gain has been realized but not recognized because of the provisions of subsection (a) (or so much of section 1031(b) as relates to subsection (a) of this section), to the extent such gain is later recognized by reason of a disposition or redemption of an obligation received in an exchange subject to such provisions, the first sentence of section 1271(c)(2) shall apply to such gain as though the obligation disposed of or redeemed were the obligation surrendered to the Government in the exchange rather than the obligation actually disposed of or redeemed. For purposes of this paragraph and subpart A of part V of subchapter P, if the obligation surrendered in the exchange is a nontransferable obligation described in subsection (a) or (c) of section 454—

(A) the aggregate amount considered, with respect to the obligation surrendered, as ordinary income shall not exceed the difference between the issue price and the stated redemption price which applies at the time of the exchange, and

INCOME TAX—NONTAXABLE EXCHANGES

(B) the issue price of the obligation received in the exchange shall be considered to be the stated redemption price of the obligation surrendered in the exchange, increased by the amount of other consideration (if any) paid to the United States as a part of the exchange.

(2) EXCHANGES OF TRANSFERABLE OBLIGATIONS ISSUED AT NOT LESS THAN PAR.—In any case in which subsection (a) (or so much of section 1031(b) or (c) as relates to subsection (a) of this section) has applied to the exchange of a transferable obligation which was issued at not less than par for another transferable obligation, the issue price of the obligation received from the Government in the exchange shall be considered for purposes of applying subpart A of part V of subchapter P to be the same as the issue price of the obligation surrendered to the Government in the exchange, increased by the amount of other consideration (if any) paid to the United States as a part of the exchange.

Amendments

• **1984, Deficit Reduction Act of 1984 (P.L. 98-369)**

P.L. 98-369, §42(a)(11):

Amended Code Sec. 1037(b) by striking out "section 1232(a)(2)(B)" in paragraph (1) and inserting in lieu thereof "section 1271(c)(2)", by striking out "section 1232" in paragraphs (1) and (2) and inserting in lieu thereof "subpart A of part Y of subchapter P", and by striking out "Section 1232" in the subsection heading and inserting in lieu thereof "Original Issue Discount Rules". **Effective** for tax years ending after 7-18-84.

• **1976, Tax Reform Act of 1976 (P.L. 94-455)**

P.L. 94-455, §1901(a)(130):

Substituted "section 1232(a)(2)(B)" for "section 1232(a)(2)(A)" in Code Sec. 1037(b)(1). **Effective** for tax years beginning after 12-31-76.

P.L. 94-455, §1901(b)(3)(I):

Substituted "ordinary income" for "gain from the sale or exchange of property which is not a capital asset" in Code Sec. 1037(b)(1)(A). **Effective** for tax years beginning after 12-31-76.

[Sec. 1037(c)]

(c) CROSS REFERENCES.—

(1) For rules relating to the recognition of gain or loss in a case where subsection (a) would apply except for the fact that the exchange was not made solely for other obligations of the United States, see subsections (b) and (c) of section 1031.

(2) For rules relating to the basis of obligations of the United States acquired in an exchange for other obligations described in subsection (a), see subsection (d) of section 1031.

Amendments

• **1959 (P.L. 86-346)**

P.L. 86-346, §201:

Added Code Sec. 1037. **Effective** for tax years ending after 9-22-59.

[Sec. 1038]

SEC. 1038. CERTAIN REACQUISITIONS OF REAL PROPERTY.

[Sec. 1038(a)]

(a) GENERAL RULE.—If—

(1) a sale of real property gives rise to indebtedness to the seller which is secured by the real property sold, and

(2) the seller of such property reacquires such property in partial or full satisfaction of such indebtedness,

then, except as provided in subsections (b) and (d), no gain or loss shall result to the seller from such reacquisition, and no debt shall become worthless or partially worthless as a result of such reacquisition.

[Sec. 1038(b)]

(b) AMOUNT OF GAIN RESULTING.—

(1) IN GENERAL.—In the case of a reacquisition of real property to which subsection (a) applies, gain shall result from such reacquisition to the extent that—

(A) the amount of money and the fair market value of other property (other than obligations of the purchaser) received, prior to such reacquisition, with respect to the sale of such property, exceeds

(B) the amount of the gain on the sale of such property returned as income for periods prior to such reacquisition.

(2) LIMITATION.—The amount of gain determined under paragraph (1) resulting from a reacquisition during any taxable year beginning after the date of the enactment of this section shall not exceed the amount by which the price at which the real property was sold exceeded its adjusted basis, reduced by the sum of—

(A) the amount of the gain on the sale of such property returned as income for periods prior to the reacquisition of such property, and

(B) the amount of money and the fair market value of other property (other than obligations of the purchaser received with respect to the sale of such property) paid or transferred by the seller in connection with the reacquisition of such property.

For purposes of this paragraph, the price at which real property is sold is the gross sales price reduced by the selling commissions, legal fees, and other expenses incident to the sale of such property which are properly taken into account in determining gain or loss on such sale.

(3) GAIN RECOGNIZED.—Except as provided in this section, the gain determined under this subsection resulting from a reacquisition to which subsection (a) applies shall be recognized, notwithstanding any other provision of this subtitle.

[Sec. 1038(c)]

(c) BASIS OF REACQUIRED REAL PROPERTY.—If subsection (a) applies to the reacquisition of any real property, the basis of such property upon such reacquisition shall be the adjusted basis of the indebtedness to the seller secured by such property (determined as of the date of reacquisition), increased by the sum of—

(1) the amount of the gain determined under subsection (b) resulting from such reacquisition, and

(2) the amount described in subsection (b)(2)(B).

If any indebtedness to the seller secured by such property is not discharged upon the reacquisition of such property, the basis of such indebtedness shall be zero.

[Sec. 1038(d)]

(d) INDEBTEDNESS TREATED AS WORTHLESS PRIOR TO REACQUISITION.—If, prior to a reacquisition of real property to which subsection (a) applies, the seller has treated indebtedness secured by such property as having become worthless or partially worthless—

(1) such seller shall be considered as receiving, upon the reacquisition of such property, an amount equal to the amount of such indebtedness treated by him as having become worthless, and

(2) the adjusted basis of such indebtedness shall be increased (as of the date of reacquisition) by an amount equal to the amount so considered as received by such seller.

[Sec. 1038(e)]

(e) PRINCIPAL RESIDENCES.—If—

(1) subsection (a) applies to a reacquisition of real property with respect to the sale of which gain was not recognized under section 121 (relating to gain on sale of principal residence); and

(2) within 1 year after the date of the reacquisition of such property by the seller, such property is resold by him,

INCOME TAX—NONTAXABLE EXCHANGES

then, under regulations prescribed by the Secretary, subsections (b), (c), and (d) of this section shall not apply to the reacquisition of such property and, for purposes of applying section 121, the resale of such property shall be treated as a part of the transaction constituting the original sale of such property.

Amendments

• **1997, Taxpayer Relief Act of 1997 (P.L. 105-34)**

P.L. 105-34, §312(d)(8):

Amended Code Sec. 1038(e). **Effective**, generally, for sales and exchanges after 5-6-97. Prior to amendment, Code Sec. 1038(e) read as follows:

(e) PRINCIPAL RESIDENCES.—If—

(1) subsection (a) applies to a reacquisition of real property with respect to the sale of which—

(A) an election under section 121 (relating to one-time exclusion of gain from sale of principal residence by individual who has attained age 55) is in effect, or

(B) gain was not recognized under section 1034 (relating to rollover of gain on sale of principal residence); and

(2) within one year after the date of the reacquisition of such property by the seller, such property is resold by him,

then, under regulations prescribed by the Secretary, subsections (b), (c), and (d) of this section shall not apply to the reacquisition of such property and, for purposes of applying sections 121 and 1034, the resale of such property shall be treated as a part of the transaction constituting the original sale of such property.

Amendments

• **1996, Small Business Job Protection Act of 1996 (P.L. 104-188)**

P.L. 104-188, §1616(b)(12):

Amended Code Sec. 1038 by striking subsection (f). **Effective** for tax years beginning after 12-31-95. Prior to amendment, Code Sec. 1038(f) read as follows:

• **1978, Revenue Act of 1978 (P.L. 95-600)**

P.L. 95-600, §404(c)(6), (d):

Amended Code Sec. 1038(e)(1)(A). **Effective** for sales or exchanges made after 7-26-78, in tax years ending after such date. Before amendment, subparagraph (A) read:

"(A) an election under section 121 (relating to gain from sale or exchange of residence of an individual who has attained age 65) is in effect, or".

P.L. 95-600, §405(c)(3):

Amended Code Sec. 1038(e)(1)(B) by substituting "(relating to rollover of gain on sale of principal residence)" for "(relating to sale or exchange of residence)".

• **1976, Tax Reform Act of 1976 (P.L. 94-455)**

P.L. 94-455, §1906(b)(13)(A):

Amended 1954 Code by substituting "Secretary" for "Secretary or his delegate" each place it appeared. **Effective** 2-1-77.

• **1964 (P.L. 88-570)**

P.L. 88-570, §2(a):

Added Code Sec. 1038. **Effective**, generally, for tax years beginning after 9-2-64. Taxpayers may elect, however, to have Sec. 1038 apply to tax years beginning after 1957, except for reacquisitions of real property in tax years closed on 9-2-64 by operation of any law or rule of law. The election must be made within one year after 9-2-64. (P.L. 88-570, §2(c)).

[Sec. 1038(f)—Stricken]

(f) REACQUISITIONS BY DOMESTIC BUILDING AND LOAN ASSOCIATIONS.—This section shall not apply to a reacquisition of real property by an organization described in section 593(a) (relating to domestic building and loan associations, etc.).

[Sec. 1038(g)]

(g) ACQUISITION BY ESTATE, ETC., OF SELLER.—Under regulations prescribed by the Secretary, if an installment obligation is indebtedness to the seller which is described in subsection (a), and if such obligation is, in the hands of the taxpayer, an obligation with respect to which section 691(a)(4)(B) applies, then—

(1) for purposes of subsection (a), acquisition of real property by the taxpayer shall be treated as reacquisition by the seller, and

(2) the basis of the real property acquired by the taxpayer shall be increased by an amount equal to the deduction under section 691(c) which would (but for this subsection) have been allowable to the taxpayer with respect to the gain on the exchange of the obligation for the real property.

Amendments

• **1980, Installment Sales Revision Act of 1980 (P.L. 96-471)**

P.L. 96-471, §4:

Added Code Sec. 1038(g). **Effective** for acquisitions of real property by the taxpayer after 10-19-80.

[Sec. 1039—Repealed]

Amendments

• **1990, Omnibus Budget Reconciliation Act of 1990 (P.L. 101-508)**

P.L. 101-508, §11801(a)(33):

Repealed Code Sec. 1039. **Effective** 11-5-90.

P.L. 101-508, §11821(b)(1)-(2), provides:

(b) SAVINGS PROVISION.—If—

(1) any provision amended or repealed by this part applied to—

(A) any transaction occurring before the date of the enactment of this Act,

(B) any property acquired before such date of enactment, or

(C) any item of income, loss, deduction, or credit taken into account before such date of enactment, and

(2) the treatment of such transaction, property, or item under such provision would (without regard to the amendments made by this part) affect liability for tax for periods ending after such date of enactment,

nothing in the amendments made by this part shall be construed to affect the treatment of such transaction, property, or item for purposes of determining liability for tax for periods ending after such date of enactment.

Prior to amendment, Code Sec. 1039 read as follows:

SEC. 1039. CERTAIN SALES OF LOW-INCOME HOUSING PROJECTS.

[Sec. 1039(a)]

(a) NONRECOGNITION OF GAIN.—If—

(1) a qualified housing project is sold or disposed of by the taxpayer in an approved disposition, and

(2) within the reinvestment period the taxpayer constructs, reconstructs, or acquires another qualified housing project,

then, at the election of the taxpayer, gain from such approved disposition shall be recognized only to the extent that the net amount realized on such approved disposition exceeds the cost of such other qualified housing project. An election

under this subsection shall be made at such time and in such manner as the Secretary prescribes by regulations.

Amendments

• **1976, Tax Reform Act of 1976 (P.L. 94-455)**

P.L. 94-455, §1906(b)(13)(A):

Amended 1954 Code by substituting "Secretary" for "Secretary or his delegate" each place it appeared. **Effective** 2-1-77.

[Sec. 1039(b)]

(b) DEFINITIONS.—For purposes of this section—

(1) QUALIFIED HOUSING PROJECT.—The term "qualified housing project" means a project to provide rental or cooperative housing for lower income families—

(A) with respect to which a mortgage is insured under section 221(d)(3) or 236 of the National Housing Act, and

(B) with respect to which the owner is, under such sections or regulations issued thereunder—

(i) limited as to the rate of return on his investment in the project, and

(ii) limited as to rentals or occupancy charges for units in the project.

(2) APPROVED DISPOSITION.—The term "approved disposition" means a sale or other disposition of a qualified housing project to the tenants or occupants of units in such project, or to a cooperative or other nonprofit organization formed solely for the benefit of such tenants or occupants, which sale or disposition is approved by the Secretary of Housing and Urban Development under section 221(d)(3) or 236 of the National Housing Act or regulations issued under such sections.

(3) REINVESTMENT PERIOD.—The reinvestment period, with respect to an approved disposition of a qualified housing project, is the period beginning one year before the date of such approved disposition and ending—

(A) one year after the close of the first taxable year in which any part of the gain from such approved disposition is realized, or

INCOME TAX—NONTAXABLE EXCHANGES

(B) subject to such terms and conditions as may be specified by the Secretary, at the close of such later date as the Secretary may designate on application by the taxpayer. Such application shall be made at such time and in such manner as the Secretary prescribes by regulations.

(4) NET AMOUNT REALIZED.—The net amount realized on an approved disposition of a qualified housing project is the amount realized reduced by—

(A) the expenses paid or incurred which are directly connected with such approved disposition, and

(B) the amount of taxes (other than income taxes) paid or incurred which are attributable to such approved disposition.

Amendments

• **1976, Tax Reform Act of 1976 (P.L. 94-455)**

P.L. 94-455, §1906(b)(13)(A):

Amended 1954 Code by substituting "Secretary" for "Secretary or his delegate" each place it appeared. **Effective** 2-1-77.

[Sec. 1039(c)]

(c) SPECIAL RULES.—For purposes of applying subsection (a)(2) with respect to an approved disposition—

(1) no property acquired by the taxpayer before the date of the approved disposition shall be taken into account unless such property is held by the taxpayer on such date, and

(2) no property acquired by the taxpayer shall be taken into account unless, except as provided in subsection (d), the unadjusted basis of such property is its cost within the meaning of section 1012.

[Sec. 1039(d)]

(d) BASIS OF OTHER QUALIFIED HOUSING PROJECT.—If the taxpayer makes an election under subsection (a) with respect to an approved disposition, the basis of the qualified housing project described in subsection (a)(2) shall be its cost reduced by an amount equal to the amount of gain not recognized by reason of the application of subsection (a).

[Sec. 1039(e)]

(e) ASSESSMENT OF DEFICIENCIES.—

(1) DEFICIENCY ATTRIBUTABLE TO GAIN.—If the taxpayer has made an election under subsection (a) with respect to an approved disposition—

(A) the statutory period for the assessment of any deficiency, for any taxable year in which any part of the gain on such approved disposition is realized, attributable to the gain on such approved disposition shall not expire prior to the expiration of 3 years from the date the Secretary is notified by the taxpayer (in such manner as the Secretary may by regulations prescribe) of the construction, reconstruction, or acquisition of another qualified housing project or of the failure to construct, reconstruct, or acquire another qualified housing project, and

(B) such deficiency may be assessed before the expiration of such 3-year period notwithstanding the provisions of section 6212(c) or the provision of any other law or rule of law which would otherwise prevent such assessment.

(2) TIME FOR ASSESSMENT OF OTHER DEFICIENCIES ATTRIBUTABLE TO ELECTION.—If a taxpayer has made an election under subsection (a) with respect to an approved disposition and another qualified housing project is constructed, reconstructed, or acquired before the beginning of the last taxable year in which any part of the gain upon such approved disposition is realized, any deficiency, to the extent resulting from such election, for any taxable year ending before such last taxable year may be assessed (notwithstanding the provisions of section 6212(c) or 6501 or the provisions of any other law or rule of law which would otherwise prevent such assessment) at any time before the expiration of the period within which a deficiency for such last taxable year may be assessed.

Amendments

• **1976, Tax Reform Act of 1976 (P.L. 94-455)**

P.L. 94-455, §1906(b)(13)(A):

Amended 1954 Code by substituting "Secretary" for "Secretary or his delegate" each place it appeared. **Effective** 2-1-77.

• **1969, Tax Reform Act of 1969 (P.L. 91-172)**

P.L. 91-172, §910(a):

Added Code Sec. 1039. **Effective** for approved dispositions of qualified housing projects within the meaning of Code Sec. 1039 after 10-9-69.

[Sec. 1040]

SEC. 1040. TRANSFER OF CERTAIN FARM, ETC., REAL PROPERTY.

[Sec. 1040(a)]

(a) GENERAL RULE.—If the executor of the estate of any decedent transfers to a qualified heir (within the meaning of section 2032A(e)(1) any property with respect to which an election was made under section 2032A, then gain on such transfer shall be recognized to the estate only to the extent that, on the date of such transfer, the fair market value of such property exceeds the value of such property for purposes of chapter 11 (determined without regard to section 2032A).

[Sec. 1040(b)]

(b) SIMILAR RULE FOR CERTAIN TRUSTS.—To the extent provided in regulations prescribed by the Secretary, a rule similar to the rule provided in subsection (a) shall apply where the trustee of a trust (any portion of which is included in the gross estate of the decedent) transfers property with respect to which an election was made under section 2032A.

[Sec. 1040(c)]

(c) BASIS OF PROPERTY ACQUIRED IN TRANSFER DESCRIBED IN SUBSECTION (a) OR (b).—The basis of property acquired in a transfer with respect to which gain realized is not recognized by reason of subsection (a) or (b) shall be the basis of such property immediately before the transfer increased by the amount of the gain recognized to the estate or trust on the transfer.

Amendments

• **2013, American Taxpayer Relief Act of 2012 (P.L. 112-240)**

P.L. 112-240, §101(a)(1)-(3), provides:

SEC. 101. PERMANENT EXTENSION AND MODIFICATION OF 2001 TAX RELIEF.

(a) PERMANENT EXTENSION.—

(1) IN GENERAL.—The Economic Growth and Tax Relief Reconciliation Act of 2001 is amended by striking title IX.

(2) CONFORMING AMENDMENT.—The Tax Relief, Unemployment Insurance Reauthorization, and Job Creation Act of 2010 is amended by striking section 304.

(3) EFFECTIVE DATE.—The amendments made by this subsection shall apply to taxable, plan, or limitation years beginning after December 31, 2012, and estates of decedents dying, gifts made, or generation skipping transfers after December 31, 2012.

• **2010, Tax Relief, Unemployment Insurance Reauthorization, and Job Creation Act of 2010 (P.L. 111-312)**

P.L. 111-312, §301(a):

Amended Code Sec. 1040 to read as such provision would read if subtitle E of title V of the Economic Growth and Tax Relief Reconciliation Act of 2001 (P.L. 107-16) had never been enacted. **Effective** for estates of decedents dying, and transfers made, after 12-31-2009. For a special rule, see Act Sec. 301(c), below. Prior to amendment by P.L. 111-312, Code Sec. 1040 read as follows:

SEC. 1040. USE OF APPRECIATED CARRYOVER BASIS PROPERTY TO SATISFY PECUNIARY BEQUEST.

(a) IN GENERAL.—If the executor of the estate of any decedent satisfies the right of any person to receive a pecuniary bequest with appreciated property, then gain on such exchange shall be recognized to the estate only to the extent that, on the date of such exchange, the fair market value of such property exceeds such value on the date of death.

(b) SIMILAR RULE FOR CERTAIN TRUSTS.—To the extent provided in regulations prescribed by the Secretary, a rule similar to the rule provided in subsection (a) shall apply where—

(1) by reason of the death of the decedent, a person has a right to receive from a trust a specific dollar amount which is the equivalent of a pecuniary bequest, and

(2) the trustee of a trust satisfies such right with property.

(c) BASIS OF PROPERTY ACQUIRED IN EXCHANGE DESCRIBED IN SUBSECTION (a) OR (b).—The basis of property acquired in an exchange with respect to which gain realized is not recognized by reason of subsection (a) or (b) shall be the basis of such property immediately before the exchange increased by the amount of the gain recognized to the estate or trust on the exchange.

P.L. 111-312, §301(c), provides:

(c) SPECIAL ELECTION WITH RESPECT TO ESTATES OF DECEDENTS DYING IN 2010.—Notwithstanding subsection (a), in the case of an estate of a decedent dying after December 31, 2009, and before January 1, 2011, the executor (within the meaning of section 2203 of the Internal Revenue Code of 1986) may elect to apply such Code as though the amendments made by subsection (a) do not apply with respect to chapter 11 of such Code and with respect to property acquired or passing from such decedent (within the meaning of section 1014(b) of such Code). Such election shall be made at such time and in such manner as the Secretary of the Treasury or the Secretary's delegate shall provide. Such an election once made shall be revocable only with the consent of the Secretary of the Treasury or the Secretary's delegate. For purposes of section 2652(a)(1) of such Code, the determination of whether any property is subject to the tax imposed by such chapter 11 shall be made without regard to any election made under this subsection.

P.L. 111-312, §304, provides [but see P.L. 112-240, §101(a)(2)-(3), above]:

SEC. 304. APPLICATION OF EGTRRA SUNSET TO THIS TITLE.

Section 901 of the Economic Growth and Tax Relief Reconciliation Act of 2001 shall apply to the amendments made by this title.

• **2001, Economic Growth and Tax Relief Reconciliation Act of 2001 (P.L. 107-16)**

P.L. 107-16, §542(d)(1):

Amended Code Sec. 1040. **Effective** for estates of decedents dying after 12-31-2009. Prior to amendment, Code Sec. 1040 read as follows:

SEC. 1040. TRANSFER OF CERTAIN FARM, ETC., REAL PROPERTY.

[Sec. 1040(a)]

(a) GENERAL RULE.—If the executor of the estate of any decedent transfers to a qualified heir (within the meaning of section 2032A(e)(1) any property with respect to which an election was made under section 2032A, then gain on such transfer shall be recognized to the estate only to the extent that, on the date of such transfer, the fair market value of such property exceeds the value of such property for purposes of chapter 11 (determined without regard to section 2032A).

Amendments

• **1983, Technical Corrections Act of 1982 (P.L. 97-448)**

P.L. 97-448, §104(b)(3)(A):

Amended Code Sec. 1040(a) by striking out "such exchange" and inserting in lieu thereof "such transfer". **Effective** as if included in the provision of P.L. 97-34 to which it relates.

• **1981, Economic Recovery Tax Act of 1981 (P.L. 97-34)**

P.L. 97-34, §421(j)(2)(B):

Amended Code Sec. 1040(a). **Effective**, generally, for estates of decedents dying after 12-31-76. Prior to amendment, Code Sec. 1040(a) read as follows:

SEC. 1040. USE OF FARM, ETC., REAL PROPERTY TO SATISFY PECUNIARY BEQUEST.

(a) GENERAL RULE.—If the executor of the estate of any decedent satisfies the right of a qualified heir (within the meaning of section 2032A(e)(1)) to receive a pecuniary bequest with property with respect to which an election was made under section 2032A, then gain on such exchange shall be recognized to the estate only to the extent that, on the date of such exchange, the fair market value of such property exceeds the value of such property for purposes of chapter 11 (determined without regard to section 2032A).

P.L. 97-34, §421(k)(5), as amended by P.L. 97-448, §104(b)(4), provides:

(5) CERTAIN AMENDMENTS MADE RETROACTIVE TO 1976.—

(A) IN GENERAL.—The amendments made by subsections (b)(1), (j)(1), and (j)(2) and the provisions of subparagraph (A) of section 2032A(c)(7) of the Internal Revenue Code of 1954 (as added by subsection (c)(2)) shall apply with respect to the estates of decedents dying after December 31, 1976.

(B) TIMELY ELECTION REQUIRED.—Subparagraph (A) shall only apply in the case of an estate if a timely election under section 2032A was made with respect to such estate. If the estate of any decedent would not qualify under section 2032A of the Internal Revenue Code of 1954 but for the amendments described in subparagraph (A) and the time for making an election under section 2032A with respect to such estate would (but for this sentence) expire after July 28, 1980, the time for making such election shall not expire before the close of February 16, 1982.

(C) REINSTATEMENT OF ELECTIONS.—If any election under section 2032A was revoked before the date of the enactment of this Act, such election may be reinstated at any time before February 17, 1982.

(D) STATUTE OF LIMITATIONS.—If on the date of the enactment of this Act (or at any time before February 17, 1982) the making of a credit or refund of any overpayment of tax resulting from the amendments described in subparagraph (A) is barred by any law or rule of law, such credit or refund shall nevertheless be made if claim therefor is made before February 17, 1982.

• **1980, Crude Oil Windfall Profit Tax Act of 1980 (P.L. 96-223)**

P.L. 96-223, §401(c)(2)(A):

Amended Code Sec. 1040(a). **Effective** with respect to decedents dying after 12-31-76. However, see the amendment note for P.L. 96-223, Act Sec. 401(a), that follows Code Sec. 1014(d) for the text of Act Sec. 401(d) that authorizes the election of the carryover basis rules in the case of a decedent dying after 12-31-76 and before 11-7-78. Prior to amendment, Code Sec. 1040(a) read:

SEC. 1040. USE OF CERTAIN APPRECIATED CARRYOVER BASIS PROPERTY TO SATISFY PECUNIARY BEQUEST.

(a) GENERAL RULE.—If the executor of the estate of any decedent satisfies the right of any person to receive a pecuniary bequest with appreciated carryover basis property (as defined in section 1023(f)(5)), then gain on such exchange shall be recognized to the estate only to the extent that, on the date of such exchange, the fair market value of such property exceeds the value of such property for purposes of chapter 11 (determined without regard to section 2032A).

• **1980, Technical Corrections Act of 1979 (P.L. 96-222)**

P.L. 96-222, §105(a)(5)(B), provides:

(B) PERIOD FOR WHICH SECTION 1040 APPLIES.—Notwithstanding section 515 of the Revenue Act of 1978, section 1040 of the Internal Revenue Code of 1954 (as amended by subparagraph (A)) shall apply with respect to the estates of decedents dying after December 31, 1976.

• **1978, Revenue Act of 1978 (P.L. 95-600)**

P.L. 95-600, §702(d)(3), (6):

Amended Code Sec. 1040(a) by adding "(determined without regard to section 2032A)" after "chapter 11". **Effective** for estates of decedents dying after 12-31-76.

• **1976, Tax Reform Act of 1976 (P.L. 94-455)**

P.L. 94-455, §2005(b), (f)(1):

Added the heading of Code Sec. 1040 and Code Sec. 1040(a). **Effective** for decedents dying after 12-31-79, as amended by P.L. 95-600, Sec. 515(6).

[Sec. 1040(b)]

(b) SIMILAR RULE FOR CERTAIN TRUSTS.—To the extent provided in regulations prescribed by the Secretary, a rule similar to the rule provided in subsection (a) shall apply where the trustee of a trust (any portion of which is included in the gross estate of the decedent) transfers property with respect to which an election was made under section 2032A.

Amendments

• **1981, Economic Recovery Tax Act of 1981 (P.L. 97-34)**

P.L. 97-34, §421(j)(2)(B):

Amended Code Sec. 1040(b). **Effective**, generally, with respect to decedents dying after 12-31-81. For special rules, see the amendment note following Code Sec. 1040(a) at §421(j)(2)(B). Prior to amendment, Code Sec. 1040(b) read as follows:

(b) SIMILAR RULE FOR CERTAIN TRUSTS.—To the extent provided in regulations prescribed by the Secretary, a rule similar to the rule provided in subsection (a) shall apply where—

(1) by reason of the death of the decedent, a qualified heir has a right to receive from a trust a specific dollar amount which is the equivalent of a pecuniary bequest, and

(2) the trustee of the trust satisfies such right with property with respect to which an election was made under section 2032A.

• **1980, Crude Oil Windfall Profit Tax Act of 1980 (P.L. 96-223)**

P.L. 96-223, §401(c)(2)(A):

Amended Code Sec. 1040(b). **Effective** with respect to decedents dying after 12-31-76. However, see the amendment note for P.L. 96-223, Act Sec. 401(a), that follows Code Sec. 1014(d) for the text of Act Sec. 401(d) that authorizes the election of the carryover basis rules in the case of a decedent dying after 12-31-76 and before 11-7-78. Prior to amendment Code Sec. 1040(b) read:

(b) SIMILAR RULE FOR CERTAIN TRUSTS.—To the extent provided in regulations prescribed by the Secretary, a rule similar to the rule provided in subsection (a) shall apply where—

(1) by reason of the death of the decedent, a person has a right to receive from a trust a specific dollar amount which is the equivalent of a pecuniary bequest, and

(2) the trustee of the trust satisfies such right with carryover basis property to which section 1023 applies.

• **1976, Tax Reform Act of 1976 (P.L. 94-455)**

P.L. 94-455, §2005(b), (f)(1):

Added Code Sec. 1040(b). **Effective** as amended by P.L. 95-600; Sec. 515(6), for decedents dying after 12-31-79.

[Sec. 1040(c)]

(c) BASIS OF PROPERTY ACQUIRED IN TRANSFER DESCRIBED IN SUBSECTION (a) OR (b).—The basis of property acquired in a transfer with respect to which gain realized is not recognized by reason of subsection (a) or (b) shall be the basis of such property immediately before the transfer increased by the amount of the gain recognized to the estate or trust on the transfer.

Amendments

• **1983, Technical Corrections Act of 1982 (P.L. 97-448)**

P.L. 97-448, §104(b)(3)(B):

Amended Code Sec. 1040(c) by striking out "an exchange" and inserting in lieu thereof "a transfer", by striking out "the exchange" each place it appears and inserting in lieu thereof "the transfer", and by striking out "EXCHANGE" in the subsection hearing and inserting in lieu thereof "TRANSFER". **Effective** as if included in the provision of P.L. 97-34 to which it relates.

• **1980, Crude Oil Windfall Profit Tax Act of 1980 (P.L. 96-223)**

P.L. 96-223, §401(c)(2)(A):

Amended Code Sec. 1040(c) and repealed Code Sec. 1040(d). **Effective** with respect to decedents dying after 12-31-76. However, see the amendment note for P.L. 96-223, Act Sec. 401(a), that follows Code Sec. 1014(d) for the text of Act Sec. 401(d) that authorizes the election of the carryover basis rules in the case of a decedent dying after 12-31-76 and before 11-7-78. Prior to amendment, Code Sec. 1040(c) and (d) read:

(c) BASIS OF PROPERTY ACQUIRED IN EXCHANGE DESCRIBED IN SUBSECTION (a) OR (b).—The basis of property acquired in an exchange with respect to which gain realized is not recognized by reason of subsection (a) or (b) shall be the basis of such property immediately before the exchange, increased by the amount of the gain recognized to the estate or trust on the exchange.

(d) APPLICATION TO SECTION 2032A PROPERTY.—For purposes of this section, references to carryover basis property shall be treated as including a reference to property the valuation of which is determined under section 2032A.

• **1980, Technical Corrections Act of 1979 (P.L. 96-222)**

P.L. 96-222, §105(a)(5):

Added Code Sec. 1040(d). **Effective** for estates of decedents dying after 12-31-76.

• **1976, Tax Reform Act of 1976 (P.L. 94-455)**

P.L. 94-455, §2005(b), (f)(1):

Added Code Sec. 1040(c). **Effective** as amended by P.L. 95-600, Sec. 515(6), for decedents dying after 12-31-79.

P.L. 107-16, §901(a)-(b), as amended by P.L. 111-312, §101(a)(1), provides [but see P.L. 112-240, §101(a)(1) and (3), above]:

SEC. 901. SUNSET OF PROVISIONS OF ACT.

(a) IN GENERAL.—All provisions of, and amendments made by, this Act shall not apply—

(1) to taxable, plan, or limitation years beginning after December 31, 2012, or

(2) in the case of title V, to estates of decedents dying, gifts made, or generation skipping transfers, after December 31, 2012.

INCOME TAX—NONTAXABLE EXCHANGES

(b) APPLICATION OF CERTAIN LAWS.—The Internal Revenue Code of 1986 and the Employee Retirement Income Security Act of 1974 shall be applied and administered to years, estates, gifts, and transfers described in subsection (a) as if the provisions and amendments described in subsection (a) had never been enacted.

[Sec. 1041]

SEC. 1041. TRANSFERS OF PROPERTY BETWEEN SPOUSES OR INCIDENT TO DIVORCE.

[Sec. 1041(a)]

(a) GENERAL RULE.—No gain or loss shall be recognized on a transfer of property from an individual to (or in trust for the benefit of)—
  (1) a spouse, or
  (2) a former spouse, but only if the transfer is incident to the divorce.

[Sec. 1041(b)]

(b) TRANSFER TREATED AS GIFT; TRANSFEREE HAS TRANSFEROR'S BASIS.—In the case of any transfer of property described in subsection (a)—
  (1) for purposes of this subtitle, the property shall be treated as acquired by the transferee by gift, and
  (2) the basis of the transferee in the property shall be the adjusted basis of the transferor.

[Sec. 1041(c)]

(c) INCIDENT TO DIVORCE.—For purposes of subsection (a)(2), a transfer of property is incident to the divorce if such transfer—
  (1) occurs within 1 year after the date on which the marriage ceases, or
  (2) is related to the cessation of the marriage.

[Sec. 1041(d)]

(d) SPECIAL RULE WHERE SPOUSE IS NONRESIDENT ALIEN.—Subsection (a) shall not apply if the spouse (or former spouse) of the individual making the transfer is a nonresident alien.

Amendments

• **1988, Technical and Miscellaneous Revenue Act of 1988 (P.L. 100-647)**

P.L. 100-647, §1018(l)(3)(A)-(B):

Amended Code Sec. 1041(d) by striking out "Paragraph (1) of subsection (a)" and inserting in lieu thereof "Subsection (a)"; and by striking out "the spouse" and inserting in lieu thereof "the spouse (or former spouse)". **Effective** with respect to transfers after 6-21-88.

[Sec. 1041(e)]

(e) TRANSFERS IN TRUST WHERE LIABILITY EXCEEDS BASIS.—Subsection (a) shall not apply to the transfer of property in trust to the extent that—
  (1) the sum of the amount of the liabilities assumed, plus the amount of the liabilities to which the property is subject, exceeds
  (2) the total of the adjusted basis of the property transferred.

Proper adjustment shall be made under subsection (b) in the basis of the transferee in such property to take into account gain recognized by reason of the preceding sentence.

Amendments

• **1986, Tax Reform Act of 1986 (P.L. 99-514)**

P.L. 99-514, §1842(b):

Amended Code Sec. 1041 by adding at the end thereof new subsection (e). **Effective** as if included in the provision of P.L. 98-369 to which it relates.

• **1984, Deficit Reduction Act of 1984 (P.L. 98-369)**

P.L. 98-369, §421(a):

Amended Part III of subchapter O of chapter 1 by adding at the end thereof a new section 1041. **Effective** for transfers after 7-18-84 in tax years ending after such date. Special rules appear in Act Sec. 421(d)(2)-(4), below.

P.L. 98-369, §421(d)(2)-(4), provides:

(2) Election To Have Amendments Apply To Transfers After 1983.—If both spouses or former spouses make an election under this paragraph, the amendments made by this section shall apply to all transfers made by such spouses (or former spouses) after December 31, 1983.

(3) Exception for Transfers Pursuant to Existing Decrees.—Except in the case of an election under paragraph (2), the amendments made by this section shall not apply to transfers under any instrument in effect on or before the date of the enactment of this Act unless both spouses (or former spouses) elect to have such amendments apply to transfers under such instrument.

(4) Election.—Any election under paragraph (2) or (3) shall be made in such manner, at such time, and subject to such conditions, as the Secretary of the Treasury or his delegate may by regulations prescribe.

[Sec. 1042]

SEC. 1042. SALES OF STOCK TO EMPLOYEE STOCK OWNERSHIP PLANS OR CERTAIN COOPERATIVES.

[Sec. 1042(a)]

(a) NONRECOGNITION OF GAIN.—If—
  (1) the taxpayer or executor elects in such form as the Secretary may prescribe the application of this section with respect to any sale of qualified securities,
  (2) the taxpayer purchases qualified replacement property within the replacement period, and
  (3) the requirements of subsection (b) are met with respect to such sale,

then the gain (if any) on such sale which would be recognized as long-term capital gain shall be recognized only to the extent that the amount realized on such sale exceeds the cost to the taxpayer of such qualified replacement property.

Amendments

• **1986, Tax Reform Act of 1986 (P.L. 99-514)**

P.L. 99-514, §1854(a)(1)(A) and (B):

Amended Code Sec. 1042(a) by striking out "gain (if any) on such sale" and inserting in lieu thereof "gain (if any) on such sale which would be recognized as long-term capital gain", and by striking out "the taxpayer elects" in paragraph (1) and inserting in lieu thereof "the taxpayer or executor elects in such form as the Secretary may prescribe". **Effective** as if included in the provision of P.L. 98-369 to which it relates.

[Sec. 1042(b)]

(b) REQUIREMENTS TO QUALIFY FOR NONRECOGNITION.—A sale of qualified securities meets the requirements of this subsection if—
  (1) SALE TO EMPLOYEE ORGANIZATIONS.—The qualified securities are sold to—
    (A) an employee stock ownership plan (as defined in section 4975(e)(7)), or
    (B) an eligible worker-owned cooperative.
  (2) PLAN MUST HOLD 30 PERCENT OF STOCK AFTER SALE.—The plan or cooperative referred to in paragraph (1) owns (after application of section 318(a)(4)), immediately after the sale, at least 30 percent of—
    (A) each class of outstanding stock of the corporation (other than stock described in section 1504(a)(4)) which issued the qualified securities, or
    (B) the total value of all outstanding stock of the corporation (other than stock described in section 1504(a)(4)).

INCOME TAX—NONTAXABLE EXCHANGES

(3) WRITTEN STATEMENT REQUIRED.—

(A) IN GENERAL.—The taxpayer files with the Secretary the written statement described in subparagraph (B).

(B) STATEMENT.—A statement is described in this subparagraph if it is a verified written statement of—

(i) the employer whose employees are covered by the plan described in paragraph (1), or

(ii) any authorized officer of the cooperative described in paragraph (1),

consenting to the application of sections 4978 and 4979A with respect to such employer or cooperative.

(4) 3-YEAR HOLDING PERIOD.—The taxpayer's holding period with respect to the qualified securities is at least 3 years (determined as of the time of the sale).

Amendments

- **1989, Omnibus Budget Reconciliation Act of 1989 (P.L. 101-239)**

P.L. 101-239, §7303(a):

Amended Code Sec. 1042(b) by adding at the end thereof a new paragraph (4). **Effective** for sales after 7-10-89.

- **1986, Tax Reform Act of 1986 (P.L. 99-514)**

P.L. 99-514, §1854(a)(2)(A):

Amended Code Sec. 1042(b)(2). For the **effective** date, see Act Sec. 1854(b)(2)(B)(i), below.

P.L. 99-514, §1854(b)(2)(B)(i), provides:

(B)(i) The requirement that section 1042(b) of the Internal Revenue Code of 1954 shall be applied with regard to section 318(a)(4) of such Code shall apply to sales after May 6, 1986.

P.L. 99-514, §1854(a)(2)(B)(ii):

Amended Code Sec. 1042(b)(2). **Effective** for sales after 7-18-84, and before 10-22-86. Prior to amendment by Act Sec. 1854(a)(2)(A) and (B)(ii), Code Sec. 1042(b)(2) read as follows:

(2) EMPLOYEES MUST OWN 30 PERCENT OF STOCK AFTER SALE.—The plan or cooperative referred to in paragraph (1) owns, immediately after the sale, at least 30 percent of the total value of the employer securities (within the meaning of section 409(l)) outstanding as of such time.

P.L. 99-514, §1854(a)(3)(B), as amended by P.L. 100-647, §1018(t)(4)(F)-(G):

Amended Code Sec. 1042(b) by striking out paragraph (3) and redesignating paragraph (4) as paragraph (3). **Effective**, generally, for sales of securities after 10-22-86. For a special rule, see Act Sec. 1854(a)(3)(C)(ii) below. Prior to amendment, Code Sec. 1042(b)(3) read as follows:

(3) PLAN MAINTAINED FOR BENEFIT OF EMPLOYEES.—No portion of the assets of the plan or cooperative attributable to employer securities (within the meaning of section 409(l)) acquired by the plan or cooperative described in paragraph (1) accrue under such plan, or are allocated by such cooperative, for the benefit of—

(A) the taxpayer,

(B) any person who is a member of the family of the taxpayer (within the meaning of section 267(c)(4)), or

(C) any other person who owns (after application of section 318(a)) more than 25 percent in value of any class of outstanding employer securities (within the meaning of section 409(l)).

P.L. 99-514, §1854(a)(3)(C)(ii), provides:

(ii) A taxpayer or executor may elect to have section 1042(b)(3) of the Internal Revenue Code of 1954 (as in effect before the amendment made by subparagraph (B)) apply to sales before the date of the enactment of this Act as if such section included the last sentence of section 409(n)(1) of the Internal Revenue Code of 1986 (as added by subparagraph (A)).

P.L. 99-514, §1854(a)(9)(B):

Amended Code Sec. 1042(b)(3)(B) by striking out "section 4978(a)" and inserting in lieu thereof "sections 4978 and 4979A". **Effective** for sales of securities after 10-22-86.

P.L. 99-514, §1854(f)(3)(B):

Amended Code Sec. 1042(b)(3)(B) by inserting "and 4979A" after "section 4978(a)". **Effective** 10-22-86.

[Sec. 1042(c)]

(c) DEFINITIONS; SPECIAL RULES.—For purposes of this section—

(1) QUALIFIED SECURITIES.—The term "qualified securities" means employer securities (as defined in section 409(l)) which—

⇒ *Caution: Code Sec. 1042(c)(1)(A), below, prior to amendment by P.L. 117-328, applies to sales on or before December 31, 2027.*

(A) are issued by a domestic C corporation that has no stock outstanding that are readily tradable on an established securities market, and

⇒ *Caution: Code Sec. 1042(c)(1)(A), below, as amended by P.L. 117-328, applies to sales after December 31, 2027.*

(A) are issued by a domestic corporation that has no stock outstanding that are readily tradable on an established securities market, and

(B) were not received by the taxpayer in—

(i) a distribution from a plan described in section 401(a), or

(ii) a transfer pursuant to an option or other right to acquire stock to which section 83, 422, or 423 applied (or to which section 422 or 424 (as in effect on the day before the date of the enactment of the Revenue Reconciliation Act of 1990) applied).

(2) ELIGIBLE WORKER-OWNED COOPERATIVE.—The term "eligible worker-owned cooperative" means any organization—

(A) to which part I of subchapter T applies,

(B) a majority of the membership of which is composed of employees of such organization,

(C) a majority of the voting stock of which is owned by members,

(D) a majority of the board of directors of which is elected by the members on the basis of 1 person 1 vote, and

(E) a majority of the allocated earnings and losses of which are allocated to members on the basis of—

(i) patronage,

(ii) capital contributions, or

(iii) some combination of clauses (i) and (ii).

(3) REPLACEMENT PERIOD.—The term "replacement period" means the period which begins 3 months before the date on which the sale of qualified securities occurs and which ends 12 months after the date of such sale.

(4) QUALIFIED REPLACEMENT PROPERTY.—

(A) IN GENERAL.— The term "qualified replacement property" means any security issued by a domestic operating corporation which—

(i) did not, for the taxable year preceding the taxable year in which such security was purchased, have passive investment income (as defined in section 1362(d)(3)(C)) in excess of 25 percent of the gross receipts of such corporation for such preceding taxable year, and

(ii) is not the corporation which issued the qualified securities which such security is replacing or a member of the same controlled group of corporations (within the meaning of section 1563(a)(1)) as such corporation.

For purposes of clause (i), income which is described in section 954(c)(3) (as in effect immediately before the Tax Reform Act of 1986) shall not be treated as passive investment income.

(B) OPERATING CORPORATION.—For purposes of this paragraph—

(i) IN GENERAL.—The term "operating corporation" means a corporation more than 50 percent of the assets of which were, at the time the security was purchased or before the close of the replacement period, used in the active conduct of the trade or business.

(ii) FINANCIAL INSTITUTIONS AND INSURANCE COMPANIES.—The term "operating corporation" shall include—

(I) any financial institution described in section 581, and

INCOME TAX—NONTAXABLE EXCHANGES

(II) an insurance company subject to tax under subchapter L.

(C) CONTROLLING AND CONTROLLED CORPORATIONS TREATED AS 1 CORPORATION.—

(i) IN GENERAL.—For purposes of applying this paragraph, if—

(I) the corporation issuing the security owns stock representing control of 1 or more other corporations,

(II) 1 or more other corporations own stock representing control of the corporation issuing the security, or

(III) both,

then all such corporations shall be treated as 1 corporation.

(ii) CONTROL.—For purposes of clause (i), the term "control" has the meaning given such term by section 304(c). In determining control, there shall be disregarded any qualified replacement property of the taxpayer with respect to the section 1042 sale being tested.

(D) SECURITY DEFINED.—For purposes of this paragraph the term "security" has the meaning given such term by section 165(g)(2), except that such term shall not include any security issued by a government or political subdivision thereof.

(5) SECURITIES SOLD BY UNDERWRITER.—No sale of securities by an underwriter to an employee stock ownership plan or eligible worker-owned cooperative in the ordinary course of his trade or business as an underwriter, whether or not guaranteed, shall be treated as a sale for purposes of subsection (a).

(6) TIME FOR FILING ELECTION.—An election under subsection (a) shall be filed not later than the last day prescribed by law (including extensions thereof) for filing the return of tax imposed by this chapter for the taxable year in which the sale occurs.

(7) SECTION NOT TO APPLY TO GAIN OF C CORPORATION.—Subsection (a) shall not apply to any gain on the sale of any qualified securities which is includible in the gross income of any C corporation.

Amendments

- **2022, SECURE 2.0 Act of 2022 (P.L. 117-328)**

P.L. 117-328, §114(a):

Amended Code Sec. 1042(c)(1)(A) by striking "domestic C corporation" and inserting "domestic corporation". **Effective** for sales after 12-31-2027.

- **1996, Small Business Job Protection Act of 1996 (P.L. 104-188)**

P.L. 104-188, §1311(b)(3):

Amended Code Sec. 1042(c)(4)(A)(i) by striking "section 1362(d)(3)(D)" and inserting "section 1362(d)(3)(C)". **Effective**, generally, for tax years beginning after 12-31-96.

P.L. 104-188, §1316(d)(3):

Amended Code Sec. 1042(c)(1)(A) by striking "domestic corporation" and inserting "domestic C corporation". **Effective** for tax years beginning after 12-31-97.

P.L. 104-188, §1616(b)(13):

Amended Code Sec. 1042(c)(4)(B)(ii)[I] by striking "or 593" after "581". **Effective**, generally, for tax years beginning after 12-31-95.

- **1990, Omnibus Budget Reconciliation Act of 1990 (P.L. 101-508)**

P.L. 101-508, §11801(c)(9)(H) (as amended by P.L. 104-188, §1704(t)(50)):

Amended Code Sec. 1042(c)(1)(B)(ii) by striking "section 83, 422, 422A, 423, or 424 applies" and inserting "section 83, 422, or 423 applied (or to which section 422 or 424 (as in effect on the day before the date of the enactment of the Revenue Reconciliation Act of 1990) applied)". **Effective** 11-5-90.

P.L. 101-508, §11821(b)(1)-(2), provides:

(b) SAVINGS PROVISION.—If—

(1) any provision amended or repealed by this part applied to—

(A) any transaction occurring before the date of the enactment of this Act,

(B) any property acquired before such date of enactment, or

(C) any item of income, loss, deduction, or credit taken into account before such date of enactment, and

(2) the treatment of such transaction, property, or item under such provision would (without regard to the amendments made by this part) affect liability for tax for periods ending after such date of enactment,

nothing in the amendments made by this part shall be construed to affect the treatment of such transaction, property, or item for purposes of determining liability for tax for periods ending after such date of enactment.

- **1988, Technical and Miscellaneous Revenue Act of 1988 (P.L. 100-647)**

P.L. 100-647, §1018(t)(4)(D):

Amended Code Sec. 1042(c)(4)(A) by inserting "(as in effect immediately before the Tax Reform Act of 1986)" after "section 954(c)(3)". **Effective** as if included in the provision of P.L. 99-514 to which it relates.

P.L. 100-647, §1018(t)(4)(E):

Amended Code Sec. 1042(c)(4)(B)(i) by striking out "placement period" and inserting in lieu thereof "replacement period". **Effective** as if included in the provision of P.L. 99-514 to which it relates.

- **1986, Tax Reform Act of 1986 (P.L. 99-514)**

P.L. 99-514, §1854(a)(4)(A)-(C):

Amended Code Sec. 1042(c)(1) by striking out "securities outstanding that are" in subparagraph (A) and inserting in lieu thereof "stock outstanding that is", by inserting "and" at the end of subparagraph (A), and by striking out subparagraph (B) and redesignating subparagraph (C) as subparagraph (B). **Effective** as if included in the provision of P.L. 98-369 to which it relates. Prior to amendment, Code Sec. 1042(c)(1)(B) read as follows:

(B) at the time of the sale described in subsection (a)(1), have been held by the taxpayer for more than 1 year.

P.L. 99-514, §1854(a)(5)(A):

Amended Code Sec. 1042(c)(4). **Effective** as if included in the provision of P.L. 98-369 to which it relates. Prior to amendment, Code Sec. 1042(c)(4) read as follows:

(4) QUALIFIED REPLACEMENT PROPERTY.—The term "qualified replacement property" means any securities (as defined in section 165(g)(2)) issued by a domestic corporation which does not, for the taxable year in which such stock is issued, have passive investment income (as defined in section 1362(d)(3)(D)) that exceeds 25 percent of the gross receipts of such corporation for such taxable year.

P.L. 99-514, §1854(a)(5)(B), provides:

(B) If—

(i) before January 1, 1987, the taxpayer acquired any security (as defined in section 165(g)(2) of the Internal Revenue Code of 1954) issued by a domestic corporation or by any State or political subdivision thereof,

(ii) the taxpayer treated such security as qualified replacement property for purposes of section 1042 of such Code, and

(iii) such property does not meet the requirements of section 1042(c)(4) of such Code (as amended by subparagraph (A)),

then, with respect to so much of any gain which the taxpayer treated as not recognized under section 1042(a) by reason of the acquisition of such property, the replacement period for purposes of such section shall not expire before January 1, 1987.

P.L. 99-514, §1854(a)(6)(A):

Amended Code Sec. 1042(c) by adding at the end thereof new paragraph (7). For the **effective** date, see Act Sec. 1854(a)(6)(B)-(D), below.

P.L. 99-514, §1854(a)(6)(B)-(D), provides:

(B) The amendment made by subparagraph (A) shall apply to sales after March 28, 1985, except that such amendment shall not apply to sales made before July 1, 1985, if made pursuant to a binding contract in effect on March 28, 1985, and at all times thereafter.

(C) The amendment made by subparagraph (A) shall not apply to any sale occurring on December 20, 1985, with respect to which—

(i) a commitment letter was issued by a bank on October 31, 1984, and

(ii) a final purchase agreement was entered into on November 5, 1985.

(D) In the case of a sale on September 27, 1985, with respect to which a preliminary commitment letter was issued on April 10, 1985, and with respect to which a commitment letter was issued by a bank on June 28, 1985, the amendment made by subparagraph (A) shall apply but such sale shall be treated as having occurred on September 27, 1986.

P.L. 99-514, §1854(a)(10)(A)-(C):

Amended Code Sec. 1042(c)(5) by striking out "acquisition" and inserting in lieu thereof "sale", by inserting "to an employee stock ownership plan or eligible worker-owned cooperative" before "in", and by striking out "ACQUIRED" in the heading thereof and inserting in lieu thereof "SOLD". **Effective** as if included in the provision of P.L. 98-369 to which it relates.

P.L. 99-514, §1854(a)(11):

Amended Code Sec. 1042 by inserting "EMPLOYEE" before "STOCK" in the heading for such section. **Effective** as if included in the provision of P.L. 98-369 to which it relates.

P.L. 99-514, §1899A(26):

Amended Code Sec. 1042(c) by striking out "this section.—" in the material preceding paragraph (1) and inserting in lieu thereof "this section—". **Effective** 10-22-86.

[Sec. 1042(d)]

(d) BASIS OF QUALIFIED REPLACEMENT PROPERTY.—The basis of the taxpayer in qualified replacement property purchased by the taxpayer during the replacement period shall be reduced by the amount of gain not recognized by reason of such purchase and the application of subsection (a). If more than one item of qualified replacement property is purchased, the basis of each of such items shall be reduced by an amount determined by multiplying the total gain not recognized by reason of such purchase and the application of subsection (a) by a fraction—

INCOME TAX—NONTAXABLE EXCHANGES

(1) the numerator of which is the cost of such item of property, and

(2) the denominator of which is the total cost of all such items of property.

Any reduction in basis under this subsection shall not be taken into account for purposes of section 1278(a)(2)(A)(ii) (relating to definition of market discount).

Amendments

• **1986, Tax Reform Act of 1986 (P.L. 99-514)**

P.L. 99-514, §1854(a)(7):

Amended Code Sec. 1042(d) by adding at the end thereof a new flush sentence. **Effective** as if included in the provision of P.L. 98-369 to which it relates.

[Sec. 1042(e)]

(e) RECAPTURE OF GAIN ON DISPOSITION OF QUALIFIED REPLACEMENT PROPERTY.—

(1) IN GENERAL.—If a taxpayer disposes of any qualified replacement property, then, notwithstanding any other provision of this title, gain (if any) shall be recognized to the extent of the gain which was not recognized under subsection (a) by reason of the acquisition by such taxpayer of such qualified replacement property.

(2) SPECIAL RULE FOR CORPORATIONS CONTROLLED BY THE TAXPAYER.—If—

(A) a corporation issuing qualified replacement property disposes of a substantial portion of its assets other than in the ordinary course of its trade or business, and

(B) any taxpayer owning stock representing control (within the meaning of section 304(c)) of such corporation at the time of such disposition holds any qualified replacement property of such corporation at such time,

then the taxpayer shall be treated as having disposed of such qualified replacement property at such time.

(3) RECAPTURE NOT TO APPLY IN CERTAIN CASES.—Paragraph (1) shall not apply to any transfer of qualified replacement property—

(A) in any reorganization (within the meaning of section 368) unless the person making the election under subsection (a)(1) owns stock representing control in the acquiring or acquired corporation and such property is substituted basis property in the hands of the transferee,

(B) by reason of the death of the person making such election,

(C) by gift, or

(D) in any transaction to which section 1042(a) applies.

Amendments

• **1986, Tax Reform Act of 1986 (P.L. 99-514)**

P.L. 99-514, §1854(a)(8)(A):

Amended Code Sec. 1042 by redesignating subsection (e) as subsection (f) and by inserting after subsection (d) new subsection (e). **Effective** for dispositions after 10-22-86, in tax years ending after such date.

[Sec. 1042(f)]

(f) STATUTE OF LIMITATIONS.—If any gain is realized by the taxpayer on the sale or exchange of any qualified securities and there is in effect an election under subsection (a) with respect to such gain, then—

(1) the statutory period for the assessment of any deficiency with respect to such gain shall not expire before the expiration of 3 years from the date the Secretary is notified by the taxpayer (in such manner as the Secretary may by regulations prescribe) of—

(A) the taxpayer's cost of purchasing qualified replacement property which the taxpayer claims results in nonrecognition of any part of such gain,

(B) the taxpayer's intention not to purchase qualified replacement property within the replacement period, or

(C) a failure to make such purchase within the replacement period, and

(2) such deficiency may be assessed before the expiration of such 3-year period notwithstanding the provisions of any other law or rule of law which would otherwise prevent such assessment.

Amendments

• **1986, Tax Reform Act of 1986 (P.L. 99-514)**

P.L. 99-514, §1854(a)(8)(A):

Amended Code Sec. 1042 by redesignating subsection (e) as subsection (f) and by inserting after subsection (d) new subsection (e). **Effective** for dispositions after 10-22-86, in tax years ending after such date.

• **1984, Deficit Reduction Act of 1984 (P.L. 98-369)**

P.L. 98-369, §541(a):

Added Code Sec. 1042. **Effective** for sales of securities in tax years beginning after 7-18-84.

[Sec. 1042(g)]

(g) APPLICATION OF SECTION TO SALES OF STOCK IN AGRICULTURAL REFINERS AND PROCESSORS TO ELIGIBLE FARM COOPERATIVES.—

(1) IN GENERAL.—This section shall apply to the sale of stock of a qualified refiner or processor to an eligible farmers' cooperative.

(2) QUALIFIED REFINER OR PROCESSOR.—For purposes of this subsection, the term "qualified refiner or processor" means a domestic corporation—

(A) substantially all of the activities of which consist of the active conduct of the trade or business of refining or processing agricultural or horticultural products, and

(B) which, during the 1-year period ending on the date of the sale, purchases more than one-half of such products to be refined or processed from—

(i) farmers who make up the eligible farmers' cooperative which is purchasing stock in the corporation in a transaction to which this subsection is to apply, or

(ii) such cooperative.

(3) ELIGIBLE FARMERS' COOPERATIVE.—For purposes of this section, the term "eligible farmers' cooperative" means an organization to which part I of subchapter T applies and which is engaged in the marketing of agricultural or horticultural products.

(4) SPECIAL RULES.—In applying this section to a sale to which paragraph (1) applies—

(A) the eligible farmers' cooperative shall be treated in the same manner as a cooperative described in subsection (b)(1)(B),

(B) subsection (b)(2) shall be applied by substituting "100 percent" for "30 percent" each place it appears,

(C) the determination as to whether any stock in the domestic corporation is a qualified security shall be made without regard to whether the stock is an employer security or to subsection (c)(1)(A), and

(D) paragraphs (2)(D) and (7) of subsection (c) shall not apply.

INCOME TAX—NONTAXABLE EXCHANGES

Amendments

• **1997, Taxpayer Relief Act of 1997 (P.L. 105-34)**

P.L. 105-34, § 968(a):

Amended Code Sec. 1042 by adding at the end a new subsection (g). **Effective** for sales after 12-31-97.

⇒ *Caution: Code Sec. 1042(h), below, as added by P.L. 117-328, applies to sales after December 31, 2027.*

[Sec. 1042(h)]

(h) APPLICATION OF SECTION TO SALE OF STOCK IN S CORPORATION.—In the case of the sale of qualified securities of an S corporation, the election under subsection (a) may be made with respect to not more than 10 percent of the amount realized on such sale for purposes of determining the amount of gain not recognized and the extent to which (if at all) the amount realized on such sale exceeds the cost of qualified replacement property. The portion of adjusted basis that is properly allocable to the portion of the amount realized with respect to which the election is made under this subsection shall be taken into account for purposes of the preceding sentence.

• **2022, SECURE 2.0 Act of 2022 (P.L. 117-328)**

P.L. 117-328, § 114(b):

Amended Code Sec. 1042 by adding at the end a new subsection (h). **Effective** for sales after 12-31-2027.

[Sec. 1043]

SEC. 1043. SALE OF PROPERTY TO COMPLY WITH CONFLICT-OF-INTEREST REQUIREMENTS.

[Sec. 1043(a)]

(a) NONRECOGNITION OF GAIN.—If an eligible person sells any property pursuant to a certificate of divestiture, at the election of the taxpayer, gain from such sale shall be recognized only to the extent that the amount realized on such sale exceeds the cost (to the extent not previously taken into account under this subsection) of any permitted property purchased by the taxpayer during the 60-day period beginning on the date of such sale.

Amendments

• **1990, Omnibus Budget Reconciliation Act of 1990 (P.L. 101-508)**

P.L. 101-508, § 11703(a)(1):

Amended Code Sec. 1043(a) by striking "reduced by any basis adjustment under subsection (c) attributable to a prior sale" and inserting "to the extent not previously taken into account under this subsection". **Effective** for sales after 11-30-89.

[Sec. 1043(b)]

(b) DEFINITIONS.—For purposes of this section—

(1) ELIGIBLE PERSON.—The term "eligible person" means—

(A) an officer or employee of the executive branch, or a judicial officer, of the Federal Government, but does not mean a special Government employee as defined in section 202 of title 18, United States Code, and

(B) any spouse or minor or dependent child whose ownership of any property is attributable under any statute, regulation, rule, judicial canon, or executive order referred to in paragraph (2) to a person referred to in subparagraph (A).

(2) CERTIFICATE OF DIVESTITURE.—The term "certificate of divestiture" means any written determination—

(A) that states that divestiture of specific property is reasonably necessary to comply with any Federal conflict of interest statute, regulation, rule, judicial canon, or executive order (including section 208 of title 18, United States Code), or requested by a congressional committee as a condition of confirmation,

(B) that has been issued by the President or the Director of the Office of Government Ethics, in the case of executive branch officers or employees, or by the Judicial Conference of the United States (or its designee), in the case of judicial officers, and

(C) that identifies the specific property to be divested.

(3) PERMITTED PROPERTY.—The term "permitted property" means any obligation of the United States or any diversified investment fund approved by regulations issued by the Office of Government Ethics.

(4) PURCHASE.—The taxpayer shall be considered to have purchased any permitted property if, but for subsection (c), the unadjusted basis of such property would be its cost within the meaning of section 1012.

(5) SPECIAL RULE FOR TRUSTS.—For purposes of this section, the trustee of a trust shall be treated as an eligible person with respect to property which is held in the trust if—

(A) any person referred to in paragraph (1)(A) has a beneficial interest in the principal or income of the trust, or

(B) any person referred to in paragraph (1)(B) has a beneficial interest in the principal or income of the trust and such interest is attributable under any statute, regulation, rule, judicial canon, or executive order referred to in paragraph (2) to a person referred to in paragraph (1)(A).

(6) JUDICIAL OFFICER.—The term "judicial officer" means the Chief Justice of the United States, the Associate Justices of the Supreme Court, and the judges of the United States courts of appeals, United States district courts, including the district courts in Guam, the Northern Mariana Islands, and the Virgin Islands, Court of Appeals for the Federal Circuit, Court of International Trade, Tax Court, Court of Federal Claims, Court of Appeals for Veterans Claims, United States Court of Appeals for the Armed Forces, and any court created by Act of Congress, the judges of which are entitled to hold office during good behavior.

Amendments

• **2006, Tax Relief and Health Care Act of 2006 (P.L. 109-432)**

P.L. 109-432, Division A, § 418(a)(1)(A)-(B):

Amended Code Sec. 1043(b)(1) by inserting ", or a judicial officer," after "an officer or employee of the executive branch" in subparagraph (A); and by inserting "judicial canon," after "any statute, regulation, rule," in subparagraph (B). **Effective** for sales after 12-20-2006.

P.L. 109-432, Division A, § 418(a)(2)(A)-(B):

Amended Code Sec. 1043(b)(2) by inserting "judicial canon," after "any Federal conflict of interest statute, regulation, rule," in subparagraph (A); and by inserting "in the case of executive branch officers or employees, or by the Judicial Conference of the United States (or its designee), in the case of judicial officers," after "the Director of the Office of Government Ethics," in subparagraph (B). **Effective** for sales after 12-20-2006.

P.L. 109-432, Division A, § 418(a)(3):

Amended Code Sec. 1043(b)(5)(B) by inserting "judicial canon," after "any statute, regulation, rule,". **Effective** for sales after 12-20-2006.

P.L. 109-432, Division A, § 418(b):

Amended Code Sec. 1043(b) by adding at the end a new paragraph (6). **Effective** for sales after 12-20-2006.

• **1990 (P.L. 101-280)**

P.L. 101-280, § 6(a)(1):

Amended Code Sec. 1043(b) by adding at the end thereof a new paragraph (5). **Effective** for sales after 11-30-89.

P.L. 101-280, § 6(a)(2), provides:

(2)(A) For purposes of section 1043 of such Code—

INCOME TAX—NONTAXABLE EXCHANGES

(i) any property sold before June 19, 1990, shall be treated as sold pursuant to a certificate of divestiture (as defined in subsection (b)(2) thereof) if such a certificate is issued with respect to such sale before such date, and

(ii) in any such case, the 60-day period referred to in subsection (a) thereof shall not expire before the end of the 60-day period beginning on the date on which the certificate of divestiture was issued.

(B) Notwithstanding subparagraph (A), section 1043 of such Code shall not apply to any sale before April 19, 1990, unless—

(i) the sale was made in order to comply with an ethics agreement or pursuant to specific direction from the appropriate agency or confirming committee, and

(ii) the justification for the sale meets the criteria set forth in subsection (b)(2)(A) thereof as implemented by the interim regulations implementing such section 1043, published on April 18, 1990.

[Sec. 1043(c)]

(c) BASIS ADJUSTMENTS.—If gain from the sale of any property is not recognized by reason of subsection (a), such gain shall be applied to reduce (in the order acquired) the basis for determining gain or loss of any permitted property which is purchased by the taxpayer during the 60-day period described in subsection (a).

Amendments

• **1989, Ethics Reform Act (P.L. 101-194)**

P.L. 101-194, § 502(a):

Amended part III of subchapter O of chapter 1 by adding at the end thereof a new section 1043. **Effective** for sales after 11-30-89.

[Sec. 1044—Stricken]

Amendments

• **2017, Tax Cuts and Jobs Act (P.L. 115-97)**

P.L. 115-97, § 13313(a):

Amended part III of subchapter O of chapter 1 by striking Code Sec. 1044. **Effective** for sales after 12-31-2017. Prior to being stricken, Code Sec. 1044 read as follows:

SEC. 1044. ROLLOVER OF PUBLICLY TRADED SECURITIES GAIN INTO SPECIALIZED SMALL BUSINESS INVESTMENT COMPANIES.

[Sec. 1044(a)]

(a) NONRECOGNITION OF GAIN.—In the case of the sale of any publicly traded securities with respect to which the taxpayer elects the application of this section, gain from such sale shall be recognized only to the extent that the amount realized on such sale exceeds—

(1) the cost of any common stock or partnership interest in a specialized small business investment company purchased by the taxpayer during the 60-day period beginning on the date of such sale, reduced by

(2) any portion of such cost previously taken into account under this section.

This section shall not apply to any gain which is treated as ordinary income for purposes of this subtitle.

[Sec. 1044(b)]

(b) LIMITATIONS.—

(1) LIMITATION ON INDIVIDUALS.—In the case of an individual, the amount of gain which may be excluded under subsection (a) for any taxable year shall not exceed the lesser of—

(A) $50,000, or

(B) $500,000, reduced by the amount of gain excluded under subsection (a) for all preceding taxable years.

(2) LIMITATION ON C CORPORATIONS.—In the case of a C corporation, the amount of gain which may be excluded under subsection (a) for any taxable year shall not exceed the lesser of—

(A) $250,000, or

(B) $1,000,000, reduced by the amount of gain excluded under subsection (a) for all preceding taxable years.

(3) SPECIAL RULES FOR MARRIED INDIVIDUALS.—For purposes of this subsection—

(A) SEPARATE RETURNS.—In the case of a separate return by a married individual, paragraph (1) shall be applied by substituting "$25,000" for "$50,000" and "$250,000" for "$500,000".

(B) ALLOCATION OF GAIN.—In the case of any joint return, the amount of gain excluded under subsection (a) for any taxable year shall be allocated equally between the spouses for purposes of applying this subsection to subsequent taxable years.

(C) MARITAL STATUS.—For purposes of this subsection, marital status shall be determined under section 7703.

(4) SPECIAL RULES FOR C CORPORATION.—For purposes of this subsection—

(A) all corporations which are members of the same controlled group of corporations (within the meaning of section 52(a)) shall be treated as 1 taxpayer, and

(B) any gain excluded under subsection (a) by a predecessor of any C corporation shall be treated as having been excluded by such C corporation.

[Sec. 1044(c)]

(c) DEFINITIONS AND SPECIAL RULES.—For purposes of this section—

(1) PUBLICLY TRADED SECURITIES.—The term "publicly traded securities" means securities which are traded on an established securities market.

(2) PURCHASE.—The taxpayer shall be considered to have purchased any property if, but for subsection (d), the unadjusted basis of such property would be its cost within the meaning of section 1012.

(3) SPECIALIZED SMALL BUSINESS INVESTMENT COMPANY.—The term "specialized small business investment company" means any partnership or corporation which is licensed by the Small Business Administration under section 301(d) of the Small Business Investment Act of 1958 (as in effect on May 13, 1993).

(4) CERTAIN ENTITIES NOT ELIGIBLE.—This section shall not apply to any estate, trust, partnership, or S corporation.

Amendments

• **1996, Small Business Job Protection Act of 1996 (P.L. 104-188)**

P.L. 104-188, § 1703(a):

Amended Code Sec. 1044(c)(2). **Effective** as if included in the provision of P.L. 103-66 to which such amendment relates. Prior to amendment, Code Sec. 1044(c)(2) read as follows:

(2) PURCHASE.—The term "purchase" has the meaning given such term by section 1043(b)(4).

[Sec. 1044(d)]

(d) BASIS ADJUSTMENTS.—If gain from any sale is not recognized by reason of subsection (a), such gain shall be applied to reduce (in the order acquired) the basis for determining gain or loss of any common stock or partnership interest in any specialized small business investment company which is purchased by the taxpayer during the 60-day period described in subsection (a). This subsection shall not apply for purposes of section 1202.

Amendments

• **1993, Omnibus Budget Reconciliation Act of 1993 (P.L. 103-66)**

P.L. 103-66, § 13114(a):

Amended Part III of subchapter O of chapter 1 by adding at the end a new section 1044. **Effective** for sales on and after 8-10-93, in tax years ending on and after such date.

[Sec. 1045]

SEC. 1045. ROLLOVER OF GAIN FROM QUALIFIED SMALL BUSINESS STOCK TO ANOTHER QUALIFIED SMALL BUSINESS STOCK.

[Sec. 1045(a)]

(a) NONRECOGNITION OF GAIN.—In the case of any sale of qualified small business stock held by a taxpayer other than a corporation for more than 6 months and with respect to which such taxpayer elects the application of this section, gain from such sale shall be recognized only to the extent that the amount realized on such sale exceeds—

(1) the cost of any qualified small business stock purchased by the taxpayer during the 60-day period beginning on the date of such sale, reduced by

(2) any portion of such cost previously taken into account under this section.

This section shall not apply to any gain which is treated as ordinary income for purposes of this title.

Amendments

• **1998, IRS Restructuring and Reform Act of 1998 (P.L. 105-206)**

P.L. 105-206, § 6005(f)(1)(A)-(B):

Amended Code Sec. 1045(a) by striking "an individual" and inserting "a taxpayer other than a corporation", and by striking "such individual" and inserting "such taxpayer". **Effective** as if included in the provision of P.L. 105-34 to which it relates [effective for sales after 8-5-97.—CCH].

[Sec. 1045(b)]

(b) DEFINITIONS AND SPECIAL RULES.—For purposes of this section—

(1) QUALIFIED SMALL BUSINESS STOCK.—The term "qualified small business stock" has the meaning given such term by section 1202(c).

(2) PURCHASE.—A taxpayer shall be treated as having purchased any property if, but for paragraph (3), the unadjusted basis of such property in the hands of the taxpayer would be its cost (within the meaning of section 1012).

INCOME TAX—SPECIAL RULES

(3) BASIS ADJUSTMENTS.—If gain from any sale is not recognized by reason of subsection (a), such gain shall be applied to reduce (in the order acquired) the basis for determining gain or loss of any qualified small business stock which is purchased by the taxpayer during the 60-day period described in subsection (a).

(4) HOLDING PERIOD.—For purposes of determining whether the nonrecognition of gain under subsection (a) applies to stock which is sold—

(A) the taxpayer's holding period for such stock and the stock referred to in subsection (a)(1) shall be determined without regard to section 1223, and

(B) only the first 6 months of the taxpayer's holding period for the stock referred to in subsection (a)(1) shall be taken into account for purposes of applying section 1202(c)(2).

(5) CERTAIN RULES TO APPLY.—Rules similar to the rules of subsections (f), (g), (h), (i), (j), and (k) of section 1202 shall apply.

Amendments

• **1998, IRS Restructuring and Reform Act of 1998 (P.L. 105-206)**

P.L. 105-206, §6005(f)(2):

Amended Code Sec. 1045(b) by adding at the end a new paragraph (5). **Effective** as if included in the provision of P.L. 105-34 to which it relates [effective for sales after 8-5-97.—CCH].

• **1997, Taxpayer Relief Act of 1997 (P.L. 105-34)**

P.L. 105-34, §313(a):

Amended part III of subchapter O of chapter 1 by adding at the end a new Code Sec. 1045. **Effective** for sales after 8-5-97.

PART IV—SPECIAL RULES

Sec. 1052.	Basis established by the Revenue Act of 1932 or 1934 or by the Internal Revenue Code of 1939.
Sec. 1053.	Property acquired before March 1, 1913.
Sec. 1054.	Certain stock of Federal National Mortgage Association.
Sec. 1055.	Redeemable ground rents.
Sec. 1058.	Transfer of securities under certain agreements.
Sec. 1059.	Corporate shareholder's basis in stock reduced by nontaxed portion of extraordinary dividends.
Sec. 1059A.	Limitation on taxpayer's basis or inventory cost in property imported from related persons.
Sec. 1060.	Special allocation rules for certain asset acquisitions.
Sec. 1061.	Partnership interests held in connection with performance of services.
Sec. 1062.	Cross references.

[Sec. 1051—Repealed]

Amendments

• **2014, Tax Technical Corrections Act of 2014 (P.L. 113-295)**

P.L. 113-295, §221(a)(78), Division A:

Repealed Code Sec. 1051. **Effective** generally 12-19-2014. For a special rule, see Act Sec. 221(b)(2), Division A, below.

P.L. 113-295, §221(b)(2), Division A, provides:

(2) SAVINGS PROVISION.—If—

(A) any provision amended or repealed by the amendments made by this section applied to—

(i) any transaction occurring before the date of the enactment of this Act,

(ii) any property acquired before such date of enactment, or

(iii) any item of income, loss, deduction, or credit taken into account before such date of enactment, and

(B) the treatment of such transaction, property, or item under such provision would (without regard to the amendments or repeals made by this section) affect the liability for tax for periods ending after date of enactment, nothing in the amendments or repeals made by this section shall be construed to affect the treatment of such transaction, property, or item for purposes of determining liability for tax for periods ending after such date of enactment.

Prior to repeal, Code Sec. 1051 read as follows:

SEC. 1051. PROPERTY ACQUIRED DURING AFFILIATION.

In the case of property acquired by a corporation, during a period of affiliation, from a corporation with which it was affiliated, the basis of such property, after such period of affiliation, shall be determined, in accordance with regulations prescribed by the Secretary, without regard to inter-company transactions in respect of which gain or loss was not recognized. For purposes of this section, the term "period of affiliation" means the period during which such corporations were affiliated (determined in accordance with the law applicable thereto) but does not include any taxable year beginning on or after January 1, 1922, unless a consolidated return was made, nor any taxable year after the taxable year 1928.

Amendments

• **1976, Tax Reform Act of 1976 (P.L. 94-455)**

P.L. 94-455, §1901(a)(131):

Struck out the last two sentences of Code Sec. 1051. **Effective** for tax years beginning after 12-31-76. Prior to striking, the last two sentences of Code Sec. 1051 read as follows:

The basis in case of property acquired by a corporation during any period, in the taxable year 1929 or any subsequent taxable year, in respect of which a consolidated return was made by such corporation under chapter 6 of this subtitle (sec. 1501 and following) or under section 141 or the Internal Revenue Code of 1939 or of the Revenue Act of 1938, 1936, 1934, 1932, or 1928 shall be determined in accordance with regulations prescribed under section 1502 or in accordance with regulations prescribed under the appropriate section 141, as the case may be. The basis in the case of property held by a corporation during any period, in the taxable year 1929 or any subsequent taxable year, in respect of which a consolidated return was made by such corporation under chapter 6 of this subtitle or such section 141 shall be adjusted in respect of any items relating to such period, in accordance with regulations prescribed under section 1502 or in accordance with regulations prescribed under the appropriate section 141, as the case may be.

P.L. 94-455, §1906(b)(13)(A):

Amended 1954 Code by substituting "Secretary" for "Secretary or his delegate" each place it appeared. **Effective** 2-1-77.

• **1976, Tax Reform Act of 1976 (P.L. 94-455)**

P.L. 94-455, §1901(a)(131):

Struck out the last two sentences of Code Sec. 1051. **Effective** for tax years beginning after 12-31-76. Prior to striking, the last two sentences of Code Sec. 1051 read as follows:

The basis in case of property acquired by a corporation during any period, in the taxable year 1929 or any subsequent taxable year, in respect of which a consolidated return was made by such corporation under chapter 6 of this subtitle (sec. 1501 and following) or under section 141 or the Internal Revenue Code of 1939 or of the Revenue Act of 1938, 1936, 1934, 1932, or 1928 shall be determined in accordance with regulations prescribed under section 1502 or in accordance with regulations prescribed under the appropriate section 141, as the case may be. The basis in case of property held by a corporation during any period, in the taxable year 1929 or any subsequent taxable year, in respect of which a consolidated return was made by such corporation under chapter 6 of this subtitle or such section 141 shall be adjusted in respect of any items relating to such period, in accordance with regulations prescribed under section 1502 or in accordance with regulations prescribed under the appropriate section 141, as the case may be.

P.L. 94-455, §1906(b)(13)(A):

Amended 1954 Code by substituting "Secretary" for "Secretary or his delegate" each place it appeared. **Effective** 2-1-77.

INCOME TAX—SPECIAL RULES

[Sec. 1052]
SEC. 1052. BASIS ESTABLISHED BY THE REVENUE ACT OF 1932 OR 1934 OR BY THE INTERNAL REVENUE CODE OF 1939.

[Sec. 1052(a)]
(a) REVENUE ACT OF 1932.—If the property was acquired, after February 28, 1913, in any taxable year beginning before January 1, 1934, and the basis thereof, for purposes of the Revenue Act of 1932 was prescribed by section 113(a)(6), (7), or (9) of such Act (47 Stat. 199), then for purposes of this subtitle the basis shall be the same as the basis therein prescribed in the Revenue Act of 1932.

[Sec. 1052(b)]
(b) REVENUE ACT OF 1934.—If the property was acquired, after February 28, 1913, in any taxable year beginning before January 1, 1936, and the basis thereof, for purposes of the Revenue Act of 1934, was prescribed by section 113(a)(6), (7), or (8) of such Act (48 Stat. 706), then for purposes of this subtitle the basis shall be the same as the basis therein prescribed in the Revenue Act of 1934.

[Sec. 1052(c)]
(c) INTERNAL REVENUE CODE OF 1939.—If the property was acquired, after February 28, 1913, in a transaction to which the Internal Revenue Code of 1939 applied, and the basis thereof, for purposes of the Internal Revenue Code of 1939, was prescribed by section 113(a)(6), (7), (8), (13), (15), (18), (19), or (23) of such code, then for purposes of this subtitle the basis shall be the same as the basis therein prescribed in the Internal Revenue Code of 1939.

[Sec. 1053]
SEC. 1053. PROPERTY ACQUIRED BEFORE MARCH 1, 1913.

In the case of property acquired before March 1, 1913, if the basis otherwise determined under this subtitle, adjusted (for the period before March 1, 1913) as provided in section 1016, is less than the fair market value of the property as of March 1, 1913, then the basis for determining gain shall be such fair market value. In determining the fair market value of stock in a corporation as of March 1, 1913, due regard shall be given to the fair market value of the assets of the corporation as of that date.

Amendments
• 1958, Technical Amendments Act of 1958 (P.L. 85-866)

P.L. 85-866, §47:
Struck out the phrase, in Sec. 1053, "under this part" and substituted the phrase "under this subtitle". **Effective** 1-1-54.

[Sec. 1054]
SEC. 1054. CERTAIN STOCK OF FEDERAL NATIONAL MORTGAGE ASSOCIATION.

In the case of a share of stock issued pursuant to section 303(c) of the Federal National Mortgage Association Charter Act (12 U.S.C., sec. 1718), the basis of such share in the hands of the initial holder shall be an amount equal to the capital contributions evidenced by such share reduced by the amount (if any) required by section 162(d) to be treated (with respect to such share) as ordinary and necessary expenses paid or incurred in carrying on a trade or business.

Amendments
P.L. 86-779, §8(b):
Redesignated Code Sec. 1054 as 1055 and added a new Code Sec. 1054. **Effective** for tax years beginning after 1959.

[Sec. 1055]
SEC. 1055. REDEEMABLE GROUND RENTS.

[Sec. 1055(a)]
(a) CHARACTER.—For purposes of this subtitle—
  (1) a redeemable ground rent shall be treated as being in the nature of a mortgage, and
  (2) real property held subject to liabilities under a redeemable ground rent shall be treated as held subject to liabilities under a mortgage.

[Sec. 1055(b)]
(b) APPLICATION OF SUBSECTION (a).—
  (1) IN GENERAL.—Subsection (a) shall take effect on the day after the date of the enactment of this section and shall apply with respect to taxable years ending after such date of enactment.
  (2) BASIS OF HOLDER.—In determining the basis of real property held subject to liabilities under a redeemable ground rent, subsection (a) shall apply whether such real property was acquired before or after the enactment of this section.
  (3) BASIS OF RESERVED REDEEMABLE GROUND RENT.—In the case of a redeemable ground rent reserved or created on or before the date of the enactment of this section in connection with a transfer of the right to hold real property subject to liabilities under such ground rent, the basis of such ground rent after such date in the hands of the person who reserved or created the ground rent shall be the amount taken into account in respect of such ground rent for Federal income tax purposes as consideration for the disposition of such real property. If no such amount was taken into account, such basis shall be determined as if this section had not been enacted.

[Sec. 1055(c)]
(c) REDEEMABLE GROUND RENT DEFINED.—For purposes of this subtitle, the term "redeemable ground rent" means only a ground rent with respect to which—
  (1) there is a lease of land which is assignable by the lessee without the consent of the lessor and which (together with periods for which the lease may be renewed at the option of the lessee) is for a term in excess of 15 years.
  (2) the leaseholder has a present or future right to terminate, and to acquire the entire interest of the lessor in the land, by payment of a determined or determinable amount, which right exists by virtue of State or local law and not because of any private agreement or privately created condition, and
  (3) the lessor's interest in the land is primarily a security interest to protect the rental payments to which the lessor is entitled under the lease.

[Sec. 1055(d)]
(d) CROSS REFERENCE.—
For treatment of rentals under redeemable ground rents as interest, see section 163(c).

INCOME TAX—SPECIAL RULES

Amendments

• **1963 (P.L. 88-9)**

P.L. 88-9, §1(b):

Redesignated Code Sec. 1055 as Code Sec. 1056 and added new Code Sec. 1055. **Effective** for tax years ending after 4-10-63.

[Sec. 1056—Repealed]

Amendments

• **2004, American Jobs Creation Act of 2004 (P.L. 108-357)**

P.L. 108-357, §886(b)(1)(A):

Repealed Code Sec. 1056. **Effective** for property acquired after 10-22-2004. Prior to repeal, Code Sec. 1056 read as follows:

SEC. 1056. BASIS LIMITATION FOR PLAYER CONTRACTS TRANSFERRED IN CONNECTION WITH THE SALE OF A FRANCHISE.

[Sec. 1056(a)]

(a) GENERAL RULE.—If a franchise to conduct any sports enterprise is sold or exchanged, and if, in connection with such sale or exchange, there is a transfer of a contract for the services of an athlete, the basis of such contract in the hands of the transferee shall not exceed the sum of—

(1) the adjusted basis of such contract in the hands of the transferor immediately before the transfer, plus

(2) the gain (if any) recognized by the transferor on the transfer of such contract.

Amendments

• **1986, Tax Reform Act of 1986 (P.L. 99-514)**

P.L. 99-514, §631(e)(13):

Amended Code Sec. 1056(a) by striking out the last sentence thereof. **Effective** for any distribution in complete liquidation, and any sale or exchange, made by a corporation after 7-31-86, unless such corporation is completely liquidated before 1-1-87, any transaction described in section 338 of the Internal Revenue Code of 1986 for which the acquisition date occurs after 12-31-86, and any distribution (not in complete liquidation) made after 12-31-86. However, see Act Sec. 633(b)-(f) under the amendment notes for Code Sec. 26. Prior to amendment, the last sentence of Code Sec. 1056(a) read as follows:

For purposes of this section, gain realized by the transferor on the transfer of such contract, but not recognized by reason of section 337(a), shall be treated as recognized to the extent recognized by the transferor's shareholders.

[Sec. 1056(b)]

(b) EXCEPTIONS.—Subsection (a) shall not apply—

(1) to an exchange described in section 1031 (relating to exchange of property held for productive use or investment), and

(2) to property in the hands of a person acquiring the property from a decedent or to whom the property passed from a decedent (within the meaning of section 1014(a)).

[Sec. 1056(c)]

(c) TRANSFEROR REQUIRED TO FURNISH CERTAIN INFORMATION.—Under regulations prescribed by the Secretary, the transfer[or] shall, at the times and in the manner provided in such regulations, furnish to the Secretary and to the transferee the following information:

(1) the amount which the transferor believes to be the adjusted basis referred to in paragraph (1) of subsection (a),

(2) the amount which the transferor believes to be the gain referred to in paragraph (2) of subsection (a), and

(3) any subsequent modification of either such amount.

To the extent provided in such regulations, the amounts furnished pursuant to the preceding sentence shall be binding on the transferor and on the transferee.

[Sec. 1056(d)]

(d) PRESUMPTION AS TO AMOUNT ALLOCABLE TO PLAYER CONTRACTS.—In the case of any sale or exchange described in subsection (a), it shall be presumed that not more than 50 percent of the consideration is allocable to contracts for the services of athletes unless it is established to the satisfaction of the Secretary that a specified amount in excess of 50 percent is properly allocable to such contracts. Nothing in the preceding sentence shall give rise to a presumption that an allocation of less than 50 percent of the consideration to contracts for the services of athletes is a proper allocation.

Amendments

• **1976, Tax Reform Act of 1976 (P.L. 94-455)**

P.L. 94-455, §212(a)(1):

Redesignated former Code Sec. 1056 as Code Sec. 1057 and added new Code Sec. 1056. **Effective** for sales or exchanges of franchises after 12-31-75, in tax years ending after such date.

[Sec. 1057—Repealed]

Amendments

• **1997, Taxpayer Relief Act of 1997 (P.L. 105-34)**

P.L. 105-34, §1131(c)[(d)](2):

Repealed Code Sec. 1057. **Effective** 8-5-97. Prior to repeal, Code Sec. 1057 read as follows:

SEC. 1057. ELECTION TO TREAT TRANSFER TO FOREIGN TRUST, ETC., AS TAXABLE EXCHANGE.

In lieu of payment of the tax imposed by section 1491, the taxpayer may elect (for purposes of this subtitle), at such time and in such manner as the Secretary may prescribe, to treat a transfer described in section 1491 as a sale or exchange of property for an amount equal in value to the fair market value of the property transferred and to recognize as gain the excess of—

(1) the fair market value of the property so transferred, over

(2) the adjusted basis (for determining gain) of such property in the hands of the transferor.

Amendments

• **1976, Tax Reform Act of 1976 (P.L. 94-455)**

P.L. 94-455, §1015(c):

Redesignated former Code Sec. 1057 as Code Sec. 1058 and added a new Code Sec. 1057. **Effective** for transfers of property after 10-2-75.

[Sec. 1058]

SEC. 1058. TRANSFER OF SECURITIES UNDER CERTAIN AGREEMENTS.

[Sec. 1058(a)]

(a) GENERAL RULE.—In the case of a taxpayer who transfers securities (as defined in section 1236(c)) pursuant to an agreement which meets the requirements of subsection (b), no gain or loss shall be recognized on the exchange of such securities by the taxpayer for an obligation under such agreement, or on the exchange of rights under such agreement by that taxpayer for securities identical to the securities transferred by that taxpayer.

[Sec. 1058(b)]

(b) AGREEMENT REQUIREMENTS.—In order to meet the requirements of this subsection, an agreement shall—

(1) provide for the return to the transferor of securities identical to the securities transferred;

(2) require that payments shall be made to the transferor of amounts equivalent to all interest, dividends, and other distributions which the owner of the securities is entitled to receive during the period beginning with the transfer of the securities by the transferor and ending with the transfer of identical securities back to the transferor;

(3) not reduce the risk of loss or opportunity for gain of the transferor of the securities in the securities transferred; and

(4) meet such other requirements as the Secretary may by regulation prescribe.

[Sec. 1058(c)]

(c) BASIS.—Property acquired by a taxpayer described in subsection (a), in a transaction described in that subsection, shall have the same basis as the property transferred by that taxpayer.

Amendments

• **1978 (P.L. 95-345)**

P.L. 95-345, §2(d)(1):

Added Code Sec. 1058. **Effective** for (1) amounts received after 12-31-76, as payments with respect to securities loans defined in Code Sec. 512(a)(5), and (2) transfers of securities under agreements described in Code Sec. 1058 occurring after such date.

INCOME TAX—SPECIAL RULES

[Sec. 1059]

SEC. 1059. CORPORATE SHAREHOLDER'S BASIS IN STOCK REDUCED BY NONTAXED PORTION OF EXTRAORDINARY DIVIDENDS.

[Sec. 1059(a)]

(a) GENERAL RULE.—If any corporation receives any extraordinary dividend with respect to any share of stock and such corporation has not held such stock for more than 2 years before the dividend announcement date—

(1) REDUCTION IN BASIS.—The basis of such corporation in such stock shall be reduced (but not below zero) by the nontaxed portion of such dividends.

(2) AMOUNTS IN EXCESS OF BASIS.—If the nontaxed portion of such dividends exceeds such basis, such excess shall be treated as gain from the sale or exchange of such stock for the taxable year in which the extraordinary dividend is received.

Amendments

- **1997, Taxpayer Relief Act of 1997 (P.L. 105-34)**

P.L. 105-34, §1011(a):

Amended Code Sec. 1059(a)(2). **Effective**, generally, for distributions after 5-3-95. For special and transitional rules, see Act Sec. 1011(d)(2)-(3), below. Prior to amendment, Code Sec. 1059(a)(2) read as follows:

(2) RECOGNITION UPON SALE OR DISPOSITION IN CERTAIN CASES.—In addition to any gain recognized under this chapter, there shall be treated as gain from the sale or exchange of any stock for the taxable year in which the sale or disposition of such stock occurs an amount equal to the aggregate nontaxed portions of any extraordinary dividends with respect to such stock which did not reduce the basis of such stock by reason of the limitation on reducing basis below zero.

P.L. 105-34, §1011(d)(2)-(3), provides:

(2) TRANSITION RULE.—The amendments made by this section shall not apply to any distribution made pursuant to the terms of—

(A) a written binding contract in effect on May 3, 1995, and at all times thereafter before such distribution, or

(B) a tender offer outstanding on May 3, 1995.

(3) CERTAIN DIVIDENDS NOT PURSUANT TO CERTAIN REDEMPTIONS.—In determining whether the amendment made by subsection (a) applies to any extraordinary dividend other than a dividend treated as an extraordinary dividend under section 1059(e)(1) of the Internal Revenue Code of 1986 (as amended by this Act), paragraphs (1) and (2) shall be applied by substituting "September 13, 1995" for "May 3, 1995".

- **1986, Tax Reform Act of 1986 (P.L. 99-514)**

P.L. 99-514, §614(a)(1):

Amended Code Sec. 1059(a). **Effective** for any dividend declared after 7-18-86, in tax years ending after such date. However, for an exception see Act Sec. 614(d)(2), below. Prior to amendment, Code Sec. 1059(a) read as follows:

(a) GENERAL RULE.—If any corporation—

(1) receives an extraordinary dividend with respect to any share of stock, and

(2) sells or otherwise disposes of such stock before such stock has been held for more than 1 year,

the basis of such corporation in such stock shall be reduced by the nontaxed portion of such dividend. If the nontaxed portion of such dividend exceeds such basis, such excess shall be treated as gain from the sale or exchange of such stock.

P.L. 99-514, §614(d)(2), provides:

(2) AGGREGATION.—For purposes of section 1059(c)(3) of the Internal Revenue Code of 1986, dividends declared after July 18, 1986, shall not be aggregated with dividends declared on or before July 18, 1986.

[Sec. 1059(b)]

(b) NONTAXED PORTION.—For purposes of this section—

(1) IN GENERAL.—The nontaxed portion of any dividend is the excess (if any) of—

(A) the amount of such dividend, over

(B) the taxable portion of such dividend.

(2) TAXABLE PORTION.—The taxable portion of any dividend is—

(A) the portion of such dividend includible in gross income, reduced by

(B) the amount of any deduction allowable with respect to such dividend under section 243[,] 245, or 245A.

Amendments

- **2017, Tax Cuts and Jobs Act (P.L. 115-97)**

P.L. 115-97, §14101(c)(2):

Amended Code Sec. 1059(b)(2)(B) by striking "or 245" and inserting "245, or 245A". **Effective** for distributions made after 12-31-2017.

- **2014, Tax Technical Corrections Act of 2014 (P.L. 113-295)**

P.L. 113-295, §221(a)(41)(G), Division A:

Amended Code Sec. 1059(b)(2)(B) by striking ", 244," following "section 243". **Effective** generally 12-19-2014. For a special rule, see Act Sec. 221(b)(2), Division A, below.

P.L. 113-295, §221(b)(2), Division A, provides:

(2) SAVINGS PROVISION.—If—

(A) any provision amended or repealed by the amendments made by this section applied to—

(i) any transaction occurring before the date of the enactment of this Act,

(ii) any property acquired before such date of enactment, or

(iii) any item of income, loss, deduction, or credit taken into account before such date of enactment, and

(B) the treatment of such transaction, property, or item under such provision would (without regard to the amendments or repeals made by this section) affect the liability for tax for periods ending after date of enactment, nothing in the amendments or repeals made by this section shall be construed to affect the treatment of such transaction, property, or item for purposes of determining liability for tax for periods ending after such date of enactment.

[Sec. 1059(c)]

(c) EXTRAORDINARY DIVIDEND DEFINED.—For purposes of this section—

(1) IN GENERAL.—The term "extraordinary dividend" means any dividend with respect to a share of stock if the amount of such dividend equals or exceeds the threshold percentage of the taxpayer's adjusted basis in such share of stock.

(2) THRESHOLD PERCENTAGE.—The term "theshold percentage" means—

(A) 5 percent in the case of stock which is preferred as to dividends, and

(B) 10 percent in the case of any other stock.

(3) AGGREGATION OF DIVIDENDS.—

(A) AGGREGATION WITHIN 85-DAY PERIOD.—All dividends—

(i) which are received by the taxpayer (or a person described in subparagraph (C)) with respect to any share of stock, and

(ii) which have ex-dividend dates within the same period of 85 consecutive days,

shall be treated as 1 dividend.

(B) AGGREGATION WITHIN 1 YEAR WHERE DIVIDENDS EXCEED 20 PERCENT OF ADJUSTED BASIS.—All dividends—

(i) which are received by the taxpayer (or a person described in subparagraph (C)) with respect to any share of stock, and

(ii) which have ex-dividend dates during the same period of 365 consecutive days,

shall be treated as extraordinary dividends if the aggregate of such dividends exceeds 20 percent of the taxpayer's adjusted basis in such stock (determined without regard to this section).

(C) SUBSTITUTED BASIS TRANSACTIONS.—In the case of any stock, a person is described in this subparagraph if—

(i) the basis of such stock in the hands of such person is determined in whole or in part by reference to the basis of such stock in the hands of the taxpayer, or

INCOME TAX—SPECIAL RULES

(ii) the basis of such stock in the hands of the taxpayer is determined in whole or in part by reference to the basis of such stock in the hands of such person.

(4) FAIR MARKET VALUE DETERMINATION.—If the taxpayer establishes to the satisfaction of the Secretary the fair market value of any share of stock as of the day before the ex-dividend date, the taxpayer may elect to apply paragraphs (1) and (3) by substituting such value for the taxpayer's adjusted basis.

Amendments

• **1986, Tax Reform Act of 1986 (P.L. 99-514)**

P.L. 99-514, § 614(b):

Amended Code Sec. 1059(c) by adding at the end thereof new paragraph (4). **Effective** for any dividend declared after 7-18-86, in tax years ending after such date. However, for an exception see Act Sec. 614(d)(2), below.

P.L. 99-514, § 614(c)(2):

Amended Code Sec. 1059(c)(1) by striking out "(determined without regard to this section)". **Effective** for any dividend declared after 7-18-86, in tax years ending after such date. However, for an exception see Act Sec. 614(d)(2), below.

P.L. 99-514, § 614(d)(2), provides:

(2) AGGREGATION.—For purposes of section 1059(c)(3) of the Internal Revenue Code of 1986, dividends declared after July 18, 1986, shall not be aggregated with dividends declared on or before July 18, 1986.

[Sec. 1059(d)]

(d) SPECIAL RULES.—For purposes of this section—

(1) TIME FOR REDUCTION.—Any reduction in basis under subsection (a)(1) shall be treated as occurring at the beginning of the ex-dividend date of the extraordinary dividend to which the reduction relates.

(2) DISTRIBUTIONS IN KIND.—To the extent any dividend consists of property other than cash, the amount of such dividend shall be treated as the fair market value of such property (as of the date of the distribution) reduced as provided in section 301(b)(2).

(3) DETERMINATION OF HOLDING PERIOD.—For purposes of determining the holding period of stock under subsection (a), rules similar to the rules of paragraphs (3) and (4) of section 246(c) shall apply and there shall not be taken into account any day which is more than 2 years after the date on which such share becomes ex-dividend.

(4) EX-DIVIDEND DATE.—The term "ex-dividend date" means the date on which the share of stock becomes ex-dividend.

(5) DIVIDEND ANNOUNCEMENT DATE.—The term "dividend announcement date" means, with respect to any dividend, the date on which the corporation declares, announces, or agrees to, the amount or payment of such dividend, whichever is the earliest.

(6) EXCEPTION WHERE STOCK HELD DURING ENTIRE EXISTENCE OF CORPORATION.—

(A) IN GENERAL.—Subsection (a) shall not apply to any extraordinary dividend with respect to any share of stock of a corporation if—

(i) such stock was held by the taxpayer during the entire period such corporation was in existence, and

(ii) except as provided in regulations, no earnings and profits of such corporation were attributable to transfers of property from (or earnings and profits of) a corporation which is not a qualified corporation.

(B) QUALIFIED CORPORATION.—For purposes of subparagraph (A), the term "qualified corporation" means any corporation (including a predecessor corporation)—

(i) with respect to which the taxpayer holds directly or indirectly during the entire period of such corporation's existence at least the same ownership interest as the taxpayer holds in the corporation distributing the extraordinary dividend, and

(ii) which has no earnings and profits—

(I) which were earned by, or

(II) which are attributable to gain on property which accrued during a period the corporation holding the property was,

a corporation not described in clause (i).

(C) APPLICATION OF PARAGRAPH.—This paragraph shall not apply to any extraordinary dividend to the extent such application is inconsistent with the purposes of this section.

Amendments

• **2018, Tax Technical Corrections Act of 2018 (P.L. 115-141)**

P.L. 115-141, § 401(a)(169), Div. U:

Amended Code Sec. 1059(d)(3) by striking "; except that" and all that follows and inserting "and there shall not be taken into account any day which is more than 2 years after the date on which such share becomes ex-dividend.". **Effective** 3-23-2018. Prior to amendment, Code Sec. 1059(d)(3) read as follows:

(3) DETERMINATION OF HOLDING PERIOD.—For purposes of determining the holding period of stock under subsection (a), rules similar to the rules of paragraphs (3) and (4) of section 246(c) shall apply; except that "2 years" shall be substituted for the number of days specified in subparagraph (B) of section 246(c)(3).

• **1997, Taxpayer Relief Act of 1997 (P.L. 105-34)**

P.L. 105-34, § 1011(c):

Amended Code Sec. 1059(d)(1). **Effective**, generally, for distributions after 5-3-95. For special and transitional rules, see Act Sec. 1011(d)(2)-(3) in the amendment notes following Code Sec. 1059(a). Prior to amendment, Code Sec. 1059(d)(1) read as follows:

(1) TIME FOR REDUCTION.—

(A) IN GENERAL.—Except as provided in subparagraph (B), any reduction in basis under subsection (a)(1) shall occur immediately before any sale or disposition of the stock.

(B) SPECIAL RULE FOR COMPUTING EXTRAORDINARY DIVIDEND.—In determining a taxpayer's adjusted basis for purposes of subsection (c)(1), any reduction in basis under subsection (a)(1) by reason of a prior distribution which was an extraordinary dividend shall be treated as occurring at the beginning of the ex-dividend date for such distribution.

P.L. 105-34, § 1604(d)(1):

Amended Code Sec. 1059(d)(3) by striking "subsection (a)(2)" and inserting "subsection (a)". **Effective** 8-5-97.

• **1988, Technical and Miscellaneous Revenue Act of 1988 (P.L. 100-647)**

P.L. 100-647, § 1006(c)(1):

Amended Code Sec. 1059(d) by striking paragraph (5) and redesignating paragraphs (6) and (7) as paragraphs (5) and (6). **Effective** as if included in the provision of P.L. 99-514 to which it relates. Prior to amendment, Code Sec. 1059(d)(5) read as follows:

(5) EXTENSION TO CERTAIN PROPERTY DISTRIBUTIONS.—In the case of any distribution of property (other than cash) to which section 301 applies—

(A) such distribution shall be treated as a dividend without regard to whether the corporation has earnings and profits, and

(B) the amount so treated shall be reduced by the amount of any reduction in basis under section 301(c)(2) by reason of such distribution.

P.L. 100-647, § 1006(c)(2):

Amended Code Sec. 1059(d)(5), as redesignated by Act Sec. 1006(c)(1), by inserting "amount or" before "payment". **Effective** as if included in the provision of P.L. 99-514 to which it relates.

P.L. 100-647, § 1006(c)(3):

Amended Code Sec. 1059(d)(6), as redesignated by Act Sec. 1006(c)(1). **Effective** as if included in the provision of P.L. 99-514 to which it relates. Prior to amendment, Code Sec. 1059(d)(6) read as follows:

(6) EXCEPTION WHERE STOCK HELD DURING ENTIRE EXISTENCE OF CORPORATION.—Subsection (a) shall not apply to any extraordinary dividend with respect to any share of stock of a corporation if—

(A) such stock was held by the taxpayer during the entire period such corporation (and any predecessor corporation) was in existence,

(B) except as provided in regulations, the only earnings and profits of such corporation were earnings and profits accumulated by such corporation (or any predecessor corporation) during such period, and

(C) the application of this paragraph to such dividend is not inconsistent with the purposes of this section.

• **1986, Tax Reform Act of 1986 (P.L. 99-514)**

P.L. 99-514, § 614(a)(2):

Amended Code Sec. 1059(d) by adding at the end thereof new paragraph (6). **Effective** for any dividend declared after 7-18-86, in tax years ending after such date. However, for an exception see Act Sec. 614(d)(2), below.

P.L. 99-514, § 614(a)(3):

Amended Code Sec. 1059(d)(3) by striking out "1 year" and inserting in lieu thereof "2 years". **Effective** for any dividend declared after 7-18-86, in tax years ending after such date. However, for an exception see Act Sec. 614(d)(2), below.

INCOME TAX—SPECIAL RULES

P.L. 99-514, § 614(c)(1):

Amended Code Sec. 1059(d)(1). **Effective** for any dividend declared after 7-18-86, in tax years ending after such date. However, for an exception see Act Sec. 614(d)(2), below. Prior to amendment, Code Sec. 1059(d)(1) read as follows:

(1) TIME FOR REDUCTION.—Any reduction in basis under subsection (a) by reason of any distribution which is an extraordinary dividend shall occur at the beginning of the ex-dividend date for such distribution.

P.L. 99-514, § 614(d):

Amended Code Sec. 1059(d) by adding at the end thereof new paragraph (7). **Effective** for any dividend declared after 7-18-86, in tax years ending after such date. However, for an exception see Act Sec. 614(d)(2), below.

P.L. 99-514, § 614(d)(2), provides:

(2) AGGREGATION.—For purposes of section 1059(c)(3) of the Internal Revenue Code of 1986, dividends declared after July 18, 1986, shall not be aggregated with dividends declared on or before July 18, 1986.

[Sec. 1059(e)]

(e) SPECIAL RULES FOR CERTAIN DISTRIBUTIONS.—

(1) TREATMENT OF PARTIAL LIQUIDATIONS AND CERTAIN REDEMPTIONS.—Except as otherwise provided in regulations—

(A) REDEMPTIONS.—In the case of any redemption of stock—

(i) which is part of a partial liquidation (within the meaning of section 302(e)) of the redeeming corporation,

(ii) which is not pro rata as to all shareholders, or

(iii) which would not have been treated (in whole or in part) as a dividend if—

(I) any options had not been taken into account under section 318(a)(4), or

(II) section 304(a) had not applied,

any amount treated as a dividend with respect to such redemption shall be treated as an extraordinary dividend to which paragraphs (1) and (2) of subsection (a) apply without regard to the period the taxpayer held such stock. In the case of a redemption described in clause (iii), only the basis in the stock redeemed shall be taken into account under subsection (a).

(B) REORGANIZATIONS, ETC.—An exchange described in section 356 which is treated as a dividend shall be treated as a redemption of stock for purposes of applying subparagraph (A).

(2) QUALIFYING DIVIDENDS.—

(A) IN GENERAL.—Except as provided in regulations, the term "extraordinary dividend" does not include any qualifying dividend (within the meaning of section 243).

(B) EXCEPTION.—Subparagraph (A) shall not apply to any portion of a dividend which is attributable to earnings and profits which—

(i) were earned by a corporation during a period it was not a member of the affiliated group, or

(ii) are attributable to gain on property which accrued during a period the corporation holding the property was not a member of the affiliated group.

(3) QUALIFIED PREFERRED DIVIDENDS.—

(A) IN GENERAL.—In the case of 1 or more qualified preferred dividends with respect to any share of stock—

(i) this section shall not apply to such dividends if the taxpayer holds such stock for more than 5 years, and

(ii) if the taxpayer disposes of such stock before it has been held for more than 5 years, the aggregate reduction under subsection (a)(1) with respect to such dividends shall not be greater than the excess (if any) of—

(I) the qualified preferred dividends paid with respect to such stock during the period the taxpayer held such stock, over

(II) the qualified preferred dividends which would have been paid during such period on the basis of the stated rate of return.

(B) RATE OF RETURN.—For the purposes of this paragraph—

(i) ACTUAL RATE OF RETURN.—The actual rate of return shall be the rate of return for the period for which the taxpayer held the stock, determined—

(I) by only taking into account dividends during such period, and

(II) by using the lesser of the adjusted basis of the taxpayer in such stock or the liquidation preference of such stock.

(ii) STATED RATE OF RETURN.—The stated rate of return shall be the annual rate of the qualified preferred dividend payable with respect to any share of stock (expressed as a percentage of the amount described in clause (i)(II)).

(C) DEFINITIONS AND SPECIAL RULES.—For purposes of this paragraph—

(i) QUALIFIED PREFERRED DIVIDEND.—The term "qualified preferred dividend" means any fixed dividend payable with respect to any share of stock which—

(I) provides for fixed preferred dividends payable not less frequently than annually, and

(II) is not in arrears as to dividends at the time the taxpayer acquires the stock.

Such term shall not include any dividend payable with respect to any share of stock if the actual rate of return on such stock exceeds 15 percent.

(ii) HOLDING PERIOD.—In determining the holding period for purposes of subparagraph (A)(ii), subsection (d)(3) shall be applied by substituting "5 years" for "2 years".

Amendments

• **1997, Taxpayer Relief Act of 1997 (P.L. 105-34)**

P.L. 105-34, § 1011(b):

Amended Code Sec. 1059(e)(1). **Effective**, generally, for distributions after 5-3-95. For special and transitional rules, see Act Sec. 1011(d)(2)-(3) in the amendment notes following Code Sec. 1059(a). Prior to amendment, Code Sec. 1059(e)(1) read as follows:

(1) TREATMENT OF PARTIAL LIQUIDATIONS AND NON-PRO RATA REDEMPTIONS.—Except as otherwise provided in regulations, in the case of any redemption of stock which is—

(A) part of a partial liquidation (within the meaning of section 302(e)) of the redeeming corporation, or

(B) not pro rata as to all shareholders,

any amount treated as a dividend under section 301 with respect to such redemption shall be treated as an extraordinary dividend to which paragraphs (1) and (2) of subsection (a) apply without regard to the period the taxpayer held such stock.

P.L. 105-34, § 1013(b):

Amended Code Sec. 1059(e)(1)(A)(iii), as amended by Act Sec. 1011(b). **Effective** for distributions and acquisitions after 6-8-97. For a transitional rule, see Act Sec. 1013(d)(2), below. Prior to amendment, Code Sec. 1059(e)(1)(A)(iii) read as follows:

(iii) which would not have been treated (in whole or in part) as a dividend if any options had not been taken into account under section 318(a)(4),

P.L. 105-34, § 1013(d)(2), provides:

(2) TRANSITION RULE.—The amendments made by this section shall not apply to any distribution or acquisition after June 8, 1997, if such distribution or acquisition is—

(A) made pursuant to a written agreement which was binding on such date and at all times thereafter,

(B) described in a ruling request submitted to the Internal Revenue Service on or before such date, or

(C) described in a public announcement or filing with the Securities and Exchange Commission on or before such date.

INCOME TAX—SPECIAL RULES

• **1988, Technical and Miscellaneous Revenue Act of 1988 (P.L. 100-647)**

P.L. 100-647, §1006(c)(4):

Amended Code Sec. 1059(e)(1) by striking out "for purposes of this section (without regard to the holding period of the stock)" and inserting in lieu thereof "to which paragraphs (1) and (2) of subsection (a) apply without regard to the period the taxpayer held such stock". **Effective** as if included in the provision of P.L. 99-514 to which it relates.

P.L. 100-647, §1006(c)(5):

Amended Code Sec. 1059(e)(2). **Effective** as if included in the provision of P.L. 99-514 to which it relates. Prior to amendment, Code Sec. 1059(e)(2) read as follows:

(2) QUALIFYING DIVIDENDS.—Except as provided in regulations, the term "extraordinary dividend" shall not include any qualifying dividend (within the meaning of section 243(b)(1)).

P.L. 100-647, §1006(c)(6):

Amended Code Sec. 1059(e)(3)(A). **Effective** as if included in the provision of P.L. 99-514 to which it relates. Prior to amendment, Code Sec. 1059(e)(3)(A) read as follows:

(A) IN GENERAL.—A qualified preferred dividend shall be treated as an extraordinary dividend—

(i) only if the actual rate of return of the taxpayer on the stock with respect to which such dividend was paid exceeds 15 percent, or

(ii) if clause (i) does not apply, and the taxpayer disposes of such stock before the taxpayer has held such stock for more than 5 years, only to the extent the actual rate of return exceeds the stated rate of return.

P.L. 100-647, §1006(c)(7)(A)-(B):

Amended Code Sec. 1059(e)(3)(C)(i) by striking out "any dividend payable" and inserting in lieu thereof "any fixed dividend payable", and by adding at the end thereof a new sentence. **Effective** as if included in the provision of P.L. 99-514 to which it relates.

P.L. 100-647, §1006(c)(8)(A)-(B):

Amended Code Sec. 1059(e)(3)(B) by striking out "subparagraph (A)" in the material preceding clause (i) and inserting in lieu thereof "this paragraph", and by striking out "subparagraph (B)(i)(II)" in clause (ii) and inserting in lieu thereof "clause (i)(II)". **Effective** as if included in the provision of P.L. 99-514 to which it relates.

• **1986, Tax Reform Act of 1986 (P.L. 99-514)**

P.L. 99-514, §614(e):

Amended Code Sec. 1059 by redesignating subsection (e) as subsection (f) and by adding after subsection (d) new subsection (e). **Effective** for dividends declared after 10-22-86, in tax years ending after such date.

[Sec. 1059(f)]

(f) TREATMENT OF DIVIDENDS ON CERTAIN PREFERRED STOCK.—

(1) IN GENERAL.—Any dividend with respect to disqualified preferred stock shall be treated as an extraordinary dividend to which paragraphs (1) and (2) of subsection (a) apply without regard to the period the taxpayer held the stock.

(2) DISQUALIFIED PREFERRED STOCK.—For purposes of this subsection, the term "disqualified preferred stock" means any stock which is preferred as to dividends if—

(A) when issued, such stock has a dividend rate which declines (or can reasonably be expected to decline) in the future,

(B) the issue price of such stock exceeds its liquidation rights or its stated redemption price, or

(C) such stock is otherwise structured—

(i) to avoid the other provisions of this section, and

(ii) to enable corporate shareholders to reduce tax through a combination of dividend received deductions and loss on the disposition of the stock.

Amendments

• **1989, Omnibus Budget Reconciliation Act of 1989 (P.L. 101-239)**

P.L. 101-239, §7206(a):

Amended Code Sec. 1059 by striking subsection (f) and inserting a new subsection (f). **Effective** for stock issued after 7-10-89, in tax years ending after such date, except as provided in Act Sec. 7206(b)(2), below. Prior to amendment, Code Sec. 1059(f) read as follows:

(f) REGULATIONS.—The Secretary shall prescribe such regulations as may be appropriate to carry out the purposes of this section, including regulations providing for the application of this section in the case of stock dividends, stock splits, reorganizations, and other similar transactions and in the case of stock held by pass-thru entities.

P.L. 101-239, §7206(b)(2), provides:

(2) BINDING CONTRACT.—The amendment made by subsection (a) shall not apply to any stock issued pursuant to a written binding contract in effect on July 10, 1989, and at all times thereafter before the stock is issued.

• **1988, Technical and Miscellaneous Revenue Act of 1988 (P.L. 100-647)**

P.L. 100-647, §1006(c)(9):

Amended Code Sec. 1059(f) by inserting before the period at the end thereof "and in the case of stock held by pass-thru entities". **Effective** as if included in the provision of P.L. 99-514 to which it relates.

• **1986, Tax Reform Act of 1986 (P.L. 99-514)**

P.L. 99-514, §614(e):

Amended Code Sec. 1059 by redesignating subsection (e) as subsection (f) and by adding after subsection (d) new subsection (e). **Effective** for dividends declared after 10-22-86, in tax years ending after such date.

• **1984, Deficit Reduction Act of 1984 (P.L. 98-369)**

P.L. 98-369, §53(a):

Amended Part IV of subchapter O of chapter 1 by redesignating Code Sec. 1059 as Code Sec. 1060 and by inserting after section 1058 a new section 1059. **Effective** for distributions after 3-1-84, in tax years ending after such date.

[Sec. 1059(g)]

(g) REGULATIONS.—The Secretary shall prescribe such regulations as may be appropriate to carry out the purposes of this section, including regulations—

(1) providing for the application of this section in the case of stock dividends, stock splits, reorganizations, and other similar transactions, in the case of stock held by pass-thru entities, and in the case of consolidated groups, and

(2) providing that the rules of subsection (f) shall apply in the case of stock which is not preferred as to dividends in cases where stock is structured to avoid the purposes of this section.

Amendments

• **1998, IRS Restructuring and Reform Act of 1998 (P.L. 105-206)**

P.L. 105-206, §6010(b):

Amended Code Sec. 1059(g)(1) by striking "and in the case of stock held by pass-thru entities" and inserting ", in the case of stock held by pass-thru entities, and in the case of consolidated groups". **Effective** as if included in the provision of P.L. 105-34 to which it relates [generally effective for distributions after 5-3-95.—CCH].

• **1989, Omnibus Budget Reconciliation Act of 1989 (P.L. 101-239)**

P.L. 101-239, §7206(a):

Amended Code Sec. 1059 by striking subsection (f) and inserting new subsections (f)-(g). **Effective** for stock issued after 7-10-89, in tax years ending after such date, except as provided in Act Sec. 7206(b)(2), below.

P.L. 101-239, §7206(b)(2), provides:

(2) BINDING CONTRACT.—The amendment made by subsection (a) shall not apply to any stock issued pursuant to a written binding contract in effect on July 10, 1989, and at all times thereafter before the stock is issued.

[Sec. 1059A]

SEC. 1059A. LIMITATION ON TAXPAYER'S BASIS OR INVENTORY COST IN PROPERTY IMPORTED FROM RELATED PERSONS.

[Sec. 1059A(a)]

(a) IN GENERAL.—If any property is imported into the United States in a transaction (directly or indirectly) between related persons (within the meaning of section 482), the amount of any costs—

(1) which are taken into account in computing the basis or inventory cost of such property by the purchaser, and

(2) which are also taken into account in computing the customs value of such property,

shall not, for purposes of computing such basis or inventory cost for purposes of this chapter, be greater than the amount of such costs taken into account in computing such customs value.

Sec. 1059(f)

INCOME TAX—SPECIAL RULES

[Sec. 1059A(b)]

(b) CUSTOMS VALUE; IMPORT.—For purposes of this section—

(1) CUSTOMS VALUE.—The term "customs value" means the value taken into account for purposes of determining the amount of any customs duties or any other duties which may be imposed on the importation of any property.

(2) IMPORT.—Except as provided in regulations, the term "import" means the entering, or withdrawal from warehouse, for consumption.

Amendments

• **1986, Tax Reform Act of 1986 (P.L. 99-514)**

P.L. 99-514, §1248(a):

Amended part IV of subchapter O of chapter 1 by inserting after section 1059 new section 1059A. **Effective** for transactions entered into after 3-18-86.

SEC. 1060. SPECIAL ALLOCATION RULES FOR CERTAIN ASSET ACQUISITIONS.

[Sec. 1060(a)]

(a) GENERAL RULE.—In the case of any applicable asset acquisition, for purposes of determining both—

(1) the transferee's basis in such assets, and

(2) the gain or loss of the transferor with respect to such acquisition,

the consideration received for such assets shall be allocated among such assets acquired in such acquisition in the same manner as amounts are allocated to assets under section 338(b)(5). If in connection with an applicable asset acquisition, the transferee and transferor agree in writing as to the allocation of any consideration, or as to the fair market value of any of the assets, such agreement shall be binding on both the transferee and transferor unless the Secretary determines that such allocation (or fair market value) is not appropriate.

Amendments

• **1990, Omnibus Budget Reconciliation Act of 1990 (P.L. 101-508)**

P.L. 101-508, §1132(a):

Amended Code Sec. 1060(a) by adding at the end thereof a new sentence. **Effective**, generally, for acquisitions after 10-9-90. For an exception, see 11323(d)(2), below.

P.L. 101-508, §11323(d)(2), provides:

(2) BINDING CONTRACT EXCEPTION.—The amendments made by this section shall not apply to any acquisition pursuant to a written binding contract in effect on October 9, 1990, and at all times thereafter before such acquisition.

[Sec. 1060(b)]

(b) INFORMATION REQUIRED TO BE FURNISHED TO SECRETARY.—Under regulations, the transferor and transferee in an applicable asset acquisition shall, at such times and in such manner as may be provided in such regulations, furnish to the Secretary the following information:

(1) The amount of the consideration received for the assets which is allocated to Section 197 intangibles.

(2) Any modification of the amount described in paragraph (1).

(3) Any other information with respect to other assets transferred in such acquisition as the Secretary deems necessary to carry out the provisions of this section.

Amendments

• **1993, Omnibus Budget Reconciliation Act of 1993 (P.L. 103-66)**

P.L. 103-66, §13261(e)(1):

Amended Code Sec. 1060(b)(1) by striking "goodwill or going concern value" and inserting "section 197 intangibles". **Effective**, generally, with respect to property acquired after 8-10-93. For special rules, see Act Sec. 13261(g)(2)-(3) in the amendment notes following Code Sec. 197.

• **1988, Technical and Miscellaneous Revenue Act of 1988 (P.L. 100-647)**

P.L. 100-647, §1006(h)(1):

Amended Code Sec. 1060(b)(3) by striking out "the Secretary may find necessary" and inserting in lieu thereof "the Secretary deems necessary". **Effective** as if included in the provision of P.L. 99-514 to which it relates.

[Sec. 1060(c)]

(c) APPLICABLE ASSET ACQUISITION.—For purposes of this section, the term "applicable asset acquisition" means any transfer (whether directly or indirectly)—

(1) of assets which constitute a trade or business, and

(2) with respect to which the transferee's basis in such assets is determined wholly by reference to the consideration paid for such assets.

A transfer shall not be treated as failing to be an applicable asset acquisition merely because section 1031 applies to a portion of the assets transferred.

Amendments

• **1986, Tax Reform Act of 1986 (P.L. 99-514)**

P.L. 99-514, §641(a):

Amended part IV of subchapter O of chapter 1 by redesignating section 1060 as section 1061 and by inserting after section 1059 new section 1060. **Effective** for any acquisition of assets after 5-6-86, unless such acquisition is pursuant to a binding contract which was in effect on 5-6-86, and at all times thereafter.

[Sec. 1060(d)]

(d) TREATMENT OF CERTAIN PARTNERSHIP TRANSACTIONS.—In the case of a distribution of partnership property or a transfer of an interest in a partnership—

(1) the rules of subsection (a) shall apply but only for purposes of determining the value of section 197 intangibles for purposes of applying section 755, and

(2) if section 755 applies, such distribution or transfer (as the case may be) shall be treated as an applicable asset acquisition for purposes of subsection (b).

Amendments

• **1993, Omnibus Budget Reconciliation Act of 1993 (P.L. 103-66)**

P.L. 103-66, §13261(e)(2):

Amended Code Sec. 1060(d)(1) by striking "goodwill or going concern value (or similar items)" and inserting "section 197 intangibles". **Effective**, generally, for property acquired after 8-10-93. For special rules, see Act Sec. 13261(g)(2)-(3) in the amendment notes following Code Sec. 197.

• **1988, Technical and Miscellaneous Revenue Act of 1988 (P.L. 100-647)**

P.L. 100-647, §1006(h)(2):

Amended Code Sec. 1060 by adding at the end thereof new subsection (d). **Effective** as if included in the provision of P.L. 99-514 to which it relates.

[Sec. 1060(e)]

(e) INFORMATION REQUIRED IN CASE OF CERTAIN TRANSFERS OF INTERESTS IN ENTITIES.—

(1) IN GENERAL.—If—

(A) a person who is a 10-percent owner with respect to any entity transfers an interest in such entity, and

(B) in connection with such transfer, such owner (or a related person) enters into an employment contract, covenant not to compete, royalty or lease agreement, or other agreement with the transferee,

Internal Revenue Code   Sec. 1060(e)(1)(B)

INCOME TAX—SPECIAL RULES

such owner and the transferee shall, at such time and in such manner as the Secretary may prescribe, furnish such information as the Secretary may require.

(2) 10-PERCENT OWNER.—For purposes of this subsection—

(A) IN GENERAL.—The term "10-percent owner" means, with respect to any entity, any person who holds 10 percent or more (by value) of the interests in such entity immediately before the transfer.

(B) CONSTRUCTIVE OWNERSHIP.—Section 318 shall apply in determining ownership of stock in a corporation. Similar principles shall apply in determining the ownership of interests in any other entity.

(3) RELATED PERSON.—For purposes of this subsection, the term "related person" means any person who is related (within the meaning of section 267(b) or 707(b)(1)) to the 10-percent owner.

Amendments

• 1990, Omnibus Budget Reconciliation Act of 1990 (P.L. 101-508)

P.L. 101-508, §11323(b)(1):

Amended Code Sec. 1060 by redesignating subsection (e) as subsection (f) and by inserting after subsection (d) a new subsection (e). **Effective**, generally, for acquisitions after 10-9-90. For an exception, see 11323(d)(2), below.

P.L. 101-508, §11323(d)(2), provides:

(2) BINDING CONTRACT EXCEPTION.—The amendments made by this section shall not apply to any acquisition pursuant to a written binding contract in effect on October 9, 1990, and at all times thereafter before such acquisition.

[Sec. 1060(f)]

(f) CROSS REFERENCE.—

For provisions relating to penalties for failure to file a return required by this section, see section 6721.

Amendments

• 1990, Omnibus Budget Reconciliation Act of 1990 (P.L. 101-508)

P.L. 101-508, §11323(b)(1):

Amended Code Sec. 1060 by redesignating subsection (e) as subsection (f). **Effective**, generally, for acquisitions after 10-9-90. For an exception, see 11323(d)(2), below.

P.L. 101-508, §11323(d)(2), provides:

(2) BINDING CONTRACT EXCEPTION.—The amendments made by this section shall not apply to any acquisition pursuant to a written binding contract in effect on October 9, 1990, and at all times thereafter before such acquisition.

• 1988, Technical and Miscellaneous Revenue Act of 1988 (P.L. 100-647)

P.L. 100-647, §1006(h)(3)(B):

Amended Code Sec. 1060 by adding at the end thereof new subsection (e). **Effective** as if included in the provision of P.L. 99-514 to which it relates.

[Sec. 1061]

SEC. 1061. PARTNERSHIP INTERESTS HELD IN CONNECTION WITH PERFORMANCE OF SERVICES.

[Sec. 1061(a)]

(a) IN GENERAL.—If one or more applicable partnership interests are held by a taxpayer at any time during the taxable year, the excess (if any) of—

(1) the taxpayer's net long-term capital gain with respect to such interests for such taxable year, over

(2) the taxpayer's net long-term capital gain with respect to such interests for such taxable year computed by applying paragraphs (3) and (4) of sections [sic] 1222 by substituting "3 years" for "1 year",

shall be treated as short-term capital gain, notwithstanding section 83 or any election in effect under section 83(b).

[Sec. 1061(b)]

(b) SPECIAL RULE.—To the extent provided by the Secretary, subsection (a) shall not apply to income or gain attributable to any asset not held for portfolio investment on behalf of third party investors.

[Sec. 1061(c)]

(c) APPLICABLE PARTNERSHIP INTEREST.—For purposes of this section—

(1) IN GENERAL.—Except as provided in this paragraph or paragraph (4), the term "applicable partnership interest" means any interest in a partnership which, directly or indirectly, is transferred to (or is held by) the taxpayer in connection with the performance of substantial services by the taxpayer, or any other related person, in any applicable trade or business. The previous sentence shall not apply to an interest held by a person who is employed by another entity that is conducting a trade or business (other than an applicable trade or business) and only provides services to such other entity.

(2) APPLICABLE TRADE OR BUSINESS.—The term "applicable trade or business" means any activity conducted on a regular, continuous, and substantial basis which, regardless of whether the activity is conducted in one or more entities, consists, in whole or in part, of—

(A) raising or returning capital, and

(B) either—

(i) investing in (or disposing of) specified assets (or identifying specified assets for such investing or disposition), or

(ii) developing specified assets.

(3) SPECIFIED ASSET.—The term "specified asset" means securities (as defined in section 475(c)(2) without regard to the last sentence thereof), commodities (as defined in section 475(e)(2)), real estate held for rental or investment, cash or cash equivalents, options or derivative contracts with respect to any of the foregoing, and an interest in a partnership to the extent of the partnership's proportionate interest in any of the foregoing.

(4) EXCEPTIONS.—The term "applicable partnership interest" shall not include—

(A) any interest in a partnership directly or indirectly held by a corporation, or

(B) any capital interest in the partnership which provides the taxpayer with a right to share in partnership capital commensurate with—

(i) the amount of capital contributed (determined at the time of receipt of such partnership interest), or

(ii) the value of such interest subject to tax under section 83 upon the receipt or vesting of such interest.

(5) THIRD PARTY INVESTOR.—The term "third party investor" means a person who—

(A) holds an interest in the partnership which does not constitute property held in connection with an applicable trade or business; and

(B) is not (and has not been) actively engaged, and is (and was) not related to a person so engaged, in (directly or indirectly) providing substantial services described in paragraph (1) for such partnership or any applicable trade or business.

Sec. 1060(e)(2)

INCOME TAX—CHANGES FOR F.C.C. POLICY

[Sec. 1061(d)]

(d) TRANSFER OF APPLICABLE PARTNERSHIP INTEREST TO RELATED PERSON.—

(1) IN GENERAL.—If a taxpayer transfers any applicable partnership interest, directly or indirectly, to a person related to the taxpayer, the taxpayer shall include in gross income (as short term capital gain) the excess (if any) of—

(A) so much of the taxpayer's long-term capital gains with respect to such interest for such taxable year attributable to the sale or exchange of any asset held for not more than 3 years as is allocable to such interest, over

(B) any amount treated as short term capital gain under subsection (a) with respect to the transfer of such interest.

(2) RELATED PERSON.—For purposes of this paragraph, a person is related to the taxpayer if—

(A) the person is a member of the taxpayer's family within the meaning of section 318(a)(1), or

(B) the person performed a service within the current calendar year or the preceding three calendar years in any applicable trade or business in which or for which the taxpayer performed a service.

[Sec. 1061(e)]

(e) REPORTING.—The Secretary shall require such reporting (at the time and in the manner prescribed by the Secretary) as is necessary to carry out the purposes of this section.

[Sec. 1061(f)]

(f) REGULATIONS.—The Secretary shall issue such regulations or other guidance as is necessary or appropriate to carry out the purposes of this section.

Amendments

• **2017, Tax Cuts and Jobs Act (P.L. 115-97)**

P.L. 115-97, §13309(a)(1)-(2):

Amended part IV of subchapter O of chapter 1 by redesignating Code Sec. 1061 as Code Sec. 1062, and by inserting after Code Sec. 1060 a new Code Sec. 1061. **Effective** for tax years beginning after 12-31-2017.

[Sec. 1062]

SEC. 1062. CROSS REFERENCES.

(1) For nonrecognition of gain in connection with the transfer of obsolete vessels to the Maritime Administration under chapter 573 of title 46, United States Code, see section 57307 of title 46.

(2) For recognition of gain or loss in connection with the construction of new vessels, see chapter 533 of title 46, United States Code.

Amendments

• **2017, Tax Cuts and Jobs Act (P.L. 115-97)**

P.L. 115-97, §13309(a)(1)-(2):

Amended part IV of subchapter O of chapter 1 by redesignating Code Sec. 1061 as Code Sec. 1062. **Effective** for tax years beginning after 12-31-2017.

• **2006 (P.L. 109-304)**

P.L. 109-304, §17(e)(5)(A)-(C):

Amended Code Sec. 1061 by striking "section 510 of the Merchant Marine Act, 1936, see subsection (e) of that section, as amended August 4, 1939 (46 U.S.C. App. 1160)" and substituting "chapter 573 of title 46, United States Code, see section 57307 of title 46" in paragraph (1); by striking "section 511 of such Act, as amended (46 U.S.C. App. 1161)" and substituting "chapter 533 of title 46, United States Code" in paragraph (2); and by striking paragraph (3). **Effective** 10-6-2006. Prior to being stricken, Code Sec. 1061(3) read as follows:

(3) For nonrecognition of gain in connection with vessels exchanged with the Maritime Administration under section 8 of the Merchant Ship Sales Act of 1946, see subsection (a) of that section (50 U. S. C. App. 1741).

• **1986, Tax Reform Act of 1986 (P.L. 99-514)**

P.L. 99-514, §641(a):

Amended part IV of subchapter O of chapter 1 by redesignating section 1060 as section 1061. **Effective** for any acquisition of assets after 5-6-86, unless such acquisition is pursuant to a binding contract which was in effect on 5-6-86, and at all times thereafter.

P.L. 99-514, §1899A(27):

Amended Code Sec. 1060 prior to its redesignation by Act Sec. 641(a) by striking out "46 U.S.C." and inserting in lieu thereof "46 U.S.C. App.". **Effective** 10-22-86.

• **1984, Deficit Reduction Act of 1984 (P.L. 98-369)**

P.L. 98-369, §53(a):

Redesignated Code Sec. 1059 as Code Sec. 1060. **Effective** for distributions after 3-1-84, in tax years ending after such date.

• **1978 (P.L. 95-345)**

P.L. 95-345, §2(d)(1):

Redesignated former Code Sec. 1058 as Code Sec. 1059. **Effective** with respect to (1) amounts received after 12-31-76, as payments with respect to securities loans defined in Code Sec. 512(a)(5), and (2) transfers of securities under agreements described in Code Sec. 1058 occurring after such date.

• **1976, Tax Reform Act of 1976 (P.L. 94-455)**

P.L. 94-455, §212(a)(1):

Redesignated former Code Sec. 1056 as Code Sec. 1057. **Effective** for sales or exchanges of franchises after 12-31-75, in tax years ending after such date.

P.L. 94-455, §1015(c):

Redesignated former Code Sec. 1057 as Code Sec. 1058. **Effective** for transfers of property after 10-2-75.

• **1963 (P.L. 88-9)**

P.L. 88-9, §1(b):

Redesignated Code Sec. 1055 as Code Sec. 1056. **Effective** 4-11-63.

• **1960 (P.L. 86-779)**

P.L. 86-779, §8(b):

Redesignated Code Sec. 1054 as Code Sec. 1055. **Effective** 1-1-60.

PART V—CHANGES TO EFFECTUATE F. C. C. POLICY—[Stricken]

[Sec. 1071—Stricken]

Amendments

• **1995, Self-Employed Health Insurance Act (P.L. 104-7)**

P.L. 104-7, §2(a):

Amended subchapter O of chapter 1 by striking part V (relating to changes to effectuate FCC policy). **Effective**, generally, for sales and exchanges on or after 1-17-95, and sales and exchanges before such date if the FCC tax certificate with respect to such sale or exchange is issued on or after such date.

P.L. 104-7, §2(d)(2)-(3), provides:

(2) BINDING CONTRACTS.—

(A) IN GENERAL.—The amendments made by this section shall not apply to any sale or exchange pursuant to a written contract which was binding on January 16, 1995, and at all times thereafter before the sale or exchange, if the FCC tax certificate with respect to such sale or exchange was applied for, or issued, on or before such date.

(B) SALES CONTINGENT ON ISSUANCE OF CERTIFICATE.—

(i) IN GENERAL.—A contract shall be treated as not binding for purposes of subparagraph (A) if the sale or exchange pursuant to such contract, or the material terms of such contract, were contingent, at any time on January 16, 1995, on the issuance of an FCC tax certificate. The preceding sentence shall not apply if the FCC tax certificate for such sale or exchange is issued on or before January 16, 1995.

(ii) MATERIAL TERMS.—For purposes of clause (i), the material terms of a contract shall not be treated as contingent on the issuance of an FCC tax certificate solely because such terms provide that the sales price would, if such certificate were not issued, be increased by an amount not greater that 10 percent of the sales price otherwise provided in the contract.

(3) FCC TAX CERTIFICATE.—For purposes of this subsection, the term "FCC tax certificate" means any certificate of the Federal Communications Commission for the effectuation of section 1071 of the Internal Revenue Code of 1986 (as in effect on the day before the date of the enactment of this Act).

Prior to being stricken, part V of subchapter O of chapter 1 read as follows:

PART V—CHANGES TO EFFECTUATE F.C.C. POLICY

SEC. 1071. GAIN FROM SALE OR EXCHANGE TO EFFECTUATE POLICIES OF F.C.C.

INCOME TAX—S.E.C. EXCHANGES

[Sec. 1071(a)]

(a) NONRECOGNITION OF GAIN OR LOSS.—If the sale or exchange of property (including stock in a corporation) is certified by the Federal Communications Commission to be necessary or appropriate to effectuate a change in a policy of, or the adoption of a new policy by, the Commission with respect to the ownership and control of radio broadcasting stations, such sale or exchange shall, if the taxpayer so elects, be treated as an involuntary conversion of such property within the meaning of section 1033. For purposes of such section as made applicable by the provisions of this section, stock of a corporation operating a radio broadcasting station, whether or not representing control of such corporation, shall be treated as property similar or related in service or use to the property so converted. The part of the gain, if any, on such sale or exchange to which section 1033 is not applied shall nevertheless not be recognized, if the taxpayer so elects, to the extent that it is applied to reduce the basis for determining gain or loss on sale or exchange of property, of a character subject to the allowance for depreciation under section 167, remaining in the hands of the taxpayer immediately after the sale or exchange, or acquired in the same taxable year. The manner and amount of such reduction shall be determined under regulations prescribed by the Secretary. Any election made by the taxpayer under this section shall be made by a statement to that effect in his return for the taxable year in which the sale or exchange takes place, and such election shall be binding for the taxable year and all subsequent taxable years.

Amendments

• **1982, Miscellaneous Revenue Act of 1982 (P.L. 97-362)**

P.L. 97-362, § 103 provides:

SEC. 103. ROLLOVER OF GAIN ON CERTAIN SALES UNDER FCC ORDER WHERE NEWSPAPERS ARE BOUGHT.

If—

(1) a corporation was ordered by the Federal Communications Commission in January 1975 to divest itself of its newspaper operations or its broadcasting operations,

(2) after the conclusion of the appellate process, the order was again issued in October 1979,

(3) the corporation sold its broadcasting operations before 1982, and

(4) on October 15, 1981, the corporation acquired 100 percent of the stock of a publishing company,

then the second sentence of section 1071(a) of the Internal Revenue Code of 1954 shall be applied with respect to sales and exchanges by such corporation before January 1, 1982, which are related to such order as if such second sentence treated stock of any corporation the principal business of which is operating newspapers and related printing operations in the same manner as stock of a corporation operating a radio broadcasting station.

• **1976, Tax Reform Act of 1976 (P.L. 94-455)**

P.L. 94-455, § 1906(b)(13)(A):

Amended 1954 Code by substituting "Secretary" for "Secretary or his delegate" each place it appeared. **Effective** 2-1-77.

• **1958, Technical Amendments Act of 1958 (P.L. 85-866)**

P.L. 85-866, § 48:

Struck out the phrase "necessary or appropriate to effectuate the policies of the Commission" where it appeared in Sec. 1071(a) and substituted the phrase "necessary or appropriate to effectuate a change in a policy of, or the adoption of a new policy by, the Commission". **Effective** for any sale or exchange after 12-31-57.

[Sec. 1071(b)]

(b) BASIS.—

For basis of property acquired on a sale or exchange treated as an involuntary conversion under subsection (a), see section 1033(b).

Amendments

• **1976, Tax Reform Act of 1976 (P.L. 94-455)**

P.L. 94-455, § 1901(b)(31)(E):

Substituted "1033(b)" for "1033(c)" in Code Sec. 1071(b). **Effective** for tax years beginning after 12-31-76.

PART VI—EXCHANGES IN OBEDIENCE TO S.E.C. ORDERS—[Repealed]

[Sec. 1081—Repealed]

Amendments

• **2005, Gulf Opportunity Zone Act of 2005 (P.L. 109-135)**

P.L. 109-135, § 402(a)(1):

Repealed part VI of subchapter O of chapter 1 (Code Secs. 1081-1083). **Effective** as if included in the provision of the Energy Policy Act of 2005 (P.L. 109-58) to which it relates [effective 6 months after 8-8-2005.—CCH]. For a special rule, see Act Sec. 402(m)(2), below.

P.L. 109-135, § 402(m)(2), provides:

(2) REPEAL OF PUBLIC UTILITY HOLDING COMPANY ACT OF 1935.—The amendments made by subsection (a) shall not apply with respect to any transaction ordered in compliance with the Public Utility Holding Company Act of 1935 before its repeal.

Prior to repeal, Code Sec. 1081 read as follows:

SEC. 1081. NONRECOGNITION OF GAIN OR LOSS ON EXCHANGES OR DISTRIBUTIONS IN OBEDIENCE TO ORDERS OF S. E. C.

[Sec. 1081(a)]

(a) EXCHANGES OF STOCK OR SECURITIES ONLY.—No gain or loss shall be recognized to the transferor if stock or securities in a corporation which is a registered holding company or a majority-owned subsidiary company are transferred to such corporation or to an associate company thereof which is a registered holding company or a majority-owned subsidiary company solely in exchange for stock or securities (other than stock or securities which are nonexempt property), and the exchange is made by the transferee corporation in obedience to an order of the Securities and Exchange Commission.

[Sec. 1081(b)]

(b) EXCHANGES AND SALES OF PROPERTY BY CORPORATIONS.—

(1) GENERAL RULE.—No gain shall be recognized to a transferor corporation which is a registered holding company or an associate company of a registered holding company, if such corporation, in obedience to an order of the Securities and Exchange Commission, transfers property in exchange for property, and such order recites that such exchange by the transferor corporation is necessary or appropriate to the integration or simplification of the holding company system of which the transferor corporation is a member. Any gain, to the extent that it cannot be applied in reduction of basis under section 1082(a)(2), shall be recognized.

(2) NONEXEMPT PROPERTY.—If any such property so received is nonexempt property, gain shall be recognized unless such nonexempt property or an amount equal to the fair market value of such property at the time of the transfer is, within 24 months of the transfer, under regulations prescribed by the Secretary, and in accordance with an order of the Securities and Exchange Commission, expended for property other than nonexempt property or is invested as a contribution to the capital, or as paid-in surplus, of another corporation, and such order recites that such expenditure or investment by the transferor corporation is necessary or appropriate to the integration or simplification of the holding company system of which the transferor corporation is a member. If the fair market value of such nonexempt property at the time of the transfer exceeds the amount expended and the amount invested, as required in the preceding sentence, the gain, if any, to the extent of such excess, shall be recognized.

(3) CANCELLATION OR REDEMPTION OF STOCK OR SECURITIES.—For purposes of this subsection, a distribution in cancellation or redemption (except a distribution having the effect of a dividend) of the whole or a part of the transferor's own stock (not acquired on the transfer) and a payment in complete or partial retirement or cancellation of securities representing indebtedness of the transferor or a complete or partial retirement or cancellation of such securities which is a part of the consideration for the transfer shall be considered an expenditure for property other than nonexempt property, and if, on the transfer, a liability of the transferor is assumed, or property of the transferor is transferred subject to a liability, the amount of such liability shall be considered to be an expenditure by the transferor for property other than nonexempt property.

(4) CONSENTS.—This subsection shall not apply unless the transferor corporation consents, at such time and in such manner as the Secretary may by regulations prescribe to the regulations prescribed under section 1082(a)(2) in effect at the time of filing its return for the taxable year in which the transfer occurs.

Amendments

• **1976, Tax Reform Act of 1976 (P.L. 94-455)**

P.L. 94-455, § 1906(b)(13)(A):

Amended 1954 Code by substituting "Secretary" for "Secretary or his delegate" each place it appeared. **Effective** 2-1-77.

[Sec. 1081(c)]

(c) DISTRIBUTION OF STOCK OR SECURITIES ONLY.—If there is distributed, in obedience to an order of the Securities and Exchange Commission, to a shareholder in a corporation which is a registered holding company or a majority-owned subsidiary company, stock or securities (other than stock or securities which are nonexempt property), without the surrender by such shareholder of stock or securities in such corporation, no gain to the distributee from the receipt of the stock or securities so distributed shall be recognized.

Amendments

• **1976, Tax Reform Act of 1976 (P.L. 94-455)**

P.L. 94-455, § 1901(a)(132)(A):

Amended Code Sec. 1081(c). **Effective** for tax years beginning after 12-31-76. Prior to amendment, Code Sec. 1081(c) read as follows:

(c) DISTRIBUTION OF STOCK OR SECURITIES ONLY.—

(1) IN GENERAL.—If there is distributed, in obedience to an order of the Securities and Exchange Commission, to a shareholder in a corporation which is a registered holding company or a majorityowned subsidiary company, stock or securities (other than stock or securities which are nonexempt property), without the surrender by such shareholder of stock or securities in such corporation, no gain to the distributee from the receipt of the stock or securities so distributed shall be recognized.

(2) SPECIAL RULE.—If—

(A) there is distributed to a shareholder in a corporation rights to acquire common stock in a second corporation without the surrender by such shareholder of stock in the first corporation,

(B) such distribution is in accordance with an arrangement forming a ground for an order of the Securities and Exchange Commission issued pursuant to Section 3 of the Public Utility Holding Company Act of 1935 (49 Stat. 810; 15 U. S. C. 79c) that such corporation is exempt from any provision or provisions of such Act, and

(C) before January 1, 1958, the first corporation disposes of all of the common stock in the second corporation which it owns,

then no gain to the distributee from the receipt of the rights so distributed shall be recognized. If the first corporation does not, before January 1, 1958, dispose of all of the common stock which it owns in the second corporation, then the periods of limitation provided in Sections 6501 and 6502 on the making of an assessment or the collection by levy or a proceeding in court shall, with respect to any deficiency (including interest and additions to the tax) resulting solely from the receipt of such rights to acquire stock, include one year immediately following the date on which the first corporation notifies the Secretary or his delegate whether or not the requirements of subparagraph (C) of the preceding sentence have been met; and such assessment and collection may be made notwithstanding any provision of law or rule of law which would otherwise prevent such assessment and collection.

[Sec. 1081(d)]

(d) TRANSFERS WITHIN SYSTEM GROUP.—

(1) GENERAL RULE.—No gain or loss shall be recognized to a corporation which is a member of a system group—

(A) if such corporation transfers property to another corporation which is a member of the same system group in exchange for other property, and the exchange by each corporation is made in obedience to an order of the Securities and Exchange Commission, or

(B) if there is distributed to such corporation as a shareholder in a corporation which is a member of the same system group, property, without the surrender by such shareholder of stock or securities in the corporation making the distribution, and the distribution is made and received in obedience to an order of the Securities and Exchange Commission.

If an exchange by or a distribution to a corporation with respect to which no gain or loss is recognized under any of the provisions of this paragraph may also be considered to be within the provisions of subsection (a), (b), or (c), then the provisions of this paragraph only shall apply.

(2) SALES OF STOCK OR SECURITIES.—If the property received on an exchange which is within any of the provisions of paragraph (1) consists in whole or in part of stock or securities issued by the corporation from which such property was received, and if in obedience to an order of the Securities and Exchange Commission such stock or securities (other than stock which is not preferred as to both dividends and assets) are sold and the proceeds derived therefrom are applied in whole or in part in the retirement or cancellation of stock or of securities of the recipient corporation outstanding at the time of such exchange, no gain or loss shall be recognized to the recipient corporation on the sale of the stock or securities with respect to which such order was made; except that if any part of the proceeds derived from the sale of such stock or securities is not so applied, or if the amount of such proceeds is in excess of the fair market value of such stock or securities at the time of such exchange, the gain, if any, shall be recognized, but in an amount not in excess of the proceeds which are not so applied, or in an amount not more than the amount by which the proceeds derived from such sale exceed such fair market value, whichever is the greater.

[Sec. 1081(e)]

(e) EXCHANGES NOT SOLELY IN KIND.—

(1) GENERAL RULE.—If an exchange (not within any of the provisions of subsection (d)) would be within the provisions of subsection (a) if it were not for the fact that property received in exchange consists not only of property permitted by such subsection to be received without the recognition of gain or loss, but also of other property or money, then the gain, if any, to the recipient shall be recognized, but in

an amount not in excess of the sum of such money and the fair market value of such other property, and the loss, if any, to the recipient shall not be recognized.

(2) DISTRIBUTION TREATED AS DIVIDEND.—If an exchange is within the provisions of paragraph (1) and if it includes a distribution which has the effect of the distribution of a taxable dividend, then there shall be taxed as a dividend to each distributee such an amount of gain recognized under such paragraph as is not in excess of his ratable share of the undistributed earnings and profits of the corporation accumulated after February 28, 1913. The remainder, if any, of the gain recognized under paragraph (1) shall be taxed as a gain from the exchange of property.

[Sec. 1081(f)]

(f) CONDITIONS FOR APPLICATION OF SECTION.—The provisions of this section shall not apply to an exchange, expenditure, investment, distribution, or sale unless—

(1) the order of the Securities and Exchange Commission in obedience to which such exchange, expenditure, investment, distribution, or sale was made recites that such exchange, expenditure, investment, distribution, or sale is necessary or appropriate to effectuate the provisions of section 11(b) of the Public Utility Holding Company Act of 1935 (15 U. S. C. 79k(b)),

(2) such order specifies and itemizes the stock and securities and other property which are ordered to be acquired, transferred, received, or sold on such exchange, acquisition, expenditure, distribution, or sale, and, in the case of an investment, the investment to be made, and

(3) such exchange, acquisition, expenditure, investment, distribution, or sale was made in obedience to such order, and was completed within the time prescribed therefor.

Amendments

• 1976, Tax Reform Act of 1976 (P.L. 94-455)

P.L. 94-455, § 1901(a)(132)(B):

Substituted "The provisions" for "Except in the case of a distribution described in subsection (c)(2), the provisions" at the beginning of Code Sec. 1081(f), and struck out "49 Stat. 820;" before "15 U.S.C. 79k(b)" in Code Sec. 1081(f)(1). **Effective** for tax years beginning after 12-31-76.

[Sec. 1081(g)]

(g) NONAPPLICATION OF OTHER PROVISIONS.—If an exchange or distribution made in obedience to an order of the Securities and Exchange Commission is within any of the provisions of this part and may also be considered to be within any of the other provisions of this subchapter or subchapter (C) (sec. 301 and following, relating to corporate distributions and adjustments), then the provisions of this part only shall apply.

Amendments

• 1976, Tax Reform Act of 1976 (P.L. 94-455)

P.L. 94-455, § 1901(a)(132)(C):

Substituted "If an" for "If a distribution described in subsection (c)(2), or an" in Code Sec. 1081(g), and deleted the comma following "Commission". **Effective** for tax years beginning after 12-31-76.

[Sec. 1082—Repealed]

Amendments

• 2005, Gulf Opportunity Zone Act of 2005 (P.L. 109-135)

P.L. 109-135, § 402(a)(1):

Repealed part VI of subchapter O of chapter 1 (Code Secs. 1081-1083). **Effective** as if included in the provision of the Energy Policy Act of 2005 (P.L. 109-58) to which it relates [**effective 6 months after 8-8-2005.—CCH**]. For a special rule, see Act Sec. 402(m)(2), below.

P.L. 109-135, § 402(m)(2), provides:

(2) REPEAL OF PUBLIC UTILITY HOLDING COMPANY ACT OF 1935.—The amendments made by subsection (a) shall not apply with respect to any transaction ordered in compliance with the Public Utility Holding Company Act of 1935 before its repeal.

Prior to repeal, Code Sec. 1082 read as follows:

SEC. 1082. BASIS FOR DETERMINING GAIN OR LOSS.

[Sec. 1082(a)]

(a) EXCHANGES GENERALLY.—

(1) EXCHANGES SUBJECT TO THE PROVISIONS OF SECTION 1081(a) OR (e).—If the property was acquired on an exchange subject to the provisions of section 1081(a) or (e), or the corresponding provisions of prior internal revenue laws, the basis shall be the same as in the case of the property exchanged, decreased in the amount of any money received by the taxpayer, and increased in the amount of gain or decreased in the amount of loss to the taxpayer that was recognized on such exchange under the law applicable to the year in which the exchange was made. If the property so acquired consisted in part of the type of property permitted by section 1081(a) to be received without the recognition of gain or loss, and in part of nonexempt property, the basis provided in this subsection shall be allocated between the properties (other than money) received, and for the purpose of the allocation there shall be assigned to such nonexempt property (other than money) an amount equivalent to its fair market value at the date of the exchange. This subsection shall not apply to property acquired by a corporation by the issuance of its stock or securities as the consideration in whole or in part for the transfer of the property to it.

(2) EXCHANGES SUBJECT TO THE PROVISIONS OF SECTION 1081(b).—The gain not recognized on a transfer by reason of section 1081(b) or the corresponding provisions of prior internal revenue laws shall be applied to reduce the basis for determining the gain or loss on sale or exchange of the following categories of property in the hands of the transferor immediately after the transfer, and property acquired within 24 months after such transfer by an expenditure or investment to which section 1081 (b) relates on account of the acquisition of which gain is not recognized under such subsection, in the following order:

(A) property of a character subject to the allowance for depreciation under section 167;

(B) property (not described in subparagraph (A)) with respect to which a deduction for amortization is allowable under section 169;

(C) property with respect to which a deduction for depletion is allowable under section 611 but not allowable under section 613;

(D) stock and securities of corporations not members of the system group of which the transferor is a member (other than stock or securities of a corporation of which the transferor is a subsidiary);

(E) securities (other than stock) of corporations which are members of the system group of which the transferor is a member (other than securities of the transferor or of a corporation of which the transferor is a subsidiary);

(F) stock of corporations which are members of the system group of which the transferor is a member (other than stock of the transferor or of a corporation of which the transferor is a subsidiary);

(G) all other remaining property of the transferor (other than stock or securities of the transferor or of a corporation of which the transferor is a subsidiary).

The manner and amount of the reduction to be applied to particular property within any of the categories described in subparagraphs (A) to (G), inclusive, shall be determined under regulations prescribed by the Secretary.

(3) BASIS IN CASE OF PRE-1942 ACQUISITION.—Notwithstanding the provisions of paragraph (1) or (2), if the property was acquired in a taxable year beginning before January 1, 1942, in any manner described in section 372 of the Internal Revenue Code of 1939 before its amendment by the Revenue Act of 1942, the basis shall be that prescribed in such section (before its amendment by such Act) with respect to such property.

Amendments

• 1990, Omnibus Budget Reconciliation Act of 1990 (P.L. 101-508)

P.L. 101-508, § 11801(c)(6)(D):

Amended Code Sec. 1082(a)(2)(B) by striking "169, 184, or 188" and inserting "169". **Effective** 11-5-90.

P.L. 101-508, § 11821(b)(1)-(2), provides:

(b) SAVINGS PROVISION.—If—

(1) any provision amended or repealed by this part applied to—

(A) any transaction occurring before the date of the enactment of this Act,

(B) any property acquired before such date of enactment, or

INCOME TAX—S.E.C. EXCHANGES

(C) any item of income, loss, deduction, or credit taken into account before such date of enactment, and

(2) the treatment of such transaction, property, or item under such provision would (without regard to the amendments made by this part) affect liability for tax for periods ending after such date of enactment,

nothing in the amendments made by this part shall be construed to affect the treatment of such transaction, property, or item for purposes of determining liability for tax for periods ending after such date of enactment.

- **1986, Tax Reform Act of 1986 (P.L. 99-514)**

P.L. 99-514, §242(b)(1):

Amended Code Sec. 1082(a)(2)(B) by striking out ", 185,". **Effective** for that portion of the basis of any property which is attributable to expenditures paid or incurred after 12-31-86. However, for a transitional rule, see Act Sec. 242(c)(2) under the amendment note to Code Sec. 185.

- **1981, Economic Recovery Tax Act of 1981 (P.L. 97-34)**

P.L. 97-34, §212(d)(2)(E):

Amended Code Sec. 1082(a)(2)(B) by striking out "188, or 191" and inserting in lieu thereof "or 188". **Effective** for expenditures incurred after 12-31-81, in tax years ending after such date.

P.L. 97-34, §212(e)(2), as amended by P.L. 97-448, §102(f)(1), provides:

(2) TRANSITIONAL RULE.—The amendments made by this section shall not apply with respect to any rehabilitation of a building if—

(A) the physical work on such rehabilitation began before January 1, 1982, and

(B) such building does not meet the requirements of paragraph (1) of section 48(g) of the Internal Revenue Code of 1954 (as amended by this Act).

- **1976, Tax Reform Act of 1976 (P.L. 94-455)**

P.L. 94-455, §1901(b)(11)(C):

Struck out "187," following "185," in Code Sec. 1082(a)(2)(B). **Effective** for tax years beginning after 12-31-76.

P.L. 94-455, §1906(b)(13)(A):

Amended 1954 Code by substituting "Secretary" for "Secretary or his delegate" each place it appeared. **Effective** 2-1-77.

P.L. 94-455, §1951(c)(2)(B):

Struck out "168," following "section" in Code Sec. 1082(a)(2)(B). **Effective** for tax years beginning after 12-31-76.

P.L. 94-455, §2124(a)(3)(C):

Substituted "188, or 191" for "or 188" in Code Sec. 1082(a)(2)(B). **Effective** for additions to capital accounts made after 6-14-76, and before 6-15-81.

- **1971, Revenue Act of 1971 (P.L. 92-178)**

P.L. 92-178, §303(c)(5):

Amended Code Sec. 1082(a)(2)(B) by substituting "187, or 188" for "or 187". **Effective** for to tax years ending after 12-31-71.

Amendments

- **2005, Gulf Opportunity Zone Act of 2005 (P.L. 109-135)**

P.L. 109-135, §402(a)(1):

Repealed part VI of subchapter O of chapter 1 (Code Secs. 1081-1083). **Effective** as if included in the provision of the Energy Policy Act of 2005 (P.L. 109-58) to which it relates [effective 6 months after 8-8-2005.—CCH]. For a special rule, see Act Sec. 402(m)(2), below.

P.L. 109-135, §402(m)(2), provides:

(2) REPEAL OF PUBLIC UTILITY HOLDING COMPANY ACT OF 1935.—The amendments made by subsection (a) shall not apply with respect to any transaction ordered in compliance with the Public Utility Holding Company Act of 1935 before its repeal.

Prior to repeal, Code Sec. 1083 read as follows:

SEC. 1083. DEFINITIONS.

[Sec. 1083(a)]

(a) ORDER OF SECURITIES AND EXCHANGE COMMISSION.—For purposes of this part, the term "order of the Securities and Exchange Commission" means an order issued after May 28, 1938, by the Securities and Exchange Commission which requires, authorizes, permits, or approves transactions described in such order to effectuate section 11(b) of the Public Utility Holding Company Act of 1935 (15 U. S. C. 79k(b)), which has become or becomes final in accordance with law.

Amendments

- **1976, Tax Reform Act of 1976 (P.L. 94-455)**

P.L. 94-455, §1901(a)(133)(A):

Struck out "49 Stat. 820;" before "15 U.S.C. 79k(b)" in Code Sec. 1083(a). **Effective** for tax years beginning after 12-31-76.

[Sec. 1083(b)]

(b) REGISTERED HOLDING COMPANY; HOLDING COMPANY SYSTEM; ASSOCIATE COMPANY.—For purposes of this part, the terms "registered holding company", "holding company system", and "associate company" shall have the meanings assigned to them by section 2 of the Public Utility Holding Company Act of 1935 (15 U. S. C. 79b(a)).

Sec. 1083—Repealed

- **1969, Tax Reform Act of 1969 (P.L. 91-172)**

P.L. 91-172, §704(b)(3):

Amended Code Sec. 1082(a)(2)(B) by striking out "or 169" and inserting in lieu thereof ", 169, 184, 185, or 187". **Effective** for tax years ending after 12-31-68.

[Sec. 1082(b)]

(b) TRANSFERS TO CORPORATIONS.—If, in connection with a transfer subject to the provisions of section 1081(a), (b), or (e) or the corresponding provisions of prior internal revenue laws, the property was acquired by a corporation, either as paid-in surplus or as a contribution to capital, or in consideration for stock or securities issued by the corporation receiving the property (including cases where part of the consideration for the transfer of such property to the corporation consisted of property or money in addition to such stock or securities), then the basis shall be the same as it would be in the hands of the transferor, increased in the amount of gain or decreased in the amount of loss recognized to the transferor on such transfer under the law applicable to the year in which the transfer was made.

[Sec. 1082(c)]

(c) DISTRIBUTIONS OF STOCK OR SECURITIES.—If the stock or securities were received in a distribution subject to the provisions of section 1081(c) or the corresponding provisions of prior internal revenue laws, then the basis in the case of the stock in respect of which the distribution was made shall be apportioned, under regulations prescribed by the Secretary, between such stock and the stock or securities distributed.

Amendments

- **1976, Tax Reform Act of 1976 (P.L. 94-455)**

P.L. 94-455, §1906(b)(13)(A):

Amended 1954 Code by substituting "Secretary" for "Secretary or his delegate" each place it appeared. **Effective** 2-1-77.

[Sec. 1082(d)]

(d) TRANSFERS WITHIN SYSTEM GROUP.—If the property was acquired by a corporation which is a member of a system group on a transfer or distribution described in section 1081(d)(1), then the basis shall be the same as it would be in the hands of the transferor; except that if such property is stock or securities issued by the corporation from which such stock or securities were received and they were issued—

(1) as the sole consideration for the property transferred to such corporation, then the basis of such stock or securities shall be either—

(A) the same as in the case of the property transferred therefor, or

(B) the fair market value of such stock or securities at the time of their receipt, whichever is the lower; or

(2) as part consideration for the property transferred to such corporation, then the basis of such stock or securities shall be either—

(A) an amount which bears the same ratio to the basis of the property transferred as the fair market value of such stock or securities at the time of their receipt bears to the total fair market value of the entire consideration received, or

(B) the fair market value of such stock or securities at the time of their receipt, whichever is the lower.

[Sec. 1083—Repealed]

Amendments

- **1976, Tax Reform Act of 1976 (P.L. 94-455)**

P.L. 94-455, §1901(a)(133)(B):

Struck out "49 Stat. 804;" before "15 U.S.C. 79b(a)" in Code Sec. 1083(b). **Effective** for tax years beginning after 12-31-76.

[Sec. 1083(c)]

(c) MAJORITY-OWNED SUBSIDIARY COMPANY.—For purposes of this part, the term "majority-owned subsidiary company" of a registered holding company means a corporation, stock of which, representing in the aggregate more than 50 percent of the total combined voting power of all classes of stock of such corporation entitled to vote (not including stock which is entitled to vote only on default or nonpayment of dividends or other special circumstances) is owned wholly by such registered holding company, or partly by such registered holding company and partly by one or more majority-owned subsidiary companies thereof, or by one or more majority-owned subsidiary companies of such registered holding company.

[Sec. 1083(d)]

(d) SYSTEM GROUP.—For purposes of this part, the term "system group" means one or more chains of corporations connected through stock ownership with a common parent corporation if—

(1) at least 90 percent of each class of the stock (other than (A) stock which is preferred as to both dividends and assets, and (B) stock which is limited and preferred as to dividends but which is not preferred as to assets but only if the total value of such stock is less than 1 percent of the aggregate value of all classes of stock which are not preferred as to both dividends and assets) of each of the corporations (except the common parent corporation) is owned directly by one or more of the other corporations; and

(2) the common parent corporation owns directly at least 90 percent of each class of the stock (other than stock, which is preferred as to both dividends and assets) of at least one of the other corporations; and

(3) each of the corporations is either a registered holding company or a majority-owned subsidiary company.

INCOME TAX—WASH SALES; STRADDLES

[Sec. 1083(e)]

(e) NONEXEMPT PROPERTY.—For purposes of this part, the term "nonexempt property" means—

(1) any consideration in the form of evidences of indebtedness owed by the transferor or a cancellation or assumption of debts or other liabilities of the transferor (including a continuance of encumbrances subject to which the property was transferred);

(2) short-term obligations (including notes, drafts, bills of exchange, and bankers' acceptances) having a maturity at the time of issuance of not exceeding 24 months, exclusive of days of grace;

(3) securities issued or guaranteed as to principal or interest by a government or subdivision thereof (including those issued by a corporation which is an instrumentality of a government or subdivision thereof);

(4) stock or securities which were acquired from a registered holding company or an associate company of a registered holding company which acquired such stock or securities after February 28, 1938, unless such stock or securities (other than obligations described as nonexempt property in paragraph (1), (2), or (3)) were acquired in obedience to an order of the Securities and Exchange Commission or were acquired with the authorization or approval of the Securities and Exchange Commission under any section of the Public Utility Holding Company Act of 1935 (15 U. S. C. 79k(b));

(5) money, and the right to receive money not evidenced by a security other than an obligation described as nonexempt property in paragraph (2) or (3).

Amendments

• **1976, Tax Reform Act of 1976 (P.L. 94-455)**

P.L. 94-455, § 1901(a)(133)(C):

Struck out "49 Stat. 820;" before "15 U.S.C. 79k(b)" in Code Sec. 1083(e)(4). **Effective** for tax years beginning after 12-31-76.

[Sec. 1083(f)]

(f) STOCK OR SECURITIES.—For purposes of this part, the term "stock or securities" means shares of stock in any corporation, certificates of stock or interest in any corporation, notes, bonds, debentures, and evidences of indebtedness (including any evidence of an interest in or right to subscribe to or purchase any of the foregoing).

PART VII—WASH SALES; STRADDLES

Sec. 1091. Loss from wash sales of stock or securities.
Sec. 1092. Straddles.

[Sec. 1091]

SEC. 1091. LOSS FROM WASH SALES OF STOCK OR SECURITIES.

[Sec. 1091(a)]

(a) DISALLOWANCE OF LOSS DEDUCTION.—In the case of any loss claimed to have been sustained from any sale or other disposition of shares of stock or securities where it appears that, within a period beginning 30 days before the date of such sale or disposition and ending 30 days after such date, the taxpayer has acquired (by purchase or by an exchange on which the entire amount of gain or loss was recognized by law), or has entered into a contract or option so to acquire, substantially identical stock or securities, then no deduction shall be allowed under section 165 unless the taxpayer is a dealer in stock or securities and the loss is sustained in a transaction made in the ordinary course of such business. For purposes of this section, the term "stock or securities" shall, except as provided in regulations, include contracts or options to acquire or sell stock or securities.

Amendments

• **1988, Technical and Miscellaneous Revenue Act of 1988 (P.L. 100-647)**

P.L. 100-647, § 5075(a):

Amended Code Sec. 1091(a) by adding at the end thereof a new sentence. **Effective** with respect to any sale after 11-10-88, in tax years ending after such date.

• **1984, Deficit Reduction Act of 1984 (P.L. 98-369)**

P.L. 98-369, § 106(b):

Amended Code Sec. 1091(a) by striking out "no deduction for the loss shall be allowed under section 165(c)(2); nor shall such deduction be allowed a corporation under section 165(a) unless it is a dealer in stocks or securities, and the loss is sustained in a transaction made in the ordinary course of its business." and inserting in lieu thereof the language following "then". **Effective** for sales after 12-31-84, in tax years ending after such date.

[Sec. 1091(b)]

(b) STOCK ACQUIRED LESS THAN STOCK SOLD.—If the amount of stock or securities acquired (or covered by the contract or option to acquire) is less than the amount of stock or securities sold or otherwise disposed of, then the particular shares of stock or securities the loss from the sale or other disposition of which is not deductible shall be determined under regulations prescribed by the Secretary.

Amendments

• **1976, Tax Reform Act of 1976 (P.L. 94-455)**

P.L. 94-455, § 1906(b)(13)(A):

Amended 1954 Code by substituting "Secretary" for "Secretary or his delegate" each place it appeared. **Effective** 2-1-77.

[Sec. 1091(c)]

(c) STOCK ACQUIRED NOT LESS THAN STOCK SOLD.—If the amount of stock or securities acquired (or covered by the contract or option to acquire) is not less than the amount of stock or securities sold or otherwise disposed of, then the particular shares of stock or securities the acquisition of which (or the contract or option to acquire which) resulted in the nondeductibility of the loss shall be determined under regulations prescribed by the Secretary.

Amendments

• **1976, Tax Reform Act of 1976 (P.L. 94-455)**

P.L. 94-455, § 1906(b)(13)(A):

Amended 1954 Code by substituting "Secretary" for "Secretary or his delegate" each place it appeared. **Effective** 2-1-77.

[Sec. 1091(d)]

(d) UNADJUSTED BASIS IN CASE OF WASH SALE OF STOCK.—If the property consists of stock or securities the acquisition of which (or the contract or option to acquire which) resulted in the nondeductibility (under this section or corresponding provisions of prior internal revenue laws) of the loss from the sale or other disposition of substantially identical stock or securities, then the basis shall be the basis of the stock or securities so sold or disposed of, increased or decreased, as the case may be, by the difference, if any, between the price at which the property was acquired and the price at which such substantially identical stock or securities were sold or otherwise disposed of.

[Sec. 1091(e)]

(e) CERTAIN SHORT SALES OF STOCK OR SECURITIES AND SECURITIES FUTURES CONTRACTS TO SELL.—Rules similar to the rules of subsection (a) shall apply to any loss realized on the closing of a short sale of (or the sale, exchange, or termination of a securities futures contract to sell) stock or securities if, within a period beginning 30 days before the date of such closing and ending 30 days after such date—

(1) substantially identical stock or securities were sold, or

(2) another short sale of (or securities futures contracts to sell) substantially identical stock or securities was entered into.

For purposes of this subsection, the term "securities futures contract" has the meaning provided by section 1234B(c).

INCOME TAX—WASH SALES; STRADDLES

Amendments

• **2002, Job Creation and Worker Assistance Act of 2002 (P.L. 107-147)**

P.L. 107-147, §412(d)(2)(A)-(D):

Amended Code Sec. 1091(e) by striking "SECURITIES.—" and inserting "SECURITIES AND SECURITIES FUTURES CONTRACTS TO SELL.—", by inserting "(or the sale, exchange, or termination of a securities futures contract to sell)" following "closing of a short sale of", by inserting in paragraph (2) "(or securities futures contracts to sell)" following "short sale of", and by adding at the end a new sentence. **Effective** as if included in the provision of P.L. 106-554 to which it relates [**effective** on 12-21-2000.—CCH].

• **1984, Deficit Reduction Act of 1984 (P.L. 98-369)**

P.L. 98-369, §106(a):

Amended Code Sec. 1091 by adding at the end thereof subsection (e). **Effective** for short sales of stock or securities after 7-18-84, in tax years ending after such date.

[Sec. 1091(f)]

(f) CASH SETTLEMENT.—This section shall not fail to apply to a contract or option to acquire or sell stock or securities solely by reason of the fact that the contract or option settles in (or could be settled in) cash or property other than such stock or securities.

Amendments

• **2000, Community Renewal Tax Relief Act of 2000 (P.L. 106-554)**

P.L. 106-554, §401(d):

Amended Code Sec. 1091 by adding at the end a new subsection (f). **Effective** 12-21-2000.

[Sec. 1092]

SEC. 1092. STRADDLES.

[Sec. 1092(a)]

(a) RECOGNITION OF LOSS IN CASE OF STRADDLES, ETC.—

(1) LIMITATION ON RECOGNITION OF LOSS.—

(A) IN GENERAL.—Any loss with respect to 1 or more positions shall be taken into account for any taxable year only to the extent that the amount of such loss exceeds the unrecognized gain (if any) with respect to 1 or more positions which were offsetting positions with respect to 1 or more positions from which the loss arose.

(B) CARRYOVER OF LOSS.—Any loss which may not be taken into account under subparagraph (A) for any taxable year shall, subject to the limitations under subparagraph (A), be treated as sustained in the succeeding taxable year.

(2) SPECIAL RULE FOR IDENTIFIED STRADDLES.—

(A) IN GENERAL.—In the case of any straddle which is an identified straddle—

(i) paragraph (1) shall not apply with respect to positions comprising the identified straddle,

(ii) if there is any loss with respect to any position of the identified straddle, the basis of each of the offsetting positions in the identified straddle shall be increased by an amount which bears the same ratio to the loss as the unrecognized gain with respect to such offsetting position bears to the aggregate unrecognized gain with respect to all such offsetting positions,

(iii) if the application of clause (ii) does not result in an increase in the basis of any offsetting position in the identified straddle, the basis of each of the offsetting positions in the identified straddle shall be increased in a manner which—

(I) is reasonable, consistent with the purposes of this paragraph, and consistently applied by the taxpayer, and

(II) results in an aggregate increase in the basis of such offsetting positions which is equal to the loss described in clause (ii), and

(iv) any loss described in clause (ii) shall not otherwise be taken into account for purposes of this title.

(B) IDENTIFIED STRADDLE.—The term "identified straddle" means any straddle—

(i) which is clearly identified on the taxpayer's records as an identified straddle before the earlier of—

(I) the close of the day on which the straddle is acquired, or

(II) such time as the Secretary may prescribe by regulations.

(ii) to the extent provided by regulations, the value of each position of which (in the hands of the taxpayer immediately before the creation of the straddle) is not less than the basis of such position in the hands of the taxpayer at the time the straddle is created, and

(iii) which is not part of a larger straddle.

A straddle shall be treated as clearly identified for purposes of clause (i) only if such identification includes an identification of the positions in the straddle which are offsetting with respect to other positions in the straddle.

(C) APPLICATION TO LIABILITIES AND OBLIGATIONS.—Except as otherwise provided by the Secretary, rules similar to the rules of clauses (ii) and (iii) of subparagraph (A) shall apply for purposes of this paragraph with respect to any position which is, or has been, a liability or obligation.

(D) REGULATIONS.—The Secretary shall prescribe such regulations or other guidance as may be necessary or appropriate to carry out the purposes of this paragraph. Such regulations or other guidance may specify the proper methods for clearly identifying a straddle as an identified straddle (and for identifying the positions comprising such straddle), the rules for the application of this section to a taxpayer which fails to comply with those identification requirements, the rules for the application of this section to a position which is or has been a liability or obligation, methods of loss allocation which satisfy the requirements of subparagraph (A)(iii), and the ordering rules in cases where a taxpayer disposes (or otherwise ceases to be the holder) of any part of any position which is part of an identified straddle.

(3) UNRECOGNIZED GAIN.—For purposes of this subsection—

(A) IN GENERAL.—The term "unrecognized gain" means—

(i) in the case of any position held by the taxpayer as of the close of the taxable year, the amount of gain which would be taken into account with respect to such position if such position were sold on the last business day of such taxable year at its fair market value, and

(ii) in the case of any position with respect to which, as of the close of the taxable year, gain has been realized but not recognized, the amount of gain so realized.

(B) SPECIAL RULE FOR IDENTIFIED STRADDLES.—For purposes of paragraph (2)(A)(ii), the unrecognized gain with respect to any offsetting position shall be the excess of the fair market value of the position at the time of the determination over the fair market value of the position at the time the taxpayer identified the position as a position in an identified straddle.

(C) REPORTING OF GAIN.—

(i) IN GENERAL.—Each taxpayer shall disclose to the Secretary, at such time and in such manner and form as the Secretary may prescribe by regulations—

(I) each position (whether or not part of a straddle) with respect to which, as of the close of the taxable year, there is unrecognized gain, and

(II) the amount of such unrecognized gain.

(ii) REPORTS NOT REQUIRED IN CERTAIN CASES.—Clause (i) shall not apply—

(I) to any position which is part of an identified straddle,

(II) to any position which, with respect to the taxpayer, is property described in paragraph (1) or (2) of section 1221(a) or to any position which is part of a hedging transaction (as defined in section 1256(e)), or

(III) with respect to any taxable year if no loss on a position (including a regulated futures contract) has been sustained during such taxable year or if the only loss sustained on such position is a loss described in subclause (II).

Amendments

• **2018, Tax Technical Corrections Act of 2018 (P.L. 115-141)**

P.L. 115-141, §401(a)(170), Div. U:

Amended Code Sec. 1092(a)(2)(B) by striking "with respect other" in the last sentence and inserting "with respect to other". **Effective** 3-23-2018.

• **2007, Tax Technical Corrections Act of 2007 (P.L. 110-172)**

P.L. 110-172, §7(d)(1):

Amended Code Sec. 1092(a)(2)(A) by striking "and" at the end of clause (ii), by redesignating clause (iii) as clause (iv), and by inserting after clause (ii) a new clause (iii). **Effective** as if included in the provision of the American Jobs Creation Act of 2004 (P.L. 108-357) to which it relates [effective for positions established on or after 10-22-2004.—CCH].

P.L. 110-172, §7(d)(2)(A):

Amended Code Sec. 1092(a)(2)(B) by adding at the end a new flush sentence. **Effective** for straddles acquired after 12-29-2007.

P.L. 110-172, §7(d)(2)(B)(i)-(iii):

Amended Code Sec. 1092(a)(2)(A) by striking "identified positions" in clause (i) and inserting "positions", by striking "identified position" in clause (ii) and inserting "position", and by striking "identified offsetting positions" in clause (ii) and inserting "offsetting positions". **Effective** as if included in the provision of the American Jobs Creation Act of 2004 (P.L. 108-357) to which it relates [effective for positions established on or after 10-22-2004.—CCH].

P.L. 110-172, §7(d)(2)(C):

Amended Code Sec. 1092(a)(3)(B) by striking "identified offsetting position" and inserting "offsetting position". **Effective** as if included in the provision of the American Jobs Creation Act of 2004 (P.L. 108-357) to which it relates [effective for positions established on or after 10-22-2004.—CCH].

P.L. 110-172, §7(d)(3):

Amended Code Sec. 1092(a)(2) by redesignating subparagraph (C) as subparagraph (D) and inserting after subparagraph (B) a new subparagraph (C). **Effective** as if included in the provision of the American Jobs Creation Act of 2004 (P.L. 108-357) to which it relates [effective for positions established on or after 10-22-2004.—CCH].

P.L. 110-172, §7(d)(4):

Amended Code Sec. 1092(a)(2)(D), as redesignated by Act Sec. 7(d)(3), by inserting "the rules for the application of this section to a position which is or has been a liability or obligation, methods of loss allocation which satisfy the requirements of subparagraph (A)(iii)," before "and the ordering rules". **Effective** as if included in the provision of the American Jobs Creation Act of 2004 (P.L. 108-357) to which it relates [effective for positions established on or after 10-22-2004.—CCH].

• **2005, Gulf Opportunity Zone Act of 2005 (P.L. 109-135)**

P.L. 109-135, §403(ii):

Amended Code Sec. 1092(a)(2) by striking the last sentence and adding at the end a new subparagraph (C). **Effective** as if included in the provision of the American Jobs Creation Act of 2004 (P.L. 108-357) to which it relates [effective for positions established on or after 10-22-2004.—CCH]. Prior to amendment, the last sentence of Code Sec. 1092(a)(2) read as follows:

The Secretary shall prescribe regulations which specify the proper methods for clearly identifying a straddle as an identified straddle (and the positions comprising such straddle), which specify the rules for the application of this section for a taxpayer which fails to properly identify the positions of an identified straddle, and which specify the ordering rules in cases where a taxpayer disposes of less than an entire position which is part of an identified straddle.

• **2004, American Jobs Creation Act of 2004 (P.L. 108-357)**

P.L. 108-357, §888(a)(1):

Amended Code Sec. 1092(a)(2)(A). **Effective** for positions established on or after 10-22-2004. Prior to amendment Code Sec. 1092(a)(2)(A) read as follows:

(A) IN GENERAL.—In the case of any straddle which is an identified straddle as of the close of any taxable year—

(i) paragraph (1) shall not apply for such taxable year, and

(ii) any loss with respect to such straddle shall be treated as sustained not earlier than the day on which all of the positions making up the straddle are disposed of.

P.L. 108-357, §888(a)(2)(A)-(B):

Amended Code Sec. 1092(a)(2)(B) by striking clause (ii) and inserting a new clause (ii), and by adding at the end a new flush sentence. **Effective** for positions established on or after 10-22-2004. Prior to amendment, Code Sec. 1092(a)(2)(B)(ii) read as follows:

(ii) all of the original positions of which (as identified by the taxpayer) are acquired on the same day and with respect to which—

(I) all of such positions are disposed of on the same day during the taxable year, or

(II) none of such positions has been disposed of as of the close of the taxable year, and

P.L. 108-357, §888(a)(3):

Amended Code Sec. 1092(a)(3) by redesignating subparagraph (B) as subparagraph (C) and by inserting after subparagraph (A) new subparagraph (B). **Effective** for positions established on or after 10-22-2004.

• **1999, Tax Relief Extension Act of 1999 (P.L. 106-170)**

P.L. 106-170, §532(c)(1)(F):

Amended Code Sec. 1092(a)(3)(B)(ii)(II) by striking "section 1221" and inserting "section 1221(a)". **Effective** for any instrument held, acquired, or entered into, any transaction entered into, and supplies held or acquired on or after 12-17-99.

• **1984, Deficit Reduction Act of 1984 (P.L. 98-369)**

P.L. 98-369, §107(a):

Amended Code Sec. 1092(a)(2)(B)(i). **Effective** for positions entered into after 7-18-84, in tax years ending after such date. Prior to amendment, Code Sec. 1092(a)(2)(B)(i) read as follows:

(i) which is clearly identified on the taxpayer's records, before the close of the day on which the straddle is acquired, as an identified straddle.

• **1983, Technical Corrections Act of 1982 (P.L. 97-448)**

P.L. 97-448, §105(a)(1)(A):

Amended Code Sec. 1092(a)(1)(A) by striking out "unrealized gain" and inserting in lieu thereof "unrecognized gain". **Effective** as if included in the provision of P.L. 97-34 to which it relates.

P.L. 97-448, §105(a)1)(B):

Amended so much of Code Sec. 1092(a)(3) as preceded subparagraph (B). **Effective** as if included in the provision of P.L. 97-34 to which it relates. Prior to amendment, the text read as follows:

(3) Unrealized gain.—For purposes of this subsection—

(A) In general.—The term "unrealized gain" means the amount of gain which would be taken into account with respect to any position held by the taxpayer as of the close of the taxable year if such position were sold on the last business day of such taxable year at its fair market value.

P.L. 97-448, §105(a)(1)(C):

Amended Code Sec. 1092(a)(3)(B)(i)(I) and (II). **Effective** as if included in the provision of P.L. 97-34 to which it relates. Prior to amendment, Code Sec. 1092(a)(3)(B)(i)(I) and (II) read as follows:

(I) each position (whether or not part of a straddle) which is held by such taxpayer as of the close of the taxable year and with respect to which there is unrealized gain, and

(II) the amount of such unrealized gain.

P.L. 97-448, §105(a)(2):

Amended Code Sec. 1092(a)(1)(A) by striking out "which—

(i) were acquired by the taxpayer before the disposition giving rise to such loss,

(ii) were offsetting positions with respect to the 1 or more positions from which the loss arose, and

(iii) were not part of an identified straddle as of the close of the taxable year."

and inserting in lieu thereof the following: "which were offsetting positions with respect to 1 or more positions from which the loss arose." **Effective** as if included in the provision of P.L. 97-34 to which it relates.

[Sec. 1092(b)]

(b) REGULATIONS.—

(1) IN GENERAL.—The Secretary shall prescribe such regulations with respect to gain or loss on positions which are a part of a straddle as may be appropriate to carry out the purposes of this section and section 263(g). To the extent consistent with such purposes, such regulations shall include rules applying the principles of subsections (a) and (d) of section 1091 and of subsections (b) and (d) of section 1233.

(2) REGULATIONS RELATING TO MIXED STRADDLES.—

(A) ELECTIVE PROVISIONS IN LIEU OF SECTION 1233(d) PRINCIPLES.—The regulations prescribed under paragraph (1) shall provide that—

(i) the taxpayer may offset gains and losses from positions which are part of mixed straddles—

(I) by straddle-by-straddle identification, or

INCOME TAX—WASH SALES; STRADDLES

(II) by the establishment (with respect to any class of activities) of a mixed straddle account for which gains and losses would be recognized (and offset) on a periodic basis,

(ii) such offsetting will occur before the application of section 1256, and section 1256(a)(3) will only apply to net gain or net loss attributable to section 1256 contracts, and

(iii) the principles of section 1233(d) shall not apply with respect to any straddle identified under clause (i)(I) or part of an account established under clause (i)(II).

(B) LIMITATION ON NET GAIN OR NET LOSS FROM MIXED STRADDLE ACCOUNT.—In the case of any mixed straddle account referred to in subparagraph (A)(i)(II)—

(i) NOT MORE THAN 50 PERCENT OF NET GAIN MAY BE TREATED AS LONG-TERM CAPITAL GAIN.—In no event shall more than 50 percent of the net gain from such account for any taxable year be treated as long-term capital gain.

(ii) NOT MORE THAN 40 PERCENT OF NET LOSS MAY BE TREATED AS SHORT-TERM CAPITAL LOSS.—In no event shall more than 40 percent of the net loss from such account for any taxable year be treated as short-term capital loss.

(C) AUTHORITY TO TREAT CERTAIN POSITIONS AS MIXED STRADDLES.—The regulations prescribed under paragraph (1) may treat as a mixed straddle positions not described in section 1256(d)(4).

(D) TIMING AND CHARACTER AUTHORITY.—The regulations prescribed under paragraph (1) shall include regulations relating to the timing and character of gains and losses in case of straddles where at least 1 position is ordinary and at least 1 position is capital.

Amendments

• **1988, Technical and Miscellaneous Revenue Act of 1988 (P.L. 100-647)**

P.L. 100-647, §6130(c):

Amended Code Sec. 1092(b)(2) by adding at the end thereof new subparagraph (D). **Effective**, generally, with respect to forward contracts, future contracts, options, and similar instruments entered into or acquired after 10-21-88.

• **1984, Deficit Reduction Act of 1984 (P.L. 98-369)**

P.L. 98-369, §103(a):

Amended Code Sec. 1092(b). **Effective** as noted in Act Sec. 103(b)-(c), below. Prior to amendment, it read as follows:

(b) Character of Gain or Loss; Wash Sales.—Under regulations prescribed by the Secretary, in the case of gain or loss with respect to any position of a straddle, rules which are similar to the rules of subsections (a) and (d) of section 1091 and of subsections (b) and (d) of section 1233 and which are consistent with the purposes of this section shall apply.

P.L. 98-369, §103(b)-(c), provides:

(b) REQUIREMENT THAT REGULATIONS BE ISSUED WITHIN 6 MONTHS AFTER THE DATE OF ENACTMENT.—The Secretary of the Treasury or his delegate shall prescribe initial regulations under section 1092(b) of the Internal Revenue Code of 1954 (including regulations relating to mixed straddles) not later than the date 6 months after the date of the enactment of this Act.

(c) EFFECTIVE DATE OF REGULATIONS WITH RESPECT TO MIXED STRADDLES.—The regulations described in subsection (b) with respect to the application of section 1233 of the Internal Revenue Code of 1954 to mixed straddles shall not apply to mixed straddles all of the positions of which were established before January 1, 1984.

[Sec. 1092(c)]

(c) STRADDLE DEFINED.—For purposes of this section—

(1) IN GENERAL.—The term "straddle" means offsetting positions with respect to personal property.

(2) OFFSETTING POSITIONS.—

(A) IN GENERAL.—A taxpayer holds offsetting positions with respect to personal property if there is a substantial diminution of the taxpayer's risk of loss from holding any position with respect to personal property by reason of his holding 1 or more other positions with respect to personal property (whether or not of the same kind).

(B) SPECIAL RULE FOR IDENTIFIED STRADDLES.—In the case of any position which is not part of an identified straddle (within the meaning of subsection (a)(2)(B)), such position shall not be treated as offsetting with respect to any position which is part of an identifed straddle.

(3) PRESUMPTION.—

(A) IN GENERAL.—For purposes of paragraph (2), 2 or more positions shall be presumed to be offsetting if—

(i) the positions are in the same personal property (whether established in such property or a contract for such property),

(ii) the positions are in the same personal property, even though such property may be in a substantially altered form,

(iii) the positions are in debt instruments of a similar maturity or other debt instruments described in regulations prescribed by the Secretary,

(iv) the positions are sold or marketed as offsetting positions (whether or not such positions are called a straddle, spread, butterfly, or any similar name),

(v) the aggregate margin requirement for such positions is lower than the sum of the margin requirements for each such position (if held separately), or

(vi) there are such other factors (or satisfaction of subjective or objective tests) as the Secretary may by regulations prescribe as indicating that such positions are offsetting.

For purposes of the preceding sentence, 2 or more positions shall be treated as described in clause (i), (ii), (iii), or (vi) only if the value of 1 or more of such positions ordinarily varies inversely with the value of 1 or more other such positions.

(B) PRESUMPTION MAY BE REBUTTED.—Any presumption established pursuant to subparagraph (A) may be rebutted.

(4) EXCEPTION FOR CERTAIN STRADDLES CONSISTING OF QUALIFIED COVERED CALL OPTIONS AND THE OPTIONED STOCK.—

(A) IN GENERAL.—If—

(i) all the offsetting positions making up any straddle consist of 1 or more qualified covered call options and the stock to be purchased from the taxpayer under such options, and

(ii) such straddle is not part of a larger straddle,

such straddle shall not be treated as a straddle for purposes of this section and section 263(g).

(B) QUALIFIED COVERED CALL OPTION DEFINED.—For purposes of subparagraph (A), the term "qualified covered call option" means any option granted by the taxpayer to purchase stock held by the taxpayer (or stock acquired by the taxpayer in connection with the granting of the option) but only if—

(i) such option is traded on a national securities exchange which is registered with the Securities and Exchange Commission or other market which the Secretary determines has rules adequate to carry out the purposes of this paragraph,

(ii) such option is granted more than 30 days before the day on which the option expires,

(iii) such option is not a deep-in-the-money option,

(iv) such option is not granted by an options dealer (within the meaning of section 1256(g)(8)) in connection with his activity of dealing in options, and

(v) gain or loss with respect to such option is not ordinary income or loss.

(C) DEEP-IN-THE-MONEY OPTION.—For purposes of subparagraph (B), the term "deep-in-the-money option" means an option having a strike price lower than the lowest qualified bench mark.

INCOME TAX—WASH SALES; STRADDLES

(D) LOWEST QUALIFIED BENCH MARK.—

(i) IN GENERAL.—Except as otherwise provided in this subparagraph, for purposes of subparagraph (C), the term "lowest qualified bench mark" means the highest available strike price which is less than the applicable stock price.

(ii) SPECIAL RULE WHERE OPTION IS FOR PERIOD MORE THAN 90 DAYS AND STRIKE PRICE EXCEEDS $50.—In the case of an option—

(I) which is granted more than 90 days before the date on which such option expires, and

(II) with respect to which the strike price is more than $50,

the lowest qualified bench mark is the second highest available strike price which is less than the applicable stock price.

(iii) 85 PERCENT RULE WHERE APPLICABLE STOCK PRICE $25 OR LESS.—If—

(I) the applicable stock price is $25 or less, and

(II) but for this clause, the lowest qualified bench mark would be less than 85 percent of the applicable stock price,

the lowest qualified bench mark shall be treated as equal to 85 percent of the applicable stock price.

(iv) LIMITATION WHERE APPLICABLE STOCK PRICE $150 OR LESS.—If—

(I) the applicable stock price is $150 or less, and

(II) but for this clause, the lowest qualified bench mark would be less than the applicable stock price reduced by $10,

the lowest qualified bench mark shall be treated as equal to the applicable stock price reduced by $10.

(E) SPECIAL YEAR-END RULE.—Subparagraph (A) shall not apply to any straddle for purposes of section 1092(a) if—

(i) the qualified covered call options referred to in such subparagraph are closed or the stock is disposed of at a loss during any taxable year,

(ii) gain on disposition of the stock to be purchased from the taxpayer under such options or gains on such options are includible in gross income for a later taxable year, and

(iii) such stock or option was not held by the taxpayer for 30 days or more after the closing of such options or the disposition of such stock.

For purposes of the preceding sentence, the rules of paragraphs (3) and (4) of section 246(c) shall apply in determining the period for which the taxpayer holds the stock.

(F) STRIKE PRICE.—For purposes of this paragraph, the term "strike price" means the price at which the option is exercisable.

(G) APPLICABLE STOCK PRICE.—For purposes of subparagraph (D), the term "applicable stock price" means, with respect to any stock for which an option has been granted—

(i) the closing price of such stock on the most recent day on which such stock was traded before the date on which such option was granted, or

(ii) the opening price of such stock on the day on which such option was granted, but only if such price is greater than 110 percent of the price determined under clause (i).

(H) REGULATIONS.—The Secretary shall prescribe such regulations as may be necessary or appropriate to carry out the purposes of this paragraph. Such regulations may include modifications to the provisions of this paragraph which are appropriate to take account of changes in the practices of option exchanges or to prevent the use of options for tax avoidance purposes.

Amendments

• **2018, Tax Technical Corrections Act of 2018 (P.L. 115-141)**

P.L. 115-141, §401(a)(171), Div. U:

Amended Code Sec. 1092(c)(4)(E) by striking "(other than subparagraph (B) thereof)" after "the rules of paragraphs (3)" in the flush left sentence. **Effective** 3-23-2018.

• **2004, American Jobs Creation Act of 2004 (P.L. 108-357)**

P.L. 108-357, §888(a)(4):

Amended Code Sec. 1092(c)(2) by striking subparagraph (B) and by redesignating subparagraph (C) as subparagraph (B). **Effective** for positions established on or after 10-22-2004. Prior to being stricken, Code Sec. 1092(c)(2)(B) read as follows:

(B) ONE SIDE LARGER THAN OTHER SIDE.—If 1 or more positions offset only a portion of 1 or more other positions, the Secretary shall by regulations prescribe the method for determining the portion of such other positions which is to be taken into account for purposes of this section.

• **1986, Tax Reform Act of 1986 (P.L. 99-514)**

P.L. 99-514, §331(a)(1)-(3):

Amended Code Sec. 1092(c)(4)(E) by inserting "or the stock is disposed of at a loss" in clause (i) after "closed", by striking out "is" in clause (ii) and inserting in lieu thereof "or gains on such options are", and by inserting "or option" after "stock" and "or the disposition of such stock" after "options" in clause (iii). **Effective** for positions established on or after 1-1-87.

• **1984, Deficit Reduction Act of 1984 (P.L. 98-369)**

P.L. 98-369, §101(a)(2):

Added Code Sec. 1092(c)(4). **Effective** for positions established after 12-31-83, in tax years ending after such date.

• **1983, Technical Corrections Act of 1982 (P.L. 97-448)**

P.L. 97-448, §105(a)(4):

Amended Code Sec. 1092(c)(2)(C) by striking out "subsection (a)(3)(B)" and inserting in lieu thereof "subsection (a)(2)(B)". **Effective** as if included in the provision of P.L. 97-34 to which it relates.

[Sec. 1092(d)]

(d) DEFINITIONS AND SPECIAL RULES.—For purposes of this section—

(1) PERSONAL PROPERTY.—The term "personal property" means any personal property of a type which is actively traded.

(2) POSITION.—The term "position" means an interest (including a futures or forward contract or option) in personal property.

(3) SPECIAL RULES FOR STOCK.—For purposes of paragraph (1)—

(A) IN GENERAL.—In the case of stock, the term "personal property" includes stock only if—

(i) such stock is of a type which is actively traded and at least 1 of the positions offsetting such stock is a position with respect to such stock or substantially similar or related property, or

(ii) such stock is of a corporation formed or availed of to take positions in personal property which offset positions taken by any shareholder.

(B) RULE FOR APPLICATION.—For purposes of determining whether subsection (e) applies to any transaction with respect to stock described in subparagraph (A)(ii), all includible corporations of an affiliated group (within the meaning of section 1504(a)) shall be treated as 1 taxpayer.

(4) POSITIONS HELD BY RELATED PERSONS, ETC.—

(A) IN GENERAL.—In determining whether 2 or more positions are offsetting, the taxpayer shall be treated as holding any position held by a related person.

(B) RELATED PERSON.—For purposes of subparagraph (A), a person is a related person to the taxpayer if with respect to any period during which a position is held by such person, such person—

INCOME TAX—WASH SALES; STRADDLES

(i) is the spouse of the taxpayer, or

(ii) files a consolidated return (within the meaning of section 1501) with the taxpayer for any taxable year which includes a portion of such period.

(C) CERTAIN FLOWTHROUGH ENTITIES.—If part or all of the gain or loss with respect to a position held by a partnership, trust, or other entity would properly be taken into account for purposes of this chapter by a taxpayer, then, except to the extent otherwise provided in regulations, such position shall be treated as held by the taxpayer.

(5) SPECIAL RULE FOR SECTION 1256 CONTRACTS.—

(A) GENERAL RULE.—In the case of a straddle at least 1 (but not all) of the positions of which are section 1256 contracts, the provisions of this section shall apply to any section 1256 contract and any other position making up such straddle.

(B) SPECIAL RULE FOR IDENTIFIED STRADDLES.—For purposes of subsection (a)(2) (relating to identified straddles), subparagraph (A) and section 1256(a)(4) shall not apply to a straddle all of the offsetting positions of which consist of section 1256 contracts.

(6) SECTION 1256 CONTRACT.—The term "section 1256 contract" has the meaning given such term by section 1256(b).

(7) SPECIAL RULES FOR FOREIGN CURRENCY.—

(A) POSITION TO INCLUDE INTEREST IN CERTAIN DEBT.—For purposes of paragraph (2), an obligor's interest in a nonfunctional currency denominated debt obligation is treated as a position in the nonfunctional currency.

(B) ACTIVELY TRADED REQUIREMENT.—For purposes of paragraph (1), foreign currency for which there is an active interbank market is presumed to be actively traded.

(8) SPECIAL RULES FOR PHYSICALLY SETTLED POSITIONS.—For purposes of subsection (a), if a taxpayer settles a position which is part of a straddle by delivering property to which the position relates (and such position, if terminated, would result in a realization of a loss), then such taxpayer shall be treated as if such taxpayer—

(A) terminated the position for its fair market value immediately before the settlement, and

(B) sold the property so delivered by the taxpayer at its fair market value.

Amendments

- **2004, American Jobs Creation Act of 2004 (P.L. 108-357)**

P.L. 108-357, §888(b):

Amended Code Sec. 1092(d) by adding at the end a new paragraph (8). **Effective** for positions established on or after 10-22-2004.

P.L. 108-357, §888(c)(1):

Amended Code Sec. 1092(d)(3). **Effective** for positions established on or after 10-22-2004. Prior to amendment, Code Sec. 1092(d)(3) read as follows:

(3) SPECIAL RULES FOR STOCK.—For purposes of paragraph (1)—

(A) IN GENERAL.—Except as provided in subparagraph (B), the term "personal property" does not include stock. The preceding sentence shall not apply to any interest in stock.

(B) EXCEPTIONS.—The term "personal property" includes—

(i) any stock which is part of a straddle at least 1 of the offsetting positions of which is—

(I) an option with respect to such stock or substantially identical stock or securities,

(II) a securities futures contract (as defined in section 1234B) with respect to such stock or substantially identical stock or securities, or

(III) under regulations, a position with respect to substantially similar or related property (other than stock), and

(ii) any stock of a corporation formed or availed of to take positions in personal property which offset positions taken by any shareholder.

(C) SPECIAL RULES.—

(i) For purposes of subparagraph (B), subsection (c) and paragraph (4) shall be applied as if stock described in clause (i) or (ii) of subparagraph (B) were personal property.

(ii) For purposes of determining whether subsection (e) applies to any transaction with respect to stock described in clause (ii) of subparagraph (B), all includible corporations of an affiliated group (within the meaning of section 1504(a)) shall be treated as 1 taxpayer.

- **2000, Community Renewal Tax Relief Act of 2000 (P.L. 106-554)**

P.L. 106-554, §401(e):

Amended Code Sec. 1092(d)(3)(B)(i) by striking "or" at the end of subclause (I), by redesignating subclause (II) as subclause (III), and by inserting after subclause (I) new subclause (II). **Effective** 12-21-2000.

- **1986, Tax Reform Act of 1986 (P.L. 99-514)**

P.L. 99-514, §1261(c):

Amended Code Sec. 1092(d) by adding at the end thereof new paragraph (7). **Effective** for tax years beginning after 12-31-86. However, see Act Sec. 1261(e)(2), below.

P.L. 99-514, §1261(e)(2), provides:

(2) SPECIAL RULES FOR PURPOSES OF SECTIONS 902 AND 960.—For purposes of applying sections 902 and 960 of the Internal Revenue Code of 1986, the amendments made by this section shall apply to—

(A) earnings and profits of the foreign corporation for taxable years beginning after December 31, 1986, and

(B) foreign taxes paid or accrued by the foreign corporation with respect to such earnings and profits.

P.L. 99-514, §1808(c):

Amended Code Sec. 1092(d)(3)(A) by adding at the end thereof a new sentence. **Effective** as if included in the provision of P.L. 98-369 to which it relates.

- **1984, Deficit Reduction Act of 1984 (P.L. 98-369)**

P.L. 98-369, §101(a)(1):

Amended Code Sec. 1092(d)(2). **Effective** for positions established after 12-31-83, in tax years ending after such date. A special rule appears in Act Sec. 101(e)(2), below. Prior to amendment, it read as follows:

(2) Position—

(A) In General—The term "position" means an interest (including a futures or forward contract or option) in personal property.

(B) Special Rule for Stock Options.—The term "position" includes any stock option which is a part of a straddle and which is an option to buy or sell stock which is actively traded, but does not include a stock option which—

(i) is traded on a domestic exchange or on a similar foreign exchange designated by the Secretary, and

(ii) is of a type with respect to which the maximum period during which such option may be exercised is less than the minimum period for which a capital asset must be held for gain to be treated as long-term capital gain under section 1222(3).

P.L. 98-369, §101(b)(1):

Amended Code Sec. 1092(d)(1) by striking out "(other than stock)". **Effective** for positions established after 12-31-83, in tax years ending after such date. A special rule appears in Act Sec. 101(e)(2), below.

P.L. 98-369, §101(b)(2):

Amended Code Sec. 1092(d) by redesignating paragraphs (3), (4), and (5) as paragraphs (4), (5), and (6), respectively, and by inserting after paragraph (2) new paragraph (3). **Effective** for positions established after 12-31-83, in tax years ending after such date. A special rule appears in Act Sec. 101(e)(2), below.

P.L. 98-369, §101(d):

Amended Code Sec. 1092(d)(4), redesignated as (d)(5) by Act Sec. 101(b)(2). **Effective** for positions established after 7-18-84, in tax years ending after such date. Prior to amendment, it read as follows:

(4) Special Rule for Regulated Futures Contracts.—In the case of a straddle at least 1 (but not all) of the positions of which are regulated futures contracts, the provisions of this section shall apply to any regulated futures contract and any other position making up such straddle.

P.L. 98-369, §101(e)(2), provides:

(2) Special Rule for Offsetting Position Stock.—In the case of any stock of a corporation formed or availed of to take positions in personal property which offset positions taken by any shareholder, the amendments made by this section shall apply to positions established on or after May 23, 1983, in taxable years ending on or after such date.

P.L. 98-369, §102(e):

Amended Code Sec. 1092(d)(5), redesignated as (d)(6) by Act Sec. 101(b)(2). **Effective** for positions established after 7-18-84, in tax years ending after such date. Prior to amendment, it read as follows:

(5) Regulated Futures Contract.—The term "regulated futures contract" has the same meaning given such term by section 1256(b).

- **1983, Technical Corrections Act of 1982 (P.L. 97-448)**

P.L. 97-448, §105(a)(3):

Amended Code Sec. 1092(d)(4). **Effective** as if included in the provision of P.L. 97-34 to which it relates. Prior to amendment, Code Sec. 1092(d)(4) read as follows:

(4) Special rule for regulated futures contracts.—In the case of a straddle—

(A) at least 1 (but not all) of the positions of which are regulated futures contracts, and

(B) with respect to which the taxpayer has elected not to have the provisions of section 1256 apply,

the provisions of this section shall apply to any regulated futures contract and any other position making up such straddle.

INCOME TAX—DISTRIBUTIONS, BANK HOLDING CO. ACT

[Sec. 1092(e)]

(e) EXCEPTION FOR HEDGING TRANSACTIONS.—This section shall not apply in the case of any hedging transaction (as defined in section 1256(e)).

[Sec. 1092(f)]

(f) TREATMENT OF GAIN OR LOSS AND SUSPENSION OF HOLDING PERIOD WHERE TAXPAYER GRANTOR OF QUALIFIED COVERED CALL OPTION.—If a taxpayer holds any stock and grants a qualified covered call option to purchase such stock with a strike price less than the applicable stock price—

(1) TREATMENT OF LOSS.—Any loss with respect to such option shall be treated as long-term capital loss if, at the time such loss is realized, gain on the sale or exchange of such stock would be treated as long-term capital gain.

(2) SUSPENSION OF HOLDING PERIOD.—The holding period of such stock shall not include any period during which the taxpayer is the grantor of such option.

Amendments

• **1997, Taxpayer Relief Act of 1997 (P.L. 105-34)**

P.L. 105-34, §1271(b)(9):

Amended Code Sec. 1092(f)(2) by striking "Except for purposes of section 851(b)(3), the" and inserting "The". **Effective** for tax years beginning after 8-5-97.

• **1984, Deficit Reduction Act of 1984 (P.L. 98-369)**

P.L. 98-369, §101(c):

Amended Code Sec. 1092 by redesignating subsection (f) as subsection (g) and by inserting after subsection (e) the new subsection (f). **Effective** for positions established after 6-30-84, in tax years ending after such date.

[Sec. 1092(g)]

(g) CROSS REFERENCE.—

For provision requiring capitalization of certain interest and carrying charges where there is a straddle, see section 263(g).

Amendments

• **1984, Deficit Reduction Act of 1984 (P.L. 98-369)**

P.L. 98-369, §101(c):

Amended Code Sec. 1092 by redesignating subsection (f) as subsection (g). **Effective** for positions established after 6-30-84, in tax years ending after such date.

• **1981, Economic Recovery Tax Act of 1981 (P.L. 97-34)**

P.L. 97-34, §501(a):

Added Code Sec. 1092. **Effective** for property acquired and positions established by the taxpayer after 6-23-81, in tax years ending after such date. A special election is provided in Act Sec. 508(c), below.

P.L. 97-34, §508(c), provides:

(c) ELECTION WITH RESPECT TO PROPERTY HELD ON JUNE 23, 1981.—If the taxpayer so elects (at such time and in such manner as the Scretary of the Treasury or his delegate shall prescribe) with respect to all regulated futures contracts or positions held by the taxpayer on June 23, 1981, the amendments made by this title shall apply to all such contracts and positions, effective for periods after such date in taxable years ending after such date. For purposes of the preceding sentence, the term "regulated futures contract" has the meaning given to such term by section 1256(b) of the Internal Revenue Code of 1954, and the term "position" has the meaning given to such term by section 1092(d)(2) of such Code.

PART VIII—DISTRIBUTIONS PURSUANT TO BANK HOLDING COMPANY ACT—[Repealed]

[Sec. 1101—Repealed]

Amendments

• **1990, Omnibus Budget Reconciliation Act of 1990 (P.L. 101-508)**

P.L. 101-508, §11801(a)(34):

Repealed Part VIII of subchapter O of chapter 1. **Effective** 11-5-90.

P.L. 101-508, §11821(b), provides:

(b) SAVINGS PROVISION.—If—

(1) any provision amended or repealed by this part applied to—

(A) any transaction occurring before the date of the enactment of this Act,

(B) any property acquired before such date of enactment, or

(C) any item of income, loss, deduction, or credit taken into account before such date of enactment, and

(2) the treatment of such transaction, property, or item under such provision would (without regard to the amendments made by this part) affect liability for tax for periods ending after such date of enactment,

nothing in the amendments made by this part shall be construed to affect the treatment of such transaction, property, or item for purposes of determining liability for tax for periods ending after such date of enactment.

Prior to repeal, Code Sec. 1101 read as follows:

SEC. 1101. DISTRIBUTIONS PURSUANT TO BANK HOLDING COMPANY ACT.

[Sec. 1101(a)]

(a) DISTRIBUTIONS OF CERTAIN NON-BANKING PROPERTY.—

(1) DISTRIBUTIONS OF PROHIBITED PROPERTY.—If—

(A) a qualified bank holding corporation distributes prohibited property (other than stock received in an exchange to which subsection (c)(2) applies)—

(i) to a shareholder (with respect to its stock held by such shareholder), without the surrender by such shareholder of stock in such corporation, or

(ii) to a shareholder, in exchange for its preferred stock, or

(iii) to a security holder, in exchange for its securities, and

(B) the Board has, before the distribution, certified that the distribution of such prohibited property is necessary or appropriate to effectuate section 4 of the Bank Holding Company Act,

then no gain to the shareholder or security holder from the receipt of such property shall be recognized.

(2) DISTRIBUTIONS OF STOCK AND SECURITIES RECEIVED IN AN EXCHANGE TO WHICH SUBSECTION (c)(2) APPLIES.—If—

(A) a qualified bank holding corporation distributes—

(i) common stock received in an exchange to which subsection (c)(2) applies to a shareholder (with respect to its stock held by such shareholder), without the surrender by such shareholder of stock in such corporation, or

(ii) common stock received in an exchange to which subsection (c)(2) applies to a shareholder, in exchange for its common stock, or

(iii) preferred stock or common stock received in an exchange to which subsection (c)(2) applies to a shareholder, in exchange for its preferred stock, or

(iv) securities or preferred or common stock received in an exchange to which subsection (c)(2) applies to a security holder in exchange for its securities, and

(B) any preferred stock received has substantially the same terms as the preferred stock exchanged, and any securities received have substantially the same terms as the securities exchanged,

then, except as provided in subsection (f), no gain to the shareholder or security holder from the receipt of such stock or such securities or such stock and securities shall be recognized.

(3) PRO RATA AND OTHER REQUIREMENTS.—

(A) IN GENERAL.—Paragraphs (1) and (2) of this subsection, or paragraphs (1) and (2) of subsection (b), as the case may be, shall apply to any distribution to the shareholders of a qualified bank holding corporation only if each distribution—

(i) which is made by such corporation to its shareholders after July 7, 1970, and on or before the date on which the Board makes its final certification under subsection (e), and

(ii) to which such paragraph (1) or (2) applies (determined without regard to this paragraph),

meets the requirements of subparagraph (B), (C), or (D).

(B) PRO RATA REQUIREMENTS.—A distribution meets the requirements of this subparagraph if the distribution is pro rata with respect to all shareholders of the distributing qualified bank holding corporation or with respect to all shareholders of common stock of such corporation.

(C) REDEMPTIONS WHEN UNIFORM OFFER IS MADE.—A distribution meets the requirements of this subparagraph if the distribution is in exchange for stock of the distributing qualified bank holding corporation and such distribution is pursuant to a good faith offer made on a uniform basis to all shareholders of the distributing qualified bank holding corporation or to all shareholders of common stock of such corporation.

(D) NON-PRO RATA DISTRIBUTIONS FROM CERTAIN CLOSELY-HELD CORPORATIONS.—A distribution meets the requirements of this subparagraph if such distribution is made by a qualified bank holding corporation which does not have more than 10 shareholders (within the meaning of section 1361(b)(1)(A)) and does not have as a shareholder a person (other than an estate) which is not an individual, and if the Board (after consultation with the Secretary) certifies that—

(i) a distribution which meets the requirements of subparagraph (B) or (C) is not appropriate to effectuate section 4 or the policies of the Bank Holding Company Act, and

(ii) the distribution being made is necessary or appropriate to effectuate section 4 of the policies of such Act.

(4) EXCEPTION.—This subsection shall not apply to any distribution by a corporation if such corporation, a corporation having control of such corporation, or a subsidiary of such corporation has made any distribution pursuant to subsection (b) or has made an election under section 6158 with respect to bank property (as defined in section 6158(f)(3)).

(5) DISTRIBUTIONS INVOLVING GIFT OR COMPENSATION.—In the case of a distribution to which paragraph (1) or (2) applies but which—

(A) results in a gift, see section 2501 and following, or

(B) has the effect of the payment of compensation, see section 61.

INCOME TAX—DISTRIBUTIONS, BANK HOLDING CO. ACT

Amendments

• **1982, Subchapter S Revision Act of 1982 (P.L. 97-354)**

P.L. 97-354, § 5(a)(34):

Amended Code Sec. 1101(a)(3)(D) by striking out "section 1371(a)(1)" and inserting in lieu thereof "section 1361(b)(1)(A)". **Effective** for tax years beginning after 12-31-82.

• **1976, Bank Holding Company Tax Act of 1976 (P.L. 94-452)**

P.L. 94-452, § 2(a):

Amended Code Sec. 1101(a) by changing Code Secs. 1101(a)(1)(B) and 1101(a)(3), (4) and (5). **Effective** 10-1-77, with respect to distributions after 7-7-70, in tax years ending after 7-7-70, but only in the case of qualified bank holding corporations. For purposes of Code Secs. 1101(a)(1)(B) and 1101(a)(3)(D), in the case of any distribution which takes place on or before 12-31-76, a certification by the Federal Reserve Board shall be treated as made before the distribution if application for such certification is made before the close of 12-31-76. Prior to amendment Code Sec. 1101(a)(1)(B) read as follows:

(B) the Board has, before the distribution, certified that the distribution of such prohibited property is necessary or appropriate to effectuate section 4 of the Bank Holding Company Act of 1956,

Prior to amendment Code Sec. 1101(a)(3)-(5) read as follows:

(3) NON PRO RATA DISTRIBUTIONS.—Paragraphs (1) and (2) shall apply to a distribution whether or not the distribution is pro rata with respect to all of the shareholders of the distributing qualified bank holding corporation.

(4) EXCEPTION.—This subsection shall not apply to any distribution by a corporation which has made any distribution pursuant to subsection (b).

(5) DISTRIBUTIONS INVOLVING GIFT OR COMPENSATION.—In the case if a distribution to which paragraph (1) or (2) applies, but which—

(A) results in a gift, see section 2501, and following, or

(B) has the effect of the payment of compensation, see section 61(a)(1).

[Sec. 1101(b)]

(b) CORPORATION CEASING TO BE A BANK HOLDING COMPANY.—

(1) DISTRIBUTIONS OF PROPERTY WHICH CAUSE A CORPORATION TO BE A BANK HOLDING COMPANY.—If—

(A) a qualified bank holding corporation distributes property (other than stock received in an exchange to which subsection (c)(3) applies)—

(i) to a shareholder (with respect to its stock held by such shareholder), without the surrender by such shareholder of stock in such corporation, or

(ii) to a shareholder, in exchange for its preferred stock, or

(iii) to a security holder, in exchange for its securities, and

(B) the Board has, before the distribution, certified that—

(i) such property is all or part of the property by reason of which such corporation controls (within the meaning of section 2(a) of the Bank Holding Company Act) a bank or bank holding company, or such property is part of the property by reason of which such corporation did control a bank or a bank holding company before any property of the same kind was distributed under this subsection or exchanged under subsection (c)(3); and

(ii) the distribution is necessary or appropriate to effectuate the policies of such Act,

then no gain to the shareholder or security holder from the receipt of such property shall be recognized.

(2) DISTRIBUTIONS OF STOCK AND SECURITIES RECEIVED IN AN EXCHANGE TO WHICH SUBSECTION (c)(3) APPLIES.—If—

(A) a qualified bank holding corporation distributes—

(i) common stock received in an exchange to which subsection (c)(3) applies to a shareholder (with respect to its stock held by such shareholder), without the surrender by such shareholder of stock in such corporation, or

(ii) common stock received in an exchange to which subsection (c)(3) applies to a shareholder, in exchange for its common stock, or

(iii) preferred stock or common stock received in an exchange to which subsection (c)(3) applies to a shareholder, in exchange for its preferred stock, or

(iv) securities or preferred or common stock received in an exchange to which subsection (c)(3) applies to a security holder, in exchange for its securities, and

(B) any preferred stock received has substantially the same terms as the preferred stock exchanged, and any securities received have substantially the same terms as the securities exchanged,

then, except as provided in subsection (f), no gain to the shareholder or security holder from the receipt of such stock or such securities or such stock and securities shall be recognized.

(3) PRO RATA AND OTHER REQUIREMENTS.—For pro rata and other requirements, see subsection (a)(3).

(4) EXCEPTION.—This subsection shall not apply to any distribution by a corporation if such corporation, a corporation having control of such corporation, or a subsidiary of such corporation has made any distribution pursuant to subsection (a) or has made an election under section 6158 with respect to prohibited property.

(5) DISTRIBUTIONS INVOLVING GIFT OR COMPENSATION.—In the case of a distribution to which paragraph (1) or (2) applies but which—

(A) results in a gift, see section 2501 and following, or

(B) has the effect of the payment of compensation, see section 61.

Amendments

• **1976, Bank Holding Company Tax Act of 1976 (P.L. 94-452)**

P.L. 94-452, § 2(a):

Amended Code Sec. 1101(b)(1)(B)(i) and (b)(3)-(5). **Effective** 10-1-77, with respect to distributions after 7-7-70, in tax years ending after 7-7-70, but only in the case of qualified bank holding corporations. For purposes of Code Sec. 1101(b)(1)(B), in the case of any distribution which takes place on or before 12-31-76, a certification by the Federal Reserve Board shall be treated as made before the distribution if application for such certification is made before the close of 12-31-76. Prior to amendment Code Sec. 1101(b)(1)(B)(i) read as follows:

(i) such property is all or part of the property by reason of which such corporation controls (within the meaning of section 2(a) of the Bank Holding Company Act of 1956) a bank or bank holding company, or such property is a part of the property by reason of which such corporation did control a bank or a bank holding company before any property of the same kind was distributed under this subsection or exchanged under subsection (c)(3); and

Prior to amendment Code Sec. 1101(b)(3)-(5) read as follows:

(3) NON PRO RATA DISTRIBUTIONS.—Paragraphs (1) and (2) shall apply to a distribution whether or not the distribution is pro rata with respect to all of the shareholders of the distributing qualified bank holding corporation.

(4) EXCEPTION.—This subsection shall not apply to any distribution by a corporation which has made any distribution pursuant to subsection (a).

(5) DISTRIBUTIONS INVOLVING GIFT OR COMPENSATION.—

In the case of a distribution to which paragraph (1) or (2) applies, but which—

(A) results in a gift, see section 2501, and following, or

(B) has the effect of the payment of compensation, see section 61(a)(1).

[Sec. 1101(c)]

(c) PROPERTY ACQUIRED AFTER JULY 7, 1970.—

(1) IN GENERAL.—Except as provided in paragraphs (2) and (3), subsection (a) or (b) shall not apply to—

(A) any property acquired by the distributing corporation after July 7, 1970, unless (i) gain to such corporation with respect to the receipt of such property was not recognized by reason of subsection (a) or (b), or (ii) such property was received by it in exchange for all of its stock in an exchange to which paragraph (2) or (3) applies, or (iii) such property was acquired by the distributing corporation in a transaction in which gain was not recognized under section 305(a) or section 332, or under section 354 or 356 (but only with respect to property permitted by section 354 or 356 to be received without the recognition of gain or loss) with respect to a reorganization described in section 368(a)(1) (A), (B), (E), or (F), or

(B) any property which was acquired by the distributing corporation in a distribution with respect to stock acquired by such corporation after July 7, 1970, unless such stock was acquired by such corporation (i) in a distribution (with respect to stock held by it on July 7, 1970, or with respect to stock in respect of which all previous applications of this clause are satisfied) with respect to which gain to it was not recognized by reason of subsection (a) or (b), or (ii) in exchange for all of its stock in an exchange to which paragraph (2) or (3) applies, or (iii) in a transaction in which gain was not recognized under section 305(a) or section 332, or under section 354 or 356 (but only with respect to property permitted by section 354 or 356 to be received without the recognition of gain or loss) with respect to a reorganization described in section 368(a)(1)(A), (B), (E), or (F), or

(C) any property acquired by the distributing corporation in a transaction in which gain was not recognized under section 332, unless such property was acquired from a corporation which, if it had been a qualified bank holding corporation, could have distributed such property under subsection (a)(1) or (b)(1), or

(D) any property acquired by the distributing corporation in a transaction in which gain was not recognized under section 354 or 356 with respect to a reorganization described in section 368(a)(1)(A) or (B), unless such property was acquired by the distributing corporation in exchange for property which the distributing corporation could have distributed under subsection (a)(1) or (b)(1).

(2) EXCHANGES INVOLVING PROHIBITED PROPERTY.—If—

(A) any qualified bank holding corporation exchanges (i) property, which, under subsection (a)(1), such corporation could distribute directly to its shareholders or security holders without the recognition of gain to such shareholders or security holders, and other property (except property described in subsection (b)(1)(B)(i)), for (ii) all of the stock of a second corporation created and availed of solely for the purpose of receiving such property.

(B) immediately after the exchange, the qualified bank holding corporation distributes all of such stock in a manner prescribed in subsection (a)(2)(A), and

(C) before such distribution, the Board has certified (with respect to the property exchanged which consists of property which, under subsection (a)(1), such corporation could distribute directly to its shareholders or security holders without the recognition of gain) that the exchange and distribution are necessary or appropriate to effectuate section 4 of the Bank Holding Company Act,

then paragraph (1) shall not apply with respect to such distribution.

(3) EXCHANGES INVOLVING INTERESTS IN BANKS.—If—

(A) any qualified bank holding corporation exchanges (i) property which, under subsection (b)(1), such corporation could distribute directly to its shareholders or security holders without the recognition of gain to such shareholders or security holders, and other property (except prohibited property), for (ii) all of the stock of a second corporation created and availed of solely for the purpose of receiving such property,

(B) immediately after the exchange, the qualified bank holding corporation distributes all of such stock in a manner prescribed in subsection (b)(2)(A), and

(C) before such distribution, the Board has certified (with respect to the property exchanged which consists of property which, under subsection (b)(1), such corporation could distribute directly to its shareholders or security holders without the recognition of gain) that—

(i) such property is all or part of the property by reason of which such corporation controls (within the meaning of section 2(a) of the Bank Holding Company Act) a bank or bank holding company, or such property is part of the property by reason of which such corporation did control a bank or a bank holding company before any property of the same kind was distributed under subsection (b)(1) or exchanged under this paragraph, and

(ii) the exchange and distribution are necessary or appropriate to effectuate the policies of such Act,

then paragraph (1) shall not apply with respect to such distribution.

Sec. 1101—Repealed

INCOME TAX—DISTRIBUTIONS, BANK HOLDING CO. ACT

Amendments

• **1976, Bank Holding Company Tax Act of 1976 (P.L. 94-452)**

P.L. 94-452, §2(a):

Amended Code Sec. 1101(c). **Effective** 10-1-77, with respect to distributions after 7-7-70, in tax years ending after 7-7-70, but only in the case of qualified bank holding corporations. For purposes of Code Secs. 1101(c)(2)(C) and 1101(c)(3)(C), in the case of any distribution which takes place on or before 12-31-76, a certification by the Federal Reserve Board shall be treated as made before the distribution if application for such certification is made before the close of 12-31-76. Prior to amendment Code Sec. 1101(c) read as follows:

(c) PROPERTY ACQUIRED AFTER MAY 15, 1955.—

(1) IN GENERAL.—Except as provided in paragraphs (2) and (3), subsection (a) or (b) shall not apply to—

(A) any property acquired by the distributing corporation after May 15, 1955, unless (i) gain to such corporation with respect to the receipt of such property was not recognized by reason of subsection (a) or (b), or (ii) such property was received by it in exchange for all of its stock in an exchange to which paragraph (2) or (3) applies, or (iii) such property was acquired by the distributing corporation in a transaction in which gain was not recognized under section 305(a) or section 332, or under section 354 with respect to a reorganization described in section 368(a)(1)(E) or (F), or

(B) any property which was acquired by the distributing corporation in a distribution with respect to stock acquired by such corporation after May 15, 1955, unless such stock was acquired by such corporation (i) in a distribution (with respect to stock held by it on May 15, 1955, or with respect to stock in respect of which all previous applications of this clause are satisfied) with respect to which gain to it was not recognized by reason of subsection (a) or (b), or (ii) in exchange for all of its stock in an exchange to which paragraph (2) or (3) applies, or (iii) in a transaction in which gain was not recognized under section 305(a) or section 332, or under section 354 with respect to a reorganization described in section 368(a)(1)(E) or (F), or

(C) any property acquired by the distributing corporation in a transaction in which gain was not recognized under section 332, unless such property was acquired from a corporation which, if it had been a qualified bank holding corporation, could have distributed such property under subsection (a)(1) or (b)(1).

(2) EXCHANGES INVOLVING PROHIBITED PROPERTY.—If—

(A) any qualified bank holding corporation exchanges (i) property, which, under subsection (a)(1), such corporation could distribute directly to its shareholders or security holders without the recognition of gain to such shareholders or security holders, and other property (except property described in subsection (b)(1)(B)(i)), for (ii) all of the stock of a second corporation created and availed of solely for the purpose of receiving such property;

(B) immediately after the exchange, the qualified bank holding corporation distributes all of such stock in a manner prescribed in subsection (a)(2)(A); and

(C) before such exchange, the Board has certified (with respect to the property exchanged which consists of property which, under subsection (a)(1), such corporation could distribute directly to its shareholders or security holders without the recognition of gain) that the exchange and distribution are necessary or appropriate to effectuate section 4 of the Bank Holding Company Act of 1956,

then paragraph (1) shall not apply with respect to such distribution.

(3) EXCHANGES INVOLVING INTERESTS IN BANKS.—If—

(A) any qualified bank holding corporation exchanges (i) property which, under subsection (b)(1), such corporation could distribute directly to its shareholders or security holders without the recognition of gain to such shareholders or security holders, and other property (except prohibited property), for (ii) all of the stock of a second corporation created and availed of solely for the purpose of receiving such property;

(B) immediately after the exchange, the qualified bank holding corporation distributes all of such stock in a manner prescribed in subsection (b)(2)(A); and

(C) before such exchange, the Board has certified (with respect to the property exchanged which consists of property which, under subsection (b)(1), such corporation could distribute directly to its shareholders or security holders without the recognition of gain) that—

(i) such property is all or part of the property by reason of which such corporation controls (within the meaning of section 2(a) of the Bank Holding Company Act of 1956) a bank or bank holding company, or such property is part of the property by reason of which such corporation did control a bank or a bank holding company before any property of the same kind was distributed under subsection (b)(1) or exchanged under this paragraph; and

(ii) the exchange and distribution are necessary or appropriate to effectuate the policies of such Act,

then paragraph (1) shall not apply with respect to such distribution.

[Sec. 1101(d)]

(d) DISTRIBUTIONS TO AVOID FEDERAL INCOME TAX.—

(1) PROHIBITED PROPERTY.—Subsection (a) shall not apply to a distribution if, in connection with such distribution, the distributing corporation retains, or transfers after July 7, 1970, to any corporation, property (other than prohibited property) as part of a plan one of the principal purposes of which is the distribution of the earnings and profits of any corporation.

(2) BANKING PROPERTY.—Subsection (b) shall not apply to a distribution if, in connection with such distribution, the distributing corporation retains, or transfers after July 7, 1970, to any corporation, property (other than property described in subsection (b)(1)(B)(i)) as part of a plan one of the principal purposes of which is the distribution of the earnings and profits of any corporation.

Amendments

• **1976, Bank Holding Company Tax Act of 1976 (P.L. 94-452)**

P.L. 94-452, §2(a):

Amended Code Sec. 1101(d). **Effective** 10-1-77, with respect to distributions after 7-7-70, in tax years ending after 7-7-70, but only in the case of qualified bank holding corporations. Prior to amendment Code Sec. 1101(d) read as follows:

(d) DISTRIBUTIONS TO AVOID FEDERAL INCOME TAX.—

(1) PROHIBITED PROPERTY.—Subsection (a) shall not apply to a distribution if, in connection with such distribution, the distributing corporation retains, or transfers after May 15, 1955, to any corporation, property (other than prohibited property) as part of a plan one of the principal purposes of which is the distribution of the earnings and profits of any corporation.

(2) BANKING PROPERTY.—Subsection (b) shall not apply to a distribution if, in connection with such distribution, the distributing corporation retains, or transfers after May 15, 1955, to any corporation, property (other than property described in subsection (b)(1)(B)(i)) as part of a plan one of the principal purposes of which is the distribution of the earnings and profits of any corporation.

(3) CERTAIN CONTRIBUTIONS TO CAPITAL.—In the case of a distribution a portion of which is attributable to a transfer which is a contribution to the capital of a corporation, made after May 15, 1955, and prior to the date of the enactment of this part, if subsection (a) or (b) would apply to such distribution but for the fact that, under paragraph (1) or (2) (as the case may be) of this subsection, such contribution to capital is part of a plan one of the principal purposes of which is to distribute the earnings and profits of any corporation, then, notwithstanding paragraph (1) or (2), subsection (a) or (b) (as the case may be) shall apply to that portion of such distribution not attributable to such contribution to capital, and shall not apply to that portion of such distribution attributable to such contribution to capital.

[Sec. 1101(e)]

(e) FINAL CERTIFICATION.—

(1) FOR SUBSECTION (a).—Subsection (a) shall not apply with respect to any distribution by a corporation unless the Board certifies, before the close of the calendar year following the calendar year in which the last distribution occurred, that the corporation has (before the expiration of the period prohibited property is permitted under the Bank Holding Company Act to be held by a bank holding company) disposed of all of the property the disposition of which is necessary or appropriate to effectuate section 4 of the Bank Holding Company Act.

(2) FOR SUBSECTION (b).—Subsection (b) shall not apply with respect to any distribution by a corporation unless the Board certifies, before the close of the calendar year following the calendar year in which the last distribution occurred, that the corporation has (before the expiration of the period prohibited property is permitted under the Bank Holding Company Act to be held by a bank holding company) ceased to be a bank holding company.

Amendments

• **1976, Bank Holding Company Tax Act of 1976 (P.L. 94-452)**

P.L. 94-452, §2(a):

Amended Code Sec. 1101(e). **Effective** 10-1-77, with respect to distributions after 7-7-70, in tax years ending after 7-7-70, but only in the case of qualified bank holding corporations. For purposes of Code Sec. 1101(e) in the case of any distribution which takes place on or before 12-31-76, a certification by the Federal Reserve Board shall be treated as made before the distribution if application for such certification is made before the close of 12-31-76. Prior to amendment Code Sec. 1101(e) read as follows:

(e) FINAL CERTIFICATION.—

(1) FOR SUBSECTION (a).—Subsection (a) shall not apply with respect to any distribution by a corporation unless the Board certifies that, before the expiration of the period permitted under section 4(a) of the Bank Holding Company Act of 1956 (including any extensions thereof granted to such corporation under such section 4(a)), the corporation has disposed of all the property the disposition of which is necessary or appropriate to effectuate section 4 of such Act (or would have been so necessary or appropriate if the corporation had continued to be a bank holding company).

(2) FOR SUBSECTION (b).—

(A) Subsection (b) shall not apply with respect to any distribution by any corporation unless the Board certifies that, before the expiration of the period specified in subparagraph (B), the corporation has ceased to be a bank holding company.

(B) The period referred to in subparagraph (A) is the period which expires 2 years after the date of the enactment of this part or 2 years after the date on which the corporation becomes a bank holding company, whichever date is later. The Board is authorized, on application by any corporation, to extend such period from time to time with respect to such corporation for not more than one year at a time if, in its judgment, such an extension would not be detrimental to the public interest; except that such period may not in any case be extended beyond the date 5 years after the date of the enactment of this part or 5 years after the date on which the corporation becomes a bank holding company, whichever date is later.

[Sec. 1101(f)]

(f) CERTAIN EXCHANGES OF SECURITIES.—In the case of an exchange described in subsection (a)(2)(A)(iv) or subsection (b)(2)(A)(iv), subsection (a) or subsection (b) (as the case may be) shall apply only to the extent that the principal amount of the securities received does not exceed the principal amount of the securities exchanged.

Amendments

• **1956, Bank Holding Company Act of 1956 (P.L. 511, 84th Cong.)**

P.L. 511, 84th Cong., §10:

Added Sec. 1101 to the 1954 Code, and amended table of parts for Subchapter O to reflect addition of new Part VIII (Secs. 1101-1103). **Effective** for tax years ending after 5-9-56.

INCOME TAX—DISTRIBUTIONS, BANK HOLDING CO. ACT

[Sec. 1102—Repealed]

Amendments

• **1990, Omnibus Budget Reconciliation Act of 1990 (P.L. 101-508)**

P.L. 101-508, §11801(a)(34):

Repealed Code Sec. 1102. **Effective** 11-5-90.

P.L. 101-508, §11821(b), provides:

(b) SAVINGS PROVISION.—If—

(1) any provision amended or repealed by this part applied to—

(A) any transaction occurring before the date of the enactment of this Act,

(B) any property acquired before such date of enactment, or

(C) any item of income, loss, deduction, or credit taken into account before such date of enactment, and

(2) the treatment of such transaction, property, or item under such provision would (without regard to the amendments made by this part) affect liability for tax for periods ending after such date of enactment,

nothing in the amendments made by this part shall be construed to affect the treatment of such transaction, property, or item for purposes of determining liability for tax for periods ending after such date of enactment.

Prior to repeal, Code Sec. 1102 read as follows:

SEC. 1102. SPECIAL RULES.

[Sec. 1102(a)]

(a) BASIS OF PROPERTY ACQUIRED IN DISTRIBUTIONS.—If, by reason of section 1101, gain is not recognized with respect to the receipt of any property, then, under regulations prescribed by the Secretary—

(1) if the property is received by a shareholder with respect to stock without the surrender by such shareholder of stock, the basis of the property received and of the stock with respect to which it is distributed shall, in the distributee's hands, be determined by allocating between such property and such stock the adjusted basis of such stock, or

(2) if the property is received by a shareholder in exchange for stock or by a security holder in exchange for securities, the basis of the property received shall, in the distributee's hands, be the same as the adjusted basis of the stock or securities exchanged, increased by the amount of gain to the taxpayer recognized on the property received.

Amendments

• **1976, Tax Reform Act of 1976 (P.L. 94-455)**

P.L. 94-455, §1906(b)(13)(A):

Amended 1954 Code by substituting "Secretary" for "Secretary or his delegate" each place it appeared. **Effective** 2-1-77.

• **1976, Bank Holding Company Tax Act of 1976 (P.L. 94-452)**

P.L. 94-452, §2(a):

Amended Code Sec. 1102(a). **Effective** 10-1-77, with respect to distributions after 7-7-70, in tax years ending after 7-7-70, but only in the case of qualified bank holding corporations. Prior to amendment Code Sec. 1102(a) read as follows:

(a) BASIS OF PROPERTY ACQUIRED IN DISTRIBUTIONS.—If, by reason of section 1101, gain is not recognized with respect to the receipt of any property, then, under regulations prescribed by the Secretary—

(1) if the property is received by a shareholder with respect to stock, without the surrender by such shareholder of stock, the basis of the property received and of the stock with respect to which it is distributed shall, in the distributee's hands, be determined by allocating between such property and such stock the adjusted basis of such stock; or

(2) if the property is received by a shareholder in exchange for stock or by a security holder in exchange for securities, the basis of the property received shall, in the distributee's hands, be the same as the adjusted basis of the stock or securities exchanged, increased by—

(A) the amount of the property received which was treated as a dividend, and

(B) the amount of gain to the taxpayer recognized on the property received (not including any portion of such gain which was treated as a dividend.)

[Sec. 1102(b)]

(b) PERIODS OF LIMITATION.—The periods of limitation provided in section 6501 (relating to limitations on assessment and collection) shall not expire, with respect to any deficiency (including interest and additions to the tax) resulting solely from the receipt of property by shareholders in a distribution which is certified by the Board under subsection (a), (b), or (c) of section 1101, until 5 years after the distributing corporation notifies the Secretary (in such manner and with such accompanying information as the Secretary may by regulations prescribe)—

(1) that the final certification required by subsection (e) of Section 1101 has been made, or

(2) that such final certification will not be made;

and such assessment may be made notwithstanding any provision of law or rule of law which would otherwise prevent such assessment.

Amendments

P.L. 94-455, §1906(b)(13)(A):

Amended 1954 Code by substituting "Secretary" for "Secretary or his delegate" each place it appeared. **Effective** 2-1-77.

Amendments

• **1990, Omnibus Budget Reconciliation Act of 1990 (P.L. 101-508)**

P.L. 101-508, §11801(a)(34):

Repealed Code Sec. 1103. **Effective** 11-5-90.

• **1976, Bank Holding Company Tax Act of 1976 (P.L. 94-452)**

P.L. 94-452, §2(a):

Amended Code Sec. 1102(b). **Effective** 10-1-77, with respect to distributions after 7-7-70, in tax years ending after 7-7-70, but only in the case of qualified bank holding corporations. Prior to amendment Code Sec. 1102(b) read as follows:

(b) PERIODS OF LIMITATION.—The periods of limitation provided in section 6501 (relating to limitations on assessment and collection) shall not expire, with respect to any deficiency (including interest and additions to the tax) resulting solely from the receipt of property by shareholders in a distribution which is certified by the Board under subsection (a), (b), or (c) of section 1101, until five years after the distributing corporation notifies the Secretary or his delegate (in such manner and with such accompanying information as the Secretary or his delegate may by regulations prescribe) that the period (including extensions thereof) prescribed in section 4(a) of the Bank Holding Company Act of 1956, or section 1101(e)(2)(B), whichever is applicable, has expired; and such assessment may be made notwithstanding any provision of law or rule of law which would otherwise prevent such assessment.

[Sec. 1102(c)]

(c) ALLOCATION OF EARNINGS AND PROFITS.—

(1) DISTRIBUTION OF STOCK IN A CONTROLLED CORPORATION.—In the case of a distribution by a qualified bank holding corporation under section 1101(a)(1) or (b)(1) of stock in a controlled corporation, proper allocation with respect to the earnings and profits of the distributing corporation and the controlled corporation shall be made under regulations prescribed by the Secretary.

(2) EXCHANGES DESCRIBED IN SECTION 1101 (c)(2) or (3).—In the case of any exchange described in section 1101(c)(2) or (3), proper allocation with respect to the earnings and profits of the corporation transferring the property and the corporation receiving such property shall be made under regulations prescribed by the Secretary.

(3) DEFINITION OF CONTROLLED CORPORATION.—For purposes of paragraph (1), the term "controlled corporation" means a corporation with respect to which at least 80 percent of the total combined voting power of all classes of stock entitled to vote and at least 80 percent of the total number of shares of all other classes of stock is owned by the distributing qualified bank holding corporation.

Amendments

• **1976, Tax Reform Act of 1976 (P.L. 94-455)**

P.L. 94-455, §1906(b)(13)(A):

Amended 1954 Code by substituting "Secretary" for "Secretary or his delegate" each place it appeared. **Effective** 2-1-77.

[Sec. 1102(d)]

(d) ITEMIZATION OF PROPERTY.—In any certification under this part, the Board shall make such specification and itemization of property as may be necessary to carry out the provisions of this part.

[Sec. 1102(e)—Repealed]

Amendments

• **1976, Bank Holding Company Tax Act of 1976 (P.L. 94-452)**

P.L. 94-452, §2(a):

Repealed Code Sec. 1102(e). **Effective** 10-1-77, with respect to distributions after 7-7-70, in tax years ending after 7-7-70, but only in the case of qualified bank holding corporations. Prior to repeal, Code Sec. 1102(e) read as follows:

(e) CERTAIN BANK HOLDING COMPANIES.—This part shall apply in respect of any company which becomes a bank holding company as a result of the enactment of the Act entitled "An Act to amend the Bank Holding Company Act of 1956", approved July 1, 1966 (Public Law 89-485), with the following modifications:

(1) Subsections (a)(3) and (b)(3) of section 1101 shall not apply.

(2) Subsections (a)(1) and (2) and (b)(1) and (2) of section 1101 shall apply in respect of distributions to shareholders of the distributing bank holding corporation only if all distributions to each class of shareholders which are made—

(A) after April 12, 1965, and

(B) on or before the date on which the Board of Governors of the Federal Reserve System makes its final certification under section 1101(e),

are pro rata. For purposes of the preceding sentence, any redemption of stock made in whole or in part with property other than money shall be treated as a distribution.

(3) In applying subsections (c) and (d) of section 1101 and subsection (b) of section 1103, the date "April 12, 1965" shall be substituted for the date "May 15, 1955".

(4) In applying subsection (d)(3) of section 1101, the date of the enactment of this subsection shall be treated as being the date of the enactment of this part.

(5) In applying subsection (b)(2)(A) of section 1103, the reference to the Bank Holding Company Act of 1956 shall be treated as referring to such Act as amended by Public Law 89-485.

• **1967 (P.L. 90-225)**

P. L. 90-225, §1:

Added Sec. 1102(e). **Effective** with respect to distributions made after 12-27-67, in tax years ending after such date.

• **1956, Bank Holding Company Act of 1956 (P.L. 511, 84th Cong.)**

P.L. 511, 84th Cong., §10:

Added Sec. 1102 to the 1954 Code. **Effective** for tax years ending after 5-9-56.

[Sec. 1103—Repealed]

P.L. 101-508, §11821(b), provides:

(b) SAVINGS PROVISION.—If—

(1) any provision amended or repealed by this part applied to—

(A) any transaction occurring before the date of the enactment of this Act,

Sec. 1102—Repealed

(B) any property acquired before such date of enactment, or

(C) any item of income, loss, deduction, or credit taken into account before such date of enactment, and

(2) the treatment of such transaction, property, or item under such provision would (without regard to the amendments made by this part) affect liability for tax for periods ending after such date of enactment,

nothing in the amendments made by this part shall be construed to affect the treatment of such transaction, property, or item for purposes of determining liability for tax for periods ending after such date of enactment.

Prior to repeal, Code Sec. 1103 read as follows:

SEC. 1103. DEFINITIONS.

[Sec. 1103(a)]

(a) BANK HOLDING COMPANY; BANK HOLDING COMPANY ACT.—For purposes of this part—

(1) BANK HOLDING COMPANY.—The term "bank holding company" means—

(A) a bank holding company within the meaning of section 2(a) of the Bank Holding Company Act, or

(B) a bank holding company subsidiary within the meaning of section 2(d) of such Act.

(2) BANK HOLDING COMPANY ACT.—The term "Bank Holding Company Act" means the Bank Holding Company Act of 1956, as amended through December 31, 1970 (12 U.S.C. 1841 et seq.).

Amendments

• **1976, Bank Holding Company Tax Act of 1976 (P.L. 94-452)**

P.L. 94-452, §2(a):

Amended Code Sec. 1103(a). **Effective** 10-1-77, with respect to distributions after 7-7-70, in tax years ending after 7-7-70, but only in the case of qualified bank holding corporations. Prior to amendment Code Sec. 1102(a) read as follows:

(a) BANK HOLDING COMPANY.—For purposes of this part, the term "bank holding company" has the meaning assigned to such term by section 2 of the Bank Holding Company Act of 1956.

[Sec. 1103(b)]

(b) QUALIFIED BANK HOLDING CORPORATION.—

(1) IN GENERAL.—Except as provided in paragraph (2), for purposes of this part the term "qualified bank holding corporation" means any corporation (as defined in section 7701(a)(3)) which is a bank holding company and which holds prohibited property acquired by it—

(A) on or before July 7, 1970,

(B) in a distribution in which gain to such corporation with respect to the receipt of such property was not recognized by reason of subsection (a) or (b) of section 1101, or

(C) in exchange for all of its stock in an exchange described in section 1101(e)(2) or (c)(3).

(2) LIMITATIONS.—

(A) A bank holding company shall not be a qualified bank holding corporation, unless it would have been a bank holding company on July 7, 1970, if the Bank Holding Company Act Amendments of 1970 had been in effect on such date, or unless it is a bank holding company determined solely by reference to—

(i) property acquired by it on or before July 7, 1970,

(ii) property acquired by it in a distribution in which gain to such corporation with respect to the receipt of such property was not recognized by reason of subsection (a) or (b) of section 1101, or

(iii) property acquired by it in exchange for all of its stock in an exchange described in section 1101(c)(2) or (3).

For purposes of this subparagraph, property held by a corporation having control of the corporation or by a subsidiary of the corporation shall be treated as held by the corporation.

(B) A bank holding company shall not be a qualified bank holding corporation by reason of property described in subparagraph (B) of paragraph (1) or clause (ii) of subparagraph (A) of this paragraph, unless such property was acquired in a distribution with respect to stock, which stock was acquired by such bank holding company—

(i) on or before July 7, 1970,

(ii) in a distribution (with respect to stock held by it on July 7, 1970, or with respect to stock in respect of which all previous applications of this clause are satisfied) with respect to which gain to it was not recognized by reason of subsection (a) or (b) of section 1101, or

(iii) in exchange for all of its stock in an exchange described in section 1101(c)(2) or (3).

(C) A corporation shall be treated as a qualified bank holding corporation only if the Board certifies that it satisfies the foregoing requirements of this subsection.

(3) CERTAIN SUCCESSOR CORPORATIONS.—For purposes of this subsection, a successor corporation in a reorganization described in section 368(a)(1)(F) shall succeed to the status of its predecessor corporation as a qualified bank holding corporation.

Amendments

• **1976, Bank Holding Company Tax Act of 1976 (P.L. 94-452)**

P.L. 94-452, §2(a):

Amended Code Sec. 1103(b). **Effective** 10-1-77, with respect to distributions after 7-7-70, in tax years ending after 7-7-70, but only in the case of qualified bank holding corporations. Prior to amendment Code Sec. 1103(b) read as follows:

(b) QUALIFIED BANK HOLDING CORPORATION.—

(1) IN GENERAL.—Except as provided in paragraph (2), for purposes of this part the term "qualified bank holding corporation" means any corporation (as defined in section 7701(a)(3)) which is a bank holding company and which holds prohibited property acquired by it—

(A) on or before May 15, 1955,

(B) in a distribution in which gain to such corporation with respect to the receipt of such property was not recognized by reason of subsection (a) or (b) of section 1101, or

(C) in exchange for all of its stock in an exchange described in section 1101(c)(2) or (c)(3).

(2) LIMITATIONS.—

(A) A bank holding company shall not be a qualified bank holding corporation, unless it would have been a bank holding company on May 15, 1955, if the Bank Holding Company Act of 1956 had been in effect on such date, or unless it is a bank holding company determined solely by reference to—

(i) property acquired by it on or before May 15, 1955,

(ii) property acquired by it in a distribution in which gain to such corporation with respect to the receipt of such property was not recognized by reason of subsection (a) or (b) of section 1101, and

(iii) property acquired by it in exchange for all of its stock in an exchange described in section 1101(c)(2) or (3).

(B) A bank holding company shall not be a qualified bank holding corporation by reason of property described in subparagraph (B) of paragraph (1) or clause (ii) of subparagraph (A) of this paragraph, unless such property was acquired in a distribution with respect to stock, which stock was acquired by such bank holding company—

(i) on or before May 15, 1955,

(ii) in a distribution (with respect to stock held by it on May 15, 1955, or with respect to stock in respect of which all previous applications of this clause are satisfied) with respect to which gain to it was not recognized by reason of subsection (a) or (b) of section 1101, or

(iii) in exchange for all of its stock in an exchange described in section 1101(c)(2) or (3).

(C) A corporation shall be treated as a qualified bank holding corporation only if the Board certifies that it satisfies the foregoing requirements of this subsection.

[Sec. 1103(c)]

(c) PROHIBITED PROPERTY.—For purposes of this part, the term "prohibited property" means, in the case of any bank holding company, property (other than nonexempt property) the disposition of which would be necessary or appropriate to effectuate section 4 of the Bank Holding Company Act if such company continued to be a bank holding company beyond the period (including any extensions thereof) specified in subsection (a) of such section. The term "prohibited property" also includes shares of any company not in excess of 5 percent of the outstanding voting shares of such company if the prohibitions of section 4 of such Act apply to the shares of such company in excess of such 5 percent.

Amendments

• **1976, Bank Holding Company Tax Act of 1976 (P.L. 94-452)**

P.L. 94-452, §2(a):

Amended Code Sec. 1103(c). **Effective** 10-1-77, with respect to distributions after 7-7-70, in tax years ending after 7-7-70, but only in the case of qualified bank holding corporations. Prior to amendment Code Sec. 1103(c) read as follows:

(c) PROHIBITED PROPERTY.—For purposes of this part, the term "prohibited property" means, in the case of any bank holding company, property (other than nonexempt property) the disposition of which would be necessary or appropriate to effectuate section 4 of the Bank Holding Company Act of 1956 if such company continued to be a bank holding company beyond the period (including any extensions thereof) specified in subsection (a) of such section or in section 1101(e)(2)(B) of this part, as the case may be. The term "prohibited property" does not include shares of any company held by a bank holding company to the extent that the prohibitions of section 4 of the Bank Holding Company Act of 1956 do not apply to the ownership by such bank holding company of such property by reason of subsection (c)(5) of such section.

[Sec. 1103(d)]

(d) NONEXEMPT PROPERTY.—For purposes of this part, the term "nonexempt property" means—

(1) obligations (including notes, drafts, bills of exchange, and bankers' acceptances) having a maturity at the time of issuance of not exceeding 24 months, exclusive of days of grace;

(2) securities issued by or guaranteed as to principal or interest by a government or subdivision thereof or by any instrumentality of a government of subdivision; or

(3) money, and the right to receive money not evidenced by a security or obligation (other than a security or obligation described in paragraph (1) or (2)).

[Sec. 1103(e)]

(e) BOARD.—For purposes of this part, the term "Board" means the Board of Governors of the Federal Reserve System.

Amendments

• **1956, Bank Holding Company Act of 1956 (P.L. 511, 84th Cong.)**

P.L. 511, 84th Cong., §10:

Added Sec. 1103 to the 1954 Code. **Effective** for tax years ending after 5-9-56.

[Sec. 1103(f)]

(f) CONTROL; SUBSIDIARY.—For purposes of this part—

(1) CONTROL.—Except as provided in section 1102(c)(3), a corporation shall be treated as having control of another corporation if such corporation has control (within the meaning of section 2(a)(2) of the Bank Holding Company Act) of such other corporation.

(2) SUBSIDIARY.—The term "subsidiary" has the meaning given to such term by section 2(d) of the Bank Holding Company Act.

INCOME TAX—CAPITAL GAINS

Amendments

• **1976, Bank Holding Company Tax Act of 1976 (P.L. 94-452)**

P.L. 94-452, §2(a):

Added Code Sec. 1103(f). **Effective** 10-1-77, with respect to distributions after 7-7-70, in tax years ending after 7-7-70, but only in the case of qualified bank holding corporations.

[Sec. 1103(g)]

(g) ELECTION TO FOREGO GRANDFATHER PROVISION FOR ALL PROPERTY REPRESENTING PRE-JUNE 30, 1968, ACTIVITIES.—Any bank holding company may elect, for purposes of this part and section 6158, to have the determination of whether property is property described in subsection (c) or is property eligible to be distributed without recognition of gain under section 1101(b)(1) made under the Bank Holding Company Act as if such Act did not contain the proviso of section 4(a)(2) thereof. Any election under this subsection shall apply to all property described in such proviso and shall be made at such time and in such manner as the Secretary or his delegate may by regulations prescribe. Any such election, once made, shall be irrevocable. An election under this subsection or subsection (h) shall not apply unless the final certification referred to in section 1101(e) or section 6158(c)(2), as the case may be, includes a certification by the Board that the bank holding company has disposed of either all banking property or all nonbanking property.

Amendments

• **1976, Bank Holding Company Tax Act of 1976 (P.L. 94-452)**

P.L. 94-452, §2(a):

Added Code Sec. 1103(g). **Effective** 10-1-77, with respect to distributions after 7-7-70, in tax years ending after 7-7-70, but only in the case of qualified bank holding corporations.

[Sec. 1103(h)]

(h) ELECTION TO DIVEST ALL BANKING OR NONBANKING PROPERTY IN CASE OF CERTAIN CLOSELY HELD BANK HOLDING COMPANIES.—Any bank holding company may elect, for purposes of this part and section 6158, to have the determination of whether property is property described in subsection (c) or is property eligible to be distributed without recognition of gain under section 1101(b)(1) made under the Bank Holding Company Act as if such Act did not contain clause (ii) of section 4(c) of such Act. Any election under this subsection shall apply to all property described in subsection (c), or to all property eligible to be distributed without recognition of gain under section 1101(b)(1), as the case may be, and shall be made at such time and in such manner as the Secretary may by regulations prescribe. Any such election, once made, shall be irrevocable.

Amendments

• **1976, Bank Holding Company Tax Act of 1976 (P.L. 94-452)**

P.L. 94-452, §2(a):

Added Code Sec. 1103(h). **Effective** 10-1-77, with respect to distributions after 7-7-70, in tax years ending after 7-7-70, but only in the case of qualified bank holding corporations.

Subchapter P—Capital Gains and Losses

Part I.	Treatment of capital gains.
Part II.	Treatment of capital losses.
Part III.	General rules for determining capital gains and losses.
Part IV.	Special rules for determining capital gains and losses.
Part V.	Special rules for bonds and other debt instruments.
Part VI.	Treatment of certain passive foreign investment companies.

PART I—TREATMENT OF CAPITAL GAINS

Sec. 1202.   Partial exclusion for gain from certain small business stock.

[Sec. 1201—Stricken]

Amendments

• **2018, Bipartisan Budget Act of 2018 (P.L. 115-123)**

P.L. 115-123, §40310, Div. D, provides:

SEC. 40310. EXTENSION OF SPECIAL RULE RELATING TO QUALIFIED TIMBER GAIN.

For purposes of applying section 1201(b) of the Internal Revenue Code of 1986 with respect to taxable years beginning during 2017, such section shall be applied by substituting "2016 or 2017" for "2016".

• **2017, Tax Cuts and Jobs Act (P.L. 115-97)**

P.L. 115-97, §13001(b)(2)(A):

Amended part I of subchapter P of chapter 1 by striking Code Sec. 1201. **Effective** for tax years beginning after 12-31-2017. Prior to being stricken, Code Sec. 1201 read as follows:

SEC. 1201. ALTERNATIVE TAX FOR CORPORATIONS.

[Sec. 1201(a)]

(a) GENERAL RULE.—If for any taxable year a corporation has a net capital gain and any rate of tax imposed by section 11, 511, or 831(a) or (b) (whichever is applicable) exceeds 35 percent (determined without regard to the last 2 sentences of section 11(b)(1)), then, in lieu of any such tax, there is hereby imposed a tax (if such tax is less than the tax imposed by such sections) which shall consist of the sum of—

(1) a tax computed on the taxable income reduced by the amount of the net capital gain, at the rates and in the manner as if this subsection had not been enacted, plus

(2) a tax of 35 percent of the net capital gain (or, if less, taxable income).

Amendments

• **1997, Taxpayer Relief Act of 1997 (P.L. 105-34)**

P.L. 105-34, §314(a):

Amended Code Sec. 1201(a)(2) by inserting before the period "(or, if less, taxable income)". **Effective** for tax years ending after 12-31-97.

• **1996, Small Business Job Protection Act of 1996 (P.L. 104-188)**

P.L. 104-188, §1703(f):

Amended Code Sec. 1201(a) by striking "last sentence" each place it appears and inserting "last 2 sentences". **Effective** as if included in the provision of P.L. 103-66 to which it relates.

• **1993, Omnibus Budget Reconciliation Act of 1993 (P.L. 103-66)**

P.L. 103-66, §13221(c)(2):

Amended Code Sec. 1201(a) by striking "34 percent" each place it appears and inserting "35 percent". **Effective** for tax years beginning on or after 1-1-93.

• **1988, Technical and Miscellaneous Revenue Act of 1988 (P.L. 100-647)**

P.L. 100-647, §1003(c)(1):

Amended Code Sec. 1201(a) by striking out "831(a)" and inserting in lieu thereof "831(a) or (b)". **Effective** as if included in the provision of P.L. 99-514 to which it relates.

P.L. 100-647, §2004(l):

Amended Code Sec. 1201(a) by striking out "section 11(b)" and inserting in lieu thereof "section 11(b)(1)". **Effective** as if included in the provision of P.L. 100-203 to which it relates.

• **1986, Tax Reform Act of 1986 (P.L. 99-514)**

P.L. 99-514, §311(a):

Amended Code Sec. 1201(a). **Effective** for tax years beginning after 12-31-86. Prior to amendment, Code Sec. 1201(a) read as follows:

(a) CORPORATIONS.—If for any taxable year a corporation has a net capital gain, then, in lieu of the tax imposed by sections 11, 511, 821(a) or (c) and 831(a), there is hereby imposed a tax (if such tax is less than the tax imposed by such sections) which shall consist of the sum of—

(1) a tax computed on the taxable income reduced by the amount of the net capital gain, at the rates and in the manner as if this subsection had not been enacted, plus

(2) a tax of 28 percent of the net capital gain.

P.L. 99-514, §311(d)(1), provides:

(d) TRANSITIONAL RULES.—

(1) TAXABLE YEARS WHICH BEGIN IN 1986 AND END IN 1987.—In the case of any taxable year which begins before January 1, 1987, and ends on or after such date, paragraph (2) of section 1201(a) of the Internal Revenue Code of 1954, as in effect on the date before the date of enactment of this Act, shall be applied as if it read as follows:

(2) the sum of—

(A) 28 percent of the lesser of—

(i) the net capital gain determined by taking into account only gain or loss which is properly taken into account for the portion of the taxable year before January 1, 1987, or

(ii) the net capital gain for the taxable year, and

(B) 34 percent of the excess (if any) of—

(i) the net capital gain for the taxable year, over

(ii) the amount of the net capital gain taken into account under subparagraph (A).

[Note: For an additional transitional rule, see Act Sec. 311(d)(2) under the amendment notes to Code Sec. 631.—CCH.]

INCOME TAX—CAPITAL GAINS

P.L. 99-514, §1024(c)(14):

Amended Code Sec. 1201(a) by striking out "821(a) or (c) and 831(a)" and inserting in lieu thereof "831(a) or (b)". **Effective** for tax years beginning after 12-31-86. However, see the transitional rules in Act Sec. 1024(d), below.

P.L. 99-514, §1024(d), provides:

(d) TRANSITIONAL RULES.—

(1) TREATMENT OF AMOUNTS IN PROTECTION AGAINST LOSS ACCOUNT.—In the case of any insurance company which had a protection against loss account for its last taxable year beginning before January 1, 1987, there shall be included in the gross income of such company for any taxable year beginning after December 31, 1986, the amount which would have been included in gross income for such taxable year under section 824 of the Internal Revenue Code of 1954 (as in effect on the day before the date of enactment of this Act). For purposes of the preceding sentence, no addition to such account shall be made for any taxable year beginning after December 31, 1986.

(2) TRANSITIONAL RULE FOR UNUSED LOSS CARRYOVER UNDER SECTION 825.—Any unused loss carryover under section 825 of the Internal Revenue Code of 1954 (as in effect on the day before the date of the enactment of this Act) which—

(A) is from a taxable year beginning before January 1, 1987, and

(B) could have been carried under such section to a taxable year beginning after December 31, 1986, but for the repeal made by subsection (a)(1),

shall be included in the net operating loss deduction under section 832(c)(10) of such Code without regard to the limitations of section 844(b) of such Code.

- **1978, Revenue Act of 1978 (P.L. 95-600)**

P.L. 95-600, §403(a):

Amended Code Sec. 1201(a)(2) by striking out "30 percent" and inserting in place thereof "28 percent". **Effective** for tax years ending after 12-31-78.

P.L. 95-600, §403(a)(3):

Amended the heading for Code Sec. 1201. **Effective** for tax years beginning after 12-31-78.

- **1976, Tax Reform Act of 1976 (P.L. 94-455)**

P.L. 94-455, §1901(a)(135)(A):

Amended Code Sec. 1201(a). **Effective** with respect to tax years beginning after 12-31-76. Prior to amendment Code Sec. 1201(a) read as follows:

(a) CORPORATIONS.—If for any taxable year a corporation has a net section 1201 gain, then, in lieu of the tax imposed by sections 11, 511, 821(a) or (c), and 831(a), there is hereby imposed a tax (if such tax is less than the tax imposed by such sections) which shall consist of the sum of a tax computed on the taxable income reduced by the amount of the net section 1201 gain, at the rates and in the manner as if this subsection had not been enacted, plus—

(1) in the case of a taxable year beginning before January 1, 1975—

(A) a tax of 25 percent of the lesser of—

(i) the amount of the subsection (d) gain, or

(ii) the amount of the net section 1201 gain,

and

(B) a tax of 30 percent (28 percent in the case of a taxable year beginning after December 31, 1969, and before January 1, 1971) of the excess (if any) of the net section 1201 gain over the subsection (d) gain; and

(2) in the case of a taxable year beginning after December 31, 1974, a tax of 30 percent of the net section 1201 gain.

- **1969, Tax Reform Act of 1969 (P.L. 91-172)**

P.L. 91-172, §511(b):

Amended Sec. 1201(a). **Effective** for tax years beginning after 12-31-69. Prior to amendment, Sec. 1201(a) read as follows:

(a) Corporations.—If for any taxable year the net long-term capital gain of any corporation exceeds the net short-term capital loss, then, in lieu of the tax imposed by sections 11, 511, 821(a) or (c), and 831(a), there is hereby imposed a tax (if such tax is less than the tax imposed by such sections) which shall consist of the sum of—

(1) a partial tax computed on the taxable income reduced by the amount of such excess, at the rates and in the manner as if this subsection had not been enacted, and

(2) an amount equal to 25 percent of such excess, or, in the case of a taxable year beginning before April 1, 1954, an amount equal to 26 percent of such excess.

In the case of a taxable year beginning before April 1, 1954, the amount under paragraph (2) shall be determined without regard to section 21 (relating to effect of change of tax rates).

- **1962, Revenue Act of 1962 (P.L. 87-834)**

P.L. 87-834, §8:

Amended Code Sec. 1201(a) by substituting "or (c)" for "(1) or (b)" after 821(a) in line 3. **Effective** 1-1-63.

- **1959, Life Insurance Company Tax Act of 1959 (P.L. 86-69)**

P.L. 86-69, §3(f)(2):

Amended Sec. 1201(a) by striking out "802(a)," where it appeared following "511,". **Effective** for tax years beginning after 12-31-57.

- **1955, Life Insurance Company Tax Act for 1955 (P.L. 429, 84th Cong.)**

P.L. 429, 84th Cong., §5(7):

Amended Sec. 1201(a) by inserting "802(a)," after "511,". **Effective** for tax years beginning after 12-31-54.

[Sec. 1201(b)]

(b) SPECIAL RATE FOR QUALIFIED TIMBER GAINS.—

(1) IN GENERAL.—If, for any taxable year beginning in 2016, a corporation has both a net capital gain and qualified timber gain—

(A) subsection (a) shall apply to such corporation for the taxable year without regard to whether the applicable tax rate exceeds 35 percent, and

(B) the tax computed under subsection (a)(2) shall be equal to the sum of—

(i) 23.8 percent of the least of—

(I) qualified timber gain,

(II) net capital gain, or

(III) taxable income, plus

(ii) 35 percent of the excess (if any) of taxable income over the sum of the amounts for which a tax was determined under subsection (a)(1) and clause (i).

(2) QUALIFIED TIMBER GAIN.—For purposes of this section, the term "qualified timber gain" means, with respect to any taxpayer for any taxable year, the excess (if any) of—

(A) the sum of the taxpayer's gains described in subsections (a) and (b) of section 631 for such year, over

(B) the sum of the taxpayer's losses described in such subsections for such year.

For purposes of subparagraphs (A) and (B), only timber held more than 15 years shall be taken into account.

Amendments

- **2015, Protecting Americans from Tax Hikes Act of 2015 (P.L. 114-113)**

P.L. 114-113, §334(a), Div. Q:

Amended Code Sec. 1201(b). **Effective** for tax years beginning after 12-31-2015. Prior to amendment, Code Sec. 1201(b) read as follows:

(b) SPECIAL RATE FOR QUALIFIED TIMBER GAINS.—

(1) IN GENERAL.—If, for any taxable year ending after the date of the enactment of the Food, Conservation, and Energy Act of 2008 and beginning on or before the date which is 1 year after such date, a corporation has both a net capital gain and qualified timber gain—

(A) subsection (a) shall apply to such corporation for the taxable year without regard to whether the applicable tax rate exceeds 35 percent, and

(B) the tax computed under subsection (a)(2) shall be equal to the sum of—

(i) 15 percent of the least of—

(I) qualified timber gain,

(II) net capital gain, or

(III) taxable income, plus

(ii) 35 percent of the excess (if any) of taxable income over the sum of the amounts for which a tax was determined under subsection (a)(1) and clause (i).

(2) QUALIFIED TIMBER GAIN.—For purposes of this section, the term "qualified timber gain" means, with respect to any taxpayer for any taxable year, the excess (if any) of—

(A) the sum of the taxpayer's gains described in subsections (a) and (b) of section 631 for such year, over

(B) the sum of the taxpayer's losses described in such subsections for such year.

For purposes of subparagraphs (A) and (B), only timber held more than 15 years shall be taken into account.

(3) COMPUTATION FOR TAXABLE YEARS IN WHICH RATE FIRST APPLIES OR ENDS.—In the case of any taxable year which includes either of the dates set forth in paragraph (1), the qualified timber gain for such year shall not exceed the qualified timber gain properly taken into account for—

(A) in the case of the taxable year including the date of the enactment of the Food, Conservation, and Energy Act of 2008, the portion of the year after such date, and

(B) in the case of the taxable year including the date which is 1 year after such date of enactment, the portion of the year on or before such later date.

- **2008, Heartland, Habitat, Harvest, and Horticulture Act of 2008 (P.L. 110-246)**

P.L. 110-246, §15311(a):

Amended Code Sec. 1201 by redesignating subsection (b) as subsection (c) and by adding after subsection (a) a new subsection (b). **Effective** for tax years ending after 5-22-2008.

[Sec. 1202]

SEC. 1202. PARTIAL EXCLUSION FOR GAIN FROM CERTAIN SMALL BUSINESS STOCK.

[Sec. 1202(a)]

(a) EXCLUSION.—

(1) IN GENERAL.—In the case of a taxpayer other than a corporation, gross income shall not include 50 percent of any gain from the sale or exchange of qualified small business stock held for more than 5 years.

INCOME TAX—CAPITAL GAINS

(2) EMPOWERMENT ZONE BUSINESSES.—

(A) IN GENERAL.—In the case of qualified small business stock acquired after the date of the enactment of this paragraph in a corporation which is a qualified business entity (as defined in section 1397C(b)) during substantially all of the taxpayer's holding period for such stock, paragraph (1) shall be applied by substituting "60 percent" for "50 percent".

(B) CERTAIN RULES TO APPLY.—Rules similar to the rules of paragraphs (5) and (7) of section 1400B(b) (as in effect before its repeal) shall apply for purposes of this paragraph.

(C) GAIN AFTER 2018 NOT QUALIFIED.—Subparagraph (A) shall not apply to gain attributable to periods after December 31, 2018.

(D) TREATMENT OF DC ZONE.—The District of Columbia Enterprise Zone shall not be treated as an empowerment zone for purposes of this paragraph.

(3) SPECIAL RULES FOR 2009 AND CERTAIN PERIODS IN 2010.—In the case of qualified small business stock acquired after the date of the enactment of this paragraph and on or before the date of the enactment of the Creating Small Business Jobs Act of 2010—

(A) paragraph (1) shall be applied by substituting "75 percent" for "50 percent", and

(B) paragraph (2) shall not apply.

In the case of any stock which would be described in the preceding sentence (but for this sentence), the acquisition date for purposes of this subsection shall be the first day on which such stock was held by the taxpayer determined after the application of section 1223.

(4) 100 PERCENT EXCLUSION FOR STOCK ACQUIRED DURING CERTAIN PERIODS IN 2010 AND THEREAFTER.—In the case of qualified small business stock acquired after the date of the enactment of the Creating Small Business Jobs Act of 2010—

(A) paragraph (1) shall be applied by substituting "100 percent" for "50 percent",

(B) paragraph (2) shall not apply, and

(C) paragraph (7) of section 57(a) shall not apply.

In the case of any stock which would be described in the preceding sentence (but for this sentence), the acquisition date for purposes of this subsection shall be the first day on which such stock was held by the taxpayer determined after the application of section 1223.

Amendments

- **2018, Tax Technical Corrections Act of 2018 (P.L. 115-141)**

P.L. 115-141, §401(d)(4)(B)(v), Div. U:

Amended Code Sec. 1202(a)(2)(B) by inserting "(as in effect before its repeal)" after "1400B(b)". **Effective** 3-23-2018. For a special rule, see Act Sec. 401(e), Div. U, below.

P.L. 115-141, §401(e), Div. U, provides:

(e) GENERAL SAVINGS PROVISION WITH RESPECT TO DEADWOOD PROVISIONS.—If—

(1) any provision amended or repealed by the amendments made by subsection (b) or (d) applied to—

(A) any transaction occurring before the date of the enactment of this Act,

(B) any property acquired before such date of enactment, or

(C) any item of income, loss, deduction, or credit taken into account before such date of enactment, and

(2) the treatment of such transaction, property, or item under such provision would (without regard to the amendments or repeals made by such subsection) affect the liability for tax for periods ending after such date of enactment,

nothing in the amendments or repeals made by this section shall be construed to affect the treatment of such transaction, property, or item for purposes of determining liability for tax for periods ending after such date of enactment.

- **2015, Protecting Americans from Tax Hikes Act of 2015 (P.L. 114-113)**

P.L. 114-113, §126(a)(1)-(2), Div. Q:

Amended Code Sec. 1202(a)(4) by striking "and before January 1, 2015" following "Creating Small Business Jobs Act of 2010", and by striking ", 2011, 2012, 2013, AND 2014" in the heading and inserting "AND THEREAFTER". **Effective** for stock acquired after 12-31-2014.

- **2014, Tax Increase Prevention Act of 2014 (P.L. 113-295)**

P.L. 113-295, §136(a)(1)-(2), Division A:

Amended Code Sec. 1202(a)(4) by striking "January 1, 2014" and inserting "January 1, 2015", and by striking "AND 2013" in the heading and inserting "2013, AND 2014". **Effective** for stock acquired after 12-31-2013.

- **2013, American Taxpayer Relief Act of 2012 (P.L. 112-240)**

P.L. 112-240, §324(a)(1)-(2):

Amended Code Sec. 1202(a)(4) by striking "January 1, 2012" and inserting "January 1, 2014", and by striking "AND 2011" and inserting ", 2011, 2012, AND 2013" in the heading thereof. **Effective** for stock acquired after 12-31-2011.

P.L. 112-240, §324(b)(1):

Amended Code Sec. 1202(a)(3) by adding at the end a new flush sentence. **Effective** as if included in section 1241(a) of division B of the American Recovery and Reinvestment Act of 2009 (P.L. 111-5) [effective for stock acquired after 2-17-2009.—CCH].

P.L. 112-240, §324(b)(2):

Amended Code Sec. 1202(a)(4) by adding at the end a new flush sentence. **Effective** as if included in section 2011(a) of the Creating Small Business Jobs Act of 2010 (P.L. 111-240) [effective for stock acquired after 9-27-2010.—CCH].

P.L. 112-240, §327(b)(1)-(2):

Amended Code Sec. 1202(a)(2)(C) by striking "December 31, 2016" and inserting "December 31, 2018"; and by striking "2016" in the heading and inserting "2018". **Effective** for periods after 12-31-2011.

- **2010, Tax Relief, Unemployment Insurance Reauthorization, and Job Creation Act of 2010 (P.L. 111-312)**

P.L. 111-312, §753(b)(1)-(2):

Amended Code Sec. 1202(a)(2)(C) by striking "December 31, 2014" and inserting "December 31, 2016"; and by striking "2014" in the heading and inserting "2016". **Effective** for periods after 12-31-2009.

P.L. 111-312, §760(a)(1)-(2):

Amended Code Sec. 1202(a)(4) by striking "January 1, 2011" and inserting "January 1, 2012", and by inserting "AND 2011" after "2010" in the heading thereof. **Effective** for stock acquired after 12-31-2010.

- **2010, Creating Small Business Jobs Act of 2010 (P.L. 111-240)**

P.L. 111-240, §2011(a):

Amended Code Sec. 1202(a) by adding at the end a new paragraph (4). **Effective** for stock acquired after 9-27-2010.

P.L. 111-240, §2011(b)(1)-(2):

Amended Code Sec. 1202(a)(3) by inserting "CERTAIN PERIODS IN" before "2010" in the heading, and by striking "before January 1, 2011" and inserting "on or before the date of the enactment of the Creating Small Business Jobs Act of 2010". **Effective** for stock acquired after 9-27-2010.

- **2009, American Recovery and Reinvestment Tax Act of 2009 (P.L. 111-5)**

P.L. 111-5, §1241(a):

Amended Code Sec. 1202(a) by adding at the end a new paragraph (3). **Effective** for stock acquired after 2-17-2009.

- **2000, Community Renewal Tax Relief Act of 2000 (P.L. 106-554)**

P.L. 106-554, §117(a):

Amended Code Sec. 1202(a). **Effective** for stock acquired after 12-21-2000. Prior to amendment, Code Sec. 1202(a) read as follows:

(a) 50-PERCENT EXCLUSION.—In the case of a taxpayer other than a corporation, gross income shall not include 50 percent of any gain from the sale or exchange of qualified small business stock held for more than 5 years.

P.L. 106-554, §117(b)(2):

Amended the section heading for Code Sec. 1202 by striking "50-PERCENT" and inserting "PARTIAL". **Effective** for stock acquired after 12-21-2000.

[Sec. 1202(b)]

(b) PER-ISSUER LIMITATION ON TAXPAYER'S ELIGIBLE GAIN.—

(1) IN GENERAL.—If the taxpayer has eligible gain for the taxable year from 1 or more dispositions of stock issued by any corporation, the aggregate amount of such gain from dispositions of stock issued by such corporation which may be taken into account under subsection (a) for the taxable year shall not exceed the greater of—

(A) $10,000,000 reduced by the aggregate amount of eligible gain taken into account by the taxpayer under subsection (a) for prior taxable years attributable to dispositions of stock issued by such corporation, or

(B) 10 times the aggregate adjusted bases of qualified small business stock issued by such corporation and disposed of by the taxpayer during the taxable year.

Sec. 1202(a)(2)

For purposes of subparagraph (B), the adjusted basis of any stock shall be determined without regard to any addition to basis after the date on which such stock was originally issued.

(2) ELIGIBLE GAIN.—For purposes of this subsection, the term "eligible gain" means any gain from the sale or exchange of qualified small business stock held for more than 5 years.

(3) TREATMENT OF MARRIED INDIVIDUALS.—

(A) SEPARATE RETURNS.—In the case of a separate return by a married individual, paragraph (1)(A) shall be applied by substituting "$5,000,000" for "$10,000,000".

(B) ALLOCATION OF EXCLUSION.—In the case of any joint return, the amount of gain taken into account under subsection (a) shall be allocated equally between the spouses for purposes of applying this subsection to subsequent taxable years.

(C) MARITAL STATUS.—For purposes of this subsection, marital status shall be determined under section 7703.

[Sec. 1202(c)]

(c) QUALIFIED SMALL BUSINESS STOCK.—For purposes of this section—

(1) IN GENERAL.—Except as otherwise provided in this section, the term "qualified small business stock" means any stock in a C corporation which is originally issued after the date of the enactment of the Revenue Reconciliation Act of 1993, if—

(A) as of the date of issuance, such corporation is a qualified small business, and

(B) except as provided in subsections (f) and (h), such stock is acquired by the taxpayer at its original issue (directly or through an underwriter)—

(i) in exchange for money or other property (not including stock), or

(ii) as compensation for services provided to such corporation (other than services performed as an underwriter of such stock).

(2) ACTIVE BUSINESS REQUIREMENT; ETC.—

(A) IN GENERAL.—Stock in a corporation shall not be treated as qualified small business stock unless, during substantially all of the taxpayer's holding period for such stock, such corporation meets the active business requirements of subsection (e) and such corporation is a C corporation.

(B) SPECIAL RULE FOR CERTAIN SMALL BUSINESS INVESTMENT COMPANIES.—

(i) WAIVER OF ACTIVE BUSINESS REQUIREMENT.—Notwithstanding any provision of subsection (e), a corporation shall be treated as meeting the active business requirements of such subsection for any period during which such corporation qualifies as a specialized small business investment company.

(ii) SPECIALIZED SMALL BUSINESS INVESTMENT COMPANY.—For purposes of clause (i), the term "specialized small business investment company" means any eligible corporation (as defined in subsection (e)(4)) which is licensed to operate under section 301(d) of the Small Business Investment Act of 1958 (as in effect on May 13, 1993).

(3) CERTAIN PURCHASES BY CORPORATION OF ITS OWN STOCK.—

(A) REDEMPTIONS FROM TAXPAYER OR RELATED PERSON.—Stock acquired by the taxpayer shall not be treated as qualified small business stock if, at any time during the 4-year period beginning on the date 2 years before the issuance of such stock, the corporation issuing such stock purchased (directly or indirectly) any of its stock from the taxpayer or from a person related (within the meaning of section 267(b) or 707(b)) to the taxpayer.

(B) SIGNIFICANT REDEMPTIONS.—Stock issued by a corporation shall not be treated as qualified business stock if, during the 2-year period beginning on the date 1 year before the issuance of such stock, such corporation made 1 or more purchases of its stock with an aggregate value (as of the time of the respective purchases) exceeding 5 percent of the aggregate value of all of its stock as of the beginning of such 2-year period.

(C) TREATMENT OF CERTAIN TRANSACTIONS.—If any transaction is treated under section 304(a) as a distribution in redemption of the stock of any corporation, for purposes of subparagraphs (A) and (B), such corporation shall be treated as purchasing an amount of its stock equal to the amount treated as such a distribution under section 304(a).

[Sec. 1202(d)]

(d) QUALIFIED SMALL BUSINESS.—For purposes of this section—

(1) IN GENERAL.—The term "qualified small business" means any domestic corporation which is a C corporation if—

(A) the aggregate gross assets of such corporation (or any predecessor thereof) at all times on or after the date of the enactment of the Revenue Reconciliation Act of 1993 and before the issuance did not exceed $50,000,000,

(B) the aggregate gross assets of such corporation immediately after the issuance (determined by taking into account amounts received in the issuance) do not exceed $50,000,000, and

(C) such corporation agrees to submit such reports to the Secretary and to shareholders as the Secretary may require to carry out the purposes of this section.

(2) AGGREGATE GROSS ASSETS.—

(A) IN GENERAL.—For purposes of paragraph (1), the term "aggregate gross assets" means the amount of cash and the aggregate adjusted bases of other property held by the corporation.

(B) TREATMENT OF CONTRIBUTED PROPERTY.—For purposes of subparagraph (A), the adjusted basis of any property contributed to the corporation (or other property with a basis determined in whole or in part by reference to the adjusted basis of property so contributed) shall be determined as if the basis of the property contributed to the corporation (immediately after such contribution) were equal to its fair market value as of the time of such contribution.

(3) AGGREGATION RULES.—

(A) IN GENERAL.—All corporations which are members of the same parent-subsidiary controlled group shall be treated as 1 corporation for purposes of this subsection.

(B) PARENT-SUBSIDIARY CONTROLLED GROUP.—For purposes of subparagraph (A), the term "parent-subsidiary controlled group" means any controlled group of corporations as defined in section 1563(a)(1), except that—

(i) "more than 50 percent" shall be substituted for "at least 80 percent" each place it appears in section 1563(a)(1), and

(ii) section 1563(a)(4) shall not apply.

[Sec. 1202(e)]

(e) ACTIVE BUSINESS REQUIREMENT.—

(1) IN GENERAL.—For purposes of subsection (c)(2), the requirements of this subsection are met by a corporation for any period if during such period—

INCOME TAX—CAPITAL GAINS

(A) at least 80 percent (by value) of the assets of such corporation are used by such corporation in the active conduct of 1 or more qualified trades or businesses, and

(B) such corporation is an eligible corporation.

(2) SPECIAL RULE FOR CERTAIN ACTIVITIES.—For purposes of paragraph (1), if, in connection with any future qualified trade or business, a corporation is engaged in—

(A) start-up activities described in section 195(c)(1)(A),

(B) activities resulting in the payment or incurring of expenditures which may be treated as research and experimental expenditures under section 174, or

(C) activities with respect to in-house research expenses described in section 41(b)(4),

assets used in such activities shall be treated as used in the active conduct of a qualified trade or business. Any determination under this paragraph shall be made without regard to whether a corporation has any gross income from such activities at the time of the determination.

(3) QUALIFIED TRADE OR BUSINESS.—For purposes of this subsection, the term "qualified trade or business" means any trade or business other than—

(A) any trade or business involving the performance of services in the fields of health, law, engineering, architecture, accounting, actuarial science, performing arts, consulting, athletics, financial services, brokerage services, or any trade or business where the principal asset of such trade or business is the reputation or skill of 1 or more of its employees,

(B) any banking, insurance, financing, leasing, investing, or similar business,

(C) any farming business (including the business of raising or harvesting trees),

(D) any business involving the production or extraction of products of a character with respect to which a deduction is allowable under section 613 or 613A, and

(E) any business of operating a hotel, motel, restaurant, or similar business.

(4) ELIGIBLE CORPORATION.—For purposes of this subsection, the term "eligible corporation" means any domestic corporation; except that such term shall not include—

(A) a DISC or former DISC,

(B) a regulated investment company, real estate investment trust, or REMIC, and

(C) a cooperative.

(5) STOCK IN OTHER CORPORATIONS.—

(A) LOOK-THRU IN CASE OF SUBSIDIARIES.—For purposes of this subsection, stock and debt in any subsidiary corporation shall be disregarded and the parent corporation shall be deemed to own its ratable share of the subsidiary's assets, and to conduct its ratable share of the subsidiary's activities.

(B) PORTFOLIO STOCK OR SECURITIES.—A corporation shall be treated as failing to meet the requirements of paragraph (1) for any period during which more than 10 percent of the value of its assets (in excess of liabilities) consists of stock or securities in other corporations which are not subsidiaries of such corporation (other than assets described in paragraph (6)).

(C) SUBSIDIARY.—For purposes of this paragraph, a corporation shall be considered a subsidiary if the parent owns more than 50 percent of the combined voting power of all classes of stock entitled to vote, or more than 50 percent in value of all outstanding stock, of such corporation.

(6) WORKING CAPITAL.—For purposes of paragraph (1)(A), any assets which—

(A) are held as a part of the reasonably required working capital needs of a qualified trade or business of the corporation, or

(B) are held for investment and are reasonably expected to be used within 2 years to finance research and experimentation in a qualified trade or business or increases in working capital needs of a qualified trade or business,

shall be treated as used in the active conduct of a qualified trade or business. For periods after the corporation has been in existence for at least 2 years, in no event may more than 50 percent of the assets of the corporation qualify as used in the active conduct of a qualified trade or business by reason of this paragraph.

(7) MAXIMUM REAL ESTATE HOLDINGS.—A corporation shall not be treated as meeting the requirements of paragraph (1) for any period during which more than 10 percent of the total value of its assets consists of real property which is not used in the active conduct of a qualified trade or business. For purposes of the preceding sentence, the ownership of, dealing in, or renting of real property shall not be treated as the active conduct of a qualified trade or business.

(8) COMPUTER SOFTWARE ROYALTIES.—For purposes of paragraph (1), rights to computer software which produces active business computer software royalties (within the meaning of section 543(d)(1)) shall be treated as an asset used in the active conduct of a trade or business.

Amendments

• **2018, Tax Technical Corrections Act of 2018 (P.L. 115-141)**

P.L. 115-141, §401(d)(1)(D)(xv), Div. U:

Amended Code Sec. 1202(e)(4) by striking subparagraph (B) and by redesignating subparagraphs (C) and (D) as subparagraphs (B) and (C), respectively. **Effective** 3-23-2018. For a special rule, see Act Sec. 401(e), Div. U, below. Prior to being stricken, Code Sec. 1202(e)(4)(B) read as follows:

(B) a corporation with respect to which an election under section 936 is in effect or which has a direct or indirect subsidiary with respect to which such an election is in effect,

P.L. 115-141, §401(e), Div. U, provides:

(e) GENERAL SAVINGS PROVISION WITH RESPECT TO DEADWOOD PROVISIONS.—If—

(1) any provision amended or repealed by the amendments made by subsection (b) or (d) applied to—

(A) any transaction occurring before the date of the enactment of this Act,

(B) any property acquired before such date of enactment, or

(C) any item of income, loss, deduction, or credit taken into account before such date of enactment, and

(2) the treatment of such transaction, property, or item under such provision would (without regard to the amendments or repeals made by such subsection) affect the liability for tax for periods ending after such date of enactment,

nothing in the amendments or repeals made by this section shall be construed to affect the treatment of such transaction, property, or item for purposes of determining liability for tax for periods ending after such date of enactment.

• **2004, American Jobs Creation Act of 2004 (P.L. 108-357)**

P.L. 108-357, §835(b)(9):

Amended Code Sec. 1202(e)(4)(C) by striking "REMIC, or FASIT" and inserting "or REMIC". For the **effective** date, see Act Sec. 835(c), below.

P.L. 108-357, §835(c), provides:

(c) EFFECTIVE DATE.—

(1) IN GENERAL.—Except as provided in paragraph (2), the amendments made by this section shall take effect on January 1, 2005.

(2) EXCEPTION FOR EXISTING FASITS.—Paragraph (1) shall not apply to any FASIT in existence on the date of the enactment of this Act [10-22-2004.—CCH] to the extent that regular interests issued by the FASIT before such date continue to remain outstanding in accordance with the original terms of issuance.

• **1996, Small Business Job Protection Act of 1996 (P.L. 104-188)**

P.L. 104-188, §1621(b)(7):

Amended Code Sec. 1202(e)(4)(C) by striking "or REMIC" and inserting "REMIC, or FASIT". **Effective** 9-1-97.

[Sec. 1202(f)]

(f) STOCK ACQUIRED ON CONVERSION OF OTHER STOCK.—If any stock in a corporation is acquired solely through the conversion of other stock in such corporation which is qualified small business stock in the hands of the taxpayer—

(1) the stock so acquired shall be treated as qualified small business stock in the hands of the taxpayer, and

(2) the stock so acquired shall be treated as having been held during the period during which the converted stock was held.

[Sec. 1202(g)]

(g) TREATMENT OF PASS-THRU ENTITIES.—

(1) IN GENERAL.—If any amount included in gross income by reason of holding an interest in a pass-thru entity meets the requirements of paragraph (2)—

(A) such amount shall be treated as gain described in subsection (a), and

(B) for purposes of applying subsection (b), such amount shall be treated as gain from a disposition of stock in the corporation issuing the stock disposed of by the pass-thru entity and the taxpayer's proportionate share of the adjusted basis of the pass-thru entity in such stock shall be taken into account.

(2) REQUIREMENTS.—An amount meets the requirements of this paragraph if—

(A) such amount is attributable to gain on the sale or exchange by the pass-thru entity of stock which is qualified small business stock in the hands of such entity (determined by treating such entity as an individual) and which was held by such entity for more than 5 years, and

(B) such amount is includible in the gross income of the taxpayer by reason of the holding of an interest in such entity which was held by the taxpayer on the date on which such pass-thru entity acquired such stock and at all times thereafter before the disposition of such stock by such pass-thru entity.

(3) LIMITATION BASED ON INTEREST ORIGINALLY HELD BY TAXPAYER.—Paragraph (1) shall not apply to any amount to the extent such amount exceeds the amount to which paragraph (1) would have applied if such amount were determined by reference to the interest the taxpayer held in the pass-thru entity on the date the qualified small business stock was acquired.

(4) PASS-THRU ENTITY.—For purposes of this subsection, the term "pass-thru entity" means—

(A) any partnership,

(B) any S corporation,

(C) any regulated investment company, and

(D) any common trust fund.

[Sec. 1202(h)]

(h) CERTAIN TAX-FREE AND OTHER TRANSFERS.—For purposes of this section—

(1) IN GENERAL.—In the case of a transfer described in paragraph (2), the transferee shall be treated as—

(A) having acquired such stock in the same manner as the transferor, and

(B) having held such stock during any continuous period immediately preceding the transfer during which it was held (or treated as held under this subsection) by the transferor.

(2) DESCRIPTION OF TRANSFERS.—A transfer is described in this subsection if such transfer is—

(A) by gift,

(B) at death, or

(C) from a partnership to a partner of stock with respect to which requirements similar to the requirements of subsection (g) are met at the time of the transfer (without regard to the 5-year holding period requirement).

(3) CERTAIN RULES MADE APPLICABLE.—Rules similar to the rules of section 1244(d)(2) shall apply for purposes of this section.

(4) INCORPORATIONS AND REORGANIZATIONS INVOLVING NONQUALIFIED STOCK.—

(A) IN GENERAL.—In the case of a transaction described in section 351 or a reorganization described in section 368, if qualified small business stock is exchanged for other stock which would not qualify as qualified small business stock but for this subparagraph, such other stock shall be treated as qualified small business stock acquired on the date on which the exchanged stock was acquired.

(B) LIMITATION.—This section shall apply to gain from the sale or exchange of stock treated as qualified small business stock by reason of subparagraph (A) only to the extent of the gain which would have been recognized at the time of the transfer described in subparagraph (A) if section 351 or 368 had not applied at such time. The preceding sentence shall not apply if the stock which is treated as qualified small business stock by reason of subparagraph (A) is issued by a corporation which (as of the time of the transfer described in subparagraph (A)) is a qualified small business.

(C) SUCCESSIVE APPLICATION.—For purposes of this paragraph, stock treated as qualified small business stock under subparagraph (A) shall be so treated for subsequent transactions or reorganizations, except that the limitation of subparagraph (B) shall be applied as of the time of the first transfer to which such limitation applied (determined after the application of the second sentence of subparagraph (B)).

(D) CONTROL TEST.—In the case of a transaction described in section 351, this paragraph shall apply only if, immediately after the transaction, the corporation issuing the stock owns directly or indirectly stock representing control (within the meaning of section 368(c)) of the corporation whose stock was exchanged.

[Sec. 1202(i)]

(i) BASIS RULES.—For purposes of this section—

(1) STOCK EXCHANGED FOR PROPERTY.—In the case where the taxpayer transfers property (other than money or stock) to a corporation in exchange for stock in such corporation—

(A) such stock shall be treated as having been acquired by the taxpayer on the date of such exchange, and

(B) the basis of such stock in the hands of the taxpayer shall in no event be less than the fair market value of the property exchanged.

(2) TREATMENT OF CONTRIBUTIONS TO CAPITAL.—If the adjusted basis of any qualified small business stock is adjusted by reason of any contribution to capital after the date on which such stock was originally issued, in determining the amount of the adjustment by reason of such contribution, the basis of the contributed property shall in no event be treated as less than its fair market value on the date of the contribution.

[Sec. 1202(j)]

(j) TREATMENT OF CERTAIN SHORT POSITIONS.—

(1) IN GENERAL.—If the taxpayer has an offsetting short position with respect to any qualified small business stock, subsection (a) shall not apply to any gain from the sale or exchange of such stock unless—

(A) such stock was held by the taxpayer for more than 5 years as of the first day on which there was such a short position, and

(B) the taxpayer elects to recognize gain as if such stock were sold on such first day for its fair market value.

INCOME TAX—CAPITAL GAINS

(2) OFFSETTING SHORT POSITION.—For purposes of paragraph (1), the taxpayer shall be treated as having an offsetting short position with respect to any qualified small business stock if—

(A) the taxpayer has made a short sale of substantially identical property,

(B) the taxpayer has acquired an option to sell substantially identical property at a fixed price, or

(C) to the extent provided in regulations, the taxpayer has entered into any other transaction which substantially reduces the risk of loss from holding such qualified small business stock.

For purposes of the preceding sentence, any reference to the taxpayer shall be treated as including a reference to any person who is related (within the meaning of section 267(b) or 707(b)) to the taxpayer.

[Sec. 1202(k)]

(k) REGULATIONS.—The Secretary shall prescribe such regulations as may be appropriate to carry out the purposes of this section, including regulations to prevent the avoidance of the purposes of this section through split-ups, shell corporations, partnerships, or otherwise.

Amendments

• **1993, Omnibus Budget Reconciliation Act of 1993 (P.L. 103-66)**

P.L. 103-66, § 13113(a):

Amended Part I of subchapter P of chapter 1 by adding at the end thereof a new section 1202. **Effective** for stock issued after 8-10-93.

[Sec. 1202—Repealed]

Amendments

• **1986, Tax Reform Act of 1986 (P.L. 99-514)**

P.L. 99-514, § 301(a):

Repealed Code Sec. 1202. **Effective** for tax years beginning after 12-31-86. Prior to repeal, Code Sec. 1202 read as follows:

SEC. 1202. DEDUCTION FOR CAPITAL GAINS.

(a) IN GENERAL.—If for any taxable year a taxpayer other than a corporation has a net capital gain, 60 percent of the amount of the net capital gain shall be a deduction from gross income.

(b) ESTATES AND TRUSTS.—In the case of an estate or trust, the deduction shall be computed by excluding the portion (if any) of the gains for the taxable year from sales or exchanges of capital assets which, under sections 652 and 662 (relating to inclusions of amounts in gross income of beneficiaries of trusts), is includible by the income beneficiaries as gain derived from the sale or exchange of capital assets.

(c) TRANSITIONAL RULE.—If for any taxable year ending after October 31, 1978, and beginning before November 1, 1979, a taxpayer other than a corporation has a net capital gain, the deduction under subsection (a) shall be the sum of—

(1) 60 percent of the lesser of—

(A) the net capital gain for the taxable year, or

(B) the net capital gain taking into account only gain or loss properly taken into account for the portion of the taxable year after October 31, 1978, plus

(2) 50 percent of the excess of—

(A) the net capital gain for the taxable year, over

(B) the amount of net capital gain taken into account under paragraph (1).

• **1981, Economic Recovery Tax Act of 1981 (P.L. 97-34)**

P.L. 97-34, § 102 provides:

SEC. 102. 20-PERCENT MAXIMUM RATE ON NET CAPITAL GAIN FOR PORTION OF 1981.

(a) IN GENERAL.—If for any taxable year ending after June 9, 1981, and beginning before January 1, 1982, a taxpayer other than a corporation has qualified net capital gain, then the tax imposed under section 1 of the Internal Revenue Code of 1954 for such taxable year shall be equal to the lesser of—

(1) the tax imposed under such section determined without regard to this subsection, or

(2) the sum of—

(A) the tax imposed under such section on the excess of—

(i) the taxable income of the taxpayer, over

(ii) 40 percent of the qualified net capital gain of the taxpayer, and

(B) 20 percent of the qualified net capital gain.

(b) APPLICATION WITH ALTERNATIVE MINIMUM TAX.—

(1) IN GENERAL.—If subsection (a) applies to any taxpayer for any taxable year, then the amount determined under section 55(a)(1) of the Internal Revenue Code of 1954 for such taxable year shall be equal to the lesser of—

(A) the amount determined under such section 55(a)(1) determined without regard to this subsection, or

(B) the sum of—

(i) the amount which would be determined under such section 55(a)(1) if the alternative minimum taxable income was the excess of—

(I) the alternative minimum taxable income (within the meaning of section 55(b)(1) of such Code) of the taxpayer, over

(II) the qualified net capital gain of the taxpayer, and

(ii) 20 percent of the qualified net capital gain.

(2) NO CREDITS ALLOWABLE.—For purposes of section 55(c) of such Code, no credit allowable under subpart A of part IV of subchapter A of chapter 1 of such Code (other than section 33(a) of such Code) shall be allowable against the amount described in paragraph (1)(B)(ii).

(c) QUALIFIED NET CAPITAL GAIN.—

(1) IN GENERAL.—For purposes of this section, the term "qualified net capital gain" means the lesser of—

(A) the net capital gain for the taxable year, or

(B) the net capital gain for the taxable year taking into account only gain or loss from sales or exchanges occurring after June 9, 1981.

(2) NET CAPITAL GAIN.—For purposes of this subsection, the term "net capital gain" has the meaning given such term by section 1222(11) of the Internal Revenue Code of 1954.

(d) SPECIAL RULE FOR PASS-THRU ENTITIES.—

(1) IN GENERAL.—In applying subsections (a), (b), and (c) with respect to any pass-thru entity, the determination of when a sale or exchange has occurred shall be made at the entity level.

(2) PASS-THRU ENTITY DEFINED.—For purposes of paragraph (1), the term "pass-thru entity" means—

(A) a regulated investment company,

(B) a real estate investment trust,

(C) an electing small business corporation,

(D) a partnership,

(E) an estate or trust, and

(F) a common trust fund.

• **1980, Technical Corrections Act of 1979 (P.L. 96-222)**

P.L. 96-222, § 104(a)(2)(A)(i):

Amended Code Sec. 1202(c) by changing "(c) TAXABLE YEARS WHICH INCLUDE NOVEMBER 1, 1978.—If for any taxable year beginning before November 1, 1978, and ending after October 31, 1978," to "(c) TRANSITIONAL RULE.—If for any taxable year ending after October 31, 1978, and beginning before November 1, 1979,". **Effective** for tax years ending after 10-31-78.

P.L. 96-222, § 104(a)(2)(A)(ii):

Amended Code Sec. 1202(c)(1)(B). **Effective** for tax years ending after 10-31-78. Prior to amendment, Code Sec. 1202(c)(1)(B) read as follows:

(B) the net capital gain taking into account only sales and exchanges after October 31, 1978, plus

For a special rule for pass-through entities, see P.L. 96-222, § 104(a)(3)(A)(ii), following Code Sec. 1201(c).

• **1978, Revenue Act of 1978 (P.L. 95-600)**

P.L. 95-600, §§ 402(a), (c)(1):

Amended Code Sec. 1202. **Effective** for tax years ending after 10-31-78. Before amendment, such code section read:

"SEC. 1202. DEDUCTION FOR CAPITAL GAINS.

If for any taxable year, a taxpayer other than a corporation has a net capital gain, 50 percent of the amount of the net capital gain shall be a deduction from gross income. In the case of an estate or trust, the deduction shall be computed by excluding the portion (if any), of the gains for the taxable year from sales or exchanges of capital assets, which, under sections 652 and 662 (relating to inclusions of amounts in gross income of beneficiaries of trusts), is includible by the income beneficiaries as gain derived from the sale or exchange of capital assets."

• **1976, Tax Reform Act of 1976 (P.L. 94-455)**

P.L. 94-455, § 1901(b)(33)(M):

Amended Code Sec. 1202 by having the first sentence read "If for any taxable year, a taxpayer other than a corporation has a net capital gain, 50 percent of the amount of the net capital gain shall be a deduction from gross income." rather than "In the case of a taxpayer other than a corporation, if for any taxable year the net long-term capital gain exceeds the net short-term capital loss, 50 percent of the amount of such excess shall be a deduction from gross income." **Effective** with respect to tax years beginning after 12-31-76.

INCOME TAX—CAPITAL LOSSES

PART II—TREATMENT OF CAPITAL LOSSES

Sec. 1211. Limitation on capital losses.
Sec. 1212. Capital loss carrybacks and carryovers.

[Sec. 1211]

SEC. 1211. LIMITATION ON CAPITAL LOSSES.

[Sec. 1211(a)]

(a) CORPORATIONS.—In the case of a corporation, losses from sales or exchanges of capital assets shall be allowed only to the extent of gains from such sales or exchanges.

[Sec. 1211(b)]

(b) OTHER TAXPAYERS.—In the case of a taxpayer other than a corporation, losses from sales or exchanges of capital assets shall be allowed only to the extent of the gains from such sales or exchanges, plus (if such losses exceed such gains) the lower of—

(1) $3,000 ($1,500 in the case of a married individual filing a separate return), or

(2) the excess of such losses over such gains.

Amendments

• **1986, Tax Reform Act of 1986 (P.L. 99-514)**

P.L. 99-514, §301(b)(10):

Amended Code Sec. 1211(b). **Effective** for tax years beginning after 12-31-86. Prior to amendment, Code Sec. 1211(b) read as follows:

(b) OTHER TAXPAYERS.—

(1) IN GENERAL.—In the case of a taxpayer other than a corporation, losses from sales or exchanges of capital assets shall be allowed only to the extent of the gains from such sales or exchanges, plus (if such losses exceed such gains) whichever of the following is smallest:

(A) the taxable income, for the taxable year reduced (but not below zero) by the zero bracket amount,

(B) the applicable amount, or

(C) the sum of—

(i) the excess of the net short-term capital loss over the net long-term capital gain, and

(ii) one-half of the excess of the net long-term capital loss over the net short-term capital gain.

(2) APPLICABLE AMOUNT.—For purposes of paragraph (1)(B), the term "applicable amount" means—

(A) $2,000 in the case of any taxable year beginning in 1977; and

(B) $3,000 in the case of any taxable year beginning after 1977.

In the case of a separate return by a husband or wife, the applicable amount shall be one-half of the amount determined under the preceding sentence.

(3) COMPUTATION OF TAXABLE INCOME.—For purposes of paragraph (1), taxable income shall be computed without regard to gains or losses from sales or exchanges of capital assets and without regard to the deductions provided in section 151 (relating to personal exemptions) or any deduction in lieu thereof.

• **1977, Tax Reduction and Simplification Act of 1977 (P.L. 95-30)**

P.L. 95-30, §102(b)(14):

Amended subparagraph (A) of Code Sec. 1211(b)(1). **Effective** for tax years beginning after 12-31-76. Prior to amendment, subparagraph (A) of Code Sec. 1211(b)(1) read as follows:

"(A) the taxable income for the taxable year,"

• **1976, Tax Reform Act of 1976 (P.L. 94-455)**

P.L. 94-455, §501(b)(6):

Amended Code Sec. 1211(b)(3) by striking out the last sentence, which read, "If the taxpayer elects to pay the optional tax imposed by section 3, `taxable income' as used in this subsection shall read as `adjusted gross income'." **Effective** for tax years beginning after 12-31-75.

P.L. 94-455, §1401(a):

Amended Code Sec. 1211(b)(1)(B) by substituting "the applicable amount" for "$1,000". **Effective** for tax years beginning after 12-31-76.

P.L. 94-455, §1401(b):

Amended Code Sec. 1211(b)(2). **Effective** for tax years beginning after 12-31-76. Prior to amendment, Code Sec. 1211(b)(2) read as follows:

(2) MARRIED INDIVIDUALS.—In the case of a husband or wife who files a separate return, the amount specified in paragraph (1)(b) shall be $500 in lieu of $1,000.

• **1969, Tax Reform Act of 1969 (P.L. 91-172)**

P.L. 91-172, §513(a):

Amended Code Sec. 1211(b). **Effective** for tax years beginning after 12-31-69. Prior to amendment, Code Sec. 1211(b) read as follows:

"(b) Other Taxpayers.—In the case of a taxpayer other than a corporation, losses from sales or exchanges of capital assets shall be allowed only to the extent of the gains from such sales or exchanges, plus the taxable income of the taxpayer or $1,000, whichever is smaller. For purposes of this subsection, taxable income shall be computed without regard to gains or losses from sales or exchanges of capital assets and without regard to the deductions provided in section 151 (relating to personal exemptions) or any deduction in lieu thereof. If the taxpayer elects to pay the optional tax imposed by section 3, `taxable income' as used in this subsection shall be read as `adjusted gross income'."

[Sec. 1212]

SEC. 1212. CAPITAL LOSS CARRYBACKS AND CARRYOVERS.

[Sec. 1212(a)]

(a) CORPORATIONS.—

(1) IN GENERAL.—If a corporation has a net capital loss for any taxable year (hereinafter in this paragraph referred to as the "loss year"), the amount thereof shall be—

(A) a capital loss carryback to each of the 3 taxable years preceding the loss year, but only to the extent—

(i) such loss is not attributable to a foreign expropriation capital loss, and

(ii) the carryback of such loss does not increase or produce a net operating loss (as defined in section 172(c)) for the taxable year to which it is being carried back;

(B) except as provided in subparagraph (C), a capital loss carryover to each of the 5 taxable years succeeding the loss year; and

(C) a capital loss carryover to each of the 10 taxable years succeeding the loss year, but only to the extent such loss is attributable to a foreign expropriation loss,

and shall be treated as a short-term capital loss in each such taxable year. The entire amount of the net capital loss for any taxable year shall be carried to the earliest of the taxable years to which such loss may be carried, and the portion of such loss which shall be carried to each of the other taxable years to which such loss may be carried shall be the excess, if any, of such loss over the total of the capital gain net income for each of the prior taxable years to which such loss may be carried. For purposes of the preceding sentence, the capital gain net income for any such prior taxable year shall be computed without regard to the net capital loss for the loss year or for any taxable year thereafter. In the case of any net capital loss which cannot be carried back in full to a preceding taxable year by reason of clause (ii) of subparagraph (A), the capital gain net income for such prior taxable year shall in no case be treated as greater than the amount of such loss which can be carried back to such preceding taxable year upon the application of such clause (ii).

(2) DEFINITIONS AND SPECIAL RULES.—

(A) FOREIGN EXPROPRIATION CAPITAL LOSS DEFINED.—For purposes of this subsection, the term "foreign expropriation capital loss" means, for any taxable year, the sum of the losses taken into account in computing the net capital loss for such year which are—

(i) losses sustained directly by reason of the expropriation, intervention, seizure, or similar taking of property by the government of any foreign country, any political subdivision thereof, or any agency or instrumentality of the foregoing, or

(ii) losses (treated under section 165(g)(1) as losses from the sale or exchange of capital assets) from securities which become worthless by reason of the expropriation, intervention, seizure, or similar taking of property by the government of any foreign country, any political subdivision thereof, or any agency or instrumentality of the foregoing.

Internal Revenue Code

Sec. 1212(a)(2)(A)(ii)

INCOME TAX—CAPITAL LOSSES

(B) PORTION OF LOSS ATTRIBUTABLE TO FOREIGN EXPROPRIATION CAPITAL LOSS.—For purposes of paragraph (1), the portion of any net capital loss for any taxable year attributable to a foreign expropriation capital loss is the amount of the foreign expropriation capital loss for such year (but not in excess of the net capital loss for such year).

(C) PRIORITY OF APPLICATION.—For purposes of paragraph (1), if a portion of a net capital loss for any taxable year is attributable to a foreign expropriation capital loss, such portion shall be considered to be a separate net capital loss for such year to be applied after the other portion of such net capital loss.

(3) REGULATED INVESTMENT COMPANIES.—

(A) IN GENERAL.—If a regulated investment company has a net capital loss for any taxable year—

(i) paragraph (1) shall not apply to such loss,

(ii) the excess of the net short-term capital loss over the net long-term capital gain for such year shall be a short-term capital loss arising on the first day of the next taxable year, and

(iii) the excess of the net long-term capital loss over the net short-term capital gain for such year shall be a long-term capital loss arising on the first day of the next taxable year.

(B) COORDINATION WITH GENERAL RULE.—If a net capital loss to which paragraph (1) applies is carried over to a taxable year of a regulated investment company—

(i) LOSSES TO WHICH THIS PARAGRAPH APPLIES.—Clauses (ii) and (iii) of subparagraph (A) shall be applied without regard to any amount treated as a short-term capital loss under paragraph (1).

(ii) LOSSES TO WHICH GENERAL RULE APPLIES.—Paragraph (1) shall be applied by substituting "net capital loss for the loss year or any taxable year thereafter (other than a net capital loss to which paragraph (3)(A) applies)" for "net capital loss for the loss year or any taxable year thereafter".

(4) SPECIAL RULES ON CARRYBACKS.—A net capital loss of a corporation shall not be carried back under paragraph (1)(A) to a taxable year—

(A) for which it is a regulated investment company (as defined in section 851), or

(B) for which it is a real estate investment trust (as defined in section 856).

Amendments

• **2010, Regulated Investment Company Modernization Act of 2010 (P.L. 111-325)**

P.L. 111-325, §101(a):

Amended Code Sec. 1212(a) by redesignating paragraph (3) as paragraph (4) and by inserting after paragraph (2) a new paragraph (3). **Effective** generally for net capital losses for tax years beginning after 12-22-2010. For a special rule, see Act Sec. 101(c)(1)-(3), below.

P.L. 111-325, §101(b)(1):

Amended Code Sec. 1212(a)(1)(C). **Effective** for net capital losses for tax years beginning after 12-22-2010. Prior to amendment, Code Sec. 1212(a)(1)(C) read as follows:

(C) a capital loss carryover—

(i) in the case of a regulated investment company (as defined in section 851) to each of the 8 taxable years succeeding the loss year, and

(ii) to the extent such loss is attributable to a foreign expropriation capital loss, to each of the 10 taxable years succeeding the loss year,

P.L. 111-325, §101(c)(1)-(3) (as amended by P.L. 113-295, §205(a)(1)(A)-(B), Division A), provides:

(1) IN GENERAL.—Except as provided in paragraphs (2) and (3), the amendments made by this section shall apply to net capital losses for taxable years beginning after the date of the enactment of this Act.

(2) COORDINATION RULES.—Subparagraph (B) of section 1212(a)(3) of the Internal Revenue Code of 1986, as added by this section, shall apply to taxable years beginning after the date of the enactment of this Act.

(3) EXCISE TAX.—

(A) IN GENERAL.—Except as provided in subparagraph (B), for purposes of section 4982 of the Internal Revenue Code of 1986, paragraphs (1) and (2) shall apply by substituting "the 1-year periods taken into account under subsection (b)(1)(B) of such section with respect to calendar years beginning after December 31, 2010" for "taxable years beginning after the date of the enactment of this Act".

(B) ELECTION.—A regulated investment company may elect to apply subparagraph (A) by substituting "2011" for "2010". Such election shall be made at such time and in such form and manner as the Secretary of the Treasury (or the Secretary's delegate) shall prescribe.

• **2004, American Jobs Creation Act of 2004 (P.L. 108-357)**

P.L. 108-357, §413(c)(20)(A):

Amended Code Sec. 1212(a)(3). **Effective** for tax years beginning after 12-31-2004. Prior to amendment, Code Sec. 1212(a)(3) read as follows:

(3) SPECIAL RULES ON CARRYBACKS.—A net capital loss of a corporation shall not be carried back under paragraph (1)(A) to a taxable year—

(A) for which it is a foreign personal holding company (as defined in section 552);

(B) for which it is a regulated investment company (as defined in section 851);

(C) for which it is a real estate investment trust (as defined in section 856); or

(D) for which an election made by it under section 1247 is applicable (relating to election by foreign investment companies to distribute income currently).

• **1982, Subchapter S Revision Act of 1982 (P.L. 97-354)**

P.L. 97-354, §5(a)(35):

Amended Code Sec. 1212(a) by striking out paragraph (3) and by redesignating paragraph (4) as paragraph (3). **Effective** for tax years beginning after 12-31-82. Prior to being stricken, paragraph (3) read as follows:

"(3) ELECTING SMALL BUSINESS CORPORATIONS.—Paragraph (1)(A) shall not apply to the net capital loss of a corporation for any taxable year for which it is an electing small business corporation under subchapter S, and a net capital loss of a corporation (for a year for which it is not such an electing small business corporation) shall not be carried back under paragraph (1)(A) to a taxable year for which it is an electing small business corporation."

• **1978, Revenue Act of 1978 (P.L. 95-600)**

P.L. 95-600, §703(k), (r):

Amended Code Sec. 1212(a)(1)(C)(ii) by striking out "exceeding the loss year" and inserting in place thereof "succeeding the loss year". **Effective** 10-4-76.

• **1976, Tax Reform Act of 1976 (P.L. 94-455)**

P.L. 94-455, §1403(a):

Amended Code Sec. 1212(a)(1) by striking out "and" at the end of subparagraph (A) and by substituting new subparagraphs (B) and (C) for former subparagraph (B). **Effective** for loss years (within the meaning of Code Sec. 1212(a)(1)) ending on or after 1-1-70. Prior to deletion, Code Sec. 1212(a)(1)(B) read as follows:

(B) a capital loss carryover to each of the 5 taxable years (10 taxable years to the extent such loss is attributable to a foreign expropriation capital loss) succeeding the loss year,

P.L. 94-455, §1901(b)(33)(O):

Substituted "capital gain net income" for "net capital gain" and, "net capital gains" in Code Sec. 1212(a)(1). **Effective** for tax years beginning after 12-31-76.

• **1969, Tax Reform Act of 1969 (P.L. 91-172)**

P.L. 91-172, §512(a):

Amended Sec. 1212(a)(1). **Effective** with respect to net capital losses sustained in tax years beginning after 12-31-69. Prior to amendment, Sec. 1212(a)(1) read as follows:

(a) Corporations.—

(1) In general.—If for any taxable year a corporation has a net capital loss, the amount thereof shall be a short-term capital loss—

(A) in each of the 5 succeeding taxable years, or

(B) to the extent such loss is attributable to a foreign expropriation capital loss, in each of the 10 succeeding taxable years,

to the extent such amount exceeds the total of any net capital gains (determined without regard to this paragraph) of any taxable years intervening between the taxable year in which the net capital loss arose and such succeeding taxable year.

P.L. 91-172, §512(b):

Amended Sec. 1212(a) by adding paragraphs (3) and (4). **Effective** with respect to net capital losses sustained in tax years beginning after 12-31-69.

[Sec. 1212(b)]

(b) OTHER TAXPAYERS.—

(1) IN GENERAL.—If a taxpayer other than a corporation has a net capital loss for any taxable year—

(A) the excess of the net short-term capital loss over the net long-term capital gain for such year shall be a short-term capital loss in the succeeding taxable year, and

(B) the excess of the net long-term capital loss over the net short-term capital gain for such year shall be a long-term capital loss in the succeeding taxable year.

Sec. 1212(a)(2)(B)

INCOME TAX—CAPITAL LOSSES

(2) TREATMENT OF AMOUNTS ALLOWED UNDER SECTION 1211(b)(1) OR (2).—

(A) IN GENERAL.—For purposes of determining the excess referred to in subparagraph (A) or (B) of paragraph (1), there shall be treated as a short-term capital gain in the taxable year an amount equal to the lesser of—

(i) the amount allowed for the taxable year under paragraph (1) or (2) of section 1211(b), or

(ii) the adjusted taxable income for such taxable year.

(B) ADJUSTED TAXABLE INCOME.—For purposes of subparagraph (A), the term "adjusted taxable income" means taxable income increased by the sum of—

(i) the amount allowed for the taxable year under paragraph (1) or (2) of section 1211(b), and

(ii) the deduction allowed for such year under section 151 or any deduction in lieu thereof.

For purposes of the preceding sentence, any excess of the deductions allowed for the taxable year over the gross income for such year shall be taken into account as negative taxable income.

Amendments

• **1988, Technical and Miscellaneous Revenue Act of 1988 (P.L. 100-647)**

P.L. 100-647, §1003(a)(3):

Amended Code Sec. 1212(b)(2). **Effective** as if included in the provision of P.L. 99-514 to which it relates. Prior to amendment, Code Sec. 1212(b)(2) read as follows:

(2) SPECIAL RULE.—For purposes of determining the excess referred to in subparagraph (A) or (B) of paragraph (1), an amount equal to the amount allowed for the taxable year under paragraph (1) or (2) of section 1211(b) shall be treated as a short-term capital gain in such year.

• **1986, Tax Reform Act of 1986 (P.L. 99-514)**

P.L. 99-514, §301(b)(11):

Amended Code Sec. 1212(b)(2). **Effective** for tax years beginning after 12-31-86. Prior to amendment, Code Sec. 1212(b)(2) read as follows:

(2) SPECIAL RULES.—

(A) For purposes of determining the excess referred to in paragraph (1)(A), an amount equal to the amount allowed for the taxable year under section 1211(b)(1)(A), (B), or (C) shall be treated as a short-term capital gain in such year.

(B) For purposes of determining the excess referred to in paragraph (1)(B), an amount equal to the sum of—

(i) the amount allowed for the taxable year under section 1211(b)(1)(A), (B), or (C), and

(ii) the excess of the amount described in clause (i) over the net short-term capital loss (determined without regard to this subsection) for such year,

shall be treated as a short-term capital gain in such year.

• **1984, Deficit Reduction Act of 1984 (P.L. 98-369)**

P.L. 98-369, §1002(a):

Repealed Code Sec. 1212(b)(3). **Effective** for tax years beginning after 12-31-86. Prior to repeal, Code Sec. 1212(b)(3) read as follows:

(3) TRANSITIONAL RULE.—In the case of any amount which, under paragraph (1) and section 1211(b) (as in effect for taxable years beginning before January 1, 1970), is treated as a capital loss in the first taxable year beginning after December 31, 1969, paragraph (1) and section 1211(b) (as in effect for taxable years beginning before January 1, 1970) shall apply (and paragraph (1) and section 1211(b) as in effect for taxable years beginning after December 31, 1969, shall not apply) to the extent such amount exceeds the total of any net capital gains (determined without regard to this subsection) of taxable years beginning after December 31, 1969.

• **1969, Tax Reform Act of 1969 (P.L. 91-172)**

P.L. 91-172, §512(f):

Amended Code Sec. 1212 heading to read **"CAPITAL LOSS CARRYBACKS AND CARRYOVERS"** instead of **"CAPITAL LOSS CARRYOVER"**. **Effective** with respect to net capital losses sustained in tax years beginning after 12-31-69.

P.L. 91-172, §513(b):

Amended Code Sec. 1212(b)(1) by striking out "beginning after December 31, 1963" at the beginning of paragraph (1) and by striking out the last sentence of paragraph (1) and all of paragraph (2) and adding new paragraphs (2) and (3). **Effective** for tax years beginning after 12-31-69. Prior to amendment, the last sentence of Code Sec. paragraphs (1) and (2) of Sec. 1212(b) read as follows:

"For purposes of this paragraph, in determining such excesses an amount equal to the excess of the sum allowed for the taxable year under section 1211(b) over the gains from sales or exchanges of capital assets (determined without regard to this sentence) shall be treated as a short-term capital gain in such year.

"(2) Transitional Rule.—In the case of a taxpayer other than a corporation, there shall be treated as a short-term capital loss in the first taxable year beginning after December 31, 1963, any amount which is treated as a short-term capital loss in such year under this subchapter as in effect immediately before the enactment of the Revenue Act of 1964."

• **1964 (P.L. 88-571)**

P.L. 88-571, §7(a):

Amended Code Sec. 1212(a). **Effective** with respect to net capital losses (to the extent attributable to foreign expropriation capital losses, as defined in Sec. 1212(a)(2)(A)) sustained in tax years ending after 12-31-58. Prior to amendment, Sec. 1212(a) read as follows:

"(a) Corporations.—If for any taxable year a corporation has a net capital loss, the amount thereof shall be a short-term capital loss in each of the 5 succeeding taxable years to the extent that such amount exceeds the total of any net capital gains of any taxable years intervening between the taxable year in which the net capital loss arose and such succeeding taxable year. For purposes of this section, a net capital gain shall be computed without regard to such net capital loss or to any net capital losses arising in any such intervening taxable years, and a net capital loss for a taxable year beginning before October 20, 1951, shall be determined under the applicable law relating to the computation of capital gains and losses in effect before such date."

• **1964, Revenue Act of 1964 (P.L. 88-272)**

P.L. 88-272, §230(a):

Added subsection (b) and amended subsection (a) in the first sentence by inserting "(a) Corporations.—If for any taxable year a corporation". **Effective** for tax years beginning after 12-31-63. Prior to amendment, the subsection read: "If for any taxable year the taxpayer".

[Sec. 1212(c)]

(c) CARRYBACK OF LOSSES FROM SECTION 1256 CONTRACTS TO OFFSET PRIOR GAINS FROM SUCH CONTRACTS.—

(1) IN GENERAL.—If a taxpayer (other than a corporation) has a net section 1256 contracts loss for the taxable year and elects to have this subsection apply to such taxable year, the amount of such net section 1256 contracts loss—

(A) shall be a carryback to each of the 3 taxable years preceding the loss year, and

(B) to the extent that, after the application of paragraphs (2) and (3), such loss is allowed as a carryback to any such preceding taxable year—

(i) 40 percent of the amount so allowed shall be treated as a short-term capital loss from section 1256 contracts, and

(ii) 60 percent of the amount so allowed shall be treated as a long-term capital loss from section 1256 contracts.

(2) AMOUNT CARRIED TO EACH TAXABLE YEAR.—The entire amount of the net section 1256 contracts loss for any taxable year shall be carried to the earliest of the taxable years to which such loss may be carried back under paragraph (1). The portion of such loss which shall be carried to each of the 2 other taxable years to which such loss may be carried back shall be the excess (if any) of such loss over the portion of such loss which, after the application of paragraph (3), was allowed as a carryback for any prior taxable year.

(3) AMOUNT WHICH MAY BE USED IN ANY PRIOR TAXABLE YEAR.—An amount shall be allowed as a carryback under paragraph (1) to any prior taxable year only to the extent—

(A) such amount does not exceed the net section 1256 contract gain for such year, and

(B) the allowance of such carryback does not increase or produce a net operating loss (as defined in section 172(c)) for such year.

(4) NET SECTION 1256 CONTRACTS LOSS.—For purposes of paragraph (1), the term "net section 1256 contracts loss" means the lesser of—

(A) the net capital loss for the taxable year determined by taking into account only gains and losses from section 1256 contracts, or

(B) the sum of the amounts which, but for paragraph (6)(A), would be treated as capital losses in the succeeding taxable year under subparagraphs (A) and (B) of subsection (b)(1).

(5) NET SECTION 1256 CONTRACT GAIN.—For purposes of paragraph (1)—

(A) IN GENERAL.—The term "net section 1256 contract gain" means the lesser of—

Internal Revenue Code   **Sec. 1212(c)(5)(A)**

INCOME TAX—CAPITAL GAINS, LOSSES

(i) the capital gain net income for the taxable year determined by taking into account only gains and losses from section 1256 contracts, or

(ii) the capital gain net income for the taxable year.

(B) SPECIAL RULE.—The net section 1256 contract gain for any taxable year before the loss year shall be computed without regard to the net section 1256 contracts loss for the loss year or for any taxable year thereafter.

(6) COORDINATION WITH CARRYFORWARD PROVISIONS OF SUBSECTION (b)(1).—

(A) CARRYFORWARD AMOUNT REDUCED BY AMOUNT USED AS CARRYBACK.—For purposes of applying subsection (b)(1), if any portion of the net section 1256 contracts loss for any taxable year is allowed as a carryback under paragraph (1) to any preceding taxable year—

(i) 40 percent of the amount allowed as a carryback shall be treated as a short-term capital gain for the loss year, and

(ii) 60 percent of the amount allowed as a carryback shall be treated as a long-term capital gain for the loss year.

(B) CARRYOVER LOSS RETAINS CHARACTER AS ATTRIBUTABLE TO SECTION 1256 CONTRACT.—Any amount carried forward as a short-term or long-term capital loss to any taxable year under subsection (b)(1) (after the application of subparagraph (A)) shall, to the extent attributable to losses from section 1256 contracts, be treated as loss from section 1256 contracts for such taxable year.

(7) OTHER DEFINITIONS AND SPECIAL RULES.—For purposes of this subsection—

(A) SECTION 1256 CONTRACT.—The term "section 1256 contract" means any section 1256 contract (as defined in section 1256(b)) to which section 1256 applies.

(B) EXCLUSION FOR ESTATES AND TRUSTS.—This subsection shall not apply to any estate or trust.

Amendments

• **1984, Deficit Reduction Act of 1984 (P.L. 98-369)**

P.L. 98-369, §102(e)(3):

Amended Code Sec. 1212(c) by striking out "net commodity futures loss" each place it appeared (including in any headings) and inserting in lieu thereof "net section 1256 contracts loss", by striking out "regulated futures contracts" and "regulated futures contract" each place it appeared (including in any headings) and inserting in lieu thereof "section 1256 contracts" and "section 1256 contract", respectively, and by striking out "net commodity futures gain" each place it appeared (including in any headings) and inserting in lieu thereof "net section 1256 contract gain". **Effective** for positions established after 7-18-84, in tax years ending after such date.

• **1983, Technical Corrections Act of 1982 (P.L. 97-448)**

P.L. 97-448, §105(c)(7):

Amended Code Sec. 1212(c)(4)(A) by striking out "and positions to which section 1256 applies". **Effective** as if included in the provision of P.L. 97-34 to which it relates.

• **1981, Economic Recovery Tax Act of 1981 (P.L. 97-34)**

P.L. 97-34, §504:

Added Code Sec. 1212(c). **Effective** for property acquired and positions established by the taxpayer after 6-23-81, in tax years ending after such date.

PART III—GENERAL RULES FOR DETERMINING CAPITAL GAINS AND LOSSES

Sec. 1221.   Capital asset defined.
Sec. 1222.   Other terms relating to capital gains and losses.
Sec. 1223.   Holding period of property.

[Sec. 1221]

SEC. 1221. CAPITAL ASSET DEFINED.

[Sec. 1221(a)]

(a) IN GENERAL.—For purposes of this subtitle, the term "capital asset" means property held by the taxpayer (whether or not connected with his trade or business), but does not include—

(1) stock in trade of the taxpayer or other property of a kind which would properly be included in the inventory of the taxpayer if on hand at the close of the taxable year, or property held by the taxpayer primarily for sale to customers in the ordinary course of his trade or business;

(2) property, used in his trade or business, of a character which is subject to the allowance for depreciation provided in section 167, or real property used in his trade or business;

(3) a patent, invention, model or design (whether or not patented), a secret formula or process, a copyright, a literary, musical, or artistic composition, a letter or memorandum, or similar property, held by—

(A) a taxpayer whose personal efforts created such property,

(B) in the case of a letter, memorandum, or similar property, a taxpayer for whom such property was prepared or produced, or

(C) a taxpayer in whose hands the basis of such property is determined, for purposes of determining gain from a sale or exchange, in whole or part by reference to the basis of such property in the hands of a taxpayer described in subparagraph (A) or (B);

(4) accounts or notes receivable acquired in the ordinary course of trade or business for services rendered or from the sale of property described in paragraph (1);

(5) a publication of the United States Government (including the Congressional Record) which is received from the United States Government or any agency thereof, other than by purchase at the price at which it is offered for sale to the public, and which is held by—

(A) a taxpayer who so received such publication, or

(B) a taxpayer in whose hands the basis of such publication is determined, for purposes of determining gain from a sale or exchange, in whole or in part by reference to the basis of such publication in the hands of a taxpayer described in subparagraph (A);

(6) any commodities derivative financial instrument held by a commodities derivatives dealer, unless—

(A) it is established to the satisfaction of the Secretary that such instrument has no connection to the activities of such dealer as a dealer, and

(B) such instrument is clearly identified in such dealer's records as being described in subparagraph (A) before the close of the day on which it was acquired, originated, or entered into (or such other time as the Secretary may by regulations prescribe);

(7) any hedging transaction which is clearly identified as such before the close of the day on which it was acquired, originated, or entered into (or such other time as the Secretary may by regulations prescribe); or

(8) supplies of a type regularly used or consumed by the taxpayer in the ordinary course of a trade or business of the taxpayer.

Amendments

• **2017, Tax Cuts and Jobs Act (P.L. 115-97)**

P.L. 115-97, §13314(a):

Amended Code Sec. 1221(a)(3) by inserting "a patent, invention, model or design (whether or not patented), a secret formula or process," before "a copyright". **Effective** for dispositions after 12-31-2017.

• **2013, American Taxpayer Relief Act of 2012 (P.L. 112-240)**

P.L. 112-240, §101(a)(1)-(3), provides:

SEC. 101. PERMANENT EXTENSION AND MODIFICATION OF 2001 TAX RELIEF.

(a) PERMANENT EXTENSION.—

(1) IN GENERAL.—The Economic Growth and Tax Relief Reconciliation Act of 2001 is amended by striking title IX.

(2) CONFORMING AMENDMENT.—The Tax Relief, Unemployment Insurance Reauthorization, and Job Creation Act of 2010 is amended by striking section 304.

(3) EFFECTIVE DATE.—The amendments made by this subsection shall apply to taxable, plan, or limitation years beginning after December 31, 2012, and estates of decedents dying, gifts made, or generation skipping transfers after December 31, 2012.

- **2010, Tax Relief, Unemployment Insurance Reauthorization, and Job Creation Act of 2010 (P.L. 111-312)**

P.L. 111-312, §301(a):

Amended Code Sec. 1221(a)(3)(C) to read as such provision would read if subtitle E of title V of the Economic Growth and Tax Relief Reconciliation Act of 2001 (P.L. 107-16) had never been enacted. **Effective** for estates of decedents dying, and transfers made, after 12-31-2009. For a special rule, see Act Sec. 301(c), below.

P.L. 111-312, §301(c), provides:

(c) SPECIAL ELECTION WITH RESPECT TO ESTATES OF DECEDENTS DYING IN 2010.—Notwithstanding subsection (a), in the case of an estate of a decedent dying after December 31, 2009, and before January 1, 2011, the executor (within the meaning of section 2203 of the Internal Revenue Code of 1986) may elect to apply such Code as though the amendments made by subsection (a) do not apply with respect to chapter 11 of such Code and with respect to property acquired or passing from such decedent (within the meaning of section 1014(b) of such Code). Such election shall be made at such time and in such manner as the Secretary of the Treasury or the Secretary's delegate shall provide. Such an election once made shall be revocable only with the consent of the Secretary of the Treasury or the Secretary's delegate. For purposes of section 2652(a)(1) of such Code, the determination of whether any property is subject to the tax imposed by such chapter 11 shall be made without regard to any election made under this subsection.

P.L. 111-312, §304, provides [but see P.L. 112-240, §101(a)(2)-(3), above]:

SEC. 304. APPLICATION OF EGTRRA SUNSET TO THIS TITLE.

Section 901 of the Economic Growth and Tax Relief Reconciliation Act of 2001 shall apply to the amendments made by this title.

- **2001, Economic Growth and Tax Relief Reconciliation Act of 2001 (P.L. 107-16)**

P.L. 107-16, §542(e)(2)(A):

Amended Code Sec. 1221(a)(3)(C) by inserting "(other than by reason of section 1022)" after "is determined". **Effective** for estates of decedents dying after 12-31-2009.

P.L. 107-16, §901(a)-(b), as amended by P.L. 111-312, §101(a)(1), provides [but see P.L. 112-240, §101(a)(1) and (3), above]:

SEC. 901. SUNSET OF PROVISIONS OF ACT.

(a) IN GENERAL.—All provisions of, and amendments made by, this Act shall not apply—

(1) to taxable, plan, or limitation years beginning after December 31, 2012, or

(2) in the case of title V, to estates of decedents dying, gifts made, or generation skipping transfers, after December 31, 2012.

(b) APPLICATION OF CERTAIN LAWS.—The Internal Revenue Code of 1986 and the Employee Retirement Income Security Act of 1974 shall be applied and administered to years, estates, gifts, and transfers described in subsection (a) as if the provisions and amendments described in subsection (a) had never been enacted.

- **1999, Tax Relief Extension Act of 1999 (P.L. 106-170)**

P.L. 106-170, §532(a)(1)-(3):

Amended Code Sec. 1221 by striking "For purposes" and inserting "(a) IN GENERAL.—For purposes", by striking the period at the end of paragraph (5) and inserting a semicolon, and by adding at the end new paragraphs (6), (7) and (8). **Effective** for any instrument held, acquired, or entered into, any transaction entered into, and supplies held or acquired on or after 12-17-99.

[Sec. 1221(b)]

(b) DEFINITIONS AND SPECIAL RULES.—

(1) COMMODITIES DERIVATIVE FINANCIAL INSTRUMENTS.—For purposes of subsection (a)(6)—

(A) COMMODITIES DERIVATIVES DEALER.—The term "commodities derivatives dealer" means a person which regularly offers to enter into, assume, offset, assign, or terminate positions in commodities derivative financial instruments with customers in the ordinary course of a trade or business.

(B) COMMODITIES DERIVATIVE FINANCIAL INSTRUMENT.—

(i) IN GENERAL.—The term "commodities derivative financial instrument" means any contract or financial instrument with respect to commodities (other than a share of stock in a corporation, a beneficial interest in a partnership or trust, a note, bond, debenture, or other evidence of indebtedness, or a section 1256 contract (as defined in section 1256(b))), the value or settlement price of which is calculated by or determined by reference to a specified index.

(ii) SPECIFIED INDEX.—The term "specified index" means any one or more or any combination of—

(I) a fixed rate, price, or amount, or

(II) a variable rate, price, or amount,

which is based on any current, objectively determinable financial or economic information with respect to commodities which is not within the control of any of the parties to the contract or instrument and is not unique to any of the parties' circumstances.

(2) HEDGING TRANSACTION.—

(A) IN GENERAL.—For purposes of this section, the term "hedging transaction" means any transaction entered into by the taxpayer in the normal course of the taxpayer's trade or business primarily—

(i) to manage risk of price changes or currency fluctuations with respect to ordinary property which is held or to be held by the taxpayer,

(ii) to manage risk of interest rate or price changes or currency fluctuations with respect to borrowings made or to be made, or ordinary obligations incurred or to be incurred, by the taxpayer, or

(iii) to manage such other risks as the Secretary may prescribe in regulations.

(B) TREATMENT OF NONIDENTIFICATION OR IMPROPER IDENTIFICATION OF HEDGING TRANSACTIONS.—Notwithstanding subsection (a)(7), the Secretary shall prescribe regulations to properly characterize any income, gain, expense, or loss arising from a transaction—

(i) which is a hedging transaction but which was not identified as such in accordance with subsection (a)(7), or

(ii) which was so identified but is not a hedging transaction.

(3) SALE OR EXCHANGE OF SELF-CREATED MUSICAL WORKS.—At the election of the taxpayer, paragraphs (1) and (3) of subsection (a) shall not apply to musical compositions or copyrights in musical works sold or exchanged by a taxpayer described in subsection (a)(3).

(4) REGULATIONS.—The Secretary shall prescribe such regulations as are appropriate to carry out the purposes of paragraph (6) and (7) of subsection (a) in the case of transactions involving related parties.

Amendments

- **2006, Tax Relief and Health Care Act of 2006 (P.L. 109-432)**

P.L. 109-432, Division A, §412(a):

Amended Code Sec. 1221(b)(3) by striking "before January 1, 2011," before "by a taxpayer". **Effective** as if included in section 204 of the Tax Increase Prevention and Reconciliation Act of 2005 (P.L. 109-222) [**effective** for sales and exchanges in tax years beginning after 5-17-2006.—CCH].

- **2006, Tax Increase Prevention and Reconciliation Act of 2005 (P.L. 109-222)**

P.L. 109-222, §204(a):

Amended Code Sec. 1221(b) by redesignating paragraph (3) as paragraph (4) and by inserting after paragraph (2) a new paragraph (3). **Effective** for sales and exchanges in tax years beginning after 5-17-2006.

- **2002, Job Creation and Worker Assistance Act of 2002 (P.L. 107-147)**

P.L. 107-147, §417(20):

Amended Code Sec. 1221(b)(1)(B)(i) by striking "1256(b))" and inserting "1256(b)))". **Effective** 3-9-2002.

- **1999, Tax Relief Extension Act of 1999 (P.L. 106-170)**

P.L. 106-170, §532(a)(3):

Amended Code Sec. 1221 by adding at the end new subsection (b). **Effective** for any instrument held, acquired, or entered into, any transaction entered into, and supplies held or acquired on or after 12-17-99.

INCOME TAX—CAPITAL GAINS, LOSSES

• **1981, Economic Recovery Tax Act of 1981 (P.L. 97-34)**

P.L. 97-34, §505(a):

Struck Code Sec. 1221(5) and redesignated Code Sec. 1221(6) as Code Sec. 1221(5). **Effective** for property acquired and positions established by the taxpayer after 6-23-81, in tax years ending after such date. Prior to being stricken, Code Sec. 1221(5) read as follows:

(5) an obligation of the United States or any of its possessions, or of a State or any political subdivision thereof, or of the District of Columbia, issued on or after March 1, 1941, on a discount basis and payable without interest at a fixed maturity date not exceeding one year from the date of issue; or

• **1976, Tax Reform Act of 1976 (P.L. 94-455)**

P.L. 94-455, §1901(c)(9):

Amended Code Sec. 1221(5) by striking out "or Territory," following the word "State". **Effective** with respect to tax years beginning after 12-31-76.

P.L. 94-455, §2132(a):

Amended Code Sec. 1221 by adding new paragraph (6). **Effective** for sales, exchanges, and contributions made after 10-4-76.

• **1969, Tax Reform Act of 1969 (P.L. 91-172)**

P.L. 91-172, §514(a):

Amended Code Sec. 1221(3). **Effective** for sales and other dispositions occuring after 7-25-69. Prior to amendment, Code Sec. 1221(3) read as follows:

"(3) a copyright, a literary, musical, or artistic composition, or similar property, held by—

"(A) a taxpayer whose personal efforts created such property, or

"(B) a taxpayer in whose hands the basis of such property is determined, for the purpose of determining gain from a sale or exchange, in whole or in part by reference to the basis of such property in the hands of the person whose personal efforts created such property;".

[Sec. 1222]

SEC. 1222. OTHER TERMS RELATING TO CAPITAL GAINS AND LOSSES.

For purposes of this subtitle—

⟫→ *Caution: P.L. 98-369, §1001(a)(1)-(2), amended Code Sec. 1222(1)-(4), below, by striking "1 year" and inserting "6 months". This amendment applies to property acquired after June 22, 1984, and before January 1, 1988.*

(1) SHORT-TERM CAPITAL GAIN.—The term "short-term capital gain" means gain from the sale or exchange of a capital asset held for not more than 6 months [1 year], if and to the extent such gain is taken into account in computing gross income.

(2) SHORT-TERM CAPITAL LOSS.—The term "short-term capital loss" means loss from the sale or exchange of a capital asset held for not more than 6 months [1 year], if and to the extent that such loss is taken into account in computing taxable income.

(3) LONG-TERM CAPITAL GAIN.—The term "long-term capital gain" means gain from the sale or exchange of a capital asset held for more than 6 months [1 year], if and to the extent such gain is taken into account in computing gross income.

(4) LONG-TERM CAPITAL LOSS.—The term "long-term capital loss" means loss from the sale or exchange of a capital asset held for more than 6 months [1 year], if and to the extent that such loss is taken into account in computing taxable income.

(5) NET SHORT-TERM CAPITAL GAIN.—The term "net short-term capital gain" means the excess of short-term capital gains for the taxable year over the short-term capital losses for such year.

(6) NET SHORT-TERM CAPITAL LOSS.—The term "net short-term capital loss" means the excess of short-term capital losses for the taxable year over the short-term capital gains for such year.

(7) NET LONG-TERM CAPITAL GAIN.—The term "net long-term capital gain" means the excess of long-term capital gains for the taxable year over the long-term capital losses for such year.

(8) NET LONG-TERM CAPITAL LOSS.—The term "net long-term capital loss" means the excess of long-term capital losses for the taxable year over the long-term capital gains for such year.

(9) CAPITAL GAIN NET INCOME.—The term "capital gain net income" means the excess of the gains from sales or exchanges of capital assets over the losses from such sales or exchanges.

(10) NET CAPITAL LOSS.—The term "net capital loss" means the excess of the losses from sales or exchanges of capital assets over the sum allowed under section 1211. In the case of a corporation, for the purpose of determining losses under this paragraph, amounts which are short-term capital losses under section 1212(a)(1) shall be excluded.

(11) NET CAPITAL GAIN.—The term "net capital gain" means the excess of the net long-term capital gain for the taxable year over the net short-term capital loss for such year.

Amendments

• **2014, Tax Technical Corrections Act of 2014 (P.L. 113-295)**

P.L. 113-295, §221(a)(79), Division A:

Amended Code Sec. 1222 by striking the last sentence. **Effective** generally 12-19-2014. For a special rule, see Act Sec. 221(b)(2), Division A, below. Prior to being stricken, the last sentence of Code Sec. 1222 read as follows:

For purposes of this subtitle, in the case of futures transactions in any commodity subject to the rules of a board of trade or commodity exchange, the length of the holding period taken into account under this section or under any other section amended by section 1402 of the Tax Reform Act of 1976 shall be determined without regard to the amendments made by subsections (a) and (b) of such section 1402.

P.L. 113-295, §221(b)(2), Division A, provides:

(2) SAVINGS PROVISION.—If—

(A) any provision amended or repealed by the amendments made by this section applied to—

(i) any transaction occurring before the date of the enactment of this Act,

(ii) any property acquired before such date of enactment, or

(iii) any item of income, loss, deduction, or credit taken into account before such date of enactment, and

(B) the treatment of such transaction, property, or item under such provision would (without regard to the amendments or repeals made by this section) affect the liability for tax for periods ending after date of enactment, nothing in the amendments or repeals made by this section shall be construed to affect the treatment of such transaction, property, or item for purposes of determining liability for tax for periods ending after such date of enactment.

• **2010, Regulated Investment Company Modernization Act of 2010 (P.L. 111-325)**

P.L. 111-325, §101(b)(2):

Amended Code Sec. 1222(10) by striking "section 1212" and inserting "section 1212(a)(1)". **Effective** for net capital losses for tax years beginning after 12-22-2010. For a special rule, see Act Sec. 101(c)(1)-(3), below.

P.L. 111-325, §101(c)(1)-(3) (as amended by P.L. 113-295, §205(a)(1)(A)-(B), Division A), provides:

(1) IN GENERAL.—Except as provided in paragraphs (2) and (3), the amendments made by this section shall apply to net capital losses for taxable years beginning after the date of the enactment of this Act.

(2) COORDINATION RULES.—Subparagraph (B) of section 1212(a)(3) of the Internal Revenue Code of 1986, as added by this section, shall apply to taxable years beginning after the date of the enactment of this Act.

(3) EXCISE TAX.—

(A) IN GENERAL.—Except as provided in subparagraph (B), for purposes of section 4982 of the Internal Revenue Code of 1986, paragraphs (1) and (2) shall apply by substituting "the 1-year periods taken into account under subsection (b)(1)(B) of such section with respect to calendar years beginning after December 31, 2010" for "taxable years beginning after the date of the enactment of this Act".

(B) ELECTION.—A regulated investment company may elect to apply subparagraph (A) by substituting "2011" for "2010". Such election shall be made at such time and in such form and manner as the Secretary of the Treasury (or the Secretary's delegate) shall prescribe.

• **1984, Deficit Reduction Act of 1984 (P.L. 98-369)**

P.L. 98-369, §1001(a)(1):

Amended Code Sec. 1222(1) and (3) by striking out "1 year" and inserting in lieu thereof "6 months". **Effective** for property acquired after 6-22-84, and before 1-1-88.

P.L. 98-369, §1001(a)(2):

Amended Code Sec. 1222(2) and (4) by striking out "1 year" and inserting in lieu thereof "6 months". **Effective** for property acquired after 6-22-84, and before 1-1-88.

• **1976, Tax Reform Act of 1976 (P.L. 94-455)**

P.L. 94-455, §1402(a)(1):

Amended Code Sec. 1222(1), (2), (3), and (4) by substituting "9 months" for "6 months". **Effective** with respect to tax years beginning in 1977.

INCOME TAX—CAPITAL GAINS, LOSSES

P.L. 94-455, § 1402(a)(2):

Amended Code Sec. 1222(1), (2), (3), and (4) by substituting "1 year" for "9 months". **Effective** with respect to tax years beginning after 12-31-77.

P.L. 94-455, § 1402(c), provides:

(c) TRANSITIONAL RULE FOR CERTAIN INSTALLMENT OBLIGATIONS.—In the case of amounts received from sales or other dispositions of capital assets pursuant to binding contracts, including sales or other dispositions the income from which is returned on the basis and in the manner prescribed in section 453(a)(1) of the Internal Revenue Code of 1954, if the gain or loss was treated as long-term for the taxable year for which the amount was realized, such gain or loss shall be treated as long-term for the taxable year for which the gain or loss is returned or otherwise recognized.

P.L. 94-455, § 1402(d):

Amended Code Sec. 1222 by adding at the end thereof a new sentence, beginning with "For purposes of this subtitle." **Effective** 10-4-76.

P.L. 94-455, § 1901(a)(136)(A):

Amended Code Sec. 1222(9). **Effective** with respect to tax years beginning after 12-31-76. Prior to amendment Code Sec. 1222(9) read:

(9) NET CAPITAL GAIN.—The term "net capital gain" means the excess of the gains from sales or exchanges of capital assets over the losses from such sales or exchanges.

P.L. 94-455, § 1901(a)(136)(B):

Amended Code Sec. 1222(11). **Effective** with respect to tax years beginning after 12-31-76. Prior to amendment Code Sec. 1222(11) read:

(11) NET SECTION 1201 GAIN.—The term "net section 1201 gain" means the excess of the net long-term capital gain for the taxable year over the net short-term capital loss for such year.

• **1969, Tax Reform Act of 1969 (P.L. 91-172)**

P.L. 91-172, § 511(a):

Added paragraph (11). **Effective** tax years beginning after 12-31-69.

P.L. 91-172, § 513(c):

Amended Code Sec. 1222(9) by striking out "In the case of a corporation, the" and inserting "The" in its place. **Effective** for tax years beginning after 12-31-69.

• **1964, Revenue Act of 1964 (P.L. 88-272)**

P.L. 88-272, § 230(b):

Amended paragraph (9). **Effective** with respect to tax years beginning after 12-31-63. Prior to amendment, paragraph (9) read as follows:

"(9) Net Capital Gain.—

"(A) Corporations.—In the case of a corporation, the term `net capital gain' means the excess of the gains from sales or exchanges of capital assets over the losses from such sales or exchanges.

"(B) Other taxpayers.—In the case of a taxpayer other than a corporation, the term `net capital gain' means the excess of—

"(i) the sum of the gains from sales or exchanges of capital assets, plus taxable income (computed without regard to the deductions provided by section 151, relating to personal exemptions or any deduction in lieu thereof) of the taxpayer or $1,000, whichever is smaller, over

"(ii) the losses from such sales or exchanges.

For purposes of this subparagraph, taxable income shall be computed without regard to gains or losses from sales or exchanges of capital assets. If the taxpayer elects to pay the optional tax under section 3, the term `taxable income' as used in this subparagraph shall be read as `adjusted gross income.'"

and amended paragraph (10) by inserting at the beginning of the second sentence the words "In the case of a corporation,". **Effective** with respect to taxable years beginning after December 31, 1963.

[Sec. 1223]

SEC. 1223. HOLDING PERIOD OF PROPERTY.

For purposes of this subtitle—

(1) In determining the period for which the taxpayer has held property received in an exchange, there shall be included the period for which he held the property exchanged if, under this chapter, the property has, for the purpose of determining gain or loss from a sale or exchange, the same basis in whole or in part in his hands as the property exchanged, and, in the case of such exchanges the property exchanged at the time of such exchange was a capital asset as defined in section 1221 or property described in section 1231. For purposes of this paragraph—

(A) an involuntary conversion described in section 1033 shall be considered an exchange of the property converted for the property acquired, and

(B) a distribution to which section 355 (or so much of section 356 as relates to section 355) applies shall be treated as an exchange.

(2) In determining the period for which the taxpayer has held property however acquired there shall be included the period for which such property was held by any other person, if under this chapter such property has, for the purpose of determining gain or loss from a sale or exchange, the same basis in whole or in part in his hands as it would have in the hands of such other person.

(3) In determining the period for which the taxpayer has held stock or securities the acquisition of which (or the contract or option to acquire which) resulted in the nondeductibility (under section 1091 relating to wash sales) of the loss from the sale or other disposition of substantially identical stock or securities, there shall be included the period for which he held the stock or securities the loss from the sale or other disposition of which was not deductible.

(4) In determining the period for which the taxpayer has held stock or rights to acquire stock received on a distribution, if the basis of such stock or rights is determined under section 307, there shall (under regulations prescribed by the Secretary) be included the period for which he held the stock in the distributing corporation before the receipt of such stock or rights upon such distribution.

(5) In determining the period for which the taxpayer has held stock or securities acquired from a corporation by the exercise of rights to acquire such stock or securities, there shall be included only the period beginning with the date on which the right to acquire was exercised.

(6) [Repealed.]

(7) In determining the period for which the taxpayer has held a commodity acquired in satisfaction of a commodity futures contract (other than a commodity futures contract to which section 1256 applies) there shall be included the period for which he held the commodity futures contract if such commodity futures contract was a capital asset in his hands.

(8) [Repealed.]

(9) In the case of a person acquiring property from a decedent or to whom property passed from a decedent (within the meaning of section 1014(b)), if—

(A) the basis of such property in the hands of such person is determined under section 1014, and

(B) such property is sold or otherwise disposed of by such person within 1 year after the decedent's death,

then such person shall be considered to have held such property for more than 1 year.

(10) If—

(A) property is acquired by any person in a transfer to which section 1040 applies,

(B) such property is sold or otherwise disposed of by such person within 1 year after the decedent's death, and

(C) such sale or disposition is to a person who is a qualified heir (as defined in section 2032A(e)(1)) with respect to the decedent,

then the person making such sale or other disposition shall be considered to have held such property for more than 1 year.

(11) In determining the period for which the taxpayer has held qualified replacement property (within the meaning of section 1042(b)) the acquisition of which resulted under section 1042 in the nonrecognition of any part of the gain realized on the sale of qualified securities (within the meaning of section 1042(b)), there shall be included the period for which such qualified securities had been held by the taxpayer.

(12) In determining the period for which the taxpayer has held property the acquisition of which resulted under section 1043 in the nonrecognition of any part of the gain realized on the sale of other property, there shall be included the period for which such other property had been held as of the date of such sale.

(13) Except for purposes of subsections (a)(2) and (c)(2)(A) of section 1202, in determining the period for which the taxpayer has held property the acquisition of which resulted under section 1045 or 1397B in the nonrecognition of any part of the gain realized on the sale of other property, there shall be included the period for which such other property has been held as of the date of such sale.

INCOME TAX—CAPITAL GAINS, LOSSES

(14) If the security to which a securities futures contract (as defined in section 1234B) relates (other than a contract to which section 1256 applies) is acquired in satisfaction of such contract, in determining the period for which the taxpayer has held such security, there shall be included the period for which the taxpayer held such contract if such contract was a capital asset in the hands of the taxpayer.

(15) CROSS REFERENCE.—

For special holding period provision relating to certain partnership distributions, see section 735(b).

Amendments

• **2018, Tax Technical Corrections Act of 2018 (P.L. 115-141)**

P.L. 115-141, §401(d)(4)(B)(vi), Div. U:

Amended Code Sec. 1223(13) by striking "sections 1202(a)(2), 1202(c)(2)(A), 1400B(b), and 1400F(b)" and inserting "subsections (a)(2) and (c)(2)(A) of section 1202". **Effective** 3-23-2018. For a special rule, see Act Sec. 401(e), Div. U, below.

P.L. 115-141, §401(e), Div. U, provides:

(e) GENERAL SAVINGS PROVISION WITH RESPECT TO DEADWOOD PROVISIONS.—If—

(1) any provision amended or repealed by the amendments made by subsection (b) or (d) applied to—

(A) any transaction occurring before the date of the enactment of this Act,

(B) any property acquired before such date of enactment, or

(C) any item of income, loss, deduction, or credit taken into account before such date of enactment, and

(2) the treatment of such transaction, property, or item under such provision would (without regard to the amendments or repeals made by such subsection) affect the liability for tax for periods ending after such date of enactment,

nothing in the amendments or repeals made by this section shall be construed to affect the treatment of such transaction, property, or item for purposes of determining liability for tax for periods ending after such date of enactment.

• **2014, Tax Technical Corrections Act of 2014 (P.L. 113-295)**

P.L. 113-295, §221(a)(80)(A), Division A:

Amended Code Sec. 1223(1) by striking "after March 1, 1954," following "and, in the case of such exchanges". **Effective** generally 12-19-2014. For a special rule, see Act Sec. 221(b)(2), Division A, below.

P.L. 113-295, §221(a)(80)(B), Division A:

Amended Code Sec. 1223(4) by striking "'[sic](or under so much of section 1052(c) as refers to section 113(a)(23) of the Internal Revenue Code of 1939)[sic]'" following "under section 307.". **Effective** generally 12-19-2014. For a special rule, see Act Sec. 221(b)(2), Division A, below.

P.L. 113-295, §221(a)(80)(C), Division A:

Repealed Code Sec. 1223(6) and (8). **Effective** generally 12-19-2014. For a special rule, see Act Sec. 221(b)(2), Division A, below. Prior to repeal, Code Sec. 1223(6) and (8) read as follows:

(6) In determining the period for which the taxpayer has held a residence, the acquisition of which resulted under section 1034 (as in effect on the day before the date of the enactment of the Taxpayer Relief Act of 1997) in the nonrecognition of any part of the gain realized on the sale or exchange of another residence, there shall be included the period for which such other residence had been held as of the date of such sale or exchange. For purposes of this paragraph, the term "sale or exchange" includes an involuntary conversion occurring after December 31, 1950, and before January 1, 1954.

(8) Any reference in this section to a provision of this title shall, where applicable, be deemed a reference to the corresponding provision of the Internal Revenue Code of 1939, or prior internal revenue laws.

P.L. 113-295, §221(b)(2), Division A, provides:

(2) SAVINGS PROVISION.—If—

(A) any provision amended or repealed by the amendments made by this section applied to—

(i) any transaction occurring before the date of the enactment of this Act,

(ii) any property acquired before such date of enactment, or

(iii) any item of income, loss, deduction, or credit taken into account before such date of enactment, and

(B) the treatment of such transaction, property, or item under such provision would (without regard to the amendments or repeals made by this section) affect the liability for tax for periods ending after date of enactment, nothing in the amendments or repeals made by this section shall be construed to affect the treatment of such transaction, property, or item for purposes of determining liability for tax for periods ending after such date of enactment.

• **2005, Gulf Opportunity Zone Act of 2005 (P.L. 109-135)**

P.L. 109-135, §402(a)(2):

Amended Code Sec. 1223 by striking paragraph (3) and by redesignating paragraphs (4) through (16) as paragraphs (3) through (15), respectively. **Effective** as if included in the provision of the Energy Policy Act of 2005 (P.L. 109-58) to which it relates [**effective** 2-8-2006.—CCH]. For a special rule, see Act Sec. 402(m)(2), below. Prior to being stricken, Code Sec. 1223(3) read as follows:

(3) In determining the period for which the taxpayer has held stock or securities received upon a distribution where no gain was recognized to the distributee under section 1081(c) (or under section 112(g) of the Revenue Act of 1928, 45 Stat. 818, or the Revenue Act of 1932, 48 Stat. 705), there shall be included the period for which he held the stock or securities in the distributing corporation before the receipt of the stock or securities on such distribution.

P.L. 109-135, §402(m)(2), provides:

(2) REPEAL OF PUBLIC UTILITY HOLDING COMPANY ACT OF 1935.—The amendments made by subsection (a) shall not apply with respect to any transaction ordered in compliance with the Public Utility Holding Company Act of 1935 before its repeal.

• **2004, American Jobs Creation Act of 2004 (P.L. 108-357)**

P.L. 108-357, §413(c)(21):

Amended Code Sec. 1223 by striking paragraph (10) and by redesignating the following paragraphs accordingly. **Effective** for tax years of foreign corporations beginning after 12-31-2004, and for tax years of United States shareholders with or within which such tax years of foreign corporations end. Prior to being stricken, Code Sec. 1223(10) read as follows:

(10) In determining the period for which the taxpayer has held trust certificates of a trust to which subsection (d) of section 1246 applies, or the period for which the taxpayer has held stock in a corporation to which subsection (d) of section 1246 applies, there shall be included the period for which the trust or corporation (as the case may be) held the stock of foreign investment companies.

• **2000, Community Renewal Tax Relief Act of 2000 (P.L. 106-554)**

P.L. 106-554, §116(b)(2):

Amended Code Sec. 1223(15). **Effective** for qualified empowerment zone assets acquired after 12-21-2000. Prior to amendment, Code Sec. 1223(15) read as follows:

(15) In determining the period for which the taxpayer has held property the acquisition of which resulted under section 1045 in the nonrecognition of any part of the gain realized on the sale of other property, there shall be included the period for which such other property has been held as of the date of such sale.

P.L. 106-554, §401(h)(1):

Amended Code Sec. 1223 by redesignating paragraph (16) as paragraph (17) and by inserting after paragraph (15) a new paragraph (16). **Effective** 12-21-2000.

• **1998, IRS Restructuring and Reform Act of 1998 (P.L. 105-206)**

P.L. 105-206, §5001(a)(5):

Amended Code Sec. 1223(11)-(12) by striking "18 months" each place it appears and inserting "1 year". **Effective** 1-1-98.

P.L. 105-206, §6005(d)(4):

Amended Code Sec. 1223(11)-(12), prior to amendment by Act Sec. 5001(a)(5), by striking "1 year" each place it appears and inserting "18 months". **Effective** as if included in the provision of P.L. 105-34 to which it relates [effective for tax years ending after 5-6-97.—CCH].

• **1997, Taxpayer Relief Act of 1997 (P.L. 105-34)**

P.L. 105-34, §312(d)(9):

Amended Code Sec. 1223(7) by inserting "(as in effect on the day before the date of the enactment of the Taxpayer Relief Act of 1997)" after "1034". **Effective**, generally, for sales and exchanges after 5-6-97.

P.L. 105-34, §313(b)(2):

Amended Code Sec. 1223 by redesignating paragraph (15) as paragraph (16) and by inserting after paragraph (14) a new paragraph (15). **Effective** for sales after 8-5-97.

• **1989, Ethics Reform Act (P.L. 101-194)**

P.L. 101-194, §502(b)(1):

Amended Code Sec. 1223 by redesignating paragraph (14) as paragraph (15) and by inserting after paragraph (13) a new paragraph (14). **Effective** for sales after 11-30-89.

• **1988, Technical and Miscellaneous Revenue Act of 1988 (P.L. 100-647)**

P.L. 100-647, §1006(e)(17):

Amended Code Sec. 1223(14). **Effective** as if included in the provision of P.L. 99-514 to which it relates. Prior to amendment, Code Sec. 1223(14) read as follows:

(14) CROSS REFERENCES.—

(A) For special holding period provision relating to certain partnership distributions, see section 735(b).

(B) For special holding period provision relating to distributions of appreciated property to corporations, see section 301(e).

• **1984, Deficit Reduction Act of 1984 (P.L. 98-369)**

P.L. 98-369, §54(c):

Amended Code Sec. 1223(13), prior to its redesignation by Act Sec. 541(b)(1). **Effective** for distributions declared after 7-18-84, in tax years ending after such date. Prior to amendment, it read:

(13) Cross Reference.—

For special holding period provision relating to certain partnership distributions, see section 735(b).

P.L. 98-369, §541(b)(1):

Amended Code Sec. 1223 by redesignating paragraph (13), as amended by Act Sec. 54(c), as paragraph (14) and inserting new paragraph (13). **Effective** for sales of securities in tax years beginning after 7-18-84.

P.L. 98-369, §1001(b)(14):

Amended Code Sec. 1223(11) and (12) by striking out "1 year" each place it appeared and inserting in lieu thereof "6 months". **Effective** for property acquired after 6-22-84, and before 1-1-88.

INCOME TAX—CAPITAL GAINS, LOSSES

- **1983, Technical Corrections Act of 1982 (P.L. 97-448)**

P.L. 97-448, §104(b)(3)(C):

Amended Code Sec. 1223 by redesignating paragraph (12) as paragraph (13) and by inserting after paragraph (11) new paragraph (12). **Effective** as if included in the provision of P.L. 97-34 to which it relates.

P.L. 97-448, §105(c)(4):

Amended Code Sec. 1223 (8) by inserting "(other than a commodity futures contract to which section 1256 applies)" after "commodity futures contract" the first place it appears. **Effective** as if included in the provision of P.L. 97-34 to which it relates.

- **1980, Crude Oil Windfall Profit Tax Act of 1980 (P.L. 96-223)**

P.L. 96-223, §401(a):

Repealed Code Sec. 1223(11)(A) as amended by P.L. 95-600, Act Sec. 702(c)(5). **Effective** with respect to decedents dying after 1976. However, see the amendment note for P.L. 96-223 §401(a) that follows Code Sec. 1014(d) for the text of Act Sec. 401(d) that authorizes the election of the carryover basis rules in the case of a decedent dying after 12-31-76 and before 11-7-78. Prior to repeal, Code Sec. 1223(11)(A) read as follows:

"(A) the basis of such property in the hands of such person is determined under section 1014 or 1023, and".

P.L. 96-223, §401(b):

Revived Code Sec. 1223(11)(A) as it read prior to amendment by P.L. 95-600, Act Sec. 702(c)(5). **Effective** with respect to decedents dying after 12-31-76. However, see the amendment note for Act Sec. 401(a).

- **1978, Revenue Act of 1978 (P.L. 95-600)**

P.L. 95-600, §702(c)(5), (10):

Amended Code Sec. 1223(11)(A). **Effective** as if included in the amendments and additions made by, and the appropriate provisions of, P.L. 94-455.

- **1976, Tax Reform Act of 1976 (P.L. 94-455)**

P. L. 94-455, §1402(b)(1)(Q):

Amended Code Sec. 1223(11) by substituting "9 months" for "6 months". **Effective** for tax years beginning in 1977.

P. L. 94-455, §1402(b)(2):

Amended Code Sec. 1223(11) by substituting "1 year" for "9 months". **Effective** with respect to tax years beginning after 12-31-77.

P.L. 94-455, §1906(b)(13)(A):

Amended the 1954 Code by substituting "Secretary" for "Secretary or his delegate" each place it appeared. **Effective** 2-1-77.

- **1970, Excise, Estate, and Gift Tax Adjustment Act of 1970 (P.L. 91-614)**

P.L. 91-614, §101(g):

Amended Code Sec. 1223 by redesignating paragraph (11) as (12) and by adding a new paragraph (11). **Effective** with respect to decedents dying after 12-31-70.

- **1962, Revenue Act of 1962 (P.L. 87-834)**

P.L. 87-834, §14(b)(3):

Amended Code Sec. 1223 by redesignating paragraph (10) as (11) and by adding a new paragraph (10). **Effective** for tax years beginning after 12-31-62.

PART IV—SPECIAL RULES FOR DETERMINING CAPITAL GAINS AND LOSSES

Sec. 1231.	Property used in the trade or business and involuntary conversions.
Sec. 1233.	Gains and losses from short sales.
Sec. 1234.	Options to buy or sell.
Sec. 1234A.	Gains or losses from certain terminations.
Sec. 1234B.	Gains or losses from securities futures contracts.
Sec. 1235.	Sale or exchange of patents.
Sec. 1236.	Dealers in securities.
Sec. 1237.	Real property subdivided for sale.
Sec. 1239.	Gain from sale of depreciable property between certain related taxpayers.
Sec. 1241.	Cancellation of lease or distributor's agreement.
Sec. 1242.	Losses on small business investment company stock.
Sec. 1243.	Loss of small business investment company.
Sec. 1244.	Losses on small business stock.
Sec. 1245.	Gain from dispositions of certain depreciable property.
Sec. 1248.	Gain from certain sales or exchanges of stock in certain foreign corporations.
Sec. 1249.	Gain from certain sales or exchanges of patents, etc., to foreign corporations.
Sec. 1250.	Gain from dispositions of certain depreciable realty.
Sec. 1252.	Gain from disposition of farm land.
Sec. 1253.	Transfers of franchises, trademarks, and trade names.
Sec. 1254.	Gain from disposition of interest in oil, gas, geothermal, or other mineral properties.
Sec. 1255.	Gain from disposition of section 126 property.
Sec. 1256.	Section 1256 contracts marked to market.
Sec. 1257.	Disposition of converted wetlands or highly erodible croplands.
Sec. 1258.	Recharacterization of gain from certain financial transactions.
Sec. 1259.	Constructive sales treatment for appreciated financial positions.
Sec. 1260.	Gains from constructive ownership transactions.

[Sec. 1231]

SEC. 1231. PROPERTY USED IN THE TRADE OR BUSINESS AND INVOLUNTARY CONVERSIONS.

⟫⟶ *Caution: P.L. 98-369, §1001(b)(15), amended Code Sec. 1231(a), below, by striking "1 year" and inserting "6 months". This amendment applies to property acquired after June 22, 1984, and before January 1, 1988.*

[Sec. 1231(a)]

(a) GENERAL RULE.—
   (1) GAINS EXCEED LOSSES.—If—
      (A) the section 1231 gains for any taxable year, exceed
      (B) the section 1231 losses for such taxable year,
such gains and losses shall be treated as long-term capital gains or long-term capital losses, as the case may be.
   (2) GAINS DO NOT EXCEED LOSSES.—If—
      (A) the section 1231 gains for any taxable year, do not exceed
      (B) the section 1231 losses for such taxable year,
such gains and losses shall not be treated as gains and losses from sales or exchanges of capital assets.
   (3) SECTION 1231 GAINS AND LOSSES.—For purposes of this subsection—

Internal Revenue Code

INCOME TAX—CAPITAL GAINS, LOSSES

(A) SECTION 1231 GAIN.—The term "section 1231 gain" means—

(i) any recognized gain on the sale or exchange of property used in the trade or business, and

(ii) any recognized gain from the compulsory or involuntary conversion (as a result of destruction in whole or in part, theft or seizure, or an exercise of the power of requisition or condemnation or the threat or imminence thereof) into other property or money of—

(I) property used in the trade or business, or

(II) any capital asset which is held for more than 6 months [1 year] and is held in connection with a trade or business or a transaction entered into for profit.

(B) SECTION 1231 LOSS.—The term "section 1231 loss" means any recognized loss from a sale or exchange or conversion described in subparagraph (A).

(4) SPECIAL RULES.—For purposes of this subsection—

(A) In determining under this subsection whether gains exceed losses—

(i) the section 1231 gains shall be included only if and to the extent taken into account in computing gross income, and

(ii) the section 1231 losses shall be included only if and to the extent taken into account in computing taxable income, except that section 1211 shall not apply.

(B) Losses (including losses not compensated for by insurance or otherwise) on the destruction, in whole or in part, theft or seizure, or requisition or condemnation of—

(i) property used in the trade or business, or

(ii) capital assets which are held for more than 6 months [1 year] and are held in connection with a trade or business or a transaction entered into for profit,

shall be treated as losses from a compulsory or involuntary conversion.

(C) In the case of any involuntary conversion (subject to the provisions of this subsection but for this sentence) arising from fire, storm, shipwreck, or other casualty, or from theft, of any—

(i) property used in the trade or business, or

(ii) any capital asset which is held for more than 6 months [1 year] and is held in connection with a trade or business or a transaction entered into for profit,

this subsection shall not apply to such conversion (whether resulting in gain or loss) if during the taxable year the recognized losses from such conversions exceed the recognized gains from such conversions.

Amendments

• **1984, Deficit Reduction Act of 1984 (P.L. 98-369)**

P.L. 98-369, §711(c)(2)(A)(iii):

Amended Code Sec. 1231(a). **Effective** for tax years beginning after 1983; Code Sec. 1231 is to be applied after Code Sec. 165(h)(1). Prior to amendment, Code Sec. 1231(a) read as follows:

(a) General Rule.—If, during the taxable year, the recognized gains on sales or exchanges of property used in the trade or business, plus the recognized gains from the compulsory or involuntary conversion (as a result of destruction in whole or in part, theft or seizure, or an exercise of the power of requisition or condemnation or the threat or imminence thereof) of property used in the trade or business and capital assets held for more than 1 year into other property or money, exceed the recognized losses from such sales, exchanges, and conversions, such gains and losses shall be considered as gains and losses from sales or exchanges of capital assets held for more than 1 year. If such gains do not exceed such losses, such gains and losses shall not be considered as gains and losses from sales or exchanges of capital assets. For purposes of this subsection—

(1) in determining under this subsection whether gains exceed losses, the gains described therein shall be included only if and to the extent taken into account in computing gross income and the losses described therein shall be included only if and to the extent taken into account in computing taxable income and the losses described therein shall be included only if and to the extent taken into account in computing taxable income, except that section 1211 shall not apply; and

(2) losses (including losses not compensated for by insurance or otherwise) upon the destruction, in whole or in part, theft or seizure, or requisition or condemnation of (A) property used in the trade or business or (B) capital assets held for more than 1 year shall be considered losses from a compulsory or involuntary conversion.

In the case of any involuntary conversion (subject to the provisions of this subsection but for this sentence) arising from fire, storm, shipwreck, or other casualty, or from theft, of any property used in the trade or business or of any capital asset held for more than 1 year, this subsection shall not apply to such conversion (whether resulting in gain or loss) if during the taxable year the recognized losses from such conversions exceed the recognized gains from such conversions.

P.L. 98-369, §1001(b)(15):

Amended Code Sec. 1231(a) by striking out "1 year" each place it appeared and inserting in lieu thereof "6 months". **Effective** for property acquired after 6-22-84, and before 1-1-88.

• **1976, Tax Reform Act of 1976 (P.L. 94-455)**

P.L. 94-455, §1402(b)(1)(R):

Amended Code Sec. 1231 by substituting "9 months" for "6 months". **Effective** for tax years beginning in 1977.

P.L. 94-455, §1402(b)(2):

Amended Code Sec. 1231 by substituting "1 year" for "9 months". **Effective** with respect to tax years beginning after 12-31-77.

• **1969, Tax Reform Act of 1969 (P.L. 91-172)**

P.L. 91-172, §516(b):

Amended Code Sec. 1231(a) by striking out all that follows paragraph (1) and adding text. **Effective** for tax years beginning after 12-31-69. Prior to amendment, Code Sec. 1231(a)(2) read as follows: "(2) losses upon the destruction, in whole or in part, theft or seizure, or requisition or condemnation of property used in the trade or business or capital assets held for more than 6 months shall be considered losses from a compulsory or involuntary conversion.

In the case of any property used in the trade or business and of any capital asset held for more than 6 months and held for the production of income, this subsection shall not apply to any loss, in respect of which the taxpayer is not compensated for by insurance in any amount, arising from fire, storm, shipwreck, or other casualty, or from theft."

• **1958, Technical Amendments Act of 1958 (P.L. 85-866)**

P. L. 85-866, §49(a):

Added the last sentence in Sec. 1231(a). **Effective** for tax years beginning after 12-31-57.

⇒ *Caution: P.L. 98-369, §1001(b)(15), amended Code Sec. 1231(b), below, by striking "1 year" and inserting "6 months". This amendment applies to property acquired after June 22, 1984, and before January 1, 1988.*

[Sec. 1231(b)]

(b) DEFINITION OF PROPERTY USED IN THE TRADE OR BUSINESS.—For purposes of this section—

(1) GENERAL RULE.—The term "property used in the trade or business" means property used in the trade or business, of a character which is subject to the allowance for depreciation provided in section 167, held for more than 6 months [1 year], and real property used in the trade or business, held for more than 6 months [1 year], which is not—

(A) property of a kind which would properly be includible in the inventory of the taxpayer if on hand at the close of the taxable year,

(B) property held by the taxpayer primarily for sale to customers in the ordinary course of his trade or business,

(C) a patent, invention, model or design (whether or not patented), a secret formula or process, a copyright, a literary, musical, or artistic composition, a letter or memorandum, or similar property, held by a taxpayer described in paragraph (3) of section 1221(a), or

(D) a publication of the United States Government (including the Congressional Record) which is received from the United States Government, or any agency thereof, other than by purchase at the price at which it is offered for sale to the public, and which is held by a taxpayer described in paragraph (5) of section 1221(a).

(2) TIMBER, COAL, OR DOMESTIC IRON ORE.—Such term includes timber, coal, and iron ore with respect to which section 631 applies.

(3) LIVESTOCK.—Such term includes—

INCOME TAX—CAPITAL GAINS, LOSSES

(A) cattle and horses, regardless of age, held by the taxpayer for draft, breeding, dairy, or sporting purposes, and held by him for 24 months or more from the date of acquisition, and

(B) other livestock, regardless of age, held by the taxpayer for draft, breeding, dairy, or sporting purposes, and held by him for 12 months or more from the date of acquisition.

Such term does not include poultry.

(4) UNHARVESTED CROP.—In the case of an unharvested crop on land used in the trade or business and held for more than 6 months [1 year], if the crop and the land are sold or exchanged (or compulsorily or involuntarily converted) at the same time and to the same person, the crop shall be considered as "property used in the trade or business."

Amendments

• **2017, Tax Cuts and Jobs Act (P.L. 115-97)**

P.L. 115-97, §13314(b):

Amended Code Sec. 1231(b)(1)(C) by inserting "a patent, invention, model or design (whether or not patented), a secret formula or process," before "a copyright". **Effective** for dispositions after 12-31-2017.

• **1999, Tax Relief Extension Act of 1999 (P.L. 106-170)**

P.L. 106-170, §532(c)(1)(G):

Amended Code Sec. 1231(b)(1)(C)-(D) by striking "section 1221" and inserting "section 1221(a)". **Effective** for any instrument held, acquired, or entered into, any transaction entered into, and supplies held or acquired on or after 12-17-99.

• **1984, Deficit Reduction Act of 1984 (P.L. 98-369)**

P.L. 98-369, §1001(b)(15):

Amended Code Sec. 1231(b) by striking out "1 year" each place it appeared and inserting in lieu thereof "6 months". **Effective** for property acquired after 6-22-84, and before 1-1-88.

• **1981, Economic Recovery Tax Act of 1981 (P.L. 97-34)**

P.L. 97-34, §505(c)(1):

Amended Code Sec. 1231(b)(1)(D) by striking out "paragraph (6)" and inserting "paragraph (5)". **Effective** for property acquired and positions established by the taxpayer after 6-23-81, in tax years ending after such date.

• **1978, Revenue Act of 1978 (P.L. 95-600)**

P.L. 95-600, §701(ee)(1)(A), (B), (C), (2):

Amended Code Sec. 1231(b)(1) by: (A) striking out "or" at the end of subparagraph (B); (B) striking out the period at the end of subparagraph (C) and inserting in place thereof ", or"; and (C) by adding subparagraph (D). **Effective** for sales, exchanges, and contributions made after 10-4-76.

• **1976, Tax Reform Act of 1976 (P.L. 94-455)**

P.L. 94-455, §1402(b)(1)(R), (b)(2):

See amendment note at Code Sec. 1231(a).

• **1969, Tax Reform Act of 1969 (P.L. 91-172)**

P.L. 91-172, §212(b):

Amended Code Sec. 1231(b)(3). **Effective** for livestock acquired after 12-31-69. Prior to amendment, Code Sec. 1231(b)(3) read as follows:

(3) Livestock.—Such term also includes livestock, regardless of age, held by the taxpayer for draft, breeding, or dairy purposes, and held by him for 12 months or more from the date of acquisition. Such term does not include poultry.

P.L. 91-172, §514(b)(2):

Amended Code Sec. 1231(b)(1)(C) by adding "a letter or memorandum," before "or similar property". **Effective** for sales and other dispositions occurring after 7-25-69.

• **1964, Revenue Act of 1964 (P.L. 88-272)**

P.L. 88-272, §227(a)(2):

Amended Code Sec. 1231(b)(2). **Effective** with respect to amounts received or accrued in tax years beginning after 12-31-63, attributable to iron ore mined in such taxable years. Prior to amendment, Code Sec. 1231(b)(2) read as follows:

"(2) Timber or coal.—Such term includes timber and coal with respect to which section 631 applies."

[Sec. 1231(c)]

(c) RECAPTURE OF NET ORDINARY LOSSES.—

(1) IN GENERAL.—The net section 1231 gain for any taxable year shall be treated as ordinary income to the extent such gain does not exceed the non-recaptured net section 1231 losses.

(2) NON-RECAPTURED NET SECTION 1231 LOSSES.—For purposes of this subsection, the term "non-recaptured net section 1231 losses" means the excess of—

(A) the aggregate amount of the net section 1231 losses for the 5 most recent preceding taxable years, over

(B) the portion of such losses taken into account under paragraph (1) for such preceding taxable years.

(3) NET SECTION 1231 GAIN.—For purposes of this subsection, the term "net section 1231 gain" means the excess of—

(A) the section 1231 gains, over

(B) the section 1231 losses.

(4) NET SECTION 1231 LOSS.—For purposes of this subsection, the term "net section 1231 loss" means the excess of—

(A) the section 1231 losses, over

(B) the section 1231 gains.

(5) SPECIAL RULES.—For purposes of determining the amount of the net section 1231 gain or loss for any taxable year, the rules of paragraph (4) of subsection (a) shall apply.

Amendments

• **2014, Tax Technical Corrections Act of 2014 (P.L. 113-295)**

P.L. 113-295, §221(a)(81), Division A:

Amended Code Sec. 1231(c)(2)(A) by striking "beginning after December 31, 1981" following "most recent preceding taxable years". **Effective** generally 12-19-2014. For a special rule, see Act Sec. 221(b)(2), Division A, below.

P.L. 113-295, §221(b)(2), Division A, provides:

(2) SAVINGS PROVISION.—If—

(A) any provision amended or repealed by the amendments made by this section applied to—

(i) any transaction occurring before the date of the enactment of this Act,

(ii) any property acquired before such date of enactment, or

(iii) any item of income, loss, deduction, or credit taken into account before such date of enactment, and

(B) the treatment of such transaction, property, or item under such provision would (without regard to the amendments or repeals made by this section) affect the liability for tax for periods ending after date of enactment, nothing in the amendments or repeals made by this section shall be construed to affect the treatment of such transaction, property, or item for purposes of determining liability for tax for periods ending after such date of enactment.

• **1984, Deficit Reduction Act of 1984 (P.L. 98-369)**

P.L. 98-369, §176(a):

Amended Code Sec. 1231 by adding at the end thereof new subsection (c). **Effective** for net section 1231 gains for tax years beginning after 12-31-84.

[Sec. 1232—Repealed]

Amendments

• **1984, Deficit Reduction Act of 1984 (P.L. 98-369)**

P.L. 98-369, §42(a)(1):

Repealed Code Sec. 1232. **Effective** for tax years ending after 7-18-84. Prior to repeal, but after the amendments by P.L. 98-369, §1001(b)(16) and (d), Code Sec. 1232 read as follows:

SEC. 1232. BONDS AND OTHER EVIDENCES OF INDEBTEDNESS.

[Sec. 1232(a)]

(a) GENERAL RULE.—For purposes of this subtitle, in the case of bonds, debentures, notes, or certificates or other evidences of indebtedness, which are capital assets in the hands of the taxpayer, and which are issued by any corporation, or by any government or political subdivision thereof—

(1) RETIREMENT.—Amounts received by the holder on retirement of such bonds or other evidences of indebtedness shall be considered as amounts received in exchange therefor (except that in the case of bonds or other evidences of indebtedness issued before January 1, 1955, this paragraph shall apply only to those issued with interest coupons or in registered form, or to those in such form on March 1, 1954).

(2) SALE OR EXCHANGE.—

(A) CORPORATE BONDS ISSUED AFTER MAY 27, 1969, AND GOVERNMENT BONDS ISSUED AFTER JULY 1, 1982.—Except as provided in subparagraph (C), on the sale or exchange of bonds or other evidences of indebtedness issued by a corporation after May 27, 1969,

INCOME TAX—CAPITAL GAINS, LOSSES

or by a government or political subdivision thereof after July 1, 1982, held by the taxpayer more than 6 months, any gain realized shall (except as provided in the following sentence) be considered gain from the sale or exchange of a capital asset held for more than 6 months. If at the time of original issue there was an intention to call the bond or other evidence of indebtedness before maturity, any gain realized on the sale or exchange thereof which does not exceed an amount equal to the original issue discount (as defined in subsection (b)) reduced by the portion of original issue discount previously includible in the gross income of any holder (without regard to subsection (a)(6) or (b)(4) of section 1232A (or the corresponding provisions of prior law)) shall be considered as ordinary income.

(B) CORPORATE BONDS ISSUED ON OR BEFORE MAY 27, 1969, AND GOVERNMENT BONDS ISSUED ON OR BEFORE JULY 1, 1982.—Except as provided in subparagraph (C), on the sale or exchange of bonds or other evidences of indebtedness issued by a government or political subdivision thereof after December 31, 1954, and on or before July 1, 1982, or by a corporation after December 31, 1954, and on or before May 27, 1969, held by the taxpayer more than 6 months, any gain realized which does not exceed—

(i) an amount equal to the original issue discount (as defined in subsection (b)), or

(ii) if at the time of original issue there was no intention to call the bond or other evidence of indebtedness before maturity, an amount which bears the same ratio to the original issue discount (as defined in subsection (b)) as the number of complete months that the bond or other evidence of indebtedness was held by the taxpayer bears to the number of complete months from the date of original issue to the date of maturity,

shall be considered as ordinary income. Gain in excess of such amount shall be considered gain from the sale or exchange of a capital asset held more than 6 months.

(C) EXCEPTIONS.—This paragraph shall not apply to—

(i) obligations the interest on which is not includible in gross income under section 103 (relating to certain governmental obligations), or

(ii) any holder who has purchased the bond or other evidence of indebtedness at a premium.

(D) DOUBLE INCLUSION IN INCOME NOT REQUIRED.—This section and sections 1232A and 1232B shall not require the inclusion of any amount previously includible in gross income.

(3) CERTAIN SHORT-TERM GOVERNMENT OBLIGATIONS.—

(A) IN GENERAL.—On the sale or exchange of any shortterm Government obligation, any gain realized which does not exceed an amount equal to the ratable share of the acquisition discount shall be treated as ordinary income. Gain in excess of such amount shall be considered gain from the sale or exchange of a capital asset.

(B) SHORT-TERM GOVERNMENT OBLIGATION.—For purposes of this paragraph, the term "shortterm Government obligation" means any obligation of the United States or any of its possessions, or of a State or any political subdivision thereof, or of the District of Columbia which is issued on a discount basis and payable without interest at a fixed maturity date not exceeding 1 year from the date of issue. Such term does not include any obligation the interest on which is not includible in gross income under section 103 (relating to certain governmental obligations).

(C) ACQUISITION DISCOUNT.—For purposes of this paragraph, the term "acquisition discount" means the excess of the stated redemption price at maturity over the taxpayer's basis for the obligation.

(D) RATABLE SHARE.—For purposes of this paragraph, the ratable share of the acquisition discount is an amount which bears the same ratio to such discount as—

(i) the number of days which the taxpayer held the obligation, bears to

(ii) the number of days after the date the taxpayer acquired the obligation and up to (and including) the date of its maturity.

Amendments

• **1984, Deficit Reduction Act of 1984 (P.L. 98-369)**

P.L. 98-369, §1001(b)(16):

Amended Code Sec. 1232(a)(2), prior to its repeal by Act Sec. 42(a)(1), by striking out "1 year" each place it appeared and inserting in lieu thereof "6 months". **Effective** for property acquired after 6-22-84, and before 1-1-88.

P.L. 98-369, §1001(d):

Amended Code Sec. 1232(a)(3)(A), prior to its repeal by Act Sec. 42(a)(1), by striking out "held less than 1 year" following "sale or exchange of a capital asset". **Effective** for property acquired after 6-22-84, and before 1-1-88.

• **1982, Tax Equity and Fiscal Responsibility Act of 1982 (P.L. 97-248)**

P.L. 97-248, §231(c)(1)(A):

Amended Code Sec. 1232(a)(2)(A) by striking out "by a corporation after May 27, 1969" and inserting in lieu thereof "by a corporation after May 27, 1969, or by a government or political subdivision thereof after July 1, 1982". **Effective** for obligations issued after 7-1-82, unless issued pursuant to a written commitment binding on 7-1-82, and at all times thereafter.

P.L. 97-248, §231(c)(1)(B):

Amended Code Sec. 1232(a)(2)(A) by striking out "as provided in paragraph (3)(B)" and inserting in lieu thereof "without regard to subsection (a)(6) or (b)(4) of section 1232A (or the corresponding provisions of prior law)". **Effective** for obligations issued after 7-1-82, unless issued pursuant to a written commitment binding on 7-1-82, and at all times thereafter.

P.L. 97-248, §231(c)(1)(C):

Amended Code Sec. 1232(a)(2)(A) by striking out the subparagraph heading "Corporate Bonds Issued After May 27, 1969.—" and inserting in lieu thereof the subparagraph heading. **Effective** for obligations issued after 7-1-82, unless issued pursuant to a written commitment binding on 7-1-82, and at all times thereafter.

P.L. 97-248, §231(c)(2)(B):

Amended Code Sec. 1232(a)(2)(B) by striking out "Government Bonds" in the subparagraph heading and inserting in lieu thereof "Government Bonds Issued On Or Before July 1, 1982." **Effective** for obligations issued after 7-1-82, unless issued pursuant to a written commitment binding on 7-1-82, and at all times thereafter.

P.L. 97-248, §231(c)(2)(A):

Amended Code Sec. 1232(a)(2)(B) by striking out "by a government or political subdivision thereof after December 31, 1954" and inserting in lieu thereof "by a government or political subdivision thereof after December 31, 1954, and on or before July 1, 1982." **Effective** for obligations issued after 7-1-82, unless issued pursuant to a written commitment binding on 7-1-82, and at all times thereafter.

P.L. 97-248, §231(c)(3):

Amended Code Sec. 1232(a)(2)(D) by striking out "This section" and inserting in lieu thereof "This section and sections 1232A and 1232B." **Effective** for obligations issued after 7-1-82, unless issued pursuant to a written commitment binding on 7-1-82, and at all times thereafter.

P.L. 97-248, §231(c)(4):

Amended Code Sec. 1232(a) by striking out paragraph (3) and by redesignating paragraph (4) as paragraph (3). For purposes of this amendment, any bonds issued pursuant to a written commitment which was binding on 7-1-82, and at all times thereafter shall be treated as issued on 7-1-82. Prior to amendment, paragraph (3) read as follows:

"(3) Inclusion in income of original issue discount on corporate bonds issued after May 27, 1969.—

(a) General rule.—There shall be included in the gross income of the holder of any bond or other evidence of indebtedness issued by a corporation after May 27, 1969, the ratable monthly portion of original issue discount multiplied by the number of complete months (plus any fractional part of a month determined in accordance with the last sentence of this subparagraph) such holder held such bond or other evidence of indebtedness during the taxable year. Except as provided in subparagraph (B), the ratable monthly portion of original issue discount shall equal the original issue discount (as defined in subsection (b)) divided by the number of complete months from the date of original issue to the stated maturity date of such bond or other evidence of indebtedness. For purposes of this section, a complete month commences with the date of original issue and the corresponding day of each succeeding calendar month (or the last day of a calendar month in which there is no corresponding day); and, in any case where a bond or other evidence of indebtedness is acquired on any other day, the ratable monthly portion of original issue discount for the complete month in which such acquisition occurs shall be allocated between the transferor and the transferee in accordance with the number of days in such complete month each held the bond or other evidence of indebtedness.

(B) Reduction in case of any subsequent holder.—For purposes of this paragraph, the ratable monthly portion of original issue discount shall not include an amount, determined at the time of any purchase after the original issue of such bond or other evidence of indebtedness, equal to the excess of—

(i) the cost of such bond or other evidence of indebtedness incurred by such holder, over

(ii) the issue price of such bond or other evidence of indebtedness increased by the portion of original discount previously includible in the gross income of any holder (computed without regard to this subparagraph),

divided by the number of complete months (plus any fractional part of a month commencing with the date of purchase) from the date of such purchase to the stated maturity date of such bond or other evidence of indebtedness.

(C) Purchase defined.—For purposes of subparagraph (B), the term 'purchase' means any acquisition of a bond or other evidence of indebtedness, but only if the basis of the bond or other evidence of indebtedness is not determined in whole or in part by reference to the adjusted basis of such bond or other evidence of indebtedness in the hands of the person from whom acquired, or under section 1014(a) (relating to property acquired from a decedent).

(D) Exceptions.—This paragraph shall not apply to any holder—

(i) who has purchased the bond or other evidence of indebtedness at a premium, or

(ii) which is a life insurance company to which section 818(b) applies.

(E) Basis adjustments.—The basis of any bond or other evidence of indebtedness in the hands of the holder thereof shall be increased by the amount included in his gross income pursuant to subparagraph (A)." **Effective** for obligations issued after July 1, 1982, unless issued pursuant to a written commitment binding on July 1, 1982, and at all times thereafter.

• **1981, Economic Recovery Tax Act of 1981 (P.L. 97-34)**

P.L. 97-34, §505(b):

Added Code Sec. 1232(a)(4). **Effective** for property acquired and positions established by the taxpayer after 6-23-81, in tax years ending after such date.

• **1976, Tax Reform Act of 1976 (P.L. 94-455)**

P.L. 94-455, §1402(b)(1)(S):

Amended Code Sec. 1232(a)(2) by substituting "9 months" for "6 months" each place it appeared. **Effective** with respect to tax years beginning in 1977.

P.L. 94-455, §1402(b)(2):

Amended Code Sec. 1232(a)(2) by substituting "1 year" for "9 months" each place it appeared. **Effective** with respect to tax years beginning after 12-31-77.

P.L. 94-455, §1901(b)(3)(I):

Amended Code Sec. 1232(a)(2)(A) and (B) by substituting "ordinary income" for "gain from the sale of property which is not a capital asset". **Effective** with respect to tax years beginning after 12-31-76.

• **1969, Tax Reform Act of 1969 (P.L. 91-172)**

P.L. 91-172, §413(a):

Amended subsection (a). **Effective** with respect to bonds and other evidences of indebtedness issued after 5-27-69 (other than evidences of indebtedness issued pursuant to a written commitment which was binding on 5-27-69, and at all times thereafter). Prior to amendment, subsection (a) read as follows:

(a) General Rule.—For purposes of this subtitle, in the case of bonds, debentures, notes, or certificates or other evidences of indebtedness, which are capital assets in

Sec. 1232—Repealed

the hands of the taxpayer, and which are issued by any corporation, or government or political subdivision thereof—

(1) Retirement.—Amounts received by the holder on retirement of such bonds or other evidences of indebtedness shall be considered as amounts received in exchange therefor (except that in the case of bonds or other evidences of indebtedness issued before January 1, 1955, this paragraph shall apply only to those issued with interest coupons or in registered form, or to those in such form on March 1, 1954).

(2) Sale or exchange.—

(A) General rule.—Except as provided in subparagraph (B), upon sale or exchange of bonds or other evidences of indebtedness issued after December 31, 1954, held by the taxpayer more than 6 months, any gain realized which does not exceed—

(i) an amount equal to the original issue discount (as defined in subsection (b)), or

(ii) if at the time of original issue there was no intention to call the bond or other evidence of indebtedness before maturity, an amount which bears the same ratio to the original issue discount (as defined in subsection (b)) as the number of complete months that the bond or other evidence of indebtedness was held by the taxpayer bears to the number of complete months from the date of original issue to the date of maturity,

shall be considered as gain from the sale or exchange of property which is not a capital asset. Gain in excess of such amount shall be considered gain from the sale or exchange of a capital asset held more than 6 months.

(B) Exceptions. — This paragraph shall not apply to—

(i) obligations the interest on which is not includible in gross income under section 103 (relating to certain governmental obligations), or

(ii) any holder who has purchased the bond or other evidence of indebtedness at a premium.

(C) Double inclusion in income not required.—This section shall not require the inclusion of any amount previously includible in gross income.

- **1959, Life Insurance Company Income Tax Act of 1959 (P.L. 86-69)**

P.L. 86-69, §3(e):

Amended Code Sec. 1232(a)(2)(C). **Effective** for tax years beginning after 12-31-57. Prior to amendment, Code Sec. 1232(a)(2)(C) read as follows:

"(C) Election as to inclusion.—In the case of obligations with respect to which the taxpayer has made an election provided by section 454(a) and (c) (relating to accounting rules for certain obligations issued at a discount), this section shall not require the inclusion of any amount previously includible in gross income."

- **1958, Technical Amendments Act of 1958 (P.L. 85-866)**

P.L. 85-866, §50(a):

Amended Sec. 1232(a)(2)(A). **Effective** for tax years ending after 12-31-57. Prior to amendment Sec. 1232(a)(2)(A) read as follows:

"(A) General rule.—Except as provided in subparagraph (B), upon sale or exchange of bonds or other evidences of indebtedness issued after December 31, 1954, held by the taxpayer more than 6 months, any gain realized which does not exceed an amount which bears the same ratio to the original issue discount (as defined in subsection (b)) as the number of complete months that the bond or other evidences of indebtedness was held by the taxpayer bears to the number of complete months from the date of original issue to the date of maturity, shall be considered as gain from the sale or exchange of property, which is not a capital asset. Gain in excess of such amount shall be considered gain from the sale or exchange of a capital asset held more than 6 months."

[Sec. 1232(b)]

(b) DEFINITIONS.—

(1) ORIGINAL ISSUE DISCOUNT.—For purposes of subsection (a), the term "original issue discount" means the difference between the issue price and the stated redemption price at maturity. If the original issue discount is less than onefourth of 1 percent of the redemption price at maturity multiplied by the number of complete years to maturity, then the issue discount shall be considered to be zero. For purposes of this paragraph, the term "stated redemption price at maturity" means the amount fixed by the last modification of the purchase agreement and includes dividends payable at that time.

(2) ISSUE PRICE.—In the case of issues of bonds or other evidences of indebtedness registered with the Securities and Exchange Commission, the term "issue price" means the initial offering price to the public (excluding bond houses and brokers) at which price a substantial amount of such bonds or other evidences of indebtedness were sold. In the case of privately placed issues of bonds or other evidence of indebtedness, the issue price of each such bond or other evidence of indebtedness is the price paid by the first buyer of such bond increased by the amount, if any, of tax paid under section 4911, as in effect before July 1, 1974 (and not credited, refunded, or reimbursed) on the acquisition of such bond or evidence of indebtedness by the first buyer. For purposes of this paragraph, the terms "initial offering price" and "price paid by the first buyer" include the aggregate payments made by the purchaser under the purchase agreement, including modifications thereof. In the case of a bond or other evidence of indebtedness and an option or other security issued together as an investment unit, the issue price for such investment unit shall be determined in accordance with the rules stated in this paragraph. Such issue price attributable to each element of the investment unit shall be that portion thereof which the fair market value of such element bears to the total fair market value of all the elements in the investment unit. The issue price of the bond or other evidence of indebtedness included in such investment unit shall be the portion so allocated to it. In the case of a bond or other evidence of indebtedness, or an investment unit as described in this paragraph, which is issued for property and which—

(A) is part of an issue a portion of which is traded on an established securities market, or

(B) is issued for stock or securities which are traded on an established securities market,

the issue price of such bond or other evidence of indebtedness or investment unit, as the case may be, shall be the fair market value of such property. Except in cases to which the preceding sentence applies, the issue price of a bond or other evidence of indebtedness (whether or not issued as a part of an investment unit) which is issued for property (other than money) shall be the stated redemption price at maturity.

(3) ISSUE DATE.—In the case of issues of bonds or other evidences of indebtedness registered with the Securities and Exchange Commission, the term "date of original issue" means the date on which the issue was first sold to the public at the issue price. In the case of privately placed issues of bonds or other evidences of indebtedness, the term "date of original issue" means the date on which each such bond or other evidence of indebtedness was sold by the issuer.

(4) SPECIAL RULE FOR EXCHANGE OF BONDS IN REORGANIZATIONS.—

(A) IN GENERAL.—If—

(i) any bond is issued pursuant to a plan of reorganization within the meaning of section 368(a)(1) for another bond (hereinafter in this paragraph referred to as the "old bond"), and

(ii) the fair market value of the old bond is less than its adjusted issue price,

then, for purposes of the next to the last sentence of paragraph (2), the fair market value of the old bond shall be treated as equal to its adjusted issue price.

(B) DEFINITIONS.—For purposes of this paragraph—

(i) BOND.—The term "bond" includes any other evidence of indebtedness and an investment unit.

(ii) ADJUSTED ISSUE PRICE.—

(I) IN GENERAL.—The adjusted issue price of the old bond is its issue price, increased by the portion of any original issue discount previously includible in the gross income of any holder (without regard to subsection (a)(6) or (b)(4) of section 1232A (or the corresponding provisions of prior law)).

(II) SPECIAL RULE FOR APPLYING SECTION 163(e).—For purposes of section 163(e), the adjusted issue price of the old bond is its issue price, increased by any original issue discount previously allowed as a deduction.

Amendments

- **1983, Technical Corrections Act of 1982 (P.L. 97-448)**

P.L. 97-448, §306(a)(9)(C)(i):

Amended the next to the last sentence of Code Sec. 1232(b)(2) by striking out "(other than a bond or other evidence of indebtedness or an investment unit issued pursuant to a plan of reorganization within the meaning of section 368(a)(1) or an insolvency reorganization within the meaning of section 371 or 374)". **Effective** for evidences of indebtedness issued after 12-31-82; except that such amendment shall not apply to any evidence of indebtedness issued after such date pursuant to a written commitment which was binding on such date and at all times thereafter.

P.L. 97-448, §306(a)(9)(C)(ii):

Added Code Sec. 1232(b)(4). **Effective** for evidences of indebtedness issued after 12-13-82; except that such amendment shall not apply to any evidence of indebtedness issued after such date pursuant to a written commitment which was binding on such date and at all times thereafter.

P.L. 97-448, §306(a)(9)(C)(iii), provides:

(iii) For purposes of paragraph (4) of section 1232(b) of the Internal Revenue Code of 1954 (as added by clause (ii)), any insolvency reorganization within the meaning of section 371 or 374 of such Code shall be treated as a reorganization within the meaning of section 368(a)(1) of such Code.

- **1976, Tax Reform Act of 1976 (P.L. 94-455)**

P.L. 94-455, §1901(b)(14)(D):

Amended Code Sec. 1232(b)(2) by substituting "section 371 or 374" for "section 371, 373, or 374". **Effective** with respect to tax years beginning after 12-31-76.

P.L. 94-455, §1904(b)(10)(C):

Amended Code Sec. 1232(b)(2) by substituting "section 4911, as in effect before July 1, 1974" for "section 4911". **Effective** 2-1-77.

- **1969, Tax Reform Act of 1969 (P.L. 91-172)**

P.L. 91-172, §413(b):

Added the last 5 sentences of paragraph (b)(2). **Effective** with respect to bonds and other evidences of indebtedness issued after 5-27-69 (other than evidences of indebtedness issued pursuant to a written commitment which was binding on 5-27-69, and at all times thereafter).

- **1964, Interest Equalization Tax Act (P.L. 88-563)**

P.L. 88-563, §5:

Amended Code Sec. 1232(b)(2) by adding the following at the end of the second sentence: "increased by the amount, if any, of tax paid under section 4911 (and not credited, refunded, or reimbursed) on the acquisition of such bond or evidence of indebtedness by the first buyer."

[Sec. 1232(c)—Stricken]

Amendments

- **1982, Tax Equity and Fiscal Responsibility Act of 1982 (P.L. 97-248)**

P.L. 97-248, §232(b):

Amended Code Sec. 1232 by striking out subsection (c). **Effective** for the purchase and sale of a stripped bond or stripped coupons after 7-1-82. Prior to amendment, Code Sec. 1232(c) read as follows:

"(c) Bond With Unmatured Coupons Detached.—If a bond or other evidence of indebtedness issued at any time with interest coupons—

(1) is purchased after August 16, 1954, and before January 1, 1958, and the purchaser does not receive all the coupons which first become payable more than 12 months after the date of the purchase, or

(2) is purchased after December 31, 1957, and the purchaser does not receive all the coupons which first become payable after the date of the purchase,

INCOME TAX—CAPITAL GAINS, LOSSES

then the gain on the sale or other disposition of such evidence of indebtedness by such purchaser (or by a person whose basis is determined by reference to the basis in the hands of such purchaser) shall be considered as ordinary income to the extent that the fair market value (determined as of the time of the purchase) of the evidence of indebtedness with coupons attached exceeds the purchase price. If this subsection and subsection (a)(2)(A) apply with respect to gain realized on the sale or exchange of any evidence of indebtedness, then subsection (a)(2)(A) shall apply with respect to that part of the gain to which this subsection does not apply."

- **1976, Tax Reform Act of 1976 (P.L. 94-455)**

P.L. 94-455, § 1901(b)(3)(I):

Substituted "ordinary income" for "gain from the sale or exchange of property which is not a capital asset" in Code Sec. 1232(c). **Effective** with respect to tax years beginning after 12-31-76.

- **1958, Technical Amendments Act of 1958 (P.L. 85-866)**

P.L. 85-866, § 51:

Amended Sec. 1232(c). **Effective** 1-1-54. Prior to amendment Sec. 1232(c) read as follows:

"(c) BOND WITH EXCESS NUMBER OF COUPONS DETACHED.—If—

"(1) a bond or other evidence of indebtedness issued at any time with interest coupons is purchased after the date of enactment of this title, and

"(2) the purchaser does not receive all the coupons which first become payable more than 12 months after the date of the purchase,

then the gain on the sale or other disposition of such evidence of indebtedness by such purchaser shall be considered as gain from the sale or exchange of property which is not a capital asset to the extent that the market value (determined as of the time of the purchase) of the evidence of indebtedness with coupons attached exceeds the purchase price. If this subsection and subsection (a)(2)(A) apply with respect to gain realized on the retirement of any bond, then subsection (a)(2)(A) shall apply with respect to that part of the gain to which this subsection does not apply.".

[Sec. 1232(c)]

(c) DENIAL OF CAPITAL GAIN TREATMENT FOR GAINS ON CERTAIN OBLIGATIONS NOT IN REGISTERED FORM.—

(1) IN GENERAL.—If any registration-required obligation is not in registered form, any gain on the sale or other disposition of such obligation shall be treated as ordinary income (unless the issuance of such obligation was subject to tax under section 4701).

Amendments

- **1984, Deficit Reduction Act of 1984 (P.L. 98-369)**

P.L. 98-369, § 42(a)(1):

Repealed Code Sec. 1232A. **Effective** for tax years ending after 7-18-84. Prior to repeal but after amendment by Act Sec. 211(b)(17), it read as follows:

SEC. 1232A. ORIGINAL ISSUE DISCOUNT.

(a) ORIGINAL ISSUE DISCOUNT ON BONDS ISSUED AFTER JULY 1, 1982, INCLUDED IN INCOME ON BASIS OF CONSTANT INTEREST RATE.—

(1) GENERAL RULE.—For purposes of this subtitle, there shall be included in the gross income of the holder of any bond having an original issue discount issued after July 1, 1982 (and which is a capital asset in the hands of the holder) an amount equal to the sum of the daily portions of the original issue discount for each day during the taxable year on which such holder held such bond.

(2) EXCEPTIONS.—Paragraph (1) shall not apply to—

(A) NATURAL PERSONS.—Any obligation issued by a natural person.

(B) TAX-EXEMPT OBLIGATIONS.—Any obligation if—

(i) the interest on such obligation is not includible in gross income under section 103, or

(ii) the interest on such obligation is exempt from tax (without regard to the identity of the holder) under any other provision of law.

(C) SHORT-TERM GOVERNMENT OBLIGATIONS.—Any short-term Government obligation (within the meaning of section 1232(a)(3)).

(D) UNITED STATES SAVINGS BONDS.—Any United States savings bond.

(3) DETERMINATION OF DAILY PORTIONS.—For purposes of paragraph (1), the daily portion of the original issue discount on any bond shall be determined by allocating to each day in any bond period its ratable portion of the increase during such bond period in the adjusted issue price of the bond. For purposes of the preceding sentence, the increase in the adjusted issue price for any bond period shall be an amount equal to the excess (if any) of—

(A) the product of—

(i) the adjusted issue price of the bond at the beginning of such bond period, and

(ii) the yield to maturity (determined on the basis of compounding at the close of each bond period), over

(B) the sum of the amounts payable as interest on such bond during such bond period.

(4) ADJUSTED ISSUE PRICE.—For purposes of this subsection, the adjusted issue price of any bond at the beginning of any bond period is the sum of—

(A) the issue price of such bond, plus

(B) the adjustments under this subsection to such issue price for all periods before the first day of such bond period.

(5) BOND PERIOD.—Except as otherwise provided in regulations prescribed by the Secretary, the term "bond period" means a 1-year period (or the shorter period to maturity) beginning on the day in the calendar year which corresponds to the date of original issue of the bond.

(6) REDUCTION IN CASE OF CERTAIN SUBSEQUENT HOLDERS.—For purposes of this subsection, in the case of any purchase of a bond to which this subsection applies after its original issue, the daily portion shall not include an amount (determined at the time of purchase) equal to the excess (if any) of—

(2) DEFINITIONS.—For purposes of this subsection—

(A) REGISTRATION-REQUIRED OBLIGATION.—The term "registration-required obligation" has the meaning given to such term by section 163(f)(2) except that clause (iv) of subparagraph (A), and subparagraph (B), of such section shall not apply.

(B) REGISTERED FORM.—The term "registered form" has the same meaning as when used in section 163(f).

Amendments

- **1983, Technical Corrections Act of 1982 (P.L. 97-448)**

P.L. 97-448, § 306(a)(9)(B):

Amended Code Sec. 1232 by redesignating subsection (d) as subsection (c). **Effective** as if included in the provision of P.L. 97-248 to which it relates.

- **1982, Tax Equity and Fiscal Responsibility Act of 1982 (P.L. 97-248)**

P.L. 97-248, § 232(b):

Amended Code Sec. 1232 by striking out subsection (d). **Effective** for the purchase and sale of a stripped bond or stripped coupons after 7-1-82. Prior to amendment, Code Sec. 1232(d) read as follows: [Note: P.L. 97-248, Act Sec. 310(b)(6), below, redesignated subsection (d).]

[Sec. 1232(d)]

(d) Cross Reference.—

For special treatment of face-amount certificates on retirement, see section 72.

Amendments

P.L. 97-248, § 310(b)(6):

Amended Code Sec. 1232 by redesignating subsection (d) as subsection (e) and by inserting a new subsection (d). [Note: P.L. 97-248, Act Sec. 232(b) struck out subsection (d).] **Effective** for obligations issued after 12-31-82. However, the amendments made by subsection (b) shall not apply to any obligations issued after 12-31-82, on the exercise of a warrant or the conversion of a convertible obligation if such warrant or obligation was offered or sold outside the United States without registration under the Securities Act of 1933 and was issued before 8-10-82. A rule similar to the rule of the preceding sentence shall also apply in the case of any regulations issued under section 163(f)(2)(C) of the Internal Revenue Code of 1954 (as added by this section) except that the date on which such regulations take effect shall be substituted for "August 10, 1982."

[Sec. 1232A—Repealed]

(A) the cost of such bond incurred by the purchaser, over

(B) the issue price of such bond, increased by the sum of the daily portions for such bond for all days before the date of purchase (computed without regard to this paragraph),

divided by the number of days beginning on the date of such purchase and ending on the day before the stated maturity date.

(7) REGULATION AUTHORITY.—The Secretary may prescribe regulations providing that where, by reason of varying rates of interest, put or call options, or other circumstances, the inclusion under paragraph (1) for the taxable year does not accurately reflect the income of the holder, the proper amount of income shall be included for such taxable year (and appropriate adjustments shall be made in the amounts included for subsequent taxable years).

(b) RATABLE INCLUSION RETAINED FOR CORPORATE BONDS ISSUED BEFORE JULY 2, 1982.—

(1) GENERAL RULE.—There shall be included in the gross income of the holder of any bond issued by corporation after May 27, 1969, and before July 2, 1982 (and which is a capital asset in the hands of the holder)—

(A) the ratable monthly portion of original issue discount, multiplied by

(B) the number of complete months (plus any fractional part of a month determined under paragraph (3)) such holder held such bond during the taxable year.

(2) DETERMINATION OF RATABLE MONTHLY PORTION.—Except as provided in paragraph (4), the ratable monthly portion of original issue discount shall equal—

(A) the original issue discount, divided by

(B) the number of complete months from the date of original issue to the stated maturity date of the bond.

(3) MONTH DEFINED.—For purposes of this subsection, a complete month commences with the date of original issue and the corresponding day of each succeeding calendar month (or the last day of a calendar month in which there is no corresponding day). In any case where a bond is acquired on any day other than a day determined under the preceding sentence, the ratable monthly portion of original issue discount for the complete month (or partial month) in which such acquisition occurs shall be allocated between the transferor and the transferee in accordance with the number of days in such complete (or partial) month each held the bond.

(4) REDUCTION IN CASE OF CERTAIN SUBSEQUENT HOLDERS.—For purposes of this subsection, the ratable monthly portion of original issue discount shall not include an amount, determined at the time of any purchase after the original issue of the bond, equal to the excess of—

(A) the cost of such bond incurred by the holder, over

(B) the issue price of such bond, increased by the portion of original discount previously includible in the gross income of any holder (computed without regard to this paragraph),

divided by the number of complete months (plus any fractional part of a month) from the date of such purchase to the stated maturity date of such bond.

(c) DEFINITIONS AND SPECIAL RULES.—

(1) BOND INCLUDES OTHER EVIDENCES OF INDEBTEDNESS.—For purposes of this section, the term "bond" means a bond, debenture, note, or certificate or other evidence of indebtedness.

(2) PURCHASE DEFINED.—For purposes of this section, the term "purchase" means any acquisition of a bond, but only if the basis of the bond is not determined in whole or in part by reference to the adjusted basis of such bond in the hands of the person

INCOME TAX—CAPITAL GAINS, LOSSES

from whom acquired, or under section 1014(a) (relating to property acquired from a decedent).

(3) ORIGINAL ISSUE DISCOUNT, ETC.—For purposes of this section, the terms "original issue discount", "issue price", and "date or original issue" shall have the respective meanings given to such terms by section 1232(b).

(4) EXCEPTIONS.—This section shall not apply to any holder—
(A) who has purchased the bond at a premium, or
(B) which is a life insurance company to which section 811(b) applies.

(5) BASIS ADJUSTMENTS.—The basis of any bond in the hands of the holder thereof shall be increased by the amount included in his gross income pursuant to this section.

• **1984, Deficit Reduction Act of 1984 (P.L. 98-369)**

P.L. 98-369, §211(b)(17):

Amended Code Sec. 1232A(c)(4) (prior to repeal by Act Sec. 42(a)(1)) by striking out "section 818(b)" and inserting in lieu thereof "section 811(b)". **Effective** for tax years beginning after 12-31-83.

Amendments

• **1984, Deficit Reduction Act of 1984 (P.L. 98-369)**

P.L. 98-369, §42(a)(1):

Repealed Code Sec. 1232B. **Effective** for tax years ending after 7-18-84. Prior to repeal, it read as follows:

SEC. 1232B. TAX TREATMENT OF STRIPPED BONDS.

(a) INCLUSION IN INCOME AS IF BOND AND COUPONS WERE ORIGINAL ISSUE DISCOUNT BONDS.—If any person purchases after July 1, 1982, a stripped bond or a stripped coupon, then such bond or coupon while held by such purchaser (or by any other person whose basis is determined by reference to the basis in the hands of such purchaser) shall be treated for purposes of section 1232A(a) as a bond originally issued by a corporation on the purchase date and having an original issue discount equal to the excess (if any) of—

(1) the stated redemption price at maturity (or, in the case of a coupon, the amount payable on the due date of such coupon), over
(2) such bond's or coupon's ratable share of the purchase price.

For purposes of paragraph (2), ratable shares shall be determined on the basis of their respective fair market values on the date of purchase.

(b) TAX TREATMENT OF PERSON STRIPPING BOND.—For purposes of this subtitle, if any person strips 1 or more coupons from a bond and after July 1, 1982, disposes of the bond or such coupon—

(1) such person shall include in gross income an amount equal to the interest accrued on such bond before the time that such coupon or bond was disposed of (to the extent such interest has not theretofore been included in such person's gross income),
(2) the basis of the bond and coupons shall be increased by the amount of the accrued interest described in paragraph (1),
(3) the basis of the bond and coupons immediately before the disposition (as adjusted pursuant to paragraph (2)) shall be allocated among the items retained by such person and the items disposed of by such person on the basis of their respective fair market values, and
(4) for purposes of subsection (a), such person shall be treated as having purchased on the date of such disposition each such item which he retains for an amount equal to the basis allocated to such item under paragraph (3).

A rule similar to the rule of paragraph (4) shall apply in the case of any person whose basis in any bond or coupon is determined by reference to the basis of the person described in the preceding sentence.

(c) RETENTION OF EXISTING LAW FOR STRIPPED BONDS PURCHASED BEFORE JULY 2, 1982.—If a bond issued at any time with interest coupons—

(1) is purchased after August 16, 1954, and before January 1, 1958, and the purchaser does not receive all the coupons which first become payable more than 12 months after the date of the purchase, or
(2) is purchased after December 31, 1957, and before July 2, 1982, and the purchaser does not receive all the coupons which first become payable after the date of the purchase,

• **1982, Tax Equity and Fiscal Responsibility Act of 1982 (P.L. 97-248)**

P.L. 97-248, §231(a):

Added Code Sec. 1232A. A transitional rule appears at Act Sec. 231(e), below.

P.L. 97-248, §231(e), provides:

(e) Transitional Rule.—For purposes of the amendments made by this section, any evidence of indebtedness issued pursuant to a written commitment which was binding on July 1, 1982, and at all times thereafter shall be treated as issued on July 1, 1982. Effective for obligations issued after July 1, 1982, unless issued pursuant to a written commitment binding on July 1, 1982, and at all times thereafter. Such a commitment would have to involve a commitment by the issuer to issue the bonds at a particular price.

[Sec. 1232B—Repealed]

then the gain on the sale or other disposition of such bond by such purchaser (or by a person whose basis is determined by reference to the basis in the hands of such purchaser) shall be considered as ordinary income to the extent that the fair market value (determined as of the time of the purchase) of the bond with coupons attached exceeds the purchase price. If this subsection and section 1232(a)(2)(A) apply with respect to gain realized on the sale or exchange of any evidence of indebtedness, then section 1232(a)(2)(A) shall apply with respect to that part of the gain to which this subsection does not apply.

(d) SPECIAL RULES FOR TAX-EXEMPT OBLIGATIONS.—In the case of any obligation the interest on which is not includible in gross income under section 103 or is exempt from tax (without regard to the identity of the holder) under any other provision of law—

(1) subsections (a) and (b)(1) shall not apply,
(2) the rules of subsection (b)(4) shall apply for purposes of subsection (c), and
(3) subsection (c) shall be applied without regard to the requirement that the bond be purchased before July 2, 1982.

(e) DEFINITIONS AND SPECIAL RULES.—For purposes of this section—

(1) BOND.—The term "bond" means a bond, debenture, note, or certificate or other evidence of indebtedness.

(2) STRIPPED BOND.—The term "stripped bond" means a bond issued at any time with interest coupons where there is a separation in ownership between the bond and any coupon which has not yet become payable.

(3) STRIPPED COUPON.—The term "stripped coupon" means any coupon relating to a stripped bond.

(4) STATED REDEMPTION PRICE AT MATURITY.—The term "stated redemption price at maturity" has the meaning given such term by the third sentence of section 12322b)(1).

(5) COUPON.—The term "coupon" includes any right to receive interest on a bond (whether or not evidenced by a coupon). This paragraph shall apply for purposes of subsection (c) only in the case of purchases after July 1, 1982.

(f) REGULATION AUTHORITY.—The Secretary may prescribe regulations providing that where, by reason of varying rates of interest, put or call options, extendable maturities, or other circumstances, the tax treatment under this section does not accurately reflect the income of the holder of a stripped coupon or stripped bond, or of the person disposing of such bond or coupon, as the case may be, for any period, such treatment shall be modified to require that the proper amount of income be included for such period.

• **1982, Tax Equity and Fiscal Responsibility Act of 1982 (P.L. 97-248)**

P.L. 97-248, §232(a):

Amended Part IV of subchapter P of chapter 1 by inserting after Code Sec. 1232A new Code Sec. 1232B. **Effective** for the purchase and sale of a stripped bond or stripped coupons after 7-1-82.

[Sec. 1233]

SEC. 1233. GAINS AND LOSSES FROM SHORT SALES.

[Sec. 1233(a)]

(a) CAPITAL ASSETS.—For purposes of this subtitle, gain or loss from the short sale of property shall be considered as gain or loss from the sale or exchange of a capital asset to the extent that the property, including a commodity future, used to close the short sale constitutes a capital asset in the hands of the taxpayer.

Amendments

• **1958, Technical Amendments Act of 1958 (P.L. 85-866)**

P.L. 85-866, §52(b):

Struck out ", other than a hedging transaction in commodity futures," where it followed the phrase "For purposes of this subtitle, gain or loss from the short sale of property" in Sec. 1233(a).

⟫→ *Caution: P.L. 98-369, §1001(b)(17), amended Code Sec. 1233(b), below, by striking "1 year" and inserting "6 months". This amendment applies to property acquired after June 22, 1984, and before January 1, 1988.*

[Sec. 1233(b)]

(b) SHORT-TERM GAINS AND HOLDING PERIODS.—If gain or loss from a short sale is considered as gain or loss from the sale or exchange of a capital asset under subsection (a) and if on the date of such short sale substantially identical property has been held by the taxpayer for not more than 6

INCOME TAX—CAPITAL GAINS, LOSSES

months [1 year] (determined without regard to the effect, under paragraph (2) of this subsection, of such short sale on the holding period), or if substantially identical property is acquired by the taxpayer after such short sale and on or before the date of the closing thereof—

(1) any gain on the closing of such short sale shall be considered as a gain on the sale or exchange of a capital asset held for not more than 6 months [1 year] (notwithstanding the period of time any property used to close such short sale has been held); and

(2) the holding period of such substantially identical property shall be considered to begin (notwithstanding section 1223, relating to the holding period of property) on the date of the closing of the short sale, or on the date of a sale, gift, or other disposition of such property, whichever date occurs first. This paragraph shall apply to such substantially identical property in the order of the dates of the acquisition of such property, but only to so much of such property as does not exceed the quantity sold short.

For purposes of this subsection, the acquisition of an option to sell property at a fixed price shall be considered as a short sale, and the exercise or failure to exercise such option shall be considered as a closing of such short sale.

Amendments

- **1984, Deficit Reduction Act of 1984 (P.L. 98-369)**

P.L. 98-369, §1001(b)(17):

Amended Code Sec. 1233(b) by striking out "1 year" each place it appeared and inserting in lieu thereof "6 months". **Effective** for property acquired after 6-22-84 and before 1-1-88.

- **1976, Tax Reform Act of 1976 (P.L. 94-455)**

P.L. 94-455, §1402(b)(1)(T):

Amended Code Sec. 1233(b) by substituting "9 months" for "6 months" each place it appeared. **Effective** with respect to tax years beginning in 1977.

P.L. 94-455, §1402(b)(2):

Amended Code Sec. 1233(b) by substituting "1 year" for "9 months" each place it appeared. **Effective** with respect to tax years beginning after 12-31-77.

[Sec. 1233(c)]

(c) CERTAIN OPTIONS TO SELL.—Subsection (b) shall not include an option to sell property at a fixed price acquired on the same day on which the property identified as intended to be used in exercising such option is acquired and which, if exercised, is exercised through the sale of the property so identified. If the option is not exercised, the cost of the option shall be added to the basis of the property with which the option is identified. This subsection shall apply only to options acquired after August 16, 1954.

Amendments

- **1976, Tax Reform Act of 1976 (P.L. 94-455)**

P.L. 94-455, §1901(a)(137):

Substituted "August 16, 1954" for "the date of enactment of this title" in Code Sec. 1233(c). **Effective** with respect to tax years beginning after 12-31-76.

⟫→ *Caution: P.L. 98-369, §1001(b)(17), amended Code Sec. 1233(d), below, by striking "1 year" and inserting "6 months". This amendment applies to property acquired after June 22, 1984, and before January 1, 1988.*

[Sec. 1233(d)]

(d) LONG-TERM LOSSES.—If on the date of such short sale substantially identical property has been held by the taxpayer for more than 6 months [1 year], any loss on the closing of such short sale shall be considered as a loss on the sale or exchange of a capital asset held for more than 6 months [1 year] (notwithstanding the period of time any property used to close such short sale has been held, and notwithstanding section 1234).

Amendments

- **1984, Deficit Reduction Act of 1984 (P.L. 98-369)**

P.L. 98-369, §1001(b)(17):

Amended Code Sec. 1233(d) by striking out "1 year" and inserting in lieu thereof "6 months". **Effective** for property acquired after 6-22-84 and before 1-1-88.

- **1976, Tax Reform Act of 1976 (P.L. 94-455)**

P.L. 94-455, §1402(b)(1)(T):

Amended Code Sec. 1233(d) by substituting "9 months" for "6 months" each place it appeared. **Effective** with respect to tax years beginning in 1977.

P.L. 94-455, §1402(b)(2):

Amended Code Sec. 1233(d) by substituting "1 year" for "9 months" each place it appeared. **Effective** with respect to tax years beginning after 12-31-77.

[Sec. 1233(e)]

(e) RULES FOR APPLICATION OF SECTION.—

(1) Subsection (b)(1) or (d) shall not apply to the gain or loss, respectively, on any quantity of property used to close such short sale which is in excess of the quantity of the substantially identical property referred to in the applicable subsection.

(2) For purposes of subsections (b) and (d)—

(A) the term "property" includes only stocks and securities (including stocks and securities dealt with on a "when issued" basis), and commodity futures, which are capital assets in the hands of the taxpayer, but does not include any position to which section 1092(b) applies;

(B) in the case of futures transactions in any commodity on or subject to the rules of a board of trade or commodity exchange, a commodity future requiring delivery in 1 calendar month shall not be considered as property substantially identical to another commodity future requiring delivery in a different calendar month;

(C) in the case of a short sale of property by an individual, the term "taxpayer", in the application of this subsection and subsections (b) and (d), shall be read as "taxpayer or his spouse"; but an individual who is legally separated from the taxpayer under a decree of divorce or of separate maintenance shall not be considered as the spouse of the taxpayer;

(D) a securities futures contract (as defined in section 1234B) to acquire substantially identical property shall be treated as substantially identical property; and

(E) entering into a securities futures contract (as so defined) to sell shall be considered to be a short sale, and the settlement of such contract shall be considered to be the closing of such short sale.

(3) Where the taxpayer enters into 2 commodity futures transactions on the same day, one requiring delivery by him in one market and the other requiring delivery to him of the same (or substantially identical) commodity in the same calendar month in a different market, and the taxpayer subsequently closes both such transactions on the same day, subsections (b) and (d) shall have no application to so much of the commodity involved in either such transaction as does not exceed in quantity the commodity involved in the other.

⟫→ *Caution: P.L. 98-369, §1001(b)(17), amended Code Sec. 1233(e)(4)(A), below, by striking "1 year" and inserting "6 months". This amendment applies to property acquired after June 22, 1984, and before January 1, 1988.*

(4)(A) In the case of a taxpayer who is a dealer in securities (within the meaning of section 1236)—

(i) if, on the date of a short sale of stock, substantially identical property which is a capital asset in the hands of the taxpayer has been held for not more than 6 months [1 year], and

(ii) if such short sale is closed more than 20 days after the date on which it was made,

subsection (b)(2) shall apply in respect of the holding period of such substantially identical property.

(B) For purposes of subparagraph (A)—

(i) the last sentence of subsection (b) applies; and

(ii) the term "stock" means any share or certificate of stock in a corporation, any bond or other evidence of indebtedness which is convertible into any such share or certificate, or any evidence of an interest in, or right to subscribe to or purchase, any of the foregoing.

Amendments

• **2002, Job Creation and Worker Assistance Act of 2002 (P.L. 107-147)**

P.L. 107-147, §412(d)(3)(A):

Amended Code Sec. 1233(e)(2) by striking "and" at the end of subparagraph (C), by striking the period and inserting "; and" at the end of subparagraph (D), and inserting after subparagraph (D) a new subparagraph (E). **Effective** as if included in the provision of P.L. 106-554 to which it relates [**effective** 12-21-2000.—CCH].

• **2000, Community Renewal Tax Relief Act of 2000 (P.L. 106-554)**

P.L. 106-554, §401(f):

Amended Code Sec. 1233(e)(2) by striking "and" at the end of subparagraph (B), by striking the period at the end of subparagraph (C) and inserting "; and", and by adding at the end a new subparagraph (D). **Effective** 12-21-2000.

• **1984, Deficit Reduction Act of 1984 (P.L. 98-369)**

P.L. 98-369, §1001(b)(17):

Amended Code Sec. 1233(e)(4)(A) by striking out "1 year" and inserting in lieu thereof "6 months". **Effective** for property acquired after 6-22-84 and before 1-1-88.

• **1981, Economic Recovery Tax Act of 1981 (P.L. 97-34)**

P.L. 97-34, §501(c):

Amended Code Sec. 1233(e)(2)(A) by inserting ", but does not include any position to which section 1092(b) applies" after "taxpayer". **Effective** for property acquired and positions established by the taxpayer after 6-23-81, in tax years ending after such date.

• **1976, Tax Reform Act of 1976 (P.L. 94-455)**

P.L. 94-455, §1402(b)(1)(T):

Amended Code Sec. 1233(e) by substituting "9 months" for "6 months". **Effective** with respect to tax years beginning in 1977.

P.L. 94-455, §1402(b)(2):

Amended Code Sec. 1233(e) by substituting "1 year" for "9 months". **Effective** with respect to tax years beginning after 12-31-77.

• **1958, Technical Amendments Act of 1958 (P.L. 85-866)**

P.L. 85-866, §52(a):

Added paragraph (4) to Sec. 1233(e). **Effective** for short sales made after 12-31-57.

[Sec. 1233(f)]

(f) ARBITRAGE OPERATIONS IN SECURITIES.—In the case of a short sale which had been entered into as an arbitrage operation, to which sale the rule of subsection (b)(2) would apply except as otherwise provided in this subsection—

(1) subsection (b)(2) shall apply first to substantially identical assets acquired for arbitrage operations held at the close of business on the day such sale is made, and only to the extent that the quantity sold short exceeds the substantially identical assets acquired for arbitrage operations held at the close of business on the day such sale is made, shall the holding period of any other such identical assets held by the taxpayer be affected;

(2) in the event that assets acquired for arbitrage operations are disposed of in such manner as to create a net short position in assets acquired for arbitrage operations, such net short position shall be deemed to constitute a short sale made on that day;

(3) for the purpose of paragraphs (1) and (2) of this subsection the taxpayer will be deemed as of the close of any business day to hold property which he is or will be entitled to receive or acquire by virtue of any other asset acquired for arbitrage operations or by virtue of any contract he has entered into in an arbitrage operation; and

(4) for the purpose of this subsection arbitrage operations are transactions involving the purchase and sale of assets for the purpose of profiting from a current difference between the price of the asset purchased and the price of the asset sold, and in which the asset purchased, if not identical to the asset sold, is such that by virtue thereof the taxpayer is, or will be, entitled to acquire assets identical to the assets sold. Such operations must be clearly identified by the taxpayer in his records as arbitrage operations on the day of the transaction or as soon thereafter as may be practicable. Assets acquired for arbitrage operations will include stocks and securities and the right to acquire stocks and securities.

Amendments

• **1955 (P.L. 385, 84th Cong.)**

P.L. 385, 84th Cong., 1st Sess., §[1]:

Added subsection (f). **Effective** only as to tax years ending after 8-12-55, and only in case of short sale of property made by taxpayer after such date.

[Sec. 1233(g)]

(g) HEDGING TRANSACTIONS.—This section shall not apply in the case of a hedging transaction in commodity futures.

Amendments

• **1958, Technical Amendments Act of 1958 (P.L. 85-866)**

P.L. 85-866, §52(b):

Added Sec. 1233(g). **Effective** 1-1-54.

[Sec. 1233(h)]

(h) SHORT SALES OF PROPERTY WHICH BECOMES SUBSTANTIALLY WORTHLESS.—

(1) IN GENERAL.—If—

(A) the taxpayer enters into a short sale of property, and

(B) such property becomes substantially worthless,

the taxpayer shall recognize gain in the same manner as if the short sale were closed when the property becomes substantially worthless. To the extent provided in regulations prescribed by the Secretary, the preceding sentence also shall apply with respect to any option with respect to property, any offsetting notional principal contract with respect to property, any futures or forward contract to deliver any property, and any other similar transaction.

(2) STATUTE OF LIMITATIONS.—If property becomes substantially worthless during a taxable year and any short sale of such property remains open at the time such property becomes substantially worthless, then—

(A) the statutory period for the assessment of any deficiency attributable to any part of the gain on such transaction shall not expire before the earlier of—

(i) the date which is 3 years after the date the Secretary is notified by the taxpayer (in such manner as the Secretary may by regulations prescribe) of the substantial worthlessness of such property, or

(ii) the date which is 6 years after the date the return for such taxable year is filed, and

(B) such deficiency may be assessed before the date applicable under subparagraph (A) notwithstanding the provisions of any other law or rule of law which would otherwise prevent such assessment.

Amendments

• **1997, Taxpayer Relief Act of 1997 (P.L. 105-34)**

P.L. 105-34, §1003(b)(1):

Amended Code Sec. 1233 by adding a new subsection (h). **Effective** for property which becomes substantially worthless after 8-5-97.

INCOME TAX—CAPITAL GAINS, LOSSES

[Sec. 1234]

SEC. 1234. OPTIONS TO BUY OR SELL.

[Sec. 1234(a)]

(a) TREATMENT OF GAIN OR LOSS IN THE CASE OF THE PURCHASER.—

(1) GENERAL RULE.—Gain or loss attributable to the sale or exchange of, or loss attributable to failure to exercise, an option to buy or sell property shall be considered gain or loss from the sale or exchange of property which has the same character as the property to which the option relates has in the hands of the taxpayer (or would have in the hands of the taxpayer if acquired by him).

(2) SPECIAL RULE FOR LOSS ATTRIBUTABLE TO FAILURE TO EXERCISE OPTION.—For purposes of paragraph (1), if loss is attributable to failure to exercise an option, the option shall be deemed to have been sold or exchanged on the day it expired.

(3) NONAPPLICATION OF SUBSECTION.—This subsection shall not apply to—

(A) an option which constitutes property described in paragraph (1) of section 1221(a);

(B) in the case of gain attributable to the sale or exchange of an option, any income derived in connection with such option which, without regard to this subsection, is treated as other than gain from the sale or exchange of a capital asset; and

(C) a loss attributable to failure to exercise an option described in section 1233(c).

Amendments

• **1999, Tax Relief Extension Act of 1999 (P.L. 106-170)**

P.L. 106-170, §532(c)(1)(H):

Amended Code Sec. 1234(a)(3)(A) by striking "section 1221" and inserting "section 1221(a)". **Effective** for any instrument held, acquired, or entered into, any transaction entered into, and supplies held or acquired on or after 12-17-99.

[Sec. 1234(b)]

(b) TREATMENT OF GRANTOR OF OPTION IN THE CASE OF STOCK, SECURITIES, OR COMMODITIES.—

▶▶▶ *Caution: P.L. 98-369, §1001(b)(18), amended Code Sec. 1234(b)(1), below, by striking "1 year" and inserting "6 months". This amendment applies to property acquired after June 22, 1984, and before January 1, 1988.*

(1) GENERAL RULE.—In the case of the grantor of the option, gain or loss from any closing transaction with respect to, and gain on lapse of, an option in property shall be treated as a gain or loss from the sale or exchange of a capital asset held not more than 6 months [1 year].

(2) DEFINITIONS.—For purposes of this subsection—

(A) CLOSING TRANSACTION.—The term "closing transaction" means any termination of the taxpayer's obligation under an option in property other than through the exercise or lapse of the option.

(B) PROPERTY.—The term "property" means stocks and securities (including stocks and securities dealt with on a "when issued" basis), commodities, and commodity futures.

(3) NONAPPLICATION OF SUBSECTION.—This subsection shall not apply to any option granted in the ordinary course of the taxpayer's trade or business of granting options.

Amendments

• **1984, Deficit Reduction Act of 1984 (P.L. 98-369)**

P.L. 98-369, §1001(b)(18):

Amended Code Sec. 1234(b)(1) by striking out "1 year" and inserting in lieu thereof "6 months". **Effective** for property acquired after 6-22-84, and before 1-1-88.

• **1976, Tax Reform Act of 1976 (P.L. 94-455)**

P.L. 94-455, §1402(b)(1)(U):

Amended Code Sec. 1234(b)(1) by substituting "9 months" for "6 months". **Effective** with respect to tax years beginning in 1977.

P.L. 94-455, §1402(b)(2):

Amended Code Sec. 1234(b)(1) by substituting "1 year" for "9 months". **Effective** with respect to tax years beginning after 12-31-77.

P.L. 94-455, §2136(a):

Amended Code Sec. 1234. **Effective** for options granted after 9-1-76. Prior to amendment Code Sec. 1234 read:

(a) TREATMENT OF GAIN OR LOSS.—Gain or loss attributable to the sale or exchange of, or loss attributable to failure to exercise, a privilege or option to buy or sell property shall be considered gain or loss from the sale or exchange of property which has the same character as the property to which the option or privilege relates has in the hands of the taxpayer (or would have in the hands of the taxpayer if acquired by him).

(b) SPECIAL RULE FOR LOSS ATTRIBUTABLE TO FAILURE TO EXERCISE OPTION.—For purposes of subsection (a), if loss is attributable to failure to exercise a privilege or option, the privilege or option shall be deemed to have been sold or exchanged on the day it expired.

(c) SPECIAL RULE FOR GRANTORS OF STRADDLES.—

(1) GAIN ON LAPSE.—In the case of gain on lapse of an option granted by the taxpayer as part of a straddle, the gain shall be deemed to be gain from the sale or exchange of a capital asset held for not more than 6 months on the day that the option expired.

(2) EXCEPTION.—This subsection shall not apply to any person who holds securities for sale to customers in the ordinary course of his trade or business.

(3) DEFINITIONS.—For purposes of this subsection—

(A) The term "straddle" means a simultaneously granted combination of an option to buy, and an option to sell, the same quantity of a security at the same price during the same period of time.

(B) The term "security" has the meaning assigned to such term by section 1236(c).

(d) NON-APPLICATION OF SECTION.—This section shall not apply to—

(1) a privilege or option which constitutes property described in paragraph (1) of section 1221;

(2) in the case of gain attributable to the sale or exchange of a privilege or option, any income derived in connection with such privilege or option which, without regard to this section, is treated as other than gain from the sale or exchange of a capital asset;

(3) a loss attributable to failure to exercise an option described in section 1233(c); or

(4) gain attributable to the sale or exchange of a privilege or option acquired by the taxpayer before March 1, 1954, if in the hands of the taxpayer such privilege or option is a capital asset.

• **1966, Foreign Investors Tax Act of 1966 (P.L. 89-809)**

P.L. 89-809, §210(a):

Redesignated former Code Sec. 1234(c) as Sec. 1234(d) and added new subsection (c). **Effective** for straddle transactions entered into after 1-25-65, in tax years ending after that date.

• **1958, Technical Amendments Act of 1958 (P.L. 85-866)**

P.L. 85-866, §53:

Amended Sec. 1234. Prior to amendment Sec. 1234 read as follows:

SEC. 1234. OPTIONS TO BUY OR SELL.

Gain or loss attributable to the sale or exchange of, or loss on failure to exercise, a privilege or option to buy or sell property which in the hands of the taxpayer constitutes (or if acquired would constitute) a capital asset shall be considered gain or loss from the sale or exchange of a capital asset; and, if the loss is attributable to failure to exercise such privilege or option, the privilege or option shall be deemed to have been sold or exchanged on the day it expired. This section shall not apply to losses on failure to exercise options described in section 1233(c).

[Sec. 1234(c)]

(c) TREATMENT OF OPTIONS ON SECTION 1256 CONTRACTS AND CASH SETTLEMENT OPTIONS.—

(1) SECTION 1256 CONTRACTS.—Gain or loss shall be recognized on the exercise of an option on a section 1256 contract (within the meaning of section 1256(b)).

(2) TREATMENT OF CASH SETTLEMENT OPTIONS.—

(A) IN GENERAL.—For purposes of subsections (a) and (b), a cash settlement option shall be treated as an option to buy or sell property.

(B) CASH SETTLEMENT OPTION.—For purposes of subparagraph (A), the term "cash settlement option" means any option which on exercise settles in (or could be settled in) cash or property other than the underlying property.

INCOME TAX—CAPITAL GAINS, LOSSES

Amendments

• **1984, Deficit Reduction Act of 1984 (P.L. 98-369)**

P.L. 98-369, §105(a):

Amended Code Sec. 1234 by adding new subsection (c). **Effective** for options purchased or granted after 10-31-83, in tax years ending after such date.

[Sec. 1234A]

SEC. 1234A. GAINS OR LOSSES FROM CERTAIN TERMINATIONS.

Gain or loss attributable to the cancellation, lapse, expiration, or other termination of—

(1) a right or obligation (other than a securities futures contract, as defined in section 1234B) with respect to property which is (or on acquisition would be) a capital asset in the hands of the taxpayer, or

(2) a section 1256 contract (as defined in section 1256) not described in paragraph (1) which is a capital asset in the hands of the taxpayer,

shall be treated as gain or loss from the sale of a capital asset. The preceding sentence shall not apply to the retirement of any debt instrument (whether or not through a trust or other participation arrangement).

Amendments

• **2002, Job Creation and Worker Assistance Act of 2002 (P.L. 107-147)**

P.L. 107-147, §412(d)(1)(A):

Amended Code Sec. 1234A by inserting "or" after the comma at the end of paragraph (1), by striking "or" at the end of paragraph (2), and by striking paragraph (3). **Effective** as if included in the provision of P.L. 106-554 to which it relates [**effective** 12-21-2000.—CCH]. Prior to being stricken, Code Sec. 1234A(3) read as follows:

(3) a securities futures contract (as so defined) which is a capital asset in the hands of the taxpayer,

• **2000, Community Renewal Tax Relief Act of 2000 (P.L. 106-554)**

P.L. 106-554, §401(b)(1)-(4):

Amended Code Sec. 1234A by inserting "(other than a securities futures contract, as defined in section 1234B)" after "right or obligation" in paragraph (1), by striking "or" at the end of paragraph (1), by adding "or" at the end of paragraph (2), and by inserting after paragraph (2) a new paragraph (3). **Effective** 12-21-2000.

• **1997, Taxpayer Relief Act of 1997 (P.L. 105-34)**

P.L. 105-34, §1003(a)(1):

Amended Code Sec. 1234A(1) by striking "personal property (as defined in section 1092(d)(1))" and inserting "property". **Effective** for terminations more than 30 days after 8-5-97.

• **1984, Deficit Reduction Act of 1984 (P.L. 98-369)**

P.L. 98-369, §102(e)(4):

Amended Code Sec. 1234A(2) by striking out "a regulated futures contract" and inserting in lieu thereof "a section 1256 contract". **Effective** for positions established after 7-18-84, in tax years ending after such date.

P.L. 98-369, §102(e)(9):

Amended Code Sec. 1234A by adding a new sentence at the end thereof. **Effective** as if included in the amendment made by section 505(a) of P.L. 97-34, as amended by section 105(e) of P.L. 97-448.

• **1983, Technical Corrections Act of 1982 (P.L. 97-448)**

P.L. 97-448, §105(e):

Amended Code Sec. 1234A. **Effective** as if included in the provision of P.L. 97-34 to which it relates. Prior to amendment, Code Sec. 1234A read as follows:

SEC. 1234A. GAINS OR LOSSES FROM CERTAIN TERMINATIONS.

Gain or loss attributable to the cancellation, lapse, expiration, or other termination of a right or obligation with respect to personal property (as defined in section 1092(d)(1)) which is (or on acquisition would be) a capital asset in the hands of the taxpayer shall be treated as gain or loss from the sale of a capital asset.

• **1981, Economic Recovery Tax Act of 1981 (P.L. 97-34)**

P.L. 97-34, §507(a):

Added Code Sec. 1234A. **Effective** for property acquired and positions established by the taxpayer after 6-23-81, in tax years ending after such date.

[Sec. 1234B]

SEC. 1234B. GAINS OR LOSSES FROM SECURITIES FUTURES CONTRACTS.

[Sec. 1234B(a)]

(a) TREATMENT OF GAIN OR LOSS.—

(1) IN GENERAL.—Gain or loss attributable to the sale, exchange, or termination of a securities futures contract shall be considered gain or loss from the sale or exchange of property which has the same character as the property to which the contract relates has in the hands of the taxpayer (or would have in the hands of the taxpayer if acquired by the taxpayer).

(2) NONAPPLICATION OF SUBSECTION.—This subsection shall not apply to—

(A) a contract which constitutes property described in paragraph (1) or (7) of section 1221(a), and

(B) any income derived in connection with a contract which, without regard to this subsection, is treated as other than gain from the sale or exchange of a capital asset.

Amendments

• **2002, Job Creation and Worker Assistance Act of 2002 (P.L. 107-147)**

P.L. 107-147, §412(d)(1)(B)(i):

Amended Code Sec. 1234B(a)(1) by striking "sale or exchange" the first place it appears and inserting "sale, exchange, or termination". **Effective** as if included in the provision of P.L. 106-554 to which it relates [**effective** on 12-21-2000.—CCH].

[Sec. 1234B(b)]

(b) SHORT-TERM GAINS AND LOSSES.—Except as provided in the regulations under section 1092(b) or this section, or in section 1233, if gain or loss on the sale, exchange, or termination of a securities futures contract to sell property is considered as gain or loss from the sale or exchange of a capital asset, such gain or loss shall be treated as short-term capital gain or loss.

Amendments

• **2002, Job Creation and Worker Assistance Act of 2002 (P.L. 107-147)**

P.L. 107-147, §412(d)(1)(B)(i):

Amended Code Sec. 1234B(b) by striking "sale or exchange" the first place it appears and inserting "sale, exchange, or termination". **Effective** as if included in the provision of P.L. 106-554 to which it relates [**effective** on 12-21-2000.—CCH].

P.L. 107-147, §412(d)(3)(B):

Amended Code Sec. 1234B(b) by inserting "or in section 1233," following "or this section,". **Effective** as if included in the provision of P.L. 106-554 to which it relates [**effective** on 12-21-2000.—CCH].

[Sec. 1234B(c)]

(c) SECURITIES FUTURES CONTRACT.—For purposes of this section, the term "securities futures contract" means any security future (as defined in section 3(a)(55)(A) of the Securities Exchange Act of 1934, as in effect on the date of the enactment of this section). The Secretary may prescribe regulations regarding the status of contracts the values of which are determined directly or indirectly by reference to any index which becomes (or ceases to be) a narrow-based security index (as defined for purposes of section 1256(g)(6)).

INCOME TAX—CAPITAL GAINS, LOSSES

Amendments

• **2004, Working Families Tax Relief Act of 2004 (P.L. 108-311)**

P.L. 108-311, § 405(a)(1):

Amended Code Sec. 1234B(c) by adding at the end a new sentence. **Effective** as if included in section 401 of the Community Renewal Tax Relief Act of 2000 (P.L. 106-554) [**effective** 12-21-2000.—CCH].

[Sec. 1234B(d)]

(d) CONTRACTS NOT TREATED AS COMMODITY FUTURES CONTRACTS.—For purposes of this title, a securities futures contract shall not be treated as a commodity futures contract.

[Sec. 1234B(e)]

(e) REGULATIONS.—The Secretary shall prescribe such regulations as may be appropriate to provide for the proper treatment of securities futures contracts under this title.

Amendments

• **2000, Community Renewal Tax Relief Act of 2000 (P.L. 106-554)**

P.L. 106-554, § 401(a):

Amended subpart IV of subchapter P of chapter 1 by inserting after Code Sec. 1234A a new Code Sec. 1234B. **Effective** 12-21-2000.

[Sec. 1234B(f)]

(f) CROSS REFERENCE.—

For special rules relating to dealer securities futures contracts, see section 1256.

Amendments

• **2002, Job Creation and Worker Assistance Act of 2002 (P.L. 107-147)**

P.L. 107-147, § 412(d)(1)(B)(ii):

Amended Code Sec. 1234B by adding at the end a new subsection (f). **Effective** as if included in the provision of P.L. 106-554 to which it relates [**effective** on 12-21-2000.—CCH].

[Sec. 1235]

SEC. 1235. SALE OR EXCHANGE OF PATENTS.

[Sec. 1235(a)]

(a) GENERAL.—A transfer (other than by gift, inheritance, or devise) of property consisting of all substantial rights to a patent, or an undivided interest therein which includes a part of all such rights, by any holder shall be considered the sale or exchange of a capital asset held for more than 1 year, regardless of whether or not payments in consideration of such transfer are—

    (1) payable periodically over a period generally coterminous with the transferee's use of the patent, or

    (2) contingent on the productivity, use, or disposition of the property transferred.

Amendments

• **1998, IRS Restructuring and Reform Act of 1998 (P.L. 105-206)**

P.L. 105-206, § 5001(a)(5):

Amended Code Sec. 1235(a) by striking "18 months" and inserting "1 year". **Effective** 1-1-98.

P.L. 105-206, § 6005(d)(4):

Amended Code Sec. 1235(a), prior to amendment by Act Sec. 5001(a)(5), by striking "1 year" and inserting "18 months". **Effective** as if included in the provision of P.L. 105-34 to which it relates [**effective** for tax years ending after 5-6-97.—CCH].

• **1984, Deficit Reduction Act of 1984 (P.L. 98-369)**

P.L. 98-369, § 1001(b)(19):

Amended Code Sec. 1235(a) by striking out "1 year" and inserting in lieu thereof "6 months". **Effective** for property acquired after 6-22-84, and before 1-1-88.

• **1976, Tax Reform Act of 1976 (P.L. 94-455)**

P.L. 94-455, § 1402(b)(1)(V):

Amended Code Sec. 1235(a) by substituting "9 months" for "6 months". **Effective** with respect to tax years beginning in 1977.

P.L. 94-455, § 1402(b)(2):

Amended Code Sec. 1235(a) by substituting "1 year" for "9 months". **Effective** with respect to tax years beginning after 12-31-77.

[Sec. 1235(b)]

(b) "HOLDER" DEFINED.—For purposes of this section, the term "holder" means—

    (1) any individual whose efforts created such property, or

    (2) any other individual who has acquired his interest in such property in exchange for consideration in money or money's worth paid to such creator prior to actual reduction to practice of the invention covered by the patent, if such individual is neither—

        (A) the employer of such creator, nor

        (B) related to such creator (within the meaning of subsection (c)).

Amendments

• **2014, Tax Technical Corrections Act of 2014 (P.L. 113-295)**

P.L. 113-295, § 221(a)(82)(B), Division A:

Amended Code Sec. 1235(b)(2)(B) by striking "subsection (d)" and inserting "subsection (c)". **Effective** generally 12-19-2014. For a special rule, see Act Sec. 221(b)(2), Division A, below.

P.L. 113-295, § 221(b)(2), Division A, provides:

(2) SAVINGS PROVISION.—If—

(A) any provision amended or repealed by the amendments made by this section applied to—

    (i) any transaction occurring before the date of the enactment of this Act,

    (ii) any property acquired before such date of enactment, or

    (iii) any item of income, loss, deduction, or credit taken into account before such date of enactment, and

(B) the treatment of such transaction, property, or item under such provision would (without regard to the amendments or repeals made by this section) affect the liability for tax for periods ending after date of enactment, nothing in the amendments or repeals made by this section shall be construed to affect the treatment of such transaction, property, or item for purposes of determining liability for tax for periods ending after such date of enactment.

[Sec. 1235(c)—Stricken]

(c) EFFECTIVE DATE.—This section shall be applicable with regard to any amounts received, or payments made, pursuant to a transfer described in subsection (a) in any taxable year to which this subtitle applies, regardless of the taxable year in which such transfer occurred.

Amendments

• **2014, Tax Technical Corrections Act of 2014 (P.L. 113-295)**

P.L. 113-295, § 221(a)(82)(A), Division A:

Amended Code Sec. 1235 by striking subsection (c) and by redesignating subsections (d) and (e) as subsections (c) and (d), respectively. **Effective** generally 12-19-2014. For a special rule, see Act Sec. 221(b)(2), Division A, below. Prior to being stricken, Code Sec. 1235(c) read as follows:

P.L. 113-295, § 221(b)(2), Division A, provides:

(2) SAVINGS PROVISION.—If—

Sec. 1234B(d)

INCOME TAX—CAPITAL GAINS, LOSSES

(A) any provision amended or repealed by the amendments made by this section applied to—

(i) any transaction occurring before the date of the enactment of this Act,

(ii) any property acquired before such date of enactment, or

(iii) any item of income, loss, deduction, or credit taken into account before such date of enactment, and

(B) the treatment of such transaction, property, or item under such provision would (without regard to the amendments or repeals made by this section) affect the liability for tax for periods ending after date of enactment, nothing in the amendments or repeals made by this section shall be construed to affect the treatment of such transaction, property, or item for purposes of determining liability for tax for periods ending after such date of enactment.

[Sec. 1235(c)]

(c) RELATED PERSONS.—Subsection (a) shall not apply to any transfer, directly or indirectly, between persons specified within any one of the paragraphs of section 267(b) or persons described in section 707(b); except that, in applying section 267(b) and (c) and section 707(b) for purposes of this section—

(1) the phrase "25 percent or more" shall be substituted for the phrase "more than 50 percent" each place it appears in section 267(b) or 707(b), and

(2) paragraph (4) of section 267(c) shall be treated as providing that the family of an individual shall include only his spouse, ancestors, and lineal descendants.

Amendments

• **2014, Tax Technical Corrections Act of 2014 (P.L. 113-295)**

P.L. 113-295, §221(a)(82)(A), Division A:

Amended Code Sec. 1235 by redesignating subsection (d) subsection (c). **Effective** generally 12-19-2014. For a special rule, see Act Sec. 221(b)(2), Division A, below.

P.L. 113-295, §221(b)(2), Division A, provides:

(2) SAVINGS PROVISION.—If—

(A) any provision amended or repealed by the amendments made by this section applied to—

(i) any transaction occurring before the date of the enactment of this Act,

(ii) any property acquired before such date of enactment, or

(iii) any item of income, loss, deduction, or credit taken into account before such date of enactment, and

(B) the treatment of such transaction, property, or item under such provision would (without regard to the amendments or repeals made by this section) affect the liability for tax for periods ending after date of enactment, nothing in the amendments or repeals made by this section shall be construed to affect the treatment of such transaction, property, or item for purposes of determining liability for tax for periods ending after such date of enactment.

• **1984, Deficit Reduction Act of 1984 (P.L. 98-369)**

P.L. 98-369, §174(b)(5)(C):

Amended Code Sec. 1235(d) by striking out "section 267(b)" in the matter preceding paragraph (1) and inserting in lieu thereof "section 267(b) or persons described in section 707(b)", by striking out "section 267(b) and (c)" and inserting in lieu thereof "section 267(b) and (c) and section 707(b)", and by striking out "section 267(b)" in paragraph (1) and inserting in lieu thereof "section 267(b) or 707(b)". **Effective** for transactions after 12-31-83, in tax years ending after such date.

• **1958, Technical Amendments Act of 1958 (P.L. 85-866)**

P.L. 85-866, §54(a):

Amended Sec. 1235(d). **Effective** for tax years ending after 9-2-58, but only for transfers after that date. Prior to amendment, Sec. 1235(d) read as follows:

(d) Related Persons.—Subsection (a) shall not apply to any sale or exchange between an individual and any other related person (as defined in section 267(b)), except brothers and sisters, whether by the whole or half blood.

[Sec. 1235(d)]

(d) CROSS REFERENCE.—

For special rule relating to nonresident aliens, see section 871(a).

• **2014, Tax Technical Corrections Act of 2014 (P.L. 113-295)**

P.L. 113-295, §221(a)(82)(A), Division A:

Amended Code Sec. 1235 by redesignating subsection (e) as subsection (d). **Effective** generally 12-19-2014. For a special rule, see Act Sec. 221(b)(2), Division A, below.

P.L. 113-295, §221(b)(2), Division A, provides:

(2) SAVINGS PROVISION.—If—

(A) any provision amended or repealed by the amendments made by this section applied to—

(i) any transaction occurring before the date of the enactment of this Act,

(ii) any property acquired before such date of enactment, or

(iii) any item of income, loss, deduction, or credit taken into account before such date of enactment, and

(B) the treatment of such transaction, property, or item under such provision would (without regard to the amendments or repeals made by this section) affect the liability for tax for periods ending after date of enactment, nothing in the amendments or repeals made by this section shall be construed to affect the treatment of such transaction, property, or item for purposes of determining liability for tax for periods ending after such date of enactment.

[Sec. 1236]

SEC. 1236. DEALERS IN SECURITIES.

[Sec. 1236(a)]

(a) CAPITAL GAINS.—Gain by a dealer in securities from the sale or exchange of any security shall in no event be considered as gain from the sale or exchange of a capital asset unless—

(1) the security was, before the close of the day on which it was acquired (or such earlier time as the Secretary may prescribe by regulations), clearly identified in the dealer's records as a security held for investment; and

(2) the security was not, at any time after the close of such day (or such earlier time), held by such dealer primarily for sale to customers in the ordinary course of his trade or business.

Amendments

• **1984, Deficit Reduction Act of 1984 (P.L. 98-369)**

P.L. 98-369, §107(b)(1):

Amended Code Sec. 1236(a)(1). **Effective** for positions entered into after 7-18-84, in tax years ending after such date. Prior to amendment, it read as follows:

(1) the security was, before the close of the day on which it was acquired (before the close of the following day in the case of an acquisition before January 1, 1982), clearly identified in the dealer's records as a security held for investment or if acquired before October 20, 1951, was so identified before November 20, 1951; and

P.L. 98-369, §107(b)(2):

Amended Code Sec. 1236(a)(2) by inserting "(or such earlier time)" after "such day". **Effective** for positions entered into after 7-18-84, in tax years ending after such date.

• **1981, Economic Recovery Tax Act of 1981 (P.L. 97-34)**

P.L. 97-34, §506(a):

Amended Code Sec. 1236(a). **Effective** for property acquired by the taxpayer after 8-13-81, in tax years ending afer such date. Prior to amendment, Code Sec. 1236(a) read as follows:

(a) CAPITAL GAINS.—Gain by a dealer in securities from the sale or exchange of any security shall in no event be considered as gain from the sale or exchange of a capital asset unless—

(1) the security was, before the expiration of the 30th day after the date of its acquisition, clearly identified in the dealer's records as a security held for investment or if acquired before October 20, 1951, was so identified before November 20, 1951; and

(2) the security was not, at any time after the expiration of such 30th day, held by such dealer primarily for sale to customers in the ordinary course of his trade or business.

[Sec. 1236(b)]

(b) ORDINARY LOSSES.—Loss by a dealer in securities from the sale or exchange of any security shall, except as otherwise provided in section 582(c) (relating to bond, etc., losses of banks), in no event be considered as an ordinary loss if at any time the security was clearly identified in the dealer's records as a security held for investment.

INCOME TAX—CAPITAL GAINS, LOSSES

Amendments

• **2014, Tax Technical Corrections Act of 2014 (P.L. 113-295)**

P.L. 113-295, §221(a)(83), Division A:

Amended Code Sec. 1236(b) by striking "after November 19, 1951," following "if at any time". **Effective** generally 12-19-2014. For a special rule, see Act Sec. 221(b)(2), Division A, below.

P.L. 113-295, §221(b)(2), Division A, provides:

(2) SAVINGS PROVISION.—If—

(A) any provision amended or repealed by the amendments made by this section applied to—

(i) any transaction occurring before the date of the enactment of this Act,

(ii) any property acquired before such date of enactment, or

(iii) any item of income, loss, deduction, or credit taken into account before such date of enactment, and

(B) the treatment of such transaction, property, or item under such provision would (without regard to the amendments or repeals made by this section) affect the liability for tax for periods ending after date of enactment, nothing in the amendments or repeals made by this section shall be construed to affect the treatment of such transaction, property, or item for purposes of determining liability for tax for periods ending after such date of enactment.

• **1976, Tax Reform Act of 1976 (P.L. 94-455)**

P.L. 94-455, §1901(b)(3)(E):

Substituted "an ordinary loss" for "loss from the sale or exchange of property which is not a capital asset" in Code Sec. 1236(b). **Effective** with respect to tax years beginning after 12-31-76.

[Sec. 1236(c)]

(c) DEFINITION OF SECURITY.—For purposes of this section, the term "security" means any share of stock in any corporation, certificate of stock or interest in any corporation, note, bond, debenture, or evidence of indebtedness, or any evidence of an interest in or right to subscribe to or purchase any of the foregoing.

[Sec. 1236(d)]

(d) SPECIAL RULE FOR FLOOR SPECIALISTS.—

(1) IN GENERAL.—In the case of a floor specialist (but only with respect to acquisitions, in connection with his duties on an exchange, of stock in which the specialist is registered with the exchange), subsection (a) shall be applied—

(A) by inserting "the 7th business day following" before "the day" the first place it appears in paragraph (1) and by inserting "7th business" before "day" in paragraph (2), and

(B) by striking the parenthetical phrase in paragraph (1).

(2) FLOOR SPECIALIST.—The term "floor specialist" means a person who is—

(A) a member of a national securities exchange,

(B) is registered as a specialist with the exchange, and

(C) meets the requirements for specialists established by the Securities and Exchange Commission.

Amendments

• **1981, Economic Recovery Tax Act of 1981 (P.L. 97-34)**

P.L. 97-34, §506(b):

Added Code Sec. 1236(d). **Effective** for property acquired by the taxpayer after 8-13-81, in tax years ending after such date.

[Sec. 1236(e)]

(e) SPECIAL RULE FOR OPTIONS.—For purposes of subsection (a), any security acquired by a dealer pursuant to an option held by such dealer may be treated as held for investment only if the dealer, before the close of the day on which the option was acquired, clearly identified the option on his records as held for investment. For purposes of the preceding sentence, the term "option" includes the right to subscribe to or purchase any security.

Amendments

• **1983, Technical Corrections Act of 1982 (P.L. 97-448)**

P.L. 97-448, §105(d)(1):

Amended Code Sec. 1236 by adding at the end thereof new subsection (e). **Effective** for securities acquired after 9-22-82, in tax years ending after such date.

[Sec. 1237]

SEC. 1237. REAL PROPERTY SUBDIVIDED FOR SALE.

[Sec. 1237(a)]

(a) GENERAL.—Any lot or parcel which is part of a tract of real property in the hands of a taxpayer other than a C corporation shall not be deemed to be held primarily for sale to customers in the ordinary course of trade or business at the time of sale solely because of the taxpayer having subdivided such tract for purposes of sale or because of any activity incident to such subdivision or sale, if—

(1) such tract, or any lot or parcel thereof, had not previously been held by such taxpayer primarily for sale to customers in the ordinary course of trade or business (unless such tract at such previous time would have been covered by this section) and, in the same taxable year in which the sale occurs, such taxpayer does not so hold any other real property; and

(2) no substantial improvement that substantially enhances the value of the lot or parcel sold is made by the taxpayer on such tract while held by the taxpayer or is made pursuant to a contract of sale entered into between the taxpayer and the buyer. For purposes of this paragraph, an improvement shall be deemed to be made by the taxpayer if such improvement was made by—

(A) the taxpayer or members of his family (as defined in section 267(c)(4)), by a corporation controlled by the taxpayer, an S corporation which included the taxpayer as a shareholder, or by a partnership which included the taxpayer as a partner; or

(B) a lessee, but only if the improvement constitutes income to the taxpayer; or

(C) Federal, State, or local government, or political subdivision thereof, but only if the improvement constitutes an addition to basis for the taxpayer; and

(3) such lot or parcel, except in the case of real property acquired by inheritance or devise, is held by the taxpayer for a period of 5 years.

Amendments

• **1996, Small Business Job Protection Act of 1996 (P.L. 104-188)**

P.L. 104-188, §1314(a):

Amended Code Sec. 1237(a) by striking "other than a corporation" in the material preceding paragraph (1) and inserting "other than a C corporation". **Effective** for tax years beginning after 12-31-96.

P.L. 104-188, §1314(b):

Amended Code Sec. 1237(a)(2)(A) by inserting "an S corporation which included the taxpayer as a shareholder," after "controlled by the taxpayer,". **Effective** for tax years beginning after 12-31-96.

• **1971 (P.L. 91-686)**

P.L. 91-686, §2(a)(1):

Amended the matter preceding paragraph (1) of Code Sec. 1237(a) by substituting "other than a corporation" for "(including corporations only if no shareholder directly or indirectly holds real property for sale to customers in the ordinary course of trade or business and only in the case of property described in the last sentence of subsection (b)(3))". **Effective** for tax years beginning after 1-12-71.

P.L. 91-686, §1, provides:

(a) For purposes of the Internal Revenue Code of 1954 any lot or parcel of real property sold or exchanged by a corporation which would, but for this Act, be

INCOME TAX—CAPITAL GAINS, LOSSES

treated as property held primarily for sale to customers in the ordinary course of trade or business shall not, except to the extent provided in (b), be so treated if—

(1) no shareholder of the corporation directly or indirectly holds real property primarily for sale to customers in the ordinary course of trade or business; and

(2)(A) such lot or parcel is part of real property (i) held for more than twenty-five years at the time of sale or exchange, and (ii) acquired before January 1, 1934, by the corporation as a result of the foreclosure of a lien (or liens) thereon which secured the payment of indebtedness held by one or more creditors who transferred one or more foreclosure bids to the corporation in exchange for all its stock (with or without other consideration), or

(B)(i) such lot or parcel is a part of additional real property acquired before January 1, 1957, by the corporation in the near vicinity of any real property to which subparagraph (A) applies, or

(ii) such lot or parcel is wholly or to some extent a part of any minor acquisition made after December 31, 1956, by the corporation to adjust boundaries, to fill gaps in previously acquired property, to facilitate the installation of streets, utilities, and other public facilities, or to facilitate the sale of adjacent property, or

(iii) such lot or parcel is wholly or to some extent a part of a reacquisition by the corporation after December 31, 1956, of property previously owned by the corporation; but only if at least 80 percent (as measured by area) of the real property sold or exchanged by the corporation within the taxable year is property described in subparagraph (A); and

(3) there were no acquisitions of real property by the corporation after December 31, 1956, other than—

(A) acquisitions described in paragraph (2)(B)(ii) and reacquisitions described in paragraph (2)(B)(iii), or

(B) acquisitions of real property used in a trade or business of the corporation or held for investment by the corporation; and

(4) the corporation did not after December 31, 1957, sell or exchange (except in condemnation or under threat of condemnation) any residential lot or parcel on which, at the time of the sale or exchange, there existed any substantial improvements (other than improvements in existence at the time the land was acquired by the corporation) except subdivision, clearing, grubbing, and grading, building or installation of water, sewer, and drainage facilities, construction of roads, streets, and sidewalks, and installation of utilities.

In any case in which a corporation referred to in paragraphs (1), (2), (3), and (4) is a member of an affiliated group as defined in section 1504(a) of the Internal Revenue Code of 1954, such affiliated group shall, for purposes of such paragraphs, be treated as a single corporation.

(b)(1) Gain from any sale or exchange described in subsection (a) shall be deemed, for purposes of such Code, to be gain from the sale of property held primarily for sale to customers in the ordinary course of trade or business to the extent of 5 percent of the selling price.

(2) For the purpose of computing gain under paragraph (1), expenditures incurred in connection with the sale or exchange of any lot or parcel shall neither be allowed as a deduction in computing taxable income, nor treated as reducing the amount realized on such sale or exchange; but so much of such expenditures as does not exceed the portion of gain deemed under paragraph (1) to be gain from the sale of property held primarily for sale to customers in the ordinary course of trade or business shall be so allowed as a deduction, and the remainder, if any, shall be treated as reducing the amount realized on such sale or exchange.

(c) The provisions of subsections (a) and (b) shall apply to taxable years beginning after December 31, 1957, and before January 1, 1984.

• **1958, Technical Amendments Act of 1958 (P.L. 85-866)**

P.L. 85-866, § 55:

Amended Code Sec. 1237(a)(1) by substituting "and, in the same taxable year" for "or, in the same taxable year". **Effective** 1-1-54.

• **1956 (P.L. 495, 84th Cong.)**

P.L. 495, 84th Cong., 2nd Sess., § [1]:

Amended Code Sec. 1237(a) by striking out the words "other than a corporation" and inserting: "(including corporations only if no shareholder directly or indirectly holds real property for sale to customers in the ordinary course of trade or business and only in the case of property described in the last sentence of subsection (b)(3))". **Effective** 1-1-55.

[Sec. 1237(b)]

(b) SPECIAL RULES FOR APPLICATION OF SECTION.—

(1) GAINS.—If more than 5 lots or parcels contained in the same tract of real property are sold or exchanged, gain from any sale or exchange (which occurs in or after the taxable year in which the sixth lot or parcel is sold or exchanged) of any lot or parcel which comes within the provisions of paragraphs (1), (2) and (3) of subsection (a) of this section shall be deemed to be gain from the sale of property held primarily for sale to customers in the ordinary course of the trade or business to the extent of 5 percent of the selling price.

(2) EXPENDITURES OF SALE.—For the purpose of computing gain under paragraph (1) of this subsection, expenditures incurred in connection with the sale or exchange of any lot or parcel shall neither be allowed as a deduction in computing taxable income, nor treated as reducing the amount realized on such sale or exchange; but so much of such expenditures as does not exceed the portion of gain deemed under paragraph (1) of this subsection to be gain from the sale of property held primarily for sale to customers in the ordinary course of trade or business shall be so allowed as a deduction, and the remainder, if any, shall be treated as reducing the amount realized on such sale or exchange.

(3) NECESSARY IMPROVEMENTS.—No improvement shall be deemed a substantial improvement for purposes of subsection (a) if the lot or parcel is held by the taxpayer for a period of 10 years and if—

(A) such improvement is the building or installation of water, sewer, or drainage facilities or roads (if such improvement would except for this paragraph constitute a substantial improvement);

(B) it is shown to the satisfaction of the Secretary that the lot or parcel, the value of which was substantially enhanced by such improvement, would not have been marketable at the prevailing local price for similar building sites without such improvement; and

(C) the taxpayer elects, in accordance with regulations prescribed by the Secretary, to make no adjustment to basis of the lot or parcel, or of any other property owned by the taxpayer, on account of the expenditures for such improvements. Such election shall not make any item deductible which would not otherwise be deductible.

Amendments

• **1976, Tax Reform Act of 1976 (P.L. 94-455)**

P.L. 94-455, § 1906(b)(13)(A):

Amended 1954 Code by substituting "Secretary" for "Secretary or his delegate" each place it appeared. **Effective** 2-1-77.

• **1971 (P.L. 91-686)**

P.L. 91-686, § 2(a)(2):

Deleted the former last sentence of Code Sec. 1237(b). **Effective** for tax years beginning after 1-12-71. See also the amendment note for P.L. 91-686, under Code Sec. 1237(a). Prior to amendment, the last sentence of Code Sec. 1237(b) read as follows:

"The requirements of subparagraphs (B) and (C) shall not apply in the case of property acquired through the foreclosure of a lien thereon which secured the payment of an indebtedness to the taxpayer or (in the case of a corporation) to a creditor who has transferred the foreclosure bid to the taxpayer in exchange for all of its stock and other consideration and in the case of property adjacent to such property if 80 percent of the real property owned by the taxpayer is property described in the first part of this sentence."

• **1956 (P.L. 495, 84th Cong.)**

P.L. 495, 84th Cong., 2nd Sess., § 2:

Amended subparagraph A of Code Sec. 1237(b)(3) by striking out the words "water or sewer facilities" and inserting in lieu thereof the words "water, sewer, or drainage facilities", and added the last sentence to Code Sec. 1237(b)(3). **Effective** 1-1-55.

[Sec. 1237(c)]

(c) TRACT DEFINED.—For purposes of this section, the term "tract of real property" means a single piece of real property, except that 2 or more pieces of real property shall be considered a tract if at any time they were contiguous in the hands of the taxpayer or if they would be contiguous except for the interposition of a road, street, railroad, stream, or similar property. If, following the sale or exchange of any lot or parcel from a tract of real property, no further sales or exchanges of any other lots or parcels from the remainder of such tract are made for a period of 5 years, such remainder shall be deemed a tract.

[Sec. 1237(d)—Repealed]

Amendments

• **1976, Tax Reform Act of 1976 (P.L. 94-455)**

P.L. 94-455, § 1901(a)(138):

Repealed Code Sec. 1237(d). **Effective** with respect to tax years beginning after 12-31-76. Prior to repeal, Code Sec. 1237(d) read as follows:

(d) EFFECTIVE DATE.—This section shall apply only with respect to sales of property occurring after December 31, 1953, except that, for purposes of subsection (c) (defining tract of real property) and for determining the number of sales under paragraph (1) of subsection (b), all sales of lots and parcels from any tract of real property during the period of 5 years before December 31, 1953, shall be taken into account, except as provided in subsection (c).

INCOME TAX—CAPITAL GAINS, LOSSES

[Sec. 1238—Repealed]

Amendments

• **1990, Omnibus Budget Reconciliation Act of 1990 (P.L. 101-508)**

P.L. 101-508, § 11801(a)(35):

Repealed Code Sec. 1238. **Effective** 11-5-90. Prior to repeal, Code Sec. 1238 read as follows:

SEC. 1238. AMORTIZATION IN EXCESS OF DEPRECIATION.

Gain from the sale or exchange of property, to the extent that the adjusted basis of such property is less than its adjusted basis determined without regard to section 168 (as in effect before its repeal by the Tax Reform Act of 1976), shall be considered as ordinary income.

P.L. 101-508, § 11821(b), provides:

(b) SAVINGS PROVISION.—If—

(1) any provision amended or repealed by this part applied to—

(A) any transaction occurring before the date of the enactment of this Act,

(B) any property acquired before such date of enactment, or

(C) any item of income, loss, deduction, or credit taken into account before such date of enactment, and

(2) the treatment of such transaction, property, or item under such provision would (without regard to the amendments made by this part) affect liability for tax for periods ending after such date of enactment,

nothing in the amendments made by this part shall be construed to affect the treatment of such transaction, property, or item for purposes of determining liability for tax for periods ending after such date of enactment.

• **1976, Tax Reform Act of 1976 (P.L. 94-455)**

P.L. 94-455, § 1901(b)(3)(K):

Amended Code Sec. 1238 by substituting "ordinary income" for "gain from the sale or exchange of property which is neither a capital asset nor property described in section 1231". **Effective** with respect to tax taxable years beginning after 12-31-76.

P.L. 94-455, § 1951(c)(2)(A):

Amended Code Sec. 1238 by substituting "(as in effect before its repeal by the Tax Reform Act of 1976)" for "(relating to amortization deduction of emergency facilities)". **Effective** with respect to tax years beginning after 12-31-76.

[Sec. 1239]

SEC. 1239. GAIN FROM SALE OF DEPRECIABLE PROPERTY BETWEEN CERTAIN RELATED TAXPAYERS.

[Sec. 1239(a)]

(a) TREATMENT OF GAIN AS ORDINARY INCOME.—In the case of a sale or exchange of property, directly or indirectly, between related persons, any gain recognized to the transferor shall be treated as ordinary income if such property is, in the hands of the transferee, of a character which is subject to the allowance for depreciation provided in section 167.

[Sec. 1239(b)]

(b) RELATED PERSONS.—For purposes of subsection (a), the term "related persons" means—

(1) a person and all entities which are controlled entities with respect to such person,

(2) a taxpayer and any trust in which such taxpayer (or his spouse) is a beneficiary, unless such beneficiary's interest in the trust is a remote contingent interest (within the meaning of section 318(a)(3)(B)(i)), and

(3) except in the case of a sale or exchange in satisfaction of a pecuniary bequest, an executor of an estate and a beneficiary of such estate.

Amendments

• **1997, Taxpayer Relief Act of 1997 (P.L. 105-34)**

P.L. 105-34, § 1308(b):

Amended Code Sec. 1239(b) by striking the period at the end of paragraph (2) and inserting ", and" and by adding at the end a new paragraph (3). **Effective** for tax years beginning after 8-5-97.

• **1986, Tax Reform Act of 1986 (P.L. 99-514)**

P.L. 99-514, § 642(a)(1)(A):

Amended Code Sec. 1239(b)(1) by striking out "80-percent owned entities" and inserting in lieu thereof "controlled entities". **Effective**, generally, for sales after 10-22-86, in tax years ending after such date. However, see Act Sec. 642(c)(2), below.

P.L. 99-514, § 642(c)(2), as amended by P.L. 100-647, § 1006(i)(3), provides:

(2) TRADITIONAL RULE FOR BINDING CONTRACTS.—The amendments made by this section shall not apply to sales made after August 14, 1986, which are made pursuant to a binding contract in effect on August 14, 1986, and at all times thereafter.

• **1984, Deficit Reduction Act of 1984 (P.L. 98-369)**

P.L. 98-369, § 175(b):

Amended Code Sec. 1239(b). **Effective** for sales or exchanges after 3-1-84, in tax years ending after such date. Prior to amendment, it read as follows:

(b) Related Persons.—For purposes of subsection (a) the term "related persons" means—

(1) a husband and wife, and

(2) a person and all entities which are 80-percent owned entities with respect to such person.

P.L. 98-369, § 421(b)(6)(A):

Amended Code Sec. 1239(b), as amended by Act Sec. 175(b), by striking out paragraph (1) and by redesignating paragraphs (2) and (3) as paragraphs (1) and (2), respectively. **Effective** for transfers after 7-18-84, in tax years ending after such date. Prior to amendment, paragraph (1) read as follows:

(1) a husband and wife,

• **1983, Technical Corrections Act of 1982 (P.L. 97-448)**

P.L. 97-448, § 301(a):

Amended Code Sec. 1239(b). **Effective** for dispositions made after 10-19-80, in tax years ending after such date. Prior to amendment, Code Sec. 1239(b) read as follows:

(b) RELATED PERSONS.—For purposes of subsection (a), the term "related persons" means—

(1) the taxpayer and the taxpayer's spouse,

(2) the taxpayer and an 80-percent owned entity, or

(3) two 80-percent owned entities.

• **1980, Installment Sales Revision Act of 1980 (P.L. 96-471)**

P.L. 96-471, § 5:

Amended Code Sec. 1239(b). **Effective** for dispositions made after 10-19-80, in tax years ending after that date. Prior to amendment, Code Sec. 1239(b) provided:

(b) RELATED PERSONS.—For purposes of subsection (a), the term "related persons" means—

(1) a husband and wife,

(2) an individual and a corporation 80 percent or more in value of the outstanding stock of which is owned, directly or indirectly, by or for such individual, or

(3) two or more corporations 80 percent or more in value of the outstanding stock of each of which is owned, directly or indirectly, by or for the same individual.

[Sec. 1239(c)]

(c) CONTROLLED ENTITY DEFINED.—

(1) GENERAL RULE.—For purposes of this section, the term "controlled entity" means, with respect to any person—

(A) a corporation more than 50 percent of the value of the outstanding stock of which is owned (directly or indirectly) by or for such person,

(B) a partnership more than 50 percent of the capital interest or profits interest in which is owned (directly or indirectly) by or for such person, or

(C) any entity which is a related person to such person under paragraph (3), (10), (11), or (12) of section 267(b).

(2) CONSTRUCTIVE OWNERSHIP.—For purposes of this section, ownership shall be determined in accordance with rules similar to the rules under section 267(c) (other than paragraph (3) thereof).

Amendments

• **1986, Tax Reform Act of 1986 (P.L. 99-514)**

P.L. 99-514, § 642(a)(1)(B)(i)(I)-(IV):

Amended Code Sec. 1239(c)(1)(A)-(C) by striking out "80-percent owned entity" and inserting in lieu thereof "controlled entity", "80 percent or more in value" in subparagraph (A) and inserting in lieu thereof "more than 50 percent of the value", by striking out "80 percent or more" in subparagraph (B) and inserting in lieu thereof "more than 50 percent", and by striking out "and" at the end of subparagraph (A), by striking out the period at the end of subparagraph (B) and inserting ", and" and by adding at the end thereof new paragraph (C). **Effective**, generally, for sales after 10-22-86, in tax years ending after such date. However, see Act Sec. 642(c)(2), below.

P.L. 99-514, § 642(a)(1)(B)(ii):

Amended Code Sec. 1239(c) by striking out "80-percent owned entity" in the heading thereof and inserting in lieu thereof "controlled entity". **Effective**, generally, for sales after 10-22-86, in tax years ending after such date. However, see Act Sec. 642(c)(2), below.

INCOME TAX—CAPITAL GAINS, LOSSES

P.L. 99-514, §642(a)(1)(C):

Amended Code Sec. 1239(c) by striking out paragraph (2) and inserting in lieu thereof new paragraph (2). **Effective**, generally, for sales after 10-22-86, in tax years ending after such date. However, see Act Sec. 642(c)(2), below: Prior to amendment, Code Sec. 1239(c)(2) read as follows:

(2) CONSTRUCTIVE OWNERSHIP.—For purposes of subparagraphs (A) and (B) of paragraph (1), the principles of section 318 shall apply, except that—

(A) the members of an individual's family shall consist only of such individual and such individual's spouse,

(B) paragraph (2)(C) of section 318(a) shall be applied without regard to the 50-percent limitation contained therein, and

(C) paragraph (3) of section 318(a) shall not apply.

P.L. 99-514, §642(c)(2), as amended by P.L. 100-647, §1006(i)(3), provides:

(2) TRANSITIONAL RULE FOR BINDING CONTRACTS.—The amendments made by this section shall not apply to sales made after August 14, 1986, which are made pursuant to a binding contract in effect on August 14, 1986, and at all times thereafter.

- **1983, Technical Corrections Act of 1982 (P.L. 97-448)**

P.L. 97-448, §301(b):

Amended Code Sec. 1239(c). **Effective** for dispositions made after 10-19-80, in tax years ending after such date. Prior to amendment, Code Sec. 1239(c) read as follows:

(c) 80-PERCENT OWNED ENTITY DEFINED.—

(1) GENERAL RULE.—For purposes of this section, the term `80-percent owned entity' means—

(A) a corporation 80 percent or more in value of the outstanding stock of which is owned (directly or indirectly) by or for the taxpayer, and

(B) a partnership 80 percent or more of the capital interest or profits interest in which is owned (directly or indirectly) by or for the taxpayer.

(2) CONSTRUCTIVE OWNERSHIP.—For purposes of subparagraphs (A) and (B) of paragraph (1), the principles of section 318 shall apply, except that—

(A) the members of an individual's family shall consist only of such individual and such individual's spouse, and

(B) paragraphs (2)(C) and (3)(C) of section 318(a) shall be applied without regard to the 50-percent limitation contained therein.

- **1980, Installment Sales Revision Act of 1980 (P.L. 96-471)**

P.L. 96-471, §5:

Amended Code Sec. 1239(c). **Effective** for dispositions made after 10-19-80, in tax years ending after that date. Prior to amendment, Code Sec. 1239(c) provided:

(c) CONSTRUCTIVE OWNERSHIP OF STOCK.—Section 318 shall apply in determining the ownership of stock for purposes of this section, except that sections 318(a)(2)(C) and 318(a)(3)(C) shall be applied without regard to the 50-percent limitation contained therein.

- **1978, Revenue Act of 1978 (P.L. 95-600)**

P.L. 95-600, §701(v)(1):

Amended Code Sec. 1239(a) by striking out "subject to the allowance for depreciation provided in section 167" and inserting in lieu thereof "of a character which is subject to the allowance for depreciation provided in section 167". **Effective** as set forth in P.L. 94-455, §2129(b), below.

- **1976, Tax Reform Act of 1976 (P.L. 94-455)**

P.L. 94-455, §2129(a):

Amended Code Sec. 1239. **Effective** as indicated in §2129(b) below. Prior to amendment, Code Sec. 1239 read as follows:

SEC. 1239. GAIN FROM SALE OF CERTAIN PROPERTY BETWEEN SPOUSES OR BETWEEN AN INDIVIDUAL AND A CONTROLLED CORPORATION.

(a) TREATMENT OF GAIN AS ORDINARY INCOME.—In the case of a sale or exchange, directly or indirectly, of property described in subsection (b)—

(1) between a husband and wife; or

(2) between an individual and a corporation more than 80 percent in value of the outstanding stock of which is owned by such individual, his spouse, and his minor children and minor grandchildren;

any gain recognized to the transferor from the sale or exchange of such property shall be considered as gain from the sale or exchange of property which is neither a capital asset nor property described in section 1231.

(b) SECTION APPLICABLE ONLY TO SALES OR EXCHANGES OF DEPRECIABLE PROPERTY.—This section shall apply only in the case of a sale or exchange by a transferor of property which in the hands of the transferee is property of a character which is subject to the allowance for depreciation provided in section 167.

(c) SECTION NOT APPLICABLE WITH RESPECT TO SALES OR EXCHANGES MADE ON OR BEFORE MAY 3, 1951.—This section shall apply only in the case of a sale or exchange made after May 3, 1951.

P.L. 94-455, §2129(b), provides:

(b) EFFECTIVE DATE.—The amendment made by this section shall apply to sales or exchanges after the date [October 4, 1976] of the enactment of this act. For purposes of the preceding sentence, a sale or exchange is considered to have occurred on or before such date of enactment if such sale or exchange is made pursuant to a binding contract entered into on or before that date.

- **1958, Technical Amendments Act of 1958 (P.L. 85-866)**

P.L. 85-866, §56:

Added Code Sec. 1239(c). **Effective** 1-1-54.

[Sec. 1239(d)]

(d) EMPLOYER AND RELATED EMPLOYEE ASSOCIATION.—For purposes of subsection (a), the term "related person" also includes—

(1) an employer and any person related to the employer (within the meaning of subsection (b)), and

(2) a welfare benefit fund (within the meaning of section 419(e)) which is controlled directly or indirectly by persons referred to in paragraph (1).

Amendments

- **1984, Deficit Reduction Act of 1984 (P.L. 98-369)**

P.L. 98-369, §557(a):

Amended Code Sec. 1239 by adding new subsection (d). **Effective** for sales or exchanges after 7-18-84, in tax years ending after such date.

[Sec. 1239(e)]

(e) PATENT APPLICATIONS TREATED AS DEPRECIABLE PROPERTY.—For purposes of this section, a patent application shall be treated as property which, in the hands of the transferee, is of a character which is subject to the allowance for depreciation provided in section 167.

Amendments

- **1984, Deficit Reduction Act of 1984 (P.L. 98-369)**

P.L. 98-369, §175(a):

Amended Code Sec. 1239 by adding new subsection (e). **Effective** for sales or exchanges after 3-1-84, in tax years ending after such date.

[Sec. 1241]

SEC. 1241. CANCELLATION OF LEASE OR DISTRIBUTOR'S AGREEMENT.

Amounts received by a lessee for the cancellation of a lease, or by a distributor of goods for the cancellation of a distributor's agreement (if the distributor has a substantial capital investment in the distributorship), shall be considered as amounts received in exchange for such lease or agreement.

[Sec. 1242]

SEC. 1242. LOSSES ON SMALL BUSINESS INVESTMENT COMPANY STOCK.

If—

(1) a loss is on stock in a small business investment company operating under the Small Business Investment Act of 1958, and

(2) such loss would (but for this section) be a loss from the sale or exchange of a capital asset,

then such loss shall be treated as an ordinary loss. For purposes of section 172 (relating to the net operating loss deduction) any amount of loss treated by reason of this section as an ordinary loss shall be treated as attributable to a trade or business of the taxpayer.

Amendments

- **1976, Tax Reform Act of 1976 (P.L. 94-455)**

P.L. 94-455, §1901(b)(3)(F):

Substituted "an ordinary loss" for "a loss from the sale or exchange of property which is not a capital asset" wherever it appeared in Code Sec. 1242. **Effective** with respect to tax years beginning after 12-31-76.

- **1958, Technical Amendments Act of 1958 (P.L. 85-866)**

P.L. 85-866, §57(a):

Added Code Sec. 1242. **Effective** for tax years beginning after 9-2-58.

INCOME TAX—CAPITAL GAINS, LOSSES

[Sec. 1243]
SEC. 1243. LOSS OF SMALL BUSINESS INVESTMENT COMPANY.

In the case of a small business investment company operating under the Small Business Investment Act of 1958, if—

(1) a loss is on stock received pursuant to the conversion privilege of convertible debentures acquired pursuant to section 304 of the Small Business Investment Act of 1958, and

(2) such loss would (but for this section) be a loss from the sale or exchange of a capital asset,

then such loss shall be treated as an ordinary loss.

Amendments

- **1976, Tax Reform Act of 1976 (P.L. 94-455)**

P.L. 94-455, §1901(b)(3)(F):

Substituted "an ordinary loss" for "a loss from the sale or exchange of property which is not a capital asset" in Code Sec. 1243. **Effective** with respect to tax years beginning after 12-31-76.

- **1969, Tax Reform Act of 1969 (P.L. 91-172)**

P.L. 91-172, §433(b):

Amended Code Sec. 1243(1). **Effective**, generally, for tax years beginning after 7-11-69. However, see P.L. 91-172, §433(d)(2), below. Prior to amendment, Code Sec. 1243(1) read as follows:

(1) a loss is on convertible debentures (including stock received pursuant to the conversion privilege) acquired pursuant to section 304 of the Small Business Investment Act of 1958, and

P.L. 91-172, §433(d)(2), provides:

(d)(2) Election for small business investment companies and business development corporations. — Notwithstanding paragraph (1) [General effective date—CCH.], in the case of a financial institution described in section 586(a) of the Internal Revenue Code of 1954, the amendments made by this section shall not apply for its taxable years beginning after July 11, 1969, and before July 11, 1974, unless the taxpayer so elects at such time and in such manner as shall be prescribed by the Secretary of the Treasury or his delegate. Such election shall be irrevocable and shall apply to all such taxable years.

- **1958, Technical Amendments Act of 1958 (P.L. 85-866)**

P.L. 85-866, §57(a):

Added Code Sec. 1243. **Effective** for tax years beginning after 9-2-58.

[Sec. 1244]
SEC. 1244. LOSSES ON SMALL BUSINESS STOCK.

[Sec. 1244(a)]

(a) GENERAL RULE.—In the case of an individual, a loss on section 1244 stock issued to such individual or to a partnership which would (but for this section) be treated as a loss from the sale or exchange of a capital asset shall, to the extent provided in this section, be treated as an ordinary loss.

Amendments

- **1976, Tax Reform Act of 1976 (P.L. 94-455)**

P.L. 94-455, §1901(b)(3)(G):

Substituted "an ordinary loss" for "a loss from the sale or exchange of an asset which is not a capital asset" in Code Sec. 1244(a). **Effective** with respect to tax years beginning after 12-31-76.

[Sec. 1244(b)]

(b) MAXIMUM AMOUNT FOR ANY TAXABLE YEAR.—For any taxable year the aggregate amount treated by the taxpayer by reason of this section as an ordinary loss shall not exceed—

(1) $50,000, or

(2) $100,000, in the case of a husband and wife filing a joint return for such year under section 6013.

Amendments

- **1978, Revenue Act of 1978 (P.L. 95-600)**

P.L. 95-600, §345(b):

Amended Code Sec. 1244(b) by striking out "$25,000" in paragraph (1) and inserting in lieu thereof "$50,000", and by striking out "$50,000" in paragraph (2) and inserting in lieu thereof "$100,000". **Effective** for stock issued after 12-6-78. See Act Sec. 345(e)(3), as added by P.L. 96-222, for a transitional rule.

P.L. 95-600, §345(e)(3), as amended by P.L. 96-222, §103(a)(9), provides:

(3) TRANSITIONAL RULE FOR SUBSECTION (b).—In the case of a taxable year which includes November 6, 1978, the amendments made by subsection (b) shall apply with respect to stock issued after such date.

- **1976, Tax Reform Act of 1976 (P.L. 94-455)**

P.L. 94-455, §1901(b)(3)(G):

Substituted "an ordinary loss" for "a loss from the sale or exchange of an asset which is not a capital asset" in Code Sec. 1244(b). **Effective** with respect to tax years beginning after 12-31-76.

[Sec. 1244(c)]

(c) SECTION 1244 STOCK DEFINED.—

(1) IN GENERAL.—For purposes of this section, the term "section 1244 stock" means stock in a domestic corporation if—

(A) at the time such stock is issued, such corporation was a small business corporation,

(B) such stock was issued by such corporation for money or other property (other than stock and securities), and

(C) such corporation, during the period of its 5 most recent taxable years ending before the date the loss on such stock was sustained, derived more than 50 percent of its aggregate gross receipts from sources other than royalties, rents, dividends, interests, annuities, and sales or exchanges of stocks or securities.

(2) RULES FOR APPLICATION OF PARAGRAPH (1)(C).—

(A) PERIOD TAKEN INTO ACCOUNT WITH RESPECT TO NEW CORPORATIONS.—For purposes of paragraph (1)(C), if the corporation has not been in existence for 5 taxable years ending before the date the loss on the stock was sustained, there shall be substituted for such 5-year period—

(i) the period of the corporation's taxable years ending before such date, or

(ii) if the corporation has not been in existence for 1 taxable year ending before such date, the period such corporation has been in existence before such date.

(B) GROSS RECEIPTS FROM SALES OF SECURITIES.—For purposes of paragraph (1)(C), gross receipts from the sales or exchanges of stock or securities shall be taken into account only to the extent of gains therefrom.

(C) NONAPPLICATION WHERE DEDUCTIONS EXCEED GROSS INCOME.—Paragraph (1)(C) shall not apply with respect to any corporation if, for the period taken into account for purposes of paragraph (1)(C), the amount of the deductions allowed by this chapter (other than by sections 172, 243, and 245) exceeds the amount of gross income.

(3) SMALL BUSINESS CORPORATION DEFINED.—

(A) IN GENERAL.—For purposes of this section, a corporation shall be treated as a small business corporation if the aggregate amount of money and other property received by the corporation for stock, as a contribution to capital, and as paid-in surplus, does not exceed

INCOME TAX—CAPITAL GAINS, LOSSES

$1,000,000. The determination under the preceding sentence shall be made as of the time of the issuance of the stock in question but shall include amounts received for such stock and for all stock theretofore issued.

(B) AMOUNT TAKEN INTO ACCOUNT WITH RESPECT TO PROPERTY.—For purposes of subparagraph (A), the amount taken into account with respect to any property other than money shall be the amount equal to the adjusted basis to the corporation of such property for determining gain, reduced by any liability to which the property was subject or which was assumed by the corporation. The determination under the preceding sentence shall be made as of the time the property was received by the corporation.

Amendments

• **2014, Tax Technical Corrections Act of 2014 (P.L. 113-295)**

P.L. 113-295, §221(a)(41)(H), Division A:

Amended Code Sec. 1244(c)(2)(C) by striking "244," following "sections 172, 243,". **Effective** generally 12-19-2014. For a special rule, see Act Sec. 221(b)(2), Division A, below.

P.L. 113-295, §221(b)(2), Division A, provides:

(2) SAVINGS PROVISION.—If—

(A) any provision amended or repealed by the amendments made by this section applied to—

(i) any transaction occurring before the date of the enactment of this Act,

(ii) any property acquired before such date of enactment, or

(iii) any item of income, loss, deduction, or credit taken into account before such date of enactment, and

(B) the treatment of such transaction, property, or item under such provision would (without regard to the amendments or repeals made by this section) affect the liability for tax for periods ending after date of enactment, nothing in the amendments or repeals made by this section shall be construed to affect the treatment of such transaction, property, or item for purposes of determining liability for tax for periods ending after such date of enactment.

• **1984, Deficit Reduction Act of 1984 (P.L. 98-369)**

P.L. 98-369, §481(a):

Amended Code Sec. 1244(c)(1) by striking out "common stock" and inserting in lieu thereof "stock". **Effective** for stock issued after 7-18-84, in tax years ending after such date.

• **1978, Revenue Act of 1978 (P.L. 95-600)**

P.L. 95-600, §345(a):

Amended Code Sec. 1244(c). **Effective** for stock issued after 11-6-78. Prior to amendment, Code Sec. 1244(c) read as follows:

(c) SECTION 1244 STOCK DEFINED.—

(1) IN GENERAL.—For purposes of this section, the term "section 1244 stock" means common stock in a domestic corporation if—

(A) such corporation adopted a plan after June 30, 1958, to offer such stock for a period (ending not later than two years after the date such plan was adopted) specified in the plan,

(B) at the time such plan was adopted, such corporation was a small business corporation,

(C) at the time such plan was adopted, no portion of a prior offering was outstanding,

(D) such stock was issued by such corporation, pursuant to such plan, for money or other property (other than stock and securities), and

(E) such corporation, during the period of its 5 most recent taxable years ending before the date the loss on such stock is sustained (or if such corporation has not been in existence for 5 taxable years ending before such date, during the period of its taxable years ending before such date, or if such corporation has not been in existence for one taxable year ending before such date, during the period such corporation has been in existence before such date), derived more than 50 percent of its aggregate gross receipts from sources other than royalties, rents, dividends, interest, annuities, and sales or exchanges of stock or securities (gross receipts from such sales or exchanges being taken into account for purposes of this subparagraph only to the extent of gains therefrom); except that this subparagraph shall not apply with respect to any corporation if, for the period referred to, the amount of the deductions allowed by this chapter (other than by sections 172, 243, 244, and 245) exceed the amount of gross income.

Such term does not include stock if issued (pursuant to the plan referred to in subparagraph (A)) after a subsequent offering of stock has been made by the corporation.

(2) SMALL BUSINESS CORPORATION DEFINED.—For purposes of this section, a corporation shall be treated as a small business corporation if at the time of the adoption of the plan—

(A) the sum of—

(i) the aggregate amount which may be offered under the plan, plus

(ii) the aggregate amount of money and other property (taken into account in an amount, as of the time received by the corporation, equal to the adjusted basis to the corporation of such property for determining gain, reduced by any liabilities to which the property was subject or which were assumed by the corporation at such time) received by the corporation after June 30, 1958, for stock, as a contribution to capital, and as paid-in surplus,

does not exceed $500,000; and

(B) the sum of—

(i) the aggregate amount which may be offered under the plan, plus

(ii) the equity capital of the corporation (determined on the date of the adoption of the plan),

does not exceed $1,000,000.

For purposes of subparagraph (B), the equity capital of a corporation is the sum of its money and other property (in an amount equal to the adjusted basis of such property for determining gain), less the amount of its indebtedness (other than indebtedness to shareholders).

• **1976, Tax Reform Act of 1976 (P.L. 94-455)**

P.L. 94-455, §1901(b)(1)(W):

Substituted "sections 172, 243" for "sections 172, 242, 243" in Code Sec. 1244(c)(1)(E). **Effective** with respect to tax years beginning after 12-31-76.

[Sec. 1244(d)]

(d) SPECIAL RULES.—

(1) LIMITATIONS ON AMOUNT OF ORDINARY LOSS.—

(A) CONTRIBUTIONS OF PROPERTY HAVING BASIS IN EXCESS OF VALUE.—If—

(i) section 1244 stock was issued in exchange for property,

(ii) the basis of such stock in the hands of the taxpayer is determined by reference to the basis in his hands of such property, and

(iii) the adjusted basis (for determining loss) of such property immediately before the exchange exceeded its fair market value at such time,

then in computing the amount of the loss on such stock for purposes of this section the basis of such stock shall be reduced by an amount equal to the excess described in clause (iii).

(B) INCREASES IN BASIS.—In computing the amount of the loss on stock for purposes of this section, any increase in the basis of such stock (through contributions to the capital of the corporation, or otherwise) shall be treated as allocable to stock which is not section 1244 stock.

(2) RECAPITALIZATIONS, CHANGES IN NAME, ETC.—To the extent provided in regulations prescribed by the Secretary, stock in a corporation, the basis of which (in the hands of a taxpayer) is determined in whole or in part by reference to the basis in his hands of stock in such corporation which meets the requirements of subsection (c)(1) (other than subparagraph (C) thereof), or which is received in a reorganization described in section 368(a)(1)(F) in exchange for stock which meets such requirements, shall be treated as meeting such requirements. For purposes of paragraphs (1)(C) and (3)(A) of subsection (c), a successor corporation in a reorganization described in section 368(a)(1)(F) shall be treated as the same corporation as its predecessor.

(3) RELATIONSHIP TO NET OPERATING LOSS DEDUCTION.—For purposes of section 172 (relating to the net operating loss deduction), any amount of loss treated by reason of this section as an ordinary loss shall be treated as attributable to a trade or business of the taxpayer.

(4) INDIVIDUAL DEFINED.—For purposes of this section, the term "individual" does not include a trust or estate.

Amendments

• **1984, Deficit Reduction Act of 1984 (P.L. 98-369)**

P.L. 98-369, §481(a):

Amended Code Sec. 1244(d)(2) by stiking out "common stock" and inserting in lieu thereof "stock". **Effective** for stock issued after 7-18-84, in tax years ending after such date.

• **1978, Revenue Act of 1978 (P.L. 95-600)**

P.L. 95-600, §345(d):

Amended Code Sec. 1244(d)(2) by striking out "subparagraph (E)" and inserting in lieu thereof "subparagraph (C)", and by striking out "paragraphs (1)(E) and (2)(A)" and inserting in lieu thereof "paragraphs (1)(C) and (3)(A)". **Effective** for stock issued after 11-6-78.

INCOME TAX—CAPITAL GAINS, LOSSES

• **1976, Tax Reform Act of 1976 (P.L. 94-455)**

P.L. 94-455, § 1901(b)(3)(G):

Substituted "an ordinary loss" for "a loss from the sale or exchange of an asset which is not a capital asset" in Code Sec. 1244(d). **Effective** with respect to tax years beginning after 12-31-76.

P.L. 94-455, § 1901(b)(13)(A):

Amended the 1954 Code by substituting "Secretary" for "Secretary or his delegate" each place it appeared. **Effective** 2-1-77.

[Sec. 1244(e)]

(e) REGULATIONS.—The Secretary shall prescribe such regulations as may be necessary to carry out the purposes of this section.

Amendments

• **1976, Tax Reform Act of 1976 (P.L. 94-455)**

P.L. 94-455, § 1906(b)(13)(A):

Amended 1954 Code by substituting "Secretary" for "Secretary or his delegate" each place it appeared. **Effective** 2-1-77.

• **1958, Technical Amendments Act of 1958 (P.L. 85-866)**

P.L. 85-866, § 202(b):

Added Sec. 1244. **Effective** 9-2-58.

[Sec. 1245]

SEC. 1245. GAIN FROM DISPOSITIONS OF CERTAIN DEPRECIABLE PROPERTY.

[Sec. 1245(a)]

(a) GENERAL RULE.—

(1) ORDINARY INCOME.—Except as otherwise provided in this section, if section 1245 property is disposed of the amount by which the lower of—

   (A) the recomputed basis of the property, or

   (B)(i) in the case of a sale, exchange, or involuntary conversion, the amount realized, or

   (ii) in the case of any other disposition, the fair market value of such property,

exceeds the adjusted basis of such property shall be treated as ordinary income. Such gain shall be recognized notwithstanding any other provision of this subtitle.

(2) RECOMPUTED BASIS.—For purposes of this section—

   (A) IN GENERAL.—The term "recomputed basis" means, with respect to any property, its adjusted basis recomputed by adding thereto all adjustments reflected in such adjusted basis on account of deductions (whether in respect of the same or other property) allowed or allowable to the taxpayer or to any other person for depreciation or amortization.

   (B) TAXPAYER MAY ESTABLISH AMOUNT ALLOWED.—For purposes of subparagraph (A), if the taxpayer can establish by adequate records or other sufficient evidence that the amount allowed for depreciation or amortization for any period was less than the amount allowable, the amount added for such period shall be the amount allowed.

   (C) CERTAIN DEDUCTIONS TREATED AS AMORTIZATION.—Any deduction allowable under section 179, 179B, 179C, 179D, 179E, 181, 190, 193, or 194 shall be treated as if it were a deduction allowable for amortization.

(3) SECTION 1245 PROPERTY.—For purposes of this section, the term "section 1245 property" means any property which is or has been property of a character subject to the allowance for depreciation provided in section 167 and is either—

   (A) personal property,

   (B) other property (not including a building or its structural components) but only if such other property is tangible and has an adjusted basis in which there are reflected adjustments described in paragraph (2) for a period in which such property (or other property)—

      (i) was used as an integral part of manufacturing, production, or extraction or of furnishing transportation, communications, electrical energy, gas, water, or sewage disposal services, or

      (ii) constituted a research facility used in connection with any of the activities referred to in clause (i), or

      (iii) constituted a facility used in connection with any of the activities referred to in clause (i) for the bulk storage of fungible commodities (including commodities in a liquid or gaseous state),

   (C) so much of any real property (other than any property described in subparagraph B)) which has an adjusted basis in which there are reflected adjustments for amortization under section 169, 179, 179B, 179C, 179D, 179E, 188 (as in effect before its repeal by the Revenue Reconciliation Act of 1990), 190, 193, or 194,

   (D) a single purpose agricultural or horticultural structure (as defined in section 168(i)(13)),

   (E) a storage facility (not including a building or its structural components) used in connection with the distribution of petroleum or any primary product of petroleum, or

   (F) any railroad grading or tunnel bore (as defined in section 168(e)(4)).

Amendments

• **2018, Tax Technical Corrections Act of 2018 (P.L. 115-141)**

P.L. 115-141, § 401(b)(31), Div. U:

Amended Code Sec. 1245(a)(3)(C) by striking ", 185" following ", 179E". **Effective** 3-23-2018. For a special rule, see Act Sec. 401(e), Div. U, below.

P.L. 115-141, § 401(e), Div. U, provides:

(e) GENERAL SAVINGS PROVISION WITH RESPECT TO DEADWOOD PROVISIONS.—If—

(1) any provision amended or repealed by the amendments made by subsection (b) or (d) applied to—

(A) any transaction occurring before the date of the enactment of this Act,

(B) any property acquired before such date of enactment, or

(C) any item of income, loss, deduction, or credit taken into account before such date of enactment, and

(2) the treatment of such transaction, property, or item under such provision would (without regard to the amendments or repeals made by such subsection) affect the liability for tax for periods ending after such date of enactment,

nothing in the amendments or repeals made by this section shall be construed to affect the treatment of such transaction, property, or item for purposes of determining liability for tax for periods ending after such date of enactment.

• **2014, Tax Technical Corrections Act of 2014 (P.L. 113-295)**

P.L. 113-295, § 221(a)(34)(H), Division A:

Amended Code Sec. 1245(a) by striking "179A," following "179," in paragraphs (2)(C) and (3)(C). **Effective** generally 12-19-2014. For a special rule, see Act Sec. 221(b)(2), Division A, below.

P.L. 113-295, § 221(b)(2), Division A, provides:

(2) SAVINGS PROVISION.—If—

(A) any provision amended or repealed by the amendments made by this section applied to—

(i) any transaction occurring before the date of the enactment of this Act,

(ii) any property acquired before such date of enactment, or

(iii) any item of income, loss, deduction, or credit taken into account before such date of enactment, and

(B) the treatment of such transaction, property, or item under such provision would (without regard to the amendments or repeals made by this section) affect the liability for tax for periods ending after date of enactment, nothing in the amendments or repeals made by this section shall be construed to affect the treatment of such transaction, property, or item for purposes of determining liability for tax for periods ending after such date of enactment.

INCOME TAX—CAPITAL GAINS, LOSSES

• **2006, Tax Relief and Health Care Act of 2006 (P.L. 109-432)**

P.L. 109-432, Division A, § 404(b)(3):

Amended Code Sec. 1245(a)(2)(C) and (3)(C) by inserting "179E," after "179D,". **Effective** for costs paid or incurred after 12-20-2006.

• **2005, Gulf Opportunity Zone Act of 2005 (P.L. 109-135)**

P.L. 109-135, § 403(e)(2):

Amended Code Sec. 1245(a)(2)(C) by inserting "181," after "179B,". **Effective** as if included in the provision of the American Jobs Creation Act of 2004 (P.L. 108-357) to which it relates [effective for qualified film and television productions commencing after 10-22-2004.—CCH].

P.L. 109-135, § 403(i)(2):

Amended Code Sec. 1245(a)(2)(C) by striking "or 193" and inserting "193, or 194". **Effective** as if included in the provision of the American Jobs Creation Act of 2004 (P.L. 108-357) to which it relates [effective for expenditures paid or incurred after 10-22-2004.—CCH].

• **2005, Energy Tax Incentives Act of 2005 (P.L. 109-58)**

P.L. 109-58, § 1323(b)(1):

Amended Code Sec. 1245(a) by inserting "179C," after "179B," both places it appears in paragraphs (2)(C) and (3)(C). **Effective** for properties placed in service after 8-8-2005.

P.L. 109-58, § 1331(b)(2):

Amended Code Sec. 1245(a), as amended by this Act, by inserting "179D," after "179C," both places it appears in paragraphs (2)(C) and (3)(C). **Effective** for property placed in service after 12-31-2005.

• **2004, American Jobs Creation Act of 2004 (P.L. 108-357)**

P.L. 108-357, § 338(b)(5):

Amended Code Sec. 1245(a)(2)(C) and (3)(C) by inserting "179B," after "179A,". **Effective** for expenses paid or incurred after 12-31-2002, in tax years ending after such date.

P.L. 108-357, § 886(b)(2):

Amended Code Sec. 1245(a) by striking paragraph (4). **Effective** for franchises acquired after 10-22-2004. Prior to being stricken, Code Sec. 1245(a)(4) read as follows:

(4) SPECIAL RULE FOR PLAYER CONTRACTS.—

(A) IN GENERAL.—For purposes of this section, if a franchise to conduct any sports enterprise is sold or exchanged, and if, in connection with such sale or exchange, there is a transfer of any player contracts, the recomputed basis of such player contracts in the hands of the transferor shall be the adjusted basis of such contracts increased by the greater of—

(i) the previously unrecaptured depreciation with respect to player contracts acquired by the transferor at the time of acquisition of such franchise, or

(ii) the previously unrecaptured depreciation with respect to the player contracts involved in such transfer.

(B) PREVIOUSLY UNRECAPTURED DEPRECIATION WITH RESPECT TO INITIAL CONTRACTS.—For purposes of subparagraph (A)(i), the term "previously unrecaptured depreciation" means the excess (if any) of—

(i) the sum of the deduction allowed or allowable to the taxpayer transferor for the depreciation attributable to periods after December 31, 1975, of any player contracts acquired by him at the time of acquisition of such franchise, plus the deduction allowed or allowable for losses incurred after December 31, 1975, with respect to such player contracts acquired at the time of such acquisition, over

(ii) the aggregate of the amounts described in clause (i) treated as ordinary income by reason of this section with respect to prior dispositions of such player contracts acquired upon acquisition of the franchise.

(C) PREVIOUSLY UNRECAPTURED DEPRECIATION WITH RESPECT TO CONTRACTS TRANSFERRED.—For purposes of subparagraph (A)(ii), the term "previously unrecaptured depreciation" means the amount of any deduction allowed or allowable to the taxpayer transferor for the depreciation of any contracts involved in such transfer.

(D) PLAYER CONTRACT.—For purposes of this paragraph, the term "player contract" means any contract for the services of an athlete which, in the hands of the taxpayer, is of a character subject to the allowance for depreciation provided in section 167.

• **1997, Taxpayer Relief Act of 1997 (P.L. 105-34)**

P.L. 105-34, § 1604(a)(3):

Amended Code Sec. 1245(a)(2)(C) and (3)(C) by inserting "179A," after "179,". **Effective** as if included in the amendments made by Act Sec. 1913 of P.L. 102-486 [effective for property placed in service after 6-30-93.—CCH].

• **1996, Small Business Job Protection Act of 1996 (P.L. 104-188)**

P.L. 104-188, § 1703(n)(6):

Amended so much of Code Sec. 1245(a)(3) as precedes subparagraph (A). **Effective** as if included in the provision of P.L. 103-66 to which it relates. Prior to amendment, Code Sec. 1245(a)(3) preceding subparagraph (A) read as follows:

(3) SECTION 1245 PROPERTY.—For purposes of this section, the term "section 1245 property" means any property which is or has been property of a character subject to the allowance for depreciation provided in section 167 (or subject to the allowance of amortization provided in section 197 and is either—

• **1993, Omnibus Budget Reconciliation Act of 1993 (P.L. 103-66)**

P.L. 103-66, § 13261(f)(4):

Amended Code Sec. 1245(a)(2)(C) by striking "193, or 1253(d)(2) or (3)" and inserting "or 193". **Effective** with respect to property acquired after 8-10-93. For special rules, see Act Sec. 13261(g)(2)-(3) in the amendment notes following Code Sec. 197.

P.L. 103-66, § 13261(f)(5):

Amended Code Sec. 1245(a)(3) by striking "section 185 or 1253(d)(2) or (3)" [and inserting "section 197"]. **Effective** with respect to property acquired after 8-10-93. For special rules, see Act Sec. 13261(g)(2)-(3) in the amendment notes following Code Sec. 197.

• **1990, Omnibus Budget Reconciliation Act of 1990 (P.L. 101-508)**

P.L. 101-508, § 11704(a)(13):

Amended Code Sec. 1245(a)(3) by striking "or (3)" in the material preceding subparagraph (A) and inserting "or (3))". **Effective** 11-5-90.

P.L. 101-508, § 11801(c)(6)(E):

Amended Code Sec. 1245(a)(3)(C) by striking "188," and inserting "188 (as in effect before its repeal by the Revenue Reconciliation Act of 1990)". **Effective** 11-5-90.

P.L. 101-508, § 11821(b), provides:

(b) SAVINGS PROVISION.—If—

(1) any provision amended or repealed by this part applied to—

(A) any transaction occurring before the date of the enactment of this Act,

(B) any property acquired before such date of enactment, or

(C) any item of income, loss, deduction, or credit taken into account before such date of enactment, and

(2) the treatment of such transaction, property, or item under such provision would (without regard to the amendments made by this part) affect liability for tax for periods ending after such date of enactment,

nothing in the amendments made by this part shall be construed to affect the treatment of such transaction, property, or item for purposes of determining liability for tax for periods ending after such date of enactment.

P.L. 101-508, § 11813(b)(21):

Amended Code Sec. 1245(a)(3)(D) by striking "section 48(p)" and inserting "section 168(i)(13)". **Effective**, generally, for property placed in service after 12-31-90. However, for exceptions, see Act Sec. 11813(c)(2) below.

P.L. 101-508, § 11813(c)(2), provides:

(2) EXCEPTIONS.—The amendments made by this section shall not apply to—

(A) any transition property (as defined in section 49(e) of the Internal Revenue Code of 1986 (as in effect on the day before the date of the enactment of this Act),

(B) any property with respect to which qualified progress expenditures were previously taken into account under section 46(d) of such Code (as so in effect), and

(C) any property described in section 46(b)(2)(C) of such Code (as so in effect).

• **1989, Omnibus Budget Reconciliation Act of 1989 (P.L. 101-239)**

P.L. 101-239, § 7622(b)[d](2)(A):

Amended Code Sec. 1245(a)(2)(C) by striking "or 193" and inserting "193, or 1253(d)(2) or (3)". **Effective** for transfers after 10-2-89. For a special rule, see Act Sec. 7622(c)[e](2), below.

P.L. 101-239, § 7622(b)[d](2)(B):

Amended Code Sec. 1245(a)(3) by striking "section 185" in the material preceding subparagraph (A) and inserting "section 185 or 1253(d)(2) or (3)". **Effective** for transfers after 10-2-89. For a special rule, see Act Sec. 7622(c)[e](2), below.

P.L. 101-239, § 7622(c)[e](2), provides:

(2) BINDING CONTRACT.—The amendments made by this section shall not apply to any transfer pursuant to a written binding contract in effect on October 2, 1989, and at all times thereafter before the transfer.

• **1988, Technical and Miscellaneous Revenue Act of 1988 (P.L. 100-647)**

P.L. 100-647, § 1002(i)(2)(I):

Amended Code Sec. 1245(a)(3) by striking out "or" at the end of subparagraph (D), by striking out the period at the end of subparagraph (E) and inserting in lieu thereof ", or", and by adding at the end thereof a new subparagraph (F). **Effective** as if included in the provision of P.L. 99-514 to which it relates.

• **1986, Tax Reform Act of 1986 (P.L. 99-514)**

P.L. 99-514, § 201(d)(11)(A):

Amended Code Sec. 1245(a)(1) by striking out "during a taxable year beginning after December 31, 1962, or section 1245 recovery property is disposed of after December 31, 1980,". **Effective**, generally, for property placed in service after 12-31-86, in tax years ending after such date. However, for special and transitional rules, see Act Sec. 203 following Code Sec. 168. Prior to amendment Code Sec. 1245(a)(1) read as follows:

(1) ORDINARY INCOME.—Except as otherwise provided in this section, if section 1245 property is disposed of during a taxable year beginning after December 31, 1962, or section 1245 recovery property is disposed of after December 31, 1980, the amount by which the lower of—

P.L. 99-514, § 201(d)(11)(B):

Amended Code Sec. 1245(a)(2). **Effective**, generally, for property placed in service after 12-31-86, in tax years ending after such date. However, for special and transitional rules, see Act Sec. 203 following Code Sec. 168. Prior to amendment, Code Sec. 1245(a)(2) read as follows:

(2) RECOMPUTED BASIS.—For purposes of this section, the term "recomputed basis" means—

(A) with respect to any property referred to in paragraph (3)(A) or (B), its adjusted basis recomputed by adding thereto all adjustments attributable to periods after December 31, 1961,

(B) with respect to any property referred to in paragraph (3)(C), its adjusted basis recomputed by adding thereto all adjustments attributable to periods after June 30, 1963,

INCOME TAX—CAPITAL GAINS, LOSSES

(C) with respect to livestock, its adjusted basis recomputed by adding thereto all adjustments attributable to periods after December 31, 1969,

(D) with respect to any property referred to in paragraph (3)(D), its adjusted basis recomputed by adding thereto all adjustments attributable to periods beginning with the first month for which a deduction for amortization is allowed under section 169, 179, 185, 190, 193, or 194, or

(E) with respect to any section 1245 recovery property, the adjusted basis of such property recomputed by adding thereto all adjustments attributable to periods for which a deduction is allowed under section 168(a) (as added by the Economic Recovery Tax Act of 1981) with respect to such property,

reflected in such adjusted basis on account of deductions (whether in respect of the same or other property) allowed or allowable to the taxpayer or to any other person for depreciation, or for amortization under section 168 (as in effect before its repeal by the Tax Reform Act of 1976), 169, 179, 184, 185, 188, 190, 193, 194, or (in the case of property described in paragraph (3)(C)) 191 (as in effect before its repeal by the Economic Recovery Tax Act of 1981). For purposes of the preceding sentence, if the taxpayer can establish by adequate records or other sufficient evidence that the amount allowed for depreciation, or for amortization under section 168 (as in effect before its repeal by the Tax Reform Act of 1976), 169, 179, 184, 185, 188, 190, 193, 194, or (in the case of property described in paragraph (3)(C)) 191 (as in effect before its repeal by the Economic Recovery Tax Act of 1981), for any period was less than the amount allowable, the amount added for such period shall be the amount allowed. For purposes of this section, any deduction allowable under section 179, 190, 193, or 194 shall be treated as if it were a deduction allowable for amortization.

P.L. 99-514, § 201(d)(11)(C):

Amended Code Sec. 1245(a)(3) by striking out subparagraph (C) and redesignating subparagraphs (D), (E), and (F) as subparagraphs (C), (D), and (E), respectively. **Effective**, generally, for property placed in service after 12-31-86, in tax years ending after such date. However, for special and transitional rules, see Act Sec. 203 following Code Sec. 168. Prior to amendment, subparagraph (C) read as follows:

an elevator or an escalator,

P.L. 99-514, § 201(d)(11)(D):

Amended Code Sec. 1245(a) by striking out paragraphs (5) and (6). **Effective**, generally, for property placed in service after 12-31-86, in tax years ending after such date. However, for special and transitional rules, see Act Sec. 203 following Code Sec. 168. Prior to amendment, Code Sec. 1245(a)(5) and (6) read as follows:

(5) SECTION 1245 RECOVERY PROPERTY.—For purposes of this section, the term "section 1245 recovery property" means recovery property (within the meaning of section 168) other than—

(A) 19-year real property and low-income housing which is residential rental property (as defined in section 167(j)(2)(B)),

(B) 19-year real property and low-income housing which is described in section 168(f)(2),

(C) 19-year real property and low-income housing with respect to which an election under subsection (b)(3) of section 168 to use a different recovery percentage is in effect, and

(D) low-income housing (within the meaning of section 168(c)(2)(F)).

If only a portion of a building (or other structure) is section 1245 recovery property, gain from any disposition of such building (or other structure) shall be allocated first to the portion of the building (or other structure) which is section 1245 recovery property (to the extent of the amount which may be treated as ordinary income under this section) and then to the portion of the building or other structure which is not section 1245 recovery property.

(6) SPECIAL RULE FOR QUALIFIED LEASED PROPERTY.—In any case in which—

(A) the lessor of qualified leased property (within the meaning of section 168(f)(8)(d)) is treated as the owner of such property for purposes of this subtitle under section 168(f)(8), and

(B) the lessee acquires such property,

the recomputed basis of the lessee under this subsection shall be determined by taking into account any adjustments which would be taken into account in determining the recomputed basis of the lessor.

• **1985 (P.L. 99-121)**

P.L. 99-121, § 103(b)(1)(D):

Amended Code Sec. 1245(a)(5)(A), (B), and (C) by striking out "18-year real property" each place it appeared in the text and headings thereof and inserting in lieu thereof "19-year real property". **Effective** with respect to property placed in service by the taxpayer after 5-8-85. However, for an exception, see Act Sec. 105(b)(2), below.

P.L. 99-121, § 105(b)(2), provides:

(2) EXCEPTION.—The amendments made by section 103 shall not apply to property placed in service by the taxpayer before January 1, 1987, if—

(A) the taxpayer or a qualified person entered into a binding contract to purchase or construct such property before May 9, 1985, or

(B) construction of such property was commenced by or for the taxpayer or a qualified person before May 9, 1985.

For purposes of this paragraph, the term "qualified person" means any person whose rights in such a contract or such property are transferred to the taxpayer, but only if such property is not placed in service before such rights are transferred to the taxpayer.

• **1984, Deficit Reduction Act of 1984 (P.L. 98-369)**

P.L. 98-369, § 111(e)(5):

Amended Code Sec. 1245(A)[(a)](5)(A), (B) and (C) by striking out "15-year real property" each place it appeared and inserting in lieu thereof "18-year real property and low-income housing". **Effective** with respect to property placed in service by the taxpayer after 3-15-84. For special rules, see Act Sec. 111(g) in the amendment notes following Code Sec. 168(f).

P.L. 98-369, § 111(e)(10):

Amended Code Sec. 1245(a)(5)(D). **Effective** with respect to property placed in service by the taxpayer after 3-15-84. For special rules, see Act Sec. 111(g) in the amendment notes following Code Sec. 168(f). Prior to amendment, it read as follows:

(D) 15-year real property which is described in clause (i), (ii), (iii), or (iv) of section 1250(a)(1)(B).

• **1983, Technical Corrections Act of 1982 (P.L. 97-448)**

P.L. 97-448, § 102(e)(2)(B):

Amended Code Sec. 1245(a)(3)(F) by inserting "(not including a building or its structural components)" after "storage facility". **Effective** as if included in the provision of P.L. 97-34 to which it relates.

P.L. 97-448, § 102(f)(1):

Amended subparagraph (B) of section 212(e)(2) of P.L. 97-34 to read as under the amendment note for P.L. 97-34, § 212(e)(2).

• **1981, Economic Recovery Tax Act of 1981 (P.L. 97-34)**

P.L. 97-34, § 201(b):

Amended Code Sec. 1245(a)(3) by striking out "or" at the end of subparagraph (C), by striking out the period at the end of subparagraph (D), and by adding at the end thereof new subparagraphs (E) and (F). **Effective** for property placed in service after 12-31-80, in tax years ending after such date.

P.L. 97-34, § 202(b):

Amended Code Sec. 1245(a) by striking out "169, 184" each place it appeared in paragraph (2) and inserting in lieu thereof "169, 179, 184"; by striking out "section 190" in paragraph (2) and inserting in lieu thereof "section 179, 190"; and by striking out "169, 185" in paragraphs (2)(D) and (3)(D) and inserting in lieu thereof "169, 179, 185". **Effective** for property placed in service after 12-31-80, in tax years ending after such date.

P.L. 97-34, § 204(a):

Amended Code Sec. 1245(a)(1) by inserting after "December 31, 1962," "or section 1245 recovery property is disposed of after December 31, 1980". **Effective** for property placed in service after 12-31-80, in tax years ending after such date.

P.L. 97-34, § 204(b):

Amended Code Sec. 1245(a)(2) by striking out "or" at the end of subparagraph (C); by inserting, "or" at the end of subparagraph (D), and by inserting immediately after subparagraph (D) new subparagraph (E). **Effective** for property placed in service after 12-31-80, in tax years ending after such date.

P.L. 97-34, § 204(c), (d):

Amended Code Sec. 1245(a) by ending at the end thereof new paragraphs (5) and (6). **Effective** for property placed in service after 12-31-80, in tax years ending after such date.

P.L. 97-34, § 212(d)(2)(F):

Amended Code Sec. 1245(a)(2) by inserting "(as in effect before its repeal by the Economic Recovery Tax Act of 1981)" after "191" each place it appeared. **Effective** for expenditures incurred after 12-31-81, in tax years ending after such date.

P.L. 97-34, § 212(e)(2), provides:

(2) TRANSITIONAL RULE.—The amendments made by this section shall not apply with respect to any rehabilitation of a building if—

(A) the physical work on such rehabilitation began before January 1, 1982, and

(B) such building does not meet the requirements of paragraph (1) of section 48(g) of the Internal Revenue Code of 1954 (as amended by this Act).

• **1980, Recreational Boating Safety and Facilities Improvement Act of 1980 (P.L. 96-451)**

P.L. 96-451, § 301(c)(1):

Amended Code Sec. 1245(a) by striking out "190, 193" each place it occurred in paragraph (2) and inserting in its place "190, 193, 194" and by striking out in paragraphs (2) and 3(D) "or 193" and inserting "193, or 194". **Effective** with respect to additions to capital account made after 12-31-79. (Note: An earlier Code Section 194 was added by P.L. 96-364, enacted on 9-26-80.)

• **1980, Crude Oil Windfall Profit Tax Act of 1980 (P.L. 96-223)**

P.L. 96-223, § 251(a)(2)(C):

Amended Code Sec. 1245(a) by striking out "or 190" each place it appeared in paragraphs (2)(D) and (3)(D) and inserting "190, or 193", by inserting "193," after "190," each place it appeared in paragraph (2) and by inserting "or 193" after "190" in the last sentence of paragraph (2). **Effective** for tax years beginning after 12-31-79.

• **1978, Revenue Act of 1978 (P.L. 95-600)**

P.L. 95-600, § 701(f)(3)(A):

Amended Code Sec. 1245(a)(2) by striking out "190 or 191" in subparagraph (D) and inserting in lieu thereof "or 190", and by striking out "190, or 191" wherever else it appeared and inserting in lieu thereof "190, or (in the case of property described in paragraph (3)(C)) 191". **Effective** with respect to additions to capital account made after 6-14-76 and before 6-15-81.

P.L. 95-600, § 701(f)(3)(B):

Amended Code Sec. 1245(a)(3)(D) by striking out "190, or 191" and inserting in lieu thereof "or 190". **Effective** with respect to additions to capital account made after 6-14-76 and before 6-15-81.

P.L. 95-600, § 701(w)(1):

Amended Code Sec. 1245(a)(4)(C). **Effective** for transfers of player contracts in connection with any sale or exchange of a franchise after 12-31-75. Prior to amendment, Code Sec. 1245(a)(4)(C) read as follows:

Sec. 1245(a)(3)(F)

INCOME TAX—CAPITAL GAINS, LOSSES

"(C) PREVIOUSLY UNRECAPTURED DEPRECIATION WITH RESPECT TO CONTRACTS TRANSFERRED.—For purposes of subparagraph (A)(ii), the term "previously unrecaptured depreciation" means—

(i) the amount of any deduction allowed or allowable to the taxpayer transferor for the depreciation of any contracts involved in such transfer, over

(ii) the aggregate of the amounts treated as ordinary income by reason of this section with respect to prior dispositions of such player contracts acquired upon acquisition of the franchise."

P.L. 95-600, §701(w)(2):

Amended Code Sec. 1245(a)(4)(B). **Effective** for transfers of player contracts in connection with any sale or exchange of a franchise after 12-31-75. Prior to amendment, Code Sec. 1245(a)(4)(B) read as follows:

(B) PREVIOUSLY UNRECAPTURED DEPRECIATION WITH RESPECT TO INITIAL CONTRACTS.—For purposes of subparagraph (A)(i), the term "previously unrecaptured depreciation" means the excess (if any) of—

(i) the sum of the deduction allowed or allowable to the taxpayer transferor for the depreciation of any player contracts acquired by him at the time of acquisition of such franchise, plus the deduction allowed or allowable for losses with respect to such player contracts acquired at the time of such acquisition, over

(ii) the aggregate of the amounts treated as ordinary income by reason of this section with respect to prior dispositions of such player contracts acquired upon acquisition of the franchise.

• **1976, Tax Reform Act of 1976 (P.L. 94-455)**

P.L. 94-455, §212(b)(1):

Added Code Sec. 1245(a)(4). **Effective** for transfers of player contracts in connection with any sale or exchange of a franchise after 12-31-75.

P.L. 94-455, §1901(b)(3)(K):

Substituted "ordinary income" for "gain from the sale or exchange of property which is neither a capital asset nor property described in section 1231" in Code Sec. 1245(a)(1). **Effective** with respect to tax years beginning after 12-31-76.

P.L. 94-455, §1901(b)(11)(D):

Deleted "187" each place it appeared in Code Sec. 1245(a)(2). **Effective** with respect to tax years beginning after 12-31-76.

P.L. 94-455, §1951(c)(2)(C):

Substituted "168 (as in effect before its repeal by the Tax Reform Act of 1976)," for "168," wherever it appeared in Code Sec. 1245(a)(2). **Effective** for tax years beginning after 12-31-76.

P.L. 94-455, §2122(b)(3)(A):

Substituted "188, or 190" for "or 188" wherever it appeared in Code Sec. 1245(a)(2) and (3). **Effective** for tax years beginning after 12-31-76, and before 1-1-80.

P.L. 94-455, §2122(b)(3)(B):

Substituted "185, or 190" for "or 185" in Code Sec. 1245(a)(2)(D). **Effective** for tax years beginning after 12-31-76, and before 1-1-80.

P.L. 94-455, §2122(b)(3)(C):

Added the following new sentence "For purposes of this section, any deduction allowable under section 190 shall be treated as if it were a deduction allowable for amortization." to the end of Code Sec. 1245(a)(2). **Effective** for tax years beginning after 12-31-76, and before 1-1-80.

P.L. 94-455, §2124(a)(2):

Substituted "190, or 191" for "or 190" wherever it appeared in Code Sec. 1245(a). **Effective** for additions to capital account made after 6-14-76 and before 6-15-81.

• **1971, Revenue Act of 1971 (P.L. 92-178)**

P.L. 92-178, §104(a)(2):

Substituted clauses (ii) and (iii) in subparagraph (B) of Code Sec. 1245(a)(3) for the following:

"(ii) constituted research or storage facilities used in connection with any of the activities referred to in clause (i)". **Effective** for property described in code Sec. 50.

P.L. 92-178, §303(c)(1):

Substituted "187, or 188" for "or 187" in the last two sentences of Code Sec. 1245(a)(2). **Effective** for tax years ending after 12-31-71.

P.L. 92-178, §303(c)(2):

Substituted ", 185, or 188" for "or 185" in subparagraph (D) of Code Sec. 1245(a)(3). **Effective** for tax years ending after 12-31-71.

• **1969, Tax Reform Act of 1969 (P.L. 91-172)**

P.L. 91-172, §212(a)(1):

Amended Code Sec. 1245(a)(2) by striking out "or" at the end of subparagraph (A) and by inserting subparagraph (C) immediately after subparagraph (B). **Effective** for tax years beginning after 12-31-69.

P.L. 91-172, §212(a)(2):

Amended Code Sec. 1245(a)(3) by striking out "(other than livestock)". **Effective** for tax years beginning after 12-31-69. Before amendment, Code Sec. 1245(a)(3) read as follows:

(3) Section 1245 property.—For purposes of this section, the term "section 1245 property" means any property (other than livestock) which is or has been property of a character subject to the allowance for depreciation provided in section 167 and is either—

(A) personal property, or

(B) other property (not including a building or its structural components) but only if such other property is tangible and has an adjusted basis in which there are reflected adjustments described in paragraph (2) for a period in which such property (or other property)—

(i) was used as an integral part of manufacturing, production, or extraction or of furnishing transportation, communications, electrical energy, gas, water, or sewage disposal services, or

(ii) constituted research or storage facilities used in connection with any of the activities referred to in clause (i), or

(C) an elevator or an escalator.

P.L. 91-172, §704(b)(4):

Amended Code Sec. 1245(a)(2) by adding Code Sec. 1245(a)(2)(D), and struck out "168" and inserted in lieu thereof "168, 169, 184, 185, or 187". **Effective** for tax years ending after 12-31-68.

P.L. 91-172, §704(b)(4):

Added Code Sec. 1245(a)(3)(D) and amended Code Sec. 1245(a)(3) by striking out "section 167" and inserting in lieu thereof "section 167 (or subject to the allowance for amortization provided in section 185)"; by striking out "or" and the end of Code Secs. 1245(a)(3)(A) and 1245(a)(3)(B) and; by striking out the period at the end of Code Sec. 1245(a)(3)(C) and substituting ",or" in place thereof. **Effective** for tax years ending after 12-31-68.

• **1964, Revenue Act of 1964 (P.L. 88-272)**

P.L. 88-272, §203(d):

Amended paragraph (2). **Effective** with respect to dispositions after 12-31-63, in tax years ending after such date. Prior to amendment, paragraph (2) read as follows:

(2) Recomputed basis.—For purposes of this section, the term "recomputed basis" means, with respect to any property, its adjusted basis recomputed by adding thereto all adjustments, attributable to periods after December 31, 1961, reflected in such adjusted basis on account of deductions (whether in respect of the same or other property) allowed or allowable to the taxpayer or to any other person for depreciation, or for amortization under section 168: For purposes of the preceding sentence, if the taxpayer can establish by adequate records or other sufficient evidence that the amount allowed for depreciation, or for amortization under section 168, for any period was less than the amount allowable, the amount added for such period shall be the amount allowed.

Amended paragraph (3) by adding subparagraph (C) thereto. The amendment is effective with respect to dispositions after December 31, 1963, in taxable years ending after such date.

[Sec. 1245(b)]

(b) EXCEPTIONS AND LIMITATIONS.—

(1) GIFTS.—Subsection (a) shall not apply to a disposition by gift.

(2) TRANSFERS AT DEATH.—Except as provided in section 691 (relating to income in respect of a decedent), subsection (a) shall not apply to a transfer at death.

(3) CERTAIN TAX-FREE TRANSACTIONS.—If the basis of property in the hands of a transferee is determined by reference to its basis in the hands of the transferor by reason of the application of section 332, 351, 361, 721, or 731, then the amount of gain taken into account by the transferor under subsection (a)(1) shall not exceed the amount of gain recognized to the transferor on the transfer of such property (determined without regard to this section). Except as provided in paragraph (6), this paragraph shall not apply to a disposition to an organization (other than a cooperative described in section 521) which is exempt from the tax imposed by this chapter.

(4) LIKE KIND EXCHANGES; INVOLUNTARY CONVERSIONS, ETC.—If property is disposed of and gain (determined without regard to this section) is not recognized in whole or in part under section 1031 or 1033, then the amount of gain taken into account by the transferor under subsection (a)(1) shall not exceed the sum of—

(A) the amount of gain recognized on such disposition (determined without regard to this section), plus

(B) the fair market value of property acquired which is not section 1245 property and which is not taken into account under subparagraph (A).

(5) PROPERTY DISTRIBUTED BY A PARTNERSHIP TO A PARTNER.—

(A) IN GENERAL.—For purposes of this section, the basis of section 1245 property distributed by a partnership to a partner shall be deemed to be determined by reference to the adjusted basis of such property to the partnership.

(B) ADJUSTMENTS ADDED BACK.—In the case of any property described in subparagraph (A), for purposes of computing the recomputed basis of such property the amount of the adjustments added back for periods before the distribution by the partnership shall be—

INCOME TAX—CAPITAL GAINS, LOSSES

(i) the amount of the gain to which subsection (a) would have applied if such property had been sold by the partnership immediately before the distribution at its fair market value at such time, reduced by

(ii) the amount of such gain to which section 751(b) applied.

(6) TRANSFERS TO TAX-EXEMPT ORGANIZATION WHERE PROPERTY WILL BE USED IN UNRELATED BUSINESS.—

(A) IN GENERAL.—The second sentence of paragraph (3) shall not apply to a disposition of section 1245 property to an organization described in section 511(a)(2) or 511(b)(2) if, immediately after such disposition, such organization uses such property in an unrelated trade or business (as defined in section 513).

(B) LATER CHANGE IN USE.—If any property with respect to the disposition of which gain is not recognized by reason of subparagraph (A) ceases to be used in an unrelated trade or business of the organization acquiring such property, such organization shall be treated for purposes of this section as having disposed of such property on the date of such cessation.

(7) TIMBER PROPERTY.—In determining, under subsection (a)(2), the recomputed basis of property with respect to which a deduction under section 194 was allowed for any taxable year, the taxpayer shall not take into account adjustments under section 194 to the extent such adjustments are attributable to the amortizable basis of the taxpayer acquired before the 10th taxable year preceding the taxable year in which gain with respect to the property is recognized.

(8) DISPOSITION OF AMORTIZABLE SECTION 197 INTANGIBLES.—

(A) IN GENERAL.—If a taxpayer disposes of more than 1 amortizable section 197 intangible (as defined in section 197(c)) in a transaction or a series of related transactions, all such amortizable 197 intangibles shall be treated as 1 section 1245 property for purposes of this section.

(B) EXCEPTION.—Subparagraph (A) shall not apply to any amortizable section 197 intangible (as so defined) with respect to which the adjusted basis exceeds the fair market value.

Amendments

• **2005, Gulf Opportunity Zone Act of 2005 (P.L. 109-135)**

P.L. 109-135, §402(a)(6)(A):

Amended Code Sec. 1245(b) by striking paragraph (5) and redesignating paragraphs (6) through (9) as paragraphs (5) through (8), respectively. **Effective** as if included in the provision of the Energy Policy Act of 2005 (P.L. 109-58) to which it relates [**effective** 2-8-2006.—CCH]. For a special rule, see Act Sec. 402(m)(2), below. Prior to being stricken, Code Sec. 1245(b)(5) read as follows:

(5) SECTION 1081 TRANSACTIONS.—Under regulations prescribed by the Secretary, rules consistent with paragraphs (3) and (4) of this subsection shall apply in the case of transactions described in section 1081 (relating to exchanges in obedience to SEC orders).

P.L. 109-135, §402(a)(6)(B):

Amended Code Sec. 1245(b)(3) by striking "paragraph (7)" and inserting "paragraph (6)". **Effective** as if included in the provision of the Energy Policy Act of 2005 (P.L. 109-58) to which it relates [**effective** 2-8-2006.—CCH]. For a special rule, see Act Sec. 402(m)(2), below.

P.L. 109-135, §402(m)(2), provides:

(2) REPEAL OF PUBLIC UTILITY HOLDING COMPANY ACT OF 1935.—The amendments made by subsection (a) shall not apply with respect to any transaction ordered in compliance with the Public Utility Holding Company Act of 1935 before its repeal.

• **2005, Energy Tax Incentives Act of 2005 (P.L. 109-58)**

P.L. 109-58, §1363(a):

Amended Code Sec. 1245(b) by adding at the end a new paragraph (9). **Effective** for dispositions of property after 8-8-2005.

• **1995, Self-Employed Health Insurance Act (P.L. 104-7)**

P.L. 104-7, §2(b)(1)-(2):

Amended Code Sec. 1245(b)(5) by striking "section 1071 (relating to gain from sale or exchange to effectuate polices [policies]of FCC) or" following "described in", and by striking "1071 AND" following "SECTION" in the heading. **Effective**, generally, for sales and exchanges on or after 1-17-95, and sales and exchanges before such date if the FCC tax certificate with respect to such sale or exchange is issued on or after such date. For special rules, see Act Sec. 2(d)(2)-(3) in the amendment notes following repealed Code Sec. 1071.

• **1990, Omnibus Budget Reconciliation Act of 1990 (P.L. 101-508)**

P.L. 101-508, §11801(c)(8)(H):

Amended Code Sec. 1245(b)(3) by striking "371(a), 374(a)," after "361". **Effective** 11-5-90.

P.L. 101-508, §1821(b), provides:

(b) SAVINGS PROVISION.—If—

(1) any provision amended or repealed by this part applied to—

(A) any transaction occurring before the date of the enactment of this Act,

(B) any property acquired before such date of enactment, or

(C) any item of income, loss, deduction, or credit taken into account before such date of enactment, and

(2) the treatment of such transaction, property, or item under such provision would (without regard to the amendments made by this part) affect liability for tax for periods ending after such date of enactment,

nothing in the amendments made by this part shall be construed to affect the treatment of such transaction, property, or item for purposes of determining liability for tax for periods ending after such date of enactment.

• **1980, Recreational Boating Safety and Facilities Improvement Act of 1980 (P.L. 96-451)**

P.L. 96-451, §301(c)(1):

Amended Code Sec. 1245(b) by adding at the end thereof paragraph (8). **Effective** with respect to additions to capital account made after 12-31-79. (Note: An earlier Code Sec. 194 was added by P.L. 96-364, enacted on 9-26-80.)

• **1976, Tax Reform Act of 1976 (P.L. 94-455)**

P.L. 94-455, §1901(a)(140):

Amended Code Sec. 1245(b)(7)(B). **Effective** with respect to tax years beginning after 12-31-76. Prior to amendment Code Sec. 1245(b)(7)(B) read as follows:

(B) LATER CHANGE IN USE.—If any property with respect to the disposition of which gain is not recognized by reason of subparagraph (A) ceases to be used in an unrelated trade or business of the organization acquiring such property, such organization acquiring such property, such organization shall be treated for purposes of this section as having disposed of such property on the date of such cessation.

P.L. 94-455, §1906(b)(13)(A):

Amended the 1954 Code by substituting "Secretary" for "Secretary or his delegate" each place it appeared. **Effective** 2-1-77.

• **1975 (P.L. 94-81)**

P.L. 94-81, §2(a):

Amended Code Sec. 1245(b) by adding "Except as provided in paragraph (7), this" in place of "This" at the beginning of the second sentence of paragraph (3) and by adding paragraph (7). **Effective** date is noted in Act Sec. 2(c), below.

P.L. 94-81, §2(c), provides:

"(c) Effective Date.—

"(1) In general.—Except as provided in paragraph (2), the amendments made by this section shall apply to dispositions after December 31, 1969, in taxable years ending after such date.

"(2) Election for past transactions.—In the case of any disposition occurring before the date of the enactment of this Act, the amendments made by this section shall apply only if the organization acquiring the property elects (in the manner provided by regulations prescribed by the Secretary of the Treasury or his delegate) within 1 year after the date of the enactment [August 9, 1975] of this Act to have such amendments apply with respect to such property."

[Sec. 1245(c)]

(c) ADJUSTMENTS TO BASIS.—The Secretary shall prescribe such regulations as he may deem necessary to provide for adjustments to the basis of property to reflect gain recognized under subsection (a).

Amendments

• **1976, Tax Reform Act of 1976 (P.L. 94-455)**

P.L. 94-455, §1906(b)(13)(A):

Amended 1954 Code by substituting "Secretary" for "Secretary or his delegate" each place it appeared. **Effective** 2-1-77.

• **1962, Revenue Act of 1962 (P.L. 87-834)**

P.L. 87-834, §13(a):

Added Code Sec. 1245. **Effective** for tax years beginning after 12-31-62.

[Sec. 1245(d)]

(d) APPLICATION OF SECTION.—This section shall apply notwithstanding any other provision of this subtitle.

INCOME TAX—CAPITAL GAINS, LOSSES

Amendments

• **1962, Revenue Act of 1962 (P.L. 87-834)**

P.L. 87-834, §13(a):

Added Code Sec. 1245(d). **Effective** for taxable years beginning after 12-31-62.

[Sec. 1246—Repealed]

Amendments

• **2013, American Taxpayer Relief Act of 2012 (P.L. 112-240)**

P.L. 112-240, §101(a)(1)-(3), provides:

SEC. 101. PERMANENT EXTENSION AND MODIFICATION OF 2001 TAX RELIEF.

(a) PERMANENT EXTENSION.—

(1) IN GENERAL.—The Economic Growth and Tax Relief Reconciliation Act of 2001 is amended by striking title IX.

(2) CONFORMING AMENDMENT.—The Tax Relief, Unemployment Insurance Reauthorization, and Job Creation Act of 2010 is amended by striking section 304.

(3) EFFECTIVE DATE.—The amendments made by this subsection shall apply to taxable, plan, or limitation years beginning after December 31, 2012, and estates of decedents dying, gifts made, or generation skipping transfers after December 31, 2012.

• **2010, Tax Relief, Unemployment Insurance Reauthorization, and Job Creation Act of 2010 (P.L. 111-312)**

P.L. 111-312, §301(a):

Amended Code Sec. 1246(e) to read as such provision would read if subtitle E of title V of the Economic Growth and Tax Relief Reconciliation Act of 2001 (P.L. 107-16) had never been enacted. **Effective** for estates of decedents dying, and transfers made, after 12-31-2009. For a special rule, see Act Sec. 301(c), below. [Note: P.L. 107-16 struck Code Sec. 1246(e). Thus, the amendment by P.L. 111-312 effectively reinstates Code Sec. 1246(e) as it read prior to being stricken by P.L. 107-16. P.L. 108-357, §413(a)(2), however, repealed Code Sec. 1246 in its entirety, so this amendment made by P.L. 111-312 cannot be made.]

P.L. 111-312, §301(c), provides:

(c) SPECIAL ELECTION WITH RESPECT TO ESTATES OF DECEDENTS DYING IN 2010.—Notwithstanding subsection (a), in the case of an estate of a decedent dying after December 31, 2009, and before January 1, 2011, the executor (within the meaning of section 2203 of the Internal Revenue Code of 1986) may elect to apply such Code as though the amendments made by subsection (a) do not apply with respect to chapter 11 of such Code and with respect to property acquired or passing from such decedent (within the meaning of section 1014(b) of such Code). Such election shall be made at such time and in such manner as the Secretary of the Treasury or the Secretary's delegate shall provide. Such an election once made shall be revocable only with the consent of the Secretary of the Treasury or the Secretary's delegate. For purposes of section 2652(a)(1) of such Code, the determination of whether any property is subject to the tax imposed by such chapter 11 shall be made without regard to any election made under this subsection.

P.L. 111-312, §304, provides [but see P.L. 112-240, §101(a)(2)-(3), above]:
SEC. 304. APPLICATION OF EGTRRA SUNSET TO THIS TITLE.

Section 901 of the Economic Growth and Tax Relief Reconciliation Act of 2001 shall apply to the amendments made by this title.

• **2004, American Jobs Creation Act of 2004 (P.L. 108-357)**

P.L. 108-357, §413(a)(2):

Repealed Code Sec. 1246. **Effective** for tax years of foreign corporations beginning after 12-31-2004, and for tax years of United States shareholders with or within which such tax years of foreign corporations end. Prior to repeal, Code Sec. 1246 read as follows:

SEC. 1246. GAIN ON FOREIGN INVESTMENT COMPANY STOCK.

[Sec. 1246(a)]

(a) TREATMENT OF GAIN AS ORDINARY INCOME.—

(1) GENERAL RULE.—In the case of a sale or exchange (or a distribution which, under section 302 or 331, is treated as an exchange of stock) after December 31, 1962, of stock in a foreign corporation which was a foreign investment company (as defined in subsection (b)) at any time during the period during which the taxpayer held such stock, any gain shall be treated as ordinary income, to the extent of the taxpayer's ratable share of the earnings and profits of such corporation accumulated for taxable years beginning after December 31, 1962.

(2) RATABLE SHARE.—For purposes of this section, the taxpayer's ratable share shall be determined under regulations prescribed by the Secretary, but shall include only his ratable share of the accumulated earnings and profits of such corporation—

(A) for the period during which the taxpayer held such stock, but

(B) excluding such earnings and profits attributable to—

(i) any amount previously included in the gross income of such taxpayer under section 951 (but only to the extent the inclusion of such amount did not result in an exclusion of any other amount from gross income under section 959), or

(ii) any taxable year during which such corporation was not a foreign investment company but only if—

(I) such corporation was not a foreign investment company at any time before such taxable year, and

(II) such corporation was treated as a foreign investment company solely by reason of subsection (b)(2).

(3) TAXPAYER TO ESTABLISH EARNINGS AND PROFITS.—Unless the taxpayer establishes the amount of the accumulated earnings and profits of the foreign investment company and the ratable share thereof for the period during which the taxpayer held such stock, all the gain from the sale or exchange of stock in such company shall be considered as ordinary income.

(4) HOLDING PERIOD OF STOCK MUST BE MORE THAN 1 YEAR.—This section shall not apply with respect to the sale or exchange of stock where the holding period of such stock as of the date of such sale or exchange is 6 months [1 year] or less.

Amendments

• **1984, Deficit Reduction Act of 1984 (P.L. 98-369)**

P.L. 98-369, §1001(b)(20):

Amended Code Sec. 1246(a)(4) by striking out "1 year" each place it appeared and inserting in lieu thereof "6 months". **Effective** for property acquired after 6-22-84 and before 1-1-88.

• **1981, Economic Recovery Tax Act of 1981 (P.L. 97-34)**

P.L. 97-34, §832(a):

Amended Code Sec. 1246(a)(2)(B). **Effective** for sales or exchanges after 8-13-81, in tax years ending after that date. Prior to amendment, Code Sec. 1246(a)(2)(B) read as follows:

(B) excluding such earnings and profits attributable to any amount previously included in the gross income of such taxpayer under section 951 (but only to the extent the inclusion of such amount did not result in an exclusion of any other amount from gross income under section 959).

• **1976, Tax Reform Act of 1976 (P.L. 94-455)**

P.L. 94-455, §1402(b)(1)(W):

Substituted "9 months" for "6 months" wherever it appeared in Code Sec. 1246(a)(4). **Effective** with respect to tax years beginning in 1977.

P.L. 94-455, §1402(b)(2):

Substituted "1 year" for "9 months" wherever it appeared in Code Sec. 1246(a)(4). **Effective** with respect to tax years beginning after 12-31-77.

P.L. 94-455, §1901(b)(3)(I):

Substituted "ordinary income" for "gain from the sale or exchange of property which is not a capital asset" wherever it appeared in Code Sec. 1246(a). **Effective** with respect to tax years beginning after 12-31-76.

P.L. 94-455, §1906(b)(13)(A):

Amended the 1954 Code by substituting "Secretary" for "Secretary or his delegate" each place it appeared. **Effective** 2-1-77.

[Sec. 1246(b)]

(b) DEFINITION OF FOREIGN INVESTMENT COMPANY.—For purposes of this section, the term "foreign investment company" means any foreign corporation which, for any taxable year beginning after December 31, 1962, is—

(1) registered under the Investment Company Act of 1940, as amended (15 U. S. C. 80a-1 to 80b-2), either as a management company or as a unit investment trust, or

(2) engaged (or holding itself out as being engaged) primarily in the business of investing, reinvesting, or trading in—

(A) securities (as defined in section 2(a)(36) of the Investment Company Act of 1940, as amended),

(B) commodities, or

(C) any interest (including a futures or forward contract or option) in property described in subparagraph (A) or (B),

at a time when 50 percent or more of the total combined voting power of all classes of stock entitled to vote, or the total value of all classes of stock, was held directly (or indirectly through applying paragraphs (2) and (3) of section 958(a) and paragraph (4) of section 318(a)) by United States persons (as defined in section 7701(a)(30)).

Amendments

• **1984, Deficit Reduction Act of 1984 (P.L. 98-369)**

P.L. 98-369, §134(a):

Amended Code Sec. 1246(b)(2). **Effective** for sales and exchanges (and distributions) on or after 9-29-83, in tax years ending on or after such date. However, see the exception provided by Act Sec. 134(b)(2), below. Prior to amendment, it read as follows:

(2) engaged (or holding itself out as being engaged) primarily in the business of investing, reinvesting, or trading in securities (within the meaning of section 3(a)(1) of such Act, as limited by paragraphs (2) through (10) (except paragraph (6)(C)) and paragraphs (12) through (15) of section 3(c) of such Act) at a time when more than 50 percent of the total combined voting power of all classes of stock entitled to vote, or of the total value of shares of all classes of stock, was held, directly or indirectly (within the meaning of section 958(a)), by United States persons (as defined in section 7701(a)(30)).

P.L. 98-369, §134(b)(2), provides:

(2) Stock Held on September 29, 1983.—In the case of a sale or exchange (or distribution) not later than the date which is 1 year after the date of the enactment of this Act, the amendment made by subsection (a) shall not apply with respect to stock held by the taxpayer continuously from September 29, 1983, to the date of such sale or exchange (or distribution).

[Sec. 1246(c)]

(c) STOCK HAVING TRANSFERRED OR SUBSTITUTED BASIS.—To the extent provided in regulations prescribed by the Secretary, stock in a foreign corporation, the basis of which (in the hands of the taxpayer selling or exchanging such stock) is determined by reference to the basis (in the hands of such taxpayer or any other person) of stock

INCOME TAX—CAPITAL GAINS, LOSSES

in a foreign investment company, shall be treated as stock of a foreign investment company and held by the taxpayer throughout the holding period for such stock (determined under section 1223).

Amendments

- **1976, Tax Reform Act of 1976 (P.L. 94-455)**

P.L. 94-455, §1906(b)(13)(A):

Amended 1954 Code by substituting "Secretary" for "Secretary or his delegate" each place it appeared. **Effective** 2-1-77.

[Sec. 1246(d)]

(d) RULES RELATING TO ENTITIES HOLDING FOREIGN INVESTMENT COMPANY STOCK.—To the extent provided in regulations prescribed by the Secretary—

(1) trust certificates of a trust to which section 677 (relating to income for benefit of grantor) applies, and

(2) stock of a domestic corporation,

shall be treated as stock of a foreign investment company and held by the taxpayer throughout the holding period for such certificates or stock (determined under section 1223) in the same proportion that the investment in stock in a foreign investment company by the trust or domestic corporation bears to the total assets of such trust or corporation.

Amendments

- **1976, Tax Reform Act of 1976 (P.L. 94-455)**

P.L. 94-455, §1906(b)(13)(A):

Amended 1954 Code by substituting "Secretary" for "Secretary or his delegate" each place it appeared. **Effective** 2-1-77.

[Sec. 1246(e)—Stricken]

Amendments

- **2001, Economic Growth and Tax Relief Reconciliation Act of 2001 (P.L. 107-16)**

P.L. 107-16, §542(e)(5)(A):

Amended Code Sec. 1246 by striking subsection (e). **Effective** for estates of decedents dying after 12-31-2009. Prior to being stricken, Code Sec. 1246(e) read as follows:

(e) RULES RELATING TO STOCK ACQUIRED FROM A DECEDENT.—

(1) BASIS.—In the case of stock of a foreign investment company acquired by bequest, devise, or inheritance (or by the decedent's estate) from a decedent dying after December 31, 1962, the basis determined under section 1014 shall be reduced (but not below the adjusted basis of such stock in the hands of the decedent immediately before his death) by the amount of the decedent's ratable share of the earnings and profits of such company accumulated after December 31, 1962. Any stock so acquired shall be treated as stock described in subsection (c).

(2) DEDUCTION FOR ESTATE TAX.—If stock to which subsection (a) applies is acquired from a decedent, the taxpayer shall, under regulations prescribed by the Secretary or his delegate, be allowed (for the taxable year of the sale or exchange) a deduction from gross income equal to that portion of the decedent's estate tax deemed paid which is attributable to the excess of (A) the value at which such stock was taken into account for purposes of determining the value of the decedent's gross estate, over (B) the value at which it would have been so taken into account if such value had been reduced by the amount described in paragraph (1).

P.L. 107-16, §901(a)-(b) [as amended by P.L. 111-312, §101(a)(1)], provides [but see P.L. 112-240, §101(a)(1) and (3), above]:

SEC. 901. SUNSET OF PROVISIONS OF ACT.

(a) IN GENERAL.—All provisions of, and amendments made by, this Act shall not apply—

(1) to taxable, plan, or limitation years beginning after December 31, 2012, or

(2) in the case of title V, to estates of decedents dying, gifts made, or generation skipping transfers, after December 31, 2012.

(b) APPLICATION OF CERTAIN LAWS.—The Internal Revenue Code of 1986 and the Employee Retirement Income Security Act of 1974 shall be applied and administered to years, estates, gifts, and transfers described in subsection (a) as if the provisions and amendments described in subsection (a) had never been enacted.

- **1980, Crude Oil Windfall Profit Tax Act of 1980 (P.L. 96-223)**

P.L. 96-223, §401(b):

Revised Code Sec. 1246(e), before its amendment by P.L. 94-455, Act Sec. 2005(a)(5). **Effective** with respect to decedents dying after 12-31-76. However, see also the amendment note for P.L. 96-223, §401(a), that follows Code Sec. 1016(d) for the election to use the carryover basis rules with respect to a decedent dying after 12-31-76 and before 11-7-78.

[Sec. 1246(f)]

(f) INFORMATION WITH RESPECT TO CERTAIN FOREIGN INVESTMENT COMPANIES.—Every United States person who, on the last day of the taxable year of a foreign investment company, owns 5 percent or more in value of the stock of such company shall furnish with respect to such company such information as the Secretary shall by regulations prescribe.

Amendments

- **1988, Technical and Miscellaneous Revenue Act of 1988 (P.L. 100-647)**

P.L. 100-647, §1012(p)(21):

Amended Code Sec. 1246 by redesignating subsections (e)-(g) as subsections (f)-(h) respectively. **Effective** as if included in the provision of P.L. 99-514 to which it relates.

Sec. 1246—Repealed

- **1980, Crude Oil Windfall Profit Tax Act of 1980 (P.L. 96-223)**

P.L. 96-223, §401(a):

Repealed the redesignation of Code Sec. 1246(f) as Code Sec. 1246(e) made by P.L. 94-455, Act Sec. 2005(a)(5). **Effective** with respect to decedents dying after 12-31-76. However, see the amendment note for P.L. 96-223, §401(b), following Code Sec. 1246(e).

- **1976, Tax Reform Act of 1976 (P.L. 94-455)**

P.L. 94-455, §1901(a)(141):

Struck the phrase "beginning after December 31, 1962" following the phrase "foreign investment company" in Code Sec. 1246(f). **Effective** with respect to tax years beginning after 12-31-76.

P.L. 94-455, §1906(b)(13)(A):

Amended the 1954 Code by substituting "Secretary" for "Secretary or his delegate" each place it appeared. **Effective** 2-1-77.

P.L. 94-455, §2005(a)(5):

Repealed former Code Sec. 1246(e) and redesignated subsections (f) and (g) as subsections (e) and (f). **Effective** for decedents dying after 12-31-79 (effective date amended by P.L. 95-600, Sec. 515(6)). Prior to repeal, Code Sec. 1246(e) read as follows:

(e) RULES RELATING TO STOCK ACQUIRED FROM A DECEDENT.—

(1) BASIS.—In the case of stock of a foreign investment company acquired by bequest, devise, or inheritance (or by the decedent's estate) from a decedent dying after December 31, 1962, the basis determined under section 1014 shall be reduced (but not below the adjusted basis of such stock in the hands of the decedent immediately before his death) by the amount of the decedent's ratable share of the earnings and profits of such company accumulated after December 31, 1962. Any stock so acquired shall be treated as stock described in subsection (c).

(2) DEDUCTION FOR ESTATE TAX.—If stock to which subsection (a) applies is acquired from a decedent, the taxpayer shall, under regulations prescribed by the Secretary or his delegate, be allowed (for the taxable year of the sale or exchange) a deduction from gross income equal to that portion of the decedent's estate tax deemed paid which is attributable to the excess of (A) the value at which such stock was taken into account for purposes of determining the value of the decedent's gross estate, over (B) the value at which it would have been so taken into account if such value had been reduced by the amount described in paragraph (1).

[Sec. 1246(g)]

(g) COORDINATION WITH SECTION 1248.—This section shall not apply to any gain to the extent such gain is treated as ordinary income under section 1248 (determined without regard to section 1248(g)(2)).

Amendments

- **1988, Technical and Miscellaneous Revenue Act of 1988 (P.L. 100-647)**

P.L. 100-647, §1012(p)(21):

Amended Code Sec. 1246 by redesignating subsections (e)-(g) as subsections (f)-(h) respectively. **Effective** as if included in the provision of P.L. 99-514 to which it relates.

P.L. 100-647, §1018((o)(2):

Amended Code Sec. 1246(g) (as redesignated) by striking out "1248(g)(3)" and inserting in lieu thereof "1248(g)(2)". **Effective** as if included in the provision of P.L. 99-514 to which it relates.

- **1986, Tax Reform Act of 1986 (P.L. 99-514)**

P.L. 99-514, §1235(b):

Amended Code Sec. 1246 by redesignating subsection (f) as subsection (g) and by inserting after subsection (e) new subsection (f). **Effective** for tax years of foreign corporations beginning after 12-31-86.

[Sec. 1246(h)]

(h) CROSS REFERENCE.—

For special rules relating to the earnings and profits of foreign investment companies, see section 312(j).

Amendments

- **1988, Technical and Miscellaneous Revenue Act of 1988 (P.L. 100-647)**

P.L. 100-647, §1012(p)(21):

Amended Code Sec. 1246 by redesignating subsections (e)-(g) as subsections (f)-(h) respectively. **Effective** as if included in the provision of P.L. 99-514 to which it relates.

- **1986, Tax Reform Act of 1986 (P.L. 99-514)**

P.L. 99-514, §1235(b):

Amended Code Sec. 1246 by redesignating subsection (f) as subsection (g) and by inserting after subsection (e) new subsection (f). **Effective** for tax years of foreign corporations beginning after 12-31-86.

- **1980, Crude Oil Windfall Profit Tax Act of 1980 (P.L. 96-223)**

P.L. 96-223, §401(a):

Repealed the redesignation of Code Sec. 1246(g) as Code Sec. 1246(f) made by P.L. 94-455, Act Sec. 2005(a)(5). **Effective** with respect to decedents dying after 12-31-76. However, see the amendment note for P.L. 96-223, §401(b), following Code Sec. 1246(e).

INCOME TAX—CAPITAL GAINS, LOSSES

• **1976, Tax Reform Act of 1976 (P.L. 94-455)**

P.L. 94-455, § 1901(b)(32)(B):

Substituted "312(j)" for "312(l)" in Code Sec. 1246(g). **Effective** with respect to tax years beginning after 12-31-76.

P.L. 94-455, § 2005(a)(5):

Renumbered former subsection (g) as (f) of Code Sec. 1246. **Effective** for decedents dying after 12-31-79 (effective date amended by P.L. 95-600, Sec. 515(6)).

Amendments

• **2004, American Jobs Creation Act of 2004 (P.L. 108-357)**

P.L. 108-357, § 413(a)(3):

Repealed Code Sec. 1247. **Effective** for tax years of foreign corporations beginning after 12-31-2004, and for tax years of United States shareholders with or within which such tax years of foreign corporations end. Prior to repeal, Code Sec. 1247 read as follows:

SEC. 1247. ELECTION BY FOREIGN INVESTMENT COMPANIES TO DISTRIBUTE INCOME CURRENTLY.

[Sec. 1247(a)]

(a) ELECTION BY FOREIGN INVESTMENT COMPANY.—

(1) IN GENERAL.—If a foreign investment company which is described in section 1246(b)(1) elects (in the manner provided in regulations prescribed by the Secretary) on or before December 31, 1962, with respect to each taxable year beginning after December 31, 1962, to—

(A) distribute to its shareholders 90 percent or more of what its taxable income would be if it were a domestic corporation;

(B) designate in a written notice mailed to its shareholders at any time before the expiration of 45 days after the close of its taxable year the pro rata amount of the amount (determined as if such corporation were a domestic corporation) of the net capital gain of the taxable year; and the portion thereof which is being distributed; and

(C) provide such information as the Secretary deems necessary to carry out the purposes of this section,

then section 1246 shall not apply with respect to the qualified shareholders of such company during any taxable year to which such election applies.

(2) SPECIAL RULES.—

(A) COMPUTATION OF TAXABLE INCOME.—For purposes of paragraph (1)(A), the taxable income of the company shall be computed without regard to—

(i) the net capital gain referred to in paragraph (1)(B),

(ii) section 172 (relating to net operating losses), and

(iii) any deduction provided by part VIII of subchapter B (other than the deduction provided by section 248, relating to organizational expenditures).

(B) DISTRIBUTIONS AFTER THE CLOSE OF THE TAXABLE YEAR.—For purposes of paragraph (1)(A), a distribution made after the close of the taxable year and on or before the 15th day of the third month of the next taxable year shall be treated as distributed during the taxable year to the extent elected by the company (in accordance with regulations prescribed by the Secretary) on or before the 15th day of such third month.

(C) CARRYOVER OF CAPITAL LOSSES FROM NONELECTION YEARS DENIED.—In computing the net capital gain referred to in paragraph (1)(B), section 1212 shall not apply to losses incurred in or with respect to taxable years before the first taxable year to which the election applies.

Amendments

• **1976, Tax Reform Act of 1976 (P.L. 94-455)**

P.L. 94-455, § 1901(b)(33)(P):

Substituted "the amount (determined as if such corporation were a domestic corporation) of the net capital gain" for "the excess (determined as if such corporation were a domestic corporation) of the net long-term capital gain over the short-term capital loss" in Code Sec. 1247(a)(1)(B). **Effective** with respect to tax years beginning after 12-31-76.

P.L. 94-455, § 1901(b)(33)(R):

Substituted "the net capital gain" for "the excess of the net long-term capital gain over the net short-term capital loss" in Code Sec. 1247(a)(2)(A)(i) and (a)(2)(C). **Effective** with respect to tax years beginning after 12-31-76.

P.L. 94-455, § 1906(b)(13)(A):

Amended the 1954 Code by substituting "Secretary" for "Secretary or his delegate" each place it appeared. **Effective** 2-1-77.

[Sec. 1247(b)]

(b) YEARS TO WHICH ELECTION APPLIES.—The election of any foreign investment company under this section shall terminate as of the close of the taxable year preceding its first taxable year in which any of the following occurs:

(1) the company fails to comply with the provisions of subparagraph (A), (B), or (C) of subsection (a)(1), unless it is shown that such failure is due to reasonable cause and not due to willful neglect,

(2) the company is a foreign personal holding company, or

(3) the company is not a foreign investment company which is described in section 1246(b)(1).

[Sec. 1247(c)]

(c) QUALIFIED SHAREHOLDERS.—For purposes of this section—

(1) IN GENERAL.—The term "qualified shareholder" means any shareholder who United States person (as defined in section 7701(a)(30)), other than a shareholder described in paragraph (2).

• **1962, Revenue Act of 1962 (P.L. 87-834)**

P.L. 87-834, § 14(a):

Added Code Sec. 1246. **Effective** for tax years beginning after 12-31-62.

[Sec. 1247—Repealed]

(2) CERTAIN UNITED STATES PERSONS EXCLUDED FROM DEFINITION.—A United States person shall not be treated as a qualified shareholder for the taxable year if for such taxable year (or for any prior taxable year) he did not include, in computing his long-term capital gains in his return for such taxable year, the amount designated by such company pursuant to subsection (a)(1)(B) as his share of the undistributed capital gains of such company for its taxable year ending within or with such taxable year of the taxpayer. The preceding sentence shall not apply with respect to any failure by the taxpayer to treat an amount as provided therein if the taxpayer shows that such failure was due to reasonable cause and not due to willful neglect.

[Sec. 1247(d)]

(d) TREATMENT OF DISTRIBUTED AND UNDISTRIBUTED CAPITAL GAINS BY A QUALIFIED SHAREHOLDER.—Every qualified shareholder of a foreign investment company for any taxable year of such company with respect to which an election pursuant to subsection (a) is in effect shall include, in computing his long-term capital gains—

(1) for his taxable year in which received, his pro rata share of the distributed portion of the net capital gain for such taxable year of such company, and

(2) for his taxable year in which or with which the taxable year of such company ends, his pro rata share of the undistributed portion of the net capital gain for such taxable year of such company.

Amendments

• **1976, Tax Reform Act of 1976 (P.L. 94-455)**

P.L. 94-455, § 1901(b)(33)(R):

Substituted "the net capital gain" for "the excess of the net long-term capital gain over the net short-term capital loss" in Code Sec. 1247(d)(1) and (2). **Effective** with respect to tax years beginning after 12-31-76.

[Sec. 1247(e)]

(e) ADJUSTMENTS.—Under regulations prescribed by the Secretary, proper adjustment shall be made—

(1) in the earnings and profits of the electing foreign investment company and a qualified shareholder's ratable share thereof, and

(2) in the adjusted basis of stock of such company held by such shareholder,

to reflect such shareholder's inclusion in gross income of undistributed capital gains.

Amendments

• **1976, Tax Reform Act of 1976 (P.L. 94-455)**

P.L. 94-455, § 1906(b)(13)(A):

Amended 1954 Code by substituting "Secretary" for "Secretary or his delegate" each place it appeared. **Effective** 2-1-77.

[Sec. 1247(f)]

(f) ELECTION BY FOREIGN INVESTMENT COMPANY WITH RESPECT TO FOREIGN TAX CREDIT.—A foreign investment company with respect to which an election pursuant to subsection (a) is in effect and more than 50 percent of the value (as defined in section 851(c)(4)) of whose total assets at the close of the taxable year consists of stock or securities in foreign corporations may, for such taxable year, elect the application of this subsection with respect to income, war profits, and excess profits taxes described in section 901(b)(1) which are paid by the foreign investment company during such taxable year to foreign countries and possessions of the United States. If such election is made—

(1) the foreign investment company—

(A) shall compute its taxable income, for purposes of subsection (a)(1)(A), without any deductions for income, war profits, or excess profits taxes paid to foreign countries or possessions of the United States, and

(B) shall treat the amount of such taxes, for purposes of subsection (a)(1)(A), as distributed to its shareholders;

(2) each qualified shareholder of such foreign investment company—

(A) shall include in gross income and treat as paid by him his proportionate share of such taxes, and

(B) shall treat, for purposes of applying subpart A of part III of subchapter N, his proportionate share of such taxes as having been paid to the country in which the foreign investment company is incorporated, and

(C) shall treat as gross income from sources within the country in which the foreign investment company is incorporated, for purposes of applying subpart A of part III of subchapter N, the sum of his proportionate share of such taxes and any dividend paid to him by such foreign investment company.

[Sec. 1247(g)]

(g) NOTICE TO SHAREHOLDERS.—The amounts to be treated by qualified shareholders, for purposes of subsection (f)(2), as their proportionate share of the taxes described in subsection (f)(1)(A) paid by a foreign investment company shall not exceed the amounts so designated by the foreign investment company in a written notice mailed to its shareholders not later than 45 days after the close of its taxable year.

INCOME TAX—CAPITAL GAINS, LOSSES

[Sec. 1247(h)]

(h) MANNER OF MAKING ELECTION AND NOTIFYING SHAREHOLDERS.—The election provided in subsection (f) and the notice to shareholders required by subsection (g) shall be made in such manner as the Secretary may prescribe by regulations.

Amendments

• **1976, Tax Reform Act of 1976 (P.L. 94-455)**

P.L. 94-455, §1906(b)(13)(A):

Amended 1954 Code by substituting "Secretary" for "Secretary or his delegate" each place it appeared. **Effective** 2-1-77.

[Sec. 1247(i)]

(i) LOSS ON SALE OR EXCHANGE OF CERTAIN STOCK HELD LESS THAN 1 YEAR.—If—

(1) under this section, any qualified shareholder treats any amount designated under subsection (a)(1)(B) with respect to a share of stock as long-term capital gain, and

(2) such share is held by the taxpayer for less than 6 months [1 year]

then any loss on the sale or exchange of such share shall, to the extent of the amount described in paragraph (1), be treated as loss from the sale or exchange of a capital asset held for more than 6 months [1 year].

Amendments

• **1984, Deficit Reduction Act of 1984 (P.L. 98-369)**

P.L. 98-369, §1001(b)(21):

Amended Code Sec. 1247(i) by striking out "1 year" each place it appeared and inserting in lieu thereof "6 months". **Effective** for property acquired after 6-22-84 and before 1-1-88.

• **1976, Tax Reform Act of 1976 (P.L. 94-455)**

P.L. 94-455, §1402(b)(1)(X):

Substituted "9 months" for "6 months" wherever it appeared in Code Sec. 1247(i). **Effective** with respect to tax years beginning in 1977.

P.L. 94-455, §1402(b)(2):

Substituted "1 year" for "9 months" wherever it appeared in Code Sec. 1247(i). **Effective** with respect to tax years beginning after 12-31-77.

• **1962, Revenue Act of 1962 (P.L. 87-834)**

P.L. 87-834, §14(a):

Added Code Sec. 1247. **Effective** for tax years beginning after 12-31-62.

[Sec. 1248]

SEC. 1248. GAIN FROM CERTAIN SALES OR EXCHANGES OF STOCK IN CERTAIN FOREIGN CORPORATIONS.

[Sec. 1248(a)]

(a) GENERAL RULE.—If—

(1) a United States person sells or exchanges stock in a foreign corporation, and

(2) such person owns, within the meaning of section 958(a), or is considered as owning by applying the rules of ownership of section 958(b), 10 percent or more of the total combined voting power of all classes of stock entitled to vote of such foreign corporation at any time during the 5-year period ending on the date of the sale or exchange when such foreign corporation was a controlled foreign corporation (as defined in section 957),

then the gain recognized on the sale or exchange of such stock shall be included in the gross income of such person as a dividend, to the extent of the earnings and profits of the foreign corporation attributable (under regulations prescribed by the Secretary) to such stock which were accumulated in taxable years of such foreign corporation beginning after December 31, 1962, and during the period or periods the stock sold or exchanged was held by such person while such foreign corporation was a controlled foreign corporation. For purposes of this section, a United States person shall be treated as having sold or exchanged any stock if, under any provision of this subtitle, such person is treated as realizing gain from the sale or exchange of such stock.

Amendments

• **1996, Small Business Job Protection Act of 1996 (P.L. 104-188)**

P.L. 104-188, §1702(g)(1)(A)(i)-(ii):

Amended Code Sec. 1248(a) by striking ", or if a United States person receives a distribution from a foreign corporation which, under section 302 or 331, is treated as an exchange of stock" before ", and" in paragraph (1), and by adding at the end a new sentence. **Effective** as if included in the provision of P.L. 101-508 to which it relates.

• **1976, Tax Reform Act of 1976 (P.L. 94-455)**

P.L. 94-455, §1906(b)(13)(A):

Amended 1954 Code by substituting "Secretary" for "Secretary or his delegate" each place it appeared. **Effective** 2-1-77.

▶▶▶ **Caution:** P.L. 98-369, §1001(b)(22), amended Code Sec. 1248(b), below, by striking "1 year" and inserting "6 months". This amendment applies to property acquired after June 22, 1984, and before January 1, 1988.

[Sec. 1248(b)]

(b) LIMITATION ON TAX APPLICABLE TO INDIVIDUALS.—In the case of an individual, if the stock sold or exchanged is a capital asset (within the meaning of section 1221) and has been held for more than 6 months [1 year], the tax attributable to an amount included in gross income as a dividend under subsection (a) shall not be greater than a tax equal to the sum of—

(1) a pro rata share of the excess of—

(A) the taxes that would have been paid by the foreign corporation with respect to its income had it been taxed under this chapter as a domestic corporation (but without allowance for deduction of, or credit for, taxes described in subparagraph (B)), for the period or periods the stock sold or exchanged was held by the United States person in taxable years beginning after December 31, 1962, while the foreign corporation was a controlled foreign corporation, adjusted for distributions and amounts previously included in gross income of a United States shareholder under section 951, over

(B) the income, war profits, or excess profits taxes paid by the foreign corporation with respect to such income; and

(2) an amount equal to the tax that would result by including in gross income, as gain from the sale or exchange of a capital asset held for more than 6 months [1 year], an amount equal to the excess of (A) the amount included in gross income as a dividend under subsection (a), over (B) the amount determined under paragraph (1).

Amendments

• **1984, Deficit Reduction Act of 1984 (P.L. 98-369)**

P.L. 98-369, §1001(b)(22):

Amended Code Sec. 1248(b) by striking out "1 year" each place it appeared and inserting in lieu thereof "6 months". **Effective** for property acquired after 6-22-84, and before 1-1-88.

• **1976, Tax Reform Act of 1976 (P.L. 94-455)**

P.L. 94-455, §1402(b)(1)(Y):

Substituted "9 months" for "6 months" wherever it appeared in Code Sec. 1248(b). **Effective** with respect to tax years beginning in 1977.

P.L. 94-455, §1402(b)(2):

Substituted "1 year" for "9 months" wherever it appeared in Code Sec. 1248(b). **Effective** with respect to tax years beginning after 12-31-77.

[Sec. 1248(c)]

(c) DETERMINATION OF EARNINGS AND PROFITS.—

(1) IN GENERAL.—Except as provided in section 312(k)(4), for purposes of this section, the earnings and profits of any foreign corporation for any taxable year shall be determined according to rules substantially similar to those applicable to domestic corporations, under regulations prescribed by the Secretary.

(2) EARNINGS AND PROFITS OF SUBSIDIARIES OF FOREIGN CORPORATIONS.—If—

(A) subsection (a) or (f) applies to a sale, exchange, or distribution by a United States person of stock of a foreign corporation and, by reason of the ownership of the stock sold or exchanged, such person owned within the meaning of section 958(a)(2) stock of any other foreign corporation; and

INCOME TAX—CAPITAL GAINS, LOSSES

(B) such person owned, within the meaning of section 958(a), or was considered as owning by applying the rules of ownership of section 958(b), 10 percent or more of the total combined voting power of all classes of stock entitled to vote of such other foreign corporation at any time during the 5-year period ending on the date of the sale or exchange when such other foreign corporation was a controlled foreign corporation (as defined in section 957),

then, for purposes of this section, the earnings and profits of the foreign corporation the stock of which is sold or exchanged which are attributable to the stock sold or exchanged shall be deemed to include the earnings and profits of such other foreign corporation which—

(C) are attributable (under regulations prescribed by the Secretary) to the stock of such other foreign corporation which such person owned within the meaning of section 958(a)(2) (by reason of his ownership within the meaning of section 958(a)(1)(A) of the stock sold or exchanged) on the date of such sale or exchange (or on the date of any sale or exchange of the stock of such other foreign corporation occurring during the 5-year period ending on the date of the sale or exchange of the stock of such foreign corporation, to the extent not otherwise taken into account under this section but not in excess of the fair market value of the stock of such other foreign corporation sold or exchanged over the basis of such stock (for determining gain) in the hands of the transferor); and

(D) were accumulated in taxable years of such other corporation beginning after December 31, 1962, and during the period or periods—

(i) such other corporation was a controlled foreign corporation, and

(ii) such person owned within the meaning of section 958(a) the stock of such other foreign corporation.

Amendments

• **1984, Deficit Reduction Act of 1984 (P.L. 98-369)**

P.L. 98-369, § 133(c):

Amended Code Sec. 1248(c)(2)(D) by striking out "section 958(a)(2)" and inserting in lieu thereof "section 958(a)". **Effective** with respect to transactions to which subsection (a) or (f) of Code Sec. 1248 applies occurring after 7-18-84. Special rules appear following Code Sec. 1248(j).

• **1983, Technical Corrections Act of 1982 (P.L. 97-448)**

P.L. 97-448, § 102(c)(1):

Amended Code Sec. 1248(c)(1) by striking out "section 312(k)(3)" and inserting in lieu thereof "section 312(k)(4)". **Effective** as if included in the provision of P.L. 97-34 to which it relates.

• **1976, Tax Reform Act of 1976 (P.L. 94-455)**

P.L. 94-455, § 1042(b):

Amended Code Sec. 1248(c)(2)(C). For **effective** dates, see Act Sec. 1042(e) below. Prior to amendment Code Sec. 1248(c)(2)(C) read as follows:

(C) are attributable (under regulations prescribed by the Secretary or his delegate) to the stock of such other foreign corporation which such person owned within the meaning of section 958(a)(2) (by reason of his ownership within the meaning of section 958(a)(1)(A) of the stock sold or exchanged) on the date of such sale or exchange; and

P.L. 94-455, § 1042(c):

Substituted "subsection (a) or (f) applies to a sale, exchange, or distribution" for "subsection (a) applies to a sale or exchange" in Code Sec. 1248(c)(2)(A). For **effective** dates, see Act Sec. 1042(e) below.

P.L. 94-455, § 1042(e), provides:

(e) EFFECTIVE DATES.—

(1) The amendments made by this section (other than by subsection (d)) shall apply to transfers beginning after October 9, 1975, and to sales, exchanges, and distributions taking place after such date. The amendments made by subsection (d) shall apply with respect to pleadings filed with the Tax Court after the date of the enactment of this Act but only with respect to transfers beginning after October 9, 1975.

(2) In the case of any exchange described in section 367 of the Internal Revenue Code of 1954 (as in effect on December 31, 1974) in any taxable year beginning after December 31, 1962, and before the date of the enactment of this Act, which does not involve the transfer of property to or from a United States person, a taxpayer shall have for purposes of such section until 183 days after the date of the enactment of this Act to file a request with the Secretary of the Treasury or his delegate seeking to establish to the satisfaction of the Secretary of the Treasury or his delegate that such exchange was not in pursuance of a plan having as one of its principal purposes the avoidance of Federal income taxes and that for purposes of such section a foreign corporation is to be treated as a foreign corporation.

P.L. 94-455, § 1901(b)(32)(B):

Substituted "312(k)(3)" for "312(m)(3)" in Code Sec. 1248(c)(1). **Effective** with respect to tax years beginning after 12-31-76.

P.L. 94-455, § 1906(b)(13)(A):

Amended the 1954 Code by substituting "Secretary" for "Secretary or his delegate" each place it appeared. **Effective** 2-1-77.

• **1969, Tax Reform Act of 1969 (P.L. 91-172)**

P.L. 91-172, § 442(b)(2):

Amended subsection (c)(1) by inserting "Except as provided in section 312(m)(3), for purposes of this section" in lieu of "For purposes of this section,". **Effective** for tax years beginning after 6-30-72.

[Sec. 1248(d)]

(d) EXCLUSIONS FROM EARNINGS AND PROFITS.—For purposes of this section, the following amounts shall be excluded, with respect to any United States person, from the earnings and profits of a foreign corporation:

(1) AMOUNTS INCLUDED IN GROSS INCOME UNDER SECTION 951.—Earnings and profits of the foreign corporation attributable to any amount previously included in the gross income of such person under section 951, with respect to the stock sold or exchanged, but only to the extent the inclusion of such amount did not result in an exclusion of an amount from gross income under section 959.

(2) [Stricken.]

(3) LESS DEVELOPED COUNTRY CORPORATIONS UNDER PRIOR LAW.—Earnings and profits of a foreign corporation which were accumulated during any taxable year beginning before January 1, 1976, while such corporation was a less developed country corporation under section 902(d) as in effect before the enactment of the Tax Reduction Act of 1975.

(4) UNITED STATES INCOME.—Any item includible in gross income of the foreign corporation under this chapter—

(A) for any taxable year beginning before January 1, 1967, as income derived from sources within the United States of a foreign corporation engaged in trade or business within the United States, or

(B) for any taxable year beginning after December 31, 1966, as income effectively connected with the conduct by such corporation of a trade or business within the United States.

This paragraph shall not apply with respect to any item which is exempt from taxation (or is subject to a reduced rate of tax) pursuant to a treaty obligation of the United States.

(5) FOREIGN TRADE INCOME.—Earnings and profits of the foreign corporation attributable to foreign trade income of a FSC (as defined in section 922) other than foreign trade income which—

(A) is section 923(a)(2) non-exempt income (within the meaning of section 927(d)(6)), or

(B) would not (but for section 923(a)(4)) be treated as exempt foreign trade income.

For purposes of the preceding sentence, the terms "foreign trade income" and "exempt foreign trade income" have the respective meanings given such terms by section 923. Any reference in this paragraph to section 922, 923, or 927 shall be treated as a reference to such section as in effect before its repeal by the FSC Repeal and Extraterritorial Income Exclusion Act of 2000.

(6) AMOUNTS INCLUDED IN GROSS INCOME UNDER SECTION 1293.—Earnings and profits of the foreign corporation attributable to any amount previously included in the gross income of such person under section 1293 with respect to the stock sold or exchanged, but only to the extent the inclusion of such amount did not result in an exclusion of an amount under section 1293(c).

INCOME TAX—CAPITAL GAINS, LOSSES

Amendments

- **2007, Tax Technical Corrections Act of 2007 (P.L. 110-172)**

P.L. 110-172, §11(g)(17)(A)-(B):

Amended Code Sec. 1248(d)(5) by inserting "(as defined in section 922)" after "a FSC", and by adding at the end a new sentence. **Effective** 12-29-2007.

- **2004, American Jobs Creation Act of 2004 (P.L. 108-357)**

P.L. 108-357, §413(c)(22):

Amended Code Sec. 1248(d) by striking paragraph (5) and by redesignating paragraphs (6) and (7) as paragraphs (5) and (6), respectively. **Effective** for tax years of foreign corporations beginning after 12-31-2004, and for tax years of United States shareholders with or within which such tax years of foreign corporations end. Prior to being stricken, Code Sec. 1248(d)(5) read as follows:

(5) AMOUNTS INCLUDED IN GROSS INCOME UNDER SECTION 1247.—If the United States person whose stock is sold or exchanged was a qualified shareholder (as defined in section 1247(c)) of a foreign corporation which was a foreign investment company (as described in section 1246(b)(1)), the earnings and profits of the foreign corporation for taxable years in which such person was a qualified shareholder.

- **1988, Technical and Miscellaneous Revenue Act of 1988 (P.L. 100-647)**

P.L. 100-647, §1006(e)(14)(A):

Amended Code Sec. 1248(d) by striking out paragraph (2). **Effective** as if included in the provision of P.L. 99-514 to which it relates. Prior to amendment, Code Sec. 1248(d)(2) read as follows:

(2) GAIN REALIZED FROM THE SALE OR EXCHANGE OF PROPERTY IN PURSUANCE OF A PLAN OF COMPLETE LIQUIDATION.—If a foreign corporation adopts a plan of complete liquidation in a taxable year of a foreign corporation beginning after December 31, 1962, and if section 337(a) would apply if such foreign corporation were a domestic corporation, earnings and profits of the foreign corporation attributable (under regulations prescribed by the Secretary) to any net gain from the sale or exchange of property.

P.L. 100-647, §1012(p)(19):

Amended Code Sec. 1248(d) by adding at the end thereof new paragraph (7). **Effective** as if included in the provision of P.L. 99-514 to which it relates.

- **1986, Tax Reform Act of 1986 (P.L. 99-514)**

P.L. 99-514, §1876(a)(2):

Amended Code Sec. 1248(d)(6). **Effective** as if included in the provision of P.L. 98-369 to which it relates. Prior to amendment, Code Sec. 1248(d)(6) read as follows:

(6) FOREIGN TRADE INCOME.—Earnings and profits of the foreign corporation attributable to foreign trade income (within the meaning of section 923(b)) of a FSC.

- **1984, Deficit Reduction Act of 1984 (P.L. 98-369)**

P.L. 98-369, §801(d)(6):

Added Code Sec. 1248(d)(6). **Effective** for transactions after 12-31-84, in tax years ending after such date. Special rules appear in Act Sec. 805(b)(2) following Code Sec. 995(f).

- **1976, Tax Reform Act of 1976 (P.L. 94-455)**

P.L. 94-455, §1022(a):

Amended Code Sec. 1248(d)(3). **Effective** for tax years beginning after 12-31-75. Prior to amendment, Code Sec. 1248(d)(3) read as follows:

(3) LESS DEVELOPED COUNTRY CORPORATIONS.—Earnings and profits accumulated by a foreign corporation while it was a less developed country corporation (as defined in section 902(d)), if the stock sold or exchanged was owned for a continuous period of at least 10 years, ending with the date of the sale or exchange, by the United States person who sold or exchanged such stock. In the case of stock sold or exchanged by a corporation, if United States persons who are individuals, estates, or trusts (each of whom owned within the meaning of section 958(a), or were considered as owning by applying the rules of ownership of section 958(b), 10 percent or more of the total combined voting power of all classes of stock entitled to vote of such corporation) owned, or were considered as owning, at any time during the 10-year period ending on the date of the sale or exchange more than 50 percent of the total combined voting power of all classes of stock entitled to vote of such corporation, this paragraph shall apply only if such United States persons owned, or were considered as owning, at all times during the remainder of such 10-year period more than 50 percent of the total combined voting power of all classes of stock entitled to vote of such corporation. For purposes of this paragraph, stock owned by a United States person who is an individual, estate, or trust which was acquired by reason of the death of the predecessor in interest of such United States person shall be considered as owned by such United States person during the period such stock was owned by such predecessor in interest, and during the period such stock was owned by any other predecessor in interest if between such United States person and such other predecessor in interest there was no transfer other than by reason of the death of an individual.

P.L. 94-455, §1906(b)(13)(A):

Amended the 1954 Code by substituting "Secretary" for "Secretary or his delegate" each place it appeared. **Effective** 2-1-77.

- **1966, Foreign Investors Tax Act of 1966 (P.L. 89-809)**

P.L. 89-809, §104(k):

Amended Code Sec. 1248(d)(4). **Effective** with respect to sales or exchanges occurring after 12-31-66. Prior to amendment, Sec. 1248(d)(4) read as follows:

(4) UNITED STATES INCOME.—Any item includible in gross income of the foreign corporation under this chapter as income derived from sources within the United States of a foreign corporation engaged in trade or business in the United States.

[Sec. 1248(e)]

(e) SALES OR EXCHANGES OF STOCK IN CERTAIN DOMESTIC CORPORATIONS.—Except as provided in regulations prescribed by the Secretary, if—

(1) a United States person sells or exchanges stock of a domestic corporation, and

(2) such domestic corporation was formed or availed of principally for the holding, directly or indirectly, of stock of one or more foreign corporations,

such sale or exchange shall, for purposes of this section, be treated as a sale or exchange of the stock of the foreign corporation or corporations held by the domestic corporation.

Amendments

- **1996, Small Business Job Protection Act of 1996 (P.L. 104-188)**

P.L. 104-188, §1702(g)(1)(B):

Amended Code Sec. 1248(e)(1) by striking ", or receives a distribution from a domestic corporation which, under section 302 or 331, is treated as an exchange of stock" after "domestic corporation". **Effective** as if included in the provision of P.L. 101-508 to which it relates.

- **1986, Tax Reform Act of 1986 (P.L. 99-514)**

P.L. 99-514, §631(d)(2)(A):

Amended Code Sec. 1248(e) by striking out "Under regulations" and inserting in lieu thereof "Except as provided in regulations". For the **effective** date, see amendment note for Act Sec. 631(d)(2)(B) following Code Sec. 1248(f).

- **1976, Tax Reform Act of 1976 (P.L. 94-455)**

P.L. 94-455, §1906(b)(13)(A):

Amended 1954 Code by substituting "Secretary" for "Secretary or his delegate" each place it appeared. **Effective** 2-1-77.

[Sec. 1248(f)]

(f) CERTAIN NONRECOGNITION TRANSACTIONS.—Except as provided in regulations prescribed by the Secretary—

(1) IN GENERAL.—If—

(A) a domestic corporation satisfies the stock ownership requirements of subsection (a)(2) with respect to a foreign corporation, and

(B) such domestic corporation distributes stock of such foreign corporation in a distribution to which section 311(a), 337, 355(c)(1), or 361(c)(1) applies,

then, notwithstanding any other provision of this subtitle, an amount equal to the excess of the fair market value of such stock over its adjusted basis in the hands of the domestic corporation shall be included in the gross income of the domestic corporation as a dividend to the extent of the earnings and profits of the foreign corporation attributable (under regulations prescribed by the Secretary) to such stock which were accumulated in taxable years of such foreign corporation beginning after December 31, 1962, and during the period or periods the stock was held by such domestic corporation while such foreign corporation was a controlled foreign corporation. For purposes of subsections (c)(2), (d), and (h), a distribution of stock to which this subsection applies shall be treated as a sale of stock to which subsection (a) applies.

(2) EXCEPTION FOR CERTAIN DISTRIBUTIONS.—In the case of any distribution of stock of a foreign corporation, paragraph (1) shall not apply if such distribution is to a domestic corporation—

(A) which is treated under this section as holding such stock for the period for which the stock was held by the distributing corporation, and

(B) which, immediately after the distribution, satisfies the stock ownership requirements of subsection (a)(2) with respect to such foreign corporation.

(3) APPLICATION TO CASES DESCRIBED IN SUBSECTION (e).—To the extent that earnings and profits are taken into account under this subsection, they shall be excluded and not taken into account for purposes of subsection (e).

INCOME TAX—CAPITAL GAINS, LOSSES

Amendments

• **1996, Small Business Job Protection Act of 1996 (P.L. 104-188)**

P.L. 104-188, §1702(g)(1)(C):

Amended Code Sec. 1248(f)(1)(B) by striking "or 361(c)(1)" and inserting "355(c)(1), or 361(c)(1)". **Effective** as if included in the provision of P.L. 101-508 to which it relates.

• **1988, Technical and Miscellaneous Revenue Act of 1988 (P.L. 100-647)**

P.L. 100-647, §1006(e)(14)(B):

Amended Code Sec. 1248(f)(1)(B). **Effective** as if included in the provision of P.L. 99-514 to which it relates. Prior to amendment, Code Sec. 1248(f)(1)(B) read as follows:

(B) such domestic corporation distributes, sells, or exchanges stock of such foreign corporation in a transaction to which section 311, 336, or 337 applies,

P.L. 100-647, §1006(e)(14)(C):

Amended Code Sec. 1248(f)(1) by striking out "distribution, sale, or exchange" in the last sentence and inserting in lieu thereof "distribution". **Effective** as if included in the provision of P.L. 99-514 to which it relates.

P.L. 100-647, §1006(e)(14)(D):

Amended Code Sec. 1248(f) by striking out paragraph (3) and by redesignating paragraph (4) as paragraph (3). **Effective** as if included in the provision of P.L. 99-514 to which it relates. Prior to amendment, Code Sec. 1248(f)(3) read as follows:

(3) NONAPPLICATION OF PARAGRAPH (1) IN CERTAIN CASES.—Paragraph (1) shall not apply to a sale or exchange to which section 337 applies if—

(A) throughout the period or periods the stock of the foreign corporation was held by the domestic corporation (or predecessor referred to in paragraph (2)) all the stock of such domestic corporation was owned by United States persons who satisfied the 10-percent stock ownership requirements of subsection (a)(2) with respect to such domestic corporation, and

(B) subsection (a) applies to the proceeds of the sale or exchange and also applied to all transactions described in subsection (e)(1) which took place during the period or periods referred to in subparagraph (A).

P.L. 100-647, §1006(e)(14)(E):

Amended Code Sec. 1248(f) by striking out "SECTION 311, 336, OR 337 TRANSACTIONS" and inserting in lieu thereof "NONRECOGNITION TRANSACTIONS" in the heading. **Effective** as if included in the provision of P.L. 99-514 to which it relates.

• **1986, Tax Reform Act of 1986 (P.L. 99-514)**

P.L. 99-514, §631(d)(2)(B):

Amended Code Sec. 1248(f) by inserting "Except as provided in regulations prescribed by the Secretary—" after the subsection heading. **Effective**, generally, for (1) any distribution in complete liquidation, and any sale or exchange, made by a corporation after 7-31-86, unless such corporation is completely liquidated before 1-1-87, (2) any transaction described in section 338 of the Internal Revenue Code of 1986 for which the acquisition date occurs after 12-31-86, and (3) any distribution (not in complete liquidation) made after 12-31-86. However, see the special rules provided by Act Sec. 633(b)-(f) following Code Sec. 26.

• **1976, Tax Reform Act of 1976 (P.L. 94-455)**

P.L. 94-455, §1042(c):

Added Code Sec. 1248(f). For **effective** dates, see Act Sec. 1042(e) in historical note to Code Sec. 1248(c).

[Sec. 1248(g)]

(g) EXCEPTIONS.—This section shall not apply to—

(1) distributions to which section 303 (relating to distributions in redemption of stock to pay death taxes) applies; or

(2) any amount to the extent that such amount is, under any other provision of this title, treated as—

(A) a dividend (other than an amount treated as a dividend under subsection (f)),

(B) ordinary income, or

⋙→ *Caution: P.L. 98-369, §1001(b)(22), amended former Code Sec. 1248(g)(3)(C), prior to its redesignation as Code Sec. 1248(g)(2)(C), below, by striking "1 year" and inserting "6 months". This amendment applies to property acquired after June 22, 1984, and before January 1, 1988.*

(C) gain from the sale of an asset held for not more than 6 months [1 year].

Amendments

• **1986, Tax Reform Act of 1986 (P.L. 99-514)**

P.L. 99-514, §1875(g)(1):

Amended Code Sec. 1248(g) by inserting "or" at the end of paragraph (1), by striking out paragraph (2), and redesignating paragraph (3) as paragraph (2). **Effective** for exchanges after 3-1-86. For a transitional rule, see Act Sec. 1875(g)(3), below. Prior to amendment, Code Sec. 1248(g)(2) read as follows:

(2) gain realized on exchanges to which section 356 (relating to receipt of additional consideration in certain reorganizations) applies; or

P.L. 99-514, §1875(g)(3), provides:

(3) TRANSITIONAL RULE.—An exchange shall be treated as occurring on or before March, 1, 1986, if—

(A) on or before such date, the taxpayer adopts a plan of reorganization to which section 356 applies, and

(B) such plan or reorganization is implemented and distributions pursuant to such plan are completed on or before the date of enactment of this Act.

• **1984, Deficit Reduction Act of 1984 (P.L. 98-369)**

P.L. 98-369, §1001(b)(22):

Amended Code Sec. 1248(g)(3)(C) by striking out "1 year" each place it appeared and inserting in lieu thereof "6 months". **Effective** for property acquired after 6-22-84 and before 1-1-88.

• **1976, Tax Reform Act of 1976 (P.L. 94-455)**

P.L. 94-455, §1042(c)(1):

Added new Code Sec. 1248(f) and renumbered former subsection (f) as (g). For **effective** dates, see Act Sec. 1042(e) in historical note to Code Sec. 1248(c).

P.L. 94-455, §1042(c)(3)(B):

Substituted "(A) a dividend (other than an amount treated as a dividend under subsection (f))," for "(A) a dividend," in Code Sec. 1248(g)(3). For **effective** dates, see Act Sec. 1042(e) in historical note to Code Sec. 1248(c).

P.L. 94-455, §1402(b)(1)(Y):

Substituted "9 months" for "6 months" in Code Sec. 1248(f)(3)(C). **Effective** with respect to tax years beginning in 1977.

P.L. 94-455, §1402(b)(2):

Substituted "1 year" for "9 months" in Code Sec. 1248(f)(3)(C). **Effective** with respect to tax years beginning after 12-31-77.

P.L. 94-455, §1901(b)(3)(H):

Substituted "ordinary income" for "gain from the sale of an asset which is not a capital asset" in redesignated Code Sec. 1248(g)(3)(B). **Effective** with respect to tax years beginning after 12-31-76.

[Sec. 1248(h)]

(h) TAXPAYER TO ESTABLISH EARNINGS AND PROFITS.—Unless the taxpayer establishes the amount of the earnings and profits of the foreign corporation to be taken into account under subsection (a) or (f), all gain from the sale or exchange shall be considered a dividend under subsection (a) or (f), and unless the taxpayer establishes the amount of foreign taxes to be taken into account under subsection (b), the limitation of such subsection shall not apply.

Amendments

• **1976, Tax Reform Act of 1976 (P.L. 94-455)**

P.L. 94-455, §1042(c)(1):

Renumbered former subsection (g) as Code Sec. 1248(h). For **effective** dates, see Act Sec. 1042(e) in historical note to Code Sec. 1248(c).

P.L. 94-455, §1042(c)(3)(C):

Substituted "subsection (a) or (f)" for "subsection (a)" wherever it appeared in redesignated Code Sec. 1248(h). For **effective** dates, see Act Sec. 1042(e) in historical note to Code Sec. 1248(c).

• **1962, Revenue Act of 1962 (P.L. 87-834)**

P.L. 87-834, §15(a):

Added Code Sec. 1248. **Effective** for sales or exchanges occurring after 12-31-62.

[Sec. 1248(i)]

(i) TREATMENT OF CERTAIN INDIRECT TRANSFERS.—

(1) IN GENERAL.—If any shareholder of a 10-percent corporate shareholder of a foreign corporation exchanges stock of the 10-percent corporate shareholder for stock of the foreign corporation, such 10-percent corporate shareholder shall recognize gain in the same manner as if the stock of the foreign corporation received in such exchange had been—

(A) issued to the 10-percent corporate shareholder, and

INCOME TAX—CAPITAL GAINS, LOSSES

(B) then distributed by the 10-percent corporate shareholder to such shareholder in redemption or liquidation (whichever is appropriate).

The amount of gain recognized by such 10-percent corporate shareholder under the preceding sentence shall not exceed the amount treated as a dividend under this section.

(2) 10-PERCENT CORPORATE SHAREHOLDER DEFINED.—For purposes of this subsection, the term "10-percent corporate shareholder" means any domestic corporation which, as of the day before the exchange referred to in paragraph (1), satisfies the stock ownership requirements of subsection (a)(2) with respect to the foreign corporation.

Amendments

• **1996, Small Business Job Protection Act of 1996 (P.L. 104-188)**

P.L. 104-188, §1702(g)(1)(D):

Amended Code Sec. 1248(i)(1). **Effective** as if included in the provision of P.L. 101-508 to which it relates. Prior to amendment, Code Sec. 1248(i)(1) read as follows:

(1) IN GENERAL.—If any shareholder of a 10-percent corporate shareholder of a foreign corporation exchanges stock of the 10-percent corporate shareholder for stock of the foreign corporation, for purposes of this section, the stock of the foreign corporation received in such exchange shall be treated as if it had been—

(A) issued to the 10-percent corporate shareholder, and

(B) then distributed by the 10-percent corporate shareholder to such shareholder in redemption or liquidation (whichever is appropriate).

• **1986, Tax Reform Act of 1986 (P.L. 99-514)**

P.L. 99-514, §1810(i)(1):

Amended Code Sec. 1248(i)(1)(B) by striking out "in redemption of his stock" and inserting in lieu thereof "in redemption or liquidation (whichever is appropriate)". **Effective** as if included in the provision of P.L. 98-369 to which it relates.

• **1984, Deficit Reduction Act of 1984 (P.L. 98-369)**

P.L. 98-369, §133(a):

Amended Code Sec. 1248 by adding new subsection (i). **Effective** for exchanges after 7-18-84, in tax years ending after such date.

[Sec. 1248(j)]

(j) COORDINATION WITH DIVIDENDS RECEIVED DEDUCTION.—In the case of the sale or exchange by a domestic corporation of stock in a foreign corporation held for 1 year or more, any amount received by the domestic corporation which is treated as a dividend by reason of this section shall be treated as a dividend for purposes of applying section 245A.

Amendments

• **2017, Tax Cuts and Jobs Act (P.L. 115-97)**

P.L. 115-97, §14102(a):

Amended Code Sec. 1248 by redesignating subsection (j) as subsection (k) and by inserting after subsection (i) a new subsection (j). **Effective** for sales or exchanges after 12-31-2017.

• **1984, Deficit Reduction Act of 1984 (P.L. 98-369)**

P.L. 98-369, §133(b)(2):

Amended Code Sec. 1248 by adding new subsection (j). **Effective** with respect to transactions to which subsection (a) or (f) of Code Sec. 1248 applies occurring after 7-18-84. Special rules appear below.

P.L. 98-369, §133(d)(2)-(3), as amended by P.L. 99-514, §1810(i) and P.L. 100-647, §1018(g)(2), provides:

(2) SUBSECTIONS (b) AND (c).—Except as provided in paragraph (3), the amendments made by subsections (b) and (c) shall apply with respect to transactions to which subsection (a) or (f) of section 1248 of the Internal Revenue Code of 1954 applies occurring after the date of the enactment of this Act.

(3) ELECTION OF EARLIER DATE FOR CERTAIN TRANSACTIONS.—

(A) IN GENERAL.—If the appropriate election is made under subparagraph (B), the amendments made by subsection (b) shall apply with respect to transactions to which subsection (a) or (f) of section 1248 of such Code applies occurring after October 9, 1975.

(B) ELECTION.—

(i) Subparagraph (A) shall apply with respect to transactions to which subsection (a) of section 1248 of such Code applies if the foreign corporation described in such subsection (or its successor in interest) so elects.

(ii) Subparagraph (A) shall apply with respect to transactions to which subsection (f) of section 1248 of such Code applies if the domestic corporation described in section 1248(f)(1) of such Code (or its successor) so elects.

(iii) Any election under clause (i) or (ii) shall be made not later than the date which is 1 year after the date of the enactment of the Tax Reform Act of 1986 and shall be made in such manner as the Secretary of the Treasury or his delegate shall prescribe.

[Sec. 1248(k)]

(k) CROSS REFERENCE.—

For provision excluding amounts previously taxed under this section from gross income when subsequently distributed, see section 959(e).

Amendments

• **2017, Tax Cuts and Jobs Act (P.L. 115-97)**

P.L. 115-97, §14102(a)(1):

Amended Code Sec. 1248 by redesignating subsection (j) as subsection (k). **Effective** for sales or exchanges after 12-31-2017.

[Sec. 1249]

SEC. 1249. GAIN FROM CERTAIN SALES OR EXCHANGES OF PATENTS, ETC., TO FOREIGN CORPORATIONS.

[Sec. 1249(a)]

(a) GENERAL RULE.—Gain from the sale or exchange of a patent, an invention, model, or design (whether or not patented), a copyright, a secret formula or process, or any other similar property right to any foreign corporation by any United States person (as defined in section 7701(a)(30)) which controls such foreign corporation shall, if such gain would (but for the provisions of this subsection) be gain from the sale or exchange of a capital asset or of property described in section 1231, be considered as ordinary income.

Amendments

• **2014, Tax Technical Corrections Act of 2014 (P.L. 113-295)**

P.L. 113-295, §221(a)(84), Division A:

Amended Code Sec. 1249(a) by striking "after December 31, 1962," following "Gain from the sale or exchange". **Effective** generally 12-19-2014. For a special rule, see Act Sec. 221(b)(2), Division A, below.

P.L. 113-295, §221(b)(2), Division A, provides:

(2) SAVINGS PROVISION.—If—

(A) any provision amended or repealed by the amendments made by this section applied to—

(i) any transaction occurring before the date of the enactment of this Act,

(ii) any property acquired before such date of enactment, or

(iii) any item of income, loss, deduction, or credit taken into account before such date of enactment, and

(B) the treatment of such transaction, property, or item under such provision would (without regard to the amendments or repeals made by this section) affect the liability for tax for periods ending after date of enactment, nothing in the amendments or repeals made by this section shall be construed to affect the treatment of such transaction, property, or item for purposes of determining liability for tax for periods ending after such date of enactment.

• **1976, Tax Reform Act of 1976 (P.L. 94-455)**

P.L. 94-455, §1901(b)(3)(K):

Substituted "ordinary income" for "gain from the sale or exchange of property which is neither a capital asset nor property described in section 1231" in Code Sec. 1249(a). **Effective** with respect to tax years beginning after 12-31-76.

• **1966, Foreign Investors Tax Act of 1966 (P.L. 89-809)**

P.L. 89-809, §104(m)(3):

Substituted "Gain" for "Except as provided in subsection (c), gain" in Code Sec. 1249(a). **Effective** 1-1-67.

INCOME TAX—CAPITAL GAINS, LOSSES

[Sec. 1249(b)]

(b) CONTROL.—For purposes of subsection (a), control means, with respect to any foreign corporation, the ownership, directly or indirectly, of stock possessing more than 50 percent of the total combined voting power of all classes of stock entitled to vote. For purposes of this subsection, the rules for determining ownership of stock prescribed by section 958 shall apply.

Amendments

- 1962, Revenue Act of 1962 (P.L. 87-834)

P.L. 87-834, §16(a):

Added Code Sec. 1249. **Effective** for tax years beginning after 12-31-62.

[Sec. 1250]

SEC. 1250. GAIN FROM DISPOSITIONS OF CERTAIN DEPRECIABLE REALTY.

[Sec. 1250(a)]

(a) GENERAL RULE.—Except as otherwise provided in this section—

(1) ADDITIONAL DEPRECIATION AFTER DECEMBER 31, 1975.—

(A) IN GENERAL.—If section 1250 property is disposed of after December 31, 1975, then the applicable percentage of the lower of—

(i) that portion of the additional depreciation (as defined in subsection (b)(1) or (4)) attributable to periods after December 31, 1975, in respect of the property, or

(ii) the excess of the amount realized (in the case of a sale, exchange, or involuntary conversion), or the fair market value of such property (in the case of any other disposition), over the adjusted basis of such property,

shall be treated as gain which is ordinary income. Such gain shall be recognized notwithstanding any other provision of this subtitle.

(B) APPLICABLE PERCENTAGE.—For purposes of subparagraph (A), the term "applicable percentage" means—

(i) in the case of section 1250 property with respect to which a mortgage is insured under section 221(d)(3) or 236 of the National Housing Act, or housing financed or assisted by direct loan or tax abatement under similar provisions of State or local laws and with respect to which the owner is subject to the restrictions described in section 1039(b)(1)(B) (as in effect on the day before the date of the enactment of the Revenue Reconciliation Act of 1990), 100 percent minus 1 percentage point for each full month the property was held after the date the property was held 100 full months;

(ii) in the case of dwelling units which, on the average, were held for occupancy by families or individuals eligible to receive subsidies under section 8 of the United States Housing Act of 1937, as amended, or under the provisions of State or local law authorizing similar levels of subsidy for lower-income families, 100 percent minus 1 percentage point for each full month the property was held after the date the property was held 100 full months;

(iii) in the case of section 1250 property with respect to which a depreciation deduction for rehabilitation expenditures was allowed under section 167(k), 100 percent minus 1 percentage point for each full month in excess of 100 full months after the date on which such property was placed in service;

(iv) in the case of section 1250 property with respect to which a loan is made or insured under title V of the Housing Act of 1949, 100 percent minus 1 percentage point for each full month the property was held after the date the property was held 100 full months; and

(v) in the case of all other section 1250 property, 100 percent.

In the case of a building (or a portion of a building devoted to dwelling units), if, on the average, 85 percent or more of the dwelling units contained in such building (or portion thereof) are units described in clause (ii), such building (or portion thereof) shall be treated as property described in clause (ii). Clauses (i), (ii), and (iv) shall not apply with respect to the additional depreciation described in subsection (b)(4) which was allowed under section 167(k).

(2) ADDITIONAL DEPRECIATION AFTER DECEMBER 31, 1969, AND BEFORE JANUARY 1, 1976.—

(A) IN GENERAL.—If section 1250 property is disposed of after December 31, 1969, and the amount determined under paragraph (1)(A)(ii) exceeds the amount determined under paragraph (1)(A)(i), then the applicable percentage of the lower of—

(i) that portion of the additional depreciation attributable to periods after December 31, 1969, and before January 1, 1976, in respect of the property, or

(ii) the excess of the amount determined under paragraph (1)(A)(ii) over the amount determined under paragraph (1)(A)(i),

shall also be treated as gain which is ordinary income. Such gain shall be recognized notwithstanding any other provision of this subtitle.

(B) APPLICABLE PERCENTAGE.—For purposes of subparagraph (A), the term "applicable percentage" means—

(i) in the case of section 1250 property disposed of pursuant to a written contract which was, on July 24, 1969, and at all times thereafter, binding on the owner of the property, 100 percent minus 1 percentage point for each full month the property was held after the date the property was held 20 full months;

(ii) in the case of section 1250 property with respect to which a mortgage is insured under section 221(d)(3) or 236 of the National Housing Act, or housing financed or assisted by direct loan or tax abatement under similar provisions of State or local laws, and with respect to which the owner is subject to the restrictions described in section 1039(b)(1)(B) (as in effect on the day before the date of the enactment of the Revenue Reconciliation Act of 1990), 100 percent minus 1 percentage point for each full month the property was held after the date the property was held 20 full months;

(iii) in the case of residential rental property (as defined in section 167(j)(2)(B)) other than that covered by clauses (i) and (ii), 100 percent minus 1 percentage point for each full month the property was held after the date the property was held 100 full months;

(iv) in the case of section 1250 property with respect to which a depreciation deduction for rehabilitation expenditures was allowed under section 167(k), 100 percent minus 1 percentage point for each full month in excess of 100 full months after the date on which such property was placed in service; and

(v) in the case of all other section 1250 property, 100 percent.

Clauses (i), (ii), and (iii) shall not apply with respect to the additional depreciation described in subsection (b)(4).

(3) ADDITIONAL DEPRECIATION BEFORE JANUARY 1, 1970.—

(A) IN GENERAL.—If section 1250 property is disposed of after December 31, 1963, and the amount determined under paragraph (1)(A)(ii) exceeds the sum of the amounts determined under paragraphs (1)(A)(i) and (2)(A)(i), then the applicable percentage of the lower of—

(i) that portion of the additional depreciation attributable to periods before January 1, 1970, in respect of the property, or

(ii) the excess of the amount determined under paragraph (1)(A)(ii) over the sum of the amounts determined under paragraphs (1)(A)(i) and (2)(A)(i),

shall also be treated as gain which is ordinary income. Such gain shall be recognized notwithstanding any other provision of this subtitle.

INCOME TAX—CAPITAL GAINS, LOSSES

(B) APPLICABLE PERCENTAGE.—For purposes of subparagraph (A), the term "applicable percentage" means 100 percent minus 1 percentage point for each full month the property was held after the date on which the property was held for 20 full months.

(4) SPECIAL RULE.—For purposes of this subsection, any reference to section 167(k) or 167(j)(2)(B) shall be treated as a reference to such section as in effect on the day before the date of the enactment of the Revenue Reconciliation Act of 1990.

(5) CROSS REFERENCE.—

For reduction in the case of corporations on capital gain treatment under this section, see section 291(a)(1).

Amendments

• **1990, Omnibus Budget Reconciliation Act of 1990 (P.L. 101-508)**

P.L. 101-508, §11801(c)(15)(A):

Amended Code Sec. 1250(a) by inserting in paragraphs (1)(A)[B](i) and (2)(B)(ii) "(as in effect on the day before the date of the enactment of the Revenue Reconciliation Act of 1990)" after "section 1039(b)(1)(B)". **Effective** 11-5-90.

P.L. 101-508, §11812(b)(11):

Amended Code Sec. 1250(a) by redesignating paragraph (4) as paragraph (5) and by inserting after paragraph (3) new paragraph (4). **Effective**, generally, for property placed in service after 11-5-90. For exceptions, see Act Sec. 11812(c)(2)-(3), below.

P.L. 101-508, §11812(c)(2)-(3), provides:

(2) EXCEPTION.—The amendments made by this section shall not apply to any property to which section 168 of the Internal Revenue Code of 1986 does not apply by reason of subsection (f)(5) thereof.

(3) EXCEPTION FOR PREVIOUSLY GRANDFATHER EXPENDITURES.—The amendments made by this section shall not apply to rehabilitation expenditures described in section 252(f)(5) of the Tax Reform Act of 1986 (as added by section 1002(l)(31) of the Technical and Miscellaneous Revenue Act of 1988).

P.L. 101-508, §1821(b), provides:

(b) SAVINGS PROVISION.—If—

(1) any provision amended or repealed by this part applied to—

(A) any transaction occurring before the date of the enactment of this Act,

(B) any property acquired before such date of enactment, or

(C) any item of income, loss, deduction, or credit taken into account before such date of enactment, and

(2) the treatment of such transaction, property, or item under such provision would (without regard to the amendments made by this part) affect liability for tax for periods ending after such date of enactment,

nothing in the amendments made by this part shall be construed to affect the treatment of such transaction, property, or item for purposes of determining liability for tax for periods ending after such date of enactment.

• **1984, Deficit Reduction Act of 1984 (P.L. 98-369)**

P.L. 98-369, §712(a)(1)(B):

Amended Code Sec. 1250(a) by adding new paragraph (4). **Effective** as if included in the provision of P.L. 97-248 to which it relates.

• **1980, Technical Corrections Act of 1979 (P.L. 96-222)**

P.L. 96-222, §107(a)(1)(D):

Amended Code Sec. 1250(a)(1)(B) by adding at the end of the sentence "which was allowed under section 167(k)". **Effective** for additions to capital accounts made after 6-14-76 and before 6-15-81.

• **1976, Tax Reform Act of 1976 (P.L. 94-455)**

P.L. 94-455, §202(a):

Amended Code Sec. 1250(a). **Effective** for tax years ending after 12-31-75. Prior to amendment Code Sec. 1250(a) read as follows:

(a) GENERAL RULE.—Except as otherwise provided in this section—

(1) ADDITIONAL DEPRECIATION AFTER DECEMBER 31, 1969.—If section 1250 property is disposed of after December 31, 1969, the applicable percentage of the lower of—

(A) that portion of the additional depreciation (as defined in subsection (b)(1) or (4)) attributable to periods after December 31, 1969, in respect of the property, or

(B) the excess of—

(i) the amount realized (in the case of a sale, exchange, or involuntary conversion), or the fair market value of such property (in the case of any other disposition), over

(ii) the adjusted basis of such property,

shall be treated as gain from the sale or exchange of property which is neither a capital asset nor property described in section 1231. Such gain shall be recognized notwithstanding any other provision of this subtitle.

(C) APPLICABLE PERCENTAGE.—For purposes of paragraph (1), the term "applicable percentage" means—

(i) in the case of section 1250 property disposed of pursuant to a written contract which was, on July 24, 1969, and at all times thereafter, binding on the owner of the property, 100 percent minus 1 percentage point for each full month the property was held after the date the property was held 20 full months;

(ii) in the case of section 1250 property constructed, reconstructed, or acquired by the taxpayer before January 1, 1976, with respect to which a mortgage is insured under section 221(d)(3) or 236 of the National Housing Act, or housing is financed or assisted by direct loan or tax abatement under similar provisions of State or local laws, and with respect to which the owner is subject to the restrictions described in section 1039(b)(1)(B), 100 percent minus one percentage point for each full month the property was held after the date the property was held 20 full months;

(iii) in the case of residential rental property (as defined in section 167(j)(2)(B)) other than that covered by clauses (i) and (ii), 100 percent minus 1 percentage point for each full month the property was held after the date the property was held 100 full months;

(iv) in the case of section 1250 property with respect to which a depreciation deduction for rehabilitation expenditures was allowed under section 167(k), 100 percent minus 1 percentage point for each full month in excess of 100 full months after the date on which such property was placed in service; and

(v) in the case of all other section 1250 property, 100 percent.

Clauses (i), (ii), and (iii) shall not apply with respect to the additional depreciation described in subsection (b)(4).

(2) ADDITIONAL DEPRECIATION BEFORE JANUARY 1, 1970.—

(A) IN GENERAL.—If section 1250 property is disposed of after December 31, 1963, and the amount determined under paragraph (1)(B) exceeds the amount determined under paragraph (1)(A), then the applicable percentage of the lower of—

(i) that portion of the additional depreciation attributable to periods before January 1, 1970, in respect of the property, or

(ii) the excess of the amount determined under paragraph (1)(B) over the amount determined under paragraph (1)(A),

shall also be treated as gain from the sale or exchange of property which is neither a capital asset nor property described in section 1231. Such gain shall be recognized notwithstanding any other provision of this subtitle.

(B) APPLICABLE PERCENTAGE.—For purposes of subparagraph (A) the term "applicable percentage" means 100 percent minus 1 percentage point for each full month the property was held after the date on which the property was held for 20 full months.

• **1975 (P.L. 93-625)**

P.L. 93-625, §5(c):

Amended Code Sec. 1250(a)(1)(C)(ii) by substituting "January 1, 1976" for "January 1, 1975". **Effective** with respect to property placed in service after 12-31-73.

• **1969, Tax Reform Act of 1969 (P.L. 91-172)**

P.L. 91-172, §521(b):

Amended Code Sec. 1250(a). **Effective** for tax years ending after 7-24-69. Prior to amendment, Code Sec. 1250(a) read as follows:

(a) General Rule.—

(1) Ordinary income.—Except as otherwise provided in this section, if section 1250 property is disposed of after December 31, 1963, the applicable percentage of the lower of—

(A) the additional depreciation (as defined in subsection (b)(1)) in respect of the property, or

(B) the excess of—

(i) the amount realized (in the case of a sale, exchange, or involuntary conversion), or the fair market value of such property (in the case of any other disposition), over

(ii) the adjusted basis of such property,

shall be treated as gain from the sale or exchange of property which is neither a capital asset nor property described in section 1231. Such gain shall be recognized notwithstanding any other provision of this subtitle.

(2) Applicable percentage.—For purposes of paragraph (1), the term "applicable percentage" means 100 percent minus one percentage point for each full month the property was held after the date on which the property was held 20 full months.

[Sec. 1250(b)]

(b) ADDITIONAL DEPRECIATION DEFINED.—For purposes of this section—

(1) IN GENERAL.—The term "additional depreciation" means, in the case of any property, the depreciation adjustments in respect of such property; except that, in the case of property held more than one year, it means such adjustments only to the extent that they exceed the amount of the depreciation adjustments which would have resulted if such adjustments had been determined for each taxable year under the straight line method of adjustment.

(2) PROPERTY HELD BY LESSEE.—In the case of a lessee, in determining the depreciation adjustments which would have resulted in respect of any building erected (or other improvement made) on the leased property, or in respect of any cost of acquiring the lease, the lease period shall be treated as including all renewal periods. For purposes of the preceding sentence—

(A) the term "renewal period" means any period for which the lease may be renewed, extended, or continued pursuant to an option exercisable by the lessee, but

(B) the inclusion of renewal periods shall not extend the period taken into account by more than $2/3$ of the period on the basis of which the depreciation adjustments were allowed.

Sec. 1250(a)(3)(B)

INCOME TAX—CAPITAL GAINS, LOSSES

(3) DEPRECIATION ADJUSTMENTS.—The term "depreciation adjustments" means, in respect of any property, all adjustments attributable to periods after December 31, 1963, reflected in the adjusted basis of such property on account of deductions (whether in respect of the same or other property) allowed or allowable to the taxpayer or to any other person for exhaustion, wear and tear, obsolescence, or amortization (other than amortization under section 168 (as in effect before its repeal by the Tax Reform Act of 1976), 169, 185 (as in effect before its repeal by the Tax Reform Act of 1986), 188 (as in effect before its repeal by the Revenue Reconciliation Act of 1990), 190, or 193). For purposes of the preceding sentence, if the taxpayer can establish by adequate records or other sufficient evidence that the amount allowed as a deduction for any period was less than the amount allowable, the amount taken into account for such period shall be the amount allowed.

(4) ADDITIONAL DEPRECIATION ATTRIBUTABLE TO REHABILITATION EXPENDITURES.—The term "additional depreciation" also means, in the case of section 1250 property with respect to which a depreciation or amortization deduction for rehabilitation expenditures was allowed under section 167(k) (as in effect on the day before the date of the enactment of the Revenue Reconciliation Act of 1990) or 1991 (as in effect before its repeal by the Economic Recovery Tax Act of 1981), the depreciation or amortization adjustments allowed under such section to the extent attributable to such property, except that, in the case of such property held for more than one year after the rehabilitation expenditures so allowed were incurred, it means such adjustments only to the extent that they exceed the amount of the depreciation adjustments which would have resulted if such adjustments had been determined under the straight line method of adjustment without regard to the useful life permitted under section 167(k) (as in effect on the day before the date of the enactment of the Revenue Reconciliation Act of 1990) or 191 (as in effect before its repeal by the Economic Recovery Tax Act of 1981).

(5) METHOD OF COMPUTING STRAIGHT LINE ADJUSTMENTS.—For purposes of paragraph (1), the depreciation adjustments which would have resulted for any taxable year under the straight line method shall be determined—

(A) in the case of property to which section 168 applies, by determining the adjustments which would have resulted for such year if the taxpayer had elected the straight line method for such year using the recovery period applicable to such property, and

(B) in the case of any property to which section 168 does not apply, if a useful life (or salvage value) was used in determining the amount allowable as a deduction for any taxable year, by using such life (or value).

Amendments

- **2005, Gulf Opportunity Zone Act of 2005 (P.L. 109-135)**

P.L. 109-135, §402(h):

Amended Code Sec. 1250(b)(3) by striking "or by section 179D" after "or 193)". **Effective** as if included in the provision of the Energy Policy Act of 2005 (P.L. 109-58) to which it relates [**effective** for property placed in service after 12-31-2005.—CCH].

- **2005, Energy Tax Incentives Act of 2005 (P.L. 109-58)**

P.L. 109-58, §1331(b)(3):

Amended Code Sec. 1250(b)(3) by inserting before the period at the end of the first sentence "or by section 179D". **Effective** for property placed in service after 12-31-2005.

- **1990, Omnibus Budget Reconciliation Act of 1990 (P.L. 101-508)**

P.L. 101-508, §11801(c)(6)(F):

Amended Code Sec. 1250(b)(3) by striking "188" and inserting "188 (as in effect before its repeal by the Revenue Reconciliation Act of 1990),". **Effective** 11-5-90.

P.L. 101-508, §11812(b)(12):

Amended Code Sec. 1250(b)(4) by striking "167(k)" each place it appears and inserting "167(k) (as in effect on the day before the date of the enactment of the Revenue Reconciliation Act of 1990)". **Effective**, generally, for property placed in service after 11-5-90. For exceptions, see Act Sec. 11812(c)(2)-(3) in the amendment notes following Code Sec. 1250(a).

P.L. 101-508, §11821(b), provides:

(b) SAVINGS PROVISION.—If—

(1) any provision amended or repealed by this part applied to—

(A) any transaction occurring before the date of the enactment of this Act,

(B) any property acquired before such date of enactment, or

(C) any item of income, loss, deduction, or credit taken into account before such date of enactment, and

(2) the treatment of such transaction, property, or item under such provision would (without regard to the amendments made by this part) affect liability for tax for periods ending after such date of enactment,

nothing in the amendments made by this part shall be construed to affect the treatment of such transaction, property, or item for purposes of determining liability for tax for periods ending after such date of enactment.

- **1989, Omnibus Budget Reconciliation Act of 1989 (P.L. 101-239)**

P.L. 101-239, §7831(b)(1)-(2):

Amended Code Sec. 1250(b)(5) by striking "in the case of recovery property" in subparagraph (A) and inserting "in the case of property to which section 168 applies", and by striking "in the case of any property which is not recovery property" in subparagraph (B) and inserting "in the case of any property to which section 168 does not apply". **Effective** as if included in the provision of P.L. 99-514 to which it relates.

- **1986, Tax Reform Act of 1986 (P.L. 99-514)**

P.L. 99-514, §242(b)(2):

Amended Code Sec. 1250(b)(3) by inserting "(as in effect before its repeal by the Tax Reform Act of 1986)" after "185". **Effective**, generally, for that portion of the basis of any property which is attributable to expenditures paid or incurred after 12-31-86. However, for transitional rules, see Act Sec. 242(c)(2), below.

P.L. 99-514, §242(c)(2), provides:

(c) EFFECTIVE DATE.—

(1) IN GENERAL.—Except as provided in paragraph (2), the amendments made by this section shall apply to that portion of the basis of any property which is attributable to expenditures paid or incurred after December 31, 1986.

(2) TRANSITIONAL RULE.—The amendments made by this section shall not apply to any expenditure incurred—

(A) pursuant to a binding contract entered into before March 2, 1986, or

(B) with respect to any improvement commenced before March 2, 1986, but only if not less than the lesser of $1,000,000 or 5 percent of the aggregate cost of such improvement has been incurred or committed before such date.

The preceding sentence shall not apply to any expenditure with respect to an improvement placed in service after December 31, 1987.

- **1983, Technical Corrections Act of 1982 (P.L. 97-448)**

P.L. 97-448, §102(a)(7)(A):

Amended Code Sec. 1250(b) by adding at the end thereof new paragraph (5). **Effective** as if included in the provision of P.L. 97-34 to which it relates.

P.L. 97-448, §102(a)(7)(B):

Amended Code Sec. 1250(b)(1) by striking out the last sentence. **Effective** as if such included in the provision of P.L. 97-34 to which it relates. Prior to amendment, the last sentence read as follows: "For purposes of the preceding sentence, if a useful life (or salvage value) was used in determining the amount allowed as a deduction for any taxable year, such life (or value) shall be used in determining the depreciation adjustments which would have resulted for such year under the straight line method."

- **1981, Economic Recovery Tax Act of 1981 (P.L. 97-34)**

P.L. 97-34, §212(d)(2)(F):

Amended Code Sec. 1250(b)(4) by inserting "(as in effect before its repeal by the Economic Recovery Tax Act of 1981)" after "191" each place it appeared. **Effective** for expenditures incurred after 12-31-81, in tax years ending after such date.

P.L. 97-34, §212(e)(2), provides:

(2) TRANSITIONAL RULE.—The amendments made by this section shall not apply with respect to any rehabilitation of a building if—

(A) the physical work on such rehabilitation began before January 1, 1982, and

(B) such building meets the requirements of paragraph (1) of section 48(g) of the Internal Revenue Code of 1954 (as in effect on the day before the date of enactment of this Act) but does not meet the requirements of such paragraph (1) (as amended by this Act).

- **1980, Crude Oil Windfall Profit Tax Act of 1980 (P.L. 96-223)**

P.L. 96-223, §251(a)(2)(D):

Amended Code Sec. 1250(b)(3) by striking out "or 190" and inserting "190, or 193". **Effective** for tax years beginning after 12-31-79.

- **1978, Revenue Act of 1978 (P.L. 95-600)**

P.L. 95-600, §701(f)(3)(C):

Amended Code Sec. 1250(b)(3) by striking out "190 or 191" and inserting in lieu thereof "or 190". **Effective** as set forth in P.L. 94-455, §2124(a)(3)(D) below.

P.L. 95-600, §701(f)(3)(E):

Amended Code Sec. 1250(b)(4) by inserting "or amortization" after "depreciation" the second and third places it appears and by inserting "or 191" after "167(k)" each place it appears. **Effective** as set forth in P.L. 94-455, §2124(a)(3)(D).

- **1976, Tax Reform Act of 1976 (P.L. 94-455)**

P.L. 94-455, §1951(c)(2)(C):

Substituted "168 (as in effect before its repeal by the Tax Reform Act of 1976)," for "168," in Code Sec. 1250(b)(3). **Effective** with respect to tax years beginning after 12-31-76.

P.L. 94-455, §2122(b)(4):

Substituted "188, or 190" for "or 188" in Code Sec. 1250(b)(3). **Effective** for tax years beginning after 12-31-76, and before 1-1-80.

P.L. 94-455, §2124(a)(3)(D):

Substituted "190 or 191" for "or 190" in Code Sec. 1250(b)(3). **Effective** with respect to Applicable with respect to additions to capital account made after 6-14-76 and before 6-15-81.

INCOME TAX—CAPITAL GAINS, LOSSES

- 1971, Revenue Act of 1971 (P.L. 92-178)

P.L. 92-178, §303(c)(3):
Amended the first sentence of Code Sec. 1250(b)(3) by substituting "185, or 188" for "or 185". **Effective** for tax years ending after 12-31-71.

- 1969, Tax Reform Act of 1969 (P.L. 91-172)

P.L. 91-172, §521(c):
Added Code Sec. 1250(b)(4). **Effective** for tax years ending after 7-24-69.

P.L. 91-172, §704(b)(5):
Amended Code Sec. 1250(b)(3) by inserting "168, 169, or 185" in place of "168". **Effective** for tax years ending after 12-31-68.

[Sec. 1250(c)]

(c) SECTION 1250 PROPERTY.—For purposes of this section, the term "section 1250 property" means any real property (other than section 1245 property, as defined in section 1245(a)(3)) which is or has been property of a character subject to the allowance for depreciation provided in section 167.

[Sec. 1250(d)]

(d) EXCEPTIONS AND LIMITATIONS.—

(1) GIFTS.—Subsection (a) shall not apply to a disposition by gift.

(2) TRANSFERS AT DEATH.—Except as provided in section 691 (relating to income in respect of a decedent), subsection (a) shall not apply to a transfer at death.

(3) CERTAIN TAX-FREE TRANSACTIONS.—If the basis of property in the hands of a transferee is determined by reference to its basis in the hands of the transferor by reason of the application of section 332, 351, 361, 721, or 731, then the amount of gain taken into account by the transferor under subsection (a) shall not exceed the amount of gain recognized to the transferor on the transfer of such property (determined without regard to this section). Except as provided in paragraph (6), this paragraph shall not apply to a disposition to an organization (other than a cooperative described in section 521) which is exempt from the tax imposed by this chapter.

(4) LIKE KIND EXCHANGES; INVOLUNTARY CONVERSIONS, ETC.—

(A) RECOGNITION LIMIT.—If property is disposed of and gain (determined without regard to this section) is not recognized in whole or in part under section 1031 or 1033, then the amount of gain taken into account by the transferor under subsection (a) shall not exceed the greater of the following:

(i) the amount of gain recognized on the disposition (determined without regard to this section), increased as provided in subparagraph (B), or

(ii) the amount determined under subparagraph (C).

(B) INCREASE FOR CERTAIN STOCK.—With respect to any transaction, the increase provided by this subparagraph is the amount equal to the fair market value of any stock purchased in a corporation which (but for this paragraph) would result in nonrecognition of gain under section 1033(a)(2)(A).

(C) ADJUSTMENT WHERE INSUFFICIENT SECTION 1250 PROPERTY IS ACQUIRED.—With respect to any transaction, the amount determined under this subparagraph shall be the excess of—

(i) the amount of gain which would (but for this paragraph) be taken into account under subsection (a), over

(ii) the fair market value (or cost in the case of a transaction described in section 1033(a)(2)) of the section 1250 property acquired in the transaction.

(D) BASIS OF PROPERTY ACQUIRED.—In the case of property purchased by the taxpayer in a transaction described in section 1033(a)(2), in applying [the last sentence of] section 1033(b)(2), such sentence shall be applied—

(i) first solely to section 1250 properties and to the amount of gain not taken into account under subsection (a) by reason of this paragraph, and

(ii) then to all purchased properties to which such sentence applies and to the remaining gain not recognized on the transaction as if the cost of the section 1250 properties were the basis of such properties computed under clause (i).

In the case of property acquired in any other transaction to which this paragraph applies, rules consistent with the preceding sentence shall be applied under regulations prescribed by the Secretary.

(E) ADDITIONAL DEPRECIATION WITH RESPECT TO PROPERTY DISPOSED OF.—In the case of any transaction described in section 1031 or 1033, the additional depreciation in respect of the section 1250 property acquired which is attributable to the section 1250 property disposed of shall be an amount equal to the amount of the gain which was not taken into account under subsection (a) by reason of the application of this paragraph.

(5) PROPERTY DISTRIBUTED BY A PARTNERSHIP TO A PARTNER.—

(A) IN GENERAL.—For purposes of this section, the basis of section 1250 property distributed by a partnership to a partner shall be deemed to be determined by reference to the adjusted basis of such property to the partnership.

(B) ADDITIONAL DEPRECIATION.—In respect of any property described in subparagraph (A), the additional depreciation attributable to periods before the distribution by the partnership shall be—

(i) the amount of the gain to which subsection (a) would have applied if such property had been sold by the partnership immediately before the distribution at its fair market value at such time and the applicable percentage for the property had been 100 percent, reduced by

(ii) if section 751(b) applied to any part of such gain, the amount of such gain to which section 751(b) would have applied if the applicable percentage for the property had been 100 percent.

(6) TRANSFERS TO TAX-EXEMPT ORGANIZATION WHERE PROPERTY WILL BE USED IN UNRELATED BUSINESS.—

(A) IN GENERAL.—The second sentence of paragraph (3) shall not apply to a disposition of section 1250 property to an organization described in section 511(a)(2) or 511(b)(2) if, immediately after such disposition, such organization uses such property in an unrelated trade or business (as defined in section 513).

(B) LATER CHANGE IN USE.—If any property with respect to the disposition of which gain is not recognized by reason of subparagraph (A) ceases to be used in an unrelated trade or business of the organization acquiring such property, such organization shall be treated for purposes of this section as having disposed of such property on the date of such cessation.

(7) FORECLOSURE DISPOSITIONS.—If any section 1250 property is disposed of by the taxpayer pursuant to a bid for such property at foreclosure or by operation of an agreement or of process of law after there was a default on indebtedness which such property secured, the applicable percentage referred to in paragraph (1)(B), (2)(B), or (3)(B) of subsection (a), as the case may be, shall be determined as if the taxpayer ceased to hold such property on the date of the beginning of the proceedings pursuant to which the disposition occurred, or, in the event there are no proceedings, such percentage shall be determined as if the taxpayer ceased to hold such property on the date, determined

INCOME TAX—CAPITAL GAINS, LOSSES

under regulations prescribed by the Secretary, on which such operation of an agreement or process of law, pursuant to which the disposition occurred, began.

Amendments

• **2018, Tax Technical Corrections Act of 2018 (P.L. 115-141)**

P.L. 115-141, § 401(a)(174), Div. U:

Amended Code Sec. 1250(d)(3) by striking "paragraph (9)" and inserting "paragraph (6)". **Effective** 3-23-2018.

• **2005, Gulf Opportunity Zone Act of 2005 (P.L. 109-135)**

P.L. 109-135, § 402(a)(7)(A):

Amended Code Sec. 1250(d) by striking paragraph (5) and redesignating paragraphs (6) through (8) as paragraphs (5) through (7), respectively. **Effective** as if included in the provision of the Energy Policy Act of 2005 (P.L. 109-58) to which it relates [effective 2-8-2006.—CCH]. For a special rule, see Act Sec. 402(m), below. Prior to being stricken, Code Sec. 1250(d)(5) read as follows:

(5) SECTION 1081 TRANSACTIONS.—Under regulations prescribed by the Secretary, rules consistent with paragraphs (3) and (4) of this subsection and with subsections (e) and (f) shall apply in the case of transactions described in section 1081 (relating to exchanges in obedience to SEC orders).

P.L. 109-135, § 402(m)(2), provides:

(2) REPEAL OF PUBLIC UTILITY HOLDING COMPANY ACT OF 1935.—The amendments made by subsection (a) shall not apply with respect to any transaction ordered in compliance with the Public Utility Holding Company Act of 1935 before its repeal.

• **1998, IRS Restructuring and Reform Act of 1998 (P.L. 105-206)**

P.L. 105-206, § 6023(12):

Amended Code Sec. 1250(d)(4)(D) by striking "the last sentence of section 1033(b)" and inserting "[the last sentence of] section 1033(b)(2)". **Effective** 7-22-98.

• **1997, Taxpayer Relief Act of 1997 (P.L. 105-34)**

P.L. 105-34, § 312(d)(10)(A):

Amended Code Sec. 1250(d) by striking paragraph (7) and by redesignating paragraphs (9) and (10) as paragraphs (7) and (8), respectively. **Effective**, generally, for sales and exchanges after 5-6-97. Prior to amendment, Code Sec. 1250(d)(7) read as follows:

(7) DISPOSITION OF PRINCIPAL RESIDENCE.—Subsection (a) shall not apply to a disposition of—

(A) property to the extent used by the taxpayer as his principal residence (within the meaning of section 1034, relating to rollover of gain on sale of principal residence), and

(B) property in respect of which the taxpayer meets the age and ownership requirements of section 121 (relating to one-time exclusion of gain from sale of principal residence by individual who has attained age 55) but only to the extent that he meets the use requirements of such section in respect of such property.

• **1995, Self-Employed Health Insurance Act (P.L. 104-7)**

P.L. 104-7, § 2(b)(1)-(2):

Amended Code Sec. 1250(d)(5) by striking "section 1071 (relating to gain from sale or exchange to effectuate polices [policies]of FCC) or" following "described in", and by striking "1071 AND" following "SECTION" in the heading. **Effective**, generally, for sales and exchanges on or after 1-17-95, and sales and exchanges before such date if the FCC tax certificate with respect to such sale or exchange is issued on or after such date. For special rules, see Act Sec. 2(d)(2)-(3) in the amendment notes following repealed Code Sec. 1071.

• **1990, Omnibus Budget Reconciliation Act of 1990 (P.L. 101-508)**

P.L. 101-508, § 11801(c)(8)(I):

Amended Code Sec. 1250(d)(3) by striking "371(a), 374(a)," after "361". **Effective** 11-5-90.

P.L. 101-508, § 11801(c)(15)(B):

Amended Code Sec. 1250(d) by striking paragraph (8). **Effective** 11-5-90. Prior to being stricken, Code Sec. 1250(d)(8) read as follows:

(8) DISPOSITION OF QUALIFIED LOW-INCOME HOUSING.—If section 1250 property is disposed of and gain (determined without regard to this section) is not recognized in whole or in part under section 1039, then—

(A) RECOGNITION LIMIT.—The amount of gain recognized by the transferor under subsection (a) shall not exceed the greater of—

(i) the amount of gain recognized on the disposition (determined without regard to this section), or

(ii) the amount determined under subparagraph (B).

(B) ADJUSTMENT WHERE INSUFFICIENT SECTION 1250 PROPERTY IS ACQUIRED.—With respect to any transaction, the amount determined under this subparagraph shall be the excess of—

(i) the amount of gain which would (but for this paragraph) be taken into account under subsection (a), over

(ii) the cost of the section 1250 property acquired in the transaction.

(C) BASIS OF PROPERTY ACQUIRED.—The basis of property acquired by the taxpayer, determined under section 1039(d), shall be allocated—

(i) first to the section 1250 property described in subparagraph (E)(i), in the amount determined under such subparagraph, reduced by the amount of gain not recognized attributable to the section 1250 property disposed of,

(ii) then to any property (other than section 1250 property) to which section 1039 applies, in the amount of its cost, reduced by the amount of gain not recognized except to the extent taken into account under clause (i), and

(iii) then to the section 1250 property described in subparagraph (E)(ii), in the amount determined thereunder, reduced by the amount of gain not recognized except to the extent taken into account under clauses (i) and (ii).

(D) ADDITIONAL DEPRECIATION WITH RESPECT TO PROPERTY DISPOSED OF.—The additional depreciation with respect to any property acquired shall include the additional depreciation with respect to the corresponding section 1250 property disposed of, reduced by the amount of gain recognized attributable to such property.

(E) PROPERTY CONSISTING OF MORE THAN ONE ELEMENT.—There shall be treated as a separate element of section 1250 property—

(i) that portion of the section 1250 property acquired the cost of which does not exceed the net amount realized (as defined in section 1039(b)) attributable to the section 1250 property disposed of, reduced by the amount of gain recognized (if any) attributable to such property, and

(ii) that portion of the section 1250 property acquired the cost of which exceeds the net amount realized (as defined in section 1039(b)) attributable to the section 1250 property disposed of.

(F) ALLOCATION RULES.—For purposes of this paragraph—

(i) the amount of gain recognized attributable to the section 1250 property disposed of shall be the net amount realized with respect to such property, reduced by the greater of the adjusted basis of the section 1250 property disposed of or the cost of the section 1250 property acquired, but shall not exceed the gain recognized in the transaction, and

(ii) if any section 1250 property is treated as consisting of more than one element by reason of the application of subparagraph (E) to a prior transaction, then the amount of gain recognized, the net amount realized, and the additional depreciation, with respect to each such element shall be allocated in accordance with regulations prescribed by the Secretary.

P.L. 101-508, § 11821(b), provides:

(b) SAVINGS PROVISION.—If—

(1) any provision amended or repealed by this part applied to—

(A) any transaction occurring before the date of the enactment of this Act,

(B) any property acquired before such date of enactment, or

(C) any item of income, loss, deduction, or credit taken into account before such date of enactment, and

(2) the treatment of such transaction, property, or item under such provision would (without regard to the amendments made by this part) affect liability for tax for periods ending after such date of enactment,

nothing in the amendments made by this part shall be construed to affect the treatment of such transaction, property, or item for purposes of determining liability for tax for periods ending after such date of enactment.

• **1988, Technical and Miscellaneous Revenue Act of 1988 (P.L. 100-647)**

P.L. 100-647, § 1002(a)(1):

Amended Code Sec. 1250(d) by striking out paragraph (11). **Effective** as if included in the provision of P.L. 99-514 to which it relates. Prior to amendment, Code Sec. 1250(d)(11) read as follows:

(11) SECTION 1245 RECOVERY PROPERTY.—Subsection (a) shall not apply to the disposition of property which is section 1245 recovery property (as defined in section 1245(a)(5)).

[Note: Code Sec. 1250(d)(11) was already stricken by P.L. 99-514, § 201(d)(11)(E).]

• **1986, Tax Reform Act of 1986 (P.L. 99-514)**

P.L. 99-514, § 201(d)(11)(E):

Amended Code Sec. 1250(d) by striking out paragraph (11). **Effective**, generally, for property placed in service after 12-31-86, in tax years ending after such date. However, for transitional rules, see Act Secs. 203, 204 and 251(d) following Code Sec. 168. Prior to amendment, Code Sec. 1250(d)(11) read as follows:

(11) SECTION 1245 RECOVERY PROPERTY.—Subsection (a) shall not apply to the disposition of property which is section 1245 recovery property (as defined in section 1245(a)(5)).

• **1981, Economic Recovery Tax Act of 1981 (P.L. 97-34)**

P.L. 97-34, § 204(e):

Amended Code Sec. 1250(d) by adding at the end thereof new paragraph (11). **Effective** for property placed in service after 12-31-80, in tax years ending after such date.

• **1978, Revenue Act of 1978 (P.L. 95-600)**

P.L. 95-600, § 404(c)(7):

Amended Code Sec. 1250(d)(7)(B) by striking out "relating to gains from sale or exchange of residence of individual who has attained the age of 65" and inserting in lieu thereof "relating to one-time exclusion of gain from sale of principal residence by individual who has attained age 55". **Effective** for sales or exchanges after 7-26-78, in tax years ending after such date.

P.L. 95-600, § 405(c)(4):

Amended Code Sec. 1250(d)(7)(A) by striking out "relating to sale or exchange of residence" and inserting in lieu thereof "relating to rollover of gain on sale of principal residence". **Effective** for sales and exchanges of residences after 7-26-78, in tax years ending after such date.

• **1976, Tax Reform Act of 1976 (P.L. 94-455)**

P.L. 94-455, § 202(b):

Added Code Sec. 1250(d)(10). **Effective** with respect to proceedings (and operations of law) referred to in Code Sec. 1250(d)(10) which begin after 12-31-75.

P.L. 94-455, § 1901(b)(31)(A):

Substituted "1033(a)(2)(A)" for "1033(a)(3)(A)" in Code Sec. 1250(d)(4)(B). **Effective** with respect to tax years beginning after 12-31-76.

INCOME TAX—CAPITAL GAINS, LOSSES

P.L. 94-455, §1901(b)(31)(B):
Substituted "1033(a)(2)" for "1033(a)(3)" in Code Sec. 1250(d)(4)(C) and (D). **Effective** with respect to tax years beginning after 12-31-76.

P.L. 94-455, §1901(b)(31)(E):
Substituted "1033(b)" for "1033(c)" in Code Sec. 1250(d)(4)(D). **Effective** with respect to tax years beginning after 12-31-76.

P.L. 94-455, §1906(b)(13)(A):
Amended the 1954 Code by substituting "Secretary" for "Secretary or his delegate" each place it appeared. **Effective** 2-1-77.

- **1975 (P.L. 94-81)**

P.L. 94-81, §2(b):
Amended Code Sec. 1250(d) by adding "Except as provided in paragraph (9), this" in place of "This" at the beginning of the second sentence of paragraph (3) and by adding paragraph (9). **Effective** date as noted in Act Sec. 2(c), as below.

P.L. 94-81, §2(c), provides:
"(c) Effective Date.—

"(1) In general.—Except as provided in paragraph (2), the amendments made by this section shall apply to dispositions after December 31, 1969, in taxable years ending after such date.

"(2) Election for past transactions.—In the case of any disposition occurring before the date of the enactment of this Act, the amendments made by this section shall apply only if the organization acquiring the property elects (in the manner provided by regulations prescribed by the Secretary of the Treasury or his delegate) within 1 year after the date of the enactment [August 9, 1975] of this Act to have such amendments apply with respect to such property."

- **1969, Tax Reform Act of 1969 (P.L. 91-172)**

P.L. 91-172, §521(e)(1):
Amended Code Sec. 1250(d) by inserting "subsection (a)" in lieu of "subsection (a)(1)" wherever it appeared. **Effective** for tax years ending after 7-24-69.

P.L. 91-172, §910(b)(1):
Amended Code Sec. 1250(d) by adding paragraph (8). **Effective** for approved dispositions of qualified housing projects within the meaning of Code Sec. 1039 after 10-9-69.

[Sec. 1250(e)]

(e) HOLDING PERIOD.—For purposes of determining the applicable percentage under this section, the provisions of section 1223 shall not apply, and the holding period of section 1250 property shall be determined under the following rules:

(1) BEGINNING OF HOLDING PERIOD.—The holding period of section 1250 property shall be deemed to begin—

(A) in the case of property acquired by the taxpayer, on the day after the date of acquisition, or

(B) in the case of property constructed, reconstructed, or erected by the taxpayer, on the first day of the month during which the property is placed in service.

(2) PROPERTY WITH TRANSFERRED BASIS.—If the basis of property acquired in a transaction described in paragraph (1), (2), or (3) of subsection (d) is determined by reference to its basis in the hands of the transferor, then the holding period of the property in the hands of the transferee shall include the holding period of the property in the hands of the transferor.

Amendments

- **2005, Gulf Opportunity Zone Act of 2005 (P.L. 109-135)**

P.L. 109-135, §402(a)(7)(B):
Amended Code Sec. 1250(e)(2) by striking "(3), or (5)" and inserting "or (3)". **Effective** as if included in the provision of the Energy Policy Act of 2005 (P.L. 109-58) to which it relates [effective 2-8-2006.—CCH]. For a special rule, see Act Sec. 402(m), below.

P.L. 109-135, §402(m)(2), provides:
(2) REPEAL OF PUBLIC UTILITY HOLDING COMPANY ACT OF 1935.—The amendments made by subsection (a) shall not apply with respect to any transaction ordered in compliance with the Public Utility Holding Company Act of 1935 before its repeal.

- **1997, Taxpayer Relief Act of 1997 (P.L. 105-34)**

P.L. 105-34, §312(d)(10)(B):
Amended Code Sec. 1250(e) by striking paragraph (3). **Effective**, generally, for sales and exchanges after 5-6-97. Prior to being stricken, paragraph Code Sec. 1250(e)(3) read as follows:

(3) PRINCIPAL RESIDENCE.—If the basis of property acquired in a transaction described in paragraph (7) of subsection (d) is determined by reference to the basis in the hands of the taxpayer of other property, then the holding period of the property acquired shall include the holding period of such other property.

- **1996, Small Business Job Protection Act of 1996 (P.L. 104-188)**

P.L. 104-188, §1702(h)(18):
Repealed Code Sec. 1250(e)(4). **Effective** as if included in the provision of P.L. 101-508 to which it relates. Prior to repeal, Code Sec. 1250(e)(4) read as follows:

(4) QUALIFIED LOW-INCOME HOUSING.—The holding period of any section 1250 property acquired which is described in subsection (d)(8)(E)(i) shall include the holding period of the corresponding element of section 1250 property disposed of.

- **1969, Tax Reform Act of 1969 (P.L. 91-172)**

P.L. 91-172, §910(b)(2):
Amended Code Sec. 1250(e) by adding paragraph (4). **Effective** for approved dispositions of qualified housing projects within the meaning of Code Sec. 1039 after 10-9-69.

[Sec. 1250(f)]

(f) SPECIAL RULES FOR PROPERTY WHICH IS SUBSTANTIALLY IMPROVED.—

(1) AMOUNT TREATED AS ORDINARY INCOME.—If, in the case of a disposition of section 1250 property, the property is treated as consisting of more than one element by reason of paragraph (3), then the amount taken into account under subsection (a) in respect of such section 1250 property as ordinary income shall be the sum of the amounts determined under paragraph (2).

(2) ORDINARY INCOME ATTRIBUTABLE TO AN ELEMENT.—For purposes of paragraph (1), the amount taken into account for any element shall be the sum of a series of amounts determined for the periods set forth in subsection (a), with the amount for any such period being determined by multiplying—

(A) the amount which bears the same ratio to the lower of the amounts specified in clause (i) or (ii) of subsection (a)(1)(A), in clause (i) or (ii) of subsection (a)(2)(A), or in clause (i) or (ii) of subsection (a)(3)(A), as the case may be, for the section 1250 property as the additional depreciation for such element attributable to such period bears to the sum of the additional depreciation for all elements attributable to such period, by

(B) the applicable percentage for such element for such period.

For purposes of this paragraph, determinations with respect to any element shall be made as if it were a separate property.

(3) PROPERTY CONSISTING OF MORE THAN ONE ELEMENT.—In applying this subsection in the case of any section 1250 property, there shall be treated as a separate element—

(A) each separate improvement,

(B) if, before completion of section 1250 property, units thereof (as distinguished from improvements) were placed in service, each such unit of section 1250 property, and

(C) the remaining property which is not taken into account under subparagraphs (A) and (B).

(4) PROPERTY WHICH IS SUBSTANTIALLY IMPROVED.—For purposes of this subsection—

(A) IN GENERAL.—The term "separate improvement" means each improvement added during the 36-month period ending on the last day of any taxable year to the capital account for the property, but only if the sum of the amounts added to such account during such period exceeds the greatest of—

(i) 25 percent of the adjusted basis of the property,

(ii) 10 percent of the adjusted basis of the property, determined without regard to the adjustments provided in paragraphs (2) and (3) of section 1016(a), or

(iii) $5,000.

For purposes of clauses (i) and (ii), the adjusted basis of the property shall be determined as of the beginning of the first day of such 36-month period, or of the holding period of the property (within the meaning of subsection (e)), whichever is the later.

Sec. 1250(e)

INCOME TAX—CAPITAL GAINS, LOSSES

(B) EXCEPTION.—Improvements in any taxable year shall be taken into account for purposes of subparagraph (A) only if the sum of the amounts added to the capital account for the property for such taxable year exceeds the greater of—

(i) $2,000, or

(ii) one percent of the adjusted basis referred to in subparagraph (A)(ii), determined, however, as of the beginning of such taxable year.

For purposes of this section, if the amount added to the capital account for any separate improvement does not exceed the greater of clause (i) or (ii), such improvement shall be treated as placed in service on the first day, of a calendar month, which is closest to the middle of the taxable year.

(C) IMPROVEMENT.—The term "improvement" means, in the case of any section 1250 property, any addition to capital account for such property after the initial acquisition or after completion of the property.

Amendments

• **1976, Tax Reform Act of 1976 (P.L. 94-455)**

P.L. 94-455, §202(c)(1):

Amended Code Sec. 1250(f)(2). **Effective** for tax years ending after 12-31-75. Prior to amendment Code Sec. 1250(f)(2) read as follows:

(2) ORDINARY INCOME ATTRIBUTABLE TO AN ELEMENT.—For purposes of paragraph (1), the amount taken into account for any element shall be the sum of—

(A) the amount (if any) determined by multiplying—

(i) the amount which bears the same ratio to the lower of the amounts specified in subparagraph (A) or (B) of subsection (a)(1) for the section 1250 property as the additional depreciation for such element attributable to periods after December 31, 1969, bears to the sum of the additional depreciation for all elements attributable to periods after December 31, 1969, by

(ii) the applicable percentage for such element, and

(B) the amount (if any) determined by multiplying—

(i) the amount which bears the same ratio to the lower of the amounts specified in subsection (a)(2)(A)(i) or (ii) for the section 1250 property as the additional depreciation for such element attributable to periods before January 1, 1970, bears to the sum of the additional depreciation for all elements attributable to periods before January 1, 1970, by

(ii) the applicable percentage for such element.

For purposes of this paragraph, determinations with respect to any element shall be made as if it were a separate property.

P.L. 94-455, §1901(b)(3)(K):

Substituted "ordinary income" for "gain from the sale or exchange of property which is neither a capital asset nor property described in section 1231" in Code Sec. 1250(f)(1). **Effective** with respect to tax years beginning after 12-31-76.

• **1969, Tax Reform Act of 1969 (P.L. 91-172)**

P.L. 91-172, §521(e)(2):

Amended Code Sec. 1250(f)(1) by inserting "subsection (a)" in lieu of "subsection (a)(1)", and amended Code Sec. 1250(f)(2). **Effective** for tax years ending after 7-24-69. Prior to amendment, Code Sec. 1250(f)(2) read as follows:

(f)(2) ORDINARY INCOME ATTRIBUTABLE TO AN ELEMENT.—For purposes of paragraph (1), the amount taken into account for any element shall be the amount determined by multiplying—

(A) the amount which bears the same ratio to the lower of the amounts specified in subparagraph (A) or (B) of subsection (a)(1) for the section 1250 property as the additional depreciation for such element bears to the sum of the additional depreciation for all elements, by

(B) the applicable percentage for such element.

For purposes of this paragraph, determinations with respect to any element shall be made as if it were a separate property.

• **1964, Revenue Act of 1964 (P.L. 88-272)**

P.L. 88-272, §231(a):

Added Code Sec. 1250. **Effective** for dispositions after 12-31-63, in tax years ending after such date.

[Sec. 1250(g)]

(g) ADJUSTMENTS TO BASIS.—The Secretary shall prescribe such regulations as he may deem necessary to provide for adjustments to the basis of property to reflect gain recognized under subsection (a).

Amendments

• **1990, Omnibus Budget Reconciliation Act of 1990 (P.L. 101-508)**

P.L. 101-508, §11801(c)(15)(C):

Amended Code Sec. 1250(g) by striking subsection (g) and by redesignating subsections (h) and (i) as subsections (g) and (h), respectively. **Effective** 11-5-90. Prior to repeal, Code Sec. 1250(g) read as follows:

(g) SPECIAL RULES FOR QUALIFIED LOW-INCOME HOUSING.—

(1) AMOUNT TREATED AS ORDINARY INCOME.—If, in the case of a disposition of section 1250 property, the property is treated as consisting of more than one element by reason of the application of subsection (d)(8)(E), and gain is recognized in whole or in part, then the amount taken into account under subsection (a) as ordinary income shall be the sum of the amounts determined under paragraph (2).

(2) ORDINARY INCOME ATTRIBUTABLE TO AN ELEMENT.—For purposes of paragraph (1), the amount taken into account for any element shall be determined in a manner similar to that provided by subsection (f)(2).

P.L. 101-508, §11821(b), provides:

(b) SAVINGS PROVISION.—If—

(1) any provision amended or repealed by this part applied to—

(A) any transaction occurring before the date of the enactment of this Act,

(B) any property acquired before such date of enactment, or

(C) any item of income, loss, deduction, or credit taken into account before such date of enactment, and

(2) the treatment of such transaction, property, or item under such provision would (without regard to the amendments made by this part) affect liability for tax for periods ending after such date of enactment,

nothing in the amendments made by this part shall be construed to affect the treatment of such transaction, property, or item for purposes of determining liability for tax for periods ending after such date of enactment.

• **1976, Tax Reform Act of 1976 (P.L. 94-455)**

P.L. 94-455, §1906(b)(13)(A):

Amended 1954 Code by substituting "Secretary" for "Secretary or his delegate" each place it appeared. **Effective** 2-1-77.

P.L. 94-455, §202(c)(2):

Amended Code Sec. 1250(g)(2). **Effective** for tax years ending after 12-31-75. Prior to amendment Code Sec. 1250(g)(2) read as follows:

(2) ORDINARY INCOME ATTRIBUTABLE TO AN ELEMENT.—For purposes of paragraph (1), the amount taken into account for any element shall be the amount determined by multiplying—

(A) the amount which bears the same ratio to the lower of the additional depreciation or the gain recognized for the section 1250 property disposed of as the additional depreciation for such element bears to the sum of the additional depreciation for all elements disposed of, by

(B) the applicable percentage for such element.

For purposes of this paragraph, determinations with respect to any element shall be made as if it were a separate property.

P.L. 94-455, §1901(b)(3)(K):

Substituted "ordinary income" for "gain from the sale or exchange of property which is neither a capital asset nor property described in section 1231" in Code Sec. 1250(g)(1). **Effective** with respect to tax years beginning after 12-31-76.

• **1969, Tax Reform Act of 1969 (P.L. 91-172)**

P.L. 91-172, §910(b)(3):

Added Code Sec. 1250(g). **Effective** for approved dispositions of qualified housing projects within the meaning of Code Sec. 1039 after 10-9-69.

P.L. 91-172, §910(b)(3):

Redesignated subsection (g) as subsection (h). **Effective** 10-10-69.

• **1964, Revenue Act of 1964 (P.L. 88-272)**

P.L. 88-272, §231(a):

Added Code Sec. 1250(g). **Effective** as to dispositions after 12-31-63, in tax years ending after such date.

[Sec. 1250(h)]

(h) APPLICATION OF SECTION.—This section shall apply notwithstanding any other provision of this subtitle.

Amendments

• **1990, Omnibus Budget Reconciliation Act of 1990 (P.L. 101-508)**

P.L. 101-508, §11801(c)(15)(C):

Amended Code Sec. 1250 by redesignating subsection (i) as subsection (h). **Effective** 11-5-90.

P.L. 101-508, §11821(b), provides:

(b) SAVINGS PROVISION.—If—

(1) any provision amended or repealed by this part applied to—

(A) any transaction occurring before the date of the enactment of this Act,

(B) any property acquired before such date of enactment, or

(C) any item of income, loss, deduction, or credit taken into account before such date of enactment, and

(2) the treatment of such transaction, property, or item under such provision would (without regard to the amendments made by this part) affect liability for tax for periods ending after such date of enactment,

INCOME TAX—CAPITAL GAINS, LOSSES

nothing in the amendments made by this part shall be construed to affect the treatment of such transaction, property, or item for purposes of determining liability for tax for periods ending after such date of enactment.

- **1969, Tax Reform Act of 1969 (P.L. 91-172)**

P.L. 91-172, § 910(b)(3):

Redesignated subsection (h) as subsection (i). **Effective** 10-10-69.

Amendments

- **1984, Deficit Reduction Act of 1984 (P.L. 98-369)**

P.L. 98-369, § 492(a):

Repealed Code Sec. 1251. **Effective** for tax years beginning after 12-31-83. Prior to repeal, Code Sec. 1251 read as follows:

SEC. 1251. GAIN FROM DISPOSITION OF PROPERTY USED IN FARMING WHERE FARM LOSSES OFFSET NONFARM INCOME.

[Sec. 1251(a)]

(a) CIRCUMSTANCES UNDER WHICH SECTION APPLIES.—This section shall apply with respect to any taxable year only if—

(1) there is a farm net loss for the taxable year, or

(2) there is a balance in the excess deductions account as of the close of the taxable year after applying subsection (b)(3)(A).

[Sec. 1251(b)]

(b) EXCESS DEDUCTIONS ACCOUNT.—

(1) REQUIREMENT.—Each taxpayer subject to this section shall, for purposes of this section, establish and maintain an excess deductions account.

(2) ADDITIONS TO ACCOUNT.—

(A) GENERAL RULE.—There shall be added to the excess deductions account for each taxable year an amount equal to the farm net loss.

(B) EXCEPTIONS.—In the case of an individual (other than a trust) and, except as provided in this subparagraph, in the case of an S corporation, subparagraph (A) shall apply for a taxable year—

(i) only if the taxpayer's nonfarm adjusted gross income for such year exceeds $50,000, and

(ii) only to the extent the taxpayer's farm net loss for such year exceeds $25,000.

This subparagraph shall not apply to an S corporation for a taxable year if on any day of such year a shareholder of such corporation is an individual who, for his taxable year with which or within which the taxable year of the corporation ends, has a farm net loss or is a shareholder of another S corporation which has a farm net loss for its taxable year ending within such taxable year of the individual. For purposes of clause (i), in the case of an S corporation the nonfarm adjusted gross income of the corporation shall be increased by the amount of the nonfarm adjusted gross income of that shareholder (on any day of the corporation's taxable year) who has the highest amount of all such shareholders of nonfarm adjusted gross income for his taxable year with which or within which the taxable year of the corporation ends.

(C) MARRIED INDIVIDUALS.—In the case of a husband or wife who files a separate return, the amount specified in subparagraph (B)(i) shall be $25,000 in lieu of $50,000, and in subparagraph (B)(ii) shall be $12,500 in lieu of $25,000. This subparagraph shall not apply if the spouse of the taxpayer does not have any nonfarm adjusted gross income for the taxable year.

(D) NONFARM ADJUSTED GROSS INCOME.—For purposes of this section, the term "nonfarm adjusted gross income" means adjusted gross income (taxable income, in the case of an S corporation) computed without regard to income or deductions attributable to the business of farming.

(E) TERMINATION OF ADDITIONS.—No amount shall be added to the excess deductions account for any taxable year beginning after December 31, 1975.

(3) SUBTRACTIONS FROM ACCOUNT.—If there is any amount in the excess deductions account at the close of any taxable year (determined before any amount is subtracted under this paragraph for such year) there shall be subtracted from the account—

(A) an amount equal to the farm net income for such year, plus the amount (determined as provided in regulations prescribed by the Secretary) necessary to adjust the account for deductions which did not result in a reduction of the taxpayer's tax under this subtitle for the taxable year or any preceding taxable year, and

(B) after applying paragraph (2) or subparagraph (A) of this paragraph (as the case may be), an amount equal to the sum of the amounts treated, solely by reason of the application of subsection (c), as ordinary income.

In the case of a corporation which has made or received a transfer described in clause (ii) of paragraph (5)(A), subtractions from the excess deductions account shall be determined, in such manner as the Secretary shall prescribe, applying this paragraph to the farm net income, and the amounts described in subparagraph (B), of the transferor corporation and the transferee corporation on an aggregate basis.

(4) EXCEPTION FOR TAXPAYERS USING CERTAIN ACCOUNTING METHODS.—

(A) GENERAL RULE.—Except to the extent that the taxpayer has succeeded to an excess deductions account as provided in paragraph (5), additions to the excess deductions account shall not be required by a taxpayer who elects to compute taxable income from farming (i) by using inventories, and (ii) by charging to capital account all expenditures paid or incurred which are properly chargeable to capital account (including such expenditures which the taxpayer may, under this chapter or regulations prescribed thereunder, otherwise treat or elect to treat as expenditures which are not chargeable to capital account).

(B) TIME, MANNER, AND EFFECT OF ELECTION.—An election under subparagraph (A) for any taxable year shall be filed within the time prescribed by law (including extensions thereof) for filing the return for such taxable year, and shall be made and filed in such manner as the Secretary shall prescribe by regulations. Such election shall be binding on the taxpayer for such taxable year and for all subsequent taxable years and may not be revoked except with the consent of the Secretary.

(C) CHANGE OF METHOD OF ACCOUNTING, ETC.—If, in order to comply with the election made under subparagraph (A), a taxpayer changes his method of accounting in

Sec. 1251—Repealed

- **1964, Revenue Act of 1964 (P.L. 88-272)**

P.L. 88-272, § 231(a):

Added Code Sec. 1250(h). **Effective** as to dispositions after 12-31-63, in tax years ending after such date.

[Sec. 1251—Repealed]

computing taxable income from the business of farming, such change shall be treated as having been made with the consent of the Secretary and for purposes of section 481(a)(2) shall be treated as a change not initiated by the taxpayer.

(5) TRANSFER OF ACCOUNT.—

(A) CERTAIN CORPORATE TRANSACTIONS.—

(i) In the case of a transfer described in subsection (d)(3) to which section 371(a), 374(a), or 381 applies, the acquiring corporation shall succeed to and take into account as of the close of the day of distribution or transfer, the excess deductions account of the transferor.

(ii) In the case of a transfer which is described in subsection (d)(3), which is in connection with a reorganization described in section 368(a)(1)(D), and which is not described in clause (i), the transferee corporation shall be deemed to have an excess deductions account in an amount equal to the amount in the excess deductions account of the transferor. The transferor's excess deductions account shall not be reduced by reason of the preceding sentence.

(B) CERTAIN GIFTS.—If—

(i) farm recapture property is disposed of by gift, and

(ii) the potential gain (as defined in subsection (e)(5)) on farm recapture property disposed of by gift during any one year period in which any such gift occurs is more than 25 percent of the potential gain on farm recapture property held by the donor immediately prior to the first of such gifts,

each donee of the property shall succeed (at the time the first of such gifts is made, but in an amount determined as of the close of the donor's taxable year in which the first of such gifts is made) to the same proportion of the donor's excess deductions account (determined, after the application of paragraphs (2) and (3) with respect to the donor, as of the close of such taxable year), as the potential gain on the property received by such donee bears to the aggregate potential gain on farm recapture property held by the donor immediately prior to the first of such gifts.

(6) JOINT RETURN.—In the case of an addition to an excess deductions account for a taxable year for which a joint return was filed under section 6013, for any subsequent taxable year for which a separate return was filed the Secretary shall provide rules for allocating any remaining amount of such addition in a manner consistent with the purposes of this section.

Amendments

- **1982, Subchapter S Revision Act of 1982 (P.L. 97-354)**

P.L. 97-354, § 5(a)(36)(A):

Amended Code Sec. 1251(b)(2)(B) by striking out "an electing small business corporation (as defined in section 1371(b))," and inserting in lieu thereof "an S corporation,", and by striking out "electing small business corporation" each place it appears in the second and third sentences and inserting in lieu thereof "S corporation." **Effective** for tax years beginning after 12-31-82.

P.L. 97-354, § 5(a)(36)(B):

Amended Code Sec. 1251(b)(2)(D) by striking out "an electing small business corporation" and inserting in lieu thereof "an S corporation". **Effective** for tax years beginning after 12-31-82.

- **1976, Tax Reform Act of 1976 (P.L. 94-455)**

P.L. 94-455, § 206(a):

Added Code Sec. 1251(b)(2)(E). **Effective** for transfers occurring after 12-31-75.

P.L. 94-455, § 206(b)(1):

Amended Code Sec. 1251(b)(5)(A). **Effective** for transfers occurring after 12-31-75. Prior to amendment Code Sec. 1251(b)(5)(A) read as follows:

(A) CERTAIN CORPORATE TRANSACTIONS.—In the case of a transfer described in subsection (d)(3) to which section 371(a), 374(a), or 381 applies, the acquiring corporation shall succeed to and take into account as of the close of the day of distribution or transfer, the excess deductions account of the transferor.

P.L. 94-455, § 206(b)(2):

Added a new sentence at the end of Code Sec. 1251(b)(3). **Effective** for transfers occurring after 12-31-75.

P.L. 94-455, § 1901(b)(3)(K):

Substituted "ordinary income" for "gain from the sale or exchange of property which is neither a capital asset nor property described in section 1231" in Code Sec. 1251(b)(3)(B). **Effective** with respect to tax years beginning after 12-31-76.

P.L. 94-455, § 1906(b)(13)(A):

Amended the 1954 Code by substituting "Secretary" for "Secretary or his delegate" each place it appeared. **Effective** 2-1-77.

- **1971, Revenue Act of 1971 (P.L. 92-178)**

P.L. 92-178, § 305(a):

Amended the last sentence of Code Sec. 1251(b)(2)(B). **Effective** for tax years ending after 12-10-71. Prior to amendment, the last sentence read as follows:

This subparagraph shall not apply to an electing small business corporation for a taxable year if on any day of such year a shareholder of such corporation is an individual who, for his taxable year with which or within which the taxable year of the corporation ends, has a farm net loss.

INCOME TAX—CAPITAL GAINS, LOSSES

• **1969, Tax Reform Act of 1969 (P.L. 91-172)**

P.L. 91-172, §211(a):

Added Code Sec. 1251(b). **Effective** as to tax years beginning after 12-31-69.

[Sec. 1251(c)]

(c) ORDINARY INCOME.—

(1) GENERAL RULE.—Except as otherwise provided in this section, if farm recapture property (as defined in subsection (e)(1)) is disposed of during a taxable year beginning after December 31, 1969, the amount by which—

(A) in the case of a sale, exchange, or involuntary conversion, the amount realized, or

(B) in the case of any other disposition, the fair market value of such property,

exceeds the adjusted basis of such property shall be treated as ordinary income. Such gain shall be recognized notwithstanding any other provision of this subtitle.

(2) LIMITATION.—

(A) AMOUNT IN EXCESS DEDUCTIONS ACCOUNT.—The aggregate of the amounts treated under paragraph (1) as ordinary income for any taxable year shall not exceed the amount in the excess deductions account at the close of the taxable year after applying subsection (b)(3)(A).

(B) DISPOSITIONS TAKEN INTO ACCOUNT.—If the aggregate of the amounts to which paragraph (1) applies is limited by the application of subparagraph (A), paragraph (1) shall apply in respect of such dispositions (and in such amounts) as provided under regulations prescribed by the Secretary.

(C) SPECIAL RULE FOR DISPOSITIONS OF LAND.—In applying subparagraph (A), any gain on the sale or exchange of land shall be taken into account only to the extent of its potential gain (as defined in subsection (e)(5)).

Amendments

• **1976, Tax Reform Act of 1976 (P.L. 94-455)**

P.L. 94-455, §1901(b)(3)(K):

Substituted "ordinary income" for "gain from the sale or exchange of property which is neither a capital asset nor property described in section 1231" in Code Sec. 1251(c)(1) and (c)(2). **Effective** with respect to tax years beginning after 12-31-76.

P.L. 94-455, §1906(b)(13)(A):

Amended the 1954 Code by substituting "Secretary" for "Secretary or his delegate" each place it appeared. **Effective** 2-1-77.

• **1969, Tax Reform Act of 1969 (P.L. 91-172)**

P.L. 91-172, §211(a):

Added Code Sec. 1251(c). **Effective** as to tax years beginning after 12-31-69.

[Sec. 1251(d)]

(d) EXCEPTIONS AND SPECIAL RULES.—

(1) GIFTS.—Subsection (c) shall not apply to a disposition by gift.

(2) TRANSFER AT DEATH.—Except as provided in section 691 (relating to income in respect of a decedent), subsection (c) shall not apply to a transfer at death.

(3) CERTAIN CORPORATE TRANSACTIONS.—If the basis of property in the hands of a transferee is determined by reference to its basis in the hands of the transferor by reason of the application of section 332, 351, 361, 371(a), or 374(a), then the amount of gain taken into account by the transferor under subsection (c)(1) shall not exceed the amount of gain recognized to the transferor on the transfer of such property (determined without regard to this section). This paragraph shall not apply to a disposition to an organization (other than a cooperative described in section 521) which is exempt from the tax imposed by this chapter.

(4) LIKE KIND EXCHANGES; INVOLUNTARY CONVERSION, ETC.—If property is disposed of and gain (determined without regard to this section) is not recognized in whole or in part under section 1031 or 1033, then the amount of gain taken into account by the transferor under subsection (c)(1) shall not exceed the sum of—

(A) the amount of gain recognized on such disposition (determined without regard to this section), plus

(B) the fair market value of property acquired with respect to which no gain is recognized under subparagraph (A), but which is not farm recapture property.

(5) PARTNERSHIPS.—

(A) IN GENERAL.—In the case of a partnership, each partner shall take into account separately his distributive share of the partnership's farm net losses, gains from dispositions of farm recapture property, and other items in applying this section to the partner.

(B) TRANSFERS TO PARTNERSHIPS.—If farm recapture property is contributed to a partnership and gain (determined without regard to this section) is not recognized under section 721, then the amount of gain taken into account by the transferor under subsection (c)(1) shall not exceed the excess of the fair market value of farm recapture property transferred over the fair market value of the partnership interest attributable to such property. If the partnership agreement provides for an allocation of gain to the contributing partner with respect to farm recapture property contributed to the partnership (as provided in section 704(c)(2)), the partnership interest of the contributing partner shall be deemed to be attributable to such property.

(6) PROPERTY TRANSFERRED TO CONTROLLED CORPORATIONS.—Except for transactions described in subsection (b)(5)(A), in the case of a transfer, described in paragraph (3), of farm recapture property to a corporation, stock or securities received by a transferor in the exchange shall be farm recapture property to the extent attributable to the fair market value of farm recapture property (or, in the case of land, if less, the adjusted basis plus the potential gain (as defined in subsection (e)(5)) on farm recapture property) contributed to the corporation by such transferor.

Amendments

• **1969, Tax Reform Act of 1969 (P.L. 91-172)**

P.L. 91-172, §211(a):

Added Code Sec. 1251(d). **Effective** as to tax years beginning after 12-31-69.

[Sec. 1251(e)]

(e) DEFINITIONS.—For purposes of this section—

(1) FARM RECAPTURE PROPERTY.—The term "farm recapture property" means—

(A) any property (other than section 1250 property) described in paragraph (1) (relating to business property held for more than 1 year), (3) (relating to livestock), or (4) (relating to an unharvested crop) of section 1231(b) which is or has been used in the trade or business of farming by the taxpayer or by a transferor in a transaction described in subsection (b)(5), and

(B) any property the basis of which in the hands of the taxpayer is determined with reference to the adjusted basis of property which was farm recapture property in the hands of the taxpayer within the meaning of subparagraph (A).

(2) FARM NET LOSS.—The term "farm net loss" means the amount by which—

(A) the deductions allowed or allowable by this chapter which are directly connected with the carrying on of the trade or business of farming, exceed

(B) the gross income derived from such trade or business.

Gains and losses on the disposition of farm recapture property referred to in section 1231(a) (determined without regard to this section or section 1245(a)) shall not be taken into account.

(3) FARM NET INCOME.—The term "farm net income" means the amount by which the amount referred to in paragraph (2)(B) exceeds the amount referred to in paragraph (2)(A).

(4) TRADE OR BUSINESS OF FARMING.—

(A) HORSE RACING.—In the case of a taxpayer engaged in the raising of horses, the term "trade or business of farming" includes the racing of horses.

(B) SEVERAL BUSINESSES OF FARMING.—If a taxpayer is engaged in more than one trade or business of farming, all such trades and businesses shall be treated as one trade or business.

(5) POTENTIAL GAIN.—The term "potential gain" means an amount equal to the excess of the fair market value of property over its adjusted basis, but limited in the case of land to the extent of the deductions allowable in respect to such land under sections 175 (relating to soil and water conservation expenditures) and 182 (relating to expenditures by farmers for clearing land) for the taxable year and the 4 preceding taxable years.

Amendments

• **1984, Deficit Reduction Act of 1984 (P.L. 98-369)**

P.L. 98-369, §1001(b)(23):

Amended Code Sec. 1251(e)(1)(A) by striking out "1 year" and inserting in lieu thereof "6 months". [Note: P.L. 98-369, §492(a), repealed Code Sec. 1251, applicable to tax years beginning after 12-31-83. Therefore, this amendment cannot be made.— CCH] **Effective** for property acquired after 6-22-84, and before 1-1-88.

• **1976, Tax Reform Act of 1976 (P.L. 94-455)**

P.L. 94-455, §1402(b)(1)(Z):

Substituted "9 months" for "6 months" in Code Sec. 1251(e)(1). **Effective** with respect to tax years beginning in 1977.

P.L. 94-455, §1402(b)(2):

Substituted "1 year" for "9 months" in Code Sec. 1251(e)(1). **Effective** with respect to tax years beginning after 12-31-77.

• **1969, Tax Reform Act of 1969 (P.L. 91-172)**

P.L. 91-172, §211(a):

Added Code Sec. 1251(e). **Effective** as to tax years beginning after 12-31-69.

[Sec. 1252]

SEC. 1252. GAIN FROM DISPOSITION OF FARM LAND.

[Sec. 1252(a)]

(a) GENERAL RULE.—

(1) ORDINARY INCOME.—Except as otherwise provided in this section, if farm land which the taxpayer has held for less than 10 years is disposed of, the lower of—

(A) the applicable percentage of the aggregate of the deductions allowed under section 175 (relating to soil and water conservation expenditures) for expenditures made by the taxpayer with respect to the farm land or

(B) the excess of—

(i) the amount realized (in the case of a sale, exchange, or involuntary conversion), or the fair market value of the farm land (in the case of any other disposition), over

(ii) the adjusted basis of such land,

shall be treated as ordinary income. Such gain shall be recognized notwithstanding any other provision of this subtitle.

INCOME TAX—CAPITAL GAINS, LOSSES

(2) Farm land.—For purposes of this section, the term "farm land" means any land with respect to which deductions have been allowed under section 175 (relating to soil and water conservation expenditures).

(3) Applicable percentage.—For purposes of this section—

If the farm land is disposed of—	The applicable percentage is—
Within 5 years after the date it was acquired	100 percent.
Within the sixth year after it was acquired	80 percent.
Within the seventh year after it was acquired	60 percent.
Within the eighth year after it was acquired	40 percent.
Within the ninth year after it was acquired	20 percent.
10 years or more years after it was acquired	0 percent.

Amendments

• **2018, Tax Technical Corrections Act of 2018 (P.L. 115-141)**

P.L. 115-141, §401(b)(32)(A), Div. U:

Amended Code Sec. 1252(a)(1) by striking "during a taxable year beginning" following "10 years is disposed of". **Effective** 3-23-2018. For a special rule, see Act Sec. 401(e), Div. U, below.

P.L. 115-141, §401(b)(32)(B)(i)-(ii), Div. U:

Amended Code Sec. 1252(a)(1)(A) by striking "sections" and inserting "section", and by striking "and 182" and all that follows through "for expenditures" and inserting "for expenditures". **Effective** 3-23-2018. For a special rule, see Act Sec. 401(e), Div. U, below. Prior to being stricken, "and 182" and all that follows through "for expenditures" in Code Sec. 1252(a)(1)(A) read as follows:

and 182 (as in effect on the day before the date of enactment of the Tax Reform Act of 1986) for expenditures

P.L. 115-141, §401(b)(32)(C)(i)-(ii), Div. U:

Amended Code Sec. 1252(a)(2) by striking "sections" and inserting "section", and by striking "or 182" and all that follows and inserting a period. **Effective** 3-23-2018. For a special rule, see Act Sec. 401(e), Div. U, below. Prior to being stricken, "or 182" and all that follows in Code Sec. 1252(a)(2) read as follows:

or 182 (relating to expenditures by farmers for clearing land).

P.L. 115-141, §401(e), Div. U, provides:

(e) General Savings Provision With Respect To Deadwood Provisions.—If—

(1) any provision amended or repealed by the amendments made by subsection (b) or (d) applied to—

(A) any transaction occurring before the date of the enactment of this Act,

(B) any property acquired before such date of enactment, or

(C) any item of income, loss, deduction, or credit taken into account before such date of enactment, and

(2) the treatment of such transaction, property, or item under such provision would (without regard to the amendments or repeals made by such subsection) affect the liability for tax for periods ending after such date of enactment,

nothing in the amendments or repeals made by this section shall be construed to affect the treatment of such transaction, property, or item for purposes of determining liability for tax for periods ending after such date of enactment.

• **2014, Tax Technical Corrections Act of 2014 (P.L. 113-295)**

P.L. 113-295, §221(a)(85)(A)-(B), Division A:

Amended Code Sec. 1252(a)(1) by striking "after December 31, 1969" the first place it appears [following "expenditures made by the taxpayer"], and by striking "after December 31, 1969," following "expenditures made by the taxpayer" in subparagraph (A). **Effective** generally 12-19-2014. For a special rule, see Act Sec. 221(b)(2), Division A, below.

P.L. 113-295, §221(b)(2), Division A, provides:

(2) Savings provision.—If—

(A) any provision amended or repealed by the amendments made by this section applied to—

(i) any transaction occurring before the date of the enactment of this Act,

(ii) any property acquired before such date of enactment, or

(iii) any item of income, loss, deduction, or credit taken into account before such date of enactment, and

(B) the treatment of such transaction, property, or item under such provision would (without regard to the amendments or repeals made by this section) affect the liability for tax for periods ending after date of enactment, nothing in the amendments or repeals made by this section shall be construed to affect the treatment of such transaction, property, or item for purposes of determining liability for tax for periods ending after such date of enactment.

• **1986, Tax Reform Act of 1986 (P.L. 99-514)**

P.L. 99-514, §402(b)(2):

Amended Code Sec. 1252(a)(1)(A) by striking out "(relating to expenditures by farmers for clearing land)" and inserting in lieu thereof "(as in effect on the day before the date of enactment of the Tax Reform Act of 1986)". **Effective** for amounts paid or incurred after 12-31-85, in tax years ending after such date.

• **1984, Deficit Reduction Act of 1984 (P.L. 98-369)**

P.L. 98-369, §492(b)(5):

Amended Code Sec. 1252(a)(1) by striking out ", except that this section shall not apply to the extent section 1251 applies to such gain" in the second sentence. **Effective** for tax years beginning after 12-31-83.

• **1976, Tax Reform Act of 1976 (P.L. 94-455)**

P.L. 94-455, §1901(b)(3)(K):

Substituted "ordinary income" for "gain from the sale or exchange of property which is neither a capital asset nor property described in section 1231" in Code Sec. 1252(a)(1). **Effective** with respect to tax years beginning after 12-31-76.

• **1969, Tax Reform Act of 1969 (P.L. 91-172)**

P.L. 91-172, §214(a):

Added Code Sec. 1251[2](a). **Effective** for tax years beginning after 12-31-69.

[Sec. 1252(b)]

(b) Special Rules.—Under regulations prescribed by the Secretary, rules similar to the rules of section 1245 shall be applied for purposes of this section.

Amendments

• **1976, Tax Reform Act of 1976 (P.L. 94-455)**

P.L. 94-455, §1906(b)(13)(A):

Amended 1954 Code by substituting "Secretary" for "Secretary or his delegate" each place it appeared. **Effective** 2-1-77.

• **1969, Tax Reform Act of 1969 (P.L. 91-172)**

P.L. 91-172, §214(a):

Added Code Sec. 1252(b). **Effective** for tax years beginning after 12-31-69.

[Sec. 1253]

SEC. 1253. TRANSFERS OF FRANCHISES, TRADEMARKS, AND TRADE NAMES.

[Sec. 1253(a)]

(a) General Rule.—A transfer of a franchise, trademark, or trade name shall not be treated as a sale or exchange of a capital asset if the transferor retains any significant power, right, or continuing interest with respect to the subject matter of the franchise, trademark, or trade name.

[Sec. 1253(b)]

(b) Definitions.—For purposes of this section—

(1) Franchise.—The term "franchise" includes an agreement which gives one of the parties to the agreement the right to distribute, sell, or provide goods, services, or facilities, within a specified area.

(2) Significant power, right, or continuing interest.—The term "significant power, right, or continuing interest" includes, but is not limited to, the following rights with respect to the interest transferred:

(A) A right to disapprove any assignment of such interest, or any part thereof.

(B) A right to terminate at will.

(C) A right to prescribe the standards of quality of products used or sold, or of services furnished, and of the equipment and facilities used to promote such products or services.

(D) A right to require that the transferee sell or advertise only products or services of the transferor.

(E) A right to require that the transferee purchase substantially all of his supplies and equipment from the transferor.

Sec. 1252(a)(2)

(F) A right to payments contingent on the productivity, use, or disposition of the subject matter of the interest transferred, if such payments constitute a substantial element under the transfer agreement.

(3) TRANSFER.—The term "transfer" includes the renewal of a franchise, trademark, or trade name.

[Sec. 1253(c)]

(c) TREATMENT OF CONTINGENT PAYMENTS BY TRANSFEROR.—Amounts received or accrued on account of a transfer, sale, or other disposition of a franchise, trademark, or trade name which are contingent on the productivity, use, or disposition of the franchise, trademark, or trade name transferred shall be treated as amounts received or accrued from the sale or other disposition of property which is not a capital asset.

[Sec. 1253(d)]

(d) TREATMENT OF PAYMENTS BY TRANSFEREE.—

(1) CONTINGENT SERIAL PAYMENTS.—

(A) IN GENERAL.—Any amount described in subparagraph (B) which is paid or incurred during the taxable year on account of a transfer, sale, or other disposition of a franchise, trademark, or trade name shall be allowed as a deduction under section 162(a) (relating to trade or business expenses).

(B) AMOUNTS TO WHICH PARAGRAPH APPLIES.—An amount is described in this subparagraph if it—

(i) is contingent on the productivity, use, or disposition of the franchise, trademark, or trade name, and

(ii) is paid as part of a series of payments—

(I) which are payable not less frequently than annually throughout the entire term of the transfer agreement, and

(II) which are substantially equal in amount (or payable under a fixed formula).

(2) OTHER PAYMENTS.—Any amount paid or incurred on account of a transfer, sale, or other disposition of a franchise, trademark, or trade name to which paragraph (1) does not apply shall be treated as an amount chargeable to capital account.

(3) RENEWALS, ETC.—For purposes of determining the term of a transfer agreement under this section, there shall be taken into account all renewal options (and any other period for which the parties reasonably expect the agreement to be renewed).

Amendments

- **1993, Omnibus Budget Reconciliation Act of 1993 (P.L. 103-66)**

P.L. 103-66, §13261(c):

Amended Code Sec. 1253(d) by striking paragraphs (2), (3), (4), and (5) and inserting new paragraphs (2)-(3). **Effective** with respect to property acquired after 8-10-93. For special rules, see Act Sec. 13261(g)(2)-(3) in the amendment notes following Code Sec. 197. Prior to amendment, Code Sec. 1253(d)(2)-(5) read as follows:

(2) CERTAIN PAYMENTS IN DISCHARGE OF PRINCIPAL SUMS.—

(A) IN GENERAL.—If a transfer of a franchise, trademark, or trade name is not (by reason of the application of subsection (a)) treated as a sale or exchange of a capital asset, any payment not described in paragraph (1) which is made in discharge of a principal sum agreed upon in the transfer agreement shall be allowed as a deduction—

(i) in the case of a single payment made in discharge of such principal sum, ratably over the taxable years in the period beginning with the taxable year in which the payment is made and ending with the ninth succeeding taxable year or ending with the last taxable year beginning in the period of the transfer agreement, whichever period is shorter;

(ii) in the case of a payment which is one of a series of approximately equal payments made in discharge of such principal sum, which are payable over—

(I) the period of the transfer agreement, or

(II) a period of more than 10 taxable years, whether ending before or after the end of the period of the transfer agreement,

in the taxable year in which the payment is made; and

(iii) in the case of any other payment, in the taxable year or years specified in regulations prescribed by the Secretary, consistently with the preceding provisions of this paragraph.

(B) $100,000 LIMITATION ON DEDUCTIBILITY OF PRINCIPAL SUM.—Subparagraph (A) shall not apply if the principal sum referred to in such subparagraph exceeds $100,000. For purposes of the preceding sentence, all payments which are part of the same transaction (or a series of related transactions) shall be taken into account as payments with respect to each such transaction.

(3) OTHER PAYMENTS.—

(A) IN GENERAL.—Any amount paid or incurred on account of a transfer, sale, or other disposition of a franchise, trademark, or trade name to which paragraph (1) or (2) does not apply shall be treated as an amount chargeable to capital account.

(B) ELECTION TO RECOVER AMOUNTS OVER 25 YEARS.—

(i) IN GENERAL.—If the taxpayer elects the application of this subparagraph, an amount chargeable to capital account—

(I) to which paragraph (1) would apply but for subparagraph (B)(ii) thereof, or

(II) to which paragraph (2) would apply but for subparagraph (B) thereof,

shall be allowed as a deduction ratably over the 25-year period beginning with the taxable year in which the transfer occurs.

(ii) CONSISTENT TREATMENT.—An election under clause (i) shall apply to all amounts which are part of the same transaction (or a series of related transactions).

(4) RENEWALS, ETC.—For purposes of determining the term of a transfer agreement under this section or any period of amortization under this subtitle for any payment described in this section, there shall be taken into account all renewal options (and any other period for which the parties reasonably expect the agreement to be renewed).

(5) CERTAIN RULES MADE APPLICABLE.—Rules similar to the rules of section 168(i)(7) shall apply for purposes of this subsection.

- **1990, Omnibus Budget Reconciliation Act of 1990 (P.L. 101-508)**

P.L. 101-508, §11701(i) (as amended by P.L. 104-188, §1704(t)(47)):

Amended Code Sec. 1253(d)(4) by striking "or any period of amortization under this subsection" and inserting "under this section or any period of amortization under this subtitle for any payment described in this section". **Effective** as if included in the provision of P.L. 101-239 to which it relates.

- **1989, Omnibus Budget Reconciliation Act of 1989 (P.L. 101-239)**

P.L. 101-239, §7622(a):

Amended Code Sec. 1253(d)(1). **Effective** for transfers after 10-2-89. For a special rule, see Act Sec. 7622(c)[e](2), below. Prior to amendment, Code Sec. 1253(d)(1) read as follows:

(1) CONTINGENT PAYMENTS.—Amounts paid or incurred during the taxable year on account of a transfer, sale, or other disposition of a franchise, trademark, or trade name which are contingent on the productivity, use, or disposition of the franchise, trademark, or trade name transferred shall be allowed as a deduction under section 162(a) (relating to trade or business expenses).

P.L. 101-239, §7622(b)(1):

Amended Code Sec. 1253(d)(2) by adding at the end thereof a new subparagraph (B). **Effective** for transfers after 10-2-89. For a special rule, see Act Sec. 7622(c)[e](2), below.

P.L. 101-239, §7622(b)(2)(A)-(B):

Amended Code Sec. 1253(d)(2). **Effective** for transfers after 10-2-89. For a special rule, see Act Sec. 7622(c)[e](2), below. Prior to amendment, Code Sec. 1253(d)(2) read as follows:

(2) OTHER PAYMENTS.—If a transfer of a franchise, trademark, or trade name is not (by reason of the application of subsection (a)) treated as a sale or exchange of a capital asset, any payment not described in paragraph (1) which is made in discharge of a principal sum agreed upon in the transfer agreement shall be allowed as a deduction—

(A) in the case of a single payment made in discharge of such principal sum, ratably over the taxable years in the period beginning with the taxable year in which the payment is made and ending with the ninth succeeding taxable year or ending with the last taxable year beginning in the period of the transfer agreement, whichever period is shorter;

(B) in the case of a payment which is one of a series of approximately equal payments made in discharge of such principal sum, which are payable over—

(i) the period of the transfer agreement, or

(ii) a period of more than 10 taxable years, whether ending before or after the end of the period of the transfer agreement,

in the taxable year in which the payment is made; and

(C) in the case of any other payment, in the taxable year or years specified in regulations prescribed by the Secretary, consistently with the preceding provisions of this paragraph.

P.L. 101-239, §7622(c):

Amended Code Sec. 1253(d), as amended by subsection (b), by adding at the end thereof new paragraphs (3)-(5). **Effective** for transfers after 10-2-89. For a special rule, see Act Sec. 7622(c)[e](2), below.

P.L. 101-239, §7622(c)[e](2), provides:

(2) BINDING CONTRACT.—The amendments made by this section shall not apply to any transfer pursuant to a written binding contract in effect on October 2, 1989, and at all times thereafter before the transfer.

- **1976, Tax Reform Act of 1976 (P.L. 94-455)**

P.L. 94-455, §1906(b)(13)(A):

Amended 1954 Code by substituting "Secretary" for "Secretary or his delegate" each place it appeared. **Effective** 2-1-77.

INCOME TAX—CAPITAL GAINS, LOSSES

Amendments

• **2004, American Jobs Creation Act of 2004 (P.L. 108-357)**

P.L. 108-357, §886(b)(3):

Amended Code Sec. 1253 by striking subsection (e). **Effective** for property acquired after 10-22-2004. Prior to being stricken, Code Sec. 1253(e) read as follows:

(e) EXCEPTION.—This section shall not apply to the transfer of a franchise to engage in professional football, basketball, baseball, or other professional sport.

[Sec. 1253(e)—Stricken]

• **1969, Tax Reform Act of 1969 (P.L. 91-172)**

P.L. 91-172, §516(c)(1):

Added Code Sec. 1253. **Effective** for transfers after 12-31-69, except that section 1253(d)(1) of the Internal Revenue Code of 1954 (as added by subsection (c)) shall, at the election of the taxpayer (made at such time and in such manner as the Secretary or his delegate may by regulations prescribe), apply to transfers before 1-1-70, but only with respect to payments made in tax years ending after 12-31-69, and beginning before 1-1-80.

[Sec. 1254]

SEC. 1254. GAIN FROM DISPOSITION OF INTEREST IN OIL, GAS, GEOTHERMAL, OR OTHER MINERAL PROPERTIES.

[Sec. 1254(a)]

(a) GENERAL RULE.—

(1) ORDINARY INCOME.—If any section 1254 property is disposed of, the lesser of—

(A) the aggregate amount of—

(i) expenditures which have been deducted by the taxpayer or any person under section 263, 616, or 617 with respect to such property and which, but for such deduction, would have been included in the adjusted basis of such property, and

(ii) the deductions for depletion under section 611 which reduced the adjusted basis of such property, or

(B) the excess of—

(i) in the case of—

(I) a sale, exchange, or involuntary conversion, the amount realized, or

(II) in the case of any other disposition, the fair market value of such property, over

(ii) the adjusted basis of such property,

shall be treated as gain which is ordinary income. Such gain shall be recognized notwithstanding any other provision of this subtitle.

(2) DISPOSITION OF PORTION OF PROPERTY.—For purposes of paragraph (1)—

(A) In the case of the disposition of a portion of section 1254 property (other than an undivided interest), the entire amount of the aggregate expenditures or deductions described in paragraph (1)(A) with respect to such property shall be treated as allocable to such portion to the extent of the amount of the gain to which paragraph (1) applies.

(B) In the case of the disposition of an undivided interest in a section 1254 property (or a portion thereof), a proportionate part of the expenditures or deductions described in paragraph (1)(A) with respect to such property shall be treated as allocable to such undivided interest to the extent of the amount of the gain to which paragraph (1) applies.

This paragraph shall not apply to any expenditures to the extent the taxpayer establishes to the satisfaction of the Secretary that such expenditures do not relate to the portion (or interest therein) disposed of.

(3) SECTION 1254 PROPERTY.—The term "section 1254 property" means any property (within the meaning of section 614) if—

(A) any expenditures described in paragraph (1)(A) are properly chargeable to such property, or

(B) the adjusted basis of such property includes adjustments for deductions for depletion under section 611.

(4) ADJUSTMENT FOR AMOUNTS INCLUDED IN GROSS INCOME UNDER SECTION 617(b)(1)(A).—The amount of the expenditures referred to in paragraph (1)(A)(i) shall be properly adjusted for amounts included in gross income under section 617(b)(1)(A).

Amendments

• **1988, Technical and Miscellaneous Revenue Act of 1988 (P.L. 100-647)**

P.L. 100-647, §1004(c):

Amended Code Sec. 1254(a) by adding at the end thereof new paragraph (4). **Effective** as if included in the provision of P.L. 99-514 to which it relates.

[Sec. 1254(b)]

(b) SPECIAL RULES UNDER REGULATIONS.—Under regulations prescribed by the Secretary—

(1) rules similar to the rule of subsection (g) of section 617 and to the rules of subsections (b) and (c) of section 1245 shall be applied for purposes of this section; and

(2) in the case of the sale or exchange of stock in an S corporation, rules similar to the rules of section 751 shall be applied to that portion of the excess of the amount realized over the adjusted basis of the stock which is attributable to expenditures referred to in subsection (a)(1)(A) of this section.

Amendments

• **1986, Tax Reform Act of 1986 (P.L. 99-514)**

P.L. 99-514, §413(a):

Amended Code Sec. 1254. **Effective**, generally, for any disposition of property which is placed in service by the taxpayer after 12-31-86. However, for an exception see Act Sec. 413(c)(2), below. Prior to amendment, Code Sec. 1254 read as follows:

CODE SEC. 1254. GAIN FROM DISPOSITION OF INTEREST IN OIL, GAS, OR GEOTHERMAL PROPERTY.

(a) GENERAL RULE.—

(1) ORDINARY INCOME.—If oil, gas, or geothermal property is disposed of after December 31, 1975, the lower of—

(A) the aggregate amount of expenditures after December 31, 1975, which are allocable to such property and which have been deducted as intangible drilling and development costs under section 263(c) by the taxpayer or any other person and which (but for being so deducted) would be reflected in the adjusted basis of such property, adjusted as provided in paragraph (4), or

(B) the excess of—

(i) the amount realized (in the case of a sale, exchange, or involuntary conversion), or the fair market value of the interest (in the case of any other disposition), over

(ii) the adjusted basis of such interest,

shall be treated as gain which is ordinary income. Such gain shall be recognized notwithstanding any other provision of this subtitle.

(2) DISPOSITION OF PORTION OF PROPERTY.—For purposes of paragraph (1)—

(A) In the case of the disposition of a portion of an oil, gas, or geothermal property (other than an undivided interest), the entire amount of the aggregate expenditures described in paragraph (1)(A) with respect to such property shall be treated as allocable to such portion to the extent of the amount of the gain to which paragraph (1) applies.

(B) In the case of the disposition of an undivided interest in an oil, gas, or geothermal property (or a portion thereof), a proportionate part of the expenditures described in paragraph (1)(A) with respect to such property shall be treated as allocable to such undivided interest to the extent of the amount of the gain to which paragraph (1) applies.

This paragraph shall not apply to any expenditures to the extent the taxpayer establishes to the satisfaction of the Secretary that such expenditures do not relate to the portion (or interest therein) disposed of.

(3) OIL, GAS, OR GEOTHERMAL PROPERTY.—The term "oil, gas, or geothermal property" means any property (within the meaning of section 614) with respect to which any expenditures described in paragraph (1)(A) are properly chargeable.

(4) SPECIAL RULE FOR PARAGRAPH (1)(A).—In applying paragraph (1)(A), the amount deducted for intangible drilling and development costs and allocable to the interest disposed of shall be reduced by the amount (if any) by which the deduction for depletion under section 611 with respect to such interest would have been increased if such costs incurred (after December 31, 1975) had been charged to capital account rather than deducted.

(b) SPECIAL RULES UNDER REGULATIONS.—Under regulations prescribed by the Secretary—

Sec. 1253(e)—Stricken

(1) rules similar to the rules of subsection (g) of section 617 and to the rules of subsection (b) and (c) of section 1245 shall be applied for purposes of this section; and

(2) in the case of the sale or exchange of stock in an S corporation, rules similar to the rules of section 751 shall be applied to that portion of the excess of the amount realized over the adjusted basis of the stock which is attributable to expenditures referred to in subsection (a)(1)(A) of this section.

P.L. 99-514, §413(c)(2), provides:

(2) EXCEPTION FOR BINDING CONTRACTS.—The amendments made by this section shall not apply to any disposition of property placed in service after December 31, 1986, if such property was acquired pursuant to a written contract which was entered into before September 26, 1985, and which was binding at all times thereafter.

- **1982, Subchapter S Revision Act of 1982 (P.L. 97-354)**

P.L. 97-354, §5(a)(37):

Amended Code Sec. 1254(b)(2) by striking out "an electing small business corporation (as defined in section 1371(b))," and inserting in lieu thereof "an S corporation,". **Effective** for tax years beginning after 12-31-82.

[Sec. 1255]

SEC. 1255. GAIN FROM DISPOSITION OF SECTION 126 PROPERTY.

[Sec. 1255(a)]

(a) GENERAL RULE.—

(1) ORDINARY INCOME.—Except as otherwise provided in this section, if section 126 property is disposed of, the lower of—

(A) the applicable percentage of the aggregate payments, with respect to such property, excluded from gross income under section 126, or

(B) the excess of—

(i) the amount realized (in the case of a sale, exchange, or involuntary conversion), or the fair market value of such section 126 property (in the case of any other disposition), over

(ii) the adjusted basis of such property,

shall be treated as ordinary income. Such gain shall be recognized notwithstanding any other provision of this subtitle, except that this section shall not apply to the extent such gain is recognized as ordinary income under any other provision of this part.

(2) SECTION 126 PROPERTY.—For purposes of this section, "section 126 property" means any property acquired, improved, or otherwise modified by the application of payments excluded from gross income under section 126.

(3) APPLICABLE PERCENTAGE.—For purposes of this section, if section 126 property is disposed of less than 10 years after the date of receipt of payments excluded from gross income under section 126, the applicable percentage is 100 percent. If section 126 property is disposed of more than 10 years after such date, the applicable percentage is 100 percent reduced (but not below zero) by 10 percent for each year or part thereof in excess of 10 years such property was held after the date of receipt of the payments.

[Sec. 1255(b)]

(b) SPECIAL RULES.—Under regulations prescribed by the Secretary—

(1) rules similar to the rules applicable under section 1245 shall be applied for purposes of this section, and

(2) for purposes of sections 170(e) and 751(c), amounts treated as ordinary income under this section shall be treated in the same manner as amounts treated as ordinary income under section 1245.

Amendments

- **2018, Tax Technical Corrections Act of 2018 (P.L. 115-141)**

P.L. 115-141, §401(a)(175), Div. U:

Amended Code Sec. 1255(b)(2) by striking "170(e)," and inserting "170(e)". **Effective** 3-23-2018.

- **2013, American Taxpayer Relief Act of 2012 (P.L. 112-240)**

P.L. 112-240, §102(a), provides:

SEC. 102. PERMANENT EXTENSION AND MODIFICATION OF 2003 TAX RELIEF.

(a) PERMANENT EXTENSION.—The Jobs and Growth Tax Relief Reconciliation Act of 2003 is amended by striking section 303.

- **2003, Jobs and Growth Tax Relief Reconciliation Act of 2003 (P.L. 108-27)**

P.L. 108-27, §302(e)(4)(B)(ii):

Amended Code Sec. 1255(b)(2) by striking ", 341(e)(12)," after "170(e)". For the **effective** date, see Act Sec. 302(f), as amended by P.L. 108-311, §402(a)(6), below.

P.L. 108-27, §302(f), as amended by P.L. 108-311, §402(a)(6), provides:

(f) EFFECTIVE DATE.—

(1) IN GENERAL.—Except as provided in paragraph (2), the amendments made by this section shall apply to taxable years beginning after December 31, 2002.

(2) PASS-THRU ENTITIES.—In the case of a pass-thru entity described in subparagraph (A), (B), (C), (D), (E), or (F) of section 1(h)(10) of the Internal Revenue Code of 1986, as amended by this Act, the amendments made by this section shall apply to taxable years ending after December 31, 2002; except that dividends received by such an entity on or before such date shall not be treated as qualified dividend income (as defined in section 1(h)(11)(B) of such Code, as added by this Act).

P.L. 108-27, §303, as amended by P.L. 109-222, §102, and P.L. 111-312, §102(a), provides [but see P.L. 112-240, §102(a), above]:

SEC. 303. SUNSET OF TITLE.

All provisions of, and amendments made by, this title shall not apply to taxable years beginning after December 31, 2012, and the Internal Revenue Code of 1986 shall be applied and administered to such years as if such provisions and amendments had never been enacted.

- **1978, Energy Tax Act of 1978 (P.L. 95-618)**

P.L. 95-618, §402(c)(1), (2), (3):

Amended Code Sec. 1254(a) by striking out the words "oil or gas property" wherever it occurred in paragraphs (1), (2), and (3) and inserting in lieu thereof "oil, gas, or geothermal property", and also amended the heading for Code Sec. 1254 by striking out "OIL OR GAS PROPERTY" and inserting in lieu thereof "OIL, GAS, OR GEOTHERMAL PROPERTY". **Effective** with respect to wells commenced on or after 10-1-78, in tax years ending on or after such date.

- **1976, Tax Reform Act of 1976 (P.L. 94-455)**

P.L. 94-455, §205(a):

Added Code Sec. 1254. **Effective** for tax years ending after 12-31-75.

- **1986, Tax Reform Act of 1986 (P.L. 99-514)**

P.L. 99-514, §511(d)[c](2)(A) (as amended by P.L. 100-647, §1005(c)(10)):

Amended Code Sec. 1255(b)(2) by striking out "163(d),". **Effective** for tax years beginning after 12-31-86.

P.L. 99-514, §631(e)(14):

Amended Code Sec. 1255(b)(2) by striking out "453B(d)(2)". **Effective** (1) to any distribution in complete liquidation, and any sale or exchange, made by a corporation after 7-31-86, unless such corporation is completely liquidated before 1-1-87, (2) any transaction described in section 338 of the Internal Revenue Code of 1986 for which the acquisition date occurs after 12-31-86, and (3) any distribution (not in complete liquidation) made after 12-31-86. For special and transitional rules, see Act Sec. 633(b)-(f) following Code Sec. 26.

- **1980, Installment Sales Revision Act of 1980 (P.L. 96-471)**

P.L. 96-471, §2(b)(6):

Amended Code Sec. 1255(b)(2) by striking out "453(d)(4)(B)" and substituting "453B(d)(2)". **Effective** for dispositions made after 10-19-80, in tax years ending after that date.

- **1980, Technical Corrections Act of 1979 (P.L. 96-222)**

P.L. 96-222, §105(a)(7)(B):

Amended all of Code Sec. 1255(a)(1)(B) that follows (i). Prior to amendment, it read as follows:

(ii) the adjusted basis of such property shall be treated as ordinary income.

P.L. 96-222, §105(a)(7)(D):

Amended Code Sec. 1255(b)(2) by changing "(2)" to "(2) for purposes of sections 163(d), 170(e), 341(e)(12), 453(d)(4)(B) and 751(c),". **Effective** with respect to grants made under the programs after 9-30-79.

- **1978, Revenue Act of 1978 (P.L. 95-600)**

P.L. 95-600, §543(c):

Added Code Sec. 1255. **Effective** for grants made under the programs after 9-30-79.

INCOME TAX—CAPITAL GAINS, LOSSES

[Sec. 1256]

SEC. 1256. SECTION 1256 CONTRACTS MARKED TO MARKET.

[Sec. 1256(a)]

(a) GENERAL RULE.—For purposes of this subtitle—

(1) each section 1256 contract held by the taxpayer at the close of the taxable year shall be treated as sold for its fair market value on the last business day of such taxable year (and any gain or loss shall be taken into account for the taxable year),

(2) proper adjustment shall be made in the amount of any gain or loss subsequently realized for gain or loss taken into account by reason of paragraph (1),

(3) any gain or loss with respect to a section 1256 contract shall be treated as—

(A) short-term capital gain or loss, to the extent of 40 percent of such gain or loss, and

(B) long-term capital gain or loss, to the extent of 60 percent of such gain or loss, and

(4) if all the offsetting positions making up any straddle consist of section 1256 contracts to which this section applies (and such straddle is not part of a larger straddle), sections 1092 and 263(g) shall not apply with respect to such straddle.

Amendments

• **1984, Deficit Reduction Act of 1984 (P.L. 98-369)**

P.L. 98-369, § 102(a)(1):

Amended Code Sec. 1256 by striking out "regulated futures contract" each place it appears and inserting in lieu thereof "section 1256 contract", and by striking out "regulated futures contracts" and inserting in lieu thereof "section 1256 contracts". **Effective** for positions established after 7-18-84, in tax years ending after such date. However, see the special rule and elections provided by Act Sec. 102(f)(2)-(g) in the notes following Code Sec. 1256(g).

P.L. 98-369, § 102(e)(5):

Amended the Code Sec. 1256 section heading by striking out **"REGULATED FUTURES CONTRACTS"** and inserting in lieu thereof **"SECTION 1256 CONTRACTS"**. **Effective** for positions established after 7-18-84, in tax years ending after such date. However, see the special rule and elections provided by Act Sec. 102(f)(2)-(g) in the notes following Code Sec. 1256(g).

• **1981, Economic Recovery Tax Act of 1981 (P.L. 97-34)**

P.L. 97-34, § 503(a):

Added Code Sec. 1256(a). **Effective** for property acquired and positions established by the taxpayer after 6-23-81, in tax years ending after such date. For special elections, see Act Sec. 508(c) and Act Sec. 509, below.

P.L. 97-34, § 508(c), provides:

(c) ELECTION WITH RESPECT TO PROPERTY HELD ON JUNE 23, 1981.—If the taxpayer so elects (at such time and in such manner as the Secretary of the Treasury or his delegate shall prescribe) with respect to all regulated futures contracts or positions held by the taxpayer on June 23, 1981, the amendments made by this title shall apply to all such contracts and positions, effective for periods after such date in taxable years ending after such date. For purposes of the preceding sentence, the term "regulated futures contract" has the meaning given to such term by section 1256(b) of the Internal Revenue Code of 1954, and the term "position" has the meaning given to such term by section 1092(d)(2) of such Code.

P.L. 97-34, § 509, as amended by P.L. 97-448, § 105(c)(6), provides:

SEC. 509. ELECTION FOR EXTENSION OF TIME FOR PAYMENT AND APPLICATION OF SECTION 1256 FOR THE TAXABLE YEAR INCLUDING JUNE 23, 1981.

(a) ELECTION.—

(1) IN GENERAL.—In the case of any taxable year beginning before June 23, 1981, and ending after June 22, 1981, the taxpayer may elect, in lieu of any election under section 508(c), to have this section apply to all regulated futures contracts held during such taxable year.

(2) APPLICATION OF SECTION 1256.—If a taxpayer elects to have the provisions of this section apply to the taxable year described in paragraph (1).—

(A) the provisions of section 1256 of the Internal Revenue Code of 1954 (other than section 1256(e)(2)(C)) shall apply to regulated futures contracts held by the taxpayer at any time during such taxable year, and

(B) for purposes of determining the rate of tax applicable to gains and losses from regulated futures contracts held at any time during such year, such gains and losses shall be treated as gain or loss from a sale or exchange occurring in a taxable year beginning in 1982.

(3) DETERMINATION OF DEFERRED TAX LIABILITY.—If the taxpayer makes an election under this subsection.—

(A) the taxpayer may pay part or all of the tax for such year in two or more (but not exceeding five) equal installments;

(B) the maximum amount of tax which may be paid in installments under this section shall be the excess of—

(i) the tax for such year, determined by taking into account paragraph (2), over

(ii) the tax for such year, determined by taking into account paragraph (2) and by treating all regulated futures contracts which were held by the taxpayer on the first day of the taxable year described in paragraph (1), and which were acquired before the first day of such taxable year, as having been acquired for a purchase price equal to their fair market value on the last business day of the preceding taxable year.

(4) DATE FOR PAYMENT OF INSTALLMENT.—

(A) If an election is made under this subsection, the first installment under subsection (a)(3)(A) shall be paid on or before the due date for filing the return for the taxable year described in paragraph (1), and each succeeding installment shall be paid on or before the date which is one year after the date prescribed for payment of the preceding installment.

(B) If a bankruptcy case or insolvency proceeding involving the taxpayer is commenced before the final installment is paid, the total amount of any unpaid installments shall be treated as due and payable on the day preceding the day on which such case or proceeding is commenced.

(5) INTEREST IMPOSED.—For purposes of section 6601 of the Internal Revenue Code of 1954, the time for payment of any tax with respect to which an election is made under this subsection shall be determined without regard to this subsection.

(b) FORM OF ELECTION.—An election under this section shall be made not later than the time for filing the return for the taxable year described in subsection (a)(1) and shall be made in the manner and form required by regulations prescribed by the Secretary. The election shall set forth—

(1) the amount determined under subsection (a)(3)(B) and the number of installments elected by the taxpayer,

(2) each regulated futures contract held by the taxpayer on the first day of the taxable year described in subsection (a)(1), and the date such contract was acquired,

(3) the fair market value on the last business day of the preceding taxable year for each regulated futures contract described in paragraph (2), and

(4) such other information for purposes of carrying out the provisions of this section as may be required by such regulations.

[Sec. 1256(b)]

(b) SECTION 1256 CONTRACT DEFINED.—

(1) IN GENERAL.—For purposes of this section, the term "section 1256 contract" means—

(A) any regulated futures contract,

(B) any foreign currency contract,

(C) any nonequity option,

(D) any dealer equity option, and

(E) any dealer securities futures contract.

(2) EXCEPTIONS.—The term "section 1256 contract" shall not include—

(A) any securities futures contract or option on such a contract unless such contract or option is a dealer securities futures contract, or

(B) any interest rate swap, currency swap, basis swap, interest rate cap, interest rate floor, commodity swap, equity swap, equity index swap, credit default swap, or similar agreement.

Amendments

• **2010, Dodd-Frank Wall Street Reform and Consumer Protection Act (P.L. 111-203)**

P.L. 111-203, § 1601(a)(1)-(3):

Amended Code Sec. 1256(b) by redesignating paragraphs (1)-(5) as subparagraphs (A)-(E), respectively, and by indenting such subparagraphs (as so redesignated) accordingly, by striking "For purposes of" and inserting "(1) IN GENERAL.—For purposes of", and by striking the last sentence and inserting new paragraph (2). **Effective** for tax years beginning after 7-21-2010. Prior to being stricken, the last sentence of Code Sec. 1256(b) read as follows:

The term "section 1256 contract" shall not include any securities futures contract or option on such a contract unless such contract or option is a dealer securities futures contract.

• **2000, Community Renewal Tax Relief Act of 2000 (P.L. 106-554)**

P.L. 106-554, § 401(g)(1)(A):

Amended Code Sec. 1256(b) by striking "and" at the end of paragraph (3), by striking the period at the end of paragraph (4) and inserting ", and", and by adding at the end new text. **Effective** 12-21-2000.

INCOME TAX—CAPITAL GAINS, LOSSES

• **1984, Deficit Reduction Act of 1984 (P.L. 98-369)**

P.L. 98-369, §102(a)(2):

Amended Code Sec. 1256(b). **Effective** for positions established after 7-18-84, in tax years ending after such date. However, see the special rule and elections provided by Act Sec. 102(f)(2)-(g) in the notes following Code Sec. 1256(g). Prior to amendment, it read as follows:

(b) Regulated Futures Contracts Defined.—For purposes of this section, the term "regulated futures contract" means a contract—

(1) with respect to which the amount required to be deposited and the amount which may be withdrawn depends on a system of marking to market; and

(2) which is traded on or subject to the rules of a domestic board of trade designated as a contract market by the Commodity Futures Trading Commission or of any board of trade or exchange which the Secretary determines has rules adequate to carry out the purposes of this section.

Such term includes any foreign currency contract.

• **1983, Technical Corrections Act of 1982 (P.L. 97-448)**

P.L. 97-448, §105(c)(5)(A):

Amended Code Sec. 1256(b) by striking out paragraph (1) and by redesignating paragraphs (2) and (3) as (1) and (2), respectively. **Effective** as if included in the provision of P.L. 97-34 to which it relates. Prior to being stricken, paragraph (1) read:

"(1) which requires delivery of personal property (as defined in section 1092(d)(1)) or an interest in such property;".

P.L. 97-448, §105(c)(5)(B):

Amended Code Sec. 1256(b), as amended by Act Sec. 105(c)(5)(A), by adding the last sentence. **Effective** with respect to contracts entered into after 5-11-82, except as provided in Act Sec. 105(c)(5)(D)(ii)-(iii) as follows:

(ii) ELECTION BY TAXPAYER OF RETROACTIVE APPLICATION.—

(I) RETROACTIVE APPLICATION.—If the taxpayer so elects, the amendments made by subparagraphs (B) and (C) shall apply as if included within the amendments made by title V of the Economic Recovery Tax Act of 1981.

(II) ADDITIONAL CHOICES WITH RESPECT TO 1981.—If the taxpayer held a foreign currency contract after December 31, 1980, and before June 24, 1981, and such taxpayer makes an election under subclause (I), such taxpayer may revoke any election made under section 508(c) or 509(a) of such Act, and may make an election under section 508(c) or 509(a) of such Act.

(III) ADDITIONAL CHOICES APPLY TO ALL REGULATED FUTURES CONTRACTS.—Except as provided in subclause (IV), in the case of any taxpayer who makes an election under subclause (I), any election under section 508(c) or 509(a) of such Act or any revocation of such an election shall apply to all regulated futures contracts (including foreign currency contracts).

(IV) SECTION 509(a)(3) AND (4) NOT TO APPLY TO FOREIGN CURRENCY CONTRACTS.—Paragraphs (3) and (4) of section 509(a) of such Act shall not apply to any foreign currency contract.

(V) TIME FOR MAKING ELECTION OR REVOCATION.—Any election under subclause (I) and any election or revocation under subclause (II) may be made only within the 90-day period beginning on the date of the enactment of this Act. Any such action, once taken, shall be irrevocable.

(VI) DEFINITIONS.—For purposes of this clause, the terms "regulated futures contract" and "foreign currency contract" have the same respective meanings as when used in section 1256 of the Internal Revenue Code of 1954 (as amended by this Act).

(iii) ELECTION BY TAXPAYER WITH RESPECT TO POSITIONS HELD DURING TAXABLE YEARS ENDING AFTER MAY 11, 1982.—In lieu of the election under clause (ii), a taxpayer may elect to have the amendments made by subparagraphs (B) and (C) applied to all positions held in taxable years ending after May 11, 1982, except that the provisions of section 509(a)(3) and (4) of the Economic Recovery Tax Act of 1981 shall not apply.

• **1981, Economic Recovery Tax Act of 1981 (P.L. 97-34)**

P.L. 97-34, §503(a):

Added Code Sec. 1256(b). **Effective** for property acquired and positions established by the taxpayer after 6-23-81, in tax years ending after such date. For special elections, see the amendment note at P.L. 97-34, following Code Sec. 1256(a).

[Sec. 1256(c)]

(c) TERMINATIONS, ETC.—

(1) IN GENERAL.—The rules of paragraphs (1), (2), and (3) of subsection (a) shall also apply to the termination (or transfer) during the taxable year of the taxpayer's obligation (or rights) with respect to a section 1256 contract by offsetting, by taking or making delivery, by exercise or being exercised, by assignment or being assigned, by lapse, or otherwise.

(2) SPECIAL RULE WHERE TAXPAYER TAKES DELIVERY ON OR EXERCISES PART OF STRADDLE.—If—

(A) 2 or more section 1256 contracts are part of a straddle (as defined in section 1092(c)), and

(B) the taxpayer takes delivery under or exercises any of such contracts,

then, for purposes of this section, each of the other such contracts shall be treated as terminated on the day on which the taxpayer took delivery.

(3) FAIR MARKET VALUE TAKEN INTO ACCOUNT.—For purposes of this subsection, fair market value at the time of the termination (or transfer) shall be taken into account.

Amendments

• **1984, Deficit Reduction Act of 1984 (P.L. 98-369)**

P.L. 98-369, §102(a)(1):

Amended Code Sec. 1256 by striking out "regulated futures contract" each place it appears and inserting in lieu thereof "section 1256 contract", and by striking out "regulated futures contracts" each place it appears and inserting in lieu thereof "section 1256 contracts". **Effective** for positions established after 7-18-84, in tax years ending after such date. However, see the special rule and elections provided by Act Sec. 102(f)(2)-(g) following Code Sec. 1256(g).

P.L. 98-369, §102(e)(1):

Amended Code Sec. 1256(c) by striking out "by taking or making delivery," in paragraph (1) and inserting in lieu thereof "by taking or making delivery, by exercise or being exercised, by assignment or being assigned, by lapse,", by striking out "takes delivery under" in paragraph (2) and inserting in lieu thereof "takes delivery under or exercises", and by striking out "Takes Delivery On" in the heading of paragraph (2) and inserting in lieu thereof "Takes Delivery On Or Exercises". **Effective** for positions established after 7-18-84, in tax years ending after such date. However, see the special rule and elections provided by Act Sec. 102(f)(2)-(g) following Code Sec. 1256(g).

• **1983, Technical Corrections Act of 1982 (P.L. 97-448)**

P.L. 97-448, §105(c)(1):

Amended Code Sec. 1256(c). **Effective** as if included in the provision of P.L. 97-34 to which it relates. Prior to amendment, Code Sec. 1256(c) read as follows:

"(c) TERMINATIONS.—The rules of paragraphs (1), (2), and (3) of subsection (a) shall also apply to the termination during the taxable year of the taxpayer's obligation with respect to a regulated futures contract by offsetting, by taking or making delivery, or otherwise. For purposes of the preceding sentence, fair market value at the time of the termination shall be taken into account."

• **1981, Economic Recovery Tax Act of 1981 (P.L. 97-34)**

P.L. 97-34, §503(a):

Added Code Sec. 1256(c). **Effective** for property acquired and positions established by the taxpayer after 6-23-81, in tax years ending after such date. For special elections, see the amendment note at P.L. 97-34, following Code Sec. 1256(a).

[Sec. 1256(d)]

(d) ELECTIONS WITH RESPECT TO MIXED STRADDLES.—

(1) ELECTION.—The taxpayer may elect to have this section not to apply to all section 1256 contracts which are part of a mixed straddle.

(2) TIME AND MANNER.—An election under paragraph (1) shall be made at such time and in such manner as the Secretary may by regulations prescribe.

(3) ELECTION REVOCABLE ONLY WITH CONSENT.—An election under paragraph (1) shall apply to the taxpayer's taxable year for which made and to all subsequent taxable years, unless the Secretary consents to a revocation of such election.

(4) MIXED STRADDLE.—For purposes of this subsection, the term "mixed straddle" means any straddle (as defined in section 1092(c))—

(A) at least 1 (but not all) of the positions of which are section 1256 contracts, and

(B) with respect to which each position forming part of such straddle is clearly identified, before the close of the day on which the first section 1256 contract forming part of the straddle is acquired (or such earlier time as the Secretary may prescribe by regulations), as being part of such straddle.

Amendments

• **1984, Deficit Reduction Act of 1984 (P.L. 98-369)**

P.L. 98-369, §102(a)(1):

Amended Code Sec. 1256 by striking out "regulated futures contract" each place it appears and inserting in lieu thereof "section 1256 contract", and by striking out "regulated futures contracts" each place it appears and inserting in lieu thereof "section 1256 contracts". **Effective** for positions established after 7-18-84, in tax years ending after such date. However, see the special rule and elections provided by Act Sec. 102(f)(2)-(g) following Code Sec. 1256(g).

INCOME TAX—CAPITAL GAINS, LOSSES

P.L. 98-369, § 107(c):

Amended Code Sec. 1256(d)(4)(B) by inserting "(or such earlier time as the Secretary may prescribe by regulations)" after "acquired". **Effective** for positions entered into after 7-18-84, in tax years ending after such date.

• **1983, Technical Corrections Act of 1982 (P.L. 97-448)**

P.L. 97-448, § 105(c)(2):

Amended Code Sec. 1256(d)(4)(B) by striking out "such position" and inserting in lieu thereof "the first regulated futures contract forming part of the straddle". **Effective** as if included in the provision of P.L. 97-34 to which it relates.

• **1981, Economic Recovery Tax Act of 1981 (P.L. 97-34)**

P.L. 97-34, § 503(a):

Added Code Sec. 1256(d). **Effective** for property acquired and positions established by the taxpayer after 6-23-81, in tax years ending after such date. For special elections, see the amendment note at P.L. 97-34, following Code Sec. 1256(a).

[Sec. 1256(e)]

(e) MARK TO MARKET NOT TO APPLY TO HEDGING TRANSACTIONS.—

(1) SECTION NOT TO APPLY.—Subsection (a) shall not apply in the case of a hedging transaction.

(2) DEFINITION OF HEDGING TRANSACTION.—For purposes of this subsection, the term "hedging transaction" means any hedging transaction (as defined in section 1221(b)(2)(A)) if, before the close of the day on which such transaction was entered into (or such earlier time as the Secretary may prescribe by regulations), the taxpayer clearly identifies such transaction as being a hedging transaction.

(3) SPECIAL RULE FOR SYNDICATES.—

(A) IN GENERAL.—Notwithstanding paragraph (2), the term "hedging transaction" shall not include any transaction entered into by or for a syndicate.

(B) SYNDICATE DEFINED.—For purposes of subparagraph (A), the term "syndicate" means any partnership or other entity (other than a corporation which is not an S corporation) if more than 35 percent of the losses of such entity during the taxable year are allocable to limited partners or limited entrepreneurs (within the meaning of section 461(k)(4)).

(C) HOLDINGS ATTRIBUTABLE TO ACTIVE MANAGEMENT.—For purposes of subparagraph (B), an interest in an entity shall not be treated as held by a limited partner or a limited entrepreneur (within the meaning of section 461(k)(4))—

(i) for any period if during such period such interest is held by an individual who actively participates at all times during such period in the management of such entity,

(ii) for any period if during such period such interest is held by the spouse, children, grandchildren, and parents of an individual who actively participates at all times during such period in the management of such entity,

(iii) if such interest is held by an individual who actively participated in the management of such entity for a period of not less than 5 years,

(iv) if such interest is held by the estate of an individual who actively participated in the management of such entity or is held by the estate of an individual if with respect to such individual such interest was at any time described in clause (ii), or

(v) if the Secretary determines (by regulations or otherwise) that such interest should be treated as held by an individual who actively participates in the management of such entity, and that such entity and such interest are not used (or to be used) for tax-avoidance purposes.

For purposes of this subparagraph, a legally adopted child of an individual shall be treated as a child of such individual by blood.

(4) LIMITATION ON LOSSES FROM HEDGING TRANSACTIONS.—

(A) IN GENERAL.—

(i) LIMITATION.—Any hedging loss for a taxable year which is allocable to any limited partner or limited entrepreneur (within the meaning of paragraph (3)) shall be allowed only to the extent of the taxable income of such limited partner or entrepreneur for such taxable year attributable to the trade or business in which the hedging transactions were entered into. For purposes of the preceding sentence, taxable income shall be determined by not taking into account items attributable to hedging transactions.

(ii) CARRYOVER OF DISALLOWED LOSS.—Any hedging loss disallowed under clause (i) shall be treated as a deduction attributable to a hedging transaction allowable in the first succeeding taxable year.

(B) EXCEPTION WHERE ECONOMIC LOSS.—Subparagraph (A)(i) shall not apply to any hedging loss to the extent that such loss exceeds the aggregate unrecognized gains from hedging transactions as of the close of the taxable year attributable to the trade or business in which the hedging transactions were entered into.

(C) EXCEPTION FOR CERTAIN HEDGING TRANSACTIONS.—In the case of any hedging transaction relating to property other than stock or securities, this paragraph shall apply only in the case of a taxpayer described in section 465(a)(1).

(D) HEDGING LOSS.—The term "hedging loss" means the excess of—

(i) the deductions allowable under this chapter for the taxable year attributable to hedging transactions (determined without regard to subparagraph (A)(i)), over

(ii) income received or accrued by the taxpayer during such taxable year from such transactions.

(E) UNRECOGNIZED GAIN.—The term "unrecognized gain" has the meaning given to such term by section 1092(a)(3).

Amendments

• **2018, Tax Technical Corrections Act of 2018 (P.L. 115-141)**

P.L. 115-141, § 401(a)(176)(A), Div. U:

Amended Code Sec. 1256(e)(3)(B) and (C) by striking "section 464(e)(2)" and inserting "section 461(k)(4)". **Effective** 3-23-2018.

• **1999, Tax Relief Extension Act of 1999 (P.L. 106-170)**

P.L. 106-170, § 532(b)(4):

Amended Code Sec. 1256(e)(2). **Effective** for any instrument held, acquired, or entered into, any transaction entered into, and supplies held or acquired on or after 12-17-99. Prior to amendment, Code Sec. 1256(e)(2) read as follows:

(2) DEFINITION OF HEDGING TRANSACTION.—For purposes of this subsection, the term "hedging transaction" means any transaction if—

(A) such transaction is entered into by the taxpayer in the normal course of the taxpayer's trade or business primarily—

(i) to reduce risk of price change or currency fluctuations with respect to property which is held or to be held by the taxpayer, or

(ii) to reduce risk of interest rate or price changes or currency fluctuations with respect to borrowings made or to be made, or obligations incurred or to be incurred, by the taxpayer,

(B) the gain or loss on such transactions is treated as ordinary income or loss, and

(C) before the close of the day on which such transaction was entered into (or such earlier time as the Secretary may prescribe by regulations), the taxpayer clearly identifies such transaction as being a hedging transaction.

• **1986, Tax Reform Act of 1986 (P.L. 99-514)**

P.L. 99-514, § 1261(c):

Amended Code Sec. 1256(e) by striking out paragraph (4) and by redesignating paragraph (5) as paragraph (4). **Effective** for tax years beginning after 12-31-86. Prior to amendment, Code Sec. 1256(e)(4) read as follows:

(4) SPECIAL RULE FOR BANKS.—In the case of a bank (as defined in section 581), subparagraph (A) of paragraph (2) shall be applied without regard to clause (i) or (ii) thereof.

• **1984, Deficit Reduction Act of 1984 (P.L. 98-369)**

P.L. 98-369, § 104(a):

Amended Code Sec. 1256(e) by adding new paragraph (5). **Effective** for tax years beginning after 12-31-84.

P.L. 98-369, § 107(d):

Amended Code Sec. 1256(e)(2)(C) by inserting "(or such earlier time as the Secretary may prescribe by regulations)" after "entered into". **Effective** for positions entered into after 7-18-84 in tax years ending after such date.

INCOME TAX—CAPITAL GAINS, LOSSES

• **1983, Technical Corrections Act of 1982 (P.L. 97-448)**

P.L. 97-448, § 105(c)(3):

Amended Code Sec. 1256(e)(3)(C)(v) by inserting "(by regulations or otherwise)" after "determines". **Effective** as if included in the provision of P.L. 97-34 to which it relates.

• **1982, Subchapter S Revision Act of 1982 (P.L. 97-354)**

P.L. 97-354, § 5(a)(38):

Amended Code Sec. 1256(e)(3)(B) by striking out "an electing small business corporation within the meaning of section 1371(b)" and inserting in lieu thereof "an S corporation". **Effective** for tax years beginning after 12-31-82.

• **1981, Economic Recovery Tax Act of 1981 (P.L. 97-34)**

P.L. 97-34, § 503(a):

Added Code Sec. 1256(e). **Effective** generally for property acquired and positions established by the taxpayer after 6-23-81, in tax years ending after such date. For the **effective** date for Code Sec. 1256(e)(2)(C), see Act Sec. 508(b)(2), below. For special elections, see the amendment note at P.L. 97-34, following Code Sec. 1256(a).

P.L. 97-34, § 508(b)(2), provides:

(2) UNDER SECTION 1256(e)(2)(C) OF CODE.—Section 1256(e)(2)(C) of the Internal Revenue Code of 1954 (as added by this title) shall apply to property acquired and positions established by the taxpayer after December 31, 1981, in taxable years ending after such date.

[Sec. 1256(f)]

(f) SPECIAL RULES.—

(1) DENIAL OF CAPITAL GAINS TREATMENT FOR PROPERTY IDENTIFIED AS PART OF A HEDGING TRANSACTION.—For purposes of this title, gain from any property shall in no event be considered as gain from the sale or exchange of a capital asset if such property was at any time personal property (as defined in section 1092(d)(1)) identified under subsection (e)(2) by the taxpayer as being part of a hedging transaction.

(2) SUBSECTION (a)(3) NOT TO APPLY TO ORDINARY INCOME PROPERTY.—Paragraph (3) of subsection (a) shall not apply to any gain or loss which, but for such paragraph, would be ordinary income or loss.

(3) CAPITAL GAIN TREATMENT FOR TRADERS IN SECTION 1256 CONTRACTS.—

(A) IN GENERAL.—For purposes of this title, gain or loss from trading of section 1256 contracts shall be treated as gain or loss from the sale or exchange of a capital asset.

(B) EXCEPTION FOR CERTAIN HEDGING TRANSACTIONS.—Subparagraph (A) shall not apply to any section 1256 contract to the extent such contract is held for purposes of hedging property if any loss with respect to such property in the hands of the taxpayer would be ordinary loss.

(C) TREATMENT OF UNDERLYING PROPERTY.—For purposes of determining whether gain or loss with respect to any property is ordinary income or loss, the fact that the taxpayer is actively engaged in dealing in or trading section 1256 contracts related to such property shall not be taken into account.

(4) SPECIAL RULE FOR DEALER EQUITY OPTIONS AND DEALER SECURITIES FUTURES CONTRACTS OF LIMITED PARTNERS OR LIMITED ENTREPRENEURS.—In the case of any gain or loss with respect to dealer equity options, or dealer securities futures contracts, which are allocable to limited partners or limited entrepreneurs (within the meaning of subsection (e)(3))—

(A) paragraph (3) of subsection (a) shall not apply to any such gain or loss, and

(B) all such gains or losses shall be treated as short-term capital gains or losses, as the case may be.

(5) SPECIAL RULE RELATED TO LOSSES.—Section 1091 (relating to loss from wash sales of stock or securities) shall not apply to any loss taken into account by reason of paragraph (1) of subsection (a).

Amendments

• **2005, Gulf Opportunity Zone Act of 2005 (P.L. 109-135)**

P.L. 109-135, § 412(oo):

Amended Code Sec. 1256(f)(1) by striking "subsection (e)(2)(C)" and inserting "subsection (e)(2)". **Effective** 12-21-2005.

• **2002, Job Creation and Worker Assistance Act of 2002 (P.L. 107-147)**

P.L. 107-147, § 416(b)(1):

Amended Code Sec. 1256(f) by adding at the end a new paragraph (5). **Effective** as if included in section 5075 of P.L. 100-647 [**effective** for sales made after 11-10-88, in tax years ending after such date.—CCH].

• **2000, Community Renewal Tax Relief Act of 2000 (P.L. 106-554)**

P.L. 106-554, § 401(g)(2)(A)-(B):

Amended Code Sec. 1256(f)(4) by inserting ", or dealer securities futures contracts," after "dealer equity options" in the text, and by inserting "AND DEALER SECURITIES FUTURES CONTRACTS" after "DEALER EQUITY OPTIONS" in the heading. **Effective** on 12-21-2000.

• **1984, Deficit Reduction Act of 1984 (P.L. 98-369)**

P.L. 98-369, § 102(b):

Amended Code Sec. 1256(f) by adding new paragraphs (3) and (4). **Effective** for positions established after 7-18-84, in tax years ending after such date. However, see the special rule and elections provided by Act Sec. 102(f)(2)-(g) following Code Sec. 1256(g).

• **1981, Economic Recovery Tax Act of 1981 (P.L. 97-34)**

P.L. 97-34, § 503(a):

Added Code Sec. 1256(f). **Effective** for property acquired and positions established by the taxpayer after 6-23-81, in tax years ending after such date. For special elections, see the amendment note at P.L. 97-34, following Code Sec. 1256(a).

[Sec. 1256(g)]

(g) DEFINITIONS.—For purposes of this section—

(1) REGULATED FUTURES CONTRACTS DEFINED.—The term "regulated futures contract" means a contract—

(A) with respect to which the amount required to be deposited and the amount which may be withdrawn depends on a system of marking to market, and

(B) which is traded on or subject to the rules of a qualified board or exchange.

(2) FOREIGN CURRENCY CONTRACT DEFINED.—

(A) FOREIGN CURRENCY CONTRACT.—The term "foreign currency contract" means a contract—

(i) which requires delivery of, or the settlement of which depends on the value of, a foreign currency which is a currency in which positions are also traded through regulated futures contracts,

(ii) which is traded in the interbank market, and

(iii) which is entered into at arm's length at a price determined by reference to the price in the interbank market.

(B) REGULATIONS.—The Secretary shall prescribe such regulations as may be necessary or appropriate to carry out the purposes of subparagraph (A), including regulations excluding from the application of subparagraph (A) any contract (or type of contract) if its application thereto would be inconsistent with such purposes.

(3) NONEQUITY OPTION.—The term "nonequity option" means any listed option which is not an equity option.

(4) DEALER EQUITY OPTION.—The term "dealer equity option" means, with respect to an options dealer, any listed option which—

(A) is an equity option,

(B) is purchased or granted by such options dealer in the normal course of his activity of dealing in options, and

(C) is listed on the qualified board or exchange on which such options dealer is registered.

(5) LISTED OPTION.—The term "listed option" means any option (other than a right to acquire stock from the issuer) which is traded on (or subject to the rules of) a qualified board or exchange.

(6) EQUITY OPTION.—The term "equity option" means any option—

Internal Revenue Code   Sec. 1256(g)(6)

INCOME TAX—CAPITAL GAINS, LOSSES

(A) to buy or sell stock, or

(B) the value of which is determined directly or indirectly by reference to any stock or any narrow-based security index (as defined in section 3(a)(55) of the Securities Exchange Act of 1934, as in effect on the date of the enactment of this paragraph).

The term "equity option" includes such an option on a group of stocks only if such group meets the requirements for a narrow-based security index (as so defined). The Secretary may prescribe regulations regarding the status of options the values of which are determined directly or indirectly by reference to any index which becomes (or ceases to be) a narrow-based security index (as so defined).

(7) QUALIFIED BOARD OR EXCHANGE.—The term "qualified board or exchange" means—

(A) a national securities exchange which is registered with the Securities and Exchange Commission,

(B) a domestic board of trade designated as a contract market by the Commodity Futures Trading Commission, or

(C) any other exchange, board of trade, or other market which the Secretary determines has rules adequate to carry out the purposes of this section.

(8) OPTIONS DEALER.—

(A) IN GENERAL.—The term "options dealer" means any person registered with an appropriate national securities exchange as a market maker or specialist in listed options.

(B) PERSONS TRADING IN OTHER MARKETS.—In any case in which the Secretary makes a determination under subparagraph (C) of paragraph (7), the term "options dealer" also includes any person whom the Secretary determines performs functions similar to the persons described in subparagraph (A). Such determinations shall be made to the extent appropriate to carry out the purposes of this section.

(9) DEALER SECURITIES FUTURES CONTRACT.—

(A) IN GENERAL.—The term "dealer securities futures contract" means, with respect to any dealer, any securities futures contract, and any option on such a contract, which—

(i) is entered into by such dealer (or, in the case of an option, is purchased or granted by such dealer) in the normal course of his activity of dealing in such contracts or options, as the case may be, and

(ii) is traded on a qualified board or exchange.

(B) DEALER.—For purposes of subparagraph (A), a person shall be treated as a dealer in securities futures contracts or options on such contracts if the Secretary determines that such person performs, with respect to such contracts or options, as the case may be, functions similar to the functions performed by persons described in paragraph (8)(A). Such determination shall be made to the extent appropriate to carry out the purposes of this section.

(C) SECURITIES FUTURES CONTRACT.—The term "securities futures contract" has the meaning given to such term by section 1234B.

Amendments

• **2004, Working Families Tax Relief Act of 2004 (P.L. 108-311)**

P.L. 108-311, §405(a)(2):

Amended Code Sec. 1256(g)(6) by adding at the end a new sentence. **Effective** as if included in section 401 of the Community Renewal Tax Relief Act of 2000 (P.L. 106-554) [effective 12-21-2000.—CCH].

• **2000, Community Renewal Tax Relief Act of 2000 (P.L. 106-554)**

P.L. 106-554, §401(g)(1)(B):

Amended Code Sec. 1256(g) by adding at the end a new paragraph (9). **Effective** 12-21-2000.

P.L. 106-554, §401(g)(3):

Amended Code Sec. 1256(g)(6). **Effective** 12-21-2000. Prior to amendment, Code Sec. 1256(g)(6) read as follows:

(6) EQUITY OPTION.—

(A) IN GENERAL.—Except as provided in subparagraph (B), the term "equity option" means any option—

(i) to buy or sell stock, or

(ii) the value of which is determined directly or indirectly by reference to any stock (or group of stocks) or stock index.

(B) EXCEPTION FOR CERTAIN OPTIONS REGULATED BY COMMODITIES FUTURES TRADING COMMISSION.—The term "equity option" does not include any option with respect to any group of stocks or stock index if—

(i) there is in effect a designation by the Commodities Futures Trading Commission of a contract market for a contract based on such group of stocks or index, or

(ii) the Secretary determines that such option meets the requirements of law for such a designation.

P.L. 106-554, §401(g)(4), provides:

(4) The Secretary of the Treasury or his delegate shall make the determinations under section 1256(g)(9)(B) of the Internal Revenue Code of 1986, as added by this Act, not later than July 1, 2001.

• **1984, Deficit Reduction Act of 1984 (P.L. 98-369)**

P.L. 98-369, §102(a)(3):

Amended Code Sec. 1256(g). **Effective** for positions established after 7-18-84, in tax years ending after such date. However, see the special rule and elections provided by Act Sec. 102(f)(2)-(j), below. Prior to amendment by §102(a)(3), but after the amendment by §722(a)(2), it read as follows:

(g) Foreign Currency Contract Defined.—

(1) Foreign Currency Contract.—For purposes of this section, the term "foreign currency contract" means a contract—

(A) which requires delivery of, or the settlement of which depends on the value of, a foreign currency which is a currency in which positions are also traded through regulated futures contracts,

(B) which is traded in the interbank market, and

(C) which is entered into at arm's length at a price determined by reference to the price in the interbank market.

(2) Regulations.—The Secretary shall prescribe such regulations as may be necessary or appropriate to carry out the purposes of paragraph (1), including regulations excluding from the application of paragraph (1) any contract (or type of contract) if its application thereto would be inconsistent with such purposes.

P.L. 98-369, §102(f)(2)-(j), as amended by P.L. 99-514, §1808, provides:

(2) Special Rule for Options on Regulated Futures Contracts.—In the case of any option with respect to a regulated futures contract (within the meaning of section 1256 of the Internal Revenue Code of 1954), the amendments made by this section shall apply to positions established after October 31, 1983, in taxable years ending after such date.

(g) Elections With Respect to Property Held on or Before the Date of the Enactment of This Act.—At the election of the taxpayer—

(1) the amendments made by this section shall apply to all section 1256 contracts held by the taxpayer on the date of enactment of this Act, effective for periods after such date in taxable years ending after such date, or

(2) in lieu of an election under paragraph (1), the amendments made by this section shall apply to all section 1256 contracts held by the taxpayer at any time during the taxable year of the taxpayer which includes the date of the enactment of this Act.

(h) Elections for Installment Payment of Tax Attributable to Stock Options.—

(1) In General.—If the taxpayer makes an election under subsection (g)(2) and under this subsection—

(A) the taxpayer may pay part or all the tax for the taxable year referred to in subsection (g)(2) in 2 or more (but not exceeding 5) equal installments, and

(B) the maximum amount of tax which may be paid in installments under this subsection shall be the excess of—

(i) the tax for such taxable year determined by taking into account subsection (g)(2), over

(ii) the tax for such taxable year determined by taking into account subsection (g)(2) and by treating—

(I) all section 1256 contracts which are stock options, and

(II) any stock which was a part of a straddle including any such stock options,

as having been acquired for a purchase price equal to their fair market value on the last business day of the preceding taxable year. Stock options and stock shall be taken into account under subparagraph (B)(ii) only if such options or stock were held on the last day of the preceding taxable year and only if income on such options or stock would have been ordinary income if such options or stock were sold at a gain on such last day.

(2) Date for Payment of Installment.—

(A) If an election is made under this subsection, the first installment under paragraph (1) shall be paid on or before the due date for filing the return for the taxable year described in paragraph (1), and each succeeding installment shall be paid on or before the date which is 1 year after the date prescribed for payment of the preceding installment.

(B) If an bankruptcy case or insolvency proceeding involving the taxpayer is commenced before the final installment is paid, the total amount of any unpaid installments shall be treated as due and payable on the day preceding the day on which such case or proceeding is commenced.

(3) Interest Imposed.—For purposes of section 6601 of the Internal Revenue Code of 1954, the time for payment of any tax with respect to which an election is made under this subsection shall be determined without regard to this subsection.

(4) Form of Election.—An election under this subsection shall be made not later than the time for filing the return for the taxable year described in paragraph (1) and

shall be made in the manner and form required by regulations prescribed by [the] Secretary of the Treasury or his delegate. The election shall set forth—

(A) the amount determined under paragraph (1)(B) and the number of installments elected by the taxpayer,

(B) the property described in paragraph (1)(B)(ii), and the date on which such property was acquired,

(C) the fair market value of the property described in paragraph (1)(B)(ii) on the last business day of the taxable year preceding the taxable year described in paragraph (1), and

(D) such other information for purposes of carrying out the provisions of this subsection as may be required by such regulations.

(5) Delay of Identification Requirement.—Section 1256(e)(2)(C) of the Internal Revenue Code of 1954 shall not apply to any stock option or stock acquired on or before the 60th day after the date of the enactment of this Act.

(i) Definitions.—For purposes of subsections (g) and (h)—

(1) Section 1256 Contract.—The term "section 1256 contract" has the meaning given to such term by section 1256(b) of the Internal Revenue Code of 1954 (as amended by this section).

(2) Stock Option.—The term "stock option" means any option to buy or sell stock.

(j) Coordination of Election Under Subsection (d)(3) with Elections Under Subsections (g) and (h).—The Secretary of the Treasury or his delegate shall prescribe such regulations as may be necessary to coordinate the election provided by subsection (d)(3) with the election provided by subsections (g) and (h).

P.L. 98-369, §722(a)(2):

Amended Code Sec. 1256(g)(1)(A) by inserting after "delivery of" the following: ", or the settlement of which depends on the value of,". **Effective** as if included in the provision of P.L. 97-448 to which it relates.

P.L. 98-369, §108, as amended by P.L. 99-514, §1808, provides:

SEC. 108. TREATMENT OF CERTAIN LOSSES ON STRADDLES ENTERED INTO BEFORE EFFECTIVE DATE OF ECONOMIC RECOVERY TAX ACT OF 1981.

(a) General Rule.—For purposes of the Internal Revenue Code of 1954, in the case of any disposition of 1 or more positions—

(1) which were entered into before 1982 and form part of a straddle, and

(2) to which the amendments made by title V of the Economic Recovery Tax Act of 1981 do not apply,

any loss from such disposition shall be allowed for the taxable year of the disposition if such loss is incurred in a trade or business, or if such loss is incurred in a transaction entered into for profit though not connected with a trade or business.

(b) Loss Incurred in a Trade or Business.—For purposes of subsection (a), any loss incurred by a commodities dealer in the trading of commodities shall be treated as a loss incurred in a trade or business.

(c) Net Loss Allowed.—If any loss with respect to a position described in paragraphs (1) and (2) of subsection (a) is not allowable as a deduction (after applying subsections (a) and (b)), such loss shall be allowed in determining the gain or loss from dispositions of other positions in the straddle to the extent required to accurately reflect the taxpayer's net gain or loss from all positions in such straddle.

(d) Other Rules.—Except as otherwise provided in subsections (a) and (c) and in sections 1233 and 1234 of such Code, the determination of whether there is recognized gain or loss with respect to a position, and the amount and timing of such gain or loss, and the treatment of such gain or loss as long-term or short-term shall be made without regard to whether such position constitutes part of a straddle.

(e) Straddle.—For purposes of this section, the term "straddle" has the meaning given to such term by section 1092(c) of the Internal Revenue Code of 1954 as in effect on the day after the date of the enactment of the Economic Recovery Tax Act of 1981, and shall include a straddle all the positions of which are regulated futures contracts.

(f) Commodities Dealer.—For purposes of this section, the term "commodities dealer" means any taxpayer who—

(1) at any time before January 1, 1982, was an individual described in section 1402(i)(2)(B) of the Internal Revenue Code of 1954 (as added by this subtitle), or

(2) was a member of the family (within of section 704(e)(3) of such Code) of an individual described in paragraph (1) to the extent such member engaged in commodities trading through an organization the members of which consisted solely of—

(A) 1 or more individuals described in paragraph (1), and

(B) 1 or more members of the families (as so defined) of such individuals.

(g) Regulated Futures Contracts.—For purposes of this section, the term "regulated futures contracts" has the meaning given to such term by section 1256(b) of the Internal Revenue Code of 1954 (as in effect before the date of enactment of this Act).

(h) Syndicates.—For purposes of this section, any loss incurred by a person (other than a commodities dealer) with respect to an interest in a syndicate (within the meaning of section 1256(e)(3)(B) of the Internal Revenue Code of 1954) shall not be considered to be a loss incurred in a trade or business.

• **1983, Technical Corrections Act of 1982 (P.L. 97-448)**

P.L. 97-448, §105(c)(5)(C):

Amended Code Sec. 1256 by adding at the end thereof new subsection (g). **Effective** with respect to contracts entered into after 5-11-82, except as noted in Act Sec. 105(c)(5)(D)(ii)-(iii), which appears in the amendment note for Act Sec. 105(c)(5)(B) following Code Sec. 1256(b).

[Sec. 1257]
SEC. 1257. DISPOSITION OF CONVERTED WETLANDS OR HIGHLY ERODIBLE CROPLANDS.

[Sec. 1257(a)]

(a) Gain Treated as Ordinary Income.—Any gain on the disposition of converted wetland or highly erodible cropland shall be treated as ordinary income. Such gain shall be recognized notwithstanding any other provision of this subtitle, except that this section shall not apply to the extent such gain is recognized as ordinary income under any other provision of this part.

[Sec. 1257(b)]

(b) Loss Treated as Long-Term Capital Loss.—Any loss recognized on the disposition of converted wetland or highly erodible cropland shall be treated as a long-term capital loss.

[Sec. 1257(c)]

(c) Definitions.—For purposes of this section—

(1) Converted wetland.—The term "converted wetland" means any converted wetland (as defined in section 1201(a)(7) of the Food Security Act of 1985 (16 U.S.C. 3801(7))) held—

(A) by the person whose activities resulted in such land being converted wetland, or

(B) by any other person who at any time used such land for farming purposes.

(2) Highly erodible cropland.—The term "highly erodible cropland" means any highly erodible cropland (as defined in section 1201(a)(10) of the Food Security Act of 1985 (16 U.S.C. 3801(10))), if at any time the taxpayer used such land for farming purposes (other than the grazing of animals).

(3) Treatment of successors.—If any land is converted wetland or highly erodible cropland in the hands of any person, such land shall be treated as converted wetland or highly erodible cropland in the hands of any other person whose adjusted basis in such land is determined (in whole or in part) by reference to the adjusted basis of such land in the hands of such person.

Amendments

• **2018, Tax Technical Corrections Act of 2018 (P.L. 115-141)**

P.L. 115-141, §401(a)(177)(A)-(B), Div. U:

Amended Code Sec. 1257(c)(1) by striking "section 1201(4)" and inserting "section 1201(a)(7)", and by striking "16 U.S.C. 3801(4)" and inserting "16 U.S.C. 3801(7)". **Effective** 3-23-2018.

P.L. 115-141, §401(a)(178)(A)-(B), Div. U:

Amended Code Sec. 1257(c)(2) by striking "section 1201(6)" and inserting "section 1201(a)(10)", and by striking "16 U.S.C. 3801(6)" and inserting "16 U.S.C. 3801(10)". **Effective** 3-23-2018.

[Sec. 1257(d)]

(d) Special Rules.—Under regulations prescribed by the Secretary, rules similar to the rules applicable under section 1245 shall apply for purposes of subsection (a). For purposes of sections 170(e) and 751(c), amounts treated as ordinary income under subsection (a) shall be treated in the same manner as amounts treated as ordinary income under section 1245.

Amendments

• **2013, American Taxpayer Relief Act of 2012 (P.L. 112-240)**

P.L. 112-240, §102(a), provides:

SEC. 102. PERMANENT EXTENSION AND MODIFICATION OF 2003 TAX RELIEF.

(a) Permanent Extension.—The Jobs and Growth Tax Relief Reconciliation Act of 2003 is amended by striking section 303.

INCOME TAX—CAPITAL GAINS, LOSSES

• 2003, Jobs and Growth Tax Relief Reconciliation Act of 2003 (P.L. 108-27)

P.L. 108-27, §302(e)(4)(B)(ii):

Amended Code Sec. 1257(d) by striking ", 341(e)(12)," after "170(e)". For the **effective** date, see Act Sec. 302(f), as amended by P.L. 108-311, §402(a)(6), below.

P.L. 108-27, §302(f), as amended by P.L. 108-311, §402(a)(6), provides:

(f) EFFECTIVE DATE.—

(1) IN GENERAL.—Except as provided in paragraph (2), the amendments made by this section shall apply to taxable years beginning after December 31, 2002.

(2) PASS-THRU ENTITIES.—In the case of a pass-thru entity described in subparagraph (A), (B), (C), (D), (E), or (F) of section 1(h)(10) of the Internal Revenue Code of 1986, as amended by this Act, the amendments made by this section shall apply to taxable years ending after December 31, 2002; except that dividends received by such an entity on or before such date shall not be treated as qualified dividend income (as defined in section 1(h)(11)(B) of such Code, as added by this Act).

P.L. 108-27, §303, as amended by P.L. 109-222, §102, and P.L. 111-312, §102(a), provides [but see P.L. 112-240, §102(a), above]:

SEC. 303. SUNSET OF TITLE.

All provisions of, and amendments made by, this title shall not apply to taxable years beginning after December 31, 2012, and the Internal Revenue Code of 1986 shall be applied and administered to such years as if such provisions and amendments had never been enacted.

• 1986, Tax Reform Act of 1986 (P.L. 99-514)

P.L. 99-514, §403(a):

Amended part IV of subchapter P of chapter 1 by adding at the end thereof new Code Sec. 1257. **Effective** for disposition of converted wetland or highly erodible cropland (as defined in section 1257(c) of the Internal Revenue Code of 1986 as added by this section) first used for farming after 3-1-86, in tax years ending after that date.

[Sec. 1258]

SEC. 1258. RECHARACTERIZATION OF GAIN FROM CERTAIN FINANCIAL TRANSACTIONS.

[Sec. 1258(a)]

(a) GENERAL RULE.—In the case of any gain—

(1) which (but for this section) would be treated as gain from the sale or exchange of a capital asset, and

(2) which is recognized on the disposition or other termination of any position which was held as part of a conversion transaction,

such gain (to the extent such gain does not exceed the applicable imputed income amount) shall be treated as ordinary income.

[Sec. 1258(b)]

(b) APPLICABLE IMPUTED INCOME AMOUNT.—For purposes of subsection (a), the term "applicable imputed income amount" means, with respect to any disposition or other termination referred to in subsection (a), an amount equal to—

(1) the amount of interest which would have accrued on the taxpayer's net investment in the conversion transaction for the period ending on the date of such disposition or other termination (or, if earlier, the date on which the requirements of subsection (c) ceased to be satisfied) at a rate equal to 120 percent of the applicable rate, reduced by

(2) the amount treated as ordinary income under subsection (a) with respect to any prior disposition or other termination of a position which was held as a part of such transaction.

The Secretary shall by regulations provide for such reductions in the applicable imputed income amount as may be appropriate by reason of amounts capitalized under section 263(g), ordinary income received, or otherwise.

[Sec. 1258(c)]

(c) CONVERSION TRANSACTION.—For purposes of this section, the term "conversion transaction" means any transaction—

(1) substantially all of the taxpayer's expected return from which is attributable to the time value of the taxpayer's net investment in such transaction, and

(2) which is—

(A) the holding of any property (whether or not actively traded), and the entering into a contract to sell such property (or substantially identical property) at a price determined in accordance with such contract, but only if such property was acquired and such contract was entered into on a substantially contemporaneous basis,

(B) an applicable straddle,

(C) any other transaction which is marketed or sold as producing capital gains from a transaction described in paragraph (1), or

(D) any other transaction specified in regulations prescribed by the Secretary.

[Sec. 1258(d)]

(d) DEFINITIONS AND SPECIAL RULES.—For purposes of this section—

(1) APPLICABLE STRADDLE.—The term "applicable straddle" means any straddle (within the meaning of section 1092(c)).

(2) APPLICABLE RATE.—The term "applicable rate" means—

(A) the applicable Federal rate determined under section 1274(d) (compounded semiannually) as if the conversion transaction were a debt instrument, or

(B) if the term of the conversion transaction is indefinite, the Federal short-term rates in effect under section 6621(b) during the period of the conversion transaction (compounded daily).

(3) TREATMENT OF BUILT-IN LOSSES.—

(A) IN GENERAL.—If any position with a built-in loss becomes part of a conversion transaction—

(i) for purposes of applying this subtitle to such position for periods after such position becomes part of such transaction, such position shall be taken into account at its fair market value as of the time it became part of such transaction, except that

(ii) upon the disposition or other termination of such position in a transaction in which gain or loss is recognized, such built-in loss shall be recognized and shall have a character determined without regard to this section.

(B) BUILT-IN LOSS.—For purposes of subparagraph (A), the term "built-in loss" means the loss (if any) which would have been realized if the position had been disposed of or otherwise terminated at its fair market value as of the time such position became part of the conversion transaction.

(4) POSITION TAKEN INTO ACCOUNT AT FAIR MARKET VALUE.—In determining the taxpayer's net investment in any conversion transaction, there shall be included the fair market value of any position which becomes part of such transaction (determined as of the time such position became part of such transaction).

(5) SPECIAL RULE FOR OPTIONS DEALERS AND COMMODITIES TRADERS.—

(A) IN GENERAL.—Subsection (a) shall not apply to transactions—

(i) of an options dealer in the normal course of the dealer's trade or business of dealing in options, or

(ii) of a commodities trader in the normal course of the trader's trade or business of trading section 1256 contracts.

(B) DEFINITIONS.—For purposes of this paragraph—

(i) OPTIONS DEALER.—The term "options dealer" has the meaning given such term by section 1256(g)(8).

INCOME TAX—CAPITAL GAINS, LOSSES

(ii) COMMODITIES TRADER.—The term "commodities trader" means any person who is a member (or, except as otherwise provided in regulations, is entitled to trade as a member) of a domestic board of trade which is designated as a contract market by the Commodity Futures Trading Commission.

(C) LIMITED PARTNERS AND LIMITED ENTREPRENEURS.—In the case of any gain from a transaction recognized by an entity which is allocable to a limited partner or limited entrepreneur (within the meaning of section 461(k)(4)), subparagraph (A) shall not apply if—

(i) substantially all of the limited partner's (or limited entrepreneur's) expected return from the entity is attributable to the time value of the partner's (or entrepreneur's) net investment in such entity,

(ii) the transaction (or the interest in the entity) was marketed or sold as producing capital gains treatment from a transaction described in subsection (c)(1), or

(iii) the transaction (or the interest in the entity) is a transaction (or interest) specified in regulations prescribed by the Secretary.

Amendments

• **2018, Tax Technical Corrections Act of 2018 (P.L. 115-141)**

P.L. 115-141, §401(a)(176)(B), Div. U:

Amended Code Sec. 1258(d)(5)(C) by striking "section 464(e)(2)" and inserting "section 461(k)(4)". **Effective** 3-23-2018.

• **2004, American Jobs Creation Act of 2004 (P.L. 108-357)**

P.L. 108-357, §888(c)(2):

Amended Code Sec. 1258(d)(1) by striking "; except that the term 'personal property' shall include stock" immediately after "section 1092(c))". **Effective** for positions established on or after 10-22-2004.

• **1993, Omnibus Budget Reconciliation Act of 1993 (P.L. 103-66)**

P.L. 103-66, §13206(a)(1):

Amended Part IV of subchapter P of chapter 1 by adding at the end thereof new section 1258. **Effective** for conversion transactions entered into after 4-30-93.

[Sec. 1259]

SEC. 1259. CONSTRUCTIVE SALES TREATMENT FOR APPRECIATED FINANCIAL POSITIONS.

[Sec. 1259(a)]

(a) IN GENERAL.—If there is a constructive sale of an appreciated financial position—

(1) the taxpayer shall recognize gain as if such position were sold, assigned, or otherwise terminated at its fair market value on the date of such constructive sale (and any gain shall be taken into account for the taxable year which includes such date), and

(2) for purposes of applying this title for periods after the constructive sale—

(A) proper adjustment shall be made in the amount of any gain or loss subsequently realized with respect to such position for any gain taken into account by reason of paragraph (1), and

(B) the holding period of such position shall be determined as if such position were originally acquired on the date of such constructive sale.

[Sec. 1259(b)]

(b) APPRECIATED FINANCIAL POSITION.—For purposes of this section—

(1) IN GENERAL.—Except as provided in paragraph (2), the term "appreciated financial position" means any position with respect to any stock, debt instrument, or partnership interest if there would be gain were such position sold, assigned, or otherwise terminated at its fair market value.

(2) EXCEPTIONS.—The term "appreciated financial position" shall not include—

(A) any position with respect to debt if—

(i) the position unconditionally entitles the holder to receive a specified principal amount,

(ii) the interest payments (or other similar amounts) with respect to such position meet the requirements of clause (i) of section 860G(a)(1)(B), and

(iii) such position is not convertible (directly or indirectly) into stock of the issuer or any related person,

(B) any hedge with respect to a position described in subparagraph (A), and

(C) any position which is marked to market under any provision of this title or the regulations thereunder.

(3) POSITION.—The term "position" means an interest, including a futures or forward contract, short sale, or option.

Amendments

• **1998, IRS Restructuring and Reform Act of 1998 (P.L. 105-206)**

P.L. 105-206, §6010(a)(1)(A)-(C):

Amended Code Sec. 1259(b)(2) by striking "debt" each place it appears in clauses (i), (ii), and (iii) of subparagraph (A) and inserting "position", by striking "and" at the end of subparagraph (A), and by redesignating subparagraph (B) as subparagraph (C) and by inserting after subparagraph (A) a new subparagraph (B). **Effective** as if included in the provision of P.L. 105-34 to which it relates [generally **effective** for constructive sales after 6-8-97.—CCH].

[Sec. 1259(c)]

(c) CONSTRUCTIVE SALE.—For purposes of this section—

(1) IN GENERAL.—A taxpayer shall be treated as having made a constructive sale of an appreciated financial position if the taxpayer (or a related person)—

(A) enters into a short sale of the same or substantially identical property,

(B) enters into an offsetting notional principal contract with respect to the same or substantially identical property,

(C) enters into a futures or forward contract to deliver the same or substantially identical property,

(D) in the case of an appreciated financial position that is a short sale or a contract described in subparagraph (B) or (C) with respect to any property, acquires the same or substantially identical property, or

(E) to the extent prescribed by the Secretary in regulations, enters into 1 or more other transactions (or acquires 1 or more positions) that have substantially the same effect as a transaction described in any of the preceding subparagraphs.

(2) EXCEPTION FOR SALES OF NONPUBLICLY TRADED PROPERTY.—A taxpayer shall not be treated as having made a constructive sale solely because the taxpayer enters into a contract for sale of any stock, debt instrument, or partnership interest which is not a marketable security (as defined in section 453(f)) if the contract settles within 1 year after the date such contract is entered into.

(3) EXCEPTION FOR CERTAIN CLOSED TRANSACTIONS.—

(A) IN GENERAL.—In applying this section, there shall be disregarded any transaction (which would otherwise cause a constructive sale) during the taxable year if—

(i) such transaction is closed on or before the 30th day after the close of such taxable year,

INCOME TAX—CAPITAL GAINS, LOSSES

(ii) the taxpayer holds the appreciated financial position throughout the 60-day period beginning on the date such transaction is closed, and

(iii) at no time during such 60-day period is the taxpayer's risk of loss with respect to such position reduced by reason of a circumstance which would be described in section 246(c)(4) if references to stock included references to such position.

(B) TREATMENT OF CERTAIN CLOSED TRANSACTIONS WHERE RISK OF LOSS ON APPRECIATED FINANCIAL POSITION DIMINISHED.—If—

(i) a transaction, which would otherwise cause a constructive sale of an appreciated financial position, is closed during the taxable year or during the 30 days thereafter, and

(ii) another transaction is entered into during the 60-day period beginning on the date the transaction referred to in clause (i) is closed—

(I) which would (but for this subparagraph) cause the requirement of subparagraph (A)(iii) not to be met with respect to the transaction described in clause (i) of this subparagraph,

(II) which is closed on or before the 30th day after the close of the taxable year in which the transaction referred to in clause (i) occurs, and

(III) which meets the requirements of clauses (ii) and (iii) of subparagraph (A),

the transaction referred to in clause (ii) shall be disregarded for purposes of determining whether the requirements of subparagraph (A)(iii) are met with respect to the transaction described in clause (i).

(4) RELATED PERSON.—A person is related to another person with respect to a transaction if—

(A) the relationship is described in section 267(b) or 707(b), and

(B) such transaction is entered into with a view toward avoiding the purposes of this section.

Amendments

- 2004, Working Families Tax Relief Act of 2004 (P.L. 108-311)

P.L. 108-311, § 406(e)(1):

Amended Code Sec. 1259(c)(2) by striking "The term 'constructive sale' shall not include any contract" and inserting "A taxpayer shall not be treated as having made a constructive sale solely because the taxpayer enters into a contract". **Effective** as if included in the provision of the Taxpayer Relief Act of 1997 (P.L. 105-34) to which it relates [**effective** for constructive sales after 6-8-97, generally.—CCH].

P.L. 108-311, § 406(e)(2):

Amended Code Sec. 1259(c)(3)(A) and (B)(i) by striking "be treated as a constructive sale" and inserting "cause a constructive sale". **Effective** as if included in the provision of the Taxpayer Relief Act of 1997 (P.L. 105-34) to which it relates [**effective** for constructive sales after 6-8-97, generally.—CCH].

P.L. 108-311, § 406(e)(3):

Amended Code Sec. 1259(c)(3)(A)(i) by striking "before the end of" and inserting "on or before". **Effective** as if included in the provision of the Taxpayer Relief Act of 1997 (P.L. 105-34) to which it relates [**effective** for constructive sales after 6-8-97, generally.—CCH].

P.L. 108-311, § 406(e)(4):

Amended Code Sec. 1259(c)(3)(B)(ii) by striking "substantially similar" following "(ii) another". **Effective** as if included in the provision of the Taxpayer Relief Act of 1997 (P.L. 105-34) to which it relates [**effective** for constructive sales after 6-8-97, generally.—CCH].

P.L. 108-311, § 406(e)(5):

Amended Code Sec. 1259(c)(3)(B)(ii)(I). **Effective** as if included in the provision of the Taxpayer Relief Act of 1997 (P.L. 105-34) to which it relates [**effective** for constructive sales after 6-8-97, generally.—CCH]. Prior to amendment, Code Sec. 1259(c)(3)(B)(ii)(I) read as follows:

(I) which also would otherwise be treated as a constructive sale of such position,

P.L. 108-311, § 406(e)(6):

Amended Code Sec. 1259(c)(3)(B)(ii)(II) by inserting "on or" before "before the 30th day". **Effective** as if included in the provision of the Taxpayer Relief Act of 1997 (P.L. 105-34) to which it relates [**effective** for constructive sales after 6-8-97, generally.—CCH].

P.L. 108-311, § 406(e)(7):

Amended the heading for Code Sec. 1259(c)(3)(B) by striking "POSITIONS WHICH ARE REESTABLISHED" and inserting "CERTAIN CLOSED TRANSACTIONS WHERE RISK OF LOSS ON APPRECIATED FINANCIAL POSITION DIMINISHED". **Effective** as if included in the provision of the Taxpayer Relief Act of 1997 (P.L. 105-34) to which it relates [**effective** for constructive sales after 6-8-97, generally.—CCH].

[Sec. 1259(d)]

(d) OTHER DEFINITIONS.—For purposes of this section—

(1) FORWARD CONTRACT.—The term "forward contract" means a contract to deliver a substantially fixed amount of property (including cash) for a substantially fixed price.

(2) OFFSETTING NOTIONAL PRINCIPAL CONTRACT.—The term "offsetting notional principal contract" means, with respect to any property, an agreement which includes—

(A) a requirement to pay (or provide credit for) all or substantially all of the investment yield (including appreciation) on such property for a specified period, and

(B) a right to be reimbursed for (or receive credit for) all or substantially all of any decline in the value of such property.

Amendments

- 1998, IRS Restructuring and Reform Act of 1998 (P.L. 105-206)

P.L. 105-206, § 6010(a)(2):

Amended Code Sec. 1259(d)(1) by inserting "(including cash)" after "property". **Effective** as if included in the provision of P.L. 105-34 to which it relates [generally **effective** for constructive sales after 6-8-97.—CCH].

[Sec. 1259(e)]

(e) SPECIAL RULES.—

(1) TREATMENT OF SUBSEQUENT SALE OF POSITION WHICH WAS DEEMED SOLD.—If—

(A) there is a constructive sale of any appreciated financial position,

(B) such position is subsequently disposed of, and

(C) at the time of such disposition, the transaction resulting in the constructive sale of such position is open with respect to the taxpayer or any related person,

solely for purposes of determining whether the taxpayer has entered into a constructive sale of any other appreciated financial position held by the taxpayer, the taxpayer shall be treated as entering into such transaction immediately after such disposition. For purposes of the preceding sentence, an assignment or other termination shall be treated as a disposition.

(2) CERTAIN TRUST INSTRUMENTS TREATED AS STOCK.—For purposes of this section, an interest in a trust which is actively traded (within the meaning of section 1092(d)(1)) shall be treated as stock unless substantially all (by value) of the property held by the trust is debt described in subsection (b)(2)(A).

(3) MULTIPLE POSITIONS IN PROPERTY.—If a taxpayer holds multiple positions in property, the determination of whether a specific transaction is a constructive sale and, if so, which appreciated financial position is deemed sold shall be made in the same manner as actual sales.

[Sec. 1259(f)]

(f) REGULATIONS.—The Secretary shall prescribe such regulations as may be necessary or appropriate to carry out the purposes of this section.

Sec. 1259(c)(3)(A)(ii)

Amendments

• 1997, Taxpayer Relief Act of 1997 (P.L. 105-34)

P.L. 105-34, §1001(a):

Amended part IV of subchapter P of chapter 1 by adding at the end a new Code Sec. 1259. **Effective**, generally, for any constructive sale after 6-8-97. For special rules, see Act Sec. 1001(d)(2)-(4), below.

P.L. 105-34, §1001(d)(2)-(4) (as amended by P.L. 105-206, §6010(a)(4)), provides:

(2) EXCEPTION FOR SALES OF POSITIONS, ETC. HELD BEFORE JUNE 9, 1997.—If—

(A) before June 9, 1997, the taxpayer entered into any transaction which is a constructive sale of any appreciated financial position, and

(B) before the close of the 30-day period beginning on the date of the enactment of this Act or before such later date as may be specified by the Secretary of the Treasury, such transaction and position are clearly identified in the taxpayer's records as offsetting, such transaction and position shall not be taken into account in determining whether any other constructive sale after June 8, 1997, has occurred. The preceding sentence shall cease to apply as of the date such transaction is closed or the taxpayer ceases to hold such position.

(3) SPECIAL RULE.—In the case of a decedent dying after June 8, 1997, if—

(A) there was a constructive sale on or before such date of any appreciated financial position,

(B) the transaction resulting in such constructive sale of such position remains open (with respect to the decedent or any related person)—

(i) for not less than 2 years after the date of such transaction (whether such period is before or after June 8, 1997), and

(ii) at any time during the 3-year period ending on the date of the decedent's death, and

(C) such transaction is not closed before the close of the 30th day after the date of the enactment of this Act,

then, for purposes of such Code, such position (and the transaction resulting in such constructive sale) shall be treated as property constituting rights to receive an item of income in respect of a decedent under section 691 of such Code. Section 1014(c) of such Code shall not apply to so much of such position's or property's value (as included in the decedent's estate for purposes of chapter 11 of such Code) as exceeds its fair market value as of the date such transaction is closed.

(4) ELECTION OF MARK TO MARKET BY SECURITIES TRADERS AND TRADERS AND DEALERS IN COMMODITIES.—

(A) IN GENERAL.—The amendments made by subsection (b) shall apply to taxable years ending after the date of the enactment of this Act.

(B) 4-YEAR SPREAD OF ADJUSTMENTS.—In the case of a taxpayer who elects under subsection (e) or (f) of section 475 of the Internal Revenue Code of 1986 (as added by this section) to change its method of accounting for the taxable year which includes the date of the enactment of this Act—

(i) any identification required under such subsection with respect to securities and commodities held on the date of the enactment of this Act shall be treated as timely made if made on or before the 30th day after such date of enactment, and

(ii) the net amount of the adjustments required to be taken into account by the taxpayer under section 481 of such Code shall be taken into account ratably over the 4-taxable year period beginning with such first taxable year.

[Sec. 1260]

SEC. 1260. GAINS FROM CONSTRUCTIVE OWNERSHIP TRANSACTIONS.

[Sec. 1260(a)]

(a) IN GENERAL.—If the taxpayer has gain from a constructive ownership transaction with respect to any financial asset and such gain would (without regard to this section) be treated as a long-term capital gain—

(1) such gain shall be treated as ordinary income to the extent that such gain exceeds the net underlying long-term capital gain, and

(2) to the extent such gain is treated as a long-term capital gain after the application of paragraph (1), the determination of the capital gain rate (or rates) applicable to such gain under section 1(h) shall be determined on the basis of the respective rate (or rates) that would have been applicable to the net underlying long-term capital gain.

[Sec. 1260(b)]

(b) INTEREST CHARGE ON DEFERRAL OF GAIN RECOGNITION.—

(1) IN GENERAL.—If any gain is treated as ordinary income for any taxable year by reason of subsection (a)(1), the tax imposed by this chapter for such taxable year shall be increased by the amount of interest determined under paragraph (2) with respect to each prior taxable year during any portion of which the constructive ownership transaction was open. Any amount payable under this paragraph shall be taken into account in computing the amount of any deduction allowable to the taxpayer for interest paid or accrued during such taxable year.

(2) AMOUNT OF INTEREST.—The amount of interest determined under this paragraph with respect to a prior taxable year is the amount of interest which would have been imposed under section 6601 on the underpayment of tax for such year which would have resulted if the gain (which is treated as ordinary income by reason of subsection (a)(1)) had been included in gross income in the taxable years in which it accrued (determined by treating the income as accruing at a constant rate equal to the applicable Federal rate as in effect on the day the transaction closed). The period during which such interest shall accrue shall end on the due date (without extensions) for the return of tax imposed by this chapter for the taxable year in which such transaction closed.

(3) APPLICABLE FEDERAL RATE.—For purposes of paragraph (2), the applicable Federal rate is the applicable Federal rate determined under section 1274(d) (compounded semiannually) which would apply to a debt instrument with a term equal to the period the transaction was open.

(4) NO CREDITS AGAINST INCREASE IN TAX.—Any increase in tax under paragraph (1) shall not be treated as tax imposed by this chapter for purposes of determining—

(A) the amount of any credit allowable under this chapter, or

(B) the amount of the tax imposed by section 55.

[Sec. 1260(c)]

(c) FINANCIAL ASSET.—For purposes of this section—

(1) IN GENERAL.—The term "financial asset" means—

(A) any equity interest in any pass-thru entity, and

(B) to the extent provided in regulations—

(i) any debt instrument, and

(ii) any stock in a corporation which is not a pass-thru entity.

(2) PASS-THRU ENTITY.—For purposes of paragraph (1), the term "pass-thru entity" means—

(A) a regulated investment company,

(B) a real estate investment trust,

(C) an S corporation,

(D) a partnership,

(E) a trust,

(F) a common trust fund,

(G) a passive foreign investment company (as defined in section 1297 without regard to subsection (d) thereof), and

(H) a REMIC.

INCOME TAX—CAPITAL GAINS, LOSSES

Amendments

• **2007, Tax Technical Corrections Act of 2007 (P.L. 110-172)**

P.L. 110-172, §11(a)(23):

Amended Code Sec. 1260(c)(2)(G) by adding "and" at the end. **Effective** 12-29-2007.

P.L. 110-172, §11(a)(24)(B):

Amended Code Sec. 1260(c)(2)(G) by striking "subsection (e)" and inserting "subsection (d)". **Effective** 12-29-2007.

• **2004, American Jobs Creation Act of 2004 (P.L. 108-357)**

P.L. 108-357, §413(c)(23):

Amended Code Sec. 1260(c)(2) by striking subparagraphs (H) and (I) and by redesignating subparagraph (J) as subparagraph (H). **Effective** for tax years of foreign corporations beginning after 12-31-2004, and for tax years of United States shareholders with or within which such tax years of foreign corporations end. Prior to being stricken, Code Sec. 1260(c)(2)(H)-(I) read as follows:

(H) a foreign personal holding company,

(I) a foreign investment company (as defined in section 1246(b)), and

[Sec. 1260(d)]

(d) CONSTRUCTIVE OWNERSHIP TRANSACTION.—For purposes of this section—

(1) IN GENERAL.—The taxpayer shall be treated as having entered into a constructive ownership transaction with respect to any financial asset if the taxpayer—

(A) holds a long position under a notional principal contract with respect to the financial asset,

(B) enters into a forward or futures contract to acquire the financial asset,

(C) is the holder of a call option, and is the grantor of a put option, with respect to the financial asset and such options have substantially equal strike prices and substantially contemporaneous maturity dates, or

(D) to the extent provided in regulations prescribed by the Secretary, enters into one or more other transactions (or acquires one or more positions) that have substantially the same effect as a transaction described in any of the preceding subparagraphs.

(2) EXCEPTION FOR POSITIONS WHICH ARE MARKED TO MARKET.—This section shall not apply to any constructive ownership transaction if all of the positions which are part of such transaction are marked to market under any provision of this title or the regulations thereunder.

(3) LONG POSITION UNDER NOTIONAL PRINCIPAL CONTRACT.—A person shall be treated as holding a long position under a notional principal contract with respect to any financial asset if such person—

(A) has the right to be paid (or receive credit for) all or substantially all of the investment yield (including appreciation) on such financial asset for a specified period, and

(B) is obligated to reimburse (or provide credit for) all or substantially all of any decline in the value of such financial asset.

(4) FORWARD CONTRACT.—The term "forward contract" means any contract to acquire in the future (or provide or receive credit for the future value of) any financial asset.

[Sec. 1260(e)]

(e) NET UNDERLYING LONG-TERM CAPITAL GAIN.—For purposes of this section, in the case of any constructive ownership transaction with respect to any financial asset, the term "net underlying long-term capital gain" means the aggregate net capital gain that the taxpayer would have had if—

(1) the financial asset had been acquired for fair market value on the date such transaction was opened and sold for fair market value on the date such transaction was closed, and

(2) only gains and losses that would have resulted from the deemed ownership under paragraph (1) were taken into account.

The amount of the net underlying long-term capital gain with respect to any financial asset shall be treated as zero unless the amount thereof is established by clear and convincing evidence.

[Sec. 1260(f)]

(f) SPECIAL RULE WHERE TAXPAYER TAKES DELIVERY.—Except as provided in regulations prescribed by the Secretary, if a constructive ownership transaction is closed by reason of taking delivery, this section shall be applied as if the taxpayer had sold all the contracts, options, or other positions which are part of such transaction for fair market value on the closing date. The amount of gain recognized under the preceding sentence shall not exceed the amount of gain treated as ordinary income under subsection (a). Proper adjustments shall be made in the amount of any gain or loss subsequently realized for gain recognized and treated as ordinary income under this subsection.

[Sec. 1260(g)]

(g) REGULATIONS.—The Secretary shall prescribe such regulations as may be necessary or appropriate to carry out the purposes of this section, including regulations—

(1) to permit taxpayers to mark to market constructive ownership transactions in lieu of applying this section, and

(2) to exclude certain forward contracts which do not convey substantially all of the economic return with respect to a financial asset.

Amendments

• **1999, Tax Relief Extension Act of 1999 (P.L. 106-170)**

P.L. 106-170, §534(a):

Amended Part IV of subchapter P of chapter 1 by inserting after Code Sec. 1259 a new Code Sec. 1260. **Effective** for transactions entered into after 7-11-99.

PART V—SPECIAL RULES FOR BONDS AND OTHER DEBT INSTRUMENTS

Subpart A.	Original issue discount.
Subpart B.	Market discount on bonds.
Subpart C.	Discount on short-term obligations.
Subpart D.	Miscellaneous provisions.

Subpart A—Original Issue Discount

Sec. 1271.	Treatment of amounts received on retirement or sale or exchange of debt instruments.
Sec. 1272.	Current inclusion in income of original issue discount.
Sec. 1273.	Determination of amount of original issue discount.
Sec. 1274.	Determination of issue price in the case of certain debt instruments issued for property.
Sec. 1274A.	Special rules for certain transactions where stated principal amount does not exceed $2,800,000.
Sec. 1275.	Other definitions and special rules.

INCOME TAX—ORIGINAL ISSUE DISCOUNT

[Sec. 1271]

SEC. 1271. TREATMENT OF AMOUNTS RECEIVED ON RETIREMENT OR SALE OR EXCHANGE OF DEBT INSTRUMENTS.

[Sec. 1271(a)]

(a) GENERAL RULE.—For purposes of this title—

(1) RETIREMENT.—Amounts received by the holder on retirement of any debt instrument shall be considered as amounts received in exchange therefor.

(2) ORDINARY INCOME ON SALE OR EXCHANGE WHERE INTENTION TO CALL BEFORE MATURITY.—

(A) IN GENERAL.—If at the time of original issue there was an intention to call a debt instrument before maturity, any gain realized on the sale or exchange thereof which does not exceed an amount equal to—

(i) the original issue discount, reduced by

(ii) the portion of original issue discount previously includible in the gross income of any holder (without regard to section 1272(a)(7) (or the corresponding provisions of prior law)),

shall be treated as ordinary income.

(B) EXCEPTIONS.—This paragraph shall not apply to—

(i) any tax-exempt obligation, or

(ii) any holder who has purchased the debt instrument at a premium.

(3) CERTAIN SHORT-TERM GOVERNMENT OBLIGATIONS.—

(A) IN GENERAL.—On the sale or exchange of any short-term Government obligation, any gain realized which does not exceed an amount equal to the ratable share of the acquisition discount shall be treated as ordinary income.

(B) SHORT-TERM GOVERNMENT OBLIGATION.—For purposes of this paragraph, the term "short-term Government obligation" means any obligation of the United States or any of its possessions, or of a State or any political subdivision thereof, or of the District of Columbia, which has a fixed maturity date not more than 1 year from the date of issue. Such term does not include any tax-exempt obligation.

(C) ACQUISITION DISCOUNT.—For purposes of this paragraph, the term "acquisition discount" means the excess of the stated redemption price at maturity over the taxpayer's basis for the obligation.

(D) RATABLE SHARE.—For purposes of this paragraph, except as provided in subparagraph (E) the ratable share of the acquisition discount is an amount which bears the same ratio to such discount as—

(i) the number of days which the taxpayer held the obligation, bears to

(ii) the number of days after the date the taxpayer acquired the obligation and up to (and including) the date of its maturity.

(E) ELECTION OF ACCRUAL ON BASIS OF CONSTANT INTEREST RATE.—At the election of the taxpayer with respect to any obligation, the ratable share of the aquisition discount is the portion of the acquisition discount accruing while the taxpayer held the obligation determined (under regulations prescribed by the Secretary) on the basis of—

(i) the taxpayer's yield to maturity based on the taxpayer's cost of acquiring the obligation, and

(ii) compounding daily.

An election under this subparagraph, once made with respect to any obligation, shall be irrevocable.

(4) CERTAIN SHORT-TERM NONGOVERNMENT OBLIGATIONS.—

(A) IN GENERAL.—On the sale or exchange of any short-term nongovernment obligation, any gain realized which does not exceed an amount equal to the ratable share of the original issue discount shall be treated as ordinary income.

(B) SHORT-TERM NONGOVERNMENT OBLIGATION.—For purposes of this paragraph, the term "short-term nongovernment obligation" means any obligation which—

(i) has a fixed maturity date not more than 1 year from the date of the issue, and

(ii) is not a short-term Government obligation (as defined in paragraph (3)(B) without regard to the last sentence thereof).

(C) RATABLE SHARE.—For purposes of this paragraph, except as provided in subparagraph (D), the ratable share of the original issue discount is an amount which bears the same ratio to such discount as—

(i) the number of days which the taxpayer held the obligation, bears to

(ii) the number of days after the date of original issue and up to (and including) the date of its maturity.

(D) ELECTION OF ACCRUAL ON BASIS OF CONSTANT INTEREST RATE.—At the election of the taxpayer with respect to any obligation, the ratable share of the original issue discount is the portion of the original issue discount accruing while the taxpayer held the obligation determined (under regulations prescribed by the Secretary) on the basis of—

(i) the yield to maturity based on the issue price of the obligation, and

(ii) compounding daily.

Any election under this subparagraph, once made with respect to any obligation, shall be irrevocable.

Amendments

- **2018, Tax Technical Corrections Act of 2018 (P.L. 115-141)**

P.L. 115-141, §401(c)(1)(A)(ii), Div. U:

Amended Code Sec. 1271(a)(2)(B) by striking "(and paragraph (2) of subsection (c))" following "This paragraph". **Effective** for debt instruments issued on or after 7-2-1982.

P.L. 115-141, §401(c)(1)(D), Div. U:

Amended Code Sec. 1271(a)(2)(A)(ii) by striking "subsection (a)(7) or (b)(4) of section 1272" and inserting "section 1272(a)(7)". **Effective** for debt instruments issued on or after 7-2-1982.

- **1988, Technical and Miscellaneous Revenue Act of 1988 (P.L. 100-647)**

P.L. 100-647, §1006(u)(4):

Amended Code Sec. 1271(a)(2)(A)(ii) by striking out "subsection (a)(6)" and inserting in lieu thereof "subsection (a)(7)". **Effective** as if included in the provision of P.L. 99-514 to which it relates.

- **1986, Tax Reform Act of 1986 (P.L. 99-514)**

P.L. 99-514, §1803(a)(1)(A):

Amended Code Sec. 1271(a) by adding at the end thereof new paragraph (4). **Effective** as if included in the provision of P.L. 98-369 to which it relates.

P.L. 99-514, §1803(a)(2)(A):

Amended Code Sec. 1271(a)(3) by adding at the end thereof new subparagraph (E). **Effective** as if included in the provision of P.L. 98-369 to which it relates.

P.L. 99-514, §1803(a)(2)(B):

Amended Code Sec. 1271(a)(3)(D) by striking out "this paragraph" and inserting in lieu thereof "this paragraph, except as provided in subparagraph (E)". **Effective** as if included in the provision of P.L. 98-369 to which it relates.

P.L. 99-514, §1803(a)(3):

Amended Code Sec. 1271(a)(3)(B). **Effective** as if included in the provision of P.L. 98-369 to which it relates. Prior to amendment, Code Sec. 1271(a)(3)(B) read as follows:

(B) SHORT-TERM GOVERNMENT OBLIGATION.—For purposes of this paragraph, the term "short-term Government obligation" means any obligation of the United States or any of its possessions, or of a State or any political subdivision thereof, or of the District of Columbia which is—

(i) issued on a discount basis, and

(ii) payable without interest at a fixed maturity date not more than 1 year from the date of issue.

Such term does not include any tax-exempt obligation.

INCOME TAX—ORIGINAL ISSUE DISCOUNT

[Sec. 1271(b)]

(b) EXCEPTION FOR CERTAIN OBLIGATIONS.—

(1) IN GENERAL.—This section shall not apply to any obligation issued by a natural person before June 9, 1997.

(2) TERMINATION.—Paragraph (1) shall not apply to any obligation purchased (within the meaning of section 1272(d)(1)) after June 8, 1997.

Amendments

• **2018, Tax Technical Corrections Act of 2018 (P.L. 115-141)**

P.L. 115-141, §401(c)(1)(E), Div. U:

Amended Code Sec. 1271(b)(1). **Effective** for debt instruments issued on or after 7-2-1982. Prior to amendment, Code Sec. 1271(b)(1) read as follows:

(1) IN GENERAL.—This section shall not apply to—

(A) any obligation issued by a natural person before June 9, 1997, and

(B) any obligation issued before July 2, 1982, by an issuer which is not a corporation and is not a government or political subdivision thereof.

• **1997, Taxpayer Relief Act of 1997 (P.L. 105-34)**

P.L. 105-34, §1003(c)(1):

Amended Code Sec. 1271(b). **Effective** for sales, exchanges, and retirements after 8-5-97. Prior to amendment, Code Sec. 1271(b) read as follows:

(b) EXCEPTIONS.—This section shall not apply to—

(1) NATURAL PERSONS.—Any obligation issued by a natural person.

(2) OBLIGATIONS ISSUED BEFORE JULY 2, 1982, BY CERTAIN ISSUERS.—Any obligation issued before July 2, 1982, by an issuer which—

(A) is not a corporation, and

(B) is not a government or political subdivision thereof.

[Sec. 1271(c)—Stricken]

Amendments

• **2018, Tax Technical Corrections Act of 2018 (P.L. 115-141)**

P.L. 115-141, §401(c)(1)(A)(i), Div. U:

Amended Code Sec. 1271 by striking subsection (c) and by redesignating subsection (d) as subsection (c). **Effective** for debt instruments issued on or after 7-2-1982. Prior to being stricken, Code Sec. 1271(c) read as follows:

(c) SPECIAL RULE FOR CERTAIN OBLIGATIONS WITH RESPECT TO WHICH ORIGINAL ISSUE DISCOUNT NOT CURRENTLY INCLUDIBLE.—

(1) IN GENERAL.—On the sale or exchange of debt instruments issued by a government or political subdivision thereof after December 31, 1954, and before July 2, 1982, or by a corporation after December 31, 1954, and on or before May 27, 1969, any gain realized which does not exceed—

(A) an amount equal to the original issue discount, or

(B) if at the time of original issue there was no intention to call the debt instrument before maturity, an amount which bears the same ratio to the original issue discount as the number of complete months that the debt instrument was held by the taxpayer bears to the number of complete months from the date of original issue to the date of maturity, shall be considered as ordinary income.

(2) SUBSECTION (a)(2)(A) NOT TO APPLY.—Subsection (a)(2)(A) shall not apply to any debt instrument referred to in paragraph (1) of this subsection.

(3) CROSS REFERENCE.—For current inclusion of original issue discount, see section 1272.

• **2014, Tax Technical Corrections Act of 2014 (P.L. 113-295)**

P.L. 113-295, §221(a)(86):

Amended Code Sec. 1271(c). **Effective** generally 12-19-2014. For a special rule, see Act Sec. 221(b)(2), Division A, below. Prior to amendment, Code Sec. 1271(c) read as follows:

(c) TRANSITION RULES.—

(1) SPECIAL RULE FOR CERTAIN OBLIGATIONS ISSUED BEFORE JANUARY 1, 1955.—Paragraph (1) of subsection (a) shall apply to a debt instrument issued before January 1, 1955, only if such instrument was issued with interest coupons or in registered form, or was in such form on March 1, 1954.

(2) SPECIAL RULE FOR CERTAIN OBLIGATIONS WITH RESPECT TO WHICH ORIGINAL ISSUE DISCOUNT NOT CURRENTLY INCLUDIBLE.—

(A) IN GENERAL.—On the sale or exchange of debt instruments issued by a government or political subdivision thereof after December 31, 1954, and before July 2, 1982, or by a corporation after December 31, 1954, and on or before May 27, 1969, any gain realized which does not exceed—

(i) an amount equal to the original issue discount, or

(ii) if at the time of original issue there was no intention to call the debt instrument before maturity, an amount which bears the same ratio to the original issue discount as the number of complete months that the debt instrument was held by the taxpayer bears to the number of complete months from the date of original issue to the date of maturity,

shall be considered as ordinary income.

(B) SUBSECTION (a)(2)(A) NOT TO APPLY.—Subsection (a)(2)(A) shall not apply to any debt instrument referred to in subparagraph (A) of this paragraph.

(C) CROSS REFERENCE.—

For current inclusion of original issue discount, see section 1272.

P.L. 113-295, §221(b)(2), Division A, provides:

(2) SAVINGS PROVISION.—If—

(A) any provision amended or repealed by the amendments made by this section applied to—

(i) any transaction occurring before the date of the enactment of this Act,

(ii) any property acquired before such date of enactment, or

(iii) any item of income, loss, deduction, or credit taken into account before such date of enactment, and

(B) the treatment of such transaction, property, or item under such provision would (without regard to the amendments or repeals made by this section) affect the liability for tax for periods ending after date of enactment, nothing in the amendments or repeals made by this section shall be construed to affect the treatment of such transaction, property, or item for purposes of determining liability for tax for periods ending after such date of enactment.

[Sec. 1271(c)]

(c) DOUBLE INCLUSION IN INCOME NOT REQUIRED.—This section and sections 1272 and 1286 shall not require the inclusion of any amount previously includible in gross income.

Amendments

• **2018, Tax Technical Corrections Act of 2018 (P.L. 115-141)**

P.L. 115-141, §401(c)(1)(A)(i), Div. U:

Amended Code Sec. 1271 by redesignating subsection (d) as subsection (c). **Effective** for debt instruments issued on or after 7-2-1982.

• **1984, Deficit Reduction Act of 1984 (P.L. 98-369)**

P.L. 98-369, §41(a):

Added Code Sec. 1271. **Effective** for tax years ending after 7-18-84.

[Sec. 1272]

SEC. 1272. CURRENT INCLUSION IN INCOME OF ORIGINAL ISSUE DISCOUNT.

[Sec. 1272(a)]

(a) ORIGINAL ISSUE DISCOUNT INCLUDED IN INCOME ON BASIS OF CONSTANT INTEREST RATE.—

(1) GENERAL RULE.—For purposes of this title, there shall be included in the gross income of the holder of any debt instrument having original issue discount an amount equal to the sum of the daily portions of the original issue discount for each day during the taxable year on which such holder held such debt instrument.

(2) EXCEPTIONS.—Paragraph (1) shall not apply to—

(A) TAX-EXEMPT OBLIGATIONS.—Any tax-exempt obligation.

(B) UNITED STATES SAVINGS BONDS.—Any United States savings bond.

(C) SHORT-TERM OBLIGATIONS.—Any debt instrument which has a fixed maturity date not more than 1 year from the date of issue.

(D) LOANS BETWEEN NATURAL PERSONS.—

(i) IN GENERAL.—Any loan made by a natural person to another natural person if—

(I) such loan is not made in the course of a trade or business of the lender, and

(II) the amount of such loan (when increased by the outstanding amount of prior loans by such natural person to such other natural person) does not exceed $10,000.

(ii) CLAUSE (i) NOT TO APPLY WHERE TAX AVOIDANCE A PRINCIPAL PURPOSE.—Clause (i) shall not apply if the loan has as 1 of its principal purposes the avoidance of any Federal tax.

INCOME TAX—ORIGINAL ISSUE DISCOUNT

(iii) TREATMENT OF HUSBAND AND WIFE.—For purposes of this subparagraph, a husband and wife shall be treated as 1 person. The preceding sentence shall not apply where the spouses lived apart at all times during the taxable year in which the loan is made.

(3) DETERMINATION OF DAILY PORTIONS.—For purposes of paragraph (1), the daily portion of the original issue discount on any debt instrument shall be determined by allocating to each day in any accrual period its ratable portion of the increase during such accrual period in the adjusted issue price of the debt instrument. For purposes of the preceding sentence, the increase in the adjusted issue price for any accrual period shall be an amount equal to the excess (if any) of—

(A) the product of—

(i) the adjusted issue price of the debt instrument at the beginning of such accrual period, and

(ii) the yield to maturity (determined on the basis of compounding at the close of each accrual period and properly adjusted for the length of the accrual period), over

(B) the sum of the amounts payable as interest on such debt instrument during such accrual period.

(4) ADJUSTED ISSUE PRICE.—For purposes of this subsection, the adjusted issue price of any debt instrument at the beginning of any accrual period is the sum of—

(A) the issue price of such debt instrument, plus

(B) the adjustments under this subsection to such issue price for all periods before the first day of such accrual period.

(5) ACCRUAL PERIOD.—Except as otherwise provided in regulations prescribed by the Secretary, the term "accrual period" means a 6-month period (or shorter period from the date of original issue of the debt instrument) which ends on a day in the calendar year corresponding to the maturity date of the debt instrument or the date 6 months before such maturity date.

(6) DETERMINATION OF DAILY PORTIONS WHERE PRINCIPAL SUBJECT TO ACCELERATION.—

(A) IN GENERAL.—In the case of any debt instrument to which this paragraph applies, the daily portion of the original issue discount shall be determined by allocating to each day in any accrual period its ratable portion of the excess (if any) of—

(i) the sum of (I) the present value determined under subparagraph (B) of all remaining payments under the debt instrument as of the close of such period, and (II) the payments during the accrual period of amounts included in the stated redemption price of the debt instrument, over

(ii) the adjusted issue price of such debt instrument at the beginning of such period.

(B) DETERMINATION OF PRESENT VALUE.—For purposes of subparagraph (A), the present value shall be determined on the basis of—

(i) the original yield to maturity (determined on the basis of compounding at the close of each accrual period and properly adjusted for the length of the accrual period),

(ii) events which have occurred before the close of the accrual period, and

(iii) a prepayment assumption determined in the manner prescribed by regulations.

(C) DEBT INSTRUMENTS TO WHICH PARAGRAPH APPLIES.—This paragraph applies to—

(i) any regular interest in a REMIC or qualified mortgage held by a REMIC,

(ii) any other debt instrument if payments under such debt instrument may be accelerated by reason of prepayments of other obligations securing such debt instrument (or, to the extent provided in regulations, by reason of other events), or

(iii) any pool of debt instruments the yield on which may be affected by reason of prepayments (or to the extent provided in regulations, by reason of other events).

To the extent provided in regulations prescribed by the Secretary, in the case of a small business engaged in the trade or business of selling tangible personal property at retail, clause (iii) shall not apply to debt instruments incurred in the ordinary course of such trade or business while held by such business.

(7) REDUCTION WHERE SUBSEQUENT HOLDER PAYS ACQUISITION PREMIUM.—

(A) REDUCTION.—For purposes of this subsection, in the case of any purchase after its original issue of a debt instrument to which this subsection applies, the daily portion for any day shall be reduced by an amount equal to the amount which would be the daily portion for such day (without regard to this paragraph) multiplied by the fraction determined under subparagraph (B).

(B) DETERMINATION OF FRACTION.—For purposes of subparagraph (A), the fraction determined under this subparagraph is a fraction—

(i) the numerator of which is the excess (if any) of—

(I) the cost of such debt instrument incurred by the purchaser, over

(II) the issue price of such debt instrument, increased by the portion of original issue discount previously includible in the gross income of any holder (computed without regard to this paragraph), and

(ii) the denominator of which is the sum of the daily portions for such debt instrument for all days after the date of such purchase and ending on the stated maturity date (computed without regard to this paragraph).

Amendments

• **2018, Tax Technical Corrections Act of 2018 (P.L. 115-141)**

P.L. 115-141, § 401(c)(1)(F)(i)-(ii), Div. U:

Amended Code Sec. 1272(a) by striking "ON DEBT INSTRUMENTS ISSUED AFTER JULY 1, 1982" following "ORIGINAL ISSUE DISCOUNT" in the heading, and by striking "issued after July 1, 1982" following "instrument having original issue discount" in paragraph (1). **Effective** for debt instruments issued on or after 7-2-1982.

P.L. 115-141, § 401(c)(3)(A), Div. U:

Amended Code Sec. 1272(a)(2) by striking subparagraph (D) and by redesignating subparagraph (E) as subparagraph (D). **Effective** for obligations issued on or after 3-2-1984. Prior to being stricken, Code Sec. 1272(a)(2)(D) read as follows:

(D) OBLIGATIONS ISSUED BY NATURAL PERSONS BEFORE MARCH 2, 1984.—Any obligation issued by a natural person before March 2, 1984.

• **1997, Taxpayer Relief Act of 1997 (P.L. 105-34)**

P.L. 105-34, § 1004(a):

Amended Code Sec. 1272(a)(6)(C) by striking "or" at the end of clause (i), by striking the period at the end of clause (ii) and inserting ", or", and by inserting after clause (ii) a new clause (iii) and a new flush sentence. **Effective**, generally, for tax years beginning after 8-5-97. For a special rule, see Act Sec. 1004(b)(2)(A)-(C).

P.L. 105-34, § 1004(b)(2)(A)-(C), provides:

(2) CHANGE IN METHOD OF ACCOUNTING.—In the case of any taxpayer required by this section to change its method of accounting for its first taxable year beginning after the date of the enactment of this Act—

(A) such change shall be treated as initiated by the taxpayer,

(B) such change shall be treated as made with the consent of the Secretary of the Treasury, and

(C) the net amount of the adjustments required to be taken into account by the taxpayer under section 481 of the Internal Revenue Code of 1986 shall be taken into account ratably over the 4-taxable year period beginning with such first taxable year.

• **1986, Tax Reform Act of 1986 (P.L. 99-514)**

P.L. 99-514, § 672:

Amended Code Sec. 1272(a) by redesignating paragraph (6) as paragraph (7) and by inserting after paragraph (5) new paragraph (6). **Effective** for debt instruments issued after 12-31-86, in tax years ending after such date.

INCOME TAX—ORIGINAL ISSUE DISCOUNT

[Sec. 1272(b)—Stricken]

Amendments

- **2018, Tax Technical Corrections Act of 2018 (P.L. 115-141)**

P.L. 115-141, §401(c)(1)(B), Div. U:

Amended Code Sec. 1272 by striking subsection (b) and by redesignating subsections (c) and (d) as subsections (b) and (c), respectively. **Effective** for debt instruments issued on or after 7-2-1982. Prior to being stricken, Code Sec. 1272(b) read as follows:

(b) RATABLE INCLUSION RETAINED FOR CORPORATE DEBT INSTRUMENTS ISSUED BEFORE JULY 2, 1982.—

(1) GENERAL RULE.—There shall be included in the gross income of the holder of any debt instrument issued by a corportion after May 27, 1969, and before July 2, 1982—

(A) the ratable monthly portion of original issue discount, multiplied by

(B) the number of complete months (plus any fractional part of a month determined under paragraph (3)) such holder held such debt instrument during the taxable year.

(2) DETERMINATION OF RATABLE MONTHLY PORTION.—Except as provided in paragraph (4), the ratable monthly portion of original issue discount shall equal—

(A) the original issue discount, divided by

(B) the number of complete months from the date of original issue to the stated maturity date of the debt instrument.

(3) MONTH DEFINED.—For purposes of this subsection—

(A) COMPLETE MONTH.—A complete month commences with the date of original issue and the corresponding day of each succeeding calendar month (or the last day of a calendar month in which there is no corresponding day).

(B) TRANSFERS DURING MONTH.—In any case where a debt instrument is acquired on any day other than a day determined under subparagraph (A), the ratable monthly portion of original issue discount for the complete month (or partial month) in which such acquisition occurs shall be allocated between the transferor and the transferee in accordance with the number of days in such complete (or partial) month each held the debt instrument.

(4) REDUCTION WHERE SUBSEQUENT HOLDER PAYS ACQUISITION PREMIUM.—

(A) REDUCTION.—For purposes of this subsection, the ratable monthly portion of original issue discount shall not include its share of the acquisition premium.

(B) SHARE OF ACQUISITION PREMIUM.—For purposes of subparagraph (A), any month's share of the acquisition premium is an amount (determined at the time of the purchase) equal to—

(i) the excess of—

(I) the cost of such debt instrument incurred by the holder, over

(II) the issue price of such debt instrument, increased by the portion of original issue discount previously includible in the gross income of any holder (computed without regard to this paragraph),

(ii) divided by the number of complete months (plus any fractional part of a month) from the date of such purchase to the stated maturity date of such debt instrument.

[Sec. 1272(b)]

(b) EXCEPTIONS.—This section shall not apply to any holder—

(1) who has purchased the debt instrument at a premium, or

(2) which is a life insurance company to which section 811(b) applies.

Amendments

- **2018, Tax Technical Corrections Act of 2018 (P.L. 115-141)**

P.L. 115-141, §401(c)(1)(B), Div. U:

Amended Code Sec. 1272 by redesignating subsection (c) as subsection (b). **Effective** for debt instruments issued on or after 7-2-1982.

[Sec. 1272(c)]

(c) DEFINITION AND SPECIAL RULE.—

(1) PURCHASE DEFINED.—For purposes of this section, the term "purchase" means—

(A) any acquisition of a debt instrument, where

(B) the basis of the debt instrument is not determined in whole or in part by reference to the adjusted basis of such debt instrument in the hands of the person from whom acquired.

(2) BASIS ADJUSTMENT.—The basis of any debt instrument in the hands of the holder thereof shall be increased by the amount included in his gross income pursuant to this section.

Amendments

- **2018, Tax Technical Corrections Act of 2018 (P.L. 115-141)**

P.L. 115-141, §401(c)(1)(B), Div. U:

Amended Code Sec. 1272 by redesignating subsection (d) as subsection (c). **Effective** for debt instruments issued on or after 7-2-1982.

- **1984, Deficit Reduction Act of 1984 (P.L. 98-369)**

P.L. 98-369, §41(a):

Added Code Sec. 1272. **Effective** for tax years ending after 7-18-84. However, Code Sec. 1272 does not apply to any obligation issued on or before 12-31-84, which is not a capital asset in the hands of the taxpayer [**effective** date changed by P.L. 99-514, §1803(b)]. For a special rule, see Act Sec. 44(i)-(j), below.

P.L. 98-369, §44(i)-(j), provides:

(i) Other Miscellaneous Changes.—

(1) Accrual Period.—In the case of any obligation issued after July 1, 1982, and before January 1, 1985, the accrual period, for purposes of section 1272(a) of the Internal Revenue Code of 1954 (as amended by section 41(a)), shall be a 1-year period (or shorter period to maturity) beginning on the day in the calendar year which corresponds to the date of original issue of the obligation.

(2) Change in Reduction for Purchase After Original Issue.—Section 1272(a)(6) of such Code (as so amended) shall not apply to any purchase on or before the date of the enactment of this Act, and the rules of section 1232A(a)(6) of such code (as in effect on the day before the date of the enactment of this Act) shall continue to apply to such purchase.

(j) Clarification That Prior Effective Date Rules Not Affected.—Nothing in the amendment made by section 41(a) shall affect the application of any effective date provision (including any transitional rule) for any provision which was a predecessor to any provision contained in part V of subchapter P of chapter 1 of the Internal Revenue Code of 1954 (as added by section 41).

[Sec. 1273]

SEC. 1273. DETERMINATION OF AMOUNT OF ORIGINAL ISSUE DISCOUNT.

[Sec. 1273(a)]

(a) GENERAL RULE.—for purposes of this subpart—

(1) IN GENERAL.—The term "original issue discount" means the excess (if any) of—

(A) the stated redemption price at maturity, over

(B) the issue price.

(2) STATED REDEMPTION PRICE AT MATURITY.—The term "stated redemption price at maturity" means the amount fixed by the last modification of the purchase agreement and includes interest and other amounts payable at that time (other than any interest based on a fixed rate, and payable unconditionally at fixed periodic intervals of 1 year or less during the entire term of the debt instrument).

(3) $1/4$ OF 1 PERCENT DE MINIMIS RULE.—If the original issue discount determined under paragraph (1) is less than—

(A) $1/4$ of 1 percent of the stated redemption price at maturity, multiplied by

(B) the number of complete years to maturity,

then the original issue discount shall be treated as zero.

[Sec. 1273(b)]

(b) ISSUE PRICE.—For purposes of this subpart—

(1) PUBLICLY OFFERED DEBT INSTRUMENTS NOT ISSUED FOR PROPERTY.—In the case of any issue of debt instruments—

(A) publicly offered, and

(B) not issued for property,

the issue price is the initial offering price to the public (excluding bond houses and brokers) at which price a substantial amount of such debt instruments was sold.

(2) OTHER DEBT INSTRUMENTS NOT ISSUED FOR PROPERTY.—In the case of any isssue of debt instruments not issued for property and not publicly offered, the issue price of each such instrument is the price paid by the first buyer of such debt instrument.

(3) DEBT INSTRUMENTS ISSUED FOR PROPERTY WHERE THERE IS PUBLIC TRADING.—In the case of a debt instrument which is issued for property and which—

(A) is part of an issue a portion of which is traded on an established securities market, or

(B)(i) is issued for stock or securities which are traded on an established securities market, or

(ii) to the extent provided in regulations, is issued for property (other than stock or securities) of a kind regularly traded on an established market,

the issue price of such debt instrument shall be the fair market value of such property.

(4) OTHER CASES.—Except in any case—

(A) to which paragraph (1), (2), or (3) of this subsection applies, or

(B) to which section 1274 applies,

the issue price of a debt instrument which is issued for property shall be the stated redemption price at maturity.

(5) PROPERTY.—In applying this subsection, the term "property" includes services and the right to use property, but such term does not include money.

Amendments

- **1986, Tax Reform Act of 1986 (P.L. 99-514)**

P.L. 99-514, §1803(a)(10):

Amended Code Sec. 1273(b)(3)(B). **Effective** as if included in the provision of P.L. 98-369 to which it relates. Prior to amendment, Code Sec. 1273(b)(3)(B) read as follows:

(B) is issued for stock or securities which are traded on an established securities market,

the issue price of such debt instrument shall be the fair market value of such property.

[Sec. 1273(c)]

(c) SPECIAL RULES FOR APPLYING SUBSECTION (b).—For purposes of subsection (b)—

(1) INITIAL OFFERING PRICE; PRICE PAID BY THE FIRST BUYER.—The terms "initial offering price" and "price paid by the first buyer" include the aggregate payments made by the purchaser under the purchase agreement, including modifications thereof.

(2) TREATMENT OF INVESTMENT UNITS.—In the case of any debt instrument and an option, security, or other property issued together as an investment unit—

(A) the issue price for such unit shall be determined in accordance with the rules of this subsection and subsection (b) as if it were a debt instrument,

(B) the issue price determined for such unit shall be allocated to each element of such unit on the basis of the relationship of the fair market value of such element to the fair market value of all elements in such unit, and

(C) the issue price of any debt instrument included in such unit shall be the portion of the issue price of the unit allocated to the debt instrument under subparagraph (B).

Amendments

- **1984, Deficit Reduction Act of 1984 (P.L. 98-369)**

P.L. 98-369, §41(a):

Added Code Sec. 1273. **Effective** for tax years ending after 7-18-84.

[Sec. 1274]

SEC. 1274. DETERMINATION OF ISSUE PRICE IN THE CASE OF CERTAIN DEBT INSTRUMENTS ISSUED FOR PROPERTY.

[Sec. 1274(a)]

(a) IN GENERAL.—In the case of any debt instrument to which this section applies, for purposes of this subpart, the issue price shall be—

(1) where there is adequate stated interest, the stated principal amount, or

(2) in any other case, the imputed principal amount.

[Sec. 1274(b)]

(b) IMPUTED PRINCIPAL AMOUNT.—For purposes of this section—

(1) IN GENERAL.—Except as provided in paragraph (3), the imputed principal amount of any debt instrument shall be equal to the sum of the present values of all payments due under such debt instrument.

(2) DETERMINATION OF PRESENT VALUE.—For purposes of paragraph (1), the present value of a payment shall be determined in the manner provided by regulations prescribed by the Secretary—

(A) as of the date of the sale or exchange, and

(B) by using a discount rate equal to the applicable Federal rate, compounded semiannually.

(3) FAIR MARKET VALUE RULE IN POTENTIALLY ABUSIVE SITUATIONS.—

(A) IN GENERAL.—In the case of any potentially abusive situation, the imputed principal amount of any debt instrument received in exchange for property shall be the fair market value of such property adjusted to take into account other consideration involved in the transaction.

(B) POTENTIALLY ABUSIVE SITUATION DEFINED.—For purposes of subparagraph (A), the term "potentially abusive situation" means—

(i) a tax shelter (as defined in section 6662(d)(2)(C)(ii), and

(ii) any other situation which, by reason of—

(I) recent sales transactions,

(II) nonrecourse financing,

(III) financing with a term in excess of the economic life of the property, or

(IV) other circumstances,

is of a type which the Secretary specifies by regulations as having potential for tax avoidance.

INCOME TAX—ORIGINAL ISSUE DISCOUNT

Amendments

• **2018, Tax Technical Corrections Act of 2018 (P.L. 115-141)**

P.L. 115-141, § 401(a)(179), Div. U:

Amended Code Sec. 1274(b)(3)(B)(i) by striking "section 6662(d)(2)(C)(iii)" and inserting "section 6662(d)(2)(C)(ii)". **Effective** 3-23-2018.

• **1996, Small Business Job Protection Act of 1996 (P.L. 104-188)**

P.L. 104-188, § 1704(t)(78):

Amended Code Sec. 1274(b)(3)(B)(i) by striking "section 6662(d)(2)(C)(ii)" and inserting "section 6662(d)(2)(C)(iii)". **Effective** 8-20-96.

• **1989, Omnibus Budget Reconciliation Act of 1989 (P.L. 101-239)**

P.L. 101-239, § 7721(c)(11):

Amended Code Sec. 1274(b)(3)(B)(i) by striking "section 6661(b)(2)(C)(ii)" and inserting "section 6662(d)(2)(C)(ii)". **Effective** for returns the due date for which (determined without regard to extensions) is after 12-31-89.

• **1985 (P.L. 99-121)**

P.L. 99-121, § 101(a)(1)(A):

Amended Code Sec. 1274(b)(2)(B) by striking out "120 percent of" after "rate equal to". **Effective** for sales and exchanges after 6-30-85, in tax years ending after such date. The amendment made by P.L. 98-612, § 2, shall not apply to sales and exchanges after 6-30-85, in tax years ending after such date. However, for a special rule see Act Sec. 104 following Code Sec. 1274(e).

[Sec. 1274(c)]

(c) DEBT INSTRUMENTS TO WHICH SECTION APPLIES.—

(1) IN GENERAL.—Except as otherwise provided in this subsection, this section shall apply to any debt instrument given in consideration for the sale or exchange of property if—

(A) the stated redemption price at maturity for such debt instrument exceeds—

(i) where there is adequate stated interest, the stated principal amount, or

(ii) in any other case, the imputed principal amount of such debt instrument determined under subsection (b), and

(B) some or all of the payments due under such debt instrument are due more than 6 months after the date of such sale or exchange.

(2) ADEQUATE STATED INTEREST.—For purposes of this section, there is adequate stated interest with respect to any debt instrument if the stated principal amount for such debt instrument is less than or equal to the imputed principal amount of such debt instrument determined under subsection (b).

(3) EXCEPTIONS.—This section shall not apply to—

(A) SALES FOR $1,000,000 OR LESS OF FARMS BY INDIVIDUALS OR SMALL BUSINESSES.—

(i) IN GENERAL.—Any debt instrument arising from the sale or exchange of a farm (within the meaning of section 6420(c)(2))—

(I) by an individual, estate, or testamentary trust,

(II) by a corporation which as of the date of the sale or exchange is a small business corporation (as defined in section 1244(c)(3)), or

(III) by a partnership which as of the date of the sale or exchange meets requirements similar to those of section 1244(c)(3).

(ii) $1,000,000 LIMITATION.—Clause (i) shall apply only if it can be determined at the time of the sale or exchange that the sales price cannot exceed $1,000,000. For purposes of the preceding sentence, all sales and exchanges which are part of the same transaction (or a series of related transactions) shall be treated as 1 sale or exchange.

(B) SALES OF PRINCIPAL RESIDENCES.—Any debt instrument arising from the sale or exchange by an individual of his principal residence (within the meaning of section 121).

(C) SALES INVOLVING TOTAL PAYMENTS OF $250,000 OR LESS.—

(i) IN GENERAL.—Any debt instrument arising from the sale or exchange of property if the sum of the following amounts does not exceed $250,000:

(I) the aggregate amount of the payments due under such debt instrument and all other debt instruments received as consideration for the sale or exchange, and

(II) the aggregate amount of any other consideration to be received for the sale or exchange.

(ii) CONSIDERATION OTHER THAN DEBT INSTRUMENT TAKEN INTO ACCOUNT AT FAIR MARKET VALUE.—For purposes of clause (i), any consideration (other than a debt instrument) shall be taken into account at its fair market value.

(iii) AGGREGATION OF TRANSACTIONS.—For purposes of this subparagraph, all sales and exchanges which are part of the same transaction (or a series of related transactions) shall be treated as 1 sale or exchange.

(D) DEBT INSTRUMENTS WHICH ARE PUBLICLY TRADED OR ISSUED FOR PUBLICLY TRADED PROPERTY.—Any debt instrument to which section 1273(b)(3) applies.

(E) CERTAIN SALES OF PATENTS.—In the case of any transfer described in section 1235(a) (relating to sale or exchange of patents), any amount contingent on the productivity, use, or disposition of the property transferred.

(F) SALES OR EXCHANGES TO WHICH SECTION 483(e) APPLIES.—Any debt instrument to the extent section 483(e) (relating to certain land transfers between related persons) applies to such instrument.

(4) EXCEPTION FOR ASSUMPTIONS.—If any person—

(A) in connection with the sale or exchange of property, assumes any debt instrument, or

(B) acquires any property subject to any debt instrument,

in determining whether this section or section 483 applies to such debt instrument, such assumption (or such acquisition) shall not be taken into account unless the terms and conditions of such debt instrument are modified (or the nature of the transaction is changed) in connection with the assumption (or acquisition).

Amendments

• **1997, Taxpayer Relief Act of 1997 (P.L. 105-34)**

P.L. 105-34, § 312(d)(1):

Amended Code Sec. 1274(c)(3)(B) by striking "section 1034" and inserting "section 121". **Effective**, generally, for sales and exchanges after 5-6-97.

• **1986, Tax Reform Act of 1986 (P.L. 99-514)**

P.L. 99-514, § 1803(a)(14)(A):

Amended Code Sec. 1274(c)(4)[3](A) by striking out "for less than $1,000,000" in the subparagraph heading and inserting in lieu thereof "for $1,000,000 or Less". **Effective** as if included in the provision of P.L. 98-369 to which it relates.

• **1985 (P.L. 99-121)**

P.L. 99-121, § 101(a)(1)(B):

Amended Code Sec. 1274(c)(1)(A)(ii). **Effective** for sales and exchanges after 6-30-85, in tax years ending after such date. The amendment made by P.L. 98-612, § 2, shall not apply to sales and exchanges after 6-30-85, in tax years ending after such date. However, for a special rule, see Act Sec. 104 following Code Sec. 1274(e). Prior to amendment, Code Sec. 1274(c)(1)(A)(ii) read as follows:

(ii) in any other case, the testing amount, and

P.L. 99-121, § 101(a)(1)(C):

Amended Code Sec. 1274(c)(2) by striking out "the testing amount" and inserting in lieu thereof "the imputed principal amount of such debt instrument determined under subsection (b)". **Effective** for sales and exchanges after 6-30-85, in tax years ending after such date. The amendment made by P.L. 98-612, § 2, shall not apply to sales and exchanges after 6-30-85, in tax years ending after such date. However, for a special rule, see Act Sec. 104 following Code Sec. 1274(e).

P.L. 99-121, § 101(a)(1)(D):

Amended Code Sec. 1274(c) by striking out paragraph (3) and by redesignating paragraph (4) as paragraph (3). **Effective** for sales and exchanges after 6-30-85, in tax years ending after such date. The amendment made by P.L. 98-612, § 2, shall not apply to sales and exchanges after 6-30-85, in tax years ending after such date. However, for a special rule, see Act Sec. 104 following Code Sec. 1274(e). Prior to amendment, Code Sec. 1274(c)(3) read as follows:

INCOME TAX—ORIGINAL ISSUE DISCOUNT

(3) TESTING AMOUNT.—For purposes of this section, the term "testing amount" means, with respect to any debt instrument, the imputed principal amount of such debt instrument which would be determined under subsection (b) (including paragraph (3) thereof) if a discount rate equal to 110 percent of the applicable Federal rate were used.

[Sec. 1274(d)]

(d) DETERMINATION OF APPLICABLE FEDERAL RATE.—For purposes of this section—

(1) APPLICABLE FEDERAL RATE.—

(A) IN GENERAL.—

In the case of a debt instrument with a term of:	The applicable Federal rate is:
Not over 3 years	The Federal short-term rate.
Over 3 years but not over 9 years	The Federal mid-term rate.
Over 9 years	The Federal long-term rate.

(B) DETERMINATION OF RATES.—During each calendar month, the Secretary shall determine the Federal short-term rate, mid-term rate, and long-term rate which shall apply during the following calendar month.

(C) FEDERAL RATE FOR ANY CALENDAR MONTH.—For purposes of this paragraph—

(i) FEDERAL SHORT-TERM RATE.—The Federal short-term rate shall be the rate determined by the Secretary based on the average market yield (during any 1-month period selected by the Secretary and ending in the calendar month in which the determination is made) on outstanding marketable obligations of the United States with remaining periods to maturity of 3 years or less.

(ii) FEDERAL MID-TERM AND LONG-TERM RATES.—The Federal mid-term and long-term rate shall be determined in accordance with the principles of clause (i).

(D) LOWER RATE PERMITTED IN CERTAIN CASES.—The Secretary may by regulations permit a rate to be used with respect to any debt instrument which is lower than the applicable Federal rate if the taxpayer establishes to the satisfaction of the Secretary that such lower rate is based on the same principles as the applicable Federal rate and is appropriate for the term of such instrument.

(2) LOWEST 3-MONTH RATE APPLICABLE TO ANY SALE OR EXCHANGE.—

(A) IN GENERAL.—In the case of any sale or exchange, the applicable Federal rate shall be the lowest 3-month rate.

(B) LOWEST 3-MONTH RATE.—For purposes of subparagraph (A), the term "lowest 3-month rate" means the lowest of the applicable Federal rates in effect for any month in the 3-calendar-month period ending with the 1st calendar month in which there is a binding contract in writing for such sale or exchange.

(3) TERM OF DEBT INSTRUMENT.—In determining the term of a debt instrument for purposes of this subsection, under regulations prescribed by the Secretary, there shall be taken into account options to renew or extend.

Amendments

• **1985 (P.L. 99-121)**

P.L. 99-121, §101(b)(1):

Amended Code Sec. 1274(d)(1) by striking out subparagraphs (B), (C), and (D) and inserting in lieu thereof new subparagraphs (B), (C), and (D). **Effective** for sales and exchanges after 6-30-85, in tax years ending after such date. The amendment made by P.L. 98-612, §2, shall not apply to sales and exchanges after 6-30-85, in tax years ending after such date. However, for a special rule see Act Sec. 104 following Code Sec. 1274(e). Prior to amendment, Code Sec. 1274(d)(1)(B)-(D) read as follows:

(B) DETERMINATION OF RATES.—Within 15 days after the close of—

(i) the 6-month period ending on September 30 of any calendar year, or

(ii) the 6-month period ending on March 31 of any calendar year,

the Secretary shall determine the Federal short-term rate, mid-term rate, and long-term rate for such 6-month period.

(C) EFFECTIVE DATE OF DETERMINATION.—Any Federal rate determined under subparagraph (A) shall—

(i) apply during the 6-month period beginning on January 1 of the succeeding calendar year in the case of a determination made under subparagraph (B)(i), and

(ii) apply during the 6-month period beginning on July 1 of the calendar year in the case of a determination made under subparagraph (B)(ii).

(D) FEDERAL RATE FOR ANY 6-MONTH PERIOD.—For purposes of this paragraph—

(i) FEDERAL SHORT-TERM RATE.—The Federal short-term rate for any 6-month period shall be the rate determined by the Secretary based on the average market yield (during such 6-month period) on outstanding marketable obligations of the United States with remaining periods to maturity of 3 years or less.

(ii) FEDERAL MID-TERM AND LONG-TERM RATES.—The Federal mid-term rate and long-term rate shall be determined in accordance with the principles of clause (i).

P.L. 99-121, §101(b)(2):

Amended Code Sec. 1274(d)(2). **Effective** for sales and exchanges after 6-30-85, in tax years ending after such date. The amendment made by P.L. 98-612, §2, shall not apply to sales and exchanges after 6-30-85, in tax years ending after such date. However, for a special rule see Act Sec. 104 following Code Sec. 1274(e). Prior to amendment, Code Sec. 1274(d)(2) read as follows:

(2) RATE APPLICABLE TO ANY SALE OR EXCHANGE.—In the case of any sale or exchange, the determination of the applicable Federal rate shall be made as of the first day on which there is a binding contract in writing for the sale or exchange.

P.L. 99-121, §105(a)(2), provides:

(2) REGULATORY AUTHORITY TO ESTABLISH LOWER RATE.—Section 1274(d)(1)(D) of the Internal Revenue Code of 1954, as added by section 101(b), shall apply as if included in the amendments made by section 41 of the Tax Reform Act of 1984.

• **1984, Deficit Reduction Act of 1984 (P.L. 98-369)**

P.L. 98-369, §41(a):

Added Code Sec. 1274. **Effective** for sales or exchanges after 12-31-84. However, Code Sec. 1274 does not apply to any sale or exchange pursuant to a written contract which was binding on 3-1-84, and at all times thereafter before the sale or exchange.

[Sec. 1274(e)]

(e) 110 PERCENT RATE WHERE SALE-LEASEBACK INVOLVED.—

(1) IN GENERAL.—In the case of any debt instrument to which this subsection applies, the discount rate used under subsection (b)(2)(B) or section 483(b) shall be 110 percent of the applicable Federal rate, compounded semiannually.

(2) LOWER DISCOUNT RATES SHALL NOT APPLY.—Section 1274A shall not apply to any debt instrument to which this subsection applies.

(3) DEBT INSTRUMENTS TO WHICH THIS SUBSECTION APPLIES.—This subsection shall apply to any debt instrument given in consideration for the sale or exchange of any property if, pursuant to a plan, the transferor or any related person leases a portion of such property after such sale or exchange.

Amendments

• **1985 (P.L. 99-121)**

P.L. 99-121, §101(c):

Amended Code Sec. 1274 by adding at the end thereof new subsection (e). **Effective** for sales and exchanges after 6-30-85, in tax years ending after such date. The amendment made by P.L. 98-612, §2, shall not apply to sales and exchanges after 6-30-85, in tax years ending after such date. However, for a special rule see Act Sec. 104.

P.L. 99-121, §102(b):

Amended Code Sec. 1274(c) by adding at the end thereof new paragraph (4). **Effective** for sales and exchanges after 6-30-85, in tax years ending after such date. The amendment made by P.L. 98-612, §2, shall not apply to sales and exchanges after 6-30-85, in tax years ending after such date. However, for a special rule, see Act Sec. 104 following Code Sec. 1274(e).

P.L. 99-121, §104, provides:

SEC. 104. SPECIAL RULE FOR CERTAIN WORKOUTS.

(a) GENERAL RULE.—Sections 483 and 1274 of the Internal Revenue Code of 1954 shall not apply to the issuance or modification of any written indebtedness if—

(1) such issuance or modification is in connection with a workout of a specified MLC loan which (as of May 31, 1985) was substantially in arrears, and

INCOME TAX—ORIGINAL ISSUE DISCOUNT

(2) the aggregate principal amount of indebtedness resulting from such workout does not exceed the sum (as of the time of the workout) of the outstanding principal amount of the specified MCL loan and any arrearages on such loan.

(b) SPECIFIED MLC LOAN.—For purposes of subsection (a), the term "specified MLC loan" means any loan which, in a submission dated June 17, 1985, on behalf of the New York State Mortgage Loan Enforcement and Administration Corporation, had one of the following loan numbers: 001, 005, 007, 012, 025, 038, 041, 042, 043, 049, 053, 064, 068, 090, 141, 180, or 188.

[Sec. 1274A]

SEC. 1274A. SPECIAL RULES FOR CERTAIN TRANSACTIONS WHERE STATED PRINCIPAL AMOUNT DOES NOT EXCEED $2,800,000.

[Sec. 1274A(a)]

(a) LOWER DISCOUNT RATE.—In the case of any qualified debt instrument, the discount rate used for purposes of sections 483 and 1274 shall not exceed 9 percent, compounded semiannually.

[Sec. 1274A(b)]

(b) QUALIFIED DEBT INSTRUMENT DEFINED.—For purposes of this section, the term "qualified debt instrument" means any debt instrument given in consideration for the sale or exchange of property (other than new section 38 property within the meaning of section 48(b), as in effect on the day before the date of enactment of the Revenue Reconciliation Act of 1990) if the stated principal amount of such instrument does not exceed $2,800,000.

Amendments
• 1990, Omnibus Budget Reconciliation Act of 1990 (P.L. 101-508)

P.L. 101-508, §11813(b)(22):

Amended Code Sec. 1274A(b) by inserting ", as in effect on the day before the date of the enactment of the Revenue Reconciliation Act of 1990" after "section 48(b)". **Effective**, generally, for property placed in service after 12-31-90. However, for exceptions see Act Sec. 11813(c)(2), below.

P.L. 101-508, §11813(c)(2), provides:

(2) EXCEPTIONS.—The amendments made by this section shall not apply to—

(A) any transition property (as defined in section 49(e) of the Internal Revenue Code of 1986 (as in effect on the day before the date of the enactment of this Act),

(B) any property with respect to which qualified progress expenditures were previously taken into account under section 46(d) of such Code (as so in effect), and

(C) any property described in section 46(b)(2)(C) of such Code (as so in effect).

[Sec. 1274A(c)]

(c) ELECTION TO USE CASH METHOD WHERE STATED PRINCIPAL AMOUNT DOES NOT EXCEED $2,000,000.—

(1) IN GENERAL.—In the case of any cash method debt instrument—

(A) section 1274 shall not apply, and

(B) interest on such debt instrument shall be taken into account by both the borrower and the lender under the cash receipts and disbursements method of accounting.

(2) CASH METHOD DEBT INSTRUMENT.—For purposes of paragraph (1), the term "cash method debt instrument" means any qualified debt instrument if—

(A) the stated principal amount does not exceed $2,000,000,

(B) the lender does not use an accrual method of accounting and is not a dealer with respect to the property sold or exchanged,

(C) section 1274 would have applied to such instrument but for an election under this subsection, and

(D) an election under this subsection is jointly made with respect to such debt instrument by the borrower and lender.

(3) SUCCESSORS BOUND BY ELECTION.—

(A) IN GENERAL.—Except as provided in subparagraph (B), paragraph (1) shall apply to any successor to the borrower or lender with respect to a cash method debt instrument.

(B) EXCEPTION WHERE LENDER TRANSFERS DEBT INSTRUMENT TO ACCRUAL METHOD TAXPAYER.—If the lender (or any successor) transfers any cash method debt instrument to a taxpayer who uses an accrual method of accounting, this paragraph shall not apply with respect to such instrument for periods after such transfer.

(4) FAIR MARKET VALUE RULE IN POTENTIALLY ABUSIVE SITUATIONS.—In the case of any cash method debt instrument, section 483 shall be applied as if it included provisions similar to the provisions of section 1274(b)(3).

Amendments
• 1996, Small Business Job Protection Act of 1996 (P.L. 104-188)

P.L. 104-188, §1704(t)(62):

Amended Code Sec. 1274A(c)(1)(B) by striking "instument" and inserting "instrument". **Effective** 8-20-96.

[Sec. 1274A(d)]

(d) OTHER SPECIAL RULES.—

(1) AGGREGATION RULES.—For purposes of this section—

(A) all sales or exchanges which are part of the same transaction (or a series of related transactions) shall be treated as 1 sale or exchange, and

(B) all debt instruments arising from the same transaction (or a series of related transactions) shall be treated as 1 debt instrument.

(2) ADJUSTMENT FOR INFLATION.—In the case of any debt instrument arising out of a sale or exchange during any calendar year after 1989, each dollar amount contained in the preceding provisions of this section shall be increased by an amount equal to—

(A) such amount, multiplied by

(B) the cost-of-living adjustment determined under section 1(f)(3) for the calendar year in which the taxable year begins, by substituting "calendar year 1988" for "calendar year 2016" in subparagraph (A)(ii) thereof.

Any increase under the preceding sentence shall be rounded to the nearest multiple of $100 (or, if such increase is a multiple of $50, such increase shall be increased to the nearest multiple of $100).

Amendments
• 2017, Tax Cuts and Jobs Act (P.L. 115-97)

P.L. 115-97, §11002(d)(10):

Amended Code Sec. 1274A(d)(2). **Effective** for tax years beginning after 12-31-2017. Prior to amendment, Code Sec. 1274A(d)(2) read as follows:

(2) INFLATION ADJUSTMENTS.—

(A) IN GENERAL.—In the case of any debt instrument arising out of a sale or exchange during any calendar year after 1989, each dollar amount contained in the preceding provisions of this section shall be increased by the inflation adjustment for such calendar year. Any increase under the preceding sentence shall be rounded to the nearest multiple of $100 (or, if such increase is a multiple of $50, such increase shall be increased to the nearest multiple of $100).

(B) INFLATION ADJUSTMENT.—For purposes of subparagraph (A), the inflation adjustment for any calendar year is the percentage (if any) by which—

(i) the CPI for the preceding calendar year exceeds

(ii) the CPI for calendar year 1988.

For purposes of the preceding sentence, the CPI for any calendar year is the average of the Consumer Price Index as of the close of the 12-month period ending on September 30 of such calendar year.

INCOME TAX—ORIGINAL ISSUE DISCOUNT

[Sec. 1274A(e)]

(e) REGULATIONS.—The Secretary shall prescribe such regulations as may be necessary to carry out the purposes of this subsection, including—

(1) regulations coordinating the provisions of this section with other provisions of this title,

(2) regulations necessary to prevent the avoidance of tax through the abuse of the provisions of subsection (c), and

(3) regulations relating to the treatment of transfers of cash method debt instruments.

- **1985 (P.L. 99-121)**

P.L. 99-121, § 102(a):

Amended subpart A of part V of subchapter P of chapter 1 by adding new Code Sec. 1274A. **Effective** for sales and exchanges after 6-30-85, in tax years ending after such date. The amendment made by P.L. 98-612, § 2, shall not apply to sales and exchanges after 6-30-85, in tax years ending after such date.

[Sec. 1275]

SEC. 1275. OTHER DEFINITIONS AND SPECIAL RULES.

[Sec. 1275(a)]

(a) DEFINITIONS.—For purposes of this subpart—

(1) DEBT INSTRUMENT.—

(A) IN GENERAL.—Except as provided in subparagraph (B), the term "debt instrument" means a bond, debenture, note, or certificate or other evidence of indebtedness.

(B) EXCEPTION FOR CERTAIN ANNUITY CONTRACTS.—The term "debt instrument" shall not include any annuity contract to which section 72 applies and which—

(i) depends (in whole or in substantial part) on the life expectancy of 1 or more individuals, or

(ii) is issued by an insurance company subject to tax under subchapter L (or by an entity described in section 501(c) and exempt from tax under section 501(a) which would be subject to tax under subchapter L were it not so exempt)—

(I) in a transaction in which there is no consideration other than cash or another annuity contract meeting the requirements of this clause,

(II) pursuant to the exercise of an election under an insurance contract by a beneficiary thereof on the death of the insured party under such contract, or

(III) in a transaction involving a qualified pension or employee benefit plan.

(2) ISSUE DATE.—

(A) PUBLICLY OFFERED DEBT INSTRUMENTS.—In the case of any debt instrument which is publicly offered, the term "date of original issue" means the date on which the issue was first issued to the public.

(B) ISSUES NOT PUBLICLY OFFERED AND NOT ISSUED FOR PROPERTY.—In the case of any debt instrument to which section 1273(b)(2) applies, the term "date of original issue" means the date on which the debt instrument was sold by the issuer.

(C) OTHER DEBT INSTRUMENTS.—In the case of any debt instrument not described in subparagraph (A) or (B), the term "date of original issue" means the date on which the debt instrument was issued in a sale or exchange.

(3) TAX-EXEMPT OBLIGATION.—The term "tax-exempt obligation" means any obligation if—

(A) the interest on such obligation is not includible in gross income under section 103, or

(B) the interest on such obligation is exempt from tax (without regard to the identity of the holder) under any other provision of law.

(4) TREATMENT OF OBLIGATIONS DISTRIBUTED BY CORPORATIONS.—Any debt obligation of a corporation distributed by such corporation with respect to its stock shall be treated as if it had been issued by such corporation for property.

Amendments

- **2000, Community Renewal Tax Relief Act of 2000 (P.L. 106-554)**

P.L. 106-554, § 318(c)(1):

Amended Code Sec. 1275(a)(1)(B)(ii) by striking "subchapter L" and inserting "subchapter L (or by an entity described in section 501(c) and exempt from tax under section 501(a) which would be subject to tax under subchapter L were it not so exempt)". **Effective** as if included in the amendments made by section 41 of P.L. 98-369 [effective for tax years ending after 7-18-84.—CCH].

- **1990, Omnibus Budget Reconciliation Act of 1990 (P.L. 101-508)**

P.L. 101-508, § 11325(a)(2):

Amended Code Sec. 1275(a) by striking paragraph (4) and redesignating paragraph (5) as paragraph (4). **Effective**, generally, for debt instruments issued, and stock transferred, after 10-9-90, in satisfaction of any indebtedness. For exceptions, see Act Sec. 11325(c)(2), below. Prior to amendment, Code Sec. 1275(a)(4) read as follows:

(4) SPECIAL RULE FOR DETERMINATION OF ISSUE PRICE IN CASE OF EXCHANGE OF DEBT INSTRUMENTS IN REORGANIZATIONS.—

(A) IN GENERAL.—If—

(i) any debt instrument is issued pursuant to a plan of reorganization (within the meaning of section 368(a)(1)) for another debt instrument (hereinafter in this paragraph referred to as the "old debt instrument"), and

(ii) the amount which (but for this paragraph) would be the issue price of the debt instrument so issued is less than the adjusted issue price of the old debt instrument,

then the issue price of the debt instrument so issued shall be treated as equal to the adjusted issue price of the old debt instrument.

(B) DEFINITIONS.—For purposes of this paragraph—

(i) DEBT INSTRUMENT.—The term "debt instrument" includes an investment unit.

(ii) ADJUSTED ISSUE PRICE.—

(I) IN GENERAL.—The adjusted issue price of the old debt instrument is its issue price, increased by the portion of any original issue discount previously includible in the gross income of any holder (without regard to subsection (a)(7) or (b)(4) of section 1272 (or the corresponding provisions of prior law)).

(II) SPECIAL RULE FOR APPLYING SECTION 163(e).—For purposes of section 163(e), the adjusted issue price of the old debt instrument is its issue price, increased by any original issue discount previously allowed as a deduction.

P.L. 101-508, § 11325(c)(2), provides:

(2) EXCEPTIONS.—The amendments made by this section shall not apply to any debt instrument issued, or stock transferred, in satisfaction of any indebtedness if such issuance or transfer (as the case may be)—

(A) is in a title 11 or similar case (as defined in section 368(a)(3)(A) of the Internal Revenue Code of 1986) which was filed on or before October 9, 1990,

(B) is pursuant to a written binding contract in effect on October 9, 1990, and at all times thereafter before such issuance or transfer,

(C) is pursuant to a transaction which was described in documents filed with the Securities and Exchange Commission on or before October 9, 1990, or

(D) is pursuant to a transaction—

(i) the material terms of which were described in a written public announcement on or before October 9, 1990,

(ii) which was the subject of a prior filing with the Securities and Exchange Commission, and

(iii) which is the subject of a subsequent filing with the Securities and Exchange Commission before January 1, 1991.

- **1988, Technical and Miscellaneous Revenue Act of 1988 (P.L. 100-647)**

P.L. 100-647, § 1006(u)(4):

Amended Code Sec. 1275(a)(4)(B)(ii)(I) by striking out "subsection (a)(6)" and inserting in lieu thereof "subsection (a)(7)". **Effective** as if included in the provision of P.L. 99-514 to which it relates.

- **1986, Tax Reform Act of 1986 (P.L. 99-514)**

P.L. 99-514, § 1804(f)(2)(A)(i) and (ii):

Amended Code Sec. 1275(a) by redesignating paragraph (4)[5], which was added by section 61 of the Tax Reform Act of 1984, as paragraph (5), and by striking out "TO CORPORATIONS" in the heading of such paragraph and inserting in lieu thereof "by Corporations". **Effective** as if included in the provision of P.L. 98-369 to which it relates.

- **1984, Deficit Reduction Act of 1984 (P.L. 98-369)**

P.L. 98-369, § 61(c)(2):

Amended Code Sec. 1275(a) by adding new paragraph (4)[(5)]. **Effective** with respect to distributions declared after 3-15-84, in tax years ending after such date.

INCOME TAX—MARKET DISCOUNT ON BONDS

[Sec. 1275(b)]

(b) TREATMENT OF BORROWER IN THE CASE OF CERTAIN LOANS FOR PERSONAL USE.—

(1) SECTIONS 1274 AND 483 NOT TO APPLY.—In the case of the obligor under any debt instrument given in consideration for the sale or exchange of property, sections 1274 and 483 shall not apply if such property is personal use property.

(2) ORIGINAL ISSUE DISCOUNT DEDUCTED ON CASH BASIS IN CERTAIN CASES.—In the case of any debt instrument, if—

(A) such instrument—

(i) is incurred in connection with the acquisition or carrying of personal use property, and

(ii) has original issue discount (determined after the application of paragraph (1)), and

(B) the obligor under such instrument uses the cash receipts and disbursements method of accounting,

notwithstanding section 163(e), the original issue discount on such instrument shall be deductible only when paid.

(3) PERSONAL USE PROPERTY.—For purposes of this subsection, the term "personal use property" means any property substantially all of the use of which by the taxpayer is not in connection with a trade or business of the taxpayer or an activity described in section 212. The determination of whether property is described in the preceding sentence shall be made as of the time of issuance of the debt instrument.

[Sec. 1275(c)]

(c) INFORMATION REQUIREMENTS.—

(1) INFORMATION REQUIRED TO BE SET FORTH ON INSTRUMENT.—

(A) IN GENERAL.—In the case of any debt instrument having original issue discount, the Secretary may by regulations require that—

(i) the amount of the original issue discount, and

(ii) the issue date,

be set forth on such instrument.

(B) SPECIAL RULE FOR INSTRUMENTS NOT PUBLICLY OFFERED.—In the case of any issue of debt instruments not publicly offered, the regulations prescribed under subparagraph (A) shall not require the information to be set forth on the debt instrument before any disposition of such instrument by the first buyer.

(2) INFORMATION REQUIRED TO BE SUBMITTED TO SECRETARY.—In the case of any issue of publicly offered debt instruments having original issue discount, the issuer shall (at such time and in such manner as the Secretary shall by regulation prescribe) furnish the Secretary the following information:

(A) The amount of the original issue discount.

(B) The issue date.

(C) Such other information with respect to the issue as the Secretary may by regulations require.

For purposes of the preceding sentence, any person who makes a public offering of stripped bonds (or stripped coupons) shall be treated as the issuer of a publicly offered debt instrument having original issue discount.

(3) EXCEPTIONS.—This subsection shall not apply to any obligation referred to in section 1272(a)(2) (relating to exceptions from current inclusion of original issue discount).

(4) CROSS REFERENCE.—

For civil penalty for failure to meet requirements of this subsection, see section 6706.

[Sec. 1275(d)]

(d) REGULATION AUTHORITY.—The Secretary may prescribe regulations providing that where, by reason of varying rates of interest, put or call options, indefinite maturities, contingent payments, assumptions of debt instruments, or other circumstances, the tax treatment under this subpart (or section 163(e)) does not carry out the purposes of this subpart (or section 163(e)), such treatment shall be modified to the extent appropriate to carry out the purposes of this subpart (or section 163(e)).

Amendments

• **1984, Deficit Reduction Act of 1984 (P.L. 98-369)**

P.L. 98-369, §41(a):

Added Code Sec. 1275. **Effective** for tax years ending after 7-18-84. Code Sec. 1275(c) is **effective** 8-17-84.

Subpart B—Market Discount on Bonds

Sec. 1276.   Disposition gain representing accrued market discount treated as ordinary income.
Sec. 1277.   Deferral of interest deduction allocable to accrued market discount.
Sec. 1278.   Definitions and special rules.

[Sec. 1276]

SEC. 1276. DISPOSITION GAIN REPRESENTING ACCRUED MARKET DISCOUNT TREATED AS ORDINARY INCOME.

[Sec. 1276(a)]

(a) ORDINARY INCOME.—

(1) IN GENERAL.—Except as otherwise provided in this section, gain on the disposition of any market discount bond shall be treated as ordinary income to the extent it does not exceed the accrued market discount on such bond. Such gain shall be recognized notwithstanding any other provision of this subtitle.

(2) DISPOSITIONS OTHER THAN SALES, ETC.—For purposes of paragraph (1), a person disposing of any market discount bond in any transaction other than a sale, exchange, or involuntary conversion shall be treated as realizing an amount equal to the fair market value of the bond.

(3) TREATMENT OF PARTIAL PRINCIPAL PAYMENTS.—

(A) IN GENERAL.—Any partial principal payment on a market discount bond shall be included in gross income as ordinary income to the extent such payment does not exceed the accrued market discount on such bond.

(B) ADJUSTMENT.—If subparagraph (A) applies to any partial principal payment on any market discount bond, for purposes of applying this section to any disposition of (or subsequent partial principal payment on) such bond, the amount of accrued market discount shall be reduced by the amount of such partial principal payment included in gross income under subparagraph (A).

(4) GAIN TREATED AS INTEREST FOR CERTAIN PURPOSES.—Except for purposes of sections 103, 871(a), 881, 1441, 1442, and 6049 (and such other provisions as may be specified in regulations), any amount treated as ordinary income under paragraph (1) or (3) shall be treated as interest for purposes of this title.

INCOME TAX—MARKET DISCOUNT ON BONDS

Amendments

• **2018, Tax Technical Corrections Act of 2018 (P.L. 115-141)**

P.L. 115-141, §401(a)(180), Div. U:

Amended Code Sec. 1276(a)(4) by striking "871(a),," and inserting "871(a),". **Effective** 3-23-2018.

• **1993, Omnibus Budget Reconciliation Act of 1993 (P.L. 103-66)**

P.L. 103-66, §13206(b)(2)(B)(i):

Amended Code Sec. 1276(a)(4) by striking "sections 871(a)" and inserting "sections 103, 871(a),". **Effective** for obligations purchased (within the meaning of Code Sec. 1272(d)(1)) after 4-30-93.

• **1986, Tax Reform Act of 1986 (P.L. 99-514)**

P.L. 99-514, §1803(a)(13)(A)(i):

Amended Code Sec. 1276(a) by redesignating paragraph (3) as paragraph (4) and by inserting after paragraph (2) new paragraph (3). **Effective** for obligations acquired after 10-22-86.

P.L. 99-514, §1803(a)(13)(A)(ii):

Amended Code Sec. 1276(a)(4), as redesignated by Act Sec. 1803(a)(13)(A)(i), by striking out "under paragraph (1)" and inserting in lieu thereof "under paragraph (1) or (3)". **Effective** for obligations acquired after 10-22-86.

[Sec. 1276(b)]

(b) ACCRUED MARKET DISCOUNT.—For purposes of this section—

(1) RATABLE ACCRUAL.—Except as otherwise provided in this subsection or subsection (c), the accrued market discount on any bond shall be an amount which bears the same ratio to the market discount on such bond as—

(A) the number of days which the taxpayer held the bond, bears to

(B) the number of days after the date the taxpayer acquired the bond and up to (and including) the date of its maturity.

(2) ELECTION OF ACCRUAL ON BASIS OF CONSTANT INTEREST RATE (IN LIEU OF RATABLE ACCRUAL).—

(A) IN GENERAL.—At the election of the taxpayer with respect to any bond, the accrued market discount on such bond shall be the aggregate amount which would have been includible in the gross income of the taxpayer under section 1272(a) (determined without regard to paragraph (2) thereof) with respect to such bond for all periods during which the bond was held by the taxpayer if such bond had been—

(i) originally issued on the date on which such bond was acquired by the taxpayer,

(ii) for an issue price equal to the basis of the taxpayer in such bond immediately after its acquisition.

(B) COORDINATION WHERE BOND HAS ORIGINAL ISSUE DISCOUNT.—In the case of any bond having original issue discount, for purposes of applying subparagraph (A)—

(i) the stated redemption price at maturity of such bond shall be treated as equal to its revised issue price, and

(ii) the determination of the portion of the original issue discount which would have been includible in the gross income of the taxpayer under section 1272(a) shall be made under regulations prescribed by the Secretary.

(C) ELECTION IRREVOCABLE.—An election under subparagraph (A), once made with respect to any bond, shall be irrevocable.

(3) SPECIAL RULE WHERE PARTIAL PRINCIPAL PAYMENTS.—In the case of a bond the principal of which may be paid in 2 or more payments, the amount of accrued market discount shall be determined under regulations prescribed by the Secretary.

Amendments

• **1988, Technical and Miscellaneous Revenue Act of 1988 (P.L. 100-647)**

P.L. 100-647, §1018(u)(46)(A)-(C):

Amended Code Sec. 1276(b) by inserting "(3)" before "Special" in the paragraph heading following paragraph (2), by inserting a 1 em dash after "payments." in the paragraph heading following paragraph (2) and by adding a period at the end thereof. **Effective** as if included in the provision of P.L. 99-514 to which it relates.

• **1986, Tax Reform Act of 1986 (P.L. 99-514)**

P.L. 99-514, §1803(a)(13)(A)(iii):

Amended Code Sec. 1276(b) by adding at the end thereof new paragraph (3). **Effective** for obligations acquired after 10-22-86.

[Sec. 1276(c)]

(c) TREATMENT OF NONRECOGNITION TRANSACTIONS.—Under regulations prescribed by the Secretary—

(1) TRANSFERRED BASIS PROPERTY.—If a market discount bond is transferred in a nonrecognition transaction and such bond is transferred basis property in the hands of the transferee, for purposes of determining the amount of the accrued market discount with respect to the transferee—

(A) the transferee shall be treated as having acquired the bond on the date on which it was acquired by the transferor for an amount equal to the basis of the transferor, and

(B) proper adjustments shall be made for gain recognized by the transferor on such transfer (and for any original issue discount or market discount included in the gross income of the transferor).

(2) EXCHANGED BASIS PROPERTY.—If any market discount bond is disposed of by the taxpayer in a nonrecognition transaction and paragraph (1) does not apply to such transaction, any accrued market discount determined with respect to the property disposed of to the extent not theretofore treated as ordinary income under subsection (a)—

(A) shall be treated as accrued market discount with respect to the exchanged basis property received by the taxpayer in such transaction if such property is a market discount bond, and

(B) shall be treated as ordinary income on the disposition of the exchanged basis property received by the taxpayer in such exchange if such property is not a market discount bond.

(3) PARAGRAPH (1) TO APPLY TO CERTAIN DISTRIBUTIONS BY CORPORATIONS OR PARTNERSHIPS.—For purposes of paragraph (1), if the basis of any market discount bond in the hands of a transferee is determined under section 732(a), or 732(b), such property shall be treated as transferred basis property in the hands of such transferee.

Amendments

• **1986, Tax Reform Act of 1986 (P.L. 99-514)**

P.L. 99-514, §631(e)(15):

Amended Code Sec. 1276(c)(3) by striking out after the words "under section" "334(c),". **Effective** for (1) any distribution in complete liquidation, and any sale or exchange, made by a corporation after 7-31-86, unless such corporation is completely liquidated before 1-1-87, (2) any transaction described in section 338 of the Internal Revenue Code of 1986 for which the acquisition date occurs after 12-31-86, and (3) any distribution (not in complete liquidation) made after 12-31-86. For special and transitional rules, see Act Sec. 633(b)-(f) following Code Sec. 26.

[Sec. 1276(d)]

(d) SPECIAL RULES.—Under regulations prescribed by the Secretary—

(1) rules similar to the rules of subsection (b) of section 1245 shall apply for purposes of this section; except that—

(A) paragraph (1) of such subsection shall not apply,

(B) an exchange qualifying under section 354(a), 355(a), or 356(a) (determined without regard to subsection (a) of this section) shall be treated as an exchange described in paragraph (3) of such subsection, and

(C) paragraph (3) of section 1245(b) shall be applied as if it did not contain a reference to section 351, and

(2) appropriate adjustments shall be made to the basis of any property to reflect gain recognized under subsection (a).

INCOME TAX—MARKET DISCOUNT ON BONDS

Amendments

• **1986, Tax Reform Act of 1986 (P.L. 99-514)**

P.L. 99-514, § 1803(a)(5):

Amended Code Sec. 1276(d)(1) by striking out "and" at the end of subparagraph (A) and by inserting after subparagraph (B) new subparagraph (C). **Effective** as if included in the provision to which it relates.

Amendments

• **1993, Omnibus Budget Reconciliation Act of 1993 (P.L. 103-66)**

P.L. 103-66, § 13206(b)(1)(A):

Repealed Code Sec. 1276(e). **Effective** for obligations purchased (within the meaning of Code Sec. 1272(d)(1)) after 4-30-93. Prior to repeal, Code Sec. 1276(e) read as follows:

(e) SECTION NOT TO APPLY TO MARKET DISCOUNT BONDS ISSUED ON OR BEFORE DATE OF ENACTMENT OF SECTION.—This section shall not apply to any market discount bond issued on or before July 18, 1984.

• **1984, Deficit Reduction Act of 1984 (P.L. 98-369)**

P.L. 98-369, § 41(a):

Added Code Sec. 1276. **Effective** for obligations issued after 7-18-84, in tax years ending after such date.

[Sec. 1276(e)—Repealed]

• **1986, Tax Reform Act of 1986 (P.L. 99-514)**

P.L. 99-514, § 1899A(28):

Amended Code Sec. 1276(e) by striking out "the date of the enactment of this section" and inserting in lieu thereof "July 18, 1984". **Effective** 10-22-86.

[Sec. 1277]

SEC. 1277. DEFERRAL OF INTEREST DEDUCTION ALLOCABLE TO ACCRUED MARKET DISCOUNT.

[Sec. 1277(a)]

(a) GENERAL RULE.—Except as otherwise provided in this section, the net direct interest expense with respect to any market discount bond shall be allowed as a deduction for the taxable year only to the extent that such expense exceeds the portion of the market discount allocable to the days during the taxable year on which such bond was held by the taxpayer (as determined under the rules of section 1276(b)).

[Sec. 1277(b)]

(b) DISALLOWED DEDUCTION ALLOWED FOR LATER YEARS.—

(1) ELECTION TO TAKE INTO ACCOUNT IN LATER YEAR WHERE NET INTEREST INCOME FROM BOND.—

(A) IN GENERAL.—If—

(i) there is net interest income for any taxable year with respect to any market discount bond, and

(ii) the taxpayer makes an election under this subparagraph with respect to such bond,

any disallowed interest expense with respect to such bond shall be treated as interest paid or accrued by the taxpayer during such taxable year to the extent such disallowed interest expense does not exceed the net interest income with respect to such bond.

(B) DETERMINATION OF DISALLOWED INTEREST EXPENSE.—For purposes of subparagraph (A), the amount of the disallowed interest expense—

(i) shall be determined as of the close of the preceding taxable year, and

(ii) shall not include any amount previously taken into account under subparagraph (A).

(C) NET INTEREST INCOME.—For purposes of this paragraph, the term "net interest income" means the excess of the amount determined under paragraph (2) of subsection (c) over the amount determined under paragraph (1) of subsection (c).

(2) REMAINDER OF DISALLOWED INTEREST EXPENSE ALLOWED FOR YEAR OF DISPOSITION.—

(A) IN GENERAL.—Except as otherwise provided in this paragraph, the amount of the disallowed interest expense with respect to any market discount bond shall be treated as interest paid or accrued by the taxpayer in the taxable year in which such bond is disposed of.

(B) NONRECOGNITION TRANSACTIONS.—If any market discount bond is disposed of in a nonrecognition transaction—

(i) the disallowed interest expense with respect to such bond shall be treated as interest paid or accrued in the year of disposition only to the extent of the amount of gain recognized on such disposition, and

(ii) the disallowed interest expense with respect to such property (to the extent not so treated) shall be treated as disallowed interest expense—

(I) in the case of a transaction described in section 1276(c)(1), of the transferee with respect to the transferred basis property, or

(II) in the case of a transaction described in section 1276(c)(2), with respect to the exchanged basis property.

(C) DISALLOWED INTEREST EXPENSE REDUCED FOR AMOUNTS PREVIOUSLY TAKEN INTO ACCOUNT UNDER PARAGRAPH (1).—For purposes of this paragraph, the amount of the disallowed interest expense shall not include any amount previously taken into account under paragraph (1).

(3) DISALLOWED INTEREST EXPENSE.—For purposes of this subsection, the term "disallowed interest expense" means the aggregate amount disallowed under subsection (a) with respect to the market discount bond.

Amendments

• **1986, Tax Reform Act of 1986 (P.L. 99-514)**

P.L. 99-514, § 1899A(29):

Amended Code Sec. 1277(b)(1)(C) by striking out "this paragraph" and inserting in lieu thereof "this paragraph". **Effective** 10-22-86.

P.L. 99-514, § 1899A(30):

Amended Code Sec. 1277(b)(2)(C) by striking out "Paragraph 1.—" and inserting in lieu thereof "Paragraph (1).—" in the heading for subparagraph (C). **Effective** 10-22-86.

[Sec. 1277(c)]

(c) NET DIRECT INTEREST EXPENSE.—For purposes of this section, the term "net direct interest expense" means, with respect to any market discount bond, the excess (if any) of—

(1) the amount of interest paid or accrued during the taxable year on indebtedness which is incurred or continued to purchase or carry such bond, over

(2) the aggregate amount of interest (including original issue discount) includible in gross income for the taxable year with respect to such bond.

In the case of any financial institution which is a bank (as defined in section 585(a)(2)), the determination of whether interest is described in paragraph (1) shall be made under principles similar to the principles of section 291(e)(1)(B)(ii). Under rules similar to the rules of section 265(a)(5), short sale expenses shall be treated as interest for purposes of determining net direct interest expense.

Sec. 1276(e)—Repealed

Amendments

● **1996, Small Business Job Protection Act of 1996 (P.L. 104-188)**

P.L. 104-188, §1616(b)(14):

Amended Code Sec. 1277(c) by striking "or to which section 593 applies" after "585(a)(2)". **Effective**, generally, for tax years beginning after 12-31-95.

● **1988, Technical and Miscellaneous Revenue Act of 1988 (P.L. 100-647)**

P.L. 100-647, §1018(u)(31):

Amended Code Sec. 1277(c) by inserting a closing parenthesis after "section 585(a)(2)". **Effective** as if included in the provision of P.L. 99-514 to which it relates.

● **1986, Tax Reform Act of 1986 (P.L. 99-514)**

P.L. 99-514, §901(d)(4)(F):

Amended Code Sec. 1277(c) by striking out "to which section 585 or 593 applies" and inserting in lieu thereof "which is a bank (as defined in section 585(a)(2)) or to which section 593 applies." **Effective** for tax years beginning after 12-31-86.

P.L. 99-514, §902(e)(2):

Amended Code Sec. 1277(c) by striking out "section 265(5)" and inserting in lieu thereof "section 265(a)(5)". **Effective**, generally, for tax years ending after 12-31-86. For transitional rules, see Act Sec. 902(f)(2)-(4) following Code Sec. 291.

● **1984, Deficit Reduction Act of 1984 (P.L. 98-369)**

P.L. 98-369, §41(a):

Added Code Sec. 1277. **Effective** for obligations acquired after 7-18-84, in tax years ending after such date.

[Sec. 1277(d)—Repealed]

Amendments

● **1993, Omnibus Budget Reconciliation Act of 1993 (P.L. 103-66)**

P.L. 103-66, §13206(b)(1)(B):

Repealed Code Sec. 1277(d). **Effective** for obligations purchased (within the meaning of Code Sec. 1272(d)(1)) after 4-30-93. Prior to repeal, Code Sec. 1277(d) read as follows:

(d) SPECIAL RULE FOR GAIN RECOGNIZED ON DISPOSITION OF MARKET DISCOUNT BONDS ISSUED ON OR BEFORE DATE OF ENACTMENT OF SECTION.—In the case of a market discount bond issued on or before July 18, 1984, any gain recognized by the taxpayer on any disposition of such bond shall be treated as ordinary income to the extent the amount of such gain does not exceed the amount allowable with respect to such bond under subsection (b)(2) for the taxable year in which such bond is disposed of.

● **1986, Tax Reform Act of 1986 (P.L. 99-514)**

P.L. 99-514, §1899A(31):

Amended Code Sec. 1277(d) by striking out "the date of the enactment of this section" and inserting in lieu thereof "July 18, 1984". **Effective** 10-22-86.

[Sec. 1278]

SEC. 1278. DEFINITIONS AND SPECIAL RULES.

[Sec. 1278(a)]

(a) IN GENERAL.—For purposes of this part—

(1) MARKET DISCOUNT BOND.—

(A) IN GENERAL.—Except as provided in subparagraph (B), the term "market discount bond" means any bond having market discount.

(B) EXCEPTIONS.—The term "market discount bond" shall not include—

▶▶▶ *Caution: P.L. 98-369, §1001(b)(24), amended Code Sec. 1278(a)(1)(B)(i), below, by striking "1 year" and inserting "6 months". This amendment applies to property acquired after June 22, 1984, and before January 1, 1988.*

(i) SHORT-TERM OBLIGATIONS.—Any obligation with a fixed maturity date not exceeding 6 months [1 year] from the date of issue.

(ii) UNITED STATES SAVINGS BONDS.—Any United States savings bond.

(iii) INSTALLMENT OBLIGATIONS.—Any installment obligation to which section 453B applies.

(C) SECTION 1277 NOT APPLICABLE TO TAX-EXEMPT OBLIGATIONS.—For purposes of section 1277, the term "market discount bond" shall not include any tax-exempt obligation (as defined in section 1275(a)(3)).

(D) TREATMENT OF BONDS ACQUIRED AT ORIGINAL ISSUE.—

(i) IN GENERAL.—Except as otherwise provided in this subparagraph or in regulations, the term "market discount bond" shall not include any bond acquired by the taxpayer at its original issue.

(ii) TREATMENT OF BONDS ACQUIRED FOR LESS THAN ISSUE PRICE.—Clause (i) shall not apply to any bond if—

(I) the basis of the taxpayer in such bond is determined under section 1012, and

(II) such basis is less than the issue price of such bond determined under subpart A of this part.

(iii) BONDS ACQUIRED IN CERTAIN REORGANIZATIONS.—Clause (i) shall not apply to any bond issued pursuant to a plan of reorganization (within the meaning of section 368(a)(1)) in exchange for another bond having market discount. Solely for purposes of section 1276, the preceding sentence shall not apply if such other bond was issued on or before July 18, 1984 (the date of the enactment of section 1276) and if the bond issued pursuant to such plan of reorganization has the same term and the same interest rate as such other bond had.

(iv) TREATMENT OF CERTAIN TRANSFERRED BASIS PROPERTY.—For purposes of clause (i), if the adjusted basis of any bond in the hands of the taxpayer is determined by reference to the adjusted basis of such bond in the hands of a person who acquired such bond at its original issue, such bond shall be treated as acquired by the taxpayer at its original issue.

(2) MARKET DISCOUNT.—

(A) IN GENERAL.—The term "market discount" means the excess (if any) of—

(i) the stated redemption price of the bond at maturity, over

(ii) the basis of such bond immediately after its acquisition by the taxpayer.

(B) COORDINATION WHERE BOND HAS ORIGINAL ISSUE DISCOUNT.—In the case of any bond having original issue discount, for purposes of subparagraph (A), the stated redemption price of such bond at maturity shall be treated as equal to its revised issue price.

(C) DE MINIMIS RULE.—If the market discount is less than $1/4$ of 1 percent of the stated redemption price of the bond at maturity multiplied by the number of complete years to maturity (after the taxpayer acquired the bond), then the market discount shall be considered to be zero.

(3) BOND.—The term "bond" means any bond, debenture, note, certificate, or other evidence of indebtedness.

(4) REVISED ISSUE PRICE.—The term "revised issue price" means the sum of—

(A) the issue price of the bond, and

(B) the aggregate amount of the original issue discount includible in the gross income of all holders for periods before the acquisition of the bond by the taxpayer (determined without regard to section 1272(a)(7)) or, in the case of a tax-exempt obligation, the aggregate amount of the original issue discount which accrued in the manner provided by section 1272(a) (determined without regard to paragraph (7) thereof) during periods before the acquisition of the bond by the taxpayer.

INCOME TAX—DISCOUNT ON SHORT-TERM OBLIGATIONS

(5) ORIGINAL ISSUE DISCOUNT, ETC.—The terms "original issue discount", "stated redemption price at maturity", and "issue price" have the respective meanings given such terms by subpart A of this part.

Amendments

• **2018, Tax Technical Corrections Act of 2018 (P.L. 115-141)**

P.L. 115-141, §401(c)(1)(G), Div. U:

Amended Code Sec. 1278(a)(4)(B) by striking "or (b)(4)" following "section 1272(a)(7)". **Effective** for debt instruments issued on or after 7-2-1982.

• **1993, Omnibus Budget Reconciliation Act of 1993 (P.L. 103-66)**

P.L. 103-66, §13206(b)(2)(A)(i)-(iii):

Amended Code Sec. 1278(a)(1) by striking clause (ii) of subparagraph (B) and redesignating subclauses (iii) and (iv) of such subparagraph as subclauses (ii) and (iii), respectively, by redesignating subparagraph (C) as subparagraph (D), and by inserting after subparagraph (B) new subparagraph (C). **Effective** for obligations puchased (within the meaning of Code Sec. 1272(d)(1)) after 4-30-93. Prior to amendment, Code Sec. 1278(a)(1)(B)(ii) read as follows:

(ii) TAX-EXEMPT OBLIGATIONS.—Any tax-exempt obligation (as defined in section 1275(a)(3)).

P.L. 103-66, §13206(b)(2)(B)(ii):

Amended Code Sec. 1278(a)(4)(B) by adding material at the end. **Effective** for obligations purchased (within the meaning of Code Sec. 1272(d)(1)) after 4-30-93.

• **1988, Technical and Miscellaneous Revenue Act of 1988 (P.L. 100-647)**

P.L. 100-647, §1006(u)(2):

Amended Code Sec. 1278(a)(4)(B) by striking out "section 1272(a)(6)" and inserting in lieu thereof "section 1272(a)(7)". **Effective** as if included in the provision of P.L. 99-514 to which it relates.

• **1986, Tax Reform Act of 1986 (P.L. 99-514)**

P.L. 99-514, §1803(a)(6):

Amended Code Sec. 1278(a)(1) by adding at the end thereof new subparagraph (C). **Effective** as if included in the provision of P.L. 98-369 to which it relates.

P.L. 99-514, §1899A(32):

Amended Code Sec. 1278(a)(4) by striking out "means of" and inserting in lieu thereof "means". **Effective** 10-22-86.

• **1984, Deficit Reduction Act of 1984 (P.L. 98-369)**

P.L. 98-369, §1001(b)(24), as added by P.L. 99-514, §1878(a):

Amended Code Sec. 1278(a)(1)(B)(i) by striking out "1 year" each place it appears and inserting in lieu thereof "6 months". Effective as if included in the provision of P.L. 98-369 to which it relates [effective for property acquired after 6-22-84, and before 1-1-88.—CCH].

[Sec. 1278(b)]

(b) ELECTION TO INCLUDE MARKET DISCOUNT CURRENTLY.—

(1) IN GENERAL.—If the taxpayer makes an election under this subsection—

(A) sections 1276 and 1277 shall not apply, and

(B) market discount on any market discount bond shall be included in the gross income of the taxpayer for the taxable years to which it is attributable (as determined under the rules of subsection (b) of section 1276).

Except for purposes of sections 103, 871(a), 881, 1441, 1442, and 6049 (and such other provisions as may be specified in regulations), any amount included in gross income under subparagraph (B) shall be treated as interest for purposes of this title.

(2) SCOPE OF ELECTION.—An election under this subsection shall apply to all market discount bonds acquired by the taxpayer on or after the 1st day of the 1st taxable year to which such election applies.

(3) PERIOD TO WHICH ELECTION APPLIES.—An election under this subsection shall apply to the taxable year for which is it made and for all subsequent taxable years, unless the taxpayer secures the consent of the Secretary to the revocation of such election.

(4) BASIS ADJUSTMENT.—The basis of any bond in the hands of the taxpayer shall be increased by the amount included in gross income pursuant to this subsection.

Amendments

• **2018, Tax Technical Corrections Act of 2018 (P.L. 115-141)**

P.L. 115-141, §401(a)(181), Div. U:

Amended Code Sec. 1278(b)(1) by striking "871(a),," and inserting "871(a),". **Effective** 3-23-2018.

• **1993, Omnibus Budget Reconciliation Act of 1993 (P.L. 103-66)**

P.L. 103-66, §13206(b)(2)(B)(i):

Amended Code Sec. 1278(b)(1) by striking "sections 871(a)" and inserting "sections 103, 871(a),". **Effective** for obligations purchased (within the meaning of Code Sec. 1272(d)(1)) after 4-30-93.

• **1988, Technical and Miscellaneous Revenue Act of 1988 (P.L. 100-647)**

P.L. 100-647, §1018(c)(3):

Amended Code Sec. 1278(b) by adding new paragraph (4). **Effective** as if included in the provision of P.L. 99-514 to which it relates.

[Sec. 1278(c)]

(c) REGULATIONS.—The Secretary shall prescribe such regulations as may be necessary to carry out the purposes of this subpart, including regulations providing proper adjustments in the case of a bond the principal of which may be paid in 2 or more payments.

Amendments

• **1988, Technical and Miscellaneous Revenue Act of 1988 (P.L. 100-647)**

P.L. 100-647, §1018(c)(2):

Amended Code Sec. 1278(c) by inserting before the period ", including regulations providing proper adjustments in the case of a bond the principal of which may be paid in 2 or more payments". **Effective** as included in the provision of P.L. 99-514 to which it relates.

• **1984, Deficit Reduction Act of 1984 (P.L. 98-369)**

P.L. 98-369, §41(a):

Added Code Sec. 1278. **Effective** for tax years ending after 7-18-84.

Subpart C—Discount on Short-Term Obligations

Sec. 1281.	Current inclusion in income of discount on certain short-term obligations.
Sec. 1282.	Deferral of interest deduction allocable to accrued discount.
Sec. 1283.	Definitions and special rules.

[Sec. 1281]

SEC. 1281. CURRENT INCLUSION IN INCOME OF DISCOUNT ON CERTAIN SHORT-TERM OBLIGATIONS.

[Sec. 1281(a)]

(a) GENERAL RULE.—In the case of any short-term obligation to which this section applies, for purposes of this title—

(1) there shall be included in the gross income of the holder an amount equal to the sum of the daily portions of the acquisition discount for each day during the taxable year on which such holder held such obligation, and

(2) any interest payable on the obligation (other than interest taken into account in determining the amount of the acquisition discount) shall be included in gross income as it accrues.

INCOME TAX—DISCOUNT ON SHORT-TERM OBLIGATIONS

Amendments

• **1986, Tax Reform Act of 1986 (P.L. 99-514)**

P.L. 99-514, § 1803(a)(8)(A):

Amended Code Sec. 1281(a). **Effective** with respect to obligations acquired after 12-31-85 [**effective** date changed by P.L. 100-647, § 1018(c)(1)]. Prior to amendment, Code Sec. 1281(a) read as follows:

(a) IN GENERAL.—In the case of any short-term obligation to which this section applies, for purposes of this title, there shall be included in the gross income of the holder an amount equal to the sum of the daily portions of the acquisition discount for each day during the taxable year on which such holder held such obligation.

[Sec. 1281(b)]

(b) SHORT-TERM OBLIGATIONS TO WHICH SECTION APPLIES.—

(1) IN GENERAL.—This section shall apply to any short-term obligation which—

(A) is held by a taxpayer using an accrual method of accounting,

(B) is held primarily for sale to customers in the ordinary course of the taxpayer's trade or business,

(C) is held by a bank (as defined in section 581),

(D) is held by a regulated investment company or a common trust fund,

(E) is identified by the taxpayer under section 1256(e)(2) as being part of a hedging transaction, or

(F) is a stripped bond or stripped coupon held by the person who stripped the bond or coupon (or by any other person whose basis is determined by reference to the basis in the hands of such person).

(2) TREATMENT OF OBLIGATIONS HELD BY PASS-THRU ENTITIES.—

(A) IN GENERAL.—This section shall apply also to—

(i) any short-term obligation which is held by a pass-thru entity which is formed or availed of for purposes of avoiding the provisions of this section, and

(ii) any short-term obligation which is acquired by a pass-thru entity (not described in clause (i)) during the required accrual period.

(B) REQUIRED ACCRUAL PERIOD.—For purposes of subparagraph (A), the term "required accrual period" means the period—

(i) which begins with the first taxable year for which the ownership test of subparagraph (C) is met with respect to the pass-thru entity (or a predecessor), and

(ii) which ends with the first taxable year after the taxable year referred to in clause (i) for which the ownership test of subparagraph (C) is not met and with respect to which the Secretary consents to the termination of the required accrual period.

(C) OWNERSHIP TEST.—The ownership test of this subparagraph is met for any taxable year if, on at least 90 days during the taxable year, 20 percent or more of the value of the interests in the pass-thru entity are held by persons described in paragraph (1) or by other pass-thru entities to which subparagraph (A) applies.

(D) PASS-THRU ENTITY.—The term "pass-thru entity" means any partnership, S corporation, trust, or other pass-thru entity.

Amendments

• **1986, Tax Reform Act of 1986 (P.L. 99-514)**

P.L. 99-514, § 1803(a)(7):

Amended Code Sec. 1281(b)(1) by striking out "or" at the end of subparagraph (D), by striking out the period at the end of subparagraph (E) and inserting in lieu thereof ", or", and by adding at the end thereof new subparagraph (F). **Effective** as if included in the provision of P.L. 98-369 to which it relates.

[Sec. 1281(c)]

(c) CROSS REFERENCE.—

For special rules limiting the application of this section to original issue discount in the case of nongovernmental obligations, see section 1283(c).

Amendments

• **1984, Deficit Reduction Act of 1984 (P.L. 98-369)**

P.L. 98-369, § 41(a):

Added Code Sec. 1281. **Effective** for obligations acquired after 7-18-84. However, see the special election provided by Act Sec. 44(e), below.

P.L. 98-369, § 44(e), provides:

(e) 5-Year Spread of Adjustments Required by Reason of Accrual of Discount on Certain Short-Term Obligations.—

(1) Election to Have Section 1281 Apply to All Obligations Held During Taxable Year.—A taxpayer may elect for his first taxable year ending after the date of the enactment of this Act to have section 1281 of the Internal Revenue Code of 1954 apply to all short-term obligations described in subsection (b) of such section which were held by the taxpayer at any time during such first taxable year.

(2) 5-Year Spread.—

(A) In General.—In the case of any taxpayer who makes an election under paragraph (1)—

(i) the provisions of section 1281 of the Internal Revenue Code of 1954 (as added by section 41) shall be treated as a change in the method of accounting of the taxpayer,

(ii) such change shall be treated as having been made with the consent of the Secretary, and

(iii) the net amount of the adjustments required by section 481(a) of such Code to be taken into account by the taxpayer in computing taxable income (hereinafter in this paragraph referred to as the "net adjustments") shall be taken into account during the spread period with the amount taken into account in each taxable year in such period determined under subparagraph (B).

(B) Amount Taken Into Account During Each Year of Spread Period.—

(i) First Year.—The amount taken into account for the first taxable year in the spread period shall be the sum of—

(I) one-fifth of the net adjustments, and

(II) the excess (if any) of—

(a) the cash basis income over the accrual basis income, over

(b) one-fifth of the net adjustments.

(ii) For Subsequent Years in Spread Period.—The amount taken into account in the second or any succeeding taxable year in the spread period shall be the sum of—

(I) the portion of the net adjustments not taken into account in the preceding taxable year of the spread period divided by the number of remaining taxable years in the spread period (including the year for which the determination is being made), and

(II) the excess (if any) of—

(a) the excess of the cash basis income over the accrual basis income, over

(b) One-fifth of the net adjustments, multiplied by 5 minus the number of years remaining in the spread period (not including the current year).

The excess described in subparagraph (B)(ii)(II)(a) shall be reduced by any amount taken into account under this subclause or clause (i)(II) in any prior year.

(C) Spread Period.—For purposes of this paragraph, the term "spread period" means the period consisting of the 5 taxable years beginning with the year for which the election is made under paragraph (1).

(D) Cash Basis Income.—For purposes of this paragraph, the term "cash basis income" means for any taxable year the aggregate amount which would be includible in the gross income of the taxpayer with respect to short-term obligations described in subsection (b) of section 1281 of such Code if the provisions of section 1281 of such Code did not apply to such taxable year and all prior taxable years within the spread period.

(E) Accrual Basis Income.—For purposes of this paragraph, the term "accrual basis income" means for any taxable year the aggregate amount includible in gross income under section 1281(a) of such Code for such a taxable year and all prior taxable years within the spread period.

[Sec. 1282]

SEC. 1282. DEFERRAL OF INTEREST DEDUCTION ALLOCABLE TO ACCRUED DISCOUNT.

[Sec. 1282(a)]

(a) GENERAL RULE.—Except as otherwise provided in this section, the net direct interest expense with respect to any short-term obligation shall be allowed as a deduction for the taxable year only to the extent such expense exceeds the sum of—

INCOME TAX—DISCOUNT ON SHORT-TERM OBLIGATIONS

(1) the daily portions of the acquisition discount for each day during the taxable year on which the taxpayer held such obligation, and

(2) the amount of any interest payable on the obligation (other than interest taken into account in determining the amount of the acquisition discount) which accrues during the taxable year while the taxpayer held such obligation (and is not included in the gross income of the taxpayer for such taxable year by reason of the taxpayer's method of accounting).

Amendments
• **1986, Tax Reform Act of 1986 (P.L. 99-514)**

P.L. 99-514, § 1803(a)(8)(B):

Amended Code Sec. 1282(a). **Effective** as if included in the provision of P.L. 98-369 to which it relates. Prior to amendment, Code Sec. 1282(a) read as follows:

(a) GENERAL RULE.—Except as otherwise provided in this section, the net direct interest expense with respect to any short-term obligation shall be allowed as a deduction for the taxable year only to the extent that such expense exceeds the sum of the daily portions of the acquisition discount for each day during the taxable year on which the taxpayer held such obligation.

[Sec. 1282(b)]

(b) SECTION NOT TO APPLY TO OBLIGATIONS TO WHICH SECTION 1281 APPLIES.—

(1) IN GENERAL.—This section shall not apply to any short-term obligation to which section 1281 applies.

(2) ELECTION TO HAVE SECTION 1281 APPLY TO ALL OBLIGATIONS.—

(A) IN GENERAL.—A taxpayer may make an election under this paragraph to have section 1281 apply to all short-term obligations acquired by the taxpayer on or after the 1st day of the 1st taxable year to which such election applies.

(B) PERIOD TO WHICH ELECTION APPLIES.—An election under this paragraph shall apply to the taxable year for which it is made and for all subsequent taxable years, unless the taxpayer secures the consent of the Secretary to the revocation of such election.

[Sec. 1282(c)]

(c) CERTAIN RULES MADE APPLICABLE.—Rules similar to the rules of subsections (b) and (c) of section 1277 shall apply for purposes of this section.

[Sec. 1282(d)]

(d) CROSS REFERENCE.—

For special rules limiting the application of this section to original issue discount in the case of nongovernmental obligations, see section 1283(c).

Amendments
• **1984, Deficit Reduction Act of 1984 (P.L. 98-369)**

P.L. 98-369, § 41(a):

Added Code Sec. 1282. **Effective** for obligations acquired after 7-18-84.

[Sec. 1283]

SEC. 1283. DEFINITIONS AND SPECIAL RULES.

[Sec. 1283(a)]

(a) DEFINITIONS.—For purposes of this subpart—

(1) SHORT-TERM OBLIGATION.—

(A) IN GENERAL.—Except as provided in subparagraph (B), the term "short-term obligation" means any bond, debenture, note, certificate, or other evidence of indebtedness which has a fixed maturity date not more than 1 year from the date of issue.

(B) EXCEPTIONS FOR TAX-EXEMPT OBLIGATIONS.—The term "short-term obligation" shall not include any tax-exempt obligation (as defined in section 1275(a)(3)).

(2) ACQUISITION DISCOUNT.—The term "acquisition discount" means the excess of—

(A) the stated redemption price at maturity (as defined in section 1273), over

(B) the taxpayer's basis for the obligation.

[Sec. 1283(b)]

(b) DAILY PORTION.—For purposes of this subpart—

(1) RATABLE ACCRUAL.—Except as otherwise provided in this subsection, the daily portion of the acquisition discount is an amount equal to—

(A) the amount of such discount, divided by

(B) the number of days after the day on which the taxpayer acquired the obligation and up to (and including) the day of its maturity.

(2) ELECTION OF ACCRUAL ON BASIS OF CONSTANT INTEREST RATE (IN LIEU OF RATABLE ACCRUAL).—

(A) IN GENERAL.—At the election of the taxpayer with respect to any obligation, the daily portion of the acquisition discount for any day is the portion of the acquisition discount accruing on such day determined (under regulations prescribed by the Secretary) on the basis of—

(i) the taxpayer's yield to maturity based on the taxpayer's cost of acquiring the obligation, and

(ii) compounding daily.

(B) ELECTION IRREVOCABLE.—An election under subparagraph (A), once made with respect to any obligation, shall be irrevocable.

[Sec. 1283(c)]

(c) SPECIAL RULES FOR NONGOVERNMENTAL OBLIGATIONS.—

(1) IN GENERAL.—In the case of any short-term obligation which is not a short-term Government obligation (as defined in section 1271(a)(3)(B))—

(A) sections 1281 and 1282 shall be applied by taking into account original issue discount in lieu of acquisition discount, and

(B) appropriate adjustments shall be made in the application of subsection (b) of this section.

(2) ELECTION TO HAVE PARAGRAPH (1) NOT APPLY.—

(A) IN GENERAL.—A taxpayer may make an election under this paragraph to have paragraph (1) not apply to all obligations acquired by the taxpayer on or after the first day of the first taxable year to which such election applies.

(B) PERIOD TO WHICH ELECTION APPLIES.—An election under this paragraph shall apply to the taxable year for which it is made and for all subsequent taxable years, unless the taxpayer secures the consent of the Secretary to the revocation of such election.

INCOME TAX—MISCELLANEOUS PROVISIONS

[Sec. 1283(d)]

(d) OTHER SPECIAL RULES.—

(1) BASIS ADJUSTMENTS.—The basis of any short-term obligation in the hands of the holder thereof shall be increased by the amount included in his gross income pursuant to section 1281.

(2) DOUBLE INCLUSION IN INCOME NOT REQUIRED.—Section 1281 shall not require the inclusion of any amount previously includible in gross income.

(3) COORDINATION WITH OTHER PROVISIONS.—Section 454(b) and paragraphs (3) and (4) of section 1271(a) shall not apply to any short-term obligation to which section 1281 applies.

Amendments

- **1986, Tax Reform Act of 1986 (P.L. 99-514)**

P.L. 99-514, §1803(a)(1)(B):

Amended Code Sec. 1283(d)(3) by striking out "section 1271(a)(3)" and inserting in lieu thereof "paragraph (3) and (4) of section 1271(a)". **Effective** as if included in the provision or P.L. 98-369 to which it relates.

- **1984, Deficit Reduction Act of 1984 (P.L. 98-369)**

P.L. 98-369, §41(a):

Added Code Sec. 1283. **Effective** for obligations acquired after 7-18-84.

Subpart D—Miscellaneous Provisions

Sec. 1286.   Tax treatment of stripped bonds.
Sec. 1287.   Denial of capital gain treatment for gains on certain obligations not in registered form.
Sec. 1288.   Treatment of original issue discount on tax-exempt obligations.

[Sec. 1286]

SEC. 1286. TAX TREATMENT OF STRIPPED BONDS.

[Sec. 1286(a)]

(a) INCLUSION IN INCOME AS IF BOND AND COUPONS WERE ORIGINAL ISSUE DISCOUNT BONDS.—If any person purchases a stripped bond or stripped coupon, then such bond or coupon while held by such purchaser (or by any other person whose basis is determined by reference to the basis in the hands of such purchaser) shall be treated for purposes of this part as a bond originally issued on the purchase date and having an original issue discount equal to the excess (if any) of—

(1) the stated redemption price at maturity (or, in the case of coupon, the amount payable on the due date of such coupon), over

(2) such bond's or coupon's ratable share of the purchase price.

For purposes of paragraph (2), ratable shares shall be determined on the basis of their respective fair market values on the date of purchase.

Amendments

- **2018, Tax Technical Corrections Act of 2018 (P.L. 115-141)**

P.L. 115-141, §401(c)(2)(B), Div. U:

Amended Code Sec. 1286(a) by striking "after July 1, 1982," following "If any person purchases". **Effective** for bonds purchased on or after 7-2-1982.

[Sec. 1286(b)]

(b) TAX TREATMENT OF PERSON STRIPPING BOND.—For purposes of this subtitle, if any person strips 1 or more coupons from a bond and disposes of the bond or such coupon—

(1) such person shall include in gross income an amount equal to the sum of—

(A) the interest accrued on such bond while held by such person and before the time such coupon or bond was disposed of (to the extent such interest has not theretofore been included in such person's gross income), and

(B) the accrued market discount on such bond determined as of the time such coupon or bond was disposed of (to the extent such discount has not theretofore been included in such person's gross income),

(2) the basis of the bond and coupons shall be increased by the amount included in gross income under paragraph (1),

(3) the basis of the bond and coupons immediately before the disposition (as adjusted pursuant to paragraph (2)) shall be allocated among the items retained by such person and the items disposed of by such person on the basis of their respective fair market values, and

(4) for purposes of subsection (a), such person shall be treated as having purchased on the date of such disposition each such item which he retains for an amount equal to the basis allocated to such item under paragraph (3).

A rule similar to the rule of paragraph (4) shall apply in the case of any person whose basis in any bond or coupon is determined by reference to the basis of the person described in the preceding sentence.

Amendments

- **2018, Tax Technical Corrections Act of 2018 (P.L. 115-141)**

P.L. 115-141, §401(c)(2)(B), Div. U:

Amended Code Sec. 1286(b) by striking "after July 1, 1982," following "coupons from a bond and". **Effective** for bonds purchased on or after 7-2-1982.

- **1986, Tax Reform Act of 1986 (P.L. 99-514)**

P.L. 99-514, §1803(a)(13)(B)(i):

Amended Code Sec. 1286(b)(1). **Effective** for obligations acquired after 10-22-86. Prior to amendment, Code Sec. 1286(b)(1) read as follows:

(1) such person shall include in gross income an amount equal to the interest accrued on such bond while held by such person and before the time that such coupon or bond was disposed of (to the extent such interest has not theretofore been included in such person's gross income),

P.L. 99-514, §1803(a)(13)(B)(ii):

Amended Code Sec. 1286(b)(2) by striking out "the amount of the accrued interest described in paragraph (1)" and inserting in lieu thereof "the amount included in gross income under paragraph (1)". **Effective** for obligations acquired after 10-22-86.

[Sec. 1286(c)—Stricken]

Amendments

- **2018, Tax Technical Corrections Act of 2018 (P.L. 115-141)**

P.L. 115-141, §401(c)(2)(A), Div. U:

Amended Code Sec. 1286, as amended by Act Sec. 401, Div. U, by striking subsection (c) and by redesignating subsections (d), (e), (f), and (g) as subsections (c), (d), (e), and (f), respectively. **Effective** for bonds purchased on or after 7-2-1982. Prior to being stricken, Code Sec. 1286(c) read as follows:

(c) RETENTION OF EXISTING LAW FOR STRIPPED BONDS PURCHASED BEFORE JULY 2, 1982.—

If a bond issued at any time with interest coupons—

(1) is purchased after August 16, 1954, and before January 1, 1958, and the purchaser does not receive all the coupons which first become payable more than 12 months after the date of the purchase, or

(2) is purchased after December 31, 1957, and before July 2, 1982, and the purchaser does not receive all the coupons which first become payable after the date of the purchase,

then the gain on the sale or other disposition of such bond by such purchaser (or by a person whose basis is determined by reference to the basis in the hands of such purchaser) shall be considered as ordinary income to the extent that the fair market value (determined as of the time of the purchase) of the bond with coupons attached exceeds the purchase price. If this subsection and section 1271(a)(2)(A) apply with respect to gain realized on the sale or exchange of any evidence of indebtedness, then section 1271(a)(2)(A) shall apply with respect to that part of the gain to which this subsection does not apply.

INCOME TAX—MISCELLANEOUS PROVISIONS

[Sec. 1286(c)]

(c) SPECIAL RULES FOR TAX-EXEMPT OBLIGATIONS.—

(1) IN GENERAL.—In the case of any tax-exempt obligation (as defined in section 1275(a)(3)) from which 1 or more coupons have been stripped—

(A) the amount of the original issue discount determined under subsection (a) with respect to any stripped bond or stripped coupon—

(i) shall be treated as original issue discount on a tax-exempt obligation to the extent such discount does not exceed the tax-exempt portion of such discount, and

(ii) shall be treated as original issue discount on an obligation which is not a tax-exempt obligation to the extent such discount exceeds the tax-exempt portion of such discount,

(B) subsection (b)(1)(A) shall not apply, and

(C) subsection (b)(2) shall be applied by increasing the basis of the bond or coupon by the sum of—

(i) the interest accrued but not paid before such bond or coupon was disposed of (and not previously reflected in basis), plus

(ii) the amount included in gross income under subsection (b)(1)(B).

(2) TAX-EXEMPT PORTION.—For purposes of paragraph (1), the tax-exempt portion of the original issue discount determined under subsection (a) is the excess of—

(A) the amount referred to in subsection (a)(1), over

(B) an issue price which would produce a yield to maturity as of the purchase date equal to the lower of—

(i) the coupon rate of interest on the obligation from which the coupons were separated, or

(ii) the yield to maturity (on the basis of the purchase price) of the stripped obligation or coupon.

The purchaser of any stripped obligation or coupon may elect to apply clause (i) by substituting "original yield to maturity of" for "coupon rate of interest on".

Amendments

• **2018, Tax Technical Corrections Act of 2018 (P.L. 115-141)**

P.L. 115-141, § 401(c)(2)(A), Div. U:

Amended Code Sec. 1286, as amended by Act Sec. 401, Div. U, by redesignating subsection (d) as subsection (c). **Effective** for bonds purchased on or after 7-2-1982.

• **1988, Technical and Miscellaneous Revenue Act of 1988 (P.L. 100-647)**

P.L. 100-647, § 1018(q)(4)(A):

Amended Code Sec. 1286(d). For the **effective** date, see Act Sec. 1018(q)(4)(B)(i)-(ii), below. Prior to amendment, Code Sec. 1286(d) read as follows:

(d) SPECIAL RULES FOR TAX-EXEMPT OBLIGATIONS.—In the case of any tax-exempt obligation (as defined in section 1275(a)(3)) from which 1 or more coupons have been stripped—

(1) the amount of original issue discount determined under subsection (a) with respect to any stripped bond or stripped coupon from such obligation shall be the amount which produces a yield to maturity (as of the purchase date) equal to the lower of—

(A) the coupon rate of interest on such obligation before the separation of coupons, or

(B) the yield to maturity (on the basis of purchase price) of the stripped obligation or coupon,

(2) the amount of original issue discount determined under paragraph (1) shall be taken into account in determining the adjusted basis of the holder under section 1288,

(3) subsection (b)(1) shall not apply, and

(4) subsection (b)(2) shall be applied by increasing the basis of the bond or coupon by the interest accrued but not paid before the time such bond or coupon was disposed of (and not previously reflected in basis).

P.L. 100-647, § 1018(q)(4)(B)(i)-(ii), provides:

(B)(i) Except as provided in clause (ii), the amendment made by subparagraph (A) shall apply to any purchase or sale after June 10, 1987, of any stripped tax-exempt obligation or stripped coupon from such an obligation.

(ii) If—

(I) any person held any obligation or coupon in stripped form on June 10, 1987, and

(II) such obligation or coupon was held by such person on such date for sale in the ordinary course of such person's trade or business,

the amendment made by subparagraph (A) shall not apply to any sale of such obligation or coupon by such person and shall not apply to any such obligation or coupon while held by another person who purchased such obligation or coupon from the person referred to in subclause (I).

• **1986, Tax Reform Act of 1986 (P.L. 99-514)**

P.L. 99-514, § 1879(s)(1):

Amended Code Sec. 1286(d). **Effective** for any purchase or sale of any stripped tax-exempt obligation or stripped coupon from such an obligation after 10-22-86. Prior to amendment, Code Sec. 1286(d) read as follows:

(d) SPECIAL RULES FOR TAX-EXEMPT OBLIGATIONS.—In the case of any tax-exempt obligation (as defined in section 1275(a)(3))—

(1) subsections (a) and (b)(1) shall not apply,

(2) the rules of subsection (b)(4) shall apply for purposes of subsection (c), and

(3) subsection (c) shall be applied without regard to the requirement that the bond be purchased before July 2, 1982.

[Sec. 1286(d)]

(d) DEFINITIONS AND SPECIAL RULES.—For purposes of this section—

(1) BOND.—The term "bond" means a bond, debenture, note, or certificate or other evidence of indebtedness.

(2) STRIPPED BOND.—The term "stripped bond" means a bond issued at any time with interest coupons where there is a separation in ownership between the bond and any coupon which has not yet become payable.

(3) STRIPPED COUPON.—The term "stripped coupon" means any coupon relating to a stripped bond.

(4) STATED REDEMPTION PRICE AT MATURITY.—The term "stated redemption price at maturity" has the meaning given such term by section 1273(a)(2).

(5) COUPON.—The term "coupon" includes any right to receive interest on a bond (whether or not evidenced by a coupon).

(6) PURCHASE.—The term "purchase" has the meaning given such term by section 1272(d)(1).

Amendments

• **2018, Tax Technical Corrections Act of 2018 (P.L. 115-141)**

P.L. 115-141, § 401(c)(2)(A), Div. U:

Amended Code Sec. 1286, as amended by Act Sec. 401, Div. U, by redesignating subsection (e) as subsection (d). **Effective** for bonds purchased on or after 7-2-1982.

P.L. 115-141, § 401(c)(2)(C), Div. U:

Amended Code Sec. 1286(d)(5), as redesignated by Act Sec. 401(c)(2)(A), by striking the last sentence. **Effective** for bonds purchased on or after 7-2-1982. Prior to being stricken, the last sentence of Code Sec. 1286(d)(5) read as follows:

This paragraph shall apply for purposes of subsection (c) only in the case of purchases after July 1, 1982.

[Sec. 1286(e)]

(e) TREATMENT OF STRIPPED INTERESTS IN BOND AND PREFERRED STOCK FUNDS, ETC.—In the case of an account or entity substantially all of the assets of which consist of bonds, preferred stock, or a combination thereof, the Secretary may by regulations provide that rules similar to the rules of this section and section 305(e), as appropriate, shall apply to interests in such account or entity to which (but for this subsection) this section or section 305(e), as the case may be, would not apply.

Amendments

• **2018, Tax Technical Corrections Act of 2018 (P.L. 115-141)**

P.L. 115-141, § 401(a)(182), Div. U:

Amended Code Sec. 1286(f) by striking "and 305(e)," and inserting "and section 305(e),". **Effective** 3-23-2018.

P.L. 115-141, § 401(c)(2)(A), Div. U:

Amended Code Sec. 1286, as amended by Act Sec. 401, Div. U, by redesignating subsection (f) as subsection (e). **Effective** for bonds purchased on or after 7-2-1982.

Sec. 1286(c)

INCOME TAX—MISCELLANEOUS PROVISIONS

• 2004, American Jobs Creation Act of 2004 (P.L. 108-357)

P.L. 108-357, § 831(a):

Amended Code Sec. 1286 by redesignating subsection (f) as subsection (g) and by inserting after subsection (e) a new subsection (f). **Effective** for purchases and dispositions after 10-22-2004.

[Sec. 1286(f)]

(f) REGULATION AUTHORITY.—The Secretary may prescribe regulations providing that where, by reason of varying rates of interest, put or call options, or other circumstances, the tax treatment under this section does not accurately reflect the income of the holder of a stripped coupon or stripped bond, or of the person disposing of such bond or coupon, as the case may be, for any period, such treatment shall be modified to require that the proper amount of income be included for such period.

Amendments

• 2018, Tax Technical Corrections Act of 2018 (P.L. 115-141)

P.L. 115-141, § 401(c)(2)(A), Div. U:

Amended Code Sec. 1286, as amended by Act Sec. 401, Div. U, by redesignating subsection (g) as subsection (f). **Effective** for bonds purchased on or after 7-2-1982.

• 2004, American Jobs Creation Act of 2004 (P.L. 108-357)

P.L. 108-357, § 831(a):

Amended Code Sec. 1286 by redesignating subsection (f) as subsection (g). **Effective** for purchases and dispositions after 10-22-2004.

• 1984, Deficit Reduction Act of 1984 (P.L. 98-369)

P.L. 98-369, § 41(a):

Added Code Sec. 1286. **Effective** for tax years ending after 7-18-84.

[Sec. 1287]

SEC. 1287. DENIAL OF CAPITAL GAIN TREATMENT FOR GAINS ON CERTAIN OBLIGATIONS NOT IN REGISTERED FORM.

[Sec. 1287(a)]

(a) IN GENERAL.—If any registration-required obligation is not in registered form, any gain on the sale or other disposition of such obligation shall be treated as ordinary income (unless the issuance of such obligation was subject to tax under section 4701).

[Sec. 1287(b)]

(b) DEFINITIONS.—For purposes of subsection (a)—

(1) REGISTRATION-REQUIRED OBLIGATION.—The term "registration-required obligation" has the meaning given to such term by section 163(f)(2).

(2) REGISTERED FORM.—the term "registered form" has the same meaning as when used in section 163(f).

Amendments

• 2010, Hiring Incentives to Restore Employment Act (P.L. 111-147)

P.L. 111-147, § 502(a)(2)(D):

Amended Code Sec. 1287(b)(1) by striking "except that clause (iv) of subparagraph (A), and subparagraph (B), of such section shall not apply" following "section 163(f)(2)". **Effective** for obligations issued after the date which is 2 years after 3-18-2010.

• 1984, Deficit Reduction Act of 1984 (P.L. 98-369)

P.L. 98-369, § 41(a):

Added Code Sec. 1287. **Effective** for tax years ending after 7-18-84.

[Sec. 1288]

SEC. 1288. TREATMENT OF ORIGINAL ISSUE DISCOUNT ON TAX-EXEMPT OBLIGATIONS.

[Sec. 1288(a)]

(a) GENERAL RULE.—Original issue discount on any tax-exempt obligation shall be treated as accruing—

(1) for purposes of section 163, in the manner provided by section 1272(a) (determined without regard to paragraph (7) thereof), and

(2) for purposes of determining the adjusted basis of the holder, in the manner provided by section 1272(a) (determined with regard to paragraph (7) thereof).

Amendments

• 1988, Technical and Miscellaneous Revenue Act of 1988 (P.L. 100-647)

P.L. 100-647, § 1006(u)(3):

Amended Code Sec. 1288(a) by striking out "paragraph (6)" each place it appears and inserting in lieu thereof "paragraph (7)". **Effective** as if included in the provision of P.L. 99-514 to which it relates.

[Sec. 1288(b)]

(b) DEFINITIONS AND SPECIAL RULES.—For purposes of this section—

(1) ORIGINAL ISSUE DISCOUNT.—The term "original issue discount" has the meaning given to such term by section 1273(a) without regard to paragraph (3) thereof. In applying section 483 or 1274, under regulations prescribed by the Secretary, appropriate adjustments shall be made to the applicable Federal rate to take into account the tax exemption for interest on the obligation.

(2) TAX-EXEMPT OBLIGATION.—The term "tax-exempt obligation" has the meaning given to such term by section 1275(a)(3).

(3) SHORT-TERM OBLIGATION.—In applying this section to obligations with maturity of 1 year or less, rules similar to the rules of section 1283(b) shall apply.

Amendments

• 1984, Deficit Reduction Act of 1984 (P.L. 98-369)

P.L. 98-369, § 41(a):

Added Code Sec. 1288. **Effective** for obligations issued after 9-3-82, and acquired after 3-1-84.

PART VI—TREATMENT OF CERTAIN PASSIVE FOREIGN INVESTMENT COMPANIES

Subpart A.	Interest on tax deferral.
Subpart B.	Treatment of qualified electing funds.
Subpart C.	Election of mark to market for marketable stock.
Subpart D.	General provisions.

Subpart A—Interest on Tax Deferral

Sec. 1291. Interest on tax deferral.

INCOME TAX—INTEREST ON TAX DEFERRAL

[Sec. 1291]

SEC. 1291. INTEREST ON TAX DEFERRAL.

[Sec. 1291(a)]

(a) TREATMENT OF DISTRIBUTIONS AND STOCK DISPOSITIONS.—

(1) DISTRIBUTIONS.—If a United States person receives an excess distribution in respect of stock in a passive foreign investment company, then—

(A) the amount of the excess distribution shall be allocated ratably to each day in the taxpayer's holding period for the stock,

(B) with respect to such excess distribution, the taxpayer's gross income for the current year shall include (as ordinary income) only the amounts allocated under subparagraph (A) to—

(i) the current year, or

(ii) any period in the taxpayer's holding period before the 1st day of the 1st taxable year of the company which begins after December 31, 1986, and for which it was a passive foreign investment company, and

(C) the tax imposed by this chapter for the current year shall be increased by the deferred tax amount (determined under subsection (c)).

(2) DISPOSITIONS.—If the taxpayer disposes of stock in a passive foreign investment company, then the rules of paragraph (1) shall apply to any gain recognized on such disposition in the same manner as if such gain were an excess distribution.

(3) DEFINITIONS.—For purposes of this section—

(A) HOLDING PERIOD.—The taxpayer's holding period shall be determined under section 1223; except that—

(i) for purposes of applying this section to an excess distribution, such holding period shall be treated as ending on the date of such distribution, and

(ii) if section 1296 applied to such stock with respect to the taxpayer for any prior taxable year, such holding period shall be treated as beginning on the first day of the first taxable year beginning after the last taxable year for which section 1296 so applied.

(B) CURRENT YEAR.—The term "current year" means the taxable year in which the excess distribution or disposition occurs.

Amendments

- **1997, Taxpayer Relief Act of 1997 (P.L. 105-34)**

P.L. 105-34, § 1122(b)(3):

Amended Code Sec. 1291(a)(3)(A). **Effective** for tax years of United States persons beginning after 12-31-97, and tax years of foreign corporations ending with or within such tax years of United States persons. Prior to amendment, Code Sec. 1291(a)(3)(A) read as follows:

(A) HOLDING PERIOD.—The taxpayer's holding period shall be determined under section 1223; except that, for purposes of applying this section to an excess distribution, such holding period shall be treated as ending on the date of such distribution.

- **1988, Technical and Miscellaneous Revenue Act of 1988 (P.L. 100-647)**

P.L. 100-647, § 1012(p)(7)(A):

Repealed Code Sec. 1291(a)(4) and (5). **Effective** as if included in the provision of P.L. 99-514 to which it relates. Prior to repeal, Code Sec. 1291(a)(4) and (5) read as follows:

(4) COORDINATION WITH SECTION 904.—Subparagraph (B) of paragraph (1) shall not apply for purposes of section 904.

(5) SECTION 902 NOT TO APPLY.—Section 902 shall not apply to any dividend paid by a passive foreign investment company unless such company is a qualified electing fund.

P.L. 100-647, § 1012(p)(12):

Amended Code Sec. 1291(a)(1)(B)(ii). **Effective** as if included in the provision of P.L. 99-514 to which it relates. Prior to amendment, Code Sec. 1291(a)(1)(B)(ii) read as follows:

(ii) any period in the taxpayer's holding period before the 1st day of the 1st taxable year of the company for which it was a passive foreign investment company (or, if later, January 1, 1987), and

P.L. 100-647, § 1012(p)(14):

Amended Code Sec. 1291(a)(3)(A) by striking out "in the case of an excess distribution" and inserting in lieu thereof "for purposes of applying this section to an excess distribution". **Effective** as if included in the provision of P.L. 99-514 to which it relates.

[Sec. 1291(b)]

(b) EXCESS DISTRIBUTION.—

(1) IN GENERAL.—For purposes of this section, the term "excess distribution" means any distribution in respect of stock received during any taxable year to the extent such distribution does not exceed its ratable portion of the total excess distribution (if any) for such taxable year.

(2) TOTAL EXCESS DISTRIBUTION.—For purposes of this subsection—

(A) IN GENERAL.—The term "total excess distribution" means the excess (if any) of—

(i) the amount of the distributions in respect of the stock received by the taxpayer during the taxable year, over

(ii) 125 percent of the average amount received in respect of such stock by the taxpayer during the 3 preceding taxable years (or, if shorter, the portion of the taxpayer's holding period before the taxable year).

For purposes of clause (ii), any excess distribution received during such 3-year period shall be taken into account only to the extent it was included in gross income under subsection (a)(1)(B).

(B) NO EXCESS FOR 1ST YEAR.—The total excess distributions with respect to any stock shall be zero for the taxable year in which the taxpayer's holding period in such stock begins.

(3) ADJUSTMENTS.—Under regulations prescribed by the Secretary—

(A) determinations under this subsection shall be made on a share-by-share basis, except that shares with the same holding period may be aggregated,

(B) proper adjustments shall be made for stock splits and stock dividends,

(C) if the taxpayer does not hold the stock during the entire taxable year, distributions received during such year shall be annualized,

(D) if the taxpayer's holding period includes periods during which the stock was held by another person, distributions received by such other person shall be taken into account as if received by the taxpayer,

(E) if the distributions are received in a foreign currency, determinations under this subsection shall be made in such currency and the amount of any excess distribution determined in such currency shall be translated into dollars,

(F) proper adjustment shall be made for amounts not includible in gross income by reason of section 959(a) or 1293(c), and

(G) if a charitable deduction was allowable under section 642(c) to a trust for any distribution of its income, proper adjustments shall be made for the deduction so allowable to the extent allocable to distributions or gain in respect of stock in a passive foreign investment company.

INCOME TAX—INTEREST ON TAX DEFERRAL

Amendments

• **2004, American Jobs Creation Act of 2004 (P.L. 108-357)**

P.L. 108-357, §413(c)(24)(A):

Amended Code Sec. 1291(b)(3)(F) by striking "551(d), 959(a)," and inserting "959(a)". **Effective** for tax years of foreign corporations beginning after 12-31-2004, and for tax years of United States shareholders with or within which such tax years of foreign corporations end.

• **1988, Technical and Miscellaneous Revenue Act of 1988 (P.L. 100-647)**

P.L. 100-647, §1012(p)(3):

Amended Code Sec. 1291(b)(3) by striking out "and" at the end of subparagraph (D), by striking out the period at the end of subparagraph (E) and inserting in lieu thereof ", and", and by adding at the end thereof new subparagraph (F). **Effective** as if included in the provision of P.L. 99-514 to which it relates.

P.L. 100-647, §1012(p)(13):

Amended Code Sec. 1291(b)(2)(A) by adding at the end thereof a new sentence. **Effective** as if included in the provision of P.L. 99-514 to which it relates.

P.L. 100-647, §1012(p)(33):

Amended Code Sec. 1291(b)(3) (as amended by paragraph (3)) by striking out "and" at the end of subparagraph (E), by striking out the period at the end of subparagraph (F) and inserting in lieu thereof ", and", and by adding at the end thereof new subparagraph (G). **Effective** as if included in the provision of P.L. 99-514 to which it relates.

[Sec. 1291(c)]

(c) DEFERRED TAX AMOUNT.—For purposes of this section—

(1) IN GENERAL.—The term "deferred tax amount" means, with respect to any distribution or disposition to which subsection (a) applies, an amount equal to the sum of—

(A) the aggregate increases in taxes described in paragraph (2), plus

(B) the aggregate amount of interest (determined in the manner provided under paragraph (3)) on such increases in tax.

Any increase in the tax imposed by this chapter for the current year under subsection (a) to the extent attributable to the amount referred to in subparagraph (B) shall be treated as interest paid under section 6601 on the due date for the current year.

(2) AGGREGATE INCREASES IN TAXES.—For purposes of paragraph (1)(A), the aggregate increases in taxes shall be determined by multiplying each amount allocated under subsection (a)(1)(A) to any taxable year (other than any taxable year referred to in subsection (a)(1)(B)) by the highest rate of tax in effect for such taxable year under section 1 or 11, whichever applies.

(3) COMPUTATION OF INTEREST.—

(A) IN GENERAL.—The amount of interest referred to in paragraph (1)(B) on any increase determined under paragraph (2) for any taxable year shall be determined for the period—

(i) beginning on the due date for such taxable year, and

(ii) ending on the due date for the taxable year with or within which the distribution or disposition occurs,

by using the rates and method applicable under section 6621 for underpayments of tax for such period.

(B) DUE DATE.—For purposes of this subsection, the term "due date" means the date prescribed by law (determined without regard to extensions) for filing the return of the tax imposed by this chapter for the taxable year.

Amendments

• **1988, Technical and Miscellaneous Revenue Act of 1988 (P.L. 100-647)**

P.L. 100-647, §1012(p)(31):

Amended Code Sec. 1291(c)(1) by adding at the end thereof a new sentence. **Effective** as if included in the provision of P.L. 99-514 to which it relates.

[Sec. 1291(d)]

(d) COORDINATION WITH SUBPARTS B AND C.—

(1) IN GENERAL.—This section shall not apply with respect to any distribution paid by a passive foreign investment company, or any disposition of stock in a passive foreign investment company, if such company is a qualified electing fund with respect to the taxpayer for each of its taxable years—

(A) which begins after December 31, 1986, and for which such company is a passive foreign investment company, and

(B) which includes any portion of the taxpayer's holding period.

Except as provided in section 1296(j), this section also shall not apply if an election under section 1296(k) is in effect for the taxpayer's taxable year. In the case of stock which is marked to market under section 475 or any other provision of this chapter, this section shall not apply, except that rules similar to the rules of section 1296(j) shall apply.

(2) ELECTION TO RECOGNIZE GAIN WHERE COMPANY BECOMES QUALIFIED ELECTING FUND.—

(A) IN GENERAL.—If—

(i) a passive foreign investment company becomes a qualified electing fund with respect to the taxpayer for a taxable year which begins after December 31, 1986,

(ii) the taxpayer holds stock in such company on the first day of such taxable year, and

(iii) the taxpayer establishes to the satisfaction of the Secretary the fair market value of such stock on such first day,

the taxpayer may elect to recognize gain as if he sold such stock on such first day for such fair market value.

(B) ADDITIONAL ELECTION FOR SHAREHOLDER OF CONTROLLED FOREIGN CORPORATIONS.—

(i) IN GENERAL.—If—

(I) a passive foreign investment company becomes a qualified electing fund with respect to the taxpayer for a taxable year which begins after December 1, 1986,

(II) the taxpayer holds stock in such company on the first day of such taxable year, and

(III) such company is a controlled foreign corporation (as defined in section 957(a)),

the taxpayer may elect to include in gross income as a dividend received on such first day an amount equal to the portion of the post-1986 earnings and profits of such company attributable (under regulations prescribed by the Secretary) to the stock in such company held by the taxpayer on such first day. The amount treated as a dividend under the preceding sentence shall be treated as a excess distribution and shall be allocated under subsection (a)(1)(A) only to days during periods taken into account in determining the post-1986 earnings and profits so attributable.

(ii) POST-1986 EARNINGS AND PROFITS.—For purposes of clause (i), the term "post-1986 earnings and profits" means earnings and profits which were accumulated in taxable years of such company beginning after December 31, 1986, and during the period or periods the stock was held by the taxpayer while the company was a passive foreign investment company.

(iii) COORDINATION WITH SECTION 959(e).—For purposes of section 959(e), any amount included in gross income under this subparagraph shall be treated as included in gross income under section 1248(a).

(C) ADJUSTMENTS.—In the case of any stock to which subparagraph (A) or (B) applies.—

INCOME TAX—INTEREST ON TAX DEFERRAL

(i) the adjusted basis of such stock shall be increased by the gain recognized under subparagraph (A) or the amount treated as a dividend under subparagraph (B), as the case may be, and

(ii) the taxpayer's holding period in such stock shall be treated as beginning on the first day referred to in such subparagraph.

Amendments

• **1998, IRS Restructuring and Reform Act of 1998 (P.L. 105-206)**

P.L. 105-206, §6011(c)(2):

Amended Code Sec. 1291(d)(1) by adding at the end a new sentence. **Effective** as if included in the provision of P.L. 105-34 to which it relates [**effective** for tax years of U.S. persons beginning after 12-31-97 and tax years of foreign corporations ending with or within such tax years of U.S. persons.—CCH].

• **1997, Taxpayer Relief Act of 1997 (P.L. 105-34)**

P.L. 105-34, §1122(b)(1):

Amended Code Sec. 1291(d)(1) by adding at the end a new flush sentence. **Effective** for tax years of United States persons beginning after 12-31-97, and tax years of foreign corporations ending with or within such tax years of United States persons.

P.L. 105-34, §1122(b)(2):

Amended Code Sec. 1291(d) by striking "Subpart B" in the heading and inserting "Subparts B and C". **Effective** for tax years of United States persons beginning after 12-31-97, and tax years of foreign corporations ending with or within such tax years of United States persons.

• **1988, Technical and Miscellaneous Revenue Act of 1988 (P.L. 100-647)**

P.L. 100-647, §1012(p)(1):

Amended Code Sec. 1291(d)(1). **Effective** as if included in the provision of P.L. 99-514 to which it relates. Prior to amendment, Code Sec. 1291(d)(1) read as follows:

(1) In general.—This section shall not apply with respect to—

(A) any distribution paid by a passive foreign investment company during a taxable year for which such company is a qualified electing fund, and

(B) any disposition of stock in a passive foreign investment company if such company is a qualified electing fund for each of its taxable years—

(i) which begins after December 31, 1986, and for which such company is a passive foreign investment company, and

(ii) which includes any portion of the taxpayer's holding period.

P.L. 100-647, §1012(p)(28):

Amended Code Sec. 1291(d)(2) by striking out subparagraph (B) and inserting in lieu thereof new subparagraphs (B)-(C). **Effective** as if included in the provision of P.L. 99-514 to which it relates. Prior to amendment, Code Sec. 1291(d)(2)(B) read as follows:

(B) Adjustments.—In the case of any stock to which subparagraph (A) applies—

(i) the adjusted basis of such stock shall be increased by the gain recognized under subparagraph (A), and

(ii) the taxpayer's holding period in such stock shall be treated as beginning on the first day referred to in subparagraph (A).

P.L. 100-647, §6127(b)(1):

Amended Code Sec. 1291(d)(1) (as amended by title I) by striking out "for each" in the material preceding subparagraph (A) and inserting in lieu thereof "with respect to the taxpayer for each". **Effective** as if included in the amendments made by section 1235 of P.L. 99-514.

P.L. 100-647, §6127(b)(2):

Amended Code Sec. 1291(d)(2)(A)(i) and (B)(i) (as amended by title I) by striking out "for a taxable year" and inserting in lieu thereof "with respect to the taxpayer for a taxable year". **Effective** as if included in the amendments made by section 1235 of P.L. 99-514.

[Sec. 1291(e)]

(e) Certain Basis, Etc., Rules Made Applicable..—Except to the extent inconsistent with the regulations prescribed under subsection (f), rules similar to the rules of subsections (c), (d), and (e) of section 1246 (as in effect on the day before the date of the enactment of the American Jobs Creation Act of 2004) shall apply for purposes of this section; except that—

(1) the reduction under subsection (e) of such section shall be the excess of the basis determined under section 1014 over the adjusted basis of the stock immediately before the decedent's death, and

(2) such a reduction shall not apply in the case of a decedent who was a nonresident alien at all times during his holding period in the stock.

Amendments

• **2018, Tax Technical Corrections Act of 2018 (P.L. 115-141)**

P.L. 115-141, §401(a)(183), Div. U:

Amended Code Sec. 1291(e) by striking "subsections (c) and (d) (e)," and inserting "subsections (c), (d), and (e)". **Effective** 3-23-2018.

• **2013, American Taxpayer Relief Act of 2012 (P.L. 112-240)**

P.L. 112-240, §101(a)(1)-(3), provides:

SEC. 101. PERMANENT EXTENSION AND MODIFICATION OF 2001 TAX RELIEF.

(a) Permanent Extension.—

(1) In general.—The Economic Growth and Tax Relief Reconciliation Act of 2001 is amended by striking title IX.

(2) Conforming amendment.—The Tax Relief, Unemployment Insurance Reauthorization, and Job Creation Act of 2010 is amended by striking section 304.

(3) Effective date.—The amendments made by this subsection shall apply to taxable, plan, or limitation years beginning after December 31, 2012, and estates of decedents dying, gifts made, or generation skipping transfers after December 31, 2012.

• **2010, Tax Relief, Unemployment Insurance Reauthorization, and Job Creation Act of 2010 (P.L. 111-312)**

P.L. 111-312, §301(a):

Amended Code Sec. 1291(e) to read as such provision would read if subtitle E of title V of the Economic Growth and Tax Relief Reconciliation Act of 2001 (P.L. 107-16) had never been enacted. **Effective** for estates of decedents dying, and transfers made, after 12-31-2009. For a special rule, see Act Sec. 301(c), below. Prior to amendment by P.L. 111-312, Code Sec. 1291(e) read as follows:

(e) Certain Basis, Etc., Rules Made Applicable.—Except to the extent inconsistent with the regulations prescribed under subsection (f), rules similar to the rules of subsections (c) and (d) of section 1246 (as in effect on the day before the date of the enactment of the American Jobs Creation Act of 2004) shall apply for purposes of this section.

P.L. 111-312, §301(c), provides:

(c) Special Election With Respect To Estates Of Decedents Dying In 2010.—Notwithstanding subsection (a), in the case of an estate of a decedent dying after December 31, 2009, and before January 1, 2011, the executor (within the meaning of section 2203 of the Internal Revenue Code of 1986) may elect to apply such Code as though the amendments made by subsection (a) do not apply with respect to chapter 11 of such Code and with respect to property acquired or passing from such decedent (within the meaning of section 1014(b) of such Code). Such election shall be made at such time and in such manner as the Secretary of the Treasury or the Secretary's delegate shall provide. Such an election once made shall be revocable only with the consent of the Secretary of the Treasury or the Secretary's delegate. For purposes of section 2652(a)(1) of such Code, the determination of whether any property is subject to the tax imposed by such chapter 11 shall be made without regard to any election made under this subsection.

P.L. 111-312, §304, provides [but see P.L. 112-240, §101(a)(2)-(3), above]:

SEC. 304. APPLICATION OF EGTRRA SUNSET TO THIS TITLE.

Section 901 of the Economic Growth and Tax Relief Reconciliation Act of 2001 shall apply to the amendments made by this title.

• **2010, Hiring Incentives to Restore Employment Act (P.L. 111-147)**

P.L. 111-147, §521(b):

Amended Code Sec. 1291(e) by striking ", (d), and (f)" and inserting "and (d)". **Effective** 3-18-2010.

• **2004, American Jobs Creation Act of 2004 (P.L. 108-357)**

P.L. 108-357, §413(c)(24)(B):

Amended Code Sec. 1291(e) by inserting "(as in effect on the day before the date of the enactment of the American Jobs Creation Act of 2004)" after "section 1246". **Effective** for tax years of foreign corporations beginning after 12-31-2004, and for tax years of United States shareholders with or within which such tax years of foreign corporations end.

• **2001, Economic Growth and Tax Relief Reconciliation Act of 2001 (P.L. 107-16)**

P.L. 107-16, §542(e)(5)(B)(i)-(ii):

Amended Code Sec. 1291(e) by striking "(e)," following "rules of subsections (c), (d),"; and by striking "; except that" and all that follows and inserting a period. **Effective** for estates of decedents dying after 12-31-2009. Prior to amendment Code Sec. 1291(e) read as follows:

(e) Certain Basis, Etc., Rules Made Applicable.—Except to the extent inconsistent with the regulations prescribed under subsection (f), rules similar to the rules of subsections (c), (d), (e), and (f) of section 1246 shall apply for purposes of this section; except that—

(1) the reduction under subsection (e) of such section shall be the excess of the basis determined under section 1014 over the adjusted basis of the stock immediately before the decedent's death, and

(2) such a reduction shall not apply in the case of a decedent who was a nonresident alien at all times during his holding period in the stock.

P.L. 107-16, §901(a)-(b), as amended by P.L. 111-312, §101(a)(1), provides [but see P.L. 112-240, §101(a)(1) and (3), above]:

SEC. 901. SUNSET OF PROVISIONS OF ACT.

(a) In General.—All provisions of, and amendments made by, this Act shall not apply—

(1) to taxable, plan, or limitation years beginning after December 31, 2012, or

(2) in the case of title V, to estates of decedents dying, gifts made, or generation skipping transfers, after December 31, 2012.

INCOME TAX—QUALIFIED ELECTING FUNDS

(b) APPLICATION OF CERTAIN LAWS.—The Internal Revenue Code of 1986 and the Employee Retirement Income Security Act of 1974 shall be applied and administered to years, estates, gifts, and transfers described in subsection (a) as if the provisions and amendments described in subsection (a) had never been enacted.

• **1988, Technical and Miscellaneous Revenue Act of 1988 (P.L. 100-647)**

P.L. 100-647, §1012(p)(6)(B):

Amended Code Sec. 1291(e) by striking out "Rules similar" and inserting in lieu thereof "Except to the extent inconsistent with the regulations prescribed under subsection (f), rules similar". **Effective** as if included in the provision of P.L. 99-514 to which it relates.

P.L. 100-647, §1012(p)(9):

Amended Code Sec. 1291(e)(2) by striking out "not" the second place it appears (before "a nonresident"). **Effective** as if included in the provision of P.L. 99-514 to which it relates.

[Sec. 1291(f)]

(f) RECOGNITION OF GAIN.—To the extent provided in regulations, in the case of any transfer of stock in a passive foreign investment company where (but for this subsection) there is not full recognition of gain, the excess (if any) of—

(1) the fair market value of such stock, over

(2) its adjusted basis,

shall be treated as gain from the sale or exchange of such stock and shall be recognized notwithstanding any provision of law. Proper adjustment shall be made to the basis of any such stock for gain recognized under the preceding sentence.

Amendments

• **1988, Technical and Miscellaneous Revenue Act of 1988 (P.L. 100-647)**

P.L. 100-647, §1012(p)(6)(A):

Amended Code Sec. 1291(f). **Effective** as if included in the provision of P.L. 99-514 to which it relates. Prior to amendment, Code Sec. 1291(f) read as follows:

(f) NONRECOGNITION PROVISIONS.—To the extent provided in regulations, gain shall be recognized on any disposition of stock in a passive foreign investment company.

• **1986, Tax Reform Act of 1986 (P.L. 99-514)**

P.L. 99-514, §1235(a):

Added Code Sec. 1291. **Effective** for tax years of foreign corporations beginning after 12-31-86.

[Sec. 1291(g)]

(g) COORDINATION WITH FOREIGN TAX CREDIT RULES.—

(1) IN GENERAL.—If there are creditable foreign taxes with respect to any distribution in respect of stock in a passive foreign investment company—

(A) the amount of such distribution shall be determined for purposes of this section with regard to section 78,

(B) the excess distribution taxes shall be allocated ratably to each day in the taxpayer's holding period for the stock, and

(C) to the extent—

(i) that such excess distribution taxes are allocated to a taxable year referred to in subsection (a)(1)(B), such taxes shall be taken into account under section 901 for the current year, and

(ii) that such excess distribution taxes are allocated to any other taxable year, such taxes shall reduce (subject to the principles of section 904(d) and not below zero) the increase in tax determined under subsection (c)(2) for such taxable year by reason of such distribution (but such taxes shall not be taken into account under section 901).

(2) DEFINITIONS.—For purposes of this subsection—

(A) CREDITABLE FOREIGN TAXES.—The term "creditable foreign taxes" means, with respect to any distribution, any withholding tax imposed with respect to such distribution, but only if the taxpayer chooses the benefits of section 901 and such taxes are creditable under section 901 (determined without regard to paragraph (1)(C)(ii)).

(B) EXCESS DISTRIBUTION TAXES.—The term "excess distribution taxes" means, with respect to any distribution, the portion of the creditable foreign taxes with respect to such distribution which is attributable (on a pro rata basis) to the portion of such distribution which is an excess distribution.

(C) SECTION 1248 GAIN.—The rules of this subsection also shall apply in the case of any gain which but for this section would be includible in gross income as a dividend under section 1248.

Amendments

• **2017, Tax Cuts and Jobs Act (P.L. 115-97)**

P.L. 115-97, §14301(c)(34):

Amended Code Sec. 1291(g)(2)(A) by striking "any distribution—"and all that follows through "but only if" and inserting "any distribution, any withholding tax imposed with respect to such distribution, but only if". **Effective** for tax years of foreign corporations beginning after 12-31-2017, and to tax years of United States shareholders in which or with which such tax years of foreign corporations end. Prior to amendment, Code Sec. 1291(g)(2)(A) read as follows:

(A) CREDITABLE FOREIGN TAXES.—The term "creditable foreign taxes" means, with respect to any distribution—

(i) any foreign taxes deemed paid under section 902 with respect to such distribution, and

(ii) any withholding tax imposed with respect to such distribution,

but only if the taxpayer chooses the benefits of section 901 and such taxes are creditable under section 901 (determined without regard to paragraph (1)(C)(ii)).

• **1988, Technical and Miscellaneous Revenue Act of 1988 (P.L. 100-647)**

P.L. 100-647, §1012(p)(7)(B):

Amended Code Sec. 1291 by adding at the end thereof new subsection (g). **Effective** as if included in the provision of P.L. 99-514 to which it relates.

Subpart B—Treatment of Qualified Electing Funds

Sec. 1293.	Current taxation of income from qualified electing funds.
Sec. 1294.	Election to extend time for payment of tax on undistributed earnings.
Sec. 1295.	Qualified electing fund.

[Sec. 1293]

SEC. 1293. CURRENT TAXATION OF INCOME FROM QUALIFIED ELECTING FUNDS.

[Sec. 1293(a)]

(a) INCLUSION.—

(1) IN GENERAL.—Every United States person who owns (or is treated under section 1298(a) as owning) stock of a qualified electing fund at any time during the taxable year of such fund shall include in gross income—

(A) as ordinary income, such shareholder's pro rata share of the ordinary earnings of such fund for such year, and

(B) as long-term capital gain, such shareholder's pro rata share of the net capital gain of such fund for such year.

(2) YEAR OF INCLUSION.—The inclusion under paragraph (1) shall be for the taxable year of the shareholder in which or with which the taxable year of the fund ends.

INCOME TAX—QUALIFIED ELECTING FUNDS

Amendments

• **1997, Taxpayer Relief Act of 1997 (P.L. 105-34)**

P.L. 105-34, § 1122(d)(3):

Amended Code Sec. 1293(a)(1) by striking "section 1297(a)" and inserting "section 1298(a)". **Effective** for tax years of United States persons beginning after 12-31-97, and tax years of foreign corporations ending with or within such tax years of United States persons.

[Sec. 1293(b)]

(b) PRO RATA SHARE.—The pro rata share referred to in subsection (a) in the case of any shareholder is the amount which would have been distributed with respect to the shareholder's stock if, on each day during the taxable year of the fund, the fund had distributed to each shareholder a pro rata share of that day's ratable share of the fund's ordinary earnings and net capital gain for such year. To the extent provided in regulations, if the fund establishes to the satisfaction of the Secretary that it uses a shorter period than the taxable year to determine shareholders' interests in the earnings of such fund, pro rata shares may be determined by using such shorter period.

Amendments

• **1988, Technical and Miscellaneous Revenue Act of 1988 (P.L. 100-647)**

P.L. 100-647, § 1012(p)(15):

Amended Code Sec. 1293(b) by adding at the end thereof a new sentence. **Effective** as if included in the provision of P.L. 99-514 to which it relates.

[Sec. 1293(c)]

(c) PREVIOUSLY TAXED AMOUNTS DISTRIBUTED TAX FREE.—If the taxpayer establishes to the satisfaction of the Secretary that any amount distributed by a passive foreign investment company is paid out of earnings and profits of the company which were included under subsection (a) in the income of any United States person, such amount shall be treated, for purposes of this chapter, as a distribution which is not a dividend; except that such distribution shall immediately reduce earnings and profits. If the passive foreign investment company is a controlled foreign corporation (as defined in section 957(a)), the preceding sentence shall not apply to any United States shareholder (as defined in section 951(b)) in such corporation, and, in applying section 959 to any such shareholder, any inclusion under this section shall be treated as an inclusion under section 951(a)(1)(A).

Amendments

• **1993, Omnibus Budget Reconciliation Act of 1993 (P.L. 103-66)**

P.L. 103-66, § 13231(c)(3):

Amended Code Sec. 1293(c) by adding at the end thereof a new sentence. **Effective** for tax years of foreign corporations beginning after 9-30-93, and to tax years of United States shareholders in which or with which such tax years of foreign corporations end.

• **1988, Technical and Miscellaneous Revenue Act of 1988 (P.L. 100-647)**

P.L. 100-647, § 1012(p)(23):

Amended Code Sec. 1293(c) by striking out "shall be treated as a distribution which is not a dividend" and inserting in lieu thereof "shall be treated, for purposes of this chapter, as a distribution which is not a dividend; except that such distribution shall immediately reduce earnings and profits". **Effective** as if included in the provision of P.L. 99-514 to which it relates.

[Sec. 1293(d)]

(d) BASIS ADJUSTMENTS.—The basis of taxpayer's stock in a passive foreign investment company shall be—

(1) increased by any amount which is included in the income of the taxpayer under subsection (a) with respect to such stock, and

(2) decreased by any amount distributed with respect to such stock which is not includible in the income of the taxpayer by reason of subsection (c).

A similar rule shall apply also in the case of any property if by reason of holding such property the taxpayer is treated under section 1298(a) as owning stock in a qualified electing fund.

Amendments

• **1997, Taxpayer Relief Act of 1997 (P.L. 105-34)**

P.L. 105-34, § 1122(d)(3):

Amended Code Sec. 1293(d) by striking "section 1297(a)" and inserting "section 1298(a)". **Effective** for tax years of United States persons beginning after 12-31-97, and tax years of foreign corporations ending with or within such tax years of United States persons.

[Sec. 1293(e)]

(e) ORDINARY EARNINGS.—For purposes of this section—

(1) ORDINARY EARNINGS.—The term "ordinary earnings" means the excess of the earnings and profits of the qualified electing fund for the taxable year over its net capital gain for such taxable year.

(2) LIMITATION ON NET CAPITAL GAIN.—A qualified electing fund's capital gain for any taxable year shall not exceed its earnings and profits for such taxable year.

(3) DETERMINATION OF EARNINGS AND PROFITS.—The earnings and profits of any qualified electing fund shall be determined without regard to paragraphs (4), (5), and (6) of section 312(n). Under regulations, the preceding sentence shall not apply to the extent it would increase earnings and profits by an amount which was previously distributed by the qualified electing fund.

Amendments

• **1988, Technical and Miscellaneous Revenue Act of 1988 (P.L. 100-647)**

P.L. 100-647, § 1012(p)(18):

Amended Code Sec. 1293(e) by adding at the end thereof new paragraph (3). **Effective** as if included in the provision of P.L. 99-514 to which it relates.

[Sec. 1293(f)]

(f) FOREIGN TAX CREDIT ALLOWED IN THE CASE OF 10-PERCENT CORPORATE SHAREHOLDER.—For purposes of section 960—

(1) any amount included in the gross income under subsection (a) shall be treated as if it were included under section 951(a),

(2) any amount excluded from gross income under subsection (c) shall be treated in the same manner as amounts excluded from gross income under section 959, and

(3) a domestic corporation which owns (or is treated under section 1298(a) as owning) stock of a qualified electing fund shall be treated in the same manner as a United States shareholder of a controlled foreign corporation (and such qualified electing fund shall be treated in the same manner as such controlled foreign corporation) if such domestic corporation meets the stock ownership requirements of subsection (a) or (b) of section 902 (as in effect before its repeal) with respect to such qualified electing fund.

Amendments

• **2017, Tax Cuts and Jobs Act (P.L. 115-97)**

P.L. 115-97, § 14301(c)(35):

Amended Code Sec. 1293(f) by striking "and" at the end of paragraph (1), by striking the period at the end of paragraph (2) and inserting ", and", and by adding at the end a new paragraph (3). **Effective** for tax years of foreign corporations beginning after 12-31-2017, and to tax years of United States shareholders in which or with which such tax years of foreign corporations end.

• **1986, Tax Reform Act of 1986 (P.L. 99-514)**

P.L. 99-514, § 1235(a):

Added Code Sec. 1293. **Effective** for tax years of foreign corporations beginning after 12-31-86.

Sec. 1293(b)

INCOME TAX—QUALIFIED ELECTING FUNDS

[Sec. 1293(g)]

(g) OTHER SPECIAL RULES.—

(1) EXCEPTION FOR CERTAIN INCOME.—For purposes of determining the amount included in the gross income of any person under this section, the ordinary earnings and net capital gain of a qualified electing fund shall not include any item of income received by such fund if—

(A) such fund is a controlled foreign corporation (as defined in section 957(a)) and such person is a United States shareholder (as defined in section 951(b)) in such fund, and

(B) such person establishes to the satisfaction of the Secretary that—

(i) such income was subject to an effective rate of income tax imposed by a foreign country greater than 90 percent of the maximum rate of tax specified in section 11, or

(ii) such income is—

(I) from sources within the United States,

(II) effectively connected with the conduct by the qualified electing fund of a trade or business in the United States, and

(III) not exempt from taxation (or subject to a reduced rate of tax) pursuant to a treaty obligation of the United States.

(2) PREVENTION OF DOUBLE INCLUSION.—The Secretary shall prescribe such adjustment to the provisions of this section as may be necessary to prevent the same item of income of a qualified electing fund from being included in the gross income of a United States person more than once.

Amendments

• **1988, Technical and Miscellaneous Revenue Act of 1988 (P.L. 100-647)**

P.L. 100-647, § 1012(p)(32):

Amended Code Sec. 1293 by adding at the end thereof a new subsection (g). **Effective** as if included in the provision of P.L. 99-514 to which it relates.

[Sec. 1294]

SEC. 1294. ELECTION TO EXTEND TIME FOR PAYMENT OF TAX ON UNDISTRIBUTED EARNINGS.

[Sec. 1294(a)]

(a) EXTENSION ALLOWED BY ELECTION.—

(1) IN GENERAL.—At the election of the taxpayer, the time for payment of any undistributed PFIC earnings tax liability of the taxpayer for the taxable year shall be extended to the extent and subject to the limitations provided in this section.

(2) ELECTION NOT PERMITTED WHERE AMOUNTS OTHERWISE INCLUDIBLE UNDER SECTION 951.—The taxpayer may not make an election under paragraph (1) with respect to the undistributed PFIC earnings tax liability attributable to a qualified electing fund for the taxable year if any amount is includible in the gross income of the taxpayer under section 951 with respect to such fund for such taxable year.

Amendments

• **2004, American Jobs Creation Act of 2004 (P.L. 108-357)**

P.L. 108-357, § 413(c)(25):

Amended Code Sec. 1294(a)(2). **Effective** for tax years of foreign corporations beginning after 12-31-2004, and for tax years of United States shareholders with or within which such tax years of foreign corporations end. Prior to amendment, Code Sec. 1294(a)(2) read as follows:

(2) ELECTION NOT PERMITTED WHERE AMOUNTS OTHERWISE INCLUDIBLE UNDER SECTION 551 OR 951.—The taxpayer may not make an election under paragraph (1) with respect to the undistributed PFIC earnings tax liability attributable to a qualified electing fund for the taxable year if—

(A) any amount is includible in the gross income of the taxpayer under section 551 with respect to such fund for such taxable year, or

(B) any amount is includible in the gross income of the taxpayer under section 951 with respect to such fund for such taxable year.

[Sec. 1294(b)]

(b) DEFINITIONS.—For purposes of this section—

(1) UNDISTRIBUTED PFIC EARNINGS TAX LIABILITY.—The term "undistributed PFIC earnings tax liability" means, in the case of any taxpayer, the excess of—

(A) the tax imposed by this chapter for the taxable year, over

(B) the tax which would be imposed by this chapter for such year without regard to the inclusion in gross income under section 1293 of the undistributed earnings of a qualified electing fund.

(2) UNDISTRIBUTED EARNINGS.—The term "undistributed earnings" means, with respect to any qualified electing fund, the excess (if any) of—

(A) the amount includible in gross income by reason of section 1293(a) for the taxable year, over

(B) the amount not includible in gross income by reason of section 1293(c) for such taxable year.

[Sec. 1294(c)]

(c) TERMINATION OF EXTENSION.—

(1) DISTRIBUTIONS.—

(A) IN GENERAL.—If a distribution is not includible in gross income for the taxable year by reason of section 1293(c), then the extension under subsection (a) for payment of the undistributed PFIC earnings tax liability with respect to the earnings to which such distribution is attributable shall expire on the last date prescribed by law (determined without regard to extensions) for filing the return of tax for such taxable year.

(B) ORDERING RULE.—For purposes of subparagraph (A), a distribution shall be treated as made from the most recently accumulated earnings and profits.

(2) TRANSFERS, ETC.—If—

(A) stock in a passive foreign investment company is transferred during the taxable year, or

(B) a passive foreign investment company ceases to be a qualified electing fund,

all extensions under subsection (a) for payment of undistributed PFIC earnings tax liability attributable to such stock (or, in the case of such a cessation, attributable to any stock in such company) which had not expired before the date of such transfer or cessation shall expire on the last date prescribed by law (determined without regard to extensions) for filing the return of tax for the taxable year in which such transfer or cessation occurs. To the extent provided in regulations, the preceding sentence shall not apply in the case of a transfer in a transaction with respect to which gain or loss is not recognized (in whole or in part), and the transferee in such transaction shall succeed to the treatment under this section of the transferor.

INCOME TAX—QUALIFIED ELECTING FUNDS

(3) JEOPARDY.—If the Secretary believes that collection of an amount to which an extension under this section relates is in jeopardy, the Secretary shall immediately terminate such extension with respect to such amount, and notice and demand shall be made by him for payment of such amount.

Amendments

• **1988, Technical and Miscellaneous Revenue Act of 1988 (P.L. 100-647)**

P.L. 100-647, § 1012(p)(4)(A)-(C):

Amended Code Sec. 1294(c)(2) by striking out "is disposed of" in subparagraph (A) and inserting in lieu thereof "is transferred", by striking out "such disposition or cessation" each place it appears and inserting in lieu thereof "such transfer or cessation", and by striking out "DISPOSITIONS" in the paragraph heading and inserting in lieu thereof "TRANSFERS". Effective as if included in the provision of P.L. 99-514 to which it relates.

P.L. 100-647, § 1012(p)(34):

Amended Code Sec. 1294(c)(2) by adding at the end thereof a new sentence. Effective as if included in the provision of P.L. 99-514 to which it relates.

[Sec. 1294(d)]

(d) ELECTION.—The election under subsection (a) shall be made not later than the time prescribed by law (including extensions) for filing the return of tax imposed by this chapter for the taxable year.

[Sec. 1294(e)]

(e) AUTHORITY TO REQUIRE BOND.—Section 6165 shall apply to any extension under this section as though the Secretary were extending the time for payment of the tax.

Amendments

• **1986, Tax Reform Act of 1986 (P.L. 99-514)**

P.L. 99-514, § 1235(a):

Added Code Sec. 1294. Effective for tax years of foreign corporations beginning after 12-31-86.

[Sec. 1294(f)]

(f) TREATMENT OF LOANS TO SHAREHOLDER.—For purposes of this section and section 1293, any loan by a qualified electing fund (directly or indirectly) to a shareholder of such fund shall be treated as a distribution to such shareholder.

Amendments

• **1988, Technical and Miscellaneous Revenue Act of 1988 (P.L. 100-647)**

P.L. 100-647, § 1012(p)(25):

Amended Code Sec. 1294 by adding at the end thereof a new subsection (f). Effective as if included in the provision of P.L. 99-514 to which it relates.

[Sec. 1294(g)]

(g) CROSS REFERENCE.—

For provisions providing for interest for the period of the extension under this section, see section 6601.

Amendments

• **1988, Technical and Miscellaneous Revenue Act of 1988 (P.L. 100-647)**

P.L. 100-647, § 1012(p)(8):

Amended Code Sec. 1294 by adding at the end thereof new subsection (g). Effective as if included in the provision of P.L. 99-514 to which it relates.

[Sec. 1295]

SEC. 1295. QUALIFIED ELECTING FUND.

[Sec. 1295(a)]

(a) GENERAL RULE.—For purposes of this part, any passive foreign investment company shall be treated as a qualified electing fund with respect to the taxpayer if—

(1) an election by the taxpayer under subsection (b) applies to such company for the taxable year, and

(2) such company complies with such requirements as the Secretary may prescribe for purposes of—

  (A) determining the ordinary earnings and net capital gain of such company, and

  (B) otherwise carrying out the purposes of this subpart.

[Sec. 1295(b)]

(b) ELECTION.—

(1) IN GENERAL.—A taxpayer may make an election under this subsection with respect to any passive foreign investment company for any taxable year of the taxpayer. Such an election, once made with respect to any company, shall apply to all subsequent taxable years of the taxpayer with respect to such company unless revoked by the taxpayer with the consent of the Secretary.

(2) WHEN MADE.—An election under this subsection may be made for any taxable year at any time on or before the due date (determined with regard to extensions) for filing the return of the tax imposed by this chapter for such taxable year. To the extent provided in regulations, such an election may be made later than as required in the preceding sentence where the taxpayer fails to make a timely election because the taxpayer reasonably believed that the company was not a passive foreign investment company.

Amendments

• **1988, Technical and Miscellaneous Revenue Act of 1988 (P.L. 100-647)**

P.L. 100-647, § 1012(p)(37)(A):

Amended Code Sec. 1295(b)(2) by adding at the end thereof the following new sentence. Effective as if included in the provision of P.L. 99-514 to which it relates.

P.L. 100-647, § 6127(a):

Amended Code Sec. 1295. Effective as if included in the amendments made by section 1235 of P.L. 99-514. See, also, Act Sec. 6127(c)(2), below. Prior to amendment, Code Sec. 1295 read as follows:

SEC. 1295. QUALIFIED ELECTING FUND.

(a) GENERAL RULE.—For purposes of this part, the term "qualified electing fund" means any passive foreign investment company if—

(1) an election under subsection (b) applies to such company for the taxable year, and

(2) such company complies for such taxable year with such requirements as the Secretary may prescribe for purposes of—

(A) determining the ordinary earnings and net capital gain of such company for the taxable year,

(B) ascertaining the ownership of its outstanding stock, and

(C) otherwise carrying out the purposes of this subpart.

To the extent provided in regulations, such an election may be made later than as required by the preceding sentence in cases where the company failed to make a timely election because it reasonably believed it was not a passive foreign investment company.

(b) ELECTION.—

(1) IN GENERAL.—A passive foreign investment company may make an election under this subsection for any taxable year. Such an election, once made, shall apply to all subsequent taxable years of such company for which such company is a passive foreign investment company unless revoked with the consent of the Secretary.

(2) WHEN MADE.—An election under this subsection may be made for any taxable year at any time before the 15th day of the 3rd month of the following taxable year. To the extent provided in regulations, such an election may be made later than as required by the preceding sentence in cases where the company failed to make a

INCOME TAX—MARK-TO-MARKET ELECTION

timely election because it reasonably believed it was not a passive foreign investment company.

P.L. 100-647, §6127(c)(2), provides:

(2) TIME FOR MAKING ELECTION.—The period during which an election under section 1295(b) of the 1986 Code may be made shall in no event expire before the date 60 days after the date of the enactment of this Act.

• 1986, Tax Reform Act of 1986 (P.L. 99-514)

P.L. 99-514, §1235(a):

Added Code Sec. 1295. **Effective** for tax years of foreign corporations beginning after 12-31-86.

Subpart C—Election of Mark to Market for Marketable Stock

Sec. 1296. Election of mark to market for marketable stock.

[Sec. 1296]

SEC. 1296. ELECTION OF MARK TO MARKET FOR MARKETABLE STOCK.

[Sec. 1296(a)]

(a) GENERAL RULE.—In the case of marketable stock in a passive foreign investment company which is owned (or treated under subsection (g) as owned) by a United States person at the close of any taxable year of such person, at the election of such person—

(1) If the fair market value of such stock as of the close of such taxable year exceeds its adjusted basis, such United States person shall include in gross income for such taxable year an amount equal to the amount of such excess.

(2) If the adjusted basis of such stock exceeds the fair market value of such stock as of the close of such taxable year, such United States person shall be allowed a deduction for such taxable year equal to the lesser of—

(A) the amount of such excess, or

(B) the unreversed inclusions with respect to such stock.

[Sec. 1296(b)]

(b) BASIS ADJUSTMENTS.—

(1) IN GENERAL.—The adjusted basis of stock in a passive foreign investment company—

(A) shall be increased by the amount included in the gross income of the United States person under subsection (a)(1) with respect to such stock, and

(B) shall be decreased by the amount allowed as a deduction to the United States person under subsection (a)(2) with respect to such stock.

(2) SPECIAL RULE FOR STOCK CONSTRUCTIVELY OWNED.—In the case of stock in a passive foreign investment company which the United States person is treated as owning under subsection (g)—

(A) the adjustments under paragraph (1) shall apply to such stock in the hands of the person actually holding such stock but only for purposes of determining the subsequent treatment under this chapter of the United States person with respect to such stock, and

(B) similar adjustments shall be made to the adjusted basis of the property by reason of which the United States person is treated as owning such stock.

[Sec. 1296(c)]

(c) CHARACTER AND SOURCE RULES.—

(1) ORDINARY TREATMENT.—

(A) GAIN.—Any amount included in gross income under subsection (a)(1), and any gain on the sale or other disposition of marketable stock in a passive foreign investment company (with respect to which an election under this section is in effect), shall be treated as ordinary income.

(B) LOSS.—Any—

(i) amount allowed as a deduction under subsection (a)(2), and

(ii) loss on the sale or other disposition of marketable stock in a passive foreign investment company (with respect to which an election under this section is in effect) to the extent that the amount of such loss does not exceed the unreversed inclusions with respect to such stock,

shall be treated as an ordinary loss. The amount so treated shall be treated as a deduction allowable in computing adjusted gross income.

(2) SOURCE.—The source of any amount included in gross income under subsection (a)(1) (or allowed as a deduction under subsection (a)(2)) shall be determined in the same manner as if such amount were gain or loss (as the case may be) from the sale of stock in the passive foreign investment company.

[Sec. 1296(d)]

(d) UNREVERSED INCLUSIONS.—For purposes of this section, the term "unreversed inclusions" means, with respect to any stock in a passive foreign investment company, the excess (if any) of—

(1) the amount included in gross income of the taxpayer under subsection (a)(1) with respect to such stock for prior taxable years, over

(2) the amount allowed as a deduction under subsection (a)(2) with respect to such stock for prior taxable years.

The amount referred to in paragraph (1) shall include any amount which would have been included in gross income under subsection (a)(1) with respect to such stock for any prior taxable year but for section 1291. In the case of a regulated investment company which elected to mark to market the stock held by such company as of the last day of the taxable year preceding such company's first taxable year for which such company elects the application of this section, the amount referred to in paragraph (1) shall include amounts included in gross income under such mark to market with respect to such stock for prior taxable years.

Amendments

• 1998, IRS Restructuring and Reform Act of 1998 (P.L. 105-206)

P.L. 105-206, §6011(c)(3):

Amended Code Sec. 1296(d) by adding at the end a new sentence. **Effective** as if included in the provision of P.L. 105-34 to which it relates [effective for tax years of U.S. persons beginning after 12-31-97 and tax years of foreign corporations ending with or within such tax years of U.S. persons.—CCH].

[Sec. 1296(e)]

(e) MARKETABLE STOCK.—For purposes of this section—

(1) IN GENERAL.—The term "marketable stock" means—

(A) any stock which is regularly traded on—

INCOME TAX—MARK-TO-MARKET ELECTION

(i) a national securities exchange which is registered with the Securities and Exchange Commission or the national market system established pursuant to section 11A of the Securities and Exchange Act of 1934, or

(ii) any exchange or other market which the Secretary determines has rules adequate to carry out the purposes of this part,

(B) to the extent provided in regulations, stock in any foreign corporation which is comparable to a regulated investment company and which offers for sale or has outstanding any stock of which it is the issuer and which is redeemable at its net asset value, and

(C) to the extent provided in regulations, any option on stock described in subparagraph (A) or (B).

(2) SPECIAL RULE FOR REGULATED INVESTMENT COMPANIES.—In the case of any regulated investment company which is offering for sale or has outstanding any stock of which it is the issuer and which is redeemable at its net asset value, all stock in a passive foreign investment company which it owns directly or indirectly shall be treated as marketable stock for purposes of this section. Except as provided in regulations, similar treatment as marketable stock shall apply in the case of any other regulated investment company which publishes net asset valuations at least annually.

[Sec. 1296(f)]

(f) TREATMENT OF CONTROLLED FOREIGN CORPORATIONS WHICH ARE SHAREHOLDERS IN PASSIVE FOREIGN INVESTMENT COMPANIES.—In the case of a foreign corporation which is a controlled foreign corporation and which owns (or is treated under subsection (g) as owning) stock in a passive foreign investment company—

(1) this section (other than subsection (c)(2)) shall apply to such foreign corporation in the same manner as if such corporation were a United States person, and

(2) for purposes of subpart F of part III of subchapter N—

(A) any amount included in gross income under subsection (a)(1) shall be treated as foreign personal holding company income described in section 954(c)(1)(A), and

(B) any amount allowed as a deduction under subsection (a)(2) shall be treated as a deduction allocable to foreign personal holding company income so described.

[Sec. 1296(g)]

(g) STOCK OWNED THROUGH CERTAIN FOREIGN ENTITIES.—Except as provided in regulations—

(1) IN GENERAL.—For purposes of this section, stock owned, directly or indirectly, by or for a foreign partnership or foreign trust or foreign estate shall be considered as being owned proportionately by its partners or beneficiaries. Stock considered to be owned by a person by reason of the application of the preceding sentence shall, for purposes of applying such sentence, be treated as actually owned by such person.

(2) TREATMENT OF CERTAIN DISPOSITIONS.—In any case in which a United States person is treated as owning stock in a passive foreign investment company by reason of paragraph (1)—

(A) any disposition by the United States person or by any other person which results in the United States person being treated as no longer owning such stock, and

(B) any disposition by the person owning such stock,

shall be treated as a disposition by the United States person of the stock in the passive foreign investment company.

[Sec. 1296(h)]

(h) COORDINATION WITH SECTION 851(b).—For purposes of section 851(b)(2), any amount included in gross income under subsection (a) shall be treated as a dividend.

Amendments

• **2004, Working Families Tax Relief Act of 2004 (P.L. 108-311)**

P.L. 108-311, § 408(a)(19):

Amended Code Sec. 1296(h) by striking "paragraphs (2) and (3) of section 851(b)" and inserting "section 851(b)(2)". **Effective** 10-4-2004.

[Sec. 1296(i)]

(i) STOCK ACQUIRED FROM A DECEDENT.—In the case of stock of a passive foreign investment company which is acquired by bequest, devise, or inheritance (or by the decedent's estate) and with respect to which an election under this section was in effect as of the date of the decedent's death, notwithstanding section 1014, the basis of such stock in the hands of the person so acquiring it shall be the adjusted basis of such stock in the hands of the decedent immediately before his death (or, if lesser, the basis which would have been determined under section 1014 without regard to this subsection).

Amendments

• **2013, American Taxpayer Relief Act of 2012 (P.L. 112-240)**

P.L. 112-240, § 101(a)(1)-(3), provides:

SEC. 101. PERMANENT EXTENSION AND MODIFICATION OF 2001 TAX RELIEF.

(a) PERMANENT EXTENSION.—

(1) IN GENERAL.—The Economic Growth and Tax Relief Reconciliation Act of 2001 is amended by striking title IX.

(2) CONFORMING AMENDMENT.—The Tax Relief, Unemployment Insurance Reauthorization, and Job Creation Act of 2010 is amended by striking section 304.

(3) EFFECTIVE DATE.—The amendments made by this subsection shall apply to taxable, plan, or limitation years beginning after December 31, 2012, and estates of decedents dying, gifts made, or generation skipping transfers after December 31, 2012.

• **2010, Tax Relief, Unemployment Insurance Reauthorization, and Job Creation Act of 2010 (P.L. 111-312)**

P.L. 111-312, § 301(a):

Amended Code Sec. 1296(i) to read as such provision would read if subtitle E of title V of the Economic Growth and Tax Relief Reconciliation Act of 2001 (P.L. 107-16) had never been enacted. **Effective** for estates of decedents dying, and transfers made, after 12-31-2009. For a special rule, see Act Sec. 301(c), below.

P.L. 111-312, § 301(c), provides:

(c) SPECIAL ELECTION WITH RESPECT TO ESTATES OF DECEDENTS DYING IN 2010.—Notwithstanding subsection (a), in the case of an estate of a decedent dying after December 31, 2009, and before January 1, 2011, the executor (within the meaning of section 2203 of the Internal Revenue Code of 1986) may elect to apply such Code as though the amendments made by subsection (a) do not apply with respect to chapter 11 of such Code and with respect to property acquired or passing from such decedent (within the meaning of section 1014(b) of such Code). Such election shall be made at such time and in such manner as the Secretary of the Treasury or the Secretary's delegate shall provide. Such an election once made shall be revocable only with the consent of the Secretary of the Treasury or the Secretary's delegate. For purposes of section 2652(a)(1) of such Code, the determination of whether any property is subject to the tax imposed by such chapter 11 shall be made without regard to any election made under this subsection.

P.L. 111-312, § 304, provides [but see P.L. 112-240, § 101(a)(2)-(3), above]:

SEC. 304. APPLICATION OF EGTRRA SUNSET TO THIS TITLE.

Section 901 of the Economic Growth and Tax Relief Reconciliation Act of 2001 shall apply to the amendments made by this title.

• **2001, Economic Growth and Tax Relief Reconciliation Act of 2001 (P.L. 107-16)**

P.L. 107-16, § 542(e)(5)(C):

Amended Code Sec. 1296 by striking subsection (i). **Effective** for estates of decedents dying after 12-31-2009. Prior to being stricken, Code Sec. 1296(i) read as follows:

(i) STOCK ACQUIRED FROM A DECEDENT.—In the case of stock of a passive foreign investment company which is acquired by bequest, devise, or inheritance (or by the decedent's estate) and with respect to which an election under this section was in effect as of the date of the decedent's death, notwithstanding section 1014, the basis of such stock in the hands of the person so acquiring it shall be the adjusted basis of such stock in the hands of the decedent immediately before his death (or, if lesser, the basis which would have been determined under section 1014 without regard to this subsection).

INCOME TAX—GENERAL PROVISIONS

P.L. 107-16, §901(a)-(b), as amended by P.L. 111-312, §101(a)(1), provides [but see P.L. 112-240, §101(a)(1) and (3), above]:

SEC. 901. SUNSET OF PROVISIONS OF ACT.

(a) IN GENERAL.—All provisions of, and amendments made by, this Act shall not apply—

(1) to taxable, plan, or limitation years beginning after December 31, 2012, or

(2) in the case of title V, to estates of decedents dying, gifts made, or generation skipping transfers, after December 31, 2012.

(b) APPLICATION OF CERTAIN LAWS.—The Internal Revenue Code of 1986 and the Employee Retirement Income Security Act of 1974 shall be applied and administered to years, estates, gifts, and transfers described in subsection (a) as if the provisions and amendments described in subsection (a) had never been enacted.

[Sec. 1296(j)]

(j) COORDINATION WITH SECTION 1291 FOR FIRST YEAR OF ELECTION.—

(1) TAXPAYERS OTHER THAN REGULATED INVESTMENT COMPANIES.—

(A) IN GENERAL.—If the taxpayer elects the application of this section with respect to any marketable stock in a corporation after the beginning of the taxpayer's holding period in such stock, and if the requirements of subparagraph (B) are not satisfied, section 1291 shall apply to—

(i) any distributions with respect to, or disposition of, such stock in the first taxable year of the taxpayer for which such election is made, and

(ii) any amount which, but for section 1291, would have been included in gross income under subsection (a) with respect to such stock for such taxable year in the same manner as if such amount were gain on the disposition of such stock.

(B) REQUIREMENTS.—The requirements of this subparagraph are met if, with respect to each of such corporation's taxable years for which such corporation was a passive foreign investment company and which begin after December 31, 1986, and included any portion of the taxpayer's holding period in such stock, such corporation was treated as a qualified electing fund under this part with respect to the taxpayer.

(2) SPECIAL RULES FOR REGULATED INVESTMENT COMPANIES.—

(A) IN GENERAL.—If a regulated investment company elects the application of this section with respect to any marketable stock in a corporation after the beginning of the taxpayer's holding period in such stock, then, with respect to such company's first taxable year for which such company elects the application of this section with respect to such stock—

(i) section 1291 shall not apply to such stock with respect to any distribution or disposition during, or amount included in gross income under this section for, such first taxable year, but

(ii) such regulated investment company's tax under this chapter for such first taxable year shall be increased by the aggregate amount of interest which would have been determined under section 1291(c)(3) if section 1291 were applied without regard to this subparagraph.

Clause (ii) shall not apply if for the preceding taxable year the company elected to mark to market the stock held by such company as of the last day of such preceding taxable year.

(B) DISALLOWANCE OF DEDUCTION.—No deduction shall be allowed to any regulated investment company for the increase in tax under subparagraph (A)(ii).

[Sec. 1296(k)]

(k) ELECTION.—This section shall apply to marketable stock in a passive foreign investment company which is held by a United States person only if such person elects to apply this section with respect to such stock. Such an election shall apply to the taxable year for which made and all subsequent taxable years unless—

(1) such stock ceases to be marketable stock, or

(2) the Secretary consents to the revocation of such election.

[Sec. 1296(l)]

(l) TRANSITION RULE FOR INDIVIDUALS BECOMING SUBJECT TO UNITED STATES TAX.—If any individual becomes a United States person in a taxable year beginning after December 31, 1997, solely for purposes of this section, the adjusted basis (before adjustments under subsection (b)) of any marketable stock in a passive foreign investment company owned by such individual on the first day of such taxable year shall be treated as being the greater of its fair market value on such first day or its adjusted basis on such first day.

Amendments

• 1997, Taxpayer Relief Act of 1997 (P.L. 105-34)

P.L. 105-34, §1122(a):

Amended part VI of subchapter P of chapter 1 by redesignating subpart C as subpart D, by redesignating Code Secs. 1296 and 1297 as Code Secs. 1297 and 1298, respectively, and by inserting after subpart B a new subpart C (Code Sec. 1296). **Effective** for tax years of United States persons beginning after 12-31-97, and to tax years of foreign corporations ending with or within such tax years of United States persons.

Subpart D—General Provisions

Sec. 1297.   Passive foreign investment company.
Sec. 1298.   Special rules.

[Sec. 1297]

SEC. 1297. PASSIVE FOREIGN INVESTMENT COMPANY.

[Sec. 1297(a)]

(a) IN GENERAL.—For purposes of this part, except as otherwise provided in this subpart, the term "passive foreign investment company" means any foreign corporation if—

(1) 75 percent or more of the gross income of such corporation for the taxable year is passive income, or

(2) the average percentage of assets (as determined in accordance with subsection (e)) held by such corporation during the taxable year which produce passive income or which are held for the production of passive income is at least 50 percent.

Amendments

• 1997, Taxpayer Relief Act of 1997 (P.L. 105-34)

P.L. 105-34, §1122(a):

Redesignated Code Sec. 1296 as Code Sec. 1297. **Effective** for tax years of United States persons beginning after 12-31-97, and to tax years of foreign corporations ending with or within such tax years of United States persons.

P.L. 105-34, §1123(b)(1)-(2):

Amended Code Sec. 1297(a), as redesignated by Act Sec. 1122(a), by striking "(by value)" and inserting "(as determined in accordance with subsection (e))", and by striking the last two sentences. **Effective** for tax years of United States persons beginning after 12-31-97, and to tax years of foreign corporations ending with or within such tax years of United States persons. Prior to amendment, the last two sentences of Code Sec. 1297(a) read as follows:

In the case of a controlled foreign corporation (or any other foreign corporation if such corporation so elects), the determination under paragraph (2) shall be based on the adjusted bases (as determined for purposes of computing earnings and profits) of its assets in lieu of their value. Such an election, once made, may be revoked only with the consent of the Secretary.

INCOME TAX—GENERAL PROVISIONS

• **1993, Omnibus Budget Reconciliation Act of 1993 (P.L. 103-66)**

P.L. 103-66, §13231(d)(1):

Amended Code Sec. 1296(a) by striking the material following paragraph (2) and inserting the new material. **Effective** for tax years of foreign corporations beginning after 9-30-93, and to tax years of United States shareholders in which or with which such tax years of foreign corporations end. Prior to amendment, the material following paragraph (2) read as follows:

A foreign corporation may elect to have the determination under paragraph (2) based on the adjusted bases of its assets in lieu of their value. Such an election, once made, may be revoked only with the consent of the Secretary.

• **1988, Technical and Miscellaneous Revenue Act of 1988 (P.L. 100-647)**

P.L. 100-647, §1012(p)(27):

Amended Code Sec. 1296(a) by adding at the end thereof two new sentences. **Effective** as if included in the provision of P.L. 99-514 to which it relates.

P.L. 100-647, §1018(u)(40):

Amended Code Sec. 1296(a) by inserting a comma after "this subpart". **Effective** as if included in the provision of P.L. 99-514 to which it relates.

[Sec. 1297(b)]

(b) PASSIVE INCOME.—For purposes of this section—

(1) IN GENERAL.—Except as provided in paragraph (2), the term "passive income" means any income which is of a kind which would be foreign personal holding company income as defined in section 954(c).

(2) EXCEPTIONS.—Except as provided in regulations, the term "passive income" does not include any income—

(A) derived in the active conduct of a banking business by an institution licensed to do business as a bank in the United States (or, to the extent provided in regulations, by any other corporation),

(B) derived in the active conduct of an insurance business by a qualifying insurance corporation (as defined in subsection (f)),

(C) which is interest, a dividend, or a rent or royalty, which is received or accrued from a related person (within the meaning of section 954(d)(3)) to the extent such amount is properly allocable (under regulations prescribed by the Secretary) to income of such related person which is not passive income, or

(D) which is export trade income of an export trade corporation (as defined in section 971).

For purposes of subparagraph (C), the term "related person" has the meaning given such term by section 954(d)(3) determined by substituting "foreign corporation" for "controlled foreign corporation" each place it appears in section 954(d)(3).

Amendments

• **2017, Tax Cuts and Jobs Act (P.L. 115-97)**

P.L. 115-97, §14501(a):

Amended Code Sec. 1297(b)(2)(B). **Effective** for tax years beginning after 12-31-2017. Prior to amendment, Code Sec. 1297(b)(2)(B) read as follows:

(B) derived in the active conduct of an insurance business by a corporation which is predominantly engaged in an insurance business and which would be subject to tax under subchapter L if it were a domestic corporation,

• **2007, Tax Technical Corrections Act of 2007 (P.L. 110-172)**

P.L. 110-172, §11(g)(18):

Amended Code Sec. 1297(b)(2)(D) by striking "foreign trade income of a FSC or" following "which is". **Effective** 12-29-2007.

• **1997, Taxpayer Relief Act of 1997 (P.L. 105-34)**

P.L. 105-34, §1122(d)(4):

Repealed Code Sec. 1297(b)(3), as redesignated by Act Sec. 1122(a). **Effective** for tax years of United States persons beginning after 12-31-97, and to tax years of foreign corporations ending with or within such tax years of United States persons. Prior to repeal, Code Sec. 1297(b)(3) read as follows:

(3) TREATMENT OF CERTAIN DEALERS IN SECURITIES.—

(A) IN GENERAL.—In the case of any foreign corporation which is a controlled foreign corporation (as defined in section 957(a)), the term "passive income" does not include any income derived in the active conduct of a securities business by such corporation if such corporation is registered as a securities broker or dealer under section 15(a) of the Securities Exchange Act of 1934 or is registered as a Government securities broker or dealer under section 15C(a) of such Act. To the extent provided in regulations, such term shall not include any income derived in the active conduct of a securities business by a controlled foreign corporation which is not so registered.

(B) APPLICATION OF LOOK-THRU RULES.—For purposes of paragraph (2)(C), rules similar to the rules of subparagraph (A) of this paragraph shall apply in determining whether any income of a related person (whether or not a corporation) is passive income.

(C) LIMITATION.—The preceding provisions of this paragraph shall only apply in the case of persons who are United States shareholders (as defined in section 951(b)) in the controlled foreign corporation.

• **1996, Small Business Job Protection Act of 1996 (P.L. 104-188)**

P.L. 104-188, §1704(r)(1):

Amended Code Sec. 1296(b)(2) by striking "or" at the end of subparagraph (B), by striking the period at the end of subparagraph (C) and inserting ", or", and by inserting after subparagraph (C) a new subparagraph (D). **Effective** as if included in the amendments made by section 1235 of P.L. 99-514.

• **1993, Omnibus Budget Reconciliation Act of 1993 (P.L. 103-66)**

P.L. 103-66, §13231(d)(3):

Amended Code Sec. 1296(b) by adding at the end thereof new paragraph (3). **Effective** for tax years of foreign corporations beginning after 9-30-93, and to tax years of United States shareholders in which or with which such tax years of foreign corporations end.

• **1988, Technical and Miscellaneous Revenue Act of 1988 (P.L. 100-647)**

P.L. 100-647, §1012(p)(5):

Amended Code Sec. 1296(b)(1). **Effective** as if included in the provision of P.L. 99-514 to which it relates. Prior to amendment, Code Sec. 1296(b)(1) read as follows:

(1) IN GENERAL.—Except as provided in paragraph (2), the term "passive income" has the meaning given such term by section 904(d)(2)(A) without regard to the exceptions contained in clause (iii) thereof.

P.L. 100-647, §1012(p)(16):

Amended Code Sec. 1296(b)(2)(B) by striking out "by a corporation which" and inserting in lieu thereof "by a corporation which is predominantly engaged in an insurance business and which". **Effective** as if included in the provision of P.L. 99-514 to which it relates.

P.L. 100-647, §1012(p)(26)(A):

Amended Code Sec. 1296(b)(2) by striking out "or" at the end of subparagraph (A), by striking out the period at the end of subparagraph (B) and inserting in lieu thereof ", or", and by adding at the end thereof a new subparagraph (C) and a new sentence. **Effective** as if included in the provision of P.L. 99-514 to which it relates.

P.L. 100-647, §1012(p)(26)(B):

Amended the paragraph heading for Code Sec. 1296(b)(2) by striking out "EXCEPTION FOR CERTAIN BANKS AND INSURANCE COMPANIES" and inserting in lieu thereof "EXCEPTIONS". **E ffective** as if included in the provision of P.L. 99-514 to which it relates.

[Sec. 1297(c)]

(c) LOOK-THRU IN THE CASE OF 25-PERCENT OWNED CORPORATIONS.—If a foreign corporation owns (directly or indirectly) at least 25 percent (by value) of the stock of another corporation, for purposes of determining whether such foreign corporation is a passive foreign investment company, such foreign corporation shall be treated as if it—

(1) held its proportionate share of the assets of such other corporation, and

(2) received directly its proportionate share of the income of such other corporation.

Amendments

• **1988, Technical and Miscellaneous Revenue Act of 1988 (P.L. 100-647)**

P.L. 100-647, §1012(p)(2):

Amended Code Sec. 1296(c) by striking out "owns at least" and inserting in lieu thereof "owns (directly or indirectly) at least". **Effective** as if included in the provision of P.L. 99-514 to which it relates.

INCOME TAX—GENERAL PROVISIONS

[Sec. 1297(d)—Stricken]

Amendments

• **2007, Tax Technical Corrections Act of 2007 (P.L. 110-172)**

P.L. 110-172, §11(a)(24)(A):

Amended Code Sec. 1297 by striking subsection (d) and by redesignating subsections (e) and (f) as subsections (d) and (e), respectively. **Effective** 12-29-2007. Prior to being stricken, Code Sec. 1297(d) read as follows:

(d) SECTION 1247 CORPORATIONS.—For purposes of this part, the term "passive foreign investment company" does not include any foreign investment company to which section 1247 applies.

• **1986, Tax Reform Act of 1986 (P.L. 99-514)**

P.L. 99-514, §1235(a):

Added Code Sec. 1296. **Effective** for tax years of foreign corporations beginning after 12-31-86.

[Sec. 1297(d)]

(d) EXCEPTION FOR UNITED STATES SHAREHOLDERS OF CONTROLLED FOREIGN CORPORATIONS.—

(1) IN GENERAL.—For purposes of this part, a corporation shall not be treated with respect to a shareholder as a passive foreign investment company during the qualified portion of such shareholder's holding period with respect to stock in such corporation.

(2) QUALIFIED PORTION.—For purposes of this subsection, the term "qualified portion" means the portion of the shareholder's holding period—

(A) which is after December 31, 1997, and

(B) during which the shareholder is a United States shareholder (as defined in section 951(b)) of the corporation and the corporation is a controlled foreign corporation.

(3) NEW HOLDING PERIOD IF QUALIFIED PORTION ENDS.—

(A) IN GENERAL.—Except as provided in subparagraph (B), if the qualified portion of a shareholder's holding period with respect to any stock ends after December 31, 1997, solely for purposes of this part, the shareholder's holding period with respect to such stock shall be treated as beginning as of the first day following such period.

(B) EXCEPTION.—Subparagraph (A) shall not apply if such stock was, with respect to such shareholder, stock in a passive foreign investment company at any time before the qualified portion of the shareholder's holding period with respect to such stock and no election under section 1298(b)(1) is made.

(4) TREATMENT OF HOLDERS OF OPTIONS.—Paragraph (1) shall not apply to stock treated as owned by a person by reason of section 1298(a)(4) (relating to the treatment of a person that has an option to acquire stock as owning such stock) unless such person establishes that such stock is owned (within the meaning of section 958(a)) by a United States shareholder (as defined in section 951(b)) who is not exempt from tax under this chapter.

Amendments

• **2007, Tax Technical Corrections Act of 2007 (P.L. 110-172)**

P.L. 110-172, §11(a)(24)(A):

Amended Code Sec. 1297 by redesignating subsection (e) as subsection (d). **Effective** 12-29-2007.

• **1998, IRS Restructuring and Reform Act of 1998 (P.L. 105-206)**

P.L. 105-206, §6011(b)(1):

Amended Code Sec. 1297(e) by adding at the end a new paragraph (4). **Effective** as if included in the provision of P.L. 105-34 to which it relates [**effective** for tax years of U.S. persons beginning after 12-31-97 and tax years of foreign corporations ending with or within such tax years of U.S. persons.—CCH].

• **1997, Taxpayer Relief Act of 1997 (P.L. 105-34)**

P.L. 105-34, §1121:

Amended Code Sec. 1296, prior to redesignation by Act Sec. 1122(a), by adding at the end a new subsection (e). **Effective** for tax years of United States persons beginning after 12-31-97, and to tax years of foreign corporations ending with or within such tax years of United States persons.

[Sec. 1297(e)]

(e) METHODS FOR MEASURING ASSETS.—

(1) DETERMINATION USING VALUE.—The determination under subsection (a)(2) shall be made on the basis of the value of the assets of a foreign corporation if—

(A) such corporation is a publicly traded corporation for the taxable year, or

(B) paragraph (2) does not apply to such corporation for the taxable year.

(2) DETERMINATION USING ADJUSTED BASES.—The determination under subsection (a)(2) shall be based on the adjusted bases (as determined for the purposes of computing earnings and profits) of the assets of a foreign corporation if such corporation is not described in paragraph (1)(A) and such corporation—

(A) is a controlled foreign corporation, or

(B) elects the application of this paragraph.

An election under subparagraph (B), once made, may be revoked only with the consent of the Secretary.

(3) PUBLICLY TRADED CORPORATION.—For purposes of this subsection, a foreign corporation shall be treated as a publicly traded corporation if the stock in the corporation is regularly traded on—

(A) a national securities exchange which is registered with the Securities and Exchange Commission or the national market system established pursuant to section 11A of the Securities and Exchange Act of 1934, or

(B) any exchange or other market which the Secretary determines has rules adequate to carry out the purposes of this subsection.

Amendments

• **2007, Tax Technical Corrections Act of 2007 (P.L. 110-172)**

P.L. 110-172, §11(a)(24)(A):

Amended Code Sec. 1297 by redesignating subsection (f) as subsection (e). **Effective** 12-29-2007.

• **1998, IRS Restructuring and Reform Act of 1998 (P.L. 105-206)**

P.L. 105-206, §6011(d):

Amended Code Sec. 1297 by redesignating subsection (e), as added by Act Sec. 1123 of P.L. 105-34, as subsection (f). **Effective** as if included in the provision of P.L. 105-34 to which it relates [**effective** for tax years of U.S. persons beginning after 12-31-97 and tax years of foreign corporations ending with or within such tax years of U.S. persons.—CCH].

• **1997, Taxpayer Relief Act of 1997 (P.L. 105-34)**

P.L. 105-34, §1123(a):

Amended Code Sec. 1297, as redesignated by Act Sec. 1122(a), by adding at the end a new subsection (e)[(f)]. **Effective** for tax years of United States persons beginning after 12-31-97, and for tax years of foreign corporations ending with or within such tax years of United States persons.

[Sec. 1297(f)]

(f) QUALIFYING INSURANCE CORPORATION.—For purposes of subsection (b)(2)(B)—

(1) IN GENERAL.—The term "qualifying insurance corporation" means, with respect to any taxable year, a foreign corporation—

(A) which would be subject to tax under subchapter L if such corporation were a domestic corporation, and

(B) the applicable insurance liabilities of which constitute more than 25 percent of its total assets, determined on the basis of such liabilities and assets as reported on the corporation's applicable financial statement for the last year ending with or within the taxable year.

INCOME TAX—GENERAL PROVISIONS

(2) ALTERNATIVE FACTS AND CIRCUMSTANCES TEST FOR CERTAIN CORPORATIONS.—If a corporation fails to qualify as a qualified insurance corporation under paragraph (1) solely because the percentage determined under paragraph (1)(B) is 25 percent or less, a United States person that owns stock in such corporation may elect to treat such stock as stock of a qualifying insurance corporation if—

    (A) the percentage so determined for the corporation is at least 10 percent, and

    (B) under regulations provided by the Secretary, based on the applicable facts and circumstances—

        (i) the corporation is predominantly engaged in an insurance business, and

        (ii) such failure is due solely to runoff-related or rating-related circumstances involving such insurance business.

(3) APPLICABLE INSURANCE LIABILITIES.—For purposes of this subsection—

    (A) IN GENERAL.—The term "applicable insurance liabilities" means, with respect to any life or property and casualty insurance business—

        (i) loss and loss adjustment expenses, and

        (ii) reserves (other than deficiency, contingency, or unearned premium reserves) for life and health insurance risks and life and health insurance claims with respect to contracts providing coverage for mortality or morbidity risks.

    (B) LIMITATIONS ON AMOUNT OF LIABILITIES.—Any amount determined under clause (i) or (ii) of subparagraph (A) shall not exceed the lesser of such amount—

        (i) as reported to the applicable insurance regulatory body in the applicable financial statement described in paragraph (4)(A) (or, if less, the amount required by applicable law or regulation), or

        (ii) as determined under regulations prescribed by the Secretary.

(4) OTHER DEFINITIONS AND RULES.—For purposes of this subsection—

    (A) APPLICABLE FINANCIAL STATEMENT.—The term "applicable financial statement" means a statement for financial reporting purposes which—

        (i) is made on the basis of generally accepted accounting principles,

        (ii) is made on the basis of international financial reporting standards, but only if there is no statement that meets the requirement of clause (i), or

        (iii) except as otherwise provided by the Secretary in regulations, is the annual statement which is required to be filed with the applicable insurance regulatory body, but only if there is no statement which meets the requirements of clause (i) or (ii).

    (B) APPLICABLE INSURANCE REGULATORY BODY.—The term "applicable insurance regulatory body" means, with respect to any insurance business, the entity established by law to license, authorize, or regulate such business and to which the statement described in subparagraph (A) is provided.

Amendments

• **2017, Tax Cuts and Jobs Act (P.L. 115-97)**

P.L. 115-97, § 14501(b):

Amended Code Sec. 1297 by adding at the end a new subsection (f). **Effective** for tax years beginning after 12-31-2017.

[Sec. 1298]

SEC. 1298. SPECIAL RULES.

[Sec. 1298(a)]

(a) ATTRIBUTION OF OWNERSHIP.—For purposes of this part—

(1) ATTRIBUTION TO UNITED STATES PERSONS.—This subsection—

    (A) shall apply to the extent that the effect is to treat stock of a passive foreign investment company as owned by a United States person, and

    (B) except to the extent provided in regulations, shall not apply to treat stock owned (or treated as owned under this subsection) by a United States person as owned by any other person.

(2) CORPORATIONS.—

    (A) IN GENERAL.—If 50 percent or more in value of the stock of a corporation is owned, directly or indirectly, by or for any person, such person shall be considered as owning the stock owned directly or indirectly by or for such corporation in that proportion which the value of the stock which such person so owns bears to the value of all stock in the corporation.

    (B) 50-PERCENT LIMITATION NOT TO APPLY TO PFIC.—For purposes of determining whether a shareholder of a passive foreign investment company is treated as owning stock owned directly or indirectly by or for such company, subparagraph (A) shall be applied without regard to the 50-percent limitation contained therein. Section 1297(d) shall not apply in determining whether a corporation is a passive foreign investment company for purposes of this subparagraph.

(3) PARTNERSHIPS, ETC.—Stock owned, directly or indirectly, by or for a partnership, estate, or trust shall be considered as being owned proportionately by its partners or beneficiaries.

(4) OPTIONS.—To the extent provided in regulations, if any person has an option to acquire stock, such stock shall be considered as owned by such person. For purposes of this paragraph, an option to acquire such an option, and each one of a series of such options, shall be considered as an option to acquire such stock.

(5) SUCCESSIVE APPLICATION.—Stock considered to be owned by a person by reason of the application of paragraph (2), (3), or (4) shall, for purposes of applying such paragraphs, be considered as actually owned by such person.

Amendments

• **2007, Tax Technical Corrections Act of 2007 (P.L. 110-172)**

P.L. 110-172, § 11(a)(24)(C):

Amended Code Sec. 1298(a)(2)(B) by striking "Section 1297(e)" and inserting "Section 1297(d)". **Effective** 12-29-2007.

• **1998, IRS Restructuring and Reform Act of 1998 (P.L. 105-206)**

P.L. 105-206, § 6011(b)(2):

Amended Code Sec. 1298(a)(2)(B) by adding at the end a new sentence. **Effective** as if included in the provision of P.L. 105-34 to which it relates [**effective** for tax years of U.S. persons beginning after 12-31-97 and tax years of foreign corporations ending with or within such tax years of U.S. persons.—CCH].

• **1997, Taxpayer Relief Act of 1997 (P.L. 105-34)**

P.L. 105-34, § 1122(a):

Redesignated Code Sec. 1297 as Code Sec. 1298. **Effective** for tax years of United States persons beginning after 12-31-97, and to tax years of foreign corporations ending with or within such tax years of United States persons.

• **1988, Technical and Miscellaneous Revenue Act of 1988 (P.L. 100-647)**

P.L. 100-647, § 1012(p)(10)(A):

Amended Code Sec. 1297(a) by redesignating paragraph (4) as paragraph (5) and by inserting after paragraph (3) new paragraph (4). **Effective** as if included in the provision of P.L. 99-514 to which it relates.

P.L. 100-647, §1012(p)(10)(B):

Amended Code Sec. 1297(a)(5) (as redesignated by Act Sec. 112(p)(10)(A)) by striking out "paragraph (2) or (3)" and inserting in lieu thereof "paragraph (2), (3), or (4)". **Effective** as if included in the provision of P.L. 99-514 to which it relates.

[Sec. 1298(b)]

(b) OTHER SPECIAL RULES.—For purposes of this part—

(1) TIME FOR DETERMINATION.—Stock held by a taxpayer shall be treated as stock in a passive foreign investment company if, at any time during the holding period of the taxpayer with respect to such stock, such corporation (or any predecessor) was a passive foreign investment company which was not a qualified electing fund. The preceding sentence shall not apply if the taxpayer elects to recognize gain (as of the last day of the last taxable year for which the company was a passive foreign investment company (determined without regard to the preceding sentence)) under rules similar to the rules of section 1291(d)(2).

(2) CERTAIN CORPORATIONS NOT TREATED AS PFIC'S DURING START-UP YEAR.—A corporation shall not be treated as a passive foreign investment company for the first taxable year such corporation has gross income (hereinafter in this paragraph referred to as the "start-up year") if—

   (A) no predecessor of such corporation was a passive foreign investment company,

   (B) it is established to the satisfaction of the Secretary that such corporation will not be a passive foreign investment company for either of the 1st 2 taxable years following the start-up year, and

   (C) such corporation is not a passive foreign investment company for either of the 1st 2 taxable years following the start-up year.

(3) CERTAIN CORPORATIONS CHANGING BUSINESSES.—A corporation shall not be treated as a passive foreign investment company for any taxable year if—

   (A) neither such corporation (nor any predecessor) was a passive foreign investment company for any prior taxable year,

   (B) it is established to the satisfaction of the Secretary that—

      (i) substantially all of the passive income of the corporation for the taxable year is attributable to proceeds from the disposition of 1 or more active trades or businesses, and

      (ii) such corporation will not be a passive foreign investment company for either of the 1st 2 taxable years following such taxable year, and

   (C) such corporation is not a passive foreign investment company for either of such 2 taxable years.

(4) SEPARATE INTERESTS TREATED AS SEPARATE CORPORATIONS.—Under regulations prescribed by the Secretary, where necessary to carry out the purposes of this part, separate classes of stock (or other interests) in a corporation shall be treated as interests in separate corporations.

(5) APPLICATION OF PART WHERE STOCK HELD BY OTHER ENTITY.—

   (A) IN GENERAL.—Under regulations, in any case in which a United States person is treated as owning stock in a passive foreign investment company by reason of subsection (a)—

      (i) any disposition by the United States person or the person owning such stock which results in the United States person being treated as no longer owning such stock, or

      (ii) any distribution of property in respect of such stock to the person holding such stock,

shall be treated as a disposition by, or distribution to, the United States person with respect to the stock in the passive foreign investment company.

   (B) AMOUNT TREATED IN SAME MANNER AS PREVIOUSLY TAXED INCOME.—Rules similar to the rules of section 959(b) shall apply to any amount described in subparagraph (A) and to any amount included in gross income under section 1293(a) (or which would have been so included but for section 951(c)) in respect of stock which the taxpayer is treated as owning under subsection (a).

(6) DISPOSITIONS.—Except as provided in regulations, if a taxpayer uses any stock in a passive foreign investment company as security for a loan, the taxpayer shall be treated as having disposed of such stock.

(7) TREATMENT OF CERTAIN FOREIGN CORPORATIONS OWNING STOCK IN 25-PERCENT OWNED DOMESTIC CORPORATION.—

   (A) IN GENERAL.—If—

      (i) a foreign corporation is subject to the tax imposed by section 531 (or waives any benefit under any treaty which would otherwise prevent the imposition of such tax), and

      (ii) such foreign corporation owns at least 25 percent (by value) of the stock of a domestic corporation,

for purposes of determining whether such foreign corporation is a passive foreign investment company, any qualified stock held by such domestic corporation shall be treated as an asset which does not produce passive income (and is not held for the production of passive income) and any amount included in gross income with respect to such stock shall not be treated as passive income.

   (B) QUALIFIED STOCK.—For purposes of subparagraph (A), the term "qualified stock" means any stock in a C corporation which is a domestic corporation and which is not a regulated investment company or real estate investment trust.

(8) TREATMENT OF CERTAIN SUBPART F INCLUSIONS.—Any amount included in gross income under section 951(a)(1)(B) shall be treated as a distribution received with respect to the stock.

Amendments

- **2018, Tax Technical Corrections Act of 2018 (P.L. 115-141)**

P.L. 115-141, §401(a)(184), Div. U:

Amended Code Sec. 1298(b)(5)(B) by striking "section 951(f)" and inserting "section 951(c)". **Effective** 3-23-2018.

- **2007, Tax Technical Corrections Act of 2007 (P.L. 110-172)**

P.L. 110-172, §11(f)(2):

Amended Code Sec. 1298(b) by striking paragraph (7) and by redesignating paragraphs (8) and (9) as paragraphs (7) and (8), respectively. **Effective** as if included in the provision of the American Jobs Creation Act of 2004 (P.L. 108-357) to which it applies [**effective** for tax years of foreign corporations beginning after 12-31-2004, and to tax years of United States shareholders with or within which such tax years of foreign corporations end.—CCH]. Prior to being stricken, Code Sec. 1298(b)(7) read as follows:

(7) COORDINATION WITH SECTION 1246.—Section 1246 shall not apply to earnings and profits of any company for any taxable year beginning after December 31, 1986, if such company is a passive foreign investment company for such taxable year.

- **1997, Taxpayer Relief Act of 1997 (P.L. 105-34)**

P.L. 105-34, §1122(e):

Amended Code Sec. 1298(b)(1), as redesignated by Act Sec. 1122(a), by inserting "(determined without regard to the preceding sentence)" after "investment company" in the last sentence. **Effective** for tax years of United States persons beginning after 12-31-97, and tax years of foreign corporations ending with or within such tax years of United States persons.

- **1996, Small Business Job Protection Act of 1996 (P.L. 104-188)**

P.L. 104-188, §1501(b)(10):

Amended Code Sec. 1297(b)(9) by striking "subparagraph (B) or (C) of section 951(a)(1)" and inserting "section 951(a)(1)(B)". **Effective** for tax years of foreign corporations beginning after 12-31-96, and to tax years of United States shareholders within which or with which such tax years of foreign corporations end.

INCOME TAX—GENERAL PROVISIONS

- **1993, Omnibus Budget Reconciliation Act of 1993 (P.L. 103-66)**

P.L. 103-66, § 13231(d)(2):

Amended Code Sec. 1297(b) by adding at the end thereof new paragraph (9). **Effective** for tax years of foreign corporations beginning after 9-30-93, and to tax years of United States shareholders in which or with which such tax years of foreign corporations end.

- **1989, Omnibus Budget Reconciliation Act of 1989 (P.L. 101-239)**

P.L. 101-239, § 7811(i)(4)(A)-(C):

Amended Code Sec. 1297(b) by inserting "stock" after "where" in the paragraph heading, by striking "any disposition of" in subparagraph (A)(ii) and inserting "any distribution of", and by striking "treated as a disposition to" in subparagraph (A) and inserting "treated as a disposition by, or distribution to". **Effective** as if included in the provision of P.L. 100-647 to which it relates.

- **1988, Technical and Miscellaneous Revenue Act of 1988 (P.L. 100-647)**

P.L. 100-647, § 1012(p)(17):

Amended Code Sec. 1297(b)(5). **Effective** as if included in the provision of P.L. 99-514 to which it relates. Prior to amendment, Code Sec. 1297(b)(5) read as follows:

(5) APPLICATION OF SECTION WHERE STOCK HELD BY OTHER ENTITY.—Under regulations, in any case in which a United States person is treated as holding stock in a passive foreign investment company by reason of subsection (a), any disposition by the United States person or the person holding such stock which results in the United States person being treated as no longer holding such stock, shall be treated as a disposition by the United States person with respect to stock in the passive foreign investment company.

P.L. 100-647, § 1012(p)(20):

Amended Code Sec. 1297(b)(6) by striking out "If a" and inserting in lieu thereof "Except as provided in regulations, if a". **Effective** as if included in the provision of P.L. 99-514 to which it relates.

P.L. 100-647, § 1012(p)(22):

Amended Code Sec. 1297(b)(3)(A). **Effective** as if included in the provision of P.L. 99-514 to which it relates. Prior to amendment, Code Sec. 1297(b)(3)(A) read as follows:

(A) such corporation (and any predecessor) was not a passive foreign investment corporation for any prior taxable year,

P.L. 100-647, § 1012(p)(24):

Amended Code Sec. 1297(b) by adding at the end thereof new paragraph (8). **Effective** as if included in the provision of P.L. 99-514 to which it relates.

P.L. 100-647, § 1012(p)(36):

Amended Code Sec. 1297(b)(1) by striking out "passive foreign investment corporation" and inserting in lieu thereof "passive foreign investment company". **Effective** as if included in the provision of P.L. 99-514 to which it relates.

[Sec. 1298(c)]

(c) TREATMENT OF STOCK HELD BY POOLED INCOME FUND.—If stock in a passive foreign investment company is owned (or treated as owned under subsection (a)) by a pooled income fund (as defined in section 642(c)(5)) and no portion of any gain from a disposition of such stock may be allocated to income under the terms of the governing instrument of such fund—

(1) section 1291 shall not apply to any gain on a disposition of such stock by such fund if (without regard to section 1291) a deduction would be allowable with respect to such gain under section 642(c)(3),

(2) section 1293 shall not apply with respect to such stock, and

(3) in determining whether section 1291 applies to any distribution in respect of such stock, subsection (d) of section 1291 shall not apply.

Amendments

- **1988, Technical and Miscellaneous Revenue Act of 1988 (P.L. 100-647)**

P.L. 100-647, § 1012(p)(35):

Amended Code Sec. 1297 by redesignating subsection (c) as subsection (d) and inserting after subsection (b) new subsection (c). **Effective** as if included in the provision of P.L. 99-514 to which it relates.

[Sec. 1298(d)]

(d) TREATMENT OF CERTAIN LEASED PROPERTY.—For purposes of this part—

(1) IN GENERAL.—Any tangible personal property with respect to which a foreign corporation is the lessee under a lease with a term of at least 12 months shall be treated as an asset actually held by such corporation.

(2) AMOUNT TAKEN INTO ACCOUNT.—

(A) IN GENERAL.—The amount taken into account under section 1297(a)(2) with respect to any asset to which paragraph (1) applies shall be the unamortized portion (as determined under regulations prescribed by the Secretary) of the present value of the payments under the lease for the use of such property.

(B) PRESENT VALUE.—For purposes of subparagraph (A), the present value of payments described in subparagraph (A) shall be determined in the manner provided in regulations prescribed by the Secretary—

(i) as of the beginning of the lease term, and

(ii) except as provided in such regulations, by using a discount rate equal to the applicable Federal rate determined under section 1274(d)—

(I) by substituting the lease term for the term of the debt instrument, and

(II) without regard to paragraph (2) or (3) thereof.

(3) EXCEPTIONS.—This subsection shall not apply in any case where—

(A) the lessor is a related person (as defined in section 954(d)(3)) with respect to the foreign corporation, or

(B) a principal purpose of leasing the property was to avoid the provisions of this part.

Amendments

- **2018, Tax Technical Corrections Act of 2018 (P.L. 115-141)**

P.L. 115-141, § 401(a)(185), Div. U:

Amended Code Sec. 1298(d)(2)(A) by striking "section 1296(a)(2)" and inserting "section 1297(a)(2)". **Effective** 3-23-2018.

- **1996, Small Business Job Protection Act of 1996 (P.L. 104-188)**

P.L. 104-188, § 1501(b)(11):

Amended Code Sec. 1297(d)(3)(B) by striking "or section 956A" before the period. **Effective** for tax years of foreign corporations beginning after 12-31-96, and to tax years of United States shareholders within which or with which such tax years of foreign corporations end.

P.L. 104-188, § 1703(i)(5)(A):

Amended Code Sec. 1297(d)(2)(A) by striking "The adjusted basis of any asset" and inserting "The amount taken into account under section 1296(a)(2) with respect to any asset". **Effective** as if included in the provision of P.L. 103-66 to which it relates.

P.L. 104-188, § 1703(i)(5)(B):

Amended the paragraph heading of Code Sec. 1297(d)(2). **Effective** as if included in the provision of P.L. 103-66 to which it relates. Prior to amendment, the paragraph heading of Code Sec. 1297(d)(2) read as follows:

(2) DETERMINATION OF ADJUSTED BASIS.—

- **1993, Omnibus Budget Reconciliation Act of 1993 (P.L. 103-66)**

P.L. 103-66, § 13231(d)(4):

Amended Code Sec. 1297 by redesignating subsection (d) as subsection (f) and by inserting after subsection (c) new subsection (d). **Effective** for tax years of foreign corporations beginning after 9-30-93, and to tax years of United States shareholders in which or with which such tax years of foreign corporations end.

[Sec. 1298(e)]

(e) SPECIAL RULES FOR CERTAIN INTANGIBLES.—For purposes of this part—

(1) RESEARCH EXPENDITURES.—The adjusted basis of the total assets of a controlled foreign corporation shall be increased by the research or experimental expenditures (within the meaning of section 174) paid or incurred by such foreign corporation during the taxable year and the preceding 2 taxable years. Any expenditure otherwise taken into account under the preceding sentence shall be reduced by the amount of any reimbursement received by the controlled foreign corporation with respect to such expenditure.

INCOME TAX—GENERAL PROVISIONS

(2) CERTAIN LICENSED INTANGIBLES.—

(A) IN GENERAL.—In the case of any intangible property (as defined in section 367(d)(4)) with respect to which a controlled foreign corporation is a licensee and which is used by such foreign corporation in the active conduct of a trade or business, the adjusted basis of the total assets of such foreign corporation shall be increased by an amount equal to 300 percent of the payments made during the taxable year by such foreign corporation for the use of such intangible property.

(B) EXCEPTIONS.—Subparagraph (A) shall not apply to—

(i) any payments to a foreign person if such foreign person is a related person (as defined in section 954(d)(3)) with respect to the controlled foreign corporation, and

(ii) any payments under a license if a principal purpose of entering into such license was to avoid the provisions of this part.

(3) CONTROLLED FOREIGN CORPORATION.—For purposes of this subsection, the term "controlled foreign corporation" has the meaning given such term by section 957(a).

Amendments

• **2018, Tax Technical Corrections Act of 2018 (P.L. 115-141)**

P.L. 115-141, §401(a)(186), Div. U:

Amended Code Sec. 1298(e)(2)(B)(ii) by striking "provisons" and inserting "provisions". **Effective** 3-23-2018.

P.L. 115-141, §401(d)(1)(D)(viii)(III), Div. U:

Amended Code Sec. 1298(e)(2)(A) by striking "section 936(h)(3)(B)" and inserting "section 367(d)(4)". **Effective** 3-23-2018. For a special rule, see Act Sec. 401(e), Div. U, below.

P.L. 115-141, §401(e), Div. U, provides:

(e) GENERAL SAVINGS PROVISION WITH RESPECT TO DEADWOOD PROVISIONS.—If—

(1) any provision amended or repealed by the amendments made by subsection (b) or (d) applied to—

(A) any transaction occurring before the date of the enactment of this Act,

(B) any property acquired before such date of enactment, or

(C) any item of income, loss, deduction, or credit taken into account before such date of enactment, and

(2) the treatment of such transaction, property, or item under such provision would (without regard to the amendments or repeals made by such subsection) affect the liability for tax for periods ending after such date of enactment,

nothing in the amendments or repeals made by this section shall be construed to affect the treatment of such transaction, property, or item for purposes of determining liability for tax for periods ending after such date of enactment.

• **1996, Small Business Job Protection Act of 1996 (P.L. 104-188)**

P.L. 104-188, §1501(b)(11):

Amended Code Sec. 1297(e)(2)(B)(ii) by striking "or section 956A" before the period. **Effective** for tax years of foreign corporations beginning after 12-31-96, and to tax years of United States shareholders within which or with which such tax years of foreign corporations end.

P.L. 104-188, §1703(i)(6):

Amended Code Sec. 1297(e) by inserting "For purposes of this part—" after the subsection heading. **Effective** as if included in the provision of P.L. 103-66 to which it relates.

• **1993, Omnibus Budget Reconciliation Act of 1993 (P.L. 103-66)**

P.L. 103-66, §13231(d)(4):

Amended Code Sec. 1297 by redesignating subsection (d) as subsection (f) and adding after subsection (c) new subsections (d) and (e). **Effective** for tax years of foreign corporations beginning after 9-30-93, and to tax years of United States shareholders in which or with which such tax years of foreign corporations end.

[Sec. 1298(f)]

(f) REPORTING REQUIREMENT.—Except as otherwise provided by the Secretary, each United States person who is a shareholder of a passive foreign investment company shall file an annual report containing such information as the Secretary may require.

Amendments

• **2010, Hiring Incentives to Restore Employment Act (P.L. 111-147)**

P.L. 111-147, §521(a):

Amended Code Sec. 1298 by redesignating subsection (f) as subsection (g) and by inserting after subsection (e) a new subsection (f). **Effective** 3-18-2010.

[Sec. 1298(g)]

(g) REGULATIONS.—The Secretary shall prescribe such regulations as may be necessary or appropriate to carry out the purposes of this part.

Amendments

• **2010, Hiring Incentives to Restore Employment Act (P.L. 111-147)**

P.L. 111-147, §521(a):

Amended Code Sec. 1298 by redesignating subsection (f) as subsection (g). **Effective** 3-18-2010.

• **1997, Taxpayer Relief Act of 1997 (P.L. 105-34)**

P.L. 105-34, §1122(a):

Redesignated Code Sec. 1297 as Code Sec. 1298. **Effective** for tax years of United States persons beginning after 12-31-97, and to tax years of foreign corporations ending with or within such tax years of United States persons.

• **1993, Omnibus Budget Reconciliation Act of 1993 (P.L. 103-66)**

P.L. 103-66, §13231(d)(4):

Amended Code Sec. 1297 by redesignating subsection (d) as subsection (f). **Effective** for tax years of foreign corporations beginning after 9-30-93, and to tax years of United States shareholders in which or with which such tax years of foreign corporations end.

• **1988, Technical and Miscellaneous Revenue Act of 1988 (P.L. 100-647)**

P.L. 100-647, §1012(p)(35):

Amended Code Sec. 1297 by redesignating subsection (c) as subsection (d). **Effective** as if included in the provision of P.L. 99-514 to which it relates.

• **1986, Tax Reform Act of 1986 (P.L. 99-514)**

P.L. 99-514, §1235(a):

Added Code Sec. 1297. **Effective** for tax years of foreign corporations beginning after 12-31-86.

Subchapter Q—Readjustment of Tax Between Years and Special Limitations

Part I.	Income averaging.
Part II.	Mitigation of effect of limitations and other provisions.
Part III.	[Repealed]
Part IV.	[Repealed]
Part V.	Claim of right.
Part VI.	[Repealed]
Part VII.	Recoveries of foreign expropriation losses.

PART I—INCOME AVERAGING

Sec. 1301.	Averaging of farm income.

INCOME TAX—INCOME AVERAGING

[Sec. 1301]

SEC. 1301. AVERAGING OF FARM INCOME.

[Sec. 1301(a)]

(a) IN GENERAL.—At the election of an individual engaged in a farming business or fishing business, the tax imposed by section 1 for such taxable year shall be equal to the sum of—

(1) a tax computed under such section on taxable income reduced by elected farm income, plus

(2) the increase in tax imposed by section 1 which would result if taxable income for each of the 3 prior taxable years were increased by an amount equal to one-third of the elected farm income.

Any adjustment under this section for any taxable year shall be taken into account in applying this section for any subsequent taxable year.

Amendments

• **2008, Tax Extenders and Alternative Minimum Tax Relief Act of 2008 (P.L. 110-343)**

P.L. 110-343, §504, provides:

SEC. 504. INCOME AVERAGING FOR AMOUNTS RECEIVED IN CONNECTION WITH THE EXXON VALDEZ LITIGATION.

(a) INCOME AVERAGING OF AMOUNTS RECEIVED FROM THE EXXON VALDEZ LITIGATION.—For purposes of section 1301 of the Internal Revenue Code of 1986—

(1) any qualified taxpayer who receives any qualified settlement income in any taxable year shall be treated as engaged in a fishing business (determined without regard to the commercial nature of the business), and

(2) such qualified settlement income shall be treated as income attributable to such a fishing business for such taxable year.

(b) CONTRIBUTIONS OF AMOUNTS RECEIVED TO RETIREMENT ACCOUNTS.—

(1) IN GENERAL.—Any qualified taxpayer who receives qualified settlement income during the taxable year may, at any time before the end of the taxable year in which such income was received, make one or more contributions to an eligible retirement plan of which such qualified taxpayer is a beneficiary in an aggregate amount not to exceed the lesser of—

(A) $100,000 (reduced by the amount of qualified settlement income contributed to an eligible retirement plan in prior taxable years pursuant to this subsection), or

(B) the amount of qualified settlement income received by the individual during the taxable year.

(2) TIME WHEN CONTRIBUTIONS DEEMED MADE.—For purposes of paragraph (1), a qualified taxpayer shall be deemed to have made a contribution to an eligible retirement plan on the last day of the taxable year in which such income is received if the contribution is made on account of such taxable year and is made not later than the time prescribed by law for filing the return for such taxable year (not including extensions thereof).

(3) TREATMENT OF CONTRIBUTIONS TO ELIGIBLE RETIREMENT PLANS.—For purposes of the Internal Revenue Code of 1986, if a contribution is made pursuant to paragraph (1) with respect to qualified settlement income, then—

(A) except as provided in paragraph (4)—

(i) to the extent of such contribution, the qualified settlement income shall not be included in taxable income, and

(ii) for purposes of section 72 of such Code, such contribution shall not be considered to be investment in the contract,

(B) the qualified taxpayer shall, to the extent of the amount of the contribution, be treated—

(i) as having received the qualified settlement income—

(I) in the case of a contribution to an individual retirement plan (as defined under section 7701(a)(37) of such Code), in a distribution described in section 408(d)(3) of such Code, and

(II) in the case of any other eligible retirement plan, in an eligible rollover distribution (as defined under section 402(f)(2) of such Code), and

(ii) as having transferred the amount to the eligible retirement plan in a direct trustee to trustee transfer within 60 days of the distribution,

(C) section 408(d)(3)(B) of the Internal Revenue Code of 1986 shall not apply with respect to amounts treated as a rollover under this paragraph, and

(D) section 408A(c)(3)(B) of the Internal Revenue Code of 1986 shall not apply with respect to amounts contributed to a Roth IRA (as defined under section 408A(b) of such Code) or a designated Roth contribution to an applicable retirement plan (within the meaning of section 402A of such Code) under this paragraph.

(4) SPECIAL RULE FOR ROTH IRAS AND ROTH 401(k)S.—For purposes of the Internal Revenue Code of 1986, if a contribution is made pursuant to paragraph (1) with respect to qualified settlement income to a Roth IRA (as defined under section 408A(b) of such Code) or as a designated Roth contribution to an applicable retirement plan (within the meaning of section 402A of such Code), then—

(A) the qualified settlement income shall be includible in taxable income, and

(B) for purposes of section 72 of such Code, such contribution shall be considered to be investment in the contract.

(5) ELIGIBLE RETIREMENT PLAN.—For purpose of this subsection, the term "eligible retirement plan" has the meaning given such term under section 402(c)(8)(B) of the Internal Revenue Code of 1986.

(c) TREATMENT OF QUALIFIED SETTLEMENT INCOME UNDER EMPLOYMENT TAXES.—

(1) SECA.—For purposes of chapter 2 of the Internal Revenue Code of 1986 and section 211 of the Social Security Act, no portion of qualified settlement income received by a qualified taxpayer shall be treated as self-employment income.

(2) FICA.—For purposes of chapter 21 of the Internal Revenue Code of 1986 and section 209 of the Social Security Act, no portion of qualified settlement income received by a qualified taxpayer shall be treated as wages.

(d) QUALIFIED TAXPAYER.—For purposes of this section, the term "qualified taxpayer" means—

(1) any individual who is a plaintiff in the civil action In re Exxon Valdez, No. 89-095-CV (HRH) (Consolidated) (D. Alaska); or

(2) any individual who is a beneficiary of the estate of such a plaintiff who—

(A) acquired the right to receive qualified settlement income from that plaintiff; and

(B) was the spouse or an immediate relative of that plaintiff.

(e) QUALIFIED SETTLEMENT INCOME.—For purposes of this section, the term "qualified settlement income" means any interest and punitive damage awards which are—

(1) otherwise includible in taxable income, and

(2) received (whether as lump sums or periodic payments) in connection with the civil action In re Exxon Valdez, No. 89-095-CV (HRH) (Consolidated) (D. Alaska) (whether pre- or post-judgment and whether related to a settlement or judgment).

• **2004, American Jobs Creation Act of 2004 (P.L. 108-357)**

P.L. 108-357, §314(b)(1):

Amended Code Sec. 1301(a) by striking "farming business" and inserting "farming business or fishing business". **Effective** for tax years beginning after 12-31-2003.

[Sec. 1301(b)]

(b) DEFINITIONS.—In this section—

(1) ELECTED FARM INCOME.—

(A) IN GENERAL.—The term "elected farm income" means so much of the taxable income for the taxable year—

(i) which is attributable to any farming business or fishing business; and

(ii) which is specified in the election under subsection (a).

(B) TREATMENT OF GAINS.—For purposes of subparagraph (A), gain from the sale or other disposition of property (other than land) regularly used by the taxpayer in such a farming business or fishing business for a substantial period shall be treated as attributable to such a farming business or fishing business.

(2) INDIVIDUAL.—The term "individual" shall not include any estate or trust.

(3) FARMING BUSINESS.—The term "farming business" has the meaning given such term by section 263A(e)(4).

(4) FISHING BUSINESS.—The term "fishing business" means the conduct of commercial fishing as defined in section 3 of the Magnuson-Stevens Fishery Conservation and Management Act (16 U.S.C. 1802).

Amendments

• **2004, American Jobs Creation Act of 2004 (P.L. 108-357)**

P.L. 108-357, §314(b)(2)(A):

Amended Code Sec. 1301(b)(1)(A)(i) by inserting "or fishing business" before the semicolon. **Effective** for tax years beginning after 12-31-2003.

P.L. 108-357, §314(b)(2)(B):

Amended Code Sec. 1301(b)(1)(B) by inserting "or fishing business" after "farming business" both places it occurs. **Effective** for tax years beginning after 12-31-2003.

P.L. 108-357, §314(b)(3):

Amended Code Sec. 1301(b) by adding at the end new paragraph (4). **Effective** for tax years beginning after 12-31-2003.

[Sec. 1301(c)]

(c) REGULATIONS.—The Secretary shall prescribe such regulations as may be appropriate to carry out the purposes of this section, including regulations regarding—

INCOME TAX—INCOME AVERAGING

(1) the order and manner in which items of income, gain, deduction, or loss, or limitations on tax, shall be taken into account in computing the tax imposed by this chapter on the income of any taxpayer to whom this section applies for any taxable year, and

(2) the treatment of any short taxable year.

Amendments

• **1997, Taxpayer Relief Act of 1997 (P.L. 105-34)**

P.L. 105-34, §933(a):

Amended subchapter Q of chapter 1 by adding a new part I (Code Sec. 1301). **Effective** for tax years beginning after 12-31-97 [effective date changed by P.L. 105-277, §2011.—CCH].

[Sec. 1301—Repealed]

Amendments

• **1986, Tax Reform Act of 1986 (P.L. 99-514)**

P.L. 99-514, §141(a):

Repealed Code Sec. 1301. **Effective** for tax years beginning after 12-31-86. Prior to repeal Code Sec. 1301 read as follows:

SEC. 1301. LIMITATION ON TAX.

If an eligible individual has averagable income for the computation year, and if the amount of such income exceeds $3,000, then the tax imposed by section 1 for the computation year which is attributable to averagable income shall be 4 times the increase in tax under such section which would result from adding 25 percent of such income to 140 percent of average base period income.

• **1984, Deficit Reduction Act of 1984 (P.L. 98-369)**

P.L. 98-369, §173(b):

Amended Code Sec. 1301 by striking out "120 percent" and inserting in lieu thereof "140 percent." **Effective** for computation years beginning after 12-31-83, and to base period years applicable to such computation years.

P.L. 98-369, §173(c)(1)(A):

Amended Code Sec. 1301 by striking out "5 times" and inserting in lieu thereof "4 times." **Effective** for computation years beginning after 12-31-83, and to base period years applicable to such computation years.

P.L. 98-369, §173(c)(1)(B):

Amended Code Sec. 1301 by striking out "20 percent" and inserting in lieu thereof "25 percent." **Effective** for computation years beginning after 12-31-83, and to base period years applicable to such computation years.

• **1969, Tax Reform Act of 1969 (P.L. 91-172)**

P.L. 91-172, §311(a):

Amended Code Sec. 1301 by substituting the phrase "20 percent of such income to 120 percent of average base period income." for "20 percent of such income to the sum of—

(1) 133$^1/_3$ percent of average base period income, and

(2) the amount (if any) of the average base period capital gain net income." **Effective** 1-1-70.

• **1964, Revenue Act of 1964 (P.L. 88-272)**

P.L. 88-272, §232(a):

Amended Code Sec. 1301. For text of Code Sec. 1301 and amendments prior to amendment by P.L. 88-272, see the comment following Code §1305. **Effective** with respect to tax years beginning after 12-31-63, except as provided in §232(g)(2) of P.L. 88-272, below.

P.L. 88-272, §232(g)(2), provides:

(2) Income from an employment.—If, in a taxable year beginning after December 31, 1963, an individual or partnership receives or accrues compensation for an employment (as defined by section 1301(b) of the Internal Revenue Code of 1954 as in effect immediately before the enactment of this Act) and the employment began before February 6, 1963, the tax attributable to such compensation may, at the election of the taxpayer, be computed under the provisions of sections 1301 and 1307 of such Code as in effect immediately before the enactment of this Act. If a taxpayer so elects (at such time and in such manner as the Secretary of the Treasury or his delegate by regulations prescribes), he may not choose for such taxable year the benefits provided by part I of subchapter Q of chapter 1 of such Code (relating to income averaging) as amended by this Act and (if he elects to have subsection (e) of such section 1307 apply) section 170(b)(5) of such Code as amended by this Act shall not apply to charitable contributions paid in such taxable year.

[Sec. 1302—Repealed]

Amendments

• **1986, Tax Reform Act of 1986 (P.L. 99-514)**

P.L. 99-514, §141(a):

Repealed Code Sec. 1302. **Effective** for tax years beginning after 12-31-86. Prior to repeal, Code Sec. 1302 read as follows:

SEC. 1302. DEFINITION OF AVERAGABLE INCOME; RELATED DEFINITIONS.

[Sec. 1302(a)]

(a) AVERAGABLE INCOME.—

(1) IN GENERAL.—For purposes of this part, the term "averagable income" means the amount by which taxable income for the computation year (reduced as provided in paragraph (2)) exceeds 140 percent of average base period income.

(2) REDUCTIONS.—The taxable income for the computation year shall be reduced by—

(A) the amount (if any) to which section 72(m)(5) or (q)(1) applies, and

(B) the amounts included in the income of a beneficiary of a trust under section 667(a).

Amendments

• **1984, Deficit Reduction Act of 1984 (P.L. 98-369)**

P.L. 98-369, §173(c)(2):

Amended Code Sec. 1302(a)(1) by striking out "120 percent" and inserting in lieu thereof "140 percent". **Effective** for computation years beginning after 12-31-83, and to base period years applicable to such computation years.

• **1982, Tax Equity and Fiscal Responsibility Act of 1982 (P.L. 97-248)**

P.L. 97-248, §265(b)(2)(B):

Amended Code Sec. 1302(a)(2)(A) by inserting "or (q)(1)" after "section 72(m)(5)". **Effective** for distributions after 12-31-82.

• **1976, Tax Reform Act of 1976 (P.L. 94-455)**

P.L. 94-455, §701(f)(1):

Substituted "667(a)" for "668(a)" in Code Sec. 1302(a)(2)(B). **Effective** for distributions made in tax years beginning after 12-31-75.

• **1969, Tax Reform Act of 1969 (P.L. 91-172)**

P.L. 91-172, §311(b):

Amended Code Sec. 1302(a). **Effective** for computation years beginning after 12-31-69 and to base period years applicable to such computation years. Prior to amendment, Code Sec. 1302(a) read as indicated in the historical note following former Code Sec. 1302(c).

• **1964, Revenue Act of 1964 (P.L. 88-272)**

P.L. 88-272, §232(a):

Amended Code Sec. 1302(a) to read as indicated in the historical note for P.L. 91-172, §311(b), following former Code Sec. 1302(c). **Effective** with respect to tax years beginning after 12-31-63, except as provided in P.L. 88-272, §232(g)(2) reproduced in the historical comment following Code Sec. 1301. For text of Code Sec. 1302 and amendments prior to P.L. 88-272, see the historical comment following former Code Sec. 1305.

[Sec. 1302(b)]

(b) AVERAGE BASE PERIOD INCOME.—For purposes of this part—

(1) IN GENERAL.—The term "average base period income" means $^1/_3$ of the sum of the base period incomes for the base period.

(2) BASE PERIOD INCOME.—The base period income for any taxable year is the taxable income for such year—

(A) increased by an amount equal to the excess of—

(i) the amount excluded from gross income under section 911 (relating to citizens or residents of the United States living abroad) and subpart D of part III of subchapter N (sec. 931 and following, relating to income from sources within possessions of the United States), over

(ii) the deductions which would have been properly allocable to or chargeable against such amount but for the exclusion of such amount from gross income; and

(B) decreased by the amounts included in the income of a beneficiary of a trust under section 667(a).

(3) TRANSITIONAL RULE FOR DETERMINING BASE PERIOD INCOME.—The base period income (determined under paragraph (2)) for any taxable year beginning before January 1, 1977, shall be increased by—

(A) $3,200 in the case of a joint return or a surviving spouse (as defined in section 2(a)),

(B) $2,200 in the case of an individual who is not married (within the meaning of section 143) and is not a surviving spouse (as so defined), or

(C) $1,600 in the case of a married individual (within the meaning of section 143) filing a separate return.

For purposes of this paragraph, filing status shall be determined as of the computation year.

INCOME TAX—INCOME AVERAGING

Amendments

- **1984, Deficit Reduction Act of 1984 (P.L. 98-369)**

P.L. 98-369, § 173(c)(3):

Amended Code Sec. 1302(b)(1) by striking out "one-fourth" and inserting in lieu thereof "$1/3$". **Effective** for computation years beginning after 12-31-83, and to base period years applicable to such computation years.

- **1981, Economic Recovery Tax Act of 1981 (P.L. 97-34)**

P.L. 97-34, § 111(b)(3):

Amended Code Sec. 1302(b)(2)(A)(i) by striking out "relating to income earned by employees in certain camps" and inserting in lieu thereof "relating to citizens or residents of the United States living abroad". **Effective** with respect to tax years beginning after 12-31-81.

- **1978, Tax Treatment Extension Act of 1978 (P.L. 95-615)**

P.L. 95-615, § 202(f)(5):

Amended Code Sec. 1302(b)(2)(A)(i) by striking out "relating to earned income from sources without the United States" and inserting in lieu thereof "relating to income earned by employees in certain camps". **Effective** for tax years beginning after 12-31-77.

- **1978, Revenue Act of 1978 (P.L. 95-600)**

P.L. 95-600, § 101(d)(2):

Amended Code Sec. 1302(b)(3). **Effective** for tax years beginning after 12-31-78. Prior to amendment, Code Sec. 1302(b)(3) read as follows:

"(3) TRANSITIONAL RULE FOR DETERMINING BASE PERIOD INCOME.—The base period income (determined under paragraph (2)) for any taxable year beginning before January 1, 1977, shall be increased by the amount of the taxpayer's zero bracket amount for the computation year."

- **1977, Tax Reduction and Simplification Act of 1977 (P.L. 95-30)**

P.L. 95-30, § 102(b)(15):

Amended Code Sec. 1302(b) by adding new paragraph (3). **Effective** for tax years beginning after 12-31-76.

- **1976, Tax Reform Act of 1976 (P.L. 94-455)**

P.L. 94-455, § 701(f)(1):

Substituted "667(a)" for "668(a)" in Code Sec. 1302(b)(2)(B). **Effective** for distributions made in tax years beginning after 12-31-75.

- **1969, Tax Reform Act of 1969 (P.L. 91-172)**

P.L. 91-172, § 311(b):

Amended Code Sec. 1302(b). **Effective** for computation years beginning after 12-31-69 and to base period years applicable to such years. Prior to amendment, Code Sec. 1302 read as indicated in the historical note following Code Sec. 1302(c).

- **1964, Revenue Act of 1964 (P.L. 88-272)**

P.L. 88-272, § 232(a):

Amended Code Sec. 1302. **Effective** with respect to tax years beginning after 12-31-63, except as provided in § 232(g)(2) reproduced in the historical comment following former Code Sec. 1301. For text of Code Sec. 1302 and amendments prior to P.L. 88-272, see the historical comment following Code Sec. 1305.

[Sec. 1302(c)]

(c) OTHER RELATED DEFINITIONS.—For purposes of this part—

(1) COMPUTATION YEAR.—The term "computation year" means the taxable year for which the taxpayer chooses the benefits of this part.

(2) BASE PERIOD.—The term "base period" means the 3 taxable years immediately preceding the computation year.

(3) BASE PERIOD YEAR.—The term "base period year" means any of the 3 taxable years immediately preceding the computation year.

(4) JOINT RETURN.—The term "joint return" means the return of a husband and wife made under section 6013.

Amendments

- **1984, Deficit Reduction Act of 1984 (P.L. 98-369)**

P.L. 98-369, § 173(a):

Amended Code Sec. 1302(c)(2) by striking out "4 taxable years" and inserting in lieu thereof "3 taxable years". **Effective** for computation years beginning after 12-31-83, and to base period years applicable to such computation years.

P.L. 98-369, § 173(c)(4):

Amended Code Sec. 1302(c)(3) by striking out "4 taxable years" and inserting in lieu thereof "3 taxable years". **Effective** for computation years beginning after 12-31-83, and to base period years applicable to such computation years.

- **1969, Tax Reform Act of 1969 (P.L. 91-172)**

P.L. 91-172, § 311(b):

Amended Code Sec. 1302. **Effective** for computation years beginning after 12-31-69 and to base period years applicable to such computation years. Prior to amendment, Code Sec. 1302 read as follows:

SEC. 1302. DEFINITION OF AVERAGABLE INCOME; RELATED DEFINITIONS.

(a) Averagable Income.—For purposes of this part—

Sec. 1302—Repealed

(1) In General.—The term "averagable income" means the amount (if any) by which adjusted taxable income exceeds $133 1/3$ percent of average base period income.

(2) Adjustment In Certain Cases For Capital Gains.—If—

(A) the average base period capital gain net income, exceeds

(B) the capital gain net income for the computation year,

then the term "averagable income" means the amount determined under paragraph (1), reduced by an amount equal to such excess.

(b) Adjusted Taxable Income.—For purposes of this part, the term "adjusted taxable income" means the taxable income for the computation year, decreased by the sum of the following amounts:

(1) Capital Gain Net Income For The Computation Year.—The amount (if any) of the capital gain net income for the computation year.

(2) Income Attributable To Gifts, Bequests, Etc.—

(A) In General.—The amount of net income attributable to an interest in property where such interest was received by the taxpayer as a gift, bequest, devise, or inheritance during the computation year or any base period year. This paragraph shall not apply to gifts, bequests, devises, or inheritances between husband and wife if they make a joint return, or if one of them makes a return as a surviving spouse (as defined in section 2(b)), for the computation year.

(B) Amount Of Net Income.—Unless the taxpayer otherwise establishes to the satisfaction of the Secretary or his delegate, the amount of net income for any taxable year attributable to an interest described in subparagraph (A) shall be deemed to be 6 percent of the fair market value of such interest (as determined in accordance with the provisions of chapter 11 or chapter 12, as the case may be).

(C) Limitation.—This paragraph shall apply only if the sum of the net incomes attributable to interests described in subparagraph (A) exceeds $3,000.

(D) Net Income.—For purposes of this paragraph, the term "net income" means, with respect to any interest, the excess of—

(i) items of gross income attributable to such interest, over

(ii) the deductions properly allocable to or chargeable against such items.

For purposes of computing such net income, capital gains and losses shall not be taken into account.

(3) Wagering Income.—The amount (if any) by which the gains from wagering transactions for the computation year exceed the losses from such transactions.

(4) Certain Amounts Received By Owner-Employees.—The amount (if any) to which section 72(m)(5) (relating to penalties applicable to certain amounts received by owner-employees) applies.

(c) Average Base Period Income.—For purposes of this part—

(1) In General.—The term "average base period income" means one-fourth of the sum of the base period incomes for the base period.

(2) Base Period Income.—The base period income for any taxable year is the taxable income for such year first increased and then decreased (but not below zero) in the following order:

(A) Taxable income shall be increased by an amount equal to the excess of—

(i) the amount excluded from gross income under section 911 (relating to earned income from sources without the United States) and subpart D of part III of subchapter N (sec. 931 and following, relating to income from sources within possessions of the United States), over

(ii) the deductions which would have been properly allocable to or chargeable against such amount for the exclusion of such amount from gross income.

(B) Taxable income shall be decreased by the capital gain net income.

(C) If the decrease provided by paragraph (2) of subsection (b) applies to the computation year, the taxable income shall be decreased under the rules of such paragraph (2) (other than the limitation contained in subparagraph (C) thereof).

(d) Capital Gain Net Income, Etc.—For purposes of this part—

(1) Capital Gain Net Income.—The term "capital gain net income" means the amount equal to 50 percent of the excess of the net long-term capital gain over the net short-term capital loss.

(2) Average Base Period Capital Gain Net Income.—The term "average base period capital gain net income" means one-fourth of the sum of the capital gain net incomes for the base period. For purposes of the preceding sentence, the capital gain net income for any base period year shall not exceed the base period income for such year computed without regard to subsection (c)(2)(B).

(e) Other Related Definitions.—For purposes of this part—

(1) Computation Year.—The term "computation year" means the taxable year for which the taxpayer chooses the benefits of this part.

(2) Base Period.—The term "base period" means the 4 taxable years immediately preceding the computation year.

(3) Base Period Year.—The term "base period year" means any of the 4 taxable years immediately preceding the computation year.

(4) Joint Return.—The term "joint return" means the return of a husband and wife made under section 6013.

- **1964, Revenue Act of 1964 (P.L. 88-272)**

P.L. 88-272, § 232(a):

Amended Code Sec. 1302. **Effective** with respect to tax years beginning after 12-31-63, except as provided in § 232(g)(2) of P.L. 88-272 reproduced in comment following former Code Sec. 1301. For text of Code Sec. 1302 and amendments prior to amendment, see the comment following Code Sec. 1305.

INCOME TAX—INCOME AVERAGING

[Sec. 1303—Repealed]

Amendments

• **1986, Tax Reform Act of 1986 (P.L. 99-514)**

P.L. 99-514, §141(a):

Repealed Code Sec. 1303. **Effective** for tax years beginning after 12-31-86. Prior to repeal, Code Sec. 1303 read as follows:

SEC. 1303. ELIGIBLE INDIVIDUALS.

[Sec. 1303(a)]

(a) GENERAL RULE.—Except as otherwise provided in this section, for purposes of this part the term "eligible individual" means any individual who is a citizen or resident of the United States throughout the computation year.

[Sec. 1303(b)]

(b) NONRESIDENT ALIEN INDIVIDUALS.—For purposes of this part, an individual shall not be an eligible individual for the computation year if, at any time during such year or the base period, such individual was a nonresident alien.

[Sec. 1303(c)]

(c) INDIVIDUALS RECEIVING SUPPORT FROM OTHERS.—

(1) IN GENERAL.—For purposes of this part, an individual shall not be an eligible individual for the computation year if, for any base period year, such individual (and his spouse) furnished less than one-half of his support.

(2) EXCEPTIONS.—Paragraph (1) shall not apply to any computation year if—

(A) more than one-half of the individual's taxable income for the computation year is attributable to work performed by him in substantial part during 2 or more of the base period years, or

(B) the individual makes a joint return for the computation year and not more than 25 percent of the aggregate adjusted gross income of such individual and his spouse for the computation year is attributable to such individual.

In applying subparagraph (B), amounts which constitute earned income (within the meaning of section 911(d)(2)) and are community income under community property laws applicable to such income shall be taken into account as if such amounts did not constitute community income.

Amendments

• **1986, Consolidated Omnibus Budget Reconciliation Act of 1985 (P.L. 99-272)**

P.L. 99-272, §13206(b)(1)-(3):

Amended Code Sec. 1303(c)(2) by striking out subparagraph (A), by redesignating subparagraphs (B) and (C) as subparagraphs (A) and (B), and by striking out "subparagraph (C)" in the second sentence and inserting in lieu thereof "subparagraph (B)". **Effective** with respect to tax years beginning after 12-31-85. Prior to amendment, Code Sec. 1303(c)(2)(A) read as follows:

(A) such year ends after the individual attained age 25, and during at least 4 of his taxable years beginning after he attained age 21 and ending with his computation year, he was not a full-time student,

• **1981, Economic Recovery Tax Act of 1981 (P.L. 97-34)**

P.L. 97-34, §111(b)(4):

Amended Code Sec. 1303(c)(2) by striking out "section 911(b)" and inserting in lieu thereof "section 911(d)(2)". **Effective** with respect to tax years beginning after 12-31-81.

• **1969, Tax Reform Act of 1969 (P.L. 91-172)**

P.L. 91-172, §311(d)(1):

Amended Sec. 1303(c)(2)(B) by inserting "taxable income" in lieu of "adjusted taxable income". **Effective** with respect to computation years within the meaning of Code Sec. 1302(c)(1) beginning after 12-31-69, and to base period years within the meaning of Code Sec. 1302(c)(3) applicable to such computation years.

[Sec. 1303(d)]

(d) ELIGIBLE INDIVIDUALS NOT TO INCLUDE FULL-TIME STUDENTS.—

(1) IN GENERAL.—For purposes of this part, an individual shall not be an eligible individual for the computation year if, at any time during any base period year, such individual was a student.

(2) EXCEPTION FOR MARRIED STUDENTS PROVIDING 25 PERCENT OR LESS OF JOINT INCOME.—Paragraph (1) shall not apply to any individual for any computation year if—

(A) the individual makes a joint return for the computation year, and

(B) not more than 25 percent of the aggregate adjusted gross income of such individual and the spouse of such individual for such computation year is attributable to such individual. In applying subparagraph (B), amounts which constitute earned income (within the meaning of section 911(d)(2)) and are community income under community property laws applicable to such income shall be taken into account as if such amounts did not constitute community income.

(3) STUDENT DEFINED.—For the purposes of this subsection, the term "student" means, with respect to a taxable year, an individual who during each of 5 calendar months during such taxable year—

(A) was a full-time student at an educational organization described in section 170(b)(1)(A)(ii); or

(B) was pursuing a full-time course of institutional on-farm training under the supervision of an accredited agent of an educational organization described in section 170(b)(1)(A)(ii) or of a State or political subdivision of a State.

• **1986, Consolidated Omnibus Budget Reconciliation Act of 1985 (P.L. 99-272)**

P.L. 99-272, §13206(a):

Amended Code Sec. 1303(d). **Effective** with respect to tax years beginning after 12-31-85. Prior to amendment, Code Sec. 1303(d) read as follows:

(d) STUDENT DEFINED.—For purposes of this section, the term "student" means, with respect to a taxable year, an individual who during each of 5 calendar months during such taxable year—

(1) was a full-time student at an educational organization described in section 170(b)(1)(A)(ii); or

(2) was pursuing a full-time course of institutional on-farm training under the supervision of an accredited agent of an educational organization described in section 170(b)(1)(A)(ii) or of a State or political subdivision of a State.

• **1976, Tax Reform Act of 1976 (P.L. 94-455)**

P.L. 94-455, §1901(b)(8)(G):

Substituted "educational organization described in section 170(b)(1)(A)(ii)" for "educational institution (as defined in section 151(e)(4))" wherever it appeared in Code Sec. 1303(d). **Effective** with respect to tax years beginning after 12-31-76.

• **1964, Revenue Act of 1964 (P.L. 88-272)**

P.L. 88-272, §232(a):

Amended Code Sec. 1303. **Effective** with respect to tax years beginning after 12-31-63, except as provided in §232(g)(2) of P.L. 88-272 reproduced in comment following former Code Sec. 1301. For text of Code Sec. 1303 and amendments prior to amendment, see the comment following Code Sec. 1305.

[Sec. 1304—Repealed]

• **1986, Tax Reform Act of 1986 (P.L. 99-514)**

P.L. 99-514, §141(a):

Repealed Code Sec. 1304. **Effective** for tax years beginning after 12-31-86. Prior to repeal, Code Sec. 1304 read as follows:

SEC. 1304. SPECIAL RULES.

[Sec. 1304(a)]

(a) TAXPAYER MUST CHOOSE BENEFITS.—This part shall apply to the taxable year only if the taxpayer chooses to have the benefits of this part for such taxable year. Such choice may be made or changed at any time before the expiration of the period prescribed for making a claim for credit or refund of the tax imposed by this chapter for the taxable year.

[Sec. 1304(b)]

(b) CERTAIN PROVISIONS INAPPLICABLE.—If the taxpayer chooses the benefits of this part for the taxable year, the following provisions shall not apply to him for such year:

(1) section 911 (relating to citizens or residents of the United States living abroad), and

(2) subpart D of part III of subchapter N (sec. 931 and following, relating to income from sources within possessions of the United States).

Amendments

• **1981, Economic Recovery Tax Act of 1981 (P.L. 97-34)**

P.L. 97-34, §101(c)(2)(B):

Amended Code Sec. 1304(b) by inserting "and" at the end of paragraph (1), by striking out ", and" at the end of paragraph (2) and inserting in lieu thereof a period, and by striking out paragraph (3). **Effective** for tax years beginning after 12-31-81. Prior to repeal, Code Sec. 1304(b)(3) read as follows:

"(3) section 1348 (relating to 50-percent maximum rate on personal service income."

P.L. 97-34, §111(b)(3):

Amended Code Sec. 1304(b)(1) by striking out "relating to income earned by employees in certain camps" and inserting in lieu thereof "relating to citizens or residents of the United States living abroad". **Effective** with respect to tax years beginning after 12-31-81.

• **1978, Tax Treatment Extension Act of 1978 (P.L. 95-615)**

P.L. 95-615, §202(f)(5):

Amended Code Sec. 1304(b)(1) by striking out "relating to earned income from sources without the United States" and inserting in lieu thereof "relating to income earned by employees in certain camps". **Effective** for tax years beginning after 12-31-77.

• **1978, Revenue Act of 1978 (P.L. 95-600)**

P.L. 95-600, §401(b)(5):

Amended Code Sec. 1304(b) by adding "and" at the end of paragraph (2), by striking out paragraph (3), and by redesignating paragraph (4) as paragraph (3). **Effective** for tax years beginning after 12-31-78. Prior to amendment, Code Sec. 1304(b)(3) read as follows:

"(3) section 1201(b) (relating to alternative capital gains tax), and"

• **1976, Tax Reform Act of 1976 (P.L. 94-455)**

P.L. 94-455, §302(c):

Substituted "personal service" for "earned" in Code Sec. 1304(b)(5). **Effective** for tax years beginning after 12-31-76.

P.L. 94-455, §501(b)(7):

Deleted paragraph (1) and redesignated paragraphs (2), (3), (4), and (5) as paragraphs (1), (2), (3), and (4) in Code Sec. 1304(b). **Effective** for tax years beginning after 12-31-75. Prior to its deletion, Code Sec. 1304(b)(1) read as follows:

INCOME TAX—INCOME AVERAGING

(1) section 3 (relating to optional tax).

• **1974, Employee Retirement Income Security Act of 1974 (P.L. 93-406)**

P.L. 93-406, § 2005(c)(6):

Amended Code Sec. 1304(b) by deleting paragraph (2) and by redesignating paragraphs (3), (4), (5), and (6) as paragraphs (2), (3), (4) and (5). **Effective** for distributions and payments made after 12-31-73 in tax years beginning after such date. Prior to being deleted, paragraph (2) read as follows:

"(2) section 72(n)(2) (relating to limitation of tax in case of total distribution),".

• **1969, Tax Reform Act of 1969 (P.L. 91-172)**

P.L. 91-172, § 311(c):

Amended Sec. 1304(b) by adding paragraphs (5) and (6). **Effective** for computation years beginning after 12-31-69 and for base period years applicable to such computation years.

P.L. 91-172, § 515(c)(4):

Amended Code Sec. 1304(b)(2). **Effective** for tax years ending after 12-31-69. Prior to amendment, Code Sec. 1304(b)(2) read as follows:

"(2) section 72(n)(2) (relating to limitation of tax in case of certain distributions with respect to contributions by self-employed individuals),".

P.L. 91-172, § 803(d)(8):

Amended Code Sec. 1304(b)(1) by striking out "if adjusted gross income is less than $5,000". **Effective** for tax years beginning after 12-31-69. Before amendment Code Sec. 1304(b)(1) read as follows:

"(1) section 3 (relating to optional tax if adjusted gross income is less than $5,000),"

[Sec. 1304(c)]

(c) FAILURE OF CERTAIN MARRIED INDIVIDUALS TO MAKE JOINT RETURN, ETC.—

(1) APPLICATION OF SUBSECTION.—Paragraphs (2) and (3) of this subsection shall apply in the case of any individual who was married for any base period year or the computation year; except that—

(A) such paragraphs shall not apply in respect of a base period year if—

(i) such individual and his spouse make a joint return, or such individual makes a return as a surviving spouse (as defined in section 2(b)), for the computation year, and

(ii) such individual was not married to any other spouse for such base period year, and

(B) paragraph (3) shall not apply in respect of the computation year if the individual and his spouse make a joint return for such year.

(2) MINIMUM BASE PERIOD INCOME.—For purposes of this part, the base period income of an individual for any base period year shall not be less than 50 percent of the base period income which would result from combining his income and deductions for such year—

(A) with the income and deductions for such year of the individual who is his spouse for the computation year, or

(B) if greater, with the income and deductions for such year of the individual who was his spouse for such base period year.

(3) COMMUNITY INCOME ATTRIBUTABLE TO SERVICES.—In the case of amounts which constitute earned income (within the meaning of section 911(d)(2)) and are community income under community property laws applicable to such income—

(A) the amount taken into account for any base period year for purposes of determining base period income shall not be less than the amount which would be taken into account if such amounts did not constitute community income, and

(B) the amount taken into account for purposes of determining taxable income for the computation year shall not exceed the amount which would be taken into account if such amounts did not constitute community income.

(4) MARITAL STATUS.—For purposes of this subsection, section 143(a) shall apply in determining whether an individual is married for any taxable year.

Amendments

• **1981, Economic Recovery Tax Act of 1981 (P.L. 97-34)**

P.L. 97-34, § 111(b)(4):

Amended Code Sec. 1304(c)(3) by striking out "section 911(b)" and inserting in lieu thereof "section 911(d)(2)". **Effective** with respect to tax years beginning after 12-31-81.

• **1969, Tax Reform Act of 1969 (P.L. 91-172)**

P.L. 91-172, § 311(d)(2):

Amended Sec. 1304(c) by deleting paragraph (3) and by redesignating paragraphs (4) and (5) as (3) and (4). **Effective** 1-1-70. Prior to amendment, Sec. 1304(c)(3) read as follows:

"(3) Minimum base period capital gain net income.—For purposes of this part, the capital gain net income of any individual for any base period year shall not be less than 50 percent of the capital gain net income which would result from combining his capital gain net income for such year (determined without regard to this paragraph) with the capital gain net income for such year (similarly determined) of the individual with whom he is required by paragraph (2) to combine his income and deductions for such year.", and by inserting "taxable income" in lieu of "adjusted taxable income" in redesignated paragraph (c)(3)(B).

P.L. 91-172, § 802(c):

Amended Code Sec. 1304(c)(4) by striking out "section 143" and inserting in lieu thereof "section 143(a)". **Effective** for tax years beginning after 12-31-69.

[Sec. 1304(d)]

(d) DOLLAR LIMITATIONS IN CASE OF JOINT RETURNS.—In the case of a joint return, the $3,000 figure contained in section 1301 shall be applied to the aggregate averagable income.

Amendments

• **1969, Tax Reform Act of 1969 (P.L. 91-172)**

P.L. 91-172, § 311(d)(2):

Amended Sec. 1304(d) by deleting ", and the $3,000 figure contained in section 1302(b)(2)(C) shall be applied to the aggregate net incomes" from the end thereof. **Effective** 1-1-70.

[Sec. 1304(e)]

(e) TREATMENT OF CERTAIN OTHER ITEMS.—

(1) SECTION 72(m) OR (q)(1).—Section 72(m)(5) (relating to penalties applicable to certain amounts received by owner-employees) or section 72(q)(1) (relating to 5-percent tax on premature distributions under annuity contracts) shall be applied as if this part had not been enacted.

(2) OTHER ITEMS.—Except as otherwise provided in this part, the order and manner in which items of income or limitations on tax shall be taken into account in computing the tax imposed by this chapter on the income of any eligible individual to whom section 1301 applies for any computation year shall be determined under regulations prescribed by the Secretary.

Amendments

• **1982, Tax Equity and Fiscal Responsibility Act of 1982 (P.L. 97-248)**

P.L. 97-248, § 265(b)(2)(C)(i)-(ii):

Amended Code Sec. 1304(e)(1) by inserting "or section 72(q)(1) (relating to 5-percent tax on premature distributions under annuity contracts)" after "owner-employees)"; and by inserting "or (q)(1)" after "SECTION 72(m)(5)" in the heading thereof. **Effective** for distributions after 12-31-82.

• **1976, Tax Reform Act of 1976 (P.L. 94-455)**

P.L. 94-455, § 1906(b)(13)(A):

Amended 1954 Code by substituting "Secretary" for "Secretary or his delegate" each place it appeared. **Effective** 2-1-77.

• **1969, Tax Reform Act of 1969 (P.L. 91-172)**

P.L. 91-172, § 311(d)(2):

Amended Sec. 1304(e). **Effective** 1-1-70. Prior to amendment, subsection (e) read as follows:

"(e) Special Rules Where There Are Capital Gains.—

"(1) Treatment of capital gains in computation year.—In the case of any taxpayer who has capital gain net income for the computation year, the tax imposed by section 1 for the computation year which is attributable to the amount of such net income shall be computed—

"(A) by adding so much of the amount thereof as does not exceed average base period capital gain net income above $133\frac{1}{3}$ percent of average base period income, and

"(B) by adding the remainder (if any) of such net income above the 20 percent of the averagable income as taken into account for purposes of computing the tax imposed by section 1 (and above the amounts (if any) referred to in subsection (f)(1)).

"(2) Computation of alternative tax.—In the case of any taxpayer who has capital gain net income for the computation year, section 1201(b) shall be treated as imposing a tax equal to the tax imposed by section 1, reduced by the amount (if any) by which—

"(A) the tax imposed by section 1 and attributable to the capital gain net income for the computation year (determined under paragraph (1)), exceeds

"(B) an amount equal to 25 percent of the excess of the net long-term capital gain over the net short-term capital loss."

[Sec. 1304(f)]

(f) SHORT TAXABLE YEARS.—In the case of any computation year or base period year which is a short taxable year, this part shall be applied in the manner provided in regulations prescribed by the Secretary.

Amendments

• **1976, Tax Reform Act of 1976 (P.L. 94-455)**

P.L. 94-455, § 1906(b)(13)(A):

Amended 1954 Code by substituting "Secretary" for "Secretary or his delegate" each place it appeared. **Effective** 2-1-77.

• **1969, Tax Reform Act of 1969 (P.L. 91-172)**

P.L. 91-172, § 311(d)(2):

Amended Sec. 1304 by deleting subsection (f) and redesignating subsection (g) as (f). **Effective** 1-1-70. Prior to deletion, subsection (f) read as follows:

"(f) Treatment of Certain Other Items.—

"(1) Gift or wagering income.—The tax imposed by section 1 for the computation year which is attributable to the amounts subtracted from taxable income under paragraphs (2) and (3) of section 1302(b) shall equal the increase in tax under section 1 which results from adding such amounts above the 20 percent of the averagable income as taken into account for purposes of computing the tax imposed thereon by section 1.

"(2) Section 72(m)(5).—Section 72(m)(5) (relating to penalties applicable to certain amounts received by owner-employees) shall be applied as if this part had not been enacted.

"(3) Other items.—Except as otherwise provided in this part, the order and manner in which items of income shall be taken into account in computing the tax imposed by this chapter on the income of any eligible individual to whom section 1301 applies for any computation year shall be determined under regulations prescribed by the Secretary or his delegate."

Sec. 1304—Repealed

INCOME TAX—INCOME AVERAGING

• **1964, Revenue Act of 1964 (P.L. 88-272)**

P.L. 88-272, § 232(a):

Amended Code Sec. 1304. **Effective** with respect to tax years beginning after 12-31-63, except as provided in § 232(g)(2) of P.L. 88-272 reproduced in comment following former Code Sec. 1301. For text of Code Sec. 1304 and amendments prior to amendment, see the comment following Code Sec. 1305.

[Sec. 1305—Repealed]

Amendments

• **1986, Tax Reform Act of 1986 (P.L. 99-514)**

P.L. 99-514, § 141(a):

Repealed Code Sec. 1305. **Effective** for tax years beginning after 12-31-86. Prior to repeal, Code Sec. 1305 read as follows:

SEC. 1305. REGULATIONS.

The Secretary shall prescribe such regulations as may be necessary to carry out the purposes of this part.

• **1976, Tax Reform Act of 1976 (P.L. 94-455)**

P.L. 94-455, § 1906(b)(13)(A):

Amended 1954 Code by substituting "Secretary" for "Secretary or his delegate" each place it appeared. **Effective** 2-1-77.

• **1964, Revenue Act of 1964 (P.L. 88-272)**

P.L. 88-272, § 232(a):

Amended Code Sec. 1305. **Effective** with respect to tax years beginning after 12-31-63. Code Secs. 1306-1307 were eliminated from the Code. Full text of Code Secs. 1301-1307 and amendments prior to amendment are set out below:

SEC. 1301. COMPENSATION FROM AN EMPLOYMENT.

(a) Limitation on Tax.—If an individual or partnership—

(1) engages in an employment as defined in subsection (b); and

(2) the employment covers a period of 36 months or more (from the beginning to the completion of such employment); and

(3) the gross compensation from the employment received or accrued in the taxable year of the individual or partnership is not less than 80 percent of the total compensation from such employment,

then the tax attributable to any part of the compensation which is included in the gross income of any individual shall not be greater than the aggregate of the taxes attributable to such part had it been included in the gross income of such individual ratably over that part of the period which precedes the date of such receipt or accrual.

(b) Definition of an Employment.—For purposes of this section, the term "an employment" means an arrangement or series of arrangements for the performance of personal services by an individual or partnership to effect a particular result, regardless of the number of sources from which compensation therefor is obtained.

(c) Rule With Respect to Partners.—An individual who is a member of a partnership receiving or accruing compensation from an employment of the type described in subsection (a) shall be entitled to the benefits of that subsection only if the individual has been a member of the partnership continuously for a period of 36 months or the period of the employment immediately preceding the receipt or accrual. In such a case the tax attributable to the part of the compensation which is includible in the gross income of the individual shall not be greater than the aggregate of the taxes which would have been attributable to that part had it been included in the gross income of the individual ratably over the period in which it was earned or the period during which the individual continuously was a member of the partnership, whichever period is the shorter. For purposes of this subsection, a member of a partnership shall be deemed to have been a member of the partnership for any period, ending immediately prior to becoming such a member, in which he was an employee of such partnership, if during the taxable year he received or accrued compensation attributable to employment by the partnership during such period.

SEC. 1302. INCOME FROM AN INVENTION OR ARTISTIC WORK.

(a) Limitation on Tax.—If—

(1) an individual includes in gross income amounts in respect of a particular invention or artistic work created by the individual; and

(2) the work on the invention or the artistic work covered a period of 24 months or more (from the beginning to the completion thereof); and

(3) the amounts in respect of the invention or the artistic work includible in gross income for the taxable year are not less than 80 percent of the gross income in respect of such invention or artistic work in the taxable year plus the gross income therefrom in previous taxable years and the 12 months immediately succeeding the close of the taxable year,

then the tax attributable to the part of such gross income of the taxable year which is not taxable as a gain from the sale or exchange of a capital asset held for more than 6 months shall not be greater than the aggregate of the taxes attributable to such part had it been received ratably over, in the case of an invention, that part of the period preceding the close of the taxable year or 60 months, whichever is shorter, or, in the case of an artistic work, that part of the period preceding the close of the taxable year but not more than 36 months.

(b) Definitions.—For purposes of this section—

(1) Invention.—The term "invention" means a patent covering an invention of the individual.

(2) Artistic work.—The term "artistic work" means a literary, musical, or artistic composition or a copyright covering a literary, musical, or artistic composition.

SEC. 1303. INCOME FROM BACK PAY.

(a) Limitation on Tax.—If the amount of the back pay received or accrued by an individual during the taxable year exceeds 15 percent of the gross income of the individual for such year, the part of the tax attributable to the inclusion of such back pay in gross income for the taxable year shall not be greater than the aggregate of the increases in the taxes which would have resulted from the inclusion of the respective portions of such back pay in gross income for the taxable years to which such portions are respectively attributable, as determined under regulations prescribed by the Secretary or his delegate.

(b) Definition of Back Pay.—For purposes of this section, the term "back pay" means amounts includible in gross income under this subtitle which are one of the following:

(1) Remuneration, including wages, salaries, retirement pay, and other similar compensation, which is received or accrued during the taxable year by an employee for services performed before the taxable year for his employer and which would have been paid before the taxable year except for the intervention of one of the following events:

(A) bankruptcy or receivership of the employer;

(B) dispute as to the liability of the employer to pay such remuneration, which is determined after the commencement of court proceedings;

(C) if the employer is the United States, a State, a Territory, or any political subdivision thereof, or the District of Columbia, or any agency or instrumentality of any of the foregoing, lack of funds appropriated to pay such remuneration; or

(D) any other event determined to be similar in nature under regulations prescribed by the Secretary or his delegate.

(2) Wages or salaries which are received or accrued during the taxable year by an employee for services performed before the taxable year for his employer and which constitute retroactive wage or salary increases ordered, recommended, or approved by any Federal or State agency, and made retroactive to any period before the taxable year.

(3) Payments which are received or accrued during the taxable year as the result of an alleged violation by an employer of any State or Federal law relating to labor standards or practices, and which are determined under regulations prescribed by the Secretary or his delegate to be attributable to a prior taxable year.

(4) Termination payments under section 5(c) or section 6(1) of the Peace Corps Act which are received or accrued by an individual during the taxable year on account of any period of service, as a volunteer or volunteer leader under the Peace Corps Act, occurring prior to the taxable year.

Amendments

• **1961, Peace Corps Act (P.L. 87-293)**

P.L. 87-293, § 201(b):

Added Code Sec. 1303(b)(4). **Effective** for tax years ending after 3-1-61.

SEC. 1304. COMPENSATORY DAMAGES FOR PATENT INFRINGEMENT.—If an amount representing compensatory damages is received or accrued by a taxpayer during a taxable year as the result of an award in a civil action for infringement of a patent issued by the United States, then the tax attributable to the inclusion of such amount in gross income for the taxable year shall not be greater than the aggregate of the increases in taxes which would have resulted if such amount had been included in gross income in equal installments for each month during which such infringement occurred.

Amendments

• **1955 (P.L. 366, 84th Cong.)**

P.L. 366, 84th Cong., § [1]:

Added a section, and renumbered the section formerly numbered "1304" as "1305." **Effective** for tax years ending after 8-11-55, but only as to amounts received or accrued after such date as the result of awards made after such date.

SEC. 1305. BREACH OF CONTRACT DAMAGES.

(a) General Rule.—If an amount representing damages is received or accrued by a taxpayer during a taxable year as a result of an award in a civil action for breach of contract or breach of a fiduciary duty or relationship, then the tax attributable to the inclusion in gross income for the taxable year of that part of such amount which would have been received or accrued by the taxpayer in a prior taxable year or years but for the breach of contract, or breach of a fiduciary duty or relationship, shall not be greater than the aggregate of the increases in taxes which would have resulted had such part been included in gross income for such prior taxable year or years.

(b) Credits and Deductions Allowed in Computation of Tax.—The taxpayer in computing said tax shall be entitled to deduct all credits and deductions for depletion, depreciation, and other items to which he would have been entitled, had such income been received or accrued by the taxpayer in the year during which he would have received or accrued it, except for such breach of contract or for such breach of a fiduciary duty or relationship. The credits, deductions, or other items referred to in the prior sentence, attributable to property, shall be allowed only with respect to that part of the award which represents the taxpayer's share of income from the actual operation of such property.

(c) Limitation.—Subsection (a) shall not apply unless the amount representing damages is $3,000 or more.

Amendments

• **1957 (P.L. 85-165)**

P.L. 85-165, §§ [1], 3:

Added a section and renumbered the section formerly numbered "1305" as "1306." **Effective** for tax years ending after 12-31-54, but only as to amounts received or accrued after such date as the result of awards made after such date.

SEC. 1306. DAMAGES FOR INJURIES UNDER THE ANTITRUST LAWS.—If an amount representing damages is received or accrued during a taxable year as a result of an award in, or settlement of, a civil action brought under section 4 of the Act entitled "An Act to supplement existing laws against unlawful restraints and monop-

INCOME TAX—MITIGATION OF LIMITATIONS

olies, and for other purposes", approved October 15, 1914 (commonly known as the Clayton Act), for injuries sustained by the taxpayer in his business or property by reason of anything forbidden in the antitrust laws, then the tax attributable to the inclusion of such amount in gross income for the taxable year shall not be greater than the aggregate of the increases in taxes which would have resulted if such amount had been included in gross income in equal installments for each month during the period in which such injuries were sustained by the taxpayer.

Amendments

- **1958, Technical Amendments Act of 1958 (P.L. 85-866)**

P.L. 85-866, § 58(a):
Added a section and renumbered the section formerly numbered "1306" as "1307." **Effective** for tax years ending after 9-2-58, but only for amounts received or accrued after that date as a result of awards or settlements made after such date.

SEC. 1307. RULES APPLICABLE TO THIS PART.

(a) Fractional Parts of a Month.—For purposes of this part, a fractional part of a month shall be disregarded unless it amounts to more than half a month, in which case it should be considered as a month.

(b) Tax on Self-Employment Income.—This part shall be applied without regard to, and shall not affect, the tax imposed by chapter 2 relating to self-employment income.

(c) Computation of Tax Attributable to Income Allocated to Prior Period.—For the purpose of computing the tax attributable to the amount of an item of gross income allocable under this part to a particular taxable year, such amount shall be considered income only of the person who would be required to include the item of gross income in a separate return filed for the taxable year in which such item was received or accrued.

(d) Effective Date of Certain Subsections.—Subsection (c) of section 1301 and subsection (c) of this section shall apply only to amounts received or accrued after March 1, 1954. Notwithstanding any other provision of this title, section 107 of the Internal Revenue Code of 1939 shall apply to amounts received or accrued as a partner on or before March 1, 1954, under this section and to the computation of tax on amounts received or accrued on or before March 1, 1954.

(e) Election With Respect to Charitable Contributions.—In the case of an individual who elects (in such manner and at such time as the Secretary or his delegate prescribes by regulations) to have the provisions of this subsection apply, an amount received or accrued to which this part applies shall be reduced, for purposes of computing the tax liability of the taxpayer under this part with respect to the amount so received or accrued, by an amount equal to that portion of (1) the amount of charitable contributions made by the taxpayer during the taxable year in which the amount is so received or accrued which are allowable as a deduction for such year under section 170 (determined without regard to this part), as (2) the amount received or accrued to which this part applies is of the adjusted gross income for the taxable year (determined without regard to this part). In any case in which the taxpayer elects to have the provisions of the preceding sentence apply, for purposes of computing the limitation on tax under this part—

(1) only the same proportion of the amount to which this part applies shall be taken into account for purposes of computing the limitations under section 170(b)(1)(A) and (B) for taxable years before the taxable year in which such amount is received or accrued as (A) the excess of the maximum amount which could, if the taxpayer had made additional contributions described in clause (i), (ii), or (iii) of section 170(b)(1)(A), have been described in clause (1) of the preceding sentence over the amount described in such clause (1), bears to (B) such maximum amount, and

(2) the portion of the amount of charitable contributions described in the preceding sentence shall not be taken into account in computing the tax for the taxable year in which the amount to which this part applies is received or accrued.

Amendments

- **1962, Revenue Act of 1962 (P.L. 87-834)**

P.L. 87-834, § 22:
Added to Code Sec. 1307 a new subsection (e). **Effective** with respect to amounts received or accrued in tax years beginning after 12-31-61.

- **1958, Technical Amendments Act of 1958 (P.L. 85-866)**

P.L. 85-866, § 58(a):
Renumbered Code Sec 1306 and designated it "1307." **Effective** for tax years beginning after 9-2-58.

- **1957 (P.L. 85-165)**

P.L. 85-165, §§ [1], 3:
Renumbered Code Sec. 1305 as 1306. **Effective** for tax years ending after 12-31-54, but only as to amounts received or accrued after such date as the result of awards made after such date.

- **1955 (P.L. 366, 84th Cong.)**

P.L. 366, 84th Cong., §[1]:
Renumbered Code Sec 1304 as 1305. **Effective** for tax years ending after 8-11-55, but only as to amounts received or accrued after such date as the result of awards made after such date.

PART II—MITIGATION OF EFFECT OF LIMITATIONS AND OTHER PROVISIONS

Sec. 1311.	Correction of error.
Sec. 1312.	Circumstances of adjustment.
Sec. 1313.	Definitions.
Sec. 1314.	Amount and method of adjustment.

[Sec. 1311]

SEC. 1311. CORRECTION OF ERROR.

[Sec. 1311(a)]

(a) GENERAL RULE.—If a determination (as defined in section 1313) is described in one or more of the paragraphs of section 1312 and, on the date of the determination, correction of the effect of the error referred to in the applicable paragraph of section 1312 is prevented by the operation of any law or rule of law, other than this part and other than section 7122 (relating to compromises), then the effect of the error shall be corrected by an adjustment made in the amount and in the manner specified in section 1314.

[Sec. 1311(b)]

(b) CONDITIONS NECESSARY FOR ADJUSTMENT.—

(1) MAINTENANCE OF AN INCONSISTENT POSITION.—Except in cases described in paragraphs (3) (B) and (4) of section 1312, an adjustment shall be made under this part only if—

(A) in case the amount of the adjustment would be credited or refunded in the same manner as an overpayment under section 1314, there is adopted in the determination a position maintained by the Secretary, or

(B) in case the amount of the adjustment would be assessed and collected in the same manner as a deficiency under section 1314, there is adopted in the determination a position maintained by the taxpayer with respect to whom the determination is made,

and the position maintained by the Secretary in the case described in subparagraph (A) or maintained by the taxpayer in the case described in subparagraph (B) is inconsistent with the erroneous inclusion, exclusion, omission, allowance, disallowance, recognition, or nonrecognition, as the case may be.

(2) CORRECTION NOT BARRED AT TIME OF ERRONEOUS ACTION.—

(A) DETERMINATION DESCRIBED IN SECTION 1312(3)(B).—In the case of a determination described in section 1312(3)(B) (relating to certain exclusions from income), adjustment shall be made under this part only if assessment of a deficiency for the taxable year in which the item is includible or against the related taxpayer was not barred, by any law or rule of law, at the time the Secretary first maintained, in a notice of deficiency sent pursuant to section 6212 or before the Tax Court, that the item described in section 1312(3)(B) should be included in the gross income of the taxpayer for the taxable year to which the determination relates.

(B) DETERMINATION DESCRIBED IN SECTION 1312(4).—In the case of a determination described in section 1312(4) (relating to disallowance of certain deductions and credits), adjustment shall be made under this part only if credit or refund of the overpayment attributable to the deduction or credit described in such section which should have been allowed to the taxpayer or related taxpayer was not barred, by any law or rule of law, at the time the taxpayer first maintained before the Secretary or before the Tax Court, in writing, that he was entitled to such deduction or credit for the taxable year to which the determination relates.

(3) EXISTENCE OF RELATIONSHIP.—In case the amount of the adjustment would be assessed and collected in the same manner as a deficiency (except for cases described in section 1312(3)(B)), the adjustment shall not be made with respect to a related taxpayer unless he stands in such relationship to the taxpayer at the time the latter first maintains the inconsistent position in a return, claim for refund, or petition (or amended

petition) to the Tax Court for the taxable year with respect to which the determination is made, or if such position is not so maintained, then at the time of the determination.

Amendments

• **1976, Tax Reform Act of 1976 (P.L. 94-455)**

P.L. 94-455, §1901(a)(142):
Substituted "Tax Court" for "Tax Court of the United States" in Code Sec. 1311(b)(2)(A), (2)(B), and (3). **Effective** with respect to tax years beginning after 12-31-76.

P.L. 94-455, §1906(b)(13)(A):
Amended the 1954 Code by substituting "Secretary" for "Secretary or his delegate" each place it appeared. **Effective** 2-1-77.

[Sec. 1312]

SEC. 1312. CIRCUMSTANCES OF ADJUSTMENT.

The circumstances under which the adjustment provided in section 1311 is authorized are as follows:

(1) DOUBLE INCLUSION OF AN ITEM OF GROSS INCOME.—The determination requires the inclusion in gross income of an item which was erroneously included in the gross income of the taxpayer for another taxable year or in the gross income of a related taxpayer.

(2) DOUBLE ALLOWANCE OF A DEDUCTION OR CREDIT.—The determination allows a deduction or credit which was erroneously allowed to the taxpayer for another taxable year or to a related taxpayer.

(3) DOUBLE EXCLUSION OF AN ITEM OF GROSS INCOME.—

(A) ITEMS INCLUDED IN INCOME.—The determination requires the exclusion from gross income of an item included in a return filed by the taxpayer or with respect to which tax was paid and which was erroneously excluded or omitted from the gross income of the taxpayer for another taxable year, or from the gross income of a related taxpayer; or

(B) ITEMS NOT INCLUDED IN INCOME.—The determination requires the exclusion from gross income of an item not included in a return filed by the taxpayer and with respect to which the tax was not paid but which is includible in the gross income of the taxpayer for another taxable year or in the gross income of a related taxpayer.

(4) DOUBLE DISALLOWANCE OF A DEDUCTION OR CREDIT.—The determination disallows a deduction or credit which should have been allowed to, but was not allowed to, the taxpayer for another taxable year, or to a related taxpayer.

(5) CORRELATIVE DEDUCTIONS AND INCLUSIONS FOR TRUSTS OR ESTATES AND LEGATEES, BENEFICIARIES, OR HEIRS.—The determination allows or disallows any of the additional deductions allowable in computing the taxable income of estates or trusts, or requires or denies any of the inclusions in the computation of taxable income of beneficiaries, heirs, or legatees, specified in subparts A to E, inclusive (secs. 641 and following, relating to estates, trusts, and beneficiaries) of part I of subchapter J of this chapter, or corresponding provisions of prior internal revenue laws, and the correlative inclusion or deduction, as the case may be, has been erroneously excluded, omitted, or included, or disallowed, omitted, or allowed, as the case may be, in respect of the related taxpayer.

(6) CORRELATIVE DEDUCTIONS AND CREDITS FOR CERTAIN RELATED CORPORATIONS.—The determination allows or disallows a deduction (including a credit) in computing the taxable income (or, as the case may be, net income, normal tax net income, or surtax net income) of a corporation, and a correlative deduction or credit has been erroneously allowed, omitted, or disallowed, as the case may be, in respect of a related taxpayer described in section 1313(c)(7).

(7) BASIS OF PROPERTY AFTER ERRONEOUS TREATMENT OF A PRIOR TRANSACTION.—

(A) GENERAL RULE.—The determination determines the basis of property, and in respect of any transaction on which such basis depends, or in respect of any transaction which was erroneously treated as affecting such basis, there occurred, with respect to a taxpayer described in subparagraph (B) of this paragraph, any of the errors described in subparagraph (C) of this paragraph.

(B) TAXPAYERS WITH RESPECT TO WHOM THE ERRONEOUS TREATMENT OCCURRED.—The taxpayer with respect to whom the erroneous treatment occurred must be—

(i) the taxpayer with respect to whom the determination is made,

(ii) a taxpayer who acquired title to the property in the transaction and from whom, mediately or immediately, the taxpayer with respect to whom the determination is made derived title, or

(iii) a taxpayer who had title to the property at the time of the transaction and from whom, mediately or immediately, the taxpayer with respect to whom the determination is made derived title, if the basis of the property in the hands of the taxpayer with respect to whom the determination is made is determined under section 1015(a) (relating to the basis of property acquired by gift).

(C) PRIOR ERRONEOUS TREATMENT.—With respect to a taxpayer described in subparagraph (B) of this paragraph—

(i) there was an erroneous inclusion in, or omission from, gross income,

(ii) there was an erroneous recognition, or nonrecognition, of gain or loss, or

(iii) there was an erroneous deduction of an item properly chargeable to capital account or an erroneous charge to capital account of an item properly deductible.

Amendments

• **1958, Technical Amendments Act of 1958 (P.L. 85-866)**

P.L. 85-866, §59(a):
Amended Code Sec. 1312 by redesignating paragraph (6) as paragraph (7) and adding a new paragraph (6). **Effective** for determinations (as defined in Code Sec. 1313(a)) made after 11-14-54.

[Sec. 1313]

SEC. 1313. DEFINITIONS.

[Sec. 1313(a)]

(a) DETERMINATION.—For purposes of this part, the term "determination" means—

(1) a decision by the Tax Court or a judgment, decree, or other order by any court of competent jurisdiction, which has become final;

(2) a closing agreement made under section 7121;

(3) a final disposition by the Secretary of a claim for refund. For purposes of this part, a claim for refund shall be deemed finally disposed of by the Secretary—

(A) as to items with respect to which the claim was allowed, on the date of allowance of refund or credit or on the date of mailing notice of disallowance (by reason of offsetting items) of the claim for refund, and

(B) as to items with respect to which the claim was disallowed, in whole or in part, or as to items applied by the Secretary in reduction of the refund or credit, on expiration of the time for instituting suit with respect thereto (unless suit is instituted before the expiration of such time); or

INCOME TAX—MITIGATION OF LIMITATIONS

(4) under regulations prescribed by the Secretary, an agreement for purposes of this part, signed by the Secretary and by any person, relating to the liability of such person (or the person for whom he acts) in respect of a tax under this subtitle for any taxable period.

Amendments

- **1976, Tax Reform Act of 1976 (P.L. 94-455)**

P.L. 94-455, §1906(b)(13)(A):

Amended 1954 Code by substituting "Secretary" for "Secretary or his delegate" each place it appeared. **Effective** 2-1-77.

[Sec. 1313(b)]

(b) TAXPAYER.—Notwithstanding section 7701(a)(14), the term "taxpayer" means any person subject to a tax under the applicable revenue law.

[Sec. 1313(c)]

(c) RELATED TAXPAYER.—For purposes of this part, the term "related taxpayer" means a taxpayer who, with the taxpayer with respect to whom a determination is made, stood, in the taxable year with respect to which the erroneous inclusion, exclusion, omission, allowance, or disallowance was made, in one of the following relationships:

(1) husband and wife,
(2) grantor and fiduciary,
(3) grantor and beneficiary,
(4) fiduciary and beneficiary, legatee, or heir,
(5) decedent and decedent's estate,
(6) partner, or
(7) member of an affiliated group of corporations (as defined in section 1504).

[Sec. 1314]

SEC. 1314. AMOUNT AND METHOD OF ADJUSTMENT.

[Sec. 1314(a)]

(a) ASCERTAINMENT OF AMOUNT OF ADJUSTMENT.—In computing the amount of an adjustment under this part there shall first be ascertained the tax previously determined for the taxable year with respect to which the error was made. The amount of the tax previously determined shall be the excess of—

(1) the sum of—

(A) the amount shown as the tax by the taxpayer on his return (determined as provided in section 6211(b)(1), (3), and (4), relating to the definition of deficiency), if a return was made by the taxpayer and an amount was shown as the tax by the taxpayer thereon, plus

(B) the amounts previously assessed (or collected without assessment) as a deficiency, over—

(2) the amount of rebates, as defined in section 6211(b)(2), made.

There shall then be ascertained the increase or decrease in tax previously determined which results solely from the correct treatment of the item which was the subject of the error (with due regard given to the effect of the item in the computation of gross income, taxable income, and other matters under this subtitle). A similar computation shall be made for any other taxable year affected, or treated as affected, by a net operating loss deduction (as defined in section 172) or by a capital loss carryback or carryover (as defined in section 1212), determined with reference to the taxable year with respect to which the error was made. The amount so ascertained (together with any amounts wrongfully collected as additions to the tax or interest, as a result of such error) for each taxable year shall be the amount of the adjustment for that taxable year.

Amendments

- **1969, Tax Reform Act of 1969 (P.L. 91-172)**

P.L. 91-172, §512(f):

Amended Code Sec. 1314(a) by inserting "capital loss carryback or carryover" in lieu of "capital loss carryover" in the next to last sentence. **Effective** with respect to net capital losses sustained in tax years beginning after 12-31-69.

- **1965, Excise Tax Reduction Act of 89-44(P.L.)**

P.L. 89-44, §809(d)(5)(B):

Amended Sec. 1314(a)(1)(A) by substituting "section 6211(b)(1), (3), and (4)" for "section 6211(b)(1) and (3)" in the text thereof. **Effective** 7-1-65.

[Sec. 1314(b)]

(b) METHOD OF ADJUSTMENT.—The adjustment authorized in section 1311(a) shall be made by assessing and collecting, or refunding or crediting, the amount thereof in the same manner as if it were a deficiency determined by the Secretary with respect to the taxpayer as to whom the error was made or an overpayment claimed by such taxpayer, as the case may be, for the taxable year or years with respect to which an amount is ascertained under subsection (a), and as if on the date of the determination one year remained before the expiration of the periods of limitation upon assessment or filing claim for refund for such taxable year or years. If, as a result of a determination described in section 1313(a)(4), an adjustment has been made by the assessment and collection of a deficiency or the refund or credit of an overpayment, and subsequently such determination is altered or revoked, the amount of the adjustment ascertained under subsection (a) of this section shall be redetermined on the basis of such alteration or revocation and any overpayment or deficiency resulting from such redetermination shall be refunded or credited, or assessed and collected, as the case may be, as an adjustment under this part. In the case of an adjustment resulting from an increase or decrease in a net operating loss or net capital loss which is carried back to the year of adjustment, interest shall not be collected or paid for any period prior to the close of the taxable year in which the net operating loss or net capital loss arises.

Amendments

- **1976, Tax Reform Act of 1976 (P.L. 94-455)**

P.L. 94-455, §1906(b)(13)(A):

Amended 1954 Code by substituting "Secretary" for "Secretary or his delegate" each place it appeared. **Effective** 2-1-77.

- **1969, Tax Reform Act of 1969 (P.L. 91-172)**

P.L. 91-172, §512(f):

Amended last sentence of Code Sec. 1314(b). **Effective** with respect to net capital losses sustained in tax years beginning after 12-31-69. Prior to amendment, the last sentence of Code Sec. 1314(b) read as follows: "In the case of an adjustment resulting from an increase or decrease in a net operating loss which is carried back to the year of adjustment, interest shall not be collected or paid for any period prior to the close of the taxable year in which the net operating loss arises."

[Sec. 1314(c)]

(c) ADJUSTMENT UNAFFECTED BY OTHER ITEMS.—The amount to be assessed and collected in the same manner as a deficiency, or to be refunded or credited in the same manner as an overpayment, under this part, shall not be diminished by any credit or set-off based upon any item other than the one which was the subject of the adjustment. The amount of the adjustment under this part, if paid, shall not be recovered by a claim or suit for refund or suit for erroneous refund based upon any item other than the one which was the subject of the adjustment.

INCOME TAX—CLAIM OF RIGHT

Amendments

• **1958, Technical Amendments Act of 1958 (P.L. 85-866)**

P.L. 85-866, § 59(b):

Struck out the phrase "Other than in the case of an adjustment resulting from a determination under section 1313(a)(4), the" where it appeared at the beginning of the second sentence in Sec. 1314(c) and substituted the word "The". **Effective** for determinations (as defined in Code Sec. 1313(a)) made after 11-14-54.

[Sec. 1314(d)—Stricken]

Amendments

• **2014, Tax Technical Corrections Act of 2014 (P.L. 113-295)**

P.L. 113-295, § 221(a)(87):

Amended Code Sec. 1314 by striking subsection (d) and by redesignating subsection (e) as subsection (d). **Effective** generally 12-19-2014. For a special rule, see Act Sec. 221(b)(2), Division A, below. Prior to being stricken, Code Sec. 1314(d) read as follows:

(d) PERIODS FOR WHICH ADJUSTMENTS MAY BE MADE.—No adjustment shall be made under this part in respect of any taxable year beginning prior to January 1, 1932.

P.L. 113-295, § 221(b)(2), Division A, provides:

(2) SAVINGS PROVISION.—If—

(A) any provision amended or repealed by the amendments made by this section applied to—

(i) any transaction occurring before the date of the enactment of this Act,

(ii) any property acquired before such date of enactment, or

(iii) any item of income, loss, deduction, or credit taken into account before such date of enactment, and

(B) the treatment of such transaction, property, or item under such provision would (without regard to the amendments or repeals made by this section) affect the liability for tax for periods ending after date of enactment, nothing in the amendments or repeals made by this section shall be construed to affect the treatment of such transaction, property, or item for purposes of determining liability for tax for periods ending after such date of enactment.

[Sec. 1314(d)]

(d) TAXES IMPOSED BY SUBTITLE C.—This part shall not apply to any tax imposed by subtitle C (sec. 3101 and following relating to employment taxes).

Amendments

• **2014, Tax Technical Corrections Act of 2014 (P.L. 113-295)**

P.L. 113-295, § 221(a)(87):

Amended Code Sec. 1314 by redesignating subsection (e) as subsection (d). **Effective** generally 12-19-2014. For a special rule, see Act Sec. 221(b)(2), Division A, below.

P.L. 113-295, § 221(b)(2), Division A, provides:

(2) SAVINGS PROVISION.—If—

(A) any provision amended or repealed by the amendments made by this section applied to—

(i) any transaction occurring before the date of the enactment of this Act,

(ii) any property acquired before such date of enactment, or

(iii) any item of income, loss, deduction, or credit taken into account before such date of enactment, and

(B) the treatment of such transaction, property, or item under such provision would (without regard to the amendments or repeals made by this section) affect the liability for tax for periods ending after date of enactment, nothing in the amendments or repeals made by this section shall be construed to affect the treatment of such transaction, property, or item for purposes of determining liability for tax for periods ending after such date of enactment.

PART V—CLAIM OF RIGHT

Sec. 1341.   Computation of tax where taxpayer restores substantial amount held under claim of right.

[Sec. 1341]

SEC. 1341. COMPUTATION OF TAX WHERE TAXPAYER RESTORES SUBSTANTIAL AMOUNT HELD UNDER CLAIM OF RIGHT.

[Sec. 1341(a)]

(a) GENERAL RULE.—If—

(1) an item was included in gross income for a prior taxable year (or years) because it appeared that the taxpayer had an unrestricted right to such item;

(2) a deduction is allowable for the taxable year because it was established after the close of such prior taxable year (or years) that the taxpayer did not have an unrestricted right to such item or to a portion of such item; and

(3) the amount of such deduction exceeds $3,000,

then the tax imposed by this chapter for the taxable year shall be the lesser of the following:

(4) the tax for the taxable year computed with such deduction; or

(5) an amount equal to—

(A) the tax for the taxable year computed without such deduction, minus

(B) the decrease in tax under this chapter (or the corresponding provisions of prior revenue laws) for the prior taxable year (or years) which would result solely from the exclusion of such item (or portion thereof) from gross income for such prior taxable year (or years).

For purposes of paragraph (5)(B), the corresponding provisions of the Internal Revenue Code of 1939 shall be chapter 1 of such code (other than subchapter E, relating to self-employment income) and subchapter E of chapter 2 of such code.

Amendments

• **1958, Technical Amendments Act of 1958 (P.L. 85-866)**

P.L. 85-866, § 60(a):

Added the phrase "and subchapter E of chapter 2 of such code." to the end of Code Sec. 1341(a). **Effective** 1-1-54.

[Sec. 1341(b)]

(b) SPECIAL RULES.—

(1) If the decrease in tax ascertained under subsection (a)(5)(B) exceeds the tax imposed by this chapter for the taxable year (computed without the deduction) such excess shall be considered to be a payment of tax on the last day prescribed by law for the payment of tax for the taxable year, and shall be refunded or credited in the same manner as if it were an overpayment for such taxable year.

(2) Subsection (a) does not apply to any deduction allowable with respect to an item which was included in gross income by reason of the sale or other disposition of stock in trade of the taxpayer (or other property of a kind which would properly have been included in the inventory of the taxpayer if on hand at the close of the prior taxable year) or property held by the taxpayer primarily for sale to customers in the ordinary course of his trade or business. This paragraph shall not apply if the deduction arises out of refunds or repayments with respect to rates made by a regulated public utility (as defined in section 7701(a)(33) without regard to the limitation contained in the last two sentences thereof) if such refunds or repayments are required to be made by the Government, political subdivision, agency, or instrumentality referred to in such section, or by an order of a court, or are made in settlement of litigation or under threat or imminence of litigation.

(3) If the tax imposed by this chapter for the taxable year is the amount determined under subsection (a)(5), then the deduction referred to in subsection (a)(2) shall not be taken into account for any purpose of this subtitle other than this section.

(4) For purposes of determining whether paragraph (4) or paragraph (5) of subsection (a) applies—

INCOME TAX—PERSONAL SERVICE INCOME

(A) in any case where the deduction referred to in paragraph (4) of subsection (a) results in a net operating loss, such loss shall, for purposes of computing the tax for the taxable year under such paragraph (4), be carried back to the same extent and in the same manner as is provided under section 172; and

(B) in any case where the exclusion referred to in paragraph (5)(B) of subsection (a) results in a net operating loss or capital loss for the prior taxable year (or years), such loss shall, for purposes of computing the decrease in tax for the prior taxable year (or years) under such paragraph (5)(B), be carried back and carried over to the same extent and in the same manner as is provided under section 172 or section 1212, except that no carryover beyond the taxable year shall be taken into account.

(5) For purposes of this chapter, the net operating loss described in paragraph (4)(A) of this subsection, or the net operating loss or capital loss described in paragraph (4)(B) of this subsection, as the case may be, shall (after the application of paragraph (4) or (5)(B) of subsection (a) for the taxable year) be taken into account under section 172 or 1212 for taxable years after the taxable year to the same extent and in the same manner as—

(A) a net operating loss sustained for the taxable year, if paragraph (4) of subsection (a) applied, or

(B) a net operating loss or capital loss sustained for the prior taxable year (or years), if paragraph (5)(B) of subsection (a) applied.

Amendments

• **1976, Tax Reform Act of 1976 (P.L. 94-455)**

P.L. 94-455, § 1901(a)(146):

Amended Code Sec. 1341(b)(2) by striking out the last sentence. **Effective** with respect to tax years beginning after 12-31-76. Prior to deletion, the last sentence of Code Sec. 1341(b)(2) read as follows:

This paragraph shall not apply if the deduction arises out of payments or repayments made pursuant to a price redetermination provision in a subcontract entered into before January 1, 1958, between persons other than those bearing the relationship set forth in section 267(b), if the subcontract containing the price redetermination provision is subject to statutory renegotiation and section 1481 (relating to mitigation of effect of renegotiation of Government contracts) does not apply to such payment or repayment solely because such payment or repayment is not paid or repaid to the United States or any agency thereof.

• **1964, Revenue Act of 1964 (P.L. 88-272)**

P.L. 88-272, § 234(b)(7):

Amended Code Sec. 1341(b)(2) by inserting "(as defined in section 7701(a)(33) without regard to the limitation contained in the last two sentences thereof)" in lieu of "(as defined in section 1503(c) without regard to paragraph (2) thereof)". **Effective** 1-1-64.

• **1962 (P.L. 87-863)**

P.L. 87-863, § 5(a):

Amended Code Sec. 1341(b) by adding paragraphs (4) and (5). **Effective** with respect to tax years beginning on or after 1-1-62.

• **1958, Technical Amendments Act of 1958 (P.L. 85-866)**

P.L. 85-866, § 60(b):

Amended the second sentence of Sec. 1341(b)(2). **Effective** for tax years beginning after 12-31-57. Prior to amendment, the last sentence of Sec. 1341(b)(2) read as follows:

"This paragraph shall not apply if the deduction arises out of refunds or repayments made by a regulated public utility (as defined in section 1503(c) without regard to paragraph (2) thereof) if such refunds or repayments are required to be made by the government, political subdivision, agency, or instrumentality referred to in such section."

P.L. 85-866, § 60(c):

Added the last sentence to Code Sec. 1341(b)(2). No interest shall be allowed or paid on any overpayment resulting from the application of the amendment made by subsection (c).

P.L. 85-866, § 60(d):

Added paragraph (3) to Sec. 1341(b).

[Sec. 1347—Repealed]

Amendments

• **1976, Tax Reform Act of 1976 (P.L. 94-455)**

P.L. 94-455, § 1951(b)(12):

Repealed Code Sec. 1347. **Effective** for tax years beginning after 12-31-76. Prior to repeal, Code Sec. 1347 read as follows:

SEC. 1347. CLAIMS AGAINST UNITED STATES INVOLVING ACQUISITION OF PROPERTY.

In the case of amounts (other than interest) received by a taxpayer from the United States with respect to a claim against the United States involving the acquisition of property and remaining unpaid for more than 15 years, the tax imposed by section 1 attributable to such receipt shall not exceed 33 percent of the amount (other than interest) so received. This section shall apply only if claim was filed with the United States before January 1, 1958.

P.L. 94-455, § 1951(b)(12)(B) provides:

Notwithstanding the repeal of Sec. 1347, if amounts received in a taxable year beginning after 1976 would have been subject to the provisions of Sec. 1347 if received in a taxable year beginning before such date, the tax imposed by Sec. 1 attributable to such receipt shall be computed as if Sec. 1347 had not been repealed.

PART VI—MAXIMUM RATE ON PERSONAL SERVICE INCOME—[Repealed]

[Sec. 1348—Repealed]

Amendments

• **1981, Economic Recovery Tax Act of 1981 (P.L. 97-34)**

P.L. 97-34, § 101(c)(1):

Repealed Part VI. **Effective** for tax years beginning after 12-31-81. Prior to repeal, Part VI read as follows:

PART VI—MAXIMUM RATE ON PERSONAL SERVICE INCOME

Sec. 1348. 50-percent maximum rate on personal service income.

SEC. 1348. 50-PERCENT MAXIMUM RATE ON PERSONAL SERVICE INCOME.

(a) GENERAL RULE.—If for any taxable year an individual has personal service taxable income which exceeds the amount of taxable income specified in paragraph (1), the tax imposed by section 1 for such year shall, unless the taxpayer chooses the benefits of part I (relating to income averaging), be the sum of—

(1) the tax imposed by section 1 on the highest amount of taxable income on which the rate of tax does not exceed 50 percent,

(2) 50 percent of the amount by which his personal service taxable income exceeds the amount of taxable income specified in paragraph (1) of this subsection, and

(3) the excess of the tax computed under section 1 without regard to this section over the tax so computed with reference solely to his personal service taxable income.

(b) DEFINITIONS.—For purposes of this section—

(1) PERSONAL SERVICE INCOME.—

(A) IN GENERAL.—The term "personal service income" means any income which is earned income within the meaning of section 401(c)(2)(C) or section 911(b) or which is an amount received as a pension or annuity which arises from an employer-employee relationship or from tax-deductible contributions to a retirement plan. For purposes of this subparagraph, section 911(b) shall be applied without regard to the phrase ", not in excess of 30 percent of his share of net profits of such trade or business,".

(B) EXCEPTIONS.—The term "personal service income" does not include any amount—

(i) to which section 72(m)(5), 402(a)(2), 402(e), 403(a)(2), 408(e)(2), 408(e)(3), 408(e)(4), 408(e)(5), 408(f), or 409(c) applies; or

(ii) which is includible in gross income under section 409(b) because of the redemption of a bond which was not tendered before the close of the taxable year in which the registered owner attained age $70^{1}/_{2}$.

(2) PERSONAL SERVICE TAXABLE INCOME.—The personal service taxable income of an individual is the excess of—

(A) the amount which bears the same ratio (but not in excess of 100 percent) to his taxable income as his personal service net income bears to his adjusted gross income, over

(B) the sum of the items of tax preference described in subsection (a) (other than paragraph (9)) of section 57 for the taxable year.

For purposes of subparagraph (A), the term "personal service net income" means personal service income reduced by any deductions allowable under section 62 which are properly allocable to or chargeable against such personal service income.

(c) MARRIED INDIVIDUALS.—This section shall apply to a married individual only if such individual and his spouse make a single return jointly for the taxable year.

• **1978, Revenue Act of 1978 (P.L. 95-600)**

P.L. 95-600, § 441(a):

Amended Code Sec. 1348(b)(2)(B) by striking out "items of tax preference (as defined in section 57)" and inserting in lieu thereof "items of tax preference described in subsection (a) (other than paragraph (9)) of section 57". **Effective** as provided in P.L. 95-600, § 441(b), below.

P.L. 95-600, § 441(b), as amended by P.L. 96-222, § 104(a)(5)(A), provides:

(b) EFFECTIVE DATE.—

(1) GENERAL RULE.—The amendment made by subsection (a) shall apply with respect to taxable years beginning after October 31, 1978.

(2) TAXABLE YEARS WHICH STRADDLE NOVEMBER 1, 1978.—In the case of a taxable year which begins before November 1, 1978, and ends after October 31, 1978, the amount taken into account under section 1348(b)(2)(B) of the Internal Revenue Code of 1954 by reason of section 57(a)(9) of such Code shall be 50 percent of the lesser of—

(A) the net capital gain for the taxable year, or

INCOME TAX—EXPROPRIATION LOSSES

(B) the net capital gain taking into account only gain or loss properly taken into account for the portion of the taxable year before November 1, 1978.

P.L. 95-600, § 442(a):

Amended Code Sec. 1348(b)(1)(A) by adding a new last sentence to the end thereof. **Effective** with respect to tax years beginning after 12-31-78.

P.L. 95-600, § 701(x)(1):

Amended Code Sec. 1348(b)(1)(A) by striking out "pension or annuity" and inserting in lieu thereof "pension or annuity which arises from an employer-employee relationship or from tax-deductible contributions to a retirement plan". **Effective** for tax years beginning after 12-31-76.

P.L. 95-600, § 701(x)(2):

Amended the last sentence of Code Sec. 1348(b) by striking out "against such earned income" and inserting in lieu thereof "against such personal service income". **Effective** for tax years beginning after 12-31-76.

- **1976, Tax Reform Act of 1976 (P.L. 94-455)**

P.L. 94-455, § 302(a):

Amended Code Sec. 1348. **Effective** for tax years beginning after 12-31-76. Prior to amendment Code Sec. 1348 read as follows:

SEC. 1348. FIFTY-PERCENT MAXIMUM RATE ON EARNED INCOME.

(a) GENERAL RULE.—If for any taxable year an individual has earned taxable income which exceeds the amount of taxable income specified in paragraph (1), the tax imposed by section 1 for such year shall, unless the taxpayer chooses the benefits of part I (relating to income averaging), be the sum of—

(1) the tax imposed by section 1 on the lowest amount of taxable income on which the rate of tax under section 1 exceeds 50 percent,

(2) 50 percent of the amount by which his earned taxable income exceeds the lowest amount of taxable income on which the rate of tax under section 1 exceeds 50 percent, and

(3) the excess of the tax computed under section 1 without regard to this section over the tax so computed with reference solely to his earned taxable income.

In applying this subsection to a taxable year beginning after December 31, 1970, and before January 1, 1972, "60 percent" shall be substituted for "50 percent" each place it appears in paragraphs (1) and (2).

(b) DEFINITIONS.—For purposes of this section—

(1) EARNED INCOME.—The term "earned income" means any income which is earned income within the meaning of section 401(c)(2)(C) or section 911(b), except that such term does not include any distribution to which section 72(m)(5), 402(a)(2), 402(e), or 403(c)(2)(A) applies or any deferred compensation within the meaning of section 404. For purposes of this paragraph, deferred compensation does not include any amount received before the end of the taxable year following the first taxable year of the recipient in which his right to receive such amount is not subject to a substantial risk of forfeiture (within the meaning of section 83(c)(1)).

(2) EARNED TAXABLE INCOME.—The earned taxable income of an individual is the excess of—

(A) the amount which bears the same ratio (but not in excess of 100 percent) to his taxable income as his earned net income bears to his adjusted gross income, over

(B) the amount by which the greater of—

(i) one-fifth of the sum of the taxpayer's items of tax preference referred to in section 57 for the taxable year and the 4 preceding taxable years, or

(ii) the sum of the items of tax preference for the taxable year, exceeds $30,000.

For purposes of subparagraph (A), the term "earned net income" means earned income reduced by any deductions allowable under section 62 which are properly allocable to or chargeable against such earned income.

(c) MARRIED INDIVIDUALS.—This section shall apply to a married individual only if such individual and his spouse make a single return jointly for the taxable year.

- **1974, Employee Retirement Income Security Act of 1974 (P.L. 93-406)**

P.L. 93-406, § 2005(c)(14):

Amended Code Sec. 1348(b)(1) by substituting "402(a)(2), 402(e)" for "72(n), 402(a)(2)". **Effective** with respect to distributions and payments made after 12-31-73 in tax years beginning after such date.

- **1969, Tax Reform Act of 1969 (P.L. 91-172)**

P.L. 91-172, § 804(a):

Added Code Sec. 1348. **Effective** for tax years beginning after 12-31-70.

PART VII—RECOVERIES OF FOREIGN EXPROPRIATION LOSSES

Sec. 1351.   Treatment of recoveries of foreign expropriation losses.

[Sec. 1351]

SEC. 1351. TREATMENT OF RECOVERIES OF FOREIGN EXPROPRIATION LOSSES.

[Sec. 1351(a)]

(a) ELECTION.—

(1) IN GENERAL.—This section shall apply only to a recovery, by a domestic corporation subject to the tax imposed by section 11 or 801, of a foreign expropriation loss sustained by such corporation and only if such corporation was subject to the tax imposed by section 11 or 801, as the case may be, for the year of the loss and elects to have the provisions of this section apply with respect to such loss.

(2) TIME, MANNER, AND SCOPE.—An election under paragraph (1) shall be made at such time and in such manner as the Secretary may prescribe by regulations. An election made with respect to any foreign expropriation loss shall apply to all recoveries in respect of such loss.

Amendments

- **1984, Deficit Reduction Act of 1984 (P.L. 98-369)**

P.L. 98-369, § 211(b)(18)(A):

Amended Code Sec. 1351(a)(1) by striking out "802" each place it appeared and inserting in lieu thereof "801". **Effective** for tax years beginning after 12-31-83.

- **1976, Tax Reform Act of 1976 (P.L. 94-455)**

P.L. 94-455, § 1906(b)(13)(A):

Amended 1954 Code by substituting "Secretary" for "Secretary or his delegate" each place it appeared. **Effective** 2-1-77.

[Sec. 1351(b)]

(b) DEFINITION OF FOREIGN EXPROPRIATION LOSS.—For purposes of this section, the term "foreign expropriation loss" means any loss sustained by reason of the expropriation, intervention, seizure, or similar taking of property by the government of any foreign country, any political subdivision thereof, or any agency or instrumentality of the foregoing. For purposes of the preceding sentence, a debt which becomes worthless shall, to the extent of any deduction allowed under section 166(a), be treated as a loss.

[Sec. 1351(c)]

(c) AMOUNT OF RECOVERY.—

(1) GENERAL RULE.—The amount of any recovery of a foreign expropriation loss is the amount of money and the fair market value of other property received in respect of such loss, determined as of the date of receipt.

(2) SPECIAL RULE FOR LIFE INSURANCE COMPANIES.—The amount of any recovery of a foreign expropriation loss includes, in the case of a life insurance company, the amount of decrease of any item taken into account under section 807(c), to the extent such decrease is attributable to the release, by reason of such loss, of its liabilities with respect to such item.

Amendments

- **1984, Deficit Reduction Act of 1984 (P.L. 98-369)**

P.L. 98-369, § 211(b)(18)(B):

Amended Code Sec. 1351(c)(2) by striking out "section 810(c)" and inserting in lieu thereof "section 807(c)". **Effective** for tax years beginning after 12-31-83.

[Sec. 1351(d)]

(d) ADJUSTMENT FOR PRIOR TAX BENEFITS.—

(1) IN GENERAL.—That part of the amount of a recovery of a foreign expropriation loss to which this section applies which, when added to the aggregate of the amounts of previous recoveries with respect to such loss, does not exceed the allowable deductions in prior taxable years on account of such loss shall be excluded from gross income for the taxable year of the recovery for purposes of computing the tax under this subtitle; but there shall be added to, and assessed and collected as a part of, the tax under this subtitle for such taxable year an amount equal to

INCOME TAX—EXPROPRIATION LOSSES

the total increase in the tax under this subtitle for all taxable years which would result by decreasing, in an amount equal to such part of the recovery so excluded, the deductions allowable in the prior taxable years on account of such loss. For purposes of this paragraph, if the loss to which the recovery relates was taken into account as a loss from the sale or exchange of a capital asset, the amount of the loss shall be treated as an allowable deduction even though there were no gains against which to allow such loss.

(2) COMPUTATION.—The increase in the tax for each taxable year referred to in paragraph (1) shall be computed in accordance with regulations prescribed by the Secretary. Such regulations shall give effect to previous recoveries of any kind (including recoveries described in section 111, relating to recovery of tax benefit items) with respect to any prior taxable year, but shall otherwise treat the tax previously determined for any taxable year in accordance with the principles set forth in section 1314(a) (relating to correction of errors). Subject to the provisions of paragraph (3), all credits allowable against the tax for any taxable year, and all carryovers and carrybacks affected by so decreasing the allowable deductions, shall be taken into account in computing the increase in the tax.

(3) FOREIGN TAXES.—For purposes of this subsection, any choice made under subpart A of part III of subchapter N (relating to foreign tax credit) for any taxable year may be changed.

(4) SUBSTITUTION OF CURRENT TAX RATE.—For purposes of this subsection, the rates of tax specified in section 11(b) for the taxable year of the recovery shall be treated as having been in effect for all prior taxable years.

Amendments

- **1986, Tax Reform Act of 1986 (P.L. 99-514)**

P.L. 99-514, §1812(a)(4):

Amended Code Sec. 1351(d)(2) by striking out "relating to recovery of bad debts, etc." and inserting in lieu thereof "relating to recovery of tax benefit items". **Effective** as if included in the provision of P.L. 98-369 to which it relates.

- **1978, Revenue Act of 1978 (P.L. 95-600)**

P.L. 95-600, §301(b)(17):

Amended Code Sec. 1351(d)(4). **Effective** for tax years beginning after 12-31-78. Prior to amendment, Code Sec. 1351(d)(4) read as follows:

"(4) SUBSTITUTION OF CURRENT NORMAL TAX AND SURTAX RATES.—For purposes of this subsection, the normal tax rate provided by section 11(b) and the surtax rate provided by section 11(c) which are in effect for the taxable year of the recovery shall be treated as having been in effect for all prior taxable years."

- **1976, Tax Reform Act of 1976 (P.L. 94-455)**

P.L. 94-455, §1031(b)(3):

Amended Code Sec. 1351(d)(3). **Effective** as indicated in P.L. 94-455, §1031(c), below. Prior to amendment, Code Sec. 1351(d)(3) read as follows:

(3) FOREIGN TAXES.—For purposes of this subsection—

(A) any choice made under subpart A of part III of subchapter N (relating to foreign tax credit) for any taxable year may be changed,

(B) subject to the provisions of section 904(b), an election to have the limitation provided by section 904(a)(2) apply may be made, and

(C) notwithstanding section 904(b)(1), an election previously made to have the limitation provided by section 904(a)(2) apply may be revoked with respect to any taxable year and succeeding taxable years.

P.L. 94-455, §1031(c) provides:

(c) EFFECTIVE DATES.—

(1) IN GENERAL.—Except as provided in paragraphs (2) and (3), the amendments made by this section shall apply to taxable years beginning after December 31, 1975.

(2) EXCEPTION FOR CERTAIN MINING OPERATIONS.—In the case of a domestic corporation or includible corporation in an affiliated group (as defined in section 1504 of the Internal Revenue Code of 1954) which has as of October 1, 1975—

(A) been engaged in the active conduct of the trade or business of the extraction of minerals (of a character with respect to which a deduction for depletion is allowable under section 613 of such Code) outside the United States or its possessions for less than 5 years preceding the date of enactment of this Act,

(B) had deductions properly apportioned or allocated to its gross income from such trade or business in excess of such gross income in at least 2 taxable years,

(C) 80 percent of its gross receipts are from the sale of such minerals, and

(D) made commitments for substantial expansion of such mineral extraction activities,

the amendments made by this section shall apply to taxable years beginning after December 31, 1978. In the case of losses sustained in taxable years beginning before January 1, 1979, by any corporation to which this paragraph applies, the provisions of section 904(f) of such Code shall be applied with respect to such losses under the principles of section 904(a)(1) of such Code as in effect before the enactment of this Act.

(3) EXCEPTION FOR INCOME FROM POSSESSIONS.—In the case of gross income from sources within a possession of the United States (and the deductions properly apportioned or allocated thereto), the amendments made by this section shall apply to taxable years beginning after December 31, 1978. In the case of losses sustained in a possession of the United States in taxable years beginning before January 1, 1979, the provisions of section 904(f) of such Code shall be applied with respect to such losses under the principles of section 904(a)(1) of such Code as in effect before the enactment of this Act.

(4) CARRYBACKS AND CARRYOVERS IN THE CASE OF MINING OPERATIONS AND INCOME FROM A POSSESSION.—In the case of a taxpayer to whom paragraph (2) or (3) of this subsection applies, section 904(e) of such Code shall apply except that "January 1, 1979" shall be substituted for "January 1, 1976" each place it appears therein. If such a taxpayer elects the overall limitation for a taxable year beginning before January 1, 1979, such section 904(e) shall be applied by substituting "the January 1, of the last year for which such taxpayer is on the per-country limitation" for "January 1, 1976" each place it appears therein.

P.L. 94-455, §1906(b)(13)(A):

Amended the 1954 Code by substituting "Secretary" for "Secretary or his delegate" each place it appeared. **Effective** 2-1-77.

[Sec. 1351(e)]

(e) GAIN ON RECOVERY.—That part of the amount of a recovery of a foreign expropriation loss to which this section applies which is not excluded from gross income under subsection (d)(1) shall be considered for the taxable year of the recovery as gain on the involuntary conversion of property as a result of its destruction or seizure and shall be recognized or not recognized as provided in section 1033.

[Sec. 1351(f)]

(f) BASIS OF RECOVERED PROPERTY.—The basis of property (other than money) received as a recovery of a foreign expropriation loss to which this section applies shall be an amount equal to its fair market value on the date of receipt, reduced by such part of the gain under subsection (e) which is not recognized as provided in section 1033.

[Sec. 1351(g)]

(g) RESTORATION OF VALUE OF INVESTMENTS.—For purposes of this section, if the value of any interest in, or with respect to, property (including any interest represented by a security, as defined in section 165(g)(2))—

(1) which became worthless by reason of the expropriation, intervention, seizure, or similar taking of such property by the government of any foreign country, any political subdivision thereof, or any agency or instrumentality of the foregoing, and

(2) which was taken into account as a loss from the sale or exchange of a captial asset or with respect to which a deduction for a loss was allowed under section 165 or a deduction for a bad debt was allowed under section 166,

is restored in whole or in part by reason of any recovery of money or other property in respect of the property which became worthless, the value so restored shall be treated as property received as a recovery in respect of such loss or such bad debt.

[Sec. 1351(h)]

(h) SPECIAL RULE FOR EVIDENCES OF INDEBTEDNESS.—Bonds or other evidences of indebtedness received as a recovery of a foreign expropriation loss to which this section applies shall not be considered to have any original issue discount within the meaning of section 1273(a).

Amendments

- **1984, Deficit Reduction Act of 1984 (P.L. 98-369)**

P.L. 98-369, §42(a)(12):

Amended Code Sec. 1351(h) by striking out "section 1232(a)(2)" and inserting in lieu thereof "section 1273(a)". **Effective** for tax years ending after 7-18-84.

[Sec. 1351(i)]

(i) ADJUSTMENTS FOR SUCCEEDING YEARS.—For purposes of this subtitle, proper adjustment shall be made, under regulations prescribed by the Secretary, in—

(1) the credit under section 27 (relating to foreign tax credit),
(2) the credit under section 38 (relating to general business credit),
(3) the net operating loss deduction under section 172,
(4) the capital loss carryover under section 1212(a), and
(5) such other items as may be specified by such regulations,

for the taxable year of a recovery of a foreign expropriation loss to which this section applies, and for succeeding taxable years, to take into account items changed in making the computations under subsection (d) for taxable years prior to the taxable year of such recovery.

Amendments

• **2017, Tax Cuts and Jobs Act (P.L. 115-97)**

P.L. 115-97, §13511(b)(8):

Amended Code Sec. 1351(i)(3) by striking "or the operations loss deduction under section 810," following "under section 172,". **Effective** for losses arising in tax years beginning after 12-31-2017.

• **1984, Deficit Reduction Act of 1984 (P.L. 98-369)**

P.L. 98-369, §211(b)(18)(C):

Amended Code Sec. 1351(i)(3) by striking out "section 812" and inserting in lieu thereof "section 810". **Effective** for tax years beginning after 12-31-83.

P.L. 98-369, §474(r)(25)(A):

Amended Code Sec. 1351(i) by striking out "section 33" and inserting in lieu thereof "section 27". **Effective** for tax years beginning after 12-31-83, and to carrybacks from such years.

P.L. 98-369, §474(r)(25)(B):

Amended Code Sec. 1351(i) by striking out "section 38 (relating to investment credit)" and inserting in lieu thereof "section 38 (relating to general business credit)". **Effective** for tax years beginning after 12-31-83, and to carrybacks from such years.

• **1976, Tax Reform Act of 1976 (P.L. 94-455)**

P.L. 94-455, §1906(b)(13)(A):

Amended 1954 Code by substituting "Secretary" for "Secretary or his delegate" each place it appeared. **Effective** 2-1-77.

• **1966 (P.L. 89-384)**

P.L. 89-384, §1(a):

Added new Part VII, Subchapter Q, consisting of Code Sec. 1351. **Effective** with respect to amounts received after 12-31-64, in respect of foreign expropriation losses sustained after 12-31-58.

Subchapter R—Election To Determine Corporate Tax on Certain International Shipping Activities Using Per Ton Rate

Sec.	
Sec. 1352.	Alternative tax on qualifying shipping activities.
Sec. 1353.	Notional shipping income.
Sec. 1354.	Alternative tax election; revocation; termination.
Sec. 1355.	Definitions and special rules.
Sec. 1356.	Qualifying shipping activities.
Sec. 1357.	Items not subject to regular tax; depreciation; interest.
Sec. 1358.	Allocation of credits, income, and deductions.
Sec. 1359.	Disposition of qualifying vessels.

[Sec. 1352]

SEC. 1352. ALTERNATIVE TAX ON QUALIFYING SHIPPING ACTIVITIES.

In the case of an electing corporation, the tax imposed by section 11 shall be the amount equal to the sum of—

(1) the tax imposed by section 11 determined after the application of this subchapter, and
(2) a tax equal to—
   (A) the highest rate of tax specified in section 11, multiplied by
   (B) the notional shipping income for the taxable year.

Amendments

• **2004, American Jobs Creation Act of 2004 (P.L. 108-357)**

P.L. 108-357, §248(a):

Amended chapter 1 by inserting after subchapter Q a new subchapter R (Code Secs. 1352-1359). **Effective** for tax years beginning after 10-22-2004.

[Sec. 1353]

SEC. 1353. NOTIONAL SHIPPING INCOME.

[Sec. 1353(a)]

(a) IN GENERAL.—For purposes of this subchapter, the notional shipping income of an electing corporation shall be the sum of the amounts determined under subsection (b) for each qualifying vessel operated by such electing corporation.

[Sec. 1353(b)]

(b) AMOUNTS.—

(1) IN GENERAL.—For purposes of subsection (a), the amount of notional shipping income of an electing corporation for each qualifying vessel for the taxable year shall equal the product of—
   (A) the daily notional shipping income, and
   (B) the number of days during the taxable year that the electing corporation operated such vessel as a qualifying vessel in United States foreign trade.

(2) TREATMENT OF VESSELS THE INCOME FROM WHICH IS NOT OTHERWISE SUBJECT TO TAX.—In the case of a qualifying vessel any of the income from which is not included in gross income by reason of section 883 or otherwise, the amount of notional shipping income from such vessel for the taxable year shall be the amount which bears the same ratio to such shipping income (determined without regard to this paragraph) as the gross income from the operation of such vessel in the United States foreign trade bears to the sum of such gross income and the income so excluded.

[Sec. 1353(c)]

(c) DAILY NOTIONAL SHIPPING INCOME.—For purposes of subsection (b), the daily notional shipping income from the operation of a qualifying vessel is—

INCOME TAX—ELECTION, INTL. SHIPPING ACTIVITIES

(1) 40 cents for each 100 tons of so much of the net tonnage of the vessel as does not exceed 25,000 net tons, and

(2) 20 cents for each 100 tons of so much of the net tonnage of the vessel as exceeds 25,000 net tons.

[Sec. 1353(d)]

(d) MULTIPLE OPERATORS OF VESSEL.—If for any period 2 or more persons are operators of a qualifying vessel, the notional shipping income from the operation of such vessel for such period shall be allocated among such persons on the basis of their respective ownership, charter, and operating agreement interests in such vessel or on such other basis as the Secretary may prescribe by regulations.

Amendments

• 2005, Gulf Opportunity Zone Act of 2005 (P.L. 109-135)

P.L. 109-135, §403(g)(1)(A):

Amended Code Sec. 1353(d) by striking "ownership and charter interests" and inserting "ownership, charter, and operating agreement interests". **Effective** as if included in the provision of the American Jobs Creation Act of 2004 (P.L. 108-357) to which it relates [**effective** for tax years beginning after 10-22-2004.—CCH].

• 2004, American Jobs Creation Act of 2004 (P.L. 108-357)

P.L. 108-357, §248(a):

Amended chapter 1 by inserting after subchapter Q a new subchapter R (Code Secs. 1352-1359). **Effective** for tax years beginning after 10-22-2004.

[Sec. 1354]

SEC. 1354. ALTERNATIVE TAX ELECTION; REVOCATION; TERMINATION.

[Sec. 1354(a)]

(a) IN GENERAL.—A qualifying vessel operator may elect the application of this subchapter.

[Sec. 1354(b)]

(b) TIME AND MANNER; YEARS FOR WHICH EFFECTIVE.—An election under this subchapter—

(1) shall be made in such form as prescribed by the Secretary, and

(2) shall be effective for the taxable year for which made and all succeeding taxable years until terminated under subsection (d).

Such election may be effective for any taxable year only if made on or before the due date (including extensions) for filing the corporation's return for such taxable year.

Amendments

• 2005, Gulf Opportunity Zone Act of 2005 (P.L. 109-135)

P.L. 109-135, §403(g)(4):

Amended the last sentence of Code Sec. 1354(b) by inserting "on or" after "only if made". **Effective** as if included in the provision of the American Jobs Creation Act of 2004 (P.L. 108-357) to which it relates [**effective** for tax years beginning after 10-22-2004.—CCH].

[Sec. 1354(c)]

(c) CONSISTENT ELECTIONS BY MEMBERS OF CONTROLLED GROUPS.—An election under subsection (a) by a member of a controlled group shall apply to all qualifying vessel operators that are members of such group.

[Sec. 1354(d)]

(d) TERMINATION.—

(1) BY REVOCATION.—

(A) IN GENERAL.—An election under subsection (a) may be terminated by revocation.

(B) WHEN EFFECTIVE.—Except as provided in subparagraph (C)—

(i) a revocation made during the taxable year and on or before the 15th day of the 4th month thereof shall be effective on the 1st day of such taxable year, and

(ii) a revocation made during the taxable year but after such 15th day shall be effective on the 1st day of the following taxable year.

(C) REVOCATION MAY SPECIFY PROSPECTIVE DATE.—If the revocation specifies a date for revocation which is on or after the day on which the revocation is made, the revocation shall be effective for taxable years beginning on and after the date so specified.

(2) BY PERSON CEASING TO BE QUALIFYING VESSEL OPERATOR.—

(A) IN GENERAL.—An election under subsection (a) shall be terminated whenever (at any time on or after the 1st day of the 1st taxable year for which the corporation is an electing corporation) such corporation ceases to be a qualifying vessel operator.

(B) WHEN EFFECTIVE.—Any termination under this paragraph shall be effective on and after the date of cessation.

(C) ANNUALIZATION.—The Secretary shall prescribe such annualization and other rules as are appropriate in the case of a termination under this paragraph.

Amendments

• 2015, Surface Transportation and Veterans Health Care Choice Improvement Act of 2015 (P.L. 114-41)

P.L. 114-41, §2006(a)(2)(C):

Amended Code Sec. 1354(d)(1)(B)(i) by striking "3d month" and inserting "4th month". **Effective** generally for returns for tax years beginning after 12-31-2015. For an exception, see Act Sec. 2006(a)(3)(B), below.

P.L. 114-41, §2006(a)(3)(B), provides:

(B) SPECIAL RULE FOR C CORPORATIONS WITH FISCAL YEARS ENDING ON JUNE 30.—In the case of any C corporation with a taxable year ending on June 30, the amendments made by this subsection shall apply to returns for taxable years beginning after December 31, 2025.

[Sec. 1354(e)]

(e) ELECTION AFTER TERMINATION.—If a qualifying vessel operator has made an election under subsection (a) and if such election has been terminated under subsection (d), such operator (and any successor operator) shall not be eligible to make an election under subsection (a) for any taxable year before its 5th taxable year which begins after the 1st taxable year for which such termination is effective, unless the Secretary consents to such election.

Amendments

• 2004, American Jobs Creation Act of 2004 (P.L. 108-357)

P.L. 108-357, §248(a):

Amended chapter 1 by inserting after subchapter Q a new subchapter R (Code Secs. 1352-1359). **Effective** for tax years beginning after 10-22-2004.

Sec. 1353(c)(1)

SEC. 1355. DEFINITIONS AND SPECIAL RULES.

[Sec. 1355(a)]

(a) DEFINITIONS.—For purposes of this subchapter—

(1) ELECTING CORPORATION.—The term "electing corporation" means any corporation for which an election is in effect under this subchapter.

(2) ELECTING GROUP; CONTROLLED GROUP.—

(A) ELECTING GROUP.—The term "electing group" means a controlled group of which one or more members is an electing corporation.

(B) CONTROLLED GROUP.—The term "controlled group" means any group which would be treated as a single employer under subsection (a) or (b) of section 52 if paragraphs (1) and (2) of section 52(a) did not apply.

(3) QUALIFYING VESSEL OPERATOR.—The term "qualifying vessel operator" means any corporation—

(A) who operates one or more qualifying vessels, and

(B) who meets the shipping activity requirement in subsection (c).

(4) QUALIFYING VESSEL.—The term "qualifying vessel" means a self-propelled (or a combination self-propelled and non-self-propelled) United States flag vessel of not less than 6,000 deadweight tons used exclusively in the United States foreign trade during the period that the election under this subchapter is in effect.

(5) UNITED STATES FLAG VESSEL.—The term "United States flag vessel" means any vessel documented under the laws of the United States.

(6) UNITED STATES DOMESTIC TRADE.—The term "United States domestic trade" means the transportation of goods or passengers between places in the United States.

(7) UNITED STATES FOREIGN TRADE.—The term "United States foreign trade" means the transportation of goods or passengers between a place in the United States and a foreign place or between foreign places.

Amendments

• **2006, Tax Relief and Health Care Act of 2006 (P.L. 109-432)**

P.L. 109-432, Division A, §413(a):

Amended Code Sec. 1355(a)(4) by striking "10,000 (6,000, in the case of taxable years beginning after December 31, 2005, and ending before January 1, 2011)" and inserting "6,000". **Effective** as if included in section 205 of the Tax Increase Prevention and Reconciliation Act of 2005 (P.L. 109-222) [**effective** for tax years beginning after 12-31-2005.—CCH].

• **2006, Tax Increase Prevention and Reconciliation Act of 2005 (P.L. 109-222)**

P.L. 109-222, §205(a):

Amended Code Sec. 1355(a)(4) by inserting "(6,000, in the case of taxable years beginning after December 31, 2005, and ending before January 1, 2011)" after "10,000". **Effective** for tax years beginning after 12-31-2005.

• **2005, Gulf Opportunity Zone Act of 2005 (P.L. 109-135)**

P.L. 109-135, §403(g)(1)(B):

Amended Code Sec. 1355(a) by striking paragraph (8). **Effective** as if included in the provision of the American Jobs Creation Act of 2004 (P.L. 108-357) to which it relates [**effective** for tax years beginning after 10-22-2004.—CCH]. Prior to being stricken, Code Sec. 1355(a)(8) read as follows:

(8) CHARTER.—The term "charter" includes an operating agreement.

[Sec. 1355(b)]

(b) OPERATING A VESSEL.—For purposes of this subchapter—

(1) IN GENERAL.—Except as provided in paragraph (2), a person is treated as operating any vessel during any period if—

(A)(i) such vessel is owned by, or chartered (including a time charter) to, the person, or

(ii) the person provides services for such vessel pursuant to an operating agreement, and

(B) such vessel is in use as a qualifying vessel during such period.

(2) BAREBOAT CHARTERS.—A person is treated as operating and using a vessel that it has chartered out on bareboat charter terms only if—

(A)(i) the vessel is temporarily surplus to the person's requirements and the term of the charter does not exceed 3 years, or

(ii) the vessel is bareboat chartered to a member of a controlled group which includes such person or to an unrelated person who subbareboats or time charters the vessel to such a member (including the owner of the vessel), and

(B) the vessel is used as a qualifying vessel by the person to whom ultimately chartered.

Amendments

• **2005, Gulf Opportunity Zone Act of 2005 (P.L. 109-135)**

P.L. 109-135, §403(g)(1)(C):

Amended Code Sec. 1355(b)(1). **Effective** as if included in the provision of the American Jobs Creation Act of 2004 (P.L. 108-357) to which it relates [**effective** for tax years beginning after 10-22-2004.—CCH]. Prior to amendment, Code Sec. 1355(b)(1) read as follows:

(1) IN GENERAL.—Except as provided in paragraph (2), a person is treated as operating any vessel during any period if such vessel is—

(A) owned by, or chartered (including a time charter) to, the person, and

(B) is in use as a qualifying vessel during such period.

[Sec. 1355(c)]

(c) SHIPPING ACTIVITY REQUIREMENT.—For purposes of this section—

(1) IN GENERAL.—Except as otherwise provided in this subsection, a corporation meets the shipping activity requirement of this subsection for any taxable year only if the requirement of paragraph (4) is met for each of the 2 preceding taxable years.

(2) SPECIAL RULE FOR 1ST YEAR OF ELECTION.—A corporation meets the shipping activity requirement of this subsection for the first taxable year for which the election under section 1354(a) is in effect only if the requirement of paragraph (4) is met for the preceding taxable year.

(3) CONTROLLED GROUPS.—A corporation who is a member of a controlled group meets the shipping activity requirement of this subsection only if such requirement is met determined by treating all members of such group as 1 person.

(4) REQUIREMENT.—The requirement of this paragraph is met for any taxable year if, on average during such year, at least 25 percent of the aggregate tonnage of qualifying vessels used by the corporation were owned by such corporation or chartered to such corporation on bareboat charter terms.

Amendments

• **2005, Gulf Opportunity Zone Act of 2005 (P.L. 109-135)**

P.L. 109-135, §403(g)(2):

Amended Code Sec. 1355(c)(3) by striking "determined—" and all that follows and inserting "determined by treating all members of such group as 1 person.". **Effective** as if included in the provision of the American Jobs Creation Act of 2004 (P.L. 108-357) to which it relates [**effective** for tax years beginning after 10-22-2004.—CCH]. Prior to amendment, Code Sec. 1355(c)(3) read as follows:

(3) CONTROLLED GROUPS.—A corporation who is a member of a controlled group meets the shipping activity requirement of this subsection only if such requirement is met determined—

(A) by treating all members of such group as 1 person, and

(B) by disregarding vessel charters between members of such group.

INCOME TAX—ELECTION, INTL. SHIPPING ACTIVITIES

[Sec. 1355(d)]

(d) ACTIVITIES CARRIED ON [BY] PARTNERSHIPS, ETC.—In applying this subchapter to a partner in a partnership—

(1) each partner shall be treated as operating vessels operated by the partnership,

(2) each partner shall be treated as conducting the activities conducted by the partnership, and

(3) the extent of a partner's ownership, charter, or operating agreement interest in any vessel operated by the partnership shall be determined on the basis of the partner's interest in the partnership.

A similar rule shall apply with respect to other pass-thru entities.

Amendments

• **2005, Gulf Opportunity Zone Act of 2005 (P.L. 109-135)**

P.L. 109-135, §403(g)(1)(D):

Amended Code Sec. 1355(d)(3). **Effective** as if included in the provision of the American Jobs Creation Act of 2004 (P.L. 108-357) to which it relates [effective for tax years beginning after 10-22-2004.—CCH]. Prior to amendment, Code Sec. 1355(d)(3) read as follows:

(3) the extent of a partner's ownership or charter interest in any vessel owned by or chartered to the partnership shall be determined on the basis of the partner's interest in the partnership.

[Sec. 1355(e)]

(e) EFFECT OF TEMPORARILY CEASING TO OPERATE A QUALIFYING VESSEL.—

(1) IN GENERAL.—For purposes of subsections (b) and (c), an electing corporation shall be treated as continuing to use a qualifying vessel during any period of temporary cessation if the electing corporation gives timely notice to the Secretary stating—

(A) that it has temporarily ceased to operate the qualifying vessel, and

(B) its intention to resume operating the qualifying vessel.

(2) NOTICE.—Notice shall be deemed timely if given not later than the due date (including extensions) for the corporation's tax return for the taxable year in which the temporary cessation begins.

(3) PERIOD DISREGARD IN EFFECT.—The period of temporary cessation under paragraph (1) shall continue until the earlier of the date on which—

(A) the electing corporation abandons its intention to resume operation of the qualifying vessel, or

(B) the electing corporation resumes operation of the qualifying vessel.

[Sec. 1355(f)]

(f) EFFECT OF TEMPORARILY OPERATING A QUALIFYING VESSEL IN THE UNITED STATES DOMESTIC TRADE.—

(1) IN GENERAL.—For purposes of this subchapter, an electing corporation shall be treated as continuing to use a qualifying vessel in the United States foreign trade during any period of temporary use in the United States domestic trade if the electing corporation gives timely notice to the Secretary stating—

(A) that it temporarily operates or has operated in the United States domestic trade a qualifying vessel which had been used in the United States foreign trade, and

(B) its intention to resume operation of the vessel in the United States foreign trade.

(2) NOTICE.—Notice shall be deemed timely if given not later than the due date (including extensions) for the corporation's tax return for the taxable year in which the temporary cessation begins.

(3) PERIOD DISREGARD IN EFFECT.—The period of temporary use under paragraph (1) continues until the earlier of the date on which—

(A) the electing corporation abandons its intention to resume operations of the vessel in the United States foreign trade, or

(B) the electing corporation resumes operation of the vessel in the United States foreign trade.

(4) NO DISREGARD IF DOMESTIC TRADE USE EXCEEDS 30 DAYS.—Paragraph (1) shall not apply to any qualifying vessel which is operated in the United States domestic trade for more than 30 days during the taxable year.

Amendments

• **2018, Tax Technical Corrections Act of 2018 (P.L. 115-141)**

P.L. 115-141, §401(a)(187), Div. U:

Amended Code Sec. 1355(f)(3) by striking "of which" and inserting "on which". **Effective** 3-23-2018.

[Sec. 1355(g)]

(g) GREAT LAKES DOMESTIC SHIPPING TO NOT DISQUALIFY VESSEL.—

(1) IN GENERAL.—If the electing corporation elects (at such time and in such manner as the Secretary may require) to apply this subsection for any taxable year to any qualifying vessel which is used in qualified zone domestic trade during the taxable year—

(A) solely for purposes of subsection (a)(4), such use shall be treated as use in United States foreign trade (and not as use in United States domestic trade), and

(B) subsection (f) shall not apply with respect to such vessel for such taxable year.

(2) EFFECT OF TEMPORARILY OPERATING VESSEL IN UNITED STATES DOMESTIC TRADE.—In the case of a qualifying vessel to which this subsection applies—

(A) IN GENERAL.—An electing corporation shall be treated as using such vessel in qualified zone domestic trade during any period of temporary use in the United States domestic trade (other than qualified zone domestic trade) if the electing corporation gives timely notice to the Secretary stating—

(i) that it temporarily operates or has operated in the United States domestic trade (other than qualified zone domestic trade) a qualifying vessel which had been used in the United States foreign trade or qualified zone domestic trade, and

(ii) its intention to resume operation of the vessel in the United States foreign trade or qualified zone domestic trade.

(B) NOTICE.—Notice shall be deemed timely if given not later than the due date (including extensions) for the corporation's tax return for the taxable year in which the temporary cessation begins.

(C) PERIOD DISREGARD IN EFFECT.—The period of temporary use under subparagraph (A) continues until the earlier of the date of which—

(i) the electing corporation abandons its intention to resume operations of the vessel in the United States foreign trade or qualified zone domestic trade, or

(ii) the electing corporation resumes operation of the vessel in the United States foreign trade or qualified zone domestic trade.

(D) NO DISREGARD IF DOMESTIC TRADE USE EXCEEDS 30 DAYS.—Subparagraph (A) shall not apply to any qualifying vessel which is operated in the United States domestic trade (other than qualified zone domestic trade) for more than 30 days during the taxable year.

(3) ALLOCATION OF INCOME AND DEDUCTIONS TO QUALIFYING SHIPPING ACTIVITIES.—In the case of a qualifying vessel to which this subsection applies, the Secretary shall prescribe rules for the proper allocation of income, expenses, losses, and deductions between the qualified shipping activities and the other activities of such vessel.

(4) QUALIFIED ZONE DOMESTIC TRADE.—For purposes of this subsection—

(A) IN GENERAL.—The term "qualified zone domestic trade" means the transportation of goods or passengers between places in the qualified zone if such transportation is in the United States domestic trade.

(B) QUALIFIED ZONE.—The term "qualified zone" means the Great Lakes Waterway and the St. Lawrence Seaway.

Amendments

• **2006, Tax Relief and Health Care Act of 2006 (P.L. 109-432)**

P.L. 109-432, Division A, §415(a):

Amended Code Sec. 1355 by redesignating subsection (g) as subsection (h) and by inserting after subsection (f) a new subsection (g). **Effective** for tax years beginning after 12-20-2006.

[Sec. 1355(h)]

(h) REGULATIONS.—The Secretary shall prescribe such regulations as may be necessary or appropriate to carry out the purposes of this section.

Amendments

• **2006, Tax Relief and Health Care Act of 2006 (P.L. 109-432)**

P.L. 109-432, Division A, §415(a):

Amended Code Sec. 1355 by redesignating subsection (g) as subsection (h). **Effective** for tax years beginning after 12-20-2006.

• **2004, American Jobs Creation Act of 2004 (P.L. 108-357)**

P.L. 108-357, §248(a):

Amended chapter 1 by inserting after subchapter Q a new subchapter R (Code Secs. 1352-1359). **Effective** for tax years beginning after 10-22-2004.

[Sec. 1356]

SEC. 1356. QUALIFYING SHIPPING ACTIVITIES.

[Sec. 1356(a)]

(a) QUALIFYING SHIPPING ACTIVITIES.—For purposes of this subchapter, the term "qualifying shipping activities" means—

(1) core qualifying activities,

(2) qualifying secondary activities, and

(3) qualifying incidental activities.

[Sec. 1356(b)]

(b) CORE QUALIFYING ACTIVITIES.—For purposes of this subchapter, the term "core qualifying activities" means activities in operating qualifying vessels in United States foreign trade.

[Sec. 1356(c)]

(c) QUALIFYING SECONDARY ACTIVITIES.—For purposes of this section—

(1) IN GENERAL.—The term "qualifying secondary activities" means secondary activities but only to the extent that, without regard to this subchapter, the gross income derived by such corporation from such activities does not exceed 20 percent of the gross income derived by the corporation from its core qualifying activities.

(2) SECONDARY ACTIVITIES.—The term "secondary activities" means—

(A) the active management or operation of vessels other than qualifying vessels in the United States foreign trade,

(B) the provision of vessel, barge, container, or cargo-related facilities or services to any person,

(C) other activities of the electing corporation and other members of its electing group that are an integral part of its business of operating qualifying vessels in United States foreign trade, including—

(i) ownership or operation of barges, containers, chassis, and other equipment that are the complement of, or used in connection with, a qualifying vessel in United States foreign trade,

(ii) the inland haulage of cargo shipped, or to be shipped, on qualifying vessels in United States foreign trade, and

(iii) the provision of terminal, maintenance, repair, logistical, or other vessel, barge, container, or cargo-related services that are an integral part of operating qualifying vessels in United States foreign trade, and

(D) such other activities as may be prescribed by the Secretary pursuant to regulations.

Such term shall not include any core qualifying activities.

Amendments

• **2005, Gulf Opportunity Zone Act of 2005 (P.L. 109-135)**

P.L. 109-135, §403(g)(3)(A)-(B):

Amended Code Sec. 1356(c) by striking paragraph (3) and by adding at the end of paragraph (2) a new flush sentence. **Effective** as if included in the provision of the American Jobs Creation Act of 2004 (P.L. 108-357) to which it relates [**effective** for tax years beginning after 10-22-2004.—CCH]. Prior to being stricken, Code Sec. 1356(c)(3) read as follows:

(3) COORDINATION WITH CORE ACTIVITIES.—

(A) IN GENERAL.—Such term shall not include any core qualifying activities.

(B) NONELECTING CORPORATIONS.—In the case of a corporation (other than an electing corporation) which is a member of an electing group, any core qualifying activities of the corporation shall be treated as qualifying secondary activities (and not as core qualifying activities).

[Sec. 1356(d)]

(d) QUALIFYING INCIDENTAL ACTIVITIES.—For purposes of this section, the term "qualified incidental activities" means shipping-related activities if—

(1) they are incidental to the corporation's core qualifying activities,

(2) they are not qualifying secondary activities, and

(3) without regard to this subchapter, the gross income derived by such corporation from such activities does not exceed 0.1 percent of the corporation's gross income from its core qualifying activities.

[Sec. 1356(e)]

(e) APPLICATION OF GROSS INCOME TESTS IN CASE OF ELECTING GROUP.—In the case of an electing group, subsections (c)(1) and (d)(3) shall be applied as if such group were 1 entity, and the limitations under such subsections shall be allocated among the corporations in such group.

INCOME TAX—ELECTION, INTL. SHIPPING ACTIVITIES

Amendments

- **2004, American Jobs Creation Act of 2004 (P.L. 108-357)**

P.L. 108-357, § 248(a):

Amended chapter 1 by inserting after subchapter Q a new subchapter R (Code Secs. 1352-1359). **Effective** for tax years beginning after 10-22-2004.

[Sec. 1357]

SEC. 1357. ITEMS NOT SUBJECT TO REGULAR TAX; DEPRECIATION; INTEREST.

[Sec. 1357(a)]

(a) EXCLUSION FROM GROSS INCOME.—Gross income of an electing corporation shall not include its income from qualifying shipping activities.

[Sec. 1357(b)]

(b) ELECTING GROUP MEMBER.—Gross income of a corporation (other than an electing corporation) which is a member of an electing group shall not include its income from qualifying shipping activities conducted by such member.

[Sec. 1357(c)]

(c) DENIAL OF LOSSES, DEDUCTIONS, AND CREDITS.—

(1) GENERAL RULE.—Subject to paragraph (2), each item of loss, deduction (other than for interest expense), or credit of any taxpayer with respect to any activity the income from which is excluded from gross income under this section shall be disallowed.

(2) DEPRECIATION.—

(A) IN GENERAL.—Notwithstanding paragraph (1), the adjusted basis (for purposes of determining gain) of any qualifying vessel shall be determined as if the deduction for depreciation had been allowed.

(B) METHOD.—

(i) IN GENERAL.—Except as provided in clause (ii), the straight-line method of depreciation shall apply to qualifying vessels the income from operation of which is excluded from gross income under this section.

(ii) EXCEPTION.—Clause (i) shall not apply to any qualifying vessel which is subject to a charter entered into before the date of the enactment of this subchapter.

(3) INTEREST.—

(A) IN GENERAL.—Except as provided in subparagraph (B), the interest expense of an electing corporation shall be disallowed in the ratio that the fair market value of such corporation's qualifying vessels bears to the fair market value of such corporation's total assets.

(B) ELECTING GROUP.—In the case of a corporation which is a member of an electing group, the interest expense of such corporation shall be disallowed in the ratio that the fair market value of such corporation's qualifying vessels bears to the fair market value of the electing group[']s total assets.

Amendments

- **2004, American Jobs Creation Act of 2004 (P.L. 108-357)**

P.L. 108-357, § 248(a):

Amended chapter 1 by inserting after subchapter Q a new subchapter R (Code Secs. 1352-1359). **Effective** for tax years beginning after 10-22-2004.

[Sec. 1358]

SEC. 1358. ALLOCATION OF CREDITS, INCOME, AND DEDUCTIONS.

[Sec. 1358(a)]

(a) QUALIFYING SHIPPING ACTIVITIES.—For purposes of this chapter, the qualifying shipping activities of an electing corporation shall be treated as a separate trade or business activity distinct from all other activities conducted by such corporation.

[Sec. 1358(b)]

(b) EXCLUSION OF CREDITS OR DEDUCTIONS.—

(1) No deduction shall be allowed against the notional shipping income of an electing corporation, and no credit shall be allowed against the tax imposed by section 1352(2).

(2) No deduction shall be allowed for any net operating loss attributable to the qualifying shipping activities of any person to the extent that such loss is carried forward by such person from a taxable year preceding the first taxable year for which such person was an electing corporation.

Amendments

- **2018, Tax Technical Corrections Act of 2018 (P.L. 115-141)**

P.L. 115-141, § 401(a)(188), Div. U:

Amended Code Sec. 1358(b)(1) by striking "section 1352(a)(2)" and inserting "section 1352(2)". **Effective** 3-23-2018.

[Sec. 1358(c)]

(c) TRANSACTIONS NOT AT ARM'S LENGTH.—Section 482 applies in accordance with this subsection to a transaction or series of transactions—

(1) as between an electing corporation and another person, or

(2) as between a person's qualifying shipping activities and other activities carried on by it.

Amendments

- **2018, Tax Technical Corrections Act of 2018 (P.L. 115-141)**

P.L. 115-141, § 401(a)(189), Div. U:

Amended Code Sec. 1358(c)(2) by striking "an person's" and inserting "a person's". **Effective** 3-23-2018.

- **2004, American Jobs Creation Act of 2004 (P.L. 108-357)**

P.L. 108-357, § 248(a):

Amended chapter 1 by inserting after subchapter Q a new subchapter R (Code Secs. 1352-1359). **Effective** for tax years beginning after 10-22-2004.

INCOME TAX—S CORPORATION DEFINED

[Sec. 1359]
SEC. 1359. DISPOSITION OF QUALIFYING VESSELS.

[Sec. 1359(a)]

(a) IN GENERAL.—If any qualifying vessel operator sells or disposes of any qualifying vessel in an otherwise taxable transaction, at the election of such operator, no gain shall be recognized if any replacement qualifying vessel is acquired during the period specified in subsection (b), except to the extent that the amount realized upon such sale or disposition exceeds the cost of the replacement qualifying vessel.

[Sec. 1359(b)]

(b) PERIOD WITHIN WHICH PROPERTY MUST BE REPLACED.—The period referred to in subsection (a) shall be the period beginning one year prior to the disposition of the qualifying vessel and ending—

(1) 3 years after the close of the first taxable year in which the gain is realized, or

(2) subject to such terms and conditions as may be specified by the Secretary, on such later date as the Secretary may designate on application by the taxpayer.

Such application shall be made at such time and in such manner as the Secretary may by regulations prescribe.

[Sec. 1359(c)]

(c) APPLICATION OF SECTION TO NONCORPORATE OPERATORS.—For purposes of this section, the term "qualifying vessel operator" includes any person who would be a qualifying vessel operator were such person a corporation.

[Sec. 1359(d)]

(d) TIME FOR ASSESSMENT OF DEFICIENCY ATTRIBUTABLE TO GAIN.—If a qualifying vessel operator has made the election provided in subsection (a), then—

(1) the statutory period for the assessment of any deficiency, for any taxable year in which any part of the gain is realized, attributable to such gain shall not expire prior to the expiration of 3 years from the date the Secretary is notified by such operator (in such manner as the Secretary may by regulations prescribe) of the replacement qualifying vessel or of an intention not to replace, and

(2) such deficiency may be assessed before the expiration of such 3-year period notwithstanding the provisions of section 6212(c) or the provisions of any other law or rule of law which would otherwise prevent such assessment.

[Sec. 1359(e)]

(e) BASIS OF REPLACEMENT QUALIFYING VESSEL.—In the case of any replacement qualifying vessel purchased by the qualifying vessel operator which resulted in the nonrecognition of any part of the gain realized as the result of a sale or other disposition of a qualifying vessel, the basis shall be the cost of the replacement qualifying vessel decreased in the amount of the gain not so recognized; and if the property purchased consists of more than one piece of property, the basis determined under this sentence shall be allocated to the purchased properties in proportion to their respective costs.

Amendments

• **2004, American Jobs Creation Act of 2004 (P.L. 108-357)**

P.L. 108-357, §248(a):

Amended chapter 1 by inserting after subchapter Q a new subchapter R (Code Secs. 1352-1359). **Effective** for tax years beginning after 10-22-2004.

Subchapter S—Tax Treatment of S Corporations and Their Shareholders

Part I.   In general.
Part II.   Tax treatment of shareholders.
Part III.   Special rules.
Part IV.   Definitions; miscellaneous.

PART I—IN GENERAL

Sec. 1361.   S corporation defined.
Sec. 1362.   Election; revocation; termination.
Sec. 1363.   Effect of election on corporation.

[Sec. 1361]
SEC. 1361. S CORPORATION DEFINED.

[Sec. 1361(a)]

(a) S CORPORATION DEFINED.—

(1) IN GENERAL.—For purposes of this title, the term "S corporation" means, with respect to any taxable year, a small business corporation for which an election under section 1362(a) is in effect for such year.

(2) C CORPORATION.—For purposes of this title, the term "C corporation" means, with respect to any taxable year, a corporation which is not an S corporation for such year.

[Sec. 1361(b)]

(b) SMALL BUSINESS CORPORATION.—

(1) IN GENERAL.—For purposes of this subchapter, the term "small business corporation" means a domestic corporation which is not an ineligible corporation and which does not—

(A) have more than 100 shareholders,

(B) have as a shareholder a person (other than an estate, a trust described in subsection (c)(2), or an organization described in subsection (c)(6) who is not an individual,

(C) have a nonresident alien as a shareholder, and

(D) have more than 1 class of stock.

(2) INELIGIBLE CORPORATION DEFINED.—For purposes of paragraph (1), the term "ineligible corporation" means any corporation which is—

(A) a financial institution which uses the reserve method of accounting for bad debts described in section 585,

INCOME TAX—S CORPORATION DEFINED

(B) an insurance company subject to tax under subchapter L, or

(C) a DISC or former DISC.

(3) TREATMENT OF CERTAIN WHOLLY OWNED SUBSIDIARIES.—

(A) IN GENERAL.—Except as provided in regulations prescribed by the Secretary, for purposes of this title—

(i) a corporation which is a qualified subchapter S subsidiary shall not be treated as a separate corporation, and

(ii) all assets, liabilities, and items of income, deduction, and credit of a qualified subchapter S subsidiary shall be treated as assets, liabilities, and such items (as the case may be) of the S corporation.

(B) QUALIFIED SUBCHAPTER S SUBSIDIARY.—For purposes of this paragraph, the term "qualified subchapter S subsidiary" means any domestic corporation which is not an ineligible corporation (as defined in paragraph (2)), if—

(i) 100 percent of the stock of such corporation is held by the S corporation, and

(ii) the S corporation elects to treat such corporation as a qualified subchapter S subsidiary.

(C) TREATMENT OF TERMINATIONS OF QUALIFIED SUBCHAPTER S SUBSIDIARY STATUS.—

(i) IN GENERAL.—For purposes of this title, if any corporation which was a qualified subchapter S subsidiary ceases to meet the requirements of subparagraph (B), such corporation shall be treated as a new corporation acquiring all of its assets (and assuming all of its liabilities) immediately before such cessation from the S corporation in exchange for its stock.

(ii) TERMINATION BY REASON OF SALE OF STOCK.—If the failure to meet the requirements of subparagraph (B) is by reason of the sale of stock of a corporation which is a qualified subchapter S subsidiary, the sale of such stock shall be treated as if—

(I) the sale were a sale of an undivided interest in the assets of such corporation (based on the percentage of the corporation's stock sold), and

(II) the sale were followed by an acquisition by such corporation of all of its assets (and the assumption by such corporation of all of its liabilities) in a transaction to which section 351 applies.

(D) ELECTION AFTER TERMINATION.—If a corporation's status as a qualified subchapter S subsidiary terminates, such corporation (and any successor corporation) shall not be eligible to make—

(i) an election under subparagraph (B)(ii) to be treated as a qualified subchapter S subsidiary, or

(ii) an election under section 1362(a) to be treated as an S corporation,

before its 5th taxable year which begins after the 1st taxable year for which such termination was effective, unless the Secretary consents to such election.

(E) INFORMATION RETURNS.—Except to the extent provided by the Secretary, this paragraph shall not apply to part III of subchapter A of chapter 61 (relating to information returns).

Amendments

• **2018, Tax Technical Corrections Act of 2018 (P.L. 115-141)**

P.L. 115-141, §401(d)(1)(D)(xvi), Div. U:

Amended Code Sec. 1361(b)(2) by adding "or" at the end of subparagraph (B), by striking subparagraph (C), and by redesignating subparagraph (D) as subparagraph (C). **Effective** 3-23-2018. For a special rule, see Act Sec. 401(e), Div. U, below. Prior to being stricken, Code Sec. 1361(b)(2)(C) read as follows:

(C) a corporation to which an election under section 936 applies, or

P.L. 115-141, §401(e), Div. U, provides:

(e) GENERAL SAVINGS PROVISION WITH RESPECT TO DEADWOOD PROVISIONS.—If—

(1) any provision amended or repealed by the amendments made by subsection (b) or (d) applied to—

(A) any transaction occurring before the date of the enactment of this Act,

(B) any property acquired before such date of enactment, or

(C) any item of income, loss, deduction, or credit taken into account before such date of enactment, and

(2) the treatment of such transaction, property, or item under such provision would (without regard to the amendments or repeals made by such subsection) affect the liability for tax for periods ending after such date of enactment,

nothing in the amendments or repeals made by this section shall be construed to affect the treatment of such transaction, property, or item for purposes of determining liability for tax for periods ending after such date of enactment.

• **2007, Small Business and Work Opportunity Tax Act of 2007 (P.L. 110-28)**

P.L. 110-28, §8234(a)(1)-(2):

Amended Code Sec. 1361(b)(3)(C) by striking "For purposes of this title" and inserting "(i) IN GENERAL.—For purposes of this title,", and by inserting at the end a new clause (ii). **Effective** for tax years beginning after 12-31-2006.

• **2005, Gulf Opportunity Zone Act of 2005 (P.L. 109-135)**

P.L. 109-135, §413(c)(1)-(2):

Amended Code Sec. 1361(b)(3) by striking "and in the case of information returns required under part III of subchapter A of chapter 61" after "Secretary" in subparagraph (A), and by adding at the end a new subparagraph (E). **Effective** as if included in the provision of the American Jobs Creation Act of 2004 (P.L. 108-357) to which it relates [**effective** for tax years beginning after 12-31-2004.—CCH].

• **2004, American Jobs Creation Act of 2004 (P.L. 108-357)**

P.L. 108-357, §232(a):

Amended Code Sec. 1361(b)(1)(A) by striking "75" and inserting "100". **Effective** for tax years beginning after 12-31-2004.

P.L. 108-357, §239(a):

Amended Code Sec. 1361(b)(3)(A) by inserting "and in the case of information returns required under part III of subchapter A of chapter 61" after "Secretary". **Effective** for tax years beginning after 12-31-2004.

• **1997, Taxpayer Relief Act of 1997 (P.L. 105-34)**

P.L. 105-34, §1601(c)(3):

Amended Code Sec. 1361(b)(3)(A) by striking "For purposes of this title" and inserting "Except as provided in regulations prescribed by the Secretary, for purposes of this title". **Effective** as if included in the provision of P.L. 104-188 to which it relates [effective for tax years beginning after 12-31-96.—CCH].

P.L. 105-34, §1601(c)(4)(C):

Amended Code Sec. 1361(b)(1)(B) by striking "subsection (c)(7)" and inserting "subsection (c)(6)". **Effective** as if included in the provision of P.L. 104-188 to which it relates [effective for tax years beginning after 12-31-96.—CCH].

• **1996, Small Business Job Protection Act of 1996 (P.L. 104-188)**

P.L. 104-188, §1301:

Amended Code Sec. 1361(b)(1)(A) by striking "35 shareholders" and inserting "75 shareholders". **Effective** for tax years beginning after 12-31-96.

P.L. 104-188, §1308(a):

Amended Code Sec. 1361(b)(2) by striking subparagraph (A) and by redesignating subparagraphs (B), (C), (D) and (E) as subparagraphs (A), (B), (C) and (D), respectively. **Effective** for tax years beginning after 12-31-96. Prior to amendment, Code Sec. 1361(b)(2)(A) read as follows:

(A) a member of an affiliated group (determined under section 1504 without regard to the exceptions contained in subsection (b) thereof),

P.L. 104-188, §1308(b):

Amended Code Sec. 1361(b) by adding at the end a new paragraph (3). **Effective** for tax years beginning after 12-31-96.

P.L. 104-188, §1315:

Amended Code Sec. 1361(b)(2)(A), as redesignated by Act Sec. 1308(a). **Effective** for tax years beginning after 12-31-96. Prior to amendment, Code Sec. 1361(b)(2)(A) read as follows:

(A) a financial institution to which section 585 applies (or would apply but for subsection (c) thereof),

P.L. 104-188, §1316(a)(1):

Amended Code Sec. 1361(b)(1)(B). **Effective** for tax years beginning after 12-31-97. Prior to amendment, Code Sec. 1361(b)(1)(B) read as follows:

(B) have as a shareholder a person (other than an estate and other than a trust described in subsection (c)(2)) who is not an individual,

P.L. 104-188, §1616(b)(15):

Amended Code Sec. 1361(b)(2)(B) by striking "or to which section 593 applies" before the comma at the end. **Effective** for tax years beginning after 12-31-95.

• **1989, Omnibus Budget Reconciliation Act of 1989 (P.L. 101-239)**

P.L. 101-239, §7811(c)(6):

Amended Code Sec. 1361(b)(2)(B). **Effective** as if included in the provision of P.L. 100-647 to which it relates. Prior to amendment, Code Sec. 1361(b)(2)(B) read as follows:

Sec. 1361(b)(2)(B)

INCOME TAX—S CORPORATION DEFINED

(B) a financial institution which is a bank (as defined in section 585(a)(2)) or to which section 593 applies,

• **1986, Tax Reform Act of 1986 (P.L. 99-514)**
P.L. 99-514, § 901(d)(4)(G):
   Amended Code Sec. 1361(b)(2)(B) by striking out "to which section 585 or 593 applies" and inserting in lieu thereof "which is a bank (as defined in section 585(a)(2)) or to which section 593 applies". **Effective** for tax years beginning after 12-31-86.

[Sec. 1361(c)]

(c) SPECIAL RULES FOR APPLYING SUBSECTION (b).—
   (1) MEMBERS OF A FAMILY TREATED AS 1 SHAREHOLDER.—
      (A) IN GENERAL.—For purposes of subsection (b)(1)(A), there shall be treated as one shareholder—
         (i) a husband and wife (and their estates), and
         (ii) all members of a family (and their estates).
      (B) MEMBERS OF A FAMILY.—For purposes of this paragraph—
         (i) IN GENERAL.—The term "members of a family" means a common ancestor, any lineal descendant of such common ancestor, and any spouse or former spouse of such common ancestor or any such lineal descendant.
         (ii) COMMON ANCESTOR.—An individual shall not be considered to be a common ancestor if, on the applicable date, the individual is more than 6 generations removed from the youngest generation of shareholders who would (but for this subparagraph) be members of the family. For purposes of the preceding sentence, a spouse (or former spouse) shall be treated as being of the same generation as the individual to whom such spouse is (or was) married.
         (iii) APPLICABLE DATE.—The term "applicable date" means the latest of—
            (I) the date the election under section 1362(a) is made,
            (II) the earliest date that an individual described in clause (i) holds stock in the S corporation, or
            (III) October 22, 2004.
      (C) EFFECT OF ADOPTION, ETC.—Any legally adopted child of an individual, any child who is lawfully placed with an individual for legal adoption by the individual, and any eligible foster child of an individual (within the meaning of section 152(f)(1)(C)), shall be treated as a child of such individual by blood.
   (2) CERTAIN TRUSTS PERMITTED AS SHAREHOLDERS.—
      (A) IN GENERAL.—For purposes of subsection (b)(1)(B), the following trusts may be shareholders:
         (i) A trust all of which is treated (under subpart E of part I of subchapter J of this chapter) as owned by an individual who is a citizen or resident of the United States.
         (ii) A trust which was described in clause (i) immediately before the death of the deemed owner and which continues in existence after such death, but only for the 2-year period beginning on the day of the deemed owner's death.
         (iii) A trust with respect to stock transferred to it pursuant to the terms of a will, but only for the 2-year period beginning on the day on which such stock is transferred to it.
         (iv) A trust created primarily to exercise the voting power of stock transferred to it.
         (v) An electing small business trust.
         (vi) In the case of a corporation which is a bank (as defined in section 581) or a depository institution holding company (as defined in section 3(w)(1) of the Federal Deposit Insurance Act (12 U.S.C. 1813(w)(1)), a trust which constitutes an individual retirement account under section 408(a), including one designated as a Roth IRA under section 408A, but only to the extent of the stock held by such trust in such bank or company as of the date of the enactment of this clause.
This subparagraph shall not apply to any foreign trust.
      (B) TREATMENT AS SHAREHOLDERS.—For purposes of subsection (b)(1)—
         (i) In the case of a trust described in clause (i) of subparagraph (A), the deemed owner shall be treated as the shareholder.
         (ii) In the case of a trust described in clause (ii) of subparagraph (A), the estate of the deemed owner shall be treated as the shareholder.
         (iii) In the case of a trust described in clause (iii) of subparagraph (A), the estate of the testator shall be treated as the shareholder.
         (iv) In the case of a trust described in clause (iv) of subparagraph (A), each beneficiary of the trust shall be treated as a shareholder.
         (v) In the case of a trust described in clause (v) of subparagraph (A), each potential current beneficiary of such trust shall be treated as a shareholder; except that, if for any period there is no potential current beneficiary of such trust, such trust shall be treated as the shareholder during such period. This clause shall not apply for purposes of subsection (b)(1)(C).
         (vi) In the case of a trust described in clause (vi) of subparagraph (A), the individual for whose benefit the trust was created shall be treated as the shareholder.
   (3) ESTATE OF INDIVIDUAL IN BANKRUPTCY MAY BE SHAREHOLDER.—For purposes of subsection (b)(1)(B), the term "estate" includes the estate of an individual in a case under title 11 of the United States Code.
   (4) DIFFERENCES IN COMMON STOCK VOTING RIGHTS DISREGARDED.—For purposes of subsection (b)(1)(D), a corporation shall not be treated as having more than 1 class of stock solely because there are differences in voting rights among the shares of common stock.
   (5) STRAIGHT DEBT SAFE HARBOR.—
      (A) IN GENERAL.—For purposes of subsection (b)(1)(D), straight debt shall not be treated as a second class of stock.
      (B) STRAIGHT DEBT DEFINED.—For purposes of this paragraph, the term "straight debt" means any written unconditional promise to pay on demand or on a specified date a sum certain in money if—
         (i) the interest rate (and interest payment dates) are not contingent on profits, the borrower's discretion, or similar factors,
         (ii) there is no convertibility (directly or indirectly) into stock, and
         (iii) the creditor is an individual (other than a nonresident alien), an estate, a trust described in paragraph (2), or a person which is actively and regularly engaged in the business of lending money.
      (C) REGULATIONS.—The Secretary shall prescribe such regulations as may be necessary or appropriate to provide for the proper treatment of straight debt under this subchapter and for the coordination of such treatment with other provisions of this title.
   (6) CERTAIN EXEMPT ORGANIZATIONS PERMITTED AS SHAREHOLDERS.—For purposes of subsection (b)(1)(B), an organization which is—
      (A) described in section 401(a) or 501(c)(3), and
      (B) exempt from taxation under section 501(a),

INCOME TAX—S CORPORATION DEFINED

may be a shareholder in an S corporation.

Amendments

• **2018, Tax Technical Corrections Act of 2018 (P.L. 115-141)**

P.L. 115-141, §109(a), Div. U:

Amended Code Sec. 1361(c)(2)(B)(vi) by striking "a shareholder" and inserting "the shareholder". **Effective** as if included in section 319 of the American Jobs Creation Act of 2004 [effective for tax years beginning after 10-22-2004.—CCH].

• **2017, Tax Cuts and Jobs Act (P.L. 115-97)**

P.L. 115-97, §13541(a):

Amended Code Sec. 1361(c)(2)(B)(v) by adding at the end a new sentence. **Effective** 1-1-2018.

• **2005, Gulf Opportunity Zone Act of 2005 (P.L. 109-135)**

P.L. 109-135, §403(b):

Amended Code Sec. 1361(c)(1). **Effective** as if included in the provision of the American Jobs Creation Act of 2004 (P.L. 108-357) to which it relates [effective for tax years beginning after 12-31-2004.—CCH]. Prior to amendment, Code Sec. 1361(c)(1) read as follows:

(1) MEMBERS OF FAMILY TREATED AS 1 SHAREHOLDER.—

(A) IN GENERAL.—For purpose of subsection (b)(1)(A)—

(i) except as provided in clause (ii), a husband and wife (and their estates) shall be treated as 1 shareholder, and

(ii) in the case of a family with respect to which an election is in effect under subparagraph (D), all members of the family shall be treated as 1 shareholder.

(B) MEMBERS OF THE FAMILY.—For purpose of subparagraph (A)(ii)—

(i) IN GENERAL.—The term "members of the family" means the common ancestor, lineal descendants of the common ancestor, and the spouses (or former spouses) of such lineal descendants or common ancestor.

(ii) COMMON ANCESTOR.—For purposes of this paragraph, an individual shall not be considered a common ancestor if, as of the later of the effective date of this paragraph or the time the election under section 1362(a) is made, the individual is more than 6 generations removed from the youngest generation of shareholders who would (but for this clause) be members of the family. For purposes of the preceding sentence, a spouse (or former spouse) shall be treated as being of the same generation as the individual to which such spouse is (or was) married.

(C) EFFECT OF ADOPTION, ETC.—In determining whether any relationship specified in subparagraph (B) exists, the rules of section 152(b)(2) shall apply.

(D) ELECTION.—An election under subparagraph (A)(ii)—

(i) may, except as otherwise provided in regulations prescribed by the Secretary, be made by any member of the family, and

(ii) shall remain in effect until terminated as provided in regulations prescribed by the Secretary.

P.L. 109-135, §413(a)(1)(A)-(B):

Amended Code Sec. 1361(c)(2)(A)(vi) by inserting "or a depository institution holding company (as defined in section 3(w)(1) of the Federal Deposit Insurance Act (12 U.S.C. 1813(w)(1))" after "a bank (as defined in section 581)", and by inserting "or company" after "such bank". **Effective** as if included in the provision of the American Jobs Creation Act of 2004 (P.L. 108-357) to which it relates [effective 10-22-2004.—CCH].

• **2004, American Jobs Creation Act of 2004 (P.L. 108-357)**

P.L. 108-357, §231(a):

Amended Code Sec. 1361(c)(1). **Effective** for tax years beginning after 12-31-2004. Prior to amendment, Code Sec. 1361(c)(1) read as follows:

(1) HUSBAND AND WIFE TREATED AS 1 SHAREHOLDER.—For purposes of subsection (b)(1)(A), a husband and wife (and their estates) shall be treated as 1 shareholder.

P.L. 108-357, §233(a):

Amended Code Sec. 1361(c)(2)(A) by inserting after clause (v) a new clause (vi). **Effective** 10-22-2004.

P.L. 108-357, §233(b):

Amended Code Sec. 1361(c)(2)(B) by adding at the end a new clause (vi). **Effective** 10-22-2004.

• **1997, Taxpayer Relief Act of 1997 (P.L. 105-34)**

P.L. 105-34, §1601(c)(4)(B):

Amended Code Sec. 1361(c) by redesignating paragraph (7) as paragraph (6). **Effective** as if included in the provision of P.L. 104-188 to which it relates [effective for tax years beginning after 12-31-97.—CCH].

• **1996, Small Business Job Protection Act of 1996 (P.L. 104-188)**

P.L. 104-188, §1302(a):

Amended Code Sec. 1361(c)(2)(A) by inserting after clause (iv) a new clause (v). **Effective** for tax years beginning after 12-31-96.

P.L. 104-188, §1302(b):

Amended Code Sec. 1361(c)(2)(B) by adding at the end a new clause (v). **Effective** for tax years beginning after 12-31-96.

P.L. 104-188, §1303(1)-(2):

Amended Code Sec. 1361(c)(2)(A) by striking "60-day period" each place it appears in clauses (ii) and (iii) and inserting "2-year period", and by striking the last sentence of clause (ii). **Effective** for tax years beginning after 12-31-96. Prior to amendment, the last sentence of Code Sec. 1361(c)(2)(A)(ii) read as follows:

If a trust is described in the preceding sentence and if the entire corpus of the trust is includible in the gross estate of the deemed owner, the preceding sentence shall be applied by substituting "2-year period" for "60-day period".

P.L. 104-188, §1304:

Amended Code Sec. 1361(c)(5)(B)(iii) by striking "or a trust described in paragraph (2)" and inserting "a trust described in paragraph (2), or a person which is actively and regularly engaged in the business of lending money". **Effective** for tax years beginning after 12-31-96.

P.L. 104-188, §1308(d)(1):

Amended Code Sec. 1361(c) by striking paragraph (6). **Effective** for tax years beginning after 12-31-96. Prior to amendment, Code Sec. 1361(c)(6) read as follows:

(6) OWNERSHIP OF STOCK IN CERTAIN INACTIVE CORPORATIONS.—For purposes of subsection (b)(2)(A), a corporation shall not be treated as a member of an affiliated group during any period within a taxable year by reason of the ownership of stock in another corporation if such other corporation—

(A) has not begun business at any time on or before the close of such period, and

(B) does not have gross income for such period.

P.L. 104-188, §1316(a)(2):

Amended Code Sec. 1361(c) by adding at the end a new paragraph (7)[6]. **Effective** for tax years beginning after 12-31-97.

• **1984, Deficit Reduction Act of 1984 (P.L. 98-369)**

P.L. 98-369, §721(c):

Amended Code Sec. 1361(c)(6). **Effective** as if included in P.L. 97-354. Prior to amendment, Code Sec. 1361(c)(6) read as follows:

(6) Ownership of Stock in Certain Inactive Corporations.—For purposes of subsection (b)(2)(A), a corporation shall not be treated as a member of an affiliated group at any time during any taxable year by reason of the ownership of stock in another corporation if such other corporation—

(A) has not begun business at any time on or after the date of its incorporation and before the close of such taxable year, and

(B) does not have taxable income for the period included within such taxable year.

[Sec. 1361(d)]

(d) SPECIAL RULE FOR QUALIFIED SUBCHAPTER S TRUST.—

(1) IN GENERAL.—In the case of a qualified subchapter S trust with respect to which a beneficiary makes an election under paragraph (2)—

(A) such trust shall be treated as a trust described in subsection (c)(2)(A)(i),

(B) for purposes of section 678(a), the beneficiary of such trust shall be treated as the owner of that portion of the trust which consists of stock in an S corporation with respect to which the election under paragraph (2) is made, and

(C) for purposes of applying sections 465 and 469 to the beneficiary of the trust, the disposition of the S corporation stock by the trust shall be treated as a disposition by such beneficiary.

(2) ELECTION.—

(A) IN GENERAL.—A beneficiary of a qualified subchapter S trust (or his legal representative) may elect to have this subsection apply.

(B) MANNER AND TIME OF ELECTION.—

(i) SEPARATE ELECTION WITH RESPECT TO EACH CORPORATION.—An election under this paragraph shall be made separately with respect to each corporation the stock of which is held by the trust.

(ii) ELECTIONS WITH RESPECT TO SUCCESSIVE INCOME BENEFICIARIES.—If there is an election under this paragraph with respect to any beneficiary, an election under this paragraph shall be treated as made by each successive beneficiary unless such beneficiary affirmatively refuses to consent to such election.

(iii) TIME, MANNER, AND FORM OF ELECTION.—Any election, or refusal, under this paragraph shall be made in such manner and form, and at such time, as the Secretary may prescribe.

(C) ELECTION IRREVOCABLE.—An election under this paragraph, once made, may be revoked only with the consent of the Secretary.

(D) GRACE PERIOD.—An election under this paragraph shall be effective up to 15 days and 2 months before the date of the election.

INCOME TAX—S CORPORATION DEFINED

(3) QUALIFIED SUBCHAPTER S TRUST.—For purposes of this subsection, the term "qualified subchapter S trust" means a trust—

(A) the terms of which require that—

(i) during the life of the current income beneficiary, there shall be only 1 income beneficiary of the trust,

(ii) any corpus distributed during the life of the current income beneficiary may be distributed only to such beneficiary,

(iii) the income interest of the current income beneficiary in the trust shall terminate on the earlier of such beneficiary's death or the termination of the trust, and

(iv) upon the termination of the trust during the life of the current income beneficiary, the trust shall distribute all of its assets to such beneficiary, and

(B) all of the income (within the meaning of section 643(b)) of which is distributed (or required to be distributed) currently to 1 individual who is a citizen or resident of the United States.

A substantially separate and independent share of a trust within the meaning of 663(c) shall be treated as a separate trust for purposes of this subsection and subsection (c).

(4) TRUST CEASING TO BE QUALIFIED.—

(A) FAILURE TO MEET REQUIREMENTS OF PARAGRAPH (3)(A).—If a qualified subchapter S trust ceases to meet any requirement of paragraph (3)(A), the provisions of this subsection shall not apply to such trust as of the date it ceases to meet such requirement.

(B) FAILURE TO MEET REQUIREMENTS OF PARAGRAPH (3)(B).—If any qualified subchapter S trust ceases to meet any requirement of paragraph (3)(B) but continues to meet the requirements of paragraph (3)(A), the provisions of this subsection shall not apply to such trust as of the first day of the first taxable year beginning after the first taxable year for which it failed to meet the requirements of paragraph (3)(B).

Amendments

- **2004, American Jobs Creation Act of 2004 (P.L. 108-357)**

P.L. 108-357, §236(a)(1)-(3):

Amended Code Sec. 1361(d)(1) by striking "and" at the end of subparagraph (A), by striking the period at the end of subparagraph (B) and inserting ", and", and by adding at the end a new subparagraph (C). **Effective** for transfers made after 12-31-2004.

- **1988, Technical and Miscellaneous Revenue Act of 1988 (P.L. 100-647)**

P.L. 100-647, §1018(q)(2):

Amended Code Sec. 1361(d)(3) by striking out "treated as a separate trust under section 663(c)" in the last sentence and inserting in lieu thereof "within the meaning of section 663(c)". **Effective** as if included in the provision of P.L. 99-514 to which it relates.

- **1986, Tax Reform Act of 1986 (P.L. 99-514)**

P.L. 99-514, §1879(m)(1)(A):

Amended Code Sec. 1361(d)(3) by adding to the end thereof the last sentence. **Effective** for tax years beginning after 12-31-82.

- **1984, Deficit Reduction Act of 1984 (P.L. 98-369)**

P.L. 98-369, §721(f)(1):

Amended Code Sec. 1361(d)(2)(D) by striking out "60 days" and inserting in lieu thereof "15 days and 2 months". **Effective** as if included in P.L. 97-354.

P.L. 98-369, §721(f)(2):

Amended Code Sec. 1361(d) by striking out paragraphs (3) and (4) and inserting in lieu thereof paragraphs (3) and (4). **Effective** as if included in P.L. 97-354. Prior to amendment, paragraphs (3) and (4) read as follows:

(3) QUALIFIED SUBCHAPTER S TRUST.—For purposes of this subsection, the term "qualified subchapter S trust" means a trust—

(A) which owns stock in 1 or more S corporations,

(B) all of the income (within the meaning of section 643(b)) of which is distributed (or required to be distributed) currently to 1 individual who is a citizen or resident of the United States, and

(C) the terms of which require that—

(i) during the life of the current income beneficiary there shall be only 1 income beneficiary of the trust,

(ii) any corpus distributed during the life of the current income beneficiary may be distributed only to such beneficiary,

(iii) the income interest of the current income beneficiary in the trust shall terminate on the earlier of such beneficiary's death or the termination of the trust, and

(iv) upon the termination of the trust during the life of the current income beneficiary, the trust shall distribute all of its assets to such beneficiary.

(4) TRUST CEASING TO BE QUALIFIED.—If a qualified subchapter S trust ceases to meet any requirement under paragraph (3), the provisions of this subsection shall not apply to such trust as of the date it ceases to meet such requirements.

P.L. 98-369, §721(f)(3):

Amended Code Sec. 1361(d)(2)(B)(i) by striking "S corporation" each place it appeared and inserting in lieu thereof "corporation". **Effective** as if included in P.L. 97-354.

- **1982, Subchapter S Revision Act of 1982 (P.L. 97-354)**

P.L. 97-354, §2:

Added Code Sec. 1361. **Effective** for tax years beginning after 12-31-82. For special rules, see Act Sec. 6(c)(2)-(4), below. For a special rule for subsidiaries that are foreign corporations or DISCs, see P.L. 97-354, §6(c)(1), below.

P.L. 97-354, §6(c)(1), provides:

(c) GRANDFATHER RULES.—

(1) SUBSIDIARIES WHICH ARE FOREIGN CORPORATIONS OR DISC'S.—In the case of any corporation which on September 28, 1982, would have been a member of the same affiliated group as an electing small business corporation but for paragraph (3) or (7) of section 1504(b) of the Internal Revenue Code of 1954, subparagraph (A) of section 1361(b)(2) of such Code (as amended by section 2) shall be applied by substituting "without regard to the exceptions contained in paragraphs (1), (2), (4), (5), and (6) of subsection (b) thereof" for "without regard to the exceptions contained in subsection (b) thereof".

P.L. 97-354, §6(c)(2)-(4), provides:

(2) CASUALTY INSURANCE COMPANIES.—

(A) IN GENERAL.—In the case of any qualified casualty insurance electing small business corporation—

(i) the amendments made by this Act shall not apply, and

(ii) subchapter S (as in effect on July 1, 1982) of chapter 1 of the Internal Revenue Code of 1954 and part III of subchapter L of chapter 1 of such Code shall apply.

(B) QUALIFIED CASUALTY INSURANCE ELECTING SMALL BUSINESS CORPORATION.—The term "qualified casualty insurance electing small business corporation" means any corporation described in section 831(a) of the Internal Revenue Code of 1954 if—

(i) as of July 12, 1982, such corporation was an electing small business corporation and was described in section 831(a) of such Code,

(ii) such corporation was formed before April 1, 1982, and proposed (through a written private offering first circulated to investors before such date) to elect to be taxed as a subchapter S corporation and to be operated on an established insurance exchange, or

(iii) such corporation is approved for membership on an established insurance exchange pursuant to a written agreement entered into before December 31, 1982, and such corporation is described in section 831(a) of such Code as of December 31, 1984.

A corporation shall not be treated as a qualified casualty insurance electing small business corporation unless an election under subchapter S of chapter 1 of such Code is in effect for its first taxable year beginning after December 31, 1984.

(3) CERTAIN CORPORATIONS WITH OIL AND GAS PRODUCTION.—

(A) IN GENERAL.—In the case of any qualified oil corporation—

(i) the amendments made by this Act shall not apply, and

(ii) subchapter S (as in effect on July 1, 1982) of chapter 1 of the Internal Revenue Code of 1954 shall apply.

(B) QUALIFIED OIL CORPORATION.—For purposes of this paragraph, the term "qualified oil corporation" means any corporation if—

(i) as of September 28, 1982, such corporation—

(I) was an electing small business corporation, or

(II) was a small business corporation which made an election under section 1372(a) after December 31, 1981, and before September 28, 1982,

(ii) for calendar year 1982, the combined average daily production of domestic crude oil or natural gas of such corporation and any one of its substantial shareholders exceeds 1,000 barrels, and

(iii) such corporation makes an election under this subparagraph at such time and in such manner as the Secretary of the Treasury or his delegate shall prescribe.

(C) AVERAGE DAILY PRODUCTION.—For purposes of subparagraph (B), the average daily production of domestic crude oil or domestic natural gas shall be determined under section 613A(c)(2) of such Code without regard to the last sentence thereof.

(D) SUBSTANTIAL SHAREHOLDER.—For purposes of subparagraph (B), the term "substantial shareholder" means any person who on July 1, 1982, owns more than 40 percent (in value) of the stock of the corporation.

(4) CONTINUITY REQUIRED.—

(A) IN GENERAL.—This subsection shall cease to apply with respect to any corporation after—

(i) any termination of the election of the corporation under subchapter S of chapter 1 of such Code, or

(ii) the first day on which more than 50 percent of the stock of the corporation is newly owned stock within the meaning of section 1378(c)(2) of such Code (as amended by this Act).

(B) SPECIAL RULES FOR PARAGRAPH (2).—

(i) Paragraph (2) shall also cease to apply with respect to any corporation after the corporation ceases to be described in section 831(a) of such Code.

(ii) For purposes of determining under subparagraph (A)(ii) whether paragraph (2) ceases to apply to any corporation, section 1378(c)(2) of such Code (as amended by this Act) shall be applied by substituting "December 31, 1984" for "December 31, 1982" each place it appears therein.

INCOME TAX—S CORPORATION DEFINED

[Sec. 1361(e)]

(e) ELECTING SMALL BUSINESS TRUST DEFINED.—

(1) ELECTING SMALL BUSINESS TRUST.—For purposes of this section—

(A) IN GENERAL.—Except as provided in subparagraph (B), the term "electing small business trust" means any trust if—

(i) such trust does not have as a beneficiary any person other than (I) an individual, (II) an estate, (III) an organization described in paragraph (2), (3), (4), or (5) of section 170(c), or (IV) an organization described in section 170(c)(1) which holds a contingent interest in such trust and is not a potential current beneficiary,

(ii) no interest in such trust was acquired by purchase, and

(iii) an election under this subsection applies to such trust.

(B) CERTAIN TRUSTS NOT ELIGIBLE.—The term "electing small business trust" shall not include—

(i) any qualified subchapter S trust (as defined in subsection (d)(3)) if an election under subsection (d)(2) applies to any corporation the stock of which is held by such trust,

(ii) any trust exempt from tax under this subtitle, and

(iii) any charitable remainder annuity trust or charitable remainder unitrust (as defined in section 664(d)).

(C) PURCHASE.—For purposes of subparagraph (A), the term "purchase" means any acquisition if the basis of the property acquired is determined under section 1012.

(2) POTENTIAL CURRENT BENEFICIARY.—For purposes of this section, the term "potential current beneficiary" means, with respect to any period, any person who at any time during such period is entitled to, or at the discretion of any person may receive, a distribution from the principal or income of the trust (determined without regard to any power of appointment to the extent such power remains unexercised at the end of such period). If a trust disposes of all of the stock which it holds in an S corporation, then, with respect to such corporation, the term "potential current beneficiary" does not include any person who first met the requirements of the preceding sentence during the 1-year period ending on the date of such disposition.

(3) ELECTION.—An election under this subsection shall be made by the trustee. Any such election shall apply to the taxable year of the trust for which made and all subsequent taxable years of such trust unless revoked with the consent of the Secretary.

(4) CROSS REFERENCE.—

For special treatment of electing small business trusts, see section 641(c).

Amendments

• **2004, American Jobs Creation Act of 2004 (P.L. 108-357)**

P.L. 108-357, §234(a)(1)-(2):

Amended Code Sec. 1361(e)(2) by inserting "(determined without regard to any power of appointment to the extent such power remains unexercised at the end of such period)" after "of the trust" in the first sentence, and by striking "60-day" and inserting "1-year" in the second sentence. **Effective** for tax years beginning after 12-31-2004.

• **2000, Community Renewal Tax Relief Act of 2000 (P.L. 106-554)**

P.L. 106-554, §316(b):

Amended Code Sec. 1361(e)(1)(A)(i) by striking "or" before "(III)" and by adding at the end new text. **Effective** as if included in the provision of P.L. 104-188 to which it relates [effective for tax years beginning after 12-31-96.—CCH].

• **1998, IRS Restructuring and Reform Act of 1998 (P.L. 105-206)**

P.L. 105-206, §6007(f)(3):

Amended Code Sec. 1361(e)(4) by striking "section 641(d)" and inserting "section 641(c)". **Effective** as if included in the provision of P.L. 105-134 to which it relates [effective for sales or exchanges after 8-5-97.—CCH].

• **1997, Taxpayer Relief Act of 1997 (P.L. 105-34)**

P.L. 105-34, §1601(c)(1):

Amended Code Sec. 1361(e)(1)(B) by striking "and" at the end of clause (i), striking the period at the end of clause (ii) and inserting ", and", and adding at the end a new clause (iii). **Effective** as if included in the provision of P.L. 104-188 to which it relates [effective for tax years beginning after 12-31-96.—CCH].

• **1996, Small Business Job Protection Act of 1996 (P.L. 104-188)**

P.L. 104-188, §1302(c):

Amended Code Sec. 1361 by adding at the end a new subsection (e). **Effective** for tax years beginning after 12-31-96.

P.L. 104-188, §1316(e):

Amended Code Sec. 1361(e)(1)(A)(i), as added by section 1302, by striking "which holds a contingent interest and is not a potential current beneficiary". **Effective** for tax years beginning after 12-31-97.

[Sec. 1361(f)]

(f) RESTRICTED BANK DIRECTOR STOCK.—

(1) IN GENERAL.—Restricted bank director stock shall not be taken into account as outstanding stock of the S corporation in applying this subchapter (other than section 1368(f)).

(2) RESTRICTED BANK DIRECTOR STOCK.—For purposes of this subsection, the term "restricted bank director stock" means stock in a bank (as defined in section 581) or a depository institution holding company (as defined in section 3(w)(1) of the Federal Deposit Insurance Act (12 U.S.C. 1813(w)(1))), if such stock—

(A) is required to be held by an individual under applicable Federal or State law in order to permit such individual to serve as a director, and

(B) is subject to an agreement with such bank or company (or a corporation which controls (within the meaning of section 368(c)) such bank or company) pursuant to which the holder is required to sell back such stock (at the same price as the individual acquired such stock) upon ceasing to hold the office of director.

(3) CROSS REFERENCE.—

For treatment of certain distributions with respect to restricted bank director stock, see section 1368(f).

Amendments

• **2018, Tax Technical Corrections Act of 2018 (P.L. 115-141)**

P.L. 115-141, §401(a)(190), Div. U:

Amended Code Sec. 1361(f)(2) by striking "1813(w)(1))," and inserting "1813(w)(1))),". **Effective** 3-23-2018.

• **2007, Small Business and Work Opportunity Tax Act of 2007 (P.L. 110-28)**

P.L. 110-28, §8232(a):

Amended Code Sec. 1361 by adding at the end a new subsection (f). **Effective** generally for tax years beginning after 12-31-2006. For a special rule, see Act Sec. 8232(c)(2), below.

P.L. 110-28, §8232(c)(2), provides:

(2) SPECIAL RULE FOR TREATMENT AS SECOND CLASS OF STOCK.—In the case of any taxable year beginning after December 31, 1996, restricted bank director stock (as defined in section 1361(f) of the Internal Revenue Code of 1986, as added by this section) shall not be taken into account in determining whether an S corporation has more than 1 class of stock.

[Sec. 1361(g)]

(g) SPECIAL RULE FOR BANK REQUIRED TO CHANGE FROM THE RESERVE METHOD OF ACCOUNTING ON BECOMING S CORPORATION.—In the case of a bank which changes from the reserve method of accounting for bad debts described in section 585 or 593 for its first taxable year for which an election

INCOME TAX—ELECTION; REVOCATION; TERMINATION

under section 1362(a) is in effect, the bank may elect to take into account any adjustments under section 481 by reason of such change for the taxable year immediately preceding such first taxable year.

Amendments

• **2007, Small Business and Work Opportunity Tax Act of 2007 (P.L. 110-28)**

P.L. 110-28, §8233(a):

Amended Code Sec. 1361, as amended by this Act, by adding at the end a new subsection (g). **Effective** for tax years beginning after 12-31-2006.

[Sec. 1362]

SEC. 1362. ELECTION; REVOCATION; TERMINATION.

[Sec. 1362(a)]

(a) ELECTION.—

(1) IN GENERAL.—Except as provided in subsection (g), a small business corporation may elect, in accordance with the provisions of this section, to be an S corporation.

(2) ALL SHAREHOLDERS MUST CONSENT TO ELECTION.—An election under this subsection shall be valid only if all persons who are shareholders in such corporation on the day on which such election is made consent to such election.

[Sec. 1362(b)]

(b) WHEN MADE.—

(1) IN GENERAL.—An election under subsection (a) may be made by a small business corporation for any taxable year—

(A) at any time during the preceding taxable year, or

(B) at any time during the taxable year and on or before the 15th day of the 3d month of the taxable year.

(2) CERTAIN ELECTIONS MADE DURING 1ST $2^1/_2$ MONTHS TREATED AS MADE FOR NEXT TAXABLE YEAR.—If—

(A) an election under subsection (a) is made for any taxable year during such year and on or before the 15th day of the 3d month of such year, but

(B) either—

(i) on 1 or more days in such taxable year before the day on which the election was made the corporation did not meet the requirements of subsection (b) of section 1361, or

(ii) 1 or more of the persons who held stock in the corporation during such taxable year and before the election was made did not consent to the election,

then such election shall be treated as made for the following taxable year.

(3) ELECTION MADE AFTER 1ST $2^1/_2$ MONTHS TREATED AS MADE FOR FOLLOWING TAXABLE YEAR.—If—

(A) a small business corporation makes an election under subsection (a) for any taxable year, and

(B) such election is made after the 15th day of the 3d month of the taxable year and on or before the 15th day of the 3rd month of the following taxable year,

then such election shall be treated as made for the following taxable year.

(4) TAXABLE YEARS OF $2^1/_2$ MONTHS OR LESS.—For purposes of this subsection, an election for a taxable year made not later than 2 months and 15 days after the first day of the taxable year shall be treated as timely made during such year.

(5) AUTHORITY TO TREAT LATE ELECTIONS, ETC., AS TIMELY.—If—

(A) an election under subsection (a) is made for any taxable year (determined without regard to paragraph (3)) after the date prescribed by this subsection for making such election for such taxable year or no such election is made for any taxable year, and

(B) the Secretary determines that there was reasonable cause for the failure to timely make such election,

the Secretary may treat such an election as timely made for such taxable year (and paragraph (3) shall not apply).

Amendments

• **1996, Small Business Job Protection Act of 1996 (P.L. 104-188)**

P.L. 104-188, §1305(b):

Amended Code Sec. 1362(b) by adding at the end a new paragraph (5). **Effective** with respect to elections for tax years beginning after 12-31-82.

• **1984, Deficit Reduction Act of 1984 (P.L. 98-369)**

P.L. 98-369, §721(l)(1):

Amended Code Sec. 1362(b) by adding paragraph (4). **Effective** for any election under section 1362 of the Internal Revenue Code of 1954 (or any corresponding provision of prior law) made after 10-19-82.

P.L. 98-369, §721(l)(2):

Amended Code Sec. 1362(b)(3) by striking out "on or before the last day of such taxable year" and inserting in lieu thereof "on or before the 15th day of the 3rd month of the following taxable year". **Effective** for any election under section 1362 of the Internal Revenue Code of 1954 (or any corresponding provision of prior law) made after 10-19-82.

[Sec. 1362(c)]

(c) YEARS FOR WHICH EFFECTIVE.—An election under subsection (a) shall be effective for the taxable year of the corporation for which it is made and for all succeeding taxable years of the corporation, until such election is terminated under subsection (d).

[Sec. 1362(d)]

(d) TERMINATION.—

(1) BY REVOCATION.—

(A) IN GENERAL.—An election under subsection (a) may be terminated by revocation.

(B) MORE THAN ONE-HALF OF SHARES MUST CONSENT TO REVOCATION.—An election may be revoked only if shareholders holding more than one-half of the shares of stock of the corporation on the day on which the revocation is made consent to the revocation.

(C) WHEN EFFECTIVE.—Except as provided in subparagraph (D)—

(i) a revocation made during the taxable year and on or before the 15th day of the 3d month thereof shall be effective on the 1st day of such taxable year, and

(ii) a revocation made during the taxable year but after such 15th day shall be effective on the 1st day of the following taxable year.

(D) REVOCATION MAY SPECIFY PROSPECTIVE DATE.—If the revocation specifies a date for revocation which is on or after the day on which the revocation is made, the revocation shall be effective on and after the date so specified.

Internal Revenue Code

Sec. 1362(d)(1)(D)

INCOME TAX—ELECTION; REVOCATION; TERMINATION

(2) BY CORPORATION CEASING TO BE SMALL BUSINESS CORPORATION.—

(A) IN GENERAL.—An election under subsection (a) shall be terminated whenever (at any time on or after the 1st day of the 1st taxable year for which the corporation is an S corporation) such corporation ceases to be a small business corporation.

(B) WHEN EFFECTIVE.—Any termination under this paragraph shall be effective on and after the date of cessation.

(3) WHERE PASSIVE INVESTMENT INCOME EXCEEDS 25 PERCENT OF GROSS RECEIPTS FOR 3 CONSECUTIVE TAXABLE YEARS AND CORPORATION HAS ACCUMULATED EARNINGS AND PROFITS.—

(A) TERMINATION.—

(i) IN GENERAL.—An election under subsection (a) shall be terminated whenever the corporation—

(I) has accumulated earnings and profits at the close of each of 3 consecutive taxable years, and

(II) has gross receipts for each of such taxable years more than 25 percent of which are passive investment income.

(ii) WHEN EFFECTIVE.—Any termination under this paragraph shall be effective on and after the first day of the first taxable year beginning after the third consecutive taxable year referred to in clause (i).

(iii) YEARS TAKEN INTO ACCOUNT.—A prior taxable year shall not be taken into account under clause (i) unless the corporation was an S corporation for such taxable year.

(B) GROSS RECEIPTS FROM THE SALES OF CERTAIN ASSETS.—For purposes of this paragraph—

(i) in the case of dispositions of capital assets (other than stock and securities), gross receipts from such dispositions shall be taken into account only to the extent of the capital gain net income therefrom, and

(ii) in the case of sales or exchanges of stock or securities, gross receipts shall be taken into account only to the extent of the gains therefrom.

(C) PASSIVE INVESTMENT INCOME DEFINED.—

(i) IN GENERAL.—Except as otherwise provided in this subparagraph, the term "passive investment income" means gross receipts derived from royalties, rents, dividends, interest, and annuities.

(ii) EXCEPTION FOR INTEREST ON NOTES FROM SALES OF INVENTORY.—The term "passive investment income" shall not include interest on any obligation acquired in the ordinary course of the corporation's trade or business from its sale of property described in section 1221(a)(1).

(iii) TREATMENT OF CERTAIN LENDING OR FINANCE COMPANIES.—If the S corporation meets the requirements of section 542(c)(6) for the taxable year, the term "passive investment income" shall not include gross receipts for the taxable year which are derived directly from the active and regular conduct of a lending or finance business (as defined in section 542(d)(1)).

(iv) TREATMENT OF CERTAIN DIVIDENDS.—If an S corporation holds stock in a C corporation meeting the requirements of section 1504(a)(2), the term "passive investment income" shall not include dividends from such C corporation to the extent such dividends are attributable to the earnings and profits of such C corporation derived from the active conduct of a trade or business.

(v) EXCEPTION FOR BANKS, ETC.—In the case of a bank (as defined in section 581) or a depository institution holding company (as defined in section 3(w)(1) of the Federal Deposit Insurance Act (12 U.S.C. 1813(w)(1))), the term "passive investment income" shall not include—

(I) interest income earned by such bank or company, or

(II) dividends on assets required to be held by such bank or company, including stock in the Federal Reserve Bank, the Federal Home Loan Bank, or the Federal Agricultural Mortgage Bank or participation certificates issued by a Federal Intermediate Credit Bank.

Amendments

- **2018, Tax Technical Corrections Act of 2018 (P.L. 115-141)**

P.L. 115-141, §401(a)(190), Div. U:

Amended Code Sec. 1362(d)(3)(C)(v) by striking "1813(w)(1))," and inserting "1813(w)(1)))," **Effective** 3-23-2018.

- **2014, Tax Technical Corrections Act of 2014 (P.L. 113-295)**

P.L. 113-295, §221(a)(88), Division A:

Amended Code Sec. 1362(d)(3)(A)(iii) by striking "unless" and all that follows and inserting "unless the corporation was an S corporation for such taxable year.". **Effective** generally 12-19-2014. For a special rule, see Act Sec. 221(b)(2), Division A, below. Prior to amendment, Code Sec. 1362(d)(3)(A)(iii) read as follows:

(iii) YEARS TAKEN INTO ACCOUNT.—A prior taxable year shall not be taken into account under clause (i) unless—

(I) such taxable year began after December 31, 1981, and

(II) the corporation was an S corporation for such taxable year.

P.L. 113-295, §221(b)(2), Division A, provides:

(2) SAVINGS PROVISION.—If—

(A) any provision amended or repealed by the amendments made by this section applied to—

(i) any transaction occurring before the date of the enactment of this Act,

(ii) any property acquired before such date of enactment, or

(iii) any item of income, loss, deduction, or credit taken into account before such date of enactment, and

(B) the treatment of such transaction, property, or item under such provision would (without regard to the amendments or repeals made by this section) affect the liability for tax for periods ending after date of enactment, nothing in the amendments or repeals made by this section shall be construed to affect the treatment of such transaction, property, or item for purposes of determining liability for tax for periods ending after such date of enactment.

- **2007, Small Business and Work Opportunity Tax Act of 2007 (P.L. 110-28)**

P.L. 110-28, §8231(a):

Amended Code Sec. 1362(d)(3) by striking subparagraphs (B)-(F) and inserting new subparagraphs (B) and (C). **Effective** for tax years beginning after 5-25-2007. Prior to being stricken, Code Sec. 1362(d)(3)(B)-(F) read as follows:

(B) GROSS RECEIPTS FROM SALES OF CAPITAL ASSETS (OTHER THAN STOCK AND SECURITIES).—For purposes of this paragraph, in the case of dispositions of capital assets (other than stock and securities), gross receipts from such dispositions shall be taken into account only to the extent of the capital gain net income therefrom.

(C) PASSIVE INVESTMENT INCOME DEFINED.—For purposes of this paragraph—

(i) IN GENERAL.—Except as otherwise provided in this subparagraph, the term "passive investment income" means gross receipts derived from royalties, rents, dividends, interest, annuities, and sales or exchanges of stock or securities (gross receipts from such sales or exchanges being taken into account for purposes of this paragraph only to the extent of gains therefrom).

(ii) EXCEPTION FOR INTEREST ON NOTES FROM SALES OF INVENTORY.—The term "passive investment income" shall not include interest on any obligation acquired in the ordinary course of the corporation's trade or business from its sale of property described in section 1221(a)(1).

(iii) TREATMENT OF CERTAIN LENDING OR FINANCE COMPANIES.—If the S corporation meets the requirements of section 542(c)(6) for the taxable year, the term "passive investment income" shall not include gross receipts for the taxable year which are derived directly from the active and regular conduct of a lending or finance business (as defined in section 542(d)(1)).

(iv) TREATMENT OF CERTAIN LIQUIDATIONS.—Gross receipts derived from sales or exchanges of stock or securities shall not include amounts received by an S corporation which are treated under section 331 (relating to corporate liquidations) as payments in exchange for stock where the S corporation owned more than 50 percent of each class of stock of the liquidating corporation.

(D) SPECIAL RULE FOR OPTIONS AND COMMODITY DEALINGS.—

(i) IN GENERAL.—In the case of any options dealer or commodities dealer, passive investment income shall be determined by not taking into account any gain or loss (in the normal course of the taxpayer's activity of dealing in or trading section 1256 contracts) from any section 1256 contract or property related to such a contract.

(ii) DEFINITIONS.—For purposes of this subparagraph—

(I) OPTIONS DEALER.—The term "options dealer" has the meaning given such term by section 1256(g)(8).

(II) COMMODITIES DEALER.—The term "commodities dealer" means a person who is actively engaged in trading section 1256 contracts and is registered with a domestic board of trade which is designated as a contract market by the Commodities Futures Trading Commission.

(III) SECTION 1256 CONTRACT.—The term "section 1256 contract" has the meaning given to such term by section 1256(b).

(E) TREATMENT OF CERTAIN DIVIDENDS.—If an S corporation holds stock in a C corporation meeting the requirements of section 1504(a)(2), the term "passive investment income" shall not include dividends from such C corporation to the extent such dividends are attributable to the earnings and profits of such C corporation derived from the active conduct of a trade or business.

(F) EXCEPTION FOR BANKS; ETC.—In the case of a bank (as defined in section 581), [or] a depository institution holding company (as defined in section 3(w)(1) of the Federal Deposit Insurance Act (12 U.S.C. 1813(w)(1)), the term "passive investment income" shall not include—

(i) interest income earned by such bank or company, or

(ii) dividends on assets required to be held by such bank or company, including stock in the Federal Reserve Bank, the Federal Home Loan Bank, or the Federal Agricultural Mortgage Bank or participation certificates issued by a Federal Intermediate Credit Bank.

• **2005, Gulf Opportunity Zone Act of 2005 (P.L. 109-135)**

P.L. 109-135, § 413(b):

Amended Code Sec. 1362(d)(3)(F) by striking "a bank holding company" and all that follows through "section 2(p) of such Act)" and inserting "[or] a depository institution holding company (as defined in section 3(w)(1) of the Federal Deposit Insurance Act (12 U.S.C. 1813(w)(1))". **Effective** as if included in the provision of the American Jobs Creation Act of 2004 (P.L. 108-357) to which it relates [effective for tax years beginning after 12-31-2004.—CCH]. Prior to amendment, Code Sec. 1362(d)(3)(F) read as follows:

(F) EXCEPTION FOR BANKS; ETC.—In the case of a bank (as defined in section 581), a bank holding company (within the meaning of section 2(a) of the Bank Holding Company Act of 1956 (12 U.S.C. 1841(a))), or a financial holding company (within the meaning of section 2(p) of such Act), the term "passive investment income" shall not include—

(i) interest income earned by such bank or company, or

(ii) dividends on assets required to be held by such bank or company, including stock in the Federal Reserve Bank, the Federal Home Loan Bank, or the Federal Agricultural Mortgage Bank or participation certificates issued by a Federal Intermediate Credit Bank.

• **2004, American Jobs Creation Act of 2004 (P.L. 108-357)**

P.L. 108-357, § 237(a):

Amended Code Sec. 1362(d)(3) by adding at the end a new subparagraph (F). **Effective** for tax years beginning after 12-31-2004.

• **1999, Tax Relief Extension Act of 1999 (P.L. 106-170)**

P.L. 106-170, § 532(c)(2)(T):

Amended Code Sec. 1362(d)(3)(C)(ii) by striking "section 1221(1)" and inserting "section 1221(a)(1)". **Effective** for any instrument held, acquired, or entered into, any transaction entered into, and supplies held or acquired on or after 12-17-99.

• **1996, Small Business Job Protection Act of 1996 (P.L. 104-188)**

P.L. 104-188, § 1308(c):

Amended Code Sec. 1362(d)(3) by adding at the end a new subparagraph (F). **Effective** for tax years beginning after 12-31-96.

P.L. 104-188, § 1311(b)(1)(A)-(C):

Amended Code Sec. 1362(d)(3) by striking "SUBCHAPTER C" in the paragraph heading and inserting "ACCUMULATED", by striking "subchapter C" in subparagraph (A)(i)(I) and inserting "accumulated", and by striking subparagraph (B) and redesignating the following subparagraphs accordingly. **Effective** for tax years beginning after 12-31-96. Prior to amendment, Code Sec. 1362(d)(3)(B) read as follows:

(B) SUBCHAPTER C EARNINGS AND PROFITS.—For purposes of subparagraph (A), the term "subchapter C earnings and profits" means earnings and profits of any corporation for any taxable year with respect to which an election under section 1362(a) (or under section 1372 of prior law) was not in effect.

• **1988, Technical and Miscellaneous Revenue Act of 1988 (P.L. 100-647)**

P.L. 100-647, § 1006(f)(6)(A)-(B):

Amended Code Sec. 1362(d)(3) by striking out clause (v) of subparagraph (D), and by adding at the end thereof new subparagraph (E). **Effective** as if included in the provision of P.L. 99-514 to which it relates. Prior to amendment, Code Sec. 1362(d)(3)(D)(v) read as follows:

(v) SPECIAL RULE FOR OPTIONS AND COMMODITIES DEALERS.—In the case of any options or commodities dealer, passive investment income shall be determined by not taking into account any gain or loss described in section 1374(c)(4)(A).

• **1984, Deficit Reduction Act of 1984 (P.L. 98-369)**

P.L. 98-369, § 102(d)(2):

Amended Code Sec. 1362(d)(3)(D) by adding new clause (v). **Effective** for positions established after 7-18-84, in tax years ending after such date. For a special rule, see Act Sec. 102(d)(3), below.

P.L. 98-369, § 102(d)(3), as amended by P.L. 99-514, § 1808(a), provides:

(3) SUBCHAPTER S ELECTION.—If a commodities dealer or an options dealer—

(A) becomes a small business corporation (as defined in section 1361(b) of the Internal Revenue Code of 1954) at any time before the close of the 75th day after the date of the enactment of this Act, and

(B) makes the election under section 1362(a) of such Code before the close of such 75th day,

then such dealer shall be treated as having received approval for and adopted a taxable year beginning on the first day during 1984 on which it was a small business corporation (as so defined) or such other day as may be permitted under regulations and ending on the date determined under section 1378 of such Code and such election shall be effective for such taxable year.

[Sec. 1362(e)]

(e) TREATMENT OF S TERMINATION YEAR.—

(1) IN GENERAL.—In the case of an S termination year, for purposes of this title—

(A) S SHORT YEAR.—The portion of such year ending before the 1st day for which the termination is effective shall be treated as a short taxable year for which the corporation is an S corporation.

(B) C SHORT YEAR.—The portion of such year beginning on such 1st day shall be treated as a short taxable year for which the corporation is a C corporation.

(2) PRO RATA ALLOCATION.—Except as provided in paragraph (3) and subparagraphs (C) and (D) of paragraph (6), the determination of which items are to be taken into account for each of the short taxable years referred to in paragraph (1) shall be made—

(A) first by determining for the S termination year—

(i) the amount of each of the items of income, loss, deduction, or credit described in section 1366(a)(1)(A), and

(ii) the amount of the nonseparately computed income or loss, and

(B) then by assigning an equal portion of each amount determined under subparagraph (A) to each day of the S termination year.

(3) ELECTION TO HAVE ITEMS ASSIGNED TO EACH SHORT TAXABLE YEAR UNDER NORMAL TAX ACCOUNTING RULES.—

(A) IN GENERAL.—A corporation may elect to have paragraph (2) not apply.

(B) SHAREHOLDERS MUST CONSENT TO ELECTION.—An election under this subsection shall be valid only if all persons who are shareholders in the corporation at any time during the S short year and all persons who are shareholders in the corporation on the first day of the C short year consent to such election.

(4) S TERMINATION YEAR.—For purposes of this subsection, the term "S termination year" means any taxable year of a corporation (determined without regard to this subsection) in which a termination of an election made under subsection (a) takes effect (other than on the 1st day thereof).

(5) TAX FOR C SHORT YEAR DETERMINED ON ANNUALIZED BASIS.—

(A) IN GENERAL.—The taxable income for the short year described in subparagraph (B) of paragraph (1) shall be placed on an annual basis by multiplying the taxable income for such short year by the number of days in the S termination year and by dividing the result by the number of days in the short year. The tax shall be the same part of the tax computed on the annual basis as the number of days in such short year is of the number of days in the S termination year.

(B) SECTION 443(d)(2) TO APPLY.—Subsection (d) of section 443 shall apply to the short taxable year described in subparagraph (B) of paragraph (1).

(6) OTHER SPECIAL RULES.—For purposes of this title—

(A) SHORT YEARS TREATED AS 1 YEAR FOR CARRYOVER PURPOSES.—The short taxable year described in subparagraph (A) of paragraph (1) shall not be taken into account for purposes of determining the number of taxable years to which any item may be carried back or carried forward by the corporation.

(B) DUE DATE FOR S YEAR.—The due date for filing the return for the short taxable year described in subparagraph (A) of paragraph (1) shall be the same as the due date for filing the return for the short taxable year described in subparagraph (B) of paragraph (1) (including extensions thereof).

INCOME TAX—ELECTION; REVOCATION; TERMINATION

(C) Paragraph (2) not to apply to items resulting from section 338.—Paragraph (2) shall not apply with respect to any item resulting from the application of section 338.

(D) Pro rata allocation for S termination year not to apply if 50-percent change in ownership.—Paragraph (2) shall not apply to an S termination year if there is a sale or exchange of 50 percent or more of the stock in such corporation during such year.

Amendments

• **1988, Technical and Miscellaneous Revenue Act of 1988 (P.L. 100-647)**

P.L. 100-647, §1007(g)(9):

Amended Code Sec. 1362(e)(5)(B) by striking out "Subsection (d)(2)" and inserting in lieu thereof "Subsection (d)". **Effective** as if included in the provision of P.L. 99-514 to which it relates.

• **1984, Deficit Reduction Act of 1984 (P.L. 98-369)**

P.L. 98-369, §721(g)(1):

Amended Code Sec. 1362(e)(6) by adding subparagraph (C). **Effective** as if included in P.L. 97-354, except as noted in Act Sec. 721(y)(3), below.

P.L. 98-369, §721(g)(2):

Amended Code Sec. 1362(e)(2) by striking out "as provided in paragraph (3)" and inserting in lieu thereof "as provided in paragraph (3) and subparagraphs (C) and (D) of paragraph (6)". **Effective** as if included in P.L. 97-354.

P.L. 98-369, §721(h):

Amended Code Sec. 1362(e)(3)(B). **Effective** as if included in P.L. 97-354. Prior to amendment, Code Sec. 1362(e)(3)(B) read as follows:

(B) All shareholders must consent to election.—An election under this paragraph shall be valid only if all persons who are shareholders in the corporation at any time during the S termination year consent to such election.

P.L. 98-369, §721(t):

Amended Code Sec. 1362(e)(6) by adding subparagraph (D). **Effective** as if included in P.L. 97-354, except as noted in Act Sec. 721(y)(5), below.

P.L. 98-369, §721(y)(3), provides:

(3) Amendment made by subsection (g)(1).—If—

(A) any portion of a qualified stock purchase is pursuant to a binding contract entered into on or after October 19, 1982, and before the date of the enactment of this Act, and

(B) the purchasing corporation establishes by clear and convincing evidence that such contract was negotiated on the contemplation that, with respect to the deemed sale under section 338 of the Internal Revenue Code of 1954, paragraph (2) of section 1362(e) of such Code would apply, then the amendment made by paragraph (1) of subsection (g) shall not apply to such qualified stock purchase.

P.L. 98-369, §721(y)(5), provides:

(5) Amendment made by subsection (t).—If—

(A) on or before the date of the enactment of this Act 50 percent or more of the stock of an S corporation has been sold or exchanged in 1 or more transactions, and

(B) the person (or persons) acquiring such stock establish by clear and convincing evidence that such acquisitions were negotiated on the contemplation that paragraph (2) of section 1362(e) of the Internal Revenue Code of 1954 would apply to the S termination year in which such sales or exchanges occur,

then the amendment made by subsection (t) shall not apply to such S termination year.

[Sec. 1362(f)]

(f) Inadvertent Invalid Elections or Terminations.—If—

(1) an election under subsection (a) or section 1361(b)(3)(B)(ii) by any corporation—

(A) was not effective for the taxable year for which made (determined without regard to subsection (b)(2)) by reason of a failure to meet the requirements of section 1361(b) or to obtain shareholder consents, or

(B) was terminated under paragraph (2) or (3) of subsection (d) or section 1361(b)(3)(C),

(2) the Secretary determines that the circumstances resulting in such ineffectiveness or termination were inadvertent,

(3) no later than a reasonable period of time after discovery of the circumstances resulting in such ineffectiveness or termination, steps were taken—

(A) so that the corporation for which the election was made or the termination occurred is a small business corporation or a qualified subchapter S subsidiary, as the case may be, or

(B) to acquire the required shareholder consents, and

(4) the corporation for which the election was made or the termination occurred, and each person who was a shareholder in such corporation at any time during the period specified pursuant to this subsection, agrees to make such adjustments (consistent with the treatment of such corporation as an S corporation or a qualified subchapter S subsidiary, as the case may be) as may be required by the Secretary with respect to such period,

then, notwithstanding the circumstances resulting in such ineffectiveness or termination, such corporation shall be treated as an S corporation or a qualified subchapter S subsidiary, as the case may be, during the period specified by the Secretary.

Amendments

• **2018, Tax Technical Corrections Act of 2018 (P.L. 115-141)**

P.L. 115-141, §401(a)(191), Div. U:

Amended Code Sec. 1362(f) by striking "may be during" and inserting "may be, during". **Effective** 3-23-2018.

• **2007, Tax Technical Corrections Act of 2007 (P.L. 110-172)**

P.L. 110-172, §11(a)(25)(A)-(B):

Amended Code Sec. 1362(f)(1) by striking ", section 1361(b)(3)(B)(ii), or section 1361(c)(1)(A)(ii)" and inserting "or section 1361(b)(3)(B)(ii)", and by striking ", section 1361(b)(3)(C), or section 1361(c)(1)(D)(iii)" in subparagraph (B) and inserting "or section 1361(b)(3)(C)". **Effective** 12-29-2007.

• **2004, American Jobs Creation Act of 2004 (P.L. 108-357)**

P.L. 108-357, §231(b)(1):

Amended Code Sec. 1362(f)(1), as amended by this Act, by inserting "or section 1361(c)(1)(A)(ii)" after "section 1361(b)(3)(B)(ii),". **Effective** for elections made and terminations made after 12-31-2004.

P.L. 108-357, §231(b)(2):

Amended Code Sec. 1362(f)(1)(B), as amended by this Act, by inserting "or section 1361(c)(1)(D)(iii)" after "section 1361(b)(3)(C),". **Effective** for elections made and terminations made after 12-31-2004.

P.L. 108-357, §238(a)(1):

Amended Code Sec. 1362(f)(1) by inserting ", section 1361(b)(3)(B)(ii)," after "subsection (a),". **Effective** for elections made and terminations made after 12-31-2004.

P.L. 108-357, §238(a)(2):

Amended Code Sec. 1362(f)(1)(B) by inserting ", section 1361(b)(3)(C)," after "subsection (d)". **Effective** for elections made and terminations made after 12-31-2004.

P.L. 108-357, §238(a)(3):

Amended Code Sec. 1362(f)(3)(A). **Effective** for elections made and terminations made after 12-31-2004. Prior to amendment, Code Sec. 1362(f)(3)(A) read as follows:

(A) so that the corporation is a small business corporation, or

P.L. 108-357, §238(a)(4):

Amended Code Sec. 1362(f)(4). **Effective** for elections made and terminations made after 12-31-2004. Prior to amendment, Code Sec. 1362(f)(4) read as follows:

(4) the corporation, and each person who was a shareholder in the corporation at any time during the period specified pursuant to this subsection, agrees to make such adjustments (consistent with the treatment of the corporation as an S corporation) as may be required by the Secretary with respect to such period,

P.L. 108-357, §238(a)(5):

Amended Code Sec. 1362(f) by inserting "or a qualified subchapter S subsidiary, as the case may be" after "S corporation" in the matter following paragraph (4). **Effective** for elections made and terminations made after 12-31-2004.

• **1996, Small Business Job Protection Act of 1996 (P.L. 104-188)**

P.L. 104-188, §1305(a):

Amended Code Sec. 1362(f). **Effective** with respect to elections for tax years beginning after 12-31-82. Prior to amendment, Code Sec. 1362(f) read as follows:

(f) Inadvertent Terminations.—If—

(1) an election under subsection (a) by any corporation was terminated under paragraph (2) or (3) of subsection (d),

(2) the Secretary determines that the termination was inadvertent,

(3) no later than a reasonable period of time after discovery of the event resulting in such termination, steps were taken so that the corporation is once more a small business corporation, and

(4) the corporation, and each person who was a shareholder of the corporation at any time during the period specified pursuant to this subsection, agrees to make such adjustments (consistent with the treatment of the corporation as an S corporation) as may be required by the Secretary with respect to such period,

then, notwithstanding the terminating event, such corporation shall be treated as continuing to be an S corporation during the period specified by the Secretary.

INCOME TAX—EFFECT OF ELECTION

[Sec. 1362(g)]

(g) ELECTION AFTER TERMINATION.—If a small business corporation has made an election under subsection (a) and if such election has been terminated under subsection (d), such corporation (and any successor corporation) shall not be eligible to make an election under subsection (a) for any taxable year before its 5th taxable year which begins after the 1st taxable year for which such termination is effective, unless the Secretary consents to such election.

Amendments

• **1996, Small Business Job Protection Act of 1996 (P.L. 104-188)**

P.L. 104-188, §1317(b), provides:

(b) TREATMENT OF CERTAIN ELECTIONS UNDER PRIOR LAW.—For purposes of section 1362(g) of the Internal Revenue Code of 1986 (relating to election after termination), any termination under section 1362(d) of such Code in a taxable year beginning before January 1, 1997, shall not be taken into account.

• **1982, Subchapter S Revision Act of 1982 (P.L. 97-354)**

P.L. 97-354, §2:

Added Code Sec. 1362. **Effective** for tax years beginning after 12-31-82, except that Code Sec. 1362(d)(3) applies to tax years beginning during 1982. See, however, the amendment note for Act Sec. 6(c)(2)-(4) following Code Sec. 1361 for special rules and exceptions concerning certain casualty insurance companies and qualified oil corporations.

P.L. 97-354, §6(b)(3), as amended by P.L. 98-369, §721(i) provides:

(3) NEW PASSIVE INCOME RULES APPLY TO TAXABLE YEARS BEGINNING DURING 1982—

(A) sections 1362(d)(3), 1366(f)(3), and 1375 of the Internal Revenue Code of 1954 (as amended by this Act) shall apply, and

(B) section 1372(e)(5) of such Code (as in effect on the day before the date of the enactment of this Act) shall not apply.

The preceding sentence shall not apply in the case of any corporation which elects (at such time and in such manner as the Secretary of the Treasury or his delegate shall prescribe) to have such sentence not apply. Subsection (e) shall not apply to any termination resulting from an election under the preceding sentence.

P.L. 97-354, §6(e), as amended by P.L. 98-369, §721(k), provides:

(e) TREATMENT OF CERTAIN ELECTIONS UNDER PRIOR LAW.—For purposes of section 1362(g) of the Internal Revenue Code of 1954, as amended by this Act (relating to no election permitted within 5 years after termination of prior election), any termination or revocation under section 1372(e) of such Code (as in effect on the day before the date of the enactment of this Act) shall not be taken into account.

[Sec. 1363]

SEC. 1363. EFFECT OF ELECTION ON CORPORATION.

[Sec. 1363(a)]

(a) GENERAL RULE.—Except as otherwise provided in this subchapter, an S corporation shall not be subject to the taxes imposed by this chapter.

Amendments

• **1986, Tax Reform Act of 1986 (P.L. 99-514)**

P.L. 99-514, §701(e)(4)(J):

Amended Code Sec. 1363(a) by striking out the words "and in section 58(d)". **Effective**, generally, for tax years beginning after 12-31-86. However, see Act Sec. 701(f)(2)-(7) following Code Sec. 56 for special rules.

[Sec. 1363(b)]

(b) COMPUTATION OF CORPORATION'S TAXABLE INCOME.—The taxable income of an S corporation shall be computed in the same manner as in the case of an individual, except that—

(1) the items described in section 1366(a)(1)(A) shall be separately stated,

(2) the deductions referred to in section 703(a)(2) shall not be allowed to the corporation,

(3) section 248 shall apply, and

(4) section 291 shall apply if the S corporation (or any predecessor) was a C corporation for any of the 3 immediately preceding taxable years.

Amendments

• **1984, Deficit Reduction Act of 1984 (P.L. 98-369)**

P.L. 98-369, §721(p):

Amended Code Sec. 1363(b) by striking out "and" at the end of paragraph (2), by striking out the period at the end of paragraph (3) and inserting in lieu thereof ", and", and by adding at the end thereof new paragraph (4). **Effective** as if included in P.L. 97-354.

[Sec. 1363(c)]

(c) ELECTIONS OF THE S CORPORATION.—

(1) IN GENERAL.—Except as provided in paragraph (2), any election affecting the computation of items derived from an S corporation shall be made by the corporation.

(2) EXCEPTIONS.—In the case of an S corporation, elections under the following provisions shall be made by each shareholder separately—

(A) section 617 (relating to deduction and recapture of certain mining exploration expenditures), and

(B) section 901 (relating to taxes of foreign countries and possessions of the United States).

Amendments

• **1986, Tax Reform Act of 1986 (P.L. 99-514)**

P.L. 99-514, §511(d)[c](2)(C):

Amended Code Sec. 1363(c)(2) by striking out subparagraph (A) and by redesignating subparagraphs (B) and (C) as subparagraphs (A) and (B), respectively. **Effective** for tax years beginning after 12-31-86. Prior to amendment, Code Sec. 1363(c)(2)(A) read as follows:

(A) section 163(d) (relating to limitation on interest on investment indebtedness),

• **1984, Deficit Reduction Act of 1984 (P.L. 98-369)**

P.L. 98-369, §721(b)(1):

Amended Code Sec. 1363(c)(2) by striking out subparagraph (A) and by redesignating subparagraphs (B), (C), and (D) as subparagraphs (A), (B), and (C), respectively. **Effective** as if included in P.L. 97-354. Prior to its deletion, Code Sec. 1363(c)(2)(A) read as follows:

(A) subsection (b)(5) or (d)(4) of section 108 (relating to income from discharge of indebtedness),

• **1982, Subchapter S Revision Act of 1982 (P.L. 97-354)**

P.L. 97-354, §2:

Added Code Sec. 1363. **Effective**, generally, for tax years beginning after 1982. See the amendment note for Act Sec. 6(c)(2)-(4) following Code Sec. 1361 for special rules and exceptions concerning certain casualty insurance companies and qualified oil corporations.

[Sec. 1363(d)—Repealed]

Amendments

• **1988, Technical and Miscellaneous Revenue Act of 1988 (P.L. 100-647)**

P.L. 100-647, §1006(f)(7):

Repealed Code Sec. 1363(d). **Effective** as if included in the provision of P.L. 99-514 to which it relates. Prior to repeal, Code Sec. 1363(d) read as follows:

(d) DISTRIBUTIONS OF APPRECIATED PROPERTY.—Except as provided in subsection (e), if—

(1) an S corporation makes a distribution of property (other than an obligation of such corporation) with respect to its stock, and

(2) the fair market value of such property exceeds its adjusted basis in the hands of the S corporation,

then, notwithstanding any other provision of this subtitle, gain shall be recognized to the S corporation on the distribution in the same manner as if it had sold such property to the distributee at its fair market value.

INCOME TAX—TREATMENT OF SHAREHOLDERS

● **1984, Deficit Reduction Act of 1984 (P.L. 98-369)**

P.L. 98-369, § 721(a)(2):

Amended Code Sec. 1363(d) by striking out "If" and inserting in lieu thereof "Except as provided in subsection (e), if". **Effective** as if included in P.L. 97-354.

[Sec. 1363(d)]

(d) RECAPTURE OF LIFO BENEFITS.—

(1) IN GENERAL.—If—

(A) an S corporation was a C corporation for the last taxable year before the first taxable year for which the election under section 1362(a) was effective, and

(B) the corporation inventoried goods under the LIFO method for such last taxable year,

the LIFO recapture amount shall be included in the gross income of the corporation for such last taxable year (and appropriate adjustments to the basis of inventory shall be made to take into account the amount included in gross income under this paragraph).

(2) ADDITIONAL TAX PAYABLE IN INSTALLMENTS.—

(A) IN GENERAL.—Any increase in the tax imposed by this chapter by reason of this subsection shall be payable in 4 equal installments.

(B) DATE FOR PAYMENT OF INSTALLMENTS.—The first installment under subparagraph (A) shall be paid on or before the due date (determined without regard to extensions) for the return of the tax imposed by this chapter for the last taxable year for which the corporation was a C corporation and the 3 succeeding installments shall be paid on or before the due date (as so determined) for the corporation's return for the 3 succeeding taxable years.

(C) NO INTEREST FOR PERIOD OF EXTENSION.—Notwithstanding section 6601(b), for purposes of section 6601, the date prescribed for the payment of each installment under this paragraph shall be determined under this paragraph.

(3) LIFO RECAPTURE AMOUNT.—For purposes of this subsection, the term "LIFO recapture amount" means the amount (if any) by which—

(A) the inventory amount of the inventory asset under the first-in, first-out method authorized by section 471, exceeds

(B) the inventory amount of such assets under the LIFO method.

For purposes of the preceding sentence, inventory amounts shall be determined as of the close of the last taxable year referred to in paragraph (1).

(4) OTHER DEFINITIONS.—For purposes of this subsection—

(A) LIFO METHOD.—The term "LIFO method" means the method authorized by section 472.

(B) INVENTORY ASSETS.—The term "inventory assets" means stock in trade of the corporation, or other property of a kind which would properly be included in the inventory of the corporation if on hand at the close of the taxable year.

(C) METHOD OF DETERMINING INVENTORY AMOUNT.—The inventory amount of assets under a method authorized by section 471 shall be determined—

(i) if the corporation uses the retail method of valuing inventories under section 472, by using such method, or

(ii) if clause (i) does not apply, by using cost or market, whichever is lower.

(D) NOT TREATED AS MEMBER OF AFFILIATED GROUP.—Except as provided in regulations, the corporation referred to in paragraph (1) shall not be treated as a member of an affiliated group with respect to the amount included in gross income under paragraph (1).

(5) SPECIAL RULE.—Sections 1367(a)(2)(D) and 1371(c)(1) shall not apply with respect to any increase in the tax imposed by reason of this subsection.

Amendments

● **2005, Gulf Opportunity Zone Act of 2005 (P.L. 109-135)**

P.L. 109-135, § 411(a):

Amended Code Sec. 1363(d) by adding at the end a new paragraph (5). **Effective** as if included in section 10227 of the Omnibus Budget Reconciliation Act of 1987 (P.L. 100-203) [effective, generally, for elections made after 12-17-87.—CCH].

● **1988, Technical and Miscellaneous Revenue Act of 1988 (P.L. 100-647)**

P.L. 100-647, § 2004(n):

Amended Code Sec. 1363(d)(4) by adding at the end thereof new subparagraph (D). **Effective** as if included in the provision of P.L. 100-203 to which it relates.

[Sec. 1363(e)—Repealed]

Amendments

● **1988, Technical and Miscellaneous Revenue Act of 1988 (P.L. 100-647)**

P.L. 100-647, § 1006(f)(7):

Repealed Code Sec. 1363(e). **Effective** as if included in the provision of P.L. 99-514 to which it relates. Prior to repeal, Code Sec. 1363(e) read as follows:

(e) SUBSECTION (d) NOT TO APPLY TO REORGANIZATIONS, ETC.—Subsection (d) shall not apply to any distribution to the extent it consists of property permitted by section 354, 355, or 356 to be received without the recognition of gain.

● **1986, Tax Reform Act of 1986 (P.L. 99-514)**

P.L. 99-514, § 632(b):

Amended Code Sec. 1363(e). **Effective**, generally, to (1) any distribution in complete liquidation, and any sale or exchanges made by a corporation after 7-31-86, unless such corporation is completely liquidated before 1-1-87, (2) any transaction

● **1987, Revenue Act of 1987 (P.L. 100-203)**

P.L. 100-203, § 10227(a):

Amended Code Sec. 1363 by adding at the end thereof new subsection (d). **Effective**, generally, in the case of elections made after 12-17-87. For an exception, see Act Sec. 10227(b)(2), below.

P.L. 100-203, § 10227(b)(2), provides:

(2) EXCEPTION.—The amendment made by subsection (a) shall not apply in the case of any election made by a corporation after December 17, 1987, and before January 1, 1989, if, on or before December 17, 1987—

(A) there was a resolution adopted by the board of directors of such corporation to make an election under subchapter S of chapter 1 of the Internal Revenue Code of 1986, or

(B) there was a ruling request with respect to the business filed with the Internal Revenue Service expressing an intent to make such an election.

described in section 338 of the Internal Revenue Code of 1986 for which the acquisition date occurs after 12-31-86, and (3) any distribution (not in complete liquidation) made after 12-31-86. For special rules, see Act Sec. 633(b)-(f) following Code Sec. 26. Prior to amendment, Code Sec. 1363(e) read as follows:

(e) SUBSECTION (d) NOT TO APPLY TO COMPLETE LIQUIDATIONS AND REORGANIZATIONS.—Subsection (d) shall not apply to any distribution—

(1) of property in complete liquidation of the corporation, or

(2) to the extent of property permitted by section 354, 355, or 356 to be received without the recognition of gain.

● **1984, Deficit Reduction Act of 1984 (P.L. 98-369)**

P.L. 98-369, § 721(a)(1):

Added Code Sec. 1363(e). **Effective** as if included in P.L. 97-354.

PART II—TAX TREATMENT OF SHAREHOLDERS

Sec. 1366.	Pass-thru of items to shareholders.
Sec. 1367.	Adjustments to basis of stock of shareholders, etc.
Sec. 1368.	Distributions.

INCOME TAX—TREATMENT OF SHAREHOLDERS

[Sec. 1366]

SEC. 1366. PASS-THRU OF ITEMS TO SHAREHOLDERS.

[Sec. 1366(a)]

(a) DETERMINATION OF SHAREHOLDER'S TAX LIABILITY.—

(1) IN GENERAL.—In determining the tax under this chapter of a shareholder for the shareholder's taxable year in which the taxable year of the S corporation ends (or for the final taxable year of a shareholder who dies, or of a trust or estate which terminates, before the end of the corporation's taxable year), there shall be taken into account the shareholder's pro rata share of the corporation's—

(A) items of income (including tax-exempt income), loss, deduction, or credit the separate treatment of which could affect the liability for tax of any shareholder, and

(B) nonseparately computed income or loss.

For purposes of the preceding sentence, the items referred to in subparagraph (A) shall include amounts described in paragraph (4) or (6) of section 702(a).

(2) NONSEPARATELY COMPUTED INCOME OR LOSS DEFINED.—For purposes of this subchapter, the term "nonseparately computed income or loss" means gross income minus the deductions allowed to the corporation under this chapter, determined by excluding all items described in paragraph (1)(A).

Amendments

• **1996, Small Business Job Protection Act of 1996 (P.L. 104-188)**

P.L. 104-188, §1302(e):

Amended Code Sec. 1366(a)(1) by inserting ", or of a trust or estate which terminates," after "who dies". **Effective** for tax years beginning after 12-31-96.

[Sec. 1366(b)]

(b) CHARACTER PASSED THRU.—The character of any item included in a shareholder's pro rata share under paragraph (1) of subsection (a) shall be determined as if such item were realized directly from the source from which realized by the corporation, or incurred in the same manner as incurred by the corporation.

[Sec. 1366(c)]

(c) GROSS INCOME OF A SHAREHOLDER.—In any case where it is necessary to determine the gross income of a shareholder for purposes of this title, such gross income shall include the shareholder's pro rata share of the gross income of the corporation.

[Sec. 1366(d)]

(d) SPECIAL RULES FOR LOSSES AND DEDUCTIONS.—

(1) CANNOT EXCEED SHAREHOLDER'S BASIS IN STOCK AND DEBT.—The aggregate amount of losses and deductions taken into account by a shareholder under subsection (a) for any taxable year shall not exceed the sum of—

(A) the adjusted basis of the shareholder's stock in the S corporation (determined with regard to paragraphs (1) and (2)(A) of section 1367(a) for the taxable year), and

(B) the shareholder's adjusted basis of any indebtedness of the S corporation to the shareholder (determined without regard to any adjustment under paragraph (2) of section 1367(b) for the taxable year).

(2) INDEFINITE CARRYOVER OF DISALLOWED LOSSES AND DEDUCTIONS.—

(A) IN GENERAL.—Except as provided in subparagraph (B), any loss or deduction which is disallowed for any taxable year by reason of paragraph (1) shall be treated as incurred by the corporation in the succeeding taxable year with respect to that shareholder.

(B) TRANSFERS OF STOCK BETWEEN SPOUSES OR INCIDENT TO DIVORCE.—In the case of any transfer described in section 1041(a) of stock of an S corporation, any loss or deduction described in subparagraph (A) with respect [to] such stock shall be treated as incurred by the corporation in the succeeding taxable year with respect to the transferee.

(3) CARRYOVER OF DISALLOWED LOSSES AND DEDUCTIONS TO POST-TERMINATION TRANSITION PERIOD.—

(A) IN GENERAL.—If for the last taxable year of a corporation for which it was an S corporation a loss or deduction was disallowed by reason of paragraph (1), such loss or deduction shall be treated as incurred by the shareholder on the last day of any post-termination transition period.

(B) CANNOT EXCEED SHAREHOLDER'S BASIS IN STOCK.—The aggregate amount of losses and deductions taken into account by a shareholder under subparagraph (A) shall not exceed the adjusted basis of the shareholder's stock in the corporation (determined at the close of the last day of the post-termination transition period and without regard to this paragraph).

(C) ADJUSTMENT IN BASIS OF STOCK.—The shareholder's basis in the stock of the corporation shall be reduced by the amount allowed as a deduction by reason of this paragraph.

(D) AT-RISK LIMITATIONS.—To the extent that any increase in adjusted basis described in subparagraph (B) would have increased the shareholder's amount at risk under section 465 if such increase had occurred on the day preceding the commencement of the post-termination transition period, rules similar to the rules described in subparagraphs (A) through (C) shall apply to any losses disallowed by reason of section 465(a).

(4) APPLICATION OF LIMITATION ON CHARITABLE CONTRIBUTIONS.—In the case of any charitable contribution of property to which the second sentence of section 1367(a)(2) applies, paragraph (1) shall not apply to the extent of the excess (if any) of—

(A) the shareholder's pro rata share of such contribution, over

(B) the shareholder's pro rata share of the adjusted basis of such property.

Amendments

• **2007, Tax Technical Corrections Act of 2007 (P.L. 110-172)**

P.L. 110-172, §3(b):

Amended Code Sec. 1366(d) by adding at the end a new paragraph (4). **Effective** as if included in the provision of the Pension Protection Act of 2006 (P.L. 109-280) to which it relates [**effective** for contributions made in tax years beginning after 12-31-2005.—CCH].

• **2004, American Jobs Creation Act of 2004 (P.L. 108-357)**

P.L. 108-357, §235(a):

Amended Code Sec. 1366(d)(2). **Effective** for transfers after 12-31-2004 [effective date amended by P.L. 109-135, §403(c)]. Prior to amendment, Code Sec. 1366(d)(2) read as follows:

(2) INDEFINITE CARRYOVER OF DISALLOWED LOSSES AND DEDUCTIONS.—Any loss or deduction which is disallowed for any taxable year by reason of paragraph (1) shall be treated as incurred by the corporation in the succeeding taxable year with respect to that shareholder.

• **1996, Small Business Job Protection Act of 1996 (P.L. 104-188)**

P.L. 104-188, §1309(a)(1):

Amended Code Sec. 1366(d)(1)(A) by striking "paragraph (1)" and inserting "paragraphs (1) and (2)(A)". **Effective** for tax years beginning after 12-31-96.

P.L. 104-188, §1312:

Amended Code Sec. 1366(d)(3) by adding at the end a new subparagraph (D). **Effective** for tax years beginning after 12-31-96.

INCOME TAX—TREATMENT OF SHAREHOLDERS

[Sec. 1366(e)]

(e) TREATMENT OF FAMILY GROUP.—If an individual who is a member of the family (within the meaning of section 704(e)(2)) of one or more shareholders of an S corporation renders services for the corporation or furnishes capital to the corporation without receiving reasonable compensation therefor, the Secretary shall make such adjustments in the items taken into account by such individual and such shareholders as may be necessary in order to reflect the value of such services or capital.

Amendments

• **2018, Tax Technical Corrections Act of 2018 (P.L. 115-141)**

P.L. 115-141, § 401(a)(192), Div. U:

Amended Code Sec. 1366(e) by striking "section 704(e)(3)" and inserting "section 704(e)(2)". **Effective** 3-23-2018.

[Sec. 1366(f)]

(f) SPECIAL RULES.—

(1) SUBSECTION (a) NOT TO APPLY TO CREDIT ALLOWABLE UNDER SECTION 34.—Subsection (a) shall not apply with respect to any credit allowable under section 34 (relating to certain uses of gasoline and special fuels).

(2) TREATMENT OF TAX IMPOSED ON BUILT-IN GAINS.—If any tax is imposed under section 1374 for any taxable year on an S corporation, for purposes of subsection (a), the amount so imposed shall be treated as a loss sustained by the S corporation during such taxable year. The character of such loss shall be determined by allocating the loss proportionately among the recognized built-in gains giving rise to such tax.

(3) REDUCTION IN PASS-THRU FOR TAX IMPOSED ON EXCESS NET PASSIVE INCOME.—If any tax is imposed under section 1375 for any taxable year on an S corporation, for purposes of subsection (a), each item of passive investment income shall be reduced by an amount which bears the same ratio to the amount of such tax as—

    (A) the amount of such item, bears to

    (B) the total passive investment income for the taxable year.

Amendments

• **1989, Omnibus Budget Reconciliation Act of 1989 (P.L. 101-239)**

P.L. 101-239, § 7811(c)(7):

Amended Code Sec. 1366(f)(2). **Effective** as if included in the provision of P.L. 100-647 to which it relates. Prior to amendment, Code Sec. 1366(f)(2) read as follows:

(2) REDUCTION IN PASS-THRU FOR TAX IMPOSED ON BUILT-IN GAINS.—If any tax is imposed under section 1374 for any taxable year on an S corporation, for purposes of subsection (a), the amount of each recognized built-in gain (within the meaning of section 1374) for such taxable year shall be reduced by its proportionate share of such tax.

• **1988, Technical and Miscellaneous Revenue Act of 1988 (P.L. 100-647)**

P.L. 100-647, § 1006(f)(5)(E):

Amended Code Sec. 1366(f)(2) by striking out "as defined in section 1374(d)(2)" and inserting in lieu thereof "within the meaning of section 1374". **Effective** as if included in the provision of P.L. 99-514 to which it relates.

• **1986, Tax Reform Act of 1986 (P.L. 99-514)**

P.L. 99-514, § 632(c)(2):

Amended Code Sec. 1366(f)(2). **Effective**, generally, for (1) any distribution in complete liquidation, and any sale or exchange, made by a corporation after 7-31-86, unless such corporation is completely liquidated before 1-1-87, (2) any transaction described in section 338 of the Internal Revenue Code of 1986 for which the acquisition date occurs after 12-31-86, and (3) any distribution (not in complete liquidation) made after 12-31-86. For special rules, see Act Sec. 633(b)-(f) following Code Sec. 26. Prior to amendment, Code Sec. 1366(f)(2) read as follows:

(2) REDUCTION IN PASS-THRU FOR TAX IMPOSED ON CAPITAL GAIN.—If any tax is imposed under section 56 or 1374 for any taxable year on an S corporation, for purposes of subsection (a)—

(A) the amount of the corporation's long-term capital gains for the taxable year shall be reduced by the amount of such tax, and

(B) if the amount of such tax exceeds the amount of such long-term capital gains, the corporation's gains from sales or exchanges of property described in section 1231 shall be reduced by the amount of such excess.

For purposes of the preceding sentence, the term "long-term capital gain" shall not include any gain from the sale or exchange of property described in section 1231.

P.L. 99-514, § 701(e)(4)(K):

Amended Code Sec. 1366(f)(2) by striking out "56 or". **Effective**, generally, for tax years beginning after 12-31-86. However, special rules in Act Sec. 701(f)(2)-(7) appear under the amendment notes to Code Sec. 56. Code Sec. 1366(f)(2), as amended by Act Sec. 701(e)(4)(J), would read:

(2) REDUCTION IN PASS-THRU FOR TAX IMPOSED ON CAPITAL GAIN.—If any tax is imposed under section 1374 for any taxable year on an S corporation, for purposes of subsection (a)—

(A) the amount of the corporation's long-term capital gains for the taxable year shall be reduced by the amount of such tax, and

(B) if the amount of such tax exceeds the amount of such long-term capital gains, the corporation's gains from sales or exchanges of property described in section 1231 shall be reduced by the amount of such excess.

For purposes of the preceding sentence, the term "long-term capital gain" shall not include any gain from the sale or exchange of property described in section 1231.

• **1984, Deficit Reduction Act of 1984 (P.L. 98-369)**

P.L. 98-369, § 474(r)(26):

Amended Code Sec. 1366(f)(1) by striking out "section 39" each place it appeared and inserting in lieu thereof "section 34". **Effective** for tax years beginning after 12-31-83, and to carrybacks from such years.

P.L. 98-369, § 735(c)(16):

Amended Code Sec. 1366(f)(1) by striking out ", special fuels, and lubricating oil" and inserting in lieu thereof "and special fuels". **Effective** as if included in the provision of the Highway Revenue Act of 1982 to which it relates.

• **1982, Subchapter S Revision Act of 1982 (P.L. 97-354)**

P.L. 97-354, § 2:

Added Code Sec. 1366. **Effective**, generally, for tax years beginning after 1982 except that Code Sec. 1366(f)(3) applies to tax years beginning during 1982. See, however, the amendment note for Act Sec. 6(c)(2)-(4) following Code Sec. 1361 for special rules and exceptions concerning certain casualty insurance companies and qualified oil corporations. See, also, Act Sec. 6(b)(3) following Code Sec. 1362 for a special rule affecting Code Sec. 1366(f).

[Sec. 1366(g)—Stricken]

(g) CROSS REFERENCE.—

For rules relating to procedures for determining the tax treatment of subchapter S items, see subchapter D of chapter 63.

Amendments

• **1996, Small Business Job Protection Act of 1996 (P.L. 104-188)**

P.L. 104-188, § 1307(c)(3)(A):

Amended Code Sec. 1366 by striking subsection (g). **Effective** for tax years beginning after 12-31-96. Prior to being stricken, Code Sec. 1366(g) read as follows:

[Sec. 1367]

SEC. 1367. ADJUSTMENTS TO BASIS OF STOCK OF SHAREHOLDERS, ETC.

[Sec. 1367(a)]

(a) GENERAL RULE.—

(1) INCREASES IN BASIS.—The basis of each shareholder's stock in an S corporation shall be increased for any period by the sum of the following items determined with respect to that shareholder for such period:

    (A) the items of income described in subparagraph (A) of section 1366(a)(1),

    (B) any nonseparately computed income determined under subparagraph (B) of section 1366(a)(1), and

    (C) the excess of the deductions for depletion over the basis of the property subject to depletion.

(2) DECREASES IN BASIS.—The basis of each shareholder's stock in an S corporation shall be decreased for any period (but not below zero) by the sum of the following items determined with respect to the shareholder for such period:

    (A) distributions by the corporation which were not includible in the income of the shareholder by reason of section 1368,

INCOME TAX—TREATMENT OF SHAREHOLDERS

(B) the items of loss and deduction described in subparagraph (A) of section 1366(a)(1),

(C) any nonseparately computed loss determined under subparagraph (B) of section 1366(a)(1),

(D) any expense of the corporation not deductible in computing its taxable income and not properly chargeable to capital account, and

(E) the amount of the shareholder's deduction for depletion for any oil and gas property held by the S corporation to the extent such deduction does not exceed the proportionate share of the adjusted basis of such property allocated to such shareholder under section 613A(c)(11)(B).

The decrease under subparagraph (B) by reason of a charitable contribution (as defined in section 170(c)) of property shall be the amount equal to the shareholder's pro rata share of the adjusted basis of such property.

Amendments

• **2015, Protecting Americans from Tax Hikes Act of 2015 (P.L. 114-113)**

P.L. 114-113, §115(a), Div. Q:

Amended Code Sec. 1367(a)(2) by striking the last sentence. **Effective** for contributions made in tax years beginning after 12-31-2014. Prior to being stricken, the last sentence of Code Sec. 1367(a)(2) read as follows:

The preceding sentence shall not apply to contributions made in taxable years beginning after December 31, 2014.

• **2014, Tax Increase Prevention Act of 2014 (P.L. 113-295)**

P.L. 113-295, §137(a), Division A:

Amended Code Sec. 1367(a)(2) by striking "December 31, 2013" and inserting "December 31, 2014". **Effective** for contributions made in tax years beginning after 12-31-2013.

• **2013, American Taxpayer Relief Act of 2012 (P.L. 112-240)**

P.L. 112-240, §325(a):

Amended Code Sec. 1367(a)(2) by striking "December 31, 2011" and inserting "December 31, 2013". **Effective** for contributions made in tax years beginning after 12-31-2011.

• **2010, Tax Relief, Unemployment Insurance Reauthorization, and Job Creation Act of 2010 (P.L. 111-312)**

P.L. 111-312, §752(a):

Amended Code Sec. 1367(a)(2) by striking "December 31, 2009" and inserting "December 31, 2011". **Effective** for contributions made in tax years beginning after 12-31-2009.

• **2008, Tax Extenders and Alternative Minimum Tax Relief Act of 2008 (P.L. 110-343)**

P.L. 110-343, Division C, §307(a):

Amended the last sentence of Code Sec. 1367(a)(2) by striking "December 31, 2007" and inserting "December 31, 2009". **Effective** for contributions made in tax years beginning after 12-31-2007.

• **2006, Pension Protection Act of 2006 (P.L. 109-280)**

P.L. 109-280, §1203(a):

Amended Code Sec. 1367(a)(2) by adding at the end a new flush sentence. **Effective** for contributions made in tax years beginning after 12-31-2005.

• **1996, Small Business Job Protection Act of 1996 (P.L. 104-188)**

P.L. 104-188, §1702(h)(14):

Amended Code Sec. 1367(a)(2)(E) by striking "section 613A(c)(13)(B)" and inserting "section 613A(c)(11)(B)". **Effective** as if included in the provision of P.L. 101-508 to which it relates.

• **1984, Deficit Reduction Act of 1984 (P.L. 98-369)**

P.L. 98-369, §722(e)(2):

Amended Code Sec. 1367(a)(2)(E). **Effective** for tax years beginning after 12-31-82. Prior to amendment, Code Sec. 1367(a)(2)(E) read as follows:

(E) the amount of the shareholder's deduction for depletion under section 611 with respect to oil and gas wells.

[Sec. 1367(b)]

(b) SPECIAL RULES.—

(1) INCOME ITEMS.—An amount which is required to be included in the gross income of a shareholder and shown on his return shall be taken into account under subparagraph (A) or (B) of subsection (a)(1) only to the extent such amount is included in the shareholder's gross income on his return, increased or decreased by any adjustment of such amount in a redetermination of the shareholder's tax liability.

(2) ADJUSTMENTS IN BASIS OF INDEBTEDNESS.—

(A) REDUCTION OF BASIS.—If for any taxable year the amounts specified in subparagraphs (B), (C), (D), and (E) of subsection (a)(2) exceed the amount which reduces the shareholder's basis to zero, such excess shall be applied to reduce (but not below zero) the shareholder's basis in any indebtedness of the S corporation to the shareholder.

(B) RESTORATION OF BASIS.—If for any taxable year beginning after December 31, 1982, there is a reduction under subparagraph (A) in the shareholder's basis in the indebtedness of an S corporation to a shareholder, any net increase (after the application of paragraphs (1) and (2) of subsection (a)) for any subsequent taxable year shall be applied to restore such reduction in basis before any of it may be used to increase the shareholder's basis in the stock of the S corporation.

(3) COORDINATION WITH SECTIONS 165(g) AND 166(d).—This section and section 1366 shall be applied before the application of sections 165(g) and 166(d) to any taxable year of the shareholder or the corporation in which the security or debt becomes worthless.

(4) ADJUSTMENTS IN CASE OF INHERITED STOCK.—

(A) IN GENERAL.—If any person acquires stock in an S corporation by reason of the death of a decedent or by bequest, devise, or inheritance, section 691 shall be applied with respect to any item of income of the S corporation in the same manner as if the decedent had held directly his pro rata share of such item.

(B) ADJUSTMENTS TO BASIS.—The basis determined under section 1014 of any stock in an S corporation shall be reduced by the portion of the value of the stock which is attributable to items constituting income in respect of the decedent.

Amendments

• **1996, Small Business Job Protection Act of 1996 (P.L. 104-188)**

P.L. 104-188, §1313(a):

Amended Code Sec. 1367(b) by adding at the end a new paragraph (4). **Effective** in the case of decedents dying after 8-20-96.

• **1984, Deficit Reduction Act of 1984 (P.L. 98-369)**

P.L. 98-369, §721(d):

Amended Code Sec. 1367(b)(3). **Effective** as if included in P.L. 97-354. Prior to amendment, Code Sec. 1367(b)(3) read as follows:

(3) COORDINATION WITH SECTION 165(g).—This section and section 1366 shall be applied before the application of section 165(g) to any taxable year of the shareholder or the corporation in which the stock becomes worthless.

P.L. 98-369, §721(w):

Amended Code Sec. 1367(b)(2)(B) by striking out "for any taxable year there is" and inserting in lieu thereof "for any taxable year beginning after December 31, 1982, there is". **Effective** as if included in P.L. 97-354.

• **1982, Subchapter S Revision Act of 1982 (P.L. 97-354)**

P.L. 97-354, §2:

Added Code Sec. 1367. **Effective**, generally, for tax years beginning after 1982. See the amendment note for Act Sec. 6(c)(2)-(4) following Code Sec. 1361 for special rules and exceptions concerning certain casualty insurance companies and qualified oil corporations.

[Sec. 1368]

SEC. 1368. DISTRIBUTIONS.

[Sec. 1368(a)]

(a) GENERAL RULE.—A distribution of property made by an S corporation with respect to its stock to which (but for this subsection) section 301(c) would apply shall be treated in the manner provided in subsection (b) or (c), whichever applies.

INCOME TAX—TREATMENT OF SHAREHOLDERS

[Sec. 1368(b)]

(b) S Corporation Having No Earnings and Profits.—In the case of a distribution described in subsection (a) by an S corporation which has no accumulated earnings and profits—

(1) Amount applied against basis.—The distribution shall not be included in gross income to the extent that it does not exceed the adjusted basis of the stock.

(2) Amount in excess of basis.—If the amount of the distribution exceeds the adjusted basis of the stock, such excess shall be treated as gain from the sale or exchange of property.

[Sec. 1368(c)]

(c) S Corporation Having Earnings and Profits.—In the case of a distribution described in subsection (a) by an S corporation which has accumulated earnings and profits—

(1) Accumulated adjustments account.—That portion of the distribution which does not exceed the accumulated adjustments account shall be treated in the manner provided by subsection (b).

(2) Dividend.—That portion of the distribution which remains after the application of paragraph (1) shall be treated as a dividend to the extent it does not exceed the accumulated earnings and profits of the S corporation.

(3) Treatment of remainder.—Any portion of the distribution remaining after the application of paragraph (2) of this subsection shall be treated in the manner provided by subsection (b).

Except to the extent provided in regulations, if the distributions during the taxable year exceed the amount in the accumulated adjustments account at the close of the taxable year, for purposes of this subsection, the balance of such account shall be allocated among such distributions in proportion to their respective sizes.

Amendments

- **1984, Deficit Reduction Act of 1984 (P.L. 98-369)**

P.L. 98-369, §721(r)(2):

Amended Code Sec. 1368(c) by adding the last sentence. **Effective** as if included in P.L. 97-354.

[Sec. 1368(d)]

(d) Certain Adjustments Taken Into Account.—Subsections (b) and (c) shall be applied by taking into account (to the extent proper)—

(1) the adjustments to the basis of the shareholder's stock described in section 1367, and

(2) the adjustments to the accumulated adjustments account which are required by subsection (e)(1).

In the case of any distribution made during any taxable year, the adjusted basis of the stock shall be determined with regard to the adjustments provided in paragraph (1) of section 1367(a) for the taxable year.

Amendments

- **2007, Small Business and Work Opportunity Tax Act of 2007 (P.L. 110-28)**

P.L. 110-28, §8235, provides:

SEC. 8235. ELIMINATION OF ALL EARNINGS AND PROFITS ATTRIBUTABLE TO PRE-1983 YEARS FOR CERTAIN CORPORATIONS.

In the case of a corporation which is—

(1) described in section 1311(a)(1) of the Small Business Job Protection Act of 1996, and

(2) not described in section 1311(a)(2) of such Act,

the amount of such corporation's accumulated earnings and profits (for the first taxable year beginning after the date of the enactment of this Act [5-25-2007.—CCH]) shall be reduced by an amount equal to the portion (if any) of such accumulated earnings and profits which were accumulated in any taxable year beginning before January 1, 1983, for which such corporation was an electing small business corporation under subchapter S of the Internal Revenue Code of 1986.

- **1996, Small Business Job Protection Act of 1996 (P.L. 104-188)**

P.L. 104-188, §1309(a)(2):

Amended Code Sec. 1368(d) by adding at the end a new flush sentence. **Effective** for tax years beginning after 12-31-96.

P.L. 104-188, §1311(a), provides:

(a) In General.—If—

(1) a corporation was an electing small business corporation under subchapter S of chapter 1 of the Internal Revenue Code of 1986 for any taxable year beginning before January 1, 1983, and

(2) such corporation is an S corporation under subchapter S of chapter 1 of such Code for its first taxable year beginning after December 31, 1996,

the amount of such corporation's accumulated earnings and profits (as of the beginning of such first taxable year) shall be reduced by an amount equal to the portion (if any) of such accumulated earnings and profits which were accumulated in any taxable year beginning before January 1, 1983, for which such corporation was an electing small business corporation under such subchapter S.

[Sec. 1368(e)]

(e) Definitions and Special Rules.—For purposes of this section—

(1) Accumulated adjustments account.—

(A) In general.—Except as otherwise provided in this paragraph, the term "accumulated adjustments account" means an account of the S corporation which is adjusted for the S period in a manner similar to the adjustments under section 1367 (except that no adjustment shall be made for income (and related expenses) which is exempt from tax under this title and the phrase "(but not below zero)" shall be disregarded in section 1367(a)(2)) and no adjustment shall be made for Federal taxes attributable to any taxable year in which the corporation was a C corporation.

(B) Amount of adjustment in the case of redemptions.—In the case of any redemption which is treated as an exchange under section 302(a) or 303(a), the adjustment in the accumulated adjustments account shall be an amount which bears the same ratio to the balance in such account as the number of shares redeemed in such redemption bears to the number of shares of stock in the corporation immediately before such redemption.

(C) Net loss for year disregarded.—

(i) In general.—In applying this section to distributions made during any taxable year, the amount in the accumulated adjustments account as of the close of such taxable year shall be determined without regard to any net negative adjustment for such taxable year.

(ii) Net negative adjustment.—For purposes of clause (i), the term "net negative adjustment" means, with respect to any taxable year, the excess (if any) of—

(I) the reductions in the account for the taxable year (other than for distributions), over

(II) the increases in such account for such taxable year.

(2) S period.—The term "S period" means the most recent continuous period during which the corporation has been an S corporation. Such period shall not include any taxable year beginning before January 1, 1983.

(3) Election to distribute earnings first.—

(A) In general.—An S corporation may, with the consent of all of its affected shareholders, elect to have paragraph (1) of subsection (c) not apply to all distributions made during the taxable year for which the election is made.

INCOME TAX—SPECIAL RULES

(B) AFFECTED SHAREHOLDER.—For purposes of subparagraph (A), the term "affected shareholder" means any shareholder to whom a distribution is made by the S corporation during the taxable year.

Amendments

• **1996, Small Business Job Protection Act of 1996 (P.L. 104-188)**

P.L. 104-188, § 1309(b):

Amended Code Sec. 1368(e)(1) by adding at the end a new subparagraph (C). **Effective** for tax years beginning after 12-31-96.

P.L. 104-188, § 1309(c)(1)-(2):

Amended Code Sec. 1368(e)(1)(A) by striking "as provided in subparagraph (B)" and inserting "as otherwise provided in this paragraph", and by striking "section 1367(b)(2)(A)" and inserting "section 1367(a)(2)". **Effective** for tax years beginning after 12-31-96.

• **1986, Tax Reform Act of 1986 (P.L. 99-514)**

P.L. 99-514, § 1879(m)(1)(B):

Amended Code Sec. 1368(e)(1) by striking out the period at the end of subparagraph (A) and inserting in lieu thereof "and no adjustment shall be made for Federal taxes attributable to any taxable year in which the corporation was a C corporation.". **Effective** for tax years beginning after 12-31-82.

• **1984, Deficit Reduction Act of 1984 (P.L. 98-369)**

P.L. 98-369, § 721(r)(1):

Amended Code Sec. 1368(e)(1)(A) by striking out "(except that no adjustment shall be made for income which is exempt from tax under this title and no adjustment shall be made for any expense not deductible in computing the corporation's taxable income and not properly chargeable to capital account.)." and inserting in lieu thereof "(except that no adjustment shall be made for income (and related expenses) which is exempt from tax under this title and the phrase `(but not below zero)' shall be disregarded in section 1367(b)(2)(A))". **Effective** as if included in P.L. 97-354.

• **1983, Technical Corrections Act of 1982 (P.L. 97-448)**

P.L. 97-448, § 305(d)(2):

Amended Code Sec. 1368(e) by adding paragraph (3). **Effective** 10-19-82.

• **1982, Subchapter S Revision Act of 1982 (P.L. 97-354)**

P.L. 97-354, § 2:

Added Code Sec. 1368. **Effective**, generally, for tax years beginning after 1982. See the amendment note for Act Sec. 6(c)(2)-(4) following Code Sec. 1361 for special rules and exceptions concerning certain casualty insurance companies and qualified oil corporations.

[Sec. 1368(f)]

(f) RESTRICTED BANK DIRECTOR STOCK.—If a director receives a distribution (not in part or full payment in exchange for stock) from an S corporation with respect to any restricted bank director stock (as defined in section 1361(f)), the amount of such distribution—

(1) shall be includible in gross income of the director, and

(2) shall be deductible by the corporation for the taxable year of such corporation in which or with which ends the taxable year in which such amount is included in the gross income of the director.

Amendments

• **2018, Tax Technical Corrections Act of 2018 (P.L. 115-141)**

P.L. 115-141, § 401(a)(193), Div. U:

Amended Code Sec. 1368(f)(2) by striking "in included" and inserting "is included". **Effective** 3-23-2018.

• **2007, Small Business and Work Opportunity Tax Act of 2007 (P.L. 110-28)**

P.L. 110-28, § 8232(b):

Amended Code Sec. 1368 by adding at the end a new subsection (f). **Effective** generally for tax years beginning after 12-31-2006. For a special rule, see Act Sec. 8232(c)(2), below.

P.L. 110-28, § 8232(c)(2), provides:

(2) SPECIAL RULE FOR TREATMENT AS SECOND CLASS OF STOCK.—In the case of any taxable year beginning after December 31, 1996, restricted bank director stock (as defined in section 1361(f) of the Internal Revenue Code of 1986, as added by this section) shall not be taken into account in determining whether an S corporation has more than 1 class of stock.

PART III—SPECIAL RULES

Sec. 1371.	Coordination with subchapter C.
Sec. 1372.	Partnership rules to apply for fringe benefit purposes.
Sec. 1373.	Foreign income.
Sec. 1374.	Tax imposed on certain built-in gains.
Sec. 1375.	Tax imposed when passive investment income of corporation having subchapter C earnings and profits exceeds 25 percent of gross receipts.

[Sec. 1371]

SEC. 1371. COORDINATION WITH SUBCHAPTER C.

[Sec. 1371(a)]

(a) APPLICATION OF SUBCHAPTER C RULES.—Except as otherwise provided in this title, and except to the extent inconsistent with this subchapter, subchapter C shall apply to an S corporation and its shareholders.

Amendments

• **1996, Small Business Job Protection Act of 1996 (P.L. 104-188)**

P.L. 104-188, § 1310:

Amended Code Sec. 1371(a). **Effective** for tax years beginning after 12-31-96. Prior to amendment, Code Sec. 1371(a) read as follows:

(a) APPLICATION OF SUBCHAPTER C RULES.—

(1) IN GENERAL.—Except as otherwise provided in this title, and except to the extent inconsistent with this subchapter, subchapter C shall apply to an S corporation and its shareholders.

(2) S CORPORATION AS SHAREHOLDER TREATED LIKE INDIVIDUAL.—For purposes of subchapter C, an S corporation in its capacity as a shareholder of another corporation shall be treated as an individual.

[Sec. 1371(b)]

(b) NO CARRYOVER BETWEEN C YEAR AND S YEAR.—

(1) FROM C YEAR TO S YEAR.—No carryforward, and no carryback, arising for a taxable year for which a corporation is a C corporation may be carried to a taxable year for which such corporation is an S corporation.

(2) NO CARRYOVER FROM S YEAR.—No carryforward, and no carryback, shall arise at the corporate level for a taxable year for which a corporation is an S corporation.

(3) TREATMENT OF S YEAR AS ELAPSED YEAR.—Nothing in paragraphs (1) and (2) shall prevent treating a taxable year for which a corporation is an S corporation as a taxable year for purposes of determining the number of taxable years to which an item may be carried back or carried forward.

[Sec. 1371(c)]

(c) EARNINGS AND PROFITS.—

(1) IN GENERAL.—Except as provided in paragraphs (2) and (3) and subsection (d)(3), no adjustment shall be made to the earnings and profits of an S corporation.

(2) ADJUSTMENTS FOR REDEMPTIONS, LIQUIDATIONS, REORGANIZATIONS, DIVISIVES, ETC.—In the case of any transaction involving the application of subchapter C to any S corporation, proper adjustment to any accumulated earnings and profits of the corporation shall be made.

INCOME TAX—SPECIAL RULES

(3) ADJUSTMENTS IN CASE OF DISTRIBUTIONS TREATED AS DIVIDENDS UNDER SECTION 1368(c)(2).—Paragraph (1) shall not apply with respect to that portion of a distribution which is treated as a dividend under section 1368(c)(2).

Amendments

• **1984, Deficit Reduction Act of 1984 (P.L. 98-369)**

P.L. 98-369, §721(e)(2):

Amended Code Sec. 1371(c)(1) by striking out "paragraphs (2) and (3)" and inserting in lieu thereof "paragraphs (2) and (3) and subsection (d)(3)". **Effective** as if included in P.L. 97-354.

[Sec. 1371(d)]

(d) COORDINATION WITH INVESTMENT CREDIT RECAPTURE.—

(1) NO RECAPTURE BY REASON OF ELECTION.—Any election under section 1362 shall be treated as a mere change in the form of conducting a trade or business for purposes of the second sentence of section 50(a)(5).

(2) CORPORATION CONTINUES TO BE LIABLE.—Notwithstanding an election under section 1362, an S corporation shall continue to be liable for any increase in tax under section 49(b) or 50(a) attributable to credits allowed for taxable years for which such corporation was not an S corporation.

(3) ADJUSTMENT TO EARNINGS AND PROFITS FOR AMOUNT OF RECAPTURE.—Paragraph (1) of subsection (c) shall not apply to any increase in tax under section 49(b) or 50(a) for which the S corporation is liable.

Amendments

• **2022, CHIPS Act of 2022 (P.L. 117-167)**

P.L. 117-167, §107(b)(3)(C), Div. A:

Amended Code Sec. 1371(d)(1) by striking "section 50(a)(4)" and inserting "section 50(a)(5)". **Effective** for property placed in service after 12-31-2022, and, for any property the construction of which begins prior to 1-1-2023, only to the extent of the basis thereof attributable to the construction, reconstruction, or erection after 8-9-2022.

• **1990, Omnibus Budget Reconciliation Act of 1990 (P.L. 101-508)**

P.L. 101-508, §11813(b)(23)(A)-(B):

Amended Code Sec. 1371(d) by striking "section 47(b)" in paragraph (1) and inserting "section 50(a)(4)", and by striking "section 47" in paragraphs (2) and (3) and inserting "section 49(b) or 50(a)". **Effective**, generally, for property placed in service after 12-31-90. However, for exceptions, see Act Sec. 11813(c)(2), below.

P.L. 101-508, §11813(c)(2), provides:

(2) EXCEPTIONS.—The amendments made by this section shall not apply to—

(A) any transition property (as defined in section 49(e) of the Internal Revenue Code of 1986 (as in effect on the day before the date of the enactment of this Act),

(B) any property with respect to which qualified progress expenditures were previously taken into account under section 46(d) of such Code (as so in effect), and

(C) any property described in section 46(b)(2)(C) of such Code (as so in effect).

• **1984, Deficit Reduction Act of 1984 (P.L. 98-369)**

P.L. 98-369, §721(e)(1):

Added Code Sec. 1371(d)(3). **Effective** as if included in P.L. 97-354.

[Sec. 1371(e)]

(e) CASH DISTRIBUTIONS DURING POST-TERMINATION TRANSITION PERIOD.—

(1) IN GENERAL.—Any distribution of money by a corporation with respect to its stock during a post-termination transition period shall be applied against and reduce the adjusted basis of the stock, to the extent that the amount of the distribution does not exceed the accumulated adjustments account (within the meaning of section 1368(e)).

(2) ELECTION TO DISTRIBUTE EARNINGS FIRST.—An S corporation may elect to have paragraph (1) not apply to all distributions made during a post-termination transition period described in section 1377(b)(1)(A). Such election shall not be effective unless all shareholders of the S corporation to whom distributions are made by the S corporation during such post-termination transition period consent to such election.

Amendments

• **1986, Tax Reform Act of 1986 (P.L. 99-514)**

P.L. 99-514, §1899A(33):

Amended Code Sec. 1371(e)(1) by inserting "(within the meaning of section 1368(e))" after "accumulated adjustments account". **Effective** 10-22-86.

P.L. 99-514, §1899A(34):

Amended Code Sec. 1371(e)(2) by striking out "(within the meaning of section 1368(e))". **Effective** 10-22-86.

• **1984, Deficit Reduction Act of 1984 (P.L. 98-369)**

P.L. 98-369, §721(o):

Amended Code Sec. 1371(e). **Effective** as if included in P.L. 97-354. Prior to amendment, Code Sec. 1371(e) read as follows:

(e) Cash Distributions During Post-Termination Transition Period.—Any distribution of money by a corporation with respect to its stock during a post-termination transition period shall be applied against and reduce the adjusted basis of the stock, to the extent that the amount of the distribution does not exceed the accumulated adjustments account.

P.L. 98-369, §721(x)(3):

Amended Code Sec. 1371(e), as amended by Act Sec. 721(o), by inserting before the period at the end thereof the following: "(within the meaning of section 1368(e))". **Effective** as if included in P.L. 97-354.

• **1982, Subchapter S Revision Act of 1982 (P.L. 97-354)**

P.L. 97-354, §2:

Amended Code Sec. 1371. **Effective**, generally, for tax years beginning after 12-31-82. See the amendment note for Act Sec. 6(c)(2)-(4) following Code Sec. 1361 for special rules and exceptions concerning certain casualty insurance companies and qualified oil corporations. Prior to amendment, the table of contents for subchapter S and Code Sec. 1371 read as follows:

Subchapter S—Election of Certain Small Business Corporations as to Taxable Status

Sec. 1371. Definitions.
Sec. 1372. Election by small business corporation.
Sec. 1373. Corporation undistributed taxable income taxed to shareholders.
Sec. 1374. Corporation net operating loss allowed to shareholders.
Sec. 1375. Special rules applicable to distributions of electing small business corporations.
Sec. 1376. Adjustment to basis of stock of, and indebtedness owing, shareholders.
Sec. 1377. Special rules applicable to earnings and profits of electing small business corporations.
Sec. 1378. Tax imposed on certain capital gains.
Sec. 1379. Certain qualified pension, etc., plans.

SEC. 1371. DEFINITIONS.

[Sec. 1371(a)]

(a) SMALL BUSINESS CORPORATION.—For purposes of this subchapter, the term "small business corporation" means a domestic corporation which is not a member of an affiliated group (as defined in section 1504) and which does not—

(1) have more than 25 shareholders;

(2) have as a shareholder a person (other than an estate and other than a trust described in subsection (e)) who is not an individual;

(3) have a nonresident alien as a shareholder; and

(4) have more than one class of stock.

Amendments

• **1981, Economic Recovery Tax Act of 1981 (P.L. 97-34)**

P.L. 97-34, §233(a):

Amended Code Sec. 1371(a)(1) by striking out "15 shareholders" and inserting in lieu thereof "25 shareholders". **Effective** with respect to tax years beginning after 12-31-81.

• **1978, Revenue Act of 1978 (P.L. 95-600)**

P.L. 95-600, §341(a):

Amended Code Sec. 1371(a)(1) by striking out "(1) have (except as provided in subsection (e)) more than 10 shareholders;" and inserting in lieu thereof "(1) have more than 15 shareholders;". **Effective** for tax years beginning after 12-31-78.

P.L. 95-600, §341(b)(2):

Amended Code Sec. 1371(a)(2) by striking out "subsection (f)" and inserting in lieu thereof "subsection (e)". **Effective** for tax years beginning after 12-31-78.

INCOME TAX—SPECIAL RULES

• **1976, Tax Reform Act of 1976 (P.L. 94-455)**

P.L. 94-455, §902(a)(1):

Amended Code Sec. 1371(a)(1). **Effective** for tax years beginning after 12-31-76. Prior to amendment Code Sec. 1371(a)(1) read:

(1) have more than 10 shareholders;

P.L. 94-455, §902(c)(2)(B):

Substituted "(other than an estate and other than a trust described in subsection (f))" for "(other than an estate)" in Code Sec. 1371(a)(2). **Effective** for tax years beginning after 12-31-76.

• **1958, Technical Amendments Act of 1958 (P.L. 85-866)**

P.L. 85-866, §64(a):

Added Code Sec. 1371(a). **Effective** for tax years beginning after 12-31-57.

[Sec. 1371(b)]

(b) ELECTING SMALL BUSINESS CORPORATION.—For purposes of this subchapter, the term "electing small business corporation" means, with respect to any taxable year, a small business corporation which has made an election under section 1372(a) which, under section 1372, is in effect for such taxable year.

Amendments

• **1959 (P.L. 86-376)**

P.L. 86-376, §2(a):

Added Code Sec. 1371(b). **Effective** for tax years beginning after 12-31-59.

[Sec. 1371(c)]

(c) STOCK OWNED BY HUSBAND AND WIFE.—For purposes of subsection (a)(1), a husband and wife (and their estates) shall be treated as one shareholder.

Amendments

• **1978, Revenue Act of 1978 (P.L. 95-600)**

P.L. 95-600, §342(a):

Amended Code Sec. 1371(c). **Effective** for tax years beginning after 12-31-78. Prior to amendment, Code Sec. 1371(c) read as follows:

(c) STOCK OWNED BY HUSBAND AND WIFE.—For purposes of subsection (a)(1) stock which—

(1) is community property of a husband and wife (or the income from which is community income) under the applicable community property law of a State,

(2) is held by a husband and wife as joint tenants, tenants by the entirety, or tenants in common,

(3) was, on the date of death of a spouse, stock described in paragraph (1) or (2), and is, by reason of such death, held by the estate of the deceased spouse and the surviving spouse, or by the estates of both spouses (by reason of their deaths on the same date), in the same proportion as held by the spouses before such death, or

(4) was, on the date of the death of a surviving spouse, stock described in paragraph (3), and is, by reason of such death, held by the estates of both spouses in the same proportion as held by the spouses before their deaths, shall be treated as owned by one shareholder.

• **1976, Tax Reform Act of 1976 (P.L. 94-455)**

P.L. 94-455, §902(c)(1):

Amended Code Sec. 1371(c). **Effective** for tax years beginning after 12-31-76. Prior to amendment, Code Sec. 1371(c) read as follows:

(c) STOCK OWNED BY HUSBAND AND WIFE.—For purposes of subsection (a)(1) stock which—

(1) is community property of a husband and wife (or the income from which is community income) under the applicable community property law of a State, or

(2) is held by a husband and wife as joint tenants, tenants by the entirety, or tenants in common,

shall be treated as owned by one shareholder.

• **1962, Revenue Act of 1962 (P.L. 87-834)**

P.L. 87-834, §23:

Changed Code Sec. 1371(c) to apply retroactively to tax years beginning after 12-31-57 and before 1-1-60, provided that: (1) the tax-option corporation makes a special election and consents to a one-year tolling of the statute of limitations on assessments of additional tax, credit, or refund, and (2) each person who is a shareholder on the date on which the corporation makes the election, and each person, who was a shareholder of the corporation during any taxable year of the corporation beginning after 1957, and ending before the date of the election, consents to the corporation's election and the one-year tolling of the statute of limitations. The election and consents must be made within one year after 10-16-62.

• **1959 (P.L. 86-376)**

P.L. 86-376, §2(a):

Added Code Sec. 1371(c). **Effective** for tax years beginning after 12-31-59.

[Sec. 1371(d)]

(d) OWNERSHIP OF CERTAIN STOCK.—For purposes of subsection (a), a corporation shall not be considered a member of an affiliated group at any time during any taxable year by reason of the ownership of stock in another corporation if such other corporation—

(1) has not begun business at any time on or after the date of its incorporation and before the close of such taxable year, and

(2) does not have taxable income for the period included within such taxable year.

Amendments

• **1964, Revenue Act of 1964 (P.L. 88-272)**

P.L. 88-272, §233(a):

Amended Code Sec. 1371 to add subdivision "(d)." **Effective** with respect to tax years of corporations beginning after 12-31-62.

[Sec. 1371(e)]

(e) CERTAIN TRUSTS PERMITTED AS SHAREHOLDERS.—

(1) IN GENERAL.—For purposes of subsection (a), the following trusts may be shareholders:

(A) A trust all of which is treated (under subpart E of part I of subchapter J of this chapter) as owned by an individual who is a citizen or resident of the United States.

(B) A trust which was described in subparagraph (A) immediately before the death of the deemed owner and which continues in existence after such death, but only for the 60-day period beginning on the day of the deemed owner's death. If a trust is described in the preceding sentence and if the entire corpus of the trust is includible in the gross estate of the deemed owner, the preceding sentence shall be applied by substituting "2-year period" for "60-day period".

(C) A trust with respect to stock transferred to it pursuant to the terms of a will, but only for the 60-day period beginning on the day on which such stock is transferred to it.

(D) A trust created primarily to exercise the voting power of stock transferred to it.

(2) TREATMENT AS SHAREHOLDERS.—For purposes of subsection (a)—

(A) In the case of a trust described in subparagraph (A) of paragraph (1), the deemed owner shall be treated as the shareholder.

(B) In the case of a trust described in subparagraph (B) of paragraph (1), the estate of the deemed owner shall be treated as the shareholder.

(C) In the case of a trust described in subparagraph (C) of paragraph (1), the estate of the testator shall be treated as the shareholder.

(D) In the case of a trust described in subparagraph (D) of paragraph (1), each beneficiary of the trust shall be treated as a shareholder.

Amendments

• **1981, Economic Recovery Tax Act of 1981 (P.L. 97-34)**

P.L. 97-34, §234(a):

Amended Code Sec. 1371(e). **Effective** for tax years beginning after 12-31-81. Prior to amendment, Code Sec. 1371(e) read as follows:

(e) CERTAIN TRUSTS PERMITTED AS SHAREHOLDERS.—For purposes of subsection (a), the following trusts may be shareholders:

(1)(A) A trust all of which is treated as owned by the grantor (who is an individual who is a citizen or resident of the United States) under subpart E of part I of subchapter J of this chapter.

(B) A trust which was described in subparagraph (A) immediately before the death of the grantor and which continues in existence after such death, but only for the 60-day period beginning on the day of the grantor's death. If a trust is described in the preceding sentence and if the entire corpus of the trust is includible in the gross estate of the grantor, the preceding sentence shall be applied by substituting "2-year period" for "60-day period".

(2) A trust created primarily to exercise the voting power of stock transferred to it.

(3) Any trust with respect to stock transferred to it pursuant to the terms of a will, but only for the 60-day period beginning on the day on which such stock is transferred to it.

In the case of a trust described in paragraph (1), the grantor shall be treated as the shareholder. In the case of a trust described in paragraph (2), each beneficiary of the trust shall, for purposes of subsection (a)(1), be treated as a shareholder.

• **1978, Revenue Act of 1978 (P.L. 95-600)**

P.L. 95-600, §341(b)(1):

Amended Code Sec. 1371 by striking out the former subsection (e) and by redesignating subsection (f) as subsection (e). **Effective** for tax years beginning after 12-31-78. Prior to being stricken, Code Sec. 1371(e) read as follows:

(e) SPECIAL SHAREHOLDER RULES.—

(1) A small business corporation which has been an electing small business corporation for a period of five consecutive taxable years may not have more than 15 shareholders.

(2) If, during the 5-year period set forth in paragraph (1), the number of shareholders of an electing small business corporation increases to an amount in excess of 10 (but not in excess of 15) solely by reason of additional shareholders who acquired their stock through inheritance, the corporation may have a number of additional shareholders equal to the number by which the inheriting shareholders cause the total number of shareholders of such corporation to exceed 10.

P.L. 95-600, §324(b):

Amended Code Sec. 1371(e) (as redesignated by P.L. 95-600, §341(b)(1)) by inserting after the first sentence "In the case of a trust described in paragraph (1), the grantor shall be treated as the shareholder.". **Effective** for tax years beginning after 12-31-78.

P.L. 95-600, §701(y)(1):

Amended Code Sec. 1371(e)(1) (as redesignated). **Effective** for tax years beginning after 12-31-76. Prior to amendment, Code Sec. 1371(e)(1) read as follows:

"(1) A trust all of which is treated as owned by the grantor under subpart E of part I of subchapter J of this chapter."

INCOME TAX—SPECIAL RULES

- **1976, Tax Reform Act of 1976 (P.L. 94-455)**

P.L. 94-455, § 902(c)(2)(A):

Added Code Sec. 1371(f). **Effective** for tax years beginning after 12-31-76.

[Sec. 1371(f)]

(f) ESTATE OF INDIVIDUAL IN TITLE 11 CASE MAY BE SHAREHOLDER.—For purposes of subsection (a)(2), the term "estate" includes the estate of an individual in a case under title 11 of the United States Code.

Amendments

- **1980, Bankruptcy Tax Act of 1980 (P.L. 96-589)**

P.L. 96-589, § 5(d):

Added Code Sec. 1371(f). **Effective** for any bankruptcy case commenced on or after 10-1-79.

[Sec. 1371(g)]

(g) SPECIAL RULE FOR QUALIFIED SUBCHAPTER S TRUST.—

(1) IN GENERAL.—In the case of a qualified subchapter S trust with respect to which a beneficiary makes an election under paragraph (2)—

(A) such trust shall be treated as a trust described in subsection (e)(1)(A), and

(B) for purposes of section 678(a), the beneficiary of such trust shall be treated as the owner of that portion of the trust which consists of stock in an electing small business corporation with respect to which the election under paragraph (2) is made.

(2) ELECTION.—

(A) IN GENERAL.—A beneficiary of a qualified subchapter S trust (or his legal representative) may elect to have this subsection apply.

(B) MANNER AND TIME OF ELECTION.—An election under this paragraph shall be made—

(i) separately with respect to each electing small business corporation the stock of which is held by the trust,

(ii) separately with respect to each successive income beneficiary of the trust, and

(iii) in such manner and form, and at such time, as the Secretary may prescribe.

(C) ELECTION IRREVOCABLE.—An election under this paragraph, once made, may be revoked only with the consent of the Secretary.

(D) GRACE PERIOD.—An election under this paragraph shall be effective up to 60 days before the date of the election.

(3) QUALIFIED SUBCHAPTER S TRUST.—For purposes of this subsection, the term "qualified subchapter S trust" means a trust—

(A) which owns stock in 1 or more electing small business corporations,

(B) all of the income (within the meaning of section 643(b)) of which is distributed (or required to be distributed) currently to 1 individual who is a citizen or resident of the United States, and

(C) the terms of which require that—

(i) at any time, there shall be only one income beneficiary of the trust,

(ii) any corpus distributed during the term of the trust may be distributed only to the current income beneficiary thereof,

(iii) each income interest in the trust shall terminate on the earlier of the death of the income beneficiary or the termination of the trust, and

(iv) upon the termination of the trust during the life of an income beneficiary, the trust shall distribute all of its assets to such income beneficiary.

(4) TRUST CEASING TO BE QUALIFIED.—If a qualified subchapter S trust ceases to meet any requirement under paragraph (3), the provisions of this subsection shall not apply to such trust as of the date it ceases to meet such requirements.

Amendments

- **1983, Technical Corrections Act of 1982 (P.L. 97-448)**

P.L. 97-448, § 102(i)(1):

Amended Code Sec. 1371(g)(3)(B) (prior to amendment by P.L. 97-354). **Effective** as if included in the provision of P.L. 97-34 to which it relates. Prior to amendment, Code Sec. 1371(g)(3)(B) read as follows:

"(B) all of the income of which is distributed currently to one individual who is a citizen or resident of the United States, and".

- **1981, Economic Recovery Tax Act of 1981 (P.L. 97-34)**

P.L. 97-34, § 234(b):

Amended Code Sec. 1371 by adding at the end thereof new subsection (g). **Effective** for tax years beginning after 12-31-81.

[Sec. 1371(f)]

(f) CASH DISTRIBUTIONS FOLLOWING POST-TERMINATION TRANSITION PERIOD.—In the case of a distribution of money by an eligible terminated S corporation (as defined in section 481(d)) after the post-termination transition period, the accumulated adjustments account shall be allocated to such distribution, and the distribution shall be chargeable to accumulated earnings and profits, in the same ratio as the amount of such accumulated adjustments account bears to the amount of such accumulated earnings and profits.

Amendments

- **2017, Tax Cuts and Jobs Act (P.L. 115-97)**

P.L. 115-97, § 13543(b):

Amended Code Sec. 1371 by adding at the end a new subsection (f). **Effective** 12-22-2017.

[Sec. 1372]

SEC. 1372. PARTNERSHIP RULES TO APPLY FOR FRINGE BENEFIT PURPOSES.

[Sec. 1372(a)]

(a) GENERAL RULE.—For purposes of applying the provisions of this subtitle which relate to employee fringe benefits—

(1) the S corporation shall be treated as a partnership, and

(2) any 2-percent shareholder of the S corporation shall be treated as a partner of such partnership.

[Sec. 1372(b)]

(b) 2-PERCENT SHAREHOLDER DEFINED.—For purposes of this section, the term "2-percent shareholder" means any person who owns (or is considered as owning within the meaning of section 318) on any day during the taxable year of the S corporation more than 2 percent of the outstanding stock of such corporation or stock possessing more than 2 percent of the total combined voting power of all stock of such corporation.

Amendments

- **1982, Subchapter S Revision Act of 1982 (P.L. 97-354)**

P.L. 97-354, § 2:

Amended Code Sec. 1372. **Effective**, generally, for tax years beginning after 12-31-82, except that:

(1) Code Sec. 1372(e)(5) as in effect on the day before the enactment of P.L. 97-354 shall not apply in the case of a tax year beginning during 1982.

(2) Special rules and exceptions apply to certain casualty insurance companies and qualified oil corporations. See the amendment note for Act Sec. 6(c)(2)-(4) following Code Sec. 1361.

See, also, Act Sec. 6(b)(3), following Code Sec. 1362, for a special rule affecting Code Sec. 1372(e)(5).

(3) Regarding the treatment of existing fringe benefit plans, see Act Sec. 6(d), below.

P.L. 97-354, § 6(d) provides:

(d) TREATMENT OF EXISTING FRINGE BENEFIT PLANS.—

(1) IN GENERAL.—In the case of existing fringe benefits of a corporation which as of September 28, 1982, was an electing small business corporation, section 1372 of the Internal Revenue Code of 1954 (as added by this Act) shall apply only with respect to taxable years beginning after December 31, 1987.

(2) REQUIREMENTS.—This subsection shall cease to apply with respect to any corporation after whichever of the following first occurs:

(A) the first day of the first taxable year beginning after December 31, 1982, with respect to which the corporation does not meet the requirements of section 1372(e)(5) of such Code (as in effect on the day before the date of the enactment of this Act),

(B) any termination after December 31, 1982, of the election of the corporation under subchapter S of chapter 1 of such Code, or

(C) the first day on which more than 50 percent of the stock of the corporation is newly owned stock within the meaning of section 1378(c)(2) of such Code (as amended by this Act).

(3) EXISTING FRINGE BENEFIT.—For purposes of this subsection, the term "existing fringe benefit" means any employee fringe benefit of a type which the corporation provided to its employees as of September 28, 1982.

Prior to amendment, Code Sec. 1372 read as follows:

SEC. 1372. ELECTION BY SMALL BUSINESS CORPORATION.

[Sec. 1372(a)]

(a) ELIGIBILITY.—Except as provided in subsection (f), any small business corporation may elect, in accordance with the provisions of this section, not to be subject to the taxes imposed by this chapter.

Such election shall be valid only if all persons who are shareholders in such corporation on the day on which such election is made consent to such election.

Amendments

- **1978 (P.L. 95-628)**

P.L. 95-628, § 5(b)(2):

Amended Code Sec. 1372(a), apparently duplicating the amendment made to Code Sec. 1372(a) by P.L. 95-600, § 343(b)(1). **Effective** for elections made after 1-9-79, for tax years beginning after such date.

INCOME TAX—SPECIAL RULES

• **1978, Revenue Act of 1978 (P.L. 95-600)**

P.L. 95-600, §343(b)(1):

Amended Code Sec. 1372(a), an amendment duplicated in P.L. 95-628, §5(b)(2). **Effective** for tax years beginning after 12-31-78. Prior to amendment, Code Sec. 1372(a) read as follows:

(a) ELIGIBILITY.—Except as provided in subsection (f), any small business corporation may elect, in accordance with the provisions of this section, not to be subject to the taxes imposed by this chapter. Such election shall be valid only if all persons who are shareholders in such corporation—

(1) on the first day of the first taxable year for which such election is effective, if such election is made on or before such first day, or

(2) on the day on which the election is made, if the election is made after such first day, consent to such election.

[Sec. 1372(b)]

(b) EFFECT.—If a small business corporation makes an election under subsection (a), then—

(1) with respect to the taxable years of the corporation for which such election is in effect, such corporation shall not be subject to the taxes imposed by this chapter (other than as provided by section 58(d)(2) and by section 1378) and, with respect to such taxable years and all succeeding taxable years, the provisions of section 1377 shall apply to such corporation, and

(2) with respect to the taxable years of a shareholder of such corporation in which or with which the taxable years of the corporation for which such election is in effect end, the provisions of sections 1373, 1374, and 1375 shall apply to such shareholder, and with respect to such taxable years and all succeeding taxable years, the provisions of section 1376 shall apply to such shareholder.

Amendments

• **1976, Tax Reform Act of 1976 (P.L. 94-455)**

P.L. 94-455, §1901(a)(149)(A):

Substituted "(other than as provided by section 58(d)(2) and by section 1378)" for "(other than the tax imposed by section 1378)" in Code Sec. 1372(b)(1). **Effective** with respect to tax years beginning after 12-31-76.

• **1966 (P.L. 89-389)**

P.L. 89-389, §2(b):

Amended Code Sec. 1372(b)(1) by inserting "(other than the tax imposed by section 1378)" immediately after "this chapter." **Effective** with respect to tax years of electing small business corporations beginning after 4-14-66, but not with respect to sales or exchanges occurring before 2-24-66.

[Sec. 1372(c)]

(c) WHEN AND HOW MADE.—

(1) IN GENERAL.—An election under subsection (a) may be made by a small business corporation for any taxable year—

(A) at any time during the preceding taxable year, or

(B) at any time during the first 75 days of the taxable year.

(2) TREATMENT OF CERTAIN LATE ELECTIONS.—If—

(A) a small business corporation makes an election under subsection (a) for any taxable year, and

(B) such election is made after the first 75 days of the taxable year and on or before the last day of such taxable year,

then such election shall be treated as made for the following taxable year.

(3) MANNER OF MAKING ELECTION.—An election under subsection (a) shall be made in such manner as the Secretary shall prescribe by regulations.

Amendments

• **1978 (P.L. 95-628)**

P.L. 95-628, §5(a):

Amended Code Sec. 1372(c), apparently duplicating the amendment to Code Sec. 1372(c) by P.L. 95-600, §343(a). **Effective** for elections made after 1-9-79, for tax years beginning after such date. The amendment has a retroactive application, as set forth in P.L. 95-628, §5(d), below.

P.L. 95-628, §5(d):

(d) RETROACTIVE APPLICATION OF "PRECEDING TAXABLE YEAR" AMENDMENT.—

(1) IN GENERAL.—If—

(A) a small business corporation has treated itself in its return as an electing small business corporation under subchapter S of chapter 1 of the Internal Revenue Code of 1954 for any taxable year beginning before the date 60 days after the date of the enactment of this Act (hereinafter in this subsection referred to as the "election year"),

(B) such treatment was pursuant to an election which such corporation made during the taxable year immediately preceding the election year and which, but for this subsection, would not be effective, and

(C) at such time and in such manner as the Secretary of the Treasury or his delegate may prescribe by regulations—

(i) such corporation makes an election under this paragraph, and

(ii) all persons (or their personal representatives) who were shareholders of such corporation at any time beginning with the first day of the election year and ending on the date of the making of such election consent to such election, consent to the application of the amendment made by subsection (a), and consent to the application of paragraph (3) of this subsection,

then paragraph (1) of the first sentence of section 1372(c) of such Code (as amended by subsection (a)) shall apply with respect to the taxable years referred to in paragraph (2) of this subsection.

(2) YEARS TO WHICH AMENDMENT APPLIES.—In the case of an election under paragraph (1) by any corporation, the taxable years referred to in this paragraph are—

(A) the election year,

(B) all subsequent taxable years of such corporation, and

(C) in the case of each person who was a shareholder of such corporation at any time during any taxable year described in subparagraph (A) or (B)—

(i) the first taxable year of such person ending with or within a taxable year described in subparagraph (A) or (B), and

(ii) all subsequent taxable years of such person.

(3) STATUTE OF LIMITATIONS FOR ASSESSMENT OF DEFICIENCY.—If the assessment of any deficiency in income tax resulting from the filing of an election under paragraph (1) for a taxable year ending before the date of such filing would be prevented, but for the application of this paragraph, before the expiration of one year after the date of such filing by any law or rule of law, then such deficiency (to the extent attributable to such election) may be assessed at any time before the expiration of such one-year period notwithstanding any law or rule of law which would otherwise prevent such assessment.

• **1978, Revenue Act of 1978 (P.L. 95-600)**

P.L. 95-600, §343(a):

Amended Code Sec. 1372(c), an amendment duplicated in P.L. 95-628, §5(a). **Effective** for tax years beginning after 12-31-78. Prior to amendment, Code Sec. 1372(c) read as follows:

(c) WHERE AND HOW MADE.—An election under subsection (a) may be made by a small business corporation for any taxable year at any time during the first month of such taxable year, or at any time during the month preceding such first month. Such election shall be made in such manner as the Secretary shall prescribe by regulations.

• **1976, Tax Reform Act of 1976 (P.L. 94-455)**

P.L. 94-455, §1901(a)(149)(B):

Amended Code Sec. 1372(c). **Effective** with respect to tax years beginning after 12-31-76. Prior to amendment Code Sec. 1372(c) read as follows:

(c) WHERE AND HOW MADE.—

(1) IN GENERAL.—An election under subsection (a) may be made by a small business corporation for any taxable year at any time during the first month of such taxable year, or at any time during the month preceding such first month. Such election shall be made in such manner as the Secretary or his delegate shall prescribe by regulations.

(2) TAXABLE YEARS BEGINNING BEFORE DATE OF ENACTMENT.—An election may be made under subsection (a) by a small business corporation for its first taxable year which begins after December 31, 1957, and on or before the date of the enactment of this subchapter, and ends after such date at any time—

(A) within the 90-day period beginning on the day after the date of the enactment of this subchapter, or

(B) if its taxable year ends within such 90-day period, before the close of such taxable year.

An election may be made pursuant to this paragraph only if the small business corporation has been a small business corporation (as defined in section 1371(a)) on each day after the date of the enactment of this subchapter and before the day of such election.

[Sec. 1372(d)]

(d) YEARS FOR WHICH EFFECTIVE.—An election under subsection (a) shall be effective for the taxable year of the corporation for which it is made and for all succeeding taxable years of the corporation, unless it is terminated, with respect to any such taxable year, under subsection (e).

[Sec. 1372(e)]

(e) TERMINATION.—

(1) NEW SHAREHOLDERS.—

(A) An election under subsection (a) made by a small business corporation shall terminate if any person who was not a shareholder in such corporation on the day on which the election is made becomes a shareholder in such corporation and affirmatively refuses (in such manner as the Secretary may by regulations prescribe) to consent to such election on or before the 60th day after the day on which he acquires the stock.

(B) If the person acquiring the stock is the estate of a decedent, the period under subparagraph (A) for affirmatively refusing to consent to the election shall expire on the 60th day after whichever of the following is the earlier:

(i) The day on which the executor or administrator of the estate qualifies; or

(ii) The last day of the taxable year of the corporation in which the decedent died.

(C) Any termination of an election under subparagraph (A) by reason of the affirmative refusal of any person to consent to such election shall be effective for the taxable year of the corporation in which such person becomes a shareholder in the corporation (or, if later, the first taxable year for which such election would otherwise have been effective) and for all succeeding taxable years of the corporation.

(2) REVOCATION.—An election under subsection (a) made by a small business corporation may be revoked by it for any taxable year of the corporation after the first taxable year for which the election is effective. An election may be revoked only if all persons who are shareholders in the corporation on the day on which the revocation is made consent to the revocation. A revocation under this paragraph shall be effective—

(A) for the taxable year in which made, if made before the close of the first month of such taxable year,

(B) for the taxable year following the taxable year in which made, if made after the close of such first month,

and for all succeeding taxable years of the corporation. Such revocation shall be made in such manner as the Secretary shall prescribe by regulations.

(3) CEASES TO BE SMALL BUSINESS CORPORATION.—An election under subsection (a) made by a small business corporation shall terminate if at any time—

(A) after the first day of the first taxable year of the corporation for which the election is effective, if such election is made on or before such first day, or

(B) after the day on which the election is made, if such election is made after such first day,

INCOME TAX—SPECIAL RULES

the corporation ceases to be a small business corporation (as defined in section 1371(a)). Such termination shall be effective for the taxable year of the corporation in which the corporation ceases to be a small business corporation and for all succeeding taxable years of the corporation.

(4) FOREIGN INCOME.—An election under subsection (a) made by a small business corporation shall terminate if for any taxable year of the corporation for which the election is in effect, such corporation derives more than 80 percent of its gross receipts from sources outside the United States. Such termination shall be effective for the taxable year of the corporation in which it derives more than 80 percent of its gross receipts from sources outside the United States, and for all succeeding taxable years of the corporation.

(5) PASSIVE INVESTMENT INCOME.—

(A) Except as provided in subparagraph (B), an election under subsection (a) made by a small business corporation shall terminate if, for any taxable year of the corporation for which the election is in effect, such corporation has gross receipts more than 20 percent of which is passive investment income. Such termination shall be effective for the taxable year of the corporation in which it has gross receipts of such amount, and for all succeeding taxable years of the corporation.

(B) Subparagraph (A) shall not apply with respect to a taxable year in which a small business corporation has gross receipts more than 20 percent of which is passive investment income, if—

(i) such taxable year is the first taxable year in which the corporation commenced the active conduct of any trade or business or the next succeeding taxable year; and

(ii) the amount of passive investment income for such taxable year is less than $3,000.

(C) For purposes of this paragraph, the term "passive investment income" means gross receipts derived from royalties, rents, dividends, interest, annuities, and sales or exchanges of stock or securities (gross receipts from such sales or exchanges being taken into account for purposes of this paragraph only to the extent of gains therefrom). Gross receipts derived from sales or exchanges of stock or securities for purposes of this paragraph shall not include amounts received by an electing small business corporation which are treated under section 331 (relating to corporate liquidations) as payments in exchange for stock where the electing small business corporation owned more than 50 percent of each class of the stock of the liquidating corporation.

Amendments

• **1978 (P.L. 95-628)**

P.L. 95-628, § 5(b)(1):

Amended Code Sec. 1372(e)(1)(A), apparently duplicating the amendment made to Code Sec. 1372 by P.L. 95-600, § 343(b)(2). **Effective** for elections made after 1-9-79, for tax years beginning after such date.

P.L. 95-628, § 5(b)(3):

Amended Code Sec. 1372(e)(1)(C) by inserting "(or, if later, the first taxable year for which such election would otherwise have been effective)" after "in the corporation". **Effective** for elections made after 1-9-79, for tax years beginning after such date. This amendment apparently duplicates the amendment made to Code Sec. 1372(e)(1)(C) by P.L. 95-600, § 343(b)(3).

• **1978, Revenue Act of 1978 (P.L. 95-600)**

P.L. 95-600, § 343(b)(2):

Amended Code Sec. 1372(e)(1)(A). **Effective** for tax years beginning after 12-31-78. Prior to amendment, Code Sec. 1372(e)(1)(A) read as follows:

(A) An election under subsection (a) made by a small business corporation shall terminate if any person who was not a shareholder in such corporation—

(i) on the first day of the first taxable year of the corporation for which the election is effective, if such election is made on or before such first day, or

(ii) on the day on which the election is made, if such election is made after such first day,

becomes a shareholder in such corporation and affirmatively refuses (in such manner as the Secretary shall by regulations prescribe) to consent to such election on or before the 60th day after the day on which he acquires the stock.

P.L. 95-600, § 343(b)(3):

Amended Code Sec. 1372(e)(1)(C) by inserting "(or, if later, the first taxable year for which such election would otherwise have been effective)" after "in the corporation". **Effective** for tax years beginning after 12-31-78.

• **1976, Tax Reform Act of 1976 (P.L. 94-455)**

P.L. 94-455, § 902(c)(3):

Amended Code Sec. 1372(e)(1). **Effective** for tax years beginning after 12-31-76. Prior to amendment, Code Sec. 1372(e)(1) read as follows:

(1) NEW SHAREHOLDERS.—An election under subsection (a) made by a small business corporation shall terminate if any person who was not a shareholder in such corporation—

(A) on the first day of the first taxable year of the corporation for which the election is effective, if such election is made on or before such first day, or

(B) on the day on which the election is made, if such election is made after such first day,

becomes a shareholder in such corporation and does not consent to such election within such time as the Secretary or his delegate shall prescribe by regulations. Such termination shall be effective for the taxable year of the corporation in which such person becomes a shareholder in the corporation and for all succeeding taxable years of the corporation.

P.L. 94-455, § 1906(b)(13)(A):

Amended the 1954 Code by substituting "Secretary" for "Secretary or his delegate" each place it appeared. **Effective** 2-1-77.

• **1971 (P.L. 91-683)**

P.L. 91-683, § 1(a):

Amended subsection 1372(e)(5) by adding the last sentence. For effective date, see Act Sec. 1(b)-(d), below.

P.L. 91-683, §§ 1(b)-(d), provides:

"(b) The amendment made by subsection (a) shall apply to taxable years of electing small business corporations ending after the date of the enactment of this Act [January 12, 1971]. Such amendment shall also apply with respect to any taxable year ending before October 7, 1970, but only if—

"(1) on such date the making of a refund or the allowance of a credit to the electing small business corporation is not prevented by any law or rule of law, and

"(2) within one year after the date of enactment of this Act and in such manner as the Secretary of the Treasury or his delegate prescribes by regulations—

"(A) the corporation elects to have such amendment so apply, and

"(B) all persons (or their personal representatives) who were shareholders of such corporation at any time during any taxable year beginning with the first taxable year to which this amendment applies and ending on or before the date of the enactment of this Act consent to such election and to the application of the amendment made by subsection (a).

"(c) If the assessment of any deficiency in income tax resulting from the filing of such election for a taxable year ending before the date of such filing is prevented before the expiration of one year after the date of such filing by any law or rule of law, such deficiency (to the extent attributable to such election) may be assessed at any time prior to the expiration of such one-year period notwithstanding any law or rule of law which would otherwise prevent such assessment.

"(d) If the election of a corporation under subsection (a) of section 1372 of the Internal Revenue Code of 1954 would have been terminated because of the application of subsection (e)(5) of such section (before the amendment made by subsection (a) of this section) but for the election by such corporation under paragraph (2) of subsection (b) (and the consent of shareholders under such paragraph), such election under section 1372(a) of such code shall not be treated as terminated for any year beginning before the date of the enactment of this Act as a result of—

"(1) such corporation filing its income tax return on a form 1120 (instead of a form 1120S), or

"(2) a new shareholder not consenting to such election of such corporation in accordance with the requirements of subsection (e)(1) of such section 1372."

• **1966 (P.L. 89-389)**

P.L. 89-389, § 3(a):

Amended Code Sec. 1372(e)(5). **Effective** for tax years of electing small business corporations ending after 4-14-66. The amendment also applies with respect to tax years beginning after 1962, and ending on or before 4-14-66, if (at such time and in such manner as the Secretary of the Treasury or his delegate prescribes by regulations)—(1) the corporation elects to have the amendment apply, and (2) all persons (or their personal representatives) who were shareholders of such corporation at any time during any tax year beginning after 1962, and ending on or before 4-14-66, consent to such election and to the application of the amendment. Prior to amendment, Sec. 1372(e)(5) read as follows:

"(5) Personal holding company income.—An election under subsection (a) made by a small business corporation shall terminate if, for any taxable year of the corporation for which the election is in effect, such corporation has gross receipts more than 20 percent of which is derived from royalties, rents, dividends, interest, annuities, and sales or exchanges of stock or securities (gross receipts from such sales or exchanges being taken into account for purposes of this paragraph only to the extent of gains therefrom). Such termination shall be effective for the taxable year of the corporation in which it has gross receipts of such amount, and for all succeeding taxable years of the corporation."

[Sec. 1372(f)]

(f) ELECTION AFTER TERMINATION.—If a small business corporation has made an election under subsection (a) and if such election has been terminated or revoked under subsection (e), such corporation (and any successor corporation) shall not be eligible to make an election under subsection (a) for any taxable year prior to its fifth taxable year which begins after the first taxable year for which such termination or revocation is effective, unless the Secretary consents to such election.

Amendments

• **1976, Tax Reform Act of 1976 (P.L. 94-455)**

P.L. 94-455, § 1906(b)(13)(A):

Amended 1954 Code by substituting "Secretary" for "Secretary or his delegate" each place it appeared. **Effective** 2-1-77.

• **1958, Technical Amendments Act of 1958 (P.L. 85-866)**

P.L. 85-866, § 64(a):

Added Code Sec. 1372. **Effective** for tax years beginning after 12-31-57.

[Sec. 1372(g)—Repealed]

Amendments

• **1976, Tax Reform Act of 1976 (P.L. 94-455)**

P.L. 94-455, § 1901(a)(149)(C):

Repealed Code Sec. 1372(g). **Effective** with respect to tax years beginning after 12-31-76. Prior to repeal, Code Sec. 1372(g) read as follows:

(g) CONSENT TO ELECTION BY CERTAIN SHAREHOLDERS OF STOCK HELD AS COMMUNITY PROPERTY.—If a husband and wife owned stock which was community property (or the income from which was community income) under the applicable community property law of a State, and if either spouse filed a timely consent to an election under subsection (a) for a taxable year beginning before January 1, 1961, the time for filing the consent of the other spouse to such election shall not expire prior to May 15, 1961.

• **1961 (P.L. 87-29)**

P.L. 87-29, §2:

Added Code Sec. 1372(g). **Effective** for tax years beginning before 1-1-61, the time for filing the consent not to expire prior to 5-15-61.

[Sec. 1373]

SEC. 1373. FOREIGN INCOME.

[Sec. 1373(a)]

(a) S CORPORATION TREATED AS PARTNERSHIP, ETC.—For purposes of subparts A and F of part III, and part V, of subchapter N (relating to income from sources without the United States)—

(1) an S corporation shall be treated as a partnership, and

(2) the shareholders of such corporation shall be treated as partners of such partnership.

[Sec. 1373(b)]

(b) RECAPTURE OF OVERALL FOREIGN LOSS.—For purposes of section 904(f) (relating to recapture of overall foreign loss), the making or termination of an election to be treated as an S corporation shall be treated as a disposition of the business.

Amendments

• **1982, Subchapter S Revision Act of 1982 (P.L. 97-354)**

P.L. 97-354, §2:

Amended Code Sec. 1373. **Effective**, generally, for tax years beginning after 12-31-82. See, however, the amendment note for Act Sec. 6(c)(2)-(4) following Code Sec. 1361 for special rules and exceptions applicable to certain casualty insurance companies and qualified oil corporations. Prior to amendment, Code Sec. 1373 read as follows:

SEC. 1373. CORPORATION UNDISTRIBUTED TAXABLE INCOME TAXED TO SHAREHOLDERS.

[Sec. 1373(a)]

(a) GENERAL RULE.—The undistributed taxable income of an electing small business corporation for any taxable year shall be included in the gross income of the shareholders of such corporation in the manner and to the extent set forth in this section.

[Sec. 1373(b)]

(b) AMOUNT INCLUDED IN GROSS INCOME.—Each person who is a shareholder of an electing small business corporation on the last day of a taxable year of such corporation shall include in his gross income, for his taxable year in which or with which the taxable year of the corporation ends, the amount he would have received as a dividend, if on such last day there had been distributed pro rata to its shareholders by such corporation an amount equal to the corporation's undistributed taxable income for the corporation's taxable year. For purposes of this chapter, the amount so included shall be treated as an amount distributed as a dividend on the last day of the taxable year of the corporation.

[Sec. 1373(c)]

(c) UNDISTRIBUTED TAXABLE INCOME DEFINED.—For purposes of this section, the term "undistributed taxable income" means taxable income (computed as provided in subsection (d)) minus the sum of (1) the taxes imposed by sections 56 and 1378(a) and (2) the amount of money distributed as dividends during the taxable year, to the extent that any such amount is a distribution out of earnings and profits of the taxable year as specified in section 316(a)(2).

Amendments

• **1969, Tax Reform Act of 1969 (P.L. 91-172)**

P.L. 91-172, §301(b)(10):

Amended Code Sec. 1373(c) by substituting the phrase "taxes imposed by sections 56 and 1378(a) for the phrase "tax imposed by section 1378(a)."

• **1966 (P.L. 89-389)**

P.L. 89-389, §2(b):

Amended Code Sec. 1373(c) by inserting "the sum of (1) the tax imposed by section 1378(a) and (2)" after "minus". **Effective** with respect to tax years of electing small business corporations beginning after 4-14-66, but not with respect to sales or exchanges occurring before 2-24-66.

[Sec. 1373(d)]

(d) TAXABLE INCOME.—For purposes of this subchapter, the taxable income of an electing small business corporation shall be determined without regard to—

(1) the deduction allowed by section 172 (relating to net operating loss deduction), and

(2) the deductions allowed by part VIII of subchapter B (other than the deduction allowed by section 248, relating to organization expenditures).

Amendments

• **1958, Technical Amendments Act of 1958 (P.L. 85-866)**

P.L. 85-866, §64(a):

Added Code Sec. 1373. **Effective** for tax years beginning after 12-31-57.

[Sec. 1374]

SEC. 1374. TAX IMPOSED ON CERTAIN BUILT-IN GAINS.

[Sec. 1374(a)]

(a) GENERAL RULE.—If for any taxable year beginning in the recognition period an S corporation has a net recognized built-in gain, there is hereby imposed a tax (computed under subsection (b)) on the income of such corporation for such taxable year.

Amendments

• **1988, Technical and Miscellaneous Revenue Act of 1988 (P.L. 100-647)**

P.L. 100-647, §1006(f)(1):

Amended Code Sec. 1374(a) by striking out "a recognized built-in gain" and inserting in lieu thereof "a net recognized built-in gain". **Effective** as if included in the provision of P.L. 99-514 to which it relates.

[Sec. 1374(b)]

(b) AMOUNT OF TAX.—

(1) IN GENERAL.—The amount of the tax imposed by subsection (a) shall be computed by applying the highest rate of tax specified in section 11(b) to the net recognized built-in gain of the S corporation for the taxable year.

(2) NET OPERATING LOSS CARRYFORWARDS FROM C YEARS ALLOWED.—Notwithstanding section 1371(b)(1), any net operating loss carryforward arising in a taxable year for which the corporation was a C corporation shall be allowed for purposes of this section as a deduction against the net recognized built-in gain of the S corporation for the taxable year. For purposes of determining the amount of any such loss which may be carried to subsequent taxable years, the amount of the net recognized built-in gain shall be treated as taxable income. Rules similar to the rules of the preceding sentences of this paragraph shall apply in the case of a capital loss carryforward arising in a taxable year for which the corporation was a C corporation.

(3) CREDITS.—

(A) IN GENERAL.—Except as provided in subparagraph (B), no credit shall be allowable under part IV of subchapter A of this chapter (other than under section 34) against the tax imposed by subsection (a).

(B) BUSINESS CREDIT CARRYFORWARDS FROM C YEARS ALLOWED.—Notwithstanding section 1371(b)(1), any business credit carryforward under section 39 arising in a taxable year for which the corporation was a C corporation shall be allowed as a credit against the tax imposed by subsection (a) in the same manner as if it were imposed by section 11.

INCOME TAX—SPECIAL RULES

Amendments

• **2017, Tax Cuts and Jobs Act (P.L. 115-97)**

P.L. 115-97, §12002(c):

Amended Code Sec. 1374(b)(3)(B) by striking the last sentence. **Effective** for tax years beginning after 12-31-2021. Prior to being stricken, the last sentence of Code Sec. 1374(b)(3)(B) read as follows:

A similar rule shall apply in the case of the minimum tax credit under section 53 to the extent attributable to taxable years for which the corporation was a C corporation.

P.L. 115-97, §13001(b)(2)(N):

Amended Code Sec. 1374(b) by striking paragraph (4). **Effective** for tax years beginning after 12-31-2017. Prior to being stricken, Code Sec. 1374(b)(4) read as follows:

(4) COORDINATION WITH SECTION 1201(a).—For purposes of section 1201(a)—

(A) the tax imposed by subsection (a) shall be treated as if it were imposed by section 11, and

(B) the amount of the net recognized built-in gain shall be treated as the taxable income.

• **1989, Omnibus Budget Reconciliation Act of 1989 (P.L. 101-239)**

P.L. 101-239, §7811(c)(8):

Amended Code Sec. 1374(b)(3)(B) by adding at the end thereof a new sentence. **Effective** as if included in the provision of P.L. 100-647 to which it relates.

• **1988, Technical and Miscellaneous Revenue Act of 1988 (P.L. 100-647)**

P.L. 100-647, §1006(f)(2):

Amended Code Sec. 1374(b) by striking out paragraphs (1) and (2) and inserting new paragraphs (1) and (2). **Effective** as if included in the provision of P.L. 99-514 to which it relates. Prior to amendment, paragraphs (1) and (2) read as follows:

(1) IN GENERAL.—The tax imposed by subsection (a) shall be a tax computed by applying the highest rate of tax specified in section 11(b) to the lesser of—

(A) the recognized built-in gains of the S corporation for the taxable year, or

(B) the amount which would be the taxable income of the corporation for such taxable year if such corporation were not an S corporation.

(2) NET OPERATING LOSS CARRYFORWARDS FROM C YEARS ALLOWED.—Notwithstanding section 1371(b)(1), any net operating loss carryforward arising in a taxable year for which the corporation was a C corporation shall be allowed as a deduction against the lesser of the amounts referred to in subparagraph (A) or (B) of paragraph (1). For purposes of determining the amount of any such loss which may be carried to subsequent taxable years, the lesser of the amounts referred to in subparagraph (A) or (B) of paragraph (1) shall be treated as taxable income.

P.L. 100-647, §1006(f)(3):

Amended Code Sec. 1374(b)(4)(B). **Effective** as if included in the provision of P.L. 99-514 to which it relates. Prior to amendment, Code Sec. 1374(b)(4)(B) read as follows:

(B) the lower of the amounts specified in subparagraphs (A) and (B) of paragraph (1) shall be treated as the taxable income.

[Sec. 1374(c)]

(c) LIMITATIONS.—

(1) CORPORATIONS WHICH WERE ALWAYS S CORPORATIONS.—Subsection (a) shall not apply to any corporation if an election under section 1362(a) has been in effect with respect to such corporation for each of its taxable years. Except as provided in regulations, an S corporation and any predecessor corporation shall be treated as 1 corporation for purposes of the preceding sentence.

(2) LIMITATION ON AMOUNT OF NET RECOGNIZED BUILT-IN GAIN.—The amount of the net recognized built-in gain taken into account under this section for any taxable year shall not exceed the excess (if any) of—

(A) the net unrealized built-in gain, over

(B) the net recognized built-in gain for prior taxable years beginning in the recognition period.

Amendments

• **1988, Technical and Miscellaneous Revenue Act of 1988 (P.L. 100-647)**

P.L. 100-647, §1006(f)(4):

Amended Code Sec. 1374(c)(2) by striking out "recognized built-in gains" each place it appears and inserting in lieu thereof "net recognized built-in gain". **Effective** as if included in the provision of P.L. 99-514 to which it relates.

[Sec. 1374(d)]

(d) DEFINITIONS AND SPECIAL RULES.—For purposes of this section—

(1) NET UNREALIZED BUILT-IN GAIN.—The term "net unrealized built-in gain" means the amount (if any) by which—

(A) the fair market value of the assets of S corporation as of the beginning of its 1st taxable year for which an election under section 1362(a) is in effect, exceeds

(B) the aggregate adjusted bases of such assets at such time.

(2) NET RECOGNIZED BUILT-IN GAIN.—

(A) IN GENERAL.—The term "net recognized built-in gain" means, with respect to any taxable year in the recognition period, the lesser of—

(i) the amount which would be taxable income of the S corporation for such taxable year if only recognized built-in gains and recognized built-in losses were taken into account, or

(ii) such corporation's taxable income for such taxable year (determined as provided in section 1375(b)(1)(B)).

(B) CARRYOVER.—If, for any taxable year described in subparagraph (A), the amount referred to in clause (i) of subparagraph (A) exceeds the amount referred to in clause (ii) of subparagraph (A), such excess shall be treated as a recognized built-in gain in the succeeding taxable year.

(3) RECOGNIZED BUILT-IN GAIN.—The term "recognized built-in gain" means any gain recognized during the recognition period on the disposition of any asset except to the extent that the S corporation establishes that—

(A) such asset was not held by the S corporation as of the beginning of the 1st taxable year for which it was an S corporation, or

(B) such gain exceeds the excess (if any) of—

(i) the fair market value of such asset as of the beginning of such 1st taxable year, over

(ii) the adjusted basis of the asset as of such time.

(4) RECOGNIZED BUILT-IN LOSSES.—The term "recognized built-in loss" means any loss recognized during the recognition period on the disposition of any asset to the extent that the S corporation establishes that—

(A) such asset was held by the S corporation as of the beginning of the 1st taxable year referred to in paragraph (3), and

(B) such loss does not exceed the excess of—

(i) the adjusted basis of such asset as of the beginning of such 1st taxable year, over

(ii) the fair market value of such asset as of such time.

(5) TREATMENT OF CERTAIN BUILT-IN ITEMS.—

(A) INCOME ITEMS.—Any item of income which is properly taken into account during the recognition period but which is attributable to periods before the 1st taxable year for which the corporation was an S corporation shall be treated as a recognized built-in gain for the taxable year in which it is properly taken into account.

(B) DEDUCTION ITEMS.—Any amount which is allowable as a deduction during the recognition period (determined without regard to any carryover) but which is attributable to periods before the 1st taxable year referred to in subparagraph (A) shall be treated as a recognized built-in loss for the taxable year for which it is allowable as a deduction.

(C) ADJUSTMENT TO NET UNREALIZED BUILT-IN GAIN.—The amount of the net unrealized built-in gain shall be properly adjusted for amounts which would be treated as recognized built-in gains or losses under this paragraph if such amounts were properly taken into account (or allowable as a deduction) during the recognition period.

(6) TREATMENT OF CERTAIN PROPERTY.—If the adjusted basis of any asset is determined (in whole or in part) by reference to the adjusted basis of any other asset held by the S corporation as of the beginning of the 1st taxable year referred to in paragraph (3)—

(A) such asset shall be treated as held by the S corporation as of the beginning of such 1st taxable year, and

(B) any determination under paragraph (3)(B) or (4)(B) with respect to such asset shall be made by reference to the fair market value and adjusted basis of such other asset as of the beginning of such 1st taxable year.

(7) RECOGNITION PERIOD.—

(A) IN GENERAL.—The term "recognition period" means the 5-year period beginning with the 1st day of the 1st taxable year for which the corporation was an S corporation. For purposes of applying this section to any amount includible in income by reason of distributions to shareholders pursuant to section 593(e), the preceding sentence shall be applied without regard to the phrase "5-year".

(B) INSTALLMENT SALES.—If an S corporation sells an asset and reports the income from the sale using the installment method under section 453, the treatment of all payments received shall be governed by the provisions of this paragraph applicable to the taxable year in which such sale was made.

(8) TREATMENT OF TRANSFER OF ASSETS FROM C CORPORATION TO S CORPORATION.—

(A) IN GENERAL.—Except to the extent provided in regulations, if—

(i) an S corporation acquires any asset, and

(ii) the S corporation's basis in such asset is determined (in whole or in part) by reference to the basis of such asset (or any other property) in the hands of a C corporation,

then a tax is hereby imposed on any net recognized built-in gain attributable to any such assets for any taxable year beginning in the recognition period. The amount of such tax shall be determined under the rules of this section as modified by subparagraph (B).

(B) MODIFICATIONS.—For purposes of this paragraph, the modifications of this subparagraph are as follows:

(i) IN GENERAL.—The preceding paragraphs of this subsection shall be applied by taking into account the day on which the assets were acquired by the S corporation in lieu of the beginning of the 1st taxable year for which the corporation was an S corporation.

(ii) SUBSECTION (c)(1) NOT TO APPLY.—Subsection (c)(1) shall not apply.

(9) REFERENCE TO 1ST TAXABLE YEAR.—Any reference in this section to the 1st taxable year for which the corporation was an S corporation shall be treated as a reference to the 1st taxable year for which the corporation was an S corporation pursuant to its most recent election under section 1362.

Amendments

- **2018, Tax Technical Corrections Act of 2018 (P.L. 115-141)**

P.L. 115-141, §401(b)(33), Div. U:

Amended Code Sec. 1374(d)(2)(B) by striking the last sentence. **Effective** 3-23-2018. For a special rule, see Act Sec. 401(e), Div. U, below. Prior to being stricken, the last sentence of Code Sec. 1374(d)(2)(B) read as follows:

The preceding sentence shall apply only in the case of a corporation treated as an S corporation by reason of an election made on or after March 31, 1988.

P.L. 115-141, §401(e), Div. U, provides:

(e) GENERAL SAVINGS PROVISION WITH RESPECT TO DEADWOOD PROVISIONS.—If—

(1) any provision amended or repealed by the amendments made by subsection (b) or (d) applied to—

(A) any transaction occurring before the date of the enactment of this Act,

(B) any property acquired before such date of enactment, or

(C) any item of income, loss, deduction, or credit taken into account before such date of enactment, and

(2) the treatment of such transaction, property, or item under such provision would (without regard to the amendments or repeals made by such subsection) affect the liability for tax for periods ending after such date of enactment,

nothing in the amendments or repeals made by this section shall be construed to affect the treatment of such transaction, property, or item for purposes of determining liability for tax for periods ending after such date of enactment.

- **2015, Protecting Americans from Tax Hikes Act of 2015 (P.L. 114-113)**

P.L. 114-113, §127(a), Div. Q:

Amended Code Sec. 1374(d)(7). **Effective** for tax years beginning after 12-31-2014. Prior to amendment, Code Sec. 1374(d)(7) read as follows:

(7) RECOGNITION PERIOD.—

(A) IN GENERAL.—The term "recognition period" means the 10-year period beginning with the 1st day of the 1st taxable year for which the corporation was an S corporation.

(B) SPECIAL RULES FOR 2009, 2010, AND 2011.—No tax shall be imposed on the net recognized built-in gain of an S corporation—

(i) in the case of any taxable year beginning in 2009 or 2010, if the 7th taxable year in the recognition period preceded such taxable year, or

(ii) in the case of any taxable year beginning in 2011, if the 5th year in the recognition period preceded such taxable year.

The preceding sentence shall be applied separately with respect to any asset to which paragraph (8) applies.

(C) SPECIAL RULE FOR 2012, 2013, AND 2014.—For purposes of determining the net recognized built-in gain for taxable years beginning in 2012, 2013, or 2014, subparagraphs (A) and (D) shall be applied by substituting "5-year" for "10-year".

(D) SPECIAL RULE FOR DISTRIBUTIONS TO SHAREHOLDERS.—For purposes of applying this section to any amount includible in income by reason of distributions to shareholders pursuant to section 593(e)—

(i) subparagraph (A) shall be applied without regard to the phrase "10-year", and

(ii) subparagraph (B) shall not apply.

(E) INSTALLMENT SALES.—If an S corporation sells an asset and reports the income from the sale using the installment method under section 453, the treatment of all payments received shall be governed by the provisions of this paragraph applicable to the taxable year in which such sale was made.

- **2014, Tax Increase Prevention Act of 2014 (P.L. 113-295)**

P.L. 113-295, §138(a)(1)-(2), Division A:

Amended Code Sec. 1374(d)(7)(C) by striking "2012 or 2013" and inserting "2012, 2013, or 2014", and by striking "2012 AND 2013" in the heading and inserting "2012, 2013, AND 2014". **Effective** for tax years beginning after 12-31-2013.

- **2013, American Taxpayer Relief Act of 2012 (P.L. 112-240)**

P.L. 112-240, §326(a)(1)-(3):

Amended Code Sec. 1374(d)(7) by redesignating subparagraph (C) as subparagraph (D), and by inserting after subparagraph (B) a new subparagraph (C), and by adding at the end a new subparagraph (E). **Effective** for tax years beginning after 12-31-2011.

P.L. 112-240, §326(b):

Amended Code Sec. 1374(d)(2)(B) by inserting "described in subparagraph (A)" after ", for any taxable year". **Effective** for tax years beginning after 12-31-2011.

- **2010, Creating Small Business Jobs Act of 2010 (P.L. 111-240)**

P.L. 111-240, §2014(a):

Amended Code Sec. 1374(d)(7)(B). **Effective** for tax years beginning after 12-31-2010. Prior to amendment, Code Sec. 1374(d)(7)(B) read as follows:

(B) SPECIAL RULE FOR 2009 AND 2010.—In the case of any taxable year beginning in 2009 or 2010, no tax shall be imposed on the net recognized built-in gain of an S corporation if the 7th taxable year in the recognition period preceded such taxable year. The preceding sentence shall be applied separately with respect to any asset to which paragraph (8) applies.

- **2009, American Recovery and Reinvestment Tax Act of 2009 (P.L. 111-5)**

P.L. 111-5, §1251(a):

Amended Code Sec. 1374(d)(7). **Effective** for tax years beginning after 12-31-2008. Prior to amendment, Code Sec. 1374(d)(7) read as follows:

(7) RECOGNITION PERIOD.—The term "recognition period" means the 10-year period beginning with the 1st day of the 1st taxable year for which the corporation was an S corporation. For purposes of applying this section to any amount includible in income by reason of section 593(e), the preceding sentence shall be applied without regard to the phrase "10-year".

- **1997, Taxpayer Relief Act of 1997 (P.L. 105-34)**

P.L. 105-34, §1601(f)(5)(B):

Amended Code Sec. 1374(d)(7) by adding at the end a new sentence. **Effective** as if included in the provision of P.L. 104-188 to which it relates [effective for tax years beginning after 12-31-95.—CCH].

- **1989, Omnibus Budget Reconciliation Act of 1989 (P.L. 101-239)**

P.L. 101-239, §7811(c)(4):

Amended Code Sec. 1374(d)(2)(A)(i) by striking "(except as provided in subsection (b)(2))" after "year if". **Effective** as if included in the provision of P.L. 100-647 to which it relates.

INCOME TAX—SPECIAL RULES

P.L. 101-239, § 7811(c)(5)(B)(i)-(ii):

Amended Code Sec. 1374(d)(5) by striking "during the recognition period" in subparagraph (B) and inserting "during the recognition period (determined without regard to any carryover)", and by striking "treated as recognized built-in gains or losses under this paragraph" in subparagraph (C) and inserting "which would be treated as recognized built-in gains or losses under this paragraph if such amounts were properly taken into account (or allowable as a deduction) during the recognition period". **Effective** as if included in the provision of P.L. 100-647 to which it relates.

- **1988, Technical and Miscellaneous Revenue Act of 1988 (P.L. 100-647)**

P.L. 100-647, § 1006(f)(5)(A):

Amended Code Sec. 1374(d) by striking out all that follows paragraph (1) and inserting in lieu thereof new paragraphs (2)-(9) and new subsection (e). **Effective** as if included in the provision of P.L. 100-647 to which it relates. Prior to amendment, all that followed Code Sec. 1374(d)(1) read as follows:

(2) RECOGNIZED BUILT-IN GAIN.—The term "recognized built-in gain" means any gain recognized during the recognition period on the disposition of any asset except to the extent that the S corporation establishes that—

(A) such asset was not held by the S corporation as of the beginning of the 1st taxable year referred to in paragraph (1), or

(B) such gain exceeds the excess (if any) of—

(i) the fair market value of such asset as of the beginning of such 1st taxable year, over

(ii) the adjusted basis of the asset as of such time.

(3) RECOGNITION PERIOD.—The term "recognition period" means the 10-year period beginning with the 1st day of the 1st taxable year for which the corporation was an S corporation.

(4) TAXABLE INCOME.—Taxable income of the corporation shall be determined under section 63(a)—

(A) without regard to the deductions allowed by part VIII of subchapter B (other than the deduction allowed by section 248, relating to organization expenditures), and

(B) without regard to the deduction under section 172.

- **1986, Tax Reform Act of 1986 (P.L. 99-514)**

P.L. 99-514, § 632(a):

Amended Code Sec. 1374. **Effective** to (1) any distribution in complete liquidation, and any sale or exchange, made by a corporation after 7-31-86, unless such corporation is completely liquidated before 1-1-87, (2) any transaction described in section 338 of the Internal Revenue Code of 1986 for which the acquisition date occurs after 12-31-86, and (3) any distribution (not in complete liquidation) made after 12-31-86. For special and transitional rules, see Act Sec. 633(b)-(f) following Code Sec. 26. Prior to amendment, Code Sec. 1374 read as follows:

SEC. 1374. TAX IMPOSED ON CERTAIN CAPITAL GAINS.

[Sec. 1374(a)]

(a) GENERAL RULE.—If for a taxable year of an S corporation—

(1) the net capital gain of such corporation exceeds $25,000, and exceeds 50 percent of its taxable income for such year, and

(2) the taxable income of such corporation for such year exceeds $25,000,

There is hereby imposed a tax (computed under subsection (b)) on the income of such corporation.

[Sec. 1374(b)]

(b) AMOUNT OF TAX.—The tax imposed by subsection (a) shall be the lower of—

(1) an amount equal to the tax, determined as provided in section 1201(a), on the amount by which the net capital gain of the corporation for the taxable year exceeds $25,000, or

(2) an amount equal to the tax which would be imposed by section 11 on the taxable income of the corporation for the taxable year if the corporation were not an S corporation.

No credit shall be allowable under part IV of subchapter A of this chapter (other than under section 34) against the tax imposed by subsection (a).

Amendments
- **1984, Deficit Reduction Act of 1984 (P.L. 98-369)**

P.L. 98-369, § 474(r)(27):

Amended Code Sec. 1374(b) by striking out "section 39" and inserting in lieu thereof "section 34". **Effective** for tax years beginning after 12-31-83, and to carrybacks from such years.

[Sec. 1374(c)]

(c) EXCEPTIONS.—

(1) IN GENERAL.—Subsection (a) shall not apply to an S corporation for any taxable year if the election under section 1362(a) which is in effect with respect to such corporation for such taxable year has been in effect for the 3 immediately preceding taxable years.

(2) NEW CORPORATIONS.—Subsection (a) shall not apply to an S corporation if—

(A) it has been in existence for less than 4 taxable years, and

(B) an election under section 1362(a) has been in effect with respect to such corporation for each of its taxable years.

To the extent provided in regulations, an S corporation and any predecessor corporation shall be treated as 1 corporation for purposes of this paragraph and paragraph (1).

(3) PROPERTY WITH SUBSTITUTED BASIS.—If—

(A) but for paragraph (1) or (2), subsection (a) would apply for the taxable year,

(B) any long-term capital gain is attributable to property acquired by the S corporation during the period beginning 3 years before the first day of the taxable year and ending on the last day of the taxable year, and

(C) the basis of such property is determined in whole or in part by reference to the basis of any property in the hands of another corporation which was not an S corporation throughout all of the period described in subparagraph (B) before the transfer by such other corporation and during which such other corporation was in existence,

then subsection (a) shall apply for the taxable year, but the amount of the tax determined under subsection (b) shall not exceed a tax, determined as provided in section 1201(a), on the net capital gain attributable to property acquired as described in subparagraph (B) and having a basis described in subparagraph (C).

(4) TREATMENT OF CERTAIN GAINS OF OPTIONS AND COMMODITIES DEALERS.—

(A) EXCLUSION OF CERTAIN CAPITAL GAINS.—For purposes of this section, the net capital gain of any options dealer or commodities dealer shall be determined by not taking into account any gain or loss (in the normal course of the taxpayer's activity of dealing in or trading section 1256 contracts) from any section 1256 contract or property related to such a contract.

(B) DEFINITIONS.—For purposes of this paragraph—

(i) OPTIONS DEALER.—The term "options dealer" has the meaning given to such term by section 1256(g)(8).

(ii) COMMODITIES DEALER.—The term "commodities dealer" means a person who is actively engaged in trading section 1256 contracts and is registered with a domestic board of trade which is designated as a contract market by the Commodities Futures Trading Commission.

(iii) SECTION 1256 CONTRACTS.—The term "section 1256 contracts" has the meaning given to such term by section 1256(b).

Amendments
- **1984, Deficit Reduction Act of 1984 (P.L. 98-369)**

P.L. 98-369, § 102(d)(1):

Amended Code Sec. 1374(c) by adding paragraph (4). **Effective** for positions established after 7-18-84, in tax years ending after such date.

P.L. 98-369, § 721(u):

Amended Code Sec. 1374(c)(2) by striking out "(and any predecessor corporation)" in subparagraph (A) and by adding the sentence at the end thereof. **Effective** as if included in P.L. 97-354.

[Sec. 1374(d)]

(d) DETERMINATION OF TAXABLE INCOME.—For purposes of this section, taxable income of the corporation shall be determined under section 63(a) without regard to—

(1) the deduction allowed by section 172 (relating to net operating loss deduction), and

(2) the deductions allowed by part VIII of subchapter B (other than the deduction allowed by section 248, relating to organization expenditures).

Amendments
- **1983, Technical Corrections Act of 1982 (P.L. 97-448)**

P.L. 97-448, § 305(d)(3):

Amended Code Sec. 1374(d) by striking out "subsections (a)(2) and (b)(2)" and inserting in lieu thereof "this section". **Effective** 10-19-82.

- **1982, Subchapter S Revision Act of 1982 (P.L. 97-354)**

P.L. 97-354, § 2:

Amended Code Sec. 1374. **Effective**, generally, for tax years beginning after 12-31-82. See, however, the amendment note for Act Sec. 6(c)(2)-(4) following Code Sec. 1361 for special rules and exceptions applicable to certain casualty insurance companies and qualified oil corporations. Prior to amendment, Code Sec. 1374 read as follows:

SEC. 1374. CORPORATION NET OPERATING LOSS ALLOWED TO SHAREHOLDERS.

[Sec. 1374(a)]

(a) GENERAL RULE.—A net operating loss of an electing small business corporation for any taxable year shall be allowed as a deduction from gross income of the shareholders of such corporation in the manner and to the extent set forth in this section.

[Sec. 1374(b)]

(b) ALLOWANCE OF DEDUCTION.—Each person who is a shareholder of an electing small business corporation at any time during a taxable year of the corporation in which it has a net operating loss shall be allowed as a deduction from gross income, for his taxable year in which or with which the taxable year of the corporation ends (or for the final taxable year of a shareholder who dies before the end of the corporation's taxable year), an amount equal to his portion of the corporation's net operating loss (as determined under subsection (c)). The deduction allowed by this subsection shall, for purposes of this chapter, be considered as a deduction attributable to a trade or business carried on by the shareholder.

Amendments
- **1976, Tax Reform Act of 1976 (P.L. 94-455)**

P.L. 94-455, § 1901(a)(150)(A):

Added the last sentence beginning "The deduction allowed by this subsection shall," to Code Sec. 1374(b). **Effective** with respect to tax years beginning after 12-31-76.

- **1962, Revenue Act of 1962 (P.L. 87-834)**

P.L. 87-834, § 30:

Changed Code Sec. 1374(b) to apply retroactively to 9-2-58.

Sec. 1374(d)(9)

INCOME TAX—SPECIAL RULES

• 1959 (P.L. 86-376)

P.L. 86-376, §2(b):

Inserted "(or for the final taxable year of a shareholder who dies before the end of the corporation's taxable year)" after "the taxable year of the corporation ends" in Code Sec. 1374(b). **Effective** 9-24-59.

[Sec. 1374(c)]

(c) DETERMINATION OF SHAREHOLDER'S PORTION.—

(1) IN GENERAL.—For purposes of this section, a shareholder's portion of the net operating loss of an electing small business corporation is his pro rata share of the corporation's net operating loss (computed as provided in section 172(c), except that the deductions provided in part VIII (except section 248) of subchapter B shall not be allowed) for his taxable year in which or with which the taxable year of the corporation ends. For purposes of this paragraph, a shareholder's pro rata share of the corporation's net operating loss is the sum of the portions of the corporation's daily net operating loss attributable on a pro rata basis to the shares held by him on each day of the taxable year. For purposes of the preceding sentence, the corporation's daily net operating loss is the corporation's net operating loss divided by the number of days in the taxable year.

(2) LIMITATION.—A shareholder's portion of the net operating loss of an electing small business corporation for any taxable year shall not exceed the sum of—

(A) the adjusted basis (determined without regard to any adjustment under section 1376 for the taxable year) of the shareholder's stock in the electing small business corporation, determined as of the close of the taxable year of the corporation, (or, in respect of stock sold or otherwise disposed of during such taxable year, as of the day before the day of such sale or other disposition), and

(B) the adjusted basis (determined without regard to any adjustment under section 1376 for the taxable year) of any indebtedness of the corporation to the shareholder, determined as of the close of the taxable year of the corporation (or, if the shareholder is not a shareholder as of the close of such taxable year, as of the close of the last day in such taxable year on which the shareholder was a shareholder in the corporation).

[Sec. 1374(d)—Repealed]

• 1976, Tax Reform Act of 1976 (P.L. 94-455)

P.L. 94-455, §1901(a)(150)(B):

Repealed Code Sec. 1374(d). **Effective** with respect to tax years beginning after 12-31-76. Prior to repeal, Code Sec. 1374(d) read as follows:

(d) APPLICATION WITH OTHER PROVISIONS.—

(1) IN GENERAL.—The deduction allowed by subsection (b) shall, for purposes of this chapter, be considered as a deduction attributable to a trade or business carried on by the shareholder.

(2) ADJUSTMENT OF NET OPERATING LOSS CARRYBACKS AND CARRYOVERS OF SHAREHOLDERS.—

For purposes of determining, under section 172, the net operating loss carrybacks to taxable years beginning before January 1, 1958, from a taxable year of the shareholder for which he is allowed a deduction under subsection (b), such deduction shall be disregarded in determining the net operating loss for such taxable year. In the case of a net operating loss for a taxable year in which a shareholder is allowed a deduction under subsection (b), the determination of the portion of such loss which may be carried to subsequent years shall be made without regard to the preceding sentence and in accordance with section 172(b)(2), but the sum of the taxable incomes for taxable years beginning before January 1, 1958, shall be deemed not to exceed the amount of the net operating loss determined with the application of the preceding sentence.

• 1958, Technical Amendments Act of 1958 (P.L. 85-866)

P.L. 85-866, §64(a):

Added Code Sec. 1374. **Effective** for tax years beginning after 12-31-57.

[Sec. 1374(e)]

(e) REGULATIONS.—The Secretary shall prescribe such regulations as may be necessary to carry out the purposes of this section including regulations providing for the appropriate treatment of successor corporations.

Amendments

• 1988, Technical and Miscellaneous Revenue Act of 1988 (P.L. 100-647)

P.L. 100-647, §1006(f)(5)(A):

Amended Code Sec. 1374 by adding at the end thereof new subsection (e). **Effective** as if included in the provision of P.L. 99-514 to which it relates.

[Sec. 1375]

SEC. 1375. TAX IMPOSED WHEN PASSIVE INVESTMENT INCOME OF CORPORATION HAVING ACCUMULATED EARNINGS AND PROFITS EXCEEDS 25 PERCENT OF GROSS RECEIPTS.

[Sec. 1375(a)]

(a) GENERAL RULE.—If for the taxable year an S corporation has—

(1) accumulated earnings and profits at the close of such taxable year, and

(2) gross receipts more than 25 percent of which are passive investment income,

then there is hereby imposed a tax on the income of such corporation for such taxable year. Such tax shall be computed by multiplying the excess net passive income by the highest rate of tax specified in section 11(b).

Amendments

• 1996, Small Business Job Protection Act of 1996 (P.L. 104-188)

P.L. 104-188, §1311(b)(2)(A):

Amended Code Sec. 1375(a)(1) by striking "subchapter C" and inserting "accumulated". **Effective** for tax years beginning after 12-31-96.

P.L. 104-188, §1311(b)(2)(C):

Amended Code Sec. 1375 by striking "**SUBCHAPTER C**" and inserting "**ACCUMULATED**" in the section heading. **Effective** for tax years beginning after 12-31-96.

[Sec. 1375(b)]

(b) DEFINITIONS.—For purposes of this section—

(1) EXCESS NET PASSIVE INCOME.—

(A) IN GENERAL.—Except as provided in subparagraph (B), the term "excess net passive income" means an amount which bears the same ratio to the net passive income for the taxable year as—

(i) the amount by which the passive investment income for the taxable year exceeds 25 percent of the gross receipts for the taxable year, bears to

(ii) the passive investment income for the taxable year.

(B) LIMITATION.—The amount of the excess net passive income for any taxable year shall not exceed the amount of the corporation's taxable income for such taxable year as determined under section 63(a)—

(i) without regard to the deductions allowed by part VIII of subchapter B (other than the deduction allowed by section 248, relating to organization expenditures), and

(ii) without regard to the deduction under section 172.

(2) NET PASSIVE INCOME.—The term "net passive income" means—

(A) passive investment income, reduced by

(B) the deductions allowable under this chapter which are directly connected with the production of such income (other than deductions allowable under section 172 and part VIII of subchapter B).

(3) PASSIVE INVESTMENT INCOME, ETC.—The terms "passive investment income" and "gross receipts" have the same respective meanings as when used in paragraph (3) of section 1362(d).

(4) COORDINATION WITH SECTION 1374.—Notwithstanding paragraph (3), the amount of passive investment income shall be determined by not taking into account any recognized built-in gain or loss of the S corporation for any taxable year in the recognition period. Terms used in the preceding sentence shall have the same respective meanings as when used in section 1374.

INCOME TAX—SPECIAL RULES

Amendments

- **1996, Small Business Job Protection Act of 1996 (P.L. 104-188)**

P.L. 104-188, §1311(b)(2)(B):

Amended Code Sec. 1375(b)(3). **Effective** for tax years beginning after 12-31-96. Prior to amendment, Code Sec. 1375(b)(3) read as follows:

(3) PASSIVE INVESTMENT INCOME; ETC.—The terms "subchapter C earnings and profits", "passive investment income", and "gross receipts" shall have the same respective meanings as when used in paragraph (3) of section 1362(d).

- **1988, Technical and Miscellaneous Revenue Act of 1988 (P.L. 100-647)**

P.L. 100-647, §1006(f)(5)(B):

Amended Code Sec. 1375(b)(1)(B). **Effective** as if included in the provision of P.L. 99-514 to which it relates. Prior to amendment, Code Sec. 1375(b)(1)(B) read as follows:

(B) LIMITATION.—The amount of the excess net passive income for any taxable year shall not exceed the corporation's taxable income for the taxable year (determined in accordance with section 1374(d)(4)).

P.L. 100-647, §1006(f)(5)(C):

Amended Code Sec. 1375(b) by adding at the end thereof new paragraph (4). **Effective** as if included in the provision of P.L. 99-514 to which it relates.

- **1986, Tax Reform Act of 1986 (P.L. 99-514)**

P.L. 99-514, §632(c)(3):

Amended Code Sec. 1375(b)(1)(B) by striking out "section 1374(d)" and inserting in lieu thereof "section 1374(d)(4)". **Effective**, generally, for (1) any distribution in complete liquidation, and any sale or exchange, made by a corporation after 7-31-86, unless such corporation is completely liquidated before 1-1-87, (2) any transaction described in section 338 of the Internal Revenue Code of 1986 for which the acquisition date occurs after 12-31-86, and (3) any distribution (not in complete liquidation) made after 12-31-86. For special rules, see Act Sec. 633(b)-(f) following Code Sec. 26.

[Sec. 1375(c)]

(c) CREDITS NOT ALLOWABLE.—No credit shall be allowed under part IV of subchapter A of this chapter (other than section 34) against the tax imposed by subsection (a).

Amendments

- **1988, Technical and Miscellaneous Revenue Act of 1988 (P.L. 100-647)**

P.L. 100-647, §1006(f)(5)(D):

Amended Code Sec. 1375(c). **Effective** as if included in the provision of P.L. 99-514 to which it relates. Prior to amendment, Code Sec. 1375(c) read as follows:

(c) SPECIAL RULES.—

(1) DISALLOWANCE OF CREDIT.—No credit shall be allowed under part IV of subchapter A of this chapter (other than section 34) against the tax imposed by subsection (a).

(2) COORDINATION WITH SECTION 1374.—If any gain—

(A) is taken into account in determining passive income for purposes of this section, and

(B) is taken into account under section 1374,

the amount of such gain taken into account under section 1374 shall be reduced by the portion of the excess net passive income for the taxable year which is attributable (on a pro rata basis) to such gain.

- **1984, Deficit Reduction Act of 1984 (P.L. 98-369)**

P.L. 98-369, §474(r)(28):

Amended Code Sec. 1375(c)(1) by striking out "section 39" and inserting in lieu thereof "section 34". **Effective** for tax years beginning after 12-31-83, and to carrybacks from such years.

- **1982, Subchapter S Revision Act of 1982 (P.L. 97-354)**

P.L. 97-354, §2:

Amended Code Sec. 1375. **Effective**, generally, for tax years beginning after 12-31-81. See, however, the amendment notes for Act Sec. 6(c)(2)-(4) following Code Sec. 1361 for special rules and exceptions pertaining to certain casualty insurance companies and qualified oil corporations. See, also, Act Sec. 6(b)(3), following Code Sec. 1362, for a special rule affecting Code Sec. 1375. Prior to amendment, Code Sec. 1375 read as follows:

SEC. 1375. SPECIAL RULES APPLICABLE TO DISTRIBUTIONS OF ELECTING SMALL BUSINESS CORPORATIONS.

[Sec. 1375(a)]

(a) CAPITAL GAINS.—

(1) TREATMENT IN HANDS OF SHAREHOLDERS.—The amount includible in the gross income of a shareholder as dividends (including amounts treated as dividends under section 1373(b)) from an electing small business corporation during any taxable year of the corporation, to the extent that such amount is a distribution of property out of earnings and profits of the taxable year as specified in section 316(a)(2), shall be treated as a longterm capital gain to the extent of the shareholder's pro rata share of the corporation's net capital gain for such taxable year. For purposes of this paragraph, such net capital gain shall be deemed not to exceed the corporation's taxable income (computed as provided in section 1373(d)) for the taxable year.

(2) DETERMINATION OF SHAREHOLDER'S PRO RATA SHARE.—A shareholder's pro rata share of such gain for any taxable year shall be an amount which bears the same ratio to such gain as the amount of dividends described in paragraph (1) includible in the shareholder's gross income bears to the entire amount of dividends described in paragraph (1) includible in the gross income of all shareholders.

(3) REDUCTION FOR TAXES IMPOSED.—For purposes of paragraphs (1) and (2), an electing small business corporation's net capital gain for a taxable year shall be reduced by an amount equal to the amount of the taxes imposed by sections 56 and 1378(a) on such corporation for such year.

Amendments

- **1978, Revenue Act of 1978 (P.L. 95-600)**

P.L. 95-600, §703(j)(6):

Amended Code Sec. 1375(a)(2) by striking out "such excess" each place it appeared and inserting in lieu thereof "such gain". **Effective** 10-4-76.

- **1976, Tax Reform Act of 1976 (P.L. 94-455)**

P.L. 94-455, §1901(b)(33)(Q)(i):

Substituted "the corporation's net capital gain" for "the excess of the corporation's net long-term capital gain over its net short-term capital loss" in Code Sec. 1375(a)(1). **Effective** with respect to tax years beginning after 12-31-76.

P.L. 94-455, §1901(b)(33)(Q)(ii):

Substituted "such net capital gain" for "such excess" in the second sentence of Code Sec. 1375(a)(1). **Effective** with respect to tax years beginning after 12-31-76.

P.L. 94-455, §1901(b)(33)(Q)(iii):

Substituted "an electing small business corporation's net capital gain" for "the excess of an electing small business corporation's net long-term capital gain over its net short-term capital loss" in Code Sec. 1375(a)(3). **Effective** with respect to tax years beginning after 12-31-76.

- **1969, Tax Reform Act of 1969 (P.L. 91-172)**

P.L. 91-172, §301(b)(11):

Amended Code Sec. 1375(a)(3) by substituting as the heading "Reduction for Taxes Imposed" for "Reduction for Tax Imposed by Section 1378," and by further substituting the phrase "taxes imposed by sections 56 and 1378(a) on" for the phrase "tax imposed by section 1378(a) on the income of".

- **1966 (P.L. 89-389)**

P.L. 89-389, §2(b):

Added Code Sec. 1375(a)(3). **Effective** with respect to tax years of electing small business corporations beginning after 4-14-66, but not with respect to sales or exchanges occurring before 2-24-66.

[Sec. 1375(b)]

(b) DIVIDENDS NOT TREATED AS SUCH FOR CERTAIN PURPOSES.—The amount includible in the gross income of a shareholder as dividends from an electing small business corporation during any taxable year of the corporation (including any amount treated as a dividend under section 1373(b)) shall not be considered a dividend for purposes of section 37 or section 116 to the extent that such amount is a distribution of property out of earnings and profits of the taxable year as specified in section 316(a)(2). For purposes of this subsection, the earnings and profits of the taxable year shall be deemed not to exceed the corporation's taxable income (computed as provided in section 1373(d)) for the taxable year.

Amendments

- **1976, Tax Reform Act of 1976 (P.L. 94-455)**

P.L. 94-455, §1901(a)(151)(A):

Substituted "Not Treated as Such for Certain Purposes" for "Received Credit Not Allowed" in the heading of Code Sec. 1375(b). **Effective** with respect to tax years beginning after 12-31-76.

- **1964, Revenue Act of 1964 (P.L. 88-272)**

P.L. 88-272, §201(d)(13):

Amended Code Sec. 1375(b) by deleting "section 34," and the comma following "section 37". **Effective** with respect to dividends received after 12-31-64, in tax years ending after such date.

[Sec. 1375(c)]

(c) TREATMENT OF FAMILY GROUPS.—Any dividend received by a shareholder from an electing small business corporation (including any amount treated as a dividend under section 1373(b)) may be apportioned or allocated by the Secretary between or among shareholders of such corporation who are members of such shareholder's family (as defined in section 704(e)(3)), if he determines that such apportionment or allocation is necessary in order to reflect the value of services rendered to the corporation by such shareholders.

[Sec. 1375(d)]

(d) DISTRIBUTIONS OF UNDISTRIBUTED TAXABLE INCOME PREVIOUSLY TAXED TO SHAREHOLDERS.—

(1) DISTRIBUTIONS NOT CONSIDERED AS DIVIDENDS.—An electing small business corporation may distribute, in accordance with regulations prescribed by the Secretary, to any shareholder all or any portion of the shareholder's net share of the corporation's undistributed taxable income for taxable years prior to the taxable year in which such distribution is made. Any such distribution shall, for purposes of this chapter, be considered a distribution which is not a dividend, but the earnings and profits of the corporation shall not be reduced by reason of any such distribution.

(2) SHAREHOLDER'S NET SHARE OF UNDISTRIBUTED TAXABLE INCOME.—For purposes of this subsection, a shareholder's net share of the undistributed taxable income of an electing small business corporation is an amount equal to—

(A) the sum of the amounts included in the gross income of the shareholder under section 1373(b) for all prior taxable years (excluding any taxable year to which the provisions of this section do not apply and all taxable years preceding such year), reduced by

(B) the sum of—

(i) the amounts allowable under section 1374(b) as a deduction from gross income of the shareholder for all prior taxable years (excluding any taxable year to which the provisions of this section do not apply and all taxable years preceding such year), and

(ii) all amounts previously distributed during the taxable year and all prior taxable years (excluding any taxable year to which the provisions of this section do not apply and all taxable years preceding such year) to the shareholder which under subsection (f) or paragraph (1) of this subsection were considered distributions which were not dividends.

Amendments

- **1976, Tax Reform Act of 1976 (P.L. 94-455)**

P.L. 94-455, § 1906(b)(13)(A):

Amended 1954 Code by substituting "Secretary" for "Secretary or his delegate" each place it appeared. **Effective** 2-1-77.

[Sec. 1375(e)—Repealed]

Amendments

- **1966 (P.L. 89-389)**

P.L. 89-389, § [1(a)]:

Repealed Sec. 1375(e) which read as follows:

(e) Certain Distributions After Close of Taxable Year.—

(1) In general.—For purposes of this chapter, if—

(A) a corporation makes a distribution of money to its shareholders on or before the 15th day of the third month following the close of a taxable year with respect to which it was an electing small business corporation, and

(B) such distribution is made pursuant to a resolution of the board of directors of the corporation, adopted before the close of such taxable year, to distribute to its shareholders all or a part of the proceeds of one or more sales of capital assets, or of property described in section 1231(b), made during such taxable year,

such distribution shall, at the election of the corporation, be treated as a distribution of money made on the last day of such taxable year.

(2) Shareholders.—An election under paragraph (1) with respect to any distribution may be made by a corporation only if each person who is a shareholder on the day the distribution is received—

(A) owns the same proportion of the stock of the corporation on such day as he owned on the last day of the taxable year of the corporation preceding the distribution, and

(B) consents to such election at such time and in such manner as the Secretary or his delegate shall prescribe by regulations.

(3) Manner and time of election.—An election under paragraph (1) shall be made in such manner as the Secretary or his delegate shall prescribe by regulations. Such election shall be made not later than the time prescribed by law for filing the return for the taxable year during which the sale was made (including extensions thereof) except that, with respect to any taxable year ending on or before the date of the enactment of the Revenue Act of 1964, such election shall be made within 120 days after such date.

- **1964, Revenue Act of 1964 (P.L. 88-272)**

P.L. 88-272, § 233(b):

Amended Code Sec. 1375 to add subdivision "(e)." **Effective** for tax years of corporations beginning 12-31-57.

[Sec. 1375(f)]

(f) DISTRIBUTIONS WITHIN 2½-MONTH PERIOD AFTER CLOSE OF TAXABLE YEAR.—

(1) DISTRIBUTIONS CONSIDERED AS DISTRIBUTIONS OF UNDISTRIBUTED TAXABLE INCOME.—Any distribution of money made by a corporation after the close of a taxable year with respect to which it was an electing small business corporation and on or before the 15th day of the third month following the close of such taxable year to a person who was a shareholder of such corporation at the close of such taxable year shall be treated as a distribution of the corporation's undistributed taxable income for such year, to the extent such distribution (when added to the sum of all prior distributions of money made to such person by such corporation following the close of such year) does not exceed such person's share of the corporation's undistributed taxable income for such year. Any distribution so treated shall, for purposes of this chapter, be considered a distribution which is not a dividend, and the earnings and profits of the corporation shall not be reduced by reason of such distribution.

(2) SHARE OF UNDISTRIBUTED TAXABLE INCOME.—For purposes of paragraph (1), a person's share of a corporation's undistributed taxable income for a taxable year is the amount required to be included in his gross income under section 1373(b) as a shareholder of such corporation for his taxable year in which or with which the taxable year of the corporation ends.

Amendments

- **1976, Tax Reform Act of 1976 (P.L. 94-455)**

P.L. 94-455, § 1901(a)(151)(B):

Repealed Code Sec. 1375(f)(3). **Effective** with respect to tax years beginning after 12-31-76. Prior to repeal Code Sec. 1375(f)(3) read as follows:

(3) ELECTION UNDER SUBSECTION (e)—Paragraph (1) shall not apply to any distribution with respect to which an election under subsection (e) applies.

- **1966 (P.L. 89-389)**

P.L. 89-389, § [1(a)]:

Added new Code Sec. 1375(f) and amended Code Sec. 1375(d)(2)(B)(ii) by substituting "under subsection (f) or paragraph (1) of this subsection" for "under paragraph (1)". **Effective**, generally, only with respect to distributions made after 4-14-66, the date of enactment. However, § [1(d)] provides special rules for the application of new Code Sec. 1375(f) and the conforming amendment of Code Sec. 1375(d)(2)(B)(ii). These special rules of § [1(d)] are reproduced below:

"(d)(1) The amendments made by subsections (a)(1) and (b) shall also apply with respect to distributions of money (other than distributions with respect to which an election under section 1375(e) of the Internal Revenue Code of 1954 applies) made by a corporation on or before the date of the enactment of this Act and on or after the date of the first distribution of money during the taxable year designated by the corporation if—

"(A) such corporation elects to have such amendments apply to all such distributions made by it, and

"(B) except as otherwise provided by this subsection, all persons (or their personal representatives) who were shareholders of such corporation at any time on or after the date of such first distribution and before the date on which the corporation files the election with the Secretary of the Treasury or his delegate consent to such election and to the application of this subsection.

"(2) An election by a corporation under this subsection, and the consent thereto of the persons who are or were shareholders of such corporation, shall be made in such manner and within such time as the Secretary of the Treasury or his delegate prescribes by regulations, but the period for making such election shall not expire before one year after the date on which the regulations prescribed under this subsection are published in the Federal Register.

"(3) In applying paragraphs (1) and (2), the consent of a person (or his personal representative) shall not be required if, under regulations prescribed under this subsection, it is shown to the satisfaction of the Secretary of the Treasury or his delegate that the liability of such person for Federal income tax for any taxable year cannot be affected by the election of the corporation of which he is or was a shareholder.

"(4) In applying this subsection, the reference in section 1375(f) of the Internal Revenue Code of 1954 (as added by subsection (a)(1)) to the 15th day of the third month following the close of the taxable year shall be treated as referring to the 15th day of the fourth month following the close of the taxable year.

"(5) The statutory period for the assessment of any deficiency for any taxable year against the corporation filing the election or any person consenting thereto, to the extent such deficiency is attributable to an election under this subsection, shall not expire before the last day of the 2-year period beginning on the date on which the regulations prescribed under this subsection are published in the Federal Register; and such deficiency may be assessed at any time before the expiration of such 2-year period, notwithstanding any law or rule of law which would otherwise prevent such assessment.

"(6) If—

"(A) credit or refund of the amount of any overpayment for any taxable year attributable to an election under this subsection is not prevented, on the date of the enactment of this Act, by the operation of any law or rule of law, and

"(B) credit or refund of the amount of such overpayment is prevented, by the operation of any law or rule of law (other than chapter 74 of the Internal Revenue Code of 1954, relating to closing agreements and compromises), at any time on or before the expiration of the 2-year period beginning on the date on which the regulations prescribed under this subsection are published in the Federal Register, credit or refund of such overpayment may, nevertheless, be allowed or made, to the extent such overpayment is attributable to such election, if claim therefor is filed before the expiration of such 2-year period.

"(7) If—

"(A)(i) one or more consecutive distributions of money made by the corporation after the close of a taxable year and on or before the 15th day of the fourth month following the close of the taxable year were substantially the same in amount as the undistributed taxable income of such corporation for such year, or

"(ii) it is established to the satisfaction of the Secretary of the Treasury or his delegate that one or more distributions of money made by the corporation during the period described in clause (i) were intended to be distributions of the undistributed taxable income of such corporation for the taxable year preceding such period, and

"(B) credit or refund of the amount of any overpayment for the taxable year in which such distribution or distributions were received is prevented on the date of enactment of this Act, by the operation of any law or rule of law (other than chapter 74 of the Internal Revenue Code of 1954, relating to closing agreements and compromises),

credit or refund of such overpayment may, nevertheless, be allowed or made, to the extent such overpayment is attributable to an election under this subsection, if claim therefor is filed before the expiration of the 2-year period beginning on the date on which the regulations prescribed under this subsection are published in the Federal Register.

"(8) No interest on any deficiency attributable to an election under this subsection shall be assessed or collected for any period before the expiration of the 2-year period beginning on the date on which the regulations prescribed under this subsection are published in the Federal Register. No interest on any overpayment attributable to an election under this subsection shall be allowed or paid for any period before the expiration of such 2-year period."

- **1958, Technical Amendments Act of 1958 (P.L. 85-866)**

P.L. 85-866, § 64(a):

Added Code Sec. 1375. **Effective** for tax years beginning after 12-31-57.

[Sec. 1375(d)]

(d) WAIVER OF TAX IN CERTAIN CASES.—If the S corporation establishes to the satisfaction of the Secretary that—

(1) it determined in good faith that it had no accumulated earnings and profits at the close of a taxable year, and

INCOME TAX—DEFINITIONS; MISCELLANEOUS

(2) during a reasonable period of time after it was determined that it did have accumulated earnings and profits at the close of such taxable year such earnings and profits were distributed,

the Secretary may waive the tax imposed by subsection (a) for such taxable year.

Amendments

• **2005, Gulf Opportunity Zone Act of 2005 (P.L. 109-135)**

P.L. 109-135, §412(qq):

Amended Code Sec. 1375(d)(1) and (2) by striking "subchapter C" and inserting "accumulated". **Effective** 12-21-2005.

• **1984, Deficit Reduction Act of 1984 (P.L. 98-369)**

P.L. 98-369, §721(v):

Amended Code Sec. 1375 by adding new subsection (d). **Effective** as if included in P.L. 97-354.

[Sec. 1376—Repealed]

Amendments

• **1982, Subchapter S Revision Act of 1982 (P.L. 97-354)**

P.L. 97-354, §2:

Repealed Code Sec. 1376. **Effective**, generally, for tax years beginning after 12-31-82. See, however, the amendment note for Act Sec. 6(c)(2)-(4) following Code Sec. 1361 for special rules and exceptions applicable to certain casualty insurance companies and qualified oil corporations. Prior to repeal, Code Sec. 1376 read as follows:

SEC. 1376. ADJUSTMENT TO BASIS OF STOCK OF, AND INDEBTEDNESS OWING, SHAREHOLDERS.

(a) INCREASE IN BASIS OF STOCK FOR AMOUNTS TREATED AS DIVIDENDS.—The basis of a shareholder's stock in an electing small business corporation shall be increased by the amount required to be included in the gross income of such shareholder under section 1373(b), but only to the extent to which such amount is included in his gross income in his return, increased or decreased by any adjustment of such amount in any redetermination of the shareholder's tax liability.

(b) REDUCTION IN BASIS OF STOCK AND INDEBTEDNESS FOR SHAREHOLDER'S PORTION OF CORPORATION NET OPERATING LOSS.—

(1) REDUCTION IN BASIS OF STOCK.—The basis of a shareholder's stock in an electing small business corporation shall be reduced (but not below zero) by an amount equal to the amount of his portion of the corporation's net operating loss for any taxable year attributable to such stock (as determined under section 1374(c)).

(2) REDUCTION IN BASIS OF INDEBTEDNESS.—The basis of any indebtedness of an electing small business corporation to a shareholder of such corporation shall be reduced (but not below zero) by an amount equal to the amount of the shareholder's portion of the corporation's net operating loss for any taxable year (as determined under section 1374(c)), but only to the extent that such amount exceeds the adjusted basis of the stock of such corporation held by the shareholder.

• **1958, Technical Amendments Act of 1958 (P.L. 85-866)**

P.L. 85-866, §64(a):

Added Sec. 1376. **Effective** for tax years beginning after 12-31-57.

PART IV—DEFINITIONS; MISCELLANEOUS

Sec. 1377.   Definitions and special rule.
Sec. 1378.   Taxable year of S corporation.
Sec. 1379.   Transitional rules on enactment.

[Sec. 1377]

SEC. 1377. DEFINITIONS AND SPECIAL RULE.

[Sec. 1377(a)]

(a) PRO RATA SHARE.—For purposes of this subchapter—

(1) IN GENERAL.—Except as provided in paragraph (2), each shareholder's pro rata share of any item for any taxable year shall be the sum of the amounts determined with respect to the shareholder—

(A) by assigning an equal portion of such item to each day of the taxable year, and

(B) then by dividing that portion pro rata among the shares outstanding on such day.

(2) ELECTION TO TERMINATE YEAR.—

(A) IN GENERAL.—Under regulations prescribed by the Secretary, if any shareholder terminates the shareholder's interest in the corporation during the taxable year and all affected shareholders and the corporation agree to the application of this paragraph, paragraph (1) shall be applied to the affected shareholders as if the taxable year consisted of 2 taxable years the first of which ends on the date of the termination.

(B) AFFECTED SHAREHOLDERS.—For purposes of subparagraph (A), the term "affected shareholders" means the shareholder whose interest is terminated and all shareholders to whom such shareholder has transferred shares during the taxable year. If such shareholder has transferred shares to the corporation, the term "affected shareholders" shall include all persons who are shareholders during the taxable year.

Amendments

• **1996, Small Business Job Protection Act of 1996 (P.L. 104-188)**

P.L. 104-188, §1306:

Amended Code Sec. 1377(a)(2). **Effective** for tax years beginning after 12-31-96. Prior to amendment, Code Sec. 1377(a)(2) read as follows:

(2) ELECTION TO TERMINATE YEAR.—Under regulations prescribed by the Secretary, if any shareholder terminates his interest in the corporation during the taxable year and all persons who are shareholders during the taxable year agree to the application of this paragraph, paragraph (1) shall be applied as if the taxable year consisted of 2 taxable years the first of which ends on the date of the termination.

[Sec. 1377(b)]

(b) POST-TERMINATION TRANSITION PERIOD.—

(1) IN GENERAL.—For purposes of this subchapter, the term "post-termination transition period" means—

(A) the period beginning on the day after the last day of the corporation's last taxable year as an S corporation and ending on the later of—

(i) the day which is 1 year after such last day, or

(ii) the due date for filing the return for such last year as an S corporation (including extensions),

(B) the 120-day period beginning on the date of any determination pursuant to an audit of the taxpayer which follows the termination of the corporation's election and which adjusts a subchapter S item of income, loss, or deduction of the corporation arising during the S period (as defined in section 1368(e)(2)), and

(C) the 120-day period beginning on the date of a determination that the corporation's election under section 1362(a) had terminated for a previous taxable year.

(2) DETERMINATION DEFINED.—For purposes of paragraph (1), the term "determination" means—

(A) a determination as defined in section 1313(a), or

(B) an agreement between the corporation and the Secretary that the corporation failed to qualify as an S corporation.

(3) SPECIAL RULES FOR AUDIT RELATED POST-TERMINATION TRANSITION PERIODS.—

(A) NO APPLICATION TO CARRYOVERS.—Paragraph (1)(B) shall not apply for purposes of section 1366(d)(3).

INCOME TAX—DEFINITIONS; MISCELLANEOUS

(B) LIMITATION ON APPLICATION TO DISTRIBUTIONS.—Paragraph (1)(B) shall apply to a distribution described in section 1371(e) only to the extent that the amount of such distribution does not exceed the aggregate increase (if any) in the accumulated adjustments account (within the meaning of section 1368(e)) by reason of the adjustments referred to in such paragraph.

Amendments

• **2004, Working Families Tax Relief Act of 2004 (P.L. 108-311)**

P.L. 108-311, §407(a):

Amended Code Sec. 1377(b) by adding at the end a new paragraph (3). **Effective** as if included in the provision of the Small Business Job Protection Act of 1996 (P.L. 104-188) to which it relates [effective for determinations made after 12-31-96.—CCH].

• **1997, Taxpayer Relief Act of 1997 (P.L. 105-34)**

P.L. 105-34, §1601(c)(2)(B), provides:

(B) In no event shall the 120-day period referred to in section 1377(b)(1)(B) of the Internal Revenue Code of 1986 (as added by such section 1307) expire before the end of the 120-day period beginning on the date of the enactment of this Act.

• **1996, Small Business Job Protection Act of 1996 (P.L. 104-188)**

P.L. 104-188, §1307(a):

Amended Code Sec. 1377(b)(1) by striking "and" at the end of subparagraph (A), by redesignating subparagraph (B) as subparagraph (C), and by inserting after subparagraph (A) a new subparagraph (B). **Effective** for determinations made after 12-31-96 (effective date amended by P.L. 105-34, §1601(c)(2)(A); for a special rule, see Act Sec. 1601(c)(2)(B), above).

P.L. 104-188, §1307(b):

Amended Code Sec. 1377(b)(2) by striking subparagraphs (A) and (B), by redesignating subparagraph (C) as subparagraph (B) and by inserting before subparagraph (B) (as so redesignated) a new subparagraph (A). **Effective** for determinations made after 12-31-96 (effective date amended by P.L. 105-34, §1601(c)(2)(A); for a special rule, see Act Sec. 1601(c)(2)(B), above). Prior to amendment, Code Sec. 1377(b)(2)(A)-(B) read as follows:

(A) a court decision which becomes final,

(B) a closing agreement, or

[Sec. 1377(c)]

(c) MANNER OF MAKING ELECTIONS, ETC.—Any election under this subchapter, and any revocation under section 1362(d)(1), shall be made in such manner as the Secretary shall by regulations prescribe.

Amendments

• **1982, Subchapter S Revision Act of 1982 (P.L. 97-354)**

P.L. 97-354, §2:

Amended Code Sec. 1377. **Effective**, generally, for tax years beginning after 12-31-82. See, however, the amendment note for Act Sec. 6(c)(2)-(4) following Code Sec. 1361 for special rules and exceptions applicable to certain casualty insurance companies and qualified oil corporations. Prior to amendment, Code Sec. 1377 read as follows:

SEC. 1377. SPECIAL RULES APPLICABLE TO EARNINGS AND PROFITS OF ELECTING SMALL BUSINESS CORPORATIONS.

[Sec. 1377(a)]

(a) REDUCTION FOR UNDISTRIBUTED TAXABLE INCOME.—The accumulated earnings and profits of an electing small business corporation as of the close of its taxable year shall be reduced to the extent that its undistributed taxable income for such year is required to be included in the gross income of the shareholders of such corporation under section 1373(b).

[Sec. 1377(b)]

(b) CURRENT EARNINGS AND PROFITS NOT REDUCED BY ANY AMOUNT NOT ALLOWABLE AS DEDUCTION.—The earnings and profits of an electing small business corporation for any taxable year (but not its accumulated earnings and profits) shall not be reduced by any amount which is not allowable as a deduction in computing its taxable income (as provided in section 1373(d)) for such taxable year.

[Sec. 1377(c)]

(c) EARNINGS AND PROFITS NOT AFFECTED BY NET OPERATING LOSS.—The earnings and profits and the accumulated earnings and profits of an electing small business corporation shall not be affected by any item of gross income or any deduction taken into account in determining the amount of any net operating loss (computed as provided in section 1374(c)) of such corporation.

[Sec. 1377(d)]

(d) DISTRIBUTIONS OF UNDISTRIBUTED TAXABLE INCOME PREVIOUSLY TAXED TO SHAREHOLDERS.—For purposes of determining whether a distribution by an electing small business corporation constitutes a distribution of such corporation's undistributed taxable income previously taxed to shareholders (as provided for in section 1375(d)), the earnings and profits of such corporation for the taxable year in which the distribution is made shall be computed without regard to section 312(k). Such computation shall be made without regard to section 312(k) only for such purposes.

Amendments

• **1958, Technical Amendments Act of 1958 (P.L. 85-866)**

P.L. 85-866, §64(a):

Added Sec. 1377. **Effective** for tax years beginning after 12-31-57.

[Sec. 1378]

SEC. 1378. TAXABLE YEAR OF S CORPORATION.

[Sec. 1378(a)]

(a) GENERAL RULE.—For purposes of this subtitle, the taxable year of an S corporation shall be a permitted year.

Amendments

• **1986, Tax Reform Act of 1986 (P.L. 99-514)**

P.L. 99-514, §806(b)(1):

Amended Code Sec. 1378(a). **Effective**, generally, for tax years beginning after 12-31-86. However, for a rule regarding change in accounting period, see Act Sec. 806(e)(2) following Code Sec. 706. Prior to amendment, Code Sec. 1378(a) read as follows:

(a) GENERAL RULE.—For purposes of this subtitle—

(1) an S corporation shall not change its taxable year to any accounting period other than a permitted year, and

(2) no corporation may make an election under section 1362(a) for any taxable year unless such taxable year is a permitted year.

[Sec. 1378(b)]

(b) PERMITTED YEAR DEFINED.—For purposes of this section, the term "permitted year" means a taxable year which—

(1) is a year ending December 31, or

(2) is any other accounting period for which the corporation establishes a business purpose to the satisfaction of the Secretary.

For purposes of paragraph (2), any deferral of income to shareholders shall not be treated as a business purpose.

Amendments

• **1986, Tax Reform Act of 1986 (P.L. 99-514)**

P.L. 99-514, §806(b)(2):

Amended Code Sec. 1378(b) by adding at the end thereof a new flush sentence. **Effective**, generally, for tax years beginning after 12-31-86. However, for a rule regarding change in accounting period, see Act Sec. 806(e)(2) following Code Sec. 706.

[Sec. 1378(c)—Stricken]

Amendments

P.L. 99-514, §806(b)(3):

Amended Code Sec. 1378 by striking out subsection (c). **Effective**, generally, for tax years beginning after 12-31-86. However, for a rule regarding change in accounting period, see Act Sec. 806(e)(2) following Code Sec. 706. Prior to amendment, Code Sec. 1378(c) read as follows:

(c) EXISTING S CORPORATIONS REQUIRED TO USE PERMITTED YEAR AFTER 50-PERCENT SHIFT IN OWNERSHIP.—

(1) IN GENERAL.—A corporation which is an S corporation for a taxable year which includes December 31, 1982 (or which is an S corporation for a taxable year beginning during 1983 by reason of an election made on or before October 19, 1982), shall not be treated as an S corporation for any subsequent taxable year beginning after the first day on which more than 50 percent of the stock is newly owned stock unless such subsequent taxable year is a permitted year.

(2) NEWLY OWNED STOCK.—For purposes of paragraph (1), the stock held by any person on any day shall be treated as newly owned stock to the extent that—

(A) the percentage of the stock of such corporation owned by such person on such day, exceeds

(B) the percentage of the stock of such corporation owned by such person on December 31, 1982.

(3) STOCK ACQUIRED BY REASON OF DEATH, GIFT FROM FAMILY MEMBER, ETC.—

(A) IN GENERAL.—For purposes of paragraph (2), if—

(i) a person acquired stock in the corporation after December 31, 1982, and

INCOME TAX—DEFINITIONS; MISCELLANEOUS

(ii) such stock was acquired by such person—

(I) by reason of the death of a qualified transferor,

(II) by reason of a gift from a qualified transferor who is a member of such person's family, or

(III) by reason of a qualified buy-sell agreement from a qualified transferor (or his estate) who was a member of such person's family,

then such stock shall be treated as held on December 31, 1982, by the person described in clause (i).

(B) QUALIFIED TRANSFEROR.—For purposes of subparagraph (A), the term "qualified transferor" means a person—

(i) who (or whose estate) held the stock in the corporation (or predecessor stock) on December 31, 1982, or

(ii) who acquired the stock in an acquisition which meets the requirements of subparagraph (A).

(C) FAMILY.—For purposes of subparagraph (A), the term "family" has the meaning given such term by section 267(c)(4).

(D) QUALIFIED BUY-SELL AGREEMENT.—For purposes of subparagraph (A), the term "qualified buy-sell agreement" means any agreement which—

(i) has been continuously in existence since September 28, 1982, and

(ii) provides that on the death of any party to such agreement, the stock in the S corporation held by such party will be sold to surviving parties to such agreement who were parties to such agreement on September 28, 1982.

• **1984, Deficit Reduction Act of 1984 (P.L. 98-369)**

P.L. 98-369, §721(m):

Amended Code Sec. 1378(c)(1) by striking out "which includes December 31, 1982" and inserting in lieu thereof "which includes December 31, 1982 (or which is an S corporation for a taxable year beginning during 1983 by reason of an election made on or before October 19, 1982)". **Effective** as if included in P.L. 97-354.

P.L. 98-369, §721(q):

Amended Code Sec. 1378(c)(3)(B)(i) by striking out "who held" and inserting in lieu thereof "who (or whose estate) held". **Effective** as if included in P.L. 97-354.

• **1983, Technical Corrections Act of 1982 (P.L. 97-448)**

P.L. 97-448, §305(d)(1)(B) provides:

(B) If—

(i) after September 30, 1982, and on or before the date of the enactment of this Act, stock or securities were transferred to a small business corporation (as defined in section 1361(b) of the Internal Revenue Code of 1954 as amended by the Subchapter S Revision Act of 1982) in a transaction to which section 351 of such Code applies, and

(ii) such corporation is liquidated under section 333 of such Code before March 1, 1983,

then such stock or securities shall not be taken into account under section 333(e)(2) of such Code.

• **1982, Subchapter S Revision Act of 1982 (P.L. 97-354)**

P.L. 97-354, §2:

Amended Code Sec. 1378. **Effective**, generally, for tax years beginning after 12-31-82. See, however, the special rules and exceptions provided in Act Sec. 6(c)(2)-(4) following Code Sec. 1361 that are applicable to certain casualty insurance companies and qualified oil corporations. Prior to amendment, Code Sec. 1378 read as follows:

SEC. 1378. TAX IMPOSED ON CERTAIN CAPITAL GAINS.

[Sec. 1378(a)]

(a) GENERAL RULE.—If for a taxable year of an electing small business corporation—

(1) the net capital gain of such corporation exceeds $25,000, and exceeds 50 percent of its taxable income for such year, and

(2) the taxable income of such corporation for such year exceeds $25,000, there is hereby imposed a tax (computed under subsection (b)) on the income of such corporation.

Amendments

• **1982, Subchapter S Revision Act of 1982 (P.L. 97-354)**

P.L. 97-354, §6(f), as added by P.L. 97-448, §305(d)(1)(A), provides:

(f) TAXABLE YEAR OF S CORPORATIONS.—Section 1378 of the Internal Revenue Code of 1954 (as added by this Act) shall take effect on the day after the date of the enactment of this Act. For purposes of applying such section, the reference in subsection (a)(2) of such section to an election under section 1362(a) shall include a reference to an election under section 1372(a) of such Code as in effect on the day before the date of the enactment of this Act.

• **1976, Tax Reform Act of 1976 (P.L. 94-455)**

P.L. 94-455, §1901(b)(33)(R):

Substituted "the net capital gain" for "the excess of the net long-term capital gain over the net short-term capital loss" in Code Sec. 1378(a)(1). **Effective** with respect tor tax years beginning after 12-31-76.

[Sec. 1378(b)]

(b) AMOUNT OF TAX.—The tax imposed by subsection (a) shall be the lower of—

(1) an amount equal to the tax, determined as provided in section 1201(a), on the amount by which the net capital gain of the corporation for the taxable year exceeds $25,000, or

(2) an amount equal to the tax which would be imposed by section 11 on the taxable income (computed as provided in section 1373(d)) of the corporation for the taxable year if the corporation was not an electing small business corporation.

No credit shall be allowable under part IV of subchapter A of this chapter (other than under section 39) against the tax imposed by subsection (a).

Amendments

• **1976, Tax Reform Act of 1976 (P.L. 94-455)**

P.L. 94-455, §1901(a)(152):

Struck out the last sentence of Code Sec. 1378(b). **Effective** with respect to tax years beginning after 12-31-76. Prior to being struck, the last sentence of Code Sec. 1378(b) read as follows:

In applying section 1201(a)(1)(A) and (B) for purposes of paragraph (1), the $25,000 limitation shall first be deducted from the amount (determined without regard to this subsection) subject to tax in accordance with section 1201(a)(1)(B), to the extent thereof, and then from the amount (determined without regard to this subsection) subject to tax in accordance with section 1201(a)(1)(A).

P.L. 94-455, §1901(b)(33)(R):

Substituted "the net capital gain" for "the excess of the net long-term capital gain over the net short-term capital loss" in Code Sec. 1378(b)(1). **Effective** with respect to tax years beginning after 12-31-76.

• **1969, Tax Reform Act of 1969 (P.L. 91-172)**

P.L. 91-172, §511(c)(4):

Amended Sec. 1378(b) by substituting the words "the tax, determined as provided in section 1201(a), on" for "25 percent of" in paragraph (1), and added the last sentence to subsection (b). **Effective** for tax years beginning after 12-31-69.

[Sec. 1378(c)]

(c) EXCEPTIONS.—

(1) IN GENERAL.—Subsection (a) shall not apply to an electing small business corporation for any taxable year if the election under section 1372(a) which is in effect with respect to such corporation for such taxable year has been in effect for the 3 immediately preceding taxable years.

(2) NEW CORPORATIONS.—Subsection (a) shall not apply to an electing small business corporation if—

(A) it has been in existence for less than 4 taxable years, and

(B) an election under section 1372(a) has been in effect with respect to such corporation for each of its taxable years.

(3) PROPERTY WITH SUBSTITUTED BASIS.—If—

(A) but for paragraph (1) or (2), subsection (a) would apply for the taxable year,

(B) any long-term capital gain is attributable to property acquired by the electing small business corporation during the period beginning 3 years before the first day of the taxable year and ending on the last day of the taxable year, and

(C) the basis of such property is determined in whole or in part by reference to the basis of any property in the hands of another corporation which was not an electing small business corporation throughout all of the period described in subparagraph (B) before the transfer by such other corporation and during which such other corporation was in existence,

then subsection (a) shall apply for the taxable year, but the amount of the tax determined under subsection (b) shall not exceed a tax, determined as provided in section 1201(a), on the net capital gain attributable to property acquired as provided in subparagraph (B) and having a basis described in subparagraph (C).

Amendments

• **1976, Tax Reform Act of 1976 (P.L. 94-455)**

P.L. 94-455, §1901(b)(33)(R):

Substituted "the net capital gain" for "the excess of the net long-term capital gain over the net short-term capital loss" in Code Sec. 1378(c)(3). **Effective** with respect to tax years beginning after 12-31-76.

• **1969, Tax Reform Act of 1969 (P.L. 91-172)**

P.L. 91-172, §501(c)(4):

Amended Sec. 1378(c)(3) by substituting the words "a tax, determined as provided in section 1201(a), on" for "25 percent of". **Effective** for tax years beginning after 12-31-69.

• **1966 (P.L. 89-389)**

P.L. 89-389, §2(a):

Added Code Sec. 1378. **Effective** with respect to tax years of electing small business corporations beginning after 4-14-66, but not with respect to sales or exchanges occurring before 2-24-66.

[Sec. 1379]

SEC. 1379. TRANSITIONAL RULES ON ENACTMENT.

[Sec. 1379(a)]

(a) OLD ELECTIONS.—Any election made under section 1372(a) (as in effect before the enactment of the Subchapter S Revision Act of 1982) shall be treated as an election made under section 1362.

INCOME TAX—DEFINITIONS; MISCELLANEOUS

[Sec. 1379(b)]

(b) REFERENCES TO PRIOR LAW INCLUDED.—Any references in this title to a provision of this subchapter shall, to the extent not inconsistent with the purposes of this subchapter, include a reference to the corresponding provision as in effect before the enactment of the Subchapter S Revision Act of 1982.

Amendments

• **1984, Deficit Reduction Act of 1984 (P.L. 98-369)**

P.L. 98-369, §713(d)(8) provides:

(8) Coordination of Repeals of Certain Sections.—Sections 404(e) and 1379(b) of the Internal Revenue Code of 1954 (as in effect on the day before the date of the enactment of the Tax Equity and Fiscal Responsibility Act of 1982) shall not apply to any plan to which section 401(j) of such Code applies (or would apply but for its repeal).

P.L. 98-369, §721(n):

Amended Code Sec. 1379(b). **Effective** as if included in P.L. 97-354. Prior to amendment, Code Sec. 1379(b) read as follows:

(b) References to Prior Law Included.—In applying this subchapter to any taxable year beginning after December 31, 1982, any reference in this subchapter to another provision of this subchapter shall, to the extent not inconsistent with the purposes of this subchapter, include a reference to the corresponding provision as in effect before the enactment of the Subchapter S Revision Act of 1982.

[Sec. 1379(c)]

(c) DISTRIBUTIONS OF UNDISTRIBUTED TAXABLE INCOME.—If a corporation was an electing small business corporation for the last preenactment year, subsections (f) and (d) of section 1375 (as in effect before the enactment of the Subchapter S Revision Act of 1982) shall continue to apply with respect to distributions of undistributed taxable income for any taxable year beginning before January 1, 1983.

[Sec. 1379(d)]

(d) CARRYFORWARDS.—If a corporation was an electing small business corporation for the last preenactment year and is an S corporation for the 1st postenactment year, any carryforward to the 1st postenactment year which arose in a taxable year for which the corporation was an electing small business corporation shall be treated as arising in the 1st postenactment year.

[Sec. 1379(e)]

(e) PREENACTMENT AND POSTENACTMENT YEARS DEFINED.—For purposes of this subsection—

(1) LAST PREENACTMENT YEAR.—The term "last preenactment year" means the last taxable year of a corporation which begins before January 1, 1983.

(2) 1ST POSTENACTMENT YEAR.—The term "1st postenactment year" means the 1st taxable year of a corporation which begins after December 31, 1982.

Amendments

• **1982, Subchapter S Revision Act of 1982 (P.L. 97-354)**

P.L. 97-354, §2:

Amended Code Sec. 1379. **Effective** for tax years beginning after 12-31-82. P.L. 97-354, §6(b)(1) provides that Code Sec. 1379 prior to amendment by §2 will be in effect for years beginning before 1984. Prior to amendment, Code Sec. 1379 read as follows:

SEC. 1379. CERTAIN QUALIFIED PENSION, ETC., PLANS.

(a) ADDITIONAL REQUIREMENT FOR QUALIFICATION OF STOCK BONUS OR PROFIT-SHARING PLANS.—A trust forming part of a stock bonus or profit-sharing plan which provides contributions or benefits for employees some or all of whom are shareholder-employees shall not constitute a qualified trust under section 401 (relating to qualified pension, profit-sharing, and stock bonus plans) unless the plan of which such trust is a part provides that forfeitures attributable to contributions deductible under section 404(a)(3) for any taxable year (beginning after December 31, 1970) of the employer with respect to which it is an electing small business corporation may not inure to the benefit of any individual who is a shareholder-employee for such taxable year. A plan shall be considered as satisfying the requirement of this subsection for the period beginning with the first day of a taxable year and ending with the 15th day of the third month following the close of such taxable year, if all the provisions of the plan which are necessary to satisfy this requirement are in effect by the end of such period and have been made effective for all purposes with respect to the whole of such period.

(b) TAXABILITY OF SHAREHOLDER-EMPLOYEE BENEFICIARIES.—

(1) INCLUSION OF EXCESS CONTRIBUTIONS IN GROSS INCOME.—Notwithstanding the provisions of section 402 (relating to taxability of beneficiary of employees' trust), section 403 (relating to taxation of employee annuities), or section 405(d) (relating to taxability of beneficiaries under qualified bond purchase plans), an individual who is a shareholder-employee of an electing small business corporation shall include in gross income, for his taxable year in which or with which the taxable year of the corporation ends, the excess of the amount of contributions paid on his behalf which is deductible under section 404(a)(1), (2), or (3) by the corporation for its taxable year over the lesser of—

(A) 15 percent of the compensation received or accrued by him from such corporation during its taxable year, or

(B) $15,000.

(2) TREATMENT OF AMOUNTS INCLUDED IN GROSS INCOME.—Any amount included in the gross income of a shareholder-employee under paragraph (1) shall be treated as consideration for the contract contributed by the shareholder-employee for purposes of section 72 (relating to annuities).

(3) DEDUCTION FOR AMOUNTS NOT RECEIVED AS BENEFITS.—If—

(A) amounts are included in the gross income of an individual under paragraph (1), and

(B) the rights of such individual (or his beneficiaries) under the plan terminate before payments under the plan which are excluded from gross income equal the amounts included in gross income under paragraph (1),

then there shall be allowed as a deduction, for the taxable year in which such rights terminate, an amount equal to the excess of the amounts included in gross income under paragraph (1) over such payments.

(c) CARRYOVER OF AMOUNTS DEDUCTIBLE.—No amount deductible shall be carried forward under the second sentence of section 404(a)(3)(A) (relating to limits on deductible contributions under stock bonus and profit-sharing trusts) to a taxable year of a corporation with respect to which it is not an electing small business corporation from a taxable year (beginning after December 31, 1970) with respect to which it is an electing small business corporation.

(d) SHAREHOLDER-EMPLOYEE.—For purposes of this section, the term "shareholder-employee" means an employee or officer of an electing small business corporation who owns (or is considered as owning within the meaning of section 318(a)(1)), on any day during the taxable year of such corporation, more than 5 percent of the outstanding stock of the corporation.

• **1982, Tax Equity and Fiscal Responsibility Act of 1982 (P.L. 97-248)**

P.L. 97-248, §238(c):

Amended Code Sec. 1379 by striking out subsections (a) and (b) and redesignating subsections (c) and (d) as subsections (a) and (b) respectively. **Effective** for years beginning after 12-31-83.

• **1981, Economic Recovery Tax Act of 1981 (P.L. 97-34)**

P.L. 97-34, §312(c)(6):

Amended Code Sec. 1379(b)(1)(B) by striking out "$7,500" and inserting "$15,000". **Effective** for tax years beginning after 12-31-81.

• **1974, Employee Retirement Income Security Act of 1974 (P.L. 93-406)**

P. L. 93-406, §2001(b):

Amended Code Sec. 1379(b) by substituting "15 percent" for "10 percent" in subparagraph (A) and by substituting "$7,500" for "$2,500" in subparagraph (B). **Effective** for tax years beginning after 12-31-73.

• **1969, Tax Reform Act of 1969 (P.L. 91-172)**

P. L. 91-172, §531(a):

Added Code Sec. 1379. **Effective** for tax years of electing small business corporations beginning after 12-31-70.

Subchapter T—Cooperatives and Their Patrons

Part I.   Tax treatment of cooperatives.
Part II.   Tax treatment by patrons of patronage dividends and per-unit retain certificates.
Part III.   Definitions; special rules.

PART I—TAX TREATMENT OF COOPERATIVES

Sec. 1381.   Organizations to which part applies.
Sec. 1382.   Taxable income of cooperatives.
Sec. 1383.   Computation of tax where cooperative redeems nonqualified written notices of allocation or nonqualified per-unit retain certificates.

INCOME TAX—COOPERATIVES

[Sec. 1381]

SEC. 1381. ORGANIZATIONS TO WHICH PART APPLIES.

[Sec. 1381(a)]

(a) IN GENERAL.—This part shall apply to—

(1) any organization exempt from tax under section 521 (relating to exemption of farmers' cooperatives from tax), and

(2) any corporation operating on a cooperative basis other than an organization—

(A) which is exempt from tax under this chapter,

(B) which is subject to the provisions of—

(i) part II of subchapter H (relating to mutual savings banks, etc.), or

(ii) subchapter L (relating to insurance companies), or

(C) which is engaged in furnishing electric energy, or providing telephone service, to persons in rural areas.

[Sec. 1381(b)]

(b) TAX ON CERTAIN FARMERS' COOPERATIVES.—An organization described in subsection (a)(1) shall be subject to the tax imposed by section 11.

Amendments

• **2017, Tax Cuts and Jobs Act (P.L. 115-97)**

P.L. 115-97, §13001(b)(2)(O):

Amended Code Sec. 1381(b) by striking "taxes imposed by section 11 or 1201" and inserting "tax imposed by section 11". **Effective** for tax years beginning after 12-31-2017.

• **1962, Revenue Act of 1962 (P.L. 87-834)**

P.L. 87-834, §17(a):

Added Code Sec. 1381. **Effective:**

(1) For Cooperatives.—Except as provided in paragraph (3) below, the amendments (made by section 17 of P. L. 87- 834) apply to tax years of organizations described in Code Section 1381(a) beginning after 12-31-62.

(2) For Patrons.—Except as provided in paragraph (3) below, Code Section 1385 applies with respect to any amount received from any organization described in Code Section 1381(a), to the extent that such amount is paid by such organization in a tax year of such organization beginning after 12-31-62.

(3) Application of Existing Law.—In the case of any money, written notice of allocation, or other property paid by any organization described in Code Section 1381(a)—

(A) before the first day of the first tax year of such organization beginning after 12-31-62, or

(B) on or after such first day with respect to patronage occurring before such first day,

the tax treatment of such money, written notice of allocation, or other property (including the tax treatment of gain or loss on the redemption, sale or other disposition of such written notice of allocation) by any person must be made under the 1954 Code without regard to subchapter T of chapter 1.

[Sec. 1381(c)]

(c) CROSS REFERENCE.—

For treatment of income from load loss transactions of organizations described in subsection (a)(2)(C), see section 501(c)(12)(H).

Amendments

• **2004, American Jobs Creation Act of 2004 (P.L. 108-357)**

P.L. 108-357, §319(d):

Amended Code Sec. 1381 by adding at the end a new subsection (c). **Effective** for tax years beginning after 10-22-2004.

[Sec. 1382]

SEC. 1382. TAXABLE INCOME OF COOPERATIVES.

[Sec. 1382(a)]

(a) GROSS INCOME.—Except as provided in subsection (b), the gross income of any organization to which this part applies shall be determined without any adjustment (as a reduction in gross receipts, an increase in cost of goods sold, or otherwise) by reason of any allocation or distribution to a patron out of the net earnings of such organization or by reason of any amount paid to a patron as a per-unit retain allocation (as defined in section 1388(f)).

Amendments

• **1966, Foreign Investors Tax Act of 1966 (P.L. 89-809)**

P.L. 89-809, §211(a)(1):

Amended Code Sec. 1382(a) by striking out the period at the end thereof and adding: "or by reason of any amount paid to a patron as a per-unit retain allocation (as defined in section 1388(f))." **Effective** as to per-unit retain allocations made during tax years of organization described in Code Sec. 1381(a) beginning after 4-30-66, with respect to products delivered during such years.

[Sec. 1382(b)]

(b) PATRONAGE DIVIDENDS AND PER-UNIT RETAIN ALLOCATIONS.—In determining the taxable income of an organization to which this part applies, there shall not be taken into account amounts paid during the payment period for the taxable year—

(1) as patronage dividends (as defined in section 1388(a)), to the extent paid in money, qualified written notices of allocation (as defined in section 1388(c)), or other property (except nonqualified written notices of allocation (as defined in section 1388(d))) with respect to patronage occurring during such taxable year;

(2) in money or other property (except written notices of allocation) in redemption of a nonqualified written notice of allocation which was paid as a patronage dividend during the payment period for the taxable year during which the patronage occurred;

(3) as per-unit retain allocations (as defined in section 1388(f)), to the extent paid in money, qualified per-unit retain certificates (as defined in section 1388(h)), or other property (except nonqualified per-unit retain certificates, as defined in section 1388(i)) with respect to marketing occurring during such taxable year; or

(4) in money or other property (except per-unit retain certificates) in redemption of a nonqualified per-unit retain certificate which was paid as a per-unit retain allocation during the payment period for the taxable year during which the marketing occurred.

For purposes of this title, any amount not taken into account under the preceding sentence shall, in the case of an amount described in paragraph (1) or (2), be treated in the same manner as an item of gross income and as a deduction therefrom, and in the case of an amount described in paragraph (3) or (4), be treated as a deduction in arriving at gross income.

Amendments

• **1969, Tax Reform Act of 1969 (P.L. 91-172)**

P.L. 91-172, §911(a):

Amended paragraph (b)(3). **Effective** for per-unit retain allocations made after 10-9-69. Prior to amendment, paragraph (b)(3) read as follows:

(3) as per-unit retain allocations, to the extent paid in qualified per-unit retain certificates (as defined in section 1388(h)) with respect to marketing occurring during such taxable year; or

INCOME TAX—COOPERATIVES

• **1966, Foreign Investors Tax Act of 1966 (P.L. 89-809)**

P.L. 89-809, § 211(a)(2):

Amended Code Sec. 1382(b) by adding "AND PER-UNIT RETAIN ALLOCATIONS" after "DIVIDENDS" in the heading; by striking out "or" at the end of paragraph (1); by substituting a semicolon for the period at the end of paragraph (2); and by striking out the sentence following paragraph (2) and inserting new paragraphs (3) and (4) and new last sentence. **Effective** as to per-unit retain allocations made during tax years of organizations described in Code Sec. 1381(a) beginning after 4-30-66, with respect to products delivered during such years. Prior to amendment, Code Sec. 1382(b) read as follows:

"(b) Patronage Dividends—In determining the taxable income of an organization to which this part applies, there shall not be taken into account amounts paid during the payment period for the taxable year—

"(1) as patronage dividends (as defined in section 1388(a)), to the extent paid in money, qualified written notices of allocation (as defined in section 1388(c)), or other property (except nonqualified written notices of allocation (as defined in section 1388(d)), with respect to patronage occurring during such taxable year; or

"(2) in money or other property (except written notices of allocation) in redemption of a nonqualified written notice of allocation which was paid as a patronage dividend during the payment period for the taxable year during which the patronage occurred.

"For purposes of this title, any amount not taken into account under the preceding sentence shall be treated in the same manner as an item of gross income and as a deduction therefrom."

[Sec. 1382(c)]

(c) DEDUCTION FOR NONPATRONAGE DISTRIBUTIONS, ETC.—In determining the taxable income of an organization described in section 1381(a)(1), there shall be allowed as a deduction (in addition to other deductions allowable under this chapter)—

(1) amounts paid during the taxable year as dividends on its capital stock; and

(2) amounts paid during the payment period for the taxable year—

(A) in money, qualified written notices of allocation, or other property (except nonqualified written notices of allocation) on a patronage basis to patrons with respect to its earnings during such taxable year which are derived from business done for the United States or any of its agencies or from sources other than patronage, or

(B) in money or other property (except written notices of allocation) in redemption of a nonqualified written notice of allocation which was paid, during the payment period for the taxable year during which the earnings were derived, on a patronage basis to a patron with respect to earnings derived from business or sources described in subparagraph (A).

[Sec. 1382(d)]

(d) PAYMENT PERIOD FOR EACH TAXABLE YEAR.—For purposes of subsections (b) and (c)(2), the payment period for any taxable year is the period beginning with the first day of such taxable year and ending with the fifteenth day of the ninth month following the close of such year. For purposes of subsections (b)(1) and (c)(2)(A), a qualified check issued during the payment period shall be treated as an amount paid in money during such period if endorsed and cashed on or before the 90th day after the close of such period.

[Sec. 1382(e)]

(e) PRODUCTS MARKETED UNDER POOLING ARRANGEMENTS.—For purposes of subsection (b), in the case of a pooling arrangement for the marketing of products—

(1) the patronage shall (to the extent provided in regulations prescribed by the Secretary) be treated as patronage occurring during the taxable year in which the pool closes, and

(2) the marketing of products shall be treated as occurring during any of the taxable years in which the pool is open.

Amendments

• **1976, Tax Reform Act of 1976 (P.L. 94-455)**

P.L. 94-455, § 1906(b)(13)(A):

Amended 1954 Code by substituting "Secretary" for "Secretary or his delegate" each place it appeared. **Effective** 2-1-77.

• **1966, Foreign Investors Tax Act of 1966 (P.L. 89-809)**

P.L. 89-809, § 211(a)(3):

Amended Code Sec. 1382(e). **Effective** as to per-unit retain allocations made during tax years of organizations described in Code Sec. 1381(a) beginning after 4-30-66, with respect to products delivered during such years. Prior to amendment, Code Sec. 1382(e) read as follows:

(e) Products Marketed Under Pooling Arrangements.—For purposes of subsection (b), in the case of a pooling arrangement for the marketing of products, the patronage shall (to the extent provided in regulations prescribed by the Secretary or his delegate) be treated as patronage occurring during the taxable year in which the pool closes.

[Sec. 1382(f)]

(f) TREATMENT OF EARNINGS RECEIVED AFTER PATRONAGE OCCURRED.—If any portion of the earnings from business done with or for patrons is includible in the organization's gross income for a taxable year after the taxable year during which the patronage occurred, then for purposes of applying paragraphs (1) and (2) of subsection (b) to such portion the patronage shall, to the extent provided in regulations prescribed by the Secretary, be considered to have occurred during the taxable year of the organization during which such earnings are includible in gross income.

[Sec. 1382(g)]

(g) USE OF COMPLETED CROP POOL METHOD OF ACCOUNTING.—

(1) IN GENERAL.—An organization described in section 1381(a) which is engaged in pooling arrangements for the marketing of products may compute its taxable income with respect to any pool opened prior to March 1, 1978, under the completed crop pool method of accounting if—

(A) the organization has computed its taxable income under such method for the 10 taxable years ending with its first taxable year beginning after December 31, 1976, and

(B) with respect to the pool, the organization has entered into an agreement with the United States or any of its agencies which includes provisions to the effect that—

(i) the United States or such agency shall provide a loan to the organization with the products comprising the pool serving as collateral for such loan,

(ii) the organization shall use an amount equal to the proceeds of such loan to make price support advances to eligible producers (as determined by the United States or such agency), to defray costs of handling, processing, and storing such products, or to pay all or part of any administrative costs associated with the price support program,

(iii) an amount equal to the net proceeds (as determined under such agreement) from the sale or exchange of the products in the pool shall be used to repay such loan until such loan is repaid in full (or all the products in the pool are disposed of), and

(iv) the net gains (as determined under such agreement) from the sale or exchange of such products shall be distributed to eligible producers, except to the extent that the United States or such agency permits otherwise.

(2) COMPLETED CROP POOL METHOD OF ACCOUNTING DEFINED.—For purposes of this subsection, the term "completed crop pool method of accounting" means a method of accounting under which gain or loss is computed separately for each crop year pool in the year in which the last of the products in the pool are disposed of.

INCOME TAX—PATRONAGE DIVIDENDS

Amendments

• **1978 (P.L. 95-345)**

P.L. 95-345, §3:

Amended Code Sec. 1382 by adding paragraph (g).

• **1976, Tax Reform Act of 1976 (P.L. 94-455)**

P.L. 94-455, §1906(b)(13)(A):

Amended 1954 Code by substituting "Secretary" for "Secretary or his delegate" each place it appeared. **Effective** 2-1-77.

• **1966, Foreign Investors Tax Act of 1966 (P.L. 89-809)**

P.L. 89-809, §211(a)(4):

Amended Code Sec. 1382(f) by inserting "paragraphs (1) and (2) of" immediately before "subsection (b)". **Effective** as to per-unit retain allocations made during tax years of organizations described in Code Sec. 1381(a) beginning after 6-30-66, with respect to products delivered during such years.

• **1962, Revenue Act of 1962 (P.L. 87-834)**

P.L. 87-834, §17(a):

Added Code Sec. 1382. For **effective** date, see amendment note for Code Sec. 1381.

[Sec. 1383]

SEC. 1383. COMPUTATION OF TAX WHERE COOPERATIVE REDEEMS NONQUALIFIED WRITTEN NOTICES OF ALLOCATION OR NONQUALIFIED PER-UNIT RETAIN CERTIFICATES.

[Sec. 1383(a)]

(a) GENERAL RULE.—If, under section 1382(b)(2) or (4), or (c)(2)(B), a deduction is allowable to an organization for the taxable year for amounts paid in redemption of nonqualified written notices of allocation or nonqualified per-unit retain certificates, then the tax imposed by this chapter on such organization for the taxable year shall be the lesser of the following:

(1) the tax for the taxable year computed with such deduction; or

(2) an amount equal to—

(A) the tax for the taxable year computed without such deduction, minus

(B) the decrease in tax under this chapter for any prior taxable year (or years) which would result solely from treating such nonqualified written notices of allocation or nonqualified per-unit retain certificates as qualified written notices of allocation or qualified per-unit retain certificates (as the case may be).

Amendments

• **1966, Foreign Investors Tax Act of 1966 (P.L. 89-809)**

P.L. 89-809, §211(a)(5), (6):

Amended the heading for Code Sec. 1383 by inserting "Or Nonqualified Per-Unit Retain Certificates" immediately after "Allocation", amended Code Sec. 1383(a) by substituting "section 1382(b)(2) or (4)," for "section 1382(b)(2)", by substituting "nonqualified written notices of allocation or nonqualified per-unit retain certificates" for "nonqualified written notices of allocation" each place it appears, and by substituting "qualified written notices of allocation or qualified per-unit retain certificates (as the case may be)" for "qualified written notices of allocation". **Effective** as to per-unit retain allocations made during tax years of organizations described in Code Sec. 1381(a) beginning after 4-30-66, with respect to products delivered during such years.

[Sec. 1383(b)]

(b) SPECIAL RULES.—

(1) If the decrease in tax ascertained under subsection (a)(2)(B) exceeds the tax for the taxable year (computed without the deduction described in subsection (a)) such excess shall be considered to be a payment of tax on the last day prescribed by law for the payment of tax for the taxable year, and shall be refunded or credited in the same manner as if it were an overpayment for such taxable year.

(2) For purposes of determining the decrease in tax under subsection (a)(2)(B), the stated dollar amount of any nonqualified written notice of allocation or nonqualified per-unit retain certificate which is to be treated under such subsection as a qualified written notice of allocation or qualified per-unit retain certificate (as the case may be) shall be the amount paid in redemption of such written notice of allocation or per-unit retain certificate which is allowable as a deduction under section 1382(b)(2) or (4), or (c)(2)(B) for the taxable year.

(3) If the tax imposed by this chapter for the taxable year is the amount determined under subsection (a)(2), then the deduction described in subsection (a) shall not be taken into account for any purpose of this subtitle other than for purposes of this section.

Amendments

• **1966, Foreign Investors Tax Act of 1966 (P.L. 89-809)**

P.L. 89-809, §211(a)(7):

Amended Code Sec. 1383(b)(2) by inserting "or nonqualified per-unit retain certificate" after "nonqualified written notice of allocation", by inserting "or qualified per-unit retain certificate (as the case may be)" after "qualified written notice of allocation", by inserting "or per-unit retain certificate" after "such written notice of allocation", and by inserting "or (4)," after "section 1382(b)(2)". **Effective** as to per-unit retain allocations made during tax years of organizations described in Code Sec. 1381(a) beginning after 4-30-66, with respect to products delivered during such years.

• **1962, Revenue Act of 1962 (P.L. 87-834)**

P.L. 87-834, §17(a):

Added Code Sec. 1383. For **effective** date, see amendment note for Code Sec. 1381.

PART II—TAX TREATMENT BY PATRONS OF PATRONAGE DIVIDENDS AND PER-UNIT RETAIN ALLOCATIONS

Sec. 1385. Amounts includible in patron's gross income.

[Sec. 1385]

SEC. 1385. AMOUNTS INCLUDIBLE IN PATRON'S GROSS INCOME.

[Sec. 1385(a)]

(a) GENERAL RULE.—Except as otherwise provided in subsection (b), each person shall include in gross income—

(1) the amount of any patronage dividend which is paid in money, a qualified written notice of allocation, or other property (except a nonqualified written notice of allocation), and which is received by him during the taxable year from an organization described in section 1381(a),

(2) any amount, described in section 1382(c)(2)(A) (relating to certain nonpatronage distributions by tax-exempt farmers' cooperatives), which is paid in money, a qualified written notice of allocation, or other property (except a nonqualified written notice of allocation), and which is received by him during the taxable year from an organization described in section 1381(a)(1), and

(3) the amount of any per-unit retain allocation which is paid in qualified per-unit retain certificates and which is received by him during the taxable year from an organization described in section 1381(a).

Amendments

• **1966, Foreign Investors Tax Act of 1966 (P.L. 89-809)**

P.L. 89-809, §211(b)(1):

Amended Code Sec. 1385(a) by striking out "and" at the end of paragraph (1), by substituting ", and" for the period at the end of paragraph (2), and by adding new paragraph (3). **Effective** as to per-unit retain allocations made during tax years of organizations described in Code Sec. 1381(a) beginning after 4-30-66, with respect to products delivered during such years.

INCOME TAX—DEFINITIONS; SPECIAL RULES

[Sec. 1385(b)]

(b) EXCLUSION FROM GROSS INCOME.—Under regulations prescribed by the Secretary, the amount of any patronage dividend, and any amount received on the redemption, sale, or other disposition of a nonqualified written notice of allocation which was paid as a patronage dividend, shall not be included in gross income to the extent that such amount—

    (1) is properly taken into account as an adjustment to basis of property, or

    (2) is attributable to personal, living, or family items.

Amendments

• **1976, Tax Reform Act of 1976 (P.L. 94-455)**

P.L. 94-455, §1906(b)(13)(A):

Amended 1954 Code by substituting "Secretary" for "Secretary or his delegate" each place it appeared. **Effective** 2-1-77.

[Sec. 1385(c)]

(c) TREATMENT OF CERTAIN NONQUALIFIED WRITTEN NOTICES OF ALLOCATION AND CERTAIN NONQUALIFIED PER-UNIT RETAIN CERTIFICATES.—

    (1) APPLICATION OF SUBSECTION.—This subsection shall apply to—

        (A) any nonqualified written notice of allocation which—

            (i) was paid as a patronage dividend, or

            (ii) was paid by an organization described in section 1381(a)(1) on a patronage basis with respect to earnings derived from business or sources described in section 1382(c)(2)(A), and

        (B) any nonqualified per-unit retain certificate which was paid as a per-unit retain allocation.

    (2) BASIS; AMOUNT OF GAIN.—In the case of any nonqualified written notice of allocation or nonqualified per-unit retain certificate to which this subsection applies, for purposes of this chapter—

        (A) the basis of such written notice of allocation or per-unit retain certificate in the hands of the patron to whom such written notice of allocation or per-unit retain certificate was paid shall be zero,

        (B) the basis of such written notice of allocation or per-unit retain certificate which was acquired from a decedent shall be its basis in the hands of the decedent, and

        (C) gain on the redemption, sale, or other disposition of such written notice of allocation or per-unit retain certificate by any person shall, to the extent that the stated dollar amount of such written notice of allocation or per-unit retain certificate exceeds its basis, be considered as ordinary income.

Amendments

• **1976, Tax Reform Act of 1976 (P.L. 94-455)**

P.L. 94-455, §1901(b)(3)(I):

Substituted "ordinary income" for "gain from the sale or exchange of property which is not a capital asset" in Code Sec. 1385(c)(2)(C). **Effective** with respect to tax years beginning after 12-31-76.

• **1966, Foreign Investors Tax Act of 1966 (P.L. 89-809)**

P.L. 89-809, §211(b)(2)-(4):

Amended the heading for Code Sec. 1385(c) by inserting "AND CERTAIN NONQUALIFIED PER-UNIT RETAIN CERTIFICATES" after "ALLOCATION", amended Code Sec. 1385(c)(1), and amended Code Sec. 1385(c)(2) by inserting "or nonqualified per-unit retain certificate" after "nonqualified written notice of allocation" and by inserting "or per-unit retain certificate" after "such written notice of allocation" each place it appears.

Effective as to per-unit retain allocations made during tax years of organizations described in Code Sec. 1381(a) beginning after 4-30-66, with respect to products delivered during such years. Prior to amendment, Code Sec. 1385(c)(1) read as follows:

(1) APPLICATION OF SUBSECTION.—This subsection shall apply to any nonqualified written notice of allocation which—

(A) was paid as a patronage dividend, or

(B) was paid by an organization described in section 1381(a)(1) on a patronage basis with respect to earnings derived from business or sources described in section 1382(c)(2)(A).

• **1962, Revenue Act of 1962 (P.L. 87-834)**

P.L. 87-834, §17(a):

Added Code Sec. 1385. For **effective** date, see amendment note for Code Sec. 1381.

PART III—DEFINITIONS; SPECIAL RULES

Sec. 1388.   Definitions; special rules.

[Sec. 1388]

SEC. 1388. DEFINITIONS; SPECIAL RULES.

[Sec. 1388(a)]

(a) PATRONAGE DIVIDEND.—For purposes of this subchapter, the term "patronage dividend" means an amount paid to a patron by an organization to which part I of this subchapter applies—

    (1) on the basis of quantity or value of business done with or for such patron,

    (2) under an obligation of such organization to pay such amount, which obligation existed before the organization received the amount so paid, and

    (3) which is determined by reference to the net earnings of the organization from business done with or for its patrons.

Such term does not include any amount paid to a patron to the extent that (A) such amount is out of earnings other than from business done with or for patrons, or (B) such amount is out of earnings from business done with or for other patrons to whom no amounts are paid, or to whom smaller amounts are paid, with respect to substantially identical transactions. For purposes of paragraph (3), net earnings shall not be reduced by amounts paid during the year as dividends on capital stock or other proprietary capital interests of the organization to the extent that the articles of incorporation or bylaws of such organization or other contract with patrons provide that such dividends are in addition to amounts otherwise payable to patrons which are derived from business done with or for patrons during the taxable year.

Amendments

• **2004, American Jobs Creation Act of 2004 (P.L. 108-357)**

P.L. 108-357, §312(a):

Amended Code Sec. 1388(a) by adding at the end a new sentence. **Effective** for distributions in tax years beginning after 10-22-2004.

[Sec. 1388(b)]

(b) WRITTEN NOTICE OF ALLOCATION.—For purposes of this subchapter, the term "written notice of allocation" means any capital stock, revolving fund certificate, retain certificate, certificate of indebtedness, letter of advice, or other written notice, which discloses to the recipient the stated dollar amount allocated to him by the organization and the portion thereof, if any, which constitutes a patronage dividend.

INCOME TAX—DEFINITIONS; SPECIAL RULES

[Sec. 1388(c)]

(c) QUALIFIED WRITTEN NOTICE OF ALLOCATION.—

(1) DEFINED.—For purposes of this subchapter, the term "qualified written notice of allocation" means—

(A) a written notice of allocation which may be redeemed in cash at its stated dollar amount at any time within a period beginning on the date such written notice of allocation is paid and ending not earlier than 90 days from such date, but only if the distributee receives written notice of the right of redemption at the time he receives such written notice of allocation; and

(B) a written notice of allocation which the distributee has consented, in the manner provided in paragraph (2), to take into account at its stated dollar amount as provided in section 1385(a).

Such term does not include any written notice of allocation which is paid as part of a patronage dividend or as part of a payment described in section 1382(c)(2)(A), unless 20 percent or more of the amount of such patronage dividend, or such payment, is paid in money or by qualified check.

(2) MANNER OF OBTAINING CONSENT.—A distributee shall consent to take a written notice of allocation into account as provided in paragraph (1)(B) only by—

(A) making such consent in writing,

(B) obtaining or retaining membership in the organization after—

(i) such organization has adopted (after October 16, 1962) a bylaw providing that membership in the organization constitutes such consent, and

(ii) he has received a written notification and copy of such bylaw, or

(C) if neither subparagraph (A) nor (B) applies, endorsing and cashing a qualified check, paid as a part of the patronage dividend or payment of which such written notice of allocation is also a part, on or before the 90th day after the close of the payment period for the taxable year of the organization for which such patronage dividend or payment is paid.

(3) PERIOD FOR WHICH CONSENT IS EFFECTIVE.—

(A) GENERAL RULE.—Except as provided in subparagraph (B)—

(i) a consent described in paragraph (2)(A) shall be a consent with respect to all patronage of the distributee with the organization occurring (determined with the application of section 1382(e)) during the taxable year of the organization during which such consent is made and all subsequent taxable years of the organization; and

(ii) a consent described in paragraph (2)(B) shall be a consent with respect to all patronage of the distributee with the organization occurring (determined without the application of section 1382(e)) after he received the notification and copy described in paragraph (2)(B)(ii).

(B) REVOCATION, ETC.—

(i) Any consent described in paragraph (2)(A) may be revoked (in writing) by the distributee at any time. Any such revocation shall be effective with respect to patronage occurring on or after the first day of the first taxable year of the organization beginning after the revocation is filed with such organization; except that in the case of a pooling arrangement described in section 1382(e), a revocation made by a distributee shall not be effective as to any pool with respect to which the distributee has been a patron before such revocation.

(ii) Any consent described in paragraph (2)(B) shall not be effective with respect to any patronage occurring (determined without the application of section 1382(e)) after the distributee ceases to be a member of the organization or after the bylaws of the organization cease to contain the provision described in paragraph (2)(B)(i).

(4) QUALIFIED CHECK.—For purposes of this subchapter, the term "qualified check" means only a check (or other instrument which is redeemable in money) which is paid as a part of a patronage dividend, or as a part of a payment described in section 1382(c)(2)(A), to a distributee who has not given consent as provided in paragraph (2)(A) or (B) with respect to such patronage dividend or payment, and on which there is clearly imprinted a statement that the endorsement and cashing of the check (or other instrument) constitutes the consent of the payee to include in his gross income, as provided in the Federal income tax laws, the stated dollar amount of the written notice of allocation which is a part of the patronage dividend or payment of which such qualified check is also a part. Such term does not include any check (or other instrument) which is paid as part of a patronage dividend or payment which does not include a written notice of allocation (other than a written notice of allocation described in paragraph (1)(A)).

Amendments

- 1976, Tax Reform Act of 1976 (P.L. 94-455)

P.L. 94-455, § 1901(a)(153)(A):

Substituted "October 16, 1962" for "the date of the enactment of the Revenue Act of 1962" in Code Sec. 1388(c)(2)(B)(i). **Effective** with respect to tax years beginning after 12-31-76.

[Sec. 1388(d)]

(d) NONQUALIFIED WRITTEN NOTICE OF ALLOCATION.—For purposes of this subchapter, the term "nonqualified written notice of allocation" means a written notice of allocation which is not described in subsection (c) or a qualified check which is not cashed on or before the 90th day after the close of the payment period for the taxable year for which the distribution of which it is a part is paid.

[Sec. 1388(e)]

(e) DETERMINATION OF AMOUNT PAID OR RECEIVED.—For purposes of this subchapter, in determining amounts paid or received—

(1) property (other than a written notice of allocation or a per-unit retain certificate) shall be taken into account at its fair market value, and

(2) a qualified written notice of allocation or qualified per-unit retain certificate shall be taken into account at its stated dollar amount.

[Sec. 1388(f)]

(f) PER-UNIT RETAIN ALLOCATION.—For purposes of this subchapter, the term "per-unit retain allocation" means any allocation, by an organization to which part I of this subchapter applies, to a patron with respect to products marketed for him, the amount of which is fixed without reference to the net earnings of the organization pursuant to an agreement between the organization and the patron.

Amendments

- 1969, Tax Reform Act of 1969 (P.L. 91-172)

P.L. 91-172, § 911(b):

Amended subparagraph (f) by deleting "other than by payment in money or other property (except per-unit retain certificates)" which appeared immediately following "part I of this chapter applies,". **Effective** for per-unit retain allocations made after 10-9-69.

INCOME TAX—DEFINITIONS; SPECIAL RULES

[Sec. 1388(g)]

(g) PER-UNIT RETAIN CERTIFICATE.—For purposes of this subchapter, the term "per-unit retain certificate" means any written notice which discloses to the recipient the stated dollar amount of a per-unit retain allocation to him by the organization.

[Sec. 1388(h)]

(h) QUALIFIED PER-UNIT RETAIN CERTIFICATE.—

(1) DEFINED.—For purposes of this subchapter, the term "qualified per-unit retain certificate" means any per-unit retain certificate which the distributee has agreed, in the manner provided in paragraph (2), to take into account at its stated dollar amount as provided in section 1385(a).

(2) MANNER OF OBTAINING AGREEMENT.—A distributee shall agree to take a per-unit retain certificate into account as provided in paragraph (1) only by—

(A) making such agreement in writing, or

(B) obtaining or retaining membership in the organization after—

(i) such organization has adopted (after November 13, 1966) a bylaw providing that membership in the organization constitutes such agreement, and

(ii) he has received a written notification and copy of such bylaw.

(3) PERIOD FOR WHICH AGREEMENT IS EFFECTIVE.—

(A) GENERAL RULE.—Except as provided in subparagraph (B)—

(i) an agreement described in paragraph (2)(A) shall be an agreement with respect to all products delivered by the distributee to the organization during the taxable year of the organization during which such agreement is made and all subsequent taxable years of the organization; and

(ii) an agreement described in paragraph (2)(B) shall be an agreement with respect to all products delivered by the distributee to the organization after he received the notification and copy described in paragraph (2)(B)(ii).

(B) REVOCATION, ETC.—

(i) Any agreement described in paragraph (2)(A) may be revoked (in writing) by the distributee at any time. Any such revocation shall be effective with respect to products delivered by the distributee on or after the first day of the first taxable year of the organization beginning after the revocation is filed with the organization; except that in the case of a pooling arrangement described in section 1382(e) a revocation made by a distributee shall not be effective as to any products which were delivered to the organization by the distributee before such revocation.

(ii) Any agreement described in paragraph (2)(B) shall not be effective with respect to any products delivered after the distributee ceases to be a member of the organization or after the bylaws of the organization cease to contain the provision described in paragraph (2)(B)(i).

Amendments

• **1976, Tax Reform Act of 1976 (P.L. 94-455)**

P.L. 94-455, §1901(a)(153)(B):

Substituted "November 13, 1966" for "the date of the enactment of this subsection" in Code Sec. 1388(h)(2)(B)(i). **Effective** with respect to tax years beginning after 12-31-76.

[Sec. 1388(i)]

(i) NONQUALIFIED PER-UNIT RETAIN CERTIFICATE.—For purposes of this subchapter, the term "nonqualified per-unit retain certificate" means a per-unit retain certificate which is not described in subsection (h).

Amendments

• **1966, Foreign Investors Tax Act of 1966 (P.L. 89-809)**

P.L. 89-809, §211(c)(1)(A)-(B):

Amended Code Sec. 1388(e)(1) by substituting "allocation or a per-unit retain certificate)" for "allocation)" and amended Code Sec. 1388(e)(2) by striking out "allocation" and inserting "allocation or qualified per-unit retain certificate". **Effective** as to per-unit retain allocations made during tax years of organizations described in Sec. 1381(a) beginning after 4-30-66, with respect to products delivered during such years. For a transition rule, see Act Sec. 211(f), below.

P.L. 89-809, §211(c)(2):

Added new Code Secs. 1388(f)-(i). **Effective** as to per-unit retain allocations made during tax years of organizations described in Sec. 1381(a) beginning after 4-30-66, with respect to products delivered during such years. For a transition rule, see Act Sec. 211(f), below.

P.L. 89-809, §211(f), provides:

(f) Transition Rule.—

(1) Except as provided in paragraph (2), a written agreement between a patron and a cooperative association—

(A) which clearly provides that the patron agrees to treat the stated dollar amounts of all per-unit retain certificates issued to him by the association as representing cash distributions which he has, of his own choice, reinvested in the cooperative association,

(B) which is revocable by the patron at any time after the close of the taxable year in which it was made,

(C) which was entered into after October 14, 1965, and before the date of the enactment of this Act, and

(D) which is in effect on the date of the enactment of this Act, and with respect to which a written notice of revocation has not been furnished to the cooperative association,

shall be effective (for the period prescribed in the agreement) for purposes of section 1388(h) as if entered into, pursuant to such section, after the date of the enactment of this Act.

(2) An agreement described in paragraphs (1)(A) and (C) which was included in a by-law of the cooperative association and which is in effect on the date of the enactment of this Act shall be effective for purposes of section 1388(h) only for taxable years of the association beginning before May 1, 1967.

• **1962, Revenue Act of 1962 (P.L. 87-834)**

P.L. 87-834, §17(a):

Added Code Sec. 1388. For **effective** date, see amendment note for Code Sec. 1381.

[Sec. 1388(j)]

(j) SPECIAL RULES FOR THE NETTING OF GAINS AND LOSSES BY COOPERATIVES.—For purposes of this subchapter, in the case of any organization to which part I of this subchapter applies—

(1) OPTIONAL NETTING OF PATRONAGE GAINS AND LOSSES PERMITTED.—The net earnings of such organization may, at its option, be determined by offsetting patronage losses (including any patronage loss carried to such year) which are attributable to 1 or more allocation units (whether such units are functional, divisional, departmental, geographic, or otherwise) against patronage earnings of 1 or more other such allocation units.

(2) CERTAIN NETTING PERMITTED AFTER SECTION 381 TRANSACTIONS.—If such an organization acquires the assets of another such organization in a transaction described in section 381(a), the acquiring organization may, in computing its net earnings for taxable years ending after the date of acquisition, offset losses of 1 or more allocation units of the acquiring or acquired organization against earnings of the acquired or acquiring organization, respectively, but only to the extent—

(A) such earnings are properly allocable to periods after the date of acquisition, and

INCOME TAX—DEFINITIONS; SPECIAL RULES

(B) such earnings could have been offset by such losses if such earnings and losses had been derived from allocation units of the same organization.

(3) NOTICE REQUIREMENTS.—

(A) IN GENERAL.—In the case of any organization which exercises its option under paragraph (1) for any taxable year, such organization shall, on or before the 15th day of the 9th month following the close of such taxable year, provide to its patrons a written notice which—

(i) states that the organization has offset earnings and losses from 1 or more of its allocation units and that such offset may have affected the amount which is being distributed to its patrons,

(ii) states generally the identity of the offsetting allocation units, and

(iii) states briefly what rights, if any, its patrons may have to additional financial information of such organization under terms of its charter, articles of incorporation, or bylaws, or under any provision of law.

(B) CERTAIN INFORMATION NEED NOT BE PROVIDED.—An organization may exclude from the information required to be provided under clause (ii) of subparagraph (A) any detailed or specific data regarding earnings or losses of such units which such organization determines would disclose commercially sensitive information which—

(i) could result in a competitive disadvantage to such organization, or

(ii) could create a competitive advantage to the benefit of a competitor of such organization.

(C) FAILURE TO PROVIDE SUFFICIENT NOTICE.—If the Secretary determines that an organization failed to provide sufficient notice under this paragraph—

(i) the Secretary shall notify such organization, and

(ii) such organization shall, upon receipt of such notification, provide to its patrons a revised notice meeting the requirements of this paragraph.

Any such failure shall not affect the treatment of the organization under any provision of this subchapter or section 521.

(4) PATRONAGE EARNINGS OR LOSSES DEFINED.—For purposes of this subsection, the terms "patronage earnings" and "patronage losses" means earnings and losses, respectively, which are derived from business done with or for patrons of the organization.

Amendments

• **1986, Consolidated Omnibus Budget Reconciliation Act of 1985 (P.L. 99-272)**

P.L. 99-272, § 13210(a):

Amended Code Sec. 1388 by redesignating subsection (j) as subsection (k) and by inserting after subsection (i) new subsection (j). For the **effective** date, see Act Sec. 13210(c), below.

P.L. 99-272, § 13210(c), provides:

(c) EFFECTIVE DATE.—

(1) IN GENERAL.—Except as provided in paragraph (2), the amendments made by this section shall apply to taxable years beginning after December 31, 1962.

(2) NOTIFICATION REQUIREMENT.—The provisions of section 1388(j)(3) of the Internal Revenue Code of 1954 (as added by subsection (a)) shall apply to taxable years beginning on or after the date of the enactment of this Act.

(3) NO INFERENCE.—Nothing in the amendments made by this section shall be construed to infer that a change in law is intended as to whether any patronage earnings may or may not be offset by nonpatronage losses, and any determination of such issue shall be made as if such amendments had not been enacted.

[Sec. 1388(k)]

(k) COOPERATIVE MARKETING INCLUDES VALUE ADDED PROCESSING INVOLVING ANIMALS.—For purposes of section 521 and this subchapter, the marketing of the products of members or other producers shall include the feeding of such products to cattle, hogs, fish, chickens, or other animals and the sale of the resulting animals or animal products.

Amendments

• **2004, American Jobs Creation Act of 2004 (P.L. 108-357)**

P.L. 108-357, § 316(a):

Amended Code Sec. 1388 by adding at the end a new subsection (k). **Effective** for tax years beginning after 10-22-2004.

[Sec. 1388(k)—Stricken]

Amendments

• **1990, Omnibus Budget Reconciliation Act of 1990 (P.L. 101-508)**

P.L. 101-508, § 11813(b)(24):

Amended Code Sec. 1388 by striking subsection (k). **Effective**, generally, for property placed in service after 12-31-90. However, for exceptions, see Act Sec. 11813(c)(2), below. Prior to being stricken, Code Sec. 1388(k) read as follows:

(k) CROSS REFERENCE.—

For provisions relating to the apportionment of the investment credit between cooperative organizations and their patrons, see section 46(h).

P.L. 101-508, § 11813(c)(2), provides:

(2) EXCEPTIONS.—The amendments made by this section shall not apply to—

(A) any transition property (as defined in section 49(e) of the Internal Revenue Code of 1986 (as in effect on the day before the date of the enactment of this Act),

(B) any property with respect to which qualified progress expenditures were previously taken into account under section 46(d) of such Code (as so in effect), and

(C) any property described in section 46(b)(2)(C) of such Code (as so in effect).

• **1986, Consolidated Omnibus Budget Reconciliation Act of 1985 (P.L. 99-272)**

P.L. 99-272, § 13210(a):

Redesignated Code Sec. 1388(j) as Code Sec. 1388(k). For the **effective** date, see Act Sec. 13210(c) in the amendment notes following Code Sec. 1388(j).

• **1978, Revenue Act of 1978 (P.L. 95-600)**

P.L. 95-600, § 316(b)(3):

Added Code Sec. 1388(j). **Effective** for tax years ending after 10-31-78.

Subchapter U—Designation and Treatment of Empowerment Zones, Enterprise Communities, and Rural Development Investment Areas

Part I.	Designation.
Part II.	Tax-exempt facility bonds for empowerment zones and enterprise communities.
Part III.	Additional incentives for empowerment zones.
Part IV.	Incentives for education zones.
Part V.	Regulations.

PART I—DESIGNATION

Sec. 1391.	Designation procedure.
Sec. 1392.	Eligibility criteria.
Sec. 1393.	Definitions and special rules.

INCOME TAX—TREATMENT OF EMPOWERMENT ZONES

[Sec. 1391]

SEC. 1391. DESIGNATION PROCEDURE.

[Sec. 1391(a)]

(a) IN GENERAL.—From among the areas nominated for designation under this section, the appropriate Secretaries may designate empowerment zones and enterprise communities.

[Sec. 1391(b)]

(b) NUMBER OF DESIGNATIONS.—

(1) ENTERPRISE COMMUNITIES.—The appropriate Secretaries may designate in the aggregate 95 nominated areas as enterprise communities under this section, subject to the availability of eligible nominated areas. Of that number, not more than 65 may be designated in urban areas and not more than 30 may be designated in rural areas.

(2) EMPOWERMENT ZONES.—The appropriate Secretaries may designate in the aggregate 11 nominated areas as empowerment zones under this section, subject to the availability of eligible nominated areas. Of that number, not more than 8 may be designated in urban areas and not more than 3 may be designated in rural areas. If 8 empowerment zones are designated in urban areas, no less than 1 shall be designated in an urban area the most populous city of which has a population of 500,000 or less and no less than 1 shall be a nominated area which includes areas in 2 States and which has a population of 50,000 or less. The Secretary of Housing and Urban Development shall designate empowerment zones located in urban areas in such a manner that the aggregate population of all such zones does not exceed 1,000,000.

Amendments

- **1997, Taxpayer Relief Act of 1997 (P.L. 105-34)**

P.L. 105-34, §951(a)(1)-(3):

Amended Code Sec. 1391(b)(2) by striking "9" and inserting "11", by striking "6" and inserting "8", and by striking "750,000" and inserting "1,000,000". **Effective** 8-5-97, except that designations of new empowerment zones made pursuant to such amendment will be made during the 180-day period beginning on 8-5-97. No designation pursuant to such amendment will take effect before 1-1-2000.

[Sec. 1391(c)]

(c) PERIOD DESIGNATIONS MAY BE MADE.—A designation may be made under subsection (a) only after 1993 and before 1996.

Amendments

- **1997, Taxpayer Relief Act of 1997 (P.L. 105-34)**

P.L. 105-34, §952(d)(2):

Amended Code Sec. 1391(c) by striking "this section" and inserting "subsection (a)". **Effective** 8-5-97.

[Sec. 1391(d)]

(d) PERIOD FOR WHICH DESIGNATION IS IN EFFECT.—

(1) IN GENERAL.—Any designation under this section shall remain in effect during the period beginning on the date of the designation and ending on the earliest of—

(A)(i) in the case of an empowerment zone, December 31, 2025, or

(ii) in the case of an enterprise community, the close of the 10th calendar year beginning on or after such date of designation,

(B) the termination date designated by the State and local governments as provided for in their nomination, or

(C) the date the appropriate Secretary revokes the designation.

(2) REVOCATION OF DESIGNATION.—The appropriate Secretary may revoke the designation under this section of an area if such Secretary determines that the local government or the State in which it is located—

(A) has modified the boundaries of the area, or

(B) is not complying substantially with, or fails to make progress in achieving the benchmarks set forth in, the strategic plan under subsection (f)(2).

Amendments

- **2020, Taxpayer Certainty and Disaster Tax Relief Act of 2020 (P.L. 116-260)**

P.L. 116-260, §118(a), Div. EE:

Amended Code Sec. 1391(d)(1)(A)(i) by striking "December 31, 2020" and inserting "December 31, 2025". **Effective** for tax years beginning after 12-31-2020. For a special rule, see Act Sec. 118(d), Div. EE, below.

P.L. 116-260, §118(d), Div. EE, provides:

(d) TREATMENT OF CERTAIN TERMINATION DATES SPECIFIED IN NOMINATIONS.—In the case of a designation of an empowerment zone the nomination for which included a termination date which is contemporaneous with the date specified in subparagraph (A)(i) of section 1391(d)(1) of the Internal Revenue Code of 1986 (as in effect before the enactment of this Act), subparagraph (B) of such section shall not apply with respect to such designation if, after the date of the enactment of this section, the entity which made such nomination amends the nomination to provide for a new termination date in such manner as the Secretary of the Treasury (or the Secretary's designee) may provide.

- **2019, Taxpayer Certainty and Disaster Tax Relief Act of 2019 (P.L. 116-94)**

P.L. 116-94, §118(a), Div. Q:

Amended Code Sec. 1391(d)(1)(A)(i) by striking "December 31, 2017" and inserting "December 31, 2020". **Effective** for tax years beginning after 12-31-2017. For a special rule, see Act Sec. 118(b), Div. Q, below.

P.L. 116-94, §118(b), Div. Q, provides:

(b) TREATMENT OF CERTAIN TERMINATION DATES SPECIFIED IN NOMINATIONS.—In the case of a designation of an empowerment zone the nomination for which included a termination date which is contemporaneous with the date specified in subparagraph (A)(i) of section 1391(d)(1) of the Internal Revenue Code of 1986 (as in effect before the enactment of this Act), subparagraph (B) of such section shall not apply with respect to such designation if, after the date of the enactment of this section, the entity which made such nomination amends the nomination to provide for a new termination date in such manner as the Secretary of the Treasury (or the Secretary's designee) may provide.

- **2018, Bipartisan Budget Act of 2018 (P.L. 115-123)**

P.L. 115-123, §40311(a)(1), Div. D:

Amended Code Sec. 1391(d)(1)(A)(i) by striking "December 31, 2016" and inserting "December 31, 2017". **Effective** for tax years beginning after 12-31-2016. For a special rule, see Act Sec. 40311(a)(2), Div. D, below.

P.L. 115-123, §40311(a)(2), Div. D, provides:

(2) TREATMENT OF CERTAIN TERMINATION DATES SPECIFIED IN NOMINATIONS.—In the case of a designation of an empowerment zone the nomination for which included a termination date which is contemporaneous with the date specified in subparagraph (A)(i) of section 1391(d)(1) of the Internal Revenue Code of 1986 (as in effect before the enactment of this Act), subparagraph (B) of such section shall not apply with respect to such designation if, after the date of the enactment of this section, the entity which made such nomination amends the nomination to provide for a new termination date in such manner as the Secretary of the Treasury (or the Secretary's designee) may provide.

- **2015, Protecting Americans from Tax Hikes Act of 2015 (P.L. 114-113)**

P.L. 114-113, §171(a)(1), Div. Q:

Amended Code Sec. 1391(d)(1)(A)(i) by striking "December 31, 2014" and inserting "December 31, 2016". **Effective** for tax years beginning after 12-31-2014. For a special rule, see Act Sec. 171(a)(2), below.

P.L. 114-113, §171(a)(2), Div. Q, provides:

(2) TREATMENT OF CERTAIN TERMINATION DATES SPECIFIED IN NOMINATIONS.—In the case of a designation of an empowerment zone the nomination for which included a termination date which is contemporaneous with the date specified in subparagraph (A)(i) of section 1391(d)(1) of the Internal Revenue Code of 1986 (as in effect before the enactment of this Act), subparagraph (B) of such section shall not apply with respect to such designation if, after the date of the enactment of this section, the entity which made such nomination amends the nomination to provide for a new termination date in such manner as the Secretary of the Treasury (or the Secretary's designee) may provide.

INCOME TAX—TREATMENT OF EMPOWERMENT ZONES

• **2014, Tax Increase Prevention Act of 2014 (P.L. 113-295)**

P.L. 113-295, §139(a), Division A:

Amended Code Sec. 1391(d)(1)(A)(i) by striking "December 31, 2013" and inserting "December 31, 2014". **Effective** for periods after 12-31-2013. For a special rule, see Act Sec. 139(b), Division A, below.

P.L. 113-295, §139(b), Division A, provides:

(b) TREATMENT OF CERTAIN TERMINATION DATES SPECIFIED IN NOMINATIONS.—In the case of a designation of an empowerment zone the nomination for which included a termination date which is contemporaneous with the date specified in subparagraph (A)(i) of section 1391(d)(1) of the Internal Revenue Code of 1986 (as in effect before the enactment of this Act), subparagraph (B) of such section shall not apply with respect to such designation if, after the date of the enactment of this section, the entity which made such nomination amends the nomination to provide for a new termination date in such manner as the Secretary of the Treasury (or the Secretary's designee) may provide.

• **2013, American Taxpayer Relief Act of 2012 (P.L. 112-240)**

P.L. 112-240, §327(a):

Amended Code Sec. 1391(d)(1)(A)(i) by striking "December 31, 2011" and inserting "December 31, 2013". **Effective** for periods after 12-31-2011.

P.L. 112-240, §327(c), provides:

(c) TREATMENT OF CERTAIN TERMINATION DATES SPECIFIED IN NOMINATIONS.—In the case of a designation of an empowerment zone the nomination for which included a termination date which is contemporaneous with the date specified in subparagraph (A)(i) of section 1391(d)(1) of the Internal Revenue Code of 1986 (as in effect before the enactment of this Act), subparagraph (B) of such section shall not apply with respect to such designation if, after the date of the enactment of this section, the entity which made such nomination amends the nomination to provide for a new termination date in such manner as the Secretary of the Treasury (or the Secretary's designee) may provide.

• **2010, Tax Relief, Unemployment Insurance Reauthorization, and Job Creation Act of 2010 (P.L. 111-312)**

P.L. 111-312, §753(a)(1):

Amended Code Sec. 1391(d)(1)(A)(i) by striking "December 31, 2009" and inserting "December 31, 2011". **Effective** for periods after 12-31-2009.

P.L. 111-312, §753(c), provides:

(c) TREATMENT OF CERTAIN TERMINATION DATES SPECIFIED IN NOMINATIONS.—In the case of a designation of an empowerment zone the nomination for which included a termination date which is contemporaneous with the date specified in subparagraph (A)(i) of section 1391(d)(1) of the Internal Revenue Code of 1986 (as in effect before the enactment of this Act), subparagraph (B) of such section shall not apply with respect to such designation if, after the date of the enactment of this section, the entity which made such nomination amends the nomination to provide for a new termination date in such manner as the Secretary of the Treasury (or the Secretary's designee) may provide.

• **2000, Community Renewal Tax Relief Act of 2010 (P.L. 106-554)**

P.L. 106-554, §112:

Amended Code Sec. 1391(d)(1)(A). **Effective** 12-21-2000. Prior to amendment, Code Sec. 1391(d)(1)(A) read as follows:

(A) the close of the 10th calendar year beginning on or after such date of designation,

[Sec. 1391(e)]

(e) LIMITATIONS ON DESIGNATIONS.—No area may be designated under this section unless—

    (1) the area is nominated by 1 or more local governments and the State or States in which it is located for designation under this section,

    (2) such State or States and the local governments have the authority—

        (A) to nominate the area for designation under this section, and

        (B) to provide the assurances described in paragraph (3),

    (3) such State or States and the local governments provide written assurances satisfactory to the appropriate Secretary that the strategic plan described in the application under subsection (f)(2) for such area will be implemented,

    (4) the appropriate Secretary determines that any information furnished is reasonably accurate, and

    (5) such State or States and local governments certify that no portion of the area nominated is already included in an empowerment zone or in an enterprise community or in an area otherwise nominated to be designated under this section.

Amendments

• **1997, Taxpayer Relief Act of 1997 (P.L. 105-34)**

P.L. 105-34, §952(d)(1):

Amended Code Sec. 1391(e) by striking "subsection (a)" and inserting "this section". **Effective** 8-5-97.

[Sec. 1391(f)]

(f) APPLICATION.—No area may be designated under this section unless the application for such designation—

    (1) demonstrates that the nominated area satisfies the eligibility criteria described in section 1392,

    (2) includes a strategic plan for accomplishing the purposes of this subchapter that—

        (A) describes the coordinated economic, human, community, and physical development plan and related activities proposed for the nominated area,

        (B) describes the process by which the affected community is a full partner in the process of developing and implementing the plan and the extent to which local institutions and organizations have contributed to the planning process,

        (C) identifies the amount of State, local, and private resources that will be available in the nominated area and the private/public partnerships to be used, which may include participation by, and cooperation with, universities, medical centers, and other private and public entities,

        (D) identifies the funding requested under any Federal program in support of the proposed economic, human, community, and physical development and related activities,

        (E) identifies baselines, methods, and benchmarks for measuring the success of carrying out the strategic plan, including the extent to which poor persons and families will be empowered to become economically self-sufficient, and

        (F) does not include any action to assist any establishment in relocating from one area outside the nominated area to the nominated area, except that assistance for the expansion of an existing business entity through the establishment of a new branch, affiliate, or subsidiary is permitted if—

            (i) the establishment of the new branch, affiliate, or subsidiary will not result in a decrease in employment in the area of original location or in any other area where the existing business entity conducts business operations, and

            (ii) there is no reason to believe that the new branch, affiliate, or subsidiary is being established with the intention of closing down the operations of the existing business entity in the area of its original location or in any other area where the existing business entity conducts business operation, and

    (3) includes such other information as may be required by the appropriate Secretary.

Amendments

• **1997, Taxpayer Relief Act of 1997 (P.L. 105-34)**

P.L. 105-34, §952(d)(1):

Amended Code Sec. 1391(f) by striking "subsection (a)" and inserting "this section". **Effective** 8-5-97.

• **1993, Omnibus Budget Reconciliation Act of 1993 (P.L. 103-66)**

P.L. 103-66, §13301(a):

Amended chapter 1 by inserting after subchapter T a new subchapter U (sections 1391-1397D). **Effective** 8-10-93.

INCOME TAX—TREATMENT OF EMPOWERMENT ZONES

[Sec. 1391(g)]

(g) ADDITIONAL DESIGNATIONS PERMITTED.—

(1) IN GENERAL.—In addition to the areas designated under subsection (a), the appropriate Secretaries may designate in the aggregate an additional 20 nominated areas as empowerment zones under this section, subject to the availability of eligible nominated areas. Of that number, not more than 15 may be designated in urban areas and not more than 5 may be designated in rural areas.

(2) PERIOD DESIGNATIONS MAY BE MADE AND TAKE EFFECT.—A designation may be made under this subsection after the date of the enactment of this subsection and before January 1, 1999.

(3) MODIFICATIONS TO ELIGIBILITY CRITERIA, ETC.—

(A) POVERTY RATE REQUIREMENT.—

(i) IN GENERAL.—A nominated area shall be eligible for designation under this subsection only if the poverty rate for each population census tract within the nominated area is not less than 20 percent and the poverty rate for at least 90 percent of the population census tracts within the nominated area is not less than 25 percent.

(ii) TREATMENT OF CENSUS TRACTS WITH SMALL POPULATIONS.—A population census tract with a population of less than 2,000 shall be treated as having a poverty rate of not less than 25 percent if—

(I) more than 75 percent of such tract is zoned for commercial or industrial use, and

(II) such tract is contiguous to 1 or more other population census tracts which have a poverty rate of not less than 25 percent (determined without regard to this clause).

(iii) EXCEPTION FOR DEVELOPABLE SITES.—Clause (i) shall not apply to up to 3 noncontiguous parcels in a nominated area which may be developed for commercial or industrial purposes. The aggregate area of noncontiguous parcels to which the preceding sentence applies with respect to any nominated area shall not exceed 2,000 acres.

(iv) CERTAIN PROVISIONS NOT TO APPLY.—Section 1392(a)(4) (and so much of paragraphs (1) and (2) of section 1392(b) as relate to section 1392(a)(4)) shall not apply to an area nominated for designation under this subsection.

(v) SPECIAL RULE FOR RURAL EMPOWERMENT ZONE.—The Secretary of Agriculture may designate not more than 1 empowerment zone in a rural area without regard to clause (i) if such area satisfies emigration criteria specified by the Secretary of Agriculture.

(B) SIZE LIMITATION.—

(i) IN GENERAL.—The parcels described in subparagraph (A)(iii) shall not be taken into account in determining whether the requirement of subparagraph (A) or (B) of section 1392(a)(3) is met.

(ii) SPECIAL RULE FOR RURAL AREAS.—If a population census tract (or equivalent division under section 1392(b)(4)) in a rural area exceeds 1,000 square miles or includes a substantial amount of land owned by the Federal, State, or local government, the nominated area may exclude such excess square mileage or governmentally owned land and the exclusion of that area will not be treated as violating the continuous boundary requirement of section 1392(a)(3)(B).

(C) AGGREGATE POPULATION LIMITATION.—The aggregate population limitation under the last sentence of subsection (b)(2) shall not apply to a designation under paragraph (1).

(D) PREVIOUSLY DESIGNATED ENTERPRISE COMMUNITIES MAY BE INCLUDED.—Subsection (e)(5) shall not apply to any enterprise community designated under subsection (a) that is also nominated for designation under this subsection.

(E) INDIAN RESERVATIONS MAY BE NOMINATED.—

(i) IN GENERAL.—Section 1393(a)(4) shall not apply to an area nominated for designation under this subsection.

(ii) SPECIAL RULE.—An area in an Indian reservation shall be treated as nominated by a State and a local government if it is nominated by the reservation governing body (as determined by the Secretary of the Interior).

Amendments

• **2018, Tax Technical Corrections Act of 2018 (P.L. 115-141)**

P.L. 115-141, §401(a)(194), Div. U:

Amended Code Sec. 1391(g)(3)(E)(ii) by striking "Interior" and inserting "the Interior". **Effective** 3-23-2018.

• **2000, Community Renewal Tax Relief Act of 2000 (P.L. 106-554)**

P.L. 106-554, §319(13):

Amended Code Sec. 1391(g)(3)(C) by striking "paragraph (1)(B)" and inserting "paragraph (1)". **Effective** 12-21-2000.

• **1997, Taxpayer Relief Act of 1997 (P.L. 105-34)**

P.L. 105-34, §952(a):

Amended Code Sec. 1391 by adding a new subsection (g). **Effective** 8-5-97.

[Sec. 1391(h)]

(h) ADDITIONAL DESIGNATIONS PERMITTED.—

(1) IN GENERAL.—In addition to the areas designated under subsections (a) and (g), the appropriate Secretaries may designate in the aggregate an additional 9 nominated areas as empowerment zones under this section, subject to the availability of eligible nominated areas. Of that number, not more than seven may be designated in urban areas and not more than 2 may be designated in rural areas.

(2) PERIOD DESIGNATIONS MAY BE MADE AND TAKE EFFECT.—A designation may be made under this subsection after the date of the enactment of this subsection and before January 1, 2002.

(3) MODIFICATIONS TO ELIGIBILITY CRITERIA, ETC.—The rules of subsection (g)(3) shall apply to designations under this subsection.

(4) EMPOWERMENT ZONES WHICH BECOME RENEWAL COMMUNITIES.—The number of areas which may be designated as empowerment zones under this subsection shall be increased by 1 for each area which ceases to be an empowerment zone by reason of section 1400E(e). Each additional area designated by reason of the preceding sentence shall have the same urban or rural character as the area it is replacing.

Amendments

• **2010, Tax Relief, Unemployment Insurance Reauthorization, and Job Creation Act of 2010 (P.L. 111-312)**

P.L. 111-312, §753(a)(2):

Amended Code Sec. 1391(h)(2) by striking the last sentence. **Effective** for periods after 12-31-2009. Prior to being stricken, the last sentence of Code Sec. 1391(h)(2) read as follows:

Subject to subparagraphs (B) and (C) of subsection (d)(1), such designations shall remain in effect during the period beginning on January 1, 2002, and ending on December 31, 2009.

• **2000, Community Renewal Tax Relief Act of 2000 (P.L. 106-554)**

P.L. 106-554, §111:

Amended Code Sec. 1391 by adding at the end a new subsection (h). **Effective** 12-21-2000.

INCOME TAX—TREATMENT OF EMPOWERMENT ZONES

[Sec. 1392]

SEC. 1392. ELIGIBILITY CRITERIA.

[Sec. 1392(a)]

(a) IN GENERAL.—A nominated area shall be eligible for designation under section 1391 only if it meets the following criteria:

(1) POPULATION.—The nominated area has a maximum population of—

(A) in the case of an urban area, the lesser of—

(i) 200,000, or

(ii) the greater of 50,000 or 10 percent of the population of the most populous city located within the nominated area, and

(B) in the case of a rural area, 30,000.

(2) DISTRESS.—The nominated area is one of pervasive poverty, unemployment, and general distress.

(3) SIZE.—The nominated area—

(A) does not exceed 20 square miles if an urban area or 1,000 square miles if a rural area,

(B) has a boundary which is continuous, or, except in the case of a rural area located in more than 1 State, consists of not more than 3 noncontiguous parcels,

(C)(i) in the case of an urban area, is located entirely within no more than 2 contiguous States, and

(ii) in the case of a rural area, is located entirely within no more than 3 contiguous States, and

(D) does not include any portion of a central business district (as such term is used for purposes of the most recent Census of Retail Trade) unless the poverty rate for each population census tract in such district is not less than 35 percent (30 percent in the case of an enterprise community).

(4) POVERTY RATE.—The poverty rate—

(A) for each population census tract within the nominated area is not less than 20 percent,

(B) for at least 90 percent of the population census tracts within the nominated area is not less than 25 percent, and

(C) for at least 50 percent of the population census tracts within the nominated area is not less than 35 percent.

[Sec. 1392(b)]

(b) SPECIAL RULES RELATING TO DETERMINATION OF POVERTY RATE.—For purposes of subsection (a)(4)—

(1) TREATMENT OF CENSUS TRACTS WITH SMALL POPULATIONS.—

(A) TRACTS WITH NO POPULATION.—In the case of a population census tract with no population—

(i) such tract shall be treated as having a poverty rate which meets the requirements of subparagraphs (A) and (B) of subsection (a)(4), but

(ii) such tract shall be treated as having a zero poverty rate for purposes of applying subparagraph (C) thereof.

(B) TRACTS WITH POPULATIONS OF LESS THAN 2,000.—A population census tract with a population of less than 2,000 shall be treated as having a poverty rate which meets the requirements of subparagraphs (A) and (B) of subsection (a)(4) if more than 75 percent of such tract is zoned for commercial or industrial use.

(2) DISCRETION TO ADJUST REQUIREMENTS FOR ENTERPRISE COMMUNITIES.—In determining whether a nominated area is eligible for designation as an enterprise community, the appropriate Secretary may, where necessary to carry out the purposes of this subchapter, reduce by 5 percentage points one of the following thresholds for not more than 10 percent of the population census tracts (or, if fewer, 5 population census tracts) in the nominated area:

(A) The 20 percent threshold in subsection (a)(4)(A).

(B) The 25 percent threshold in subsection (a)(4)(B).

(C) The 35 percent threshold in subsection (a)(4)(C).

If the appropriate Secretary elects to reduce the threshold under subparagraph (C), such Secretary may (in lieu of applying the preceding sentence) reduce by 10 percentage points the threshold under subparagraph (C) for 3 population census tracts.

(3) EACH NONCONTIGUOUS AREA MUST SATISFY POVERTY RATE RULE.—A nominated area may not include a noncontiguous parcel unless such parcel separately meets (subject to paragraphs (1) and (2)) the criteria set forth in subsection (a)(4).

(4) AREAS NOT WITHIN CENSUS TRACTS.—In the case of an area which is not tracted for population census tracts, the equivalent county divisions (as defined by the Bureau of the Census for purposes of defining poverty areas) shall be used for purposes of determining poverty rates.

[Sec. 1392(c)]

(c) FACTORS TO CONSIDER.—From among the nominated areas eligible for designation under section 1391 by the appropriate Secretary, such appropriate Secretary shall make designations of empowerment zones and enterprise communities on the basis of—

(1) the effectiveness of the strategic plan submitted pursuant to section 1391(f)(2) and the assurances made pursuant to section 1391(e)(3), and

(2) criteria specified by the appropriate Secretary.

Amendments

• **1993, Omnibus Budget Reconciliation Act of 1993 (P.L. 103-66)**

P.L. 103-66, § 13301(a):

Added new Code Sec. 1392. **Effective** 8-10-93.

[Sec. 1392(d)]

(d) SPECIAL ELIGIBILITY FOR NOMINATED AREAS LOCATED IN ALASKA OR HAWAII.—A nominated area in Alaska or Hawaii shall be treated as meeting the requirements of paragraphs (2), (3), and (4) of subsection (a) if for each census tract or block group within such area 20 percent or more of the families have income which is 50 percent or less of the statewide median family income (as determined under section 143).

Amendments

• **1997, Taxpayer Relief Act of 1997 (P.L. 105-34)**

P.L. 105-34, § 954:

Amended Code Sec. 1392 by adding at the end a new subsection (d). **Effective** 8-5-97.

INCOME TAX—TREATMENT OF EMPOWERMENT ZONES

[Sec. 1393]
SEC. 1393. DEFINITIONS AND SPECIAL RULES.

[Sec. 1393(a)]
(a) IN GENERAL.—For purposes of this subchapter—
  (1) APPROPRIATE SECRETARY.—The term "appropriate Secretary" means—
    (A) the Secretary of Housing and Urban Development in the case of any nominated area which is located in an urban area, and
    (B) the Secretary of Agriculture in the case of any nominated area which is located in a rural area.
  (2) RURAL AREA.—The term "rural area" means any area which is—
    (A) outside of a metropolitan statistical area (within the meaning of section 143(k)(2)(B)), or
    (B) determined by the Secretary of Agriculture, after consultation with the Secretary of Commerce, to be a rural area.
  (3) URBAN AREA.—The term "urban area" means an area which is not a rural area.
  (4) SPECIAL RULES FOR INDIAN RESERVATIONS.—
    (A) IN GENERAL.—No empowerment zone or enterprise community may include any area within an Indian reservation.
    (B) INDIAN RESERVATION DEFINED.—The term "Indian reservation" has the meaning given such term by section 168(j)(6).
  (5) LOCAL GOVERNMENT.—The term "local government" means—
    (A) any county, city, town, township, parish, village, or other general purpose political subdivision of a State, and
    (B) any combination of political subdivisions described in subparagraph (A) recognized by the appropriate Secretary.
  (6) NOMINATED AREA.—The term "nominated area" means an area which is nominated by 1 or more local governments and the State or States in which it is located for designation under section 1391.
  (7) GOVERNMENTS.—If more than 1 State or local government seeks to nominate an area under this part, any reference to, or requirement of, this subchapter shall apply to all such governments.
  (8) SPECIAL RULE.—An area shall be treated as nominated by a State and a local government if it is nominated by an economic development corporation chartered by the State.
  (9) USE OF CENSUS DATA.—Population and poverty rate shall be determined by the most recent decennial census data available.

[Sec. 1393(b)]
(b) EMPOWERMENT ZONE; ENTERPRISE COMMUNITY.—For purposes of this title, the terms "empowerment zone" and "enterprise community" mean areas designated as such under section 1391.

Amendments
• 1993, Omnibus Budget Reconciliation Act of 1993 (P.L. 103-66)
P.L. 103-66, § 13301(a):
  Added new Code Sec. 1393. Effective 8-10-93.

PART II—TAX-EXEMPT FACILITY BONDS FOR EMPOWERMENT ZONES AND ENTERPRISE COMMUNITIES

Sec. 1394.   Tax-exempt enterprise zone facility bonds.

[Sec. 1394]
SEC. 1394. TAX-EXEMPT ENTERPRISE ZONE FACILITY BONDS.

[Sec. 1394(a)]
(a) IN GENERAL.—For purposes of part IV of subchapter B of this chapter (relating to tax exemption requirements for State and local bonds), the term "exempt facility bond" includes any bond issued as part of an issue 95 percent or more of the net proceeds (as defined in section 150(a)(3)) of which are to be used to provide any enterprise zone facility.

[Sec. 1394(b)]
(b) ENTERPRISE ZONE FACILITY.—For purposes of this section—
  (1) IN GENERAL.—The term "enterprise zone facility" means any qualified zone property the principal user of which is an enterprise zone business, and any land which is functionally related and subordinate to such property.
  (2) QUALIFIED ZONE PROPERTY.—The term "qualified zone property" has the meaning given such term by section 1397D; except that—
    (A) the references to empowerment zones shall be treated as including references to enterprise communities, and
    (B) section 1397D(a)(2) shall be applied by substituting "an amount equal to 15 percent of the adjusted basis" for "an amount equal to the adjusted basis".
  (3) ENTERPRISE ZONE BUSINESS.—
    (A) IN GENERAL.—Except as modified in this paragraph, the term "enterprise zone business" has the meaning given such term by section 1397C.
    (B) MODIFICATIONS.—In applying section 1397C for purposes of this section—
      (i) BUSINESSES IN ENTERPRISE COMMUNITIES ELIGIBLE.—
        (I) IN GENERAL.—Except as provided in subclause (II), references in section 1397C to empowerment zones shall be treated as including references to enterprise communities.
        (II) SPECIAL RULE FOR EMPLOYEE RESIDENCE TEST.—For purposes of subsections (b)(6) and (c)(5) of section 1397C, an employee shall be treated as a resident of an empowerment zone if such employee is a resident of an empowerment zone, an enterprise community, or a qualified low-income community within an applicable nominating jurisdiction.
      (ii) WAIVER OF REQUIREMENTS DURING STARTUP PERIOD.—A business shall not fail to be treated as an enterprise zone business during the startup period if—
        (I) as of the beginning of the startup period, it is reasonably expected that such business will be an enterprise zone business (as defined in section 1397C as modified by this paragraph) at the end of such period, and
        (II) such business makes bona fide efforts to be such a business.

INCOME TAX—TREATMENT OF EMPOWERMENT ZONES

(iii) REDUCED REQUIREMENTS AFTER TESTING PERIOD.—A business shall not fail to be treated as an enterprise zone business for any taxable year beginning after the testing period by reason of failing to meet any requirement of subsection (b) or (c) of section 1397C if at least 35 percent of the employees of such business for such year are residents of an empowerment zone, an enterprise community, or a qualified low-income community within an applicable nominating jurisdiction. The preceding sentence shall not apply to any business which is not a qualified business by reason of paragraph (1), (4), or (5) of section 1397C(d).

(C) QUALIFIED LOW-INCOME COMMUNITY.—For purposes of subparagraph (B)—

(i) IN GENERAL.—The term "qualified low-income community" means any population census tract if—

(I) the poverty rate for such tract is at least 20 percent, or

(II) the median family income for such tract does not exceed 80 percent of statewide median family income (or, in the case of a tract located within a metropolitan area, metropolitan area median family income if greater).

Subclause (II) shall be applied using possessionwide median family income in the case of census tracts located within a possession of the United States.

(ii) TARGETED POPULATIONS.—The Secretary shall prescribe regulations under which 1 or more targeted populations (within the meaning of section 103(20) of the Riegle Community Development and Regulatory Improvement Act of 1994) may be treated as qualified low-income communities.

(iii) AREAS NOT WITHIN CENSUS TRACTS.—In the case of an area which is not tracted for population census tracts, the equivalent county divisions (as defined by the Bureau of the Census for purposes of defining poverty areas) shall be used for purposes of determining poverty rates and median family income.

(iv) MODIFICATION OF INCOME REQUIREMENT FOR CENSUS TRACTS WITHIN HIGH MIGRATION RURAL COUNTIES.—

(I) IN GENERAL.—In the case of a population census tract located within a high migration rural county, clause (i)(II) shall be applied to areas not located within a metropolitan area by substituting "85 percent" for "80 percent".

(II) HIGH MIGRATION RURAL COUNTY.—For purposes of this clause, the term "high migration rural county" means any county which, during the 20-year period ending with the year in which the most recent census was conducted, has a net out-migration of inhabitants from the county of at least 10 percent of the population of the county at the beginning of such period.

(D) OTHER DEFINITIONS RELATING TO SUBPARAGRAPH (B).—For purposes of subparagraph (B)—

(i) STARTUP PERIOD.—The term "startup period" means, with respect to any property being provided for any business, the period before the first taxable year beginning more than 2 years after the later of—

(I) the date of issuance of the issue providing such property, or

(II) the date such property is first placed in service after such issuance (or, if earlier, the date which is 3 years after the date described in subclause (I)).

(ii) TESTING PERIOD.—The term "testing period" means the first 3 taxable years beginning after the startup period.

(iii) APPLICABLE NOMINATING JURISDICTION.—The term "applicable nominating jurisdiction" means, with respect to any empowerment zone or enterprise community, any local government that nominated such community for designation under section 1391.

(E) PORTIONS OF BUSINESS MAY BE ENTERPRISE ZONE BUSINESS.—The term "enterprise zone business" includes any trades or businesses which would qualify as an enterprise zone business (determined after the modifications of subparagraph (B)) if such trades or businesses were separately incorporated.

Amendments

• **2018, Tax Technical Corrections Act of 2018 (P.L. 115-141)**

P.L. 115-141, §401(a)(195), Div. U:

Amended Code Sec. 1394(b)(3)(B)(i)(II) by striking "subsection" and inserting "subsections". **Effective** 3-23-2018.

• **2015, Protecting Americans from Tax Hikes Act of 2015 (P.L. 114-113)**

P.L. 114-113, §171(b)(1)-(2), Div. Q:

Amended Code Sec. 1394(b)(3)(B)(i) by striking "References" and inserting

"(I) IN GENERAL.—Except as provided in subclause (II), references",

and by adding at the end a new subclause (II). **Effective** for bonds issued after 12-31-2015.

P.L. 114-113, §171(c)(1), Div. Q:

Amended Code Sec. 1394(b)(3) by redesignating subparagraphs (C)-(D) as subparagraphs (D)-(E), respectively, and by inserting after subparagraph (B) a new subparagraph (C). **Effective** for bonds issued after 12-31-2015.

P.L. 114-113, §171(c)(2), Div. Q:

Amended Code Sec. 1394(b)(3)(D), as redesignated by Act Sec. 171(c)(1), by adding at the end a new clause (iii). **Effective** for bonds issued after 12-31-2015.

P.L. 114-113, §171(d)(1), Div. Q:

Amended Code Sec. 1394(b)(3)(B)(iii) by striking "or an enterprise community" and inserting ", an enterprise community, or a qualified low-income community within an applicable nominating jurisdiction". **Effective** for bonds issued after 12-31-2015.

P.L. 114-113, §171(d)(2), Div. Q:

Amended Code Sec. 1394(b)(3)(D), as redesignated by Act Sec. 171(c)(1), by striking "DEFINITIONS" and inserting "OTHER DEFINITIONS". **Effective** for bonds issued after 12-31-2015.

• **2000, Community Renewal Tax Relief Act of 2000 (P.L. 106-554)**

P.L. 106-554, §116(b)(3)(A)-(B):

Amended Code Sec. 1394(b)(2) by striking "section 1397C" and inserting "section 1397D", and by striking "section 1397C(a)(2)" and inserting "section 1397D(a)(2)". **Effective** for qualified empowerment zone assets acquired after 12-21-2000.

P.L. 106-554, §116(b)(4)(A)-(B):

Amended Code Sec. 1394(b)(3) by striking "section 1397B" each place it appears and inserting "section 1397C", and by striking "section 1397B(d)" and inserting "section 1397C(d)". **Effective** for qualified empowerment zone assets acquired after 12-21-2000.

• **1997, Taxpayer Relief Act of 1997 (P.L. 105-34)**

P.L. 105-34, §955(a):

Amended Code Sec. 1394(b)(3). **Effective** for obligations issued after 8-5-97. Prior to amendment, Code Sec. 1394(b)(3) read as follows:

(3) ENTERPRISE ZONE BUSINESS.—The term "enterprise zone business" has the meaning given to such term by section 1397B, except that—

(A) references to empowerment zones shall be treated as including references to enterprise communities, and

(B) such term includes any trades or businesses which would qualify as an enterprise zone business (determined after the modification of subparagraph (A)) if such trades or businesses were separately incorporated.

P.L. 105-34, §955(b):

Amended Code Sec. 1394(b)(2). **Effective** for obligations issued after 8-5-97. Prior to amendment, Code Sec. 1394(b)(2) read as follows:

(2) QUALIFIED ZONE PROPERTY.—The term "qualified zone property" has the meaning given such term by section 1397C; except that the references to empowerment zones shall be treated as including references to enterprise communities.

[Sec. 1394(c)]

(c) LIMITATION ON AMOUNT OF BONDS.—

(1) IN GENERAL.—Subsection (a) shall not apply to any issue if the aggregate amount of outstanding enterprise zone facility bonds allocable to any person (taking into account such issue) exceeds—

(A) $3,000,000 with respect to any 1 empowerment zone or enterprise community, or

(B) $20,000,000 with respect to all empowerment zones and enterprise communities.

(2) AGGREGATE ENTERPRISE ZONE FACILITY BOND BENEFIT.—For purposes of paragraph (1), the aggregate amount of outstanding enterprise zone facility bonds allocable to any person shall be determined under rules similar to the rules of section 144(a)(10), taking into account only bonds to which subsection (a) applies.

INCOME TAX—TREATMENT OF EMPOWERMENT ZONES

Amendments

• **2002, Job Creation and Worker Assistance Act of 2002 (P.L. 107-147)**

P.L. 107-147, § 417(16):

Amended Code Sec. 1394(c)(2) by striking "subparagraph (A)" and inserting "paragraph (1)". **Effective** 3-9-2002.

[Sec. 1394(d)]

(d) ACQUISITION OF LAND AND EXISTING PROPERTY PERMITTED.—The requirements of sections 147(c)(1)(A) and 147(d) shall not apply to any bond described in subsection (a).

[Sec. 1394(e)]

(e) PENALTY FOR CEASING TO MEET REQUIREMENTS.—

(1) FAILURES CORRECTED.—An issue which fails to meet 1 or more of the requirements of subsections (a) and (b) shall be treated as meeting such requirements if—

(A) the issuer and any principal user in good faith attempted to meet such requirements, and

(B) any failure to meet such requirements is corrected within a reasonable period after such failure is first discovered.

(2) LOSS OF DEDUCTIONS WHERE FACILITY CEASES TO BE QUALIFIED.—No deduction shall be allowed under this chapter for interest on any financing provided from any bond to which subsection (a) applies with respect to any facility to the extent such interest accrues during the period beginning on the first day of the calendar year which includes the date on which—

(A) substantially all of the facility with respect to which the financing was provided ceases to be used in an empowerment zone or enterprise community, or

(B) the principal user of such facility ceases to be an enterprise zone business (as defined in subsection (b)).

(3) EXCEPTION IF ZONE CEASES.—Paragraphs (1) and (2) shall not apply solely by reason of the termination or revocation of a designation as an empowerment zone or an enterprise community.

(4) EXCEPTION FOR BANKRUPTCY.—Paragraphs (1) and (2) shall not apply to any cessation resulting from bankruptcy.

Amendments

• **1996, Small Business Job Protection Act of 1996 (P.L. 104-188)**

P.L. 104-188, § 1703(n)(7)(A)-(B):

Amended Code Sec. 1394(e)(2) by striking "(i)" and inserting "(A)", and by striking "(ii)" and inserting "(B)". **Effective** as if included in the provision of P.L. 103-66 to which it relates.

• **1993, Omnibus Budget Reconciliation Act of 1993 (P.L. 103-66)**

P.L. 103-66, § 13301(a):

Added new Code Sec. 1394. **Effective** 8-10-93.

[Sec. 1394(f)]

(f) BONDS FOR EMPOWERMENT ZONES.—

(1) IN GENERAL.—In the case of an empowerment zone facility bond—

(A) such bond shall not be treated as a private activity bond for purposes of section 146, and

(B) subsection (c) of this section shall not apply.

(2) LIMITATION ON AMOUNT OF BONDS.—

(A) IN GENERAL.—Paragraph (1) shall apply to an empowerment zone facility bond only if such bond is designated for purposes of this subsection by the local government which nominated the area to which such bond relates.

(B) LIMITATION ON BONDS DESIGNATED.—The aggregate face amount of bonds which may be designated under subparagraph (A) with respect to any empowerment zone shall not exceed—

(i) $60,000,000 if such zone is in a rural area,

(ii) $130,000,000 if such zone is in an urban area and the zone has a population of less than 100,000, and

(iii) $230,000,000 if such zone is in an urban area and the zone has a population of at least 100,000.

(C) SPECIAL RULES.—

(i) COORDINATION WITH LIMITATION IN SUBSECTION (c).—Bonds to which paragraph (1) applies shall not be taken into account in applying the limitation of subsection (c) to other bonds.

(ii) CURRENT REFUNDING NOT TAKEN INTO ACCOUNT.—In the case of a refunding (or series of refundings) of a bond designated under this paragraph, the refunding obligation shall be treated as designated under this paragraph (and shall not be taken into account in applying subparagraph (B)) if—

(I) the amount of the refunding bond does not exceed the outstanding amount of the refunded bond, and

(II) the refunded bond is redeemed not later than 90 days after the date of issuance of the refunding bond.

(3) EMPOWERMENT ZONE FACILITY BOND.—For purposes of this subsection, the term "empowerment zone facility bond" means any bond which would be described in subsection (a) if—

(A) in the case of obligations issued before January 1, 2002, only empowerment zones designated under section 1391(g) were taken into account under sections 1397C and 1397D, and

(B) in the case of obligations issued after December 31, 2001, all empowerment zones (other than the District of Columbia Enterprise Zone) were taken into account under sections 1397C and 1397D.

Amendments

• **2014, Tax Technical Corrections Act of 2014 (P.L. 113-295)**

P.L. 113-295, § 220(o), Division A:

Amended the heading for Code Sec. 1394(f) by striking "DESIGNATED UNDER SECTION 1391(g)" following "BONDS FOR EMPOWERMENT ZONES". **Effective** 12-19-2014.

P.L. 113-295, § 220(p), Division A:

Amended Code Sec. 1394(f)(1) and (2)(A) by striking "a new empowerment zone facility bond" and inserting "an empowerment zone facility bond". **Effective** 12-19-2014.

• **2000, Community Renewal Tax Relief Act of 2000 (P.L. 106-554)**

P.L. 106-554, § 115(a):

Amended Code Sec. 1394(f)(3). **Effective** for obligations issued after 12-31-2001. Prior to amendment, Code Sec. 1394(f)(3) read as follows:

(3) NEW EMPOWERMENT ZONE FACILITY BOND.—For purposes of this subsection, the term "new empowerment zone facility bond" means any bond which would be described in subsection (a) if only empowerment zones designated under section 1391(g) were taken into account under sections 1397B and 1397C.

• **1997, Taxpayer Relief Act of 1997 (P.L. 105-34)**

P.L. 105-34, § 953(a):

Amended Code Sec. 1394 by adding a new subsection (f). **Effective** for obligations issued after 8-5-97.

INCOME TAX—TREATMENT OF EMPOWERMENT ZONES

PART III—ADDITIONAL INCENTIVES FOR EMPOWERMENT ZONES

SUBPART A.   Empowerment zone employment credit.
SUBPART B.   Additional expensing.
SUBPART C.   Nonrecognition of gain on rollover of empowerment zone investments.
SUBPART D.   General provisions.

Subpart A—Empowerment Zone Employment Credit

Sec. 1396.   Empowerment zone employment credit.
Sec. 1397.   Other definitions and special rules.

[Sec. 1396]

SEC. 1396. EMPOWERMENT ZONE EMPLOYMENT CREDIT.

[Sec. 1396(a)]

(a) AMOUNT OF CREDIT.—For purposes of section 38, the amount of the empowerment zone employment credit determined under this section with respect to any employer for any taxable year is the applicable percentage of the qualified zone wages paid or incurred during the calendar year which ends with or within such taxable year.

[Sec. 1396(b)]

(b) APPLICABLE PERCENTAGE.—For purposes of this section, the applicable percentage is 20 percent.

Amendments

• **2000, Community Renewal Tax Relief Act of 2000 (P.L. 106-554)**

P.L. 106-554, § 113(a):

Amended Code Sec. 1396(b). **Effective** for wages paid or incurred after 12-31-2001. Prior to amendment, Code Sec. 1396(b) read as follows:

(b) APPLICABLE PERCENTAGE.—For purposes of this section—

(1) IN GENERAL.—Except as provided in paragraph (2), the term "applicable percentage" means the percentage determined in accordance with the following table:

In the case of wages paid or incurred during calendar year:	The applicable percentage is:
1994 through 2001	20
2002	15
2003	10
2004	5

(2) SPECIAL RULE.—With respect to each empowerment zone designated pursuant to the amendments made by the Taxpayer Relief Act of 1997 to section 1391(b)(2), the following table shall apply in lieu of the table in paragraph (1):

In the case of wages paid or incurred during calendar year—	The applicable percentage is—
2000 through 2004	20
2005	15
2006	10
2007	5

• **1997, Taxpayer Relief Act of 1997 (P.L. 105-34)**

P.L. 105-34, § 951(b)(1)-(2):

Amended Code Sec. 1396(b) by striking so much of the subsection as precedes the table and inserting new material, and by adding at the end a new paragraph (2). **Effective** 8-5-97, except that designations of new empowerment zones made pursuant to such amendment will be made during the 180-day period beginning on 8-5-97. No designation pursuant to such amendment will take effect before 1-1-2000. Prior to amendment, the material in subsection (b) preceding the table read as follows:

(b) APPLICABLE PERCENTAGE.—For purposes of this section, the term "applicable percentage" means the percentage determined in accordance with the following table:

[Sec. 1396(c)]

(c) QUALIFIED ZONE WAGES.—

(1) IN GENERAL.—For purposes of this section, the term "qualified zone wages" means any wages paid or incurred by an employer for services performed by an employee while such employee is a qualified zone employee.

(2) ONLY FIRST $15,000 OF WAGES PER YEAR TAKEN INTO ACCOUNT.—With respect to each qualified zone employee, the amount of qualified zone wages which may be taken into account for a calendar year shall not exceed $15,000.

(3) COORDINATION WITH WORK OPPORTUNITY CREDIT.—

(A) IN GENERAL.—The term "qualified zone wages" shall not include wages taken into account in determining the credit under section 51.

(B) COORDINATION WITH PARAGRAPH (2).—The $15,000 amount in paragraph (2) shall be reduced for any calendar year by the amount of wages paid or incurred during such year which are taken into account in determining the credit under section 51.

Amendments

• **1996, Small Business Job Protection Act of 1996 (P.L. 104-188)**

P.L. 104-188, § 1201(e)(4):

Amended Code Sec. 1396(c)(3) by striking "TARGETED JOBS CREDIT" in the heading and inserting "WORK OPPORTUNITY CREDIT". **Effective** for individuals who begin work for the employer after 9-30-96.

[Sec. 1396(d)]

(d) QUALIFIED ZONE EMPLOYEE.—For purposes of this section—

(1) IN GENERAL.—Except as otherwise provided in this subsection, the term "qualified zone employee" means, with respect to any period, any employee of an employer if—

(A) substantially all of the services performed during such period by such employee for such employer are performed within an empowerment zone in a trade or business of the employer, and

(B) the principal place of abode of such employee while performing such services is within such empowerment zone.

(2) CERTAIN INDIVIDUALS NOT ELIGIBLE.—The term "qualified zone employee" shall not include—

(A) any individual described in subparagraph (A), (B), or (C) of section 51(i)(1),

(B) any 5-percent owner (as defined in section 416(i)(1)(B)),

(C) any individual employed by the employer for less than 90 days,

(D) any individual employed by the employer at any facility described in section 144(c)(6)(B), and

(E) any individual employed by the employer in a trade or business the principal activity of which is farming (within the meaning of subparagraphs (A) or (B) of section 2032A(e)(5)), but only if, as of the close of the taxable year, the sum of—

Sec. 1396

(i) the aggregate unadjusted bases (or, if greater, the fair market value) of the assets owned by the employer which are used in such a trade or business, and

(ii) the aggregate value of assets leased by the employer which are used in such a trade or business (as determined under regulations prescribed by the Secretary),

exceeds $500,000.

(3) SPECIAL RULES RELATED TO TERMINATION OF EMPLOYMENT.—

(A) IN GENERAL.—Paragraph (2)(C) shall not apply to—

(i) a termination of employment of an individual who before the close of the period referred to in paragraph (2)(C) becomes disabled to perform the services of such employment unless such disability is removed before the close of such period and the taxpayer fails to offer reemployment to such individual, or

(ii) a termination of employment of an individual if it is determined under the applicable State unemployment compensation law that the termination was due to the misconduct of such individual.

(B) CHANGES IN FORM OF BUSINESS.—For purposes of paragraph (2)(C), the employment relationship between the taxpayer and an employee shall not be treated as terminated—

(i) by a transaction to which section 381(a) applies if the employee continues to be employed by the acquiring corporation, or

(ii) by reason of a mere change in the form of conducting the trade or business of the taxpayer if the employee continues to be employed in such trade or business and the taxpayer retains a substantial interest in such trade or business.

Amendments

• 1993, Omnibus Budget Reconciliation Act of 1993 (P.L. 103-66)

P.L. 103-66, §13301(a):

Added new Code Sec. 1396. Effective 8-10-93.

[Sec. 1396(e)—Stricken]

Amendments

• 2000, Community Renewal Tax Relief Act of 2000 (P.L. 106-554)

P.L. 106-554, §113(b):

Amended Code Sec. 1396 by striking subsection (e). Effective for wages paid or incurred after 12-31-2001. Prior to being stricken, Code Sec. 1396(e) read as follows:

(e) CREDIT NOT TO APPLY TO EMPOWERMENT ZONES DESIGNATED UNDER SECTION 1391(g).—This section shall be applied without regard to any empowerment zone designated under section 1391(g).

• 1997, Taxpayer Relief Act of 1997 (P.L. 105-34)

P.L. 105-34, §952(b):

Amended Code Sec. 1396 by adding at the and a new subsection (e). Effective 8-5-97.

[Sec. 1397]

SEC. 1397. OTHER DEFINITIONS AND SPECIAL RULES.

[Sec. 1397(a)]

(a) WAGES.—For purposes of this subpart—

(1) IN GENERAL.—The term "wages" has the same meaning as when used in section 51.

(2) CERTAIN TRAINING AND EDUCATIONAL BENEFITS.—

(A) IN GENERAL.—The following amounts shall be treated as wages paid to an employee:

(i) Any amount paid or incurred by an employer which is excludable from the gross income of an employee under section 127, but only to the extent paid or incurred to a person not related to the employer.

(ii) In the case of an employee who has not attained the age of 19, any amount paid or incurred by an employer for any youth training program operated by such employer in conjunction with local education officials.

(B) RELATED PERSON.—A person is related to any other person if the person bears a relationship to such other person specified in section 267(b) or 707(b)(1), or such person and such other person are engaged in trades or businesses under common control (within the meaning of subsections (a) and (b) of section 52). For purposes of the preceding sentence, in applying section 267(b) or 707(b)(1), "10 percent" shall be substituted for "50 percent".

[Sec. 1397(b)]

(b) CONTROLLED GROUPS.—For purposes of this subpart—

(1) all employers treated as a single employer under subsection (a) or (b) of section 52 shall be treated as a single employer for purposes of this subpart, and

(2) the credit (if any) determined under section 1396 with respect to each such employer shall be its proportionate share of the wages giving rise to such credit.

[Sec. 1397(c)]

(c) CERTAIN OTHER RULES MADE APPLICABLE.—For purposes of this subpart, rules similar to the rules of section 51(k) and subsections (c), (d), and (e) of section 52 shall apply.

Amendments

• 1993, Omnibus Budget Reconciliation Act of 1993 (P.L. 103-66)

P.L. 103-66, §13301(a):

Added new Code Sec. 1397. Effective 8-10-93.

Subpart B—Additional Expensing

Sec. 1397A.   Increase in expensing under section 179.

[Sec. 1397A]

SEC. 1397A. INCREASE IN EXPENSING UNDER SECTION 179.

[Sec. 1397A(a)]

(a) GENERAL RULE.—In the case of an enterprise zone business, for purposes of section 179—

(1) the limitation under section 179(b)(1) shall be increased by the lesser of—

(A) $35,000, or

INCOME TAX—TREATMENT OF EMPOWERMENT ZONES

(B) the cost of section 179 property which is qualified zone property placed in service during the taxable year, and

(2) the amount taken into account under section 179(b)(2) with respect to any section 179 property which is qualified zone property shall be 50 percent of the cost thereof.

Amendments

• **2000, Community Renewal Tax Relief Act of 2000 (P.L. 106-554)**

P.L. 106-554, §114(a):

Amended Code Sec. 1397A(a)(1)(A) by striking "$20,000" and inserting "$35,000". **Effective** for tax years beginning after 12-31-2001.

[Sec. 1397A(b)]

(b) RECAPTURE.—Rules similar to the rules under section 179(d)(10) shall apply with respect to any qualified zone property which ceases to be used in an empowerment zone by an enterprise zone business.

Amendments

• **1993, Omnibus Budget Reconciliation Act of 1993 (P.L. 103-66)**

P.L. 103-66, §13301(a):

Added new Code Sec. 1397A. **Effective** 8-10-93.

[Sec. 1397A(c)]

(c) TERMINATION.—This section shall not apply to any property placed in service in taxable years beginning after December 31, 2020.

Amendments

• **2020, Taxpayer Certainty and Disaster Tax Relief Act of 2020 (P.L. 116-260)**

P.L. 116-260, §118(b), Div. EE:

Amended Code Sec. 1397A by adding at the end a new subsection (c). **Effective** for tax years beginning after 12-31-2020.

[Sec. 1397A(c)—Stricken]

• **2000, Community Renewal Tax Relief Act of 2000 (P.L. 106-554)**

P.L. 106-554, §114(b):

Amended Code Sec. 1397A by striking subsection (c). **Effective** for tax years beginning after 12-31-2001. Prior to being stricken, Code Sec. 1397A(c) read as follows:

(c) LIMITATION.—For purposes of this section, qualified zone property shall not include any property substantially all of the use of which is in any parcel described in section 1391(g)(3)(A)(iii).

• **1997, Taxpayer Relief Act of 1997 (P.L. 105-34)**

P.L. 105-34, §952(c):

Amended Code Sec. 1397A by adding at the end a new subsection (c). **Effective** 8-5-97.

Subpart C—Nonrecognition of Gain on Rollover of Empowerment Zone Investments

Sec. 1397B. Nonrecognition of gain on rollover of empowerment zone investments.

[Sec. 1397B]

SEC. 1397B. NONRECOGNITION OF GAIN ON ROLLOVER OF EMPOWERMENT ZONE INVESTMENTS.

[Sec. 1397B(a)]

(a) NONRECOGNITION OF GAIN.—In the case of any sale of a qualified empowerment zone asset held by the taxpayer for more than 1 year and with respect to which such taxpayer elects the application of this section, gain from such sale shall be recognized only to the extent that the amount realized on such sale exceeds—

(1) the cost of any qualified empowerment zone asset (with respect to the same zone as the asset sold) purchased by the taxpayer during the 60-day period beginning on the date of such sale, reduced by

(2) any portion of such cost previously taken into account under this section.

[Sec. 1397B(b)]

(b) DEFINITIONS AND SPECIAL RULES.—For purposes of this section—

(1) QUALIFIED EMPOWERMENT ZONE ASSET.—

(A) IN GENERAL.—The term "qualified empowerment zone asset" means any property which would be a qualified community asset (as defined in section 1400F) if in section 1400F—

(i) references to empowerment zones were substituted for references to renewal communities,

(ii) references to enterprise zone businesses (as defined in section 1397C) were substituted for references to renewal community businesses,

(iii) the date of the enactment of this paragraph were substituted for "December 31, 2001" each place it appears, and

(iv) the day after the date set forth in section 1391(d)(1)(A)(i) were substituted for "January 1, 2010" each place it appears.

(B) REFERENCES.—Any reference in this paragraph to section 1400F shall be treated as reference to such section before its repeal.

(2) CERTAIN GAIN NOT ELIGIBLE FOR ROLLOVER.—This section shall not apply to—

(A) any gain which is treated as ordinary income for purposes of this subtitle, and

(B) any gain which is attributable to real property, or an intangible asset, which is not an integral part of an enterprise zone business.

(3) PURCHASE.—A taxpayer shall be treated as having purchased any property if, but for paragraph (4), the unadjusted basis of such property in the hands of the taxpayer would be its cost (within the meaning of section 1012).

(4) BASIS ADJUSTMENTS.—If gain from any sale is not recognized by reason of subsection (a), such gain shall be applied to reduce (in the order acquired) the basis for determining gain or loss of any qualified empowerment zone asset which is purchased by the taxpayer during the 60-day period described in subsection (a). This paragraph shall not apply for purposes of section 1202.

(5) HOLDING PERIOD.—For purposes of determining whether the nonrecognition of gain under subsection (a) applies to any qualified empowerment zone asset which is sold, the taxpayer's holding period for such asset and the asset referred to in subsection (a)(1) shall be determined without regard to section 1223.

INCOME TAX—TREATMENT OF EMPOWERMENT ZONES

Amendments

• **2018, Tax Technical Corrections Act of 2018 (P.L. 115-141)**

P.L. 115-141, § 401(d)(4)(B)(vii), Div. U:

Amended Code Sec. 1397B(b)(1) by striking subparagraph (B). **Effective** 3-23-2018. For a special rule, see Act Sec. 401(e), Div. U, below. Prior to being stricken, Code Sec. 1397B(b)(1)(B) read as follows:

(B) TREATMENT OF DC ZONE.—The District of Columbia Enterprise Zone shall not be treated as an empowerment zone for purposes of this section.

P.L. 115-141, § 401(d)(5)(B)(iv), Div. U:

Amended Code Sec. 1397B(b)(1), as amended by the preceding provisions of this Act, by adding at the end a new subparagraph (B). **Effective** 3-23-2018. For a special rule, see Act Sec. 401(e), Div. U, below.

P.L. 115-141, § 401(d)(5)(B)(v), Div. U:

Amended Code Sec. 1397B(b)(5) by striking "which is sold—"and all that follows and inserting "which is sold, the taxpayer's holding period for such asset and the asset referred to in subsection (a)(1) shall be determined without regard to section 1223.". **Effective** 3-23-2018. For a special rule, see Act Sec. 401(e), Div. U, below. Prior to amendment, Code Sec. 1397B(b)(5) read as follows:

(5) HOLDING PERIOD.—For purposes of determining whether the nonrecognition of gain under subsection (a) applies to any qualified empowerment zone asset which is sold—

(A) the taxpayer's holding period for such asset and the asset referred to in subsection (a)(1) shall be determined without regard to section 1223, and

(B) only the first year of the taxpayer's holding period for the asset referred to in subsection (a)(1) shall be taken into account for purposes of paragraphs (2)(A)(iii), (3)(C), and (4)(A)(iii) of section 1400F(b).

P.L. 115-141, § 401(e), Div. U, provides:

(e) GENERAL SAVINGS PROVISION WITH RESPECT TO DEADWOOD PROVISIONS.—If—

(1) any provision amended or repealed by the amendments made by subsection (b) or (d) applied to—

(A) any transaction occurring before the date of the enactment of this Act,

(B) any property acquired before such date of enactment, or

(C) any item of income, loss, deduction, or credit taken into account before such date of enactment, and

(2) the treatment of such transaction, property, or item under such provision would (without regard to the amendments or repeals made by such subsection) affect the liability for tax for periods ending after such date of enactment,

nothing in the amendments or repeals made by this section shall be construed to affect the treatment of such transaction, property, or item for purposes of determining liability for tax for periods ending after such date of enactment.

• **2014, Tax Technical Corrections Act of 2014 (P.L. 113-295)**

P.L. 113-295, § 206(c), Division A:

Amended Code Sec. 1397B(b)(1)(A)(ii)-(iii) by striking "and" at the end of clause (ii), by striking the period at the end of clause (iii) and inserting ", and", and by adding at the end a new clause (iv). **Effective** as if included in the provision of the Tax Relief, Unemployment Insurance Reauthorization, and Job Creation Act of 2010 (P.L. 111-312) to which it relates [**effective** for periods after 12-31-2009.—CCH].

• **2000, Community Renewal Tax Relief Act of 2000 (P.L. 106-554)**

P.L. 106-554, § 116(a)(2)-(3):

Amended part III of subchapter U of chapter 1 by redesignating subpart C as subpart D, by redesignating Code Secs. 1397B and 1397C as Code Secs. 1397C and 1397D, respectively, and by inserting after subpart B a new subpart C (Code Sec. 1397B). **Effective** for qualified empowerment zone assets acquired after 12-21-2000.

[Sec. 1397B(c)]

(c) TERMINATION.—This section shall not apply to sales in taxable years beginning after December 31, 2020.

Amendments

• **2020, Taxpayer Certainty and Disaster Tax Relief Act of 2020 (P.L. 116-260)**

P.L. 116-260, § 118(c), Div. EE:

Amended Code Sec. 1397B by adding at the end a new subsection (c). **Effective** for tax years beginning after 12-31-2020.

Subpart D—General Provisions

Sec. 1397C. Enterprise zone business defined.
Sec. 1397D. Qualified zone property defined.

[Sec. 1397C]

SEC. 1397C. ENTERPRISE ZONE BUSINESS DEFINED.

[Sec. 1397C(a)]

(a) IN GENERAL.—For purposes of this part, the term "enterprise zone business" means—

(1) any qualified business entity, and

(2) any qualified proprietorship.

[Sec. 1397C(b)]

(b) QUALIFIED BUSINESS ENTITY.—For purposes of this section, the term "qualified business entity" means, with respect to any taxable year, any corporation or partnership if for such year—

(1) every trade or business of such entity is the active conduct of a qualified business within an empowerment zone,

(2) at least 50 percent of the total gross income of such entity is derived from the active conduct of such business,

(3) a substantial portion of the use of the tangible property of such entity (whether owned or leased) is within an empowerment zone,

(4) a substantial portion of the intangible property of such entity is used in the active conduct of any such business,

(5) a substantial portion of the services performed for such entity by its employees are performed in an empowerment zone,

(6) at least 35 percent of its employees are residents of an empowerment zone,

(7) less than 5 percent of the average of the aggregate unadjusted bases of the property of such entity is attributable to collectibles (as defined in section 408(m)(2)) other than collectibles that are held primarily for sale to customers in the ordinary course of such business, and

(8) less than 5 percent of the average of the aggregate unadjusted bases of the property of such entity is attributable to nonqualified financial property.

Amendments

• **1997, Taxpayer Relief Act of 1997 (P.L. 105-34)**

P.L. 105-34, § 956(a)(1)-(3):

Amended Code Sec. 1397B(b) by striking "80 percent" in paragraph (2) and inserting "50 percent", by striking "substantially all" each place it appears and inserting "a substantial portion", and by striking ", and exclusively related to," after "is used in," in paragraph (4). **Effective**, generally, for tax years beginning on or after 8-5-97. For a special rule, see Act Sec. 956(b)(2), below.

P.L. 105-34, § 956(b)(2), provides:

(2) SPECIAL RULE FOR ENTERPRISE ZONE FACILITY BONDS.—For purposes of section 1394(b) of the Internal Revenue Code of 1986, the amendments made by this section shall apply to obligations issued after the date of the enactment of this Act.

[Sec. 1397C(c)]

(c) QUALIFIED PROPRIETORSHIP.—For purposes of this section, the term "qualified proprietorship" means, with respect to any taxable year, any qualified business carried on by an individual as a proprietorship if for such year—

(1) at least 50 percent of the total gross income of such individual from such business is derived from the active conduct of such business in an empowerment zone,

(2) a substantial portion of the use of the tangible property of such individual in such business (whether owned or leased) is within an empowerment zone,

(3) a substantial portion of the intangible property of such business is used in the active conduct of such business,

INCOME TAX—TREATMENT OF EMPOWERMENT ZONES

(4) a substantial portion of the services performed for such individual in such business by employees of such business are performed in an empowerment zone,

(5) at least 35 percent of such employees are residents of an empowerment zone,

(6) less than 5 percent of the average of the aggregate unadjusted bases of the property of such individual which is used in such business is attributable to collectibles (as defined in section 408(m)(2)) other than collectibles that are held primarily for sale to customers in the ordinary course of such business, and

(7) less than 5 percent of the average of the aggregate unadjusted bases of the property of such individual which is used in such business is attributable to nonqualified financial property.

For purposes of this subsection, the term "employee" includes the proprietor.

Amendments

• **1997, Taxpayer Relief Act of 1997 (P.L. 105-34)**

P.L. 105-34, §956(a)(1)-(3):

Amended Code Sec. 1397B(c) by striking "80 percent" in paragraph (1) and inserting "50 percent", by striking "substantially all" each place it appears and inserting "a substantial portion", and by striking ", and exclusively related to," after "is used in," in paragraph (3). **Effective**, generally, for tax years beginning on or after 8-5-97. For a special rule, see Act Sec. 956(b)(2), below.

P.L. 105-34, §956(b)(2), provides:

(2) SPECIAL RULE FOR ENTERPRISE ZONE FACILITY BONDS.—For purposes of section 1394(b) of the Internal Revenue Code of 1986, the amendments made by this section shall apply to obligations issued after the date of the enactment of this Act.

[Sec. 1397C(d)]

(d) QUALIFIED BUSINESS.—For purposes of this section—

(1) IN GENERAL.—Except as otherwise provided in this subsection, the term "qualified business" means any trade or business.

(2) RENTAL OF REAL PROPERTY.—The rental to others of real property located in an empowerment zone shall be treated as a qualified business if and only if—

(A) the property is not residential rental property (as defined in section 168(e)(2)), and

(B) at least 50 percent of the gross rental income from the real property is from enterprise zone businesses.

For purposes of subparagraph (B), the lessor of the property may rely on a lessee's certification that such lessee is an enterprise zone business.

(3) RENTAL OF TANGIBLE PERSONAL PROPERTY.—The rental to others of tangible personal property shall be treated as a qualified business if and only if at least 50 percent of the rental of such property is by enterprise zone businesses or by residents of an empowerment zone.

(4) TREATMENT OF BUSINESS HOLDING INTANGIBLES.—The term "qualified business" shall not include any trade or business consisting predominantly of the development or holding of intangibles for sale or license.

(5) CERTAIN BUSINESSES EXCLUDED.—The term "qualified business" shall not include—

(A) any trade or business consisting of the operation of any facility described in section 144(c)(6)(B), and

(B) any trade or business the principal activity of which is farming (within the meaning of subparagraph (A) or (B) of section 2032A(e)(5)), but only if, as of the close of the taxable year, the sum of—

(i) the aggregate unadjusted bases (or, if greater, the fair market value) of the assets owned by the taxpayer which are used in such a trade or business, and

(ii) the aggregate value of assets leased by the taxpayer which are used in such a trade or business,

exceeds $500,000.

For purposes of subparagraph (B), rules similar to the rules of section 1397(b) shall apply.

Amendments

• **2018, Tax Technical Corrections Act of 2018 (P.L. 115-141)**

P.L. 115-141, §401(a)(196), Div. U:

Amended Code Sec. 1397C(d)(5)(B) by striking "subparagraphs (A) or (B)" and inserting "subparagraph (A) or (B)". **Effective** 3-23-2018.

• **1997, Taxpayer Relief Act of 1997 (P.L. 105-34)**

P.L. 105-34, §956(a)(4)-(5):

Amended Code Sec. 1397B(d) by adding at the end of paragraph (2) a new flush sentence, and by striking "substantially all" in paragraph (3) and inserting "at least 50 percent". **Effective**, generally, for tax years beginning on or after 8-5-97. For a special rule, see Act Sec. 956(b)(2), below.

P.L. 105-34, §956(b)(2), provides:

(2) SPECIAL RULE FOR ENTERPRISE ZONE FACILITY BONDS.—For purposes of section 1394(b) of the Internal Revenue Code of 1986, the amendments made by this section shall apply to obligations issued after the date of the enactment of this Act.

• **1996, Small Business Job Protection Act of 1996 (P.L. 104-188)**

P.L. 104-188, §1703(m):

Amended Code Sec. 1397B(d)(5)(B) by striking "preceding" before "taxable year". **Effective** as if included in the provision of P.L. 103-66 to which it relates.

[Sec. 1397C(e)]

(e) NONQUALIFIED FINANCIAL PROPERTY.—For purposes of this section, the term "nonqualified financial property" means debt, stock, partnership interests, options, futures contracts, forward contracts, warrants, notional principal contracts, annuities, and other similar property specified in regulations; except that such term shall not include—

(1) reasonable amounts of working capital held in cash, cash equivalents, or debt instruments with a term of 18 months or less, or

(2) debt instruments described in section 1221(a)(4).

Amendments

• **1999, Tax Relief Extension Act of 1999 (P.L. 106-170)**

P.L. 106-170, §532(c)(4):

Amended Code Sec. 1397B(e)(2) by striking "section 1221(4)" and inserting "section 1221(a)(4)". **Effective** for any instrument held, acquired, or entered into, any transaction entered into, and supplies held or acquired on or after 12-17-99.

• **1993, Omnibus Budget Reconciliation Act of 1993 (P.L. 103-66)**

P.L. 103-66, §13301(a):

Added new Code Sec. 1397B. **Effective** 8-10-93.

[Sec. 1397C(f)]

(f) TREATMENT OF BUSINESSES STRADDLING CENSUS TRACT LINES.—For purposes of this section, if—

(1) a business entity or proprietorship uses real property located within an empowerment zone,

(2) the business entity or proprietorship also uses real property located outside the empowerment zone,

(3) the amount of real property described in paragraph (1) is substantial compared to the amount of real property described in paragraph (2), and

(4) the real property described in paragraph (2) is contiguous to part or all of the real property described in paragraph (1), then all the services performed by employees, all business activities, all tangible property, and all intangible property of the business entity or proprietorship that occur in or is located on the real property described in paragraphs (1) and (2) shall be treated as occurring or situated in an empowerment zone.

INCOME TAX—TREATMENT OF EMPOWERMENT ZONES

Amendments

● **2000, Community Renewal Tax Relief Act of 2000 (P.L. 106-554)**

P.L. 106-554, §116(a)(2):

Amended part III of subchapter U of chapter 1 by redesignating Code Secs. 1397B and 1397C as Code Secs. 1397C and 1397D, respectively. **Effective** for qualified empowerment zone assets acquired after 12-21-2000.

● **1997, Taxpayer Relief Act of 1997 (P.L. 105-34)**

P.L. 105-34, §956(a)(6):

Amended Code Sec. 1397B by adding at the end a new subsection (f). **Effective**, generally, for tax years beginning on or after 8-5-97. For a special rule, see Act Sec. 956(b)(2), below.

P.L. 105-34, §956(b)(2), provides:

(2) SPECIAL RULE FOR ENTERPRISE ZONE FACILITY BONDS.—For purposes of section 1394(b) of the Internal Revenue Code of 1986, the amendments made by this section shall apply to obligations issued after the date of the enactment of this Act.

[Sec. 1397D]

SEC. 1397D. QUALIFIED ZONE PROPERTY DEFINED.

[Sec. 1397D(a)]

(a) GENERAL RULE.—For purposes of this part—

(1) IN GENERAL.—The term "qualified zone property" means any property to which section 168 applies (or would apply but for section 179) if—

(A) such property was acquired by the taxpayer by purchase (as defined in section 179(d)(2)) after the date on which the designation of the empowerment zone took effect,

(B) the original use of which in an empowerment zone commences with the taxpayer, and

(C) substantially all of the use of which is in an empowerment zone and is in the active conduct of a qualified business by the taxpayer in such zone.

(2) SPECIAL RULE FOR SUBSTANTIAL RENOVATIONS.—In the case of any property which is substantially renovated by the taxpayer, the requirements of subparagraphs (A) and (B) of paragraph (1) shall be treated as satisfied. For purposes of the preceding sentence, property shall be treated as substantially renovated by the taxpayer if, during any 24-month period beginning after the date on which the designation of the empowerment zone took effect, additions to basis with respect to such property in the hands of the taxpayer exceed the greater of (i) an amount equal to the adjusted basis at the beginning of such 24-month period in the hands of the taxpayer, or (ii) $5,000.

[Sec. 1397D(b)]

(b) SPECIAL RULES FOR SALE-LEASEBACKS.—For purposes of subsection (a)(1)(B), if property is sold and leased back by the taxpayer within 3 months after the date such property was originally placed in service, such property shall be treated as originally placed in service not earlier than the date on which such property is used under the leaseback.

Amendments

● **2000, Community Renewal Tax Relief Act of 2000 (P.L. 106-554)**

P.L. 106-554, §116(a)(2):

Amended part III of subchapter U of chapter 1 by redesignating Code Secs. 1397B and 1397C as Code Secs. 1397C and 1397D, respectively. **Effective** for qualified empowerment zone assets acquired after 12-21-2000.

● **1993, Omnibus Budget Reconciliation Act of 1993 (P.L. 103-66)**

P.L. 103-66, §13301(a):

Added new Code Sec. 1397C. **Effective** 8-10-93.

PART IV—INCENTIVES FOR EDUCATION ZONES

[Sec. 1397E—Stricken]

Amendments

● **2017, Tax Cuts and Jobs Act (P.L. 115-97)**

P.L. 115-97, §13404(c)(1):

Amended part IV of subchapter U of chapter 1 by striking Code Sec. 1397E. **Effective** for bonds issued after 12-31-2017. Prior to being stricken, Code Sec. 1397E read as follows:

SEC. 1397E. CREDIT TO HOLDERS OF QUALIFIED ZONE ACADEMY BONDS.

[Sec. 1397E(a)]

(a) ALLOWANCE OF CREDIT.—In the case of an eligible taxpayer who holds a qualified zone academy bond on the credit allowance date of such bond which occurs during the taxable year, there shall be allowed as a credit against the tax imposed by this chapter for such taxable year the amount determined under subsection (b).

[Sec. 1397E(b)]

(b) AMOUNT OF CREDIT.—

(1) IN GENERAL.—The amount of the credit determined under this subsection with respect to any qualified zone academy bond is the amount equal to the product of—

(A) the credit rate determined by the Secretary under paragraph (2) for the month in which such bond was issued, multiplied by

(B) the face amount of the bond held by the taxpayer on the credit allowance date.

(2) DETERMINATION.—During each calendar month, the Secretary shall determine a credit rate which shall apply to bonds issued during the following calendar month. The credit rate for any month is the percentage which the Secretary estimates will permit the issuance of qualified zone academy bonds without discount and without interest cost to the issuer.

[Sec. 1397E(c)]

(c) LIMITATION BASED ON AMOUNT OF TAX.—The credit allowed under subsection (a) for any taxable year shall not exceed the excess of—

(1) the sum of the regular tax liability (as defined in section 26(b)) plus the tax imposed by section 55, over

(2) the sum of the credits allowable under part IV of subchapter A (other than subpart C thereof, relating to refundable credits, and subparts H, I, and J thereof).

Amendments

● **2009, American Recovery and Reinvestment Tax Act of 2009 (P.L. 111-5)**

P.L. 111-5, §1531(c)(3):

Amended Code Sec. 1397E(c)(2) by striking "and I" and inserting ", I, and J". **Effective** for obligations issued after 2-17-2009.

● **2008, Heartland, Habitat, Harvest, and Horticulture Act of 2008 (P.L. 110-246)**

P.L. 110-246, §15316(c)(2):

Amended Code Sec. 1397E(c)(2) by striking "subpart H" and inserting "subparts H and I". **Effective** for obligations issued after 5-22-2008.

● **2005, Energy Tax Incentives Act of 2005 (P.L. 109-58)**

P.L. 109-58, §1303(c)(2):

Amended Code Sec. 1397E(c)(2) by inserting ", and subpart H thereof" after "refundable credits". **Effective** for tax years beginning after 12-31-2005 [effective date amended by P.L. 109-135, §402(c)(2)].

[Sec. 1397E(d)]

(d) QUALIFIED ZONE ACADEMY BOND.—For purposes of this section—

(1) IN GENERAL.—The term "qualified zone academy bond" means any bond issued as part of an issue if—

(A) 95 percent or more of the proceeds of such issue are to be used for a qualified purpose with respect to a qualified zone academy established by an eligible local education agency,

(B) the bond is issued by a State or local government within the jurisdiction of which such academy is located,

(C) the issuer—

(i) designates such bond for purposes of this section,

(ii) certifies that it has written assurances that the private business contribution requirement of paragraph (2) will be met with respect to such academy, and

INCOME TAX—TREATMENT OF EMPOWERMENT ZONES

(iii) certifies that it has the written approval of the eligible local education agency for such bond issuance,

(D) the term of each bond which is part of such issue does not exceed the maximum term permitted under paragraph (3), and

(E) the issue meets the requirements of subsections (f), (g), and (h).

(2) PRIVATE BUSINESS CONTRIBUTION REQUIREMENT.—

(A) IN GENERAL.—For purposes of paragraph (1), the private business contribution requirement of this paragraph is met with respect to any issue if the eligible local education agency that established the qualified zone academy has written commitments from private entities to make qualified contributions having a present value (as of the date of issuance of the issue) of not less than 10 percent of the proceeds of the issue.

(B) QUALIFIED CONTRIBUTIONS.—For purposes of subparagraph (A), the term "qualified contribution" means any contribution (of a type and quality acceptable to the eligible local education agency) of—

(i) equipment for use in the qualified zone academy (including state-of-the-art technology and vocational equipment),

(ii) technical assistance in developing curriculum or in training teachers in order to promote appropriate market driven technology in the classroom,

(iii) services of employees as volunteer mentors,

(iv) internships, field trips, or other educational opportunities outside the academy for students, or

(v) any other property or service specified by the eligible local education agency.

(3) TERM REQUIREMENT.—During each calendar month, the Secretary shall determine the maximum term permitted under this paragraph for bonds issued during the following calendar month. Such maximum term shall be the term which the Secretary estimates will result in the present value of the obligation to repay the principal on the bond being equal to 50 percent of the face amount of the bond. Such present value shall be determined using as a discount rate the average annual interest rate of tax-exempt obligations having a term of 10 years or more which are issued during the month. If the term as so determined is not a multiple of a whole year, such term shall be rounded to the next highest whole year.

(4) QUALIFIED ZONE ACADEMY.—

(A) IN GENERAL.—The term "qualified zone academy" means any public school (or academic program within a public school) which is established by and operated under the supervision of an eligible local education agency to provide education or training below the postsecondary level if—

(i) such public school or program (as the case may be) is designed in cooperation with business to enhance the academic curriculum, increase graduation and employment rates, and better prepare students for the rigors of college and the increasingly complex workforce,

(ii) students in such public school or program (as the case may be) will be subject to the same academic standards and assessments as other students educated by the eligible local education agency,

(iii) the comprehensive education plan of such public school or program is approved by the eligible local education agency, and

(iv)(I) such public school is located in an empowerment zone or enterprise community (including any such zone or community designated after the date of the enactment of this section), or

(II) there is a reasonable expectation (as of the date of issuance of the bonds) that at least 35 percent of the students attending such school or participating in such program (as the case may be) will be eligible for free or reduced-cost lunches under the school lunch program established under the Richard B. Russell National School Lunch Act.

(B) ELIGIBLE LOCAL EDUCATION AGENCY.—The term "eligible local education agency" means any local educational agency as defined in section 8101 of the Elementary and Secondary Education Act of 1965.

(5) QUALIFIED PURPOSE.—The term "qualified purpose" means, with respect to any qualified zone academy—

(A) rehabilitating or repairing the public school facility in which the academy is established,

(B) providing equipment for use at such academy,

(C) developing course materials for education to be provided at such academy, and

(D) training teachers and other school personnel in such academy.

(6) ELIGIBLE TAXPAYER.—The term "eligible taxpayer" means—

(A) a bank (within the meaning of section 581),

(B) an insurance company to which subchapter L applies, and

(C) a corporation actively engaged in the business of lending money.

Amendments

• **2015, Every Student Succeeds Act (P.L. 114-95)**

P.L. 114-95, §9215(uu)(3):

Amended Code Sec. 1397E(d)(4)(B) by striking "section 9101 of the Elementary and Secondary Education Act of 1965" and inserting "section 8101 of the Elementary and Secondary Education Act of 1965". **Effective** 12-10-2015.

• **2006, Tax Relief and Health Care Act of 2006 (P.L. 109-432)**

P.L. 109-432, Division A, §107(b)(1)(A):

Amended Code Sec. 1397E(d)(1) by striking "and" at the end of subparagraph (C)(iii), by striking the period at the end of subparagraph (D) and inserting ", and", and by adding at the end a new subparagraph (E). **Effective** for obligations issued after 12-20-2006 pursuant to allocations of the national zone academy bond limitation for calendar years after 2005.

• **2002, No Child Left Behind Act of 2001 (P.L. 107-110)**

P.L. 107-110, §1076(t):

Amended Code Sec. 1397E(d)(4)(B) by striking "14101" and inserting "9101". **Effective** 1-8-2002.

• **1999, Agriculture, Rural Development, Food and Drug Administration, and Related Agencies Appropriation Act, 2000 (P.L. 106-78)**

P.L. 106-78, §752(b)(11):

Amended Code Sec. 1397E(d)(4)(A)(iv)(II) by striking "National School Lunch Act" and inserting "Richard B. Russell National School Lunch Act". **Effective** 10-22-99.

• **1998, IRS Restructuring and Reform Act of 1998 (P.L. 105-206)**

P.L. 105-206, §6004(g)(2):

Amended Code Sec. 1397E(d)(4)(B) by striking "local education agency as defined" and inserting "local educational agency as defined". **Effective** as if included in the provision of P.L. 105-34, to which it relates [effective for obligations issued after 12-31-97.—CCH].

[Sec. 1397E(e)]

(e) LIMITATION ON AMOUNT OF BONDS DESIGNATED.—

(1) NATIONAL LIMITATION.—There is a national zone academy bond limitation for each calendar year. Such limitation is $400,000,000 for 1998, 1999, 2000, 2001, 2002, 2003, 2004, 2005, 2006, and 2007, and, except as provided in paragraph (4), zero thereafter.

(2) ALLOCATION OF LIMITATION.—The national zone academy bond limitation for a calendar year shall be allocated by the Secretary among the States on the basis of their respective populations of individuals below the poverty line (as defined by the Office of Management and Budget). The limitation amount allocated to a State under the preceding sentence shall be allocated by the State education agency to qualified zone academies within such State.

(3) DESIGNATION SUBJECT TO LIMITATION AMOUNT.—The maximum aggregate face amount of bonds issued during any calendar year which may be designated under subsection (d)(1) with respect to any qualified zone academy shall not exceed the limitation amount allocated to such academy under paragraph (2) for such calendar year.

(4) CARRYOVER OF UNUSED LIMITATION.—If for any calendar year—

(A) the limitation amount for any State, exceeds

(B) the amount of bonds issued during such year which are designated under subsection (d)(1) with respect to qualified zone academies within such State, the limitation amount for such State for the following calendar year shall be increased by the amount of such excess.

Any carryforward of a limitation amount may be carried only to the first 2 years (3 years for carryforwards from 1998 or 1999) following the unused limitation year. For purposes of the preceding sentence, a limitation amount shall be treated as used on a first-in first-out basis.

Amendments

• **2006, Tax Relief and Health Care Act of 2006 (P.L. 109-432)**

P.L. 109-432, Division A, §107(a):

Amended Code Sec. 1397E(e)(1) by striking "and 2005" and inserting "2005, 2006, and 2007". **Effective** for obligations issued after 12-31-2005.

• **2004, Working Families Tax Relief Act of 2004 (P.L. 108-311)**

P.L. 108-311, §304(a):

Amended Code Sec. 1397E(e)(1) by striking "and 2003" and inserting "2003, 2004, and 2005". **Effective** for obligations issued after 12-31-2003.

• **2002, Job Creation and Worker Assistance Act of 2002 (P.L. 107-147)**

P.L. 107-147, §608(a):

Amended Code Sec. 1397E(e)(1) by striking "2000, and 2001" and inserting "2000, 2001, 2002, and 2003". **Effective** for obligations issued after 3-9-2002.

• **1999, Tax Relief Extension Act of 1999 (P.L. 106-170)**

P.L. 106-170, §509(a):

Amended Code Sec. 1397E(e)(1) by striking "and 1999" and inserting ", 1999, 2000, and 2001". **Effective** 12-17-99.

P.L. 106-170, §509(b):

Amended Code Sec. 1397E(e)(4) by adding at the end flush sentences. **Effective** 12-17-99.

[Sec. 1397E(f)]

(f) SPECIAL RULES RELATING TO EXPENDITURES.—

(1) IN GENERAL.—An issue shall be treated as meeting the requirements of this subsection if, as of the date of issuance, the issuer reasonably expects—

(A) at least 95 percent of the proceeds from the sale of the issue are to be spent for 1 or more qualified purposes with respect to qualified zone academies within the 5-year period beginning on the date of issuance of the qualified zone academy bond,

(B) a binding commitment with a third party to spend at least 10 percent of the proceeds from the sale of the issue will be incurred within the 6-month period beginning on the date of issuance of the qualified zone academy bond, and

(C) such purposes will be completed with due diligence and the proceeds from the sale of the issue will be spent with due diligence.

(2) EXTENSION OF PERIOD.—Upon submission of a request prior to the expiration of the period described in paragraph (1)(A), the Secretary may extend such period if the

Sec. 1397E—Stricken

INCOME TAX—REGULATIONS

issuer establishes that the failure to satisfy the 5-year requirement is due to reasonable cause and the related purposes will continue to proceed with due diligence.

(3) FAILURE TO SPEND REQUIRED AMOUNT OF BOND PROCEEDS WITHIN 5 YEARS.—To the extent that less than 95 percent of the proceeds of such issue are expended by the close of the 5-year period beginning on the date of issuance (or if an extension has been obtained under paragraph (2), by the close of the extended period), the issuer shall redeem all of the nonqualified bonds within 90 days after the end of such period. For purposes of this paragraph, the amount of the nonqualified bonds required to be redeemed shall be determined in the same manner as under section 142.

Amendments

• 2006, Tax Relief and Health Care Act of 2006 (P.L. 109-432)

P.L. 109-432, Division A, §107(b)(1)(B):

Amended Code Sec. 1397E by redesignating subsections (f), (g), (h), and (i) as subsections (i), (j), (k), and (l), respectively, and by inserting after subsection (e) new subsections (f), (g), and (h). **Effective** for obligations issued after 12-20-2006 pursuant to allocations of the national zone academy bond limitation for calendar years after 2005.

[Sec. 1397E(g)]

(g) SPECIAL RULES RELATING TO ARBITRAGE.—An issue shall be treated as meeting the requirements of this subsection if the issuer satisfies the arbitrage requirements of section 148 with respect to proceeds of the issue.

Amendments

• 2006, Tax Relief and Health Care Act of 2006 (P.L. 109-432)

P.L. 109-432, Division A, §107(b)(1)(B):

Amended Code Sec. 1397E by redesignating subsections (f), (g), (h), and (i) as subsections (i), (j), (k), and (l), respectively, and by inserting after subsection (f) a new subsection (g). **Effective** for obligations issued after 12-20-2006 pursuant to allocations of the national zone academy bond limitation for calendar years after 2005.

[Sec. 1397E(h)]

(h) REPORTING.—Issuers of qualified academy zone bonds shall submit reports similar to the reports required under section 149(e).

Amendments

• 2006, Tax Relief and Health Care Act of 2006 (P.L. 109-432)

P.L. 109-432, Division A, §107(b)(1)(B):

Amended Code Sec. 1397E by redesignating subsections (f), (g), (h), and (i) as subsections (i), (j), (k), and (l), respectively, and by inserting after subsection (g) a new subsection (h). **Effective** for obligations issued after 12-20-2006 pursuant to allocations of the national zone academy bond limitation for calendar years after 2005.

[Sec. 1397E(i)]

(i) OTHER DEFINITIONS.—For purposes of this section—

(1) CREDIT ALLOWANCE DATE.—The term "credit allowance date" means, with respect to any issue, the last day of the 1-year period beginning on the date of issuance of such issue and the last day of each successive 1-year period thereafter.

(2) BOND.—The term "bond" includes any obligation.

(3) STATE.—The term "State" includes the District of Columbia and any possession of the United States.

Amendments

• 2006, Tax Relief and Health Care Act of 2006 (P.L. 109-432)

P.L. 109-432, Division A, §107(b)(1)(B):

Amended Code Sec. 1397E by redesignating subsection (f) as subsection (i). **Effective** for obligations issued after 12-20-2006 pursuant to allocations of the national zone academy bond limitation for calendar years after 2005.

[Sec. 1397E(j)]

(j) CREDIT INCLUDED IN GROSS INCOME.—Gross income includes the amount of the credit allowed to the taxpayer under this section (determined without regard to subsection (c)).

Amendments

• 2006, Tax Relief and Health Care Act of 2006 (P.L. 109-432)

P.L. 109-432, Division A, §107(b)(1)(B):

Amended Code Sec. 1397E by redesignating subsection (g) as subsection (j). **Effective** for obligations issued after 12-20-2006 pursuant to allocations of the national zone academy bond limitation for calendar years after 2005.

• 1998, IRS Restructuring and Reform Act of 1998 (P.L. 105-206)

P.L. 105-206, §6004(g)(4):

Amended Code Sec. 1397E(g) by inserting "(determined without regard to subsection (c))" after "section". **Effective** as if included in the provision of P.L. 105-34 to which it relates [effective for obligations issued after 12-31-97.—CCH].

[Sec. 1397E(k)]

(k) CREDIT TREATED AS NONREFUNDABLE BONDHOLDER CREDIT.—For purposes of this title, the credit allowed by this section shall be treated as a credit allowable under subpart H of part IV of subchapter A of this chapter.

Amendments

• 2006, Tax Relief and Health Care Act of 2006 (P.L. 109-432)

P.L. 109-432, Division A, §107(b)(1)(B):

Amended Code Sec. 1397E by redesignating subsection (h) as subsection (k). **Effective** for obligations issued after 12-20-2006 pursuant to allocations of the national zone academy bond limitation for calendar years after 2005.

• 2005, Energy Tax Incentives Act of 2005 (P.L. 109-58)

P.L. 109-58, §1303(c)(3):

Amended Code Sec. 1397E(h). **Effective** for tax years beginning after 12-31-2005 [effective date changed by P.L. 109-135, §402(c)(2)]. Prior to amendment, Code Sec. 1397E(h) read as follows:

(h) CREDIT TREATED AS ALLOWED UNDER PART IV OF SUBCHAPTER A.—For purposes of subtitle F, the credit allowed by this section shall be treated as a credit allowable under part IV of subchapter A of this chapter.

• 1998, IRS Restructuring and Reform Act of 1998 (P.L. 105-206)

P.L. 105-206, §6004(g)(3):

Amended Code Sec. 1397E by adding at the end a new subsection (h). **Effective** as if included in the provision of P.L. 105-34 to which it relates [effective for obligations issued after 12-31-97.—CCH].

• 1997, Taxpayer Relief Act of 1997 (P.L. 105-34)

P.L. 105-34, §226(a) (as amended by P.L. 105-206, §6004(g)(1)):

Amended subchapter U of chapter 1 by redesignating part IV as part V, by redesignating Code Sec. 1397D as Code Sec. 1397F, and by inserting after part III a new part IV (Code Sec. 1397E). **Effective** for obligations issued after 12-31-97.

[Sec. 1397E(l)]

(l) S CORPORATIONS.—In the case of a qualified zone academy bond held by an S corporation which is an eligible taxpayer—

(1) each shareholder shall take into account such shareholder's pro rata share of the credit, and

(2) no basis adjustments to the stock of the corporation shall be made under section 1367 on account of this section.

Amendments

• 2006, Tax Relief and Health Care Act of 2006 (P.L. 109-432)

P.L. 109-432, Division A, §107(b)(1)(B):

Amended Code Sec. 1397E by redesignating subsection (i) as subsection (l). **Effective** for obligations issued after 12-20-2006 pursuant to allocations of the national zone academy bond limitation for calendar years after 2005.

• 2004, Working Families Tax Relief Act of 2004 (P.L. 108-311)

P.L. 108-311, §406(c):

Amended Code Sec. 1397E by adding at the end a new subsection (i). **Effective** as if included in the provision of the Taxpayer Relief Act of 1997 (P.L. 105-34) to which it relates [**effective** for obligations issued after 12-31-1997.—CCH].

[Sec. 1397E(m)]

(m) TERMINATION.—This section shall not apply to any obligation issued after the date of the enactment of the Tax Extenders and Alternative Minimum Tax Relief Act of 2008.

Amendments

• 2008, Tax Extenders and Alternative Minimum Tax Relief Act of 2008 (P.L. 110-343)

P.L. 110-343, Division C, §313(b)(3):

Amended Code Sec. 1397E by adding at the end a new subsection (m). **Effective** for obligations issued after 10-3-2008.

PART V—REGULATIONS

Sec. 1397F.   Regulations.

[Sec. 1397F]

SEC. 1397F. REGULATIONS.

The Secretary shall prescribe such regulations as may be necessary or appropriate to carry out the purposes of parts II and III, including—

(1) regulations limiting the benefit of parts II and III in circumstances where such benefits, in combination with benefits provided under other Federal programs, would result in an activity being 100 percent or more subsidized by the Federal Government,

(2) regulations preventing abuse of the provisions of parts II and III, and

(3) regulations dealing with inadvertent failures of entities to be enterprise zone businesses.

INCOME TAX—GENERAL STOCK OWNERSHIP CORPS.

Amendments

• **1997, Taxpayer Relief Act of 1997 (P.L. 105-34)**

P.L. 105-34, § 226(a) (as amended by P.L. 105-206, § 6004(g)(1)):

Redesignated Code Sec. 1397D as Code Sec. 1397F. **Effective** for obligations issued after 12-31-97.

• **1993, Omnibus Budget Reconciliation Act of 1993 (P.L. 103-66)**

P.L. 103-66, § 13301(a):

Added new Code Sec. 1397D. **Effective** 8-10-93.

Subchapter U—General Stock Ownership Corporations—[Repealed]

[Sec. 1391—Repealed]

Amendments

• **1986, Tax Reform Act of 1986 (P.L. 99-514)**

P.L. 99-514, § 1303(a):

Repealed Code Sec. 1391. **Effective** 10-22-86. Prior to repeal, Code Sec. 1391 read as follows:

SEC. 1391. DEFINITIONS.

[Sec. 1391(a)]

(a) GENERAL STOCK OWNERSHIP CORPORATION.—For purposes of this subchapter, the term "general stock ownership corporation" (hereinafter referred to as a "GSOC") means a domestic corporation which—

(1) is not a member of an affiliated group (as defined in section 1504);

(2) is chartered and organized after December 31, 1978, and before January 1, 1984;

(3) is chartered by an act of a State legislature or as a result of a State-wide referendum;

(4) has a charter providing—

(A) for the issuance of only 1 class of stocks,

(B) for the issuance of shares only to eligible individuals (as defined in subsection (c));

(C) for the issuance of at least one share to each eligible individual, unless such eligible individual elects within one year after the date of issuance not to receive such share;

(D) that no share of stock shall be transferable—

(i) by a shareholder other than by will or the laws of descent and distribution until after the expiration of 5 years from the date such stock is issued by the GSOC except where the shareholder ceases to be a resident of the State;

(ii) to any person other than a resident individual of the chartering State or the estate of a deceased shareholder; or

(iii) to any individual who, after the transfer, would own more than 10 shares of the GSOC; and

(E) that such corporation shall qualify as a GSOC under the Internal Revenue Code; and

(5) is empowered to invest in properties (but not in properties acquired by it or for its benefit through the right of eminent domain).

For purposes of this subsection, section 1504(a) shall be applied by substituting "20 percent" for "80 percent" wherever it appears.

Amendments

• **1980 (P.L. 96-595)**

P.L. 96-595, § 3(a)(1):

Amended Code Sec. 1391(a)(4)(D)(ii) by inserting " or the estate of a deceased shareholder" following "State". **Effective** for corporations chartered after 1978 and before 1984.

[Sec. 1391(b)]

(b) ELECTING GSOC.—For purposes of this subchapter, the term "electing GSOC" means a GSOC which files an election under section 1392 which, under section 1392, is in effect for such taxable year.

[Sec. 1391(c)]

(c) ELIGIBLE INDIVIDUAL.—For purposes of subsection (a), the term "eligible individual" means an individual who is, as of a date specified in the State's enabling legislation for the GSOC, a resident of the chartering State and who remains a resident of such State between that date and the date of issuance.

Amendments

• **1980 (P.L. 96-595)**

P.L. 96-595, § 3(a)(2):

Amended the paragraph heading of subsection 1391(c) by striking out "INDIVIDUALS" and inserting in lieu thereof "INDIVIDUAL". **Effective** for corporations chartered after 1978 and before 1984.

[Sec. 1391(d)]

(d) TREATED AS PRIVATE CORPORATION.—For purposes of this title, a GSOC shall be treated as a private corporation and not as a governmental unit.

[Sec. 1391(e)]

(e) STUDY OF GENERAL STOCK OWNERSHIP CORPORATIONS.—The staff of the Joint Committee on Taxation shall prepare a report on the operation and effects of this subchapter relating to GSOC's. An interim report shall be filed within two years after the first GSOC is formed and a final report shall be filed by September 30, 1983.

Amendments

• **1980, Technical Corrections Act of 1979 (P.L. 96-222)**

P.L. 96-222, § 106(a)(4):

Amended Code Sec. 1391(a) by deleting ", and" from paragraph (a)(1) and inserting a semicolon, by adding "or" to the end of paragraph (a)(4)(D)(ii), by adding "and" to the end of paragraph (a)(4)(D)(iii), and by adding "and" to the end of paragraph (a)(4)(E). **Effective** with respect to corporations chartered afer 12-31-78, and before 1-1-84.

• **1978, Revenue Act of 1978 (P.L. 95-600)**

P.L. 95-600, § 601(a):

Added Code Sec. 1391. **Effective** with respect to corporations chartered after 12-31-78, and before 1-1-84.

[Sec. 1392—Repealed]

Amendments

• **1986, Tax Reform Act of 1986 (P.L. 99-514)**

P.L. 99-514, § 1303(a):

Repealed Code Sec. 1392. **Effective** 10-22-86. Prior to repeal, Code Sec. 1392 read as follows:

SEC. 1392. ELECTION BY GSOC.

[Sec. 1392(a)]

(a) ELIGIBILITY.—Except as provided in section 1396(b), any GSOC may elect, in accordance with the provisions of this section, not to be subject to the taxes imposed by this chapter.

Amendments

• **1980 (P.L. 96-595)**

P.L. 96-595, § 3(a)(3):

Amended Code Sec. 1392(a) by striking out "1393" and inserting in lieu thereof "1396(b)". **Effective** for corporations chartered after 1978 and before 1984.

[Sec. 1392(b)]

(b) EFFECT.—If a GSOC makes an election under subsection (a) then—

(1) with respect to the taxable years of the GSOC for which such election is in effect, such corporation shall not be subject to the taxes imposed by this chapter and, with respect to such taxable years, the provisions of section 1396 shall apply to such GSOC, and

(2) with respect to each such taxable year, the provisions of sections 1393, 1394, and 1395 shall apply to the shareholders of such GSOC.

Amendments

• **1980 (P.L. 96-595)**

P.L. 96-595, § 3(a)(4):

Amended Code Sec. 1392(b)(1) by striking out "and all succeeding taxable years" after "taxable years". **Effective** for corporations chartered after 1978 and before 1984.

[Sec. 1392(c)]

(c) WHEN AND HOW MADE.—An election under subsection (a) may be made by a GSOC at such time and in such manner as the Secretary shall prescribe by regulations.

[Sec. 1392(d)]

(d) YEARS FOR WHICH EFFECTIVE.—An election under subsection (a) shall be effective for the taxable year of the GSOC for which it is made and for all succeeding taxable years of the GSOC, unless it is terminated under subsection (f).

[Sec. 1392(e)]

(e) TAXABLE YEAR.—The taxable year of a GSOC shall end on October 31 unless the Secretary consents to a different taxable year.

[Sec. 1392(f)]

(f) TERMINATION.—The election of a GSOC under subsection (a) shall terminate for any taxable year during which it ceases to be a GSOC and for all succeeding taxable years. The election of a GSOC under subsection (a) may be terminated at any other time with the consent of the Secretary, effective for the first taxable year with respect to which the Secretary consents and for all succeeding taxable years.

Amendments

• **1980, Technical Corrections Act of 1979 (P.L. 96-222)**

P.L. 96-222, § 106(a)(5):

Amended Code Sec. 1392(c) by changing "Where" to "When". **Effective** with respect to corporations chartered after 12-31-78, and before 1-1-84.

• **1978, Revenue Act of 1978 (P.L. 95-600)**

P.L. 95-600, § 601(a):

Added Code Sec. 1392. **Effective** with respect to corporations chartered after 12-31-78, and before 1-1-84.

INCOME TAX—GENERAL STOCK OWNERSHIP CORPS.

[Sec. 1393—Repealed]

Amendments

• **1986, Tax Reform Act of 1986 (P.L. 99-514)**

P.L. 99-514, §1303(a):

Repealed Code Sec. 1393. **Effective** 10-22-86. Prior to repeal, Code Sec. 1393 read as follows:

SEC. 1393. GSOC TAXABLE INCOME TAXED TO SHAREHOLDERS.

[Sec. 1393(a)]

(a) GENERAL RULE.—The taxable income of an electing GSOC for any taxable year shall be included in the gross income of the shareholders of such GSOC in the manner and to the extent set forth in this subsection.

(1) AMOUNT INCLUDED IN GROSS INCOME.—Each shareholder of an electing GSOC on any day of a taxable year of such GSOC shall include in his gross income for the taxable year with or within which the taxable year of the GSOC ends the amount he would have received if, on each day of such taxable year, there had been distributed pro rata to its shareholders by such GSOC an amount equal to the taxable income of the GSOC for its taxable year divided by the number of days in the GSOC's taxable year.

(2) TAXABLE INCOME DEFINED.—For purposes of this subchapter, the taxable income of an electing GSOC shall be determined without regard to the deductions allowed by part VIII of subchapter B (other than deductions allowed by section 248, relating to organizational expenditures).

Amendments

• **1980 (P.L. 96-595)**

P.L. 96-595, §3(a)(5), (6):

Amended Code Sec. 1393(a)(2) by striking out "section, the term `taxable income'" and inserting in lieu thereof "subchapter, the taxable income", and by striking out "a GSOC" and inserting in lieu thereof "an electing GSOC". **Effective** for corporations chartered after 1978 and before 1984.

[Sec. 1393(b)]

(b) SPECIAL RULE FOR INVESTMENT CREDIT.—The investment credit of an electing GSOC for any taxable year shall be allowed as a credit to the shareholders of such corporation in the manner and to the extent set forth in this subsection.

(1) CREDIT.—There shall be apportioned among the shareholders a credit equal to the amount each shareholder would have received if, on each day of such taxable year, there had been distributed pro rata to the shareholders the electing GSOC's net investment credit divided by the number of days in the GSOC's taxable year.

(2) NET INVESTMENT CREDIT.—For purposes of this paragraph the term "net investment credit" means the investment credit of the electing GSOC for its taxable year less any tax from recomputing a prior year's investment credit in accordance with section 47.

(3) RECAPTURE.—There shall be apportioned among the shareholders of an electing GSOC, in the manner described in paragraph (1), an additional tax equal to the excess of any tax resulting from recomputing a prior year's investment credit in accordance with section 47 over the investment credit of an electing GSOC for its taxable year.

Amendments

• **1980 (P.L. 96-595)**

P.L. 96-595, §3(a)(6), (8):

Amended Code Sec. 1393(b)(3) by striking out "a GSOC" and inserting in lieu thereof "an electing GSOC" and by striking out "the GSOC" and inserting in lieu thereof "an electing GSOC". **Effective** for corporations chartered after 1978 and before 1984.

• **1978, Revenue Act of 1978 (P.L. 95-600)**

P.L. 95-600, §601(a):

Added Code Sec. 1393. **Effective** with respect to orporations chartered after 12-31-78, and before 1-1-84.

[Sec. 1394—Repealed]

Amendments

• **1986, Tax Reform Act of 1986 (P.L. 99-514)**

P.L. 99-514, §1303(a):

Repealed Code Sec. 1394. **Effective** 10-22-86. Prior to repeal, Code Sec. 1394 read as follows:

SEC. 1394. RULES APPLICABLE TO DISTRIBUTIONS OF AN ELECTING GSOC.

[Sec. 1394(a)]

(a) SHAREHOLDER INCOME ACCOUNT.—An electing GSOC shall establish and maintain a shareholder income account which account shall be—

(1) increased at the close of the GSOC's taxable year by an amount equal to the GSOC's taxable income for such year, and

(2) decreased, but not below zero, on the first day of the GSOC's taxable year by the amount of any GSOC distribution to the shareholders of such GSOC made or treated as made during the prior taxable year.

Amendments

• **1980 (P.L. 96-595)**

P.L. 96-595, §3(a)(7):

Amended the heading of Code Sec. 1394. **Effective** for corporations chartered after 1978 and before 1984. Prior to amendment, the heading of Code Sec. 1394 read:

SEC. 1394. RULES APPLICABLE TO DISTRIBUTIONS OF ELECTING GSOCs.

[Sec. 1394(b)]

(b) TAXATION OF DISTRIBUTIONS.—Distributions by an electing GSOC shall be treated as—

(1) a distribution of previously taxed income to the extent such distribution does not exceed the balance of the shareholder income account as of the close of the taxable year of the GSOC, and

(2) a distribution to which section 301(a) applies but only to the extent such distribution exceeds the balance of the shareholder income account as of the close of the taxable year of the GSOC.

[Sec. 1394(c)]

(c) DISTRIBUTIONS NOT TREATED AS A DIVIDEND.—Any amounts includible in the gross income of any individual by reason of ownership of stock in an electing GSOC shall not be considered as a dividend for purposes of section 116.

Amendments

• **1980 (P.L. 96-595)**

P.L. 96-595, §3(a)(6):

Amended Code Sec. 1394(c) by striking out "a GSOC" and inserting in lieu thereof "an electing GSOC". **Effective** for corporations chartered after 1978 and before 1984.

[Sec. 1394(d)]

(d) REGULATIONS.—The Secretary shall have authority to prescribe by regulation, rules for treatment of distributions in respect of shares of stock of an electing GSOC that have been transferred during the taxable year.

Amendments

• **1980 (P.L. 96-595)**

P.L. 96-595, §3(a)(8):

Amended Code Sec. 1394(d) by striking out "the GSOC" and inserting in lieu thereof "an electing GSOC". **Effective** for corporations chartered after 1978 and before 1984.

• **1978, Revenue Act of 1978 (P.L. 95-600)**

P.L. 95-600, §601(a):

Added Code Sec. 1394. **Effective** with respect to corporations chartered after 12-31-78, and before 1-1-84.

[Sec. 1395—Repealed]

Amendments

• **1986, Tax Reform Act of 1986 (P.L. 99-514)**

P.L. 99-514, §1303(a):

Repealed Code Sec. 1395. **Effective** 10-22-86. Prior to repeal, Code Sec. 1395 read as follows:

SEC. 1395. ADJUSTMENTS TO BASIS OF STOCK OF SHAREHOLDERS.

The basis of a shareholder's stock in an electing GSOC shall be increased by the amount includible in the gross income of such shareholder under section 1393, but only to the extent to which such amount is actually included in the gross income of such shareholder.

• **1978, Revenue Act of 1978 (P.L. 95-600)**

P.L. 95-600, §601(a):

Added Code Sec. 1395. **Effective** with respect to corporations chartered after 12-31-78, and before 1-1-84.

[Sec. 1396—Repealed]

Amendments

• **1986, Tax Reform Act of 1986 (P.L. 99-514)**

P.L. 99-514, §1303(a):

Repealed Code Sec. 1396. **Effective** 10-22-86. Prior to repeal, Code Sec. 1396 read as follows:

SEC. 1396. MINIMUM DISTRIBUTIONS.

[Sec. 1396(a)]

(a) GENERAL RULE.—An electing GSOC shall distribute at least 90 percent of its taxable income for any taxable year by January 31 following the close of such taxable year. Any distribution made on or before January 31 shall be treated as made as of the close of the preceding taxable year.

Amendments

• **1980 (P.L. 96-595)**

P.L. 96-595, §3(a)(9):

Amended Code Sec. 1396(a) by striking out "A GSOC" and inserting in lieu thereof "An electing GSOC". **Effective** for corporations chartered after 1978 and before 1984.

INCOME TAX—TITLE 11 CASES

[Sec. 1396(b)]

(b) IMPOSITION OF TAX IN CASE OF FAILURE TO MAKE MINIMUM DISTRIBUTIONS.—If an electing GSOC fails to make the minimum distribution requirements described in subsection (a), there is hereby imposed a tax equal to 20 percent of the excess of the amount required to be distributed over the amount actually distributed. Such tax shall be deductible as an ordinary and necessary expense of the corporation under section 162.

Amendments

- **1980 (P.L. 96-595)**

P.L. 96-595, §3(a)(6), (10):

Amended Code Sec. 1396(b) by striking out "a GSOC" and inserting in lieu thereof "an electing GSOC", and by adding a new last sentence. **Effective** for corporations chartered after 1978 and before 1984.

- **1978, Revenue Act of 1978 (P.L. 95-600)**

P.L. 95-600, §601(a):

Added Code Sec. 1396. **Effective** with respect to corporations chartered after 12-31-78, and before 1-1-84.

[Sec. 1397—Repealed]

Amendments

- **1986, Tax Reform Act of 1986 (P.L. 99-514)**

P.L. 99-514, §1303(a):

Repealed Code Sec. 1397. **Effective** 10-22-86. Prior to repeal, Code Sec. 1397 read as follows:

SEC. 1397. SPECIAL RULES APPLICABLE TO AN ELECTING GSOC.

[Sec. 1397(a)]

(a) GENERAL RULE.—The current earnings and profits of an electing GSOC as of the close of its taxable year shall not include the amount of taxable income for such year which is required to be included in the gross income of the shareholders of such GSOC under section 1393(a).

[Sec. 1397(b)]

(b) SPECIAL RULE FOR AUDIT ADJUSTMENTS.—

(1) TAXABLE INCOME.—Taxable income of an electing GSOC shall, in the year of final determination, be increased or decreased, as the case might be, by any adjustment to taxable income for a prior taxable year.

(2) INVESTMENT CREDIT.—The net investment credit of an electing GSOC shall, in the year of final determination, be increased or decreased, as the case might be, by any adjustment to the net investment credit for a prior taxable year.

(3) METHOD OF MAKING ADJUSTMENTS.—An electing GSOC shall include in gross income for the year of an adjustment the amount described in paragraph (1) and shall take into account the adjustment described in paragraph (2), and shall be liable for payment of interest in the amount that would have been payable by the GSOC under section 6601 (relating to interest on underpayment, nonpayment or extensions of time for payment, of tax) or receivable by the GSOC under section 6611 (relating to interest on overpayments) if such GSOC had been a corporation other than an electing GSOC.

- **1978, Revenue Act of 1978 (P.L. 95-600)**

P.L. 95-600, §601(a):

Added Code Sec. 1397. **Effective** with respect to corporations chartered after 12-31-78, and before 1-1-84.

Subchapter V—Title 11 Cases

Sec. 1398. Rules relating to individuals' title 11 cases.
Sec. 1399. No separate taxable entities for partnerships, corporations, etc.

[Sec. 1398]

SEC. 1398. RULES RELATING TO INDIVIDUALS' TITLE 11 CASES.

[Sec. 1398(a)]

(a) CASES TO WHICH SECTION APPLIES.—Except as provided in subsection (b), this section shall apply to any case under chapter 7 (relating to liquidations) or chapter 11 (relating to reorganizations) of title 11 of the United States Code in which the debtor is an individual.

[Sec. 1398(b)]

(b) EXCEPTIONS WHERE CASE IS DISMISSED, ETC.—

(1) SECTION DOES NOT APPLY WHERE CASE IS DISMISSED.—This section shall not apply if the case under chapter 7 or 11 of title 11 of the United States Code is dismissed.

(2) SECTION DOES NOT APPLY AT PARTNERSHIP LEVEL.—For purposes of subsection (a), a partnership shall not be treated as an individual, but the interest in a partnership of a debtor who is an individual shall be taken into account under this section in the same manner as any other interest of the debtor.

[Sec. 1398(c)]

(c) COMPUTATION AND PAYMENT OF TAX; BASIC STANDARD DEDUCTION.—

(1) COMPUTATION AND PAYMENT OF TAX.—Except as otherwise provided in this section, the taxable income of the estate shall be computed in the same manner as for an individual. The tax shall be computed on such taxable income and shall be paid by the trustee.

(2) TAX RATES.—The tax on the taxable income of the estate shall be determined under subsection (d) of section 1.

(3) BASIC STANDARD DEDUCTION.—In the case of an estate which does not itemize deductions, the basic standard deduction for the estate for the taxable year shall be the same as for a married individual filing a separate return for such year.

Amendments

- **1986, Tax Reform Act of 1986 (P.L. 99-514)**

P.L. 99-514, §104(b)(14)(A)-(B):

Amended Code Sec. 1398(c) by striking out "Zero Bracket Amount" in the subsection heading and inserting in lieu thereof "Basic Standard Deduction", and by striking out paragraph (3) and inserting in lieu thereof new paragraph (3). **Effective** for tax years beginning after 12-31-86. Prior to amendment, Code Sec. 1398(c)(3) read as follows:

(3) AMOUNT OF ZERO BRACKET AMOUNT.—The amount of the estate's zero bracket amount for the taxable year shall be the same as for a married individual filing a separate return for such year.

[Sec. 1398(d)]

(d) TAXABLE YEAR OF DEBTORS.—

(1) GENERAL RULE.—Except as provided in paragraph (2), the taxable year of the debtor shall be determined without regard to the case under title 11 of the United States Code to which this section applies.

(2) ELECTION TO TERMINATE DEBTOR'S YEAR WHEN CASE COMMENCES.—

(A) IN GENERAL.—Notwithstanding section 442, the debtor may (without the approval of the Secretary) elect to treat the debtor's taxable year which includes the commencement date as 2 taxable years—

(i) the first of which ends on the day before the commencement date, and

(ii) the second of which begins on the commencement date.

(B) SPOUSE MAY JOIN IN ELECTION.—In the case of a married individual (within the meaning of section 7703), the spouse may elect to have the debtor's election under subparagraph (A) also apply to the spouse, but only if the debtor and the spouse file a joint return for the taxable year referred to in subparagraph (A)(i).

(C) NO ELECTION WHERE DEBTOR HAS NO ASSETS.—No election may be made under subparagraph (A) by a debtor who has no assets other than property which the debtor may treat as exempt property under section 522 of title 11 of the United States Code.

Sec. 1397—Repealed

INCOME TAX—TITLE 11 CASES

(D) TIME FOR MAKING ELECTION.—An election under subparagraph (A) or (B) may be made only on or before the due date for filing the return for the taxable year referred to in subparagraph (A)(i). Any such election, once made, shall be irrevocable.

(E) RETURNS.—A return shall be made for each of the taxable years specified in subparagraph (A).

(F) ANNUALIZATION.—For purposes of subsections (b), (c), and (d) of section 443, a return filed for either of the taxable years referred to in subparagraph (A) shall be treated as a return made under paragraph (1) of subsection (a) of section 443.

(3) COMMENCEMENT DATE DEFINED.—For purposes of this subsection, the term "commencement date" means the day on which the case under title 11 of the United States Code to which this section applies commences.

Amendments
• **1986, Tax Reform Act of 1986 (P.L. 99-514)**
P.L. 99-514, § 1301(j)(8):
Amended Code Sec. 1398(d)(2) by striking out "section 143" and inserting in lieu thereof "section 7703". **Effective** for bonds issued after 8-15-86.

[Sec. 1398(e)]

(e) TREATMENT OF INCOME, DEDUCTIONS, AND CREDITS.—

(1) ESTATE'S SHARE OF DEBTOR'S INCOME.—The gross income of the estate for each taxable year shall include the gross income of the debtor to which the estate is entitled under title 11 of the United States Code. The preceding sentence shall not apply to any amount received or accrued by the debtor before the commencement date (as defined in subsection (d)(3)).

(2) DEBTOR'S SHARE OF DEBTOR'S INCOME.—The gross income of the debtor for any taxable year shall not include any item to the extent that such item is included in the gross income of the estate by reason of paragraph (1).

(3) RULE FOR MAKING DETERMINATIONS WITH RESPECT TO DEDUCTIONS, CREDITS, AND EMPLOYMENT TAXES.—Except as otherwise provided in this section, the determination of whether or not any amount paid or incurred by the estate—

(A) is allowable as a deduction or credit under this chapter, or

(B) is wages for purposes of subtitle C,

shall be made as if the amount were paid or incurred by the debtor and as if the debtor were still engaged in the trades and businesses, and in the activities, the debtor was engaged in before the commencement of the case.

[Sec. 1398(f)]

(f) TREATMENT OF TRANSFERS BETWEEN DEBTOR AND ESTATE.—

(1) TRANSFER TO ESTATE NOT TREATED AS DISPOSITION.—A transfer (other than by sale or exchange) of an asset from the debtor to the estate shall not be treated as a disposition for purposes of any provision of this title assigning tax consequences to a disposition, and the estate shall be treated as the debtor would be treated with respect to such asset.

(2) TRANSFER FROM ESTATE TO DEBTOR NOT TREATED AS DISPOSITION.—In the case of a termination of the estate, a transfer (other than by sale or exchange) of an asset from the estate to the debtor shall not be treated as a disposition for purposes of any provision of this title assigning tax consequences to a disposition, and the debtor shall be treated as the estate would be treated with respect to such asset.

[Sec. 1398(g)]

(g) ESTATE SUCCEEDS TO TAX ATTRIBUTES OF DEBTOR.—The estate shall succeed to and take into account the following items (determined as of the first day of the debtor's taxable year in which the case commences) of the debtor—

(1) NET OPERATING LOSS CARRYOVERS.—The net operating loss carryovers determined under section 172.

(2) CHARITABLE CONTRIBUTIONS CARRYOVERS.—The carryover of excess charitable contributions determined under section 170(d)(1).

(3) RECOVERY OF TAX BENEFIT ITEMS.—Any amount to which section 111 (relating to recovery of tax benefit items) applies.

(4) CREDIT CARRYOVERS, ETC.—The carryovers of any credit, and all other items which, but for the commencement of the case, would be required to be taken into account by the debtor with respect to any credit.

(5) CAPITAL LOSS CARRYOVERS.—The capital loss carryover determined under section 1212.

(6) BASIS, HOLDING PERIOD, AND CHARACTER OF ASSETS.—In the case of any asset acquired (other than by sale or exchange) by the estate from the debtor, the basis, holding period, and character it had in the hands of the debtor.

(7) METHOD OF ACCOUNTING.—The method of accounting used by the debtor.

(8) OTHER ATTRIBUTES.—Other tax attributes of the debtor, to the extent provided in regulations prescribed by the Secretary as necessary or appropriate to carry out the purposes of this section.

Amendments
• **1986, Tax Reform Act of 1986 (P.L. 99-514)**
P.L. 99-514, § 1812(a)(5):
Amended Code Sec. 1398(g)(3). **Effective** as if included in the provision of P.L. 98-369 to which it relates. Prior to amendment, Code Sec. 1398(g)(3) read as follows:

(3) RECOVERY EXCLUSION.—Any recovery exclusion under section 111 (relating to recovery of bad debts, prior taxes, and delinquency amounts).

[Sec. 1398(h)]

(h) ADMINISTRATION, LIQUIDATION, AND REORGANIZATION EXPENSES; CARRYOVERS AND CARRYBACKS OF CERTAIN EXCESS EXPENSES.—

(1) ADMINISTRATION, LIQUIDATION, AND REORGANIZATION EXPENSES.—Any administrative expense allowed under section 503 of title 11 of the United States Code, and any fee or charge assessed against the estate under chapter 123 of title 28 of the United States Code, to the extent not disallowed under any other provision of this title, shall be allowed as a deduction.

(2) CARRYBACK AND CARRYOVER OF EXCESS ADMINISTRATIVE COSTS, ETC., TO ESTATE TAXABLE YEARS.—

(A) DEDUCTION ALLOWED.—There shall be allowed as a deduction for the taxable year an amount equal to the aggregate of (i) the administrative expense carryovers to such year, plus (ii) the administrative expense carrybacks to such year.

(B) ADMINISTRATIVE EXPENSE LOSS, ETC.—If a net operating loss would be created or increased for any estate taxable year if section 172(c) were applied without the modification contained in paragraph (4) of section 172(d), then the amount of the net operating loss so created (or the amount of the increase in the net operating loss) shall be an administrative expense loss for such taxable year which shall be an administrative expense carryback to each of the 3 preceding taxable years and an administrative expense carryover to each of the 7 succeeding taxable years.

(C) DETERMINATION OF AMOUNT CARRIED TO EACH TAXABLE YEAR.—The portion of any administrative expense loss which may be carried to any other taxable year shall be determined under section 172(b)(2), except that for each taxable year the computation under section 172(b)(2) with respect to the net operating loss shall be made before the computation under this paragraph.

INCOME TAX—DC ENTERPRISE ZONE

(D) ADMINISTRATIVE EXPENSE DEDUCTIONS ALLOWED ONLY TO ESTATE.—The deductions allowable under this chapter solely by reason of paragraph (1), and the deduction provided by subparagraph (A) of this paragraph, shall be allowable only to the estate.

[Sec. 1398(i)]

(i) DEBTOR SUCCEEDS TO TAX ATTRIBUTES OF ESTATE.—In the case of a termination of an estate, the debtor shall succeed to and take into account the items referred to in paragraphs (1), (2), (3), (4), (5), and (6) of subsection (g) in a manner similar to that provided in such paragraphs (but taking into account that the transfer is from the estate to the debtor instead of from the debtor to the estate). In addition, the debtor shall succeed to and take into account the other tax attributes of the estate, to the extent provided in regulations prescribed by the Secretary as necessary or appropriate to carry out the purposes of this section.

[Sec. 1398(j)]

(j) OTHER SPECIAL RULES.—

(1) CHANGE OF ACCOUNTING PERIOD WITHOUT APPROVAL.—Notwithstanding section 442, the estate may change its annual accounting period one time without the approval of the Secretary.

(2) TREATMENT OF CERTAIN CARRYBACKS.—

(A) CARRYBACKS FROM ESTATE.—If any carryback year of the estate is a taxable year before the estate's first taxable year, the carryback to such carryback year shall be taken into account for the debtor's taxable year corresponding to the carryback year.

(B) CARRYBACKS FROM DEBTOR'S ACTIVITIES.—The debtor may not carry back to a taxable year before the debtor's taxable year in which the case commences any carryback from a taxable year ending after the case commences.

(C) CARRYBACK AND CARRYBACK YEAR DEFINED.—For purposes of this paragraph—

(i) CARRYBACK.—The term "carryback" means a net operating loss carryback under section 172 or a carryback of any credit provided by part IV of subchapter A.

(ii) CARRYBACK YEAR.—The term "carryback year" means the taxable year to which a carryback is carried.

Amendments

• **1980, Bankruptcy Tax Act of 1980 (P.L. 96-589)**

P.L. 96-589, §3(a)(1):

Added Code Sec. 1398. **Effective** for bankruptcy cases commencing on or after 3-25-81.

[Sec. 1399]

SEC. 1399. NO SEPARATE TAXABLE ENTITIES FOR PARTNERSHIPS, CORPORATIONS, ETC.

Except in any case to which section 1398 applies, no separate taxable entity shall result from the commencement of a case under title 11 of the United States Code.

Amendments

• **1980, Bankruptcy Tax Act of 19080 (P.L. 96-589)**

P.L. 96-589, §3(a)(1):

Added Code Sec. 1399. **Effective** for bankruptcy cases commencing on or after 3-25-81.

Subchapter W—District of Columbia Enterprise Zone—[Stricken]

[Sec. 1400—Stricken]

Amendments

• **2018, Tax Technical Corrections Act of 2018 (P.L. 115-141)**

P.L. 115-141, §401(d)(4)(A), Div. U:

Amended chapter 1 by striking subchapter W (Code Secs. 1400-1400C). **Effective** 3-23-2018. For a special rule, see Act Sec. 401(e), Div. U, below. Prior to being stricken, Code Sec. 1400 read as follows:

SEC. 1400. ESTABLISHMENT OF DC ZONE.

[Sec. 1400(a)]

(a) IN GENERAL.—For purposes of this title—

(1) the applicable DC area is hereby designated as the District of Columbia Enterprise Zone, and

(2) except as otherwise provided in this subchapter, the District of Columbia Enterprise Zone shall be treated as an empowerment zone designated under subchapter U.

[Sec. 1400(b)]

(b) APPLICABLE DC AREA.—For purposes of subsection (a), the term "applicable DC area" means the area consisting of—

(1) the census tracts located in the District of Columbia which are part of an enterprise community designated under subchapter U before the date of the enactment of this subchapter, and

(2) all other census tracts—

(A) which are located in the District of Columbia, and

(B) for which the poverty rate is not less than than 20 percent as determined on the basis of the 1990 census.

Amendments

• **1998, IRS Restructuring and Reform Act of 1998 (P.L. 105-206)**

P.L. 105-206, §6008(a):

Amended Code Sec. 1400(b)(2)(B) by inserting "as determined on the basis of the 1990 census" after "percent". **Effective** as if included in the provision of P.L. 105-34 to which it relates [effective 8-5-97.—CCH].

[Sec. 1400(c)]

(c) DISTRICT OF COLUMBIA ENTERPRISE ZONE.—For purposes of this subchapter, the terms "District of Columbia Enterprise Zone" and "DC Zone" mean the District of Columbia Enterprise Zone designated by subsection (a).

[Sec. 1400(d)]

(d) SPECIAL RULE FOR APPLICATION OF EMPLOYMENT CREDIT.—With respect to the DC Zone, section 1396(d)(1)(B) (relating to empowerment zone employment credit) shall be applied by substituting "the District of Columbia" for "such empowerment zone".

Amendments

• **2000, Community Renewal Tax Relief Act of 2000 (P.L. 106-554)**

P.L. 106-554, §113(c):

Amended Code Sec. 1400(d). **Effective** for wages paid or incurred after 12-31-2001. Prior to amendment, Code Sec. 1400(d) read as follows:

(d) SPECIAL RULES FOR APPLICATION OF EMPLOYMENT CREDIT.—

(1) EMPLOYEES WHOSE PRINCIPAL PLACE OF ABODE IS IN DISTRICT OF COLUMBIA.—With respect to the DC Zone, section 1396(d)(1)(B) (relating to empowerment zone employment credit) shall be applied by substituting "the District of Columbia" for "such empowerment zone".

(2) NO DECREASE OF PERCENTAGE IN 2002.—In the case of the DC Zone, section 1396 (relating to empowerment zone employment credit) shall be applied by substituting "20" for "15" in the table contained in section 1396(b). The preceding sentence shall apply only with respect to qualified zone employees, as defined in section 1396(d), determined by treating no area other than the DC Zone as an empowerment zone or enterprise community.

[Sec. 1400(e)]

(e) SPECIAL RULE FOR APPLICATION OF ENTERPRISE ZONE BUSINESS DEFINITION.—For purposes of this subchapter and for purposes of applying subchapter U with respect to the DC Zone, section 1397C shall be applied without regard to subsections (b)(6) and (c)(5) thereof.

Amendments

• **2000, Community Renewal Tax Relief Act of 2000 (P.L. 106-554)**

P.L. 106-554, §116(b)(5):

Amended Code Sec. 1400(e) by striking "section 1397B" and inserting "section 1397C". **Effective** for qualified empowerment zone assets acquired after 12-21-2000.

[Sec. 1400(f)]

(f) TIME FOR WHICH DESIGNATION APPLICABLE.—

(1) IN GENERAL.—The designation made by subsection (a) shall apply for the period beginning on January 1, 1998, and ending on December 31, 2011.

INCOME TAX—DC ENTERPRISE ZONE

(2) COORDINATION WITH DC ENTERPRISE COMMUNITY DESIGNATED UNDER SUBCHAPTER U.—The designation under subchapter U of the census tracts referred to in subsection (b)(1) as an enterprise community shall terminate on December 31, 2011.

Amendments

• **2010, Tax Relief, Unemployment Insurance Reauthorization, and Job Creation Act of 2010 (P.L. 111-312)**

P.L. 111-312, §754(a):

Amended Code Sec. 1400(f) by striking "December 31, 2009" each place it appears and inserting "December 31, 2011". **Effective** for periods after 12-31-2009.

• **2008, Tax Extenders and Alternative Minimum Tax Relief Act of 2008 (P.L. 110-343)**

P.L. 110-343, Division C, §322(a)(1):

Amended Code Sec. 1400(f) by striking "2007" both places it appears and inserting "2009". **Effective** for periods beginning after 12-31-2007.

• **2006, Tax Relief and Health Care Act of 2006 (P.L. 109-432)**

P.L. 109-432, Division A, §110(a)(1):

Amended Code Sec. 1400(f) by striking "2005" both places it appears and inserting "2007". **Effective** for periods beginning after 12-31-2005.

• **2004, Working Families Tax Relief Act of 2004 (P.L. 108-311)**

P.L. 108-311, §310(a):

Amended Code Sec. 1400(f) by striking "December 31, 2003" both places it appears and inserting "December 31, 2005". **Effective** on 1-1-2004.

[Sec. 1400A—Stricken]

Amendments

• **2018, Tax Technical Corrections Act of 2018 (P.L. 115-141)**

P.L. 115-141, §401(d)(4)(A), Div. U:

Amended chapter 1 by striking subchapter W (Code Secs. 1400-1400C). **Effective** 3-23-2018. For special rules, see Act Sec. 401(d)(4)(C)(i), Div. U, and Act Sec. 401(e), Div. U, below. Prior to being stricken, Code Sec. 1400A read as follows:

SEC. 1400A. TAX-EXEMPT ECONOMIC DEVELOPMENT BONDS.

[Sec. 1400A(a)]

(a) IN GENERAL.—In the case of the District of Columbia Enterprise Zone, subparagraph (A) of section 1394(c)(1) (relating to limitation on amount of bonds) shall be applied by substituting "$15,000,000" for "$3,000,000" and section 1394(b)(3)(B)(iii) shall be applied without regard to the employee residency requirement.

Amendments

• **1998, IRS Restructuring and Reform Act of 1998 (P.L. 105-206)**

P.L. 105-206, §6008(b):

Amended Code Sec. 1400A(a) by inserting before the period "and section 1394(b)(3)(B)(iii) shall be applied without regard to the employee residency requirement". **Effective** as if included in the provision of P.L. 105-34 to which it relates [effective 8-5-97.—CCH].

[Sec. 1400A(b)]

(b) PERIOD OF APPLICABILITY.—This section shall apply to bonds issued during the period beginning on January 1, 1998, and ending on December 31, 2011.

Amendments

• **2010, Tax Relief, Unemployment Insurance Reauthorization, and Job Creation Act of 2010 (P.L. 111-312)**

P.L. 111-312, §754(b):

Amended Code Sec. 1400A(b) by striking "December 31, 2009" and inserting "December 31, 2011". **Effective** for bonds issued after 12-31-2009.

• **2008, Tax Extenders and Alternative Minimum Tax Relief Act of 2008 (P.L. 110-343)**

P.L. 110-343, Division C, §322(b)(1):

Amended Code Sec. 1400A(b) by striking "2007" and inserting "2009". **Effective** for bonds issued after 12-31-2007.

• **2006, Tax Relief and Health Care Act of 2006 (P.L. 109-432)**

P.L. 109-432, Division A, §110(b)(1):

Amended Code Sec. 1400A(b) by striking "2005" and inserting "2007". **Effective** for bonds issued after 12-31-2005.

• **2004, Working Families Tax Relief Act of 2004 (P.L. 108-311)**

P.L. 108-311, §310(b):

Amended Code Sec. 1400A(b) by striking "December 31, 2003" and inserting "December 31, 2005". **Effective** for obligations issued after 10-4-2004.

• **2000, Community Renewal Tax Relief Act of 2000 (P.L. 106-554)**

P.L. 106-554, §164(a)(1):

Amended Code Sec. 1400(f) by striking "2002" each place it appears and inserting "2003". **Effective** 12-21-2000.

• **1997, Taxpayer Relief Act of 1997 (P.L. 105-34)**

P.L. 105-34, §701(a):

Amended chapter 1 by adding a new subchapter W (Code Secs. 1400-1400C). **Effective** 8-5-97.

P.L. 115-141, §401(e), Div. U, provides:

(e) GENERAL SAVINGS PROVISION WITH RESPECT TO DEADWOOD PROVISIONS.—If—

(1) any provision amended or repealed by the amendments made by subsection (b) or (d) applied to—

(A) any transaction occurring before the date of the enactment of this Act,

(B) any property acquired before such date of enactment, or

(C) any item of income, loss, deduction, or credit taken into account before such date of enactment, and

(2) the treatment of such transaction, property, or item under such provision would (without regard to the amendments or repeals made by such subsection) affect the liability for tax for periods ending after such date of enactment,

nothing in the amendments or repeals made by this section shall be construed to affect the treatment of such transaction, property, or item for purposes of determining liability for tax for periods ending after such date of enactment.

• **2006, Tax Relief and Health Care Act of 2006 (P.L. 109-432)**

P.L. 109-432, Division A, §110(b)(1):

Amended Code Sec. 1400A(b) by striking "2005" and inserting "2007". **Effective** for bonds issued after 12-31-2005.

• **2004, Working Families Tax Relief Act of 2004 (P.L. 108-311)**

P.L. 108-311, §310(b):

Amended Code Sec. 1400A(b) by striking "December 31, 2003" and inserting "December 31, 2005". **Effective** for obligations issued after 10-4-2004.

• **2000, Community Renewal Tax Relief Act of 2000 (P.L. 106-554)**

P.L. 106-554, §164(a)(2):

Amended Code Sec. 1400A(b) by striking "2002" and inserting "2003". **Effective** 12-21-2000.

• **1997, Taxpayer Relief Act of 1997 (P.L. 105-34)**

P.L. 105-34, §701(a):

Added a new Code Sec. 1400A. **Effective** 8-5-97.

P.L. 115-141, §401(d)(4)(C)(i), Div. U, provides:

(C) SAVINGS PROVISIONS.—The amendments made by this paragraph shall not apply to—

(i) in the case of the repeal of section 1400A of the Internal Revenue Code of 1986, obligations described in section 1394 of such Code (as in effect before its repeal) which were issued before January 1, 2012,

P.L. 115-141, §401(e), Div. U, provides:

(e) GENERAL SAVINGS PROVISION WITH RESPECT TO DEADWOOD PROVISIONS.—If—

(1) any provision amended or repealed by the amendments made by subsection (b) or (d) applied to—

(A) any transaction occurring before the date of the enactment of this Act,

(B) any property acquired before such date of enactment, or

(C) any item of income, loss, deduction, or credit taken into account before such date of enactment, and

(2) the treatment of such transaction, property, or item under such provision would (without regard to the amendments or repeals made by such subsection) affect the liability for tax for periods ending after such date of enactment,

nothing in the amendments or repeals made by this section shall be construed to affect the treatment of such transaction, property, or item for purposes of determining liability for tax for periods ending after such date of enactment.

[Sec. 1400B—Stricken]

Amendments

• **2018, Tax Technical Corrections Act of 2018 (P.L. 115-141)**

P.L. 115-141, §401(d)(4)(A), Div. U:

Amended chapter 1 by striking subchapter W (Code Secs. 1400-1400C). **Effective** 3-23-2018. For special rules, see Act Sec. 401(d)(4)(C)(ii), Div. U, and Act Sec. 401(e), Div. U, below. Prior to being stricken, Code Sec. 1400B read as follows:

SEC. 1400B. ZERO PERCENT CAPITAL GAINS RATE.

[Sec. 1400B(a)]

(a) EXCLUSION.—Gross income shall not include qualified capital gain from the sale or exchange of any DC Zone asset held for more than 5 years.

[Sec. 1400B(b)]

(b) DC ZONE ASSET.—For purposes of this section—

(1) IN GENERAL.—The term "DC Zone asset" means—

(A) any DC Zone business stock,

(B) any DC Zone partnership interest, and

(C) any DC Zone business property.

(2) DC ZONE BUSINESS STOCK.—

(A) IN GENERAL.—The term "DC Zone business stock" means any stock in a domestic corporation which is originally issued after December 31, 1997, if—

(i) such stock is acquired by the taxpayer, before January 1, 2012, at its original issue (directly or through an underwriter) solely in exchange for cash,

(ii) as of the time such stock was issued, such corporation was a DC Zone business (or, in the case of a new corporation, such corporation was being organized for purposes of being a DC Zone business), and

(iii) during substantially all of the taxpayer's holding period for such stock, such corporation qualified as a DC Zone business.

(B) REDEMPTIONS.—A rule similar to the rule of section 1202(c)(3) shall apply for purposes of this paragraph.

(3) DC ZONE PARTNERSHIP INTEREST.—The term "DC Zone partnership interest" means any capital or profits interest in a domestic partnership which is originally issued after December 31, 1997, if—

(A) such interest is acquired by the taxpayer, before January 1, 2012, from the partnership solely in exchange for cash,

INCOME TAX—DC ENTERPRISE ZONE

(B) as of the time such interest was acquired, such partnership was a DC Zone business (or, in the case of a new partnership, such partnership was being organized for purposes of being a DC Zone business), and

(C) during substantially all of the taxpayer's holding period for such interest, such partnership qualified as a DC Zone business.

A rule similar to the rule of paragraph (2)(B) shall apply for purposes of this paragraph.

(4) DC ZONE BUSINESS PROPERTY.—

(A) IN GENERAL.—The term "DC Zone business property" means tangible property if—

(i) such property was acquired by the taxpayer by purchase (as defined in section 179(d)(2)) after December 31, 1997, and before January 1, 2012,

(ii) the original use of such property in the DC Zone commences with the taxpayer, and

(iii) during substantially all of the taxpayer's holding period for such property, substantially all of the use of such property was in a DC Zone business of the taxpayer.

(B) SPECIAL RULE FOR BUILDINGS WHICH ARE SUBSTANTIALLY IMPROVED.—

(i) IN GENERAL.—The requirements of clauses (i) and (ii) of subparagraph (A) shall be treated as met with respect to—

(I) property which is substantially improved by the taxpayer before January 1, 2012, and

(II) any land on which such property is located.

(ii) SUBSTANTIAL IMPROVEMENT.—For purposes of clause (i), property shall be treated as substantially improved by the taxpayer only if, during any 24-month period beginning after December 31, 1997, additions to basis with respect to such property in the hands of the taxpayer exceed the greater of—

(I) an amount equal to the adjusted basis of such property at the beginning of such 24-month period in the hands of the taxpayer, or

(II) $5,000.

(5) TREATMENT OF DC ZONE TERMINATION.—The termination of the designation of the DC Zone shall be disregarded for purposes of determining whether any property is a DC Zone asset.

(6) TREATMENT OF SUBSEQUENT PURCHASERS, ETC.—The term "DC Zone asset" includes any property which would be a DC Zone asset but for paragraph (2)(A)(i), (3)(A), or (4)(A)(i) or (ii) in the hands of the taxpayer if such property was a DC Zone asset in the hands of a prior holder.

(7) 5-YEAR SAFE HARBOR.—If any property ceases to be a DC Zone asset by reason of paragraph (2)(A)(iii), (3)(C), or (4)(A)(iii) after the 5-year period beginning on the date the taxpayer acquired such property, such property shall continue to be treated as meeting the requirements of such paragraph; except that the amount of gain to which subsection (a) applies on any sale or exchange of such property shall not exceed the amount which would be qualified capital gain had such property been sold on the date of such cessation.

Amendments

• **2010, Tax Relief, Unemployment Insurance Reauthorization, and Job Creation Act of 2010 (P.L. 111-312)**

P.L. 111-312, §754(c)(1):

Amended Code Sec. 1400B(b)(2)(A)(i), (3)(A), (4)(A)(i), and (4)(B)(i)(I) by striking "January 1, 2010" and inserting "January 1, 2012". **Effective** for property acquired or substantially improved after 12-31-2009.

• **2008, Tax Extenders and Alternative Minimum Tax Relief Act of 2008 (P.L. 110-343)**

P.L. 110-343, Division C, §322(c)(1):

Amended Code Sec. 1400B(b) by striking "2008" each place it appears and inserting "2010". **Effective** for acquisitions after 12-31-2007.

• **2006, Tax Relief and Health Care Act of 2006 (P.L. 109-432)**

P.L. 109-432, Division A, §110(c)(1):

Amended Code Sec. 1400B(b) by striking "2006" each place it appears and inserting "2008". **Effective** for acquisitions after 12-31-2005.

• **2004, Working Families Tax Relief Act of 2004 (P.L. 108-311)**

P.L. 108-311, §310(c)(1):

Amended Code Sec. 1400B(b) by striking "January 1, 2004" each place it appears and inserting "January 1, 2006". **Effective** on 1-1-2004.

• **2000, Community Renewal Tax Relief Act of 2000 (P.L. 106-554)**

P.L. 106-554, §164(b)(1):

Amended Code Sec. 1400B by striking "2003" each place it appears and inserting "2004". **Effective** 12-21-2000.

P.L. 105-206, §6008(c)(1):

Amended Code Sec. 1400B(b) by inserting after paragraph (4) a new paragraph (5). **Effective** as if included in the provision of P.L. 105-34 to which it relates [effective 8-5-97.—CCH].

P.L. 105-206, §6008(c)(2):

Amended Code Sec. 1400B(b)(6) by striking "(4)(A)(ii)" and inserting "(4)(A)(i) or (ii)". **Effective** as if included in the provision of P.L. 105-34 to which it relates [effective 8-5-97.—CCH].

[Sec. 1400B(c)]

(c) DC ZONE BUSINESS.—For purposes of this section, the term "DC Zone business" means any enterprise zone business (as defined in section 1397C), determined—

(1) after the application of section 1400(e),

(2) by substituting "80 percent" for "50 percent" in subsections (b)(2) and (c)(1) of section 1397C, and

(3) by treating no area other than the DC Zone as an empowerment zone or enterprise community.

Amendments

• **2000, Community Renewal Tax Relief Act of 2000 (P.L. 106-554)**

P.L. 106-554, §116(b)(5):

Amended Code Sec. 1400B(c) by striking "section 1397B" each place it appears and inserting "section 1397C". **Effective** for qualified empowerment zone assets acquired after 12-21-2000.

• **1998, IRS Restructuring and Reform Act of 1998 (P.L. 105-206)**

P.L. 105-206, §6008(c)(3):

Amended Code Sec. 1400B(c) by striking "entity which is an" before "enterprise zone business". **Effective** as if included in the provision of P.L. 105-34 to which it relates [effective 8-5-97.—CCH].

[Sec. 1400B(d)]

(d) TREATMENT OF ZONE AS INCLUDING CENSUS TRACTS WITH 10 PERCENT POVERTY RATE.—For purposes of applying this section (and for purposes of applying this subchapter and subchapter U with respect to this section), the DC Zone shall be treated as including all census tracts—

(1) which are located in the District of Columbia, and

(2) for which the poverty rate is not less than 10 percent as determined on the basis of the 1990 census.

Amendments

• **1998, IRS Restructuring and Reform Act of 1998 (P.L. 105-206)**

P.L. 105-206, §6008(c)(4):

Amended Code Sec. 1400B(d)(2) by inserting "as determined on the basis of the 1990 census" after "percent". **Effective** as if included in the provision of P.L. 105-34 to which it relates [effective 8-5-97.—CCH].

[Sec. 1400B(e)]

(e) OTHER DEFINITIONS AND SPECIAL RULES.—For purposes of this section—

(1) QUALIFIED CAPITAL GAIN.—Except as otherwise provided in this subsection, the term "qualified capital gain" means any gain recognized on the sale or exchange of—

(A) a capital asset, or

(B) property used in the trade or business (as defined in section 1231(b)).

(2) GAIN BEFORE 1998 OR AFTER 2016 NOT QUALIFIED.—The term "qualified capital gain" shall not include any gain attributable to periods before January 1, 1998, or after December 31, 2016.

(3) CERTAIN GAIN NOT QUALIFIED.—The term "qualified capital gain" shall not include any gain which would be treated as ordinary income under section 1245 or under section 1250 if section 1250 applied to all depreciation rather than the additional depreciation.

(4) INTANGIBLES AND LAND NOT INTEGRAL PART OF DC ZONE BUSINESS.—The term "qualified capital gain" shall not include any gain which is attributable to real property, or an intangible asset, which is not an integral part of a DC Zone business.

(5) RELATED PARTY TRANSACTIONS.—The term "qualified capital gain" shall not include any gain attributable, directly or indirectly, in whole or in part, to a transaction with a related person. For purposes of this paragraph, persons are related to each other if such persons are described in section 267(b) or 707(b)(1).

Amendments

• **2010, Tax Relief, Unemployment Insurance Reauthorization, and Job Creation Act of 2010 (P.L. 111-312)**

P.L. 111-312, §754(c)(2)(A)(i)-(ii):

Amended Code Sec. 1400B(e)(2) by striking "December 31, 2014" and inserting "December 31, 2016"; and by striking "2014" in the heading and inserting "2016". **Effective** for property acquired or substantially improved after 12-31-2009.

• **2008, Tax Extenders and Alternative Minimum Tax Relief Act of 2008 (P.L. 110-343)**

P.L. 110-343, Division C, §322(c)(2)(A)(i)-(ii):

Amended Code Sec. 1400B(e)(2) by striking "2012" and inserting "2014", and by striking "2012" in the heading thereof and inserting "2014". **Effective** 10-3-2008.

• **2006, Tax Relief and Health Care Act of 2006 (P.L. 109-432)**

P.L. 109-432, Division A, §110(c)(2)(A)(i)-(ii):

Amended Code Sec. 1400B(e)(2) by striking "2010" and inserting "2012", and by striking "2010" in the heading thereof and inserting "2012". **Effective** 12-20-2006.

• **2004, Working Families Tax Relief Act of 2004 (P.L. 108-311)**

P.L. 108-311, §310(c)(2)(A)(i)-(ii):

Amended Code Sec. 1400B(e)(2) by striking "December 31, 2008" and inserting "December 31, 2010", and by striking "2008" in the heading and inserting "2010". **Effective** on 1-1-2004.

• **2000, Community Renewal Tax Relief Act of 2000 (P.L. 106-554)**

P.L. 106-554, §164(b)(2):

Amended Code Sec. 1400B by striking "2007" each place it appears and inserting "2008". **Effective** 12-21-2000.

Sec. 1400B—Stricken

INCOME TAX—DC ENTERPRISE ZONE

[Sec. 1400B(f)]

(f) CERTAIN OTHER RULES TO APPLY.—Rules similar to the rules of subsections (g), (h), (i)(2), and (j) of section 1202 shall apply for purposes of this section.

[Sec. 1400B(g)]

(g) SALES AND EXCHANGES OF INTERESTS IN PARTNERSHIPS AND S CORPORATIONS WHICH ARE DC ZONE BUSINESSES.—In the case of the sale or exchange of an interest in a partnership, or of stock in an S corporation, which was a DC Zone business during substantially all of the period the taxpayer held such interest or stock, the amount of qualified capital gain shall be determined without regard to—

(1) any gain which is attributable to real property, or an intangible asset, which is not an integral part of a DC Zone business, and

(2) any gain attributable to periods before January 1, 1998, or after December 31, 2016.

Amendments

• **2010, Tax Relief, Unemployment Insurance Reauthorization, and Job Creation Act of 2010 (P.L. 111-312)**

P.L. 111-312, §754(c)(2)(B):

Amended Code Sec. 1400B(g)(2) by striking "December 31, 2014" and inserting "December 31, 2016". **Effective** for property acquired or substantially improved after 12-31-2009.

• **2008, Tax Extenders and Alternative Minimum Tax Relief Act of 2008 (P.L. 110-343)**

P.L. 110-343, Division C, §322(c)(2)(B):

Amended Code Sec. 1400B(g)(2) by striking "2012" and inserting "2014". **Effective** 10-3-2008.

• **2006, Tax Relief and Health Care Act of 2006 (P.L. 109-432)**

P.L. 109-432, Division A, §110(c)(2)(B):

Amended Code Sec. 1400B(g)(2) by striking "2010" and inserting "2012". **Effective** 12-20-2006.

• **2004, Working Families Tax Relief Act of 2004 (P.L. 108-311)**

P.L. 108-311, §310(c)(2)(B):

Amended Code Sec. 1400B(g)(2) by striking "December 31, 2008" and inserting "December 31, 2010". **Effective** on 1-1-2004.

• **2000, Community Renewal Tax Relief Act of 2000 (P.L. 106-554)**

P.L. 106-554, §164(b)(2):

Amended Code Sec. 1400B by striking "2007" each place it appears and inserting "2008". **Effective** 12-21-2000.

• **1997, Taxpayer Relief Act of 1997 (P.L. 105-34)**

P.L. 105-34, §701(a):

Added a new Code Sec. 1400B. **Effective** 8-5-97.

P.L. 115-141, §401(d)(4)(C)(ii), Div. U, provides:

(C) SAVINGS PROVISIONS.—The amendments made by this paragraph shall not apply to—

* * *

(ii) in the case of the repeal of section 1400B of such Code, DC Zone assets (as defined in such section, as in effect before its repeal) which were acquired by the taxpayer before January 1, 2012, and

P.L. 115-141, §401(e), Div. U, provides:

(e) GENERAL SAVINGS PROVISION WITH RESPECT TO DEADWOOD PROVISIONS.—If—

(1) any provision amended or repealed by the amendments made by subsection (b) or (d) applied to—

(A) any transaction occurring before the date of the enactment of this Act,

(B) any property acquired before such date of enactment, or

(C) any item of income, loss, deduction, or credit taken into account before such date of enactment, and

(2) the treatment of such transaction, property, or item under such provision would (without regard to the amendments or repeals made by such subsection) affect the liability for tax for periods ending after such date of enactment,

nothing in the amendments or repeals made by this section shall be construed to affect the treatment of such transaction, property, or item for purposes of determining liability for tax for periods ending after such date of enactment.

[Sec. 1400C—Stricken]

Amendments

• **2018, Tax Technical Corrections Act of 2018 (P.L. 115-141)**

P.L. 115-141, §401(d)(4)(A), Div. U:

Amended chapter 1 by striking subchapter W (Code Secs. 1400-1400C). **Effective** 3-23-2018. For special rules, see Act Sec. 401(d)(4)(C)(iii), Div. U, and Act Sec. 401(e), Div. U, below. Prior to being stricken, Code Sec. 1400C read as follows:

SEC. 1400C. FIRST-TIME HOMEBUYER CREDIT FOR DISTRICT OF COLUMBIA.

[Sec. 1400C(a)]

(a) ALLOWANCE OF CREDIT.—In the case of an individual who is a first-time homebuyer of a principal residence in the District of Columbia during any taxable year, there shall be allowed as a credit against the tax imposed by this chapter for the taxable year an amount equal to so much of the purchase price of the residence as does not exceed $5,000.

[Sec. 1400C(b)]

(b) LIMITATION BASED ON MODIFIED ADJUSTED GROSS INCOME.—

(1) IN GENERAL.—The amount allowable as a credit under subsection (a) (determined without regard to this subsection and subsection (d)) for the taxable year shall be reduced (but not below zero) by the amount which bears the same ratio to the credit so allowable as—

(A) the excess (if any) of—

(i) the taxpayer's modified adjusted gross income for such taxable year, over

(ii) $70,000 ($110,000 in the case of a joint return), bears to

(B) $20,000.

(2) MODIFIED ADJUSTED GROSS INCOME.—For purposes of paragraph (1), the term "modified adjusted gross income" means the adjusted gross income of the taxpayer for the taxable year increased by any amount excluded from gross income under section 911, 931, or 933.

Amendments

• **1998, IRS Restructuring and Reform Act of 1998 (P.L. 105-206)**

P.L. 105-206, §6008(d)(1):

Amended Code Sec. 1400C(b)(1) by inserting "and subsection (d)" after "this subsection". **Effective** as if included in the provision of P.L. 105-34 to which it relates [effective 8-5-97.—CCH].

[Sec. 1400C(c)]

(c) FIRST-TIME HOMEBUYER.—For purposes of this section—

(1) IN GENERAL.—The term "first-time homebuyer" means any individual if such individual (and if married, such individual's spouse) had no present ownership interest in a principal residence in the District of Columbia during the 1-year period ending on the date of the purchase of the principal residence to which this section applies.

(2) ONE-TIME ONLY.—If an individual is treated as a first-time homebuyer with respect to any principal residence, such individual may not be treated as a first-time homebuyer with respect to any other principal residence.

(3) PRINCIPAL RESIDENCE.—The term "principal residence" has the same meaning as when used in section 121.

Amendments

• **1998, IRS Restructuring and Reform Act of 1998 (P.L. 105-206)**

P.L. 105-206, §6008(d)(2):

Amended Code Sec. 1400C(c)(1). **Effective** as if included in the provision of P.L. 105-34 to which it relates [effective 8-5-97.—CCH]. Prior to amendment, Code Sec. 1400C(c)(1) read as follows:

(1) IN GENERAL.—The term "first-time homebuyer" has the same meaning as when used in section 72(t)(8)(D)(i), except that "principal residence in the District of Columbia during the 1-year period" shall be substituted for "principal residence during the 2-year period" in subclause (I) thereof.

[Sec. 1400C(d)]

(d) CARRYFORWARD OF UNUSED CREDIT.—If the credit allowable under subsection (a) exceeds the limitation imposed by section 26(a) for such taxable year reduced by the sum of the credits allowable under subpart A of part IV of subchapter A (other than this section and section 25D), such excess shall be carried to the succeeding taxable year and added to the credit allowable under subsection (a) for such succeeding year.

Amendments

• **2013, American Taxpayer Relief Act of 2012 (P.L. 112-240)**

P.L. 112-240, §101(a)(1) and (3), provides:

SEC. 101. PERMANENT EXTENSION AND MODIFICATION OF 2001 TAX RELIEF.

(a) PERMANENT EXTENSION.—

(1) IN GENERAL.—The Economic Growth and Tax Relief Reconciliation Act of 2001 is amended by striking title IX.

* * *

(3) EFFECTIVE DATE.—The amendments made by this subsection shall apply to taxable, plan, or limitation years beginning after December 31, 2012, and estates of decedents dying, gifts made, or generation skipping transfers after December 31, 2012.

P.L. 112-240, §104(c)(2)(L):

Amended Code Sec. 1400C(d). **Effective** for tax years beginning after 12-31-2011. Prior to amendment, Code Sec. 1400C(d) read as follows:

(d) CARRYFORWARD OF UNUSED CREDIT.—

(1) RULE FOR YEARS IN WHICH ALL PERSONAL CREDITS ALLOWED AGAINST REGULAR AND ALTERNATIVE MINIMUM TAX.—In the case of a taxable year to which section 26(a)(2) applies, if the credit allowable under subsection (a) exceeds the limitation imposed by section 26(a)(2) for such taxable year reduced by the sum of the credits allowable under subpart A of part IV of subchapter A (other than this section and section 25D), such excess shall be carried to the succeeding taxable year and added to the credit allowable under subsection (a) for such taxable year.

(2) RULE FOR OTHER YEARS.—In the case of a taxable year to which section 26(a)(2) does not apply, if the credit allowable under subsection (a) exceeds the limitation imposed by section 26(a)(1) for such taxable year reduced by the sum of the credits allowable under subpart A of part IV of subchapter A (other than this section and sections 23, 24, 25A(i), 25B, 25D, 30, and 30B, and 30D), such excess shall be carried to the succeeding taxable year and added to the credit allowable under subsection (a) for such taxable year.

INCOME TAX—DC ENTERPRISE ZONE

• **2010, Tax Relief, Unemployment Insurance Reauthorization, and Job Creation Act of 2010 (P.L. 111-312)**

P.L. 111-312, §101(b)(1):

Amended Code Sec. 1400C(d)[(2)] to read as such provision would read if section 10909 of the Patient Protection and Affordable Care Act (P.L. 111-148) had never been enacted. **Effective** for tax years beginning after 12-31-2011.

• **2010, Patient Protection and Affordable Care Act (P.L. 111-148)**

P.L. 111-148, §10909(b)(2)(M):

Amended Code Sec. 1400C(d)[(2)] by striking "23," before "24". **Effective** for tax years beginning after 12-31-2009.

P.L. 111-148, §10909(c), as amended by P.L. 111-312, §101(b)(1), provides:

(c) SUNSET PROVISION.—Each provision of law amended by this section is amended to read as such provision would read if this section had never been enacted. The amendments made by the preceding sentence shall apply to taxable years beginning after December 31, 2011.

• **2009, American Recovery and Reinvestment Tax Act of 2009 (P.L. 111-5)**

P.L. 111-5, §1004(b)(6):

Amended Code Sec. 1400C(d)(2) by inserting "25A(i)," after "24,". **Effective** for tax years beginning after 12-31-2008.

P.L. 111-5, §1142(b)(1)(F):

Amended Code Sec. 1400C(d)(2) by striking "and [sic] 25D" and inserting "25D, and 30". **Effective** for vehicles acquired after 2-17-2009. For a transitional rule, see Act Sec. 1142(d) in the amendment notes for Code Sec. 30.

P.L. 111-5, §1144(b)(1)(F):

Amended Code Sec. 1400C(d)(2), as amended by this Act, by striking "and 30" and inserting "30, and 30B". **Effective** for tax years beginning after 12-31-2008.

• **2008, Energy Improvement and Extension Act of 2008 (P.L. 110-343)**

P.L. 110-343, Division B, §205(d)(1)(E):

Amended Code Sec. 1400C(d)(2) by striking "and 25D" and inserting "25D, and 30D". **Effective** for tax years beginning after 12-31-2008.

• **2006, Pension Protection Act of 2006 (P.L. 109-280)**

P.L. 109-280, §811, provides:

SEC. 811. PENSIONS AND INDIVIDUAL RETIREMENT ARRANGEMENT PROVISIONS OF ECONOMIC GROWTH AND TAX RELIEF RECONCILIATION ACT OF 2001 MADE PERMANENT.

Title IX of the Economic Growth and Tax Relief Reconciliation Act of 2001 [P.L. 107-16] shall not apply to the provisions of, and amendments made by, subtitles A through F of title VI [§§601-666]of such Act (relating to pension and individual retirement arrangement provisions).

• **2005, Gulf Opportunity Zone Act of 2005 (P.L. 109-135)**

P.L. 109-135, §402(i)(3)(F):

Amended Code Sec. 1400C(d). **Effective** for tax years beginning after 12-31-2005. Prior to amendment, Code Sec. 1400C(d) read as follows:

(d) CARRYOVER OF CREDIT.—If the credit allowable under subsection (a) exceeds the limitation imposed by section 26(a) for such taxable year reduced by the sum of the credits allowable under subpart A of part IV of subchapter A (other than this section and sections 23, 24, and 25B), such excess shall be carried to the succeeding taxable year and added to the credit allowable under subsection (a) for such taxable year.

P.L. 109-135, §402(i)(3)(H), provides:

(H) APPLICATION OF EGTRRA SUNSET.—The amendments made by this paragraph (and each part thereof) shall be subject to title IX of the Economic Growth and Tax Relief Reconciliation Act of 2001 [P.L. 107-16] in the same manner as the provisions of such Act to which such amendment (or part thereof) relates.

P.L. 109-135, §402(i)(4):

Amended Act Sec. 1335(b) of P.L. 109-58 by striking paragraphs (1), (2) and (3) and provided that the Internal Revenue Code of 1986 shall be applied and administered as if the amendments made by such paragraphs had never been enacted. **Effective** as if included in the provision of the Energy Policy Act of 2005 (P.L. 109-58) to which it relates. P.L. 109-58, §1335(b)(3), amended Code Sec. 1400C(d) by striking "this section" and inserting "this section and section 25D". This amendment reinstates the language "this section" to Code Sec. 1400C(d).

• **2005, Energy Tax Incentives Act of 2005 (P.L. 109-58)**

P.L. 109-58, §1335(b)(3) [stricken by P.L. 109-135, §402(i)(4)]:

Amended Code Sec. 1400C(d) by striking "this section" and inserting "this section and section 25D". **Effective** for property placed in service after 12-31-2005, in tax years ending after such date. [Note, this amendment cannot be made to the version of Code Sec. 1400C(d) in effect on January 1, 2006.—CCH]

• **2004, Working Families Tax Relief Act of 2004 (P.L. 108-311)**

P.L. 108-311, §312(b)(2), provides:

(2) The amendments made by sections 201(b), 202(f), and 618(b) of the Economic Growth and Tax Relief Reconciliation Act of 2001 shall not apply to taxable years beginning during 2004 or 2005.

• **2002, Job Creation and Worker Assistance Act of 2002 (P.L. 107-147)**

P.L. 107-147, §601(b)(2), provides:

(2) The amendments made by sections 201(b), 202(f), and 618(b) of the Economic Growth and Tax Relief Reconciliation Act of 2001 shall not apply to taxable years beginning during 2002 and 2003.

• **2001, Economic Growth and Tax Relief Reconciliation Act of 2001 (P.L. 107-16)**

P.L. 107-16, §201(b)(2)(H):

Amended Code Sec. 1400C(d) by inserting "and section 24" after "this section". **Effective** for tax years beginning after 12-31-2001. [But, see P.L. 107-147, §601(b)(2), and P.L. 108-311, §312(b)(2), above.—CCH].

P.L. 107-16, §202(f)(2)(C):

Amended Code Sec. 1400C(d), as amended by Act Sec. 201(b)(2)(H), by striking "section 24" and inserting "sections 23 and 24". **Effective** for tax years beginning after 12-31-2001. [But, see P.L. 107-147, §601(b)(2), and P.L. 108-311, §312(b)(2), above.—CCH].

P.L. 107-16, §618(b)(2)(E) (as amended by P.L. 107-147, §417(23)(B)):

Amended Code Sec. 1400C(d), as amended by Act Secs. 201(b)(2)(H) and 202(f), by striking "and 24" and inserting ", 24, and 25B". **Effective** for tax years beginning after 12-31-2001. [But, see P.L. 107-147, §601(b)(2), and P.L. 108-311, §312(b)(2), above.—CCH].

P.L. 107-16, §901(a)-(b), as amended by P.L. 111-312, §101(a), provides [but see P.L. 109-280, §811, and P.L. 111-148, §10909(c), as amended by P.L. 111-312, §101(b)(1), and P.L. 112-240, §101(a)(1) and (3), above]:

SEC. 901. SUNSET OF PROVISIONS OF ACT.

(a) IN GENERAL.—All provisions of, and amendments made by, this Act shall not apply—

(1) to taxable, plan, or limitation years beginning after December 31, 2012, or

(2) in the case of title V, to estates of decedents dying, gifts made, or generation skipping transfers, after December 31, 2012.

(b) APPLICATION OF CERTAIN LAWS.—The Internal Revenue Code of 1986 and the Employee Retirement Income Security Act of 1974 shall be applied and administered to years, estates, gifts, and transfers described in subsection (a) as if the provisions and amendments described in subsection (a) had never been enacted.

[Sec. 1400C(e)]

(e) SPECIAL RULES.—For purposes of this section—

(1) ALLOCATION OF DOLLAR LIMITATION.—

(A) MARRIED INDIVIDUALS FILING SEPARATELY.—In the case of a married individual filing a separate return, subsection (a) shall be applied by substituting "$2,500" for "$5,000".

(B) OTHER TAXPAYERS.—If 2 or more individuals who are not married purchase a principal residence, the amount of the credit allowed under subsection (a) shall be allocated among such individuals in such manner as the Secretary may prescribe, except that the total amount of the credits allowed to all such individuals shall not exceed $5,000.

(2) PURCHASE.—

(A) IN GENERAL.—The term "purchase" means any acquisition, but only if—

(i) the property is not acquired from a person whose relationship to the person acquiring it would result in the disallowance of losses under section 267 or 707(b) (but, in applying section 267(b) and (c) for purposes of this section, paragraph (4) of section 267(c) shall be treated as providing that the family of an individual shall include only his spouse, ancestors, and lineal descendants), and

(ii) the basis of the property in the hands of the person acquiring it is not determined—

(I) in whole or in part by reference to the adjusted basis of such property in the hands of the person from whom acquired, or

(II) under section 1014(a) (relating to property acquired from a decedent).

(B) CONSTRUCTION.—A residence which is constructed by the taxpayer shall be treated as purchased by the taxpayer on the date the taxpayer first occupies such residence.

(3) PURCHASE PRICE.—The term "purchase price" means the adjusted basis of the principal residence on the date such residence is purchased.

(4) COORDINATION WITH NATIONAL FIRST-TIME HOMEBUYERS CREDIT.—No credit shall be allowed under this section to any taxpayer with respect to the purchase of a residence after December 31, 2008, if a credit under section 36 is allowable to such taxpayer (or the taxpayer's spouse) with respect to such purchase.

Amendments

• **2009, Worker, Homeownership, and Business Assistance Act of 2009 (P.L. 111-92)**

P.L. 111-92, §11(i):

Amended Code Sec. 1400C(e)(4) by striking "and before December 1, 2009," after "December 31, 2008,". **Effective** for residences purchased after 11-30-2009.

• **2009, American Recovery and Reinvestment Act of 2009 (P.L. 111-5)**

P.L. 111-5, §1006(d)(1):

Amended Code Sec. 1400C(e) by adding at the end new paragraph (4). **Effective** for residences purchased after 12-31-2008.

• **1998, IRS Restructuring and Reform Act of 1998 (P.L. 105-206)**

P.L. 105-206, §6008(d)(3):

Amended Code Sec. 1400C(e)(2)(B) by inserting before the period "on the date the taxpayer first occupies such residence". **Effective** as if included in the provision of P.L. 105-34 to which it relates [effective 8-5-97.—CCH].

P.L. 105-206, §6008(d)(4):

Amended Code Sec. 1400C(e)(3) by striking all that follows "principal residence" and inserting "on the date such residence is purchased." **Effective** as if included in

INCOME TAX—DC ENTERPRISE ZONE

the provision of P.L. 105-34 to which it relates [effective 8-5-97.—CCH]. Prior to amendment, Code Sec. 1400C(e)(3) read as follows:

(3) PURCHASE PRICE.—The term "purchase price" means the adjusted basis of the principal residence on the date of acquisition (within the meaning of section 72(t)(8)(D)(iii)).

[Sec. 1400C(f)]

(f) REPORTING.—If the Secretary requires information reporting under section 6045 by a person described in subsection (e)(2) thereof to verify the eligibility of taxpayers for the credit allowable by this section, the exception provided by section 6045(e)(5) shall not apply.

[Sec. 1400C(g)]

(g) CREDIT TREATED AS NONREFUNDABLE PERSONAL CREDIT.—For purposes of this title, the credit allowed by this section shall be treated as a credit allowable under subpart A of part IV of subchapter A of this chapter.

[Sec. 1400C(h)]

(h) BASIS ADJUSTMENT.—For purposes of this subtitle, if a credit is allowed under this section with respect to the purchase of any residence, the basis of such residence shall be reduced by the amount of the credit so allowed.

[Sec. 1400C(i)]

(i) APPLICATION OF SECTION.—This section shall apply to property purchased after August 4, 1997, and before January 1, 2012.

Amendments

- **2010, Tax Relief, Unemployment Insurance Reauthorization, and Job Creation Act of 2010 (P.L. 111-312)**

P.L. 111-312, §754(d):

Amended Code Sec. 1400C(i) by striking "January 1, 2010" and inserting "January 1, 2012". **Effective** for homes purchased after 12-31-2009.

- **2008, Tax Extenders and Alternative Minimum Tax Relief Act of 2008 (P.L. 110-343)**

P.L. 110-343, Division C, §322(d)(1):

Amended Code Sec. 1400C(i) by striking "2008" and inserting "2010". **Effective** for property purchased after 12-31-2007.

- **2006, Tax Relief and Health Care Act of 2006 (P.L. 109-432)**

P.L. 109-432, Division A, §110(d)(1):

Amended Code Sec. 1400C(i) by striking "2006" and inserting "2008". **Effective** for property purchased after 12-31-2005.

- **2004, Working Families Tax Relief Act of 2004 (P.L. 108-311)**

P.L. 108-311, §310(d):

Amended Code Sec. 1400C(i) by striking "January 1, 2004" and inserting "January 1, 2006". **Effective** on 1-1-2004.

- **2000, Community Renewal Tax Relief Act of 2000 (P.L. 106-554)**

P.L. 106-554, §163:

Amended Code Sec. 1400C(i) by striking "2002" and inserting "2004". **Effective** 12-21-2000.

- **1999, Tax Relief Extension Act of 1999 (P.L. 106-170)**

P.L. 106-170, §510:

Amended Code Sec. 1400C(i) by striking "2001" and inserting "2002". **Effective** 12-17-99.

- **1998, IRS Restructuring and Reform Act of 1998 (P.L. 105-206)**

P.L. 105-206, §6008(d)(5):

Amended Code Sec. 1400C(i). **Effective** as if included in the provision of P.L. 105-34 to which it relates [effective 8-5-97.—CCH]. Prior to amendment, Code Sec. 1400C(i) read as follows:

(i) TERMINATION.—This section shall not apply to any property purchased after December 31, 2000.

- **1997, Taxpayer Relief Act of 1997 (P.L. 105-34)**

P.L. 105-34, §701(a):

Added a new Code Sec. 1400C. **Effective** 8-5-97.

P.L. 115-141, §401(d)(4)(C)(iii), Div. U, provides:

(C) SAVINGS PROVISIONS.—The amendments made by this paragraph shall not apply to—

* * *

(iii) in the case of the repeal of section 1400C of such Code, principal residences acquired before January 1, 2012.

P.L. 115-141, §401(e), Div. U, provides:

(e) GENERAL SAVINGS PROVISION WITH RESPECT TO DEADWOOD PROVISIONS.—If—

(1) any provision amended or repealed by the amendments made by subsection (b) or (d) applied to—

(A) any transaction occurring before the date of the enactment of this Act,

(B) any property acquired before such date of enactment, or

(C) any item of income, loss, deduction, or credit taken into account before such date of enactment, and

(2) the treatment of such transaction, property, or item under such provision would (without regard to the amendments or repeals made by such subsection) affect the liability for tax for periods ending after such date of enactment,

nothing in the amendments or repeals made by this section shall be construed to affect the treatment of such transaction, property, or item for purposes of determining liability for tax for periods ending after such date of enactment.

Subchapter X—Renewal Communities—[Stricken]

PART I—DESIGNATION—[STRICKEN]

[Sec. 1400E—Stricken]

Amendments

- **2018, Tax Technical Corrections Act of 2018 (P.L. 115-141)**

P.L. 115-141, §401(d)(5)(A), Div. U:

Amended chapter 1 by striking subchapter X (Code Secs. 1400E-1400J). **Effective** 3-23-2018. For a special rule, see Act Sec. 401(e), Div. U, below. Prior to being stricken, Code Sec. 1400E read as follows:

SEC. 1400E. DESIGNATION OF RENEWAL COMMUNITIES.

[Sec. 1400E(a)]

(a) DESIGNATION.—

(1) DEFINITIONS.—For purposes of this title, the term "renewal community" means any area—

(A) which is nominated by 1 or more local governments and the State or States in which it is located for designation as a renewal community (hereafter in this section referred to as a "nominated area"), and

(B) which the Secretary of Housing and Urban Development designates as a renewal community, after consultation with—

(i) the Secretaries of Agriculture, Commerce, Labor, and the Treasury; the Director of the Office of Management and Budget, and the Administrator of the Small Business Administration, and

(ii) in the case of an area on an Indian reservation, the Secretary of the Interior.

(2) NUMBER OF DESIGNATIONS.—

(A) IN GENERAL.—Not more than 40 nominated areas may be designated as renewal communities.

(B) MINIMUM DESIGNATION IN RURAL AREAS.—Of the areas designated under paragraph (1), at least 12 must be areas—

(i) which are within a local government jurisdiction or jurisdictions with a population of less than 50,000,

(ii) which are outside of a metropolitan statistical area (within the meaning of section 143(k)(2)(B)), or

(iii) which are determined by the Secretary of Housing and Urban Development, after consultation with the Secretary of Commerce, to be rural areas.

(3) AREAS DESIGNATED BASED ON DEGREE OF POVERTY, ETC.—

(A) IN GENERAL.—Except as otherwise provided in this section, the nominated areas designated as renewal communities under this subsection shall be those nominated areas with the highest average ranking with respect to the criteria described in subparagraphs (B), (C), and (D) of subsection (c)(3). For purposes of the preceding sentence, an area shall be ranked within each such criterion on the basis of the amount by which the area exceeds such criterion, with the area which exceeds such criterion by the greatest amount given the highest ranking.

(B) EXCEPTION WHERE INADEQUATE COURSE OF ACTION, ETC.—An area shall not be designated under subparagraph (A) if the Secretary of Housing and Urban Development determines that the course of action described in subsection (d)(2) with respect to such area is inadequate.

(C) PREFERENCE FOR ENTERPRISE COMMUNITIES AND EMPOWERMENT ZONES.—With respect to the first 20 designations made under this section, a preference shall be provided to those nominated areas which are enterprise communities or empowerment zones (and are otherwise eligible for designation under this section).

(4) LIMITATION ON DESIGNATIONS.—

(A) PUBLICATION OF REGULATIONS.—The Secretary of Housing and Urban Development shall prescribe by regulation no later than 4 months after the date of the enactment of this section, after consultation with the officials described in paragraph (1)(B)—

(i) the procedures for nominating an area under paragraph (1)(A),

(ii) the parameters relating to the size and population characteristics of a renewal community, and

(iii) the manner in which nominated areas will be evaluated based on the criteria specified in subsection (d).

(B) TIME LIMITATIONS.—The Secretary of Housing and Urban Development may designate nominated areas as renewal communities only during the period beginning on the first day of the first month following the month in which the regulations described in subparagraph (A) are prescribed and ending on December 31, 2001.

(C) PROCEDURAL RULES.—The Secretary of Housing and Urban Development shall not make any designation of a nominated area as a renewal community under paragraph (2) unless—

INCOME TAX—DC ENTERPRISE ZONE

(i) the local governments and the States in which the nominated area is located have the authority—

(I) to nominate such area for designation as a renewal community,

(II) to make the State and local commitments described in subsection (d), and

(III) to provide assurances satisfactory to the Secretary of Housing and Urban Development that such commitments will be fulfilled,

(ii) a nomination regarding such area is submitted in such a manner and in such form, and contains such information, as the Secretary of Housing and Urban Development shall by regulation prescribe, and

(iii) the Secretary of Housing and Urban Development determines that any information furnished is reasonably accurate.

(5) NOMINATION PROCESS FOR INDIAN RESERVATIONS.—For purposes of this subchapter, in the case of a nominated area on an Indian reservation, the reservation governing body (as determined by the Secretary of the Interior) shall be treated as being both the State and local governments with respect to such area.

[Sec. 1400E(b)]

(b) PERIOD FOR WHICH DESIGNATION IS IN EFFECT.—

(1) IN GENERAL.—Any designation of an area as a renewal community shall remain in effect during the period beginning on January 1, 2002, and ending on the earliest of—

(A) December 31, 2009,

(B) the termination date designated by the State and local governments in their nomination, or

(C) the date the Secretary of Housing and Urban Development revokes such designation.

(2) REVOCATION OF DESIGNATION.—The Secretary of Housing and Urban Development may revoke the designation under this section of an area if such Secretary determines that the local government or the State in which the area is located—

(A) has modified the boundaries of the area, or

(B) is not complying substantially with, or fails to make progress in achieving, the State or local commitments, respectively, described in subsection (d).

(3) EARLIER TERMINATION OF CERTAIN BENEFITS IF EARLIER TERMINATION OF DESIGNATION.—If the designation of an area as a renewal community terminates before December 31, 2009, the day after the date of such termination shall be substituted for "January 1, 2010" each place it appears in sections 1400F and 1400J with respect to such area.

[Sec. 1400E(c)]

(c) AREA AND ELIGIBILITY REQUIREMENTS.—

(1) IN GENERAL.—The Secretary of Housing and Urban Development may designate a nominated area as a renewal community under subsection (a) only if the area meets the requirements of paragraphs (2) and (3) of this subsection.

(2) AREA REQUIREMENTS.—A nominated area meets the requirements of this paragraph if—

(A) the area is within the jurisdiction of one or more local governments,

(B) the boundary of the area is continuous, and

(C) the area—

(i) has a population of not more than 200,000 and at least—

(I) 4,000 if any portion of such area (other than a rural area described in subsection (a)(2)(B)(ii)) is located within a metropolitan statistical area (within the meaning of section 143(k)(2)(B)) which has a population of 50,000 or greater, or

(II) 1,000 in any other case, or

(ii) is entirely within an Indian reservation (as determined by the Secretary of the Interior).

(3) ELIGIBILITY REQUIREMENTS.—A nominated area meets the requirements of this paragraph if the State and the local governments in which it is located certify in writing (and the Secretary of Housing and Urban Development, after such review of supporting data as he deems appropriate, accepts such certification) that—

(A) the area is one of pervasive poverty, unemployment, and general distress,

(B) the unemployment rate in the area, as determined by the most recent available data, was at least $1^{1}/_{2}$ times the national unemployment rate for the period to which such data relate,

(C) the poverty rate for each population census tract within the nominated area is at least 20 percent, and

(D) in the case of an urban area, at least 70 percent of the households living in the area have incomes below 80 percent of the median income of households within the jurisdiction of the local government (determined in the same manner as under section 119(b)(2) of the Housing and Community Development Act of 1974).

(4) CONSIDERATION OF OTHER FACTORS.—The Secretary of Housing and Urban Development, in selecting any nominated area for designation as a renewal community under this section—

(A) shall take into account—

(i) the extent to which such area has a high incidence of crime, or

(ii) if such area has census tracts identified in the May 12, 1998, report of the Government Accountability Office regarding the identification of economically distressed areas, and

(B) with respect to 1 of the areas to be designated under subsection (a)(2)(B), may, in lieu of any criteria described in paragraph (3), take into account the existence of outmigration from the area.

Amendments

• **2005, Gulf Opportunity Zone Act of 2005 (P.L. 109-135)**

P.L. 109-135, §412(rr)(1):

Amended Code Sec. 1400E(c)(4)(A)(ii) by striking "General Accounting Office" each place it appears therein and inserting "Government Accountability Office". **Effective** 12-21-2005.

Sec. 1400E—Stricken

[Sec. 1400E(d)]

(d) REQUIRED STATE AND LOCAL COMMITMENTS.—

(1) IN GENERAL.—The Secretary of Housing and Urban Development may designate any nominated area as a renewal community under subsection (a) only if—

(A) the local government and the State in which the area is located agree in writing that, during any period during which the area is a renewal community, such governments will follow a specified course of action which meets the requirements of paragraph (2) and is designed to reduce the various burdens borne by employers or employees in such area, and

(B) the economic growth promotion requirements of paragraph (3) are met.

(2) COURSE OF ACTION.—

(A) IN GENERAL.—A course of action meets the requirements of this paragraph if such course of action is a written document, signed by a State (or local government) and neighborhood organizations, which evidences a partnership between such State or government and community-based organizations and which commits each signatory to specific and measurable goals, actions, and timetables. Such course of action shall include at least 4 of the following:

(i) A reduction of tax rates or fees applying within the renewal community.

(ii) An increase in the level of efficiency of local services within the renewal community.

(iii) Crime reduction strategies, such as crime prevention (including the provision of crime prevention services by nongovernmental entities).

(iv) Actions to reduce, remove, simplify, or streamline governmental requirements applying within the renewal community.

(v) Involvement in the program by private entities, organizations, neighborhood organizations, and community groups, particularly those in the renewal community, including a commitment from such private entities to provide jobs and job training for, and technical, financial, or other assistance to, employers, employees, and residents from the renewal community.

(vi) The gift (or sale at below fair market value) of surplus real property (such as land, homes, and commercial or industrial structures) in the renewal community to neighborhood organizations, community development corporations, or private companies.

(B) RECOGNITION OF PAST EFFORTS.—For purposes of this section, in evaluating the course of action agreed to by any State or local government, the Secretary of Housing and Urban Development shall take into account the past efforts of such State or local government in reducing the various burdens borne by employers and employees in the area involved.

(3) ECONOMIC GROWTH PROMOTION REQUIREMENTS.—The economic growth promotion requirements of this paragraph are met with respect to any nominated area if the local government and the State in which such area is located certify in writing that such government and State (respectively) have repealed or reduced, will not enforce, or will reduce within the nominated area at least 4 of the following:

(A) Licensing requirements for occupations that do not ordinarily require a professional degree.

(B) Zoning restrictions on home-based businesses which do not create a public nuisance.

(C) Permit requirements for street vendors who do not create a public nuisance.

(D) Zoning or other restrictions that impede the formation of schools or child care centers.

(E) Franchises or other restrictions on competition for businesses providing public services, including taxicabs, jitneys, cable television, or trash hauling.

This paragraph shall not apply to the extent that such regulation of businesses and occupations is necessary for and well-tailored to the protection of health and safety.

[Sec. 1400E(e)]

(e) COORDINATION WITH TREATMENT OF EMPOWERMENT ZONES AND ENTERPRISE COMMUNITIES.—For purposes of this title, the designation under section 1391 of any area as an empowerment zone or enterprise community shall cease to be in effect as of the date that the designation of any portion of such area as a renewal community takes effect.

[Sec. 1400E(f)]

(f) DEFINITIONS AND SPECIAL RULES.—For purposes of this subchapter—

(1) GOVERNMENTS.—If more than one government seeks to nominate an area as a renewal community, any reference to, or requirement of, this section shall apply to all such governments.

(2) LOCAL GOVERNMENT.—The term "local government" means—

(A) any county, city, town, township, parish, village, or other general purpose political subdivision of a State, and

(B) any combination of political subdivisions described in subparagraph (A) recognized by the Secretary of Housing and Urban Development.

(3) APPLICATION OF RULES RELATING TO CENSUS TRACTS.—The rules of section 1392(b)(4) shall apply.

(4) CENSUS DATA.—Population and poverty rate shall be determined by using 1990 census data.

Amendments

• **2000, Community Renewal Tax Relief Act of 2000 (P.L. 106-554)**

P.L. 106-554, §101(a):

Amended chapter 1 by adding at the end a new subchapter X (Code Secs. 1400E-1400J). **Effective** 12-21-2000. For a special rule, see Act Sec. 101(c), below.

P.L. 106-554, §101(c), provides:

(c) AUDIT AND REPORT.—Not later than January 31 of 2004, 2007, and 2010, the Comptroller General of the United States shall, pursuant to an audit of the renewal community program established under section 1400E of the Internal Revenue Code of 1986 (as added by subsection (a)) and the empowerment zone and enterprise

INCOME TAX—DC ENTERPRISE ZONE

community program under subchapter U of chapter 1 of such Code, report to Congress on such program and its effect on poverty, unemployment, and economic growth within the designated renewal communities, empowerment zones, and enterprise communities.

[Sec. 1400E(g)]

(g) EXPANSION OF DESIGNATED AREA BASED ON 2000 CENSUS.—

(1) IN GENERAL.—At the request of all governments which nominated an area as a renewal community, the Secretary of Housing and Urban Development may expand the area of such community to include any census tract if—

(A)(i) at the time such community was nominated, such community would have met the requirements of this section using 1990 census data even if such tract had been included in such community, and

(ii) such tract has a poverty rate using 2000 census data which exceeds the poverty rate for such tract using 1990 census data, or

(B)(i) such community would be described in subparagraph (A)(i) but for the failure to meet one or more of the requirements of paragraphs (2)(C)(i), (3)(C), and (3)(D) of subsection (c) using 1990 census data,

(ii) such community, including such tract, has a population of not more than 200,000 using either 1990 census data or 2000 census data,

(iii) such tract meets the requirement of subsection (c)(3)(C) using 2000 census data, and

(iv) such tract meets the requirement of subparagraph (A)(ii).

(2) EXCEPTION FOR CERTAIN CENSUS TRACTS WITH LOW POPULATION IN 1990.—In the case of any census tract which did not have a poverty rate determined by the Bureau of the Census using 1990 census data, paragraph (1)(B) shall be applied without regard to clause (iv) thereof.

(3) SPECIAL RULE FOR CERTAIN CENSUS TRACTS WITH LOW POPULATION IN 2000.—At the request of all governments which nominated an area as a renewal community, the Secretary of Housing and Urban Development may expand the area of such community to include any census tract if—

(A) either—

(i) such tract has no population using 2000 census data, or

(ii) no poverty rate for such tract is determined by the Bureau of the Census using 2000 census data,

(B) such tract is one of general distress, and

(C) such community, including such tract, meets the requirements of subparagraphs (A) and (B) of subsection (c)(2).

(4) PERIOD IN EFFECT.—Any expansion under this subsection shall take effect as provided in subsection (b).

Amendments

• **2004, American Jobs Creation Act of 2004 (P.L. 108-357)**

P.L. 108-357, § 222(a):

Amended Code Sec. 1400E by adding at the end a new subsection (g). **Effective** as if included in the amendments made by section 101 of the Community Renewal Tax Relief Act of 2000 [**effective** 12-21-2000.—CCH].

P.L. 115-141, §401(e), Div. U, provides:

(e) GENERAL SAVINGS PROVISION WITH RESPECT TO DEADWOOD PROVISIONS.—If—

(1) any provision amended or repealed by the amendments made by subsection (b) or (d) applied to—

(A) any transaction occurring before the date of the enactment of this Act,

(B) any property acquired before such date of enactment, or

(C) any item of income, loss, deduction, or credit taken into account before such date of enactment, and

(2) the treatment of such transaction, property, or item under such provision would (without regard to the amendments or repeals made by such subsection) affect the liability for tax for periods ending after such date of enactment,

nothing in the amendments or repeals made by this section shall be construed to affect the treatment of such transaction, property, or item for purposes of determining liability for tax for periods ending after such date of enactment.

PART II—RENEWAL COMMUNITY CAPITAL GAIN; RENEWAL COMMUNITY BUSINESS—[STRICKEN]

[Sec. 1400F—Stricken]

Amendments

• **2018, Tax Technical Corrections Act of 2018 (P.L. 115-141)**

P.L. 115-141, § 401(d)(5)(A), Div. U:

Amended chapter 1 by striking subchapter X (Code Secs. 1400E-1400J). **Effective** 3-23-2018. For special rules, see Act Sec. 401(d)(5)(C)(i), Div. U, and Act Sec. 401(e), Div. U, below. Prior to being stricken, Code Sec. 1400F read as follows:

SEC. 1400F. RENEWAL COMMUNITY CAPITAL GAIN.

[Sec. 1400F(a)]

(a) GENERAL RULE.—Gross income does not include any qualified capital gain from the sale or exchange of a qualified community asset held for more than 5 years.

[Sec. 1400F(b)]

(b) QUALIFIED COMMUNITY ASSET.—For purposes of this section—

(1) IN GENERAL.—The term "qualified community asset" means—

(A) any qualified community stock,

(B) any qualified community partnership interest, and

(C) any qualified community business property.

(2) QUALIFIED COMMUNITY STOCK.—

(A) IN GENERAL.—Except as provided in subparagraph (B), the term "qualified community stock" means any stock in a domestic corporation if—

(i) such stock is acquired by the taxpayer after December 31, 2001, and before January 1, 2010, at its original issue (directly or through an underwriter) from the corporation solely in exchange for cash,

(ii) as of the time such stock was issued, such corporation was a renewal community business (or, in the case of a new corporation, such corporation was being organized for purposes of being a renewal community business), and

(iii) during substantially all of the taxpayer's holding period for such stock, such corporation qualified as a renewal community business.

(B) REDEMPTIONS.—A rule similar to the rule of section 1202(c)(3) shall apply for purposes of this paragraph.

(3) QUALIFIED COMMUNITY PARTNERSHIP INTEREST.—The term "qualified community partnership interest" means any capital or profits interest in a domestic partnership if—

(A) such interest is acquired by the taxpayer after December 31, 2001, and before January 1, 2010, from the partnership solely in exchange for cash,

(B) as of the time such interest was acquired, such partnership was a renewal community business (or, in the case of a new partnership, such partnership was being organized for purposes of being a renewal community business), and

(C) during substantially all of the taxpayer's holding period for such interest, such partnership qualified as a renewal community business.

A rule similar to the rule of paragraph (2)(B) shall apply for purposes of this paragraph.

(4) QUALIFIED COMMUNITY BUSINESS PROPERTY.—

(A) IN GENERAL.—The term "qualified community business property" means tangible property if—

(i) such property was acquired by the taxpayer by purchase (as defined in section 179(d)(2)) after December 31, 2001, and before January 1, 2010,

(ii) the original use of such property in the renewal community commences with the taxpayer, and

(iii) during substantially all of the taxpayer's holding period for such property, substantially all of the use of such property was in a renewal community business of the taxpayer.

(B) SPECIAL RULE FOR SUBSTANTIAL IMPROVEMENTS.—The requirements of clauses (i) and (ii) of subparagraph (A) shall be treated as satisfied with respect to—

(i) property which is substantially improved by the taxpayer before January 1, 2010, and

(ii) any land on which such property is located.

The determination of whether a property is substantially improved shall be made under clause (ii) of section 1400B(b)(4)(B), except that "December 31, 2001" shall be substituted for "December 31, 1997" in such clause.

[Sec. 1400F(c)]

(c) QUALIFIED CAPITAL GAIN.—For purposes of this section—

(1) IN GENERAL.—Except as otherwise provided in this subsection, the term "qualified capital gain" means any gain recognized on the sale or exchange of—

(A) a capital asset, or

(B) property used in the trade or business (as defined in section 1231(b)).

(2) GAIN BEFORE 2002 OR AFTER 2014 NOT QUALIFIED.—The term "qualified capital gain" shall not include any gain attributable to periods before January 1, 2002, or after December 31, 2014.

(3) CERTAIN RULES TO APPLY.—Rules similar to the rules of paragraphs (3), (4), and (5) of section 1400B(e) shall apply for purposes of this subsection.

[Sec. 1400F(d)]

(d) CERTAIN RULES TO APPLY.—For purposes of this section, rules similar to the rules of paragraphs (5), (6), and (7) of subsection (b), and subsections (f) and (g), of section 1400B shall apply; except that for such purposes section 1400B(g)(2) shall be applied by substituting "January 1, 2002" for "January 1, 1998" and "December 31, 2014" for "December 31, 2014" [sic].

Amendments

• **2008, Tax Extenders and Alternative Minimum Tax Relief Act of 2008 (P.L. 110-343)**

P.L. 110-343, Division C, § 322(c)(2)(C):

Amended Code Sec. 1400F(d) by striking "2012" and inserting "2014". **Effective** 10-3-2008.

• **2006, Tax Relief and Health Care Act of 2006 (P.L. 109-432)**

P.L. 109-432, Division A, § 110(c)(2)(C):

Amended Code Sec. 1400F(d) by striking "2010" and inserting "2012". **Effective** 12-20-2006.

• **2004, Working Families Tax Relief Act of 2004 (P.L. 108-311)**

P.L. 108-311, § 310(c)(2)(C):

Amended Code Sec. 1400F(d) by striking "December 31, 2008" and inserting "December 31, 2010". **Effective** on 1-1-2004.

INCOME TAX—DC ENTERPRISE ZONE

[Sec. 1400F(e)]

(e) REGULATIONS.—The Secretary shall prescribe such regulations as may be appropriate to carry out the purposes of this section, including regulations to prevent the abuse of the purposes of this section.

Amendments

- **2000, Community Renewal Tax Relief Act of 2000 (P.L. 106-554)**

P.L. 106-554, § 101(a):

Amended chapter 1 by adding at the end a new subchapter X (Code Secs. 1400E-1400J). **Effective** 12-21-2000.

P.L. 115-141, § 401(d)(5)(C)(i), Div. U, provides:

(C) SAVINGS PROVISIONS.—The amendments made by this paragraph shall not apply to—

(i) in the case of the repeal of section 1400F of the Internal Revenue Code of 1986, qualified community assets (as defined in such section, as in effect before its repeal) which were acquired by the taxpayer before January 1, 2010,

P.L. 115-141, § 401(e), Div. U, provides:

(e) GENERAL SAVINGS PROVISION WITH RESPECT TO DEADWOOD PROVISIONS.—If—

(1) any provision amended or repealed by the amendments made by subsection (b) or (d) applied to—

(A) any transaction occurring before the date of the enactment of this Act,

(B) any property acquired before such date of enactment, or

(C) any item of income, loss, deduction, or credit taken into account before such date of enactment, and

(2) the treatment of such transaction, property, or item under such provision would (without regard to the amendments or repeals made by such subsection) affect the liability for tax for periods ending after such date of enactment,

nothing in the amendments or repeals made by this section shall be construed to affect the treatment of such transaction, property, or item for purposes of determining liability for tax for periods ending after such date of enactment.

[Sec. 1400G—Stricken]

Amendments

- **2018, Tax Technical Corrections Act of 2018 (P.L. 115-141)**

P.L. 115-141, § 401(d)(5)(A), Div. U:

Amended chapter 1 by striking subchapter X (Code Secs. 1400E-1400J). **Effective** 3-23-2018. For a special rule, see Act Sec. 401(e), Div. U, below. Prior to being stricken, Code Sec. 1400G read as follows:

SEC. 1400G. RENEWAL COMMUNITY BUSINESS DEFINED.

For purposes of this subchapter, the term "renewal community business" means any entity or proprietorship which would be a qualified business entity or qualified proprietorship under section 1397C if references to renewal communities were substituted for references to empowerment zones in such section.

Amendments

- **2000, Community Renewal Tax Relief Act of 2000 (P.L. 106-554)**

P.L. 106-554, § 101(a):

Amended chapter 1 by adding at the end a new subchapter X (Code Secs. 1400E-1400J). **Effective** 12-21-2000.

P.L. 115-141, § 401(e), Div. U, provides:

(e) GENERAL SAVINGS PROVISION WITH RESPECT TO DEADWOOD PROVISIONS.—If—

(1) any provision amended or repealed by the amendments made by subsection (b) or (d) applied to—

(A) any transaction occurring before the date of the enactment of this Act,

(B) any property acquired before such date of enactment, or

(C) any item of income, loss, deduction, or credit taken into account before such date of enactment, and

(2) the treatment of such transaction, property, or item under such provision would (without regard to the amendments or repeals made by such subsection) affect the liability for tax for periods ending after such date of enactment,

nothing in the amendments or repeals made by this section shall be construed to affect the treatment of such transaction, property, or item for purposes of determining liability for tax for periods ending after such date of enactment.

PART III—ADDITIONAL INCENTIVES—[STRICKEN]

[Sec. 1400H—Stricken]

Amendments

- **2018, Tax Technical Corrections Act of 2018 (P.L. 115-141)**

P.L. 115-141, § 401(d)(5)(A), Div. U:

Amended chapter 1 by striking subchapter X (Code Secs. 1400E-1400J). **Effective** 3-23-2018. For special rules, see Act Sec. 401(d)(5)(C)(ii), Div. U, and Act Sec. 401(e), Div. U, below. Prior to being stricken, Code Sec. 1400H read as follows:

SEC. 1400H. RENEWAL COMMUNITY EMPLOYMENT CREDIT.

[Sec. 1400H(a)]

(a) IN GENERAL.—Subject to the modification in subsection (b), a renewal community shall be treated as an empowerment zone for purposes of section 1396 with respect to wages paid or incurred after December 31, 2001.

[Sec. 1400H(b)]

(b) MODIFICATION.—In applying section 1396 with respect to renewal communities—

(1) the applicable percentage shall be 15 percent, and

(2) subsection (c) thereof shall be applied by substituting "$10,000" for "$15,000" each place it appears.

Amendments

- **2000, Community Renewal Tax Relief Act of 2000 (P.L. 106-554)**

P.L. 106-554, § 101(a):

Amended chapter 1 by adding at the end a new subchapter X (Code Secs. 1400E-1400J). **Effective** 12-21-2000.

P.L. 115-141, § 401(d)(5)(C)(ii), Div. U, provides:

(C) SAVINGS PROVISIONS.—The amendments made by this paragraph shall not apply to—

* * *

(ii) in the case of the repeal [of] section 1400H of such Code, wages paid or incurred before January 1, 2010,

P.L. 115-141, § 401(e), Div. U, provides:

(e) GENERAL SAVINGS PROVISION WITH RESPECT TO DEADWOOD PROVISIONS.—If—

(1) any provision amended or repealed by the amendments made by subsection (b) or (d) applied to—

(A) any transaction occurring before the date of the enactment of this Act,

(B) any property acquired before such date of enactment, or

(C) any item of income, loss, deduction, or credit taken into account before such date of enactment, and

(2) the treatment of such transaction, property, or item under such provision would (without regard to the amendments or repeals made by such subsection) affect the liability for tax for periods ending after such date of enactment,

nothing in the amendments or repeals made by this section shall be construed to affect the treatment of such transaction, property, or item for purposes of determining liability for tax for periods ending after such date of enactment.

[Sec. 1400I—Stricken]

Amendments

- **2018, Tax Technical Corrections Act of 2018 (P.L. 115-141)**

P.L. 115-141, § 401(d)(5)(A), Div. U:

Amended chapter 1 by striking subchapter X (Code Secs. 1400E-1400J). **Effective** 3-23-2018. For special rules, see Act Sec. 401(d)(5)(C)(iii), Div. U, and Act Sec. 401(e), Div. U, below. Prior to being stricken, Code Sec. 1400I read as follows:

SEC. 1400I. COMMERCIAL REVITALIZATION DEDUCTION.

[Sec. 1400I(a)]

(a) GENERAL RULE.—At the election of the taxpayer, either—

(1) one-half of any qualified revitalization expenditures chargeable to capital account with respect to any qualified revitalization building shall be allowable as a deduction for the taxable year in which the building is placed in service, or

(2) a deduction for all such expenditures shall be allowable ratably over the 120-month period beginning with the month in which the building is placed in service.

[Sec. 1400I(b)]

(b) QUALIFIED REVITALIZATION BUILDINGS AND EXPENDITURES.—For purposes of this section—

(1) QUALIFIED REVITALIZATION BUILDING.—The term "qualified revitalization building" means any building (and its structural components) if—

(A) the building is placed in service by the taxpayer in a renewal community and the original use of the building begins with the taxpayer, or

(B) in the case of such building not described in subparagraph (A), such building—

(i) is substantially rehabilitated (within the meaning of section 47(c)(1)(C)) by the taxpayer, and

(ii) is placed in service by the taxpayer after the rehabilitation in a renewal community.

(2) QUALIFIED REVITALIZATION EXPENDITURE.—

(A) IN GENERAL.—The term "qualified revitalization expenditure" means any amount properly chargeable to capital account for property for which depreciation is allowable under section 168 (without regard to this section) and which is—

(i) nonresidential real property (as defined in section 168(e)), or

(ii) section 1250 property (as defined in section 1250(c)) which is functionally related and subordinate to property described in clause (i).

(B) CERTAIN EXPENDITURES NOT INCLUDED.—

(i) ACQUISITION COST.—In the case of a building described in paragraph (1)(B), the cost of acquiring the building or interest therein shall be treated as a qualified revitalization expenditure only to the extent that such cost does not exceed 30 percent of the aggregate qualified revitalization expenditures (determined without regard to such cost) with respect to such building.

(ii) CREDITS.—The term "qualified revitalization expenditure" does not include any expenditure which the taxpayer may take into account in computing any credit allowable under this title unless the taxpayer elects to take the expenditure into account only for purposes of this section.

[Sec. 1400I(c)]

(c) DOLLAR LIMITATION.—The aggregate amount which may be treated as qualified revitalization expenditures with respect to any qualified revitalization building shall not exceed the lesser of—

(1) $10,000,000, or

(2) the commercial revitalization expenditure amount allocated to such building under this section by the commercial revitalization agency for the State in which the building is located.

[Sec. 1400I(d)]

(d) COMMERCIAL REVITALIZATION EXPENDITURE AMOUNT.—

(1) IN GENERAL.—The aggregate commercial revitalization expenditure amount which a commercial revitalization agency may allocate for any calendar year is the amount of the State commercial revitalization expenditure ceiling determined under this paragraph for such calendar year for such agency.

(2) STATE COMMERCIAL REVITALIZATION EXPENDITURE CEILING.—The State commercial revitalization expenditure ceiling applicable to any State—

(A) for each calendar year after 2001 and before 2010 is $12,000,000 for each renewal community in the State, and

(B) for each calendar year thereafter is zero.

(3) COMMERCIAL REVITALIZATION AGENCY.—For purposes of this section, the term "commercial revitalization agency" means any agency authorized by a State to carry out this section.

(4) TIME AND MANNER OF ALLOCATIONS.—Allocations under this section shall be made at the same time and in the same manner as under paragraphs (1) and (7) of section 42(h).

[Sec. 1400I(e)]

(e) RESPONSIBILITIES OF COMMERCIAL REVITALIZATION AGENCIES.—

(1) PLANS FOR ALLOCATION.—Notwithstanding any other provision of this section, the commercial revitalization expenditure amount with respect to any building shall be zero unless—

(A) such amount was allocated pursuant to a qualified allocation plan of the commercial revitalization agency which is approved (in accordance with rules similar to the rules of section 147(f)(2) (other than subparagraph (B)(ii) thereof)) by the governmental unit of which such agency is a part, and

(B) such agency notifies the chief executive officer (or its equivalent) of the local jurisdiction within which the building is located of such allocation and provides such individual a reasonable opportunity to comment on the allocation.

(2) QUALIFIED ALLOCATION PLAN.—For purposes of this subsection, the term "qualified allocation plan" means any plan—

(A) which sets forth selection criteria to be used to determine priorities of the commercial revitalization agency which are appropriate to local conditions,

(B) which considers—

(i) the degree to which a project contributes to the implementation of a strategic plan that is devised for a renewal community through a citizen participation process,

(ii) the amount of any increase in permanent, full-time employment by reason of any project, and

(iii) the active involvement of residents and nonprofit groups within the renewal community, and

(C) which provides a procedure that the agency (or its agent) will follow in monitoring compliance with this section.

[Sec. 1400I(f)]

(f) SPECIAL RULES.—

(1) DEDUCTION IN LIEU OF DEPRECIATION.—The deduction provided by this section for qualified revitalization expenditures shall—

(A) with respect to the deduction determined under subsection (a)(1), be in lieu of any depreciation deduction otherwise allowable on account of one-half of such expenditures, and

(B) with respect to the deduction determined under subsection (a)(2), be in lieu of any depreciation deduction otherwise allowable on account of all of such expenditures.

(2) BASIS ADJUSTMENT, ETC.—For purposes of sections 1016 and 1250, the deduction under this section shall be treated in the same manner as a depreciation deduction. For purposes of section 1250(b)(5), the straight line method of adjustment shall be determined without regard to this section.

(3) SUBSTANTIAL REHABILITATIONS TREATED AS SEPARATE BUILDINGS.—A substantial rehabilitation (within the meaning of section 47(c)(1)(C)) of a building shall be treated as a separate building for purposes of subsection (a).

(4) CLARIFICATION OF ALLOWANCE OF DEDUCTION UNDER MINIMUM TAX.—Notwithstanding section 56(a)(1), the deduction under this section shall be allowed in determining alternative minimum taxable income under section 55.

[Sec. 1400I(g)]

(g) TERMINATION.—This section shall not apply to any building placed in service after December 31, 2009.

Amendments

• **2000, Community Renewal Tax Relief Act of 2000 (P.L. 106-554)**

P.L. 106-554, §101(a):

Amended chapter 1 by adding at the end a new subchapter X (Code Secs. 1400E-1400J). **Effective** 12-21-2000.

P.L. 115-141, §401(d)(5)(C)(iii), Div. U, provides:

(C) SAVINGS PROVISIONS.—The amendments made by this paragraph shall not apply to—

* * *

(iii) in the case of the repeal of section 1400I of such Code, qualified revitalization buildings (as defined in such section, as in effect before its repeal) which were placed in service before January 1, 2010, and

P.L. 115-141, §401(e), Div. U, provides:

(e) GENERAL SAVINGS PROVISION WITH RESPECT TO DEADWOOD PROVISIONS.—If—

(1) any provision amended or repealed by the amendments made by subsection (b) or (d) applied to—

(A) any transaction occurring before the date of the enactment of this Act,

(B) any property acquired before such date of enactment, or

(C) any item of income, loss, deduction, or credit taken into account before such date of enactment, and

(2) the treatment of such transaction, property, or item under such provision would (without regard to the amendments or repeals made by such subsection) affect the liability for tax for periods ending after such date of enactment,

nothing in the amendments or repeals made by this section shall be construed to affect the treatment of such transaction, property, or item for purposes of determining liability for tax for periods ending after such date of enactment.

[Sec. 1400J—Stricken]

Amendments

• **2018, Tax Technical Corrections Act of 2018 (P.L. 115-141)**

P.L. 115-141, §401(d)(5)(A), Div. U:

Amended chapter 1 by striking subchapter X (Code Secs. 1400E-1400J). **Effective** 3-23-2018. For special rules, see Act Sec. 401(d)(5)(C)(iv), Div. U, and Act Sec. 401(e), Div. U, below. Prior to being stricken, Code Sec. 1400J read as follows:

SEC. 1400J. INCREASE IN EXPENSING UNDER SECTION 179.

[Sec. 1400J(a)]

(a) IN GENERAL.—For purposes of section 1397A—

(1) a renewal community shall be treated as an empowerment zone,

(2) a renewal community business shall be treated as an enterprise zone business, and

(3) qualified renewal property shall be treated as qualified zone property.

[Sec. 1400J(b)]

(b) QUALIFIED RENEWAL PROPERTY.—For purposes of this section—

(1) IN GENERAL.—The term "qualified renewal property" means any property to which section 168 applies (or would apply but for section 179) if—

(A) such property was acquired by the taxpayer by purchase (as defined in section 179(d)(2)) after December 31, 2001, and before January 1, 2010, and

(B) such property would be qualified zone property (as defined in section 1397D) if references to renewal communities were substituted for references to empowerment zones in section 1397D.

(2) CERTAIN RULES TO APPLY.—The rules of subsections (a)(2) and (b) of section 1397D shall apply for purposes of this section.

Amendments

• **2000, Community Renewal Tax Relief Act of 2000 (P.L. 106-554)**

P.L. 106-554, §101(a):

Amended chapter 1 by adding at the end a new subchapter X (Code Secs. 1400E-1400J). **Effective** 12-21-2000.

P.L. 115-141, §401(d)(5)(C)(iv), Div. U, provides:

(C) SAVINGS PROVISIONS.—The amendments made by this paragraph shall not apply to—

* * *

(iv) in the case of the repeal of section 1400J of such Code, property acquired before January 1, 2010.

P.L. 115-141, §401(e), Div. U, provides:

(e) GENERAL SAVINGS PROVISION WITH RESPECT TO DEADWOOD PROVISIONS.—If—

(1) any provision amended or repealed by the amendments made by subsection (b) or (d) applied to—

(A) any transaction occurring before the date of the enactment of this Act,

(B) any property acquired before such date of enactment, or

(C) any item of income, loss, deduction, or credit taken into account before such date of enactment, and

(2) the treatment of such transaction, property, or item under such provision would (without regard to the amendments or repeals made by such subsection) affect the liability for tax for periods ending after such date of enactment,

nothing in the amendments or repeals made by this section shall be construed to affect the treatment of such transaction, property, or item for purposes of determining liability for tax for periods ending after such date of enactment.

Subchapter Y—Short-Term Regional Benefits—[Stricken]

PART I—TAX BENEFITS FOR NEW YORK LIBERTY ZONE—[STRICKEN]

[Sec. 1400L—Stricken]

Amendments

• **2018, Tax Technical Corrections Act of 2018 (P.L. 115-141)**

P.L. 115-141, §401(d)(6)(A), Div. U:

Amended chapter 1 by striking subchapter Y (Code Secs. 1400L-1400U-3). **Effective** 3-23-2018. For special rules, see Act Sec. 401(d)(6)(C)(i)-(vi), Div. U, and Act Sec. 401(e), Div. U, below. Prior to being stricken, Code Sec. 1400L read as follows:

SEC. 1400L. TAX BENEFITS FOR NEW YORK LIBERTY ZONE.

[Sec. 1400L(a)]

(a) EXPANSION OF WORK OPPORTUNITY TAX CREDIT.—

(1) IN GENERAL.—For purposes of section 51, a New York Liberty Zone business employee shall be treated as a member of a targeted group.

(2) NEW YORK LIBERTY ZONE BUSINESS EMPLOYEE.—For purposes of this subsection—

(A) IN GENERAL.—The term "New York Liberty Zone business employee" means, with respect to any period, any employee of a New York Liberty Zone business if substantially all the services performed during such period by such employee for such business are performed in the New York Liberty Zone.

(B) INCLUSION OF CERTAIN EMPLOYEES OUTSIDE THE NEW YORK LIBERTY ZONE.—

(i) IN GENERAL.—In the case of a New York Liberty Zone business described in subclause (II) of subparagraph (C)(i), the term "New York Liberty Zone business employee" includes any employee of such business (not described in subparagraph (A)) if substantially all the services performed during such period by such employee for such business are performed in the City of New York, New York.

(ii) LIMITATION.—The number of employees of such a business that are treated as New York Liberty Zone business employees on any day by reason of clause (i) shall not exceed the excess of—

(I) the number of employees of such business on September 11, 2001, in the New York Liberty Zone, over

(II) the number of New York Liberty Zone business employees (determined without regard to this subparagraph) of such business on the day to which the limitation is being applied.

The Secretary may require any trade or business to have the number determined under subclause (I) verified by the New York State Department of Labor.

(C) NEW YORK LIBERTY ZONE BUSINESS.—

(i) IN GENERAL.—The term "New York Liberty Zone business" means any trade or business which is—

(I) located in the New York Liberty Zone, or

(II) located in the City of New York, New York, outside the New York Liberty Zone, as a result of the physical destruction or damage of such place of business by the September 11, 2001, terrorist attack.

(ii) CREDIT NOT ALLOWED FOR LARGE BUSINESSES.—The term "New York Liberty Zone business" shall not include any trade or business for any taxable year if such trade or business employed an average of more than 200 employees on business days during the taxable year.

(D) SPECIAL RULES FOR DETERMINING AMOUNT OF CREDIT.—For purposes of applying subpart F of part IV of subchapter A of this chapter to wages paid or incurred to any New York Liberty Zone business employee—

(i) section 51(a) shall be applied by substituting "qualified wages" for "qualified first-year wages",

(ii) the rules of section 52 shall apply for purposes of determining the number of employees under this paragraph,

(iii) subsections (c)(4) and (i)(2) of section 51shall not apply, and

(iv) in determining qualified wages, the following shall apply in lieu of section 51(b):

(I) QUALIFIED WAGES.—The term "qualified wages" means wages paid or incurred by the employer to individuals who are New York Liberty Zone business employees of such employer for work performed during calendar year 2002 or 2003.

(II) ONLY FIRST $6,000 OF WAGES PER CALENDAR YEAR TAKEN INTO ACCOUNT.—The amount of the qualified wages which may be taken into account with respect to any individual shall not exceed $6,000 per calendar year.

Amendments

• **2004, Working Families Tax Relief Act of 2004 (P.L. 108-311)**

P.L. 108-311, §403(c)(1)(A)-(B):

Amended Code Sec. 1400L(a)(2)(D) by striking "subchapter B" and inserting "subchapter A", and by striking "subparagraph (B)" and inserting "this paragraph" in clause (ii). **Effective** as if included in the provision of the Job Creation and Worker Assistance Act of 2002 (P.L. 107-147) to which it relates [**effective** 3-9-2002.—CCH].

[Sec. 1400L(b)]

(b) SPECIAL ALLOWANCE FOR CERTAIN PROPERTY ACQUIRED AFTER SEPTEMBER 10, 2001.—

(1) ADDITIONAL ALLOWANCE.—In the case of any qualified New York Liberty Zone property—

(A) the depreciation deduction provided by section 167(a) for the taxable year in which such property is placed in service shall include an allowance equal to 30 percent of the adjusted basis of such property, and

(B) the adjusted basis of the qualified New York Liberty Zone property shall be reduced by the amount of such deduction before computing the amount otherwise allowable as a depreciation deduction under this chapter for such taxable year and any subsequent taxable year.

(2) QUALIFIED NEW YORK LIBERTY ZONE PROPERTY.—For purposes of this subsection—

(A) IN GENERAL.—The term "qualified New York Liberty Zone property" means property—

(i)(I) which is described in section 168(k)(2)(A)(i), or

(II) which is nonresidential real property, or residential rental property, which is described in subparagraph (B),

(ii) substantially all of the use of which is in the New York Liberty Zone and is in the active conduct of a trade or business by the taxpayer in such Zone,

(iii) the original use of which in the New York Liberty Zone commences with the taxpayer after September 10, 2001,

(iv) which is acquired by the taxpayer by purchase (as defined in section 179(d)) after September 10, 2001, but only if no written binding contract for the acquisition was in effect before September 11, 2001, and

(v) which is placed in service by the taxpayer on or before the termination date.

The term "termination date" means December 31, 2006 (December 31, 2009, in the case of nonresidential real property and residential rental property).

(B) ELIGIBLE REAL PROPERTY.—Nonresidential real property or residential rental property is described in this subparagraph only to the extent it rehabilitates real property damaged, or replaces real property destroyed or condemned, as a result of the September 11, 2001, terrorist attack. For purposes of the preceding sentence, property shall be treated as replacing real property destroyed or condemned if, as part of an integrated plan, such property replaces real property which is included in a continuous area which includes real property destroyed or condemned.

(C) EXCEPTIONS.—

(i) BONUS DEPRECIATION PROPERTY UNDER SECTION 168(k).—Such term shall not include property to which section 168(k) applies.

(ii) ALTERNATIVE DEPRECIATION PROPERTY.—The term "qualified New York Liberty Zone property" shall not include any property described in section 168(k)(2)(D)(i).

(iii) QUALIFIED NEW YORK LIBERTY ZONE LEASEHOLD IMPROVEMENT PROPERTY.—Such term shall not include any qualified New York Liberty Zone leasehold improvement property.

(iv) ELECTION OUT.—For purposes of this subsection, rules similar to the rules of section 168(k)(2)(D)(iii) shall apply.

(D) SPECIAL RULES.—For purposes of this subsection, rules similar to the rules of section 168(k)(2)(E) shall apply, except that clause (i) thereof shall be applied without regard to "and before January 1, 2015", and clause (iv) thereof shall be applied by substituting "qualified New York Liberty Zone property" for "qualified property".

(E) ALLOWANCE AGAINST ALTERNATIVE MINIMUM TAX.—For purposes of this subsection, rules similar to the rules of section 168(k)(2)(G) shall apply.

Amendments

• **2014, Tax Increase Prevention Act of 2014 (P.L. 113-295)**

P.L. 113-295, §125(d)(4), Division A:

Amended Code Sec. 1400L(b)(2)(D) by striking "January 1, 2014" and inserting "January 1, 2015". **Effective** for property placed in service after 12-31-2013, in tax years ending after such date.

• **2013, American Taxpayer Relief Act of 2012 (P.L. 112-240)**

P.L. 112-240, §331(e)(4):

Amended Code Sec. 1400L(b)(2)(D) by striking "January 1, 2013" and inserting "January 1, 2014". **Effective** for property placed in service after 12-31-2012, in tax years ending after such date.

• **2010, Tax Relief, Unemployment Insurance Reauthorization, and Job Creation Act of 2010 (P.L. 111-312)**

P.L. 111-312, §401(d)(6):

Amended Code Sec. 1400L(b)(2)(D) by striking "January 1, 2011" and inserting "January 1, 2013". **Effective** for property placed in service after 12-31-2010, in tax years ending after such date.

• **2010, Creating Small Business Jobs Act of 2010 (P.L. 111-240)**

P.L. 111-240, §2022(b)(6):

Amended Code Sec. 1400L(b)(2)(D) by striking "January 1, 2010" and inserting "January 1, 2011". **Effective** for property placed in service after 12-31-2009, in tax years ending after such date.

• **2008, Economic Stimulus Act of 2008 (P.L. 110-185)**

P.L. 110-185, §103(c)(8):

Amended Code Sec. 1400L(b)(2)(D) by striking "January 1, 2005" and inserting "January 1, 2010 [2009]". **Effective** for property placed in service after 12-31-2007, in tax years ending after such date.

• **2005, Gulf Opportunity Zone Act of 2005 (P.L. 109-135)**

P.L. 109-135, §405(a)(2):

Amended Code Sec. 1400L(b)(2)(D) by striking "September 11, 2004" and inserting "January 1, 2005". **Effective** as if included in section 201 of the Jobs and Growth Tax Relief Reconciliation Act of 2003 (P.L. 108-27) [**effective** for tax years ending after 5-3-2003.—CCH].

P.L. 109-135, §412(ss)(1):

Amended Code Sec. 1400L(b)(2)(C)(ii) by striking "section 168(k)(2)(C)(i)" and inserting "section 168(k)(2)(D)(i)". **Effective** 12-21-2005.

P.L. 109-135, §412(ss)(2):

Amended Code Sec. 1400L(b)(2)(C)(iv) by striking "section 168(k)(2)(C)(iii)" and inserting "section 168(k)(2)(D)(iii)". **Effective** 12-21-2005.

P.L. 109-135, §412(ss)(3):

Amended Code Sec. 1400L(b)(2)(D) by striking "section 168(k)(2)(D)" and inserting "section 168(k)(2)(E)". **Effective** 12-21-2005.

P.L. 109-135, §412(ss)(4):

Amended Code Sec. 1400L(b)(2)(E) by striking "section 168(k)(2)(F)" and inserting "section 168(k)(2)(G)". **Effective** 12-21-2005.

• **2004, Working Families Tax Relief Act of 2004 (P.L. 108-311)**

P.L. 108-311, §403(c)(2):

Amended Code Sec. 1400L(b)(2)(D) by inserting ", and clause (iv) thereof shall be applied by substituting 'qualified New York Liberty Zone property' for 'qualified property'" before the period at the end. **Effective** as if included in the provision of the Job Creation and Worker Assistance Act of 2002 (P.L. 107-147) to which it relates [effective 3-9-2002.—CCH].

• **2003, Jobs and Growth Tax Relief Reconciliation Act of 2003 (P.L. 108-27)**

P.L. 108-27, §201(c)(2):

Amended the heading for Code Sec. 1400L(b)(2)(C)(i) by striking "30-PERCENT ADDITIONAL ALLOWANCE PROPERTY" and inserting "BONUS DEPRECIATION PROPERTY UNDER SECTION 168(k)". **Effective** for tax years ending after 5-5-2003.

[Sec. 1400L(c)]

(c) 5-YEAR RECOVERY PERIOD FOR DEPRECIATION OF CERTAIN LEASEHOLD IMPROVEMENTS.—

(1) IN GENERAL.—For purposes of section 168, the term "5-year property" includes any qualified New York Liberty Zone leasehold improvement property.

(2) QUALIFIED NEW YORK LIBERTY ZONE LEASEHOLD IMPROVEMENT PROPERTY.—For purposes of this section, the term "qualified New York Liberty Zone leasehold improvement property" means qualified leasehold improvement property (as defined in section 168(k)(3)) if—

(A) such building is located in the New York Liberty Zone,

(B) such improvement is placed in service after September 10, 2001, and before January 1, 2007, and

(C) no written binding contract for such improvement was in effect before September 11, 2001.

(3) REQUIREMENT TO USE STRAIGHT LINE METHOD.—The applicable depreciation method under section 168 shall be the straight line method in the case of qualified New York Liberty Zone leasehold improvement property.

(4) 9-YEAR RECOVERY PERIOD UNDER ALTERNATIVE SYSTEM.—For purposes of section 168(g), the class life of qualified New York Liberty Zone leasehold improvement property shall be 9 years.

(5) ELECTION OUT.—For purposes of this subsection, rules similar to the rules of section 168(k)(2)(D)(iii) shall apply.

Amendments

• **2005, Gulf Opportunity Zone Act of 2005 (P.L. 109-135)**

P.L. 109-135, §412(ss)(5):

Amended Code Sec. 1400L(c)(5) by striking "section 168(k)(2)(C)(iii)" and inserting "section 168(k)(2)(D)(iii)". **Effective** 12-21-2005.

• **2004, Working Families Tax Relief Act of 2004 (P.L. 108-311)**

P.L. 108-311, §403(c)(3):

Amended Code Sec. 1400L(c) by adding at the end a new paragraph (5). **Effective** as if included in the provision of the Job Creation and Worker Assistance Act of 2002 (P.L. 107-147) to which it relates [effective 3-9-2002.—CCH].

[Sec. 1400L(d)]

(d) TAX-EXEMPT BOND FINANCING.—

(1) IN GENERAL.—For purposes of this title, any qualified New York Liberty Bond shall be treated as an exempt facility bond.

(2) QUALIFIED NEW YORK LIBERTY BOND.—For purposes of this subsection, the term "qualified New York Liberty Bond" means any bond issued as part of an issue if—

(A) 95 percent or more of the net proceeds (as defined in section 150(a)(3)) of such issue are to be used for qualified project costs,

(B) such bond is issued by the State of New York or any political subdivision thereof,

(C) the Governor or the Mayor designates such bond for purposes of this section, and

(D) such bond is issued after the date of the enactment of this section and before January 1, 2014.

(3) LIMITATIONS ON AMOUNT OF BONDS.—

(A) AGGREGATE AMOUNT DESIGNATED.—The maximum aggregate face amount of bonds which may be designated under this subsection shall not exceed $8,000,000,000, of which not to exceed $4,000,000,000 may be designated by the Governor and not to exceed $4,000,000,000 may be designated by the Mayor.

(B) SPECIFIC LIMITATIONS.—The aggregate face amount of bonds issued which are to be used for—

(i) costs for property located outside the New York Liberty Zone shall not exceed $2,000,000,000,

(ii) residential rental property shall not exceed $1,600,000,000, and

(iii) costs with respect to property used for retail sales of tangible property and functionally related and subordinate property shall not exceed $800,000,000.

The limitations under clauses (i), (ii), and (iii) shall be allocated proportionately between the bonds designated by the Governor and the bonds designated by the Mayor in proportion to the respective amounts of bonds designated by each.

(C) MOVABLE PROPERTY.—No bonds shall be issued which are to be used for movable fixtures and equipment.

(4) QUALIFIED PROJECT COSTS.—For purposes of this subsection—

(A) IN GENERAL.—The term "qualified project costs" means the cost of acquisition, construction, reconstruction, and renovation of—

(i) nonresidential real property and residential rental property (including fixed tenant improvements associated with such property) located in the New York Liberty Zone, and

(ii) public utility property (as defined in section 168(i)(10)) located in the New York Liberty Zone.

(B) COSTS FOR CERTAIN PROPERTY OUTSIDE ZONE INCLUDED.—Such term includes the cost of acquisition, construction, reconstruction, and renovation of nonresidential real property (including fixed tenant improvements associated with such property) located outside the New York Liberty Zone but within the City of New York, New York, if such property is part of a project which consists of at least 100,000 square feet of usable office or other commercial space located in a single building or multiple adjacent buildings.

(5) SPECIAL RULES.—In applying this title to any qualified New York Liberty Bond, the following modifications shall apply:

(A) Section 146 (relating to volume cap) shall not apply.

(B) Section 147(d) (relating to acquisition of existing property not permitted) shall be applied by substituting "50 percent" for "15 percent" each place it appears.

(C) Section 148(f)(4)(C) (relating to exception from rebate for certain proceeds to be used to finance construction expenditures) shall apply to the available construction proceeds of bonds issued under this section.

(D) Repayments of principal on financing provided by the issue—

(i) may not be used to provide financing, and

(ii) must be used not later than the close of the 1st semiannual period beginning after the date of the repayment to redeem bonds which are part of such issue.

The requirement of clause (ii) shall be treated as met with respect to amounts received within 10 years after the date of issuance of the issue (or, in the case of a refunding bond, the date of issuance of the original bond) if such amounts are used by the close of such 10 years to redeem bonds which are part of such issue.

(E) Section 57(a)(5) shall not apply.

(6) SEPARATE ISSUE TREATMENT OF PORTIONS OF AN ISSUE.—This subsection shall not apply to the portion of an issue which (if issued as a separate issue) would be treated as a qualified bond or as a bond that is not a private activity bond (determined without regard to paragraph (1)), if the issuer elects to so treat such portion.

Amendments

• **2013, American Taxpayer Relief Act of 2012 (P.L. 112-240)**

P.L. 112-240, §328(a):

Amended Code Sec. 1400L(d)(2)(D) by striking "January 1, 2012" and inserting "January 1, 2014". **Effective** for bonds issued after 12-31-2011.

• **2010, Tax Relief, Unemployment Insurance Reauthorization, and Job Creation Act of 2010 (P.L. 111-312)**

P.L. 111-312, §761(a):

Amended Code Sec. 1400L(d)(2)(D) by striking "January 1, 2010" and inserting "January 1, 2012". **Effective** for bonds issued after 12-31-2009.

• **2004, Working Families Tax Relief Act of 2004 (P.L. 108-311)**

P.L. 108-311, §309(a):

Amended Code Sec. 1400L(d)(2)(D) by striking "2005" and inserting "2010". **Effective** 10-4-2004.

[Sec. 1400L(e)]

(e) ADVANCE REFUNDINGS OF CERTAIN TAX-EXEMPT BONDS.—

(1) IN GENERAL.—With respect to a bond described in paragraph (2) issued as part of an issue 90 percent (95 percent in the case of a bond described in paragraph (2)(C)) or more of the net proceeds (as defined in section 150(a)(3)) of which were used to finance facilities located within the City of New York, New York (or property which is functionally related and subordinate to facilities located within the City of New York for the furnishing of water), one additional advanced refunding after the date of the enactment of this section and before January 1, 2006, shall be allowed under the applicable rules of section 149(d) if—

(A) the Governor or the Mayor designates the advance refunding bond for purposes of this subsection, and

(B) the requirements of paragraph (4) are met.

(2) BONDS DESCRIBED.—A bond is described in this paragraph if such bond was outstanding on September 11, 2001, and is—

(A) a State or local bond (as defined in section 103(c)(1)) which is a general obligation of the City of New York, New York,

(B) a State or local bond (as so defined) other than a private activity bond (as defined in section 141(a)) issued by the New York Municipal Water Finance Authority or the Metropolitan Transportation Authority of the State of New York or the Municipal Assistance Corporation, or

(C) a qualified 501(c)(3) bond (as defined in section 145(a)) which is a qualified hospital bond (as defined in section 145(c)) issued by or on behalf of the State of New York or the City of New York, New York.

(3) AGGREGATE LIMIT.—For purposes of paragraph (1), the maximum aggregate face amount of bonds which may be designated under this subsection by the Governor shall not exceed $4,500,000,000 and the maximum aggregate face amount of bonds

INCOME TAX—DC ENTERPRISE ZONE

which may be designated under this subsection by the Mayor shall not exceed $4,500,000,000.

(4) ADDITIONAL REQUIREMENTS.—The requirements of this paragraph are met with respect to any advance refunding of a bond described in paragraph (2) if—

(A) no advance refundings of such bond would be allowed under any provision of law after September 11, 2001,

(B) the advance refunding bond is the only other outstanding bond with respect to the refunded bond, and

(C) the requirements of section 148 are met with respect to all bonds issued under this subsection.

Amendments

• **2004, Working Families Tax Relief Act of 2004 (P.L. 108-311)**

P.L. 108-311, § 309(b):

Amended Code Sec. 1400L(e)(1) by striking "2005" and inserting "2006". **Effective** on the date of the enactment of this Act.

P.L. 108-311, § 309(c):

Amended Code Sec. 1400L(e)(2)(B) by striking ", or" and inserting "or the Municipal Assistance Corporation, or". **Effective** as if included in the amendments made by section 301 of the Job Creation and Worker Assistance Act of 2002 (P.L. 107-147) [**effective** 3-9-2002.—CCH].

[Sec. 1400L(f)]

(f) INCREASE IN EXPENSING UNDER SECTION 179.—

(1) IN GENERAL.—For purposes of section 179—

(A) the limitation under section 179(b)(1) shall be increased by the lesser of—

(i) $35,000, or

(ii) the cost of section 179 property which is qualified New York Liberty Zone property placed in service during the taxable year, and

(B) the amount taken into account under section 179(b)(2) with respect to any section 179 property which is qualified New York Liberty Zone property shall be 50 percent of the cost thereof.

(2) QUALIFIED NEW YORK LIBERTY ZONE PROPERTY.—For purposes of this subsection, the term "qualified New York Liberty Zone property" has the meaning given such term by subsection (b)(2), determined without regard to subparagraph (C)(i) thereof.

(3) RECAPTURE.—Rules similar to the rules under section 179(d)(10) shall apply with respect to any qualified New York Liberty Zone property which ceases to be used in the New York Liberty Zone.

Amendments

• **2004, Working Families Tax Relief Act of 2004 (P.L. 108-311)**

P.L. 108-311, § 403(c)(4):

Amended Code Sec. 1400L(f)(2) by inserting before the period ", determined without regard to subparagraph (C)(i) thereof". **Effective** as if included in the provision of the Job Creation and Worker Assistance Act of 2002 (P.L. 107-147) to which it relates [**effective** 3-9-2002.—CCH].

[Sec. 1400L(g)]

(g) EXTENSION OF REPLACEMENT PERIOD FOR NONRECOGNITION OF GAIN.—Notwithstanding subsections (g) and (h) of section 1033, clause (i) of section 1033(a)(2)(B) shall be applied by substituting "5 years" for "2 years" with respect to property which is compulsorily or involuntarily converted as a result of the terrorist attacks on September 11, 2001, in the New York Liberty Zone but only if substantially all of the use of the replacement property is in the City of New York, New York.

[Sec. 1400L(h)]

(h) NEW YORK LIBERTY ZONE.—For purposes of this section, the term "New York Liberty Zone" means the area located on or south of Canal Street, East Broadway (east of its intersection with Canal Street), or Grand Street (east of its intersection with East Broadway) in the Borough of Manhattan in the City of New York, New York.

[Sec. 1400L(i)]

(i) REFERENCES TO GOVERNOR AND MAYOR.—For purposes of this section, the terms "Governor" and "Mayor" mean the Governor of the State of New York and the Mayor of the City of New York, New York, respectively.

Amendments

• **2002, Job Creation and Worker Assistance Act of 2002 (P.L. 107-147)**

P.L. 107-147, § 301(a):

Amended chapter 1 by adding at the end a new subchapter Y (Code Sec. 1400L). **Effective** 3-9-2002.

P.L. 115-141, § 401(d)(6)(C)(i)-(vi), Div. U, provides:

(C) SAVINGS PROVISIONS.—The amendments made by this paragraph shall not apply to—

(i) in the case of the repeal of section 1400L(a) of the Internal Revenue Code of 1986, qualified wages (as defined in such section, as in effect before its repeal) which were paid or incurred before January 1, 2004,

(ii) in the case of the repeal of subsections (b) and (f) of section 1400L of such Code, qualified New York Liberty Zone property (as defined in section 1400L(b) of such Code, as in effect before its repeal) placed in service before January 1, 2010,

(iii) in the case of the repeal of section 1400L(c) of such Code, qualified New York Liberty Zone leasehold improvement property (as defined in such section, as in effect before its repeal) placed in service before January 1, 2007,

(iv) in the case of the repeal of section 1400L(d) of such Code, qualified New York Liberty bonds (as defined in such section, as in effect before its repeal) issued before January 1, 2014,

(v) in the case of the repeal of section 1400L(e) of such Code, advanced refundings before January 1, 2006,

(vi) in the case of the repeal of section 1400L(g) of such Code, property which is compulsorily or involuntarily converted as a result of the terrorist attacks on September 11, 2001,

P.L. 115-141, § 401(e), Div. U, provides:

(e) GENERAL SAVINGS PROVISION WITH RESPECT TO DEADWOOD PROVISIONS.—If—

(1) any provision amended or repealed by the amendments made by subsection (b) or (d) applied to—

(A) any transaction occurring before the date of the enactment of this Act,

(B) any property acquired before such date of enactment, or

(C) any item of income, loss, deduction, or credit taken into account before such date of enactment, and

(2) the treatment of such transaction, property, or item under such provision would (without regard to the amendments or repeals made by such subsection) affect the liability for tax for periods ending after such date of enactment,

nothing in the amendments or repeals made by this section shall be construed to affect the treatment of such transaction, property, or item for purposes of determining liability for tax for periods ending after such date of enactment.

PART II—TAX BENEFITS FOR GO ZONES—[STRICKEN]

[Sec. 1400M—Stricken]

Amendments

• **2018, Tax Technical Corrections Act of 2018 (P.L. 115-141)**

P.L. 115-141, § 401(d)(6)(A), Div. U:

Amended chapter 1 by striking subchapter Y (Code Secs. 1400L-1400U-3). **Effective** 3-23-2018. For a special rule, see Act Sec. 401(e), below. Prior to being stricken, Code Sec. 1400M read as follows:

SEC. 1400M. DEFINITIONS.

For purposes of this part—

(1) GULF OPPORTUNITY ZONE.—The terms "Gulf Opportunity Zone" and "GO Zone" mean that portion of the Hurricane Katrina disaster area determined by the President to warrant individual or individual and public assistance from the Federal Government under the Robert T. Stafford Disaster Relief and Emergency Assistance Act by reason of Hurricane Katrina.

(2) HURRICANE KATRINA DISASTER AREA.—The term "Hurricane Katrina disaster area" means an area with respect to which a major disaster has been declared by the President before September 14, 2005, under section 401 of such Act by reason of Hurricane Katrina.

(3) RITA GO ZONE.—The term "Rita GO Zone" means that portion of the Hurricane Rita disaster area determined by the President to warrant individual or individual and public assistance from the Federal Government under such Act by reason of Hurricane Rita.

(4) HURRICANE RITA DISASTER AREA.—The term "Hurricane Rita disaster area" means an area with respect to which a major disaster has been declared by the President before October 6, 2005, under section 401 of such Act by reason of Hurricane Rita.

(5) WILMA GO ZONE.—The term "Wilma GO Zone" means that portion of the Hurricane Wilma disaster area determined by the President to warrant individual or individual and public assistance from the Federal Government under such Act by reason of Hurricane Wilma.

(6) HURRICANE WILMA DISASTER AREA.—The term "Hurricane Wilma disaster area" means an area with respect to which a major disaster has been declared by the President before November 14, 2005, under section 401 of such Act by reason of Hurricane Wilma.

Amendments

• **2005, Gulf Opportunity Zone Act of 2005 (P.L. 109-135)**

P.L. 109-135, § 101(a):

Amended subchapter Y of chapter 1 by adding at the end a new part II containing Code Secs. 1400M and 1400N. **Effective** for tax years ending on or after 8-28-2005.

P.L. 115-141, § 401(e), Div. U, provides:

(e) GENERAL SAVINGS PROVISION WITH RESPECT TO DEADWOOD PROVISIONS.—If—

(1) any provision amended or repealed by the amendments made by subsection (b) or (d) applied to—

(A) any transaction occurring before the date of the enactment of this Act,

(B) any property acquired before such date of enactment, or

(C) any item of income, loss, deduction, or credit taken into account before such date of enactment, and

(2) the treatment of such transaction, property, or item under such provision would (without regard to the amendments or repeals made by such subsection) affect the liability for tax for periods ending after such date of enactment,

nothing in the amendments or repeals made by this section shall be construed to affect the treatment of such transaction, property, or item for purposes of determining liability for tax for periods ending after such date of enactment.

INCOME TAX—DC ENTERPRISE ZONE

[Sec. 1400N—Stricken]

Amendments

• **2018, Tax Technical Corrections Act of 2018 (P.L. 115-141)**

P.L. 115-141, §401(d)(6)(A), Div. U:

Amended chapter 1 by striking subchapter Y (Code Secs. 1400L-1400U-3). **Effective** 3-23-2018. For special rules, see Act Sec. 401(d)(6)(C)(vii)-(xiv), Div. U, and Act Sec. 401(e), Div. U, below. Prior to being stricken, Code Sec. 1400N read as follows:

SEC. 1400N. TAX BENEFITS FOR GULF OPPORTUNITY ZONE.

[Sec. 1400N(a)]

(a) TAX-EXEMPT BOND FINANCING.—

(1) IN GENERAL.—For purposes of this title—

(A) any qualified Gulf Opportunity Zone Bond described in paragraph (2)(A)(i) shall be treated as an exempt facility bond, and

(B) any qualified Gulf Opportunity Zone Bond described in paragraph (2)(A)(ii) shall be treated as a qualified mortgage bond.

(2) QUALIFIED GULF OPPORTUNITY ZONE BOND.—For purposes of this subsection, the term "qualified Gulf Opportunity Zone Bond" means any bond issued as part of an issue if—

(A)(i) 95 percent or more of the net proceeds (as defined in section 150(a)(3)) of such issue are to be used for qualified project costs, or

(ii) such issue meets the requirements of a qualified mortgage issue, except as otherwise provided in this subsection,

(B) such bond is issued by the State of Alabama, Louisiana, or Mississippi, or any political subdivision thereof,

(C) such bond is designated for purposes of this section by—

(i) in the case of a bond which is required under State law to be approved by the bond commission of such State, such bond commission, and

(ii) in the case of any other bond, the Governor of such State,

(D) such bond is issued after the date of the enactment of this section and before January 1, 2012, and

(E) no portion of the proceeds of such issue is to be used to provide any property described in section 144(c)(6)(B).

(3) LIMITATIONS ON BONDS.—

(A) AGGREGATE AMOUNT DESIGNATED.—The maximum aggregate face amount of bonds which may be designated under this subsection with respect to any State shall not exceed the product of $2,500 multiplied by the portion of the State population which is in the Gulf Opportunity Zone (as determined on the basis of the most recent census estimate of resident population released by the Bureau of Census before August 28, 2005).

(B) MOVABLE PROPERTY.—No bonds shall be issued which are to be used for movable fixtures and equipment.

(4) QUALIFIED PROJECT COSTS.—For purposes of this subsection, the term "qualified project costs" means—

(A) the cost of any qualified residential rental project (as defined in section 142(d)) located in the Gulf Opportunity Zone, and

(B) the cost of acquisition, construction, reconstruction, and renovation of—

(i) nonresidential real property (including fixed improvements associated with such property) located in the Gulf Opportunity Zone, and

(ii) public utility property (as defined in section 168(i)(10)) located in the Gulf Opportunity Zone.

(5) SPECIAL RULES.—In applying this title to any qualified Gulf Opportunity Zone Bond, the following modifications shall apply:

(A) Section 142(d)(1) (defining qualified residential rental project) shall be applied—

(i) by substituting "60 percent" for "50 percent" in subparagraph (A) thereof, and

(ii) by substituting "70 percent" for "60 percent" in subparagraph (B) thereof.

(B) Section 143 (relating to mortgage revenue bonds: qualified mortgage bond and qualified veterans' mortgage bond) shall be applied—

(i) only with respect to owner-occupied residences in the Gulf Opportunity Zone,

(ii) by treating any such residence in the Gulf Opportunity Zone as a targeted area residence,

(iii) by applying subsection (f)(3) thereof without regard to subparagraph (A) thereof, and

(iv) by substituting "$150,000" for "$15,000" in subsection (k)(4) thereof.

(C) Except as provided in section 143, repayments of principal on financing provided by the issue of which such bond is a part may not be used to provide financing.

(D) Section 146 (relating to volume cap) shall not apply.

(E) Section 147(d)(2) (relating to acquisition of existing property not permitted) shall be applied by substituting "50 percent" for "15 percent" each place it appears.

(F) Section 148(f)(4)(C) (relating to exception from rebate for certain proceeds to be used to finance construction expenditures) shall apply to the available construction proceeds of bonds which are part of an issue described in paragraph (2)(A)(i).

(G) Section 57(a)(5) (relating to tax-exempt interest) shall not apply.

(6) SEPARATE ISSUE TREATMENT OF PORTIONS OF AN ISSUE.—This subsection shall not apply to the portion of an issue which (if issued as a separate issue) would be treated as a qualified bond or as a bond that is not a private activity bond (determined without regard to paragraph (1)), if the issuer elects to so treat such portion.

(7) SPECIAL RULE FOR REPAIRS AND RECONSTRUCTIONS.—

(A) IN GENERAL.—For purposes of section 143 and this subsection, any qualified GO Zone repair or reconstruction shall be treated as a qualified rehabilitation.

(B) QUALIFIED GO ZONE REPAIR OR RECONSTRUCTION.—For purposes of subparagraph (A), the term "qualified GO Zone repair or reconstruction" means any repair of damage caused by Hurricane Katrina, Hurricane Rita, or Hurricane Wilma to a building located in the Gulf Opportunity Zone, the Rita GO Zone, or the Wilma GO Zone (or reconstruction of such building in the case of damage constituting destruction) if the expenditures for such repair or reconstruction are 25 percent or more of the mortgagor's adjusted basis in the residence. For purposes of the preceding sentence, the mortgagor's adjusted basis shall be determined as of the completion of the repair or reconstruction or, if later, the date on which the mortgagor acquires the residence.

(C) TERMINATION.—This paragraph shall apply only to owner-financing provided after the date of the enactment of this paragraph and before January 1, 2012.

(8) INCLUSION OF CERTAIN COUNTIES.—For purposes of this subsection, the Gulf Opportunity Zone includes Colbert County, Alabama and Dallas County, Alabama.

Amendments

• **2010, Tax Relief, Unemployment Insurance Reauthorization, and Job Creation Act of 2010 (P.L. 111-312)**

P.L. 111-312, §764(a):

Amended Code Sec. 1400N(a)(2)(D) and (7)(C) by striking "January 1, 2011" and inserting "January 1, 2012". **Effective** on the date of the enactment of this Act.

• **2008, Heartland Disaster Tax Relief Act of 2008 (P.L. 110-343)**

P.L. 110-343, Division C, §702 [as amended by P.L. 111-312, §764(b)], provides:

SEC. 702. TEMPORARY TAX RELIEF FOR AREAS DAMAGED BY 2008 MIDWESTERN SEVERE STORMS, TORNADOS, AND FLOODING.

(a) IN GENERAL.—Subject to the modifications described in this section, the following provisions of or relating to the Internal Revenue Code of 1986 shall apply to any Midwestern disaster area in addition to the areas to which such provisions otherwise apply:

(1) GO ZONE BENEFITS.—

(A) Section 1400N (relating to tax benefits) other than subsections (b), (d), (e), (i), (j), (m), and (o) thereof.

(B) Section 1400O (relating to education tax benefits).

(C) Section 1400P (relating to housing tax benefits).

(D) Section 1400Q (relating to special rules for use of retirement funds).

(E) Section 1400R(a) (relating to employee retention credit for employers).

(F) Section 1400S (relating to additional tax relief) other than subsection (d) thereof.

(G) Section 1400T (relating to special rules for mortgage revenue bonds).

(2) OTHER BENEFITS INCLUDED IN KATRINA EMERGENCY TAX RELIEF ACT OF 2005.—Sections 302, 303, 304, 401, and 405 of the Katrina Emergency Tax Relief Act of 2005.

(b) MIDWESTERN DISASTER AREA.—

(1) IN GENERAL.—For purposes of this section and for applying the substitutions described in subsections (d) and (e), the term "Midwestern disaster area" means an area—

(A) with respect to which a major disaster has been declared by the President on or after May 20, 2008, and before August 1, 2008, under section 401 of the Robert T. Stafford Disaster Relief and Emergency Assistance Act by reason of severe storms, tornados, or flooding occurring in any of the States of Arkansas, Illinois, Indiana, Iowa, Kansas, Michigan, Minnesota, Missouri, Nebraska, and Wisconsin, and

(B) determined by the President to warrant individual or individual and public assistance from the Federal Government under such Act with respect to damages attributable to such severe storms, tornados, or flooding.

(2) CERTAIN BENEFITS AVAILABLE TO AREAS ELIGIBLE ONLY FOR PUBLIC ASSISTANCE.—For purposes of applying this section to benefits under the following provisions, paragraph (1) shall be applied without regard to subparagraph (B):

(A) Sections 1400Q, 1400S(b), and 1400S(d) of the Internal Revenue Code of 1986.

(B) Sections 302, 401, and 405 of the Katrina Emergency Tax Relief Act of 2005.

(c) REFERENCES.—

(1) AREA.—Any reference in such provisions to the Hurricane Katrina disaster area or the Gulf Opportunity Zone shall be treated as a reference to any Midwestern disaster area and any reference to the Hurricane Katrina disaster area or the Gulf Opportunity Zone within a State shall be treated as a reference to all Midwestern disaster areas within the State.

(2) ITEMS ATTRIBUTABLE TO DISASTER.—Any reference in such provisions to any loss, damage, or other item attributable to Hurricane Katrina shall be treated as a reference to any loss, damage, or other item attributable to the severe storms, tornados, or flooding giving rise to any Presidential declaration described in subsection (b)(1)(A).

(3) APPLICABLE DISASTER DATE.—For purposes of applying the substitutions described in subsections (d) and (e), the term "applicable disaster date" means, with respect to any Midwestern disaster area, the date on which the severe storms, tornados, or flooding giving rise to the Presidential declaration described in subsection (b)(1)(A) occurred.

(d) MODIFICATIONS TO 1986 CODE.—The following provisions of the Internal Revenue Code of 1986 shall be applied with the following modifications:

(1) TAX-EXEMPT BOND FINANCING.—Section 1400N(a)—

(A) by substituting "qualified Midwestern disaster area bond" for "qualified Gulf Opportunity Zone Bond" each place it appears, except that in determining whether a bond is a qualified Midwestern disaster area bond—

(i) paragraph (2)(A)(i) shall be applied by only treating costs as qualified project costs if—

(I) in the case of a project involving a private business use (as defined in section 141(b)(6)), either the person using the property suffered a loss in a trade or business attributable to the severe storms, tornados, or flooding giving rise to any Presidential declaration described in subsection (b)(1)(A) or is a person designated for purposes of this section by the Governor of the State in which the project is located as a person carrying on a trade or business replacing a trade or business with respect to which another person suffered such a loss, and

INCOME TAX—DC ENTERPRISE ZONE

(II) in the case of a project relating to public utility property, the project involves repair or reconstruction of public utility property damaged by such severe storms, tornados, or flooding, and

(ii) paragraph (2)(A)(ii) shall be applied by treating an issue as a qualified mortgage issue only if 95 percent or more of the net proceeds (as defined in section 150(a)(3)) of the issue are to be used to provide financing for mortgagors who suffered damages to their principal residences attributable to such severe storms, tornados, or flooding.

(B) by substituting "any State in which a Midwestern disaster area is located" for "the State of Alabama, Louisiana, or Mississippi" in paragraph (2)(B),

(C) by substituting "designated for purposes of this section (on the basis of providing assistance to areas in the order in which such assistance is most needed)" for "designated for purposes of this section" in paragraph (2)(C),

(D) by substituting "January 1, 2013" for "January 1, 2012" in paragraph (2)(D),

(E) in paragraph (3)(A)—

(i) by substituting "$1,000" for "$2,500", and

(ii) by substituting "before the earliest applicable disaster date for Midwestern disaster areas within the State" for "before August 28, 2005",

(F) by substituting "qualified Midwestern disaster area repair or construction" for "qualified GO Zone repair or construction" each place it appears,

(G) by substituting "after the date of the enactment of the Heartland Disaster Tax Relief Act of 2008 and before January 1, 2013" for "after the date of the enactment of this paragraph and before January 1, 2012" in paragraph (7)(C), and

(H) by disregarding paragraph (8) thereof.

(2) LOW-INCOME HOUSING CREDIT.—Section 1400N(c)—

(A) only with respect to calendar years 2008, 2009, and 2010,

(B) by substituting "Disaster Recovery Assistance housing amount" for "Gulf Opportunity housing amount" each place it appears,

(C) in paragraph (1)(B)—

(i) by substituting "$8.00" for "$18.00", and

(ii) by substituting "before the earliest applicable disaster date for Midwestern disaster areas within the State" for "before August 28, 2005", and

(D) determined without regard to paragraphs (2), (3), (4), (5), and (6) thereof.

(3) EXPENSING FOR CERTAIN DEMOLITION AND CLEAN-UP COSTS.—Section 1400N(f)—

(A) by substituting "qualified Disaster Recovery Assistance clean-up cost" for "qualified Gulf Opportunity Zone clean-up cost" each place it appears,

(B) by substituting "beginning on the applicable disaster date and ending on December 31, 2010" for "beginning on August 28, 2005, and ending on December 31, 2007" in paragraph (2), and

(C) by treating costs as qualified Disaster Recovery Assistance clean-up costs only if the removal of debris or demolition of any structure was necessary due to damage attributable to the severe storms, tornados, or flooding giving rise to any Presidential declaration described in subsection (b)(1)(A).

(4) EXTENSION OF EXPENSING FOR ENVIRONMENTAL REMEDIATION COSTS.—Section 1400N(g)—

(A) by substituting "the applicable disaster date" for "August 28, 2005" each place it appears,

(B) by substituting "January 1, 2011" for "January 1, 2008" in paragraph (1),

(C) by substituting "December 31, 2010" for "December 31, 2007" in paragraph (1), and

(D) by treating a site as a qualified contaminated site only if the release (or threat of release) or disposal of a hazardous substance at the site was attributable to the severe storms, tornados, or flooding giving rise to any Presidential declaration described in subsection (b)(1)(A).

(5) INCREASE IN REHABILITATION CREDIT.—Section 1400N(h), as amended by this Act—

(A) by substituting "the applicable disaster date" for "August 28, 2005",

(B) by substituting "December 31, 2011" for "December 31, 2009" in paragraph (1), and

(C) by only applying such subsection to qualified rehabilitation expenditures with respect to any building or structure which was damaged or destroyed as a result of the severe storms, tornados, or flooding giving rise to any Presidential declaration described in subsection (b)(1)(A).

(6) TREATMENT OF NET OPERATING LOSSES ATTRIBUTABLE TO DISASTER LOSSES.—Section 1400N(k)—

(A) by substituting "qualified Disaster Recovery Assistance loss" for "qualified Gulf Opportunity Zone loss" each place it appears,

(B) by substituting "after the day before the applicable disaster date, and before January 1, 2011" for "after August 27, 2005, and before January 1, 2008" each place it appears,

(C) by substituting "the applicable disaster date" for "August 28, 2005" in paragraph (2)(B)(ii)(I),

(D) by substituting "qualified Disaster Recovery Assistance property" for "qualified Gulf Opportunity Zone property" in paragraph (2)(B)(iv), and

(E) by substituting "qualified Disaster Recovery Assistance casualty loss" for "qualified Gulf Opportunity Zone casualty loss" each place it appears.

(7) CREDIT TO HOLDERS OF TAX CREDIT BONDS.—Section 1400N(l)—

(A) by substituting "Midwestern tax credit bond" for "Gulf tax credit bond" each place it appears,

(B) by substituting "any State in which a Midwestern disaster area is located or any instrumentality of the State" for "the State of Alabama, Louisiana, or Mississippi" in paragraph (4)(A)(i),

(C) by substituting "after December 31, 2008 and before January 1, 2010" for "after December 31, 2005, and before January 1, 2007",

(D) by substituting "shall not exceed $100,000,000 for any State with an aggregate population located in all Midwestern disaster areas within the State of at least 2,000,000, $50,000,000 for any State with an aggregate population located in all Midwestern disaster areas within the State of at least 1,000,000 but less than 2,000,000, and zero for any other State. The population of a State within any area shall be determined on the basis of the most recent census estimate of resident population released by the Bureau of Census before the earliest applicable disaster date for Midwestern disaster areas within the State." for "shall not exceed" and all that follows in paragraph (4)(C), and

(E) by substituting "the earliest applicable disaster date for Midwestern disaster areas within the State" for "August 28, 2005" in paragraph (5)(A).

(8) EDUCATION TAX BENEFITS.—Section 1400O, by substituting "2008 or 2009" for "2005 or 2006".

(9) HOUSING TAX BENEFITS.—Section 1400P, by substituting "the applicable disaster date" for "August 28, 2005" in subsection (c)(1).

(10) SPECIAL RULES FOR USE OF RETIREMENT FUNDS.—Section 1400Q—

(A) by substituting "qualified Disaster Recovery Assistance distribution" for "qualified hurricane distribution" each place it appears,

(B) by substituting "on or after the applicable disaster date and before January 1, 2010" for "on or after August 25, 2005, and before January 1, 2007" in subsection (a)(4)(A)(i),

(C) by substituting "the applicable disaster date" for "August 28, 2005" in subsections (a)(4)(A)(i) and (c)(3)(B),

(D) by disregarding clauses (ii) and (iii) of subsection (a)(4)(A) thereof,

(E) by substituting "qualified storm damage distribution" for "qualified Katrina distribution" each place it appears,

(F) by substituting "after the date which is 6 months before the applicable disaster date and before the date which is the day after the applicable disaster date" for "after February 28, 2005, and before August 29, 2005" in subsection (b)(2)(B)(ii),

(G) by substituting "the Midwestern disaster area, but not so purchased or constructed on account of severe storms, tornados, or flooding giving rise to the designation of the area as a disaster area" for "the Hurricane Katrina disaster area, but not so purchased or constructed on account of Hurricane Katrina" in subsection (b)(2)(B)(iii),

(H) by substituting "beginning on the applicable disaster date and ending on the date which is 5 months after the date of the enactment of the Heartland Disaster Tax Relief Act of 2008" for "beginning on August 25, 2005, and ending on February 28, 2006" in subsection (b)(3)(A),

(I) by substituting "qualified storm damage individual" for "qualified Hurricane Katrina individual" each place it appears,

(J) by substituting "December 31, 2009" for "December 31, 2006" in subsection (c)(2)(A),

(K) by disregarding subparagraphs (C) and (D) of subsection (c)(3) thereof,

(L) by substituting "beginning on the date of the enactment of the Heartland Disaster Tax Relief Act of 2008 and ending on December 31, 2009" for "beginning on September 24, 2005, and ending on December 31, 2006" in subsection (c)(4)(A)(i),

(M) by substituting "the applicable disaster date" for "August 25, 2005" in subsection (c)(4)(A)(ii), and

(N) by substituting "January 1, 2010" for "January 1, 2007" in subsection (d)(2)(A)(ii).

(11) EMPLOYEE RETENTION CREDIT FOR EMPLOYERS AFFECTED BY SEVERE STORMS, TORNADOS, AND FLOODING.—Section 1400R(a)—

(A) by substituting "the applicable disaster date" for "August 28, 2005" each place it appears,

(B) by substituting "January 1, 2009" for "January 1, 2006" both places it appears, and

(C) only with respect to eligible employers who employed an average of not more than 200 employees on business days during the taxable year before the applicable disaster date.

(12) TEMPORARY SUSPENSION OF LIMITATIONS ON CHARITABLE CONTRIBUTIONS.—Section 1400S(a), by substituting the following paragraph for paragraph (4) thereof:

"(4) QUALIFIED CONTRIBUTIONS.—

"(A) IN GENERAL.—For purposes of this subsection, the term 'qualified contribution' means any charitable contribution (as defined in section 170(c)) if—

"(i) such contribution—

"(I) is paid during the period beginning on the earliest applicable disaster date for all States and ending on December 31, 2008, in cash to an organization described in section 170(b)(1)(A), and

"(II) is made for relief efforts in 1 or more Midwestern disaster areas,

"(ii) the taxpayer obtains from such organization contemporaneous written acknowledgment (within the meaning of section 170(f)(8)) that such contribution was used (or is to be used) for relief efforts in 1 or more Midwestern disaster areas, and

"(iii) the taxpayer has elected the application of this subsection with respect to such contribution.

"(B) EXCEPTION.—Such term shall not include a contribution by a donor if the contribution is—

"(i) to an organization described in section 509(a)(3), or

"(ii) for establishment of a new, or maintenance of an existing, donor advised fund (as defined in section 4966(d)(2)).

"(C) APPLICATION OF ELECTION TO PARTNERSHIPS AND S CORPORATIONS.—In the case of a partnership or S corporation, the election under subparagraph (A)(iii) shall be made separately by each partner or shareholder.".

(13) SUSPENSION OF CERTAIN LIMITATIONS ON PERSONAL CASUALTY LOSSES.—Section 1400S(b)(1), by substituting "the applicable disaster date" for "August 25, 2005".

(14) SPECIAL RULE FOR DETERMINING EARNED INCOME.—Section 1400S(d)—

(A) by treating an individual as a qualified individual if such individual's principal place of abode on the applicable disaster date was located in a Midwestern disaster area,

(B) by treating the applicable disaster date with respect to any such individual as the applicable date for purposes of such subsection, and

Sec. 1400N—Stricken

(C) by treating an area as described in paragraph (2)(B)(ii) thereof if the area is a Midwestern disaster area only by reason of subsection (b)(2) of this section (relating to areas eligible only for public assistance).

(15) ADJUSTMENTS REGARDING TAXPAYER AND DEPENDENCY STATUS.—Section 1400S(e), by substituting "2008 or 2009" for "2005 or 2006".

(e) MODIFICATIONS TO KATRINA EMERGENCY TAX RELIEF ACT OF 2005.—The following provisions of the Katrina Emergency Tax Relief Act of 2005 shall be applied with the following modifications:

(1) ADDITIONAL EXEMPTION FOR HOUSING DISPLACED INDIVIDUAL.—Section 302—

(A) by substituting "2008 or 2009" for "2005 or 2006" in subsection (a) thereof,

(B) by substituting "Midwestern displaced individual" for "Hurricane Katrina displaced individual" each place it appears, and

(C) by treating an area as a core disaster area for purposes of applying subsection (c) thereof if the area is a Midwestern disaster area without regard to subsection (b)(2) of this section (relating to areas eligible only for public assistance).

(2) INCREASE IN STANDARD MILEAGE RATE.—Section 303, by substituting "beginning on the applicable disaster date and ending on December 31, 2008" for "beginning on August 25, 2005, and ending on December 31, 2006".

(3) MILEAGE REIMBURSEMENTS FOR CHARITABLE VOLUNTEERS.—Section 304—

(A) by substituting "beginning on the applicable disaster date and ending on December 31, 2008" for "beginning on August 25, 2005, and ending on December 31, 2006" in subsection (a), and

(B) by substituting "the applicable disaster date" for "August 25, 2005" in subsection (a).

(4) EXCLUSION OF CERTAIN CANCELLATION OF INDEBTEDNESS INCOME.—Section 401—

(A) by treating an individual whose principal place of abode on the applicable disaster date was in a Midwestern disaster area (determined without regard to subsection (b)(2) of this section) as an individual described in subsection (b)(1) thereof, and by treating an individual whose principal place of abode on the applicable disaster date was in a Midwestern disaster area solely by reason of subsection (b)(2) of this section as an individual described in subsection (b)(2) thereof,

(B) by substituting "the applicable disaster date" for "August 28, 2005" both places it appears, and

(C) by substituting "January 1, 2010" for "January 1, 2007" in subsection (e).

(5) EXTENSION OF REPLACEMENT PERIOD FOR NONRECOGNITION OF GAIN.—Section 405, by substituting "on or after the applicable disaster date" for "on or after August 25, 2005".

P.L. 110-343, Division C, §704(a) [as amended by P.L. 111-312, §764(b)] and (c), provides:

SEC. 704. TEMPORARY TAX-EXEMPT BOND FINANCING AND LOW-INCOME HOUSING TAX RELIEF FOR AREAS DAMAGED BY HURRICANE IKE.

(a) TAX-EXEMPT BOND FINANCING.—Section 1400N(a) of the Internal Revenue Code of 1986 shall apply to any Hurricane Ike disaster area in addition to any other area referenced in such section, but with the following modifications:

(1) By substituting "qualified Hurricane Ike disaster area bond" for "qualified Gulf Opportunity Zone Bond" each place it appears, except that in determining whether a bond is a qualified Hurricane Ike disaster area bond—

(A) paragraph (2)(A)(i) shall be applied by only treating costs as qualified project costs if—

(i) in the case of a project involving a private business use (as defined in section 141(b)(6)), either the person using the property suffered a loss in a trade or business attributable to Hurricane Ike or is a person designated for purposes of this section by the Governor of the State in which the project is located as a person carrying on a trade or business replacing a trade or business with respect to which another person suffered such a loss, and

(ii) in the case of a project relating to public utility property, the project involves repair or reconstruction of public utility property damaged by Hurricane Ike, and

(B) paragraph (2)(A)(ii) shall be applied by treating an issue as a qualified mortgage issue only if 95 percent or more of the net proceeds (as defined in section 150(a)(3)) of the issue are to be used to provide financing for mortgagors who suffered damages to their principal residences attributable to Hurricane Ike.

(2) By substituting "any State in which any Hurricane Ike disaster area is located" for "the State of Alabama, Louisiana, or Mississippi" in paragraph (2)(B).

(3) By substituting "designated for purposes of this section (on the basis of providing assistance to areas in the order in which such assistance is most needed)" for "designated for purposes of this section" in paragraph (2)(C).

(4) By substituting "January 1, 2013" for "January 1, 2012" in paragraph (2)(D).

(5) By substituting the following for subparagraph (A) of paragraph (3):

"(A) AGGREGATE AMOUNT DESIGNATED.—The maximum aggregate face amount of bonds which may be designated under this subsection with respect to any State shall not exceed the product of $2,000 multiplied by the portion of the State population which is in—

"(i) in the case of Texas, the counties of Brazoria, Chambers, Galveston, Jefferson, and Orange, and

"(ii) in the case of Louisiana, the parishes of Calcasieu and Cameron,

(as determined on the basis of the most recent census estimate of resident population released by the Bureau of Census before September 13, 2008).".

(6) By substituting "qualified Hurricane Ike disaster area repair or construction" for "qualified GO Zone repair or construction" each place it appears.

(7) By substituting "after the date of the enactment of the Heartland Disaster Tax Relief Act of 2008 and before January 1, 2013" for "after the date of the enactment of this paragraph and before January 1, 2012" in paragraph (7)(C).

(8) By disregarding paragraph (8) thereof.

(9) By substituting "any Hurricane Ike disaster area" for "the Gulf Opportunity Zone" each place it appears.

* * *

(c) HURRICANE IKE DISASTER AREA.—For purposes of this section and for applying the substitutions described in subsections (a) and (b), the term "Hurricane Ike disaster area" means an area in the State of Texas or Louisiana—

(1) with respect to which a major disaster has been declared by the President on September 13, 2008, under section 401 of the Robert T. Stafford Disaster Relief and Emergency Assistance Act by reason of Hurricane Ike, and

(2) determined by the President to warrant individual or individual and public assistance from the Federal Government under such Act with respect to damages attributable to Hurricane Ike.

• 2008, Housing Assistance Tax Act of 2008 (P.L. 110-289)

P.L. 110-289, §3082(c)(1):

Amended Code Sec. 1400N(a) by adding at the end a new paragraph (8). **Effective** as if included in the provisions of the Gulf Opportunity Zone Act of 2005 (P.L. 109-135) to which it relates [**effective**, generally, for tax years ending on or after 8-28-2005.—CCH].

• 2007, Small Business and Work Opportunity Tax Act of 2007 (P.L. 110-28)

P.L. 110-28, §8223:

Amended Code Sec. 1400N(a) by adding at the end a new paragraph (7). **Effective** 5-25-2007.

[Sec. 1400N(b)]

(b) ADVANCE REFUNDINGS OF CERTAIN TAX-EXEMPT BONDS.—

(1) IN GENERAL.—With respect to a bond described in paragraph (3), one additional advance refunding after the date of the enactment of this section and before January 1, 2011, shall be allowed under the applicable rules of section 149(d) if—

(A) the Governor of the State designates the advance refunding bond for purposes of this subsection, and

(B) the requirements of paragraph (5) are met.

(2) CERTAIN PRIVATE ACTIVITY BONDS.—With respect to a bond described in paragraph (3) which is an exempt facility bond described in paragraph (1) or (2) of section 142(a), one advance refunding after the date of the enactment of this section and before January 1, 2011, shall be allowed under the applicable rules of section 149(d) (notwithstanding paragraph (2) thereof) if the requirements of subparagraphs (A) and (B) of paragraph (1) are met.

(3) BONDS DESCRIBED.—A bond is described in this paragraph if such bond was outstanding on August 28, 2005, and is issued by the State of Alabama, Louisiana, or Mississippi, or a political subdivision thereof.

(4) AGGREGATE LIMIT.—The maximum aggregate face amount of bonds which may be designated under this subsection by the Governor of a State shall not exceed—

(A) $4,500,000,000 in the case of the State of Louisiana,

(B) $2,250,000,000 in the case of the State of Mississippi, and

(C) $1,125,000,000 in the case of the State of Alabama.

(5) ADDITIONAL REQUIREMENTS.—The requirements of this paragraph are met with respect to any advance refunding of a bond described in paragraph (3) if—

(A) no advance refundings of such bond would be allowed under this title on or after August 28, 2005,

(B) the advance refunding bond is the only other outstanding bond with respect to the refunded bond, and

(C) the requirements of section 148 are met with respect to all bonds issued under this subsection.

(6) USE OF PROCEEDS REQUIREMENT.—This subsection shall not apply to any advance refunding of a bond which is issued as part of an issue if any portion of the proceeds of such issue (or any prior issue) was (or is to be) used to provide any property described in section 144(c)(6)(B).

[Sec. 1400N(c)]

(c) LOW-INCOME HOUSING CREDIT.—

(1) ADDITIONAL HOUSING CREDIT DOLLAR AMOUNT FOR GULF OPPORTUNITY ZONE.—

(A) IN GENERAL.—For purposes of section 42, in the case of calendar years 2006, 2007, and 2008, the State housing credit ceiling of each State, any portion of which is located in the Gulf Opportunity Zone, shall be increased by the lesser of—

(i) the aggregate housing credit dollar amount allocated by the State housing credit agency of such State to buildings located in the Gulf Opportunity Zone for such calendar year, or

(ii) the Gulf Opportunity housing amount for such State for such calendar year.

(B) GULF OPPORTUNITY HOUSING AMOUNT.—For purposes of subparagraph (A), the term "Gulf Opportunity housing amount" means, for any calendar year, the amount equal to the product of $18.00 multiplied by the portion of the State population which is in the Gulf Opportunity Zone (as determined on the basis of the most recent census estimate of resident population released by the Bureau of Census before August 28, 2005).

(C) ALLOCATIONS TREATED AS MADE FIRST FROM ADDITIONAL ALLOCATION AMOUNT FOR PURPOSES OF DETERMINING CARRYOVER.—For purposes of determining the unused State housing credit ceiling under section 42(h)(3)(C) for any calendar year, any increase in the State housing credit ceiling under subparagraph (A) shall be treated as an amount described in clause (ii) of such section.

(2) ADDITIONAL HOUSING CREDIT DOLLAR AMOUNT FOR TEXAS AND FLORIDA.—For purposes of section 42, in the case of calendar year 2006, the State housing credit ceiling of Texas and Florida shall each be increased by $3,500,000.

(3) DIFFICULT DEVELOPMENT AREA.—

(A) IN GENERAL.—For purposes of section 42, in the case of property placed in service during the period beginning on January 1, 2006, and ending on December 31, 2010, the Gulf Opportunity Zone, the Rita GO Zone, and the Wilma GO Zone—

INCOME TAX—DC ENTERPRISE ZONE

(i) shall be treated as difficult development areas designated under subclause (I) of section 42(d)(5)(B)(iii), and

(ii) shall not be taken into account for purposes of applying the limitation under subclause (II) of such section.

(B) APPLICATION.—Subparagraph (A) shall apply only to—

(i) housing credit dollar amounts allocated during the period beginning on January 1, 2006, and ending on December 31, 2008, and

(ii) buildings placed in service during the period described in subparagraph (A) to the extent that paragraph (1) of section 42(h) does not apply to any building by reason of paragraph (4) thereof, but only with respect to bonds issued after December 31, 2005.

(4) SPECIAL RULE FOR APPLYING INCOME TESTS.—In the case of property placed in service—

(A) during 2006, 2007, or 2008,

(B) in the Gulf Opportunity Zone, and

(C) in a nonmetropolitan area (as defined in section 42(d)(5)(C)(iv)(IV)),

section 42 shall be applied by substituting "national nonmetropolitan median gross income (determined under rules similar to the rules of section 142(d)(2)(B))" for "area median gross income" in subparagraphs (A) and (B) of section 42(g)(1).

(5) TIME FOR MAKING LOW-INCOME HOUSING CREDIT ALLOCATIONS.—Section 42(h)(1)(B) shall not apply to an allocation of housing credit dollar amount to a building located in the Gulf Opportunity Zone, the Rita GO Zone, or the Wilma GO Zone, if such allocation is made in 2006, 2007, or 2008, and such building is placed in service before January 1, 2012.

(6) COMMUNITY DEVELOPMENT BLOCK GRANTS NOT TAKEN INTO ACCOUNT IN DETERMINING IF BUILDINGS ARE FEDERALLY SUBSIDIZED.—For purpose of applying section 42(i)(2)(D) to any building which is placed in service in the Gulf Opportunity Zone, the Rita GO Zone, or the Wilma GO Zone during the period beginning on January 1, 2006, and ending on December 31, 2010, a loan shall not be treated as a below market Federal loan solely by reason of any assistance provided under section 106, 107, or 108 of the Housing and Community Development Act of 1974 by reason of section 122 of such Act or any provision of the Department of Defense Appropriations Act, 2006, or the Emergency Supplemental Appropriations Act for Defense, the Global War on Terror, and Hurricane Recovery, 2006.

(7) DEFINITIONS.—Any term used in this subsection which is also used in section 42 shall have the same meaning as when used in such section.

Amendments

- **2014, Tax Technical Corrections Act of 2014 (P.L. 113-295)**

P.L. 113-295, §220(q), Division A:

Amended Code Sec. 1400N(c)(3)(A)(i) by striking "section 42(d)(5)(C)(iii)" and inserting "section 42(d)(5)(B)(iii)". **Effective** 12-19-2014.

- **2010, Tax Relief, Unemployment Insurance Reauthorization, and Job Creation Act of 2010 (P.L. 111-312)**

P.L. 111-312, §763:

Amended Code Sec. 1400N(c)(5) by striking "January 1, 2011" and inserting "January 1, 2012". **Effective** on the date of the enactment of this Act.

- **2008, Heartland Disaster Tax Relief Act of 2008 (P.L. 110-343)**

P.L. 110-343, Division C, §702, provides:

For a special rule, see Division C, Act Sec. 702, in the amendment notes for Code Sec. 1400N(a).

P.L. 110-343, Division C, §704(b)-(c), provides:

SEC. 704. TEMPORARY TAX-EXEMPT BOND FINANCING AND LOW-INCOME HOUSING TAX RELIEF FOR AREAS DAMAGED BY HURRICANE IKE.

* * *

(b) LOW-INCOME HOUSING CREDIT.—Section 1400N(c) of the Internal Revenue Code of 1986 shall apply to any Hurricane Ike disaster area in addition to any other area referenced in such section, but with the following modifications:

(1) Only with respect to calendar years 2008, 2009, and 2010.

(2) By substituting "any Hurricane Ike disaster area" for "the Gulf Opportunity Zone" each place it appears.

(3) By substituting "Hurricane Ike Recovery Assistance housing amount" for "Gulf Opportunity housing amount" each place it appears.

(4) By substituting the following for subparagraph (B) of paragraph (1):

" (B) HURRICANE IKE HOUSING AMOUNT.—For purposes of subparagraph (A), the term 'Hurricane Ike housing amount' means, for any calendar year, the amount equal to the product of $16.00 multiplied by the portion of the State population which is in—

"(i) in the case of Texas, the counties of Brazoria, Chambers, Galveston, Jefferson, and Orange, and

"(ii) in the case of Louisiana, the parishes of Calcasieu and Cameron,

(as determined on the basis of the most recent census estimate of resident population released by the Bureau of Census before September 13, 2008).".

(5) Determined without regard to paragraphs (2), (3), (4), (5), and (6) thereof.

(c) HURRICANE IKE DISASTER AREA.—For purposes of this section and for applying the substitutions described in subsections (a) and (b), the term "Hurricane Ike disaster area" means an area in the State of Texas or Louisiana—

(1) with respect to which a major disaster has been declared by the President on September 13, 2008, under section 401 of the Robert T. Stafford Disaster Relief and Emergency Assistance Act by reason of Hurricane Ike, and

(2) determined by the President to warrant individual or individual and public assistance from the Federal Government under such Act with respect to damages attributable to Hurricane Ike.

Sec. 1400N—Stricken

- **2007, Small Business and Work Opportunity Tax Act of 2007 (P.L. 110-28)**

P.L. 110-28, §8222(a):

Amended Code Sec. 1400N(c) by redesignating paragraph (5) as paragraph (6) and by inserting after paragraph (4) a new paragraph (5). **Effective** 5-25-2007.

P.L. 110-28, §8222(b)(1):

Amended Code Sec. 1400N(c)(3)(A) by striking "2006, 2007, or 2008" and inserting "the period beginning on January 1, 2006, and ending on December 31, 2010". **Effective** 5-25-2007.

P.L. 110-28, §8222(b)(2):

Amended Code Sec. 1400N(c)(3)(B)(ii) by striking "such period" and inserting "the period described in subparagraph (A)". **Effective** 5-25-2007.

P.L. 110-28, §8222(c):

Amended Code Sec. 1400N(c), as amended by this Act, by redesignating paragraph (6) as paragraph (7) and by inserting after paragraph (5) a new paragraph (6). **Effective** 5-25-2007.

[Sec. 1400N(d)]

(d) SPECIAL ALLOWANCE FOR CERTAIN PROPERTY ACQUIRED ON OR AFTER AUGUST 28, 2005.—

(1) ADDITIONAL ALLOWANCE.—In the case of any qualified Gulf Opportunity Zone property—

(A) the depreciation deduction provided by section 167(a) for the taxable year in which such property is placed in service shall include an allowance equal to 50 percent of the adjusted basis of such property, and

(B) the adjusted basis of the qualified Gulf Opportunity Zone property shall be reduced by the amount of such deduction before computing the amount otherwise allowable as a depreciation deduction under this chapter for such taxable year and any subsequent taxable year.

(2) QUALIFIED GULF OPPORTUNITY ZONE PROPERTY.—For purposes of this subsection—

(A) IN GENERAL.—The term "qualified Gulf Opportunity Zone property" means property—

(i)(I) which is described in section 168(k)(2)(A)(i), or

(II) which is nonresidential real property or residential rental property,

(ii) substantially all of the use of which is in the Gulf Opportunity Zone and is in the active conduct of a trade or business by the taxpayer in such Zone,

(iii) the original use of which in the Gulf Opportunity Zone commences with the taxpayer on or after August 28, 2005,

(iv) which is acquired by the taxpayer by purchase (as defined in section 179(d)) on or after August 28, 2005, but only if no written binding contract for the acquisition was in effect before August 28, 2005, and

(v) which is placed in service by the taxpayer on or before December 31, 2007 (December 31, 2008, in the case of nonresidential real property and residential rental property).

(B) EXCEPTIONS.—

(i) ALTERNATIVE DEPRECIATION PROPERTY.—Such term shall not include any property described in section 168(k)(2)(D)(i).

(ii) TAX-EXEMPT BOND-FINANCED PROPERTY.—Such term shall not include any property any portion of which is financed with the proceeds of any obligation the interest on which is exempt from tax under section 103.

(iii) QUALIFIED REVITALIZATION BUILDINGS.—Such term shall not include any qualified revitalization building with respect to which the taxpayer has elected the application of paragraph (1) or (2) of section 1400I(a).

(iv) ELECTION OUT.—If a taxpayer makes an election under this clause with respect to any class of property for any taxable year, this subsection shall not apply to all property in such class placed in service during such taxable year.

(3) SPECIAL RULES.—For purposes of this subsection, rules similar to the rules of subparagraph (E) of section 168(k)(2) shall apply, except that such subparagraph shall be applied—

(A) by substituting "August 27, 2005" for "December 31, 2007" each place it appears therein,

(B) without regard to "and before January 1, 2015" in clause (i) thereof, and

(C) by substituting "qualified Gulf Opportunity Zone property" for "qualified property" in clause (iv) thereof.

(4) ALLOWANCE AGAINST ALTERNATIVE MINIMUM TAX.—For purposes of this subsection, rules similar to the rules of section 168(k)(2)(G) shall apply.

(5) RECAPTURE.—For purposes of this subsection, rules similar to the rules under section 179(d)(10) shall apply with respect to any qualified Gulf Opportunity Zone property which ceases to be qualified Gulf Opportunity Zone property.

(6) EXTENSION FOR CERTAIN PROPERTY.—

(A) IN GENERAL.—In the case of any specified Gulf Opportunity Zone extension property, paragraph (2)(A) shall be applied without regard to clause (v) thereof.

(B) SPECIFIED GULF OPPORTUNITY ZONE EXTENSION PROPERTY.—For purposes of this paragraph, the term "specified Gulf Opportunity Zone extension property" means property—

(i) substantially all of the use of which is in one or more specified portions of the GO Zone, and

(ii) which is—

(I) nonresidential real property or residential rental property which is placed in service by the taxpayer on or before December 31, 2011, or

(II) in the case of a taxpayer who places a building described in subclause (I) in service on or before December 31, 2011, property described in section 168(k)(2)(A)(i) if substantially all of the use of such property is in such building and such property is placed in service by the taxpayer not later than 90 days after such building is placed in service.

(C) SPECIFIED PORTIONS OF THE GO ZONE.—For purposes of this paragraph, the term "specified portions of the GO Zone" means those portions of the GO Zone which are in any county or parish which is identified by the Secretary as being a county or parish in which hurricanes occurring during 2005 damaged (in the aggregate) more than 60 percent of the housing units in such county or parish which were occupied (determined according to the 2000 Census).

(D) ONLY PRE-JANUARY 1, 2012, BASIS OF REAL PROPERTY ELIGIBLE FOR ADDITIONAL ALLOWANCE.—In the case of property which is qualified Gulf Opportunity Zone property solely by reason of subparagraph (B)(ii)(I), paragraph (1) shall apply only to the extent of the adjusted basis thereof attributable to manufacture, construction, or production before January 1, 2012.

(E) EXCEPTION FOR BONUS DEPRECIATION PROPERTY UNDER SECTION 168(k).—The term "specified Gulf Opportunity Zone extension property" shall not include any property to which section 168(k) applies.

Amendments

• **2014, Tax Increase Prevention Act of 2014 (P.L. 113-295)**

P.L. 113-295, §125(d)(5), Division A:

Amended Code Sec. 1400N(d)(3)(B) by striking "January 1, 2014" and inserting "January 1, 2015". **Effective** for property placed in service after 12-31-2013, in tax years ending after such date.

• **2013, American Taxpayer Relief Act of 2012 (P.L. 112-240)**

P.L. 112-240, §331(e)(5):

Amended Code Sec. 1400N(d)(3)(B) by striking "January 1, 2013" and inserting "January 1, 2014". **Effective** for property placed in service after 12-31-2012, in tax years ending after such date.

• **2010, Tax Relief, Unemployment Insurance Reauthorization, and Job Creation Act of 2010 (P.L. 111-312)**

P.L. 111-312, §401(d)(7):

Amended Code Sec. 1400N(d)(3)(B) by striking "January 1, 2011" and inserting "January 1, 2013". **Effective** for property placed in service after 12-31-2010, in tax years ending after such date.

P.L. 111-312, §765(a)(1)-(2):

Amended Code Sec. 1400N(d)(6) by striking "December 31, 2010" both places it appears in subparagraph (B) and inserting "December 31, 2011", and by striking "January 1, 2010" in the heading and the text of subparagraph (D) and inserting "January 1, 2012". **Effective** for property placed in service after 12-31-2009.

• **2010, Creating Small Business Jobs Act of 2010 (P.L. 111-240)**

P.L. 111-240, §2022(b)(7):

Amended Code Sec. 1400N(d)(3)(B) by striking "January 1, 2010" and inserting "January 1, 2011". **Effective** for property placed in service after 12-31-2009, in tax years ending after such date.

• **2009, American Recovery and Reinvestment Tax Act of 2009 (P.L. 111-5)**

P.L. 111-5, §1201(a)(2)(E):

Amended Code Sec. 1400N(d)(3)(B) by striking "January 1, 2009" and inserting "January 1, 2010". **Effective** for property placed in service after 12-31-2008, in tax years ending after such date.

• **2008, Housing Assistance Tax Act of 2008 (P.L. 110-289)**

P.L. 110-289, §3082(b)(1):

Amended Code Sec. 1400N(d)(3)(B). **Effective** for property placed in service after 12-31-2007. Prior to amendment, Code Sec. 1400N(d)(3)(B) read as follows:

(B) by substituting "January 1, 2008" for "January 1, 2009" in clause (i) thereof, and

• **2008, Heartland, Habitat, Harvest, and Horticulture Act of 2008 (P.L. 110-246)**

P.L. 110-246, §15345, provides:

SEC. 15345. TEMPORARY TAX RELIEF FOR KIOWA COUNTY, KANSAS AND SURROUNDING AREA.

(a) IN GENERAL.—Subject to the modifications described in this section, the following provisions of or relating to the Internal Revenue Code of 1986 shall apply to the Kansas disaster area in addition to the areas to which such provisions otherwise apply:

(1) Section 1400N(d) of such Code (relating to special allowance for certain property).

(2) Section 1400N(e) of such Code (relating to increase in expensing under section 179).

(3) Section 1400N(f) of such Code (relating to expensing for certain demolition and clean-up costs).

(4) Section 1400N(k) of such Code (relating to treatment of net operating losses attributable to storm losses).

(5) Section 1400N(n) of such Code (relating to treatment of representations regarding income eligibility for purposes of qualified rental project requirements).

(6) Section 1400N(o) of such Code (relating to treatment of public utility property disaster losses).

(7) Section 1400Q of such Code (relating to special rules for use of retirement funds).

(8) Section 1400R(a) of such Code (relating to employee retention credit for employers).

(9) Section 1400S(b) of such Code (relating to suspension of certain limitations on personal casualty losses).

(10) Section 405 of the Katrina Emergency Tax Relief Act of 2005 (relating to extension of replacement period for nonrecognition of gain).

(b) KANSAS DISASTER AREA.—For purposes of this section, the term "Kansas disaster area" means an area with respect to which a major disaster has been declared by the President under section 401 of the Robert T. Stafford Disaster Relief and Emergency Assistance Act (FEMA-1699-DR, as in effect on the date of the enactment of this Act) by reason of severe storms and tornados beginning on May 4, 2007, and determined by the President to warrant individual or individual and public assistance from the Federal Government under such Act with respect to damages attributable to such storms and tornados.

(c) REFERENCES TO AREA OR LOSS.—

(1) AREA.—Any reference in such provisions to the Katrina disaster area or the Gulf Opportunity Zone shall be treated as a reference to the Kansas disaster area.

(2) LOSS.—Any reference in such provisions to any loss or damage attributable to Hurricane Katrina shall be treated as a reference to any loss or damage attributable to the May 4, 2007, storms and tornados.

(d) REFERENCES TO DATES, ETC.—

(1) SPECIAL ALLOWANCE FOR CERTAIN PROPERTY ACQUIRED ON OR AFTER MAY 5, 2007.—Section 1400N(d) of such Code—

(A) by substituting "qualified Recovery Assistance property" for "qualified Gulf Opportunity Zone property" each place it appears,

(B) by substituting "May 5, 2007" for "August 28, 2005" each place it appears,

(C) by substituting "December 31, 2008" for "December 31, 2007" in paragraph (2)(A)(v),

(D) by substituting "December 31, 2009" for "December 31, 2008" in paragraph (2)(A)(v),

(E) by substituting "May 4, 2007" for "August 27, 2005" in paragraph (3)(A),

(F) by substituting "January 1, 2009" for "January 1, 2008" in paragraph (3)(B), and

(G) determined without regard to paragraph (6) thereof.

(2) INCREASE IN EXPENSING UNDER SECTION 179.—Section 1400N(e) of such Code, by substituting "qualified section 179 Recovery Assistance property" for "qualified section 179 Gulf Opportunity Zone property" each place it appears.

(3) EXPENSING FOR CERTAIN DEMOLITION AND CLEAN-UP COSTS.—Section 1400N(f) of such Code—

(A) by substituting "qualified Recovery Assistance clean-up cost" for "qualified Gulf Opportunity Zone clean-up cost" each place it appears, and

(B) by substituting "beginning on May 4, 2007, and ending on December 31, 2009" for "beginning on August 28, 2005, and ending on December 31, 2007" in paragraph (2) thereof.

(4) TREATMENT OF NET OPERATING LOSSES ATTRIBUTABLE TO STORM LOSSES.—Section 1400N(k) of such Code—

(A) by substituting "qualified Recovery Assistance loss" for "qualified Gulf Opportunity Zone loss" each place it appears,

(B) by substituting "after May 3, 2007, and before on January 1, 2010" for "after August 27, 2005, and before January 1, 2008" each place it appears,

(C) by substituting "May 4, 2007" for "August 28, 2005" in paragraph (2)(B)(ii)(I) thereof,

(D) by substituting "qualified Recovery Assistance property" for "qualified Gulf Opportunity Zone property" in paragraph (2)(B)(iv) thereof, and

(E) by substituting "qualified Recovery Assistance casualty loss" for "qualified Gulf Opportunity Zone casualty loss" each place it appears.

(5) SPECIAL RULES FOR USE OF RETIREMENT FUNDS.—Section 1400Q of such Code—

(A) by substituting "qualified Recovery Assistance distribution" for "qualified hurricane distribution" each place it appears,

(B) by substituting "on or after May 4, 2007, and before January 1, 2009" for "on or after August 25, 2005, and before January 1, 2007" in subsection (a)(4)(A)(i),

(C) by substituting "May 4, 2007" for "August 28, 2005" in subsections (a)(4)(A)(i) and (c)(3)(B),

(D) disregarding clauses (ii) and (iii) of subsection (a)(4)(A),

(E) by substituting "qualified storm distribution" for "qualified Katrina distribution" each place it appears,

(F) by substituting "after November 4, 2006, and before May 5, 2007" for "after February 28, 2005, and before August 29, 2005" in subsection (b)(2)(B)(ii),

(G) by substituting "the Kansas disaster area (as defined in section 15345(b) of the Food, Conservation, and Energy Act of 2008) but which was not so purchased or constructed on account of the May 4, 2007, storms and tornados" for "the Hurricane Katrina disaster area, but not so purchased or constructed on account of Hurricane Katrina" in subsection (b)(2)(B)(iii),

(H) by substituting "beginning on May 4, 2007, and ending on the date which is 5 months after the date of the enactment of the Heartland, Habitat, Harvest, and Horticulture Act of 2008" for "beginning on August 25, 2005, and ending on February 28, 2006" in subsection (b)(3)(A),

(I) by substituting "qualified storm individual" for "qualified Hurricane Katrina individual" each place it appears,

(J) by substituting "December 31, 2008" for "December 31, 2006" in subsection (c)(2)(A),

(K) by substituting "beginning on the date of the enactment of the Food, Conservation, and Energy Act of 2008 and ending on December 31, 2008" for "beginning on September 24, 2005, and ending on December 31, 2006" in subsection (c)(4)(A)(i),

(L) by substituting "May 4, 2007" for "August 25, 2005" in subsection (c)(4)(A)(ii), and

(M) by substituting "January 1, 2009" for "January 1, 2007" in subsection (d)(2)(A)(ii).

(6) EMPLOYEE RETENTION CREDIT FOR EMPLOYERS AFFECTED BY MAY 4 STORMS AND TORNADOS.—Section 1400R(a) of the Internal Revenue Code of 1986—

(A) by substituting "May 4, 2007" for "August 28, 2005" each place it appears,

INCOME TAX—DC ENTERPRISE ZONE

(B) by substituting "January 1, 2008" for "January 1, 2006" both places it appears, and

(C) only with respect to eligible employers who employed an average of not more than 200 employees on business days during the taxable year before May 4, 2007.

(7) SUSPENSION OF CERTAIN LIMITATIONS ON PERSONAL CASUALTY LOSSES.—Section 1400S(b)(1) of the Internal Revenue Code of 1986, by substituting "May 4, 2007" for "August 25, 2005".

(8) EXTENSION OF REPLACEMENT PERIOD FOR NONRECOGNITION OF GAIN.—Section 405 of the Katrina Emergency Tax Relief Act of 2005, by substituting "on or after May 4, 2007" for "on or after August 25, 2005".

- **2008, Economic Stimulus Act of 2008 (P.L. 110-185)**

P.L. 110-185, §103(c)(9)(A)-(B):

Amended Code Sec. 1400N(d)(3) by striking "September 10, 2001" in subparagraph (A) and inserting "December 31, 2007", and by striking "January 1, 2005" in subparagraph (B) and inserting "January 1, 2009". **Effective** for property placed in service after 12-31-2007, in tax years ending after such date.

P.L. 110-185, §103(c)(10):

Amended Code Sec. 1400N(d)(6) by adding at the end a new subparagraph (E). **Effective** for property placed in service after 12-31-2007, in tax years ending after such date.

- **2006, Tax Relief and Health Care Act of 2006 (P.L. 109-432)**

P.L. 109-432, Division A, §120(a):

Amended Code Sec. 1400N(d) by adding at the end a new paragraph (6). **Effective** as if included in section 101 of the Gulf Opportunity Zone Act of 2005 (P.L. 109-135) [**effective** for tax years ending on or after 8-28-2005.—CCH].

[Sec. 1400N(e)]

(e) INCREASE IN EXPENSING UNDER SECTION 179.—

(1) IN GENERAL.—For purposes of section 179—

(A) the dollar amount in effect under section 179(b)(1) for the taxable year shall be increased by the lesser of—

(i) $100,000, or

(ii) the cost of qualified section 179 Gulf Opportunity Zone property placed in service during the taxable year, and

(B) the dollar amount in effect under section 179(b)(2) for the taxable year shall be increased by the lesser of—

(i) $600,000, or

(ii) the cost of qualified section 179 Gulf Opportunity Zone property placed in service during the taxable year.

(2) QUALIFIED SECTION 179 GULF OPPORTUNITY ZONE PROPERTY.—For purposes of this subsection—

(A) IN GENERAL.—The term "qualified section 179 Gulf Opportunity Zone property" means section 179 property (as defined in section 179(d)) which is qualified Gulf Opportunity Zone property (as defined in subsection (d)(2) without regard to subsection (d)(6)).

(B) EXTENSION FOR CERTAIN PROPERTY.—In the case of property substantially all of the use of which is in one or more specified portions of the GO Zone (as defined by subsection (d)(6)), such term shall include section 179 property (as so defined) which is described in subsection (d)(2), determined—

(i) without regard to subsection (d)(6), and

(ii) by substituting "2008" for "2007" in subparagraph (A)(v) thereof.

(3) COORDINATION WITH EMPOWERMENT ZONES AND RENEWAL COMMUNITIES.—For purposes of sections 1397A and 1400J, qualified section 179 Gulf Opportunity Zone property shall not be treated as qualified zone property or qualified renewal property, unless the taxpayer elects not to take such qualified section 179 Gulf Opportunity Zone property into account for purposes of this subsection.

(4) RECAPTURE.—For purposes of this subsection, rules similar to the rules under section 179(d)(10) shall apply with respect to any qualified section 179 Gulf Opportunity Zone property which ceases to be qualified section 179 Gulf Opportunity Zone property.

Amendments

- **2008, Heartland, Habitat, Harvest, and Horticulture Act of 2008 (P.L. 110-246)**

P.L. 110-246, §15345, provides:

For a special rule, see Act Sec. 15345 in the amendment notes for Code Sec. 1400N(d).

- **2007, Small Business and Work Opportunity Tax Act of 2007 (P.L. 110-28)**

P.L. 110-28, §8221(1)-(2):

Amended Code Sec. 1400N(e)(2) by striking "this subsection, the term" and inserting "this subsection—"

"(A) IN GENERAL.—The term",

and by adding at the end a new subparagraph (B). **Effective** 5-25-2007.

- **2006, Tax Relief and Health Care Act of 2006 (P.L. 109-432)**

P.L. 109-432, Division A, §120(b):

Amended Code Sec. 1400N(e)(2) by inserting "without regard to subsection (d)(6)" after "subsection (d)(2)". **Effective** as if included in section 101 of the Gulf Opportunity Zone Act of 2005 (P.L. 109-135) [**effective** for tax years ending on or after 8-28-2005.—CCH].

[Sec. 1400N(f)]

(f) EXPENSING FOR CERTAIN DEMOLITION AND CLEAN-UP COSTS.—

(1) IN GENERAL.—A taxpayer may elect to treat 50 percent of any qualified Gulf Opportunity Zone clean-up cost as an expense which is not chargeable to capital account. Any cost so treated shall be allowed as a deduction for the taxable year in which such cost is paid or incurred.

(2) QUALIFIED GULF OPPORTUNITY ZONE CLEAN-UP COST.—For purposes of this subsection, the term "qualified Gulf Opportunity Zone clean-up cost" means any amount paid or incurred during the period beginning on August 28, 2005, and ending on December 31, 2007, for the removal of debris from, or the demolition of structures on, real property which is located in the Gulf Opportunity Zone and which is—

(A) held by the taxpayer for use in a trade or business or for the production of income, or

(B) property described in section 1221(a)(1) in the hands of the taxpayer.

For purposes of the preceding sentence, amounts paid or incurred shall be taken into account only to the extent that such amount would (but for paragraph (1)) be chargeable to capital account.

Amendments

- **2008, Heartland Disaster Tax Relief Act of 2008 (P.L. 110-343)**

P.L. 110-343, Division C, §702, provides:

For a special rule, see Division C, Act Sec. 702, in the amendment notes for Code Sec. 1400N(a).

- **2008, Heartland, Habitat, Harvest, and Horticulture Act of 2008 (P.L. 110-246)**

P.L. 110-246, §15345, provides:

For a special rule, see Act Sec. 15345 in the amendment notes for Code Sec. 1400N(d).

[Sec. 1400N(g)]

(g) EXTENSION OF EXPENSING FOR ENVIRONMENTAL REMEDIATION COSTS.—With respect to any qualified environmental remediation expenditure (as defined in section 198(b)) paid or incurred on or after August 28, 2005, in connection with a qualified contaminated site located in the Gulf Opportunity Zone, section 198 (relating to expensing of environmental remediation costs) shall be applied—

(1) in the case of expenditures paid or incurred on or after August 28, 2005, and before January 1, 2008, by substituting "December 31, 2007" for the date contained in section 198(h), and

(2) except as provided in section 198(d)(2), by treating petroleum products (as defined in section 4612(a)(3)) as a hazardous substance.

Amendments

- **2008, Heartland Disaster Tax Relief Act of 2008 (P.L. 110-343)**

P.L. 110-343, Division C, §702, provides:

For a special rule, see Division C, Act Sec. 702, in the amendment notes for Code Sec. 1400N(a).

[Sec. 1400N(h)]

(h) INCREASE IN REHABILITATION CREDIT.—In the case of qualified rehabilitation expenditures (as defined in section 47(c)) paid or incurred during the period beginning on August 28, 2005, and ending on December 31, 2011, with respect to any qualified rehabilitated building or certified historic structure (as defined in section 47(c)) located in the Gulf Opportunity Zone, subsection (a) of section 47 (relating to rehabilitation credit) shall be applied—

(1) by substituting "13 percent" for "10 percent" in paragraph (1) thereof, and

(2) by substituting "26 percent" for "20 percent" in paragraph (2) thereof.

Amendments

- **2010, Tax Relief, Unemployment Insurance Reauthorization, and Job Creation Act of 2010 (P.L. 111-312)**

P.L. 111-312, §762(a):

Amended Code Sec. 1400N(h) by striking "December 31, 2009" and inserting "December 31, 2011". **Effective** for amounts paid or incurred after 12-31-2009.

- **2008, Tax Extenders and Alternative Minimum Tax Relief Act of 2008 (P.L. 110-343)**

P.L. 110-343, Division C, §320(a):

Amended Code Sec. 1400N(h) by striking "December 31, 2008" and inserting "December 31, 2009". **Effective** for expenditures paid or incurred after 10-3-2008.

- **2008, Heartland Disaster Tax Relief Act of 2008 (P.L. 110-343)**

P.L. 110-343, Division C, §702, provides:

For a special rule, see Division C, Act Sec. 702, in the amendment notes for Code Sec. 1400N(a).

[Sec. 1400N(i)]

(i) SPECIAL RULES FOR SMALL TIMBER PRODUCERS.—

(1) INCREASED EXPENSING FOR QUALIFIED TIMBER PROPERTY.—In the case of qualified timber property any portion of which is located in the Gulf Opportunity Zone, in that portion of the Rita GO Zone which is not part of the Gulf Opportunity Zone, or in the Wilma GO Zone, the limitation under subparagraph (B) of section 194(b)(1) shall be increased by the lesser of—

(A) the limitation which would (but for this subsection) apply under such subparagraph, or

Sec. 1400N—Stricken

(B) the amount of reforestation expenditures (as defined in section 194(c)(3)) paid or incurred by the taxpayer with respect to such qualified timber property during the specified portion of the taxable year.

(2) 5 YEAR NOL CARRYBACK OF CERTAIN TIMBER LOSSES.—For purposes of determining any farming loss under section 172(i), income and deductions which are allocable to the specified portion of the taxable year and which are attributable to qualified timber property any portion of which is located in the Gulf Opportunity Zone, in that portion of the Rita GO Zone which is not part of the Gulf Opportunity Zone, or in the Wilma GO Zone shall be treated as attributable to farming businesses.

(3) RULES NOT APPLICABLE TO CERTAIN ENTITIES.—Paragraphs (1) and (2) shall not apply to any taxpayer which—

(A) is a corporation the stock of which is publicly traded on an established securities market, or

(B) is a real estate investment trust.

(4) RULES NOT APPLICABLE TO LARGE TIMBER PRODUCERS.—

(A) EXPENSING.—Paragraph (1) shall not apply to any taxpayer if such taxpayer holds more than 500 acres of qualified timber property at any time during the taxable year.

(B) NOL CARRYBACK.—Paragraph (2) shall not apply with respect to any qualified timber property unless—

(i) such property was held by the taxpayer—

(I) on August 28, 2005, in the case of qualified timber property any portion of which is located in the Gulf Opportunity Zone,

(II) on September 23, 2005, in the case of qualified timber property (other than property described in subclause (I)) any portion of which is located in that portion of the Rita GO Zone which is not part of the Gulf Opportunity Zone, or

(III) on October 23, 2005, in the case of qualified timber property (other than property described in subclause (I) or (II)) any portion of which is located in the Wilma GO Zone, and

(ii) such taxpayer held not more than 500 acres of qualified timber property on such date.

(5) DEFINITIONS.—For purposes of this subsection—

(A) SPECIFIED PORTION.—

(i) IN GENERAL.—The term "specified portion" means—

(I) in the case of qualified timber property any portion of which is located in the Gulf Opportunity Zone, that portion of the taxable year which is on or after August 28, 2005, and before the termination date,

(II) in the case of qualified timber property (other than property described in clause (i)) any portion of which is located in the Rita GO Zone, that portion of the taxable year which is on or after September 23, 2005, and before the termination date, or

(III) in the case of qualified timber property (other than property described in clause (i) or (ii)) any portion of which is located in the Wilma GO Zone, that portion of the taxable year which is on or after October 23, 2005, and before the termination date.

(ii) TERMINATION DATE.—The term "termination date" means—

(I) for purposes of paragraph (1), January 1, 2008, and

(II) for purposes of paragraph (2), January 1, 2007.

(B) QUALIFIED TIMBER PROPERTY.—The term "qualified timber property" has the meaning given such term in section 194(c)(1).

[Sec. 1400N(j)]

(j) SPECIAL RULE FOR GULF OPPORTUNITY ZONE PUBLIC UTILITY CASUALTY LOSSES.—

(1) IN GENERAL.—The amount described in section 172(f)(1)(A) for any taxable year shall be increased by the Gulf Opportunity Zone public utility casualty loss for such taxable year.

(2) GULF OPPORTUNITY ZONE PUBLIC UTILITY CASUALTY LOSS.—For purposes of this subsection, the term "Gulf Opportunity Zone public utility casualty loss" means any casualty loss of public utility property (as defined in section 168(i)(10)) located in the Gulf Opportunity Zone if—

(A) such loss is allowed as a deduction under section 165 for the taxable year,

(B) such loss is by reason of Hurricane Katrina, and

(C) the taxpayer elects the application of this subsection with respect to such loss.

(3) REDUCTION FOR GAINS FROM INVOLUNTARY CONVERSION.—The amount of any Gulf Opportunity Zone public utility casualty loss which would (but for this paragraph) be taken into account under paragraph (1) for any taxable year shall be reduced by the amount of any gain recognized by the taxpayer for such year from the involuntary conversion by reason of Hurricane Katrina of public utility property (as so defined) located in the Gulf Opportunity Zone.

(4) COORDINATION WITH GENERAL DISASTER LOSS RULES.—Subsection (k) and section 165(i) shall not apply to any Gulf Opportunity Zone public utility casualty loss to the extent such loss is taken into account under paragraph (1).

(5) ELECTION.—Any election under paragraph (2)(C) shall be made in such manner as may be prescribed by the Secretary and shall be made by the due date (including extensions of time) for filing the taxpayer's return for the taxable year of the loss. Such election, once made for any taxable year, shall be irrevocable for such taxable year.

[Sec. 1400N(k)]

(k) TREATMENT OF NET OPERATING LOSSES ATTRIBUTABLE TO GULF OPPORTUNITY ZONE LOSSES.—

(1) IN GENERAL.—If a portion of any net operating loss of the taxpayer for any taxable year is a qualified Gulf Opportunity Zone loss, the following rules shall apply:

(A) EXTENSION OF CARRYBACK PERIOD.—Section 172(b)(1) shall be applied with respect to such portion—

(i) by substituting "5 taxable years" for "2 taxable years" in subparagraph (A)(i), and

(ii) by not taking such portion into account in determining any eligible loss of the taxpayer under subparagraph (F) thereof for the taxable year.

(B) SUSPENSION OF 90 PERCENT AMT LIMITATION.—Section 56(d)(1) shall be applied by increasing the amount determined under subparagraph (A)(ii)(I) thereof by the sum of the carrybacks and carryovers of any net operating loss attributable to such portion.

(2) QUALIFIED GULF OPPORTUNITY ZONE LOSS.—For purposes of paragraph (1), the term "qualified Gulf Opportunity Zone loss" means the lesser of—

(A) the excess of—

(i) the net operating loss for such taxable year, over

(ii) the specified liability loss for such taxable year to which a 10-year carryback applies under section 172(b)(1)(C), or

(B) the aggregate amount of the following deductions to the extent taken into account in computing the net operating loss for such taxable year:

(i) Any deduction for any qualified Gulf Opportunity Zone casualty loss.

(ii) Any deduction for moving expenses paid or incurred after August 27, 2005, and before January 1, 2008, and allowable under this chapter to any taxpayer in connection with the employment of any individual—

(I) whose principal place of abode was located in the Gulf Opportunity Zone before August 28, 2005,

(II) who was unable to remain in such abode as the result of Hurricane Katrina, and

(III) whose principal place of employment with the taxpayer after such expense is located in the Gulf Opportunity Zone.

For purposes of this clause, the term "moving expenses" has the meaning given such term by section 217(b), except that the taxpayer's former residence and new residence may be the same residence if the initial vacating of the residence was as the result of Hurricane Katrina.

(iii) Any deduction allowable under this chapter for expenses paid or incurred after August 27, 2005, and before January 1, 2008, to temporarily house any employee of the taxpayer whose principal place of employment is in the Gulf Opportunity Zone.

(iv) Any deduction for depreciation (or amortization in lieu of depreciation) allowable under this chapter with respect to any qualified Gulf Opportunity Zone property (as defined in subsection (d)(2), but without regard to subparagraph (B)(iv) thereof)) for the taxable year such property is placed in service.

(v) Any deduction allowable under this chapter for repair expenses (including expenses for removal of debris) paid or incurred after August 27, 2005, and before January 1, 2008, with respect to any damage attributable to Hurricane Katrina and in connection with property which is located in the Gulf Opportunity Zone.

(3) QUALIFIED GULF OPPORTUNITY ZONE CASUALTY LOSS.—

(A) IN GENERAL.—For purposes of paragraph (2)(B)(i), the term "qualified Gulf Opportunity Zone casualty loss" means any uncompensated section 1231 loss (as defined in section 1231(a)(3)(B)) of property located in the Gulf Opportunity Zone if—

(i) such loss is allowed as a deduction under section 165 for the taxable year, and

(ii) such loss is by reason of Hurricane Katrina.

(B) REDUCTION FOR GAINS FROM INVOLUNTARY CONVERSION.—The amount of qualified Gulf Opportunity Zone casualty loss which would (but for this subparagraph) be taken into account under subparagraph (A) for any taxable year shall be reduced by the amount of any gain recognized by the taxpayer for such year from the involuntary conversion by reason of Hurricane Katrina of property located in the Gulf Opportunity Zone.

(C) COORDINATION WITH GENERAL DISASTER LOSS RULES.—Section 165(i) shall not apply to any qualified Gulf Opportunity Zone casualty loss to the extent such loss is taken into account under this subsection.

(4) SPECIAL RULES.—For purposes of paragraph (1), rules similar to the rules of paragraphs (2) and (3) of section 172(i) shall apply with respect to such portion.

Amendments

• 2008, Heartland Disaster Tax Relief Act of 2008 (P.L. 110-343)

P.L. 110-343, Division C, §702, provides:

For a special rule, see Division C, Act Sec. 702, in the amendment notes for Code Sec. 1400N(a).

• 2008, Heartland, Habitat, Harvest, and Horticulture Act of 2008 (P.L. 110-246)

P.L. 110-246, §15345, provides:

For a special rule, see Act Sec. 15345 in the amendment notes for Code Sec. 1400N(d).

[Sec. 1400N(l)]

(l) CREDIT TO HOLDERS OF GULF TAX CREDIT BONDS.—

(1) ALLOWANCE OF CREDIT.—If a taxpayer holds a Gulf tax credit bond on one or more credit allowance dates of the bond occurring during any taxable year, there shall be allowed as a credit against the tax imposed by this chapter for the taxable year an amount equal to the sum of the credits determined under paragraph (2) with respect to such dates.

(2) AMOUNT OF CREDIT.—

(A) IN GENERAL.—The amount of the credit determined under this paragraph with respect to any credit allowance date for a Gulf tax credit bond is 25 percent of the annual credit determined with respect to such bond.

(B) ANNUAL CREDIT.—The annual credit determined with respect to any Gulf tax credit bond is the product of—

(i) the credit rate determined by the Secretary under subparagraph (C) for the day on which such bond was sold, multiplied by

(ii) the outstanding face amount of the bond.

INCOME TAX—DC ENTERPRISE ZONE

(C) DETERMINATION.—For purposes of subparagraph (B), with respect to any Gulf tax credit bond, the Secretary shall determine daily or cause to be determined daily a credit rate which shall apply to the first day on which there is a binding, written contract for the sale or exchange of the bond. The credit rate for any day is the credit rate which the Secretary or the Secretary's designee estimates will permit the issuance of Gulf tax credit bonds with a specified maturity or redemption date without discount and without interest cost to the issuer.

(D) CREDIT ALLOWANCE DATE.—For purposes of this subsection, the term "credit allowance date" means March 15, June 15, September 15, and December 15. Such term also includes the last day on which the bond is outstanding.

(E) SPECIAL RULE FOR ISSUANCE AND REDEMPTION.—In the case of a bond which is issued during the 3-month period ending on a credit allowance date, the amount of the credit determined under this paragraph with respect to such credit allowance date shall be a ratable portion of the credit otherwise determined based on the portion of the 3-month period during which the bond is outstanding. A similar rule shall apply when the bond is redeemed or matures.

(3) LIMITATION BASED ON AMOUNT OF TAX.—The credit allowed under paragraph (1) for any taxable year shall not exceed the excess of—

(A) the sum of the regular tax liability (as defined in section 26(b)) plus the tax imposed by section 55, over

(B) the sum of the credits allowable under part IV of subchapter A (other than subparts C, I, and J and this subsection).

(4) GULF TAX CREDIT BOND.—For purposes of this subsection—

(A) IN GENERAL.—The term "Gulf tax credit bond" means any bond issued as part of an issue if—

(i) the bond is issued by the State of Alabama, Louisiana, or Mississippi,

(ii) 95 percent or more of the proceeds of such issue are to be used to—

(I) pay principal, interest, or premiums on qualified bonds issued by such State or any political subdivision of such State, or

(II) make a loan to any political subdivision of such State to pay principal, interest, or premiums on qualified bonds issued by such political subdivision,

(iii) the Governor of such State designates such bond for purposes of this subsection,

(iv) the bond is a general obligation of such State and is in registered form (within the meaning of section 149(a)),

(v) the maturity of such bond does not exceed 2 years, and

(vi) the bond is issued after December 31, 2005, and before January 1, 2007.

(B) STATE MATCHING REQUIREMENT.—A bond shall not be treated as a Gulf tax credit bond unless—

(i) the issuer of such bond pledges as of the date of the issuance of the issue an amount equal to the face amount of such bond to be used for payments described in subclause (I) of subparagraph (A)(ii), or loans described in subclause (II) of such subparagraph, as the case may be, with respect to the issue of which such bond is a part, and

(ii) any such payment or loan is made in equal amounts from the proceeds of such issue and from the amount pledged under clause (i).

The requirement of clause (ii) shall be treated as met with respect to any such payment or loan made during the 1-year period beginning on the date of the issuance (or any successor 1-year period) if such requirement is met when applied with respect to the aggregate amount of such payments and loans made during such period.

(C) AGGREGATE LIMIT ON BOND DESIGNATIONS.—The maximum aggregate face amount of bonds which may be designated under this subsection by the Governor of a State shall not exceed—

(i) $200,000,000 in the case of the State of Louisiana,

(ii) $100,000,000 in the case of the State of Mississippi, and

(iii) $50,000,000 in the case of the State of Alabama.

(D) SPECIAL RULES RELATING TO ARBITRAGE.—A bond which is part of an issue shall not be treated as a Gulf tax credit bond unless, with respect to the issue of which the bond is a part, the issuer satisfies the arbitrage requirements of section 148 with respect to proceeds of the issue and any loans made with such proceeds.

(5) QUALIFIED BOND.—For purposes of this subsection—

(A) IN GENERAL.—The term "qualified bond" means any obligation of a State or political subdivision thereof which was outstanding on August 28, 2005.

(B) EXCEPTION FOR PRIVATE ACTIVITY BONDS.—Such term shall not include any private activity bond.

(C) EXCEPTION FOR ADVANCE REFUNDINGS.—Such term shall not include any bond with respect to which there is any outstanding refunded or refunding bond during the period in which a Gulf tax credit bond is outstanding with respect to such bond.

(D) USE OF PROCEEDS REQUIREMENT.—Such term shall not include any bond issued as part of an issue if any portion of the proceeds of such issue was (or is to be) used to provide any property described in section 144(c)(6)(B).

(6) CREDIT INCLUDED IN GROSS INCOME.—Gross income includes the amount of the credit allowed to the taxpayer under this subsection (determined without regard to paragraph (3)) and the amount so included shall be treated as interest income.

(7) OTHER DEFINITIONS AND SPECIAL RULES.—For purposes of this subsection—

(A) BOND.—The term "bond" includes any obligation.

(B) PARTNERSHIP; S CORPORATION; AND OTHER PASS-THRU ENTITIES.—

(i) IN GENERAL.—Under regulations prescribed by the Secretary, in the case of a partnership, trust, S corporation, or other pass-thru entity, rules similar to the rules of section 41(g) shall apply with respect to the credit allowable under paragraph (1).

(ii) NO BASIS ADJUSTMENT.—In the case of a bond held by a partnership or an S corporation, rules similar to the rules under section 1397E(l) shall apply.

(C) BONDS HELD BY REGULATED INVESTMENT COMPANIES.—If any Gulf tax credit bond is held by a regulated investment company, the credit determined under paragraph (1) shall be allowed to shareholders of such company under procedures prescribed by the Secretary.

(D) REPORTING.—Issuers of Gulf tax credit bonds shall submit reports similar to the reports required under section 149(e).

(E) CREDIT TREATED AS NONREFUNDABLE BONDHOLDER CREDIT.—For purposes of this title, the credit allowed by this subsection shall be treated as a credit allowable under subpart H of part IV of subchapter A of this chapter.

Amendments

• **2009, American Recovery and Reinvestment Tax Act of 2009 (P.L. 111-5)**

P.L. 111-5, §1531(c)(3):

Amended Code Sec. 1400N(l)(3)(B) by striking "and I" and inserting ", I, and J". **Effective** for obligations issued after 2-17-2009.

• **2008, Heartland Disaster Tax Relief Act of 2008 (P.L. 110-343)**

P.L. 110-343, Division C, §702, provides:

For a special rule, see Division C, Act Sec. 702, in the amendment notes for Code Sec. 1400N(a).

• **2008, Heartland, Habitat, Harvest, and Horticulture Act of 2008 (P.L. 110-246)**

P.L. 110-246, §15316(c)(1):

Amended Code Sec. 1400N(l)(3)(B) by striking "subpart C" and inserting "subparts C and I". **Effective** for obligations issued after 5-22-2008.

• **2006, Tax Relief and Health Care Act of 2006 (P.L. 109-432)**

P.L. 109-432, Division A, §107(b)(2):

Amended Code Sec. 1400N(l)(7)(B)(ii) by striking "section 1397E(i)" and inserting "section 1397E(l)". **Effective** for obligations issued after 12-20-2006 pursuant to allocations of the national zone academy bond limitation for calendar years after 2005.

[Sec. 1400N(m)]

(m) APPLICATION OF NEW MARKETS TAX CREDIT TO INVESTMENTS IN COMMUNITY DEVELOPMENT ENTITIES SERVING GULF OPPORTUNITY ZONE.—For purposes of section 45D—

(1) a qualified community development entity shall be eligible for an allocation under subsection (f)(2) thereof of the increase in the new markets tax credit limitation described in paragraph (2) only if a significant mission of such entity is the recovery and redevelopment of the Gulf Opportunity Zone,

(2) the new markets tax credit limitation otherwise determined under subsection (f)(1) thereof shall be increased by an amount equal to—

(A) $300,000,000 for 2005 and 2006, to be allocated among qualified community development entities to make qualified low-income community investments within the Gulf Opportunity Zone, and

(B) $400,000,000 for 2007, to be so allocated, and

(3) subsection (f)(3) thereof shall be applied separately with respect to the amount of the increase under paragraph (2).

[Sec. 1400N(n)]

(n) TREATMENT OF REPRESENTATIONS REGARDING INCOME ELIGIBILITY FOR PURPOSES OF QUALIFIED RESIDENTIAL RENTAL PROJECT REQUIREMENTS.—For purposes of determining if any residential rental project meets the requirements of section 142(d)(1) and if any certification with respect to such project meets the requirements under section 142(d)(7), the operator of the project may rely on the representations of any individual applying for tenancy in such project that such individual's income will not exceed the applicable income limits of section 142(d)(1) upon commencement of the individual's tenancy if such tenancy begins during the 6-month period beginning on and after the date such individual was displaced by reason of Hurricane Katrina.

Amendments

• **2008, Heartland Disaster Tax Relief Act of 2008 (P.L. 110-343)**

P.L. 110-343, Division C, §702, provides:

For a special rule, see Division C, Act Sec. 702, in the amendment notes for Code Sec. 1400N(a).

• **2008, Heartland, Habitat, Harvest, and Horticulture Act of 2008 (P.L. 110-246)**

P.L. 110-246, §15345, provides:

For a special rule, see Act Sec. 15345 in the amendment notes for Code Sec. 1400N(d).

[Sec. 1400N(o)]

(o) TREATMENT OF PUBLIC UTILITY PROPERTY DISASTER LOSSES.—

(1) IN GENERAL.—Upon the election of the taxpayer, in the case of any eligible public utility property loss—

(A) section 165(i) shall be applied by substituting "the fifth taxable year immediately preceding" for "the taxable year immediately preceding",

(B) an application for a tentative carryback adjustment of the tax for any prior taxable year affected by the application of subparagraph (A) may be made under section 6411, and

(C) section 6611 shall not apply to any overpayment attributable to such loss.

(2) ELIGIBLE PUBLIC UTILITY PROPERTY LOSS.—For purposes of this subsection—

(A) IN GENERAL.—The term "eligible public utility property loss" means any loss with respect to public utility property located in the Gulf Opportunity Zone and attributable to Hurricane Katrina.

(B) PUBLIC UTILITY PROPERTY.—The term "public utility property" has the meaning given such term by section 168(i)(10) without regard to the matter following subparagraph (D) thereof.

Sec. 1400N—Stricken

INCOME TAX—DC ENTERPRISE ZONE

(3) WAIVER OF LIMITATIONS.—If refund or credit of any overpayment of tax resulting from the application of paragraph (1) is prevented at any time before the close of the 1-year period beginning on the date of the enactment of this section by the operation of any law or rule of law (including res judicata), such refund or credit may nevertheless be made or allowed if claim therefor is filed before the close of such period.

Amendments

• **2008, Heartland, Habitat, Harvest, and Horticulture Act of 2008 (P.L. 110-246)**

P.L. 110-246, §15345, provides:

For a special rule, see Act Sec. 15345 in the amendment notes for Code Sec. 1400N(d).

[Sec. 1400N(p)]

(p) TAX BENEFITS NOT AVAILABLE WITH RESPECT TO CERTAIN PROPERTY.—

(1) QUALIFIED GULF OPPORTUNITY ZONE PROPERTY.—For purposes of subsections (d), (e), and (k)(2)(B)(iv), the term "qualified Gulf Opportunity Zone property" shall not include any property described in paragraph (3).

(2) QUALIFIED GULF OPPORTUNITY ZONE CASUALTY LOSSES.—For purposes of subsection (k)(2)(B)(i), the term "qualified Gulf Opportunity Zone casualty loss" shall not include any loss with respect to any property described in paragraph (3).

(3) PROPERTY DESCRIBED.—

(A) IN GENERAL.—For purposes of this subsection, property is described in this paragraph if such property is—

(i) any property used in connection with any private or commercial golf course, country club, massage parlor, hot tub facility, suntan facility, or any store the principal business of which is the sale of alcoholic beverages for consumption off premises, or

(ii) any gambling or animal racing property.

(B) GAMBLING OR ANIMAL RACING PROPERTY.—For purposes of subparagraph (A)(ii)—

(i) IN GENERAL.—The term "gambling or animal racing property" means—

(I) any equipment, furniture, software, or other property used directly in connection with gambling, the racing of animals, or the on-site viewing of such racing, and

(II) the portion of any real property (determined by square footage) which is dedicated to gambling, the racing of animals, or the on-site viewing of such racing.

(ii) DE MINIMIS PORTION.—Clause (i)(II) shall not apply to any real property if the portion so dedicated is less than 100 square feet.

Amendments

• **2008, Heartland Disaster Tax Relief Act of 2008 (P.L. 110-343)**

P.L. 110-343, Division C, §702, provides:

For a special rule, see Division C, Act Sec. 702, in the amendment notes for Code Sec. 1400N(a).

[Sec. 1400O—Stricken]

Amendments

• **2018, Tax Technical Corrections Act of 2018 (P.L. 115-141)**

P.L. 115-141, §401(d)(6)(A), Div. U:

Amended chapter 1 by striking subchapter Y (Code Secs. 1400L-1400U-3). **Effective** 3-23-2018. For a special rule, see Act Sec. 401(e), below. Prior to being stricken, Code Sec. 1400O read as follows:

SEC. 1400O. EDUCATION TAX BENEFITS.

In the case of an individual who attends an eligible educational institution (as defined in section 25A(f)(2)) located in the Gulf Opportunity Zone for any taxable year beginning during 2005 or 2006—

(1) in applying section 25A, the term "qualified tuition and related expenses" shall include any costs which are qualified higher education expenses (as defined in section 529(e)(3)),

(2) each of the dollar amounts in effect under subparagraphs (A) and (B) of section 25A(b)(1) shall be twice the amount otherwise in effect before the application of this subsection, and

(3) section 25A(c)(1) shall be applied by substituting "40 percent" for "20 percent".

Amendments

• **2008, Heartland Disaster Tax Relief Act of 2008 (P.L. 110-343)**

P.L. 110-343, Division C, §702, provides:

For a special rule, see Division C, Act Sec. 702, in the amendment notes for Code Sec. 1400N(a).

• **2005, Gulf Opportunity Zone Act of 2005 (P.L. 109-135)**

P.L. 109-135, §101(a):

Amended subchapter Y of chapter 1 by adding at the end a new part II (Code Secs. 1400M and 1400N). **Effective**, generally, for tax years ending on or after 8-28-2005. For a special rule, see Act Sec. 101(c)(2), below.

P.L. 109-135, §101(c)(2), provides:

(2) CARRYBACKS.—Subsections (i)(2), (j), and (k) of section 1400N of the Internal Revenue Code of 1986 (as added by this section) shall apply to losses arising in such taxable years.

P.L. 115-141, §401(d)(6)(C)(vii)-(xiv), Div. U, provides:

(C) SAVINGS PROVISIONS.—The amendments made by this paragraph shall not apply to—

* * *

(vii) in the case of the repeal of section 1400N(a) of such Code, obligations issued before January 1, 2012,

(viii) in the case of the repeal of section 1400N(b) of such Code, advanced refundings before January 1, 2011,

(ix) in the case of the repeal of section 1400N(d) of such Code, property placed in service before January 1, 2012,

(x) in the case of the repeal of section 1400N(e) of such Code, property placed in service before January 1, 2009,

(xi) in the case of the repeal of subsections (f) and (g) of section 1400N of such Code, amounts paid or incurred before January 1, 2008,

(xii) in the case of the repeal of section 1400N(h) of such Code, amounts paid or incurred before January 1, 2012,

(xiii) in the case of the repeal of section 1400N(k)(1)(B) of such Code, losses arising in taxable years beginning before January 1, 2008,

(xiv) in the case of the repeal of section 1400N(l) of such Code, bonds issued before January 1, 2007,

P.L. 115-141, §401(e), Div. U, provides:

(e) GENERAL SAVINGS PROVISION WITH RESPECT TO DEADWOOD PROVISIONS.—If—

(1) any provision amended or repealed by the amendments made by subsection (b) or (d) applied to—

(A) any transaction occurring before the date of the enactment of this Act,

(B) any property acquired before such date of enactment, or

(C) any item of income, loss, deduction, or credit taken into account before such date of enactment, and

(2) the treatment of such transaction, property, or item under such provision would (without regard to the amendments or repeals made by such subsection) affect the liability for tax for periods ending after such date of enactment,

nothing in the amendments or repeals made by this section shall be construed to affect the treatment of such transaction, property, or item for purposes of determining liability for tax for periods ending after such date of enactment.

• **2007, Tax Technical Corrections Act of 2007 (P.L. 110-172)**

P.L. 110-172, §11(a)(26):

Amended Code Sec. 1400O(2) by striking "under of" and inserting "under". **Effective** 12-29-2007.

• **2005, Gulf Opportunity Zone Act of 2005 (P.L. 109-135)**

P.L. 109-135, §102(a):

Amended part II of subchapter Y of chapter 1 by adding at the end a new Code Sec. 1400O. **Effective** 12-21-2005.

P.L. 115-141, §401(e), Div. U, provides:

(e) GENERAL SAVINGS PROVISION WITH RESPECT TO DEADWOOD PROVISIONS.—If—

(1) any provision amended or repealed by the amendments made by subsection (b) or (d) applied to—

(A) any transaction occurring before the date of the enactment of this Act,

(B) any property acquired before such date of enactment, or

(C) any item of income, loss, deduction, or credit taken into account before such date of enactment, and

(2) the treatment of such transaction, property, or item under such provision would (without regard to the amendments or repeals made by such subsection) affect the liability for tax for periods ending after such date of enactment,

nothing in the amendments or repeals made by this section shall be construed to affect the treatment of such transaction, property, or item for purposes of determining liability for tax for periods ending after such date of enactment.

[Sec. 1400P—Stricken]

Amendments

• **2018, Tax Technical Corrections Act of 2018 (P.L. 115-141)**

P.L. 115-141, §401(d)(6)(A), Div. U:

Amended chapter 1 by striking subchapter Y (Code Secs. 1400L-1400U-3). **Effective** 3-23-2018. For a special rule, see Act Sec. 401(e), below. Prior to being stricken, Code Sec. 1400P read as follows:

SEC. 1400P. HOUSING TAX BENEFITS.

[Sec. 1400P(a)]

(a) EXCLUSION OF EMPLOYER PROVIDED HOUSING FOR INDIVIDUAL AFFECTED BY HURRICANE KATRINA.—

(1) IN GENERAL.—Gross income of a qualified employee shall not include the value of any lodging furnished in-kind to such employee (and such employee's spouse or any of such employee's dependents) by or on behalf of a qualified employer for any month during the taxable year.

(2) LIMITATION.—The amount which may be excluded under paragraph (1) for any month for which lodging is furnished during the taxable year shall not exceed $600.

(3) TREATMENT OF EXCLUSION.—The exclusion under paragraph (1) shall be treated as an exclusion under section 119 (other than for purposes of sections 3121(a)(19) and 3306(b)(14)).

[Sec. 1400P(b)]

(b) EMPLOYER CREDIT FOR HOUSING EMPLOYEES AFFECTED BY HURRICANE KATRINA.—For purposes of section 38, in the case of a qualified employer, the Hurricane Katrina housing credit for any month during the taxable year is an amount equal to 30 percent of any amount which is excludable from the gross income of a qualified

INCOME TAX—DC ENTERPRISE ZONE

employee of such employer under subsection (a) and not otherwise excludable under section 119.

[Sec. 1400P(c)]

(c) QUALIFIED EMPLOYEE.—For purposes of this section, the term "qualified employee" means, with respect to any month, an individual—

(1) who had a principal residence (as defined in section 121) in the Gulf Opportunity Zone on August 28, 2005, and

(2) who performs substantially all employment services—

(A) in the Gulf Opportunity Zone, and

(B) for the qualified employer which furnishes lodging to such individual.

[Sec. 1400P(d)]

(d) QUALIFIED EMPLOYER.—For purposes of this section, the term "qualified employer" means any employer with a trade or business located in the Gulf Opportunity Zone.

[Sec. 1400P(e)]

(e) CERTAIN RULES TO APPLY.—For purposes of this subsection, rules similar to the rules of sections 51(i)(1) and 52 shall apply.

[Sec. 1400P(f)]

(f) APPLICATION OF SECTION.—This section shall apply to lodging furnished during the period—

(1) beginning on the first day of the first month beginning after the date of the enactment of this section, and

(2) ending on the date which is 6 months after the first day described in paragraph (1).

Amendments

• 2019, Taxpayer Certainty and Disaster Tax Relief Act of 2019 (P.L. 116-94)

P.L. 116-94, §§ 201-202, Div. Q, provides:

SEC. 201. DEFINITIONS.

For purposes of this title—

(1) QUALIFIED DISASTER AREA.—

(A) IN GENERAL.—The term "qualified disaster area" means any area with respect to which a major disaster was declared, during the period beginning on January 1, 2018, and ending on the date which is 60 days after the date of the enactment of this Act, by the President under section 401 of the Robert T. Stafford Disaster Relief and Emergency Assistance Act if the incident period of the disaster with respect to which such declaration is made begins on or before the date of the enactment of this Act.

(B) DENIAL OF DOUBLE BENEFIT.—Such term shall not include the California wildfire disaster area (as defined in section 20101 of subdivision 2 of division B of the Bipartisan Budget Act of 2018).

(2) QUALIFIED DISASTER ZONE.—The term "qualified disaster zone" means that portion of any qualified disaster area which was determined by the President, during the period beginning on January 1, 2018, and ending on the date which is 60 days after the date of the enactment of this Act, to warrant individual or individual and public assistance from the Federal Government under the Robert T. Stafford Disaster Relief and Emergency Assistance Act by reason of the qualified disaster with respect to such disaster area.

(3) QUALIFIED DISASTER.—The term "qualified disaster" means, with respect to any qualified disaster area, the disaster by reason of which a major disaster was declared with respect to such area.

(4) INCIDENT PERIOD.—The term "incident period" means, with respect to any qualified disaster, the period specified by the Federal Emergency Management Agency as the period during which such disaster occurred (except that for purposes of this title such period shall not be treated as beginning before January 1, 2018, or ending after the date which is 30 days after the date of the enactment of this Act).

SEC. 202. SPECIAL DISASTER-RELATED RULES FOR USE OF RETIREMENT FUNDS.

(a) TAX-FAVORED WITHDRAWALS FROM RETIREMENT PLANS.—

(1) IN GENERAL.—Section 72(t) of the Internal Revenue Code of 1986 shall not apply to any qualified disaster distribution.

(2) AGGREGATE DOLLAR LIMITATION.—

(A) IN GENERAL.—For purposes of this subsection, the aggregate amount of distributions received by an individual which may be treated as qualified disaster distributions for any taxable year shall not exceed the excess (if any) of—

(i) $100,000, over

(ii) the aggregate amounts treated as qualified disaster distributions received by such individual for all prior taxable years.

(B) TREATMENT OF PLAN DISTRIBUTIONS.—If a distribution to an individual would (without regard to subparagraph (A)) be a qualified disaster distribution, a plan shall not be treated as violating any requirement of the Internal Revenue Code of 1986 merely because the plan treats such distribution as a qualified disaster distribution, unless the aggregate amount of such distributions from all plans maintained by the employer (and any member of any controlled group which includes the employer) to such individual exceeds $100,000.

(C) CONTROLLED GROUP.—For purposes of subparagraph (B), the term "controlled group" means any group treated as a single employer under subsection (b), (c), (m), or (o) of section 414 of the Internal Revenue Code of 1986.

(D) SPECIAL RULE FOR INDIVIDUALS AFFECTED BY MORE THAN ONE DISASTER.—The limitation of subparagraph (A) shall be applied separately with respect to distributions made with respect to each qualified disaster.

(3) AMOUNT DISTRIBUTED MAY BE REPAID.—

(A) IN GENERAL.—Any individual who receives a qualified disaster distribution may, at any time during the 3-year period beginning on the day after the date on

Amendments

• 2008, Heartland Disaster Tax Relief Act of 2008 (P.L. 110-343)

P.L. 110-343, Division C, § 702, provides:

For a special rule, see Division C, Act Sec. 702, in the amendment notes for Code Sec. 1400N(a).

• 2005, Gulf Opportunity Zone Act of 2005 (P.L. 109-135)

P.L. 109-135, § 103(a):

Amended part II of subchapter Y of chapter 1 by adding at the end a new Code Sec. 1400P. **Effective** 12-21-2005.

P.L. 115-141, § 401(e), Div. U, provides:

(e) GENERAL SAVINGS PROVISION WITH RESPECT TO DEADWOOD PROVISIONS.—If—

(1) any provision amended or repealed by the amendments made by subsection (b) or (d) applied to—

(A) any transaction occurring before the date of the enactment of this Act,

(B) any property acquired before such date of enactment, or

(C) any item of income, loss, deduction, or credit taken into account before such date of enactment, and

(2) the treatment of such transaction, property, or item under such provision would (without regard to the amendments or repeals made by such subsection) affect the liability for tax for periods ending after such date of enactment,

nothing in the amendments or repeals made by this section shall be construed to affect the treatment of such transaction, property, or item for purposes of determining liability for tax for periods ending after such date of enactment.

[Sec. 1400Q—Stricken]

which such distribution was received, make 1 or more contributions in an aggregate amount not to exceed the amount of such distribution to an eligible retirement plan of which such individual is a beneficiary and to which a rollover contribution of such distribution could be made under section 402(c), 403(a)(4), 403(b)(8), 408(d)(3), or 457(e)(16), [sic] of the Internal Revenue Code of 1986, [sic] as the case may be.

(B) TREATMENT OF REPAYMENTS OF DISTRIBUTIONS FROM ELIGIBLE RETIREMENT PLANS OTHER THAN IRAS.—For purposes of the Internal Revenue Code of 1986, if a contribution is made pursuant to subparagraph (A) with respect to a qualified disaster distribution from an eligible retirement plan other than an individual retirement plan, then the taxpayer shall, to the extent of the amount of the contribution, be treated as having received the qualified disaster distribution in an eligible rollover distribution (as defined in section 402(c)(4) of such Code) and as having transferred the amount to the eligible retirement plan in a direct trustee to trustee transfer within 60 days of the distribution.

(C) TREATMENT OF REPAYMENTS OF DISTRIBUTIONS FROM IRAS.—For purposes of the Internal Revenue Code of 1986, if a contribution is made pursuant to subparagraph (A) with respect to a qualified disaster distribution from an individual retirement plan (as defined by section 7701(a)(37) of such Code), then, to the extent of the amount of the contribution, the qualified disaster distribution shall be treated as a distribution described in section 408(d)(3) of such Code and as having been transferred to the eligible retirement plan in a direct trustee to trustee transfer within 60 days of the distribution.

(4) DEFINITIONS.—For purposes of this subsection—

(A) QUALIFIED DISASTER DISTRIBUTION.— Except as provided in paragraph (2), the term "qualified disaster distribution" means any distribution from an eligible retirement plan made—

(i) on or after the first day of the incident period of a qualified disaster and before the date which is 180 days after the date of the enactment of this Act, and

(ii) to an individual whose principal place of abode at any time during the incident period of such qualified disaster is located in the qualified disaster area with respect to such qualified disaster and who has sustained an economic loss by reason of such qualified disaster.

(B) ELIGIBLE RETIREMENT PLAN.—The term "eligible retirement plan" shall have the meaning given such term by section 402(c)(8)(B) of the Internal Revenue Code of 1986.

(5) INCOME INCLUSION SPREAD OVER 3-YEAR PERIOD.—

(A) IN GENERAL.—In the case of any qualified disaster distribution, unless the taxpayer elects not to have this paragraph apply for any taxable year, any amount required to be included in gross income for such taxable year shall be so included ratably over the 3-taxable-year period beginning with such taxable year.

(B) SPECIAL RULE.—For purposes of subparagraph (A), rules similar to the rules of subparagraph (E) of section 408A(d)(3) of the Internal Revenue Code of 1986 shall apply.

(6) SPECIAL RULES.—

(A) EXEMPTION OF DISTRIBUTIONS FROM TRUSTEE TO TRUSTEE TRANSFER AND WITHHOLDING RULES.—For purposes of sections 401(a)(31), 402(f), and 3405 of the Internal Revenue Code of 1986, qualified disaster distributions shall not be treated as eligible rollover distributions.

(B) QUALIFIED DISASTER DISTRIBUTIONS TREATED AS MEETING PLAN DISTRIBUTION REQUIREMENTS.—For purposes [of] the Internal Revenue Code of 1986, a qualified disaster distribution shall be treated as meeting the requirements of sections 401(k)(2)(B)(i), 403(b)(7)(A)(ii), 403(b)(11), and 457(d)(1)(A) of such Code.

(b) RECONTRIBUTIONS OF WITHDRAWALS FOR HOME PURCHASES.—

(1) RECONTRIBUTIONS.—

(A) IN GENERAL.—Any individual who received a qualified distribution may, during the applicable period, make 1 or more contributions in an aggregate amount not to exceed the amount of such qualified distribution to an eligible retirement plan (as defined in section 402(c)(8)(B) of the Internal Revenue Code of 1986) of which such individual is a beneficiary and to which a rollover contribution of such distribution could be made under section 402(c), 403(a)(4), 403(b)(8), or 408(d)(3), [sic] of such Code, as the case may be.

(B) TREATMENT OF REPAYMENTS.—Rules similar to the rules of subparagraphs (B) and (C) of subsection (a)(3) shall apply for purposes of this subsection.

(2) QUALIFIED DISTRIBUTION.—For purposes of this subsection, the term "qualified distribution" means any distribution—

(A) described in section 401(k)(2)(B)(i)(IV), 403(b)(7)(A)(ii) (but only to the extent such distribution relates to financial hardship), 403(b)(11)(B), or 72(t)(2)(F), [sic] of the Internal Revenue Code of 1986,

(B) which was to be used to purchase or construct a principal residence in a qualified disaster area, but which was not so used on account of the qualified disaster with respect to such area, and

(C) which was received during the period beginning on the date which is 180 days before the first day of the incident period of such qualified disaster and ending on the date which is 30 days after the last day of such incident period.

(3) APPLICABLE PERIOD.—For purposes of this subsection, the term "applicable period" means, in the case of a principal residence in a qualified disaster area with respect to any qualified disaster, the period beginning on the first day of the incident period of such qualified disaster and ending on the date which is 180 days after the date of the enactment of this Act.

(c) LOANS FROM QUALIFIED PLANS.—

(1) INCREASE IN LIMIT ON LOANS NOT TREATED AS DISTRIBUTIONS.—In the case of any loan from a qualified employer plan (as defined under section 72(p)(4) of the Internal Revenue Code of 1986) to a qualified individual made during the 180-day period beginning on the date of the enactment of this Act—

(A) clause (i) of section 72(p)(2)(A) of such Code shall be applied by substituting "$100,000" for "$50,000", and

(B) clause (ii) of such section shall be applied by substituting "the present value of the nonforfeitable accrued benefit of the employee under the plan" for "one-half of the present value of the nonforfeitable accrued benefit of the employee under the plan".

(2) DELAY OF REPAYMENT.—In the case of a qualified individual (with respect to any qualified disaster) with an outstanding loan (on or after the first day of the incident period of such qualified disaster) from a qualified employer plan (as defined in section 72(p)(4) of the Internal Revenue Code of 1986)—

(A) if the due date pursuant to subparagraph (B) or (C) of section 72(p)(2) of such Code for any repayment with respect to such loan occurs during the period beginning on the first day of the incident period of such qualified disaster and ending on the date which is 180 days after the last day of such incident period, such due date shall be delayed for 1 year (or, if later, until the date which is 180 days after the date of the enactment of this Act),

(B) any subsequent repayments with respect to any such loan shall be appropriately adjusted to reflect the delay in the due date under subparagraph (A) and any interest accruing during such delay, and

(C) in determining the 5-year period and the term of a loan under subparagraph (B) or (C) of section 72(p)(2) of such Code, the period described in subparagraph (A) of this paragraph shall be disregarded.

(3) QUALIFIED INDIVIDUAL.—For purposes of this subsection, the term "qualified individual" means any individual—

(A) whose principal place of abode at any time during the incident period of any qualified disaster is located in the qualified disaster area with respect to such qualified disaster, and

(B) who has sustained an economic loss by reason of such qualified disaster.

(d) PROVISIONS RELATING TO PLAN AMENDMENTS.—

(1) IN GENERAL.—If this subsection applies to any amendment to any plan or annuity contract, such plan or contract shall be treated as being operated in accordance with the terms of the plan during the period described in paragraph (2)(B)(i).

(2) AMENDMENTS TO WHICH SUBSECTION APPLIES.—

(A) IN GENERAL.—This subsection shall apply to any amendment to any plan or annuity contract which is made—

(i) pursuant to any provision of this section, or pursuant to any regulation issued by the Secretary or the Secretary of Labor under any provision of this section, and

(ii) on or before the last day of the first plan year beginning on or after January 1, 2020, or such later date as the Secretary may prescribe.

In the case of a governmental plan (as defined in section 414(d) of the Internal Revenue Code of 1986), clause (ii) shall be applied by substituting the date which is 2 years after the date otherwise applied under clause (ii).

(B) CONDITIONS.—This subsection shall not apply to any amendment unless—

(i) during the period—

(I) beginning on the date that this section or the regulation described in subparagraph (A)(i) takes effect (or in the case of a plan or contract amendment not required by this section or such regulation, the effective date specified by the plan), and

(II) ending on the date described in subparagraph (A)(ii) (or, if earlier, the date the plan or contract amendment is adopted),

the plan or contract is operated as if such plan or contract amendment were in effect, and

(ii) such plan or contract amendment applies retroactively for such period.

- **2018, Tax Technical Corrections Act of 2018 (P.L. 115-141)**

P.L. 115-141, § 401(d)(6)(A), Div. U:

Amended chapter 1 by striking subchapter Y (Code Secs. 1400L-1400U-3). **Effective** 3-23-2018. For special rules, see Act Sec. 401(d)(6)(C)(xv)-(xvii), Div. U, and Act Sec. 401(e), Div. U, below. Prior to being stricken, Code Sec. 1400Q read as follows:

SEC. 1400Q. SPECIAL RULES FOR USE OF RETIREMENT FUNDS.

[Sec. 1400Q(a)]

(a) TAX-FAVORED WITHDRAWALS FROM RETIREMENT PLANS.—

(1) IN GENERAL.—Section 72(t) shall not apply to any qualified hurricane distribution.

(2) AGGREGATE DOLLAR LIMITATION.—

(A) IN GENERAL.—For purposes of this subsection, the aggregate amount of distributions received by an individual which may be treated as qualified hurricane distributions for any taxable year shall not exceed the excess (if any) of—

(i) $100,000, over

(ii) the aggregate amounts treated as qualified hurricane distributions received by such individual for all prior taxable years.

(B) TREATMENT OF PLAN DISTRIBUTIONS.—If a distribution to an individual would (without regard to subparagraph (A)) be a qualified hurricane distribution, a plan shall not be treated as violating any requirement of this title merely because the plan treats such distribution as a qualified hurricane distribution, unless the aggregate amount of such distributions from all plans maintained by the employer (and any member of any controlled group which includes the employer) to such individual exceeds $100,000.

(C) CONTROLLED GROUP.—For purposes of subparagraph (B), the term "controlled group" means any group treated as a single employer under subsection (b), (c), (m), or (o) of section 414.

(3) AMOUNT DISTRIBUTED MAY BE REPAID.—

(A) IN GENERAL.—Any individual who receives a qualified hurricane distribution may, at any time during the 3-year period beginning on the day after the date on which such distribution was received, make one or more contributions in an aggregate amount not to exceed the amount of such distribution to an eligible retirement plan of which such individual is a beneficiary and to which a rollover contribution of such distribution could be made under section 402(c), 403(a)(4), 403(b)(8), 408(d)(3), or 457(e)(16), as the case may be.

(B) TREATMENT OF REPAYMENTS OF DISTRIBUTIONS FROM ELIGIBLE RETIREMENT PLANS OTHER THAN IRAS.—For purposes of this title, if a contribution is made pursuant to subparagraph (A) with respect to a qualified hurricane distribution from an eligible retirement plan other than an individual retirement plan, then the taxpayer shall, to the extent of the amount of the contribution, be treated as having received the qualified hurricane distribution in an eligible rollover distribution (as defined in section 402(c)(4)) and as having transferred the amount to the eligible retirement plan in a direct trustee to trustee transfer within 60 days of the distribution.

(C) TREATMENT OF REPAYMENTS FOR DISTRIBUTIONS FROM IRAS.—For purposes of this title, if a contribution is made pursuant to subparagraph (A) with respect to a qualified hurricane distribution from an individual retirement plan (as defined by section 7701(a)(37)), then, to the extent of the amount of the contribution, the qualified hurricane distribution shall be treated as a distribution described in section 408(d)(3) and as having been transferred to the eligible retirement plan in a direct trustee to trustee transfer within 60 days of the distribution.

(4) DEFINITIONS.—For purposes of this subsection—

(A) QUALIFIED HURRICANE DISTRIBUTION.—Except as provided in paragraph (2), the term "qualified hurricane distribution" means—

(i) any distribution from an eligible retirement plan made on or after August 25, 2005, and before January 1, 2007, to an individual whose principal place of abode on August 28, 2005, is located in the Hurricane Katrina disaster area and who has sustained an economic loss by reason of Hurricane Katrina,

(ii) any distribution (which is not described in clause (i)) from an eligible retirement plan made on or after September 23, 2005, and before January 1, 2007, to an individual whose principal place of abode on September 23, 2005, is located in the Hurricane Rita disaster area and who has sustained an economic loss by reason of Hurricane Rita, and

(iii) any distribution (which is not described in clause (i) or (ii)) from an eligible retirement plan made on or after October 23, 2005, and before January 1, 2007, to an individual whose principal place of abode on October 23, 2005, is located in the Hurricane Wilma disaster area and who has sustained an economic loss by reason of Hurricane Wilma.

(B) ELIGIBLE RETIREMENT PLAN.—The term "eligible retirement plan" shall have the meaning given such term by section 402(c)(8)(B).

(5) INCOME INCLUSION SPREAD OVER 3-YEAR PERIOD.—

(A) IN GENERAL.—In the case of any qualified hurricane distribution, unless the taxpayer elects not to have this paragraph apply for any taxable year, any amount required to be included in gross income for such taxable year shall be so included ratably over the 3-taxable year period beginning with such taxable year.

(B) SPECIAL RULE.—For purposes of subparagraph (A), rules similar to the rules of subparagraph (E) of section 408A(d)(3) shall apply.

(6) SPECIAL RULES.—

(A) EXEMPTION OF DISTRIBUTIONS FROM TRUSTEE TO TRUSTEE TRANSFER AND WITHHOLDING RULES.—For purposes of sections 401(a)(31), 402(f), and 3405, qualified hurricane distributions shall not be treated as eligible rollover distributions.

(B) QUALIFIED HURRICANE DISTRIBUTIONS TREATED AS MEETING PLAN DISTRIBUTION REQUIREMENTS.—For purposes [of] this title, a qualified hurricane distribution shall be treated as meeting the requirements of sections 401(k)(2)(B)(i), 403(b)(7)(A)(ii), 403(b)(11), and 457(d)(1)(A).

INCOME TAX—DC ENTERPRISE ZONE

Amendments

- **2018, Bipartisan Budget Act of 2018 (P.L. 115-123)**

P.L. 115-123, § 20102(a), Div. B, provides:

(a) TAX-FAVORED WITHDRAWALS FROM RETIREMENT PLANS.—

(1) IN GENERAL.—Section 72(t) of the Internal Revenue Code of 1986 shall not apply to any qualified wildfire distribution.

(2) AGGREGATE DOLLAR LIMITATION.—

(A) IN GENERAL.—For purposes of this subsection, the aggregate amount of distributions received by an individual which may be treated as qualified wildfire distributions for any taxable year shall not exceed the excess (if any) of—

(i) $100,000, over

(ii) the aggregate amounts treated as qualified wildfire distributions received by such individual for all prior taxable years.

(B) TREATMENT OF PLAN DISTRIBUTIONS.—If a distribution to an individual would (without regard to subparagraph (A)) be a qualified wildfire distribution, a plan shall not be treated as violating any requirement of the Internal Revenue Code of 1986 merely because the plan treats such distribution as a qualified wildfire distribution, unless the aggregate amount of such distributions from all plans maintained by the employer (and any member of any controlled group which includes the employer) to such individual exceeds $100,000.

(C) CONTROLLED GROUP.—For purposes of subparagraph (B), the term "controlled group" means any group treated as a single employer under subsection (b), (c), (m), or (o) of section 414 of the Internal Revenue Code of 1986.

(3) AMOUNT DISTRIBUTED MAY BE REPAID.—

(A) IN GENERAL.—Any individual who receives a qualified wildfire distribution may, at any time during the 3-year period beginning on the day after the date on which such distribution was received, make one or more contributions in an aggregate amount not to exceed the amount of such distribution to an eligible retirement plan of which such individual is a beneficiary and to which a rollover contribution of such distribution could be made under section 402(c), 403(a)(4), 403(b)(8), 408(d)(3), or 457(e)(16), [sic] of the Internal Revenue Code of 1986, as the case may be.

(B) TREATMENT OF REPAYMENTS OF DISTRIBUTIONS FROM ELIGIBLE RETIREMENT PLANS OTHER THAN IRAS.—For purposes of the Internal Revenue Code of 1986, if a contribution is made pursuant to subparagraph (A) with respect to a qualified wildfire distribution from an eligible retirement plan other than an individual retirement plan, then the taxpayer shall, to the extent of the amount of the contribution, be treated as having received the qualified wildfire distribution in an eligible rollover distribution (as defined in section 402(c)(4) of such Code) and as having transferred the amount to the eligible retirement plan in a direct trustee to trustee transfer within 60 days of the distribution.

(C) TREATMENT OF REPAYMENTS FOR DISTRIBUTIONS FROM IRAS.—For purposes of the Internal Revenue Code of 1986, if a contribution is made pursuant to subparagraph (A) with respect to a qualified wildfire distribution from an individual retirement plan (as defined by section 7701(a)(37) of such Code), then, to the extent of the amount of the contribution, the qualified wildfire distribution shall be treated as a distribution described in section 408(d)(3) of such Code and as having been transferred to the eligible retirement plan in a direct trustee to trustee transfer within 60 days of the distribution.

(4) DEFINITIONS.—For purposes of this subsection—

(A) QUALIFIED WILDFIRE DISTRIBUTION.—Except as provided in paragraph (2), the term "qualified wildfire distribution" means any distribution from an eligible retirement plan made on or after October 8, 2017, and before January 1, 2019, to an individual whose principal place of abode during any portion of the period from October 8, 2017, to December 31, 2017, is located in the California wildfire disaster area and who has sustained an economic loss by reason of the wildfires to which the declaration of such area relates.

(B) ELIGIBLE RETIREMENT PLAN.—The term "eligible retirement plan" shall have the meaning given such term by section 402(c)(8)(B) of the Internal Revenue Code of 1986.

(5) INCOME INCLUSION SPREAD OVER 3-YEAR PERIOD.—

(A) IN GENERAL.—In the case of any qualified wildfire distribution, unless the taxpayer elects not to have this paragraph apply for any taxable year, any amount required to be included in gross income for such taxable year shall be so included ratably over the 3-taxable-year period beginning with such taxable year.

(B) SPECIAL RULE.—For purposes of subparagraph (A), rules similar to the rules of subparagraph (E) of section 408A(d)(3) of the Internal Revenue Code of 1986 shall apply.

(6) SPECIAL RULES.—

(A) EXEMPTION OF DISTRIBUTIONS FROM TRUSTEE TO TRUSTEE TRANSFER AND WITHHOLDING RULES.—For purposes of sections 401(a)(31), 402(f), and 3405 of the Internal Revenue Code of 1986, qualified wildfire distributions shall not be treated as eligible rollover distributions.

(B) QUALIFIED WILDFIRE DISTRIBUTIONS TREATED AS MEETING PLAN DISTRIBUTION REQUIREMENTS.—For purposes [of] the Internal Revenue Code of 1986, a qualified wildfire distribution shall be treated as meeting the requirements of sections 401(k)(2)(B)(i), 403(b)(7)(A)(ii), 403(b)(11), and 457(d)(1)(A) of such Code.

- **2017, Tax Cuts and Jobs Act (P.L. 115-97)**

P.L. 115-97, § 11028(a) and (b)(1), provides:

SEC. 11028. RELIEF FOR 2016 DISASTER AREAS.

(a) IN GENERAL.—For purposes of this section, the term "2016 disaster area" means any area with respect to which a major disaster has been declared by the President under section 401 of the Robert T. Stafford Disaster Relief and Emergency Assistance Act during calendar year 2016.

(b) SPECIAL RULES FOR USE OF RETIREMENT FUNDS WITH RESPECT TO AREAS DAMAGED BY 2016 DISASTERS.—

(1) TAX-FAVORED WITHDRAWALS FROM RETIREMENT PLANS.—

(A) IN GENERAL.—Section 72(t) of the Internal Revenue Code of 1986 shall not apply to any qualified 2016 disaster distribution.

(B) AGGREGATE DOLLAR LIMITATION.—

(i) IN GENERAL.—For purposes of this subsection, the aggregate amount of distributions received by an individual which may be treated as qualified 2016 disaster distributions for any taxable year shall not exceed the excess (if any) of—

(I) $100,000, over

(II) the aggregate amounts treated as qualified 2016 disaster distributions received by such individual for all prior taxable years.

(ii) TREATMENT OF PLAN DISTRIBUTIONS.—If a distribution to an individual would (without regard to clause (i)) be a qualified 2016 disaster distribution, a plan shall not be treated as violating any requirement of this title merely because the plan treats such distribution as a qualified 2016 disaster distribution, unless the aggregate amount of such distributions from all plans maintained by the employer (and any member of any controlled group which includes the employer) to such individual exceeds $100,000.

(iii) CONTROLLED GROUP.—For purposes of clause (ii), the term "controlled group" means any group treated as a single employer under subsection (b), (c), (m), or (o) of section 414 of the Internal Revenue Code of 1986.

(C) AMOUNT DISTRIBUTED MAY BE REPAID.—

(i) IN GENERAL.—Any individual who receives a qualified 2016 disaster distribution may, at any time during the 3-year period beginning on the day after the date on which such distribution was received, make one or more contributions in an aggregate amount not to exceed the amount of such distribution to an eligible retirement plan of which such individual is a beneficiary and to which a rollover contribution of such distribution could be made under section 402(c), 403(a)(4), 403(b)(8), 408(d)(3), or 457(e)(16) of the Internal Revenue Code of 1986, as the case may be.

(ii) TREATMENT OF REPAYMENTS OF DISTRIBUTIONS FROM ELIGIBLE RETIREMENT PLANS OTHER THAN IRAS.—For purposes of the Internal Revenue Code of 1986, if a contribution is made pursuant to clause (i) with respect to a qualified 2016 disaster distribution from an eligible retirement plan other than an individual retirement plan, then the taxpayer shall, to the extent of the amount of the contribution, be treated as having received the qualified 2016 disaster distribution in an eligible rollover distribution (as defined in section 402(c)(4) of the Internal Revenue Code of 1986) and as having transferred the amount to the eligible retirement plan in a direct trustee to trustee transfer within 60 days of the distribution.

(iii) TREATMENT OF REPAYMENTS FOR DISTRIBUTIONS FROM IRAS.—For purposes of the Internal Revenue Code of 1986, if a contribution is made pursuant to clause (i) with respect to a qualified 2016 disaster distribution from an individual retirement plan (as defined by section 7701(a)(37) of the Internal Revenue Code of 1986), then, to the extent of the amount of the contribution, the qualified 2016 disaster distribution shall be treated as a distribution described in section 408(d)(3) of such Code and as having been transferred to the eligible retirement plan in a direct trustee to trustee transfer within 60 days of the distribution.

(D) DEFINITIONS.—For purposes of this paragraph—

(i) QUALIFIED 2016 DISASTER DISTRIBUTION.—Except as provided in subparagraph (B), the term "qualified 2016 disaster distribution" means any distribution from an eligible retirement plan made on or after January 1, 2016, and before January 1, 2018, to an individual whose principal place of abode at any time during calendar year 2016 was located in a disaster area described in subsection (a) and who has sustained an economic loss by reason of the events giving rise to the Presidential declaration described in subsection (a) which was applicable to such area.

(ii) ELIGIBLE RETIREMENT PLAN.— The term "eligible retirement plan" shall have the meaning given such term by section 402(c)(8)(B) of the Internal Revenue Code of 1986.

(E) INCOME INCLUSION SPREAD OVER 3-YEAR PERIOD.—

(i) IN GENERAL.—In the case of any qualified 2016 disaster distribution, unless the taxpayer elects not to have this subparagraph apply for any taxable year, any amount required to be included in gross income for such taxable year shall be so included ratably over the 3-taxable-year period beginning with such taxable year.

(ii) SPECIAL RULE.—For purposes of clause (i), rules similar to the rules of subparagraph (E) of section 408A(d)(3) of the Internal Revenue Code of 1986 shall apply.

(F) SPECIAL RULES.—

(i) EXEMPTION OF DISTRIBUTIONS FROM TRUSTEE TO TRUSTEE TRANSFER AND WITHHOLDING RULES.—For purposes of sections 401(a)(31), 402(f), and 3405 of the Internal Revenue Code of 1986, qualified 2016 disaster distribution shall not be treated as eligible rollover distributions.

(ii) QUALIFIED 2016 DISASTER DISTRIBUTIONS TREATED AS MEETING PLAN DISTRIBUTION REQUIREMENTS.—For purposes of the Internal Revenue Code of 1986, a qualified 2016 disaster distribution shall be treated as meeting the requirements of sections 401(k)(2)(B)(i), 403(b)(7)(A)(ii), 403(b)(11), and 457(d)(1)(A) of the Internal Revenue Code of 1986.

- **2017, Disaster Tax Relief and Airport and Airway Extension Act of 2017 (P.L. 115-63)**

P.L. 115-63, § 502(a), provides:

(a) TAX-FAVORED WITHDRAWALS FROM RETIREMENT PLANS.—

(1) IN GENERAL.—Section 72(t) of the Internal Revenue Code of 1986 shall not apply to any qualified hurricane distribution.

(2) AGGREGATE DOLLAR LIMITATION.—

(A) IN GENERAL.—For purposes of this subsection, the aggregate amount of distributions received by an individual which may be treated as qualified hurricane distributions for any taxable year shall not exceed the excess (if any) of—

(i) $100,000, over

(ii) the aggregate amounts treated as qualified hurricane distributions received by such individual for all prior taxable years.

(B) TREATMENT OF PLAN DISTRIBUTIONS.—If a distribution to an individual would (without regard to subparagraph (A)) be a qualified hurricane distribution, a plan shall not be treated as violating any requirement of the Internal Revenue Code of 1986 merely because the plan treats such distribution as a qualified hurricane distribution, unless the aggregate amount of such distributions from all plans main-

Sec. 1400Q—Stricken

tained by the employer (and any member of any controlled group which includes the employer) to such individual exceeds $100,000.

(C) CONTROLLED GROUP.—For purposes of subparagraph (B), the term "controlled group" means any group treated as a single employer under subsection (b), (c), (m), or (o) of section 414 of the Internal Revenue Code of 1986.

(3) AMOUNT DISTRIBUTED MAY BE REPAID.—

(A) IN GENERAL.—Any individual who receives a qualified hurricane distribution may, at any time during the 3-year period beginning on the day after the date on which such distribution was received, make one or more contributions in an aggregate amount not to exceed the amount of such distribution to an eligible retirement plan of which such individual is a beneficiary and to which a rollover contribution of such distribution could be made under section 402(c), 403(a)(4), 403(b)(8), 408(d)(3), or 457(e)(16), of the Internal Revenue Code of 1986, as the case may be.

(B) TREATMENT OF REPAYMENTS OF DISTRIBUTIONS FROM ELIGIBLE RETIREMENT PLANS OTHER THAN IRAS.—For purposes of the Internal Revenue Code of 1986, if a contribution is made pursuant to subparagraph (A) with respect to a qualified hurricane distribution from an eligible retirement plan other than an individual retirement plan, then the taxpayer shall, to the extent of the amount of the contribution, be treated as having received the qualified hurricane distribution in an eligible rollover distribution (as defined in section 402(c)(4) of such Code) and as having transferred the amount to the eligible retirement plan in a direct trustee to trustee transfer within 60 days of the distribution.

(C) TREATMENT OF REPAYMENTS FOR DISTRIBUTIONS FROM IRAS.—For purposes of the Internal Revenue Code of 1986, if a contribution is made pursuant to subparagraph (A) with respect to a qualified hurricane distribution from an individual retirement plan (as defined by section 7701(a)(37) of such Code), then, to the extent of the amount of the contribution, the qualified hurricane distribution shall be treated as a distribution described in section 408(d)(3) of such Code and as having been transferred to the eligible retirement plan in a direct trustee to trustee transfer within 60 days of the distribution.

(4) DEFINITIONS.—For purposes of this subsection—

(A) QUALIFIED HURRICANE DISTRIBUTION.—Except as provided in paragraph (2), the term "qualified hurricane distribution" means—

(i) any distribution from an eligible retirement plan made on or after August 23, 2017, and before January 1, 2019, to an individual whose principal place of abode on August 23, 2017, is located in the Hurricane Harvey disaster area and who has sustained an economic loss by reason of Hurricane Harvey,

(ii) any distribution (which is not described in clause (i)) from an eligible retirement plan made on or after September 4, 2017, and before January 1, 2019, to an individual whose principal place of abode on September 4, 2017, is located in the Hurricane Irma disaster area and who has sustained an economic loss by reason of Hurricane Irma, and

(iii) any distribution (which is not described in clause (i) or (ii)) from an eligible retirement plan made on or after September 16, 2017, and before January 1, 2019, to an individual whose principal place of abode on September 16, 2017, is located in the Hurricane Maria disaster area and who has sustained an economic loss by reason of Hurricane Maria.

(B) ELIGIBLE RETIREMENT PLAN.—The term "eligible retirement plan" shall have the meaning given such term by section 402(c)(8)(B) of the Internal Revenue Code of 1986.

(5) INCOME INCLUSION SPREAD OVER 3-YEAR PERIOD.—

(A) IN GENERAL.—In the case of any qualified hurricane distribution, unless the taxpayer elects not to have this paragraph apply for any taxable year, any amount required to be included in gross income for such taxable year shall be so included ratably over the 3-taxable-year period beginning with such taxable year.

(B) SPECIAL RULE.—For purposes of subparagraph (A), rules similar to the rules of subparagraph (E) of section 408A(d)(3) of the Internal Revenue Code of 1986 shall apply.

(6) SPECIAL RULES.—

(A) EXEMPTION OF DISTRIBUTIONS FROM TRUSTEE TO TRUSTEE TRANSFER AND WITHHOLDING RULES.—For purposes of sections 401(a)(31), 402(f), and 3405 of the Internal Revenue Code of 1986, qualified hurricane distributions shall not be treated as eligible rollover distributions.

(B) QUALIFIED HURRICANE DISTRIBUTIONS TREATED AS MEETING PLAN DISTRIBUTION REQUIREMENTS.—For purposes [of] the Internal Revenue Code of 1986, a qualified hurricane distribution shall be treated as meeting the requirements of sections 401(k)(2)(B)(i), 403(b)(7)(A)(ii), 403(b)(11), and 457(d)(1)(A) of such Code.

[Sec. 1400Q(b)]

(b) RECONTRIBUTIONS OF WITHDRAWALS FOR HOME PURCHASES.—

(1) RECONTRIBUTIONS.—

(A) IN GENERAL.—Any individual who received a qualified distribution may, during the applicable period, make one or more contributions in an aggregate amount not to exceed the amount of such qualified distribution to an eligible retirement plan (as defined in section 402(c)(8)(B)) of which such individual is a beneficiary and to which a rollover contribution of such distribution could be made under section 402(c), 403(a)(4), 403(b)(8), or 408(d)(3), as the case may be.

(B) TREATMENT OF REPAYMENTS.—Rules similar to the rules of subparagraphs (B) and (C) of subsection (a)(3) shall apply for purposes of this subsection.

(2) QUALIFIED DISTRIBUTION.—For purposes of this subsection—

(A) IN GENERAL.—The term "qualified distribution" means any qualified Katrina distribution, any qualified Rita distribution, and any qualified Wilma distribution.

(B) QUALIFIED KATRINA DISTRIBUTION.—The term "qualified Katrina distribution" means any distribution—

(i) described in section 401(k)(2)(B)(i)(IV), 403(b)(7)(A)(ii) (but only to the extent such distribution relates to financial hardship), 403(b)(11)(B), or 72(t)(2)(F),

(ii) received after February 28, 2005, and before August 29, 2005, and

(iii) which was to be used to purchase or construct a principal residence in the Hurricane Katrina disaster area, but which was not so purchased or constructed on account of Hurricane Katrina.

(C) QUALIFIED RITA DISTRIBUTION.—The term "qualified Rita distribution" means any distribution (other than a qualified Katrina distribution)—

(i) described in section 401(k)(2)(B)(i)(IV), 403(b)(7)(A)(ii) (but only to the extent such distribution relates to financial hardship), 403(b)(11)(B), or 72(t)(2)(F),

(ii) received after February 28, 2005, and before September 24, 2005, and

(iii) which was to be used to purchase or construct a principal residence in the Hurricane Rita disaster area, but which was not so purchased or constructed on account of Hurricane Rita.

(D) QUALIFIED WILMA DISTRIBUTION.—The term "qualified Wilma distribution" means any distribution (other than a qualified Katrina distribution or a qualified Rita distribution)—

(i) described in section 401(k)(2)(B)(i)(IV), 403(b)(7)(A)(ii) (but only to the extent such distribution relates to financial hardship), 403(b)(11)(B), or 72(t)(2)(F),

(ii) received after February 28, 2005, and before October 24, 2005, and

(iii) which was to be used to purchase or construct a principal residence in the Hurricane Wilma disaster area, but which was not so purchased or constructed on account of Hurricane Wilma.

(3) APPLICABLE PERIOD.—For purposes of this subsection, the term "applicable period" means—

(A) with respect to any qualified Katrina distribution, the period beginning on August 25, 2005, and ending on February 28, 2006,

(B) with respect to any qualified Rita distribution, the period beginning on September 23, 2005, and ending on February 28, 2006, and

(C) with respect to any qualified Wilma distribution, the period beginning on October 23, 2005, and ending on February 28, 2006.

Amendments

• **2018, Bipartisan Budget Act of 2018 (P.L. 115-123)**

P.L. 115-123, §20102(b), Div. B, provides:

(b) RECONTRIBUTIONS OF WITHDRAWALS FOR HOME PURCHASES.—

(1) RECONTRIBUTIONS.—

(A) IN GENERAL.—Any individual who received a qualified distribution may, during the period beginning on October 8, 2017, and ending on June 30, 2018, make one or more contributions in an aggregate amount not to exceed the amount of such qualified distribution to an eligible retirement plan (as defined in section 402(c)(8)(B) of the Internal Revenue Code of 1986) of which such individual is a beneficiary and to which a rollover contribution of such distribution could be made under section 402(c), 403(a)(4), 403(b)(8), or 408(d)(3), [sic] of such Code, as the case may be.

(B) TREATMENT OF REPAYMENTS.—Rules similar to the rules of subparagraphs (B) and (C) of subsection (a)(3) shall apply for purposes of this subsection.

(2) QUALIFIED DISTRIBUTION.—For purposes of this subsection, the term "qualified distribution" means any distribution—

(A) described in section 401(k)(2)(B)(i)(IV), 403(b)(7)(A)(ii) (but only to the extent such distribution relates to financial hardship), 403(b)(11)(B), or 72(t)(2)(F), [sic] of the Internal Revenue Code of 1986,

(B) received after March 31, 2017, and before January 15, 2018, and

(C) which was to be used to purchase or construct a principal residence in the California wildfire disaster area, but which was not so purchased or constructed on account of the wildfires to which the declaration of such area relates.

• **2017, Disaster Tax Relief and Airport and Airway Extension Act of 2017 (P.L. 115-63)**

P.L. 115-63, §502(b), provides:

(b) RECONTRIBUTIONS OF WITHDRAWALS FOR HOME PURCHASES.—

(1) RECONTRIBUTIONS.—

(A) IN GENERAL.—Any individual who received a qualified distribution may, during the period beginning on August 23, 2017, and ending on February 28, 2018, make one or more contributions in an aggregate amount not to exceed the amount of such qualified distribution to an eligible retirement plan (as defined in section 402(c)(8)(B) of the Internal Revenue Code of 1986) of which such individual is a beneficiary and to which a rollover contribution of such distribution could be made under section 402(c), 403(a)(4), 403(b)(8), or 408(d)(3), [sic] of such Code, as the case may be.

(B) TREATMENT OF REPAYMENTS.—Rules similar to the rules of subparagraphs (B) and (C) of subsection (a)(3) shall apply for purposes of this subsection.

(2) QUALIFIED DISTRIBUTION.—For purposes of this subsection, the term "qualified distribution" means any distribution—

(A) described in section 401(k)(2)(B)(i)(IV), 403(b)(7)(A)(ii) (but only to the extent such distribution relates to financial hardship), 403(b)(11)(B), or 72(t)(2)(F), [sic] of the Internal Revenue Code of 1986,

(B) received after February 28, 2017, and before September 21, 2017, and

(C) which was to be used to purchase or construct a principal residence in the Hurricane Harvey disaster area, the Hurricane Irma disaster area, or the Hurricane Maria disaster area, but which was not so purchased or constructed on account of Hurricane Harvey, Hurricane Irma, or Hurricane Maria.

[Sec. 1400Q(c)]

(c) LOANS FROM QUALIFIED PLANS.—

(1) INCREASE IN LIMIT ON LOANS NOT TREATED AS DISTRIBUTIONS.—In the case of any loan from a qualified employer plan (as defined under section 72(p)(4)) to a qualified individual made during the applicable period—

(A) clause (i) of section 72(p)(2)(A) shall be applied by substituting "$100,000" for "$50,000", and

(B) clause (ii) of such section shall be applied by substituting "the present value of the nonforfeitable accrued benefit of the employee under the plan" for "one-half of the present value of the nonforfeitable accrued benefit of the employee under the plan".

INCOME TAX—DC ENTERPRISE ZONE

(2) DELAY OF REPAYMENT.—In the case of a qualified individual with an outstanding loan on or after the qualified beginning date from a qualified employer plan (as defined in section 72(p)(4))—

(A) if the due date pursuant to subparagraph (B) or (C) of section 72(p)(2) for any repayment with respect to such loan occurs during the period beginning on the qualified beginning date and ending on December 31, 2006, such due date shall be delayed for 1 year,

(B) any subsequent repayments with respect to any such loan shall be appropriately adjusted to reflect the delay in the due date under paragraph (1) and any interest accruing during such delay, and

(C) in determining the 5-year period and the term of a loan under subparagraph (B) or (C) of section 72(p)(2), the period described in subparagraph (A) shall be disregarded.

(3) QUALIFIED INDIVIDUAL.—For purposes of this subsection—

(A) IN GENERAL.—The term "qualified individual" means any qualified Hurricane Katrina individual, any qualified Hurricane Rita individual, and any qualified Hurricane Wilma individual.

(B) QUALIFIED HURRICANE KATRINA INDIVIDUAL.—The term "qualified Hurricane Katrina individual" means an individual whose principal place of abode on August 28, 2005, is located in the Hurricane Katrina disaster area and who has sustained an economic loss by reason of Hurricane Katrina.

(C) QUALIFIED HURRICANE RITA INDIVIDUAL.—The term "qualified Hurricane Rita individual" means an individual (other than a qualified Hurricane Katrina individual) whose principal place of abode on September 23, 2005, is located in the Hurricane Rita disaster area and who has sustained an economic loss by reason of Hurricane Rita.

(D) QUALIFIED HURRICANE WILMA INDIVIDUAL.—The term "qualified Hurricane Wilma individual" means an individual (other than a qualified Hurricane Katrina individual or a qualified Hurricane Rita individual) whose principal place of abode on October 23, 2005, is located in the Hurricane Wilma disaster area and who has sustained an economic loss by reason of Hurricane Wilma.

(4) APPLICABLE PERIOD; QUALIFIED BEGINNING DATE.—For purposes of this subsection—

(A) HURRICANE KATRINA.—In the case of any qualified Hurricane Katrina individual—

(i) the applicable period is the period beginning on September 24, 2005, and ending on December 31, 2006, and

(ii) the qualified beginning date is August 25, 2005.

(B) HURRICANE RITA.—In the case of any qualified Hurricane Rita individual—

(i) the applicable period is the period beginning on the date of the enactment of this subsection and ending on December 31, 2006, and

(ii) the qualified beginning date is September 23, 2005.

(C) HURRICANE WILMA.—In the case of any qualified Hurricane Wilma individual—

(i) the applicable period is the period beginning on the date of the enactment of this subparagraph and ending on December 31, 2006, and

(ii) the qualified beginning date is October 23, 2005.

Amendments

- **2018, Bipartisan Budget Act of 2018 (P.L. 115-123)**

P.L. 115-123, §20102(c), Div. B, provides:

(c) LOANS FROM QUALIFIED PLANS.—

(1) INCREASE IN LIMIT ON LOANS NOT TREATED AS DISTRIBUTIONS.—In the case of any loan from a qualified employer plan (as defined under section 72(p)(4) of the Internal Revenue Code of 1986) to a qualified individual made during the period beginning on the date of the enactment of this Act and ending on December 31, 2018—

(A) clause (i) of section 72(p)(2)(A) of such Code shall be applied by substituting "$100,000" for "$50,000", and

(B) clause (ii) of such section shall be applied by substituting "the present value of the nonforfeitable accrued benefit of the employee under the plan" for "one-half of the present value of the nonforfeitable accrued benefit of the employee under the plan".

(2) DELAY OF REPAYMENT.—In the case of a qualified individual with an outstanding loan on or after October 8, 2017, from a qualified employer plan (as defined in section 72(p)(4) of the Internal Revenue Code of 1986)—

(A) if the due date pursuant to subparagraph (B) or (C) of section 72(p)(2) of such Code for any repayment with respect to such loan occurs during the period beginning on October 8, 2017, and ending on December 31, 2018, such due date shall be delayed for 1 year,

(B) any subsequent repayments with respect to any such loan shall be appropriately adjusted to reflect the delay in the due date under paragraph (1) and any interest accruing during such delay, and

(C) in determining the 5-year period and the term of a loan under subparagraph (B) or (C) of section 72(p)(2) of such Code, the period described in subparagraph (A) shall be disregarded.

(3) QUALIFIED INDIVIDUAL.—For purposes of this subsection, the term "qualified individual" means any individual whose principal place of abode during any portion of the period from October 8, 2017, to December 31, 2017, is located in the California wildfire disaster area and who has sustained an economic loss by reason of wildfires to which the declaration of such area relates.

- **2017, Disaster Tax Relief and Airport and Airway Extension Act of 2017 (P.L. 115-63)**

P.L. 115-63, §502(c), provides:

(c) LOANS FROM QUALIFIED PLANS.—

(1) INCREASE IN LIMIT ON LOANS NOT TREATED AS DISTRIBUTIONS.—In the case of any loan from a qualified employer plan (as defined under section 72(p)(4) of the Internal Revenue Code of 1986) to a qualified individual made during the period beginning on the date of the enactment of this Act and ending on December 31, 2018—

(A) clause (i) of section 72(p)(2)(A) of such Code shall be applied by substituting "$100,000" for "$50,000", and

(B) clause (ii) of such section shall be applied by substituting "the present value of the nonforfeitable accrued benefit of the employee under the plan" for "one-half of the present value of the nonforfeitable accrued benefit of the employee under the plan".

(2) DELAY OF REPAYMENT.—In the case of a qualified individual with an outstanding loan on or after the qualified beginning date from a qualified employer plan (as defined in section 72(p)(4) of the Internal Revenue Code of 1986)—

(A) if the due date pursuant to subparagraph (B) or (C) of section 72(p)(2) of such Code for any repayment with respect to such loan occurs during the period beginning on the qualified beginning date and ending on December 31, 2018, such due date shall be delayed for 1 year,

(B) any subsequent repayments with respect to any such loan shall be appropriately adjusted to reflect the delay in the due date under paragraph (1) and any interest accruing during such delay, and

(C) in determining the 5-year period and the term of a loan under subparagraph (B) or (C) of section 72(p)(2) of such Code, the period described in subparagraph (A) shall be disregarded.

(3) QUALIFIED INDIVIDUAL.—For purposes of this subsection—

(A) IN GENERAL.—The term "qualified individual" means any qualified Hurricane Harvey individual, any qualified Hurricane Irma individual, and any qualified Hurricane Maria individual.

(B) QUALIFIED HURRICANE HARVEY INDIVIDUAL.—The term "qualified Hurricane Harvey individual" means an individual whose principal place of abode on August 23, 2017, is located in the Hurricane Harvey disaster area and who has sustained an economic loss by reason of Hurricane Harvey.

(C) QUALIFIED HURRICANE IRMA INDIVIDUAL.—The term "qualified Hurricane Irma individual" means an individual (other than a qualified Hurricane Harvey individual) whose principal place of abode on September 4, 2017, is located in the Hurricane Irma disaster area and who has sustained an economic loss by reason of Hurricane Irma.

(D) QUALIFIED HURRICANE MARIA INDIVIDUAL.—The term "qualified Hurricane Maria individual" means an individual (other than a qualified Hurricane Harvey individual or a qualified Hurricane Irma individual) whose principal place of abode on September 16, 2017, is located in the Hurricane Maria disaster area and who has sustained an economic loss by reason of Hurricane Maria.

(4) QUALIFIED BEGINNING DATE.—For purposes of this subsection, the qualified beginning date is—

(A) in the case of any qualified Hurricane Harvey individual, August 23, 2017,

(B) in the case of any qualified Hurricane Irma individual, September 4, 2017, and

(C) in the case of any qualified Hurricane Maria individual, September 16, 2017.

[Sec. 1400Q(d)]

(d) PROVISIONS RELATING TO PLAN AMENDMENTS.—

(1) IN GENERAL.—If this subsection applies to any amendment to any plan or annuity contract, such plan or contract shall be treated as being operated in accordance with the terms of the plan during the period described in paragraph (2)(B)(i).

(2) AMENDMENTS TO WHICH SUBSECTION APPLIES.—

(A) IN GENERAL.—This subsection shall apply to any amendment to any plan or annuity contract which is made—

(i) pursuant to any provision of this section, or pursuant to any regulation issued by the Secretary or the Secretary of Labor under any provision of this section, and

(ii) on or before the last day of the first plan year beginning on or after January 1, 2007, or such later date as the Secretary may prescribe.

In the case of a governmental plan (as defined in section 414(d)), clause (ii) shall be applied by substituting the date which is 2 years after the date otherwise applied under clause (ii).

(B) CONDITIONS.—This subsection shall not apply to any amendment unless—

(i) during the period—

(I) beginning on the date that this section or the regulation described in subparagraph (A)(i) takes effect (or in the case of a plan or contract amendment not required by this section or such regulation, the effective date specified by the plan), and

(II) ending on the date described in subparagraph (A)(ii) (or, if earlier, the date the plan or contract amendment is adopted),

the plan or contract is operated as if such plan or contract amendment were in effect; and

(ii) such plan or contract amendment applies retroactively for such period.

Amendments

- **2018, Bipartisan Budget Act of 2018 (P.L. 115-123)**

P.L. 115-123, §20102(d), Div. B, provides:

(d) PROVISIONS RELATING TO PLAN AMENDMENTS.—

(1) IN GENERAL.—If this subsection applies to any amendment to any plan or annuity contract, such plan or contract shall be treated as being operated in accordance with the terms of the plan during the period described in paragraph (2)(B)(i).

(2) AMENDMENTS TO WHICH SUBSECTION APPLIES.—

(A) IN GENERAL.—This subsection shall apply to any amendment to any plan or annuity contract which is made—

(i) pursuant to any provision of this section, or pursuant to any regulation issued by the Secretary or the Secretary of Labor under any provision of this section, and

(ii) on or before the last day of the first plan year beginning on or after January 1, 2019, or such later date as the Secretary may prescribe.

In the case of a governmental plan (as defined in section 414(d) of the Internal Revenue Code of 1986), clause (ii) shall be applied by substituting the date which is 2 years after the date otherwise applied under clause (ii).

Sec. 1400Q—Stricken

(B) CONDITIONS.—This subsection shall not apply to any amendment unless—

(i) during the period—

(I) beginning on the date that this section or the regulation described in subparagraph (A)(i) takes effect (or in the case of a plan or contract amendment not required by this section or such regulation, the effective date specified by the plan), and

(II) ending on the date described in subparagraph (A)(ii) (or, if earlier, the date the plan or contract amendment is adopted),

the plan or contract is operated as if such plan or contract amendment were in effect, and

(ii) such plan or contract amendment applies retroactively for such period.

• **2017, Tax Cuts and Jobs Act (P.L. 115-97)**

P.L. 115-97, §11028(a) and (b)(2), provides:

SEC. 11028. RELIEF FOR 2016 DISASTER AREAS.

(a) IN GENERAL.—For purposes of this section, the term "2016 disaster area" means any area with respect to which a major disaster has been declared by the President under section 401 of the Robert T. Stafford Disaster Relief and Emergency Assistance Act during calendar year 2016.

(b) SPECIAL RULES FOR USE OF RETIREMENT FUNDS WITH RESPECT TO AREAS DAMAGED BY 2016 DISASTERS.—

* * *

(2) PROVISIONS RELATING TO PLAN AMENDMENTS.—

(A) IN GENERAL.—If this paragraph applies to any amendment to any plan or annuity contract, such plan or contract shall be treated as being operated in accordance with the terms of the plan during the period described in subparagraph (B)(ii)(I).

(B) AMENDMENTS TO WHICH SUBSECTION APPLIES.—

(i) IN GENERAL.—This paragraph shall apply to any amendment to any plan or annuity contract which is made—

(I) pursuant to any provision of this section, or pursuant to any regulation under any provision of this section, and

(II) on or before the last day of the first plan year beginning on or after January 1, 2018, or such later date as the Secretary prescribes.

In the case of a governmental plan (as defined in section 414(d) of the Internal Revenue Code of 1986), subclause (II) shall be applied by substituting the date which is 2 years after the date otherwise applied under subclause (II).

(ii) CONDITIONS.—This paragraph shall not apply to any amendment to a plan or contract unless such amendment applies retroactively for such period, and shall not apply to any such amendment unless the plan or contract is operated as if such amendment were in effect during the period—

(I) beginning on the date that this section or the regulation described in clause (i)(I) takes effect (or in the case of a plan or contract amendment not required by this section or such regulation, the effective date specified by the plan), and

(II) ending on the date described in clause (i)(II) (or, if earlier, the date the plan or contract amendment is adopted).

• **2017, Disaster Tax Relief and Airport and Airway Extension Act of 2017 (P.L. 115-63)**

P.L. 115-63, §502(d), provides:

(d) PROVISIONS RELATING TO PLAN AMENDMENTS.—

(1) IN GENERAL.—If this subsection applies to any amendment to any plan or annuity contract, such plan or contract shall be treated as being operated in accordance with the terms of the plan during the period described in paragraph (2)(B)(i).

(2) AMENDMENTS TO WHICH SUBSECTION APPLIES.—

(A) IN GENERAL.—This subsection shall apply to any amendment to any plan or annuity contract which is made—

(i) pursuant to any provision of this section, or pursuant to any regulation issued by the Secretary or the Secretary of Labor under any provision of this section, and

(ii) on or before the last day of the first plan year beginning on or after January 1, 2019, or such later date as the Secretary may prescribe.

In the case of a governmental plan (as defined in section 414(d) of the Internal Revenue Code of 1986), clause (ii) shall be applied by substituting the date which is 2 years after the date otherwise applied under clause (ii).

(B) CONDITIONS.—This subsection shall not apply to any amendment unless—

(i) during the period—

(I) beginning on the date that this section or the regulation described in subparagraph (A)(i) takes effect (or in the case of a plan or contract amendment not required by this section or such regulation, the effective date specified by the plan), and

(II) ending on the date described in subparagraph (A)(ii) (or, if earlier, the date the plan or contract amendment is adopted),

the plan or contract is operated as if such plan or contract amendment were in effect, and

(ii) such plan or contract amendment applies retroactively for such period.

• **2008, Heartland Disaster Tax Relief Act of 2008 (P.L. 110-343)**

P.L. 110-343, Division C, §702, provides:

For a special rule, see Division C, Act Sec. 702, in the amendment notes for Code Sec. 1400N(a).

• **2008, Heartland, Habitat, Harvest, and Horticulture Act of 2008 (P.L. 110-246)**

P.L. 110-246, §15345, provides:

For a special rule, see Act Sec. 15345 in the amendment notes for Code Sec. 1400N(d).

• **2005, Gulf Opportunity Zone Act of 2005 (P.L. 109-135)**

P.L. 109-135, §201(a):

Amended part II of subchapter Y of chapter 1 by adding at the end a new Code Sec. 1400Q. **Effective** 12-21-2005.

P.L. 115-141, §401(d)(6)(C)(xv)-(xvii), Div. U, provides:

(C) SAVINGS PROVISIONS.—The amendments made by this paragraph shall not apply to—

* * *

(xv) in the case of the repeal of section 1400Q(a) of such Code, distributions before January 1, 2007,

(xvi) in the case of the repeal of section 1400Q(b) of such Code, contributions before March 1, 2006,

(xvii) in the case of the repeal of section 1400Q(c) of such Code, loans made before January 1, 2007,

P.L. 115-141, §401(e), Div. U, provides:

(e) GENERAL SAVINGS PROVISION WITH RESPECT TO DEADWOOD PROVISIONS.—If—

(1) any provision amended or repealed by the amendments made by subsection (b) or (d) applied to—

(A) any transaction occurring before the date of the enactment of this Act,

(B) any property acquired before such date of enactment, or

(C) any item of income, loss, deduction, or credit taken into account before such date of enactment, and

(2) the treatment of such transaction, property, or item under such provision would (without regard to the amendments or repeals made by such subsection) affect the liability for tax for periods ending after such date of enactment,

nothing in the amendments or repeals made by this section shall be construed to affect the treatment of such transaction, property, or item for purposes of determining liability for tax for periods ending after such date of enactment.

[Sec. 1400R—Stricken]

(C) QUALIFIED WAGES.—The term "qualified wages" means wages (as defined in section 51(c)(1), but without regard to section 3306(b)(2)(B)) paid or incurred by an eligible employer with respect to an eligible employee on any day after August 28, 2005, and before January 1, 2006, which occurs during the period—

(i) beginning on the date on which the trade or business described in subparagraph (A) first became inoperable at the principal place of employment of the employee immediately before Hurricane Katrina, and

(ii) ending on the date on which such trade or business has resumed significant operations at such principal place of employment.

Such term shall include wages paid without regard to whether the employee performs no services, performs services at a different place of employment than such principal place of employment, or performs services at such principal place of employment before significant operations have resumed.

(3) CERTAIN RULES TO APPLY.—For purposes of this subsection, rules similar to the rules of sections 51(i)(1) and 52 shall apply.

(4) EMPLOYEE NOT TAKEN INTO ACCOUNT MORE THAN ONCE.—An employee shall not be treated as an eligible employee for purposes of this subsection for any period with respect to any employer if such employer is allowed a credit under section 51 with respect to such employee for such period.

Amendments

• **2018, Tax Technical Corrections Act of 2018 (P.L. 115-141)**

P.L. 115-141, §401(d)(6)(A), Div. U:

Amended chapter 1 by striking subchapter Y (Code Secs. 1400L-1400U-3). **Effective** 3-23-2018. For special rules, see Act Sec. 401(d)(6)(C)(xviii), Div. U, and Act Sec. 401(e), Div. U, below. Prior to being stricken, Code Sec. 1400R read as follows:

SEC. 1400R. EMPLOYMENT RELIEF.

[Sec. 1400R(a)]

(a) EMPLOYEE RETENTION CREDIT FOR EMPLOYERS AFFECTED BY HURRICANE KATRINA.—

(1) IN GENERAL.—For purposes of section 38, in the case of an eligible employer, the Hurricane Katrina employee retention credit for any taxable year is an amount equal to 40 percent of the qualified wages with respect to each eligible employee of such employer for such taxable year. For purposes of the preceding sentence, the amount of qualified wages which may be taken into account with respect to any individual shall not exceed $6,000.

(2) DEFINITIONS.—For purposes of this subsection—

(A) ELIGIBLE EMPLOYER.—The term "eligible employer" means any employer—

(i) which conducted an active trade or business on August 28, 2005, in the GO Zone, and

(ii) with respect to whom the trade or business described in clause (i) is inoperable on any day after August 28, 2005, and before January 1, 2006, as a result of damage sustained by reason of Hurricane Katrina.

(B) ELIGIBLE EMPLOYEE.—The term "eligible employee" means with respect to an eligible employer an employee whose principal place of employment on August 28, 2005, with such eligible employer was in the GO Zone.

Amendments

• **2008, Heartland Disaster Tax Relief Act of 2008 (P.L. 110-343)**

P.L. 110-343, Division C, §702, provides:

For a special rule, see Division C, Act Sec. 702, in the amendment notes for Code Sec. 1400N(a).

INCOME TAX—DC ENTERPRISE ZONE

- **2008, Heartland, Habitat, Harvest, and Horticulture Act of 2008 (P.L. 110-246)**

P.L. 110-246, § 15345, provides:

For a special rule, see Act Sec. 15345 in the amendment notes for Code Sec. 1400N(d).

[Sec. 1400R(b)]

(b) EMPLOYEE RETENTION CREDIT FOR EMPLOYERS AFFECTED BY HURRICANE RITA.—

(1) IN GENERAL.—For purposes of section 38, in the case of an eligible employer, the Hurricane Rita employee retention credit for any taxable year is an amount equal to 40 percent of the qualified wages with respect to each eligible employee of such employer for such taxable year. For purposes of the preceding sentence, the amount of qualified wages which may be taken into account with respect to any individual shall not exceed $6,000.

(2) DEFINITIONS.—For purposes of this subsection—

(A) ELIGIBLE EMPLOYER.—The term "eligible employer" means any employer—

(i) which conducted an active trade or business on September 23, 2005, in the Rita GO Zone, and

(ii) with respect to whom the trade or business described in clause (i) is inoperable on any day after September 23, 2005, and before January 1, 2006, as a result of damage sustained by reason of Hurricane Rita.

(B) ELIGIBLE EMPLOYEE.—The term "eligible employee" means with respect to an eligible employer an employee whose principal place of employment on September 23, 2005, with such eligible employer was in the Rita GO Zone.

(C) QUALIFIED WAGES.—The term "qualified wages" means wages (as defined in section 51(c)(1), but without regard to section 3306(b)(2)(B)) paid or incurred by an eligible employer with respect to an eligible employee on any day after September 23, 2005, and before January 1, 2006, which occurs during the period—

(i) beginning on the date on which the trade or business described in subparagraph (A) first became inoperable at the principal place of employment of the employee immediately before Hurricane Rita, and

(ii) ending on the date on which such trade or business has resumed significant operations at such principal place of employment.

Such term shall include wages paid without regard to whether the employee performs no services, performs services at a different place of employment than such principal place of employment, or performs services at such principal place of employment before significant operations have resumed.

(3) CERTAIN RULES TO APPLY.—For purposes of this subsection, rules similar to the rules of sections 51(i)(1) and 52 shall apply.

(4) EMPLOYEE NOT TAKEN INTO ACCOUNT MORE THAN ONCE.—An employee shall not be treated as an eligible employee for purposes of this subsection for any period with respect to any employer if such employer is allowed a credit under subsection (a) or section 51 with respect to such employee for such period.

[Sec. 1400R(c)]

(c) EMPLOYEE RETENTION CREDIT FOR EMPLOYERS AFFECTED BY HURRICANE WILMA.—

(1) IN GENERAL.—For purposes of section 38, in the case of an eligible employer, the Hurricane Wilma employee retention credit for any taxable year is an amount equal to 40 percent of the qualified wages with respect to each eligible employee of such employer for such taxable year. For purposes of the preceding sentence, the amount of qualified wages which may be taken into account with respect to any individual shall not exceed $6,000.

(2) DEFINITIONS.—For purposes of this subsection—

(A) ELIGIBLE EMPLOYER.—The term "eligible employer" means any employer—

(i) which conducted an active trade or business on October 23, 2005, in the Wilma GO Zone, and

(ii) with respect to whom the trade or business described in clause (i) is inoperable on any day after October 23, 2005, and before January 1, 2006, as a result of damage sustained by reason of Hurricane Wilma.

(B) ELIGIBLE EMPLOYEE.—The term "eligible employee" means with respect to an eligible employer an employee whose principal place of employment on October 23, 2005, with such eligible employer was in the Wilma GO Zone.

(C) QUALIFIED WAGES.—The term "qualified wages" means wages (as defined in section 51(c)(1), but without regard to section 3306(b)(2)(B)) paid or incurred by an eligible employer with respect to an eligible employee on any day after October 23, 2005, and before January 1, 2006, which occurs during the period—

(i) beginning on the date on which the trade or business described in subparagraph (A) first became inoperable at the principal place of employment of the employee immediately before Hurricane Wilma, and

(ii) ending on the date on which such trade or business has resumed significant operations at such principal place of employment.

Such term shall include wages paid without regard to whether the employee performs no services, performs services at a different place of employment than such principal place of employment, or performs services at such principal place of employment before significant operations have resumed.

(3) CERTAIN RULES TO APPLY.—For purposes of this subsection, rules similar to the rules of sections 51(i)(1) and 52 shall apply.

(4) EMPLOYEE NOT TAKEN INTO ACCOUNT MORE THAN ONCE.—An employee shall not be treated as an eligible employee for purposes of this subsection for any period with respect to any employer if such employer is allowed a credit under subsection (a) or (b) or section 51 with respect to such employee for such period.

Amendments

- **2018, Bipartisan Budget Act of 2018 (P.L. 115-123)**

P.L. 115-123, § 20103, Div. B, provides:

SEC. 20103. EMPLOYEE RETENTION CREDIT FOR EMPLOYERS AFFECTED BY CALIFORNIA WILDFIRES.

(a) IN GENERAL.—For purposes of section 38 of the Internal Revenue Code of 1986, in the case of an eligible employer, the California wildfire employee retention credit shall be treated as a credit listed in subsection (b) of such section. For purposes of this subsection, the California wildfire employee retention credit for any taxable year is an amount equal to 40 percent of the qualified wages with respect to each eligible employee of such employer for such taxable year. For purposes of the preceding sentence, the amount of qualified wages which may be taken into account with respect to any individual shall not exceed $6,000.

(b) DEFINITIONS.—For purposes of this section—

(1) ELIGIBLE EMPLOYER.—The term "eligible employer" means any employer—

(A) which conducted an active trade or business on October 8, 2017, in the California wildfire disaster zone, and

(B) with respect to whom the trade or business described in subparagraph (A) is inoperable on any day after October 8, 2017, and before January 1, 2018, as a result of damage sustained by reason of the wildfires to which such declaration of such area relates.

(2) ELIGIBLE EMPLOYEE.—The term "eligible employee" means with respect to an eligible employer an employee whose principal place of employment on October 8, 2017, with such eligible employer was in the California wildfire disaster zone.

(3) QUALIFIED WAGES.—The term "qualified wages" means wages (as defined in section 51(c)(1) of the Internal Revenue Code of 1986, but without regard to section 3306(b)(2)(B) of such Code) paid or incurred by an eligible employer with respect to an eligible employee on any day after October 8, 2017, and before January 1, 2018, which occurs during the period—

(A) beginning on the date on which the trade or business described in paragraph (1) first became inoperable at the principal place of employment of the employee immediately before the wildfires to which the declaration of the California wildfire disaster area relates, and

(B) ending on the date on which such trade or business has resumed significant operations at such principal place of employment.

Such term shall include wages paid without regard to whether the employee performs no services, performs services at a different place of employment than such principal place of employment, or performs services at such principal place of employment before significant operations have resumed.

(c) CERTAIN RULES TO APPLY.—For purposes of this section, rules similar to the rules of sections 51(i)(1), 52, and 280C(a) of the Internal Revenue Code of 1986, shall apply.

(d) EMPLOYEE NOT TAKEN INTO ACCOUNT MORE THAN ONCE.—An employee shall not be treated as an eligible employee for purposes of this section for any period with respect to any employer if such employer is allowed a credit under section 51 of the Internal Revenue Code of 1986 with respect to such employee for such period.

- **2017, Disaster Tax Relief and Airport and Airway Extension Act of 2017 (P.L. 115-63)**

P.L. 115-63, § 503 (as amended by P.L. 115-123, § 20201(b), Div. D), provides:

SEC. 503. DISASTER-RELATED EMPLOYMENT RELIEF.

(a) EMPLOYEE RETENTION CREDIT FOR EMPLOYERS AFFECTED BY HURRICANE HARVEY.—

(1) IN GENERAL.—For purposes of section 38 of the Internal Revenue Code of 1986, in the case of an eligible employer, the Hurricane Harvey employee retention credit shall be treated as a credit listed in subsection (b) of such section. For purposes of this subsection, the Hurricane Harvey employee retention credit for any taxable year is an amount equal to 40 percent of the qualified wages with respect to each eligible employee of such employer for such taxable year. For purposes of the preceding sentence, the amount of qualified wages which may be taken into account with respect to any individual shall not exceed $6,000.

(2) DEFINITIONS.—For purposes of this subsection—

(A) ELIGIBLE EMPLOYER.—The term "eligible employer" means any employer—

(i) which conducted an active trade or business on August 23, 2017, in the Hurricane Harvey disaster zone, and

(ii) with respect to whom the trade or business described in clause (i) is inoperable on any day after August 23, 2017, and before January 1, 2018, as a result of damage sustained by reason of Hurricane Harvey.

(B) ELIGIBLE EMPLOYEE.—The term "eligible employee" means with respect to an eligible employer an employee whose principal place of employment on August 23, 2017, with such eligible employer was in the Hurricane Harvey disaster zone.

(C) QUALIFIED WAGES.—The term "qualified wages" means wages (as defined in section 51(c)(1) of the Internal Revenue Code of 1986, but without regard to section 3306(b)(2)(B) of such Code) paid or incurred by an eligible employer with respect to an eligible employee on any day after August 23, 2017, and before January 1, 2018, which occurs during the period—

(i) beginning on the date on which the trade or business described in subparagraph (A) first became inoperable at the principal place of employment of the employee immediately before Hurricane Harvey, and

(ii) ending on the date on which such trade or business has resumed significant operations at such principal place of employment.

Such term shall include wages paid without regard to whether the employee performs no services, performs services at a different place of employment than such principal place of employment, or performs services at such principal place of employment before significant operations have resumed.

(3) CERTAIN RULES TO APPLY.—For purposes of this subsection, rules similar to the rules of sections 51(i)(1), 52, and 280C(a), [sic] of the Internal Revenue Code of 1986, [sic] shall apply.

(4) EMPLOYEE NOT TAKEN INTO ACCOUNT MORE THAN ONCE.—An employee shall not be treated as an eligible employee for purposes of this subsection for any period with respect to any employer if such employer is allowed a credit under section 51 of the Internal Revenue Code of 1986 with respect to such employee for such period.

(b) EMPLOYEE RETENTION CREDIT FOR EMPLOYERS AFFECTED BY HURRICANE IRMA.—

(1) IN GENERAL.—For purposes of section 38 of the Internal Revenue Code of 1986, in the case of an eligible employer, the Hurricane Irma employee retention credit shall be treated as a credit listed in subsection (b) of such section. For purposes of this subsection, the Hurricane Irma employee retention credit for any taxable year is an amount equal to 40 percent of the qualified wages with respect to each eligible

Sec. 1400R—Stricken

employee of such employer for such taxable year. For purposes of the preceding sentence, the amount of qualified wages which may be taken into account with respect to any individual shall not exceed $6,000.

(2) DEFINITIONS.—For purposes of this subsection—

(A) ELIGIBLE EMPLOYER.—The term "eligible employer" means any employer—

(i) which conducted an active trade or business on September 4, 2017, in the Hurricane Irma disaster zone, and

(ii) with respect to whom the trade or business described in clause (i) is inoperable on any day after September 4, 2017, and before January 1, 2018, as a result of damage sustained by reason of Hurricane Irma.

(B) ELIGIBLE EMPLOYEE.—The term "eligible employee" means with respect to an eligible employer an employee whose principal place of employment on September 4, 2017, with such eligible employer was in the Hurricane Irma disaster zone.

(C) QUALIFIED WAGES.—The term "qualified wages" means wages (as defined in section 51(c)(1) of the Internal Revenue Code of 1986, but without regard to section 3306(b)(2)(B) of such Code) paid or incurred by an eligible employer with respect to an eligible employee on any day after September 4, 2017, and before January 1, 2018, which occurs during the period—

(i) beginning on the date on which the trade or business described in subparagraph (A) first became inoperable at the principal place of employment of the employee immediately before Hurricane Irma, and

(ii) ending on the date on which such trade or business has resumed significant operations at such principal place of employment.

Such term shall include wages paid without regard to whether the employee performs no services, performs services at a different place of employment than such principal place of employment, or performs services at such principal place of employment before significant operations have resumed.

(3) CERTAIN RULES TO APPLY.—For purposes of this subsection, rules similar to the rules of sections 51(i)(1), 52, and 280C(a), [sic] of the Internal Revenue Code of 1986, [sic] shall apply.

(4) EMPLOYEE NOT TAKEN INTO ACCOUNT MORE THAN ONCE.—An employee shall not be treated as an eligible employee for purposes of this subsection for any period with respect to any employer if such employer is allowed a credit under subsection (a) or section 51 of the Internal Revenue Code of 1986, with respect to such employee for such period.

(c) EMPLOYEE RETENTION CREDIT FOR EMPLOYERS AFFECTED BY HURRICANE MARIA.—

(1) IN GENERAL.—For purposes of section 38 of the Internal Revenue Code of 1986, in the case of an eligible employer, the Hurricane Maria employee retention credit shall be treated as a credit listed in subsection (b) of such section. For purposes of this subsection, the Hurricane Maria employee retention credit for any taxable year is an amount equal to 40 percent of the qualified wages with respect to each eligible employee of such employer for such taxable year. For purposes of the preceding sentence, the amount of qualified wages which may be taken into account with respect to any individual shall not exceed $6,000.

(2) DEFINITIONS.—For purposes of this subsection—

(A) ELIGIBLE EMPLOYER.—The term "eligible employer" means any employer—

(i) which conducted an active trade or business on September 16, 2017, in the Hurricane Maria disaster zone, and

(ii) with respect to whom the trade or business described in clause (i) is inoperable on any day after September 16, 2017, and before January 1, 2018, as a result of damage sustained by reason of Hurricane Maria.

[Sec. 1400S—Stricken]

Amendments

• **2019, Taxpayer Certainty and Disaster Tax Relief Act of 2019 (P.L. 116-94)**

P.L. 116-94, §§ 201 and 204, Div. Q, provides:

SEC. 201. DEFINITIONS.

For purposes of this title—

(1) QUALIFIED DISASTER AREA.—

(A) IN GENERAL.—The term "qualified disaster area" means any area with respect to which a major disaster was declared, during the period beginning on January 1, 2018, and ending on the date which is 60 days after the date of the enactment of this Act, by the President under section 401 of the Robert T. Stafford Disaster Relief and Emergency Assistance Act if the incident period of the disaster with respect to which such declaration is made begins on or before the date of the enactment of this Act.

(B) DENIAL OF DOUBLE BENEFIT.—Such term shall not include the California wildfire disaster area (as defined in section 20101 of subdivision 2 of division B of the Bipartisan Budget Act of 2018).

(2) QUALIFIED DISASTER ZONE.—The term "qualified disaster zone" means that portion of any qualified disaster area which was determined by the President, during the period beginning on January 1, 2018, and ending on the date which is 60 days after the date of the enactment of this Act, to warrant individual or individual and public assistance from the Federal Government under the Robert T. Stafford Disaster Relief and Emergency Assistance Act by reason of the qualified disaster with respect to such disaster area.

(3) QUALIFIED DISASTER.—The term "qualified disaster" means, with respect to any qualified disaster area, the disaster by reason of which a major disaster was declared with respect to such area.

(4) INCIDENT PERIOD.—The term "incident period" means, with respect to any qualified disaster, the period specified by the Federal Emergency Management Agency as the period during which such disaster occurred (except that for purposes of this title such period shall not be treated as beginning before January 1, 2018, or ending after the date which is 30 days after the date of the enactment of this Act).

SEC. 204. OTHER DISASTER-RELATED TAX RELIEF PROVISIONS.

(a) TEMPORARY INCREASE IN LIMITATION ON QUALIFIED CONTRIBUTIONS.—

(B) ELIGIBLE EMPLOYEE.—The term "eligible employee" means with respect to an eligible employer an employee whose principal place of employment on September 16, 2017, with such eligible employer was in the Hurricane Maria disaster zone.

(C) QUALIFIED WAGES.—The term "qualified wages" means wages (as defined in section 51(c)(1) of the Internal Revenue Code of 1986, but without regard to section 3306(b)(2)(B) of such Code) paid or incurred by an eligible employer with respect to an eligible employee on any day after September 16, 2017, and before January 1, 2018, which occurs during the period—

(i) beginning on the date on which the trade or business described in subparagraph (A) first became inoperable at the principal place of employment of the employee immediately before Hurricane Maria, and

(ii) ending on the date on which such trade or business has resumed significant operations at such principal place of employment.

Such term shall include wages paid without regard to whether the employee performs no services, performs services at a different place of employment than such principal place of employment, or performs services at such principal place of employment before significant operations have resumed.

(3) CERTAIN RULES TO APPLY.—For purposes of this subsection, rules similar to the rules of sections 51(i)(1), 52, and 280C(a), [sic] of the Internal Revenue Code of 1986, [sic] shall apply.

(4) EMPLOYEE NOT TAKEN INTO ACCOUNT MORE THAN ONCE.—An employee shall not be treated as an eligible employee for purposes of this subsection for any period with respect to any employer if such employer is allowed a credit under subsection (a) or (b), or section 51 of the Internal Revenue Code of 1986, with respect to such employee for such period.

• **2005, Gulf Opportunity Zone Act of 2005 (P.L. 109-135)**

P.L. 109-135, § 201(a):

Amended part II of subchapter Y of chapter 1 by adding at the end a new Code Sec. 1400R. **Effective** 12-21-2005.

P.L. 115-141, § 401(d)(6)(C)(xviii), Div. U, provides:

(C) SAVINGS PROVISIONS.—The amendments made by this paragraph shall not apply to—

* * *

(xviii) in the case of the repeal of section 1400R of such Code, wages paid or incurred before January 1, 2006,

P.L. 115-141, § 401(e), Div. U, provides:

(e) GENERAL SAVINGS PROVISION WITH RESPECT TO DEADWOOD PROVISIONS.—If—

(1) any provision amended or repealed by the amendments made by subsection (b) or (d) applied to—

(A) any transaction occurring before the date of the enactment of this Act,

(B) any property acquired before such date of enactment, or

(C) any item of income, loss, deduction, or credit taken into account before such date of enactment, and

(2) the treatment of such transaction, property, or item under such provision would (without regard to the amendments or repeals made by such subsection) affect the liability for tax for periods ending after such date of enactment,

nothing in the amendments or repeals made by this section shall be construed to affect the treatment of such transaction, property, or item for purposes of determining liability for tax for periods ending after such date of enactment.

(1) SUSPENSION OF CURRENT LIMITATION.—Except as otherwise provided in paragraph (2), qualified contributions shall be disregarded in applying subsections (b) and (d) of section 170 of the Internal Revenue Code of 1986.

(2) APPLICATION OF INCREASED LIMITATION.—For purposes of section 170 of the Internal Revenue Code of 1986—

(A) IN GENERAL.—In the case of an individual—

(i) LIMITATION.—Any qualified contribution shall be allowed as a deduction only to the extent that the aggregate of such contributions does not exceed the excess of the taxpayer's contribution base (as defined in subparagraph (H) of section 170(b)(1) of such Code) over the amount of all other charitable contributions allowed under section 170(b)(1) of such Code.

(ii) CARRYOVER.—If the aggregate amount of qualified contributions made in the contribution year (within the meaning of section 170(d)(1) of such Code) exceeds the limitation of clause (i), such excess shall be added to the excess described in section 170(b)(1)(G)(ii).

(B) CORPORATIONS.—In the case of a corporation—

(i) LIMITATION.—Any qualified contribution shall be allowed as a deduction only to the extent that the aggregate of such contributions does not exceed the excess of the taxpayer's taxable income (as determined under paragraph (2) of section 170(b) of such Code) over the amount of all other charitable contributions allowed under such paragraph.

(ii) CARRYOVER.—If the aggregate amount of qualified contributions made in the contribution year (within the meaning of section 170(d)(2) of such Code) exceeds the limitation of clause (i), such excess shall be appropriately taken into account under section 170(d)(2) subject to the limitations thereof.

(3) QUALIFIED CONTRIBUTIONS.—

(A) IN GENERAL For purposes of this subsection, the term "qualified contribution" means any charitable contribution (as defined in section 170(c) of the Internal Revenue Code of 1986) if—

(i) such contribution—

(I) is paid, during the period beginning on January 1, 2018, and ending on the date which is 60 days after the date of the enactment of this Act, in cash to an organization described in section 170(b)(1)(A) of such Code, and

INCOME TAX—DC ENTERPRISE ZONE

(II) is made for relief efforts in one or more qualified disaster areas,

(ii) the taxpayer obtains from such organization contemporaneous written acknowledgment (within the meaning of section 170(f)(8) of such Code) that such contribution was used (or is to be used) for relief efforts described in clause (i)(II), and

(iii) the taxpayer has elected the application of this subsection with respect to such contribution.

(B) EXCEPTION.—Such term shall not include a contribution by a donor if the contribution is—

(i) to an organization described in section 509(a)(3) of the Internal Revenue Code of 1986, or

(ii) for the establishment of a new, or maintenance of an existing, donor advised fund (as defined in section 4966(d)(2) of such Code).

(C) APPLICATION OF ELECTION TO PARTNERSHIPS AND S CORPORATIONS.—In the case of a partnership or S corporation, the election under subparagraph (A)(iii) shall be made separately by each partner or shareholder.

(b) SPECIAL RULES FOR QUALIFIED DISASTER-RELATED PERSONAL CASUALTY LOSSES.—

(1) IN GENERAL.—If an individual has a net disaster loss for any taxable year—

(A) the amount determined under section 165(h)(2)(A)(ii) of the Internal Revenue Code of 1986 shall be equal to the sum of—

(i) such net disaster loss, and

(ii) so much of the excess referred to in the matter preceding clause (i) of section 165(h)(2)(A) of such Code (reduced by the amount in clause (i) of this subparagraph) as exceeds 10 percent of the adjusted gross income of the individual,

(B) section 165(h)(1) of such Code shall be applied by substituting "$500" for "$500 ($100 for taxable years beginning after December 31, 2009)",

(C) the standard deduction determined under section 63(c) of such Code shall be increased by the net disaster loss, and

(D) section 56(b)(1)(E) of such Code (section 56(b)(1)(D) of such Code in the case of taxable years ending after December 31, 2018) shall not apply to so much of the standard deduction as is attributable to the increase under subparagraph (C) of this paragraph.

(2) NET DISASTER LOSS.—For purposes of this subsection, the term "net disaster loss" means the excess of qualified disaster-related personal casualty losses over personal casualty gains (as defined in section 165(h)(3)(A) of the Internal Revenue Code of 1986).

(3) QUALIFIED DISASTER-RELATED PERSONAL CASUALTY LOSSES.—For purposes of this subsection, the term "qualified disaster-related personal casualty losses" means losses described in section 165(c)(3) of the Internal Revenue Code of 1986 which arise in a qualified disaster area on or after the first day of the incident period of the qualified disaster to which such area relates, and which are attributable to such qualified disaster.

(c) SPECIAL RULE FOR DETERMINING EARNED INCOME.—

(1) IN GENERAL.—In the case of a qualified individual, if the earned income of the taxpayer for the applicable taxable year is less than the earned income of the taxpayer for the preceding taxable year, the credits allowed under sections 24(d) and 32 of the Internal Revenue Code of 1986 may, at the election of the taxpayer, be determined by substituting—

(A) such earned income for the preceding taxable year, for

(B) such earned income for the applicable taxable year.

(2) QUALIFIED INDIVIDUAL.—For purposes of this subsection, the term "qualified individual" means any individual whose principal place of abode at any time during the incident period of any qualified disaster was located—

(A) in the qualified disaster zone with respect to such qualified disaster, or

(B) in the qualified disaster area with respect to such qualified disaster (but outside the qualified disaster zone with respect to such qualified disaster) and such individual was displaced from such principal place of abode by reason of such qualified disaster.

(3) APPLICABLE TAXABLE YEAR.—For purposes of this subsection, the term "applicable taxable year" means—

(A) in the case of a qualified individual other than an individual described in subparagraph (B), any taxable year which includes any portion of the incident period of the qualified disaster to which the qualified disaster area referred to in paragraph (2)(A) relates, or

(B) in the case of a qualified individual described in subparagraph (B) of paragraph (2), any taxable year which includes any portion of the period described in such subparagraph.

(4) EARNED INCOME.—For purposes of this subsection, the term "earned income" has the meaning given such term under section 32(c) of the Internal Revenue Code of 1986.

(A) APPLICATION TO JOINT RETURNS.—For purposes of paragraph (1), in the case of a joint return for an applicable taxable year—

(i) such paragraph shall apply if either spouse is a qualified individual, and

(ii) the earned income of the taxpayer for the preceding taxable year shall be the sum of the earned income of each spouse for such preceding taxable year.

(B) UNIFORM APPLICATION OF ELECTION.—Any election made under paragraph (1) shall apply with respect to both sections 24(d) and 32 of the Internal Revenue Code of 1986.

(C) ERRORS TREATED AS MATHEMATICAL ERROR.— For purposes of section 6213 of the Internal Revenue Code of 1986, an incorrect use on a return of earned income pursuant to paragraph (1) shall be treated as a mathematical or clerical error.

(D) NO EFFECT ON DETERMINATION OF GROSS INCOME, ETC.—Except as otherwise provided in this subsection, the Internal Revenue Code of 1986 shall be applied without regard to any substitution under paragraph (1).

Sec. 1400S—Stricken

- **2018, Tax Technical Corrections Act of 2018 (P.L. 115-141)**

P.L. 115-141, § 401(d)(6)(A), Div. U:

Amended chapter 1 by striking subchapter Y (Code Secs. 1400L-1400U-3). **Effective** 3-23-2018. For special rules, see Act Sec. 401(d)(6)(C)(xix), Div. U, and Act Sec. 401(e), Div. U, below. Prior to being stricken, Code Sec. 1400S read as follows:

SEC. 1400S. ADDITIONAL TAX RELIEF PROVISIONS.

[Sec. 1400S(a)]

(a) TEMPORARY SUSPENSION OF LIMITATIONS ON CHARITABLE CONTRIBUTIONS.—

(1) IN GENERAL.—Except as otherwise provided in paragraph (2), section 170(b) shall not apply to qualified contributions and such contributions shall not be taken into account for purposes of applying subsections (b) and (d) of section 170 to other contributions.

(2) TREATMENT OF EXCESS CONTRIBUTIONS.—For purposes of section 170—

(A) INDIVIDUALS.—In the case of an individual—

(i) LIMITATION.—Any qualified contribution shall be allowed only to the extent that the aggregate of such contributions does not exceed the excess of the taxpayer's contribution base (as defined in subparagraph (G) of section 170(b)(1)) over the amount of all other charitable contributions allowed under section 170(b)(1).

(ii) CARRYOVER.—If the aggregate amount of qualified contributions made in the contribution year (within the meaning of section 170(d)(1)) exceeds the limitation of clause (i), such excess shall be added to the excess described in the portion of subparagraph (A) of such section which precedes clause (i) thereof for purposes of applying such section.

(B) CORPORATIONS.—In the case of a corporation—

(i) LIMITATION.—Any qualified contribution shall be allowed only to the extent that the aggregate of such contributions does not exceed the excess of the taxpayer's taxable income (as determined under paragraph (2) of section 170(b)) over the amount of all other charitable contributions allowed under such paragraph.

(ii) CARRYOVER.—Rules similar to the rules of subparagraph (A)(ii) shall apply for purposes of this subparagraph.

(3) EXCEPTION TO OVERALL LIMITATION ON ITEMIZED DEDUCTIONS.—So much of any deduction allowed under section 170 as does not exceed the qualified contributions paid during the taxable year shall not be treated as an itemized deduction for purposes of section 68.

(4) QUALIFIED CONTRIBUTIONS.—

(A) IN GENERAL.—For purposes of this subsection, the term "qualified contribution" means any charitable contribution (as defined in section 170(c)) if—

(i) such contribution is paid during the period beginning on August 28, 2005, and ending on December 31, 2005, in cash to an organization described in section 170(b)(1)(A) (other than an organization described in section 509(a)(3)),

(ii) in the case of a contribution paid by a corporation, such contribution is for relief efforts related to Hurricane Katrina, Hurricane Rita, or Hurricane Wilma, and

(iii) the taxpayer has elected the application of this subsection with respect to such contribution.

(B) EXCEPTION.—Such term shall not include a contribution if the contribution is for establishment of a new, or maintenance in an existing, segregated fund or account with respect to which the donor (or any person appointed or designated by such donor) has, or reasonably expects to have, advisory privileges with respect to distributions or investments by reason of the donor's status as a donor.

(C) APPLICATION OF ELECTION TO PARTNERSHIPS AND S CORPORATIONS.—In the case of a partnership or S corporation, the election under subparagraph (A)(iii) shall be made separately by each partner or shareholder.

Amendments

- **2018, Bipartisan Budget Act of 2018 (P.L. 115-123)**

P.L. 115-123, § 20104(a), Div. B, provides:

(a) TEMPORARY SUSPENSION OF LIMITATIONS ON CHARITABLE CONTRIBUTIONS.—

(1) IN GENERAL.—Except as otherwise provided in paragraph (2), subsection (b) of section 170 of the Internal Revenue Code of 1986 shall not apply to qualified contributions and such contributions shall not be taken into account for purposes of applying subsections (b) and (d) of such section to other contributions.

(2) TREATMENT OF EXCESS CONTRIBUTIONS.—For purposes of section 170 of the Internal Revenue Code of 1986—

(A) INDIVIDUALS.—In the case of an individual—

(i) LIMITATION.—Any qualified contribution shall be allowed only to the extent that the aggregate of such contributions does not exceed the excess of the taxpayer's contribution base (as defined in subparagraph (H) of section 170(b)(1) of such Code) over the amount of all other charitable contributions allowed under section 170(b)(1) of such Code.

(ii) CARRYOVER.—If the aggregate amount of qualified contributions made in the contribution year (within the meaning of section 170(d)(1) of such Code) exceeds the limitation of clause (i), such excess shall be added to the excess described in the portion of subparagraph (A) of such section which precedes clause (i) thereof for purposes of applying such section.

(B) CORPORATIONS.—In the case of a corporation—

(i) LIMITATION.—Any qualified contribution shall be allowed only to the extent that the aggregate of such contributions does not exceed the excess of the taxpayer's taxable income (as determined under paragraph (2) of section 170(b) of such Code) over the amount of all other charitable contributions allowed under such paragraph.

(ii) CARRYOVER.—Rules similar to the rules of subparagraph (A)(ii) shall apply for purposes of this subparagraph.

(3) EXCEPTION TO OVERALL LIMITATION ON ITEMIZED DEDUCTIONS.—So much of any deduction allowed under section 170 of the Internal Revenue Code of 1986 as does

not exceed the qualified contributions paid during the taxable year shall not be treated as an itemized deduction for purposes of section 68 of such Code.

(4) QUALIFIED CONTRIBUTIONS.—

(A) IN GENERAL.—For purposes of this subsection, the term "qualified contribution" means any charitable contribution (as defined in section 170(c) of the Internal Revenue Code of 1986) if—

(i) such contribution—

(I) is paid during the period beginning on October 8, 2017, and ending on December 31, 2018, in cash to an organization described in section 170(b)(1)(A) of such Code, and

(II) is made for relief efforts in the California wildfire disaster area,

(ii) the taxpayer obtains from such organization contemporaneous written acknowledgment (within the meaning of section 170(f)(8) of such Code) that such contribution was used (or is to be used) for relief efforts described in clause (i)(II), and

(iii) the taxpayer has elected the application of this subsection with respect to such contribution.

(B) EXCEPTION.—Such term shall not include a contribution by a donor if the contribution is—

(i) to an organization described in section 509(a)(3) of the Internal Revenue Code of 1986, or

(ii) for the establishment of a new, or maintenance of an existing, donor advised fund (as defined in section 4966(d)(2) of such Code).

(C) APPLICATION OF ELECTION TO PARTNERSHIPS AND S CORPORATIONS.—In the case of a partnership or S corporation, the election under subparagraph (A)(iii) shall be made separately by each partner or shareholder.

• **2017, Disaster Tax Relief and Airport and Airway Extension Act of 2017 (P.L. 115-63)**

P.L. 115-63, § 504(a), provides:

(a) TEMPORARY SUSPENSION OF LIMITATIONS ON CHARITABLE CONTRIBUTIONS.—

(1) IN GENERAL.—Except as otherwise provided in paragraph (2), subsection (b) of section 170 of the Internal Revenue Code of 1986 shall not apply to qualified contributions and such contributions shall not be taken into account for purposes of applying subsections (b) and (d) of such section to other contributions.

(2) TREATMENT OF EXCESS CONTRIBUTIONS.—For purposes of section 170 of the Internal Revenue Code of 1986—

(A) INDIVIDUALS.—In the case of an individual—

(i) LIMITATION.—Any qualified contribution shall be allowed only to the extent that the aggregate of such contributions does not exceed the excess of the taxpayer's contribution base (as defined in subparagraph (G) of section 170(b)(1) of such Code) over the amount of all other charitable contributions allowed under section 170(b)(1) of such Code.

(ii) CARRYOVER.—If the aggregate amount of qualified contributions made in the contribution year (within the meaning of section 170(d)(1) of such Code) exceeds the limitation of clause (i), such excess shall be added to the excess described in the portion of subparagraph (A) of such section which precedes clause (i) thereof for purposes of applying such section.

(B) CORPORATIONS.—In the case of a corporation—

(i) LIMITATION.—Any qualified contribution shall be allowed only to the extent that the aggregate of such contributions does not exceed the excess of the taxpayer's taxable income (as determined under paragraph (2) of section 170(b) of such Code) over the amount of all other charitable contributions allowed under such paragraph.

(ii) CARRYOVER.—Rules similar to the rules of subparagraph (A)(ii) shall apply for purposes of this subparagraph.

(3) EXCEPTION TO OVERALL LIMITATION ON ITEMIZED DEDUCTIONS.—So much of any deduction allowed under section 170 of the Internal Revenue Code of 1986 as does not exceed the qualified contributions paid during the taxable year shall not be treated as an itemized deduction for purposes of section 68 of such Code.

(4) QUALIFIED CONTRIBUTIONS.—

(A) IN GENERAL.—For purposes of this subsection, the term "qualified contribution" means any charitable contribution (as defined in section 170(c) of the Internal Revenue Code of 1986) if—

(i) such contribution—

(I) is paid during the period beginning on August 23, 2017, and ending on December 31, 2017, in cash to an organization described in section 170(b)(1)(A) of such Code, and

(II) is made for relief efforts in the Hurricane Harvey disaster area, the Hurricane Irma disaster area, or the Hurricane Maria disaster area,

(ii) the taxpayer obtains from such organization contemporaneous written acknowledgment (within the meaning of section 170(f)(8) of such Code) that such contribution was used (or is to be used) for relief efforts described in clause (i)(II), and

(iii) the taxpayer has elected the application of this subsection with respect to such contribution.

(B) EXCEPTION.—Such term shall not include a contribution by a donor if the contribution is—

(i) to an organization described in section 509(a)(3) of the Internal Revenue Code of 1986, or

(ii) for the establishment of a new, or maintenance of an existing, donor advised fund (as defined in section 4966(d)(2) of such Code).

(C) APPLICATION OF ELECTION TO PARTNERSHIPS AND S CORPORATIONS.—In the case of a partnership or S corporation, the election under subparagraph (A)(iii) shall be made separately by each partner or shareholder.

• **2008, Heartland Disaster Tax Relief Act of 2008 (P.L. 110-343)**

P.L. 110-343, Division C, § 702, provides:

For a special rule, see Division C, Act Sec. 702, in the amendment notes for Code Sec. 1400N(a).

• **2007, Tax Technical Corrections Act of 2007 (P.L. 110-172)**

P.L. 110-172, § 11(a)(14)(C):

Amended Code Sec. 1400S(a)(2)(A)(i) by striking "subparagraph (F)" and inserting "subparagraph (G)". **Effective** 12-29-2007.

[Sec. 1400S(b)]

(b) SUSPENSION OF CERTAIN LIMITATIONS ON PERSONAL CASUALTY LOSSES.—Paragraphs (1) and (2)(A) of section 165(h) shall not apply to losses described in section 165(c)(3)—

(1) which arise in the Hurricane Katrina disaster area on or after August 25, 2005, and which are attributable to Hurricane Katrina,

(2) which arise in the Hurricane Rita disaster area on or after September 23, 2005, and which are attributable to Hurricane Rita, or

(3) which arise in the Hurricane Wilma disaster area on or after October 23, 2005, and which are attributable to Hurricane Wilma.

In the case of any other losses, section 165(h)(2)(A) shall be applied without regard to the losses referred to in the preceding sentence.

Amendments

• **2018, Bipartisan Budget Act of 2018 (P.L. 115-123)**

P.L. 115-123, § 20104(b), Div. B, provides:

(b) SPECIAL RULES FOR QUALIFIED DISASTER-RELATED PERSONAL CASUALTY LOSSES.—

(1) IN GENERAL.—If an individual has a net disaster loss for any taxable year—

(A) the amount determined under section 165(h)(2)(A)(ii) of the Internal Revenue Code of 1986 shall be equal to the sum of—

(i) such net disaster loss, and

(ii) so much of the excess referred to in the matter preceding clause (i) of section 165(h)(2)(A) of such Code (reduced by the amount in clause (i) of this subparagraph) as exceeds 10 percent of the adjusted gross income of the individual,

(B) section 165(h)(1) of such Code shall be applied by substituting "$500" for "$500 ($100 for taxable years beginning after December 31, 2009)",

(C) the standard deduction determined under section 63(c) of such Code shall be increased by the net disaster loss, and

(D) section 56(b)(1)(E) of such Code shall not apply to so much of the standard deduction as is attributable to the increase under subparagraph (C) of this paragraph.

(2) NET DISASTER LOSS.—For purposes of this subsection, the term "net disaster loss" means the excess of qualified disaster-related personal casualty losses over personal casualty gains (as defined in section 165(h)(3)(A) of the Internal Revenue Code of 1986).

(3) QUALIFIED DISASTER-RELATED PERSONAL CASUALTY LOSSES.—For purposes of this subsection, the term "qualified disaster-related personal casualty losses" means losses described in section 165(c)(3) of the Internal Revenue Code of 1986 which arise in the California wildfire disaster area on or after October 8, 2017, and which are attributable to the wildfires to which the declaration of such area relates.

• **2017, Tax Cuts and Jobs Act (P.L. 115-97)**

P.L. 115-97, § 11028(a) and (c), provides:

SEC. 11028. RELIEF FOR 2016 DISASTER AREAS.

(a) IN GENERAL.—For purposes of this section, the term "2016 disaster area" means any area with respect to which a major disaster has been declared by the President under section 401 of the Robert T. Stafford Disaster Relief and Emergency Assistance Act during calendar year 2016.

* * *

(c) SPECIAL RULES FOR PERSONAL CASUALTY LOSSES RELATED TO 2016 MAJOR DISASTER.—

(1) IN GENERAL.—If an individual has a net disaster loss for any taxable year beginning after December 31, 2015, and before January 1, 2018—

(A) the amount determined under section 165(h)(2)(A)(ii) of the Internal Revenue Code of 1986 shall be equal to the sum of—

(i) such net disaster loss, and

(ii) so much of the excess referred to in the matter preceding clause (i) of section 165(h)(2)(A) of such Code (reduced by the amount in clause (i) of this subparagraph) as exceeds 10 percent of the adjusted gross income of the individual,

(B) section 165(h)(1) of such Code shall be applied by substituting "$500" for "$500 ($100 for taxable years beginning after December 31, 2009)",

(C) the standard deduction determined under section 63(c) of such Code shall be increased by the net disaster loss, and

(D) section 56(b)(1)(E) of such Code shall not apply to so much of the standard deduction as is attributable to the increase under subparagraph (C) of this paragraph.

(2) NET DISASTER LOSS.—For purposes of this subsection, the term "net disaster loss" means the excess of qualified disaster-related personal casualty losses over personal casualty gains (as defined in section 165(h)(3)(A) of the Internal Revenue Code of 1986).

(3) QUALIFIED DISASTER-RELATED PERSONAL CASUALTY LOSSES.—For purposes of this paragraph, the term "qualified disaster-related personal casualty losses" means losses described in section 165(c)(3) of the Internal Revenue Code of 1986 which arise in a disaster area described in subsection (a) on or after January 1, 2016, and which are attributable to the events giving rise to the Presidential declaration described in subsection (a) which was applicable to such area.

INCOME TAX—DC ENTERPRISE ZONE

- **2017, Disaster Tax Relief and Airport and Airway Extension Act of 2017 (P.L. 115-63)**

P.L. 115-63, §504(b), provides:

(b) SPECIAL RULES FOR QUALIFIED DISASTER-RELATED PERSONAL CASUALTY LOSSES.—

(1) IN GENERAL.—If an individual has a net disaster loss for any taxable year—

(A) the amount determined under section 165(h)(2)(A)(ii) of the Internal Revenue Code of 1986 shall be equal to the sum of—

(i) such net disaster loss, and

(ii) so much of the excess referred to in the matter preceding clause (i) of section 165(h)(2)(A) of such Code (reduced by the amount in clause (i) of this subparagraph) as exceeds 10 percent of the adjusted gross income of the individual,

(B) section 165(h)(1) of such Code shall be applied by substituting "$500" for "$500 ($100 for taxable years beginning after December 31, 2009)",

(C) the standard deduction determined under section 63(c) of such Code shall be increased by the net disaster loss, and

(D) section 56(b)(1)(E) of such Code shall not apply to so much of the standard deduction as is attributable to the increase under subparagraph (C) of this paragraph.

(2) NET DISASTER LOSS.—For purposes of this subsection, the term "net disaster loss" means the excess of qualified disaster-related personal casualty losses over personal casualty gains (as defined in section 165(h)(3)(A) of the Internal Revenue Code of 1986).

(3) QUALIFIED DISASTER-RELATED PERSONAL CASUALTY LOSSES.—For purposes of this subsection, the term "qualified disaster-related personal casualty losses" means losses described in section 165(c)(3) of the Internal Revenue Code of 1986—

(A) which arise in the Hurricane Harvey disaster area on or after August 23, 2017, and which are attributable to Hurricane Harvey,

(B) which arise in the Hurricane Irma disaster area on or after September 4, 2017, and which are attributable to Hurricane Irma, or

(C) which arise in the Hurricane Maria disaster area on or after September 16, 2017, and which are attributable to Hurricane Maria.

- **2008, Heartland Disaster Tax Relief Act of 2008 (P.L. 110-343)**

P.L. 110-343, Division C, §702, provides:

For a special rule, see Division C, Act Sec. 702, in the amendment notes for Code Sec. 1400N(a).

- **2008, Housing Assistance Tax Act of 2008 (P.L. 110-289)**

P.L. 110-289, §3082(a), provides:

(a) USE OF AMENDED INCOME TAX RETURNS TO TAKE INTO ACCOUNT RECEIPT OF CERTAIN HURRICANE-RELATED CASUALTY LOSS GRANTS BY DISALLOWING PREVIOUSLY TAKEN CASUALTY LOSS DEDUCTIONS.—

(1) IN GENERAL.—Notwithstanding any other provision of the Internal Revenue Code of 1986, if a taxpayer claims a deduction for any taxable year with respect to a casualty loss to a principal residence (within the meaning of section 121 of such Code) resulting from Hurricane Katrina, Hurricane Rita, or Hurricane Wilma and in a subsequent taxable year receives a grant under Public Law 109-148, 109-234, or 110-116 as reimbursement for such loss, such taxpayer may elect to file an amended income tax return for the taxable year in which such deduction was allowed (and for any taxable year to which such deduction is carried) and reduce (but not below zero) the amount of such deduction by the amount of such reimbursement.

(2) TIME OF FILING AMENDED RETURN.—Paragraph (1) shall apply with respect to any grant only if any amended income tax returns with respect to such grant are filed not later than the later of—

(A) the date for filing the tax return for the taxable year in which the taxpayer receives such grant, or

(B) the date which is 1 year after the date of the enactment of this Act.

(3) WAIVER OF PENALTIES AND INTEREST.—Any underpayment of tax resulting from the reduction under paragraph (1) of the amount otherwise allowable as a deduction shall not be subject to any penalty or interest under such Code if such tax is paid not later than 1 year after the filing of the amended return to which such reduction relates.

- **2008, Heartland, Habitat, Harvest, and Horticulture Act of 2008 (P.L. 110-246)**

P.L. 110-246, §15345, provides:

For a special rule, see Act Sec. 15345 in the amendment notes for Code Sec. 1400N(d).

[Sec. 1400S(c)]

(c) REQUIRED EXERCISE OF AUTHORITY UNDER SECTION 7508A.—In the case of any taxpayer determined by the Secretary to be affected by the Presidentially declared disaster relating to Hurricane Katrina, Hurricane Rita, or Hurricane Wilma, any relief provided by the Secretary under section 7508A shall be for a period ending not earlier than February 28, 2006.

Amendments

- **2008, Heartland Disaster Tax Relief Act of 2008 (P.L. 110-343)**

P.L. 110-343, Division C, §702, provides:

For a special rule, see Division C, Act Sec. 702, in the amendment notes for Code Sec. 1400N(a).

[Sec. 1400S(d)]

(d) SPECIAL RULE FOR DETERMINING EARNED INCOME.—

(1) IN GENERAL.—In the case of a qualified individual, if the earned income of the taxpayer for the taxable year which includes the applicable date is less than the earned income of the taxpayer for the preceding taxable year, the credits allowed under sections 24(d) and 32 may, at the election of the taxpayer, be determined by substituting—

(A) such earned income for the preceding taxable year, for

(B) such earned income for the taxable year which includes the applicable date.

(2) QUALIFIED INDIVIDUAL.—For purposes of this subsection—

(A) IN GENERAL.—The term "qualified individual" means any qualified Hurricane Katrina individual, any qualified Hurricane Rita individual, and any qualified Hurricane Wilma individual.

(B) QUALIFIED HURRICANE KATRINA INDIVIDUAL.—The term "qualified Hurricane Katrina individual" means any individual whose principal place of abode on August 25, 2005, was located—

(i) in the GO Zone, or

(ii) in the Hurricane Katrina disaster area (but outside the GO Zone) and such individual was displaced from such principal place of abode by reason of Hurricane Katrina.

(C) QUALIFIED HURRICANE RITA INDIVIDUAL.—The term "qualified Hurricane Rita individual" means any individual (other than a qualified Hurricane Katrina individual) whose principal place of abode on September 23, 2005, was located—

(i) in the Rita GO Zone, or

(ii) in the Hurricane Rita disaster area (but outside the Rita GO Zone) and such individual was displaced from such principal place of abode by reason of Hurricane Rita.

(D) QUALIFIED HURRICANE WILMA INDIVIDUAL.—The term "qualified Hurricane Wilma individual" means any individual whose principal place of abode on October 23, 2005, was located—

(i) in the Wilma GO Zone, or

(ii) in the Hurricane Wilma disaster area (but outside the Wilma GO Zone) and such individual was displaced from such principal place of abode by reason of Hurricane Wilma.

(3) APPLICABLE DATE.—For purposes of this subsection, the term "applicable date" means—

(A) in the case of a qualified Hurricane Katrina individual, August 25, 2005,

(B) in the case of a qualified Hurricane Rita individual, September 23, 2005, and

(C) in the case of a qualified Hurricane Wilma individual, October 23, 2005.

(4) EARNED INCOME.—For purposes of this subsection, the term "earned income" has the meaning given such term under section 32(c).

(5) SPECIAL RULES.—

(A) APPLICATION TO JOINT RETURNS.—For purposes of paragraph (1), in the case of a joint return for a taxable year which includes the applicable date—

(i) such paragraph shall apply if either spouse is a qualified individual, and

(ii) the earned income of the taxpayer for the preceding taxable year shall be the sum of the earned income of each spouse for such preceding taxable year.

(B) UNIFORM APPLICATION OF ELECTION.—Any election made under paragraph (1) shall apply with respect to both section 24(d) and section 32.

(C) ERRORS TREATED AS MATHEMATICAL ERROR.—For purposes of section 6213, an incorrect use on a return of earned income pursuant to paragraph (1) shall be treated as a mathematical or clerical error.

(D) NO EFFECT ON DETERMINATION OF GROSS INCOME, ETC.—Except as otherwise provided in this subsection, this title shall be applied without regard to any substitution under paragraph (1).

Amendments

- **2018, Bipartisan Budget Act of 2018 (P.L. 115-123)**

P.L. 115-123, §20104(c), Div. B, provides:

(c) SPECIAL RULE FOR DETERMINING EARNED INCOME.—

(1) IN GENERAL.—In the case of a qualified individual, if the earned income of the taxpayer for the taxable year which includes any portion of the period from October 8, 2017, to December 31, 2017, is less than the earned income of the taxpayer for the preceding taxable year, the credits allowed under sections 24(d) and 32 of the Internal Revenue Code of 1986 may, at the election of the taxpayer, be determined by substituting—

(A) such earned income for the preceding taxable year, for

(B) such earned income for the taxable year which includes any portion of the period from October 8, 2017, to December 31, 2017.

(2) QUALIFIED INDIVIDUAL.—For purposes of this subsection, the term "qualified individual" means any individual whose principal place of abode during any portion of the period from October 8, 2017, to December 31, 2017, was located—

(A) in the California wildfire disaster zone, or

(B) in the California wildfire disaster area (but outside the California wildfire disaster zone) and such individual was displaced from such principal place of abode by reason of the wildfires to which the declaration of such area relates.

(3) EARNED INCOME.—For purposes of this subsection, the term "earned income" has the meaning given such term under section 32(c) of the Internal Revenue Code of 1986.

(4) SPECIAL RULES.—

(A) APPLICATION TO JOINT RETURNS.— For purposes of paragraph (1), in the case of a joint return for a taxable year which includes any portion of the period from October 8, 2017, to December 31, 2017—

(i) such paragraph shall apply if either spouse is a qualified individual, and

(ii) the earned income of the taxpayer for the preceding taxable year shall be the sum of the earned income of each spouse for such preceding taxable year.

(B) UNIFORM APPLICATION OF ELECTION.—Any election made under paragraph (1) shall apply with respect to both sections 24(d) and 32, of the Internal Revenue Code of 1986.

(C) ERRORS TREATED AS MATHEMATICAL ERROR.—For purposes of section 6213 of the Internal Revenue Code of 1986, an incorrect use on a return of earned income pursuant to paragraph (1) shall be treated as a mathematical or clerical error.

Sec. 1400S—Stricken

(D) No effect on determination of gross income, etc.—Except as otherwise provided in this subsection, the Internal Revenue Code of 1986 shall be applied without regard to any substitution under paragraph (1).

- **2017, Disaster Tax Relief and Airport and Airway Extension Act of 2017 (P.L. 115-63)**

P.L. 115-63, §504(c), provides:

(c) Special Rule for Determining Earned Income.—

(1) In general.—In the case of a qualified individual, if the earned income of the taxpayer for the taxable year which includes the applicable date is less than the earned income of the taxpayer for the preceding taxable year, the credits allowed under sections 24(d) and 32 of the Internal Revenue Code of 1986 may, at the election of the taxpayer, be determined by substituting—

(A) such earned income for the preceding taxable year, for

(B) such earned income for the taxable year which includes the applicable date.

In the case of a resident of Puerto Rico determining the credit allowed under section 24(d)(1)(B)(ii) of such Code, the preceding sentence shall be applied by substituting "social security taxes (as defined in section 24(d)(2)(A) of the Internal Revenue Code of 1986)" for "earned income" each place it appears.

(2) Qualified individual.—For purposes of this subsection—

(A) In general.—The term "qualified individual" means any qualified Hurricane Harvey individual, any qualified Hurricane Irma individual, and any qualified Hurricane Maria individual.

(B) Qualified hurricane harvey individual.—The term "qualified Hurricane Harvey individual" means any individual whose principal place of abode on August 23, 2017, was located—

(i) in the Hurricane Harvey disaster zone, or

(ii) in the Hurricane Harvey disaster area (but outside the Hurricane Harvey disaster zone) and such individual was displaced from such principal place of abode by reason of Hurricane Harvey.

(C) Qualified hurricane irma individual.—The term "qualified Hurricane Irma individual" means any individual (other than a qualified Hurricane Harvey individual) whose principal place of abode on September 4, 2017, was located—

(i) in the Hurricane Irma disaster zone, or

(ii) in the Hurricane Irma disaster area (but outside the Hurricane Irma disaster zone) and such individual was displaced from such principal place of abode by reason of Hurricane Irma.

(D) Qualified hurricane maria individual.—The term "qualified Hurricane Maria individual" means any individual (other than a qualified Hurricane Harvey individual or a qualified Hurricane Irma individual) whose principal place of abode on September 16, 2017, was located—

(i) in the Hurricane Maria disaster zone, or

(ii) in the Hurricane Maria disaster area (but outside the Hurricane Maria disaster zone) and such individual was displaced from such principal place of abode by reason of Hurricane Maria.

(3) Applicable date.—For purposes of this subsection, the term "applicable date" means—

(A) in the case of a qualified Hurricane Harvey individual, August 23, 2017,

(B) in the case of a qualified Hurricane Irma individual, September 4, 2017, and

(C) in the case of a qualified Hurricane Maria individual, September 16, 2017.

(4) Earned income.—For purposes of this subsection, the term "earned income" has the meaning given such term under section 32(c) of the Internal Revenue Code of 1986.

(5) Special rules.—

(A) Application to joint returns.—For purposes of paragraph (1), in the case of a joint return for a taxable year which includes the applicable date—

(i) such paragraph shall apply if either spouse is a qualified individual, and

(ii) the earned income of the taxpayer for the preceding taxable year shall be the sum of the earned income of each spouse for such preceding taxable year.

(B) Uniform application of election.—Any election made under paragraph (1) shall apply with respect to both sections 24(d) and 32, [sic] of the Internal Revenue Code of 1986.

(C) Errors treated as mathematical error.—For purposes of section 6213 of the Internal Revenue Code of 1986, an incorrect use on a return of earned income pursuant to paragraph (1) shall be treated as a mathematical or clerical error.

(D) No effect on determination of gross income, etc.—Except as otherwise provided in this subsection, the Internal Revenue Code of 1986 shall be applied without regard to any substitution under paragraph (1).

- **2008, Heartland Disaster Tax Relief Act of 2008 (P.L. 110-343)**

P.L. 110-343, Division C, §702, provides:

For a special rule, see Division C, Act Sec. 702, in the amendment notes for Code Sec. 1400N(a).

[Sec. 1400S(e)]

(e) Secretarial Authority to Make Adjustments Regarding Taxpayer and Dependency Status.—With respect to taxable years beginning in 2005 or 2006, the Secretary may make such adjustments in the application of the internal revenue laws as may be necessary to ensure that taxpayers do not lose any deduction or credit or experience a change of filing status by reason of temporary relocations by reason of Hurricane Katrina, Hurricane Rita, or Hurricane Wilma. Any adjustments made under the preceding sentence shall ensure that an individual is not taken into account by more than one taxpayer with respect to the same tax benefit.

Amendments

- **2008, Heartland Disaster Tax Relief Act of 2008 (P.L. 110-343)**

P.L. 110-343, Division C, §702, provides:

For a special rule, see Division C, Act Sec. 702, in the amendment notes for Code Sec. 1400N(a).

- **2005, Gulf Opportunity Zone Act of 2005 (P.L. 109-135)**

P.L. 109-135, §201(a):

Amended part II of subchapter Y of chapter 1 by adding at the end a new Code Sec. 1400S. Effective 12-21-2005.

P.L. 115-141, §401(d)(6)(C)(xix), Div. U, provides:

(C) Savings provisions.—The amendments made by this paragraph shall not apply to—

* * *

(xix) in the case of the repeal of section 1400S(a) of such Code, contributions paid before January 1, 2006,

P.L. 115-141, §401(e), Div. U, provides:

(e) General Savings Provision With Respect To Deadwood Provisions.—If—

(1) any provision amended or repealed by the amendments made by subsection (b) or (d) applied to—

(A) any transaction occurring before the date of the enactment of this Act,

(B) any property acquired before such date of enactment, or

(C) any item of income, loss, deduction, or credit taken into account before such date of enactment, and

(2) the treatment of such transaction, property, or item under such provision would (without regard to the amendments or repeals made by such subsection) affect the liability for tax for periods ending after such date of enactment,

nothing in the amendments or repeals made by this section shall be construed to affect the treatment of such transaction, property, or item for purposes of determining liability for tax for periods ending after such date of enactment.

[Sec. 1400T—Stricken]

- **2018, Tax Technical Corrections Act of 2018 (P.L. 115-141)**

P.L. 115-141, §401(d)(6)(A), Div. U:

Amended chapter 1 by striking subchapter Y (Code Secs. 1400L–1400U-3). Effective 3-23-2018. For special rules, see Act Sec. 401(d)(6)(C)(xx), Div. U, and Act Sec. 401(e), Div. U, below. Prior to being stricken, Code Sec. 1400T read as follows:

SEC. 1400T. SPECIAL RULES FOR MORTGAGE REVENUE BONDS.

[Sec. 1400T(a)]

(a) In General.—In the case of financing provided with respect to owner-occupied residences in the GO Zone, the Rita GO Zone, or the Wilma GO Zone, section 143 shall be applied—

(1) by treating any such residence in the Rita GO Zone or the Wilma GO Zone as a targeted area residence,

(2) by applying subsection (f)(3) thereof without regard to subparagraph (A) thereof, and

(3) by substituting "$150,000" for "$15,000" in subsection (k)(4) thereof.

[Sec. 1400T(b)]

(b) Application.—Subsection (a) shall not apply to financing provided after December 31, 2010.

Amendments

- **2008, Heartland Disaster Tax Relief Act of 2008 (P.L. 110-343)**

P.L. 110-343, Division C, §702, provides:

For a special rule, see Division C, Act Sec. 702, in the amendment notes for Code Sec. 1400N(a).

- **2005, Gulf Opportunity Zone Act of 2005 (P.L. 109-135)**

P.L. 109-135, §201(a):

Amended part II of subchapter Y of chapter 1 by adding at the end a new Code Sec. 1400T. Effective 12-21-2005.

P.L. 115-141, §401(d)(6)(C)(xx), Div. U, provides:

(C) Savings provisions.—The amendments made by this paragraph shall not apply to—

* * *

(xx) in the case of the repeal of section 1400T of such Code, financing provided before January 1, 2011, and

P.L. 115-141, §401(e), Div. U, provides:

(e) General Savings Provision With Respect To Deadwood Provisions.—If—

(1) any provision amended or repealed by the amendments made by subsection (b) or (d) applied to—

(A) any transaction occurring before the date of the enactment of this Act,

(B) any property acquired before such date of enactment, or

(C) any item of income, loss, deduction, or credit taken into account before such date of enactment, and

(2) the treatment of such transaction, property, or item under such provision would (without regard to the amendments or repeals made by such subsection) affect the liability for tax for periods ending after such date of enactment,

nothing in the amendments or repeals made by this section shall be construed to affect the treatment of such transaction, property, or item for purposes of determining liability for tax for periods ending after such date of enactment.

INCOME TAX—DC ENTERPRISE ZONE

PART III—RECOVERY ZONE BONDS—[STRICKEN]

[Sec. 1400U-1—Stricken]

Amendments

• **2018, Tax Technical Corrections Act of 2018 (P.L. 115-141)**

P.L. 115-141, § 401(d)(6)(A), Div. U:

Amended chapter 1 by striking subchapter Y (Code Secs. 1400L-1400U-3). **Effective** 3-23-2018. For special rules, see Act Sec. 401(d)(6)(C)(xxi), Div. U, and Act Sec. 401(e), Div. U, below. Prior to being stricken, Code Sec. 1400U-1 read as follows:

SEC. 1400U-1. ALLOCATION OF RECOVERY ZONE BONDS.

[Sec. 1400U-1(a)]

(a) ALLOCATIONS.—

(1) IN GENERAL.—

(A) GENERAL ALLOCATION.—The Secretary shall allocate the national recovery zone economic development bond limitation and the national recovery zone facility bond limitation among the States in the proportion that each such State's 2008 State employment decline bears to the aggregate of the 2008 State employment declines for all of the States.

(B) MINIMUM ALLOCATION.—The Secretary shall adjust the allocations under subparagraph (A) for any calendar year for each State to the extent necessary to ensure that no State receives less than 0.9 percent of the national recovery zone economic development bond limitation and 0.9 percent of the national recovery zone facility bond limitation.

(2) 2008 STATE EMPLOYMENT DECLINE.—For purposes of this subsection, the term "2008 State employment decline" means, with respect to any State, the excess (if any) of—

(A) the number of individuals employed in such State determined for December 2007, over

(B) the number of individuals employed in such State determined for December 2008.

(3) ALLOCATIONS BY STATES.—

(A) IN GENERAL.—Each State with respect to which an allocation is made under paragraph (1) shall reallocate such allocation among the counties and large municipalities in such State in the proportion to each such county's or municipality's 2008 employment decline bears to the aggregate of the 2008 employment declines for all the counties and municipalities in such State. A county or municipality may waive any portion of an allocation made under this subparagraph.

(B) LARGE MUNICIPALITIES.—For purposes of subparagraph (A), the term "large municipality" means a municipality with a population of more than 100,000.

(C) DETERMINATION OF LOCAL EMPLOYMENT DECLINES.—For purposes of this paragraph, the employment decline of any municipality or county shall be determined in the same manner as determining the State employment decline under paragraph (2), except that in the case of a municipality any portion of which is in a county, such portion shall be treated as part of such municipality and not part of such county.

(4) NATIONAL LIMITATIONS.—

(A) RECOVERY ZONE ECONOMIC DEVELOPMENT BONDS.—There is a national recovery zone economic development bond limitation of $10,000,000,000.

Amendments

• **2018, Tax Technical Corrections Act of 2018 (P.L. 115-141)**

P.L. 115-141, § 401(d)(6)(A), Div. U:

Amended chapter 1 by striking subchapter Y (Code Secs. 1400L-1400U-3). **Effective** 3-23-2018. For special rules, see Act Sec. 401(d)(6)(C)(xxi), Div. U, and Act Sec. 401(e), Div. U, below. Prior to being stricken, Code Sec. 1400U-2 read as follows:

SEC. 1400U-2. RECOVERY ZONE ECONOMIC DEVELOPMENT BONDS.

[Sec. 1400U-2(a)]

(a) IN GENERAL.—In the case of a recovery zone economic development bond—

(1) such bond shall be treated as a qualified bond for purposes of section 6431, and

(2) subsection (b) of such section shall be applied by substituting "45 percent" for "35 percent".

[Sec. 1400U-2(b)]

(b) RECOVERY ZONE ECONOMIC DEVELOPMENT BOND.—

(1) IN GENERAL.—For purposes of this section, the term "recovery zone economic development bond" means any build America bond (as defined in section 54AA(d)) issued before January 1, 2011, as part of issue if—

(A) 100 percent of the excess of—

(i) the available project proceeds (as defined in section 54A) of such issue, over

(ii) the amounts in a reasonably required reserve (within the meaning of section 150(a)(3)) with respect to such issue, are to be used for one or more qualified economic development purposes, and

(B) the issuer designates such bond for purposes of this section.

(2) LIMITATION ON AMOUNT OF BONDS DESIGNATED.—The maximum aggregate face amount of bonds which may be designated by any issuer under paragraph (1) shall not exceed the amount of the recovery zone economic development bond limitation allocated to such issuer under section 1400U-1.

[Sec. 1400U-2(c)]

(c) QUALIFIED ECONOMIC DEVELOPMENT PURPOSE.—For purposes of this section, the term "qualified economic development purpose" means expenditures for purposes of promoting development or other economic activity in a recovery zone, including—

(B) RECOVERY ZONE FACILITY BONDS.—There is a national recovery zone facility bond limitation of $15,000,000,000.

[Sec. 1400U-1(b)]

(b) RECOVERY ZONE.—For purposes of this part, the term "recovery zone" means—

(1) any area designated by the issuer as having significant poverty, unemployment, rate of home foreclosures, or general distress,

(2) any area designated by the issuer as economically distressed by reason of the closure or realignment of a military installation pursuant to the Defense Base Closure and Realignment Act of 1990, and

(3) any area for which a designation as an empowerment zone or renewal community is in effect.

Amendments

• **2009, American Recovery and Reinvestment Tax Act of 2009 (P.L. 111-5)**

P.L. 111-5, § 1401(a):

Amended subchapter Y of chapter 1 by adding at the end a new part III (Code Secs. 1400U-1—1400U-3). **Effective** for obligations issued after 2-17-2009.

P.L. 115-141, § 401(d)(6)(C)(xxi), Div. U, provides:

(C) SAVINGS PROVISIONS.—The amendments made by this paragraph shall not apply to—

* * *

(xxi) in the case of the repeal of part III of subchapter Y of chapter 1 of such Code, obligations issued before January 1, 2011.

P.L. 115-141, § 401(e), Div. U, provides:

(e) GENERAL SAVINGS PROVISION WITH RESPECT TO DEADWOOD PROVISIONS.—If—

(1) any provision amended or repealed by the amendments made by subsection (b) or (d) applied to—

(A) any transaction occurring before the date of the enactment of this Act,

(B) any property acquired before such date of enactment, or

(C) any item of income, loss, deduction, or credit taken into account before such date of enactment, and

(2) the treatment of such transaction, property, or item under such provision would (without regard to the amendments or repeals made by such subsection) affect the liability for tax for periods ending after such date of enactment,

nothing in the amendments or repeals made by this section shall be construed to affect the treatment of such transaction, property, or item for purposes of determining liability for tax for periods ending after such date of enactment.

[Sec. 1400U-2—Stricken]

(1) capital expenditures paid or incurred with respect to property located in such zone,

(2) expenditures for public infrastructure and construction of public facilities, and

(3) expenditures for job training and educational programs.

Amendments

• **2009, American Recovery and Reinvestment Tax Act of 2009 (P.L. 111-5)**

P.L. 111-5, § 1401(a):

Amended subchapter Y of chapter 1 by adding at the end a new part III (Code Secs. 1400U-1—1400U-3). **Effective** for obligations issued after 2-17-2009.

P.L. 115-141, § 401(d)(6)(C)(xxi), Div. U, provides:

(C) SAVINGS PROVISIONS.—The amendments made by this paragraph shall not apply to—

* * *

(xxi) in the case of the repeal of part III of subchapter Y of chapter 1 of such Code, obligations issued before January 1, 2011.

P.L. 115-141, § 401(e), Div. U, provides:

(e) GENERAL SAVINGS PROVISION WITH RESPECT TO DEADWOOD PROVISIONS.—If—

(1) any provision amended or repealed by the amendments made by subsection (b) or (d) applied to—

(A) any transaction occurring before the date of the enactment of this Act,

(B) any property acquired before such date of enactment, or

(C) any item of income, loss, deduction, or credit taken into account before such date of enactment, and

(2) the treatment of such transaction, property, or item under such provision would (without regard to the amendments or repeals made by such subsection) affect the liability for tax for periods ending after such date of enactment,

nothing in the amendments or repeals made by this section shall be construed to affect the treatment of such transaction, property, or item for purposes of determining liability for tax for periods ending after such date of enactment.

OPPORTUNITY ZONES

[Sec. 1400U-3—Stricken]

Amendments

• **2018, Tax Technical Corrections Act of 2018 (P.L. 115-141)**

P.L. 115-141, § 401(d)(6)(A), Div. U:

Amended chapter 1 by striking subchapter Y (Code Secs. 1400L-1400U-3). **Effective** 3-23-2018. For special rules, see Act Sec. 401(d)(6)(C)(xxi), Div. U, and Act Sec. 401(e), Div. U, below. Prior to being stricken, Code Sec. 1400U-3 read as follows:

SEC. 1400U-3. RECOVERY ZONE FACILITY BONDS.

[Sec. 1400U-3(a)]

(a) IN GENERAL.—For purposes of part IV of subchapter B (relating to tax exemption requirements for State and local bonds), the term "exempt facility bond" includes any recovery zone facility bond.

[Sec. 1400U-3(b)]

(b) RECOVERY ZONE FACILITY BOND.—

(1) IN GENERAL.—For purposes of this section, the term "recovery zone facility bond" means any bond issued as part of an issue if—

(A) 95 percent or more of the net proceeds (as defined in section 150(a)(3)) of such issue are to be used for recovery zone property,

(B) such bond is issued before January 1, 2011, and

(C) the issuer designates such bond for purposes of this section.

(2) LIMITATION ON AMOUNT OF BONDS DESIGNATED.—The maximum aggregate face amount of bonds which may be designated by any issuer under paragraph (1) shall not exceed the amount of recovery zone facility bond limitation allocated to such issuer under section 1400U-1.

[Sec. 1400U-3(c)]

(c) RECOVERY ZONE PROPERTY.—For purposes of this section—

(1) IN GENERAL.—The term "recovery zone property" means any property to which section 168 applies (or would apply but for section 179) if—

(A) such property was constructed, reconstructed, renovated, or acquired by purchase (as defined in section 179(d)(2)) by the taxpayer after the date on which the designation of the recovery zone took effect,

(B) the original use of which in the recovery zone commences with the taxpayer, and

(C) substantially all of the use of which is in the recovery zone and is in the active conduct of a qualified business by the taxpayer in such zone.

(2) QUALIFIED BUSINESS.—The term "qualified business" means any trade or business except that—

(A) the rental to others of real property located in a recovery zone shall be treated as a qualified business only if the property is not residential rental property (as defined in section 168(e)(2)), and

(B) such term shall not include any trade or business consisting of the operation of any facility described in section 144(c)(6)(B).

(3) SPECIAL RULES FOR SUBSTANTIAL RENOVATIONS AND SALE-LEASEBACK.—Rules similar to the rules of subsections (a)(2) and (b) of section 1397D shall apply for purposes of this subsection.

[Sec. 1400U-3(d)]

(d) NONAPPLICATION OF CERTAIN RULES.—Sections 146 (relating to volume cap) and 147(d) (relating to acquisition of existing property not permitted) shall not apply to any recovery zone facility bond.

Amendments

• **2009, American Recovery and Reinvestment Tax Act of 2009 (P.L. 111-5)**

P.L. 111-5, § 1401(a):

Amended subchapter Y of chapter 1 by adding at the end a new part III (Code Secs. 1400U-1—1400U-3). **Effective** for obligations issued after 2-17-2009.

P.L. 115-141, § 401(d)(6)(C)(xxi), Div. U, provides:

(C) SAVINGS PROVISIONS.—The amendments made by this paragraph shall not apply to—

* * *

(xxi) in the case of the repeal of part III of subchapter Y of chapter 1 of such Code, obligations issued before January 1, 2011.

P.L. 115-141, § 401(e), Div. U, provides:

(e) GENERAL SAVINGS PROVISION WITH RESPECT TO DEADWOOD PROVISIONS.—If—

(1) any provision amended or repealed by the amendments made by subsection (b) or (d) applied to—

(A) any transaction occurring before the date of the enactment of this Act,

(B) any property acquired before such date of enactment, or

(C) any item of income, loss, deduction, or credit taken into account before such date of enactment, and

(2) the treatment of such transaction, property, or item under such provision would (without regard to the amendments or repeals made by such subsection) affect the liability for tax for periods ending after such date of enactment,

nothing in the amendments or repeals made by this section shall be construed to affect the treatment of such transaction, property, or item for purposes of determining liability for tax for periods ending after such date of enactment.

Subchapter Z—Opportunity Zones

Sec. 1400Z-1.   Designation.
Sec. 1400Z-2.   Special rules for capital gains invested in opportunity zones.

[Sec. 1400Z-1]

SEC. 1400Z-1. DESIGNATION.

[Sec. 1400Z-1(a)]

(a) QUALIFIED OPPORTUNITY ZONE DEFINED.—For the purposes of this subchapter, the term "qualified opportunity zone" means a population census tract that is a low-income community that is designated as a qualified opportunity zone.

[Sec. 1400Z-1(b)]

(b) DESIGNATION.—

(1) IN GENERAL.—For purposes of subsection (a), a population census tract that is a low-income community is designated as a qualified opportunity zone if—

(A) not later than the end of the determination period, the chief executive officer of the State in which the tract is located—

(i) nominates the tract for designation as a qualified opportunity zone, and

(ii) notifies the Secretary in writing of such nomination, and

(B) the Secretary certifies such nomination and designates such tract as a qualified opportunity zone before the end of the consideration period.

(2) EXTENSION OF PERIODS.—A chief executive officer of a State may request that the Secretary extend either the determination or consideration period, or both (determined without regard to this subparagraph), for an additional 30 days.

(3) SPECIAL RULE FOR PUERTO RICO.—Each population census tract in Puerto Rico that is a low-income community shall be deemed to be certified and designated as a qualified opportunity zone, effective on the date of the enactment of Public Law 115-97.

Amendments

• **2018, Bipartisan Budget Act of 2018 (P.L. 115-123)**

P.L. 115-123, § 41115(a), Div. D:

Amended Code Sec. 1400Z-1(b) by adding at the end a new paragraph (3). **Effective** 2-9-2018.

[Sec. 1400Z-1(c)]

(c) OTHER DEFINITIONS.—For purposes of this subsection—

(1) LOW-INCOME COMMUNITIES.—The term "low-income community" has the same meaning as when used in section 45D(e).

(2) DEFINITION OF PERIODS.—

(A) CONSIDERATION PERIOD.—The term "consideration period" means the 30-day period beginning on the date on which the Secretary receives notice under subsection (b)(1)(A)(ii), as extended under subsection (b)(2).

OPPORTUNITY ZONES

(B) DETERMINATION PERIOD.—The term "determination period" means the 90-day period beginning on the date of the enactment of the Tax Cuts and Jobs Act, as extended under subsection (b)(2).

(3) STATE.—For purposes of this section, the term "State" includes any possession of the United States.

[Sec. 1400Z-1(d)]

(d) NUMBER OF DESIGNATIONS.—

(1) IN GENERAL.—Except as provided by paragraph (2) and subsection (b)(3), the number of population census tracts in a State that may be designated as qualified opportunity zones under this section may not exceed 25 percent of the number of low-income communities in the State.

(2) EXCEPTION.—If the number of low-income communities in a State is less than 100, then a total of 25 of such tracts may be designated as qualified opportunity zones.

Amendments

• **2018, Bipartisan Budget Act of 2018 (P.L. 115-123)**

P.L. 115-123, §41115(b), Div. D:

Amended Code Sec. 1400Z-1(d)(1) by inserting "and subsection (b)(3)" after "paragraph (2)". **Effective** 2-9-2018.

[Sec. 1400Z-1(e)]

(e) DESIGNATION OF TRACTS CONTIGUOUS WITH LOW-INCOME COMMUNITIES.—

(1) IN GENERAL.—A population census tract that is not a low-income community may be designated as a qualified opportunity zone under this section if—

(A) the tract is contiguous with the low-income community that is designated as a qualified opportunity zone, and

(B) the median family income of the tract does not exceed 125 percent of the median family income of the low-income community with which the tract is contiguous.

(2) LIMITATION.—Not more than 5 percent of the population census tracts designated in a State as a qualified opportunity zone may be designated under paragraph (1).

[Sec. 1400Z-1(f)]

(f) PERIOD FOR WHICH DESIGNATION IS IN EFFECT.—A designation as a qualified opportunity zone shall remain in effect for the period beginning on the date of the designation and ending at the close of the 10th calendar year beginning on or after such date of designation.

• **2017, Tax Cuts and Jobs Act (P.L. 115-97)**

P.L. 115-97, §13823(a):

Amended chapter 1 by adding at the end a new subchapter Z (Code Secs. 1400Z-1 and 1400Z-2). **Effective** 12-22-2017.

[Sec. 1400Z-2]

SEC. 1400Z-2. SPECIAL RULES FOR CAPITAL GAINS INVESTED IN OPPORTUNITY ZONES.

[Sec. 1400Z-2(a)]

(a) IN GENERAL.—

(1) TREATMENT OF GAINS.—In the case of gain from the sale to, or exchange with, an unrelated person of any property held by the taxpayer, at the election of the taxpayer—

(A) gross income for the taxable year shall not include so much of such gain as does not exceed the aggregate amount invested by the taxpayer in a qualified opportunity fund during the 180-day period beginning on the date of such sale or exchange,

(B) the amount of gain excluded by subparagraph (A) shall be included in gross income as provided by subsection (b), and

(C) subsection (c) shall apply.

(2) ELECTION.—No election may be made under paragraph (1)—

(A) with respect to a sale or exchange if an election previously made with respect to such sale or exchange is in effect, or

(B) with respect to any sale or exchange after December 31, 2026.

[Sec. 1400Z-2(b)]

(b) DEFERRAL OF GAIN INVESTED IN OPPORTUNITY ZONE PROPERTY.—

(1) YEAR OF INCLUSION.—Gain to which subsection (a)(1)(B) applies shall be included in income in the taxable year which includes the earlier of—

(A) the date on which such investment is sold or exchanged, or

(B) December 31, 2026.

(2) AMOUNT INCLUDIBLE.—

(A) IN GENERAL.—The amount of gain included in gross income under subsection (a)(1)(A) shall be the excess of—

(i) the lesser of the amount of gain excluded under paragraph (1) or the fair market value of the investment as determined as of the date described in paragraph (1), over

(ii) the taxpayer's basis in the investment.

(B) DETERMINATION OF BASIS.—

(i) IN GENERAL.—Except as otherwise provided in this clause or subsection (c), the taxpayer's basis in the investment shall be zero.

(ii) INCREASE FOR GAIN RECOGNIZED UNDER SUBSECTION (a)(1)(B).—The basis in the investment shall be increased by the amount of gain recognized by reason of subsection (a)(1)(B) with respect to such property.

(iii) INVESTMENTS HELD FOR 5 YEARS.—In the case of any investment held for at least 5 years, the basis of such investment shall be increased by an amount equal to 10 percent of the amount of gain deferred by reason of subsection (a)(1)(A).

(iv) INVESTMENTS HELD FOR 7 YEARS.—In the case of any investment held by the taxpayer for at least 7 years, in addition to any adjustment made under clause (iii), the basis of such property shall be increased by an amount equal to 5 percent of the amount of gain deferred by reason of subsection (a)(1)(A).

OPPORTUNITY ZONES

[Sec. 1400Z-2(c)]

(c) SPECIAL RULE FOR INVESTMENTS HELD FOR AT LEAST 10 YEARS.—In the case of any investment held by the taxpayer for at least 10 years and with respect to which the taxpayer makes an election under this clause, the basis of such property shall be equal to the fair market value of such investment on the date that the investment is sold or exchanged.

[Sec. 1400Z-2(d)]

(d) QUALIFIED OPPORTUNITY FUND.—For purposes of this section—

(1) IN GENERAL.—The term "qualified opportunity fund" means any investment vehicle which is organized as a corporation or a partnership for the purpose of investing in qualified opportunity zone property (other than another qualified opportunity fund) that holds at least 90 percent of its assets in qualified opportunity zone property, determined by the average of the percentage of qualified opportunity zone property held in the fund as measured—

(A) on the last day of the first 6-month period of the taxable year of the fund, and

(B) on the last day of the taxable year of the fund.

(2) QUALIFIED OPPORTUNITY ZONE PROPERTY.—

(A) IN GENERAL.—The term "qualified opportunity zone property" means property which is—

(i) qualified opportunity zone stock,

(ii) qualified opportunity zone partnership interest, or

(iii) qualified opportunity zone business property.

(B) QUALIFIED OPPORTUNITY ZONE STOCK.—

(i) IN GENERAL.—Except as provided in clause (ii), the term "qualified opportunity zone stock" means any stock in a domestic corporation if—

(I) such stock is acquired by the qualified opportunity fund after December 31, 2017, at its original issue (directly or through an underwriter) from the corporation solely in exchange for cash,

(II) as of the time such stock was issued, such corporation was a qualified opportunity zone business (or, in the case of a new corporation, such corporation was being organized for purposes of being a qualified opportunity zone business), and

(III) during substantially all of the qualified opportunity fund's holding period for such stock, such corporation qualified as a qualified opportunity zone business.

(ii) REDEMPTIONS.—A rule similar to the rule of section 1202(c)(3) shall apply for purposes of this paragraph.

(C) QUALIFIED OPPORTUNITY ZONE PARTNERSHIP INTEREST.—The term "qualified opportunity zone partnership interest" means any capital or profits interest in a domestic partnership if—

(i) such interest is acquired by the qualified opportunity fund after December 31, 2017, from the partnership solely in exchange for cash,

(ii) as of the time such interest was acquired, such partnership was a qualified opportunity zone business (or, in the case of a new partnership, such partnership was being organized for purposes of being a qualified opportunity zone business), and

(iii) during substantially all of the qualified opportunity fund's holding period for such interest, such partnership qualified as a qualified opportunity zone business.

(D) QUALIFIED OPPORTUNITY ZONE BUSINESS PROPERTY.—

(i) IN GENERAL.—The term "qualified opportunity zone business property" means tangible property used in a trade or business of the qualified opportunity fund if—

(I) such property was acquired by the qualified opportunity fund by purchase (as defined in section 179(d)(2)) after December 31, 2017,

(II) the original use of such property in the qualified opportunity zone commences with the qualified opportunity fund or the qualified opportunity fund substantially improves the property, and

(III) during substantially all of the qualified opportunity fund's holding period for such property, substantially all of the use of such property was in a qualified opportunity zone.

(ii) SUBSTANTIAL IMPROVEMENT.—For purposes of subparagraph (A)(ii), property shall be treated as substantially improved by the qualified opportunity fund only if, during any 30-month period beginning after the date of acquisition of such property, additions to basis with respect to such property in the hands of the qualified opportunity fund exceed an amount equal to the adjusted basis of such property at the beginning of such 30-month period in the hands of the qualified opportunity fund.

(iii) RELATED PARTY.—For purposes of subparagraph (A)(i), the related person rule of section 179(d)(2) shall be applied pursuant to paragraph (8) of this subsection in lieu of the application of such rule in section 179(d)(2)(A).

(3) QUALIFIED OPPORTUNITY ZONE BUSINESS.—

(A) IN GENERAL.—The term "qualified opportunity zone business" means a trade or business—

(i) in which substantially all of the tangible property owned or leased by the taxpayer is qualified opportunity zone business property (determined by substituting "qualified opportunity zone business" for "qualified opportunity fund" each place it appears in paragraph (2)(D)),

(ii) which satisfies the requirements of paragraphs (2), (4), and (8) of section 1397C(b), and

(iii) which is not described in section 144(c)(6)(B).

(B) SPECIAL RULE.—For purposes of subparagraph (A), tangible property that ceases to be a qualified opportunity zone business property shall continue to be treated as a qualified opportunity zone business property for the lesser of—

(i) 5 years after the date on which such tangible property ceases to be so qualified, or

(ii) the date on which such tangible property is no longer held by the qualified opportunity zone business.

[Sec. 1400Z-2(e)]

(e) APPLICABLE RULES.—

(1) TREATMENT OF INVESTMENTS WITH MIXED FUNDS.—In the case of any investment in a qualified opportunity fund only a portion of which consists of investments of gain to which an election under subsection (a) is in effect—

(A) such investment shall be treated as 2 separate investments, consisting of—

(i) one investment that only includes amounts to which the election under subsection (a) applies, and

(ii) a separate investment consisting of other amounts, and

(B) subsections (a), (b), and (c) shall only apply to the investment described in subparagraph (A)(i).

INCOME TAX—SELF-EMPLOYMENT INCOME

(2) RELATED PERSONS.—For purposes of this section, persons are related to each other if such persons are described in section 267(b) or 707(b)(1), determined by substituting "20 percent" for "50 percent" each place it occurs in such sections.

(3) DECEDENTS.—In the case of a decedent, amounts recognized under this section shall, if not properly includible in the gross income of the decedent, be includible in gross income as provided by section 691.

(4) REGULATIONS.—The Secretary shall prescribe such regulations as may be necessary or appropriate to carry out the purposes of this section, including—

(A) rules for the certification of qualified opportunity funds for the purposes of this section,

(B) rules to ensure a qualified opportunity fund has a reasonable period of time to reinvest the return of capital from investments in qualified opportunity zone stock and qualified opportunity zone partnership interests, and to reinvest proceeds received from the sale or disposition of qualified opportunity zone property, and

(C) rules to prevent abuse.

[Sec. 1400Z-2(f)]

(f) FAILURE OF QUALIFIED OPPORTUNITY FUND TO MAINTAIN INVESTMENT STANDARD.—

(1) IN GENERAL.—If a qualified opportunity fund fails to meet the 90-percent requirement of subsection (c)(1), the qualified opportunity fund shall pay a penalty for each month it fails to meet the requirement in an amount equal to the product of—

(A) the excess of—

(i) the amount equal to 90 percent of its aggregate assets, over

(ii) the aggregate amount of qualified opportunity zone property held by the fund, multiplied by

(B) the underpayment rate established under section 6621(a)(2) for such month.

(2) SPECIAL RULE FOR PARTNERSHIPS.—In the case that the qualified opportunity fund is a partnership, the penalty imposed by paragraph (1) shall be taken into account proportionately as part of the distributive share of each partner of the partnership.

(3) REASONABLE CAUSE EXCEPTION.—No penalty shall be imposed under this subsection with respect to any failure if it is shown that such failure is due to reasonable cause.

Amendments

• **2017, Tax Cuts and Jobs Act (P.L. 115-97)**

P.L. 115-97, §13823(a):

Amended chapter 1 by adding at the end a new subchapter Z (Code Secs. 1400Z-1 and 1400Z-2). **Effective** 12-22-2017.

CHAPTER 2—TAX ON SELF-EMPLOYMENT INCOME

Sec. 1401.   Rate of tax.
Sec. 1402.   Definitions.
Sec. 1403.   Miscellaneous provisions.

[Sec. 1401]

SEC. 1401. RATE OF TAX.

[Sec. 1401(a)]

(a) OLD-AGE, SURVIVORS, AND DISABILITY INSURANCE.—In addition to other taxes, there shall be imposed for each taxable year, on the self-employment income of every individual, a tax equal to 12.4 percent of the amount of the self-employment income for such taxable year.

Amendments

• **2021, American Rescue Plan Act of 2021 (P.L. 117-2)**

P.L. 117-2, §9642, provides:

SEC. 9642. CREDIT FOR SICK LEAVE FOR CERTAIN SELF-EMPLOYED INDIVIDUALS.

(a) IN GENERAL.—In the case of an eligible self-employed individual, there shall be allowed as a credit against the tax imposed by chapter 1 of the Internal Revenue Code of 1986 for any taxable year in an amount equal to the qualified sick leave equivalent amount with respect to the individual.

(b) ELIGIBLE SELF-EMPLOYED INDIVIDUAL.—For purposes of this section—

(1) IN GENERAL.—The term "eligible self-employed individual" means an individual who—

(A) regularly carries on any trade or business within the meaning of section 1402 of the Internal Revenue Code of 1986, and

(B) would be entitled to receive paid leave during the taxable year pursuant to the Emergency Paid Sick Leave Act if—

(i) the individual were an employee of an employer (other than himself or herself), and

(ii) such Act applied after March 31, 2021.

(2) RULES OF APPLICATION.—For purposes of paragraph (1)(B), in determining whether an individual would be entitled to receive paid leave under the Emergency Paid Sick Leave Act, such Act shall be applied—

(A) by inserting ", the employee is seeking or awaiting the results of a diagnostic test for, or a medical diagnosis of, COVID-19 and such employee has been exposed to COVID-19 or is unable to work pending the results of such test or diagnosis, or the employee is obtaining immunization related to COVID-19 or recovering from any injury, disability, illness, or condition related to such immunization" after "medical diagnosis" in section 5102(a)(3) of such Act, and

(B) by applying section 5102(b)(1) of such Act separately with respect to each taxable year.

(c) QUALIFIED SICK LEAVE EQUIVALENT AMOUNT.—For purposes of this section—

(1) IN GENERAL.—The term "qualified sick leave equivalent amount" means, with respect to any eligible self-employed individual, an amount equal to—

(A) the number of days during the taxable year (but not more than 10) that the individual is unable to perform services in any trade or business referred to in section 1402 of the Internal Revenue Code of 1986 for a reason with respect to which such individual would be entitled to receive sick leave as described in subsection (b), multiplied by

(B) the lesser of—

(i) $200 ($511 in the case of any day of paid sick time described in paragraph (1), (2), or (3) of section 5102(a) of the Emergency Paid Sick Leave Act, applied with the modification described in subsection (b)(2)(A)) of this section, or

(ii) 67 percent (100 percent in the case of any day of paid sick time described in paragraph (1), (2), or (3) of section 5102(a) of the Emergency Paid Sick Leave Act) of the average daily self-employment income of the individual for the taxable year.

(2) AVERAGE DAILY SELF-EMPLOYMENT INCOME.—For purposes of this subsection, the term "average daily self-employment income" means an amount equal to—

(A) the net earnings from self-employment of the individual for the taxable year, divided by

(B) 260.

(3) ELECTION TO USE PRIOR YEAR NET EARNINGS FROM SELF-EMPLOYMENT INCOME.—In the case of an individual who elects (at such time and in such manner as the Secretary may provide) the application of this paragraph, paragraph (2)(A) shall be applied by substituting "the prior taxable year" for "the taxable year".

(4) ELECTION TO NOT TAKE DAYS INTO ACCOUNT.—Any day shall not be taken into account under paragraph (1)(A) if the eligible self-employed individual elects (at such time and in such manner as the Secretary may prescribe) to not take such day into account for purposes of such paragraph.

(d) CREDIT REFUNDABLE.—

(1) IN GENERAL.—The credit determined under this section shall be treated as a credit allowed to the taxpayer under subpart C of part IV of subchapter A of chapter 1 of such Code.

(2) TREATMENT OF PAYMENTS.—For purposes of section 1324 of title 31, United States Code, any refund due from the credit determined under this section shall be treated in the same manner as a refund due from a credit provision referred to in subsection (b)(2) of such section.

(e) SPECIAL RULES.—

(1) DOCUMENTATION.—No credit shall be allowed under this section unless the individual maintains such documentation as the Secretary may prescribe to establish such individual as an eligible self-employed individual.

(2) DENIAL OF DOUBLE BENEFIT.—In the case of an individual who receives wages (as defined in section 3121(a) of the Internal Revenue Code of 1986) or compensation (as

INCOME TAX—SELF-EMPLOYMENT INCOME

defined in section 3231(e) of such Code) paid by an employer which are required to be paid by reason of the Emergency Paid Sick Leave Act, the qualified sick leave equivalent amount otherwise determined under subsection (c) of this section shall be reduced (but not below zero) to the extent that the sum of the amount described in such subsection and in section 3131(b)(1) of such Code exceeds $2,000 ($5,110 in the case of any day any portion of which is paid sick time described in paragraph (1), (2), or (3) of section 5102(a) of the Emergency Paid Sick Leave Act).

(f) APPLICATION OF SECTION.—Only days occurring during the period beginning on April 1, 2021, and ending on September 30, 2021, may be taken into account under subsection (c)(1)(A).

* * *

(h) REGULATIONS.—The Secretary shall prescribe such regulations or other guidance as may be necessary to carry out the purposes of this section, including—

(1) regulations or other guidance to effectuate the purposes of this section, and

(2) regulations or other guidance to minimize compliance and record-keeping burdens under this section.

P.L. 117-2, §9643, provides:
SEC. 9643. CREDIT FOR FAMILY LEAVE FOR CERTAIN SELF-EMPLOYED INDIVIDUALS.

(a) IN GENERAL.—In the case of an eligible self-employed individual, there shall be allowed as a credit against the tax imposed by chapter 1 of the Internal Revenue Code of 1986 for any taxable year an amount equal to 100 percent of the qualified family leave equivalent amount with respect to the individual.

(b) ELIGIBLE SELF-EMPLOYED INDIVIDUAL.—For purposes of this section—

(1) IN GENERAL.—The term "eligible self-employed individual" means an individual who—

(A) regularly carries on any trade or business within the meaning of section 1402 of the Internal Revenue Code of 1986, and

(B) would be entitled to receive paid leave during the taxable year pursuant to the Emergency Family and Medical Leave Expansion Act if—

(i) the individual were an employee of an employer (other than himself or herself),

(ii) section 102(a)(1)(F) of the Family and Medical Leave Act of 1993 applied after March 31, 2021.

(2) RULES OF APPLICATION.—For purposes of paragraph (1)(B), in determining whether an individual would be entitled to receive paid leave under the Emergency Family and Medical Leave Act—

(A) section 110(a)(2)(A) of the Family and Medical Leave Act of 1993 shall be applied by inserting "or any reason for leave described in section 5102(a) of the Families First Coronavirus Response Act, or the employee is seeking or awaiting the results of a diagnostic test for, or a medical diagnosis of, COVID–19 and such employee has been exposed to COVID–19 or is unable to work pending the results of such test or diagnosis, or the employee is obtaining immunization related to COVID–19 or recovering from any injury, disability, illness, or condition related to such immunization" after "public health emergency", and

(B) section 110(b) of such Act shall be applied—

(i) without regard to paragraph (1) thereof, and

(ii) by striking "after taking leave after such section for 10 days" in paragraph (2)(A) thereof.

(c) QUALIFIED FAMILY LEAVE EQUIVALENT AMOUNT.—For purposes of this section—

(1) IN GENERAL.—The term "qualified family leave equivalent amount" means, with respect to any eligible self-employed individual, an amount equal to the product of—

(A) the number of days (not to exceed 60) during the taxable year that the individual is unable to perform services in any trade or business referred to in section 1402 of the Internal Revenue Code of 1986 for a reason with respect to which such individual would be entitled to receive paid leave as described in subsection (b) of this section, multiplied by

(B) the lesser of—

(i) 67 percent of the average daily self-employment income of the individual for the taxable year, or

(ii) $200.

(2) AVERAGE DAILY SELF-EMPLOYMENT INCOME.—For purposes of this subsection, the term "average daily self-employment income" means an amount equal to—

(A) the net earnings from self-employment income of the individual for the taxable year, divided by

(B) 260.

(3) ELECTION TO USE PRIOR YEAR NET EARNINGS FROM SELF-EMPLOYMENT INCOME.—In the case of an individual who elects (at such time and in such manner as the Secretary may provide) the application of this paragraph, paragraph (2)(A) shall be applied by substituting "the prior taxable year" for "the taxable year".

(4) COORDINATION WITH CREDIT FOR SICK LEAVE.—Any day taken into account in determining the qualified sick leave equivalent amount with respect to any eligible-self employed individual under section 9642 shall not be take into account in determining the qualified family leave equivalent amount with respect to such individual under this section.

(d) CREDIT REFUNDABLE.—

(1) IN GENERAL.—The credit determined under this section shall be treated as a credit allowed to the taxpayer under subpart C of part IV of subchapter A of chapter 1 of such Code.

* * *

(e) SPECIAL RULES.—

(1) DOCUMENTATION.—No credit shall be allowed under this section unless the individual maintains such documentation as the Secretary may prescribe to establish such individual as an eligible self-employed individual.

(2) DENIAL OF DOUBLE BENEFIT.—In the case of an individual who receives wages (as defined in section 3121(a) of the Internal Revenue Code of 1986) or compensation (as defined in section 3231(e) of such Code) paid by an employer which are required to be paid by reason of the Emergency Family and Medical Leave Expansion Act, the qualified family leave equivalent amount otherwise described in subsection (c) of this section shall be reduced (but not below zero) to the extent that the sum of the amount described in such subsection and in section 3132(b)(1) of such Code exceeds $12,000.

(3) REFERENCES TO EMERGENCY FAMILY AND MEDICAL LEAVE EXPANSION ACT.—Any reference in this section to the Emergency Family and Medical Leave Expansion Act shall be treated as including a reference to the amendments made by such Act.

(f) APPLICATION OF SECTION.—Only days occurring during the period beginning on April 1, 2021 and ending on September 30, 2021, may be taken into account under subsection (c)(1)(A).

* * *

(h) REGULATIONS.—The Secretary shall prescribe such regulations or other guidance as may be necessary to carry out the purposes of this section, including—

(1) regulations or other guidance to prevent the avoidance of the purposes of this section, and

(2) regulations or other guidance to minimize compliance and record-keeping burdens under this section.

• 2020, Coronavirus Aid, Relief, and Economic Security (CARES) Act (P.L. 116-136)

P.L. 116-136, §2302, provides:
SEC. 2302. DELAY OF PAYMENT OF EMPLOYER PAYROLL TAXES.

* * *

(b) SECA.—

(1) IN GENERAL.—Notwithstanding any other provision of law, the payment for 50 percent of the taxes imposed under section 1401(a) of the Internal Revenue Code of 1986 for the payroll tax deferral period shall not be due before the applicable date.

(2) ESTIMATED TAXES.—For purposes of applying section 6654 of the Internal Revenue Code of 1986 to any taxable year which includes any part of the payroll tax deferral period, 50 percent of the taxes imposed under section 1401(a) of such Code for the payroll tax deferral period shall not be treated as taxes to which such section 6654 applies.

* * *

(d) DEFINITIONS.—For purposes of this section—

* * *

(2) PAYROLL TAX DEFERRAL PERIOD.—The term "payroll tax deferral period" means the period beginning on the date of the enactment of this Act and ending before January 1, 2021.

(3) APPLICABLE DATE.—The term "applicable date" means—

(A) December 31, 2021, with respect to 50 percent of the amounts to which subsection (a) or (b), as the case may be, apply, and

(B) December 31, 2022, with respect to the remaining such amounts.

* * *

(f) REGULATORY AUTHORITY.—The Secretary shall issue such regulations or other guidance as necessary to carry out the purposes of this section, including rules for the administration and enforcement of subsection (c).

• 2020, Families First Coronavirus Response Act (P.L. 116-127)

P.L. 116-127, §7002 (as amended by P.L. 116-260, §286(a) and (b)(2), 287(a), Div. N), provides:
SEC. 7002. CREDIT FOR SICK LEAVE FOR CERTAIN SELF-EMPLOYED INDIVIDUALS.

(a) CREDIT AGAINST SELF-EMPLOYMENT TAX.—In the case of an eligible self-employed individual, there shall be allowed as a credit against the tax imposed by subtitle A of the Internal Revenue Code of 1986 for any taxable year an amount equal to the qualified sick leave equivalent amount with respect to the individual.

(b) ELIGIBLE SELF-EMPLOYED INDIVIDUAL.—For purposes of this section, the term "eligible self-employed individual" means an individual who—

(1) regularly carries on any trade or business within the meaning of section 1402 of such Code, and

(2) either—

(A) would be entitled to receive paid leave during the taxable year pursuant to the Emergency Paid Sick Leave Act if the individual were an employee of an employer (other than himself or herself), or

(B) would be so entitled if—

(i) such Act were applied by substituting "March 31, 2021" for "'December 31, 2020" in section 5109 thereof, and

(ii) the individual were an employee of an employer (other than himself or herself).

(c) QUALIFIED SICK LEAVE EQUIVALENT AMOUNT.—For purposes of this section—

(1) IN GENERAL.—The term "qualified sick leave equivalent amount" means, with respect to any eligible self-employed individual, an amount equal to—

(A) the number of days during the taxable year (but not more than the applicable number of days) that the individual is unable to perform services in any trade or business referred to in section 1402 of such Code for a reason with respect to which such individual would be entitled to receive sick leave as described in subsection (b), multiplied by

(B) the lesser of—

(i) $200 ($511 in the case of any day of paid sick time described in paragraph (1), (2), or (3) of section 5102(a) of the Emergency Paid Sick Leave Act), or

(ii) 67 percent (100 percent in the case of any day of paid sick time described in paragraph (1), (2), or (3) of section 5102(a) of the Emergency Paid Sick Leave Act) of the average daily self-employment income of the individual for the taxable year.

(2) AVERAGE DAILY SELF-EMPLOYMENT INCOME.—For purposes of this subsection, the term "average daily self-employment income" means an amount equal to—

(A) the net earnings from self-employment of the individual for the taxable year, divided by

INCOME TAX—SELF-EMPLOYMENT INCOME

(B) 260.

(3) APPLICABLE NUMBER OF DAYS.—For purposes of this subsection, the term "applicable number of days" means, with respect to any taxable year, the excess (if any) of 10 days over the number of days taken into account under paragraph (1)(A) in all preceding taxable years.

(4) ELECTION TO USE PRIOR YEAR NET EARNINGS FROM SELF-EMPLOYMENT INCOME.—In the case of an individual who elects (at such time and in such manner as the Secretary, or the Secretary's delegate, may provide) the application of this paragraph, paragraph (2)(A) shall be applied by substituting "the prior taxable year" for "the taxable year".

(d) SPECIAL RULES.—

(1) CREDIT REFUNDABLE.—

(A) IN GENERAL.—The credit determined under this section shall be treated as a credit allowed to the taxpayer under subpart C of part IV of subchapter A of chapter 1 of such Code.

(B) TREATMENT OF PAYMENTS.—For purposes of section 1324 of title 31, United States Code, any refund due from the credit determined under this section shall be treated in the same manner as a refund due from a credit provision referred to in subsection (b)(2) of such section.

(2) DOCUMENTATION.—No credit shall be allowed under this section unless the individual maintains such documentation as the Secretary of the Treasury (or the Secretary's delegate) may prescribe to establish such individual as an eligible self-employed individual.

(3) DENIAL OF DOUBLE BENEFIT.—In the case of an individual who receives wages (as defined in section 3121(a) of the Internal Revenue Code of 1986) or compensation (as defined in section 3231(e) of the Internal Revenue Code) paid by an employer which are required to be paid by reason of the Emergency Paid Sick Leave Act, the qualified sick leave equivalent amount otherwise determined under subsection (c) shall be reduced (but not below zero) to the extent that the sum of the amount described in such subsection and in section 7001(b)(1) exceeds $2,000 ($5,110 in the case of any day any portion of which is paid sick time described in paragraph (1), (2), or (3) of section 5102(a) of the Emergency Paid Sick Leave Act).

(4) CERTAIN TERMS.—Any term used in this section which is also used in chapter 2 of the Internal Revenue Code of 1986 shall have the same meaning as when used in such chapter.

(e) APPLICATION OF SECTION.—Only days occurring during the period beginning on a date selected by the Secretary of the Treasury (or the Secretary's delegate) which is during the 15-day period beginning on the date of the enactment of this Act, and ending on March 31, 2021, may be taken into account under subsection (c)(1)(A).

(f) APPLICATION OF CREDIT IN CERTAIN POSSESSIONS.—

(1) PAYMENTS TO POSSESSIONS WITH MIRROR CODE TAX SYSTEMS.—The Secretary of the Treasury (or the Secretary's delegate) shall pay to each possession of the United States which has a mirror code tax system amounts equal to the loss (if any) to that possession by reason of the application of the provisions of this section. Such amounts shall be determined by the Secretary of the Treasury (or the Secretary's delegate) based on information provided by the government of the respective possession.

(2) PAYMENTS TO OTHER POSSESSIONS.—The Secretary of the Treasury (or the Secretary's delegate) shall pay to each possession of the United States which does not have a mirror code tax system amounts estimated by the Secretary of the Treasury (or the Secretary's delegate) as being equal to the aggregate benefits (if any) that would have been provided to residents of such possession by reason of the provisions of this section if a mirror code tax system had been in effect in such possession. The preceding sentence shall not apply unless the respective possession has a plan, which has been approved by the Secretary of the Treasury (or the Secretary's delegate), under which such possession will promptly distribute such payments to its residents.

(3) MIRROR CODE TAX SYSTEM.—For purposes of this section, the term "mirror code tax system" means, with respect to any possession of the United States, the income tax system of such possession if the income tax liability of the residents of such possession under such system is determined by reference to the income tax laws of the United States as if such possession were the United States.

(4) TREATMENT OF PAYMENTS.—For purposes of section 1324 of title 31, United States Code, the payments under this section shall be treated in the same manner as a refund due from a credit provision referred to in subsection (b)(2) of such section.

(g) REGULATIONS.—The Secretary of the Treasury (or the Secretary's delegate) shall prescribe such regulations or other guidance as may be necessary to carry out the purposes of this section, including—

(1) regulations or other guidance to effectuate the purposes of this Act, and

(2) regulations or other guidance to minimize compliance and record-keeping burdens under this section.

P.L. 116-127, §7004 (as amended by P.L. 116-260, §286(a) and (b)(4), and §287(b), Div. N), provides:

SEC. 7004. CREDIT FOR FAMILY LEAVE FOR CERTAIN SELF-EMPLOYED INDIVIDUALS.

(a) CREDIT AGAINST SELF-EMPLOYMENT TAX.—In the case of an eligible self-employed individual, there shall be allowed as a credit against the tax imposed by subtitle A of the Internal Revenue Code of 1986 for any taxable year an amount equal to 100 percent of the qualified family leave equivalent amount with respect to the individual.

(b) ELIGIBLE SELF-EMPLOYED INDIVIDUAL.—For purposes of this section, the term "eligible self-employed individual" means an individual who—

(1) regularly carries on any trade or business within the meaning of section 1402 of such Code, and

(2) either—

(A) would be entitled to receive paid leave during the taxable year pursuant to the Emergency Family and Medical Leave Expansion Act if the individual were an employee of an employer (other than himself or herself), or

(B) would be so entitled if—

(i) section 102(a)(1)(F) of the Family and Medical Leave Act of 1993, as amended by the Emergency Family and Medical Leave Expansion Act, were applied by substituting "March 31, 2021" for "December 31, 2020", and

(ii) the individual were an employee of an employer (other than himself or herself).

(c) QUALIFIED FAMILY LEAVE EQUIVALENT AMOUNT.—For purposes of this section—

(1) IN GENERAL.—The term "qualified family leave equivalent amount" means, with respect to any eligible self-employed individual, an amount equal to the product of—

(A) the number of days (not to exceed 50) during the taxable year that the individual is unable to perform services in any trade or business referred to in section 1402 of such Code for a reason with respect to which such individual would be entitled to receive paid leave as described in subsection (b), multiplied by

(B) the lesser of—

(i) 67 percent of the average daily self-employment income of the individual for the taxable year, or

(ii) $200.

(2) AVERAGE DAILY SELF-EMPLOYMENT INCOME.—For purposes of this subsection, the term "average daily self-employment income" means an amount equal to—

(A) the net earnings from self-employment income of the individual for the taxable year, divided by

(B) 260.

(4) ELECTION TO USE PRIOR YEAR NET EARNINGS FROM SELF-EMPLOYMENT INCOME.—In the case of an individual who elects (at such time and in such manner as the Secretary, or the Secretary's delegate, may provide) the application of this paragraph, paragraph (2)(A) shall be applied by substituting "the prior taxable year" for "the taxable year".

(d) SPECIAL RULES.—

(1) CREDIT REFUNDABLE.—

(A) IN GENERAL.—The credit determined under this section shall be treated as a credit allowed to the taxpayer under subpart C of part IV of subchapter A of chapter 1 of such Code.

(B) TREATMENT OF PAYMENTS.—For purposes of section 1324 of title 31, United States Code, any refund due from the credit determined under this section shall be treated in the same manner as a refund due from a credit provision referred to in subsection (b)(2) of such section.

(2) DOCUMENTATION.—No credit shall be allowed under this section unless the individual maintains such documentation as the Secretary of the Treasury (or the Secretary's delegate) may prescribe to establish such individual as an eligible self-employed individual.

(3) DENIAL OF DOUBLE BENEFIT.—In the case of an individual who receives wages (as defined in section 3121(a) of the Internal Revenue Code of 1986) or compensation (as defined in section 3231(e) of the Internal Revenue Code) paid by an employer which are required to be paid by reason of the Emergency Family and Medical Leave Expansion Act, the qualified family leave equivalent amount otherwise described in subsection (c) shall be reduced (but not below zero) to the extent that the sum of the amount described in such subsection and in section 7003(b)(1) exceeds $10,000.

(4) CERTAIN TERMS.—Any term used in this section which is also used in chapter 2 of the Internal Revenue Code of 1986 shall have the same meaning as when used in such chapter.

(5) REFERENCES TO EMERGENCY FAMILY AND MEDICAL LEAVE EXPANSION ACT.—Any reference in this section to the Emergency Family and Medical Leave Expansion Act shall be treated as including a reference to the amendments made by such Act.

(e) APPLICATION OF SECTION.—Only days occurring during the period beginning on a date selected by the Secretary of the Treasury (or the Secretary's delegate) which is during the 15-day period beginning on the date of the enactment of this Act, and ending on March 31, 2021, may be taken into account under subsection (c)(1)(A).

(f) APPLICATION OF CREDIT IN CERTAIN POSSESSIONS.—

(1) PAYMENTS TO POSSESSIONS WITH MIRROR CODE TAX SYSTEMS.—The Secretary of the Treasury (or the Secretary's delegate) shall pay to each possession of the United States which has a mirror code tax system amounts equal to the loss (if any) to that possession by reason of the application of the provisions of this section. Such amounts shall be determined by the Secretary of the Treasury (or the Secretary's delegate) based on information provided by the government of the respective possession.

(2) PAYMENTS TO OTHER POSSESSIONS.—The Secretary of the Treasury (or the Secretary's delegate) shall pay to each possession of the United States which does not have a mirror code tax system amounts estimated by the Secretary of the Treasury (or the Secretary's delegate) as being equal to the aggregate benefits (if any) that would have been provided to residents of such possession by reason of the provisions of this section if a mirror code tax system had been in effect in such possession. The preceding sentence shall not apply unless the respective possession has a plan, which has been approved by the Secretary of the Treasury (or the Secretary's delegate), under which such possession will promptly distribute such payments to its residents.

(3) MIRROR CODE TAX SYSTEM.—For purposes of this section, the term "mirror code tax system" means, with respect to any possession of the United States, the income tax system of such possession if the income tax liability of the residents of such possession under such system is determined by reference to the income tax laws of the United States as if such possession were the United States.

(4) TREATMENT OF PAYMENTS.—For purposes of section 1324 of title 31, United States Code, the payments under this section shall be treated in the same manner as a refund due from a credit provision referred to in subsection (b)(2) of such section.

(e) [(g)] REGULATIONS.—The Secretary of the Treasury (or the Secretary's delegate) shall prescribe such regulations or other guidance as may be necessary to carry out the purposes of this section, including—

(1) regulations or other guidance to prevent the avoidance of the purposes of this Act, and

(2) regulations or other guidance to minimize compliance and record-keeping burdens under this section.

INCOME TAX—SELF-EMPLOYMENT INCOME

• 2014, Tax Technical Corrections Act of 2014 (P.L. 113-295)

P.L. 113-295, § 221(a)(89), Division A:

Amended Code Sec. 1401(a) by striking "the following percent" and all that follows and inserting "12.4 percent of the amount of the self-employment income for such taxable year.". **Effective** generally 12-19-2014. For a special rule, see Act Sec. 221(b)(2), Division A, below. Prior to amendment, Code Sec. 1401(a) read as follows:

(a) In addition to other taxes, there shall be imposed for each taxable year, on the self-employment income of every individual, a tax equal to the following percent of the amount of the self-employment income for such taxable year:

In the case of a taxable year

Beginning after:	And before:	Percent
December 31, 1983	January 1, 1988	11.40
December 31, 1987	January 1, 1990	12.12
December 31, 1989		12.40

P.L. 113-295, § 221(b)(2), Division A, provides:

(2) SAVINGS PROVISION.—If—

(A) any provision amended or repealed by the amendments made by this section applied to—

(i) any transaction occurring before the date of the enactment of this Act,

(ii) any property acquired before such date of enactment, or

(iii) any item of income, loss, deduction, or credit taken into account before such date of enactment, and

(B) the treatment of such transaction, property, or item under such provision would (without regard to the amendments or repeals made by this section) affect the liability for tax for periods ending after date of enactment, nothing in the amendments or repeals made by this section shall be construed to affect the treatment of such transaction, property, or item for purposes of determining liability for tax for periods ending after such date of enactment.

• 2010, Tax Relief, Unemployment Insurance Reauthorization, and Job Creation Act of 2010 (P.L. 111-312)

P.L. 111-312, § 601 [as amended by P.L. 112-78, § 101(a)-(d), and P.L. 112-96, § 1001(a)-(b)], provides:

(a) IN GENERAL.—Notwithstanding any other provision of law—

(1) with respect to any taxable year which begins in the payroll tax holiday period, the rate of tax under section 1401(a) of the Internal Revenue Code of 1986 shall be 10.40 percent, and

(2) with respect to remuneration received during the payroll tax holiday period, the rate of tax under 3101(a) of such Code shall be 4.2 percent (including for purposes of determining the applicable percentage under section 3201(a) and 3211(a)(1) of such Code).

(b) COORDINATION WITH DEDUCTIONS FOR EMPLOYMENT TAXES.—

(1) DEDUCTION IN COMPUTING NET EARNINGS FROM SELF-EMPLOYMENT.—For purposes of applying section 1402(a)(12) of the Internal Revenue Code of 1986, the rate of tax imposed by subsection 1401(a) of such Code shall be determined without regard to the reduction in such rate under this section.

(2) INDIVIDUAL DEDUCTION.—In the case of the taxes imposed by section 1401 of such Code for any taxable year which begins in the payroll tax holiday period, the deduction under section 164(f) of such Code with respect to such taxes shall be equal to the sum of—

(A) 59.6 percent of the portion of such taxes attributable to the tax imposed by section 1401(a) of such Code (determined after the application of this section), plus

(B) one-half of the portion of such taxes attributable to the tax imposed by section 1401(b) of such Code.

(c) PAYROLL TAX HOLIDAY PERIOD.—The term "payroll tax holiday period" means calendar years 2011 and 2012.

(d) EMPLOYER NOTIFICATION.—The Secretary of the Treasury shall notify employers of the payroll tax holiday period in any manner the Secretary deems appropriate.

* * *

[Note: Act Sec. 601(f)-(g) of P.L. 111-312, below, was added by P.L. 112-78, § 101(b)-(c), and stricken by P.L. 112-96, § 1001(b), applicable to remuneration received, and tax years beginning, after 12-31-2011.—CCH.]

(f) SPECIAL RULES FOR 2012.—

(1) LIMITATION ON SELF-EMPLOYMENT INCOME.—In the case of any taxable year beginning in 2012, subsection (a)(1) shall only apply with respect to so much of the taxpayer's self-employment income (as defined in section 1402(b) of the Internal Revenue Code of 1986) as does not exceed the excess (if any) of—

(A) $18,350, over

(B) the amount of wages and compensation received during the portion of the payroll tax holiday period occurring during 2012 subject to tax under section 3101(a) of such Code or section 3201(a) of such Code.

(2) COORDINATION WITH DEDUCTION FOR EMPLOYMENT TAXES.—In the case of a taxable year beginning in 2012, subparagraph (A) of subsection (b)(2) shall be applied as if it read as follows:

"(A) the sum of—

"(i) 59.6 percent of the portion of such taxes attributable to the tax imposed by section 1401(a) of such Code (determined after the application of this section) on so much of self-employment income (as defined in section 1402(b) of such Code) as does not exceed the amount of self-employment income described in paragraph (1), plus

"(ii) one-half of the portion of such taxes attributable to the tax imposed by section 1401(a) of such Code (determined without regard to this section) on self-employment income (as so defined) in excess of such amount, plus".

(g) RECAPTURE OF EXCESS BENEFIT.—

(1) IN GENERAL.—There is hereby imposed on the income of every individual a tax equal to 2 percent of the sum of wages (within the meaning of section 3121(a)(1) of the Internal Revenue Code of 1986) and compensation (to which section 3201(a) of such Code applies) received during the period beginning January 1, 2012, and ending February 29, 2012, to the extent the amount of such sum exceeds $18,350.

(2) REGULATIONS.—The Secretary of the Treasury or the Secretary's delegate shall prescribe such regulations or other guidance as may be necessary or appropriate to carry out this subsection, including guidance for payment by the employee of the tax imposed by paragraph (1).

• 1983, Social Security Amendments of 1983 (P.L. 98-21)

P.L. 98-21, § 124(a):

Amended Code Sec. 1401(a). **Effective** for tax years beginning after 1983. Prior to amendment, Code Sec. 1401(a) read as follows:

(a) OLD-AGE, SURVIVORS, AND DISABILITY INSURANCE.—In addition to other taxes, there shall be imposed for each taxable year, on the self-employment income of every individual, a tax as follows:

(1) in the case of any taxable year beginning before January 1, 1978, the tax shall be equal to 7.0 percent of the amount of the self-employment income for such taxable year;

(2) in the case of any taxable year beginning after December 31, 1977, and before January 1, 1979, the tax shall be equal to 7.10 percent of the amount of the self-employment income for such taxable year;

(3) in the case of any taxable year beginning after December 31, 1978, and before January 1, 1981, the tax shall be equal to 7.05 percent of the amount of the self-employment income for such taxable year;

(4) in the case of any taxable year beginning after December 31, 1980, and before January 1, 1982, the tax shall be equal to 8.00 percent of the amount of the self-employment income for such taxable year;

(5) in the case of any taxable year beginning after December 31, 1981, and before January 1, 1985, the tax shall be equal to 8.05 percent of the amount of the self-employment income for such taxable year;

(6) in the case of any taxable year beginning after December 31, 1984, and before January 1, 1990, the tax shall be equal to 8.55 percent of the amount of the self-employment income for such taxable year; and

(7) in the case of any taxable year beginning after December 31, 1989, the tax shall be equal to 9.30 percent of the amount of the self-employment income for such taxable year.

• 1977 (P.L. 95-216)

P.L. 95-216, § 101(a)(3):

Amended Code Sec. 1401(a). **Effective** for remuneration paid or received, and tax years beginning after 1977. Prior to amendment, paragraph (a) read as follows:

(a) Old-age, survivors, and disability insurance.—In addition to other taxes, there shall be imposed for each taxable year, on the self-employment income of every individual, a tax equal to 7.0 percent of the amount of the self-employment income for such taxable year.

• 1976, Tax Reform Act of 1976 (P.L. 94-455)

P.L. 94-455, § 1901(a)(154)(A):

Amended Code Sec. 1401(a). **Effective** for tax years beginning after 12-31-76. Prior to amendment Code Sec. 1401(a) read as follows:

(a) OLD-AGE, SURVIVORS, AND DISABILITY INSURANCE.—In addition to other taxes, there shall be imposed for each taxable year, on the self-employment income of every individual, a tax as follows:

(1) in the case of any taxable year beginning after December 31, 1967, a nd before January 1, 1969, the tax shall be equal to 5.8 percent of the amount of the self-employment income for such taxable year;

(2) in the case of any taxable year beginning after December 31, 1968, and before January 1, 1971, the tax shall be equal to 6.3 percent of the amount of the self-employment income for such taxable year;

(3) in the case of any taxable year beginning after December 31, 1970, and before January 1, 1973, the tax shall be equal to 6.9 percent of the amount of the self-employment income for such taxable year;

(4) in the case of any taxable year beginning after December 31, 1972, the tax shall be equal to 7.0 percent of the amount of the self-employment income for such taxable year.

[Sec. 1401(b)]

(b) HOSPITAL INSURANCE.—

(1) IN GENERAL.—In addition to the tax imposed by the preceding subsection, there shall be imposed for each taxable year, on the self-employment income of every individual, a tax equal to 2.9 percent of the amount of the self-employment income for such taxable year.

INCOME TAX—SELF-EMPLOYMENT INCOME

(2) ADDITIONAL TAX.—

(A) IN GENERAL.—In addition to the tax imposed by paragraph (1) and the preceding subsection, there is hereby imposed on every taxpayer (other than a corporation, estate, or trust) for each taxable year beginning after December 31, 2012, a tax equal to 0.9 percent of the self-employment income for such taxable year which is in excess of—

(i) in the case of a joint return, $250,000,

(ii) in the case of a married taxpayer (as defined in section 7703) filing a separate return, $1/2$ of the dollar amount determined under clause (i), and

(iii) in any other case, $200,000.

(B) COORDINATION WITH FICA.—The amounts under clause (i), (ii), or (iii) (whichever is applicable) of subparagraph (A) shall be reduced (but not below zero) by the amount of wages taken into account in determining the tax imposed under section 3121(b)(2) with respect to the taxpayer.

Amendments

• **2014, Tax Technical Corrections Act of 2014 (P.L. 113-295)**

P.L. 113-295, §221(a)(90), Division A:

Amended Code Sec. 1401(b)(1) by striking "the following percent" and all that follows and inserting "2.9 percent of the amount of the self-employment income for such taxable year.". **Effective** generally 12-19-2014. For a special rule, see Act Sec. 221(b)(2), Division A, below. Prior to amendment, Code Sec. 1401(b)(1) read as follows:

(1) In addition to the tax imposed by the preceding subsection, there shall be imposed for each taxable year, on the self-employment income of every individual, a tax equal to the following percent of the amount of the self-employment income for such taxable year:

In the case of a taxable year		
Beginning after:	And before:	Percent
December 31, 1983	January 1, 1985	2.60
December 31, 1984	January 1, 1986	2.70
December 31, 1985		2.90

P.L. 113-295, §221(b)(2), Division A, provides:

(2) SAVINGS PROVISION.—If—

(A) any provision amended or repealed by the amendments made by this section applied to—

(i) any transaction occurring before the date of the enactment of this Act,

(ii) any property acquired before such date of enactment, or

(iii) any item of income, loss, deduction, or credit taken into account before such date of enactment, and

(B) the treatment of such transaction, property, or item under such provision would (without regard to the amendments or repeals made by this section) affect the liability for tax for periods ending after date of enactment, nothing in the amendments or repeals made by this section shall be construed to affect the treatment of such transaction, property, or item for purposes of determining liability for tax for periods ending after such date of enactment.

• **2010, Health Care and Education Reconciliation Act of 2010 (P.L. 111-152)**

P.L. 111-152, §1402(b)(1)(B)(i)-(ii):

Amended Code Sec. 1401(b)(2), as added by Act Sec. 9015 of the Patient Protection and Affordable Care Act (P.L. 111-148), and amended by Act Sec. 10906 of such Act, by striking "and" at the end of clause (i), by redesignating clause (ii) as clause (iii), and by inserting after clause (i) a new clause (ii) in subparagraph (A); by striking "under clauses (i) and (ii)" and inserting "under clause (i), (ii), or (iii) (whichever is applicable)" in subparagraph (B). **Effective** with respect to remuneration received, and tax years beginning after, 12-31-2012.

• **2010, Patient Protection and Affordable Care Act (P.L. 111-148)**

P.L. 111-148, §9015(b)(1)(A)-(B):

Amended Code Sec. 1401(b) by striking "In addition" and inserting:

"(1) IN GENERAL.—In addition",

and by adding at the end a new paragraph (2). **Effective** with respect to remuneration received, and tax years beginning, after 12-31-2012.

P.L. 111-148, §10906(b):

Amended Code Sec. 1401(b)(2)(A), as added by Act Sec. 9015(b)(1), by striking "0.5 percent" and inserting "0.9 percent". **Effective** with respect to remuneration received, and tax years beginning, after 12-31-2012.

• **1983, Social Security Amendments of 1983 (P.L. 98-21)**

P.L. 98-21, §124(a):

Amended Code Sec. 1401(b). **Effective** for tax years beginning after 1983. Prior to amendment, Code Sec. 1401(b) read as follows:

(b) HOSPITAL INSURANCE.—In addition to the tax imposed by the preceding subsection, there shall be imposed for each taxable year, on the self-employment income of every individual, a tax as follows:

(1) in the case of any taxable year beginning after December 31, 1973, and before January 1, 1978, the tax shall be equal to 0.90 percent of the amount of the self-employment income for such taxable year;

(2) in the case of any taxable year beginning after December 31, 1977, and before January 1, 1979, the tax shall be equal to 1.00 percent of the amount of the self-employment income for such taxable year;

(3) in the case of any taxable year beginning after December 31, 1978, and before January 1, 1981, the tax shall be equal to 1.05 percent of the amount of the self-employment income for such taxable year;

(4) in the case of any taxable year beginning after December 31, 1980, and before January 1, 1985, the tax shall be equal to 1.30 percent of the amount of the self-employment income for such taxable year;

(5) in the case of any taxable year beginning after December 31, 1984, and before January 1, 1986, the tax shall be equal to 1.35 percent of the amount of the self-employment income for such taxable year; and

(6) in the case of any taxable year beginning after December 31, 1985, the tax shall be equal to 1.45 percent of the amount of the self-employment income for such taxable year.

• **1977 (P.L. 95-216)**

P.L. 95-216, §101(b)(3):

Amended paragraphs (1) through (4) and added (5) and (6). **Effective** for remuneration paid or received, and tax years beginning, after 1977. Prior to amendment, paragraphs (1) through (4) read as follows:

(1) in the case of any taxable year beginning after December 31, 1973, and before January 1, 1978, the tax shall be equal to 0.90 percent of the amount of the self-employment income for such taxable year;

(2) in the case of any taxable year beginning after December 31, 1977, and before January 1, 1981, the tax shall be equal to 1.10 percent of the amount of the self-employment income for such taxable year;

(3) in the case of any taxable year beginning after December 31, 1980, and before January 1, 1986, the tax shall be equal to 1.35 percent of the amount of the self-employment income for such taxable year; and

(4) in the case of any taxable year beginning after December 31, 1985, the tax shall be equal to 1.50 percent of the self-employment income for such taxable year.

• **1976, Tax Reform Act of 1976 (P.L. 94-455)**

P.L. 94-455, §1901(a)(154)(B):

Struck out paragraphs (1) and (2) and redesignated paragraphs (3), (4), (5), and (6), as paragraphs (1), (2), (3), and (4) in Code Sec. 1401(b). **Effective** with respect to tax years beginning after 12-31-76. Prior to being struck, paragraphs (1) and (2) of Code Sec. 1401(b) read as follows:

(1) in the case of any taxable year beginning after December 31, 1967, and before January 1, 1973, the tax shall be equal to 0.60 percent of the amount of the self-employment income for such taxable year;

(2) in the case of any taxable year beginning after December 31, 1972, and before January 1, 1974, the tax shall be equal to 1.0 percent of the amount of the self-employment income for such taxable year;

• **1973 (P.L. 93-233)**

P.L. 93-233, §6(b)(1):

Amended paragraphs (2) through (5) of Code Sec. 1401(b) and added new paragraph (6). **Effective** only with respect to tax years beginning after 1973. Prior to amendment, Code Sec. 1401(b)(2)-(5) read as follows:

"(2) in the case of any taxable year beginning after December 31, 1972, and before January 1, 1978, the tax shall be equal to 1.0 percent of the amount of the self-employment income for such taxable year;

"(3) in the case of any taxable year beginning after December 31, 1977, and before January 1, 1981, the tax shall be equal to 1.25 percent of the amount of the self-employment income for such taxable year;

"(4) in the case of any taxable year beginning after December 31, 1980, and before January 1, 1986, the tax shall be equal to 1.35 percent of the amount of the self-employment income for such taxable year;

"(5) in the case of any taxable year beginning after December 31, 1985, the tax shall be equal to 1.45 percent of the amount of the self-employment income for such taxable year."

• **1972, Social Security Amendments of 1972 (P.L. 92-603)**

P.L. 92-603, §§135(a)(1), 135(b)(1):

Amended Code Sec. 1401. **Effective** only with respect to tax years beginning after 12-31-72. Prior to amendment, said section read as follows:

"SEC. 1401. RATE OF TAX.

"(a) Old-Age, Survivors, and Disability Insurance.—In addition to other taxes, there shall be imposed for each taxable year, on the self-employment income of every individual, a tax as follows:

"(1) in the case of any taxable year beginning after December 31, 1967, and before January 1, 1969, the tax shall be equal to 5.8 percent of the amount of the self-employment income for such taxable year;

"(2) in the case of any taxable year beginning after December 31, 1968, and before January 1, 1971, the tax shall be equal to 6.3 percent of the amount of the self-employment income for such taxable year;

INCOME TAX—SELF-EMPLOYMENT INCOME

"(3) in the case of any taxable year beginning after December 31, 1970, and before January 1, 1978, the tax shall be equal to 6.9 percent of the amount of the self-employment income for such taxable year;

"(4) in the case of any taxable year beginning after December 31, 1977, and before January 1, 2011, the tax shall be equal to 6.7 percent of the amount of the self-employment income for such taxable year; and

"(5) in the case of any taxable year beginning after December 31, 2010, the tax shall be equal to 7.0 percent of the amount of the self-employment income for such taxable year.

"(b) Hospital Insurance.—In addition to the tax imposed by the preceding subsection, there shall be imposed for each taxable year, on the self-employment income of every individual, a tax as follows:

"(1) in the case of any taxable year beginning after December 31, 1967, and before January 1, 1973, the tax shall be equal to 0.60 percent of the amount of the self-employment income for such taxable year;

"(2) in the case of any taxable year beginning after December 31, 1972, and before January 1, 1978, the tax shall be equal to 0.9 percent of the amount of the self-employment income for such taxable year;

"(3) in the case of any taxable year beginning after December 31, 1977, and before January 1, 1986, the tax shall be equal to 1.0 percent of the amount of the self-employment income for such taxable year;

"(4) in the case of any taxable year beginning after December 31, 1985, and before January 1, 1993, the tax shall be equal to 1.1 percent of the amount of the self-employment income for such taxable year; and

"(5) in the case of any taxable year beginning after December 31, 1992, the tax shall be equal to 1.2 percent of the amount of the self-employment income for such taxable year."

- **1972 (P.L. 92-336)**

P.L. 92-336, §204(a)(1), 204(b)(1):

Amended Sec. 1401. **Effective** only for tax years beginning after 12-31-72. Prior to amendment, Sec. 1401 read as follows:

SEC. 1401. RATE OF TAX.

(a) Old-Age, Survivors, and Disability Insurance.—In addition to other taxes, there shall be imposed for each taxable year, on the self-employment income of every individual, a tax as follows:

(1) in the case of any taxable year beginning after December 31, 1967, and before January 1, 1969, the tax shall be equal to 5.8 percent of the amount of the self-employment income for such taxable year;

(2) in the case of any taxable year beginning after December 31, 1968, and before January 1, 1971, the tax shall be equal to 6.3 percent of the amount of the self-employment income for such taxable year;

(3) in the case of any taxable year beginning after December 31, 1970, and before January 1, 1973, the tax shall be equal to 6.9 percent of the amount of the self-employment income for such taxable year; and

(4) in the case of any taxable year beginning after December 31, 1972, the tax shall be equal to 7.0 percent of the amount of the self-employment income for such taxable year.

(b) Hospital Insurance.—In addition to the tax imposed by the preceding subsection, there shall be imposed for each taxable year, on the self-employment income of every individual, a tax as follows:

(1) in the case of any taxable year beginning after December 31, 1967, and before January 1, 1976, the tax shall be equal to 0.60 percent of the amount of the self-employment income for such taxable year;

(2) in the case of any taxable year beginning after December 31, 1972, and before January 1, 1967, the tax shall be equal to 0.65 percent of the amount of the self-employment income for such taxable year;

(3) in the case of any taxable year beginning after December 31, 1975, and before January 1, 1980, the tax shall be equal to 0.70 percent of the amount of the self-employment income for such taxable year;

(4) in the case of any taxable year beginning after December 31, 1979, and before January 1, 1987, the tax shall be equal to 0.80 percent of the amount of the self-employment income for such taxable year; and

(5) in the case of any taxable year beginning after December 31, 1986, the tax shall be equal to 0.90 percent of the amount of the self-employment income for such taxable year.

- **1968, Social Security Amendments of 1967 (P.L. 90-248)**

P.L. 90-248, §109(a)(1), (b)(1):

Amended Sec. 1401. **Effective** only for tax years beginning after 12-31-67. Prior to amendment, Sec. 1401 read as follows:

SEC. 1401. RATE OF TAX.

(a) Old-Age, Survivors, and Disability Insurance—In addition to other taxes, there shall be imposed for each taxable year, on the self-employment income of every individual, a tax as follows:

(1) in the case of any taxable year beginning after December 31, 1965, and before January 1, 1967, the tax shall be equal to 5.8 percent of the amount of the self-employment income for such taxable year;

(2) in the case of any taxable year beginning after December 31, 1966, and before January 1, 1969, the tax shall be equal to 5.9 percent of the amount of the self-employment income for such taxable year;

(3) in the case of any taxable year beginning after December 31, 1968, and before January 1, 1973, the tax shall be equal to 6.6 percent of the amount of the self-employment income for such taxable year; and

(4) in the case of any taxable year beginning after December 31, 1972, the tax shall be equal to 7.0 percent of the amount of the self-employment income for such taxable year.

(b) Hospital Insurance.—In addition to the tax imposed by the preceding subsection, there shall be imposed for each taxable year, on the self-employment income of every individual, a tax as follows:

(1) in the case of any taxable year beginning after December 31, 1965, and before January 1, 1967, the tax shall be equal to 0.35 percent of the amount of the self-employment income for such taxable year;

(2) in the case of any taxable year beginning after December 31, 1966, and before January 1, 1973, the tax shall be equal to 0.50 percent of the amount of the self-employment income for such taxable year;

(3) in the case of any taxable year beginning after December 31, 1972, and before January 1, 1976, the tax shall be equal to 0.55 percent of the amount of the self-employment income for such taxable year;

(4) in the case of any taxable year beginning after December 31, 1975, and before January 1, 1980, the tax shall be equal to 0.60 percent of the amount of the self-employment income for such taxable year;

(5) in the case of any taxable year beginning after December 31, 1979, and before January 1, 1987, the tax shall be equal to 0.70 percent of the amount of the self-employment income for such taxable year; and

(6) in the case of any taxable year beginning after December 31, 1986, the tax shall be equal to 0.80 percent of the amount of the self-employment income for such taxable year.

- **1965, Social Security Amendments of 1965 (P.L. 89-97)**

P.L. 89-97, §§111(c), 321(a):

Amended Sec. 1401. **Effective** with respect to tax years beginning after 12-31-65. Prior to amendment, Sec. 1401 read as follows:

SEC. 1401. RATE OF TAX.

In addition to other taxes, there shall be imposed for each taxable year, on the self-employment income of every individual, a tax as follows:

(1) in the case of any taxable year beginning after December 31, 1961, and before January 1, 1963, the tax shall be equal to 4.7 percent of the amount of the self-employment income for such taxable year;

(2) in the case of any taxable year beginning after December 31, 1962, and before January 1, 1966, the tax shall be equal to 5.4 percent of the amount of the self-employment income for such taxable year;

(3) in the case of any taxable year beginning after December 31, 1965, and before January 1, 1968, the tax shall be equal to 6.2 percent of the amount of the self-employment income for such taxable year; and

(4) in the case of any taxable year beginning after December 31, 1967, the tax shall be equal to 6.9 percent of the self-employment income for such taxable year.

- **1961, Social Security Amendments of 1961 (P.L. 87-64)**

P.L. 87-64, §201(a):

Amended Code Sec. 1401. **Effective** for tax years beginning after 1961. Prior to amendment, Sec. 1401 read as follows:

"**SEC. 1401. RATE OF TAX.**

"In addition to other taxes, there shall be imposed for each taxable year, on the self-employment income of every individual, a tax as follows:

"(1) in the case of any taxable year beginning after December 31, 1958, and before January 1, 1960, the tax shall be equal to $3^{3}/_{4}$ percent of the amount of the self-employment income for such taxable year;

"(2) in the case of any taxable year beginning after December 31, 1959, and before January 1, 1963, the tax shall be equal to $4^{1}/_{2}$ percent of the amount of the self-employment income for such taxable year;

"(3) in the case of any taxable year beginning after December 31, 1962, and before January 1, 1966, the tax shall be equal to $5^{1}/_{4}$ percent of the amount of the self-employment income for such taxable year;

"(4) in the case of any taxable year beginning after December 31, 1965, and before January 1, 1969, the tax shall be equal to 6 percent of the amount of the self-employment income for such taxable year; and

"(5) in the case of any taxable year beginning after December 31, 1968, the tax shall be equal to $6^{3}/_{4}$ percent of the amount of the self-employment income for such taxable year."

- **1958, Social Security Amendments of 1958 (P.L. 85-840)**

P.L. 85-840, §401(a):

Amended Sec. 1401. **Effective** for tax years beginning after 12-31-58. Prior to amendment, Sec. 1401 read as follows:

"**SEC. 1401. RATE OF TAX.**

"In addition to other taxes, there shall be imposed for each taxable year, on the self-employment income of every individual, a tax as follows:

"(1) in the case of any taxable year beginning after December 31, 1956, and before January 1, 1960, the tax shall be equal to $3^{3}/_{8}$ percent of the amount of the self-employment income for such taxable year;

"(2) in the case of any taxable year beginning after December 31, 1959, and before January 1, 1965, the tax shall be equal to $4^{1}/_{8}$ percent of the amount of the self-employment income for such taxable year;

"(3) in the case of any taxable year beginning after December 31, 1964, and before January 1, 1970, the tax shall be equal to $4^{7}/_{8}$ percent of the amount of the self-employment income for such taxable year;

"(4) in the case of any taxable year beginning after December 31, 1969, and before January 1, 1975, the tax shall be equal to $5^{5}/_{8}$ percent of the amount of the self-employment income for such taxable year; and

INCOME TAX—SELF-EMPLOYMENT INCOME

"(5) in the case of any taxable year beginning after December 31, 1974, the tax shall be equal to $6^{3}/_{8}$ percent of the amount of the self-employment income for such taxable year."

• **1956, Social Security Amendments of 1956 (P.L. 880, 84th Cong.)**

P.L. 880, 84th Cong., § 202(a):

Amended Sec. 1401. **Effective** for tax years beginning after 12-31-56. Prior to amendment Sec. 1401 read as follows:

"SEC. 1401. RATE OF TAX.

"In addition to other taxes, there shall be imposed for each taxable year, on the self-employment income of every individual, a tax as follows:

"(1) in the case of any taxable year beginning before January 1, 1960, the tax shall be equal to 3 percent of the amount of the self-employment income for such taxable year;

"(2) in the case of any taxable year beginning after December 31, 1959, and before January 1, 1965, the tax shall be equal to $3^{3}/_{4}$ percent of the amount of the self-employment income for such taxable year;

"(3) in the case of any taxable year beginning after December 31, 1964, and before January 1, 1970, the tax shall be equal to $4^{1}/_{2}$ percent of the amount of the self-employment income for such taxable year;

"(4) in the case of any taxable year beginning after December 31, 1969, and before January 1, 1975, the tax shall be equal to $5^{1}/_{4}$ percent of the amount of the self-employment income for such taxable year; and

Amendments

• **1990, Omnibus Budget Reconciliation Act of 1990 (P.L. 101-508)**

P.L. 101-508, § 11801(a)(36):

Repealed Code Sec. 1401(c). **Effective** 11-5-90. Prior to repeal, Code Sec. 1401(c) read as follows:

(c) CREDIT AGAINST TAXES IMPOSED BY THIS SECTION.—

(1) IN GENERAL.—In the case of a taxable year beginning before 1990, there shall be allowed as a credit against the taxes imposed by this section for any taxable year an amount equal to the applicable percentage of the self-employment income of the individual for such taxable year.

(2) APPLICABLE PERCENTAGE.—For purposes of paragraph (1), the applicable percentage shall be determined in accordance with the following table:

In the case of taxable years beginning in:	The applicable percentage is:
1984	2.7
1985	2.3
1986, 1987, 1988, or 1989	2.0

[Sec. 1401(c)]

(c) RELIEF FROM TAXES IN CASES COVERED BY CERTAIN INTERNATIONAL AGREEMENTS.—During any period in which there is in effect an agreement entered into pursuant to section 233 of the Social Security Act with any foreign country, the self-employment income of an individual shall be exempt from the taxes imposed by this section to the extent that such self-employment income is subject under such agreement exclusively to the laws applicable to the social security system of such foreign country.

Amendments

• **2004, Social Security Protection Act of 2004 (P.L. 108-203)**

P.L. 108-203, § 415:

Amended Code Sec. 1401(c) by striking "to taxes or contributions for similar purposes under" and inserting "exclusively to the laws applicable to". **Effective** 3-2-2004.

• **1990, Omnibus Budget Reconciliation Act of 1990 (P.L. 101-508)**

P.L. 101-508, § 11801(c)(16):

Amended Code Sec. 1401 by redesignating subsection (d) as subsection (c). **Effective** 11-5-90.

P.L. 101-508, § 11821(b), provides:

(b) SAVINGS PROVISION.—If—

(1) any provision amended or repealed by this part applied to—

(A) any transaction occurring before the date of the enactment of this Act,

(B) any property acquired before such date of enactment, or

"(5) in the case of any taxable year beginning after December 31, 1974, the tax shall be equal to 6 percent of the amount of the self-employment income for such taxable year."

• **1954, Social Security Amendments of 1954 (P.L. 761, 83rd Cong.)**

P.L. 761, 83rd Cong., § 208(a):

Amended Sec. 1401. **Effective** 1-1-55. Prior to amendment, Sec. 1401 read as follows:

"SEC. 1401. RATE OF TAX.

"In addition to other taxes, there shall be imposed for each taxable year, on the self-employment income of every individual, a tax as follows:

"(1) in the case of any taxable year beginning before January 1, 1960, the tax shall be equal to 3 percent of the amount of the self-employment income for such taxable year;

"(2) in the case of any taxable year beginning after December 31, 1959, and before January 1, 1965, the tax shall be equal to $3^{3}/_{4}$ percent of the amount of the self-employment income for such taxable year;

"(3) in the case of any taxable year beginning after December 31, 1964, and before January 1, 1970, the tax shall be equal to $4^{1}/_{2}$ percent of the amount of the self-employment income for such taxable year;

"(4) in the case of any taxable year beginning after December 31, 1969, the tax shall be equal to $4^{7}/_{8}$ percent of the amount of the self-employment income for such taxable year."

[Sec. 1401(c)—Repealed]

P.L. 101-508, § 11821(b), provides:

(b) SAVINGS PROVISION.—If—

(1) any provision amended or repealed by this part applied to—

(A) any transaction occurring before the date of the enactment of this Act,

(B) any property acquired before such date of enactment, or

(C) any item of income, loss, deduction, or credit taken into account before such date of enactment, and

(2) the treatment of such transaction, property, or item under such provision would (without regard to the amendments made by this part) affect liability for tax for periods ending after such date of enactment,

nothing in the amendments made by this part shall be construed to affect the treatment of such transaction, property, or item for purposes of determining liability for tax for periods ending after such date of enactment.

• **1983, Social Security Amendments of 1983 (P.L. 98-21)**

P.L. 98-21, § 124(b):

Added new Code Sec. 1401(c). **Effective** for tax years beginning after 1983.

(C) any item of income, loss, deduction, or credit taken into account before such date of enactment, and

(2) the treatment of such transaction, property, or item under such provision would (without regard to the amendments made by this part) affect liability for tax for periods ending after such date of enactment,

nothing in the amendments made by this part shall be construed to affect the treatment of such transaction, property, or item for purposes of determining liability for tax for periods ending after such date of enactment.

• **1983, Social Security Amendments of 1983 (P.L. 98-21)**

P.L. 98-21, § 124(b):

Redesignated former Code Sec. 1401(c) as Code Sec. 1401(d). **Effective** for tax years beginning after 1983.

• **1977 (P.L. 95-216)**

P.L. 95-216, § 317(b)(1):

Added Code Sec. 1401(c).

[Sec. 1402]

SEC. 1402. DEFINITIONS.

[Sec. 1402(a)]

(a) NET EARNINGS FROM SELF-EMPLOYMENT.—The term "net earnings from self-employment" means the gross income derived by an individual from any trade or business carried on by such individual, less the deductions allowed by this subtitle which are attributable to such trade or business, plus his distributive share (whether or not distributed) of income or loss described in section 702(a)(8) from any trade or business carried on by a partnership of which he is a member; except that in computing such gross income and deductions and such distributive share of partnership ordinary income or loss—

(1) there shall be excluded rentals from real estate and from personal property leased with the real estate (including such rentals paid in crop shares, and including payments under section 1233(a)(2) of the Food Security Act of 1985 (16 U.S.C. 3833(a)(2)) to individuals receiving benefits under section 202 or 223 of the Social Security Act) together with the deductions attributable thereto, unless such rentals are received in the course of a trade or business as a real estate dealer; except that the preceding provisions of this paragraph shall not apply to any income derived by the owner or tenant of land if (A) such income is derived under an arrangement, between the owner or tenant and another individual, which provides that such other individual shall produce agricultural or horticultural commodities (including livestock, bees,

poultry, and fur-bearing animals and wildlife) on such land, and that there shall be material participation by the owner or tenant (as determined without regard to any activities of an agent of such owner or tenant) in the production or the management of the production of such agricultural or horticultural commodities, and (B) there is material participation by the owner or tenant (as determined without regard to any activities of an agent of such owner or tenant) with respect to any such agricultural or horticultural commodity;

(2) there shall be excluded dividends on any share of stock, and interest on any bond, debenture, note, or certificate, or other evidence of indebtedness, issued with interest coupons or in registered form by any corporation (including one issued by a government or political subdivision thereof), unless such dividends and interest are received in the course of a trade or business as a dealer in stocks or securities;

(3) there shall be excluded any gain or loss—

(A) which is considered as gain or loss from the sale or exchange of a capital asset,

(B) from the cutting of timber, or the disposal of timber, coal, or iron ore, if section 631 applies to such gain or loss, or

(C) from the sale, exchange, involuntary conversion, or other disposition of property if such property is neither—

(i) stock in trade or other property of a kind which would properly be includible in inventory if on hand at the close of the taxable year, nor

(ii) property held primarily for sale to customers in the ordinary course of the trade or business;

(4) the deduction for net operating losses provided in section 172 shall not be allowed;

(5) if—

(A) any of the income derived from a trade or business (other than a trade or business carried on by a partnership) is community income under community property laws applicable to such income, the gross income and deductions attributable to such trade or business shall be treated as the gross income and deductions of the spouse carrying on such trade or business or, if such trade or business is jointly operated, treated as the gross income and deductions of each spouse on the basis of their respective distributive share of the gross income and deductions; and

(B) any portion of a partner's distributive share of the ordinary income or loss from a trade or business carried on by a partnership is community income or loss under the community property laws applicable to such share, all of such distributive share shall be included in computing the net earnings from self-employment of such partner, and no part of such share shall be taken into account in computing the net earnings from self-employment of the spouse of such partner;

(6) a resident of Puerto Rico shall compute his net earnings from self-employment in the same manner as a citizen of the United States but without regard to section 933;

(7) the deduction for personal exemptions provided in section 151 shall not be allowed;

(8) an individual who is a duly ordained, commissioned, or licensed minister of a church or a member of a religious order shall compute his net earnings from self-employment derived from the performance of service described in subsection (c)(4) without regard to section 107 (relating to rental value of parsonages), section 119 (relating to meals and lodging furnished for the convenience of the employer), and section 911 (relating to citizens or residents of the United States living abroad), but shall not include in such net earnings from self-employment the rental value of any parsonage or any parsonage allowance (whether or not excludable under section 107) provided after the individual retires, or any other retirement benefit received by such individual from a church plan (as defined in section 414(e)) after the individual retires;

(9) the exclusion from gross income provided by section 931 shall not apply;

(10) there shall be excluded amounts received by a partner pursuant to a written plan of the partnership, which meets such requirements as are prescribed by the Secretary, and which provides for payments on account of retirement, on a periodic basis, to partners generally or to a class or classes of partners, such payments to continue at least until such partner's death, if—

(A) such partner rendered no services with respect to any trade or business carried on by such partnership (or its successors) during the taxable year of such partnership (or its successors), ending within or with his taxable year, in which such amounts were received, and

(B) no obligation exists (as of the close of the partnership's taxable year referred to in subparagraph (A)) from the other partners to such partner except with respect to retirement payments under such plan, and

(C) such partner's share, if any, of the capital of the partnership has been paid to him in full before the close of the partnership's taxable year referred to in subparagraph (A);

(11) the exclusion from gross income provided by section 911(a)(1) shall not apply;

(12) in lieu of the deduction provided by section 164(f) (relating to deduction for one-half of self-employment taxes), there shall be allowed a deduction equal to the product of—

(A) the taxpayer's net earnings from self-employment for the taxable year (determined without regard to this paragraph), and

(B) one-half of the sum of the rates imposed by subsections (a) and (b) of section 1401 for such year (determined without regard to the rate imposed under paragraph (2) of section 1401(b));

(13) there shall be excluded the distributive share of any item of income or loss of a limited partner, as such, other than guaranteed payments described in section 707(c) to that partner for services actually rendered to or on behalf of the partnership to the extent that those payments are established to be in the nature of remuneration for those services;

(14) in the case of church employee income, the special rules of subsection (j)(1) shall apply;

(15) in the case of a member of an Indian tribe, the special rules of section 7873 (relating to income derived by Indians from exercise of fishing rights) shall apply;

(16) the deduction provided by section 199 shall not be allowed; and

(17) notwithstanding the preceding provisions of this subsection, each spouse's share of income or loss from a qualified joint venture shall be taken into account as provided in section 761(f) in determining net earnings from self-employment of such spouse.

If the taxable year of a partner is different from that of the partnership, the distributive share which he is required to include in computing his net earnings from self-employment shall be based on the ordinary income or loss of the partnership for any taxable year of the partnership ending within or with his taxable year. In the case of any trade or business which is carried on by an individual or by a partnership and in which, if such trade or business were carried on exclusively by employees, the major portion of the services would constitute agricultural labor as defined in section 3121(g)—

(i) in the case of an individual, if the gross income derived by him from such trade or business is not more than the upper limit, the net earnings from self-employment derived by him from such trade or business may, at his option, be deemed to be $66^2/_3$ percent of such gross income; or

(ii) in the case of an individual, if the gross income derived by him from such trade or business is more than the upper limit and the net earnings from self-employment derived by him from such trade or business (computed under this subsection without regard to this sentence) are less than the lower limit, the net earnings from self-employment derived by him from such trade or business may, at his option, be deemed to be the lower limit; and

INCOME TAX—SELF-EMPLOYMENT INCOME

    (iii) in the case of a member of a partnership, if his distributive share of the gross income of the partnership derived from such trade or business (after such gross income has been reduced by the sum of all payments to which section 707(c) applies) is not more than the upper limit, his distributive share of income described in section 702(a)(8) derived from such trade or business may, at his option, be deemed to be an amount equal to 66²/₃ percent of his distributive share of such gross income (after such gross income has been so reduced); or

    (iv) in the case of a member of a partnership, if his distributive share of the gross income of the partnership derived from such trade or business (after such gross income has been reduced by the sum of all payments to which section 707(c) applies) is more than the upper limit and his distributive share (whether or not distributed) of income described in section 702(a)(8) derived from such trade or business (computed under this subsection without regard to this sentence) is less than the lower limit, his distributive share of income described in section 702(a)(8) derived from such trade or business may, at his option, be deemed to be the lower limit.

For purposes of the preceding sentence, gross income means—

    (v) in the case of any such trade or business in which the income is computed under a cash receipts and disbursements method, the gross receipts from such trade or business reduced by the cost or other basis of property which was purchased and sold in carrying on such trade or business, adjusted (after such reduction) in accordance with the provisions of paragraphs (1) through (7) and paragraph (9) of this subsection; and

    (vi) in the case of any such trade or business in which the income is computed under an accrual method, the gross income from such trade or business, adjusted in accordance with the provisions of paragraphs (1) through (7) and paragraph (9) of this subsection;

and, for purposes of such sentence, if an individual (including a member of a partnership) derives gross income from more than one such trade or business, such gross income (including his distributive share of the gross income of any partnership derived from any such trade or business) shall be deemed to have been derived from one trade or business.

  The preceding sentence and clauses (i) through (iv) of the second preceding sentence shall also apply in the case of any trade or business (other than a trade or business specified in such second preceding sentence) which is carried on by an individual who is self-employed on a regular basis as defined in subsection (h), or by a partnership of which an individual is a member on a regular basis as defined in subsection (h), but only if such individual's net earnings from self-employment as determined without regard to this sentence in the taxable year are less than the lower limit and less than 66²/₃ percent of the sum (in such taxable year) of such individual's gross income derived from all trades or businesses carried on by him and his distributive share of the income or loss from all trades or businesses carried on by all the partnerships of which he is a member; except that this sentence shall not apply to more than 5 taxable years in the case of any individual, and in no case in which an individual elects to determine the amount of his net earnings from self-employment for a taxable year under the provisions of the two preceding sentences with respect to a trade or business to which the second preceding sentence applies and with respect to a trade or business to which this sentence applies shall such net earnings for such years exceed the lower limit.

Amendments

- **2018, Tax Technical Corrections Act of 2018 (P.L. 115-141)**

P.L. 115-141, §401(a)(197)(A)-(B), Div. U:

Amended Code Sec. 1402(a)(1) by striking "section 1233(2)" and inserting "section 1233(a)(2)", and by striking "16 U.S.C. 3833(2)" and inserting "16 U.S.C. 3833(a)(2)". **Effective** 3-23-2018.

- **2010, Tax Relief, Unemployment Insurance Reauthorization, and Job Creation Act of 2010 (P.L. 111-312)**

P.L. 111-312, §601(a)-(d), provides:

(a) IN GENERAL.—Notwithstanding any other provision of law—

(1) with respect to any taxable year which begins in the payroll tax holiday period, the rate of tax under section 1401(a) of the Internal Revenue Code of 1986 shall be 10.40 percent, and

(2) with respect to remuneration received during the payroll tax holiday period, the rate of tax under 3101(a) of such Code shall be 4.2 percent (including for purposes of determining the applicable percentage under section 3201(a) and 3211(a)(1) of such Code).

(b) COORDINATION WITH DEDUCTIONS FOR EMPLOYMENT TAXES.—

(1) DEDUCTION IN COMPUTING NET EARNINGS FROM SELFEMPLOYMENT.—For purposes of applying section 1402(a)(12) of the Internal Revenue Code of 1986, the rate of tax imposed by subsection 1401(a) of such Code shall be determined without regard to the reduction in such rate under this section.

(2) INDIVIDUAL DEDUCTION.—In the case of the taxes imposed by section 1401 of such Code for any taxable year which begins in the payroll tax holiday period, the deduction under section 164(f) with respect to such taxes shall be equal to the sum of—

(A) 59.6 percent of the portion of such taxes attributable to the tax imposed by section 1401(a) (determined after the application of this section), plus

(B) one-half of the portion of such taxes attributable to the tax imposed by section 1401(b).

(c) PAYROLL TAX HOLIDAY PERIOD.—The term "payroll tax holiday period" means calendar year 2011.

(d) EMPLOYER NOTIFICATION.—The Secretary of the Treasury shall notify employers of the payroll tax holiday period in any manner the Secretary deems appropriate.

- **2010, Patient Protection and Affordable Care Act (P.L. 111-148)**

P.L. 111-148, §9015(b)(2)(B):

Amended Code Sec. 1402(a)(12)(B) by inserting "(determined without regard to the rate imposed under paragraph (2) of section 1401(b))" after "for such year". **Effective** with respect to remuneration received, and for tax years beginning, after 12-31-2012.

- **2008, Heartland, Habitat, Harvest, and Horticulture Act of 2008 (P.L. 110-246)**

P.L. 110-246, §15301(a):

Amended Code Sec. 1402(a)(1) by inserting "; and including payments under section 1233(2) of the Food Security Act of 1985 (16 U.S.C. 3833(2)) to individuals receiving benefits under section 202 or 223 of the Social Security Act" after "crop shares". **Effective** for payments made after 12-31-2007.

P.L. 110-246, §15352(a)(1)(A)-(B):

Amended the matter following Code Sec. 1402(a)(17) by striking "$2,400" each place it appears and inserting "the upper limit", and by striking "$1,600" each place it appears and inserting "the lower limit". **Effective** for tax years beginning after 12-31-2007.

- **2007, Small Business and Work Opportunity Tax Act of 2007 (P.L. 110-28)**

P.L. 110-28, §8215(b)(1):

Amended Code Sec. 1402(a) by striking ", and" at the end of paragraph (15) and inserting a semicolon, by striking the period at the end of paragraph (16) and inserting "; and", and by inserting after paragraph (16) a new paragraph (17). **Effective** for tax years beginning after 12-31-2006.

- **2004, American Jobs Creation Act of 2004 (P.L. 108-357)**

P.L. 108-357, §102(d)(7):

Amended Code Sec. 1402(a) by striking "and" at the end of paragraph (14), by striking the period at the end of paragraph (15) and inserting ", and", and by inserting after paragraph (15) a new paragraph (16). **Effective** for tax years beginning after 12-31-2004.

- **2004, Social Security Protection Act of 2004 (P.L. 108-203)**

P.L. 108-203, §425(b):

Amended Code Sec. 1402(a)(5)(A) by striking "all of the gross income" and all that follows and inserting "the gross income and deductions attributable to such trade or business shall be treated as the gross income and deductions of the spouse carrying on such trade or business or, if such trade or business is jointly operated, treated as the gross income and deductions of each spouse on the basis of their respective distributive share of the gross income and deductions; and". **Effective** 3-2-2004. Prior to amendment, Code Sec. 1402(a)(5)(A) read as follows:

(A) any of the income derived from a trade or business (other than a trade or business carried on by a partnership) is community income under community property laws applicable to such income, all of the gross income and deductions attributable to such trade or business shall be treated as the gross income and deductions of the husband unless the wife exercises substantially all of the management and control of such trade or business, in which case all of such gross income and deductions shall be treated as the gross income and deductions of the wife; and

- **1997, Taxpayer Relief Act of 1997 (P.L. 105-34)**

P.L. 105-34, §935, provides:

No temporary or final regulation with respect to the definition of a limited partner under section 1402(a)(13) of the Internal Revenue Code of 1986 may be issued or made effective before July 1, 1998.

- **1996, Small Business Job Protection Act of 1996 (P.L. 104-188)**

P.L. 104-188, §1456(a):

Amended Code Sec. 1402(a)(8) by inserting ", but shall not include in such net earnings from self-employment the rental value of any parsonage or any parsonage allowance (whether or not excludable under section 107) provided after the individual retires, or any other retirement benefit received by such individual from a church plan (as defined in section 414(e)) after the individual retires" before the semicolon at the end. **Effective** for years beginning before, on, or after 12-31-94.

- **1990, Omnibus Budget Reconciliation Act of 1990 (P.L. 101-508)**

P.L. 101-508, §5123(a)(3):

Amended Code Sec. 1402(a) by repealing the last undesignated paragraph (as added by section 9022(h) of the Omnibus Budget Reconciliation Act of 1987). **Effec-

INCOME TAX—SELF-EMPLOYMENT INCOME

tive with respect to income received for services performed in tax years beginning after 12-31-90. Prior to repeal, the last paragraph read as follows:

Any income of an individual which results from or is attributable to the performance of services by such indivdual as a director of a corporation during any taxable year shall be deemed to have been derived and received by such individual in that year at the time the services were performed regardless of when the income is actually paid to or received by such individual unless it was actually paid and recovered prior to that year.

• **1988, Technical and Miscellaneous Revenue Act of 1988 (P.L. 100-647)**

P.L. 100-647, §3043(c)(1):

Amended Code Sec. 1402(a) by striking out "and" at end of paragraph (13), by striking out the period at the end of paragraph (14) and inserting in lieu thereof "; and", and by inserting after paragraph (14) a new paragraph (15). **Effective** for all periods beginning before, on, or after 11-5-90. See, also, Act Sec. 3044(b), below.

P.L. 100-647, §3044(b), provides:

(b) NO INFERENCE CREATED.—Nothing in the amendments made by this subtitle shall create any inference as to the existence or non-existence or scope of any exemption from tax for income derived from fishing rights secured as of 3-17-88, by any treaty, law, or Executive Order.

• **1987, Revenue Act of 1987 (P.L. 100-203)**

P.L. 100-203, §9022(b):

Amended Code Sec. 1402(a) by adding at the end thereof a new paragraph. **Effective** for services performed in tax years beginning on or after 1-1-88.

• **1986, Tax Reform Act of 1986 (P.L. 99-514)**

P.L. 99-514, §1272(d)(8):

Amended Code Sec. 1402(a)(8) by striking out "and section 931 (relating to income from sources within possessions of the United States)"after "abroad" and by inserting "and" after "of the employer,". **Effective**, generally, for tax years beginning after 12-31-86. However, for special rules and exceptions, see Act Sec. 1277(b)-(e) following Code Sec. 48. Prior to amendment, Code Sec. 1402(a)(8) read as follows:

(8) an individual who is a duly ordained, commissioned, or licensed minister of a church or a member of a religious order shall compute his net earnings from self-employment derived from the performance of service described in subsection (c)(4) without regard to section 107 (relating to rental value of parsonages), section 119 (relating to meals and lodging furnished for the convenience of the employer), section 911 (relating to citizens or residents of the United States living abroad) and section 931 (relating to income from sources within possessions of the United States);

P.L. 99-514, §1272(d)(9):

Amended Code Sec. 1402(a)(9). **Effective**, generally, for tax years beginning after 12-31-86. However, for special rules and exceptions, see Act Sec. 1277(b)-(e) following Code Sec. 48. Prior to amendment, Code Sec. 1402(a)(9) read as follows:

(9) the term "possession of the United States" as used in sections 931 (relating to income from sources within possessions of the United States) and 932 (relating to citizens of possessions of the United States) shall be deemed not to include the Virgin Islands, Guam, or American Samoa;

P.L. 99-514, §1882(b)(1)(B)(i):

Amended Code Sec. 1402(a)(14). **Effective** for remuneration paid or derived in tax years beginning after 12-31-85. Prior to amendment, Code Sec. 1402(a)(14) read as follows:

(14) with respect to remuneration for services which are treated as services in a trade or business under subsection (c)(2)(G)—

(A) no deduction for trade or business expenses provided under this Code (other than the deduction under paragraph (12)) shall apply;

(B) the provisions of subsection (b)(2) shall not apply; and

(C) if the amount of such remuneration from an employer for the taxable year is less than $100, such remuneration from that employer shall not be included in self-employment income.

• **1984, Deficit Reduction Act of 1984 (P.L. 98-369)**

P.L. 98-369, §2603(d)(2):

Amended Code Sec. 1402(a) by striking out "and" at the end of paragraph (12); by striking out the period at the end of paragraph (13) and inserting in lieu thereof "; and"; and by adding new paragraph (14). **Effective** for service performed after 12-31-83.

• **1983, Social Security Amendments of 1983 (P.L. 98-21)**

P.L. 98-21, §124(c)(2):

Amended Code Sec. 1402(a) by striking out "and" at the end of paragraph (11), by redesignating paragraph (12) as paragraph (13), and by inserting after paragraph (11) a new paragraph (12). **Effective** for tax years beginning after 1989.

P.L. 98-21, §323(b)(1):

Amended Code Sec. 1402(a)(11) by striking out "in the case of an individual described in section 911(d)(1)(B)," **Effective** for tax years beginning after 1983.

• **1981, Economic Recovery Tax Act of 1981 (P.L. 97-34)**

P.L. 97-34, §111(b)(3), (5):

Amended Code Sec. 1402(a)(8) by striking out "relating to income earned by employees in certain camps" and inserting in lieu thereof "relating to citizens or residents of the United States living abroad" and amended Code Sec. 1402(a)(11). **Effective** with respect to tax years beginning after 12-31-81. Prior to amendment, Code Sec. 1402(a)(11) read as follows:

(11) in the case of an individual who has been a resident of the United States during the entire taxable year, the exclusion from gross income provided by section 911(a)(2) shall not apply.

• **1978, Tax Treatment Extension Act of 1978 (P.L. 95-615)**

P.L. 95-615, §§202(f)(5), 209:

Amended Code Sec. 1402(a)(8) by striking out "relating to earned income from sources without the United States" and inserting in place thereof "relating to income earned by employees in certain camps". **Effective**, generally, for tax years beginning after 12-31-77, except as provided in Act Sec. 209(c), below.

P.L. 95-615, §209(c), provides:

(c) ELECTION OF PRIOR LAW.—

(1) A taxpayer may elect not to have the amendments made by this title apply with respect to any taxable year beginning after December 31, 1977, and before January 1, 1979.

(2) An election under this subsection shall be filed with a taxpayer's timely filed return for the first taxable year beginning after December 31, 1977.

• **1978, Revenue Act of 1978 (P.L. 95-600)**

P.L. 95-600, §§703(j)(8)(A), (r):

Amended the last paragraph of Code Sec. 1402(a) by striking out "subsection (i)" each place it appeared and inserting in place thereof "subsection (h)". **Effective** 10-4-76.

• **1977 (P.L. 95-216)**

P.L. 95-216, §313(b):

Amended Code Sec. 1402(a) by striking out "and" at the end of paragraph (10); by striking out the period at the end of paragraph (11) and inserting in lieu thereof "; and"; and by inserting after paragraph (11), a new paragraph (12). **Effective** for tax years beginning after 12-31-77.

• **1976, Tax Reform Act of 1976 (P.L. 94-455)**

P.L. 94-455, §1901(b)(1)(I)(iii):

Substituted "702(a)(8)" for "702(a)(9)" wherever it appeared in Code Sec. 1402(a). **Effective** with respect to tax years beginning after 12-31-76.

P.L. 94-455, §1901(b)(1)(X):

Struck out "(other than interest described in section 35)" following the words "unless such dividends and interest" in Code Sec. 1402(a)(2). **Effective** with respect to tax years beginning after 12-31-76.

P.L. 94-455, §1906(b)(13)(A):

Amended the 1954 Code by substituting "Secretary" for "Secretary or his delegate" each place it appeared. **Effective** 2-1-77.

• **1974 (P.L. 93-368)**

P.L. 93-368, §10(b):

Amended Code Sec. 1402(a)(1) by inserting after "material participation by the owner or tenant" in the two places it occurs the following: "(as determined without regard to any activities of an agent of such owner or tenant)". **Effective** for tax years beginning after 12-31-73.

• **1972, Social Security Amendments of 1972 (P.L. 92-603)**

P.L. 92-603, §121(b)(1):

Added the last sentence to paragraph (10). **Effective** for tax years beginning after 12-31-72.

P.L. 92-603, §124(b):

Added paragraph (11). **Effective** tax years beginning after 12-31-72.

P.L. 92-603, §140(b):

Amended paragraph (8) of Code Sec. 1402(a). **Effective** for tax years beginning after 12-31-72. Prior to amendment, paragraph (8) read as follows:

"(8) an individual who is a duly ordained, commissioned, or licensed minister of a church or a member of a religious order, shall compute his net earnings from self-employment derived from the performance of service described in subsection (c)(4) without regard to section 107 (relating to rental value of parsonages) and section 119 (relating to meals and lodging furnished for the convenience of the employer) and, in addition, if he is a citizen of the United States performing such service as an employee of an American employer (as defined in section 3121(h)) or as a minister in a foreign country who has a congregation which is composed predominantly of citizens of the United States, without regard to section 911 (relating to earned income from sources without the United States) and section 931 (relating to income from sources within possessions of the United States);"

• **1968, Social Security Amendments of 1967 (P.L. 90-248)**

P. L. 90-248, §118(a):

Amended Section 1402(a) by deleting "and" at the end of paragraph (8), by substituting "; and" for the period at the end of paragraph (9), and by adding new paragraph (10). **Effective** only with respect to tax years ending on or after 12-31-67.

• **1965, Social Security Amendments of 1965 (P.L. 89-97)**

P.L. 89-97, §312(b):

Amended the second sentence following Sec. 1402(a)(9) by substituting "$2,400" for "$1,800" each place it appears and by substituting "$1,600" for "$1,200" each place it appears. **Effective** with respect to tax years beginning after 12-31-65.

• **1964, Revenue Act of 1964 (P.L. 88-272)**

P.L. 88-272, §227(b)(6):

Amended Code Sec. 1402(a)(3)(B). **Effective** for tax years beginning after 12-31-63. Prior to amendment, Code Sec. 1402(a)(3)(B) read as follows:

"(B) from the cutting of timber, or the disposal of timber or coal, if section 631 applies to such gain or loss, or"

INCOME TAX—SELF-EMPLOYMENT INCOME

- **1960, Social Security Amendments of 1960 (P.L. 86-778)**

P.L. 86-778, §103(k):

Amended Code Sec. 1402(a) by adding paragraph (9) and by inserting "and paragraph (9)" in clause (v) and clause (vi) of the last sentence. **Effective** only in the case of tax years beginning after 1960, except that insofar as they involve the nonapplication of section 932 of the Internal Revenue Code of 1954 to the Virgin Islands for purposes of subchapter 2 of such Code, such amendments shall be effective in the case of all tax years with respect to which such chapter 2 (and corresponding provisions of prior law) are applicable.

- **1957 (P.L. 85-239)**

P.L. 85-239, §5:

Amended paragraph (8). **Effective** for tax years ending on or after 12-31-57, except, that, for purposes of the retirement test under old-age and survivors insurance, the amendment is effective for tax years beginning after August 1957. Prior to amendment, paragraph (8) read as follows:

"(8) an individual who is—

"(A) a duly ordained, commissioned, or licensed minister of a church or a member of a religious order; and

"(B) a citizen of the United States performing service described in subsection (c)(4) as an employee of an American employer (as defined in section 3121 (h)) or as a minister in a foreign country who has a congregation which is composed predominantly of citizens of the United States, shall compute his net earnings from self-employment derived from the performance of service described in subsection (c)(4) without regard to section 911 (relating to earned income from sources without the United States) and section 931 (relating to income from sources within possessions of the United States)."

- **1956, Social Security Amendments of 1956 (P.L. 880, 84th Cong.)**

P.L. 880, 84th Cong., §§201(e)(2), (g), (i):

Amended Sec. 1402(a)(1) by adding the provisions following the words "real estate dealer;". **Effective** for tax years ending after 1955.

P.L. 880, 84th Cong., §§201(e)(2), (g), (i):

Amended Sec. 1402(a)(8)(B) by adding: "or as a minister in a foreign country who has a congregation which is predominantly of citizens of the United States,". The **effective** date provision of §201(m)(2) provides:

"(2)(A) Except as provided in subparagraph (B), the amendment made by subsection (g) shall apply only with respect to taxable years ending after 1956.

"(B) Any individual who, for a taxable year ending after 1954 and prior to 1957, had income which by reason of the amendment made by subsection (g) would have been included within the meaning of "net earnings from self-employment" (as such term is defined in section 1402(a) of the Internal Revenue Code of 1954), if such income had been derived in a taxable year ending after 1956 by an individual who had filed a waiver certificate under section 1402(e) of such Code, may elect to have the amendment made by subsection (g) apply to his taxable years ending after 1954 and prior to 1957. No election made by any individual under this subparagraph shall be valid unless such individual has filed a waiver certificate under section 1402(e) of such Code prior to the making of such election or files a waiver certificate at the time he makes such election.

"(C) Any individual described in subparagraph (B) who has filed a waiver certificate under section 1402(e) of such Code prior to the date of enactment of this Act, or who files a waiver certificate under such section on or before the due date or his return (including any extension thereof) for his last taxable year ending prior to 1957, must make such election on or before the due date of his return (including any extension thereof) for his last taxable year ending prior to 1957, or before April 16, 1957, whichever is the later

"(D) Any individual described in subparagraph (B) who has not filed a waiver certificate under section 1402(e) of such Code on or before the due date of his return (including any extension thereof) for his last taxable year ending prior to 1957 must make such election on or before the due date of his return (including any extension thereof) for his first taxable year ending after 1956. Any individual described in this subparagraph whose period for filing a waiver certificate under section 1402(e) of such Code has expired at the time he makes such election may, notwithstanding the provisions of paragraph (2) of such section, file a waiver certificate at the time he makes such election.

"(E) An election under subparagraph (B) shall be made in such manner as the Secretary of the Treasury or his delegate shall prescribe by regulations. Notwithstanding the provisions of paragraph (3) of section 1402(e) of such Code, the waiver certificate filed by an individual who makes an election under subparagraph (B) (regardless of when filed) shall be effective for such individual's first taxable year ending after 1954 in which he had income which by reason of the amendment made by subsection (g) would have been included within the meaning of "net earnings from self-employment" (as such term is defined in section 1402(a) of such Code), if such income had been derived in a taxable year ending after 1956 by an individual who had filed a waiver certificate under section 1402(e) of such Code, or for the taxable year prescribed by such paragraph (3) of section 1402(e) if such taxable year is earlier, and for all succeeding taxable years.

"(F) No interest or penalty shall be assessed or collected for failure to file a return within the time prescribed by law, if such failure arises solely by reason of an election made by an individual under subparagraph (B), or for any underpayment of the tax imposed by section 1401 of such Code arising solely by reason of such election, for the period ending with the date such individual makes an election under subparagraph (B)."

P.L. 880, 84th Cong., §§201(e)(2), (g), (i):

Amended Sec. 1402(a) by striking out the last two sentences and inserting in their place the provisions containing the $1,800 and $1,200 optional provisions applicable to farmers. **Effective** for tax years ending on or after 12-31-56. Prior to the amendment, the deleted sentences read as follows:

"In the case of any trade or business which is carried on by an individual who reports his income on a cash receipts and disbursements basis, and in which, if it were carried on exclusively by employees, the major portion of the services would constitute agricultural labor as defined in section 3121(g), (i) if the gross income derived from such trade or business by such individual is not more than $1,800, the net earnings from self-employment derived by him therefrom may, at his option, be deemed to be 50 percent of such gross income in lieu of his net earnings from self-employment from such trade or business computed as provided under the preceding provisions of this subsection, or (ii) if the gross income derived from such trade or business by such individual is more than $1,800 and the net earnings from self-employment derived by him therefrom, as computed under the preceding provisions of this subsection, are less than $900, such net earnings may instead, at the option of such individual, be deemed to be $900. For the purpose of the preceding sentence, gross income derived from such trade or business shall mean the gross receipts from such trade or business reduced by the cost or other basis of property which was purchased and sold in carrying on such trade or business, adjusted (after such reduction) in accordance with the preceding provisions of this subsection." Amendment made by §201(i) is applicable for taxable years ending on or after 12-31-56.

- **1954, Social Security Amendments of 1954 (P.L. 761, 83rd Cong.)**

P.L. 761, 83rd Cong., §201(a):

Amended paragraph (1) to read as prior to amendment by P.L. 880, deleted former paragraph (2), renumbered paragraphs (3) to (8), inclusive, as paragraphs (2) to (7), inclusive, and added the last two sentences of the subsection as they read prior to amendment by P.L. 880. **Effective** with respect to tax years ending after 1954. Prior to amendment by P.L. 761, paragraph (1) read as follows:

"(1) there shall be excluded rentals from real estate (including personal property leased with the real estate) and deductions attributable thereto, unless such rentals are received in the course of a trade or business as a real estate dealer;".

Prior to deletion, paragraph (2) read as follows:

"(2) there shall be excluded income derived from any trade or business in which, if the trade or business were carried on exclusively by employees, the major portion of the services would constitute agricultural labor as defined in section 3121(g); and there shall be excluded all deductions attributable to such income;".

P.L. 761, 83rd Cong., §201(c):

Added new paragraph (8).

[Sec. 1402(b)]

(b) SELF-EMPLOYMENT INCOME.—The term "self-employment income" means the net earnings from self-employment derived by an individual (other than a nonresident alien individual, except as provided by an agreement under section 233 of the Social Security Act) during any taxable year; except that such term shall not include—

(1) in the case of the tax imposed by section 1401(a), that part of the net earnings from self-employment which is in excess of (i) an amount equal to the contribution and benefit base (as determined under section 230 of the Social Security Act) which is effective for the calendar year in which such taxable year begins, minus (ii) the amount of the wages paid to such individual during such taxable years; or

(2) the net earnings from self-employment, if such net earnings for the taxable year are less than $400.

For purposes of paragraph (1), the term "wages" (A) includes such remuneration paid to an employee for services included under an agreement entered into pursuant to the provisions of section 3121 (1) (relating to coverage of citizens of the United States who are employees of foreign affiliates of American employers), as would be wages under section 3121(a) if such services constituted employment under section 3121(b), and (B) includes compensation which is subject to the tax imposed by section 3201 or 3211. An individual who is not a citizen of the United States but who is a resident of the Commonwealth of Puerto Rico, the Virgin Islands, Guam, or American Samoa shall not, for purposes of this chapter be considered to be a nonresident alien individual. In the case of church employee income, the special rules of subsection (j)(2) shall apply for purposes of paragraph (2).

Amendments

- **2018, Tax Technical Corrections Act of 2018 (P.L. 115-141)**

P.L. 115-141, §401(a)(198), Div. U:

Amended Code Sec. 1402(b) by striking "3211,." and inserting "3211.". **Effective** 3-23-2018.

- **1993, Omnibus Budget Reconciliation Act of 1993 (P.L. 103-66)**

P.L. 103-66, §13207(b)(1)(A)-(D):

Amended Code Sec. 1402(b) by striking "that part of the net" in paragraph (1) and inserting "in the case of the tax imposed by section 1401(a), that part of the net", by striking "applicable contribution base (as determined under subsection (k))" in

INCOME TAX—SELF-EMPLOYMENT INCOME

paragraph (1) and inserting "contribution and benefit base (as determined under section 230 of the Social Security Act)", by inserting "and" after "section 3121(b),", and by striking "and (C) includes" and all that follows through "3111(b)". **Effective** for 1994 and later calendar years. Prior to amendment, Code Sec. 1402(b) read as follows:

(b) SELF-EMPLOYMENT INCOME.—The term "self-employment income" means the net earnings from self-employment derived by an individual (other than a nonresident alien individual, except as provided by an agreement under section 233 of the Social Security Act) during any taxable year; except that such term shall not include—

(1) that part of the net earnings from self-employment which is in excess of (i) an amount equal to the applicable contribution base (as determined under subsection (k)) which is effective for the calendar year in which such taxable year begins, minus (ii) the amount of the wages paid to such individual during such taxable year; or

(2) the net earnings from self-employment, if such net earnings for the taxable year are less than $400.

For purposes of paragraph (1), the term "wages" (A) includes such remuneration paid to an employee for services included under an agreement entered into pursuant to the provisions of section 3121 (l) (relating to coverage of citizens of the United States who are employees of foreign affiliates of American employers), as would be wages under section 3121(a) if such services constituted employment under section 3121(b), (B) includes compensation which is subject to the tax imposed by section 3201 or 3211, and (C) includes, but only with respect to the tax imposed by section 1401(b), remuneration paid for medicare qualified government employment (as defined in section 3121(u)(3)) which is subject to the taxes imposed by sections 3101(b) and 3111(b). An individual who is not a citizen of the United States but who is a resident of the Commonwealth of Puerto Rico, the Virgin Islands, Guam, or American Samoa shall not, for purposes of this chapter be considered to be a nonresident alien individual. In the case of church employee income, the special rules of subsection (j)(2) shall apply for purposes of paragraph (2).

• **1990, Omnibus Budget Reconciliation Act of 1990 (P.L. 101-508)**

P.L. 101-508, §11331(b)(1):

Amended Code Sec. 1402(b) by striking "the contribution and benefit base (as determined under section 230 of the Social Security Act)" and inserting "the applicable contribution base (as determined under subsection (k))". **Effective** for 1991 and later calendar years.

• **1986, Tax Reform Act of 1986 (P.L. 99-514)**

P.L. 99-514, §1882(b)(1)(B)(ii):

Amended Code Sec. 1402(b) by adding at the end thereof a new sentence. **Effective** for remuneration paid or derived in tax years beginning after 12-31-85.

P.L. 99-514, §1882(b)(1)(B)(iii):

Amended Code Sec. 1402(b) by striking out "clause (1)" and inserting in lieu thereof "paragraph (1)" in the second sentence. **Effective** for remuneration paid or derived in tax years beginning after 12-31-85.

• **1986, Omnibus Budget Reconciliation Act of 1986 (P.L. 99-509)**

P.L. 99-509, §9002(b)(1)(B):

Amended Code Sec. 1402(b) in the flush sentence immediately following paragraph (2) by striking out "under agreement entered into pursuant to the provisions of section 218 of the Social Security Act (relating to coverage of State employees), or" following "for services included". For the **effective** date, see Act Sec. 9002(d), below.

P.L. 99-509, §9002(d), provides:

(d) EFFECTIVE DATE.—The amendments made by this section are effective with respect to payments due with respect to wages paid after December 31, 1986, including wages paid after such date by a State (or political subdivision thereof) that modified its agreement pursuant to the provisions of section 218(e)(2) of the Social Security Act prior to the date of the enactment of this Act; except that in cases where, in accordance with the currently applicable schedule, deposits of taxes due under an agreement entered into pursuant to section 218 of the Social Security Act would be required within 3 days after the close of an eight-monthly period, such 3-day requirement shall be changed to a 7-day requirement for wages paid prior to October 1, 1987, and to a 5-day requirement for wages paid after september 30, 1987, and prior to October 1, 1988. For wages paid prior to October 1, 1988, the deposit schedule for taxes imposed under sections 3101 and 3111 shall be determined separately from the deposit schedule for taxes withheld under section 3402 if the taxes imposed under sections 3101 and 3111 are due with respect to service included under an agreement entered into pursuant to section 218 of the Social Security Act.

• **1986, Consolidated Omnibus Budget Reconciliation Act of 1985 (P.L. 99-272)**

P.L. 99-272, §13205(a)(2)(B):

Amended Code Sec. 1402(b) by striking out "medicare qualified Federal employment (as defined in section 3121(u)(2))" and inserting in lieu thereof "medicare qualified government employment (as defined in section 3121(u)(3))". **Effective** for services performed after 3-31-86.

• **1983, Social Security Amendments of 1983 (P.L. 98-21)**

P.L. 98-21, §321(e)(83):

Amended clause (A) of the second sentence of Code Sec. 1402(b) by striking out "employees of foreign subsidiaries of domestic corporations" and inserting in place thereof "employees of foreign affiliates of American employers". **Effective**, generally, for agreements entered into after 4-20-83. Under a special election provided in Act Sec. 321(f)(1)(B), such amendments may apply to agreements executed on or before 4-20-83. For the text of Act Sec. 321(f)(1)(B) see the amendment notes following Code Sec. 406(a). For the text of Code Sec. 1402(b) before amendment, see below.

P.L. 98-21, §322(b)(2):

Amended the first sentence of Code Sec. 1402(b) by inserting after "nonresident alien individual": ", except as provided by an agreement under section 233 of the Social Security Act". **Effective** for tax years beginning on or after 4-20-83. Prior to amendment by Act Secs. 321(e)(3) and 322(b)(2), Code Sec. 1402(b) read as follows:

(b) SELF-EMPLOYMENT INCOME.—The term "self-employment income" means the net earnings from self-employment derived by an individual (other than a nonresident alien individual) during any taxable year; except that such term shall not include—

(1) that part of the net earnings from self-employment which is in excess of (i) an amount equal to the contribution and benefit base (as determined under section 230 of the Social Security Act) which is effective for the calendar year in which such taxable year begins, minus (ii) the amount of the wages paid to such individual during such taxable years; or

(2) the net earnings from self-employment, if such net earnings for the taxable year are less than $400.

For purposes of clause (1), the term "wages" (A) includes such remuneration paid to an employee for services included under an agreement entered into pursuant to the provisions of section 218 of the Social Security Act (relating to coverage of State employees), or under an agreement entered into pursuant to the provisions of section 3121(l) (relating to coverage of citizens of the United States who are employees of foreign subsidiaries of domestic corporations), as would be wages under section 3121(a) if such services constituted employment under section 3121(b), (B) includes compensation which is subject to the tax imposed by section 3201 or 3211, and (C) includes, but only with respect to the tax imposed by section 1401(b), remuneration paid for medicare qualified Federal employment (as defined in section 3121(u)(2)) which is subject to the taxes imposed by sections 3101(b) and 3111(b). An individual who is not a citizen of the United States but who is a resident of the Commonwealth of Puerto Rico, the Virgin Islands, Guam, or American Samoa shall not, for purposes of this chapter be considered to be a nonresident alien individual.

• **1982, Tax Equity and Fiscal Responsibility Act of 1982 (P.L. 97-248)**

P.L. 97-248, §278(a)(2):

Amended Code Sec. 1402(b) by striking out "and" before "(B)" in the second sentence and by inserting ", and (C) includes, but only with respect to the tax imposed by section 1401(b), remuneration paid for medicare qualified Federal employment (as defined in section 3121(u)(2)) which is subject to the taxes imposed by sections 3101(b) and 3111(b)" before the period. **Effective** with respect to remuneration paid after 12-31-82.

• **1976, Tax Reform Act of 1976 (P.L. 94-455)**

P.L. 94-455, §1901(a)(155)(A):

Amended Code Sec. 1402(b)(1). **Effective** with respect to tax years beginning after 12-31-76. Prior to amendment Code Sec. 1402(b)(1) read as follows:

(1) that part of the net earnings from self-employment which is in excess of—

(A) for any taxable year ending prior to 1955, (i) $3,600, minus (ii) the amount of the wages paid to such individual during the taxable year; and

(B) for any taxable year ending after 1954 and before 1959, (i) $4,200, minus (ii) the amount of the wages paid to such individual during the taxable year; and

(C) for any taxable year ending after 1958 and before 1966, (i) $4,800, minus (ii) the amount of the wages paid to such individual during the taxable year; and

(D) for any taxable year ending after 1965 and before 1968, (i) $6,600, minus (ii) the amount of wages paid to such individual during the taxable year; and

(E) for any taxable year ending after 1967 and beginning before 1972, (i) $7,800, minus (ii) the amount of the wages paid to such individual during the taxable year; and

(F) for any taxable year beginning after 1971 and before 1973, (i) $9,000, minus (ii) the amount of the wages paid to such individual during the taxable year; and

(G) for any taxable year beginning after 1972 and before 1974, (i) $10,800, minus (ii) the amount of wages paid to such individual during the taxable year; and

(H) for any taxable year beginning after 1973 and before 1975, (i) $13,200, minus (ii) the amount of the wages paid to such individual during the taxable year; and

(I) for any taxable year beginning in any calendar year after 1974, (i) an amount equal to the contribution and benefit base (as determined under section 230 of the Social Security Act) which is effective for such calendar year, minus (ii) the amount of the wages paid to such individual during such taxable year; or

• **1975 (P.L. 94-92)**

P.L. 94-92, §203(a) and (c):

Amended the last paragraph of Code Sec. 1402(b) by striking out ", but solely with respect to the tax imposed by section 1401(b)," from item (B) of the second sentence thereof. **Effective** 1-1-75, and only with respect to compensation paid for services rendered on or after that date. Prior to amendment item (B) read as follows:

(B) includes, but solely with respect to the tax imposed by section 1401(b), compensation which is subject to the tax imposed by section 3201 or 3211.

• **1973 (P.L. 93-233)**

P.L. 93-233, §5(b)(1):

Amended Code Sec. 1402(b)(1)(H) by substituting "$13,200" for "$12,600."

• **1973 (P.L. 93-66)**

P.L. 93-66, §203(b)(1):

Amended Code Sec. 1402(b)(1)(H) by substituting "$12,600" for "$12,000." (But see P.L. 93-233, above.)

• **1972 (P.L. 92-336)**

P.L. 92-336, §203(b)(1)(A) and (B):

Amended Code Sec. 1402(b)(1)(F) and added new subparagraphs (G) through (I). **Effective** only for tax years beginning after 1972. Prior to amendment Code Sec. 1402(b)(1)(F) read as follows:

(F) for any taxable year beginning after 1971, (i) $9,000, minus (ii) the amount of the wages paid to such individual during the taxable year; or

INCOME TAX—SELF-EMPLOYMENT INCOME

- **1971 (P.L. 92-5)**

P.L. 92-5, § 203(b)(1):

Amended Code Sec. 1402(b)(1) by inserting "and beginning before 1972" after "1967" in subparagraph (E) and by substituting "; and" for "; or" at the end, and by adding subparagraph (F). **Effective** only with respect to tax years beginning after 1971.

- **1968, Social Security Amendments of 1967 (P.L. 90-248)**

P.L. 90-248, § 108(b)(1):

Amended Code Sec. 1402(b)(1) by inserting "and before 1968" after "1965" in subparagraph (D), by substituting "and" for "or" at the end of said subparagraph, and by adding new subparagraph (E). **Effective** only with respect to tax years ending after 1967.

P.L. 90-248, § 502(b):

Amended the second sentence of Sec. 1402(b) by adding "(A)" after "wages" and by adding at the end thereof the material beginning with "and (B)". **Effective** only with respect to tax years ending on or after 12-31-68.

- **1965, Social Security Amendments of 1965 (P.L. 89-97)**

P.L. 89-97, § 320(b):

Amended Sec. 1402(b)(1)(C) by inserting "and before 1966" after "1958" and by striking out "; or" and inserting in lieu thereof "; and". **Effective** with respect to tax years ending after 1965.

P.L. 89-97, § 320(b):

Amended Sec. 1402(b)(1) by adding subparagraph (D). **Effective** with respect to tax years ending after 1965.

- **1960, Social Security Amendments of 1960 (P.L. 86-778)**

P.L. 86-778, § 103(1):

Amended Code Sec. 1402(b) by striking out "the Virgin Islands or a resident of Puerto Rico" and by substituting "the Commonwealth of Puerto Rico, the Virgin Islands, Guam, or American Samoa". **Effective** for tax years beginning after 1960.

- **1958, Social Security Amendments of 1958 (P.L. 85-840)**

P.L. 85-840, § 402(a):

Amended subparagraph (B) of Sec. 1402(b)(1) and added subparagraph (C). Prior to amendment, subparagraph (B) read as follows:

(B) for any taxable year ending after 1954, (i) $4,200, minus (ii) the amount of the wages paid to such individual during the taxable year; or.

- **1954, Social Security Amendments of 1954 (P.L. 761, 83rd Cong.)**

P.L. 761, 83rd Cong., § 201(b):

Amended subparagraph (A) of Sec. 1402(b)(1) and subparagraph (B) to read as reproduced in the amendment note for P.L. 85-840. Prior to amendment subparagraphs (A) and (B) read as follows:

(A) $3,600 minus

(B) the amount of the wages paid to such individual during the taxable year; or.

Added the comma and the language following the words "State employees)" in the second sentence.

[Sec. 1402(c)]

(c) TRADE OR BUSINESS.—The term "trade or business", when used with reference to self-employment income or net earnings from self-employment, shall have the same meaning as when used in section 162 (relating to trade or business expenses), except that such term shall not include—

(1) the performance of the functions of a public office, other than the functions of a public office of a State or a political subdivision thereof with respect to fees received in any period in which the functions are performed in a position compensated solely on a fee basis and in which such functions are not covered under an agreement entered into by such State and the Commissioner of Social Security pursuant to section 218 of the Social Security Act;

(2) the performance of service by an individual as an employee, other than—

(A) service described in section 3121(b)(14)(B) performed by an individual who has attained the age of 18,

(B) service described in section 3121(b)(16),

(C) service described in section 3121(b)(11), (12), or (15) performed in the United States (as defined in section 3121(e)(2)) by a citizen of the United States except service which constitutes "employment" under section 3121(y),

(D) service described in paragraph (4) of this subsection,

(E) service performed by an individual as an employee of a State or a political subdivision thereof in a position compensated solely on a fee basis with respect to fees received in any period in which such service is not covered under an agreement entered into by such State and the Commissioner of Social Security pursuant to section 218 of the Social Security Act,

(F) service described in section 3121(b)(20), and

(G) service described in section 3121(b)(8)(B);

(3) the performance of service by an individual as an employee or employee representative as defined in section 3231;

(4) the performance of service by a duly ordained, commissioned, or licensed minister of a church in the exercise of his ministry or by a member of a religious order in the exercise of duties required by such order;

(5) the performance of service by an individual in the exercise of his profession as a Christian Science practitioner; or

(6) the performance of service by an individual during the period for which an exemption under subsection (g) is effective with respect to him.

The provisions of paragraph (4) or (5) shall not apply to service (other than service performed by a member of a religious order who has taken a vow of poverty as a member of such order) performed by an individual unless an exemption under subsection (e) is effective with respect to him.

Amendments

- **1994, Social Security Independence and Program Improvements Act of 1994 (P.L. 103-296)**

P.L. 103-296, § 108(h)(1):

Amended Code Sec. 1402(c)(1) and (c)(2)(E) by striking "Secretary of Health and Human Services" each place it appears and inserting "Commissioner of Social Security". **Effective** 3-31-95.

P.L. 103-296, § 306 provides:

SEC. 306. LIMITED EXEMPTION FOR CANADIAN MINISTERS FROM CERTAIN SELF-EMPLOYMENT TAX LIABILITY.

(a) IN GENERAL.—Notwithstanding any other provision of law, if—

(1) an individual performed services described in section 1402(c)(4) of the Internal Revenue Code of 1986 which are subject to tax under section 1401 of such Code,

(2) such services were performed in Canada at a time when no agreement between the United States and Canada pursuant to section 233 of the Social Security Act was in effect, and

(3) such individual was required to pay contributions on the earnings from such services under the social insurance system of Canada,

then such individual may file a certificate under this section in such form and manner, and with such official, as may be prescribed in regulations issued under chapter 2 of such Code. Upon the filing of such certificate, notwithstanding any judgment which has been entered to the contrary, such individual shall be exempt from payment of such tax with respect to services described in paragraphs (1) and (2) and from any penalties or interest for failure to pay such tax or to file a self-employment tax return as required under section 6017 of such Code.

(b) PERIOD FOR FILING.—A certificate referred to in subsection (a) may be filed only during the 180-day period commencing with the date on which the regulations referred to in subsection (a) are issued.

(c) TAXABLE YEARS AFFECTED BY CERTIFICATE.—A certificate referred to in subsection (a) shall be effective for taxable years ending after December 31, 1978, and before January 1, 1985.

(d) RESTRICTION ON CREDITING OF EXEMPT SELF-EMPLOYMENT INCOME.—In any case in which an individual is exempt under this section from paying a tax imposed under section 1401 of the Internal Revenue Code of 1986, any income on which such tax would have been imposed but for such exemption shall not constitute self-employment income under section 211(b) of the Social Security Act (42 U.S.C. 411(b)), and, if such individual's primary insurance amount has been determined under section 215 of such Act (42 U.S.C. 415), notwithstanding section 215(f)(1) of such Act, the Secretary of Health and Human Services (prior to March 31, 1995) or the Commissioner of Social Security (after March 30, 1995) shall recompute such primary insurance amount so as to take into account the provisions of this subsection. The recomputation under this subsection shall be effective with respect to benefits for months following approval of the certificate of exemption.

P.L. 103-296, § 319(a)(4):

Amended Code Sec. 1402(c)(2)(C) by adding at the end "except service which constitutes 'employment' under section 3121(y)". **Effective** with respect to service performed after the calendar quarter following the calendar quarter containing 8-15-94.

INCOME TAX—SELF-EMPLOYMENT INCOME

• **1986, Tax Reform Act of 1986 (P.L. 99-514)**

P.L. 99-514, §1883(a)(11)(A):

Amended Code Sec. 1402(c)(2) by indenting subparagraph (G) two additional ems so as to align its left margin with the margins of the other subparagraphs in such section. **Effective** 10-22-86.

• **1984, Deficit Reduction Act of 1984 (P.L. 98-369)**

P.L. 98-369, §2603(c)(2):

Amended Code Sec. 1402(c)(2) by striking out "and" at the end of subparagraph (E); by striking out the semicolon at the end of subparagraph (F) and inserting in lieu thereof ", and" and by adding new subparagraph (G). **Effective** for service performed after 12-31-83. However, see Act Sec. 2603(f), below, for special rules.

P.L. 98-369, §2603(f), provides:

(f) In any case where a church or qualified church-controlled organization makes an election under section 3121(w) of the Internal Revenue Code of 1954, the Secretary of the Treasury shall refund (without interest) to such church or organization any taxes paid under sections 3101 and 3111 of such Code with respect to service performed after December 31, 1983, which is covered under such election. The refund shall be conditional upon the church or organization agreeing to pay to each employee (or former employee) the portion of the refund attributable to the tax imposed on such employee (or former employee) under section 3101, and such employee (or former employee) may not receive any other refund payment of such taxes.

P.L. 98-369, §2663(j)(5)(B):

Amended Code Sec. 1402(c)(1) and (c)(2)(E), by striking out "Health, Education, and Welfare" each place it appeared and inserting in lieu thereof "Health and Human Services". **Effective** as if included in P.L. 98-21.

• **1978, Revenue Act of 1978 (P.L. 95-600)**

P.L. 95-600, §§703(j)(8)(B), (r):

Amended Code Sec. 1402(c)(6) by striking out "subsection (h)" and inserting in place thereof "subsection (g)". **Effective** 10-4-76.

• **1976, Tax Reform Act of 1976 (P.L. 94-455)**

P.L. 94-455, §1207(e)(1)(B), (f)(4):

Added Code Sec. 1402(c)(2)(F). **Effective** for tax years ending after 12-31-54. But see Act Sec. 1207(f)(4), as amended by P.L. 95-600, Sec. 701(z)(1), (2), below, for special rules.

P.L. 94-455, §1207(f)(4)(B), as amended by P.L. 95-600, Sec. 701(z)(1), (2), provided:

(B) Notwithstanding subparagraph (A), if the owner or operator of any boat treated a share of the boat's catch of fish or other aquatic animal life (or a share of the proceeds therefrom) received by an individual after December 31, 1954, and before the date of the enactment of this Act for services performed by such individual after December 31, 1954, on such boat as being subject to the tax under chapter 21 of the Internal Revenue Code of 1954, then the amendments made by paragraphs (1)(A) and (B) and (2) of subsection (e) shall not apply with respect to such services performed by such individual (and the share of the catch, or proceeds therefrom, received by him for such services).

• **1968, Social Security Amendments of 1967 (P.L. 90-248)**

P.L. 90-248, §115(b)(1):

Amended Sec. 1402(c) in the last sentence by substituting "unless an exemption under subsection (e) is effective with respect to him" for "during the period for which a certificate filed by him under subsection (e) is in effect". **Effective** only with respect to tax years ending after 1967.

P.L. 90-248, §122(b):

Amended Sec. 1402(c)(1) and amended Code Sec. 1402(c)(2) by striking out "and" at the end of subparagraph (C), by substituting ", and" for a semicolon at the end of subparagraph (D) and by adding a new subparagraph (E). **Effective** with respect to fees received after 1967. But see, also Sec. 122(c), below. Prior to amendment Sec. 1402(c)(1) read as follows:

"(1) the performance of the functions of a public office;"

P.L. 90-248, §122(c), provides:

"Notwithstanding the provisions of subsections (a) and (b) of this section, any individual who in 1968 is in a position to which the amendments made by such subsections apply may make an irrevocable election not to have such amendments apply to the fees he receives in 1968 and every year thereafter, if on or before the due date of his income tax return for 1968 (including any extensions thereof) he files with the Secretary of the Treasury or his delegate, in such manner as the Secretary of the Treasury or his delegate shall by regulations prescribe, a certificate of election of exemption from such amendments."

• **1965, Social Security Amendments of 1965 (P.L. 89-97)**

P.L. 89-97, §311:

Amended Sec. 1402(c)(5) by deleting "doctor of medicine or" and amended the last two sentences of Sec. 1402(c). **Effective** with respect to tax years ending on or after 12-31-65. Prior to amendment, the last two sentences read as follows:

"The provisions of paragraph (4) shall not apply to service (other than service performed by a member of a religious order who has taken a vow of poverty as a member of such order) performed by an individual during the period for which a certificate filed by such individual under subsection (e) is in effect. The provisions of paragraph (5) shall not apply to service performed by an individual in the exercise of his profession as a Christian Science practitioner during the period for which a certificate filed by him under subsection (e) is in effect."

P.L. 89-97, §319(a):

Amended Sec. 1402(c) by striking out "or" at the end of paragraph (4), by striking out the period at the end of paragraph (5) and inserting in lieu thereof "; or", and by adding new paragraph (6). **Effective** with respect to tax years beginning after 12-31-50. If refund or credit of any overpayment resulting from enactment of this amendment is prevented on 7-30-65 or at any time on or before 4-15-66, by the operation of any law or rule of law, refund or credit may nevertheless be made or allowed if claim therefore is filed on or before 4-15-66. No interest shall be allowed or paid on any overpayment resulting from enactment of this amendment.

• **1960, Social Security Amendments of 1960 (P.L. 86-778)**

P.L. 86-778, §106(b):

Amended Code Sec. 1402(c)(2). **Effective** for tax years ending on or after 12-31-60. Prior to amendment, it read as follows:

(2) the performance of service by an individual as an employee (other than service described in section 3121(b)(14)(B) performed by an individual who has attained the age of 18, service described in section 3121(b)(16), and service described in paragraph (4) of this subsection);.

• **1956, Social Security Amendments of 1956 (P.L. 880, 84th Cong.)**

P.L. 880, 84th Cong., §201(e)(3), (f):

Amended Sec. 1402(c)(2) by adding after the words "age of 18": "service described in section 3121(b)(16)," and by deleting the words "other than" preceding the words "service described in paragraph (4)". **Effective** for tax years ending after 1954.

P.L. 880, 84th Cong., §201(e)(3), (f):

Amended Sec. 1402(c)(5) by substituting the words "doctor of medicine" for "physician, lawyer, dentist, osteopath, veterinarian, chiropractor, naturopath, optometrist,". **Effective** for tax years ending after 1955.

• **1954, Social Security Amendments of 1954 (P.L. 761, 83rd Cong.)**

P.L. 761, 83rd Cong., §201(c):

Added the words "and other than service described in paragraph (4) of this subsection" after "18" in paragraph (2). amended paragraph (5) by inserting "or" preceding "Christian Science practitioner" and deleting "architect, certified public accountant, accountant registered or licensed as an accountant under State or municipal law, full-time practicing public accountant, funeral director, or professional engineer" following "Christian Science practitioner.", and added the last two sentences to subsection (c). **Effective** only with respect to tax years ending after 1954.

[Sec. 1402(d)]

(d) EMPLOYEE AND WAGES.—The term "employee" and the term "wages" shall have the same meaning as when used in chapter 21 (sec. 3101 and following, relating to Federal Insurance Contributions Act).

[Sec. 1402(e)]

(e) MINISTERS, MEMBERS OF RELIGIOUS ORDERS, AND CHRISTIAN SCIENCE PRACTITIONERS.—

(1) EXEMPTION.—Subject to paragraph (2), any individual who is (A) a duly ordained, commissioned, or licensed minister of a church or a member of a religious order (other than a member of a religious order who has taken a vow of poverty as a member of such order) or (B) a Christian Science practitioner, upon filing an application (in such form and manner, and with such official, as may be prescribed by regulations made under this chapter) together with a statement that either he is conscientiously opposed to, or because of religious principles he is opposed to, the acceptance (with respect to services performed by him as such minister, member, or practitioner) of any public insurance which makes payments in the event of death, disability, old age, or retirement or makes payments toward the cost of, or provides services for, medical care (including the benefits of any insurance system established by the Social Security Act) and in the case of an individual described in subparagraph (A), that he has informed the ordaining, commissioning, or licensing body of the church or order that he is opposed to such insurance, shall receive an exemption from the tax imposed by this chapter with respect to services performed by him as such minister, member, or practitioner. Notwithstanding the preceding sentence, an exemption may not be granted to an individual under this subsection if he had filed an effective waiver certificate under this section as it was in effect before its amendment in 1967.

(2) VERIFICATION OF APPLICATION.—The Secretary may approve an application for an exemption filed pursuant to paragraph (1) only if the Secretary has verified that the individual applying for the exemption is aware of the grounds on which the individual may receive an exemption pursuant to this subsection and that the individual seeks exemption on such grounds. The Secretary (or the Commissioner of Social Security under an agreement with the Secretary) shall make such verification by such means as prescribed in regulations.

(3) TIME FOR FILING APPLICATION.—Any individual who desires to file an application pursuant to paragraph (1) must file such application on or before the due date of the return (including any extension thereof) for the second taxable year for which he has net earnings from self-

INCOME TAX—SELF-EMPLOYMENT INCOME

employment (computed without regard to subsections (c)(4) and (c)(5)) of $400 or more, any part of which was derived from the performance of service described in subsection (c)(4) or (c)(5).

(4) EFFECTIVE DATE OF EXEMPTION.—An exemption received by an individual pursuant to this subsection shall be effective for the first taxable year for which he has net earnings from self-employment (computed without regard to subsections (c)(4) and (c)(5)) of $400 or more, any part of which was derived from the performance of service described in subsection (c)(4) or (c)(5), and for all succeeding taxable years. An exemption received pursuant to this subsection shall be irrevocable.

Amendments

• **2014, Tax Technical Corrections Act of 2014 (P.L. 113-295)**

P.L. 113-295, §221(a)(91)(A)-(B), Division A:

Amended Code Sec. 1402(e)(3) by striking "whichever of the following dates is later: (A)" following "on or before", and by striking "; or (B)" and all that follows and inserting a period. **Effective** generally 12-19-2014. For a special rule, see Act Sec. 221(b)(2), Division A, below. Prior to being stricken, all that follows "; or (B)" read as follows:

the due date of the return (including any extension thereof) for his second taxable year ending after 1967.

P.L. 113-295, §221(b)(2), Division A, provides:

(2) SAVINGS PROVISION.—If—

(A) any provision amended or repealed by the amendments made by this section applied to—

(i) any transaction occurring before the date of the enactment of this Act,

(ii) any property acquired before such date of enactment, or

(iii) any item of income, loss, deduction, or credit taken into account before such date of enactment, and

(B) the treatment of such transaction, property, or item under such provision would (without regard to the amendments or repeals made by this section) affect the liability for tax for periods ending after date of enactment, nothing in the amendments or repeals made by this section shall be construed to affect the treatment of such transaction, property, or item for purposes of determining liability for tax for periods ending after such date of enactment.

• **1999, Tax Relief Extension Act of 1999 (P.L. 106-170)**

P.L. 106-170, §403, provides:

SEC. 403. REVOCATION BY MEMBERS OF THE CLERGY OF EXEMPTION FROM SOCIAL SECURITY COVERAGE.

(a) IN GENERAL.—Notwithstanding section 1402(e)(4) of the Internal Revenue Code of 1986, any exemption which has been received under section 1402(e)(1) of such Code by a duly ordained, commissioned, or licensed minister of a church, a member of a religious order, or a Christian Science practitioner, and which is effective for the taxable year in which this Act is enacted, may be revoked by filing an application therefor (in such form and manner, and with such official, as may be prescribed by the Commissioner of Internal Revenue), if such application is filed no later than the due date of the Federal income tax return (including any extension thereof) for the applicant's second taxable year beginning after December 31, 1999. Any such revocation shall be effective (for purposes of chapter 2 of the Internal Revenue Code of 1986 and title II of the Social Security Act (42 U.S.C. 401 et seq.)), as specified in the application, either with respect to the applicant's first taxable year beginning after December 31, 1999, or with respect to the applicant's second taxable year beginning after such date, and for all succeeding taxable years; and the applicant for any such revocation may not thereafter again file application for an exemption under such section 1402(e)(1). If the application is filed after the due date of the applicant's Federal income tax return for a taxable year and is effective with respect to that taxable year, it shall include or be accompanied by payment in full of an amount equal to the total of the taxes that would have been imposed by section 1401 of the Internal Revenue Code of 1986 with respect to all of the applicant's income derived in that taxable year which would have constituted net earnings from self-employment for purposes of chapter 2 of such Code (notwithstanding paragraphs (4) and (5) of section 1402(c)) except for the exemption under section 1402(e)(1) of such Code.

(b) EFFECTIVE DATE.—Subsection (a) shall apply with respect to service performed (to the extent specified in such subsection) in taxable years beginning after December 31, 1999, and with respect to monthly insurance benefits payable under title II on the basis of the wages and self-employment income of any individual for months in or after the calendar year in which such individual's application for revocation (as described in such subsection) is effective (and lump-sum death payments payable under such title on the basis of such wages and self-employment income in the case of deaths occurring in or after such calendar year).

• **1994, Social Security Independence and Program Improvements Act of 1994 (P.L. 103-296)**

P.L. 103-296, §108(h)(1):

Amended Code Sec. 1402(e)(2) by striking "Secretary of Health and Human Services" each place it appears and inserting "Commissioner of Social Security". **Effective** 3-31-95.

• **1986, Tax Reform Act of 1986 (P.L. 99-514)**

P.L. 99-514, §1704(a)(1):

Amended Code Sec. 1402(e)(1) by inserting "and, in the case of an individual described in subparagraph (A), that he has informed the ordaining, commissioning, or licensing body of the church or order that he is opposed to such insurance" after "Act". **Effective** for applications filed after 12-31-86.

P.L. 99-514, §1704(a)(2):

Amended Code Sec. 1402(e), as amended by Act Sec. 1882A(a)(1), by striking out "Any individual" in paragraph (1) and inserting in lieu thereof "Subject to paragraph (2), any individual", and by redesignating paragraphs (2) and (3) as paragraphs (3) and (4), respectively, and by inserting after paragraph (1) new paragraph (2). **Effective** for applications filed after 12-31-86.

P.L. 99-514, §1704(b), provides:

(b) REVOCATION OF EXEMPTION.

(1) IN GENERAL.—Notwithstanding section 1402(e)(3) of the Internal Revenue Code of 1986, as redesignated by subsection (a)(2)(B) of this section, any exemption which has been received under section 1402(e)(1) of such Code by a duly ordained, commissioned, or licensed minister of a church, a member of a religious order, or a Christian Science practitioner, and which is effective for the taxable year in which this Act is enacted, may be revoked by filing an application therefor (in such form and manner, and with such official, as may be prescribed in regulations made under chapter 2 of subtitle A of such Code), if such application is filed—

(A) before the applicant becomes entitled to benefits under section 202(a) or 223 of the Social Security Act (without regard to section 202(j)(1) or 223(b) of such Act), and

(B) no later than the due date of the Federal income tax return (including any extension thereof) for the applicant's first taxable year beginning after the date of the enactment of this Act.

Any such revocation shall be effective (for purposes of chapter 2 of subtitle A of the Internal Revenue Code of 1986 and title II of the Social Security Act), as specified in the application, either with respect to the applicant's first taxable year ending on or after the date of the enactment of this Act or with respect to the applicant's first taxable year beginning after such date, and for all succeeding taxable years; and the applicant for any such revocation may not thereafter again file application for an exemption under such section 1402(e)(1). If the application is filed on or after the due date of the Federal income tax return for the applicant's first taxable year ending on or after the date of the enactment of this Act and is effective with respect to that taxable year, it shall include or be accompanied by payment in full of an amount equal to the total of the taxes that would have been imposed by section 1401 of the Internal Revenue Code of 1986 with respect to all of the applicant's income derived in that taxable year which would have constituted net earnings from self-employment for purposes of chapter 2 of subtitle A of such Code (notwithstanding paragraph (4) or (5) of section 1402(c) of such Code) but for the exemption under section 1402(e)(1) of such Code.

(2) EFFECTIVE DATE.—Paragraph (1) of this subsection shall apply with respect to service performed (to the extent specified in such paragraph) in taxable years ending on or after the date of the enactment of this Act and with respect to monthly insurance benefits payable under title II of the Social Security Act on the basis of the wages and self-employment income of any individual for months in or after the calendar year in which such individual's application for revocation (as described in such paragraph) is effective (and lump-sum death payments payable under such title on the basis of such wages and self-employment income in the case of deaths occurring in or after such calendar year).

• **1977 (P.L. 95-216)**

P.L. 95-216, §316, provides:

SEC. 316. (a) Notwithstanding section 1402(e)(3) of the Internal Revenue Code of 1954, any exemption which has been received under section 1402(e)(1) of such Code by a duly ordained, commissioned, or licensed minister of a church or a Christian Science practitioner, and which is effective for the taxable year in which this Act is enacted, may be revoked by filing an application therefor (in such form and manner, and with such official, as may be prescribed in regulations made under chapter 2 of such Code), if such application is filed—

(1) before the applicant becomes entitled to benefits under section 202(a) or 223 of the Social Security Act (without regard to section 202(j)(1) or 223(b) of such Act), and

(2) no later than the due date of the Federal income tax return (including any extension thereof) for the applicant's first taxable year beginning after the date of the enactment of this Act.

Any such revocation shall be effective (for purposes of chapter 2 of the Internal Revenue Code of 1954 and title II of the Social Security Act), as specified in the application, either with respect to the applicant's first taxable year ending on or after the date of the enactment of this Act or with respect to the applicant's first taxable year beginning after such date, and for all succeeding taxable years; and the applicant for any such revocation may not thereafter again file application for an exemption under such section 1402(e)(1). If the application is filed on or after the due date of the applicant's first taxable year ending on or after the date of the enactment of this Act and is effective with respect to that taxable year, it shall include or be accompanied by payment in full of an amount equal to the total of the taxes that would have been imposed by section 1401 of the Internal Revenue Code of 1954 with respect to all of the applicant's income derived in that taxable year which would have constituted net earnings from self-employment for purposes of chapter 2 of such Code (notwithstanding section 1402(c)(4) or (c)(5) of such Code) except for the exemption under section 1402(e)(1) of such Code.

(b) Subsection (a) shall apply with respect to service performed (to the extent specified in such subsection) in taxable years ending on or after the date of the enactment of this Act, and with respect to monthly insurance benefits payable under title II of the Social Security Act on the basis of the wages and self-employment income of any individual for months in or after the calendar year in which such individual's application for revocation (as described in such subsection) is filed (and lump-sum death payments payable under such title on the basis of such wages and slef-employment income in the case of deaths occurring in or after such calendar year).

Effective 12-20-77.

• **1968, Social Security Amendments of 1967 (P.L. 90-248)**

P.L. 90-248, §115(b)(2):

Amended Sec. 1402(e). **Effective** only with respect to tax years ending after 1967. Prior to amendment Sec. 1402(e) read as follows:

"(e) Ministers, Members of Religious Orders, and Christian Science Practitioners.—

INCOME TAX—SELF-EMPLOYMENT INCOME

"(1) Waiver certificate.—Any individual who is (A) a duly ordained, commissioned, or licensed minister of a church or a member of a religious order (other than a member of a religious order who has taken a vow of poverty as a member of such order) or (B) a Christian Science practitioner may file a certificate (in such form and manner, and with such official, as may be prescribed by regulations made under this chapter) certifying that he elects to have the insurance system established by title II of the Social Security Act extended to service described in subsection (c)(4) or (c)(5) performed by him.

"(2) Time for filing certificate.—Any individual who desires to file a certificate pursuant to paragraph (1) must file such certificate on or before whichever of the following dates is later: (A) the due date of the return (including any extension thereof) for his second taxable year ending after 1954 for which he has net earnings from self-employment (computed without regard to subsection (c)(4) and (c)(5)) of $400 or more, any part of which was derived from the performance of service described in subsection (c)(4) or (c)(5); or (B) the due date of the return (including any extension thereof) for his second taxable year ending after 1963.

"(3)(A) Effective date of certificate.—A certificate filed pursuant to this subsection shall be effective for the taxable year immediately preceding the earliest taxable year for which, at the time the certificate is filed, the period for filing a return (including any extension thereof) has not expired, and for all succeeding taxable years. An election made pursuant to this subsection shall be irrevocable.

"(B) Notwithstanding the first sentence of subparagraph (A), if an individual filed a certificate on or before the date of enactment of this subparagraph which (but for this subparagraph) is effective only for the first taxable year ending after 1956 and all succeeding taxable years, such certificate shall be effective for his first taxable year ending after 1955 and all succeeding taxable years if—

"(i) such individual files a supplemental certificate after the date of enactment of this subparagraph and on or before April 15, 1962,

"(ii) the tax under section 1401 in respect of all such individual's self-employment income (except for underpayments of tax attributable to errors made in good faith) for his first taxable year ending after 1955 is paid on or before April 15, 1962, and

"(iii) in any case where refund has been made of any such tax which (but for this subparagraph) is an overpayment, the amount refunded (including any interest paid under section 6611) is repaid on or before April 15, 1962.

The provisions of section 6401 shall not apply to any payment or repayment described in this subparagraph.

"(C) Notwithstanding the first sentence of subparagraph (A), if an individual files a certificate after the date of enactment of this subparagraph and on or before the due date of the return (including any extension thereof) for his second taxable year ending after 1962, such certificate shall be effective for his first taxable year ending after 1961 and all succeeding years.

"(D) Notwithstanding the first sentence of subparagraph (A), if an individual files a certificate after the date of the enactment of this subparagraph and on or before the due date of the return (including any extension thereof) for his second taxable year ending after 1963, such certificate shall be effective for his first taxable year ending after 1962 and all succeeding years.

"(E) For purposes of sections 6015 and 6654, a waiver certificate described in paragraph (1) shall be treated as taking effect on the first day of the first taxable year beginning after the date on which such certificate is filed.

"(4) Treatment of certain remuneration paid in 1955 and 1956 as wages.—If—

"(A) in 1955 or 1956 an individual was paid remuneration for service described in section 3121(b)(8)(A) which was erroneously treated by the organization employing him (under a certificate filed by such organization pursuant to section 3121(k) or the corresponding section of prior law) as employment (within the meaning of chapter 21), and

"(B) on or before the date of the enactment of this paragraph the taxes imposed by sections 3101 and 3111 were paid (in good faith and upon the assumption that the insurance system established by title II of the Social Security Act had been extended to such service) with respect to any part of the remuneration paid to such individual for such service,

then the remuneration with respect to which such taxes were paid, and with respect to which no credit or refund of such taxes (other than a credit or refund which would be allowable if such service had constituted employment) has been obtained on or before the date of the enactment of this paragraph, shall be deemed (for purposes of this chapter and chapter 21) to constitute remuneration paid for employment and not net earnings from self-employment.

"(5) Optional provision for certain certificates filed on or before April 15, 1967.—Notwithstanding any other provision of this section, in any case where an individual has derived earnings in any taxable year ending after 1954 from the performance of service described in subsection (c)(4), or in subsection (c)(5) insofar as it related to the performance of service by an individual in the exercise of his profession as a Christian Science practitioner, and has reported such earnings as self-employment income on a return filed on or before the due date prescribed for filing such return (including any extension thereof)—

"(A) a certificate filed by such individual on or before April 15, 1966, which (but for this subparagraph) is ineffective for the first taxable year ending after 1954 for which such a return was filed shall be effective for such first taxable year and for all succeeding taxable years, provided a supplemental certificate is filed by such individual (or a fiduciary acting for such individual or his estate, or his survivor within the meaning of section 205(c)(1)(C) of the Social Security Act) after the date of enactment of the Social Security Amendments of 1965 and on or before April 15, 1967, and

"(B) a certificate filed after the date of enactment of the Social Security Amendments of 1965 and on or before April 15, 1967, by a survivor (within the meaning of section 205(c)(1)(C) of the Social Security Act) of such an individual who died on or before April 15, 1966, may be effective, at the election of the person filing such a certificate, for the first taxable year ending after 1954 for which such a return was filed and for all succeeding years,

but only if—

"(i) the tax under section 1401 in respect to all such individual's self-employment income (except for underpayments of tax attributable to errors made in good faith),

for each such year described in subparagraphs (A) and (B) ending before January 1, 1966, is paid on or before April 15, 1967, and

"(ii) in any case where refund has been made of any such tax which (but for this paragraph) is an overpayment, the amount refunded (including any interest paid under section 6611) is repaid on or before April 15, 1967.

The provisions of section 6401 shall not apply to any payment or repayment described in this paragraph."

- **1966, Tax Adjustment Act of 1966 (P.L. 89-368)**

P. L. 89-368, §102(c):

Added Code Sec. 1402(e)(3)(E). **Effective** 1-1-67.

- **1965, Social Security Amendments of 1965 (P.L. 89-97)**

P.L. 89-97, §311:

Amended Sec. 1402(e)(1) by striking out "extended to service" and all that follows and inserting in lieu thereof "extended to service described in subsection (c)(4) or (c)(5) performed by him"; amended Sec. 1402(e)(2)(A). **Effective** with respect to tax years ending on or after 12-31-65.

P.L. 89-97, §331(a):

Amended Sec. 1402(e) by striking out paragraphs (5) and (6) and inserting new paragraph (5). **Effective** with respect to (except as otherwise specifically provided in the subsections) only for certificates which supplemental certificates are filed pursuant to section 1402(e)(5)(A) after 7-30-65, and to certificates filed pursuant to section 1402(e)(5)(B) after such date; except that no monthly benefits under title II of the Social Security Act for the month in which this Act is enacted (July 1965) or any prior month shall be payable or increased by reason of such amendments, and no lump-sum death payment under such title shall be payable or increased by reason of such amendments in the case of any individual who died prior to 7-30-65. Prior Code Sec. 1402(e)(5) and (6) is applicable to any certificate filed pursuant thereto before such date if a supplemental certificate is not filed with respect to such certificate as provided in this section. Prior to amendment, Sec. 1402(e)(5) and (6) read as follows:

"(5) Optional provision for certain certificates filed on or before April 15, 1962.—In any case where an individual has derived earnings, in any taxable year ending after 1954 and before 1960, from the performance of service described in subsection (c)(4), or in subsection (c)(5) (as in effect prior to the enactment of this paragraph) insofar as it related to the performance of service by an individual in the exercise of his profession as a Christian Science practitioner, and has reported such earnings as self-employment income on a return filed on or before the date of the enactment of this paragraph and on or before the due date prescribed for filing such return (including any extension thereof)—

"(A) a certificate filed by such individual (or a fiduciary acting for such individual or his estate, or his survivor within the meaning of section 205(c)(1)(C) of the Social Security Act) after the date of enactment of this paragraph and on or before April 15, 1962, may be effective, at the election of the person filing such certificate, for the first taxable year ending after 1954 and before 1960 for which such a return was filed, and for all succeeding taxable years, rather than for the period prescribed in paragraph (3), and

"(B) a certificate by such individual on or before the date of the enactment of this paragraph which (but for this subparagraph) is ineffective for the first taxable year ending after 1954 and before 1959 for which such a return was filed shall be effective for such first taxable year, and for all succeeding taxable years, provided a supplemental certificate is filed by such individual (or a fiduciary acting for such individual or his estate, or his survivor within the meaning of section 205(c)(1)(C) of the Social Security Act) after the date of enactment of this paragraph and on or before April 15, 1962,

but only if—

"(i) the tax under section 1401 in respect of all such individual's self-employment income (except for underpayments of tax attributable to errors made in good faith), for each such year ending before 1960 in the case of a certificate described in subparagraph (A) or of each such year ending before 1959 in the case of a certificate described in subparagraph (B), is paid on or before April 15, 1962, and

"(ii) in any case where refund has been made of any such tax which (but for this paragraph) is an overpayment, the amount refunded (including any interest paid under section 6611) is repaid on or before April 15, 1962.

The provisions of section 6401 shall not apply to any payment or repayment described in this paragraph.

"(6) Certificate filed by fiduciaries or survivors on or before April 15, 1962.—In any case where an individual, whose death has occurred after September 12, 1960, and before April 16, 1962, derived earnings from the performance of services described in subsection (c)(4), or in subsection (c)(5) insofar as it relates to the performance of service by an individual in the exercise of his profession as a Christian Science practitioner, a certificate may be filed after the date of enactment of this paragraph, and on or before April 15, 1962, by a fiduciary acting for such individual's estate or by such individual's survivor within the meaning of section 205(c)(1)(C) of the Social Security Act. Such certificate shall be effective for the period prescribed in paragraph (3)(A) as if filed by the individual on the day of his death."

P.L. 89-97, §341(a)-(b):

Amended Sec. 1402(e)(2)(B) by substituting "1963" for "1962" and amended Sec. 1402(e)(3) by adding new subparagraph (D). **Effective** with respect to certificates filed pursuant to Sec. 1402(e) after 7-30-65, except that no monthly benefits under title II of the Social Security Act for the month in which this Act is enacted (July 1965) or any prior month shall be payable or increased by reason of such amendments.

- **1964 (P.L. 88-650)**

P.L. 88-650, §2:

Amended Code Sec. 1402(e)(2)(B) by substituting "1962" for "1959" and amended Code Sec. 1402(e)(3) by adding new subparagraph (C). **Effective** with respect to certificates filed after 10-13-64, the date of enactment, except that no monthly benefits

INCOME TAX—SELF-EMPLOYMENT INCOME

under title II of the Social Security Act for the month in which this Act is enacted or any prior month shall be payable or increased by reason of such amendments.

- **1961, Social Security Amendments of 1961 (P.L. 87-64)**

P.L. 87-64, §202(a):

Added paragraph (6) to Code Sec. 1402(e). **Effective** as noted in Act Sec. 202(b), below.

P.L. 97-64, §202(b), provides:

"(b) The amendment made by subsection (a) shall take effect on the date of enactment of this Act (6-30-61—CCH.); except that no monthly benefits under title II of the Social Security Act for the month in which this Act is enacted or any prior month shall be payable or increased by reason of such amendment, and no lump-sum death payment under such title shall be payable or increased by reason of such amendment in the case of any individual who died prior to the date of enactment of this Act."

- **1960, Social Security Amendments of 1960 (P.L. 86-778)**

P.L. 86-778, §101(a):

Struck out "1956" at the end of paragraph (2) of Code Sec. 1402(e) and substituted "1959". **Effective** 9-14-60.

P.L. 86-778, §101(b):

Amended paragraph (3) of Code Sec. 1402(e). **Effective** 9-14-60. Prior to amendment, it read as follows:

"(3) Effective Date of Certificate.—A certificate filed pursuant to this subsection shall be effective for the first taxable year with respect to which it is filed (but in no case shall the certificate be effective for a taxable year with respect to which the period for filing a return has expired, or for a taxable year ending prior to 1955) and all succeeding taxable years. An election made pursuant to this subsection shall be irrevocable. Notwithstanding the first sentence of this paragraph—

"(A) A certificate filed by an individual after the date of the enactment of this subparagraph but on or before the due date of the return (including any extension thereof) for his second taxable year ending after 1956 shall be effective for the first taxable year ending after 1955 and all succeeding taxable years.

"(B) If an individual filed a certificate on or before the date of the enactment of this subparagraph which (but for this subparagraph) is effective only for the third or fourth taxable year ending after 1954 and all succeeding taxable years, such certificate shall be effective for his first taxable year ending after 1955 and all succeeding taxable years if such individual files a supplemental certificate after the date of the enactment of this subparagraph and on or before the due date of the return (including any extension thereof) for his second taxable year ending after 1956.

"(C) A certificate filed by an individual after the due date of the return (including any extension thereof) for his second taxable year ending after 1956 shall be effective for the taxable year immediately preceding the taxable year with respect to which it is filed and all succeeding taxable years."

P.L. 86-778, §101(c):

§101(c) added a new paragraph (5) to Code Sec. 1402(e). **Effective** as noted in Act Sec. 101(d)-(f), below.

P.L. 86-778, §101(d)-(f), provide:

"(d) In the case of a certificate or supplemental certificate filed pursuant to section 1402(e)(3)(B) or (5) of the Internal Revenue Code of 1954—

"(1) for purposes of computing interest, the due date for the payment of the tax under section 1401 which is due for any taxable year ending before 1959 solely by reason of the filing of a certificate which is effective under such section 1402(e)(3)(B) or (5) shall be April 15, 1962;

"(2) the statutory period for the assessment of any tax for any such year which is attributable to the filing of such certificate shall not expire before the expiration of 3 years from such due date; and

"(3) for purposes of section 6651 of such Code (relating to addition to tax for failure to file tax return), the amount of tax required to be shown on the return shall not include such tax under section 1401.

"(e) The provisions of section 205(c)(5)(F) of the Social Security Act, insofar as they prohibit inclusion in the records of the Secretary of Health, Education, and Welfare of self-employment income for a taxable year when the return or statement including such income is filed after the time limitation following such taxable year, shall not be applicable to earnings which are derived in any taxable year ending before 1960 and which constitute self-employment income solely by reason of the filing of a certificate which is effective under section 1402(e)(3)(B) or (5) of the Internal Revenue Code of 1954.

"(f) The amendments made by this section shall be applicable (except as otherwise specifically indicated therein) only with respect to certificates (and supplemental certificates) filed pursuant to section 1402(e) of the Internal Revenue Code of 1954 after the date of the enactment of this Act; except that no monthly benefits under title II of the Social Security Act for the month in which this Act is enacted or any prior month shall be payable or increased by reason of such amendments, and no lump-sum death payment under such title shall be payable or increased by reason of such amendments in the case of any individual who died prior to the date of the enactment of this Act."

- **1957 (P.L. 85-239)**

P.L. 85-239, §[1] and 2:

Amended paragraph (2) of Code Sec. 1402(e) by adding the words "whichever of the following dates is later: (A)" after the phrase "on or before" and by adding the phrase "; or (B) the due date of the return (including any extension thereof) for his second taxable year ending after 1956" after the phrase "as the case may be." Also added all of subparagraph (3) following the phrase "shall be irrevocable." Also added paragraph (4). **Effective** 8-30-57.

- **1954, Social Security Amendments of 1954 (P.L. 761, 83rd Cong.)**

P.L. 761, 83rd Cong., §201(c):

Added subsection (e). **Effective** 1-1-55.

[Sec. 1402(f)]

(f) PARTNER'S TAXABLE YEAR ENDING AS THE RESULT OF DEATH.—In computing a partner's net earnings from self-employment for his taxable year which ends as a result of his death (but only if such taxable year ends within, and not with, the taxable year of the partnership), there shall be included so much of the deceased partner's distributive share of the partnership's ordinary income or loss for the partnership taxable year as is not attributable to an interest in the partnership during any period beginning on or after the first day of the first calendar month following the month in which such partner died. For purposes of this subsection—

(1) in determining the portion of the distributive share which is attributable to any period specified in the preceding sentence, the ordinary income or loss of the partnership shall be treated as having been realized or sustained ratably over the partnership taxable year; and

(2) the term "deceased partner's distributive share" includes the share of his estate or of any other person succeeding, by reason of his death, to rights with respect to his partnership interest.

Amendments

- **1958, Social Security Amendments of 1958 (P.L. 85-840)**

P.L. 85-840, §403(a):

Added subsection (f) to Sec. 1402. For the **effective** date, see Act Sec. 403(b), below.

P.L. 85-840, §403(b), provides:

(b)(1) Except as provided in paragraph (2), the amendment made by subsection (a) shall apply only with respect to individuals who die after the date of the enactment of this Act.

(2) In the case of an individual who died after 1955 and on or before the date of the enactment of this Act, the amendment made by subsection (a) shall apply only if—

(A) before January 1, 1960, there is filed a return (or amended return) of the tax imposed by chapter 2 of the Internal Revenue Code of 1954 for the taxable year ending as a result of his death, and

(B) in any case where the return is filed solely for the purpose of reporting net earnings from self-employment resulting from the amendment made by subsection (a), the return is accompanied by the amount of tax attributable to such net earnings.

In any case described in the preceding sentence, no interest or penalty shall be assessed or collected on the amount of any tax due under chapter 2 of such Code solely by reason of the operation of section 1402(f) of such Code.

[Sec. 1402(g)]

(g) MEMBERS OF CERTAIN RELIGIOUS FAITHS.—

(1) EXEMPTION.—Any individual may file an application (in such form and manner, and with such official, as may be prescribed by regulations under this chapter) for an exemption from the tax imposed by this chapter if he is a member of a recognized religious sect or division thereof and is an adherent of established tenets or teachings of such sect or division by reason of which he is conscientiously opposed to acceptance of the benefits of any private or public insurance which makes payments in the event of death, disability, old-age, or retirement or makes payments toward the cost of, or provides services for, medical care (including the benefits of any insurance system established by the Social Security Act). Such exemption may be granted only if the application contains or is accompanied by—

(A) such evidence of such individual's membership in, and adherence to the tenets or teachings of, the sect or division thereof as the Secretary may require for purposes of determining such individual's compliance with the preceding sentence, and

(B) his waiver of all benefits and other payments under titles II and XVIII of the Social Security Act on the basis of his wages and self-employment income as well as all such benefits and other payments to him on the basis of the wages and self-employment income of any other person,

and only if the Commissioner of Social Security finds that—

Sec. 1402(f)

INCOME TAX—SELF-EMPLOYMENT INCOME

(C) such sect or division thereof has the established tenets or teachings referred to in the preceding sentence,

(D) it is the practice, and has been for a period of time which he deems to be substantial, for members of such sect or division thereof to make provision for their dependent members which in his judgment is reasonable in view of their general level of living, and

(E) such sect or division thereof has been in existence at all times since December 31, 1950.

An exemption may not be granted to any individual if any benefit or other payment referred to in subparagraph (B) became payable (or, but for section 203 or 222(b) of the Social Security Act, would have become payable) at or before the time of the filing of such waiver.

(2) PERIOD FOR WHICH EXEMPTION EFFECTIVE.—An exemption granted to any individual pursuant to this subsection shall apply with respect to all taxable years beginning after December 31, 1950, except that such exemption shall not apply for any taxable year—

(A) beginning (i) before the taxable year in which such individual first met the requirements of the first sentence of paragraph (1), or (ii) before the time as of which the Commissioner of Social Security finds that the sect or division thereof of which such individual is a member met the requirements of subparagraphs (C) and (D), or

(B) ending (i) after the time such individual ceases to meet the requirements of the first sentence of paragraph (1), or (ii) after the time as of which the Commissioner of Social Security finds that the sect or division thereof of which he is a member ceases to meet the requirements of subparagraph (C) or (D).

(3) SUBSECTION TO APPLY TO CERTAIN CHURCH EMPLOYEES.—This subsection shall apply with respect to services which are described in subparagraph (B) of section 3121(b)(8) (and are not described in subparagraph (A) of such section).

Amendments

• **1994, Social Security Independence and Program Improvements Act of 1994 (P.L. 103-296)**

P.L. 103-296, §108(h)(1):

Amended Code Sec. 1402(g)(1) and (g)(2)(A)-(B) by striking "Secretary of Health and Human Services" each place it appears and inserting "Commissioner of Social Security". **Effective** 3-31-95.

• **1989, Omnibus Budget Reconciliation Act of 1989 (P.L. 101-239)**

P.L. 101-239, §10204(a)(1)(A)-(B):

Amended Code Sec. 1402(g)(3) by striking "not to apply" and inserting "to apply" in the heading, and by striking "shall not" and inserting "shall". **Effective** with respect to tax years beginning after 12-31-89.

• **1988, Technical and Miscellaneous Revenue Act of 1988 (P.L. 100-647)**

P.L. 100-647, §8007(c)(1)-(2):

Amended Code Sec. 1402(g) by striking paragraphs (2) and (4); and by redesignating paragraphs (3) and (5) paragraphs (2) and (3), respectively. **Effective** for applications for exemptions filed on or after 11-10-88. Prior to amendment, Code Sec. 1402(g)(2) and (4) read as follows:

(2) TIME FOR FILING APPLICATION.—For purposes of this subsection, an application must be filed on or before the time prescribed for filing the return (including any extension thereof) for the first taxable year for which the individual has self-employment income (determined without regard to this subsection or subsection (c)(6)), except that an application filed after such date but on or before the last day of the third calendar month following the calendar month in which the taxpayer is first notified in writing by the Secretary that a timely application for an exemption from the tax imposed by this chapter has not been filed by him shall be deemed to be filed timely.

* * *

(4) APPLICATION BY FIDUCIARIES OR SURVIVORS.—In any case where an individual who has self-employment income dies before the expiration of the time prescribed by paragraph (2) for filing an application for exemption pursuant to this subsection, such an application may be filed with respect to such individual within such time by a fiduciary acting for such individual's estate or by such individual's survivor (within the meaning of section 205(c)(1)(C) of the Social Security Act).

• **1986, Tax Reform Act of 1986 (P.L. 99-514)**

P.L. 99-514, §1882(a):

Amended Code Sec. 1402(g) by adding at the end thereof new paragraph (5). **Effective** 10-22-86.

• **1984, Deficit Reduction Act of 1984 (P.L. 98-369)**

P.L. 98-369, §2663(j)(5)(B):

Amended Code Sec. 1402(g)(1), (g)(3)(A) and (g)(3)(B) by striking out "Health, Education, and Welfare" each place it appeared and inserting in lieu thereof "Health and Human Services". **Effective** as if included in P.L. 98-21.

• **1976, Tax Reform Act of 1976 (P.L. 94-455)**

P.L. 94-455, §1901(a)(155)(B):

Repealed Code Sec. 1402(g) and redesignated subsection (h) as subsection (g). **Effective** with respect to tax years beginning after 12-31-76. Prior to repeal, Code Sec. 1402(g) read as follows:

(g) TREATMENT OF CERTAIN REMUNERATION ERRONEOUSLY REPORTED AS NET EARNINGS FROM SELF-EMPLOYMENT.—If—

(1) an amount is erroneously paid as tax under section 1401, for any taxable year ending after 1954 and before 1962, with respect to remuneration for service described in section 3121(b)(8) (other than service described in section 3121(b)(8)(A)), and such remuneration is reported as self-employment income on a return filed on or before the due date prescribed for filing such return (including any extension thereof),

(2) the individual who paid such amount (or a fiduciary acting for such individual or his estate, or his survivor (within the meaning of section 205(c)(1)(C) of the Social Security Act)) requests that such remuneration be deemed to constitute net earnings from self-employment,

(3) such request is filed after the date of the enactment of this paragraph and on or before April 15, 1962,

(4) such remuneration was paid to such individual for services performed in the employ of an organization which, on or before the date on which such request is filed, has filed a certificate pursuant to section 3121(k), and

(5) no credit or refund of any portion of the amount erroneously paid for such taxable year as tax under section 1401 (other than a credit or refund which would be allowable if such tax were applicable with respect to such remuneration) has been obtained before the date on which such request is filed or, if obtained, the amount credited or refunded (including any interest under section 6611) is repaid on or before such date,

then, for purposes of this chapter and chapter 21, any amount of such remuneration which is paid to such individual before the calendar quarter in which such request is filed (or before the succeeding quarter if such certificate first becomes effective with respect to services performed by such individual in such succeeding quarter), and with respect to which no tax (other than an amount erroneously paid as tax) has been paid under chapter 21, shall be deemed to constitute net earnings from self-employment and not remuneration for employment. For purposes of section 3121(b)(8)(B)(ii) and (iii), if the certificate filed by such organization pursuant to section 3121(k) is not effective with respect to services performed by such individual on or before the first day of the calendar quarter in which the request is filed, such individual shall be deemed to have become an employee of such organization (or to have become a member of a group described in section 3121(k)(1)(E)) on the first day of the succeeding quarter.

P.L. 94-455, §1901(a)(155)(C):

Amended redesignated Code Sec. 1402(g)(2). **Effective** with respect to tax years beginning after 12-31-76. Prior to amendment Code Sec. 1402(g)(2) read as follows:

(2) TIME FOR FILING APPLICATION.—For purposes of this subsection, an application must be filed—

(A) In the case of an individual who has self-employment income (determined without regard to this subsection and subsection (c)(6)) for any taxable year ending before December 31, 1967, on or before December 31, 1968, and

(B) In any other case, on or before the time prescribed for filing the return (including any extension thereof) for the first taxable year ending on or after December 31, 1967, for which he has self-employment income (as so determined), except that an application filed after such date but on or before the last day of the third calendar month following the calendar month in which the taxpayer is first notified in writing by the Secretary or his delegate that a timely application for an exemption from the tax imposed by this chapter has not been filed by him shall be deemed to be filed timely.

P.L. 94-455, §1906(b)(13)(A):

Amended the 1954 Code by substituting "Secretary" for "Secretary or his delegate" each place it appeared. **Effective** 2-1-77.

• **1968, Social Security Amendments of 1967 (P.L. 90-248)**

P.L. 90-248, §501(a):

Amended Sec. 1402(h)(2). **Effective** with respect to tax years beginning after 12-31-50. For such purpose, chapter 2 of the Internal Revenue Code of 1954 shall be treated as applying to all tax years beginning after such date. See, also, §501(c), below. Prior to amendment, Sec. 1402(h)(2) read as follows:

"(2) Time for filing application.—For purposes of this subsection, an application must be filed—

"(A) In the case of an individual who has self-employment income (determined without regard to this subsection and subsection (c)(6)) for any taxable year ending before December 31, 1965, on or before April 15, 1966, and

"(B) In any other case, on or before the time prescribed for filing the return (including any extension thereof) for the first taxable year ending on or after December 31, 1965, for which he has self-employment income as so determined."

P.L. 90-248, §501(c), provides:

"(c) If refund or credit of any overpayment resulting from the enactment of this section is prevented on the date of the enactment of this Act or any time on or before December 31, 1968, by the operation of any law or rule of law, refund or credit of such overpayment may, nevertheless, be made or allowed if claim therefore is filed on or before December 31, 1968. No interest shall be allowed or paid on any overpayment resulting from the enactment of this section."

• **1965, Social Security Amendments of 1965 (P.L. 89-97)**

P.L. 89-97, §319(c):

Added Code Sec. 1402(h). **Effective** for tax years beginning after 12-31-50. If refund or credit of any overpayment resulting from the enactment of this provision is prevented on 7-30-65 or at any time on or before 4-15-66, by the operation of any law or rule of law, refund or credit of such overpayment may nevertheless be made or allowed if claim therefore is filed on or before 4-15-66. No interest shall be allowed or paid on any overpayment resulting from enactment of this provision.

INCOME TAX—SELF-EMPLOYMENT INCOME

• **1960, Social Security Amendments of 1960 (P.L. 86-778)**

P.L. 86-778, §105(c):

Added Code Sec. 1402(g).

[Sec. 1402(h)]

(h) REGULAR BASIS.—An individual shall be deemed to be self-employed on a regular basis in a taxable year, or to be a member of a partnership on a regular basis in such year, if he had net earnings from self-employment, as defined in the first sentence of subsection (a), of not less than $400 in at least two of the three consecutive taxable years immediately preceding such taxable year from trades or businesses carried on by such individual or such partnership.

Amendments

• **1976, Tax Reform Act of 1976 (P.L. 94-455)**

P.L. 94-455, §1901(a)(155)(B):

Redesignated former subsection (i) as Code Sec. 1402(h). **Effective** with respect to tax years beginning after 12-31-76.

• **1972, Social Security Amendments of 1972 (P.L. 92-603)**

P.L. 92-603, §121(b)(2):

Added Code Sec. 1402(i). **Effective** for tax years beginning after 12-31-72.

[Sec. 1402(i)]

(i) SPECIAL RULES FOR OPTIONS AND COMMODITIES DEALERS.—

(1) IN GENERAL.—Notwithstanding subsection (a)(3)(A), in determining the net earnings from self-employment of any options dealer or commodities dealer, there shall not be excluded any gain or loss (in the normal course of the taxpayer's activity of dealing in or trading section 1256 contracts) from section 1256 contracts or property related to such contracts.

(2) DEFINITIONS.—For purposes of this subsection—

(A) OPTIONS DEALER.—The term "options dealer" has the meaning given such term by section 1256(g)(8).

(B) COMMODITIES DEALER.—The term "commodities dealer" means a person who is actively engaged in trading section 1256 contracts and is registered with a domestic board of trade which is designated as a contract market by the Commodities Futures Trading Commission.

(C) SECTION 1256 CONTRACTS.—The term "section 1256 contract" has the meaning given to such term by section 1256(b).

Amendments

• **1986, Tax Reform Act of 1986 (P.L. 99-514)**

P.L. 99-514, §301(b)(12):

Amended Code Sec. 1402(i)(1). **Effective** for tax years beginning after 12-31-86. Prior to amendment, Code Sec. 1402(i)(1) read as follows:

(1) IN GENERAL.—In determining the net earnings from self-employment of any options dealer or commodities dealer—

(A) notwithstanding subsection (a)(3)(A), there shall not be excluded any gain or loss (in the normal course of the taxpayer's activity of dealing in or trading section 1256 contracts) from section 1256 contracts or property related to such contracts, and

(B) the deduction provided by section 1202 shall not apply.

• **1984, Deficit Reduction Act of 1984 (P.L. 98-369)**

P.L. 98-369, §102(c)(1):

Amended Code Sec. 1402 by adding new subsection (i). **Effective** for tax years beginning after 7-18-84. However, see Act Sec. 102(g) under the amendment notes for Code Sec. 1256 for special rules.

[Sec. 1402(j)]

(j) SPECIAL RULES FOR CERTAIN CHURCH EMPLOYEE INCOME.—

(1) COMPUTATION OF NET EARNINGS.—In applying subsection (a)—

(A) church employee income shall not be reduced by any deduction;

(B) church employee income and deductions attributable to such income shall not be taken into account in determining the amount of other net earnings from self-employment.

(2) COMPUTATION OF SELF-EMPLOYMENT INCOME.—

(A) SEPARATE APPLICATION OF SUBSECTION (b)(2).—Paragraph (2) of subsection (b) shall be applied separately—

(i) to church employee income, and

(ii) to other net earnings from self-employment.

(B) $100 FLOOR.—In applying paragraph (2) of subsection (b) to church employee income, "$100" shall be substituted for "$400".

(3) COORDINATION WITH SUBSECTION (a)(12).—Paragraph (1) shall not apply to any amount allowable as a deduction under subsection (a)(12), and paragraph (1) shall be applied before determining the amount so allowable.

(4) CHURCH EMPLOYEE INCOME DEFINED.—For purposes of this section, the term "church employee income" means gross income for services which are described in section 3121(b)(8)(B) (and are not described in section 3121(b)(8)(A)).

Amendments

• **1986, Tax Reform Act of 1986 (P.L. 99-514)**

P.L. 99-514, §1882(b)(1)(A):

Amended Code Sec. 1402 by adding at the end thereof new subsection (j). **Effective** for remuneration paid or derived in tax years beginning after 12-31-85.

[Sec. 1402(k)]

(k) CODIFICATION OF TREATMENT OF CERTAIN TERMINATION PAYMENTS RECEIVED BY FORMER INSURANCE SALESMEN.—Nothing in subsection (a) shall be construed as including in the net earnings from self-employment of an individual any amount received during the taxable year from an insurance company on account of services performed by such individual as an insurance salesman for such company if—

(1) such amount is received after termination of such individual's agreement to perform such services for such company,

(2) such individual performs no services for such company after such termination and before the close of such taxable year,

(3) such individual enters into a covenant not to compete against such company which applies to at least the 1-year period beginning on the date of such termination, and

(4) the amount of such payment—

(A) depends primarily on policies sold by or credited to the account of such individual during the last year of such agreement or the extent to which such policies remain in force for some period after such termination, or both, and

(B) does not depend to any extent on length of service or overall earnings from services performed for such company (without regard to whether eligibility for payment depends on length of service).

INCOME TAX—MEDICARE TAX ON UNEARNED INCOME

Amendments

• **1997, Taxpayer Relief Act of 1997 (P.L. 105-34)**

P.L. 105-34, § 922(a):

Amended Code Sec. 1402 by adding a new subsection (k). **Effective** for payments after 12-31-97.

• **1993, Omnibus Budget Reconciliation Act of 1993 (P.L. 103-66)**

P.L. 103-66, § 13207(b)(2):

Amended Code Sec. 1402 by striking subsection (k). **Effective** for 1994 and later calendar years. Prior to being stricken, Code Sec. 1402(k) read as follows:

(k) APPLICABLE CONTRIBUTION BASE.—For purposes of this chapter—

(1) OLD-AGE, SURVIVORS, AND DISABILITY INSURANCE.—For purposes of the tax imposed by section 1401(a), the applicable contribution base for any calendar year is the contribution and benefit base determined under section 230 of the Social Security Act for such calendar year.

(2) HOSPITAL INSURANCE.—For purposes of the tax imposed by section 1401(b), the applicable contribution base for any calendar year is the applicable contribution base determined under section 3121(x)(2) for such calendar year.

• **1990, Omnibus Budget Reconciliation Act of 1990 (P.L. 101-508)**

P.L. 101-508, § 11331(b)(2):

Amended Code Sec. 1402 by adding at the end thereof a new subsection (k). **Effective** for 1991 and later calendar years.

[Sec. 1402(l)]

(l) UPPER AND LOWER LIMITS.—For purposes of subsection (a)—

(1) LOWER LIMIT.—The lower limit for any taxable year is the sum of the amounts required under section 213(d) of the Social Security Act for a quarter of coverage in effect with respect to each calendar quarter ending with or within such taxable year.

(2) UPPER LIMIT.—The upper limit for any taxable year is the amount equal to 150 percent of the lower limit for such taxable year.

Amendments

• **2008, Heartland, Habitat, Harvest, and Horticulture Act of 2008 (P.L. 110-246)**

P.L. 110-246, § 15352(a)(2):

Amended Code Sec. 1402 by adding at the end a new subsection (l). **Effective** for tax years beginning after 12-31-2007.

[Sec. 1403]

SEC. 1403. MISCELLANEOUS PROVISIONS.

[Sec. 1403(a)]

(a) TITLE OF CHAPTER.—This chapter may be cited as the "Self-Employment Contributions Act of 1954".

[Sec. 1403(b)]

(b) CROSS REFERENCES.—

(1) For provisions relating to returns, see section 6017.

(2) For provisions relating to collection of taxes in Virgin Islands, Guam, American Samoa, and Puerto Rico, see section 7651.

Amendments

• **1984, Deficit Reduction Act of 1984 (P.L. 98-369)**

P.L. 98-369, § 412(b)(2):

Amended Code Sec. 1403(b) by striking out paragraph (3). **Effective** with respect to tax years beginning after 12-31-84. Prior to deletion, paragraph (3) read as follows:

(3) For provisions relating to declarations of estimated tax on self-employment income, see section 6015.

• **1966 (P.L. 89-368)**

P.L. 89-368, § 102(b)(6):

Added Code Sec. 1403(b)(3). **Effective** 1-1-67.

• **1960, Social Security Amendments of 1960 (P.L. 86-778)**

P.L. 86-778, § 103(m):

Added ", Guam, American Samoa," following "Virgin Islands" in Code Sec. 1403(b)(2).

CHAPTER 2A—UNEARNED INCOME MEDICARE CONTRIBUTION

Sec. 1411. Imposition of tax.

[Sec. 1411]

SEC. 1411. IMPOSITION OF TAX.

[Sec. 1411(a)]

(a) IN GENERAL.—Except as provided in subsection (e)—

(1) APPLICATION TO INDIVIDUALS.—In the case of an individual, there is hereby imposed (in addition to any other tax imposed by this subtitle) for each taxable year a tax equal to 3.8 percent of the lesser of—

(A) net investment income for such taxable year, or

(B) the excess (if any) of—

(i) the modified adjusted gross income for such taxable year, over

(ii) the threshold amount.

(2) APPLICATION TO ESTATES AND TRUSTS.—In the case of an estate or trust, there is hereby imposed (in addition to any other tax imposed by this subtitle) for each taxable year a tax of 3.8 percent of the lesser of—

(A) the undistributed net investment income for such taxable year, or

(B) the excess (if any) of—

(i) the adjusted gross income (as defined in section 67(e)) for such taxable year, over

(ii) the dollar amount at which the highest tax bracket in section 1(e) begins for such taxable year.

[Sec. 1411(b)]

(b) THRESHOLD AMOUNT.—For purposes of this chapter, the term "threshold amount" means—

(1) in the case of a taxpayer making a joint return under section 6013 or a surviving spouse (as defined in section 2(a)), $250,000,

(2) in the case of a married taxpayer (as defined in section 7703) filing a separate return, ½ of the dollar amount determined under paragraph (1), and

(3) in any other case, $200,000.

[Sec. 1411(c)]

(c) NET INVESTMENT INCOME.—For purposes of this chapter—

INCOME TAX—WITHHOLDING—NONRESIDENT ALIENS

(1) IN GENERAL.—The term "net investment income" means the excess (if any) of—
　(A) the sum of—
　　(i) gross income from interest, dividends, annuities, royalties, and rents, other than such income which is derived in the ordinary course of a trade or business not described in paragraph (2),
　　(ii) other gross income derived from a trade or business described in paragraph (2), and
　　(iii) net gain (to the extent taken into account in computing taxable income) attributable to the disposition of property other than property held in a trade or business not described in paragraph (2), over
　(B) the deductions allowed by this subtitle which are properly allocable to such gross income or net gain.
(2) TRADES AND BUSINESSES TO WHICH TAX APPLIES.—A trade or business is described in this paragraph if such trade or business is—
　(A) a passive activity (within the meaning of section 469) with respect to the taxpayer, or
　(B) a trade or business of trading in financial instruments or commodities (as defined in section 475(e)(2)).
(3) INCOME ON INVESTMENT OF WORKING CAPITAL SUBJECT TO TAX.—A rule similar to the rule of section 469(e)(1)(B) shall apply for purposes of this subsection.
(4) EXCEPTION FOR CERTAIN ACTIVE INTERESTS IN PARTNERSHIPS AND S CORPORATIONS.—In the case of a disposition of an interest in a partnership or S corporation—
　(A) gain from such disposition shall be taken into account under clause (iii) of paragraph (1)(A) only to the extent of the net gain which would be so taken into account by the transferor if all property of the partnership or S corporation were sold for fair market value immediately before the disposition of such interest, and
　(B) a rule similar to the rule of subparagraph (A) shall apply to a loss from such disposition.
(5) EXCEPTION FOR DISTRIBUTIONS FROM QUALIFIED PLANS.—The term "net investment income" shall not include any distribution from a plan or arrangement described in section 401(a), 403(a), 403(b), 408, 408A, or 457(b).
(6) SPECIAL RULE.—Net investment income shall not include any item taken into account in determining self-employment income for such taxable year on which a tax is imposed by section 1401(b).

[Sec. 1411(d)]

(d) MODIFIED ADJUSTED GROSS INCOME.—For purposes of this chapter, the term "modified adjusted gross income" means adjusted gross income increased by the excess of—
(1) the amount excluded from gross income under section 911(a)(1), over
(2) the amount of any deductions (taken into account in computing adjusted gross income) or exclusions disallowed under section 911(d)(6) with respect to the amounts described in paragraph (1).

[Sec. 1411(e)]

(e) NONAPPLICATION OF SECTION.—This section shall not apply to—
(1) a nonresident alien, or
(2) a trust all of the unexpired interests in which are devoted to one or more of the purposes described in section 170(c)(2)(B).

Amendments

• **2010, Health Care and Education Reconciliation Act of 2010 (P.L. 111-152)**

P.L. 111-152, § 1402(a)(1):
Amended subtitle A by inserting after chapter 2 a new chapter 2A (Code Sec. 1411).
Effective for tax years beginning after 12-31-2012.

CHAPTER 3—WITHHOLDING OF TAX ON NONRESIDENT ALIENS AND FOREIGN CORPORATIONS

SUBCHAPTER A.	Nonresident aliens and foreign corporations.
SUBCHAPTER B.	Application of withholding provisions.

Subchapter A—Nonresident Aliens and Foreign Corporations

Sec. 1441.	Withholding of tax on nonresident aliens.
Sec. 1442.	Withholding of tax on foreign corporations.
Sec. 1443.	Foreign tax-exempt organizations.
Sec. 1444.	Withholding on Virgin Islands source income.
Sec. 1445.	Withholding of tax on dispositions of United States real property interests.
Sec. 1446.	Withholding tax on foreign partners' share of effectively connected income.

[Sec. 1441]

SEC. 1441. WITHHOLDING OF TAX ON NONRESIDENT ALIENS.

[Sec. 1441(a)]

(a) GENERAL RULE.—Except as otherwise provided in subsection (c), all persons, in whatever capacity acting (including lessees or mortgagors of real or personal property, fiduciaries, employers, and all officers and employees of the United States) having the control, receipt, custody, disposal, or payment of any of the items of income specified in subsection (b) (to the extent that any of such items constitutes gross income from sources within the United States), of any nonresident alien individual or of any foreign partnership shall (except as otherwise provided in regulations prescribed by the Secretary under section 874) deduct and withhold from such items a tax equal to 30 percent thereof, except that in the case of any item of income specified in the second sentence of subsection (b), the tax shall be equal to 14 percent of such item.

Amendments

• **1984, Deficit Reduction Act of 1984 (P.L. 98-369)**

P.L. 98-369, § 474(r)(29)(G):
Amended Code Sec. 1441(a) by striking out "except in the cases provided for in section 1451 and" in the parenthetical material following "foreign partnership shall".

Effective for tax years beginning after 12-31-83, and to carrybacks from such years but does not apply with respect to obligations issued before 1-1-84.

INCOME TAX—WITHHOLDING—NONRESIDENT ALIENS

• **1976, Tax Reform Act of 1976 (P.L. 94-455)**

P.L. 94-455, §1906(b)(13)(A):

Amended 1954 Code by substituting "Secretary" for "Secretary or his delegate" each place it appeared. **Effective** 2-1-77.

• **1966, Foreign Investors Tax Act of 1966 (P.L. 89-809)**

P.L. 89-809, §103(h)(1):

Amended Code Sec. 1441(a) by substituting "or of any foreign partnership" for ", or of any partnership not engaged in trade or business within the United States and composed in whole or in part of nonresident aliens,". **Effective** with respect to payments made in tax years of recipients beginning after 12-31-66.

• **1964, Revenue Act of 1964 (P.L. 88-272)**

P.L. 88-272, §302(c):

Amended Code Sec. 1441(a) by changing "18 percent" to "14 percent". **Effective** with respect to payments made after 3-4-64, the seventh day following the date of enactment of P. L. 88-272.

• **1961, Mutual Educational and Cultural Exchange Act of 1961 (P.L. 87-256)**

P.L. 87-256, §110(d)(1):

Added the material beginning with the second to the last comma in Code Sec. 1441(a). **Effective** for payments made after 1961.

[Sec. 1441(b)]

(b) INCOME ITEMS.—The items of income referred to in subsection (a) are interest (other than original issue discount as defined in section 1273), dividends, rent, salaries, wages, premiums, annuities, compensations, remunerations, emoluments, or other fixed or determinable annual or periodical gains, profits, and income, gains described in section 631(b) or (c), amounts subject to tax under section 871(a)(1)(C), and gains subject to tax under section 871(a)(1)(D). The items of income referred to in subsection (a) from which tax shall be deducted and withheld at the rate of 14 percent are amounts which are received by a nonresident alien individual who is temporarily present in the United States as a nonimmigrant under subparagraph (F), (J), (M), or (Q) of section 101(a)(15) of the Immigration and Nationality Act and which are—

(1) incident to a qualified scholarship to which section 117(a) applies, but only to the extent includible in gross income; or

(2) in the case of an individual who is not a candidate for a degree at an educational organization described in section 170(b)(1)(A)(ii), granted by—

    (A) an organization described in section 501(c)(3) which is exempt from tax under section 501(a),

    (B) a foreign government,

    (C) an international organization, or a binational or multinational educational and cultural foundation or commission created or continued pursuant to the Mutual Educational and Cultural Exchange Act of 1961, or

    (D) the United States, or an instrumentality or agency thereof, or a State, or a possession of the United States, or any political subdivision thereof, or the District of Columbia,

as a scholarship or fellowship for study, training, or research in the United States.

In the case of a nonresident alien individual who is a member of a domestic partnership, the items of income referred to in subsection (a) shall be treated as referring to items specified in this subsection included in his distributive share of the income of such partnership.

Amendments

• **2014, Tax Technical Corrections Act of 2014 (P.L. 113-295)**

P.L. 113-295, §221(a)(92), Division A:

Amended the first sentence of Code Sec. 1441(b) by striking "gains subject to tax" and all that follows through "October 4, 1966" and inserting "and gains subject to tax under section 871(a)(1)(D)". **Effective** generally 12-19-2014. For a special rule, see Act Sec. 221(b)(2), Division A, below. Prior to being stricken, "gains subject to tax" and all that follows through "October 4, 1966" read as follows:

gains subject to tax under section 871(a)(1)(D), and gains on transfers described in section 1235 made on or before October 4, 1966

P.L. 113-295, §221(b)(2), Division A, provides:

(2) SAVINGS PROVISION.—If—

(A) any provision amended or repealed by the amendments made by this section applied to—

(i) any transaction occurring before the date of the enactment of this Act,

(ii) any property acquired before such date of enactment, or

(iii) any item of income, loss, deduction, or credit taken into account before such date of enactment, and

(B) the treatment of such transaction, property, or item under such provision would (without regard to the amendments or repeals made by this section) affect the liability for tax for periods ending after date of enactment, nothing in the amendments or repeals made by this section shall be construed to affect the treatment of such transaction, property, or item for purposes of determining liability for tax for periods ending after such date of enactment.

• **1994, Social Security Independence and Program Improvements Act of 1994 (P.L. 103-296)**

P.L. 103-296, §320(a)(1)(B):

Amended Code Sec. 1441(b) by striking "(J), or (M)" each place it appears and inserting "(J), (M), or (Q)". **Effective** with the calendar quarter following 8-15-94.

• **1992, Unemployment Compensation Amendments of 1992 (P.L. 102-318)**

P.L. 102-318, §521(b)(32):

Amended Code Sec. 1441(b) by striking "402(a)(2), 403(a)(2), or" after "described in section". **Effective** for distributions after 12-31-92.

• **1990, Omnibus Budget Reconciliation Act of 1990 (P.L. 101-508)**

P.L. 101-508, §11704(a)(14):

Amended Code Sec. 1441(b)(2) by inserting "section" before "170(b)(1)(A)(ii)". **Effective** 11-5-90.

• **1988, Technical and Miscellaneous Revenue Act of 1988 (P.L. 100-647)**

P.L. 100-647, §1001(d)(2)(A):

Amended the second sentence of Code Sec. 1441(b). **Effective** as if included in the provision of P.L. 99-514 to which it relates. Prior to amendment, the second sentence of Code Sec. 1441(b) read as follows:

The items of income referred to in subsection (a) from which tax shall be deducted and withheld at the rate of 14 percent are amounts which are received by a nonresident alien individual who is temporarily present in the United States as a nonimmigrant under subparagraph (F) or (J) of section 101(a)(15) of the Immigration and Nationality Act and which are incident to a qualified scholarship to which section 117(a) applies, but only to the extent such amounts are includible in gross income.

• **1986, Tax Reform Act of 1986 (P.L. 99-514)**

P.L. 99-514, §123(b)(2):

Amended the second sentence of Code Sec. 1441(b). **Effective** for tax years beginning after 12-31-86, but only in the case of scholarships and fellowships granted after 8-16-86. Prior to amendment, Code Sec. 1441(b) read as follows:

(b) INCOME ITEMS.—The items of income referred to in subsection (a) are interest (other than original issue discount as defined in section 1273), dividends, rent, salaries, wages, premiums, annuities, compensations, remunerations, emoluments, or other fixed or determinable annual or periodical gains, profits, and income, gains described in section 402(a)(2), 403(a)(2), or 631(b) or (c), amounts subject to tax under section 871(a)(1)(C), gains subject to tax under section 871(a)(1)(D), gains on transfers described in section 1235 made on or before October 4, 1966. The items of income referred to in subsection (a) from which tax shall be deducted and withheld at the rate of 14 percent are—

(1) that portion of any scholarship or fellowship grant which is received by a nonresident alien individual who is temporarily present in the United States as a nonimmigrant under subparagraph (F) or (J) of section 101(a)(15) of the Immigration and Nationality Act, as amended, and which is not excluded from gross income under section 117(a)(1) solely by reason of section 117(b)(2)(B); and

(2) amounts described in subparagraphs (A), (B), (C), and (D) of section 117(a)(2) which are received by any such nonresident alien individual and which are incident to a scholarship or fellowship grant to which section 117(a)(1) applies, but only to the extent such amounts are includible in gross income.

In the case of a nonresident alien individual who is a member of a domestic partnership, the items of income referred to in subsection (a) shall be treated as referring to items specified in this subsection included in his distributive share of the income of such partnership.

• **1984, Deficit Reduction Act of 1984 (P.L. 98-369)**

P.L. 98-369, §42(a)(13):

Amended Code Sec. 1441(b) by striking out "section 1232(b)" and inserting in lieu thereof "section 1273". **Effective** for tax years ending after 7-18-84.

• **1971, Revenue Act of 1971 (P.L. 92-178)**

P.L. 92-178, §313(a):

Added "(other than original issue discount as defined in section 1232(b))" after "interest" in the first sentence of Code Sec. 1441(b). **Effective** for payments occurring on or after 4-1-72.

• **1966, Foreign Investors Tax Act of 1966 (P.L. 89-809)**

P.L. 89-809, §103(h)(2):

Amended Code Sec. 1441(b) by striking out "(except interest on deposits with persons carrying on the banking business paid to persons not engaged in business in the United States)". **Effective** with respect to payments made in tax years of recipients beginning after 12-31-66.

P.L. 89-809, §103(h)(3):

Amended Code Sec. 1441(b) by substituting "gains described in section 402(a)(2), 403(a)(2), or 631(b) or (c), amounts subject to tax under section 871(a)(1)(C), gains subject to tax under section 871(a)(1)(D), and gains on transfers described in section 1235 made on or before October 4, 1966" for "and amounts described in section

INCOME TAX—WITHHOLDING—NONRESIDENT ALIENS

402(a)(2), section 403(a)(2), section 631(b) and (c), and section 1235, which are considered to be gains from the sale or exchange of capital assets" in the first sentence. **Effective** with respect to payments made in tax years of recipients beginning after 12-31-66.

P.L. 89-809, § 103(h)(4):

Amended Code Sec. 1441(b) by adding the last sentence. **Effective** with respect to payments made in tax years of recipients beginning after 12-31-66.

• **1964, Revenue Act of 1964 (P.L. 88-272)**

P.L. 88-272, § 302(c):

Amended Code Sec. 1441(b) by changing "18 percent" to "14 percent". **Effective** with respect to payments made after 3-4-64, the seventh day following the date of enactment of P. L. 88-272.

• **1961, Mutual Educational and Cultural Exchange Act of 1961 (P.L. 87-256)**

P.L. 87-256, § 110(d)(2):

Added the last sentence to Code Sec. 1441(b). **Effective** for payments made after 1961.

• **1958, Technical Amendments Act of 1958 (P.L. 85-866)**

P.L. 85-866, § 40(b):

Amended Code Sec. 1441(b) by adding the phrase "section 403(a)(2)," after the phrase "section 402(a)(2),". **Effective** 9-3-58.

[Sec. 1441(c)]

(c) EXCEPTIONS.—

(1) INCOME CONNECTED WITH UNITED STATES BUSINESS.—No deduction or withholding under subsection (a) shall be required in the case of any item of income (other than compensation for personal services) which is effectively connected with the conduct of a trade or business within the United States and which is included in the gross income of the recipient under section 871(b)(2) for the taxable year.

(2) OWNER UNKNOWN.—The Secretary may authorize the tax under subsection (a) to be deducted and withheld from the interest upon any securities the owners of which are not known to the withholding agent.

(3) BONDS WITH EXTENDED MATURITY DATES.—The deduction and withholding in the case of interest on bonds, mortgages, or deeds of trust or other similar obligations of a corporation, within subsections (a), (b), and (c) of section 1451 (as in effect before its repeal by the Tax Reform Act of 1984) were it not for the fact that the maturity date of such obligations has been extended on or after January 1, 1934, and the liability assumed by the debtor exceeds $27^{1}/_{2}$ percent of the interest, shall not exceed the rate of $27^{1}/_{2}$ percent per annum.

(4) COMPENSATION OF CERTAIN ALIENS.—Under regulations prescribed by the Secretary, compensation for personal services may be exempted from deduction and withholding under subsection (a).

(5) SPECIAL ITEMS.—In the case of gains described in section 631(b) or (c), and gains subject to tax under section 871(a)(1)(D), the amount required to be deducted and withheld shall, if the amount of such gain is not known to the withholding agent, be such amount, not exceeding 30 percent of the amount payable, as may be necessary to assure that the tax deducted and withheld shall not be less than 30 percent of such gain.

(6) PER DIEM OF CERTAIN ALIENS.—No deduction or withholding under subsection (a) shall be required in the case of amounts of per diem for subsistence paid by the United States Government (directly or by contract) to any nonresident alien individual who is engaged in any program of training in the United States under the Mutual Security Act of 1954, as amended.

(7) CERTAIN ANNUITIES RECEIVED UNDER QUALIFIED PLANS.—No deduction or withholding under subsection (a) shall be required in the case of any amount received as an annuity if such amount is, under section 871(f), exempt from the tax imposed by section 871(a).

(8) ORIGINAL ISSUE DISCOUNT.—The Secretary may prescribe such regulations as may be necessary for the deduction and withholding of the tax on original issue discount subject to tax under section 871(a)(1)(C) including rules for the deduction and withholding of the tax on original issue discount from payments of interest.

(9) INTEREST INCOME FROM CERTAIN PORTFOLIO DEBT INVESTMENTS.—In the case of portfolio interest (within the meaning of 871(h)), no tax shall be required to be deducted and withheld from such interest unless the person required to deduct and withhold tax from such interest knows, or has reason to know, that such interest is not portfolio interest by reason of section 871(h)(3) or (4).

(10) EXCEPTION FOR CERTAIN INTEREST AND DIVIDENDS.—No tax shall be required to be deducted and withheld under subsection (a) from any amount described in section 871(i)(2).

(11) CERTAIN GAMBLING WINNINGS.—No tax shall be required to be deducted and withheld under subsection (a) from any amount exempt from the tax imposed by section 871(a)(1)(A) by reason of section 871(j).

(12) CERTAIN DIVIDENDS RECEIVED FROM REGULATED INVESTMENT COMPANIES.—

(A) IN GENERAL.—No tax shall be required to be deducted and withheld under subsection (a) from any amount exempt from the tax imposed by section 871(a)(1)(A) by reason of section 871(k).

(B) SPECIAL RULE.—For purposes of subparagraph (A), clause (i) of section 871(k)(1)(B) shall not apply to any dividend unless the regulated investment company knows that such dividend is a dividend referred to in such clause. A similar rule shall apply with respect to the exception contained in section 871(k)(2)(B).

Amendments

• **2014, Tax Technical Corrections Act of 2014 (P.L. 113-295)**

P.L. 113-295, § 221(a)(92), Division A:

Amended the first sentence of Code Sec. 1441(c)(5) by striking "gains subject to tax" and all that follows through "October 4, 1966" and inserting "and gains subject to tax under section 871(a)(1)(D)". **Effective** generally 12-19-2014. For a special rule, see Act Sec. 221(b)(2), Division A, below. Prior to being stricken, "gains subject to tax" and all that follows through "October 4, 1966" read as follows:

gains subject to tax under section 871(a)(1)(D), and gains on transfers described in section 1235 made on or before October 4, 1966

P.L. 113-295, § 221(b)(2), Division A, provides:

(2) SAVINGS PROVISION.—If—

(A) any provision amended or repealed by the amendments made by this section applied to—

(i) any transaction occurring before the date of the enactment of this Act,

(ii) any property acquired before such date of enactment, or

(iii) any item of income, loss, deduction, or credit taken into account before such date of enactment, and

(B) the treatment of such transaction, property, or item under such provision would (without regard to the amendments or repeals made by this section) affect the liability for tax for periods ending after date of enactment, nothing in the amendments or repeals made by this section shall be construed to affect the treatment of such transaction, property, or item for purposes of determining liability for tax for periods ending after such date of enactment.

• **2004, American Jobs Creation Act of 2004 (P.L. 108-357)**

P.L. 108-357, § 411(a)(3)(A):

Amended Code Sec. 1441(c) by adding at the end a new paragraph (12). **Effective** for dividends with respect to tax years of regulated investment companies beginning after 12-31-2004.

• **1993, Omnibus Budget Reconciliation Act of 1993 (P.L. 103-66)**

P.L. 103-66, § 13237(c)(4):

Amended Code Sec. 1441(c)(9) by striking "section 871(h)(3)" and inserting "section 871(h)(3) or (4)". **Effective** for interest received after 12-31-93.

• **1992, Unemployment Compensation Amendments of 1992 (P.L. 102-318)**

P.L. 102-318, § 521(b)(33):

Amended Code Sec. 1441(c)(5) by striking "402(a)(2), 403(a)(2), or" after "described in section". **Effective** for distributions after 12-31-92.

• **1988, Technical and Miscellaneous Revenue Act of 1988 (P.L. 100-647)**

P.L. 100-647, § 6134(a)(2):

Amended Code Sec. 1441(c) by adding at the end thereof new paragraph (11). **Effective** 11-10-88.

INCOME TAX—WITHHOLDING—NONRESIDENT ALIENS

- **1986, Tax Reform Act of 1986 (P.L. 99-514)**

P.L. 99-514, §1214(c)(3):

Amended Code Sec. 1441(c) by adding at the end thereof new paragraph (10). **Effective**, generally, for payments after 12-31-86. However, for a special and transitional rule, see Act Sec. 1214(d)(2)-(4) following Code Sec. 861.

P.L. 99-514, §1810(d)(3)(D):

Amended Code Sec. 1441(c)(9) by striking out "871(h)(2)" and inserting in lieu thereof "section 871(h)". **Effective** as if included in the provision of P.L. 98-369 to which it relates.

- **1984, Deficit Reduction Act of 1984 (P.L. 98-369)**

P.L. 98-369, §127(e)(1):

Amended Code Sec. 1441(c) by adding paragraph (9). **Effective** for interest received after 7-18-84, with respect to obligations issued after such date, in tax years ending after such date.

P.L. 98-369, §474(r)(29)(H):

Amended Code Sec. 1441(c)(3) by striking out "section 1451" and inserting in lieu thereof "section 1451 (as in effect before its repeal by the Tax Reform Act of 1984)". **Effective** for tax years beginning after 12-31-83, and to carrybacks from such years but does not apply with respect to obligations issued before 1-1-84.

- **1976, Tax Reform Act of 1976 (P.L. 94-455)**

P.L. 94-455, §1906(b)(13)(A):

Amended 1954 Code by substituting "Secretary" for "Secretary or his delegate" each place it appeared. **Effective** 2-1-77.

- **1971, Revenue Act of 1971 (P.L. 92-178)**

P.L. 92-178, §313(d):

Added paragraph (8) in Code Sec. 1441(c). **Effective** for payments occurring on or after 4-1-72.

- **1966, Foreign Investors Tax Act of 1966 (P.L. 89-809)**

P.L. 89-809, §103(h)(5):

Amended Code Sec. 1441(c)(1). **Effective** with respect to payments made in tax years of recipients beginning after 12-31-66. Prior to amendment, Sec. 1441(c)(1) read as follows:

"(1) Dividends of foreign corporations.—No deduction or withholding under subsection (a) shall be required in the case of dividends paid by a foreign corporation unless (A) such corporation is engaged in trade or business within the United States, and (B) more than 85 percent of the gross income of such corporation for the 3-year period ending with the close of its taxable year preceding the declaration of such dividends (or for such part of such period as the corporation has been in existence) was derived from sources within the United States as determined under part I of subchapter N of chapter 1."

P.L. 89-809, §103(h)(6):

Amended Code Sec. 1441(c)(4). **Effective** with respect to payments made in tax years of recipients beginning after 12-31-66. Prior to amendment, Sec. 1441(c)(4) read as follows:

"(4) Compensation of certain aliens.—Under regulations prescribed by the Secretary or his delegate, there may be exempted from deduction and withholding under subsection (a) the compensation for personal services of—

"(A) nonresident alien individuals who enter and leave the United States at frequent intervals, and

"(B) a nonresident alien individual for the period he is temporarily present in the United States as a nonimmigrant under subparagraph (F) or (J) of section 101(a)(15) of the Immigration and Nationality Act, as amended."

P.L. 89-809, §103(h)(7):

Amended Code Sec. 1441(c)(5). **Effective** with respect to payments made in tax years of recipients beginning after 12-31-66. Prior to amendment, Sec. 1441(c)(5) read as follows:

"(5) Special items.—In the case of amounts described in section 402(a)(2), section 403(a)(2), section 631(b) and (c), and section 1235, which are considered to be gains from the sale or exchange of capital assets, the amount required to be deducted and withheld shall, if the amount of such gain is not known to the withholding agent, be such amount, not exceeding 30 percent of the proceeds from such sale or exchange, as may be necessary to assure that the tax deducted and withheld shall not be less than 30 percent of such gain."

P.L. 89-809, §103(h)(8):

Added new Code Sec. 1441(c)(7). **Effective** with respect to payments made in tax years of recipients beginning after 12-31-66.

- **1961, Mutual Educational and Cultural Exchange Act of 1961 (P.L. 87-256)**

P.L. 87-256, §110(d)(3):

Amended Code Sec. 1441(c)(4). **Effective** for payments made after 1961. Prior to amendment it read as follows:

"(4) Compensation of certain aliens.—Under regulations prescribed by the Secretary or his delegate, there may be exempted from deduction and withholding under subsection (a) the compensation for personal services of nonresident alien individuals who enter and leave the United States at frequent intervals."

- **1958, Technical Amendments Act of 1958 (P.L. 85-866)**

P.L. 85-866, §40(b):

Amended Code Sec. 1441(c)(5) by adding the phrase "section 403(a)(2)" following the phrase "section 402(a)(2)". **Effective** 9-3-58.

- **1956, Mutual Security Act of 1956 (P.L. 726, 84th Cong.)**

P.L. 726, 84th Cong., §11:

Added paragraph (6) to subsection (c). **Effective** 7-18-56.

[Sec. 1441(d)]

(d) EXEMPTION OF CERTAIN FOREIGN PARTNERSHIPS.—Subject to such terms and conditions as may be provided by regulations prescribed by the Secretary, subsection (a) shall not apply in the case of a foreign partnership engaged in trade or business within the United States if the Secretary determines that the requirements of subsection (a) impose an undue administrative burden and that the collection of the tax imposed by section 871(a) on the members of such partnership who are nonresident alien individuals will not be jeopardized by the exemption.

Amendments

- **1976, Tax Reform Act of 1976 (P.L. 94-455)**

P.L. 94-455, §1906(b)(13)(A):

Amended 1954 Code by substituting "Secretary" for "Secretary or his delegate" each place it appeared. **Effective** 2-1-77.

- **1966, Foreign Investors Tax Act of 1966 (P.L. 89-809)**

P.L. 89-809, §103(h)(9):

Redesignated former Code Sec. 1441(d) as Sec. 1441(e) and added new Code Sec. 1441(d). **Effective** with respect to payments made in tax years of recipients beginning after 12-31-66.

[Sec. 1441(e)]

(e) ALIEN RESIDENT OF PUERTO RICO.—For purposes of this section, the term "nonresident alien individual" includes an alien resident of Puerto Rico.

Amendments

- **1966, Foreign Investors Tax Act of 1966 (P.L. 89-809)**

P.L. 89-809, §103(h)(9):

Redesignated former Code Sec. 1441(d) as Sec. 1441(e). **Effective** with respect to payments made in tax years of recipients beginning after 12-31-66.

[Sec. 1441(f)]

(f) CONTINENTAL SHELF AREAS.—For sources of income derived from, or for services performed with respect to, the exploration or exploitation of natural resources on submarine areas adjacent to the territorial waters of the United States, see section 638.

Amendments

- **1982, Tax Equity and Fiscal Responsibility Act of 1982 (P.L. 97-248)**

P.L. 97-248, §342 provides:

SEC. 342. WITHHOLDING OF TAX ON NONRESIDENT ALIENS AND FOREIGN CORPORATIONS.

Not later than 2 years after the date of the enactment of this Act, the Secretary of the Treasury or his delegate shall prescribe regulations establishing certification procedures, refund procedures, or other procedures which ensure that any benefit of any treaty relating to withholding of tax under sections 1441 and 1442 of the Internal Revenue Code of 1954 is available only to persons entitled to such benefit.

- **1969, Tax Reform Act of 1969 (P.L. 91-172)**

P.L. 91-172, §505(b):

Added subsection 1441(f). **Effective** 12-31-69.

[Sec. 1441(g)]

(g) CROSS REFERENCE.—

For provision treating 85 percent of social security benefits as subject to withholding under this section, see section 871(a)(3).

INCOME TAX—WITHHOLDING—FOREIGN CORPS.

Amendments

• **1997, Taxpayer Relief Act of 1997 (P.L. 105-34)**

P.L. 105-34, § 1604(g)(3):

Amended Code Sec. 1441(g) by striking "one-half" and inserting "85 percent". **Effective** 8-5-97.

• **1983, Social Security Amendments of 1983 (P.L. 98-21)**

P.L. 98-21, § 121(c)(2):

Added Code Sec. 1441(g). **Effective** for benefits received after 1983 in tax years ending after 1983.

[Sec. 1442]

SEC. 1442. WITHHOLDING OF TAX ON FOREIGN CORPORATIONS.

[Sec. 1442(a)]

(a) GENERAL RULE.—In the case of foreign corporations subject to taxation under this subtitle, there shall be deducted and withheld at the source in the same manner and on the same items of income as is provided in section 1441 a tax equal to 30 percent thereof. For purposes of the preceding sentence, the references in section 1441(b) to sections 871(a)(1)(C) and (D) shall be treated as referring to sections 881(a)(3) and (4), the reference in section 1441(c)(1) to section 871(b)(2) shall be treated as referring to section 842 or section 882(a)(2), as the case may be, the reference in section 1441(c)(5) to section 871(a)(1)(D) shall be treated as referring to section 881(a)(4), the reference in section 1441(c)(8) to section 871(a)(1)(C) shall be treated as referring to section 881(a)(3), the references in section 1441(c)(9) to sections 871(h) and 871(h)(3) or (4) shall be treated as referring to sections 881(c) and 881(c)(3) or (4), the reference in section 1441(c)(10) to section 871(i)(2) shall be treated as referring to section 881(d), and the references in section 1441(c)(12) to sections 871(a) and 871(k) shall be treated as referring to sections 881(a) and 881(e) (except that for purposes of applying subparagraph (A) of section 1441(c)(12), as so modified, clause (ii) of section 881(e)(1)(B) shall not apply to any dividend unless the regulated investment company knows that such dividend is a dividend referred to in such clause).

Amendments

• **2004, American Jobs Creation Act of 2004 (P.L. 108-357)**

P.L. 108-357, § 411(a)(3)(B)(i)-(ii):

Amended Code Sec. 1442(a) by striking "and the reference[s]in section 1441(c)(10)" and inserting "the reference in section 1441(c)(10)", and by inserting before the period at the end the following: ", and the references in section 1441(c)(12) to sections 871(a) and 871(k) shall be treated as referring to sections 881(a) and 881(e) (except that for purposes of applying subparagraph (A) of section 1441(c)(12), as so modified, clause (ii) of section 881(e)(1)(B) shall not apply to any dividend unless the regulated investment company knows that such dividend is a dividend referred to in such clause)". **Effective** for dividends with respect to tax years of regulated investment companies beginning after 12-31-2004.

• **1993, Omnibus Budget Reconciliation Act of 1993 (P.L. 103-66)**

P.L. 103-66, § 13237(c)(5)(A)-(B):

Amended Code Sec. 1442(a) by striking "871(h)(3)" and inserting "871(h)(3) or (4)", and by striking "881(c)(3)" and inserting "881(c)(3) or (4)". **Effective** for interest received after 12-31-93.

• **1988, Technical and Miscellaneous Revenue Act of 1988 (P.L. 100-647)**

P.L. 100-647, § 1012(g)(7)(A)-(B):

Amended Code Sec. 1442(a) by striking out "and the references in" and inserting in lieu thereof "the references in", and by inserting before the period at the end thereof the following: ", and the references in section 1441(c)(10) to section 871(i)(2) shall be treated as referring to section 881(d)". **Effective** as if included in the provision of P.L. 99-514 to which it relates.

• **1986, Tax Reform Act of 1986 (P.L. 99-514)**

P.L. 99-514, § 1810(d)(3)(E)(i)-(iii):

Amended Code Sec. 1442(a) by striking out "sections 871(h)(2)" and inserting in lieu thereof "sections 871(h)", by striking out "sections 881(c)(2)"and inserting in lieu thereof "sections 881(c)", and by striking out "section 1449(c)(9)" and inserting in lieu thereof "section 1441(c)(9)". **Effective** as if included in the provision of P.L. 98-369 to which it relates.

P.L. 99-514, § 127(e)(2):

Amended the last sentence of Code Sec. 1442(a) by striking out "and" after "section 881(a)(4)," and by inserting before the period at the end thereof the following: ", and the references in section 1449(c)(9) to sections 871(h)(2) and 871(h)(3) shall be treated as referring to sections 881(c)(2) and 881(c)(3)". **Effective** for interest received after 7-18-84 with respect to obligations issued after such date, in tax years ending after such date.

• **1984, Deficit Reduction Act of 1984 (P.L. 98-369)**

P.L. 98-369, § 474(r)(29)(I):

Amended Code Sec. 1442(a) by striking out of the first sentence "or section 1451" following "section 1441" and by striking out "; except that, in the case of interest described in section 1451 (relating to tax-free covenant bonds), the deduction and withholding shall be at the rate specified therein" following "a tax equal to 30 percent thereof". **Effective** for tax years beginning after 12-31-83, and to carrybacks from such years but does not apply with respect to obligations issued before 1-1-84.

• **1971, Revenue Act of 1971 (P.L. 92-178)**

P.L. 92-178, § 313(e):

Amended the last sentence of Code Sec. 1442(a). **Effective** for payments occurring on or after 4-1-72. Prior to amendment, the last sentence read as follows:

For purposes of the preceding sentence, the references in section 1441(b) to sections 871(a)(1)(C) and (D) shall be treated as referring to sections 881(a)(3) and (4), the reference in section 1441(c)(1) to section 871(b)(2) shall be treated as referring to section 842 or section 882(a)(2), as the case may be, and the reference in section 1441(c)(5) to section 871(a)(1)(D) shall be treated as referring to section 881(a)(4).

[Sec. 1442(b)]

(b) EXEMPTION.—Subject to such terms and conditions as may be provided by regulations prescribed by the Secretary, subsection (a) shall not apply in the case of a foreign corporation engaged in trade or business within the United States if the Secretary determines that the requirements of subsection (a) impose an undue administrative burden and that the collection of the tax imposed by section 881 on such corporation will not be jeopardized by the exemption.

Amendments

• **1976, Tax Reform Act of 1976 (P.L. 94-455)**

P.L. 94-455, § 1906(b)(13)(A):

Amended 1954 Code by substituting "Secretary" for "Secretary or his delegate" each place it appeared. **Effective** 2-1-77.

[Sec. 1442(c)]

(c) EXCEPTION FOR CERTAIN POSSESSIONS CORPORATIONS.—

(1) GUAM, AMERICAN SAMOA, THE NORTHERN MARIANA ISLANDS, AND THE VIRGIN ISLANDS.—For purposes of this section, the term "foreign corporation" does not include a corporation created or organized in Guam, American Samoa, the Northern Mariana Islands, or the Virgin Islands or under the law of any such possession if the requirements of subparagraphs (A), (B), and (C) of section 881(b)(1) are met with respect to such corporation.

(2) COMMONWEALTH OF PUERTO RICO.—

(A) IN GENERAL.—If dividends are received during a taxable year by a corporation—

(i) created or organized in, or under the law of, the Commonwealth of Puerto Rico, and

(ii) with respect to which the requirements of subparagraphs (A), (B), and (C) of section 881(b)(1) are met for the taxable year,

subsection (a) shall be applied for such taxable year by substituting "10 percent" for "30 percent".

(B) APPLICABILITY.—If, on or after the date of the enactment of this paragraph, an increase in the rate of the Commonwealth of Puerto Rico's withholding tax which is generally applicable to dividends paid to United States corporations not engaged in a trade or business in the Commonwealth to a rate greater than 10 percent takes effect, this paragraph shall not apply to dividends received on or after the effective date of the increase.

INCOME TAX—WITHHOLDING—U.S. PROPERTY

Amendments

• **2004, American Jobs Creation Act of 2004 (P.L. 108-357)**

P.L. 108-357, § 420(b)(1)-(2):

Amended Code Sec. 1442(c) by striking "For purposes" and inserting "(1) GUAM, AMERICAN SAMOA, THE NORTHERN MARIANA ISLANDS, AND THE VIRGIN ISLANDS.—For purposes", and by adding at the end a new paragraph (2). **Effective** for dividends paid after 10-22-2004.

• **1986, Tax Reform Act of 1986 (P.L. 99-514)**

P.L. 99-514, § 1273(b)(2)(B):

Amended Code Sec. 1442(c). **Effective**, generally, for tax years beginning after 12-31-86. However, for special rules and exceptions, see Act Sec. 1277(b)-(e) under the amendment notes to Code Sec. 48. Prior to amendment, Code Sec. 1442(c) read as follows:

(c) EXCEPTION FOR CERTAIN GUAM AND VIRGIN ISLANDS CORPORATIONS.—

(1) IN GENERAL.—For purposes of this section, the term "foreign corporation" does not include a corporation created or organized in Guam or the Virgin Islands or under the law of Guam or the Virgin Islands if the requirements of subparagraphs (A) and (B) of section 881(b)(1) are met with respect to such corporation.

(2) PARAGRAPH (1) NOT TO APPLY TO TAX IMPOSED IN GUAM.—For purposes of applying this subsection with respect to income tax liability incurred to Guam—

(A) paragraph (1) shall not apply, and

(B) for purposes of this section, the term "foreign corporation" does not include a corporation created or organized in Guam or under the law of Guam.

(3) CROSS REFERENCE.—

For tax imposed in the Virgin Islands, see sections 934 and 934A.

• **1984, Deficit Reduction Act of 1984 (P.L. 98-369)**

P.L. 98-369, § 130(b):

Amended Code Sec. 1442(c). **Effective** for payments made after 3-1-84, in tax years ending after such date. Prior to amendment, it read as follows:

(c) Exception for Guam Corporations.—For purposes of this section, the term "foreign corporation" does not include a corporation created or organized in Guam or under the law of Guam.

• **1972 (P.L. 92-606)**

P.L. 92-606, § 1(e)(2):

Added Code Sec. 1442(c). **Effective** 11-1-72.

• **1966, Foreign Investors Tax Act of 1966 (P.L. 89-809)**

P.L. 89-809, § 104(c):

Amended Code Sec. 1442. **Effective** 1-1-67. Prior to amendment, Code Sec. 1442 read as follows:

SEC. 1442. WITHHOLDING OF TAX ON FOREIGN CORPORATIONS.

In the case of foreign corporations subject to taxation under this subtitle not engaged in trade or business within the United States, there shall be deducted and withheld at the source in the same manner and on the same items of income as is provided in section 1441 or section 1451 a tax equal to 30 percent thereof; except that, in the case of interest described in section 1451 (relating to tax-free covenant bonds), the deduction and withholding shall be at the rate specified therein.

[Sec. 1443]

SEC. 1443. FOREIGN TAX-EXEMPT ORGANIZATIONS.

[Sec. 1443(a)]

(a) INCOME SUBJECT TO SECTION 511.—In the case of income of a foreign organization subject to the tax imposed by section 511, this chapter shall apply to income includible under section 512 in computing its unrelated business taxable income, but only to the extent and subject to such conditions as may be provided under regulations prescribed by the Secretary.

Amendments

• **1976, Tax Reform Act of 1976 (P.L. 94-455)**

P.L. 94-455, § 1906(b)(13)(A):

Amended 1954 Code by substituting "Secretary" for "Secretary or his delegate" each place it appeared. **Effective** 2-1-77.

• **1969, Tax Reform Act of 1969 (P.L. 91-172)**

P.L. 91-172, § 101(j)(22):

Added the heading for Code Sec. 1443(a). **Effective** 1-1-70.

P.L. 91-172, § 121(d)(2)(C):

Substituted "income includible" for "rents includible" in Code Sec. 1443(a). **Effective** 1-1-70.

[Sec. 1443(b)]

(b) INCOME SUBJECT TO SECTION 4948.—In the case of income of a foreign organization subject to the tax imposed by section 4948(a), this chapter shall apply, except that the deduction and withholding shall be at the rate of 4 percent and shall be subject to such conditions as may be provided under regulations prescribed by the Secretary.

Amendments

• **1976, Tax Reform Act of 1976 (P.L. 94-455)**

P.L. 94-455, § 1906(b)(13)(A):

Amended 1954 Code by substituting "Secretary" for "Secretary or his delegate" each place it appeared. **Effective** 2-1-77.

• **1969, Tax Reform Act of 1969 (P.L. 91-172)**

P.L. 91-172, § 101(j)(22):

Added Code Sec. 1443(b). **Effective** 1-1-70.

[Sec. 1444]

SEC. 1444. WITHHOLDING ON VIRGIN ISLANDS SOURCE INCOME.

For purposes of determining the withholding tax liability incurred in the Virgin Islands pursuant to this title (as made applicable to the Virgin Islands) with respect to amounts received from sources within the Virgin Islands by citizens and resident alien individuals of the United States, and corporations organized in the United States, the rate of withholding tax under sections 1441 and 1442 on income subject to tax under section 871(a)(1) or 881 shall not exceed the rate of tax on such income under section 871(a)(1) or 881, as the case may be.

Amendments

• **1988, Technical and Miscellaneous Revenue Act of 1988 (P.L. 100-647)**

P.L. 100-647, § 1012(x):

Amended Code Sec. 1444 by striking out "(as modified by section 934A)" before "shall not exceed". **Effective** as if included in the provision of P.L. 99-514 to which it relates.

• **1983 (P.L. 97-455)**

P.L. 97-455, § 1(b):

Added Code Sec. 1444. **Effective** for payments made after 1-12-83.

[Sec. 1445]

SEC. 1445. WITHHOLDING OF TAX ON DISPOSITIONS OF UNITED STATES REAL PROPERTY INTERESTS.

[Sec. 1445(a)]

(a) GENERAL RULE.—Except as otherwise provided in this section, in the case of any disposition of a United States real property interest (as defined in section 897(c)) by a foreign person, the transferee shall be required to deduct and withhold a tax equal to 15 percent of the amount realized on the disposition.

Amendments

• **2015, Protecting Americans from Tax Hikes Act of 2015 (P.L. 114-113)**

P.L. 114-113, § 324(a), Div. Q:

Amended Code Sec. 1445(a) by striking "10 percent" and inserting "15 percent". **Effective** for dispositions after the date which is 60 days after 12-18-2015.

[Sec. 1445(b)]

(b) EXEMPTIONS.—

(1) IN GENERAL.—No person shall be required to deduct and withhold any amount under subsection (a) with respect to a disposition if paragraph (2), (3), (4), (5), or (6) applies to the transaction.

INCOME TAX—WITHHOLDING—U.S. PROPERTY

(2) TRANSFEROR FURNISHES NONFOREIGN AFFIDAVIT.—Except as provided in paragraph (7), this paragraph applies to the disposition if the transferor furnishes to the transferee an affidavit by the transferor stating, under penalty of perjury, the transferor's United States taxpayer identification number and that the transferor is not a foreign person.

(3) NONPUBLICLY TRADED DOMESTIC CORPORATION FURNISHES AFFIDAVIT THAT INTEREST IN CORPORATION NOT UNITED STATES REAL PROPERTY INTERESTS.—Except as provided in paragraph (7), this paragraph applies in the case of a disposition of any interest in any domestic corporation if the domestic corporation furnishes to the transferee an affidavit by the domestic corporation stating, under penalty of perjury, that—

(A) the domestic corporation is not and has not been a United States real property holding corporation (as defined in section 897(c)(2)) during the applicable period specified in section 897(c)(1)(A)(ii), or

(B) as of the date of the disposition, interests in such corporation are not United States real property interests by reason of section 897(c)(1)(B).

(4) TRANSFEREE RECEIVES QUALIFYING STATEMENT.—

(A) IN GENERAL.—This paragraph applies to the disposition if the transferee receives a qualifying statement at such time, in such manner, and subject to such terms and conditions as the Secretary may by regulations prescribe.

(B) QUALIFYING STATEMENT.—For purposes of subparagraph (A), the term "qualifying statement" means a statement by the Secretary that—

(i) the transferor either—

(I) has reached agreement with the Secretary (or such agreement has been reached by the transferee) for the payment of any tax imposed by section 871(b)(1) or 882(a)(1) on any gain recognized by the transferor on the disposition of the United States real property interest, or

(II) is exempt from any tax imposed by section 871(b)(1) or 882(a)(1) on any gain recognized by the transferor on the disposition of the United States real property interest, and

(ii) the transferor or transferee has satisfied any transferor's unsatisfied withholding liability or has provided adequate security to cover such liability.

(5) RESIDENCE WHERE AMOUNT REALIZED DOES NOT EXCEED $300,000.—This paragraph applies to the disposition if—

(A) the property is acquired by the transferee for use by him as a residence, and

(B) the amount realized for the property does not exceed $300,000.

(6) STOCK REGULARLY TRADED ON ESTABLISHED SECURITIES MARKET.—This paragraph applies if the disposition is of a share of a class of stock that is regularly traded on an established securities market.

(7) SPECIAL RULES FOR PARAGRAPHS (2), (3), AND (9).—Paragraph (2), (3), or (9) (as the case may be) shall not apply to any disposition—

(A) if—

(i) the transferee or qualified substitute has actual knowledge that the affidavit referred to in such paragraph, or the statement referred to in paragraph (9)(A)(ii), is false, or

(ii) the transferee or qualified substitute receives a notice (as described in subsection (d)) from a transferor's agent, transferee's agent, or qualified substitute that such affidavit or statement is false, or

(B) if the Secretary by regulations requires the transferee or qualified substitute to furnish a copy of such affidavit or statement to the Secretary and the transferee or qualified substitute fails to furnish a copy of such affidavit or statement to the Secretary at such time and in such manner as required by such regulations.

(8) APPLICABLE WASH SALES TRANSACTIONS.—No person shall be required to deduct and withhold any amount under subsection (a) with respect to a disposition which is treated as a disposition of a United States real property interest solely by reason of section 897(h)(5).

(9) ALTERNATIVE PROCEDURE FOR FURNISHING NONFOREIGN AFFIDAVIT.—For purposes of paragraphs (2) and (7)—

(A) IN GENERAL.—Paragraph (2) shall be treated as applying to a transaction if, in connection with a disposition of a United States real property interest—

(i) the affidavit specified in paragraph (2) is furnished to a qualified substitute, and

(ii) the qualified substitute furnishes a statement to the transferee stating, under penalty of perjury, that the qualified substitute has such affidavit in his possession.

(B) REGULATIONS.—The Secretary shall prescribe such regulations as may be necessary or appropriate to carry out this paragraph.

Amendments

• **2008, Housing Assistance Tax Act of 2008 (P.L. 110-289)**

P.L. 110-289, §3024(a):

Amended Code Sec. 1445(b) by adding at the end a new paragraph (9). **Effective** for dispositions of United States real property interests after 7-30-2008.

P.L. 110-289, §3024(c)(1):

Amended Code Sec. 1445(b)(7). **Effective** for dispositions of United States real property interests after 7-30-2008. Prior to amendment, Code Sec. 1445(b)(7) read as follows:

(7) SPECIAL RULES FOR PARAGRAPHS (2) AND (3).—Paragraph (2) or (3) (as the case may be) shall not apply to any disposition—

(A) if—

(i) the transferee has actual knowledge that the affidavit referred to in such paragraph is false, or

(ii) the transferee receives a notice (as described in subsection (d)) from a transferor's agent or a transferee's agent that such affidavit is false, or

(B) if the Secretary by regulations requires the transferee to furnish a copy of such affidavit to the Secretary and the transferee fails to furnish a copy of such affidavit to the Secretary at such time and in such manner as required by such regulations.

• **2006, Tax Increase Prevention and Reconciliation Act of 2005 (P.L. 109-222)**

P.L. 109-222, §506(b):

Amended Code Sec. 1445(b) by adding at the end a new paragraph (8). **Effective** for tax years beginning after 12-31-2005, except that such amendment shall not apply to any distribution, or substitute dividend payment, occurring before the date that is 30 days after 5-17-2006.

• **1986, Tax Reform Act of 1986 (P.L. 99-514)**

P.L. 99-514, §1810(f)(2):

Amended Code Sec. 1445(b)(3). **Effective** as if included in the provision of P.L. 98-369 to which it relates. Prior to amendment, Code Sec. 1445(b)(3) read as follows:

(3) NONPUBLICLY TRADED DOMESTIC CORPORATION FURNISHES AFFIDAVIT THAT IT IS NOT A UNITED STATES REAL PROPERTY HOLDING CORPORATION.—Except as provided in paragraph (7), this paragraph applies in the case of a disposition of any interest in any domestic corporation, if the domestic corporation furnishes to the transferee an affidavit by the domestic corporation stating, under penalty of perjury, that the domestic corporation is not and has not been a United States real property holding corporation (as defined in section 897(c)(2)) during applicable period specified in section 897(c)(1)(A)(ii).

[Sec. 1445(c)]

(c) LIMITATIONS ON AMOUNT REQUIRED TO BE WITHHELD.—

(1) CANNOT EXCEED TRANSFEROR'S MAXIMUM TAX LIABILITY.—

(A) IN GENERAL.—The amount required to be withheld under this section with respect to any disposition shall not exceed the amount (if any) determined under subparagraph (B) as the transferor's maximum tax liability.

(B) REQUEST.—At the request of the transferor or transferee, the Secretary shall determine, with respect to any disposition, the transferor's maximum tax liability.

(C) REFUND OF EXCESS AMOUNTS WITHHELD.—Subject to such terms and conditions as the Secretary may by regulations prescribe, a transferor may seek and obtain a refund of any amounts withheld under this section in excess of the transferor's maximum tax liability.

(2) AUTHORITY OF SECRETARY TO PRESCRIBE REDUCED AMOUNT.—At the request of the transferor or transferee, the Secretary may prescribe a reduced amount to be withheld under this section if the Secretary determines that to substitute such reduced amount will not jeopardize the collection of the tax imposed by section 871(b)(1) or 882(a)(1).

(3) PROCEDURAL RULES.—

(A) REGULATIONS.—Request for—

(i) qualifying statements under subsection (b)(4),

(ii) determinations of transferor's maximum tax liability under paragraph (1), and

(iii) reductions under paragraph (2) in the amount required to be withheld,

shall be made at the time and manner, and shall include such information, as the Secretary shall prescribe by regulations.

(B) REQUESTS TO BE HANDLED WITHIN 90 DAYS.—The Secretary shall take action with respect to any request described in subparagraph (A) within 90 days after the Secretary receives the request.

(4) REDUCED RATE OF WITHHOLDING FOR RESIDENCE WHERE AMOUNT REALIZED DOES NOT EXCEED $1,000,000.—In the case of a disposition—

(A) of property which is acquired by the transferee for use by the transferee as a residence,

(B) with respect to which the amount realized for such property does not exceed $1,000,000, and

(C) to which subsection (b)(5) does not apply,

subsection (a) shall be applied by substituting "10 percent" for "15 percent".

Amendments

• **2015, Protecting Americans from Tax Hikes Act of 2015 (P.L. 114-113)**

P.L. 114-113, § 324(b), Div. Q:

Amended Code Sec. 1445(c) by adding at the end a new paragraph (4). **Effective** for dispositions after the date which is 60 days after 12-18-2015.

[Sec. 1445(d)]

(d) LIABILITY OF TRANSFEROR'S AGENTS, TRANSFEREE'S AGENTS, OR QUALIFIED SUBSTITUTES.—

(1) NOTICE OF FALSE AFFIDAVIT; FOREIGN CORPORATIONS.—If—

(A) the transferor furnishes the transferee or qualified substitute an affidavit described in paragraph (2) of subsection (b) or a domestic corporation furnishes the transferee an affidavit described in paragraph (3) of subsection (b), and

(B) in the case of—

(i) any transferor's agent—

(I) such agent has actual knowledge that such affidavit is false, or

(II) in the case of an affidavit described in subsection (b)(2) furnished by a corporation, such corporation is a foreign corporation, or

(ii) any transferee's agent or qualified substitute, such agent or substitute has actual knowledge that such affidavit is false, such agent or qualified substitute shall so notify the transferee at such time and in such manner as the Secretary shall require by regulations.

(2) FAILURE TO FURNISH NOTICE.—

(A) IN GENERAL.—If any transferor's agent, transferee's agent, or qualified substitute is required by paragraph (1) to furnish notice, but fails to furnish such notice at such time or times and in such manner as may be required by regulations, such agent or substitute shall have the same duty to deduct and withhold that the transferee would have had if such agent or substitute had complied with paragraph (1).

(B) LIABILITY LIMITED TO AMOUNT OF COMPENSATION.—An agent's or substitute's liability under subparagraph (A) shall be limited to the amount of compensation the agent or substitute derives from the transaction.

(3) TRANSFEROR'S AGENT.—For purposes of this subsection, the term "transferor's agent" means any person who represents the transferor—

(A) in any negotiation with the transferee or any transferee's agent related to the transaction, or

(B) in settling the transaction.

(4) TRANSFEREE'S AGENT.—For purposes of this subsection, the term "transferee's agent" means any person who represents the transferee—

(A) in any negotiation with the transferor or any transferor's agent related to the transaction, or

(B) in settling the transaction.

(5) SETTLEMENT OFFICER NOT TREATED AS TRANSFEROR'S AGENT.—For purposes of this subsection, a person shall not be treated as a transferor's agent or transferee's agent with respect to any transaction merely because such person performs 1 or more of the following acts:

(A) The receipt and the disbursement of any portion of the consideration for the transaction.

(B) The recording of any document in connection with the transaction.

Amendments

• **2008, Housing Assistance Tax Act of 2008 (P.L. 110-289)**

P.L. 110-289, § 3024(c)(2)(A):

Amended Code Sec. 1445(d)(1). **Effective** for dispositions of United States real property interests after 7-30-2008. Prior to amendment, Code Sec. 1445(d)(1) read as follows:

(1) NOTICE OF FALSE AFFIDAVIT; FOREIGN CORPORATIONS.—If—

(A) the transferor furnishes the transferee an affidavit described in paragraph (2) of subsection (b) or a domestic corporation furnishes the transferee an affidavit described in paragraph (3) of subsection (b), and

(B) in the case of—

(i) any transferor's agent—

(I) such agent has actual knowledge that such affidavit is false, or

(II) in the case of an affidavit described in subsection (b)(2) furnished by a corporation, such corporation is a foreign corporation, or

(ii) any transferee's agent, such agent has actual knowledge that such affidavit is false,

such agent shall so notify the transferee at such time and in such manner as the Secretary shall require by regulations.

P.L. 110-289, § 3024(c)(2)(B):

Amended Code Sec. 1445(d)(2). **Effective** for dispositions of United States real property interests after 7-30-2008. Prior to amendment, Code Sec. 1445(d)(2) read as follows:

(2) FAILURE TO FURNISH NOTICE.—

(A) IN GENERAL.—If any transferor's agent or transferee's agent is required by paragraph (1) to furnish notice, but fails to furnish such notice at such time or times and in such manner as may be required by regulations, such agent shall have the same duty to deduct and withhold that the transferee would have had if such agent had complied with paragraph (1).

(B) LIABILITY LIMITED TO AMOUNT OF COMPENSATION.—An agent's liability under subparagraph (A) shall be limited to the amount of compensation the agent derives from the transaction.

P.L. 110-289, § 3024(c)(2)(C):

Amended the heading for Code Sec. 1445(d) by striking "OR TRANSFEREE'S AGENTS" and inserting ", TRANSFEREE'S AGENTS, OR QUALIFIED SUBSTITUTES". **Effective** for dispositions of United States real property interests after 7-30-2008.

INCOME TAX—WITHHOLDING—U.S. PROPERTY

• **1986, Tax Reform Act of 1986 (P.L. 99-514)**

P.L. 99-514, § 1810(f)(3)(A):

Amended Code Sec. 1445(d)(1)(B)(i). **Effective** as if included in the provision of P.L. 98-369 to which it relates. Prior to amendment, Code Sec. 1445(d)(1)(B)(i) read as follows:

(i) any transferor's agent, the transferor is a foreign corporation or such agent has actual knowledge that such affidavit is false, or

P.L. 99-514, § 1810(f)(3)(B):

Amended Code Sec. 1445(d)(1) by striking out "described in paragraph (2)(A)" and inserting in lieu thereof "described in paragraph (2)". **Effective** as if included in the provision of P.L. 98-369 to which it relates.

[Sec. 1445(e)]

(e) SPECIAL RULES RELATING TO DISTRIBUTIONS, ETC., BY CORPORATIONS, PARTNERSHIPS, TRUSTS, OR ESTATES.—

(1) CERTAIN DOMESTIC PARTNERSHIPS, TRUSTS, AND ESTATES.—In the case of any disposition of a United States real property interest as defined in section 897(c) (other than a disposition described in paragraph (4) or (5)) by a domestic partnership, domestic trust, or domestic estate, such partnership, the trustee or such trust, or the executor of such estate (as the case may be) shall be required to deduct and withhold under subsection (a) a tax equal to the highest rate of tax in effect for the taxable year under section 11(b) (or, to the extent provided in regulations, 20 percent) multiplied by the gain realized to the extent such gain—

(A) is allocable to a foreign person who is a partner or beneficiary of such partnership, trust, or estate, or

(B) is allocable to a portion of the trust treated as owned by a foreign person under subpart E of Part I of subchapter J.

(2) CERTAIN DISTRIBUTIONS BY FOREIGN CORPORATIONS.—In the case of any distribution by a foreign corporation on which gain is recognized under subsection (d) or (e) of section 897, the foreign corporation shall deduct and withhold under subsection (a) a tax equal to the highest rate of tax in effect for the taxable year under section 11(b) multiplied by the amount of gain recognized on such distribution under such subsection.

(3) DISTRIBUTIONS BY CERTAIN DOMESTIC CORPORATIONS TO FOREIGN SHAREHOLDERS.—If a domestic corporation which is or has been a United States real property holding corporation (as defined in section 897(c)(2)) during the applicable period specified in section 897(c)(1)(A)(ii) distributes property to a foreign person in a transaction to which section 302 or part II of subchapter C applies, such corporation shall deduct and withhold under subsection (a) a tax equal to 15 percent of the amount realized by the foreign shareholder. The preceding sentence shall not apply if, as of the date of the distribution, interests in such corporation are not United States real property interests by reason of section 897(c)(1)(B). Rules similar to the rules of the preceding provisions of this paragraph shall apply in the case of any distribution to which section 301 applies and which is not made out of the earnings and profits of such a domestic corporation.

(4) TAXABLE DISTRIBUTIONS BY DOMESTIC OR FOREIGN PARTNERSHIPS, TRUSTS, OR ESTATES.—A domestic or foreign partnership, the trustee of a domestic or foreign trust, or the executor of a domestic or foreign estate shall be required to deduct and withhold under subsection (a) a tax equal to 15 percent of the fair market value (as of the time of the taxable distribution) of any United States real property interest distributed to a partner of the partnership or a beneficiary of the trust or estate, as the case may be, who is a foreign person in a transaction which would constitute a taxable distribution under the regulations promulgated by the Secretary pursuant to section 897.

(5) RULES RELATING TO DISPOSITIONS OF INTEREST IN PARTNERSHIPS, TRUSTS, OR ESTATES.—To the extent provided in regulations, the transferee of a partnership interest or of a beneficial interest in a trust or estate shall be required to deduct and withhold under subsection (a) a tax equal to 15 percent of the amount realized on the disposition.

(6) DISTRIBUTIONS BY REGULATED INVESTMENT COMPANIES AND REAL ESTATE INVESTMENT TRUSTS.—If any portion of a distribution from a qualified investment entity (as defined in section 897(h)(4)) to a nonresident alien individual or a foreign corporation is treated under section 897(h)(1) as gain realized by such individual or corporation from the sale or exchange of a United States real property interest, the qualified investment entity shall deduct and withhold under subsection (a) a tax equal to the highest rate of tax in effect for the taxable year under section 11(b) (or, to the extent provided in regulations, 20 percent) multiplied by the amount so treated.

(7) REGULATIONS.—The Secretary shall prescribe such regulations as may be necessary to carry out the purposes of this subsection, including regulations providing for exceptions from provisions of this subsection and regulations for the application of this subsection in the case of payments through 1 or more entities.

Amendments

• **2017, Tax Cuts and Jobs Act (P.L. 115-97)**

P.L. 115-97, § 13001(b)(3)(A)(i)-(ii):

Amended Code Sec. 1445(e)(1) by striking "35 percent" and inserting "the highest rate of tax in effect for the taxable year under section 11(b)", and by striking "of the gain" and inserting "multiplied by the gain". **Effective** for distributions made after 12-31-2017.

P.L. 115-97, § 13001(b)(3)(B):

Amended Code Sec. 1445(e)(2) by striking "35 percent of the amount" and inserting "the highest rate of tax in effect for the taxable year under section 11(b) multiplied by the amount". **Effective** for distributions made after 12-31-2017.

P.L. 115-97, § 13001(b)(3)(C)(i)-(ii):

Amended Code Sec. 1445(e)(6) by striking "35 percent" and inserting "the highest rate of tax in effect for the taxable year under section 11(b)", and by striking "of the amount" and inserting "multiplied by the amount". **Effective** for distributions made after 12-31-2017.

• **2015, Protecting Americans from Tax Hikes Act of 2015 (P.L. 114-113)**

P.L. 114-113, § 324(a), Div. Q:

Amended Code Sec. 1445(e)(3)-(5) by striking "10 percent" each place it appears and inserting "15 percent". **Effective** for dispositions after the date which is 60 days after 12-18-2015.

• **2013, American Taxpayer Relief Act of 2012 (P.L. 112-240)**

P.L. 112-240, § 102(a), provides:

SEC. 102. PERMANENT EXTENSION AND MODIFICATION OF 2003 TAX RELIEF.

(a) PERMANENT EXTENSION.—The Jobs and Growth Tax Relief Reconciliation Act of 2003 is amended by striking section 303.

P.L. 112-240, § 102(c)(1)(C):

Amended Code Sec. 1445(e)(1) by striking "15 percent" and inserting "20 percent". **Effective** for amounts paid on or after 1-1-2013.

P.L. 112-240, § 102(c)(3):

Amended Code Sec. 1445(e)(6) by striking "15 percent (20 percent in the case of taxable years beginning after December 31, 2010)" and inserting "20 percent". **Effective** for amounts paid on or after 1-1-2013.

• **2006, Tax Increase Prevention and Reconciliation Act of 2005 (P.L. 109-222)**

P.L. 109-222, § 505(b):

Amended Code Sec. 1445(e) by redesignating paragraph (6) as paragraph (7) and by inserting after paragraph (5) a new paragraph (6). **Effective** for tax years of qualified investment entities beginning after 12-31-2005, except that no amount shall be required to be withheld under Code Sec. 1441, 1442, or 1445 with respect to any distribution before 5-17-2006 if such amount was not otherwise required to be withheld under any such section as in effect before such amendments.

• **2003, Jobs and Growth Tax Relief Reconciliation Act of 2003 (P.L. 108-27)**

P.L. 108-27, § 301(a)(2)(C):

Amended Code Sec. 1445(e)(1) by striking "20 percent" and inserting "15 percent". **Effective** for amounts paid after 5-28-2003.

P.L. 108-27, § 303, as amended by P.L. 109-222, § 102, and P.L. 111-312, § 102(a), provides [but see P.L. 112-240, § 102(a), above]:

SEC. 303. SUNSET OF TITLE.

All provisions of, and amendments made by, this title shall not apply to taxable years beginning after December 31, 2012, and the Internal Revenue Code of 1986 shall be applied and administered to such years as if such provisions and amendments had never been enacted.

• **1997, Taxpayer Relief Act of 1997 (P.L. 105-34)**

P.L. 105-34, § 311(c)(1):

Amended Code Sec. 1445(e)(1) by striking "28 percent" and inserting "20 percent". **Effective** only for amounts paid after 8-5-97.

INCOME TAX—WITHHOLDING—PARTNERSHIPS

• **1996, Small Business Job Protection Act of 1996 (P.L. 104-188)**

P.L. 104-188, §1704(c)(1):

Amended Code Sec. 1445(e)(3) by adding at the end a new sentence. **Effective** for distributions after 8-20-96.

• **1993, Omnibus Budget Reconciliation Act of 1993 (P.L. 103-66)**

P.L. 103-66, §13221(c)(3):

Amended Code Sec. 1445(e)(1)-(2) by striking "34 percent" and inserting "35 percent". **Effective** 8-10-93.

• **1988, Technical and Miscellaneous Revenue Act of 1988 (P.L. 100-647)**

P.L. 100-647, §1003(b)(3):

Amended Code Sec. 1445(e)(1) by striking out "34 percent" and inserting in lieu thereof "34 percent (or, to the extent provided in regulations, 28 percent)". **Effective** for tax years beginning after 12-31-87.

• **1986, Tax Reform Act of 1986 (P.L. 99-514)**

P.L. 99-514, §311(b)(4):

Amended Code Sec. 1445(e)(1) and (2) by striking out "28 percent" and inserting in lieu thereof "34 percent". **Effective** for payments made after 12-31-86 [effective date changed by P.L. 100-647, §1003(c)(2)].

P.L. 99-514, §1810(f)(4)(A):

Amended Code Sec. 1445(e)(1). **Effective** for dispositions after the day 30 days after 10-22-86. Prior to amendment, Code Sec. 1445(e)(1) read as follows:

(1) CERTAIN DOMESTIC PARTNERSHIPS, TRUSTS, AND ESTATES.—A domestic partnership, the trustee of a domestic trust, or the executor of a domestic estate shall be required to deduct and withhold under subsection (a) a tax equal to 10 percent of any amount of which such partnership, trustee, or executor has custody which is—

(A) attributable to the disposition of a United States real property interest (as defined in section 897(c), other than a disposition described in paragraph (4) or (5)), and

(B) either—

(i) includible in the distributive share of a partner of the partnership who is a foreign person,

(ii) includible in the income of a beneficiary of the trust or estate who is a foreign person, or

(iii) includible in the income of a foreign person under the provisions of section 671.

P.L. 99-514, §1810(f)(5):

Amended Code Sec. 1445(e)(3) by adding at the end thereof a new sentence. **Effective** as if included in the provision of P.L. 98-369 to which it relates.

P.L. 99-514, §1810(f)(6):

Amended Code Sec. 1445(e)(4) by striking out "section 897(g)" and inserting in lieu thereof "section 897". **Effective** as if included in the provision of P.L. 98-369 to which it relates.

P.L. 99-514, §1810(f)(8):

Amended Code Sec. 1445(e)(6) by inserting "and regulations for the application of this subsection in the case of payments through 1 or more entities" before the period at the end thereof. **Effective** as if included in the provision of P.L. 98-369 to which it relates.

[Sec. 1445(f)]

(f) DEFINITIONS.—For purposes of this section—

(1) TRANSFEROR.—The term "transferor" means the person disposing of the United States real property interest.

(2) TRANSFEREE.—The term "transferee" means the person acquiring the United States real property interest.

(3) FOREIGN PERSON.—The term "foreign person" means any person other than—

(A) a United States person, and

(B) except as otherwise provided by the Secretary, an entity with respect to which section 897 does not apply by reason of subsection (l) thereof.

(4) TRANSFEROR'S MAXIMUM TAX LIABILITY.—The term "transferor's maximum tax liability" means, with respect to the disposition of any interest, the sum of—

(A) the maximum amount which the Secretary determines could be imposed as tax under section 871(b)(1) or 882(a)(1) by reason of the disposition, plus

(B) the amount the Secretary determines to be the transferor's unsatisfied withholding liability with respect to such interest.

(5) TRANSFEROR'S UNSATISFIED WITHHOLDING LIABILITY.—The term "transferor's unsatisfied withholding liability" means the withholding obligation imposed by this section on the transferor's acquisition of the United States real property interest or on the acquisition of a predecessor interest, to the extent such obligation has not been satisfied.

(6) QUALIFIED SUBSTITUTE.—The term "qualified substitute" means, with respect to a disposition of a United States real property interest—

(A) the person (including any attorney or title company) responsible for closing the transaction, other than the transferor's agent, and

(B) the transferee's agent.

Amendments

• **2015, Protecting Americans from Tax Hikes Act of 2015 (P.L. 114-113)**

P.L. 114-113, §323(b), Div. Q:

Amended Code Sec. 1445(f)(3) by striking "any person" and all that follows and inserting "any person other than—"and new subparagraphs (A)-(B). **Effective** for dispositions and distributions after 12-18-2015. Prior to being stricken, "any person" and all that follows in Code Sec. 1445(f)(3) read as follows:

any person other than a United States person.

• **2008, Housing Assistance Tax Act of 2008 (P.L. 110-289)**

P.L. 110-289, §3024(b):

Amended Code Sec. 1445(f) by adding at the end a new paragraph (6). **Effective** for dispositions of United States real property interests after 7-30-2008.

• **1984, Deficit Reduction Act of 1984 (P.L. 98-369)**

P.L. 98-369, §129(a)(1):

Added Code Sec. 1445. **Effective** for any disposition on or after 1-1-85.

[Sec. 1446]

SEC. 1446. WITHHOLDING OF TAX ON FOREIGN PARTNERS' SHARE OF EFFECTIVELY CONNECTED INCOME.

[Sec. 1446(a)]

(a) GENERAL RULE.—If—

(1) a partnership has effectively connected taxable income for any taxable year, and

(2) any portion of such income is allocable under section 704 to a foreign partner,

such partnership shall pay a withholding tax under this section at such time and in such manner as the Secretary shall by regulations prescribe.

Amendments

• **2018, Tax Technical Corrections Act of 2018 (P.L. 115-141)**

P.L. 115-141, §401(a)(199), Div. U:

Amended the heading of Code Sec. 1446 by striking "**WITHHOLDING TAX**" in the heading and inserting "**WITHHOLDING OF TAX**". **Effective** 3-23-2018.

[Sec. 1446(b)]

(b) AMOUNT OF WITHHOLDING TAX.—

(1) IN GENERAL.—The amount of the withholding tax payable by any partnership under subsection (a) shall be equal to the applicable percentage of the effectively connected taxable income of the partnership which is allocable under section 704 to foreign partners.

(2) APPLICABLE PERCENTAGE.—For purposes of paragraph (1), the term "applicable percentage" means—

(A) the highest rate of tax specified in section 1 in the case of the portion of the effectively connected taxable income which is allocable under section 704 to foreign partners who are not corporations, and

INCOME TAX—WITHHOLDING—PARTNERSHIPS

  (B) the highest rate of tax specified in section 11(b) in the case of the portion of the effectively connected taxable income which is allocable under section 704 to foreign partners which are corporations.

Amendments

• **2017, Tax Cuts and Jobs Act (P.L. 115-97)**

P.L. 115-97, §13001(b)(3)(D):

Amended Code Sec. 1446(b)(2)(B) by striking "section 11(b)(1)" and inserting "section 11(b)". **Effective** for distributions made after 12-31-2017.

• **1989, Omnibus Budget Reconciliation Act of 1989 (P.L. 101-239)**

P.L. 101-239, §7811(i)(6)(A):

Amended Code Sec. 1446(b)(2)(B) by striking "section 11(b)" and inserting "section 11(b)(1)". **Effective** as if included in the provision of P.L. 100-647 to which it relates.

[Sec. 1446(c)]

(c) EFFECTIVELY CONNECTED TAXABLE INCOME.—For purposes of this section, the term "effectively connected taxable income" means the taxable income of the partnership which is effectively connected (or treated as effectively connected) with the conduct of a trade or business in the United States computed with the following adjustments:

  (1) Paragraph (1) [of] section 703(a) shall not apply.

  (2) The partnership shall be allowed a deduction for depletion with respect to oil and gas wells but the amount of such deduction shall be determined without regard to sections 613 and 613A.

  (3) There shall not be taken into account any item of income, gain, loss, or deduction to the extent allocable under section 704 to any partner who is not a foreign partner.

[Sec. 1446(d)]

(d) TREATMENT OF FOREIGN PARTNERS.—

  (1) ALLOWANCE OF CREDIT.—Each foreign partner of a partnership shall be allowed a credit under section 33 for such partner's share of the withholding tax paid by the partnership under this section. Such credit shall be allowed for the partner's taxable year in which (or with which) the partnership taxable year (for which such tax was paid) ends.

  (2) CREDIT TREATED AS DISTRIBUTED TO PARTNER.—Except as provided in regulations, a foreign partner's share of any withholding tax paid by the partnership under this section shall be treated as distributed to such partner by such partnership on the earlier of—

    (A) the day on which such tax was paid by the partnership, or

    (B) the last day of the partnership's taxable year for which such tax was paid.

Amendments

• **1989, Omnibus Budget Reconciliation Act of 1989 (P.L. 101-239)**

P.L. 101-239, §7811(i)(6)(B):

Amended Code Sec. 1446(d)(2). **Effective** as if included in the provision of P.L. 100-647 to which it relates. Prior to amendment, Code Sec. 1446(d)(2) read as follows:

(2) CREDIT TREATED AS DISTRIBUTED TO PARTNER.—A foreign partner's share of any withholding tax paid by the partnership under this section shall be treated as distributed to such partner by such partnership on the last day of the partnership's taxable year (for which such tax was paid).

[Sec. 1446(e)]

(e) FOREIGN PARTNER.—For purposes of this section, the term "foreign partner" means any partner who is not a United States person.

[Sec. 1446(f)]

(f) SPECIAL RULES FOR WITHHOLDING ON DISPOSITIONS OF PARTNERSHIP INTERESTS.—

  (1) IN GENERAL.—Except as provided in this subsection, if any portion of the gain (if any) on any disposition of an interest in a partnership would be treated under section 864(c)(8) as effectively connected with the conduct of a trade or business within the United States, the transferee shall be required to deduct and withhold a tax equal to 10 percent of the amount realized on the disposition.

  (2) EXCEPTION IF NONFOREIGN AFFIDAVIT FURNISHED.—

    (A) IN GENERAL.—No person shall be required to deduct and withhold any amount under paragraph (1) with respect to any disposition if the transferor furnishes to the transferee an affidavit by the transferor stating, under penalty of perjury, the transferor's United States taxpayer identification number and that the transferor is not a foreign person.

    (B) FALSE AFFIDAVIT.—Subparagraph (A) shall not apply to any disposition if—

      (i) the transferee has actual knowledge that the affidavit is false, or the transferee receives a notice (as described in section 1445(d)) from a transferor's agent or transferee's agent that such affidavit or statement is false, or

      (ii) the Secretary by regulations requires the transferee to furnish a copy of such affidavit or statement to the Secretary and the transferee fails to furnish a copy of such affidavit or statement to the Secretary at such time and in such manner as required by such regulations.

    (C) RULES FOR AGENTS.—The rules of section 1445(d) shall apply to a transferor's agent or transferee's agent with respect to any affidavit described in subparagraph (A) in the same manner as such rules apply with respect to the disposition of a United States real property interest under such section.

  (3) AUTHORITY OF SECRETARY TO PRESCRIBE REDUCED AMOUNT.—At the request of the transferor or transferee, the Secretary may prescribe a reduced amount to be withheld under this section if the Secretary determines that to substitute such reduced amount will not jeopardize the collection of the tax imposed under this title with respect to gain treated under section 864(c)(8) as effectively connected with the conduct of a trade or business with in [sic] the United States.

  (4) PARTNERSHIP TO WITHHOLD AMOUNTS NOT WITHHELD BY THE TRANSFEREE.—If a transferee fails to withhold any amount required to be withheld under paragraph (1), the partnership shall be required to deduct and withhold from distributions to the transferee a tax in an amount equal to the amount the transferee failed to withhold (plus interest under this title on such amount).

  (5) DEFINITIONS.—Any term used in this subsection which is also used under section 1445 shall have the same meaning as when used in such section.

  (6) REGULATIONS.—The Secretary shall prescribe such regulations or other guidance as may be necessary to carry out the purposes of this subsection, including regulations providing for exceptions from the provisions of this subsection.

Amendments

• **2017, Tax Cuts and Jobs Act (P.L. 115-97)**

P.L. 115-97, §13501(b):

Amended Code Sec. 1446 by redesignating subsection (f) as subsection (g) and by inserting after subsection (e) a new subsection (f). **Effective** for sales, exchanges, and dispositions after 12-31-2017.

[Sec. 1446(g)]

(g) REGULATIONS.—The Secretary shall prescribe such regulations as may be necessary to carry out the purposes of this section, including—

  (1) regulations providing for the application of this section in the case of publicly traded partnerships, and

INCOME TAX—WITHHOLDING PROVISIONS

(2) regulations providing—

(A) that, for purposes of section 6655, the withholding tax imposed under this section shall be treated as a tax imposed by section 11 and any partnership required to pay such tax shall be treated as a corporation, and

(B) appropriate adjustments in applying section 6655 with respect to such withholding tax.

Amendments

• **2017, Tax Cuts and Jobs Act (P.L. 115-97)**

P.L. 115-97, §13501(b):

Amended Code Sec. 1446 by redesignating subsection (f) as subsection (g). **Effective** for sales, exchanges, and dispositions after 12-31-2017.

• **1989, Omnibus Budget Reconciliation Act of 1989 (P.L. 101-239)**

P.L. 101-239, §7811(i)(6)(C):

Amended Code Sec. 1446(f). **Effective** as if included in the provision of P.L. 100-647 to which it relates. Prior to amendment, Code Sec. 1446(f) read as follows:

(f) REGULATIONS.—The Secretary shall prescribe such regulations as may be necessary to carry out the purposes of this section, including regulations providing for the application of this section in the case of publicly traded partnerships.

• **1988, Technical and Miscellaneous Revenue Act of 1988 (P.L. 100-647)**

P.L. 100-647, §1012(s)(1)(A):

Amended Code Sec. 1446. **Effective** for tax years beginning after 12-31-87. No amount shall be required to be deducted and withheld under section 1446 of the 1986 Code (as in effect before the amendment made by subparagraph (A)). Prior to amendment, Code Sec. 1446 read as follows:

SEC. 1446. WITHHOLDING TAX ON AMOUNTS PAID BY PARTNERSHIPS TO FOREIGN PARTNERS.

(a) GENERAL RULE.—Except as provided in this section, if a partnership has any income, gain, or loss which is effectively connected or treated as effectively connected with the conduct of a trade or business within the United States, any person described in section 1441(a) shall be required to deduct and withhold a tax equal to 20 percent of any amount distributed to a partner which is not a United States person.

(b) LIMITATION IF LESS THAN 80 PERCENT OF GROSS INCOME IS EFFECTIVELY CONNECTED WITH UNITED STATES TRADE OR BUSINESS.—

(1) IN GENERAL.—If the effectively connected percentage is less than 80 percent, only the effectively connected percentage of any distribution shall be taken into account under subsection (a).

(2) EFFECTIVELY CONNECTED PERCENTAGE.—For purposes of paragraph (1) the term "effectively connected percentage" means the percentage of the gross income of the partnership for the 3 taxable years preceding the taxable year of the distribution which is effectively connected (or treated as effectively connected) with the conduct of a trade or business within the United States.

(c) EXCEPTIONS.—

(1) AMOUNTS ON WHICH TAX WITHHELD.—Subsection (a) shall not apply to that portion of any distribution with respect to which a tax is required to be deducted and withheld under section 1441 or 1442 (or would be required to be deducted and withheld but for a treaty).

(2) PARTNERSHIPS WITH CERTAIN ALLOCATIONS.—Except as provided in regulations, subsection (a) shall not apply to any partnership with respect to which substantially all income from sources within the United States and substantially all income which is effectively connected with the conduct of a trade or business within the United States is properly allocated to United States persons.

(3) COORDINATION WITH SECTION 1445.—Under regulations proper adjustments shall be made in the amount required to be deducted and withheld under subsection (a) for amounts deducted and withheld under section 1445.

(d) REGULATIONS.—The Secretary shall prescribe such regulations as may be necessary or appropriate to carry out the purposes of this section.

• **1986, Tax Reform Act of 1986 (P.L. 99-514)**

P.L. 99-514, §1246(a):

Added new Code Sec. 1446. **Effective** for distributions after 12-31-87, (or, if earlier, the effective date (which shall not be earlier than 1-1-87) of the initial regulations issued under section 1446 of the Internal Revenue Code of 1986 as added by this section).

[Sec. 1451—Stricken]

Amendments

• **1984, Deficit Reduction Act of 1984 (P.L. 98-369)**

P.L. 98-369, §474(r)(29)(A):

Amended chapter 3 by striking out subchapter B and redesignating subchapter C as subchapter B. **Effective** for tax years beginning after 12-31-83, and to carrybacks from such years but does not apply with respect to obligations issued before 1-1-84. Prior to deletion, subchapter B, which consisted of Code Sec. 1451, read as follows:

SEC. 1451. TAX-FREE COVENANT BONDS.

(a) REQUIREMENT OF WITHHOLDING.—In any case where bonds, mortgages, or deeds of trust, or other similar obligations of a corporation, issued before January 1, 1934, contain a contract or provision by which the obligor agrees to pay any portion of the tax imposed by this subtitle on the obligee, or to reimburse the obligee for any portion of the tax, or to pay the interest without deduction for any tax which the obligor may be required or permitted to pay thereon, or to retain therefrom under any law of the United States, the obligor shall deduct and withhold a tax equal to 2 percent (regardless of whether the liability assumed by the obligor is less than, equal to, or greater than 2 percent) of the interest on such bonds, mortgages, deeds of trust, or other obligations, whether such interest is payable annually or at shorter or longer periods, if payable to—

(1) an individual,

(2) a partnership, or

(3) a foreign corporation not engaged in trade or business within the United States.

(b) PAYMENTS TO FOREIGNERS.—Notwithstanding subsection (a), if the liability assumed by the obligor does not exceed 2 percent of the interest, then the deduction and withholding shall be at the rate of 30 percent in the case of—

(1) a nonresident alien individual,

(2) any partnership not engaged in trade or business within the United States and composed in whole or in part of nonresident aliens, and

(3) a foreign corporation not engaged in trade or business within the United States.

(c) OWNER UNKNOWN.—If the owners of such obligations are not known to the withholding agent, the Secretary may authorize such deduction and withholding to be at the rate of 2 percent, or, if the liability assumed by the obligor does not exceed 2 percent of the interest, then at the rate of 30 percent.

(d) BENEFIT OF PERSONAL EXEMPTIONS.—Deduction and withholding under this section shall not be required in the case of a citizen or resident entitled to receive such interest, if he files with the withholding agent on or before February 1 a signed notice in writing claiming the benefit of the deduction for personal exemptions provided in section 151; nor in the case of a nonresident alien individual if so provided for in regulations prescribed by the Secretary under section 874.

(e) ALIEN RESIDENTS OF PUERTO RICO.—For purposes of this section, the term "nonresident alien individual" includes an alien resident of Puerto Rico.

(f) INCOME OF OBLIGOR AND OBLIGEE.—The obligor shall not be allowed a deduction for the payment of the tax imposed by this subtitle, or any other tax paid pursuant to the tax-free covenant clause; nor shall such tax be included in the gross income of the obligee.

• **1976, Tax Reform Act of 1976 (P.L. 94-455)**

P.L. 94-455, §1906(b)(13)(A):

Amended 1954 Code by substituting "Secretary" for "Secretary or his delegate" each place it appeared. **Effective** 2-1-77.

Subchapter B—Application of Withholding Provisions

Sec. 1461.	Liability for withheld tax.
Sec. 1462.	Withheld tax as credit to recipient of income.
Sec. 1463.	Tax paid by recipient of income.
Sec. 1464.	Refunds and credits with respect to withheld tax.

[Sec. 1461]

SEC. 1461. LIABILITY FOR WITHHELD TAX.

Every person required to deduct and withhold any tax under this chapter is hereby made liable for such tax and is hereby indemnified against the claims and demands of any person for the amount of any payments made in accordance with the provisions of this chapter.

Amendments

• **1966, Foreign Investors Tax Act of 1966 (P.L. 89-809)**

P.L. 89-809, §103(i):

Amended Code Sec. 1461. **Effective** for payments occurring after 12-31-66. Prior to amendment, Sec. 1461 read as follows:

SEC. 1461. RETURN AND PAYMENT OF WITHHELD TAX.

Every person required to deduct and withhold any tax under this chapter shall, on or before March 15 of each year, make return thereof and pay the tax to the officer designated in section 6151. Every such person is hereby made liable for such tax and is hereby indemnified against the claims and demands of any person for the amount of any payments made in accordance with the provisions of this chapter.

INCOME TAX—WITHHOLDING PROVISIONS

[Sec. 1462]

SEC. 1462. WITHHELD TAX AS CREDIT TO RECIPIENT OF INCOME.

Income on which any tax is required to be withheld at the source under this chapter shall be included in the return of the recipient of such income, but any amount of tax so withheld shall be credited against the amount of income tax as computed in such return.

[Sec. 1463]

SEC. 1463. TAX PAID BY RECIPIENT OF INCOME.

If—

(1) any person, in violation of the provisions of this chapter, fails to deduct and withhold any tax under this chapter, and

(2) thereafter the tax against which such tax may be credited is paid,

the tax so required to be deducted and withheld shall not be collected from such person; but this section shall in no case relieve such person from liability for interest or any penalties or additions to the tax otherwise applicable in respect of such failure to deduct and withhold.

Amendments

- **1996, Small Business Job Protection Act of 1996 (P.L. 104-188)**

P.L. 104-188, §1704(t)(9):

Amended Code Sec. 1463 by striking "this subsection" and inserting "this section". **Effective** 8-20-96.

- **1989, Omnibus Budget Reconciliation Act of 1989 (P.L. 101-239)**

P.L. 101-239, §7743:

Amended Code Sec. 1463. **Effective** for failures after 12-31-89. Prior to amendment, Code Sec. 1463 read as follows:

SEC. 1463. TAX PAID BY RECIPIENT OF INCOME.

If any tax required under this chapter to be deducted and withheld is paid by the recipient of the income, it shall not be re-collected from the withholding agent; nor in cases in which the tax is so paid shall any penalty be imposed on or collected from the recipient of the income or the withholding agent for failure to return or pay the same, unless such failure was fraudulent and for the purpose of evading payment.

[Sec. 1464]

SEC. 1464. REFUNDS AND CREDITS WITH RESPECT TO WITHHELD TAX.

Where there has been an overpayment of tax under this chapter, any refund or credit made under chapter 65 shall be made to the withholding agent unless the amount of such tax was actually withheld by the withholding agent.

CHAPTER 4—TAXES TO ENFORCE REPORTING ON CERTAIN FOREIGN ACCOUNTS

Sec. 1471.	Withholdable payments to foreign financial institutions.
Sec. 1472.	Withholdable payments to other foreign entities.
Sec. 1473.	Definitions.
Sec. 1474.	Special rules.

[Sec. 1471]

SEC. 1471. WITHHOLDABLE PAYMENTS TO FOREIGN FINANCIAL INSTITUTIONS.

[Sec. 1471(a)]

(a) IN GENERAL.—In the case of any withholdable payment to a foreign financial institution which does not meet the requirements of subsection (b), the withholding agent with respect to such payment shall deduct and withhold from such payment a tax equal to 30 percent of the amount of such payment.

[Sec. 1471(b)]

(b) REPORTING REQUIREMENTS, ETC.—

(1) IN GENERAL.—The requirements of this subsection are met with respect to any foreign financial institution if an agreement is in effect between such institution and the Secretary under which such institution agrees—

(A) to obtain such information regarding each holder of each account maintained by such institution as is necessary to determine which (if any) of such accounts are United States accounts,

(B) to comply with such verification and due diligence procedures as the Secretary may require with respect to the identification of United States accounts,

(C) in the case of any United States account maintained by such institution, to report on an annual basis the information described in subsection (c) with respect to such account,

(D) to deduct and withhold a tax equal to 30 percent of—

(i) any passthru payment which is made by such institution to a recalcitrant account holder or another foreign financial institution which does not meet the requirements of this subsection, and

(ii) in the case of any passthru payment which is made by such institution to a foreign financial institution which has in effect an election under paragraph (3) with respect to such payment, so much of such payment as is allocable to accounts held by recalcitrant account holders or foreign financial institutions which do not meet the requirements of this subsection,

(E) to comply with requests by the Secretary for additional information with respect to any United States account maintained by such institution, and

(F) in any case in which any foreign law would (but for a waiver described in clause (i)) prevent the reporting of any information referred to in this subsection or subsection (c) with respect to any United States account maintained by such institution—

(i) to attempt to obtain a valid and effective waiver of such law from each holder of such account, and

(ii) if a waiver described in clause (i) is not obtained from each such holder within a reasonable period of time, to close such account.

Any agreement entered into under this subsection may be terminated by the Secretary upon a determination by the Secretary that the foreign financial institution is out of compliance with such agreement.

(2) FINANCIAL INSTITUTIONS DEEMED TO MEET REQUIREMENTS IN CERTAIN CASES.—A foreign financial institution may be treated by the Secretary as meeting the requirements of this subsection if—

(A) such institution—

(i) complies with such procedures as the Secretary may prescribe to ensure that such institution does not maintain United States accounts, and

INCOME TAX—WITHHOLDING PROVISIONS

(ii) meets such other requirements as the Secretary may prescribe with respect to accounts of other foreign financial institutions maintained by such institution, or

(B) such institution is a member of a class of institutions with respect to which the Secretary has determined that the application of this section is not necessary to carry out the purposes of this section.

(3) ELECTION TO BE WITHHELD UPON RATHER THAN WITHHOLD ON PAYMENTS TO RECALCITRANT ACCOUNT HOLDERS AND NONPARTICIPATING FOREIGN FINANCIAL INSTITUTIONS.—In the case of a foreign financial institution which meets the requirements of this subsection and such other requirements as the Secretary may provide and which elects the application of this paragraph—

(A) the requirements of paragraph (1)(D) shall not apply,

(B) the withholding tax imposed under subsection (a) shall apply with respect to any withholdable payment to such institution to the extent such payment is allocable to accounts held by recalcitrant account holders or foreign financial institutions which do not meet the requirements of this subsection, and

(C) the agreement described in paragraph (1) shall—

(i) require such institution to notify the withholding agent with respect to each such payment of the institution's election under this paragraph and such other information as may be necessary for the withholding agent to determine the appropriate amount to deduct and withhold from such payment, and

(ii) include a waiver of any right under any treaty of the United States with respect to any amount deducted and withheld pursuant to an election under this paragraph.

To the extent provided by the Secretary, the election under this paragraph may be made with respect to certain classes or types of accounts of the foreign financial institution.

[Sec. 1471(c)]

(c) INFORMATION REQUIRED TO BE REPORTED ON UNITED STATES ACCOUNTS.—

(1) IN GENERAL.—The agreement described in subsection (b) shall require the foreign financial institution to report the following with respect to each United States account maintained by such institution:

(A) The name, address, and TIN of each account holder which is a specified United States person and, in the case of any account holder which is a United States owned foreign entity, the name, address, and TIN of each substantial United States owner of such entity.

(B) The account number.

(C) The account balance or value (determined at such time and in such manner as the Secretary may provide).

(D) Except to the extent provided by the Secretary, the gross receipts and gross withdrawals or payments from the account (determined for such period and in such manner as the Secretary may provide).

(2) ELECTION TO BE SUBJECT TO SAME REPORTING AS UNITED STATES FINANCIAL INSTITUTIONS.—In the case of a foreign financial institution which elects the application of this paragraph—

(A) subparagraphs (C) and (D) of paragraph (1) shall not apply, and

(B) the agreement described in subsection (b) shall require such foreign financial institution to report such information with respect to each United States account maintained by such institution as such institution would be required to report under sections 6041, 6042, 6045, and 6049 if—

(i) such institution were a United States person, and

(ii) each holder of such account which is a specified United States person or United States owned foreign entity were a natural person and citizen of the United States.

An election under this paragraph shall be made at such time, in such manner, and subject to such conditions as the Secretary may provide.

(3) SEPARATE REQUIREMENTS FOR QUALIFIED INTERMEDIARIES.—In the case of a foreign financial institution which is treated as a qualified intermediary by the Secretary for purposes of section 1441 and the regulations issued thereunder, the requirements of this section shall be in addition to any reporting or other requirements imposed by the Secretary for purposes of such treatment.

[Sec. 1471(d)]

(d) DEFINITIONS.—For purposes of this section—

(1) UNITED STATES ACCOUNT.—

(A) IN GENERAL.—The term "United States account" means any financial account which is held by one or more specified United States persons or United States owned foreign entities.

(B) EXCEPTION FOR CERTAIN ACCOUNTS HELD BY INDIVIDUALS.—Unless the foreign financial institution elects to not have this subparagraph apply, such term shall not include any depository account maintained by such financial institution if—

(i) each holder of such account is a natural person, and

(ii) with respect to each holder of such account, the aggregate value of all depository accounts held (in whole or in part) by such holder and maintained by the same financial institution which maintains such account does not exceed $50,000.

To the extent provided by the Secretary, financial institutions which are members of the same expanded affiliated group shall be treated for purposes of clause (ii) as a single financial institution.

(C) ELIMINATION OF DUPLICATIVE REPORTING REQUIREMENTS.—Such term shall not include any financial account in a foreign financial institution if—

(i) such account is held by another financial institution which meets the requirements of subsection (b), or

(ii) the holder of such account is otherwise subject to information reporting requirements which the Secretary determines would make the reporting required by this section with respect to United States accounts duplicative.

(2) FINANCIAL ACCOUNT.—Except as otherwise provided by the Secretary, the term "financial account" means, with respect to any financial institution—

(A) any depository account maintained by such financial institution,

(B) any custodial account maintained by such financial institution, and

(C) any equity or debt interest in such financial institution (other than interests which are regularly traded on an established securities market).

Any equity or debt interest which constitutes a financial account under subparagraph (C) with respect to any financial institution shall be treated for purposes of this section as maintained by such financial institution.

(3) UNITED STATES OWNED FOREIGN ENTITY.—The term "United States owned foreign entity" means any foreign entity which has one or more substantial United States owners.

INCOME TAX—WITHHOLDING PROVISIONS

(4) FOREIGN FINANCIAL INSTITUTION.—The term "foreign financial institution" means any financial institution which is a foreign entity. Except as otherwise provided by the Secretary, such term shall not include a financial institution which is organized under the laws of any possession of the United States.

(5) FINANCIAL INSTITUTION.—Except as otherwise provided by the Secretary, the term "financial institution" means any entity that—

(A) accepts deposits in the ordinary course of a banking or similar business,

(B) as a substantial portion of its business, holds financial assets for the account of others, or

(C) is engaged (or holding itself out as being engaged) primarily in the business of investing, reinvesting, or trading in securities (as defined in section 475(c)(2) without regard to the last sentence thereof), partnership interests, commodities (as defined in section 475(e)(2)), or any interest (including a futures or forward contract or option) in such securities, partnership interests, or commodities.

(6) RECALCITRANT ACCOUNT HOLDER.—The term "recalcitrant account holder" means any account holder which—

(A) fails to comply with reasonable requests for the information referred to in subsection (b)(1)(A) or (c)(1)(A), or

(B) fails to provide a waiver described in subsection (b)(1)(F) upon request.

(7) PASSTHRU PAYMENT.—The term "passthru payment" means any withholdable payment or other payment to the extent attributable to a withholdable payment.

[Sec. 1471(e)]

(e) AFFILIATED GROUPS.—

(1) IN GENERAL.—The requirements of subsections (b) and (c)(1) shall apply—

(A) with respect to United States accounts maintained by the foreign financial institution, and

(B) except as otherwise provided by the Secretary, with respect to United States accounts maintained by each other foreign financial institution (other than any foreign financial institution which meets the requirements of subsection (b)) which is a member of the same expanded affiliated group as such foreign financial institution.

(2) EXPANDED AFFILIATED GROUP.—For purposes of this section, the term "expanded affiliated group" means an affiliated group as defined in section 1504(a), determined—

(A) by substituting "more than 50 percent" for "at least 80 percent" each place it appears, and

(B) without regard to paragraphs (2) and (3) of section 1504(b).

A partnership or any other entity (other than a corporation) shall be treated as a member of an expanded affiliated group if such entity is controlled (within the meaning of section 954(d)(3)) by members of such group (including any entity treated as a member of such group by reason of this sentence).

[Sec. 1471(f)]

(f) EXCEPTION FOR CERTAIN PAYMENTS.—Subsection (a) shall not apply to any payment to the extent that the beneficial owner of such payment is—

(1) any foreign government, any political subdivision of a foreign government, or any wholly owned agency or instrumentality of any one or more of the foregoing,

(2) any international organization or any wholly owned agency or instrumentality thereof,

(3) any foreign central bank of issue, or

(4) any other class of persons identified by the Secretary for purposes of this subsection as posing a low risk of tax evasion.

Amendments

• 2010, Hiring Incentives to Restore Employment Act (P.L. 111-147)

P.L. 111-147, § 501(a):

Amended [subtitle A of] the Internal Revenue Code of 1986 by inserting after chapter 3 a new chapter 4 (Code Secs. 1471-1474). **Effective** generally for payments made after 12-31-2012. For a special rule, see Act Sec. 501(d)(2), below.

P.L. 111-147, § 501(d)(2), provides:

(2) GRANDFATHERED TREATMENT OF OUTSTANDING OBLIGATIONS.—The amendments made by this section shall not require any amount to be deducted or withheld from any payment under any obligation outstanding on the date which is 2 years after the date of the enactment of this Act or from the gross proceeds from any disposition of such an obligation.

[Sec. 1472]

SEC. 1472. WITHHOLDABLE PAYMENTS TO OTHER FOREIGN ENTITIES.

[Sec. 1472(a)]

(a) IN GENERAL.—In the case of any withholdable payment to a non-financial foreign entity, if—

(1) the beneficial owner of such payment is such entity or any other non-financial foreign entity, and

(2) the requirements of subsection (b) are not met with respect to such beneficial owner,

then the withholding agent with respect to such payment shall deduct and withhold from such payment a tax equal to 30 percent of the amount of such payment.

[Sec. 1472(b)]

(b) REQUIREMENTS FOR WAIVER OF WITHHOLDING.—The requirements of this subsection are met with respect to the beneficial owner of a payment if—

(1) such beneficial owner or the payee provides the withholding agent with either—

(A) a certification that such beneficial owner does not have any substantial United States owners, or

(B) the name, address, and TIN of each substantial United States owner of such beneficial owner,

(2) the withholding agent does not know, or have reason to know, that any information provided under paragraph (1) is incorrect, and

(3) the withholding agent reports the information provided under paragraph (1)(B) to the Secretary in such manner as the Secretary may provide.

[Sec. 1472(c)]

(c) EXCEPTIONS.—Subsection (a) shall not apply to—

(1) except as otherwise provided by the Secretary, any payment beneficially owned by—

(A) any corporation the stock of which is regularly traded on an established securities market,

(B) any corporation which is a member of the same expanded affiliated group (as defined in section 1471(e)(2) without regard to the last sentence thereof) as a corporation described in subparagraph (A),

(C) any entity which is organized under the laws of a possession of the United States and which is wholly owned by one or more bona fide residents (as defined in section 937(a)) of such possession,

Sec. 1471(d)(4)

(D) any foreign government, any political subdivision of a foreign government, or any wholly owned agency or instrumentality of any one or more of the foregoing,

(E) any international organization or any wholly owned agency or instrumentality thereof,

(F) any foreign central bank of issue, or

(G) any other class of persons identified by the Secretary for purposes of this subsection, and

(2) any class of payments identified by the Secretary for purposes of this subsection as posing a low risk of tax evasion.

[Sec. 1472(d)]

(d) NON-FINANCIAL FOREIGN ENTITY.—For purposes of this section, the term "non-financial foreign entity" means any foreign entity which is not a financial institution (as defined in section 1471(d)(5)).

Amendments

• **2010, Hiring Incentives to Restore Employment Act (P.L. 111-147)**

P.L. 111-147, § 501(a):

Amended [subtitle A of] the Internal Revenue Code of 1986 by inserting after chapter 3 a new chapter 4 (Code Secs. 1471-1474). **Effective** generally for payments made after 12-31-2012. For a special rule, see Act Sec. 501(d)(2), below.

P.L. 111-147, § 501(d)(2), provides:

(2) GRANDFATHERED TREATMENT OF OUTSTANDING OBLIGATIONS.—The amendments made by this section shall not require any amount to be deducted or withheld from any payment under any obligation outstanding on the date which is 2 years after the date of the enactment of this Act or from the gross proceeds from any disposition of such an obligation.

[Sec. 1473]

SEC. 1473. DEFINITIONS.

For purposes of this chapter—

(1) WITHHOLDABLE PAYMENT.—Except as otherwise provided by the Secretary—

(A) IN GENERAL.—The term "withholdable payment" means—

(i) any payment of interest (including any original issue discount), dividends, rents, salaries, wages, premiums, annuities, compensations, remunerations, emoluments, and other fixed or determinable annual or periodical gains, profits, and income, if such payment is from sources within the United States, and

(ii) any gross proceeds from the sale or other disposition of any property of a type which can produce interest or dividends from sources within the United States.

(B) EXCEPTION FOR INCOME CONNECTED WITH UNITED STATES BUSINESS.—Such term shall not include any item of income which is taken into account under section 871(b)(1) or 882(a)(1) for the taxable year.

(C) SPECIAL RULE FOR SOURCING INTEREST PAID BY FOREIGN BRANCHES OF DOMESTIC FINANCIAL INSTITUTIONS.—Subparagraph (B) of section 861(a)(1) shall not apply.

(2) SUBSTANTIAL UNITED STATES OWNER.—

(A) IN GENERAL.—The term "substantial United States owner" means—

(i) with respect to any corporation, any specified United States person which owns, directly or indirectly, more than 10 percent of the stock of such corporation (by vote or value),

(ii) with respect to any partnership, any specified United States person which owns, directly or indirectly, more than 10 percent of the profits interests or capital interests in such partnership, and

(iii) in the case of a trust—

(I) any specified United States person treated as an owner of any portion of such trust under subpart E of part I of subchapter J of chapter 1, and

(II) to the extent provided by the Secretary in regulations or other guidance, any specified United States person which holds, directly or indirectly, more than 10 percent of the beneficial interests of such trust.

(B) SPECIAL RULE FOR INVESTMENT VEHICLES.—In the case of any financial institution described in section 1471(d)(5)(C), clauses (i), (ii), and (iii) of subparagraph (A) shall be applied by substituting "0 percent" for "10 percent".

(3) SPECIFIED UNITED STATES PERSON.—Except as otherwise provided by the Secretary, the term "specified United States person" means any United States person other than—

(A) any corporation the stock of which is regularly traded on an established securities market,

(B) any corporation which is a member of the same expanded affiliated group (as defined in section 1471(e)(2) without regard to the last sentence thereof) as a corporation the stock of which is regularly traded on an established securities market,

(C) any organization exempt from taxation under section 501(a) or an individual retirement plan,

(D) the United States or any wholly owned agency or instrumentality thereof,

(E) any State, the District of Columbia, any possession of the United States, any political subdivision of any of the foregoing, or any wholly owned agency or instrumentality of any one or more of the foregoing,

(F) any bank (as defined in section 581),

(G) any real estate investment trust (as defined in section 856),

(H) any regulated investment company (as defined in section 851),

(I) any common trust fund (as defined in section 584(a)), and

(J) any trust which—

(i) is exempt from tax under section 664(c), or

(ii) is described in section 4947(a)(1).

(4) WITHHOLDING AGENT.—The term "withholding agent" means all persons, in whatever capacity acting, having the control, receipt, custody, disposal, or payment of any withholdable payment.

(5) FOREIGN ENTITY.—The term "foreign entity" means any entity which is not a United States person.

Amendments

• **2010, Hiring Incentives to Restore Employment Act (P.L. 111-147)**

P.L. 111-147, § 501(a):

Amended [subtitle A of] the Internal Revenue Code of 1986 by inserting after chapter 3 a new chapter 4 (Code Secs. 1471-1474). **Effective** generally for payments made after 12-31-2012. For a special rule, see Act Sec. 501(d)(2), below.

P.L. 111-147, § 501(d)(2), provides:

(2) GRANDFATHERED TREATMENT OF OUTSTANDING OBLIGATIONS.—The amendments made by this section shall not require any amount to be deducted or withheld from any payment under any obligation outstanding on the date which is 2 years after the date of the enactment of this Act or from the gross proceeds from any disposition of such an obligation.

INCOME TAX—RECOVERY OF EXCESSIVE PROFITS

[Sec. 1474]

SEC. 1474. SPECIAL RULES.

[Sec. 1474(a)]

(a) LIABILITY FOR WITHHELD TAX.—Every person required to deduct and withhold any tax under this chapter is hereby made liable for such tax and is hereby indemnified against the claims and demands of any person for the amount of any payments made in accordance with the provisions of this chapter.

[Sec. 1474(b)]

(b) CREDITS AND REFUNDS.—

(1) IN GENERAL.—Except as provided in paragraph (2), the determination of whether any tax deducted and withheld under this chapter results in an overpayment by the beneficial owner of the payment to which such tax is attributable shall be made as if such tax had been deducted and withheld under subchapter A of chapter 3.

(2) SPECIAL RULE WHERE FOREIGN FINANCIAL INSTITUTION IS BENEFICIAL OWNER OF PAYMENT.—

(A) IN GENERAL.—In the case of any tax properly deducted and withheld under section 1471 from a specified financial institution payment—

(i) if the foreign financial institution referred to in subparagraph (B) with respect to such payment is entitled to a reduced rate of tax with respect to such payment by reason of any treaty obligation of the United States—

(I) the amount of any credit or refund with respect to such tax shall not exceed the amount of credit or refund attributable to such reduction in rate, and

(II) no interest shall be allowed or paid with respect to such credit or refund, and

(ii) if such foreign financial institution is not so entitled, no credit or refund shall be allowed or paid with respect to such tax.

(B) SPECIFIED FINANCIAL INSTITUTION PAYMENT.—The term "specified financial institution payment" means any payment if the beneficial owner of such payment is a foreign financial institution.

(3) REQUIREMENT TO IDENTIFY SUBSTANTIAL UNITED STATES OWNERS.—No credit or refund shall be allowed or paid with respect to any tax properly deducted and withheld under this chapter unless the beneficial owner of the payment provides the Secretary such information as the Secretary may require to determine whether such beneficial owner is a United States owned foreign entity (as defined in section 1471(d)(3)) and the identity of any substantial United States owners of such entity.

[Sec. 1474(c)]

(c) CONFIDENTIALITY OF INFORMATION.—

(1) IN GENERAL.—For purposes of this chapter, rules similar to the rules of section 3406(f) shall apply.

(2) DISCLOSURE OF LIST OF PARTICIPATING FOREIGN FINANCIAL INSTITUTIONS PERMITTED.—The identity of a foreign financial institution which meets the requirements of section 1471(b) shall not be treated as return information for purposes of section 6103.

[Sec. 1474(d)]

(d) COORDINATION WITH OTHER WITHHOLDING PROVISIONS.—The Secretary shall provide for the coordination of this chapter with other withholding provisions under this title, including providing for the proper crediting of amounts deducted and withheld under this chapter against amounts required to be deducted and withheld under such other provisions.

[Sec. 1474(e)]

(e) TREATMENT OF WITHHOLDING UNDER AGREEMENTS.—Any tax deducted and withheld pursuant to an agreement described in section 1471(b) shall be treated for purposes of this title as a tax deducted and withheld by a withholding agent under section 1471(a).

[Sec. 1474(f)]

(f) REGULATIONS.—The Secretary shall prescribe such regulations or other guidance as may be necessary or appropriate to carry out the purposes of, and prevent the avoidance of, this chapter.

Amendments

• 2010, Hiring Incentives to Restore Employment Act (P.L. 111-147)

P.L. 111-147, § 501(a):

Amended [subtitle A of] the Internal Revenue Code of 1986 by inserting after chapter 3 a new chapter 4 (Code Secs. 1471-1474). **Effective** generally for payments made after 12-31-2012. For a special rule, see Act Sec. 501(d)(2), below.

P.L. 111-147, § 501(d)(2), provides:

(2) GRANDFATHERED TREATMENT OF OUTSTANDING OBLIGATIONS.—The amendments made by this section shall not require any amount to be deducted or withheld from any payment under any obligation outstanding on the date which is 2 years after the date of the enactment of this Act or from the gross proceeds from any disposition of such an obligation.

CHAPTER 4—RULES APPLICABLE TO RECOVERY OF EXCESSIVE PROFITS ON GOVERNMENT CONTRACTS—[Repealed]

SUBCHAPTER A.   [Repealed]
SUBCHAPTER B.   [Repealed]

[Sec. 1471—Repealed]

Amendments

• 1976, Tax Reform Act of 1976 (P.L. 94-455)

P.L. 94-455, § 1951(b)(13):

Repealed Code Sec. 1471. **Effective** for tax years beginning after 12-31-76. Prior to repeal, Sec. 1471 read as follows:

SEC. 1471. RECOVERY OF EXCESSIVE PROFITS ON GOVERNMENT CONTRACTS.

(a) METHOD OF COLLECTION.—If the amount of profit required to be paid into the Treasury under section 3 of the Act of March 27, 1934, as amended (34 U.S.C. 496), with respect to contracts completed within taxable years subject to this code is not voluntarily paid, the Secretary or his delegate shall collect the same under the methods employed to collect taxes under this subtitle.

(b) LAWS APPLICABLE.—All provisions of law (including penalties) applicable with respect to the taxes imposed by this subtitle and not inconsistent with section 3 of the Act of March 27, 1934, as amended, shall apply with respect to the assessment, collection, or payment of excess profits to the Treasury as provided by subsection (a), and to refunds by the Treasury of overpayments of excess profits into the Treasury.

P.L. 94-455, § 1951(b)(13)(B), provides:

(B) SAVINGS PROVISION.—If the amount of profit required to be paid into the Treasury under section 2382 or 7300 of title 10, United States Code, is not voluntarily paid, the Secretary of the Treasury or his delegate shall collect the same under the methods employed to collect taxes under subtitle A. All provisions of law (including penalties) applicable with respect to such taxes and not inconsistent with section 2382 or 7300 of title 10 of such Code shall apply with respect to the assessment, collection, or payment of excess profits to the Treasury as provided in the preceding sentence, and to refunds by the Treasury of overpayments of excess profits into the Treasury.

INCOME TAX—RECOVERY OF EXCESSIVE PROFITS

[Sec. 1481—Repealed]

Amendments

• **1990, Omnibus Budget Reconciliation Act of 1990 (P.L. 101-508)**

P.L. 101-508, §11801(a)(37):

Repealed Chapter 4. **Effective** 11-5-90.

P.L. 101-508, §11821(b) provides:

(b) SAVINGS PROVISION.—If—

(1) any provision amended or repealed by this part applied to—

(A) any transaction occurring before the date of the enactment of this Act,

(B) any property acquired before such date of enactment, or

(C) any item of income, loss, deduction, or credit taken into account before such date of enactment, and

(2) the treatment of such transaction, property, or item under such provision would (without regard to the amendments made by this part) affect liability for tax for periods ending after such date of enactment,

nothing in the amendments made by this part shall be construed to affect the treatment of such transaction, property, or item for purposes of determining liability for tax for periods ending after such date of enactment.

Prior to repeal, Code Sec. 1481 read as follows:

SEC. 1481. MITIGATION OF EFFECT OF RENEGOTIATION OF GOVERNMENT CONTRACTS.

[Sec. 1481(a)]

(a) REDUCTION FOR PRIOR TAXABLE YEAR.—

(1) EXCESSIVE PROFITS ELIMINATED FOR PRIOR TAXABLE YEAR.—In the case of a contract with the United States or any agency thereof, or any subcontract thereunder, which is made by the taxpayer, if a renegotiation is made in respect of such contract or subcontract and an amount of excessive profits received or accrued under such contract or subcontract for a taxable year (referred to in this section as "prior taxable year") is eliminated and, the taxpayer is required to pay or repay to the United States or any agency thereof the amount of excessive profits eliminated or the amount of excessive profits eliminated is applied as an offset against other amounts due the taxpayer, the part of the contract or subcontract price which was received or was accrued for the prior taxable year shall be reduced by the amount of excessive profits eliminated. For purposes of this section—

(A) The term "renegotiation" includes any transaction which is a renegotiation within the meaning of the Renegotiation Act of 1951, as amended (U.S.C. App. 1211 and following), any modification of one or more contracts with the United States or any agency thereof, and any agreement with the United States or any agency thereof in respect of one or more such contracts or subcontracts thereunder.

(B) The term "excessive profits" includes any amount which constitutes excessive profits within the meaning assigned to such term by the Renegotiation Act of 1951, as amended, any part of the contract price of a contract with the United States or any agency thereof, any part of the subcontract price of a subcontract under such a contract, and any profits derived from one or more such contracts or subcontracts.

(C) The term "subcontract" includes any purchase order or agreement which is a subcontract within the meaning assigned to such term by the Renegotiation Act of 1951, as amended.

(2) REDUCTION OF REIMBURSEMENT FOR PRIOR TAXABLE YEAR.—In the case of a cost-plus-a-fixed-fee contract between the United States or any agency thereof and the taxpayer, if an item for which the taxpayer has been reimbursed is disallowed as an item of cost chargeable to such contract and the taxpayer is required to repay the United States or any agency thereof the amount disallowed or the amount disallowed is applied as an offset against other amounts due the taxpayer, the amount of the reimbursement of the taxpayer under the contract for the taxable year in which the reimbursement for such item was received or was accrued shall be reduced by the amount disallowed.

(3) DEDUCTION DISALLOWED.—The amount of the payment, repayment, or offset described in paragraph (1) or paragraph (2) shall not constitute a deduction for the year in which paid or incurred.

(4) EXCEPTION.—The foregoing provisions of this subsection shall not apply in respect of any contract if the taxpayer shows to the satisfaction of the Secretary that a different method of accounting for the amount of the payment, repayment, or disallowance clearly reflects income, and in such case the payment, repayment, or disallowance shall be accounted for with respect to the taxable year provided for under such method, which for the purposes of subsections (b) and (c) shall be considered a prior taxable year.

Amendments

• **1976, Tax Reform Act of 1976 (P.L. 94-455)**

P.L. 94-455, §1901(a)(157)(A):

Substituted "within the meaning of the Renegotiation Act of 1951, as amended (50 U.S.C. App. 1211 and following)" for "within the meaning of the Federal renegotiation act applicable to such transaction" in Code Sec. 1481(a)(1)(A). **Effective** with respect to tax years beginning after 12-31-76.

P.L. 94-455, §1901(a)(157)(B):

Repealed Code Sec. 1481(a)(1)(D). **Effective** with respect to tax years beginning after 12-31-76. Prior to repeal Code Sec. 1481(a)(1)(D) read as follows:

(D) The term "Federal renegotiation act" includes section 403 of the Sixth Supplemental National Defense Appropriation Act (Public Law 528, 77th Cong., 2d Sess.), as amended or supplemented, the Renegotiation Act of 1948, as amended or supplemented, and the Renegotiation Act of 1951, as amended or supplemented.

P.L. 94-455, §1901(a)(157)(C):

Substituted "Renegotiation Act of 1951, as amended" for "applicable Federal renegotiation act" in Code Sec. 1481(a)(1)(B) and (C). **Effective** with respect to tax years beginning after 12-31-76.

P.L. 94-455, §1906(b)(13)(A):

Amended the 1954 Code by substituting "Secretary" for "Secretary or his delegate" each place it appeared. **Effective** 2-1-77.

[Sec. 1481(b)]

(b) CREDIT AGAINST REPAYMENT ON ACCOUNT OF RENEGOTIATION OR ALLOWANCE.—

(1) GENERAL RULE.—There shall be credited against the amount of excessive profits eliminated the amount by which the tax for the prior taxable year under this subtitle is decreased by reason of the application of paragraph (1) of subsection (a); and there shall be credited against the amount disallowed the amount by which the tax for the prior taxable year under this subtitle is decreased by reason of the application of paragraph (2) of subsection (a).

(2) CREDIT FOR BARRED YEAR.—If at the time of the payment, repayment, or offset described in paragraph (1) or paragraph (2) of subsection (a), refund or credit of tax under this subtitle for the prior taxable year is prevented (except for the provisions of section 1311) by any provision of the internal revenue laws other than section 7122, or by rule of law, the amount by which the tax for such year under this subtitle is decreased by the application of paragraph (1) or paragraph (2) of subsection (a) shall be computed under this paragraph. There shall first be ascertained the tax previously determined for the prior taxable year.. The amount of the tax previously determined shall be the excess of—

(A) the sum of—

(i) the amount shown as the tax by the taxpayer on his return (determined as provided in section 6211 (b) (1), (3), and (4)), if a return was made by the taxpayer and an amount was shown as the tax by the taxpayer thereon, plus

(ii) the amounts previously assessed (or collected without assessment) as a deficiency, over—

(B) the amount of rebates, as defined in section 6211 (b) (2), made.

There shall then be ascertained the decrease in tax previously determined which results solely from the application of paragraph (1) or paragraph (2) of subsection (a) to the prior taxable year. The amount so ascertained, together with any amounts collected as additions to the tax or interest, as a result of paragraph (1) or paragraph (2) of subsection (a) not having been applied to the prior taxable year, shall be the amount by which such tax is decreased.

(3) INTEREST.—In determining the amount of the credit under this subsection no interest shall be allowed with respect to the amount ascertained under paragraph (1); except that if interest is charged by the United States or the agency thereof on account of the disallowance for any period before the date of the payment, repayment, or offset, the credit shall be increased by an amount equal to interest on the amount ascertained under such paragraph at the same rate and for the period (prior to the date of the payment, repayment, or offset) as interest is so charged.

Amendments

• **1965, Excise Tax Reduction Act of 1965 (P.L. 89-44)**

P. L. 89-44, §809(d)(5)(B):

Amended Sec. 1481(b)(2)(A)(i) by substituting "section 6211(b)(1), (3), and (4)" for "section 6211(b)(1) and (3)" in the text thereof. **Effective** 7-1-65.

[Sec. 1481(c)]

(c) CREDIT IN LIEU OF OTHER CREDIT OR REFUND.—If a credit is allowed under subsection (b) with respect to a prior taxable year no other credit or refund under the internal revenue laws founded on the application of subsection (a) shall be made on account of the amount allowed with respect to such taxable year. If the amount allowable as a credit under subsection (b) exceeds the amount allowed under such subsection, the excess shall, for purposes of the internal revenue laws relating to credit or refund of tax, be treated as an overpayment for the prior taxable year which was made at the time the payment, repayment, or offset was made.

[Sec. 1481(d)—Repealed]

Amendments

• **1976, Tax Reform Act of 1976 (P.L. 94-455)**

P.L. 94-455, §1951(b)(14)(A), (B):

Repealed Code Sec. 1481(d). **Effective** with respect to tax years beginning after 12-31-76, except for the savings provision quoted in §1951(b)(14)(B) below. Prior to repeal, Code Sec. 1481(d) read as follows:

(d) RENEGOTIATION OF GOVERNMENT CONTRACTS AFFECTING TAXABLE YEARS PRIOR TO 1954—If a recovery of excessive profits through renegotiation as described in this section relates to profits of a taxable year subject to the Internal Revenue Code of 1939, the adjustments in respect of such renegotiation shall be made under section 3806 of such Code.

P.L. 94-455, §1951(b)(14)(B), provides:

(B) SAVINGS PROVISION.—If, during a taxable year beginning after December 31, 1976, a recovery of excessive profits through renegotiation which relates to profits of a taxable year subject to the Internal Revenue Code of 1939, the adjustments in respect to such renegotiation shall be made under section 3806 of such Code.

[Sec. 1482—Repealed]

Amendments

• **1990, Omnibus Budget Reconciliation Act of 1990 (P.L. 101-508)**

P.L. 101-508, §11801(a)(37):

Repealed Code Sec. 1482. **Effective** 11-5-90.

P.L. 101-508, §11821(b) provides:

(b) SAVINGS PROVISION.—If—

(1) any provision amended or repealed by this part applied to—

(A) any transaction occurring before the date of the enactment of this Act,

INCOME TAX—TAX ON TRANSFERS TO AVOID TAX

(B) any property acquired before such date of enactment, or

(C) any item of income, loss, deduction, or credit taken into account before such date of enactment, and

(2) the treatment of such transaction, property, or item under such provision would (without regard to the amendments made by this part) affect liability for tax for periods ending after such date of enactment,

nothing in the amendments made by this part shall be construed to affect the treatment of such transaction, property, or item for purposes of determining liability for tax for periods ending after such date of enactment.

Prior to repeal, Code Sec. 1482 read as follows:

SEC. 1482. READJUSTMENT FOR REPAYMENTS MADE PURSUANT TO PRICE REDETERMINATIONS.

(a) GENERAL RULE.—If, pursuant to a price redetermination provision in a subcontract to which this section applies, a repayment with respect to an amount paid under the subcontract is made by one party to the subcontract (hereinafter referred to as the "payor") to another party to the subcontract (hereinafter referred to as the "payee"), then—

(1) the tax of the payor for prior taxable years shall be recomputed as if the amount received or accrued by him with respect to which the repayment is made did not include an amount equal to the amount of the repayment, and

(2) the tax of the payee for prior taxable years shall be recomputed as if the amount paid or incurred by him with respect to which the repayment is made did not include an amount equal to the amount of the repayment.

(b) SUBCONTRACTS TO WHICH SECTION APPLIES.—Subsection (a) shall apply only to a subcontract which is subject to renegotiation under the applicable Federal renegotiation act.

(c) LIMITATION.—Subsection (a) shall not apply to any repayment to the extent that section 1481 applies to the amount repaid.

(d) TREATMENT IN YEAR OF REPAYMENT.—The amount of any repayment to which subsection (a) applies shall not be taken into account by the payor or payee for the taxable year in which the repayment is made; but any overpayment or underpayment of tax resulting from the application of subsection (a) shall be treated as if it were an overpayment or underpayment for the taxable year in which the repayment is made.

- **1958, Technical Amendments Act of 1958 (P.L. 85-866)**

P.L. 85-866, §62(a):

Added Sec. 1482. **Effective** only for subcontracts entered into after 12-31-57.

CHAPTER 5—TAX ON TRANSFERS TO AVOID INCOME TAX—[Repealed]

[Sec. 1491—Repealed]

Amendments

- **1997, Taxpayer Relief Act of 1997 (P.L. 105-34)**

P.L. 105-34, §1131(a):

Repealed Chapter 5 (Code Secs. 1491-1494). **Effective** 8-5-97. Prior to repeal, Code Sec. 1491 read as follows:

SEC. 1491. IMPOSITION OF TAX.

There is hereby imposed on the transfer of property by a citizen or resident of the United States, or by a domestic corporation or partnership, or by an estate or trust which is not a foreign estate or trust, to a foreign corporation as paid-in surplus or as a contribution to capital, or to a foreign estate or trust, or to a foreign partnership, an excise tax equal to 35 percent of the excess of—

(1) the fair market value of the property so transferred, over

(2) the sum of—

(A) the adjusted basis (for determining gain) of such property in the hands of the transferor, plus

(B) the amount of the gain recognized to the transferor at the time of the transfer.

If a trust which is not a foreign trust becomes a foreign trust, such trust shall be treated for purposes of this section as having transferred, immediately before becoming a foreign trust, all of its assets to a foreign trust.

- **1996, Small Business Job Protection Act of 1996 (P.L. 104-188)**

P.L. 104-188, §1907(b)(1):

Amended Code Sec. 1491 by adding at the end a new flush sentence. **Effective** 8-20-96.

- **1978, Revenue Act of 1978 (P.L. 95-600)**

P.L. 95-600, §701(u)(14)(A), (C):

Amended Code Sec. 1491, by striking out "trust" each place it appeared and inserting in place thereof "estate or trust". **Effective** for transfers after 10-2-75.

- **1976, Tax Reform Act of 1976 (P.L. 94-455)**

P.L. 94-455, §1015(a):

Amended Code Sec. 1491. **Effective** for transfers of property after 10-2-75. Prior to amendment Code Sec. 1491 read as follows:

There is hereby imposed on the transfer of stock or securities by a citizen or resident of the United States, or by a domestic corporation or partnership, or by a trust which is not a foreign trust, to a foreign corporation as paid-in surplus or as a contribution to capital, or to a foreign trust, or to a foreign partnership, an excise tax equal to $27^1/_2$ percent of the excess of—

(1) the value of the stock of securities so transferred, over

(2) its adjusted basis (for determining gain) in the hands of the transferor.

[Sec. 1492—Repealed]

Amendments

- **1997, Taxpayer Relief Act of 1997 (P.L. 105-34)**

P.L. 105-34, §1131(a):

Repealed Code Sec. 1492. **Effective** 8-5-97. Prior to repeal, Code Sec. 1492 read as follows:

SEC. 1492. NONTAXABLE TRANSFERS.

The tax imposed by section 1491 shall not apply—

(1) If the transferee is an organization exempt from income tax under part I of subchapter F of chapter 1 (other than an organization described in section 401(a)); or

(2) To a transfer—

(A) described in section 367, or

(B) not described in section 367 but with respect to which the taxpayer elects (before the transfer) the application of principles similar to the principles of section 367, or

(3) To a transfer for which an election has been made under section 1057.

- **1984, Deficit Reduction Act of 1984 (P.L. 98-369)**

P.L. 98-369, §131(f)(1):

Amended Code Sec. 1492 by striking out paragraphs (2) and (3) and inserting in lieu thereof new paragraph (2), and by redesignating paragraph (4) as paragraph (3). **Effective** for transfers or exchanges after 12-31-84, in tax years ending after such date. Prior to amendment, paragraphs (2) and (3) read as follows:

(2) If before the transfer it has been established to the satisfaction of the Secretary that such transfer is not in pursuance of a plan having as one of its principal purposes the avoidance of Federal income taxes; or

(3) To a transfer described in section 367; or

- **1978, Revenue Act of 1978 (P.L. 95-600)**

P.L. 95-600, §701(u)(14)(B), (C):

Amended Code Sec. 1492(3). **Effective** for transfers after 10-2-75. Prior to amendment, Code Sec. 1492(3) read:

(3) To a transfer to which section 367 applies; or

- **1976, Tax Reform Act of 1976 (P.L. 94-455)**

P.L. 94-455, §1015(b)(1):

Substituted "section 367 applies; or" for "section 367(d) applies." in Code Sec. 1492(3). **Effective** for transfers of property after 10-2-75.

P.L. 94-455, §1015(b)(2):

Added Code Sec. 1492(4). **Effective** for transfers of property after 10-2-75.

P.L. 94-455, §1906(b)(13)(A):

Amended the 1954 Code by substituting "Secretary" for "Secretary or his delegate" each place it appeared. **Effective** 2-1-77.

- **1971 (P.L. 91-681)**

P.L. 91-681, §1(b):

Amended Code Sec. 1492 by substituting "; or" in place of the period at the end of paragraph (2) and by adding paragraph (3). **Effective** only for transfers made after 12-31-70.

[Sec. 1494—Repealed]

Amendments

- **1997, Taxpayer Relief Act of 1997 (P.L. 105-34)**

P.L. 105-34, §1131(a):

Repealed Code Sec. 1494. **Effective** 8-5-97. Prior to repeal, Code Sec. 1494 read as follows:

SEC. 1494. PAYMENT AND COLLECTION.

[Sec. 1494(a)]

(a) TIME FOR PAYMENT.—The tax imposed by section 1491 shall, without assessment or notice and demand, be due and payable by the transferor at the time of the transfer, and shall be assessed, collected, and paid under regulations prescribed by the Secretary.

- **1976, Tax Reform Act of 1976 (P.L. 94-455)**

P.L. 94-455, §1906(b)(13)(A):

Amended 1954 Code by substituting "Secretary" for "Secretary or his delegate" each place it appeared. **Effective** 2-1-77.

[Sec. 1494(b)]

(b) ABATEMENT OR REFUND.—Under regulations prescribed by the Secretary, the tax may be abated, remitted, or refunded if the taxpayer, after the transfer, elects the application of principles similar to the principles of section 367.

INCOME TAX—CONSOLIDATED RETURNS

Amendments

● **1984, Deficit Reduction Act of 1984 (P.L. 98-369)**

P.L. 98-369, § 131(f)(2):

Amended Code Sec. 1494(b). **Effective** for transfers or exchanges after 12-31-84, in tax years ending after such date. Prior to amendment, Code Sec. 1494(b) read as follows:

(b) ABATEMENT OR REFUND.—Under regulations prescribed by the Secretary, the tax may be abated, remitted, or refunded if after the transfer it has been established to the satisfaction of the Secretary that such transfer was not in pursuance of a plan having as one of its principal purposes the avoidance of Federal income taxes.

● **1976, Tax Reform Act of 1976 (P.L. 94-455)**

P.L. 94-455, § 1906(b)(13)(A):

Amended 1954 Code by substituting "Secretary" for "Secretary or his delegate" each place it appeared. **Effective** 2-1-77.

[Sec. 1494(c)]

(c) PENALTY.—In the case of any failure to file a return required by the Secretary with respect to any transfer described in section 1491, the person required to file such return shall be liable for the penalties provided in section 6677 in the same manner as if such failure were a failure to file a notice under section 6048(a).

Amendments

● **1996, Small Business Job Protection Act of 1996 (P.L. 104-188)**

P.L. 104-188, § 1902(a):

Amended Code Sec. 1494 by adding at the end a new subsection (c). **Effective** for transfers after 8-20-96.

CHAPTER 6—CONSOLIDATED RETURNS

SUBCHAPTER A.   Returns and payment of tax.
SUBCHAPTER B.   Related rules.

Subchapter A—Returns and Payment of Tax

Sec. 1501.   Privilege to file consolidated returns.
Sec. 1502.   Regulations.
Sec. 1503.   Computation and payment of tax.
Sec. 1504.   Definitions.
Sec. 1505.   Cross references.

[Sec. 1501]

SEC. 1501. PRIVILEGE TO FILE CONSOLIDATED RETURNS.

An affiliated group of corporations shall, subject to the provisions of this chapter, have the privilege of making a consolidated return with respect to the income tax imposed by chapter 1 for the taxable year in lieu of separate returns. The making of a consolidated return shall be upon the condition that all corporations which at any time during the taxable year have been members of the affiliated group consent to all the consolidated return regulations prescribed under section 1502 prior to the last day prescribed by law for the filing of such return. The making of a consolidated return shall be considered as such consent. In the case of a corporation which is a member of the affiliated group for a fractional part of the year, the consolidated return shall include the income of such corporation for such part of the year as it is a member of the affiliated group.

[Sec. 1502]

SEC. 1502. REGULATIONS.

The Secretary shall prescribe such regulations as he may deem necessary in order that the tax liability of any affiliated group of corporations making a consolidated return and of each corporation in the group, both during and after the period of affiliation, may be returned, determined, computed, assessed, collected, and adjusted, in such manner as clearly to reflect the income tax liability and the various factors necessary for the determination of such liability, and in order to prevent avoidance of such tax liability. In carrying out the preceding sentence, the Secretary may prescribe rules that are different from the provisions of chapter 1 that would apply if such corporations filed separate returns.

Amendments

● **2004, American Jobs Creation Act of 2004 (P.L. 108-357)**

P.L. 108-357, § 844(a):

Amended Code Sec. 1502 by adding at the end a new sentence. **Effective** for tax years beginning before, on, or after 10-22-2004. For a special rule, see Act Sec. 844(b), below.

P.L. 108-357, § 844(b), provides:

(b) RESULT NOT OVERTURNED.—Notwithstanding the amendment made by subsection (a), the Internal Revenue Code of 1986 shall be construed by treating Treasury Regulation § 1.1502-20(c)(1)(iii) (as in effect on January 1, 2001) as being inapplicable to the factual situation in Rite Aid Corporation and Subsidiary Corporations v. United States, 255 F.3d 1357 (Fed. Cir. 2001).

● **1976, Tax Reform Act of 1976 (P.L. 94-455)**

P.L. 94-455, § 1906(b)(13)(A):

Amended 1954 Code by substituting "Secretary" for "Secretary or his delegate" each place it appeared. **Effective** 2-1-77.

[Sec. 1503]

SEC. 1503. COMPUTATION AND PAYMENT OF TAX.

[Sec. 1503(a)]

(a) GENERAL RULE.—In any case in which a consolidated return is made or is required to be made, the tax shall be determined, computed, assessed, collected, and adjusted in accordance with the regulations under section 1502 prescribed before the last day prescribed by law for the filing of such return.

[Sec. 1503(b)—Repealed]

Amendments

● **1976, Tax Reform Act of 1976 (P.L. 94-455)**

P.L. 94-455, § 1052(c)(5):

Repealed Code Sec. 1503(b). Prior to repeal, Code Sec. 1503(b) read as follows:

(b) SPECIAL RULE FOR APPLICATION OF FOREIGN TAX CREDIT WHEN OVERALL LIMITATION APPLIES.—

(1) IN GENERAL.—If the affiliated group includes one or more Western Hemisphere trade corporations (as defined in section 921), then the amount of taxes paid or accrued to foreign countries and possessions of the United States by such Western Hemisphere trade corporations which may be taken into account for purposes of section 901 shall be reduced by the amount (if any) by which—

(A) the amount of such taxes (or, if smaller, the amount of the tax which would be computed under subsection (a), if such corporations were not Western Hemisphere trade corporations, with respect to the portion of the consolidated taxable income attributable to such corporations), exceeds

(B) the amount of the tax computed under subsection (a) with respect to the portion of the consolidated taxable income attributable to such corporations.

(2) ADJUSTMENT IN CASE OF CERTAIN PUBLIC UTILITIES.—So much of any reduction under paragraph (1) as is attributable to taxes paid or accrued to foreign countries and possessions of the United States by one or more corporations which are both Western Hemisphere trade corporations and regulated public utilities shall be decreased by the excess of—

(A) the amount of tax computed under subsection (a) with respect to the portion of the consolidated taxable income attributable to income derived, by the corporations in the affiliated group which are not Western Hemisphere trade corporations, from sources within the foreign countries referred to in paragraph (3) (B), over

(B) the amount of taxes paid or accrued to such foreign countries by the corporations referred to in subparagraph (A).

This paragraph shall apply only if the corporations described in subparagraph (A) derive 80 percent or more, of the gross income (computed without regard to capital

INCOME TAX—CONSOLIDATED RETURNS

gains and losses) which they derive from sources within the foreign countries described in paragraph (3)(B), from regulated public utilities and from operations as regulated public utilities.

(3) SPECIAL RULES.—

(A) For purposes of paragraph (2), a corporation is a regulated public utility only if it is a regulated public utility within the meaning of subparagraph (A) (other than clauses (ii) and (iii) thereof) or (D) of section 7701(a)(33). For purposes of the preceding sentence, the limitation contained in the last two sentences of section 7701(a)(33) shall be applied as if subparagraphs (A) through (F), inclusive, of section 7701(a)(33) were limited to subparagraphs (A)(i) and (D) thereof.

(B) For purposes of paragraph (2), the foreign countries referred to in this subparagraph include only any country from which any public utility referred to in the first sentence of paragraph (2) derives the principal part of its income.

[Sec. 1503(c)[b]]

(c) [b] SPECIAL RULE FOR APPLICATION OF CERTAIN LOSSES AGAINST INCOME OF INSURANCE COMPANIES TAXED UNDER SECTION 801.—

(1) IN GENERAL.—If an election under section 1504(c)(2) is in effect for the taxable year and the consolidated taxable income of the members of the group not taxed under section 801 results in a consolidated net operating loss for such taxable year, then under regulations prescribed by the Secretary, the amount of such loss which cannot be absorbed in the applicable carryback periods against the taxable income of such members not taxed under section 801 shall be taken into account in determining the consolidated taxable income of the affiliated group for such taxable year to the extent of 35 percent of such loss or 35 percent of the taxable income of the members taxed under section 801, whichever is less. The unused portion of such loss shall be available as a carryover, subject to the same limitations (applicable to the sum of the loss for the carryover year and the loss (or losses) carried over to such year), in applicable carryover years.

(2) LOSSES OF RECENT NONLIFE AFFILIATES.—Notwithstanding the provisions of paragraph (1), a net operating loss for a taxable year of a member of the group not taxed under section 801 shall not be taken into account in determining the taxable income of a member taxed under section 801 (either for the taxable year or as a carryover or carryback) if such taxable year precedes the sixth taxable year such members have been members of the same affiliated group (determined without regard to section 1504(b)(2)).

Amendments

- **1990, Omnibus Budget Reconciliation Act of 1990 (P.L. 101-508)**

P.L. 101-508, §11802(f)(4):

Amended Code Sec. 1503(c)(1) by striking the last two sentences. **Effective** 11-5-90. Prior to repeal, the last two sentences of Code Sec. 1503(c)(1) read as follows:

For taxable years ending with or within calendar year 1981, "25 percent" shall be substituted for "35 percent" each place it appears in the first sentence of this subsection. For taxable years ending with or within calendar year 1982, "30 percent" shall be substituted for "35 percent" each place it appears in that sentence.

P.L. 101-508, §11821(b) provides:

(b) SAVINGS PROVISION.—If—

(1) any provision amended or repealed by this part applied to—

(A) any transaction occurring before the date of the enactment of this Act,

(B) any property acquired before such date of enactment, or

(C) any item of income, loss, deduction, or credit taken into account before such date of enactment, and

(2) the treatment of such transaction, property, or item under such provision would (without regard to the amendments made by this part) affect liability for tax for periods ending after such date of enactment,

nothing in the amendments made by this part shall be construed to affect the treatment of such transaction, property, or item for purposes of determining liability for tax for periods ending after such date of enactment.

- **1984, Deficit Reduction Act of 1984 (P.L. 98-369)**

P.L. 98-369, §211(b)(19)(A):

Amended Code Sec. 1503(c) by striking out "section 802" each place it appeared and inserting in lieu thereof "section 801". **Effective** for tax years beginning after 12-31-83.

P.L. 98-369, §211(b)(19)(B):

Amended Code Sec. 1503(c)(1) by striking out the third sentence. **Effective** for tax years beginning after 12-31-83. Prior to its deletion, the third sentence of Code Sec. 1503(c)(1) read as follows:

For purposes of this subsection, in determining the taxable income of each insurance company subject to tax under section 802, section 802(b)(3) shall not be taken into account.

P.L. 98-369, §211(b)(19)(C):

Amended the subsection heading of Code Sec. 1503(c) by striking out "Section 802" and inserting in lieu thereof "Section 801". **Effective** for tax years beginning after 12-31-83.

- **1976, Tax Reform Act of 1976 (P.L. 94-455)**

P.L. 94-455, §1031(b)(4):

Deleted ", and if for the taxable year an election under section 904(b)(1) (relating to election of overall limitation on foreign tax credit) is in effect" as appearing after "(as defined in section 921)" in Code Sec. 1503(b)(1). **Effective** for tax years beginning after 12-31-75, except for certain mining operations and income from possessions (see §1031(c) in the historical note to Code Sec. 1351(d)).

P.L. 94-455, §1052(c)(5):

Amended Code Sec. 1503 by striking out "(a) General Rule—" and by striking out Code Sec. 1503(b). **Effective** with respect to tax years beginning after 12-31-79.

P.L. 94-455, §1507(b)(3):

Added Code Sec. 1503(c). **Effective** for tax years beginning after 12-31-80, but see transition rules of §1507(c)(2), below.

P.L. 94-455, §1507(c)(2) provides:

(2) TRANSITION RULES WITH RESPECT TO CARRYOVERS OR CARRYBACKS RELATING TO PRE-ELECTION TAXABLE YEARS AND NONTERMINATION OF GROUP.—

(A) LIMITATIONS ON CARRYOVERS OR CARRYBACKS FOR GROUPS ELECTING UNDER SECTION 1504(c)(2).—If an affiliated group elects to file a consolidated return pursuant to section 1504(c)(2) of the Internal Revenue Code of 1954, a carryover of a loss or credit from a taxable year ending before January 1, 1981, and losses or credits which may be carried back to taxable years ending before such date shall be taken into account as if this section had not been enacted.

(B) NONTERMINATION OF AFFILIATED GROUP.—The mere election to file a consolidated return pursuant to such section 1504(c)(2) shall not cause the termination of an affiliated group filing consolidated returns.

P.L. 94-455, §1901(b)(1)(Y):

Repealed Code Sec. 1503(b)(3)(C). **Effective** with respect to tax years beginning after 12-31-76. Prior to repeal Code Sec. 1503(b)(3)(C) read as follows:

(C) For purposes of this subsection, the term "consolidated taxable income" means the consolidated taxable income computed without regard to the deduction provided by section 242 for partially tax-exempt interest.

- **1964, Revenue Act of 1964 (P.L. 88-272)**

P.L. 88-272, §234(a):

Amended Code Sec. 1503(a). **Effective** with respect to tax years beginning after 12-31-63. Prior to amendment, subsection (a) read as follows:

"(a) General Rule.—In any case in which a consolidated return is made or is required to be made, the tax shall be determined, computed, assessed, collected, and adjusted in accordance with the regulations under section 1502 prescribed prior to the last day prescribed by law for the filing of such return; except that the tax imposed under section 11(c) or section 831 shall be increased for any taxable year by 2 percent of the consolidated taxable income of the affiliated group of includible corporations. For purposes of this section, the term "consolidated taxable income" means the consolidated taxable income computed without regard to the deduction provided by section 242 for partially tax-exempt interest."

P.L. 88-272, §234(b)(1), (2):

Amended Code Sec. 1503 by deleting subsections (b) and (c) by redesignating subsection (d) as (b), and by amending paragraph (3) of subsection (b), as redesignated. **Effective** with respect to tax years beginning after 12-31-63. Prior to amendment, old subsections (b) and (c) and redesignated paragraph (b)(3) read as follows:

"(b) Limitation.—If the affiliated group includes one or more Western Hemisphere trade corporations (as defined in section 921) or one or more regulated public utilities (as defined in subsection (c)), the increase of 2 percent provided in subsection (a) shall be applied only on the amount by which the consolidated taxable income of the affiliated group exceeds the portion (if any) of the consolidated taxable income attributable to the Western Hemisphere trade corporations and regulated public utilities included in such group."

"(c) Regulated Public Utility Defined.—

"(1) In general.—For purposes of subsection (b), the term 'regulated public utility' means—

"(A) A corporation engaged in the furnishing or sale of—

"(i) electric energy, gas, water, or sewerage disposal services, or

"(ii) transportation (not included in subparagraph (C) on an intrastate, suburban, municipal, or interurban electric railroad, on an intrastate, municipal, or suburban trackless trolley system, or on a municipal or suburban bus system, or

"(iii) transportation (not included in clause (ii)) by motor vehicle—

if the rates for such furnishing or sale, as the case may be, have been established or approved by a State or political subdivision thereof, by an agency or instrumentality of the United States, by a public service or public utility commission or other similar body of the District of Columbia or of any State or political subdivision thereof, or by a foreign country or an agency or instrumentality or political subdivision thereof.

"(B) A corporation engaged as a common carrier in the furnishing or sale of transportation of gas by pipe line, if subject to the jurisdiction of the Federal Power Commission.

"(C) A corporation engaged as a common carrier (i) in the furnishing or sale of transportation by railroad, if subject to the jurisdiction of the Interstate Commerce Commission, or (ii) in the furnishing or sale of transportation of oil or other petroleum products (including shale oil) by pipe line, if subject to the jurisdiction of the Interstate Commerce Commission or if the rates for such furnishing or sale are subject to the jurisdiction of a public service or public utility commission or other similar body of the District of Columbia or of any State.

"(D) A corporation engaged in the furnishing or sale of telephone or telegraph service, if the rates for such furnishing or sale meet the requirements of subparagraph (A).

"(E) A corporation engaged in the furnishing or sale of transportation as a common carrier by air, subject to the jurisdiction of the Civil Aeronautics Board.

INCOME TAX—CONSOLIDATED RETURNS

"(F) A corporation engaged in the furnishing or sale of transportation by common carrier by water, subject to the jurisdiction of the Interstate Commerce Commission under part III of the Interstate Commerce Act, or subject to the jurisdiction of the Federal Maritime Board under the Intercoastal Shipping Act, 1933.

"(2) Limitation.—For purposes of subsection (b), the term 'regulated public utility' does not (except as provided in paragraph (3)) include a corporation described in paragraph (1) unless 80 percent or more of its gross income (computed without regard to dividends and capital gains and losses) for the taxable year is derived from sources described in paragraph (1). If the taxpayer establishes to the satisfaction of the Secretary or his delegate that—

"(A) its revenue from regulated rates described in paragraph (1)(A) or (D) and its revenue derived from unregulated rates are derived from its operation of a single interconnected and coordinated system or from the operation of more than one such system, and

"(B) the unregulated rates have been and are substantially as favorable to users and consumers as are the regulated rates.

such revenue from such unregulated rates shall be considered, for purposes of this paragraph, as income derived from sources described in paragraph (1)(A) or (D).

"(3) Certain railroad corporations.—

"(A) Lessor corporation.—For purposes of subsection (b), the term 'regulated public utility' shall also include a railroad corporation subject to part I of the Interstate Commerce Act, if (i) substantially all of its railroad properties have been leased to another such railroad corporation or corporations by an agreement or agreements entered into prior to January 1, 1954, (ii) each lease is for a term of more than 20 years, and (iii) at least 80 percent or more of its gross income (computed without regard to dividends and capital gains and losses) for the taxable year is derived from such leases and from sources described in paragraph (1). For purposes of the preceding sentence, an agreement for lease of railroad properties entered into prior to January 1, 1954, shall be considered to be a lease including such term as the total number of years of such agreement may, unless sooner terminated, be renewed or continued under the terms of the agreement, and any such renewal or continuance under such agreement shall be considered part of the lease entered into prior to January 1, 1954.

"(B) Common parent corporation.—For purposes of subsection (b), the term 'regulated public utility' also includes a common parent corporation which is a common carrier by railroad subject to part I of the Interstate Commerce Act if at least 80 percent of its gross income (computed without regard to capital gains or losses) is derived directly or indirectly from sources described in paragraph (1). For purposes of the preceding sentence, dividends and interest, and income from leases described in subparagraph (A), received from a regulated public utility shall be considered as derived from sources described in paragraph (1) if the regulated public utility is a member of an affiliated group (as defined in section 1504) which includes the common parent corporation."

[Sec. 1503(d) [now (b)](3)]

"(3) Special rules.—

"(A) For purposes of paragraph (2), a corporation is a regulated public utility only if it is a regulated public utility within the meaning of subparagraph (A) (other than clauses (ii) and (iii) thereof) or (D) of subsection (c)(1). For purposes of the preceding sentence, subsection (c)(2) shall be applied as if subsection (c)(1) were limited to subparagraphs (A)(i) and (D) thereof.

"(B) For purposes of paragraph (2), the foreign countries referred to in this subparagraph include only any country from which any public utility referred to in the first sentence of paragraph (2) derives the principal part of its income.

"(C) For purposes of paragraph (1)(A), the amount of tax which would be computed with respect to the portion of the consolidated taxable income attributable to any corporation or corporations shall be determined without regard to the increase of 2 percent provided in subsection (a)."

• 1960 (P.L. 86-780)

P.L. 86-780, §2:

Added subsection (d) now (b). **Effective** for tax years beginning after 12-31-60.

[Sec. 1503(d)[c]]

(d) [c] DUAL CONSOLIDATED LOSS.—

(1) IN GENERAL.—The dual consolidated loss for any taxable year of any corporation shall not be allowed to reduce the taxable income of any other member of the affiliated group for the taxable year or any other taxable year.

(2) DUAL CONSOLIDATED LOSS.—For purposes of this section—

(A) IN GENERAL.—Except as provided in subparagraph (B), the term "dual consolidated loss" means any net operating loss of a domestic corporation which is subject to an income tax of a foreign country on its income without regard to whether such income is from sources in or outside of such foreign country, or is subject to such a tax on a residence basis.

(B) SPECIAL RULE WHERE LOSS NOT USED UNDER FOREIGN LAW.—To the extent provided in regulations, the term "dual consolidated loss" shall not include any loss which, under the foreign income tax law, does not offset the income of any foreign corporation.

(3) TREATMENT OF LOSSES OF SEPARATE BUSINESS UNITS.—To the extent provided in regulations, any loss of a separate unit of a domestic corporation shall be subject to the limitations of this subsection in the same manner as if such unit were a wholly owned subsidiary of such corporation.

(4) INCOME ON ASSETS ACQUIRED AFTER THE LOSS.—The Secretary shall prescribe such regulations as may be necessary or appropriate to prevent the avoidance of the purposes of this subsection by contributing assets to the corporation with the dual consolidated loss after such loss was sustained.

Amendments

• 1988, Technical and Miscellaneous Revenue Act of 1988 (P.L. 100-647)

P.L. 100-647, §1012(u):

Amended Code Sec. 1503(d)[c] by adding at the end thereof new paragraphs (3)-(4). **Effective** as if included in the provision of P.L. 99-514 to which it relates.

• 1986, Tax Reform Act of 1986 (P.L. 99-514)

P.L. 99-514, §1249(a):

Added new subsection 1503(d)[c]. **Effective** for net operating losses for tax years beginning after 12-31-86.

[Sec. 1503(e)[d]]

(e) [d] SPECIAL RULE FOR DETERMINING ADJUSTMENTS TO BASIS.—

(1) IN GENERAL.—Solely for purposes of determining gain or loss on the disposition of intragroup stock and the amount of any inclusion by reason of an excess loss account, in determining the adjustments to the basis of such intragroup stock on account of the earnings and profits of any member of an affiliated group for any consolidated year (and in determining the amount in such account)—

(A) such earnings and profits shall be determined as if section 312 were applied for such taxable year (and all preceding consolidated years of the member with respect to such group) without regard to subsections (k) and (n) thereof, and

(B) earnings and profits shall not include any amount excluded from gross income under section 108 to the extent the amount so excluded was not applied to reduce tax attributes (other than basis in property).

(2) DEFINITIONS.—For purposes of this subsection—

(A) INTRAGROUP STOCK.—The term "intragroup stock" means any stock which—

(i) is in a corporation which is or was a member of an affiliated group of corporations, and

(ii) is held by another corporation which is or was a member of such group.

Such term includes any other property the basis of which is determined (in whole or in part) by reference to the basis of stock described in the preceding sentence.

(B) CONSOLIDATED YEAR.—The term "consolidated year" means any taxable year for which the affiliated group makes a consolidated return.

(C) APPLICATION OF SECTION 312(n)(7) NOT AFFECTED.—The reference in paragraph (1) to subsection (n) of section 312 shall be treated as not including a reference to paragraph (7) of such subsection.

(3) ADJUSTMENTS.—Under regulations prescribed by the Secretary, proper adjustments shall be made in the application of paragraph (1)—

(A) in the case of any property acquired by the corporation before consolidation, for the difference between the adjusted basis of such property for purposes of computing taxable income and its adjusted basis for purposes of computing earnings and profits, and

(B) in the case of any property, for any basis adjustment under section 50(c).

INCOME TAX—CONSOLIDATED RETURNS

(4) ELIMINATION OF ELECTION TO REDUCE BASIS OF INDEBTEDNESS.—Nothing in the regulations prescribed under section 1502 shall permit any reduction in the amount otherwise included in gross income by reason of an excess loss account if such reduction is on account of a reduction in the basis of indebtedness.

Amendments

• **1990, Omnibus Budget Reconciliation Act of 1990 (P.L. 101-508)**

P.L. 101-508, §11813(b)(25):

Amended Code Sec. 1503(e)(3)(B) by striking "section 48(q)" and inserting "section 50(c)". **Effective**, generally, for property placed in service after 12-31-90. However, for exceptions, see Act Sec. 11813(c)(2) below.

P.L. 101-508, §11813(c)(2) provides:

(2) EXCEPTIONS.—The amendments made by this section shall not apply to—

(A) any transition property (as defined in section 49(e) of the Internal Revenue Code of 1986 (as in effect on the day before the date of the enactment of this Act)),

(B) any property with respect to which qualified progress expenditures were previously taken into account under section 46(d) of such Code (as so in effect), and

(C) any property described in section 46(b)(2)(C) of such Code (as so in effect).

• **1989, Omnibus Budget Reconciliation Act of 1989 (P.L. 101-239)**

P.L. 101-239, §7207(a):

Amended Code Sec. 1503(e) by adding at the end thereof a new paragraph (4). **Effective**, generally, for dispositions after 7-10-89, in tax years ending after such date. However, for an exception, see Act Sec. 7207(b)(2), below.

P.L. 101-239, §7207(b)(2) provides:

(2) BINDING CONTRACT.—The amendment made by subsection (a) shall not apply to any disposition pursuant to a written binding contract in effect on July 10, 1989, and at all times thereafter before such disposition.

P.L. 101-239, §7821(c):

Amended Code Sec. 1503(e)(2)(A)(ii) by striking "another member" and inserting "another corporation which is or was a member". **Effective** as if included in the provision of P.L. 100-203 to which it relates.

• **1988, Technical and Miscellaneous Revenue Act of 1988 (P.L. 100-647)**

P.L. 100-647, §2004(j)(1)(A):

Amended Code Sec. 1503(e)[d](1) by striking out so much of such paragraph as precedes subparagraph (A) thereof and inserting new material to precede subparagraph (A). **Effective** as if included in the provision of P.L. 100-203 to which it relates. Prior to amendment, the material preceding subparagraph (A) in Code Sec. 1503(e)[d](1) read as follows:

(1) IN GENERAL.—Solely for purposes of determining gain or loss on the disposition of intragroup stock, in determining the adjustments to the basis of such intragroup stock on account of the earnings and profits of any member of an affiliated group for any consolidated year—

P.L. 100-647, §2004(j)(2):

Amended Code Sec. 1503(e)[d] by adding at the end thereof a new paragraph (3). **Effective** as if included in the provision of P.L. 100-203 to which it relates.

P.L. 100-647, §2004(j)(3)(A):

Amended Code Sec. 1503(e)[d](2) by adding at the end thereof a new subparagraph (C). **Effective** as if included in the provision of P.L. 100-203 to which it relates.

• **1987, Revenue Act of 1987 (P.L. 100-203)**

P.L. 100-203, §10222(a)(1):

Amended Code Sec. 1503 by adding at the end thereof new subsection (e)[d]. **Effective** as specified in Act Sec. 10222(a)(2), below.

P.L. 100-203, §10222(a)(2), as amended by P.L. 100-647, §2004(j)(1)(B), provides:

(2) EFFECTIVE DATE.—

(A) IN GENERAL.—Except as provided in subparagraph (B), the amendment made by paragraph (1) shall apply to any intragroup stock disposed of after December 15, 1987. For purposes of determining the adjustments to the basis of such stock, such amendment shall be deemed to have been [in] effect for all periods whether before, on, or after December 15, 1987.

(B) EXCEPTION.—The amendment made by paragraph (1) shall not apply to any intragroup stock disposed of after December 15, 1987, and before January 1, 1989, if such disposition is pursuant to a written binding contract, governmental order, letter of intent or preliminary agreement, or stock acquisition agreement, in effect on or before December 15, 1987.

(C) TREATMENT OF CERTAIN EXCESS LOSS ACCOUNTS.—

(i) IN GENERAL.—If—

(I) any disposition on or before December 15, 1987, of stock resulted in an inclusion of an excess loss account (or would have so resulted if the amendments made by paragraph (1) had applied to such disposition), and

(II) there is an unrecaptured amount with respect to such disposition,

the portion of such unrecaptured amount allocable to stock disposed of in a disposition to which the amendment made by paragraph (1) applies shall be taken into account as negative basis. To the extent permitted by the Secretary of the Treasury or his delegate, the preceding sentence shall not apply to the extent the taxpayer elects to reduce its basis in indebtedness of the corporation with respect to which there would have been an excess loss account.

(ii) SPECIAL RULES.—For purposes of this subparagraph—

(I) UNRECAPTURED AMOUNT.—The term "unrecaptured amount" means the amount by which the inclusion referred to in clause (i)(I) would have been increased if the amendment made by paragraph (1) had applied to the disposition.

(II) COORDINATION WITH BINDING CONTRACT EXCEPTION.—A disposition shall be treated as occurring on or before December 15, 1987, if the amendment made by paragraph (1) does not apply to such disposition by reason of subparagraph (B).

[Sec. 1503(f)[e]]

(f) [e] LIMITATION ON USE OF GROUP LOSSES TO OFFSET INCOME OF SUBSIDIARY PAYING PREFERRED DIVIDENDS.—

(1) IN GENERAL.—In the case of any subsidiary distributing during any taxable year dividends on any applicable preferred stock—

(A) no group loss item shall be allowed to reduce the disqualified separately computed income of such subsidiary for such taxable year, and

(B) no group credit item shall be allowed against the tax imposed by this chapter on such disqualified separately computed income.

(2) GROUP ITEMS.—For purposes of this subsection—

(A) GROUP LOSS ITEM.—The term "group loss item" means any of the following items of any other member of the affiliated group which includes the subsidiary:

(i) Any net operating loss and any net operating loss carryover or carryback under section 172.

(ii) Any loss from the sale or exchange of any capital asset and any capital loss carryover or carryback under section 1212.

(B) GROUP CREDIT ITEM.—The term "group credit item" means any credit allowable under part IV of subchapter A of chapter 1 (other than section 34) to any other member of the affiliated group which includes the subsidiary and any carryover or carryback of any such credit.

(3) OTHER DEFINITIONS.—For purposes of this subsection—

(A) DISQUALIFIED SEPARATELY COMPUTED INCOME.—The term "disqualified separately computed income" means the portion of the separately computed taxable income of the subsidiary which does not exceed the dividends distributed by the subsidiary during the taxable year on applicable preferred stock.

(B) SEPARATELY COMPUTED TAXABLE INCOME.—The term "separately computed taxable income" means the separate taxable income of the subsidiary for the taxable year determined—

(i) by taking into account gains and losses from the sale or exchange of a capital asset and section 1231 gains and losses,

(ii) without regard to any net operating loss or capital loss carryover or carryback, and

(iii) with such adjustments as the Secretary may prescribe.

(C) SUBSIDIARY.—The term "subsidiary" means any corporation which is a member of an affiliated group filing a consolidated return other than the common parent.

(D) APPLICABLE PREFERRED STOCK.—The term "applicable preferred stock" means stock described in section 1504(a)(4) in the subsidiary which is—

(i) issued after November 17, 1989, and

(ii) held by a person other than a member of the same affiliated group as the subsidiary.

(4) REGULATIONS.—The Secretary shall prescribe such regulations as may be necessary or appropriate to carry out the provisions of this subsection, including regulations—

INCOME TAX—CONSOLIDATED RETURNS

(A) to prevent the avoidance of this subsection through the transfer of built-in losses to the subsidiary,

(B) to provide rules for cases in which the subsidiary owns (directly or indirectly) stock in another member of the affiliated group, and

(C) to provide for the application of this subsection where dividends are not paid currently, where the redemption and liquidation rights of the applicable preferred stock exceed the issue price for such stock, or where the stock is otherwise structured to avoid the purposes of this subsection.

Amendments

• **1989, Omnibus Budget Reconciliation Act of 1989 (P.L. 101-239)**

P.L. 101-239, §7201(a):

Amended Code Sec. 1503 by adding at the end thereof a new subsection (f)[e]. **Effective,** generally, for tax years ending after 11-17-89. However, for special rules, see Act Sec. 7201(b)(2)-(6), below.

P.L. 101-239, §7201(b)(2)-(6) provides:

(2) BINDING CONTRACT EXCEPTION.—For purposes of section 1503(f)(3)(D) of the Internal Revenue Code of 1986, stock issued after November 17, 1989, pursuant to a written binding contract in effect on November 17, 1989, and at all times thereafter before such issuance, shall be treated as issue on November 17, 1989.

(3) SPECIAL RULE WHEN SUBSIDIARY LEAVES GROUP.—If, by reason of a transaction after November 17, 1989, a corporation ceases to be, or becomes, a member of an affiliated group, the stock of such corporation shall be treated, for purposes of section 1503(f)(3)(D) of such Code, as issued on the date of such cessation or commencement, unless such transaction is of a kind which would not result in the recognition of any deferred intercompany gain under the consolidated return regulations by reason of the acquisition of the entire group.

(4) RETIRED STOCK.—

(A) Except as provided in subparagraph (B), if stock issued before November 18, 1989, (or described in paragraph (2)), is retired or acquired after November 17, 1989, by the corporation or another member of the same affiliated group, such stock shall be treated, for purposes of section 1503(f)(3)(D) of such Code, as issued on the date of such retirement or acquisition.

(B) Subparagraph (A) shall not apply to any retirement or acquisition pursuant to any obligation to reissue under a binding written contract in effect on November 17, 1989, and at all times thereafter before such retirement or acquisition.

(5) AUCTION RATE PREFERRED.—For purposes of section 1503(f)(3)(D) of such Code, auction rate preferred stock shall be treated as issued when the contract requiring the auction became binding.

(6) SPECIAL RULE FOR CERTAIN AUCTION RATE PREFERRED.—For purposes of section 1503(f)(3)(D) of the Internal Revenue Code of 1986, any auction rate preferred stock shall be treated as issued before November 18, 1989, if—

(A) a subsidiary was incorporated before July 10, 1989 for the special purpose of issuing such stock,

(B) a rating agency was retained before July 10, 1989, and

(C) such stock is issued before the date 30 days after the date of the enactment of this Act.

[Sec. 1504]

SEC. 1504. DEFINITIONS.

[Sec. 1504(a)]

(a) AFFILIATED GROUP DEFINED.—For purposes of this subtitle—

(1) IN GENERAL.—The term "affiliated group" means—

(A) 1 or more chains of includible corporations connected through stock ownership with a common parent corporation which is an includible corporation, but only if—

(B) (i) the common parent owns directly stock meeting the requirements of paragraph (2) in at least 1 of the other includible corporations, and

(ii) stock meeting the requirements of paragraph (2) in each of the includible corporations (except the common parent) is owned directly by 1 or more of the other includible corporations.

(2) 80-PERCENT VOTING AND VALUE TEST.—The ownership of stock of any corporation meets the requirements of this paragraph if it—

(A) possesses at least 80 percent of the total voting power of the stock of such corporation, and

(B) has a value equal to at least 80 percent of the total value of the stock of such corporation.

(3) 5 YEARS MUST ELAPSE BEFORE RECONSOLIDATION.—

(A) IN GENERAL.—If—

(i) a corporation is included (or required to be included) in a consolidated return filed by an affiliated group, and

(ii) such corporation ceases to be a member of such group,

with respect to periods after such cessation, such corporation (and any successor of such corporation) may not be included in any consolidated return filed by the affiliated group (or by another affiliated group with the same common parent or a successor of such common parent) before the 61st month beginning after its first taxable year in which it ceased to be a member of such affiliated group.

(B) SECRETARY MAY WAIVE APPLICATION OF SUBPARAGRAPH (A).—The Secretary may waive the application of subparagraph (A) to any corporation for any period subject to such conditions as the Secretary may prescribe.

(4) STOCK NOT TO INCLUDE CERTAIN PREFERRED STOCK.—For purposes of this subsection, the term "stock" does not include any stock which—

(A) is not entitled to vote,

(B) is limited and preferred as to dividends and does not participate in corporate growth to any significant extent,

(C) has redemption and liquidation rights which do not exceed the issue price of such stock (except for a reasonable redemption or liquidation premium), and

(D) is not convertible into another class of stock.

(5) REGULATIONS.—The Secretary shall prescribe such regulations as may be necessary or appropriate to carry out the purposes of this subsection, including (but not limited to) regulations—

(A) which treat warrants, obligations convertible into stock, and other similar interests as stock, and stock as not stock,

(B) which treat options to acquire or sell stock as having been exercised,

(C) which provide that the requirements of paragraph (2)(B) shall be treated as met if the affiliated group, in reliance on a good faith determination of value, treated such requirements as met,

(D) which disregard an inadvertent ceasing to meet the requirements of paragraph (2)(B) by reason of changes in relative values of different classes of stock,

(E) which provide that transfers of stock within the group shall not be taken into account in determining whether a corporation ceases to be a member of an affiliated group, and

(F) which disregard changes in voting power to the extent such changes are disproportionate to related changes in value.

Amendments

• **2014, Tax Technical Corrections Act of 2014 (P.L. 113-295)**

P.L. 113-295, §221(a)(93), Division A:

Amended Code Sec. 1504(a)(3)(A) by striking "for a taxable year which includes any period after December 31, 1984" following "affiliated group" in clause (i) and by striking "in a taxable year beginning after December 31, 1984" following "such group" in clause (ii). **Effective** generally 12-19-2014. For a special rule, see Act Sec. 221(b)(2), Division A, below.

P.L. 113-295, §221(b)(2), Division A, provides:

(2) SAVINGS PROVISION.—If—

(A) any provision amended or repealed by the amendments made by this section applied to—

(i) any transaction occurring before the date of the enactment of this Act,

(ii) any property acquired before such date of enactment, or

INCOME TAX—CONSOLIDATED RETURNS

(iii) any item of income, loss, deduction, or credit taken into account before such date of enactment, and

(B) the treatment of such transaction, property, or item under such provision would (without regard to the amendments or repeals made by this section) affect the liability for tax for periods ending after date of enactment, nothing in the amendments or repeals made by this section shall be construed to affect the treatment of such transaction, property, or item for purposes of determining liability for tax for periods ending after such date of enactment.

• **1988, Technical and Miscellaneous Revenue Act of 1988 (P.L. 100-647)**

P.L. 100-647, § 5021, as amended by P.L. 101-239, § 7815(b), provides:

SEC. 5021. REPEAL OF RULES PERMITTING LOSS TRANSFERS BY ALASKA NATIVE CORPORATIONS.

(a) GENERAL RULE.—Nothing in section 60(b)(5) of the Tax Reform Act of 1984 (as amended by section 1804(e)(4) of the Tax Reform Act of 1986)—

(1) shall allow any loss (or credit) of any corporation which arises after April 26, 1988, to be used to offset the income (or tax) of another corporation if such use would not be allowable without regard to such section 60(b)(5) as so amended, or

(2) shall allow any loss (or credit) of any corporation which arises on or before such date to be used to offset disqualified income (or tax attributable to such income) of another corporation if such use would not be allowable without regard to such section 60(b)(5) as so amended.

(b) EXCEPTION FOR EXISTING CONTRACTS.—

(1) IN GENERAL.—Subsection (a) shall not apply to any loss (or credit) of any corporation if—

(A) such corporation was in existence on April 26, 1988, and

(B) such loss (or credit) is used to offset income assigned (or attributable to property contributed) pursuant to a binding contract entered into before July 26, 1988.

(2) $40,000,000 LIMITATION.—The aggregate amount of losses (and the deduction equivalent of credits as determined in the same manner as under section 469(j)(5) of the 1986 Code) to which paragraph (1) applies with respect to any corporation shall not exceed $40,000,000. For purposes of this paragraph, a Native Corporation and all other corporations all of the stock of which is owned directly by such corporation shall be treated as 1 corporation.

(3) SPECIAL RULE FOR CORPORATIONS UNDER TITLE 11.—In the case of a corporation which on April 26, 1988, was under the jurisdiction of a Federal district court under title 11 of the United States Code—

(A) paragraph (1)(B) shall be applied by substituting the date 1 year after the date of the enactment of this Act for "July 26, 1988",

(B) paragraph (1) shall not apply to any loss or credit which arises on or after the date 1 year after the date of the enactment of this Act, and

(C) paragraph (2) shall be applied by substituting "99,000,000" for "$40,000,000".

(c) SPECIAL ADMINISTRATIVE RULES.—

(1) NOTICE TO NATIVE CORPORATIONS OF PROPOSED TAX ADJUSTMENTS.—Notwithstanding section 6103 of the 1986 Code, the Secretary of the Treasury or his delegate shall notify a Native Corporation or its designated representative of any proposed adjustment—

(A) of the tax liability of a taxpayer which has contracted with the Native Corporation (or other corporation all of the stock of which is owned directly by the Native Corporation) for the use of losses of such Native Corporation (or such other corporation), and

(B) which is attributable to an asserted overstatement of losses by, or misassignment of income (or income attributable to property contributed) to, an affiliated group of which the Native Corporation (or such other corporation) is a member.

Such notice shall only include information with respect to the transaction between the taxpayer and the Native Corporation.

(2) RIGHTS OF NATIVE CORPORATION.—

(A) IN GENERAL.—If a Native Corporation receives a notice under paragraph (1), the Native Corporation shall have the right to—

(i) submit to the Secretary of the Treasury or his delegate a written statement regarding the proposed adjustment, and

(ii) meet with the Secretary of the Treasury or his delegate with respect to such proposed adjustment.

The Secretary of the Treasury or his delegate may discuss such proposed adjustment with the Native Corporation or its designated representative.

(B) EXTENSION OF STATUTE OF LIMITATIONS.—Subparagraph (A) shall not apply if the Secretary of the Treasury or his delegate determines that an extension of the statute of limitation is necessary to permit the participation described in subparagraph (A) and the taxpayer and the Secretary or his delegate have not agreed to such extension.

(3) JUDICIAL PROCEEDINGS.—In the case of any proceeding in a Federal court or the United States Tax Court involving a proposed adjustment under paragraph (1), the Native Corporation, subject to the rules of such court, may file an amicus brief concerning such adjustment.

(4) FAILURES.—For purposes of the 1966 Code, any failure by the Secretary of the Treasury or his delegate to comply with the provisions of this subsection shall not affect the validity of the determination of the Internal Revenue Service of any adjustment of tax liability of any taxpayer described in paragraph (1).

(d) DISQUALIFIED INCOME DEFINED.—For purposes of subsection (a), the term "disqualified income" means any income assigned (or attributable to property contributed) after April 26, 1988, by a person who is not a Native Corporation or a corporation all the stock of which is owned directly by a Native Corporation.

(e) BASIS DETERMINATION.—For purposes of determining basis for Federal tax purposes, no provision in any law enacted after the date of the enactment of this Act shall affect the date on which the transfer to the Native Corporation is made. The preceding sentence shall apply to all taxable years whether beginning before, on, or after such date of enactment.

• **1986, Tax Reform Act of 1986 (P.L. 99-514)**

P.L. 99-514, § 1804(e)(1):

Amended Code Sec. 1504(a)(4)(C). **Effective** as if included in the provision of P.L. 98-369 to which it relates. Prior to amendment, Code Sec. 1504(a)(4)(C) read as follows:

(C) has redemption and liquidation rights which do not exceed the paid-in capital or par value represented by such stock (except for a reasonable redemption premium in excess of such paid-in capital or par value), and

• **1984, Deficit Reduction Act of 1984 (P.L. 98-369)**

P.L. 98-369, § 60(a):

Amended Code Sec. 1504(a). **Effective** for tax years beginning after 12-31-84. A special rule appears in Act Sec. 60(b)(2)-(9), below. Prior to amendment, § 1504(a) read as follows:

(a) Definition of "Affiliated Group".—As used in this chapter, the term "affiliated group" means one or more chains of includible corporations connected through stock ownership with a common parent corporation which is an includible corporation if—

(1) Stock possessing at least 80 percent of the voting power of all classes of stock and at least 80 percent of each class of the nonvoting stock of each of the includible corporations (except the common parent corporation) is owned directly by one or more of the other includible corporations; and

(2) The common parent corporation owns directly stock possessing at least 80 percent of the voting power of all classes of stock and at least 80 percent of each class of the nonvoting stock of at least one of the other includible corporations.

As used in this subsection, the term "stock" does not include nonvoting stock which is limited and preferred as to dividends, employer securities (within the meaning for [of] section 409A(1)) while such securities are held under a tax credit employee stock ownership plan, or qualifying employer securities (within the meaning of section 4975(e)(8)) while such securities are held under an employee stock ownership plan which meets the requirements of section 4975(e)(7).

• **1984, Deficit Reduction Act of 1984 (P.L. 98-369)**

P.L. 98-369, § 60(b)(2)-(9), as amended by P.L. 99-514, § 1804, provides:

(2) Special Rule for Corporations Affiliated on June 22, 1984.—In the case of a corporation which on June 22, 1984, is a member of an affiliated group which files a consolidated return for such corporation's taxable year which includes June 22, 1984, for purposes of determining whether such corporation continues to be a member of such group for taxable years beginning before January 1, 1988, the amendment made by subsection (a) shall not apply. The preceding sentence shall cease to apply as of the first day after June 22, 1984, on which such corporation does not qualify as a member of such group under section 1504(a) of the Internal Revenue Code of 1954 (as in effect on the day before the enactment of this Act).

(3) Special Rule Not to Apply to Certain Sell-Downs After June 22, 1984.—If—

(A) the requirements of paragraph (2) are satisfied with respect to a corporation,

(B) more than a de minimis amount of the stock of such corporation—

(i) is sold or exchanged (including in a redemption), or

(ii) is issued,

after June 22, 1984 (other than in the ordinary course of business), and

(C) the requirements of the amendment made by subsection (a) are not satisfied after such sale, exchange, or issuance,

then the amendment made by subsection (a) shall apply for purposes of determining whether such corporation continues to be a member of the group. The preceding sentence shall not apply to any transaction if such transaction does not reduce the percentage of the fair market value of the stock of the corporation referred to in the preceding sentence held by members of the group determined without regard to this paragraph.

(4) Exception for Certain Sell-Downs.—Subsection (b)(2) (and not subsection (b)(3)) will apply to a corporation if such corporation issues or sells stock after June 22, 1984, pursuant to a registration statement filed with the Securities and Exchange Commission on or before June 22, 1984, but only if the requirements of the amendment made by subsection (a) (substituting "more than 50 percent" for "at least 80 percent" in paragraph (2)(B) of section 1504(a) of the Internal Revenue Code of 1954) are satisfied immediately after such issuance or sale and at all times thereafter until the first day of the first taxable year beginning after December 31, 1987. For purposes of the preceding sentence, if there is a letter of intent between a corporation and a securities underwriter entered into on or before June 22, 1984, and the subsequent issuance or sale is effected pursuant to a registration statement filed with the Securities and Exchange Commission, such stock shall be treated as issued or sold pursuant to a registration statement filed with the Securities and Exchange Commission on or before June 22, 1984.

(5) Native Corporations.—

(A) In the case of a Native Corporation established under the Alaska Native Claims Settlement Act (43 U.S.C. 1601 et seq.), or a corporation all of whose stock is owned directly by such a corporation, during any taxable year (beginning after the effective date of these amendments and before 1992), or any part thereof, in which the Native Corporation is subject to the provisions of section 7(h)(1) of such Act (43 U.S.C. 1606(h)(1))—

(i) the amendment made by subsection (a) shall not apply, and

(ii) the requirements for affiliation under section 1504(a) of the Internal Revenue Code of 1986 before the amendment made by subsection (a) shall be applied solely according to the provisions expressly contained therein, without regard to escrow arrangements, redemption rights, or similar provisions.

(B) Except as provided in subparagraph (C), during the period described in subparagraph (A), no provision of the Internal Revenue Code of 1986 (including sections 269 and 482) or principle of law shall apply to deny the benefit or use of losses incurred or credits earned by a corporation described in subparagraph (A) to the affiliated group of which the Native Corporation is the common parent.

Sec. 1504(a)(5)(F)

INCOME TAX—CONSOLIDATED RETURNS

(C) Losses incurred or credits earned by a corporation described in subparagraph (A) shall be subject to the general consolidated return regulations, including the provisions relating to separate return limitations years, and to sections 382 and 383 of the Internal Revenue Code of 1986.

(D) Losses incurred and credits earned by a corporation which is affiliated with a corporation described in subparagraph (A) shall be treated as having been incurred or earned in a separate return limitation year, unless the corporation incurring the losses or earning the credits satisfies the affiliation requirements of section 1504(a) without application of subparagraph (A).

(6) Treatment of Certain Corporations Affiliated on June 22, 1984.—In the case of an affiliated group which—

(A) has as its common parent a Minnesota corporation incorporated on April 23, 1940, and

(B) has a member which is a New York corporation incorporated on November 13, 1969,

for purposes of determining whether such New York corporation continues to be a member of such group, paragraph (2) shall be applied by substituting for "January 1, 1988," the earlier of January 1, 1994, or the date on which the voting power of the preferred stock in such New York corporation terminates.

(7) Election to Have Amendments Apply for Years Beginning After 1983.—If the common parent of any group makes an election under this paragraph, notwithstanding any other provision of this subsection, the amendments made by subsection (a) shall apply to such group for taxable years beginning after December 31, 1983. Any such election, once made, shall be irrevocable.

(8) Treatment of Certain Affiliated Groups.—If—

(A) a corporation (hereinafter in this paragraph referred to as the "parent") was incorporated in 1968 and filed consolidated returns as the parent of an affiliated group for each of its taxable years ending after 1969 and before 1985,

(B) another corporation (hereinafter in this paragraph referred to as the "subsidiary") became a member of the parent's affiliated roup in 1978 by reason of a recapitalization pursuant to which the parent increased its voting interest in the subsidiary from not less than 56 percent to not less than 85 percent, and

(C) such subsidiary is engaged (or was on September 27, 1985, engaged) in manufacturing and distributing a broad line of business systems and related supplies for binding, laminating, shredding, graphics, and providing secure identification,

then, for purposes of determining whether such subsidiary corporation is a member of the parent's affiliated group under section 1504(a) of the Internal Revenue Code of 1954 (as amended by subsection (a)), paragraph (2)(B) of such section 1504(a) shall be applied by substituting "55 percent" for "80 percent".

(9) Treatment of Certain Corporations Affiliated During 1971.—In the case of a group of corporations which filed a consolidated Federal income tax return for the taxable year beginning during 1971 and which—

(A) included as a common parent on December 31, 1971, a Delaware corporation incorporated on August 26, 1969, and

(B) included as a member thereof a Delaware corporation incorporated on November 8, 1971,

for taxable years beginning after December 31, 1970, and ending before January 1, 1988, the requirements for affiliation for each member of such group under section 1504(a) of the Internal Revenue Code of 1954 (before the amendment made by subsection (a)) shall be limited solely to the provisions expressly contained therein and by reference to stock issued under State law as common or preferred stock. During the period described in the preceding sentence, no provision of the Internal Revenue Code of 1986 (including sections 269 and 482) or principle of law, except the general consolidated return regulations (including the provisions relating to separate return limitation years) and sections 382 and 383 of such Code, shall apply to deny the benefit or use of losses incurred or credits earned by members of such group.

• **1980, Technical Corrections Act of 1979 (P.L. 96-222)**

P.L. 96-222, §101(a)(7)(B):

Amended Act Sec. 141 of P.L. 95-600 by revising paragraph (g) which relates to the effective dates for amendments concerning tax credit employee stock ownership plans. For the effective dates, see the amendment note at §101(a)(7)(B), P.L. 96-222, following the text of Code Sec. 409A(n).

P.L. 96-222, §101(a)(7)(L)(i)(VIII) and (iv)(II):

Amended the last sentence of Code Sec. 1504(a) by striking out "an ESOP" and inserting "a tax credit employee stock ownership plan" and by striking out "leveraged employee stock ownership plan" and inserting "employee stock ownership plan". **Effective** for tax years beginning after 12-31-78.

• **1978, Revenue Act of 1978 (P.L. 95-600)**

P.L. 95-600, §141(f)(4), (g)(1):

Amended the last sentence of Code Sec. 1504(a). **Effective** for qualified investment for tax years beginning after 12-31-78. Prior to amendment, the last sentence read:

As used in this subsection, the term "stock" does not include nonvoting stock which is limited and preferred as to dividends, employer securities within the meaning of section 301(d)(9)(A) of the Tax Reduction Act of 1975, or qualifying employer securities within the meaning of section 4975(e)(8) while such securities are held under an employee stock ownership plan which meets the requirements of section 301(d) of such Act or section 4975(e)(7), respectively.

• **1976, Tax Reform Act of 1976 (P.L. 94-455)**

P.L. 94-455, §803(b)(3):

Amended the last sentence of Code Sec. 1504(a). **Effective** for tax years beginning after 12-31-74. Prior to amendment, the last sentence of Code Sec. 1504(a) read as follows:

As used in this subsection, the term "stock" does not include nonvoting stock which is limited and preferred as to dividends.

[Sec. 1504(b)]

(b) DEFINITION OF "INCLUDIBLE CORPORATION".—As used in this chapter, the term "includible corporation" means any corporation except—

(1) Corporations exempt from taxation under section 501.

(2) Insurance companies subject to taxation under section 801.

(3) Foreign corporations.

(4) Regulated investment companies and real estate investment trusts subject to tax under subchapter M of chapter 1.

(5) A DISC (as defined in section 992(a)(1)).

(6) An S corporation.

Amendments

• **2018, Tax Technical Corrections Act of 2018 (P.L. 115-141)**

P.L. 115-141, §401(d)(1)(D)(xvii)(I), Div. U:

Amended Code Sec. 1504(b) by striking paragraph (4) and by redesignating paragraphs (6), (7), and (8) as paragraphs (4), (5), and (6), respectively. **Effective** 3-23-2018. For a special rule, see Act Sec. 401(e), Div. U, below. Prior to being stricken, Code Sec. 1504(b)(4) read as follows:

(4) Corporations with respect to which an election under section 936 (relating to possession tax credit) is in effect for the taxable year.

P.L. 115-141, §401(e), Div. U, provides:

(e) GENERAL SAVINGS PROVISION WITH RESPECT TO DEADWOOD PROVISIONS.—If—

(1) any provision amended or repealed by the amendments made by subsection (b) or (d) applied to—

(A) any transaction occurring before the date of the enactment of this Act,

(B) any property acquired before such date of enactment, or

(C) any item of income, loss, deduction, or credit taken into account before such date of enactment, and

(2) the treatment of such transaction, property, or item under such provision would (without regard to the amendments or repeals made by such subsection) affect the liability for tax for periods ending after such date of enactment,

nothing in the amendments or repeals made by this section shall be construed to affect the treatment of such transaction, property, or item for purposes of determining liability for tax for periods ending after such date of enactment.

• **1996, Small Business Job Protection Act of 1996 (P.L. 104-188)**

P.L. 104-188, §1308(d)(2):

Amended Code Sec. 1504(b) by adding at the end a new paragraph (8). **Effective** for tax years beginning after 12-31-96.

• **1988, Technical and Miscellaneous Revenue Act of 1988 (P.L. 100-647)**

P.L. 100-647, §1018(d)(10)(A):

Amended Code Sec. 1504(b)(7). **Effective** as if included in the provision of P.L. 99-514 to which it relates. Prior to amendment Code Sec. 1504(b)(7) read as follows:

(7) A DISC (as defined in section 992(a)(1)), or any other corporation which has accumulated DISC income which is derived after December 31, 1984.

• **1986, Tax Reform Act of 1986 (P.L. 99-514)**

P.L. 99-514, §1024(c)(15):

Amended Code Sec. 1504(b)(2) by striking out "or 821". **Effective** for tax years beginning after 12-31-86. However, for transitional rules, see Act Sec. 1024(d) following Code Sec. 1504(c).

P.L. 99-514, §1804(e)(10):

Amended Code Sec. 1504(b)(7). **Effective** as if included in the provision of P.L. 98-369 to which it relates. Prior to amendment, Code Sec. 1504(b)(7) read as follows:

(7) A DISC or former DISC (as defined in section 992(a)).

• **1984, Deficit Reduction Act of 1984 (P.L. 98-369)**

P.L. 98-369, §211(b)(20):

Amended Code Sec. 1504(b)(2) by striking out "section 802" and inserting in lieu thereof "section 801". **Effective** for tax years beginning after 12-31-83.

• **1976, Tax Reform Act of 1976 (P.L. 94-455)**

P.L. 94-455, §1051(g):

Amended Code Sec. 1504(b)(4). **Effective** as indicated in §1051(i) reproduced below. Prior to amendment, Code Sec. 1504(b)(4) read as follows:

INCOME TAX—CONSOLIDATED RETURNS

(4) Corporations entitled to the benefits of section 931, by reason of receiving a large percentage of their income from sources within possessions of the United States.

P.L. 94-455, § 1051(i) reads as follows:

(i) EFFECTIVE DATE.—

(1) Except as provided by paragraph (2), the amendments made by this section shall apply to taxable years beginning after December 31, 1975, except that "qualified possession source investment income" as defined in section 936(d)(2) of the Internal Revenue Code of 1954 shall include income from any source outside the United States if the taxpayer establishes to the satisfaction of the Secretary of the Treasury or his delegate that the income from such sources was earned before October 1, 1976.

(2) The amendment made by subsection (d)(2) shall not apply to any tax imposed by a possession of the United States with respect to the complete liquidation occurring before January 1, 1979, of a corporation to the extent that such tax is attributable to earnings and profits accumulated by such corporation during periods ending before January 1, 1976.

P.L. 94-455, § 1053(d)(2):

Repealed Code Sec. 1504(b)(5). **Effective** for tax years beginning after 12-31-77. Prior to repeal, Code Sec. 1504(b)(5) read as follows:

(5) Corporations organized under the China Trade Act, 1922.

• **1971, Revenue Act of 1971 (P.L. 92-178)**

P.L. 92-178, § 502(e):

Amended Code Sec. 1504(b) by adding paragraph (7). **Effective** date is governed by the effective date for Code Sec. 992.

• **1966 (P.L. 89-389)**

P.L. 89-389, § 4(b):

Deleted Code Sec. 1504(b)(7). **Effective** 1-1-69.

• **1960 (P.L. 86-779)**

P.L. 86-779, § 10(j):

Amended paragraph (6) of Code Sec. 1504(b) by adding "and real estate investment trusts" following "Regulated investment companies". **Effective** 1-1-61.

• **1959 (P.L. 86-376)**

P.L. 86-376, § 2(c):

Amended Code Sec. 1504(b) by striking out paragraph (8). **Effective** 9-24-59. Prior to repeal, paragraph (8) read as follows:

(8) An electing small business corporation (as defined in section 1371(b)).

• **1959, Life Insurance Company Income Tax Act of 1959 (P.L. 86-69)**

P.L. 86-69, § 3(f)(1):

Amended Sec. 1504(b)(2) by striking out ", 811," where it appeared following "802". **Effective** for tax years beginning after 12-31-57.

• **1958, Technical Amendments Act of 1958 (P.L. 85-866)**

P.L. 85-866, § 64(d)(3):

Added paragraph (8) to Sec. 1504(b). **Effective** for tax years beginning after 12-31-57.

• **1956, Life Insurance Company Tax Act for 1955 (P.L. 429, 84th Cong.)**

P.L. 429, 84th Cong., § 5(8):

Amended Sec. 1504(b)(2) by substituting for "802 or 821" the words and figures "802, 811, or 821". **Effective** for tax years beginning after 12-31-54.

[Sec. 1504(c)]

(c) INCLUDIBLE INSURANCE COMPANIES.—Notwithstanding the provisions of paragraph (2) of subsection (b)—

(1) Two or more domestic insurance companies each of which is subject to tax under section 801 shall be treated as includible corporations for purposes of applying subsection (a) to such insurance companies alone.

(2) (A) If an affiliated group (determined without regard to subsection (b)(2)) includes one or more domestic insurance companies taxed under section 801, the common parent of such group may elect (pursuant to regulations prescribed by the Secretary) to treat all such companies as includible corporations for purposes of applying subsection (a) except that no such company shall be so treated until it has been a member of the affiliated group for the 5 taxable years immediately preceding the taxable year for which the consolidated return is filed.

(B) If an election under this paragraph is in effect for a taxable year—

(i) section 243(b)(3) and the exception provided under section 243(b)(2) with respect to subsections (b)(2) and (c) of this section,

(ii) section 542(b)(5), and

(iii) subsection (a)(4) and (b)(2)(D) of section 1563, and the reference to section 1563(b)(2)(D) contained in section 1563(b)(3)(C),

shall not be effective for such taxable year.

Amendments

• **1996, Small Business Job Protection Act of 1996 (P.L. 104-188)**

P.L. 104-188, § 1702(h)(6):

Amended Code Sec. 1504(c)(2)(B)(i) by inserting "section" before "243(b)(2)". **Effective** as if included in the provision of P.L. 101-508 to which it relates.

• **1990, Omnibus Budget Reconciliation Act of 1990 (P.L. 101-508)**

P.L. 101-508, § 11814(b):

Amended Code Sec. 1504(c)(2)(B)(i) by striking "section 243(b)(6)" and inserting "section 243(b)(3)", and by striking "section 243(b)(5)" and inserting "243(b)(2)". **Effective**, generally, for tax years beginning after 12-31-90.

P.L. 101-508, § 11814(c)(2) provides:

(2) TREATMENT OF OLD ELECTIONS.—For purposes of section 243(b)(3) of the Internal Revenue Code of 1986 (as amended by subsection (a)), any reference to an election under such section shall be treated as including a reference to an election under section 243(b) of such Code (as in effect on the day before the date of the enactment of this Act).

• **1986, Tax Reform Act of 1986 (P.L. 99-514)**

P.L. 99-514, § 1024(c)(16):

Amended Code Sec. 1504(c)(2)(A) by striking out "or 821". **Effective** for tax years beginning after 12-31-86. However, for transitional rules, see Act Sec. 1024(d), below.

P.L. 99-514, § 1024(d), as amended by P.L. 100-647, § 1010(f)(8), provides:

(1) TREATMENT OF AMOUNTS IN PROTECTION AGAINST LOSS ACCOUNT.—In the case of any insurance company which had a protection against loss account for its last taxable year beginning before January 1, 1987, there shall be included in the gross income of such company for any taxable year beginning after December 31, 1986, the amount which would have been included in gross income for such taxable year under section 824 of the Internal Revenue Code of 1954 (as in effect on the date before the date of the enactment of this Act). For purposes of the preceding sentence, no addition to such account shall be made for any taxable year beginning after December 31, 1986.

In the case of a company taxable under section 831(b) of the Internal Revenue Code of 1986 (as amended by subsection (a)), any amount included in gross income under this paragraph shall be treated as gross investment income.

(2) TRANSITIONAL RULE FOR UNUSED LOSS CARRYOVER UNDER SECTION 825.—Any unused loss carryover under section 825 of the Internal Revenue Code of 1954 (as in effect on the day before the date of the enactment of this Act) which—

(A) is from a taxable year beginning before January 1, 1987, and

(B) could have been carried under such section to a taxable year beginning after December 31, 1986, but for the repeal made by subsection (a)(1),

shall be included in the net operating loss deduction under section 832(c)(10) of such Code without regard to the limitations of section 844(b) of such Code.

P.L. 99-514, § 1899A(35):

Amended Code Sec. 1504(c)(2)(A) by striking out "subsection (b)(2) includes" and inserting in lieu thereof "subsection (b)(2)) includes". **Effective** 10-22-86.

• **1984, Deficit Reduction Act of 1984 (P.L. 98-369)**

P.L. 98-369, § 211(b)(20):

Amended Code Sec. 1504(c)(1) and (c)(2)(A) by striking out "section 802" and inserting in lieu thereof "section 801". **Effective** for tax years beginning after 12-31-83.

• **1976, Tax Reform Act of 1976 (P.L. 94-455)**

P.L. 94-455, § 1507(a):

Amended Code Sec. 1504(c). **Effective** for tax years beginning after 12-31-80, but see transition rules of § 1507(c)(2) in historical note to Code Sec. 1503(b). Prior to amendment, Code Sec. 1504(c) read as follows:

(c) INCLUDIBLE INSURANCE COMPANIES.—Despite the provisions of paragraph (2) of subsection (b), two or more domestic insurance companies each of which is subject to taxation under the same section of this subtitle shall be considered as includible corporations for the purpose of the application of subsection (a) to such insurance companies alone.

[Sec. 1504(d)]

(d) SUBSIDIARY FORMED TO COMPLY WITH FOREIGN LAW.—In the case of a domestic corporation owning or controlling, directly or indirectly, 100 percent of the capital stock (exclusive of directors' qualifying shares) of a corporation organized under the laws of a contiguous foreign country and maintained solely for the purpose of complying with the laws of such country as to title and operation of property, such foreign corporation may, at the option of the domestic corporation, be treated for the purpose of this subtitle as a domestic corporation.

INCOME TAX—CONSOLIDATED RETURNS

[Sec. 1504(e)]

(e) INCLUDIBLE TAX-EXEMPT ORGANIZATIONS.—Despite the provisions of paragraph (1) of subsection (b), two or more organizations exempt from taxation under section 501, one or more of which is described in section 501(c)(2) and the others of which derive income from such 501(c)(2) organizations, shall be considered as includible corporations for the purpose of the application of subsection (a) to such organizations alone.

Amendments

• **1969, Tax Reform Act of 1969 (P.L. 91-172)**

P.L. 91-172, §121(a)(4):

Added Code Sec. 1504(e). **Effective** 1-1-70.

[Sec. 1504(f)]

(f) SPECIAL RULE FOR CERTAIN AMOUNTS DERIVED FROM A CORPORATION PREVIOUSLY TREATED AS A DISC.—In determining the consolidated taxable income of an affiliated group for any taxable year beginning after December 31, 1984, a corporation which had been a DISC and which would otherwise be a member of such group shall not be treated as such a member with respect to—

(1) any distribution (or deemed distribution) of accumulated DISC income which was not treated as previously taxed income under section 805(b)(2)(A) of the Tax Reform Act of 1984, and

(2) any amount treated as received under section 805(b)(3) of such Act.

Amendments

• **1988, Technical and Miscellaneous Revenue Act of 1988 (P.L. 100-647)**

P.L. 100-647, §1018(d)(10)(B):

Amended Code Sec. 1504 by adding at the end thereof a new subsection (f). **Effective** as if included in the provision of P.L. 99-514 to which it relates.

[Sec. 1505]

SEC. 1505. CROSS REFERENCES.

(1) For suspension of running of statute of limitations when notice in respect of a deficiency is mailed to one corporation, see section 6503(a)(1).

(2) For allocation of income and deductions of related trades or businesses, see section 482.

Subchapter B—Related Rules

Part I.   In general.
Part II. Certain controlled corporations.

PART I—IN GENERAL

Sec. 1552.   Earnings and profits.

[Sec. 1551—Stricken]

Amendments

• **2017, Tax Cuts and Jobs Act (P.L. 115-97)**

P.L. 115-97, §13001(b)(5)(A):

Amended part I of subchapter B of chapter 5 by striking Code Sec. 1551. **Effective** for tax years beginning after 12-31-2017. Prior to being stricken, Code Sec. 1551 read as follows:

SEC. 1551. DISALLOWANCE OF THE BENEFITS OF THE GRADUATED CORPORATE RATES AND ACCUMULATED EARNINGS CREDIT.

[Sec. 1551(a)]

(a) IN GENERAL.—If—

(1) any corporation transfers, directly or indirectly, all or part of its property (other than money) to a transferee corporation, or

(2) five or fewer individuals who are in control of a corporation transfer, directly or indirectly, property (other than money) to a transferee corporation,

and the transferee corporation was created for the purpose of acquiring such property or was not actively engaged in business at the time of such acquisition, and if after such transfer the transferor or transferors are in control of such transferee corporation during any part of the taxable year of such transferee corporation, then for such taxable year of such transferee corporation the Secretary may (except as may be otherwise determined under subsection (c)) disallow the benefits of the rates contained in section 11(b) which are lower than the highest rate specified in such section, or the accumulated earnings credit provided in paragraph (2) or (3) of section 535(c), unless such transferee corporation shall establish by the clear preponderance of the evidence that the securing of such benefits or credit was not a major purpose of such transfer.

Amendments

• **2014, Tax Technical Corrections Act of 2014 (P.L. 113-295)**

P.L. 113-295, §221(a)(94)(A)(i)-(ii), Division A:

Amended Code Sec. 1551(a) by striking paragraph (1) and by redesignating paragraphs (2) and (3) as paragraphs (1) and (2), respectively, and by striking "after June 12, 1963," each place it appears [following "directly or indirectly,"]. **Effective** generally 12-19-2014. For a special rule, see Act Sec. 221(b)(2), Division A, below. Prior to being stricken, Code Sec. 1551(a)(1) read as follows:

(1) any corporation transfers, on or after January 1, 1951, and on or before June 12, 1963, all or part of its property (other than money) to a transferee corporation,

P.L. 113-295, §221(b)(2), Division A, provides:

(2) SAVINGS PROVISION.—If—

(A) any provision amended or repealed by the amendments made by this section applied to—

(i) any transaction occurring before the date of the enactment of this Act,

(ii) any property acquired before such date of enactment, or

(iii) any item of income, loss, deduction, or credit taken into account before such date of enactment, and

(B) the treatment of such transaction, property, or item under such provision would (without regard to the amendments or repeals made by this section) affect the liability for tax for periods ending after date of enactment, nothing in the amendments or repeals made by this section shall be construed to affect the treatment of such transaction, property, or item for purposes of determining liability for tax for periods ending after such date of enactment.

• **1981, Economic Recovery Tax Act of 1981 (P.L. 97-34)**

P.L. 97-34, §232(b)(2):

Amended Code Sec. 1551(a) by striking out "150,000". **Effective** for tax years beginning after 12-31-81.

• **1978, Revenue Act of 1978 (P.L. 95-600)**

P.L. 95-600, §301(b)(18)(A)(i), (ii), 301(b)(18)(B), 301(c):

Amended the heading of Code Sec. 1551. **Effective** for tax years beginning after 12-31-78. Prior to amendment, Code Sec. 1551(a) read as follows:

SEC. 1551. DISALLOWANCE OF SURTAX EXEMPTION AND ACCUMULATED EARNINGS CREDIT.

(a) IN GENERAL.—If—

(1) any corporation transfers, on or after January 1, 1951, and on or before June 12, 1963, all or part of its property (other than money) to a transferee corporation,

(2) any corporation transfers, directly or indirectly, after June 12, 1963, all or part of its property (other than money) to a transferee corporation, or

(3) five or fewer individuals who are in control of a corporation transfer, directly or indirectly, after June 12, 1963, property (other than money) to a transferee corporation,

and the transferee corporation was created for the purpose of acquiring such property or was not actively engaged in business at the time of such acquisition, and if after such transfer the transferor or transferors are in control of such transferee corporation during any part of the taxable year of such transferee corporation, then for such taxable year of such transferee corporation the Secretary may (except as may be otherwise determined under subsection (c)) disallow the surtax exemption (as defined in section 11(d)), or the $150,000 accumulated earnings credit provided in paragraph (2) or (3) of section 535(c), unless such transferee corporation shall establish by the clear preponderance of the evidence that the securing of such exemption or credit was not a major purpose of such transfer.

• **1976, Tax Reform Act of 1976 (P.L. 94-455)**

P.L. 94-455, §1901(a)(158):

Substituted "determined under subsection (c)" for "determined under subsection (d)" in Code Sec. 1551(a). **Effective** for tax years beginning after 12-31-76.

INCOME TAX—CONSOLIDATED RETURNS

P.L. 94-455, §1906(b)(13)(A):

Substituted "Secretary" for "Secretary or his delgate" each place it appeared. **Effective** 2-1-77.

• **1975, Tax Reduction Act of 1975 (P.L. 94-12)**

P.L. 94-12, §304(b):

Amended Code Sec. 1551(a) by substituting "$150,000" for "$100,000". **Effective** for tax years beginning after 12-31-74.

[Sec. 1551(b)]

(b) CONTROL.—For purposes of subsection (a), the term "control" means—

(1) With respect to a transferee corporation described in subsection (a)(1), the ownership by the transferor corporation, its shareholders, or both, of stock possessing at least 80 percent of the total combined voting power of all classes of stock entitled to vote or at least 80 percent of the total value of shares of all classes of the stock; or

(2) With respect to each corporation described in subsection (a)(2), the ownership by the five or fewer individuals described in such subsection of stock possessing—

(A) at least 80 percent of the total combined voting power of all classes of stock entitled to vote or at least 80 percent of the total value of shares of all classes of the stock of each corporation, and

(B) more than 50 percent of the total combined voting power of all classes of stock entitled to vote or more than 50 percent of the total value of shares of all classes of stock of each corporation, taking into account the stock ownership of each such individual only to the extent such stock ownership is identical with respect to each such corporation.

For purposes of this subsection, section 1563(e) shall apply in determining the ownership of stock.

Amendments

• **2014, Tax Technical Corrections Act of 2014 (P.L. 113-295)**

P.L. 113-295, §221(a)(94)(B)(i)-(ii), Division A:

Amended Code Sec. 1551(b) by striking "or (2)" following "described in subsection (a)(1)" in paragraph (1), and by striking "(a)(3)" in paragraph (2) and inserting "(a)(2)". **Effective** generally 12-19-2014. For a special rule, see Act Sec. 221(b)(2), Division A, below.

P.L. 113-295, §221(b)(2), Division A, provides:

(2) SAVINGS PROVISION.—If—

(A) any provision amended or repealed by the amendments made by this section applied to—

(i) any transaction occurring before the date of the enactment of this Act,

(ii) any property acquired before such date of enactment, or

(iii) any item of income, loss, deduction, or credit taken into account before such date of enactment, and

(B) the treatment of such transaction, property, or item under such provision would (without regard to the amendments or repeals made by this section) affect the liability for tax for periods ending after date of enactment, nothing in the amendments or repeals made by this section shall be construed to affect the treatment of such transaction, property, or item for purposes of determining liability for tax for periods ending after such date of enactment.

[Sec. 1551(c)]

(c) AUTHORITY OF THE SECRETARY UNDER THIS SECTION.—The provisions of section 269(c), and the authority of the Secretary under such section, shall, to the extent not inconsistent with the provisions of this section, be applicable to this section.

Amendments

• **1986, Tax Reform Act of 1986 (P.L. 99-514)**

P.L. 99-514, §1899A(36):

Amended Code Sec. 1551(c) by striking out "section 269(b)" and inserting in lieu thereof "section 269(c)". **Effective** 10-22-86.

• **1976, Tax Reform Act of 1976 (P.L. 94-455)**

P.L. 94-455, §1906(b)(13)(A):

Amended the 1954 Code by substituting "Secretary" for "Secretary or his delegate" each place it appeared. **Effective** 2-1-77.

• **1964, Revenue Act of 1964 (P.L. 88-272)**

P.L. 88-272, §235(b):

Amended Sec. 1551. **Effective** with respect to transfers made after 6-12-63. Prior to amendment, Sec. 1551 read as follows:

SEC. 1551. DISALLOWANCE OF SURTAX EXEMPTION AND ACCUMULATED EARNINGS CREDIT.

If any corporation transfers, on or after January 1, 1951, all or part of its property (other than money) to another corporation which was created for the purpose of acquiring such property or which was not actively engaged in business at the time of such acquisition, and if after such transfer the transferor corporation or its stockholders, or both, are in control of such transferee corporation during any part of the taxable year of such transferee corporation, then such transferee corporation shall not for such taxable year (except as may be otherwise determined under section 269(b)) be allowed either the $25,000 exemption from surtax provided in section 11(c) or the $100,000 accumulated earnings credit provided in paragraph (2) or (3) of section 535(c), unless such transferee corporation shall establish by the clear preponderance of the evidence that the securing of such exemption or credit was not a major purpose of such transfer. For purposes of this section, control means the ownership of stock possessing at least 80 percent of the total combined voting power of all classes of stock entitled to vote or at least 80 percent of the total value of shares of all classes of stock of the corporation. In determining the ownership of stock for the purpose of this section, the ownership of stock shall be determined in accordance with the provisions of section 544, except that constructive ownership under section 544(a)(2) shall be determined only with respect to the individual's spouse and minor children. The provisions of section 269(b), and the authority of the Secretary under such section, shall, to the extent not inconsistent with the provisions of this section, be applicable to this section.

• **1958, Technical Amendments Act of 1958 (P.L. 85-866)**

P.L. 85-866, §205(a):

Struck out "$60,000" where it preceded the phrase "accumulated earnings credit" in Sec. 1551 and substituted "$100,000". **Effective** 1-1-58.

SEC. 1552. EARNINGS AND PROFITS.

[Sec. 1552(a)]

(a) GENERAL RULE.—Pursuant to regulations prescribed by the Secretary the earnings and profits of each member of an affiliated group required to be included in a consolidated return for such group filed for a taxable year shall be determined by allocating the tax liability of the group for such year among the members of the group in accord with whichever of the following methods the group shall elect in its first consolidated return filed for such a taxable year:

(1) The tax liability shall be apportioned among the members of the group in accordance with the ratio which that portion of the consolidated taxable income attributable to each member of the group having taxable income bears to the consolidated taxable income.

(2) The tax liability of the group shall be allocated to the several members of the group on the basis of the percentage of the total tax which the tax of such member if computed on a separate return would bear to the total amount of the taxes for all members of the group so computed.

(3) The tax liability of the group (excluding the tax increases arising from the consolidation) shall be allocated on the basis of the contribution of each member of the group to the consolidated taxable income of the group. Any tax increases arising from the consolidation shall be distributed to the several members in direct proportion to the reduction in tax liability resulting to such members from the filing of the consolidated return as measured by the difference between their tax liabilities determined on a separate return basis and their tax liabilities based on their contributions to the consolidated taxable income.

(4) The tax liability of the group shall be allocated in accord with any other method selected by the group with the approval of the Secretary.

[Sec. 1552(b)]

(b) FAILURE TO ELECT.—If no election is made in such first return, the tax liability shall be allocated among the several members of the group pursuant to the method prescribed in subsection (a)(1).

Amendments

• **1976, Tax Reform Act of 1976 (P.L. 94-455)**

P.L. 94-455, §1901(a)(159):

Struck out "beginning after December 31, 1953, and ending after the date of the enactment of this title," following "filed for a taxable year" in the first sentence of Code Sec. 1552(a). **Effective** with respect to tax years beginning after 12-31-76.

P.L. 94-455, §1906(b)(13)(A):

Amended the 1954 Code by substituting "Secretary" for "Secretary or his delegate" each place it appeared. **Effective** 2-1-77.

• **1964, Revenue Act of 1964 (P.L. 88-272)**

P.L. 88-272, §234(b)(8):

Amended Code Sec. 1552(a)(3) to delete "(determined without regard to the 2 percent increase provided by section 1503(a))." **Effective** with respect to tax years beginning after 12-31-63.

INCOME TAX—CONSOLIDATED RETURNS

PART II—CERTAIN CONTROLLED CORPORATIONS

Sec. 1561. Limitations on accumulated earnings credit in the case of certain controlled corporations.
Sec. 1563. Definitions and special rules.

[Sec. 1561]

SEC. 1561. LIMITATION ON ACCUMULATED EARNINGS CREDIT IN THE CASE OF CERTAIN CONTROLLED CORPORATIONS.

[Sec. 1561(a)]

(a) IN GENERAL.—The component members of a controlled group of corporations on a December 31 shall, for their taxable years which include such December 31, be limited for purposes of this subtitle to one $250,000 ($150,000 if any component member is a corporation described in section 535(c)(2)(B)) amount for purposes of computing the accumulated earnings credit under section 535(c)(2) and (3). Such amount shall be divided equally among the component members of such group on such December 31 unless the Secretary prescribes regulations permitting an unequal allocation of such amount.

[Sec. 1561(b)]

(b) CERTAIN SHORT TAXABLE YEARS.—If a corporation has a short taxable year which does not include a December 31 and is a component member of a controlled group of corporations with respect to such taxable year, then for purposes of this subtitle, the amount to be used in computing the accumulated earnings credit under section 535(c)(2) and (3) of such corporation for such taxable year shall be the amount specified in subsection (a) with respect to such group, divided by the number of corporations which are component members of such group on the last day of such taxable year. For purposes of the preceding sentence, section 1563(b) shall be applied as if such last day were substituted for December 31.

Amendments

- **2017, Tax Cuts and Jobs Act (P.L. 115-97)**

P.L. 115-97, §13001(b)(6)(A):

Amended Code Sec. 1561, as amended by Act Sec. 12001. **Effective** for transfers made after 12-31-2017. Prior to amendment, Code Sec. 1561 read as follows:

SEC. 1561. LIMITATIONS ON CERTAIN MULTIPLE TAX BENEFITS IN THE CASE OF CERTAIN CONTROLLED CORPORATIONS.

[Sec. 1561(a)]

(a) GENERAL RULE.—The component members of a controlled group of corporations on a December 31 shall, for their taxable years which include such December 31, be limited for purposes of this subtitle from—

(1) amounts in each taxable income bracket in the tax table in section 11(b)(1) which do not aggregate more than the maximum amount in such bracket to which a corporation which is not a component member of a controlled group is entitled, and

(2) one $250,000 ($150,000 if any component member is a corporation described in section 535(c)(2)(B)) amount for purposes of computing the accumulated earnings credit under section 535(c)(2) and (3).

The amounts specified in paragraph (1) and the amount specified in paragraph (3) shall be divided equally among the component members of such group on such December 31 unless all of such component members consent (at such time and in such manner as the Secretary shall by regulations prescribe) to an apportionment plan providing for an unequal allocation of such amounts. The amounts specified in paragraph (2) shall be divided equally among the component members of such group on such December 31 unless the Secretary prescribes regulations permitting an unequal allocation of such amounts. Notwithstanding paragraph (1), in applying the last 2 sentences of section 11(b)(1) to such component members, the taxable income of all such component members shall be taken into account and any increase in tax under such last 2 sentences shall be divided among such component members in the same manner as amounts under paragraph (1).

Amendments

- **2017, Tax Cuts and Jobs Act (P.L. 115-97)**

P.L. 115-97, §12001(b)(16)(A):

Amended Code Sec. 1561(a) by inserting "and" at the end of paragraph (1), by striking ", and" at the end of paragraph (2) and inserting a period, and by striking paragraph (3). **Effective** for tax years beginning after 12-31-2017. Prior to being stricken, Code Sec. 1561(a)(3) read as follows:

(3) one $40,000 exemption amount for purposes of computing the amount of the minimum tax.

P.L. 115-97, §12001(b)(16)(B):

Amended Code Sec. 1561(a) by striking the last sentence. **Effective** for tax years beginning after 12-31-2017. Prior to being stricken, the last sentence of Code Sec. 1561(a) read as follows:

In applying section 55(d)(3), the alternative minimum taxable income of all component members shall be taken into account and any decrease in the exemption amount shall be allocated to the component members in the same manner as under paragraph (3).

- **2014, Tax Technical Corrections Act of 2014 (P.L. 113-295)**

P.L. 113-295, §221(a)(12)(H)(i)-(ii), Division A:

Amended Code Sec. 1561(a) by inserting "and" at the end of paragraph (2), by striking ", and" at the end of paragraph (3) and inserting a period, and by striking paragraph (4), and by striking ", the amount specified in paragraph (3), and the amount specified in paragraph (4)" and inserting "and the amount specified in paragraph (3)". **Effective** generally 12-19-2014. For a special rule, see Act Sec. 221(b)(2), Division A, below. Prior to being stricken, Code Sec. 1561(a)(4) read as follows:

(4) one $2,000,000 amount for purposes of computing the tax imposed by section 59A.

P.L. 113-295, §221(b)(2), Division A, provides:

(2) SAVINGS PROVISION.—If—

(A) any provision amended or repealed by the amendments made by this section applied to—

(i) any transaction occurring before the date of the enactment of this Act,

(ii) any property acquired before such date of enactment, or

(iii) any item of income, loss, deduction, or credit taken into account before such date of enactment, and

(B) the treatment of such transaction, property, or item under such provision would (without regard to the amendments or repeals made by this section) affect the liability for tax for periods ending after date of enactment, nothing in the amendments or repeals made by this section shall be construed to affect the treatment of such transaction, property, or item for purposes of determining liability for tax for periods ending after such date of enactment.

- **1996, Small Business Job Protection Act of 1996 (P.L. 104-188)**

P.L. 104-188, §1703(f):

Amended Code Sec. 1561(a) by striking "last sentence" each place it appears and inserting "last 2 sentences". **Effective** as if included in the provision of P.L. 103-66 to which it relates.

- **1988, Technical and Miscellaneous Revenue Act of 1988 (P.L. 100-647)**

P.L. 100-647, §2004(l):

Amended Code Sec. 1561(a) by striking out "section 11(b)" and inserting in lieu thereof "section 11(b)(1)". **Effective** as if included in the provision of P.L. 100-203 to which it relates.

- **1986, Tax Reform Act of 1986 (P.L. 99-514)**

P.L. 99-514, §701(e)(2)(A)-(C):

Amended Code Sec. 1561(a) by striking out "and" at the end of paragraph (1), by striking out the period at the end of paragraph (2) and inserting in lieu thereof ", and" and by inserting after paragraph (2) new paragraph (3), by striking out "amounts specified in paragraph (1)" and inserting in lieu thereof "amounts specified in paragraph (1) (and the amount specified in paragraph (3))" and by adding at the end a new sentence. **Effective**, generally, for tax years beginning after 12-31-86. However, for special rules and exceptions, see Act Sec. 701(f)(2)-(7) following Code Sec. 56.

- **1986, Superfund Amendments and Reauthorization Act of 1986 (P.L. 99-499)**

P.L. 99-499, §516(b)(3)(A)-(B):

Amended Code Sec. 1561(a) by striking out "and" at the end of paragraph (2), by striking out the period at the end of paragraph (3) and inserting in lieu thereof ", and", and by inserting after paragraph (3) new paragraph (4), and by striking out "(and the amount specified in paragraph (3))" and inserting in lieu thereof ", the amount specified in paragraph (3), and the amount specified in paragraph (4)". **Effective** for tax years beginning after 12-31-86.

- **1984, Deficit Reduction Act of 1984 (P.L. 98-369)**

P.L. 98-369, §66(b):

Amended Code Sec. 1561(a) by adding a new sentence at the end. **Effective** for tax years beginning after 12-31-83 but shall not be treated as a change in a rate of tax for purposes of section 21 of the Internal Revenue Code of 1954.

P.L. 98-369, §211(b)(21)(A)(i):

Amended Code Sec. 1561(a) by striking out paragraphs (3) and (4), by adding "and" at the end of paragraph 1, and by striking out the comma at the end of paragraph (2) and inserting in lieu thereof a period. **Effective** for tax years beginning after 12-31-83. Prior to deletion, paragraphs (3) and (4) read as follows:

(3) one $25,000 amount for purposes of computing the limitation on the small business deduction of life insurance companies under sections 804(a)(3) and 809(d)(10), and

(4) one $1,000,000 amount (adjusted as provided in section 809(f)(3)) for purposes of computing the limitation under paragraph (1) or (2) of section 809(f).

P.L. 98-369, §211(b)(21)(A)(ii):

Amended Code Sec. 1561(a) by striking out "paragraphs (2), (3), and (4)" in the last sentence and inserting in lieu thereof "paragraph (2)". **Effective** for tax years beginning after 12-31-83.

INCOME TAX—CONSOLIDATED RETURNS

• **1982, Tax Equity and Fiscal Responsibility Act of 1982 (P.L. 97-248)**

P.L. 97-248, §259(b):

Amended Sec. 1561(a) by striking out "and" at the end of paragraph (2); by striking out the period at the end of paragraph (3) and inserting in lieu thereof a comma and "and"; by inserting after paragraph (3) new paragraph (4); and by striking out "(2) and (3)" and inserting in lieu thereof "(2), (3), and (4)". **Effective** for tax years beginning after 12-31-81 and before 1-1-84. See also amendment notes for P.L. 97-248 following Code Sec. 1561(b) for special rules.

• **1981, Economic Recovery Tax Act of 1981 (P.L. 97-34)**

P.L. 97-34, §232(b)(3):

Amended Code Sec. 1561(a)(2) by striking out "$150,000" and inserting in lieu thereof "$250,000 ($150,000 if any component member is a corporation described in section 535(c)(2)(B))". **Effective** for tax years beginning after 12-31-81.

• **1978, Revenue Act of 1978 (P.L. 95-600)**

P.L. 95-600, §301(b)(19)(A)(i)-(iii), 301(c):

Amended Code Sec. 1561(a). **Effective** for tax years beginning after 12-31-78. Prior to amendment, Code Sec. 1561(a) read as follows:

(a) GENERAL RULE.—The component members of a controlled group of corporations on a December 31 shall, for their taxable years which include such December 31, be limited for purposes of this subtitle to—

(1) one surtax exemption under section 11(d),

(2) one $150,000 amount for purposes of computing the accumulated earnings credit under section 535(c)(2) and (3), and

(3) one $25,000 amount for purposes of computing the limitation on the small business deduction of life insurance companies under sections 804(a)(3) and 809(d)(10).

The amount specified in paragraph (1) shall be divided equally among the component members of such group on such December 31 unless all of such component members consent (at such time and in such manner as the Secretary shall by regulations prescribe) to an apportionment plan providing for an unequal allocation of such amount. The amounts specified in paragraphs (2) and (3) shall be divided equally among the component members of such group on such December 31 unless the Secretary prescribes regulations permitting an unequal allocation of such amounts. In applying section 11(b)(2), the first $25,000 of taxable income and the second $25,000 of taxable income shall each be allocated among the component members of a controlled group of corporations in the same manner as the surtax exemption is allocated.

• **1976, Tax Reform Act of 1976 (P.L. 94-455)**

P.L. 94-455, §901(c)(1)(J)(v):

Added "In applying section 11(b)(2), ..." as a new last sentence of Code Sec. 1561(a). **Effective** for tax years after 12-31-75.

P.L. 94-455, §1901(b)(1)(J)(v):

Substituted "sections 804(a)(3)" for "sections 804(a)(4)" in Code Sec. 1561(a)(3). **Effective** with respect to tax years beginning after 12-31-76.

P.L. 94-455, §1906(b)(13)(A):

Amended 1954 Code by substituting "Secretary" for "Secretary or his delegate" each place it appeared. **Effective** 2-1-77.

• **1975, Revenue Adjustment Act of 1975 (P.L. 94-164)**

P.L. 94-164, §4(d):

Amended Sec. 1561(a)(1) by striking out "$50,000". **Effective** for tax years ending after 12-31-75.

• **1975, Tax Reduction Act of 1975 (P.L. 94-12)**

P.L. 94-12, §303(c):

Amended Sec. 1561(a)(1) by substituting "$50,000" for "$25,000". **Effective** for tax years ending after 12-31-74, but ceases to apply for tax years ending after 12-31-75. In applying Sec. 11(b)(2) of Sec. 11, the first $25,000 of taxable income and the second $25,000 of taxable income shall each be allocated among the component members of a controlled group of corporations in the same manner as the surtax exemption is allocated.

P.L. 94-12, §304(b):

Amended Sec. 1561(a)(2) by substituting "$150,000" for "$100,000". **Effective** for tax years beginning after 12-31-74.

• **1969, Tax Reform Act of 1969 (P.L. 91-172)**

P.L. 91-172, §401(a)(1):

Amended Code Sec. 1561(a). **Effective** for tax years beginning after 12-31-74. Prior to amendment, Code Sec. 1561(a) read as follows:

"(a) General Rule.—If a corporation is a component member of a controlled group of corporations on a December 31, then for purposes of this subtitle the surtax exemption of such corporation for the taxable year which includes such December 31 shall be an amount equal to—

"(1) $25,000 divided by the number of corporations which are component members of such group on such December 31, or

"(2) if all such component members consent (at such time and in such manner as the Secretary or his delegate shall by regulations prescribe) to an apportionment plan, such portion of $25,000 as is apportioned to such member in accordance with such plan.

The sum of the amounts apportioned under paragraph (2) among the component members of any controlled group shall not exceed $25,000."

• **1964, Revenue Act of 1964 (P.L. 88-272)**

P.L. 88-272, §235(a):

Added Code Sec. 1561(a). **Effective** for tax years ending after 12-31-63.

[Sec. 1561(b)]

(b) CERTAIN SHORT TAXABLE YEARS.—If a corporation has a short taxable year which does not include a December 31 and is a component member of a controlled group of corporations with respect to such taxable year, then for purposes of this subtitle—

(1) the amount in each taxable income bracket in the tax table in section 11(b), and

(2) the amount to be used in computing the accumulated earnings credit under section 535(c)(2) and (3),

of such corporation for such taxable year shall be the amount specified in subsection (a)(1) or (2), as the case may be, divided by the number of corporations which are component members of such group on the last day of such taxable year. For purposes of the preceding sentence, section 1563(b) shall be applied as if such last day were substituted for December 31.

Amendments

• **1984, Deficit Reduction Act of 1984 (P.L. 98-369)**

P.L. 98-369, §211(b)(21)(B)(i):

Amended Code Sec. 1561(b) by striking out paragraphs (3) and (4) and by adding "and" at the end of paragraph (1). **Effective** for tax years beginning after 12-31-83. Prior to deletion, paragraphs (3) and (4) read as follows:

(3) the amount to be used in computing the limitation on the small business deduction of life insurance companies under sections 804(a)(3) and 809(d)(10), and

(4) the amount (adjusted as provided in section 809(f)(3)) to be used in computing the limitation under paragraph (1) or (2) of section 809(f),

P.L. 98-369, §211(b)(21)(B)(ii):

Amended Code Sec. 1561(b) by striking out ", (2), (3), or (4)" and inserting in lieu thereof "or (2)". **Effective** for tax years beginning after 12-31-83.

• **1982, Tax Equity and Fiscal Responsibility Act of 1982 (P.L. 97-248)**

P.L. 97-248, §259(c):

Amended Code Sec. 1561(b) by striking out "and" at the end of paragraph (2); by striking out the comma at the end of paragraph (3) and inserting in lieu thereof a comma and "and"; by inserting after paragraph (3) the new paragraph (4); and by striking out "(2), or (3)" and inserting in lieu thereof "(2), (3), or (4)". **Effective** for tax years beginning after 12-31-81 and before 1-1-84. The following special rules apply for certain transactions in tax years beginning before 1-1-82.

"Special Rules for Certain Transactions in Taxable Years Beginning Before January 1, 1982.—

(1) Certain interest and premiums.—

(A) In general.—In the case of any taxable year beginning before January 1, 1982, if a taxpayer, on his return of tax for such taxable year, treated—

(i) any amount described in subparagraph (B) as an amount which was not a dividend to policyholders (within the meaning of section 811 of the Internal Revenue Code of 1954), or

(ii) any amount described in subparagraph (C) as not described in section 809(c)(1), then such amounts shall be so treated for purposes of the Internal Revenue Code of 1954.

(B) Certain interest.—An amount is described in this subparagraph if such amount is in the nature of interest accrued for the taxable year on an insurance or annuity contract pursuant to—

(i) an interest rate guaranteed or fixed before the period of payment of such amount begins, or

(ii) any other method (fixed before such period begins) the terms of which during the period are beyond the control and are independent of the experience of the company, whether or not the interest rate or other method was guaranteed or fixed for any specified period of time.

(C) Amounts not treated as premiums.—An amount is described in this subparagraph if such amount represents the difference between—

(i) the amount of premiums received or mortality charges made under rates fixed in advance of the premium or mortality charge due date, and

(ii) the maximum premium or mortality charge which could be charged under the terms of the insurance or annuity contract.

(D) No inference.—The provisions of this paragraph shall constitute no inference with respect to the treatment of any item in taxable years beginning after December 31, 1981.

(2) Consolidated returns.—The provisions of section 818(f) of such Code, as amended by section 262, shall apply to any taxable year beginning before January 1, 1982, if the taxpayer filed a consolidated return before July 1, 1982 for such taxable year under section 1501 of such Code which, on such date (determined without regard to any amended return filed after June 30, 1982), was consistent with the provisions of section 818(f) of such Code, as so amended. In the case of a taxable year beginning in 1981, the preceding sentence shall be applied by substituting "September 16" for "July 1" and "September 15" for "June 30".

(3) Taxable years where period of limitation has run.—This subsection shall not apply to any taxable year with respect to which the statute of limitations for filing a claim for credit or refund has expired under any provision of law or by operation of law."

• **1978, Revenue Act of 1978 (P.L. 95-600)**

P.L. 95-600, §§301(b)(19)(B), (c):

Amended Code Sec. 1561(b)(1). **Effective** for tax years beginning after 12-31-78. Prior to amendment, Code Sec. 1561(b)(1) read:

(1) the surtax exemption under section 11(d),

P.L. 95-600, §§703(j)(7), (r):

Amended Code Sec. 1561(b)(3) by striking out "804(a)(4)" and inserting in place thereof "804(a)(3)". **Effective** 10-4-76.

Sec. 1561(b)

INCOME TAX—CONSOLIDATED RETURNS

• **1969, Tax Reform Act of 1969 (P.L. 91-172)**

P.L. 91-172, § 401(a)(1):

Amended Code Sec. 1561. **Effective** for tax years beginning after 12-31-74. Prior to amendment, Code Sec. 1561(b) read as follows:

"(b) CERTAIN SHORT TAXABLE YEARS.—If a corporation—

"(1) has a short taxable year which does not include a December 31, and

"(2) is a component member of a controlled group of corporations with respect to such taxable year,

then for purposes of this subtitle the surtax exemption of such corporation for such taxable year shall be an amount equal to $25,000 divided by the number of corporations which are component members of such group on the last day of such taxable year. For purposes of the preceding sentence, section 1563(b) shall be applied as if such last day were substituted for December 31."

• **1964, Revenue Act of 1964 (P.L. 88-272)**

P.L. 88-272, § 235(a):

Added Code Sec. 1561(b). **Effective** for tax years ending after 12-31-63.

[Sec. 1562—Repealed]

Amendments

• **1969, Tax Reform Act of 1969 (P.L. 91-172)**

P.L. 91-172, § 401(a)(2):

Repealed Sec. 1562. **Effective** for tax years beginning after 12-31-74. Prior to amendment, Sec. 1562 read as follows:

"SEC. 1562. PRIVILEGE OF GROUPS TO ELECT MULTIPLE SURTAX EXEMPTIONS

"(a) ELECTION OF MULTIPLE SURTAX EXEMPTIONS.—

"(1) IN GENERAL.—A controlled group of corporations shall (subject to the provisions of this section) have the privilege of electing to have each of its component members make its returns without regard to section 1561. Such election shall be made with respect to a specified December 31 and shall be valid only if—

"(A) each corporation which is a component member of such group on such December 31, and

"(B) each other corporation which is a component member of such group on any succeeding December 31 before the day on which the election is filed,

consents to such election.

"(2) YEARS FOR WHICH EFFECTIVE.—An election by a controlled group of corporations under paragraph (1) shall be effective with respect to the taxable year of each component member of such group which includes the specified December 31, and each taxable year of each corporation which is a component member of such group (or a successor group) on a succeeding December 31 included within such taxable year, unless the election is terminated under subsection (c).

"(3) EFFECT OF ELECTION.—If an election by a controlled group of corporations under paragraph (1) is effective with respect to any taxable year of a corporation—

"(A) section 1561 shall not apply to such corporation for such taxable year, but

"(B) the additional tax imposed by subsection (b) shall apply to such corporation for such taxable year.

"(b) ADDITIONAL TAX IMPOSED.—

"(1) GENERAL RULE.—If an election under subsection (a)(1) by a controlled group of corporations is effective with respect to the taxable year of a corporation, there is hereby imposed for such taxable year on the taxable income of such corporation a tax equal to 6 percent of so much of such corporation's taxable income for such taxable year as does not exceed the amount of such corporation's surtax exemption for such taxable year. This paragraph shall not apply to the taxable year of a corporation if—

"(A) such corporation is the only component member of such controlled group on the December 31 included in such corporation's taxable year which has taxable income for a taxable year including such December 31, or

"(B) such corporation's surtax exemption is disallowed for such taxable year under any provision of this subtitle.

"(2) TAX TREATED AS IMPOSED BY SECTION 11 ETC.—If for the taxable year of a corporation a tax is imposed by section 11 on the taxable income of such corporation, the additional tax imposed by this subsection shall be treated for purposes of this title as a tax imposed by section 11. If for the taxable year of a corporation a tax is imposed on the taxable income of such corporation which is computed under any other section by reference to section 11, the additional tax imposed by this subsection shall be treated for purposes of this title as imposed by such other section.

"(3) TAXABLE INCOME DEFINED.—For purposes of this subsection, the term "taxable income" means—

"(A) in the case of a corporation subject to tax under section 511, its unrelated business taxable income (within the meaning of section 512);

"(B) in the case of a life insurance company, its life insurance company taxable income (within the meaning of section 802(b));

"(C) in the case of a regulated investment company, its investment company taxable income (within the meaning of section 852(b)(2)); and

"(D) in the case of a real estate investment trust, its real estate investment trust taxable income (within the meaning of section 857(b)(2)).

"(4) SPECIAL RULES.—If for the taxable year an additional tax is imposed on the taxable income of a corporation by this subsection, then sections 244 (relating to dividends received on certain preferred stock), 247 (relating to dividends paid on certain preferred stock of public utilities), 804(a)(3) (relating to deduction for partially tax-exempt interest in the case of a life insurance company), and 922 (relating to special deduction for Western Hemisphere trade corporations) shall be applied without regard to the additional tax imposed by this subsection.

"(c) TERMINATION OF ELECTION.—An election by a controlled group of corporations under subsection (a) shall terminate with respect to such group—

"(1) CONSENT OF THE MEMBERS.—If such group files a termination of such election with respect to a specified December 31, and—

"(A) each corporation which is a component member of such group on such December 31, and

"(B) each other corporation which is a component member of such group on any succeeding December 31 before the day on which the termination is filed,

consents to such termination.

"(2) REFUSAL BY NEW MEMBER TO CONSENT.—If on December 31 of any year such group includes a component member which—

"(A) on the immediately preceding January 1 was not a member of such group, and

"(B) within the time and in the manner provided by regulations prescribed by the Secretary or his delegate, files a statement that it does not consent to the election.

"(3) CONSOLIDATED RETURNS.—If—

"(A) a corporation is a component member (determined without regard to section 1563(b)(3)) of such group on a December 31 included within a taxable year ending on or after January 1, 1964, and

"(B) such corporation is a member of an affiliated group of corporations which makes a consolidated return under this chapter (sec. 1501 and following) for such taxable year.

"(4) CONTROLLED GROUP NO LONGER IN EXISTENCE.—If such group is considered as no longer in existence with respect to any December 31.

Such termination shall be effective with respect to the December 31 referred to in paragraph (1)(A), (2), (3), or (4), as the case may be.

"(d) ELECTION AFTER TERMINATION.—If an election by a controlled group of corporations is terminated under subsection (c), such group (and any successor group) shall not be eligible to make an election under subsection (a) with respect to any December 31, before the sixth December 31 after the December 31 with respect to which such termination was effective.

"(e) MANNER AND TIME OF GIVING CONSENT AND MAKING ELECTION, ETC.—An election under subsection (a)(1) or a termination under subsection (c)(1) (and the consent of each member of a controlled group of corporations which is required with respect to such election or termination) shall be made in such manner as the Secretary or his delegate shall by regulations prescribe, and shall be made at any time before the expiration of 3 years after—

"(1) in the case of such an election, the date when the income tax return for the taxable year of the component member of the controlled group which has the taxable year ending first on or after the specified December 31 is required to be filed (without regard to any extensions of time), and

"(2) in the case of such a termination, the specified December 31 with respect to which such termination was made.

Any consent to such an election or termination, and a failure by a component member to file a statement that it does not consent to an election under this section, shall be deemed to be a consent to the application of subsection (g)(1) (relating to tolling of statute of limitations on assessment of deficiencies).

"(f) SPECIAL RULES.—For purposes of this section—

"(1) CONTINUING AND SUCCESSOR CONTROLLED GROUPS.—The determination of whether a controlled group of corporations—

"(A) is considered as no longer in existence with respect to any December 31, or

"(B) is a successor to another controlled group of corporations (and the effect of such determination with respect to any election or termination),

shall be made under regulations prescribed by the Secretary or his delegate. For purposes of subparagraph (B), such regulations shall be based on the continuation (or termination) of predominant equitable ownership.

"(2) CERTAIN SHORT TAXABLE YEARS.—If one or more corporations have short taxable years which do not include a December 31 and are component members of a controlled group of corporations with respect to such taxable years (determined by applying section 1563(b) as if the last day of each such taxable year were substituted for December 31), then an election by such group under this section shall apply with respect to such corporations with respect to such taxable years if—

"(A) such election is in effect with respect to both the December 31 immediately preceding such taxable years and the December 31 immediately succeeding such taxable years, or

"(B) such election is in effect with respect to the December 31 immediately preceding or succeeding such taxable years and each such corporation files a consent to the application of such election to its short taxable year at such time and in such manner as the Secretary or his delegate shall prescribe by regulations.

"(g) TOLLING OF STATUTE OF LIMITATIONS.—In any case in which a controlled group of corporations makes an election or termination under this section, the statutory period—

"(1) for assessment of any deficiency against a corporation which is a component member of such group for any taxable year, to the extent such deficiency is attributable to the application of this part, shall not expire before the expiration of one year after the date such election or termination is made; and

"(2) for allowing or making credit or refund of any overpayment of tax by a corporation which is a component member of such group for any taxable year, to the extent such credit or refund is attributable to the application of this part, shall not expire before the expiration of one year after the date such election or termination is made."

• **1969, Tax Reform Act of 1969 (P.L. 91-172)**

P.L. 91-172, § 401(b)(2)(A):

Amended Sec. 1562(b)(1) by inserting "the amount of such corporation's surtax exemption for such taxable year" in lieu of "$25,000". **Effective** for tax years beginning after 12-31-69.

P.L. 91-172, § 401(g), provides:

"Retroactive Termination of Section 1562 Elections.—If an affiliated group of corporations makes a consolidated return for the taxable year which includes December 31, 1970 (hereinafter in this subsection referred to as "1970 consolidated return

INCOME TAX—CONSOLIDATED RETURNS

year"), then on or before the due date prescribed by law (including any extensions thereof) for filing such consolidated return such affiliated group of corporations may terminate the election under section 1562 of the Internal Revenue Code of 1954 with respect to any prior December 31 which is included in a taxable year of any of such corporations from which there is a net operating loss carryover to the 1970 consolidated return year. A termination of an election under this subsection shall be valid only if it meets the requirements of sections 1562(c)(1) and 1562(e) of such Code (other than making the termination before the expiration of the 3-year period specified in section 1562(e))."

• **1964, Revenue Act of 1964 (P.L. 88-272)**

P.L. 88-272, §235(a):

Added Code Sec. 1562. **Effective** for tax years ending after 12-31-63.

[Sec. 1563]

SEC. 1563. DEFINITIONS AND SPECIAL RULES.

[Sec. 1563(a)]

(a) CONTROLLED GROUP OF CORPORATIONS.—For purposes of this part, the term "controlled group of corporations" means any group of—

(1) PARENT-SUBSIDIARY CONTROLLED GROUP.—One or more chains of corporations connected through stock ownership with a common parent corporation if—

(A) stock possessing at least 80 percent of the total combined voting power of all classes of stock entitled to vote or at least 80 percent of the total value of shares of all classes of stock of each of the corporations, except the common parent corporation, is owned (within the meaning of subsection (d)(1)) by one or more of the other corporations; and

(B) the common parent corporation owns (within the meaning of subsection (d)(1)) stock possessing at least 80 percent of the total combined voting power of all classes of stock entitled to vote or at least 80 percent of the total value of shares of all classes of stock of at least one of the other corporations, excluding, in computing such voting power or value, stock owned directly by such other corporations.

(2) BROTHER-SISTER CONTROLLED GROUP.—Two or more corporations if 5 or fewer persons who are individuals, estates, or trusts own (within the meaning of subsection (d)(2)) stock possessing more than 50 percent of the total combined voting power of all classes of stock entitled to vote or more than 50 percent of the total value of shares of all classes of stock of each corporation, taking into account the stock ownership of each such person only to the extent such stock ownership is identical with respect to each such corporation.

(3) COMBINED GROUP.—Three or more corporations each of which is a member of a group of corporations described in paragraph (1) or (2), and one of which—

(A) is a common parent corporation included in a group of corporations described in paragraph (1), and also

(B) is included in a group of corporations described in paragraph (2).

(4) CERTAIN INSURANCE COMPANIES.—Two or more insurance companies subject to taxation under section 801 which are members of a controlled group of corporations described in paragraph (1), (2), or (3). Such insurance companies shall be treated as a controlled group of corporations separate from any other corporations which are members of the controlled group of corporations described in paragraph (1), (2), or (3).

Amendments

• **2004, American Jobs Creation Act of 2004 (P.L. 108-357)**

P.L. 108-357, §900(a):

Amended Code Sec. 1563(a)(2) by striking "possessing—" and all that follows through "(B)" and inserting "possessing". **Effective** for tax years beginning after 10-22-2004. Prior to amendment, Code Sec. 1563(a)(2) read as follows:

(2) BROTHER-SISTER CONTROLLED GROUP.—Two or more corporations if 5 or fewer persons who are individuals, estates, or trusts own (within the meaning of subsection (d)(2)) stock possessing—

(A) at least 80 percent of the total combined voting power of all classes of stock entitled to vote or at least 80 percent of the total value of shares of all classes of the stock of each corporation, and

(B) more than 50 percent of the total combined voting power of all classes of stock entitled to vote or more than 50 percent of the total value of shares of all classes of stock of each corporation, taking into account the stock ownership of each such person only to the extent such stock ownership is identical with respect to each such corporation.

• **1984, Deficit Reduction Act of 1984 (P.L. 98-369)**

P.L. 98-369, §211(b)(22):

Amended Code Sec. 1563(a)(4) by striking out "section 802" and inserting in lieu thereof "section 801". **Effective** for tax years beginning after 12-31-83.

• **1969, Tax Reform Act of 1969 (P.L. 91-172)**

P.L. 91-172, §401(c):

Amended paragraph (a)(2). **Effective** for tax years ending on or after 12-31-70. Prior to amendment, paragraph (a)(2) read as follows:

(a)(2) Brother-Sister Controlled Group.—Two or more corporations if stock possessing at least 80 percent of the total combined voting power of all classes of stock entitled to vote or at least 80 percent of the total value of shares of all classes of stock of each of the corporations is owned (within the meaning of subsection (d)(2)) by one person who is an individual, estate, or trust.

[Sec. 1563(b)]

(b) COMPONENT MEMBER.—

(1) GENERAL RULE.—For purposes of this part, a corporation is a component member of a controlled group of corporations on a December 31 of any taxable year (and with respect to the taxable year which includes such December 31) if such corporation—

(A) is a member of such controlled group of corporations on the December 31 included in such year and is not treated as an excluded member under paragraph (2), or

(B) is not a member of such controlled group of corporations on the December 31 included in such year but is treated as an additional member under paragraph (3).

(2) EXCLUDED MEMBERS.—A corporation which is a member of a controlled group of corporations on December 31 of any taxable year shall be treated as an excluded member of such group for the taxable year including such December 31 if such corporation—

(A) is a member of such group for less than one-half the number of days in such taxable year which precede such December 31,

(B) is exempt from taxation under section 501(a) (except a corporation which is subject to tax on its unrelated business taxable income under section 511) for such taxable year,

(C) is a foreign corporation subject to tax under section 881 for such taxable year,

(D) is an insurance company subject to taxation under section 801 (other than an insurance company which is a member of a controlled group described in subsection (a)(4)), or

(E) is a franchised corporation, as defined in subsection (f)(4).

(3) ADDITIONAL MEMBERS.—A corporation which—

(A) was a member of a controlled group of corporations at any time during a calendar year,

(B) is not a member of such group on December 31 of such calendar year, and

(C) is not described, with respect to such group, in subparagraph (B), (C), (D), or (E) of paragraph (2),

shall be treated as an additional member of such group on December 31 for its taxable year including such December 31 if it was a member of such group for one-half (or more) of the number of days in such taxable year which precede such December 31.

(4) OVERLAPPING GROUPS.—If a corporation is a component member of more than one controlled group of corporations with respect to any taxable year, such corporation shall be treated as a component member of only one controlled group. The determination as to the group of

INCOME TAX—CONSOLIDATED RETURNS

which such corporation is a component member shall be made under regulations prescribed by the Secretary which are consistent with the purposes of this part.

Amendments

• **1986, Tax Reform Act of 1986 (P.L. 99-514)**

P.L. 99-514, § 1024(c)(17):

Amended Code Sec. 1563(b)(2)(D) by striking out "or section 821". **Effective** for tax years beginning after 12-31-86. For transitional rules, see Act Sec. 1024(d) following Code Sec. 1504. Prior to amendment, Code Sec. 1563(b)(2)(D) read as follows:

(D) is an insurance company subject to taxation under section 801 or section 821 (other than an insurance company which is a member of a controlled group described in subsection (a)(4)), or

• **1984, Deficit Reduction Act of 1984 (P.L. 98-369)**

P.L. 98-369, § 211(b)(22):

Amended Code Sec. 1563(b)(2)(D) by striking out "section 802" and inserting in lieu thereof "section 801". **Effective** for tax years beginning after 12-31-83.

• **1976, Tax Reform Act of 1976 (P.L. 94-455)**

P.L. 94-455, § 1906(b)(13)(A):

Amended 1954 Code by substituting "Secretary" for "Secretary or his delegate" each place it appeared. **Effective** 2-1-77.

[Sec. 1563(c)]

(c) CERTAIN STOCK EXCLUDED.—

(1) GENERAL RULE.—For purposes of this part, the term "stock" does not include—

(A) nonvoting stock which is limited and preferred as to dividends,

(B) treasury stock, and

(C) stock which is treated as "excluded stock" under paragraph (2).

(2) STOCK TREATED AS "EXCLUDED STOCK".—

(A) PARENT-SUBSIDIARY CONTROLLED GROUP.—For purposes of subsection (a)(1), if a corporation (referred to in this paragraph as "parent corporation") owns (within the meaning of subsections (d)(1) and (e)(4)), 50 percent or more of the total combined voting power of all classes of stock entitled to vote or 50 percent or more of the total value of shares of all classes of stock in another corporation (referred to in this paragraph as "subsidiary corporation"), the following stock of the subsidiary corporation shall be treated as excluded stock—

(i) stock in the subsidiary corporation held by a trust which is part of a plan of deferred compensation for the benefit of the employees of the parent corporation or the subsidiary corporation,

(ii) stock in the subsidiary corporation owned by an individual (within the meaning of subsection (d)(2)) who is a principal stockholder or officer of the parent corporation. For purposes of this clause, the term "principal stockholder" of a corporation means an individual who owns (within the meaning of subsection (d)(2)) 5 percent or more of the total combined voting power of all classes of stock entitled to vote or 5 percent or more of the total value of shares of all classes of stock in such corporation,

(iii) stock in the subsidiary corporation owned (within the meaning of subsection (d)(2)) by an employee of the subsidiary corporation if such stock is subject to conditions which run in favor of such parent (or subsidiary) corporation and which substantially restrict or limit the employee's right (or if the employee constructively owns such stock, the direct owner's right) to dispose of such stock, or

(iv) stock in the subsidiary corporation owned (within the meaning of subsection (d)(2)) by an organization (other than the parent corporation) to which section 501 (relating to certain educational and charitable organizations which are exempt from tax) applies and which is controlled directly or indirectly by the parent corporation or subsidiary corporation, by an individual, estate, or trust that is a principal stockholder (within the meaning of clause (ii)) of the parent corporation, by an officer of the parent corporation, or by any combination thereof.

(B) BROTHER-SISTER CONTROLLED GROUP.—For purposes of subsection (a)(2), if 5 or fewer persons who are individuals, estates, or trusts (referred to in this subparagraph as "common owners") own (within the meaning of subsection (d)(2)), 50 percent or more of the total combined voting power of all classes of stock entitled to vote or 50 percent or more of the total value of shares of all classes of stock in a corporation, the following stock of such corporation shall be treated as excluded stock—

(i) stock in such corporation held by an employees' trust described in section 401(a) which is exempt from tax under section 501(a), if such trust is for the benefit of the employees of such corporation,

(ii) stock in such corporation owned (within the meaning of subsection (d)(2)) by an employee of the corporation if such stock is subject to conditions which run in favor of any of such common owners (or such corporation) and which substantially restrict or limit the employee's right (or if the employee constructively owns such stock, the direct owner's right) to dispose of such stock. If a condition which limits or restricts the employee's right (or the direct owner's right) to dispose of such stock also applies to the stock held by any of the common owners pursuant to a bona fide reciprocal stock purchase arrangement, such condition shall not be treated as one which restricts or limits the employee's right to dispose of such stock, or

(iii) stock in such corporation owned (within the meaning of subsection (d)(2)) by an organization to which section 501 (relating to certain educational and charitable organizations which are exempt from tax) applies and which is controlled directly or indirectly by such corporation, by an individual, estate, or trust that is a principal stockholder (within the meaning of subparagraph (A)(ii)) of such corporation, by an officer of such corporation, or by any combination thereof.

Amendments

• **1969, Tax Reform Act of 1969 (P.L. 91-172)**

P.L. 91-172, § 401(d)(1):

Amended subparagraph (c)(2)(A) by striking out "or" at the end of subdivision (ii), by inserting "stock, or" in lieu of "stock." at the end of subdivision (iii), and by adding new subdivision (iv). **Effective** for tax years ending on or after 12-31-70.

P.L. 91-172, § 401(d)(2):

Amended subparagraph (c)(2)(B) by inserting "5 or fewer persons who are individuals, estates, or trusts (referred to in this subparagraph as 'common owners') own" in lieu of "a person who is an individual, estate, or trust (referred to in this paragraph as 'common owner') owns" in that portion of subparagraph (c)(2)(B) which precedes subdivision (i), by striking out "or" at the end of subdivision (i), by striking out in subdivision (ii) "such common owner", "the common owner", and "stock." and inserting in lieu thereof "any of such common owners", "any of the common owners", and "stock, or", respectively, and by adding new subdivision (c)(2)(B)(iii). **Effective** for tax years ending on or after 12-31-70.

[Sec. 1563(d)]

(d) RULES FOR DETERMINING STOCK OWNERSHIP.—

(1) PARENT-SUBSIDIARY CONTROLLED GROUP.—For purposes of determining whether a corporation is a member of a parent-subsidiary controlled group of corporations (within the meaning of subsection (a)(1)), stock owned by a corporation means—

(A) stock owned directly by such corporation, and

(B) stock owned with the application of paragraphs (1), (2), and (3) of subsection (e).

(2) BROTHER-SISTER CONTROLLED GROUP.—For purposes of determining whether a corporation is a member of a brother-sister controlled group of corporations (within the meaning of subsection (a)(2)), stock owned by a person who is an individual, estate, or trust means—

(A) stock owned directly by such person, and

(B) stock owned with the application of subsection (e).

INCOME TAX—CONSOLIDATED RETURNS

Amendments

• 1988, Technical and Miscellaneous Revenue Act of 1988 (P.L. 100-647)

P.L. 100-647, § 1018(s)(3)(A):

Amended Code Sec. 1563(d)(1)(B) by striking out "subsection (e)(1)" and inserting in lieu thereof "paragraphs (1), (2), and (3) of subsection (e)". **Effective** for tax years beginning after 11-10-88.

[Sec. 1563(e)]

(e) CONSTRUCTIVE OWNERSHIP.—

(1) OPTIONS.—If any person has an option to acquire stock, such stock shall be considered as owned by such person. For purposes of this paragraph, an option to acquire such an option, and each one of a series of such options, shall be considered as an option to acquire such stock.

(2) ATTRIBUTION FROM PARTNERSHIPS.—Stock owned, directly or indirectly, by or for a partnership shall be considered as owned by any partner having an interest of 5 percent or more in either the capital or profits of the partnership in proportion to his interest in capital or profits, whichever such proportion is the greater.

(3) ATTRIBUTION FROM ESTATES OR TRUSTS.—

(A) Stock owned, directly or indirectly, by or for an estate or trust shall be considered as owned by any beneficiary who has an actuarial interest of 5 percent or more in such stock, to the extent of such actuarial interest. For purposes of this subparagraph, the actuarial interest of each beneficiary shall be determined by assuming the maximum exercise of discretion by the fiduciary in favor of such beneficiary and the maximum use of such stock to satisfy his rights as a beneficiary.

(B) Stock owned, directly or indirectly, by or for any portion of a trust of which a person is considered the owner under subpart E of part I of subchapter J (relating to grantors and others treated as substantial owners) shall be considered as owned by such person.

(C) This paragraph shall not apply to stock owned by any employees' trust described in section 401(a) which is exempt from tax under section 501(a).

(4) ATTRIBUTION FROM CORPORATIONS.—Stock owned, directly or indirectly, by or for a corporation shall be considered as owned by any person who owns (within the meaning of subsection (d)) 5 percent or more in value of its stock in that proportion which the value of the stock which such person so owns bears to the value of all the stock in such corporation.

(5) SPOUSE.—An individual shall be considered as owning stock in a corporation owned, directly or indirectly, by or for his spouse (other than a spouse who is legally separated from the individual under a decree of divorce whether interlocutory or final, or a decree of separate maintenance), except in the case of a corporation with respect to which each of the following conditions is satisfied for its taxable year—

(A) The individual does not, at any time during such taxable year, own directly any stock in such corporation;

(B) The individual is not a director or employee and does not participate in the management of such corporation at any time during such taxable year;

(C) Not more than 50 percent of such corporation's gross income for such taxable year was derived from royalties, rents, dividends, interest, and annuities; and

(D) Such stock in such corporation is not, at any time during such taxable year, subject to conditions which substantially restrict or limit the spouse's right to dispose of such stock and which run in favor of the individual or his children who have not attained the age of 21 years.

(6) CHILDREN, GRANDCHILDREN, PARENTS, AND GRANDPARENTS.—

(A) MINOR CHILDREN.—An individual shall be considered as owning stock owned, directly or indirectly, by or for his children who have not attained the age of 21 years, and, if the individual has not attained the age of 21 years, the stock owned, directly or indirectly, by or for his parents.

(B) ADULT CHILDREN AND GRANDCHILDREN.—An individual who owns (within the meaning of subsection (d)(2), but without regard to this subparagraph) more than 50 percent of the total combined voting power of all classes of stock entitled to vote or more than 50 percent of the total value of shares of all classes of stock in a corporation shall be considered as owning the stock in such corporation owned, directly or indirectly, by or for his parents, grandparents, grandchildren, and children who have attained the age of 21 years.

(C) ADOPTED CHILD.—For purposes of this section, a legally adopted child of an individual shall be treated as a child of such individual by blood.

[Sec. 1563(f)]

(f) OTHER DEFINITIONS AND RULES.—

(1) EMPLOYEE DEFINED.—For purposes of this section the term "employee" has the same meaning such term is given by paragraphs (1) and (2) of section 3121(d).

(2) OPERATING RULES.—

(A) IN GENERAL.—Except as provided in subparagraph (B), stock constructively owned by a person by reason of the application of paragraph (1), (2), (3), (4), (5), or (6) of subsection (e) shall, for purposes of applying such paragraphs, be treated as actually owned by such person.

(B) MEMBERS OF FAMILY.—Stock constructively owned by an individual by reason of the application of paragraph (5) or (6) of subsection (e) shall not be treated as owned by him for purposes of again applying such paragraphs in order to make another the constructive owner of such stock.

(3) SPECIAL RULES.—For purposes of this section—

(A) If stock may be considered as owned by a person under subsection (e)(1) and under any other paragraph of subsection (e), it shall be considered as owned by him under subsection (e)(1).

(B) If stock is owned (within the meaning of subsection (d)) by two or more persons, such stock shall be considered as owned by the person whose ownership of such stock results in the corporation being a component member of a controlled group. If by reason of the preceding sentence, a corporation would (but for this sentence) become a component member of two controlled groups, it shall be treated as a component member of one controlled group. The determination as to the group of which such corporation is a component member shall be made under regulations prescribed by the Secretary which are consistent with the purposes of this part.

(C) If stock is owned by a person within the meaning of subsection (d) and such ownership results in the corporation being a component member of a controlled group, such stock shall not be treated as excluded stock under subsection (c)(2), if by reason of treating such stock as excluded stock the result is that such corporation is not a component member of a controlled group of corporations.

(4) FRANCHISED CORPORATION.—If—

(A) a parent corporation (as defined in subsection (c)(2)(A)), or a common owner (as defined in subsection (c)(2)(B)), of a corporation which is a member of a controlled group of corporations is under a duty (arising out of a written agreement) to sell stock of such corporation (referred to in this paragraph as "franchised corporation") which is franchised to sell the products of another member, or the common owner, of such controlled group;

(B) such stock is to be sold to an employee (or employees) of such franchised corporation pursuant to a bona fide plan designed to eliminate the stock ownership of the parent corporation or of the common owner in the franchised corporation;

(C) such plan—

(i) provides a reasonable selling price for such stock, and

(ii) requires that a portion of the employee's share of the profits of such corporation (whether received as compensation or as a dividend) be applied to the purchase of such stock (or the purchase of notes, bonds, debentures or other similar evidence of indebtedness of such franchised corporation held by such parent corporation or common owner);

(D) such employee (or employees) owns directly more than 20 percent of the total value of shares of all classes of stock in such franchised corporation;

(E) more than 50 percent of the inventory of such franchised corporation is acquired from members of the controlled group, the common owner, or both; and

(F) all of the conditions contained in subparagraphs (A), (B), (C), (D), and (E) have been met for one-half (or more) of the number of days preceding the December 31 included within the taxable year (or if the taxable year does not include December 31, the last day of such year) of the franchised corporation.

then such franchised corporation shall be treated as an excluded member of such group, under subsection (b)(2), for such taxable year.

(5) BROTHER-SISTER CONTROLLED GROUP DEFINITION FOR PROVISIONS OTHER THAN THIS PART.—

(A) IN GENERAL.—Except as specifically provided in an applicable provision, subsection (a)(2) shall be applied to an applicable provision as if it read as follows:

(2) "BROTHER-SISTER CONTROLLED GROUP.—Two or more corporations if 5 or fewer persons who are individuals, estates, or trusts own (within the meaning of subsection (d)(2) stock possessing—

(A) "at least 80 percent of the total combined voting power of all classes of stock entitled to vote, or at least 80 percent of the total value of shares of all classes of stock, of each corporation, and

(B) "more than 50 percent of the total combined voting power of all classes of stock entitled to vote or more than 50 percent of the total value of shares of all classes of stock of each corporation, taking into account the stock ownership of each such person only to the extent such stock ownership is identical with respect to each such corporation."

(B) APPLICABLE PROVISION.—For purposes of this paragraph, an applicable provision is any provision of law (other than this part) which incorporates the definition of controlled group of corporations under subsection (a).

Amendments

• **2004, American Jobs Creation Act of 2004 (P.L. 108-357)**

P.L. 108-357, § 900(b):

Amended Code Sec. 1563(f) by adding at the end a new paragraph (5). **Effective** for tax years beginning after 10-22-2004.

• **1976, Tax Reform Act of 1976 (P.L. 94-455)**

P.L. 94-455, § 1906(b)(13)(A):

Amended 1954 Code by substituting "Secretary" for "Secretary or his delegate" each place it appeared. **Effective** 2-1-77.

• **1970, Employment Security Amendments of 1970 (P.L. 91-373)**

P.L. 91-373, § 102(b):

Amended Code Sec. 1563(f)(1) by substituting "by paragraphs (1) and (2) of section 3121(d)" for "in section 3306(i)". **Effective** 8-10-70.

• **1964, Revenue Act of 1964 (P.L. 88-272)**

P.L. 88-272, § 235(a):

Added Code Sec. 1563. **Effective** for tax years ending after 12-31-63.

[Sec. 1564—Repealed]

Amendments

• **1990, Omnibus Budget Reconciliation Act of 1990 (P.L. 101-508)**

P.L. 101-508, § 11801(a)(38):

Repealed Code Sec. 1564. **Effective** 11-5-90.

P.L. 101-508, § 11821(b) provides:

(b) SAVINGS PROVISION.—If—

(1) any provision amended or repealed by this part applied to—

(A) any transaction occurring before the date of the enactment of this Act,

(B) any property acquired before such date of enactment, or

(C) any item of income, loss, deduction, or credit taken into account before such date of enactment, and

(2) the treatment of such transaction, property, or item under such provision would (without regard to the amendments made by this part) affect liability for tax for periods ending after such date of enactment,

nothing in the amendments made by this part shall be construed to affect the treatment of such transaction, property, or item for purposes of determining liability for tax for periods ending after such date of enactment.

Prior to repeal, Code Sec. 1564 read as follows:

SEC. 1564. TRANSITIONAL RULES IN THE CASE OF CERTAIN CONTROLLED CORPORATIONS.

[Sec. 1564(a)]

(a) LIMITATION ON ADDITIONAL BENEFITS.—

(1) IN GENERAL.—With respect to any December 31 after 1969 and before 1975, the amount of—

(A) each additional $25,000 surtax exemption under section 1562 in excess of the first such exemption,

(B) each additional $100,000 amount under section 535(c)(2) and (3) in excess of the first such amount, and

(C) each additional $25,000 limitation on the small business deduction of life insurance companies under sections 804(a)(3) and 809(d)(10) in excess of the first such limitation,

otherwise allowed to the component members of a controlled group of corporations for their taxable years which include such December 31 shall be reduced to the amount set forth in the following schedule:

Taxable years including—	Surtax exemption	Amount under sec. 535(c)(2) and (3)	Small business deduction limitation
Dec. 31, 1970	$20,833	83,333	$20,833
Dec. 31, 1971	16,667	66,667	16,667
Dec. 31, 1972	12,500	50,000	12,500
Dec. 31, 1973	8,333	33,333	8,333
Dec. 31, 1974	4,167	16,667	4,167

(2) ELECTION.—With respect to any December 31 after 1969 and before 1975, the component members of a controlled group of corporations shall elect (at such time and in such manner as the Secretary shall by regulations prescribe) which component member of such group shall be allowed for its taxable year which includes such December 31 the surtax exemption, the amount under section 535(c)(2) and (3), or the small business deduction limitation which is not reduced under paragraph (1).

INCOME TAX—CONSOLIDATED RETURNS

Amendments
- **1976, Tax Reform Act of 1976 (P.L. 94-455)**

P.L. 94-455, § 1901(b)(1)(J)(vi):

Substituted "section 804(a)(3)" for "sections 804(a)(4)" in Code Sec. 1564(a)(1)(C). **Effective** with respect to tax years beginning after 12-31-76.

P.L. 94-455, § 1906(b)(13)(A):

Amended the 1954 Code by substituting "Secretary" for "Secretary or his delegate" each place it appeared. **Effective** 2-1-77.

- **1969, Tax Reform Act of 1969 (P.L. 91-172)**

P.L. 91-172, § 401(b)(1):

Added Code Sec. 1564(a). **Effective** for tax years beginning after 12-31-69.

[Sec. 1564(b)]

(b) DIVIDENDS RECEIVED BY CORPORATIONS.—

(1) GENERAL RULE.—If—

(A) an election of a controlled group of corporations (as defined in paragraph (1), or in so much of paragraph (4) as relates to paragraph (1), of section 1563(a)) under section 1562(a) (relating to privilege of a controlled group of corporations to elect to have each of its component members make its returns without regard to section 1561) was made on or before April 22, 1969, and

(B) such election is effective with respect to the taxable year of each component member of such group which includes December 31, 1969,

then, with respect to a dividend distributed on or before December 31, 1977, out of earnings and profits of a taxable year which includes a December 31 after 1969 and before 1975, subsections (a)(3) and (b) of section 243 (relating to dividends received by corporations) shall be applied to such component members comprising an affiliated group (as defined in section 243(b)(5)) in the manner set forth in paragraph (2).

(2) SPECIAL RULES.—

(A) An election under section 243(b)(2) may be made for a taxable year which includes a December 31 after 1969 and before 1975, notwithstanding that an election under section 1562(a) is in effect for the taxable year.

(B) Section 243(b)(1)(B)(ii) shall not apply with respect to a dividend distributed on or before December 31, 1977, out of earnings and profits of a taxable year which includes a December 31 after 1969 and before 1975 for which an election under section 1562(a) is in effect, and in lieu of the percentage specified in section 243(a)(3) with respect to such dividend, the percentage shall be the percentage set forth in the following schedule:

If the dividend is distributed out of the earnings and profits of the distributing corporation's taxable year which includes—	The percentage shall be—
December 31, 1970	$87^1/_2$ percent
December 31, 1971	90 percent
December 31, 1972	$92^1/_2$ percent
December 31, 1973	95 percent
December 31, 1974	$97^1/_2$ percent

(C) For taxable years which include a December 31 after 1969 for which an election under section 1562(a) is in effect, section 243(b)(3)(C)(iv) shall not be applied to limit the number of surtax exemptions.

Amendments
- **1976, Tax Reform Act of 1976 (P.L. 94-455)**

P.L. 94-455, § 1901(b)(21)(A)(ii):

Substituted "243(b)(3)(C)(iv)" for "section 243(b)(3)(C)(v)" in Code Sec. 1564(b)(2)(C). **Effective** with respect to tax years beginning after 12-31-76.

- **1969, Tax Reform Act of 1969 (P.L. 91-172)**

P.L. 91-172, § 401(b)(1):

Added Code Sec. 1564(b). **Effective** for tax years beginning after 12-31-69.

[Sec. 1564(c)]

(c) CERTAIN SHORT TAXABLE YEARS.—If—

(1) a corporation has a short taxable year beginning after December 31, 1969, and ending before December 31, 1974, which does not include a December 31, and

(2) such corporation is a component member of a controlled group of corporations with respect to such taxable year (determined by applying section 1563(b) as if the last day of such taxable year were substituted for December 31),

then subsections (a) and (b) shall be applied as if the last day of such taxable year were the nearest December 31 to such day.

Amendments
- **1969, Tax Reform Act of 1969 (P.L. 91-172)**

P.L. 91-172, § 401(b)(1):

Added Code Sec. 1564(c). **Effective** for tax years beginning after 12-31-69.

[The next page is 3301.]

Sec. 1564—Repealed

Subtitle B—Estate and Gift Taxes

Chapter 11.	Estate tax.
Chapter 12.	Gift tax.
Chapter 13.	Tax on generation-skipping transfers.
Chapter 14.	Special valuation rules.
Chapter 15.	Gifts and bequests from expatriates.

CHAPTER 11—ESTATE TAX

Subchapter A.	Estates of citizens or residents.
Subchapter B.	Estates of nonresidents not citizens.
Subchapter C.	Miscellaneous.

Subchapter A—Estates of Citizens or Residents

Part I.	Tax imposed.
Part II.	Credits against tax.
Part III.	Gross estate.
Part IV.	Taxable estate.

PART I—TAX IMPOSED

| Sec. 2001. | Imposition and rate of tax. |
| Sec. 2002. | Liability for payment. |

[Sec. 2001]

SEC. 2001. IMPOSITION AND RATE OF TAX.

[Sec. 2001(a)]

(a) IMPOSITION.—A tax is hereby imposed on the transfer of the taxable estate of every decedent who is a citizen or resident of the United States.

[Sec. 2001(b)]

(b) COMPUTATION OF TAX.—The tax imposed by this section shall be the amount equal to the excess (if any) of—

(1) a tentative tax computed under subsection (c) on the sum of—

(A) the amount of the taxable estate, and

(B) the amount of the adjusted taxable gifts, over

(2) the aggregate amount of tax which would have been payable under chapter 12 with respect to gifts made by the decedent after December 31, 1976, if the modifications described in subsection (g) had been applicable at the time of such gifts.

For purposes of paragraph (1)(B), the term "adjusted taxable gifts" means the total amount of the taxable gifts (within the meaning of section 2503) made by the decedent after December 31, 1976, other than gifts which are includible in the gross estate of the decedent.

Amendments

• **2013, American Taxpayer Relief Act of 2012 (P.L. 112-240)**

P.L. 112-240, §101(a)(1)-(3), provides:

SEC. 101. PERMANENT EXTENSION AND MODIFICATION OF 2001 TAX RELIEF.

(a) PERMANENT EXTENSION.—

(1) IN GENERAL.—The Economic Growth and Tax Relief Reconciliation Act of 2001 is amended by striking title IX.

(2) CONFORMING AMENDMENT.—The Tax Relief, Unemployment Insurance Reauthorization, and Job Creation Act of 2010 is amended by striking section 304.

(3) EFFECTIVE DATE.—The amendments made by this subsection shall apply to taxable, plan, or limitation years beginning after December 31, 2012, and estates of decedents dying, gifts made, or generation skipping transfers after December 31, 2012.

• **2010, Tax Relief, Unemployment Insurance Reauthorization, and Job Creation Act of 2010 (P.L. 111-312)**

P.L. 111-312, §302(d)(1)(A):

Amended Code Sec. 2001(b)(2) by striking "if the provisions of subsection (c) (as in effect at the decedent's death)" and inserting "if the modifications described in subsection (g)". **Effective** for estates of decedents dying, generation-skipping transfers, and gifts made, after 12-31-2009.

P.L. 111-312, §304, provides [but see P.L. 112-240, §101(a)(2)-(3), above]:
SEC. 304. APPLICATION OF EGTRRA SUNSET TO THIS TITLE.

Section 901 of the Economic Growth and Tax Relief Reconciliation Act of 2001 shall apply to the amendments made by this title.

• **2001, Economic Growth and Tax Relief Reconciliation Act of 2001 (P.L. 107-16)**

P.L. 107-16, §901(a)-(b), as amended by P.L. 111-312, §101(a)(1), provides [but see P.L. 112-240, §101(a)(1) and (3), above]:

SEC. 901. SUNSET OF PROVISIONS OF ACT.

(a) IN GENERAL.—All provisions of, and amendments made by, this Act shall not apply—

(1) to taxable, plan, or limitation years beginning after December 31, 2012, or

(2) in the case of title V, to estates of decedents dying, gifts made, or generation skipping transfers, after December 31, 2012.

(b) APPLICATION OF CERTAIN LAWS.—The Internal Revenue Code of 1986 and the Employee Retirement Income Security Act of 1974 shall be applied and administered to years, estates, gifts, and transfers described in subsection (a) as if the provisions and amendments described in subsection (a) had never been enacted.

• **1987, Revenue Act of 1987 (P.L. 100-203)**

P.L. 100-203, §10401(b)(2)(A)(i)-(ii):

Amended Code Sec. 2001(b) by striking out "in accordance with the rate schedule set forth in subsection (c)" in paragraph (1) and inserting in lieu thereof "under subsection (c)", and by striking out "the rate schedule set forth in subsection (c) (as in effect at the decedent's death)" in paragraph (2) and inserting in lieu thereof "the provisions of subsection (c) (as in effect at the decedent's death)". **Effective** in the case of decedents dying, and gifts made, after 12-31-87.

[Sec. 2001(c)]

(c) RATE SCHEDULE.—

If the amount with respect to which the tentative tax to be computed is:	The tentative tax is:
Not over $10,000	18 percent of such amount.
Over $10,000 but not over $20,000	$1,800, plus 20 percent of the excess of such amount over $10,000.
Over $20,000 but not over $40,000	$3,800, plus 22 percent of the excess of such amount over $20,000.
Over $40,000 but not over $60,000	$8,200, plus 24 percent of the excess of such amount over $40,000.

ESTATE TAX—TAX IMPOSED

If the amount with respect to which the tentative tax to be computed is:	The tentative tax is:
Over $60,000 but not over $80,000	$13,000, plus 26 percent of the excess of such amount over $60,000.
Over $80,000 but not over $100,000	$18,200, plus 28 percent of the excess of such amount over $80,000.
Over $100,000 but not over $150,000	$23,800, plus 30 percent of the excess of such amount over $100,000.
Over $150,000 but not over $250,000	$38,800, plus 32 percent of the excess of such amount over $150,000.
Over $250,000 but not over $500,000	$70,800, plus 34 percent of the excess of such amount over $250,000.
Over $500,000 but not over $750,000	$155,800, plus 37 percent of the excess of such amount over $500,000.
Over $750,000 but not over $1,000,000	$248,300, plus 39 percent of the excess of such amount over $750,000.
Over $1,000,000	$345,800, plus 40 percent of the excess of such amount over $1,000,000.

Amendments

- **2013, American Taxpayer Relief Act of 2012 (P.L. 112-240)**

P.L. 112-240, §101(a)(1)-(3), provides:

SEC. 101. PERMANENT EXTENSION AND MODIFICATION OF 2001 TAX RELIEF.

(a) PERMANENT EXTENSION.—

(1) IN GENERAL.—The Economic Growth and Tax Relief Reconciliation Act of 2001 is amended by striking title IX.

(2) CONFORMING AMENDMENT.—The Tax Relief, Unemployment Insurance Reauthorization, and Job Creation Act of 2010 is amended by striking section 304.

(3) EFFECTIVE DATE.—The amendments made by this subsection shall apply to taxable, plan, or limitation years beginning after December 31, 2012, and estates of decedents dying, gifts made, or generation skipping transfers after December 31, 2012.

P.L. 112-240, §101(c)(1):

Amended the table contained in Code Sec. 2001(c), as amended by section 302(a)(2) of the Tax Relief, Unemployment Insurance Reauthorization, and Job Creation Act of 2010 (P.L. 111-312), by striking "Over $500,000" and all that follows and inserting three new table entries. **Effective** for estates of decedents dying, generation-skipping transfers, and gifts made, after 12-31-2012. Prior to being stricken, "Over $500,000" and all that followed read as follows:

Over $500,000	$155,800 plus 35 percent of the excess of such amount over $500,000.

- **2010, Tax Relief, Unemployment Insurance Reauthorization, and Job Creation Act of 2010 (P.L. 111-312)**

P.L. 111-312, §302(a)(2)(A)-(C):

Amended Code Sec. 2001(c) by striking "Over $500,000" and all that follows in the table contained in paragraph (1) and inserting a new table row, by striking "(1) IN GENERAL.—" before the table, and by striking paragraph (2). **Effective** for estates of decedents dying, generation-skipping transfers, and gifts made, after 12-31-2009. Prior to amendment, Code Sec. 2001(c)(1) and (2) read as follows:

(1) IN GENERAL.—

If the amount with respect to which the tentative tax to be computed is:	The tentative tax is:
Not over $10,000	18 percent of such amount.
Over $10,000 but not over $20,000	$1,800, plus 20 percent of the excess of such amount over $10,000.
Over $20,000 but not over $40,000	$3,800, plus 22 percent of the excess of such amount over $20,000.
Over $40,000 but not over $60,000	$8,200, plus 24 percent of the excess of such amount over $40,000.
Over $60,000 but not over $80,000	$13,000, plus 26 percent of the excess of such amount over $60,000.
Over $80,000 but not over $100,000	$18,200, plus 28 percent of the excess of such amount over $80,000.
Over $100,000 but not over $150,000	$23,800, plus 30 percent of the excess of such amount over $100,000.
Over $150,000 but not over $250,000	$38,800, plus 32 percent of the excess of such amount over $150,000.
Over $250,000 but not over $500,000	$70,800, plus 34 percent of the excess of such amount over $250,000.
Over $500,000	$155,800, plus 35 percent of the excess of such amount over $500,000.
Over $500,000 but not over $750,000	$155,800, plus 37 percent of the excess of such amount over $500,000.
Over $750,000 but not over $1,000,000	$248,300, plus 39 percent of the excess of such amount over $750,000.
Over $1,000,000 but not over $1,250,000	$345,800, plus 41 percent of the excess of such amount over $1,000,000.

If the amount with respect to which the tentative tax to be computed is:	The tentative tax is:
Over $1,250,000 but not over $1,500,000	$448,300, plus 43 percent of the excess of such amount over $1,250,000.
Over $1,500,000 but not over $2,000,000	$555,800, plus 45 percent of the excess of such amount over $1,500,000.
Over $2,000,000 but not over $2,500,000	$780,800, plus 49 percent of the excess of such amount over $2,000,000.
Over $2,500,000	$1,025,800, plus 50% of the excess over $2,500,000.

(2) PHASEDOWN OF MAXIMUM RATE OF TAX.—

(A) IN GENERAL.—In the case of estates of decedents dying, and gifts made, in calendar years after 2002 and before 2010, the tentative tax under this subsection shall be determined by using a table prescribed by the Secretary (in lieu of using the table contained in paragraph (1)) which is the same as such table; except that—

(i) the maximum rate of tax for any calendar year shall be determined in the table under subparagraph (B), and

(ii) the brackets and the amounts setting forth the tax shall be adjusted to the extent necessary to reflect the adjustments under subparagraph (A).

(B) MAXIMUM RATE.—

In calendar year:	The maximum rate is:
2003	49 percent
2004	48 percent
2005	47 percent
2006	46 percent
2007, 2008, and 2009	45 percent.

P.L. 111-312, §304, provides [but see P.L. 112-240, §101(a)(2)-(3), above]:

SEC. 304. APPLICATION OF EGTRRA SUNSET TO THIS TITLE.

Section 901 of the Economic Growth and Tax Relief Reconciliation Act of 2001 shall apply to the amendments made by this title.

- **2001, Economic Growth and Tax Relief Reconciliation Act of 2001 (P.L. 107-16)**

P.L. 107-16, §511(a):

Amended the table contained in Code Sec. 2001(c)(1) by striking the two highest brackets and inserting a new bracket. **Effective** for estates of decedents dying, and gifts made, after 12-31-2001. Prior to amendment, the two highest brackets in the table read as follows:

Over $2,500,000 but not over $3,000,000	$1,025,800, plus 53% of the excess over $2,500,000.
Over $3,000,000	$1,290,800, plus 55% of the excess over $3,000,000

P.L. 107-16, §511(b):

Amended Code Sec. 2001(c) by striking paragraph (2). **Effective** for estates of decedents dying, and gifts made, after 12-31-2001. Prior to being stricken, Code Sec. 2001(c)(2) read as follows:

(1) (2) PHASEOUT OF GRADUATED RATES AND UNIFIED CREDIT.—The tentative tax determined under paragraph (1) shall be increased by an amount equal to 5 percent of so much of the amount (with respect to which the tentative tax is to be computed) as exceeds $10,000,000 but does not exceed the amount at which the average tax rate under this section is 55 percent.

P.L. 107-16, §511(c):

Amended Code Sec. 2001(c), as amended by Act Sec. 511(b), by adding at the end a new paragraph (2). **Effective** for estates of decedents dying, and gifts made, after 12-31-2002.

P.L. 107-16, §901(a)-(b), as amended by P.L. 111-312, §101(a)(1), provides [but see P.L. 112-240, §101(a)(1) and (3), above]:

SEC. 901. SUNSET OF PROVISIONS OF ACT.

(a) IN GENERAL.—All provisions of, and amendments made by, this Act shall not apply—

Sec. 2001(c)

ESTATE TAX—TAX IMPOSED

(1) to taxable, plan, or limitation years beginning after December 31, 2012, or

(2) in the case of title V, to estates of decedents dying, gifts made, or generation skipping transfers, after December 31, 2012.

(b) APPLICATION OF CERTAIN LAWS.—The Internal Revenue Code of 1986 and the Employee Retirement Income Security Act of 1974 shall be applied and administered to years, estates, gifts, and transfers described in subsection (a) as if the provisions and amendments described in subsection (a) had never been enacted.

• **1997, Taxpayer Relief Act of 1997 (P.L. 105-34)**

P.L. 105-34, §501(a)(1)(D):

Amended Code Sec. 2001(c)(2) by striking "$21,040,000" and inserting "the amount at which the average tax rate under this section is 55 percent". **Effective** for the estates of decedents dying, and gifts made, after 12-31-97.

• **1993, Omnibus Budget Reconciliation Act of 1993 (P.L. 103-66)**

P.L. 103-66, §13208(a):

Amended Code Sec. 2001(c)(1) by striking the last item and inserting two new items. **Effective** in the case of decedents dying and gifts made after 12-31-92. Prior to amendment, the last item in Code Sec. 2001(c)(1) read as follows:

If the amount with respect to which the tentative tax to be computed is:	The tentative tax is:
Over $2,500,000	$1,025,800, plus 50% of the excess of such amount over $2,500,000.

P.L. 103-66, §13208(b)(1):

Amended Code Sec. 2001(c) by striking paragraph (2) and redesignating paragraph (3) as paragraph (2). **Effective** in the case of decedents dying and gifts made after 12-31-92. Prior to being stricken, Code Sec. 2001(c)(2) read as follows:

(2) PHASE-IN OF 50 PERCENT MAXIMUM RATE.—

(A) IN GENERAL.—In the case of decedents dying, and gifts made, before 1993, there shall be substituted for the last item in the schedule contained in paragraph (1) the items determined under this paragraph.

(B) FOR 1982.—In the case of decedents dying, and gifts made, in 1982, the substitution under this paragraph shall be as follows:

If the amount with respect to which the tentative tax to be computed is:	The tentative tax is:
Over $2,500,000 But not over $3,000,000	$1,025,800, plus 53% of the excess over $2,500,000.
Over $3,000,000 But not over $3,500,000	$1,290,800, plus 57% of the excess over $3,000,000.
Over $3,500,000 But not over $4,000,000	$1,575,800, plus 61% of the excess over $3,500,000.
Over $4,000,000	$1,880,800, plus 65% of the excess over $4,000,000.

(C) FOR 1983.—In the case of decedents dying, and gifts made, in 1983, the substitution under this paragraph shall be as follows:

If the amount with respect to which the tentative tax to be computed is:	The tentative tax is:
Over $2,500,000 But not over $3,000,000	$1,025,800, plus 53% of the excess over $2,500,000.
Over $3,000,000 But not over $3,500,000	$1,290,800, plus 57% of the excess over $3,000,000.
Over $3,500,000	$1,575,800, plus 60% of the excess over $3,500,000.

(D) AFTER 1983 AND BEFORE 1993.—In the case of decedents dying, and gifts made, after 1983 and before 1993 the substitution under this paragraph shall be as follows:

If the amount with respect to which the tentative tax to be computed is:	The tentative tax is:
Over $2,500,000 But not over $3,000,000	$1,025,800, plus 53% of the excess over $2,500,000.
Over $3,000,000	$1,290,800, plus 55% of the excess over $3,000,000.

P.L. 103-66, §13208(b)(2):

Amended Code Sec. 2001(c)(2) (as redesignated) by striking "($18,340,000 in the case of decedents dying, and gifts made, after 1992)" before the period. **Effective** in the case of decedents dying and gifts made after 12-31-92.

• **1987, Revenue Act of 1987 (P.L. 100-203)**

P.L. 100-203, §10401(a)(1)-(3):

Amended Code Sec. 2001(c)(2) by striking out "1988" in subparagraph (A) and inserting in lieu thereof "1993", by striking out "in 1984, 1985, 1986, or 1987" in the text of subparagraph (D) and inserting in lieu thereof "after 1983 and before 1993", and by amending the heading of subparagraph (D). **Effective** in the case of decedents dying, or gifts made, after 12-31-87. Prior to amendment, the heading for subparagraph (D) read as follows:

(D) FOR 1984, 1985, 1986, OR 1987.—

P.L. 100-203, §10401(b)(1):

Amended Code Sec. 2001(c) by adding at the end thereof new paragraph (3). **Effective** in the case of decedents dying, or gifts made, after 12-31-87.

• **1984, Deficit Reduction Act of 1984 (P.L. 98-369)**

P.L. 98-369, §21(a):

Amended Code Sec. 2001(c)(2) by striking out "1985", in subparagraph (A) and inserting in lieu thereof "1988", and by striking out "1984" each place it appears in subparagraph (D) and inserting in lieu thereof "1984, 1985, 1986, or 1987". **Effective** for estates of decedents dying after, and gifts made after, 12-31-83.

[Sec. 2001(d)]

(d) ADJUSTMENT FOR GIFT TAX PAID BY SPOUSE.—For purposes of subsection (b)(2), if—

(1) the decedent was the donor of any gift one-half of which was considered under section 2513 as made by the decedent's spouse, and

(2) the amount of such gift is includible in the gross estate of the decedent,

any tax payable by the spouse under chapter 12 on such gift (as determined under section 2012(d)) shall be treated as a tax payable with respect to a gift made by the decedent.

Amendments

• **1981, Economic Recovery Tax Act of 1981 (P.L. 97-34)**

P.L. 97-34, §402(a):

Amended Code Sec. 2001(c) by striking out the item beginning "Over $2,500,000" and all that follows and inserting "Over $2,500,000 ... $1,025,800, plus 50% of the excess over $2,500,000". **Effective** for estates of decedents dying after, and gifts made after, 12-31-81. (For the text of Code Sec. 2001(c) prior to amendment, see the amendment note at Act Sec. 402(b), below.)

P.L. 97-34, §402(b):

Amended Code Sec. 2001(c) by striking out "(c) Rate Schedule.—" and inserting "(c) Rate Schedule.—(1) In General.—" and by adding a paragraph (2). **Effective** for estates of decedents dying after, and gifts made after, 12-31-81. Prior to amendment, Code Sec. 2001(c) read as follows:

(c) RATE SCHEDULE.—

If the amount with respect to which the tentative tax to be computed is:	The tentative tax is:
Not over $10,000	18 percent of such amount.
Over $10,000 but not over $20,000	$1,800, plus 20 percent of the excess of such amount over $10,000.
Over $20,000 but not over $40,000	$3,800, plus 22 percent of the excess of such amount over $20,000.
Over $40,000 but not over $60,000	$8,200, plus 24 percent of the excess of such amount over $40,000.
Over $60,000 but not over $80,000	$13,000, plus 26 percent of the excess of such amount over $60,000.
Over $80,000 but not over $100,000	$18,200, plus 28 percent of the excess of such amount over $80,000.
Over $100,000 but not over $150,000	$23,800, plus 30 percent of the excess of such amount over $100,000.
Over $150,000 but not over $250,000	$38,800, plus 32 percent of the excess of such amount over $150,000.

ESTATE TAX—TAX IMPOSED

Taxable estate	Tax
Over $250,000 but not over $500,000	$70,800, plus 34 percent of the excess of such amount over $250,000.
Over $500,000 but not over $750,000	$155,800, plus 37 percent of the excess of such amount over $500,000.
Over $750,000 but not over $1,000,000	$248,300, plus 39 percent of the excess of such amount over $750,000.
Over $1,000,000 but not over $1,250,000	$345,800, plus 41 percent of the excess of such amount over $1,000,000.
Over $1,250,000 but not over $1,500,000	$448,300, plus 43 percent of the excess of such amount over $1,250,000.
Over $1,500,000 but not over $2,000,000	$555,800, plus 45 percent of the excess of such amount over $1,500,000.
Over $2,000,000 but not over $2,500,000	$780,800, plus 49 percent of the excess of such amount over $2,000,000.
Over $2,500,000 but not over $3,000,000	$1,025,800, plus 53 percent of the excess of such amount over $2,500,000.
Over $3,000,000 but not over $3,500,000	$1,290,800, plus 57 percent of the excess of such amount over $3,000,000.
Over $3,500,000 but not over $4,000,000	$1,575,800, plus 61 percent of the excess of such amount over $3,500,000.
Over $4,000,000 but not over $4,500,000	$1,880,800, plus 65 percent of the excess of such amount over $4,000,000.
Over $4,500,000 but not over $5,000,000	$2,205,800, plus 69 percent of the excess of such amount over $4,500,000.
Over $5,000,000	$2,550,800, plus 70 percent of the excess of such amount over $5,000,000.

P.L. 97-34, § 402(c):

Amended Code Sec. 2001(b)(2). **Effective** for estates of decedents dying after, and gifts made after, 12-31-81. Prior to amendment, Code Sec. 2001(b)(2) read as follows:

(2) the aggregate amount of tax payable under chapter 12 with respect to gifts made by the decedent after December 31, 1976.

• **1976, Tax Reform Act of 1976 (P.L. 94-455)**

P.L. 94-455, § 2001(a)(1), (d)(1):

Amended Code Sec. 2001. **Effective** for estates of decedents dying after 12-31-76. Prior to amendment, Code Sec. 2001 read as follows:

SEC. 2001. RATE OF TAX.

A tax computed in accordance with the following table is hereby imposed on the transfer of the taxable estate, determined as provided in section 2051, of every decedent, citizen or resident of the United States dying after the date of enactment of this title:

If the taxable estate is:	The tax shall be:
Not over $5,000	3% of the taxable estate.
Over $5,000 but not over $10,000	$150, plus 7% of excess over $5,000.
Over $10,000 but not over $20,000	$500, plus 11% of excess over $10,000.
Over $20,000 but not over $30,000	$1,600, plus 14% of excess over $20,000.
Over $30,000 but not over $40,000	$3,000, plus 18% of excess over $30,000.
Over $40,000 but not over $50,000	$4,800, plus 22% of excess over $40,000.
Over $50,000 but not over $60,000	$7,000, plus 25% of excess over $50,000.
Over $60,000 but not over $100,000	$9,500, plus 28% of excess over $60,000.
Over $100,000 but not over $250,000	$20,700, plus 30% of excess over $100,000.
Over $250,000 but not over $500,000	$65,700, plus 32% of excess over $250,000.
Over $500,000 but not over $750,000	$145,700, plus 35% of excess over $500,000.
Over $750,000 but not over $1,000,000	$233,200, plus 37% of excess over $750,000.
Over $1,000,000 but not over $1,250,000	$325,700, plus 39% of excess over $1,000,000.
Over $1,250,000 but not over $1,500,000	$423,200, plus 42% of excess over $1,250,000.
Over $1,500,000 but not over $2,000,000	$528,200, plus 45% of excess over $1,500,000.
Over $2,000,000 but not over $2,500,000	$753,200, plus 49% of excess over $2,000,000.
Over $2,500,000 but not over $3,000,000	$998,200, plus 53% of excess over $2,500,000.
Over $3,000,000 but not over $3,500,000	$1,263,200, plus 56% of excess over $3,000,000.
Over $3,500,000 but not over $4,000,000	$1,543,200, plus 59% of excess over $3,500,000.
Over $4,000,000 but not over $5,000,000	$1,838,200, plus 63% of excess over $4,000,000.
Over $5,000,000 but not over $6,000,000	$2,468,200, plus 67% of excess over $5,000,000.
Over $6,000,000 but not over $7,000,000	$3,138,200, plus 70% of excess over $6,000,000.
Over $7,000,000 but not over $8,000,000	$3,838,200, plus 73% of excess over $7,000,000.
Over $8,000,000 but not over $10,000,000	$4,568,200, plus 76% of excess over $8,000,000.
Over $10,000,000	$6,088,200, plus 77% of excess over $10,000,000.

[Sec. 2001(e)]

(e) COORDINATION OF SECTIONS 2513 AND 2035.—If—

(1) the decedent's spouse was the donor of any gift one-half of which was considered under section 2513 as made by the decedent, and

(2) the amount of such gift is includible in the gross estate of the decedent's spouse by reason of section 2035,

such gift shall not be included in the adjusted taxable gifts of the decedent for purposes of subsection (b)(1)(B), and the aggregate amount determined under subsection (b)(2) shall be reduced by the amount (if any) determined under subsection (d) which was treated as a tax payable by the decedent's spouse with respect to such gift.

ESTATE TAX—TAX IMPOSED

Amendments

• **1978, Revenue Act of 1978 (P.L. 95-600)**

P.L. 95-600, §702(h)(1):

Added Code Sec. 2001(e). **Effective** for estates of decedents dying after 12-31-76, except that such subsection shall not apply to transfers made before 1-1-77.

[Sec. 2001(f)]

(f) VALUATION OF GIFTS.—

(1) IN GENERAL.—If the time has expired under section 6501 within which a tax may be assessed under chapter 12 (or under corresponding provisions of prior laws) on—

(A) the transfer of property by gift made during a preceding calendar period (as defined in section 2502(b)); or

(B) an increase in taxable gifts required under section 2701(d),

the value thereof shall, for purposes of computing the tax under this chapter, be the value as finally determined for purposes of chapter 12.

(2) FINAL DETERMINATION.—For purposes of paragraph (1), a value shall be treated as finally determined for purposes of chapter 12 if—

(A) the value is shown on a return under such chapter and such value is not contested by the Secretary before the expiration of the time referred to in paragraph (1) with respect to such return;

(B) in a case not described in subparagraph (A), the value is specified by the Secretary and such value is not timely contested by the taxpayer; or

(C) the value is determined by a court or pursuant to a settlement agreement with the Secretary.

For purposes of subparagraph (A), the value of an item shall be treated as shown on a return if the item is disclosed in the return, or in a statement attached to the return, in a manner adequate to apprise the Secretary of the nature of such item.

Amendments

• **1998, Tax and Trade Relief Extension Act of 1998 (P.L. 105-277)**

P.L. 105-277, §4003(c):

Amended Code Sec. 2001(f)(2) by adding at the end a new sentence. **Effective** as if included in the provision of P.L. 105-34 to which it relates [effective for gifts made after 8-5-97.—CCH].

• **1998, IRS Restructuring and Reform Act of 1998 (P.L. 105-206)**

P.L. 105-206, §6007(e)(2)(B):

Amended Code Sec. 2001(f). **Effective** as if included in the provision of P.L. 105-34 to which it relates [effective for gifts made after 8-5-97.—CCH]. Prior to amendment, Code Sec. 2001(f) read as follows:

(f) VALUATION OF GIFTS.—If—

(1) the time has expired within which a tax may be assessed under chapter 12 (or under corresponding provisions of prior laws) on the transfer of property by gift made during a preceding calendar period (as defined in section 2502(b)), and

(2) the value of such gift is shown on the return for such preceding calendar period or is disclosed in such return, or in a statement attached to the return, in a manner adequate to apprise the Secretary of the nature of such gift, the value of such gift shall, for purposes of computing the tax under this chapter, be the value of such gift as finally determined for purposes of chapter 12.

• **1997, Taxpayer Relief Act of 1997 (P.L. 107-34)**

P.L. 105-34, §506(a):

Amended Code Sec. 2001 by adding at the end a new subsection (f). **Effective** for gifts made after 8-5-97.

[Sec. 2001(g)]

(g) MODIFICATIONS TO TAX PAYABLE.—

(1) MODIFICATIONS TO GIFT TAX PAYABLE TO REFLECT DIFFERENT TAX RATES.—For purposes of applying subsection (b)(2) with respect to 1 or more gifts, the rates of tax under subsection (c) in effect at the decedent's death shall, in lieu of the rates of tax in effect at the time of such gifts, be used both to compute—

(A) the tax imposed by chapter 12 with respect to such gifts, and

(B) the credit allowed against such tax under section 2505, including in computing—

(i) the applicable credit amount under section 2505(a)(1), and

(ii) the sum of the amounts allowed as a credit for all preceding periods under section 2505(a)(2).

(2) MODIFICATIONS TO ESTATE TAX PAYABLE TO REFLECT DIFFERENT BASIC EXCLUSION AMOUNTS.—The Secretary shall prescribe such regulations as may be necessary or appropriate to carry out this section with respect to any difference between—

(A) the basic exclusion amount under section 2010(c)(3) applicable at the time of the decedent's death, and

(B) the basic exclusion amount under such section applicable with respect to any gifts made by the decedent.

Amendments

• **2017, Tax Cuts and Jobs Act (P.L. 115-97)**

P.L. 115-97, §11061(b):

Amended Code Sec. 2001(g). **Effective** for estates of decedents dying and gifts made after 12-31-2017. Prior to amendment, Code Sec. 2001(g) read as follows:

(g) MODIFICATIONS TO GIFT TAX PAYABLE TO REFLECT DIFFERENT TAX RATES.—For purposes of applying subsection (b)(2) with respect to 1 or more gifts, the rates of tax under subsection (c) in effect at the decedent's death shall, in lieu of the rates of tax in effect at the time of such gifts, be used both to compute—

(1) the tax imposed by chapter 12 with respect to such gifts, and

(2) the credit allowed against such tax under section 2505, including in computing—

(A) the applicable credit amount under section 2505(a)(1), and

(B) the sum of the amounts allowed as a credit for all preceding periods under section 2505(a)(2).

• **2013, American Taxpayer Relief Act of 2012 (P.L. 112-240)**

P.L. 112-240, §101(a)(1)-(3), provides:

SEC. 101. PERMANENT EXTENSION AND MODIFICATION OF 2001 TAX RELIEF.

(a) PERMANENT EXTENSION.—

(1) IN GENERAL.—The Economic Growth and Tax Relief Reconciliation Act of 2001 is amended by striking title IX.

(2) CONFORMING AMENDMENT.—The Tax Relief, Unemployment Insurance Reauthorization, and Job Creation Act of 2010 is amended by striking section 304.

(3) EFFECTIVE DATE.—The amendments made by this subsection shall apply to taxable, plan, or limitation years beginning after December 31, 2012, and estates of decedents dying, gifts made, or generation skipping transfers after December 31, 2012.

• **2010, Tax Relief, Unemployment Insurance Reauthorization, and Job Creation Act of 2010 (P.L. 111-312)**

P.L. 111-312, §302(d)(1)(B):

Amended Code Sec. 2001 by adding at the end a new subsection (g). **Effective** for estates of decedents dying, generation-skipping transfers, and gifts made, after 12-31-2009.

P.L. 111-312, §304, provides [but see P.L. 112-240, §101(a)(2)-(3), above]:

SEC. 304. APPLICATION OF EGTRRA SUNSET TO THIS TITLE.

Section 901 of the Economic Growth and Tax Relief Reconciliation Act of 2001 shall apply to the amendments made by this title.

• **2001, Economic Growth and Tax Relief Reconciliation Act of 2001 (P.L. 107-16)**

P.L. 107-16, §901(a)-(b), as amended by P.L. 111-312, §101(a)(1), provides [but see P.L. 112-240, §101(a)(1) and (3), above]:

SEC. 901. SUNSET OF PROVISIONS OF ACT.

(a) IN GENERAL.—All provisions of, and amendments made by, this Act shall not apply—

(1) to taxable, plan, or limitation years beginning after December 31, 2012, or

(2) in the case of title V, to estates of decedents dying, gifts made, or generation skipping transfers, after December 31, 2012.

(b) APPLICATION OF CERTAIN LAWS.—The Internal Revenue Code of 1986 and the Employee Retirement Income Security Act of 1974 shall be applied and administered to years, estates, gifts, and transfers described in subsection (a) as if the provisions and amendments described in subsection (a) had never been enacted.

ESTATE TAX—CREDITS AGAINST TAX

[Sec. 2002]

SEC. 2002. LIABILITY FOR PAYMENT.

The tax imposed by this chapter shall be paid by the executor.

Amendments

• **1989, Omnibus Budget Reconciliation Act of 1989 (P.L. 101-239)**

P.L. 101-239, § 7304(b)(2)(A):

Amended Code Sec. 2002 by striking "Except as provided in section 2210, the" and inserting "The". **Effective** for estates of decedents dying after 7-12-89.

• **1984, Deficit Reduction Act of 1984 (P.L. 98-369)**

P.L. 98-369, § 544(b)(1):

Amended Code Sec. 2002. **Effective** for those estates of decedents which are required to file returns on a date (including any extensions) after 7-18-84. Prior to amendment, Code Sec. 2002 read as follows:

SEC. 2002. LIABILITY FOR PAYMENT.

The tax imposed by this chapter shall be paid by the executor.

PART II—CREDITS AGAINST TAX

Sec. 2010.	Unified credit against estate tax.
Sec. 2012.	Credit for gift tax.
Sec. 2013.	Credit for tax on prior transfers.
Sec. 2014.	Credit for foreign death taxes.
Sec. 2015.	Credit for death taxes on remainders.
Sec. 2016.	Recovery of taxes claimed as credit.

[Sec. 2010]

SEC. 2010. UNIFIED CREDIT AGAINST ESTATE TAX.

[Sec. 2010(a)]

(a) GENERAL RULE.—A credit of the applicable credit amount shall be allowed to the estate of every decedent against the tax imposed by section 2001.

Amendments

• **1997, Taxpayer Relief Act of 1997 (P.L. 105-34)**

P.L. 105-34, § 501(a)(1)(A):

Amended Code Sec. 2010(a) by striking "$192,800" and inserting "the applicable credit amount". **Effective** for estates of decedents dying, and gifts made, after 12-31-97.

• **1981, Economic Recovery Tax Act of 1981 (P.L. 97-34)**

P.L. 97-34, § 401(a)(1):

Amended Code Sec. 2010(a) by striking out "$47,000" and inserting "$192,800". **Effective** for estates of decedents dying after 12-31-81.

[Sec. 2010(b)]

(b) ADJUSTMENT TO CREDIT FOR CERTAIN GIFTS MADE BEFORE 1977.—The amount of the credit allowable under subsection (a) shall be reduced by an amount equal to 20 percent of the aggregate amount allowed as a specific exemption under section 2521 (as in effect before its repeal by the Tax Reform Act of 1976) with respect to gifts made by the decedent after September 8, 1976.

Amendments

• **1990, Omnibus Budget Reconciliation Act of 1990 (P.L. 101-508)**

P.L. 101-508, § 11801(c)(19)(A):

Amended Code Sec. 2010 by redesignating subsection (c) as subsection (b). **Effective** 11-5-90.

P.L. 101-508, § 11821(b), provides:

(b) SAVINGS PROVISIONS.—If—

(1) any provision amended or repealed by this part applied to—

(A) any transaction occurring before the date of the enactment of this Act,

(B) any property acquired before such date of enactment, or

(C) any item of income, loss, deduction, or credit taken into account before such date of enactment, and

(2) the treatment of such transaction, property, or item under such provision would (without regard to the amendments made by this part) affect liability for tax for periods ending after such date of enactment,

nothing in the amendments made by this part shall be construed to affect the treatment of such transaction, property, or item for purposes of determining liability for tax for periods ending after such date of enactment.

[Sec. 2010(b)—Repealed]

Amendments

• **1990, Omnibus Budget Reconciliation Act of 1990 (P.L. 101-508)**

P.L. 101-508, § 11801(a)(39):

Repealed Code Sec. 2010(b). **Effective** 11-5-90. Prior to repeal, Code Sec. 2010(b) read as follows:

(b) PHASE-IN OF CREDIT.—

In the case of decedents dying in:	Subsection (a) shall be applied by substituting for "$192,800" the following amount:
1982	$62,800
1983	79,300
1984	96,300
1985	121,800
1986	155,800

P.L. 101-508, § 11821(b), provides:

(b) SAVINGS PROVISIONS.—If—

(1) any provision amended or repealed by this part applied to—

(A) any transaction occurring before the date of the enactment of this Act,

(B) any property acquired before such date of enactment, or

(C) any item of income, loss, deduction, or credit taken into account before such date of enactment, and

(2) the treatment of such transaction, property, or item under such provision would (without regard to the amendments made by this part) affect liability for tax for periods ending after such date of enactment,

nothing in the amendments made by this part shall be construed to affect the treatment of such transaction, property, or item for purposes of determining liability for tax for periods ending after such date of enactment.

• **1981, Economic Recovery Tax Act of 1981 (P.L. 97-34)**

P.L. 97-34, § 401(a)(2)(A):

Amended Code Sec. 2010(b). **Effective** for estates of decedents dying after 12-31-81. Prior to amendment, Code Sec. 2010(b) read as follows:

(b) PHASE-IN of $47,000 CREDIT.—

In the case of decedents dying in:	Subsection (a) shall be applied by substituting for "$47,000" the following amount:
1977	$30,000
1978	34,000
1979	38,000
1980	42,500

[Sec. 2010(c)]

(c) APPLICABLE CREDIT AMOUNT.—

(1) IN GENERAL.—For purposes of this section, the applicable credit amount is the amount of the tentative tax which would be determined under section 2001(c) if the amount with respect to which such tentative tax is to be computed were equal to the applicable exclusion amount.

(2) APPLICABLE EXCLUSION AMOUNT.—For purposes of this subsection, the applicable exclusion amount is the sum of—

ESTATE TAX—CREDITS AGAINST TAX

(A) the basic exclusion amount, and

(B) in the case of a surviving spouse, the deceased spousal unused exclusion amount.

(3) BASIC EXCLUSION AMOUNT.—

(A) IN GENERAL.—For purposes of this subsection, the basic exclusion amount is $5,000,000.

(B) INFLATION ADJUSTMENT.—In the case of any decedent dying in a calendar year after 2011, the dollar amount in subparagraph (A) shall be increased by an amount equal to—

(i) such dollar amount, multiplied by

(ii) the cost-of-living adjustment determined under section 1(f)(3) for such calendar year by substituting "calendar year 2010" for "calendar year 2016" in subparagraph (A)(ii) thereof.

If any amount as adjusted under the preceding sentence is not a multiple of $10,000, such amount shall be rounded to the nearest multiple of $10,000.

(C) INCREASE IN BASIC EXCLUSION AMOUNT.—In the case of estates of decedents dying or gifts made after December 31, 2017, and before January 1, 2026, subparagraph (A) shall be applied by substituting "$10,000,000" for "$5,000,000".

(4) DECEASED SPOUSAL UNUSED EXCLUSION AMOUNT.—For purposes of this subsection, with respect to a surviving spouse of a deceased spouse dying after December 31, 2010, the term "deceased spousal unused exclusion amount" means the lesser of—

(A) the basic exclusion amount, or

(B) the excess of—

(i) the applicable exclusion amount of the last such deceased spouse of such surviving spouse, over

(ii) the amount with respect to which the tentative tax is determined under section 2001(b)(1) on the estate of such deceased spouse.

(5) SPECIAL RULES.—

(A) ELECTION REQUIRED.—A deceased spousal unused exclusion amount may not be taken into account by a surviving spouse under paragraph (2) unless the executor of the estate of the deceased spouse files an estate tax return on which such amount is computed and makes an election on such return that such amount may be so taken into account. Such election, once made, shall be irrevocable. No election may be made under this subparagraph if such return is filed after the time prescribed by law (including extensions) for filing such return.

(B) EXAMINATION OF PRIOR RETURNS AFTER EXPIRATION OF PERIOD OF LIMITATIONS WITH RESPECT TO DECEASED SPOUSAL UNUSED EXCLUSION AMOUNT.—Notwithstanding any period of limitation in section 6501, after the time has expired under section 6501 within which a tax may be assessed under chapter 11 or 12 with respect to a deceased spousal unused exclusion amount, the Secretary may examine a return of the deceased spouse to make determinations with respect to such amount for purposes of carrying out this subsection.

(6) REGULATIONS.—The Secretary shall prescribe such regulations as may be necessary or appropriate to carry out this subsection.

Amendments

- **2017, Tax Cuts and Jobs Act (P.L. 115-97)**

P.L. 115-97, §11002(d)(1)(CC):

Amended Code Sec. 2010(c)(3)(B)(ii) by striking "for 'calendar year 1992' in subparagraph (B)" and inserting "for 'calendar year 2016' in subparagraph (A)(ii)". **Effective** for tax years beginning after 12-31-2017.

P.L. 115-97, §11061(a):

Amended Code Sec. 2010(c)(3) by adding at the end a new subparagraph (C). **Effective** for estates of decedents dying and gifts made after 12-31-2017.

- **2013, American Taxpayer Relief Act of 2012 (P.L. 112-240)**

P.L. 112-240, §101(a)(1)-(3), provides:

SEC. 101. PERMANENT EXTENSION AND MODIFICATION OF 2001 TAX RELIEF.

(a) PERMANENT EXTENSION.—

(1) IN GENERAL.—The Economic Growth and Tax Relief Reconciliation Act of 2001 is amended by striking title IX.

(2) CONFORMING AMENDMENT.—The Tax Relief, Unemployment Insurance Reauthorization, and Job Creation Act of 2010 is amended by striking section 304.

(3) EFFECTIVE DATE.—The amendments made by this subsection shall apply to taxable, plan, or limitation years beginning after December 31, 2012, and estates of decedents dying, gifts made, or generation skipping transfers after December 31, 2012.

P.L. 112-240, §101(c)(2):

Amended Code Sec. 2010(c)(4)(B)(i) by striking "basic exclusion amount" and inserting "applicable exclusion amount". **Effective** as if included in the amendments made by section 303 of the Tax Relief, Unemployment Insurance Reauthorization, and Job Creation Act of 2010 (P.L. 111-312) [effective for estates of decedents dying and gifts made after 12-31-2010.—CCH].

- **2010, Tax Relief, Unemployment Insurance Reauthorization, and Job Creation Act of 2010 (P.L. 111-312)**

P.L. 111-312, §302(a)(1):

Amended Code Sec. 2010(c). **Effective** for estates of decedents dying, generation-skipping transfers, and gifts made, after 12-31-2009. Prior to amendment, Code Sec. 2010(c) read as follows:

(c) APPLICABLE CREDIT AMOUNT.—For purposes of this section, the applicable credit amount is the amount of the tentative tax which would be determined under the rate schedule set forth in section 2001(c) if the amount with respect to which such tentative tax is to be computed were the applicable exclusion amount determined in accordance with the following table:

In the case of estates of decedents dying during:	The applicable exclusion amount is:
2002 and 2003	$1,000,000
2004 and 2005	$1,500,000
2006, 2007, and 2008	$2,000,000
2009	$3,500,000

P.L. 111-312, §303(a):

Amended Code Sec. 2010(c), as amended by Act Sec. 302(a), by striking paragraph (2) and inserting new paragraphs (2)-(6). **Effective** for estates of decedents dying and gifts made after 12-31-2010. Prior to being stricken, Code Sec. 2010(c)(2) read as follows:

(2) APPLICABLE EXCLUSION AMOUNT.—

(A) IN GENERAL.—For purposes of this subsection, the applicable exclusion amount is $5,000,000.

(B) INFLATION ADJUSTMENT.—In the case of any decedent dying in a calendar year after 2011, the dollar amount in subparagraph (A) shall be increased by an amount equal to—

(i) such dollar amount, multiplied by

(ii) the cost-of-living adjustment determined under section 1(f)(3) for such calendar year by substituting "calendar year 2010" for "calendar year 1992" in subparagraph (B) thereof.

If any amount as adjusted under the preceding sentence is not a multiple of $10,000, such amount shall be rounded to the nearest multiple of $10,000.

P.L. 111-312, §304, provides [but see P.L. 112-240, §101(a)(2)-(3), above]:

SEC. 304. APPLICATION OF EGTRRA SUNSET TO THIS TITLE.

Section 901 of the Economic Growth and Tax Relief Reconciliation Act of 2001 shall apply to the amendments made by this title.

- **2001, Economic Growth and Tax Relief Reconciliation Act of 2001 (P.L. 107-16)**

P.L. 107-16, §521(a):

Amended Code Sec. 2010(c) by striking the table and inserting a new table. **Effective** for estates of decedents dying, and gifts made, after 12-31-2001. Prior to being stricken, the table read as follows:

In the case of estates of decedents dying, and gifts made, during:	The applicable exclusion amount is:
1998	$625,000
1999	$650,000
2000 and 2001	$675,000
2002 and 2003	$700,000
2004	$850,000
2005	$950,000
2006 or thereafter	$1,000,000

ESTATE TAX—CREDITS AGAINST TAX

P.L. 107-16, §901(a)-(b), as amended by P.L. 111-312, §101(a)(1), provides [but see P.L. 112-240, §101(a)(1) and (3), above]:

SEC. 901. SUNSET OF PROVISIONS OF ACT.

(a) IN GENERAL.—All provisions of, and amendments made by, this Act shall not apply—

(1) to taxable, plan, or limitation years beginning after December 31, 2012, or

(2) in the case of title V, to estates of decedents dying, gifts made, or generation skipping transfers, after December 31, 2012.

(b) APPLICATION OF CERTAIN LAWS.—The Internal Revenue Code of 1986 and the Employee Retirement Income Security Act of 1974 shall be applied and administered to years, estates, gifts, and transfers described in subsection (a) as if the provisions and amendments described in subsection (a) had never been enacted.

• **1997, Taxpayer Relief Act of 1997 (P.L. 105-34)**

P.L. 105-34, §501(a)(1)(B):

Amended Code Sec. 2010 by redesignating subsection (c) as subsection (d) and by inserting after subsection (b) a new subsection (c). **Effective** for estates of decedents dying, and gifts made, after 12-31-97.

[Sec. 2010(d)]

(d) LIMITATION BASED ON AMOUNT OF TAX.—The amount of the credit allowed by subsection (a) shall not exceed the amount of the tax imposed by section 2001.

Amendments

• **1997, Taxpayer Relief Act of 1997 (P.L. 105-34)**

P.L. 105-34, §501(a)(1)(B):

Amended Code Sec. 2010 by redesignating subsection (c) as subsection (d). **Effective** for estates of decedents dying, and gifts made, after 12-31-97.

• **1990, Omnibus Budget Reconciliation Act of 1990 (P.L. 101-508)**

P.L. 101-508, §11801(c)(19)(A):

Amended Code Sec. 2010 by redesignating subsection (d) as subsection (c). **Effective** 11-5-90.

P.L. 101-508, §11821(b), provides:

(b) SAVINGS PROVISION.—If—

(1) any provision amended or repealed by this part applied to—

(A) any transaction occurring before the date of the enactment of this Act,

(B) any property acquired before such date of enactment, or

(C) any item of income, loss, deduction, or credit taken into account before such date of enactment, and

(2) the treatment of such transaction, property, or item under such provision would (without regard to the amendments made by this part) affect liability for tax for periods ending after such date of enactment,

nothing in the amendments made by this part shall be construed to affect the treatment of such transaction, property, or item for purposes of determining liability for tax for periods ending after such date of enactment.

• **1976, Tax Reform Act of 1976 (P.L. 94-455)**

P.L. 94-455, §2001(a)(2), (d)(1):

Added Code Sec. 2010. **Effective** for estates of decedents dying after 12-31-76.

[Sec. 2011—Stricken]

Amendments

• **2014, Tax Technical Corrections Act of 2014 (P.L. 113-295)**

P.L. 113-295, §221(a)(95)(A)(i), Division A:

Amended part II of subchapter A of chapter 11 by striking Code Sec. 2011. **Effective** generally 12-19-2014. For a special rule, see Act Sec. 221(b)(2), Division A, below.

P.L. 113-295, §221(b)(2), Division A, provides:

(2) SAVINGS PROVISION.—If—

(A) any provision amended or repealed by the amendments made by this section applied to—

(i) any transaction occurring before the date of the enactment of this Act,

(ii) any property acquired before such date of enactment, or

(iii) any item of income, loss, deduction, or credit taken into account before such date of enactment, and

(B) the treatment of such transaction, property, or item under such provision would (without regard to the amendments or repeals made by this section) affect the liability for tax for periods ending after date of enactment, nothing in the amendments or repeals made by this section shall be construed to affect the treatment of such transaction, property, or item for purposes of determining liability for tax for periods ending after such date of enactment.

Prior to being stricken, Code Sec. 2011 read as follows:

SEC. 2011. CREDIT FOR STATE DEATH TAXES.

[Sec. 2011(a)]

(a) IN GENERAL.—The tax imposed by section 2001 shall be credited with the amount of any estate, inheritance, legacy, or succession taxes actually paid to any State or the District of Columbia, in respect of any property included in the gross estate (not including any such taxes paid with respect to the estate of a person other than the decedent).

Amendments

• **1976, Tax Reform Act of 1976 (P.L. 94-455)**

P.L. 94-455, §1902(a)(12)(B), (c)(2):

Deleted "or Territory" in Code Sec. 2011(a). **Effective** for gifts made after 12-31-76.

• **1958, Technical Amendments Act of 1958 (P.L. 85-866)**

P.L. 85-866, §102(c), (d):

Amended Code Sec. 2011(a) by striking the words "or any possession of the United States," after the words "District of Columbia". **Effective** for estates of decedents dying after 9-2-58.

[Sec. 2011(b)]

(b) AMOUNT OF CREDIT.—

(1) IN GENERAL.—Except as provided in paragraph (2), the credit allowed by this section shall not exceed the appropriate amount stated in the following table:

If the adjusted taxable estate is:	The maximum tax credit shall be:
Not over $90,000	8/10ths of 1% of the amount by which the adjusted taxable estate exceeds $40,000.
Over $90,000 but not over $140,000	$400 plus 1.6% of the excess over $90,000.
Over $140,000 but not over $240,000	$1,200 plus 2.4% of the excess over $140,000.
Over $240,000 but not over $440,000	$3,600 plus 3.2% of the excess over $240,000.
Over $440,000 but not over $640,000	$10,000 plus 4% of the excess over $440,000.
Over $640,000 but not over $840,000	$18,000 plus 4.8% of the excess over $640,000.
Over $840,000 but not over $1,040,000	$27,600 plus 5.6% of the excess over $840,000.
Over $1,040,000 but not over $1,540,000	$38,800 plus 6.4% of the excess over $1,040,000.
Over $1,540,000 but not over $2,040,000	$70,800 plus 7.2% of the excess over $1,540,000.
Over $2,040,000 but not over $2,540,000	$106,800 plus 8% of the excess over $2,040,000.
Over $2,540,000 but not over $3,040,000	$146,800 plus 8.8% of the excess over $2,540,000.
Over $3,040,000 but not over $3,540,000	$190,800 plus 9.6% of the excess over $3,040,000.
Over $3,540,000 but not over $4,040,000	$238,800 plus 10.4% of the excess over $3,540,000.
Over $4,040,000 but not over $5,040,000	$290,800 plus 11.2% of the excess over $4,040,000.
Over $5,040,000 but not over $6,040,000	$402,800 plus 12% of the excess over $5,040,000.
Over $6,040,000 but not over $7,040,000	$522,800 plus 12.8% of the excess over $6,040,000.
Over $7,040,000 but not over $8,040,000	$650,800 plus 13.6% of the excess over $7,040,000.
Over $8,040,000 but not over $9,040,000	$786,800 plus 14.4% of the excess over $8,040,000.
Over $9,040,000 but not over $10,040,000	$930,800 plus 15.2% of the excess over $9,040,000.
Over $10,040,000	$1,082,800 plus 16% of the excess over $10,040,000.

(2) REDUCTION OF MAXIMUM CREDIT.—

(A) IN GENERAL.—In the case of estates of decedents dying after December 31, 2001, the credit allowed by this section shall not exceed the applicable percentage of the credit otherwise determined under paragraph (1).

(B) APPLICABLE PERCENTAGE.—

In the case of estates of decedents dying during:	The applicable percentage is:
2002	75 percent
2003	50 percent
2004	25 percent

(3) ADJUSTED TAXABLE ESTATE.—For purposes of this section, the term "adjusted taxable estate" means the taxable estate reduced by $60,000.

ESTATE TAX—CREDITS AGAINST TAX

Amendments

• **2013, American Taxpayer Relief Act of 2012 (P.L. 112-240)**

P.L. 112-240, § 101(a)(1) and (3), provides:

SEC. 101. PERMANENT EXTENSION AND MODIFICATION OF 2001 TAX RELIEF.

(a) PERMANENT EXTENSION.—

(1) IN GENERAL.—The Economic Growth and Tax Relief Reconciliation Act of 2001 is amended by striking title IX.

* * *

(3) EFFECTIVE DATE.—The amendments made by this subsection shall apply to taxable, plan, or limitation years beginning after December 31, 2012, and estates of decedents dying, gifts made, or generation skipping transfers after December 31, 2012.

• **2001, Economic Growth and Tax Relief Reconciliation Act of 2001 (P.L. 107-16)**

P.L. 107-16, § 531(a)(1)-(3):

Amended Code Sec. 2011(b) by striking "CREDIT.—The credit allowed" and inserting "CREDIT.—(1) IN GENERAL.—Except as provided in paragraph (2), the credit allowed", by striking "For purposes" and inserting "(3) ADJUSTED TAXABLE ESTATE.—For purposes", and by inserting after paragraph (1) a new paragraph (2). **Effective** for estates of decedents dying after 12-31-2001.

P.L. 107-16, § 901(a)-(b), as amended by P.L. 111-312, § 101(a)(1), provides [but see P.L. 112-240, § 101(a)(1) and (3), above]:

SEC. 901. SUNSET OF PROVISIONS OF ACT.

(a) IN GENERAL.—All provisions of, and amendments made by, this Act shall not apply—

(1) to taxable, plan, or limitation years beginning after December 31, 2012, or

(2) in the case of title V, to estates of decedents dying, gifts made, or generation skipping transfers, after December 31, 2012.

(b) APPLICATION OF CERTAIN LAWS.—The Internal Revenue Code of 1986 and the Employee Retirement Income Security Act of 1974 shall be applied and administered to years, estates, gifts, and transfers described in subsection (a) as if the provisions and amendments described in subsection (a) had never been enacted.

• **1976, Tax Reform Act of 1976 (P.L. 94-455)**

P.L. 94-455, § 2001(c)(1)(A), (d)(1):

Substituted "adjusted taxable estate" for "taxable estate" each place it appeared in Code Sec. 2011(b); and added at the end of such section a new sentence. **Effective** for estates of decedents dying after 12-31-76.

[Sec. 2011(c)]

(c) PERIOD OF LIMITATIONS ON CREDIT.—The credit allowed by this section shall include only such taxes as were actually paid and credit therefor claimed within 4 years after the filing of the return required by section 6018, except that—

(1) If a petition for redetermination of a deficiency has been filed with the Tax Court within the time prescribed in section 6213(a), then within such 4-year period or before the expiration of 60 days after the decision of the Tax Court becomes final.

(2) If, under section 6161, or 6166 an extension of time has been granted for payment of the tax shown on the return, or of a deficiency, then within such 4-year period or before the date of the expiration of the period of the extension.

(3) If a claim for refund or credit of an overpayment of tax imposed by this chapter has been filed within the time prescribed in section 6511, then within such 4-year period or before the expiration of 60 days from the date of mailing by certified mail or registered mail by the Secretary to the taxpayer of a notice of the disallowance of any part of such claim, or before the expiration of 60 days after a decision by any court of competent jurisdiction becomes final with respect to a timely suit instituted upon such claim, whichever is later.

Refund based on the credit may (despite the provisions of sections 6511 and 6512) be made if claim therefor is filed within the period above provided. Any such refund shall be made without interest.

Amendments

• **1981, Economic Recovery Tax Act of 1981 (P.L. 97-34)**

P.L. 97-34, § 422(e)(2):

Amended Code Sec. 2011(c)(2) by striking out "6161, 6166 or 6166A" and inserting "6161 or 6166". **Effective** for estates of decedents dying after 12-31-81.

• **1976, Tax Reform Act of 1976 (P.L. 94-455)**

P.L. 94-455, § 1906(b)(13)(A):

Amended 1954 Code by substituting "Secretary" for "Secretary or his delegate" each place it appeared. **Effective** 2-1-77.

P.L. 94-455, § 2004(f)(3):

Amended Code Sec. 2011(c)(2) by striking out "section 6161" and inserting in lieu thereof "6166 or 6166A". **Effective** for estates of decedents dying after 12-31-76.

• **1958, Technical Amendments Act of 1958 (P.L. 85-866)**

P.L. 85-866, § 65(a):

Amended Code Sec. 2011(c) by adding paragraph (3). **Effective** for estates of decedents dying after 8-16-54.

[Sec. 2011(d)]

(d) LIMITATION IN CASES INVOLVING DEDUCTION UNDER SECTION 2053(d).—In any case where a deduction is allowed under section 2053(d) for an estate, succession, legacy, or inheritance tax imposed by a State or the District of Columbia upon a transfer for public, charitable, or religious uses described in section 2055 or 2106(a)(2), the allowance of the credit under this section shall be subject to the following conditions and limitations:

(1) The taxes described in subsection (a) shall not include any estate, succession, legacy, or inheritance tax for which such deduction is allowed under section 2053(d).

(2) The credit shall not exceed the lesser of—

(A) the amount stated in subsection (b) on a [an] adjusted taxable estate determined by allowing such deduction authorized by section 2053(d), or

(B) that proportion of the amount stated in subsection (b) on a [an] adjusted taxable estate determined without regard to such deduction authorized by section 2053(d) as (i) the amount of the taxes described in subsection (a), as limited by the provisions of paragraph (1) of this subsection, bears to (ii) the amount of the taxes described in subsection (a) before applying the limitation contained in paragraph (1) of this subsection.

(3) If the amount determined under subparagraph (B) of paragraph (2) is less than the amount determined under subparagraph (A) of that paragraph, then for purposes of subsection (d) such lesser amount shall be the maximum credit provided by subsection (b).

Amendments

• **2002, Victims of Terrorism Tax Relief Act of 2001 (P.L. 107-134)**

P.L. 107-134, § 103(b)(1):

Amended Code Sec. 2011 by striking subsection (d) and redesignating subsection (e) as subsection (d). **Effective** for estates of decedents dying on or after 9-11-2001; and in the case of individuals dying as a result of the 4-19-95 terrorist attack, dying on or after 4-19-95. For a waiver of limitations, see Act Sec. 103(d)(2), below.

P.L. 107-134, § 103(d)(2), provides:

(2) WAIVER OF LIMITATIONS.—If refund or credit of any overpayment of tax resulting from the amendments made by this section is prevented at any time before the close of the 1-year period beginning on the date of the enactment of this Act by the operation of any law or rule of law (including res judicata), such refund or credit may nevertheless be made or allowed if claim therefor is filed before the close of such period.

• **1976, Tax Reform Act of 1976 (P.L. 94-455)**

P.L. 94-455, § 1902(a)(12)(B), (c):

Deleted "or Territory" in Code Sec. 2011(e). **Effective** for gifts made after 12-31-76.

P.L. 94-455, § 2001(c)(1)(A):

Substituted "adjusted taxable estate" for "taxable estate" each place it appeared in Code Sec. 2011(e). **Effective** for estates of decedents dying after 12-31-76.

• **1959 (P.L. 86-175)**

P.L. 86-175, § 3:

Amended 1954 Code Sec. 2011(e) by striking out "imposed upon a transfer" and by substituting "imposed by a State or Territory or the District of Columbia upon a transfer"; by striking out "for which a deduction" in paragraph (1) and substituting "for which such deduction"; and by striking out "the deduction authorized by" each place it appeared in paragraph (2) and by substituting "such deduction authorized by". **Effective** with respect to the estates of decedents dying on or after 7-1-55.

• **1956 (P.L. 414, 84th Cong.)**

P.L. 414, 84th Cong., § 3:

Amended Section 2011 by adding after subsection (d) a new subsection (e). **Effective** for the estates of all decedents dying after 12-31-53.

[Sec. 2011(d)—Stricken]

Amendments

• **2002, Victims of Terrorism Tax Relief Act of 2001 (P.L. 107-134)**

P.L. 107-134, § 103(b)(1):

Amended Code Sec. 2011 by striking subsection (d) and by redesignating subsections (e), (f), and (g) as subsections (d), (e), and (f), respectively. **Effective** for estates of decedents dying on or after 9-11-2001; and in the case of individuals dying as a result of the 4-19-95 terrorist attack, dying on or after 4-19-95. For a waiver of limitations, see Act Sec. 103(d)(2) in the amendment notes for Code Sec. 2011(d). Prior to being stricken, Code Sec. 2011(d) read as follows:

(d) BASIC ESTATE TAX.—The basic estate tax and the estate tax imposed by the Revenue Act of 1926 shall be 125 percent of the amount determined to be the maximum credit provided by subsection (b). The additional estate tax shall be the difference between the tax imposed by section 2001 or 2101 and the basic estate tax.

[Sec. 2011(e)]

(e) LIMITATION BASED ON AMOUNT OF TAX.—The credit provided by this section shall not exceed the amount of the tax imposed by section 2001, reduced by the amount of the unified credit provided by section 2010.

Amendments

• **2002, Victims of Terrorism Tax Relief Act of 2001 (P.L. 107-134)**

P.L. 107-134, § 103(b)(1):

Amended Code Sec. 2011 by redesignating subsection (f) as subsection (e). **Effective** for estates of decedents dying on or after 9-11-2001; and in the case of individuals dying as a result of the 4-19-95 terrorist attack, dying on or after 4-19-95. For a waiver of limitations, see Act Sec. 103(d)(2) in the amendment notes for Code Sec. 2011(d).

• **1976, Tax Reform Act of 1976 (P.L. 94-455)**

P.L. 94-455, § 2001(c)(1)(A), (d)(1):

Added new Code Sec. 2011(f). **Effective** for estates of decedents dying after 12-31-76.

[Sec. 2011(f)]

(f) TERMINATION.—This section shall not apply to the estates of decedents dying after December 31, 2004.

ESTATE TAX—CREDITS AGAINST TAX

Amendments

• **2013, American Taxpayer Relief Act of 2012 (P.L. 112-240)**

P.L. 112-240, §101(a)(1) and (3), provides:

SEC. 101. PERMANENT EXTENSION AND MODIFICATION OF 2001 TAX RELIEF.

(a) PERMANENT EXTENSION.—

(1) IN GENERAL.—The Economic Growth and Tax Relief Reconciliation Act of 2001 is amended by striking title IX.

* * *

(3) EFFECTIVE DATE.—The amendments made by this subsection shall apply to taxable, plan, or limitation years beginning after December 31, 2012, and estates of decedents dying, gifts made, or generation skipping transfers after December 31, 2012.

• **2002, Victims of Terrorism Tax Relief Act of 2001 (P.L. 107-134)**

P.L. 107-134, §103(b)(1):

Amended Code Sec. 2011 by redesignating subsection (g) as subsection (f). **Effective** for estates of decedents dying on or after 9-11-2001; and in the case of individuals dying as a result of the 4-19-95 terrorist attack, dying on or after 4-19-95. For a waiver of limitations, see Act Sec. 103(d)(2) in the amendment notes for Code Sec. 2011(d).

• **2001, Economic Growth and Tax Relief Reconciliation Act of 2001 (P.L. 107-16)**

P.L. 107-16, §532(a):

Amended Code Sec. 2011 by adding at the end a new subsection (g). **Effective** for estates of decedents dying, and generation-skipping transfers, after 12-31-2004.

P.L. 107-16, §901(a)-(b), as amended by P.L. 111-312, §101(a)(1), provides [but see P.L. 112-240, §101(a)(1) and (3), above]:

SEC. 901. SUNSET OF PROVISIONS OF ACT.

(a) IN GENERAL.—All provisions of, and amendments made by, this Act shall not apply—

(1) to taxable, plan, or limitation years beginning after December 31, 2012, or

(2) in the case of title V, to estates of decedents dying, gifts made, or generation skipping transfers, after December 31, 2012.

(b) APPLICATION OF CERTAIN LAWS.—The Internal Revenue Code of 1986 and the Employee Retirement Income Security Act of 1974 shall be applied and administered to years, estates, gifts, and transfers described in subsection (a) as if the provisions and amendments described in subsection (a) had never been enacted.

[Sec. 2012]

SEC. 2012. CREDIT FOR GIFT TAX.

[Sec. 2012(a)]

(a) IN GENERAL.—If a tax on a gift has been paid under chapter 12 (sec. 2501 and following), or under corresponding provisions of prior laws, and thereafter on the death of the donor any amount in respect of such gift is required to be included in the value of the gross estate of the decedent for purposes of this chapter, then there shall be credited against the tax imposed by section 2001 the amount of the tax paid on a gift under chapter 12, or under corresponding provisions of prior laws, with respect to so much of the property which constituted the gift as is included in the gross estate, except that the amount of such credit shall not exceed an amount which bears the same ratio to the tax imposed by section 2001 (after deducting from such tax the unified credit provided by section 2010) as the value (at the time of the gift or at the time of the death, whichever is lower) of so much of the property which constituted the gift as is included in the gross estate bears to the value of the entire gross estate reduced by the aggregate amount of the charitable and marital deductions allowed under sections 2055, 2056, and 2106(a)(2).

Amendments

• **2013, American Taxpayer Relief Act of 2012 (P.L. 112-240)**

P.L. 112-240, §101(a)(1) and (3), provides:

SEC. 101. PERMANENT EXTENSION AND MODIFICATION OF 2001 TAX RELIEF.

(a) PERMANENT EXTENSION.—

(1) IN GENERAL.—The Economic Growth and Tax Relief Reconciliation Act of 2001 is amended by striking title IX.

* * *

(3) EFFECTIVE DATE.—The amendments made by this subsection shall apply to taxable, plan, or limitation years beginning after December 31, 2012, and estates of decedents dying, gifts made, or generation skipping transfers after December 31, 2012.

• **2001, Economic Growth and Tax Relief Reconciliation Act of 2001 (P.L. 107-16)**

P.L. 107-16, §532(c)(1):

Amended Code Sec. 2012(a) by striking "the credit for State death taxes provided by section 2011 and" following "(after deducting from such tax". **Effective** for estates of decedents dying, and generation-skipping transfers, after 12-31-2004.

P.L. 107-16, §901(a)-(b), as amended by P.L. 111-312, §101(a)(1), provides [but see P.L. 112-240, §101(a)(1) and (3), above]:

SEC. 901. SUNSET OF PROVISIONS OF ACT.

(a) IN GENERAL.—All provisions of, and amendments made by, this Act shall not apply—

(1) to taxable, plan, or limitation years beginning after December 31, 2012, or

(2) in the case of title V, to estates of decedents dying, gifts made, or generation skipping transfers, after December 31, 2012.

(b) APPLICATION OF CERTAIN LAWS.—The Internal Revenue Code of 1986 and the Employee Retirement Income Security Act of 1974 shall be applied and administered to years, estates, gifts, and transfers described in subsection (a) as if the provisions and amendments described in subsection (a) had never been enacted.

• **1976, Tax Reform Act of 1976 (P.L. 94-455)**

P.L. 94-455, §2001(c)(1)(B):

Amended Code Sec. 2012(a) by adding "and the unified credit provided by section 2010" after "section 2011". **Effective** for estates of decedents dying after 12-31-76.

[Sec. 2012(b)]

(b) VALUATION REDUCTIONS.—In applying, with respect to any gift, the ratio stated in subsection (a), the value at the time of the gift or at the time of the death, referred to in such ratio, shall be reduced—

(1) by such amount as will properly reflect the amount of such gift which was excluded in determining (for purposes of section 2503(a)), or of corresponding provisions of prior laws, the total amount of gifts made during the calendar quarter (or calendar year if the gift was made before January 1, 1971) in which the gift was made;

(2) if a deduction with respect to such gift is allowed under section 2056(a) (relating to marital deduction), then by the amount of such value, reduced as provided in paragraph (1); and

(3) if a deduction with respect to such gift is allowed under sections 2055 or 2106(a)(2) (relating to charitable deduction), then by the amount of such value, reduced as provided in paragraph (1) of this subsection.

Amendments

• **1981, Economic Recovery Tax Act of 1981 (P.L. 97-34)**

P.L. 97-34, §403(a)(2)(A):

Amended Code Sec. 2012(b)(2). **Effective** for estates of decedents dying after 12-31-81. Prior to amendment, Code Sec. 2012(b)(2) read as follows:

(2) if a deduction with respect to such gift is allowed under section 2056(a) (relating to marital deduction), then by an amount which bears the same ratio to such value (reduced as provided in paragraph (1) of this subsection) as the aggregate amount of the marital deductions allowed under section 2056 (a) bears to the aggregate amount of such marital deductions computed without regard to subsection (c) thereof; and

• **1976, Tax Reform Act of 1976 (P.L. 94-455)**

P.L. 94-455, §1902(a)(1)(A), (c)(1):

Added the heading "VALUATION REDUCTIONS.—" to Code Sec. 2012(b); and substituted "deduction), then" for "deduction)—then" in paragraphs (2) and (3) of Code Sec. 2012(b). **Effective** for estates of decedents dying after 10-4-76.

• **1970, Excise, Estate, and Gift Tax Adjustment Act of 1970 (P.L. 91-614)**

P.L. 91-614, §102(d)(2)(A):

Amended Code Sec. 2012(b)(1) by substituting "the calendar quarter (or calendar year if the gift was made before January 1, 1971)" for "the year." **Effective** for gifts made after 12-31-70.

[Sec. 2012(c)]

(c) WHERE GIFT CONSIDERED MADE ONE-HALF BY SPOUSE.—Where the decedent was the donor of the gift but, under the provisions of section 2513, or corresponding provisions of prior laws, the gift was considered as made one-half by his spouse—

(1) the term "the amount of the tax paid on a gift under chapter 12", as used in subsection (a), includes the amounts paid with respect to each half of such gift, the amount paid with respect to each being computed in the manner provided in subsection (d); and

ESTATE TAX—CREDITS AGAINST TAX

(2) in applying, with respect to such gift, the ratio stated in subsection (a), the value at the time of the gift or at the time of the death, referred to in such ratio, includes such value with respect to each half of such gift, each such value being reduced as provided in paragraph (1) of subsection (b).

Amendments

• **1976, Tax Reform Act of 1976 (P.L. 94-455)**

P.L. 94-455, §1902(a)(1)(B), (c)(1):

Added the heading "WHERE GIFT CONSIDERED MADE ONE-HALF BY SPOUSE.—" to Code Sec. 2012(c). **Effective** for estates of decedents dying after 10-4-76.

[Sec. 2012(d)]

(d) COMPUTATION OF AMOUNT OF GIFT TAX PAID.—

(1) AMOUNT OF TAX.—For purposes of subsection (a), the amount of tax paid on a gift under chapter 12, or under corresponding provisions of prior laws, with respect to any gift shall be an amount which bears the same ratio to the total tax paid for the calendar quarter (or calendar year if the gift was made before January 1, 1971) in which the gift was made as the amount of such gift bears to the total amount of taxable gifts (computed without deduction of the specific exemption) for such quarter or year.

(2) AMOUNT OF GIFT.—For purposes of paragraph (1), the "amount of such gift" shall be the amount included with respect to such gift in determining (for the purposes of section 2503(a), or of corresponding provisions of prior laws) the total amount of gifts made during such quarter or year, reduced by the amount of any deduction allowed with respect to such gift under section 2522, or under corresponding provisions of prior laws (relating to charitable deduction), or under section 2523 (relating to marital deduction).

Amendments

• **1976, Tax Reform Act of 1976 (P.L. 94-455)**

P.L. 94-455, §1902(a)(1):

Added the heading "COMPUTATION OF AMOUNT OF GIFT TAX PAID.—(1) AMOUNT OF TAX." to Code Sec. 2012(d)(1); and added the heading "AMOUNT OF GIFT.—" to Code Sec. 2012(d)(2). **Effective** for estates of decedents dying after 10-4-76.

• **1970, Excise, Estate, and Gift Tax Adjustment Act of 1970 (P.L. 91-614)**

P.L. 91-614, §102(d)(2)(A), (B):

Amended Code Sec. 2012(d)(1) by substituting "the calendar quarter (or calendar year if the gift was made before January 1, 1971)" for "the year" and by substituting "such quarter or year" for "such year." Also amended Code Sec. 2012(d)(2) by substituting "such quarter or year" for "such year.". **Effective** for gifts made after 12-31-70.

[Sec. 2012(e)]

(e) SECTION INAPPLICABLE TO GIFTS MADE AFTER DECEMBER 31, 1976.—No credit shall be allowed under this section with respect to the amount of any tax paid under chapter 12 on any gift made after December 31, 1976.

Amendments

• **1976, Tax Reform Act of 1976 (P.L. 94-455)**

P.L. 94-455, §2001(a)(3), (d)(1):

Added Code Sec. 2012(e). **Effective** for estates of decedents dying after 12-31-76.

[Sec. 2013]

SEC. 2013. CREDIT FOR TAX ON PRIOR TRANSFERS.

[Sec. 2013(a)]

(a) GENERAL RULE.—The tax imposed by section 2001 shall be credited with all or a part of the amount of the Federal estate tax paid with respect to the transfer of property (including property passing as a result of the exercise or non-exercise of a power of appointment) to the decedent by or from a person (herein designated as a "transferor") who died within 10 years before, or within 2 years after, the decedent's death. If the transferor died within 2 years of the death of the decedent, the credit shall be the amount determined under subsections (b) and (c). If the transferor predeceased the decedent by more than 2 years, the credit shall be the following percentage of the amount so determined—

(1) 80 percent, if within the third or fourth years preceding the decedent's death;

(2) 60 percent, if within the fifth or sixth years preceding the decedent's death;

(3) 40 percent, if within the seventh or eighth years preceding the decedent's death; and

(4) 20 percent, if within the ninth or tenth years preceding the decedent's death.

[Sec. 2013(b)]

(b) COMPUTATION OF CREDIT.—Subject to the limitation prescribed in subsection (c), the credit provided by this section shall be an amount which bears the same ratio to the estate tax paid (adjusted as indicated hereinafter) with respect to the estate of the transferor as the value of the property transferred bears to the taxable estate of the transferor (determined for purposes of the estate tax) decreased by any death taxes paid with respect to such estate. For purposes of the preceding sentence, the estate tax paid shall be the Federal estate tax paid increased by any credits allowed against such estate tax under section 2012, or corresponding provisions of prior laws, on account of gift tax, and for any credits allowed against such estate tax under this section on account of prior transfers where the transferor acquired property from a person who died within 10 years before the death of the decedent.

Amendments

• **1976, Tax Reform Act of 1976 (P.L. 94-455)**

P.L. 94-455, §2001(c)(1)(C), (d)(1):

Deleted "and increased by the exemption provided for by 2052 or section 2106(a)(3), or the corresponding provisions of prior laws, in determining the taxable estate of the transferor for purposes of the estate tax" at the end of the first sentence of Code Sec. 2013(b). **Effective** for estates of decedents dying after 12-31-76.

[Sec. 2013(c)]

(c) LIMITATION ON CREDIT.—

(1) IN GENERAL.—The credit provided in this section shall not exceed the amount by which—

(A) the estate tax imposed by section 2001 or section 2101 (after deducting the credits provided for in sections 2010, 2012, and 2014) computed without regard to this section, exceeds

(B) such tax computed by excluding from the decedent's gross estate the value of such property transferred and, if applicable, by making the adjustment hereinafter indicated.

If any deduction is otherwise allowable under section 2055 or section 2106(a)(2) (relating to charitable deduction) then, for the purpose of the computation indicated in subparagraph (B), the amount of such deduction shall be reduced by that part of such deduction which the value of such property transferred bears to the decedent's entire gross estate reduced by the deductions allowed under sections 2053 and 2054, or section 2106(a)(1) (relating to deduction for expenses, losses, etc.). For purposes of this section, the value of such property transferred shall be the value as provided for in subsection (d) of this section.

(2) TWO OR MORE TRANSFERORS.—If the credit provided in this section relates to property received from 2 or more transferors, the limitation provided in paragraph (1) of this subsection shall be computed by aggregating the value of the property so transferred to the decedent. The

ESTATE TAX—CREDITS AGAINST TAX

aggregate limitation so determined shall be apportioned in accordance with the value of the property transferred to the decedent by each transferor.

Amendments

• **2013, American Taxpayer Relief Act of 2012 (P.L. 112-240)**

P.L. 112-240, §101(a)(1) and (3), provides:

SEC. 101. PERMANENT EXTENSION AND MODIFICATION OF 2001 TAX RELIEF.

(a) PERMANENT EXTENSION.—

(1) IN GENERAL.—The Economic Growth and Tax Relief Reconciliation Act of 2001 is amended by striking title IX.

* * *

(3) EFFECTIVE DATE.—The amendments made by this subsection shall apply to taxable, plan, or limitation years beginning after December 31, 2012, and estates of decedents dying, gifts made, or generation skipping transfers after December 31, 2012.

• **2001, Economic Growth and Tax Relief Reconciliation Act of 2001 (P.L. 107-16)**

P.L. 107-16, §532(c)(2):

Amended Code Sec. 2013(c)(1)(A) by striking "2011," following "in sections 2010,". **Effective** for estates of decedents dying, and generation-skipping transfers, after 12-31-2004.

P.L. 107-16, §901(a)-(b), as amended by P.L. 111-312, §101(a)(1), provides [but see P.L. 112-240, §101(a)(1) and (3), above]:

SEC. 901. SUNSET OF PROVISIONS OF ACT.

(a) IN GENERAL.—All provisions of, and amendments made by, this Act shall not apply—

(1) to taxable, plan, or limitation years beginning after December 31, 2012, or

(2) in the case of title V, to estates of decedents dying, gifts made, or generation skipping transfers, after December 31, 2012.

(b) APPLICATION OF CERTAIN LAWS.—The Internal Revenue Code of 1986 and the Employee Retirement Income Security Act of 1974 shall be applied and administered to years, estates, gifts, and transfers described in subsection (a) as if the provisions and amendments described in subsection (a) had never been enacted.

• **1976, Tax Reform Act of 1976 (P.L. 94-455)**

P.L. 94-455, §2001(c)(1)(C), (d)(1):

Amended Code Sec. 2013(c)(1)(A). **Effective** for estates of decedents dying after 12-31-76. Prior to amendment such section read as follows:

(A) the estate tax imposed by section 2001 or section 2101 (after deducting the credits for State death taxes, gift tax, and foreign death taxes provided for in sections 2011, 2012, and 2014) computed without regard to this section, exceeds.

[Sec. 2013(d)]

(d) VALUATION OF PROPERTY TRANSFERRED.—The value of property transferred to the decedent shall be the value used for the purpose of determining the Federal estate tax liability of the estate of the transferor but—

(1) there shall be taken into account the effect of the tax imposed by section 2001 or 2101, or any estate, succession, legacy, or inheritance tax, on the net value to the decedent of such property;

(2) where such property is encumbered in any manner, or where the decedent incurs any obligation imposed by the transferor with respect to such property, such encumbrance or obligation shall be taken into account in the same manner as if the amount of a gift to the decedent of such property was being determined; and

(3) if the decedent was the spouse of the transferor at the time of the transferor's death, the net value of the property transferred to the decedent shall be reduced by the amount allowed under section 2056 (relating to marital deductions) as a deduction from the gross estate of the transferor.

Amendments

• **1976, Tax Reform Act of 1976 (P.L. 94-455)**

P.L. 94-455, §1902(a)(2), (c)(1):

Deleted ", or the corresponding provision of prior law," in Code Sec. 2013(d)(3). **Effective** for estates of decedents dying after 10-4-76.

[Sec. 2013(e)]

(e) PROPERTY DEFINED.—For purposes of this section, the term "property" includes any beneficial interest in property, including a general power of appointment (as defined in section 2041).

[Sec. 2013(f)]

(f) TREATMENT OF ADDITIONAL TAX IMPOSED UNDER SECTION 2032A.—If section 2032A applies to any property included in the gross estate of the transferor and an additional tax is imposed with respect to such property under section 2032A(c) before the date which is 2 years after the date of decedent's death, for purposes of this section—

(1) the additional tax imposed by section 2032A(c) shall be treated as a Federal estate tax payable with respect to the estate of the transferor; and

(2) the value of such property and the amount of the taxable estate of the transferor shall be determined as if section 2032A did not apply with respect to such property.

Amendments

• **1976, Tax Reform Act of 1976 (P.L. 94-455)**

P.L. 94-455, §2003(c), (e):

Added Code Sec. 2013(f). **Effective** for estates of decedents dying after 12-31-76.

[Sec. 2013(g)—Stricken]

Amendments

• **1997, Taxpayer Relief Act of 1997 (P.L. 105-34)**

P.L. 105-34, §1073(b)(2):

Amended Code Sec. 2013 by striking subsection (g). **Effective** for estates of decedents dying after 12-31-96. Prior to being stricken, Code Sec. 2013(g) read as follows:

(g) TREATMENT OF ADDITIONAL TAX UNDER SECTION 4980A.—For purposes of this section, the estate tax paid shall not include any portion of such tax attributable to section 4980A(d).

• **1988, Technical and Miscellaneous Revenue Act of 1988 (P.L. 100-647)**

P.L. 100-647, §1011A(g)(7):

Amended Code Sec. 2013 by adding at the end thereof new subsection (g). **Effective** as if included in the provision of P.L. 99-514 to which it relates.

[Sec. 2013(g)—Repealed]

Amendments

• **1986, Tax Reform Act of 1986 (P.L. 99-514)**

P.L. 99-514, §1432(c)(2):

Amended Code Sec. 2013 by repealing subsection (g). **Effective**, generally, for any generation-skipping transfer (within the meaning of Code Sec. 2611) made after 10-22-86. However, for special rules see Act Sec. 1433(b)-(d) in the amendments for Code Sec. 2601. Prior to repeal, Code Sec. 2013(g) read as follows:

(g) TREATMENT OF TAX IMPOSED ON CERTAIN GENERATION-SKIPPING TRANSFERS.—If any property was transferred to the decedent in a transfer which is taxable under section 2601 (relating to tax imposed on generation-skipping transfers) and if the deemed transferor (as defined in section 2612) is not alive at the time of such transfer, for purposes of this section—

(1) such property shall be deemed to have passed to the decedent from the deemed transferor;

(2) the tax payable under section 2601 on such transfer shall be treated as a Federal estate tax payable with respect to the estate of the deemed transferor; and

(3) the amount of the taxable estate of the deemed transferor shall be increased by the value of such property as determined for purposes of the tax imposed by section 2601 on the transfer.

ESTATE TAX—CREDITS AGAINST TAX

• **1976, Tax Reform Act of 1976 (P.L. 94-455)**

P.L. 94-455, § 2006(b)(2):

Added Code Sec. 2013(g). For **effective** date, see Act Sec. 2006(c), below.

P.L. 94-455, § 2006(c), as amended by P.L. 95-600, § 702(n)(1), provides:

(c) EFFECTIVE DATES.—

(1) IN GENERAL.—Except as provided in paragraph (2), the amendments made by this section shall apply to any generation-skipping transfer (within the meaning of section 2611(a) of the Internal Revenue Code of 1954) made after June 11, 1976.

(2) EXCEPTIONS.—The amendments made by this section shall not apply to any generation-skipping transfer—

(A) under a trust which was irrevocable on June 11, 1976, but only to the extent that the transfer is not made out of corpus added to the trust after June 11, 1976, or

(B) in the case of a decedent dying before January 1, 1982, pursuant to a will (or revocable trust) which was in existence on June 11, 1976, and was not amended at any time after that date in any respect which will result in the creation of, or increasing the amount of, any generation-skipping transfer.

For purposes of subparagraph (B), if the decedent on June 11, 1976, was under a mental disability to change the disposition of his property, the period set forth in such subparagraph shall not expire before the date which is 2 years after the date on which he first regains his competence to dispose of such property.

(3) TRUST EQUIVALENTS.—For purposes of paragraph (2), in the case of a trust equivalent within the meaning of subsection (d) of section 2611 of the Internal Revenue Code of 1954, the provisions of such subsection (d) shall apply.

[Sec. 2014]

SEC. 2014. CREDIT FOR FOREIGN DEATH TAXES.

[Sec. 2014(a)]

(a) IN GENERAL.—The tax imposed by section 2001 shall be credited with the amount of any estate, inheritance, legacy, or succession taxes actually paid to any foreign country in respect of any property situated within such foreign country and included in the gross estate (not including any such taxes paid with respect to the estate of a person other than the decedent). The determination of the country within which property is situated shall be made in accordance with the rules applicable under subchapter B (sec. 2101 and following) in determining whether property is situated within or without the United States.

Amendments

• **1966, Foreign Investors Tax Act of 1966 (P.L. 89-809)**

P.L. 89-809, § 106(b)(3):

Amended Code Sec. 2014(a) by deleting the second sentence. **Effective** with respect to estates of decedents dying after 11-13-66. Prior to deletion, the second sentence read as follows:

"If the decedent at the time of his death was not a citizen of the United States, credit shall not be allowed under this section unless the foreign country of which such decedent was a citizen or subject, in imposing such taxes, allows a similar credit in the case of a citizen of the United States resident in such country."

[Sec. 2014(b)]

(b) LIMITATIONS ON CREDIT.—The credit provided in this section with respect to such taxes paid to any foreign country—

(1) shall not, with respect to any such tax, exceed an amount which bears the same ratio to the amount of such tax actually paid to such foreign country as the value of property which is—

(A) situated within such foreign country,

(B) subjected to such tax, and

(C) included in the gross estate

bears to the value of all property subjected to such tax; and

(2) shall not, with respect to all such taxes, exceed an amount which bears the same ratio to the tax imposed by section 2001 (after deducting from such tax the credits provided by sections 2010 and 2012) as the value of property which is—

(A) situated within such foreign country,

(B) subjected to the taxes of such foreign country, and

(C) included in the gross estate

bears to the value of the entire gross estate reduced by the aggregate amount of the deductions allowed under sections 2055 and 2056.

Amendments

• **2013, American Taxpayer Relief Act of 2012 (P.L. 112-240)**

P.L. 112-240, § 101(a)(1) and (3), provides:

SEC. 101. PERMANENT EXTENSION AND MODIFICATION OF 2001 TAX RELIEF.

(a) PERMANENT EXTENSION.—

(1) IN GENERAL.—The Economic Growth and Tax Relief Reconciliation Act of 2001 is amended by striking title IX.

* * *

(3) EFFECTIVE DATE.—The amendments made by this subsection shall apply to taxable, plan, or limitation years beginning after December 31, 2012, and estates of decedents dying, gifts made, or generation skipping transfers after December 31, 2012.

• **2001, Economic Growth and Tax Relief Reconciliation Act of 2001 (P.L. 107-16)**

P.L. 107-16, § 532(c)(3):

Amended Code Sec. 2014(b)(2) by striking ", 2011," following "provided by sections 2010". **Effective** for estates of decedents dying, and generation-skipping transfers, after 12-31-2004.

P.L. 107-16, § 901(a)-(b), as amended by P.L. 111-312, § 101(a)(1), provides [but see P.L. 112-240, § 101(a)(1) and (3), above]:

SEC. 901. SUNSET OF PROVISIONS OF ACT.

(a) IN GENERAL.—All provisions of, and amendments made by, this Act shall not apply—

(1) to taxable, plan, or limitation years beginning after December 31, 2012, or

(2) in the case of title V, to estates of decedents dying, gifts made, or generation skipping transfers, after December 31, 2012.

(b) APPLICATION OF CERTAIN LAWS.—The Internal Revenue Code of 1986 and the Employee Retirement Income Security Act of 1974 shall be applied and administered to years, estates, gifts, and transfers described in subsection (a) as if the provisions and amendments described in subsection (a) had never been enacted.

• **1976, Tax Reform Act of 1976 (P.L. 94-455)**

P.L. 94-455, § 2001(c)(1)(G), (d)(1):

Substituted "sections 2010, 2011, and 2012" for "sections 2011 and 2012" in Code Sec. 2014(b)(2). **Effective** for estates of decedents dying after 12-31-76.

[Sec. 2014(c)]

(c) VALUATION OF PROPERTY.—

(1) The values referred to in the ratio stated in subsection (b)(1) are the values determined for purposes of the tax imposed by such foreign country.

(2) The values referred to in the ratio stated in subsection (b)(2) are the values determined under this chapter; but, in applying such ratio, the value of any property described in subparagraphs (A), (B), and (C) thereof shall be reduced by such amount as will properly reflect, in accordance with regulations prescribed by the Secretary, the deductions allowed in respect of such property under sections 2055 and 2056 (relating to charitable and marital deductions).

Amendments

• **1976, Tax Reform Act of 1976 (P.L. 94-455)**

P.L. 94-455, § 1906(b)(13)(A):

Amended 1954 Code by substituting "Secretary" for "Secretary or his delegate" each place it appeared. **Effective** 2-1-77.

ESTATE TAX—CREDITS AGAINST TAX

[Sec. 2014(d)]

(d) PROOF OF CREDIT.—The credit provided in this section shall be allowed only if the taxpayer establishes to the satisfaction of the Secretary—

(1) the amount of taxes actually paid to the foreign country,

(2) the amount and date of each payment thereof,

(3) the description and value of the property in respect of which such taxes are imposed, and

(4) all other information necessary for the verification and computation of the credit.

[Sec. 2014(e)]

(e) PERIOD OF LIMITATION.—The credit provided in this section shall be allowed only for such taxes as were actually paid and credit therefor claimed within 4 years after the filing of the return required by section 6018, except that—

(1) If a petition for redetermination of a deficiency has been filed with the Tax Court within the time prescribed in section 6213(a), then within such 4-year period or before the expiration of 60 days after the decision of the Tax Court becomes final.

(2) If, under section 6161, an extension of time has been granted for payment of the tax shown on the return, or of a deficiency, then within such 4-year period or before the date of the expiration of the period of the extension.

Refund based on such credit may (despite the provisions of sections 6511 and 6512) be made if claim therefor is filed within the period above provided. Any such refund shall be made without interest.

[Sec. 2014(f)]

(f) ADDITIONAL LIMITATION IN CASES INVOLVING A DEDUCTION UNDER SECTION 2053(d).—In any case where a deduction is allowed under section 2053(d) for an estate, succession, legacy, or inheritance tax imposed by and actually paid to any foreign country upon a transfer by the decedent for public, charitable, or religious uses described in section 2055, the property described in subparagraphs (A), (B), and (C) of paragraphs (1) and (2) of subsection (b) of this section shall not include any property in respect of which such deduction is allowed under section 2053(d).

Amendments

- 1959 (P.L. 86-175)

P.L. 86-175, § 2:

Amended 1954 Code Sec. 2014 by adding new subsection (f). **Effective** with respect to estates of decedents dying on or after 7-1-55.

[Sec. 2014(g)]

(g) POSSESSION OF UNITED STATES DEEMED A FOREIGN COUNTRY.—For purposes of the credits authorized by this section, each possession of the United States shall be deemed to be a foreign country.

Amendments

- 1959 (P.L. 86-175)

P.L. 86-175, § 2:

Amended 1954 Code Sec. 2014 by relettering subsection (f) as subsection (g). **Effective** with respect to the estates of decedents dying on or after 7-1-55.

- 1958, Technical Amendments Act of 1958 (P.L. 85-866)

P.L. 85-866, § 102(c), (d):

Added Code Sec. 2014(f). **Effective** for estates of decedents dying after 9-2-58.

[Sec. 2014(h)]

(h) SIMILAR CREDIT REQUIRED FOR CERTAIN ALIEN RESIDENTS.—Whenever the President finds that—

(1) a foreign country, in imposing estate, inheritance, legacy, or succession taxes, does not allow to citizens of the United States resident in such foreign country at the time of death a credit similar to the credit allowed under subsection (a),

(2) such foreign country, when requested by the United States to do so has not acted to provide such a similar credit in the case of citizens of the United States resident in such foreign country at the time of death, and

(3) it is in the public interest to allow the credit under subsection (a) in the case of citizens or subjects of such foreign country only if it allows such a similar credit in the case of citizens of the United States resident in such foreign country at the time of death,

the President shall proclaim that, in the case of citizens or subjects of such foreign country dying while the proclamation remains in effect, the credit under subsection (a) shall be allowed only if such foreign country allows such a similar credit in the case of citizens of the United States resident in such foreign country at the time of death.

Amendments

- 1966, Foreign Investors Tax Act of 1966 (P.L. 89-809)

P.L. 89-809, § 106(b)(3):

Added new Code Sec. 2014(h). **Effective** with respect to estates of decedents dying after 11-13-66.

[Sec. 2015]

SEC. 2015. CREDIT FOR DEATH TAXES ON REMAINDERS.

Where an election is made under section 6163(a) to postpone payment of the tax imposed by section 2001 or 2101, such part of any estate, inheritance, legacy, or succession taxes allowable as a credit under section 2014, as is attributable to a reversionary or remainder interest may be allowed as a credit against the tax attributable to such interest, subject to the limitations on the amount of the credit contained in such sections, if such part is paid, and credit therefor claimed, at any time before the expiration of the time for payment of the tax imposed by section 2001 or 2101 as postponed and extended under section 6163.

Amendments

- 2013, American Taxpayer Relief Act of 2012 (P.L. 112-240)

P.L. 112-240, § 101(a)(1) and (3), provides:

SEC. 101. PERMANENT EXTENSION AND MODIFICATION OF 2001 TAX RELIEF.

(a) PERMANENT EXTENSION.—

(1) IN GENERAL.—The Economic Growth and Tax Relief Reconciliation Act of 2001 is amended by striking title IX.

* * *

(3) EFFECTIVE DATE.—The amendments made by this subsection shall apply to taxable, plan, or limitation years beginning after December 31, 2012, and estates of decedents dying, gifts made, or generation skipping transfers after December 31, 2012.

- 2001, Economic Growth and Tax Relief Reconciliation Act of 2001 (P.L. 107-16)

P.L. 107-16, § 532(c)(4):

Amended Code Sec. 2015 by striking "2011 or" following "a credit under section". **Effective** for estates of decedents dying, and generation-skipping transfers, after 12-31-2004.

P.L. 107-16, § 901(a)-(b), as amended by P.L. 111-312, § 101(a)(1), provides [but see P.L. 112-240, § 101(a)(1) and (3), above]:

SEC. 901. SUNSET OF PROVISIONS OF ACT.

(a) IN GENERAL.—All provisions of, and amendments made by, this Act shall not apply—

(1) to taxable, plan, or limitation years beginning after December 31, 2012, or

ESTATE TAX—GROSS ESTATE

(2) in the case of title V, to estates of decedents dying, gifts made, or generation skipping transfers, after December 31, 2012.

(b) APPLICATION OF CERTAIN LAWS.—The Internal Revenue Code of 1986 and the Employee Retirement Income Security Act of 1974 shall be applied and administered to years, estates, gifts, and transfers described in subsection (a) as if the provisions and amendments described in subsection (a) had never been enacted.

• 1958, Technical Amendments Act of 1958 (P.L. 85-866)

P.L. 85-866, § 66(a):

Amended Code Sec. 2015 by substituting the phrase "the time for payment of the tax imposed by section 2001 or 2101 as postponed and extended under section 6163" in lieu of the phrase "60 days after the termination of the precedent interest or interests in the property". **Effective** in the case of any reversionary or remainder interest in property only if the precedent interest or interests in the property did not terminate before the beginning of the 60-day period which ends on 9-2-58.

[Sec. 2016]

SEC. 2016. RECOVERY OF TAXES CLAIMED AS CREDIT.

If any tax claimed as a credit under section 2014 is recovered from any foreign country, the executor, or any other person or persons recovering such amount, shall give notice of such recovery to the Secretary at such time and in such manner as may be required by regulations prescribed by him, and the Secretary shall (despite the provisions of section 6501) redetermine the amount of the tax under this chapter and the amount, if any, of the tax due on such redetermination, shall be paid by the executor or such person or persons, as the case may be, on notice and demand. No interest shall be assessed or collected on any amount of tax due on any redetermination by the Secretary resulting from a refund to the executor of tax claimed as a credit under section 2014, for any period before the receipt of such refund, except to the extent interest was paid by the foreign country on such refund.

Amendments

• 2013, American Taxpayer Relief Act of 2012 (P.L. 112-240)

P.L. 112-240, § 101(a)(1) and (3), provides:

SEC. 101. PERMANENT EXTENSION AND MODIFICATION OF 2001 TAX RELIEF.

(a) PERMANENT EXTENSION.—

(1) IN GENERAL.—The Economic Growth and Tax Relief Reconciliation Act of 2001 is amended by striking title IX.

* * *

(3) EFFECTIVE DATE.—The amendments made by this subsection shall apply to taxable, plan, or limitation years beginning after December 31, 2012, and estates of decedents dying, gifts made, or generation skipping transfers after December 31, 2012.

• 2002, Job Creation and Worker Assistance Act of 2002 (P.L. 107-147)

P.L. 107-147, § 411(h):

Amended Code Sec. 2016 by striking "any State, any possession of the United States, or the District of Columbia," following "any foreign country,". **Effective** as if included in the provision of P.L. 107-16 to which it relates [applicable to estates of decedents dying, and generation-skipping transfers, after 12-31-2004.—CCH].

• 2001, Economic Growth and Tax Relief Reconciliation Act of 2001 (P.L. 107-16)

P.L. 107-16, § 532(c)(4):

Amended Code Sec. 2016 by striking "2011 or" following "If any tax claimed as a credit under section". **Effective** for estates of decedents dying, and generation-skipping transfers, after 12-31-2004.

P.L. 107-16, § 901(a)-(b), as amended by P.L. 111-312, § 101(a)(1), provides [but see P.L. 112-240, § 101(a)(1) and (3), above]:

SEC. 901. SUNSET OF PROVISIONS OF ACT.

(a) IN GENERAL.—All provisions of, and amendments made by, this Act shall not apply—

(1) to taxable, plan, or limitation years beginning after December 31, 2012, or

(2) in the case of title V, to estates of decedents dying, gifts made, or generation skipping transfers, after December 31, 2012.

(b) APPLICATION OF CERTAIN LAWS.—The Internal Revenue Code of 1986 and the Employee Retirement Income Security Act of 1974 shall be applied and administered to years, estates, gifts, and transfers described in subsection (a) as if the provisions and amendments described in subsection (a) had never been enacted.

• 1976, Tax Reform Act of 1976 (P.L. 94-455)

P.L. 94-455, § 1902(a)(12)(C):

Deleted "Territory or" in Code Sec. 2016. **Effective** for gifts made after 12-31-76.

P.L. 94-455, § 1906(b)(13)(A):

Amended 1954 Code by substituting "Secretary" for "Secretary or his delegate" each place it appeared. **Effective** 2-1-77.

PART III—GROSS ESTATE

Sec. 2031.	Definition of gross estate.
Sec. 2032.	Alternate valuation.
Sec. 2032A.	Valuation of certain farm, etc., real property.
Sec. 2033.	Property in which the decedent had an interest.
Sec. 2034.	Dower or curtesy interests.
Sec. 2035.	Adjustments for certain gifts made within 3 years of decedent's death.
Sec. 2036.	Transfers with retained life estate.
Sec. 2037.	Transfers taking effect at death.
Sec. 2038.	Revocable transfers.
Sec. 2039.	Annuities.
Sec. 2040.	Joint interests.
Sec. 2041.	Powers of appointment.
Sec. 2042.	Proceeds of life insurance.
Sec. 2043.	Transfers for insufficient consideration.
Sec. 2044.	Certain property for which marital deduction was previously allowed.
Sec. 2045.	Prior interests.
Sec. 2046.	Disclaimers.

[Sec. 2031]

SEC. 2031. DEFINITION OF GROSS ESTATE.

[Sec. 2031(a)]

(a) GENERAL.—The value of the gross estate of the decedent shall be determined by including to the extent provided for in this part, the value at the time of his death of all property, real or personal, tangible or intangible, wherever situated.

Amendments

• 1962, Revenue Act of 1962 (P.L. 87-834)

P.L. 87-834, § 18(a)(1):

Amended Code Sec. 2031(a) by deleting ", except real property situated outside of the United States". **Effective**, generally, for estates of decedents dying after 10-16-62. For exceptions, see Act Sec. 18(b), below.

P.L. 87-834, § 18(b), provides:

(b) EFFECTIVE DATE.—

(1) Except as provided in paragraph (2), the amendments made by subsection (a) shall apply to the estates of decedents dying after the date of the enactment of this Act.

ESTATE TAX—GROSS ESTATE

(2) In the case of a decedent dying after the date of the enactment of this Act and before July 1, 1964, the value of real property situated outside of the United States shall not be included in the gross estate (as defined in section 2031(a)) of the decedent—

(A) under section 2033, 2034, 2035(a), 2036(a), 2037(a), or 2038(a) to the extent the real property, or the decedent's interest in it, was acquired by the decedent before February 1, 1962;

(B) under section 2040 to the extent such property or interest was acquired by the decedent before February 1, 1962, or was held by the decedent and the survivor in a joint tenancy or tenancy by the entirety before February 1, 1962; or

(C) under section 2041(a) to the extent that before February 1, 1962, such property or interest was subject to a general power of appointment (as defined in section 2041) possessed by the decedent.

In the case of real property, or an interest therein, situated outside of the United States (including a general power of appointment in respect of such property or interest, and including property held by the decedent and the survivor in a joint tenancy or tenancy by the entirety) which was acquired by the decedent after January 31, 1962, by gift within the meaning of section 2511, or from a prior decedent by devise or inheritance, or by reason of death, form of ownership, or other conditions (including the exercise or nonexercise of a power of appointment), for purposes of this paragraph such property or interest therein shall be deemed to have been acquired by the decedent before February 1, 1962, if before that date the donor or prior decedent had acquired the property or his interest therein or had possessed a power of appointment in respect of the property or interest.

[Sec. 2031(b)]

(b) VALUATION OF UNLISTED STOCK AND SECURITIES.—In the case of stock and securities of a corporation the value of which, by reason of their not being listed on an exchange and by reason of the absence of sales thereof, cannot be determined with reference to bid and asked prices or with reference to sales prices, the value thereof shall be determined by taking into consideration, in addition to all other factors, the value of stock or securities of corporations engaged in the same or a similar line of business which are listed on an exchange.

[Sec. 2031(c)]

(c) ESTATE TAX WITH RESPECT TO LAND SUBJECT TO A QUALIFIED CONSERVATION EASEMENT.—

(1) IN GENERAL.—If the executor makes the election described in paragraph (6), then, except as otherwise provided in this subsection, there shall be excluded from the gross estate the lesser of—

(A) the applicable percentage of the value of land subject to a qualified conservation easement, reduced by the amount of any deduction under section 2055(f) with respect to such land, or

(B) $500,000.

(2) APPLICABLE PERCENTAGE.—For purposes of paragraph (1), the term "applicable percentage" means 40 percent reduced (but not below zero) by 2 percentage points for each percentage point (or fraction thereof) by which the value of the qualified conservation easement is less than 30 percent of the value of the land (determined without regard to the value of such easement and reduced by the value of any retained development right (as defined in paragraph (5))). The values taken into account under the preceding sentence shall be such values as of the date of the contribution referred to in paragraph (8)(B).

(3) [Stricken.]

(4) TREATMENT OF CERTAIN INDEBTEDNESS.—

(A) IN GENERAL.—The exclusion provided in paragraph (1) shall not apply to the extent that the land is debt-financed property.

(B) DEFINITIONS.—For purposes of this paragraph—

(i) DEBT-FINANCED PROPERTY.—The term "debt-financed property" means any property with respect to which there is an acquisition indebtedness (as defined in clause (ii)) on the date of the decedent's death.

(ii) ACQUISITION INDEBTEDNESS.—The term "acquisition indebtedness" means, with respect to debt-financed property, the unpaid amount of—

(I) the indebtedness incurred by the donor in acquiring such property,

(II) the indebtedness incurred before the acquisition of such property if such indebtedness would not have been incurred but for such acquisition,

(III) the indebtedness incurred after the acquisition of such property if such indebtedness would not have been incurred but for such acquisition and the incurrence of such indebtedness was reasonably foreseeable at the time of such acquisition, and

(IV) the extension, renewal, or refinancing of an acquisition indebtedness.

(5) TREATMENT OF RETAINED DEVELOPMENT RIGHT.—

(A) IN GENERAL.—Paragraph (1) shall not apply to the value of any development right retained by the donor in the conveyance of a qualified conservation easement.

(B) TERMINATION OF RETAINED DEVELOPMENT RIGHT.—If every person in being who has an interest (whether or not in possession) in the land executes an agreement to extinguish permanently some or all of any development rights (as defined in subparagraph (D)) retained by the donor on or before the date for filing the return of the tax imposed by section 2001, then any tax imposed by section 2001 shall be reduced accordingly. Such agreement shall be filed with the return of the tax imposed by section 2001. The agreement shall be in such form as the Secretary shall prescribe.

(C) ADDITIONAL TAX.—Any failure to implement the agreement described in subparagraph (B) not later than the earlier of—

(i) the date which is 2 years after the date of the decedent's death, or

(ii) the date of the sale of such land subject to the qualified conservation easement,

shall result in the imposition of an additional tax in the amount of the tax which would have been due on the retained development rights subject to such agreement. Such additional tax shall be due and payable on the last day of the 6th month following such date.

(D) DEVELOPMENT RIGHT DEFINED.—For purposes of this paragraph, the term "development right" means any right to use the land subject to the qualified conservation easement in which such right is retained for any commercial purpose which is not subordinate to and directly supportive of the use of such land as a farm for farming purposes (within the meaning of section 2032A(e)(5)).

(6) ELECTION.—The election under this subsection shall be made on or before the due date (including extensions) for filing the return of tax imposed by section 2001 and shall be made on such return.

(7) CALCULATION OF ESTATE TAX DUE.—An executor making the election described in paragraph (6) shall, for purposes of calculating the amount of tax imposed by section 2001, include the value of any development right (as defined in paragraph (5)) retained by the donor in the conveyance of such qualified conservation easement. The computation of tax on any retained development right prescribed in this paragraph shall be done in such manner and on such forms as the Secretary shall prescribe.

(8) DEFINITIONS.—For purposes of this subsection—

(A) LAND SUBJECT TO A QUALIFIED CONSERVATION EASEMENT.—The term "land subject to a qualified conservation easement" means land—

(i) which is located in the United States or any possession of the United States,

(ii) which was owned by the decedent or a member of the decedent's family at all times during the 3-year period ending on the date of the decedent's death, and

(iii) with respect to which a qualified conservation easement has been made by an individual described in subparagraph (C), as of the date of the election described in paragraph (6).

(B) QUALIFIED CONSERVATION EASEMENT.—The term "qualified conservation easement" means a qualified conservation contribution (as defined in section 170(h)(1)) of a qualified real property interest (as defined in section 170(h)(2)(C)), except that clause (iv) of section 170(h)(4)(A) shall not apply, and the restriction on the use of such interest described in section 170(h)(2)(C) shall include a prohibition on more than a de minimis use for a commercial recreational activity.

(C) INDIVIDUAL DESCRIBED.—An individual is described in this subparagraph if such individual is—

(i) the decedent,

(ii) a member of the decedent's family,

(iii) the executor of the decedent's estate, or

(iv) the trustee of a trust the corpus of which includes the land to be subject to the qualified conservation easement.

(D) MEMBER OF FAMILY.—The term "member of the decedent's family" means any member of the family (as defined in section 2032A(e)(2)) of the decedent.

(9) TREATMENT OF EASEMENTS GRANTED AFTER DEATH.—In any case in which the qualified conservation easement is granted after the date of the decedent's death and on or before the due date (including extensions) for filing the return of tax imposed by section 2001, the deduction under section 2055(f) with respect to such easement shall be allowed to the estate but only if no charitable deduction is allowed under chapter 1 to any person with respect to the grant of such easement.

(10) APPLICATION OF THIS SECTION TO INTERESTS IN PARTNERSHIPS, CORPORATIONS, AND TRUSTS.—This section shall apply to an interest in a partnership, corporation, or trust if at least 30 percent of the entity is owned (directly or indirectly) by the decedent, as determined under the rules described in section 2057(e)(3) (as in effect before its repeal).

Amendments

• **2018, Tax Technical Corrections Act of 2018 (P.L. 115-141)**

P.L. 115-141, §401(a)(200), Div. U:

Amended Code Sec. 2031(c)(1) by striking all that follows subparagraph (A) and inserting

"(B) $500,000.".

Effective 3-23-2018. Prior to be stricken, all that follows subparagraph (A) read as follows:

(II) [(B)] $500,000.

P.L. 115-141, §401(a)(201), Div. U:

Amended Code Sec. 2031(c)(2) by striking "paragraph (5))." and inserting "paragraph (5))).". **Effective** 3-23-2018.

• **2014, Tax Technical Corrections Act of 2014 (P.L. 113-295)**

P.L. 113-295, §221(a)(96), Division A:

Amended Code Sec. 2031(c) by striking paragraph (3) and by amending paragraph (1)(B). **Effective** generally 12-19-2014. For a special rule, see Act Sec. 221(b)(2), Division A, below. Prior to being amended and stricken, respectively, Code Sec. 2031(c)(1)(B) and (3) read as follows:

(B) the exclusion limitation.

* * *

(3) EXCLUSION LIMITATION.—For purposes of paragraph (1), the exclusion limitation is the limitation determined in accordance with the following table:

In the case of estates of decedents dying during:	The exclusion limitation is:
1998	$100,000
1999	$200,000
2000	$300,000
2001	$400,000
2002 or thereafter	$500,000

P.L. 113-295, §221(a)(97)(B), Division A:

Amended Code Sec. 2031(c)(10) by inserting "(as in effect before its repeal)" immediately before the period at the end thereof. **Effective** generally 12-19-2014. For a special rule, see Act Sec. 221(b)(2), Division A, below.

P.L. 113-295, §221(b)(2), Division A, provides:

(2) SAVINGS PROVISION.—If—

(A) any provision amended or repealed by the amendments made by this section applied to—

(i) any transaction occurring before the date of the enactment of this Act,

(ii) any property acquired before such date of enactment, or

(iii) any item of income, loss, deduction, or credit taken into account before such date of enactment, and

(B) the treatment of such transaction, property, or item under such provision would (without regard to the amendments or repeals made by this section) affect the liability for tax for periods ending after date of enactment, nothing in the amendments or repeals made by this section shall be construed to affect the treatment of such transaction, property, or item for purposes of determining liability for tax for periods ending after such date of enactment.

• **2013, American Taxpayer Relief Act of 2012 (P.L. 112-240)**

P.L. 112-240, §101(a)(1) and (3), provides:

SEC. 101. PERMANENT EXTENSION AND MODIFICATION OF 2001 TAX RELIEF.

(a) PERMANENT EXTENSION.—

(1) IN GENERAL.—The Economic Growth and Tax Relief Reconciliation Act of 2001 is amended by striking title IX.

* * *

(3) EFFECTIVE DATE.—The amendments made by this subsection shall apply to taxable, plan, or limitation years beginning after December 31, 2012, and estates of decedents dying, gifts made, or generation skipping transfers after December 31, 2012.

• **2001, Economic Growth and Tax Relief Reconciliation Act of 2001 (P.L. 107-16)**

P.L. 107-16, §551(a):

Amended Code Sec. 2031(c)(8)(A)(i). **Effective** for estates of decedents dying after 12-31-2000. Prior to amendment, Code Sec. 2031(c)(8)(A)(i) read as follows:

(i) which is located—

(I) in or within 25 miles of an area which, on the date of the decedent's death, is a metropolitan area (as defined by the Office of Management and Budget),

(II) in or within 25 miles of an area which, on the date of the decedent's death, is a national park or wilderness area designated as part of the National Wilderness Preservation System (unless it is determined by the Secretary that land in or within 25 miles of such a park or wilderness area is not under significant development pressure), or

(III) in or within 10 miles of an area which, on the date of the decedent's death, is an Urban National Forest (as designated by the Forest Service),

P.L. 107-16, §551(b):

Amended Code Sec. 2031(c)(2) by adding at the end a new sentence. **Effective** for estates of decedents dying after 12-31-2000.

P.L. 107-16, §901(a)-(b), as amended by P.L. 111-312, §101(a)(1), provides [but see P.L. 112-240, §101(a)(1) and (3), above]:

SEC. 901. SUNSET OF PROVISIONS OF ACT.

(a) IN GENERAL.—All provisions of, and amendments made by, this Act shall not apply—

(1) to taxable, plan, or limitation years beginning after December 31, 2012, or

(2) in the case of title V, to estates of decedents dying, gifts made, or generation skipping transfers, after December 31, 2012.

(b) APPLICATION OF CERTAIN LAWS.—The Internal Revenue Code of 1986 and the Employee Retirement Income Security Act of 1974 shall be applied and administered to years, estates, gifts, and transfers described in subsection (a) as if the provisions and amendments described in subsection (a) had never been enacted.

• **1998, Tax and Trade Relief Extension Act of 1998 (P.L. 105-277)**

P.L. 105-277, §4006(c)(3):

Amended Code Sec. 2031(c)(10) by striking "section 2033A(e)(3)" and inserting "section 2057(e)(3)". **Effective** 10-21-98.

• **1998, IRS Restructuring and Reform Act of 1998 (P.L. 105-206)**

P.L. 105-206, §6007(g)(1):

Amended Code Sec. 2031(c) by redesignating paragraph (9) as paragraph (10) and by inserting after paragraph (8) a new paragraph (9). **Effective** as if included in the provision of P.L. 105-34 to which it relates [**effective** for estates of decedents dying after 12-31-97.—CCH].

P.L. 105-206, §6007(g)(2):

Amended the first sentence of Code Sec. 2031(c)(6) by striking all that follows "shall be made" and inserting "on or before the due date (including extensions) for filing the return of tax imposed by section 2001 and shall be made on such return." **Effective** as if included in the provision of P.L. 105-34 to which it relates [**effective** for estates of decedents dying after 12-31-97.—CCH]. Prior to amendment, the first sentence of Code Sec. 2031(c)(6) read as follows:

(6) ELECTION.—The election under this subsection shall be made on the return of the tax imposed by section 2001.

• **1997, Taxpayer Relief Act of 1997 (P.L. 105-34)**

P.L. 105-34, §508(a):

Amended Code Sec. 2031 by redesignating subsection (c) as subsection (d) and by inserting after subsection (b) a new subsection (c). **Effective** for estates of decedents dying after 12-31-97.

ESTATE TAX—GROSS ESTATE

[Sec. 2031(d)]

(d) Cross Reference.—

For executor's right to be furnished on request a statement regarding any valuation made by the Secretary within the gross estate, see section 7517.

Amendments

• **1997, Taxpayer Relief Act of 1997 (P.L. 105-34)**

P.L. 105-34, § 508(a):

Amended Code Sec. 2031 by redesignating subsection (c) as subsection (d). **Effective** for estates of decedents dying after 12-31-97.

• **1976, Tax Reform Act of 1976 (P.L. 94-455)**

P.L. 94-455, § 2008(a)(2):

Added Code Sec. 2031(c). For the **effective** date, see Act Sec. 2008(d)(1), below.

P.L. 94-455, § 2008(d)(1), provides:

(d) Effective Dates.—

(1) The amendments made by subsection (a)—

(A) insofar as they relate to the tax imposed under chapter 11 of the Internal Revenue Code of 1954, shall apply to the estates of decedents dying after December 31, 1976, and

(B) insofar as they relate to the tax imposed under chapter 12 of such Code, shall apply to gifts made after December 31, 1976.

[Sec. 2032]

SEC. 2032. ALTERNATE VALUATION.

[Sec. 2032(a)]

(a) General.—The value of the gross estate may be determined, if the executor so elects, by valuing all the property included in the gross estate as follows:

(1) In the case of property distributed, sold, exchanged, or otherwise disposed of, within 6 months after the decedent's death such property shall be valued as of the date of distribution, sale, exchange, or other disposition.

(2) In the case of property not distributed, sold, exchanged, or otherwise disposed of, within 6 months after the decedent's death such property shall be valued as of the date 6 months after the decedent's death.

(3) Any interest or estate which is affected by mere lapse of time shall be included at its value as of the time of death (instead of the later date) with adjustment for any difference in its value as of the later date not due to mere lapse of time.

Amendments

• **1970, Excise, Estate, and Gift Tax Adjustment Act of 1970 (P.L. 91-614)**

P.L. 91-614, § 101(a):

Amended paragraphs (1) and (2) of Code Sec. 2032(a) by substituting "6 months" for "1 year" each place it appeared. **Effective** with respect to decedents dying after 12-31-70.

[Sec. 2032(b)]

(b) Special Rules.—No deduction under this chapter of any item shall be allowed if allowance for such item is in effect given by the alternate valuation provided by this section. Wherever in any other subsection or section of this chapter reference is made to the value of property at the time of the decedent's death, such reference shall be deemed to refer to the value of such property used in determining the value of the gross estate. In case of an election made by the executor under this section, then—

(1) for purposes of the charitable deduction under section 2055 or 2106(a)(2), any bequest, legacy, devise, or transfer enumerated therein, and

(2) for the purpose of the marital deduction under section 2056, any interest in property passing to the surviving spouse,

shall be valued as of the date of the decedent's death with adjustment for any difference in value (not due to mere lapse of time or the occurrence or nonoccurrence of a contingency) of the property as of the date 6 months after the decedent's death (substituting, in the case of property distributed by the executor or trustee, or sold, exchanged, or otherwise disposed of, during such 6-month period, the date thereof).

Amendments

• **1970, Excise, Estate, and Gift Tax Adjustment Act of 1970 (P.L. 91-614)**

P.L. 91-614, § 101(a):

Amended Code Sec. 2032(b) by substituting "6 months" for "1 year" and "6-month period" for "1-year period" in the last sentence thereof. **Effective** with respect to decedents dying after 12-31-70.

[Sec. 2032(c)]

(c) Election Must Decrease Gross Estate and Estate Tax.—No election may be made under this section with respect to an estate unless such election will decrease—

(1) the value of the gross estate, and

(2) the sum of the tax imposed by this chapter and the tax imposed by chapter 13 with respect to property includible in the decedent's gross estate (reduced by credits allowable against such taxes).

Amendments

• **1986, Tax Reform Act of 1986 (P.L. 99-514)**

P.L. 99-514, § 1432(c)(1):

Amended Code Sec. 2032(c)(2). **Effective**, generally, for any generation-skipping transfer (within the meaning of Code Sec. 2611) made after 10-22-86. However, for special rules see Act Sec. 1433(b)-(d) in the amendment notes following Code Sec. 2601. Prior to amendment, Code Sec. 2032(c)(2) read as follows:

(2) the amount of the tax imposed by this chapter (reduced by credits allowable against such tax).

• **1984, Deficit Reduction Act of 1984 (P.L. 98-369)**

P.L. 98-369, § 1023(a):

Amended Code Sec. 2032 by redesignating subsection (c) as subsection (d) and by inserting after subsection (b) a new subsection (c). **Effective** with respect to the estates of decedents dying after 7-18-84. For a transitional rule, see Act Sec. 1024(b)(2) in the amendment notes following Code Sec. 2032(d).

[Sec. 2032(d)]

(d) Election.—

(1) In General.—The election provided for in this section shall be made by the executor on the return of the tax imposed by this chapter. Such election, once made, shall be irrevocable.

(2) Exception.—No election may be made under this section if such return is filed more than 1 year after the time prescribed by law (including extensions) for filing such return.

Amendments

• **1984, Deficit Reduction Act of 1984 (P.L. 98-369)**

P.L. 98-369, § 1023(a):

Amended Code Sec. 2032 by redesignating subsection (c) as subsection (d). **Effective** with respect to the estates of decedents dying after 7-18-84. For a transitional rule, see Act Sec. 1024(b)(2), below.

P.L. 98-369, § 1024(a):

Amended Code Sec. 2032(d), as redesignated by Act Sec. 1023. **Effective** with respect to the estates of decedents dying after 7-18-84. For a transitional rule, see Act Sec. 1024(b)(2), below. Prior to amendment, it read as follows:

(c) TIME OF ELECTION.—The election provided for in this section shall be exercised by the executor on his return if filed within the time prescribed by law or before the expiration of any extension of time granted pursuant to law for the filing of the return.

P.L. 98-369, § 1024(b)(2), provides:

(2) Transitional Rule.—In the case of an estate of a decedent dying before the date of the enactment of this Act if—

(A) a credit or refund of the tax imposed by chapter 11 of the Internal Revenue Code of 1954 is not prevented on the date of the enactment of this Act by the operation of any law or rule of law,

(B) the election under section 2032 of the Internal Revenue Code of 1954 would have met the requirements of such section (as amended by this section and section 1023) had the decedent died after the date of enactment of this Act, and

(C) a claim for credit or refund of such tax with respect to such estate is filed not later than the 90th day after the date of the enactment of this Act,

then such election shall be treated as a valid election under such section 2032. The statutory period for the assessment of any deficiency which is attributable to an election under this paragraph shall not expire before the close of the 2-year period beginning on the date of the enactment of this Act.

[Sec. 2032A]

SEC. 2032A. VALUATION OF CERTAIN FARM, ETC., REAL PROPERTY.

[Sec. 2032A(a)]

(a) VALUE BASED ON USE UNDER WHICH PROPERTY QUALIFIES.—

(1) GENERAL RULE.—If—

(A) the decedent was (at the time of his death) a citizen or resident of the United States, and

(B) the executor elects the application of this section and files the agreement referred to in subsection (d)(2),

then, for purposes of this chapter, the value of qualified real property shall be its value for the use under which it qualifies, under subsection (b), as qualified real property.

(2) LIMITATION ON AGGREGATE REDUCTION IN FAIR MARKET VALUE.—The aggregate decrease in the value of qualified real property taken into account for purposes of this chapter which results from the application of paragraph (1) with respect to any decedent shall not exceed $750,000.

(3) INFLATION ADJUSTMENT.—In the case of estates of decedents dying in a calendar year after 1998, the $750,000 amount contained in paragraph (2) shall be increased by an amount equal to—

(A) $750,000, multiplied by

(B) the cost-of-living adjustment determined under section 1(f)(3) for such calendar year by substituting "calendar year 1997" for "calendar year 2016" in subparagraph (A)(ii) thereof.

If any amount as adjusted under the preceding sentence is not a multiple of $10,000, such amount shall be rounded to the next lowest multiple of $10,000.

Amendments

• **2017, Tax Cuts and Jobs Act (P.L. 115-97)**

P.L. 115-97, § 11002(d)(1)(DD):

Amended Code Sec. 2032A(a)(3)(B) by striking "for 'calendar year 1992' in subparagraph (B)" and inserting "for 'calendar year 2016' in subparagraph (A)(ii)". **Effective** for tax years beginning after 12-31-2017.

• **1997, Taxpayer Relief Act of 1997 (P.L. 105-34)**

P.L. 105-34, § 501(b):

Amended Code Sec. 2032A(a) by adding a new paragraph (3). **Effective** for the estates of decedents dying, and gifts made, after 12-31-97.

• **1990, Omnibus Budget Reconciliation Act of 1990 (P.L. 101-508)**

P.L. 101-508, § 11802(f)(5):

Amended Code Sec. 2032A(a)(2). **Effective** 11-5-90. Prior to amendment, Code Sec. 2032A(a)(2) read as follows:

(2) LIMIT ON AGGREGATE REDUCTION IN FAIR MARKET VALUE.—The aggregate decrease in the value of qualified real property taken into account for purposes of this chapter which results from the application of paragraph (1) with respect to any decedent shall not exceed the applicable limit set forth in the following table:

In the case of decedents dying in:	The applicable limit is:
1981	$600,000
1982	700,000
1983	750,000

P.L. 101-508, § 11821(b), provides:

(b) SAVINGS PROVISION.—If—

(1) any provision amended or repealed by this part applied to—

(A) any transaction occurring before the date of the enactment of this Act,

(B) any property acquired before such date of enactment, or

(C) any item of income, loss, deduction, or credit taken into account before such date of enactment, and

(2) the treatment of such transaction, property, or item under such provision would (without regard to the amendments made by this part) affect liability for tax for periods ending after such date of enactment,

nothing in the amendments made by this part shall be construed to affect the treatment of such transaction, property, or item for purposes of determining liability for tax for periods ending after such date of enactment.

• **1981, Economic Recovery Tax Act of 1981 (P.L. 97-34)**

P.L. 97-34, § 421(a):

Amended Code Sec. 2032A(a)(2). **Effective** with respect to the estates of decedents dying after 12-31-80. Prior to amendment, Code Sec. 2032A(a)(2) read as follows:

(2) LIMITATION.—The aggregate decrease in the value of qualified real property taken into account for purposes of this chapter which results from the application of paragraph (1) with respect to any decedent shall not exceed $500,000.

[Sec. 2032A(b)]

(b) QUALIFIED REAL PROPERTY.—

(1) IN GENERAL.—For purposes of this section, the term "qualified real property" means real property located in the United States which was acquired from or passed from the decedent to a qualified heir of the decedent and which, on the date of the decedent's death, was being used for a qualified use by the decedent or a member of the decedent's family, but only if—

(A) 50 percent or more of the adjusted value of the gross estate consists of the adjusted value of real or personal property which—

(i) on the date of the decedent's death, was being used for a qualified use by the decedent or a member of the decedent's family, and

(ii) was acquired from or passed from the decedent to a qualified heir of the decedent.

(B) 25 percent or more of the adjusted value of the gross estate consists of the adjusted value of real property which meets the requirements of subparagraphs (A)(ii) and (C),

(C) during the 8-year period ending on the date of the decedent's death there have been periods aggregating 5 years or more during which—

(i) such real property was owned by the decedent or a member of the decedent's family and used for a qualified use by the decedent or a member of the decedent's family, and

(ii) there was material participation by the decedent or a member of the decedent's family in the operation of the farm or other business, and

(D) such real property is designated in the agreement referred to in subsection (d)(2).

ESTATE TAX—GROSS ESTATE

(2) QUALIFIED USE.—For purposes of this section, the term "qualified use" means the devotion of the property to any of the following:

(A) use as a farm for farming purposes, or

(B) use in a trade or business other than the trade or business of farming.

(3) ADJUSTED VALUE.—For purposes of paragraph (1), the term "adjusted value" means—

(A) in the case of the gross estate, the value of the gross estate for purposes of this chapter (determined without regard to this section), reduced by any amounts allowable as a deduction under paragraph (4) of section 2053(a), or

(B) in the case of any real or personal property, the value of such property for purposes of this chapter (determined without regard to this section), reduced by any amounts allowable as a deduction in respect to such property under paragraph (4) of section 2053(a).

(4) DECEDENTS WHO ARE RETIRED OR DISABLED.—

(A) IN GENERAL.—If, on the date of the decedent's death the requirements of paragraph (1)(C)(ii) with respect to the decedent for any property are not met, and the decedent—

(i) was receiving old-age benefits under title II of the Social Security Act for a continuous period ending on such date, or

(ii) was disabled for a continuous period ending on such date,

then paragraph (1)(C)(ii) shall be applied with respect to such property by substituting "the date on which the longer of such continuous periods began" for "the date of the decedent's death" in paragraph (1)(C).

(B) DISABLED DEFINED.—For purposes of subparagraph (A), an individual shall be disabled if such individual has a mental or physical impairment which renders him unable to materially participate in the operation of the farm or other business.

(C) COORDINATION WITH RECAPTURE.—For purposes of subsection (c)(6)(B)(i), if the requirements of paragraph (1)(C)(ii) are met with respect to any decedent by reason of subparagraph (A), the period ending on the date on which the continuous period taken into account under subparagraph (A) began shall be treated as the period immediately before the decedent's death.

(5) SPECIAL RULES FOR SURVIVING SPOUSES.—

(A) IN GENERAL.—If property is qualified real property with respect to a decedent (hereinafter in this paragraph referred to as the "first decedent") and such property was acquired from or passed from the first decedent to the surviving spouse of the first decedent, for purposes of applying this subsection and subsection (c) in the case of the estate of such surviving spouse, active management of the farm or other business by the surviving spouse shall be treated as material participation by such surviving spouse in the operation of such farm or business.

(B) SPECIAL RULE.—For the purposes of subparagraph (A), the determination of whether property is qualified real property with respect to the first decedent shall be made without regard to subparagraph (D) of paragraph (1) and without regard to whether an election under this section was made.

(C) COORDINATION WITH PARAGRAPH (4).—In any case in which to do so will enable the requirements of paragraph (1)(C)(ii) to be met with respect to the surviving spouse, this subsection and subsection (c) shall be applied by taking into account any application of paragraph (4).

Amendments

- **1997, Taxpayer Relief Act of 1997 (P.L. 105-34)**

P.L. 105-34, § 504(b):

Amended Code Sec. 2032A(b)(5)(A) is amended by striking the last sentence. **Effective** with respect to leases entered into after 12-31-76. Prior to being stricken, the last sentence of Code Sec. 2032A(b)(5)(A) read as follows:

For purposes of subsection (c), such surviving spouse shall not be treated as failing to use such property in a qualified use solely because such spouse rents such property to a member of such spouse's family on a net cash basis.

- **1988, Technical and Miscellaneous Revenue Act of 1988 (P.L. 100-647)**

P.L. 100-647, § 6151(a):

Amended Code Sec. 2032A(b)(5)(A) by adding at the end thereof a new sentence. **Effective**, generally, with respect to rentals occurring after 12-31-76. See, also, Act Sec. 6151(b)(2), below.

P.L. 100-647, § 6151(b)(2), provides:

(2) WAIVER OF STATUTE OF LIMITATIONS.—If on the date of the enactment of this Act (or at any time within 1 year after such date of enactment) refund or credit of any overpayment of tax resulting from the application of the amendment made by subsection (a) is barred by any law or rule of law, refund or credit of such overpayment shall, nevertheless, be made or allowed if claim therefore is filed before the date 1 year after the date of the enactment of this Act.

- **1983, Technical Corrections Act of 1982 (P.L. 97-448)**

P.L. 97-448, § 104(b)(1):

Amended Code Sec. 2032A(b)(5) by adding at the end thereof new subparagraph (C). **Effective** as if included in the provision of P.L. 97-34 to which it relates.

- **1981, Economic Recovery Tax Act of 1981 (P.L. 97-34)**

P.L. 97-34, § 421(b)(1):

Amended Code Sec. 2032A(b)(1) by inserting "by the decedent or a member of the decedent's family" after "qualified use" each place it appears. **Effective** with respect to estates of decedents dying after 12-31-76. For special rules, see P.L. 97-34, § 421(k)(5), below.

P.L. 97-34, § 421(b)(2):

Added Code Sec. 2032A(b)(4) and (5). **Effective** with respect to decedents dying after 12-31-81.

P.L. 97-34, § 421(k)(5), as amended by P.L. 97-448, § 104(b)(4), provides:

(5) CERTAIN AMENDMENTS MADE RETROACTIVE TO 1976.—

(A) IN GENERAL.—The amendments made by subsections (b)(1), (j)(1), and (j)(2) and the provisions of subparagraph (A) of section 2032A(c)(7) of the Internal Revenue Code of 1954 (as added by subsection (c)(2)) shall apply with respect to the estates of decedents dying after December 31, 1976.

(B) TIMELY ELECTION REQUIRED.—Subparagraph (A) shall only apply in the case of an estate if a timely election under section 2032A was made with respect to such estate. If the estate of any decedent would not qualify under section 2032A of the Internal Revenue Code of 1954 but for the amendments described in subparagraph (A) and the time for making an election under section 2032A with respect to such estate would (but for this sentence) expire after July 28, 1980, the time for making such election shall not expire before the close of February 16, 1982.

(C) REINSTATEMENT OF ELECTIONS.—If any election under section 2032A was revoked before the date of the enactment of this Act, such election may be reinstated at any time before February 17, 1982.

(D) STATUTE OF LIMITATIONS.—If on the date of the enactment of this Act (or at any time before February 17, 1982) the making of a credit or refund of any overpayment of tax resulting from the amendments described in subparagraph (A) is barred by any law or rule of law, such credit or refund shall nevertheless be made if claim therefor is made before February 17, 1982.

- **1978, Revenue Act of 1978 (P.L. 95-600)**

P.L. 95-600, § 702(d)(1):

Amended Code Sec. 2032A(b)(1) by adding the phrase "which was acquired from or passed to a qualified heir of the decedent and", after "real property located in the United States". **Effective** for estates of decedents dying after 12-31-76.

[Sec. 2032A(c)]

(c) TAX TREATMENT OF DISPOSITIONS AND FAILURES TO USE FOR QUALIFIED USE.—

(1) IMPOSITION OF ADDITIONAL ESTATE TAX.—If, within 10 years after the decedent's death and before the death of the qualified heir—

(A) the qualified heir disposes of any interest in qualified real property (other than by a disposition to a member of his family), or

(B) the qualified heir ceases to use for the qualified use the qualified real property which was acquired (or passed) from the decedent,

then there is hereby imposed an additional estate tax.

(2) AMOUNT OF ADDITIONAL TAX.—

(A) IN GENERAL.—The amount of the additional tax imposed by paragraph (1) with respect to any interest shall be the amount equal to the lesser of—

(i) the adjusted tax difference attributable to such interest, or

(ii) the excess of the amount realized with respect to the interest (or, in any case other than a sale or exchange at arm's length, the fair market value of the interest) over the value of the interest determined under subsection (a).

ESTATE TAX—GROSS ESTATE

(B) ADJUSTED TAX DIFFERENCE ATTRIBUTABLE TO INTEREST.—For purposes of subparagraph (A), the adjusted tax difference attributable to an interest is the amount which bears the same ratio to the adjusted tax difference with respect to the estate (determined under subparagraph (C)) as—

(i) the excess of the value of such interest for purposes of this chapter (determined without regard to subsection (a)) over the value of such interest determined under subsection (a), bears to

(ii) a similar excess determined for all qualified real property.

(C) ADJUSTED TAX DIFFERENCE WITH RESPECT TO THE ESTATE.—For purposes of subparagraph (B), the term "adjusted tax difference with respect to the estate" means the excess of what would have been the estate tax liability but for subsection (a) over the estate tax liability. For purposes of this subparagraph, the term "estate tax liability" means the tax imposed by section 2001 reduced by the credits allowable against such tax.

(D) PARTIAL DISPOSITIONS.—For purposes of this paragraph, where the qualified heir disposes of a portion of the interest acquired by (or passing to) such heir (or a predecessor qualified heir) or there is a cessation of use of such a portion—

(i) the value determined under subsection (a) taken into account under subparagraph (A)(ii) with respect to such portion shall be its pro rata share of such value of such interest, and

(ii) the adjusted tax difference attributable to the interest taken into account with respect to the transaction involving the second or any succeeding portion shall be reduced by the amount of the tax imposed by this subsection with respect to all prior transactions involving portions of such interest.

(E) SPECIAL RULE FOR DISPOSITION OF TIMBER.—In the case of qualified woodland to which an election under subsection (e)(13)(A) applies, if the qualified heir disposes of (or severs) any standing timber on such qualified woodland—

(i) such disposition (or severance) shall be treated as a disposition of a portion of the interest of the qualified heir in such property, and

(ii) the amount of the additional tax imposed by paragraph (1) with respect to such disposition shall be an amount equal to the lesser of—

(I) the amount realized on such disposition (or, in any case other than a sale or exchange at arm's length, the fair market value of the portion of the interest disposed or severed), or

(II) the amount of additional tax determined under this paragraph (without regard to this subparagraph) if the entire interest of the qualified heir in the qualified woodland had been disposed of, less the sum of the amount of the additional tax imposed with respect to all prior transactions involving such woodland to which this subparagraph applied.

For purposes of the preceding sentence, the disposition of a right to sever shall be treated as the disposition of the standing timber. The amount of additional tax imposed under paragraph (1) in any case in which a qualified heir disposes of his entire interest in the qualified woodland shall be reduced by any amount determined under this subparagraph with respect to such woodland.

(3) ONLY 1 ADDITIONAL TAX IMPOSED WITH RESPECT TO ANY 1 PORTION.—In the case of an interest acquired from (or passing from) any decedent, if subparagraph (A) or (B) of paragraph (1) applies to any portion of an interest, subparagraph (B) or (A), as the case may be, of paragraph (1) shall not apply with respect to the same portion of such interest.

(4) DUE DATE.—The additional tax imposed by this subsection shall become due and payable on the day which is 6 months after the date of the disposition or cessation referred to in paragraph (1).

(5) LIABILITY FOR TAX; FURNISHING OF BOND.—The qualified heir shall be personally liable for the additional tax imposed by this subsection with respect to his interest unless the heir has furnished bond which meets the requirements of subsection (e)(11).

(6) CESSATION OF QUALIFIED USE.—For purposes of paragraph (1)(B), real property shall cease to be used for the qualified use if—

(A) such property ceases to be used for the qualified use set forth in subparagraph (A) or (B) of subsection (b)(2) under which the property qualified under subsection (b), or

(B) during any period of 8 years ending after the date of the decedent's death and before the date of the death of the qualified heir, there had been periods aggregating more than 3 years during which—

(i) in the case of periods during which the property was held by the decedent, there was no material participation by the decedent or any member of his family in the operation of the farm or other business, and

(ii) in the case of periods during which the property was held by any qualified heir, there was no material participation by such qualified heir or any member of his family in the operation of the farm or other business.

(7) SPECIAL RULES.—

(A) NO TAX IF USE BEGINS WITHIN 2 YEARS.—If the date on which the qualified heir begins to use the qualified real property (hereinafter in this subparagraph referred to as the commencement date) is before the date 2 years after the decedent's death—

(i) no tax shall be imposed under paragraph (1) by reason of the failure by the qualified heir to so use such property before the commencement date, and

(ii) the 10-year period under paragraph (1) shall be extended by the period after the decedent's death and before the commencement date.

(B) ACTIVE MANAGEMENT BY ELIGIBLE QUALIFIED HEIR TREATMENT AS MATERIAL PARTICIPATION.—For purposes of paragraph (6)(B)(ii), the active management of a farm or other business by—

(i) an eligible qualified heir, or

(ii) a fiduciary of an eligible qualified heir described in clause (ii) or (iii) of subparagraph (C),

shall be treated as material participation by such eligible qualified heir in the operation of such farm or business. In the case of an eligible qualified heir described in clause (ii), (iii), or (iv) of subparagraph (C), the preceding sentence shall apply only during periods during which such heir meets the requirements of such clause.

(C) ELIGIBLE QUALIFIED HEIR.—For purposes of this paragraph, the term "eligible qualified heir" means a qualified heir who—

(i) is the surviving spouse of the decedent,

(ii) has not attained the age of 21,

(iii) is disabled (within the meaning of subsection (b)(4)(B)), or

(iv) is a student.

(D) STUDENT.—For purposes of subparagraph (C), an individual shall be treated as a student with respect to periods during any calendar year if (and only if) such individual is a student (within the meaning of section 152(f)(2)) for such calendar year.

(E) CERTAIN RENTS TREATED AS QUALIFIED USE.—For purposes of this subsection, a surviving spouse or lineal descendant of the decedent shall not be treated as failing to use qualified real property in a qualified use solely because such spouse or descendant rents such property to a member of the family of such spouse or descendant on a net cash basis. For purposes of the preceding sentence, a legally adopted child of an individual shall be treated as the child of such individual by blood.

ESTATE TAX—GROSS ESTATE

(8) QUALIFIED CONSERVATION CONTRIBUTION IS NOT A DISPOSITION.—A qualified conservation contribution (as defined in section 170(h)) by gift or otherwise shall not be deemed a disposition under subsection (c)(1)(A).

Amendments

• **2004, Working Families Tax Relief Act of 2004 (P.L. 108-311)**

P.L. 108-311, § 207(22):

Amended Code Sec. 2032A(c)(7)(D) by striking "section 151(c)(4)" and inserting "section 152(f)(2)". **Effective** for tax years beginning after 12-31-2004.

• **2001, Economic Growth and Tax Relief Reconciliation Act of 2001 (P.L. 107-16)**

P.L. 107-16, § 581, provides:

SEC. 581. WAIVER OF STATUTE OF LIMITATION FOR TAXES ON CERTAIN FARM VALUATIONS.

If on the date of the enactment of this Act (or at any time within 1 year after the date of the enactment) a refund or credit of any overpayment of tax resulting from the application of section 2032A(c)(7)(E) of the Internal Revenue Code of 1986 is barred by any law or rule of law, the refund or credit of such overpayment shall, nevertheless, be made or allowed if claim therefor is filed before the date 1 year after the date of the enactment of this Act.

• **1997, Taxpayer Relief Act of 1997 (P.L. 105-34)**

P.L. 105-34, § 504(a):

Amended Code Sec. 2032A(c)(7) by adding a new subparagraph (E). **Effective** with respect to leases entered into after 12-31-76.

P.L. 105-34, § 508(c):

Amended Code Sec. 2032A(c) by adding a new paragraph (8). **Effective** for easements granted after 12-31-97.

• **1986, Tax Reform Act of 1986 (P.L. 99-514)**

P.L. 99-514, § 104(b)(3):

Amended Code Sec. 2032A(c)(7)(D) by striking out "section 151(e)(4)" and inserting in lieu thereof "section 151(c)(4)". **Effective** for tax years beginning after 12-31-86.

P.L. 99-514, § 1421, as amended by P.L. 100-647, § 1014(f), provides:

SEC. 1421. INFORMATION NECESSARY FOR VALID SPECIAL USE VALUATION ELECTION.

(a) IN GENERAL.—In the case of any decedent dying before January 1, 1986, if the executor—

(1) made an election under section 2032A of the Internal Revenue Code of 1954 on the return of tax imposed by section 2001 of such Code, and

(2) provided substantially all the information with respect to such election required on such return of tax,

such election shall be a valid election for purposes of section 2032A of such Code.

(b) EXECUTOR MUST PROVIDE INFORMATION.—An election described in subsection (a) shall not be valid if the Secretary of the Treasury or his delegate after the date of the enactment of this Act requests information from the executor with respect to such election and the executor does not provide such information within 90 days of receipt of such request.

(c) EFFECTIVE DATE.—The provisions of this section shall not apply to the estate of any decedent if before the date of the enactment of this Act the statute of limitations has expired with respect to—

(1) the return of tax imposed by section 2001 of the Internal Revenue Code of 1954, and

(2) the period during which a claim for credit or refund may be timely filed.

(d) SPECIAL RULE FOR CERTAIN ESTATE.—Notwithstanding subsection (a)(2), the provisions of this section shall apply to the estate of an individual who died on January 30, 1984, and with respect to which—

(1) a Federal estate tax return was filed on October 30, 1984, electing current use valuation, and

(2) the agreement required under section 2032A was filed on November 9, 1984.

• **1983, Technical Corrections Act of 1982 (P.L. 97-448)**

P.L. 97-448, § 104(b)(4)(A):

Amended subparagraph (A) of section 421(k)(5) (relating to effective dates) of P.L. 97-34 by striking out "subsections (b)(1), (c)(2), (j)(1), and (j)(2)" and inserting "subsections (b)(1), (j)(1), and (j)(2) and the provisions of subparagraph (A) of section 2032A(c)(7) of the Internal Revenue Code of 1954 (as added by subsection (c)(2))". [Therefore, the amendment made by P.L. 97-34, § 421(c)(2)(B)(ii), is **effective** with respect to estates of decedents dying after 12-31-81.—CCH.]

• **1981, Economic Recovery Tax Act of 1981 (P.L. 97-34)**

P.L. 97-34, § 421(c)(1)(A):

Amended Code Sec. 2032A(c)(1) by striking out "15 years" and inserting "10 years". **Effective** with respect to the estates of decedents dying after 12-31-81.

P.L. 97-34, § 421(c)(1)(B)(i):

Repealed Code Sec. 2032A(c)(3) and redesignated paragraphs (4) through (7) as (3) through (6), respectively. **Effective** with respect to the estates of decedents dying after 12-31-81. Prior to its repeal, Code Sec. 2032A(c)(3) read as follows:

(3) PHASEOUT OF ADDITIONAL TAX BETWEEN 10TH AND 15TH YEARS.—If the date of the disposition or cessation referred to in paragraph (1) occurs more than 120 months and less than 180 months after the date of the death of the decedent, the amount of the tax imposed by this subsection shall be reduced (but not below zero) by an amount determined by multiplying the amount of such tax (determined without regard to this paragraph) by a fraction—

(A) the numerator of which is the number of full months after such death in excess of 120, and

(B) the denominator of which is 60.

P.L. 97-34, § 421(c)(2)(A):

Added Code Sec. 2032A(c)(7). **Effective**, generally, with respect to the estates of decedents dying after 12-31-76. For special rules applicable here relating to certain amendments made retroactive to 1976, see P.L. 97-34, § 421(k)(5), as amended by P.L. 97-448, § 104(b)(4), in the amendment notes following Code Sec. 2032A(b).

P.L. 97-34, § 421(c)(2)(B)(ii):

Amended Code Sec. 2032A(c)(6), after its redesignation by P.L. 97-34, by striking out "3 years or more" and inserting "more than 3 years". **Effective** with respect to estates of decedents dying after 12-31-81.

P.L. 97-34, § 421(h)(2):

Added Code Sec. 2032A(c)(2)(E). **Effective** with respect to estates of decedents dying after 12-31-81.

• **1978, Revenue Act of 1978 (P.L. 95-600)**

P.L. 95-600, § 702(d)(5)(A):

Amended Code Sec. 2032A(c)(6). **Effective** for estates of decedents dying after 12-31-76. Prior to amendment, Code Sec. 2032A(c)(6) read as follows:

"(6) LIABILITY FOR TAX.—The qualified heir shall be personally liable for the additional tax imposed by this subsection with respect to his interest."

[Sec. 2032A(d)]

(d) ELECTION; AGREEMENT.—

(1) ELECTION.—The election under this section shall be made on the return of the tax imposed by section 2001. Such election shall be made in such manner as the Secretary shall by regulations prescribe. Such an election, once made, shall be irrevocable.

(2) AGREEMENT.—The agreement referred to in this paragraph is a written agreement signed by each person in being who has an interest (whether or not in possession) in any property designated in such agreement consenting to the application of subsection (c) with respect to such property.

(3) MODIFICATION OF ELECTION AND AGREEMENT TO BE PERMITTED.—The Secretary shall prescribe procedures which provide that in any case in which the executor makes an election under paragraph (1) (and submits the agreement referred to in paragraph (2)) within the time prescribed therefor, but—

(A) the notice of election, as filed, does not contain all required information, or

(B) signatures of 1 or more persons required to enter into the agreement described in paragraph (2) are not included on the agreement as filed, or the agreement does not contain all required information,

the executor will have a reasonable period of time (not exceeding 90 days) after notification of such failures to provide such information or signatures.

Amendments

• **1997, Taxpayer Relief Act of 1997 (P.L. 105-34)**

P.L. 105-34, § 1313(a):

Amended Code Sec. 2032A(d)(3). **Effective** for estates of decedents dying after 8-5-97. Prior to amendment, Code Sec. 2032A(d)(3) read as follows:

(3) MODIFICATION OF ELECTION AND AGREEMENT TO BE PERMITTED.—The Secretary shall prescribe procedures which provide that in any case in which—

(A) the executor makes an election under paragraph (1) within the time prescribed for filing such election, and

(B) substantially complies with the regulations prescribed by the Secretary with respect to such election, but—

(i) the notice of election, as filed, does not contain all required information, or

(ii) signatures of 1 or more persons required to enter into the agreement described in paragraph (2) are not included on the agreement as filed, or the agreement does not contain all required information,

the executor will have a reasonable period of time (not exceeding 90 days) after notification of such failures to provide such information or agreements.

• **1984, Deficit Reduction Act of 1984 (P.L. 98-369)**

P.L. 98-369, § 1025(a):

Amended Code Sec. 2032A(d) by adding paragraph (3). **Effective** for estates of decedents dying after 12-31-76. For a special rule, see Act Sec. 1025(b)(2), below.

ESTATE TAX—GROSS ESTATE

P.L. 98-369, § 1025(b)(2), provides:

(2) REFUND OR CREDIT OR OVERPAYMENT BARRED BY STATUTE OF LIMITATIONS.—Notwithstanding section 6511(a) of the Internal Revenue Code of 1954 or any other period of limitation or lapse of time, a claim for credit or refund of overpayment of the tax imposed by such Code which arises by reason of this section may be filed by any person at any time within the 1-year period beginning on the date of the enactment of this Act. Sections 6511(b) and 6514 of such Code shall not apply to any claim for credit or refund filed under this subsection within such 1-year period.

• **1981, Economic Recovery Tax Act of 1981 (P.L. 97-34)**

P.L. 97-34, § 421(j)(3):

Amended Code Sec. 2032A(d)(1). **Effective** for the estates of decedents dying after 12-31-81. Prior to amendment, Code Sec. 2032A(d)(1) read as follows:

(1) ELECTION.—The election under this section shall be made not later than the time prescribed by section 6075(a) for filing the return of tax imposed by section 2001 (including extensions thereof), and shall be made in such manner as the Secretary shall by regulations prescribe.

[Sec. 2032A(e)]

(e) DEFINITIONS; SPECIAL RULES.—For purposes of this section—

(1) QUALIFIED HEIR.—The term "qualified heir" means, with respect to any property, a member of the decedent's family who acquired such property (or to whom such property passed) from the decedent. If a qualified heir disposes of any interest in qualified real property to any member of his family, such member shall thereafter be treated as the qualified heir with respect to such interest.

(2) MEMBER OF FAMILY.—The term "member of the family" means, with respect to any individual, only—

(A) an ancestor of such individual,

(B) the spouse of such individual,

(C) a lineal descendant of such individual, of such individual's spouse, or of a parent of such individual, or

(D) the spouse of any lineal descendant described in subparagraph (C).

For purposes of the preceding sentence, a legally adopted child of an individual shall be treated as the child of such individual by blood.

(3) CERTAIN REAL PROPERTY INCLUDED.—In the case of real property which meets the requirements of subparagraph (C) of subsection (b)(1), residential buildings and related improvements on such real property occupied on a regular basis by the owner or lessee of such real property or by persons employed by such owner or lessee for the purpose of operating or maintaining such real property, and roads, buildings, and other structures and improvements functionally related to the qualified use shall be treated as real property devoted to the qualified use.

(4) FARM.—The term "farm" includes stock, dairy, poultry, fruit, furbearing animal, and truck farms, plantations, ranches, nurseries, ranges, greenhouses or other similar structures used primarily for the raising of agricultural or horticultural commodities, and orchards and woodlands.

(5) FARMING PURPOSES.—The term "farming purposes" means—

(A) cultivating the soil or raising or harvesting any agricultural or horticultural commodity (including the raising, shearing, feeding, caring for, training, and management of animals) on a farm;

(B) handling, drying, packing, grading, or storing on a farm any agricultural or horticultural commodity in its unmanufactured state, but only if the owner, tenant, or operator of the farm regularly produces more than one-half of the commodity so treated; and

(C) (i) the planting, cultivating, caring for, or cutting of trees, or

(ii) the preparation (other than milling) of trees for market.

(6) MATERIAL PARTICIPATION.—Material participation shall be determined in a manner similar to the manner used for purposes of paragraph (1) of section 1402(a) (relating to net earnings from self-employment).

(7) METHOD OF VALUING FARMS.—

(A) IN GENERAL.—Except as provided in subparagraph (B), the value of a farm for farming purposes shall be determined by dividing—

(i) the excess of the average annual gross cash rental for comparable land used for farming purposes and located in the locality of such farm over the average annual State and local real estate taxes for such comparable land, by

(ii) the average annual effective interest rate for all new Federal Land Bank loans.

For purposes of the preceding sentence, each average annual computation shall be made on the basis of the 5 most recent calendar years ending before the date of the decedent's death.

(B) VALUE BASED ON NET SHARE RENTAL IN CERTAIN CASES.—

(i) IN GENERAL.—If there is no comparable land from which the average annual gross cash rental may be determined but there is comparable land from which the average net share rental may be determined, subparagraph (A)(i) shall be applied by substituting "average annual net share rental" for "average annual gross cash rental".

(ii) NET SHARE RENTAL.—For purposes of this paragraph, the term "net share rental" means the excess of—

(I) the value of the produce received by the lessor of the land on which such produce is grown, over

(II) the cash operating expenses of growing such produce which, under the lease, are paid by the lessor.

(C) EXCEPTION.—The formula provided by subparagraph (A) shall not be used—

(i) where it is established that there is no comparable land from which the average annual gross cash rental may be determined and that there is no comparable land from which the average net share rental may be determined, or

(ii) where the executor elects to have the value of the farm for farming purposes determined under paragraph (8).

(8) METHOD OF VALUING CLOSELY HELD BUSINESS INTERESTS, ETC.—In any case to which paragraph (7)(A) does not apply, the following factors shall apply in determining the value of any qualified real property:

(A) The capitalization of income which the property can be expected to yield for farming or closely held business purposes over a reasonable period of time under prudent management using traditional cropping patterns for the area, taking into account soil capacity, terrain configuration, and similar factors,

(B) The capitalization of the fair rental value of the land for farmland or closely held business purposes,

(C) Assessed land values in a State which provides a differential or use value assessment law for farmland or closely held business,

(D) Comparable sales of other farm or closely held business land in the same geographical area far enough removed from a metropolitan or resort area so that nonagricultural use is not a significant factor in the sales price, and

(E) Any other factor which fairly values the farm or closely held business value of the property.

(9) PROPERTY ACQUIRED FROM DECEDENT.—Property shall be considered to have been acquired from or to have passed from the decedent if—

(A) such property is so considered under section 1014(b) (relating to basis of property acquired from a decedent),

(B) such property is acquired by any person from the estate, or

(C) such property is acquired by any person from a trust (to the extent such property is includible in the gross estate of the decedent).

(10) COMMUNITY PROPERTY.—If the decedent and his surviving spouse at any time held qualified real property as community property, the interest of the surviving spouse in such property shall be taken into account under this section to the extent necessary to provide a result under

ESTATE TAX—GROSS ESTATE

this section with respect to such property which is consistent with the result which would have obtained under this section if such property had not been community property.

(11) BOND IN LIEU OF PERSONAL LIABILITY.—If the qualified heir makes written application to the Secretary for determination of the maximum amount of the additional tax which may be imposed by subsection (c) with respect to the qualified heir's interest, the Secretary (as soon as possible, and in any event within 1 year after the making of such application) shall notify the heir of such maximum amount. The qualified heir, on furnishing a bond in such amount and for such period as may be required, shall be discharged from personal liability for any additional tax imposed by subsection (c) and shall be entitled to a receipt or writing showing such discharge.

(12) ACTIVE MANAGEMENT.—The term "active management" means the making of the management decisions of a business (other than the daily operating decisions).

(13) SPECIAL RULES FOR WOODLANDS.—

(A) IN GENERAL.—In the case of any qualified woodland with respect to which the executor elects to have this subparagraph apply, trees growing on such woodland shall not be treated as a crop.

(B) QUALIFIED WOODLAND.—The term "qualified woodland" means any real property which—

(i) is used in timber operations, and

(ii) is an identifiable area of land such as an acre or other area for which records are normally maintained in conducting timber operations.

(C) TIMBER OPERATIONS.—The term "timber operations" means—

(i) the planting, cultivating, caring for, or cutting of trees, or

(ii) the preparation (other than milling) of trees for market.

(D) ELECTION.—An election under subparagraph (A) shall be made on the return of the tax imposed by section 2001. Such election shall be made in such manner as the Secretary shall by regulations prescribe. Such an election, once made, shall be irrevocable.

(14) TREATMENT OF REPLACEMENT PROPERTY ACQUIRED IN SECTION 1031 OR 1033 TRANSACTIONS.—

(A) IN GENERAL.—In the case of any qualified replacement property, any period during which there was ownership, qualified use, or material participation with respect to the replaced property by the decedent or any member of his family shall be treated as a period during which there was such ownership, use, or material participation (as the case may be) with respect to the qualified replacement property.

(B) LIMITATION.—Subparagraph (A) shall not apply to the extent that the fair market value of the qualified replacement property (as of the date of its acquisition) exceeds the fair market value of the replaced property (as of the date of its disposition).

(C) DEFINITIONS.—For purposes of this paragraph—

(i) QUALIFIED REPLACEMENT PROPERTY.—The term "qualified replacement property" means any real property which is—

(I) acquired in an exchange which qualifies under section 1031, or

(II) the acquisition of which results in the non-recognition of gain under section 1033.

Such term shall only include property which is used for the same qualified use as the replaced property was being used before the exchange.

(ii) REPLACED PROPERTY.—The term "replaced property" means—

(I) the property transferred in the exchange which qualifies under section 1031, or

(II) the property compulsorily or involuntarily converted (within the meaning of section 1033).

Amendments

• **1981, Economic Recovery Tax Act of 1981 (P.L. 97-34)**

P.L. 97-34, § 421(c)(2)(B)(i):

Added Code Sec. 2032A(e)(12). **Effective** with respect to the estates of decedents dying after 12-31-81. (For the amendment made to section 421(k)(5) of P.L. 97-34 (relating to effective dates), see the amendment note for P.L. 97-448, § 104(b)(4)(A), following Code Sec. 2032A(c).)

P.L. 97-34, § 421(f)(1):

Amended Code Sec. 2032A(e)(7) by redesignating subparagraph (B) as (C) and by inserting a new subparagraph (B). **Effective** for the estates of decedents dying after 12-31-81.

P.L. 97-34, § 421(f)(2):

Amended Code Sec. 2032A(e)(7)(C), after its redesignation by P.L. 97-34, by inserting after "determined" the following: "and that there is no comparable land from which the average net share rental may be determined". **Effective** with respect to the estates of decedents dying after 12-31-81.

P.L. 97-34, § 421(h)(1):

Added Code Sec. 2032A(e)(13). **Effective** with respect to the estates of decedents dying after 12-31-81.

P.L. 97-34, § 421(i):

Amended Code Sec. 2032A(e)(2). **Effective** with respect to the estates of decedents dying after 12-31-81. Prior to amendment, Code Sec. 2032A(e)(2) read as follows:

(2) MEMBER OF FAMILY.—The term "member of the family" means, with respect to any individual, only such individual's ancestor or lineal descendant, a lineal descendant of a grandparent of such individual, the spouse of such individual, or the spouse of any such descendant. For purposes of the preceding sentence, a legally adopted child of an individual shall be treated as a child of such individual by blood.

P.L. 97-34, § 421(j)(2)(A):

Amended Code Sec. 2032A(e)(9)(B) and (C). **Effective**, generally, with respect to the estates of decedents dying after 12-31-76. For special rules applicable here relating to certain amendments made retroactive to 1976, see P.L. 97-34, § 412(k)(5), as amended by P.L. 97-448, § 104(b)(4), in the amendment notes following Code Sec. 2032A(b). Prior to amendment, Code Sec. 2032A(e)(9)(B) and (C) read as follows:

(B) such property is acquired by any person from the estate in satisfaction of the right of such person to a pecuniary bequest, or

(C) such property is acquired by any person from a trust in satisfaction of a right (which such person has by reason of the death of the decedent) to receive from the trust a specific dollar amount which is the equivalent of a pecuniary bequest.

P.L. 97-34, § 421(j)(4):

Added Code Sec. 2032A(e)(14). **Effective** with respect to the estates of decedents dying after 12-3-81.

• **1978, Revenue Act of 1978 (P.L. 95-600)**

P.L. 95-600, § 702(d)(2), (4), (5)(B):

Added Code Sec. 2032A(e)(9), (10), and (11). **Effective** for estates of decedents dying after 12-31-76.

[Sec. 2032A(f)]

(f) STATUTE OF LIMITATIONS.—If qualified real property is disposed of or ceases to be used for a qualified use, then—

(1) The statutory period for the assessment of any additional tax under subsection (c) attributable to such disposition or cessation shall not expire before the expiration of 3 years from the date the Secretary is notified (in such manner as the Secretary may by regulations prescribe) of such disposition or cessation (or if later in the case of an involuntary conversion or exchange to which subsection (h) or (i) applies, 3 years from the date the Secretary is notified of the replacement of the converted property or of an intention not to replace or of the exchange of property, and

(2) such additional tax may be assessed before the expiration of such 3-year period notwithstanding the provisions of any other law or rule of law which would otherwise prevent such assessment.

ESTATE TAX—GROSS ESTATE

Amendments
• **1981, Economic Recovery Tax Act of 1981 (P.L. 97-34)**

P.L. 97-34, §421(d)(2)(A):

Amended Code Sec. 2032A(f)(1) by inserting "or exchange" after "conversion", by inserting "or (i)" after "(h)", and by inserting "or of the exchange of property" after "replace". **Effective** with respect to exchanges after 12-31-81.

P.L. 97-34, §421(e)(2):

Amended Code Sec. 2032A(f)(1) by striking out "to which an election under subsection (h)" and inserting "to which subsection (h)". **Effective** with respect to involuntary conversions after 12-31-81.

• **1978 (P.L. 95-472)**

P.L. 95-472, §4(c), (d):

Amended Code Sec. 2032A(f)(1) by inserting "(or if later in the case of an involuntary conversion to which an election under subsection (h) applies, 3 years from the date the Secretary is notified of the replacement of the converted property or of an intention not to replace)" immediately before ", and". **Effective** for involuntary conversions after 1976.

• **1976, Tax Reform Act of 1976 (P.L. 94-455)**

P.L. 94-455, §2003(a), (e):

Added Code Sec. 2032A(f). **Effective** for estates of decedents dying after 1976.

[Sec. 2032A(g)]

(g) APPLICATION OF THIS SECTION AND SECTION 6324B TO INTERESTS IN PARTNERSHIPS, CORPORATIONS AND TRUSTS.—The Secretary shall prescribe regulations setting forth the application of this section and section 6324B in the case of an interest in a partnership, corporation, or trust which, with respect to the decedent, is an interest in a closely held business (within the meaning of paragraph (1) of section 6166(b)). For purposes of the preceding sentence, an interest in a discretionary trust all the beneficiaries of which are qualified heirs shall be treated as a present interest.

Amendments
• **1981, Economic Recovery Tax Act of 1981 (P.L. 97-34)**

P.L. 97-34, §421(j)(1):

Amended Code Sec. 2032A(g) by adding at the end a new sentence. **Effective**, generally, with respect to estates of decedents dying after 12-31-76. For special rules applicable here relating to certain amendments made retroactive to 1976, see P.L. 97-34, §421(k)(5), as amended by P.L. 97-448, §104(b)(4), in the amendment notes, following Code Sec. 2032A(b).

• **1976, Tax Reform Act of 1976 (P.L. 94-455)**

P.L. 94-455, §2003(a), (e):

Added Code Sec. 2032A(g). **Effective** for estates of decedents dying after 12-31-76.

[Sec. 2032A(h)]

(h) SPECIAL RULES FOR INVOLUNTARY CONVERSIONS OF QUALIFIED REAL PROPERTY.—

(1) TREATMENT OF CONVERTED PROPERTY.—

(A) IN GENERAL.—If there is an involuntary conversion of an interest in qualified real property—

(i) no tax shall be imposed by subsection (c) on such conversion if the cost of the qualified replacement property equals or exceeds the amount realized on such conversion, or

(ii) if clause (i) does not apply, the amount of the tax imposed by subsection (c) on such conversion shall be the amount determined under subparagraph (B).

(B) AMOUNT OF TAX WHERE THERE IS NOT COMPLETE REINVESTMENT.—The amount determined under this subparagraph with respect to any involuntary conversion is the amount of the tax which (but for this subsection) would have been imposed on such conversion reduced by an amount which—

(i) bears the same ratio to such tax, as

(ii) the cost of the qualified replacement property bears to the amount realized on the conversion.

(2) TREATMENT OF REPLACEMENT PROPERTY.—For purposes of subsection (c)—

(A) any qualified replacement property shall be treated in the same manner as if it were a portion of the interest in qualified real property which was involuntarily converted; except that with respect to such qualified replacement property the 10-year period under paragraph (1) of subsection (c) shall be extended by any period, beyond the 2-year period referred to in section 1033(a)(2)(B)(i), during which the qualified heir was allowed to replace the qualified real property,

(B) any tax imposed by subsection (c) on the involuntary conversion shall be treated as a tax imposed on a partial disposition, and

(C) paragraph (6) of subsection (c) shall be applied—

(i) by not taking into account periods after the involuntary conversion and before the acquisition of the qualified replacement property, and

(ii) by treating material participation with respect to the converted property as material participation with respect to the qualified replacement property.

(3) DEFINITIONS AND SPECIAL RULES.—For purposes of this subsection—

(A) INVOLUNTARY CONVERSION.—The term "involuntary conversion" means a compulsory or involuntary conversion within the meaning of section 1033.

(B) QUALIFIED REPLACEMENT PROPERTY.—The term "qualified replacement property" means—

(i) in the case of an involuntary conversion described in section 1033(a)(1), any real property into which the qualified real property is converted, or

(ii) in the case of an involuntary conversion described in section 1033(a)(2), any real property purchased by the qualified heir during the period specified in section 1033(a)(2)(B) for purposes of replacing the qualified real property.

Such term only includes property which is to be used for the qualified use set forth in subparagraph (A) or (B) of subsection (b)(2) under which the qualified real property qualified under subsection (a).

(4) CERTAIN RULES MADE APPLICABLE.—The rules of the last sentence of section 1033(a)(2)(A) shall apply for purposes of paragraph (3)(B)(ii).

Amendments
• **1981, Economic Recovery Tax Act of 1981 (P.L. 97-34)**

P.L. 97-34, §421(c)(1)(B)(ii):

Amended Code Sec. 2032A(h)(2)(A). **Effective** with respect to the estates of decedents dying after 12-31-81. Prior to amendment, Code Sec. 2032A(h)(2)(A) read as follows:

(2) TREATMENT OF REPLACEMENT PROPERTY.—For purposes of subsection (c)—

(A) any qualified replacement property shall be treated in the same manner as if it were a portion of the interest in qualified real property which was involuntarily converted, except that with respect to such qualified replacement property—

(i) the 15-year period under paragraph (1) of subsection (c) shall be extended by any period, beyond the 2-year period referred to in section 1033(a)(2)(B)(i), during which the qualified heir was allowed to replace the qualified real property, and

(ii) the phaseout period under paragraph (3) of subsection (c) shall be appropriately adjusted to take into account the extension referred to in clause (i),

P.L. 97-34, §421(c)(1)(B)(iii):

Amended Code Sec. 2032A(h)(2)(C) by striking out "(7)" and inserting "(6)". **Effective** with respect to decedents dying after 12-31-81.

P.L. 97-34, §421(e)(1)(A):

Amended Code Sec. 2032A(h)(A) by striking out "and the qualified heir makes an election under this subsection". **Effective** with respect to involuntary conversions after 12-31-81.

P.L. 97-34, §421(e)(1)(B):

Repealed Code Sec. 2032A(h)(5). **Effective** with respect to involuntary conversions after 12-31-81. Prior to its repeal, Code Sec. 2032A(h)(5) read as follows:

(5) ELECTION.—Any election under this subsection shall be made at such time and in such manner as the Secretary may by regulations prescribe.

• **1978 (P.L. 95-472)**

P.L. 95-472, §4(a):

Added Code Sec. 2032A(h). **Effective** for involuntary conversions after 1976.

ESTATE TAX—GROSS ESTATE

[Sec. 2032A(i)]

(i) Exchanges of Qualified Real Property.—

(1) Treatment of property exchanged.—

(A) Exchanges solely for qualified exchange property.—If an interest in qualified real property is exchanged solely for an interest in qualified exchange property in a transaction which qualifies under section 1031, no tax shall be imposed by subsection (c) by reason of such exchange.

(B) Exchanges where other property received.—If an interest in qualified real property is exchanged for an interest in qualified exchange property and other property in a transaction which qualifies under section 1031, the amount of the tax imposed by subsection (c) by reason of such exchange shall be the amount of tax which (but for this subparagraph) would have been imposed on such exchange under subsection (c)(1), reduced by an amount which—

(i) bears the same ratio to such tax, as

(ii) the fair market value of the qualified exchange property bears to the fair market value of the qualified real property exchanged.

For purposes of clause (ii) of the preceding sentence, fair market value shall be determined as of the time of the exchange.

(2) Treatment of qualified exchange property.—For purposes of subsection (c)—

(A) any interest in qualified exchange property shall be treated in the same manner as if it were a portion of the interest in qualified real property which was exchanged,

(B) any tax imposed by subsection (c) by reason of the exchange shall be treated as a tax imposed on a partial disposition, and

(C) paragraph (6) of subsection (c) shall be applied by treating material participation with respect to the exchanged property as material participation with respect to the qualified exchange property.

(3) Qualified exchange property.—For purposes of this subsection, the term "qualified exchange property" means real property which is to be used for the qualified use set forth in subparagraph (A) or (B) of subsection (b)(2) under which the real property exchanged therefor originally qualified under subsection (a).

Amendments

• **1983, Technical Corrections Act of 1982 (P.L. 97-448)**

P.L. 97-448, § 104(b)(2)(A):

Amended Code Sec. 2032A(i)(1)(B)(ii) by striking out "the other property" and inserting in lieu thereof "the qualified exchange property". **Effective** as if included in the provision of P.L. 97-34 to which it relates.

P.L. 97-448, § 104(b)(2)(B):

Amended Code Sec. 2032A(i)(3) by striking out "subparagraph (A), (B), or (C)" and inserting in lieu thereof "subparagraph (A) or (B)". **Effective** as if included in the provision of P.L. 97-34 to which it relates.

• **1981, Economic Recovery Tax Act of 1981 (P.L. 97-34)**

P.L. 97-34, § 421(d)(1):

Added Code Sec. 2032A(i). **Effective** with respect to exchanges after 12-31-81.

[Sec. 2033]

SEC. 2033. PROPERTY IN WHICH THE DECEDENT HAD AN INTEREST.

The value of the gross estate shall include the value of all property to the extent of the interest therein of the decedent at the time of his death.

Amendments

• **1962, Revenue Act of 1962 (P.L. 87-834)**

P.L. 87-834, § 18(a)(2):

Amended Code Sec. 2033 by deleting "(except real property situated outside of the United States)". **Effective**, generally, for estates of decedents dying after 10-16-62. For exceptions, see Act Sec. 18(b) in the amendment notes for Code Sec. 2031(a).

[Sec. 2034]

SEC. 2034. DOWER OR CURTESY INTERESTS.

The value of the gross estate shall include the value of all property to the extent of any interest therein of the surviving spouse, existing at the time of the decedent's death as dower or curtesy, or by virtue of a statute creating an estate in lieu of dower or curtesy.

Amendments

• **1962, Revenue Act of 1962 (P.L. 87-834)**

P.L. 87-834, § 18(a)(2):

Amended Code Sec. 2034 by deleting "(except real property situated outside of the United States)". **Effective**, generally, for estates of decedents dying after 10-16-62. For exceptions, see Act Sec. 18(b) in the amendment notes for Code Sec. 2031(a).

[Sec. 2035]

SEC. 2035. ADJUSTMENTS FOR CERTAIN GIFTS MADE WITHIN 3 YEARS OF DECEDENT'S DEATH.

[Sec. 2035(a)]

(a) Inclusion of Certain Property in Gross Estate.—If—

(1) the decedent made a transfer (by trust or otherwise) of an interest in any property, or relinquished a power with respect to any property, during the 3-year period ending on the date of the decedent's death, and

(2) the value of such property (or an interest therein) would have been included in the decedent's gross estate under section 2036, 2037, 2038, or 2042 if such transferred interest or relinquished power had been retained by the decedent on the date of his death, the value of the gross estate shall include the value of any property (or interest therein) which would have been so included.

[Sec. 2035(b)]

(b) Inclusion of Gift Tax on Gifts Made During 3 Years Before Decedent's Death.—The amount of the gross estate (determined without regard to this subsection) shall be increased by the amount of any tax paid under chapter 12 by the decedent or his estate on any gift made by the decedent or his spouse during the 3-year period ending on the date of the decedent's death.

[Sec. 2035(c)]

(c) Other Rules Relating to Transfers Within 3 Years of Death.—

(1) In general.—For purposes of—

(A) section 303(b) (relating to distributions in redemption of stock to pay death taxes),

(B) section 2032A (relating to special valuation of certain farms, etc., real property), and

(C) subchapter C of chapter 64 (relating to lien for taxes),

ESTATE TAX—GROSS ESTATE

the value of the gross estate shall include the value of all property to the extent of any interest therein of which the decedent has at any time made a transfer, by trust or otherwise, during the 3-year period ending on the date of the decedent's death.

(2) COORDINATION WITH SECTION 6166.—An estate shall be treated as meeting the 35 percent of adjusted gross estate requirement of section 6166(a)(1) only if the estate meets such requirement both with and without the application of subsection (a).

(3) MARITAL AND SMALL TRANSFERS.—Paragraph (1) shall not apply to any transfer (other than a transfer with respect to a life insurance policy) made during a calendar year to any donee if the decedent was not required by section 6019 (other than by reason of section 6019(2)) to file any gift tax return for such year with respect to transfers to such donee.

Amendments

• **2000, Community Renewal Tax Relief Act of 2000 (P.L. 106-554)**

P.L. 106-554, §319(14)(A):

Amended Code Sec. 2035(c)(2) by striking "paragraph (1)" and inserting "subsection (a)". **Effective** 12-21-2000.

[Sec. 2035(d)]

(d) EXCEPTION.—Subsection (a) and paragraph (1) of subsection (c) shall not apply to any bona fide sale for an adequate and full consideration in money or money's worth.

Amendments

• **2000, Community Renewal Tax Relief Act of 2000 (P.L. 106-554)**

P.L. 106-554, §319(14)(B):

Amended Code Sec. 2035(d) by inserting "and paragraph (1) of subsection (c)" after "Subsection (a)". **Effective** 12-21-2000.

[Sec. 2035(e)]

(e) TREATMENT OF CERTAIN TRANSFERS FROM REVOCABLE TRUSTS.—For purposes of this section and section 2038, any transfer from any portion of a trust during any period that such portion was treated under section 676 as owned by the decedent by reason of a power in the grantor (determined without regard to section 672(e)) shall be treated as a transfer made directly by the decedent.

Amendments

• **1997, Taxpayer Relief Act of 1997 (P.L. 105-34)**

P.L. 105-34, §1310(a):

Amended Code Sec. 2035. **Effective** for the estates of decedents dying after 8-5-97. Prior to amendment, Code Sec. 2035 read as follows:

SEC. 2035. ADJUSTMENTS FOR GIFTS MADE WITHIN 3 YEARS OF DECEDENT'S DEATH.

[Sec. 2035(a)]

(a) INCLUSION OF GIFTS MADE BY DECEDENT.—Except as provided in subsection (b), the value of the gross estate shall include the value of all property to the extent of any interest therein of which the decedent has at any time made a transfer, by trust or otherwise, during the 3-year period ending on the date of the decedent's death.

Amendments

• **1976, Tax Reform Act of 1976 (P.L. 94-455)**

P.L. 94-455, §2001(a)(5), (d)(1):

Amended Code Sec. 2035(a). **Effective** for estates of decedents dying after 12-31-76, except that it does not apply to transfers made before 1-1-77. Prior to amendment, Code Sec. 2035(a) read as follows:

(a) GENERAL RULE—The value of the gross estate shall include the value of all property to the extent of any interest therein of which the decedent has at any time made a transfer (except in case of a bona fide sale for an adequate and full consideration in money or money's worth), by trust or otherwise, in contemplation of his death.

• **1962, Revenue Act of 1962 (P.L. 87-834)**

P.L. 87-834, §18(a)(2):

Amended Code Sec. 2035(a) by deleting "(except real property situated outside of the United States)". **Effective,** generally, for estates of decedents dying after 10-16-62. For exceptions, see Act Sec. 18(b) in the amendment notes for Code Sec. 2031(a).

[Sec. 2035(b)]

(b) EXCEPTIONS.—Subsection (a) shall not apply—

(1) to any bona fide sale for an adequate and full consideration in money or money's worth, and

(2) to any gift to a donee made during a calendar year if the decedent was not required by section 6019 (other than by reason of section 6019(2)) to file any gift tax return for such year with respect to gifts to such donee. Paragraph (2) shall not apply to any transfer with respect to a life insurance policy.

Amendments

• **1983, Technical Corrections Act of 1982 (P.L. 97-448)**

P.L. 97-448, §104(a)(9):

Amended Code Sec. 2035(b)(2) by striking out "section 6019(a)(2)" and inserting in lieu thereof "section 6019(2)". **Effective** as if included in the provision of P.L. 97-34 to which it relates.

• **1981, Economic Recovery Tax Act of 1981 (P.L. 97-34)**

P.L. 97-34, §403(b)(3)(B):

Amended Code Sec. 2035(b)(2) by inserting after "section 6019" the phrase "(other than by reason of section 6019(a)(2))". **Effective** for estates of decedents dying after 12-31-81.

• **1980, Technical Corrections Act of 1979 (P.L. 96-222)**

P.L. 96-222, §107(a)(2)(F)(i)-(ii), provides:

(F)(i) If the executor elects the benefits of this subparagraph with respect to any estate, section 2035(b) of the Internal Revenue Code of 1954 (relating to adjustments for gifts made within 3 years of decedent's death) shall be applied with respect to transfers made by the decedent during 1977 as if paragraph (2) of such section 2035(b) read as follows:

"(2) to any gift to a donee made during 1977 to the extent of the amount of such gift which was excludable in computing taxable gifts by reason of section 2503(b) (relating to $3,000 annual exclusion for purposes of the gift tax) determined without regard to section 2513(a)."

(ii) The election under clause (i) with respect to any estate shall be made on or before the later of—

(I) the due date for filing the estate tax return, or

(II) the day which is 120 days after the date of the enactment of this Act.

• **1978, Revenue Act of 1978 (P.L. 95-600)**

P.L. 95-600, §702(f)(1):

Amended Code Sec. 2035(b). **Effective** for estates of decedents dying after 12-31-76. Prior to amendment, Code Sec. 2035(b) read as follows:

"(b) EXCEPTIONS.—Subsection (a) shall not apply to—

"(1) any bona fide sale for an adequate and full consideration in money or money's worth, and

"(2) any gift excludable in computing taxable gifts by reason of section 2503(b) (relating to $3,000 annual exclusion for purposes of the gift tax) determined without regard to section 2513(a)."

• **1976, Tax Reform Act of 1976 (P.L. 94-455)**

P.L. 94-455, §2001(a)(5), (d)(1):

Amended Code Sec. 2035(b). **Effective** for estates of decedents dying after 12-31-76, except that it does not apply to transfers made before 1-1-77. Prior to amendment, Code Sec. 2035(b) read as follows:

(b) APPLICATION OF GENERAL RULE.—If the decedent within a period of 3 years ending with the date of his death (except in case of a bona fide sale for an adequate and full consideration in money or money's worth) transferred an interest in property, relinquished a power, or exercised or released a general power of appointment, such transfer, relinquishment, exercise, or release shall, unless shown to the contrary, be deemed to have been made in contemplation of death within the meaning of this section and sections 2038 and 2041 (relating to revocable transfers and powers of appointment); but no such transfer, relinquishment, exercise, or release made before such 3-year period shall be treated as having been made in contemplation of death.

[Sec. 2035(c)]

(c) INCLUSION OF GIFT TAX ON CERTAIN GIFTS MADE DURING 3 YEARS BEFORE DECEDENT'S DEATH.—The amount of the gross estate (determined without regard to this subsection) shall be increased by the amount of any tax paid under chapter 12 by the decedent or his estate on any gift made by the decedent or his spouse after December 31, 1976, and during the 3-year period ending on the date of the decedent's death.

Amendments

• **1976, Tax Reform Act of 1976 (P.L. 94-455)**

P.L. 94-455, §2001(a)(5), (d)(1):

Added Code Sec. 2035(c). **Effective** for estates of decedents dying after 12-31-76, except that it does not apply to transfers made before 1-1-77.

[Sec. 2035(d)]

(d) DECEDENTS DYING AFTER 1981.—

(1) IN GENERAL.—Except as otherwise provided in this subsection, subsection (a) shall not apply to the estate of a decedent dying after December 31, 1981.

(2) EXCEPTIONS FOR CERTAIN TRANSFERS.—Paragraph (1) of this subsection and paragraph (2) of subsection (b) shall not apply to a transfer of an interest in property which is included in the value of the gross estate under section 2036, 2037, 2038, or 2042 or would have been included under any of such sections if such interest had been retained by the decedent.

ESTATE TAX—GROSS ESTATE

(3) 3-YEAR RULE RETAINED FOR CERTAIN PURPOSES.—Paragraph (1) shall not apply for purposes of—

(A) section 303(b) (relating to distributions in redemption of stock to pay death taxes),

(B) section 2032A (relating to special valuation of certain farm, etc., real property), and

(C) subchapter C of chapter 64 (relating to lien for taxes).

(4) COORDINATION OF 3-YEAR RULE WITH SECTION 6166(a)(1).—An estate shall be treated as meeting the 35-percent of adjusted gross estate requirement of section 6166(a)(1) only if the estate meets such requirement both with and without the application of paragraph (1).

Amendments

• **1983, Technical Corrections Act of 1982 (P.L. 97-448)**

P.L. 97-448, §104(d)(1)(A):

Amended Code Sec. 2035(d) by adding at the end thereof new paragraph (4). **Effective** as if included in the provision of P.L. 97-34 to which it relates.

P.L. 97-448, §104(d)(1)(C):

Amended Code Sec. 2035(d)(3) by striking out subparagraph (C), by adding "and" at the end of subparagraph (B), and by redesignating subparagraph (D) as subparagraph (C). **Effective** as if included in the provision of P.L. 97-34 to which it relates. Prior to amendment, subparagraph (C) read as follows:

(C) section 6166 (relating to extension of time for payment of estate tax where estate consists largely of interest in closely held business), and.

P.L. 97-448, §104(d)(2):

Amended Code Sec. 2035(d)(2) by inserting "of this subsection and paragraph (2) of subsection (b)" after "Paragraph (1)", and by striking out "2041,". **Effective** as if included in the provision of P.L. 97-34 to which it relates.

P.L. 97-448, §104(d)(3), provides:

(3) ELECTION TO HAVE AMENDMENTS NOT APPLY.—

(A) In the case of any decedent—

(i) who dies before August 13, 1984, and

(ii) who made a gift (before August 13, 1981, and during the 3-year period ending on the date of the decedent's death) on which tax imposed by chapter 12 of the Internal Revenue Code of 1954 has been paid before April 16, 1982,

such decedent's executor may make an election to have subtitle B of such Code (relating to estate and gift taxes) applied with respect to such decedent without regard to any of the amendments made by title IV of the Economic Recovery Tax Act of 1981.

(B) An election under subparagraph (A) shall be made at such time and in such manner as the Secretary of the Treasury or his delegate shall prescribe.

(C) An election under subparagraph (A), once made, shall be irrevocable.

• **1981, Economic Recovery Tax Act of 1981 (P.L. 97-34)**

P.L. 97-34, §424(a):

Added Code Sec. 2035(d). **Effective** for estates of decedents dying after 12-31-81.

[Sec. 2036]

SEC. 2036. TRANSFERS WITH RETAINED LIFE ESTATE.

[Sec. 2036(a)]

(a) GENERAL RULE.—The value of the gross estate shall include the value of all property to the extent of any interest therein of which the decedent has at any time made a transfer (except in case of a bona fide sale for an adequate and full consideration in money or money's worth), by trust or otherwise, under which he has retained for his life or for any period not ascertainable without reference to his death or for any period which does not in fact end before his death—

(1) the possession or enjoyment of, or the right to the income from, the property, or

(2) the right, either alone or in conjunction with any person, to designate the persons who shall possess or enjoy the property or the income therefrom.

Amendments

• **1978, Revenue Act of 1978 (P.L. 95-600)**

P.L. 95-600, §702(i)(2):

Amended Code Sec. 2036(a) by deleting from the end thereof the following: "For purposes of paragraph (1), the retention of voting rights in retained stock shall be considered to be a retention of the enjoyment of such stock." **Effective** for transfers made after 6-22-76.

• **1976, Tax Reform Act of 1976 (P.L. 94-455)**

P.L. 94-455, §2009(a), (e)(1):

Added the last sentence to Code Sec. 2036(a). **Effective** for transfers made after 6-22-76.

• **1962, Revenue Act of 1962 (P.L. 87-834)**

P.L. 87-834, §18(a)(2):

Amended Code Sec. 2036(a) by deleting "(except real property situated outside of the United States)". **Effective**, generally, for estates of decedents dying after 10-16-62. For exceptions, see Act Sec. 18(b) in the amendment notes for Code Sec. 2031(a).

[Sec. 2036(b)]

(b) VOTING RIGHTS.—

(1) IN GENERAL.—For purposes of subsection (a)(1), the retention of the right to vote (directly or indirectly) shares of stock of a controlled corporation shall be considered to be a retention of the enjoyment of transferred property.

(2) CONTROLLED CORPORATION.—For purposes of paragraph (1), a corporation shall be treated as a controlled corporation if, at any time after the transfer of the property and during the 3-year period ending on the date of the decedent's death, the decedent owned (with the application of section 318), or had the right (either alone or in conjunction with any person) to vote stock possessing at least 20 percent of the total combined voting power of all classes of stock.

(3) COORDINATION WITH SECTION 2035.—For purposes of applying section 2035 with respect to paragraph (1), the relinquishment or cessation of voting rights shall be treated as a transfer of property made by the decedent.

Amendments

• **1978, Revenue Act of 1978 (P.L. 95-600)**

P.L. 95-600, §702(i)(1):

Added new Code Sec. 2036(b). **Effective** for transfers made after 6-22-76. Prior Code Sec. 2036(b) was redesignated Code Sec. 2036(c).

[Sec. 2036(c)]

(c) LIMITATION ON APPLICATION OF GENERAL RULE.—This section shall not apply to a transfer made before March 4, 1931; nor to a transfer made after March 3, 1931, and before June 7, 1932, unless the property transferred would have been includible in the decedent's gross estate by reason of the amendatory language of the joint resolution of March 3, 1931 (46 Stat. 1516).

Amendments

• **1990, Omnibus Budget Reconciliation Act of 1990 (P.L. 101-508)**

P.L. 101-508, §11601(a):

Amended Code Sec. 2036 by striking subsection (c) and by redesignating subsection (d) as subsection (c). **Effective** for property transferred after 12-17-87. Prior to being stricken, subsection (c) read as follows:

(c) INCLUSION RELATED TO VALUATION FREEZES.—

(1) IN GENERAL.—For purposes of subsection (a), if—

(A) any person holds a substantial interest in an enterprise, and

(B) such person in effect transfers after December 17, 1987, property having a disproportionately large share of the potential appreciation in such person's interest in the enterprise while retaining an interest in the income of, or rights in, the enterprise,

then the retention of the retained interest shall be considered to be a retention of the enjoyment of the transferred property.

(2) SPECIAL RULES FOR CONSIDERATION FURNISHED BY FAMILY MEMBERS.—

(A) IN GENERAL.—The exception contained in subsection (a) for a bona fide sale shall not apply to a transfer described in paragraph (1) if such transfer is to a member of the transferor's family.

(B) TREATMENT OF CONSIDERATION.—

(i) IN GENERAL.—In the case of a transfer described in paragraph (1), if—

ESTATE TAX—GROSS ESTATE

(I) a member of the transferor's family provides consideration in money or money's worth for such member's interest in the enterprise, and

(II) it is established to the satisfaction of the Secretary that such consideration originally belonged to such member and was never received or acquired (directly or indirectly) by such member from the transferor for less than full and adequate consideration in money or money's worth,

paragraph (1) shall not apply to the applicable fraction of the portion of the enterprise which would (but for this subparagraph) have been included in the gross estate of the transferor by reason of this subsection (determined without regard to any reduction under paragraph (5) for the value of the retained interest).

(ii) APPLICABLE FRACTION.—For purposes of clause (i), the applicable fraction is a fraction—

(I) the numerator of which is the amount of the consideration referred to in clause (i), and

(II) the denominator of which is the value of the portion referred to in clause (i) immediately after the transfer described in paragraph (1).

(iii) SECTION 2043 NOT TO APPLY.—The provisions of this subparagraph shall be in lieu of any adjustment under section 2043.

(3) DEFINITIONS.—For purposes of this subsection—

(A) SUBSTANTIAL INTEREST.—A person holds a substantial interest in an enterprise if such person owns (directly or indirectly) 10 percent or more of the voting power or income stream, or both, in such enterprise. For purposes of the preceding sentence, an individual shall be treated as owning any interest in an enterprise which is owned (directly or indirectly) by any member of such individual's family.

(B) FAMILY.—The term "family" means, with respect to any individual, such individual's spouse, any lineal descendant of such individual or of such individual's spouse, any parent or grandparent of such individual, and any spouse of any of the foregoing. For purposes of the preceding sentence, a relationship by legal adoption shall be treated as a relationship by blood.

(C) TREATMENT OF SPOUSE.—Except as provided in regulations, an individual and such individual's spouse shall be treated as 1 person.

(4) TREATMENT OF CERTAIN TRANSFERS.—

(A) IN GENERAL.—For purposes of this subtitle, if, before the death of the original transferor—

(i) the original transferor transfers all (or any portion of) the retained interest referred to in paragraph (1), or

(ii) the original transferee transfers all (or any portion of) the transferred property referred to in paragraph (1) to a person who is not a member of the original transferor's family,

the original transferor shall be treated as having made a transfer by gift of property to the original transferee equal to the paragraph (1) inclusion (or proportionate amount thereof). Proper adjustments shall be made in the amount treated as a gift by reason of the preceding sentence to take into account prior transfers to which this subparagraph applied and take into account any right of recovery (whether or not exercised) under section 2207B.

(B) COORDINATION WITH PARAGRAPH (1).—In any case to which subparagraph (A) applies, nothing in paragraph (1) or section 2035(d)(2) shall require the inclusion of the transferred property (or proportionate amount thereof).

(C) SPECIAL RULE WHERE PROPERTY RETRANSFERRED.—In the case of a transfer described in subparagraph (A)(ii) from the original transferee to the original transferor, the paragraph (1) inclusion (or proportion thereof) shall be reduced by the excess (if any) of—

(i) the fair market value of the property so transferred, over

(ii) the amount of the consideration paid by the original transferor in exchange for such property.

(D) DEFINITIONS.—For purposes of this paragraph—

(i) ORIGINAL TRANSFEROR.—The term "original transferor" means the person making the transfer referred to in paragraph (1).

(ii) ORIGINAL TRANSFEREE.—The term "original transferee" means the person to whom the transfer referred to in paragraph (1) is made. Such term includes any member of the original transferor's family to whom the property is subsequently transferred.

(iii) PARAGRAPH (1) INCLUSION.—The term "paragraph (1) inclusion" means the amount which would have been included in the gross estate of the original transferor under subsection (a) by reason of paragraph (1) (determined without regard to sections 2032 and 2032A) if the original transferor died immediately before the transfer referred to in subparagraph (A). The amount determined under the preceding sentence shall be reduced by the amount (if any) of the taxable gift resulting from the transfer referred to in paragraph (1)(B).

(iv) TRANSFERS TO INCLUDE TERMINATIONS, ETC.—Terminations, lapses, and other changes in any interest in property of the original transferor or original transferee shall be treated as transfers.

(E) CONTINUING INTEREST IN TRANSFERRED PROPERTY MAY NOT BE RETAINED.—A transfer (to which subparagraph (A) would otherwise apply) shall not be taken into account under subparagraph (A) if the original transferor or the original transferee (as the case may be) retains a direct or indirect continuing interest in the property transferred in such transfer.

(5) ADJUSTMENTS.—Appropriate adjustments shall be made in the amount included in the gross estate by reason of this subsection for the value of the retained interest, extraordinary distributions, and changes in the capital structure of the enterprise after the transfer described in paragraph (1).

(6) TREATMENT OF CERTAIN GRANTOR RETAINED INTEREST TRUSTS.—

(A) IN GENERAL.—For purposes of this subsection, any retention of a qualified trust income interest shall be disregarded and the property with respect to which such interest exists shall be treated as held by the transferor while such income interest continues.

(B) QUALIFIED TRUST INCOME INTEREST.—For purposes of subparagraph (A), the term "qualified trust income interest" means any right to receive amounts determined solely by reference to the income from property held in trust if—

(i) such right is for a period not exceeding 10 years,

(ii) the person holding such right transferred the property to the trust, and

(iii) such person is not a trustee of such trust.

(7) EXCEPTIONS.—

(A) IN GENERAL.—Paragraph (1) shall not apply to a transaction solely by reason of 1 or more of the following:

(i) The receipt (or retention) of qualified debt.

(ii) Except as provided in regulations, the existence of an agreement for the sale or lease of goods or other property to be used in the enterprise or the providing of services and—

(I) the agreement is an arm's length agreement for fair market value, and

(II) the agreement does not otherwise involve any change in interests in the enterprise.

(iii) An option or other agreement to buy or sell property at the fair market value of such property as of the time the option is (or the rights under the agreement are) exercised.

(B) LIMITATIONS.—

(i) SERVICES PERFORMED AFTER TRANSFER.—In the case of compensation for services performed after the transfer referred to in paragraph (1)(B), clause (ii) of subparagraph (A) shall not apply if such services were performed under an agreement providing for the performance of services over a period greater than 3 years after the date of the transfer. For purposes of the preceding sentence, the term of any agreement includes any period for which the agreement may be extended at the option of the service provider.

(ii) AMOUNTS MUST NOT BE CONTINGENT ON PROFITS, ETC.—Clause (ii) of subparagraph (A) shall not apply to any amount determined (in whole or in part) by reference to gross receipts, income, profits, or similar items of the enterprise.

(C) QUALIFIED DEBT.—For purposes of this paragraph, except as provided in subparagraph (D), the term "qualified debt" means any indebtedness if—

(i) such indebtedness—

(I) unconditionally requires the payment of a sum certain in money in 1 or more fixed payments on specified dates, and

(II) has a fixed maturity date not more than 15 years from the date of issue (or, in the case of indebtedness secured by real property, not more than 30 years from the date of issue).

(ii) the only other amount payable under such indebtedness is interest determined at—

(I) a fixed rate, or

(II) a rate which bears a fixed relationship to a specified market interest rate,

(iii) the interest payment dates are fixed,

(iv) such indebtedness is not by its terms subordinated to the claims of general creditors,

(v) except in a case where such indebtedness is in default as to interest or principal, such indebtedness does not grant voting rights to the person to whom the debt is owed or place any limitation on the exercise of voting rights by others, and

(vi) such indebtedness—

(I) is not (directly or indirectly) convertible into an interest in the enterprise which would not be qualified debt, and

(II) does not otherwise grant any right to acquire such an interest.

The requirement of clause (i)(I) that the principal be payable on 1 or more specified dates and the requirement of clause (i)(II) shall not apply to indebtedness payable on demand if such indebtedness is issued in return for cash to be used to meet normal business needs of the enterprise.

(D) SPECIAL RULE FOR STARTUP DEBT.—

(i) IN GENERAL.—For purposes of this paragraph, the term "qualified debt" includes any qualified startup debt.

(ii) QUALIFIED STARTUP DEBT.—For purposes of clause (i), the term "qualified startup debt" means any indebtedness if—

(I) such indebtedness unconditionally requires the payment of a sum certain in money,

(II) such indebtedness was received in exchange for cash to be used in any enterprise involving the active conduct of a trade or business,

(III) the person to whom the indebtedness is owed has not at any time (whether before, on, or after the exchange referred to in subclause (II)) transferred any property (including goodwill) which was not cash to the enterprise or transferred customers or other business opportunities to the enterprise,

(IV) the person to whom the indebtedness is owed has not at any time (whether before, on, or after the exchange referred to in subclause (II)) held any interest in the enterprise (including an interest as an officer, director, or employee)[)] which was not qualified startup debt,

(V) any person who (but for subparagraph (A)(i)) would have been an original transferee (as defined in paragraph (4)(C)) participates in the active management (as defined in section 2032A(e)(12)) of the enterprise, and

(VI) such indebtedness meets the requirements of clauses (v) and (vi) of subparagraph (C).

(8) REGULATIONS.—The Secretary shall prescribe such regulations as may be necessary or appropriate to carry out the purposes of this subsection, including such regulations as may be necessary or appropriate to prevent avoidance of the purposes of this subsection through distributions or otherwise.

• **1988, Technical and Miscellaneous Revenue Act of 1988 (P.L. 100-647)**
P.L. 100-647, § 3031(a)(1):

Amended Code Sec. 2036(c)(4). **Effective** in cases where the transfer referred to in section 2036(c)(1)(B) of the 1986 Code is on or after 6-21-88. Prior to amendment, Code Sec. 2036(c)(4) read as follows:

ESTATE TAX—GROSS ESTATE

(4) COORDINATION WITH SECTION 2035.—For purposes of applying section 2035, any transfer of the retained interest referred to in paragraph (1) shall be treated as a transfer of an interest in the transferred property referred to in paragraph (1).

P.L. 100-647, § 3031(b):

Amended Code Sec. 2036(c) by adding at the end thereof a new paragraph (6). For the **effective** date, see Act Sec. 3031(h), below.

P.L. 100-647, § 3031(b)[c]:

Amended Code Sec. 2036(c) by adding at the end thereof new paragraphs (7)-(8). For the **effective** date, see Act Sec. 3031(h), below.

P.L. 100-647, § 3031(d):

Amended Code Sec. 2036(c)(3)(C) by striking out "An individual" and inserting in lieu thereof "Except as provided in regulations, an individual". For the **effective** date, see Act Sec. 3031(h), below.

P.L. 100-647, § 3031(e):

Amended Code Sec. 2036(c)(1)(B) by striking out "while" and all that follows down through the comma at the end of such subparagraph and inserting in lieu thereof "while retaining an interest in the income of, or rights in, the enterprise,". For the **effective** date, see Act Sec. 3031(h), below. Prior to amendment, Code Sec. 2036(c)(1)(B) read as follows:

(B) such person in effect transfers after December 17, 1987, property having a disproportionately large share of the potential appreciation in such person's interest in the enterprise while retaining a disproportionately large share in the income of, or rights in, the enterprise,

P.L. 100-647, § 3031(g)(1):

Amended Code Sec. 2036(c)(2). For the **effective** date, see Act Sec. 3031(h), below. Prior to amendment, Code Sec. 2036(c)(2) read as follows:

(2) SPECIAL RULE FOR SALES TO FAMILY MEMBERS.—The exception contained in subsection (a) for a bona fide sale shall not apply to a transfer described in paragraph (1) if such transfer is to a member of the transferor's family.

P.L. 100-647, § 3031(g)(2):

Amended Code Sec. 2036(c)(5). For the **effective** date, see Act Sec. 3031(h), below. Prior to amendment, Code Sec. 2036(c)(5) read as follows:

(5) COORDINATION WITH SECTION 2043.—In lieu of applying section 2043, appropriate adjustments shall be made for the value of the retained interest.

P.L. 100-647, § 3031(h), provides:

(h) EFFECTIVE DATE.—

(1) IN GENERAL.—Except as provided in this subsection, any amendment made by this section shall take effect as if included in the provisions of the Revenue Act of 1987 to which such amendment relates.

(2) SUBSECTION (a).—The amendments made by subsection (a) shall apply in cases where the transfer referred to in section 2036(c)(1)(B) of the 1986 Code is on or after June 21, 1988.

(3) SUBSECTION (f).—If an amount is included in the gross estate of a decedent under section 2036 of the 1986 Code other than solely by reason of section 2036(c) of the 1986 Code, the amendments made by subsection (f) shall apply to such amount only with respect to property transferred after the date of the enactment of this Act.

(4) CORRECTION PERIOD.—If section 2036(c)(1) of the 1986 Code would (but for this paragraph) apply to any interest arising from a transaction entered into during the period beginning after December 17, 1987, and ending before January 1, 1990, such section shall not apply to such interest if—

(A) during such period, such actions are taken as are necessary to have such section 2036(c)(1) not apply to such transaction (and any such interest), or

(B) the original transferor and his spouse on January 1, 1990 (or, if earlier, the date of the original transferor's death), does not hold any interest in the enterprise involved.

(5) CLARIFICATION OF EFFECTIVE DATE.—For purposes of section 10402(b) of the Revenue Act of 1987, with respect to property transferred on or before December 17, 1987—

(A) any failure to exercise a right of conversion,

(B) any failure to pay dividends, and

(c) [C] failures to exercise other rights specified in regulations,

shall not be treated as a subsequent transfer.

- **1987, Revenue Act of 1987 (P.L. 100-203)**

P.L. 100-203, § 10402(a):

Amended Code Sec. 2036 by redesignating subsection (c) as subsection (d) and by inserting after subsection (b) new subsection (c). **Effective** for estates of decedents dying after 12-31-87, but only in the case of property transferred after 12-17-87.

P.L. 100-203, § 10402(a):

Amended Code Sec. 2036 by redesignating subsection (c) as subsection (d). **Effective** for estates of decedents dying after 12-31-87, but only in the case of property transferred after 12-17-87.

[Sec. 2037]

SEC. 2037. TRANSFERS TAKING EFFECT AT DEATH.

[Sec. 2037(a)]

(a) GENERAL RULE.—The value of the gross estate shall include the value of all property to the extent of any interest therein of which the decedent has at any time after September 7, 1916, made a transfer (except in case of a bona fide sale for an adequate and full consideration in money or money's worth), by trust or otherwise, if—

(1) possession or enjoyment of the property can, through ownership of such interest, be obtained only by surviving the decedent, and

(2) the decedent has retained a reversionary interest in the property (but in the case of a transfer made before October 8, 1949, only if such reversionary interest arose by the express terms of the instrument of transfer), and the value of such reversionary interest immediately before the death of the decedent exceeds 5 percent of the value of such property.

Amendments

- **1962, Revenue Act of 1962 (P.L. 87-834)**

P.L. 87-834, § 18(a)(2):

Amended Code Sec. 2037(a) by deleting "(except real property situated outside of the United States)". **Effective**, generally, for estates of decedents dying after 10-16-62. For exceptions, see Act Sec. 18(b) in the amendment notes for Code Sec. 2031(a).

[Sec. 2037(b)]

(b) SPECIAL RULES.—For purposes of this section, the term "reversionary interest" includes a possibility that property transferred by the decedent—

(1) may return to him or his estate, or

(2) may be subject to a power of disposition by him,

but such term does not include a possibility that the income alone from such property may return to him or become subject to a power of disposition by him. The value of a reversionary interest immediately before the death of the decedent shall be determined (without regard to the fact of the decedent's death) by usual methods of valuation, including the use of tables of mortality and actuarial principles, under regulations prescribed by the Secretary. In determining the value of a possibility that property may be subject to a power of disposition by the decedent, such possibility shall be valued as if it were a possibility that such property may return to the decedent or his estate. Notwithstanding the foregoing, an interest so transferred shall not be included in the decedent's gross estate under this section if possession or enjoyment of the property could have been obtained by any beneficiary during the decedent's life through the exercise of a general power of appointment (as defined in section 2041) which in fact was exercisable immediately before the decedent's death.

Amendments

- **1976, Tax Reform Act of 1976 (P.L. 94-455)**

P.L. 94-455, § 1906(b)(13)(A):

Amended 1954 Code by substituting "Secretary" for "Secretary or his delegate" each place it appeared. **Effective** 2-1-77.

[Sec. 2038]

SEC. 2038. REVOCABLE TRANSFERS.

[Sec. 2038(a)]

(a) IN GENERAL.—The value of the gross estate shall include the value of all property—

(1) TRANSFERS AFTER JUNE 22, 1936.—To the extent of any interest therein of which the decedent has at any time made a transfer (except in case of a bona fide sale for an adequate and full consideration in money or money's worth), by trust or otherwise, where the enjoyment thereof was subject at the date of his death to any change through the exercise of a power (in whatever capacity exercisable) by the decedent alone or

ESTATE TAX—GROSS ESTATE

by the decedent in conjunction with any other person (without regard to when or from what source the decedent acquired such power), to alter, amend, revoke, or terminate, or where any such power is relinquished during the 3-year period ending on the date of the decedent's death.

(2) TRANSFERS ON OR BEFORE JUNE 22, 1936.—To the extent of any interest therein of which the decedent has at any time made a transfer (except in case of a bona fide sale for an adequate and full consideration in money or money's worth), by trust or otherwise, where the enjoyment thereof was subject at the date of his death to any change through the exercise of a power, either by the decedent alone or in conjunction with any person, to alter, amend, or revoke, or where the decedent relinquished any such power during the 3-year period ending on the date of the decedent's death. Except in the case of transfers made after June 22, 1936, no interest of the decedent of which he has made a transfer shall be included in the gross estate under paragraph (1) unless it is includible under this paragraph.

Amendments

• **1976, Tax Reform Act of 1976 (P.L. 94-455)**

P.L. 94-455, § 2001(c)(1)(K), (d)(1):

Substituted "during the 3-year period ending on the date of the decedent's death" for "in contemplation of decedent's death" in Code Sec. 2038(a)(1); and substituted "during the 3-year period ending on the date of the decedent's death" for "in contemplation of his death" in Code Sec. 2038(a)(2). **Effective** for estates of decedents dying after 12-31-76, except that the amendments shall not apply to transfers made before 1-1-77.

• **1962, Revenue Act of 1962 (P.L. 87-834)**

P.L. 87-834, § 18(a)(2):

Amended Code Sec. 2038(a) by deleting "(except real property situated outside of the United States)". **Effective**, generally, for estates of decedents dying after 10-16-62. For exceptions, see Act Sec. 18(b) in the amendment notes for Code Sec. 2031(a).

[Sec. 2038(b)]

(b) DATE OF EXISTENCE OF POWER.—For purposes of this section, the power to alter, amend, revoke, or terminate shall be considered to exist on the date of the decedent's death even though the exercise of the power is subject to a precedent giving of notice or even though the alteration, amendment, revocation, or termination takes effect only on the expiration of a stated period after the exercise of the power, whether or not on or before the date of the decedent's death notice has been given or the power has been exercised. In such cases proper adjustment shall be made representing the interests which would have been excluded from the power if the decedent had lived, and for such purpose, if the notice has not been given or the power has not been exercised on or before the date of his death, such notice shall be considered to have been given, or the power exercised, on the date of his death.

[Sec. 2038(c)—Repealed]

Amendments

• **1976, Tax Reform Act of 1976 (P.L. 94-455)**

P.L. 94-455, § 1902(a)(3), (c)(1):

Repealed Code Sec. 2038(c). **Effective** for estates of decedents dying after 10-4-76. Prior to repeal, Code Sec. 2038(c) read as follows:

(c) EFFECT OF DISABILITY IN CERTAIN CASES.—For purposes of this section, in the case of a decedent who was (for a continuous period beginning not less than 3 months before December 31, 1947, and ending with his death) under a mental disability to relinquish a power, the term "power" shall not include a power the relinquishment of which on or after January 1, 1940, and on or before December 31, 1947, would, by reason of section 1000(e) of the Internal Revenue Code of 1939, be deemed not to be a transfer of property for purposes of chapter 4 of the Internal Revenue Code of 1939.

• **1959 (P.L. 86-141)**

P.L. 86-141, § [1]:

Amended 1954 Code Sec. 2038 by adding Sec. 2038(c). **Effective** only with respect to estates of decedents dying after 8-16-54. No interest shall be allowed or paid on any overpayment resulting from the application of the amendment with respect to any payment made before the date of the enactment of the Act [8-7-59.—CCH].

[Sec. 2039]

SEC. 2039. ANNUITIES.

[Sec. 2039(a)]

(a) GENERAL.—The gross estate shall include the value of an annuity or other payment receivable by any beneficiary by reason of surviving the decedent under any form of contract or agreement entered into after March 3, 1931 (other than as insurance under policies on the life of the decedent), if, under such contract or agreement, an annuity or other payment was payable to the decedent, or the decedent possessed the right to receive such annuity or payment, either alone or in conjunction with another for his life or for any period not ascertainable without reference to his death or for any period which does not in fact end before his death.

[Sec. 2039(b)]

(b) AMOUNT INCLUDIBLE.—Subsection (a) shall apply to only such part of the value of the annuity or other payment receivable under such contract or agreement as is proportionate to that part of the purchase price therefor contributed by the decedent. For purposes of this section, any contribution by the decedent's employer or former employer to the purchase price of such contract or agreement (whether or not to an employee's trust or fund forming part of a pension, annuity, retirement, bonus or profit-sharing plan) shall be considered to be contributed by the decedent if made by reason of his employment.

[Sec. 2039(c)—Repealed]

Amendments

• **1986, Tax Reform Act of 1986 (P.L. 99-514)**

P.L. 99-514, § 1852(e)(1)(A):

Repealed Code Sec. 2039(c). **Effective** for estates of decedents dying after 10-22-86. Prior to repeal, Code Sec. 2039(c) read as follows:

(c) EXCEPTION OF CERTAIN ANNUITY INTERESTS CREATED BY COMMUNITY PROPERTY LAWS.—

(1) IN GENERAL.—In the case of an employee on whose behalf contributions or payments were made by his employer or former employer under a trust, plan, or contract to which this subsection applies, if the spouse of such employee predeceases such employee, then notwithstanding any provision of law, there shall be excluded from the gross estate of such spouse the value of any interest of such spouse in such trust, plan, or contract, to the extent such interest—

(A) is attributable to such contributions or payments, and

(B) arises solely by reason of such spouse's interest in community income under the community property laws of a State.

(2) TRUSTS, PLANS, AND CONTRACTS TO WHICH SUBSECTION APPLIES.—This subsection shall apply to—

(A) any trust, plan, or contract which at the time of the decedent's separation from employment (by death or otherwise), or if earlier, at the time of termination of the plan—

(i) formed part of a plan which met the requirements of section 401(a), or

(ii) was purchased pursuant to a plan described in section 403(a), or

(B) a retirement annuity contract purchased for an employee by an employer which is—

(i) an organization referred to in clause (ii) or (vi) of section 170(b)(1)(A), or

(ii) a religious organization (other than a trust) exempt from taxation under section 501(a).

(3) AMOUNT CONTRIBUTED BY EMPLOYEE.—For purposes of this subsection—

(A) contributions or payments made by the decedent's employer or former employer under a trust, plan, or contract described in paragraph (2)(A) shall not be considered to be contributed by the decedent, and

(B) contributions or payments made by the decedent's employer or former employer toward the purchase of an annuity contract described in paragraph (2)(B) shall not be considered to be contributed by the decedent to the extent excludable from gross income under section 403(b).

• **1984, Deficit Reduction Act of 1984 (P.L. 98-369)**

P.L. 98-369, § 525(a):

Amended Code Sec. 2039 by striking out subsections (c)-(g) and inserting in lieu thereof subsection (c). **Effective** for the estates of decedents dying after 12-31-84. The amendment does not, however, apply to the estate of any decedent who was a

ESTATE TAX—GROSS ESTATE

participant in any plan who was in pay status on 12-31-84, and who irrevocably elected before 7-18-84 the form of benefit. Prior to amendment, subsection (c) read as follows:

(c) Exemption of Annuities Under Certain Trusts and Plans.—Subject to the limitation of subsection (g), notwithstanding any other provision of this section or of any provision of law, there shall be excluded from the gross estate the value of an annuity or other payment (other than an amount described in subsection (f)) receivable by any beneficiary (other than the executor) under—

(1) An employees' trust (or under a contract purchased by an employees' trust) forming part of a pension, stock bonus, or profit-sharing plan which, at the time of the decedent's separation from employment (whether by death or otherwise), or at the time of termination of the plan if earlier, met the requirements of section 401(a);

(2) A retirement annuity contract purchased by an employer (and not by an employees' trust) pursuant to a plan which, at the time of decedent's separation from employment (by death or otherwise), or at the time of termination of the plan if earlier, was a plan described in section 403(a);

(3) A retirement annuity contract purchased for an employee by an employer which is an organization referred to in section 170(b)(1)(A)(ii) or (vi), or which is a religious organization (other than a trust), and which is exempt from tax under section 501(a); or

(4) Chapter 73 of title 10 of the United States Code.

If such amounts payable after the death of the decedent under a plan described in paragraph (1) or (2), under a contract described in paragraph (3), or under chapter 73 of title 10 of the United States Code are attributable to any extent to payments or contributions made by the decedent, no exclusion shall be allowed for that part of the value of such amounts in the proportion that the total payments or contributions made by the decedent bears to the total payments or contributions made. For purposes of this subsection, contributions or payments made by the decedent's employer or former employer under a trust or plan described in paragraph (1) or (2) shall not be considered to be contributed by the decedent, and contributions or payments made by the decedent's employer or former employer toward the purchase of an annuity contract described in paragraph (3) shall, to the extent excludable from gross income under section 403(b), not be considered to be contributed by the decedent. The subsection shall apply to all decedents dying after December 31, 1953. For purposes of this subsection, contributions or payments on behalf of the decedent while he was an employee within the meaning of section 401(c)(1) made under a trust or plan described in paragraph (1) or (2) shall, to the extent allowable as a deduction under section 404, be considered to be made by a person other than the decedent and, to the extent not so allowable, shall be considered to be made by the decedent. For purposes of this subsection, amounts payable under chapter 73 of title 10 of the United States Code are attributable to payments or contributions made by the decedent only to the extent of amounts deposited by him pursuant to section 1438 or 1452(d) of such title 10. For purposes of this subsection, any deductible employee contributions (within the meaning of paragraph (5) of section 72(o)) shall be considered as made by a person other than the decedent.

• **1982, Tax Equity and Fiscal Responsibility Act of 1982 (P.L. 97-248)**

P.L. 97-248, § 245(b):

Amended Code Sec. 2039(c) by striking out "Notwithstanding the provisions of this section", and inserting "Subject to the limitation of subsection (g), notwithstanding any other provision of this section". **Effective** for estates of decedents dying after 12-31-82, except that such amendments shall not apply to the estate of any decedent who was a participant in any plan, who was in pay status on 12-31-82, and who irrevocably elected before 1-1-83, the form of benefit [effective date changed by P.L. 98-369].

• **1981, Economic Recovery Tax Act of 1981 (P.L. 97-34)**

P.L. 97-34, § 311(d)(1):

Amended Code Sec. 2039(c) by adding at the end the following new sentence: "For purposes of this subsection, any deductible employee contributions (within the meaning of paragraph (5) of section 72(o)) shall be made by a person other than the decedent.". **Effective** for estates of decedents dying after 12-31-81 [effective date changed by P.L. 97-448, § 103(c)(11).—CCH]. The transitional rule provides that, for purposes of the 1954 Code, any amount allowed as a deduction under section 220 of the Code (as in effect before its repeal by P.L. 97-34) shall be treated as if it were allowed by section 219 of the Code.

• **1978, Revenue Act of 1978 (P.L. 95-600)**

P.L. 95-600, § 142(a):

Amended the first sentence of Code Sec. 2039(c) by substituting "(other than an amount described in subsection (f))" for "(other than a lump sum distribution described in section 402(e)(4), determined without regard to the next to the last sentence of section 402(e)(4)(A))". **Effective** for estates of decedents dying after 12-31-78.

• **1976, Tax Reform Act of 1976 (P.L. 94-455)**

P.L. 94-455, § 2009(c)(2):

Substituted the fifth sentence of Code Sec. 2039(c). **Effective** for estates of decedents dying after 12-31-76. Prior to amendment, such sentence read as follows:

For purposes of this subsection, contributions or payments on behalf of the decedent while he was an employee within the meaning of section 401(c)(1) made under a trust or plan described in paragraph (1) or (2) shall be considered to be contributions or payments made by the decedent.

P.L. 94-455, § 2009(c)(3):

Inserted "(other than a lump sum distribution described in section 402(e)(4), determined without regard to the next to the last sentence of section 402(e)(4)(A))" after "payment" in the first sentence of Code Sec. 2039(c). **Effective** for estates of decedents dying after 12-31-76.

• **1974, Employee Retirement Income Security Act of 1974 (P.L. 93-406)**

P.L. 93-406, § 2008(b)(4):

Amended Code Sec. 2039(c) by substituting "section 1438 or 1452(d)" for "section 1438". **Effective** for tax years ending on or after 9-21-72.

• **1969, Tax Reform Act of 1969 (P.L. 91-172)**

P.L. 91-172, § 101(j)(23):

Amended Code Sec. 2039(c)(3) by substituting "section 170(b)(1)(A)(ii) or (vi), or which is a religious organization (other than a trust)," for "section 503(b)(1), (2), or (3),". **Effective** 1-1-70.

• **1966 (P.L. 89-365)**

P.L. 89-365, § 2:

Amended Code Sec. 2039(c) by striking out "or" at the end of paragraph (2), by substituting "; or" for the period at the end of paragraph (3), by adding a new paragraph (4), by substituting ", under a contract described in paragraph (3), or under chapter 73 of title 10 of the United States Code" for "or under a contract described in paragraph (3)" in the second sentence, and by adding the last sentence. **Effective** with respect to decedents dying after 12-31-65.

• **1962, Self-Employed Individuals Tax Retirement Act of 1962 (P.L. 87-792)**

P.L. 87-792, § 7:

Amended Code Sec. 2039 by striking out in subsection (c)(2) "met the requirements of section 401(a)(3), (4), (5), and (6)" and inserting in lieu thereof "was a plan described in section 403(a)"; and by adding after the period in line 28 of subsection (c) a new sentence. **Effective** 1-1-63.

• **1958, Technical Amendments Act of 1958 (P.L. 85-866)**

P.L. 85-866, § 23(e)(1):

Struck out the word "or" at the end of paragraph (1) of Sec. 2039(c), struck out the period at the end of paragraph (2) of Sec. 2039(c) and inserted in lieu thereof ", (4), (5), and (6); or". **Effective** for the estates of decedents dying after 12-31-57.

P.L. 85-866, § 23(e)(2):

Added paragraph (3) to Sec. 2039(c). **Effective** for the estates of decedents dying after 12-31-57.

P.L. 85-866, § 23(e)(3):

Added after the phrase "under a plan described in paragraph (1) or (2)" in the second sentence of Sec. 2039(c) the phrase "or under a contract described in paragraph (3)". **Effective** for the estates of decedents dying after 12-31-57.

P.L. 85-866, § 23(e)(4):

Amended the second to last sentence of Sec. 2039(c). **Effective** for the estates of decedents dying after 12-31-57. Prior to amendment, this sentence read as follows:

For purposes of this subsection, contributions or payments made by the decedent's employer or former employer under a trust or plan described in this subsection shall not be considered to be contributed by the decedent.

P.L. 85-866, § 67(a):

Amended Code Sec. 2039(c)(2) by striking out "section 401(a)(3)" and substituting in lieu thereof "section 401(a)(3), (4), (5), and (6)". **Effective** with respect to estates of decedents dying after 12-31-53.

[Sec. 2039(d)—Stricken]

Amendments

• **1984, Deficit Reduction Act of 1984 (P.L. 98-369)**

P.L. 98-369, § 525(a):

Amended Code Sec. 2039 by striking out subsection (d). **Effective** for the estates of decedents dying after 12-31-84. The amendment does not, however, apply to the estate of any decedent who was a participant in any plan who was in pay status on 12-31-84, and who irrevocably elected before 7-18-84 the form of benefit. Prior to being stricken, Code Sec. 2039(d) read as follows:

(d) EXEMPTION OF CERTAIN ANNUITY INTERESTS CREATED BY COMMUNITY PROPERTY LAWS.—In the case of an employee on whose behalf contributions or payments were made by his employer or former employer under a trust or plan described in subsection (c)(1) or (2), or toward the purchase of a contract described in subsection (c)(3), which under subsection (c) are not considered as contributed by the employee, if the spouse of such employee predeceases him, then, notwithstanding the provisions of this section or of any other provision of law, there shall be excluded from the gross estate of such spouse the value of any interest of such spouse in such trust or plan or such contract, to the extent such interest—

(1) is attributable to such contributions or payments, and

(2) arises solely by reason of such spouse's interest in community income under the community property laws of a State.

• **1972 (P.L. 92-580)**

P.L. 92-580, § 2(a):

Added Code Sec. 2039(d). **Effective** with respect to estates of decedents for which the period prescribed for filing of a claim for credit or refund of an overpayment of estate tax ends on or after 10-27-72. No interest shall be allowed or paid on any overpayment of estate tax resulting from the application of the new section for any period prior to 4-25-73.

ESTATE TAX—GROSS ESTATE

[Sec. 2039(e)—Stricken]

Amendments

• **1986, Tax Reform Act of 1986 (P.L. 99-514)**

P.L. 99-514, §1848(d):

Amended Code Sec. 2039(e) by striking out "or a bond described in paragraph (3)" in the second sentence. **Effective** as if included in the provision of P.L. 98-369 to which it relates. Prior to amendment, Code Sec. 2039(e) read as follows:

(e) EXCLUSION OF INDIVIDUAL RETIREMENT ACCOUNTS, ETC.—Subject to the limitation of subsection (g), notwithstanding any other provision of this section or of any other provision of law, there shall be excluded from the value of the gross estate the value of an annuity receivable by any beneficiary (other than the executor) under—

(1) an individual retirement account described in section 408(a), or

(2) an individual retirement annuity described in section 408(b).

If any payment to an account described in paragraph (1) or for an annuity described in paragraph (2) or a bond described in paragraph (3) [sic—paragraph (3) is repealed] was not allowable as a deduction under section 219 and was not a rollover contribution described in section 402(a)(5), 403(a)(4), section 403(b)(8) (but only to the extent such contribution is attributable to a distribution from a contract described in section (c)(3)), or 408(d)(3), the preceding sentence shall not apply to that portion of the value of the amount receivable under such account or annuity (as the case may be) which bears the same ratio to the total value of the amount so receivable as the total amount which was paid to or for such account or annuity and which was not allowable as a deduction under section 219 and was not such a rollover contribution bears to the total amount paid to or for such account or annuity. For purposes of this subsection, the term "annuity" means an annuity contract or other arrangement providing for a series of substantially equal periodic payments to be made to a beneficiary (other than the executor) for his life or over a period extending for at least 36 months after the date of the decedent's death.

• **1984, Deficit Reduction Act of 1984 (P.L. 98-369)**

P.L. 98-369, §491(d)(34):

Amended Code Sec. 2039(e) by striking out paragraph (3), by striking out ", or" at the end of paragraph (2) and inserting in lieu thereof a period, by adding "or" at the end of paragraph (1), by striking out "405(d)(3), 408(d)(3), or 409(b)(3)(C)" and inserting in lieu thereof "or 408(d)(3)", and by striking out ", annuity, or bond" each place it appears and inserting in lieu thereof "or annuity". **Effective** for obligations issued after 12-31-83. Prior to amendment Code Sec. 2039(e)(3) read as follows:

(3) a retirement bond described in section 409(a).

P.L. 98-369, §525(a):

Amended Code Sec. 2039 by striking out subsection (e). **Effective** for the estates of decedents dying after 12-31-84. The amendment does not, however, apply to the estate of any decedent who was a participant in any plan who was in pay status on 12-31-84, and who irrevocably elected before 7-18-84 the form of benefit. Prior to being stricken, Code Sec. 2039(e) read as follows:

(e) EXCLUSION OF INDIVIDUAL RETIREMENT ACCOUNTS, ETC.—Subject to the limitation of subsection (g), notwithstanding any other provision of this section or of any other provision of law, there shall be excluded from the value of the gross estate the value of an annuity receivable by any beneficiary (other than the executor) under—

(1) an individual retirement account described in section 408(a), or

(2) an individual retirement annuity described in section 408(b).

If any payment to an account described in paragraph (1) or for an annuity described in paragraph (2) was not allowable as a deduction under section 219 and was not a rollover contribution described in section 402(a)(5), 403(a)(4), section 403(b)(8) (but only to the extent such contribution is attributable to a distribution from a contract described in subsection (c)(3)), or 408(d)(3), the preceding sentence shall not apply to that portion of the value of the amount receivable under such account or annuity (as the case may be) which bears the same ratio to the total value of the amount so receivable as the total amount which was paid to or for such account or annuity and which was not allowable as a deduction under section 219 and was not such a rollover contribution bears to the total amount paid to or for such account or annuity. For purposes of this subsection, the term "annuity" means an annuity contract or other arrangement providing for a series of substantially equal periodic payments to be made to a beneficiary (other than the executor) for his life or over a period extending for at least 36 months after the date of the decedent's death.

• **1982, Tax Equity and Fiscal Responsibility Act of 1982 (P.L. 97-248)**

P.L. 97-248, §245(b):

Amended Code Sec. 2039(e) by striking out "Notwithstanding the provisions of this section", and inserting "Subject to the limitation of subsection (g), notwithstanding any other provision of this section". **Effective** for estates of decedents dying after 12-31-82, except that such amendment shall not apply to the estate of any decedent who was a participant in any plan who was in pay status on 12-31-82, and who irrevocably elected before 1-1-83 the form of benefit [**effective** date changed by P.L. 98-369].

• **1981, Economic Recovery Tax Act of 1981 (P.L. 97-34)**

P.L. 97-34, §311(h)(4):

Amended Code Sec. 2039(e) by striking out "section 219 or 220" each place it appears and inserting "section 219". **Effective** for estates of decedents dying after 12-31-81 [**effective** date changed by P.L. 97-448, §103(c)(11).—CCH]. The transitional rule provides that, for purposes of the 1954 Code, any amount allowed as a deduction under section 220 of the Code (as in effect before its repeal by P.L. 97-34) shall be treated as if it were allowed by Code Sec. 219.

P.L. 97-34, §313(b)(3):

Amended Code Sec. 2039(e) by inserting "405(d)(3)" after "a contract described in subsection (c)(3))," **Effective** for redemptions after 8-13-81 in tax years ending after 8-31-81.

• **1978, Revenue Act of 1978 (P.L. 95-600)**

P.L. 95-600, §156(c)(4):

Amended the second sentence of Code Sec. 2039(e) by adding after "403(a)(4)" the following: "section 403(b)(8) (but only to the extent such contribution is attributable to a distribution from a contract described in subsection (c)(3))," **Effective** for distributions or transfers made after 12-31-77, in tax years beginning after such date [**effective** date changed by P.L. 96-222, §101(a)(13)(A).—CCH].

P.L. 95-600, §702(j)(1):

Amended the second sentence of Code Sec. 2039(e) by adding "or 220" after "section 219" in the two places the latter phrase appears. **Effective** for estates of decedents dying after 1976.

• **1976, Tax Reform Act of 1976 (P.L. 94-455)**

P.L. 94-455, §2009(c)(1), (e)(3):

Added Code Sec. 2039(e). **Effective** for estates of decedents dying after 12-31-76.

[Sec. 2039(f)—Stricken]

Amendments

• **1984, Deficit Reduction Act of 1984 (P.L. 98-369)**

P.L. 98-369, §525(a):

Amended Code Sec. 2039 by striking out subsection (f). **Effective** for estates of decedents dying after 12-31-84. The amendment does not, however, apply to the estate of any decedent who was a participant in any plan who was in pay status on 12-31-84, and who irrevocably elected before 7-18-84 the form of benefit. Prior to being stricken, Code Sec. 2039(f) read as follows:

(f) LUMP SUM DISTRIBUTIONS—

(1) IN GENERAL—An amount is described in this subsection if—

(A) it is a lump sum distribution described in section 402(e)(4) (determined without regard to the third sentence of section 402(e)(4)(A)), or

(B) it is an amount attributable to accumulated deductible employee contributions (as defined in section 72(o)(5)(B)) in any plan taken into account for purposes of determining whether the distribution described in subparagraph (A) qualifies as a lump sum distribution.

(2) EXCEPTION WHERE RECIPIENT ELECTS NOT TO TAKE 10-YEAR AVERAGING—An amount described in paragraph (1) shall be treated as not described in this subsection if the recipient elects irrevocably (at such time and in such manner as the Secretary may by regulations prescribe) to treat the distribution as taxable under section 402(a) (without the application of paragraph (2) thereof) except to the extent that section 402(e)(4)(J) applies to such distribution.

• **1983, Technical Corrections Act of 1982 (P.L. 97-448)**

P.L. 97-448, §103(c)(9)(A):

Amended Code Sec. 2039(f)(1). **Effective** with respect to tax years beginning after 12-31-81. Prior to amendment, Code Sec. 2039(f)(1) read as follows:

(1) IN GENERAL.—An amount is described in this subsection if it is a lump sum distribution described in section 402(e)(4) (determined without regard to the next to the last sentence of section 402(e)(4)(A)).

P.L. 97-448, §103(c)(9)(B):

Amended Code Sec. 2039(f)(2) by striking out "A lump sum distribution" and inserting in lieu thereof "An amount". **Effective** as if included in the provision of P.L. 97-34 to which it relates.

• **1980, Technical Corrections Act of 1979 (P.L. 96-222)**

P.L. 96-222, §101(a)(8)(B):

Amended Code Sec. 2039(f)(2) by striking out "without the application of paragraph (2) thereof" and inserting "(without the application of paragraph (2) thereof), except to the extent that section 402(e)(4)(J) applies to such distribution". **Effective** for estates of decedents dying after 12-31-78.

• **1978, Revenue Act of 1978 (P.L. 95-600)**

P.L. 95-600, §142(b):

Added Code Sec. 2039(f). **Effective** for estates of decedents dying after 12-31-78.

[Sec. 2039(g)—Stricken]

(g) $100,000 LIMITATION ON EXCLUSIONS UNDER SUBSECTIONS (c) AND (e).—The aggregate amount excluded from the gross estate of any decedent under subsections (c) and (e) of this section shall not exceed $100,000.

• **1982, Tax Equity and Fiscal Responsibility Act of 1982 (P.L. 97-248)**

P.L. 97-248, §245(a):

Amended Code Sec. 2039 by adding subsection (g). **Effective** for estates of decedents dying after 12-31-82.

Amendments

• **1984, Deficit Reduction Act of 1984 (P.L. 98-369)**

P.L. 98-369, §525(a):

Amended Code Sec. 2039 by striking out subsection (g). **Effective** for estates of decedents dying after 12-31-84. The amendment does not, however, apply to the estate of any decedent who was a participant in any plan who was in pay status on 12-31-84, and who irrevocably elected before 7-18-84 the form of benefit.

Prior to being stricken, Code Sec. 2039(g) read as follows:

ESTATE TAX—GROSS ESTATE

[Sec. 2040]

SEC. 2040. JOINT INTERESTS.

[Sec. 2040(a)]

(a) GENERAL RULE.—The value of the gross estate shall include the value of all property to the extent of the interest therein held as joint tenants with right of survivorship by the decedent and any other person, or as tenants by the entirety by the decedent and spouse, or deposited, with any person carrying on the banking business, in their joint names and payable to either or the survivor, except such part thereof as may be shown to have originally belonged to such other person and never to have been received or acquired by the latter from the decedent for less than an adequate and full consideration in money or money's worth: *Provided*, That where such property or any part thereof, or part of the consideration with which such property was acquired, is shown to have been at any time acquired by such other person from the decedent for less than an adequate and full consideration in money or money's worth, there shall be excepted only such part of the value of such property as is proportionate to the consideration furnished by such other person: *Provided further*, That where any property has been acquired by gift, bequest, devise, or inheritance, as a tenancy by the entirety by the decedent and spouse, then to the extent of one-half of the value thereof, or, where so acquired by the decedent and any other person as joint tenants with right of survivorship and their interests are not otherwise specified or fixed by law, then to the extent of the value of a fractional part to be determined by dividing the value of the property by the number of joint tenants with right of survivorship.

Amendments

• **1981, Economic Recovery Tax Act of 1981 (P.L. 97-34)**

P.L. 97-34, §403(c)(2):

Amended Code Sec. 2040(a) by inserting "with right of survivorship" after "joint tenants" each place it appears. **Effective** for estates of decedents dying after 12-31-81.

• **1976, Tax Reform Act of 1976 (P.L. 94-455)**

P.L. 94-455, §2002(c)(3), (d)(3):

Substituted "(a) GENERAL RULE.—The value" for "The value" in Code Sec. 2040. **Effective** for joint interests created after 12-31-76.

• **1962, Revenue Act of 1962 (P.L. 87-834)**

P.L. 87-834, §18(a)(2):

Amended Code Sec. 2040 by deleting "(except real property situated outside of the United States)". **Effective**, generally, for estates of decedents dying after 10-16-62. For exceptions, see Act Sec. 18(b) in the amendment notes for Code Sec. 2031(a).

[Sec. 2040(b)]

(b) CERTAIN JOINT INTERESTS OF HUSBAND AND WIFE.—

(1) INTERESTS OF SPOUSE EXCLUDED FROM GROSS ESTATE.—Notwithstanding subsection (a), in the case of any qualified joint interest, the value included in the gross estate with respect to such interest by reason of this section is one-half of the value of such qualified joint interest.

(2) QUALIFIED JOINT INTEREST DEFINED.—For purposes of paragraph (1), the term "qualified joint interest" means any interest in property held by the decedent and the decedent's spouse as—

(A) tenants by the entirety, or

(B) joint tenants with right of survivorship, but only if the decedent and the spouse of the decedent are the only joint tenants.

Amendments

• **1981, Economic Recovery Tax Act of 1981 (P.L. 97-34)**

P.L. 97-34, §403(c)(1):

Amended Code Sec. 2040(b)(2). **Effective** for estates of decedents dying after 12-31-81. Prior to amendment, Code Sec. 2040(b)(2) read as follows:

(2) QUALIFIED JOINT INTEREST DEFINED.—For purposes of paragraph (1), the term "qualified joint interest" means any interest in property held by the decedent and the decedent's spouse as joint tenants or as tenants by the entirety, but only if—

(A) such joint interest was created by the decedent, the decedent's spouse, or both,

(B)(i) in the case of personal property, the creation of such joint interest constituted in whole or in part a gift for purposes of chapter 12, or

(ii) in the case of real property, an election under section 2515 applies with respect to the creation of such joint interest, and

(C) in the case of a joint tenancy, only the decedent and the decedent's spouse are joint tenants.

• **1976, Tax Reform Act of 1976 (P.L. 94-455)**

P.L. 94-455, §2002(c)(1), (d)(3):

Added Code Sec. 2040(b). **Effective** for joint interests created after 12-31-76.

[Sec. 2040(c)—Repealed]

Amendments

• **1981, Economic Recovery Tax Act of 1981 (P.L. 97-34)**

P.L. 97-34, §403(c)(3)(A):

Repealed Code Sec. 2040(c). **Effective** for estates of decedents dying after 12-31-81. Prior to its repeal, Code Sec. 2040(c) read as follows:

(c) VALUE WHERE SPOUSE OF DECEDENT MATERIALLY PARTICIPATED IN FARM OR OTHER BUSINESS.—

(1) IN GENERAL.—Notwithstanding subsection (a), in the case of an eligible joint interest in section 2040(c) property, the value included in the gross estate with respect to such interest by reason of this section shall be—

(A) the value of such interest, reduced by

(B) the sum of—

(i) the section 2040(c) value of such interest, and

(ii) the adjusted consideration furnished by the decedent's spouse.

(2) LIMITATIONS.—

(A) AT LEAST 50 PERCENT OF VALUE TO BE INCLUDED.—Paragraph (1) shall in no event result in the inclusion in the decedent's gross estate of less than 50 percent of the value of the eligible joint interest.

(B) AGGREGATE REDUCTION.—The aggregate decrease in the value of the decedent's gross estate resulting from the application of this subsection shall not exceed $500,000.

(C) AGGREGATE ADJUSTED CONSIDERATION MUST BE LESS THAN VALUE.—Paragraph (1) shall not apply if the sum of—

(i) the adjusted consideration furnished by the decedent, and

(ii) the adjusted consideration furnished by the decedent's spouse, equals or exceeds the value of the interest.

(3) ELIGIBLE JOINT INTEREST DEFINED.—For purposes of paragraph (1) the term "eligible joint interest" means any interest in property held by the decedent and the decedent's spouse as joint tenants or as tenants by the entirety, but only if—

(A) such joint interest was created by the decedent, the decedent's spouse, or both, and

(B) in the case of a joint tenancy, only the decedent and the decedent's spouse are joint tenants.

(4) SECTION 2040(c) PROPERTY DEFINED.—For purposes of paragraph (1), the term "section 2040(c) property" means any interest in any real or tangible personal property which is devoted to use as a farm or used for farming purposes (within the meaning of paragraphs (4) and (5) of section 2032A(e)) or is used in any other trade or business.

(5) SECTION 2040(c) VALUE.—For purposes of paragraph (1), the term "section 2040(c) value" means—

(A) the excess of the value of the eligible joint interest over the adjusted consideration furnished by the decedent, the decedent's spouse, or both, multiplied by

(B) 2 percent for each taxable year in which the spouse materially participated in the operation of the farm or other trade or business but not to exceed 50 percent.

(6) ADJUSTED CONSIDERATION.—For the purpose of this subsection, the term "adjusted consideration" means—

(A) the consideration furnished by the individual concerned (not taking into account any consideration in the form of income or gain from the business of which the section 2040(c) property is a part) determined under rules similar to the rules set forth in subsection (a), and

(B) an amount equal to the amount of interest which the consideration referred to in subparagraph (A) would have earned over the period in which it was invested in the farm or other business if it had been earning interest throughout such period at 6 percent simple interest.

(7) MATERIAL PARTICIPATION.—For purposes of paragraph (1), material participation shall be determined in a manner similar to the manner used for purposes of paragraph (1) of section 1402(a) (relating to net earnings from self-employment).

(8) VALUE.—For purposes of this subsection, except where the context clearly indicates otherwise, the term "value" means value determined without regard to this subsection.

(9) ELECTION TO HAVE SUBSECTION APPLY.—This subsection shall apply with respect to a joint interest only if the estate of the decedent elects to have this subsection apply to such interest. Such an election shall be made not later than the time prescribed by section 6075(a) for filing the return of tax imposed by section 2001 (including extensions thereof), and shall be made in such manner as the Secretary shall by regulations prescribe.

ESTATE TAX—GROSS ESTATE

• 1980, Technical Corrections Act of 1979 (P.L. 96-222)

P.L. 96-222, §105(a)(3)(A):

Amended Code Sec. 2040(c)(2) by adding paragraph (c)(2)(C). **Effective** for estates of decedents dying after 12-31-78.

P.L. 96-222, §105(a)(3)(B):

Amended Code Sec. 2040(c)(1) by changing "subsections (a)" to "subsection (a)". **Effective** for estates of decedents dying after 12-31-78.

Amendments

• 1981, Economic Recovery Tax Act of 1981 (P.L. 97-34)

P.L. 97-34, §403(c)(3)(A):

Repealed Code Sec. 2040(d). **Effective** for estates of decedents dying after 12-31-81. Prior to its repeal, Code Sec. 2040(d) read as follows:

(d) JOINT INTERESTS OF HUSBAND AND WIFE CREATED BEFORE 1977.—Under regulations prescribed by the Secretary—

(1) IN GENERAL.—In the case of any joint interest created before January 1, 1977, which (if created after December 31, 1976) would have constituted a qualified joint interest under subsection (b)(2) (determined without regard to clause (ii) of subsection (b)(2)(B)), the donor may make an election under this subsection to have paragraph (1) of subsection (b) apply with respect to such joint interest.

(2) TIME FOR MAKING ELECTION.—An election under this subsection with respect to any property shall be made for the calendar quarter in 1977, 1978, or 1979 selected by the donor in a gift tax return filed within the time prescribed by law for filing a gift tax return for such quarter. Such an election may be made irrespective of whether or not the amount involved exceeds the exclusion provided by section 2503(b); but no election may be made under this subsection after the death of the donor.

(3) TAX EFFECTS OF ELECTION.—In the case of any property with respect to which an election has been made under this subsection, for purposes of this title—

(A) the donor shall be treated as having made a gift at the close of the calendar quarter selected under paragraph (2), and

(B) the amount of the gift shall be determined under paragraph (4).

[Sec. 2040(e)—Repealed]

Amendments

• 1981, Economic Recovery Tax Act of 1981 (P.L. 97-34)

P.L. 97-34, §403(c)(3)(A):

Repealed Code Sec. 2040(e). **Effective** for estates of decedents dying after 12-31-81. Prior to its repeal, Code Sec. 2040(e) read as follows:

(e) TREATMENT OF CERTAIN POST-1976 TERMINATIONS.—

(1) IN GENERAL.—If—

(A) before January 1, 1977, a husband and wife had a joint interest in property with right of survivorship,

(B) after December 31, 1976, such joint interest was terminated, and

(C) after December 31, 1976, a joint interest of such husband and wife in such property (or in property the basis of which in whole or in part reflects the basis of such property) was created,

• 1978, Revenue Act of 1978 (P.L. 95-600)

P.L. 95-600, §511(a):

Added Code Sec. 2040(c). **Effective** for estates of decedents dying after 12-31-78.

[Sec. 2040(d)—Repealed]

(4) AMOUNT OF GIFT.—For purposes of paragraph (3)(B), the amount of any gift is one-half of the amount—

(A) which bears the same ratio to the excess of (i) the value of the property on the date of the deemed making of the gift under paragraph (3)(A), over (ii) the value of such property on the date of the creation of the joint interest, as

(B) the excess of (i) the consideration furnished by the donor at the time of the creation of the joint interest, over (ii) the consideration furnished at such time by the donor's spouse, bears to the total consideration furnished by both spouses at such time.

(5) SPECIAL RULE FOR PARAGRAPH (4)(A).—For purposes of paragraph (4)(A)—

(A) in the case of real property, if the creation was not treated as a gift at the time of the creation, or

(B) in the case of personal property, if the gift was required to be included on a gift tax return but was not so included, and the period of limitations on assessment under section 6501 has expired with respect to the tax (if any) on such gift,

then the value of the property on the date of the creation of the joint interest shall be treated as zero.

(6) SUBSTANTIAL IMPROVEMENTS.—For purposes of this subsection, a substantial improvement of any property shall be treated as the creation of a separate joint interest.

• 1978, Revenue Act of 1978 (P.L. 95-600)

P.L. 95-600, §702(k)(2):

Added Code Sec. 2040(d). **Effective** 11-6-78.

then paragraph (1) of subsection (b) shall apply to the joint interest described in subparagraph (C) only if an election is made under subsection (d).

(2) SPECIAL RULES.—For purposes of applying subsection (d) to property described in paragraph (1) of this subsection—

(A) if the creation described in paragraph (1)(C) occurs after December 31, 1979, the election may be made only with respect to the calendar quarter in which such creation occurs, and

(B) the creation of the joint interest described in paragraphs (4) and (5) of subsection (d) is the creation of the joint interest described in paragraph (1)(A) of this subsection.

• 1978, Revenue Act of 1978 (P.L. 95-600)

P.L. 95-600, §702(k)(2):

Added Code Sec. 2040(e). **Effective** 11-6-78.

[Sec. 2041]

SEC. 2041. POWERS OF APPOINTMENT.

[Sec. 2041(a)]

(a) IN GENERAL.—The value of the gross estate shall include the value of all property—

(1) POWERS OF APPOINTMENT CREATED ON OR BEFORE OCTOBER 21, 1942.—To the extent of any property with respect to which a general power of appointment created on or before October 21, 1942, is exercised by the decedent—

(A) by will, or

(B) by a disposition which is of such nature that if it were a transfer of property owned by the decedent, such property would be includible in the decedent's gross estate under sections 2035 to 2038, inclusive;

but the failure to exercise such a power or the complete release of such a power shall not be deemed an exercise thereof. If a general power of appointment created on or before October 21, 1942, has been partially released so that it is no longer a general power of appointment, the exercise of such power shall not be deemed to be the exercise of a general power of appointment if—

(i) such partial release occurred before November 1, 1951, or

(ii) the donee of such power was under a legal disability to release such power on October 21, 1942, and such partial release occurred not later than 6 months after the termination of such legal disability.

(2) POWERS CREATED AFTER OCTOBER 21, 1942.—To the extent of any property with respect to which the decedent has at the time of his death a general power of appointment created after October 21, 1942, or with respect to which the decedent has at any time exercised or released such a power of appointment by a disposition which is of such nature that if it were a transfer of property owned by the decedent, such property would be includible in the decedent's gross estate under sections 2035 to 2038, inclusive. For purposes of this paragraph (2), the power of appointment shall be considered to exist on the date of the decedent's death even though the exercise of the power is subject to a precedent giving of notice or even though the exercise of the power takes effect only on the expiration of a stated period after its exercise, whether or not on or before the date of the decedent's death notice has been given or the power has been exercised.

(3) CREATION OF ANOTHER POWER IN CERTAIN CASES.—To the extent of any property with respect to which the decedent—

(A) by will, or

(B) by a disposition which is of such nature that if it were a transfer of property owned by the decedent such property would be includible in the decedent's gross estate under section 2035, 2036, or 2037,

exercises a power of appointment created after October 21, 1942, by creating another power of appointment which under the applicable local law can be validly exercised so as to postpone the vesting of any estate or interest in such property, or suspend the absolute ownership or power of alienation of such property, for a period ascertainable without regard to the date of the creation of the first power.

Internal Revenue Code   **Sec. 2041(a)(3)(B)**

ESTATE TAX—GROSS ESTATE

Amendments

• **1976, Tax Reform Act of 1976 (P.L. 94-455)**

P.L. 94-455, § 2009(b)(4), (e)(2):

Deleted the second sentence of Code Sec. 2041(a)(2). **Effective** for transfers creating an interest in the person disclaiming made after 12-31-76. Prior to deletion, such sentence read as follows: "A disclaimer or renunciation of such a power of appointment shall not be deemed a release of such power."

• **1962, Revenue Act of 1962 (P.L. 87-834)**

P.L. 87-834, § 18(a)(2):

Amended Code Sec. 2041(a) by deleting "(except real property situated outside of the United States)". **Effective**, generally, for estates of decedents dying after 10-16-62. For exceptions, see Act Sec. 18(b) in the amendment notes for Code Sec. 2031(a).

[Sec. 2041(b)]

(b) DEFINITIONS.—For purposes of subsection (a)—

(1) GENERAL POWER OF APPOINTMENT.—The term "general power of appointment" means a power which is exercisable in favor of the decedent, his estate, his creditors, or the creditors of his estate; except that—

(A) A power to consume, invade, or appropriate property for the benefit of the decedent which is limited by an ascertainable standard relating to the health, education, support, or maintenance of the decedent shall not be deemed a general power of appointment.

(B) A power of appointment created on or before October 21, 1942, which is exercisable by the decedent only in conjunction with another person shall not be deemed a general power of appointment.

(C) In the case of a power of appointment created after October 21, 1942, which is exercisable by the decedent only in conjunction with another person—

(i) If the power is not exercisable by the decedent except in conjunction with the creator of the power—such power shall not be deemed a general power of appointment.

(ii) If the power is not exercisable by the decedent except in conjunction with a person having a substantial interest in the property, subject to the power, which is adverse to exercise of the power in favor of the decedent—such power shall not be deemed a general power of appointment. For the purposes of this clause a person who, after the death of the decedent, may be possessed of a power of appointment (with respect to the property subject to the decedent's power) which he may exercise in his own favor shall be deemed as having an interest in the property and such interest shall be deemed adverse to such exercise of the decedent's power.

(iii) If (after the application of clauses (i) and (ii)) the power is a general power of appointment and is exercisable in favor of such other person—such power shall be deemed a general power of appointment only in respect of a fractional part of the property subject to such power, such part to be determined by dividing the value of such property by the number of such persons (including the decedent) in favor of whom such power is exercisable.

For purposes of clauses (ii) and (iii), a power shall be deemed to be exercisable in favor of a person if it is exercisable in favor of such person, his estate, his creditors, or the creditors of his estate.

(2) LAPSE OF POWER.—The lapse of a power of appointment created after October 21, 1942, during the life of the individual possessing the power shall be considered a release of such power. The preceding sentence shall apply with respect to the lapse of powers during any calendar year only to the extent that the property, which could have been appointed by exercise of such lapsed powers, exceeded in value, at the time of such lapse, the greater of the following amounts:

(A) $5,000, or

(B) 5 percent of the aggregate value, at the time of such lapse, of the assets out of which, or the proceeds of which, the exercise of the lapsed powers could have been satisfied.

(3) DATE OF CREATION OF POWER.—For purposes of this section, a power of appointment created by a will executed on or before October 21, 1942, shall be considered a power created on or before such date if the person executing such will dies before July 1, 1949, without having republished such will, by codicil or otherwise, after October 21, 1942.

[Sec. 2042]

SEC. 2042. PROCEEDS OF LIFE INSURANCE.

The value of the gross estate shall include the value of all property—

(1) RECEIVABLE BY THE EXECUTOR.—To the extent of the amount receivable by the executor as insurance under policies on the life of the decedent.

(2) RECEIVABLE BY OTHER BENEFICIARIES.—To the extent of the amount receivable by all other beneficiaries as insurance under policies on the life of the decedent with respect to which the decedent possessed at his death any of the incidents of ownership, exercisable either alone or in conjunction with any other person. For purposes of the preceding sentence, the term "incident of ownership" includes a reversionary interest (whether arising by the express terms of the policy or other instrument or by operation of law) only if the value of such reversionary interest exceeded 5 percent of the value of the policy immediately before the death of the decedent. As used in this paragraph, the term "reversionary interest" includes a possibility that the policy, or the proceeds of the policy, may return to the decedent or his estate, or may be subject to a power of disposition by him. The value of a reversionary interest at any time shall be determined (without regard to the fact of the decedent's death) by usual methods of valuation, including the use of tables of mortality and actuarial principles, pursuant to regulations prescribed by the Secretary. In determining the value of a possibility that the policy or proceeds thereof may be subject to a power of disposition by the decedent, such possibility shall be valued as if it were a possibility that such policy or proceeds may return to the decedent or his estate.

Amendments

• **1976, Tax Reform Act of 1976 (P.L. 94-455)**

P.L. 94-455, § 1906(b)(13)(A):

Amended 1954 Code by substituting "Secretary" for "Secretary or his delegate" each place it appeared. **Effective** 2-1-77.

[Sec. 2043]

SEC. 2043. TRANSFERS FOR INSUFFICIENT CONSIDERATION.

[Sec. 2043(a)]

(a) IN GENERAL.—If any one of the transfers, trusts, interests, rights, or powers enumerated and described in sections 2035 to 2038, inclusive, and section 2041 is made, created, exercised, or relinquished for a consideration in money or money's worth, but is not a bona fide sale for an adequate and full consideration in money or money's worth, there shall be included in the gross estate only the excess of the fair market value at the time of death of the property otherwise to be included on account of such transaction, over the value of the consideration received therefor by the decedent.

ESTATE TAX—GROSS ESTATE

[Sec. 2043(b)]

(b) MARITAL RIGHTS NOT TREATED AS CONSIDERATION.—

(1) IN GENERAL.—For purposes of this chapter, a relinquishment or promised relinquishment of dower or curtesy, or of a statutory estate created in lieu of dower or curtesy, or of other marital rights in the decedent's property or estate, shall not be considered to any extent a consideration "in money or money's worth".

(2) EXCEPTION.—For purposes of section 2053 (relating to expenses, indebtedness, and taxes), a transfer of property which satisfies the requirements of paragraph (1) of section 2516 (relating to certain property settlements) shall be considered to be made for an adequate and full consideration in money or money's worth.

Amendments

• 1984, Deficit Reduction Act of 1984 (P.L. 98-369)

P.L. 98-369, § 425(a)(1):

Amended Code Sec. 2043(b). **Effective** for estates of decedents dying after 7-18-84. Prior to amendment, Code Sec. 2043(b) read as follows:

(b) Marital Rights Not Treated as Consideration.—For purposes of this chapter, a relinquishment or promised relinquishment of dower or curtesy, or of a statutory estate created in lieu of dower or curtesy, or of other marital rights in the decedent's property or estate, shall not be considered to any extent a consideration "in money or money's worth."

[Sec. 2044]

SEC. 2044. CERTAIN PROPERTY FOR WHICH MARITAL DEDUCTION WAS PREVIOUSLY ALLOWED.

[Sec. 2044(a)]

(a) GENERAL RULE.—The value of the gross estate shall include the value of any property to which this section applies in which the decedent had a qualifying income interest for life.

[Sec. 2044(b)]

(b) PROPERTY TO WHICH THIS SECTION APPLIES.—This section applies to any property if—

(1) a deduction was allowed with respect to the transfer of such property to the decedent—

(A) under section 2056 by reason of subsection (b)(7) thereof, or

(B) under section 2523 by reason of subsection (f) thereof, and

(2) section 2519 (relating to dispositions of certain life estates) did not apply with respect to a disposition by the decedent of part or all of such property.

Amendments

• 1981, Economic Recovery Tax Act of 1981 (P.L. 97-34)

P.L. 97-34, § 403(d)(3)(A)(i):

Added Code Sec. 2044. **Effective** for estates of decedents dying after 12-31-81.

[Sec. 2044(c)]

(c) PROPERTY TREATED AS HAVING PASSED FROM DECEDENT.—For purposes of this chapter and chapter 13, property includible in the gross estate of the decedent under subsection (a) shall be treated as property passing from the decedent.

Amendments

• 1983, Technical Corrections Act of 1982 (P.L. 97-448)

P.L. 97-448, § 104(a)(1)(B):

Amended Code Sec. 2044 by adding at the end thereof new subsection (c). **Effective** as if included in the provision of P.L. 97-34 to which it relates.

[Sec. 2045]

SEC. 2045. PRIOR INTERESTS.

Except as otherwise specifically provided by law, sections 2034 to 2042, inclusive, shall apply to the transfers, trusts, estates, interests, rights, powers, and relinquishment of powers, as severally enumerated and described therein, whenever made, created, arising, existing, exercised, or relinquished.

Amendments

• 1981, Economic Recovery Tax Act of 1981 (P.L. 97-34)

P.L. 97-34, § 403(d)(3)(A)(i):

Redesignated Code Sec. 2044 as Code Sec. 2045. **Effective** for estates of decedents dying after 12-31-81.

• 1976, Tax Reform Act of 1976 (P.L. 94-455)

P.L. 94-455, § 2001(c)(1)(M):

Substituted "specifically provided by law" for "specifically provided therein" in Code Sec. 2044. **Effective** for estates of decedents dying after 12-31-76.

[Sec. 2046]

SEC. 2046. DISCLAIMERS.

For provisions relating to the effect of a qualified disclaimer for purposes of this chapter, see section 2518.

Amendments

• 1981, Economic Recovery Tax Act of 1981 (P.L. 97-34)

P.L. 97-34, § 403(d)(3)(A)(i):

Redesignated Code Sec. 2045 as Code Sec. 2046. **Effective** for estates of decedents dying after 12-31-81.

• 1976, Tax Reform Act of 1976 (P.L. 94-455)

P.L. 94-455, § 2009(b)(2):

Added Code Sec. 2045. **Effective** for transfers creating an interest in the person disclaiming made after 12-31-76.

PART IV—TAXABLE ESTATE

Sec. 2051.	Definition of taxable estate.
Sec. 2053.	Expenses, indebtedness, and taxes.
Sec. 2054.	Losses.
Sec. 2055.	Transfers for public, charitable, and religious uses.
Sec. 2056.	Bequests, etc., to surviving spouse.
Sec. 2056A.	Qualified domestic trust.
Sec. 2058.	State death taxes.

ESTATE TAX—TAXABLE ESTATE

[Sec. 2051]

SEC. 2051. DEFINITION OF TAXABLE ESTATE.

For purposes of the tax imposed by section 2001, the value of the taxable estate shall be determined by deducting from the value of the gross estate the deductions provided for in this part.

Amendments

• **1978, Revenue Act of 1978 (P.L. 95-600)**

P.L. 95-600, § 702(r)(2):

Amended Code Sec. 2051 by deleting "exemption and" after "value of the gross estate the". **Effective** for estates of decedents dying after 1976.

[Sec. 2052—Repealed]

SEC. 2052. EXEMPTION.

For purposes of the tax imposed by section 2001, the value of the taxable estate shall be determined by deducting from the value of the gross estate an exemption of $60,000.

Amendments

• **1976, Tax Reform Act of 1976 (P.L. 94-455)**

P.L. 94-455, § 2001(a)(4):

Repealed Code Sec. 2052. **Effective** with respect to estates of decedents dying after 12-31-76. Prior to repeal, Code Sec. 2052 read as follows:

SEC. 2053. EXPENSES, INDEBTEDNESS, AND TAXES.

[Sec. 2053(a)]

(a) GENERAL RULE.—For purposes of the tax imposed by section 2001, the value of the taxable estate shall be determined by deducting from the value of the gross estate such amounts—

(1) for funeral expenses,

(2) for administration expenses,

(3) for claims against the estate, and

(4) for unpaid mortgages on, or any indebtedness in respect of, property where the value of the decedent's interest therein, undiminished by such mortgage or indebtedness, is included in the value of the gross estate,

as are allowable by the laws of the jurisdiction, whether within or without the United States, under which the estate is being administered.

[Sec. 2053(b)]

(b) OTHER ADMINISTRATION EXPENSES.—Subject to the limitations in paragraph (1) of subsection (c), there shall be deducted in determining the taxable estate amounts representing expenses incurred in administering property not subject to claims which is included in the gross estate to the same extent such amounts would be allowable as a deduction under subsection (a) if such property were subject to claims, and such amounts are paid before the expiration of the period of limitation for assessment provided in section 6501.

[Sec. 2053(c)]

(c) LIMITATIONS.—

(1) LIMITATIONS APPLICABLE TO SUBSECTIONS (a) AND (b).—

(A) CONSIDERATION FOR CLAIMS.—The deduction allowed by this section in the case of claims against the estate, unpaid mortgages, or any indebtedness shall, when founded on a promise or agreement, be limited to the extent that they were contracted bona fide and for an adequate and full consideration in money or money's worth; except that in any case in which any such claim is founded on a promise or agreement of the decedent to make a contribution or gift to or for the use of any donee described in section 2055 for the purposes specified therein, the deduction for such claims shall not be so limited, but shall be limited to the extent that it would be allowable as a deduction under section 2055 if such promise or agreement constituted a bequest.

(B) CERTAIN TAXES.—Any income taxes on income received after the death of the decedent, or property taxes not accrued before his death, or any estate, succession, legacy, or inheritance taxes, shall not be deductible under this section.

(C) CERTAIN CLAIMS BY REMAINDERMEN.—No deduction shall be allowed under this section for a claim against the estate by a remainderman relating to any property described in section 2044.

(D) SECTION 6166 INTEREST.—No deduction shall be allowed under this section for any interest payable under section 6601 on any unpaid portion of the tax imposed by section 2001 for the period during which an extension of time for payment of such tax is in effect under section 6166.

(2) LIMITATIONS APPLICABLE ONLY TO SUBSECTION (a).—In the case of the amounts described in subsection (a), there shall be disallowed the amount by which the deductions specified therein exceed the value, at the time of the decedent's death, of property subject to claims, except to the extent that such deductions represent amounts paid before the date prescribed for the filing of the estate tax return. For purposes of this section, the term "property subject to claims" means property includible in the gross estate of the decedent which, or the avails of which, would under the applicable law, bear the burden of the payment of such deductions in the final adjustment and settlement of the estate, except that the value of the property shall be reduced by the amount of the deduction under section 2054 attributable to such property.

Amendments

• **1997, Taxpayer Relief Act of 1997 (P.L. 105-34)**

P.L. 105-34, § 503(b)(1):

Amended Code Sec. 2053(c)(1) by adding a new subparagraph (D). **Effective**, generally, for estates of decedents dying after 12-31-97. For a special rule, see Act Sec. 503(d)(2), below.

P.L. 105-34, § 503(d)(2), provides:

(2) ELECTION.—In the case of the estate of any decedent dying before January 1, 1998, with respect to which there is an election under section 6166 of the Internal Revenue Code of 1986, the executor of the estate may elect to have the amendments made by this section apply with respect to installments due after the effective date of the election; except that the 2-percent portion of such installments shall be equal to the amount which would be the 4-percent portion of such installments without regard to such election. Such an election shall be made before January 1, 1999 in the manner prescribed by the Secretary of the Treasury and, once made, is irrevocable.

P.L. 105-34, § 1073(b)(3):

Amended Code Sec. 2053(c)(1)(B) by striking the last sentence. **Effective** for estates of decedents dying after 12-31-96. Prior to being stricken, the last sentence of Code Sec. 2053(c)(1)(B) read as follows:

This subparagraph shall not apply to any increase in the tax imposed by this chapter by reason of section 4980A(d).

• **1988, Technical and Miscellaneous Revenue Act of 1988 (P.L. 100-647)**

P.L. 100-647, § 1011A(g)(11):

Amended Code Sec. 2053(c)(1)(B) by adding at the end thereof a new sentence. **Effective** as if included in the provision of P.L. 99-514 to which it relates.

• **1984, Deficit Reduction Act of 1984 (P.L. 98-369)**

P.L. 98-369, § 1027(b):

Amended Code Sec. 2053(c)(1) by adding subparagraph (C). **Effective** as if included in the amendment made by section 403 of P.L. 97-34.

ESTATE TAX—TAXABLE ESTATE

[Sec. 2053(d)]

(d) CERTAIN FOREIGN DEATH TAXES.—

(1) IN GENERAL.—Notwithstanding the provisions of subsection (c)(1)(B), for purposes of the tax imposed by section 2001, the value of the taxable estate may be determined, if the executor so elects before the expiration of the period of limitation for assessment provided in section 6501, by deducting from the value of the gross estate the amount (as determined in accordance with regulations prescribed by the Secretary) of any estate, succession, legacy, or inheritance tax imposed by and actually paid to any foreign country, in respect of any property situated within such foreign country and included in the gross estate of a citizen or resident of the United States, upon a transfer by the decedent for public, charitable, or religious uses described in section 2055. The determination under this paragraph of the country within which property is situated shall be made in accordance with the rules applicable under subchapter B (sec. 2101 and following) in determining whether property is situated within or without the United States. Any election under this paragraph shall be exercised in accordance with regulations prescribed by the Secretary.

(2) CONDITION FOR ALLOWANCE OF DEDUCTION.—No deduction shall be allowed under paragraph (1) for a foreign death tax specified therein unless the decrease in the tax imposed by section 2001 which results from the deduction provided in paragraph (1) will inure solely for the benefit of the public, charitable, or religious transferees described in section 2055 or section 2106(a)(2). In any case where the tax imposed by section 2001 is equitably apportioned among all the transferees of property included in the gross estate, including those described in sections 2055 and 2106(a)(2) (taking into account any exemptions, credits, or deductions allowed by this chapter), in determining such decrease, there shall be disregarded any decrease in the Federal estate tax which any transferees other than those described in sections 2055 and 2106(a)(2) are required to pay.

(3) EFFECT ON CREDIT FOR FOREIGN DEATH TAXES OF DEDUCTION UNDER THIS SUBSECTION.—

(A) ELECTION.—An election under this subsection shall be deemed a waiver of the right to claim a credit, against the Federal estate tax, under a death tax convention with any foreign country for any tax or portion thereof in respect of which a deduction is taken under this subsection.

(B) CROSS REFERENCE.—

See section 2011(d) for the effect of a deduction taken under this paragraph on the credit for foreign death taxes.

Amendments

- **2013, American Taxpayer Relief Act of 2012 (P.L. 112-240)**

P.L. 112-240, §101(a)(1) and (3), provides:

SEC. 101. PERMANENT EXTENSION AND MODIFICATION OF 2001 TAX RELIEF.

(a) PERMANENT EXTENSION.—

(1) IN GENERAL.—The Economic Growth and Tax Relief Reconciliation Act of 2001 is amended by striking title IX.

* * *

(3) EFFECTIVE DATE.—The amendments made by this subsection shall apply to taxable, plan, or limitation years beginning after December 31, 2012, and estates of decedents dying, gifts made, or generation skipping transfers after December 31, 2012.

- **2002, Victims of Terrorism Tax Relief Act of 2001 (P.L. 107-134)**

P.L. 107-134, §103(b)(2):

Amended Code Sec. 2053(d)(3)(B) by striking "section 2011(e)" and inserting "section 2011(d)". **Effective** for estates of decedents dying on or after 9-11-2001; and in the case of individuals dying as a result of the 4-19-95 terrorist attack, dying on or after 4-19-95. For a waiver of limitations, see Act Sec. 103(d)(2), below.

P.L. 107-134, §103(d)(2), provides:

(2) WAIVER OF LIMITATIONS.—If refund or credit of any overpayment of tax resulting from the amendments made by this section is prevented at any time before the close of the 1-year period beginning on the date of the enactment of this Act by the operation of any law or rule of law (including res judicata), such refund or credit may nevertheless be made or allowed if claim therefor is filed before the close of such period.

- **2001, Economic Growth and Tax Relief Reconciliation Act of 2001 (P.L. 107-16)**

P.L. 107-16, §532(c)(5):

Amended Code Sec. 2053(d). **Effective** for estates of decedents dying, and generation-skipping transfers, after 12-31-2004. Prior to amendment, Code Sec. 2053(d) read as follows:

(d) CERTAIN STATE AND FOREIGN DEATH TAXES.—

(1) GENERAL RULE.—Notwithstanding the provisions of subsection (c)(1)(B) of this section, for purposes of the tax imposed by section 2001 the value of the taxable estate may be determined, if the executor so elects before the expiration of the period of limitation for assessment provided in section 6501, by deducting from the value of the gross estate the amount (as determined in accordance with regulations prescribed by the Secretary) of—

(A) any estate, succession, legacy, or inheritance tax imposed by a State or the District of Columbia upon a transfer by the decedent for public, charitable, or religious uses described in section 2055 or 2106(a)(2), and

(B) any estate, succession, legacy, or inheritance tax imposed by and actually paid to any foreign country, in respect of any property situated within such foreign country and included in the gross estate of a citizen or resident of the United States, upon a transfer by the decedent for public, charitable, or religious uses described in section 2055.

The determination under subparagraph (B) of the country within which property is situated shall be made in accordance with the rules applicable under subchapter B (sec. 2101 and following) in determining whether property is situated within or without the United States. Any election under this paragraph shall be exercised in accordance with regulations prescribed by the Secretary.

(2) CONDITION FOR ALLOWANCE OF DEDUCTION.—No deduction shall be allowed under paragraph (1) for a State death tax or a foreign death tax specified therein unless the decrease in the tax imposed by section 2001 which results from the deduction provided in paragraph (1) will inure solely for the benefit of the public, charitable, or religious transferees described in section 2055 or section 2106(a)(2). In any case where the tax imposed by section 2001 is equitably apportioned among all the transferees of property included in the gross estate, including those described in sections 2055 and 2106(a)(2) (taking into account any exemptions, credits, or deductions allowed by this chapter), in determining such decrease, there shall be disregarded any decrease in the Federal estate tax which any transferees other than those described in sections 2055 and 2106(a)(2) are required to pay.

(3) EFFECT ON CREDITS FOR STATE AND FOREIGN DEATH TAXES OF DEDUCTION UNDER THIS SUBSECTION.—

(A) ELECTION.—An election under this subsection shall be deemed a waiver of the right to claim a credit, against the Federal estate tax, under a death tax convention with any foreign country for any tax or portion thereof in respect of which a deduction is taken under this subsection.

(B) CROSS REFERENCES.—

See section 2011(e) for the effect of a deduction taken under this subsection on the credit for State death taxes, and see section 2014(f) for the effect of a deduction taken under this subsection on the credit for foreign death taxes.

P.L. 107-16, §901(a)-(b), as amended by P.L. 111-312, §101(a)(1), provides [but see P.L. 112-240, §101(a)(1) and (3), above]:

SEC. 901. SUNSET OF PROVISIONS OF ACT.

(a) IN GENERAL.—All provisions of, and amendments made by, this Act shall not apply—

(1) to taxable, plan, or limitation years beginning after December 31, 2012, or

(2) in the case of title V, to estates of decedents dying, gifts made, or generation skipping transfers, after December 31, 2012.

(b) APPLICATION OF CERTAIN LAWS.—The Internal Revenue Code of 1986 and the Employee Retirement Income Security Act of 1974 shall be applied and administered to years, estates, gifts, and transfers described in subsection (a) as if the provisions and amendments described in subsection (a) had never been enacted.

- **1976, Tax Reform Act of 1976 (P.L. 94-455)**

P.L. 94-455, §1902(a)(12)(B):

Deleted "or Territory" in Code Sec. 2053(d). **Effective** for gifts made after 12-31-76.

P.L. 94-455, §1906(b)(13)(A):

Amended 1954 Code by substituting "Secretary" for "Secretary or his delegate" each place it appeared. **Effective** 2-1-77.

- **1959 (P.L. 86-175)**

P.L. 86-175, §[1]:

Amended 1954 Code Sec. 2053(d). **Effective** with respect to the estates of decedents dying on or after 7-1-55. Prior to amendment, Code Sec. 2053(d) read as follows:

(d) Certain State Death Taxes.—

(1) General rule.—Notwithstanding the provisions of subsection (c)(1)(B) of this section, for purposes of the tax imposed by section 2001 the value of the taxable estate may be determined, if the executor so elects before the expiration of the period of limitation for assessment provided in section 6501, by deducting from the value of the gross estate the amount (as determined in accordance with regulations prescribed by the Secretary or his delegate) of any estate, succession, legacy or inheritance tax imposed by a State or Territory or the District of Columbia, upon a transfer by the decedent for public, charitable, or religious uses described in section 2055 or 2106(a)(2). The election shall be exercised in accordance with regulations prescribed by the Secretary or his delegate.

(2) Condition for allowance of deduction.—No deduction shall be allowed under paragraph (1) for a State death tax specified therein unless the decrease in the tax imposed by section 2001 which results from the deduction provided for in paragraph (1) will inure solely for the benefit of the public, charitable, or religious transferees described in section 2055 or section 2106(a)(2). In any case where the tax imposed by section 2001 is equitably apportioned among all the transferees of property included in the gross estate, including those described in sections 2055 and 2106(a)(2) (taking into account any exemptions, credits, or deductions allowed by this chapter), in

ESTATE TAX—TAXABLE ESTATE

determining such decrease, there shall be disregarded any decrease in the Federal estate tax which any transferees other than those described in sections 2055 and 2106(a)(2) are required to pay.

(3) Effect of deduction on credit for state death taxes.—See section 2011(e) for the effect of a deduction taken under this subsection on the credit for State death taxes.

• **1958, Technical Amendments Act of 1958 (P.L. 85-866)**

P.L. 85-866, § 102(c):

Amended Code Sec. 2053(d)(1) by striking the words "or any possession of the United States," following the words "District of Columbia". **Effective** for estates of decedents dying after 9-2-58.

• **1956 (P.L. 414, 84th Cong.)**

P.L. 414, 84th Cong., § 2:

Amended Code Sec. 2053 by redesignating subsection (d) as subsection (e) and by adding after subsection (c) a new subsection (d). **Effective** for estates of all decedents dying after 12-31-53.

[Sec. 2053(e)]

(e) MARITAL RIGHTS.—

For provisions treating certain relinquishments of marital rights as consideration in money or money's worth, see section 2043(b)(2).

Amendments

• **1984, Deficit Reduction Act of 1984 (P.L. 98-369)**

P.L. 98-369, § 425(a)(2):

Amended Code Sec. 2053(e). **Effective** for estates of decedents dying after 7-18-84. Prior to amendment, Code Sec. 2053(e) read as follows:

(e) Marital Rights.—

For provisions that relinquishment of marital rights shall not be deemed a consideration "in money or money's worth," see section 2043(b).

[Sec. 2054]

SEC. 2054. LOSSES.

For purposes of the tax imposed by section 2001, the value of the taxable estate shall be determined by deducting from the value of the gross estate losses incurred during the settlement of estates arising from fires, storms, shipwrecks, or other casualties, or from theft, when such losses are not compensated for by insurance or otherwise.

[Sec. 2055]

SEC. 2055. TRANSFERS FOR PUBLIC, CHARITABLE, AND RELIGIOUS USES.

[Sec. 2055(a)]

(a) IN GENERAL.—For purposes of the tax imposed by section 2001, the value of the taxable estate shall be determined by deducting from the value of the gross estate the amount of all bequests, legacies, devises, or transfers—

(1) to or for the use of the United States, any State, any political subdivision thereof, or the District of Columbia, for exclusively public purposes;

(2) to or for the use of any corporation organized and operated exclusively for religious, charitable, scientific, literary, or educational purposes, including the encouragement of art, or to foster national or international amateur sports competition (but only if no part of its activities involve the provision of athletic facilities or equipment), and the prevention of cruelty to children or animals, no part of the net earnings of which inures to the benefit of any private stockholder or individual, which is not disqualified for tax exemption under section 501(c)(3) by reason of attempting to influence legislation, and which does not participate in, or intervene in (including the publishing or distributing of statements), any political campaign on behalf of (or in opposition to) any candidate for public office;

(3) to a trustee or trustees, or a fraternal society, order, or association operating under the lodge system, but only if such contributions or gifts are to be used by such trustee or trustees, or by such fraternal society, order, or association, exclusively for religious, charitable, scientific, literary, or educational purposes, or for the prevention of cruelty to children or animals, such trust, fraternal society, order, or association would not be disqualified for tax exemption under section 501(c)(3) by reason of attempting to influence legislation, and such trustee or trustees, or such fraternal society, order, or association, does not participate in, or intervene in (including the publishing or distributing of statements), any political campaign on behalf of (or in opposition to) any candidate for public office;

(4) to or for the use of any veterans' organization incorporated by Act of Congress, or of its departments or local chapters or posts, no part of the net earnings of which inures to the benefit of any private shareholder or individual; or

(5) to an employee stock ownership plan if such transfer qualifies as a qualified gratuitous transfer of qualified employer securities within the meaning of section 664(g).

For purposes of this subsection, the complete termination before the date prescribed for the filing of the estate tax return of a power to consume, invade, or appropriate property for the benefit of an individual before such power has been exercised by reason of the death of such individual or for any other reason shall be considered and deemed to be a qualified disclaimer with the same full force and effect as though he had filed such qualified disclaimer. Rules similar to the rules of section 501(j) shall apply for purposes of paragraph (2).

Amendments

• **1997, Taxpayer Relief Act of 1997 (P.L. 105-34)**

P.L. 105-34, § 1530(c)(7)(i)-(iii):

Amended Code Sec. 2055(a) by striking "or" at the end of paragraph (3), by striking the period at the end of paragraph (4) and inserting "; or", and by inserting after paragraph (4) a new paragraph (5). **Effective** for transfers made by trusts to, or for the use of, an employee stock ownership plan after 8-5-97.

• **1987, Revenue Act of 1987 (P.L. 100-203)**

P.L. 100-203, § 10711(a)(3):

Amended Code Sec. 2055(a)(2) and (3) by striking out "on behalf of any candidate" and inserting in lieu thereof "on behalf of (or in opposition to) any candidate". **Effective** with respect to activities after 12-22-87.

• **1982, Tax Equity and Fiscal Responsibility Act of 1982 (P.L. 97-248)**

P.L. 97-248, § 286(b)(2):

Amended Code Sec. 2055(a) by adding a sentence at the end thereof. **Effective** 10-5-76.

• **1976, Tax Reform Act of 1976 (P.L. 94-455)**

P.L. 94-455, § 1307(d)(1)(B):

Substituted "which is not disqualified for tax exemption under section 501(c)(3) by reason of attempting to influence legislation," for "no substantial part of the activities of which is carrying on propaganda, or otherwise attempting, to influence legislation (except as otherwise provided in subsection (h))," in Code Sec. 2055(a)(2). **Effective** for tax years beginning after 12-31-76.

P.L. 94-455, § 1307(d)(1)(C):

Substituted "such trust, fraternal society, order, or association would not be disqualified for tax exemption under section 501(c)(3) by reason of attempting to influence legislation," for "no substantial part of the activities of such trustee or trustees, or of such fraternal society, order, or association, is carrying on propaganda, or otherwise attempting, to influence legislation," in Code Sec. 2055(a)(3). **Effective** for estates of decedents dying after 12-31-76.

P.L. 94-455, § 1313(b)(2):

Added ", or to foster national or international amateur sports competition (but only if no part of its activities involve the provision of athletic facilities or equipment)," after "the encouragement of art" in Code Sec. 2055(a)(2). **Effective** 10-5-76.

P.L. 94-455, § 1902(a)(12)(A):

Deleted "Territory" in Code Sec. 2055(a)(1). **Effective** for gifts made after 12-31-76.

P.L. 94-455, § 2009(b)(4)(B):

Deleted "(including the interest which falls into any such bequest, legacy, devise, or transfer as a result of an irrevocable disclaimer of a bequest, legacy, devise, transfer, or power, if the disclaimer is made before the date prescribed for the filing of the estate tax return)" in the first sentence of Code Sec. 2055(a). **Effective** for transfers creating an interest in the person disclaiming made after 12-31-76.

P.L. 94-455, § 2009(b)(4)(C):

Substituted "a qualified" for "an irrevocable" and substituted "such qualified" for "such irrevocable" in the second sentence of Code Sec. 2055(a). **Effective** for transfers creating an interest in the person disclaiming made after 12-31-76.

ESTATE TAX—TAXABLE ESTATE

• 1969, Tax Reform Act of 1969 (P.L. 91-172)

P.L. 91-172, § 201(d)(4)(A):

Amended paragraphs (2) and (3) of Code Sec. 2055(a). **Effective** with respect to gifts and transfers in trust made after 12-31-69. Prior to amendment, paragraphs (2) and (3) read as follows:

(2) to or for the use of any corporation organized and operated exclusively for religious, charitable, scientific, literary, or educational purposes, including the encouragement of art and the prevention of cruelty to children or animals, no part of the net earnings of which inures to the benefit of any private stockholder or individual, and no substantial part of the activities of which is carrying on propaganda, or otherwise attempting, to influence legislation;

(3) to a trustee or trustees, or a fraternal society, order, or association operating under the lodge system, but only if such contributions or gifts are to be used by such trustee or trustees, or by such fraternal society, order, or association, exclusively for religious, charitable, scientific, literary, or educational purposes, or for the prevention of cruelty to children or animals, and no substantial part of the activities of such trustee or trustees, or of such fraternal society, order, or association, is carrying on propaganda, or otherwise attempting, to influence legislation; or

[Sec. 2055(b)]

(b) POWERS OF APPOINTMENT.—Property includible in the decedent's gross estate under section 2041 (relating to powers of appointment) received by a donee described in this section shall, for purposes of this section, be considered a bequest of such decedent.

Amendments

• 1976, Tax Reform Act of 1976 (P.L. 94-455)

P.L. 94-455, § 1902(a)(4)(A), (c)(1):

Amended Code Sec. 2055(b). **Effective** for estates of decedents dying after 10-4-76. Prior to amendment, Code Sec. 2055(b) read as follows:

(b) POWERS OF APPOINTMENT.—

(1) GENERAL RULE.—Property includible in the decedent's gross estate under section 2041 (relating to powers of appointment) received by a donee described in this section shall, for purposes of this section, be considered a bequest of such decedent.

(2) SPECIAL RULE FOR CERTAIN BEQUESTS SUBJECT TO POWER OF APPOINTMENT.—For purposes of this section, in the case of a bequest in trust, if the surviving spouse of the decedent is entitled for life to all of the net income from the trust and such surviving spouse has a power of appointment over the corpus of such trust exercisable by will in favor of, among others, organizations described in subsection (a)(2), such bequests in trust, reduced by the value of the life estate, shall, to the extent such power is exercised in favor of such organizations, be deemed a transfer to such organizations by the decedent if—

(A) no part of the corpus of such trust is distributed to a beneficiary during the life of the surviving spouse;

(B) such surviving spouse was over 80 years of age at the date of the decedent's death;

(C) such surviving spouse by affidavit executed within 6 months after the death of the decedent specifies the organizations described in subsection (a)(2) in favor of which he intends to exercise the power of appointment and indicates the amount or proportion each such organization is to receive; and

(D) the power of appointment is exercised in favor of such organization and in the amounts or proportions specified in the affidavit required under subparagraph (C).

The affidavit referred to in subparagraph (C) shall be attached to the estate tax return of the decedent and shall constitute a sufficient basis for the allowance of the deduction under this paragraph in the first instance subject to a later disallowance of the deduction if the conditions herein specified are not complied with.

• 1970, Excise, Estate, and Gift Tax Adjustment Act of 1970 (P.L. 91-614)

P.L. 91-614, § 101(c):

Amended Code Sec. 2055(b)(2)(C) by substituting "6 months" for "one year." **Effective** with respect to decedents dying after 12-31-70.

• 1956 (P.L. 1011, 84th Cong.)

P.L. 1011, 84th Cong., §[1]:

Amended Sec. 2055(b) by adding "(1) General rule.—" before the word "Property", and by adding paragraph (2). **Effective** in the case of decedents dying after 8-16-54.

[Sec. 2055(c)]

(c) DEATH TAXES PAYABLE OUT OF BEQUESTS.—If the tax imposed by section 2001, or any estate, succession, legacy, or inheritance taxes, are, either by the terms of the will, by the law of the jurisdiction under which the estate is administered, or by the law of the jurisdiction imposing the particular tax, payable in whole or in part out of the bequests, legacies, or devises otherwise deductible under this section, then the amount deductible under this section shall be the amount of such bequests, legacies, or devises reduced by the amount of such taxes.

[Sec. 2055(d)]

(d) LIMITATION ON DEDUCTION.—The amount of the deduction under this section for any transfer shall not exceed the value of the transferred property required to be included in the gross estate.

[Sec. 2055(e)]

(e) DISALLOWANCE OF DEDUCTIONS IN CERTAIN CASES.—

(1) No deduction shall be allowed under this section for a transfer to or for the use of an organization or trust described in section 508(d) or 4948(c)(4) subject to the conditions specified in such sections.

(2) Where an interest in property (other than an interest described in section 170(f)(3)(B)) passes or has passed from the decedent to a person, or for a use, described in subsection (a), and an interest (other than an interest which is extinguished upon the decedent's death) in the same property passes or has passed (for less than an adequate and full consideration in money or money's worth) from the decedent to a person, or for a use, not described in subsection (a), no deduction shall be allowed under this section for the interest which passes or has passed to the person, or for the use, described in subsection (a) unless—

(A) in the case of a remainder interest, such interest is in a trust which is a charitable remainder annuity trust or a charitable remainder unitrust (described in section 664) or a pooled income fund (described in section 642(c)(5)), or

(B) in the case of any other interest, such interest is in the form of a guaranteed annuity or is a fixed percentage distributed yearly of the fair market value of the property (to be determined yearly).

(3) REFORMATIONS TO COMPLY WITH PARAGRAPH (2).—

(A) IN GENERAL.—A deduction shall be allowed under subsection (a) in respect of any qualified reformation.

(B) QUALIFIED REFORMATION.—For purposes of this paragraph, the term "qualified reformation" means a change of a governing instrument by reformation, amendment, construction, or otherwise which changes a reformable interest into a qualified interest but only if—

(i) any difference between—

(I) the actuarial value (determined as of the date of the decedent's death) of the qualified interest, and

(II) the actuarial value (as so determined) of the reformable interest,

does not exceed 5 percent of the actuarial value (as so determined) of the reformable interest,

(ii) in the case of—

(I) a charitable remainder interest, the nonremainder interest (before and after the qualified reformation) terminated at the same time, or

(II) any other interest, the reformable interest and the qualified interest are for the same period, and

(iii) such change is effective as of the date of the decedent's death.

A nonremainder interest (before reformation) for a term of years in excess of 20 years shall be treated as satisfying subclause (I) of clause (ii) if such interest (after reformation) is for a term of 20 years.

(C) REFORMABLE INTEREST.—For purposes of this paragraph—

(i) IN GENERAL.—The term "reformable interest" means any interest for which a deduction would be allowable under subsection (a) at the time of the decedent's death but for paragraph (2).

Internal Revenue Code   Sec. 2055(e)(3)(C)(i)

ESTATE TAX—TAXABLE ESTATE

(ii) BENEFICIARY'S INTEREST MUST BE FIXED.—The term "reformable interest" does not include any interest unless, before the remainder vests in possession, all payments to persons other than an organization described in subsection (a) are expressed either in specified dollar amounts or a fixed percentage of the fair market value of the property. For purposes of determining whether all such payments are expressed as a fixed percentage of the fair market value of the property, section 664(d)(3) shall be taken into account.

(iii) SPECIAL RULE WHERE TIMELY COMMENCEMENT OF REFORMATION.—Clause (ii) shall not apply to any interest if a judicial proceeding is commenced to change such interest into a qualified interest not later than the 90th day after—

(I) if an estate tax return is required to be filed, the last date (including extensions) for filing such return, or

(II) if no estate tax return is required to be filed, the last date (including extensions) for filing the income tax return for the 1st taxable year for which such a return is required to be filed by the trust.

(iv) SPECIAL RULE FOR WILL EXECUTED BEFORE JANUARY 1, 1979, ETC.—In the case of any interest passing under a will executed before January 1, 1979, or under a trust created before such date, clause (ii) shall not apply.

(D) QUALIFIED INTEREST.—For purposes of this paragraph, the term "qualified interest" means an interest for which a deduction is allowable under subsection (a).

(E) LIMITATION.—The deduction referred to in subparagraph (A) shall not exceed the amount of the deduction which would have been allowable for the reformable interest but for paragraph (2).

(F) SPECIAL RULE WHERE INCOME BENEFICIARY DIES.—If (by reason of the death of any individual, or by termination or distribution of a trust in accordance with the terms of the trust instrument) by the due date for filing the estate tax return (including any extension thereof) a reformable interest is in a wholly charitable trust or passes directly to a person or for a use described in subsection (a), a deduction shall be allowed for such reformable interest as if it had met the requirements of paragraph (2) on the date of the decedent's death. For purposes of the preceding sentence, the term "wholly charitable trust" means a charitable trust which, upon the allowance of a deduction, would be described in section 4947(a)(1).

(G) STATUTE OF LIMITATIONS.—The period for assessing any deficiency of any tax attributable to the application of this paragraph shall not expire before the date 1 year after the date on which the Secretary is notified that such reformation (or other proceeding pursuant to subparagraph (J)) has occurred.

(H) REGULATIONS.—The Secretary shall prescribe such regulations as may be necessary to carry out the purposes of this paragraph, including regulations providing such adjustments in the application of the provisions of section 508 (relating to special rules relating to section 501(c)(3) organizations), subchapter J (relating to estates, trusts, beneficiaries, and decedents), and chapter 42 (relating to private foundations) as may be necessary by reason of the qualified reformation.

(I) REFORMATIONS PERMITTED IN CASE OF REMAINDER INTERESTS IN RESIDENCE OR FARM, POOLED INCOME FUNDS, ETC.—The Secretary shall prescribe regulations (consistent with the provisions of this paragraph) permitting reformations in the case of any failure—

(i) to meet the requirements of section 170(f)(3)(B) (relating to remainder interests in personal residence or farm, etc.), or

(ii) to meet the requirements of section 642(c)(5).

(J) VOID OR REFORMED TRUST IN CASES OF INSUFFICIENT REMAINDER INTERESTS.—In the case of a trust that would qualify (or could be reformed to qualify pursuant to subparagraph (B)) but for failure to satisfy the requirement of paragraph (1)(D) or (2)(D) of section 664(d), such trust may be—

(i) declared null and void ab initio, or

(ii) changed by reformation, amendment, or otherwise to meet such requirement by reducing the payout rate or the duration (or both) of any noncharitable beneficiary's interest to the extent necessary to satisfy such requirement,

pursuant to a proceeding that is commenced within the period required in subparagraph (C)(iii). In a case described in clause (i), no deduction shall be allowed under this title for any transfer to the trust and any transactions entered into by the trust prior to being declared void shall be treated as entered into by the transferor.

(4) WORKS OF ART AND THEIR COPYRIGHTS TREATED AS SEPARATE PROPERTIES IN CERTAIN CASES.—

(A) IN GENERAL.—In the case of a qualified contribution of a work of art, the work of art and the copyright on such work of art shall be treated as separate properties for purposes of paragraph (2).

(B) WORK OF ART DEFINED.—For purposes of this paragraph, the term "work of art" means any tangible personal property with respect to which there is a copyright under Federal law.

(C) QUALIFIED CONTRIBUTION DEFINED.—For purposes of this paragraph, the term "qualified contribution" means any transfer of property to a qualified organization if the use of the property by the organization is related to the purpose or function constituting the basis for its exemption under section 501.

(D) QUALIFIED ORGANIZATION DEFINED.—For purposes of this paragraph, the term "qualified organization" means any organization described in section 501(c)(3) other than a private foundation (as defined in section 509). For purposes of the preceding sentence, a private operating foundation (as defined in section 4942(j)(3)) shall not be treated as a private foundation.

(5) CONTRIBUTIONS TO DONOR ADVISED FUNDS.—A deduction otherwise allowed under subsection (a) for any contribution to a donor advised fund (as defined in section 4966(d)(2)) shall only be allowed if—

(A) the sponsoring organization (as defined in section 4966(d)(1)) with respect to such donor advised fund is not—

(i) described in paragraph (3) or (4) of subsection (a), or

(ii) a type III supporting organization (as defined in section 4943(f)(5)(A)) which is not a functionally integrated type III supporting organization (as defined in section 4943(f)(5)(B)), and

(B) the taxpayer obtains a contemporaneous written acknowledgment (determined under rules similar to the rules of section 170(f)(8)(C)) from the sponsoring organization (as so defined) of such donor advised fund that such organization has exclusive legal control over the assets contributed.

Amendments

• **2018, Tax Technical Corrections Act of 2018 (P.L. 115-141)**

P.L. 115-141, § 401(a)(202), Div. U:

Amended Code Sec. 2055(e)(3)(G) by striking "subparagraph (J)" and inserting "subparagraph (J))". **Effective** 3-23-2018.

• **2006, Pension Protection Act of 2006 (P.L. 109-280)**

P.L. 109-280, § 1234(b):

Amended Code Sec. 2055(e) by adding at the end a new paragraph (5). **Effective** for contributions made after the date which is 180 days after 8-17-2006.

• **1997, Taxpayer Relief Act of 1997 (P.L. 105-34)**

P.L. 105-34, § 1089(b)(3):

Amended Code Sec. 2055(e)(3) by adding at the end a new subparagraph (J). **Effective** for transfers in trust after 7-28-97. For a special rule, see Act Sec. 1089(b)(6)(B), below.

P.L. 105-34, § 1089(b)(5):

Amended Code Sec. 2055(e)(3)(G) by inserting "(or other proceeding pursuant to subparagraph (J)[)]" after "reformation". **Effective** for transfers in trust after 7-28-97. For a special rule, see Act Sec. 1089(b)(6)(B), below.

ESTATE TAX—TAXABLE ESTATE

P.L. 105-34, § 1089(b)(6)(B), provides:

(B) SPECIAL RULES FOR CERTAIN DECEDENTS.—The amendments made by this subsection shall not apply to transfers in trust under the terms of a will (or other testamentary instrument) executed on or before July 28, 1997, if the decedent—

(i) dies before January 1, 1999, without having republished the will (or amended such instrument) by codicil or otherwise, or

(ii) was on July 28, 1997, under a mental disability to change the disposition of his property and did not regain his competence to dispose of such property before the date of his death.

• **1984, Deficit Reduction Act of 1984 (P.L. 98-369)**

P.L. 98-369, § 1022(a):

Amended Code Sec. 2055(e)(3). **Effective** for reformations after 12-31-78; except that it does not apply to any reformation to which Code Sec. 2055(e)(3) (as in effect on 7-17-84) applies. For purposes of applying Code Sec. 2055(e)(3)(C)(iii) (as amended by Act Sec. 1022), the 90th day described in such clause shall be treated as not occurring before the 90th day after 7-18-84. For statute of limitations provisions, see Act Sec. 1022(e)(3), under the amendment notes for Code Sec. 664(f). Prior to amendment, Code Sec. 2055(e)(3) read as follows:

(3) In the case of a will executed before December 31, 1978, or a trust created before such date, if a deduction is not allowable at the time of the decedent's death because of the failure of an interest in property which passes from the decedent to a person, or for a use described in subsection (a), to meet the requirements of subparagraph (A) or (B) of paragraph (2) of this subsection, and if the governing instrument is amended or conformed on or before December 31, 1981, or, if later, on or before the 30th day after the date on which judicial proceedings begun on or before December 31, 1981 (which are required to amend or conform the governing instrument), become final, so that the interest is in a trust which meets the requirements of such subparagraph (A) or (B) (as the case may be), a deduction shall nevertheless be allowed. The Secretary may, by regulation, provide for the application of the provisions of this paragraph to trusts whose governing instruments are amended or conformed in accordance with this paragraph, and such regulations may provide for any adjustments in the application of the provisions of section 508 (relating to special rules with respect to section 501(c)(3) organizations), subchapter J (relating to estates, trusts, beneficiaries, and decedents), and chapter 42 (relating to private foundations), to such trusts made necessary by the application of this paragraph. If, by the due date for the filing of an estate tax return (including any extension thereof), the interest is in a charitable trust which, upon allowance of a deduction, would be described in section 4947(a)(1), or the interest passes directly to a person or for a use described in subsection (a), a deduction shall be allowed as if the governing instrument was amended or conformed under this paragraph. If the amendment or conformation of the governing instrument is made after the due date for the filing of the estate tax return (including any extension thereof), the deduction shall be allowed upon the filing of a timely claim for credit or refund (as provided for in section 6511) of an overpayment resulting from the application of this paragraph. In the case of a credit or refund as a result of an amendment or conformation made pursuant to this paragraph, no interest shall be allowed for the period prior to the expiration of the 180th day after the date on which the claim for credit or refund is filed.

• **1981, Economic Recovery Tax Act of 1981 (P.L. 97-34)**

P.L. 97-34, § 423(a):

Added Code Sec. 2055(e)(4). **Effective** for estates of decedents dying after 12-31-81.

• **1980, Miscellaneous Revenue Act of 1980 (P.L. 96-605)**

P.L. 96-605, § 301(a)(1) and (2):

Amended the first sentence of Code Sec. 2055(e)(3): (1) by striking out "December 31, 1977" and inserting in lieu thereof "December 31, 1978"; and (2) by striking out "December 31, 1978" each place it appeared and inserting in lieu thereof "December 31, 1981". **Effective** with respect to decedents dying after 12-31-69.

P.L. 95-600, § 301(b), provides:

CHARITABLE LEAD TRUSTS AND CHARITABLE REMAINDER TRUSTS IN THE CASE OF INCOME AND GIFT TAXES.—Section 514(b) (and section 514(c) insofar as it relates to section 514(b)) of the Revenue Act of 1978 shall be applied as if the amendment made by subsection (a) [P.L. 96-605, § 301(a)(1) and (2), above] had been included in the amendment made by section 514(a) of such Act.

• **1980, Technical Corrections Act of 1979 (P.L. 96-222)**

P.L. 96-222, § 105(a)(4)(A):

Amended Code Sec. 2055(e)(3) by changing "subparagraph (a) or (B)" to "subparagraph (A) or (B)" and by changing "so that interest" to "so that the interest". For **effective** date, see below.

• **1978, Revenue Act of 1978 (P.L. 95-600)**

P.L. 95-600, § 514(a):

Amended the first sentence of Code Sec. 2055(e)(3). **Effective** as noted in Act Sec. 514(c), below. Prior to amendment, such sentence read as follows:

"In the case of a will executed before December 31, 1977, or a trust created before such date, if a deduction is not allowable at the time of the decedent's death because of the failure of an interest in property which passes from the decedent to a person, or for a use, described in subsection (a), to meet the requirements of subparagraph (A) or (B) of paragraph (2) of this subsection, and if the governing instrument is amended or conformed on or before December 31, 1977, or, if later, on or before the 30th day after the date on which judicial proceedings begun on or before December 31, 1977 (which are required to amend or conform the governing instrument), become final, so that the interest is in a trust which is a charitable remainder annuity trust, a charitable remainder unitrust (described in section 664), or a pooled income fund (described in section 642(c)(5)), a deduction shall nevertheless be allowed."

P.L. 95-600, § 514(b), provides:

(b) CHARITABLE LEAD TRUSTS AND CHARITABLE REMAINDER TRUSTS IN THE CASE OF INCOME AND GIFT TAXES.—Under regulations prescribed by the Secretary of the Treasury or his delegate, in the case of trusts created before December 31, 1977, provisions comparable to section 2055(e)(3) of the Internal Revenue Code of 1954 (as amended by subsection (a) [P.L. 95-600, § 514(a), above]) shall be deemed to be included in sections 170 and 2522 of the Internal Revenue Code of 1954.

P.L. 95-600, § 514(c), as added by P.L. 96-222, § 105(a)(4)(B), provides:

(c) EFFECTIVE DATES.—

(1) FOR SUBSECTION (a).—The amendment made by subsection (a) shall apply in the case of decedents dying after December 31, 1969.

(2) FOR SUBSECTION (b).—Subsection (b)—

(A) insofar as it relates to section 170 of the Internal Revenue Code of 1954 shall apply to transfers in trust and contributions made after July 31, 1969, and

(B) insofar as it relates to section 2522 of the Internal Revenue Code of 1954 shall apply to transfers made after December 31, 1969.

• **1976, Tax Reform Act of 1976 (P.L. 94-455)**

P.L. 94-455, § 1304(a):

Substituted "December 31, 1977," for "September 21, 1974," and substituted "December 31, 1977" for "December 31, 1975" each place it appeared in Code Sec. 2055(e)(3).

P.L. 94-455, § 1304(b), provides:

(b) EXTENSION OF PERIOD FOR FILING CLAIM FOR REFUND OF ESTATE TAX PAID.—A claim for refund or credit of an overpayment of the tax imposed by section 2001 of the Internal Revenue Code of 1954 allowable under section 2055(e)(3) of such Code (as amended by subsection (a)) shall not be denied because of the expiration of the time for filing such a claim under section 6511(a) if such claim is filed not later than June 30, 1978.

P.L. 94-455, § 1304(c), provides:

The amendments made by this section are **effective** for decedents dying after 12-31-69.

P.L. 94-455, § 1906(b)(13)(A):

Amended 1954 Code by substituting "Secretary" for "Secretary or his delegate" each place it appeared. **Effective** 2-1-77.

P.L. 94-455, § 2124(e) (as amended by P.L. 95-30, § 309(b)(2)):

Substituted "(other than an interest described in section 170(f)(3)(B))" for "(other than a remainder interest in a personal residence or farm or an undivided portion of the decedent's entire interest in property)" in Code Sec. 2055(e)(2). **Effective** for contributions or transfers made after 6-13-76, and before 6-14-77. However, P.L. 95-30, § 309(b)(2), changed this latter date to 6-14-81.

• **1974 (P.L. 93-483)**

P.L. 93-483, § 3:

Amended Code Sec. 2055(e) by adding paragraph (3). **Effective** with respect to decedents dying after 12-31-69.

• **1969, Tax Reform Act of 1969 (P.L. 91-172)**

P.L. 91-172, § 201(d)(1):

Amended Code Sec. 2055(e). **Effective** in the case of decedents dying after 12-31-69. However, such amendments shall not apply in the case of property passing under the terms of a will executed on or before 10-9-69—

(i) if the decedent dies before October 9, 1972, without having republished the will after October 9, 1969, by codicil or otherwise,

(ii) if the decedent at no time after October 9, 1969, had the right to change the portions of the will which pertain to the passing of the property to, or for the use of, an organization described in section 2055(a), or

(iii) if the will is not republished by codicil or otherwise before October 9, 1972, and the decedent is on such date and at all times thereafter under a mental disability to republish the will by codicil or otherwise.

Such amendment shall not apply in the case of property transferred in trust on or before October 9, 1969—

(i) if the decedent dies before October 9, 1972, without having amended after October 9, 1969, the instrument governing the disposition of the property,

(ii) if the property transferred was an irrevocable interest to, or for the use of, an organization described in section 2055(a), or

(iii) if the instrument governing the disposition of the property was not amended by the decedent before October 9, 1972, and the decedent is on such date and at all times thereafter under a mental disability to change the disposition of the property.

Prior to amendment, Code Sec. 2055(e) read as follows:

(e) Disallowance of Deductions in Certain Cases.—

For disallowance of certain charitable, etc., deductions otherwise allowable under this section, see sections 503 and 681.

• **1958, Technical Amendments Act of 1958 (P.L. 85-866)**

P.L. 85-866, § 30(d):

Amended Code Sec. 2055(e) by substituting "503" for "504". **Effective** 1-1-54.

[Sec. 2055(f)]

(f) SPECIAL RULE FOR IRREVOCABLE TRANSFERS OF EASEMENTS IN REAL PROPERTY.—A deduction shall be allowed under subsection (a) in respect of any transfer of a qualified real property interest (as defined in section 170(h)(2)(C)) which meets the requirements of section 170(h) (without regard to paragraph (4)(A) thereof).

Internal Revenue Code   **Sec. 2055(f)**

ESTATE TAX—TAXABLE ESTATE

Amendments

- **1986, Tax Reform Act of 1986 (P.L. 99-514)**

P.L. 99-514, §1422(a)(1) and (2):

Amended Code Sec. 2055 by redesignating subsection (f) as subsection (g), and by inserting after subsection (e) new subsection (f). **Effective** for transfers and contributions made after 12-31-86.

[Sec. 2055(g)—Stricken]

Amendments

- **2007, Tax Technical Corrections Act of 2007 (P.L. 110-172)**

P.L. 110-172, §3(d)(1):

Amended Code Sec. 2055 by striking subsection (g) and by redesignating subsection (h) as subsection (g). **Effective** as if included in the provision of the Pension Protection Act of 2006 (P.L. 109-280) to which it relates [**effective** for contributions, bequests, and gifts made after 8-17-2006.—CCH]. Prior to being stricken, Code Sec. 2055(g) read as follows:

(g) VALUATION OF SUBSEQUENT GIFTS.—

(1) IN GENERAL.—In the case of any additional contribution, the fair market value of such contribution shall be determined by using the lesser of—

(A) the fair market value of the property at the time of the initial fractional contribution, or

(B) the fair market value of the property at the time of the additional contribution.

(2) DEFINITIONS.—For purposes of this paragraph—

(A) ADDITIONAL CONTRIBUTION.—The term "additional contribution" means a bequest, legacy, devise, or transfer described in subsection (a) of any interest in a property with respect to which the decedent had previously made an initial fractional contribution.

(B) INITIAL FRACTIONAL CONTRIBUTION.—The term "initial fractional contribution" means, with respect to any decedent, any charitable contribution of an undivided portion of the decedent's entire interest in any tangible personal property for which a deduction was allowed under section 170.

- **2006, Pension Protection Act of 2006 (P.L. 109-280)**

P.L. 109-280, §1218(b):

Amended Code Sec. 2055 by redesignating subsection (g) as subsection (h) and by inserting after subsection (f) a new subsection (g). **Effective** for contributions, bequests, and gifts made after 8-17-2006.

[Sec. 2055(g)]

(g) CROSS REFERENCES.—

(1) For option as to time for valuation for purpose of deduction under this section, see section 2032.

(2) For treatment of certain organizations providing child care, see section 501(k).

(3) For exemption of gifts and bequests to or for the benefit of Library of Congress, see section 5 of the Act of March 3, 1925, as amended (2 U.S.C. 161).

(4) For treatment of gifts and bequests for the benefit of the Naval Historical Center as gifts or bequests to or for the use of the United States, see section 8622 of title 10, United States Code.

(5) For treatment of gifts and bequests to or for the benefit of National Park Foundation as gifts or bequests to or for the use of the United States, see section 8 of the Act of December 18, 1967 (16 U.S.C. 191).

(6) For treatment of gifts, devises, or bequests accepted by the Secretary of State, the Director of the International Communication Agency, or the Director of the United States International Development Cooperation Agency as gifts, devises, or bequests to or for the use of the United States, see section 25 of the State Department Basic Authorities Act of 1956.

(7) For treatment of gifts or bequests of money accepted by the Attorney General for credit to "Commissary Funds, Federal Prisons" as gifts or bequests to or for the use of the United States, see section 4043 of title 18, United States Code.

(8) For payment of tax on gifts and bequests of United States obligations to the United States, see section 3113(e) of title 31, United States Code.

(9) For treatment of gifts and bequests for benefit of the Naval Academy as gifts or bequests to or for the use of the United States, see section 8473 of title 10, United States Code.

(10) For treatment of gifts and bequests for benefit of the Naval Academy Museum as gifts or bequests to or for the use of the United States, see section 8474 of title 10, United States Code.

(11) For exemption of gifts and bequests received by National Archives Trust Fund Board, see section 2308 of title 44, United States Code.

(12) For treatment of gifts and bequests to or for the use of Indian tribal governments (or their subdivisions), see section 7871.

Amendments

- **2018, John S. McCain National Defense Authorization Act for Fiscal Year 2019 (P.L. 115-232)**

P.L. 115-232, §809(h)(2)(A), Div. A:

Amended Code Sec. 2055(g)(4) by striking "section 7222 of title 10, United States Code" and inserting "section 8622 of title 10, United States Code". **Effective** 8-13-2018.

P.L. 115-232, §809(h)(2)(B), Div. A:

Amended Code Sec. 2055(g)(9) by striking "section 6973 of title 10, United States Code" and inserting "section 8473 of title 10, United States Code". **Effective** 8-13-2018.

P.L. 115-232, §809(h)(2)(C), Div. A:

Amended Code Sec. 2055(g)(10) by striking "section 6974 of title 10, United States Code" and inserting "section 8474 of title 10, United States Code". **Effective** 8-13-2018.

- **2007, Tax Technical Corrections Act of 2007 (P.L. 110-172)**

P.L. 110-172, §3(d)(1):

Amended Code Sec. 2055 by redesignating subsection (h) as subsection (g). **Effective** as if included in the provision of the Pension Protection Act of 2006 (P.L. 109-280) to which it relates [**effective** for contributions, bequests, and gifts made after 8-17-2006.—CCH].

- **2006, Pension Protection Act of 2006 (P.L. 109-280)**

P.L. 109-280, §1218(b):

Amended Code Sec. 2055 by redesignating subsection (g) as subsection (h). **Effective** for contributions, bequests, and gifts made after 8-17-2006.

- **1996, National Defense Authorization Act for Fiscal Year 1997 (P.L. 104-201)**

P.L. 104-201, §1073(b)(3):

Amended Code Sec. 2055(h)(4). **Effective** 9-23-96. Prior to amendment, Code Sec. 2055(h)(4) read as follows:

(4) For treatment of gifts and bequests for the benefit of the Office of Naval Records and History as gifts or bequests to or for the use of the United States, see section 7222 of title 10, United States Code.

- **1986, Tax Reform Act of 1986 (P.L. 99-514)**

P.L. 99-514, §1422(a)(1)-(2):

Redesignated subsection (f) as subsection (g). **Effective** for transfers and contributions made after 12-31-86.

- **1984, Deficit Reduction Act of 1984 (P.L. 98-369)**

P.L. 98-369, §1032(b)(2):

Amended Code Sec. 2055(f) by redesignating paragraphs (2) through (11) as paragraphs (3) through (12), respectively, and by inserting after paragraph (1) a new paragraph (2). **Effective** for tax years beginning after 7-18-84.

- **1983 (P.L. 97-473)**

P.L. 97-473, §202(b)(5):

Amended Code Sec. 2055(f) by adding subparagraph (11). For the **effective** date, see the amendment note for Act Sec. 204, following Code Sec. 7871.

- **1982 (P.L. 97-258)**

P.L. 97-258, §3(f)(1):

Amended Code Sec. 2055(f)(6) by striking out "section 2 of the Act of May 15, 1952, as amended by the Act of July 9, 1952 (31 U.S.C. 725s-4)" and substituting "section 4043 of title 18, United States Code". **Effective** 9-13-82.

P.L. 97-258, §3(f)(2):

Amended Code Sec. 2055(f)(7) by striking out "section 24 of the Second Liberty Bond Act (31 U.S.C. 757e)" and substituting "section 3113(e) of title 31, United States Code". **Effective** 9-13-82.

- **1980, Foreign Service Act of 1980 (P.L. 96-465)**

P.L. 96-465, §2206(e)(4):

Amended Code Sec. 2055(f)(5). **Effective** 2-15-81. Prior to amendment, paragraph (5) read as follows:

Sec. 2055(g)—Stricken

ESTATE TAX—TAXABLE ESTATE

"(5) For treatment of gifts, devises, or bequests accepted by the Secretary of State under the Foreign Service Act of 1946 as gifts, devises, or bequests to or for the use of the United States, see section 1021(e) of that Act (22 U.S.C. 809(e)).".

• **1976, Tax Reform Act of 1976 (P.L. 94-455)**

P.L. 94-455, §1902(a)(4)(B), (c)(1):

Amended Code Sec. 2055(f). **Effective** for estates of decedents dying after 10-4-76. Prior to amendment, Code Sec. 2055(f) read as follows:

(f) OTHER CROSS REFERENCES.—

(1) For option as to time for valuation for purpose of deduction under this section, see section 2032.

(2) For exemption of bequests to or for benefit of Library of Congress, see section 5 of the Act of March 3, 1925, as amended (56 Stat. 765; 2 U.S.C. 161).

(3) For construction of bequests for benefit of the library of the Post Office Department as bequests to or for the use of the United States, see section 2 of the Act of August 8, 1946 (60 Stat. 924; 5 U.S.C. 393).

(4) For exemption of bequests for benefit of Office of Naval Records and Library, Navy Department, see section 2 of the Act of March 4, 1937 (50 Stat. 25; 5 U.S.C. 419b).

(5) For exemption of bequests to or for benefit of National Park Service, see section 5 of the Act of July 10, 1935 (49 Stat. 478; 16 U.S.C. 19c).

(6) For construction of devises or bequests accepted by the Secretary of State under the Foreign Service Act of 1946 as devises or bequests to or for the use of the United States, see section 1021(e) of that Act (60 Stat. 1032; 22 U.S.C. 809).

(7) For construction of gifts or bequests of money accepted by the Attorney General for credit to "Commissary Funds, Federal Prisons" as gifts or bequests to or for the use of the United States, see section 2 of the Act of May 15, 1952, 66 Stat. 73, as amended by the Act of July 9, 1952, 66 Stat. 479 (31 U.S.C. 725s-4).

(8) For payment of tax on bequests of United States obligations to the United States, see section 24 of the Second Liberty Bond Act, as amended (59 Stat. 48, §4; 31 U.S.C. 757e).

(9) For construction of bequests for benefit of or use in connection with the Naval Academy as bequests to or for the use of the United States, see section 3 of the Act of March 31, 1944 (58 Stat. 135; 34 U.S.C. 1115b).

(10) For exemption of bequests for benefit of Naval Academy Museum, see section 4 of the Act of March 26, 1938 (52 Stat. 119; 34 U.S.C. 1119).

(11) For exemption of bequests received by National Archives Trust Fund Board, see section 7 of the National Archives Trust Fund Board Act (55 Stat. 582; 44 U.S.C. 300gg).

[Sec. 2056]

SEC. 2056. BEQUESTS, ETC., TO SURVIVING SPOUSE.

[Sec. 2056(a)]

(a) ALLOWANCE OF MARITAL DEDUCTION.—For purposes of the tax imposed by section 2001, the value of the taxable estate shall, except as limited by subsection (b), be determined by deducting from the value of the gross estate an amount equal to the value of any interest in property which passes or has passed from the decedent to his surviving spouse, but only to the extent that such interest is included in determining the value of the gross estate.

Amendments

• **1981, Economic Recovery Tax Act of 1981 (P.L. 97-34)**

P.L. 97-34, §403(a)(1)(B):

Amended Code Sec. 2056(a) by striking out "subsections (b) and (c)" and inserting "subsection (b)". **Effective** for estates of decedents dying after 12-31-81.

• **1976, Tax Reform Act of 1976 (P.L. 94-455)**

P.L. 94-455, §2009(b)(4)(E), (e)(2):

Substituted "subsections (b) and (c)" for "subsections (b), (c), and (d)" in Code Sec. 2056(a). **Effective** for transfers creating an interest in the person disclaiming made after 12-31-76.

[Sec. 2056(b)]

(b) LIMITATION IN THE CASE OF LIFE ESTATE OR OTHER TERMINABLE INTEREST.—

(1) GENERAL RULE.—Where, on the lapse of time, on the occurrence of an event or contingency, or on the failure of an event or contingency to occur, an interest passing to the surviving spouse will terminate or fail, no deduction shall be allowed under this section with respect to such interest—

(A) if an interest in such property passes or has passed (for less than an adequate and full consideration in money or money's worth) from the decedent to any person other than such surviving spouse (or the estate of such spouse); and

(B) if by reason of such passing such person (or his heirs or assigns) may possess or enjoy any part of such property after such termination or failure of the interest so passing to the surviving spouse;

and no deduction shall be allowed with respect to such interest (even if such deduction is not disallowed under subparagraphs (A) and (B))—

(C) if such interest is to be acquired for the surviving spouse, pursuant to directions of the decedent, by his executor or by the trustee of a trust.

For purposes of this paragraph, an interest shall not be considered as an interest which will terminate or fail merely because it is the ownership of a bond, note, or similar contractual obligation, the discharge of which would not have the effect of an annuity for life or for a term.

(2) INTEREST IN UNIDENTIFIED ASSETS.—Where the assets (included in the decedent's gross estate) out of which, or the proceeds of which, an interest passing to the surviving spouse may be satisfied include a particular asset or assets with respect to which no deduction would be allowed if such asset or assets passed from the decedent to such spouse, then the value of such interest passing to such spouse shall, for purposes of subsection (a), be reduced by the aggregate value of such particular assets.

(3) INTEREST OF SPOUSE CONDITIONAL ON SURVIVAL FOR LIMITED PERIOD.—For purposes of this subsection, an interest passing to the surviving spouse shall not be considered as an interest which will terminate or fail on the death of such spouse if—

(A) such death will cause a termination or failure of such interest only if it occurs within a period not exceeding 6 months after the decedent's death, or only if it occurs as a result of a common disaster resulting in the death of the decedent and the surviving spouse, or only if it occurs in the case of either such event; and

(B) such termination or failure does not in fact occur.

(4) VALUATION OF INTEREST PASSING TO SURVIVING SPOUSE.—In determining for purposes of subsection (a) the value of any interest in property passing to the surviving spouse for which a deduction is allowed by this section—

(A) there shall be taken into account the effect which the tax imposed by section 2001, or any estate, succession, legacy, or inheritance tax, has on the net value to the surviving spouse of such interest; and

(B) where such interest or property is encumbered in any manner, or where the surviving spouse incurs any obligation imposed by the decedent with respect to the passing of such interest, such encumbrance or obligation shall be taken into account in the same manner as if the amount of a gift to such spouse of such interest were being determined.

(5) LIFE ESTATE WITH POWER OF APPOINTMENT IN SURVIVING SPOUSE.—In the case of an interest in property passing from the decedent, if his surviving spouse is entitled for life to all the income from the entire interest, or all the income from a specific portion thereof, payable annually or at more frequent intervals, with power in the surviving spouse to appoint the entire interest, or such specific portion (exercisable in favor of such surviving spouse, or of the estate of such surviving spouse, or in favor of either, whether or not in each case the power is exercisable in favor of others), and with no power in any other person to appoint any part of the interest, or such specific portion, to any person other than the surviving spouse—

(A) the interest or such portion thereof so passing shall, for purposes of subsection (a), be considered as passing to the surviving spouse, and

(B) no part of the interest so passing shall, for purposes of paragraph (1)(A), be considered as passing to any person other than the surviving spouse.

ESTATE TAX—TAXABLE ESTATE

This paragraph shall apply only if such power in the surviving spouse to appoint the entire interest, or such specific portion thereof, whether exercisable by will or during life, is exercisable by such spouse alone and in all events.

(6) LIFE INSURANCE OR ANNUITY PAYMENTS WITH POWER OF APPOINTMENT IN SURVIVING SPOUSE.—In the case of an interest in property passing from the decedent consisting of proceeds under a life insurance, endowment, or annuity contract, if under the terms of the contract such proceeds are payable in installments or are held by the insurer subject to an agreement to pay interest thereon (whether the proceeds, on the termination of any interest payments, are payable in a lump sum or in annual or more frequent installments), and such installment or interest payments are payable annually or at more frequent intervals, commencing not later than 13 months after the decedent's death, and all amounts, or a specific portion of all such amounts, payable during the life of the surviving spouse are payable only to such spouse, and such spouse has the power to appoint all amounts, or such specific portion, payable under such contract (exercisable in favor of such surviving spouse, or of the estate of such surviving spouse, or in favor of either, whether or not in each case the power is exercisable in favor of others), with no power in any other person to appoint such amounts to any person other than the surviving spouse—

(A) such amounts shall, for purposes of subsection (a), be considered as passing to the surviving spouse, and

(B) no part of such amounts shall, for purposes of paragraph (1)(A), be considered as passing to any person other than the surviving spouse.

This paragraph shall apply only if, under the terms of the contract, such power in the surviving spouse to appoint such amounts, whether exercisable by will or during life, is exercisable by such spouse alone and in all events.

(7) ELECTION WITH RESPECT TO LIFE ESTATE FOR SURVIVING SPOUSE.—

(A) IN GENERAL.—In the case of qualified terminable interest property—

(i) for purposes of subsection (a), such property shall be treated as passing to the surviving spouse, and

(ii) for purposes of paragraph (1)(A), no part of such property shall be treated as passing to any person other than the surviving spouse.

(B) QUALIFIED TERMINABLE INTEREST PROPERTY DEFINED.—For purposes of this paragraph—

(i) IN GENERAL.—The term "qualified terminable interest property" means property—

(I) which passes from the decedent,

(II) in which the surviving spouse has a qualifying income interest for life, and

(III) to which an election under this paragraph applies.

(ii) QUALIFYING INCOME INTEREST FOR LIFE.—The surviving spouse has a qualifying income interest for life if—

(I) the surviving spouse is entitled to all the income from the property, payable annually or at more frequent intervals, or has a usufruct interest for life in the property, and

(II) no person has a power to appoint any part of the property to any person other than the surviving spouse.

Subclause (II) shall not apply to a power exercisable only at or after the death of the surviving spouse. To the extent provided in regulations, an annuity shall be treated in a manner similar to an income interest in property (regardless of whether the property from which the annuity is payable can be separately identified).

(iii) PROPERTY INCLUDES INTEREST THEREIN.—The term "property" includes an interest in property.

(iv) SPECIFIC PORTION TREATED AS SEPARATE PROPERTY.—A specific portion of property shall be treated as separate property.

(v) ELECTION.—An election under this paragraph with respect to any property shall be made by the executor on the return of tax imposed by section 2001. Such an election, once made, shall be irrevocable.

(C) TREATMENT OF SURVIVOR ANNUITIES.—In the case of an annuity included in the gross estate of the decedent under section 2039 (or, in the case of an interest in an annuity arising under the community property laws of a State, included in the gross estate of the decedent under section 2033) where only the surviving spouse has the right to receive payments before the death of such surviving spouse—

(i) the interest of such surviving spouse shall be treated as a qualifying income interest for life, and

(ii) the executor shall be treated as having made an election under this subsection with respect to such annuity unless the executor otherwise elects on the return of tax imposed by section 2001.

An election under clause (ii), once made, shall be irrevocable.

(8) SPECIAL RULE FOR CHARITABLE REMAINDER TRUSTS.—

(A) IN GENERAL.—If the surviving spouse of the decedent is the only beneficiary of a qualified charitable remainder trust who is not a charitable beneficiary nor an ESOP beneficiary, paragraph (1) shall not apply to any interest in such trust which passes or has passed from the decedent to such surviving spouse.

(B) DEFINITIONS.—For purposes of subparagraph (A)—

(i) CHARITABLE BENEFICIARY.—The term "charitable beneficiary" means any beneficiary which is an organization described in section 170(c).

(ii) ESOP BENEFICIARY.—The term "ESOP beneficiary" means any beneficiary which is an employee stock ownership plan (as defined in section 4975(e)(7)) that holds a remainder interest in qualified employer securities (as defined in section 664(g)(4)) to be transferred to such plan in a qualified gratuitous transfer (as defined in section 664(g)(1)).

(iii) QUALIFIED CHARITABLE REMAINDER TRUST.—The term "qualified charitable remainder trust" means a charitable remainder annuity trust or a charitable remainder unitrust (described in section 664).

(9) DENIAL OF DOUBLE DEDUCTION.—Nothing in this section or any other provision of this chapter shall allow the value of any interest in property to be deducted under this chapter more than once with respect to the same decedent.

(10) SPECIFIC PORTION.—For purposes of paragraphs (5), (6), and (7)(B)(iv), the term "specific portion" only includes a portion determined on a fractional or percentage basis.

Amendments

- **1997, Taxpayer Relief Act of 1997 (P.L. 105-34)**

P.L. 105-34, § 1311(a):

Amended Code Sec. 2056(b)(7)(C) by inserting "(or, in the case of an interest in an annuity arising under the community property laws of a State, included in the gross estate of the decedent under section 2033)" after "section 2039". **Effective** for estates of decedents dying after 8-5-97.

P.L. 105-34, § 1530(c)(8):

Amended Code Sec. 2056(b)(8). **Effective** for transfers made by trusts to, or for the use of, an employee stock ownership plan after 8-5-97. Prior to amendment, Code Sec. 2056(b)(8) read as follows:

(8) SPECIAL RULE FOR CHARITABLE REMAINDER TRUSTS.—

(A) IN GENERAL.—If the surviving spouse of the decedent is the only noncharitable beneficiary of a qualified charitable remainder trust, paragraph (1) shall not apply to any interest in such trust which passes or has passed from the decedent to such surviving spouse.

(B) DEFINITIONS.—For purposes of subparagraph (A)—

(i) NONCHARITABLE BENEFICIARY.—The term "noncharitable beneficiary" means any beneficiary of the qualified charitable remainder trust other than an organization described in section 170(c).

(ii) QUALIFIED CHARITABLE REMAINDER TRUST.—The term "qualified charitable remainder trust" means a charitable remainder annuity trust or charitable remainder unitrust (described in section 664)."

Sec. 2056(b)(6)

ESTATE TAX—TAXABLE ESTATE

• **1992, Energy Policy Act of 1992 (P.L. 102-486)**

P.L. 102-486, §1941(a):

Amended Code Sec. 2056(b) by adding at the end thereof new paragraph (10). For the **effective** date, see Act Sec. 1941(c)(1), below.

P.L. 102-486, §1941(c)(1), provides:

(c) EFFECTIVE DATES.—

(1) SUBSECTION (a).—

(A) IN GENERAL.—Except as provided in subparagraph (B), the amendment made by subsection (a) shall apply to the estates of decedents dying after the date of the enactment of this Act.

(B) EXCEPTION.—The amendment made by subsection (a) shall not apply to any interest in property which passes (or has passed) to the surviving spouse of the decedent pursuant to a will (or revocable trust) in existence on the date of the enactment of this Act if—

(i) the decedent dies on or before the date 3 years after such date of enactment, or

(ii) the decedent was, on such date of enactment, under a mental disability to change the disposition of his property and did not regain his competence to dispose of such property before the date of his death.

The preceding sentence shall not apply if such will (or revocable trust) is amended at any time after such date of enactment in any respect which will increase the amount of the interest which so passes or alters the terms of the transfer by which the interest so passes.

• **1989, Omnibus Budget Reconciliation Act of 1989 (P.L. 101-239)**

P.L. 101-239, §7816(q):

Amended Code Sec. 2056(b)(7)(C) by striking "an annuity" and inserting "an annuity included in the gross estate of the decedent under section 2039". **Effective** as if included in the provision of P.L. 100-647 to which it relates.

• **1988, Technical and Miscellaneous Revenue Act of 1988 (P.L. 100-647)**

P.L. 100-647, §6152(a):

Amended Code Sec. 2056(b)(7) by adding at the end thereof new subparagraph (C). **Effective**, generally, with respect to decedents dying after 12-31-81. See, also, Act Sec. 6152(c)(2)-(3), below.

Amendments

• **1981, Economic Recovery Tax Act of 1981 (P.L. 97-34)**

P.L. 97-34, §403(a)(1)(A):

Repealed Code Sec. 2056(c). **Effective** for estates of decedents dying after 12-31-81. For a transitional rule, see Act Sec. 403(e)(3), below. Prior to its repeal, Code Sec. 2056(c) read as follows:

(c) LIMITATION ON AGGREGATE OF DEDUCTIONS.—

(1) LIMITATION.—

(A) IN GENERAL.—The aggregate amount of the deductions allowed under this section (computed without regard to this subsection) shall not exceed the greater of—

(i) $250,000, or

(ii) 50 percent of the value of the adjusted gross estate (as defined in paragraph (2)).

(B) ADJUSTMENT FOR CERTAIN GIFTS TO SPOUSE.—If a deduction is allowed to the decedent under section 2523 with respect to any gift made to his spouse after December 31, 1976, the limitation provided by subparagraph (A) (determined without regard to this subparagraph) shall be reduced (but not below zero) by the excess (if any) of—

(i) the aggregate of the deductions allowed to the decedent under section 2523 with respect to gifts made after December 31, 1976, over

(ii) the aggregate of the deductions which would have been allowable under section 2523 with respect to gifts made after December 31, 1976, if the amount deductible under such section with respect to any gift required to be included in a gift tax return were 50 percent of its value.

For purposes of this subparagraph, a gift which is includible in the gross estate of the donor by reason of section 2035 shall not be taken into account.

(C) COMMUNITY PROPERTY ADJUSTMENT.—The $250,000 amount set forth in subparagraph (A)(i) shall be reduced by the excess (if any) of—

(i) the amount of the subtraction determined under clauses (i), (ii), and (iii) of paragraph (2)(B), over

(ii) the excess of the aggregate of the deductions allowed under sections 2053 and 2054 over the amount taken into account with respect to such deductions under clause (iv) of paragraph (2)(B).

(2) COMPUTATION OF ADJUSTED GROSS ESTATE.—

(A) GENERAL RULE.—Except as provided in subparagraph (B) of this paragraph, the adjusted gross estate shall, for purposes of subsection (c)(1), be computed by subtracting from the entire value of the gross estate the aggregate amount of the deductions allowed by sections 2053 and 2054.

(B) SPECIAL RULE IN CASES INVOLVING COMMUNITY PROPERTY.—If the decedent and his surviving spouse at any time, held property as community property under the law of any State, or possession of the United States, or of any foreign country, then the adjusted gross estate shall, for purposes of subsection (c)(1), be determined by subtracting from the entire value of the gross estate the sum of—

(i) the value of property which is at the time of the death of the decedent held as such community property; and

(ii) the value of property transferred by the decedent during his life, if at the time of such transfer the property was held as such community property; and

(iii) the amount receivable as insurance under policies on the life of the decedent, to the extent purchased with premiums or other consideration paid out of property held as such community property; and

(iv) an amount which bears the same ratio to the aggregate of the deductions allowed under sections 2053 and 2054 which the value of the property included in the gross estate, diminished by the amount subtracted under clauses (i), (ii), and (iii) of this subparagraph, bears to the entire value of the gross estate.

For purposes of clauses (i), (ii), and (iii), community property (except property which is considered as community property solely by reason of the provisions of subparagraph (C) of this paragraph) shall be considered as not "held as such community property" as of any moment of time, if, in case of the death of the decedent at such moment, such property (and not merely one-half thereof) would be or would have been includible in determining the value of his gross estate without regard to the provisions of section 402(b) of the Revenue Act of 1942. The amount to be subtracted under clauses (i), (ii), or (iii) shall not exceed the value of the interest in the property described therein which is included in determining the value of the gross estate.

(C) COMMUNITY PROPERTY-CONVERSION INTO SEPARATE PROPERTY.—

(i) AFTER DECEMBER 31, 1941.—If after December 31, 1941, property held as such community property (unless considered by reason of subparagraph (B) of this paragraph as not so held) was by the decedent and the surviving spouse converted, by one transaction or a series of transactions, into separate property of the decedent and his spouse (including any form of coownership by them), the separate property so acquired by the decedent and any property acquired at any time by the decedent in exchange therefor (by one exchange or a series of exchanges) shall, for the purposes of clauses (i), (ii), and (iii) of subparagraph (B), be considered as "held as such community property."

(ii) LIMITATION.—Where the value (at the time of such conversion) of the separate property so acquired by the decedent exceeded the value (at such time) of the separate property so acquired by the decedent's spouse, the rule in clause (i) shall be applied only with respect to the same portion of such separate property of the decedent as the portion which the value (as of such time) of such separate property so acquired by the decedent's spouse is of the value (as of such time) of the separate property so acquired by the decedent.

P.L. 97-34, §403(e)(3), provides:

(3) If—

(A) the decedent dies after December 31, 1981,

(B) by reason of the death of the decedent property passes from the decedent or is acquired from the decedent under a will executed before the date which is 30 days after the date of the enactment of this Act, or a trust created before such date, which contains a formula expressly providing that the spouse is to receive the maximum amount of property qualifying for the marital deduction allowable by Fedeeral law,

(C) the formula referred to in subparagraph (B) was not amended to refer specifically to an unlimited marital deduction at any time after the date which is 30 days after the date of enactment of this Act, and before the death of the decedent, and

(D) the State does not enact a statute applicable to such estate which construes this type of formula as referring to the marital deduction allowable by Federal law as amended by subsection (a),

then the amendment made by subsection (a) shall not apply to the estate of such decedent.

• **1978, Revenue Act of 1978 (P.L. 95-600)**

P.L. 95-600, §702(g)(1)-(2):

Amended Code Sec. 2056(c)(1)(B) by adding "required to be included in a gift tax return" in clause (ii) and by adding the last sentence in the subparagraph. **Effective** for estates of decedents dying after 1976.

P.L. 100-647, §6152(c)(2)-(3), provides:

(2) NOT TO APPLY TO EXTENT INCONSISTENT WITH PRIOR RETURN.—In the case of any estate or gift tax return filed before the date of the enactment of this Act, the amendments made by this section shall not apply to the extent such amendments would be inconsistent with the treatment of the annuity on such return unless the executor or donor (as the case may be) otherwise elects under this paragraph before the day 2 years after the date of the enactment of this Act.

(3) EXTENSION OF TIME FOR ELECTION OUT.—The time for making an election under section 2056(b)(7)(C)(ii) or 2523(f)(6)(B) of the 1986 Code (as added by this subsection) shall not expire before the day 2 years after the date of the enactment of this Act (and, if such election is made within the time permitted under this paragraph, the requirement of such section 2056(b)(7)(C)(ii) that it be made on the return shall not apply).

• **1984, Deficit Reduction Act of 1984 (P.L. 98-369)**

P.L. 98-369, §1027(a):

Amended Code Sec. 2056(b)(7)(B)(ii)(1)[(I)] by inserting ", or has a usufruct interest for life in the property" after "intervals". **Effective** as if included in the amendment made by Act Sec. 403 of P.L. 97-34.

• **1983, Technical Corrections Act of 1982 (P.L. 97-448)**

P.L. 97-448, §104(a)(2)(A):

Amended Code Sec. 2056(b) by adding at the end thereof new paragraph (9). **Effective** as if included in the provision of P.L. 97-34 to which it relates.

P.L. 97-448, §104(a)(8):

Amended Code Sec. 2056(b)(7)(B)(ii) by adding the sentence at the end thereof. **Effective** as if included in the provision of P.L. 97-34 to which it relates.

• **1981, Economic Recovery Tax Act of 1981 (P.L. 97-34)**

P.L. 97-34, §403(d)(1):

Added Code Sec. 2056(b)(7) and (8). **Effective** for estates of decedents dying after 12-31-81.

[Sec. 2056(c)—Repealed]

ESTATE TAX—TAXABLE ESTATE

• **1976, Tax Reform Act of 1976 (P.L. 94-455)**

P.L. 94-455, §1902(a)(12)(A):

Deleted "Territory" in Code Sec. 2056(c)(2)(B). **Effective** for gifts made after 12-31-76.

P.L. 94-455, §2002(a):

Amended Code Sec. 2056(c)(1). For the **effective** date, see Act Sec. 2002(d)(1), below. Prior to amendment, Code Sec. 2056(c)(1) read as follows:

(1) GENERAL RULE.—The aggregate amount of the deductions allowed under this section (computed without regard to this subsection) shall not exceed 50 percent of the value of the adjusted gross estate, as defined in paragraph (2).

P.L. 94-455, §2002(d)(1), provides:

(d) EFFECTIVE DATES.—

(1)(A) Except as provided in subparagraph (B), the amendment made by subsection (a) shall apply with respect to the estates of decedents dying after December 31, 1976.

(B) If—

(i) the decedent dies after December 31, 1976, and before January 1, 1979,

(ii) by reason of the death of the decedent property passes from the decedent or is acquired from the decedent under a will executed before January 1, 1977, or a trust created before such date, which contains a formula expressly providing that the spouse is to receive the maximum amount of property qualifying for the marital deduction allowable by Federal law,

(iii) the formula referred to in clause (ii) was not amended at any time after December 31, 1976, and before the death of the decedent, and

(iv) the State does not enact a statute applicable to such estate which construes this type of formula as referring to the marital deduction allowable by Federal law as amended by subsection (a),

then the amendment made by subsection (a) shall not apply to the estate of such decedent.

[Sec. 2056(c)]

(c) DEFINITION.—For purposes of this section, an interest in property shall be considered as passing from the decedent to any person if and only if—

(1) such interest is bequeathed or devised to such person by the decedent;

(2) such interest is inherited by such person from the decedent;

(3) such interest is the dower or curtesy interest (or statutory interest in lieu thereof) of such person as surviving spouse of the decedent;

(4) such interest has been transferred to such person by the decedent at any time;

(5) such interest was, at the time of the decedent's death, held by such person and the decedent (or by them and any other person) in joint ownership with right of survivorship;

(6) the decedent had a power (either alone or in conjunction with any person) to appoint such interest and if he appoints or has appointed such interest to such person, or if such person takes such interest in default on the release or nonexercise of such power; or

(7) such interest consists of proceeds of insurance on the life of the decedent receivable by such person.

Except as provided in paragraph (5) or (6) of subsection (b), where at the time of the decedent's death it is not possible to ascertain the particular person or persons to whom an interest in property may pass from the decedent, such interest shall, for purposes of subparagraphs (A) and (B) of subsection (b)(1), be considered as passing from the decedent to a person other than the surviving spouse.

Amendments

• **1981, Economic Recovery Tax Act of 1981 (P.L. 97-34)**

P.L. 97-34, §403(a)(1)(A):

Redesignated Code Sec. 2056(d) as Code Sec. 2056(c). **Effective** for estates of decedents dying after 12-31-81.

Amendments

• **1976, Tax Reform Act of 1976 (P.L. 94-455)**

P.L. 94-455, §2009(b)(4)(D):

Struck Code Sec. 2056(d) and redesignated Code Sec. 2056(e) as Code Sec. 2056(d). **Effective** for transfers creating an interest in the person disclaiming made after 12-31-76. Prior to being stricken, Code Sec. 2056(d) read as follows:

(d) DISCLAIMERS.—

(1) BY SURVIVING SPOUSE.—If under this section an interest would, in the absence of a disclaimer by the surviving spouse, be considered as passing from the decedent to such spouse, and if a disclaimer of such interest is made by such spouse, then such interest shall, for the purposes of this section, be considered as passing to the person or persons entitled to receive such interest as a result of the disclaimer.

(2) BY ANY OTHER PERSON.—If under this section an interest would, in the absence of a disclaimer by any person other than the surviving spouse, be considered as passing from the decedent to such person, and if a disclaimer of such interest is made by such person and as a result of such disclaimer the surviving spouse is entitled to receive such interest, then—

(A) if the disclaimer of such interest is made by such person before the date prescribed for the filing of the estate tax return and if such person does not accept such interest before making the disclaimer, such interest shall, for purposes of this section, be considered as passing from the decedent to the surviving spouse, and

(B) if subparagraph (A) does not apply, such interest shall, for purposes of this section, be considered as passing, not to the surviving spouse, but to the person who made the disclaimer, in the same manner as if the disclaimer had not been made.

• **1966 (P.L. 89-621)**

P.L. 89-621, §[1]:

Amended Code Sec. 2056(d)(2). Except as provided, the amendment is **effective** with respect to estates of decedents dying on or after 10-4-66. However, in the case of

• **1976, Tax Reform Act of 1976 (P.L. 94-455)**

P.L. 94-455, §2009(b)(4)(D), (e)(2):

Redesignated Code Sec. 2056(e) as Code Sec. 2056(d). **Effective** for transfers creating an interest in the person disclaiming made after 12-31-76.

[Sec. 2056(d)—Stricken]

the estate of a decedent dying before 10-4-66 for which the date prescribed for the filing of the estate tax return (determined without regard to any extension of time for filing) occurs on or after 1-1-65, if, under section 2056 of the Internal Revenue Code of 1954, an interest would, in the absence of a disclaimer by any person other than the surviving spouse, be considered as passing from the decedent to such person, and if a disclaimer of such interest is made by such person and as a result of such disclaimer the surviving spouse is entitled to receive such interest, then such interest shall, for purposes of such section, be considered as passing from the decedent to the surviving spouse, if—

(1) the interest disclaimed was bequeathed or devised to such person,

(2) before the date prescribed for the filing of the estate tax return such person disclaimed all bequests and devises under such will, and

(3) such person did not accept any property under any such bequest or devise before making the disclaimer.

The amount of the deductions allowable under section 2056 of such Code by reason of this subsection, when added to the amount of the deductions allowable under such section without regard to this subsection, shall not exceed the greater of (A) the amount of the deductions which would be allowable under such section without regard to the disclaimer if the surviving spouse elected to take against the will, or (B) an amount equal to one-third of the adjusted gross estate (within the meaning of subsection (c)(2) of such section). Prior to amendment, Sec. 2056(d)(2) read as follows:

"(2) BY ANY OTHER PERSON.—If under this section an interest would, in the absence of a disclaimer by any person other than the surviving spouse, be considered as passing from the decedent to such person, and if a disclaimer of such interest is made by such person and as a result of such disclaimer the surviving spouse is entitled to receive such interest, then such interest shall, for purposes of this section, be considered as passing, not to the surviving spouse, but to the person who made the disclaimer, in the same manner as if the disclaimer had not been made."

[Sec. 2056(d)]

(d) DISALLOWANCE OF MARITAL DEDUCTION WHERE SURVIVING SPOUSE NOT UNITED STATES CITIZEN.—

(1) IN GENERAL.—Except as provided in paragraph (2), if the surviving spouse of the decedent is not a citizen of the United States—

(A) no deduction shall be allowed under subsection (a), and

(B) section 2040(b) shall not apply.

(2) MARITAL DEDUCTION ALLOWED FOR CERTAIN TRANSFERS IN TRUST.—

(A) IN GENERAL.—Paragraph (1) shall not apply to any property passing to the surviving spouse in a qualified domestic trust.

(B) SPECIAL RULE.—If any property passes from the decedent to the surviving spouse of the decedent, for purposes of subparagraph (A), such property shall be treated as passing to such spouse in a qualified domestic trust if—

(i) such property is transferred to such a trust before the date on which the return of the tax imposed by this chapter is made, or

ESTATE TAX—TAXABLE ESTATE

(ii) such property is irrevocably assigned to such a trust under an irrevocable assignment made on or before such date which is enforceable under local law.

(3) ALLOWANCE OF CREDIT TO CERTAIN SPOUSES.—If—

(A) property passes to the surviving spouse of the decedent (hereinafter in this paragraph referred to as the "first decedent"),

(B) without regard to this subsection, a deduction would be allowable under subsection (a) with respect to such property, and

(C) such surviving spouse dies and the estate of such surviving spouse is subject to the tax imposed by this chapter,

the Federal estate tax paid (or treated as paid under section 2056A(b)(7) by the first decedent with respect to such property shall be allowed as a credit under section 2013 to the estate of such surviving spouse and the amount of such credit shall be determined under such section without regard to when the first decedent died and without regard to subsection (d)(3) of such section.

(4) SPECIAL RULE WHERE RESIDENT SPOUSE BECOMES CITIZEN.—Paragraph (1) shall not apply if—

(A) the surviving spouse of the decedent becomes a citizen of the United States before the day on which the return of the tax imposed by this chapter is made, and

(B) such spouse was a resident of the United States at all times after the date of the death of the decedent and before becoming a citizen of the United States.

(5) REFORMATIONS PERMITTED.—

(A) IN GENERAL.—In the case of any property with respect to which a deduction would be allowable under subsection (a) but for this subsection, the determination of whether a trust is a qualified domestic trust shall be made—

(i) as of the date on which the return of the tax imposed by this chapter is made, or

(ii) if a judicial proceeding is commenced on or before the due date (determined with regard to extensions) for filing such return to change such trust into a trust which is a qualified domestic trust, as of the time when the changes pursuant to such proceeding are made.

(B) STATUTE OF LIMITATIONS.—If a judicial proceeding described in subparagraph (A)(ii) is commenced with respect to any trust, the period for assessing any deficiency of tax attributable to any failure of such trust to be a qualified domestic trust shall not expire before the date 1 year after the date on which the Secretary is notified that the trust has been changed pursuant to such judicial proceeding or that such proceeding has been terminated.

Amendments

• **1990, Omnibus Budget Reconciliation Act of 1990 (P.L. 101-508)**

P.L. 101-508, § 11701(l)(1):

Amended Code Sec. 2056(d) by redesignating paragraph (4)[5]as paragraph (5). **Effective** as if included in the provision of P.L. 101-239 to which it relates.

P.L. 101-508, § 11701(l)(2), provides:

(2) The period during which a proceeding may be commenced under section 2056(d)(5)(A)(ii) of the Internal Revenue Code of 1986 (as redesignated by paragraph (1)) shall not expire before the date 6 months after the date of the enactment of this Act.

P.L. 101-508, § 11702(g)(5):

Amended Code Sec. 2056(d)(3) by striking "section 2056A(b)(6)" and inserting "section 2056A(b)(7)". **Effective** as if included in the provision of P.L. 100-647 to which it relates.

• **1989, Omnibus Budget Reconciliation Act of 1989 (P.L. 101-239)**

P.L. 101-239, § 7815(d)(4)(A):

Amended Code Sec. 2056(d)(2)(B). **Effective** as if included in the provision of P.L. 100-647 to which it relates. Prior to amendment, Code Sec. 2056(d)(2)(B) read as follows:

(B) PROPERTY PASSING OUTSIDE OF PROBATE ESTATE.—If any property passes from the decedent to the surviving spouse of the decedent outside of the decedent's probate estate, for purposes of subparagraph (A), such property shall be treated as passing to such spouse in a qualified domestic trust if such property is transferred to such a trust before the day on which the return of the tax imposed by section 2001 is made.

P.L. 101-239, § 7815(d)(5):

Amended Code Sec. 2056(d) by adding at the end thereof a new paragraph (4). **Effective** as if included in the provision of P.L. 100-647 to which it relates.

P.L. 101-239, § 7815(d)(6)(A)-(B):

Amended Code Sec. 2056(d)(3) by striking "section 2001" and inserting "this chapter", and by inserting "and without regard to subsection (d)(3) of such section" before the period at the end thereof. **Effective** as if included in the provision of P.L. 100-647 to which it relates.

P.L. 101-239, § 7815(d)(8):

Amended Code Sec. 2056(d) by adding at the end thereof a new paragraph (4)[5]. **Effective** as if included in the provision of P.L. 100-647 to which it relates.

P.L. 101-239, § 7815(d)(4)(B), provides:

(B) In the case of the estate of a decedent dying before the date of the enactment of this Act, the period during which the transfer (or irrevocable assignment) referred to in section 2056(d)(2)(B) of the Internal Revenue Code of 1986 (as amended by subparagraph (A)) may be made shall not expire before the date 1 year after such date of enactment.

P.L. 101-239, § 7815(d)(16), provides:

(16) For purposes of applying section 2040(a) of the Internal Revenue Code of 1986 with respect to any joint interest to which section 2040(b) of such Code does not apply solely by reason of section 2056(d)(1)(B) of such Code, any consideration furnished before July 14, 1988, by the decedent for such interest to the extent treated as a gift to the spouse of the decedent for purposes of chapter 12 of such Code (or would have been so treated if the donor were a citizen of the United States) shall be treated as consideration originally belonging to such spouse and never acquired by such spouse from the decedent.

• **1988, Technical and Miscellaneous Revenue Act of 1988 (P.L. 100-647)**

P.L. 100-647, § 5033(a)(1):

Amended Code Sec. 2056 by adding at the end thereof a new subsection (d). **Effective** for estates of decedents dying after the date of enactment of this Act.

SEC. 2056A. QUALIFIED DOMESTIC TRUST.

(a) QUALIFIED DOMESTIC TRUST DEFINED.—For purposes of this section and section 2056(d), the term "qualified domestic trust" means, with respect to any decedent, any trust if—

(1) the trust instrument—

(A) except as provided in regulations prescribed by the Secretary, requires that at least 1 trustee of the trust be an individual citizen of the United States or a domestic corporation, and

(B) provides that no distribution (other than a distribution of income) may be made from the trust unless a trustee who is an individual citizen of the United States or domestic corporation has the right to withhold from such distribution the tax imposed by this section on such distribution,

(2) such trust meets such requirements as the Secretary may by regulations prescribe to ensure the collection of any tax imposed by subsection (b), and

(3) an election under this section by the executor of the decedent applies to such trust.

Amendments

• **1997, Taxpayer Relief Act of 1997 (P.L. 105-34)**

P.L. 105-34, § 1303, provides:

SEC. 1303. TRANSITIONAL RULE UNDER SECTION 2056A.

(a) GENERAL RULE.—In the case of any trust created under an instrument executed before the date of the enactment of the Revenue Reconciliation Act of 1990, such trust shall be treated as meeting the requirements of paragraph (1) of section 2056A(a) of the Internal Revenue Code of 1986 if the trust instrument requires that all trustees of the trust be individual citizens of the United States or domestic corporations.

(b) EFFECTIVE DATE.—The provisions of subsection (a) shall take effect as if included in the provisions of section 11702(g) of the Revenue Reconciliation Act of 1990.

ESTATE TAX—TAXABLE ESTATE

P.L. 105-34, § 1314(a):

Amended Code Sec. 2056A(a)(1)(A) by inserting "except as provided in regulations prescribed by the Secretary," before "requires". **Effective** for estates of decedents dying after 8-5-97.

• **1990, Omnibus Budget Reconciliation Act of 1990 (P.L. 101-508)**

P.L. 101-508, § 11702(g)(2)(A):

Amended Code Sec. 2056A(a)(1). **Effective** as if included in the provision of P.L. 100-647 to which it relates. Prior to amendment, paragraph (1) read as follows:

(1) the trust instrument requires that at least 1 trustee of the trust be an individual citizen of the United States or a domestic corporation and that no distribution from the trust may be made without the approval of such a trustee,

• **1989, Omnibus Budget Reconciliation Act of 1989 (P.L. 101-239)**

P.L. 101-239, § 7815(d)(7)(A)(i)-(ii):

Amended Code Sec. 2056A(a) by amending paragraph (1), and by striking paragraph (2) and redesignating paragraphs (3) and (4) as paragraphs (2) and (3), respectively. **Effective** as if included in the provision of P.L. 100-647 to which it relates. Prior to amendment, Code Sec. 2056A(a)(1)-(2) read as follows:

(1) the trust instrument requires that all trustees of the trust be individual citizens of the United States or domestic corporations,

(2) the surviving spouse of the decedent is entitled to all the income from the property in such trust, payable annually or at more frequent intervals,

[Sec. 2056A(b)]

(b) TAX TREATMENT OF TRUST.—

(1) IMPOSITION OF ESTATE TAX.—There is hereby imposed an estate tax on—

(A) any distribution before the date of the death of the surviving spouse from a qualified domestic trust, and

(B) the value of the property remaining in a qualified domestic trust on the date of the death of the surviving spouse.

(2) AMOUNT OF TAX.—

(A) IN GENERAL.—In the case of any taxable event, the amount of the estate tax imposed by paragraph (1) shall be the amount equal to—

(i) the tax which would have been imposed under section 2001 on the estate of the decedent if the taxable estate of the decedent had been increased by the sum of—

(I) the amount involved in such taxable event, plus

(II) the aggregate amount involved in previous taxable events with respect to qualified domestic trusts of such decedent, reduced by

(ii) the tax which would have been imposed under section 2001 on the estate of the decedent if the taxable estate of the decedent had been increased by the amount referred to in clause (i)(II).

(B) TENTATIVE TAX WHERE TAX OF DECEDENT NOT FINALLY DETERMINED.—

(i) IN GENERAL.—If the tax imposed on the estate of the decedent under section 2001 is not finally determined before the taxable event, the amount of the tax imposed by paragraph (1) on such event shall be determined by using the highest rate of tax in effect under section 2001 as of the date of the decedent's death.

(ii) REFUND OF EXCESS WHEN TAX FINALLY DETERMINED.—If—

(I) the amount of the tax determined under clause (i), exceeds

(II) the tax determined under subparagraph (A) on the basis of the final determination of the tax imposed by section 2001 on the estate of the decedent,

such excess shall be allowed as a credit or refund (with interest) if claim therefor is filed not later than 1 year after the date of such final determination.

(C) SPECIAL RULE WHERE DECEDENT HAS MORE THAN 1 QUALIFIED DOMESTIC TRUST.—If there is more than 1 qualified domestic trust with respect to any decedent, the amount of the tax imposed by paragraph (1) with respect to such trusts shall be determined by using the highest rate of tax in effect under section 2001 as of the date of the decedent's death (and the provisions of paragraph (3)(B) shall not apply) unless, pursuant to a designation made by the decedent's executor, there is 1 person—

(i) who is an individual citizen of the United States or a domestic corporation and is responsible for filing all returns of tax imposed under paragraph (1) with respect to such trusts and for paying all tax so imposed, and

(ii) who meets such requirements as the Secretary may by regulations prescribe.

(3) CERTAIN LIFETIME DISTRIBUTIONS EXEMPT FROM TAX.—

(A) INCOME DISTRIBUTIONS.—No tax shall be imposed by paragraph (1)(A) on any distribution of income to the surviving spouse.

(B) HARDSHIP EXEMPTION.—No tax shall be imposed by paragraph (1)(A) on any distribution to the surviving spouse on account of hardship.

(4) TAX WHERE TRUST CEASES TO QUALIFY.—If any qualified domestic trust ceases to meet the requirements of paragraphs (1) and (2) of subsection (a), the tax imposed by paragraph (1) shall apply as if the surviving spouse died on the date of such cessation.

(5) DUE DATE.—

(A) TAX ON DISTRIBUTIONS.—The estate tax imposed by paragraph (1)(A) shall be due and payable on the 15th day of the 4th month following the calendar year in which the taxable event occurs; except that the estate tax imposed by paragraph (1)(A) on distributions during the calendar year in which the surviving spouse dies shall be due and payable not later than the date on which the estate tax imposed by paragraph (1)(B) is due and payable.

(B) TAX AT DEATH OF SPOUSE.—The estate tax imposed by paragraph (1)(B) shall be due and payable on the date 9 months after the date of such death.

(6) LIABILITY FOR TAX.—Each trustee shall be personally liable for the amount of the tax imposed by paragraph (1). Rules similar to the rules of section 2204 shall apply for purposes of the preceding sentence.

(7) TREATMENT OF TAX.—For purposes of section 2056(d), any tax paid under paragraph (1) shall be treated as a tax paid under section 2001 with respect to the estate of the decedent.

(8) LIEN FOR TAX.—For purposes of section 6324, any tax imposed by paragraph (1) shall be treated as an estate tax imposed under this chapter with respect to a decedent dying on the date of the taxable event (and the property involved shall be treated as the gross estate of such decedent).

(9) TAXABLE EVENT.—The term "taxable event" means the event resulting in tax being imposed under paragraph (1).

(10) CERTAIN BENEFITS ALLOWED.—

(A) IN GENERAL.—If any property remaining in the qualified domestic trust on the date of the death of the surviving spouse is includible in the gross estate of such spouse for purposes of this chapter (or would be includible if such spouse were a citizen or resident of the United States), any benefit which is allowable (or would be allowable if such spouse were a citizen or resident of the United States) with respect to such property to the estate of such spouse under section 2014, 2032, 2032A, 2055, 2056, 2058, or 6166 shall be allowed for purposes of the tax imposed by paragraph (1)(B).

ESTATE TAX—TAXABLE ESTATE

(B) SECTION 303.—If the estate of the surviving spouse meets the requirements of section 303 with respect to any property described in subparagraph (A), for purposes of section 303, the tax imposed by paragraph (1)(B) with respect to such property shall be treated as a Federal estate tax payable with respect to the estate of the surviving spouse.

(C) SECTION 6161(a)(2).—The provisions of section 6161(a)(2) shall apply with respect to the tax imposed by paragraph (1)(B), and the reference in such section to the executor shall be treated as a reference to the trustees of the trust.

(11) SPECIAL RULE WHERE DISTRIBUTION TAX PAID OUT OF TRUST.—For purposes of this subsection, if any portion of the tax imposed by paragraph (1)(A) with respect to any distribution is paid out of the trust, an amount equal to the portion so paid shall be treated as a distribution described in paragraph (1)(A).

(12) SPECIAL RULE WHERE SPOUSE BECOMES CITIZEN.—If the surviving spouse of the decedent becomes a citizen of the United States and if—

(A) such spouse was a resident of the United States at all times after the date of the death of the decedent and before such spouse becomes a citizen of the United States,

(B) no tax was imposed by paragraph (1)(A) with respect to any distribution before such spouse becomes such a citizen, or

(C) such spouse elects—

(i) to treat any distribution on which tax was imposed by paragraph (1)(A) as a taxable gift made by such spouse for purposes of—

(I) section 2001, and

(II) determining the amount of the tax imposed by section 2501 on actual taxable gifts made by such spouse during the year in which the spouse becomes a citizen or any subsequent year, and

(ii) to treat any reduction in the tax imposed by paragraph (1)(A) by reason of the credit allowable under section 2010 with respect to the decedent as a credit allowable to such surviving spouse under section 2505 for purposes of determining the amount of the credit allowable under section 2505 with respect to taxable gifts made by the surviving spouse during the year in which the spouse becomes a citizen or any subsequent year,

paragraph (1)(A) shall not apply to any distributions after such spouse becomes such a citizen (and paragraph (1)(B) shall not apply).

(13) COORDINATION WITH SECTION 1015.—For purposes of section 1015, any distribution on which tax is imposed by paragraph (1)(A) shall be treated as a transfer by gift, and any tax paid under paragraph (1)(A) shall be treated as a gift tax.

(14) COORDINATION WITH TERMINABLE INTEREST RULES.—Any interest in a qualified domestic trust shall not be treated as failing to meet the requirements of paragraph (5) or (7) of section 2056(b) merely by reason of any provision of the trust instrument permitting the withholding from any distribution of an amount to pay the tax imposed by paragraph (1) on such distribution.

(15) NO TAX ON CERTAIN DISTRIBUTIONS.—No tax shall be imposed by paragraph (1) on any distribution to the surviving spouse to the extent such distribution is to reimburse such surviving spouse for any tax imposed by subtitle A on any item of income of the trust to which such surviving spouse is not entitled under the terms of the trust.

Amendments

• **2013, American Taxpayer Relief Act of 2012 (P.L. 112-240)**

P.L. 112-240, §101(a)(1) and (3), provides:

SEC. 101. PERMANENT EXTENSION AND MODIFICATION OF 2001 TAX RELIEF.

(a) PERMANENT EXTENSION.—

(1) IN GENERAL.—The Economic Growth and Tax Relief Reconciliation Act of 2001 is amended by striking title IX.

***

(3) EFFECTIVE DATE.—The amendments made by this subsection shall apply to taxable, plan, or limitation years beginning after December 31, 2012, and estates of decedents dying, gifts made, or generation skipping transfers after December 31, 2012.

• **2001, Economic Growth and Tax Relief Reconciliation Act of 2001 (P.L. 107-16)**

P.L. 107-16, §532(c)(6)(A)-(B):

Amended Code Sec. 2056A(b)(10)(A) by striking "2011," following "spouse under section", and by inserting "2058," after "2056,". **Effective** for estates of decedents dying, and generation-skipping transfers, after 12-31-2004.

P.L. 107-16, §901(a)-(b), as amended by P.L. 111-312, §101(a)(1), provides [but see P.L. 112-240, §101(a)(1) and (3), above]:

SEC. 901. SUNSET OF PROVISIONS OF ACT.

(a) IN GENERAL.—All provisions of, and amendments made by, this Act shall not apply—

(1) to taxable, plan, or limitation years beginning after December 31, 2012, or

(2) in the case of title V, to estates of decedents dying, gifts made, or generation skipping transfers, after December 31, 2012.

(b) APPLICATION OF CERTAIN LAWS.—The Internal Revenue Code of 1986 and the Employee Retirement Income Security Act of 1974 shall be applied and administered to years, estates, gifts, and transfers described in subsection (a) as if the provisions and amendments described in subsection (a) had never been enacted.

• **1990, Omnibus Budget Reconciliation Act of 1990 (P.L. 101-508)**

P.L. 101-508, §11702(g)(2)(B):

Amended Code Sec. 2056A(b) by adding new paragraphs (14) and (15). **Effective** as if included in the provision of P.L. 100-647 to which it relates.

P.L. 101-508, §11702(g)(4):

Amended Code Sec. 2056A(b)(10)(A) by striking "section 2032" and inserting "section 2011, 2014, 2032". **Effective** as if included in the provision of P.L. 100-647 to which it relates.

P.L. 101-508, §11704(a)(15):

Amended Code Sec. 2056A(b)(2)(B)(ii) by striking "therefore" and inserting "therefor". **Effective** 11-5-90.

• **1989, Omnibus Budget Reconciliation Act of 1989 (P.L. 101-239)**

P.L. 101-239, §7815(d)(7)(B):

Amended Code Sec. 2056A(b) by redesignating paragraphs (3) through (8) as paragraphs (4) through (9), respectively, and by inserting after paragraph (2) a new paragraph (3). **Effective** as if included in the provision of P.L. 100-647 to which it relates.

P.L. 101-239, §7815(d)(7)(C):

Amended Code Sec. 2056A(b)(1)(A) by striking "other than a distribution of income required under subsection (a)(2)" after "domestic trust". **Effective** as if included in the provision of P.L. 100-647 to which it relates.

P.L. 101-239, §7815(d)(7)(D):

Amended Code Sec. 2056A(b)(4), as redesignated by subparagraph (B). **Effective** as if included in the provision of P.L. 100-647 to which it relates. Prior to amendment, Code Sec. 2056A(b)(4) read as follows:

(4) TAX IMPOSED WHERE TRUST CEASES TO QUALIFY.—If any person other than an individual citizen of the United States or a domestic corporation becomes a trustee of a qualified domestic trust (or such trust ceases to meet the requirements of subsection (a)(3)), the tax imposed by paragraph (1) shall apply as if the surviving spouse died on the date on which such person became such a trustee or the date of such cessation, as the case may be.

P.L. 101-239, §7815(d)(9):

Amended Code Sec. 2056A(b) by adding at the end thereof new paragraphs (10)-(13). **Effective** as if included in the provision of P.L. 100-647 to which it relates.

P.L. 101-239, §7815(d)(11):

Amended Code Sec. 2056A(b)(2)(B)(ii) by striking "as a credit or refund" and inserting "as a credit or refund (with interest)". **Effective** as if included in the provision of P.L. 100-647 to which it relates.

P.L. 101-239, §7815(d)(12):

Amended Code Sec. 2056A(b)(2) by adding at the end thereof a new subparagraph (C). **Effective** as if included in the provision of P.L. 100-647 to which it relates.

P.L. 101-239, §7815(d)(15):

Amended Code Sec. 2056A(b)(5), as redesignated by section (7)(B). **Effective** as if included in the provision of P.L. 100-647 to which it relates. Prior to amendment, Code Sec. 2056A(b)(5) read as follows:

(5) DUE DATE.—The estate tax imposed by paragraph (1) shall be due and payable on the 15th day of the 4th month following the calendar year in which the taxable event occurs.

[Sec. 2056A(c)]

(c) DEFINITIONS.—For purposes of this section—

(1) PROPERTY INCLUDES INTEREST THEREIN.—The term "property" includes an interest in property.

(2) INCOME.—Except as provided in regulations, the term "income" has the meaning given to such term by section 643(b).

ESTATE TAX—TAXABLE ESTATE

(3) TRUST.—To the extent provided in regulations prescribed by the Secretary, the term "trust" includes other arrangements which have substantially the same effect as a trust.

Amendments

• **1997, Taxpayer Relief Act of 1997 (P.L. 105-34)**

P.L. 105-34, §1312(a):

Amended Code Sec. 2056A(c) by adding at the end a new paragraph (3). **Effective** for estates of decedents dying after 8-5-97.

• **1989, Omnibus Budget Reconciliation Act of 1989 (P.L. 101-239)**

P.L. 101-239, §7815(d)(10):

Amended Code Sec. 2056A(c)(2) by striking "The term" and inserting "Except as provided in regulations, the term". **Effective** as if included in the provision of P.L. 100-647 to which it relates.

[Sec. 2056A(d)]

(d) ELECTION.—An election under this section with respect to any trust shall be made by the executor on the return of the tax imposed by section 2001. Such an election, once made, shall be irrevocable. No election may be made under this section on any return if such return is filed more than one year after the time prescribed by law (including extensions) for filing such return.

Amendments

• **1990, Omnibus Budget Reconciliation Act of 1990 (P.L. 101-508)**

P.L. 101-508, §11702(g)(3)(A):

Amended Code Sec. 2056A(d) by adding at the end thereof a new sentence. Not **effective** for any election made before the date 6 months after 11-5-90.

• **1988, Technical and Miscellaneous Revenue Act of 1988 (P.L. 100-647)**

P.L. 100-647, §5033(a)(2):

Amended Part IV of subchapter A of chapter 11 by inserting after section 2056 a new section 2056A. **Effective** for estates of decedents dying after 11-10-88.

[Sec. 2056A(e)]

(e) REGULATIONS.—The Secretary shall prescribe such regulations as may be necessary or appropriate to carry out the purposes of this section, including regulations under which there may be treated as a qualified domestic trust any annuity or other payment which is includible in the decedent's gross estate and is by its terms payable for life or a term of years.

Amendments

• **1989, Omnibus Budget Reconciliation Act of 1989 (P.L. 101-239)**

P.L. 101-239, §7815(d)(13):

Amended Code Sec. 2056A by adding at the end thereof a new subsection (e). **Effective** as if included in the provision of P.L. 100-647 to which it relates.

P.L. 101-239, §7815(d)(14), provides:

(14) In the case of the estate of, or gift by, an individual who was not a citizen or resident of the United States but was a resident of a foreign country with which the United States has a tax treaty with respect to estate, inheritance, or gift taxes, the amendments made by section 5033 of the 1988 Act shall not apply to the extent such amendments would be inconsistent with the provisions of such treaty relating to estate, inheritance, or gift tax marital deductions. In the case of the estate of an individual dying before the date 3 years after the date of the enactment of this Act, or a gift by an individual before the date 3 years after the date of the enactment of this Act, the requirement of the preceding sentence that the individual not be a citizen or resident of the United States shall not apply.

[Sec. 2057—Stricken]

Amendments

• **2014, Tax Technical Corrections Act of 2014 (P.L. 113-295)**

P.L. 113-295, §221(a)(97)(A), Division A:

Amended part IV of subchapter A of chapter 11 by striking Code Sec. 2057. **Effective** generally 12-19-2014. For a special rule, see Act Sec. 221(b)(2), Division A, below.

P.L. 113-295, §221(b)(2), Division A, provides:

(2) SAVINGS PROVISION.—If—

(A) any provision amended or repealed by the amendments made by this section applied to—

(i) any transaction occurring before the date of the enactment of this Act,

(ii) any property acquired before such date of enactment, or

(iii) any item of income, loss, deduction, or credit taken into account before such date of enactment, and

(B) the treatment of such transaction, property, or item under such provision would (without regard to the amendments or repeals made by this section) affect the liability for tax for periods ending after date of enactment, nothing in the amendments or repeals made by this section shall be construed to affect the treatment of such transaction, property, or item for purposes of determining liability for tax for periods ending after such date of enactment.

Prior to being stricken, Code Sec. 2057 read as follows:

SEC. 2057. FAMILY-OWNED BUSINESS INTERESTS.

[Sec. 2057(a)]

(a) GENERAL RULE.—

(1) ALLOWANCE OF DEDUCTION.—For purposes of the tax imposed by section 2001, in the case of an estate of a decedent to which this section applies, the value of the taxable estate shall be determined by deducting from the value of the gross estate the adjusted value of the qualified family-owned business interests of the decedent which are described in subsection (b)(2).

(2) MAXIMUM DEDUCTION.—The deduction allowed by this section shall not exceed $675,000.

(3) COORDINATION WITH UNIFIED CREDIT.—

(A) IN GENERAL.—Except as provided in subparagraph (B), if this section applies to an estate, the applicable exclusion amount under section 2010 shall be $625,000.

(B) INCREASE IN UNIFIED CREDIT IF DEDUCTION IS LESS THAN $675,000.—If the deduction allowed by this section is less than $675,000, the amount of the applicable exclusion amount under section 2010 shall be increased (but not above the amount which would apply to the estate without regard to this section) by the excess of $675,000 over the amount of the deduction allowed.

Amendments

• **1998, IRS Restructuring and Reform Act of 1998 (P.L. 105-206)**

P.L. 105-206, §6007(b)(1)(A):

Amended Code Sec. 2033A by moving it to the end of part IV of subchapter A of chapter 11 and redesignating it as Code Sec. 2057. **Effective** as if included in the provision of P.L. 105-34 to which it relates [**effective** for estates of decedents dying after 12-31-97.—CCH].

P.L. 105-206, §6007(b)(1)(B):

Amended so much of Code Sec. 2057 (as redesignated) as precedes subsection (b). **Effective** as if included in the provision of P.L. 105-34 to which it relates [**effective** for estates of decedents dying after 12-31-97.—CCH]. Prior to amendment, so much of Code Sec. 2057, as redesignated, as precedes subsection (b) read as follows:

SEC. 2033A. FAMILY-OWNED BUSINESS EXCLUSION.

(a) IN GENERAL.—In the case of an estate of a decedent to which this section applies, the value of the gross estate shall not include the lesser of—

(1) the adjusted value of the qualified family-owned business interests of the decedent otherwise includible in the estate, or

(2) the excess of $1,300,000 over the applicable exclusion amount under section 2010(c) with respect to such estate.

[Sec. 2057(b)]

(b) ESTATES TO WHICH SECTION APPLIES.—

(1) IN GENERAL.—This section shall apply to an estate if—

(A) the decedent was (at the date of the decedent's death) a citizen or resident of the United States,

(B) the executor elects the application of this section and files the agreement referred to in subsection (h),

(C) the sum of—

(i) the adjusted value of the qualified family-owned business interests described in paragraph (2), plus

(ii) the amount of the gifts of such interests determined under paragraph (3),

exceeds 50 percent of the adjusted gross estate, and

(D) during the 8-year period ending on the date of the decedent's death there have been periods aggregating 5 years or more during which—

(i) such interests were owned by the decedent or a member of the decedent's family, and

(ii) there was material participation (within the meaning of section 2032A(e)(6)) by the decedent or a member of the decedent's family in the operation of the business to which such interests relate.

(2) INCLUDIBLE QUALIFIED FAMILY-OWNED BUSINESS INTERESTS.—The qualified family-owned business interests described in this paragraph are the interests which—

(A) are included in determining the value of the gross estate, and

(B) are acquired by any qualified heir from, or passed to any qualified heir from, the decedent (within the meaning of section 2032A(e)(9)).

(3) INCLUDIBLE GIFTS OF INTERESTS.—The amount of the gifts of qualified family-owned business interests determined under this paragraph is the sum of—

(A) the amount of such gifts from the decedent to members of the decedent's family taken into account under section 2001(b)(1)(B), plus

(B) the amount of such gifts otherwise excluded under section 2503(b),

to the extent such interests are continuously held by members of such family (other than the decedent's spouse) between the date of the gift and the date of the decedent's death.

Amendments

• **1998, IRS Restructuring and Reform Act of 1998 (P.L. 105-206)**

P.L. 105-206, §6007(b)(1)(C):

Amended Code Sec. 2057(b)(2)(A) (as redesignated) by striking "(without regard to this section)" after "the value of the gross estate". **Effective** as if included in the provision of P.L. 105-34 to which it relates [**effective** for estates of decedents dying after 12-31-97.—CCH].

P.L. 105-206, § 6007(b)(2):

Amended Code Sec. 2057(b)(3) (as redesignated). **Effective** as if included in the provision of P.L. 105-34 to which it relates [**effective** for estates of decedents dying after 12-31-97.—CCH]. Prior to amendment, Code Sec. 2057(b)(3) read as follows:

(3) INCLUDIBLE GIFTS OF INTERESTS.—The amount of the gifts of qualified family-owned business interests determined under this paragraph is the excess of—

(A) the sum of—

(i) the amount of such gifts from the decedent to members of the decedent's family taken into account under subsection 2001(b)(1)(B), plus

(ii) the amount of such gifts otherwise excluded under section 2503(b),

to the extent such interests are continuously held by members of such family (other than the decedent's spouse) between the date of the gift and the date of the decedent's death, over

(B) the amount of such gifts from the decedent to members of the decedent's family otherwise included in the gross estate.

[Sec. 2057(c)]

(c) ADJUSTED GROSS ESTATE.—For purposes of this section, the term "adjusted gross estate" means the value of the gross estate—

(1) reduced by any amount deductible under paragraph (3) or (4) of section 2053(a), and

(2) increased by the excess of—

(A) the sum of—

(i) the amount of gifts determined under subsection (b)(3), plus

(ii) the amount (if more than de minimis) of other transfers from the decedent to the decedent's spouse (at the time of the transfer) within 10 years of the date of the decedent's death, plus

(iii) the amount of other gifts (not included under clause (i) or (ii)) from the decedent within 3 years of such date, other than gifts to members of the decedent's family otherwise excluded under section 2503(b), over

(B) the sum of the amounts described in clauses (i), (ii), and (iii) of subparagraph (A) which are otherwise includible in the gross estate.

For purposes of the preceding sentence, the Secretary may provide that de minimis gifts to persons other than members of the decedent's family shall not be taken into account.

Amendments

- **1998, IRS Restructuring and Reform Act of 1998 (P.L. 105-206)**

P.L. 105-206, § 6007(b)(1)(D):

Amended Code Sec. 2057(c) (as redesignated) by striking "(determined without regard to this section)" after "the value of the gross estate". **Effective** as if included in the provision of P.L. 105-34 to which it relates [**effective** for estates of decedents dying after 12-31-97.—CCH].

[Sec. 2057(d)]

(d) ADJUSTED VALUE OF THE QUALIFIED FAMILY-OWNED BUSINESS INTERESTS.—For purposes of this section, the adjusted value of any qualified family-owned business interest is the value of such interest for purposes of this chapter (determined without regard to this section), reduced by the excess of—

(1) any amount deductible under paragraph (3) or (4) of section 2053(a), over

(2) the sum of—

(A) any indebtedness on any qualified residence of the decedent the interest on which is deductible under section 163(h)(3), plus

(B) any indebtedness to the extent the taxpayer establishes that the proceeds of such indebtedness were used for the payment of educational and medical expenses of the decedent, the decedent's spouse, or the decedent's dependents (within the meaning of section 152, determined without regard to subsections (b)(1), (b)(2), and (d)(1)(B) thereof), plus

(C) any indebtedness not described in subparagraph (A) or (B), to the extent such indebtedness does not exceed $10,000.

Amendments

- **2004, Working Families Tax Relief Act of 2004 (P.L. 108-311)**

P.L. 108-311, § 207(23):

Amended Code Sec. 2057(d)(2)(B) by inserting ", determined without regard to subsections (b)(1), (b)(2), and (d)(1)(B) thereof" after "section 152". **Effective** for tax years beginning after 12-31-2004.

[Sec. 2057(e)]

(e) QUALIFIED FAMILY-OWNED BUSINESS INTEREST.—

(1) IN GENERAL.—For purposes of this section, the term "qualified family-owned business interest" means—

(A) an interest as a proprietor in a trade or business carried on as a proprietorship, or

(B) an interest in an entity carrying on a trade or business, if—

(i) at least—

(I) 50 percent of such entity is owned (directly or indirectly) by the decedent and members of the decedent's family,

(II) 70 percent of such entity is so owned by members of 2 families, or

(III) 90 percent of such entity is so owned by members of 3 families, and

(ii) for purposes of subclause (II) or (III) of clause (i), at least 30 percent of such entity is so owned by the decedent and members of the decedent's family.

For purposes of the preceding sentence, a decedent shall be treated as engaged in a trade or business if any member of the decedent's family is engaged in such trade or business.

(2) LIMITATION.—Such term shall not include—

(A) any interest in a trade or business the principal place of business of which is not located in the United States,

(B) any interest in an entity, if the stock or debt of such entity or a controlled group (as defined in section 267(f)(1)) of which such entity was a member was readily tradable on an established securities market or secondary market (as defined by the Secretary) at any time within 3 years of the date of the decedent's death,

(C) any interest in a trade or business not described in section 542(c)(2), if more than 35 percent of the adjusted ordinary gross income of such trade or business for the taxable year which includes the date of the decedent's death would qualify as personal holding company income (as defined in section 543(a) without regard to paragraph (2)(B) thereof) if such trade or business were a corporation,

(D) that portion of an interest in a trade or business that is attributable to—

(i) cash or marketable securities, or both, in excess of the reasonably expected day-to-day working capital needs of such trade or business, and

(ii) any other assets of the trade or business (other than assets used in the active conduct of a trade or business described in section 542(c)(2)), which produce, or are held for the production of, personal holding company income (as defined in subparagraph (C)) or income described in section 954(c)(1) (determined without regard to subparagraph (A) thereof and by substituting "trade or business" for "controlled foreign corporation").

In the case of a lease of property on a net cash basis by the decedent to a member of the decedent's family, income from such lease shall not be treated as personal holding company income for purposes of subparagraph (C), and such property shall not be treated as an asset described in subparagraph (D)(ii), if such income and property would not be so treated if the lessor had engaged directly in the activities engaged in by the lessee with respect to such property.

(3) RULES REGARDING OWNERSHIP.—

(A) OWNERSHIP OF ENTITIES.—For purposes of paragraph (1)(B)—

(i) CORPORATIONS.—Ownership of a corporation shall be determined by the holding of stock possessing the appropriate percentage of the total combined voting power of all classes of stock entitled to vote and the appropriate percentage of the total value of shares of all classes of stock.

(ii) PARTNERSHIPS.—Ownership of a partnership shall be determined by the owning of the appropriate percentage of the capital interest in such partnership.

(B) OWNERSHIP OF TIERED ENTITIES.—For purposes of this section, if by reason of holding an interest in a trade or business, a decedent, any member of the decedent's family, any qualified heir, or any member of any qualified heir's family is treated as holding an interest in any other trade or business—

(i) such ownership interest in the other trade or business shall be disregarded in determining if the ownership interest in the first trade or business is a qualified family-owned business interest, and

(ii) this section shall be applied separately in determining if such interest in any other trade or business is a qualified family-owned business interest.

(C) INDIVIDUAL OWNERSHIP RULES.—For purposes of this section, an interest owned, directly or indirectly, by or for an entity described in paragraph (1)(B) shall be considered as being owned proportionately by or for the entity's shareholders, partners, or beneficiaries. A person shall be treated as a beneficiary of any trust only if such person has a present interest in such trust.

Amendments

- **1998, IRS Restructuring and Reform Act of 1998 (P.L. 105-206)**

P.L. 105-206, § 6007(b)(3)(A):

Amended Code Sec. 2057(e)(2)(C) (as redesignated) by striking "(as defined in section 543(a))" and inserting "(as defined in section 543(a) without regard to paragraph (2)(B) thereof) if such trade or business were a corporation". **Effective** as if included in the provision of P.L. 105-34 to which it relates [**effective** for estates of decedents dying after 12-31-97.—CCH].

P.L. 105-206, § 6007(b)(3)(B):

Amended Code Sec. 2057(e)(2)(D)(ii) (as redesignated) by striking "income of which is described in section 543(a) or" and inserting "personal holding company income (as defined in subparagraph (C)) or income described". **Effective** as if included in the provision of P.L. 105-34 to which it relates [**effective** for estates of decedents dying after 12-31-97.—CCH].

P.L. 105-206, § 6007(b)(3)(C):

Amended Code Sec. 2057(e)(2) (as redesignated) by adding at the end a new flush sentence. **Effective** as if included in the provision of P.L. 105-34 to which it relates [**effective** for estates of decedents dying after 12-31-97.—CCH].

P.L. 105-206, § 6007(b)(5)(A):

Amended Code Sec. 2057(e)(1) (as redesignated) by adding at the end a new flush sentence. **Effective** as if included in the provision of P.L. 105-34 to which it relates [**effective** for estates of decedents dying after 12-31-97.—CCH].

[Sec. 2057(f)]

(f) TAX TREATMENT OF FAILURE TO MATERIALLY PARTICIPATE IN BUSINESS OR DISPOSITIONS OF INTERESTS.—

(1) IN GENERAL.—There is imposed an additional estate tax if, within 10 years after the date of the decedent's death and before the date of the qualified heir's death—

(A) the material participation requirements described in section 2032A(c)(6)(B) are not met with respect to the qualified family-owned business interest which was acquired (or passed) from the decedent,

(B) the qualified heir disposes of any portion of a qualified family-owned business interest (other than by a disposition to a member of the qualified heir's family or through a qualified conservation contribution under section 170(h)),

(C) the qualified heir loses United States citizenship (within the meaning of section 877) or with respect to whom an event described in subparagraph (A) or (B) of section 877(e)(1) occurs, and such heir does not comply with the requirements of subsection (g), or

(D) the principal place of business of a trade or business of the qualified family-owned business interest ceases to be located in the United States.

ESTATE TAX—TAXABLE ESTATE

(2) ADDITIONAL ESTATE TAX.—

(A) IN GENERAL.—The amount of the additional estate tax imposed by paragraph (1) shall be equal to—

(i) the applicable percentage of the adjusted tax difference attributable to the qualified family-owned business interest, plus

(ii) interest on the amount determined under clause (i) at the underpayment rate established under section 6621 for the period beginning on the date the estate tax liability was due under this chapter and ending on the date such additional estate tax is due.

(B) APPLICABLE PERCENTAGE.—For purposes of this paragraph, the applicable percentage shall be determined under the following table:

If the event described in paragraph (1) occurs in the following year of material participation:	The applicable percentage is:
1 through 6	100
7	80
8	60
9	40
10	20

(C) ADJUSTED TAX DIFFERENCE.—For purposes of subparagraph (A)—

(i) IN GENERAL.—The adjusted tax difference attributable to a qualified family-owned business interest is the amount which bears the same ratio to the adjusted tax difference with respect to the estate (determined under clause (ii)) as the value of such interest bears to the value of all qualified family-owned business interests described in subsection (b)(2).

(ii) ADJUSTED TAX DIFFERENCE WITH RESPECT TO THE ESTATE.—For purposes of clause (i), the term "adjusted tax difference with respect to the estate" means the excess of what would have been the estate tax liability but for the election under this section over the estate tax liability. For purposes of this clause, the term "estate tax liability" means the tax imposed by section 2001 reduced by the credits allowable against such tax.

(3) USE IN TRADE OR BUSINESS BY FAMILY MEMBERS.—A qualified heir shall not be treated as disposing of an interest described in subsection (e)(1)(A) by reason of ceasing to be engaged in a trade or business so long as the property to which such interest relates is used in a trade or business by any member of such individual's family.

Amendments

• **1998, IRS Restructuring and Reform Act of 1998 (P.L. 105-206)**

P.L. 105-206, §6007(b)(4)(A)-(B):

Amended Code Sec. 2057(f)(2) (as redesignated) by striking "(as determined under rules similar to the rules of section 2032A(c)(2)(B))" before ", plus", and by adding at the end a new subparagraph (C). **Effective** as if included in the provision of P.L. 105-34 to which it relates [**effective** for estates of decedents dying after 12-31-97.—CCH].

P.L. 105-206, §6007(b)(5)(B):

Amended Code Sec. 2057(f) (as redesignated) by adding at the end a new paragraph (3). **Effective** as if included in the provision of P.L. 105-34 to which it relates [**effective** for estates of decedents dying after 12-31-97.—CCH].

[Sec. 2057(g)]

(g) SECURITY REQUIREMENTS FOR NONCITIZEN QUALIFIED HEIRS.—

(1) IN GENERAL.—Except upon the application of subparagraph (F) of subsection (i)(3), if a qualified heir is not a citizen of the United States, any interest under this section passing to or acquired by such heir (including any interest held by such heir at a time described in subsection (f)(1)(C)) shall be treated as a qualified family-owned business interest only if the interest passes or is acquired (or is held) in a qualified trust.

(2) QUALIFIED TRUST.—The term "qualified trust" means a trust—

(A) which is organized under, and governed by, the laws of the United States or a State, and

(B) except as otherwise provided in regulations, with respect to which the trust instrument requires that at least 1 trustee of the trust be an individual citizen of the United States or a domestic corporation.

Amendments

• **1998, IRS Restructuring and Reform Act of 1998 (P.L. 105-206)**

P.L. 105-206, §6007(b)(6):

Amended Code Sec. 2057(g)(1) (as redesignated) by striking "or (M)" after "subparagraph (F)". **Effective** as if included in the provision of P.L. 105-34 to which it relates [**effective** for estates of decedents dying after 12-31-97.—CCH].

[Sec. 2057(h)]

(h) AGREEMENT.—The agreement referred to in this subsection is a written agreement signed by each person in being who has an interest (whether or not in possession) in any property designated in such agreement consenting to the application of subsection (f) with respect to such property.

[Sec. 2057(i)]

(i) OTHER DEFINITIONS AND APPLICABLE RULES.—For purposes of this section—

(1) QUALIFIED HEIR.—The term "qualified heir"—

(A) has the meaning given to such term by section 2032A(e)(1), and

(B) includes any active employee of the trade or business to which the qualified family-owned business interest relates if such employee has been employed by such trade or business for a period of at least 10 years before the date of the decedent's death.

(2) MEMBER OF THE FAMILY.—The term "member of the family" has the meaning given to such term by section 2032A(e)(2).

(3) APPLICABLE RULES.—Rules similar to the following rules shall apply:

(A) Section 2032A(b)(4) (relating to decedents who are retired or disabled).

(B) Section 2032A(b)(5) (relating to special rules for surviving spouses).

(C) Section 2032A(c)(2)(D) (relating to partial dispositions).

(D) Section 2032A(c)(3) (relating to only 1 additional tax imposed with respect to any 1 portion).

(E) Section 2032A(c)(4) (relating to due date).

(F) Section 2032A(c)(5) (relating to liability for tax; furnishing of bond).

(G) Section 2032A(c)(7) (relating to no tax if use begins within 2 years; active management by eligible qualified heir treated as material participation).

(H) Paragraphs (1) and (3) of section 2032A(d) (relating to election; agreement).

(I) Section 2032A(e)(10) (relating to community property).

(J) Section 2032A(e)(14) (relating to treatment of replacement property acquired in section 1031 or 1033 transactions).

(K) Section 2032A(f) (relating to statute of limitations).

(L) Section 2032A(g) (relating to application to interests in partnerships, corporations, and trusts).

(M) Subsections (h) and (i) of section 2032A.

(N) Section 6166(b)(3) (relating to farmhouses and certain other structures taken into account).

(O) Subparagraphs (B), (C), and (D) of section 6166(g)(1) (relating to acceleration of payment).

(P) Section 6324B (relating to special lien for additional estate tax).

Amendments

• **1998, IRS Restructuring and Reform Act of 1998 (P.L. 105-206)**

P.L. 105-206, §6007(b)(1)(A):

Amended Code Sec. 2033A by moving it to the end of part IV of subchapter A of chapter 11 and redesignating it as Code Sec. 2057. **Effective** as if included in the provision of P.L. 105-34 to which it relates [**effective** for estates of decedents dying after 12-31-97.—CCH].

P.L. 105-206, §6007(b)(7):

Amended Code Sec. 2057(i)(3) (as redesignated) by redesignating subparagraphs (L), (M), and (N) as subparagraphs (N), (O), and (P), respectively, and by inserting after subparagraph (K) new subparagraphs (L) and (M). **Effective** as if included in the provision of P.L. 105-34 to which it relates [**effective** for estates of decedents dying after 12-31-97.—CCH].

• **1997, Taxpayer Relief Act of 1997 (P.L. 105-34)**

P.L. 105-34, §502(a):

Amended part III of subchapter A of chapter 11 by inserting after Code Sec. 2033 a new Code Sec. 2033A. **Effective** for estates of decedents dying after 12-31-97.

[Sec. 2057(j)]

(j) TERMINATION.—This section shall not apply to the estates of decedents dying after December 31, 2003.

Amendments

• **2013, American Taxpayer Relief Act of 2012 (P.L. 112-240)**

P.L. 112-240, §101(a)(1) and (3), provides:

SEC. 101. PERMANENT EXTENSION AND MODIFICATION OF 2001 TAX RELIEF.

(a) PERMANENT EXTENSION.—

(1) IN GENERAL.—The Economic Growth and Tax Relief Reconciliation Act of 2001 is amended by striking title IX.

* * *

(3) EFFECTIVE DATE.—The amendments made by this subsection shall apply to taxable, plan, or limitation years beginning after December 31, 2012, and estates of decedents dying, gifts made, or generation skipping transfers after December 31, 2012.

• **2001, Economic Growth and Tax Relief Reconciliation Act of 2001 (P.L. 107-16)**

P.L. 107-16, §521(d):

Amended Code Sec. 2057 by adding at the end a new subsection (j). **Effective** for estates of decedents dying, and generation-skipping transfers, after 12-31-2003.

P.L. 107-16, §901(a)-(b), as amended by P.L. 111-312, §101(a)(1), provides [but see P.L. 112-240, §101(a)(1) and (3), above]:

SEC. 901. SUNSET OF PROVISIONS OF ACT.

(a) IN GENERAL.—All provisions of, and amendments made by, this Act shall not apply—

(1) to taxable, plan, or limitation years beginning after December 31, 2012, or

(2) in the case of title V, to estates of decedents dying, gifts made, or generation skipping transfers, after December 31, 2012.

(b) APPLICATION OF CERTAIN LAWS.—The Internal Revenue Code of 1986 and the Employee Retirement Income Security Act of 1974 shall be applied and administered to years, estates, gifts, and transfers described in subsection (a) as if the provisions and amendments described in subsection (a) had never been enacted.

Sec. 2057—Stricken

ESTATE TAX—TAXABLE ESTATE

[Sec. 2057—Repealed]

Amendments

• **1989, Omnibus Budget Reconciliation Act of 1989 (P.L. 101-239)**

P.L. 101-239, § 7304(a)(1):

Repealed Code Sec. 2057. **Effective** for estates of decedents dying after 12-19-89. Prior to repeal, Code Sec. 2057 read as follows:

SEC. 2057. SALES OF EMPLOYER SECURITIES TO EMPLOYEE STOCK OWNERSHIP PLANS OR WORKER-OWNED COOPERATIVES.

(a) GENERAL RULE.—For purposes of the tax imposed by section 2001, the value of the taxable estate shall be determined by deducting from the value of the gross estate an amount equal to 50 percent of the proceeds of any sale of any qualified employer securities to—

(1) an employee stock ownership plan, or

(2) an eligible worker-owned cooperative.

(b) LIMITATIONS.—

(1) MAXIMUM REDUCTION IN TAX LIABILITY.—The amount allowable as a deduction under subsection (a) shall not exceed the amount which would result in an aggregate reduction in the tax imposed by section 2001 (determined without regard to any credit allowable against such tax) equal to $750,000.

(2) DEDUCTION SHALL NOT EXCEED 50 PERCENT OF TAXABLE ESTATE.—The amount of the deduction allowable under subsection (a) shall not exceed 50 percent of the taxable estate (determined without regard to this section).

(c) LIMITATIONS ON PROCEEDS WHICH MAY BE TAKEN INTO ACCOUNT.—

(1) DISPOSITIONS BY PLAN OR COOPERATIVE WITHIN 1 YEAR OF SALE.—

(A) IN GENERAL.—Proceeds from a sale which are taken into account under subsection (a) shall be reduced (but not below zero) by the net sale amount.

(B) NET SALE AMOUNT.—For purposes of subparagraph (A), the term "net sale amount" means the excess (if any) of—

(i) the proceeds of the plan or cooperative from the disposition of employer securities during the 1-year period immediately preceding such sale, over

(ii) the cost of employer securities purchased by such plan or cooperative during such 1-year period.

(C) EXCEPTIONS.—For purposes of subparagraph (B)(i), there shall not be taken into account any proceeds of a plan or cooperative from a disposition described in section 4978A(e).

(D) AGGREGATION RULES.—For purposes of this paragraph, all employee stock ownership plans maintained by an employer shall be treated as 1 plan.

(2) SECURITIES MUST BE ACQUIRED BY PLAN FROM ASSETS WHICH ARE NOT TRANSFERRED ASSETS.—

(A) IN GENERAL.—Proceeds from a sale shall not be taken into account under subsection (a) to the extent that such proceeds (as under paragraph (1)) are attributable to transferred assets. For purposes of the preceding sentence, all assets of a plan or cooperative (other than qualified employer securities) shall be treated as first acquired out of transferred assets.

(B) TRANSFERRED ASSETS.—For purposes of subparagraph (A)—

(i) IN GENERAL.—The term "transferred assets" means assets of an employee stock ownership plan which—

(I) are attributable to assets held by a plan exempt from tax under section 501(a) and meeting the requirements of section 401(a) (other than an employee stock ownership plan of the employer), or

(II) were held by the plan when it was not an employee stock ownership plan.

(ii) EXCEPTION FOR ASSETS HELD ON FEBRUARY 26, 1987.—The term "transferred assets" shall not include any asset held by the employee stock ownership plan on February 26, 1987.

(iii) SECRETARIAL AUTHORITY TO WAIVE TREATMENT AS TRANSFERRED ASSET.—The Secretary may provide that assets or a class of assets shall not be treated as transferred assets if the Secretary finds such treatment is not necessary to carry out the purposes of this paragraph.

(3) OTHER PROCEEDS.—The following proceeds shall not be taken into account under subsection (a):

(A) PROCEEDS FROM SALE AFTER DUE DATE FOR RETURN.—Any proceeds from a sale which occurs after the date on which the return of the tax imposed by section 2001 is required to be filed (determined by taking into account any extension of time for filing).

(B) PROCEEDS FROM SALE OF CERTAIN SECURITIES.—Any proceeds from a sale of employer securities which were received by the decedent—

(i) in a distribution from a plan exempt from tax under section 501(a) and meeting the requirements of section 401(a), or

(ii) as a transfer pursuant to an option or other right to acquire stock to which section 83, 422, 422A, 423, or 424 applies.

Any employer security the basis of which is determined by reference to any employer security described in the preceding sentence shall be treated as an employer security to which this subparagraph applies.

(d) QUALIFIED EMPLOYER SECURITIES.—

(1) IN GENERAL.—The term "qualified employer securities" means employer securities—

(A) which are issued by a domestic corporation which has no stock outstanding which is readily tradable on an established securities market,

(B) which are includible in the gross estate of the decedent,

(C) which would have been includible in the gross estate of the decedent if the decedent had died at any time during the shorter of—

(i) the 5-year period ending on the date of death, or

(ii) the period beginning on October 22, 1986, and ending on the date of death, and

(D) with respect to which the executor elects the application of this section.

Subparagraph (C) shall not apply if the decedent died on or before October 22, 1986.

(2) CERTAIN ASSETS HELD BY SPOUSE.—For purposes of paragraph (1)(C), any employer security which would have been includible in the gross estate of the spouse of a decedent during any period if the spouse had died during such period shall be treated as includible in the gross estate of the decedent during such period.

(3) PERIODS DURING WHICH DECEDENT NOT AT RISK.—For purposes of paragraph (1)(C), employer securities shall not be treated as includible in the gross estate of the decedent during any period described in section 246(c)(4).

(e) WRITTEN STATEMENT REQUIRED.—

(1) IN GENERAL.—No deduction shall be allowed under subsection (a) unless the executor of the estate of the decedent files with the Secretary the statement described in paragraph (2).

(2) STATEMENT.—A statement is described in this paragraph if it is a verified written statement—

(A) which is made by—

(i) the employer whose employees are covered by the employee stock ownership plan, or

(ii) any authorized officer of the eligible worker-owned cooperative, and

(B) which—

(i) acknowledges that the sale of employer securities to the plan or cooperative is a sale to which sections 4978A and 4979A apply, and

(ii) certifies—

(I) the net sale amount for purposes of subsection (c)(1), and

(II) the amount of assets which are not transferred assets for purposes of subsection (c)(2).

(f) OTHER DEFINITIONS AND SPECIAL RULES.—For purposes of this section—

(1) EMPLOYER SECURITIES.—The term "employer securities" has the meaning given such term by section 409(1).

(2) EMPLOYEE STOCK OWNERSHIP PLAN.—The term "employee stock ownership plan" means—

(A) a tax credit employee stock ownership plan (within the meaning of section 409(a)), or

(B) a plan described in section 4975(e)(7).

(3) ELIGIBLE WORKER-OWNED COOPERATIVE.—The term "eligible worker-owned cooperative" has the meaning given such term by section 1042(c).

(4) EMPLOYER.—Except to the extent provided in regulations, the term "employer" includes any person treated as an employer under subsections (b), (c), (m), and (o) of section 414.

(g) TERMINATION.—This section shall not apply to any sale after December 31, 1991.

• **1988, Technical and Miscellaneous Revenue Act of 1988 (P.L. 100-647)**

P.L. 100-647, § 1011B(g)(3):

Amended Code Sec. 2057(b)(1) by striking out "is" after "plan". **Effective** as if included in the provision of P.L. 99-514 to which it relates.

• **1987, Revenue Act of 1987 (P.L. 100-203)**

P.L. 100-203, § 10411(a):

Amended Code Sec. 2057 by redesignating subsections (d), (e), and (f) as subsections (e), (f), and (g), respectively, and by inserting after subsection (c) new subsection (d). **Effective** as if included in the amendments made by section 1172 of P.L. 99-514.

P.L. 100-203, § 10412(a):

Amended Code Sec. 2057. **Effective**, generally, for sales after 2-26-87. However, see Act Sec. 10412(b)(2)-(4), below, for special provisions. Prior to amendment, Code Sec. 2057 read as follows:

SEC. 2057. SALES OF EMPLOYER SECURITIES TO EMPLOYEE STOCK OWNERSHIP PLANS OR WORKER-OWNED COOPERATIVES.

(a) GENERAL RULE.—For purposes of the tax imposed by section 2001, the value of the taxable estate shall be determined by deducting from the value of the gross estate an amount equal to 50 percent of the qualified proceeds of a qualified sale of employer securities.

(b) QUALIFIED SALE.—For purposes of this section, the term "qualified sale" means any sale of employer securities by the executor of an estate to—

(1) an employee stock ownership plan described in section 4975(e)(7), or

(2) an eligible worker-owned cooperative (within the meaning of section 1042(c)).

(c) QUALIFIED PROCEEDS.—For purposes of this section—

(1) IN GENERAL.—The term "qualified proceeds" means the amount received by the estate from the sale of employer securities at any time before the date on which the return of the tax imposed by section 2001 is required to be filed (including any extensions).

(2) PROCEEDS FROM CERTAIN SECURITIES NOT QUALIFIED.—The term "qualified proceeds" shall not include the proceeds from the sale of any employer securities if such securities were received by the decedent—

(A) in a distribution from a plan exempt from tax under section 501(a) which meets the requirements of section 401(a), or

(B) as a transfer pursuant to an option or other right to acquire stock to which section 83, 422, 422A, 423, or 424 applies.

(d) QUALIFED PROCEEDS FROM QUALIFIED SALES.—

(1) IN GENERAL.—For purposes of this section, the proceeds of a sale of employer securities by an executor to an employee stock ownership plan or an eligible worker-owned cooperative shall not be treated as qualified proceeds from a qualified sale unless—

(A) the decedent directly owned the securities immediately before death, and

(B) after the sale, the employer securities—

(i) are allocated to participants, or

ESTATE TAX—TAXABLE ESTATE

(ii) are held for future allocation in connection with—

(I) an exempt loan under the rules of section 4975, or

(II) a transfer of assets under the rules of section 4980(c)(3).

(2) No SUBSTITUTION PERMITTED.—For purposes of paragraph (1)(B), except as in the case of a bona fide business transaction (e.g., a substitution of employer securities in connection with a merger of employers), employer securities shall not be treated as allocated or held for future allocation to the extent that such securities are allocated or held for future allocation in substitution of other employer securities that had been allocated or held for future allocation.

(e) WRITTEN STATEMENT REQUIRED.—

(1) IN GENERAL.—No deduction shall be allowed under subsection (a) unless the executor of the estate of the decedent files with the Secretary the statement described in paragraph (2).

(2) STATEMENT.—A statement is described in this paragraph if it is a verified written statement of—

(A) the employer whose employees are covered by the plan described in subsection (b)(1), or

(B) any authorized officer of the cooperative described in subsection (b)(2),

consenting to the application of section 4979A with respect to such employer or cooperative.

(f) EMPLOYER SECURITIES.—For purposes of this section, the term "employer securities" has the meaning given such term by section 409(l).

(g) TERMINATION.—This section shall not apply to any sale after December 31, 1991.

Amendments

• **1981, Economic Recovery Tax Act of 1981 (P.L. 97-34)**

P.L. 97-34, §427(a):

Repealed Code Sec. 2057. **Effective** for estates of decedents dying after 12-31-81. Prior to its repeal, Code Sec. 2057 read as follows:

SEC. 2057. BEQUESTS, ETC., TO CERTAIN MINOR CHILDREN.

(a) ALLOWANCE OF DEDUCTION.—For purposes of the tax imposed by section 2001, if—

(1) the decedent does not have a surviving spouse, and

(2) the decedent is survived by a minor child who, immediately after the death of the decedent, has no known parent,

then the value of the taxable estate shall be determined by deducting from the value of the gross estate an amount equal to the value of any interest in property which passes or has passed from the decedent to such child, but only to the extent that such interest is included in determining the value of the gross estate.

(b) LIMITATION.—The aggregate amount of the deductions allowed under this section (computed without regard to this subsection) with respect to interests in property passing to any minor child shall not exceed an amount equal to $5,000 multiplied by the excess of 21 over the age (in years) which such child has attained on the date of the decedent's death.

(c) LIMITATION IN THE CASE OF LIFE ESTATE OR OTHER TERMINABLE INTEREST.—A deduction shall be allowed under this section with respect to any interest in property passing to a minor child only to the extent that a deduction would have been allowable under section 2056(b) if such interest had passed to a surviving spouse of the decedent. For purposes of this subsection, an interest shall not be treated as terminable solely because the property will pass to another person if the child dies before the youngest child of the decedent attains age 23.

(d) QUALIFIED MINORS' TRUST.—

(1) IN GENERAL.—For purposes of subsection (a), the interest of a minor child in a qualified minors' trust shall be treated as an interest in property which passes or has passed from the decedent to such child.

(2) QUALIFIED MINORS' TRUST.—For purposes of paragraph (1), the term "qualified minors' trust" means a trust—

(A) except as provided in subparagraph (d), all of the beneficiaries of which are minor children of the decedent,

(B) the corpus of which is property which passes or has passed from the decedent to such trust,

(C) except as provided in paragraph (3), all distributions from which to the beneficiaries of the trust before the termination of their interests will be pro rata,

(D) on the death of any beneficiary of which before the termination of the trust, the beneficiary's pro rata share of the corpus and accumulated income remains in the trust for the benefit of the minor children of the decedent who survive the beneficiary or vests in any person, and

(E) on the termination of which, each beneficiary will receive a pro rata share of the corpus and accumulated income.

(3) CERTAIN DISPROPORTIONATE DISTRIBUTIONS PERMITTED.—A trust shall not be treated as failing to meet the requirements of paragraph (2)(C) solely by reason of the fact that the governing instrument of the trust permits the making of disproportionate distributions which are limited by an ascertainable standard relating to the health, education, support, or maintenance of the beneficiaries.

(4) TRUSTEE MAY ACCUMULATE INCOME.—A trust which otherwise qualifies as a qualified minors' trust shall not be disqualified solely by reason of the fact that the trustee has power to accumulate income.

(5) COORDINATION WITH SUBSECTION (c).—In applying subsection (c) to a qualified minors' trust, those provisions of section 2056(b) which are inconsistent with paragraph (3) or (4) of this subsection shall not apply.

(6) DEATH OF BENEFICIARY BEFORE YOUNGEST CHILD REACHES AGE 23.—Nothing in this subsection shall be treated as disqualifying an interest of a minor child in a trust solely because such interest will pass to another person if the child dies before the youngest child of the decedent attains age 23.

(e) DEFINITIONS.—For purposes of this section—

(1) MINOR CHILD.—The term "minor child" means any child of the decedent who has not attained the age of 21 before the date of the decedent's death.

(2) ADOPTED CHILDREN.—A relationship by legal adoption shall be treated as replacing a relationship by blood.

(3) PROPERTY PASSING FROM THE DECEDENT.—The determination of whether an interest in property passes from the decedent to any person shall be made in accordance with section 2056(d).

P.L. 100-203, §10412(b)(2)-(4), provides:

(2) PROVISIONS TAKING EFFECT AS IF INCLUDED IN THE TAX REFORM ACT OF 1986.—The following provisions shall take effect as if included in the amendments made by section 1172 of the Tax Reform Act of 1986:

(A) Section 2057(f)(2) of the Internal Revenue Code of 1986, as added, by this section.

(B) The repeal of the requirement that a sale be made by the executor of an estate to qualify for purposes of section 2057 of such Code.

(3) DIRECT OWNERSHIP REQUIREMENT.—If the requirements of section 2057(d)(1)(B) of such Code (as modified by section 2057(d)(2) of such Code), as in effect after the amendments made by this section, are met with respect to any employer securities sold after October 22, 1986, and before February 27, 1987, such securities shall be treated as having been directly owned by the decedent for purposes of section 2057 of such Code, as in effect before such amendments.

(4) REDUCTION FOR SALES ON OR BEFORE FEBRUARY 26, 1987.—In applying the limitations of subsection (b) of section 2057 of such Code to sales after February 26, 1987, there shall be taken into account sales on or before February 26, 1987, to which section 2057 of such Code applied.

• **1986, Tax Reform Act of 1986 (P.L. 99-514)**

P.L. 99-514, §1172(a):

Amended Part IV of Subchapter A of chapter 11 by adding new Code Sec. 2057 at the end thereof. **Effective** for sales after 10-22-86 with respect to which an election is made by the executor of an estate who is required to file the return of the tax imposed by the Internal Revenue Code of 1986 on a date (including extensions) after the date of the enactment of this Act.

[Sec. 2057—Repealed]

• **1978, Revenue Act of 1978 (P.L. 95-600)**

P.L. 95-600, §702(l)(1):

Redesignated Code Sec. 2057(d) as Code Sec. 2057(e) and added new Code Sec. 2057(d). **Effective** for estates of decedents dying after 1976.

P.L. 95-600, §702(l)(2):

Amended the last sentence of Code Sec. 2057(c) by substituting "23" for "21". **Effective** for estates of decedents dying after 1976.

• **1976, Tax Reform Act of 1976 (P.L. 94-455)**

P.L. 94-455, §2007(a), (c):

Added Code Sec. 2057. **Effective** for estates of decedents dying after 12-31-76.

[Sec. 2058]

SEC. 2058. STATE DEATH TAXES.

[Sec. 2058(a)]

(a) ALLOWANCE OF DEDUCTION.—For purposes of the tax imposed by section 2001, the value of the taxable estate shall be determined by deducting from the value of the gross estate the amount of any estate, inheritance, legacy, or succession taxes actually paid to any State or the District of Columbia, in respect of any property included in the gross estate (not including any such taxes paid with respect to the estate of a person other than the decedent).

[Sec. 2058(b)]

(b) PERIOD OF LIMITATIONS.—The deduction allowed by this section shall include only such taxes as were actually paid and deduction therefor claimed before the later of—

(1) 4 years after the filing of the return required by section 6018, or

(2) if—

(A) a petition for redetermination of a deficiency has been filed with the Tax Court within the time prescribed in section 6213(a), the expiration of 60 days after the decision of the Tax Court becomes final,

ESTATE TAX—ESTATES OF NONRESIDENTS NOT CITIZENS

(B) an extension of time has been granted under section 6161 or 6166 for payment of the tax shown on the return, or of a deficiency, the date of the expiration of the period of the extension, or

(C) a claim for refund or credit of an over-payment of tax imposed by this chapter has been filed within the time prescribed in section 6511, the latest of the expiration of—

(i) 60 days from the date of mailing by certified mail or registered mail by the Secretary to the taxpayer of a notice of the disallowance of any part of such claim,

(ii) 60 days after a decision by any court of competent jurisdiction becomes final with respect to a timely suit instituted upon such claim, or

(iii) 2 years after a notice of the waiver of disallowance is filed under section 6532(a)(3).

Notwithstanding sections 6511 and 6512, refund based on the deduction may be made if the claim for refund is filed within the period provided in the preceding sentence. Any such refund shall be made without interest.

Amendments

• **2013, American Taxpayer Relief Act of 2012 (P.L. 112-240)**

P.L. 112-240, § 101(a)(1) and (3), provides:

SEC. 101. PERMANENT EXTENSION AND MODIFICATION OF 2001 TAX RELIEF.

(a) PERMANENT EXTENSION.—

(1) IN GENERAL.—The Economic Growth and Tax Relief Reconciliation Act of 2001 is amended by striking title IX.

***

(3) EFFECTIVE DATE.—The amendments made by this subsection shall apply to taxable, plan, or limitation years beginning after December 31, 2012, and estates of decedents dying, gifts made, or generation skipping transfers after December 31, 2012.

• **2001, Economic Growth and Tax Relief Reconciliation Act of 2001 (P.L. 107-16)**

P.L. 107-16, § 532(b):

Amended part IV of subchapter A of chapter 11 by adding at the end a new Code Sec. 2058. **Effective** for estates of decedents dying, and generation-skipping transfers, after 12-31-2004.

P.L. 107-16, § 901(a)-(b), as amended by P.L. 111-312, § 101(a)(1), provides [but see P.L. 112-240, § 101(a)(1) and (3), above]:

SEC. 901. SUNSET OF PROVISIONS OF ACT.

(a) IN GENERAL.—All provisions of, and amendments made by, this Act shall not apply—

(1) to taxable, plan, or limitation years beginning after December 31, 2012, or

(2) in the case of title V, to estates of decedents dying, gifts made, or generation skipping transfers, after December 31, 2012.

(b) APPLICATION OF CERTAIN LAWS.—The Internal Revenue Code of 1986 and the Employee Retirement Income Security Act of 1974 shall be applied and administered to years, estates, gifts, and transfers described in subsection (a) as if the provisions and amendments described in subsection (a) had never been enacted.

Subchapter B—Estates of Nonresidents Not Citizens

Sec. 2101.	Tax imposed.
Sec. 2102.	Credits against tax.
Sec. 2103.	Definition of gross estate.
Sec. 2104.	Property within the United States.
Sec. 2105.	Property without the United States.
Sec. 2106.	Taxable estate.
Sec. 2107.	Expatriation to avoid tax.
Sec. 2108.	Application of pre-1967 estate tax provisions.

[Sec. 2101]

SEC. 2101. TAX IMPOSED.

[Sec. 2101(a)]

(a) IMPOSITION.—Except as provided in section 2107, a tax is hereby imposed on the transfer of the taxable estate (determined as provided in section 2106) of every decedent nonresident not a citizen of the United States.

Amendments

• **1976, Tax Reform Act of 1976 (P.L. 94-455)**

P.L. 94-455, § 2001(c)(1)(D), (d)(1):

Amended Code Sec. 2101(a). **Effective** for estates of decedents dying after 12-31-76. Prior to amendment, Code Sec. 2101(a) read as follows:

(a) RATE OF TAX.—Except as provided in section 2107, a tax computed in accordance with the following table is hereby imposed on the transfer of the taxable estate, determined as provided in section 2106, of every decedent nonresident not a citizen of the United States:

If the taxable estate is:	The tax shall be:
Not over $100,000	5% of the taxable estate.
Over $100,000 but not over $500,000	$5,000, plus 10% of excess over $100,000.
Over $500,000 but not over $1,000,000	$45,000, plus 15% of excess over $500,000.
Over $1,000,000 but not over $2,000,000	$120,000, plus 20% of excess over $1,000,000.
Over $2,000,000	$320,000, plus 25% of excess over $2,000,000.

• **1966, Foreign Investors Tax Act of 1966 (P.L. 89-809)**

P.L. 89-809, § 108(a):

Amended Code Sec. 2101(a). **Effective** with respect to estates of decedents dying after 11-13-66, the date of enactment. Prior to amendment, Sec. 2101(a) read as follows:

(a) In General.—A tax computed in accordance with the table contained in section 2001 is hereby imposed on the transfer of the taxable estate, determined as provided in section 2106, of every decedent nonresident not a citizen of the United States dying after the date of enactment of this title.

[Sec. 2101(b)]

(b) COMPUTATION OF TAX.—The tax imposed by this section shall be the amount equal to the excess (if any) of—

(1) a tentative tax computed under section 2001(c) on the sum of—

(A) the amount of the taxable estate, and

(B) the amount of the adjusted taxable gifts, over

(2) a tentative tax computed under section 2001(c) on the amount of the adjusted taxable gifts.

For purposes of the preceding sentence, there shall be appropriate adjustments in the application of section 2001(c)(2) to reflect the difference between the amount of the credit provided under section 2102(c) and the amount of the credit provided under section 2010.

ESTATE TAX—ESTATES OF NONRESIDENTS NOT CITIZENS

Amendments

• **2013, American Taxpayer Relief Act of 2012 (P.L. 112-240)**

P.L. 112-240, §101(a)(1) and (3), provides:

SEC. 101. PERMANENT EXTENSION AND MODIFICATION OF 2001 TAX RELIEF.

(a) PERMANENT EXTENSION.—

(1) IN GENERAL.—The Economic Growth and Tax Relief Reconciliation Act of 2001 is amended by striking title IX.

* * *

(3) EFFECTIVE DATE.—The amendments made by this subsection shall apply to taxable, plan, or limitation years beginning after December 31, 2012, and estates of decedents dying, gifts made, or generation skipping transfers after December 31, 2012.

• **2002, Job Creation and Worker Assistance Act of 2002 (P.L. 107-147)**

P.L. 107-147, §411(g)(2):

Amended Code Sec. 2101(b) by striking the last sentence. **Effective** as if included in the provision of P.L. 107-16 to which it relates [**effective** for estates of decedents dying, and gifts made, after 12-31-2001.—CCH]. Prior to being stricken, the last sentence of Code Sec. 2101(b) read as follows:

For purposes of the preceding sentence, there shall be appropriate adjustments in the application of section 2001(c)(2) to reflect the difference between the amount of the credit provided under section 2102(c) and the amount of the credit provided under section 2010.

• **2001, Economic Growth and Tax Relief Reconciliation Act of 2001 (P.L. 107-16)**

P.L. 107-16, §901(a)-(b), as amended by P.L. 111-312, §101(a)(1), provides [but see P.L. 112-240, §101(a)(1) and (3), above]:

SEC. 901. SUNSET OF PROVISIONS OF ACT.

(a) IN GENERAL.—All provisions of, and amendments made by, this Act shall not apply—

(1) to taxable, plan, or limitation years beginning after December 31, 2012, or

(2) in the case of title V, to estates of decedents dying, gifts made, or generation skipping transfers, after December 31, 2012.

(b) APPLICATION OF CERTAIN LAWS.—The Internal Revenue Code of 1986 and the Employee Retirement Income Security Act of 1974 shall be applied and administered to years, estates, gifts, and transfers described in subsection (a) as if the provisions and amendments described in subsection (a) had never been enacted.

• **1993, Omnibus Budget Reconciliation Act of 1993 (P.L. 103-66)**

P.L. 103-66, §13208(b)(3):

Amended Code Sec. 2101(b) by striking "section 2001(c)(3)" and inserting "section 2001(c)(2)". **Effective** in the case of decedents dying and gifts made after 12-31-92.

• **1989, Omnibus Budget Reconciliation Act of 1989 (P.L. 101-239)**

P.L. 101-239, §7815(c):

Amended Code Sec. 2101(b) by adding at the end thereof a new sentence. **Effective** as if included in the provision of P.L. 100-647 to which it relates.

• **1988, Technical and Miscellaneous Revenue Act of 1988 (P.L. 100-647)**

P.L. 100-647, §5032(a):

Amended Code Sec. 2101(b) by striking out "a tentative tax computed in accordance with the rate schedule set forth in subsection (d)" each place it appears and inserting in lieu thereof "a tentative tax computed under section 2001(c)". **Effective** for estates of decedents dying after the date of enactment of this Act.

• **1976, Tax Reform Act of 1976 (P.L. 94-455)**

P.L. 94-455, §2001(c)(1)(D), (d)(1):

Amended Code Sec. 2101(b). **Effective** for estates of decedents dying after 12-31-76. Prior to amendment, Code Sec. 2101(b) read as follows:

(b) PROPERTY HELD BY ALIEN PROPERTY CUSTODIAN.—

For taxes in connection with property or interests transferred to or vested in the Alien Property Custodian, see section 36 of the Trading with the Enemy Act, as added by the Act of August 8, 1946 (60 Stat. 929; 50 U.S.C. App. 36).

[Sec. 2101(c)]

(c) ADJUSTMENTS FOR TAXABLE GIFTS.—

(1) ADJUSTED TAXABLE GIFTS DEFINED.—For purposes of this section, the term "adjusted taxable gifts" means the total amount of the taxable gifts (within the meaning of section 2503 as modified by section 2511) made by the decedent after December 31, 1976, other than gifts which are includible in the gross estate of the decedent.

(2) ADJUSTMENT FOR CERTAIN GIFT TAX.—For purposes of this section, the rules of section 2001(d) shall apply.

Amendments

• **1976, Tax Reform Act of 1976 (P.L. 94-455)**

P.L. 94-455, §2001(c)(1)(D), (d)(1):

Added Code Sec. 2101(c). **Effective** for estates of decedents dying after 12-31-76.

[Sec. 2101(d)—Repealed]

Amendments

• **1988, Technical and Miscellaneous Revenue Act of 1988 (P.L. 100-647)**

P.L. 100-647, §5032(c):

Repealed Code Sec. 2101(d). **Effective** for estates of decedents dying after 11-10-88. Prior to repeal, Code Sec. 2101(d) read as follows:

(d) RATE SCHEDULE.—

If the amount with respect to which the tentative tax to be computed is:	The tentative tax is:
Not over $100,000	6% of such amount.
Over $100,000 but not over $500,000	$6,000, plus 12% of excess over $100,000.
Over $500,000 but not over $1,000,000	$54,000, plus 18% of excess over $500,000.
Over $1,000,000 but not over $2,000,000	$144,000, plus 24% of excess over $1,000,000.
Over $2,000,000	$384,000, plus 30% of excess over $2,000,000.

• **1976, Tax Reform Act of 1976 (P.L. 94-455)**

P.L. 94-455, §2001(c)(1)(D), (d)(1):

Added Code Sec. 2101(d). **Effective** for estates of decedents dying after 12-31-76.

[Sec. 2102]

SEC. 2102. CREDITS AGAINST TAX.

[Sec. 2102(a)]

(a) IN GENERAL.—The tax imposed by section 2101 shall be credited with the amounts determined in accordance with sections 2012 and 2013 (relating to gift tax and tax on prior transfers).

Amendments

• **2013, American Taxpayer Relief Act of 2012 (P.L. 112-240)**

P.L. 112-240, §101(a)(1) and (3), provides:

SEC. 101. PERMANENT EXTENSION AND MODIFICATION OF 2001 TAX RELIEF.

(a) PERMANENT EXTENSION.—

(1) IN GENERAL.—The Economic Growth and Tax Relief Reconciliation Act of 2001 is amended by striking title IX.

* * *

(3) EFFECTIVE DATE.—The amendments made by this subsection shall apply to taxable, plan, or limitation years beginning after December 31, 2012, and estates of decedents dying, gifts made, or generation skipping transfers after December 31, 2012.

• **2001, Economic Growth and Tax Relief Reconciliation Act of 2001 (P.L. 107-16)**

P.L. 107-16, §532(c)(7)(A):

Amended Code Sec. 2102(a). **Effective** for estates of decedents dying, and generation-skipping transfers, after 12-31-2004. Prior to amendment, Code Sec. 2102(a) read as follows:

(a) IN GENERAL.—The tax imposed by section 2101 shall be credited with the amounts determined in accordance with sections 2011 to 2013, inclusive (relating to State death taxes, gift tax, and tax on prior transfers), subject to the special limitation provided in subsection (b).

ESTATE TAX—ESTATES OF NONRESIDENTS NOT CITIZENS

P.L. 107-16, § 901(a)-(b), as amended by P.L. 111-312, § 101(a)(1), provides [but see P.L. 112-240, § 101(a)(1) and (3), above]:

SEC. 901. SUNSET OF PROVISIONS OF ACT.

(a) IN GENERAL.—All provisions of, and amendments made by, this Act shall not apply—

(1) to taxable, plan, or limitation years beginning after December 31, 2012, or

(2) in the case of title V, to estates of decedents dying, gifts made, or generation skipping transfers, after December 31, 2012.

(b) APPLICATION OF CERTAIN LAWS.—The Internal Revenue Code of 1986 and the Employee Retirement Income Security Act of 1974 shall be applied and administered to years, estates, gifts, and transfers described in subsection (a) as if the provisions and amendments described in subsection (a) had never been enacted.

Amendments

• **2013, American Taxpayer Relief Act of 2012 (P.L. 112-240)**

P.L. 112-240, § 101(a)(1) and (3), provides:

SEC. 101. PERMANENT EXTENSION AND MODIFICATION OF 2001 TAX RELIEF.

(a) PERMANENT EXTENSION.—

(1) IN GENERAL.—The Economic Growth and Tax Relief Reconciliation Act of 2001 is amended by striking title IX.

* * *

(3) EFFECTIVE DATE.—The amendments made by this subsection shall apply to taxable, plan, or limitation years beginning after December 31, 2012, and estates of decedents dying, gifts made, or generation skipping transfers after December 31, 2012.

• **2001, Economic Growth and Tax Relief Reconciliation Act of 2001 (P.L. 107-16)**

P.L. 107-16, § 532(c)(7)(B):

Amended Code Sec. 2102 by striking subsection (b) and by redesignating subsection (c) as subsection (b). **Effective** for estates of decedents dying, and generation-skipping transfers, after 12-31-2004. Prior to being stricken, Code Sec. 2102(b) read as follows:

[Sec. 2102(b)]

(b) SPECIAL LIMITATION.—The maximum credit allowed under section 2011 against the tax imposed by section 2101 for State death taxes paid shall be an amount which bears the same ratio to the credit computed as provided in section 2011(b) as the value of the property, as determined for purposes of this chapter, upon which State death taxes were paid and which is included in the gross estate under section 2103 bears to the value of the total gross estate under section 2103. For purposes of this subsection, the term "State death taxes" means the taxes described in section 2011(a).

P.L. 107-16, § 901(a)-(b), as amended by P.L. 111-312, § 101(a)(1), provides [but see P.L. 112-240, § 101(a)(1) and (3), above]:

SEC. 901. SUNSET OF PROVISIONS OF ACT.

(a) IN GENERAL.—All provisions of, and amendments made by, this Act shall not apply—

(1) to taxable, plan, or limitation years beginning after December 31, 2012, or

(2) in the case of title V, to estates of decedents dying, gifts made, or generation skipping transfers, after December 31, 2012.

(b) APPLICATION OF CERTAIN LAWS.—The Internal Revenue Code of 1986 and the Employee Retirement Income Security Act of 1974 shall be applied and administered to years, estates, gifts, and transfers described in subsection (a) as if the provisions and amendments described in subsection (a) had never been enacted.

[Sec. 2102(b)]

(b) UNIFIED CREDIT.—

(1) IN GENERAL.—A credit of $13,000 shall be allowed against the tax imposed by section 2101.

(2) RESIDENTS OF POSSESSIONS OF THE UNITED STATES.—In the case of a decedent who is considered to be a "nonresident not a citizen of the United States" under section 2209, the credit under this subsection shall be the greater of—

(A) $13,000, or

(B) that proportion of $46,800 which the value of that part of the decedent's gross estate which at the time of his death is situated in the United States bears to the value of his entire gross estate wherever situated.

(3) SPECIAL RULES.—

(A) COORDINATION WITH TREATIES.—To the extent required under any treaty obligation of the United States, the credit allowed under this subsection shall be equal to the amount which bears the same ratio to the applicable credit amount in effect under section 2010(c) for the calendar year which includes the date of death as the value of the part of the decedent's gross estate which at the time of his death is situated in the United States bears to the value of his entire gross estate wherever situated. For purposes of the preceding sentence, property shall not be treated as situated in the United States if such property is exempt from the tax imposed by this subchapter under any treaty obligation of the United States.

(B) COORDINATION WITH GIFT TAX UNIFIED CREDIT.—If a credit has been allowed under section 2505 with respect to any gift made by the decedent, each dollar amount contained in paragraph (1) or (2) or subparagraph (A) of this paragraph (whichever applies) shall be reduced by the amount so allowed.

(4) LIMITATION BASED ON AMOUNT OF TAX.—The credit allowed under this subsection shall not exceed the amount of the tax imposed by section 2101.

(5) APPLICATION OF OTHER CREDITS.—For purposes of subsection (a), sections 2012 and 2013 shall be applied as if the credit allowed under this subsection were allowed under section 2010.

Amendments

• **2013, American Taxpayer Relief Act of 2012 (P.L. 112-240)**

P.L. 112-240, § 101(a)(1) and (3), provides:

SEC. 101. PERMANENT EXTENSION AND MODIFICATION OF 2001 TAX RELIEF.

(a) PERMANENT EXTENSION.—

(1) IN GENERAL.—The Economic Growth and Tax Relief Reconciliation Act of 2001 is amended by striking title IX.

* * *

(3) EFFECTIVE DATE.—The amendments made by this subsection shall apply to taxable, plan, or limitation years beginning after December 31, 2012, and estates of decedents dying, gifts made, or generation skipping transfers after December 31, 2012.

• **2001, Economic Growth and Tax Relief Reconciliation Act of 2001 (P.L. 107-16)**

P.L. 107-16, § 532(c)(7)(B):

Amended Code Sec. 2102 by striking subsection (b) and by redesignating subsection (c) as subsection (b). **Effective** for estates of decedents dying, and generation-skipping transfers, after 12-31-2004. Prior to being stricken, Code Sec. 2102(b) read as follows:

(b) SPECIAL LIMITATION.—The maximum credit allowed under section 2011 against the tax imposed by section 2101 for State death taxes paid shall be an amount which bears the same ratio to the credit computed as provided in section 2011(b) as the value of the property, as determined for purposes of this chapter, upon which State death taxes were paid and which is included in the gross estate under section 2103 bears to the value of the total gross estate under section 2103. For purposes of this subsection, the term "State death taxes" means the taxes described in section 2011(a).

P.L. 107-16, § 532(c)(7)(C):

Amended Code Sec. 2102(b)(5), as redesignated by Act Sec. 532(c)(7)(B), by striking "2011 to 2013, inclusive," and inserting "2012 and 2013". **Effective** for estates of decedents dying, and generation-skipping transfers, after 12-31-2004.

P.L. 107-16, § 901(a)-(b), as amended by P.L. 111-312, § 101(a)(1), provides [but see P.L. 112-240, § 101(a)(1) and (3), above]:

SEC. 901. SUNSET OF PROVISIONS OF ACT.

(a) IN GENERAL.—All provisions of, and amendments made by, this Act shall not apply—

(1) to taxable, plan, or limitation years beginning after December 31, 2012, or

(2) in the case of title V, to estates of decedents dying, gifts made, or generation skipping transfers, after December 31, 2012.

(b) APPLICATION OF CERTAIN LAWS.—The Internal Revenue Code of 1986 and the Employee Retirement Income Security Act of 1974 shall be applied and administered to years, estates, gifts, and transfers described in subsection (a) as if the provisions and amendments described in subsection (a) had never been enacted.

• **1997, Taxpayer Relief Act of 1997 (P.L. 105-34)**

P.L. 105-34, § 501(a)(1)(E):

Amended Code Sec. 2102(c)(3)(A) by striking "$192,800" and inserting "the applicable credit amount in effect under section 2010(c) for the calendar year which includes the date of death". **Effective** for estates of decedents dying, and gifts made, after 12-31-97.

• **1996, Small Business Job Protection Act of 1996 (P.L. 104-188)**

P.L. 104-188, § 1704(f)(1):

Amended Code Sec. 2102(c)(3)(A) by adding at the end thereof a new sentence. **Effective** 8-20-96.

ESTATE TAX—ESTATES OF NONRESIDENTS NOT CITIZENS

• **1988, Technical and Miscellaneous Revenue Act of 1988 (P.L. 100-647)**

P.L. 100-647, § 5032(b)(1)(A)-(B):

Amended Code Sec. 2102(c) by striking out "$3,600" in paragraph (1) and (2)(A) and inserting in lieu thereof "$13,000", and by striking out "$15,075" in paragraph (2)(B) and inserting in lieu thereof "$46,800". **Effective** for estates of decedents dying after 11-10-88.

P.L. 100-647, § 5032(b)(2):

Amended Code Sec. 2102(c)(3). **Effective** for estates of decedents dying after 11-10-88. Prior to amendment, Code Sec. 2102(c)(3) read as follows:

(3) PHASE-IN OF PARAGRAPH (2)(B) AMOUNT.—In the case of a decedent dying before 1979, paragraph (2)(B) shall be applied—

(A) in the case of a decedent dying during 1977, by substituting "$8,480" for "$15,075",

(B) in the case of a decedent dying during 1978, by substituting "$10,080" for "$15,075",

(C) in the case of a decedent dying during 1979, by substituting "$11,680" for "$15,075", and

(D) in the case of a decedent dying during 1980, by substituting "$13,388" for "$15,075".

• **1976, Tax Reform Act of 1976 (P.L. 94-455)**

P.L. 94-455, § 2001(c)(1)(E), (d)(1):

Added Code Sec. 2102(c). **Effective** for estates of decedents dying after 12-31-76.

• **1966, Foreign Investors Tax Act of 1966 (P.L. 89-809)**

P.L. 89-809, § 108(b):

Amended Code Sec. 2102 by designating Sec. 2102 as Sec. 2102(a), amending it, and adding Sec. 2102(b). **Effective** with respect to estates of decedents dying after 11-13-66. Prior to amendment, Sec. 2102 read as follows:

SEC. 2102. CREDITS AGAINST TAX.

The tax imposed by section 2101 shall be credited with the amounts determined in accordance with sections 2011 to 2013, inclusive (relating to State death taxes, gift tax, and tax on prior transfers).

[Sec. 2103]

SEC. 2103. DEFINITION OF GROSS ESTATE.

For the purpose of the tax imposed by section 2101, the value of the gross estate of every decedent nonresident not a citizen of the United States shall be that part of his gross estate (determined as provided in section 2031) which at the time of his death is situated in the United States.

[Sec. 2104]

SEC. 2104. PROPERTY WITHIN THE UNITED STATES.

[Sec. 2104(a)]

(a) STOCK IN CORPORATION.—For purposes of this subchapter shares of stock owned and held by a nonresident not a citizen of the United States shall be deemed property within the United States only if issued by a domestic corporation.

[Sec. 2104(b)]

(b) REVOCABLE TRANSFERS AND TRANSFERS WITHIN 3 YEARS OF DEATH.—For purposes of this subchapter, any property of which the decedent has made a transfer, by trust or otherwise, within the meaning of sections 2035 to 2038, inclusive, shall be deemed to be situated in the United States, if so situated either at the time of the transfer or at the time of the decedent's death.

Amendments

• **1976, Tax Reform Act of 1976 (P.L. 94-455)**

P.L. 94-455, § 2001(c)(1)(L), (d)(1):

Substituted "AND TRANSFERS WITHIN 3 YEARS OF DEATH" for "AND TRANSFERS IN CONTEMPLATION OF DEATH" in the heading of Code Sec. 2104(b). **Effective** for estates of decedents dying after 12-31-76, except that the amendment shall not apply to transfers made before 1-1-77.

[Sec. 2104(c)]

(c) DEBT OBLIGATIONS.—For purposes of this subchapter, debt obligations of—

(1) a United States person, or

(2) the United States, a State or any political subdivision thereof, or the District of Columbia,

owned and held by a nonresident not a citizen of the United States shall be deemed property within the United States. Deposits with a domestic branch of a foreign corporation, if such branch is engaged in the commercial banking business, shall, for purposes of this subchapter, be deemed property within the United States. This subsection shall not apply to a debt obligation to which section 2105(b) applies.

Amendments

• **2014, Tax Technical Corrections Act of 2014 (P.L. 113-295)**

P.L. 113-295, § 221(a)(98), Division A:

Amended Code Sec. 2104(c) by striking "With respect to estates of decedents dying after December 31, 1969, deposits" and inserting "Deposits". **Effective** generally 12-19-2014. For a special rule, see Act Sec. 221(b)(2), Division A, below.

P.L. 113-295, § 221(b)(2), Division A, provides:

(2) SAVINGS PROVISION.—If—

(A) any provision amended or repealed by the amendments made by this section applied to—

(i) any transaction occurring before the date of the enactment of this Act,

(ii) any property acquired before such date of enactment, or

(iii) any item of income, loss, deduction, or credit taken into account before such date of enactment, and

(B) the treatment of such transaction, property, or item under such provision would (without regard to the amendments or repeals made by this section) affect the liability for tax for periods ending after date of enactment, nothing in the amendments or repeals made by this section shall be construed to affect the treatment of such transaction, property, or item for purposes of determining liability for tax for periods ending after such date of enactment.

• **2010, (P.L. 111-226)**

P.L. 111-226, § 217(c)(3):

Amended Code Sec. 2104(c) in the last sentence by striking "or to a debt obligation of a domestic corporation" and all that follows and inserting a period. **Effective** generally for tax years beginning after 12-31-2010. For a grandfather rule, see Act Sec. 217(d)(2), below. Prior to being stricken, "or to a debt obligation of a domestic corporation" and all that followed in the last sentence of Code Sec. 2104(c) read as follows:

or to a debt obligation of a domestic corporation if any interest on such obligation, were such interest received by the decedent at the time of his death, would be treated by reason of section 861(a)(1)(A) as income from sources without the United States.

P.L. 111-226, § 217(d)(2), provides:

(2) GRANDFATHER RULE FOR OUTSTANDING DEBT OBLIGATIONS.—

(A) IN GENERAL.—The amendments made by this section shall not apply to payments of interest on obligations issued before the date of the enactment of this Act.

(B) EXCEPTION FOR RELATED PARTY DEBT.—Subparagraph (A) shall not apply to any interest which is payable to a related person (determined under rules similar to the rules of section 954(d)(3)).

(C) SIGNIFICANT MODIFICATIONS TREATED AS NEW ISSUES.—For purposes of subparagraph (A), a significant modification of the terms of any obligation (including any extension of the term of such obligation) shall be treated as a new issue.

• **1996, Small Business Job Protection Act of 1996 (P.L. 104-188)**

P.L. 104-188, § 1704(t)(38):

Amended Code Sec. 2104(c) by striking "subparagraph (A), (C), or (D) of section 861(a)(1)" and inserting "section 861(a)(1)(A)". **Effective** 8-20-96.

• **1988, Technical and Miscellaneous Revenue Act of 1988 (P.L. 100-647)**

P.L. 100-647, § 1012(q)(11):

Amended Code Sec. 2104(c) by striking out "section 861(a)(1)(B), section 861(a)(1)(G), or section 861(a)(1)(H)" and inserting in lieu thereof "subparagraph (A), (C), or (D) of section 861(a)(1)". **Effective** as if included in the provision of P.L. 99-514 to which it relates.

• **1975 (P.L. 93-625)**

P.L. 93-625, § 9(b):

Amended the last sentence of Code Sec. 2104(c) by adding ", or section 861(a)(1)(H)". **Effective** with respect to estates of decedents dying after 1-3-75.

• **1973, Interest Equalization Tax Extension Act of 1973 (P.L. 93-17)**

P.L. 93-17, § 3(a):

Amended Code Sec. 2104(c) by adding "or section 861(a)(1)(G)" in the last sentence thereof. **Effective** with respect to estates of decedents dying after 12-31-72, except that in the case of the assumption of a debt obligation of a foreign corporation which is treated as issued under section 4912(c)(2) after 12-31-72, and before 1-1-74, the amendment applies with respect to estates of decedents dying after 12-31-73.

ESTATE TAX—ESTATES OF NONRESIDENTS NOT CITIZENS

• **1969, Tax Reform Act of 1969 (P.L. 91-172)**

P.L. 91-172, §435(b):

Amended the second sentence of Sec. 2104(c) by inserting "December 31, 1969" in lieu of "December 31, 1972".

• **1966, Foreign Investors Tax Act of 1966 (P.L. 89-809)**

P.L. 89-809, §108(c):

Added Code Sec. 2104(c). **Effective** with respect to estates of decedents dying after 11-13-66.

[Sec. 2105]

SEC. 2105. PROPERTY WITHOUT THE UNITED STATES.

[Sec. 2105(a)]

(a) PROCEEDS OF LIFE INSURANCE.—For purposes of this subchapter, the amount receivable as insurance on the life of a nonresident not a citizen of the the United States shall not be deemed property within the United States.

[Sec. 2105(b)]

(b) BANK DEPOSITS AND CERTAIN OTHER DEBT OBLIGATIONS.—For purposes of this subchapter, the following shall not be deemed property within the United States.—

(1) amounts described in section 871(i)(3), if any interest thereon would not be subject to tax by reason of section 871(i)(1) were such interest received by the decedent at the time of his death,

(2) deposits with a foreign branch of domestic corporation or domestic partnership, if such branch is engaged in the commercial banking business,

(3) debt obligations, if, without regard to whether a statement meeting the requirements of section 871(h)(5) has been received, any interest thereon would be eligible for the exemption from tax under section 871(h)(1) were such interest received by the decedent at the time of his death, and

(4) obligations which would be original issue discount obligations as defined in section 871(g)(1) but for subparagraph (B)(i) thereof, if any interest thereon (were such interest received by the decedent at the time of his death) would not be effectively connected with the conduct of a trade or business within the United States.

Notwithstanding the preceding sentence, if any portion of the interest on an obligation referred to in paragraph (3) would not be eligible for the exemption referred to in paragraph (3) by reason of section 871(h)(4) if the interest were received by the decedent at the time of his death, then an appropriate portion (as determined in a manner prescribed by the Secretary) of the value (as determined for purposes of this chapter) of such debt obligation shall be deemed property within the United States.

Amendments

• **1997, Taxpayer Relief Act of 1997 (P.L. 105-34)**

P.L. 105-34, §1304(a):

Amended Code Sec. 2105(b) by striking "and" at the end of paragraph (2), by striking the period at the end of paragraph (3) and inserting ", and", and by inserting after paragraph (3) a new paragraph (4). **Effective** for estates of decedents dying after 8-5-97.

• **1993, Omnibus Budget Reconciliation Act of 1993 (P.L. 103-66)**

P.L. 103-66, §13237(b)(1)-(2):

Amended Code Sec. 2105(b) by striking "this subchapter" in the material preceding paragraph (1) and inserting "this subchapter, the following shall not be deemed property within the United States", and by striking paragraph (3) and all that follows down through the period at the end thereof and inserting new paragraph (3) and a flush sentence. **Effective** for estates of decedents dying after 12-31-93. Prior to amendment, paragraph (3) and all that followed read as follows:

(3) debt obligations, if, without regard to whether a statement meeting the requirements of section 871(h)(4) has been received, any interest thereon would be eligible for the exemption from tax under section 871(h)(1) were such interest received by the decedent at the time of his death,

shall not be deemed property within the United States.

• **1988, Technical and Miscellaneous Revenue Act of 1988 (P.L. 100-647)**

P.L. 100-647, §1012(g)(4):

Amended Code Sec. 2105(b)(1) by striking out "section 861(c), if any interest thereon would be treated by reason of section 861(a)(1)(A) as income from sources without the United States" and inserting in lieu thereof "section 871(i)(3), if any interest thereon would not be subject to tax by reason of section 871(i)(1)". **Effective** as if included in the provision of P.L. 99-514 to which it relates.

• **1984, Deficit Reduction Act of 1984 (P.L. 98-369)**

P.L. 98-369, §127(d):

Amended Code Sec. 2105(b). **Effective** for obligations issued after 7-18-84 with respect to estates of decedents dying after such date. Prior to amendment, Code Sec. 2105(b) read as follows:

(b) Certain Bank Deposits, Etc.—For purposes of this subchapter—

(1) amounts described in section 861(c) if any interest thereon, were such interest received by the decedent at the time of his death, would be treated by reason of section 861(a)(1)(A) as income from sources without the United States, and

(2) deposits with a foreign branch of a domestic corporation or domestic partnership, if such branch is engaged in the commercial banking business,

shall not be deemed property within the United States.

• **1966, Foreign Investors Tax Act of 1966 (P.L. 89-809)**

P.L. 89-809, §108(d):

Amended Code Sec. 2105(b). **Effective** with respect to estates of decedents dying after 11-13-66, the date of enactment. Prior to amendment, Code Sec. 2105(b) read as follows:

(b) BANK DEPOSITS.—For purposes of this subchapter, any moneys deposited with any person carrying on the banking business, by or for a nonresident not a citizen of the United States who was not engaged in business in the United States at the time of his death shall not be deemed property within the United States.

[Sec. 2105(c)]

(c) WORKS OF ART ON LOAN FOR EXHIBITION.—For purposes of this subchapter, works of art owned by a nonresident not a citizen of the United States shall not be deemed property within the United States if such works of art are—

(1) imported into the United States solely for exhibition purposes,

(2) loaned for such purposes, to a public gallery or museum, no part of the net earnings of which inures to the benefit of any private stockholder or individual, and

(3) at the time of the death of the owner, on exhibition, or en route to or from exhibition, in such a public gallery or museum.

[Sec. 2105(d)]

(d) STOCK IN A RIC.—

(1) IN GENERAL.—For purposes of this subchapter, stock in a regulated investment company (as defined in section 851) owned by a nonresident not a citizen of the United States shall not be deemed property within the United States in the proportion that, at the end of the quarter of such investment company's taxable year immediately preceding a decedent's date of death (or at such other time as the Secretary may designate in regulations), the assets of the investment company that were qualifying assets with respect to the decedent bore to the total assets of the investment company.

(2) QUALIFYING ASSETS.—For purposes of this subsection, qualifying assets with respect to a decedent are assets that, if owned directly by the decedent, would have been—

(A) amounts, deposits, or debt obligations described in subsection (b) of this section,

(B) debt obligations described in the last sentence of section 2104(c), or

(C) other property not within the United States.

(3) TERMINATION.—This subsection shall not apply to estates of decedents dying after December 31, 2011.

Internal Revenue Code Sec. 2105(d)(3)

ESTATE TAX—ESTATES OF NONRESIDENTS NOT CITIZENS

Amendments

• **2010, Tax Relief, Unemployment Insurance Reauthorization, and Job Creation Act of 2010 (P.L. 111-312)**

P.L. 111-312, § 726(a):

Amended Code Sec. 2105(d)(3) by striking "December 31, 2009" and inserting "December 31, 2011". **Effective** for estates of decedents dying after 12-31-2009.

• **2008, Tax Extenders and Alternative Minimum Tax Relief Act of 2008 (P.L. 110-343)**

P.L. 110-343, Division C, § 207(a):

Amended Code Sec. 2105(d)(3) by striking "December 31, 2007" and inserting "December 31, 2009". **Effective** for decedents dying after 12-31-2007.

• **2004, American Jobs Creation Act of 2004 (P.L. 108-357)**

P.L. 108-357, § 411(b):

Amended Code Sec. 2105 by adding at the end a new subsection (d). **Effective** for estates of decedents dying after 12-31-2004.

[Sec. 2106]

SEC. 2106. TAXABLE ESTATE.

[Sec. 2106(a)]

(a) DEFINITION OF TAXABLE ESTATE.—For purposes of the tax imposed by section 2101, the value of the taxable estate of every decedent nonresident not a citizen of the United States shall be determined by deducting from the value of that part of his gross estate which at the time of his death is situated in the United States—

(1) EXPENSES, LOSSES, INDEBTEDNESS, AND TAXES.—That proportion of the deductions specified in sections 2053 and 2054 (other than the deductions described in the following sentence) which the value of such part bears to the value of his entire gross estate, wherever situated. Any deduction allowable under section 2053 in the case of a claim against the estate which was founded on a promise or agreement but was not contracted for an adequate and full consideration in money or money's worth shall be allowable under this paragraph to the extent that it would be allowable as a deduction under paragraph (2) if such promise or agreement constituted a bequest.

(2) TRANSFERS FOR PUBLIC, CHARITABLE, AND RELIGIOUS USES.—

(A) IN GENERAL.—The amount of all bequests, legacies, devises, or transfers (including the interest which falls into any such bequest, legacy, devise, or transfer as a result of an irrevocable disclaimer of a bequest, legacy, devise, transfer, or power, if the disclaimer is made before the date prescribed for the filing of the estate tax return)—

(i) to or for the use of the United States, any State, any political subdivision thereof, or the District of Columbia, for exclusively public purposes;

(ii) to or for the use of any domestic corporation organized and operated exclusively for religious, charitable, scientific, literary, or educational purposes, including the encouragement of art and the prevention of cruelty to children or animals, no part of the net earnings of which inures to the benefit of any private stockholder or individual, which is not disqualified for tax exemption under section 501(c)(3) by reason of attempting to influence legislation, and which does not participate in, or intervene in (including the publishing or distributing of statements), any political campaign on behalf of (or in opposition to) any candidate for public office; or

(iii) to a trustee or trustees, or a fraternal society, order, or association operating under the lodge system, but only if such contributions of gifts are to be used within the United States by such trustee or trustees, or by such fraternal society, order, or association, exclusively for religious, charitable, scientific, literary, or educational purposes, or for the prevention of cruelty to children or animals, such trust, fraternal society, order, or association would not be disqualified for tax exemption under section 501(c)(3) by reason of attempting to influence legislation, and such trustee or trustees, or such fraternal society, order, or association, does not participate in, or intervene in (including the publishing or distributing of statements), any political campaign on behalf of (or in opposition to) any candidate for public office.

(B) POWERS OF APPOINTMENT.—Property includible in the decedent's gross estate under section 2041 (relating to powers of appointment) received by a donee described in this paragraph shall, for purposes of this paragraph, be considered a bequest of such decedent.

(C) DEATH TAXES PAYABLE OUT OF BEQUESTS.—If the tax imposed by section 2101, or any estate, succession, legacy, or inheritance taxes, are, either by the terms of the will, by the law of the jurisdiction under which the estate is administered, or by the law of the jurisdiction imposing the particular tax, payable in whole or in part out of the bequest, legacies, or devises otherwise deductible under this paragraph, then the amount deductible under this paragraph shall be the amount of such bequests, legacies, or devises reduced by the amount of such taxes.

(D) LIMITATION ON DEDUCTION.—The amount of the deduction under this paragraph for any transfer shall not exceed the value of the transferred property required to be included in the gross estate.

(E) DISALLOWANCE OF DEDUCTIONS IN CERTAIN CASES.—The provisions of section 2055(e) shall be applied in the determination of the amount allowable as a deduction under this paragraph.

(F) CROSS REFERENCES.—

(i) For option as to time for valuation for purposes of deduction under this section, see section 2032.

(ii) For exemption of certain bequests for the benefit of the United States and for rules of construction for certain bequests, see section 2055(g).

(iii) For treatment of gifts and bequests to or for the use of Indian tribal governments (or their subdivisions), see section 7871.

(3) MARITAL DEDUCTION.—The amount which would be deductible with respect to property situated in the United States at the time of the decedent's death under the principles of section 2056.

(4) STATE DEATH TAXES.—The amount which bears the same ratio to the State death taxes as the value of the property, as determined for purposes of this chapter, upon which State death taxes were paid and which is included in the gross estate under section 2103 bears to the value of the total gross estate under section 2103. For purposes of this paragraph, the term "State death taxes" means the taxes described in section 2058(a).

Amendments

• **2018, Tax Technical Corrections Act of 2018 (P.L. 115-141)**

P.L. 115-141, § 401(a)(203), Div. U:

Amended Code Sec. 2106(a)(4) by inserting "section" before "2058(a)". **Effective** 3-23-2018.

• **2014, Tax Technical Corrections Act of 2014 (P.L. 113-295)**

P.L. 113-295, § 221(a)(95)(A)(ii), Division A:

Amended Code Sec. 2106(a)(4) by striking "section 2011(a)" and inserting "[section] 2058(a)". **Effective** generally 12-19-2014. For a special rule, see Act Sec. 221(b)(2), Division A, below.

P.L. 113-295, § 221(b)(2), Division A, provides:

(2) SAVINGS PROVISION.—If—

(A) any provision amended or repealed by the amendments made by this section applied to—

(i) any transaction occurring before the date of the enactment of this Act,

(ii) any property acquired before such date of enactment, or

(iii) any item of income, loss, deduction, or credit taken into account before such date of enactment, and

(B) the treatment of such transaction, property, or item under such provision would (without regard to the amendments or repeals made by this section) affect the liability for tax for periods ending after date of enactment, nothing in the amendments or repeals made by this section shall be construed to affect the treatment of such transaction, property, or item for purposes of determining liability for tax for periods ending after such date of enactment.

- **2013, American Taxpayer Relief Act of 2012 (P.L. 112-240)**

P.L. 112-240, §101(a)(1) and (3), provides:

SEC. 101. PERMANENT EXTENSION AND MODIFICATION OF 2001 TAX RELIEF.

(a) PERMANENT EXTENSION.—

(1) IN GENERAL.—The Economic Growth and Tax Relief Reconciliation Act of 2001 is amended by striking title IX.

* * *

(3) EFFECTIVE DATE.—The amendments made by this subsection shall apply to taxable, plan, or limitation years beginning after December 31, 2012, and estates of decedents dying, gifts made, or generation skipping transfers after December 31, 2012.

- **2001, Economic Growth and Tax Relief Reconciliation Act of 2001 (P.L. 107-16)**

P.L. 107-16, §532(c)(8):

Amended Code Sec. 2106(a) by adding at the end a new paragraph (4). **Effective** for estates of decedents dying, and generation-skipping transfers, after 12-31-2004.

P.L. 107-16, §901(a)-(b), as amended by P.L. 111-312, §101(a)(1), provides [but see P.L. 112-240, §101(a)(1) and (3), above]:

SEC. 901. SUNSET OF PROVISIONS OF ACT.

(a) IN GENERAL.—All provisions of, and amendments made by, this Act shall not apply—

(1) to taxable, plan, or limitation years beginning after December 31, 2012, or

(2) in the case of title V, to estates of decedents dying, gifts made, or generation skipping transfers, after December 31, 2012.

(b) APPLICATION OF CERTAIN LAWS.—The Internal Revenue Code of 1986 and the Employee Retirement Income Security Act of 1974 shall be applied and administered to years, estates, gifts, and transfers described in subsection (a) as if the provisions and amendments described in subsection (a) had never been enacted.

- **1989, Omnibus Budget Reconciliation Act of 1989 (P.L. 101-239)**

P.L. 101-239, §7815(d)(3):

Amended Code Sec. 2106(a)(3) by striking "ALLOWED WHERE SPOUSE IS CITIZEN" after "MARITAL DEDUCTION". **Effective** as if included in the provision of P.L. 100-647 to which it relates.

- **1988, Technical and Miscellaneous Revenue Act of 1988 (P.L. 100-647)**

P.L. 100-647, §5033(c):

Amended Code Sec. 2106(a) by adding at the end thereof a new paragraph (3). **Effective** for estates of decedents dying after 11-10-88.

- **1987, Revenue Act of 1987 (P.L. 100-203)**

P.L. 100-203, §10711(a)(4):

Amended Code Sec. 2106(a)(2)(A)(ii) and (iii) by striking out "on behalf of any candidate" and inserting in lieu thereof "on behalf of (or in opposition to) any candidate". **Effective** with respect to activities after 12-22-87.

- **1986, Tax Reform Act of 1986 (P.L. 99-514)**

P.L. 99-514, §1422(c):

Amended Code Sec. 2106(a)(2)(F)(ii) by striking out "section 2055(f)" and inserting in lieu thereof "section 2055(g)". **Effective** for transfers and contributions made after 12-31-86.

- **1983 (P.L. 97-473)**

P.L. 97-473, §202(b)(6):

Amended Code Sec. 2106(a)(2)(F). For the **effective** date, see the amendment note for P.L. 97-473, Act Sec. 204, following Code Sec. 7871. Prior to amendment, Code Sec. 2106(a)(2)(F) read as follows:

(F) CROSS REFERENCES.—

(1) For option as to time for valuation for purposes of deduction under this section, see section 2032.

(2) For exemption of certain bequests for the benefit of the United States and for rules of construction for certain bequests, see section 2055(f).

- **1976, Tax Reform Act of 1976 (P.L. 94-455)**

P.L. 94-455, §1307(d)(1)(B):

Substituted "which is not disqualified for tax exemption under section 501(c)(3) by reason of attempting to influence legislation," for "no substantial part of the activities of which is carrying on propaganda, or otherwise attempting, to influence legislation," in Code Sec. 2106(a)(2)(A)(ii). **Effective** for estates of decedents dying after 12-31-76.

P.L. 94-455, §1307(d)(1)(C):

Substituted "such trust, fraternal society, order, or association would not be disqualified for tax exemption under section 501(c)(3) by reason of attempting to influence legislation," for "no substantial part of the activities of such trustee or trustees, or of such fraternal society, order, or association, is carrying on propaganda, or otherwise attempting, to influence legislation," in Code Sec. 2106(a)(2)(A)(iii). **Effective** for estates of decedents dying after 12-31-76.

P.L. 94-455, §1902(a)(5)(A):

Amended Code Sec. 2106(a)(2)(F). **Effective** for estates of decedents dying after 10-4-76. Prior to amendment, Code Sec. 2106(a)(2)(F) read as follows:

(F) OTHER CROSS REFERENCES.—

(1) For option as to time for valuation for purpose of deduction under this paragraph [section], see section 2032.

(2) For exemption of bequests to or for benefit of Library of Congress, see section 5 of the Act of March 3, 1925, as amended (56 Stat. 765; 2 U.S.C. 161).

(3) For construction of bequests for benefit of the library of the Post Office Department as bequests to or for the use of the United States, see section 2 of the Act of August 8, 1946 (60 Stat. 924; 5 U.S.C. 393).

(4) For exemption of bequests for benefit of Office of Naval Records and Library, Navy Department, see section 2 of the Act of March 4, 1937 (50 Stat. 25; 5 U.S.C. 419b).

(5) For exemption of bequests to or for benefit of National Park Service, see section 5 of the Act of July 10, 1935 (49 Stat. 478; 16 U.S.C. 19c).

(6) For construction of devises or bequests accepted by the Secretary of State under the Foreign Service Act of 1946 as devises or bequests to or for the use of the United States, see section 1021(e) of that Act (60 Stat. 1032; 22 U.S.C. 809).

(7) For construction of gifts or bequests of money accepted by the Attorney General for credit to "Commissary Funds, Federal Prisons" as gifts or bequests to or for the use of the United States, see section 2 of the Act of May 15, 1952, 66 Stat. 73, as amended by the Act of July 9, 1952, 66 Stat. 479 (31 U.S.C. 725s-4).

(8) For payment of tax on bequests of United States obligations to the United States, see section 24 of the Second Liberty Bond Act, as amended (59 Stat. 48, §4; 31 U.S.C. 757e).

(9) For construction of bequests for benefit of or use in connection with the Naval Academy as bequests to or for the use of the United States, see section 3 of the Act of March 31, 1944 (58 Stat. 135; 34 U.S.C. 1115b).

(10) For exemption of bequests for benefit of Naval Academy Museum, see section 4 of the Act of March 26, 1938 (52 Stat. 119; 34 U.S.C. 1119).

(11) For exemption of bequests received by National Archives Trust Fund Board, see section 7 of the National Archives Trust Fund Board Act (55 Stat. 582; 44 U.S.C. 300gg).

P.L. 94-455, §1902(a)(12):

Deleted "Territory" in Code Sec. 2106(a)(2)(A)(i). **Effective** for gifts made after 12-31-76.

P.L. 94-455, §2001(c)(1)(F):

Repealed paragraph (3) of Code Sec. 2106(a). **Effective** for estates of decedents dying after 12-31-76. Prior to repeal, paragraph (3) read as follows:

(3) EXEMPTION.—

(A) GENERAL RULE.—An exemption of $30,000.

(B) RESIDENTS OF POSSESSIONS OF THE UNITED STATES.—In the case of a decedent who is considered to be a "nonresident not a citizen of the United States" under the provisions of section 2209, the exemption shall be the greater of (i) $30,000, or (ii) that proportion of the exemption authorized by section 2052 which the value of that part of the decedent's gross estate which at the time of his death is situated in the United States bears to the value of his entire gross estate wherever situated.

- **1969, Tax Reform Act of 1969 (P.L. 91-172)**

P.L. 91-172, §201(d)(2):

Amended Code Sec. 2106(a)(2)(E). **Effective** in the case of decedents dying after 12-31-69. For exceptions, see Act Sec. 201(g)(4)(B)-(C), below.

P.L. 91-172, §201(g)(4)(B)-(C), provides:

(B) Such amendments shall not apply in the case of property passing under the terms of a will executed on or before October 9, 1969—

(i) if the decedent dies before October 9, 1972, without having republished the will after October 9, 1969, by codicil or otherwise,

(ii) if the decedent at no time after October 9, 1969, had the right to change the portions of the will which pertain to the passing of the property to, or for the use of, an organization described in section 2055(a), or

(iii) if the will is not republished by codicil or otherwise.

(C) Such amendment shall not apply in the case of property transferred in trust on or before October 9, 1969—

(i) if the decedent dies before October 9, 1972, without having amended after October 9, 1969, the instrument governing the disposition of the property,

(ii) if the property transferred was an irrevocable interest to, or for the use of, an organization described in section 2055(a), or

(iii) if the instrument governing the disposition of the property was not amended by the decedent before October 9, 1972, and the decedent is on such date and at all times thereafter under a mental disability to change the disposition of the property.

Prior to amendment, Code Sec. 2106(a)(2)(E) read as follows:

"(E) Disallowance of Deductions in Certain Cases.—

"For disallowance of certain charitable, etc., deductions otherwise allowable under this paragraph [section]. See sections 503 and 681."

P.L. 91-172, §201(d)(4)(B):

Amended subparagraphs (A)(ii) and (A)(iii) of Code Sec. 2106(a)(2). **Effective** with respect to gifts and transfers made after 12-31-69. Prior to amendment, subparagraphs (A)(ii) and (A)(iii) of Code Sec. 2106(a)(2) read as follows:

"(ii) to or for the use of any domestic corporation organized and operated exclusively for religious, charitable, scientific, literary, or educational purposes, including the encouragement of art and the prevention of cruelty to children or animals, no part of the net earnings of which inures to the benefit of any private stockholder or individual, and no substantial part of the activities of which is carrying on propaganda, or otherwise attempting, to influence legislation; or

"(iii) to a trustee or trustees, or a fraternal society, order, or association operating under the lodge system, but only if such contributions or gifts are to be used within the United States by such trustee or trustees, or by such fraternal society, order, or association, exclusively for religious, charitable, scientific, literary, or educational purposes, or for the prevention of cruelty to children or animals, and no substantial part of the activities of such trustee or trustees, or of such fraternal society, order, or

ESTATE TAX—ESTATES OF NONRESIDENTS NOT CITIZENS

association, is carrying on propaganda, or otherwise attempting, to influence legislation."

• **1966, Foreign Investors Tax Act of 1966 (P.L. 89-809)**

P.L. 89-809, § 108(e):

Amended Code Sec. 2106(a)(3). **Effective** with respect to estates of decedents dying after 11-13-66. Prior to amendment, Sec. 2106(a)(3) read as follows:

(3) EXEMPTION.—

(A) GENERAL RULE.—An exemption of $2,000.

(B) RESIDENTS OF POSSESSIONS OF THE UNITED STATES.—In the case of a decedent who is considered to be a 'nonresident not a citizen of the United States' under the provisions of section 2209, the exemption shall be the greater of (i) $2,000, or (ii) that proportion of the exemption authorized by section 2052 which the value of that part of the decedent's gross estate which at the time of his death is situated in the United States bears to the value of his entire gross estate wherever situated.

• **1960 (P.L. 86-779)**

P.L. 86-779, § 4(c):

Amended Code Sec. 2106(a)(3). **Effective** for estates of decedents dying after 9-14-60. Prior to amendment, Code Sec. 2106(a)(3) read as follows:

(3) EXEMPTION.—An exemption of $2,000.

• **1958, Technical Amendments Act of 1958 (P.L. 85-866)**

P.L. 85-866, § 30(d):

Amended Code Sec. 2106(a)(2)(E) by substituting "503" for "504". **Effective** 1-1-54.

[Sec. 2106(b)]

(b) CONDITION OF ALLOWANCE OF DEDUCTIONS.—No deduction shall be allowed under paragraphs (1) and (2) of subsection (a) in the case of a nonresident not a citizen of the United States unless the executor includes in the return required to be filed under section 6018 the value at the time of his death of that part of the gross estate of such nonresident not situated in the United States.

[Sec. 2106(c)—Repealed]

Amendments

• **1976, Tax Reform Act of 1976 (P.L. 94-455)**

P.L. 94-455, § 1902(a)(5)(B), (c)(1):

Repealed Code Sec. 2106(c). **Effective** for estates of decedents dying after 10-4-76. Prior to repeal, Code Sec. 2106(c) read as follows:

(c) UNITED STATES BONDS.—For purposes of section 2103, the value of the gross estate (determined as provided in section 2031) of a decedent who was not engaged in business in the United States at the time of his death—

(1) shall not include obligations issued by the United States before March 1, 1941; and

(2) shall include obligations issued by the United States on or after March 1, 1941.

[Sec. 2107]

SEC. 2107. EXPATRIATION TO AVOID TAX.

[Sec. 2107(a)]

(a) TREATMENT OF EXPATRIATES.—A tax computed in accordance with the table contained in section 2001 is hereby imposed on the transfer of the taxable estate, determined as provided in section 2106, of every decedent nonresident not a citizen of the United States if the date of death occurs during a taxable year with respect to which the decedent is subject to tax under section 877(b).

Amendments

• **2004, American Jobs Creation Act of 2004 (P.L. 108-357)**

P.L. 108-357, § 804(a)(3):

Amended Code Sec. 2107(a). **Effective** for individuals who expatriate after 6-3-2004. Prior to amendment, Code Sec. 2107(a) read as follows:

(a) TREATMENT OF EXPATRIATES.—

(1) RATE OF TAX.—A tax computed in accordance with the table contained in section 2001 is hereby imposed on the transfer of the taxable estate, determined as provided in section 2106, of every decedent nonresident not a citizen of the United States if, within the 10-year period ending with the date of death, such decedent lost United States citizenship, unless such loss did not have for 1 of its principal purposes the avoidance of taxes under this subtitle or subtitle A.

(2) CERTAIN INDIVIDUALS TREATED AS HAVING TAX AVOIDANCE PURPOSE.—

(A) IN GENERAL.—For purposes of paragraph (1), an individual shall be treated as having a principal purpose to avoid such taxes if such individual is so treated under section 877(a)(2).

(B) EXCEPTION.—Subparagraph (A) shall not apply to a decedent meeting the requirements of section 877(c)(1).

• **1996, Health Insurance Portability and Accountability Act of 1996 (P.L. 104-191)**

P.L. 104-191, § 511(e)(1)(A):

Amended Code Sec. 2107(a). For the **effective** date, see Act Sec. 511(g), below. Prior to amendment, Code Sec. 2107(a) read as follows:

(a) RATE OF TAX.—A tax computed in accordance with the table contained in section 2001 is hereby imposed on the transfer of the taxable estate, determined as provided in section 2106, of every decedent nonresident not a citizen of the United States dying after November 13, 1966, if after March 8, 1965, and within the 10-year period ending with the date of death such decedent lost United States citizenship, unless such loss did not have for one of its principal purposes the avoidance of taxes under this subtitle or subtitle A.

P.L. 104-191, § 511(g), provides:

(g) EFFECTIVE DATE.—

(1) IN GENERAL.—The amendments made by this section shall apply to—

(A) individuals losing United States citizenship (within the meaning of section 877 of the Internal Revenue Code of 1986) on or after February 6, 1995, and

(B) long-term residents of the United States with respect to whom an event described in subparagraph (A) or (B) of section 877(e)(1) of such Code occurs on or after February 6, 1995.

(2) RULING REQUESTS.—In no event shall the 1-year period referred to in section 877(c)(1)(B) of such Code, as amended by this section, expire before the date which is 90 days after the date of the enactment of this Act.

(3) SPECIAL RULE.—

(A) IN GENERAL.—In the case of an individual who performed an act of expatriation specified in paragraph (1), (2), (3), or (4) of section 349(a) of the Immigration and Nationality Act (8 U.S.C. 1481(a)(1)-(4)) before February 6, 1995, but who did not, on or before such date, furnish to the United States Department of State a signed statement of voluntary relinquishment of United States nationality confirming the performance of such act, the amendments made by this section and section 512 shall apply to such individual except that the 10-year period described in section 877(a) of such Code shall not expire before the end of the 10-year period beginning on the date such statement is so furnished.

(B) EXCEPTION.—Subparagraph (A) shall not apply if the individual establishes to the satisfaction of the Secretary of the Treasury that such loss of United States citizenship occurred before February 6, 1994.

• **1976, Tax Reform Act of 1976 (P.L. 94-455)**

P.L. 94-455, § 1902(a)(6), (c)(1):

Substituted "November 13, 1966" for "the date of enactment of this section" in Code Sec. 2107(a). **Effective** for estates of decedents dying after 10-4-76.

[Sec. 2107(b)]

(b) GROSS ESTATE.—For purposes of the tax imposed by subsection (a), the value of the gross estate of every decedent to whom subsection (a) applies shall be determined as provided in section 2103, except that—

(1) if such decedent owned (within the meaning of section 958(a)) at the time of his death 10 percent or more of the total combined voting power of all classes of stock entitled to vote of a foreign corporation, and

(2) if such decedent owned (within the meaning of section 958(a)), or is considered to have owned (by applying the ownership rules of section 958(b)), at the time of his death, more than 50 percent of—

(A) the total combined voting power of all classes of stock entitled to vote of such corporation, or

(B) the total value of the stock of such corporation,

then that proportion of the fair market value of the stock of such foreign corporation owned (within the meaning of section 958(a)) by such decedent at the time of his death, which the fair market value of any assets owned by such foreign corporation and situated in the United States, at the time of his death, bears to the total fair market value of all assets owned by such foreign corporation at the time of his death, shall be included in the gross estate of such decedent. For purposes of the preceding sentence, a decedent shall be treated as owning stock of a foreign corporation at the time of his death if, at the time of a transfer, by trust or otherwise, within the meaning of sections 2035 to 2038, inclusive, he owned such stock.

Sec. 2106(b)

ESTATE TAX—ESTATES OF NONRESIDENTS NOT CITIZENS

Amendments

• **1996, Health Insurance Portability and Accountability Act of 1996 (P.L. 104-191)**

P.L. 104-191, § 511(e)(1)(C):

Amended Code Sec. 2107(b)(2) by striking "more than 50 percent of" and all that follows and inserting "more than 50 percent of—" and new subparagraphs (A) and (B). For the **effective** date, see Act Sec. 511(g), in the amendment notes following Code Sec. 2107(a). Prior to amendment, Code Sec. 2107(b)(2) read as follows:

(2) if such decedent owned (within the meaning of section 958(a)), or is considered to have owned (by applying the ownership rules of section 958(b)), at the time of his death, more than 50 percent of the total combined voting power of all classes of stock entitled to vote of such foreign corporation,

[Sec. 2107(c)]

(c) CREDITS.—

(1) UNIFIED CREDIT.—

(A) IN GENERAL.—A credit of $13,000 shall be allowed against the tax imposed by subsection (a).

(B) LIMITATION BASED ON AMOUNT OF TAX.—The credit allowed under this paragraph shall not exceed the amount of the tax imposed by subsection (a).

(2) CREDIT FOR FOREIGN DEATH TAXES.—

(A) IN GENERAL.—The tax imposed by subsection (a) shall be credited with the amount of any estate, inheritance, legacy, or succession taxes actually paid to any foreign country in respect of any property which is included in the gross estate solely by reason of subsection (b).

(B) LIMITATION ON CREDIT.—The credit allowed by subparagraph (A) for such taxes paid to a foreign country shall not exceed the lesser of—

(i) the amount which bears the same ratio to the amount of such taxes actually paid to such foreign country as the value of the property subjected to such taxes by such foreign country and included in the gross estate solely by reason of subsection (b) bears to the value of all property subjected to such taxes by such foreign country, or

(ii) such property's proportionate share of the excess of—

(I) the tax imposed by subsection (a), over

(II) the tax which would be imposed by section 2101 but for this section.

(C) PROPORTIONATE SHARE.—In the case of property which is included in the gross estate solely by reason of subsection (b), such property's proportionate share is the percentage which the value of such property bears to the total value of all property included in the gross estate solely by reason of subsection (b).

(3) OTHER CREDITS.—The tax imposed by subsection (a) shall be credited with the amounts determined in accordance with subsections (a) and (b) of section 2102. For purposes of subsection (a) of section 2102, sections 2012 and 2013 shall be applied as if the credit allowed under paragraph (1) were allowed under section 2010.

Amendments

• **2013, American Taxpayer Relief Act of 2012 (P.L. 112-240)**

P.L. 112-240, § 101(a)(1) and (3), provides:

SEC. 101. PERMANENT EXTENSION AND MODIFICATION OF 2001 TAX RELIEF.

(a) PERMANENT EXTENSION.—

(1) IN GENERAL.—The Economic Growth and Tax Relief Reconciliation Act of 2001 is amended by striking title IX.

* * *

(3) EFFECTIVE DATE.—The amendments made by this subsection shall apply to taxable, plan, or limitation years beginning after December 31, 2012, and estates of decedents dying, gifts made, or generation skipping transfers after December 31, 2012.

• **2001, Economic Growth and Tax Relief Reconciliation Act of 2001 (P.L. 107-16)**

P.L. 107-16, § 532(c)(7)(C):

Amended Code Sec. 2107(c)(3) by striking "2011 to 2013, inclusive," and inserting "2012 and 2013". **Effective** for estates of decedents dying, and generation-skipping transfers, after 12-31-2004.

P.L. 107-16, § 901(a)-(b), as amended by P.L. 111-312, § 101(a)(1), provides [but see P.L. 112-240, § 101(a)(1) and (3), above]:

SEC. 901. SUNSET OF PROVISIONS OF ACT.

(a) IN GENERAL.—All provisions of, and amendments made by, this Act shall not apply—

(1) to taxable, plan, or limitation years beginning after December 31, 2012, or

(2) in the case of title V, to estates of decedents dying, gifts made, or generation skipping transfers, after December 31, 2012.

(b) APPLICATION OF CERTAIN LAWS.—The Internal Revenue Code of 1986 and the Employee Retirement Income Security Act of 1974 shall be applied and administered to years, estates, gifts, and transfers described in subsection (a) as if the provisions and amendments described in subsection (a) had never been enacted.

• **1997, Taxpayer Relief Act of 1997 (P.L. 105-34)**

P.L. 105-34, § 1602(g)(6)(A):

Amended Code Sec. 2107(c)(2)(B)(i) by striking "such foreign country in respect of property included in the gross estate as the value of the property" and inserting "such foreign country as the value of the property subjected to such taxes by such foreign country and". **Effective** as if included in the provision of P.L. 104-191 to which such amendment relates [**effective**, generally, for individuals losing U.S. citizenship on or after 2-6-95, and long-term U.S. residents who end U.S. residency or begin foreign residency on or after 2-6-95.—CCH].

P.L. 105-34, § 1602(g)(6)(B):

Amended Code Sec. 2107(c)(2)(C). **Effective** as if included in the provision of P.L. 104-191 to which such amendment relates [**effective**, generally, for individuals losing U.S. citizenship or begin foreign residency on or after 2-6-95.—CCH]. Prior to amendment, Code Sec. 2107(c)(2)(C) read as follows:

(C) PROPORTIONATE SHARE.—For purposes of subparagraph (B), a property's proportionate share is the percentage of the value of the property which is included in the gross estate solely by reason of subsection (b) bears to the total value of the gross estate.

• **1996, Health Insurance Portability and Accountability Act of 1996 (P.L. 104-191)**

P.L. 104-191, § 511(e)(1)(B):

Amended Code Sec. 2107(c) by redesignating paragraph (2) as paragraph (3) and by inserting after paragraph (1) a new paragraph (2). For the **effective** date, see Act Sec. 511(g) in the amendment notes following Code Sec. 2107(a).

• **1976, Tax Reform Act of 1976 (P.L. 94-455)**

P.L. 94-455, § 2001(c)(1)(E)(ii):

Amended Code Sec. 2107(c). **Effective** for estates of decedents dying after 12-31-76. Prior to amendment, Code Sec. 2107(c) read as follows:

(c) CREDITS.—The tax imposed by subsection (a) shall be credited with the amounts determined in accordance with section 2102.

[Sec. 2107(d)]

(d) BURDEN OF PROOF.—If the Secretary establishes that it is reasonable to believe that an individual's loss of United States citizenship would, but for this section, result in a substantial reduction in the estate, inheritance, legacy, and succession taxes in respect of the transfer of his estate, the burden of proving that such loss of citizenship did not have for one of its principal purposes the avoidance of taxes under this subtitle or subtitle A shall be on the executor of such individual's estate.

Amendments

• **1996, Health Insurance Portability and Accountability Act of 1996 (P.L. 104-191)**

P.L. 104-191, § 511(f)(2)(A):

Amended Code Sec. 2107 by striking subsection (d) and by redesignating subsection (e) as subsection (d). For the **effective** date, see Act Sec. 511(g) in the amendment notes following Code Sec. 2107(a). Prior to being stricken, subsection (d) read as follows:

(d) EXCEPTION FOR LOSS OF CITIZENSHIP FOR CERTAIN CAUSES.—Subsection (a) shall not apply to the transfer of the estate of a decedent whose loss of United States citizenship resulted from the application of section 301(b), 350, or 355 of the Immigration and Nationality Act, as amended (8 U.S.C. 1401(b), 1482, or 1487).

ESTATE TAX—ESTATES OF NONRESIDENTS NOT CITIZENS

[Sec. 2107(e)]

(e) CROSS REFERENCE.—

For comparable treatment of long-term lawful permanent residents who ceased to be taxed as residents, see section 877(e).

Amendments

• **1996, Health Insurance Portability and Accountability Act of 1996 (P.L. 104-191)**

P.L. 104-191, § 511(f)(2)(A):

Amended Code Sec. 2107 by striking subsection (d), by redesignating subsection (e) as subsection (d), and by inserting after subsection (d) (as so redesignated) a new subsection (e). For the **effective** date, see Act Sec. 511(g) in the amendment notes following Code Sec. 2107(a).

• **1976, Tax Reform Act of 1976 (P.L. 94-455)**

P.L. 94-455, § 1906(b)(13)(A):

Amended 1954 Code by substituting "Secretary" for "Secretary or his delegate" each place it appeared. **Effective** 2-1-77.

• **1966, Foreign Investors Tax Act of 1966 (P.L. 89-809)**

P.L. 89-809, § 108(f):

Added Code Sec. 2107. **Effective** with respect to estates of decedents dying after 11-13-66.

[Sec. 2108]

SEC. 2108. APPLICATION OF PRE-1967 ESTATE TAX PROVISIONS.

[Sec. 2108(a)]

(a) IMPOSITION OF MORE BURDENSOME TAX BY FOREIGN COUNTRY.—Whenever the President finds that—

(1) under the laws of any foreign country, considering the tax system of such foreign country, a more burdensome tax is imposed by such foreign country on the transfer of estates of decedents who were citizens of the United States and not residents of such foreign country than the tax imposed by this subchapter on the transfer of estates of decedents who were residents of such foreign country,

(2) such foreign country, when requested by the United States to do so, has not acted to revise or reduce such tax so that it is no more burdensome than the tax imposed by this subchapter on the transfer of estates of decedents who were residents of such foreign country, and

(3) it is in the public interest to apply pre-1967 tax provisions in accordance with this section to the transfer of estates of decedents who were residents of such foreign country,

the President shall proclaim that the tax on the transfer of the estate of every decedent who was a resident of such foreign country at the time of his death shall, in the case of decedents dying after the date of such proclamation, be determined under this subchapter without regard to amendments made to sections 2101 (relating to tax imposed), 2102 (relating to credits against tax), 2106 (relating to taxable estate), and 6018 (relating to estate tax returns) on or after November 13, 1966.

Amendments

• **1976, Tax Reform Act of 1976 (P.L. 94-455)**

P.L. 94-455, § 1902(a)(6):

Substituted "November 13, 1966" for "the date of enactment of this section" in Code Sec. 2108(a). **Effective** for estates of decedents dying after 10-4-76.

[Sec. 2108(b)]

(b) ALLEVIATION OF MORE BURDENSOME TAX.—Whenever the President finds that the laws of any foreign country with respect to which the President has made a proclamation under subsection (a) have been modified so that the tax on the transfer of estates of decedents who were citizens of the United States and not residents of such foreign country is no longer more burdensome than the tax imposed by this subchapter on the transfer of estates of decedents who were residents of such foreign country, he shall proclaim that the tax on the transfer of the estate of every decedent who was a resident of such foreign country at the time of his death shall, in the case of decedents dying after the date of such proclamation, be determined under this subchapter without regard to subsection (a).

[Sec. 2108(c)]

(c) NOTIFICATION OF CONGRESS REQUIRED.—No proclamation shall be issued by the President pursuant to this section unless, at least 30 days prior to such proclamation, he has notified the Senate and the House of Representatives of his intention to issue such proclamation.

[Sec. 2108(d)]

(d) IMPLEMENTATION BY REGULATIONS.—The Secretary shall prescribe such regulations as may be necessary or appropriate to implement this section.

Amendments

• **1976, Tax Reform Act of 1976 (P.L. 94-455)**

P.L. 94-455, § 1906(b)(13)(A):

Amended 1954 Code by substituting "Secretary" for "Secretary or his delegate" each place it appeared. **Effective** 2-1-77.

• **1966, Foreign Investors Tax Act of 1966 (P.L. 89-809)**

P.L. 89-809, § 108(f):

Added Code Sec. 2108. **Effective** with respect to estates of decedents dying after 11-13-66.

Subchapter C—Miscellaneous

Sec. 2201.	Combat zone-related deaths of members of the Armed Forces, deaths of astronauts, and deaths of victims of certain terrorist attacks.
Sec. 2203.	Definition of executor.
Sec. 2204.	Discharge of fiduciary from personal liability.
Sec. 2205.	Reimbursement out of estate.
Sec. 2206.	Liability of life insurance beneficiaries.
Sec. 2207.	Liability of recipient of property over which decedent had power of appointment.
Sec. 2207A.	Right of recovery in the case of certain marital deduction property.
Sec. 2207B.	Right of recovery where decedent retained interest.
Sec. 2208.	Certain residents of possessions considered citizens of the United States.
Sec. 2209.	Certain residents of possessions considered nonresidents not citizens of the United States.
Sec. 2210.	Termination.

ESTATE TAX—MISCELLANEOUS

[Sec. 2201]

SEC. 2201. COMBAT ZONE-RELATED DEATHS OF MEMBERS OF THE ARMED FORCES, DEATHS OF ASTRONAUTS, AND DEATHS OF VICTIMS OF CERTAIN TERRORIST ATTACKS.

[Sec. 2201(a)]

(a) IN GENERAL.—Unless the executor elects not to have this section apply, in applying sections 2001 and 2101 to the estate of a qualified decedent, the rate schedule set forth in subsection (c) shall be deemed to be the rate schedule set forth in section 2001(c).

Amendments

• **2003, Military Family Tax Relief Act of 2003 (P.L. 108-121)**

P.L. 108-121, § 110(c)(2)(A):

Amended the heading of Code Sec. 2201 by inserting ", **DEATHS OF ASTRONAUTS**," after "**FORCES**". **Effective** for estates of decedents dying after 12-31-2002.

[Sec. 2201(b)]

(b) QUALIFIED DECEDENT.—For purposes of this section, the term "qualified decedent" means—

(1) any citizen or resident of the United States dying while in active service of the Armed Forces of the United States, if such decedent—

(A) was killed in action while serving in a combat zone, as determined under section 112(c), or

(B) died as a result of wounds, disease, or injury suffered while serving in a combat zone (as determined under section 112(c)), and while in the line of duty, by reason of a hazard to which such decedent was subjected as an incident of such service,

(2) any specified terrorist victim (as defined in section 692(d)(4)), and

(3) any astronaut whose death occurs in the line of duty.

Amendments

• **2003, Military Family Tax Relief Act of 2003 (P.L. 108-121)**

P.L. 108-121, § 110(c)(1):

Amended Code Sec. 2201(b) by striking "and" at the end of paragraph (1)(B), by striking the period at the end of paragraph (2) and inserting ", and", and by adding at the end a new paragraph (3). **Effective** for estates of decedents dying after 12-31-2002.

[Sec. 2201(c)]

(c) RATE SCHEDULE.—

If the amount with respect to which the tentative tax to be computed is:	The tentative tax is:
Not over $150,000	1 percent of the amount by which such amount exceeds $100,000.
Over $150,000 but not over $200,000	$500 plus 2 percent of the excess over $150,000.
Over $200,000 but not over $300,000	$1,500 plus 3 percent of the excess over $200,000.
Over $300,000 but not over $500,000	$4,500 plus 4 percent of the excess over $300,000.
Over $500,000 but not over $700,000	$12,500 plus 5 percent of the excess over $500,000.
Over $700,000 but not over $900,000	$22,500 plus 6 percent of the excess over $700,000.
Over $900,000 but not over $1,100,000	$34,500 plus 7 percent of the excess over $900,000.
Over $1,100,000 but not over $1,600,000	$48,500 plus 8 percent of the excess over $1,100,000.
Over $1,600,000 but not over $2,100,000	$88,500 plus 9 percent of the excess over $1,600,000.
Over $2,100,000 but not over $2,600,000	$133,500 plus 10 percent of the excess over $2,100,000.
Over $2,600,000 but not over $3,100,000	$183,500 plus 11 percent of the excess over $2,600,000.
Over $3,100,000 but not over $3,600,000	$238,500 plus 12 percent of the excess over $3,100,000.
Over $3,600,000 but not over $4,100,000	$298,500 plus 13 percent of the excess over $3,600,000.
Over $4,100,000 but not over $5,100,000	$363,500 plus 14 percent of the excess over $4,100,000.
Over $5,100,000 but not over $6,100,000	$503,500 plus 15 percent of the excess over $5,100,000.
Over $6,100,000 but not over $7,100,000	$653,500 plus 16 percent of the excess over $6,100,000.
Over $7,100,000 but not over $8,100,000	$813,500 plus 17 percent of the excess over $7,100,000.
Over $8,100,000 but not over $9,100,000	$983,500 plus 18 percent of the excess over $8,100,000.
Over $9,100,000 but not over $10,100,000	$1,163,500 plus 19 percent of the excess over $9,100,000.
Over $10,100,000	$1,353,500 plus 20 percent of the excess over $10,100,000.

[Sec. 2201(d)]

(d) DETERMINATION OF UNIFIED CREDIT.—In the case of an estate to which this section applies, subsection (a) shall not apply in determining the credit under section 2010.

Amendments

• **2017, Tax Cuts and Jobs Act (P.L. 115-97)**

P.L. 115-97, § 11026, provides:

For a special rule, see Act Sec. 11026 in the amendment notes for Code Sec. 112(c).

• **2002, Victims of Terrorism Tax Relief Act of 2001 (P.L. 107-134)**

P.L. 107-134, § 103(a):

Amended Code Sec. 2201. **Effective** for estates of decedents dying on or after 9-11-2001; and in the case of individuals dying as a result of the 4-19-95 terrorist attack, dying on or after 4-19-95. For a waiver of limitations, see Act Sec. 103(d)(2), below. Prior to amendment, Code Sec. 2201 read as follows:

SEC. 2201. MEMBERS OF THE ARMED FORCES DYING IN COMBAT ZONE OR BY REASON OF COMBAT-ZONE-INCURRED WOUNDS, ETC.

The additional estate tax as defined in section 2011(d) shall not apply to the transfer of the taxable estate of a citizen or resident of the United States dying while in active service as a member of the Armed Forces of the United States, if such decedent—

(1) was killed in action while serving in a combat zone, as determined under section 112(c); or

(2) died as a result of wounds, disease, or injury suffered, while serving in a combat zone (as determined under section 112(c)), and while in line of duty, by reason of a hazard to which he was subjected as an incident of such service.

P.L. 107-134, § 103(b)(3):

Retroactively repealed paragraph (9) of section 532(c) of P.L. 107-16, and it never took effect.

P.L. 107-134, § 103(d)(2), provides:

(2) WAIVER OF LIMITATIONS.—If refund or credit of any overpayment of tax resulting from the amendments made by this section is prevented at any time before the close of the 1-year period beginning on the date of the enactment of this Act by the operation of any law or rule of law (including res judicata), such refund or credit may nevertheless be made or allowed if claim therefor is filed before the close of such period.

• **2001, Economic Growth and Tax Relief Reconciliation Act of 2001 (P.L. 107-16)**

P.L. 107-16, § 532(c)(9)(A)-(B) (repealed by P.L. 107-134, § 103(b)(3)):

Amended Code Sec. 2201 by striking "as defined in section 2011(d)" following "The additional estate tax", and by adding at the end a new flush sentence. **Effective** for estates of decedents dying, and generation-skipping transfers, after 12-31-2004.

P.L. 107-16, § 901(a)-(b), as amended by P.L. 111-312, § 101(a)(1), provides:

SEC. 901. SUNSET OF PROVISIONS OF ACT.

(a) IN GENERAL.—All provisions of, and amendments made by, this Act shall not apply—

ESTATE TAX—MISCELLANEOUS

(1) to taxable, plan, or limitation years beginning after December 31, 2012, or

(2) in the case of title V, to estates of decedents dying, gifts made, or generation skipping transfers, after December 31, 2012.

(b) APPLICATION OF CERTAIN LAWS.—The Internal Revenue Code of 1986 and the Employee Retirement Income Security Act of 1974 shall be applied and administered to years, estates, gifts, and transfers described in subsection (a) as if the provisions and amendments described in subsection (a) had never been enacted.

• **1999 (P.L. 106-21)**

P.L. 106-21, § 1(a)(4), (b) and (d)(1), provide:

SECTION 1. AVAILABILITY OF CERTAIN TAX BENEFITS FOR SERVICES AS PART OF OPERATION ALLIED FORCE.

(a) GENERAL RULE.—For purposes of the following provisions of the Internal Revenue Code of 1986, a qualified hazardous duty area shall be treated in the same manner as if it were a combat zone (as determined under section 112 of such Code):

* * *

(4) Section 2201 (relating to members of the Armed Forces dying in combat zone or by reason of combat-zone-incurred wounds, etc.).

* * *

(b) QUALIFIED HAZARDOUS DUTY AREA.—For purposes of this section, the term "qualified hazardous duty area" means any area of the Federal Republic of Yugoslavia (Serbia/Montenegro), Albania, the Adriatic Sea, and the northern Ionian Sea (above the 39th parallel) during the period (which includes the date of the enactment of this Act) that any member of the Armed Forces of the United States is entitled to special pay under section 310 of title 37, United States Code (relating to special pay; duty subject to hostile fire or imminent danger) for services performed in such area.

* * *

(d) EFFECTIVE DATES.—

(1) IN GENERAL.—Except as provided in paragraph (2), this section shall take effect on March 24, 1999.

• **1996 (P.L. 104-117)**

P.L. 104-117, § 1(a)(4), (b) and (e)(1), provide:

SECTION 1. TREATMENT OF CERTAIN INDIVIDUALS PERFORMING SERVICES IN CERTAIN HAZARDOUS DUTY AREAS.

(a) GENERAL RULE.—For purposes of the following provisions of the Internal Revenue Code of 1986, a qualified hazardous duty area shall be treated in the same manner as if it were a combat zone (as determined under section 112 of such Code):

* * *

(4) Section 2201 (relating to members of the Armed Forces dying in combat zone or by reason of combat-zone-incurred wounds, etc.).

* * *

(b) QUALIFIED HAZARDOUS DUTY AREA.—For purposes of this section, the term "qualified hazardous duty area" means Bosnia and Herzegovina, Croatia, or Macedonia, if as of the date of the enactment of this section any member of the Armed Forces of the United States is entitled to special pay under section 310 of title 37, United States Code (relating to special pay; duty subject to hostile fire or imminent danger) for services performed in such country. Such term includes any such country only during the period such entitlement is in effect. Solely for purposes of applying section 7508 of the Internal Revenue Code of 1986, in the case of an individual who is performing services as part of Operation Joint Endeavor outside the United States while deployed away from such individual's permanent duty station, the term "qualified hazardous duty area" includes, during the period for which such entitlement is in effect, any area in which such services are performed.

* * *

(e) EFFECTIVE DATE.—

(1) IN GENERAL.—Except as provided in paragraph (2), the provisions of and amendments made by this section shall take effect on November 21, 1995.

• **1975 (P.L. 93-597)**

P.L. 93-597, § 6(b):

Amended Code Sec. 2201 by deleting "during an induction period (as defined in sec. 112(c)(5))," that formerly appeared after the word "dying" and by amending the heading of the section. **Effective** 7-1-73. Prior to amendment, the heading read as follows: **"MEMBERS OF THE ARMED FORCES DYING DURING AN INDUCTION PERIOD."**.

[Sec. 2203]

SEC. 2203. DEFINITION OF EXECUTOR.

The term "executor" wherever it is used in this title in connection with the estate tax imposed by this chapter means the executor or administrator of the decedent, or, if there is no executor or administrator appointed, qualified, and acting within the United States, then any person in actual or constructive possession of any property of the decedent.

[Sec. 2204]

SEC. 2204. DISCHARGE OF FIDUCIARY FROM PERSONAL LIABILITY.

[Sec. 2204(a)]

(a) GENERAL RULE.—If the executor makes written application to the Secretary for determination of the amount of the tax and discharge from personal liability therefor, the Secretary (as soon as possible, and in any event within 9 months after the making of such application, or, if the application is made before the return is filed, then within 9 months after the return is filed, but not after the expiration of the period prescribed for the assessment of the tax in section 6501) shall notify the executor of the amount of the tax. The executor, on payment of the amount of which he is notified (other than any amount the time for payment of which is extended under section 6161, 6163, or 6166), and on furnishing any bond which may be required for any amount for which the time for payment is extended, shall be discharged from personal liability for any deficiency in tax thereafter found to be due and shall be entitled to a receipt or writing showing such discharge.

Amendments

• **1981, Economic Recovery Tax Act of 1981 (P.L. 97-34)**

P.L. 97-34, § 422(e)(3):

Amended Code Sec. 2204(a) by striking out "6166 or 6166A" and inserting "or 6166". **Effective** for estates of decedents dying after 12-31-81.

• **1976, Tax Reform Act of 1976 (P.L. 94-455)**

P.L. 94-455, § 1906(b)(13)(A):

Amended 1954 Code by substituting "Secretary" for "Secretary or his delegate" each place it appeared. **Effective** 2-1-77.

P.L. 94-455, § 2004(f)(6):

Amended Code Sec. 2204(a) by substituting "6166 or 6166A" for "or 6166". **Effective** for estates of decedents dying after 12-31-76.

• **1970, Excise, Estate, and Gift Tax Adjustment Act of 1970 (P.L. 91-614)**

P.L. 91-614, § 101(d)(1):

Amended Code Sec. 2204. **Effective** with respect to decedents dying after 12-31-70. Prior to amendment, Code Sec. 2204 read as follows:

SEC. 2204. DISCHARGE OF EXECUTOR FROM PERSONAL LIABILITY.

"If the executor makes written application to the Secretary or his delegate for determination of the amount of the tax and discharge from personal liability therefor, the Secretary or his delegate (as soon as possible, and in any event within 1 year after the making of such application, or, if the application is made before the return is filed, then within 1 year after the return is filed, but not after the expiration of the period prescribed for the assessment of the tax in section 6501) shall notify the executor of the amount of the tax. The executor, on payment of the amount of which he is notified, shall be discharged from personal liability for any deficiency in tax thereafter found to be due and shall be entitled to a receipt or writing showing such discharge.

P.L. 91-614, § 101(f):

Amended Code Sec. 2204(a) by substituting "9 months" for "1 year." **Effective** with respect to estates of decedents dying after 12-31-73.

[Sec. 2204(b)]

(b) FIDUCIARY OTHER THAN THE EXECUTOR.—If a fiduciary (not including a fiduciary in respect of the estate of a nonresident decedent) other than the executor makes written application to the Secretary for determination of the amount of any estate tax for which the fiduciary may be personally liable, and for discharge from personal liability therefor, the Secretary upon the discharge of the executor from personal liability under subsection (a), or upon the expiration of 6 months after the making of such application by the fiduciary, if later, shall notify the fiduciary (1) of the amount of such tax for which it has been determined the fiduciary is liable, or (2) that it has been determined that the fiduciary is not liable for any such tax. Such application shall be accompanied by a copy of the instrument, if any, under which such fiduciary is acting, a description of the property held by the fiduciary, and such other information for purposes of carrying out the provisions of this section as the Secretary may require by regulations. On payment of the amount of such tax for which it has been determined the fiduciary is liable (other than any amount the time for payment of which has been extended under section 6161, 6163, or 6166), and on furnishing any bond which may be required for any amount for which the time for payment has been extended, or on receipt by him of notification of a determination that he is not liable for any such tax, the fiduciary shall be

ESTATE TAX—MISCELLANEOUS

discharged from personal liability for any deficiency in such tax thereafter found to be due and shall be entitled to a receipt or writing evidencing such discharge.

Amendments

• **1981, Economic Recovery Tax Act of 1981 (P.L. 97-34)**

P.L. 97-34, § 422(e)(3):

Amended Code Sec. 2204(b) by striking out "6166 or 6166A" and inserting "or 6166". **Effective** for estates of decedents dying after 12-31-81.

• **1976, Tax Reform Act of 1976 (P.L. 94-455)**

P.L. 94-455, § 1902(a)(9):

Substituted "has been" for "has not been" in the last sentence of Code Sec. 2204(b). **Effective** for estates of decedents dying after 10-4-76.

P.L. 94-455, § 1906(b)(13)(A):

Amended the 1954 Code by substituting "Secretary" for "Secretary or his delegate" each place it appeared. **Effective** 2-1-77.

P.L. 94-455, § 2004(f)(4):

Substituted "has been extended under" for "has not been extended under" in the last sentence of Code Sec. 2204(b). **Effective** for estates of decedents dying after 12-31-76.

P.L. 94-455, § 2004(f)(6):

Substituted "6166 or 6166A" for "or 6166". **Effective** for estates of decedents dying after 12-31-76.

• **1970, Excise, Estate, and Gift Tax Adjustment Act of 1970 (P.L. 91-614)**

P.L. 91-614, § 101(d)(1):

Amended Code Sec. 2204. **Effective** with respect to decedents dying after 12-31-70. For prior text, see note under Code Sec. 2204(a).

[Sec. 2204(c)]

(c) SPECIAL LIEN UNDER SECTION 6324A.—For purposes of the second sentence of subsection (a) and the last sentence of subsection (b), an agreement which meets the requirements of section 6324A (relating to special lien for estate tax deferred under section 6166) shall be treated as the furnishing of bond with respect to the amount for which the time for payment has been extended under section 6166.

Amendments

• **1981, Economic Recovery Tax Act of 1981 (P.L. 97-34)**

P.L. 97-34, § 422(e)(1):

Amended Code Sec. 2204(c) by striking out "or 6166A" each place it appears. **Effective** for estates of decedents dying after 12-31-81.

• **1976, Tax Reform Act of 1976 (P.L. 94-455)**

P.L. 94-455, § 2004(d)(2), (g):

Added Code Sec. 2204(c). **Effective** for estates of decedents dying after 12-31-76.

[Sec. 2204(d)]

(d) GOOD FAITH RELIANCE ON GIFT TAX RETURNS.—If the executor in good faith relies on gift tax returns furnished under section 6103(e)(3) for determining the decedent's adjusted taxable gifts, the executor shall be discharged from personal liability with respect to any deficiency of the tax imposed by this chapter which is attributable to adjusted taxable gifts which—

(1) are made more than 3 years before the date of the decedent's death, and

(2) are not shown on such returns.

Amendments

• **1978, Revenue Act of 1978 (P.L. 95-600)**

P.L. 95-600, § 702(p)(1):

Added Code Sec. 2204(d). **Effective** for estates of decedents dying after 1976.

[Sec. 2205]

SEC. 2205. REIMBURSEMENT OUT OF ESTATE.

If the tax or any part thereof is paid by, or collected out of, that part of the estate passing to or in the possession of any person other than the executor in his capacity as such, such person shall be entitled to reimbursement out of any part of the estate still undistributed or by a just and equitable contribution by the persons whose interest in the estate of the decedent would have been reduced if the tax had been paid before the distribution of the estate or whose interest is subject to equal or prior liability for the payment of taxes, debts, or other charges against the estate, it being the purpose and intent of this chapter that so far as is practicable and unless otherwise directed by the will of the decedent the tax shall be paid out of the estate before its distribution.

[Sec. 2206]

SEC. 2206. LIABILITY OF LIFE INSURANCE BENEFICIARIES.

Unless the decedent directs otherwise in his will, if any part of the gross estate on which tax has been paid consists of proceeds of policies of insurance on the life of the decedent receivable by a beneficiary other than the executor, the executor shall be entitled to recover from such beneficiary such portion of the total tax paid as the proceeds of such policies bear to the taxable estate. If there is more than one such beneficiary, the executor shall be entitled to recover from such beneficiaries in the same ratio. In the case of such proceeds receivable by the surviving spouse of the decedent for which a deduction is allowed under section 2056 (relating to marital deduction), this section shall not apply to such proceeds except as to the amount thereof in excess of the aggregate amount of the marital deductions allowed under such section.

Amendments

• **1976, Tax Reform Act of 1976 (P.L. 94-455)**

P.L. 94-455, § 2001(c)(1)(H), (d)(1):

Substituted "the taxable estate" for "the sum of the taxable estate and the amount of the exemption allowed in computing the taxable estate, determined under section 2051" in the first sentence of Code Sec. 2206. **Effective** for estates of decedents dying after 12-31-76.

[Sec. 2207]

SEC. 2207. LIABILITY OF RECIPIENT OF PROPERTY OVER WHICH DECEDENT HAD POWER OF APPOINTMENT.

Unless the decedent directs otherwise in his will, if any part of the gross estate on which the tax has been paid consists of the value of property included in the gross estate under section 2041, the executor shall be entitled to recover from the person receiving such property by reason of the exercise, nonexercise, or release of a power of appointment such portion of the total tax paid as the value of such property bears to the taxable estate. If there is more than one such person, the executor shall be entitled to recover from such persons in the same ratio. In the case of such property received by the surviving spouse of the decedent for which a deduction is allowed under section 2056 (relating to marital deduction), this section shall not apply to such property except as to the value thereof reduced by an amount equal to the excess of the aggregate amount of the marital deductions allowed under section 2056 over the amount of proceeds of insurance upon the life of the decedent receivable by the surviving spouse for which proceeds a marital deduction is allowed under such section.

Amendments

• **1976, Tax Reform Act of 1976 (P.L. 94-455)**

P.L. 94-455, § 2001(c)(1)(I), (d)(1):

Substituted "the taxable estate" for "the sum of the taxable estate and the amount of the exemption allowed in computing the taxable estate, determined under section 2052, or section 2106(a), as the case may be" in the first sentence of Code Sec. 2207. **Effective** for estates of decedents dying after 12-31-76.

ESTATE TAX—MISCELLANEOUS

[Sec. 2207A]

SEC. 2207A. RIGHT OF RECOVERY IN THE CASE OF CERTAIN MARITAL DEDUCTION PROPERTY.

[Sec. 2207A(a)]

(a) RECOVERY WITH RESPECT TO ESTATE TAX.—

(1) IN GENERAL.—If any part of the gross estate consists of property the value of which is includible in the gross estate by reason of section 2044 (relating to certain property for which marital deduction was previously allowed), the decedent's estate shall be entitled to recover from the person receiving the property the amount by which—

(A) the total tax under this chapter which has been paid, exceeds

(B) the total tax under this chapter which would have been payable if the value of such property had not been included in the gross estate.

(2) DECEDENT MAY OTHERWISE DIRECT.—Paragraph (1) shall not apply with respect to any property to the extent that the decedent in his will (or a revocable trust) specifically indicates an intent to waive any right of recovery under this subchapter with respect to such property.

Amendments

• **1997, Taxpayer Relief Act of 1997 (P.L. 105-34)**

P.L. 105-34, § 1302(a):

Amended Code Sec. 2207A(a)(2). **Effective** with respect to the estates of decedents dying after 8-5-97. Prior to amendment, Code Sec. 2207A(a)(2) read as follows:

(2) DECEDENT MAY OTHERWISE DIRECT BY WILL.—Paragraph (1) shall not apply if the decedent otherwise directs by will.

[Sec. 2207A(b)]

(b) RECOVERY WITH RESPECT TO GIFT TAX.—If for any calendar year tax is paid under chapter 12 with respect to any person by reason of property treated as transferred by such person under section 2519, such person shall be entitled to recover from the person receiving the property the amount by which—

(1) the total tax for such year under chapter 12, exceeds

(2) the total tax which would have been payable under such chapter for such year if the value of such property had not been taken into account for purposes of chapter 12.

[Sec. 2207A(c)]

(c) MORE THAN ONE RECIPIENT OF PROPERTY.—For purposes of this section, if there is more than one person receiving the property, the right of recovery shall be against each such person.

[Sec. 2207A(d)]

(d) TAXES AND INTEREST.—In the case of penalties and interest attributable to additional taxes described in subsections (a) and (b), rules similar to subsections (a), (b), and (c) shall apply.

Amendments

• **1983, Technical Corrections Act of 1982 (P.L. 97-448)**

P.L. 97-448, § 104(a)(10):

Amended paragraph (2) of section 403(e) of P.L. 97-34 (relating to effective date) by striking out "and paragraphs (2) and (3)(B) of subsection (d)" and inserting "paragraphs (2) and (3)(B) of subsection (d), and paragraph (4)(A) of subsection (d) (to the extent related to the tax imposed by chapter 12 [gift tax] of the Internal Revenue Code of 1954)". (For the amendment made by P.L. 97-34, Act Sec. 403(d)(4)(A), see below.)

• **1981, Economic Recovery Tax Act of 1981 (P.L. 97-34)**

P.L. 97-34, § 403(d)(4)(A):

Added Code Sec. 2207A. **Effective**, generally, for gifts made after 12-31-81. For a special rule applicable to certain wills or trusts executed or created before 9-12-81, see Act Sec. 403(e)(3), below.

P.L. 97-34, § 403(e)(3), provides:

(3) If—

(A) the decedent dies after December 31, 1981,

(B) by reason of the death of the decedent property passes from the decedent or is acquired from the decedent under a will executed before the date which is 30 days after the date of the enactment of this Act, or a trust created before such date, which contains a formula expressly providing that the spouse is to receive the maximum amount of property qualifying for the marital deduction allowable by Federal law,

(C) the formula referred to in subparagraph (B) was not amended to refer specifically to an unlimited marital deduction at any time after the date which is 30 days after the date of enactment of this Act, and before the death of the decedent, and

(D) the State does not enact a statute applicable to such estate which construes this type of formula as referring to the marital deduction allowable by Federal law as amended by subsection (a),

then the amendment made by subsection (a) [relating to the unlimited marital deduction (Code Sec. 2056, as amended by P.L. 97-34)] shall not apply to the estate of such decedent.

[Sec. 2207B]

SEC. 2207B. RIGHT OF RECOVERY WHERE DECEDENT RETAINED INTEREST.

[Sec. 2207B(a)]

(a) ESTATE TAX.—

(1) IN GENERAL.—If any part of the gross estate on which tax has been paid consists of the value of property included in the gross estate by reason of section 2036 (relating to transfers with retained life estate), the decedent's estate shall be entitled to recover from the person receiving the property the amount which bears the same ratio to the total tax under this chapter which has been paid as—

(A) the value of such property, bears to

(B) the taxable estate.

(2) DECEDENT MAY OTHERWISE DIRECT.—Paragraph (1) shall not apply with respect to any property to the extent that the decedent in his will (or a revocable trust) specifically indicates an intent to waive any right of recovery under this subchapter with respect to such property.

Amendments

• **1997, Taxpayer Relief Act of 1997 (P.L. 105-34)**

P.L. 105-34, § 1302(b):

Amended Code Sec. 2207B(a)(2). **Effective** with respect to the estates of decedents dying after 8-5-97. Prior to amendment, Code Sec. 2207B(a)(2) read as follows:

(2) DECEDENT MAY OTHERWISE DIRECT BY WILL.—Paragraph (1) shall not apply if the decedent otherwise directs in a provision of his will (or a revocable trust) specifically referring to this section.

[Sec. 2207B(b)]

(b) MORE THAN ONE RECIPIENT.—For purposes of this section, if there is more than 1 person receiving the property, the right of recovery shall be against each such person.

ESTATE TAX—MISCELLANEOUS

Amendments

• 1990, Omnibus Budget Reconciliation Act of 1990 (P.L. 101-508)

P.L. 101-508, §11601(b)(1)(A):

Amended Code Sec. 2207B by striking subsection (b) and redesignating subsections (c), (d), and (e) as subsections (b), (c), and (d), respectively. **Effective** in the case of property transferred after 12-17-87. Prior to amendment, Code Sec. 2207B(b) read as follows:

(b) GIFT TAX.—If for any calendar year tax is paid under chapter 12 with respect to any person by reason of property treated as transferred by such person under section 2036(c)(4), such person shall be entitled to recover from the original transferee (as defined in section 2036(c)(4)(C)(ii)) the amount which bears the same ratio to the total tax for such year under chapter 12 as—

(1) the value of such property for purposes of chapter 12, bears to

(2) the total amount of the taxable gifts for such year.

[Sec. 2207B(c)]

(c) PENALTIES AND INTEREST.—In the case of penalties and interest attributable to the additional taxes described in subsection (a), rules similar to the rules of subsections (a) and (b) shall apply.

Amendments

• 1990, Omnibus Budget Reconciliation Act of 1990 (P.L. 101-508)

P.L. 101-508, §11601(b)(1)(A):

Redesignated Code Sec. 2207B(d) as subsection (c). **Effective** in the case of property transferred after 12-17-87.

P.L. 101-508, §11601(b)(1)(B):

Amended Code Sec. 2207B(c) (as so redesignated) by striking "subsections (a) and (b)" and inserting "subsection (a)". **Effective** in the case of property transferred after 12-17-87.

P.L. 101-508, §11601(b)(1)(C):

Amended Code Sec. 2207B(c) (as so redesignated) by striking "subsections (a), (b), and (c)" and inserting "subsections (a) and (b)". **Effective** in the case of property transferred after 12-17-87.

[Sec. 2207B(d)]

(d) NO RIGHT OF RECOVERY AGAINST CHARITABLE REMAINDER TRUSTS.—No person shall be entitled to recover any amount by reason of this section from a trust to which section 664 applies (determined without regard to this section).

Amendments

• 1990, Omnibus Budget Reconciliation Act of 1990 (P.L. 101-508)

P.L. 101-508, §11601(b)(1)(A):

Redesignated Code Sec. 2207B(e) as subsection (d). **Effective** in the case of property transferred after 12-17-87.

• 1988, Technical and Miscellaneous Revenue Act of 1988 (P.L. 100-647)

P.L. 100-647, §3031(f)(1):

Amended Subchapter C of chapter 11 by inserting after section 2207A a new section 2207B. **Effective**, generally, as if included in the provision of P.L. 99-514 to which it relates. For a special rule, see Act Sec. 3031(h)(3), below.

P.L. 100-647, §3031(h)(3), provides:

(3) SUBSECTION (f).—If an amount is included in the gross estate of a decedent under section 2036 of the 1986 Code other than solely by reason of section 2036(c) of the 1986 Code, the amendments made by subsection (f) shall apply to such amount only with respect to property transferred after the date of the enactment of this Act.

[Sec. 2208]

SEC. 2208. CERTAIN RESIDENTS OF POSSESSIONS CONSIDERED CITIZENS OF THE UNITED STATES.

A decedent who was a citizen of the United States and a resident of a possession thereof at the time of his death shall, for purposes of the tax imposed by this chapter, be considered a "citizen" of the United States within the meaning of that term wherever used in this title unless he acquired his United States citizenship solely by reason of (1) his being a citizen of such possession of the United States, or (2) his birth or residence within such possession of the United States.

Amendments

• 1958, Technical Amendments Act of 1958 (P.L. 85-866)

P.L. 85-866, §102(a):

Added Code Sec. 2208. **Effective** for estates of decedents dying after 9-2-58.

[Sec. 2209]

SEC. 2209. CERTAIN RESIDENTS OF POSSESSIONS CONSIDERED NONRESIDENTS NOT CITIZENS OF THE UNITED STATES.

A decedent who was a citizen of the United States and a resident of a possession thereof at the time of his death shall, for purposes of the tax imposed by this chapter, be considered a "nonresident not a citizen of the United States" within the meaning of that term wherever used in this title, but only if such person acquired his United States citizenship solely by reason of (1) his being a citizen of such possession of the United States, or (2) his birth or residence within such possession of the United States.

Amendments

• 1960 (P.L. 86-779)

P.L. 86-779, §4(b):

Added Code Sec. 2209. **Effective** for estates of decedents dying after 9-14-60.

[Sec. 2210]

SEC. 2210. TERMINATION.

[Sec. 2210(a)]

(a) IN GENERAL.—Except as provided in subsection (b), this chapter shall not apply to the estates of decedents dying after December 31, 2009.

[Sec. 2210(b)]

(b) CERTAIN DISTRIBUTIONS FROM QUALIFIED DOMESTIC TRUSTS.—In applying section 2056A with respect to the surviving spouse of a decedent dying before January 1, 2010—

(1) section 2056A(b)(1)(A) shall not apply to distributions made after December 31, 2020, and

(2) section 2056A(b)(1)(B) shall not apply after December 31, 2009.

Amendments

• 2010, Tax Relief, Unemployment Insurance Reauthorization, and Job Creation Act of 2010 (P.L. 111-312)

P.L. 111-312, §301(a):

Amended Code Sec. 2210 to read as such provision would read if subtitle A of title V of the Economic Growth and Tax Relief Reconciliation Act of 2001 (P.L. 107-16) had never been enacted. **Effective** for estates of decedents dying, and transfers made, after 12-31-2009. For a special rule, see Act Sec. 301(c), below.

P.L. 111-312, §301(c), provides:

(c) SPECIAL ELECTION WITH RESPECT TO ESTATES OF DECEDENTS DYING IN 2010.—Notwithstanding subsection (a), in the case of an estate of a decedent dying after December 31, 2009, and before January 1, 2011, the executor (within the meaning of section 2203 of the Internal Revenue Code of 1986) may elect to apply such Code as though the amendments made by subsection (a) do not apply with respect to chapter 11 of such Code and with respect to property acquired or passing from such decedent (within the meaning of section 1014(b) of such Code). Such election shall be made at

ESTATE TAX—MISCELLANEOUS

such time and in such manner as the Secretary of the Treasury or the Secretary's delegate shall provide. Such an election once made shall be revocable only with the consent of the Secretary of the Treasury or the Secretary's delegate. For purposes of section 2652(a)(1) of such Code, the determination of whether any property is subject to the tax imposed by such chapter 11 shall be made without regard to any election made under this subsection.

P.L. 111-312, § 304, provides:

SEC. 304. APPLICATION OF EGTRRA SUNSET TO THIS TITLE.

Section 901 of the Economic Growth and Tax Relief Reconciliation Act of 2001 shall apply to the amendments made by this title.

Amendments

• **2001, Economic Growth and Tax Relief Reconciliation Act of 2001 (P.L. 107-16)**

P.L. 107-16, § 501(a):

Amended subchapter C of chapter 11 of subtitle B by adding at the end a new Code Sec. 2210. **Effective** for the estates of decedents dying, and generation-skipping transfers, after 12-31-2009.

Amendments

• **1989, Omnibus Budget Reconciliation Act of 1989 (P.L. 101-239)**

P.L. 101-239, § 7304(b)(1):

Repealed Code Sec. 2210. **Effective** for estates of decedents dying after 7-12-89. Prior to repeal, Code Sec. 2210 read as follows:

SEC. 2210. LIABILITY FOR PAYMENT IN CASE OF TRANSFER OF EMPLOYER SECURITIES TO AN EMPLOYEE STOCK OWNERSHIP PLAN OR A WORKER-OWNED COOPERATIVE.

[Sec. 2210(a)]

(a) IN GENERAL.—If—

(1) employer securities—

(A) are acquired from the decedent by an employee stock ownership plan or by an eligible worker-owned cooperative from any decedent,

(B) pass from the decedent to such a plan or cooperative, or

(C) are transferred by the executor to such a plan or cooperative,

(2) the executor of the estate of the decedent may (without regard to this section) make an election under section 6166 with respect to that portion of the tax imposed by section 2001 which is attributable to employer securities, and

(3) the executor elects the application of this section and files the agreements described in subsection (e) before the due date (including extensions) for filing the return of tax imposed by section 2001,

then the executor is relieved of liability for payment of that portion of the tax imposed by section 2001 which such employee stock ownership plan or cooperative is required to pay under subsection (b).

Amendments

• **1986, Tax Reform Act of 1986 (P.L. 99-514)**

P.L. 99-514, § 1854(d)(1)(A):

Amended Code Sec. 2210(a) by striking out "and" at the end of paragraph (1), by redesignating paragraph (2) as paragraph (3), and by inserting after paragraph (1) new paragraph (2). **Effective** for the estates of decedents dying after 9-27-85.

[Sec. 2210(b)]

(b) PAYMENT OF TAX BY EMPLOYEE STOCK OWNERSHIP PLAN OR COOPERATIVE.—

(1) IN GENERAL.—An employee stock ownership plan or eligible worker-owned cooperative—

(A) which has acquired employer securities from the decedent, or to which such securities have passed from the decedent or been transferred by the executor, and

(B) with respect to which an agreement described in subsection (e)(1) is in effect,

shall pay that portion of the tax imposed by section 2001 with respect to the taxable estate of the decedent which is described in paragraph (2).

(2) AMOUNT OF TAX TO BE PAID.—The portion of the tax imposed by section 2001 with respect to the taxable estate of the decedent that is referred to in paragraph (1) is equal to the lesser of—

(A) the value of the employer securities described in subsection (a)(1) which is included in the gross estate of the decedent, or

(B) the tax imposed by section 2001 with respect to such taxable estate reduced by the sum of the credits allowable against such tax.

[Sec. 2210(c)]

(c) INSTALLMENT PAYMENTS.—

(1) IN GENERAL.—If—

(A) the executor of the estate of the decedent (without regard to this section) elects to have the provisions of section 6166 (relating to extensions of time for payment of estate tax where estate consists largely of interest in closely held business) apply to payment of that portion of the tax imposed by section 2001 with respect to such estate which is attributable to employer securities, and

(B) the plan administrator or the cooperative provides to the executor the agreement described in subsection (e)(1),

then the plan administrator or any authorized officer of the cooperative may elect, before the due date (including extensions) for filing the return of such tax, to pay all or part of the tax described in subsection (b)(2) in installments under the provisions of section 6166.

(2) INTEREST ON INSTALLMENTS.—In determining the 4-percent portion for purposes of section 6601(j)—

(A) the portion of the tax imposed by section 2001 with respect to an estate for which the executor is liable, and

P.L. 107-16, § 901(a)-(b), as amended by P.L. 111-312, § 101(a)(1), provides:

SEC. 901. SUNSET OF PROVISIONS OF ACT.

(a) IN GENERAL.—All provisions of, and amendments made by, this Act shall not apply—

(1) to taxable, plan, or limitation years beginning after December 31, 2012, or

(2) in the case of title V, to estates of decedents dying, gifts made, or generation skipping transfers, after December 31, 2012.

(b) APPLICATION OF CERTAIN LAWS.—The Internal Revenue Code of 1986 and the Employee Retirement Income Security Act of 1974 shall be applied and administered to years, estates, gifts, and transfers described in subsection (a) as if the provisions and amendments described in subsection (a) had never been enacted.

[Sec. 2210—Repealed]

(B) the portion of such tax for which an employee stock ownership plan or an eligible worker-owned cooperative is liable,

shall be aggregated.

(3) SPECIAL RULES FOR APPLICATION OF SECTION 6166(g).—In the case of any transfer of employer securities to an employee stock ownership plan or eligible worker-owned cooperative to which this section applies—

(A) TRANSFER DOES NOT TRIGGER ACCELERATION.—Such transfer shall not be treated as a disposition or withdrawal to which section 6166(g) applies.

(B) SEPARATE APPLICATION TO ESTATE AND PLAN INTERESTS.—Section 6166(g) shall be applied separately to the interests held after such transfer by the estate and such plan or cooperative.

(C) REQUIRED DISTRIBUTION NOT TAKEN INTO ACCOUNT.—In the case of any distribution of such securities by such plan which is described in section 4978(d)(1)—

(i) such distribution shall not be treated as a disposition or withdrawal for purposes of section 6166(g), and

(ii) such securities shall not be taken into account in applying section 6166(g) to any subsequent disposition or withdrawal.

Amendments

• **1986, Tax Reform Act of 1986 (P.L. 99-514)**

P.L. 99-514, § 1854(d)(2):

Amended Code Sec. 2210(c) by adding at the end thereof new paragraph (3). **Effective** as if included in the provision of P.L. 98-369 to which it relates.

P.L. 99-514, § 1854(d)(4):

Amended Code Sec. 2210(c)(1) by inserting "any authorized officer of" before "the cooperative" in the matter following subparagraph (B). **Effective** as if included in the provision of P.L. 98-369 to which it relates.

[Sec. 2210(d)]

(d) GUARANTEE OF PAYMENTS.—Any employer—

(1) whose employees are covered by an employee stock ownership plan, and

(2) who has entered into an agreement described in subsection (e)(2) which is in effect,

and any eligible worker-owned cooperative shall guarantee (in such manner as the Secretary may prescribe) the payment of any amount such plan or cooperative, repectively, is required to pay under subsection (b).

Amendments

• **1986, Tax Reform Act of 1986 (P.L. 99-514)**

P.L. 99-514, § 1854(d)(5)(A)-(C):

Amended Code Sec. 2210(d) by inserting "and any eligible worker-owned cooperative" before "shall guarantee" in the matter following paragraph (2), by striking out "such plan" and inserting in lieu thereof "such plan or cooperative, respectively,", and by striking out ", including any interest payable under section 6601 which is attributable to such amount". **Effective** as if included in the provision of P.L. 98-369 to which it relates.

P.L. 99-514, § 1899A(37):

Amended Code Sec. 2210(d) by striking out "may prescibe" and inserting in lieu thereof "may prescribe". **Effective** 10-22-86.

[Sec. 2210(e)]

(e) AGREEMENTS.—The agreements described in this subsection are as follows:

(1) A written agreement signed by the plan administrator, or by any authorized officer of the eligible worker-owned cooperative, consenting to the application of subsection (b) to such plan or cooperative.

(2) A written agreement signed by the employer whose employees are covered by the plan described in subsection (b) consenting to the application of subsection (d).

[Sec. 2210(f)]

(f) EXEMPTION FROM TAX ON PROHIBITED TRANSACTIONS.—The assumption under this section by an employee stock ownership plan of any portion of the liability for the tax imposed by section 2001 shall be treated as a loan described in section 4975(d)(3).

[Sec. 2210(g)]

(g) DEFINITIONS.—For purposes of this section—

(1) EMPLOYER SECURITIES.—The term "employer securities" has the meaning given such term by section 409(l).

(2) EMPLOYEE STOCK OWNERSHIP PLAN.—The term "employee stock ownership plan" has the meaning given such term by section 4975(e)(7).

(3) ELIGIBLE WORKER-OWNED COOPERATIVE.—The term "eligible worker-owned cooperative" has the meaning given to such term by section 1041(c)(2).

(4) PLAN ADMINISTRATOR.—The term "plan administrator" has the meaning given such term by section 414(g).

(5) TAX IMPOSED BY SECTION 2001.—The term "tax imposed by section 2001" includes any interest, penalty, addition to tax, or additional amount relating to any tax imposed by section 2001.

Amendments

• **1986, Tax Reform Act of 1986 (P.L. 99-514)**

P.L. 99-514, § 1854(d)(3):

Amended Code Sec. 2210(g) by adding at the end thereof new paragraph (5). **Effective** as if included in the provision of P.L. 98-369 to which it relates.

P.L. 99-514, § 1854(d)(6):

Amended Code Sec. 2210(g)(3) by striking out "section 1041(b)(2)" and inserting in lieu thereof "section 1042(c)(2)". **Effective** as if included in the provision of P.L. 98-369 to which it relates.

• **1984, Deficit Reduction Act of 1984 (P.L. 98-369)**

P.L. 98-369, § 544(a):

Added Code Sec. 2210. **Effective** for those estates of decedents which are required to file returns on a date (including any extensions) after 7-18-84.

CHAPTER 12—GIFT TAX

SUBCHAPTER A.   Determination of tax liability.
SUBCHAPTER B.   Transfers.
SUBCHAPTER C.   Deductions.

Subchapter A—Determination of Tax Liability

Sec. 2501.   Imposition of tax.
Sec. 2502.   Rate of tax.
Sec. 2503.   Taxable gifts.
Sec. 2504.   Taxable gifts for preceding calendar periods.
Sec. 2505.   Unified credit against gift tax.

[Sec. 2501]

SEC. 2501. IMPOSITION OF TAX.

[Sec. 2501(a)]

(a) TAXABLE TRANSFERS.—

(1) GENERAL RULE.—A tax, computed as provided in section 2502, is hereby imposed for each calendar year on the transfer of property by gift during such calendar year by any individual, resident or nonresident.

(2) TRANSFERS OF INTANGIBLE PROPERTY.—Except as provided in paragraph (3), paragraph (1) shall not apply to the transfer of intangible property by a nonresident not a citizen of the United States.

(3) EXCEPTION.—

(A) CERTAIN INDIVIDUALS.—Paragraph (2) shall not apply in the case of a donor to whom section 877(b) applies for the taxable year which includes the date of the transfer.

(B) CREDIT FOR FOREIGN GIFT TAXES.—The tax imposed by this section solely by reason of this paragraph shall be credited with the amount of any gift tax actually paid to any foreign country in respect of any gift which is taxable under this section solely by reason of this paragraph.

(4) TRANSFERS TO POLITICAL ORGANIZATIONS.—Paragraph (1) shall not apply to the transfer of money or other property to a political organization (within the meaning of section 527(e)(1)) for the use of such organization.

(5) TRANSFERS OF CERTAIN STOCK.—

(A) IN GENERAL.—In the case of a transfer of stock in a foreign corporation described in subparagraph (B) by a donor to whom section 877(b) applies for the taxable year which includes the date of the transfer—

(i) section 2511(a) shall be applied without regard to whether such stock is situated within the United States, and

(ii) the value of such stock for purposes of this chapter shall be its U.S.-asset value determined under subparagraph (C).

(B) FOREIGN CORPORATION DESCRIBED.—A foreign corporation is described in this subparagraph with respect to a donor if—

(i) the donor owned (within the meaning of section 958(a)) at the time of such transfer 10 percent or more of the total combined voting power of all classes of stock entitled to vote of the foreign corporation, and

(ii) such donor owned (within the meaning of section 958(a)), or is considered to have owned (by applying the ownership rules of section 958(b)), at the time of such transfer, more than 50 percent of—

(I) the total combined voting power of all classes of stock entitled to vote of such corporation, or

(II) the total value of the stock of such corporation.

(C) U.S.-ASSET VALUE.—For purposes of subparagraph (A), the U.S.-asset value of stock shall be the amount which bears the same ratio to the fair market value of such stock at the time of transfer as—

(i) the fair market value (at such time) of the assets owned by such foreign corporation and situated in the United States, bears to

(ii) the total fair market value (at such time) of all assets owned by such foreign corporation.

(6) TRANSFERS TO CERTAIN EXEMPT ORGANIZATIONS.—Paragraph (1) shall not apply to the transfer of money or other property to an organization described in paragraph (4), (5), or (6) of section 501(c) and exempt from tax under section 501(a), for the use of such organization.

Amendments

• **2015, Protecting Americans from Tax Hikes Act of 2015 (P.L. 114-113)**

P.L. 114-113, § 408(a), Div. Q:

Amended Code Sec. 2501(a) by adding at the end a new paragraph (6). **Effective** for gifts made after 12-18-2015. For a special rule, see Act Sec. 408(c), below.

P.L. 114-113, § 408(c), Div. Q, provides:

(c) NO INFERENCE.—Nothing in the amendment made by subsection (a) shall be construed to create any inference with respect to whether any transfer of property (whether made before, on, or after the date of the enactment of this Act) to an organization described in paragraph (4), (5), or (6) of section 501(c) of the Internal Revenue Code of 1986 is a transfer of property by gift for purposes of chapter 12 of such Code.

• **2004, American Jobs Creation Act of 2004 (P.L. 108-357)**

P.L. 108-357, § 804(d)(1):

Amended Code Sec. 2501(a) by striking paragraph (4), by redesignating paragraph (5) as paragraph (4), and by striking paragraph (3) and inserting a new paragraph (3). **Effective** for individuals who expatriate after 6-3-2004. Prior to being stricken, Code Sec. 2501(a)(3)-(4) read as follows:

(3) EXCEPTION.—

(A) CERTAIN INDIVIDUALS.—Paragraph (2) shall not apply in the case of a donor who, within the 10-year period ending with the date of transfer, lost United States citizenship, unless such loss did not have for 1 of its principal purposes the avoidance of taxes under this subtitle or subtitle A.

GIFT TAX—LIABILITY

(B) CERTAIN INDIVIDUALS TREATED AS HAVING TAX AVOIDANCE PURPOSE.—For purposes of subparagraph (A), an individual shall be treated as having a principal purpose to avoid such taxes if such individual is so treated under section 877(a)(2).

(C) EXCEPTION FOR CERTAIN INDIVIDUALS.—Subparagraph (B) shall not apply to a donor meeting the requirements of section 877(c)(1).

(D) CREDIT FOR FOREIGN GIFT TAXES.—The tax imposed by this section solely by reason of this paragraph shall be credited with the amount of any gift tax actually paid to any foreign country in respect of any gift which is taxable under this section solely by reason of this paragraph.

(E) CROSS REFERENCE.—For comparable treatment of long-term lawful permanent residents who ceased to be taxed as residents, see section 877(e).

(4) BURDEN OF PROOF.—If the Secretary establishes that it is reasonable to believe that an individual's loss of United States citizenship would, but for paragraph (3), result in a substantial reduction for the calendar year in the taxes on the transfer of property by gift, the burden of proving that such loss of citizenship did not have for one of its principal purposes the avoidance of taxes under this subtitle or subtitle A shall be on such individual.

P.L. 108-357, §804(d)(2):

Amended Code Sec. 2501(a) by adding at the end a new paragraph (5). **Effective** for individuals who expatriate after 6-3-2004.

• **1997, Taxpayer Relief Act of 1997 (P.L. 105-34)**

P.L. 105-34, §1602(g)(5):

Amended Code Sec. 2501(a)(3)(C) by striking "decedent" and inserting "donor". **Effective** as if included in the provision of P.L. 104-191 to which it relates [effective, generally, for individuals losing U.S. citizenship on or after 2-6-95, and long-term U.S. residents who end U.S. residency or begin foreign residency on or after 2-6-95.—CCH].

• **1996, Health Insurance Portability and Accountability Act of 1996 (P.L. 104-191)**

P.L. 104-191, §511(e)(2)(A):

Amended Code Sec. 2501(a)(3). For the **effective** date, see Act Sec. 511(g), below. Prior to amendment, Code Sec. 2501(a)(3) read as follows:

(3) EXCEPTIONS.—Paragraph (2) shall not apply in the case of a donor who at any time after March 8, 1965, and within the 10-year period ending with the date of transfer lost United States citizenship unless—

(A) such donor's loss of United States citizenship resulted from the application of section 301(b), 350, or 355 of the Immigration and Nationality Act, as amended (8 U. S. C. 1401(b), 1482, or 1487), or

(B) such loss did not have for one of its principal purposes the avoidance of taxes under this subtitle or subtitle A.

P.L. 104-191, §511(f)(2)(B):

Amended Code Sec. 2501(a)(3) (as amended by Act Sec. 511(e)) by adding at the end a new subparagraph (E). For the **effective** date, see Act Sec. 511(g), below.

P.L. 104-191, §511(g), provides:

(g) EFFECTIVE DATE.—

(1) IN GENERAL.—The amendments made by this section shall apply to—

(A) individuals losing United States citizenship (within the meaning of section 877 of the Internal Revenue Code of 1986) on or after February 6, 1995, and

(B) long-term residents of the United States with respect to whom an event described in subparagraph (A) or (B) of section 877(e)(1) of such Code occurs on or after February 6, 1995.

(2) RULING REQUESTS.—In no event shall the 1-year period referred to in section 877(c)(1)(B) of such Code, as amended by this section, expire before the date which is 90 days after the date of the enactment of this Act.

(3) SPECIAL RULE.—

(A) IN GENERAL.—In the case of an individual who performed an act of expatriation specified in paragraph (1), (2), (3), or (4) of section 349(a) of the Immigration and Nationality Act (8 U.S.C. 1481(a)(1)-(4)) before February 6, 1995, but who did not, on or before such date, furnish to the United States Department of State a signed statement of voluntary relinquishment of United States nationality confirming the performance of such act, the amendments made by this section and section 512 shall apply to such individual except that the 10-year period described in section 877(a) of such Code shall not expire before the end of the 10-year period beginning on the date such statement is so furnished.

(B) EXCEPTION.—Subparagraph (A) shall not apply if the individual establishes to the satisfaction of the Secretary of the Treasury that such loss of United States citizenship occurred before February 6, 1994.

• **1981, Economic Recovery Tax Act of 1981 (P.L. 97-34)**

P.L. 97-34, §442(a)(1):

Amended Code Sec. 2501(a)(1) and (4) by striking out "calendar quarter" and inserting "calendar year". **Effective** with respect to gifts made after 12-31-81.

• **1976, Tax Reform Act of 1976 (P.L. 94-455)**

P.L. 94-455, §1902(a)(10):

Amended Code Sec. 2501(a)(1). **Effective** for estates of decedents dying after 10-4-76. Prior to amendment, Code Sec. 2501(a)(1) read as follows:

(1) GENERAL RULE.—For the first calendar quarter of the calendar year 1971 and each calendar quarter thereafter a tax, computed as provided in section 2502, is hereby imposed on the transfer of property by gift during such calendar quarter by any individual, resident or nonresident.

P.L. 94-455, §1906(b)(13)(A):

Amended 1954 Code by substituting "Secretary" for "Secretary or his delegate" each place it appeared. **Effective** 2-1-77.

• **1975 (P.L. 93-625)**

P.L. 93-625, §14(a):

Amended Code Sec. 2501(a) by adding paragraph (5). **Effective** with respect to transfers made after 5-7-74.

• **1970, Excise, Estate, and Gift Tax Adjustment Act of 1970 (P.L. 91-614)**

P.L. 91-614, §102(a)(1), (2):

Amended paragraph (1) of Code Sec. 2501(a) by substituting "the first calendar quarter of the calendar year 1971 and each calendar quarter thereafter" for "the calendar year 1955 and each calendar year thereafter" and by substituting "during such calendar quarter" for "during such calendar year." Also amended paragraph (4) by substituting "calendar quarter" for "calendar year.". **Effective** for gifts made after 12-31-70.

• **1966, Foreign Investors Tax Act of 1966 (P.L. 89-809)**

P.L. 89-809, §109(a):

Amended Code Sec. 2501(a). **Effective** for the calendar year 1967 and all calendar years thereafter. Prior to amendment, Code Sec. 2501(a) read as follows:

(a) GENERAL RULE.—For the calendar year 1955 and each calendar year thereafter a tax, computed as provided in section 2502, is hereby imposed on the transfer of property by gift during such calendar year by any individual, resident or nonresident, except transfers of intangible property by a nonresident not a citizen of the United States who was not engaged in business in the United States during such calendar year."

• **1960 (P.L. 86-779)**

P.L. 86-779, §4(d)(2):

Amended Code Sec. 2501(a) by striking out "nonresident who is not a citizen of the United States and" and by substituting "nonresident not a citizen of the United States". **Effective** for gifts made after 9-14-60.

[Sec. 2501(b)]

(b) CERTAIN RESIDENTS OF POSSESSIONS CONSIDERED CITIZENS OF THE UNITED STATES.—A donor who is a citizen of the United States and a resident of a possession thereof shall, for purposes of the tax imposed by this chapter, be considered a "citizen" of the United States within the meaning of that term wherever used in this title unless he acquired his United States citizenship solely by reason of (1) his being a citizen of such possession of the United States, or (2) his birth or residence within such possession of the United States.

Amendments

• **1958, Technical Amendments Act of 1958 (P.L. 85-866)**

P.L. 85-866, §102(b), (d):

Redesignated former Code Sec. 2501(b) as 2501(c) (now (d)) and added new subsection (b). **Effective** for gifts made after 9-2-58.

[Sec. 2501(c)]

(c) CERTAIN RESIDENTS OF POSSESSIONS CONSIDERED NONRESIDENTS NOT CITIZENS OF THE UNITED STATES.—A donor who is a citizen of the United States and a resident of a possession thereof shall, for purposes of the tax imposed by this chapter, be considered a "nonresident not a citizen of the United States" within the meaning of that term wherever used in this title, but only if such donor acquired his United States citizenship solely by reason of (1) his being a citizen of such possession of the United States, or (2) his birth or residence within such possession of the United States.

Amendments

• **1960 (P.L. 86-779)**

P.L. 86-779, §4(d)(1):

Redesignated former Code Sec. 2501(c) as 2501(d) and added a new subsection (c). **Effective** for gifts made after 9-14-60.

GIFT TAX—LIABILITY

[Sec. 2501(d)]

(d) CROSS REFERENCES.—
(1) For increase in basis of property acquired by gift for gift tax paid, see section 1015(d).
(2) For exclusion of transfers of property outside the United States by a nonresident who is not a citizen of the United States, see section 2511(a).

Amendments

• **1990, Omnibus Budget Reconciliation Act of 1990 (P.L. 101-508)**

P.L. 101-508, §11601(b)(2):

Amended Code Sec. 2051(d) by striking paragraph (3). **Effective** in the case of property transferred after 12-17-87. Prior to being stricken, paragraph (3) read as follows:

(3) For treatment of certain transfers related to estate tax valuation freezes as gifts to which this chapter applies, see section 2036(c)(4).

• **1988, Technical and Miscellaneous Revenue Act of 1988 (P.L. 100-647)**

P.L. 100-647, §3031(a)(2):

Amended Code Sec. 2501(d) by adding at the end thereof a new paragraph (3). **Effective** in cases where the Code Sec. 2036(c)(1)(B) transfer is on or after 6-21-88.

• **1960 (P.L. 86-779)**

P.L. 86-779, §4(d)(1):

Redesignated former Code Sec. 2501(c) as 2501(d). **Effective** for gifts made after 9-14-60.

• **1958, Technical Amendments Act of 1958 (P.L. 85-866)**

P.L. 85-866, §43(b):

Amended former Code Sec. 2501(b). **Effective** 1-1-54. Prior to amendment, Code Sec. 2501(b) read as follows:

"(b) CROSS REFERENCE.—
"For exclusion of transfers of property outside the United States by a nonresident who is not a citizen of the United States, see section 2511(a)."

P.L. 85-866, §102(b):

Redesignated subsection (b) as subsection (c). **Effective** 9-3-58.

[Sec. 2502]

SEC. 2502. RATE OF TAX.

[Sec. 2502(a)]

(a) COMPUTATION OF TAX.—The tax imposed by section 2501 for each calendar year shall be an amount equal to the excess of—
(1) a tentative tax, computed under section 2001(c), on the aggregate sum of the taxable gifts for such calendar year and for each of the preceding calendar periods, over
(2) a tentative tax, computed under such section, on the aggregate sum of the taxable gifts for each of the preceding calendar periods.

Amendments

• **2010, Tax Relief, Unemployment Insurance Reauthorization, and Job Creation Act of 2010 (P.L. 111-312)**

P.L. 111-312, §302(b)(2):

Amended Code Sec. 2502(a) to read as such subsection would read if section 511(d) of the Economic Growth and Tax Relief Reconciliation Act of 2001 (P.L. 107-16) had never been enacted. **Effective** on and after 1-1-2011. Prior to amendment by P.L. 111-312, Code Sec. 2502(a) read as follows:

(a) COMPUTATION OF TAX.—
(1) IN GENERAL.—The tax imposed by section 2501 for each calendar year shall be an amount equal to the excess of—
(A) a tentative tax, computed under paragraph (2), on the aggregate sum of the taxable gifts for such calendar year and for each of the preceding calendar periods, over
(B) a tentative tax, computed under paragraph (2), on the aggregate sum of the taxable gifts for each of the preceding calendar periods.
(2) RATE SCHEDULE.—

If the amount with respect to which the tentative tax to be computed is:	The tentative tax is:
Not over $10,000	18% of such amount.
Over $10,000 but not over $20,000	$1,800, plus 20% of the excess over $10,000.
Over $20,000 but not over $40,000	$3,800, plus 22% of the excess over $20,000.
Over $40,000 but not over $60,000	$8,200, plus 24% of the excess over $40,000.
Over $60,000 but not over $80,000	$13,000, plus 26% of the excess over $60,000.
Over $80,000 but not over $100,000	$18,200, plus 28% of the excess over $80,000.
Over $100,000 but not over $150,000	$23,800, plus 30% of the excess over $100,000.
Over $150,000 but not over $250,000	$38,800, plus 32% of the excess over $150,000.
Over $250,000 but not over $500,000	$70,800, plus 34% of the excess over $250,000.
Over $500,000	$155,800, plus 35% of the excess over $500,000.

P.L. 111-312, §304, provides:

SEC. 304. APPLICATION OF EGTRRA SUNSET TO THIS TITLE.

Section 901 of the Economic Growth and Tax Relief Reconciliation Act of 2001 shall apply to the amendments made by this title.

• **2001, Economic Growth and Tax Relief Reconciliation Act of 2001 (P.L. 107-16)**

P.L. 107-16, §511(d):

Amended Code Sec. 2502(a). **Effective** for gifts made after 12-31-2009. Prior to amendment, Code Sec. 2502(a) read as follows:

(a) COMPUTATION OF TAX.—The tax imposed by section 2501 for each calendar year shall be an amount equal to the excess of—

(1) a tentative tax, computed under section 2001(c), on the aggregate sum of the taxable gifts for such calendar year and for each of the preceding calendar periods, over

(2) a tentative tax, computed under such section, on the aggregate sum of the taxable gifts for each of the preceding calendar periods.

P.L. 107-16, §901(a)-(b), as amended by P.L. 111-312, §101(a)(1), provides:

SEC. 901. SUNSET OF PROVISIONS OF ACT.

(a) IN GENERAL.—All provisions of, and amendments made by, this Act shall not apply—

(1) to taxable, plan, or limitation years beginning after December 31, 2012, or

(2) in the case of title V, to estates of decedents dying, gifts made, or generation skipping transfers, after December 31, 2012.

(b) APPLICATION OF CERTAIN LAWS.—The Internal Revenue Code of 1986 and the Employee Retirement Income Security Act of 1974 shall be applied and administered to years, estates, gifts, and transfers described in subsection (a) as if the provisions and amendments described in subsection (a) had never been enacted.

• **1987, Revenue Act of 1987 (P.L. 100-203)**

P.L. 100-203, §10401(b)(2)(B)(i)-(ii):

Amended Code Sec. 2502(a) by striking out "in accordance with the rate schedule set forth in section 2001(c)" in paragraph (1) and inserting in lieu thereof "under section 2001(c)", and by striking out "in accordance with such rate schedule" in paragraph (2) and inserting in lieu thereof "under such section". **Effective** in the case of decedents dying, and gifts made, after 12-31-87.

• **1981, Economic Recovery Tax Act of 1981 (P.L. 97-34)**

P.L. 97-34, §442(a)(2):

Amended Code Sec. 2502(a). **Effective** with respect to gifts made after 12-31-81. Prior to amendment, Code Sec. 2502(a) read as follows:

(a) COMPUTATION OF TAX.—The tax imposed by section 2501 for each calendar quarter shall be an amount equal to the excess of—

(1) a tentative tax, computed in accordance with the rate schedule set forth in Section 2001(c), on the aggregate sum of the taxable gifts for such calendar quarter and for each of the preceding calendar years and calendar quarters, over

(2) a tentative tax, computed in accordance with such rate schedule, on the aggregate sum of the taxable gifts for each of the preceding calendar years and calendar quarters.

• **1976, Tax Reform Act of 1976 (P.L. 94-455)**

P.L. 94-455, §2001(b)(1), (d)(2):

Amended Code Sec. 2502(a). **Effective** for gifts made after 12-31-76. Prior to amendment, Code Sec. 2502(a) read as follows:

(a) COMPUTATION OF TAX.—The tax imposed by section 2501 for each calendar quarter shall be an amount equal to the excess of—

(1) a tax, computed in accordance with the rate schedule set forth in this subsection, on the aggregate sum of the taxable gifts for such calendar quarter and for each of the preceding calendar years and calendar quarters, over

(2) a tax, computed in accordance with such rate schedule, on the aggregate sum of the taxable gifts for each of the preceding calendar years and calendar quarters.

RATE SCHEDULE

If the taxable gifts are:	The tax shall be:
Not over $5,000	2¼% of the taxable gifts.

GIFT TAX—LIABILITY

Over $5,000 but not over $10,000	$112.50, plus 5¼% of excess over $5,000.	Over $3,500,000 but not over $4,000,000	$1,157,400, plus 44¼% of excess over $3,500,000.
Over $10,000 but not over $20,000	$375, plus 8¼% of excess over $10,000.	Over $4,000,000 but not over $5,000,000	$1,378,650, plus 47¼% of excess over $4,000,000.
Over $20,000 but not over $30,000	$1,200, plus 10½% of excess over $20,000.	Over $5,000,000 but not over $6,000,000	$1,851,150, plus 50¼% of excess over $5,000,000.
Over $30,000 but not over $40,000	$2,250, plus 13½% of excess over $30,000.	Over $6,000,000 but not over $7,000,000	$2,353,650, plus 52½% of excess over $6,000,000.
Over $40,000 but not over $50,000	$3,600, plus 16½% of excess over $40,000.	Over $7,000,000 but not over $8,000,000	$2,878,650, plus 54¾% of excess over $7,000,000.
Over $50,000 but not over $60,000	$5,250, plus 18¾% of excess over $50,000.	Over $8,000,000 but not over $10,000,000	$3,426,150, plus 57% of excess over $8,000,000.
Over $60,000 but not over $100,000	$7,125, plus 21% of excess over $60,000.	Over $10,000,000	$4,566,150, plus 57¾% of excess over $10,000,000.
Over $100,000 but not over $250,000	$15,525, plus 22½% of excess over $100,000.		
Over $250,000 but not over $500,000	$49,275, plus 24% of excess over $250,000.		
Over $500,000 but not over $750,000	$109,275, plus 26¼% of excess over $500,000.		
Over $750,000 but not over $1,000,000	$174,900, plus 27¾% of excess over $750,000.		
Over $1,000,000 but not over $1,250,000	$244,275, plus 29¼% of excess over $1,000,000.		
Over $1,250,000 but not over $1,500,000	$317,400, plus 31½% of excess over $1,250,000.		
Over $1,500,000 but not over $2,000,000	$396,150, plus 33¾% of excess over $1,500,000.		
Over $2,000,000 but not over $2,500,000	$564,900, plus 36¾% of excess over $2,000,000.		
Over $2,500,000 but not over $3,000,000	$748,650, plus 39¾% of excess over $2,500,000.		
Over $3,000,000 but not over $3,500,000	$947,400, plus 42% of excess over $3,000,000.		

• **1970, Excise, Estate, and Gift Tax Adjustment Act of 1970 (P.L. 91-614)**

P.L. 91-614, §102(a)(2)(A):

Amended the matter preceding the tax rate schedule in Code Sec. 2502. **Effective** for gifts made after 12-31-70. Prior to amendment, this matter read as follows:

"(a) Computation of Tax.—The tax imposed by section 2501 for each calendar year shall be an amount equal to the excess of—

"(1) a tax, computed in accordance with the rate schedule set forth in this subsection, on the aggregate sum of the taxable gifts for such calendar year and for each of the preceding calendar years, over

"(2) a tax, computed in accordance with such rate schedule, on the aggregate sum of the taxable gifts for each of the preceding calendar years."

[Sec. 2502(b)]

(b) PRECEDING CALENDAR PERIOD.—Whenever used in this title in connection with the gift tax imposed by this chapter, the term "preceding calendar period" means—

(1) calendar years 1932 and 1970 and all calendar years intervening between calendar year 1932 and calendar year 1970,

(2) the first calendar quarter of calendar year 1971 and all calendar quarters intervening between such calendar quarter and the first calendar quarter of calendar year 1982, and

(3) all calendar years after 1981 and before the calendar year for which the tax is being computed.

For purposes of paragraph (1), the term "calendar year 1932" includes only that portion of such year after June 6, 1932.

Amendments

• **1981, Economic Recovery Tax Act of 1981 (P.L. 97-34)**

P.L. 97-34, §442(a)(2):

Amended Code Sec. 2502(b). **Effective** with respect to gifts made after 12-31-81. Prior to amendment Code Sec. 2502(b) read as follows:

(b) CALENDAR QUARTER.—Wherever used in this title in connection with the gift tax imposed by this chapter, the term "calendar quarter" includes only the first calendar quarter of the calendar year 1971 and succeeding calendar quarters.

• **1970, Excise, Estate, and Gift Tax Adjustment Act of 1970 (P.L. 91-614)**

P.L. 91-614, §102(a)(2)(B):

Amended Code Sec. 2502(b). **Effective** for gifts made after 12-31-70. Prior to amendment, Code Sec. 2502(b) read as follows:

"(b) Calendar Year.—The term `calendar year' includes only the calendar year 1932 and succeeding calendar years, and, in the case of the calendar year 1932, includes only the portion of such year after June 6, 1932."

[Sec. 2502(c)]

(c) TAX TO BE PAID BY DONOR.—The tax imposed by section 2501 shall be paid by the donor.

Amendments

• **1981, Economic Recovery Tax Act of 1981 (P.L. 97-34)**

P.L. 97-34, §442(a)(2):

Amended Code Sec. 2502(c). **Effective** with respect to gifts made after 12-31-81. Prior to amendment, Code Sec. 2502(c) read as follows:

(c) PRECEDING CALENDAR YEARS AND QUARTERS.—Wherever used in this title in connection with the gift tax imposed by this chapter—

(1) The term "preceding calendar years" means calendar years 1932 and 1970 and all calendar years intervening between calendar year 1932 and calendar year 1970. The term "calendar year 1932" includes only the portion of such year after June 6, 1932.

(2) The term "preceding calendar quarters" means the first calendar quarter of calendar year 1971 and all calendar quarters intervening between such calendar quarter and the calendar quarter for which the tax is being computed.

• **1970, Excise, Estate, and Gift Tax Adjustment Act of 1970 (P.L. 91-614)**

P.L. 91-614, §102(a)(2)(B):

Amended Code Sec. 2502(c). **Effective** for gifts made after 12-31-70. Prior to amendment, Code Sec. 2502(c) read as follows:

"(c) Preceding Calendar Years.—The term `preceding calendar years' means the calendar year 1932 and all calendar years intervening between the calendar year 1932 and the calendar year for which the tax is being computed."

[Sec. 2502(d)—Repealed]

Amendments

• **1981, Economic Recovery Tax Act of 1981 (P.L. 97-34)**

P.L. 97-34, §442(a)(2):

Amended Code Sec. 2502. **Effective** with respect to gifts made after 12-31-81. Code Sec. 2502, as amended, does not include Code Sec. 2502(d). Prior to repeal, Code Sec. 2502(d) read as follows:

(d) TAX TO BE PAID BY DONOR.—The tax imposed by section 2501 shall be paid by the donor.

[Sec. 2503]

SEC. 2503. TAXABLE GIFTS.

[Sec. 2503(a)]

(a) GENERAL DEFINITION.—The term "taxable gifts" means the total amount of gifts made during the calendar year, less the deductions provided in subchapter C (section 2522 and following).

GIFT TAX—LIABILITY

Amendments

• **1981, Economic Recovery Tax Act of 1981 (P.L. 97-34)**

P.L. 97-34, §442(a)(3)(A):

Amended Code Sec. 2503(a). **Effective** with respect to gifts made after 12-31-81. Prior to amendment, Code Sec. 2503(a) read as follows:

(a) GENERAL DEFINITION.—The term "taxable gifts" means, in the case of gifts made after December 31, 1970, the total amount of gifts made during the calendar quarter, less the deductions provided in subchapter C (sec. 2521 and following). In the case of gifts made before January 1, 1971, such term means the total amount of gifts made during the calendar year, less the deductions provided in subchapter C.

• **1970, Excise, Estate, and Gift Tax Adjustment Act of 1970 (P.L. 91-614)**

P.L. 91-614, §102(a)(3)(A):

Amended Code Sec. 2503(a). **Effective** for gifts made after 12-31-70. Prior to amendment, the section read as follows:

"(a) General Definition.—The term 'taxable gifts' means the total amount of gifts made during the calendar year, less the deductions provided in subchapter C (sec. 2521 and following)."

[Sec. 2503(b)]

(b) EXCLUSIONS FROM GIFTS.—

(1) IN GENERAL.—In the case of gifts (other than gifts of future interests in property) made to any person by the donor during the calendar year, the first $10,000 of such gifts to such person shall not, for purposes of subsection (a), be included in the total amount of gifts made during such year. Where there has been a transfer to any person of a present interest in property, the possibility that such interest may be diminished by the exercise of a power shall be disregarded in applying this subsection, if no part of such interest will at any time pass to any other person.

(2) INFLATION ADJUSTMENT.—In the case of gifts made in a calendar year after 1998, the $10,000 amount contained in paragraph (1) shall be increased by an amount equal to—

(A) $10,000, multiplied by

(B) the cost-of-living adjustment determined under section 1(f)(3) for such calendar year by substituting "calendar year 1997" for "calendar year 2016" in subparagraph (A)(ii) thereof.

If any amount as adjusted under the preceding sentence is not a multiple of $1,000, such amount shall be rounded to the next lowest multiple of $1,000.

Amendments

• **2017, Tax Cuts and Jobs Act (P.L. 115-97)**

P.L. 115-97, §11002(d)(1)(EE):

Amended Code Sec. 2503(b)(2)(B) by striking "for 'calendar year 1992' in subparagraph (B)" and inserting "for 'calendar year 2016' in subparagraph (A)(ii)". **Effective** for tax years beginning after 12-31-2017.

• **1997, Taxpayer Relief Act of 1997 (P.L. 105-34)**

P.L. 105-34, §501(c)(1)-(3):

Amended Code Sec. 2503(b) by striking the subsection heading and inserting "(b) EXCLUSIONS FROM GIFTS.—(1) IN GENERAL.—", by moving the text 2 ems to the right, and by adding a new paragraph (2). **Effective** for estates of decedents dying, and gifts made, after 12-31-97. Prior to amendment, the heading for Code Sec. 2503(b) read as follows:

(b) EXCLUSIONS FROM GIFTS.—

• **1981, Economic Recovery Tax Act of 1981 (P.L. 97-34)**

P.L. 97-34, §441(a):

Amended Code Sec. 2503(b) by striking out "$3,000" and inserting "$10,000". **Effective**, generally, for transfers made after 12-31-81. There is also a special rule applicable to certain instruments creating powers of appointment before 9-12-81.

P.L. 97-34, §441(c), provides:

(c) EFFECTIVE DATES.—

(1) IN GENERAL.—Except as provided in paragraph (2), the amendments made by this section shall apply to transfers after December 31, 1981.

(2) TRANSITIONAL RULE.—If—

(A) an instrument executed before the date which is 30 days after the date of the enactment of this Act provides for a power of appointment which may be exercised during any period after December 31, 1981,

(B) such power of appointment is expressly defined in terms of, or by reference to, the amount of the gift tax exclusion under section 2503(b) of the Internal Revenue Code of 1954 (or the corresponding provision of prior law),

(C) the instrument described in subparagraph (A) has not been amended on or after the date which is 30 days after the date of the enactment of this Act, and

(D) the State has not enacted a statute applicable to such gift under which such power of appointment is to be construed as being defined in terms of, or by reference to, the amount of the exclusion under such section 2503(b) after its amendment by subsection (a),

then the amendment made by subsection (a) shall not apply to such gift.

P.L. 97-34, §442(a)(3)(B):

Amended the first sentence of Code Sec. 2503(b). **Effective** with respect to gifts made after 12-31-81. Prior to amendment, the sentence read as follows:

In computing taxable gifts for the calendar quarter, in the case of gifts (other than gifts of future interests in property) made to any person by the donor during the calendar year 1971 and subsequent calendar years, $3,000 of such gifts to such person less the aggregate of the amounts of such gifts to such person during all preceding calendar quarters of the calendar year shall not, for purposes of subsection (a), be included in the total amount of gifts made during such quarter.

• **1970, Excise, Estate, and Gift Tax Adjustment Act of 1970 (P.L. 91-614)**

P.L. 91-614, §102(a)(3)(B):

Amended the first sentence of Code Sec. 2503(b). **Effective** for gifts made after 12-31-70. Prior to amendment, the first sentence read as follows:

"In the case of gifts (other than gifts of future interests in property) made to any person by the donor during the calendar year 1955 and subsequent calendar years, the first $3,000 of such gifts to such person shall not, for purposes of subsection (a), be included in the total amount of gifts made during such year."

[Sec. 2503(c)]

(c) TRANSFER FOR THE BENEFIT OF MINOR.—No part of a gift to an individual who has not attained the age of 21 years on the date of such transfer shall be considered a gift of a future interest in property for purposes of subsection (b) if the property and the income therefrom—

(1) may be expended by, or for the benefit of, the donee before his attaining the age of 21 years, and

(2) will to the extent not so expended—

(A) pass to the donee on his attaining the age of 21 years, and

(B) in the event the donee dies before attaining the age of 21 years, be payable to the estate of the donee or as he may appoint under a general power of appointment as defined in section 2514(c).

[Sec. 2503(d)—Repealed]

Amendments

• **1981, Economic Recovery Tax Act of 1981 (P.L. 97-34)**

P.L. 97-34, §311(h)(5):

Repealed Code Sec. 2503(d). **Effective** for transfers after 12-31-81 [effective date changed by P.L. 97-448, §103(c)(11).—CCH]. The transitional rule provides that, for purposes of the 1954 Code, any amount allowed as a deduction under section 220 of the Code (as in effect before its repeal by P.L. 97-34) shall be treated as if it were allowed by Code Sec. 219. Prior to repeal, Code Sec. 2503(d) read as follows:

(d) INDIVIDUAL RETIREMENT ACCOUNTS, ETC., FOR SPOUSE.—For purposes of subsection (b), any payment made by an individual for the benefit of his spouse—

(1) to an individual retirement account described in section 408(a),

(2) for an individual retirement annuity described in section 408(b), or

(3) for a retirement bond described in section 409,

shall not be considered a gift of a future interest in property to the extent that such payment is allowable as a deduction under section 220.

• **1978, Revenue Act of 1978 (P.L. 95-600)**

P.L. 95-600, §702(j)(2):

Added Code Sec. 2503(d). **Effective** for transfers made after 12-31-76.

[Sec. 2503(e)]

(e) EXCLUSION FOR CERTAIN TRANSFERS FOR EDUCATIONAL EXPENSES OR MEDICAL EXPENSES.—

(1) IN GENERAL.—Any qualified transfer shall not be treated as a transfer of property by gift for purposes of this chapter.

(2) QUALIFIED TRANSFER.—For purposes of this subsection, the term "qualified transfer" means any amount paid on behalf of an individual—

GIFT TAX—LIABILITY

(A) as tuition to an educational organization described in section 170(b)(1)(A)(ii) for the education or training of such individual, or

(B) to any person who provides medical care (as defined in section 213(d)) with respect to such individual as payment for such medical care.

Amendments

• **1988, Technical and Miscellaneous Revenue Act of 1988 (P.L. 100-647)**

P.L. 100-647, §1018(u)(52):

Amended Code Sec. 2503(e)(2)(B) by striking out "section 213(e)" and inserting in lieu thereof "section 213(d)". **Effective** as if included in the provision of P.L. 99-514 to which it relates.

• **1981, Economic Recovery Tax Act of 1981 (P.L. 97-34)**

P.L. 97-34, §441(b):

Added Code Sec. 2503(e). **Effective** for transfers made after 12-31-81.

[Sec. 2503(f)]

(f) WAIVER OF CERTAIN PENSION RIGHTS.—If any individual waives, before the death of a particpant, any survivor benefit, or right to such benefit, under section 401(a)(11) or 417, such waiver shall not be treated as a transfer of property by gift for purposes of this chapter.

Amendments

• **1986, Tax Reform Act of 1986 (P.L. 99-514)**

P.L. 99-514, §1898(h)(1)(B):

Amended Code Sec. 2503 by adding at the end thereof new subsection (f). **Effective** as if included in the provision of P.L. 98-397 to which it relates.

[Sec. 2503(g)]

(g) TREATMENT OF CERTAIN LOANS OF ARTWORKS.—

(1) IN GENERAL.—For purposes of this subtitle, any loan of a qualified work of art shall not be treated as a transfer (and the value of such qualified work of art shall be determined as if such loan had not been made) if—

(A) such loan is to an organization described in section 501(c)(3) and exempt from tax under section 501(c) (other than a private foundation), and

(B) the use of such work by such organization is related to the purpose or function constituting the basis for its exemption under section 501.

(2) DEFINITIONS.—For purposes of this section—

(A) QUALIFIED WORK OF ART.—The term "qualified work of art" means any archaelogical, historic, or creative tangible personal property.

(B) PRIVATE FOUNDATION.—The term "private foundation" has the meaning given such term by section 509, except that such term shall not include any private operating foundation (as defined in section 4942(j)(3)).

Amendments

• **1989, Omnibus Budget Reconciliation Act of 1989 (P.L. 101-239)**

P.L. 101-239, §7811(m)(1):

Amended Code Sec. 2503 by redesignating subsection (f), as added by §1018 of P.L. 100-647, as subsection (g). **Effective** as if included in the provision of P.L. 100-647 to which it relates.

• **1988, Technical and Miscellaneous Revenue Act of 1988 (P.L. 100-647)**

P.L. 100-647, §1018(s)(2)(A):

Amended Code Sec. 2503 by adding at the end thereof a new subsection (f)[(g)]. **Effective** for loans after 7-31-69.

[Sec. 2504]

SEC. 2504. TAXABLE GIFTS FOR PRECEDING CALENDAR PERIODS.

[Sec. 2504(a)]

(a) IN GENERAL.—In computing taxable gifts for preceding calendar periods for purposes of computing the tax for any calendar year—

(1) there shall be treated as gifts such transfers as were considered to be gifts under the gift tax laws applicable to the calendar period in which the transfers were made,

(2) there shall be allowed such deductions as were provided for under such laws, and

(3) the specific exemption in the amount (if any) allowable under section 2521 (as in effect before its repeal by the Tax Reform Act of 1976) shall be applied in all computations in respect of preceding calendar periods ending before January 1, 1977, for purposes of computing the tax for any calendar year.

Amendments

• **1981, Economic Recovery Tax Act of 1981 (P.L. 97-34)**

P.L. 97-34, §442(a)(4)(A):

Amended Code Sec. 2504(a). **Effective** with respect to gifts made after 12-31-81. Prior to amendment, Code Sec. 2504(a) read as follows:

(a) IN GENERAL.—In computing taxable gifts for preceding calendar years or calendar quarters for the purpose of computing the tax for any calendar quarter, there shall be treated as gifts such transfers as were considered to be gifts under the gift tax laws applicable to the years or calendar quarters in which the transfers were made and there shall be allowed such deductions as were provided for under such laws; except that the specific exemption in the amount, if any, allowable under section 2521 (as in effect before its repeal by the Tax Reform Act of 1976) shall be applied in all computations in respect of calendar years or calendar quarters ending before January 1, 1977, for purposes of computing the tax for any calendar quarter.

P.L. 97-34, §442(a)(4)(D):

Amended the section heading for Code Sec. 2504 by striking out "PRECEDING YEARS AND QUARTERS" and inserting "PRECEDING CALENDAR PERIODS". **Effective** with respect to gifts made after 12-31-81.

• **1976, Tax Reform Act of 1976 (P.L. 94-455)**

P.L. 94-455, §2001(c)(2)(A), (d)(2):

Substituted "section 2521 (as in effect before its repeal by the Tax Reform Act of 1976) shall be applied in all computations in respect of calendar years or calendar quarters ending before January 1, 1977, for purposes of computing the tax for any calendar quarter" for "section 2521 shall be applied in all computations in respect of previous calendar years or calendar quarters for the purpose of computing the tax for any calendar year or calendar quarter" in Code Sec. 2504(a). **Effective** for gifts made after 12-31-76.

[Sec. 2504(b)]

(b) EXCLUSIONS FROM GIFTS FOR PRECEDING CALENDAR PERIODS.—In the case of gifts made to any person by the donor during preceding calendar periods, the amount excluded, if any, by the provisions of gift tax laws applicable to the periods in which the gifts were made shall not, for purposes of subsection (a), be included in the total amount of the gifts made during such preceding calendar periods.

Amendments

• **1981, Economic Recovery Tax Act of 1981 (P.L. 97-34)**

P.L. 97-34, §442(a)(4)(B):

Amended Code Sec. 2504(b) by striking out "preceding calendar years and calendar quarters" and inserting "preceding calendar periods", by striking out "the years and calendar quarters" and inserting "such preceding calendar periods", and by striking out "PRECEDING YEARS AND QUARTERS" in the subsection heading and inserting "PRECEDING CALENDAR PERIODS". **E**ffective with respect to gifts made after 12-31-81.

[Sec. 2504(c)]

(c) VALUATION OF GIFTS.—If the time has expired under section 6501 within which a tax may be assessed under this chapter 12 (or under corresponding provisions of prior laws) on—

Sec. 2503(e)(2)(A)

GIFT TAX—LIABILITY

(1) the transfer of property by gift made during a preceding calendar period (as defined in section 2502(b)); or

(2) an increase in taxable gifts required under section 2701(d),

the value thereof shall, for purposes of computing the tax under this chapter, be the value as finally determined (within the meaning of section 2001(f)(2)) for purposes of this chapter.

Amendments

• **1998, IRS Restructuring and Reform Act of 1998 (P.L. 105-206)**

P.L. 105-206, §6007(e)(2)(B)[(C)]:

Amended Code Sec. 2504(c). **Effective** as if included in the provision of P.L. 105-34 to which it relates [**effective** for gifts made after 8-5-97.—CCH]. Prior to amendment, Code Sec. 2504(c) read as follows:

(c) VALUATION OF CERTAIN GIFTS FOR PRECEDING CALENDAR PERIODS.—If the time has expired within which a tax may be assessed under this chapter or under corresponding provisions of prior laws on the transfer of property by gift made during a preceding calendar period, as defined in section 2502(b), the value of such gift made in such preceding calendar period shall, for purposes of computing the tax under this chapter for any calendar year, be the value of such gift which was used in computing the tax for the last preceding calendar period for which a tax under this chapter or under corresponding provisions of prior laws was assessed or paid.

• **1997, Taxpayer Relief Act of 1997 (P.L. 105-34)**

P.L. 105-34, §506(d):

Amended Code Sec. 2504(c) by striking ", and if a tax under this chapter or under corresponding provisions of prior laws has been assessed or paid for such preceding calendar period" after "section 2502(b)". **Effective** for gifts made after 8-5-97 [effective date changed by P.L. 105-206, §6007(e)(1)].

• **1981, Economic Recovery Tax Act of 1981 (P.L. 97-34)**

P.L. 97-34, §442(a)(4)(C):

Amended Code Sec. 2504(c) by striking out "preceding calendar year or calendar quarter" each place it appears and inserting "preceding calendar period", by striking out "under this chapter for any calendar quarter" and inserting "under this chapter for any calendar year", by striking out "section 2502(c)" and inserting "section 2502(b)", and by striking out "PRECEDING CALENDAR YEARS AND QUARTERS" in the subsection heading and inserting "PRECEDING CALENDAR PERIODS". **Effective** with respect to gifts made after 12-31-81.

[Sec. 2504(d)]

(d) NET GIFTS.—The term "net gifts" as used in corresponding provisions of prior laws shall be read as "taxable gifts" for purposes of this chapter.

Amendments

• **1970, Excise, Estate, and Gift Tax Adjustment Act of 1970 (P.L. 91-614)**

P.L. 91-614, §102(a)(4)(A):

Amended Code Sec. 2504. **Effective** 1-1-71. Prior to amendment, the section read as follows:

Sec. 2504. Taxable Gifts for Preceding Years.

(a) In General.—In computing taxable gifts for the calendar year 1954 and preceding calendar years for the purpose of computing the tax for the calendar year 1955 or any calendar year thereafter, there shall be treated as gifts such transfers as were considered to be gifts under the gift tax laws applicable to the years in which the transfers were made and there shall be allowed such deductions as were provided for under such laws, except that specific exemption in the amount, if any, allowable under section 2521 shall be applied in all computations in respect of the calendar year 1954 and previous calendar years for the purpose of computing the tax for the calendar year 1955 or any calendar year thereafter.

(b) Exclusions From Gifts for Preceding Years.—In the case of gifts made to any person by the donor during the calendar year 1954 and preceding calendar years, the amount excluded, if any, by the provisions of gift tax laws applicable to the years in which the gifts were made shall not, for purposes of subsection (a), be included in the total amount of the gifts made during such year.

(c) Valuation of Certain Gifts for Preceding Calendar Years.—If the time has expired within which a tax may be assessed under this chapter or under corresponding provisions of prior laws, on the transfer of property by gift made during a preceding calendar year, as defined in section 2502(c), and if a tax under this chapter or under corresponding provisions of prior laws has been assessed or paid for such preceding calendar year, the value of such gift made in such preceding calendar year shall, for purposes of computing the tax under this chapter for the calendar year 1955 and subsequent calendar years, be the value of such gift which was used in computing the tax for the last preceding calendar year, for which a tax under this chapter or under corresponding provisions of prior laws was assessed or paid.

(d) Net Gifts.—For years before the calendar year 1955, the term "net gifts" as used in corresponding provisions of prior laws shall be read as "taxable gifts" for purposes of this chapter.

[Sec. 2505]

SEC. 2505. UNIFIED CREDIT AGAINST GIFT TAX.

[Sec. 2505(a)]

(a) GENERAL RULE.—In the case of a citizen or resident of the United States, there shall be allowed as a credit against the tax imposed by section 2501 for each calendar year an amount equal to—

(1) the applicable credit amount in effect under section 2010(c) which would apply if the donor died as of the end of the calendar year, reduced by

(2) the sum of the amounts allowable as a credit to the individual under this section for all preceding calendar periods.

For purposes of applying paragraph (2) for any calendar year, the rates of tax in effect under section 2502(a)(2) for such calendar year shall, in lieu of the rates of tax in effect for preceding calendar periods, be used in determining the amounts allowable as a credit under this section for all preceding calendar periods.

Amendments

• **2010, Tax Relief, Unemployment Insurance Reauthorization, and Job Creation Act of 2010 (P.L. 111-312)**

P.L. 111-312, §301(b):

Amended Code Sec. 2505(a)(1) to read as such paragraph would read if section 521(b)(2) of the Economic Growth and Tax Relief Reconciliation Act of 2001 (P.L. 107-16) had never been enacted. **Effective** on and after 1-1-2011. Prior to amendment by P.L. 111-312, Code Sec. 2505(a)(1) read as follows:

(1) the amount of the tentative tax which would be determined under the rate schedule set forth in section 2502(a)(2) if the amount with respect to which such tentative tax is to be computed were $1,000,000, reduced by

P.L. 111-312, §302(b)(1)(A):

Amended Code Sec. 2505(a)(1), after the application of Act Sec. 301(b), by striking "(determined as if the applicable exclusion amount were $1,000,000)" after "such calendar year". **Effective** for gifts made after 12-31-2010.

P.L. 111-312, §302(d)(2):

Amended Code Sec. 2505(a) by adding at the end a new flush sentence. **Effective** for estates of decedents dying, generation-skipping transfers, and gifts made, after 12-31-2009.

P.L. 111-312, §303(b)(1):

Amended Code Sec. 2505(a)(1), as amended by Act Sec. 302(b)(1). **Effective** for estates of decedents dying and gifts made after 12-31-2010. Prior to amendment, Code Sec. 2505(a)(1) read as follows:

(1) the applicable credit amount in effect under section 2010(c) for such calendar year, reduced by

P.L. 111-312, §304, provides:

SEC. 304. APPLICATION OF EGTRRA SUNSET TO THIS TITLE.

Section 901 of the Economic Growth and Tax Relief Reconciliation Act of 2001 shall apply to the amendments made by this title.

• **2001, Economic Growth and Tax Relief Reconciliation Act of 2001 (P.L. 107-16)**

P.L. 107-16, §521(b)(1):

Amended Code Sec. 2505(a)(1) by inserting "(determined as if the applicable exclusion amount were $1,000,000)" after "calendar year". **Effective** for estates of decedents dying, and gifts made, after 12-31-2001.

P.L. 107-16, §521(b)(2):

Amended Code Sec. 2505(a)(1), as amended by Act Sec. 521(b)(1). **Effective** for gifts made after 12-31-2009. Prior to amendment, Code Sec. 2505(a)(1) read as follows:

(1) the applicable credit amount in effect under section 2010(c) for such calendar year (determined as if the applicable exclusion amount were $1,000,000), reduced by

P.L. 107-16, §901(a)-(b), as amended by P.L. 111-312, §101(a)(1), provides:

SEC. 901. SUNSET OF PROVISIONS OF ACT.

(a) IN GENERAL.—All provisions of, and amendments made by, this Act shall not apply—

(1) to taxable, plan, or limitation years beginning after December 31, 2012, or

(2) in the case of title V, to estates of decedents dying, gifts made, or generation skipping transfers, after December 31, 2012.

(b) APPLICATION OF CERTAIN LAWS.—The Internal Revenue Code of 1986 and the Employee Retirement Income Security Act of 1974 shall be applied and administered to years, estates, gifts, and transfers described in subsection (a) as if the provisions and amendments described in subsection (a) had never been enacted.

GIFT TAX—LIABILITY

• **1997, Taxpayer Relief Act of 1997 (P.L. 105-34)**

P.L. 105-34, § 501(a)(2):

Amended Code Sec. 2505(a)(1) by striking "$192,800" and inserting "the applicable credit amount in effect under section 2010(c) for such calendar year". **Effective** for estates of decedents dying, and gifts made, after 12-31-97.

• **1981, Economic Recovery Tax Act of 1981 (P.L. 97-34)**

P.L. 97-34, § 401(b)(1):

Amended Code Sec. 2505(a) by striking out "$47,000" and inserting "$192,800". **Effective** for gifts made after 12-31-81.

[Sec. 2505(b)—Repealed]

Amendments

• **1990, Omnibus Budget Reconciliation Act of 1990 (P.L. 101-508)**

P.L. 101-508, § 11801(a)(40):

Repealed Code Sec. 2505(b). **Effective** 11-5-90. Prior to repeal, Code Sec. 2505(b) read as follows:

(b) PHASE-IN OF CREDIT.—

In the case of gifts made in:	Subsection (a)(1) shall be applied by substituting for "$192,800" the following amount:
1982	$ 62,800
1983	79,300
1984	96,300
1985	121,800
1986	155,800

P.L. 101-508, § 11821(b), provides:

(b) SAVINGS PROVISION.—If—

(1) any provision amended or repealed by this part applied to—

(A) any transaction occurring before the date of the enactment of this Act,

(B) any property acquired before such date of enactment, or

(C) any item of income, loss, deduction, or credit taken into account before such date of enactment, and

(2) the treatment of such transaction, property, or item under such provision would (without regard to the amendments made by this part) affect liability for tax for periods ending after such date of enactment,

nothing in the amendments made by this part shall be construed to affect the treatment of such transaction, property, or item for purposes of determining liability for tax for periods ending after such date of enactment.

• **1981, Economic Recovery Tax Act of 1981 (P.L. 97-34)**

P.L. 97-34, § 401(b)(2):

Amended Code Sec. 2505(b). **Effective** for gifts made after 12-31-81. Prior to amendment, Code Sec. 2505(b) read as follows:

(b) PHASE-IN OF $47,000 CREDIT.—

In the case of gifts made in:	Subsection (a)(1) shall be applied by substituting for "$192,800" the following amount:
After December 31, 1976, and before July 1, 1977	$ 6,000
After June 30, 1977, and before January 1, 1978	30,000
After December 31, 1977, and before January 1, 1979	34,000
After December 31, 1978, and before January 1, 1980	38,000
After December 31, 1979, and before January 1, 1981	42,500

[Sec. 2505(b)]

(b) ADJUSTMENT TO CREDIT FOR CERTAIN GIFTS MADE BEFORE 1977.—The amount allowable under subsection (a) shall be reduced by an amount equal to 20 percent of the aggregate amount allowed as a specific exemption under section 2521 (as in effect before its repeal by the Tax Reform Act of 1976) with respect to gifts made by the individual after September 8, 1976.

Amendments

• **1990, Omnibus Budget Reconciliation Act of 1990 (P.L. 101-508)**

P.L. 101-508, § 11801(c)(19)(B):

Amended Code Sec. 2505 by redesignating subsection (c) as subsection (b). **Effective** 11-5-90.

P.L. 101-508, § 11821(b), provides:

(b) SAVINGS PROVISION.—If—

(1) any provision amended or repealed by this part applied to—

(A) any transaction occurring before the date of the enactment of this Act,

(B) any property acquired before such date of enactment, or

(C) any item of income, loss, deduction, or credit taken into account before such date of enactment, and

(2) the treatment of such transaction, property, or item under such provision would (without regard to the amendments made by this part) affect liability for tax for periods ending after such date of enactment,

nothing in the amendments made by this part shall be construed to affect the treatment of such transaction, property, or item for purposes of determining liability for tax for periods ending after such date of enactment.

[Sec. 2505(c)]

(c) LIMITATION BASED ON AMOUNT OF TAX.—The amount of the credit allowed under subsection (a) for any calendar year shall not exceed the amount of the tax imposed by section 2501 for such calendar year.

Amendments

• **1990, Omnibus Budget Reconciliation Act of 1990 (P.L. 101-508)**

P.L. 101-508, § 11801(c)(19)(B):

Amended Code Sec. 2505 by redesignating subsection (d) as subsection (c). **Effective** 11-5-90.

P.L. 101-508, § 11821(b), provides:

(b) SAVINGS PROVISION.—If—

(1) any provision amended or repealed by this part applied to—

(A) any transaction occurring before the date of the enactment of this Act,

(B) any property acquired before such date of enactment, or

(C) any item of income, loss, deduction, or credit taken into account before such date of enactment, and

(2) the treatment of such transaction, property, or item under such provision would (without regard to the amendments made by this part) affect liability for tax for periods ending after such date of enactment,

nothing in the amendments made by this part shall be construed to affect the treatment of such transaction, property, or item for purposes of determining liability for tax for periods ending after such date of enactment.

P.L. 97-34, § 442(a)(5)(A):

Amended Code Sec. 2505(a) by striking out "each calendar quarter" and inserting "each calendar year" and by striking out "preceding calendar quarters" and inserting "preceding calendar periods". **Effective** for gifts made after 12-31-81.

• **1981, Economic Recovery Tax Act of 1981 (P.L. 97-34)**

P.L. 97-34, § 442(a)(5)(B):

Amended Code Sec. 2505(d) by striking out "calendar quarter" each place it appears and inserting "calendar year". **Effective** with respect to gifts made after 12-31-81.

• **1976, Tax Reform Act of 1976 (P.L. 94-455)**

P.L. 94-455, § 2001(b)(2), (d)(2):

Added Code Sec. 2505. **Effective** for gifts made after 12-31-76.

Subchapter B—Transfers

Sec. 2511.	Transfers in general.
Sec. 2512.	Valuation of gifts.
Sec. 2513.	Gift by husband or wife to third party.

Sec. 2505(b)—Repealed

GIFT TAX—TRANSFERS

Sec. 2514.   Powers of appointment.
Sec. 2515.   Treatment of generation-skipping transfer tax.
Sec. 2516.   Certain property settlements.
Sec. 2518.   Disclaimers.
Sec. 2519.   Dispositions of certain life estates.

[Sec. 2511]

SEC. 2511. TRANSFERS IN GENERAL.

[Sec. 2511(a)]

(a) SCOPE.—Subject to the limitations contained in this chapter, the tax imposed by section 2501 shall apply whether the transfer is in trust or otherwise, whether the gift is direct or indirect, and whether the property is real or personal, tangible or intangible; but in the case of a nonresident not a citizen of the United States, shall apply to a transfer only if the property is situated within the United States.

[Sec. 2511(b)]

(b) INTANGIBLE PROPERTY.—For purposes of this chapter, in the case of a nonresident not a citizen of the United States who is excepted from the application of section 2501(a)(2)—

    (1) shares of stock issued by a domestic corporation, and

    (2) debt obligations of—

        (A) a United States person, or

        (B) the United States, a State or any political subdivision thereof, or the District of Columbia,

which are owned and held by such nonresident shall be deemed to be property situated within the United States.

Amendments

• **1966, Foreign Investors Tax Act of 1966 (P.L. 89-809)**

P.L. 89-809, §109(b):

Amended Code Sec. 2511(b). **Effective** for the calendar year 1967 and all calendar years thereafter. Prior to amendment, Sec. 2511(b) read as follows:

"(b) Stock in Corporation.—Shares of stock owned and held by a nonresident not a citizen of the United States shall be deemed property within the United States only if issued by a domestic corporation."

[Sec. 2511(c)—Stricken]

Amendments

• **2013, American Taxpayer Relief Act of 2012 (P.L. 112-240)**

P.L. 112-240, §101(a)(1) and (3), provides:

SEC. 101. PERMANENT EXTENSION AND MODIFICATION OF 2001 TAX RELIEF.

(a) PERMANENT EXTENSION.—

(1) IN GENERAL.—The Economic Growth and Tax Relief Reconciliation Act of 2001 is amended by striking title IX.

(2) CONFORMING AMENDMENT.—The Tax Relief, Unemployment Insurance Reauthorization, and Job Creation Act of 2010 is amended by striking section 304.

(3) EFFECTIVE DATE.—The amendments made by this subsection shall apply to taxable, plan, or limitation years beginning after December 31, 2012, and estates of decedents dying, gifts made, or generation skipping transfers after December 31, 2012.

• **2010, Tax Relief, Unemployment Insurance Reauthorization, and Job Creation Act of 2010 (P.L. 111-312)**

P.L. 111-312, §302(e):

Amended Code Sec. 2511 by striking subsection (c). **Effective** for estates of decedents dying, generation-skipping transfers, and gifts made, after 12-31-2009. Prior to being stricken, Code Sec. 2511(c) read as follows:

(c) TREATMENT OF CERTAIN TRANSFERS IN TRUST.—Notwithstanding any other provision of this section and except as provided in regulations, a transfer in trust shall be treated as a transfer of property by gift, unless the trust is treated as wholly owned by the donor or the donor's spouse under subpart E of part I of subchapter J of chapter 1.

P.L. 111-312, §304, provides [but see P.L. 112-240, §101(a)(2)-(3), above]:
SEC. 304. APPLICATION OF EGTRRA SUNSET TO THIS TITLE.

Section 901 of the Economic Growth and Tax Relief Reconciliation Act of 2001 shall apply to the amendments made by this title.

• **2002, Job Creation and Worker Assistance Act of 2002 (P.L. 107-147)**

P.L. 107-147, §411(g)(1):

Amended Code Sec. 2511(c) by striking "taxable gift under section 2503," and inserting "transfer of property by gift,". **Effective** as if included in the provision of P.L. 107-16 to which it relates [**effective** for gifts made after 12-31-2009.—CCH].

• **2001, Economic Growth and Tax Relief Reconciliation Act of 2001 (P.L. 107-16)**

P.L. 107-16, §511(e):

Amended Code Sec. 2511 by adding at the end a new subsection (c). **Effective** for gifts made after 12-31-2009.

P.L. 107-16, §901(a)-(b), as amended by P.L. 111-312, §101(a)(1), provides [but see P.L. 112-240, §101(a)(1) and (3), above]:

SEC. 901. SUNSET OF PROVISIONS OF ACT.

(a) IN GENERAL.—All provisions of, and amendments made by, this Act shall not apply—

(1) to taxable, plan, or limitation years beginning after December 31, 2012, or

(2) in the case of title V, to estates of decedents dying, gifts made, or generation skipping transfers, after December 31, 2012.

(b) APPLICATION OF CERTAIN LAWS.—The Internal Revenue Code of 1986 and the Employee Retirement Income Security Act of 1974 shall be applied and administered to years, estates, gifts, and transfers described in subsection (a) as if the provisions and amendments described in subsection (a) had never been enacted.

[Sec. 2512]

SEC. 2512. VALUATION OF GIFTS.

[Sec. 2512(a)]

(a) If the gift is made in property, the value thereof at the date of the gift shall be considered the amount of the gift.

[Sec. 2512(b)]

(b) Where property is transferred for less than an adequate and full consideration in money or money's worth, then the amount by which the value of the property exceeded the value of the consideration shall be deemed a gift, and shall be included in computing the amount of gifts made during the calendar year.

Amendments

• **1981, Economic Recovery Tax Act of 1981 (P.L. 97-34)**

P.L. 97-34, §442(b)(1):

Amended Code Sec. 2512(b) by striking out "calendar quarter" and inserting "calendar year". **Effective** with respect to gifts made after 12-31-81.

• **1970, Excise, Estate, and Gift Tax Adjustment Act of 1970 (P.L. 91-614)**

P.L. 91-614, §102(b)(1):

Amended Code Sec. 2512(b) by substituting "calendar quarter" for "calendar year". **Effective** for gifts made after 12-31-70.

[Sec. 2512(c)]

(c) CROSS REFERENCE.—

For individual's right to be furnished on request a statement regarding any valuation made by the Secretary of a gift by that individual, see section 7517.

GIFT TAX—TRANSFERS

Amendments

• **1976, Tax Reform Act of 1976 (P.L. 94-455)**

P.L. 94-455, § 2008(a)(2)(B), (d)(1)(B):

Added Code Sec. 2512(c). **Effective** for gifts made after 12-31-76.

[Sec. 2513]

SEC. 2513. GIFT BY HUSBAND OR WIFE TO THIRD PARTY.

[Sec. 2513(a)]

(a) CONSIDERED AS MADE ONE-HALF BY EACH.—

(1) IN GENERAL.—A gift made by one spouse to any person other than his spouse shall, for the purposes of this chapter, be considered as made one-half by him and one-half by his spouse, but only if at the time of the gift each spouse is a citizen or resident of the United States. This paragraph shall not apply with respect to a gift by a spouse of an interest in property if he creates in his spouse a general power of appointment, as defined in section 2514(c), over such interest. For purposes of this section, an individual shall be considered as the spouse of another individual only if he is married to such individual at the time of the gift and does not remarry during the remainder of the calendar year.

(2) CONSENT OF BOTH SPOUSES.—Paragraph (1) shall apply only if both spouses have signified (under the regulations provided for in subsection (b)) their consent to the application of paragraph (1) in the case of all such gifts made during the calendar year by either while married to the other.

Amendments

• **1981, Economic Recovery Tax Act of 1981 (P.L. 97-34)**

P.L. 97-34, § 442(b)(2)(A):

Amended Code Sec. 2513(a) by striking out "calendar quarter" each place it appears and inserting "calendar year". **Effective** with respect to gifts made after 12-31-81.

• **1970, Excise, Estate, and Gift Tax Adjustment Act of 1970 (P.L. 91-614)**

P.L. 91-614, § 102(b)(2)(A):

Amended Code Sec. 2513(a) by substituting "calendar quarter" for "calendar year" in the last line of both paragraphs (1) and (2). **Effective** for gifts made after 12-31-70.

[Sec. 2513(b)]

(b) MANNER AND TIME OF SIGNIFYING CONSENT.—

(1) MANNER.—A consent under this section shall be signified in such manner as is provided under regulations prescribed by the Secretary.

(2) TIME.—Such consent may be so signified at any time after the close of the calendar year in which the gift was made, subject to the following limitations—

(A) The consent may not be signified after the 15th day of April following the close of such year, unless before such 15th day no return has been filed for such year by either spouse, in which case the consent may not be signified after a return for such year is filed by either spouse.

(B) The consent may not be signified after a notice of deficiency with respect to the tax for such year has been sent to either spouse in accordance with section 6212(a).

Amendments

• **1981, Economic Recovery Tax Act of 1981 (P.L. 97-34)**

P.L. 97-34, § 442(b)(2)(B):

Amended Code Sec. 2513(b)(2) by striking out "calendar quarter" and inserting "calendar year". **Effective** with respect to gifts made after 12-31-81.

P.L. 97-34, § 442(b)(2)(C):

Amended Code Sec. 2513(b)(2)(A). **Effective** with respect to gifts made after 12-31-81. Prior to amendment, Code Sec. 2513(b)(2)(A) read as follows:

(A), the consent may not be signified after the 15th day of the second month following the close of such calendar quarter, unless before such 15th day no return has been filed for such calendar quarter by either spouse, in which case the consent may not be signified after a return for such calendar quarter is filed by either spouse;

P.L. 97-34, § 442(b)(2)(D):

Amended Code Sec. 2513(b)(2)(B) by striking out "the consent" and inserting "The consent", and by striking out "such calendar quarter" and inserting "such year". **Effective** with respect to gifts made after 12-31-81.

• **1976, Tax Reform Act of 1976 (P.L. 94-455)**

P.L. 94-455, § 1906(b)(13)(A):

Amended 1954 Code by substituting "Secretary" for "Secretary or his delegate" each place it appeared. **Effective** 2-1-77.

• **1970, Excise, Estate, and Gift Tax Adjustment Act of 1970 (P.L. 91-614)**

P.L. 91-614, § 102(b)(2)(A)-(C):

Amended Code Sec. 2513(b)(2). **Effective** for gifts made after 12-31-70. Prior to amendment, Code Sec. 2513(b)(2) read as follows:

"(2) Time.—Such consent may be so signified at any time after the close of the calendar year in which the gift was made, subject to the following limitations—

"(A) the consent may not be signified after the 15th day of April following the close of such year, unless before such 15th day no return has been filed for such year by either spouse, in which case the consent may not be signified after a return for such year is filed by either spouse;

"(B) the consent may not be signified after a notice of deficiency with respect to the tax for such year has been sent to either spouse in accordance with section 6212(a)."

[Sec. 2513(c)]

(c) REVOCATION OF CONSENT.—Revocation of a consent previously signified shall be made in such manner as is provided under regulations prescribed by the Secretary, but the right to revoke a consent previously signified with respect to a calendar year—

(1) shall not exist after the 15th day of April following the close of such year if the consent was signified on or before such 15th day; and

(2) shall not exist if the consent was not signified until after such 15th day.

Amendments

• **1981, Economic Recovery Tax Act of 1981 (P.L. 97-34)**

P.L. 97-34, § 442(b)(2)(E):

Amended Code Sec. 2513(c) by striking out "calendar quarter" and inserting "calendar year", and by striking out "15th day of the second month following the close of such quarter" and inserting "15th day of April following the close of such year". **Effective** with respect to estates of decedents dying after 12-31-81.

• **1976, Tax Reform Act of 1976 (P.L. 94-455)**

P.L. 94-455, § 1906(b)(13)(A):

Amended 1954 Code by substituting "Secretary" for "Secretary or his delegate" each place it appeared. **Effective** 2-1-77.

• **1970, Excise, Estate, and Gift Tax Adjustment Act of 1970 (P.L. 91-614)**

P.L. 91-614, § 102(b)(2)(A), (D):

Amended Code Sec. 2513(c). **Effective** for gifts made after 12-31-70. Prior to amendment, the section read as follows:

"(c) Revocation of Consent.—Revocation of a consent previously signified shall be made in such manner as is provided under regulations prescribed by the Secretary or his delegate, but the right to revoke a consent previously signified with respect to a calendar year—

"(1) shall not exist after the 15th day of April following the close of such year if the consent was signified on or before such 15th day; and

"(2) shall not exist if the consent was not signified until after such 15th day."

[Sec. 2513(d)]

(d) JOINT AND SEVERAL LIABILITY FOR TAX.—If the consent required by subsection (a)(2) is signified with respect to a gift made in any calendar year, the liability with respect to the entire tax imposed by this chapter of each spouse for such year shall be joint and several.

GIFT TAX—TRANSFERS

Amendments

- **1981, Economic Recovery Tax Act of 1981 (P.L. 97-34)**

P.L. 97-34, §442(b)(2)(F):

Amended Code Sec. 2513(d) by striking out "any calendar quarter" and inserting "any calendar year", and by striking out "such calendar quarter" and inserting "such year". **Effective** with respect to estates of decedents dying after 12-31-81.

- **1970, Excise, Estate, and Gift Tax Adjustment Act of 1970 (P.L. 91-614)**

P.L. 91-614, §102(b)(2)(E):

Amended Code Sec. 2513(d) by substituting "calendar quarter" for "calendar year" and by substituting "for such calendar quarter" for "for such year." **Effective** for gifts made after 12-31-70.

[Sec. 2514]

SEC. 2514. POWERS OF APPOINTMENT.

[Sec. 2514(a)]

(a) POWERS CREATED ON OR BEFORE OCTOBER 21, 1942.—An exercise of a general power of appointment created on or before October 21, 1942, shall be deemed a transfer of property by the individual possessing such power; but the failure to exercise such a power or the complete release of such a power shall not be deemed an exercise thereof. If a general power of appointment created on or before October 21, 1942, has been partially released so that it is no longer a general power of appointment, the subsequent exercise of such power shall not be deemed to be the exercise of a general power of appointment if—

   (1) such partial release occurred before November 1, 1951, or

   (2) the donee of such power was under a legal disability to release such power on October 21, 1942, and such partial release occurred not later than six months after the termination of such legal disability.

[Sec. 2514(b)]

(b) POWERS CREATED AFTER OCTOBER 21, 1942.—The exercise or release of a general power of appointment created after October 21, 1942, shall be deemed a transfer of property by the individual possessing such power.

Amendments

- **1976, Tax Reform Act of 1976 (P.L. 94-455)**

P.L. 94-455, §2009(b)(4)(F), (e)(2):

Deleted the second sentence of Code Sec. 2514(b). **Effective** for transfers creating an interest in the person disclaiming made after 12-31-76. Prior to deletion, such sentence read as follows:

"A disclaimer or renunciation of such a power of appointment shall not be deemed a release of such power."

[Sec. 2514(c)]

(c) DEFINITION OF GENERAL POWER OF APPOINTMENT.—For purposes of this section, the term "general power of appointment" means a power which is exercisable in favor of the individual possessing the power (hereafter in this subsection referred to as the "possessor"), his estate, his creditors, or the creditors of his estate; except that—

   (1) A power to consume, invade, or appropriate property for the benefit of the possessor which is limited by an ascertainable standard relating to the health, education, support, or maintenance of the possessor shall not be deemed a general power of appointment.

   (2) A power of appointment created on or before October 21, 1942, which is exercisable by the possessor only in conjunction with another person shall not be deemed a general power of appointment.

   (3) In the case of a power of appointment created after October 21, 1942, which is exercisable by the possessor only in conjunction with another person—

      (A) if the power is not exercisable by the possessor except in conjunction with the creator of the power—such power shall not be deemed a general power of appointment;

      (B) if the power is not exercisable by the possessor except in conjunction with a person having a substantial interest in the property subject to the power, which is adverse to exercise of the power in favor of the possessor—such power shall not be deemed a general power of appointment. For the purposes of this subparagraph a person who, after the death of the possessor, may be possessed of a power of appointment (with respect to the property subject to the possessor's power) which he may exercise in his own favor shall be deemed as having an interest in the property and such interest shall be deemed adverse to such exercise of the possessor's power;

      (C) if (after the application of subparagraphs (A) and (B)) the power is a general power of appointment and is exercisable in favor of such other person—such power shall be deemed a general power of appointment only in respect of a fractional part of the property subject to such power, such part to be determined by dividing the value of such property by the number of such persons (including the possessor) in favor of whom such power is exercisable.

For purposes of subparagraphs (B) and (C), a power shall be deemed to be exercisable in favor of a person if it is exercisable in favor of such person, his estate, his creditors, or the creditors of his estate.

[Sec. 2514(d)]

(d) CREATION OF ANOTHER POWER IN CERTAIN CASES.—If a power of appointment created after October 21, 1942, is exercised by creating another power of appointment which, under the applicable local law, can be validly exercised so as to postpone the vesting of any estate or interest in the property which was subject to the first power, or suspend the absolute ownership or power of alienation of such property, for a period ascertainable without regard to the date of the creation of the first power, such exercise of the first power shall, to the extent of the property subject to the second power, be deemed a transfer of property by the individual possessing such power.

[Sec. 2514(e)]

(e) LAPSE OF POWER.—The lapse of a power of appointment created after October 21, 1942, during the life of the individual possessing the power shall be considered a release of such power. The rule of the preceding sentence shall apply with respect to the lapse of powers during any calendar year only to the extent that the property which could have been appointed by exercise of such lapsed powers exceeds in value the greater of the following amounts:

   (1) $5,000, or

   (2) 5 percent of the aggregate value of the assets out of which, or the proceeds of which, the exercise of the lapsed powers could be satisfied.

[Sec. 2514(f)]

(f) DATE OF CREATION OF POWER.—For purposes of this section a power of appointment created by a will executed on or before October 21, 1942, shall be considered a power created on or before such date if the person executing such will dies before July 1, 1949, without having republished such will, by codicil or otherwise, after October 21, 1942.

GIFT TAX—TRANSFERS

[Sec. 2515]

SEC. 2515. TREATMENT OF GENERATION-SKIPPING TRANSFER TAX.

In the case of any taxable gift which is a direct skip (within the meaning of chapter 13), the amount of such gift shall be increased by the amount of any tax imposed on the transferor under chapter 13 with respect to such gift.

Amendments

• **1986, Tax Reform Act of 1986 (P.L. 99-514)**

P.L. 99-514, § 1432(d)(1):

Amended Subchapter B of chapter 12 by inserting after Code Sec. 2514 new Code Sec. 2515. **Effective**, generally, for any generation-skipping transfer (within the meaning of section 2611 of the Internal Revenue Code of 1986) made after the date of the enactment of this Act. However, for special rules see Act Sec. 1433(b)-(d) in the amendments for Code Sec. 2601.

[Sec. 2515—Repealed]

Amendments

• **1981, Economic Recovery Tax Act of 1981 (P.L. 97-34)**

P.L. 97-34, § 403(c)(3)(B):

Repealed Code Sec. 2515. **Effective**, generally, for gifts made after 12-31-81. For special rules, see Act Sec. 403(e)(3), below. Prior to its repeal, Code Sec. 2515 read as follows:

SEC. 2515. TENANCIES BY THE ENTIRETY IN REAL PROPERTY.

(a) CREATION.—The creation of a tenancy by the entirety in real property, either by one spouse alone or by both spouses, and additions to the value thereof in the form of improvements, reductions in the indebtedness thereon, or otherwise, shall not be deemed transfers of property for purposes of this chapter, regardless of the proportion of the consideration furnished by each spouse, unless the donor elects to have such creation of a tenancy by the entirety treated as a transfer, as provided in subsection (c).

(b) TERMINATION.—In the case of the termination of a tenancy by the entirety, other than by reason of the death of a spouse, the creation of which, or additions to which, were not deemed to be transfers by reason of subsection (a), a spouse shall be deemed to have made a gift to the extent that the proportion of the total consideration furnished by such spouse multiplied by the proceeds of such termination (whether in form of cash, property, or interests in property) exceeds the value of such proceeds of termination received by such spouse.

(c) EXERCISE OF ELECTION.—

(1) IN GENERAL.—The election provided by subsection (a) shall be exercised by including such creation of a tenancy by the entirety as a transfer by gift, to the extent such transfer constitutes a gift (determined without regard to this section), in the gift tax return of the donor for the calendar quarter in which such tenancy by the entirety was created, filed within the time prescribed by law, irrespective of whether or not the gift exceeds the exclusion provided by section 2503(b).

(2) SUBSEQUENT ADDITIONS IN VALUE.—If the election provided by subsection (a) has been made with respect to the creation of any tenancy by the entirety, such election shall also apply to each addition made to the value of such tenancy by the entirety.

(3) CERTAIN ACTUARIAL COMPUTATIONS NOT REQUIRED.—In the case of any election under subsection (a) with respect to any property, the retained interest of each spouse shall be treated as one-half of the value of their joint interest.

(d) CERTAIN JOINT TENANCIES INCLUDED.—For purposes of this section, the term "tenancy by the entirety" includes a joint tenancy between husband and wife with right of survivorship.

Amendments

• **1981, Economic Recovery Tax Act of 1981 (P.L. 97-34)**

P.L. 97-34, § 403(c)(3)(B):

Repealed Code Sec. 2515A. **Effective**, generally, for gifts made after 12-31-81. For special rules, see Act Sec. 403(e)(3), below. Prior to its repeal, Code Sec. 2515A read as follows:

SEC. 2515A. TENANCIES BY THE ENTIRETY IN PERSONAL PROPERTY.

(a) CERTAIN ACTUARIAL COMPUTATIONS NOT REQUIRED.—In the case of—

(1) the creation (either by one spouse alone or by both spouses) of a joint interest of a husband and wife in personal property with right of survivorship, or

(2) additions to the value thereof in the form of improvements, reductions in the indebtedness thereof, or otherwise,

the retained interest of each spouse shall be treated as one-half of the value of their joint interest.

(b) EXCEPTION.—Subsection (a) shall not apply with respect to any joint interest in property if the fair market value of the interest or of the property (determined as if each spouse had a right to sever) cannot reasonably be ascertained except by reference to the life expectancy of one or both spouses.

P.L. 97-34, § 403(e)(3), provides:

(3) If—

P.L. 97-34, § 403(e)(3), provides:

(3) If—

(A) the decedent dies after December 31, 1981,

(B) by reason of the death of the decedent property passes from the decedent or is acquired from the decedent under a will executed before the date which is 30 days after the date of the enactment of this Act, or a trust created before such date, which contains a formula expressly providing that the spouse is to receive the maximum amount of property qualifying for the marital deduction allowable by Federal law,

(C) the formula referred to in subparagraph (B) was not amended to refer specifically to an unlimited marital deduction at any time after the date which is 30 days after the date of enactment of this Act, and before the death of the decedent, and

(D) the State does not enact a statute applicable to such estate which construes this type of formula as referring to the marital deduction allowable by Federal law as amended by subsection (a),

then the amendment made by subsection (a) [relating to the unlimited marital deduction (Code Sec. 2056, as amended by P.L. 97-34)] shall not apply to the estate of such decedent.

• **1976, Tax Reform Act of 1976 (P.L. 94-455)**

P.L. 94-455, § 2002(c)(2):

Amended Code Sec. 2515(c). **Effective** for joint interests created after 12-31-76. Prior to amendment, Code Sec. 2515(c) read as follows:

(c) EXERCISE OF ELECTION.—The election provided by subsection (a) shall be exercised by including such creation of a tenancy by the entirety or additions made to the value thereof as a transfer by gift, to the extent such transfer constitutes a gift, determined without regard to this section, in the gift tax return of the donor for the calendar quarter in which such tenancy by the entirety was created or additions made to the value thereof, filed within the time prescribed by law, irrespective of whether or not the gift exceeds the exclusion provided by section 2503(b).

• **1970, Excise, Estate, and Gift Tax Adjustment Act of 1970 (P.L. 91-614)**

P.L. 91-614, § 102(b)(3):

Amended Code Sec. 2515(c) by substituting "calendar quarter" for "calendar year." **Effective** for gifts made after 12-31-70.

[Sec. 2515A—Repealed]

(A) the decedent dies after December 31, 1981,

(B) by reason of the death of the decedent property passes from the decedent or is acquired from the decedent under a will executed before the date which is 30 days after the date of the enactment of this Act, or a trust created before such date, which contains a formula expressly providing that the spouse is to receive the maximum amount of property qualifying for the marital deduction allowable by Federal law,

(C) the formula referred to in subparagraph (B) was not amended to refer specifically to an unlimited marital deduction at any time after the date which is 30 days after the date of enactment of this Act, and before the death of the decedent, and

(D) the State does not enact a statute applicable to such estate which construes this type of formula as referring to the marital deduction allowable by Federal law as amended by subsection (a),

then the amendment made by subsection (a) shall not apply to the estate of such decedent.

• **1978, Revenue Act of 1978 (P.L. 95-600)**

P.L. 95-600, § 702(k)(1)(A):

Added Code Sec. 2515A. **Effective** for joint interests created after 12-31-76.

[Sec. 2516]

SEC. 2516. CERTAIN PROPERTY SETTLEMENTS.

Where husband and wife enter into a written agreement relative to their marital and property rights and divorce occurs within the 3-year period beginning on the date 1 year before such agreement is entered into (whether or not such agreement is approved by the divorce decree), any transfers of property or interests in property made pursuant to such agreement—

(1) to either spouse in settlement of his or her marital or property rights, or

(2) to provide a reasonable allowance for the support of issue of the marriage during minority,

shall be deemed to be transfers made for a full and adequate consideration in money or money's worth.

GIFT TAX—TRANSFERS

Amendments
• **1984, Deficit Reduction Act of 1984 (P.L. 98-369)**

P.L. 98-369, §425(b):

Amended Code Sec. 2516 by striking out so much of such section as preceded paragraph (1) thereof and inserting in lieu thereof new material. **Effective** for transfers after 7-18-84. Prior to amendment the material preceding paragraph (1) of Code Sec. 2516 read as follows:

Where husband and wife enter into a written agreement relative to their marital and property rights and divorce occurs within 2 years thereafter (whether or not such agreement is approved by the divorce decree), any transfers of property or interests in property made pursuant to such agreement—

[Sec. 2517—Repealed]

Amendments
• **1986, Tax Reform Act of 1986 (P.L. 99-514)**

P.L. 99-514, §1852(e)(2)(A):

Repealed Code Sec. 2517. **Effective** for transfers after 10-22-86. Prior to repeal, Code Sec. 2517 read as follows:

SEC. 2517. CERTAIN ANNUITIES UNDER QUALIFIED PLANS.

[Sec. 2517(a)]

(a) GENERAL RULE.—The exercise or nonexercise by an employee of an election or option whereby an annuity or other payment will become payable to any beneficiary at or after the employee's death shall not be considered a transfer for purposes of this chapter if the option or election and annuity or other payment is provided for under—

(1) an employees' trust (or under a contract purchased by an employees' trust) forming part of a pension, stock bonus, or profit-sharing plan which, at the time of such exercise or nonexercise, or at the time of termination of the plan if earlier, met the requirements of section 401(a);

(2) a retirement annuity contract purchased by an employer (and not by an employees' trust) pursuant to a plan which, at the time of such exercise or nonexercise, or at the time of termination of the plan if earlier, was a plan described in section 403(a);

(3) a retirement annuity contract purchased for an employee by an employer which is an organization referred to in section 170 (b)(1)(A)(ii) or (vi), or which is a religious organization (other than a trust), and which is exempt from tax under section 501(a);

(4) chapter 73 of title 10 of the United States Code; or

(5) an individual retirement account described in section 408(a) or an individual retirement annuity described in section 408(b).

Amendments
• **1984, Deficit Reduction Act of 1984 (P.L. 98-369)**

P.L. 98-369, §491(d)(35):

Amended Code Sec. 2517(a)(5) by striking out ", an individual retirement annuity described in section 408(b), or a retirement bond described in section 409(a)" and inserting in lieu thereof "or an individual retirement annuity described in section 408(b)". **Effective** for obligations issued after 12-31-83.

• **1976, Tax Reform Act of 1976 (P.L. 94-455)**

P.L. 94-455, §2009(c)(4)(A), (e)(3)(B):

Amended Code Sec. 2517(a) by striking out "or" at the end of paragraph (3); by striking out the period at the end of paragraph (4) and inserting in lieu thereof "; or"; and by adding after paragraph (4) a new paragraph (5). **Effective** for transfers made after 12-31-76.

• **1969, Tax Reform Act of 1969 (P.L. 91-172)**

P.L. 91-172, §101(j)(24):

Amended Code Sec. 2517(a)(3) by substituting "section 170(b)(1)(A)(ii) or (vi), or which is a religious organization (other than a trust)," for "section 503(b)(1), (2), or (3),". **Effective** 1-1-70.

• **1966 (P.L. 89-365)**

P.L. 89-365, §2:

Amended Code Sec. 2517(a) by striking out "or" at the end of paragraph (2), by substituting "; or" for the period at the end of paragraph (3), and by adding new paragraph (4). **Effective** for calendar years after 1965.

• **1962, Self-Employed Individuals Tax Retirement Act of 1962 (P.L. 87-792)**

P.L. 87-792, §7:

Amended Code Sec. 2517(a) by striking out in paragraph (2) "met the requirements of section 401(a)(3), (4), (5), and (6)" and inserting in lieu thereof "was a plan described in section 403(a)". **Effective** 1-1-63.

[Sec. 2517(b)]

(b) TRANSFERS ATTRIBUTABLE TO EMPLOYEE CONTRIBUTIONS.—If the annuity or other payment referred to in subsection (a) (other than paragraphs (4) and (5)) is attributable to any extent to payments or contributions made by the employee, then subsection (a) shall not apply to that part of the value of such annuity or other payment which bears the same proportion to the total value of the annuity or other payment as the total payments or contributions made by the employee bear to the total payments or contributions made. For purposes of the preceding sentence, payments or contributions made by the employee's employer or former employer toward the purchase of an annuity contract described in subsection (a)(3) shall, to the extent not excludable from gross income under section 403(b), be considered to have been made by the employee. For purposes of this subsection, contributions or payments on behalf of an individual while he was an employee within the meaning of section 401(c)(1) made under a trust or plan described in paragraph (1) or (2) of subsection (a) shall, to the extent allowable as a deduction under section 404, be considered to be made by a person other than such individual and, to the extent not so allowable, shall be considered to be made by such individual. For purposes of this subsection, any deductible employee contributions (within the meaning of paragraph (5) of section 72(o)) shall be considered as made by a person other than the employee.

Amendments
• **1983, Technical Corrections Act of 1982 (P.L. 97-448)**

P.L. 97-448, §103(c)(11):

Amended subsection (i) of section 311 of P.L. 97-34 so that the amendment made by subsection (d)(2) is **effective** for transfers made after 12-31-81.

• **1981, Economic Recovery Tax Act of 1981 (P.L. 97-34)**

P.L. 97-34, §311(d)(2):

Amended Code Sec. 2517(b) by adding at the end the following new sentence: "For purposes of this subsection, any deductible employee contributions (within the meaning of paragraph (5) of section 72(o)) shall be considered as made by a person other than the employee.". **Effective** for transfers after 12-31-81. The transitional rule provides that, for purposes of the 1954 Code, any amount allowed as a deduction under section 220 of the Code (as in effect before its repeal by P. L. 97-34) shall be treated as if it were allowed by section 219 of the Code.

• **1976, Tax Reform Act of 1976 (P.L. 94-455)**

P.L. 94-455, §2009(c)(4)(A):

Substituted "other than paragraphs (4) and (5)" for "other than paragraph (4)" in Code Sec. 2517(b). **Effective** for transfers made after 12-31-76.

P.L. 94-455, §2009(c)(4)(B):

Amended the last sentence of Code Sec. 2517(b). **Effective** for transfers made after 12-31-76. Prior to amendment, such sentence read as follows:

"For purposes of this subsection, payments or contributions on behalf of an individual while he was an employee within the meaning of section 401(c)(1) made under a trust or plan described in subsection (a)(1) or (2) shall be considered to be payments or contributions made by the employee."

• **1966 (P.L. 89-365)**

P.L. 89-365, §2:

Amended Code Sec. 2517(b) by inserting "(other than paragraph (4))" immediately after "referred to in subsection (a)" in the first sentence. **Effective** for calendar years after 1965.

• **1962, Self-Employed Individuals Tax Retirement Act of 1962 (P.L. 87-792)**

P.L. 87-792, §7:

Amended Code Sec. 2517(b) by adding after the period in line 11 a new sentence. **Effective** 1-1-63.

[Sec. 2517(c)]

(c) EXEMPTION OF CERTAIN ANNUITY INTERESTS CREATED BY COMMUNITY PROPERTY LAWS.—Notwithstanding any other provision of law, in the case of an employee on whose behalf contributions or payments are made—

(1) by his employer or former employer under a trust or plan described in paragraph (1) or (2) of subsection (a), or toward the purchase of a contract described in paragraph (3) of subsection (a), which under subsection (b) are not considered as contributed by the employee, or

(2) by the employee to a retirement plan described in paragraph (5) of subsection (a),

a transfer of benefits attributable to such contributions or payments shall, for purposes of this chapter, not be considered as a transfer by the spouse of the employee to the extent that the value of any interest of such spouse in such contributions or payments or in such trust or plan or such contract—

(A) is attributable to such contribution or payments, and

(B) arises solely by reason of such spouse's interest in community income under the community property laws of the State.

Amendments
• **1976, Tax Reform Act of 1976 (P.L. 94-455)**

P.L. 94-455, §2009(c)(5), (e)(3)(B):

Redesignated Code Sec. 2517(c) (as amended by paragraph (4)(A)(iii)) as Code Sec. 2517(d) and added after Code Sec. 2517(b) a new subsection (c). **Effective** for transfers made after 12-31-76.

[Sec. 2517(d)]

(d) EMPLOYEE DEFINED.—For purposes of this section, the term "employee" includes a former employee. In the case of a retirement plan described in paragraph (5) of subsection (a), such term means the individual for whose benefit the plan was established.

Amendments
• **1976, Tax Reform Act of 1976 (P.L. 94-455)**

P.L. 94-455, §2009(c)(4)(A):

Added a new sentence at the end of Code Sec. 2517(c). **Effective** for transfers made after 12-31-76.

P.L. 94-455, §2009(c)(5):

Redesignated Code Sec. 2517(c) (as amended by paragraph (4)(A)(iii)) as Code Sec. 2517(d). **Effective** for transfers made after 12-31-76.

GIFT TAX—TRANSFERS

• **1958, Technical Amendments Act of 1958 (P.L. 85-866)**

P.L. 85-866, § 68(a):

Added Sec. 2517 to the Code.

P.L. 85-866, § 68(c), provides:

"The amendments made by this section shall apply with respect to the calendar year 1955 and all calendar years thereafter. For calendar years before 1955, the determination as to whether the exercise or nonexercise by an employee of an election or option described in section 2517 of the Internal Revenue Code of 1954 (as added by subsection (a)) is a transfer for purposes of chapter 4 of the Internal Revenue Code of 1939 shall be made as if this section had not been enacted and without inferences drawn from the fact that this section is not made applicable with respect to calendar years before 1955."

P.L. 85-866, § 23(f), (g):

Amended Code Sec. 2517, as added by § 68(a) of P.L. 85-866, by striking out "or" at the end of subsection (a)(1), and by striking out the period at the end of subsection (a)(2) and inserting in lieu thereof "; or", and by inserting after subsection (a)(2) paragraph (3). **Effective** for calendar years after 1957.

[Sec. 2518]

SEC. 2518. DISCLAIMERS.

[Sec. 2518(a)]

(a) GENERAL RULE.—For purposes of this subtitle, if a person makes a qualified disclaimer with respect to any interest in property, this subtitle shall apply with respect to such interest as if the interest had never been transferred to such person.

[Sec. 2518(b)]

(b) QUALIFIED DISCLAIMER DEFINED.—For purposes of subsection (a), the term "qualified disclaimer" means an irrevocable and unqualified refusal by a person to accept an interest in property but only if—

(1) such refusal is in writing,

(2) such writing is received by the transferor of the interest, his legal representative, or the holder of the legal title to the property to which the interest relates not later than the date which is 9 months after the later of—

(A) the date on which the transfer creating the interest in such person is made, or

(B) the day on which such person attains age 21,

(3) such person has not accepted the interest or any of its benefits, and

(4) as a result of such refusal, the interest passes without any direction on the part of the person making the disclaimer and passes either—

(A) to the spouse of the decedent, or

(B) to a person other than the person making the disclaimer.

Amendments

• **2010, Tax Relief, Unemployment Insurance Reauthorization, and Job Creation Act of 2010 (P.L. 111-312)**

P.L. 111-312, § 301(d)(1), provides:

(1) ESTATE TAX.—In the case of the estate of a decedent dying after December 31, 2009, and before the date of the enactment of this Act, the due date for—

(A) filing any return under section 6018 of the Internal Revenue Code of 1986 (including any election required to be made on such a return) as such section is in effect after the date of the enactment of this Act without regard to any election under subsection (c),

(B) making any payment of tax under chapter 11 of such Code, and

(C) making any disclaimer described in section 2518(b) of such Code of an interest in property passing by reason of the death of such decedent,

shall not be earlier than the date which is 9 months after the date of the enactment of this Act.

• **1978, Revenue Act of 1978 (P.L. 95-600)**

P.L. 95-600, § 702(m)(1):

Amended paragraph (4) of Code Sec. 2518(b). **Effective** for transfers creating an interest in the person disclaiming made after 1976. Prior to amendment, paragraph (4) read as follows:

"(4) as a result of such refusal, the interest passes to a person other than the person making the disclaimer (without any direction on the part of the person making the disclaimer)."

[Sec. 2518(c)]

(c) OTHER RULES.—For purposes of subsection (a)—

(1) DISCLAIMER OF UNDIVIDED PORTION OF INTEREST.—A disclaimer with respect to an undivided portion of an interest which meets the requirements of the preceding sentence shall be treated as a qualified disclaimer of such portion of the interest.

(2) POWERS.—A power with respect to property shall be treated as an interest in such property.

(3) CERTAIN TRANSFERS TREATED AS DISCLAIMERS.—A written transfer of the transferor's entire interest in the property—

(A) which meets requirements similar to the requirements of paragraphs (2) and (3) of subsection (b), and

(B) which is to a person or persons who would have received the property had the transferor made a qualified disclaimer (within the meaning of subsection (b)), shall be treated as a qualified disclaimer.

Amendments

• **1983, Technical Corrections Act of 1982 (P.L. 97-448)**

P.L. 97-448, § 104(e):

Amended Code Sec. 2518(c)(3) by striking out "For purposes of subsection (a), a" and inserting in lieu thereof "A". **Effective** as if included in the provision of P.L. 97-34 to which it relates.

• **1981, Economic Recovery Tax Act of 1981 (P.L. 97-34)**

P.L. 97-34, § 426(a):

Added Code Sec. 2518(c)(3). **Effective** for transfers creating an interest in the person disclaiming made after 12-31-81.

• **1976, Tax Reform Act of 1976 (P.L. 94-455)**

P.L. 94-455, § 2009(b)(1), (e)(2):

Added Code Sec. 2518. **Effective** for transfers creating an interest in the person disclaiming made after 12-31-76.

[Sec. 2519]

SEC. 2519. DISPOSITIONS OF CERTAIN LIFE ESTATES.

[Sec. 2519(a)]

(a) GENERAL RULE.—For purposes of this chapter and chapter 11, any disposition of all or part of a qualifying income interest for life in any property to which this section applies shall be treated as a transfer of all interests in such property other than the qualifying income interest.

[Sec. 2519(b)]

(b) PROPERTY TO WHICH THIS SUBSECTION APPLIES.—This section applies to any property if a deduction was allowed with respect to the transfer of such property to the donor—

(1) under section 2056 by reason of subsection (b)(7) thereof, or

(2) under section 2523 by reason of subsection (f) thereof.

GIFT TAX—DEDUCTIONS

[Sec. 2519(c)]

(c) CROSS REFERENCE.—

For right of recovery for gift tax in the case of property treated as transferred under this section, see section 2207A(b).

Amendments

• **1983, Technical Corrections Act of 1982 (P.L. 97-448)**

P.L. 97-448, §104(a)(3)(A):

Amended Code Sec. 2519(a). **Effective** as if included in the provision of P.L. 97-34 to which it relates. Prior to amendment, Code Sec. 2519(a) read as follows:

"(a) GENERAL RULE.—Any disposition of all or part of a qualifying income interest for life in any property to which this section applies shall be treated as a transfer of such property."

P.L. 97-448, §104(a)(7):

Amended Code Sec. 2519 by adding at the end thereof new subsection (c). **Effective** as if included in the provision of P.L. 97-34 to which it relates.

• **1981, Economic Recovery Tax Act of 1981 (P.L. 97-34)**

P.L. 97-34, §403(d)(3)(B)(i):

Added Code Sec. 2519. **Effective**, generally, for gifts made after 12-31-81. See Act Sec. 403(e)(3), below, for a special rule applicable to certain wills and trusts, executed or created, before 9-12-81.

P.L. 97-34, §403(e)(3), provides:

(3) If—

(A) the decedent dies after December 31, 1981,

(B) by reason of the death of the decedent property passes from the decedent or is acquired from the decedent under a will executed before the date which is 30 days after the date of the enactment of this Act, or a trust created before such date, which contains a formula expressly providing that the spouse is to receive the maximum amount of property qualifying for the marital deduction allowable by Federal law,

(C) the formula referred to in subparagraph (B) was not amended to refer specifically to an unlimited marital deduction at any time after the date which is 30 days after the date of enactment of this Act, and before the death of the decedent, and

(D) the State does not enact a statute applicable to such estate which construes this type of formula as referring to the marital deduction allowable by Federal law as amended by subsection (a),

then the amendment made by subsection (a) [relating to the unlimited marital deduction (Code Sec. 2056, as amended by P.L. 97-34)] shall not apply to the estate of such decedent.

Subchapter C—Deductions

Sec. 2522.   Charitable and similar gifts.
Sec. 2523.   Gift to spouse.
Sec. 2524.   Extent of deductions.

[Sec. 2521—Repealed]

Amendments

• **1976, Tax Reform Act of 1976 (P.L. 94-455)**

P.L. 94-455, §2001(b)(3):

Repealed Code Sec. 2521. **Effective** for gifts made after 12-31-76. Prior to repeal, Code Sec. 2521 read as follows:

"SEC. 2521. SPECIFIC EXEMPTION.

"In computing taxable gifts for a calendar quarter, there shall be allowed as a deduction in the case of a citizen or resident an exemption of $30,000, less the aggregate of the amounts claimed and allowed as specific exemption in the computation of gift taxes for the calendar year 1932 and all calendar years and calendar quarters intervening between that calendar year and the calendar quarter for which the tax is being computed under the laws applicable to such years or calendar quarters."

[Sec. 2522]

SEC. 2522. CHARITABLE AND SIMILAR GIFTS.

[Sec. 2522(a)]

(a) CITIZENS OR RESIDENTS.—In computing taxable gifts for the calendar year, there shall be allowed as a deduction in the case of a citizen or resident the amount of all gifts made during such year to or for the use of—

(1) the United States, any State, or any political subdivision thereof, or the District of Columbia, for exclusively public purposes;

(2) a corporation, or trust, or community chest, fund, or foundation, organized and operated exclusively for religious, charitable, scientific, literary, or educational purposes, or to foster national or international amateur sports competition (but only if no part of its activities involve the provision of athletic facilities or equipment), including the encouragement of art and the prevention of curelty to children or animals, no part of the net earnings of which inures to the benefit of any private shareholder or individual, which is not disqualified for tax exemption under section 501(c)(3) by reason of attempting to influence legislation, and which does not participate in, or intervene in (including the publishing or distributing of statements), any political campaign on behalf of (or in opposition to) any candidate for public office;

(3) a fraternal society, order, or association, operating under the lodge system, but only if such gifts are to be used exclusively for religious, charitable, scientific, literary, or educational purposes, including the encouragement of art and the prevention of cruelty to children or animals;

(4) posts or organizations of war veterans, or auxiliary units or societies of any such posts or organizations, if such posts, organizations, units, or societies are organized in the United States or any of its possessions, and if no part of their net earnings inures to the benefit of any private shareholder or individual.

Rules similar to the rules of section 501(j) shall apply for purposes of paragraph (2).

Amendments

• **1987, Revenue Act of 1987 (P.L. 100-203)**

P.L. 100-203, §10711(a)(5):

Amended Code Sec. 2522(a)(2) by striking out "on behalf of any candidate" and inserting in lieu thereof "on behalf of (or in opposition to) any candidate". **Effective** with respect to activities after 12-22-87.

• **1982, Tax Equity and Fiscal Responsibility Act of 1982 (P.L. 97-248)**

P.L. 97-248, §286(b)(3):

Amended Code Sec. 2522(a) by adding a new sentence at the end thereof. **Effective** 10-5-76.

• **1981, Economic Recovery Tax Act of 1981 (P.L. 97-34)**

P.L. 97-34, §442(c):

Amended Code Sec. 2522(a) by striking out "quarter" and inserting "year". **Effective** with respect to estates of decedents dying after 12-31-81.

• **1976, Tax Reform Act of 1976 (P.L. 94-455)**

P.L. 94-455, §1307(d)(1)(B)(iv):

Substituted "which is not disqualified for tax exemption under section 501(c)(3) by reason of attempting to influence legislation" for "no substantial part of the activities of which is carrying on propaganda, or otherwise attempting, to influence legislation" in Code Sec. 2522(a)(2). **Effective** for gifts in calendar years beginning after 12-31-76.

P.L. 94-455, §1313(b)(3):

Added after "educational purposes" in Code Sec. 2522(a)(2) the following:", or to foster national or international amateur sports competition (but only if no part of its activities involved the provision of athletic facilities or equipment)". **Effective** 10-5-76.

P.L. 94-455, §1902(a)(12)(D):

Deleted "Territory" in Code Sec. 2522(a)(1). **Effective** for gifts made after 12-31-76.

• **1970, Excise, Estate, and Gift Tax Adjustment Act of 1970 (P.L. 91-614)**

P.L. 91-614, §102(c)(2):

Amended Code Sec. 2522(a) by substituting "quarter" for "year" in the line preceding paragraph (1). **Effective** for gifts made after 12-31-70.

• **1969, Tax Reform Act of 1969 (P.L. 91-172)**

P.L. 91-172, §201(d)(4)(C):

Amended Code Sec. 2522(a)(2). **Effective** with respect to gifts and transfers made after 12-31-69. Prior to amendment, Code Sec. 2522(a)(2) read as follows:

"(2) a corporation, or trust, or community chest, fund, or foundation, organized and operated exclusively for religious, charitable, scientific, literary, or educational purposes, including the encouragement of art and the prevention of cruelty to children or animals, no part of the net earnings of which inures to the benefit of any private shareholder or individual, and no substantial part of the activities of which is carrying on propaganda, or otherwise attempting, to influence legislation;".

GIFT TAX—DEDUCTIONS

[Sec. 2522(b)]

(b) NONRESIDENTS.—In the case of a nonresident not a citizen of the United States, there shall be allowed as a deduction the amount of all gifts made during such year to or for the use of—

(1) the United States, any State, or any political subdivision thereof, or the District of Columbia, for exclusively public purposes;

(2) a domestic corporation organized and operated exclusively for religious, charitable, scientific, literary, or educational purposes, including the encouragement of art and the prevention of cruelty to children or animals, no part of the net earnings of which inures to the benefit of any private shareholder or individual, which is not disqualified for tax exemption under section 501(c)(3) by reason of attempting to influence legislation, and which does not participate in, or intervene in (including the publishing or distributing of statements), any political campaign on behalf of (or in opposition to) any candidate for public office;

(3) a trust, or community chest, fund, or foundation, organized and operated exclusively for religious, charitable, scientific, literary, or educational purposes, including the encouragement of art and the prevention of cruelty to children or animals, no substantial part of the activities of which is carrying on propaganda, or otherwise attempting, to influence legislation, and which does not participate in, or intervene in (including the publishing or distributing of statements), any political campaign on behalf of (or in opposition to) any candidate for public office; but only if such gifts are to be used within the United States exclusively for such purposes;

(4) a fraternal society, order, or association, operating under the lodge system, but only if such gifts are to be used within the United States exclusively for religious, charitable, scientific, literary, or educational purposes, including the encouragement of art and the prevention of cruelty to children or animals;

(5) posts or organizations of war veterans, or auxiliary units or societies of any such posts or organizations, if such posts, organizations, units, or societies are organized in the United States or any of its possessions, and if no part of their net earnings inures to the benefit of any private shareholder or individual.

Amendments

• **1987, Revenue Act of 1987 (P.L. 100-203)**

P.L. 100-203, §10711(a)(6):

Amended Code Sec. 2522(b)(2) and (3) by striking out "on behalf of any candidate" and inserting in lieu thereof "on behalf of (or in opposition to) any candidate". **Effective** with respect to activities after 12-22-87.

• **1981, Economic Recovery Tax Act of 1981 (P.L. 97-34)**

P.L. 97-34, §442(c):

Amended Code Sec. 2522(b) by striking out "quarter" and inserting "year". **Effective** with respect to estates of decedents dying after 12-31-81.

• **1976, Tax Reform Act of 1976 (P.L. 94-455)**

P.L. 94-455, §1307(d)(1)(B)(v):

Substituted "which is not disqualified for tax exemption under section 501(c)(3) by reason of attempting to influence legislation" for "no substantial part of the activities of which is carrying on propaganda, or otherwise attempting, to influence legislation" in Code Sec. 2522(b)(2). **Effective** for gifts in calendar years beginning after 12-31-76.

P.L. 94-455, §1902(a)(12)(D):

Deleted "territory" in Code Sec. 2522(b)(1). **Effective** for gifts made after 12-31-76.

• **1970, Excise, Estate, and Gift Tax Adjustment Act of 1970 (P.L. 91-614)**

P.L. 91-614, §102(c)(2):

Amended Code Sec. 2522(b) by substituting "quarter" for "year" in the line preceding paragraph (1). **Effective** for gifts made after 12-31-70.

• **1969, Tax Reform Act of 1969 (P.L. 91-172)**

P.L. 91-172, §201(d)(4)(D):

Amended Code Sec. 2522(b)(2) and (3). **Effective** with respect to gifts and transfers made after 12-31-69. Prior to Amendment, Code Sec. 2522(b)(2) and (3) read as follows:

"(2) a domestic corporation organized and operated exclusively for religious, charitable, scientific, literary, or educational purposes, including the encouragement of art and the prevention of cruelty to children or animals, no part of the net earnings of which inures to the benefit of any private shareholder or individual, and no substantial part of the activities of which is carrying on propaganda, or otherwise attempting, to influence legislation;

(3) a trust, or community chest, fund, or foundation, organized and operated exclusively for religious, charitable, scientific, literary, or educational purposes, including the encouragement of art and the prevention of cruelty to children or animals, no substantial part of the activities of which is carrying on propaganda, or otherwise attempting, to influence legislation; but only if such gifts are to be used within the United States exclusively for such purposes;".

[Sec. 2522(c)]

(c) DISALLOWANCE OF DEDUCTIONS IN CERTAIN CASES.—

(1) No deduction shall be allowed under this section for a gift to or for the use of an organization or trust described in section 508(d) or 4948(c)(4) subject to the conditions specified in such sections.

(2) Where a donor transfers an interest in property (other than an interest described in section 170(f)(3)(B)) to a person, or for a use, described in subsection (a) or (b) and an interest in the same property is retained by the donor, or is transferred or has been transferred (for less than an adequate and full consideration in money or money's worth) from the donor to a person, or for a use, not described in subsection (a) or (b), no deduction shall be allowed under this section for the interest which is, or has been transferred to the person, or for the use, described in subsection (a) or (b), unless—

(A) in the case of a remainder interest, such interest is in a trust which is a charitable remainder annuity trust or a charitable remainder unitrust (described in section 664) or a pooled income fund (described in section 642(c)(5)), or

(B) in the case of any other interest, such interest is in the form of a guaranteed annuity or is a fixed percentage distributed yearly of the fair market value of the property (to be determined yearly).

(3) Rules similar to the rules of section 2055(e)(4) shall apply for purposes of paragraph (2).

(4) REFORMATIONS TO COMPLY WITH PARAGRAPH (2).—

(A) IN GENERAL.—A deduction shall be allowed under subsection (a) in respect of any qualified reformation (within the meaning of section 2055(e)(3)(B)).

(B) RULES SIMILAR TO SECTION 2055(e)(3) TO APPLY.—For purposes of this paragraph, rules similar to the rules of section 2055(e)(3) shall apply.

(5) CONTRIBUTIONS TO DONOR ADVISED FUNDS.—A deduction otherwise allowed under subsection (a) for any contribution to a donor advised fund (as defined in section 4966(d)(2)) shall only be allowed if—

(A) the sponsoring organization (as defined in section 4966(d)(1)) with respect to such donor advised fund is not—

(i) described in paragraph (3) or (4) of subsection (a), or

(ii) a type III supporting organization (as defined in section 4943(f)(5)(A)) which is not a functionally integrated type III supporting organization (as defined in section 4943(f)(5)(B)), and

(B) the taxpayer obtains a contemporaneous written acknowledgment (determined under rules similar to the rules of section 170(f)(8)(C)) from the sponsoring organization (as so defined) of such donor advised fund that such organization has exclusive legal control over the assets contributed.

Amendments

• **2018, Tax Technical Corrections Act of 2018 (P.L. 115-141)**

P.L. 115-141, §401(a)(204), Div. U:

Amended Code Sec. 2522(c)(1) by striking "to of for" and inserting "to or for". **Effective** 3-23-2018.

• **2006, Pension Protection Act of 2006 (P.L. 109-280)**

P.L. 109-280, §1234(c):

Amended Code Sec. 2522(c) by adding at the end a new paragraph (5). **Effective** for contributions made after the date which is 180 days after 8-17-2006.

GIFT TAX—DEDUCTIONS

- **1984, Deficit Reduction Act of 1984 (P.L. 98-369)**

P.L. 98-369, §1022(c):

Amended Code Sec. 2522(c) by adding at the end thereof a new paragraph (4). **Effective** for reformations after 12-31-78, except that such amendments shall not apply to any reformation to which Code Sec. 2055(e)(3) (as in effect on the day before 7-18-84) applies. For purposes of applying Code Sec. 2055(e)(3)(C)(iii) (as amended by this section), the 90th day described in such clause shall be treated as not occurring before the 90th day after 7-18-84.

- **1981, Economic Recovery Tax Act of 1981 (P.L. 97-34)**

P.L. 97-34, §423(b):

Added Code Sec. 2522(c)(3). **Effective** for transfers after 12-31-81.

- **1976, Tax Reform Act of 1976 (P.L. 94-455)**

P.L. 94-455, §2124(e)(3)-(4) (as amended by P.L. 95-30, §309(b)(2)):

Substituted "(other than an interest described in section 170(f)(3)(B))" for "(other than a remainder interest in a personal residence or farm or an undivided portion of the donor's entire interest in property)" in Code Sec. 2522(c)(2). **Effective** for contributions or transfers made after 6-13-76, and before 6-14-77. However, P.L. 95-30, §309(b)(2), changed this latter date to 6-14-81.

- **1969, Tax Reform Act of 1969 (P.L. 91-172)**

P.L. 91-172, §201(d)(3):

Amended Code Sec. 2522(c). **Effective** for gifts made after 12-31-69, except the amendments made to section 2522(c)(2) shall apply to gifts made after 7-31-69. Prior to amendment, Code Sec. 2522(c) read as follows:

"(c) Disallowance of Deductions in Certain Cases.—

"For disallowance of certain charitable, etc., deductions otherwise allowable under this section, see sections 503 and 681."

- **1958, Technical Amendments Act of 1958 (P.L. 85-866)**

P.L. 85-866, §30(d):

Amended Code Sec. 2522(c) by substituting "503" for "504". **Effective** 1-1-54.

[Sec. 2522(d)]

(d) SPECIAL RULE FOR IRREVOCABLE TRANSFERS OF EASEMENTS IN REAL PROPERTY.—A deduction shall be allowed under subsection (a) in respect of any transfer of a qualified real property interest (as defined in section 170(h)(2)(C)) which meets the requirements of section 170(h) (without regard to paragraph (4)(A) thereof).

Amendments

- **1986, Tax Reform Act of 1986 (P.L. 99-514)**

P.L. 99-514, §1422(b):

Amended Code Sec. 2522 by redesignating subsection (d) as subsection (e) and by inserting after subsection (c) new subsection (d). **Effective** for transfers and contributions made after 12-31-86.

[Sec. 2522(e)]

(e) SPECIAL RULES FOR FRACTIONAL GIFTS.—

(1) DENIAL OF DEDUCTION IN CERTAIN CASES.—

(A) IN GENERAL.—No deduction shall be allowed for a contribution of an undivided portion of a taxpayer's entire interest in tangible personal property unless all interests in the property are held immediately before such contribution by—

(i) the taxpayer, or

(ii) the taxpayer and the donee.

(B) EXCEPTIONS.—The Secretary may, by regulation, provide for exceptions to subparagraph (A) in cases where all persons who hold an interest in the property make proportional contributions of an undivided portion of the entire interest held by such persons.

(2) RECAPTURE OF DEDUCTION IN CERTAIN CASES; ADDITION TO TAX.—

(A) IN GENERAL.—The Secretary shall provide for the recapture of an amount equal to any deduction allowed under this section (plus interest) with respect to any contribution of an undivided portion of a taxpayer's entire interest in tangible personal property—

(i) in any case in which the donor does not contribute all of the remaining interests in such property to the donee (or, if such donee is no longer in existence, to any person described in section 170(c)) on or before the earlier of—

(I) the date that is 10 years after the date of the initial fractional contribution, or

(II) the date of the death of the donor, and

(ii) in any case in which the donee has not, during the period beginning on the date of the initial fractional contribution and ending on the date described in clause (i)—

(I) had substantial physical possession of the property, and

(II) used the property in a use which is related to a purpose or function constituting the basis for the organizations' exemption under section 501.

(B) ADDITION TO TAX.—The tax imposed under this chapter for any taxable year for which there is a recapture under subparagraph (A) shall be increased by 10 percent of the amount so recaptured.

(C) INITIAL FRACTIONAL CONTRIBUTION.—For purposes of this paragraph, the term "initial fractional contribution" means, with respect to any donor, the first gift of an undivided portion of the donor's entire interest in any tangible personal property for which a deduction is allowed under subsection (a) or (b).

Amendments

- **2007, Tax Technical Corrections Act of 2007 (P.L. 110-172)**

P.L. 110-172, §3(d)(2)(A)-(C):

Amended Code Sec. 2522(e) by striking paragraphs (2) and (4), by redesignating paragraph (3) as paragraph (2), and by adding at the end of paragraph (2), as so redesignated, a new subparagraph (C). **Effective** as if included in the provision of the Pension Protection Act of 2006 (P.L. 109-280) to which it relates [effective for contributions, bequests, and gifts made after 8-17-2006.—CCH]. Prior to being stricken, Code Sec. 2522(e)(2) and (4) read as follows:

(2) VALUATION OF SUBSEQUENT GIFTS.—In the case of any additional contribution, the fair market value of such contribution shall be determined by using the lesser of—

(A) the fair market value of the property at the time of the initial fractional contribution, or

(B) the fair market value of the property at the time of the additional contribution.

* * *

(4) DEFINITIONS.—For purposes of this subsection—

(A) ADDITIONAL CONTRIBUTION.—The term "additional contribution" means any gift for which a deduction is allowed under subsection (a) or (b) of any interest in a property with respect to which the donor has previously made an initial fractional contribution.

(B) INITIAL FRACTIONAL CONTRIBUTION.—The term "initial fractional contribution" means, with respect to any donor, the first gift of an undivided portion of the donor's entire interest in any tangible personal property for which a deduction is allowed under subsection (a) or (b).

P.L. 110-172, §11(a)(16)(A):

Amended Code Sec. 2522(e)(1)(A) by striking "all interest in the property is" and inserting "all interests in the property are". **Effective** 12-29-2007.

P.L. 110-172, §11(a)(16)(B)(i)-(ii):

Amended Code Sec. 2522(e)(2)(A)(i) (as redesignated by Act Sec. 3(d)(2)) by striking "interest" and inserting "interests", and by striking "before" and inserting "on or before". **Effective** 12-29-2007.

- **2006, Pension Protection Act of 2006 (P.L. 109-280)**

P.L. 109-280, §1218(c):

Amended Code Sec. 2522 by redesignating subsection (e) as subsection (f) and by inserting after subsection (d) a new subsection (e). **Effective** for contributions, bequests, and gifts made after 8-17-2006.

[Sec. 2522(f)]

(f) CROSS REFERENCES.—

(1) For treatment of certain organizations providing child care, see section 501(k).

GIFT TAX—DEDUCTIONS

(2) For exemption of certain gifts to or for the benefit of the United States and for rules of construction with respect to certain bequests, see section 2055(f).

(3) For treatment of gifts to or for the use of Indian tribal governments (or their subdivisions), see section 7871.

Amendments

- **2006, Pension Protection Act of 2006 (P.L. 109-280)**

P.L. 109-280, § 1218(c):

Amended Code Sec. 2522 by redesignating subsection (e) as subsection (f). **Effective** for contributions, bequests, and gifts made after 8-17-2006.

- **1986, Tax Reform Act of 1986 (P.L. 99-514)**

P.L. 99-514, § 1422(b):

Redesignated subsection (d) as subsection (e). **Effective** for transfers and contributions made after 12-31-86.

- **1984, Deficit Reduction Act of 1984 (P.L. 98-369)**

P.L. 98-369 § 1032(b)(3):

Amended Code Sec. 2522(d) by redesignating paragraphs (1) and (2) as paragraphs (2) and (3), respectively, and by inserting before paragraph (2) (as so redesignated) a new paragraph (1). **Effective** for tax years beginning after 7-18-84.

- **1983 (P.L. 97-473)**

P.L. 97-473, § 202(b)(7):

Amended Code Sec. 2522(d). For the **effective** date, see the amendment note for P.L. 97-473, Act Sec. 204, following Code Sec. 7871. Prior to amendment, Code Sec. 2522(d) read as follows:

"(d) CROSS REFERENCES.—

For exemption of certain gifts to or for the benefit of the United States and for rules of construction with respect to certain gifts, see section 2055(f)."

- **1976, Tax Reform Act of 1976 (P.L. 94-455)**

P.L. 94-455, § 1902(a)(11), (c)(1):

Amended Code Sec. 2522(d). **Effective** for estates of decedents dying after 12-31-70. Prior to amendment, Code Sec. 2522(d) read as follows:

(d) OTHER CROSS REFERENCES.—

(1) For exemption of gifts to or for benefit of Library of Congress, see section 5 of the Act of March 3, 1925, as amended (56 Stat. 765; 2 U.S.C. 161).

(2) For construction of gifts for benefit of library of Post Office Department as gifts to or for the use of the United States, see section 2 of the Act of August 8, 1946 (60 Stat. 924; 5 U.S.C. 393).

(3) For exemption of gifts for benefit of Office of Naval Records and Library, Navy Department, see section 2 of the Act of March 4, 1937 (50 Stat. 25; 5 U.S.C. 419b).

(4) For exemption of gifts to or for benefit of National Park Service, see section 5 of the Act of July 10, 1935 (49 Stat. 478; 16 U.S.C. 19c).

(5) For construction of gifts accepted by the Secretary of State under the Foreign Service Act of 1946 as gifts to or for the use of the United States, see section 1021 (e) of that Act (60 Stat. 1032; 22 U.S.C. 809).

(6) For construction of gifts or bequests of money accepted by the Attorney General for credit to "Commissary Funds, Federal Prisons" as gifts or bequests to or for the use of the United States, see section 2 of the Act of May 15, 1952, 66 Stat. 73, as amended by the Act of July 9, 1952, 66 Stat. 479 (31 U.S.C. 725s-4).

(7) For payment of tax on gifts of United States obligations to the United States, see section 24 of the Second Liberty Bond Act, as amended (59 Stat. 48, § 4; 31 U.S.C. 757e).

(8) For construction of gifts for benefit of or use in connection with Naval Academy as gifts to or for the use of the United States, see section 3 of the Act of March 31, 1944 (58 Stat. 135; 34 U.S.C. 1115b).

(9) For exemption of gifts for benefit of Naval Academy Museum, see section 4 of the Act of March 26, 1938 (52 Stat. 119; 34 U.S.C. 1119).

(10) For exemption of gifts received by National Archives Trust Fund Board, see section 7 of the National Archives Trust Fund Board Act (55 Stat. 582; 44 U.S.C. 300gg).

[Sec. 2523]

SEC. 2523. GIFT TO SPOUSE.

[Sec. 2523(a)]

(a) ALLOWANCE OF DEDUCTION.—Where a donor transfers during the calendar year by gift an interest in property to a donee who at the time of the gift is the donor's spouse, there shall be allowed as a deduction in computing taxable gifts for the calendar year an amount with respect to such interest equal to its value.

Amendments

- **1989, Omnibus Budget Reconciliation Act of 1989 (P.L. 101-239)**

P.L. 101-239, § 7815(d)(2):

Amended Code Sec. 2523(a) by striking "who is a citizen or resident" after "Where a donor". **Effective** as if included in the provision of P.L. 100-647 to which it relates.

- **1981, Economic Recovery Tax Act of 1981 (P.L. 97-34)**

P.L. 97-34, § 403(b)(1):

Amended Code Sec. 2523(a). **Effective**, generally, for gifts made after 12-31-81. For special rules, see Act Sec. 403(e)(3), below. Prior to amendment, Code Sec. 2523(a) read as follows:

(a) ALLOWANCE OF DEDUCTION.—

(1) IN GENERAL.—Where a donor who is a citizen or resident transfers during the calendar quarter by gift an interest in property to a donee who at the time of the gift is the donor's spouse, there shall be allowed as a deduction in computing taxable gifts for the calendar quarter an amount with respect to such interest equal to its value.

(2) LIMITATION.—The aggregate of the deductions allowed under paragraph (1) for any calendar quarter shall not exceed the sum of—

(A) $100,000 reduced (but not below zero) by the aggregate of the deductions allowed under this section for preceding calendar quarters beginning after December 31, 1976; plus

(B) 50 percent of the lessor of—

(i) the amount of the deductions allowable under paragraph (1) for such calendar quarter (determined without regard to this paragraph); or

(ii) the amount (if any) by which the aggregate of the amounts determined under clause (i) for the calendar quarter and for each preceding calendar quarter beginning after December 31, 1976, exceeds $200,000.

P.L. 97-34, § 403(e)(3), provides:

(3) If—

(A) the decedent dies after December 31, 1981,

(B) by reason of the death of the decedent property passes from the decedent or is acquired from the decedent under a will executed before the date which is 30 days after the date of the enactment of this Act, or a trust created before such date, which contains a formula expressly providing that the spouse is to receive the maximum amount of property qualifying for the marital deduction allowable by Federal law,

(C) the formula referred to in subparagraph (B) was not amended to refer specifically to an unlimited marital deduction at any time after the date which is 30 days after the date of enactment of this Act, and before the death of the decedent, and

(D) the State does not enact a staute applicable to such estate which construes this type of formula as referring to the marital deduction allowable by Federal law as amended by subsection (a),

then the amendment made by subsection (a) [relating to the unlimited marital deduction (Code Sec. 2056, as amended by P.L. 97-34)] shall not apply to the estate of such decedent.

- **1976, Tax Reform Act of 1976 (P.L. 94-455)**

P.L. 94-455, § 2002(b), (d)(2):

Amended Code Sec. 2523(a). **Effective** for gifts made after 12-31-76. Prior to amendment, Code Sec. 2523(a) read as follows:

(a) IN GENERAL.—Where a donor who is a citizen or resident transfers during the calendar quarter by gift an interest in property to a donee who at the time of the gift is the donor's spouse, there shall be allowed as a deduction in computing taxable gifts for the calendar quarter an amount with respect to such interest equal to one-half of its value.

- **1970, Excise, Estate, and Gift Tax Adjustment Act of 1970 (P.L. 91-614)**

P.L. 91-614, § 102(c)(3):

Amended Code Sec. 2523(a) by substituting "calendar quarter" for "calendar year" in the two places such term appears. **Effective** for gifts made after 12-31-70.

[Sec. 2523(b)]

(b) LIFE ESTATE OR OTHER TERMINABLE INTEREST.—Where, on the lapse of time, on the occurrence of an event or contingency, or on the failure of an event or contingency to occur, such interest transferred to the spouse will terminate or fail, no deduction shall be allowed with respect to such interest—

(1) if the donor retains in himself, or transfers or has transferred (for less than an adequate and full consideration in money or money's worth) to any person other than such donee spouse (or the estate of such spouse), an interest in such property, and if by reason of such retention or transfer the donor (or his heirs or assigns) or such person (or his heirs or assigns) may possess or enjoy any part of such property after such termination or failure of the interest transferred to the donee spouse; or

(2) if the donor immediately after the transfer to the donee spouse has a power to appoint an interest in such property which he can exercise (either alone or in conjunction with any person) in such manner that the appointee may possess or enjoy any part of such property after such termination or failure of the interest transferred to the donee spouse. For purposes of this paragraph, the donor shall be considered

GIFT TAX—DEDUCTIONS

as having immediately after the transfer to the donee spouse such power to appoint even though such power cannot be exercised until after the lapse of time, upon the occurrence of an event or contingency, or on the failure of an event or contingency to occur.

An exercise or release at any time by the donor, either alone or in conjunction with any person, of a power to appoint an interest in property, even though not otherwise a transfer, shall, for purposes of paragraph (1), be considered as a transfer by him. Except as provided in subsection (e), where at the time of the transfer it is impossible to ascertain the particular person or persons who may receive from the donor an interest in property so transferred by him, such interest shall, for purposes of paragraph (1), be considered as transferred to a person other than the donee spouse.

[Sec. 2523(c)]

(c) INTEREST IN UNIDENTIFIED ASSETS.—Where the assets out of which, or the proceeds of which, the interest transferred to the donee spouse may be satisfied include a particular asset or assets with respect to which no deduction would be allowed if such asset or assets were transferred from the donor to such spouse, then the value of the interest transferred to such spouse shall, for purposes of subsection (a), be reduced by the aggregate value of such particular assets.

[Sec. 2523(d)]

(d) JOINT INTERESTS.—If the interest is transferred to the donee spouse as sole joint tenant with the donor or as tenant by the entirety, the interest of the donor in the property which exists solely by reason of the possibility that the donor may survive the donee spouse, or that there may occur a severance of the tenancy, shall not be considered for purposes of subsection (b) as an interest retained by the donor in himself.

[Sec. 2523(e)]

(e) LIFE ESTATE WITH POWER OF APPOINTMENT IN DONEE SPOUSE.—Where the donor transfers an interest in property, if by such transfer his spouse is entitled for life to all of the income from the entire interest, or all the income from a specific portion thereof, payable annually or at more frequent intervals, with power in the donee spouse to appoint the entire interest, or such specific portion (exercisable in favor of such donee spouse, or of the estate of such donee spouse, or in favor of either, whether or not in each case the power is exercisable in favor of others), and with no power in any other person to appoint any part of such interest, or such portion, to any person other than the donee spouse—

(1) the interest, or such portion, so transferred shall, for purposes of subsection (a) be considered as transferred to the donee spouse, and

(2) no part of the interest, or such portion, so transferred shall, for purposes of subsection (b)(1), be considered as retained in the donor or transferred to any person other than the donee spouse.

This subsection shall apply only if, by such transfer, such power in the donee spouse to appoint the interest, or such portion, whether exercisable by will or during life, is exercisable by such spouse alone and in all events. For purposes of this subsection, the term "specific portion" only includes a portion determined on a fractional or percentage basis.

Amendments

- **1992, Energy Policy Act of 1992 (P.L. 102-486)**

P.L. 102-486, § 1941(b)(1):

Amended Code Sec. 2523(e) by adding at the end thereof a new sentence. **Effective** for gifts made after 10-24-92.

[Sec. 2523(f)—Repealed]

Amendments

- **1981, Economic Recovery Tax Act of 1981 (P.L. 97-34)**

P.L. 97-34, § 403(b)(2):

Repealed Code Sec. 2523(f). **Effective**, generally, for gifts made after 12-31-81. Prior to its repeal, Code Sec. 2523(f) read as follows:

(f) COMMUNITY PROPERTY.—

(1) A deduction otherwise allowable under this section shall be allowed only to the extent that the transfer can be shown to represent a gift of property which is not, at the time of the gift, held as community property under the law of any State, possession of the United States, or of any foreign country.

(2) For purposes of paragraph (1), community property (except property which is considered as community property solely by reason of paragraph (3)) shall not be considered as "held as community property" if the entire value of such property (and not merely one-half thereof) is treated as the amount of the gift.

(3) If during the calendar year 1942 or in succeeding calendar years, property held as such community property (unless considered by reason of paragraph (2) as not so held) was by the donor and the donee spouse converted, by one transaction or a series of transactions, into separate property of the donor and such spouse (including any form of coownership by them), the separate property so acquired by the donor and any property acquired at any time by the donor in exchange therefor (by one exchange or a series of exchanges) shall, for purposes of paragraph (1), be considered as "held as community property."

(4) Where the value (at the time of such conversion) of the separate property so acquired by the donor exceeded the value (at such time) of the separate property so acquired by such spouse, paragraph (3) shall apply only with respect to the same portion of such separate property of the donor as the portion which the value (as of such time) of such separate property so acquired by such spouse is of the value (as of such time) of the separate property so acquired by the donor.

For the special rule applicable to certain wills or trusts, executed or created, before September 12, 1981, see the historical comment following Code Sec. 2523(a), at P.L. 97-34, § 403(b)(1), above.

- **1976, Tax Reform Act of 1976 (P.L. 94-455)**

P.L. 94-455, § 1902(a)(12)(E), (c)(2):

Deleted "Territory, or" in Code Sec. 2523(f)(1). **Effective** for gifts made after 12-31-76.

[Sec. 2523(f)]

(f) ELECTION WITH RESPECT TO LIFE ESTATE FOR DONEE SPOUSE.—

(1) IN GENERAL.—In the case of qualified terminable interest property—

(A) for purposes of subsection (a), such property shall be treated as transferred to the donee spouse, and

(B) for purposes of subsection (b)(1), no part of such property shall be considered as retained in the donor or transferred to any person other than the donee spouse.

(2) QUALIFIED TERMINABLE INTEREST PROPERTY.—For purposes of this subsection, the term "qualified terminable interest property" means any property—

(A) which is transferred by the donor spouse,

(B) in which the donee spouse has a qualifying income interest for life, and

(C) to which an election under this subsection applies.

(3) CERTAIN RULES MADE APPLICABLE.—For purposes of this subsection, rules similar to the rules of clauses (ii), (iii), and (iv) of section 2056(b)(7)(B) shall apply and the rules of section 2056(b)(10) shall apply.

(4) ELECTION.—

(A) TIME AND MANNER.—An election under this subsection with respect to any property shall be made on or before the date prescribed by section 6075(b) for filing a gift tax return with respect to the transfer (determined without regard to section 6019(2)) and shall be made in such manner as the Secretary shall by regulations prescribe.

(B) ELECTION IRREVOCABLE.—An election under this subsection, once made, shall be irrevocable.

(5) TREATMENT OF INTEREST RETAINED BY DONOR SPOUSE.—

(A) IN GENERAL.—In the case of any qualified terminable interest property—

GIFT TAX—DEDUCTIONS

        (i) such property shall not be includible in the gross estate of the donor spouse, and

        (ii) any subsequent transfer by the donor spouse of an interest in such property shall not be treated as a transfer for purposes of this chapter.

    (B) SUBPARAGRAPH (A) NOT TO APPLY AFTER TRANSFER BY DONEE SPOUSE.—Subparagraph (A) shall not apply with respect to any property after the donee spouse is treated as having transferred such property under section 2519, or such property is includible in the donee spouse's gross estate under section 2044.

  (6) TREATMENT OF JOINT AND SURVIVOR ANNUITIES.—In the case of a joint and survivor annuity where only the donor spouse and donee spouse have the right to receive payments before the death of the last spouse to die—

    (A) the donee spouse's interest shall be treated as a qualifying income interest for life,

    (B) the donor spouse shall be treated as having made an election under this subsection with respect to such annuity unless the donor spouse otherwise elects on or before the date specified in paragraph (4)(A),

    (C) paragraph (5) and section 2519 shall not apply to the donor spouse's interest in the annuity, and

    (D) if the donee spouse dies before the donor spouse, no amount shall be includible in the gross estate of the donee spouse under section 2044 with respect to such annuity. An election under subparagraph (B), once made, shall be irrevocable.

Amendments

• **1992, Energy Policy Act of 1992 (P.L. 102-486)**

P.L. 102-486, § 1941(b)(2):

Amended Code Sec. 2523(f)(3) by inserting "and the rules of section 2056(b)(10) shall apply" before the period at the end thereof. **Effective** for gifts made after the date of the enactment of this Act.

• **1988, Technical and Miscellaneous Revenue Act of 1988 (P.L. 100-647)**

P.L. 100-647, § 6152(b):

Amended Code Sec. 2523(f) by adding at the end thereof new paragraph (6). **Effective**, generally, for transfers made after 12-31-81. However, Act Sec. 6152(c)(2) and (3) provide special rules.

P.L. 100-647, § 6152(c)(2)-(3), provide:

(2) NOT TO APPLY TO EXTENT INCONSISTENT WITH PRIOR RETURN.—In the case of any estate or gift tax return filed before the date of the enactment of this Act, the amendments made by this section shall not apply to the extent such amendments would be inconsistent with the treatment of the annuity on such return unless the executor or donor (as the case may be) otherwise elects under this paragraph before the day 2 years after the date of the enactment of this Act.

(3) EXTENSION OF TIME FOR ELECTION OUT.—The time for making an election under section 2056(b)(7)(C)(ii) or 2523(f)(6)(B) of the 1986 Code (as added by this subsection) shall not expire before the day 2 years after the date of the enactment of this Act (and, if such election is made within the time permitted under this paragraph, the requirement of such section 2056(b)(7)(C)(ii) that it be made on the return shall not apply).

• **1986, Tax Reform Act of 1986 (P.L. 99-514)**

P.L. 99-514, § 1879(n)(1):

Amended Code Sec. 2523(f)(4)(A). **Effective** for transfers made after 12-31-85. For a special rule, see Act Sec. 1879(n)(3), below. Prior to amendment, Code Sec. 2523(f)(4)(A) read as follows:

(A) TIME AND MANNER.—An election under this subsection with respect to any property shall be made on or before the first April 15th after the calendar year in which the interest was transferred and shall be made in such manner as the Secretary shall by regulations prescribe.

P.L. 99-514, § 1879(n)(3), provides:

(3) SPECIAL RULE FOR CERTAIN TRANSFERS IN OCTOBER 1984.—An election under section 2523(f) of the Internal Revenue Code of 1954 with respect to an interest in property which—

(A) was transferred during October 1984, and

(B) was transferred pursuant to a trust instrument stating that the grantor's intention was that the property of the trust would constitute qualified terminable interest property as to which a Federal gift tax marital deduction would be allowed upon the grantor's election,

shall be made on the return of tax imposed by section 2501 of such Code for the calendar year 1984 which is filed on or before the due date of such return or, if a timely return is not filed, on the first such return filed after the due date of such return and before December 31, 1986.

• **1983, Technical Corrections Act of 1982 (P.L. 97-448)**

P.L. 97-448, § 104(a)(4):

Amended Code Sec. 2523(f)(4). **Effective** as if included in the provision of P.L. 97-34 to which it relates. Prior to amendment, Code Sec. 2523(f)(4) read as follows:

"(4) ELECTION.—An election under this subsection with respect to any property shall be made on the return of the tax imposed by section 2501 for the calendar year in which the interest was transferred. Such an election, once made, shall be irrevocable."

P.L. 97-448, § 104(a)(5):

Amended Code Sec. 2523(f) by adding at the end thereof new paragraph (5). **Effective** as if included in the provision of P.L. 97-34 to which it relates.

P.L. 97-448, § 104(a)(6):

Amended Code Sec. 2523(f)(3) by striking out "the rules of" and inserting in lieu thereof "rules similar to the rules of". **Effective** as if included in the provision of P.L. 97-34 to which it relates.

• **1981, Economic Recovery Tax Act of 1981 (P.L. 97-34)**

P.L. 97-34, § 403(d)(2):

Added Code Sec. 2523(f). **Effective**, generally, for gifts made after 12-31-81. See Act Sec. 403(e)(3), below, for a special rule applicable to certain wills and trusts, executed or created, before 9-12-81.

P.L. 97-34, § 403(e)(3), provides:

(3) If—

(A) the decedent dies after December 31, 1981,

(B) by reason of the death of the decedent property passes from the decedent or is acquired from the decedent under a will executed before the date which is 30 days after the date of the enactment of this Act, or a trust created before such date, which contains a formula expressly providing that the spouse is to receive the maximum amount of property qualifying for the marital deduction allowable by Federal law,

(C) the formula referred to in subparagraph (B) was not amended to refer specifically to an unlimited marital deduction at any time after the date which is 30 days after the date of enactment of this Act, and before the death of the decedent, and

(D) the State does not enact a statute applicable to such estate which construes this type of formula as referring to the marital deduction allowable by Federal law as amended by subsection (a),

then the amendment made by subsection (a) [relating to the unlimited marital deduction (Code Sec. 2056, as amended by P.L. 97-34)] shall not apply to the estate of such decedent.

[Sec. 2523(g)]

  (g) SPECIAL RULE FOR CHARITABLE REMAINDER TRUSTS.—

    (1) IN GENERAL.—If, after the transfer, the donee spouse is the only beneficiary who is not a charitable beneficiary (other than the donor) of a qualified charitable remainder trust, subsection (b) shall not apply to the interest in such trust which is transferred to the donee spouse.

    (2) DEFINITIONS.—For purposes of paragraph (1), the terms "charitable beneficiary" and "qualified charitable remainder trust" have the meanings given to such terms by section 2056(b)(8)(B).

Amendments

• **2018, Tax Technical Corrections Act of 2018 (P.L. 115-141)**

P.L. 115-141, § 401(a)(205), Div. U:

Amended Code Sec. 2523(g)(1) by striking "noncharitable beneficiary" and inserting "beneficiary who is not a charitable beneficiary". **Effective** 3-23-2018.

P.L. 115-141, § 401(a)(206), Div. U:

Amended Code Sec. 2523(g)(2) by striking "noncharitable" and inserting "charitable". **Effective** 3-23-2018.

• **1997, Taxpayer Relief Act of 1997 (P.L. 105-34)**

P.L. 105-34, § 1604(g)(4):

Amended Code Sec. 2523(g)(1) by striking "qualified remainder trust" and inserting "qualified charitable remainder trust". **Effective** 8-5-97.

• **1981, Economic Recovery Tax Act of 1981 (P.L. 97-34)**

P.L. 97-34, § 403(d)(2):

Added Code Sec. 2523(g). **Effective**, generally, for gifts made after 12-31-81. For the special rule applicable to certain wills and trusts, executed or created, before 9-12-81, see the amendment note following Code Sec. 2523(f).

[Sec. 2523(h)]

  (h) DENIAL OF DOUBLE DEDUCTION.—Nothing in this section or any other provision of this chapter shall allow the value of any interest in property to be deducted under this chapter more than once with respect to the same donor.

Amendments

• **1983, Technical Corrections Act of 1982 (P.L. 97-448)**

P.L. 97-448, §104(a)(2)(B):

Added Code Sec. 2523(h). **Effective** as if included in the provision of P.L. 97-34 to which it relates.

[Sec. 2523(i)]

(i) DISALLOWANCE OF MARITAL DEDUCTION WHERE SPOUSE NOT CITIZEN.—If the spouse of the donor is not a citizen of the United States—

(1) no deduction shall be allowed under this section,

(2) section 2503(b) shall be applied with respect to gifts which are made by the donor to such spouse and with respect to which a deduction would be allowable under this section but for paragraph (1) by substituting "$100,000" for "$10,000", and

(3) the principles of sections 2515 and 2515A (as such sections were in effect before their repeal by the Economic Recovery Tax Act of 1981) shall apply, except that the provisions of such section 2515 providing for an election shall not apply.

This subsection shall not apply to any transfer resulting from the acquisition of rights under a joint and survivor annuity described in subsection (f)(6).

Amendments

• **1990, Omnibus Budget Reconciliation Act of 1990 (P.L. 101-508)**

P.L. 101-508, §11702(g)(1):

Amended Code Sec. 2523(i) by adding at the end thereof a new sentence. **Effective** as if included in the provision of P.L. 100-647 to which it relates.

• **1989, Omnibus Budget Reconciliation Act of 1989 (P.L. 101-239)**

P.L. 101-239, §7815(d)(1)(A):

Amended Code Sec. 2523(i)(2) by striking "made by the donor to such spouse" and inserting "which are made by the donor to such spouse and with respect to which a deduction would be allowable under this section but for paragraph (1)". **Effective** with respect to gifts made after 6-29-89.

• **1988, Technical and Miscellaneous Revenue Act of 1988 (P.L. 100-647)**

P.L. 100-647, §5033(b):

Amended Code Sec. 2523 by adding at the end thereof a new subsection (i). **Effective** for gifts on or after 7-14-88.

[Sec. 2524]

SEC. 2524. EXTENT OF DEDUCTIONS.

The deductions provided in sections 2522 and 2523 shall be allowed only to the extent that the gifts therein specified are included in the amount of gifts against which such deductions are applied.

CHAPTER 13—TAX ON GENERATION-SKIPPING TRANSFERS

SUBCHAPTER A.	Tax imposed.
SUBCHAPTER B.	Generation-skipping transfers.
SUBCHAPTER C.	Taxable amount.
SUBCHAPTER D.	GST exemption.
SUBCHAPTER E.	Applicable rate; inclusion ratio.
SUBCHAPTER F.	Other definitions and special rules.
SUBCHAPTER G.	Administration.

Subchapter A—Tax Imposed

Sec. 2601.	Tax imposed.
Sec. 2602.	Amount of tax.
Sec. 2603.	Liability for tax.

[Sec. 2601]

SEC. 2601. TAX IMPOSED.

A tax is hereby imposed on every generation-skipping transfer (within the meaning of subchapter B).

Amendments

• **1990, Omnibus Budget Reconciliation Act of 1990 (P.L. 101-508)**

P.L. 101-508, §11703(c)(3), provides:

(3) Subparagraph (C) of section 1433(b)(2) of the Tax Reform Act of 1986 shall not exempt any generation-skipping transfer from the amendments made by subtitle D of title XVI of such Act to the extent such transfer is attributable to property transferred by gift or by reason of the death of another person to the decedent (or trust) referred to in such subparagraph after August 3, 1990.

• **1988, Technical and Miscellaneous Revenue Act of 1988 (P.L. 100-647)**

P.L. 100-647, §1014(h)(3)(B) and (h)(5), provide:

(3)(B) Clause (iii) of section 1443[1433](b)(3)(B) of the Reform Act (as amended by subparagraph (A)) shall apply only to transfers after June 10, 1987.

* * *

(5) Subparagraph (C) of section 1433(b)(2) of the Reform Act shall not exempt any direct skip from the amendments made by subtitle D of title XIV of the Reform Act if—

(A) such direct skip results from the application of section 2044 of the 1986 Code, and

(B) such direct skip is attributable to property transferred to the trust after October 21, 1988.

• **1986, Tax Reform Act of 1986 (P.L. 99-514)**

P.L. 99-514, §1431(a):

Amended chapter 13 (Code Secs. 2601-2602). **Effective**, generally, for any generation-skipping transfer (within the meaning of section 2611 of the Internal Revenue Code of 1986) made after 10-22-86. However, for special rules, see Act Sec. 1433(b)-(d), below. Prior to amendment by P.L. 99-514, Code Sec. 2601 read as follows:

SEC. 2601. TAX IMPOSED.

A tax is hereby imposed on every generation-skipping transfer in the amount determined under section 2602.

P.L. 99-514, §1433(b)-(d), as amended by P.L. 100-647, §1014(h)(2)-(4), provides:

(b) SPECIAL RULES.—

(1) TREATMENT OF CERTAIN INTER VIVOS TRANSFERS MADE AFTER SEPTEMBER 25, 1985.—For purposes of subsection (a) (and chapter 13 of the Internal Revenue Code of 1986 as amended by this part), any inter vivos transfer after September 25, 1985, and on or before the date of the enactment of this Act shall be treated as if it were made on the 1st day after the date of enactment of this Act.

(2) EXCEPTIONS.—The amendments made by this subtitle shall not apply to—

(A) any generation-skipping transfer under a trust which was irrevocable on September 25, 1985, but only to the extent that such transfer is not made out of corpus added to the trust after September 25, 1985 (or out of income attributable to corpus so added),

(B) any generation-skipping transfer under a will or revocable trust executed before the date of the enactment of this Act if the decedent dies before January 1, 1987, and

(C) any generation-skipping transfer—

(i) under a trust to the extent such trust consists of property included in the gross estate of a decedent (other than property transferred by the decedent during his life after the date of the enactment of this Act), or reinvestments thereof, or

(ii) which is a direct skip which occurs by reason of the death of any decedent;

but only if such decedent was, on the date of the enactment of this Act, under a mental disability to change the disposition of his property and did not regain his competence to dispose of such property before the date of his death.

(3) TREATMENT OF CERTAIN TRANSFERS TO GRANDCHILDREN.—

GENERATION-SKIPPING TRANSFERS

(A) IN GENERAL.—For purposes of chapter 13 of the Internal Revenue Code of 1986, the term "direct skip" shall not include any transfer before January 1, 1990, from a transferor to a grandchild of the transferor to the extent the aggregate transfers from such transferor to such grandchild do not exceed $2,000,000.

(B) TREATMENT OF TRANSFERS IN TRUST.—For purposes of subparagraph (A), a transfer in trust for the benefit of a grandchild shall be treated as a transfer to such grandchild if (and only if)—

(i) during the life of the grandchild, no portion of the corpus or income of the trust may be distributed to (or for the benefit of) any person other than such grandchild.

(ii) the assets of the trust will be includible in the gross estate of the grandchild if the grandchild dies before the trust is terminated, and

(iii) all of the income of the trust for periods after the grandchild has attained age 21 will be distributed to (or for the benefit of) such grandchild not less frequently than annually.

(C) COORDINATION WITH SECTION 2653(a) OF THE 1986 CODE.—In the case of any transfer which would be a generation-skipping transfer but for subparagraph (A), the rules of section 2653(a) of the Internal Revenue Code of 1986 shall apply as if such transfer were a generation-skipping transfer.

(D) COORDINATION WITH TAXABLE TERMINATIONS AND TAXABLE DISTRIBUTIONS.—For purposes of chapter 13 of the Internal Revenue Code of 1986, the terms "taxable termination" and "taxable distribution" shall not include any transfer which would be a direct skip but for subparagraph (A).

(4) DEFINITIONS.—Terms used in this section shall have the same respective meanings as when used in chapter 13 of the Internal Revenue Code of 1986; except that section 2612(c)(2) of such Code shall not apply in determining whether an individual is a grandchild of the transferor.

(c) REPEAL OF EXISTING TAX ON GENERATION-SKIPPING TRANSFERS.—

(1) IN GENERAL.—In the case of any tax imposed by chapter 13 of the Internal Revenue Code of 1954 (as in effect on the day before the date of the enactment of this Act), such tax (including interest, additions to tax, and additional amounts) shall not be assessed and if assessed, the assessment shall be abated, and if collected, shall be credited or refunded (with interest) as an overpayment.

(2) WAIVER OF STATUTE OF LIMITATIONS.—If on the date of the enactment of this Act (or at any time within 1 year after such date of enactment) refund or credit of any overpayment of tax resulting from the application of paragraph (1) is barred by any law or rule of law, refund or credit of such overpayment shall, nevertheless, be made or allowed if claim therefore is filed before the date 1 year after the date of the enactment of this Act.

(d) ELECTION FOR CERTAIN TRANSFERS BENEFITING GRANDCHILDREN.—

(1) IN GENERAL.—For purposes of chapter 13 of the Internal Revenue Code of 1986 (as amended by this Act) and subsection (b) of this section, any transfer in trust for the benefit of a grandchild of a transferor shall be treated as a direct skip to such grandchild if—

(A) the transfer occurs before the date of enactment of this Act,

(B) the transfer would be a direct skip to a grandchild except for the fact that the trust instrument provides that, if the grandchild dies before vesting of the interest transferred, the interest is transferred to the grandchild's heir (rather than the grandchild's estate), and

(C) an election under this subsection applies to such transfer.

Any transfer treated as a direct skip by reason of the preceding sentence shall be subject to Federal estate tax on the grandchild's death in the same manner as if the contingent gift over had been to the grandchild's estate. Unless the grandchild otherwise directs by will, the estate of such grandchild shall be entitled to recover from the person receiving the property on the death of the grandchild any increase in Federal estate tax on the estate of the grandchild by reason of the preceding sentence.

(2) ELECTION.—An election under paragraph (1) shall be made at such time and in such manner as the Secretary of the Treasury or his delegate may prescribe.

• **1976, Tax Reform Act of 1976 (P.L. 94-455)**

P.L. 94-455, § 2006(a), (c):

Added Code Sec. 2601. **Effective** as noted in Act Sec. 2006(c), below.

P.L. 94-455, § 2006(c) (as amended by P.L. 95-600, § 702(n)(1) and P.L. 97-34, § 428), provides:

(c) EFFECTIVE DATES.—

(1) IN GENERAL.—Except as provided in paragraph (2), the amendments made by this section shall apply to any generation-skipping transfer (within the meaning of section 2611(a) of the Internal Revenue Code of 1954) made after June 11, 1976.

(2) EXCEPTIONS.—The amendments made by this section shall not apply to any generation-skipping transfer—

(A) under a trust which was irrevocable on June 11, 1976, but only to the extent that the transfer is not made out of corpus added to the trust after June 11, 1976, or

(B) in the case of a decedent dying before January 1, 1983, pursuant to a will (or revocable trust) which was in existence on June 11, 1976, and was not amended at any time after that date in any respect which will result in the creation of, or increasing the amount of, any generation-skipping transfer.

For purposes of subparagraph (B), if the decedent on June 11, 1976, was under a mental disability to change the disposition of his property, the period set forth in such subparagraph shall not expire before the date which is 2 years after the date on which he first regains his competence to dispose of such property.

(3) TRUST EQUIVALENTS.—For purposes of paragraph (2), in the case of a trust equivalent within the meaning of subsection (d) of section 2611 of the Internal Revenue Code of 1954, the provisions of such subsection (d) shall apply.

[Sec. 2602]

SEC. 2602. AMOUNT OF TAX.

The amount of the tax imposed by section 2601 is—

(1) the taxable amount (determined under subchapter C), multiplied by

(2) the applicable rate (determined under subchapter E).

Amendments

• **1986, Tax Reform Act of 1986 (P.L. 99-514)**

P.L. 99-514, § 1431(a):

Amended Chapter 13 by amending Code Sec. 2602. **Effective**, generally, for any generation-skipping transfer (within the meaning of section 2511 of the Internal Revenue Code of 1986) made after the date of enactment. However, for special rules, see Act Sec. 1433(b)-(d) following Code Sec. 2601. Prior to amendment, Code Sec. 2602 read as follows:

SEC. 2602. AMOUNT OF TAX.

[Sec. 2602(a)]

(a) GENERAL RULE.—The amount of the tax imposed by section 2601 with respect to any transfer shall be the excess of—

(1) a tentative tax computed in accordance with the rate schedule set forth in section 2001(c) (as in effect on the date of transfer) on the sum of—

(A) the fair market value of the property transferred determined as of the date of transfer (or in the case of an election under subsection (d), as of the applicable valuation date prescribed by section 2032),

(B) the aggregate fair market value (determined for purposes of this chapter) of all prior transfers of the deemed transferor to which this chapter applied,

(C) the amount of the adjusted taxable gifts (within the meaning of section 2001(b), as modified by section 2001(e)) made by the deemed transferor before this transfer, and

(D) if the deemed transferor has died at the same time as, or before, this transfer, the taxable estate of the deemed transferor, over

(2) a tentative tax (similarly computed) on the sum of the amounts determined under subparagraphs (B), (C), and (D) of paragraph (1).

Amendments

• **1978, Revenue Act of 1978 (P.L. 95-600)**

P.L. 95-600, § 702(h)(2):

Amended Code Sec. 2602(a)(C) by adding after section 2001(b) ", as modified by section 2001(e)". **Effective** for estates of decedents dying after 1976, except that such amendment shall not apply to transfers made before 1977.

[Sec. 2602(b)]

(b) MULTIPLE SIMULTANEOUS TRANSFERS.—If two or more transfers which are taxable under section 2601 and which have the same deemed transferor occur by reason of the same event, the tax imposed by section 2601 on each such transfer shall be the amount which bears the same ratio to—

(1) the amount of the tax which would be imposed by section 2601 if the aggregate of such transfers were a single transfer, as

(2) the fair market value of the property transferred in such transfer bears to the aggregate fair market value of all property transferred in such transfers.

[Sec. 2602(c)]

(c) DEDUCTIONS, CREDITS, ETC.—

(1) GENERAL RULE.—Except as otherwise provided in this subsection, no deduction, exclusion, exemption, or credit shall be allowed against the tax imposed by section 2601.

(2) CHARITABLE DEDUCTIONS ALLOWED.—The deduction under section 2055, 2106(a)(2), or 2522, whichever is appropriate, shall be allowed in determining the tax imposed by section 2601.

(3) UNUSED PORTION OF UNIFIED CREDIT.—If the generation-skipping transfer occurs at the same time as, or after, the death of the deemed transferor, then the portion of the credit under section 2010(a) (relating to unified credit) which exceeds the sum of—

(A) the tax imposed by section 2001, and

(B) the taxes theretofore imposed by section 2601 with respect to this deemed transferor,

shall be allowed as a credit against the tax imposed by section 2601. The amount of the credit allowed by the preceding sentence shall not exceed the amount of the tax imposed by section 2601.

(4) CREDIT FOR TAX ON PRIOR TRANSFERS.—The credit under section 2013 (relating to credit for tax on prior transfers) shall be allowed against the tax imposed by section 2601. For purposes of the preceding sentence, section 2013 shall be applied as if so much of the property subject to tax under section 2601 as is not taken into account for purposes of determining the credit allowable by section 2013 with respect to the estate of the deemed transferor passed from the transferor (as defined in section 2013) to the deemed transferor.

(5) COORDINATION WITH ESTATE TAX.—

(A) CERTAIN EXPENSES ATTRIBUTABLE TO GENERATION-SKIPPING TRANSFER.—If the generation-skipping transfer occurs at the same time as, or after, the death of the deemed transferor, for purposes of this section, the amount taken into account with respect to such transfer shall be reduced—

(i) in the case of a taxable termination, by any item referred to in section 2053 or 2054 to the extent that a deduction would have been allowable under such section for such item if the amount of the trust had been includible in the deemed transferor's gross estate and if the deemed transferor had died immediately before such transfer, or

GENERATION-SKIPPING TRANSFERS

(ii) in the case of a taxable distribution, by any expense incurred in connection with the determination, collection, or refund of the tax imposed by section 2601 on such transfer.

(B) CREDIT FOR STATE INHERITANCE TAX.—If the generation-skipping transfer occurs at the same time as, or after, the death of the deemed transferor, there shall be allowed as a credit against the tax imposed by section 2601 an amount equal to that portion of the estate, inheritance, legacy, or succession tax actually paid to any State or the District of Columbia in respect of any property included in the generation-skipping transfer, but only to the extent of the lesser of—

(i) that portion of such taxes which is levied on such transfer, or

(ii) the excess of the limitation applicable under section 2011(b) if the adjusted taxable estate of the decedent had been increased by the amount of the transfer and all prior generation-skipping transfers to which this subparagraph applied which had the same deemed transferor, over the sum of the amount allowable as a credit under section 2011 with respect to the estate of the decedent plus the aggregate amounts allowable under this subparagraph with respect to such prior generation-skipping transfers.

Amendments

- **1981, Economic Recovery Tax Act of 1981 (P.L. 97-34)**

P.L. 97-34, §403(a)(2)(B):

Amended Code Sec. 2602(c)(5) by striking out subparagraph (A) and by redesignating subparagraphs (B) and (C) as (A) and (B), respectively. **Effective** for estates of decedents dying after 12-31-81. Prior to deletion, Code Sec. 2602(c)(5)(A) read as follows:

(A) ADJUSTMENTS TO MARITAL DEDUCTION.—If the generation-skipping transfer occurs at the same time as, or within 9 months after, the death of the deemed transferor, for purposes of section 2056 (relating to bequests, etc., to surviving spouse), the value of the gross estate of the deemed transferor shall be deemed to be increased by the amount of such transfer.

[Sec. 2602(d)]

(d) ALTERNATE VALUATION.—

(1) IN GENERAL.—In the case of—

(A) 1 or more generation-skipping transfers from the same trust which have the same deemed transferor and which are taxable terminations occurring at the same time as the death of such deemed transferor (or at the same time as the death of a beneficiary of the trust assigned to a higher generation than such deemed transferor); or

(B) 1 or more generation-skipping transfers from the same trust with different deemed transferors—

(i) which are taxable terminations occurring on the same day; and

(ii) which would, but for section 2613(b)(2), have occurred at the same time as the death of the individuals who are the deemed transferors with respect to the transfers;

the trustee may elect to value all of the property transferred in such transfers in accordance with section 2032.

(2) SPECIAL RULES.—If the trustee makes an election under paragraph (1) with respect to any generation-skipping transfer, section 2032 shall be applied by taking into account (in lieu of the date of the decedent's death) the following date:

(A) in the case of any generation-skipping transfer described in paragraph (1)(A), the date of the death of the deemed transferor (or beneficiary) described in such paragraph, or

(B) in the case of any generation-skipping transfer described in paragraph (1)(B), the date on which such transfer occurred.

Amendments

- **1978, Revenue Act of 1978 (P.L. 95-600)**

P.L. 95-600, §702(n)(4):

Amended Code Sec. 2602(d) by adding "(or at the same time as the death of a beneficiary of the trust assigned to a higher generation than such deemed transferor)" in subparagraph (1)(A) and by adding "(or beneficiary)" in subparagraph (2)(A). **Effective** as if included in chapter 13 (Code Secs. 2601-2603), as added by Sec. 2006 of the Tax Reform Act of 1976.

[Sec. 2602(e)]

(e) TRANSFERS WITHIN 3 YEARS OF DEATH OF DEEMED TRANSFEROR.—Under regulations prescribed by the Secretary, the principles of section 2035 shall apply with respect to transfers made during the 3-year period ending on the date of the deemed transferor's death. In the case of any transfer to which this subsection applies, the amount of the tax imposed by this chapter shall be determined as if the transfer occurred after the death of the deemed transferor and appropriate adjustments shall be made with respect to the amount of any prior transfer which is taken into account under subparagraph (B) or (C) of subsection (a)(1).

Amendments

- **1976, Tax Reform Act of 1976 (P.L. 94-455)**

P.L. 94-455, §2006(a):

Added Code Sec. 2602. For **effective** date, see Act Sec. 2006(c) under Code Sec. 2601.

[Sec. 2603]

SEC. 2603. LIABILITY FOR TAX.

[Sec. 2603(a)]

(a) PERSONAL LIABILITY.—

(1) TAXABLE DISTRIBUTIONS.—In the case of a taxable distribution, the tax imposed by section 2601 shall be paid by the transferee.

(2) TAXABLE TERMINATION.—In the case of a taxable termination or a direct skip from a trust, the tax shall be paid by the trustee.

(3) DIRECT SKIP.—In the case of a direct skip (other than a direct skip from a trust), the tax shall be paid by the transferor.

[Sec. 2603(b)]

(b) SOURCE OF TAX.—Unless otherwise directed pursuant to the governing instrument by specific reference to the tax imposed by this chapter, the tax imposed by this chapter on a generation-skipping transfer shall be charged to the property constituting such transfer.

[Sec. 2603(c)]

(c) CROSS REFERENCE.—

For provisions making estate and gift tax provisions with respect to transferee liability, liens, and related matters applicable to the tax imposed by section 2601, see section 2661.

Amendments

- **1986, Tax Reform Act of 1986 (P.L. 99-514)**

P.L. 99-514, §1431(a):

Amended Chapter 13 by amending Code Sec. 2603. **Effective**, generally, for any generation-skipping transfer (within the meaning of section 2611 of the Internal Revenue Code of 1986) made after 10-22-86. However, for special rules, see Act Sec. 1433(b)-(d) following Code Sec. 2601. Prior to amendment, Code Sec. 2603 read as follows:

SEC. 2603. LIABILITY FOR TAX.

(a) PERSONAL LIABILITY.—

(1) IN GENERAL.—If the tax imposed by section 2601 is not paid, when due then—

(A) except to the extent provided in paragraph (2), the trustee shall be personally liable for any portion of such tax which is attributable to a taxable termination, and

(B) the distributee of the property shall be personally liable for such tax to the extent provided in paragraph (3).

(2) LIMITATION OF PERSONAL LIABILITY OF TRUSTEE WHO RELIES ON CERTAIN INFORMATION FURNISHED BY THE SECRETARY.—

(A) INFORMATION WITH RESPECT TO RATES.—The trustee shall not be personally liable for any increase in the tax imposed by section 2601 which is attributable to the application to the transfer of rates of tax which exceed the rates of tax furnished by the Secretary to the trustee as being the rates at which the transfer may reasonably be expected to be taxed.

(B) AMOUNT OF REMAINING EXCLUSION.—The trustee shall not be personally liable for any increase in the tax imposed by section 2601 which is attributable to the fact that—

(i) the amount furnished by the Secretary to the trustee as being the amount of the exclusion for a transfer to a grandchild of the grantor of the trust which may reasonably be expected to remain with respect to the deemed transferor, is less than

(ii) the amount of such exclusion remaining with respect to such deemed transferor.

(3) LIMITATION OF PERSONAL LIABILITY OF DISTRIBUTEE.—The distributee of the property shall be personally liable for the tax imposed by section 2601 only to the extent of an amount equal to the fair market value (determined as of the time of the distribution) of the property received by the distributee in the distribution.

(b) LIEN.—The tax imposed by section 2601 on any transfer shall be a lien on the property transferred until the tax is paid in full or becomes unenforceable by reason of lapse of time.

- **1976, Tax Reform Act of 1976 (P.L. 94-455)**

P.L. 94-455, §2006(a):

Added Code Sec. 2603. For **effective** date, see Act Sec. 2006(c) under Code Sec. 2601.

GENERATION-SKIPPING TRANSFERS

[Sec. 2604—Stricken]

Amendments

• **2014, Tax Technical Corrections Act of 2014 (P.L. 113-295)**

P.L. 113-295, §221(a)(95)(B)(i), Division A:

Amended subchapter A of chapter 13 by striking Code Sec. 2604. **Effective** generally 12-19-2014. For a special rule, see Act Sec. 221(b)(2), Division A, below.

P.L. 113-295, §221(b)(2), Division A, provides:

(2) SAVINGS PROVISION.—If—

(A) any provision amended or repealed by the amendments made by this section applied to—

(i) any transaction occurring before the date of the enactment of this Act,

(ii) any property acquired before such date of enactment, or

(iii) any item of income, loss, deduction, or credit taken into account before such date of enactment, and

(B) the treatment of such transaction, property, or item under such provision would (without regard to the amendments or repeals made by this section) affect the liability for tax for periods ending after date of enactment, nothing in the amendments or repeals made by this section shall be construed to affect the treatment of such transaction, property, or item for purposes of determining liability for tax for periods ending after such date of enactment.

Prior to being stricken, Code Sec. 2604 read as follows:

SEC. 2604. CREDIT FOR CERTAIN STATE TAXES.

[Sec. 2604(a)]

(a) GENERAL RULE.—If a generation-skipping transfer (other than a direct skip) occurs at the same time as and as a result of the death of an individual, a credit against the tax imposed by section 2601 shall be allowed in an amount equal to the generation-skipping transfer tax actually paid to any State in respect to any property included in the generation-skipping transfer.

[Sec. 2604(b)]

(b) LIMITATION.—The aggregate amount allowed as a credit under this section with respect to any transfer shall not exceed 5 percent of the amount of the tax imposed by section 2601 on such transfer.

Amendments

• **1986, Tax Reform Act of 1986 (P.L. 99-514)**

P.L. 99-514, §1431(a):

Amended Chapter 13 by adding Code Sec. 2604. **Effective**, generally, for any generation-skipping transfer (within the meaning of section 2611 of the Internal Revenue Code of 1986) made after 10-22-86. However, for special rules, see Act Sec. 1433(b)-(d) following Code Sec. 2601.

[Sec. 2604(c)]

(c) TERMINATION.—This section shall not apply to the generation-skipping transfers after December 31, 2004.

Amendments

• **2013, American Taxpayer Relief Act of 2012 (P.L. 112-240)**

P.L. 112-240, §101(a)(1) and (3), provides:

SEC. 101. PERMANENT EXTENSION AND MODIFICATION OF 2001 TAX RELIEF.

(a) PERMANENT EXTENSION.—

(1) IN GENERAL.—The Economic Growth and Tax Relief Reconciliation Act of 2001 is amended by striking title IX.

* * *

(3) EFFECTIVE DATE.—The amendments made by this subsection shall apply to taxable, plan, or limitation years beginning after December 31, 2012, and estates of decedents dying, gifts made, or generation skipping transfers after December 31, 2012.

• **2001, Economic Growth and Tax Relief Reconciliation Act of 2001 (P.L. 107-16)**

P.L. 107-16, §532(c)(10):

Amended Code Sec. 2604 by adding at the end a new subsection (c). **Effective** for estates of decedents dying, and generation-skipping transfers, after 12-31-2004.

P.L. 107-16, §901(a)-(b), as amended by P.L. 111-312, §101(a)(1), provides [but see P.L. 112-240, §101(a)(1) and (3), above]:

SEC. 901. SUNSET OF PROVISIONS OF ACT.

(a) IN GENERAL.—All provisions of, and amendments made by, this Act shall not apply—

(1) to taxable, plan, or limitation years beginning after December 31, 2012, or

(2) in the case of title V, to estates of decedents dying, gifts made, or generation skipping transfers, after December 31, 2012.

(b) APPLICATION OF CERTAIN LAWS.—The Internal Revenue Code of 1986 and the Employee Retirement Income Security Act of 1974 shall be applied and administered to years, estates, gifts, and transfers described in subsection (a) as if the provisions and amendments described in subsection (a) had never been enacted.

Subchapter B—Generation-Skipping Transfers

Sec. 2611.   Generation-skipping transfer defined.
Sec. 2612.   Taxable termination; taxable distribution; direct skip.
Sec. 2613.   Skip person and non-skip person defined.

[Sec. 2611]

SEC. 2611. GENERATION-SKIPPING TRANSFER DEFINED.

[Sec. 2611(a)]

(a) IN GENERAL.—For purposes of this chapter, the term "generation-skipping transfer" means—

(1) a taxable distribution,

(2) a taxable termination, and

(3) a direct skip.

Amendments

• **1988, Technical and Miscellaneous Revenue Act of 1988 (P.L. 100-647)**

P.L. 100-647, §1014(g)(1):

Amended Code Sec. 2611(a) by striking out "generation-skipping transfers" and inserting in lieu thereof "generation-skipping transfer". **Effective** as if included in the provision of P.L. 99-514 to which it relates.

P.L. 100-647, §1018(u)(43):

Amended Code Sec. 2611(a) by striking out "mean" and inserting in lieu thereof "means". **Effective** as if included in the provision of P.L. 99-514 to which it relates.

[Sec. 2611(b)]

(b) CERTAIN TRANSFERS EXCLUDED.—The term "generation-skipping transfer" does not include—

(1) any transfer which, if made inter vivos by an individual, would not be treated as a taxable gift by reason of section 2503(e) (relating to exclusion of certain transfers for educational or medical expenses), and

(2) any transfer to the extent—

(A) the property transferred was subject to a prior tax imposed under this chapter,

(B) the transferee in the prior transfer was assigned to the same generation as (or a lower generation than) the generation assignment of the transferee in this transfer, and

(C) such transfers do not have the effect of avoiding tax under this chapter with respect to any transfer.

Amendments

• **1988, Technical and Miscellaneous Revenue Act of 1988 (P.L. 100-647)**

P.L. 100-647, §1014(g)(2):

Amended Code Sec. 2611(b) by striking out paragraph (1) and by redesignating paragraphs (2) and (3) as paragraphs (1) and (2) respectively. **Effective** as if included in the provision of P.L. 99-514 to which it relates. Prior to amendment Code Sec. 2611(b)(1) read as follows:

(1) any transfer (other than a direct skip) from a trust, to the extent such transfer is subject to a tax imposed by chapter 11 or 12 with respect to a person in the 1st generation below that of the grantor, and

• **1986, Tax Reform Act of 1986 (P.L. 99-514)**

P.L. 99-514, §1431(a):

Amended Chapter 13 by amending Code Sec. 2611. **Effective**, generally, for any generation-skipping transfer (within the meaning of section 2611 of the Internal Revenue Code of 1986) made after 10-22-86. However, for special rules, see Act Sec. 1433(b)-(d) following Code Sec. 2601. Prior to amendment, the table of contents for former subchapter B and Code Sec. 2611 read as follows:

GENERATION-SKIPPING TRANSFERS

Subchapter B—Definitions and Special Rules

Sec. 2611. Generation-skipping transfer.
Sec. 2612. Deemed transferor.
Sec. 2613. Other definitions.
Sec. 2614. Special rules.

SEC. 2611. GENERATION-SKIPPING TRANSFER.

(a) GENERATION-SKIPPING TRANSFER DEFINED.—For purposes of this chapter, the terms "generation-skipping transfer" and "transfer" mean any taxable distribution or taxable termination with respect to a generation-skipping trust or trust equivalent.

(b) GENERATION-SKIPPING TRUST.—For purposes of this chapter, the term "generation-skipping trust" means any trust having younger generation beneficiaries (within the meaning of section 2613(c)(1)) who are assigned to more than one generation.

(c) ASCERTAINMENT OF GENERATION.—For purposes of this chapter, the generation to which any person (other than the grantor) belongs shall be determined in accordance with the following rules:

(1) an individual who is a lineal descendant of a grandparent of the grantor shall be assigned to that generation which results from comparing the number of generations between the grandparent and such individual with the number of generations between the grandparent and the grantor,

(2) an individual who has been at any time married to a person described in paragraph (1) shall be assigned to the generation of the person so described and an individual who has been at any time married to the grantor shall be assigned to the grantor's generation,

(3) a relationship by the half blood shall be treated as a relationship by the whole blood,

(4) a relationship by legal adoption shall be treated as a relationship by blood,

(5) an individual who is not assigned to a generation by reason of the foregoing paragraphs shall be assigned to a generation on the basis of the date of such individual's birth, with—

(A) an individual born not more than $12\frac{1}{2}$ years after the date of the birth of the grantor assigned to the grantor's generation,

(B) an individual born more than $12\frac{1}{2}$ years but not more than $37\frac{1}{2}$ years after the date of the birth of the grantor assigned to the first generation younger than the grantor, and

(C) similar rules for a new generation every 25 years,

(6) an individual who, but for this paragraph, would be assigned to more than one generation shall be assigned to the youngest such generation, and

(7) if any beneficiary of the trust is an estate or a trust, partnership, corporation, or other entity (other than an organization described in section 511(a)(2) and other than a charitable trust described in section 511(b)(2)), each individual having an indirect interest or power in the trust through such entity shall be treated as a beneficiary of the trust and shall be assigned to a generation under the foregoing provisions of this subsection.

(d) GENERATION-SKIPPING TRUST EQUIVALENT.—

(1) IN GENERAL.—For purposes of this chapter, the term "generation-skipping trust equivalent" means any arrangement which, although not a trust, has substantially the same effect as a generation-skipping trust.

(2) EXAMPLES OF ARRANGEMENTS TO WHICH SUBSECTION RELATES.—Arrangements to be taken into account for purposes of determining whether or not paragraph (1) applies include (but are not limited to) arrangements involving life estates and remainders, estates for years, insurance and annuities, and split interests.

(3) REFERENCES TO TRUST INCLUDE REFERENCES TO TRUST EQUIVALENTS.—Any reference in this chapter in respect of a generation-skipping trust shall include the appropriate reference in respect of a generation-skipping trust equivalent.

• **1976, Tax Reform Act of 1976 (P.L. 94-455)**

P.L. 94-455, § 2006(a):

Added Code Sec. 2611. For **effective** date, see Act Sec. 2006(c) under Code Sec. 2601.

[Sec. 2612]

SEC. 2612. TAXABLE TERMINATION; TAXABLE DISTRIBUTION; DIRECT SKIP.

[Sec. 2612(a)]

(a) TAXABLE TERMINATION.—

(1) GENERAL RULE.—For purposes of this chapter, the term "taxable termination" means the termination (by death, lapse of time, release of power, or otherwise) of an interest in property held in a trust unless—

(A) immediately after such termination, a non-skip person has an interest in such property, or

(B) at no time after such termination may a distribution (including distributions on termination) be made from such trust to a skip person.

(2) CERTAIN PARTIAL TERMINATIONS TREATED AS TAXABLE.—If, upon the termination of an interest in property held in trust by reason of the death of a lineal descendant of the transferor, a specified portion of the trust's assets are distributed to 1 or more skip persons (or 1 or more trusts for the exclusive benefit of such persons), such termination shall constitute a taxable termination with respect to such portion of the trust property.

Amendments

• **1988, Technical and Miscellaneous Revenue Act of 1988 (P.L. 100-647)**

P.L. 100-647, § 1014(g)(15):

Amended Code Sec. 2612(a)(2). **Effective** as if included in the provision of P.L. 99-514 to which it relates. Prior to amendment, Code Sec. 2612(a)(2) read as follows:

(2) CERTAIN PARTIAL TERMINATIONS TREATED AS TAXABLE.—If, upon the termination of an interest in property held in a trust, a specified portion of the trust assets are distributed to skip persons who are lineal descendants of the holder of such interest (or to 1 or more trusts for the exclusive benefit of such persons), such termination shall constitute a taxable termination with respect to such portion of the trust property.

[Sec. 2612(b)]

(b) TAXABLE DISTRIBUTION.—For purposes of this chapter, the term "taxable distribution" means any distribution from a trust to a skip person (other than a taxable termination or a direct skip).

[Sec. 2612(c)]

(c) DIRECT SKIP.—For purposes of this chapter—

(1) IN GENERAL.—The term "direct skip" means a transfer subject to a tax imposed by chapter 11 or 12 of an interest in property to a skip person.

(2) LOOK-THRU RULES NOT TO APPLY.—Solely for purposes of determining whether any transfer to a trust is a direct skip, the rules of section 2651(f)(2) shall not apply.

Amendments

• **1997, Taxpayer Relief Act of 1997 (P.L. 105-34)**

P.L. 105-34, § 511(b)(1):

Amended Code Sec. 2612(c) by striking paragraph (2) and by redesignating paragraph (3) as paragraph (2). **Effective** for terminations, distributions, and transfers occurring after 12-31-97. Prior to being stricken, Code Sec. 2612(c)(2) read as follows:

(2) SPECIAL RULE FOR TRANSFERS TO GRANDCHILDREN.—For purposes of determining whether any transfer is a direct skip, if—

(A) an individual is a grandchild of the transferor (or the transferor's spouse or former spouse), and

(B) as of the time of the transfer, the parent of such individual who is a lineal descendant of the transferor (or the transferor's spouse or former spouse) is dead,

such individual shall be treated as if such individual were a child of the transferor and all of that grandchild's children shall be treated as if they were grandchildren of the transferor. In the case of lineal descendants below a grandchild, the preceding sentence may be reapplied. If any transfer of property to a trust would be a direct skip but for this paragraph, any generation assignment under this paragraph shall apply also for purposes of applying this chapter to transfers from the portion of the trust attributable to such property.

P.L. 105-34, § 511(b)(2):

Amended Code Sec. 2612(c)(2), as redesignated by Act Sec. 511(b)(1), by striking "section 2651(e)(2)" and inserting "section 2651(f)(2)". **Effective** for terminations, distributions, and transfers occurring after 12-31-97.

• **1988, Technical and Miscellaneous Revenue Act of 1988 (P.L. 100-647)**

P.L. 100-647, § 1014(g)(5)(B):

Amended Code Sec. 2612(c) by adding at the end thereof new paragraph (3). **Effective** as if included in the provision of P.L. 99-514 to which it relates.

P.L. 100-647, § 1014(g)(7):

Amended Code Sec. 2612(c)(2) adding at the end thereof a new sentence. **Effective** as if included in the provision of P.L. 99-514 to which it relates.

• **1986, Tax Reform Act of 1986 (P.L. 99-514)**

P.L. 99-514, § 1431(a):

Amended Chapter 13 by amending Code Sec. 2612. **Effective**, generally, for any generation-skipping transfer (within the meaning of section 2611 of the Internal Revenue Code of 1986) made after 10-22-86. However, for special rules, see Act Sec.

GENERATION-SKIPPING TRANSFERS

1433(b)-(d) following Code Sec. 2601. Prior to amendment, Code Sec. 2612 read as follows:

SEC. 2612. DEEMED TRANSFEROR.

(a) GENERAL RULE.—For purposes of this chapter, the deemed transferor with respect to a transfer is—

(1) except as provided in paragraph (2), the parent of the transferee of the property who is more closely related to the grantor of the trust than the other parent of such transferee (or if neither parent is related to such grantor, the parent having a closer affinity to the grantor), or

(2) if the parent described in paragraph (1) is not a younger generation beneficiary of the trust but 1 or more ancestors of the transferee is a younger generation beneficiary related by blood or adoption to the grantor of the trust, the youngest of such ancestors.

(b) DETERMINATION OF RELATIONSHIP.—For purposes of subsection (a), a parent related to the grantor of the trust by blood or adoption is more closely related than a parent related to such grantor by marriage.

• **1976, Tax Reform Act of 1976 (P.L. 94-455)**

P.L. 94-455, §2006(a):

Added Code Sec. 2612. For **effective** date, see Act Sec. 2006(c) under Code Sec. 2601.

[Sec. 2613]

SEC. 2613. SKIP PERSON AND NON-SKIP PERSON DEFINED.

[Sec. 2613(a)]

(a) SKIP PERSON.—For purposes of this chapter, the term "skip person" means—

(1) a natural person assigned to a generation which is 2 or more generations below the generation assignment of the transferor, or

(2) a trust—

(A) if all interests in such trust are held by skip persons, or

(B) if—

(i) there is no person holding an interest in such trust, and

(ii) at no time after such transfer may a distribution (including distributions on termination) be made from such trust to a non-skip person.

[Sec. 2613(b)]

(b) NON-SKIP PERSON.—For purposes of this chapter, the term "non-skip person" means any person who is not a skip person.

Amendments

• **1988, Technical and Miscellaneous Revenue Act of 1988 (P.L. 100-647)**

P.L. 100-647, §1014(g)(5)(A):

Amended Code Sec. 2613(a)(1) by striking out "a person assigned" and inserting in lieu thereof "a natural person assigned". **Effective** as if included in the provision of P.L. 99-514 to which it relates.

• **1986, Tax Reform Act of 1986 (P.L. 99-514)**

P.L. 99-514, §1431(a):

Amended Chapter 13 by amending Code Sec. 2613. **Effective**, generally, for any generation-skipping transfer (within the meaning of section 2611 of the Internal Revenue Code of 1986) made after 10-22-86. However, for special rules, see Act Sec. 1433(b)-(d) following Code Sec. 2601. Prior to amendment, Code Sec. 2613 read as follows:

SEC. 2613. OTHER DEFINITIONS.

[Sec. 2613(a)]

(a) TAXABLE DISTRIBUTION.—For purposes of this chapter—

(1) IN GENERAL.—The term "taxable distribution" means any distribution which is not out of the income of the trust (within the meaning of section 643(b)) from a generation-skipping trust to any younger generation beneficiary who is assigned to a generation younger than the generation assignment of any other person who is a younger generation beneficiary. For purposes of the preceding sentence, an individual who at no time has had anything other than a future interest or future power (or both) in the trust shall not be considered as a younger generation beneficiary.

(2) SOURCE OF DISTRIBUTION.—If, during the taxable year of the trust, there are distributions out of the income of the trust (within the meaning of section 643(b)) and out of other amounts, for purposes of paragraph (1) the distributions of such income shall be deemed to have been made to the beneficiaries (to the extent of the aggregate distributions made to each such beneficiary during such year) in descending order of generations, beginning with the beneficiaries assigned to the oldest generation.

(3) PAYMENT OF TAX.—If any portion of the tax imposed by this chapter with respect to any transfer is paid out of the income or corpus of the trust, an amount equal to the portion so paid shall be deemed to be a generation-skipping transfer.

(4) CERTAIN DISTRIBUTIONS EXCLUDED FROM TAX.—The term "taxable distribution" does not include—

(A) any transfer to the extent such transfer is to a grandchild of the grantor of the trust and does not exceed the limitation provided by subsection (b)(6), and

(B) any transfer to the extent such transfer is subject to a tax imposed by chapter 11 or 12.

[Sec. 2613(b)]

(b) TAXABLE TERMINATION.—For purposes of this chapter—

(1) IN GENERAL.—The term "taxable termination" means the termination (by death, lapse of time, exercise or nonexercise, or otherwise) of the interest or power in a generation-skipping trust of any younger generation beneficiary who is assigned to any generation older than the generation assignment of any other person who is a younger generation beneficiary of that trust. Such term does not include a termination of the interest or power of any person who at no time has had anything other than a future interest or future power (or both) in the trust.

(2) TIME CERTAIN TERMINATIONS DEEMED TO OCCUR.—

(A) WHERE 2 OR MORE BENEFICIARIES ARE ASSIGNED TO SAME GENERATION.—In any case where 2 or more younger generation beneficiaries of a trust are assigned to the same generation, except to the extent provided in regulations prescribed by the Secretary, the transfer constituting the termination with respect to each such beneficiary shall be treated as occurring at the time when the last such termination occurs.

(B) SAME BENEFICIARY HAS MORE THAN 1 PRESENT INTEREST OR PRESENT POWER.—In any case where a younger generation beneficiary of a trust has both a present interest and a present power, or more than 1 present interest or present power, in the trust, except to the extent provided in regulations prescribed by the Secretary, the termination with respect to each such present interest or present power shall be treated as occurring at the time when the last such termination occurs.

(C) UNUSUAL ORDER OF TERMINATION.—

(i) IN GENERAL.—If—

(I) but for this subparagraph, there would have been a termination (determined after the application of subparagraphs (A) and (B)) of an interest or power of a younger generation beneficiary (hereinafter in this subparagraph referred to as the "younger beneficiary"), and

(II) at the time such termination would have occurred, a beneficiary (hereinafter in this subparagraph referred to as the "older beneficiary") of the trust assigned to a higher generation than the generation of the younger beneficiary has a present interest or power in the trust,

then, except to the extent provided in regulations prescribed by the Secretary, the transfer constituting the termination with respect to the younger beneficiary shall be treated as occurring at the time when the termination of the last present interest or power of the older beneficiary occurs.

(ii) SPECIAL RULES.—If clause (i) applies with respect to any younger beneficiary—

(I) this chapter shall be applied first to the termination of the interest or power of the older beneficiary as if such termination occurred before the termination of the power or interest of the younger beneficiary; and

(II) the value of the property taken into account for purposes of determining the tax (if any) imposed by this chapter with respect to the termination of the interest or power of the younger beneficiary shall be reduced by the tax (if any) imposed by this chapter with respect to the termination of the interest or power of the older beneficiary.

(D) SPECIAL RULE.—Subparagraphs (A) and (C) shall also apply where a person assigned to the same generation as, or a higher generation than, the person whose power or interest terminates has a present power or interest immediately after the termination and such power or interest arises as a result of such termination.

(3) DEEMED TRANSFEREES OF CERTAIN TERMINATIONS.—Where, at the time of any termination, it is not clear who will be the transferee of any portion of the property transferred, except to the extent provided in regulations prescribed by the Secretary, such portion shall be deemed transferred pro rata to all beneficiaries of the trust in accordance with the amount which each of them would receive under a maximum exercise of discretion on his behalf. For purposes of the preceding sentence, where it is not clear whether discretion will be exercised per stirpes or per capita, it shall be presumed that the discretion will be exercised per stirpes.

(4) TERMINATION OF POWER.—In the case of the termination of any power, the property transferred shall be deemed to be the property subject to the power immediately before the termination (determined without the application of paragraph (2)).

(5) CERTAIN TERMINATIONS EXCLUDED FROM TAX.—The term "taxable termination" does not include—

(A) any transfer to the extent such transfer is to a grandchild of the grantor of the trust and does not exceed the limitation provided by paragraph (6), and

(B) any transfer to the extent such transfer is subject to a tax imposed by chapter 11 or 12.

(6) $250,000 LIMIT ON EXCLUSION OF TRANSFERS TO GRANDCHILDREN.—In the case of any deemed transferor, the maximum amount excluded from the terms "taxable distribution" and "taxable termination" by reason of provisions exempting from such terms transfers to the grandchildren of the grantor of the trust shall be $250,000. The preceding sentence shall be applied to transfers from one or more trusts in the order in which such transfers are made or deemed made.

(7) COORDINATION WITH SUBSECTION (a).—

(A) TERMINATIONS TAKE PRECEDENCE OVER DISTRIBUTIONS.—If—

(i) the death of an individual or any other occurrence is a taxable termination with respect to any property, and

GENERATION-SKIPPING TRANSFERS

(ii) such occurrence also requires the distribution of part or all of such property in a distribution which would (but for this subparagraph) be a taxable distribution,

then a taxable distribution shall be deemed not to have occurred with respect to the portion described in clause (i).

(B) CERTAIN PRIOR TRANSFERS.—To the extent that—

(i) the deemed transferor in any prior transfer of the property of the trust being transferred in this transfer was assigned to the same generation as (or a lower generation than) the generation assignment of the deemed transferor in this transfer,

(ii) the transferee in such prior transfer was assigned to the same generation as (or a higher generation than) the generation assignment of the transferee in this transfer, and

(iii) such transfers do not have the effect of avoiding tax under this chapter with respect to any transfer,

the terms "taxable termination" and "taxable distribution" do not include this later transfer.

Amendments

- **1978, Revenue Act of 1978 (P.L. 95-600)**

P.L. 95-600, § 702(n)(3):

Amended Code Sec. 2613(b)(2)(B) by substituting "a present interest and a present power" for "an interest and a power" and by substituting "present interest of present power" for "interest or power" in the text and heading. **Effective** as if included in chapter 13 (Code Secs. 2601-2603) as added by Act Sec. 2006 of the Tax Reform Act of 1976.

[Sec. 2613(c)]

(c) YOUNGER GENERATION BENEFICIARY; BENEFICIARY.—For purposes of this chapter—

(1) YOUNGER GENERATION BENEFICIARY.—The term "younger generation beneficiary" means any beneficiary who is assigned to a generation younger than the grantor's generation.

(2) TIME FOR ASCERTAINING YOUNGER GENERATION BENEFICIARIES.—A person is a younger generation beneficiary of a trust with respect to any transfer only if such person was a younger generation beneficiary of the trust immediately before the transfer (or, in the case of a series of related transfers, only if such person was a younger generation beneficiary of the trust immediately before the first of such transfers).

(3) BENEFICIARY.—The term "beneficiary" means any person who has a present or future interest or power in the trust.

[Sec. 2613(d)]

(d) INTEREST OR POWER.—For purposes of this chapter—

(1) INTEREST.—A person has an interest in a trust if such person—

(A) has a right to receive income or corpus from the trust, or

(B) is a permissible recipient of such income or corpus.

(2) POWER.—The term "power" means any power to establish or alter beneficial enjoyment of the corpus or income of the trust.

[Sec. 2613(e)]

(e) CERTAIN POWERS NOT TAKEN INTO ACCOUNT.—

(1) LIMITED POWER TO APPOINT AMONG LINEAL DESCENDANTS OF THE GRANTOR.—For purposes of this chapter, an individual shall be treated as not having any power in a trust if such individual does not have any present or future power in the trust other than a power to dispose of the corpus of the trust or the income therefrom to a beneficiary or a class of beneficiaries who are lineal descendants of the grantor assigned to a generation younger than the generation assignment of such individual.

(2) POWERS OF INDEPENDENT TRUSTEES.—

(A) IN GENERAL.—For purposes of this chapter, an individual shall be treated as not having any power in a trust if such individual—

(i) is a trustee who has no interest in the trust (other than as a potential appointee under a power of appointment held by another),

(ii) is not a related or subordinate trustee, and

(iii) does not have any present or future power in the trust other than a power to dispose of the corpus of the trust or the income therefrom to a beneficiary or a class of beneficiaries designated in the trust instrument.

(B) RELATED OR SUBORDINATE TRUSTEE DEFINED.—For purposes of subparagraph (A), the term "related or subordinate trustee" means any trustee who is assigned to a younger generation than the grantor's generation and who is—

(i) the spouse of the grantor or of any beneficiary,

(ii) the father, mother, lineal descendant, brother, or sister of the grantor or of any beneficiary,

(iii) an employee of the grantor or of any beneficiary,

(iv) an employee of a corporation in which the stockholdings of the grantor, the trust, and the beneficiaries of the trust are significant from the viewpoint of voting control,

(v) an employee of a corporation in which the grantor or any beneficiary of the trust is an executive,

(vi) a partner of a partnership in which the interest of the grantor, the trust, and the beneficiaries of the trust are significant from the viewpoint of operating control or distributive share of partnership income, or

(vii) an employee of a partnership in which the grantor or any beneficiary of the trust is a partner.

Amendments

- **1980, Technical Corrections Act of 1979 (P.L. 96-222)**

P.L. 96-222, § 107(a)(2)(B)(i):

Amended Code Sec. 2613(e)(2)(A)(i) by inserting after "the trust" the phrase "(other than as a potential appointee under a power of appointment held by another)". **Effective** for any generation-skipping transfer made after 6-11-76.

P.L. 96-222, § 107(a)(2)(B)(ii):

Amended Code Sec. 2613(e)(2)(B) by inserting after clause (ii) a new clause, by striking out clause (vi), by redesignating clauses (iii), (iv) and (v) as clauses (iv), (v) and (vi), and by inserting "or" at the end of redesignated clause (vi). **Effective** for any generation-skipping transfer made after 6-11-76. Prior to deletion, clause (vi) read as follows:

(vi) an employee of a corporation in which the grantor or any beneficiary of the trust is an executive, or

- **1978, Revenue Act of 1978 (P.L. 95-600)**

P.L. 95-600, § 702(n)(2):

Amended Code Sec. 2613(e). **Effective** as if included in chapter 13 (Code Secs. 2601-2603) as added by Act Sec. 2006 of P.L. 94-455. Prior to amendment, Code Sec. 2613(e) read as follows:

"(e) LIMITED POWER TO APPOINT AMONG LINEAL DESCENDANTS OF GRANTOR NOT TAKEN INTO ACCOUNT IN CERTAIN CASES.—For purposes of this chapter, if any individual does not have any present or future power in the trust other than a power to dispose of the corpus of the trust or the income therefrom to a beneficiary or a class of beneficiaries who are lineal descendants of the grantor assigned to a generation younger than the generation assignment of such individual, then such individual shall be treated as not having any power in the trust."

[Sec. 2613(f)]

(f) EFFECT OF ADOPTION.—For purposes of this chapter, a relationship by legal adoption shall be treated as a relationship by blood.

Amendments

- **1976, Tax Reform Act of 1976 (P.L. 94-455)**

P.L. 94-455, § 2006(a):

Added Code Sec. 2613. For **effective** date, see Act Sec. 2006(c) under Code Sec. 2601.

[Sec. 2614—Repealed]

Amendments

- **1986, Tax Reform Act of 1986 (P.L. 99-514)**

P.L. 99-514, § 1431(a):

Amended Chapter 13 and removed Code Sec. 2614. **Effective**, generally, for any generation-skipping transfer (within the meaning of section 2611 of the Internal Revenue Code of 1986) made after 10-22-86. However, for special rules, see Act Sec. 1433(b)-(d) following Code Sec. 2601. Prior to amendment, Code Sec. 2614 read as follows:

SEC. 2614. SPECIAL RULES.

[Sec. 2614(a)]

(a) BASIS ADJUSTMENT.—If property is transferred to any person pursuant to a generation-skipping transfer which occurs before the death of the deemed transferor, the basis of such property in the hands of the transferee shall be increased (but not above the fair market value of such property) by an amount equal to that portion of the tax imposed by section 2601 with respect to the transfer which is attributable to the excess of the fair market value of such property over its adjusted basis immediately before the transfer. If property is transferred in a generation-skipping transfer subject to tax under this chapter which occurs at the same time as, or after, the death of the deemed transferor, the basis of such property shall be adjusted in a manner similar to the manner provided under section 1014(a).

Amendments

- **1980, Crude Oil Windfall Profit Tax Act of 1980 (P.L. 96-223)**

P.L. 96-223, § 401(c)(3):

Amended the last sentence of Code Sec. 2614(a). **Effective** with respect to decedents dying after 12-31-76. However, see the amendment note for P.L. 96-223, Act Sec. 401(a), that follows Code Sec. 1014(d) for the text of Code Sec. 401(d) that authorizes the election of the carryover basis rules in the case of a decedent dying after 12-31-76 and before 11-7-78. Prior to amendment Code Sec. 2614(a) read:

(a) BASIS ADJUSTMENT.—If property is transferred to any person pursuant to a generation-skipping transfer which occurs before the death of the deemed transferor, the basis of such property in the hands of the transferee shall be increased (but not above the fair market value of such property) by an amount equal to that portion of the tax imposed by section 2601 with respect to the transfer which is attributable to the excess of the fair market value of such property over its adjusted basis immediately before the transfer. If property is transferred in a generation-skipping transfer subject to tax under this chapter which occurs at the same time as, or after, the death of the deemed transferor, the basis of the property shall be adjusted—

(1) in the case of such a transfer occurring after June 11, 1976 and before January 1, 1980, in a manner similar to the manner provided under section 1014(a), and

(2) in the case of such a transfer occurring after December 31, 1979, in a manner similar to the manner provided by section 1023 without regard to subsection (d) thereof (relating to basis of property passing from a decedent dying after December 31, 1979).

- **1978, Revenue Act of 1978 (P.L. 95-600)**

P.L. 95-600, § 700(c)(1)(B):

Amended Code Sec. 2614(a). **Effective** as if part of P.L. 94-455. Prior to amendment, Code Sec. 2614(a) read as follows:

"(a) BASIS ADJUSTMENT.—If property is transferred to any person pursuant to a generation-skipping transfer which occurs before the death of the deemed transferor, the basis of such property in the hands of the transferee shall be increased (but not above the fair market value of such property) by an amount equal to that portion of the tax imposed by section 2601 with respect to the transfer which is attributable to the excess of the fair market value of such property over its adjusted basis immedi-

GENERATION-SKIPPING TRANSFERS

ately before the transfer. If property is transferred in a generation-skipping transfer subject to tax under this chapter which occurs at the same time as, or after, the death of the deemed transferor, the basis of such property shall be adjusted in a manner similar to the manner provided by section 1023 without regard to subsection (d) thereof (relating to basis of property passing from a decedent dying after December 31, 1976)."

[Sec. 2614(b)]

(b) NONRESIDENTS NOT CITIZENS OF THE UNITED STATES.—If the deemed transferor of any transfer is, at the time of the transfer, a nonresident not a citizen of the United States and—

(1) if the deemed transferor is alive at the time of the transfer, there shall be taken into account only property which would be taken into account for purposes of chapter 12, or

(2) if the deemed transferor has died at the same time as, or before, the transfer, there shall be taken into account only property which would be taken into account for purposes of chapter 11.

[Sec. 2614(c)]

(c) DISCLAIMERS.—

For provisions relating to the effect of a qualified disclaimer for purposes of this chapter, see section 2518.

Amendments

• **1976, Tax Reform Act of 1976 (P.L. 94-455)**

P.L. 94-455, § 2006(a):

Added Code Sec. 2614. For **effective** date, see Act Sec. 2006(c) under Code Sec. 2601.

Subchapter C—Taxable Amount

Sec. 2621.	Taxable amount in case of taxable distribution.
Sec. 2622.	Taxable amount in case of taxable termination.
Sec. 2623.	Taxable amount in case of direct skip.
Sec. 2624.	Valuation.

[Sec. 2621]

SEC. 2621. TAXABLE AMOUNT IN CASE OF TAXABLE DISTRIBUTION.

[Sec. 2621(a)]

(a) IN GENERAL.—For purposes of this chapter, the taxable amount in the case of any taxable distribution shall be—

(1) the value of the property received by the transferee, reduced by

(2) any expense incurred by the transferee in connection with the determination, collection, or refund of the tax imposed by this chapter with respect to such distribution.

[Sec. 2621(b)]

(b) PAYMENT OF GST TAX TREATED AS TAXABLE DISTRIBUTION.—For purposes of this chapter, if any of the tax imposed by this chapter with respect to any taxable distribution is paid out of the trust, an amount equal to the portion so paid shall be treated as a taxable distribution.

Amendments

• **1986, Tax Reform Act of 1986 (P.L. 99-514)**

P.L. 99-514, § 1431(a):

Amended Chapter 13 by amending Code Sec. 2621. **Effective**, generally, for any generation-skipping transfer (within the meaning of section 2611 of the Internal Revenue Code of 1986) made after 10-22-86. However, for special rules, see Act Sec. 1433(b)-(d) following Code Sec. 2601. Prior to amendment, the table of contents for former subchapter C and Code Sec. 2621 read as follows:

Subchapter C—Administration

Sec. 2621. Administration.

Sec. 2622. Regulations.

[Sec. 2621]

SEC. 2621. ADMINISTRATION.

[Sec. 2621(a)]

(a) GENERAL RULE.—Insofar as applicable and not inconsistent with the provisions of this chapter—

(1) if the deemed transferor is not alive at the time of the transfer, all provisions of subtitle F (including penalties) applicable to chapter 11 or section 2001 are hereby made applicable in respect of this chapter or section 2601, as the case may be, and

(2) if the deemed transferor is alive at the time of the transfer, all provisions of subtitle F (including penalties) applicable to chapter 12 or section 2501 are hereby made applicable in respect of this chapter or section 2601, as the case may be.

[Sec. 2621(b)]

(b) SECTION 6166 NOT APPLICABLE.—For purposes of this chapter, section 6166 (relating to extension of time for payment of estate tax where estate consists largely of interest in closely held business) shall not apply.

Amendments

• **1981, Economic Recovery Tax Act of 1981 (P.L. 97-34)**

P.L. 97-34, § 422(e)(4)(A):

Amended Code Sec. 2621(b) by striking out "sections 6166 and 6166A (relating to extensions" and inserting "section 6166 (relating to extension". **Effective** for estates of decedents dying after 12-31-81.

P.L. 97-34, § 422(e)(4)(B):

Amended Code Sec. 2621(b) by striking out in the heading "SECTIONS 6166 AND 6166A" and inserting "SECTION 6166". **Effective** for estates of decedents dying after 12-31-81.

[Sec. 2621(c)]

(c) RETURN REQUIREMENTS.—

(1) IN GENERAL.—The Secretary shall prescribe by regulations the person who is required to make the return with respect to the tax imposed by this chapter and the time by which any such return must be filed. To the extent practicable, such regulations shall provide that—

(A) the person who is required to make such return shall be—

(i) in the case of a taxable distribution, the distributee, or

(ii) in the case of a taxable termination, the trustee; and

(B) the return shall be filed—

(i) in the case of a generation-skipping transfer occurring before the death of the deemed transferor, on or before the 90th day after the close of the taxable year of the trust in which such transfer occurred, or

(ii) in the case of a generation-skipping transfer occurring at the same time as, or after, the death of the deemed transferor, on or before the 90th day after the last day prescribed by law (including extensions) for filing the return of tax under chapter 11 with respect to the estate of the deemed transferor (or if later, the day which is 9 months after the day on which such generation-skipping transfer occurred).

(2) INFORMATION RETURNS.—The Secretary may by regulations require the trustee to furnish the Secretary with such information as he determines to be necessary for purposes of this chapter.

Amendments

• **1976, Tax Reform Act of 1976 (P.L. 94-455)**

P.L. 94-455, § 2006(a):

Added Code Sec. 2621. For **effective** date, see Act Sec. 2006(c) under Code Sec. 2601.

[Sec. 2622]

SEC. 2622. TAXABLE AMOUNT IN CASE OF TAXABLE TERMINATION.

[Sec. 2622(a)]

(a) IN GENERAL.—For purposes of this chapter, the taxable amount in the case of a taxable termination shall be—

(1) the value of all property with respect to which the taxable termination has occurred, reduced by

(2) any deduction allowed under subsection (b).

GENERATION-SKIPPING TRANSFERS

[Sec. 2622(b)]

(b) DEDUCTION FOR CERTAIN EXPENSES.—For purposes of subsection (a), there shall be allowed a deduction similar to the deduction allowed by section 2053 (relating to expenses, indebtedness, and taxes) for amounts attributable to the property with respect to which the taxable termination has occurred.

Amendments

• **1986, Tax Reform Act of 1986 (P.L. 99-514)**

P.L. 99-514, §1431(a):

Amended Chapter 13 by amending Code Sec. 2622. **Effective**, generally, for any generation-skipping transfer (within the meaning of section 2611 of the Internal Revenue Code of 1986) made after 10-22-86. However, for special rules, see Act Sec. 1433(b)-(d) following Code Sec. 2601. Prior to amendment, Code Sec. 2622 read as follows:

SEC. 2622. REGULATIONS.

The Secretary shall prescribe such regulations as may be necessary or appropriate to carry out the purposes of this chapter, including regulations providing the extent to which substantially separate and independent shares of different beneficiaries in the trust shall be treated as separate trusts.

• **1976, Tax Reform Act of 1976 (P.L. 94-455)**

P.L. 94-455, §2006(a):

Added Code Sec. 2622. For **effective** date, see Act Sec. 2006(c) under Code Sec. 2601.

[Sec. 2623]

SEC. 2623. TAXABLE AMOUNT IN CASE OF DIRECT SKIP.

For purposes of this chapter, the taxable amount in the case of a direct skip shall be the value of the property received by the transferee.

Amendments

• **1986, Tax Reform Act of 1986 (P.L. 99-514)**

P.L. 99-514, §1431(a):

Added Code Sec. 2623. **Effective**, generally, for any generation-skipping transfer (within the meaning of section 2611 of the Internal Revenue Code of 1986) made after 10-22-86. However, for special rules, see Act Sec. 1433(b)-(d) following Code Sec. 2601.

[Sec. 2624]

SEC. 2624. VALUATION.

[Sec. 2624(a)]

(a) GENERAL RULE.—Except as otherwise provided in this chapter, property shall be valued as of the time of the generation-skipping transfer.

[Sec. 2624(b)]

(b) ALTERNATE VALUATION AND SPECIAL USE VALUATION ELECTIONS APPLY TO CERTAIN DIRECT SKIPS.—In the case of any direct skip of property which is included in the transferor's gross estate, the value of such property for purposes of this chapter shall be the same as its value for purposes of chapter 11 (determined with regard to sections 2032 and 2032A).

[Sec. 2624(c)]

(c) ALTERNATE VALUATION ELECTION PERMITTED IN THE CASE OF TAXABLE TERMINATIONS OCCURRING AT DEATH.—If 1 or more taxable terminations with respect to the same trust occur at the same time as and as a result of the death of an individual, an election may be made to value all of the property included in such terminations in accordance with section 2032.

[Sec. 2624(d)]

(d) REDUCTION FOR CONSIDERATION PROVIDED BY TRANSFEREE.—For purposes of this chapter, the value of the property transferred shall be reduced by the amount of any consideration provided by the transferee.

Amendments

• **1986, Tax Reform Act of 1986 (P.L. 99-514)**

P.L. 99-514, §1431(a):

Added Code Sec. 2624. **Effective**, generally, for any generation-skipping transfer (within the meaning of section 2611 of the Internal Revenue Code of 1986) made after 10-22-86. However, for special rules, see Act Sec. 1433(b)-(d) following Code Sec. 2601.

Subchapter D—GST Exemption

Sec. 2631.   GST exemption.
Sec. 2632.   Special rules for allocation of GST exemption.

[Sec. 2631]

SEC. 2631. GST EXEMPTION.

[Sec. 2631(a)]

(a) GENERAL RULE.—For purposes of determining the inclusion ratio, every individual shall be allowed a GST exemption amount which may be allocated by such individual (or his executor) to any property with respect to which such individual is the transferor.

Amendments

• **2013, American Taxpayer Relief Act of 2012 (P.L. 112-240)**

P.L. 112-240, §101(a)(1) and (3), provides:

SEC. 101. PERMANENT EXTENSION AND MODIFICATION OF 2001 TAX RELIEF.

(a) PERMANENT EXTENSION.—

(1) IN GENERAL.—The Economic Growth and Tax Relief Reconciliation Act of 2001 is amended by striking title IX.

* * *

(3) EFFECTIVE DATE.—The amendments made by this subsection shall apply to taxable, plan, or limitation years beginning after December 31, 2012, and estates of decedents dying, gifts made, or generation skipping transfers after December 31, 2012.

• **2001, Economic Growth and Tax Relief Reconciliation Act of 2001 (P.L. 107-16)**

P.L. 107-16, §521(c)(1):

Amended Code Sec. 2631(a) by striking "of $1,000,000" and inserting "amount". **Effective** for estates of decedents dying, and generation-skipping transfers, after 12-31-2003.

P.L. 107-16, §901(a)-(b), as amended by P.L. 111-312, §101(a)(1), provides [but see P.L. 112-240, §101(a)(1) and (3), above]:

SEC. 901. SUNSET OF PROVISIONS OF ACT.

(a) IN GENERAL.—All provisions of, and amendments made by, this Act shall not apply—

(1) to taxable, plan, or limitation years beginning after December 31, 2012, or

(2) in the case of title V, to estates of decedents dying, gifts made, or generation skipping transfers, after December 31, 2012.

(b) APPLICATION OF CERTAIN LAWS.—The Internal Revenue Code of 1986 and the Employee Retirement Income Security Act of 1974 shall be applied and administered to years, estates, gifts, and transfers described in subsection (a) as if the provisions and amendments described in subsection (a) had never been enacted.

GENERATION-SKIPPING TRANSFERS

[Sec. 2631(b)]

(b) ALLOCATIONS IRREVOCABLE.—Any allocation under subsection (a), once made, shall be irrevocable.

Amendments

• **1986, Tax Reform Act of 1986 (P.L. 99-514)**

P.L. 99-514, §1431(a):

Added Code Sec. 2631. **Effective**, generally, for any generation-skipping transfer (within the meaning of section 2611 of the Internal Revenue Code of 1986) made after 10-22-86. However, for special rules, see Act Sec. 1433(b)-(d) following Code Sec. 2601.

[Sec. 2631(c)]

(c) GST EXEMPTION AMOUNT.—For purposes of subsection (a), the GST exemption amount for any calendar year shall be equal to the basic exclusion amount under section 2010(c) for such calendar year.

Amendments

• **2013, American Taxpayer Relief Act of 2012 (P.L. 112-240)**

P.L. 112-240, §101(a)(1)-(3), provides:

SEC. 101. PERMANENT EXTENSION AND MODIFICATION OF 2001 TAX RELIEF.

(a) PERMANENT EXTENSION.—

(1) IN GENERAL.—The Economic Growth and Tax Relief Reconciliation Act of 2001 is amended by striking title IX.

(2) CONFORMING AMENDMENT.—The Tax Relief, Unemployment Insurance Reauthorization, and Job Creation Act of 2010 is amended by striking section 304.

(3) EFFECTIVE DATE.—The amendments made by this subsection shall apply to taxable, plan, or limitation years beginning after December 31, 2012, and estates of decedents dying, gifts made, or generation skipping transfers after December 31, 2012.

• **2010, Tax Relief, Unemployment Insurance Reauthorization, and Job Creation Act of 2010 (P.L. 111-312)**

P.L. 111-312, §303(b)(2):

Amended Code Sec. 2631(c) by striking "the applicable exclusion amount" and inserting "the basic exclusion amount". **Effective** for generation-skipping transfers after 12-31-2010.

P.L. 111-312, §304, provides [but see P.L. 112-240, §101(a)(2)-(3), above]:

SEC. 304. APPLICATION OF EGTRRA SUNSET TO THIS TITLE.

Section 901 of the Economic Growth and Tax Relief Reconciliation Act of 2001 shall apply to the amendments made by this title.

• **2001, Economic Growth and Tax Relief Reconciliation Act of 2001 (P.L. 107-16)**

P.L. 107-16, §521(c)(2):

Amended Code Sec. 2631(c). **Effective** for estates of decedents dying, and generation-skipping transfers, after 12-31-2003. Prior to amendment, Code Sec. 2631(c) read as follows:

(c) INFLATION ADJUSTMENT.—

(1) IN GENERAL.—In the case of any calendar year after 1998, the $1,000,000 amount contained in subsection (a) shall be increased by an amount equal to—

(A) $1,000,000, multiplied by

(B) the cost-of-living adjustment determined under section 1(f)(3) for such calendar year by substituting "calendar year 1997" for "calendar year 1992" in subparagraph (B) thereof.

If any amount as adjusted under the preceding sentence is not a multiple of $10,000, such amount shall be rounded to the next lowest multiple of $10,000.

(2) ALLOCATION OF INCREASE.—Any increase under paragraph (1) for any calendar year shall apply only to generation-skipping transfers made during or after such calendar year; except that no such increase for calendar years after the calendar year in which the transferor dies shall apply to transfers by such transferor.

P.L. 107-16, §901(a)-(b), as amended by P.L. 111-312, §101(a)(1), provides [but see P.L. 112-240, §101(a)(1) and (3), above]:

SEC. 901. SUNSET OF PROVISIONS OF ACT.

(a) IN GENERAL.—All provisions of, and amendments made by, this Act shall not apply—

(1) to taxable, plan, or limitation years beginning after December 31, 2012, or

(2) in the case of title V, to estates of decedents dying, gifts made, or generation skipping transfers, after December 31, 2012.

(b) APPLICATION OF CERTAIN LAWS.—The Internal Revenue Code of 1986 and the Employee Retirement Income Security Act of 1974 shall be applied and administered to years, estates, gifts, and transfers described in subsection (a) as if the provisions and amendments described in subsection (a) had never been enacted.

• **1998, IRS Restructuring and Reform Act of 1998 (P.L. 105-206)**

P.L. 105-206, §6007(a)(1):

Amended Code Sec. 2631(c). **Effective** as if included in the provision of P.L. 105-34 to which it relates [effective on 8-5-97.—CCH]. Prior to amendment, Code Sec. 2631(c) read as follows:

(c) INFLATION ADJUSTMENT.—In the case of an individual who dies in any calendar year after 1998, the $1,000,000 amount contained in subsection (a) shall be increased by an amount equal to—

(1) $1,000,000, multiplied by

(2) the cost-of-living adjustment determined under section 1(f)(3) for such calendar year by substituting "calendar year 1997" for "calendar year 1992" in subparagraph (B) thereof.

If any amount as adjusted under the preceding sentence is not a multiple of $10,000, such amount shall be rounded to the next lowest multiple of $10,000.

• **1997, Taxpayer Relief Act of 1997 (P.L. 105-34)**

P.L. 105-34, §501(d):

Amended Code Sec. 2631 by adding a new subsection (c). **Effective** 8-5-97 [effective date changed by P.L. 105-206, §6007(a)(2)].

[Sec. 2632]

SEC. 2632. SPECIAL RULES FOR ALLOCATION OF GST EXEMPTION.

[Sec. 2632(a)]

(a) TIME AND MANNER OF ALLOCATION.—

(1) TIME.—Any allocation by an individual of his GST exemption under section 2631(a) may be made at any time on or before the date prescribed for filing the estate tax return for such individual's estate (determined with regard to extensions), regardless of whether such a return is required to be filed.

(2) MANNER.—The Secretary shall prescribe by forms or regulations the manner in which any allocation referred to in paragraph (1) is to be made.

[Sec. 2632(b)]

(b) DEEMED ALLOCATION TO CERTAIN LIFETIME DIRECT SKIPS.—

(1) IN GENERAL.—If any individual makes a direct skip during his lifetime, any unused portion of such individual's GST exemption shall be allocated to the property transferred to the extent necessary to make the inclusion ratio for such property zero. If the amount of the direct skip exceeds such unused portion, the entire unused portion shall be allocated to the property transferred.

(2) UNUSED PORTION.—For purposes of paragraph (1), the unused portion of an individual's GST exemption is that portion of such exemption which has not previously been allocated by such individual (or treated as allocated under paragraph (1) or subsection (c)(1)).

(3) SUBSECTION NOT TO APPLY IN CERTAIN CASES.—An individual may elect to have this subsection not apply to a transfer.

Amendments

• **2013, American Taxpayer Relief Act of 2012 (P.L. 112-240)**

P.L. 112-240, §101(a)(1) and (3), provides:

SEC. 101. PERMANENT EXTENSION AND MODIFICATION OF 2001 TAX RELIEF.

(a) PERMANENT EXTENSION.—

(1) IN GENERAL.—The Economic Growth and Tax Relief Reconciliation Act of 2001 is amended by striking title IX.

* * *

(3) EFFECTIVE DATE.—The amendments made by this subsection shall apply to taxable, plan, or limitation years beginning after December 31, 2012, and estates of decedents dying, gifts made, or generation skipping transfers after December 31, 2012.

GENERATION-SKIPPING TRANSFERS

- **2001, Economic Growth and Tax Relief Reconciliation Act of 2001 (P.L. 107-16)**

P.L. 107-16, § 561(b):

Amended Code Sec. 2632(b)(2) by striking "with respect to a prior direct skip" and inserting "or subsection (c)(1)". **Effective** for transfers subject to chapter 11 or 12 made after 12-31-2000, and to estate tax inclusion periods ending after 12-31-2000.

P.L. 107-16, § 901(a)-(b), as amended by P.L. 111-312, § 101(a)(1), provides [but see P.L. 112-240, § 101(a)(1) and (3), above]:

SEC. 901. SUNSET OF PROVISIONS OF ACT.

(a) IN GENERAL.—All provisions of, and amendments made by, this Act shall not apply—

(1) to taxable, plan, or limitation years beginning after December 31, 2012, or

(2) in the case of title V, to estates of decedents dying, gifts made, or generation skipping transfers, after December 31, 2012.

(b) APPLICATION OF CERTAIN LAWS.—The Internal Revenue Code of 1986 and the Employee Retirement Income Security Act of 1974 shall be applied and administered to years, estates, gifts, and transfers described in subsection (a) as if the provisions and amendments described in subsection (a) had never been enacted.

- **1988, Technical and Miscellaneous Revenue Act of 1988 (P.L. 100-647)**

P.L. 100-647, § 1014(g)(16):

Amended Code Sec. 2632(b)(2) by striking out "paragraph (1)) with respect to a prior direct skip" and inserting in lieu thereof "paragraph (1) with respect to a prior direct skip)". **Effective** as if included in the provision of P.L. 99-514 to which it relates.

[Sec. 2632(c)]

(c) DEEMED ALLOCATION TO CERTAIN LIFETIME TRANSFERS TO GST TRUSTS.—

(1) IN GENERAL.—If any individual makes an indirect skip during such individual's lifetime, any unused portion of such individual's GST exemption shall be allocated to the property transferred to the extent necessary to make the inclusion ratio for such property zero. If the amount of the indirect skip exceeds such unused portion, the entire unused portion shall be allocated to the property transferred.

(2) UNUSED PORTION.—For purposes of paragraph (1), the unused portion of an individual's GST exemption is that portion of such exemption which has not previously been—

(A) allocated by such individual,

(B) treated as allocated under subsection (b) with respect to a direct skip occurring during or before the calendar year in which the indirect skip is made, or

(C) treated as allocated under paragraph (1) with respect to a prior indirect skip.

(3) DEFINITIONS.—

(A) INDIRECT SKIP.—For purposes of this subsection, the term "indirect skip" means any transfer of property (other than a direct skip) subject to the tax imposed by chapter 12 made to a GST trust.

(B) GST TRUST.—The term "GST trust" means a trust that could have a generation-skipping transfer with respect to the transferor unless—

(i) the trust instrument provides that more than 25 percent of the trust corpus must be distributed to or may be withdrawn by one or more individuals who are non-skip persons—

(I) before the date that the individual attains age 46,

(II) on or before one or more dates specified in the trust instrument that will occur before the date that such individual attains age 46, or

(III) upon the occurrence of an event that, in accordance with regulations prescribed by the Secretary, may reasonably be expected to occur before the date that such individual attains age 46,

(ii) the trust instrument provides that more than 25 percent of the trust corpus must be distributed to or may be withdrawn by one or more individuals who are non-skip persons and who are living on the date of death of another person identified in the instrument (by name or by class) who is more than 10 years older than such individuals,

(iii) the trust instrument provides that, if one or more individuals who are non-skip persons die on or before a date or event described in clause (i) or (ii), more than 25 percent of the trust corpus either must be distributed to the estate or estates of one or more of such individuals or is subject to a general power of appointment exercisable by one or more of such individuals,

(iv) the trust is a trust any portion of which would be included in the gross estate of a non-skip person (other than the transferor) if such person died immediately after the transfer,

(v) the trust is a charitable lead annuity trust (within the meaning of section 2642(e)(3)(A)) or a charitable remainder annuity trust or a charitable remainder unitrust (within the meaning of section 664(d)), or

(vi) the trust is a trust with respect to which a deduction was allowed under section 2522 for the amount of an interest in the form of the right to receive annual payments of a fixed percentage of the net fair market value of the trust property (determined yearly) and which is required to pay principal to a non-skip person if such person is alive when the yearly payments for which the deduction was allowed terminate.

For purposes of this subparagraph, the value of transferred property shall not be considered to be includible in the gross estate of a non-skip person or subject to a right of withdrawal by reason of such person holding a right to withdraw so much of such property as does not exceed the amount referred to in section 2503(b) with respect to any transferor, and it shall be assumed that powers of appointment held by non-skip persons will not be exercised.

(4) AUTOMATIC ALLOCATIONS TO CERTAIN GST TRUSTS.—For purposes of this subsection, an indirect skip to which section 2642(f) applies shall be deemed to have been made only at the close of the estate tax inclusion period. The fair market value of such transfer shall be the fair market value of the trust property at the close of the estate tax inclusion period.

(5) APPLICABILITY AND EFFECT.—

(A) IN GENERAL.—An individual—

(i) may elect to have this subsection not apply to—

(I) an indirect skip, or

(II) any or all transfers made by such individual to a particular trust, and

(ii) may elect to treat any trust as a GST trust for purposes of this subsection with respect to any or all transfers made by such individual to such trust.

(B) ELECTIONS.—

(i) ELECTIONS WITH RESPECT TO INDIRECT SKIPS.—An election under subparagraph (A)(i)(I) shall be deemed to be timely if filed on a timely filed gift tax return for the calendar year in which the transfer was made or deemed to have been made pursuant to paragraph (4) or on such later date or dates as may be prescribed by the Secretary.

(ii) OTHER ELECTIONS.—An election under clause (i)(II) or (ii) of subparagraph (A) may be made on a timely filed gift tax return for the calendar year for which the election is to become effective.

GENERATION-SKIPPING TRANSFERS

Amendments

- **2013, American Taxpayer Relief Act of 2012 (P.L. 112-240)**

P.L. 112-240, § 101(a)(1) and (3), provides:

SEC. 101. PERMANENT EXTENSION AND MODIFICATION OF 2001 TAX RELIEF.

(a) PERMANENT EXTENSION.—

(1) IN GENERAL.—The Economic Growth and Tax Relief Reconciliation Act of 2001 is amended by striking title IX.

* * *

(3) EFFECTIVE DATE.—The amendments made by this subsection shall apply to taxable, plan, or limitation years beginning after December 31, 2012, and estates of decedents dying, gifts made, or generation skipping transfers after December 31, 2012.

- **2001, Economic Growth and Tax Relief Reconciliation Act of 2001 (P.L. 107-16)**

P.L. 107-16, § 561(a):

Amended Code Sec. 2632 by redesignating subsection (c) as subsection (e) and by inserting after subsection (b) a new subsection (c). **Effective** for transfers subject to chapter 11 or 12 made after 12-31-2000, and to estate tax inclusion periods ending after 12-31-2000.

P.L. 107-16, § 901(a)-(b), as amended by P.L. 111-312, § 101(a)(1), provides [but see P.L. 112-240, § 101(a)(1) and (3), above]:

SEC. 901. SUNSET OF PROVISIONS OF ACT.

(a) IN GENERAL.—All provisions of, and amendments made by, this Act shall not apply—

(1) to taxable, plan, or limitation years beginning after December 31, 2012, or

(2) in the case of title V, to estates of decedents dying, gifts made, or generation skipping transfers, after December 31, 2012.

(b) APPLICATION OF CERTAIN LAWS.—The Internal Revenue Code of 1986 and the Employee Retirement Income Security Act of 1974 shall be applied and administered to years, estates, gifts, and transfers described in subsection (a) as if the provisions and amendments described in subsection (a) had never been enacted.

[Sec. 2632(d)]

(d) RETROACTIVE ALLOCATIONS.—

(1) IN GENERAL.—If—

(A) a non-skip person has an interest or a future interest in a trust to which any transfer has been made,

(B) such person—

(i) is a lineal descendant of a grandparent of the transferor or of a grandparent of the transferor's spouse or former spouse, and

(ii) is assigned to a generation below the generation assignment of the transferor, and

(C) such person predeceases the transferor,

then the transferor may make an allocation of any of such transferor's unused GST exemption to any previous transfer or transfers to the trust on a chronological basis.

(2) SPECIAL RULES.—If the allocation under paragraph (1) by the transferor is made on a gift tax return filed on or before the date prescribed by section 6075(b) for gifts made within the calendar year within which the non-skip person's death occurred—

(A) the value of such transfer or transfers for purposes of section 2642(a) shall be determined as if such allocation had been made on a timely filed gift tax return for each calendar year within which each transfer was made,

(B) such allocation shall be effective immediately before such death, and

(C) the amount of the transferor's unused GST exemption available to be allocated shall be determined immediately before such death.

(3) FUTURE INTEREST.—For purposes of this subsection, a person has a future interest in a trust if the trust may permit income or corpus to be paid to such person on a date or dates in the future.

Amendments

- **2013, American Taxpayer Relief Act of 2012 (P.L. 112-240)**

P.L. 112-240, § 101(a)(1) and (3), provides:

SEC. 101. PERMANENT EXTENSION AND MODIFICATION OF 2001 TAX RELIEF.

(a) PERMANENT EXTENSION.—

(1) IN GENERAL.—The Economic Growth and Tax Relief Reconciliation Act of 2001 is amended by striking title IX.

* * *

(3) EFFECTIVE DATE.—The amendments made by this subsection shall apply to taxable, plan, or limitation years beginning after December 31, 2012, and estates of decedents dying, gifts made, or generation skipping transfers after December 31, 2012.

- **2001, Economic Growth and Tax Relief Reconciliation Act of 2001 (P.L. 107-16)**

P.L. 107-16, § 561(a):

Amended Code Sec. 2632 by redesignating subsection (c) as subsection (e) and by inserting after new subsection (c), as added by Act Sec. 561(a), a new subsection (d). **Effective** for deaths of non-skip persons occurring after 12-31-2000.

P.L. 107-16, § 901(a)-(b), as amended by P.L. 111-312, § 101(a)(1), provides [but see P.L. 112-240, § 101(a)(1) and (3), above]:

SEC. 901. SUNSET OF PROVISIONS OF ACT.

(a) IN GENERAL.—All provisions of, and amendments made by, this Act shall not apply—

(1) to taxable, plan, or limitation years beginning after December 31, 2012, or

(2) in the case of title V, to estates of decedents dying, gifts made, or generation skipping transfers, after December 31, 2012.

(b) APPLICATION OF CERTAIN LAWS.—The Internal Revenue Code of 1986 and the Employee Retirement Income Security Act of 1974 shall be applied and administered to years, estates, gifts, and transfers described in subsection (a) as if the provisions and amendments described in subsection (a) had never been enacted.

[Sec. 2632(e)]

(e) ALLOCATION OF UNUSED GST EXEMPTION.—

(1) IN GENERAL.—Any portion of an individual's GST exemption which has not been allocated within the time prescribed by subsection (a) shall be deemed to be allocated as follows—

(A) first, to property which is the subject of a direct skip occurring at such individual's death, and

(B) second, to trusts with respect to which such individual is the transferor and from which a taxable distribution or a taxable termination might occur at or after such individual's death.

(2) ALLOCATION WITHIN CATEGORIES.—

(A) IN GENERAL.—The allocation under paragraph (1) shall be made among the properties described in subparagraph (A) thereof and the trust described in subparagraph (B) thereof, as the case may be, in proportion to the respective amounts (at the time of allocation) of the nonexempt portions of such properties or trusts.

(B) NONEXEMPT PORTION.—For purposes of subparagraph (A), the term "nonexempt portion" means the value (at the time of allocation) of the property or trust, multiplied by the inclusion ratio with respect to such property or trust.

Amendments

- **2013, American Taxpayer Relief Act of 2012 (P.L. 112-240)**

P.L. 112-240, § 101(a)(1) and (3), provides:

SEC. 101. PERMANENT EXTENSION AND MODIFICATION OF 2001 TAX RELIEF.

(a) PERMANENT EXTENSION.—

(1) IN GENERAL.—The Economic Growth and Tax Relief Reconciliation Act of 2001 is amended by striking title IX.

* * *

(3) EFFECTIVE DATE.—The amendments made by this subsection shall apply to taxable, plan, or limitation years beginning after December 31, 2012, and estates of

decedents dying, gifts made, or generation skipping transfers after December 31, 2012.

• **2001, Economic Growth and Tax Relief Reconciliation Act of 2001 (P.L. 107-16)**

P.L. 107-16, §561(a):

Amended Code Sec. 2632 by redesignating subsection (c) as subsection (e). **Effective** 6-7-2001.

P.L. 107-16, §901(a)-(b), as amended by P.L. 111-312, §101(a)(1), provides [but see P.L. 112-240, §101(a)(1) and (3), above]:

SEC. 901. SUNSET OF PROVISIONS OF ACT.

(a) IN GENERAL.—All provisions of, and amendments made by, this Act shall not apply—

(1) to taxable, plan, or limitation years beginning after December 31, 2012, or

(2) in the case of title V, to estates of decedents dying, gifts made, or generation skipping transfers, after December 31, 2012.

(b) APPLICATION OF CERTAIN LAWS.—The Internal Revenue Code of 1986 and the Employee Retirement Income Security Act of 1974 shall be applied and administered to years, estates, gifts, and transfers described in subsection (a) as if the provisions and amendments described in subsection (a) had never been enacted.

• **1986, Tax Reform Act of 1986 (P.L. 99-514)**

P.L. 99-514, §1431(a):

Added Code Sec. 2632. **Effective**, generally, for any generation-skipping transfer (within the meaning of section 2611 of the Internal Revenue Code of 1986) made after 10-22-86. However, for special rules, see Act Sec. 1433(b)-(d) following Code Sec. 2601.

Subchapter E—Applicable Rate; Inclusion Ratio

Sec. 2641.   Applicable rate.
Sec. 2642.   Inclusion ratio.

[Sec. 2641]

SEC. 2641. APPLICABLE RATE.

[Sec. 2641(a)]

(a) GENERAL RULE.—For purposes of this chapter, the term "applicable rate" means, with respect to any generation-skipping transfer, the product of—

(1) the maximum Federal estate tax rate, and

(2) the inclusion ratio with respect to the transfer.

Amendments

• **2010, Tax Relief, Unemployment Insurance Reauthorization, and Job Creation Act of 2010 (P.L. 111-312)**

P.L. 111-312, §302(c), provides:

(c) MODIFICATION OF GENERATION-SKIPPING TRANSFER TAX.—In the case of any generation-skipping transfer made after December 31, 2009, and before January 1, 2011, the applicable rate determined under section 2641(a) of the Internal Revenue Code of 1986 shall be zero.

[Sec. 2641(b)]

(b) MAXIMUM FEDERAL ESTATE TAX RATE.—For purposes of subsection (a), the term "maximum Federal estate tax rate" means the maximum rate imposed by section 2001 on the estates of decedents dying at the time of the taxable distribution, taxable termination, or direct skip, as the case may be.

Amendments

• **1986, Tax Reform Act of 1986 (P.L. 99-514)**

P.L. 99-514, §1431(a):

Added Code Sec. 2641. **Effective**, generally, for any generation-skipping transfer (within the meaning of section 2611 of the Internal Revenue Code of 1986) made after 10-22-86. However, for special rules, see Act Sec. 1433(b)-(d) following Code Sec. 2601.

[Sec. 2642]

SEC. 2642. INCLUSION RATIO.

[Sec. 2642(a)]

(a) INCLUSION RATIO DEFINED.—For purposes of this chapter—

(1) IN GENERAL.—Except as otherwise provided in this section, the inclusion ratio with respect to any property transferred in a generation-skipping transfer shall be the excess (if any) of 1 over—

(A) except as provided in subparagraph (B), the applicable fraction determined for the trust from which such transfer is made, or

(B) in the case of a direct skip, the applicable fraction determined for such skip.

(2) APPLICABLE FRACTION.—For purposes of paragraph (1), the applicable fraction is a fraction—

(A) the numerator of which is the amount of the GST exemption allocated to the trust (or in the case of a direct skip, allocated to the property transferred in such skip), and

(B) the denominator of which is—

(i) the value of the property transferred to the trust (or involved in the direct skip), reduced by

(ii) the sum of—

(I) any Federal estate tax or State death tax actually recovered from the trust attributable to such property, and

(II) any charitable deduction allowed under section 2055 or 2522 with respect to such property.

(3) SEVERING OF TRUSTS.—

(A) IN GENERAL.—If a trust is severed in a qualified severance, the trusts resulting from such severance shall be treated as separate trusts thereafter for purposes of this chapter.

(B) QUALIFIED SEVERANCE.—For purposes of subparagraph (A)—

(i) IN GENERAL.—The term "qualified severance" means the division of a single trust and the creation (by any means available under the governing instrument or under local law) of two or more trusts if—

(I) the single trust was divided on a fractional basis, and

(II) the terms of the new trusts, in the aggregate, provide for the same succession of interests of beneficiaries as are provided in the original trust.

(ii) TRUSTS WITH INCLUSION RATIO GREATER THAN ZERO.—If a trust has an inclusion ratio of greater than zero and less than 1, a severance is a qualified severance only if the single trust is divided into two trusts, one of which receives a fractional share of the total value of all trust assets equal to the applicable fraction of the single trust immediately before the severance. In such case, the trust receiving such fractional share shall have an inclusion ratio of zero and the other trust shall have an inclusion ratio of 1.

GENERATION-SKIPPING TRANSFERS

(iii) REGULATIONS.—The term "qualified severance" includes any other severance permitted under regulations prescribed by the Secretary.

(C) TIMING AND MANNER OF SEVERANCES.—A severance pursuant to this paragraph may be made at any time. The Secretary shall prescribe by forms or regulations the manner in which the qualified severance shall be reported to the Secretary.

Amendments

• **2013, American Taxpayer Relief Act of 2012 (P.L. 112-240)**

P.L. 112-240, §101(a)(1) and (3), provides:

SEC. 101. PERMANENT EXTENSION AND MODIFICATION OF 2001 TAX RELIEF.

(a) PERMANENT EXTENSION.—

(1) IN GENERAL.—The Economic Growth and Tax Relief Reconciliation Act of 2001 is amended by striking title IX.

***

(3) EFFECTIVE DATE.—The amendments made by this subsection shall apply to taxable, plan, or limitation years beginning after December 31, 2012, and estates of decedents dying, gifts made, or generation skipping transfers after December 31, 2012.

• **2001, Economic Growth and Tax Relief Reconciliation Act of 2001 (P.L. 107-16)**

P.L. 107-16, §562(a):

Amended Code Sec. 2642(a) by adding at the end a new paragraph (3). **Effective** for severances after 12-31-2000.

P.L. 107-16, §901(a)-(b), as amended by P.L. 111-312, §101(a)(1), provides [but see P.L. 112-240, §101(a)(1) and (3), above]:

SEC. 901. SUNSET OF PROVISIONS OF ACT.

(a) IN GENERAL.—All provisions of, and amendments made by, this Act shall not apply—

(1) to taxable, plan, or limitation years beginning after December 31, 2012, or

(2) in the case of title V, to estates of decedents dying, gifts made, or generation skipping transfers, after December 31, 2012.

(b) APPLICATION OF CERTAIN LAWS.—The Internal Revenue Code of 1986 and the Employee Retirement Income Security Act of 1974 shall be applied and administered to years, estates, gifts, and transfers described in subsection (a) as if the provisions and amendments described in subsection (a) had never been enacted.

• **1988, Technical and Miscellaneous Revenue Act of 1988 (P.L. 100-647)**

P.L. 100-647, §1014(g)(4)(B):

Amended Code Sec. 2642(a)(2) by striking out the last sentence. **Effective** as if included in the provision of P.L. 99-514 to which it relates. Prior to amendment, the last sentence of Code Sec. 2642(a)(2) read as follows:

Except as provided in paragraphs (3) and (4) of subsection (b), the value determined under subparagraph (B)(i) shall be of the property as of the time of the transfer to the trust (or the direct skip).

[Sec. 2642(b)]

(b) VALUATION RULES, ETC.—Except as provided in subsection (f)—

(1) GIFTS FOR WHICH GIFT TAX RETURN FILED OR DEEMED ALLOCATION MADE.—If the allocation of the GST exemption to any transfers of property is made on a gift tax return filed on or before the date prescribed by section 6075(b) for such transfer or is deemed to be made under section 2632(b)(1) or (c)(1)—

(A) the value of such property for purposes of subsection (a) shall be its value as finally determined for purposes of chapter 12 (within the meaning of section 2001(f)(2)), or, in the case of an allocation deemed to have been made at the close of an estate tax inclusion period, its value at the time of the close of the estate tax inclusion period, and

(B) such allocation shall be effective on and after the date of such transfer, or, in the case of an allocation deemed to have been made at the close of an estate tax inclusion period, on and after the close of such estate tax inclusion period.

(2) TRANSFERS AND ALLOCATIONS AT OR AFTER DEATH.—

(A) TRANSFERS AT DEATH.—If property is transferred as a result of the death of the transferor, the value of such property for purposes of subsection (a) shall be its value as finally determined for purposes of chapter 11; except that, if the requirements prescribed by the Secretary respecting allocation of post-death changes in value are not met, the value of such property shall be determined as of the time of the distribution concerned.

(B) ALLOCATIONS TO PROPERTY TRANSFERRED AT DEATH OF TRANSFEROR.—Any allocation to property transferred as a result of the death of the transferor shall be effective on and after the date of the death of the transferor.

(3) ALLOCATIONS TO INTER VIVOS TRANSFERS NOT MADE ON TIMELY FILED GIFT TAX RETURN.—If any allocation of the GST exemption to any property not transferred as a result of the death of the transferor is not made on a gift tax return filed on or before the date prescribed by section 6075(b) and is not deemed to be made under section 2632(b)(1)—

(A) the value of such property for purposes of subsection (a) shall be determined as of the time such allocation is filed with the Secretary, and

(B) such allocation shall be effective on and after the date on which such allocation is filed with the Secretary.

(4) QTIP TRUSTS.—If the value of property is included in the estate of a spouse by virtue of section 2044, and if such spouse is treated as the transferor of such property under section 2652(a), the value of such property for purposes of subsection (a) shall be its value for purposes of chapter 11 in the estate of such spouse.

Amendments

• **2013, American Taxpayer Relief Act of 2012 (P.L. 112-240)**

P.L. 112-240, §101(a)(1) and (3), provides:

SEC. 101. PERMANENT EXTENSION AND MODIFICATION OF 2001 TAX RELIEF.

(a) PERMANENT EXTENSION.—

(1) IN GENERAL.—The Economic Growth and Tax Relief Reconciliation Act of 2001 is amended by striking title IX.

***

(3) EFFECTIVE DATE.—The amendments made by this subsection shall apply to taxable, plan, or limitation years beginning after December 31, 2012, and estates of decedents dying, gifts made, or generation skipping transfers after December 31, 2012.

• **2001, Economic Growth and Tax Relief Reconciliation Act of 2001 (P.L. 107-16)**

P.L. 107-16, §563(a):

Amended Code Sec. 2642(b)(1). **Effective** for transfers subject to chapter 11 or 12 of the Internal Revenue Code of 1986 made after 12-31-2000. Prior to amendment, Code Sec. 2642(b)(1) read as follows:

(1) GIFTS FOR WHICH GIFT TAX RETURN FILED OR DEEMED ALLOCATION MADE.—If the allocation of the GST exemption to any property is made on a gift tax return filed on or before the date prescribed by section 6075(b) or is deemed to be made under section 2632(b)(1)—

(A) the value of such property for purposes of subsection (a) shall be its value for purposes of chapter 12, and

(B) such allocation shall be effective on and after the date of such transfer.

P.L. 107-16, §563(b):

Amended Code Sec. 2642(b)(2)(A). **Effective** for transfers subject to chapter 11 or 12 of the Internal Revenue Code of 1986 made after 12-31-2000. Prior to amendment, Code Sec. 2642(b)(2)(A) read as follows:

(A) TRANSFERS AT DEATH.—If property is transferred as a result of the death of the transferor, the value of such property for purposes of subsection (a) shall be its value for purposes of chapter 11; except that, if the requirements prescribed by the Secretary respecting allocation of post-death changes in value are not met, the value of such property shall be determined as of the time of the distribution concerned.

P.L. 107-16, §901(a)-(b), as amended by P.L. 111-312, §101(a)(1), provides [but see P.L. 112-240, §101(a)(1) and (3), above]:

SEC. 901. SUNSET OF PROVISIONS OF ACT.

(a) IN GENERAL.—All provisions of, and amendments made by, this Act shall not apply—

(1) to taxable, plan, or limitation years beginning after December 31, 2012, or

(2) in the case of title V, to estates of decedents dying, gifts made, or generation skipping transfers, after December 31, 2012.

(b) APPLICATION OF CERTAIN LAWS.—The Internal Revenue Code of 1986 and the Employee Retirement Income Security Act of 1974 shall be applied and administered to years, estates, gifts, and transfers described in subsection (a) as if the provisions and amendments described in subsection (a) had never been enacted.

• **1989, Omnibus Budget Reconciliation Act of 1989 (P.L. 101-239)**

P.L. 101-239, §7811(j)(4):

Amended Code Sec. 2642(b)(1) and (3) by striking "a timely filed gift tax return required by section 6019" and inserting "a gift tax return filed on or before the date

GENERATION-SKIPPING TRANSFERS

prescribed by section 6075(b)". **Effective** as if included in the provision of P.L. 100-647 to which it relates.

• **1988, Technical and Miscellaneous Revenue Act of 1988 (P.L. 100-647)**

P.L. 100-647, §1014(g)(4)(C):

Amended Code Sec. 2642(b)(2)(A) by inserting before the period at the end thereof the following: "; except that, if the requirements prescribed by the Secretary respecting allocation of post-death changes in value are not met, the value of such property shall be determined as of the time of the distribution concerned." **Effective** as if included in the provision of P.L. 99-514 to which it relates.

P.L. 100-647, §1014(g)(4)(D):

Amended Code Sec. 2642(b) by inserting "Except as provided in subsection (f)—" immediately after the subsection heading. **Effective** as if included in the provision of P.L. 99-514 to which it relates.

P.L. 100-647, §1014(g)(4)(E)(i)-(ii):

Amended Code Sec. 2642(b)(2)(B) by striking out "at or after the death of the transferor" and inserting in lieu thereof "to property transferred as a result of the death of the transferor"; and by striking out "AT OR AFTER DEATH" in the subparagraph heading and inserting in lieu thereof "TO PROPERTY TRANSFERRED AT DEATH". **Effective** as if included in the provision of P.L. 99-514 to which it relates.

P.L. 100-647, §1014(g)(4)(F)(i)-(ii):

Amended Code Sec. 2642(b)(3) by striking out "to any property is made during the life of the transferor but is" and inserting in lieu thereof "to any property not transferred as a result of the death of the transferor is"; and by striking out "Inter vivos allocations" in the subparagraph heading and inserting in lieu thereof "Allocations to inter vivos transfers". **Effective** as if included in the provision of P.L. 99-514 to which it relates.

[Sec. 2642(c)]

(c) TREATMENT OF CERTAIN DIRECT SKIPS WHICH ARE NONTAXABLE GIFTS.—

(1) IN GENERAL.—In the case of a direct skip which is a nontaxable gift, the inclusion ratio shall be zero.

(2) EXCEPTION FOR CERTAIN TRANSFERS IN TRUST.—Paragraph (1) shall not apply to any transfer to a trust for the benefit of an individual unless—

(A) during the life of such individual, no portion of the corpus or income of the trust may be distributed to (or for the benefit of) any person other than such individual, and

(B) if the trust does not terminate before the individual dies, the assets of such trust will be includible in the gross estate of such individual.

Rules similar to the rules of section 2652(c)(3) shall apply for purposes of subparagraph (A).

(3) NONTAXABLE GIFT.—For purposes of this subsection, the term "nontaxable gift" means any transfer of property to the extent such transfer is not treated as a taxable gift by reason of—

(A) section 2503(b) (taking into account the application of section 2513), or

(B) section 2503(e).

Amendments

• **1990, Omnibus Budget Reconciliation Act of 1990 (P.L. 101-508)**

P.L. 101-508, §11703(c)(1):

Amended Code Sec. 2642(c)(2)(B) by striking "such individual dies before the trust is terminated" and inserting "the trust does not terminate before the individual dies". **Effective** for transfers after 3-31-88.

P.L. 101-508, §11703(c)(2):

Amended Code Sec. 2642(c)(2) by adding at the end thereof a new sentence. **Effective** for transfers after 3-31-88.

• **1988, Technical and Miscellaneous Revenue Act of 1988 (P.L. 100-647)**

P.L. 100-647, §1014(g)(17)(A):

Amended Code Sec. 2642(c). **Effective** for transfers after 3-31-88. Prior to amendment, Code Sec. 2642(c) read as follows:

(c) TREATMENT OF CERTAIN NONTAXABLE GIFTS.—

(1) DIRECT SKIPS.—In the case of any direct skip which is a nontaxable gift, the inclusion ratio shall be zero.

(2) TREATMENT OF NONTAXABLE GIFTS MADE TO TRUSTS.—

(A) IN GENERAL.—Except as provided in subparagraph (B), any nontaxable gift which is not a direct skip and which is made to a trust shall not be taken into account under subsection (a)(2)(B).

(B) DETERMINATION OF 1ST TRANSFER TO TRUST.—In the case of any nontaxable gift referred to in subparagraph (A) which is the 1st transfer to the trust, the inclusion ratio for such trust shall be zero.

(3) NONTAXABLE GIFT.—For purposes of this section, the term "nontaxable gift" means any transfer of property to the extent such transfer is not treated as a taxable gift by reason of—

(A) section 2503(b) (taking into account the application of section 2513), or

(B) section 2503(e).

[Sec. 2642(d)]

(d) SPECIAL RULES WHERE MORE THAN 1 TRANSFER MADE TO TRUST.—

(1) IN GENERAL.—If a transfer of property is made to a trust in existence before such transfer, the applicable fraction for such trust shall be recomputed as of the time of such transfer in the manner provided in paragraph (2).

(2) APPLICABLE FRACTION.—In the case of any such transfer, the recomputed applicable fraction is a fraction—

(A) the numerator of which is the sum of—

(i) the amount of the GST exemption allocated to property involved in such transfer, plus

(ii) the nontax portion of such trust immediately before such transfer, and

(B) the denominator of which is the sum of—

(i) the value of the property involved in such transfer reduced by the sum of—

(I) any Federal estate tax or State death tax actually recovered from the trust attributable to such property, and

(II) any charitable deduction allowed under section 2055 or 2522 with respect to such property, and

(ii) the value of all of the property in the trust (immediately before such transfer).

(3) NONTAX PORTION.—For purposes of paragraph (2), the term "nontax portion" means the product of—

(A) the value of all of the property in the trust, and

(B) the applicable fraction in effect for such trust.

(4) SIMILAR RECOMPUTATION IN CASE OF CERTAIN LATE ALLOCATIONS.—If—

(A) any allocation of the GST exemption to property transferred to a trust is not made on a timely filed gift tax return required by section 6019, and

(B) there was a previous allocation with respect to property transferred to such trust,

the applicable fraction for such trust shall be recomputed as of the time of such allocation under rules similar to the rules of paragraph (2).

Amendments

• **1990, Omnibus Budget Reconciliation Act of 1990 (P.L. 101-508)**

P.L. 101-508, §11074(a)(17):

Amended Code Sec. 2642(d)(2)(B)(i)(I) by striking "state" and inserting "State". **Effective** 11-5-90.

• **1988, Technical and Miscellaneous Revenue Act of 1988 (P.L. 100-647)**

P.L. 100-647, §1014(g)(17)(B):

Amended Code Sec. 2642(d)(1) by striking out "(other than a nontaxable gift)" after "property". **Effective** for transfers after 3-31-88.

P.L. 100-647, §1014(g)(18):

Amended Code Sec. 2642(d)(2)(B)(i). **Effective** as if included in the provision of P.L. 99-514 to which it relates. Prior to amendment, Code Sec. 2642(d)(2)(B)(i) read as follows:

(i) the value of the property involved in such transfer, reduced by any charitable deduction allowed under section 2055 or 2522 with respect to such property, and

GENERATION-SKIPPING TRANSFERS

• **1986, Tax Reform Act of 1986 (P.L. 99-514)**
P.L. 99-514, § 1431(a):
Added Code Sec. 2642. **Effective,** generally, for any generation-skipping transfer (within the meaning of section 2611 of the Internal Revenue Code of 1986) made after 10-22-86. However, for special rules, see Act Sec. 1433(b)-(d) following Code Sec. 2601.

[Sec. 2642(e)]

(e) SPECIAL RULES FOR CHARITABLE LEAD ANNUITY TRUSTS.—

(1) IN GENERAL.—For purposes of determining the inclusion ratio for any charitable lead annuity trust, the applicable fraction shall be a fraction—

(A) the numerator of which is the adjusted GST exemption, and

(B) the denominator of which is the value of all of the property in such trust immediately after the termination of the charitable lead annuity.

(2) ADJUSTED GST EXEMPTION.—For purposes of paragraph (1), the adjusted GST exemption is an amount equal to the GST exemption allocated to the trust increased by interest determined—

(A) at the interest rate used in determining the amount of the deduction under section 2055 or 2522 (as the case may be) for the charitable lead annuity, and

(B) for the actual period of the charitable lead annuity.

(3) DEFINITIONS.—For purposes of this subsection—

(A) CHARITABLE LEAD ANNUITY TRUST.—The term "charitable lead annuity trust" means any trust in which there is a charitable lead annuity.

(B) CHARITABLE LEAD ANNUITY.—The term "charitable lead annuity" means any interest in the form of a guaranteed annuity with respect to which a deduction was allowed under section 2055 or 2522 (as the case may be).

(4) COORDINATION WITH SUBSECTION (d).—Under regulations, appropriate adjustments shall be made in the application of subsection (d) to take into account the provisions of this subsection.

Amendments

• **1988, Technical and Miscellaneous Revenue Act of 1988 (P.L. 100-647)**
P.L. 100-647, § 1014(g)(3)(A):
Amended Code Sec. 2642 by adding at the end thereof new subsection (e). **Effective** for purposes of determining the inclusion ratio with respect to property transferred after 10-13-87.

[Sec. 2642(f)]

(f) SPECIAL RULES FOR CERTAIN INTER VIVOS TRANSFERS.—Except as provided in regulations—

(1) IN GENERAL.—For purposes of determining the inclusion ratio, if—

(A) an individual makes an inter vivos transfer of property, and

(B) the value of such property would be includible in the gross estate of such individual under chapter 11 if such individual died immediately after making such transfer (other than by reason of section 2035),

any allocation of GST exemption to such property shall not be made before the close of the estate tax inclusion period (and the value of such property shall be determined under paragraph (2)). If such transfer is a direct skip, such skip shall be treated as occurring as of the close of the estate tax inclusion period.

(2) VALUATION.—In the case of any property to which paragraph (1) applies, the value of such property shall be—

(A) if such property is includible in the gross estate of the transferor (other than by reason of section 2035), its value for purposes of chapter 11, or

(B) if subparagraph (A) does not apply, its value as of the close of the estate tax inclusion period (or, if any allocation of GST exemption to such property is not made on a timely filed gift tax return for the calendar year in which such period ends, its value as of the time such allocation is filed with the Secretary).

(3) ESTATE TAX INCLUSION PERIOD.—For purposes of this subsection, the term "estate tax inclusion period" means any period after the transfer described in paragraph (1) during which the value of the property involved in such transfer would be includible in the gross estate of the transferor under chapter 11 if he died. Such period shall in no event extend beyond the earlier of—

(A) the date on which there is a generation-skipping transfer with respect to such property, or

(B) the date of the death of the transferor.

(4) TREATMENT OF SPOUSE.—Except as provided in regulations, any reference in this subsection to an individual or transferor shall be treated as including a reference to the spouse of such individual or transferor.

(5) COORDINATION WITH SUBSECTION (d).—Under regulations, appropriate adjustments shall be made in the application of subsection (d) to take into account the provisions of this subsection.

Amendments

• **1988, Technical and Miscellaneous Revenue Act of 1988 (P.L. 100-647)**
P.L. 100-647, § 1014(g)(4)(A):
Amended Code Sec. 2642 by adding at the end thereof new subsection (f). **Effective** as if included in the provision of P.L. 99-514 to which it relates.

[Sec. 2642(g)]

(g) RELIEF PROVISIONS.—

(1) RELIEF FROM LATE ELECTIONS.—

(A) IN GENERAL.—The Secretary shall by regulation prescribe such circumstances and procedures under which extensions of time will be granted to make—

(i) an allocation of GST exemption described in paragraph (1) or (2) of subsection (b), and

(ii) an election under subsection (b)(3) or (c)(5) of section 2632.

Such regulations shall include procedures for requesting comparable relief with respect to transfers made before the date of the enactment of this paragraph.

(B) BASIS FOR DETERMINATIONS.—In determining whether to grant relief under this paragraph, the Secretary shall take into account all relevant circumstances, including evidence of intent contained in the trust instrument or instrument of transfer and such other factors as the Secretary deems relevant. For purposes of determining whether to grant relief under this paragraph, the time for making the allocation (or election) shall be treated as if not expressly prescribed by statute.

(2) SUBSTANTIAL COMPLIANCE.—An allocation of GST exemption under section 2632 that demonstrates an intent to have the lowest possible inclusion ratio with respect to a transfer or a trust shall be deemed to be an allocation of so much of the transferor's unused GST exemption as produces the lowest possible inclusion ratio. In determining whether there has been substantial compliance, all relevant circumstances shall be taken into account, including evidence of intent contained in the trust instrument or instrument of transfer and such other factors as the Secretary deems relevant.

Amendments

• **2013, American Taxpayer Relief Act of 2012 (P.L. 112-240)**

P.L. 112-240, §101(a)(1) and (3), provides:

SEC. 101. PERMANENT EXTENSION AND MODIFICATION OF 2001 TAX RELIEF.

(a) PERMANENT EXTENSION.—

(1) IN GENERAL.—The Economic Growth and Tax Relief Reconciliation Act of 2001 is amended by striking title IX.

***

(3) EFFECTIVE DATE.—The amendments made by this subsection shall apply to taxable, plan, or limitation years beginning after December 31, 2012, and estates of decedents dying, gifts made, or generation skipping transfers after December 31, 2012.

• **2001, Economic Growth and Tax Relief Reconciliation Act of 2001 (P.L. 107-16)**

P.L. 107-16, §564(a):

Amended Code Sec. 2642 by adding at the end a new subsection (g). For the **effective** date, see Act Sec. 564(b)(1)-(2), below.

P.L. 107-16, §564(b)(1)-(2), provides:

(b) EFFECTIVE DATES.—

(1) RELIEF FROM LATE ELECTIONS.—Section 2642(g)(1) of the Internal Revenue Code of 1986 (as added by subsection (a)) shall apply to requests pending on, or filed after, December 31, 2000.

(2) SUBSTANTIAL COMPLIANCE.—Section 2642(g)(2) of such Code (as so added) shall apply to transfers subject to chapter 11 or 12 of the Internal Revenue Code of 1986 made after December 31, 2000. No implication is intended with respect to the availability of relief from late elections or the application of a rule of substantial compliance on or before such date.

P.L. 107-16, §901(a)-(b), as amended by P.L. 111-312, §101(a)(1), provides [but see P.L. 112-240, §101(a)(1) and (3), above]:

SEC. 901. SUNSET OF PROVISIONS OF ACT.

(a) IN GENERAL.—All provisions of, and amendments made by, this Act shall not apply—

(1) to taxable, plan, or limitation years beginning after December 31, 2012, or

(2) in the case of title V, to estates of decedents dying, gifts made, or generation skipping transfers, after December 31, 2012.

(b) APPLICATION OF CERTAIN LAWS.—The Internal Revenue Code of 1986 and the Employee Retirement Income Security Act of 1974 shall be applied and administered to years, estates, gifts, and transfers described in subsection (a) as if the provisions and amendments described in subsection (a) had never been enacted.

Subchapter F—Other Definitions and Special Rules

Sec. 2651.	Generation assignment.
Sec. 2652.	Other definitions.
Sec. 2653.	Taxation of multiple skips.
Sec. 2654.	Special rules.

[Sec. 2651]

SEC. 2651. GENERATION ASSIGNMENT.

[Sec. 2651(a)]

(a) IN GENERAL.—For purposes of this chapter, the generation to which any person (other than the transferor) belongs shall be determined in accordance with the rules set forth in this section.

[Sec. 2651(b)]

(b) LINEAL DESCENDANTS.—

(1) IN GENERAL.—An individual who is a lineal descendant of a grandparent of the transferor shall be assigned to that generation which results from comparing the number of generations between the grandparent and such individual with the number of generations between the grandparent and the transferor.

(2) ON SPOUSE'S SIDE.—An individual who is a lineal descendant of a grandparent of a spouse (or former spouse) of the transferor (other than such spouse) shall be assigned to that generation which results from comparing the number of generations between such grandparent and such individual with the number of generations between such grandparent and such spouse.

(3) TREATMENT OF LEGAL ADOPTIONS, ETC.—For purposes of this subsection—

(A) LEGAL ADOPTIONS.—A relationship by legal adoption shall be treated as a relationship by blood.

(B) RELATIONSHIPS BY HALF-BLOOD.—A relationship by the half-blood shall be treated as a relationship of the whole-blood.

Amendments

• **1988, Technical and Miscellaneous Revenue Act of 1988 (P.L. 100-647)**

P.L. 100-647, §1014(g)(19):

Amended Code Sec. 2651(b)(2) by striking out "a spouse of the transferor" and inserting in lieu thereof "a spouse (or former spouse) of the transferor". **Effective** as if included in the provision of P.L. 99-514 to which it relates.

[Sec. 2651(c)]

(c) MARITAL RELATIONSHIP.—

(1) MARRIAGE TO TRANSFEROR.—An individual who has been married at any time to the transferor shall be assigned to the transferor's generation.

(2) MARRIAGE TO OTHER LINEAL DESCENDANTS.—An individual who has been married at any time to an individual described in subsection (b) shall be assigned to the generation of the individual so described.

[Sec. 2651(d)]

(d) PERSONS WHO ARE NOT LINEAL DESCENDANTS.—An individual who is not assigned to a generation by reason of the foregoing provisions of this section shall be assigned to a generation on the basis of the date of such individual's birth with—

(1) an individual born not more than 12½ years after the date of the birth of the transferor assigned to the transferor's generation,

(2) an individual born more than 12½ years but not more than 37½ years after the date of the birth of the transferor assigned to the first generation younger than the transferor, and

(3) similar rules for a new generation every 25 years.

GENERATION-SKIPPING TRANSFERS

[Sec. 2651(e)]

(e) SPECIAL RULE FOR PERSONS WITH A DECEASED PARENT.—

(1) IN GENERAL.—For purposes of determining whether any transfer is a generation-skipping transfer, if—

(A) an individual is a descendant of a parent of the transferor (or the transferor's spouse or former spouse), and

(B) such individual's parent who is a lineal descendant of the parent of the transferor (or the transferor's spouse or former spouse) is dead at the time the transfer (from which an interest of such individual is established or derived) is subject to a tax imposed by chapter 11 or 12 upon the transferor (and if there shall be more than 1 such time, then at the earliest such time),

such individual shall be treated as if such individual were a member of the generation which is 1 generation below the lower of the transferor's generation or the generation assignment of the youngest living ancestor of such individual who is also a descendant of the parent of the transferor (or the transferor's spouse or former spouse), and the generation assignment of any descendant of such individual shall be adjusted accordingly.

(2) LIMITED APPLICATION OF SUBSECTION TO COLLATERAL HEIRS.—This subsection shall not apply with respect to a transfer to any individual who is not a lineal descendant of the transferor (or the transferor's spouse or former spouse) if, at the time of the transfer, such transferor has any living lineal descendant.

Amendments

• **1997, Taxpayer Relief Act of 1997 (P.L. 105-34)**

P.L. 105-34, § 511(a):

Amended Code Sec. 2651 by redesignating subsection (e) as subsection (f) and by inserting after subsection (d) a new subsection (e). **Effective** for terminations, distributions, and transfers occurring after 12-31-97.

[Sec. 2651(f)]

(f) OTHER SPECIAL RULES.—

(1) INDIVIDUALS ASSIGNED TO MORE THAN 1 GENERATION.—Except as provided in regulations, an individual who, but for this subsection, would be assigned to more than 1 generation shall be assigned to the youngest such generation.

(2) INTEREST THROUGH ENTITIES.—Except as provided in paragraph (3), if an estate, trust, partnership, corporation, or other entity has an interest in property, each individual having a beneficial interest in such entity shall be treated as having an interest in such property and shall be assigned to a generation under the foregoing provisions of this subsection.

(3) TREATMENT OF CERTAIN CHARITABLE ORGANIZATIONS AND GOVERNMENTAL ENTITIES.—Any—

(A) organization described in section 511(a)(2),

(B) charitable trust described in section 511(b)(2), and

(C) governmental entity,

shall be assigned to the transferor's generation.

Amendments

• **1997, Taxpayer Relief Act of 1997 (P.L. 105-34)**

P.L. 105-34, § 511(a):

Amended Code Sec. 2651 by redesignating subsection (e) as subsection (f). **Effective** for terminations, distributions, and transfers occurring after 12-31-97.

• **1988, Technical and Miscellaneous Revenue Act of 1988 (P.L. 100-647)**

P.L. 100-647, § 1014(g)(11):

Amended Code Sec. 2651(e)(3). **Effective** as if included in the provision of P.L. 99-514 to which it relates. Prior to amendment, Code Sec. 2651(e)(3) read as follows:

(3) TREATMENT OF CERTAIN CHARITABLE ORGANIZATIONS.—Any organization described in section 511(a)(2) and any charitable trust described in section 511(b)(2) shall be assigned to the transferor's generation.

• **1986, Tax Reform Act of 1986 (P.L. 99-514)**

P.L. 99-514, § 1431(a):

Added Code Sec. 2651. **Effective**, generally, for any generation-skipping transfer (within the meaning of section 2611 of the Internal Revenue Code of 1986) made after 10-22-86. However, for special rules, see Act Sec. 1433(b)-(d) following Code Sec. 2601.

[Sec. 2652]

SEC. 2652. OTHER DEFINITIONS.

[Sec. 2652(a)]

(a) TRANSFEROR.—For purposes of this chapter—

(1) IN GENERAL.—Except as provided in this subsection or section 2653(a), the term "transferor" means—

(A) in the case of any property subject to the tax imposed by chapter 11, the decedent, and

(B) in the case of any property subject to the tax imposed by chapter 12, the donor.

An individual shall be treated as transferring any property with respect to which such individual is the transferor.

(2) GIFT-SPLITTING BY MARRIED COUPLES.—If, under section 2513, one-half of a gift is treated as made by an individual and one-half of such gift is treated as made by the spouse of such individual, such gift shall be so treated for purposes of this chapter.

(3) SPECIAL ELECTION FOR QUALIFIED TERMINABLE INTEREST PROPERTY.—In the case of—

(A) any trust with respect to which a deduction is allowed to the decedent under section 2056 by reason of subsection (b)(7) thereof, and

(B) any trust with respect to which a deduction to the donor spouse is allowed under section 2523 by reason of subsection (f) thereof,

the estate of the decedent or the donor spouse, as the case may be may elect to treat all of the property in such trust for purposes of this chapter as if the election to be treated as qualified terminable interest property had not been made.

Amendments

• **2010, Tax Relief, Unemployment Insurance Reauthorization, and Job Creation Act of 2010 (P.L. 111-312)**

P.L. 111-312, § 301(c), provides:

(c) SPECIAL ELECTION WITH RESPECT TO ESTATES OF DECEDENTS DYING IN 2010.—Notwithstanding subsection (a), in the case of an estate of a decedent dying after December 31, 2009, and before January 1, 2011, the executor (within the meaning of section 2203 of the Internal Revenue Code of 1986) may elect to apply such Code as though the amendments made by subsection (a) do not apply with respect to chapter 11 of such Code and with respect to property acquired or passing from such decedent (within the meaning of section 1014(b) of such Code). Such election shall be made at such time and in such manner as the Secretary of the Treasury or the Secretary's delegate shall provide. Such an election once made shall be revocable only with the consent of the Secretary of the Treasury or the Secretary's delegate. For purposes of section 2652(a)(1) of such Code, the determination of whether any property is subject to the tax imposed by such chapter 11 shall be made without regard to any election made under this subsection.

• **1988, Technical and Miscellaneous Revenue Act of 1988 (P.L. 100-647)**

P.L. 100-647, § 1014(g)(9)(A)-(B):

Amended Code Sec. 2652(a)(1) by striking out "a transfer of a kind" each place it appears and inserting in lieu thereof "any property", and by adding at the end thereof a new sentence. **Effective** as if included in the provision of P.L. 99-514 to which it relates.

P.L. 100-647, § 1014(g)(14)(A)-(B):

Amended Code Sec. 2652(a)(3) by striking out "any property" in subparagraphs (A) and (B) and inserting in lieu thereof "any trust", and by striking out "may elect to treat such property" and inserting in lieu thereof "may elect to treat all of the property in such trust". **Effective** as if included in the provision of P.L. 99-514 to which it relates.

GENERATION-SKIPPING TRANSFERS

[Sec. 2652(b)]

(b) TRUST AND TRUSTEE.—

(1) TRUST.—The term "trust" includes any arrangement (other than an estate) which, although not a trust, has substantially the same effect as a trust.

(2) TRUSTEE.—In the case of an arrangement which is not a trust but which is treated as a trust under this subsection, the term "trustee" shall mean the person in actual or constructive possession of the property subject to such arrangement.

(3) EXAMPLES.—Arrangements to which this subsection applies include arrangements involving life estates and remainders, estates for years, and insurance and annuity contracts.

Amendments

• **1998, IRS Restructuring and Reform Act of 1998 (P.L. 105-206)**

P.L. 105-206, § 6013(a)(3):

Amended Code Sec. 2652(b)(1) by striking "section 646". and inserting "section 645". **Effective** as if included in the provision of P.L. 105-34 to which it relates [**effective** for estates of decedents dying after 8-5-97.—CCH].

P.L. 105-206, § 6013(a)(4)(A):

Amended Code Sec. 2652(b)(1) [as amended by Act Sec. 6013(a)(3)]by striking the second sentence. **Effective** as if included in the provision of P.L. 105-34 to which it relates [**effective** for estates of decedents dying after 8-5-97.—CCH]. Prior to being stricken, the second sentence of Code Sec. 2652(b)(1) read as follows:

Such term shall not include any trust during any period the trust is treated as part of an estate under section 645.

• **1997, Taxpayer Relief Act of 1997 (P.L. 105-34)**

P.L. 105-34, § 1305(b):

Amended Code Sec. 2652(b)(1) by adding at the end a new sentence. **Effective** for estates of decedents dying after 8-5-97.

[Sec. 2652(c)]

(c) INTEREST.—

(1) IN GENERAL.—A person has an interest in property held in trust if (at the time the determination is made) such person—

(A) has a right (other than a future right) to receive income or corpus from the trust,

(B) is a permissible current recipient of income or corpus from the trust and is not described in section 2055(a), or

(C) is described in section 2055(a) and the trust is—

(i) a charitable remainder annuity trust,

(ii) a charitable remainder unitrust within the meaning of section 664, or

(iii) a pooled income fund within the meaning of section 642(c)(5).

(2) CERTAIN INTERESTS DISREGARDED.—For purposes of paragraph (1), an interest which is used primarily to postpone or avoid any tax imposed by this chapter shall be disregarded.

(3) CERTAIN SUPPORT OBLIGATIONS DISREGARDED.—The fact that income or corpus of the trust may be used to satisfy an obligation of support arising under State law shall be disregarded in determining whether a person has an interest in the trust, if—

(A) such use is discretionary, or

(B) such use is pursuant to the provisions of any State law substantially equivalent to the Uniform Gifts to Minors Act.

Amendments

• **1988, Technical and Miscellaneous Revenue Act of 1988 (P.L. 100-647)**

P.L. 100-647, § 1014(g)(6):

Amended Code Sec. 2652(c) by adding at the end thereof new paragraph (3). **Effective** as if included in the provision of P.L. 99-514 to which it relates.

P.L. 100-647, § 1014(g)(8)(A)-(B):

Amended Code Sec. 2652(c)(2) by striking out "NOMINAL INTERESTS" in the paragraph heading and inserting in lieu thereof "INTERESTS", and by striking out "the tax" and inserting in lieu thereof "any tax". **Effective** as if included in the provision of P.L. 99-514 to which it relates.

• **1986, Tax Reform Act of 1986 (P.L. 99-514)**

P.L. 99-514, § 1431(a):

Added Code Sec. 2652. **Effective**, generally, for any generation-skipping transfer (within the meaning of section 2611 of the Internal Revenue Code of 1986) made after 10-22-86. However, for special rules, see Act Sec. 1433(b)-(d) following Code Sec. 2601.

[Sec. 2652(d)]

(d) EXECUTOR.—For purposes of this chapter, the term "executor" has the meaning given such term by section 2203.

Amendments

• **1988, Technical and Miscellaneous Revenue Act of 1988 (P.L. 100-647)**

P.L. 100-647, § 1014(g)(20):

Amended Code Sec. 2652 by adding at the end thereof new subsection (d). **Effective** as if included in the provision of P.L. 99-514 to which it relates.

[Sec. 2653]

SEC. 2653. TAXATION OF MULTIPLE SKIPS.

[Sec. 2653(a)]

(a) GENERAL RULE.—For purposes of this chapter, if—

(1) there is a generation-skipping transfer of any property, and

(2) immediately after such transfer such property is held in trust,

for purposes of applying this chapter (other than section 2651) to subsequent transfers from the portion of such trust attributable to such property, the trust will be treated as if the transferor of such property were assigned to the 1st generation above the highest generation of any person who has an interest in such trust immediately after the transfer.

[Sec. 2653(b)]

(b) TRUST RETAINS INCLUSION RATIO.—

(1) IN GENERAL.—Except as provided in paragraph (2), the provisions of subsection (a) shall not affect the inclusion ratio determined with respect to any trust. Under regulations prescribed by the Secretary, notwithstanding the preceding sentence, proper adjustment shall be made to the inclusion ratio with respect to such trust to take into account any tax under this chapter borne by such trust which is imposed by this chapter on the transfer described in subsection (a).

(2) SPECIAL RULE FOR POUR-OVER TRUST.—

(A) IN GENERAL.—If the generation-skipping transfer referred to in subsection (a) involves the transfer of property from 1 trust to another trust (hereinafter in this paragraph referred to as the "pour-over trust"), the inclusion ratio for the pour-over trust shall be determined by treating the nontax portion of such distribution as if it were a part of a GST exemption allocated to such trust.

(B) NONTAX PORTION.—For purposes of subparagraph (A), the nontax portion of any distribution is the amount of such distribution multiplied by the applicable fraction which applies to such distribution.

GENERATION-SKIPPING TRANSFERS

Amendments
- **1986, Tax Reform Act of 1986 (P.L. 99-514)**

P.L. 99-514, § 1431(a):

Added Code Sec. 2653. **Effective**, generally, for any generation-skipping transfer (within the meaning of section 2611 of the Internal Revenue Code of 1986) made after 10-22-86. However, for special rules, see Act Sec. 1433(b)-(d) following Code Sec. 2601.

[Sec. 2654]

SEC. 2654. SPECIAL RULES.

[Sec. 2654(a)]

(a) BASIS ADJUSTMENT.—

(1) IN GENERAL.—Except as provided in paragraph (2), if property is transferred in a generation-skipping transfer, the basis of such property shall be increased (but not above the fair market value of such property) by an amount equal to that portion of the tax imposed by section 2601 with respect to the transfer which is attributable to the excess of the fair market value of such property over its adjusted basis immediately before the transfer. The preceding shall be applied after any basis adjustment under section 1015 with respect to transfer.

(2) CERTAIN TRANSFERS AT DEATH.—If property is transferred in a taxable termination which occurs at the same time as and as a result of the death of an individual, the basis of such property shall be adjusted in a manner similar to the manner provided under section 1014(a); except that, if the inclusion ratio with respect to such property is less than 1, any increase or decrease in basis shall be limited by multiplying such increase or decrease (as the case may be) by the inclusion ratio.

Amendments
- **2014, Tax Technical Corrections Act of 2014 (P.L. 113-295)**

P.L. 113-295, § 221(a)(95)(B)(iii), Division A:

Amended Code Sec. 2654(a)(1) by striking "(computed without regard to section 2604)" following "section 2601". **Effective** generally 12-19-2014. For a special rule, see Act Sec. 221(b)(2), Division A, below.

P.L. 113-295, § 221(b)(2), Division A, provides:

(2) SAVINGS PROVISION.—If—

(A) any provision amended or repealed by the amendments made by this section applied to—

(i) any transaction occurring before the date of the enactment of this Act,

(ii) any property acquired before such date of enactment, or

(iii) any item of income, loss, deduction, or credit taken into account before such date of enactment, and

(B) the treatment of such transaction, property, or item under such provision would (without regard to the amendments or repeals made by this section) affect the liability for tax for periods ending after date of enactment, nothing in the amendments or repeals made by this section shall be construed to affect the treatment of such transaction, property, or item for purposes of determining liability for tax for periods ending after such date of enactment.

- **1989, Omnibus Budget Reconciliation Act of 1989 (P.L. 101-239)**

P.L. 101-239, § 7811(j)(2):

Amended Code Sec. 2654(a)(1) by adding at the end thereof a new sentence. **Effective** as if included in the provision of P.L. 100-647 to which it relates.

- **1988, Technical and Miscellaneous Revenue Act of 1988 (P.L. 100-647)**

P.L. 100-647, § 1014(g)(12)(A)-(B):

Amended Code Sec. 2654(a)(2) by striking out "any increase" and inserting in lieu thereof "any increase or decrease", and by striking out "such increase" and inserting in lieu thereof "such increase or decrease (as the case may be)". **Effective** as if included in the provision of P.L. 99-514 to which it relates.

[Sec. 2654(b)]

(b) CERTAIN TRUSTS TREATED AS SEPARATE TRUSTS.—For purposes of this chapter—

(1) the portions of a trust attributable to transfers from different transferors shall be treated as separate trusts, and

(2) substantially separate and independent shares of different beneficiaries in a trust shall be treated as separate trusts.

Except as provided in the preceding sentence, nothing in this chapter shall be construed as authorizing a single trust to be treated as 2 or more trusts. For purposes of this subsection, a trust shall be treated as part of an estate during any period that the trust is so treated under section 645.

Amendments
- **1998, IRS Restructuring and Reform Act of 1998 (P.L. 105-206)**

P.L. 105-206, § 6013(a)(4)(B):

Amended Code Sec. 2654(b) by adding at the end a new sentence. **Effective** as if included in the provision of P.L. 105-34 to which it relates [effective for estates of decedents dying after 8-5-97.—CCH].

- **1988, Technical and Miscellaneous Revenue Act of 1988 (P.L. 100-647)**

P.L. 100-647, § 1014(g)(13):

Amended Code Sec. 2654(b). **Effective** as if included in the provision of P.L. 99-514 to which it relates. Prior to amendment, Code Sec. 2654(b) read as follows:

(b) SEPARATE SHARES TREATED AS SEPARATE TRUSTS.—Substantially separate and independent shares of different beneficiaries in a trust shall be treated as separate trusts.

[Sec. 2654(c)]

(c) DISCLAIMERS.—

For provisions relating to the effect of a qualified disclaimer for purposes of this chapter, see section 2518.

[Sec. 2654(d)]

(d) LIMITATION ON PERSONAL LIABILITY OF TRUSTEE.—A trustee shall not be personally liable for any increase in the tax imposed by section 2601 which is attributable to the fact that—

(1) section 2642(c) (relating to exemption of certain nontaxable gifts) does not apply to a transfer to the trust which was made during the life of the transferor and for which a gift tax return was not filed, or

(2) the inclusion ratio with respect to the trust is greater than the amount of such ratio as computed on the basis of the return on which was made (or was deemed made) an allocation of the GST exemption to property transferred to such trust.

The preceding sentence shall not apply if the trustee has knowledge of facts sufficient reasonably to conclude that a gift tax return was required to be filed or that the inclusion ratio was erroneous.

Amendments
- **1986, Tax Reform Act of 1986 (P.L. 99-514)**

P.L. 99-514, § 1431(a):

Added Code Sec. 2654. **Effective** for any generation-skipping transfer (within the meaning of section 2611 of the Internal Revenue Code of 1986) made after 10-22-86. However, for special rules, see Act Sec. 1433(b)-(d) following Code Sec. 2601.

Subchapter G—Administration

Sec. 2661.	Administration.
Sec. 2662.	Return requirements.
Sec. 2663.	Regulations.
Sec. 2664.	Termination.

GENERATION-SKIPPING TRANSFERS

[Sec. 2661]

SEC. 2661. ADMINISTRATION.

Insofar as applicable and not inconsistent with the provisions of this chapter—

(1) except as provided in paragraph (2), all provisions of subtitle F (including penalties) applicable to the gift tax, to chapter 12, or to section 2501, are hereby made applicable in respect of the generation-skipping transfer tax, this chapter, or section 2601, as the case may be, and

(2) in the case of a generation-skipping transfer occurring at the same time as and as a result of the death of an individual, all provisions of subtitle F (including penalties) applicable to the estate tax, to chapter 11, or to section 2001 are hereby made applicable in respect of the generation-skipping transfer tax, this chapter, or section 2601 (as the case may be).

Amendments

• **1986, Tax Reform Act of 1986 (P.L. 99-514)**

P.L. 99-514, §1431(a):

Added Code Sec. 2661. **Effective**, generally, for any generation-skipping transfer (within the meaning of section 2611 of the Internal Revenue Code of 1986) made after 10-22-86. However, for special rules, see Act Sec. 1433(b)-(d) following Code Sec. 2601.

[Sec. 2662]

SEC. 2662. RETURN REQUIREMENTS.

[Sec. 2662(a)]

(a) IN GENERAL.—The Secretary shall prescribe by regulations the person who is required to make the return with respect to the tax imposed by this chapter and the time by which any such return must be filed. To the extent practicable, such regulations shall provide that—

(1) the person who is required to make such return shall be the person liable under section 2603(a) for payment of such tax, and

(2) the return shall be filed—

(A) in the case of a direct skip (other than from a trust), on or before the date on which an estate or gift tax return is required to be filed with respect to the transfer, and

(B) in all other cases, on or before the 15th day of the 4th month after the close of the taxable year of the person required to make such return in which such transfer occurs.

Amendments

• **2010, Tax Relief, Unemployment Insurance Reauthorization, and Job Creation Act of 2010 (P.L. 111-312)**

P.L. 111-312, §301(d)(2), provides:

(2) GENERATION-SKIPPING TAX.—In the case of any generation-skipping transfer made after December 31, 2009, and before the date of the enactment of this Act, the due date for filing any return under section 2662 of the Internal Revenue Code of 1986 (including any election required to be made on such a return) shall not be earlier than the date which is 9 months after the date of the enactment of this Act.

[Sec. 2662(b)]

(b) INFORMATION RETURNS.—The Secretary may by regulations require a return to be filed containing such information as he determines to be necessary for purposes of this chapter.

Amendments

• **1986, Tax Reform Act of 1986 (P.L. 99-514)**

P.L. 99-514, §1431(a):

Added Code Sec. 2662. **Effective** for any generation-skipping transfer (within the meaning of section 2611 of the Internal Revenue Code of 1986) made after 10-22-86. However, for special rules, see Act Sec. 1433(b)-(d) following Code Sec. 2601.

[Sec. 2663]

SEC. 2663. REGULATIONS.

The Secretary shall prescribe such regulations as may be necessary or appropriate to carry out the purposes of this chapter, including—

(1) such regulations as may be necessary to coordinate the provisions of this chapter with the recapture tax imposed under section 2032A(c),

(2) regulations (consistent with the principles of chapters 11 and 12) providing for the application of this chapter in the case of transferors who are nonresidents not citizens of the United States, and

(3) regulations providing for such adjustments as may be necessary to the application of this chapter in the case of any arrangement which, although not a trust, is treated as a trust under section 2652(b).

Amendments

• **1988, Technical and Miscellaneous Revenue Act of 1988 (P.L. 100-647)**

P.L. 100-647, §1014(g)(10):

Amended Code Sec. 2663 by striking out "and" at the end of paragraph (1), by striking out the period at the end of paragraph (2) and inserting in lieu thereof ", and", and by adding at the end thereof new paragraph (3). **Effective** as if included in the provision of P.L. 99-514 to which it relates.

• **1986, Tax Reform Act of 1986 (P.L. 99-514)**

P.L. 99-514, §1431(a):

Added Code Sec. 2663. **Effective**, generally, for any generation-skipping transfer (within the meaning of section 2611 of the Internal Revenue Code of 1986) made after 10-22-86. However, for special rules, see Act Sec. 1433(b)-(d) following Code Sec. 2601.

[Sec. 2664]

SEC. 2664. TERMINATION.

This chapter shall not apply to generation-skipping transfers after December 31, 2009.

Amendments

• **2010, Tax Relief, Unemployment Insurance Reauthorization, and Job Creation Act of 2010 (P.L. 111-312)**

P.L. 111-312, §301(a):

Amended Code Sec. 2664 to read as such provision would read if subtitle A of title V of the Economic Growth and Tax Relief Reconciliation Act of 2001 (P.L. 107-16) had never been enacted. **Effective** for estates of decedents dying, and transfers made, after 12-31-2009. For a special rule, see Act Sec. 301(c), below. Prior to amendment by P.L. 111-312, Code Sec. 2664 read as follows:

SEC. 2664. TERMINATION.

This chapter shall not apply to generation-skipping transfers after December 31, 2009.

P.L. 111-312, §301(c), provides:

(c) SPECIAL ELECTION WITH RESPECT TO ESTATES OF DECEDENTS DYING IN 2010.—Notwithstanding subsection (a), in the case of an estate of a decedent dying after December 31, 2009, and before January 1, 2011, the executor (within the meaning of section 2203 of the Internal Revenue Code of 1986) may elect to apply such Code as though the amendments made by subsection (a) do not apply with respect to chapter 11 of such Code and with respect to property acquired or passing from such decedent (within the meaning of section 1014(b) of such Code). Such election shall be made at such time and in such manner as the Secretary of the Treasury or the Secretary's delegate shall provide. Such an election once made shall be revocable only with the consent of the Secretary of the Treasury or the Secretary's delegate. For purposes of section 2652(a)(1) of such Code, the determination of whether any property is subject

SPECIAL VALUATION RULES

to the tax imposed by such chapter 11 shall be made without regard to any election made under this subsection.

P.L. 111-312, § 304, provides:

SEC. 304. APPLICATION OF EGTRRA SUNSET TO THIS TITLE.

Section 901 of the Economic Growth and Tax Relief Reconciliation Act of 2001 shall apply to the amendments made by this title.

- **2001, Economic Growth and Tax Relief Reconciliation Act of 2001 (P.L. 107-16)**

P.L. 107-16, § 501(b):

Amended subchapter G of chapter 13 of subtitle B by adding at the end a new Code Sec. 2664. **Effective** for the estates of decedents dying, and generation-skipping transfers, after 12-31-2009.

P.L. 107-16, § 901(a)-(b), as amended by P.L. 111-312, § 101(a)(1), provides:

SEC. 901. SUNSET OF PROVISIONS OF ACT.

(a) IN GENERAL.—All provisions of, and amendments made by, this Act shall not apply—

(1) to taxable, plan, or limitation years beginning after December 31, 2012, or

(2) in the case of title V, to estates of decedents dying, gifts made, or generation skipping transfers, after December 31, 2012.

(b) APPLICATION OF CERTAIN LAWS.—The Internal Revenue Code of 1986 and the Employee Retirement Income Security Act of 1974 shall be applied and administered to years, estates, gifts, and transfers described in subsection (a) as if the provisions and amendments described in subsection (a) had never been enacted.

CHAPTER 14—SPECIAL VALUATION RULES

Sec. 2701.	Special valuation rules in case of transfers of certain interests in corporations or partnerships.
Sec. 2702.	Special valuation rules in case of transfers of interests in trusts.
Sec. 2703.	Certain rights and restrictions disregarded.
Sec. 2704.	Treatment of certain lapsing rights and restrictions.

[Sec. 2701]

SEC. 2701. SPECIAL VALUATION RULES IN CASE OF TRANSFERS OF CERTAIN INTERESTS IN CORPORATIONS OR PARTNERSHIPS.

[Sec. 2701(a)]

(a) VALUATION RULES.—

(1) IN GENERAL.—Solely for purposes of determining whether a transfer of an interest in a corporation or partnership to (or for the benefit of) a member of the transferor's family is a gift (and the value of such transfer), the value of any right—

(A) which is described in subparagraph (A) or (B) of subsection (b)(1), and

(B) which is with respect to any applicable retained interest that is held by the transferor or an applicable family member immediately after the transfer,

shall be determined under paragraph (3). This paragraph shall not apply to the transfer of any interest for which market quotations are readily available (as of the date of transfer) on an established securities market.

(2) EXCEPTIONS FOR MARKETABLE RETAINED INTERESTS, ETC.—Paragraph (1) shall not apply to any right with respect to an applicable retained interest if—

(A) market quotations are readily available (as of the date of the transfer) for such interest on an established securities market,

(B) such interest is of the same class as the transferred interest, or

(C) such interest is proportionally the same as the transferred interest, without regard to nonlapsing differences in voting power (or, for a partnership, nonlapsing differences with respect to management and limitations on liability).

Subparagraph (C) shall not apply to any interest in a partnership if the transferor or an applicable family member has the right to alter the liability of the transferee of the transferred property. Except as provided by the Secretary, any difference described in subparagraph (C) which lapses by reason of any Federal or State law shall be treated as a nonlapsing difference for purposes of such subparagraph.

(3) VALUATION OF RIGHTS TO WHICH PARAGRAPH (1) APPLIES.—

(A) IN GENERAL.—The value of any right described in paragraph (1), other than a distribution right which consists of a right to receive a qualified payment, shall be treated as being zero.

(B) VALUATION OF CERTAIN QUALIFIED PAYMENTS.—If—

(i) any applicable retained interest confers a distribution right which consists of the right to a qualified payment, and

(ii) there are 1 or more liquidation, put, call, or conversion rights with respect to such interest,

the value of all such rights shall be determined as if each liquidation, put, call, or conversion right were exercised in the manner resulting in the lowest value being determined for all such rights.

(C) VALUATION OF QUALIFIED PAYMENTS WHERE NO LIQUIDATION, ETC. RIGHTS.—In the case of an applicable retained interest which is described in subparagraph (B)(i) but not subparagraph (B)(ii), the value of the distribution right shall be determined without regard to this section.

(4) MINIMUM VALUATION OF JUNIOR EQUITY.—

(A) IN GENERAL.—In the case of a transfer described in paragraph (1) of a junior equity interest in a corporation or partnership, such interest shall in no event be valued at an amount less than the value which would be determined if the total value of all of the junior equity interests in the entity were equal to 10 percent of the sum of—

(i) the total value of all of the equity interests in such entity, plus

(ii) the total amount of indebtedness of such entity to the transferor (or an applicable family member).

(B) DEFINITIONS.—For purposes of this paragraph—

(i) JUNIOR EQUITY INTEREST.—The term "junior equity interest" means common stock or, in the case of a partnership, any partnership interest under which the rights as to income and capital (or, to the extent provided in regulations, the rights as to either income or capital) are junior to the rights of all other classes of equity interests.

(ii) EQUITY INTEREST.—The term "equity interest" means stock or any interest as a partner, as the case may be.

Amendments

- **1996, Small Business Job Protection Act of 1996 (P.L. 104-188)**

P.L. 104-188, § 1702(f)(1)(A):

Amended Code Sec. 2701(a)(3) by adding at the end thereof a new subparagraph (C). **Effective** as if included in the provision of P.L. 101-508 to which it relates.

P.L. 104-188, § 1702(f)(1)(B):

Amended Code Sec. 2701(a)(3)(B) by inserting "CERTAIN" before "QUALIFIED" in the section heading. **Effective** as if included in the provision of P.L. 101-508 to which it relates.

P.L. 104-188, § 1702(f)(2):

Amended Code Sec. 2701(a)(4)(B)(i) by inserting "(or, to the extent provided in regulations, the rights as to either income or capital)" after "income and capital". **Effective** as if included in the provision of P.L. 101-508 to which it relates.

SPECIAL VALUATION RULES

[Sec. 2701(b)]

(b) APPLICABLE RETAINED INTERESTS.—For purposes of this section—

(1) IN GENERAL.—The term "applicable retained interest" means any interest in an entity with respect to which there is—

(A) a distribution right, but only if, immediately before the transfer described in subsection (a)(1), the transferor and applicable family members hold (after application of subsection (e)(3)) control of the entity, or

(B) a liquidation, put, call, or conversion right.

(2) CONTROL.—For purposes of paragraph (1)—

(A) CORPORATIONS.—In the case of a corporation, the term "control" means the holding of at least 50 percent (by vote or value) of the stock of the corporation.

(B) PARTNERSHIPS.—In the case of a partnership, the term "control" means—

(i) the holding of at least 50 percent of the capital or profits interests in the partnership, or

(ii) in the case of a limited partnership, the holding of any interest as a general partner.

(C) APPLICABLE FAMILY MEMBER.—For purposes of this subsection, the term "applicable family member" includes any lineal descendant of any parent of the transferor or the transferor's spouse.

Amendments

- **1996, Small Business Job Protection Act of 1996 (P.L. 104-188)**

P.L. 104-188, § 1702(f)(3)(A):

Amended Code Sec. 2701(b)(2) by adding at the end a new subparagraph (C).
Effective as if included in the provision of P.L. 101-508 to which it relates.

[Sec. 2701(c)]

(c) DISTRIBUTION AND OTHER RIGHTS; QUALIFIED PAYMENTS.—For purposes of this section—

(1) DISTRIBUTION RIGHT.—

(A) IN GENERAL.—The term "distribution right" means—

(i) a right to distributions from a corporation with respect to its stock, and

(ii) a right to distributions from a partnership with respect to a partner's interest in the partnership.

(B) EXCEPTIONS.—The term "distribution right" does not include—

(i) a right to distributions with respect to any interest which is junior to the rights of the transferred interest,

(ii) any liquidation, put, call, or conversion right, or

(iii) any right to receive any guaranteed payment described in section 707(c) of a fixed amount.

(2) LIQUIDATION, ETC. RIGHTS.—

(A) IN GENERAL.—The term "liquidation, put, call, or conversion right" means any liquidation, put, call, or conversion right, or any similar right, the exercise or nonexercise of which affects the value of the transferred interest.

(B) EXCEPTION FOR FIXED RIGHTS.—

(i) IN GENERAL.—The term "liquidation, put, call, or conversion right" does not include any right which must be exercised at a specific time and at a specific amount.

(ii) TREATMENT OF CERTAIN RIGHTS.—If a right is assumed to be exercised in a particular manner under subsection (a)(3)(B), such right shall be treated as so exercised for purposes of clause (i).

(C) EXCEPTION FOR CERTAIN RIGHTS TO CONVERT.—The term "liquidation, put, call, or conversion right" does not include any right which—

(i) is a right to convert into a fixed number (or a fixed percentage) of shares of the same class of stock in a corporation as the transferred stock in such corporation under subsection (a)(1) (or stock which would be of the same class but for nonlapsing differences in voting power),

(ii) is nonlapsing,

(iii) is subject to proportionate adjustments for splits, combinations, reclassifications, and similar changes in the capital stock, and

(iv) is subject to adjustments similar to the adjustments under subsection (d) for accumulated but unpaid distributions.

A rule similar to the rule of the preceding sentence shall apply for partnerships.

(3) QUALIFIED PAYMENT.—

(A) IN GENERAL.—Except as otherwise provided in this paragraph, the term "qualified payment" means any dividend payable on a periodic basis under any cumulative preferred stock (or a comparable payment under any partnership interest) to the extent that such dividend (or comparable payment) is determined at a fixed rate.

(B) TREATMENT OF VARIABLE RATE PAYMENTS.—For purposes of subparagraph (A), a payment shall be treated as fixed as to rate if such payment is determined at a rate which bears a fixed relationship to a specified market interest rate.

(C) ELECTIONS.—

(i) IN GENERAL.—Payments under any interest held by a transferor which (without regard to this subparagraph) are qualified payments shall be treated as qualified payments unless the transferor elects not to treat such payments as qualified payments. Payments described in the preceding sentence which are held by an applicable family member shall be treated as qualified payments only if such member elects to treat such payments as qualified payments.

(ii) ELECTION TO HAVE INTEREST TREATED AS QUALIFIED PAYMENT.—A transferor or applicable family member holding any distribution right which (without regard to this subparagraph) is not a qualified payment may elect to treat such right as a qualified payment, to be paid in the amounts and at the times specified in such election. The preceding sentence shall apply only to the extent that the amounts and times so specified are not inconsistent with the underlying legal instrument giving rise to such right.

(iii) ELECTIONS IRREVOCABLE.—Any election under this subparagraph with respect to an interest shall, once made, be irrevocable.

Amendments

- **1996, Small Business Job Protection Act of 1996 (P.L. 104-188)**

P.L. 104-188, § 1702(f)(4):

Amended Code Sec. 2701(c)(1)(B)(i). **Effective** as if included in the provision of P.L. 101-508 to which it relates. For a special rule, see Act Sec. 1702(f)(5)(C), below. Prior to amendment, Code Sec. 2701(c)(1)(B)(i) read as follows:

(i) a right to distributions with respect to any junior equity interest (as defined in subsection (a)(4)(B)(i));

P.L. 104-188, § 1702(f)(5)(A):

Amended Code Sec. 2701(c)(3)(C)(i). **Effective** as if included in the provision of P.L. 101-508 to which it relates. For a special rule, see Act Sec. 1702(f)(5)(C), below. Prior to amendment, Code Sec. 2701(c)(3)(C)(i) read as follows:

SPECIAL VALUATION RULES

(i) WAIVER OF QUALIFIED PAYMENT TREATMENT.—A transferor or applicable family member may elect with respect to payments under any interest specified in such election to treat such payments as payments which are not qualified payments.

P.L. 104-188, § 1702(f)(5)(B):

Amended the first sentence of Code Sec. 2701(c)(3)(C)(ii). **Effective** as if included in the provision of P.L. 101-508 to which it relates. For a special rule, see Act Sec. 1702(f)(5)(C), below. Prior to amendment, the first sentence of Code Sec. 2701(c)(3)(C)(ii) read as follows:

A transferor or any applicable family member may elect to treat any distribution right as a qualified payment, to be paid in the amounts and at the times specified in such election.

P.L. 104-188, § 1702(f)(5)(C), provides:

(C) The time for making an election under the second sentence of section 2701(c)(3)(C)(i) of the Internal Revenue Code of 1986 (as amended by subparagraph (A)) shall not expire before the due date (including extensions) for filing the transferor's return of the tax imposed by section 2501 of such Code for the first calendar year ending after August 20, 1996.

[Sec. 2701(d)]

(d) TRANSFER TAX TREATMENT OF CUMULATIVE BUT UNPAID DISTRIBUTIONS.—

(1) IN GENERAL.—If a taxable event occurs with respect to any distribution right to which subsection (a)(3)(B) or (C) applied, the following shall be increased by the amount determined under paragraph (2):

(A) The taxable estate of the transferor in the case of a taxable event described in paragraph (3)(A)(i).

(B) The taxable gifts of the transferor for the calendar year in which the taxable event occurs in the case of a taxable event described in paragraph (3)(A)(ii) or (iii).

(2) AMOUNT OF INCREASE.—

(A) IN GENERAL.—The amount of the increase determined under this paragraph shall be the excess (if any) of—

(i) the value of the qualified payments payable during the period beginning on the date of the transfer under subsection (a)(1) and ending on the date of the taxable event determined as if—

(I) all such payments were paid on the date payment was due, and

(II) all such payments were reinvested by the transferor as of the date of payment at a yield equal to the discount rate used in determining the value of the applicable retained interest described in subsection (a)(1), over

(ii) the value of such payments paid during such period computed under clause (i) on the basis of the time when such payments were actually paid.

(B) LIMITATION ON AMOUNT OF INCREASE.—

(i) IN GENERAL.—The amount of the increase under subparagraph (A) shall not exceed the applicable percentage of the excess (if any) of—

(I) the value (determined as of the date of the taxable event) of all equity interests in the entity which are junior to the applicable retained interest, over

(II) the value of such interests (determined as of the date of the transfer to which subsection (a)(1) applied).

(ii) APPLICABLE PERCENTAGE.—For purposes of clause (i), the applicable percentage is the percentage determined by dividing—

(I) the number of shares in the corporation held (as of the date of the taxable event) by the transferor which are applicable retained interests of the same class, by

(II) the total number of shares in such corporation (as of such date) which are of the same class as the class described in subclause (I).

A similar percentage shall be determined in the case of interests in a partnership.

(iii) DEFINITION.—For purposes of this subparagraph, the term "equity interest" has the meaning given such term by subsection (a)(4)(B).

(C) GRACE PERIOD.—For purposes of subparagraph (A), any payment of any distribution during the 4-year period beginning on its due date shall be treated as having been made on such due date.

(3) TAXABLE EVENTS.—For purposes of this subsection—

(A) IN GENERAL.—The term "taxable event" means any of the following:

(i) The death of the transferor if the applicable retained interest conferring the distribution right is includible in the estate of the transferor.

(ii) The transfer of such applicable retained interest.

(iii) At the election of the taxpayer, the payment of any qualified payment after the period described in paragraph (2)(C), but only with respect to such payment.

(B) EXCEPTION WHERE SPOUSE IS TRANSFEREE.—

(i) DEATHTIME TRANSFERS.—Subparagraph (A)(i) shall not apply to any interest includible in the gross estate of the transferor if a deduction with respect to such interest is allowable under section 2056 or 2106(a)(3).

(ii) LIFETIME TRANSFERS.—A transfer to the spouse of the transferor shall not be treated as a taxable event under subparagraph (A)(ii) if such transfer does not result in a taxable gift by reason of—

(I) any deduction allowed under section 2523, or the exclusion under section 2503(b), or

(II) consideration for the transfer provided by the spouse.

(iii) SPOUSE SUCCEEDS TO TREATMENT OF TRANSFEROR.—If an event is not treated as a taxable event by reason of this subparagraph, the transferee spouse or surviving spouse (as the case may be) shall be treated in the same manner as the transferor in applying this subsection with respect to the interest involved.

(4) SPECIAL RULES FOR APPLICABLE FAMILY MEMBERS.—

(A) FAMILY MEMBER TREATED IN SAME MANNER AS TRANSFEROR.—For purposes of this subsection, an applicable family member shall be treated in the same manner as the transferor with respect to any distribution right retained by such family member to which subsection (a)(3)(B) or (C) applied.

(B) TRANSFER TO APPLICABLE FAMILY MEMBER.—In the case of a taxable event described in paragraph (3)(A)(ii) involving the transfer of an applicable retained interest to an applicable family member (other than the spouse of the transferor), the applicable family member shall be treated in the same manner as the transferor in applying this subsection to distributions accumulating with respect to such interest after such taxable event.

(C) TRANSFER TO TRANSFERORS.—In the case of a taxable event described in paragraph (3)(A)(ii) involving a transfer of an applicable retained interest from an applicable family member to a transferor, this subsection shall continue to apply to the transferor during any period the transferor holds such interest.

(5) TRANSFER TO INCLUDE TERMINATION.—For purposes of this subsection, any termination of an interest shall be treated as a transfer.

Amendments

• **1996, Small Business Job Protection Act of 1996 (P.L. 104-188)**

P.L. 104-188, §1702(f)(1)(C):

Amended Code Sec. 2701(d)(1) and (d)(4)[A] by striking "subsection (a)(3)(B)" and inserting "subsection (a)(3)(B) or (C)". **Effective** as if included in the provision of P.L. 101-508 to which it relates.

P.L. 104-188, §1702(f)(6):

Amended Code Sec. 2701(d)(3)(A)(iii) by striking "the period ending on the date of" before "such payment". **Effective** as if included in the provision of P.L. 101-508 to which it relates.

P.L. 104-188, §1702(f)(7):

Amended Code Sec. 2701(d)(3)(B)(ii)(I) by inserting "or the exclusion under section 2503(b)," after "section 2523,". **Effective** as if included in the provision of P.L. 101-508 to which it relates.

P.L. 104-188, §1702(f)(9):

Amended Code Sec. 2701(d)(4) by adding at the end thereof a new subparagraph (C). **Effective** as if included in the provision of P.L. 101-508 to which it relates.

[Sec. 2701(e)]

(e) OTHER DEFINITIONS AND RULES.—For purposes of this section—

(1) MEMBER OF THE FAMILY.—The term "member of the family" means, with respect to any transferor—

(A) the transferor's spouse,

(B) a lineal descendant of the transferor or the transferor's spouse, and

(C) the spouse of any such descendant.

(2) APPLICABLE FAMILY MEMBER.—The term "applicable family member" means, with respect to any transferor—

(A) the transferor's spouse,

(B) an ancestor of the transferor or the transferor's spouse, and

(C) the spouse of any such ancestor.

(3) ATTRIBUTION OF INDIRECT HOLDINGS AND TRANSFERS.—An individual shall be treated as holding any interest to the extent such interest is held indirectly by such individual through a corporation, partnership, trust, or other entity. If any individual is treated as holding any interest by reason of the preceding sentence, any transfer which results in such interest being treated as no longer held by such individual shall be treated as a transfer of such interest.

(4) EFFECT OF ADOPTION.—A relationship by legal adoption shall be treated as a relationship by blood.

(5) CERTAIN CHANGES TREATED AS TRANSFERS.—Except as provided in regulations, a contribution to capital or a redemption, recapitalization, or other change in the capital structure of a corporation or partnership shall be treated as a transfer of an interest in such entity to which this section applies if the taxpayer or an applicable family member—

(A) receives an applicable retained interest in such entity pursuant to such transaction, or

(B) under regulations, otherwise holds, immediately after such transaction, an applicable retained interest in such entity.

This paragraph shall not apply to any transaction (other than a contribution to capital) if the interests in the entity held by the transferor, applicable family members, and members of the transferor's family before and after the transaction are substantially identical.

(6) ADJUSTMENTS.—Under regulations prescribed by the Secretary, if there is any subsequent transfer, or inclusion in the gross estate, of any applicable retained interest which was valued under the rules of subsection (a), appropriate adjustments shall be made for purposes of chapter 11, 12, or 13 to reflect the increase in the amount of any prior taxable gift made by the transferor or decedent by reason of such valuation or to reflect the application of subsection (d).

(7) TREATMENT AS SEPARATE INTERESTS.—The Secretary may by regulation provide that any applicable retained interest shall be treated as 2 or more separate interests for purposes of this section.

Amendments

• **1996, Small Business Job Protection Act of 1996 (P.L. 104-188)**

P.L. 104-188, §1702(f)(3)(B)(i)-(ii):

Amended Code Sec. 2701(e)(3) by striking subparagraph (B), and by striking so much of paragraph (3) as precedes "shall be treated as holding" and inserting "(3) ATTRIBUTION OF INDIRECT HOLDINGS AND TRANSFERS.—An individual". **Effective** as if included in the provision of P.L. 101-508 to which it relates. Prior to amendment, Code Sec. 2701(e)(3) read as follows:

(3) ATTRIBUTION RULES.—

(A) INDIRECT HOLDINGS AND TRANSFERS.—An individual shall be treated as holding any interest to the extent such interest is held indirectly by such individual through a corporation, partnership, trust, or other entity. If any individual is treated as holding any interest by reason of the preceding sentence, any transfer which results in such interest being treated as no longer held by such individual shall be treated as a transfer of such interest.

(B) CONTROL.—For purposes of subsections (b)(1), an individual shall be treated as holding any interest held by the individual's brothers, sisters, or lineal descendants.

P.L. 104-188, §1702(f)(8)(A)-(B):

Amended Code Sec. 2701(e)(5) by striking "such contribution to capital or such redemption, recapitalization, or other change" in subparagraph (A) and inserting "such transaction", and by striking "the transfer" in subparagraph (B) and inserting "such transaction". **Effective** as if included in the provision of P.L. 101-508 to which it relates.

P.L. 104-188, §1702(f)(10):

Amended Code Sec. 2701(e)(6) by inserting "or to reflect the application of subsection (d)" before the period at the end thereof. **Effective** as if included in the provision of P.L. 101-508 to which it relates.

• **1990, Omnibus Budget Reconciliation Act of 1990 (P.L. 101-508)**

P.L. 101-508, §11602(a):

Amended Subtitle B by adding new Code Sec. 2701. For the **effective** date, see Act Sec. 11602(e)(1), below.

P.L. 101-508, §11602(e)(1), provides:

(e) EFFECTIVE DATES.—

(1) SUBSECTION (a).—

(A) IN GENERAL.—The amendments made by subsection (a)—

(i) to the extent such amendments relate to sections 2701 and 2702 of the Internal Revenue Code of 1986 (as added by such amendments), shall apply to transfers after October 8, 1990,

(ii) to the extent such amendments relate to section 2703 of such Code (as so added), shall apply to—

(I) agreements, options, rights, or restrictions entered into or granted after October 8, 1990, and

(II) agreements, options, rights, or restrictions which are substantially modified after October 8, 1990, and

(iii) to the extent such amendments relate to section 2704 of such Code (as so added), shall apply to restrictions or rights (or limitations on rights) created after October 8, 1990.

(B) EXCEPTION.—For purposes of subparagraph (A)(i), with respect to property transferred before October 9, 1990—

(i) any failure to exercise a right of conversion,

(ii) any failure to pay dividends, and

(iii) any failure to exercise other rights specified in regulations,

shall not be treated as a subsequent transfer.

[Sec. 2702]

SEC. 2702. SPECIAL VALUATION RULES IN CASE OF TRANSFERS OF INTERESTS IN TRUSTS.

[Sec. 2702(a)]

(a) VALUATION RULES.—

(1) IN GENERAL.—Solely for purposes of determining whether a transfer of an interest in trust to (or for the benefit of) a member of the transferor's family is a gift (and the value of such transfer), the value of any interest in such trust retained by the transferor or any applicable family member (as defined in section 2701(e)(2)) shall be determined as provided in paragraph (2).

(2) VALUATION OF RETAINED INTERESTS.—

(A) IN GENERAL.—The value of any retained interest which is not a qualified interest shall be treated as being zero.

SPECIAL VALUATION RULES

(B) VALUATION OF QUALIFIED INTEREST.—The value of any retained interest which is a qualified interest shall be determined under section 7520.

(3) EXCEPTIONS.—

(A) IN GENERAL.—This subsection shall not apply to any transfer—

(i) if such transfer is an incomplete gift,

(ii) if such transfer involves the transfer of an interest in trust all the property in which consists of a residence to be used as a personal residence by persons holding term interests in such trust, or

(iii) to the extent that regulations provide that such transfer is not inconsistent with the purposes of this section.

(B) INCOMPLETE GIFT.—For purposes of subparagraph (A), the term "incomplete gift" means any transfer which would not be treated as a gift whether or not consideration was received for such transfer.

Amendments

• **1996, Small Business Job Protection Act of 1996 (P.L. 104-188)**

P.L. 104-188, §1702(f)(11)(A)(i)-(iv):

Amended Code Sec. 2702(a)(3)(A) by striking "to the extent" and inserting "if" in clause (i), by striking "or" at the end of clause (i), by striking the period at the end of clause (ii) and inserting ", or", and by adding at the end thereof a new clause (iii). **Effective** as if included in the provision of P.L. 101-508 to which it relates.

P.L. 104-188, §1702(f)(11)(B)(i):

Amended Code Sec. 2702(a)(3) by striking "incomplete transfer" each place it appears and inserting "incomplete gift". **Effective** as if included in the provision of P.L. 101-508 to which it relates.

P.L. 104-188, §1702(f)(11)(B)(ii):

Amended Code Sec. 2702(a)(3)(B) by striking "INCOMPLETE TRANSFER" in the heading and inserting "INCOMPLETE GIFT". **Effective** as if included in the provision of P.L. 101-508 to which it relates.

[Sec. 2702(b)]

(b) QUALIFIED INTEREST.—For purposes of this section, the term "qualified interest" means—

(1) any interest which consists of the right to receive fixed amounts payable not less frequently than annually,

(2) any interest which consists of the right to receive amounts which are payable not less frequently than annually and are a fixed percentage of the fair market value of the property in the trust (determined annually), and

(3) any noncontingent remainder interest if all of the other interests in the trust consist of interests described in paragraph (1) or (2).

[Sec. 2702(c)]

(c) CERTAIN PROPERTY TREATED AS HELD IN TRUST.—For purposes of this section—

(1) IN GENERAL.—The transfer of an interest in property with respect to which there is 1 or more term interests shall be treated as a transfer of an interest in a trust.

(2) JOINT PURCHASES.—If 2 or more members of the same family acquire interests in any property described in paragraph (1) in the same transaction (or a series of related transactions), the person (or persons) acquiring the term interests in such property shall be treated as having acquired the entire property and then transferred to the other persons the interests acquired by such other persons in the transaction (or series of transactions). Such transfer shall be treated as made in exchange for the consideration (if any) provided by such other persons for the acquisition of their interests in such property.

(3) TERM INTEREST.—The term "term interest" means—

(A) a life interest in property, or

(B) an interest in property for a term of years.

(4) VALUATION RULE FOR CERTAIN TERM INTERESTS.—If the nonexercise of rights under a term interest in tangible property would not have a substantial effect on the valuation of the remainder interest in such property—

(A) subparagraph (A) of subsection (a)(2) shall not apply to such term interest, and

(B) the value of such term interest for purposes of applying subsection (a)(1) shall be the amount which the holder of the term interest establishes as the amount for which such interest could be sold to an unrelated third party.

[Sec. 2702(d)]

(d) TREATMENT OF TRANSFERS OF INTERESTS IN PORTION OF TRUST.—In the case of a transfer of an income or remainder interest with respect to a specified portion of the property in a trust, only such portion shall be taken into account in applying this section to such transfer.

[Sec. 2702(e)]

(e) MEMBER OF THE FAMILY.—For purposes of this section, the term "member of the family" shall have the meaning given such term by section 2704(c)(2).

Amendments

• **1990, Omnibus Budget Reconciliation Act of 1990 (P.L. 101-508)**

P.L. 101-508, §11602(a):

Amended Subtitle B by adding new Code Sec. 2702. For the **effective** date, see Act Sec. 11602(e)(1), below.

P.L. 101-508, §11602(e)(1), provides:

(e) EFFECTIVE DATES.—

(1) SUBSECTION (a).—

(A) IN GENERAL.—The amendments made by subsection (a)—

(i) to the extent such amendments relate to sections 2701 and 2702 of the Internal Revenue Code of 1986 (as added by such amendments), shall apply to transfers after October 8, 1990,

(ii) to the extent such amendments relate to section 2703 of such Code (as so added), shall apply to—

(I) agreements, options, rights, or restrictions entered into or granted after October 8, 1990, and

(II) agreements, options, rights, or restrictions which are substantially modified after October 8, 1990, and

(iii) to the extent such amendments relate to section 2704 of such Code (as so added), shall apply to restrictions or rights (or limitations on rights) created after October 8, 1990.

(B) EXCEPTION.—For purposes of subparagraph (A)(i), with respect to property transferred before October 9, 1990—

(i) any failure to exercise a right of conversion,

(ii) any failure to pay dividends, and

(iii) any failure to exercise other rights specified in regulations,

shall not be treated as a subsequent transfer.

[Sec. 2703]

SEC. 2703. CERTAIN RIGHTS AND RESTRICTIONS DISREGARDED.

[Sec. 2703(a)]

(a) GENERAL RULE.—For purposes of this subtitle, the value of any property shall be determined without regard to—

(1) any option, agreement, or other right to acquire or use the property at a price less than the fair market value of the property (without regard to such option, agreement, or right), or

(2) any restriction on the right to sell or use such property.

SPECIAL VALUATION RULES

[Sec. 2703(b)]

(b) EXCEPTIONS.—Subsection (a) shall not apply to any option, agreement, right, or restriction which meets each of the following requirements:

(1) It is a bona fide business arrangement.

(2) It is not a device to transfer such property to members of the decedent's family for less than full and adequate consideration in money or money's worth.

(3) Its terms are comparable to similar arrangements entered into by persons in an arms' length transaction.

Amendments

• **1990, Omnibus Budget Reconciliation Act of 1990 (P.L. 101-508)**

P.L. 101-508, § 11602(a):

Amended Subtitle B by adding new Code Sec. 2703. For the **effective** date, see Act Sec. 11602(e)(1), below.

P.L. 101-508, § 11602(e)(1), provides:

(e) EFFECTIVE DATES.—

(1) SUBSECTION (a).—

(A) IN GENERAL.—The amendments made by subsection (a)—

(i) to the extent such amendments relate to sections 2701 and 2702 of the Internal Revenue Code of 1986 (as added by such amendments), shall apply to transfers after October 8, 1990,

(ii) to the extent such amendments relate to section 2703 of such Code (as so added), shall apply to—

(I) agreements, options, rights, or restrictions entered into or granted after October 8, 1990, and

(II) agreements, options, rights, or restrictions which are substantially modified after October 8, 1990, and

(iii) to the extent such amendments relate to section 2704 of such Code (as so added), shall apply to restrictions or rights (or limitations on rights) created after October 8, 1990.

(B) EXCEPTION.—For purposes of subparagraph (A)(i), with respect to property transferred before October 9, 1990—

(i) any failure to exercise a right of conversion,

(ii) any failure to pay dividends, and

(iii) any failure to exercise other rights specified in regulations,

shall not be treated as a subsequent transfer.

[Sec. 2704]

SEC. 2704. TREATMENT OF CERTAIN LAPSING RIGHTS AND RESTRICTIONS.

[Sec. 2704(a)]

(a) TREATMENT OF LAPSED VOTING OR LIQUIDATION RIGHTS.—

(1) IN GENERAL.—For purposes of this subtitle, if—

(A) there is a lapse of any voting or liquidation right in a corporation or partnership, and

(B) the individual holding such right immediately before the lapse and members of such individual's family hold, both before and after the lapse, control of the entity,

such lapse shall be treated as a transfer by such individual by gift, or a transfer which is includible in the gross estate of the decedent, whichever is applicable, in the amount determined under paragraph (2).

(2) AMOUNT OF TRANSFER.—For purposes of paragraph (1), the amount determined under this paragraph is the excess (if any) of—

(A) the value of all interests in the entity held by the individual described in paragraph (1) immediately before the lapse (determined as if the voting and liquidation rights were nonlapsing), over

(B) the value of such interests immediately after the lapse.

(3) SIMILAR RIGHTS.—The Secretary may by regulations apply this subsection to rights similar to voting and liquidation rights.

[Sec. 2704(b)]

(b) CERTAIN RESTRICTIONS ON LIQUIDATION DISREGARDED.—

(1) IN GENERAL.—For purposes of this subtitle, if—

(A) there is a transfer of an interest in a corporation or partnership to (or for the benefit of) a member of the transferor's family, and

(B) the transferor and members of the transferor's family hold, immediately before the transfer, control of the entity,

any applicable restriction shall be disregarded in determining the value of the transferred interest.

(2) APPLICABLE RESTRICTION.—For purposes of this subsection, the term "applicable restriction" means any restriction—

(A) which effectively limits the ability of the corporation or partnership to liquidate, and

(B) with respect to which either of the following applies:

(i) The restriction lapses, in whole or in part, after the transfer referred to in paragraph (1).

(ii) The transferor or any member of the transferor's family, either alone or collectively, has the right after such transfer to remove, in whole or in part, the restriction.

(3) EXCEPTIONS.—The term "applicable restriction" shall not include—

(A) any commercially reasonable restriction which arises as part of any financing by the corporation or partnership with a person who is not related to the transferor or transferee, or a member of the family of either, or

(B) any restriction imposed, or required to be imposed, by any Federal or State law.

(4) OTHER RESTRICTIONS.—The Secretary may by regulations provide that other restrictions shall be disregarded in determining the value of the transfer of any interest in a corporation or partnership to a member of the transferor's family if such restriction has the effect of reducing the value of the transferred interest for purposes of this subtitle but does not ultimately reduce the value of such interest to the transferee.

[Sec. 2704(c)]

(c) DEFINITIONS AND SPECIAL RULES.—For purposes of this section—

(1) CONTROL.—The term "control" has the meaning given such term by section 2701(b)(2).

(2) MEMBER OF THE FAMILY.—The term "member of the family" means, with respect to any individual—

(A) such individual's spouse,

(B) any ancestor or lineal descendant of such individual or such individual's spouse,

(C) any brother or sister of the individual, and

(D) any spouse of any individual described in subparagraph (B) or (C).

(3) ATTRIBUTION.—The rule of section 2701(e)(3) shall apply for purposes of determining the interests held by any individual.

Amendments

• **1996, Small Business Job Protection Act of 1996 (P.L. 104-188)**

P.L. 104-188, § 1702(f)(3)(C):

Amended Code Sec. 2704(c)(3) by striking "section 2701(e)(3)(A)" and inserting "section 2701(e)(3)". **Effective** as if included in the provision of P.L. 101-508 to which it relates.

• **1990, Omnibus Budget Reconciliation Act of 1990 (P.L. 101-508)**

P.L. 101-508, § 11602(a):

Amended Subtitle B by adding new Code Sec. 2704. For the **effective** date, see Act Sec. 11602(e)(1), below.

GIFTS AND BEQUESTS FROM EXPATRIATES

P.L. 101-508, §11602(e)(1), provides:

(e) EFFECTIVE DATES.—

(1) SUBSECTION (a).—

(A) IN GENERAL.—The amendments made by subsection (a)—

(i) to the extent such amendments relate to sections 2701 and 2702 of the Internal Revenue Code of 1986 (as added by such amendments), shall apply to transfers after October 8, 1990,

(ii) to the extent such amendments relate to section 2703 of such Code (as so added), shall apply to—

(I) agreements, options, rights, or restrictions entered into or granted after October 8, 1990, and

(II) agreements, options, rights, or restrictions which are substantially modified after October 8, 1990, and

(iii) to the extent such amendments relate to section 2704 of such Code (as so added), shall apply to restrictions or rights (or limitations on rights) created after October 8, 1990.

(B) EXCEPTION.—For purposes of subparagraph (A)(i), with respect to property transferred before October 9, 1990—

(i) any failure to exercise a right of conversion,

(ii) any failure to pay dividends, and

(iii) any failure to exercise other rights specified in regulations,

shall not be treated as a subsequent transfer.

CHAPTER 15—GIFTS AND BEQUESTS FROM EXPATRIATES

Sec. 2801. Imposition of tax.

[Sec. 2801]

SEC. 2801. IMPOSITION OF TAX.

[Sec. 2801(a)]

(a) IN GENERAL.—If, during any calendar year, any United States citizen or resident receives any covered gift or bequest, there is hereby imposed a tax equal to the product of—

(1) the highest rate of tax specified in the table contained in section 2001(c) as in effect on the date of such receipt, and

(2) the value of such covered gift or bequest.

Amendments

• **2014, Tax Technical Corrections Act of 2014 (P.L. 113-295)**

P.L. 113-295, §206(b)(1), Division A:

Amended Code Sec. 2801(a)(1) by striking "(or, if greater, the highest rate of tax specified in the table applicable under section 2502(a) as in effect on the date)" following "such receipt". **Effective** as if included in the provision of the Tax Relief, Unemployment Insurance Reauthorization, and Job Creation Act of 2010 (P.L. 111-312) to which it relates [**effective** for estates of decedents dying, generation-skipping transfers, and gifts made, after 12-31-2001.—CCH].

[Sec. 2801(b)]

(b) TAX TO BE PAID BY RECIPIENT.—The tax imposed by subsection (a) on any covered gift or bequest shall be paid by the person receiving such gift or bequest.

[Sec. 2801(c)]

(c) EXCEPTION FOR CERTAIN GIFTS.—Subsection (a) shall apply only to the extent that the value of covered gifts and bequests received by any person during the calendar year exceeds the dollar amount in effect under section 2503(b) for such calendar year.

[Sec. 2801(d)]

(d) TAX REDUCED BY FOREIGN GIFT OR ESTATE TAX.—The tax imposed by subsection (a) on any covered gift or bequest shall be reduced by the amount of any gift or estate tax paid to a foreign country with respect to such covered gift or bequest.

[Sec. 2801(e)]

(e) COVERED GIFT OR BEQUEST.—

(1) IN GENERAL.—For purposes of this chapter, the term "covered gift or bequest" means—

(A) any property acquired by gift directly or indirectly from an individual who, at the time of such acquisition, is a covered expatriate, and

(B) any property acquired directly or indirectly by reason of the death of an individual who, immediately before such death, was a covered expatriate.

(2) EXCEPTIONS FOR TRANSFERS OTHERWISE SUBJECT TO ESTATE OR GIFT TAX.—Such term shall not include—

(A) any property shown on a timely filed return of tax imposed by chapter 12 which is a taxable gift by the covered expatriate, and

(B) any property included in the gross estate of the covered expatriate for purposes of chapter 11 and shown on a timely filed return of tax imposed by chapter 11 of the estate of the covered expatriate.

(3) EXCEPTIONS FOR TRANSFERS TO SPOUSE OR CHARITY.—Such term shall not include any property with respect to which a deduction would be allowed under section 2055, 2056, 2522, or 2523, whichever is appropriate, if the decedent or donor were a United States person.

(4) TRANSFERS IN TRUST.—

(A) DOMESTIC TRUSTS.—In the case of a covered gift or bequest made to a domestic trust—

(i) subsection (a) shall apply in the same manner as if such trust were a United States citizen, and

(ii) the tax imposed by subsection (a) on such gift or bequest shall be paid by such trust.

(B) FOREIGN TRUSTS.—

(i) IN GENERAL.—In the case of a covered gift or bequest made to a foreign trust, subsection (a) shall apply to any distribution attributable to such gift or bequest from such trust (whether from income or corpus) to a United States citizen or resident in the same manner as if such distribution were a covered gift or bequest.

(ii) DEDUCTION FOR TAX PAID BY RECIPIENT.—There shall be allowed as a deduction under section 164 the amount of tax imposed by this section which is paid or accrued by a United States citizen or resident by reason of a distribution from a foreign trust, but only to the extent such tax is imposed on the portion of such distribution which is included in the gross income of such citizen or resident.

(iii) ELECTION TO BE TREATED AS DOMESTIC TRUST.—Solely for purposes of this section, a foreign trust may elect to be treated as a domestic trust. Such an election may be revoked with the consent of the Secretary.

[Sec. 2801(f)]

(f) COVERED EXPATRIATE.—For purposes of this section, the term "covered expatriate" has the meaning given to such term by section 877A(g)(1).

Amendments

• **2008, Heroes Earnings Assistance and Relief Tax Act of 2008 (P.L. 110-245)**

P.L. 110-245, §301(b)(1):

Amended subtitle B by inserting after chapter 14 a new chapter 15 (Code Sec. 2801). **Effective** for covered gifts and bequests (as defined in Code Sec. 2801, as so added) received on or after 6-17-2008 from transferors (or from the estates of transferors) whose expatriation date is on or after 6-17-2008.

[The next page is 3501.]

Subtitle C—Employment Taxes

Chapter 21.	Federal insurance contributions act.
Chapter 22.	Railroad retirement tax act.
Chapter 23.	Federal unemployment tax act.
Chapter 23A.	Railroad unemployment repayment tax.
Chapter 24.	Collection of income tax at source on wages.
Chapter 25.	General provisions relating to employment taxes.

CHAPTER 21—FEDERAL INSURANCE CONTRIBUTIONS ACT

Subchapter A.	Tax on employees.
Subchapter B.	Tax on employers.
Subchapter C.	General provisions.
Subchapter D.	Credits.

Subchapter A—Tax on Employees

Sec. 3101.	Rate of tax.
Sec. 3102.	Deduction of tax from wages.

[Sec. 3101]

SEC. 3101. RATE OF TAX.

[Sec. 3101(a)]

(a) OLD-AGE, SURVIVORS, AND DISABILITY INSURANCE.—In addition to other taxes, there is hereby imposed on the income of every individual a tax equal to 6.2 percent of the wages (as defined in section 3121(a)) received by the individual with respect to employment (as defined in section 3121(b)).

Amendments

• **2020, COVID-related Tax Relief Act of 2020 (P.L. 116-260)**

P.L. 116-260, §274, Div. N, provides:

SEC. 274. EXTENSION OF CERTAIN DEFERRED PAYROLL TAXES.

The Secretary of the Treasury (or the Secretary's delegate) shall ensure that Internal Revenue Service Notice 2020-65 [I.R.B. 2020-38, 567] (entitled "Relief with Respect to Employment Tax Deadlines Applicable to Employers Affected by the Ongoing Coronavirus (COVID-19) Disease 2019 Pandemic") and any successor or related regulation, notice, or guidance is applied—

(1) by substituting "December 31, 2021" for "April 30, 2021" each place it appears therein, and

(2) by substituting "January 1, 2022" for "May 1, 2021" each place it appears therein.

• **2018, Tax Technical Corrections Act of 2018 (P.L. 115-141)**

P.L. 115-141, §401(a)(207), Div. U:

Amended Code Sec. 3101(a) by adding a period at the end. **Effective** 3-23-2018.

• **2014, Tax Technical Corrections Act of 2014 (P.L. 113-295)**

P.L. 113-295, §221(a)(99)(A), Division A:

Amended Code Sec. 3101(a) by striking "the following percentages" and all that follows and inserting "6.2 percent of the wages (as defined in section 3121(a)) received by the individual with respect to employment (as defined in section 3121(b))". **Effective** generally 12-19-2014. For a special rule, see Act Sec. 221(b)(2), Division A, below. Prior to amendment, Code Sec. 3101(a) read as follows:

(a) OLD-AGE, SURVIVORS, AND DISABILITY INSURANCE.—In addition to other taxes, there is hereby imposed on the income of every individual a tax equal to the following percentages of the wages (as defined in section 3121(a)) received by him with respect to employment (as defined in section 3121(b))—

In cases of wages received during:	The rate shall be:
1984, 1985, 1986, or 1987	5.7 percent
1988 or 1989	6.06 percent
1990 or thereafter	6.2 percent.

P.L. 113-295, §221(b)(2), Division A, provides:

(2) SAVINGS PROVISION.—If—

(A) any provision amended or repealed by the amendments made by this section applied to—

(i) any transaction occurring before the date of the enactment of this Act,

(ii) any property acquired before such date of enactment, or

(iii) any item of income, loss, deduction, or credit taken into account before such date of enactment, and

(B) the treatment of such transaction, property, or item under such provision would (without regard to the amendments or repeals made by this section) affect the liability for tax for periods ending after date of enactment, nothing in the amendments or repeals made by this section shall be construed to affect the treatment of such transaction, property, or item for purposes of determining liability for tax for periods ending after such date of enactment.

• **2010, Tax Relief, Unemployment Insurance Reauthorization, and Job Creation Act of 2010 (P.L. 111-312)**

P.L. 111-312, §601(a)-(e), provides:

(a) IN GENERAL.—Notwithstanding any other provision of law—

(1) with respect to any taxable year which begins in the payroll tax holiday period, the rate of tax under section 1401(a) of the Internal Revenue Code of 1986 shall be 10.40 percent, and

(2) with respect to remuneration received during the payroll tax holiday period, the rate of tax under 3101(a) of such Code shall be 4.2 percent (including for purposes of determining the applicable percentage under section 3201(a) and 3211(a)(1) of such Code).

(b) COORDINATION WITH DEDUCTIONS FOR EMPLOYMENT TAXES.—

(1) DEDUCTION IN COMPUTING NET EARNINGS FROM SELFEMPLOYMENT.—For purposes of applying section 1402(a)(12) of the Internal Revenue Code of 1986, the rate of tax imposed by subsection 1401(a) of such Code shall be determined without regard to the reduction in such rate under this section.

(2) INDIVIDUAL DEDUCTION.—In the case of the taxes imposed by section 1401 of such Code for any taxable year which begins in the payroll tax holiday period, the deduction under section 164(f) with respect to such taxes shall be equal to the sum of—

(A) 59.6 percent of the portion of such taxes attributable to the tax imposed by section 1401(a) (determined after the application of this section), plus

(B) one-half of the portion of such taxes attributable to the tax imposed by section 1401(b).

(c) PAYROLL TAX HOLIDAY PERIOD.—The term "payroll tax holiday period" means calendar year 2011.

(d) EMPLOYER NOTIFICATION.—The Secretary of the Treasury shall notify employers of the payroll tax holiday period in any manner the Secretary deems appropriate.

(e) TRANSFERS OF FUNDS.—

(1) TRANSFERS TO FEDERAL OLD-AGE AND SURVIVORS INSURANCE TRUST FUND.—There are hereby appropriated to the Federal Old-Age and Survivors Trust Fund and the Federal Disability Insurance Trust Fund established under section 201 of the Social Security Act (42 U.S.C. 401) amounts equal to the reduction in revenues to the Treasury by reason of the application of subsection (a). Amounts appropriated by the preceding sentence shall be transferred from the general fund at such times and in such manner as to replicate to the extent possible the transfers which would have occurred to such Trust Fund had such amendments not been enacted.

(2) TRANSFERS TO SOCIAL SECURITY EQUIVALENT BENEFIT ACCOUNT.—There are hereby appropriated to the Social Security Equivalent Benefit Account established under section 15A(a) of the Railroad Retirement Act of 1974 (45 U.S.C. 231n–1(a)) amounts equal to the reduction in revenues to the Treasury by reason of the application of subsection (a)(2). Amounts appropriated by the preceding sentence shall be transferred from the general fund at such times and in such manner as to replicate to the extent possible the transfers which would have occurred to such Account had such amendments not been enacted.

(3) COORDINATION WITH OTHER FEDERAL LAWS.—For purposes of applying any provision of Federal law other than the provisions of the Internal Revenue Code of 1986, the rate of tax in effect under section 3101(a) of such Code shall be determined without regard to the reduction in such rate under this section.

• **1983, Social Security Amendments of 1983 (P.L. 98-21)**

P.L. 98-21, §123(a)(1), (3):

Amended Code Sec. 3101(a) by striking out paragraphs (1) through (7) and inserting in lieu thereof a chart. **Effective** for remuneration paid after 12-31-83. Prior to amendment, Code Sec. 3101(a)(1)-(7) read as follows:

(1) with respect to wages received during the calendar years 1974 through 1977, the rate shall be 4.95 percent;

(2) with respect to wages received during the calendar year 1978, the rate shall be 5.05 percent;

(3) with respect to wages received during the calendar years 1979 and 1980, the rate shall be 5.08 percent;

EMPLOYMENT TAX—EMPLOYEES

(4) with respect to wages received during the calendar year 1981, the rate shall be 5.35 percent;

(5) with respect to wages received during the calendar years 1982 through 1984, the rate shall be 5.40 percent;

(6) with respect to wages received during the calendar years 1985 through 1989, the rate shall be 5.70 percent; and

(7) with respect to wages received after December 31, 1989, the rate shall be 6.20 percent.

- **1977 (P.L. 95-216)**

P.L. 95-216, §101(a)(1):

Amended Code Sec. 3101(a)(1) and (2) and added paragraphs (3) through (7). **Effective** for remuneration paid or received, and tax years beginning, after 1977. Prior to amendment, paragraphs (1) and (2) read as follows:

(1) with respect to wages received during the calendar years 1974 through 2010, the rate shall be 4.95 percent; and

(2) with respect to wages received after December 31, 2010, the rate shall be 5.95 percent.

- **1976, Tax Reform Act of 1976 (P.L. 94-455)**

P.L. 94-455, §1903(a)(1)(A):

Deleted paragraphs (1), (2), (3), and (4) of Code Sec. 3101(a) and redesignated paragraphs (5) and (6) as paragraphs (1) and (2), respectively. **Effective** for wages paid after 12-31-76. Prior to amendment, paragraphs (1), (2), (3), and (4) read as follows:

(1) with respect to wages received during the calendar year 1968, the rate shall be 3.8 percent;

(2) with respect to wages received during the calendar years 1969 and 1970, the rate shall be 4.2 percent;

(3) with respect to wages received during the calendar years 1971 and 1972, the rate shall be 4.6 percent;

(4) with respect to wages received during the calendar year 1973, the rate shall be 4.85 percent;

- **1973 (P.L. 93-233)**

P.L. 93-233, §6(a)(1):

Amended Code Sec. 3101(a)(4)-(6). **Effective** for remuneration paid after 1973. Prior to amendment, Code Sec. 3101(a)(4)-(6) read as follows:

"(4) with respect to wages received during the calendar years 1973, 1974, 1975, 1976, and 1977, the rate shall be 4.85 percent;

"(5) with respect to wages received during the calendar years 1978 through 2010, the rate shall be 4.80 percent; and

"(6) with respect to wages received after December 31, 2010, the rate shall be 5.85 percent."

[Sec. 3101(b)]

(b) HOSPITAL INSURANCE.—

(1) IN GENERAL.—In addition to the tax imposed by the preceding subsection, there is hereby imposed on the income of every individual a tax equal to 1.45 percent of the wages (as defined in section 3121(a)) received by him with respect to employment (as defined in section 3121(b)).

(2) ADDITIONAL TAX.—In addition to the tax imposed by paragraph (1) and the preceding subsection, there is hereby imposed on every taxpayer (other than a corporation, estate, or trust) a tax equal to 0.9 percent of wages which are received with respect to employment (as defined in section 3121(b)) during any taxable year beginning after December 31, 2012, and which are in excess of—

(A) in the case of a joint return, $250,000,

(B) in the case of a married taxpayer (as defined in section 7703) filing a separate return, 1/2 of the dollar amount determined under subparagraph (A), and

(C) in any other case, $200,000.

Amendments

- **2010, Health Care and Education Reconciliation Act of 2010 (P.L. 111-152)**

P.L. 111-152, §1402(b)(1)(A):

Amended Code Sec. 3101(b)(2), as added by section 9015 of the Patient Protection and Affordable Care Act (P.L. 111-148), and amended by section 10906 of such Act, by striking "and" at the end of subparagraph (A), by redesignating subparagraph (B) as subparagraph (C), and by inserting after subparagraph (A) a new subparagraph (B). **Effective** with respect to remuneration received, and tax years beginning after, 12-31-2012.

- **2010, Patient Protection and Affordable Care Act (P.L. 111-148)**

P.L. 111-148, §9015(a)(1)(A)-(D):

Amended Code Sec. 3101(b) by striking "In addition" and inserting:

"(1) IN GENERAL.—In addition",

by striking "the following percentages of the" and inserting "1.45 percent of the", by striking "(as defined in section 3121(b))—"and all that follows and inserting "(as defined in section 3121(b)).", and by adding at the end a new paragraph (2). **Effective** with respect to remuneration received, and tax years beginning, after 12-31-2012. Prior to amendment, Code Sec. 3101(b) read as follows:

(b) HOSPITAL INSURANCE.—In addition to the tax imposed by the preceding subsection, there is hereby imposed on the income of every individual a tax equal to the following percentages of the wages (as defined in section 3121(a)) received by him with respect to employment (as defined in section 3121(b))—

(1) with respect to wages received during the calendar years 1974 through 1977, the rate shall be 0.90 percent;

(2) with respect to wages received during the calendar year 1978, the rate shall be 1.00 percent;

(3) with respect to wages received during the calendar years 1979 and 1980, the rate shall be 1.05 percent;

(4) with respect to wages received during the calendar years 1981 through 1984, the rate shall be 1.30 percent;

(5) with respect to wages received during the calendar year 1985, the rate shall be 1.35 percent; and

(6) with respect to wages received after December 31, 1985, the rate shall be 1.45 percent.

P.L. 111-148, §10906(a):

Amended Code Sec. 3101(b)(2), as added by Act Sec. 9015(a)(1), by striking "0.5 percent" and inserting "0.9 percent". **Effective** with respect to remuneration received, and tax years beginning, after 12-31-2012.

- **1977 (P.L. 95-216)**

P.L. 95-216, §101(b)(1):

Amended Code Sec. 3101(b)(1) through (4) and added (5) and (6). **Effective** for remuneration paid or received, and tax years beginning after 1977. Prior to amendment, paragraphs (1) through (4) read as follows:

(1) with respect to wages received during the calendar years 1974 through 1977, the rate shall be 0.90 percent;

(2) with respect to wages received during the calendar years 1978 through 1980, the rate shall be 1.10 percent;

(3) with respect to wages received during the calendar years 1981 through 1985, the rate shall be 1.35 percent; and

(4) with respect to wages received after December 31, 1985, the rate shall be 1.50 percent.

- **1976, Tax Reform Act of 1976 (P.L. 94-455)**

P.L. 94-455, §1903(a)(1)(B):

Deleted paragraphs (1) and (2) of Code Sec. 3101(b) and redesignated paragraphs (3), (4), (5), and (6) as paragraphs (1), (2), (3), and (4), respectively. **Effective** for wages paid after 12-31-76. Prior to amendment, paragraphs (1) and (2) read as follows:

(1) with respect to wages paid during the calendar years 1968, 1969, 1970, 1971, and 1972, the rate shall be 0.60 percent;

(2) with respect to wages paid during the calendar year 1973, the rate shall be 1.0 percent;

- **1973 (P.L. 93-233)**

P.L. 93-233, §6(b)(2):

Amended paragraphs (2) through (5) (plus new paragraph (6)) of Code Sec. 3101(b). **Effective** for remuneration paid after 1973. Prior to amendment, Code Sec. 3101(b)(2)-(5) read as follows:

"(2) with respect to wages received during the calendar years 1973, 1974, 1975, 1976, and 1977, the rate shall be 1.0 percent;

"(3) with respect to wages received during the calendar years 1978, 1979, and 1980, the rates shall be 1.25 percent;

"(4) with respect to wages paid during the calendar years 1981, 1982, 1983, 1984, and 1985, the rate shall be 1.35 percent; and

"(5) with respect to wages paid after December 31, 1985, the rate shall be 1.45 percent."

- **1972, Social Security Amendments of 1972 (P.L. 92-603)**

P.L. 92-603, §§135(a)(2), 135(b)(2):

Amended Code Sec. 3101. **Effective** for remuneration paid after 12-31-72. Prior to amendment, said section read as follows:

"SEC. 3101. RATE OF TAX.

"(a) Old-Age, Survivors, and Disability Insurance. — In addition to other taxes, there is hereby imposed on the income of every individual a tax equal to the following percentages of the wages (as defined in section 3121(a)) received by him with respect to employment (as defined in section 3121(b))—

"(1) with respect to wages received during the calendar year 1968, the rate shall be 3.8 percent;

"(2) with respect to wages received during the calendar years 1969 and 1970, the rate shall be 4.2 percent;

"(3) with respect to wages received during any of the calendar years 1971 through 1977, the rate shall be 4.6 percent;

EMPLOYMENT TAX—EMPLOYEES

"(4) with respect to wages received during any of the calendar years 1978 through 2010, the rate shall be 4.5 percent; and

"(5) with respect to wages received after December 31, 2010, the rate shall be 5.35 percent.

"(b) Hospital Insurance.—In addition to the tax imposed by the preceding subsection, there is hereby imposed on the income of every individual a tax equal to the following percentages of the wages (as defined in section 3121(a)) received by him with respect to employment (as defined in section 3121(b))—

"(1) with respect to wages paid during the calendar years 1968, 1969, 1970, 1971, and 1972, the rate shall be 0.60 percent;

"(2) with respect to wages received during the calendar years 1973, 1974, 1975, 1976, and 1977, the rate shall be 0.9 percent;

"(3) with respect to wages received during the calendar years 1978, 1979, 1980, 1981, 1982, 1983, 1984, and 1985, the rate shall be 1.0 percent;

"(4) with respect to wages received during the calendar years 1986, 1987, 1988, 1989, 1990, 1991, and 1992, the rate shall be 1.1 percent; and

"(5) with respect to wages received after December 31, 1992, the rate shall be 1.2 percent."

• **1972 (P.L. 92-336)**

P.L. 92-336, §§ 204(a)(2), 204(b)(1)-(2):

Amended Sec. 3101(a)(3) and (4)-(5). **Effective** only for remuneration paid after 12-31-72. Prior to amendment Code Sec. 3101(a)(3) and (4)-(5) read as follows:

"(3) with respect to wages received during the calendar years 1971 and 1972, the rate shall be 4.6 percent;"

"(4) with respect to wages received during the calendar years 1973, 1974, 1975, the rate shall be 5.0 percent; and

"(5) with respect to wages received after December 31, 1975, the rate shall be 5.15 percent."

Amended Sec. 3101(b)(2)-(5). **Effective** only for remuneration paid after 12-31-72. Prior to amendment, Code Sec. 3101(b)(2)-(5) read as follows:

"(2) with respect to wages received during the calendar years 1973, 1974, and 1975, the rate shall be 0.65 percent;

"(3) with respect to wages received during the calendar years 1976, 1977, 1978, and 1979, the rate shall be 0.70 percent;

"(4) with respect to wages received during the calendar years 1980, 1981, 1982, 1983, 1984, 1985, and 1986, the rate shall be 0.80 percent; and

"(5) with respect to wages received after December 31, 1986, the rate shall be 0.90 percent."

• **1971 (P.L. 92-5)**

P.L. 92-5, § 204(a)(1):

Amended Sec. 3101(a) by amending subparagraph (4) and by adding subparagraph (5). **Effective** for tax years beginning after 12-31-71. Prior to amendment, subparagraph (4) read as follows:

"(4) with respect to wages received after December 31, 1972, the rate shall be 5.0 percent."

• **1968, Social Security Amendments of 1967 (P.L. 90-248)**

P.L. 90-248, § 109(a)(2), (b)(2):

Amended Sec. 3101. **Effective** only with respect to remuneration paid after 12-31-67. Prior to amendment, Sec. 3101 read as follows:

"SEC. 3101. RATE OF TAX.

"(a) Old-Age, Survivors, and Disability Insurance.—In addition to other taxes, there is hereby imposed on the income of every individual a tax equal to the following percentages of the wages (as defined in section 3121(a)) received by him with respect to employment (as defined in section 3121(b))—

"(1) with respect to wages received during the calendar year 1966, the rate shall be 3.85 percent;

"(2) with respect to wages received during the calendar years 1967 and 1968, the rate shall be 3.9 percent;

"(3) with respect to wages received during the calendar years 1969, 1970, 1971, and 1972, the rate shall be 4.4 percent; and

"(4) with respect to wages received after December 31, 1972, the rate shall be 4.85 percent.

"(b) Hospital Insurance.—In addition to the tax imposed by the preceding subsection, there is hereby imposed on the income of every individual a tax equal to the following percentages of the wages (as defined in section 3121(a)) received by him with respect to employment (as defined in section 3121(b))—

"(1) with respect to wages received during the calendar year 1966, the rate shall be 0.35 percent;

"(2) with respect to wages received during the calendar years 1967, 1968, 1969, 1970, 1971, and 1972, the rate shall be 0.50 percent;

"(3) with respect to wages received during the calendar years 1973, 1974, and 1975, the rate shall be 0.55 percent;

"(4) with respect to wages received during the calendar years 1976, 1977, 1978, and 1979, the rate shall be 0.60 percent;

"(5) with respect to wages received during the calendar years 1980, 1981, 1982, 1983, 1984, 1985, and 1986, the rate shall be 0.70 percent; and

"(6) with respect to wages received after December 31, 1986, the rate shall be 0.80 percent."

• **1965, Social Security Amendments of 1965 (P.L. 89-97)**

P.L. 89-97, § 320(b):

Amended Sec. 3101. **Effective** with respect to remuneration paid after 12-31-65. Prior to amendment, Sec. 3101 read as follows:

"SEC. 3101. RATE OF TAX.

"In addition to other taxes, there is hereby imposed on the income of every individual a tax equal to the following percentages of the wages (as defined in section 3121(a)) received by him with respect to employment (as defined in section 3121(b))—

"(1) with respect to wages received during the calendar year 1962, the rate shall be $3^{1}/_{8}$ percent;

"(2) with respect to wages received during the calendar years 1963 to 1965, both inclusive, the rate shall be $3^{5}/_{8}$ percent;

"(3) with respect to wages received during the calendar years 1966 to 1967, both inclusive, the rate shall be $4^{1}/_{8}$ percent; and

"(4) with respect to wages received after December 31, 1967, the rate shall be $4^{5}/_{8}$ percent."

• **1961, Social Security Amendments of 1961 (P.L. 87-64)**

P.L. 87-64, § 201(b):

Amended Code Sec. 3101. **Effective** for remuneration paid after 1961. Prior to amendment, Sec. 3101 read as follows:

"SEC. 3101. RATE OF TAX.

"In addition to other taxes, there is hereby imposed on the income of every individual a tax equal to the following percentages of the wages (as defined in section 3121(a)) received by him with respect to employment (as defined in section 3121(b))—

"(1) with respect to wages received during the calendar year 1959, the rate shall be $2^{1}/_{2}$ percent;

"(2) with respect to wages received during the calendar years 1960 to 1962, both inclusive, the rate shall be 3 percent;

"(3) with respect to wages received during the calendar years 1963 to 1965, both inclusive, the rate shall be $3^{1}/_{2}$ percent;

"(4) with respect to wages received during the calendar years 1966 to 1968, both inclusive, the rate shall be 4 percent; and

"(5) with respect to wages received after December 31, 1968, the rate shall be $4^{1}/_{2}$ percent."

• **1958, Social Security Amendments of 1958 (P.L. 85-840)**

P.L. 85-840, § 401(b):

Amended Sec. 3101. **Effective** for remuneration paid after 12-31-58. Prior to amendment, Sec. 3101 read as follows:

"SEC. 3101. RATE OF TAX.

"In addition to other taxes, there is hereby imposed on the income of every individual a tax equal to the following percentages of the wages (as defined in section 3121(a)) received by him with respect to employment (as defined in section 3121(b))—

"(1) with respect to wages received during the calendar years 1957 to 1959, both inclusive, the rate shall be $2^{1}/_{4}$ percent;

"(2) with respect to wages received during the calendar years 1960 to 1964, both inclusive, the rate shall be $2^{3}/_{4}$ percent;

"(3) with respect to wages received during the calendar years 1965 to 1969, both inclusive, the rate shall be $3^{1}/_{4}$ percent;

"(4) with respect to wages received during the calendar years 1970 to 1974, both inclusive, the rate shall be $3^{3}/_{4}$ percent; and

"(5) with respect to wages received after December 31, 1974, the rate shall be $4^{1}/_{4}$ percent."

• **1956, Social Security Amendments of 1956 (P.L. 880, 84th Cong.)**

P.L. 880, 84th Cong., § 202(b), (d):

Amended Sec. 3101. **Effective** for remuneration paid after 12-31-56. Prior to amendment, Sec. 3101 read as follows:

"SEC. 3101. RATE OF TAX.

"In addition to other taxes, there is hereby imposed on the income of every individual a tax equal to the following percentages of the wages (as defined in section 3121(a)) received by him with respect to employment (as defined in section 3121(b))—

"(1) with respect to wages received during the calendar years 1955 to 1959, both inclusive, the rate shall be 2 percent;

"(2) with respect to wages received during the calendar years 1960 to 1964, both inclusive, the rate shall be $2^{1}/_{2}$ percent;

"(3) with respect to wages received during the calendar years 1965 to 1969, both inclusive, the rate shall be 3 percent;

"(4) with respect to wages received during the calendar years 1970 to 1974, both inclusive, the rate shall be $3^{1}/_{2}$ percent; and

"(5) with respect to wages received after December 31, 1974, the rate shall be 4 percent."

• **1954, Social Security Amendments of 1954 (P.L. 761, 83rd Cong.)**

P.L. 761, 83rd Cong., § 208(b):

Amended Sec. 3101. **Effective** 9-1-54. Prior to amendment, Sec. 3101 read as follows:

"SEC. 3101. RATE OF TAX.

"In addition to other taxes, there is hereby imposed on the income of every individual a tax equal to the following percentages of the wages (as defined in section 3121(a)) received by him with respect to employment (as defined in section 3121(b))—

"(1) with respect to wages received during the calendar years 1955 to 1959, both inclusive, the rate shall be 2 percent;

EMPLOYMENT TAX—EMPLOYEES

"(2) with respect to wages received during the calendar years 1960 to 1964, both inclusive, the rate shall be 2½ percent;

"(3) with respect to wages received during the calendar years 1965 to 1969, both inclusive, the rate shall be 3 percent;

"(4) with respect to wages received after December 31, 1969, the rate shall be 3¼ percent."

[Sec. 3101(c)]

(c) RELIEF FROM TAXES IN CASES COVERED BY CERTAIN INTERNATIONAL AGREEMENTS.—During any period in which there is in effect an agreement entered into pursuant to section 233 of the Social Security Act with any foreign country, wages received by or paid to an individual shall be exempt from the taxes imposed by this section to the extent that such wages are subject under such agreement exclusively to the laws applicable to the social security system of such foreign country.

Amendments

• **2004, Social Security Protection Act of 2004 (P.L. 108-203)**

P.L. 108-203, §415:

Amended Code Sec. 3101(c) by striking "to taxes or contributions for similar purposes under" and inserting "exclusively to the laws applicable to". **Effective** 3-2-2004.

• **1977 (P.L. 95-216)**

P.L. 95-216, §317(b)(2):

Added Code Sec. 3101(c). **Effective** 12-20-77.

SEC. 3102. DEDUCTION OF TAX FROM WAGES.

[Sec. 3102(a)]

(a) REQUIREMENT.—The tax imposed by section 3101 shall be collected by the employer of the taxpayer, by deducting the amount of the tax from the wages as and when paid. An employer who in any calendar year pays to an employee cash remuneration to which paragraph (7)(B) of section 3121(a) is applicable may deduct an amount equivalent to such tax from any such payment of remuneration, even though at the time of payment the total amount of such remuneration paid to the employee by the employer in the calendar year is less than the applicable dollar threshold (as defined in section 3121(x)) for such year; and an employer who in any calendar year pays to an employee cash remuneration to which paragraph (7)(C) or (10) of section 3121(a) is applicable may deduct an amount equivalent to such tax from any such payment of remuneration, even though at the time of payment the total amount of such remuneration paid to the employee by the employer in the calendar year is less than $100; and an employer who in any calendar year pays to an employee cash remuneration to which paragraph (8)(B) of section 3121(a) is applicable may deduct an amount equivalent to such tax from any such payment of remuneration, even though at the time of payment the total amount of such remuneration paid to the employee by the employer in the calendar year is less than $150; and an employer who is furnished by an employee a written statement of tips (received in a calendar month) pursuant to section 6053(a) to which paragraph (12)(B) of section 3121(a) is applicable may deduct an amount equivalent to such tax with respect to such tips from any wages of the employee (exclusive of tips) under his control, even though at the time such statement is furnished the total amount of the tips included in statements furnished to the employer as having been received by the employee in such calendar month in the course of his employment by such employer is less than $20.

Amendments

• **2004, Social Security Protection Act of 2004 (P.L. 108-203)**

P.L. 108-203, §424(b):

Amended Code Sec. 3102(a) by striking "and the employee has not performed agricultural labor for the employer on 20 days or more in the calendar year for cash remuneration computed on a time basis" following "less than $150". **Effective** 3-2-2004.

• **1994, Social Security Domestic Employment Reform Act of 1994 (P.L. 103-387)**

P.L. 103-387, §2(a)(1)(D)(i)-(ii):

Amended the second sentence of Code Sec. 3102(a) by striking "calendar quarter" each place it appears and inserting "calendar year", and by striking "$50" and inserting "the applicable dollar threshold (as defined in section 3121(x)) for such year". **Effective** for remuneration paid after 12-31-93.

• **1977 (P.L. 95-216)**

P.L. 95-216, §355(a):

Amended Code Sec. 3102(a). **Effective** for remuneration paid and tips received after 1977. Before amendment, paragraph (a) read as follows:

(a) REQUIREMENT.—The tax imposed by section 3101 shall be collected by the employer of the taxpayer by deducting the amount of the tax from the wages as and when paid. An employer who in any calendar quarter pays to an employee cash remuneration to which paragraph (7)(B) or (C) or (10) of section 3121(a) is applicable may deduct an amount equivalent to such tax from any such payment of remuneration, even though at the time of payment the total amount of such remuneration paid to the employee by the employer in the calendar quarter is less than $50; and an employer who in any calendar year pays to an employee cash remuneration to which paragraph (8)(B) of section 3121(a) is applicable may deduct an amount equivalent to such tax from any such payment of remuneration, even though at the time of payment the total amount of such remuneration paid to the employee by the employer in the calendar year is less than $150 and the employee has not performed agricultural labor for the employer on 20 days or more in the calendar year for cash remuneration computed on a time basis; and an employer who is furnished by an employee a written statement of tips (received in a calendar month) pursuant to section 6053(a) to which paragraph (12)(B) of section 3121(a) is applicable may deduct an amount equivalent to such tax with respect to such tips from any wages of the employee (exclusive of tips) under his control, even though at the time such statement is furnished the total amount of the tips included in statements furnished to the employer as having been received by the employee in such calendar month in the course of his employment by such employer is less than $20.

• **1965, Social Security Amendments of 1965 (P.L. 89-97)**

P.L. 89-97, §313(c):

Amended Sec. 3102(a) by deleting the period at the end thereof and adding the semicolon and all that follows. **Effective** with respect to tips received by employees after 1965.

• **1956, Social Security Amendments of 1956 (P.L. 880, 84th Cong.)**

P.L. 880, 84th Cong., 2d Sess., §201(h)(3):

Amended Sec. 3102(a) by striking "$100" in the last sentence and substituting "$150", plus the words which follow to the end of the sentence. **Effective** for remuneration paid after 1956.

• **1954, Social Security Amendments of 1954 (P.L. 761, 83rd Cong.)**

P.L. 761, 83rd Cong., §205A:

Amended subsection (a). **Effective** 9-1-54. Prior to amendment, subsection (a) read as follows:

"(a) Requirement.—The tax imposed by section 3101 shall be collected by the employer of the taxpayer, by deducting the amount of the tax from the wages as and when paid."

[Sec. 3102(b)]

(b) INDEMNIFICATION OF EMPLOYER.—Every employer required so to deduct the tax shall be liable for the payment of such tax, and shall be indemnified against the claims and demands of any person for the amount of any such payment made by such employer.

[Sec. 3102(c)]

(c) SPECIAL RULE FOR TIPS.—

(1) In the case of tips which constitute wages, subsection (a) shall be applicable only to such tips as are included in a written statement furnished to the employer pursuant to section 6053(a), and only to the extent that collection can be made by the employer, at or after the time such statement is so furnished and before the close of the 10th day following the calendar month (or, if paragraph (3) applies, the 30th day following the year) in which the tips were deemed paid, by deducting the amount of the tax from such wages of the employee (excluding tips, but including funds turned over by the employee to the employer pursuant to paragraph (2)) as are under control of the employer.

(2) If the tax imposed by section 3101, with respect to tips which are included in written statements furnished in any month to the employer pursuant to section 6053(a), exceeds the wages of the employee (excluding tips) from which the employer is required to collect the tax under paragraph (1), the employee may furnish to the employer on or before the 10th day of the following month (or, if paragraph (3) applies, on or before the 30th day of the following year) an amount of money equal to the amount of the excess.

(3) The Secretary may, under regulations prescribed by him, authorize employers—

EMPLOYMENT TAX—EMPLOYEES

   (A) to estimate the amount of tips that will be reported by the employee pursuant to section 6053(a) in any calendar year,

   (B) to determine the amount to be deducted upon each payment of wages (exclusive of tips) during such year as if the tips so estimated constituted the actual tips so reported, and

   (C) to deduct upon any payment of wages (other than tips, but including funds turned over by the employee to the employer pursuant to paragraph (2)) to such employee during such year (and within 30 days thereafter) such amount as may be necessary to adjust the amount actually deducted upon such wages of the employee during the quarter to the amount required to be deducted in respect of tips included in written statements furnished to the employer during the year.

   (4) If the tax imposed by section 3101 with respect to tips which constitute wages exceeds the portion of such tax which can be collected by the employer from the wages of the employee pursuant to paragraph (1) or paragraph (3), such excess shall be paid by the employee.

Amendments

• **1977 (P.L. 95-216)**

P.L. 95-216, §355(b):

Amended Code Sec. 3102(c)(1) through (3). **Effective** for remuneration paid and tips received after 1977. Before amendment, paragraphs (c)(1) through (3) read as follows:

(c) SPECIAL RULE FOR TIPS.—

(1) In the case of tips which constitute wages, subsection (a) shall be applicable only to such tips as are included in a written statement furnished to the employer pursuant to section 6053(a), and only to the extent that collection can be made by the employer, at or after the time such statement is so furnished and before the close of the 10th day following the calendar month (or, if paragraph (3) applies, the 30th day following the quarter) in which the tips were deemed paid, by deducting the amount of the tax from such wages of the employee (excluding tips, but including funds turned over by the employee to the employer pursuant to paragraph (2) as are under control of the employer.

(2) If the tax imposed by section 3101 with respect to tips which are included in written statements furnished in any month to the employer pursuant to section 6053(a), exceeds the wages of the employee (excluding tips) from which the employer is required to collect the tax under paragraph (1), the employee may furnish to the employer on or before the 10th day of the following month (or, if paragraph (3) applies, on or before the 30th day of the following quarter) an amount of money equal to the amount of the excess.

(3) The Secretary may, under regulations prescribed by him, authorize employers—

   (A) to estimate the amount of tips that will be reported by the employee pursuant to section 6053(a) in any quarter of the calendar year,

   (B) to determine the amount to be deducted upon each payment of wages (exclusive of tips) during such quarter as if the tips so estimated constituted the actual tips so reported, and

   (C) to deduct upon any payment of wages (other than tips, but including funds turned over by the employee to the employer pursuant to paragraph (2)) to such employee during such quarter (and within 30 days thereafter) such amount as may be necessary to adjust the amount actually deducted upon such wages of the employee during the quarter to the amount required to be deducted in respect of tips included in written statements furnished to the employer during the quarter.

• **1976, Tax Reform Act of 1976 (P.L. 94-455)**

P.L. 94-455, §1906(b)(13)(A):

Amended 1954 Code by substituting "Secretary" for "Secretary or his delegate" each place it appeared. **Effective** 2-1-77.

• **1965, Social Security Amendments of 1965 (P.L. 89-97)**

P.L. 89-97, §313(c):

Added Sec. 3102(c). **Effective** for tips received by employees after 1965.

[Sec. 3102(d)]

(d) SPECIAL RULE FOR CERTAIN TAXABLE GROUP-TERM LIFE INSURANCE BENEFITS.—

   (1) IN GENERAL.—In the case of any payment for group-term life insurance to which this subsection applies—

      (A) subsection (a) shall not apply,

      (B) the employer shall separately include on the statement required under section 6051—

         (i) the portion of the wages which consists of payments for group-term life insurance to which this subsection applies, and

         (ii) the amount of the tax imposed by section 3101 on such payments, and

      (C) the tax imposed by section 3101 on such payments shall be paid by the employee.

   (2) BENEFITS TO WHICH SUBSECTION APPLIES.—This subsection shall apply to any payment for group-term life insurance to the extent—

      (A) such payment constitutes wages, and

      (B) such payment is for coverage for periods during which an employment relationship no longer exists between the employee and the employer.

Amendments

• **1990, Omnibus Budget Reconciliation Act of 1990 (P.L. 101-508)**

P.L. 101-508, §5124(a):

Amended Code Sec. 3102 by adding at the end thereof a new subsection (d). **Effective** for coverage provided after 12-31-90.

[Sec. 3102(e)]

(e) SPECIAL RULE FOR CERTAIN TRANSFERRED FEDERAL EMPLOYEES.—In the case of any payments of wages for service performed in the employ of an international organization pursuant to a transfer to which the provisions of section 3121(y) are applicable—

   (1) subsection (a) shall not apply,

   (2) the head of the Federal agency from which the transfer was made shall separately include on the statement required under section 6051—

      (A) the amount determined to be the amount of the wages for such service, and

      (B) the amount of the tax imposed by section 3101 on such payments, and

   (3) the tax imposed by section 3101 on such payments shall be paid by the employee.

Amendments

• **1994, Social Security Independence and Program Improvements Act of 1994 (P.L. 103-296)**

P.L. 103-296, §319(a)(3):

Amended Code Sec. 3102 by adding at the end a new subsection (e). **Effective** with respect to service performed after the calendar quarter following the calendar quarter containing 8-15-94.

[Sec. 3102(f)]

(f) SPECIAL RULES FOR ADDITIONAL TAX.—

   (1) IN GENERAL.—In the case of any tax imposed by section 3101(b)(2), subsection (a) shall only apply to the extent to which the taxpayer receives wages from the employer in excess of $200,000, and the employer may disregard the amount of wages received by such taxpayer's spouse.

   (2) COLLECTION OF AMOUNTS NOT WITHHELD.—To the extent that the amount of any tax imposed by section 3101(b)(2) is not collected by the employer, such tax shall be paid by the employee.

   (3) TAX PAID BY RECIPIENT.—If an employer, in violation of this chapter, fails to deduct and withhold the tax imposed by section 3101(b)(2) and thereafter the tax is paid by the employee, the tax so required to be deducted and withheld shall not be collected from the employer, but

EMPLOYMENT TAX—EMPLOYERS

this paragraph shall in no case relieve the employer from liability for any penalties or additions to tax otherwise applicable in respect of such failure to deduct and withhold.

Amendments

• **2010, Patient Protection and Affordable Care Act (P.L. 111-148)**

P.L. 111-148, §9015(a)(2):

Amended Code Sec. 3102 by adding at the end a new subsection (f). **Effective** with respect to remuneration received, and tax years beginning, after 12-31-2012.

Subchapter B—Tax on Employers

Sec. 3111.   Rate of tax.
Sec. 3112.   Instrumentalities of the United States.

[Sec. 3111]

SEC. 3111. RATE OF TAX.

[Sec. 3111(a)]

(a) OLD-AGE, SURVIVORS, AND DISABILITY INSURANCE.—In addition to other taxes, there is hereby imposed on every employer an excise tax, with respect to having individuals in his employ, equal to 6.2 percent of the wages (as defined in section 3121(a)) paid by the employer with respect to employment (as defined in section 3121(b)).

Amendments

• **2020, Taxpayer Certainty and Disaster Tax Relief Act of 2020 (116-260)**

P.L. 116-260, §206(e)(2), Div. EE, provides:

(2) SPECIAL RULE.—

(A) IN GENERAL.—For purposes of section 2301 of the CARES Act, an employer who has filed a return of tax with respect to applicable employment taxes (as defined in section 2301(c)(1) of division A of such Act) before the date of the enactment of this Act [12-27-2020.--CCH] may elect (in such manner as the Secretary of the Treasury (or the Secretary's delegate) shall prescribe) to treat any applicable amount as an amount paid in the calendar quarter which includes the date of the enactment of this Act.

(B) APPLICABLE AMOUNT.—For purposes of subparagraph (A), the term "applicable amount" means the amount of wages which—

(i) are—

(I) described in section 2301(c)(5)(B) of the CARES Act, as added by the amendments made by subsection (b), or

(II) permitted to be treated as qualified wages under guidance issued pursuant to section 2301(g)(2) of the CARES Act (as added by subsection (c)), and

(ii) were—

(I) paid in a calendar quarter beginning after December 31, 2019, and before October 1, 2020, and

(II) not taken into account by the taxpayer in calculating the credit allowed under section 2301(a) of division A of such Act for such calendar quarter.

P.L. 116-260, §303(d)-(f), Div. EE, provides:

(d) PAYROLL TAX CREDIT FOR CERTAIN TAX-EXEMPT ORGANIZATIONS.—

(1) IN GENERAL.—In the case of any qualified tax-exempt organization, there shall be allowed as a credit against the tax imposed by section 3111(a) of the Internal Revenue Code of 1986 on wages paid with respect to employment of all employees of the organization during the calendar quarter an amount equal to 40 percent of the qualified wages paid to eligible employees of such organization during such calendar quarter.

(2) APPLICATION OF AGGREGATE DOLLAR LIMITATION PER EMPLOYEE.—The amount of qualified wages with respect to any employee which may be taken into account under this subsection by the employer for any calendar quarter shall not exceed $6,000 (reduced by the amount of qualified wages with respect to which credit was allowed under this subsection for any prior calendar quarter with respect to such employee).

(3) OVERALL LIMITATION.—

(A) IN GENERAL.—The aggregate amount allowed as a credit under this subsection for all eligible employees of any employer for any calendar quarter shall not exceed the amount of the tax imposed by section 3111(a) of the Internal Revenue Code of 1986 on wages paid with respect to employment of all employees of such employer during such calendar quarter (reduced by any credits allowed under subsections (e) and (f) of section 3111 of such Code for such quarter).

(B) CARRYFORWARD.—If the amount of the credit under paragraph (1) exceeds the limitation of subparagraph (A) for any calendar quarter, such excess shall be carried to the succeeding calendar quarter and allowed as a credit under paragraph (1) for such quarter.

* * *

(4) DEFINITIONS.—

(A) QUALIFIED TAX-EXEMPT ORGANIZATION.—For purposes of this subsection, the term "qualified tax-exempt organization" means an organization described in section 501(c) of the Internal Revenue Code of 1986 and exempt from taxation under section 501(a) of such Code if such organization would be an eligible employer if the activities of such organization were an active trade or business.

(B) APPLICATION OF CERTAIN TERMS WITH RESPECT TO QUALIFIED TAX-EXEMPT ORGANIZATIONS.—For purposes of this subsection, the terms "eligible employee" and "qualified wages" shall be applied with respect to any qualified tax-exempt organization—

(i) by treating the activities of such organization as an active trade or business, and

(ii) by substituting "wages (within the meaning of subsection (d)(4)(C))" for "wages (as defined in section 51(c)(1) of the Internal Revenue Code of 1986, but without regard to section 3306(b)(2)(B) of such Code)" in subsection (b)(3).

(C) OTHER TERMS.—Except as otherwise provided in this subsection, any term used in this subsection which is also used in chapter 21 or 22 of the Internal Revenue Code of 1986 shall have the same meaning as when used in such chapter.

* * *

(6) TREATMENT OF DEPOSITS.—The Secretary shall waive any penalty under section 6656 of such Code for any failure to make a deposit of applicable employment taxes if the Secretary determines that such failure was due to the anticipation of the credit allowed under this subsection.

(7) THIRD PARTY PAYORS.—Any credit allowed under this subsection shall be treated as a credit described in section 3511(d)(2) of such Code.

(8) COORDINATION WITH SUBSECTION (a) CREDIT.—Any wages taken into account in determining the credit allowed under this subsection shall not be take into account as wages for purposes of subsection (a).

(9) REGULATIONS AND GUIDANCE.—The Secretary shall issue such forms, instructions, regulations, and guidance as are necessary—

(A) to allow the advance payment of the credit under paragraph (1), subject to the limitations provided in this subsection, based on such information as the Secretary shall require,

(B) regulations or other guidance to provide for the reconciliation of such advance payment with the amount of the credit under this subsection at the time of filing the return of tax for the applicable quarter or taxable year,

(C) with respect to the application of the credit under paragraph (1) to third party payors (including professional employer organizations, certified professional employer organizations, or agents under section 3504 of the Internal Revenue Code of 1986), including regulations or guidance allowing such payors to submit documentation necessary to substantiate the eligible employer status of employers that use such payors, and

(D) for recapturing the benefit of credits determined under this subsection in cases where there is a subsequent adjustment to the credit determined under paragraph (1).

(e) ELECTION TO NOT TAKE CERTAIN WAGES INTO ACCOUNT.—

(1) IN GENERAL.—This section shall not apply to qualified wages paid by an eligible employer with respect to which such employer makes an election (at such time and in such manner as the Secretary may prescribe) to have this section not apply to such wages.

* * *

(f) CERTAIN GOVERNMENTAL EMPLOYERS.—

(1) IN GENERAL.—The credits under this section shall not apply to the Government of the United States, the government of any State or political subdivision thereof, or any agency or instrumentality of any of the foregoing.

(2) EXCEPTION.—Paragraph (1) shall not apply to—

(A) any organization described in section 501(c)(1) of the Internal Revenue Code of 1986 and exempt from tax under section 501(a) of such Code, or

(B) any entity described in paragraph (1) if —

(i) such entity is a college or university, or

(ii) the principal purpose or function of such entity is providing medical or hospital care.

An entity described in subparagraph (B) shall be treated for purposes of this section in the same manner as an organization described in section 501(c) of the Internal Revenue Code of 1986 and exempt from tax under section 501(a) of such Code.

• **2020, Coronavirus Aid, Relief, and Economic Security (CARES) Act (P.L. 116-136)**

P.L. 116-136, §2301 (as amended by P.L. 116-260, §206(a)-(b), (c)(2)(A), (c)(2)(B)(i)-(ii), and (d), Div. EE, §207(a)(1)-(2), (b)-(c), (d)(1)(A)-(B), (d)(2)(A)-(B), (d)(3)(A)-(B), (e)(1)-(2), (f), (g)(1)-(2), (h), and (j), Div. EE, and §303(d)(3)(C)(iii), Div. EE), provides:

SEC. 2301. EMPLOYEE RETENTION CREDIT FOR EMPLOYERS SUBJECT TO CLOSURE DUE TO COVID–19.

(a) IN GENERAL.—In the case of an eligible employer, there shall be allowed as a credit against applicable employment taxes for each calendar quarter an amount equal to 70 percent of the qualified wages with respect to each employee of such employer for such calendar quarter.

(b) LIMITATIONS AND REFUNDABILITY.—

(1) WAGES TAKEN INTO ACCOUNT.—The amount of qualified wages with respect to any employee which may be taken into account under subsection (a) by the eligible employer for any calendar quarter shall not exceed $10,000.

(2) CREDIT LIMITED TO EMPLOYMENT TAXES.—The credit allowed by subsection (a) with respect to any calendar quarter shall not exceed the applicable employment taxes (reduced by any credits allowed under subsections (e) and (f) of section 3111 of the Internal Revenue Code of 1986, sections 7001 and 7003 of the Families First Coronavirus Response Act, and section 303(d) of the Taxpayer Certainty and Disaster Tax Relief Act of 2020) on the wages paid with respect to the employment of all the employees of the eligible employer for such calendar quarter.

(3) REFUNDABILITY OF EXCESS CREDIT.—

(A) IN GENERAL.—If the amount of the credit under subsection (a) exceeds the limitation of paragraph (2) for any calendar quarter, such excess shall be treated as an overpayment that shall be refunded under sections 6402(a) and 6413(b) of the Internal Revenue Code of 1986.

(B) TREATMENT OF PAYMENTS.—For purposes of section 1324 of title 31, United States Code, any amounts due to the employer under this paragraph shall be treated in the same manner as a refund due from a credit provision referred to in subsection (b)(2) of such section.

(c) DEFINITIONS.—For purposes of this section—

(1) APPLICABLE EMPLOYMENT TAXES.—The term "applicable employment taxes" means the following:

(A) The taxes imposed under section 3111(a) of the Internal Revenue Code of 1986.

(B) So much of the taxes imposed under section 3221(a) of such Code as are attributable to the rate in effect under section 3111(a) of such Code.

(2) ELIGIBLE EMPLOYER.—

(A) IN GENERAL.—The term "eligible employer" means any employer—

(i) which was carrying on a trade or business during the calendar quarter for which the credit is determined under subsection (a), and

(ii) with respect to any calendar quarter, for which—

(I) the operation of the trade or business described in clause (i) is fully or partially suspended during the calendar quarter due to orders from an appropriate governmental authority limiting commerce, travel, or group meetings (for commercial, social, religious, or other purposes) due to the coronavirus disease 2019 (COVID–19), or

(II) the gross receipts (within the meaning of section 448(c) of the Internal Revenue Code of 1986) of such employer for such calendar quarter are less than 80 percent of the gross receipts of such employer for the same calendar quarter in calendar year 2019.

With respect to any employer for any calendar quarter, if such employer was not in existence as of the beginning of the same calendar quarter in calendar year 2019, clause (ii)(II) shall be applied by substituting "2020" for "2019".

(B) ELECTION TO USE ALTERNATIVE QUARTER.—At the election of the employer—

(i) subparagraph (A)(ii)(II) shall be applied—

(I) by substituting "for the immediately preceding calendar quarter" for "for such calendar quarter", and

(II) by substituting "the corresponding calendar quarter in calendar year 2019" for "the same calendar quarter in calendar year 2019", and

(ii) the last sentence of subparagraph (A) shall be applied by substituting "the corresponding calendar quarter in calendar year 2019" for "the same calendar quarter in calendar year 2019".

An election under this subparagraph shall be made at such time and in such manner as the Secretary may prescribe.

(C) TAX-EXEMPT ORGANIZATIONS.—In the case of an organization which is described in section 501(c) of the Internal Revenue Code of 1986 and exempt from tax under section 501(a) of such Code—

(i) clauses (i) and (ii)(I) of subparagraph (A) shall apply to all operations of such organization, and

(ii) any reference in this section to gross receipts shall be treated as a reference to gross receipts within the meaning of section 6033 of such Code.

(3) QUALIFIED WAGES.—

(A) IN GENERAL.—The term "qualified wages" means—

(i) in the case of an eligible employer for which the average number of full-time employees (within the meaning of section 4980H of the Internal Revenue Code of 1986) employed by such eligible employer during 2019 was greater than 500, wages paid by such eligible employer with respect to which an employee is not providing services due to circumstances described in subclause (I) or (II) of paragraph (2)(A)(ii), or

(ii) in the case of an eligible employer for which the average number of full-time employees (within the meaning of section 4980H of the Internal Revenue Code of 1986) employed by such eligible employer during 2019 was not greater than 500—

(I) with respect to an eligible employer described in subclause (I) of paragraph (2)(A)(ii), wages paid by such eligible employer with respect to an employee during any period described in such clause, or

(II) with respect to an eligible employer described in subclause (II) of such paragraph, wages paid by such eligible employer with respect to an employee during such quarter.

(B) EXCEPTION.—The term "qualified wages" shall not include any wages taken into account under section 7001 or section 7003 of the Families First Coronavirus Response Act.

(4) SECRETARY.—The term "Secretary" means the Secretary of the Treasury or the Secretary's delegate.

(5) WAGES.—

(A) IN GENERAL.—The term "wages" means wages (as defined in section 3121(a) of the Internal Revenue Code of 1986) and compensation (as defined in section 3231(e) of such Code). For purposes of the preceding sentence, in the case of any organization or entity described in subsection (f)(2), wages as defined in section 3121(a) of the Internal Revenue Code of 1986 shall be determined without regard to paragraphs (5), (6), (7), (10), and (13) of section 3121(b) of such Code (except with respect to services performed in a penal institution by an inmate thereof).

(B) ALLOWANCE FOR CERTAIN HEALTH PLAN EXPENSES.—

(i) IN GENERAL.—Such term shall include amounts paid by the eligible employer to provide and maintain a group health plan (as defined in section 5000(b)(1) of the Internal Revenue Code of 1986), but only to the extent that such amounts are excluded from the gross income of employees by reason of section 106(a) of such Code.

(ii) ALLOCATION RULES.—For purposes of this section, amounts treated as wages under clause (i) shall be treated as paid with respect to any employee (and with respect to any period) to the extent that such amounts are properly allocable to such employee (and to such period) in such manner as the Secretary may prescribe. Except as otherwise provided by the Secretary, such allocation shall be treated as properly made if made on the basis of being pro rata among periods of coverage.

(6) OTHER TERMS.—Any term used in this section which is also used in chapter 21 or 22 of the Internal Revenue Code of 1986 shall have the same meaning as when used in such chapter.

(d) AGGREGATION RULE.—All persons treated as a single employer under subsection (a) or (b) of section 52 of the Internal Revenue Code of 1986, or subsection (m) or (o) of section 414 of such Code, shall be treated as one employer for purposes of this section.

(e) CERTAIN RULES TO APPLY.—For purposes of this section, rules similar to the rules of sections 51(i)(1) and 280C(a) of the Internal Revenue Code of 1986 shall apply.

(f) CERTAIN GOVERNMENTAL EMPLOYERS.—

(1) IN GENERAL.—This credit shall not apply to the Government of the United States, the government of any State or political subdivision thereof, or any agency or instrumentality of any of the foregoing.

(2) EXCEPTION.—Paragraph (1) shall not apply to—

(A) any organization described in section 501(c)(1) of the Internal Revenue Code of 1986 and exempt from tax under section 501(a) of such Code, or

(B) any entity described in paragraph (1) if—

(i) such entity is a college or university, or

(ii) the principal purpose or function of such entity is providing medical or hospital care.

In the case of any entity described in subparagraph (B), such entity shall be treated as satisfying the requirements of subsection (c)(2)(A)(i):

(g) ELECTION TO NOT TAKE CERTAIN WAGES INTO ACCOUNT.—

(1) IN GENERAL.—This section shall not apply to so much of the qualified wages paid by an eligible employer as such employer elects (at such time and in such manner as the Secretary may prescribe) to not take into account for purposes of this section.

(2) COORDINATION WITH PAYCHECK PROTECTION PROGRAM.—The Secretary, in consultation with the Administrator of the Small Business Administration, shall issue guidance providing that payroll costs paid during the covered period shall not fail to be treated as qualified wages under this section by reason of an election under paragraph (1) to the extent that a covered loan of the eligible employer is not forgiven by reason of a decision under section 7A(g) of the Small Business Act or the application of section 7(a)(37)(J) of the Small Business Act. Terms used in the preceding sentence which are also used in section 7A(g) or 7(a)(37)(J) of the Small Business Act shall, when applied in connection with either such section, have the same meaning as when used in such section, respectively.

(h) SPECIAL RULES.—

(1) DENIAL OF DOUBLE BENEFIT.—Any wages taken into account in determining the credit allowed under this section shall not be taken into account as wages for purposes of sections 41, 45A, 45P, 45S, 51, and 1396 of the Internal Revenue Code of 1986.

(2) THIRD PARTY PAYORS.—Any credit allowed under this section shall be treated as a credit described in section 3511(d)(2) of such Code.

* * *

(j) ADVANCE PAYMENTS.—

(1) IN GENERAL.—Except as provided in paragraph (2), no advance payment of the credit under subsection (a) shall be allowed.

(2) ADVANCE PAYMENTS TO SMALL EMPLOYERS.—

(A) IN GENERAL.—Under rules provided by the Secretary, an eligible employer for which the average number of full-time employees (within the meaning of section 4980H of the Internal Revenue Code of 1986) employed by such eligible employer during 2019 was not greater than 500 may elect for any calendar quarter to receive an advance payment of the credit under subsection (a) for such quarter in an amount not to exceed 70 percent of the average quarterly wages paid by the employer in calendar year 2019.

(B) SPECIAL RULE FOR SEASONAL EMPLOYERS.—In the case of any employer who employs seasonal workers (as defined in section 45R(d)(5)(B) of the Internal Revenue Code of 1986), the employer may elect to substitute "the wages for the calendar quarter in 2019 which corresponds to the calendar quarter to which the election relates" for "the average quarterly wages paid by the employer in calendar year 2019".

(C) SPECIAL RULE FOR EMPLOYERS NOT IN EXISTENCE IN 2019.—In the case of any employer that was not in existence in 2019, subparagraphs (A) and (B) shall each be applied by substituting "2020" for "2019" each place it appears.

(3) RECONCILIATION OF CREDIT WITH ADVANCE PAYMENTS.—

(A) IN GENERAL.—The amount of credit which would (but for this subsection) be allowed under this section shall be reduced (but not below zero) by the aggregate payment allowed to the taxpayer under paragraph (2). Any failure to so reduce the credit shall be treated as arising out of a mathematical or clerical error and assessed according to section 6213(b)(1) of the Internal Revenue Code of 1986.

(B) EXCESS ADVANCE PAYMENTS.—If the advance payments to a taxpayer under paragraph (2) for a calendar quarter exceed the credit allowed by this section (determined without regard to subparagraph (A)), the tax imposed by chapter 21 or 22 of the Internal Revenue Code of 1986 (whichever is applicable) for the calendar quarter shall be increased by the amount of such excess.

(k) TREATMENT OF DEPOSITS.—The Secretary shall waive any penalty under section 6656 of the Internal Revenue Code of 1986 for any failure to make a deposit of any

EMPLOYMENT TAX—EMPLOYERS

applicable employment taxes if the Secretary determines that such failure was due to the reasonable anticipation of the credit allowed under this section.

(l) REGULATIONS AND GUIDANCE.—The Secretary shall issue such forms, instructions, regulations, and guidance as are necessary—

(1) to allow the advance payment of the credit under subsection (a) as provided in paragraph (j)(2), subject to the limitations provided in this section, based on such information as the Secretary shall require,

(2) with respect to the application of the credit under subsection (a) to third party payors (including professional employer organizations, certified professional employer organizations, or agents under section 3504 of the Internal Revenue Code of 1986), including regulations or guidance allowing such payors to submit documentation necessary to substantiate the eligible employer status of employers that use such payors, and

(3) to prevent the avoidance of the purposes of the limitations under this section, including through the leaseback of employees.

Any forms, instructions, regulations, or guidance described in paragraph (2) shall require the customer to be responsible for the accounting of the credit and for any liability for improperly claimed credits and shall require the certified professional employer organization or other third party payor to accurately report such tax credits based on the information provided by the customer.

(m) APPLICATION.—This section shall only apply to wages paid after March 12, 2020, and before July 1, 2021.

* * *

P.L. 116-136, §2302, provides:
SEC. 2302. DELAY OF PAYMENT OF EMPLOYER PAYROLL TAXES.

(a) IN GENERAL.—

(1) TAXES.—Notwithstanding any other provision of law, the payment for applicable employment taxes for the payroll tax deferral period shall not be due before the applicable date.

(2) DEPOSITS.—Notwithstanding section 6302 of the Internal Revenue Code of 1986, an employer shall be treated as having timely made all deposits of applicable employment taxes that are required to be made (without regard to this section) for such taxes during the payroll tax deferral period if all such deposits are made not later than the applicable date.

(3) EXCEPTION.—This subsection shall not apply to any taxpayer if such taxpayer has had indebtedness forgiven under section 1106 of this Act with respect to a loan under paragraph (36) of section 7(a) of the Small Business Act (15 U.S.C. 636(a)), as added by section 1102 of this Act, or indebtedness forgiven under section 1109 of this Act. [Stricken by P.L. 116-142, §4(a), **effective** as if included in the CARES Act (P.L. 116-136) and applicable to any loan made pursuant to section 7(a)(36) of the Small Business Act (15 U.S.C. 636(a)(36)) or section 1109 of the CARES Act.]

(b) SECA.—

(1) IN GENERAL.—Notwithstanding any other provision of law, the payment for 50 percent of the taxes imposed under section 1401(a) of the Internal Revenue Code of 1986 for the payroll tax deferral period shall not be due before the applicable date.

(2) ESTIMATED TAXES.—For purposes of applying section 6654 of the Internal Revenue Code of 1986 to any taxable year which includes any part of the payroll tax deferral period, 50 percent of the taxes imposed under section 1401(a) of such Code for the payroll tax deferral period shall not be treated as taxes to which such section 6654 applies.

(c) LIABILITY OF THIRD PARTIES.—

(1) ACTS TO BE PERFORMED BY AGENTS.—For purposes of section 3504 of the Internal Revenue Code of 1986, in the case of any person designated pursuant to such section (and any regulations or other guidance issued by the Secretary with respect to such section) to perform acts otherwise required to be performed by an employer under such Code, if such employer directs such person to defer payment of any applicable employment taxes during the payroll tax deferral period under this section, such employer shall be solely liable for the payment of such applicable employment taxes before the applicable date for any wages paid by such person on behalf of such employer during such period.

(2) CERTIFIED PROFESSIONAL EMPLOYER ORGANIZATIONS.—For purposes of section 3511, in the case of a certified professional employer organization (as defined in subsection (a) of section 7705 of the Internal Revenue Code of 1986) that has entered into a service contract described in subsection (e)(2) of such section with a customer, if such customer directs such organization to defer payment of any applicable employment taxes during the payroll tax deferral period under this section, such customer shall, notwithstanding subsections (a) and (c) of section 3511, be solely liable for the payment of such applicable employment taxes before the applicable date for any wages paid by such organization to any work site employee performing services for such customer during such period.

(d) DEFINITIONS.—For purposes of this section—

(1) APPLICABLE EMPLOYMENT TAXES.—The term "applicable employment taxes" means the following:

(A) The taxes imposed under section 3111(a) of the Internal Revenue Code of 1986.

(B) So much of the taxes imposed under section 3211(a) of such Code as are attributable to the rate in effect under section 3111(a) of such Code.

(C) So much of the taxes imposed under section 3221(a) of such Code as are attributable to the rate in effect under section 3111(a) of such Code.

(2) PAYROLL TAX DEFERRAL PERIOD.—The term "payroll tax deferral period" means the period beginning on the date of the enactment of this Act and ending before January 1, 2021.

(3) APPLICABLE DATE.—The term "applicable date" means—

(A) December 31, 2021, with respect to 50 percent of the amounts to which subsection (a) or (b), as the case may be, apply, and

(B) December 31, 2022, with respect to the remaining such amounts.

(4) SECRETARY.—The term "Secretary" means the Secretary of the Treasury (or the Secretary's delegate).

* * *

(f) REGULATORY AUTHORITY.—The Secretary shall issue such regulations or other guidance as necessary to carry out the purposes of this section, including rules for the administration and enforcement of subsection (c).

- **2020, Families First Coronavirus Response Act (P.L. 116-127)**

P.L. 116-127, §7001 (as amended by P.L. 116-136, §3606(a)(1)-(3); P.L. 116-260, §286(a) and (b)(1), Div. N, §288(a)(1)-(2), and (b)-(c), Div. N, and §303(d)(3)(C)(i), Div. EE), provides:

SEC. 7001. PAYROLL CREDIT FOR REQUIRED PAID SICK LEAVE.

(a) IN GENERAL.—In the case of an employer, there shall be allowed as a credit against the tax imposed by section 3111(a) or 3221(a) of the Internal Revenue Code of 1986 for each calendar quarter an amount equal to 100 percent of the qualified sick leave wages paid by such employer with respect to such calendar quarter.

(b) LIMITATIONS AND REFUNDABILITY.—

(1) WAGES TAKEN INTO ACCOUNT.—The amount of qualified sick leave wages taken into account under subsection (a) with respect to any individual shall not exceed $200 ($511 in the case of any day any portion of which is paid sick time described in paragraph (1), (2), or (3) of section 5102(a) of the Emergency Paid Sick Leave Act) for any day (or portion thereof) for which the individual is paid qualified sick leave wages.

(2) OVERALL LIMITATION ON NUMBER OF DAYS TAKEN INTO ACCOUNT.—The aggregate number of days taken into account under paragraph (1) for any calendar quarter shall not exceed the excess (if any) of—

(A) 10, over

(B) the aggregate number of days so taken into account for all preceding calendar quarters.

(3) CREDIT LIMITED TO CERTAIN EMPLOYMENT TAXES.—The credit allowed by subsection (a) with respect to any calendar quarter shall not exceed the tax imposed by section 3111(a) or 3221(a) of such Code for such calendar quarter (reduced by any credits allowed under subsections (e) and (f) of section 3111 of such Code, and section 303(d) of the Taxpayer Certainty and Disaster Tax Relief Act of 2020, for such quarter) on the wages paid with respect to the employment of all employees of the employer.

(4) REFUNDABILITY OF EXCESS CREDIT.—

(A)(i) CREDIT IS REFUNDABLE.—If the amount of the credit under subsection (a) exceeds the limitation of paragraph (3) for any calendar quarter, such excess shall be treated as an overpayment that shall be refunded under sections 6402(a) and 6413(b) of such Code.

(ii) ADVANCING CREDIT.—In anticipation of the credit, including the refundable portion under clause (i), the credit may be advanced, according to forms and instructions provided by the Secretary, up to an amount calculated under subsection (a), subject to the limits under subsection (b), both calculated through the end of the most recent payroll period in the quarter.

(B) TREATMENT OF PAYMENTS.—For purposes of section 1324 of title 31, United States Code, any amounts due to an employer under this paragraph shall be treated in the same manner as a refund due from a credit provision referred to in subsection (b)(2) of such section.

(c) QUALIFIED SICK LEAVE WAGES.—For purposes of this section, the term "qualified sick leave wages" means wages (as defined in section 3121(a) of the Internal Revenue Code of 1986, determined without regard to paragraphs (1) through (22) of section 3121(b) of such Code and section 7005(a) of this Act, [sic] and compensation (as defined in section 3231(e) of the Internal Revenue Code, determined without regard to the sentence in paragraph (1) thereof which begins "Such term does not include remuneration" and without regard to section 7005(a) of this Act) paid by an employer—

(1) which are required to be paid by reason of the Emergency Paid Sick Leave Act, or

(2) both—

(A) which would be so required to be paid if such Act were applied—

(i) by substituting "March 31, 2021" for "December 31, 2020" in section 5109 thereof, and

(ii) without regard to section 5102(b)(3) thereof, and

(B) with respect to which all requirements of such Act (other than subsections (a) and (b) of section 5105 thereof, and determined by substituting "To be compliant with section 5102, an employer may not" for "It shall be unlawful for any employer to" in section 5104 thereof) which would apply if so required are satisfied.

(d) ALLOWANCE OF CREDIT FOR CERTAIN HEALTH PLAN EXPENSES.—

(1) IN GENERAL.—The amount of the credit allowed under subsection (a) shall be increased by so much of the employer's qualified health plan expenses as are properly allocable to the qualified sick leave wages for which such credit is so allowed.

(2) QUALIFIED HEALTH PLAN EXPENSES.—For purposes of this subsection, the term "qualified health plan expenses" means amounts paid or incurred by the employer to provide and maintain a group health plan (as defined in section 5000(b)(1) of the Internal Revenue Code of 1986), but only to the extent that such amounts are excluded from the gross income of employees by reason of section 106(a) of such Code.

(3) ALLOCATION RULES.—For purposes of this section, qualified health plan expenses shall be allocated to qualified sick leave wages in such manner as the Secretary of the Treasury (or the Secretary's delegate) may prescribe. Except as otherwise provided by the Secretary, such allocation shall be treated as properly made if made on the basis of being pro rata among covered employees and pro rata on the basis of periods of coverage (relative to the time periods of leave to which such wages relate).

(e) SPECIAL RULES.—

(1) DENIAL OF DOUBLE BENEFIT.—For purposes of chapter 1 of such Code, the gross income of the employer, for the taxable year which includes the last day of any calendar quarter with respect to which a credit is allowed under this section, shall be increased by the amount of such credit. Any wages taken into account in determining the credit allowed under this section shall not be taken into account for purposes of determining the credit allowed under section 45S of such Code.

(2) ELECTION NOT TO HAVE SECTION APPLY.—This section shall not apply with respect to any employer for any calendar quarter if such employer elects (at such time and in such manner as the Secretary of the Treasury (or the Secretary's delegate) may prescribe) not to have this section apply.

(3) CERTAIN TERMS.—Except as otherwise provided in this section, any term used in this section which is also used in chapter 21 of such Code shall have the same meaning as when used in such chapter.

(4) CERTAIN GOVERNMENTAL EMPLOYERS.—This credit shall not apply to the Government of the United States, the government of any State or political subdivision thereof, or any agency or instrumentality of any of the foregoing.

(4) [(5)] REFERENCES TO RAILROAD RETIREMENT TAX.—Any reference in this section to the tax imposed by section 3221(a) of the Internal Revenue Code of 1986 shall be treated as a reference to so much of such tax as is attributable to the rate in effect under section 3111(a) of such Code.

(f) REGULATIONS.—The Secretary of the Treasury (or the Secretary's delegate) shall prescribe such regulations or other guidance as may be necessary to carry out the purposes of this section, including—

(1) regulations or other guidance to prevent the avoidance of the purposes of the limitations under this section,

(2) regulations or other guidance to minimize compliance and record-keeping burdens under this section,

(3) regulations or other guidance providing for waiver of penalties for failure to deposit amounts in anticipation of the allowance of the credit allowed under this section,

(4) regulations or other guidance for recapturing the benefit of credits determined under this section in cases where there is a subsequent adjustment to the credit determined under subsection (a),

(5) regulations or other guidance to ensure that the wages taken into account under this section conform with the paid sick time required to be provided under the Emergency Paid Sick Leave Act, and

(6) regulations or other guidance to permit the advancement of the credit determined under subsection (a).

(g) APPLICATION OF SECTION.—This section shall apply only to wages paid with respect to the period beginning on a date selected by the Secretary of the Treasury (or the Secretary's delegate) which is during the 15-day period beginning on the date of the enactment of this Act, and ending on March 31, 2021.

* * *

(i) TREATMENT OF DEPOSITS.—The Secretary of the Treasury (or the Secretary's delegate) shall waive any penalty under section 6656 of the Internal Revenue Code of 1986 for any failure to make a deposit of the tax imposed by section 3111(a) or 3221(a) of such Code if the Secretary determines that such failure was due to the anticipation of the credit allowed under this section.

P.L. 116-127, §7003 (as amended by P.L. 116-136, §3606(b)-(c); P.L. 116-260, §286(a) and (b)(3), Div. N, §288(a)(1)-(2), and (b)-(c), Div. N, and §303(d)(3)(C)(ii), Div. EE), provides:

SEC. 7003. PAYROLL CREDIT FOR REQUIRED PAID FAMILY LEAVE.

(a) IN GENERAL.—In the case of an employer, there shall be allowed as a credit against the tax imposed by section 3111(a) or 3221(a) of the Internal Revenue Code of 1986 for each calendar quarter an amount equal to 100 percent of the qualified family leave wages paid by such employer with respect to such calendar quarter.

(b) LIMITATIONS AND REFUNDABILITY.—

(1) WAGES TAKEN INTO ACCOUNT.—The amount of qualified family leave wages taken into account under subsection (a) with respect to any individual shall not exceed—

(A) for any day (or portion thereof) for which the individual is paid qualified family leave wages, $200, and

(B) in the aggregate with respect to all calendar quarters, $10,000.

(2) CREDIT LIMITED TO CERTAIN EMPLOYMENT TAXES.—The credit allowed by subsection (a) with respect to any calendar quarter shall not exceed the tax imposed by section 3111(a) or 3221(a) of such Code for such calendar quarter (reduced by any credits allowed under subsections (e) and (f) of section 3111 of such Code, section 7001 of this Act, and section 303(d) of the Taxpayer Certainty and Disaster Tax Relief Act of 2020, for such quarter) on the wages paid with respect to the employment of all employees of the employer.

(3) REFUNDABILITY OF EXCESS CREDIT.—

(A) CREDIT IS REFUNDABLE.—If the amount of the credit under subsection (a) exceeds the limitation of paragraph (2) for any calendar quarter, such excess shall be treated as an overpayment that shall be refunded under sections 6402(a) and 6413(b) of such Code.

(B) ADVANCING CREDIT.—In anticipation of the credit, including the refundable portion under subparagraph (A), the credit may be advanced, according to forms and instructions provided by the Secretary, up to an amount calculated under subsection (a), subject to the limits under subsection (b), both calculated through the end of the most recent payroll period in the quarter.

(c) QUALIFIED FAMILY LEAVE WAGES.—For purposes of this section, the term "qualified family leave wages" means wages (as defined in section 3121(a) of such Code) and compensation (as defined in section 3231(e) of the Internal Revenue Code, determined without regard to the sentence in paragraph (1) thereof which begins "Such term does not include remuneration") and without regard to section 7005(a) of this Act) paid by an employer—[P.L. 116-260, §288(a)(1)(A) and (b)(1), Div. N, amendments cannot be made because the text "as defined in section 3121(a) of the Internal Revenue Code of 1986" does not exist.—CCH]

(1) which are required to be paid by reason of the Emergency Family and Medical Leave Expansion Act (including the amendments made by such Act), or

(2) both—

(A) which would be so required to be paid if section 102(a)(1)(F) of the Family and Medical Leave Act of 1993, as amended by the Emergency Family and Medical Leave Expansion Act, were applied by substituting "March 31, 2021" for "December 31, 2020", and

(B) with respect to which all requirements of the Family and Medical Leave Act of 1993 (other than section 107 thereof, and determined by substituting "To be compliant with section 102(a)(1)(F), an employer may not" for "It shall be unlawful for any employer to" each place it appears in subsection (a) of section 105 thereof, by substituting "made unlawful in this title or described in this section" for "made unlawful by this title", in paragraph (2) of such subsection, and by substituting "To be compliant with section 102(a)(1)(F), an employer may not" for "It shall be unlawful for any person to" in subsection (b) of such section) which relate to such section 102(a)(1)(F), and which would apply if so required, are satisfied.

(d) ALLOWANCE OF CREDIT FOR CERTAIN HEALTH PLAN EXPENSES.—

(1) IN GENERAL.—The amount of the credit allowed under subsection (a) shall be increased by so much of the employer's qualified health plan expenses as are properly allocable to the qualified family leave wages for which such credit is so allowed.

(2) QUALIFIED HEALTH PLAN EXPENSES.—For purposes of this subsection, the term "qualified health plan expenses" means amounts paid or incurred by the employer to provide and maintain a group health plan (as defined in section 5000(b)(1) of the Internal Revenue Code of 1986), but only to the extent that such amounts are excluded from the gross income of employees by reason of section 106(a) of such Code.

(3) ALLOCATION RULES.—For purposes of this section, qualified health plan expenses shall be allocated to qualified family leave wages in such manner as the Secretary of the Treasury (or the Secretary's delegate) may prescribe. Except as otherwise provided by the Secretary, such allocation shall be treated as properly made if made on the basis of being pro rata among covered employees and pro rata on the basis of periods of coverage (relative to the time periods of leave to which such wages relate).

(e) SPECIAL RULES.—

(1) DENIAL OF DOUBLE BENEFIT.—For purposes of chapter 1 of such Code, the gross income of the employer, for the taxable year which includes the last day of any calendar quarter with respect to which a credit is allowed under this section, shall be increased by the amount of such credit. Any wages taken into account in determining the credit allowed under this section shall not be taken into account for purposes of determining the credit allowed under section 45S of such Code.

(2) ELECTION NOT TO HAVE SECTION APPLY.—This section shall not apply with respect to any employer for any calendar quarter if such employer elects (at such time and in such manner as the Secretary of the Treasury (or the Secretary's delegate) may prescribe) not to have this section apply.

(3) CERTAIN TERMS.—Except as otherwise provided in this section, any term used in this section which is also used in chapter 21 of such Code shall have the same meaning as when used in such chapter.

(4) CERTAIN GOVERNMENTAL EMPLOYERS.—This credit shall not apply to the Government of the United States, the government of any State or political subdivision thereof, or any agency or instrumentality of any of the foregoing.

(4) [(5)] REFERENCES TO RAILROAD RETIREMENT TAX.—Any reference in this section to the tax imposed by section 3221(a) of the Internal Revenue Code of 1986 shall be treated as a reference to so much of such tax as is attributable to the rate in effect under section 3111(a) of such Code.

(f) REGULATIONS.—The Secretary of the Treasury (or the Secretary's delegate) shall prescribe such regulations or other guidance as may be necessary to carry out the purposes of this section, including—

(1) regulations or other guidance to prevent the avoidance of the purposes of the limitations under this section,

(2) regulations or other guidance to minimize compliance and record-keeping burdens under this section,

(3) regulations or other guidance providing for waiver of penalties for failure to deposit amounts in anticipation of the allowance of the credit allowed under this section,

(4) regulations or other guidance for recapturing the benefit of credits determined under this section in cases where there is a subsequent adjustment to the credit determined under subsection (a),

(5) regulations or other guidance to ensure that the wages taken into account under this section conform with the paid leave required to be provided under the Emergency Family and Medical Leave Expansion Act (including the amendments made by such Act), and

(6) regulations or other guidance to permit the advancement of the credit determined under subsection (a).

(g) APPLICATION OF SECTION.—This section shall apply only to wages paid with respect to the period beginning on a date selected by the Secretary of the Treasury (or the Secretary's delegate) which is during the 15-day period beginning on the date of the enactment of this Act, and ending on March 31, 2021.

* * *

(i) TREATMENT OF DEPOSITS.—The Secretary of the Treasury (or the Secretary's delegate) shall waive any penalty under section 6656 of the Internal Revenue Code of 1986 for any failure to make a deposit of the tax imposed by section 3111(a) or 3221(a) of such Code if the Secretary determines that such failure was due to the anticipation of the credit allowed under this section.

P.L. 116-127, §7005(a)-(b) (as amended by P.L. 116-260, §286(b)(5), Div. N, and §288(d)-(e), Div. N) provides:

SEC. 7005. SPECIAL RULE RELATED TO TAX ON EMPLOYERS.

(a) IN GENERAL.—Any wages required to be paid by reason of the Emergency Paid Sick Leave Act and the Emergency Family and Medical Leave Expansion Act (or, in the case of wages paid after December 31, 2020, and before April 1, 2021, with respect to which a credit is allowed under section 7001 or 7003) shall not be considered wages for purposes of section 3111(a) of the Internal Revenue Code of 1986 or compensation for purposes of section 3221(a) of such Code. Any reference in this subsection to the tax imposed by section 3221(a) of such Code shall be treated as a reference to so much of the tax as is attributable to the rate in effect under section 3111(a) of such Code.

EMPLOYMENT TAX—EMPLOYERS

(b) ALLOWANCE OF CREDIT FOR HOSPITAL INSURANCE TAXES.—

(1) IN GENERAL.—The credit allowed by section 7001 and the credit allowed by section 7003 shall each be increased by the amount of the tax imposed by section 3111(b) of the Internal Revenue Code of 1986 and so much of the taxes imposed under section 3221(a) of such Code as are attributable to the rate in effect under section 3111(b) of such Code on qualified sick leave wages, or qualified family leave wages, for which credit is allowed under such section 7001 or 7003 (respectively).

(2) DENIAL OF DOUBLE BENEFIT.—For denial of double benefit with respect to the credit increase under paragraph (1), see sections 7001(e)(1) and 7003(e)(1).

- **2014, Tax Technical Corrections Act of 2014 (P.L. 113-295)**

P.L. 113-295, §221(a)(99)(B)(i), Division A:

Amended Code Sec. 3111(a) by striking "the following percentages" and all that follows and inserting "6.2 percent of the wages (as defined in section 3121(a)) paid by the employer with respect to employment (as defined in section 3121(b))". **Effective** generally 12-19-2014. For a special rule, see Act Sec. 221(b)(2), Division A, below. Prior to amendment, Code Sec. 3111(a) read as follows:

(a) OLD-AGE, SURVIVORS, AND DISABILITY INSURANCE.—In addition to other taxes, there is hereby imposed on every employer an excise tax, with respect to having individuals in his employ, equal to the following percentages of the wages (as defined in section 3121(a)) paid by him with respect to employment (as defined in section 3121(b))—

In cases of wages paid during:	The rate shall be:
1984, 1985, 1986, or 1987	5.7 percent
1988 or 1989	6.06 percent
1990 or thereafter	6.2 percent.

P.L. 113-295, §221(b)(2), Division A, provides:

(2) SAVINGS PROVISION.—If—

(A) any provision amended or repealed by the amendments made by this section applied to—

(i) any transaction occurring before the date of the enactment of this Act,

(ii) any property acquired before such date of enactment, or

(iii) any item of income, loss, deduction, or credit taken into account before such date of enactment, and

(B) the treatment of such transaction, property, or item under such provision would (without regard to the amendments or repeals made by this section) affect the liability for tax for periods ending after date of enactment, nothing in the amendments or repeals made by this section shall be construed to affect the treatment of such transaction, property, or item for purposes of determining liability for tax for periods ending after such date of enactment.

- **1987, Revenue Act of 1987 (P.L. 100-203)**

P.L. 100-203, §9006(b)(1):

Amended Code Sec. 3111(a) by striking out "and (t)" after "section 3121(a)". **Effective** with respect to tips received (and wages paid) on and after 1-1-88.

- **1983, Social Security Amendments of 1983 (P.L. 98-21)**

P.L. 98-21, §123(a)(2):

Amended Code Sec. 3111(a) by striking out paragraphs (1) through (7) and inserting in lieu thereof a chart. **Effective** for remuneration paid after 12-31-83. Prior to amendment, Code Sec. 3111(a)(1)-(7) read as follows:

(1) with respect to wages paid during the calendar years 1974 through 1977, the rate shall be 4.95 percent;

(2) with respect to wages paid during the calendar year 1978, the rate shall be 5.05 percent;

(3) with respect to wages paid during the calendar years 1979 and 1980, the rate shall be 5.08 percent;

(4) with respect to wages paid during the calendar year 1981, the rate shall be 5.35 percent;

(5) with respect to wages paid during the calendar years 1982 through 1984, the rate shall be 5.40 percent;

(6) with respect to wages paid during the calendar years 1985 through 1989, the rate shall be 5.70 percent; and

(7) with respect to wages paid after December 31, 1989, the rate shall be 6.20 percent.

- **1977 (P.L. 95-216)**

P.L. 95-216, §101(a)(2):

Amended Code Sec. 3111(a)(1) and (2), and added paragraphs (3) through (7). **Effective** for remuneration paid or received, and tax years beginning after 1977. Prior to amendment, paragraphs (1) and (2) read as follows:

(1) with respect to wages paid during the calendar years 1974 through 2010, the rate shall be 4.95 percent; and

(2) with respect to wages paid after December 31, 2010, the rate shall be 5.95 percent.

P.L. 95-216, §315(b):

Amended Code Sec. 3111 by inserting "and (t)" after "3121(a)" in subsection (a). **Effective** for wages paid for employment performed after 1977.

- **1976, Tax Reform Act of 1976 (P.L. 94-455)**

P.L. 94-455, §1903(a)(1)(A), (d):

Deleted paragraphs (1), (2), (3), and (4) of Code Sec. 3111(a) and redesignated paragraphs (5) and (6) as paragraphs (1) and (2), respectively. **Effective** for wages paid after 12-31-76. Prior to amendment, paragraphs (1), (2), (3), and (4) read as follows:

(1) with respect to wages paid during the calendar year 1968, the rate shall be 3.8 percent;

(2) with respect to wages paid during the calendar years 1969 and 1970, the rate shall be 4.2 percent;

(3) with respect to wages paid during the calendar years 1971 and 1972, the rate shall be 4.6 percent;

(4) with respect to wages paid during the calendar year 1973, the rate shall be 4.85 percent;

- **1973 (P.L. 93-233)**

P.L. 93-233, §6(a)(2):

Amended Code Sec. 3111(a)(2)-(5). **Effective** for remuneration paid after 1973. Prior to amendment, Code Sec. 3111(a)(2)-(5) read as follows:

"(4) with respect to wages paid during the calendar years 1973, 1974, 1975, 1976, and 1977, the rate shall be 4.85%;

"(5) with respect to wages paid during the calendar years 1978 through 2010, the rate shall be 4.80 percent; and

"(6) with respect to wages paid after December 31, 2010, the rate shall be 5.85 percent."

- **1972, Social Security Amendments of 1972 (P.L. 92-336)**

P.L. 92-336, §204(a)(3):

Amended Sec. 3111(a)(3)-(5). **Effective** only for remuneration paid after 12-31-72. Prior to amendment Sec. 3111(a)(3)-(5) read as follows:

"(3) with respect to wages paid during the calendar years 1971 and 1972, the rate shall be 4.6 percent;

"(4) with respect to wages paid during the calendar years 1973, 1974, and 1975, the rate shall be 5.0 percent; and

"(5) with respect to wages paid after December 31, 1975, the rate shall be 5.15 percent."

- **1971 (P.L. 92-5)**

P.L. 92-5, §204(a)(2):

Amended Sec. 3111(a) by amending subparagraph (4) and by adding subparagraph (5). **Effective** for remuneration paid after 12-31-71. Prior to amendment, subparagraph (4) read as follows:

"(4) with respect to wages paid after December 31, 1972, the rate shall be 5.0 percent."

[Sec. 3111(b)]

(b) HOSPITAL INSURANCE.—In addition to the tax imposed by the preceding subsection, there is hereby imposed on every employer an excise tax, with respect to having individuals in his employ, equal to 1.45 percent of the wages (as defined in section 3121(a)) paid by the employer with respect to employment (as defined in section 3121(b)).

Amendments

- **2014, Tax Technical Corrections Act of 2014 (P.L. 113-295)**

P.L. 113-295, §221(a)(99)(B)(ii), Division A:

Amended Code Sec. 3111(b) by striking "the following percentages" and all that follows and inserting "1.45 percent of the wages (as defined in section 3121(a)) paid by the employer with respect to employment (as defined in section 3121(b)).". **Effective** generally 12-19-2014. For a special rule, see Act Sec. 221(b)(2), Division A, below. Prior to amendment, Code Sec. 3111(b) read as follows:

(b) HOSPITAL INSURANCE.—In addition to the tax imposed by the preceding subsection, there is hereby imposed on every employer an excise tax, with respect to having individuals in his employ, equal to the following percentages of the wages (as defined in section 3121(a)) paid by him with respect to employment (as defined in section 3121(b))—

(1) with respect to wages paid during the calendar years 1974 through 1977, the rate shall be 0.90 percent;

(2) with respect to wages paid during the calendar year 1978, the rate shall be 1.00 percent;

(3) with respect to wages paid during the calendar years 1979 and 1980, the rate shall be 1.05 percent;

(4) with respect to wages paid during the calendar years 1981 through 1984, the rate shall be 1.30 percent;

(5) with respect to wages paid during the calendar year 1985, the rate shall be 1.35 percent; and

(6) with respect to wages paid after December 31, 1985, the rate shall be 1.45 percent.

P.L. 113-295, §221(b)(2), Division A, provides:

(2) SAVINGS PROVISION.—If—

(A) any provision amended or repealed by the amendments made by this section applied to—

(i) any transaction occurring before the date of the enactment of this Act,

(ii) any property acquired before such date of enactment, or

(iii) any item of income, loss, deduction, or credit taken into account before such date of enactment, and

(B) the treatment of such transaction, property, or item under such provision would (without regard to the amendments or repeals made by this section) affect the liability for tax for periods ending after date of enactment, nothing in the amendments or repeals made by this section shall be construed to affect the treatment of such transaction, property, or item for purposes of determining liability for tax for periods ending after such date of enactment.

• **1987, Revenue Act of 1987 (P.L. 100-203)**

P.L. 100-203, § 9006(b)(1):

Amended Code Sec. 3111(b) by striking out "and (t)" after "section 3121(a)". **Effective** with respect to tips received (and wages paid) on and after 1-1-88.

• **1977 (P.L.95-216)**

P.L. 95-216, § 101(b)(2):

Amended paragraphs (1) through (4), and added (5) and (6). **Effective** for remuneration paid or received, and tax years beginning, after 1977. Before amendment, paragraphs (1) through (4) read as follows:

(1) with respect to wages paid during the calendar years 1974 through 1977, the rate shall be 0.90 percent;

(2) with respect to wages paid during the calendar years 1978 through 1980, the rate shall be 1.10 percent;

(3) with respect to wages paid during the calendar years 1981 through 1985, the rate shall be 1.35 percent; and

(4) with respect to wages paid after December 31, 1985, the rate shall be 1.50 percent.

P.L. 95-216, § 315(b):

Amended Code Sec. 3111 by inserting "and (t)" after "3121(a)" in subsection (b). **Effective** for wages paid for employment performed after 1977.

• **1976, Tax Reform Act of 1976 (P.L. 94-455)**

P.L. 94-455, § 1903(a)(1)(B), (d):

Deleted paragraphs (1) and (2) of Code Sec. 3111(b) and redesignated paragraphs (3), (4), (5), and (6) as paragraphs (1), (2), (3), and (4), respectively. **Effective** for wages paid after 12-31-76. Prior to amendment, paragraphs (1) and (2) read as follows:

(1) with respect to wages paid during the calendar years 1968, 1969, 1970, 1971, and 1972, the rate shall be 0.60 percent;

(2) with respect to wages paid during the calendar year 1973, the rate shall be 1.0 percent;

• **1973 (P.L. 93-233)**

P.L. 93-233, § 6(b)(3):

Amended paragraphs (2) through (5) (plus new paragraph (6)) of Code Sec. 3111(b). **Effective** for remuneration paid after 1973. Prior to amendment, Code Sec. 3111(b)(2)-(5) read as follows:

"(2) with respect to wages paid during the calendar years 1973, 1974, 1975, 1976, and 1977, the rate shall be 1.0 percent;

"(3) with respect to wages received during the calendar years 1978, 1979, and 1980, the rate shall be 1.25 percent;

"(4) with respect to wages received during the calendar years 1981, 1982, 1983, 1984, and 1985, the rate shall be 1.35 percent; and

"(5) with respect to wages received after December 31, 1985, the rate shall be 1.45 percent."

• **1972, Social Security Amendments of 1972 (P.L. 92-603)**

P.L. 92-603, §§ 135(a)(3), 135(b)(3):

Amended Code Sec. 3111. **Effective** for remuneration paid after 12-31-72. Prior to amendment, said section read as follows:

"SEC. 3111. RATE OF TAX.

"(a) Old-Age, Survivors, and Disability Insurance.—In addition to other taxes, there is hereby imposed on every employer an excise tax, with respect to having individuals in his employ, equal to the following percentages of the wages (as defined in section 3121(a)) paid by him with respect to employment (as defined in section 3121(b))—

"(1) with respect to wages paid during the calendar year 1968, the rate shall be 3.8 percent;

"(2) with respect to wages paid during the calendar years 1969 and 1970, the rate shall be 4.2 percent;

"(3) with respect to wages paid during any of the calendar years 1971 through 1977, the rate shall be 4.6 percent;

"(4) with respect to wages paid during any of the calendar years 1978 through 2010, the rate shall be 4.5 percent; and

"(5) with respect to wages paid after December 31, 2010, the rate shall be 5.35 percent.

"(b) Hospital Insurance.—In addition to the tax imposed by the preceding subsection, there is hereby imposed on every employer an excise tax, with respect to having individuals in his employ, equal to the following percentages of the wages (as defined in section 3121(a)) paid by him with respect to employment (as defined in section 3121(b))—

"(1) with respect to wages paid during the calendar years 1968, 1969, 1970, 1971, and 1972, the rate shall be 0.60 percent;

"(2) with respect to wages paid during the calendar years 1973, 1974, 1975, 1976, and 1977, the rate shall be 0.9 percent;

"(3) with respect to wages paid during the calendar years 1978, 1979, 1980, 1981, 1982, 1983, 1984, and 1985, the rate shall be 1.0 percent;

"(4) with respect to wages paid during the calendar years 1986, 1987, 1988, 1989, 1990, 1991, and 1992, the rate shall be 1.1 percent; and

"(5) with respect to wages paid after December 31, 1992, the rate shall be 1.2 percent."

• **1972, Social Security Amendments of 1972 (P.L. 92-336)**

P.L. 92-336, § 204(a)(3):

Amended Sec. 3111(b)(2)-(5). **Effective** only for remuneration paid after 12-31-72. Prior to amendment Sec. 3111(b)(2)-(5) read as follows:

"(2) with respect to wages paid during the calendar years 1973, 1974, and 1975, the rate shall be 0.65 percent;

"(3) with respect to wages paid during the calendar years 1976, 1977, 1978, and 1979, the rate shall be 0.70 percent;

"(4) with respect to wages paid during the calendar years 1980, 1981, 1982, 1983, 1984, 1985, and 1986, the rate shall be 0.80 percent; and

"(5) with respect to wages paid after December 31, 1986, the rate shall be 0.90 percent."

• **1968, Social Security Amendments of 1967 (P.L. 90-248)**

P.L. 90-248, § 109(a)(3), (b)(3):

Amended Sec. 3111. **Effective** only with respect to remuneration paid after 12-31-67. Prior to amendment, Sec. 3111 read as follows:

"SEC. 3111. RATE OF TAX.

"(a) Old-Age, Survivors, and Disability Insurance.—In addition to other taxes, there is hereby imposed on every employer an excise tax, with respect to having individuals in his employ, equal to the following percentages of the wages (as defined in section 3121(a)) paid by him with respect to employment (as defined in section 3121(b))—

"(1) with respect to wages paid during the calendar year 1966, the rate shall be 3.85 percent;

"(2) with respect to wages paid during the calendar years 1967 and 1968, the rate shall be 3.9 percent;

"(3) with respect to wages paid during the calendar years 1969, 1970, 1971, and 1972, the rate shall be 4.4 percent; and

"(4) with respect to wages paid after December 31, 1972, the rate shall be 4.85 percent.

"(b) Hospital Insurance.—In addition to the tax imposed by the preceding subsection, there is hereby imposed on every employer an excise tax, with respect to having individuals in his employ, equal to the following percentages of the wages (as defined in section 3121(a)) paid by him with respect to employment (as defined in section 3121(b))—

"(1) with respect to wages paid during the calendar year 1966, the rate shall be 0.35 percent;

"(2) with respect to wages paid during the calendar years 1967, 1968, 1969, 1970, 1971, and 1972, the rate shall be 0.50 percent;

"(3) with respect to wages paid during the calendar years 1973, 1974, and 1975, the rate shall be 0.55 percent;

"(4) with respect to wages paid during the calendar years 1976, 1977, 1978, and 1979, the rate shall be 0.60 percent;

"(5) with respect to wages paid during the calendar years 1980, 1981, 1982, 1983, 1984, 1985, and 1986, the rate shall be 0.70 percent;

"(6) with respect to wages paid after December 31, 1986, the rate shall be 0.80 percent."

• **1965, Social Security Amendments of 1965 (P.L. 89-97)**

P.L. 89-97, § 320(c):

Amended Sec. 3111. **Effective** with respect to remuneration paid after 12-31-65. Prior to amendment, Sec. 3111 read as follows:

"SEC. 3111. RATE OF TAX.

"In addition to other taxes, there is hereby imposed on every employer an excise tax, with respect to having individuals in his employ, equal to the following percentages of the wages (as defined in section 3121(a)) paid by him with respect to employment (as defined in section 3121(b))—

"(1) with respect to wages paid during the calendar year 1962, the rate shall be $3^1/8$ percent;

"(2) with respect to wages paid during the calendar years 1963 to 1965, both inclusive, the rate shall be $3^5/8$ percent;

"(3) with respect to wages paid during the calendar years 1966 to 1967, both inclusive, the rate shall be $4^1/8$ percent; and

"(4) with respect to wages paid after December 31, 1967, the rate shall be $4^5/8$ percent."

• **1961, Social Security Amendments of 1961 (P.L. 87-64)**

P.L. 87-64, § 201(c):

Amended Code Sec. 3111. **Effective** for remuneration paid after 1961. Prior to amendment, Sec. 3111 read as follows:

"SEC. 3111. RATE OF TAX.

"In addition to other taxes, there is hereby imposed on every employer an excise tax with respect to having individuals in his employ, equal to the following percentages of the wages (as defined in section 3121(a)) paid by him with respect to employment (as defined in section 3121(b))—

"(1) with respect to wages paid during the calendar year 1959, the rate shall be $2^1/2$ percent;

"(2) with respect to wages paid during the calendar years 1960 to 1962, both inclusive, the rate shall be 3 percent;

"(3) with respect to wages paid during the calendar years 1963 to 1965, both inclusive, the rate shall be $3^1/2$ percent;

EMPLOYMENT TAX—EMPLOYERS

"(4) with respect to wages paid during the calendar years 1966 to 1968, both inclusive, the rate shall be 4 percent; and

"(5) with respect to wages paid after December 31, 1968, the rate shall be $4^{1}/_{2}$ percent."

• **1958, Social Security Amendments of 1958 (P.L. 85-840)**

P.L. 85-840, §401(c):

Amended Sec. 3111. **Effective** for remuneration paid after 12-31-58. Prior to amendment, Sec. 3111 read as follows:

"SEC. 3111. RATE OF TAX.

"In addition to other taxes, there is hereby imposed on every employer an excise tax, with respect to having individuals in his employ, equal to the following percentages of the wages (as defined in section 3121(a)) paid by him with respect to employment (as defined in section 3121(b))—

"(1) with respect to wages paid during the calendar years 1957 to 1959, both inclusive, the rate shall be $2^{1}/_{4}$ percent;

"(2) with respect to wages paid during the calendar years 1960 to 1964, both inclusive, the rate shall be $2^{3}/_{4}$ percent;

"(3) with respect to wages paid during the calendar years 1965 to 1969, both inclusive, the rate shall be $3^{1}/_{4}$ percent;

"(4) with respect to wages paid during the calendar years 1970 to 1974, both inclusive, the rate shall be $3^{3}/_{4}$ percent; and

"(5) with respect to wages paid after December 31, 1974, the rate shall be $4^{1}/_{4}$ percent."

• **1956, Social Security Amendments of 1956 (P.L. 880, 84th Cong.)**

P.L. 880, 84th Cong., §202(c):

Amended Sec. 3111 to read as reproduced in the amendment note for P.L. 85-840. **Effective** for remuneration paid after 12-31-56. Prior to amendment, Sec. 3111 read as follows:

"SEC. 3111. RATE OF TAX.

"In addition to other taxes, there is hereby imposed on every employer an excise tax, with respect to having individuals in his employ, equal to the following percentages of the wages (as defined in section 3121(a)) paid by him with respect to employment (as defined in section 3121(b))—

"(1) with respect to wages paid during the calendar years 1955 to 1959, both inclusive, the rate shall be 2 percent;

"(2) with respect to wages paid during the calendar years 1960 to 1964, both inclusive, the rate shall be $2^{1}/_{2}$ percent;

"(3) with respect to wages paid during the calendar years 1965 to 1969, both inclusive, the rate shall be 3 percent;

"(4) with respect to wages paid during the calendar years 1970 to 1974, both inclusive, the rate shall be $3^{1}/_{2}$ percent; and

"(5) with respect to wages paid after December 31, 1974, the rate shall be 4 percent."

• **1954, Social Security Amendments of 1954 (P.L. 761, 83rd Cong.)**

P.L. 761, 83rd Cong., §208(c):

Amended Sec. 3111. **Effective** 9-1-54. Prior to amendment, Sec. 3111 read as follows:

"SEC. 3111. RATE OF TAX.

"In addition to other taxes, there is hereby imposed on every employer an excise tax, with respect to having individuals in his employ, equal to the following percentages of the wages (as defined in section 3121(a)) paid by him with respect to employment (as defined in section 3121(b))—

"(1) with respect to wages paid during the calendar years 1955 to 1959, both inclusive, the rate shall be 2 percent;

"(2) with respect to wages paid during the calendar years 1960 to 1964, both inclusive, the rate shall be $2^{1}/_{2}$ percent;

"(3) with respect to wages paid during the calendar years 1965 to 1969, both inclusive, the rate shall be 3 percent;

"(4) with respect to wages paid after December 31, 1969, the rate shall be $3^{1}/_{4}$ percent."

[Sec. 3111(c)]

(c) RELIEF FROM TAXES IN CASES COVERED BY CERTAIN INTERNATIONAL AGREEMENTS.—During any period in which there is in effect an agreement entered into pursuant to section 233 of the Social Security Act with any foreign country, wages received by or paid to an individual shall be exempt from the taxes imposed by this section to the extent that such wages are subject under such agreement exclusively to the laws applicable to the social security system of such foreign country.

Amendments

• **2004, Social Security Protection Act of 2004 (P.L. 108-203)**

P.L. 108-203, §415:

Amended Code Sec. 3111(c) by striking "to taxes or contributions for similar purposes under" and inserting "exclusively to the laws applicable to". **Effective** 3-2-2004.

• **1977 (P.L. 95-216)**

P.L. 95-216, §317(b)(2):

Added Code Sec. 3111(c). **Effective** 12-20-77.

[Sec. 3111(d)—Stricken]

Amendments

• **2018, Tax Technical Corrections Act of 2018 (P.L. 115-141)**

P.L. 115-141, §401(b)(34), Div. U:

Amended Code Sec. 3111 by striking subsection (d). **Effective** 3-23-2018. For a special rule, see Act Sec. 401(e), Div. U, below. Prior to being stricken, Code Sec. 3111(d) read as follows:

(d) SPECIAL EXEMPTION FOR CERTAIN INDIVIDUALS HIRED IN 2010.—

(1) IN GENERAL.—Subsection (a) shall not apply to wages paid by a qualified employer with respect to employment during the period beginning on the day after the date of the enactment of this subsection and ending on December 31, 2010, of any qualified individual for services performed—

(A) in a trade or business of such qualified employer, or

(B) in the case of a qualified employer exempt from tax under section 501(a), in furtherance of the activities related to the purpose or function constituting the basis of the employer's exemption under section 501.

(2) QUALIFIED EMPLOYER.—For purposes of this subsection—

(A) IN GENERAL.—The term "qualified employer" means any employer other than the United States, any State, or any political subdivision thereof, or any instrumentality of the foregoing.

(B) TREATMENT OF EMPLOYEES OF POSTSECONDARY EDUCATIONAL INSTITUTIONS.—Notwithstanding subparagraph (A), the term "qualified employer" includes any employer which is a public institution of higher education (as defined in section 101(b) of the Higher Education Act of 1965).

(3) QUALIFIED INDIVIDUAL.—For purposes of this subsection, the term "qualified individual" means any individual who—

(A) begins employment with a qualified employer after February 3, 2010, and before January 1, 2011,

(B) certifies by signed affidavit, under penalties of perjury, that such individual has not been employed for more than 40 hours during the 60-day period ending on the date such individual begins such employment,

(C) is not employed by the qualified employer to replace another employee of such employer unless such other employee separated from employment voluntarily or for cause, and

(D) is not an individual described in section 51(i)(1) (applied by substituting "qualified employer" for "taxpayer" each place it appears).

(4) ELECTION.—A qualified employer may elect to have this subsection not apply. Such election shall be made in such manner as the Secretary may require.

(5) SPECIAL RULE FOR FIRST CALENDAR QUARTER OF 2010.—

(A) NONAPPLICATION OF EXEMPTION DURING FIRST QUARTER.—Paragraph (1) shall not apply with respect to wages paid during the first calendar quarter of 2010.

(B) CREDITING OF FIRST QUARTER EXEMPTION DURING SECOND QUARTER.—The amount by which the tax imposed under subsection (a) would (but for subparagraph (A)) have been reduced with respect to wages paid by a qualified employer during the first calendar quarter of 2010 shall be treated as a payment against the tax imposed under subsection (a) with respect to the qualified employer for the second calendar quarter of 2010 which is made on the date that such tax is due.

P.L. 115-141, §401(e), Div. U, provides:

(e) GENERAL SAVINGS PROVISION WITH RESPECT TO DEADWOOD PROVISIONS.—If—

(1) any provision amended or repealed by the amendments made by subsection (b) or (d) applied to—

(A) any transaction occurring before the date of the enactment of this Act,

(B) any property acquired before such date of enactment, or

(C) any item of income, loss, deduction, or credit taken into account before such date of enactment, and

(2) the treatment of such transaction, property, or item under such provision would (without regard to the amendments or repeals made by such subsection) affect the liability for tax for periods ending after such date of enactment,

nothing in the amendments or repeals made by this section shall be construed to affect the treatment of such transaction, property, or item for purposes of determining liability for tax for periods ending after such date of enactment.

• **2010, Hiring Incentives to Restore Employment Act (P.L. 111-147)**

P.L. 111-147, §101(a):

Amended Code Sec. 3111 by adding at the end a new subsection (d). **Effective** for wages paid after 3-18-2010.

[Sec. 3111(e)]

(e) CREDIT FOR EMPLOYMENT OF QUALIFIED VETERANS.—

(1) IN GENERAL.—If a qualified tax-exempt organization hires a qualified veteran with respect to whom a credit would be allowable under section 38 by reason of section 51 if the organization were not a qualified tax-exempt organization, then there shall be allowed as a credit

against the tax imposed by subsection (a) on wages paid with respect to employment of all employees of the organization during the applicable period an amount equal to the credit determined under section 51 (after application of the modifications under paragraph (3)) with respect to wages paid to such qualified veteran during such period.

(2) OVERALL LIMITATION.—The aggregate amount allowed as a credit under this subsection for all qualified veterans for any period with respect to which tax is imposed under subsection (a) shall not exceed the amount of the tax imposed by subsection (a) on wages paid with respect to employment of all employees of the organization during such period.

(3) MODIFICATIONS.—For purposes of paragraph (1), section 51 shall be applied—

(A) by substituting "26 percent" for "40 percent" in subsection (a) thereof,

(B) by substituting "16.25 percent" for "25 percent" in subsection (i)(3)(A) thereof, and

(C) by only taking into account wages paid to a qualified veteran for services in furtherance of the activities related to the purpose or function constituting the basis of the organization's exemption under section 501.

(4) APPLICABLE PERIOD.—The term "applicable period" means, with respect to any qualified veteran, the 1-year period beginning with the day such qualified veteran begins work for the organization.

(5) DEFINITIONS.—For purposes of this subsection—

(A) the term "qualified tax-exempt organization" means an employer that is an organization described in section 501(c) and exempt from taxation under section 501(a), and

(B) the term "qualified veteran" has the meaning given such term by section 51(d)(3).

Amendments

• **2018, Tax Technical Corrections Act of 2018 (P.L. 115-141)**

P.L. 115-141, §401(a)(208), Div. U:

Amended Code Sec. 3111(e)(5)(B) by inserting "the" before "meaning". **Effective** 3-23-2018.

• **2011, VOW to Hire Heroes Act of 2011 (P.L. 112-56)**

P.L. 112-56, §261(e)(2):

Amended Code Sec. 3111 by adding at the end a new subsection (e). **Effective** for individuals who begin work for the employer after 11-21-2011.

[Sec. 3111(f)]

(f) CREDIT FOR RESEARCH EXPENDITURES OF QUALIFIED SMALL BUSINESSES.—

(1) IN GENERAL.—In the case of a taxpayer who has made an election under section 41(h) for a taxable year—

(A) there shall be allowed as a credit against the tax imposed by subsection (a) for the first calendar quarter which begins after the date on which the taxpayer files the return specified in section 41(h)(4)(A)(ii) an amount equal to so much of the payroll tax credit portion determined under section 41(h)(2) as does not exceed the limitation of subclause (I) of section 41(h)(4)(B)(i) (applied without regard to subclause (II) thereof), and

(B) there shall be allowed as a credit against the tax imposed by subsection (b) for the first calendar quarter which begins after the date on which the taxpayer files the return specified in section 41(h)(4)(A)(ii) an amount equal to so much of the payroll tax credit portion determined under section 41(h)(2) as is not allowed as a credit under subparagraph (A).

(2) LIMITATION.—The credit allowed by paragraph (1)(A) shall not exceed the tax imposed by subsection (a) for any calendar quarter, and the credit allowed by paragraph (1)(B) shall not exceed the tax imposed by subsection (b) for any calendar quarter, on the wages paid with respect to the employment of all individuals in the employ of the employer.

(3) CARRYOVER OF UNUSED CREDIT.—If the amount of any credit under paragraph (1) exceeds the limitation of paragraph (2) for any calendar quarter, such excess shall be carried to the succeeding calendar quarter and allowed as a credit under paragraph (1) for such quarter.

(4) DEDUCTION ALLOWED FOR CREDITED AMOUNTS.—The credits allowed under paragraph (1) shall not be taken into account for purposes of determining the amount of any deduction allowed under chapter 1 for taxes imposed under subsection (a) or (b).

Amendments

• **2022, Inflation Reduction Act of 2022 (P.L. 117-169)**

P.L. 117-169, §13902(b)(1)(A)-(D):

Amended Code Sec. 3111(f)(1) by striking "for a taxable year, there shall be allowed" and inserting "for a taxable year—

(A) there shall be allowed",

by striking "equal to the" and inserting "equal to so much of the", by striking the period at the end and inserting "as does not exceed the limitation of subclause (I) of section 41(h)(4)(B)(i) (applied without regard to subclause (II) thereof), and", and by adding at the end a new subparagraph (B). **Effective** for tax years beginning after 12-31-2022.

P.L. 117-169, §13902(b)(2)(A)-(B):

Amended Code Sec. 3111(f)(2) by striking "paragraph (1)" and inserting "paragraph (1)(A)", and by inserting ", and the credit allowed by paragraph (1)(B) shall not exceed the tax imposed by subsection (b) for any calendar quarter," after "calendar quarter". **Effective** for tax years beginning after 12-31-2022.

P.L. 117-169, §13902(b)(3):

Amended Code Sec. 3111(f)(3) by striking "the credit" and inserting "any credit". **Effective** for tax years beginning after 12-31-2022.

P.L. 117-169, §13902(b)(4)(A)-(B):

Amended Code Sec. 3111(f)(4) by striking "credit" and inserting "credits", and by striking "subsection (a)" and inserting "subsection (a) or (b)". **Effective** for tax years beginning after 12-31-2022.

• **2015, Protecting Americans from Tax Hikes Act of 2015 (P.L. 114-113)**

P.L. 114-113, §121(c)(2), Div. Q:

Amended Code Sec. 3111 by adding at the end a new subsection (f). **Effective** for tax years beginning after 12-31-2015.

[Sec. 3112]

SEC. 3112. INSTRUMENTALITIES OF THE UNITED STATES.

Notwithstanding any other provision of law (whether enacted before or after the enactment of this section) which grants to any instrumentality of the United States an exemption from taxation, such instrumentality shall not be exempt from the tax imposed by section 3111 unless such other provision of law grants a specific exemption, by reference to section 3111 (or the corresponding section of prior law), from the tax imposed by such section.

Subchapter C—General Provisions

Sec. 3121.	Definitions.
Sec. 3122.	Federal service.
Sec. 3123.	Deductions as constructive payments.
Sec. 3124.	Estimate of revenue reduction.
Sec. 3125.	Returns in the case of governmental employees in States, Guam, American Samoa, and the District of Columbia.
Sec. 3126.	Return and payment by governmental employer.
Sec. 3127.	Exemption for employers and their employees where both are members of religious faiths opposed to participation in social security act programs.
Sec. 3128.	Short title.

EMPLOYMENT TAX—GENERAL PROVISIONS

[Sec. 3121]

SEC. 3121. DEFINITIONS.

[Sec. 3121(a)]

(a) WAGES.—For purposes of this chapter, the term "wages" means all remuneration for employment, including the cash value of all remuneration (including benefits) paid in any medium other than cash; except that such term shall not include—

(1) in the case of taxes imposed by sections 3101(a) and 3111(a) that part of the remuneration which, after remuneration (other than remuneration referred to in the succeeding paragraphs of this subsection) equal to the contribution and benefit base (as determined under section 230 of the Social Security Act) with respect to employment has been paid to an individual by an employer during the calendar year with respect to which such contribution and benefit base is effective, is paid to such individual by such employer during such calendar year. If an employer (hereinafter referred to as successor employer) during any calendar year acquires substantially all the property used in a trade or business of another employer (hereinafter referred to as a predecessor), or used in a separate unit of a trade or business of a predecessor, and immediately after the acquisition employs in his trade or business an individual who immediately prior to the acquisition was employed in the trade or business of such predecessor, then, for the purpose of determining whether the successor employer has paid remuneration (other than remuneration referred to in the succeeding paragraphs of this subsection) with respect to employment equal to the contribution and benefit base (as determined under section 230 of the Social Security Act) to such individual during such calendar year, any remuneration (other than remuneration referred to in the succeeding paragraph of this subsection) with respect to employment paid (or considered under this paragraph as having been paid) to such individual by such predecessor during such calendar year and prior to such acquisition shall be considered as having been paid by such successor employer;

(2) the amount of any payment (including any amount paid by an employer for insurance or annuities, or into a fund, to provide for any such payment) made to, or on behalf of, an employee or any of his dependents under a plan or system established by an employer which makes provision for his employees generally (or for his employees generally and their dependents) or for a class or classes of his employees (or for a class or classes of his employees and their dependents), on account of—

(A) sickness or accident disability (but, in the case of payments made to an employee or any of his dependents, this subparagraph shall exclude from the term "wages" only payments which are received under a workmen's compensation law), or

(B) medical or hospitalization expenses in connection with sickness or accident disability, or

(C) death, except that this paragraph does not apply to a payment for group-term life insurance to the extent that such payment is includible in the gross income of the employee,

(3) [Stricken.]

(4) any payment on account of sickness or accident disability, or medical or hospitalization expenses in connection with sickness or accident disability, made by an employer to, or on behalf of, an employee after the expiration of 6 calendar months following the last calendar month in which the employee worked for such employer;

(5) any payment made to, or on behalf of, an employee or his beneficiary—

(A) from or to a trust described in section 401(a) which is exempt from tax under section 501(a) at the time of such payment unless such payment is made to an employee of the trust as remuneration for services rendered as such employee and not as a beneficiary of the trust,

(B) under or to an annuity plan which, at the time of such payment, is a plan described in section 403(a),

(C) under a simplified employee pension (as defined in section 408(k)(1)), other than any contributions described in section 408(k)(6),

(D) under or to an annuity contract described in section 403(b), other than a payment for the purchase of such contract which is made by reason of a salary reduction agreement (whether evidenced by a written instrument or otherwise),

(E) under or to an exempt governmental deferred compensation plan (as defined in subsection (v)(3)),

(F) to supplement pension bnefits under a plan or trust described in any of the foregoing provisions of this paragraph to take into account some portion or all of the increase in the cost of living (as determined by the Secretary of Labor) since retirement but only if such supplemental payments are under a plan which is treated as a welfare plan under section 3(2)(B)(ii) of the Employee Retirement Income Security Act of 1974,

(G) under a cafeteria plan (within the meaning of section 125) if such payment would not be treated as wages without regard to such plan and it is reasonable to believe that (if section 125 applied for purposes of this section) section 125 would not treat any wages as constructively received,

(H) under an arrangement to which section 408(p) applies, other than any elective contributions under paragraph (2)(A)(i) thereof, or

(I) under a plan described in section 457(e)(11)(A)(ii) and maintained by an eligible employer (as defined in section 457(e)(1));

(6) the payment by an employer (without deduction from the remuneration of the employee)—

(A) of the tax imposed upon an employee under section 3101, or

(B) of any payment required from an employee under a State unemployment compensation law,

with respect to remuneration paid to an employee for domestic service in a private home of the employer or for agricultural labor;

(7)(A) remuneration paid in any medium other than cash to an employee for service not in the course of the employer's trade or business or for domestic service in a private home of the employer;

(B) cash remuneration paid by an employer in any calendar year to an employee for domestic service in a private home of the employer (including domestic service on a farm operated for profit), if the cash remuneration paid in such year by the employer to the employee for such service is less than the applicable dollar threshold (as defined in subsection (x)) for such year;

(C) cash remuneration paid by an employer in any calendar year to an employee for service not in the course of the employer's trade or business, if the cash remuneration paid in such year by the employer to the employee for such service is less than $100. As used in this subparagraph, the term "service not in the course of the employer's trade or business" does not include domestic service in a private home of the employer and does not include service described in subsection (g) (5);

(8)(A) remuneration paid in any medium other than cash for agricultural labor;

(B) cash remuneration paid by an employer in any calendar year to an employee for agricultural labor unless—

(i) the cash remuneration paid in such year by the employer to the employee for such labor is $150 or more, or

(ii) the employer's expenditures for agricultural labor in such year equal or exceed $2,500,

except that clause (ii) shall not apply in determining whether remuneration paid to an employee constitutes "wages" under this section if such employee (I) is employed as a hand harvest laborer and is paid on a piece rate basis in an operation which has been, and is customarily and generally recognized as having been, paid on a piece rate basis in the region of employment, (II) commutes daily from his permanent residence to the farm on which he is so employed, and (III) has been employed in agriculture less than 13 weeks during the preceding calendar year;

(9) [Stricken.]

(10) remuneration paid by an employer in any calendar year to an employee for service described in subsection (d)(3)(C) (relating to home workers), if the cash remuneration paid in such year by the employer to the employee for such service is less than $100;

(11) remuneration paid to or on behalf of an employee if (and to the extent that) at the time of the payment of such remuneration it is reasonable to believe that a corresponding deduction is allowable under section 217 (determined without regard to section 274(n)),

(12)(A) tips paid in any medium other than cash;

(B) cash tips received by an employee in any calendar month in the course of his employment by an employer unless the amount of such cash tips is $20 or more;

(13) any payment or series of payments by an employer to an employee or any of his dependents which is paid—

(A) upon or after the termination of an employee's employment relationship because of (i) death, or (ii) retirement for disability, and

(B) under a plan established by the employer which makes provision for his employees generally or a class or classes of his employees (or for such employees or class or classes of employees and their dependents),

other than such payment or series of payments which would have been paid if the employee's employment relationship had not been so terminated;

(14) any payment made by an employer to a survivor or the estate of a former employee after the calendar year in which such employee died;

(15) any payment made by an employer to an employee, if at the time such payment is made such employee is entitled to disability insurance benefits under section 223(a) of the Social Security Act and such entitlement commenced prior to the calendar year in which such payment is made, and if such employee did not perform any services for such employer during the period for which such payment is made;

(16) remuneration paid by an organization exempt from income tax under section 501(a) (other than an organization described in section 401(a)) or under section 521 in any calendar year to an employee for service rendered in the employ of such organization, if the remuneration paid in such year by the organization to the employee for such service is less than $100;

(17) [Stricken.]

(18) any payment made, or benefit furnished, to or for the benefit of an employee if at the time of such payment or such furnishing it is reasonable to believe that the employee will be able to exclude such payment or benefit from income under section 127, 129, 134(b)(4), or 134(b)(5);

(19) the value of any meals or lodging furnished by or on behalf of the employer if at the time of such furnishing it is reasonable to believe that the employee will be able to exclude such items from income under section 119;

(20) any benefit provided to or on behalf of an employee if at the time such benefit is provided it is reasonable to believe that the employee will be able to exclude such benefit from income under section 74(c), 108(f)(4), 117, or 132;

(21) in the case of a member of an Indian tribe, any remuneration on which no tax is imposed by this chapter by reason of section 7873 (relating to income derived by Indians from exercise of fishing rights);

(22) remuneration on account of—

(A) a transfer of a share of stock to any individual pursuant to an exercise of an incentive stock option (as defined in section 422(b)) or under an employee stock purchase plan (as defined in section 423(b)), or

(B) any disposition by the individual of such stock; or

(23) any benefit or payment which is excludable from the gross income of the employee under section [sic]section 139B(a).

Nothing in the regulations prescribed for purposes of chapter 24 (relating to income tax withholding) which provides an exclusion from "wages" as used in such chapter shall be construed to require a similar exclusion from "wages" in the regulations prescribed for purposes of this chapter.

Except as otherwise provided in regulations prescribed by the Secretary, any third party which makes a payment included in wages solely by reason of the parenthetical matter contained in subparagraph (A) of paragraph (2) shall be treated for purposes of this chapter and chapter 22 as the employer with respect to such wages.

Amendments

• **2019, Setting Every Community Up for Retirement Enhancement Act of 2019 (P.L. 116-94)**

P.L. 116-94, §301(c), Div. O:

Amended Code Sec. 3121(a)(23) by striking "139B(b)" and inserting "section 139B(a)". **Effective** for tax years beginning after 12-31-2019.

• **2014, Tax Technical Corrections Act of 2014 (P.L. 113-295)**

P.L. 113-295, §221(a)(19)(B)(iv), Division A:

Amended Code Sec. 3121(a) by striking paragraph (17). **Effective** generally 12-19-2014. For a special rule, see Act Sec. 221(b)(2), Division A, below. Prior to being stricken, Code Sec. 3121(a)(17) read as follows:

(17) any contribution, payment, or service provided by an employer which may be excluded from the gross income of an employee, his spouse, or his dependents, under the provisions of section 120 (relating to amounts received under qualified group legal services plans);

P.L. 113-295, §221(b)(2), Division A, provides:

(2) SAVINGS PROVISION.—If—

(A) any provision amended or repealed by the amendments made by this section applied to—

(i) any transaction occurring before the date of the enactment of this Act,

(ii) any property acquired before such date of enactment, or

(iii) any item of income, loss, deduction, or credit taken into account before such date of enactment, and

(B) the treatment of such transaction, property, or item under such provision would (without regard to the amendments or repeals made by this section) affect the liability for tax for periods ending after date of enactment, nothing in the amendments or repeals made by this section shall be construed to affect the treatment of such transaction, property, or item for purposes of determining liability for tax for periods ending after such date of enactment.

• **2008, Heroes Earnings Assistance and Relief Tax Act of 2008 (P.L. 110-245)**

P.L. 110-245, §115(a)(1):

Amended Code Sec. 3121(a) by striking "or" at the end of paragraph (21), by striking the period at the end of paragraph (22) and inserting "; or", and by inserting after paragraph (22) a new paragraph (23). **Effective** as if included in section 5 of the Mortgage Forgiveness Debt Relief Act of 2007 (P.L. 110-142) [**effective** for tax years beginning after 12-31-2007.—CCH].

• **2004, Ronald W. Reagan National Defense Authorization Act for Fiscal Year 2005 (P.L. 108-375)**

P.L. 108-375, §585(b)(2)(B):

Amended Code Sec. 3121(a)(18) by striking "or 134(b)(4)" and inserting "134(b)(4), or 134(b)(5)". **Effective** for travel benefits provided after 10-28-2004.

• **2004, American Jobs Creation Act of 2004 (P.L. 108-357)**

P.L. 108-357, §251(a)(1)(A):

Amended Code Sec. 3121(a) by striking "or" at the end of paragraph (20), by striking the period at the end of paragraph (21) and inserting "; or", and by inserting after paragraph (21) a new paragraph (22). **Effective** for stock acquired pursuant to options exercised after 10-22-2004.

P.L. 108-357, §320(b)(1):

Amended Code Sec. 3121(a)(20) by inserting "108(f)(4)," after "74(c),". **Effective** for amounts received by an individual in tax years beginning after 12-31-2003.

• **2004, Social Security Protection Act of 2004 (P.L. 108-203)**

P.L. 108-203, §423(a):

Amended Code Sec. 3121(a)(7)(B) by striking "described in subsection (g)(5)" and inserting "on a farm operated for profit". **Effective** 3-2-2004.

• **2003, Military Family Tax Relief Act of 2003 (P.L. 108-121)**

P.L. 108-121, §106(b)(2):

Amended Code Sec. 3121(a)(18) by striking "or 129" and inserting ", 129, or 134(b)(4)". **Effective** for tax years beginning after 12-31-2002. For a special rule, see Act Sec. 106(d), below.

P.L. 108-121, §106(d), provides:

(d) NO INFERENCE.—No inference may be drawn from the amendments made by this section with respect to the tax treatment of any amounts under the program described in section 134(b)(4) of the Internal Revenue Code of 1986 (as added by this section) for any taxable year beginning before January 1, 2003.

EMPLOYMENT TAX—GENERAL PROVISIONS

• **2000, Community Renewal Tax Relief Act of 2000 (P.L. 106-554)**

P.L. 106-554, §319(15):

Amended Code Sec. 3121(a)(5) by striking the semicolon at the end of subparagraph (G) and inserting a comma. **Effective** 12-21-2000.

• **1998, IRS Restructuring and Reform Act of 1998 (P.L. 105-206)**

P.L. 105-206, §6023(13)(A)-(C):

Amended Code Sec. 3121(a)(5) by striking the semicolon at the end of subparagraph (F) and inserting a comma, by striking "or" at the end of subparagraph (G), and by striking the period at the end of subparagraph (I) and inserting a semicolon. **Effective** 7-22-98.

• **1996, Small Business Job Protection Act of 1996 (P.L. 104-188)**

P.L. 104-188, §1421(b)(8)(A):

Amended Code Sec. 3121(a)(5) by striking "or" at the end of subparagraph (F), by inserting "or" at the end of subparagraph (G), and by adding at the end a new subparagraph (H). **Effective** for tax years beginning after 12-31-96.

P.L. 104-188, §1458(b)(1):

Amended Code Sec. 3121(a)(5), as amended by Act Sec. 1421(b)(8)(A), by striking "(or)" ["or"] at the end of subparagraph (G), by inserting "or" at the end of subparagraph (H), and by adding at the end a new subparagraph (I). **Effective** for remuneration paid after 12-31-96. For a special rule, see Act Sec. 1802, below.

P.L. 104-188, §1802, provides:

ACT SEC. 1802. TREATMENT OF CERTAIN UNIVERSITY ACCOUNTS.

(a) IN GENERAL.—For purposes of subsection (s) of section 3121 of the Internal Revenue Code of 1986 (relating to concurrent employment by 2 or more employers)—

(1) the following entities shall be deemed to be related corporations that concurrently employ the same individual:

(A) a State university which employs health professionals as faculty members at a medical school, and

(B) an agency account of a State university which is described in subparagraph (A) and from which there is distributed to such faculty members payments forming a part of the compensation that the State, or such State university, as the case may be, agrees to pay to such faculty members, but only if—

(i) such agency account is authorized by State law and receives the funds for such payments from a faculty practice plan described in section 501(c)(3) of such Code and exempt from tax under section 501(a) of such Code,

(ii) such payments are distributed by such agency account to such faculty members who render patient care at such medical school, and

(iii) such faculty members comprise at least 30 percent of the membership of such faculty practice plan, and

(2) remuneration which is disbursed by such agency account to any such faculty member of the medical school described in paragraph (1)(A) shall be deemed to have been actually disbursed by the State, or such State university, as the case may be, as a common paymaster and not to have been actually disbursed by such agency account.

(b) EFFECTIVE DATE.—The provisions of subsection (a) shall apply to remuneration paid after December 31, 1996.

• **1994, Social Security Domestic Employment Reform Act of 1994 (P.L. 103-387)**

P.L. 103-387, §2(a)(1)(A):

Amended Code Sec. 3121(a)(7)(B). **Effective** for remuneration paid after 12-31-93. Prior to amendment, Code Sec. 3121(a)(7)(B) read as follows:

(B) Cash remuneration paid by an employer in any calendar quarter to an employee for domestic service in a private home of the employer, if the cash remuneration paid in such quarter by the employer to the employee for such service is less than $50. As used in this subparagraph, the term "domestic service in a private home of the employer" does not include service described in subsection (g)(5);

P.L. 103-387, §2(a)(4), provides:

(4) NO LOSS OF SOCIAL SECURITY COVERAGE FOR 1994: CONTINUATION OF W-2 FILING REQUIREMENT.—Notwithstanding the amendments made by this subsection, if the wages (as defined in section 3121(a) of the Internal Revenue Code of 1986) paid during 1994 to an employee for domestic service in a private home of the employer are less than $1,000—

(A) the employer shall file any return or statement required under section 6051 of such Code with respect to such wages (determined without regard to such amendments), and

(B) the employee shall be entitled to credit under section 209 of the Social Security Act with respect to any such wages required to be included on any such return or statement.

• **1993, Omnibus Budget Reconciliation Act of 1993 (P.L. 103-66)**

P.L. 103-66, §13207(a)(1)(A)-(C):

Amended Code Sec. 3121(a)(1) by inserting "in the case of taxes imposed by sections 3101(a) and 3111(a)" after "(1)", by striking "applicable contribution base (as determined under subsection (x))" each place it appears and inserting "contribution and benefit base (as determined under section 230 of the Social Security Act)", and by striking "such applicable contribution base" and inserting "such contribution and benefit base". **Effective** for 1994 and later calendar years.

• **1990, Omnibus Budget Reconciliation Act of 1990 (P.L. 101-508)**

P.L. 101-508, §11331(a)(1)(A)(B):

Amended Code Sec. 3121(a)(1) by striking "contribution and benefit base (as determined under section 230 of the Social Security Act)" each place it appears and inserting "applicable contribution base (as determined under subsection (x))", and by striking "such contribution and benefit base" and inserting "such applicable contribution base". **Effective** for 1991 and later calendar years.

• **1989 (P.L. 101-136)**

P.L. 101-136, §528, provides:

SEC. 528. No monies appropriated by this Act may be used to implement or enforce section 1151 of the Tax Reform Act of 1986 or the amendments made by such section.

• **1988, Technical and Miscellaneous Revenue Act of 1988 (P.L. 100-647)**

P.L. 100-647, §1001(g)(4)(B)(i):

Amended Code Sec. 3121(a)(11) by striking out "section 217" and inserting in lieu thereof "section 217 (determined without regard to section 274(n))". **Effective** as if included in the provision of P.L. 99-514 to which it relates.

P.L. 100-647, §1011B(a)(23)(A):

Amended Code Sec. 3121(a)(5)(G) by inserting "if such payment would not be treated as wages without regard to such plan and it is reasonable to believe that (if section 125 applied for purposes of this section) section 125 would not treat any wages as constructively received" after "section 125)". **Effective** as if included in the provision of P.L. 99-514 to which it relates.

P.L. 100-647, §3043(c)(2):

Amended Code Sec. 3121(a) by striking out "or" at the end of paragraph (19), by striking out the period at the end of paragraph (20) and inserting in lieu thereof "; or", and by inserting after paragraph (20) new paragraph (21). **Effective** for all periods beginning before, on, or after 11-10-88.

P.L. 100-647, §3044(b), provides:

(b) NO INFERENCE CREATED.—Nothing in the amendments made by this subtitle shall create any inference as to the existence or non-existence or scope of any exemption from tax for income derived from fishing rights secured as of March 17, 1988, by any treaty, law, or Executive Order.

P.L. 100-647, §8017(b):

Amended Code Sec. 3121(a)(8)(B). **Effective** as if included in the provision of P.L. 100-203 to which it relates. Prior to amendment, Code Sec. 3121(a)(8)(B) read as follows:

(B) cash remuneration paid by an employer in any calendar year to an employee for agricultural labor unless (i) the cash remuneration paid in such year by the employer to the employee for such labor is $150 or more, or (ii) the employer's expenditures for agricultural labor in such year equal or exceed $2,500;

• **1987, Revenue Act of 1987 (P.L. 100-203)**

P.L. 100-203, §9002(b):

Amended Code Sec. 3121(a)(8)(B) by striking out clause (ii) and inserting a new clause (ii). **Effective** with respect to remuneration for agricultural labor paid after 12-31-87. Prior to amendment, Code Sec. 3121(a)(8)(B)(ii) read as follows:

(ii) the employee performs agricultural labor for the employer on 20 days or more during such year for cash remuneration computed on a time basis;

P.L. 100-203, §9003(a)(2):

Amended Code Sec. 3121(a)(2)(C) by striking out "death" and inserting "death, except that this paragraph does not apply to a payment for group term life insurance to the extent that such payment is includible in the gross income of the employee". **Effective** with respect to group term life insurance coverage in effect after 12-31-87, except that it shall not apply with respect to payments by the employer (or a successor of such employer) for group-term life insurance for such employer's former employees who separated from employment with the employer on or before 12-31-88, to the extent that such employee payments are not for coverage for any period for which such employee is employed by such employer (or a successor of such employer) after the date of such separation [effective date changed by P.L. 100-647, §8013(a)].

• **1986, Tax Reform Act of 1986 (P.L. 99-514)**

P.L. 99-514, §122(e)(1):

Amended Code Sec. 3121(a)(20) by striking out "117 or" and inserting in lieu thereof "74(c), 117, or". **Effective** for prizes and awards granted after 12-31-86.

P.L. 99-514, §1108(g)(7):

Amended Code Sec. 3121(a)(5) by striking out subparagraph (C) and inserting in lieu thereof new subparagraph (C). **Effective** for years beginning after 12-31-86. Prior to amendment, Code Sec. 3121(a)(5)(C) read as follows:

(C) under a simplified employee pension if, at the time of the payment, it is reasonable to believe that the employee will be entitled to a deduction under section 219(b)(2) for such payment,

P.L. 99-514, §1151(d)(2)(A):

Amended Code Sec. 3121(a)(5) by striking out "or" at the end of subparagraph (E), by inserting "or" at the end of subparagraph (F), and by inserting after subparagraph (F) new subparagraph (G). **Effective** for tax years beginning after 12-31-83.

P.L. 99-514, §1883(a)(11)(B):

Amended Code Sec. 3121(a)(8) by moving subparagraph (B) two ems to the left, so that its left margin is in flush alignment with the margin of subparagraph (A) of such section. **Effective** 10-22-86.

• **1984, Deficit Reduction Act of 1984 (P.L. 98-369)**

P.L. 98-369, §491(d)(36):

Amended Code Sec. 3121(a)(5) by striking out subparagraph (C) and by redesignating subparagraphs (D) through (G) as subparagraphs (C) through (F), respectively. **Effective** for obligations issued after 12-31-83. Prior to amendment, subparagraph (C) read as follows:

(C) under or to a bond purchase plan which, at the time of such payment, is a qualified bond purchase plan described in section 405(a),

Sec. 3121(a)(23)

EMPLOYMENT TAX—GENERAL PROVISIONS

P.L. 98-369, § 531(d)(1)(A):

Amended Code Sec. 3121(a) by striking out "all remuneration paid in any medium" in the material preceding paragraph (1) and inserting in lieu thereof "all remuneration (including benefits) paid in any medium", and by striking out "or" at the end of paragraph (18), by striking out the period at the end of paragraph (19) and inserting in lieu thereof "; or", and by inserting after paragraph (19) new paragraph (20). **Effective** 1-1-85.

• **1983, Social Security Amendments of 1983 (P.L. 98-21)**

P.L. 98-21, § 324(a)(2):

Amended Code Sec. 3121(a)(5). **Effective** with respect to remuneration paid after 12-31-83. P.L. 98-21, § 324(d)(1), as amended by P.L. 98-369, § 2662(f)(2), provides that for purposes of applying such amendments to remuneration paid after 12-31-83, which would have been taken into account before 1-1-84, if such amendments had applied to periods before 1-1-84, such remuneration shall be taken into account when paid (or, at the election of the payor, at the time which would be appropriate if such amendments had applied). Prior to amendment, Code Sec. 3121(a)(5) read as follows:

(5) any payment made to, or on behalf of, an employee or his beneficiary—

(A) from or to a trust described in section 401(a) which is exempt from tax under section 501(a) at the time of such payment unless such payment is made to an employee of the trust as remuneration for services rendered as such employee and not as a beneficiary of the trust,

(B) under or to an annuity plan which, at the time of such payment, is a plan described in section 403(a),

(C) under or to a bond purchase plan which, at the time of such payment, is a qualified bond purchase plan described in section 405(a), or

(D) under a simplified employee pension if, at the time of the payment, it is reasonable to believe that the employee will be entitled to a deduction under section 219 for such payment;

P.L. 98-21, § 324(d)(3)-(4), provides:

(3) The amendments made by this section shall not apply to employer contributions made during 1984 and attributable to services performed during 1983 under a qualified cash or deferred arrangement (as defined in section 3121(k) of the Internal Revenue Code of 1954) if, under the terms of such arrangement as in effect on March 24, 1983—

(A) the employee makes an election with respect to such contribution before January 1, 1984, and

(B) the employer identifies the amount of such contribution before January 1, 1984.

* * *

(4) In the case of an agreement in existence on March 24, 1983, between a nonqualified deferred compensation plan (as defined in section 3121(v)(2)(C) of the Internal Revenue Code of 1954, as added by this section) and an individual—

(A) the amendments made by this section ***shall apply with respect to services performed by such individual after December 31, 1983, and ***

The preceding sentence shall not apply in the case of a plan to which section 457(a) of such Code applies. For purposes of this paragraph, any plan or agreement to make payments described in paragraph (2), (3), or (13)(A)(iii) of section 3121(a) of such Code (as in effect on the day before the date of the enactment of this Act) shall be treated as a nonqualified deferred compensation plan. [Last sentence added by P.L. 98-369, § 2662 (f)(2)(C).]

P.L. 98-21, § 324(a)(3):

Amended Code Sec. 3121(a) by: striking out in paragraph (2) subparagraph (A) and redesignating subparagraphs (B), (C), and (D) as subparagraphs (A), (B), and (C), respectively; by striking out paragraphs (3) and (9); by inserting in paragraph (13)(A) "or" after "death," and by striking out "or (iii) retirement after attaining an age specified in the plan referred to in subparagraph (B) or in a pension plan of the employer,"; and by striking out "subparagraph (B)" in the last sentence thereof and inserting in lieu thereof "subparagraph (A)". **Effective** with respect to remuneration paid after 12-31-83. But see § 324(d)(3) and (4) of P.L. 98-21. Prior to amendment, Code Sec. 3121(a)(2)(A), (3) and (9) read as follows:

(A) retirement, or

(3) any payment made to an employee (including any amount paid by an employer for insurance or annuities, or into a fund, to provide for any such payment) on account of retirement;

(9) any payment (other than vacation or sick pay) made to an employee after the month in which he attains age 62, if such employee did not work for the employer in the period for which such payment is made;

P.L. 98-21, § 327(a)(1):

Amended Code Sec. 3121(a) by striking out "or" at the end of paragraph (17), by striking out the period at the end of paragraph (18) and inserting in lieu thereof "; or", and by adding paragraph (19). **Effective** with respect to remuneration paid after 12-31-83.

P.L. 98-21, § 327(b)(1):

Amended Code Sec. 3121(a) by inserting the flush sentence after and below Code Sec. 3121(a)(19). **Effective** for remuneration (other than amounts excluded under Code Sec. 119) paid after 3-4-83, and to any such remuneration paid on or before such date which the employer treated as wages when paid. [**Effective** date changed by P.L. 98-369, § 2662(z).]

P.L. 98-21, § 328(a):

Amended Code Sec. 3121(a)(5)(D) by striking out "section 219" and inserting in lieu thereof "section 219(b)(2)". **Effective** with respect to remuneration paid after 12-31-83.

• **1981 (P.L. 97-123)**

P.L. 97-123, § 3(b)(1):

Amended Code Sec. 3121(a)(2)(B). **Effective** with respect to remuneration paid after 12-31-81. Prior to amendment, Code Sec. 3121(a)(2)(B) read as follows: "(B) sickness or accident disability, or".

P.L. 97-123, § 3(b)(2):

Amended Code Sec. 3121(a) by adding the last sentence at the end thereof. **Effective** with respect to remuneration paid after 12-31-81. But, see § 3(g)(2) of P.L. 97-123.

P.L. 97-123, § 3(d)-(f), provides:

(d)(1) The regulations prescribed under the last sentence of section 3121(a) of the Internal Revenue Code of 1954, and the regulations prescribed under subparagraph (D) of section 3231(e)(4) of such Code, shall provide procedures under which, if (with respect to any employee) the third party promptly—

(A) withholds the employee portion of the taxes involved,

(B) deposits such portion under section 6302 of such Code, and

(C) notifies the employer of the amount of the wages or compensation involved,

the employer (and not the third party) shall be liable for the employer portion of the taxes involved and for meeting the requirements of section 6041 of such Code (relating to receipts for employees) with respect to the wages or compensation involved.

(2) For purposes of paragraph (1)—

(A) the term "employer" means the employer for whom services are normally rendered,

(B) the term "taxes involved" means, in the case of any employee, the taxes under chapters 21 and 22 which are payable solely by reason of the parenthetical matter contained in subparagraph (B) of section 3121(a)(2) of such Code, or solely by reason of paragraph (4) of section 3231(e) of such Code, and

(C) the term "wages or compensation involved" means, in the case of any employee, wages or compensation with respect to which taxes described in subparagraph (B) are imposed.

(e) For purposes of applying section 209 of the Social Security Act, section 3121(a) of the Internal Revenue Code of 1954, and section 3231(e) of such Code with respect to the parenthetical matter contained in section 209(b)(2) of the Social Security Act or section 3121(a)(2)(B) of the Internal Revenue Code of 1954, or with respect to section 3231(e)(4) of such Code (as the case may be), payments under a State temporary disability law shall be treated as remuneration for service.

(f) Notwithstanding any other provision of law, no penalties or interest shall be assessed on account of any failure to make timely payment of taxes, imposed by section 3101, 3111, 3201(b), 3211, or 3221(b) of the Internal Revenue Code of 1954 with respect to payments made for the period beginning January 1, 1982, and ending June 30, 1982, to the extent that such taxes are attributable to this section (or the amendments made by this section) and that such failure is due to reasonable cause and not to willful neglect.

P.L. 97-123, § 3(g)(2), provides:

(2) This section (and the amendments made by this section) shall not apply with respect to any payment made by a third party to an employee pursuant to a contractual relationship of an employer with such third party entered into before December 14, 1981, if—

(A) coverage by such third party for the group in which such employee falls ceases before March 1, 1982, and

(B) no payment by such third party is made to such employee under such relationship after February 28, 1982.

• **1981, Economic Recovery Tax Act of 1981 (P.L. 97-34)**

P.L. 97-34, § 124(e)(2):

Amended Code Sec. 3121(a)(18) by striking out "section 127" and inserting in lieu thereof "section 127 or 129". **Effective** with respect to remuneration paid after 12-31-81.

• **1980, Omnibus Reconciliation Act of 1980 (P.L. 96-499)**

P.L. 96-499, § 1141(a)(1):

Amended Code Sec. 3121(a)(6). **Effective**, generally, for remuneration paid after 12-31-80, however, in the case of state and local governments, see P.L. 96-499, § 1141(c)(2), below. Prior to amendment, Code Sec. 3121(a)(6) provided:

(6) the payment by an employer (without deduction from the remuneration of the employee)—

(A) of the tax imposed upon an employee under section 3101 (or the corresponding section of prior law), or

(B) of any payment required from an employee under a State unemployment compensation law;

P.L. 96-499, § 1141(c)(2), provides:

(2) EXCEPTION FOR STATE AND LOCAL GOVERNMENTS.—

(A) the amendments made by this section (insofar as they affect the application of section 218 of the Social Security Act) shall not apply to any payment made before January 1, 1984, by any governmental unit for positions of a kind for which all or a substantial portion of the social security employee taxes were paid by such governmental unit (without deduction from the remuneration of the employee) under the practices of such governmental unit in effect on October 1, 1980.

(B) For purposes of subparagraph (A), the term `social security employee taxes' means the amount required to be paid under section 218 of the Social Security Act as the equivalent of the taxes imposed by section 3101 of the Internal Revenue Code of 1954.

(C) For purposes of subparagraph (A), the term `governmental unit' means a State or political subdivision thereof within the meaning of section 218 of the Social Security Act".

• **1980, Technical Corrections Act of 1979 (P.L. 96-222)**

P.L. 96-222, § 101(a)(10)(B)(i):

Amended Code Sec. 3121(a)(5) by adding paragraph (5). **Effective** for payments made on or after 1-1-79.

EMPLOYMENT TAX—GENERAL PROVISIONS

- **1978, Revenue Act of 1978 (P.L. 95-600)**

P.L. 95-600, §164(b)(3)(A), (B), (C), (d):

Amended Code Sec. 3121(a). **Effective** for tax years beginning after 12-31-78, by: (A) striking out "or" at the end of paragraph (16); (B) striking out the period at the end of paragraph (17) and inserting in place thereof "; or"; and (C) adding paragraph (18).

- **1978 (P.L. 95-472)**

P.L. 95-472, §3(b), (d):

Added Code Sec. 3121(a)(17). **Effective** for tax years beginning after 1976.

- **1977 (P.L. 95-216)**

P.L. 95-216, §356(a):

Amended Code Sec. 3121(a)(7)(C). **Effective** for remuneration paid and services rendered after 12-31-77. Prior to amendment, Code Sec. 3121(a)(7)(C) read as follows:

(C) cash remuneration paid by an employer in any calendar quarter to an employee for service not in the course of the employer's trade or business, if the cash remuneration paid in such quarter by the employer to the employee for such service is less than $50. As used in this subparagraph, the term "service not in the course of the employer's trade or business" does not include domestic service in a private home of the employer and does not include service described in subsection (g) (5);

P.L. 95-216, §356(a):

Amended Code Sec. 3121(a)(10). **Effective** for remuneration paid and services rendered after 12-31-77. Prior to amendment, Code Sec. 3121(a)(10) read as follows:

(10) remuneration paid by an employer in any calendar quarter to an employee for service described in subsection (d)(3)(C) (relating to home workers), if the cash remuneration paid in such quarter by the employer to the employee for such service is less than $50;

P.L. 95-216, §356(b):

Amended Code Sec. 3121(a) by striking out "or" at the end of paragraph (14), by striking out the period at the end of paragraph (15) and inserting in lieu thereof "; or", and by adding paragraph (16). **Effective** for remuneration paid and services rendered after 12-31-77.

- **1973 (P.L. 93-233)**

P.L. 93-233, §5(b)(2):

Amended Code Sec. 3121(a)(1) by substituting "$13,200" for "$10,800." **Effective** with respect to remuneration paid after 1973.

- **1973 (P.L. 93-66)**

P.L. 93-66, §203(b)(2):

Amended Code Sec. 3121(a)(1) by substituting "$12,600" for "$12,000." **Effective** with respect to remuneration paid in 1974 (but see P.L. 93-233, above).

- **1972, Social Security Amendments of 1972 (P.L. 92-603)**

P.L. 92-603, §104(i):

Amended Code Sec. 3121(a)(9). **Effective** with respect to payments after 1974. Prior to amendment, Code Sec. 3121(a)(9) read as follows:

"(9) any payment (other than vacation or sick pay) made to an employee after the month in which—

"(A) in the case of a man, he attains the age of 65, or

"(B) in the case of a woman, she attains the age of 62, if such employee did not work for the employer in the period for which such payment is made;".

P.L. 92-603, §122(b):

Added paragraph (14). **Effective** in the case of any payment made after 12-31-72.

P.L. 92-603, §138(b):

Added paragraph (15). **Effective** in the case of any payment made after 12-31-72.

- **1972 (P.L. 92-336)**

P.L. 92-336, §203(b)(2)(A) (as amended by P.L. 93-233, §5(d)):

Amended Code Sec. 3121(a)(1) by striking out $9,000 each place it appeared and inserting in lieu thereof $10,800 with respect to remuneration paid after December 1972. **Effective** with respect to remuneration paid after 1973, Sec. 3121(a)(1) is amended by striking out $10,800 each place it appears and inserting in lieu thereof "$12,000". (But see P.L. 93-66, above.) **Effective** with respect to remuneration paid after 1974, Sec. 3121 is amended: (i) by striking out $13,200 each place it appears and inserting in lieu thereof "the contribution and benefit base (as determined under section 230 of the Social Security Act)", and (ii) by striking out "by an employer during any calendar year", and inserting in lieu thereof "by an employer during the calendar year with respect to which such contribution and benefit base is effective".

- **1971 (P.L. 92-5)**

P.L. 92-5, §203(b)(2):

Amended Code Sec. 3121(a)(1). **Effective** with respect to remuneration paid after 12-31-71, by substituting "$9,000" for "$7,800" each place that such figure appears.

- **1968, Social Security Amendments of 1967 (P.L. 90-248)**

P.L. 90-248, §108(b)(2):

Amended Sec. 3121(a)(1) by substituting "$7,800" for "$6,600" in each place it appeared. **Effective** only with respect to remuneration paid after 12-31-67.

P.L. 90-248, §504(a):

Amended Sec. 3121(a) by deleting "or" at the end of paragraph (11), by substituting "; or" for the period at the end of paragraph (12), and by adding new paragraph (13). **Effective** with respect to remuneration paid after 1-2-68.

- **1965, Social Security Amendments of 1965 (P.L. 89-97)**

P.L. 89-97, §313(c):

Added Sec. 3121(a)(12). **Effective** with respect to tips received by employees after 1965.

P.L. 89-97, §320(b):

Amended Sec. 3121(a)(1) by substituting "$6,600" for "$4,800" in each place it appeared. **Effective** with respect to remuneration paid after 12-31-65.

- **1964 (P.L. 88-650)**

P.L. 88-650, §4(b):

Added Code Sec. 3121(a)(11). **Effective** with respect to remuneration paid on or after the first day of the first calendar month which begins more than 10 days after 10-13-64.

- **1964, Revenue Act of 1964 (P.L. 88-272)**

P.L. 88-272, §220(c)(2):

Amended subparagraph (B) of subsection (a)(5). **Effective** only with respect to remuneration paid after 1962. Prior to amendment, subparagraph (B) read as follows:

"(B) under or to an annuity plan which, at the time of such payment, meets the requirements of section 401(a)(3), (4), (5), and (6);"

- **1958, Social Security Amendments of 1958 (P.L. 85-840)**

P.L. 85-840, §402(b):

Amended Sec. 3121(a) by substituting "$4,800" for "$4,200" wherever it appeared. **Effective** for remuneration paid after 1958.

- **1956, Social Security Amendments of 1956 (P.L. 880, 84th Cong.)**

P.L. 880, 84th Cong., §201(b):

Amended Sec. 3121(a)(9). **Effective** for remuneration paid after 10-31-56. Prior to the amendment Sec. 3121(a)(9) read as follows:

"(9) any payment (other than vacation or sick pay) made to an employee after the month in which he attains the age of 65, if he did not work for the employer in the period for which such payment is made; or".

P.L. 880, 84th Cong., 2d Sess., §201(h)(1):

Amended Sec. 3121(a)(8)(B). **Effective** for remuneration paid after 1956. Prior to amendment, Sec. 3121(a)(8)(B) read as follows:

"(B) cash remuneration paid by an employer in any calendar year to an employee for agricultural labor, if the cash remuneration paid in such year by the employer to the employee for such labor is less than $100;".

- **1954, Social Security Amendments of 1954 (P.L. 761, 83rd Cong.)**

P.L. 761, 83rd Cong., §204(a), (b):

Substituted "$4,200" wherever it appeared in paragraph (1) for "$3,600", added subparagraph (C) to paragraph (7), inserted "(A)" after "(8)" in paragraph (8), added subparagraph (B) to paragraph (8), and amended subparagraph (7)(B). **Effective** 1-1-55. Prior to amendment, subparagraph (7)(B) read as follows:

"(B) cash remuneration paid by an employer in any calendar quarter to an employee for domestic service in a private home of the employer, if the cash remuneration paid in the quarter for such service is less than $50 or the employee is not regularly employed by the employer in such quarter of payment. For purposes of this subparagraph, an employee shall be deemed to be regularly employed by an employer during a calendar quarter only if—

"(i) on each of some 24 days during the quarter the employee performs for the employer for some portion of the day domestic service in a private home of the employer, or

"(ii) the employee was regularly employed (as determined under clause (i)) by the employer in the performance of such service during the preceding calendar quarter.

"As used in this subparagraph, the term `domestic service in a private home of the employer' does not include service described in subsection (g)(5);".

[Sec. 3121(b)]

(b) EMPLOYMENT.—For purposes of this chapter, the term "employment" means any service, of whatever nature, performed (A) by an employee for the person employing him, irrespective of the citizenship or residence of either, (i) within the United States, or (ii) on or in connection with an American vessel or American aircraft under a contract of service which is entered into within the United States or during the performance of which and while the employee is employed on the vessel or aircraft it touches at a port in the United States, if the employee is employed on and in connection with such vessel or aircraft when outside the United States, or (B) outside the United States by a citizen of the United States [a citizen or resident of the United States (effective for remuneration paid after December 31, 1983)] as an employee for an American employer (as defined in subsection (h)), or (C) if it is service, regardless of where or by whom performed, which is designated as employment or recognized as equivalent to employment under an agreement entered into under section 233 of the Social Security Act; except that such term shall not include—

(1) service performed by foreign agricultural workers lawfully admitted to the United States from the Bahamas, Jamaica, and the other British West Indies, or from any other foreign country or possession thereof, on a temporary basis to perform agricultural labor;

EMPLOYMENT TAX—GENERAL PROVISIONS

(2) domestic service performed in a local college club, or local chapter of a college fraternity or sorority, by a student who is enrolled and is regularly attending classes at a school, college, or university;

(3)(A) service performed by a child under the age of 18 in the employ of his father or mother;

(B) service not in the course of the employer's trade or business, or domestic service in a private home of the employer, performed by an individual under the age of 21 in the employ of his father or mother, or performed by an individual in the employ of his spouse or son or daughter; except that the provisions of this subparagraph shall not be applicable to such domestic service performed by an individual in the employ of his son or daughter if—

(i) the employer is a surviving spouse or a divorced individual and has not remarried, or has a spouse living in the home who has a mental or physical condition which results in such spouse's being incapable of caring for a son, daughter, stepson, or stepdaughter (referred to in clause (ii)) for at least 4 continuous weeks in the calendar quarter in which the service is rendered, and

(ii) a son, daughter, stepson, or stepdaughter of such employer is living in the home, and

(iii) the son, daughter, stepson, or stepdaughter (referred to in clause (ii)) has not attained age 18 or has a mental or physical condition which requires the personal care and supervision of an adult for at least 4 continuous weeks in the calendar quarter in which the service is rendered;

(4) service performed by an individual on or in connection with a vessel not an American vessel, or on or in connection with an aircraft not an American aircraft, if (A) the individual is employed on and in connection with such vessel or aircraft, when outside the United States and (B) (i) such individual is not a citizen of the United States or (ii) the employer is not an American employer;

(5) service performed in the employ of the United States or any instrumentality of the United States, if such service—

(A) would be excluded from the term "employment" for purposes of this title if the provisions of paragraphs (5) and (6) of this subsection as in effect in January 1983 had remained in effect, and

(B) is performed by an individual who—

(i) has been continuously performing service described in subparagraph (A) since December 31, 1983, and for purposes of this clause—

(I) if an individual performing service described in subparagraph (A) returns to the performance of such service after being separated therefrom for a period of less than 366 consecutive days, regardless of whether the period began before, on, or after December 31, 1983, then such service shall be considered continuous,

(II) if an individual performing service described in subparagraph (A) returns to the performance of such service after being detailed or transferred to an international organization as described under section 3343 of subchapter III of chapter 33 of title 5, United States Code, or under section 3581 of chapter 35 of such title, then the service performed for that organization shall be considered service described in subparagraph (A),

(III) if an individual performing service described in subparagraph (A) is reemployed or reinstated after being separated from such service for the purpose of accepting employment with the American Institute in Taiwan as provided under section 3310 of chapter 48 of title 22, United States Code, then the service performed for that Institute shall be considered service described in subparagraph (A),

(IV) if an individual performing service described in subparagraph (A) returns to the performance of such service after performing service as a member of a uniformed service (including, for purposes of this clause, service in the National Guard and temporary service in the Coast Guard Reserve) and after exercising restoration or reemployment rights as provided under chapter 43 of title 38, United States Code, then the service so performed as a member of a uniformed service shall be considered service described in subparagraph (A), and

(V) if an individual performing service described in subparagraph (A) returns to the performance of such service after employment (by a tribal organization) to which section 104(e)(2) of the Indian Self-Determination Act applies, then the service performed for that tribal organization shall be considered service described in subparagraph (A); or

(ii) is receiving an annuity from the Civil Service Retirement and Disability Fund, or benefits (for service as an employee) under another retirement system established by a law of the United States for employees of the Federal Government (other than for members of the uniformed service);

except that this paragraph shall not apply with respect to any such service performed on or after any date on which such individual performs—

(C) service performed as the President or Vice President of the United States,

(D) service performed—

(i) in a position placed in the Executive Schedule under Sections 5312 through 5317 of title 5, United States Code,

(ii) as a noncareer appointee in the Senior Executive Service or a noncareer member of the Senior Foreign Service, or

(iii) in a position to which the individual is appointed by the President (or his designee) or the Vice President under section 105(a)(1), 106(a)(1), or 107(a)(1) or (b)(1) of title 3, United States Code, if the maximum rate of basic pay for such position is at or above the rate for level V of the Executive Schedule,

(E) service performed as the Chief Justice of the United States, an Associate Justice of the Supreme Court, a judge of a United States court of appeals, a judge or of a United States district court (including the district court of a territory), a judge of the United States Court of Federal Claims, a judge of the United States Court of International Trade, a judge or special trial judge of the United States Tax Court, a United States magistrate, or a referee in bankruptcy or United States bankruptcy judge,

(F) service performed as a Member, Delegate, or Resident Commissioner of or to the Congress,

(G) any other service in the legislative branch of the Federal Government if such service—

(i) is performed by an individual who was not subject to subchapter III of chapter 83 of title 5, United States Code, or to another retirement system established by a law of the United States for employees of the Federal Government (other than for members of the uniformed services), on December 31, 1983, or

(ii) is performed by an individual who has, at any time after December 31, 1983, received a lump-sum payment under section 8342(a) of title 5, United States Code, or under the corresponding provision of the law establishing the other retirement system described in clause (i), or

(iii) is performed by an individual after such individual has otherwise ceased to be subject to subchapter III of chapter 83 of title 5, United States Code (without having an application pending for coverage under such subchapter), while performing service in the legislative branch (determined without regard to the provisions of subparagraph (B) relating to continuity of employment), for any period of time after December 31, 1983,

and for purposes of this subparagraph (G) an individual is subject to such subchapter III or to any such other retirement system at any time only if (a) such individual's pay is subject to deductions, contributions, or similar payments (concurrent with the service being performed at that time) under section 8334(a) of such title 5 or the corresponding provision of the law establishing such other

EMPLOYMENT TAX—GENERAL PROVISIONS

system, or (in a case to which section 8332(k)(1) of such title applies) such individual is making payments of amounts equivalent to such deductions, contributions, or similar payments while on leave without pay, or (b) such individual is receiving an annuity from the Civil Service Retirement and Disability Fund, or is receiving benefits (for service as an employee) under another retirement system established by a law of the United States for employees of the Federal Government (other than for members of the uniformed services), or

(H) service performed by an individual—

(i) on or after the effective date of an election by such individual, under section 301 of the Federal Employees' Retirement System Act of 1986, section 307 of the Central Intelligence Agency Retirement Act (50 U.S.C. 2157), or the Federal Employees' Retirement System Open Enrollment Act of 1997, to become subject to the Federal Employees' Retirement System provided in chapter 84 of title 5, United States Code, or

(ii) on or after the effective date of an election by such individual, under regulations issued under section 860 of the Foreign Service Act of 1980, to become subject to the Foreign Service Pension System provided in subchapter II of chapter 8 of title I of such Act;

(6) service performed in the employ of the United States or any instrumentality of the United States if such service is performed—

(A) in a penal institution of the United States by an inmate thereof;

(B) by any individual as an employee included under section 5351(2) of title 5, United States Code (relating to certain interns, student nurses, and other student employees of hospitals of the Federal Government), other than as a medical or dental intern or a medical or dental resident in training; or

(C) by any individual as an employee serving on a temporary basis in case of fire, storm, earthquake, flood, or other similar emergency;

(7) service performed in the employ of a State, or any political subdivision thereof, or any instrumentality of any one or more of the foregoing which is wholly owned thereby, except that this paragraph shall not apply in the case of—

(A) service which, under subsection (j), constitutes covered transportation service,

(B) service in the employ of the Government of Guam or the Government of American Samoa or any political subdivision thereof, or of any instrumentality of any one or more of the foregoing which is wholly owned thereby, performed by an officer or employee thereof (including a member of the legislature of any such Government or political subdivision), and, for purposes of this title with respect to the taxes imposed by this chapter—

(i) any person whose service as such an officer or employee is not covered by a retirement system established by a law of the United States shall not, with respect to such service, be regarded as an employee of the United States or any agency or instrumentality thereof, and

(ii) the remuneration for service described in clause (i) (including fees paid to a public official) shall be deemed to have been paid by the Government of Guam or the Government of American Samoa or by a political subdivision thereof or an instrumentality of any one or more of the foregoing which is wholly owned thereby, whichever is appropriate,

(C) service performed in the employ of the District of Columbia or any instrumentality which is wholly owned thereby, if such service is not covered by a retirement system established by a law of the United States (other than the Federal Employees Retirement System provided in chapter 84 of title 5, United States Code); except that the provisions of this subparagraph shall not be applicable to service performed—

(i) in a hospital or penal institution by a patient or inmate thereof;

(ii) by any individual as an employee included under section 5351(2) of title 5, United States Code (relating to certain interns, student nurses, and other student employees of hospitals of the District of Columbia Government), other than as a medical or dental intern or as a medical or dental resident in training;

(iii) by any individual as an employee serving on a temporary basis in case of fire, storm, snow, earthquake, flood or other similar emergency; or

(iv) by a member of a board, committee, or council of the District of Columbia, paid on a per diem, meeting, or other fee basis,

(D) service performed in the employ of the Government of Guam (or any instrumentality which is wholly owned by such Government) by an employee properly classified as a temporary or intermittent employee, if such service is not covered by a retirement system established by a law of Guam; except that (i) the provisions of this subparagraph shall not be applicable to services performed by an elected official or a member of the legislature or in a hospital or penal institution by a patient or inmate thereof, and (ii) for purposes of this subparagraph, clauses (i) and (ii) of subparagraph (B) shall apply,

(E) service included under an agreement entered into pursuant to section 218 of the Social Security Act, or

(F) service in the employ of a State (other than the District of Columbia, Guam, or American Samoa), of any political subdivision thereof, or of any instrumentality of any one or more of the foregoing which is wholly owned thereby, by an individual who is not a member of a retirement system of such State, political subdivision, or instrumentality, except that the provisions of this subparagraph shall not be applicable to service performed—

(i) by an individual who is employed to relieve such individual from unemployment;

(ii) in a hospital, home, or other institution by a patient or inmate thereof;

(iii) by any individual as an employee serving on a temporary basis in case of fire, storm, snow, earthquake, flood, or other similar emergency;

(iv) by an election official or election worker if the remuneration paid in a calendar year for such service is less than $1,000 with respect to service performed during any calendar year commencing on or after January 1, 1995, ending on or before December 31, 1999, and the adjusted amount determined under section 218(c)(8)(B) of the Social Security Act for any calendar year commencing on or after January 1, 2000, with respect to service performed during such calendar year; or

(v) by an employee in a position compensated solely on a fee basis which is treated pursuant to section 1402(c)(2)(E) as a trade or business for purposes of inclusion of such fees in net earnings from self-employment; for purposes of this subparagraph, except as provided in regulations prescribed by the Secretary, the term "retirement system" has the meaning given such term by section 218(b)(4) of the Social Security Act;

(8)(A) service performed by a duly ordained, commissioned, or licensed minister of a church in the exercise of his ministry or by a member of a religious order in the exercise of duties required by such order, except that this subparagraph shall not apply to service performed by a member of such an order in the exercise of such duties, if an election of coverage under subsection (r) is in effect with respect to such order, or with respect to the autonomous subdivision thereof to which such member belongs;

(B) service performed in the employ of a church or qualified church-controlled organization if such church or organization has in effect an election under subsection (w), other than service in an unrelated trade or business (within the meaning of section 513(a));

(9) service performed by an individual as an employee or employee representative as defined in section 3231;

(10) service performed in the employ of—

(A) a school, college, or university, or

(B) an organization described in section 509(a)(3) if the organization is organized, and at all times thereafter is operated, exclusively for the benefit of, to perform the functions of, or to carry out the purposes of a school, college, or university and is operated, supervised, or controlled by or in connection with such school, college, or university unless it is a school, college, or university of a State or a political subdivision thereof and the services performed in its employ by a student referred to in section 218(c)(5) of the Social Security Act are covered under the agreement between the Commissioner of Social Security and such State entered into pursuant to section 218 of such Act;

if such service is performed by a student who is enrolled and regularly attending classes at such school, college, or university;

(11) service performed in the employ of a foreign government (including service as a consular or other officer or employee or a nondiplomatic representative);

(12) service performed in the employ of an instrumentality wholly owned by a foreign government—

(A) if the service is of a character similar to that performed in foreign countries by employees of the United States Government or of an instrumentality thereof; and

(B) if the Secretary of State shall certify to the Secretary of the Treasury that the foreign government, with respect to whose instrumentality and employees thereof exemption is claimed, grants an equivalent exemption with respect to similar service performed in the foreign country by employees of the United States Government and of instrumentalities thereof;

(13) service performed as a student nurse in the employ of a hospital or a nurses' training school by an individual who is enrolled and is regularly attending classes in a nurses' training school chartered or approved pursuant to State law;

(14)(A) service performed by an individual under the age of 18 in the delivery or distribution of newspapers or shopping news, not including delivery or distribution to any point for subsequent delivery or distribution;

(B) service performed by an individual in, and at the time of, the sale of newspapers or magazines to ultimate consumers, under an arrangement under which the newspapers or magazines are to be sold by him at a fixed price, his compensation being based on the retention of the excess of such price over the amount at which the newspapers or magazines are charged to him, whether or not he is guaranteed a minimum amount of compensation for such service, or is entitled to be credited with the unsold newspapers or magazines turned back;

(15) service performed in the employ of an international organization, except service which constitutes "employment" under subsection (y);

(16) service performed by an individual under an arrangement with the owner or tenant of land pursuant to which—

(A) such individual undertakes to produce agricultural or horticultural commodities (including livestock, bees, poultry, and fur-bearing animals and wildlife) on such land,

(B) the agricultural or horticultural commodities produced by such individual, or the proceeds therefrom, are to be divided between such individual and such owner or tenant, and

(C) the amount of such individual's share depends on the amount of the agricultural or horticultural commodities produced;

(17) [Stricken.]

(18) service performed in Guam by a resident of the Republic of the Philippines while in Guam on a temporary basis as a nonimmigrant alien admitted to Guam pursuant to section 101(a)(15)(H)(ii) of the Immigration and Nationality Act (8 U.S.C. 1101(a)(15)(H)(ii));

(19) service which is performed by a nonresident alien individual for the period he is temporarily present in the United States as a nonimmigrant under subparagraph (F), (J), (M), or (Q) of section 101(a)(15) of the Immigration and Nationality Act, as amended, and which is performed to carry out the purpose specified in subparagraph (F), (J), (M), or (Q), as the case may be;

(20) service (other than service described in paragraph (3)(A)) performed by an individual on a boat engaged in catching fish or other forms of aquatic animal life under an arrangement with the owner or operator of such boat pursuant to which—

(A) such individual does not receive any cash remuneration other than as provided in subparagraph (B) and other than cash remuneration—

(i) which does not exceed $100 per trip;

(ii) which is contingent on a minimum catch; and

(iii) which is paid solely for additional duties (such as mate, engineer, or cook) for which additional cash remuneration is traditional in the industry,

(B) such individual receives a share of the boat's (or the boats' in the case of a fishing operation involving more than one boat) catch of fish or other forms of aquatic animal life or a share of the proceeds from the sale of such catch, and

(C) the amount of such individual's share depends on the amount of the boat's (or the boats' in the case of a fishing operation involving more than one boat) catch of fish or other forms of aquatic animal life,

but only if the operating crew of such boat (or each boat from which the individual receives a share in the case of a fishing operation involving more than one boat) is normally made up of fewer than 10 individuals;

(21) domestic service in a private home of the employer which—

(A) is performed in any year by an individual under the age of 18 during any portion of such year; and

(B) is not the principal occupation of such employee; or

(22) service performed by members of Indian tribal councils as tribal council members in the employ of an Indian tribal government, except that this paragraph shall not apply in the case of service included under an agreement under section 218A of the Social Security Act.

For purposes of paragraph (20), the operating crew of a boat shall be treated as normally made up of fewer than 10 individuals if the average size of the operating crew on trips made during the preceding 4 calendar quarters consisted of fewer than 10 individuals.

Amendments

• **2022, SECURE 2.0 Act of 2022 (P.L. 117-328)**

P.L. 117-328, §702(b)(1):

Amended Code Sec. 3121(b)(5)(E) by inserting "or special trial judge" before "of the United States Tax Court". For the **effective** date, see Act Sec. 702(d), below.

P.L. 117-328, §702(d), provides:

(d) EFFECTIVE DATE.—The amendments made by this section shall take effect on the date of the enactment of this Act, except that section 7447A(e) of the Internal Revenue Code of 1986 (as added by this section) shall take effect on the date that is 180 days after such date of enactment. Special trial judges retiring on or after the date of the enactment of this Act, and before the date that is 180 days after the date of such enactment, may file an election under such section not later than 60 days after such date.

• **2018, Tribal Social Security Fairness Act of 2018 (P.L. 115-243)**

P.L. 115-243, §2(b)(2)(A)(i)-(iii):

Amended Code Sec. 3121(b) by striking "or" at the end in paragraph (20), by striking the period at the end in paragraph (21) and inserting "; or"; and by inserting after paragraph (21) a new paragraph (22). **Effective** 9-20-2018.

P.L. 115-243, §2(c), provides:

(c) RULE OF CONSTRUCTION.—Nothing in this Act or the amendments made by this Act shall be construed to affect application of any Federal income tax withholding requirements under the Internal Revenue Code of 1986.

EMPLOYMENT TAX—GENERAL PROVISIONS

• **2018, Tax Technical Corrections Act of 2018 (P.L. 115-141)**

P.L. 115-141, § 401(a)(209), Div. U:

Amended Code Sec. 3121(b)(5)(B)(i)(V) by striking "section 105(e)(2)" and inserting "section 104(e)(2)". **Effective** 3-23-2018.

P.L. 115-141, § 401(a)(210), Div. U:

Amended Code Sec. 3121(b)(5)(H)(i) by striking "1997" and inserting "1997,". **Effective** 3-23-2018.

P.L. 115-141, § 401(a)(325)(A), Div. U:

Amended Code Sec. 3121(b)(5)(E) by striking "United States Claims Court" and inserting "United States Court of Federal Claims". [Note: Code Sec. 3121(b)(5)(E) does not contain the text "United States Claims Court". Therefore, this amendment cannot be made.—CCH] **Effective** 3-23-2018.

• **2014, Tax Technical Corrections Act of 2014 (P.L. 113-295)**

P.L. 113-295, § 221(a)(99)(C)(i):

Amended Code Sec. 3121(b) by striking paragraph (17). **Effective** generally 12-19-2014. For a special rule, see Act Sec. 221(b)(2), Division A, below. Prior to being stricken, Code Sec. 3121(b)(17) read as follows:

(17) service in the employ of any organization which is performed (A) in any year during any part of which such organization is registered, or there is in effect a final order of the Subversive Activities Control Board requiring such organization to register, under the Internal Security Act of 1950, as amended, as a Communist-action organization, a Communist-front organization, or a Communist-infiltrated organization, and (B) after June 30, 1956;

P.L. 113-295, § 221(b)(2), Division A, provides:

(2) SAVINGS PROVISION.—If—

(A) any provision amended or repealed by the amendments made by this section applied to—

(i) any transaction occurring before the date of the enactment of this Act,

(ii) any property acquired before such date of enactment, or

(iii) any item of income, loss, deduction, or credit taken into account before such date of enactment, and

(B) the treatment of such transaction, property, or item under such provision would (without regard to the amendments or repeals made by this section) affect the liability for tax for periods ending after date of enactment, nothing in the amendments or repeals made by this section shall be construed to affect the treatment of such transaction, property, or item for purposes of determining liability for tax for periods ending after such date of enactment.

• **2008, Worker, Retiree, and Employer Recovery Act of 2008 (P.L. 110-458)**

P.L. 110-458, § 108(k)(1):

Amended Code Sec. 3121(b)(5)(E) by striking "or special trial judge" before "of the United States Tax Court". **Effective** as if included in the provision of the 2006 Act to which the amendment relates [**effective** 8-17-2006.—CCH].

• **2006, Pension Protection Act of 2006 (P.L. 109-280)**

P.L. 109-280, § 854(c)(8):

Amended Code Sec. 3121(b)(5)(E) by inserting "or special trial judge" before "of the United States Tax Court". **Effective** 8-17-2006.

• **1997, Treasury and General Government Appropriations Act, 1998 (P.L. 105-61)**

P.L. 105-61, § 642(d)(2)(A)-(B):

Amended Code Sec. 3121(b)(5)(H)(i) by striking "or" after "1986" and inserting a comma, and by inserting "or the Federal Employees' Retirement System Open Enrollment Act of 1997" after "(50 U.S.C. 2157),". **Effective** 10-10-97.

• **1997, Balanced Budget Act of 1997 (P.L. 105-33)**

P.L. 105-33, § 11246(b)(2) (as amended by P.L. 105-277, Div. A, § 802(a)(2)):

Amended Code Sec. 3121(b)(7)(C) by inserting "(other than the Federal Employees Retirement System provided in chapter 84 of title 5, United States Code)" after "law of the United States". **Effective** as if included in the enactment of title XI of P.L. 105-33.

• **1996, Small Business Job Protection Act of 1996 (P.L. 104-188)**

P.L. 104-188, § 1116(a)(1)(A):

Amended Code Sec. 3121(b) by adding at the end a new sentence. For the **effective** date, see Act Sec. 1116(a)(3)(A), below.

P.L. 104-188, § 1116(a)(1)(B):

Amended Code Sec. 3121(b)(20)(A). For the **effective** date, see Act Sec. 1116(a)(3)(A), below. Prior to amendment, Code Sec. 3121(b)(20)(A) read as follows:

(A) such individual does not receive any cash remuneration (other than as provided in subparagraph (B)),

P.L. 104-188, § 1116(a)(3)(A), provides:

(A) IN GENERAL.—The amendments made by this subsection shall apply to remuneration paid—

(i) after December 31, 1994, and

(ii) after December 31, 1984, and before January 1, 1995, unless the payor treated such remuneration (when paid) as being subject to tax under chapter 21 of the Internal Revenue Code of 1986.

• **1994, Social Security Domestic Employment Reform Act of 1994 (P.L. 103-387)**

P.L. 103-387, § 2(a)(1)(C)(i)-(iii):

Amended Code Sec. 3121(b) by striking "or" at the end of paragraph (19), by striking the period at the end of paragraph (20) and inserting "; or", and by adding at the end a new paragraph (21). **Effective** for services performed after 12-31-94.

• **1994, Social Security Independence and Program Improvements Act of 1994 (P.L. 103-296)**

P.L. 103-296, § 108(h)(2):

Amended Code Sec. 3121(b)(10)(B) by striking "Secretary of Health and Human Services" each place it appears and inserting "Commissioner of Social Security". **Effective** 3-31-95.

P.L. 103-296, § 303(a)(2):

Amended Code Sec. 3121(b)(7)(F)(iv) by striking "$100" and inserting "$1,000 with respect to service performed during any calendar year commencing on or after January 1, 1995, ending on or before December 31, 1999, and the adjusted amount determined under section 218(c)(8)(B) of the Social Security Act for any calendar year commencing on or after January 1, 2000, with respect to service performed during such calendar year". **Effective** with respect to service performed on or after 1-1-95.

P.L. 103-296, § 319(a)(5):

Amended Code Sec. 3121(b)(15) by inserting ", except service which constitutes 'employment' under subsection (y)" after "organization". **Effective** with respect to service performed after the calendar quarter following the calendar quarter containing 8-15-94.

P.L. 103-296, § 320(a)(1)(C):

Amended Code Sec. 3121(b)(19) by striking "(J), or (M)" each place it appears and inserting "(J), (M), or (Q)". **Effective** for the calendar quarter following 8-15-94.

• **1993, Intelligence Authorization Act for Fiscal Year 1994 (P.L. 103-178)**

P.L. 103-178, § 204(c):

Amended Code Sec. 3121(b)(5)(H)(i) by striking "section 307 of the Central Intelligence Agency Retirement Act of 1964 for Certain Employees" and inserting in lieu thereof "section 307 of the Central Intelligence Agency Retirement Act (50 U.S.C. 2157)". **Effective** 12-3-93.

• **1992, Court of Federal Claims Technical and Procedural Improvements Act of 1992 (P.L. 102-572)**

P.L. 102-572, § 902(b)(1):

Amended Code Sec. 3121(b)(5)(E) by striking "United States Claims Court" and inserting "United States Court of Federal Claims". **Effective** 10-29-92.

• **1990, Omnibus Budget Reconciliation Act of 1990 (P.L. 101-508)**

P.L. 101-508, § 11332(b)(1):

Amended Code Sec. 3121(b)(7) by striking "or" at the end of subparagraph (D). **Effective** with respect to service performed after 7-1-91.

P.L. 101-508, § 11332(b)(2):

Amended Code Sec. 3121(b)(7)(E) by striking the semicolon at the end thereof and inserting ", or". **Effective** with respect to service performed after 7-1-91.

P.L. 101-508, § 11332(b)(3):

Amended Code Sec. 3121(b)(7) by adding at the end thereof a new subparagraph (F). **Effective** with respect to service performed after 7-1-91.

• **1988, Technical and Miscellaneous Revenue Act of 1988 (P.L. 100-647)**

P.L. 100-647, § 1001(d)(2)(C)(i):

Amended Code Sec. 3121(b)(19) by striking out "(F) or (J)" each place it appears and inserting in lieu thereof "(F), (J), or (M)". **Effective** as if included in the provision of P.L. 99-514 to which it relates.

P.L. 100-647, § 8015(b)(2):

Amended Code Sec. 3121(b)(5)(H). **Effective** as if included or reflected in section 304 of the Federal Employees' Retirement System Act of 1986 (100 Stat. 606) at the time of its enactment. Prior to amendment, Code Sec. 3121(b)(5)(H) read as follows:

(H) service performed by an individual on or after the effective date of an election by such individual under section 301(a) of the Federal Employees' Retirement System Act of 1986, or under regulations issued under section 860 of the Foreign Service Act of 1980 or section 307 of the Central Intelligence Agency Retirement Act of 1964 for Certain Employees, to become subject to chapter 84 of title 5, United States Code;

P.L. 100-647, § 8015(c)(2):

Amended Code Sec. 3121(b)(5) in the matter following subparagraph (B)(ii), by inserting after "with respect to" "any such service performed on or after any date on which such individual performs". **Effective** for any individual only upon the performance by such individual of service described in subparagraph (C), (D), (E), (F), (G), or (H) of section 210(a)(5) of the Social Security Act (42 U.S.C. 410(a)(5)) on or after 11-10-88.

• **1987, Revenue Act of 1987 (P.L. 100-203)**

P.L. 100-203, § 9004(b)(1):

Amended Code Sec. 3121(b)(3)(A) by striking "performed by an individual in the employ of his spouse, and service" before "performed". **Effective** with respect to remuneration paid after 12-31-87.

Sec. 3121(b)(22)

EMPLOYMENT TAX—GENERAL PROVISIONS

P.L. 100-203, §9004(b)(2):

Amended Code Sec. 3121(b)(3) by striking so much of subparagraph (B) as precedes clause (i) and inserting the new material that precedes clause (i). **Effective** with respect to remuneration paid after 12-31-87. Prior to amendment, the material preceding clause (i) read as follows:

(B) service not in the course of the employer's trade or business, or domestic service in a private home of the employer, performed by an individual in the employ of his son or daughter; except that the provisions of this subparagraph shall not be applicable to such domestic service if—

P.L. 100-203, §9005(b)(1):

Amended Code Sec. 3121(b)(3)(A) by striking out "21" and inserting "18". **Effective** with respect to remuneration paid after 12-31-87.

P.L. 100-203, §9005(b)(2):

Amended Code Sec. 3121(b)(3)(B) by inserting "under the age of 21 in the employ of his father or mother, or performed by an individual" after "individual" the first place it appears. **Effective** with respect to remuneration paid after 12-31-87.

- **1986, Omnibus Budget Reconciliation Act of 1986 (P.L. 99-509)**

P.L. 99-509, §9002(b)(1)(A)(i)-(iii):

Amended Code Sec. 3121(b)(7) by striking out "; or" at the end of subparagraph (C) and inserting in lieu thereof a comma, by striking out the semicolon at the end of subparagraph (D) and inserting in lieu thereof ", or", and by adding after subparagraph (D) new subparagraph (E) For the **effective** date, see Act Sec. 9002(d), below.

P.L. 99-509, §9002(d), provides:

(d) EFFECTIVE DATE.—The amendments made by this section are effective with respect to payments due with respect to wages paid after December 31, 1986, including wages paid after such date by a State (or political subdivision thereof) that modified its agreement pursuant to the provisions of section 218(e)(2) of the Social Security Act prior to the date of the enactment of this Act; except that in cases where, in accordance with the currently applicable schedule, deposits of taxes due under an agreement entered into pursuant to section 218 of the Social Security Act would be required within 3 days after the close of an eighth-monthly period, such 3-day requirement shall be changed to a 7-day requirement for wages paid prior to October 1, 1987, and to a 5-day requirement for wages paid after September 30, 1987, and prior to October 1, 1988. For wages paid prior to October 1, 1988, the deposit schedule for taxes imposed under sections 3101 and 3111 shall be determined separately from the deposit schedule for taxes withheld under section 3402 if the taxes imposed under sections 3101 and 3111 are due with respect to service included under an agreement entered into pursuant to section 218 of the Social Security Act.

- **1986 (P.L. 99-335)**

P.L. 99-335, §304(b)(1)-(3):

Amended Code Sec. 3121(b)(5) by striking out "or" at the end of subparagraph (F); by striking out the semicolon at the end of subparagraph (G) and inserting in lieu thereof ", or"; and adding at the end new subparagraph. **Effective** 6-6-86.

- **1986, Consolidated Omnibus Budget Reconciliation Act of 1985 (P.L. 99-272)**

P.L. 99-272, §13303(c)(2):

Amended Code Sec. 3121(b)(20) by inserting "(other than service described in paragraph (3)(A))" before "performed". **Effective** 4-7-86.

- **1985, Cherokee Leasing Act (P.L. 99-221)**

P.L. 99-221, §(3)(b)(1)-(3):

Amended Code Sec. 3121(b)(5)(B)(i) by striking out "and" at the end of subclause (III), by striking out "; or" at the end of the subclause (IV) and inserting in lieu thereof ", and", and by adding after subclause (IV) new subclause (V). **Effective** for any return to the performance of service in the employ of the United States, or of an instrumentality thereof, after 1983.

- **1984, Deficit Reduction Act of 1984 (P.L. 98-369)**

P.L. 98-369, §2601(b)(1):

Amended Code Sec. 3121(b)(5)(B). **Effective** with respect to service performed after 12-31-83. Special rules appear in Act Sec. 2601(c)-(e), below. Prior to amendment, Code Sec. 3121(b)(5)(B) reads as follows:

(B) is performed by an individual who (i) has been continuously in the employ of the United States or an instrumentality thereof since December 31, 1983 (and for this purpose an individual who returns to the performance of such service after being separated therefrom following a previous period of such service shall nevertheless be considered upon such return as having been continuously in the employ of the United States or an instrumentality thereof, regardless of whether the period of such separation began before, on, or after December 31, 1983, if the period of such separation does not exceed 365 consecutive days), or (ii) is receiving an annuity from the Civil Service Retirement and Disability Fund, or benefits (for service as an employee) under another retirement system established by law of the United States for employees of the Federal Government other than for members of the uniformed services);

P.L. 98-369, §2601(b)(2):

Further amended Code Sec. 3121(b)(5) (in the matter which follows "except that this paragraph shall not apply with respect to —") by striking out "(i)", "(ii)", "(iii)", "(iv)", and "(v)" and inserting in lieu thereof "(C)", "(D)", "(E)", "(F)", and "(G)", respectively; by striking out "(I)", "(II)", and "(III)", and inserting in lieu thereof "(i)", "(ii)", and "(iii)", respectively; and by striking out subparagraph (G) (as redesignated by subparagraph (A) of this paragraph) and inserting in lieu thereof new paragraph (G). **Effective** with respect to service performed after 12-31-83. Special rules appear in Act Sec. 2601(e), below. Prior to amendment, subparagraph (G) ((v), prior to redesignation) read as follows:

(v) any other service in the legislative branch of the Federal Government if such service is performed by an individual who, on December 31, 1983, is not subject to subchapter III of chapter 83 of title 5, United States Code;

P.L. 98-369, §2601(c)-(e), provides:

(c) For purposes of section 210(a)(5)(G) of the Social Security Act and section 3121(b)(5)(G) of the Internal Revenue Code of 1954, an individual shall not be considered to be subject to subchapter III of chapter 83 of title 5, United States Code or to another retirement system established by a law of the United States for employees of the Federal Government (other than for members of the uniformed services), if he is contributing a reduced amount by reason of the Federal Employees' Retirement Contribution Temporary Adjustment Act of 1983.

(d)(1) Any individual who—

(A) was subject to subchapter III of chapter 83 of title 5, United States Code, or to another retirement system established by a law of the United States for employees of the Federal Government (other than for members of the uniformed services), on December 31, 1983 (as determined for purposes of section 210(a)(5)(G) of the Social Security Act), and

(B)(i) received a lump-sum payment under section 8342(a) of such title 5, or under the corresponding provision of the law establishing the other retirement system described in subparagraph (A), after December 31, 1983, and prior to June 15, 1984, or received such a payment on or after June 15, 1984, pursuant to an application which was filed in accordance with such section 8342(a) or the corresponding provision of the law establishing such other retirement system prior to that date, or

(ii) otherwise ceased to be subject to subchapter III of chapter 83 of title 5, United States Code, for a period after December 31, 1983, to which section 210(a)(5)(G)(iii) of the Social Security Act applies,

shall, if such individual again becomes subject to subchapter III of chapter 83 of title 5 (or effectively applies for coverage under such subchapter) after the date on which he last ceased to be subject to such subchapter but prior to, or within 30 days after, the date of the enactment of this Act, requalify for the exemption from social security coverage and taxes under section 210(a)(5) of the Social Security Act and section 3121(b)(5) of the Internal Revenue Code of 1954 as if the cessation of coverage under title 5 had not occurred.

(2) An individual meeting the requirements of subparagraphs (A) and (B) of paragraph (1) who is not in the employ of the United States or an instrumentality thereof on the date of the enactment of this Act may requalify for such exemptions in the same manner as under paragraph (1) if such individual again becomes subject to subchapter III of chapter 83 of title 5 (or effectively applies for coverage under such subchapter) within 30 days after the date on which he first returns to service in the legislative branch after such date of enactment, if such date (on which he returns to service) is within 365 days after he was last in the employ of the United States or an instrumentality thereof.

(3) If an individual meeting the requirements of subparagraphs (A) and (B) of paragraph (1) does not again become subject to subchapter III of chapter 83 of title 5 (or effectively apply for coverage under such subchapter) prior to the date of the enactment of this Act or within the relevant 30-day period as provided in paragraph (1) or (2), social security coverage and taxes by reason of section 210(a)(5)(G) of the Social Security Act and section 3121(b)(5)(G) of the Internal Revenue Code of 1954 shall, with respect to such individual's service in the legislative branch of the Federal Government, become effective with the first month beginning after such 30-day period.

(4) The provisions of paragraphs (1) and (2) shall apply only for purposes of reestablishing an exemption from social security coverage and taxes, and do not affect the amount of service to be credited to an individual for purposes of title 5, United States Code.

(e)(1) For purposes of section 210(a)(5) of the Social Security Act (as in effect in January 1983 and as in effect on and after January 1, 1984) and section 3121(b)(5) of the Internal Revenue Code of 1954 (as so in effect), service performed in the employ of a non-profit organization described in section 501(c)(3) of the Internal Revenue Code of 1954 by an employee who is required by law to be subject to subchapter III of chapter 83 of title 5, United States Code, with respect to such service, shall be considered to be service performed in the employ of an instrumentality of the United States.

(2) For purposes of section 203 of the Federal Employees' Retirement Contribution Temporary Adjustment Act of 1983, service described in paragraph (1) which is also "employment" for purposes of title II of the Social Security Act, shall be considered to be "covered service".

P.L. 98-369, §2603(a)(2):

Amended Code Sec. 3121(b)(8) by inserting "(A)" after "(8)", by striking out "this paragraph" and inserting in lieu thereof "this subparagraph", and by adding at the end thereof new subparagraph (B). **Effective** for service performed after 12-31-83. A special rule appears in Act Sec. 2603(f), below.

P.L. 98-369, §2603(f), provides:

(f) In any case where a church or qualified church-controlled organization makes an election under section 3121(w) of the Internal Revenue Code of 1954, the Secretary of the Treasury shall refund (without interest) to such church or organization any taxes paid under sections 3101 and 3111 of such Code with respect to service performed after December 31, 1983, which is covered under such election. The refund shall be conditional upon the church or organization agreeing to pay to each employee (or former employee) the portion of the refund attributable to the tax imposed on such employee (or former employee) under section 3101, and such employee (or former employee) may not receive any other refund payment of such taxes.

P.L. 98-369, §2663(i)(1):

Amended Code Sec. 3121(b)(1) by striking out "(A)" and all that follows down through "or (B)". **Effective** on 7-18-84, but shall not be construed as changing or affecting any right, liability, status, or interpretation which existed (under the provisions of law involved) before that date. Prior to amendment, paragraph (1) of Code Sec. 3121(b) read as follows:

(1) service performed by foreign agricultural workers (A) under contracts entered into in accordance with title V of the Agricultural Act of 1949, as amended (7 U.S.C. 1461-1468), or (B) lawfully admitted to the United States from the Bahamas, Jamaica, and the other British West Indies, or from any other foreign country or possession thereof, on a temporary basis to perform agricultural labor;

EMPLOYMENT TAX—GENERAL PROVISIONS

P.L. 98-369, §2663(j)(5)(C):

Amended Code Sec. 3121(b)(10)(B) by striking out "Health, Education, and Welfare" and inserting in lieu thereof "Health and Human Services". **Effective** on 7-18-84, but shall not be construed as changing or affecting any right, liability, status, or interpretation which existed (under the provisions of law involved) before that date.

- **1983, Social Security Amendments of 1983 (P.L. 98-21)**

P.L. 98-21, §101(b)(1):

Amended Code Secs. 3121(b)(5) and (6). **Effective** with respect to service performed after 12-31-83. Prior to amendment, Code Sec. 3121(b)(5)-(6) read as follows:

(5) service performed in the employ of any instrumentality of the United States, if such instrumentality is exempt from the tax imposed by section 3111 by virtue of any provision of law which specifically refers to such section (or the corresponding section of prior law) in granting such exemption;

(6)(A) service performed in the employ of the United States or in the employ of any instrumentality of the United States, if such service is covered by a retirement system established by a law of the United States;

(B) service performed by an individual in the employ of an instrumentality of the United States if such an instrumentality was exempt from the tax imposed by section 1410 of the Internal Revenue Code of 1939 on December 31, 1950, and if such service is covered by a retirement system established by such instrumentality; except that the provisions of this subparagraph shall not be applicable to—

(i) service performed in the employ of a corporation which is wholly owned by the United States;

(ii) service performed in the employ of a Federal land bank, a Federal intermediate credit bank, a bank for cooperatives, a Federal land bank association, a production credit association, a Federal Reserve Bank, a Federal Home Loan Bank, or a Federal Credit Union;

(iii) service performed in the employ of a State, county, or community committee under the Commodity Stabilization Service;

(iv) service performed by a civilian employee, not compensated from funds appropriated by the Congress, in the Army and Air Force Exchange Service, Army and Air Force Motion Picture Service, Navy Exchanges, Marine Corps Exchanges, or other activities, conducted by an instrumentality of the United States subject to the jurisdiction of the Secretary of Defense, at installations of the Department of Defense for the comfort, pleasure, contentment, and mental and physical improvement of personnel of such Department; or

(v) service performed by a civilian employee, not compensated from funds appropriated by the Congress, in the Coast Guard Exchanges or other activities, conducted by an instrumentality of the United States subject to the jurisdiction of the Secretary of Transportation, at installations of the Coast Guard for the comfort, pleasure, contentment, and mental and physical improvement of personnel of the Coast Guard;

(C) service performed in the employ of the United States or in the employ of any instrumentality of the United States, if such service is performed—

(i) as the President or Vice President of the United States or as a Member, Delegate, or Resident Commissioner of or to the Congress;

(ii) in the legislative branch;

(iii) in a penal institution of the United States by an inmate thereof;

(iv) by any individual as an employee included under section 5351(2) of title 5, United States Code (relating to certain interns, student nurses, and other student employees of hospitals of the Federal Government) other than as a medical or dental intern or a medical or dental resident in training;

(v) by any individual as an employee serving on a temporary basis in case of fire, storm, earthquake, flood, or other similar emergency; or

(vi) by any individual to whom subchapter III of chapter 83 of title 5, United States Code, does not apply because such individual is subject to another retirement system (other than the retirement system of the Tennessee Valley Authority).

P.L. 98-21, §102(b)(1):

Amended Code Sec. 3121(b)(8). **Effective** with respect to service performed after 12-31-83. Prior to amendment, Code Sec. 3121(b)(8) read as follows:

(8)(A) service performed by a duly ordained, commissioned, or licensed minister of a church in the exercise of his ministry or by a member of a religious order in the exercise of duties required by such order, except that this subparagraph shall not apply to service performed by a member of such an order in the exercise of such duties, if an election of coverage under subsection (r) is in effect with respect to such order, or with respect to the autonomous subdivision thereof to which such member belongs;

(B) service performed in the employ of a religious, charitable, educational, or other organization described in section 501(c)(3) which is exempt from income tax under section 501(a), but this subparagraph shall not apply to service performed during the period for which a certificate, filed pursuant to subsection (k) (or the corresponding subsection of prior law) or deemed to have been so filed under paragraph (4) or (5) of such subsection, is in effect if such service is performed by an employee—

(i) whose signature appears on the list filed (or deemed to have been filed) by such organization under subsection (k) (or the corresponding subsection of prior law);

(ii) who became an employee of such organization after the calendar quarter in which the certificate (other than a certificate referred to in clause (iii)) was filed (or deemed to have been filed), or

(iii) who, after the calendar quarter in which the certificate was (or deemed to have been filed) filed with respect to a group described in section 3121(k)(1)(E), became a member of such group,

except that this subparagraph shall apply with respect to service performed by an employee as a member of a group described in section 3121(k)(1)(E) with respect to which no certificate is (or is deemed to be) in effect;

P.L. 98-21, §322(a)(2):

Amended the material preceding paragraph (1) in Code Sec. 3121(b) by striking out "either" before "(A)", and by inserting before "; except" the following: ", or (C) if it is service, regardless of where or by whom performed, which is designated as employment or recognized as equivalent to employment under an agreement entered into under section 233 of the Social Security Act". **Effective** with respect to tax years beginning on or after 4-20-83.

P.L. 98-21, §323(a)(1):

Amended the material preceding paragraph (1) in Code Sec. 3121(b) by striking out "a citizen of the United States" and inserting in lieu thereof "a citizen or resident of the United States". **Effective** for remuneration paid after 12-31-83.

- **1977 (P.L. 95-216)**

P.L. 95-216, §356(c):

Amended Code Sec. 3121(b)(10). **Effective** for remuneration paid and services rendered after 1977. Before amendment, paragraph (b)(10) read as follows:

(10)(A) service performed in any calendar quarter in the employ of any organization exempt from income tax under section 501(a) (other than an organization described in section 401(a)) or under section 521, if the remuneration for such service is less than $50;

(B) service performed in the employ of—

(i) a school, college, or university, or

(ii) an organization described in section 509(a)(3) if the organization is organized, and at all times thereafter is operated, exclusively for the benefit of, to perform the functions of, or to carry out the purposes of a school, college, or university and is operated, supervised, or controlled by or in connection with such school, college, or university unless it is a school, college, or university of a State or a political subdivision thereof and the services performed in its employ by a student referred to in section 218(c)(5) of the Social Security Act are covered under the agreement between the Secretary of Health, Education, and Welfare and such State entered into pursuant to section 218 of such Act;

if such service is performed by a student who is enrolled and regularly attending classes at such school, college, or university;

P.L. 95-216, §356(d):

Amended Code Sec. 3121(b)(17). **Effective** for remuneration paid and services rendered after 1977. Before amendment, paragraph (b)(17) read as follows:

(17) service in the employ of any organization which is performed (A) in any quarter during any part of which such organization is registered, or there is in effect a final order of the Subversive Activities Control Board requiring such organization to register, under the Internal Security Act of 1950, as amended, as a Communist-action organization, a Communist-front organization, or a Communist-infiltrated organization, and (B) after June 30, 1956;

- **1976 (P.L. 94-563)**

P.L. 94-563, §1(b),(d):

Amended Code Sec. 3121(b)(8) by inserting after "filed pursuant to subsection (k) (or the corresponding subsection of prior law)" in the matter preceding clause (i): "or deemed to have been so filed under paragraph (4) or (5) of such subsection"; by inserting after "filed" in clauses (i), (ii), and (iii) the following: "(or deemed to have been filed)"; and by substituting "is (or is deemed to be) in effect" for "is in effect" in the matter following clause (iii). **Effective** for services performed after 1950, to the extent covered by waiver certificates filed or deemed to have been filed under section 3121(k)(4) or (5) of the Internal Revenue Code of 1954 (as added by such amendments).

- **1976, Tax Reform Act of 1976 (P.L. 94-455)**

P.L. 94-455, §1207(e)(1)(A):

Amended Code Sec. 3121(b) by striking out "or" at the end of paragraph (18); by striking out the period at the end of paragraph (19) and inserting in lieu thereof "; or"; and by adding a new paragraph (20).

P.L. 94-455, §1207(f)(4), as amended by P.L. 95-600, §701(z)(1), (2), provides:

(4) SUBSECTION (e).—

(A) The amendments made by paragraphs (1)(A) and (2)(A) of subsection (e) shall apply to services performed after December 31, 1954. The amendments made by paragraphs (1)(B), (1)(C), and (2)(B) of such subsection shall apply to taxable years ending after December 31, 1954. The amendments made by paragraph (3) of such subsection shall apply to calendar years beginning after the date of the enactment of this Act.

(B) Notwithstanding subparagraph (A), if the owner or operator of any boat treated a share of the boat's catch of fish or other aquatic animal life (or a share of the proceeds therefrom) received by an individual after December 31, 1954, and before the date of the enactment of this Act for services performed by such individual after December 31, 1954, on such boat as being subject to the tax under chapter 21 of the Internal Revenue Code of 1954, then the amendments made by paragraphs (1)(A) and (B) and (2) of subsection (e) shall not apply with respect to such services performed by such individual (and the share of the catch, or proceeds therefrom, received by him for such services).

P.L. 94-455, §1903(a)(3)(A):

Substituted ", of whatever nature, performed" for "performed after 1936 and prior to 1955 which was employment for purposes of subchapter A of chapter 9 of the Internal Revenue Code of 1939 under the law applicable to the period in which such service was performed, and any service, of whatever nature, performed after 1954"; and deleted ", in the case of service performed after 1954," in Code Sec. 3121(b). **Effective** for wages paid after 12-31-76.

P.L. 94-455, §1903(a)(3)(B):

Deleted "65 Stat. 119;" in Code Sec. 3121(b)(1). **Effective** for wages paid after 12-31-76.

P.L. 94-455, §1903(a)(3)(A)(C):

Substituted "Secretary of Transportation" for "Secretary of the Treasury" in Code Sec. 3121(b)(6)(B)(v). **Effective** for wages paid after 12-31-76.

Sec. 3121(b)(22)

EMPLOYMENT TAX—GENERAL PROVISIONS

P.L. 94-455, §1906(b)(13)(C):

Substituted "to the Secretary of the Treasury" for "to the Secretary" in Code Sec. 3121(b)(12)(B). **Effective** 2-1-77.

• **1972, Social Security Amendments of 1972 (P.L. 92-603)**

P.L. 92-603, §123(a)(2):

Added at the end of Code Sec. 3121(b)(8)(A): ", except that this subparagraph shall not apply to service performed by a member of such an order in the exercise of such duties, if an election of coverage under subsection (r) is in effect with respect to such order, or with respect to the autonomous subdivision thereof to which such member belongs". For **effective** date, see Code Sec. 3121(r).

P.L. 92-603, §125(a), provides:

"The provisions of section 210(a)(6)(B)(ii) of the Social Security Act and section 3121(b)(6)(B)(ii) of the Internal Revenue Code of 1954, insofar as they relate to service performed in the employ of a Federal home loan bank, shall be effective—

"(1) with respect to all service performed in the employ of a Federal home loan bank on and after the first day of the first calendar quarter which begins on or after the date of the enactment of this Act [October 30, 1972]; and

"(2) in the case of individuals who are in the employ of a Federal home loan bank on such first day, with respect to any service performed in the employ of a Federal home loan bank after the last day of the sixth calendar year preceding the year in which this Act is enacted: but this paragraph shall be effective only if an amount equal to the taxes imposed by sections 3101 and 3111 of such Code with respect to the services of all such individuals performed in the employ of Federal home loan banks after the last day of the sixth calendar year preceding the year in which this Act is enacted are paid under the provisions of section 3122 of such Code by July 1, 1973, or by such later date as may be provided in an agreement entered into before such date with the Secretary of the Treasury or his delegate for purposes of this paragraph."

P.L. 92-603, §128(b):

Added Code Sec. 3121(b)(7)(D). **Effective** for service performed on and after 1-1-73.

P.L. 92-603, §129(a)(2):

Amended Code Sec. 3121(b)(10)(B). **Effective** for services performed after 12-31-72. Prior to amendment, said section read as follows:

"(B) service performed in the employ of a school, college, or university if such service is performed by a student who is enrolled and is regularly attending classes at such school, college, or university."

• **1968, Social Security Amendments of 1967 (P.L. 90-248)**

P.L. 90-248, §123(b):

Amended Sec. 3121(b)(3)(B). **Effective** with respect to services performed after 12-31-67. Prior to amendment, Sec. 3121(b)(3)(B) read as follows:

"(B) service not in the course of the employer's trade or business, or domestic service in a private home of the employer, performed by an individual in the employ of his son or daughter;"

P.L. 90-248, §403(i):

Amended Secs. 3121(b)(6)(C)(iv) and 3121(b)(7)(C)(ii) by substituting "under section 5351(2) of title 5, United States Code" for "under section 2 of the Act of August 4, 1947" and by deleting "; 5 U.S.C. 1052" which formerly appeared after the word "Government," in both Code sections. Also amended Sec. 3121(b)(6)(C)(vi) by substituting "subchapter III of chapter 83 of title 5, United States Code" for "the Civil Service Retirement Act".

• **1965, Social Security Amendments of 1965 (P.L. 89-97)**

P.L. 89-97, §103(o):

Amended Code Sec. 3121(b) by striking out "or" at the end of paragraph (16), by striking out the period at the end of paragraph (17) and substituting "; or", and by adding a new paragraph (18). **Effective** for service performed after 1960.

P.L. 89-97, §104(b):

Amended paragraph (3) of Code Sec. 3121(b). **Effective** for services performed after 1960. Prior to amendment, it read as follows:

"(3) service performed by an individual in the employ of his son, daughter, or spouse, and service performed by a child under the age of 21 in the employ of his father or mother;".

P.L. 89-97, §§311, 317(b):

Amended Sec. 3121(b)(6)(C)(iv) by inserting before the semicolon at the end ", other than as a medical or dental intern or a medical or dental resident in training"; Amended Sec. 3121(b)(13) by striking out all that followed the first semicolon, "and thereof, or any instrumentality of any one or more of the foregoing wholly owned thereby, which is performed after 1960 and after the calendar quarter in which the Secretary of the Treasury receives a certification by the Governor of American Samoa that the Government of American Samoa desires to have the insurance system established by such title II extended to the officers and employees of such Government and such political subdivisions and instrumentalities."

• **1959, Farm Credit Act of 1959 (P.L. 86-168)**

P.L. 86-168, §104(h):

Amended Code Sec. 3121(b)(6)(B)(ii) by substituting "Federal land bank association" for "national farm loan association". **Effective** 12-31-59.

P.L. 86-168, §202(a):

Amended Code Sec. 3121(b)(6)(B)(ii) by adding "a Federal land bank, a Federal intermediate credit bank, a bank for cooperatives,". **Effective** 1-1-60.

• **1958, Social Security Amendments of 1958 (P.L. 85-840)**

P.L. 85-840, §404(a):

Amended Sec. 3121(b)(1). **Effective** for service performed after 1958. Prior to amendment Sec. 3121(b)(1) read as follows:

"(1)(A) service performed in connection with the production or harvesting of any commodity defined as an agricultural commodity in section 15(g) of the Agricultural Marketing Act, as amended (46 Stat. 1550 §3; 12 U. S. C. 1141j);

"(B) service performed by foreign agricultural workers (i) under contracts entered into in accordance with title V of the Agricultural Act of 1949, as amended (65 Stat. 119; 7 U. S. C. 1461-1468), or (ii) lawfully admitted to the United States from the Bahamas, Jamaica, and the other British West Indies, or from any other foreign country or possession thereof, on a temporary basis to perform agricultural labor;".

P.L. 85-840, §405(b):

Amended Sec. 3121(b)(8)(B). **Effective** for certificates filed under Sec. 3121(k)(1) after 8-28-58 and requests filed under subparagraph (F) of that section after that date. Prior to amendment, Sec. 3121(b)(8)(B) read as follows:

"(B) service performed in the employ of a religious, charitable, educational, or other organization described in section 501(c)(3) which is exempt from income tax under section 501(a), but this subparagraph shall not apply to service performed during the period for which a certificate, filed pursuant to subsection (k) (or the corresponding subsection of prior law), is in effect if such service is performed by an employee—

"(i) whose signature appears on the list filed by such organization under subsection (k) (or the corresponding subsection of prior law), or

"(ii) who became an employee of such organization after the calendar quarter in which the certificate was filed;".

• **1956, Social Security Amendments of 1956 (P.L. 880, 84th Cong.)**

P.L. 880, 84th Cong., 2d Sess., §201(c):

Amended Sec. 3121(b)(1). **Effective** for service performed after 1956. Prior to amendment Sec. 3121(b)(1) read as follows:

"(1)(A) service performed in connection with the production or harvesting of any commodity defined as an agricultural commodity in section 15(g) of the Agricultural Marketing Act, as amended (46 Stat. 1550 §3; 12 U. S. C. 1141j);

"(B) service performed by foreign agricultural workers (i) under contracts entered into in accordance with title V of the Agricultural Act of 1949, as amended (65 Stat. 119; 7 U. S. C. 1461-1468), or (ii) lawfully admitted to the United States from the Bahamas, Jamaica, and the other British West Indies on a temporary basis to perform agricultural labor;".

P.L. 880, 84th Cong., 2d Sess., §201(d)(1):

Amended Sec. 3121(b)(6)(B)(ii) by adding the following: "a Federal Home Loan Bank,". §201(d)(2) amended Sec. 3121(b)(6)(C)(vi) by deleting "of 1930" following the words "Civil Service Retirement Act" and by adding the following: "(other than the retirement system of the Tennessee Valley Authority)". These amendments are identical with the amendments made by §104(b) of P.L. 880 to Social Security Act Sec. 210 and the **effective** dates in §104(i) of P.L. 880 apply. These provide as follows:

"(2)(A) Except as provided in subparagraphs (B) and (C), the amendments made by subsection (b) shall apply only with respect to service performed after June 30, 1957, and only if—

"(i) in the case of the amendment made by paragraph (1) of such subsection, the conditions prescribed in subparagraph (B) are met; and

"(ii) in the case of the amendment made by paragraph (2) of such subsection, the conditions prescribed in subparagraph (C) are met.

"(B) the amendment made by paragraph (1) of subsection (b) shall be effective only if—

"(i) the Federal Home Loan Bank Board submits to the Secretary of Health, Education, and Welfare, and the Secretary approves, before July 1, 1957, a plan, with respect to employees of Federal Home Loan Banks, for the coordination, on an equitable basis, of the benefits provided by the retirement system applicable to such employees with the benefits provided by title II of the Social Security Act; and

"(ii) such plan specifies, as the effective date of the plan July 1, 1957, or the first day of a prior calendar quarter beginning not earlier than January 1, 1956.

If the plan specifies as the effective date of the plan a day before July 1, 1957, the amendment made by paragraph (1) of subsection (b) shall apply with respect to service performed on or after such effective date; except that, if such effective date is prior to the day on which the Secretary approves the plan, such amendment shall not apply with respect to service performed, prior to the day on which the Secretary approves the plan, by an individual who is not an employee of a Federal Home Loan Bank on such day.

"(C) The amendment made by paragraph (2) of subsection (b) shall be effective only if—

"(i) the Board of Directors of the Tennessee Valley Authority submits to the Secretary of Health, Education, and Welfare, and the Secretary approves, before July 1, 1957, a plan, with respect to employees of the Tennessee Valley Authority, for the coordination, on an equitable basis, of the benefits provided by the retirement system applicable to such employees with the benefits provided by title II of the Social Security Act; and

"(ii) such plan specifies as the effective date of the plan July 1, 1957, or the first day of a prior calendar quarter beginning not earlier than January 1, 1956.

If the plan specifies as the effective date of the plan a day before July 1, 1957, the amendment made by paragraph (2) of subsection (b) shall apply with respect to service performed on or after such effective date; except that, if such effective date is prior to the day on which the Secretary approves the plan, such amendment shall not apply with respect to service performed, prior to the day on which the Secretary approves the plan, by an individual who is not an employee of the Tennessee Valley Authority on such day.

"(D) The Secretary of Health, Education, and Welfare shall, on or before July 31, 1957, submit a report to the Congress setting forth the details of any plan approved by him under subparagraph (B) or (C)."

EMPLOYMENT TAX—GENERAL PROVISIONS

P.L. 880, 84th Cong., 2d Sess., §201(e)(1):

Amended Sec. 3121(b) by deleting the "or" after paragraph (14); substituting a semicolon for the period after paragraph (15); and by adding paragraph (16). **Effective** for service performed after 1954.

P.L. 880, 84th Cong., 2d Sess., §121(d):

Amended Sec. 3121(b) by adding paragraph (17).

- **1954, Social Security Amendments of 1954 (P.L. 761, 83rd Cong.)**

P.L. 761, 83rd Cong., §205(a):

Amended paragraph (1). Prior to amendment, paragraph (1) read as follows:

"(1)(A) agricultural labor (as defined in subsection (g)) performed in any calendar quarter by an employee, unless the cash remuneration paid for such labor (other than service described in subparagraph (B)) is $50 or more and such labor is performed for an employer by an individual who is regularly employed by such employer to perform such agricultural labor. For purposes of this subparagraph, an individual shall be deemed to be regularly employed by an employer during a calendar quarter only if—

"(i) such individual performs agricultural labor (other than service described in subparagraph (B)) for such employer on a full-time basis on 60 days during such quarter, and

"(ii) the quarter was immediately preceded by a qualifying quarter.

For purposes of the preceding sentence, the term 'qualifying quarter' means—

"(I) any quarter during all of which such individual was continuously employed by such employer, or

"(II) any subsequent quarter which meets the test of clause (i) if, after the last quarter during all of which such individual was continuously employed by such employer, each intervening quarter met the test of clause (i).

Notwithstanding the preceding provisions of this subparagraph, an individual shall also be deemed to be regularly employed by an employer during a calendar quarter if such individual was regularly employed (upon application of clauses (i) and (ii)) by such employer during the preceding calendar quarter;

"(B) service performed in connection with the production or harvesting of any commodity defined as an agricultural commodity in section 15(g) of the Agricultural Marketing Act, as amended (46 Stat. 1550, §3; 12 U. S. C. 1141j), or in connection with the ginning of cotton;

"(C) service performed by foreign agricultural workers under contracts entered into in accordance with title V of the Agricultural Act of 1949, as amended (65 Stat. 119; 7 U. S. C. 1461-1468);".

P.L. 761, 83rd Cong., §205(b):

Deleted paragraph (3) and renumbered paragraphs (4), (5), (6), (7), (8), (9), (10), (11), (12), (13), and (14), as paragraphs (3), (4), (5), (6), (7), (8), (9), (10), (11), (12), and (13), respectively. Prior to deletion, former paragraph (3) read as follows:

"(3) service not in the course of the employer's trade or business performed in any calendar quarter by an employee, unless the cash remuneration paid for such service is $50 or more and such service is performed by an individual who is regularly employed by such employer to perform such service. For purposes of this paragraph, an individual shall be deemed to be regularly employed by an employer during a calendar quarter only if—

"(A) on each of some 24 days during such quarter such individual performs for such employer for some portion of the day service not in the course of the employer's trade or business, or

"(B) such individual was regularly employed (as determined under subparagraph (A)) by such employer in the performance of such service during the preceding calendar quarter.

As used in this paragraph, the term 'service not in the course of the employer's trade or business' does not include domestic service in a private home of the employer and does not include service described in subsection (g)(5);".

P.L. 761, 83rd Cong., §205(c):

Amended the redesignated paragraph (4) by substituting the language "if (A) the individual is employed on and in connection with such vessel or aircraft, when outside the United States and (B)(i) such individual is not a citizen of the United States or (ii) the employer is not an American employer" for the language "if the individual is employed on and in connection with such vessel or aircraft when outside the United States".

P.L. 761, 83rd Cong., §205(d)(1)(A):

Amended the redesignated subparagraph (6)(B) by inserting "by an individual" after "service performed", and by inserting "and if such service is covered by a retirement system established by such instrumentality;" after "December 31, 1950,".

P.L. 761, 83rd Cong., §205(d)(1)(B):

Amended the redesignated subparagraph (6)(B) by deleting "or" at the end of clause (iii), by adding "or" at the end of clause (iv), and by adding clause (v).

P.L. 761, 83rd Cong., §205(d)(2):

Amended subparagraph (6)(C). Prior to amendment, subparagraph (6)(C) read as follows:

"(C) service performed in the employ of the United States or in the employ of any instrumentality of the United States, if such service is performed—

"(i) as the President or Vice President of the United States or as a Member, Delegate, or Resident Commissioner, of or to the Congress;

"(ii) in the legislative branch;

"(iii) in the field service of the Post Office Department unless performed by any individual as an employee who is excluded by Executive order from the operation of the Civil Service Retirement Act of 1930 (46 Stat. 470; 5 U. S. C. 693) because he is serving under a temporary appointment pending final determination of eligibility for permanent or indefinite appointment;

"(iv) in or under the Bureau of the Census of the Department of Commerce by temporary employees employed for the taking of any census;

"(v) by any individual as an employee who is excluded by Executive order from the operation of the Civil Service Retirement Act of 1930 (46 Stat. 470; 5 U. S. C. 693) because he is paid on a contract or fee basis;

"(vi) by any individual as an employee receiving nominal compensation of $12 or less per annum;

"(vii) in a hospital, home, or other institution of the United States by a patient or inmate thereof;

"(viii) by any individual as a consular agent appointed under authority of section 551 of the Foreign Service Act of 1946 (60 Stat. 1011; 22 U. S. C. 951);

"(ix) by any individual as an employee included under section 2 of the Act of August 4, 1947 (relating to certain interns, student nurses, and other student employees of hospitals of the Federal Government) (61 Stat. 727; 5 U.S.C. 1052);

"(x) by any individual as an employee serving on a temporary basis in case of fire, storm, earthquake, flood, or other similar emergency;

"(xi) by any individual as an employee who is employed under a Federal relief program to relieve him from unemployment;

"(xii) as a member of a State, county, or community committee under the Commodity Stabilization Service or of any other board, council, committee, or other similar body, unless such board, council, committee, or other body is composed exclusively of individuals otherwise in the full-time employ of the United States; or

"(xiii) by an individual to whom the Civil Service Retirement Act of 1930 (46 Stat. 470; 5 U. S. C. 693) does not apply because such individual is subject to another retirement system;".

P.L. 761, 83rd Cong., §205(e):

Deleted paragraph (15) and renumbered paragraphs (16) and (17) as paragraphs (15) and (16), respectively. Prior to deletion, former paragraph (15) read as follows:

"(15) service performed by an individual in (or as an officer or member of the crew of a vessel while it is engaged in) the catching, taking, harvesting, cultivating, or farming of any kind of fish, shellfish, crustacea, sponges, seaweeds, or other aquatic forms of animal and vegetable life (including service performed by any such individual as an ordinary incident to any such activity), except—

"(A) service performed in connection with the catching or taking of salmon or halibut, for commercial purposes, and

"(B) service performed on or in connection with a vessel of more than 10 net tons (determined in the manner provided for determining the register tonnage of merchant vessels under the laws of the United States);".

[Sec. 3121(c)]

(c) INCLUDED AND EXCLUDED SERVICE.—For purposes of this chapter, if the services performed during one-half or more of any pay period by an employee for the person employing him constitute employment, all the services of such employee for such period shall be deemed to be employment; but if the services performed during more than one-half of any such pay period by an employee for the person employing him do not constitute employment, then none of the services of such employee for such period shall be deemed to be employment. As used in this subsection, the term "pay period" means a period (of not more than 31 consecutive days) for which a payment of remuneration is ordinarily made to the employee by the person employing him. This subsection shall not be applicable with respect to services performed in a pay period by an employee for the person employing him, where any of such service is excepted by subsection (b)(9).

[Sec. 3121(d)]

(d) EMPLOYEE.—For purposes of this chapter, the term "employee" means—

(1) any officer of a corporation; or

(2) any individual who, under the usual common law rules applicable in determining the employer-employee relationship, has the status of an employee; or

(3) any individual (other than an individual who is an employee under paragraph (1) or (2)) who performs services for remuneration for any person—

(A) as an agent-driver or commission-driver engaged in distributing meat products, vegetable products, bakery products, beverages (other than milk), or laundry or dry-cleaning services, for his principal;

(B) as a full-time life insurance salesman;

(C) as a home worker performing work, according to specifications furnished by the person for whom the services are performed, on materials or goods furnished by such person which are required to be returned to such person or a person designated by him; or

(D) as a traveling or city salesman, other than as an agent-driver or commission-driver, engaged upon a full-time basis in the solicitation on behalf of, and the transmission to, his principal (except for side-line sales activities on behalf of some other person) of orders from wholesalers, retailers, contractors, or operators of hotels, restaurants, or other similar establishments for merchandise for resale or supplies for use in their business operations;

if the contract of service contemplates that substantially all of such services are to be performed personally by such individual; except that an individual shall not be included in the term "employee" under the provisions of this paragraph if such individual has a substantial investment in facilities used in connection with the performance of such services (other than in facilities for transportation), or if the services are in the nature of a single transaction not part of a continuing relationship with the person for whom the services are performed; or

(4) any individual who performs services that are included under an agreement entered into pursuant to section 218 or 218A of the Social Security Act.

Amendments

• 2018, Tribal Social Security Fairness Act of 2018 (P.L. 115-243)

P.L. 115-243, §2(b)(2)(B):

Amended Code Sec. 3121(d)(4) by inserting "or 218A" after "section 218". **Effective** 9-20-2018.

P.L. 115-243, §2(c), provides:

(c) RULE OF CONSTRUCTION.—Nothing in this Act or the amendments made by this Act shall be construed to affect application of any Federal income tax withholding requirements under the Internal Revenue Code of 1986.

• 1997, Taxpayer Relief Act of 1997 (P.L. 105-34)

P.L. 105-34, §921, provides:

ACT SEC. 921. CLARIFICATION OF STANDARD TO BE USED IN DETERMINING EMPLOYMENT TAX STATUS OF SECURITIES BROKERS.

(a) IN GENERAL.—In determining for purposes of the Internal Revenue Code of 1986 whether a registered representative of a securities broker-dealer is an employee (as defined in section 3121(d) of the Internal Revenue Code of 1986), no weight shall be given to instructions from the service recipient which are imposed only in compliance with investor protection standards imposed by the Federal Government, any State government, or a governing body pursuant to a delegation by a Federal or State agency.

(b) EFFECTIVE DATE.—Subsection (a) shall apply to services performed after December 31, 1997.

• 1988, Technical and Miscellaneous Revenue Act of 1988 (P.L. 100-647)

P.L. 100-647, §8016(a)(3)(A)(i)-(ii):

Amended Code Sec. 3121(d) by redesignating paragraph (3) as paragraph (4), by striking "; or" at the end of such paragraph and inserting a period, and by moving such paragraph (as so redesignated and amended) to the end of the subsection; and by redesignating paragraph (4) as paragraph (3), and by striking the period at the end and inserting "; or". For the **effective** date, see Act Sec. 8016(b), below.

P.L. 100-647, §8016(b), provides:

(b) EFFECTIVE DATE.—(1) Except as provided in paragraph (2), the amendments made by this section shall be effective on the date of the enactment of this Act.

(2) Any amendment made by this section to a provision of a particular Public Law which is referred to by its number, or to a provision of the Social Security Act or the Internal Revenue Code of 1986 as added or amended by a provision of a particular Public Law which is so referred to, shall be effective as though it had been included or reflected in the relevant provisions of that Public Law at the time of its enactment.

• 1986, Omnibus Budget Reconciliation Act of 1986 (P.L. 99-509)

P.L. 99-509, §9002(b)(2)(A):

Amended Code Sec. 3121(d) by redesignating paragraph (3) as paragraph (4), and by inserting after paragraph (2) new paragraph (3). For the **effective** date, see Act Sec. 9002(d), below.

P.L. 99-509, §9002(d), provides:

(d) EFFECTIVE DATE.—The amendments made by this section are effective with respect to payments due with respect to wages paid after December 31, 1986, including wages paid after such date by a State (or political subdivision thereof) that modified its agreement pursuant to the provisions of section 218(e)(2) of the Social Security Act prior to the date of the enactment of this Act; except that in cases where, in accordance with the currently applicable schedule, deposits of taxes due under an agreement entered into pursuant to section 218 of the Social Security Act would be required within 3 days after the close of an eighth-monthly period, such 3-day requirement shall be changed to a 7-day requirement for wages paid prior to October 1, 1987, and to a 5-day requirement for wages paid after September 30, 1987, and prior to October 1, 1988. For wages paid prior to October 1, 1988, the deposit schedule for taxes imposed under sections 3101 and 3111 shall be determined separately from the deposit schedule for taxes withheld under section 3402 if the taxes imposed under sections 3101 and 3111 are due with respect to service included under an agreement entered into pursuant to section 218 of the Social Security Act.

• 1954, Social Security Amendments of 1954 (P.L. 761, 83rd Cong.)

P.L. 761, 83rd Cong., §206(a):

Amended subparagraph (C) by deleting ", if the performance of such services is subject to licensing requirements under the laws of the State in which such services are performed" following "designated by him". **Effective** 1-1-55.

[Sec. 3121(e)]

(e) STATE, UNITED STATES, AND CITIZEN.—For purposes of this chapter—

(1) STATE.—The term "State" includes the District of Columbia, the Commonwealth of Puerto Rico, the Virgin Islands, Guam, and American Samoa.

(2) UNITED STATES.—The term "United States" when used in a geographical sense includes the Commonwealth of Puerto Rico, the Virgin Islands, Guam, and American Samoa.

An individual who is a citizen of the Commonwealth of Puerto Rico (but not otherwise a citizen of the United States) shall be considered, for purposes of this section, as a citizen of the United States.

Amendments

• 1960, Social Security Amendments of 1960 (P.L. 86-778)

P.L. 86-778, §103(p):

Amended Code Sec. 3121(e). **Effective** for service performed after 1960. Prior to amendment it read as follows:

"(e) State, United States, and Citizen.—For purposes of this chapter—

"(1) State.—The term 'State' includes Hawaii, the District of Columbia, Puerto Rico, and the Virgin Islands.

"(2) United States.—The term 'United States' when used in a geographical sense includes Puerto Rico and the Virgin Islands.

An individual who is a citizen of Puerto Rico (but not otherwise a citizen of the United States) shall be considered, for purposes of this section, as a citizen of the United States."

• 1960, Hawaii Omnibus Act (P.L. 86-624)

P.L. 86-624, §18(c):

Amended 1954 Code Sec. 3121(e)(1) by striking out "Hawaii," where it appeared following "includes". **Effective** 8-21-59.

• 1959, Alaska Omnibus Bill (P.L. 86-70)

P.L. 86-70, §22(a):

Amended 1954 Code Sec. 3121(e)(1) by striking out "Alaska," where it appeared following "includes". **Effective** 1-3-59.

[Sec. 3121(f)]

(f) AMERICAN VESSEL AND AIRCRAFT.—For purposes of this chapter, the term "American vessel" means any vessel documented or numbered under the laws of the United States; and includes any vessel which is neither documented or numbered under the laws of the United States nor documented under the laws of any foreign country, if its crew is employed solely by one or more citizens or residents of the United States or corporations organized under the laws of the United States or of any State; and the term "American aircraft" means an aircraft registered under the laws of the United States.

[Sec. 3121(g)]

(g) AGRICULTURAL LABOR.—For purposes of this chapter, the term "agricultural labor" includes all service performed—

(1) on a farm, in the employ of any person, in connection with cultivating the soil, or in connection with raising or harvesting any agricultural or horticultural commodity, including the raising, shearing, feeding, caring for, training, and management of livestock, bees, poultry, and fur-bearing animals and wildlife;

EMPLOYMENT TAX—GENERAL PROVISIONS

   (2) in the employ of the owner or tenant or other operator of a farm, in connection with the operation, management, conservation, improvement, or maintenance of such farm and its tools and equipment, or in salvaging timber or clearing land of brush and other debris left by a hurricane, if the major part of such service is performed on a farm;

   (3) in connection with the production or harvesting of any commodity defined as an agricultural commodity in section 15(g) of the Agricultural Marketing Act, as amended (12 U.S.C. 1141(j), or in connection with the ginning of cotton, or in connection with the operation or maintenance of ditches, canals, reservoirs, or waterways, not owned or operated for profit, used exclusively for supplying and storing water for farming purposes;

   (4)(A) in the employ of the operator of a farm in handling, planting, drying, packing, packaging, processing, freezing, grading, storing, or delivering to storage or to market or to a carrier for transportation to market, in its unmanufactured state, any agricultural or horticultural commodity; but only if such operator produced more than one-half of the commodity with respect to which such service is performed;

   (B) in the employ of a group of operators of farms (other than a co-operative organization) in the performance of service described in subparagraph (A), but only if such operators produced all of the commodity with respect to which such service is performed. For purposes of this subparagraph, any unincorporated group of operators shall be deemed a cooperative organization if the number of operators comprising such group is more than 20 at any time during the calendar year in which such service is performed;

   (C) the provisions of subparagraphs (A) and (B) shall not be deemed to be applicable with respect to service performed in connection with commercial canning or commercial freezing or in connection with any agricultural or horticultural commodity after its delivery to a terminal market for distribution for consumption; or

   (5) on a farm operated for profit if such service is not in the course of the employer's trade or business.

As used in this subsection, the term "farm" includes stock, dairy, poultry, fruit, fur-bearing animal, and truck farms, plantations, ranches, nurseries, ranges, greenhouses or other similar structures used primarily for the raising of agricultural or horticultural commodities, and orchards.

Amendments

• **2004, Social Security Protection Act of 2004 (P.L. 108-203)**

P.L. 108-203, §423(c):

Amended Code Sec. 3121(g)(5) by striking "or is domestic service in a private home of the employer" before the period. **Effective** 3-2-2004.

• **1977 (P.L. 95-216)**

P.L. 95-216, §356(d):

Amended Code Sec. 3121(g)(4)(B). **Effective** for remuneration paid and services rendered after 1977. Before amendment, paragraph (g)(4)(B) read as follows:

(B) in the employ of a group of operators of farms (other than a co-operative organization) in the performance of service described in subparagraph (A), but only if such operators produced all of the commodity with respect to which such service is performed. For purposes of this subparagraph, any unincorporated group of operators shall be deemed a cooperative organization if the number of operators comprising such group is more than 20 at any time during the calendar quarter in which such service is performed;

• **1976, Tax Reform Act of 1976 (P.L. 94-455)**

P.L. 94-455, §1903(a)(3)(D), (d):

Deleted "46 Stat. 1550, §3;" in Code Sec. 3121(g)(3). **Effective** for wages paid after 12-31-76.

[Sec. 3121(h)]

   (h) AMERICAN EMPLOYER.—For purposes of this chapter, the term "American employer" means an employer which is—

   (1) the United States or any instrumentality thereof,

   (2) an individual who is a resident of the United States,

   (3) a partnership, if two-thirds or more of the partners are residents of the United States,

   (4) a trust, if all of the trustees are residents of the United States, or

   (5) a corporation organized under the laws of the United States or of any State.

[Sec. 3121(i)]

   (i) COMPUTATION OF WAGES IN CERTAIN CASES.—

   (1) DOMESTIC SERVICE.—For purposes of this chapter, in the case of domestic service described in subsection (a)(7)(B), any payment of cash remuneration for such service which is more or less than a whole-dollar amount shall, under such conditions and to such extent as may be prescribed by regulations made under this chapter, be computed to the nearest dollar. For the purpose of the computation to the nearest dollar, the payment of a fractional part of a dollar shall be disregarded unless it amounts to one-half dollar or more, in which case it shall be increased to $1. The amount of any payment of cash remuneration so computed to the nearest dollar shall, in lieu of the amount actually paid, be deemed to constitute the amount of cash remuneration for purposes of subsection (a)(7)(B).

   (2) SERVICE IN THE UNIFORMED SERVICES.—For purposes of this chapter, in the case of an individual performing service, as a member of a uniformed service, to which the provisions of subsection (m)(1) are applicable, the term "wages" shall, subject to the provisions of subsection (a)(1) of this section, include as such individual's remuneration for such service only (A) his basic pay as described in chapter 3 and section 1009 of title 37, United States Code, in the case of an individual performing services to which subparagraph (A) of such subsection (m)(1) applies, or (B) his compensation for such service as determined under Section 206(a) of title 37, United States Code, in the case of an individual performing service to which subparagraph (B) of such subsection (m)(1) applies.

   (3) PEACE CORPS VOLUNTEER SERVICE.—For purposes of this chapter, in the case of an individual performing service, as a volunteer or volunteer leader within the meaning of the Peace Corps Act, to which the provisions of section 3121(p) are applicable, the term "wages" shall, subject to the provisions of subsection (a)(1) of this section, include as such individual's remuneration for such service only amounts paid pursuant to section 5(c) or 6(1) of the Peace Corps Act.

   (4) SERVICE PERFORMED BY CERTAIN MEMBERS OF RELIGIOUS ORDERS.—For purposes of this chapter, in any case where an individual is a member of a religious order (as defined in subsection (r)(2)) performing service in the exercise of duties required by such order, and an election of coverage under subsection (r) is in effect with respect to such order or with respect to the autonomous subdivision thereof to which such member belongs, the term "wages" shall, subject to the provisions of subsection (a)(1), include as such individual's remuneration for such service the fair market value of any board, lodging, clothing, and other perquisites furnished to such member by such order or subdivision thereof or by any other person or organization pursuant to an agreement with such order or subdivision, except that the amount included as such individual's remuneration under this paragraph shall not be less than $100 a month.

   (5) SERVICE PERFORMED BY CERTAIN RETIRED JUSTICES AND JUDGES.—For purposes of this chapter, in the case of an individual performing service under the provisions of section 294 of title 28, United States Code (relating to assignment of retired justices and judges to active duty), the term "wages" shall not include any payment under section 371(b) of such title 28 which is received during the period of such service.

Amendments

• **1987, Revenue Act of 1987 (P.L. 100-203)**

P.L. 100-203, §9001(b)(2):

Amended Code Sec. 3121(i)(2) by striking "only his basic pay" and all that follows and inserting "only (A) his basic pay as described in chapter 3 and section 1009 of title 37, United States Code, in the case of an individual performing service to which subparagraph (A) of such subsection (m)(1) applies, or (B) his compensation for such service as determined under section 206(a) of title 37, United States Code, in the case of an individual performing service to which subparagraph (B) of such subsection (m)(1) applies." **Effective** with respect to renumeration paid after 12-31-87.

EMPLOYMENT TAX—GENERAL PROVISIONS

• **1986, Consolidated Omnibus Budget Reconciliation Act of 1985 (P.L. 99-272)**

P.L. 99-272, § 12112(b):

Amended Code Sec. 3121(i)(5) by striking out "shall, subject to the provisions of subsection (a)(1) of this section, include" and inserting in lieu thereof "shall not include". **Effective** with respect to service performed after 12-31-83.

• **1984, Deficit Reduction Act of 1984 (P.L. 98-369)**

P.L. 98-369, § 2663(i)(2):

Amended Code Sec. 3121(i)(2) by striking out "section 102(10) of the Servicemen's and Veterans' Survivor Benefits Act" and inserting in lieu thereof "chapter 3 and section 1009 of title 37, United States Code". **Effective** 7-18-84, but it shall not be construed as changing or affecting any right, liability, status, or interpretation which existed (under the provisions of law involved) before that date.

• **1983, Social Security Act of 1983 (P.L. 98-21)**

P.L. 98-21, § 101(c)(2):

Added paragraph (5) to Code Sec. 3121(i). **Effective** with respect to service performed after 12-31-83.

• **1972, Social Security Amendments of 1972 (P.L. 92-603)**

P.L. 92-603, § 123(c)(2):

Added paragraph (4) to Code Sec. 3121(i). **Effective** 10-30-72.

• **1961, Peace Corps Act (P.L. 87-293)**

P.L. 87-293, § 202(a)(1):

Added Code Sec. 1321(i)(3). **Effective** with respect to services performed after 9-22-61.

• **1956, Servicemen's and Veterans' Survivor Benefits Act (P.L. 881, 84th cong.)**

P.L. 881, 84th Cong., § 410:

Amended Sec. 3121(i) by inserting "(1) Domestic Service.—" preceding the first sentence and by adding paragraph (2). **Effective** 1-1-57.

[Sec. 3121(j)]

(j) COVERED TRANSPORTATION SERVICE.—For purposes of this chapter—

(1) EXISTING TRANSPORTATION SYSTEMS—GENERAL RULE.—Except as provided in in paragraph (2), all service performed in the employ of a State or political subdivision in connection with its operation of a public transportation system shall constitute covered transportation service if any part of the transportation system was acquired from private ownership after 1936 and prior to 1951.

(2) EXISTING TRANSPORTATION SYSTEMS—CASES IN WHICH NO TRANSPORTATION EMPLOYEES, OR ONLY CERTAIN EMPLOYEES, ARE COVERED.—Service performed in the employ of a State or political subdivision in connection with the operation of its public transportation system shall not constitute covered transportation service if—

(A) any part of the transportation system was acquired from private ownership after 1936 and prior to 1951, and substantially all service in connection with the operation of the transportation system was, on December 31, 1950, covered under a general retirement system providing benefits which, by reason of a provision of the State constitution dealing specifically with retirement systems of the State or political subdivisions thereof, cannot be diminished or impaired; or

(B) no part of the transportation system operated by the State or political subdivision on December 31, 1950, was acquired from private ownership after 1936 and prior to 1951;

except that if such State or political subdivision makes an acquisition after 1950 from private ownership of any part of its transportation system, then, in the case of any employee who—

(C) became an employee of such State or political subdivision in connection with and at the time of its acquisition after 1950 of such part, and

(D) prior to such acquisition rendered service in employment (including as employment service covered by an agreement under section 218 of the Social Security Act) in connection with the operation of such part of the transportation system acquired by the State or political subdivision,

the service of such employee in connection with the operation of the transportation system shall constitute covered transportation service, commencing with the first day of the third calendar quarter following the calendar quarter in which the acquisition of such part took place, unless on such first day such service of such employee is covered by a general retirement system which does not, with respect to such employee, contain special provisions applicable only to employees described in subparagraph (C).

(3) TRANSPORTATION SYSTEMS ACQUIRED AFTER 1950.—All service performed in the employ of a State or political subdivision thereof in connection with its operation of a public transportation system shall constitute covered transportation service if the transportation system was not operated by the State or political subdivision prior to 1951 and, at the time of its first acquisition (after 1950) from private ownership of any part of its transportation system, the State or political subdivision did not have a general retirement system covering substantially all service performed in connection with the operation of the transportation system.

(4) DEFINITIONS.—For purposes of this subsection—

(A) The term "general retirement system" means any pension, annuity, retirement, or similar fund or system established by a State or by a political subdivision thereof for employees of the State, political subdivision, or both; but such terms shall not include such a fund or system which covers only service performed in positions connected with the operation of its public transportation system.

(B) A transportation system or a part thereof shall be considered to have been acquired by a State or political subdivision from private ownership if prior to the acquisition service performed by employees in connection with the operation of the system or part thereof acquired constituted employment under this chapter or subchapter A of chapter 9 of the Internal Revenue Code of 1939 or was covered by an agreement made pursuant to section 218 of the Social Security Act and some of such employees became employees of the State or political subdivision in connection with and at the time of such acquisition.

(C) The term "political subdivision" includes an instrumentality of—

(i) a State,

(ii) one or more political subdivisions of a State, or

(iii) a State and one or more of its political subdivisions.

[Sec. 3121(k)—Repealed]

Amendments

• **1983, Social Security Act of 1983 (P.L. 98-21)**

P.L. 98-21, § 102(b)(2):

Repealed Code Sec. 3121(k). **Effective** with respect to service performed after 12-31-83. The period for which a certificate is in effect under Code Sec. 3121(k) may not be terminated under paragraph (1)(D) or (2) of § 3121(k) on or after 3-31-83, but no such certificate shall be effective with respect to any service to which the amendments made by Act Sec. 102 apply.

If any individual, (1) on 1-1-84, is age 55 or over, and is an employee of an organization described in § 210(a)(8)(B) of the Social Security Act (a) which does not have in effect (on that date) a waiver certificate under Code Sec. 3121(k) and (b) to the employees of which social security coverage is extended on 1-1-84, solely by reason of enactment of this section, and (2) after 12-31-83, acquires the number of quarters of coverage (within the meaning of § 213 of the Social Security Act) which is required for purposes of this subparagraph under paragraph (2) then such individual shall be deemed to be a fully insured individual for all of the purposes of title II of such Act.

Prior to repeal, Code Sec. 3121(k) read as follows:

(k) EXEMPTION OF RELIGIOUS, CHARITABLE, AND CERTAIN OTHER ORGANIZATIONS.—

(1) WAIVER OF EXEMPTION BY ORGANIZATION.—

(A) An organization described in section 501(c)(3) which is exempt from income tax under section 501(a) may file a certificate (in such form and manner, and with such official, as may be prescribed by regulations made under this chapter) certifying that it desires to have the insurance system established by title II of the Social Security Act extended to service performed by its employees. Such certificate may be filed only if it is accompanied by a list containing the signature, address, and social security account number (if any) of each employee (if any) who concurs in the filing of the certificate. Such list may be amended at any time prior to the expiration of the twenty-fourth month following the calendar quarter in which the certificate is filed

Internal Revenue Code   Sec. 3121(k)—Repealed

EMPLOYMENT TAX—GENERAL PROVISIONS

by filing with the prescribed official a supplemental list or lists containing the signature, address, and social security account number (if any) of each additional employee who concurs in the filing of the certificate. The list and any supplemental list shall be filed in such form and manner as may be prescribed by regulations made under this chapter.

(B) The certificate shall be in effect (for purposes of subsection (b)(8)(B) and for purposes of section 210(a)(8)(B) of the Social Security Act) for the period beginning with whichever of the following may be designated by the organization:

(i) the first day of the calendar quarter in which the certificate is filed,

(ii) the first day of the calendar quarter succeeding such quarter, or

(iii) the first day of any calendar quarter preceding the calendar quarter in which the certificate is filed, except that such date may not be earlier than the first day of the twentieth calendar quarter preceding the quarter in which such certificate is filed.

(C) In the case of service performed by an employee whose name appears on a supplemental list filed after the first month following the calendar quarter in which the certificate is filed, the certificate shall be in effect (for purposes of subsection (b)(8)(B) and for purposes of section 210(a)(8)(B) of the Social Security Act) only with respect to service performed by such individual for the period beginning with the first day of the calendar quarter in which such supplemental list is filed.

(D) The period for which a certificate filed pursuant to this subsection or the corresponding subsection of prior law is effective may be terminated by the organization, effective at the end of a calendar quarter, upon giving 2 years' advance notice in writing, but only if, at the time of the receipt of such notice, the certificate has been in effect for a period of not less than 8 years. The notice of termination may be revoked by the organization by giving, prior to the close of the calendar quarter specified in the notice of termination, a written notice of such revocation. Notice of termination or revocation thereof shall be filed in such form and manner, and with such official, as may be prescribed by regulations made under this chapter.

(E) If an organization described in subparagraph (A) employs both individuals who are in positions covered by a pension, annuity, retirement, or similar fund or system established by a State or by a political subdivision thereof and individuals who are not in such positions, the organization shall divide its employees into two separate groups. One group shall consist of all employees who are in positions covered by such a fund or system and (i) are members of such fund or system, or (ii) are not members of such fund or system but are eligible to become members thereof; and the other group shall consist of all remaining employees. An organization which has so divided its employees into two groups may file a certificate pursuant to subparagraph (A) with respect to the employees in either group, or may file a separate certificate pursuant to such subparagraph with respect to the employees in each group.

(F) If a certificate filed pursuant to this paragraph is effective for one or more calendar quarters prior to the quarter in which the certificate is filed, then—

(i) for purposes of computing interest and for purposes of section 6651 (relating to addition to tax for failure to file tax return or pay tax), the due date for the return and payment of the tax for such prior calendar quarters resulting from the filing of such certificate shall be the last day of the calendar month following the calendar quarter in which the certificate is filed; and

(ii) the statutory period for the assessment of such tax shall not expire before the expiration of 3 years from such due date.

(2) TERMINATION OF WAIVER PERIOD BY SECRETARY.—If the Secretary finds that any organization which filed a certificate pursuant to this subsection or the corresponding subsection of prior law has failed to comply substantially with the requirements applicable with respect to the taxes imposed by this chapter or the corresponding provisions of prior law or is no longer able to comply with the requirements applicable with respect to the taxes imposed by this chapter, the Secretary shall give such organization not less than 60 days' advance notice in writing that the period covered by such certificate will terminate at the end of the calendar quarter specified in such notice. Such notice of termination may be revoked by the Secretary by giving, prior to the close of the calendar quarter specified in the notice of termination, written notice of such revocation to the organization. No notice of termination or of revocation thereof shall be given under this paragraph to an organization without the prior concurrence of the Secretary of Health, Education, and Welfare.

(3) NO RENEWAL OF WAIVER.—In the event the period covered by a certificate filed pursuant to this subsection or the corresponding subsection of prior law is terminated by the organization, no certificate may again be filed by such organization pursuant to this subsection.

(4) CONSTRUCTIVE FILING OF CERTIFICATE WHERE NO REFUND OR CREDIT OF TAXES HAS BEEN MADE.—

(A) In any case where—

(i) an organization described in section 501(c)(3) which is exempt from income tax under section 501(a) has not filed a valid waiver certificate under paragraph (1) of this subsection (or under the corresponding provision of prior law) as of the date of the enactment of this paragraph or, if later, as of the earliest date on which it satisfies clause (ii of this subparagraph[.]), but

(ii) the taxes imposed by sections 3101 and 3111 have been paid with respect to the remuneration paid by such organization to its employees, as though such a certificate had been filed, during any period (subject to subparagraph (B)(i)) of not less than three consecutive calendar quarters,

such organization shall be deemed (except as provided in subparagraph (B) of this paragraph) for purposes of subsection (b)(8)(B) and section 210(a)(8)(B) of the Social Security Act, to have filed a valid waiver under paragraph (1) of this subsection (or under the corresponding provision of prior law) on the first day of the period described in clause (ii) of this subparagraph effective (subject to subparagraph (c)) on the first day of the calendar quarter in which such period began, and to have accompanied such certificate with a list containing the signature, address, and social security number (if any) of each employee with respect to whom the taxes described in such subparagraph were paid (and each such employee shall be deemed for such purposes to have concurred in the filing of the certificate). or

(B) Subparagraph (A) shall not apply with respect to any organization if—

(i) the period referred to in clause (ii) of such subparagraph (in the case of that organization) terminated before the end of the earliest calendar quarter falling wholly or partly within the time limitation (as defined in section 205(c)(1)(B) of the Social Security Act) immediately preceding the date of the enactment of this paragraph, or

(ii) a refund or credit of any part of the taxes which were paid as described in clause (ii) of such subparagraph with respect to remuneration for services performed on or after the first day of the earliest calendar quarter falling wholly or partly within the time limitation (as defined in section 205(c)(1)(B) of the Social Security Act) immediately preceding the first day of the calendar quarter other than a refund or credit which would have been allowed if a valid waiver certificate filed under paragraph (1) had been in effect) has been obtained by the organization or its employees prior to September 9, 1976, or

(iii) the organization, prior to the end of the period referred to in clause (ii) of such subparagraph (and, in the case of an organization organized on or before October 9, 1969, prior to October 19, 1976), had applied for a ruling or determination letter acknowledging it to be exempt from income tax under section 501(c)(3), and it subsequently received such ruling or determination letter and did not pay any taxes under sections 3101 and 3111 with respect to any employee with respect to any quarter ending after the twelfth month following the date of mailing or such ruling or determination letter and did not pay any such taxes with respect to any quarter beginning after the later of (I) December 31, 1975 or (II) the date on which such ruling or determination letter was issued.

(C) In the case of any organization which is deemed under this paragraph to have filed a valid waiver certificate under paragraph (1), if—

(i) the period with respect to which the taxes imposed by sections 3101 and 3111 were paid by such organization (as described in subparagraph (A)(ii)) terminated prior to October 1, 1976, or

(ii) the taxes imposed by sections 3101 and 3111 were not paid during the period referred to in clause (i) (whether such period has terminated or not) with respect to remuneration paid by such organization to individuals who became its employees after the close of the calendar quarter in which such period began,

taxes under sections 3101 and 3111—

(iii) in the case of an organization which meets the requirements of this subparagraph by reason of clause (i), with respect to remuneration paid by such organization after the termination of the period referred to in clause (i) and prior to July 1, 1977; or

(iv) in the case of an organization which meets the requirements of this subparagraph by reason of clause (ii), with respect to remuneration paid prior to July 1, 1977, to individuals who became its employees after the close of the calendar quarter in which the period referred to in clause (i) began,

which remain unpaid on the date of the enactment of this subparagraph, or which were paid after October 19, 1976, but prior to the date of the enactment of this subparagraph, shall not be due or payable (or, if paid, shall be refunded); and the certificate which such organization is deemed under this paragraph to have filed shall not apply to any service with respect to the remuneration for which the taxes imposed by sections 3101 and 3111 (which remain unpaid on the date of the enactment of this subparagraph, or were paid after October 19, 1976, but prior to the date of the enactment of this subparagraph) are not due and payable (or are refunded) by reason of the preceding provisions of this subparagraph. In applying this subparagraph for purposes of title II of the Social Security Act, the period during which reports of wages subject to the taxes imposed by section 3101 and 3111 were made by any organization may be conclusively treated as the period (described in subparagraph (A)(ii)) during which the taxes imposed by such sections were paid by such organization.

(5) CONSTRUCTIVE FILING OF CERTIFICATE WHERE REFUND OR CREDIT HAS BEEN MADE AND NEW CERTIFICATE IS NOT FILED.—In any case where—

(A) an organization described in section 501(c)(3) which is exempt from income tax under section 501(a) would be deemed under paragraph (4) of this subsection to have filed a valid waiver certificate under paragraph (1) if it were not excluded from such paragraph (4) (pursuant to subparagraph (B)(ii) thereof) because a refund or credit of all or a part of the taxes described in paragraph (4)(A)(ii) was obtained prior to September 9, 1976; and

(B) such organization has not, prior to April 1, 1978, filed a valid waiver certificate under paragraph (1) which is effective for a period beginning on or before the first day of the first calendar quarter with respect to which such refund or credit was made (or, if later, with the first day of the earliest calendar quarter for which such certificate may be in effect under paragraph (1)(B)(iii)) and which is accompanied by the list described in paragraph (1)(A),

such organization shall be deemed, for purposes of subsection (b)(8)(B) and section 210(a)(8)(B) of the Social Security Act, to have filed a valid waiver certificate under paragraph (1) of this subsection on April 1, 1978, effective for the period beginning on the first day of the first calendar quarter with respect to which the refund or credit referred to in subparagraph (A) of this paragraph was made (or, if later, with the first day of the earliest calendar quarter falling wholly or partly within the time limitation (as defined in section 205(c)(1)(B) of the Social Security Act) immediately preceding the date of the enactment of this paragraph), and to have accompanied such certificate with a list containing the signature, address, and social security number (if any) of each employee described in subparagraph (A) of paragraph (4) including any employee with respect to whom taxes were refunded or credited as described in subparagraph (A) of this paragraph (and each such employee shall be deemed for such purposes to have concurred in the filing of the certificate). A certificate which is deemed to have been filed by an organization on April 1, 1978, shall supersede any certificate which may have been actually filed by such organization prior to that day except to the extent prescribed by the Secretary.

(6) APPLICATION OF CERTAIN PROVISIONS TO CASES OF CONSTRUCTIVE FILING.—All of the provisions of this subsection (other than subparagraphs (B), (F), and (H) of paragraph (1)), including the provisions requiring payment of taxes under sections 3101 and 3111 with respect to the services involved (except as provided in paragraph (4)(c)) shall apply with respect to any certificate which is deemed to have been filed by an organization on any day under paragraph (4) or (5), in the same way they would apply if the certificate had been actually filed on that day under paragraph (1); except that—

Sec. 3121(k)—Repealed

EMPLOYMENT TAX—GENERAL PROVISIONS

(A) the provisions relating to the filing of supplemental lists of concurring employees in the third sentence of paragraph (1)(A), and in paragraph (1)(C), shall apply to the extent prescribed by the Secretary;

(B) the provisions of paragraph (1)(E) shall not apply unless the taxes described in paragraph (4)(A)(ii) were paid by the organization as though a separate certificate had been filed with respect to one or both of the groups to which such provisions relate; and

(C) the action of the organization in obtaining the refund or credit described in paragraph (5)(A) shall not be considered a termination of such organization's coverage period for purposes of paragraph (3). Any organization which is deemed to have filed a waiver certificate under paragraph (4) or (5) shall be considered for purposes of section 3102(b) to have been required to deduct the taxes imposed by section 3101 with respect to the services involved.

(7) BOTH EMPLOYEE AND EMPLOYER TAXES PAYABLE BY ORGANIZATION FOR RETROACTIVE PERIOD IN CASES OF CONSTRUCTIVE FILING.—Notwithstanding any other provision of this chapter, in any case where an organization described in paragraph (5)(A) has not filed a valid waiver certificate under paragraph (1) prior to April 1, 1978, and is accordingly deemed under paragraph (5) to have filed such a certificate on April 1, 1978, the taxes due under section 3101, with respect to services constituting employment by reason of such certificate for any period prior to that date (along with the taxes due under section 3111 with respect to such services and the amount of any interest paid in connection with the refund or credit described in paragraph (5)(A)) shall be paid by such organization from its own funds and without any deduction from the wages of the individuals who performed such services; and those individuals shall have no liability for the payment of such taxes.

(8) EXTENDED PERIOD FOR PAYMENT OF TAXES FOR RETROACTIVE COVERAGE.—Notwithstanding any other provision of this title, in any case where—

(A) an organization is deemed under paragraph (4) to have filed a valid waiver certificate under paragraph (1), but the applicable period described in paragraph (4)(A)(ii) has terminated and part or all of the taxes imposed by sections 3101 and 3111 with respect to remuneration paid by such organization to its employees after the close of such period remains payable notwithstanding paragraph (4)(C), or

(B) an organization described in paragraph (5)(A) files a valid waiver certificate under paragraph (1) by March 31, 1978, as described in paragraph (5)(B), or (not having filed such a certificate by that date) is deemed under paragraph (5) to have filed such a certificate on April 1, 1978, or

(C) an individual files a request under section 3 of Public Law 94-563, or under section 312(c) of the Social Security Amendments of 1977, to have service treated as constituting remuneration for employment (as defined in section 3121(b) and in section 210(a) of the Social Security Act).

the taxes due under sections 3101 and 3111 with respect to services constituting employment by reason of such certificate for any period prior to the first day of the calendar quarter in which the date of such filing or constructive filing occurs, or with respect to service constituting employment by reason of such request, may be paid in installments over an appropriate period of time, as determined under regulations prescribed by the Secretary, rather than in a lump sum.

- **1977 (P.L. 95-216)**

P.L. 95-216, §312(a)(1):

Amended Code Sec. 3121(k)(5). **Effective** as indicated in §312(h), below. Prior to amendment, paragraph (k)(5) read as follows:

(5) CONSTRUCTIVE FILING OF CERTIFICATE WHERE REFUND OR CREDIT HAS BEEN MADE AND NEW CERTIFICATE IS NOT FILED.—In any case where—

(A) an organization described in section 501(c)(3) which is exempt from income tax under section 501(a) would be deemed under paragraph (4) of this subsection to have filed a valid waiver certificate under paragraph (1) if it were not excluded from such paragraph (4) (pursuant to subparagraph (B)(ii) thereof) because a refund or credit of all or a part of the taxes described in paragraph (4)(A)(ii) was obtained prior to September 9, 1976; and

(B) such organization has not, prior to the expiration of 180 days after the date of the enactment of this paragraph, filed a valid waiver certificate under paragraph (1) which is effective for a period beginning on or before the first day of the first calendar quarter with respect to which such refund or credit was made (or, if later, with the first day of the earliest calendar quarter for which such certificate may be in effect under paragraph (1)(B)(iii)) and which is accompanied by the list described in paragraph (1)(A),

such organization shall be deemed, for purposes of subsection (b)(8)(B) and section 210(a)(8)(B) of the Social Security Act, to have filed a valid waiver certificate under paragraph (1) of this subsection on the 181st day after the date of the enactment of this paragraph, effective for the period beginning on the first day of the first calendar quarter with respect to which the refund or credit referred to in subparagraph (A) of this paragraph was made (or, if later, with the first day of the earliest calendar quarter falling wholly or partly within the time limitation (as defined in section 205(c)(1)(B) of the Social Security Act) immediately preceding the date of the enactment of this paragraph), and to have accompanied such certificate with a list containing the signature, address, and social security number (if any) of each employee described in subparagraph (A) of paragraph (4) including any employee with respect to whom taxes were refunded or credited as described in subparagraph (A) of this paragraph (and each such employee shall be deemed for such purposes to have concurred in the filing of the certificate). A certificate which is deemed to have been filed by an organization on such 181st day shall supersede any certificate which may have been actually filed by such organization prior to that day except to the extent prescribed by the Secretary.

P.L. 95-216, §312(a)(2)(A), (B), and (C):

Amended Code Sec. 3121(k)(7) by striking out "prior to the expiration of 180 days after the date of the enactment of this paragraph" and inserting in lieu thereof "prior to April 1, 1978,"; by striking out "the 181st day after such date," and inserting in lieu thereof "April 1, 1978,"; and by striking out "prior to the first day of the calendar quarter in which such 181st day occurs" and inserting in lieu thereof "prior to that date". **Effective** as indicated in §312(h), below. Prior to amendment, paragraph (k)(7) read as follows:

(7) BOTH EMPLOYEE AND EMPLOYER TAXES PAYABLE BY ORGANIZATION FOR RETROACTIVE PERIOD IN CASES OF CONSTRUCTIVE FILING.—Notwithstanding any other provision of this chapter, in any case where an organization described in paragraph (5)(A) has not filed a valid waiver certificate under paragraph (1) prior to the expiration of 180 days after the date of the enactment of this paragraph and is accordingly deemed under paragraph (5) to have filed such a certificate on the 181st day after such date, the taxes due under section 3101, with respect to services constituting employment by reason of such certificate for any period prior to the first day of the calendar quarter in which such 181st day occurs (along with the taxes due under section 3111 with respect to such services and the amount of any interest paid in connection with the refund or credit described in paragraph (5)(A)) shall be paid by such organization from its own funds and without any deduction from the wages of the individuals who performed such services; and those individuals shall have no liability for the payment of such taxes.

P.L. 95-216, §312(a)(3):

Amended paragraph (k)(8) by striking out "by the end of the 180-day period following the date of the enactment of this paragraph" and inserting in lieu thereof "prior to April 1, 1978,"; by striking out "within that period" and inserting in lieu thereof "prior to April 1, 1978"; and by striking out "on the 181st day following that date" and inserting in lieu thereof "on that date". **Effective** as indicated in §312(h), below. Prior to amendment, paragraph (k)(8) read as follows:

(8) EXTENDED PERIOD FOR PAYMENT OF TAXES FOR RETROACTIVE COVERAGE.—Notwithstanding any other provision of this title, in any case where an organization described in paragraph (5)(A) files a valid waiver certificate under paragraph (1) by the end of the 180-day period following the date of the enactment of this paragraph as described in paragraph (5)(B), or (not having filed such a certificate within that period) is deemed under paragraph (5) to have filed such a certificate on the 181st day following that date, the taxes due under sections 3101 and 3111 with respect to services constituting employment by reason of such certificate for any period prior to the first day of the calendar quarter in which the date of such filing or constructive filing occurs may be paid in installments over an appropriate period of time, as determined under regulations prescribed by the Secretary, rather than in a lump sum.

P.L. 95-216, §312(b)(1):

Added a new subparagraph (k)(4)(C). **Effective** as indicated in §312(h), below.

P.L. 95-216, §312(b)(2):

Amended subparagraph (k)(4)(A) by inserting "(subject to subparagraph (C))" after "effective" in the matter following clause (ii). **Effective** as indicated in §312(h), below.

P.L. 95-216, §312(b)(3):

Amended Code Sec. 3121(k)(6) by inserting "(except as provided in paragraph (4)(C))" after "services involved" in the matter preceding subparagraph (A). **Effective** as indicated in §312(h), below.

P.L. 95-216, §312(b)(4):

Amended paragraph (k)(4) by striking out "date of enactment of this paragraph" in subparagraph (B)(ii) and inserting in lieu thereof "first day of the calendar quarter". **Effective** as indicated in §312(h), below.

P.L. 95-216, §312(d):

Amended paragraph (k)(8), as amended by §312(a)(3). **Effective** as indicated in §312(h), below.

P.L. 95-216 §312(e):

Amended the first sentence of Section 3 of P.L. 94-563 (in the matter following paragraph(3)) by inserting "on or before April 15, 1980," after "filed"; and by inserting "(or by satisfactory evidence that appropriate arrangements have been made for the repayment of such taxes in installments as provided in section 3121(k)(8) of such Code)" after "so refunded or credited". **Effective** as indicated in §312(h), below.

P.L. 95-216, §312(f):

Amended paragraph (k)(4)(A)(i) by striking out "or any subsequent date" and inserting in lieu thereof "(or, if later, as of the earliest date on which it satisfies clause (ii) of this subparagraph [.])". **Effective** as indicated in §312(h), below.

P.L. 95-216, §312(g)(1)-(2):

Amended paragraph (k)(4)(B) by striking out the period at the end of clause (ii) and inserting in lieu thereof ", or"; and by adding after clause (ii) a clause (iii). **Effective** as indicated in §312(h), below. Prior to amendment, paragraph (k)(4) read as follows:

(4) CONSTRUCTIVE FILING OF CERTIFICATE WHERE NO REFUND OR CREDIT OF TAXES HAS BEEN MADE.—

(A) In any case where—

(i) an organization described in section 501(c)(3) which is exempt from income tax under section 501(a) has not filed a valid waiver certificate under paragraph (1) of this subsection (or under the corresponding provision of prior law) as of the date of the enactment of this paragraph or any subsequent date, but

(ii) the taxes imposed by sections 3101 and 3111 have been paid with respect to the remuneration paid by such organization to its employees, as though such a certificate had been filed, during any period (subject to subparagraph (B)(ii)) of not less than three consecutive calendar quarters,

such organization shall be deemed (except as provided in subparagraph (B) of this paragraph) for purposes of subsection (b)(8)(B) and section 210(a)(8)(B) of the Social Security Act, to have filed a valid waiver certificate under paragraph (1) of this subsection (or under the corresponding provision of prior law) on the first day of the period described in clause (ii) of this subparagraph effective on the first day of the calendar quarter in which such period began, and to have accompanied such certificate with a list containing the signature, address, and social security number (if any) of each employee with respect to whom the taxes described in such subparagraph were paid (and each such employee shall be deemed for such purposes to have concurred in the filing of the certificate).

(B) Subparagraph (A) shall not apply with respect to any organization if—

EMPLOYMENT TAX—GENERAL PROVISIONS

(i) the period referred to in clause (ii) of such subparagraph (in the case of that organization) terminated before the end of the earliest calendar quarter falling wholly or partly within the time limitation (as defined in section 205(c)(1)(B) of the Social Security Act) immediately preceding the date of the enactment of this paragraph, or

(ii) a refund or credit of any part of the taxes which were paid as described in clause (ii) of such subparagraph with respect to remuneration for services performed on or after the first day of the earliest calendar quarter falling wholly or partly within the time limitation (as defined in section 205(c)(1)(B) of the Social Security Act) immediately preceding the date of enactment of this paragraph (other than a refund or credit which would have been allowed if a valid waiver certificate filed under paragraph (1) had been in effect) has been obtained by the organization or its employees prior to September 9, 1976.

P.L. 95-216, §312(h), provides:

The amendments made by subsections (a), (b), (d), (e), (f), and (g) of this section shall be effective as though they had been included as a part of the amendments made to section 3121(k) of the Internal Revenue Code of 1954 by the first section of Public Law 94-563 (or, in the case of the amendments made by subsection (e), as a part of section 3 of such Public Law).

- **1976 (P.L. 94-563)**

P.L. 94-563, §1(c):

Added paragraphs (4), (5), (6), (7), and (8) at the end of Code Sec. 3121(k). **Effective** for services performed after 1950, to the extent covered by waiver certificates filed or deemed to have been filed under section 3121(k)(4) or (5) of the Internal Revenue Code of 1954 (as added by such amendments).

P.L. 94-563, §2, provides:

SEC. 2. Notwithstanding any other provision of law, no refund or credit of any tax paid under section 3101 or 3111 of the Internal Revenue Code of 1954 by an organization described in section 501(c)(3) of such Code which is exempt from income tax under section 501(a) of such Code shall be made on or after September 9, 1976, by reason of such organization's failure to file a waiver certificate under section 3121(k)(1) of such Code (or the corresponding provision of prior law), if such organization is deemed to have filed such a certificate under section 3121(k)(4) of such Code (as added by the first section of this Act).

P.L. 94-563, §3 (as amended by P.L. 95-216), provides:

SEC. 3. In any case where—

(1) an individual performed service, as an employee of an organization which is deemed under section 3121(k)(5) of the Internal Revenue Code of 1954 to have filed a waiver certificate under section 3121(k)(1) of such Code, at any time prior to the period for which such certificate is effective;

(2) the taxes imposed by sections 3101 and 3111 of such Code were paid with respect to remuneration paid for such service, but such service (or any part thereof) does not constitute employment (as defined in section 210(a) of the Social Security Act and section 3121(b) of such Code) because the applicable taxes so paid were refunded or credited (otherwise than through a refund or credit which would have been allowed if a valid waiver certificate filed under section 3121(k)(1) of such Code had been in effect) prior to September 9, 1976; and

(3) any portion of such service (with respect to which taxes were paid and refunded or credited as described in paragraph (2)) would constitute employment (as so defined) if the organization had actually filed under section 3121(k)(1) of such Code a valid waiver certificate effective as provided in section 3121(k)(5)(B) thereof (with such individual's signature appearing on the accompanying list),

the remuneration paid for the portion of such service described in paragraph (3) shall, upon the request of such individual (filed on or before April 15, 1980, in such manner and form, and with such official, as may be prescribed by regulations made under title II of the Social Security Act) accompanied by full repayment of the taxes which were paid under section 3101 of such Code with respect to such remuneration and so refunded or credited (or by satisfactory evidence that appropriate arrangements have been made for repayment of such taxes in installments as provided in section 3121 (k)(8) of such Code), be deemed to constitute remuneration for employment as so defined. In any case where remuneration paid by an organization to an individual is deemed under the preceding sentence to constitute remuneration for employment, such organization shall be liable (notwithstanding any other provision of such Code) for repayment of any taxes which it paid under section 3111 of such Code with respect to such remuneration and which were refunded or credited to it.

- **1976, Tax Reform Act of 1976 (P.L. 94-455)**

P.L. 94-455, §1903(a)(3)(E):

Deleted subparagraphs (F) and (H) of Code Sec. 3121(k)(1) and redesignated subparagraph (G) as subparagraph (F). **Effective** for wages paid after 12-31-76. Prior to amendment, subparagraphs (F) and (H) read as follows:

(F) An organization which filed a certificate under this subsection after 1955 but prior to the enactment of this subparagraph may file a request at any time before 1960 to have such certificate effective, with respect to the service of individuals who concurred in the filing of such certificate (initially or through the filing of a supplemental list) prior to enactment of this subparagraph and who concur in the filing of such new request, for the period beginning with the first day of any calendar quarter preceding the first calendar quarter for which it was effective and following the last calendar quarter of 1955. Such request shall be filed with such official and in such form and manner as may be prescribed by regulations made under this chapter. If a request is filed pursuant to this subparagraph—

(i) for purposes of computing interest and for purposes of section 6651 (relating to addition to tax for failure to file tax return or pay tax), the due date for the return and payment of the tax for any calendar quarter resulting from the filing of such request shall be the last day of the calendar month following the calendar quarter in which the request is filed; and

(ii) the statutory period for the assessment of such tax shall not expire before the expiration of 3 years from such due date.

* * *

Sec. 3121(k)—Repealed

(H) An organization which files a certificate under subparagraph (A) before 1966 may amend such certificate during 1965 or 1966 to make the certificate effective with the first day of any calendar quarter preceding the quarter for which such certificate originally became effective, except that such date may not be earlier than the first day of the twentieth calendar quarter preceding the quarter in which such certificate is so amended. If an organization amends its certificate pursuant to the preceding sentence, such amendment shall be effective with respect to the service of individuals who concurred in the filing of such certificate (initially or through the filing of a supplemental list) and who concur in the filing of such amendment. An amendment to a certificate filed pursuant to this subparagraph shall be filed with such official and in such form and manner as may be prescribed by regulations made under this chapter. If an amendment is filed pursuant to this subparagraph—

(i) for purposes of computing interest and for purposes of section 6651 (relating to addition to tax for failure to file tax return or pay tax), the due date for the return and payment of the tax for any calendar quarter resulting from the filing of such an amendment shall be the last day of the calendar month following the calendar quarter in which the amendment is filed; and

(ii) the statutory period for the assessment of such tax shall not expire before the expiration of three years from such due date.

P.L. 94-455, §1906(b)(13)(A):

Amended 1954 Code by substituting "Secretary" for "Secretary or his delegate" each place it appeared. **Effective** 2-1-77.

- **1969, Tax Reform Act of 1969 (P.L. 91-172)**

P.L. 91-172, §943(c)(1)-(3):

Amended subparagraphs (k)(1)(F)(i), (G)(i) and (H)(i) by inserting "or pay tax" immediately after "tax return" in each instance. **Effective** with respect to returns the date prescribed by law (without regard to any extension of time) for filing of which is after 12-31-69, and with respect to notices and demands for payment of tax made after 12-31-69.

- **1965, Social Security Amendments of 1965 (P.L. 89-97)**

P.L. 89-97, §316(a), (b):

Amended Sec. 3121(k)(1)(B)(iii) and amended Sec. 3121(k)(l) by adding subparagraph (H). **Effective** with respect to certificates filed under Sec. 3121(k)(1)(A) after 7-30-65.

- **1960, Social Security Amendments of 1960 (P.L. 86-778)**

P.L. 86-778, §105(a):

Amended Code Sec. 3121(k) by: (1) striking out, in the first sentence of paragraph (1)(A), the phrase "and that at least two-thirds of its employees concur in the filing of the certificate" where it appeared at the end of that sentence; (2) inserting "(if any)" following "each employee" in the second sentence of paragraph (1)(A); and (3) striking out the last two sentences of paragraph (1)(E) and substituting the present last sentence of that paragraph. **Effective** with respect to certificates filed under Code Sec. 3121(k)(1) after 9-13-60. Prior to deletion, the last two sentences read as follows: "An organization which has so divided its employees into two groups may file a certificate pursuant to subparagraph (A) with respect to the employees in one of the groups if at least two-thirds of the employees in such groups concur in the filing of the certificate. The organization may also file such a certificate with respect to the employees in the other group if at least two-thirds of the employees in such other group concur in the filing of such certificate."

- **1958, Social Security Amendments of 1958 (P.L. 85-840)**

P.L. 85-840, §405(a):

Amended Sec. 3121(k)(1), except for the amendments added by P.L. 86-778. **Effective** for certificates filed under Sec. 3121(k)(1) after 8-28-58 and requests filed under subparagraph (F) of that section after that date. Prior to amendment, Sec. 3121(k)(1) read as follows:

"(1) Waiver of exemption by organization.—An organization described in section 501(c)(3) which is exempt from income tax under section 501(a) may file a certificate (in such form and manner, and with such official, as may be prescribed by regulations made under this chapter) certifying that it desires to have the insurance system established by title II of the Social Security Act extended to service performed by its employees and that at least two-thirds of its employees concur in the filing of the certificate. Such certificate may be filed only if it is accompanied by a list containing the signature, address, and social security account number (if any) of each employee who concurs in the filing of the certificate. Such list may be amended at any time prior to the expiration of the twenty-fourth month following the first calendar quarter for which the certificate is in effect, or at any time prior to January 1, 1959, whichever is the later, by filing with the prescribed official a supplemental list or lists containing the signature, address, and social security number (if any) of each additional employee who concurs in the filing of the certificate. The list and any supplemental list shall be filed in such form and manner as may be prescribed by regulations made under this chapter. The certificate shall be in effect (for purposes of subsection (b)(8)(B) and for purposes of section 210(a)(8)(B) of the Social Security Act) for the period beginning with the first day of the calendar quarter in which such certificate is filed or the first day of the succeeding calendar quarter, as may be specified in the certificate, except that, in the case of service performed by an individual whose name appears on a supplemental list filed after the first month following the first calendar quarter for which the certificate is in effect, the certificate shall be in effect, for purposes of such subsection (b)(8) and for purposes of section 210(a)(8) of the Social Security Act, only with respect to service performed by such individual after the calendar quarter in which such supplemental list is filed. The period for which a certificate filed pursuant to this subsection or the corresponding subsection of prior law is effective may be terminated by the organization, effective at the end of a calendar quarter, upon giving 2 years' advance notice in writing, but only if, at the time of the receipt of such notice, the certificate has been in effect for a period of not less than 8 years. The notice of termination may be revoked by the organization by giving, prior to the close of the calendar quarter specified in the

EMPLOYMENT TAX—GENERAL PROVISIONS

notice of termination, a written notice of such revocation. Notice of termination or revocation thereof shall be filed in such form and manner, and with such official, as may be prescribed by regulations made under this chapter."

• **1956, Social Security Amendments of 1956 (P.L. 880, 84th Cong.)**

P.L. 880, 84th Cong., 2d Sess., § 201(k), (l):

Amended Sec. 3121(k)(1). **Effective** for certificates filed after 1956 under Sec. 3121(k). Prior to amendment, Sec. 3121(k)(1) read as follows:

"(1) Waiver of exemption by organization.—An organization described in section 501(c)(3) which is exempt from income tax under section 501(a) may file a certificate (in such form and manner, and with such official, as may be prescribed by regulations made under this chapter) certifying that it desires to have the insurance system established by title II of the Social Security Act extended to service performed by its employees and that at least two-thirds of its employees concur in the filing of the certificate. Such certificate may be filed only if it is accompanied by a list containing the signature, address, and social security account number (if any) of each employee who concurs in the filing of the certificate. Such list may be amended at any time prior to the expiration of the twenty-fourth month following the first calendar quarter for which the certificate is in effect by filing with the prescribed official a supplemental list or lists containing the signature, address, and social security account number (if any) of each additional employee who concurs in the filing of the certificate. The list and any supplemental list shall be filed in such form and manner as may be prescribed by regulations made under this chapter. The certificate shall be in effect (for purposes of subsection (b)(8)(B) and for purposes of section 210(a)(8)(B) of the Social Security Act) for the period beginning with the first day following the close of the calendar quarter in which such certificate is filed, except that, in the case of service performed by an individual whose name appears on a supplemental list filed after the first month following the first calendar quarter for which the certificate is in effect, the certificate shall be in effect, for purposes of such subsection (b)(8) and for purposes of section 210(a)(8) of the Social Security Act, only with respect to service performed by such individual after the calendar quarter in which such supplemental list is filed. The period for which a certificate filed pursuant to this subsection or the corresponding subsection of prior law is effective may be terminated by the organization, effective at the end of a calendar quarter, upon giving 2 years' advance notice in writing, but only if, at the time of the receipt of such notice, the certificate has been in effect for a period of not less than 8 years. The notice of termination may be revoked by the organization by giving, prior to the close of the calendar quarter specified in the notice of termination, a written notice of such revocation. Notice of termination or revocation thereof shall be filed in such form and manner, and with such official, as may be prescribed by the regulations made under this chapter."

• **1954, Social Security Amendments of 1954 (P.L. 761, 83rd Cong.)**

P.L. 761, 83rd Cong., § 207(a), (b):

Amended Sec. 3121(k)(1). **Effective** 9-1-54. Prior to amendment Sec. 3121(k)(1) read as follows:

"(1) Waiver of exemption by organization.—An organization described in section 501(c)(3) which is exempt from income tax under section 501(a) may file a certificate (in such form and manner, and with such official, as may be prescribed by regulations made under this chapter) certifying that it desires to have the insurance system established by title II of the Social Security Act extended to service performed by its employees and that at least two-thirds of its employees concur in the filing of the certificate. Such certificate may be filed only if it is accompanied by a list containing the signature, address, and social security account number (if any) of each employee who concurs in the filing of the certificate. Such list may be amended at any time prior to the expiration of the first month following the first calendar quarter for which the certificate is in effect, by filing with such official a supplemental list or lists containing the signature, address, and social security account number (if any) of each additional employee who concurs in the filing of the certificate. The list and any supplemental list shall be filed in such form and manner as may be prescribed by regulations made under this chapter. The certificate shall be in effect (for purposes of subsection (b)(8)(B) and for purposes of section 210(a)(8)(B) of the Social Security Act) for the period beginning with the first day of the calendar quarter in which such certificate is filed. The period for which a certificate filed pursuant to this subsection or the corresponding subsection of prior law is effective may be terminated by the organization, effective at the end of a calendar quarter, upon giving 2 years' advance notice in writing, but only if, at the time of the receipt of such notice, the certificate has been in effect for a period of not less than 8 years. The notice of termination may be revoked by the organization by giving, prior to the close of the calendar quarter specified in the notice of termination, a written notice of such revocation. Notice of termination or revocation thereof shall be filed in such form and manner, and with such official, as may be prescribed by regulations made under this chapter."

[Sec. 3121(l)]

(l) AGREEMENTS ENTERED INTO BY AMERICAN EMPLOYERS WITH RESPECT TO FOREIGN AFFILIATES.—

(1) AGREEMENT WITH RESPECT TO CERTAIN EMPLOYEES OF FOREIGN AFFILIATE.—The Secretary shall, at the American employer's request, enter into an agreement (in such manner and form as may be prescribed by the Secretary) with any American employer (as defined in subsection (h)) who desires to have the insurance system established by title II of the Social Security Act extended to service performed outside the United States in the employ of any 1 or more of such employer's foreign affiliates (as defined in paragraph (6)) by all employees who are citizens or residents of the United States, except that the agreement shall not apply to any service performed by, or remuneration paid to, an employee if such service or remuneration would be excluded from the term "employment" or "wages", as defined in this section, had the service been performed in the United States. Such agreement may be amended at any time so as to be made applicable, in the same manner and under the same conditions, with respect to any other foreign affiliate of such American employer. Such agreement shall be applicable with respect to citizens or residents of the United States who, on or after the effective date of the agreement, are employees of and perform services outside the United States for any foreign affiliate specified in the agreement. Such agreement shall provide—

(A) that the American employer shall pay to the Secretary, at such time or times as the Secretary may by regulations prescribe, amounts equivalent to the sum of the taxes which would be imposed by sections 3101 and 3111 (including amounts equivalent to the interest, additions to the taxes, additional amounts, and penalties which would be applicable) with respect to the remuneration which would be wages if the services covered by the agreement constituted employment as defined in this section; and

(B) that the American employer will comply with such regulations relating to payments and reports as the Secretary may prescribe to carry out the purposes of this subsection.

(2) EFFECTIVE PERIOD OF AGREEMENT.—An agreement entered into pursuant to paragraph (1) shall be in effect for the period beginning with the first day of the calendar quarter in which such agreement is entered into or the first day of the succeeding calendar quarter, as may be specified in the agreement; except that in case such agreement is amended to include the services performed for any other affiliate and such amendment is executed after the first month following the first calendar quarter for which the agreement is in effect, the agreement shall be in effect with respect to service performed for such other affiliate only after the calendar quarter in which such amendment is executed. Notwithstanding any other provision of this subsection, the period for which any such agreement is effective with respect to any foreign entity shall terminate at the end of any calendar quarter in which the foreign entity, at any time in such quarter, ceases to be a foreign affiliate as defined in paragraph (6).

(3) NO TERMINATION OF AGREEMENT.—No agreement under this subsection may be terminated, either in its entirety or with respect to any foreign affiliate, on or after June 15, 1989.

(4) DEPOSITS IN TRUST FUNDS.—For purposes of section 201 of the Social Security Act, relating to appropriations to the Federal Old-Age and Survivors Insurance Trust Fund and the Federal Disability Insurance Trust Fund, such remuneration—

(A) paid for services covered by an agreement entered into pursuant to paragraph (1) as would be wages if the services constituted employment, and

(B) as is reported to the Secretary pursuant to the provisions of such agreement or of the regulations issued under this subsection,

shall be considered wages subject to the taxes imposed by this chapter.

(5) OVERPAYMENTS AND UNDERPAYMENTS.—

(A) If more or less than the correct amount due under an agreement entered into pursuant to this subsection is paid with respect to any payment of remuneration, proper adjustments with respect to the amounts due under such agreement shall be made, without interest, in such manner and at such times as may be required by regulations prescribed by the Secretary.

(B) If an overpayment cannot be adjusted under subparagraph (A), the amount thereof shall be paid by the Secretary, through the Fiscal Service of the Treasury Department, but only if a claim for such overpayment is filed with the Secretary within two years from the time such overpayment was made.

(6) FOREIGN AFFILIATE DEFINED.—For purposes of this subsection and section 210(a) of the Social Security Act—

(A) IN GENERAL.—A foreign affiliate of an American employer is any foreign entity in which such American employer has not less than a 10-percent interest.

EMPLOYMENT TAX—GENERAL PROVISIONS

(B) DETERMINATION OF 10-PERCENT INTEREST.—For purposes of subparagraph (A), an American employer has a 10-percent interest in any entity if such employer has such an interest directly (or through one or more entities)—

(i) in the case of a corporation, in the voting stock thereof, and

(ii) in the case of any other entity, in the profits thereof.

(7) AMERICAN EMPLOYER AS SEPARATE ENTITY.—Each American employer which enters into an agreement pursuant to paragraph (1) of this subsection shall, for purposes of this subsection and section 6413(c)(2)(C), relating to special refunds in the case of employees of certain foreign entities, be considered an employer in its capacity as a party to such agreement separate and distinct from its identity as a person employing individuals on its own account.

(8) REGULATIONS.—Regulations of the Secretary to carry out the purposes of this subsection shall be designed to make the requirements imposed on American employers with respect to services covered by an agreement entered into pursuant to this subsection the same, so far as practicable, as those imposed upon employers pursuant to this title with respect to the taxes imposed by this chapter.

Amendments

• **1989, Omnibus Budget Reconciliation Act of 1989 (P.L. 101-239)**

P.L. 101-239, § 10201(a)(1)-(4):

Amended Code Sec. 3121(l) by adding at the end of paragraph (2) a new sentence, by striking paragraphs (3), (4), and (5), by inserting after paragraph (2) a new paragraph (3), and by redesignating paragraphs (6) through (10) as paragraphs (4) through (8) respectively. **Effective** with respect to any agreement in effect under section 3121(l) of the Internal Revenue Code of 1986 on or after 6-15-89, with respect to which no notice of termination is in effect on such date. Prior to amendment, Code Sec. 3121(l)(3)-(5) read as follows:

(3) TERMINATION OF PERIOD BY AN AMERICAN EMPLOYER.—The period for which an agreement entered into pursuant to paragraph (1) of this subsection is effective may be terminated with respect to any one or more of its foreign affiliates by the American employer, effective at the end of a calendar quarter, upon giving two years' advance notice in writing, but only if, at the time of the receipt of such notice, the agreement has been in effect for a period of not less than eight years. The notice of termination may be revoked by the American employer by giving, prior to the close of the calendar quarter specified in the notice of termination, a written notice of such revocation. Notice of termination or revocation thereof shall be filed in such form and manner as may be prescribed by regulations. Notwithstanding any other provision of this subsection, the period for which any such agreement is effective with respect to any foreign entity shall terminate at the end of any calendar quarter in which the foreign entity, at any time in such quarter, ceases to be a foreign affiliate as defined in paragraph (8).

(4) TERMINATION OF PERIOD BY SECRETARY.—If the Secretary finds that any American employer which entered into an agreement pursuant to this subsection has failed to comply substantially with the terms of such agreement, the Secretary shall give such American employer not less than sixty days' advance notice in writing and the period covered by such agreement will terminate at the end of the calendar quarter specified in such notice. Such notice of termination may be revoked by the Secretary by giving, prior to the close of the calendar quarter specified in the notice of termination, written notice of such revocation to the American employer. No notice of termination or of revocation thereof shall be given under this paragraph to an American employer without the prior concurrence of the Secretary of Health, Education, and Welfare.

(5) NO RENEWAL OF AGREEMENT.—If any agreement entered into pursuant to paragraph (1) of this subsection is terminated in its entirety (A) by a notice of termination filed by the American employer pursuant to paragraph (3), or (B) by a notice of termination given by the Secretary pursuant to paragraph (4), the American employer may not again enter into an agreement pursuant to paragraph (1). If any such agreement is terminated with respect to any foreign affiliate, such agreement may not thereafter be amended so as again to make it applicable with respect to such affiliate.

P.L. 101-239, § 10201(b)(3):

Amended Code Sec. 3121(l)(1) by striking "paragraph (8)" and inserting "paragraph (6)" in the matter preceding subparagraph (A). **Effective** with respect to any agreement in effect under section 3121(l) of the Internal Revenue Code of 1986 on or after 6-15-89, with respect to which no notice of termination is in effect on such date.

• **1983, Social Security Act of 1983 (P.L. 98-21)**

P.L. 98-21, § 321(a)(1):

Amended that part of Code Sec. 3121(l) which preceded the second sentence of paragraph (1). **Effective** with respect to agreements entered into after 4-20-83. Prior to amendment, the material read as follows:

"(l) AGREEMENTS ENTERED INTO BY DOMESTIC CORPORATIONS WITH RESPECT TO FOREIGN SUBSIDIARIES.—

(1) AGREEMENT WITH RESPECT TO CERTAIN EMPLOYEES OF FOREIGN SUBSIDIARIES.—The Secretary shall, at the request of any domestic corporation, enter into an agreement (in such form and manner as may be prescribed by the Secretary) with any such corporation which desires to have the insurance system established by title II of the Social Security Act extended to service performed outside the United States in the employ of any one or more of its foreign subsidiaries (as defined in paragraph (8)) by all employees who are citizens of the United States, except that the agreement shall not be applicable to any service performed by, or remuneration paid to, an employee if such service or remuneration would be excluded from the term `employment' or `wages', as defined in this section, had the service been performed in the United States."

P.L. 98-21, § 321(a)(2):

Amended Code Sec. 3121(l)(8). **Effective** with respect to agreements entered into after 4-20-83. Prior to amendment, Code Sec. 3121(l)(8) read as follows:

"(8) DEFINITION OF FOREIGN SUBSIDIARY.—For purposes of this subsection and section 210(a) of the Social Security Act, a foreign subsidiary of a domestic corporation is—

(A) a foreign corporation not less than 20 percent of the voting stock of which is owned by such domestic corporation; or

(B) a foreign corporation more than 50 percent of the voting stock of which is owned by the foreign corporation described in subparagraph (A)."

P.L. 98-21, § 321(e)(1):

Amended Code Sec. 3121(l) (not otherwise amended by P.L. 98-21) by striking out "domestic corporation" and inserting in lieu thereof "American employer"; by striking out "domestic corporations" and inserting in lieu thereof "American employers"; by striking out "subsidiary" and inserting in lieu thereof "affiliate"; by striking out "subsidiaries" and inserting in lieu thereof "affiliates"; by striking out "foreign corporation" and inserting in lieu thereof "foreign entity"; by striking out "foreign corporations" and inserting in lieu thereof "foreign entities"; by striking out "citizens" and inserting in lieu thereof "citizens or residents" and by striking out "a" where it appeared before "domestic" and inserting in lieu thereof "an". **Effective** for agreements entered into after 4-20-83.

• **1976, Tax Reform Act of 1976 (P.L. 94-455)**

P.L. 94-455, § 1903(a)(3)(F):

Deleted ", but in no case prior to January 1, 1955" in Code Sec. 3121(l)(2). **Effective** for wages paid after 12-31-76.

P.L. 94-455, § 1906(b)(13)(A):

Amended 1954 Code by substituting "Secretary" for "Secretary or his delegate" each place it appeared. **Effective** 2-1-77.

• **1958, Technical Amendments Act of 1958 (P.L. 85-866)**

P.L. 85-866, § 69:

Amended the heading of Sec. 3121(l)(3) by striking out "BE" and substituting "BY". Prior to amendment the heading read: "TERMINATION OF PERIOD BE A DOMESTIC CORPORATION". **Effective** 1-1-54.

• **1956, Social Security Amendments of 1956 (P.L. 880, 84th Cong.)**

P.L. 880, 84th Cong., § 103(j), 201(j):

Amended Sec. 3121(l)(6) by striking "Fund" in the heading and inserting in its place "Funds"; by inserting after "Federal Old-Age and Survivors Insurance Trust Fund" the following: "and the Federal Disability Insurance Trust Fund". Sec. 3121(l)(8)(A) was amended by substituting the phrase "not less than 20" for "more than 50". **Effective** 8-1-56.

• **1954, Social Security Amendments of 1954 (P.L. 761, 83rd Cong.)**

P.L. 761, 83rd Cong., § 209:

Amended Sec. 3121 by adding subsection (l). **Effective** 9-1-54.

[Sec. 3121(m)]

(m) SERVICE IN THE UNIFORMED SERVICES.—For purposes of this chapter—

(1) INCLUSION OF SERVICE.—The term "employment" shall, notwithstanding the provisions of subsection (b) of this section, include—

(A) service performed by an individual as a member of a uniformed service on active duty, but such term shall not include any such service which is performed while on leave without pay, and

(B) service performed by an individual as a member of a uniformed service on inactive duty training.

(2) ACTIVE DUTY.—The term "active duty" means "active duty" as described in paragraph (21) of section 101 of title 38, United States Code and, except that it shall also include "active duty for training" as described in paragraph (22) of such section.

(3) INACTIVE DUTY TRAINING.—The term "inactive duty training" means "inactive duty training" as described in paragraph (23) of such section 101.

Amendments

• **1987, Revenue Act of 1987 (P.L. 100-203)**

P.L. 100-203, § 9001(b)(1):

Amended Code Sec. 3121(m)(1). **Effective** with respect to remuneration paid after 12-31-87. Prior to amendment, Code Sec. 3121(m)(1) read as follows:

(1) INCLUSION OF SERVICE.—The term "employment" shall, notwithstanding the provisions of subsection (b) of this section, include service performed by an individual as a member of a uniformed service on active duty; but such term shall not include any such service which is performed while on leave without pay.

EMPLOYMENT TAX—GENERAL PROVISIONS

• **1984, Deficit Reduction Act of 1984 (P.L. 98-369)**

P.L. 98-369, §2663(i)(3):

Amended Code Sec. 3121(m)(2) by striking out "section 102 of the Servicemen's and Veterans' Survivor Benefits Act" and inserting in lieu thereof "paragraph (21) of section 101 of title 38, United States Code"; and by striking out "such section" and inserting in lieu thereof "paragraph (22) of such section". **Effective** 7-18-84, but shall not be construed as changing or affecting any right, liability, status, or interpretation which existed (under the provisions of law involved) before that date.

P.L. 98-369, §2663(i)(4):

Amended Code Section 3121(m)(3) by striking out "such section 102" and inserting in lieu thereof "paragraph (23) of such section 101". **Effective** 7-18-84, but shall not be construed as changing or affecting any right, liability, status, or interpretation which existed (under the provisions of law involved) before that date.

• **1976, Tax Reform Act of 1976 (P.L. 94-455)**

P.L. 94-455, §1903(a)(3)(G), (d):

Deleted "after December 1956" in Code Sec. 3121(m)(1). **Effective** for wages paid after 12-31-76.

• **1956, Servicemen's and Veterans' Survivor Benefits Act (P.L. 881, 84th Cong.)**

P.L. 881, 84th Cong., §411(a):

Amended Sec. 3121 by adding subsection (m). **Effective** under §603(a) of P.L. 881.

[Sec. 3121(n)]

(n) MEMBER OF A UNIFORMED SERVICE.—For purposes of this chapter, the term "member of a uniformed service" means any person appointed, enlisted, or inducted in a component of the Army, Navy, Air Force, Marine Corps, or Coast Guard (including a reserve component as defined in section 101(27) of title 38, United States Code), or in one of those services without specification of component, or as a commissioned officer of the Coast and Geodetic Survey, the National Oceanic and Atmospheric Administration Corps, or the Regular or Reserve Corps of the Public Health Service, and any person serving in the Army or Air Force under call or conscription. The term includes—

(1) a retired member of any of those services;

(2) a member of the Fleet Reserve or Fleet Marine Corps Reserve;

(3) a cadet at the United States Military Academy, a midshipman at the United States Naval Academy, and a cadet at the United States Coast Guard Academy or United States Air Force Academy;

(4) a member of the Reserve Officers' Training Corps, the Naval Reserve Officers' Training Corps, or the Air Force Reserve Officers' Training Corps, when ordered to annual training duty for fourteen days or more, and while performing authorized travel to and from that duty; and

(5) any person while en route to or from, or at, a place for final acceptance or for entry upon active duty in the military, naval, or air service—

(A) who has been provisionally accepted for such duty; or

(B) who, under the Military Selective Service Act, has been selected for active military, naval, or air service;

and has been ordered or directed to proceed to such place. The term does not include a temporary member of the Coast Guard Reserve.

Amendments

• **1984, Deficit Reduction Act of 1984 (P.L. 98-369)**

P.L. 98-369, §2663(i)(5):

Amended Code Sec. 3121(n) by striking out "a reserve component of a uniformed service as defined in section 102(3) of the Servicemen's and Veterans' Survivor Benefits Act" in the first sentence and inserting in lieu thereof "a reserve component as defined in section 101(27) of title 38, United States Code"; by inserting ", the National Oceanic and Atmospheric Administration Corps," after "Coast and Geodetic Survey" in the first sentence; by striking out "military or naval" each place it appears in paragraph (5) and inserting in lieu thereof "military, naval, or air"; and by striking out "Universal Military Training and Service Act" in paragraph (5)(B) and inserting in lieu thereof "Military Selective Service Act". **Effective** 7-18-84, but shall not be construed as changing or affecting any right, liability, status, or interpretation which existed (under the provisions of law involved) before that date.

• **1956, Servicemen's and Veterans' Survivor Benefits Act (P.L. 881, 84th Cong.)**

P.L. 881, 84th Cong., §411(a):

Amended Sec. 3121 by adding subsection (n). **Effective** under §603(a) of P.L. 881.

[Sec. 3121(o)]

(o) CREW LEADER.—For purposes of this chapter, the term "crew leader" means an individual who furnishes individuals to perform agricultural labor for another person, if such individual pays (either on his own behalf or on behalf of such person) the individuals so furnished by him for the agricultural labor performed by them and if such individual has not entered into a written agreement with such person whereby such individual has been designated as an employee of such person; and such individuals furnished by the crew leader to perform agricultural labor for another person shall be deemed to be the employees of such crew leader. For purposes of this chapter and chapter 2, a crew leader shall, with respect to service performed in furnishing individuals to perform agricultural labor for another person and service performed as a member of the crew, be deemed not to be an employee of such other person.

Amendments

• **1956, Social Security Amendments of 1956 (P.L. 880, 84th Cong.)**

P.L. 880, 84th Cong., 2d Sess., §201(h)(2):

Amended Sec. 3121 by adding subsection (o). **Effective** for service performed after 1956.

[Sec. 3121(p)]

(p) PEACE CORPS VOLUNTEER SERVICE.—For purposes of this chapter, the term "employment" shall, notwithstanding the provisions of subsection (b) of this section, include service performed by an individual as a volunteer or volunteer leader within the meaning of the Peace Corps Act.

Amendments

• **1961, Peace Corps Act (P.L. 87-293)**

P.L. 87-293, §202(a)(2):

Added Code Sec. 3121(p). **Effective** for services performed after 9-22-61.

[Sec. 3121(q)]

(q) TIPS INCLUDED FOR BOTH EMPLOYEE AND EMPLOYER TAXES.—For purposes of this chapter, tips received by an employee in the course of his employment shall be considered remuneration for such employment (and deemed to have been paid by the employer for purposes of subsections (a) and (b) of section 3111). Such remuneration shall be deemed to be paid at the time a written statement including such tips is furnished to the employer pursuant to section 6053(a) or (if no statement including such tips is so furnished) at the time received; except that, in determining the employer's liability in connection with the taxes imposed by section 3111 with respect to such tips in any case where no statement including such tips was so furnished (or to the extent that the statement so furnished was inaccurate or incomplete), such remuneration shall be deemed for purposes of subtitle F to be paid on the date on which notice and demand for such taxes is made to the employer by the Secretary.

Amendments

• **1987, Revenue Act of 1987 (P.L. 100-203)**

P.L. 100-203, §9006(a)(1)-(4):

Amended Code Sec. 3121(q) by striking out "Employee Taxes" in the heading and inserting "Both Employee and Employer Taxes", by striking out "other than for purposes of the taxes imposed by section 3111" after "this chapter", by striking out "remuneration for employment" and inserting "remuneration for such employment (and deemed to have been paid by the employer for purposes of subsections (a) and (b) of section 3111)", and by inserting after "at the time received" the following "; except that, in determining the employer's liability in connection with the taxes imposed by section 3111 with respect to such tips in any case where no statement

EMPLOYMENT TAX—GENERAL PROVISIONS

including such tips was so furnished (or to the extent that the statement so furnished was inaccurate or incomplete), such remuneration shall be deemed for purposes of subtitle F to be paid on the date on which notice an demand for such taxes is made to the employer by the Secretary." **Effective** with respect to tips received (and wages paid) on and after 1-1-88.

- **1965, Social Security Amendments of 1965 (P.L. 89-97)**

P.L. 89-97, §313(c):

Added Sec. 3121(q). **Effective** with respect to tips received by employees after 1965.

[Sec. 3121(r)]

(r) ELECTION OF COVERAGE BY RELIGIOUS ORDERS.—

(1) CERTIFICATE OF ELECTION BY ORDER.—A religious order whose members are required to take a vow of poverty, or any autonomous subdivision of such order, may file a certificate (in such form and manner, and with such official, as may be prescribed by regulations under this chapter) electing to have the insurance system established by title II of the Social Security Act extended to services performed by its members in the exercise of duties required by such order or such subdivision thereof. Such certificate of election shall provide that—

(A) such election of coverage by such order or subdivision shall be irrevocable;

(B) such election shall apply to all current and future members of such order, or in the case of a subdivision thereof to all current and future members of such order who belong to such subdivision;

(C) all services performed by a member of such an order or subdivision in the exercise of duties required by such order or subdivision shall be deemed to have been performed by such member as an employee of such order or subdivision; and

(D) the wages of each member, upon which such order or subdivision shall pay the taxes imposed by sections 3101 and 3111, will be determined as provided in subsection (i)(4).

(2) DEFINITION OF MEMBER.—For purposes of this subsection, a member of a religious order means any individual who is subject to a vow of poverty as a member of such order and who performs tasks usually required (and to the extent usually required) of an active member of such order and who is not considered retired because of old age or total disability.

(3) EFFECTIVE DATE FOR ELECTION.—

(A) A certificate of election of coverage shall be in effect, for purposes of subsection (b)(8) and for purposes of section 210(a)(8) of the Social Security Act, for the period beginning with whichever of the following may be designated by the order or subdivision thereof:

(i) the first day of the calendar quarter in which the certificate is filed,

(ii) the first day of the calendar quarter succeeding such quarter, or

(iii) the first day of any calendar quarter preceding the calendar quarter in which the certificate is filed, except that such date may not be earlier than the first day of the twentieth calendar quarter preceding the quarter in which such certificate is filed.

Whenever a date is designated under clause (iii), the election shall apply to services performed before the quarter in which the certificate is filed only if the member performing such services was a member at the time such services were performed and is living on the first day of the quarter in which such certificate is filed.

(B) If a certificate of election filed pursuant to this subsection is effective for one or more calendar quarters prior to the quarter in which such certificate is filed, then—

(i) for purposes of computing interest and for purposes of section 6651 (relating to addition to tax for failure to file tax return), the due date for the return and payment of the tax for such prior calendar quarters resulting from the filing of such certificate shall be the last day of the calendar month following the calendar quarter in which the certificate is filed; and

(ii) the statutory period for the assessment of such tax shall not expire before the expiration of 3 years from such due date.

Amendments

- **1983, Social Security Act of 1983 (P.L. 98-21)**

P.L. 98-21, §102(b)(3):

Amended Code Sec. 3121(r) by striking out "subsection (b)(8)(A)" and "section 210(a)(8)(A) in paragraph (3) and inserting in lieu thereof "subsection (b)(8)" and "section 210(a)(8)", respectively; and by striking out paragraph (4). **Effective** with respect to service performed after 12-31-83. The period for which a certificate is in effect under Code Sec. 3121(k) may not be terminated under §3121(k)(1)(D) or 3121(k)(2) on or after 3-31-83, but no such certificate shall be effective for any service to which the amendments made by §102 of P.L. 98-21 apply. If any individual, (1) on 1-1-84, is age 55 or over, and is an employee of an organization described in §210(a)(8)(B) of the Social Security Act (a) which does not have in effect (on that date) a waiver certificate under Code Sec. 3121(k) and (b) to the employees of which social security coverage is extended on 1-1-84, solely by reason of enactment of this section, and (2) after 12-31-83, acquires the number of quarters of coverage (within the meaning of §213 of the Social Security Act) which is required for purposes of this subparagraph under paragraph (2), then such individual shall be deemed to be a fully insured individual for all of the purposes of title II of such act. Prior to amendment, Code Sec. 3121(r)(4) read as follows:

(4) COORDINATION WITH COVERAGE OF LAY EMPLOYEES.—Notwithstanding the preceding provisions of this subsection, no certificate of election shall become effective with respect to an order or subdivision thereof, unless—

(A) if at the time the certificate of election is filed a certificate of waiver of exemption under subsection (k) is in effect with respect to such order or subdivision, such order or subdivision amends such certificate of waiver of exemption (in such form and manner as may be prescribed by regulations made under this chapter) to provide that it may not be revoked, or

(B) if at the time the certificate of election is filed a certificate of waiver of exemption under such subsection is not in effect with respect to such order or subdivision, such order or subdivision files such certificate of waiver of exemption under the provisions of such subsection except that such certificate of waiver of exemption cannot become effective at a later date than the certificate of election and such certificate of waiver of exemption must specify that such certificate of waiver of exemption may not be revoked. The certificate of waiver of exemption required under this subparagraph shall be filed notwithstanding the provisions of subsection (k)(3).

- **1972, Social Security Amendments of 1972 (P.L. 92-603)**

P.L. 92-603, §123(b):

Added Code Sec. 3121(r). **Effective** 10-30-72.

[Sec. 3121(s)]

(s) CONCURRENT EMPLOYMENT BY TWO OR MORE EMPLOYERS.—For purposes of sections 3102, 3111 and 3121(a)(1), if two or more related corporations concurrently employ the same individual and compensate such individual through a common paymaster which is one of such corporations, each such corporation shall be considered to have paid as remuneration to such individual only the amounts actually disbursed by it to such individual and shall not be considered to have paid as remuneration to such individual amounts actually disbursed to such individual by another of such corporations.

Amendments

- **1983, Social Security Act of 1983 (P.L. 98-21)**

P.L. 98-21, §125, provides:

SEC. 125. TREATMENT OF CERTAIN FACULTY PRACTICE PLANS.

(a) GENERAL RULE.—For purposes of subsection (s) of section 3121 of the Internal Revenue Code of 1954 (relating to concurrent employment by 2 or more employers)—

(1) the following entities shall be deemed to be related corporations:

(A) a State university which employs health professionals as faculty members at a medical school, and

(B) a faculty practice plan described in section 501(c)(3) of such Code and exempt from tax under section 501(a) of such Code—

(i) which employs faculty members of such medical school, and

(ii) 30 percent or more of the employees of which are concurrently employed by such medical school; and

(2) remuneration which is disbursed by such faculty practice plan to a health professional employed by both such entities shall be deemed to have been actually disbursed by such university as a common paymaster and not to have been actually disbursed by such faculty practice plan.

(b) EFFECTIVE DATE.—The provisions of subsection (a) shall apply to remuneration paid after December 31, 1983.

- **1977 (P.L. 95-216)**

P.L. 95-216, §314(a), (c):

Added Code Sec. 3121(s). **Effective** for wages paid after 12-31-78.

EMPLOYMENT TAX—GENERAL PROVISIONS

[Sec. 3121(t)—Repealed]

Amendments

• **1987, Revenue Act of 1987 (P.L. 100-203)**

P.L. 100-203, § 9006(b)(2):

Repealed Code Sec. 3121(t). **Effective** with respect to tips received (and wages paid) on and after 1-1-88. Prior to repeal, Code Sec. 3121(t) read as follows:

(t) SPECIAL RULE FOR DETERMINING WAGES SUBJECT TO EMPLOYER TAX IN CASE OF CERTAIN EMPLOYERS WHOSE EMPLOYEES RECEIVE INCOME FROM TIPS.—If the wages paid by an employer with respect to the employment during any month of an individual who (for services performed in connection with such employment) receives tips which constitute wages, and to which section 3102(a) applies, are less than the total amount which would be payable (with respect to such employment) at the minimum wage rate applicable to such individual under section 6(a)(1) of the Fair Labor Standards Act of 1938 (determined without regard to section 3(m) of such Act), the wages so paid shall be deemed for purposes of section 3111 to be equal to such total amount.

• **1977 (P.L. 95-216)**

P.L. 95-216, § 315(a):

Added Code Sec. 3121(t). **Effective** for wages paid for employment performed after 1977.

[Sec. 3121(u)]

(u) APPLICATION OF HOSPITAL INSURANCE TAX TO FEDERAL, STATE, AND LOCAL EMPLOYMENT.—

(1) FEDERAL EMPLOYMENT.—For purposes of the taxes imposed by sections 3101(b) and 3111(b), subsection (b) shall be applied without regard to paragraph (5) thereof.

(2) STATE AND LOCAL EMPLOYMENT.—For purposes of the taxes imposed by sections 3101(b) and 3111(b)—

(A) IN GENERAL.—Except as provided in subparagraphs (B) and (C), subsection (b) shall be applied without regard to paragraph (7) thereof.

(B) EXCEPTION FOR CERTAIN SERVICES.—Service shall not be treated as employment by reason of subparagraph (A) if—

(i) the service is included under an agreement under section 218 of the Social Security Act, or

(ii) the service is performed—

(I) by an individual who is employed by a State or political subdivision thereof to relieve him from unemployment,

(II) in a hospital, home, or other institution by a patient or inmate thereof as an employee of a State or political subdivision thereof or of the District of Columbia,

(III) by an individual, as an employee of a State or political subdivision thereof or of the District of Columbia, serving on a temporary basis in case of fire, storm, snow, earthquake, flood or other similar emergency,

(IV) by any individual as an employee included under section 5351(2) of title 5, United States Code (relating to certain interns, student nurses, and other student employees of hospitals of the District of Columbia Government), other than as a medical or dental intern or a medical or dental resident in training,

(V) by an election official or election worker if the remuneration paid in a calendar year for such service is less than $1,000 with respect to service performed during any calendar year commencing on or after January 1, 1995, ending on or before December 31, 1999, and the adjusted amount determined under section 218(c)(8)(B) of the Social Security Act for any calendar year commencing on or after January 1, 2000, with respect to service performed during such calendar year, or

(VI) by an individual in a position described in section 1402(c)(2)(E).

As used in this subparagraph, the terms "State" and "political subdivision" have the meanings given those terms in section 218(b) of the Social Security Act.

(C) EXCEPTION FOR CURRENT EMPLOYMENT WHICH CONTINUES.—Service performed for an employer shall not be treated as employment by reason of subparagraph (A) if—

(i) such service would be excluded from the term "employment" for purposes of this chapter if subparagraph (A) did not apply;

(ii) such service is performed by an individual—

(I) who was performing substantial and regular service for remuneration for that employer before April 1, 1986,

(II) who is a bona fide employee of that employer on March 31, 1986, and

(III) whose employment relationship with that employer was not entered into for purposes of meeting the requirements of this subparagraph; and

(iii) the employment relationship with that employer has not been terminated after March 31, 1986.

(D) TREATMENT OF AGENCIES AND INSTRUMENTALITIES.—For purposes of subparagraph (C), under regulations—

(i) All agencies and instrumentalities of a State (as defined in section 218(b) of the Social Security Act) or of the District of Columbia shall be treated as a single employer.

(ii) All agencies and instrumentalities of a political subdivision of a State (as so defined) shall be treated as a single employer and shall not be treated as described in clause (i).

(3) MEDICARE QUALIFIED GOVERNMENT EMPLOYMENT.—For purposes of this chapter, the term "medicare qualified government employment" means service which—

(A) is employment (as defined in subsection (b)) with the application of paragraphs (1) and (2), but

(B) would not be employment (as so defined) without the application of such paragraphs.

Amendments

• **1994, Social Security Independence and Program Improvements Act of 1994 (P.L. 103-296)**

P.L. 103-296, § 303(b)(2):

Amended Code Sec. 3121(u)(2)(B)(ii)(V) by striking out "$100" and inserting "$1,000 with respect to service performed during any calendar year commencing on or after January 1, 1995, ending on or before December 31, 1999, and the adjusted amount determined under section 218(c)(8)(B) of the Social Security Act for any calendar year commencing on or after January 1, 2000, with respect to service performed during such calendar year". **Effective** with respect to service performed on or after 1-1-95.

• **1988, Technical and Miscellaneous Revenue Act of 1988 (P.L. 100-647)**

P.L. 100-647, § 1018(r)(2)(A):

Amended Code Sec. 3121(u)(2)(B)(ii) by striking out "or" at the end of subclause (IV), by striking out the period at the end of subclause (V) and inserting in lieu thereof ", or", and by inserting after subclause (V) new subclause (VI). **Effective** for services performed after 3-31-86.

• **1986, Tax Reform Act of 1986 (P.L. 99-514)**

P.L. 99-514, § 1895(b)(18)(A):

Amended Code Sec. 3121(u)(2)(B)(ii) by striking out "or" at the end of subclause (III), by striking out the period at the end of subclause (IV) and inserting in lieu thereof ", or", and by adding at the end thereof new subclause (V). **Effective** as if included in the enactment of P.L. 99-272.

• **1986, Consolidated Omnibus Budget Reconciliation Act of 1985 (P.L. 99-272)**

P.L. 99-272, § 13205(a)(1):

Amended Code Sec. 3121(u). **Effective** for services performed after 3-31-86. Prior to amendment, Code Sec. 3121(u) read as follows:

(u) APPLICATION OF HOSPITAL INSURANCE TAX TO FEDERAL EMPLOYMENT.—

(1) IN GENERAL.—For purposes of the taxes imposed by sections 3101(b) and 3111(b), subsection (b) shall be applied without regard to paragraph (5) thereof.

EMPLOYMENT TAX—GENERAL PROVISIONS

(2) MEDICARE QUALIFIED FEDERAL EMPLOYMENT.—For purposes of this chapter, the term "medicare qualified Federal employment" means service which—

(A) is employment (as defined in subsection (b)) with the application of paragraph (1), but

(B) would not be employment (as so defined) without the application of paragraph (1).

• **1983, Social Security Act of 1983 (P.L. 98-21)**

P.L. 98-21, § 101(b)(2):

Amended Code Sec. 3121(u)(1). **Effective** with respect to service performed after 12-31-83. Prior to amendment Code Sec. 3121(u)(1) read as follows:

(1) IN GENERAL.—For purposes of the taxes imposed by sections 3101(b) and 3111(b)—

(A) paragraph (6) of subsection (b) shall be applied without regard to subparagraphs (A), (B), and (C)(i), (ii), and (vi) thereof, and

(B) paragraph (5) of subsection (b) (and the provisions of law referred to therein) shall not apply.

• **1982, Tax Equity and Fiscal Responsibility Act of 1982 (P.L. 97-248)**

P.L. 97-248, § 278(a)(1):

Added Code Sec. 3121(u). **Effective** for remuneration paid after 12-31-82.

[Sec. 3121(v)]

(v) TREATMENT OF CERTAIN DEFERRED COMPENSATION AND SALARY REDUCTION ARRANGEMENTS.—

(1) CERTAIN EMPLOYER CONTRIBUTIONS TREATED AS WAGES.—Nothing in any paragraph of subsection (a) (other than paragraph (1)) shall exclude from the term "wages"—

(A) any employer contribution under a qualified cash or deferred arrangement (as defined in section 401(k)) to the extent not included in gross income by reason of section 402(e)(3) or consisting of designated Roth contributions (as defined in section 402A(c)), or

(B) any amount treated as an employer contribution under section 414(h)(2) where the pickup referred to in such section is pursuant to a salary reduction agreement (whether evidenced by a written instrument or otherwise).

(2) TREATMENT OF CERTAIN NONQUALIFIED DEFERRED COMPENSATION PLANS.—

(A) IN GENERAL.—Any amount deferred under a nonqualified deferred compensation plan shall be taken into account for purposes of this chapter as of the later of—

(i) when the services are performed, or

(ii) when there is no substantial risk of forfeiture of the rights to such amount.

The preceding sentence shall not apply to any excess parachute payment (as defined in section 280G(b)) or to any specified stock compensation (as defined in section 4985) on which tax is imposed by section 4985.

(B) TAXED ONLY ONCE.—Any amount taken into account as wages by reason of subparagraph (A) (and the income attributable thereto) shall not thereafter be treated as wages for purposes of this chapter.

(C) NONQUALIFIED DEFERRED COMPENSATION PLAN.—For purposes of this paragraph, the term "nonqualified deferred compensation plan" means any plan or other arrangement for deferral of compensation other than a plan described in subsection (a)(5).

(3) EXEMPT GOVERNMENTAL DEFERRED COMPENSATION PLAN.—For purposes of subsection (a)(5), the term "exempt governmental deferred compensation plan" means any plan providing for deferral of compensation established and maintained for its employees by the United States, by a State or political subdivision thereof, or by an agency or instrumentality of any of the foregoing. Such term shall not include—

(A) any plan to which section 83, 402(b), 403(c), 457(a), or 457(f)(1) applies,

(B) any annuity contract described in section 403(b), and

(C) the Thrift Savings Fund (within the meaning of subchapter III of chapter 84 of title 5, United States Code).

Amendments

• **2007, Tax Technical Corrections Act of 2007 (P.L. 110-172)**

P.L. 110-172, § 8(a)(2):

Amended Code Sec. 3121(v)(1)(A) by inserting "or consisting of designated Roth contributions (as defined in section 402A(c)" before the comma at the end. **Effective** as if included in the provision of the Economic Growth and Tax Relief Reconciliation Act of 2001 (P.L. 107-16) to which it relates [**effective** for tax years beginning after 12-31-2005.—CCH].

• **2004, American Jobs Creation Act of 2004 (P.L. 108-357)**

P.L. 108-357, § 802(c)(1):

Amended the last sentence of Code Sec. 3121(v)(2)(A) by inserting before the period "or to any specified stock compensation (as defined in section 4985) on which tax is imposed by section 4985". For the **effective** date, see Act Sec. 802(d), below.

P.L. 108-357, § 802(d), provides:

(d) EFFECTIVE DATE.—The amendments made by this section shall take effect on March 4, 2003; except that periods before such date shall not be taken into account in applying the periods in subsections (a) and (e)(1) of section 4985 of the Internal Revenue Code of 1986, as added by this section.

• **1992, Unemployment Compensation Amendments of 1992 (P.L. 102-318)**

P.L. 102-318, § 521(b)(34):

Amended Code Sec. 3121(v)(1)(A) by striking "section 402(a)(8)" and inserting "section 402(e)(3)". **Effective** for distributions after 12-31-92.

• **1988, Technical and Miscellaneous Revenue Act of 1988 (P.L. 100-647)**

P.L. 100-647, § 1011(e)(8):

Amended Code Sec. 3121(v)(3)(A) by striking out "457(e)(1)" and inserting in lieu thereof "457(f)(1)". **Effective** as if included in the provision of P.L. 99-514 to which it relates.

P.L. 100-647, § 1018(u)(35):

Amended Code Sec. 3121(v)(3)(C) by striking out "Saving" and inserting in lieu thereof "Savings". **Effective** as if included in the provision of P.L. 99-514 to which it relates.

• **1986, Tax Reform Act of 1986 (P.L. 99-514)**

P.L. 99-514, § 1147(b):

Amended Code Sec. 3121(v)(3) by striking out "and" at the end of subparagraph (A), by striking out the period at the end of subparagraph (B), and inserting in lieu thereof ", and", and by inserting after subparagraph (B) the new subparagraph (C). **Effective** 10-22-86.

P.L. 99-514, § 1899A(38):

Amended Code Sec. 3121(v)(2)(A)(ii) by striking out "forfeiture" and inserting in lieu thereof "forfeiture". **Effective** 10-22-86.

• **1984, Deficit Reduction Act of 1984 (P.L. 98-369)**

P.L. 98-369, § 67(c):

Amended Code Sec. 3121(v)(2)(A) by adding the sentence at the end thereof. **Effective** for payments under agreements entered into or renewed after 6-14-84, in tax years ending after such date. A special rule appears below.

P.L. 98-369, § 67(e)(2), provides:

(2) Special Rule for Contract Amendments.—In the case of any contract entered into before June 15, 1984, any amendment to such contract after June 14, 1984, which amends such contract in any significant relevant aspect shall be treated as a new contract.

P.L. 98-369, § 2661(o)(3):

Amended Code Sec. 3121(v)(1)(B). **Effective** 1-1-84. Prior to amendment, subparagraph (B) read as follows:

(B) any amount treated as an employer contribution under section 414(h)(2).

• **1983, Social Security Act of 1983 (P.L. 98-21)**

P.L. 98-21, § 324(a)(1):

Added Code Sec. 3121(v). **Effective**, generally, for remuneration paid after 12-31-83; it shall not apply, however, to employer contributions made during 1984 and attributable to services performed during 1983 under a qualified cash or deferred arrangement (as defined in Code Sec. 401(k)) if, under the terms of such arrangement as in effect on 3-24-83, (A) the employee makes an election with respect to such contribution before 1-1-84, and (B) the employer identifies the amount of such contribution before 1-1-84. In the case of an agreement in existence on 3-24-83, between a nonqualified deferred compensation plan (as defined in Code Sec. 3121(v)(2)(C), as added by P.L. 98-21), and an individual, (A) the amendments made by Act Sec. 324(a) (which includes new Code Sec. 3121(v)) and (c) shall apply with respect to services performed by such individual after 12-31-83. The preceding sentence shall not apply in the case of a plan to which Code Sec. 457(a) applies. P.L. 98-21, § 324(d)(1), as amended by P.L. 98-369, § 2662(f)(2), provides that for purposes of applying such amendments to remuneration paid after 12-31-83, which would have been taken into account before 1-1-84, if such remuneration had applied to periods before 1-1-84, such remuneration shall be taken into account when paid (or, at the election of the payor, at the time which would be appropriate if such amendments had applied). P.L. 98-21, § 324(d)(4), as amended by P.L. 98-369, § 2662(f)(2)(C), provides that for, purposes of this paragraph, any plan or agreement to make payments described in paragraph (2), (3), or (13)(A)(iii) of section 3121(a) of such Code (as in effect on the day before the date of the enactment of this Act) shall be treated as a nonqualified deferred compensation plan.

EMPLOYMENT TAX—GENERAL PROVISIONS

[Sec. 3121(w)]

(w) EXEMPTION OF CHURCHES AND QUALIFIED CHURCH-CONTROLLED ORGANIZATIONS.—

(1) GENERAL RULE.—Any church or qualified church-controlled organization (as defined in paragraph (3)) may make an election within the time period described in paragraph (2), in accordance with such procedures as the Secretary determines to be appropriate, that services performed in the employ of such church or organization shall be excluded from employment for purposes of title II of the Social Security Act and this chapter. An election may be made under this subsection only if the church or qualified church-controlled organization states that such church or organization is opposed for religious reasons to the payment of the tax imposed under section 3111.

(2) TIMING AND DURATION OF ELECTION.—An election under this subsection must be made prior to the first date, more than 90 days after July 18, 1984, on which a quarterly employment tax return for the tax imposed under section 3111 is due, or would be due but for the election, from such church or organization. An election under this subsection shall apply to current and future employees, and shall apply to service performed after December 31, 1983. The election may be revoked by the church or organization under regulations prescribed by the Secretary. The election shall be revoked by the Secretary if such church or organization fails to furnish the information required under section 6051 to the Secretary for a period of 2 years or more with respect to remuneration paid for such services by such church or organization, and, upon request by the Secretary, fails to furnish all such previously unfurnished information for the period covered by the election. Any revocation under the preceding sentence shall apply retroactively to the beginning of the 2-year period for which the information was not furnished.

(3) DEFINITIONS—

(A) For purposes of this subsection, the term "church" means a church, a convention or association of churches, or an elementary or secondary school which is controlled, operated, or principally supported by a church or by a convention or association of churches.

(B) For purposes of this subsection, the term "qualified church-controlled organization" means any church-controlled tax-exempt organization described in section 501(c)(3), other than an organization which—

(i) offers goods, services, or facilities for sale, other than on an incidental basis, to the general public, other than goods, services, or facilities which are sold at a nominal charge which is substantially less than the cost of providing such goods, services, or facilities; and

(ii) normally receives more than 25 percent of its support from either (I) governmental sources, or (II) receipts from admissions, sales of merchandise, performance of services, or furnishing of facilities, in activities which are not unrelated trades or businesses, or both.

Amendments

• **1986, Tax Reform Act of 1986 (P.L. 99-514)**

P.L. 99-514, §1882(c):

Amended Code Sec. 3121(w)(2) by striking out the last two sentences and inserting in lieu thereof three new sentences. **Effective** 10-22-86. Prior to amendment, the last two sentences read as follows:

The election may not be revoked by the church or organization, but shall be permanently revoked by the Secretary if such church or organization fails to furnish the information required under section 6051 to the Secretary for a period of 2 years or more with respect to remuneration paid for such services by such church or organization, and, upon request by the Secretary, fails to furnish all such previously unfurnished information for the period covered by the election. Such revocation shall apply retroactively to the beginning of the 2-year period for which the information was not furnished.

P.L. 99-514, §1899A(39):

Amended the first sentence of paragraph (1) of Code Sec. 3121(w) by striking out "chapter 21 of this Code" and inserting in lieu thereof "this chapter". **Effective** 10-22-86.

P.L. 99-514, §1899A(40):

Amended Code Sec. 3121(w)(2) by striking out "the date of the enactment of this subsection" and inserting in lieu thereof "July 18, 1984". **Effective** 10-22-86.

• **1984, Deficit Reduction Act of 1984 (P.L. 98-369)**

P.L. 98-369, §2603(b):

Amended Code Sec. 3121 by adding at the end thereof new subsection (w). **Effective** for service performed after 12-31-83. A special rule appears below.

P.L. 98-369, §2603(f), provides:

(f) In any case where a church or qualified church controlled organization makes an election under section 3121(w) of the Internal Revenue Code of 1954, the Secretary of the Treasury shall refund (without interest) to such church or organization any taxes paid under sections 3101 and 3111 of such Code with respect to service performed after December 31, 1983, which is covered under such election. The refund shall be conditional upon the church or organization agreeing to pay to each employee (or former employee) the portion of the refund attributable to the tax imposed on such employee (or former employee) under section 3101, and such employee (or former employee) may not receive any other refund payment of such taxes.

[Sec. 3121(x)]

(x) APPLICABLE DOLLAR THRESHOLD.—For purposes of subsection (a)(7)(B), the term "applicable dollar threshold" means $1,000. In the case of calendar years after 1995, the Commissioner of Social Security shall adjust such $1,000 amount at the same time and in the same manner as under section 215(a)(1)(B)(ii) of the Social Security Act with respect to the amounts referred to in section 215(a)(1)(B)(i) of such Act, except that, for purposes of this paragraph, 1993 shall be substituted for the calendar year referred to in section 215(a)(1)(B)(ii)(II) of such Act. If any amount as adjusted under the preceding sentence is not a multiple of $100, such amount shall be rounded to the next lowest multiple of $100.

Amendments

• **1994, Social Security Domestic Employment Reform Act of 1994 (P.L. 103-387)**

P.L. 103-387, §2(a)(1)(B):

Amended Code Sec. 3121 by adding at the end thereof [sic] a new subsection (x). **Effective** for remuneration paid after 12-31-93.

[Sec. 3121(x)—Stricken]

Amendments

• **1993, Omnibus Budget Reconciliation Act of 1993 (P.L. 103-66)**

P.L. 103-66, §13207(a)(2):

Amended Code Sec. 3121 by striking subsection (x). **Effective** for 1994 and later calendar years. Prior to amendment, Code Sec. 3121(x) read as follows:

(x) APPLICABLE CONTRIBUTION BASE.—For purposes of this chapter—

(1) OLD-AGE, SURVIVORS, AND DISABILITY INSURANCE.—For purposes of the taxes imposed by sections 3101(a) and 3111(a), the applicable contribution base for any calendar year is the contribution and benefit base determined under section 230 of the Social Security Act for such calendar year.

(2) HOSPITAL INSURANCE.—For purposes of the taxes imposed by section 3101(b) and 3111(b), the applicable contribution base is—

(A) $125,000 for calendar year 1991, and

(B) for any calendar year after 1991, the applicable contribution base for the preceding year adjusted in the same manner as is used in adjusting the contribution and benefit base under section 230(b) of the Social Security Act.

• **1990, Omnibus Budget Reconciliation Act of 1990 (P.L. 101-508)**

P.L. 101-508, §11331(a)(2):

Amended Code Sec. 3121 by adding at the end thereof a new subsection (x). **Effective** for 1991 and later calendar years.

• **1989 (P.L. 101-140)**

P.L. 101-140, §203(a)(2), provides:

Code Sec. 3121(x) as added by Section 1011B(a)(22)(A) of the Technical and Miscellaneous Revenue Act of 1988 (P.L. 100-647) shall be applied as if the amendment made by such section has not been enacted. Code Sec. 3121(x), as added by Act Sec. 1011B(a)(22)(A) of P.L. 100-647, read as follows:

(x) Benefits Provided Under Certain Employee Benefit Plans.—Notwithstanding any paragraph of subsection (a) (other than paragraph (1)), the term "wages" shall include any amount which is includible in gross income by reason of section 89. **Effective** as if included in section 1151 of P.L. 99-514.

• **1988, Technical and Miscellaneous Revenue Act of 1988 (P.L. 100-647)**

P.L. 100-647, §1011B(a)(22)(A):

Amended Code Sec. 3121 by adding at the end thereof new subsection (x). Not **effective** for any individual who separated from service with the employer before 1-1-89.

EMPLOYMENT TAX—GENERAL PROVISIONS

[Sec. 3121(y)]

(y) SERVICE IN THE EMPLOY OF INTERNATIONAL ORGANIZATIONS BY CERTAIN TRANSFERRED FEDERAL EMPLOYEES.—

(1) IN GENERAL.—For purposes of this chapter, service performed in the employ of an international organization by an individual pursuant to a transfer of such individual to such international organization pursuant to section 3582 of title 5, United States Code, shall constitute "employment" if—

(A) immediately before such transfer, such individual performed service with a Federal agency which constituted "employment" under subsection (b) for purposes of the taxes imposed by sections 3101(a) and 3111(a), and

(B) such individual would be entitled, upon separation from such international organization and proper application, to reemployment with such Federal agency under such section 3582.

(2) DEFINITIONS.—For purposes of this subsection—

(A) FEDERAL AGENCY.—The term "Federal agency" means an agency, as defined in section 3581(1) of title 5, United States Code.

(B) INTERNATIONAL ORGANIZATION.—The term "international organization" has the meaning provided such term by section 3581(3) of title 5, United States Code.

Amendments

• **1994, Social Security Independence and Program Improvements Act of 1994 (P.L. 103-296)**

P.L. 103-296, §319(a)(1):

Amended Code Sec. 3121 by adding at the end thereof a new subsection (y). **Effective** with respect to service performed after the calendar quarter following the calendar quarter containing 8-15-94.

[Sec. 3121(z)]

(z) TREATMENT OF CERTAIN FOREIGN PERSONS AS AMERICAN EMPLOYERS.—

(1) IN GENERAL.—If any employee of a foreign person is performing services in connection with a contract between the United States Government (or any instrumentality thereof) and any member of any domestically controlled group of entities which includes such foreign person, such foreign person shall be treated for purposes of this chapter as an American employer with respect to such services performed by such employee.

(2) DOMESTICALLY CONTROLLED GROUP OF ENTITIES.—For purposes of this subsection—

(A) IN GENERAL.—The term "domestically controlled group of entities" means a controlled group of entities the common parent of which is a domestic corporation.

(B) CONTROLLED GROUP OF ENTITIES.—The term "controlled group of entities" means a controlled group of corporations as defined in section 1563(a)(1), except that—

(i) "more than 50 percent" shall be substituted for "at least 80 percent" each place it appears therein, and

(ii) the determination shall be made without regard to subsections (a)(4) and (b)(2) of section 1563.

A partnership or any other entity (other than a corporation) shall be treated as a member of a controlled group of entities if such entity is controlled (within the meaning of section 954(d)(3)) by members of such group (including any entity treated as a member of such group by reason of this sentence).

(3) LIABILITY OF COMMON PARENT.—In the case of a foreign person who is a member of any domestically controlled group of entities, the common parent of such group shall be jointly and severally liable for any tax under this chapter for which such foreign person is liable by reason of this subsection, and for any penalty imposed on such person by this title with respect to any failure to pay such tax or to file any return or statement with respect to such tax or wages subject to such tax. No deduction shall be allowed under this title for any liability imposed by the preceding sentence.

(4) PROVISIONS PREVENTING DOUBLE TAXATION.—

(A) AGREEMENTS.—Paragraph (1) shall not apply to any services which are covered by an agreement under subsection (l).

(B) EQUIVALENT FOREIGN TAXATION.—Paragraph (1) shall not apply to any services if the employer establishes to the satisfaction of the Secretary that the remuneration paid by such employer for such services is subject to a tax imposed by a foreign country which is substantially equivalent to the taxes imposed by this chapter.

(5) CROSS REFERENCE.—For relief from taxes in cases covered by certain international agreements, see sections 3101(c) and 3111(c).

Amendments

• **2008, Heroes Earnings Assistance and Relief Tax Act of 2008 (P.L. 110-245)**

P.L. 110-245, §302(a):

Amended Code Sec. 3121 by adding at the end a new subsection (z). **Effective** for services performed in calendar months beginning more than 30 days after 6-17-2008.

[Sec. 3122]

SEC. 3122. FEDERAL SERVICE.

In the case of the taxes imposed by this chapter with respect to service performed in the employ of the United States or in the employ of any instrumentality which is wholly owned by the United States, including such service which is medicare qualified government employment (as defined in section 3121(u)(3)), including service, performed as a member of a uniformed service, to which the provisions of section 3121(m)(1) are applicable, and including service, performed as a volunteer or volunteer leader within the meaning of the Peace Corps Act, to which the provisions of section 3121(p) are applicable, the determination of the amount of renumeration for such service, and the return and payment of the taxes imposed by this chapter, shall be made by the head of the Federal agency or instrumentality having the control of such service, or by such agents as such head may designate. In the case of the taxes imposed by this chapter with respect to service performed in the employ of an international organization pursuant to a transfer to which the provisions of section 3121(y) are applicable, the determination of the amount of renumeration for such service, and the return and payment of the taxes imposed by this chapter, shall be made by the head of the Federal agency from which the transfer was made. Nothing in this paragraph shall be construed to affect the Secretary's authority to determine under subsections (a) and (b) of section 3121 whether any such service constitutes employment, the periods of such employment, and whether remuneration paid for any such service constitutes wages. The person making such return may, for convenience of administration, make payments of the tax imposed under section 3111 with respect to such service without regard to the contribution and benefit base limitation in section 3121(a)(1), and he shall not be required to obtain a refund of the tax paid under section 3111 on that part of the remuneration not included in wages by reason of section 3121(a)(1). Payments of the tax imposed under section 3111 with respect to service, performed by an individual as a member of a uniformed service, to which the provisions of section 3121(m)(1) are applicable, shall be made from appropriations available for the pay of members of such uniformed service. The provisions of this section shall be applicable in the case of service performed by a civilian employee, not compensated from funds apopropriated by the Congress, in the Army and Air Force Exchange Service, Army and Air Force Motion Picture Service, Navy Exchanges, Marine Corps Exchanges, or other activities, conducted by an instrumentality of the United States subject to the jurisdiction of the Secretary of Defense, at installations of the Department of Defense for the comfort, pleasure, contentment, and mental and physical improvement of personnel of such Department; and for purposes of this section the Secretary of Defense shall be deemed to be the head of such instrumentality. The provisions of this section shall be applicable also in the case of service performed by a civilian employee, not compensated from funds appropriated by the Congress, in the Coast Guard Exchanges or other activities, conducted by an instrumentality of the United States subject to the jurisdiction of the Secretary of the Department in which the Coast Guard is operating, at installations of the Coast Guard for the comfort, pleasure, contentment, and mental and physical improvement of personnel of the Coast Guard; and for purposes of this section the Secretary of the Department in which the Coast Guard is operating shall be deemed to be the head of such instrumentality.

Amendments

- **2006, Coast Guard and Maritime Transportation Act of 2006 (P.L. 109-241)**

P.L. 109-241, §902(i):

Amended Code Sec. 3122 by striking "Secretary of Transportation" each place it appears and inserting "Secretary of the Department in which the Coast Guard is operating". **Effective** 7-11-2006.

- **1994, Social Security Independence and Program Improvements Act of 1994 (P.L. 103-296)**

P.L. 103-296, §319(a)(2):

Amended Code Sec. 3122 by inserting after the first sentence a new sentence. **Effective** with respect to service performed after the calendar quarter following the calendar quarter containing 8-15-94.

- **1993, Omnibus Budget Reconciliation Act of 1993 (P.L. 103-66)**

P.L. 103-66, §13207(d)(4):

Amended Code Sec. 3122 by striking "applicable contribution base limitation" and inserting "contribution and benefit base limitation". **Effective** for 1994 and later calendar years.

- **1990, Omnibus Budget Reconciliation Act of 1990 (P.L. 101-508)**

P.L. 101-508, §11331(d)(2):

Amended Code Sec. 3122 by striking "contribution and benefit base limitation" each place it appears and inserting "applicable contribution base limitation". **Effective** for 1991 and later calendar years.

- **1988, Technical and Miscellaneous Revenue Act of 1988 (P.L. 100-647)**

P.L. 100-647, §8015(a)(2)(A)-(C):

Amended Code Sec. 3122 by striking "the determination whether an individual has performed service which constitutes employment as defined in section 3121(b)," following the phrase "to which the provisions of section 3121(p) are applicable," in the first sentence; by striking "which constitutes wages as defined in section 3121(a)" following the phrase "the determination of the amount of remuneration for such service" in the first sentence; and by inserting after the first sentence a new sentence. **Effective** for determinations relating to service commenced in any position on or after 11-10-88.

- **1986, Consolidated Omnibus Budget Reconciliation Act of 1985 (P.L. 99-272)**

P.L. 99-272, §13205(a)(2)(C):

Amended Code Sec. 3122 by striking out "including service which is medicare qualified Federal employment (as defined in section 3121(u)(2))" and inserting in lieu thereof "including such service which is medicare qualified government employment (as defined in section 3121(u)(3))". **Effective** for services performed after 3-31-86.

- **1982, Tax Equity and Fiscal Responsibility Act of 1982 (P.L. 97-248)**

P.L. 97-248, §278(a)(3):

Amended Code Sec. 3122 by adding "including service which is medicare qualified Federal employment (as defined in section 3121(u)(2))," in the first sentence after "wholly owned by the United States,". **Effective** with respect to remuneration paid after 12-31-82.

- **1976, Tax Reform Act of 1976 (P.L. 94-455)**

P.L. 94-455, §1903(a)(4), (d):

Substituted "Secretary of Transportation" for "Secretary" each place it appeared in the last sentence of Code Sec. 3122. **Effective** for wages paid after 12-31-76.

- **1973 (P.L. 93-233)**

P.L. 93-233, §5(b)(3):

Amended Code Sec. 3122 by substituting "$13,200" for "$10,800." **Effective** with respect to remuneration paid after 1973.

- **1973 (P.L. 93-66)**

P.L. 93-66, §203(b)(3):

Amended Code Sec. 3122 by substituting "$12,600" for "$12,000." **Effective** with respect to remuneration paid after 1973. (But see P.L. 93-233, above.)

- **1972 (P.L. 92-336)**

P.L. 92-336, §203(b)(3)(A) (as amended by P.L. 93-233, §5(d)):

Amended Sec. 3122 by striking out "$9,000" and inserting in lieu thereof "$10,800". **Effective** with respect to remuneration paid after 1972. Amended the second sentence of Sec. 3122 by striking out "$10,800" and inserting in lieu thereof "12,000". **Effective** with respect to remuneration paid after 1973. (But see P.L. 93-66.) Amended the second sentence of Sec. 3122 by striking out "the $13,200 limitation" and inserting in lieu thereof "the contribution and benefit base limitation". **Effective** with respect to remuneration paid after 1974.

- **1971 (P.L. 92-5)**

P.L. 92-5, §203(b)(3):

Amended Code Sec. 3122. **Effective** with respect to remuneration paid after 12-31-71, by substituting "$9,000" for "$7,800".

- **1968, Social Security Amendments of 1967 (P.L. 90-248)**

P.L. 90-248, §108(b)(3):

Amended Sec. 3122 by substituting "$7,800" for "$6,600" in the second sentence. **Effective** only with respect to remuneration paid after December 1967.

- **1965, Social Security Amendments of 1965 (P.L. 89-97)**

P.L. 89-97, §320(b):

Amended Sec. 3122 by substituting "$6,600" for "$4,800" in the second sentence. **Effective** for remuneration paid after December 1965.

- **1961, Peace Corps Act (P.L. 87-293)**

P.L. 87-293, §202(a)(3):

Amended Sec. 3122 by adding (first sentence) after "section 3121(m)(1) are applicable," the words "and including service, performed as a volunteer or volunteer leader within the meaning of the Peace Corps Act, to which the provisions of section 3121(p) are applicable,". **Effective** with respect to services performed after 9-22-61.

- **1958, Technical Amendments Act of 1958 (P.L. 85-866)**

P.L. 85-866, §70:

Struck out, in the last sentence of Sec. 3122, the phrase "this subsection" wherever it appeared and substituted the phrase "this section". **Effective** 1-1-54.

- **1958, Social Security Amendments of 1958 (P.L. 85-840)**

P.L. 85-840, §402(c):

Amended Sec. 3122 by substituting "$4,800" for "$4,200" wherever it appeared. **Effective** 1-1-59.

- **1956, Servicemen's and Veterans' Survivor Benefits Act (P.L. 881, 84th Cong.)**

P.L. 881, 84th Cong., §411(b), (c):

Amended Sec. 3122 by inserting in the first sentence the words "including service, performed as a member of a uniformed service, to which the provisions of section 3121(m)(1) are applicable,", and by inserting after the second sentence the following sentence: "Payments of tax imposed under section 3111 . . . for the pay of members of such uniformed service." **Effective** under §603(a) of P.L. 881.

- **1954, Social Security Amendments of 1954 (P.L. 761, 83rd Cong.)**

P.L. 761, 83rd Cong., §202(c):

Amended Sec. 3122 by substituting "$4,200" in place of "$3,600". **Effective** 1-1-55.

P.L. 761, 83rd Cong., §203(a):

Added the last sentence to Sec. 3122. **Effective** 1-1-55.

[Sec. 3123]

SEC. 3123. DEDUCTIONS AS CONSTRUCTIVE PAYMENTS.

Whenever under this chapter or any act of Congress, or under the law of any State, an employer is required or permitted to deduct any amount from the remuneration of an employee and to pay the amount deducted to the United States, a State, or any political subdivision thereof, then for purposes of this chapter the amount so deducted shall be considered to have been paid to the employee at the time of such deduction.

[Sec. 3124]

SEC. 3124. ESTIMATE OF REVENUE REDUCTION.

The Secretary at intervals of not longer than 3 years shall estimate the reduction in the amount of taxes collected under this chapter by reason of the operation of section 3121(b)(9) and shall include such estimate in his annual report.

EMPLOYMENT TAX—GENERAL PROVISIONS

Amendments
- **1976, Tax Reform Act of 1976 (P.L. 94-455)**

P.L. 94-455, §1906(b)(13)(A):
Amended 1954 Code by substituting "Secretary" for "Secretary or his delegate" each place it appeared. **Effective** 2-1-77.

[Sec. 3125]
SEC. 3125. RETURNS IN THE CASE OF GOVERNMENTAL EMPLOYEES IN STATES, GUAM, AMERICAN SAMOA, AND THE DISTRICT OF COLUMBIA.

[Sec. 3125(a)]
(a) STATES.—Except as otherwise provided in this section, in the case of the taxes imposed by sections 3101(b) and 3111(b) with respect to service performed in the employ of a State or any political subdivision thereof (or any instrumentality of any one or more of the foregoing which is wholly owned thereby), the return and payment of such taxes may be made by the head of the agency or instrumentality having the control of such service, or by such agents as such head may designate. The person making such return may, for convenience of administration, make payments of the tax imposed under section 3111 with respect to the service of such individuals without regard to the contribution and benefit base limitation in section 3121(a)(1).

Amendments
- **1993, Omnibus Budget Reconciliation Act of 1993 (P.L. 103-66)**

P.L. 103-66, §13207(d)(4):
Amended Code Sec. 3125 by striking "applicable contribution base limitation" and inserting "contribution and benefit base limitation". **Effective** for 1994 and later calendar years.

[Sec. 3125(b)]
(b) GUAM.—The return and payment of the taxes imposed by this chapter on the income of individuals who are officers or employees of the Government of Guam or any political subdivision thereof or of any instrumentality of any one or more of the foregoing which is wholly owned thereby, and those imposed on such Government or political subdivision or instrumentality with respect to having such individuals in its employ, may be made by the Governor of Guam or by such agents as he may designate. The person making such return may, for convenience of administration, make payments of the tax imposed under section 3111 with respect to the service of such individuals without regard to the contribution and benefit base limitation in section 3121(a)(1).

Amendments
- **1993, Omnibus Budget Reconciliation Act of 1993 (P.L. 103-66)**

P.L. 103-66, §13207(d)(4):
Amended Code Sec. 3125 by striking "applicable contribution base limitation" and inserting "contribution and benefit base limitation". **Effective** for 1994 and later calendar years.

[Sec. 3125(c)]
(c) AMERICAN SAMOA.—The return and payment of the taxes imposed by this chapter on the income of individuals who are officers or employees of the Government of American Samoa or any political subdivision thereof or of any instrumentality of any one or more of the foregoing which is wholly owned thereby, and those imposed on such Government or political subdivision or instrumentality with respect to having such individuals in its employ, may be made by the Governor of American Samoa or by such agents as he may designate. The person making such return may, for convenience of administration, make payments of the tax imposed under section 3111 with respect to the service of such individuals without regard to the contribution and benefit base limitation in section 3121(a)(1).

Amendments
- **1993, Omnibus Budget Reconciliation Act of 1993 (P.L. 103-66)**

P.L. 103-66, §13207(d)(4):
Amended Code Sec. 3125 by striking "applicable contribution base limitation" and inserting "contribution and benefit base limitation". **Effective** for 1994 and later calendar years.

[Sec. 3125(d)]
(d) DISTRICT OF COLUMBIA.—In the case of the taxes imposed by this chapter with respect to service performed in the employ of the District of Columbia or in the employ of any instrumentality which is wholly owned thereby, the return and payment of the taxes may be made by the Mayor of the District of Columbia or such agents as he may designate. The person making such return may, for convenience of administration, make payments of the tax imposed by section 3111 with respect to such service without regard to the contribution and benefit base limitation in section 3121(a)(1).

Amendments
- **1993, Omnibus Budget Reconciliation Act of 1993 (P.L. 103-66)**

P.L. 103-66, §13207(d)(4):
Amended Code Sec. 3125 by striking "applicable contribution base limitation" and inserting "contribution and benefit base limitation". **Effective** for 1994 and later calendar years.

- **1990, Omnibus Budget Reconciliation Act of 1990 (P.L. 101-508)**

P.L. 101-508, §11331(d)(2):
Amended Code Sec. 3125 by striking "contribution and benefit base limitation" each place it appears and inserting "applicable contribution base limitation". **Effective** for 1991 and later calendar years.

- **1986, Consolidated Omnibus Budget Reconciliation Act of 1985 (P.L. 99-272)**

P.L. 99-272, §13205(a)(2)(A)(i):
Amended Code Sec. 3125 by redesignating subsections (a), (b), and (c) as subsections (b), (c), and (d), respectively, and by inserting before subsection (b) (as so redesignated) new subsection (a). **Effective** for services performed after 3-31-86.

P.L. 99-272, §13205(a)(2)(A)(ii):
Amended Code Sec. 3125 by inserting "States," before "Guam" in the section heading. **Effective** for services performed after 3-31-86.

- **1976, Tax Reform Act of 1976 (P.L. 94-455)**

P.L. 94-455, §1903(a)(5), (d):
Substituted "Mayor of the District of Columbia or such agents as he may designate" for "Commissioners of the District of Columbia or such agents as they may designate" in Code Sec. 3125(c). **Effective** for wages paid after 12-31-76.

- **1973 (P.L. 93-233)**

P.L. 93-233, §5(b)(4):
Amended the limitation figure in Code Sec. 3125(a), (b) and (c) by substituting "$13,200" for "$10,800." **Effective** with respect to remuneration paid after 1973.

- **1973 (P.L. 93-66)**

P.L. 93-66, §203(b)(4):
Amended the limitation figure of Code Sec. 3125 by changing "$12,000" to "$12,600,". **Effective** for remuneration paid after 1973. (But see P.L. 93-233, above.)

- **1972 (P.L. 92-336)**

P.L. 92-336, §203(b)(4)(A), (c) (as amended by P.L. 93-233, §5(d)):
Amended the limitation figure of Code Sec. 3125 by changing "$9,000" to "$10,800,". **Effective** for remuneration paid after 1972. A $12,000 limitation was adopted, but this was pre-empted by the $12,600 limitation adopted by P.L. 93-66. **Effective** for remuneration paid after 1973. Substituted "contribution and benefit

EMPLOYMENT TAX—GENERAL PROVISIONS

base" for the limitation figure in Code Sec. 3125(a), (b) and (c). **Effective** for remuneration paid after 1974.

• **1971 (P.L. 92-5)**

P.L. 92-5, § 203(b)(4):

Amended the limitation figure of Code Sec. 3125 by changing "$7,800" to "$9,000,". **Effective** for remuneration paid after 1971.

• **1968, Social Security Amendments of 1967 (P.L. 90-248)**

P.L. 90-248, § 108(b)(4):

Amended the limitation figure of Code Sec. 3125 by changing "$6,600" to "$7,800,". **Effective** for remuneration paid after 1967.

• **1965, Social Security Amendments of 1965 (P.L. 89-97)**

P.L. 89-97, § 320(b):

Amended the limitation figure of Code Sec. 3125 by changing "$4,800" to "$6,600,". **Effective** for remuneration paid after 1965.

• **1960, Social Security Amendments of 1960 (P.L. 86-778)**

P.L. 86-778, § 103(q):

Redesignated former Code Sec. 3125 to be new Code Sec. 3126 and added new Code Sec. 3125. **Effective** 1-1-61.

Code Sec. 3125 applies only with respect to service in the employ of the Governments of Guam or American Samoa or any political subdivision thereof, or any instrumentality of any one or more of the foregoing wholly owned thereby. Code Sec. 3125 applies to service performed after 1960 and after the calendar quarter in which the Secretary of the Treasury receives a certification from Guam or American Samoa expressing its desire to have social security coverage extended to its officers and employees.

[Sec. 3126]

SEC. 3126. RETURN AND PAYMENT BY GOVERNMENTAL EMPLOYER.

If the employer is a State or political subdivision thereof, or an agency or instrumentality of any one or more of the foregoing, the return of the amount deducted and withheld upon any wages under section 3101 and the amount of the tax imposed by section 3111 may be made by any officer or employee of such State or political subdivision or such agency or instrumentality, as the case may be, having control of the payment of such wages, or appropriately designated for that purpose.

Amendments

• **1986, Omnibus Budget Reconciliation Act of 1986 (P.L. 99-509)**

P.L. 99-509, § 9002(a):

Amended subchapter C of chapter 21 of the Internal Revenue Code of 1954 by redesignating Code Sec. 3126 as Code Sec. 3127, and by inserting after Code Sec. 3125 new Code Sec. 3126. For the **effective** date, see Act Sec. 9002(d), below.

P.L. 99-509, § 9002(d), provides:

(d) EFFECTIVE DATE.—The amendments made by this section are effective with respect to payments due with respect to wages paid after December 31, 1986, including wages paid after such date by a State (or political subdivision thereof) that modified its agreement pursuant to the provisions of section 218(e)(2) of the Social Security Act prior to the date of the enactment of this Act; except that in cases where, in accordance with the currently applicable schedule, deposits of taxes due under an agreement entered into pursuant to section 218 of the Social Security Act would be required within 3 days after the close of an eighth-monthly period, such 3-day requirement shall be changed to a 7-day requirement for wages paid prior to October 1, 1987, and to a 5-day requirement for wages paid after September 30, 1987, and prior to October 1, 1988. For wages paid prior to October 1, 1988, the deposit schedule for taxes imposed under sections 3101 and 3111 shall be determined separately from the deposit schedule for taxes withheld under section 3402 if the taxes imposed under sections 3101 and 3111 are due with respect to service included under an agreement entered into pursuant to section 218 of the Social Security Act.

[Sec. 3127]

SEC. 3127. EXEMPTION FOR EMPLOYERS AND THEIR EMPLOYEES WHERE BOTH ARE MEMBERS OF RELIGIOUS FAITHS OPPOSED TO PARTICIPATION IN SOCIAL SECURITY ACT PROGRAMS.

[Sec. 3127(a)]

(a) IN GENERAL.—Notwithstanding any other provision of this chapter (and under regulations prescribed to carry out this section), in any case where—

(1) an employer (or, if the employer is a partnership, each partner therein) is a member of a recognized religious sect or division thereof described in section 1402(g)(1) and an adherent of established tenets or teachings of such sect or division as described in such section, and has filed and had approved under subsection (b) an application (in such form and manner, and with such official, as may be prescribed by such regulations) for an exemption from the taxes imposed by section 3111, and

(2) an employee of such employer who is also a member of such a religious sect or division and an adherent of its established tenets or teachings has filed and had approved under subsection (b) an identical application for exemption from the taxes imposed by section 3101,

such employer shall be exempt from the taxes imposed by section 3111 with respect to wages paid to each of the employees thereof who meets the requirements of paragraph (2) and each such employee shall be exempt from the taxes imposed by section 3101 with respect to such wages paid to him by such employer.

Amendments

• **1989, Omnibus Budget Reconciliation Act of 1989 (P.L. 101-239)**

P.L. 101-239, § 10204(b)(1)(A):

Amended Code Sec. 3127(a)(1) by inserting "(or, if the employer is a partnership, each partner therein)" after "an employer". **Effective** as if included in the amendments made by section 8007(a)(1) of P.L. 100-647.

P.L. 101-239, § 10204(b)(1)(B):

Amended Code Sec. 3127(a) by striking "his employees" and inserting "the employees thereof" in the matter following paragraph (2). **Effective** as if included in the amendments made by section 8007(a)(1) of P.L. 100-647.

[Sec. 3127(b)]

(b) APPROVAL OF APPLICATION.—An application for exemption filed by an employer (or a partner) under subsection (a)(1) or by an employee under subsection (a)(2) shall be approved only if—

(1) such application contains or is accompanied by the evidence described in section 1402(g)(1)(A) and a waiver described in section 1402(g)(1)(B),

(2) the Commissioner of Social Security makes the findings (with respect to such sect or division) described in section 1402(g)(1)(C), (D), and (E), and

(3) no benefit or other payment referred to in section 1402(g)(1)(B) became payable (or, but for section 203 of the Social Security Act, would have become payable) to the individual filing the application at or before the time of such filing.

Amendments

• **2018, Tax Technical Corrections Act of 2018 (P.L. 115-141)**

P.L. 115-141, § 401(b)(35), Div. U:

Amended Code Sec. 3127(b)(3) by striking "or 222(b)" following "section 203". **Effective** 3-23-2018. For a special rule, see Act Sec. 401(e), Div. U, below.

P.L. 115-141, § 401(e), Div. U, provides:

(e) GENERAL SAVINGS PROVISION WITH RESPECT TO DEADWOOD PROVISIONS.—If—

(1) any provision amended or repealed by the amendments made by subsection (b) or (d) applied to—

(A) any transaction occurring before the date of the enactment of this Act,

(B) any property acquired before such date of enactment, or

(C) any item of income, loss, deduction, or credit taken into account before such date of enactment, and

(2) the treatment of such transaction, property, or item under such provision would (without regard to the amendments or repeals made by such subsection) affect the liability for tax for periods ending after such date of enactment,

nothing in the amendments or repeals made by this section shall be construed to affect the treatment of such transaction, property, or item for purposes of determining liability for tax for periods ending after such date of enactment.

• **1994, Social Security Independence and Program Improvements Act of 1994 (P.L. 103-296)**

P.L. 103-296, § 108(h)(3):

Amended Code Sec. 3127 by striking "Secretary of Health and Human Services" each place it appears and inserting "Commissioner of Social Security". **Effective** 3-31-95.

EMPLOYMENT TAX—GENERAL PROVISIONS

• **1989, Omnibus Budget Reconciliation Act of 1989 (P.L. 101-239)**

P.L. 101-239, § 10204(b)(1)(C):

Amended Code Sec. 3127(b) by inserting "(or a partner)" after "an employer". **Effective** as if included in the amendments made by section 8007(a)(1) of P.L. 100-647.

[Sec. 3127(c)]

(c) EFFECTIVE PERIOD OF EXEMPTION.—An exemption granted under this section to any employer with respect to wages paid to any of the employees thereof, or granted to any such employee, shall apply with respect to wages paid by such employer during the period—

(1) commencing with the first day of the first calendar quarter, after the quarter in which such application is filed, throughout which such employer (or, if the employer is a partnership, each partner therein) or employee meets the applicable requirements specified in subsections (a) and (b), and

(2) ending with the last day of the calendar quarter preceding the first calendar quarter thereafter in which (A) such employer (or, if the employer is a partnership, any partner therein) or the employee involved does not meet the applicable requirements of subsection (a), or (B) the sect or division thereof of which such employer (or, if the employer is a partnership, any partner therein) or employee is a member is found by the Commissioner of Social Security to have ceased to meet the requirements of subsection (b)(2).

Amendments

• **1994, Social Security Independence and Program Improvements Act of 1994 (P.L. 103-296)**

P.L. 103-296, § 108(h)(3):

Amended Code Sec. 3127 by striking "Secretary of Health and Human Services" each place it appears and inserting "Commissioner of Social Security". **Effective** 3-31-95.

• **1989, Omnibus Budget Reconciliation Act of 1989 (P.L. 101-239)**

P.L. 101-239, § 10204(b)(1)(D):

Amended Code Sec. 3127(c) by striking "his employees" and inserting "the employees thereof". **Effective** as if included in the amendments made by section 8007(a)(1) of P.L. 100-647.

P.L. 101-239, § 10204(b)(1)(E):

Amended Code Sec. 3127(c)(1) by inserting "(or, if the employer is a partnership, each partner therein)" after "such employer". **Effective** as if included in the amendments made by section 8007(a)(1) of P.L. 100-647.

P.L. 101-239, § 10204(b)(1)(F):

Amended Code Sec. 3127(c)(2) by striking "such employer or the employee involved ceases to meet" and inserting "such employer (or, if the employer is a partnership, any partner therein) or the employee involved does not meet", and inserting "(or, if the employer is a partnership, any partner therein)" after "such employer" the second place it appears. **Effective** as if included in the amendments made by section 8007(a)(1) of P.L. 100-647.

• **1988, Technical and Miscellaneous Revenue Act of 1988 (P.L. 100-647)**

P.L. 100-647, § 8007(a)(1):

Amended Subchapter C of chapter 21 by redesignating Code Sec. 3127 as Code Sec. 3128 and inserting after Code Sec. 3126 new Code Sec. 3127. **Effective** for wages paid after 12-31-88.

[Sec. 3128]

SEC. 3128. SHORT TITLE.

This chapter may be cited as the "Federal Insurance Contributions Act."

Amendments

• **1988, Technical and Miscellaneous Revenue Act of 1988 (P.L. 100-647)**

P.L. 100-647, § 8007(a)(1):

Amended Subchapter C of chapter 21 by redesignating section 3127 as 3128. **Effective** for wages paid after 12-31-88.

• **1986, Omnibus Budget Reconciliation Act of 1986 (P.L. 99-509)**

P.L. 99-509, § 9002(a):

Amended subchapter C of chapter 21 of the Internal Revenue Code of 1954 by redesignating Code Sec. 3126 as Code Sec. 3127. For the **effective** date, see Act Sec. 9002(d) reproduced under the amendment notes for Code Sec. 3216.

• **1960, Social Security Amendments of 1960 (P.L. 86-778)**

P.L. 86-778, § 103(q):

Redesignated Code Sec. 3215 as Code Sec. 3126. **Effective** 1-1-61.

Subchapter D—Credits

Sec. 3131.   Credit for paid sick leave.
Sec. 3132.   Payroll credit for paid family leave.
Sec. 3133.   Special rule related to tax on employers.
Sec. 3134.   Employee retention credit for employers subject to closure due to COVID–19.

[Sec. 3131]

SEC. 3131. CREDIT FOR PAID SICK LEAVE.

[Sec. 3131(a)]

(a) IN GENERAL.—In the case of an employer, there shall be allowed as a credit against applicable employment taxes for each calendar quarter an amount equal to 100 percent of the qualified sick leave wages paid by such employer with respect to such calendar quarter.

[Sec. 3131(b)]

(b) LIMITATIONS AND REFUNDABILITY.—

(1) WAGES TAKEN INTO ACCOUNT.—The amount of qualified sick leave wages taken into account under subsection (a), plus any increases under subsection (e), with respect to any individual shall not exceed $200 ($511 in the case of any day any portion of which is paid sick time described in paragraph (1), (2), or (3) of section 5102(a) of the Emergency Paid Sick Leave Act, applied with the modification described in subsection (c)(2)(A)(i)) for any day (or portion thereof) for which the individual is paid qualified sick leave wages.

(2) OVERALL LIMITATION ON NUMBER OF DAYS TAKEN INTO ACCOUNT.—The aggregate number of days taken into account under paragraph (1) for any calendar quarter shall not exceed the excess (if any) of—

(A) 10, over

(B) the aggregate number of days so taken into account during preceding calendar quarters in such calendar year (other than the first quarter of calendar year 2021).

(3) CREDIT LIMITED TO CERTAIN EMPLOYMENT TAXES.—The credit allowed by subsection (a) with respect to any calendar quarter shall not exceed the applicable employment taxes for such calendar quarter on the wages paid with respect to the employment of all employees of the employer.

(4) REFUNDABILITY OF EXCESS CREDIT.—

(A) CREDIT IS REFUNDABLE.—If the amount of the credit under subsection (a) exceeds the limitation of paragraph (3) for any calendar quarter, such excess shall be treated as an overpayment that shall be refunded under sections 6402(a) and 6413(b).

(B) ADVANCING CREDIT.—In anticipation of the credit, including the refundable portion under subparagraph (A), the credit shall be advanced, according to forms and instructions provided by the Secretary, up to an amount calculated under subsection (a), subject to the limits under paragraph[s] (1) and (2), all calculated through the end of the most recent payroll period in the quarter.

[Sec. 3131(c)]

(c) QUALIFIED SICK LEAVE WAGES.—For purposes of this section—

(1) IN GENERAL.—The term "qualified sick leave wages" means wages paid by an employer which would be required to be paid by reason of the Emergency Paid Sick Leave Act as if such Act applied after March 31, 2021.

(2) RULES OF APPLICATION.—For purposes of determining whether wages are qualified sick leave wages under paragraph (1)—

(A) IN GENERAL.—The Emergency Paid Sick Leave Act shall be applied—

(i) by inserting ", the employee is seeking or awaiting the results of a diagnostic test for, or a medical diagnosis of, COVID–19 and such employee has been exposed to COVID–19 or the employee's employer has requested such test or diagnosis, or the employee is obtaining immunization related to COVID–19 or recovering from any injury, disability, illness, or condition related to such immunization" after "medical diagnosis" in section 5102(a)(3) thereof, and

(ii) by applying section 5102(b)(1) of such Act separately with respect to each calendar year after 2020 (and, in the case of calendar year 2021, without regard to the first quarter thereof).

(B) LEAVE MUST MEET REQUIREMENTS.—If an employer fails to comply with any requirement of such Act (determined without regard to section 5109 thereof) with respect to paid sick time (as defined in section 5110 of such Act), amounts paid by such employer with respect to such paid sick time shall not be taken into account as qualified sick leave wages. For purposes of the preceding sentence, an employer which takes an action described in section 5104 of such Act shall be treated as failing to meet a requirement of such Act.

[Sec. 3131(d)]

(d) ALLOWANCE OF CREDIT FOR CERTAIN HEALTH PLAN EXPENSES.—

(1) IN GENERAL.—The amount of the credit allowed under subsection (a) shall be increased by so much of the employer's qualified health plan expenses as are properly allocable to the qualified sick leave wages for which such credit is so allowed.

(2) QUALIFIED HEALTH PLAN EXPENSES.—For purposes of this subsection, the term "qualified health plan expenses" means amounts paid or incurred by the employer to provide and maintain a group health plan (as defined in section 5000(b)(1)), but only to the extent that such amounts are excluded from the gross income of employees by reason of section 106(a).

(3) ALLOCATION RULES.—For purposes of this section, qualified health plan expenses shall be allocated to qualified sick leave wages in such manner as the Secretary may prescribe. Except as otherwise provided by the Secretary, such allocation shall be treated as properly made if made on the basis of being pro rata among covered employees and pro rata on the basis of periods of coverage (relative to the time periods of leave to which such wages relate).

[Sec. 3131(e)]

(e) ALLOWANCE OF CREDIT FOR AMOUNTS PAID UNDER CERTAIN COLLECTIVELY BARGAINED AGREEMENTS.—

(1) IN GENERAL.—The amount of the credit allowed under subsection (a) shall be increased by the sum of—

(A) so much of the employer's collectively bargained defined benefit pension plan contributions as are properly allocable to the qualified sick leave wages for which such credit is so allowed, plus

(B) so much of the employer's collectively bargained apprenticeship program contributions as are properly allocable to the qualified sick leave wages for which such credit is so allowed.

(2) COLLECTIVELY BARGAINED DEFINED BENEFIT PENSION PLAN CONTRIBUTIONS.—For purposes of this subsection—

(A) IN GENERAL.—The term "collectively bargained defined benefit pension plan contributions" means, with respect to any calendar quarter, contributions which—

(i) are paid or incurred by an employer during the calendar quarter on behalf of its employees to a defined benefit plan (as defined in section 414(j)), which meets the requirements of section 401(a),

(ii) are made based on a pension contribution rate, and

(iii) are required to be made pursuant to the terms of a collective bargaining agreement in effect with respect to such calendar quarter.

(B) PENSION CONTRIBUTION RATE.—The term "pension contribution rate" means the contribution rate that the employer is obligated to pay on behalf of its employees under the terms of a collective bargaining agreement for benefits under a defined benefit plan under such agreement, as such rate is applied to contribution base units (as defined by section 4001(a)(11) of the Employee Retirement Income Security Act of 1974 (29 U.S.C. 1301(a)(11)).

(C) ALLOCATION RULES.—The amount of collectively bargained defined benefit pension plan contributions allocated to qualified sick leave wages for any calendar quarter shall be the product of—

(i) the pension contribution rate (expressed as an hourly rate), and

(ii) the number of hours for which qualified sick leave wages were provided to employees covered under the collective bargaining agreement described in subparagraph (A)(iii) during the calendar quarter.

(3) COLLECTIVELY BARGAINED APPRENTICESHIP PROGRAM CONTRIBUTIONS.—For purposes of this section—

(A) IN GENERAL.—The term "collectively bargained apprenticeship program contributions" means, with respect to any calendar quarter, contributions which—

(i) are paid or incurred by an employer on behalf of its employees with respect to the calendar quarter to a registered apprenticeship program,

(ii) are made based on an apprenticeship program contribution rate, and

(iii) are required to be made pursuant to the terms of a collective bargaining agreement that is in effect with respect to such calendar quarter.

(B) REGISTERED APPRENTICESHIP PROGRAM.—The term "registered apprenticeship program" means an apprenticeship registered under the Act of August 16, 1937 (commonly known as the "National Apprenticeship Act"; 50 Stat. 664, chapter 663; 29 U.S.C. 50 et seq.) that meets the standards of subpart A of part 29 and part 30 of title 29, Code of Federal Regulations.

(C) APPRENTICESHIP PROGRAM CONTRIBUTION RATE.—The term "apprenticeship program contribution rate" means the contribution rate that the employer is obligated to pay on behalf of its employees under the terms of a collective bargaining agreement for benefits under a registered apprenticeship program under such agreement, as such rate is applied to contribution base units (as defined by section 4001(a)(11) of the Employee Retirement Income Security Act of 1974 (29 U.S.C. 1301(a)(11)).

EMPLOYMENT TAX—GENERAL PROVISIONS

(D) ALLOCATION RULES.—The amount of collectively bargained apprenticeship program contributions allocated to qualified sick leave wages for any calendar quarter shall be the product of—

(i) the apprenticeship program contribution rate (expressed as an hourly rate), and

(ii) the number of hours for which qualified sick leave wages were provided to employees covered under the collective bargaining agreement described in subparagraph (A)(iii) during the calendar quarter.

[Sec. 3131(f)]

(f) DEFINITIONS AND SPECIAL RULES.—

(1) APPLICABLE EMPLOYMENT TAXES.—For purposes of this section, the term "applicable employment taxes" means the following:

(A) The taxes imposed under section 3111(b).

(B) So much of the taxes imposed under section 3221(a) as are attributable to the rate in effect under section 3111(b).

(2) WAGES.—For purposes of this section, the term "wages" means wages (as defined in section 3121(a), determined without regard to paragraphs (1) through (22) of section 3121(b)) and compensation (as defined in section 3231(e), determined without regard to the sentence in paragraph (1) thereof which begins "Such term does not include remuneration").

(3) DENIAL OF DOUBLE BENEFIT.—For purposes of chapter 1, the gross income of the employer, for the taxable year which includes the last day of any calendar quarter with respect to which a credit is allowed under this section, shall be increased by the amount of such credit. Any wages taken into account in determining the credit allowed under this section shall not be taken into account for purposes of determining the credit allowed under sections 45A, 45P, 45S, 51, 3132, and 3134. In the case of any credit allowed under section 2301 of the CARES Act or section 41 with respect to wages taken into account under this section, the credit allowed under this section shall be reduced by the portion of the credit allowed under such section 2301 or section 41 which is attributable to such wages.

(4) ELECTION TO NOT TAKE CERTAIN WAGES INTO ACCOUNT.—This section shall not apply to so much of the qualified sick leave wages paid by an eligible employer as such employer elects (at such time and in such manner as the Secretary may prescribe) to not take into account for purposes of this section.

(5) CERTAIN GOVERNMENTAL EMPLOYERS.—No credit shall be allowed under this section to the Government of the United States or to any agency or instrumentality thereof. The preceding sentence shall not apply to any organization described in section 501(c)(1) and exempt from tax under section 501(a).

(6) EXTENSION OF LIMITATION ON ASSESSMENT.—Notwithstanding section 6501, the limitation on the time period for the assessment of any amount attributable to a credit claimed under this section shall not expire before the date that is 5 years after the later of—

(A) the date on which the original return which includes the calendar quarter with respect to which such credit is determined is filed, or

(B) the date on which such return is treated as filed under section 6501(b)(2).

(7) COORDINATION WITH CERTAIN PROGRAMS.—

(A) IN GENERAL.—This section shall not apply to so much of the qualified sick leave wages paid by an eligible employer as are taken into account as payroll costs in connection with—

(i) a covered loan under section 7(a)(37) or 7A of the Small Business Act,

(ii) a grant under section 324 of the Economic Aid to Hard-Hit Small Businesses, Non-Profits, and Venues Act, or

(iii) a restaurant revitalization grant under section 5003 of the American Rescue Plan Act of 2021.

(B) APPLICATION WHERE PPP LOANS NOT FORGIVEN.—The Secretary shall issue guidance providing that payroll costs paid during the covered period shall not fail to be treated as qualified sick leave wages under this section by reason of subparagraph (A)(i) to the extent that—

(i) a covered loan of the taxpayer under section 7(a)(37) of the Small Business Act is not forgiven by reason of a decision under section 7(a)(37)(J) of such Act, or

(ii) a covered loan of the taxpayer under section 7A of the Small Business Act is not forgiven by reason of a decision under section 7A(g) of such Act.

Terms used in the preceding sentence which are also used in section 7A(g) or 7(a)(37)(J) of the Small Business Act shall, when applied in connection with either such section, have the same meaning as when used in such section, respectively.

[Sec. 3131(g)]

(g) REGULATIONS.—The Secretary shall prescribe such regulations or other guidance as may be necessary to carry out the purposes of this section, including—

(1) regulations or other guidance to prevent the avoidance of the purposes of the limitations under this section,

(2) regulations or other guidance to minimize compliance and record-keeping burdens under this section,

(3) regulations or other guidance providing for waiver of penalties for failure to deposit amounts in anticipation of the allowance of the credit allowed under this section,

(4) regulations or other guidance for recapturing the benefit of credits determined under this section in cases where there is a subsequent adjustment to the credit determined under subsection (a),

(5) regulations or other guidance to ensure that the wages taken into account under this section conform with the paid sick time required to be provided under the Emergency Paid Sick Leave Act,

(6) regulations or other guidance to permit the advancement of the credit determined under subsection (a), and

(7) regulations or other guidance with respect to the allocation, reporting, and substantiation of collectively bargained defined benefit pension plan contributions and collectively bargained apprenticeship program contributions.

[Sec. 3131(h)]

(h) APPLICATION OF SECTION.—This section shall apply only to wages paid with respect to the period beginning on April 1, 2021, and ending on September 30, 2021.

[Sec. 3131(i)]

(i) TREATMENT OF DEPOSITS.—The Secretary shall waive any penalty under section 6656 for any failure to make a deposit of applicable employment taxes if the Secretary determines that such failure was due to the anticipation of the credit allowed under this section.

[Sec. 3131(j)]

(j) NON-DISCRIMINATION REQUIREMENT.—No credit shall be allowed under this section to any employer for any calendar quarter if such employer, with respect to the availability of the provision of qualified sick leave wages to which this section otherwise applies for such calendar quarter, discriminates in favor of highly compensated employees (within the meaning of section 414(q)), full-time employees, or employees on the basis of employment tenure with such employer.

Amendments

• 2021, American Rescue Plan Act of 2021 (P.L. 117-2)

P.L. 117-2, § 9641(a):

Amended chapter 21 by adding at the end a new subchapter D (Code Secs. 3131-3133). **Effective** for amounts paid with respect to calendar quarters beginning after 3-31-2021.

[Sec. 3132]

SEC. 3132. PAYROLL CREDIT FOR PAID FAMILY LEAVE.

[Sec. 3132(a)]

(a) IN GENERAL.—In the case of an employer, there shall be allowed as a credit against applicable employment taxes for each calendar quarter an amount equal to 100 percent of the qualified family leave wages paid by such employer with respect to such calendar quarter.

[Sec. 3132(b)]

(b) LIMITATIONS AND REFUNDABILITY.—

(1) WAGES TAKEN INTO ACCOUNT.—The amount of qualified family leave wages taken into account under subsection (a), plus any increases under subsection (e), with respect to any individual shall not exceed—

(A) for any day (or portion thereof) for which the individual is paid qualified family leave wages, $200, and

(B) in the aggregate with respect to all calendar quarters, $12,000.

(2) CREDIT LIMITED TO CERTAIN EMPLOYMENT TAXES.—The credit allowed by subsection (a) with respect to any calendar quarter shall not exceed the applicable employment taxes for such calendar quarter (reduced by any credits allowed under section 3131) on the wages paid with respect to the employment of all employees of the employer.

(3) REFUNDABILITY OF EXCESS CREDIT.—

(A) CREDIT IS REFUNDABLE.—If the amount of the credit under subsection (a) exceeds the limitation of paragraph (2) for any calendar quarter, such excess shall be treated as an overpayment that shall be refunded under sections 6402(a) and 6413(b).

(B) ADVANCING CREDIT.—In anticipation of the credit, including the refundable portion under subparagraph (A), the credit shall be advanced, according to forms and instructions provided by the Secretary, up to an amount calculated under subsection (a), subject to the limits under paragraph[s] (1) and (2), all calculated through the end of the most recent payroll period in the quarter.

[Sec. 3132(c)]

(c) QUALIFIED FAMILY LEAVE WAGES.—

(1) IN GENERAL.—For purposes of this section, the term "qualified family leave wages" means wages paid by an employer which would be required to be paid by reason of the Emergency Family and Medical Leave Expansion Act (including the amendments made by such Act) as if such Act (and amendments made by such Act) applied after March 31, 2021.

(2) RULES OF APPLICATION.—

(A) IN GENERAL.—For purposes of determining whether wages are qualified family leave wages under paragraph (1)—

(i) section 110(a)(2)(A) of the Family and Medical Leave Act of 1993 shall be applied by inserting "or any reason for leave described in section 5102(a) of the Families First Coronavirus Response Act, or the employee is seeking or awaiting the results of a diagnostic test for, or a medical diagnosis of, COVID–19 and such employee has been exposed to COVID–19 or the employee's employer has requested such test or diagnosis, or the employee is obtaining immunization related to COVID–19 or recovering from any injury, disability, illness, or condition related to such immunization" after "public health emergency", and

(ii) section 110(b) of such Act shall be applied—

(I) without regard to paragraph (1) thereof,

(II) by striking "after taking leave after such section for 10 days" in paragraph (2)(A) thereof, and

(III) by substituting "$12,000" for "$10,000" in paragraph (2)(B)(ii) thereof.

(B) LEAVE MUST MEET REQUIREMENTS.—For purposes of determining whether wages would be required to be paid under paragraph (1), if an employer fails to comply with any requirement of the Family and Medical Leave Act of 1993 or the Emergency Family and Medical Leave Expansion Act (determined without regard to any time limitation under section 102(a)(1)(F) of the Family and Medical Leave Act of 1994) with respect to any leave provided for a qualifying need related to a public health emergency (as defined in section 110 of such Act, applied as described in subparagraph (A)(i)), amounts paid by such employer with respect to such leave shall not be taken into account as qualified family leave wages. For purposes of the preceding sentence, an employer which takes an action described in section 105 of the Family and Medical Leave Act of 1993 shall be treated as failing to meet a requirement of such Act.

[Sec. 3132(d)]

(d) ALLOWANCE OF CREDIT FOR CERTAIN HEALTH PLAN EXPENSES.—

(1) IN GENERAL.—The amount of the credit allowed under subsection (a) shall be increased by so much of the employer's qualified health plan expenses as are properly allocable to the qualified family leave wages for which such credit is so allowed.

(2) QUALIFIED HEALTH PLAN EXPENSES.—For purposes of this subsection, the term "qualified health plan expenses" means amounts paid or incurred by the employer to provide and maintain a group health plan (as defined in section 5000(b)(1)), but only to the extent that such amounts are excluded from the gross income of employees by reason of section 106(a).

(3) ALLOCATION RULES.—For purposes of this section, qualified health plan expenses shall be allocated to qualified family leave wages in such manner as the Secretary may prescribe. Except as otherwise provided by the Secretary, such allocation shall be treated as properly made if made on the basis of being pro rata among covered employees and pro rata on the basis of periods of coverage (relative to the time periods of leave to which such wages relate).

[Sec. 3132(e)]

(e) ALLOWANCE OF CREDIT FOR AMOUNTS PAID UNDER CERTAIN COLLECTIVELY BARGAINED AGREEMENTS.—

(1) IN GENERAL.—The amount of the credit allowed under subsection (a) shall be increased by so much of the sum of—

(A) so much of the employer's collectively bargained defined benefit pension plan contributions as are properly allocable to the qualified family leave wages for which such credit is so allowed, plus

(B) so much of the employer's collectively bargained apprenticeship program contributions as are properly allocable to the qualified family leave wages for which such credit is so allowed.

(2) COLLECTIVELY BARGAINED DEFINED BENEFIT PENSION PLAN CONTRIBUTIONS.—For purposes of this subsection—

(A) IN GENERAL.—The term "collectively bargained defined benefit pension plan contributions" has the meaning given such term under section 3131(e)(2).

(B) ALLOCATION RULES.—The amount of collectively bargained defined benefit pension plan contributions allocated to qualified family leave wages for any calendar quarter shall be the product of—

(i) the pension contribution rate (as defined in section 3131(e)(2)), expressed as an hourly rate, and

(ii) the number of hours for which qualified family leave wages were provided to employees covered under the collective bargaining agreement described in section 3131(e)(2)(A)(iii) during the calendar quarter.

(3) COLLECTIVELY BARGAINED APPRENTICESHIP PROGRAM CONTRIBUTIONS.—For purposes of this section—

(A) IN GENERAL.—The term "collectively bargained apprenticeship program contributions" has the meaning given such term under section 3131(e)(3).

(B) ALLOCATION RULES.—For purposes of this section, the amount of collectively bargained apprenticeship program contributions allocated to qualified family leave wages for any calendar quarter shall be the product of—

(i) the apprenticeship contribution rate (as defined in section 3131(e)(3)), expressed as an hourly rate, and

(ii) the number of hours for which qualified family leave wages were provided to employees covered under the collective bargaining agreement described in section 3131(e)(3)(A)(iii) during the calendar quarter.

[Sec. 3132(f)]

(f) DEFINITIONS AND SPECIAL RULES.—

(1) APPLICABLE EMPLOYMENT TAXES.—For purposes of this section, the term "applicable employment taxes" means the following:

(A) The taxes imposed under section 3111(b).

(B) So much of the taxes imposed under section 3221(a) as are attributable to the rate in effect under section 3111(b).

(2) WAGES.—For purposes of this section, the term "wages" means wages (as defined in section 3121(a), determined without regard to paragraphs (1) through (22) of section 3121(b)) and compensation (as defined in section 3231(e), determined without regard to the sentence in paragraph (1) thereof which begins "Such term does not include remuneration").

(3) DENIAL OF DOUBLE BENEFIT.—For purposes of chapter 1, the gross income of the employer, for the taxable year which includes the last day of any calendar quarter with respect to which a credit is allowed under this section, shall be increased by the amount of such credit. Any wages taken into account in determining the credit allowed under this section shall not be taken into account for purposes of determining the credit allowed under sections 45A, 45P, 45S, 51, 3131, and 3134. In the case of any credit allowed under section 2301 of the CARES Act or section 41 with respect to wages taken into account under this section, the credit allowed under this section shall be reduced by the portion of the credit allowed under such section 2301 or section 41 which is attributable to such wages.

(4) ELECTION TO NOT TAKE CERTAIN WAGES INTO ACCOUNT.—This section shall not apply to so much of the qualified family leave wages paid by an eligible employer as such employer elects (at such time and in such manner as the Secretary may prescribe) to not take into account for purposes of this section.

(5) CERTAIN GOVERNMENTAL EMPLOYERS.—No credit shall be allowed under this section to the Government of the United States or to any agency or instrumentality thereof. The preceding sentence shall not apply to any organization described in section 501(c)(1) and exempt from tax under section 501(a).

(6) EXTENSION OF LIMITATION ON ASSESSMENT.—Notwithstanding section 6501, the limitation on the time period for the assessment of any amount attributable to a credit claimed under this section shall not expire before the date that is 5 years after the later of—

(A) the date on which the original return which includes the calendar quarter with respect to which such credit is determined is filed, or

(B) the date on which such return is treated as filed under section 6501(b)(2).

(7) COORDINATION WITH CERTAIN PROGRAMS.—

(A) IN GENERAL.—This section shall not apply to so much of the qualified family leave wages paid by an eligible employer as are taken into account as payroll costs in connection with—

(i) a covered loan under section 7(a)(37) or 7A of the Small Business Act,

(ii) a grant under section 324 of the Economic Aid to Hard-Hit Small Businesses, Non-Profits, and Venues Act, or

(iii) a restaurant revitalization grant under section 5003 of the American Rescue Plan Act of 2021.

(B) APPLICATION WHERE PPP LOANS NOT FORGIVEN.—The Secretary shall issue guidance providing that payroll costs paid during the covered period shall not fail to be treated as qualified family leave wages under this section by reason of subparagraph (A)(i) to the extent that—

(i) a covered loan of the taxpayer under section 7(a)(37) of the Small Business Act is not forgiven by reason of a decision under section 7(a)(37)(J) of such Act, or

(ii) a covered loan of the taxpayer under section 7A of the Small Business Act is not forgiven by reason of a decision under section 7A(g) of such Act.

Terms used in the preceding sentence which are also used in section 7A(g) or 7(a)(37)(J) of the Small Business Act shall, when applied in connection with either such section, have the same meaning as when used in such section, respectively.

[Sec. 3132(g)]

(g) REGULATIONS.—The Secretary shall prescribe such regulations or other guidance as may be necessary to carry out the purposes of this section, including—

(1) regulations or other guidance to prevent the avoidance of the purposes of the limitations under this section,

(2) regulations or other guidance to minimize compliance and record-keeping burdens under this section,

(3) regulations or other guidance providing for waiver of penalties for failure to deposit amounts in anticipation of the allowance of the credit allowed under this section,

(4) regulations or other guidance for recapturing the benefit of credits determined under this section in cases where there is a subsequent adjustment to the credit determined under subsection (a),

(5) regulations or other guidance to ensure that the wages taken into account under this section conform with the paid leave required to be provided under the Emergency Family and Medical Leave Expansion Act (including the amendments made by such Act),

(6) regulations or other guidance to permit the advancement of the credit determined under subsection (a), and

[Sec. 3132(h)]

(h) APPLICATION OF SECTION.—This section shall apply only to wages paid with respect to the period beginning on April 1, 2021, and ending on September 30, 2021.

[Sec. 3132(i)]

(i) TREATMENT OF DEPOSITS.—The Secretary shall waive any penalty under section 6656 for any failure to make a deposit of applicable employment taxes if the Secretary determines that such failure was due to the anticipation of the credit allowed under this section.

[Sec. 3132(j)]

(j) NON-DISCRIMINATION REQUIREMENT.—No credit shall be allowed under this section to any employer for any calendar quarter if such employer, with respect to the availability of the provision of qualified family leave wages to which this section otherwise applies for such calendar quarter, discriminates in favor of highly compensated employees (within the meaning of section 414(q)), full-time employees, or employees on the basis of employment tenure with such employer.

Amendments

• 2021, American Rescue Plan Act of 2021 (P.L. 117-2)

P.L. 117-2, § 9641(a):

Amended chapter 21 by adding at the end a new subchapter D (Code Secs. 3131-3133). **Effective** for amounts paid with respect to calendar quarters beginning after 3-31-2021.

[Sec. 3133]

SEC. 3133. SPECIAL RULE RELATED TO TAX ON EMPLOYERS.

[Sec. 3133(a)]

(a) IN GENERAL.—The credit allowed by section 3131 and the credit allowed by section 3132 shall each be increased by the amount of the taxes imposed by subsections (a) and (b) of section 3111 and section 3221(a) on qualified sick leave wages, or qualified family leave wages, for which credit is allowed under such section 3131 or 3132 (respectively).

[Sec. 3133(b)]

(b) DENIAL OF DOUBLE BENEFIT.—For denial of double benefit with respect to the credit increase under subsection (a), see sections 3131(f)(3) and 3132(f)(3).

Amendments

• 2021, American Rescue Plan Act of 2021 (P.L. 117-2)

P.L. 117-2, § 9641(a):

Amended chapter 21 by adding at the end a new subchapter D (Code Secs. 3131-3133). **Effective** for amounts paid with respect to calendar quarters beginning after 3-31-2021.

[Sec. 3134]

SEC. 3134. EMPLOYEE RETENTION CREDIT FOR EMPLOYERS SUBJECT TO CLOSURE DUE TO COVID–19.

[Sec. 3134(a)]

(a) IN GENERAL.—In the case of an eligible employer, there shall be allowed as a credit against applicable employment taxes for each calendar quarter an amount equal to 70 percent of the qualified wages with respect to each employee of such employer for such calendar quarter.

[Sec. 3134(b)]

(b) LIMITATIONS AND REFUNDABILITY.—

(1) IN GENERAL.—

(A) WAGES TAKEN INTO ACCOUNT.—The amount of qualified wages with respect to any employee which may be taken into account under subsection (a) by the eligible employer for any calendar quarter shall not exceed $10,000.

(B) RECOVERY STARTUP BUSINESSES.—In the case of an eligible employer which is a recovery startup business (as defined in subsection (c)(5)), the amount of the credit allowed under subsection (a) (after application of subparagraph (A)) for any calendar quarter shall not exceed $50,000.

(2) CREDIT LIMITED TO EMPLOYMENT TAXES.—The credit allowed by subsection (a) with respect to any calendar quarter shall not exceed the applicable employment taxes (reduced by any credits allowed under sections 3131 and 3132) on the wages paid with respect to the employment of all the employees of the eligible employer for such calendar quarter.

(3) REFUNDABILITY OF EXCESS CREDIT.—If the amount of the credit under subsection (a) exceeds the limitation of paragraph (2) for any calendar quarter, such excess shall be treated as an overpayment that shall be refunded under sections 6402(a) and 6413(b).

[Sec. 3134(c)]

(c) DEFINITIONS.—For purposes of this section—

(1) APPLICABLE EMPLOYMENT TAXES.—The term "applicable employment taxes" means the following:

(A) The taxes imposed under section 3111(b).

(B) So much of the taxes imposed under section 3221(a) as are attributable to the rate in effect under section 3111(b).

(2) ELIGIBLE EMPLOYER.—

(A) IN GENERAL.—The term "eligible employer" means any employer—

(i) which was carrying on a trade or business during the calendar quarter for which the credit is determined under subsection (a), and

(ii) with respect to any calendar quarter, for which—

(I) the operation of the trade or business described in clause (i) is fully or partially suspended during the calendar quarter due to orders from an appropriate governmental authority limiting commerce, travel, or group meetings (for commercial, social, religious, or other purposes) due to the coronavirus disease 2019 (COVID–19),

EMPLOYMENT TAX—GENERAL PROVISIONS

(II) the gross receipts (within the meaning of section 448(c)) of such employer for such calendar quarter are less than 80 percent of the gross receipts of such employer for the same calendar quarter in calendar year 2019, or

(III) the employer is a recovery startup business (as defined in paragraph (5)).

With respect to any employer for any calendar quarter, if such employer was not in existence as of the beginning of the same calendar quarter in calendar year 2019, clause (ii)(II) shall be applied by substituting "2020" for "2019".

(B) ELECTION TO USE ALTERNATIVE QUARTER.—At the election of the employer—

(i) subparagraph (A)(ii)(II) shall be applied—

(I) by substituting "for the immediately preceding calendar quarter" for "for such calendar quarter", and

(II) by substituting "the corresponding calendar quarter in calendar year 2019" for "the same calendar quarter in calendar year 2019", and

(ii) the last sentence of subparagraph (A) shall be applied by substituting "the corresponding calendar quarter in calendar year 2019" for "the same calendar quarter in calendar year 2019".

An election under this subparagraph shall be made at such time and in such manner as the Secretary shall prescribe.

(C) TAX-EXEMPT ORGANIZATIONS.—In the case of an organization which is described in section 501(c) and exempt from tax under section 501(a)—

(i) clauses (i) and (ii)(I) of subparagraph (A) shall apply to all operations of such organization, and

(ii) any reference in this section to gross receipts shall be treated as a reference to gross receipts within the meaning of section 6033.

(3) QUALIFIED WAGES.—

(A) IN GENERAL.—The term "qualified wages" means—

(i) in the case of an eligible employer for which the average number of full-time employees (within the meaning of section 4980H) employed by such eligible employer during 2019 was greater than 500, wages paid by such eligible employer with respect to which an employee is not providing services due to circumstances described in subclause (I) or (II) of paragraph (2)(A)(ii), or

(ii) in the case of an eligible employer for which the average number of full-time employees (within the meaning of section 4980H) employed by such eligible employer during 2019 was not greater than 500—

(I) with respect to an eligible employer described in subclause (I) of paragraph (2)(A)(ii), wages paid by such eligible employer with respect to an employee during any period described in such clause, or

(II) with respect to an eligible employer described in subclause (II) of such paragraph, wages paid by such eligible employer with respect to an employee during such quarter.

(B) SPECIAL RULE FOR EMPLOYERS NOT IN EXISTENCE IN 2019.—In the case of any employer that was not in existence in 2019, subparagraph (A) shall be applied by substituting "2020" for "2019" each place it appears.

(C) SEVERELY FINANCIALLY DISTRESSED EMPLOYERS.—

(i) IN GENERAL.—Notwithstanding subparagraph (A)(i), in the case of a severely financially distressed employer, the term "qualified wages" means wages paid by such employer with respect to an employee during any calendar quarter.

(ii) DEFINITION.—The term "severely financially distressed employer" means an eligible employer as defined in paragraph (2), determined by substituting "less than 10 percent" for "less than 80 percent" in subparagraph (A)(ii)(II) thereof.

(D) EXCEPTION.—The term "qualified wages" shall not include any wages taken into account under sections 41, 45A, 45P, 45S, 51, 1396, 3131, and 3132.

(4) WAGES.—

(A) IN GENERAL.—The term "wages" means wages (as defined in section 3121(a)) and compensation (as defined in section 3231(e)). For purposes of the preceding sentence, in the case of any organization or entity described in subsection (f)(2), wages as defined in section 3121(a) shall be determined without regard to paragraphs (5), (6), (7), (10), and (13) of section 3121(b) (except with respect to services performed in a penal institution by an inmate thereof).

(B) ALLOWANCE FOR CERTAIN HEALTH PLAN EXPENSES.—

(i) IN GENERAL.—Such term shall include amounts paid by the eligible employer to provide and maintain a group health plan (as defined in section 5000(b)(1)), but only to the extent that such amounts are excluded from the gross income of employees by reason of section 106(a).

(ii) ALLOCATION RULES.—For purposes of this section, amounts treated as wages under clause (i) shall be treated as paid with respect to any employee (and with respect to any period) to the extent that such amounts are properly allocable to such employee (and to such period) in such manner as the Secretary may prescribe. Except as otherwise provided by the Secretary, such allocation shall be treated as properly made if made on the basis of being pro rata among periods of coverage.

(5) RECOVERY STARTUP BUSINESS.—The term "recovery startup business" means any employer—

(A) which began carrying on any trade or business after February 15, 2020, and

(B) for which the average annual gross receipts of such employer (as determined under rules similar to the rules under section 448(c)(3)) for the 3-taxable-year period ending with the taxable year which precedes the calendar quarter for which the credit is determined under subsection (a) does not exceed $1,000,000.

(6) OTHER TERMS.—Any term used in this section which is also used in this chapter or chapter 22 shall have the same meaning as when used in such chapter.

Amendments

• 2021, Infrastructure Investment and Jobs Act (P.L. 117-58)

P.L. 117-58, § 80604(a)(1)(A)-(C), Div. H:

Amended Code Sec. 3134(c)(5) by adding "and" at the end in subparagraph (A), by striking ", and" at the end and inserting a period in subparagraph (B), and by striking subparagraph (C). **Effective** for calendar quarters beginning after 9-30-2021. Prior to being stricken, Code Sec. 3134(c)(5)(C) reads as follows:

(C) which, with respect to such calendar quarter, is not described in subclause (I) or (II) of paragraph (2)(A)(ii).

[Sec. 3134(d)]

(d) AGGREGATION RULE.—All persons treated as a single employer under subsection (a) or (b) of section 52, or subsection (m) or (o) of section 414, shall be treated as one employer for purposes of this section.

[Sec. 3134(e)]

(e) CERTAIN RULES TO APPLY.—For purposes of this section, rules similar to the rules of sections 51(i)(1) and 280C(a) shall apply.

EMPLOYMENT TAX—GENERAL PROVISIONS

[Sec. 3134(f)]

(f) CERTAIN GOVERNMENTAL EMPLOYERS.—

(1) IN GENERAL.—This credit shall not apply to the Government of the United States, the government of any State or political subdivision thereof, or any agency or instrumentality of any of the foregoing.

(2) EXCEPTION.—Paragraph (1) shall not apply to—

(A) any organization described in section 501(c)(1) and exempt from tax under section 501(a), or

(B) any entity described in paragraph (1) if—

(i) such entity is a college or university, or

(ii) the principal purpose or function of such entity is providing medical or hospital care.

In the case of any entity described in subparagraph (B), such entity shall be treated as satisfying the requirements of subsection (c)(2)(A)(i).

[Sec. 3134(g)]

(g) ELECTION TO NOT TAKE CERTAIN WAGES INTO ACCOUNT.—This section shall not apply to so much of the qualified wages paid by an eligible employer as such employer elects (at such time and in such manner as the Secretary may prescribe) to not take into account for purposes of this section.

[Sec. 3134(h)]

(h) COORDINATION WITH CERTAIN PROGRAMS.—

(1) IN GENERAL.—This section shall not apply to so much of the qualified wages paid by an eligible employer as are taken into account as payroll costs in connection with—

(A) a covered loan under section 7(a)(37) or 7A of the Small Business Act,

(B) a grant under section 324 of the Economic Aid to Hard-Hit Small Businesses, Non-Profits, and Venues Act, or

(C) a restaurant revitalization grant under section 5003 of the American Rescue Plan Act of 2021.

(2) APPLICATION WHERE PPP LOANS NOT FORGIVEN.—The Secretary shall issue guidance providing that payroll costs paid during the covered period shall not fail to be treated as qualified wages under this section by reason of paragraph (1) to the extent that—

(A) a covered loan of the taxpayer under section 7(a)(37) of the Small Business Act is not forgiven by reason of a decision under section 7(a)(37)(J) of such Act, or

(B) a covered loan of the taxpayer under section 7A of the Small Business Act is not forgiven by reason of a decision under section 7A(g) of such Act.

Terms used in the preceding sentence which are also used in section 7A(g) or 7(a)(37)(J) of the Small Business Act shall, when applied in connection with either such section, have the same meaning as when used in such section, respectively.

[Sec. 3134(i)]

(i) THIRD PARTY PAYORS.—Any credit allowed under this section shall be treated as a credit described in section 3511(d)(2).

[Sec. 3134(j)]

(j) ADVANCE PAYMENTS.—

(1) IN GENERAL.—Except as provided in paragraph (2), no advance payment of the credit under subsection (a) shall be allowed.

(2) ADVANCE PAYMENTS TO SMALL EMPLOYERS.—

(A) IN GENERAL.—Under rules provided by the Secretary, an eligible employer for which the average number of full-time employees (within the meaning of section 4980H) employed by such eligible employer during 2019 was not greater than 500 may elect for any calendar quarter to receive an advance payment of the credit under subsection (a) for such quarter in an amount not to exceed 70 percent of the average quarterly wages paid by the employer in calendar year 2019.

(B) SPECIAL RULE FOR SEASONAL EMPLOYERS.—In the case of any employer who employs seasonal workers (as defined in section 45R(d)(5)(B)), the employer may elect to apply subparagraph (A) by substituting "the wages for the calendar quarter in 2019 which corresponds to the calendar quarter to which the election relates" for "the average quarterly wages paid by the employer in calendar year 2019".

(C) SPECIAL RULE FOR EMPLOYERS NOT IN EXISTENCE IN 2019.—In the case of any employer that was not in existence in 2019, subparagraphs (A) and (B) shall each be applied by substituting "2020" for "2019" each place it appears.

(3) RECONCILIATION OF CREDIT WITH ADVANCE PAYMENTS.—

(A) IN GENERAL.—The amount of credit which would (but for this subsection) be allowed under this section shall be reduced (but not below zero) by the aggregate payment allowed to the taxpayer under paragraph (2). Any failure to so reduce the credit shall be treated as arising out of a mathematical or clerical error and assessed according to section 6213(b)(1).

(B) EXCESS ADVANCE PAYMENTS.—If the advance payments to a taxpayer under paragraph (2) for a calendar quarter exceed the credit allowed by this section (determined without regard to subparagraph (A)), the tax imposed under section 3111(b) or so much of the tax imposed under section 3221(a) as is attributable to the rate in effect under section 3111(b) (whichever is applicable) for the calendar quarter shall be increased by the amount of such excess.

[Sec. 3134(k)]

(k) TREATMENT OF DEPOSITS.—The Secretary shall waive any penalty under section 6656 for any failure to make a deposit of any applicable employment taxes if the Secretary determines that such failure was due to the reasonable anticipation of the credit allowed under this section.

[Sec. 3134(l)]

(l) EXTENSION OF LIMITATION ON ASSESSMENT.—Notwithstanding section 6501, the limitation on the time period for the assessment of any amount attributable to a credit claimed under this section shall not expire before the date that is 5 years after the later of—

(1) the date on which the original return which includes the calendar quarter with respect to which such credit is determined is filed, or

(2) the date on which such return is treated as filed under section 6501(b)(2).

[Sec. 3134(m)]

(m) REGULATIONS AND GUIDANCE.—The Secretary shall issue such forms, instructions, regulations, and other guidance as are necessary—

(1) to allow the advance payment of the credit under subsection (a) as provided in subsection (j)(2), subject to the limitations provided in this section, based on such information as the Secretary shall require,

RAILROAD RETIREMENT TAX—EMPLOYEES

(2) with respect to the application of the credit under subsection (a) to third party payors (including professional employer organizations, certified professional employer organizations, or agents under section 3504), including regulations or guidance allowing such payors to submit documentation necessary to substantiate the eligible employer status of employers that use such payors, and

(3) to prevent the avoidance of the purposes of the limitations under this section, including through the leaseback of employees.

Any forms, instructions, regulations, or other guidance described in paragraph (2) shall require the customer to be responsible for the accounting of the credit and for any liability for improperly claimed credits and shall require the certified professional employer organization or other third party payor to accurately report such tax credits based on the information provided by the customer.

[Sec. 3134(n)]

(n) APPLICATION.—This section shall only apply to wages paid after June 30, 2021, and before October 1, 2021 (or, in the case of wages paid by an eligible employer which is a recovery startup business, January 1, 2022).

Amendments

• **2021, Infrastructure Investment and Jobs Act (P.L. 117-58)**

P.L. 117-58, § 80604(a)(2), Div. H:

Amended Code Sec. 3134(n) by striking "January 1, 2022" and inserting "October 1, 2021 (or, in the case of wages paid by an eligible employer which is a recovery startup business, January 1, 2022)". **Effective** for calendar quarters beginning after 9-30-2021.

• **2021, American Rescue Plan Act of 2021 (P.L. 117-2)**

P.L. 117-2, § 9651(a):

Amended subchapter D of chapter 21 of subtitle C, as added by Act Sec. 9641, by adding at the end Code Sec. 3134. **Effective** for calendar quarters beginning after 6-30-2021.

CHAPTER 22—RAILROAD RETIREMENT TAX ACT

SUBCHAPTER A.	Tax on employees.
SUBCHAPTER B.	Tax on employee representatives.
SUBCHAPTER C.	Tax on employers.
SUBCHAPTER D.	General provisions.
SUBCHAPTER E.	Tier 2 tax rate determination.

Subchapter A—Tax on Employees

Sec. 3201.	Rate of tax.
Sec. 3202.	Deduction of tax from compensation.

[Sec. 3201]

SEC. 3201. RATE OF TAX.

[Sec. 3201(a)]

(a) TIER 1 TAX.—In addition to other taxes, there is hereby imposed on the income of each employee a tax equal to the applicable percentage of the compensation received during any calendar year by such employee for services rendered by such employee. For purposes of the preceding sentence, the term "applicable percentage" means the percentage equal to the sum of the rates of tax in effect under subsections (a) and (b) of section 3101 for the calendar year.

Amendments

• **2020, COVID-related Tax Relief Act of 2020 (P.L. 116-260)**

P.L. 116-260, § 274, Div. N, provides:

SEC. 274. EXTENSION OF CERTAIN DEFERRED PAYROLL TAXES.

The Secretary of the Treasury (or the Secretary's delegate) shall ensure that Internal Revenue Service Notice 2020-65 [I.R.B. 2020-38, 567] (entitled "Relief with Respect to Employment Tax Deadlines Applicable to Employers Affected by the Ongoing Coronavirus (COVID-19) Disease 2019 Pandemic") and any successor or related regulation, notice, or guidance is applied—

(1) by substituting "December 31, 2021" for "April 30, 2021" each place it appears therein, and

(2) by substituting "January 1, 2022" for "May 1, 2021" each place it appears therein.

• **1990, Omnibus Budget Reconciliation Act of 1990 (P.L. 101-508)**

P.L. 101-508, § 5125(a)(1)-(2):

Amended Code Sec. 3201(a) by striking "following" and inserting "applicable", and by striking "employee:" and all that follows and inserting "employee. For purposes of the preceding sentence, the term `applicable percentage' means the percentage equal to the sum of the rates of the tax in effect under subsections (a) and (b) of section 3101 for the calendar year." **Effective** 11-5-90. Prior to amendment, Code Sec. 3201(a) read as follows:

(a) TIER 1 TAX.—In addition to other taxes, there is hereby imposed on the income of each employee a tax equal to the following percentage of the compensation received during any calendar year by such employee for services rendered by such employee:

In the case of compensation received during:	The rate shall be:
1985	7.05
1986 or 1987	7.15
1988 or 1989	7.51
1990 or thereafter	7.65

• **1989, Omnibus Budget Reconciliation Act of 1989 (P.L. 101-239)**

P.L. 101-239, § 10202(b), provides:

(b) RAILROAD RETIREMENT PROGRAM.—For purposes of chapter 22 of the Internal Revenue Code of 1986, the term "compensation" shall not include the amount of any refund required under section 421 of the Medicare Catastrophic Coverage Act of 1988.

[Sec. 3201(b)]

(b) TIER 2 TAX.—In addition to other taxes, there is hereby imposed on the income of each employee a tax equal to the percentage determined under section 3241 for any calendar year of the compensation received during such calendar year by such employee for services rendered by such employee.

Amendments

• **2014, Tax Technical Corrections Act of 2014 (P.L. 113-295)**

P.L. 113-295, § 221(a)(100)(A), Division A:

Amended Code Sec. 3201(b). **Effective** generally 12-19-2014. For a special rule, see Act Sec. 221(b)(2), Division A, below. Prior to amendment, Code Sec. 3201(b) read as follows:

(b) TIER 2 TAX.—

(1) IN GENERAL.—In addition to other taxes, there is hereby imposed on the income of each employee a tax equal to the applicable percentage of the compensation received during any calendar year by such employee for services rendered by such employee.

(2) APPLICABLE PERCENTAGE.—For purposes of paragraph (1), the term "applicable percentage" means—

(A) 4.90 percent in the case of compensation received during 2002 or 2003, and

(B) in the case of compensation received during any calendar year after 2003, the percentage determined under section 3241 for such calendar year.

P.L. 113-295, § 221(b)(2), Division A, provides:

(2) SAVINGS PROVISION.—If—

(A) any provision amended or repealed by the amendments made by this section applied to—

(i) any transaction occurring before the date of the enactment of this Act,

(ii) any property acquired before such date of enactment, or

(iii) any item of income, loss, deduction, or credit taken into account before such date of enactment, and

RAILROAD RETIREMENT TAX—EMPLOYEES

• **2001, Railroad Retirement and Survivors' Improvement Act of 2001 (P.L. 107-90)**

P.L. 107-90, §204(c):

Amended Code Sec. 3201(b). **Effective** for calendar years beginning after 12-31-2001. Prior to amendment, Code Sec. 3201(b) read as follows:

(b) TIER 2 TAX.—In addition to other taxes, there is hereby imposed on the income of each employee a tax equal to 4.90 percent of the compensation received during any calendar year by such employee for services rendered by such employee.

[Sec. 3201(c)]

(c) CROSS REFERENCE.—

For application of different contribution bases with respect to the taxes imposed by subsections (a) and (b), see section 3231(e)(2).

Amendments

• **1983, Railroad Retirement Solvency Act of 1983 (P.L. 98-76)**

P.L. 98-76, §221:

Amended Code Sec. 3201. **Effective** for remuneration paid after 1984. Prior to amendment, Code Sec. 3201 read as follows:

SEC. 3201. RATE OF TAX.

[Sec. 3201(a)]

(a) In addition to other taxes, there is hereby imposed on the income of each employee a tax equal to 2.75 percent of so much of the compensation paid in any calendar month to such employee for services rendered by him as is not in excess of an amount equal to one-twelfth of the current maximum annual taxable "wages" as defined in section 3121 for any month.

[Sec. 3201(b)]

(b) The rate of tax imposed by subsection (a) shall be increased by the rate of the tax imposed with respect to wages by section 3101(a) plus the rate imposed by section 3101(b) of so much of the compensation paid in any calendar month to such employee for services rendered by him as is not in excess of an amount equal to one-twelfth of the current maximum annual taxable "wages" as defined in section 3121 for any month.

Amendments

• **1983, Railroad Retirement Solvency Act of 1983 (P.L. 98-76)**

P.L. 98-76, §§211(a), 225(c)(1)(A), (c)(2):

Amended Code Sec. 3201. **Effective** with respect to compensation paid for services rendered after 12-31-83, and before 1-1-85. Prior to amendment, Code Sec. 3201 read as follows:

SEC. 3201. RATE OF TAX.

[Sec. 3201(a)]

(a) In addition to other taxes, there is hereby imposed on the income of each employee a tax equal to 2.0 percent of so much of the compensation paid in any calendar month to such employee for services rendered by him as is not in excess of an amount equal to one-twelfth of the current maximum annual taxable "wages" as defined in section 3121 for any month.

[Sec. 3201(b)]

(b) The rate of tax imposed by subsection (a) shall be increased by the rate of the tax imposed with respect to wages by section 3101(a) plus the rate imposed by section 3101(b) of so much of the compensation paid in any calendar month to such employee for services rendered by him as is not in excess of an amount equal to one-twelfth of the current maximum annual taxable "wages" as defined in section 3121 for any month.

Amendments

• **1981, Economic Recovery Tax Act of 1981 (P.L. 97-34)**

P.L. 97-34, §741(a):

Amended Code Sec. 3201. **Effective** for compensation paid for services rendered after 9-30-81. Prior to amendment, Code Sec. 3201 read as follows:

In addition to other taxes, there is hereby imposed on the income of every employee a tax equal to the rate of tax imposed with respect to wages by section 3101(a) plus the rate imposed by section 3101(b) of so much of the compensation paid in any calendar month to such employee for services rendered by him as is not in excess of an amount equal to one-twelfth of the current maximum annual taxable "wages" as defined in section 3121 for any month.

• **1976, Tax Reform Act of 1976 (P.L. 94-455)**

P.L. 94-455, §1903(a)(6), (d):

Amended Code Sec. 3201 by deleting "of the Internal Revenue Code of 1954" each place it appeared; by deleting "of such Code"; by substituting "as is" for "after September 30, 1973, as is"; and by substituting "any month" for "any month after September 30, 1973." **Effective** with respect to compensation paid for services rendered after 12-31-76.

• **1975 (P.L. 94-93)**

P.L. 94-93, §§201 and 207:

Amended Code Sec. 3201 by striking out "compensation paid to such employee" and inserting in lieu thereof "compensation paid in any calendar month to such employee". **Effective** for tax years ending on or after 8-9-75 and for tax years ending before 8-9-75 as to which the period for assessment and collection of tax or the filing of a claim for credit or refund has not expired on 8-9-75.

• **1987, Revenue Act of 1987 (P.L. 100-203)**

P.L. 100-203, §9031(a):

Amended Code Sec. 3201(b). **Effective** with respect to compensation received after 12-31-87. Prior to amendment, Code Sec. 3201(b) read as follows:

(b) TIER 2 TAX.—In addition to other taxes, there is hereby imposed on the income of each employee a tax equal to the following percentage of the compensation received during any calendar year by such employee for services rendered by such employee:

In the case of compensation received during:	The rate shall be:
1985	3.50
1986 or thereafter	4.25

• **1973 (P.L. 93-69)**

P.L. 93-69, §102(a):

Amended Code Sec. 3201. **Effective** 10-1-73 and applicable only to compensation paid for services rendered on or after that date. However, the amendment is not applicable to any dock company, common carrier railroad, or railway labor organization described in section 1(a) of the Railroad Retirement Act of 1937, with respect to those of its employees covered as of 10-1-73, by a private supplemental pension plan established through collective bargaining, where a moratorium in an agreement made on or before 3-8-73, is applicable to changes in rates of pay contained in the current collective bargaining agreement covering such employees, until the earliest of (1) the date as of which such moratorium expires, or (2) the date as of which such dock company, common carrier railroad, or railway labor organization agrees through collective bargaining to make the provisions of such amendments applicable. Prior to amendment, Code Sec. 3201 read as follows:

"In addition to other taxes, there is hereby imposed on the income of every employee a tax equal to—

"(1) $6\frac{1}{4}$ percent of so much of the compensation paid to such employee for services rendered by him after September 30, 1965,

"(2) $6\frac{1}{2}$ percent of so much of the compensation paid to such employee for services rendered by him after December 31, 1965,

"(3) 7 percent of so much of the compensation paid to such employee for services rendered by him after December 31, 1966,

"(4) $7\frac{1}{4}$ percent of so much of the compensation paid to such employee for services rendered by him after December 31, 1967, and

"(5) $7\frac{1}{2}$ percent of so much of the compensation paid to such employee for services rendered by him after December 31, 1968,

as is not in excess of (i) $450, or (ii) an amount equal to one-twelfth of the current maximum annual taxable `wages' as defined in section 3121 of the Internal Revenue Code of 1954 whichever is greater, for any month after September 30, 1965. *Provided*, That the rate of tax imposed by this section shall be increased, with respect to compensation paid for services rendered after September 30, 1965, by a number of percentage points (including fractional points) equal at any given time to the number of percentage points (including fractional points) by which the rate of the tax imposed with respect to wages by section 3101(a) plus the rate imposed by section 3101(b) at such time exceeds $2\frac{3}{4}$ percent (the rate provided by paragraph (2) of section 3101 as amended by the Social Security Amendments of 1956)."

• **1966 (P.L. 89-700)**

P.L. 89-700, §301(vi):

Amended the proviso of Code Sec. 3201 by substituting "after September 30, 1965" for "December 31, 1964". **Effective** 11-1-66.

P.L. 89-700, §301(v):

Amended Code Sec. 3201 by deleting "$400 for any calendar month before the calendar month next following the month in which this provision was amended in 1963, or $450 for any calendar month after the month in which this provision was so amended and before the calendar month next following the calendar month in which this provision was amended in 1965, or" immediately after "as is not in excess of" and by substituting "September 30, 1965" for "the month in which this provision was so amended" in (ii). **Effective** 11-1-66.

• **1966 (P.L. 89-699)**

P.L. 89-699, §301(a):

Amended Code Sec. 3201 by substituting "7 percent" for "$6\frac{3}{4}$ percent" in subdivision (3), by substituting "$7\frac{1}{4}$ percent" for "7 percent" in subdivision (4), and by substituting "$7\frac{1}{2}$ percent" for "$7\frac{1}{4}$ percent" in subdivision (5). **Effective** 1-1-67.

• **1965 (P.L. 89-212)**

P.L. 89-212, §4:

Amended Code Sec. 3201 by inserting "and before the calendar month next following the calendar month in which this provision was amended in 1965, or (i) $450, or (ii) an amount equal to one-twelfth of the current maximum annual taxable `wages' as defined in section 3121 of the Internal Revenue Code of 1954, whichever is greater, for any month after the month in which this provision was so amended" immediately after "or $450 for any calendar month after the month in which this provision was so amended". **Effective** only with respect to calendar months after September 1965.

Internal Revenue Code | Sec. 3201(c)

RAILROAD RETIREMENT TAX—EMPLOYEES

P.L. 89-212, § 5:

Amended Code Sec. 3201 by substituting new paragraphs (1)-(5) for old paragraphs (1) and (2). **Effective** only with respect to compensation paid for services rendered after 9-30-65. Prior to amendment, paragraphs (1) and (2) read as follows:

"(1) 6¾ percent of so much of the compensation paid to such employee for services rendered by him after the month in which this provision was amended in 1959, and before January 1, 1962, and

"(2) 7¼ percent of so much of the compensation paid to such employee for services rendered by him after December 31, 1961,".

- **1965, Social Security Amendments of 1965 (P.L. 89-97)**

P.L. 89-97, §§ 105(b), 111(c):

Amended Sec. 3201 by striking out "the rate of the tax imposed with respect to wages by section 3101 at such time exceeds the rate provided by paragraph (2) of such section 3101 as amended by the Social Security Amendments of 1956" and inserting in lieu thereof "the rate of the tax imposed with respect to wages by section 3101(a) plus the rate imposed by section 3101(b) at such time exceeds 2¾ percent (the rate provided by paragraph (2) of section 3101 as amended by the Social Security Amendments of 1956)." **Effective** with respect to compensation paid for services rendered after 12-31-65.

- **1963 (P.L. 88-133)**

P.L. 88-133, § 201:

Amended Sec. 3201 by inserting before the colon the following: "before the calendar month next following the month in which this provision was amended in 1963, or $450 for any calendar month after the month in which this provision was so amended". **Effective** 11-1-63.

- **1959 (P.L. 86-28)**

P.L. 86-28, § 201(a):

Amended Sec. 3201. **Effective** 6-1-59. Prior to amendment Sec. 3201 read as follows:

"In addition to other taxes, there is hereby imposed on the income of every employee a tax equal to 6¼ percent of so much of the compensation paid to such employee after December 31, 1954, for services rendered by him after such date as is not in excess of $350 for any calendar month."

Sec. 202 provides that the amendments made by Sec. 201 shall, except as otherwise provided in such amendments, be effective as of the first day of the calendar month next following the month in which this Act was enacted [May, 1959], and shall apply only with respect to compensation paid after the month of such enactment, for services rendered after such month of enactment.

- **1954 (P.L. 746, 83rd Cong.)**

P.L. 746, 83rd Cong., §§ 206(a), 407:

Amended Code § 3201 by substituting "$350" for "$300". **Effective** as if enacted as a part of the 1954 Code [effective with respect to remuneration paid after 12-31-54 which is for services performed after such date.—CCH]. **Effective** 1-1-55.

[Sec. 3202]

SEC. 3202. DEDUCTION OF TAX FROM COMPENSATION.

[Sec. 3202(a)]

(a) REQUIREMENT.—The taxes imposed by section 3201 shall be collected by the employer of the taxpayer by deducting the amount of the taxes from the compensation of the employee as and when paid. An employer who is furnished by an employee a written statement of tips (received in a calendar month) pursuant to section 6053(a) to which paragraph (3) of section 3231(e) is applicable may deduct an amount equivalent to such taxes with respect to such tips from any compensation of the employee (exclusive of tips) under his control, even though at the time such statement is furnished the total amount of the tips included in statements furnished to the employer as having been received by the employee in such calendar month in the course of his employment by such employer is less than $20.

Amendments

- **1983, Railroad Retirement Solvency Act of 1983 (P.L. 98-76)**

P.L. 98-76, § 225(c)(1)(A), (2):

Amended Code Sec. 3202(a). **Effective** for remuneration paid after 12-31-84.

- **1976, Tax Reform Act of 1976 (P.L. 94-455)**

P.L. 94-455, § 1903(a)(7)(A), (d):

Amended the second sentence of Code Sec. 3202(a) by deleting "after September 30, 1973," each place it appeared, by substituting "and the aggregate" for "after September 30, 1973 and the aggregate", by deleting "of the Internal Revenue Code of 1954" each place it appeared, and by inserting a comma immediately after "for any month" each place it appeared. **Effective** with respect to compensation paid for services rendered after 12-31-76.

- **1973 (P.L. 93-69)**

P.L. 93-69, § 102(b):

Amended Code Sec. 3202(a). (The **effective** date is the same as that for Code Sec. 3201. See the historical comment for P.L. 93-69 under Code Sec. 3201.) Prior to amendment, Code Sec. 3202(a) read as follows:

"(a) Requirement.—The tax imposed by section 3201 shall be collected by the employer of the taxpayer by deducting the amount of the tax from the compensation of the employee as and when paid. If an employee is paid compensation after September 30, 1965, by more than one employer for services rendered during any calendar month after September 30, 1965 and the aggregate of such compensation is in excess of (i) $450, or (ii) an amount equal to one-twelfth of the current maximum annual taxable `wages' as defined in section 3121 of the Internal Revenue Code of 1954, whichever is greater, for any month after September 30, 1965, the tax to be deducted by each employer other than a subordinate unit of a national railway-labor-organization employer from the compensation paid by him with respect to such compensation paid by all such employers which the compensation paid by him after September 30, 1965, to the employee for services rendered during such month bears to the total compensation paid by all such employers after September 30, 1965, to such employee for services rendered during such month; and in the event that the compensation so paid by such employers to the employee for services rendered during such month is less than (i) $450, or (ii) an amount equal to one-twelfth of the current maximum annual taxable `wages' as defined in section 3121 of the Internal Revenue Code of 1954, whichever is greater, for any month after September 30, 1965, each subordinate unit of a national railway-labor-organization employer shall deduct such proportion of any additional tax as the compensation paid by such employer after September 30, 1965, to such employee for services rendered during such month bears to the total compensation paid by all such employers after September 30, 1965, to such employee for services rendered during such month. An employer who is furnished by an employee a written statement of tips (received in a calendar month) pursuant to section 6053(a) to which paragraph (3) of section 3231(e) is applicable may deduct an amount equivalent to such tax with respect to such tips from any compensation of the employee (exclusive of tips) under his control, even though at the time such statement is furnished the total amount of the tips included in statements furnished to the employer as having been received by the employee in such calendar month in the course of his employment by such employer is less than $20."

- **1966 (P.L. 89-700)**

P.L. 89-700, § 301(v):

Amended Code Sec. 3202(a) by deleting "$400 for any calender month before the calendar month next following the month in which this provision was amended in 1963, or $450 for any calendar month after the month in which this provision was so amended and before the calendar month next following the calendar month in which this provision was amended in 1965, or" each place it appears and by substituting "September 30, 1965" for "the month in which this provision was so amended" in (ii) each time it appears. **Effective** 11-1-66.

P.L. 89-700, § 301(iii):

Amended Code Sec. 3202(a) by substituting "after September 30, 1965" for "after the month in which this provision was amended in 1959" each place it appears. **Effective** 11-1-66.

- **1965 (P.L. 89-212)**

P.L. 89-212, § 2(a)(1):

Amended Code Sec. 3202(a) by adding the last sentence. **Effective** only with respect to tips received after 1965.

P.L. 89-212, § 4:

Amended Code Sec. 3202(a) by inserting "and before the calendar month next following the calendar month in which this provision was amended in 1965, or (i) $450, or (ii) an amount equal to one-twelfth of the current maximum annual taxable `wages' as defined in section 3121 of the Internal Revenue Code of 1954, whichever is greater, for any month after the month in which this provision was so amended" immediately after "or $450 for any calendar month after the month in which this provision was so amended". **Effective** only with respect to calendar months after September 1965.

- **1963 (P.L. 88-133)**

P.L. 88-133, § 202:

Amended Sec. 3202 by inserting the following immediately after "$400" each place it appears: "for any calendar month before the calendar month next following the month in which this provision was amended in 1963, or $450 for any calendar month after the month in which this provision was so amended". **Effective** 11-1-63.

- **1958 (P.L. 86-28)**

P.L. 86-28, § 201(b):

Amended Sec. 3202(a) by striking out the phrases "after December 31, 1954" and "after 1954" wherever they appeared and substituting the phrase "after the month in which this provision was amended in 1959", and by striking out "$350" wherever it appeared and substituting "$400.". **Effective**, except as otherwise provided, as of the first day of the calendar month next following the month in which this Act was enacted [May, 1959], and shall apply only with respect to compensation paid after the month of such enactment, for services rendered after such month of enactment.

- **1954 (P.L. 83rd Cong.)**

P.L. 746, 83rd Cong., §§ 206(a), 407:

Amended Code § 3202(a) by substituting $350 for $300 in each place where the former amount now appears. **Effective** as if enacted as a part of the 1954 Code [effective with respect to remuneration paid after 12-31-54 which is for services performed after such date.—CCH].

RAILROAD RETIREMENT TAX—EMPLOYEES

[Sec. 3202(b)]

(b) INDEMNIFICATION OF EMPLOYER.—Every employer required under subsection (a) to deduct the tax shall be liable for the payment of such tax and shall not be liable to any person for the amount of any such payment.

Amendments

• **1976, Tax Reform Act of 1976 (P.L. 94-455)**

P.L. 94-455, §1903(a)(7)(B), (d):

Deleted "made" in Code Sec. 3202(b). **Effective** with respect to compensation paid for services rendered after 12-31-76.

[Sec. 3202(c)]

(c) SPECIAL RULE FOR TIPS.—

(1) In the case of tips which constitute compensation, subsection (a) shall be applicable only to such tips as are included in a written statement furnished to the employer pursuant to section 6053(a), and only to the extent that collection can be made by the employer, at or after the time such statement is so furnished and before the close of the 10th day following the calendar month (or, if paragraph (3) applies, the 30th day following the quarter) in which the tips were deemed paid, by deducting the amount of the tax from such compensation of the employee (excluding tips, but including funds turned over by the employee to the employer pursuant to paragraph (2)) as are under control of the employer.

(2) If the taxes imposed by section 3201, with respect to tips which are included in written statements furnished in any month to the employer pursuant to section 6053(a), exceed the compensation of the employee (excluding tips) from which the employer is required to collect the taxes under paragraph (1), the employee may furnish to the employer on or before the 10th day of the following month (or, if paragraph (3) applies, on or before the 30th day of the following quarter) an amount of money equal to the amount of the excess.

(3) The Secretary may, under regulations prescribed by him, authorize employers—

(A) to estimate the amount of tips that will be reported by the employee pursuant to section 6053(a) in any quarter of the calendar year,

(B) to determine the amount to be deducted upon each payment of compensation (exclusive of tips) during such quarter as if the tips so estimated constituted actual tips so reported, and

(C) to deduct upon any payment of compensation (other than tips, but including funds turned over by the employee to the employer pursuant to paragraph (2)) to such employee during such quarter (and within 30 days thereafter) such amount as may be necessary to adjust the amount actually deducted upon such compensation of the employee during the quarter to the amount required to be deducted in respect of tips included in written statements furnished to the employer during the quarter.

(4) If the taxes imposed by section 3201 with respect to tips which constitute compensation exceed the portion of such taxes which can be collected by the employer from the compensation of the employee pursuant to paragraph (1) or paragraph (3), such excess shall be paid by the employee.

Amendments

• **1983, Railroad Retirement Solvency Act of 1983 (P.L. 98-76)**

P.L. 98-76, §225(c)(1)(B), (3)-(5):

Amended Code Sec. 3202(c). **Effective** for remuneration paid after 12-31-84. Prior to amendment, Code Sec. 3202(c) read as follows:

(c) SPECIAL RULE FOR TIPS.—

(1) In the case of tips which constitute compensation, subsection (a) shall be applicable only to such tips as are included in a written statement furnished to the employer pursuant to section 6053(a), and only to the extent that collection can be made by the employer, at or after the time such statement is so furnished and before the close of the 10th day following the calendar month (or, if paragraph (3) applies, the 30th day following the quarter) in which the tips were deemed paid, by deducting the amount of the tax from such compensation of the employee (excluding tips, but including funds turned over by the employee to the employer pursuant to paragraph (2)) as are under control of the employer.

(2) If the tax imposed by section 3201, with respect to tips which are included in written statements furnished in any month to the employer pursuant to section 6053(a), exceeds the compensation of the employee (excluding tips) from which the employer is required to collect the tax under paragraph (1), the employee may furnish to the employer on or before the 10th day of the following month (or, if paragraph (3) applies, on or before the 30th day of the following quarter) an amount of money equal to the amount of the excess.

(3) The Secretary may, under regulations prescribed by him, authorize employers—

(A) to estimate the amount of tips that will be reported by the employee pursuant to section 6053(a) in any quarter of the calendar year,

(B) to determine the amount to be deducted upon each payment of compensation (exclusive of tips) during such quarter as if the tips so estimated constituted actual tips so reported, and

(C) to deduct upon any payment of compensation (other than tips, but including funds turned over by the employee to the employer pursuant to paragraph (2)) to such employee during such quarter (and within 30 days thereafter) such amount as may be necessary to adjust the amount actually deducted upon such compensation of the employee during the quarter to the amount required to be deducted in respect of tips included in written statements furnished to the employer during the quarter.

(4) If the tax imposed by section 3201 with respect to tips which constitute compensation exceeds the portion of such tax which can be collected by the employer from the compensation of the employee pursuant to paragraph (1) or paragraph (3), such excess shall be paid by the employee.

• **1976, Tax Reform Act of 1976 (P.L. 94-455)**

P.L. 94-455, §1906(b)(13)(A):

Amended 1954 Code by substituting "Secretary" for "Secretary or his delegate" each place it appeared. **Effective** 2-1-77.

• **1965 (P.L. 89-212)**

P.L. 89-212, §2(a)(2):

Added Code Sec. 3202(c). **Effective** with respect to tips received after 1965.

[Sec. 3202(d)]

(d) SPECIAL RULE FOR CERTAIN TAXABLE GROUP-TERM LIFE INSURANCE BENEFITS.—

(1) IN GENERAL.—In the case of any payment for group-term life insurance to which this subsection applies—

(A) subsection (a) shall not apply,

(B) the employer shall separately include on the statement required under section 6051—

(i) the portion of the compensation which consists of payments for group-term life insurance to which this subsection applies, and

(ii) the amount of the tax imposed by section 3201 on such payments, and

(C) the tax imposed by section 3201 on such payments shall be paid by the employee.

(2) BENEFITS TO WHICH SUBSECTION APPLIES.—This subsection shall apply to any payment for group-term life insurance to the extent—

(A) such payment constitutes compensation, and

(B) such payment is for coverage for periods during which an employment relationship no longer exists between the employee and the employer.

Amendments

• **1990, Omnibus Budget Reconciliation Act of 1990 (P.L. 101-508)**

P.L. 101-508, §5124(b):

Amended Code Sec. 3202 by adding at the end thereof a new subsection (d). **Effective** for coverage provided after 12-31-90.

RAILROAD RETIREMENT TAX—EMPLOYEE REPS.

Subchapter B—Tax on Employee Representatives

Sec. 3211. Rate of tax.
Sec. 3212. Determination of compensation.

[Sec. 3211]

SEC. 3211. RATE OF TAX.

[Sec. 3211(a)]

(a) TIER 1 TAX.—In addition to other taxes, there is hereby imposed on the income of each employee representative a tax equal to the applicable percentage of the compensation received during any calendar year by such employee representative for services rendered by such employee representative. For purposes of the preceding sentence, the term "applicable percentage" means the percentage equal to the sum of the rates of tax in effect under subsections (a) and (b) of section 3101 and subsections (a) and (b) of section 3111 for the calendar year.

Amendments

- **2020, Coronavirus Aid, Relief, and Economic Security (CARES) Act (P.L. 116-136)**

P.L. 116-136, § 2302, provides:

SEC. 2302. DELAY OF PAYMENT OF EMPLOYER PAYROLL TAXES.

(a) IN GENERAL.—

(1) TAXES.—Notwithstanding any other provision of law, the payment for applicable employment taxes for the payroll tax deferral period shall not be due before the applicable date.

(2) DEPOSITS.—Notwithstanding section 6302 of the Internal Revenue Code of 1986, an employer shall be treated as having timely made all deposits of applicable employment taxes that are required to be made (without regard to this section) for such taxes during the payroll tax deferral period if all such deposits are made not later than the applicable date.

(3) EXCEPTION.—This subsection shall not apply to any taxpayer if such taxpayer has had indebtedness forgiven under section 1106 of this Act with respect to a loan under paragraph (36) of section 7(a) of the Small Business Act (15 U.S.C. 636(a)), as added by section 1102 of this Act, or indebtedness forgiven under section 1109 of this Act. [Stricken by P.L. 116-142, § 4(a), **effective** as if included in the CARES Act (P.L. 116-136) and applicable to any loan made pursuant to section 7(a)(36) of the Small Business Act (15 U.S.C. 636(a)(36)) or section 1109 of the CARES Act.]

(b) SECA.—

(1) IN GENERAL.—Notwithstanding any other provision of law, the payment for 50 percent of the taxes imposed under section 1401(a) of the Internal Revenue Code of 1986 for the payroll tax deferral period shall not be due before the applicable date.

(2) ESTIMATED TAXES.—For purposes of applying section 6654 of the Internal Revenue Code of 1986 to any taxable year which includes any part of the payroll tax deferral period, 50 percent of the taxes imposed under section 1401(a) of such Code for the payroll tax deferral period shall not be treated as taxes to which such section 6654 applies.

(c) LIABILITY OF THIRD PARTIES.—

(1) ACTS TO BE PERFORMED BY AGENTS.—For purposes of section 3504 of the Internal Revenue Code of 1986, in the case of any person designated pursuant to such section (and any regulations or other guidance issued by the Secretary with respect to such section) to perform acts otherwise required to be performed by an employer under such Code, if such employer directs such person to defer payment of any applicable employment taxes during the payroll tax deferral period under this section, such employer shall be solely liable for the payment of such applicable employment taxes before the applicable date for any wages paid by such person on behalf of such employer during such period.

(2) CERTIFIED PROFESSIONAL EMPLOYER ORGANIZATIONS.—For purposes of section 3511, in the case of a certified professional employer organization (as defined in subsection (a) of section 7705 of the Internal Revenue Code of 1986) that has entered into a service contract described in subsection (e)(2) of such section with a customer, if such customer directs such organization to defer payment of any applicable employment taxes during the payroll tax deferral period under this section, such customer shall, notwithstanding subsections (a) and (c) of section 3511, be solely liable for the payment of such applicable employment taxes before the applicable date for any wages paid by such organization to any work site employee performing services for such customer during such period.

(d) DEFINITIONS.—For purposes of this section—

(1) APPLICABLE EMPLOYMENT TAXES.—The term "applicable employment taxes" means the following:

(A) The taxes imposed under section 3111(a) of the Internal Revenue Code of 1986.

(B) So much of the taxes imposed under section 3211(a) of such Code as are attributable to the rate in effect under section 3111(a) of such Code.

(C) So much of the taxes imposed under section 3221(a) of such Code as are attributable to the rate in effect under section 3111(a) of such Code.

(2) PAYROLL TAX DEFERRAL PERIOD.—The term "payroll tax deferral period" means the period beginning on the date of the enactment of this Act and ending before January 1, 2021.

(3) APPLICABLE DATE.—The term "applicable date" means—

(A) December 31, 2021, with respect to 50 percent of the amounts to which subsection (a) or (b), as the case may be, apply, and

(B) December 31, 2022, with respect to the remaining such amounts.

(4) SECRETARY.—The term "Secretary" means the Secretary of the Treasury (or the Secretary's delegate).

* * *

(f) REGULATORY AUTHORITY.—The Secretary shall issue such regulations or other guidance as necessary to carry out the purposes of this section, including rules for the administration and enforcement of subsection (c).

- **2001, Railroad Retirement and Survivors' Improvement Act of 2001 (P.L. 107-90)**

P.L. 107-90, § 204(b):

Amended Code Sec. 3211, as amended by Act Sec. 203[(a)], by striking subsection (a) and inserting a new subsection (a). **Effective** for calendar years beginning after 12-31-2001. Prior to being stricken, Code Sec. 3211(a) read as follows:

(a) IMPOSITION OF TAXES.—

(1) TIER 1 TAX.—In addition to other taxes, there is hereby imposed on the income of each employee representative a tax equal to the applicable percentage of the compensation received during any calendar year by such employee representative for services rendered by such employee representative. For purposes of the preceding sentence, the term "applicable percentage" means the percentage equal to the sum of the rates of the tax in effect under subsections (a) and (b) of section 3101 and subsections (a) and (b) of section 3111 for the calendar year.

(2) TIER 2 TAX.—In addition to other taxes, there is hereby imposed on the income of each employee representative a tax equal to the following percentage of the compensation received during any calendar year by such employee representatives for services rendered by such employee representative:

In the case of compensation received during:	The rate shall be:
1985	13.75
1986 or thereafter	14.75

(3) CROSS REFERENCE.—

For application of different contribution bases with respect to the taxes imposed by paragraphs (1) and (2), see section 3231(e)(2).

- **1990, Omnibus Budget Reconciliation Act of 1990 (P.L. 101-508)**

P.L. 101-508, § 5125(b)(1)-(2):

Amended Code Sec. 3211(a)(1) by striking "following" and inserting "applicable", and by striking "representative:" and all that follows and inserting "representative. For purposes of the preceding sentence, the term `applicable percentage' means the percentage equal to the sum of the rates of the tax in effect under subsections (a) and (b) of section 3101 and subsections (a) and (b) of section 3111 for the calendar year." **Effective** 11-5-90. Prior to amendment, Code Sec. 3211(a)(1) read as follows:

(a) IMPOSITION OF TAXES.—

(1) TIER 1 TAX.—In addition to other taxes, there is hereby imposed on the income of each employee representative a tax equal to the following percentage of the compensation received during any calendar year by such employee representative for services rendered by such employee representative:

In the case of compensation received during:	The rate shall be:
1985	14.10
1986 or 1987	14.30
1988 or 1989	15.02
1990 or thereafter	15.30

- **1983, Railroad Retirement Solvency Act of 1983 (P.L. 98-76)**

P.L. 98-76, § 211(c):

Amended Code Sec. 3211(a). **Effective** for compensation paid for services rendered after 12-31-83, and before 1-1-85. Prior to amendment, Code Sec. 3211(a) read as follows:

(a) In addition to other taxes, there is hereby imposed on the income of each employee representative a tax equal to 11.75 percent plus the sum of the rates of tax imposed with respect to wages by sections 3101(a), 3101(b), 3111(a), and 3111(b) of so much of the compensation paid in any calendar month to such employee representative for services rendered by him as is not in excess of an amount equal to one-twelfth of the current maximum annual taxable "wages" as defined in section 3121 for any month.

P.L. 98-76, § 223:

Amended Code Sec. 3211(a). **Effective** for remuneration paid after 12-31-84. Prior to amendment, Code Sec. 3211(a) read as follows:

(a) In addition to other taxes, there is hereby imposed on the income of each employee representative a tax equal to 12.75 percent plus the sum of the rates of tax imposed with respect to wages by sections 3101(a), 3101(b), 3111(a), and 3111(b) of so much of the compensation paid in any calendar month to such employee representa-

RAILROAD RETIREMENT TAX—EMPLOYEE REPS.

tive for services rendered by him as is not in excess of an amount equal to one-twelfth of the current maximum annual taxable "wages" as defined in section 3121 for any month.

• **1981, Economic Recovery Tax Act of 1981 (P.L. 97-34)**

P.L. 97-34, §741(b):

Amended Code Sec. 3211(a) by striking out "9.5 percent" and inserting "11.75 percent". **Effective** for compensation paid for services rendered after 9-30-81.

[Sec. 3211(b)]

(b) TIER 2 TAX.—In addition to other taxes, there is hereby imposed on the income of each employee representative a tax equal to the percentage determined under section 3241 for any calendar year of the compensation received during such calendar year by such employee representative for services rendered by such employee representative.

Amendments

• **2014, Tax Technical Corrections Act of 2014 (P.L. 113-295)**

P.L. 113-295, §221(a)(100)(B), Division A:

Amended Code Sec. 3211(b). **Effective** generally 12-19-2014. For a special rule, see Act Sec. 221(b)(2), Division A, below. Prior to amendment, Code Sec. 3211(b) read as follows:

(b) TIER 2 TAX.—

(1) IN GENERAL.—In addition to other taxes, there is hereby imposed on the income of each employee representative a tax equal to the applicable percentage of the compensation received during any calendar year by such employee representatives for services rendered by such employee representative.

(2) APPLICABLE PERCENTAGE.—For purposes of paragraph (1), the term "applicable percentage" means—

(A) 14.75 percent in the case of compensation received during 2002,

(B) 14.20 percent in the case of compensation received during 2003, and

(C) in the case of compensation received during any calendar year after 2003, the percentage determined under section 3241 for such calendar year.

P.L. 113-295, §221(b)(2), Division A, provides:

(2) SAVINGS PROVISION.—If—

(A) any provision amended or repealed by the amendments made by this section applied to—

(i) any transaction occurring before the date of the enactment of this Act,

(ii) any property acquired before such date of enactment, or

(iii) any item of income, loss, deduction, or credit taken into account before such date of enactment, and

(B) the treatment of such transaction, property, or item under such provision would (without regard to the amendments or repeals made by this section) affect the liability for tax for periods ending after date of enactment, nothing in the amendments or repeals made by this section shall be construed to affect the treatment of such transaction, property, or item for purposes of determining liability for tax for periods ending after such date of enactment.

• **2001, Railroad Retirement and Survivors' Improvement Act of 2001 (P.L. 107-90)**

P.L. 107-90, §203(a):

Amended Code Sec. 3211 by striking subsection (b). **Effective** for calendar years beginning after 12-31-2001. Prior to being stricken, Code Sec. 3211(b) read as follows:

(b) In addition to other taxes, there is hereby imposed on the income of each employee representative a tax at a rate equal to the rate of excise tax imposed on every employer, provided for in section 3221(c), for each man-hour for which compensation is paid to him for services rendered as an employee representative.

P.L. 107-90, §204(b):

Amended Code Sec. 3211, as amended by Act Sec. 203[(a)], by inserting a new subsection (b). **Effective** for calendar years beginning after 12-31-2001.

• **1975 (P.L. 94-93)**

P.L. 94-93, §§202 and 207:

Amended Code Sec. 3211(a) by striking out "compensation paid to such employee representative" and inserting in lieu thereof "compensation paid in any calendar month to such employee representative". **Effective** for tax years ending on or after 8-9-75, and for tax years ending before 8-9-75, as to which the period for assessment and collection of tax or the filing of a claim for credit or refund has not expired on 8-9-75.

• **1973 (P.L. 93-69)**

P.L. 93-69, §102(c):

Amended Code Sec. 3211(a). (The **effective** date is the same as that for Code Sec. 3201. See the historical comment for P.L. 93-69 under Code Sec. 3201.) Prior to amendment, Code Sec. 3211(a) read as follows:

"(a) In addition to other taxes, there is hereby imposed on the income of each employee representative a tax equal to—

"(1) 12½ percent of so much of the compensation paid to such employee representative for services rendered by him after September 30, 1965,

"(2) 13 percent of so much of the compensation paid to such employee representative for services rendered by him after December 31, 1965,

"(3) 14 percent of so much of the compensation paid to such employee representative for services rendered by him after December 31, 1966,

"(4) 14½ percent of so much of the compensation paid to such employee representative for services rendered by him after December 31, 1967, and

"(5) 15 percent of so much of the compensation paid to such employee representative for services rendered by him after December 31, 1968.

as is not in excess of (i) $450, or (ii) an amount equal to one-twelfth of the current maximum annual taxable `wages' as defined in section 3121 of the Internal Revenue Code of 1954, whichever is greater, for any month after September 30, 1965: *Provided*, That the rate of tax imposed by this section shall be increased, with respect to compensation paid for services rendered after September 30, 1965, by a number of percentage points (including fractional points) equal at any given time to twice the number of percentage points (including fractional points) by which the rate of the tax imposed with respect to wages by section 3101(a) plus the rate imposed by section 3101(b) at such time exceeds 2¾ percent (the rate provided by paragraph (2) of section 3101 as amended by the Social Security Amendments of 1956)."

• **1976, Tax Reform Act of 1976 (P.L. 94-455)**

P.L. 94-455, §1903(a)(8), (d):

Amended Code Sec. 3211(a) by substituting "3111(a), and 3111(b)" for "3111(a), 3111(b)"; by deleting "of the Internal Revenue Code of 1954" each place it appeared; by substituting "rendered by him" for "rendered by him after September 30, 1973,"; and by deleting "after September 30, 1973". **Effective** with respect to compensation paid for services rendered after 12-31-76. For prior amendments, see amendment note under Code Sec. 3211(b).

• **1970 (P.L. 91-215)**

P.L. 91-215, §4:

Amended Code Sec. 3211(b). **Effective** 3-18-70. Prior to amendment, this section read as follows:

"(b) In addition to other taxes, there is hereby imposed on the income of each employee representative a tax equal to 2 cents for each man-hour for which compensation is paid to him for services rendered as an employee representative."

• **1966 (P.L. 89-700)**

P.L. 89-700, §301(vi):

Amended the proviso in Code Sec. 3211(a) by substituting "after September 30, 1965" for "after December 31, 1964". **Effective** 11-1-66.

P.L. 89-700, §301(v):

Amended Code Sec. 3211(a) by deleting "$400 for any calendar month before the calendar month next following the month in which this provision was amended in 1963, or $450 for any calendar month after the month in which this provision was so amended and before the calendar month next following the calendar month in which this provision was amended in 1965, or" and by substituting "September 30, 1965" for "the month in which this provision was so amended" in (1). **Effective** 11-1-66.

• **1966 (P.L. 89-699)**

P.L. 89-699, §301(b):

Amended Code Sec. 3211 by substituting "14 percent" for "13½ percent" in subdivision (3), by substituting "14½ percent" for "14 percent" in subdivision (4), and by substituting "15 percent" for "14½ percent" in subdivision (5). **Effective** 1-1-67.

P.L. 89-699, §301(d):

Amended Code Sec. 3211 by inserting "(a)" before the first paragraph and by adding new subsection (b). **Effective** with respect to man-hours, for sixty months beginning with November 1966, for which compensation is paid.

• **1965 (P.L. 89-212)**

P.L. 89-212, §4:

Amended Code Sec. 3211 by inserting "and before the calendar month next following the calendar month in which this provision was amended in 1965, or (i) $450, or (ii) an amount equal to one-twelfth of the current maximum annual taxable `wages' as defined in section 3121 of the Internal Revenue Code of 1954, whichever is greater, for any month after the month in which this provision was so amended" immediately after "or $450 for any calendar month after the month in which this provision was so amended". **Effective** only with respect to calendar months after September 1965.

P.L. 89-212, §5:

Amended Code Sec. 3211 by substituting new paragraphs (1)-(5) for old paragraphs (1) and (2). **Effective** only with respect to compensation paid for services rendered after 9-30-65. Prior to amendment, paragraphs (1) and (2) read as follows:

"(1) 13½ percent of so much of the compensation paid to such employee representative for services rendered by him after the month in which this provision was amended in 1959, and before January 1, 1962, and

"(2) 14½ percent of so much of the compensation paid to such employee representative for services rendered by him after December 31, 1961."

• **1965, Social Security Amendments of 1965 (P.L. 89-97)**

P.L. 89-97, §§105(b), 111(c):

Amended Sec. 3211 by striking out "the rate of the tax imposed with respect to wages by section 3101 at such time exceeds the rate provided by paragraph (2) of section 3101 as amended by the Social Security Amendments of 1956" and inserting in lieu thereof "the rate of the tax imposed with respect to wages by section 3101(a) plus the rate imposed by section 3101(b) at such time exceeds 2¾ percent (the rate provided by paragraph (2) of section 3101 as amended by the Social Security Amendments of 1956." **Effective** with respect to compensation paid for services rendered after 12-31-65.

• **1963 (P.L. 88-133)**

P.L. 88-133, §201:

Amended Sec. 3211 by inserting before the colon the following: "before the calendar month next following the month in which this provision was amended in

RAILROAD RETIREMENT TAX—EMPLOYERS

1963, or $450 for any calendar month after the month in which this provision was so amended". **Effective** 11-1-63.

- **1959 (P.L. 86-28)**

P.L. 86-28, §201(c):

Amended Sec. 3211. **Effective**, except as otherwise provided, as of the first day of the calendar month next following the month in which this Act was enacted [May, 1959], and shall apply only with respect to compensation paid after the month of such enactment, for services rendered after such month of enactment. Prior to amendment Sec. 3211 read as follows:

(c) CROSS REFERENCE.—

For application of different contribution bases with respect to the taxes imposed by subsections (a) and (b), see section 3231(e)(2).

Amendments

- **2001, Railroad Retirement and Survivors' Improvement Act of 2001 (P.L. 107-90)**

P.L. 107-90, §204(b):

Amended Code Sec. 3211, as amended by Act Sec. 203[(a)], by inserting a new subsection (c). **Effective** for calendar years beginning after 12-31-2001.

"In addition to other taxes, there is hereby imposed on the income of each employee representative a tax equal to $12\frac{1}{2}$ percent of so much of the compensation, paid to such employee representative after December 31, 1954, for services rendered by him after such date as is not in excess of $350 for any calendar month."

- **1954 (P.L. 83rd Cong.)**

P.L. 746, 83rd Cong., §§206(a), 407:

Amended Code §3211 by substituting $350 for $300. **Effective** as if enacted as a part of the 1954 Code [**effective** with respect to remuneration paid after 12-31-54 which is for services performed after such date.—CCH].

[Sec. 3211(c)]

[Sec. 3212]

SEC. 3212. DETERMINATION OF COMPENSATION.

The compensation of an employee representative for the purpose of ascertaining the tax thereon shall be determined in the same manner and with the same effect as if the employee organization by which such employee representative is employed were an employer as defined in section 3231(a).

Subchapter C—Tax on Employers

Sec. 3221.   Rate of tax.

[Sec. 3221]

SEC. 3221. RATE OF TAX.

[Sec. 3221(a)]

(a) TIER 1 TAX.—In addition to other taxes, there is hereby imposed on every employer an excise tax, with respect to having individuals in his employ, equal to the applicable percentage of compensation paid during any calendar year by such employer for services rendered to such employer. For purposes of the preceding sentence, the term "applicable percentage" means the percentage equal to the sum of the rates of tax in effect under subsections (a) and (b) of section 3111 for the calendar year.

Amendments

- **2020, Taxpayer Certainty and Disaster Tax Relief Act of 2020 (P.L. 116-260)**

P.L. 116-260, §206(e)(2), Div. EE, provides:

(2) SPECIAL RULE.—

(A) IN GENERAL.—For purposes of section 2301 of the CARES Act, an employer who has filed a return of tax with respect to applicable employment taxes (as defined in section 2301(c)(1) of division A of such Act) before the date of the enactment of this Act [12-27-2020.--CCH] may elect (in such manner as the Secretary of the Treasury (or the Secretary's delegate) shall prescribe) to treat any applicable amount as an amount paid in the calendar quarter which includes the date of the enactment of this Act.

(B) APPLICABLE AMOUNT.—For purposes of subparagraph (A), the term "applicable amount" means the amount of wages which—

(i) are—

(I) described in section 2301(c)(5)(B) of the CARES Act, as added by the amendments made by subsection (b), or

(II) permitted to be treated as qualified wages under guidance issued pursuant to section 2301(g)(2) of the CARES Act (as added by subsection (c)), and

(ii) were—

(I) paid in a calendar quarter beginning after December 31, 2019, and before October 1, 2020, and

(II) not taken into account by the taxpayer in calculating the credit allowed under section 2301(a) of division A of such Act for such calendar quarter.

- **2020, Coronavirus Aid, Relief, and Economic Security (CARES) Act (P.L. 116-136)**

P.L. 116-136, §2301 (as amended by P.L. 116-260, §206(a)-(b), (c)(2)(A), (c)(2)(B)(i)-(ii), and (d), Div. EE, §207(a)(1)-(2), (b)-(c), (d)(1)(A)-(B), (d)(2)(A)-(B), (d)(3)(A)-(B), (e)(1)-(2), (f), (g)(1)-(2), (h), and (j), Div. EE, and §303(d)(3)(C)(iii), Div. EE), provides:

SEC. 2301. EMPLOYEE RETENTION CREDIT FOR EMPLOYERS SUBJECT TO CLOSURE DUE TO COVID–19.

(a) IN GENERAL.—In the case of an eligible employer, there shall be allowed as a credit against applicable employment taxes for each calendar quarter an amount equal to 70 percent of the qualified wages with respect to each employee of such employer for such calendar quarter.

(b) LIMITATIONS AND REFUNDABILITY.—

(1) WAGES TAKEN INTO ACCOUNT.—The amount of qualified wages with respect to any employee which may be taken into account under subsection (a) by the eligible employer for any calendar quarter shall not exceed $10,000.

(2) CREDIT LIMITED TO EMPLOYMENT TAXES.—The credit allowed by subsection (a) with respect to any calendar quarter shall not exceed the applicable employment taxes (reduced by any credits allowed under subsections (e) and (f) of section 3111 of the Internal Revenue Code of 1986, sections 7001 and 7003 of the Families First Coronavirus Response Act, and section 303(d) of the Taxpayer Certainty and Disaster Tax Relief Act of 2020) on the wages paid with respect to the employment of all the employees of the eligible employer for such calendar quarter.

(3) REFUNDABILITY OF EXCESS CREDIT.—

(A) IN GENERAL.—If the amount of the credit under subsection (a) exceeds the limitation of paragraph (2) for any calendar quarter, such excess shall be treated as an overpayment that shall be refunded under sections 6402(a) and 6413(b) of the Internal Revenue Code of 1986.

(B) TREATMENT OF PAYMENTS.—For purposes of section 1324 of title 31, United States Code, any amounts due to the employer under this paragraph shall be treated in the same manner as a refund due from a credit provision referred to in subsection (b)(2) of such section.

(c) DEFINITIONS.—For purposes of this section—

(1) APPLICABLE EMPLOYMENT TAXES.—The term "applicable employment taxes" means the following:

(A) The taxes imposed under section 3111(a) of the Internal Revenue Code of 1986.

(B) So much of the taxes imposed under section 3221(a) of such Code as are attributable to the rate in effect under section 3111(a) of such Code.

(2) ELIGIBLE EMPLOYER.—

(A) IN GENERAL.—The term "eligible employer" means any employer—

(i) which was carrying on a trade or business during the calendar quarter for which the credit is determined under subsection (a), and

(ii) with respect to any calendar quarter, for which—

(I) the operation of the trade or business described in clause (i) is fully or partially suspended during the calendar quarter due to orders from an appropriate governmental authority limiting commerce, travel, or group meetings (for commercial, social, religious, or other purposes) due to the coronavirus disease 2019 (COVID–19), or

(II) the gross receipts (within the meaning of section 448(c) of the Internal Revenue Code of 1986) of such employer for such calendar quarter are less than 80 percent of the gross receipts of such employer for the same calendar quarter in calendar year 2019.

With respect to any employer for any calendar quarter, if such employer was not in existence as of the beginning of the same calendar quarter in calendar year 2019, clause (ii)(II) shall be applied by substituting "2020" for "2019".

(B) ELECTION TO USE ALTERNATIVE QUARTER.—At the election of the employer—

(i) subparagraph (A)(ii)(II) shall be applied—

(I) by substituting "for the immediately preceding calendar quarter" for "for such calendar quarter", and

(II) by substituting "the corresponding calendar quarter in calendar year 2019" for "the same calendar quarter in calendar year 2019", and

(ii) the last sentence of subparagraph (A) shall be applied by substituting "the corresponding calendar quarter in calendar year 2019" for "the same calendar quarter in calendar year 2019".

An election under this subparagraph shall be made at such time and in such manner as the Secretary shall prescribe.

(C) TAX-EXEMPT ORGANIZATIONS.—In the case of an organization which is described in section 501(c) of the Internal Revenue Code of 1986 and exempt from tax under section 501(a) of such Code—

(i) clauses (i) and (ii)(I) of subparagraph (A) shall apply to all operations of such organization, and

(ii) any reference in this section to gross receipts shall be treated as a reference to gross receipts within the meaning of section 6033 of such Code.

(3) QUALIFIED WAGES.—

(A) IN GENERAL.—The term "qualified wages" means—

(i) in the case of an eligible employer for which the average number of full-time employees (within the meaning of section 4980H of the Internal Revenue Code of 1986) employed by such eligible employer during 2019 was greater than 500, wages paid by such eligible employer with respect to which an employee is not providing services due to circumstances described in subclause (I) or (II) of paragraph (2)(A)(ii), or

(ii) in the case of an eligible employer for which the average number of full-time employees (within the meaning of section 4980H of the Internal Revenue Code of 1986) employed by such eligible employer during 2019 was not greater than 500—

(I) with respect to an eligible employer described in subclause (I) of paragraph (2)(A)(ii), wages paid by such eligible employer with respect to an employee during any period described in such clause, or

(II) with respect to an eligible employer described in subclause (II) of such paragraph, wages paid by such eligible employer with respect to an employee during such quarter.

(B) EXCEPTION.—The term "qualified wages" shall not include any wages taken into account under section 7001 or section 7003 of the Families First Coronavirus Response Act.

(4) SECRETARY.—The term "Secretary" means the Secretary of the Treasury or the Secretary's delegate.

(5) WAGES.—

(A) IN GENERAL.—The term "wages" means wages (as defined in section 3121(a) of the Internal Revenue Code of 1986) and compensation (as defined in section 3231(e) of such Code). For purposes of the preceding sentence, in the case of any organization or entity described in subsection (f)(2), wages as defined in section 3121(a) of the Internal Revenue Code of 1986 shall be determined without regard to paragraphs (5), (6), (7), (10), and (13) of section 3121(b) of such Code (except with respect to services performed in a penal institution by an inmate thereof).

(B) ALLOWANCE FOR CERTAIN HEALTH PLAN EXPENSES.—

(i) IN GENERAL.—Such term shall include amounts paid by the eligible employer to provide and maintain a group health plan (as defined in section 5000(b)(1) of the Internal Revenue Code of 1986), but only to the extent that such amounts are excluded from the gross income of employees by reason of section 106(a) of such Code.

(ii) ALLOCATION RULES.—For purposes of this section, amounts treated as wages under clause (i) shall be treated as paid with respect to any employee (and with respect to any period) to the extent that such amounts are properly allocable to such employee (and to such period) in such manner as the Secretary may prescribe. Except as otherwise provided by the Secretary, such allocation shall be treated as properly made if made on the basis of being pro rata among periods of coverage.

(6) OTHER TERMS.—Any term used in this section which is also used in chapter 21 or 22 of the Internal Revenue Code of 1986 shall have the same meaning as when used in such chapter.

(d) AGGREGATION RULE.—All persons treated as a single employer under subsection (a) or (b) of section 52 of the Internal Revenue Code of 1986, or subsection (m) or (o) of section 414 of such Code, shall be treated as one employer for purposes of this section.

(e) CERTAIN RULES TO APPLY.—For purposes of this section, rules similar to the rules of sections 51(i)(1) and 280C(a) of the Internal Revenue Code of 1986 shall apply.

(f) CERTAIN GOVERNMENTAL EMPLOYERS.—

(1) IN GENERAL.—This credit shall not apply to the Government of the United States, the government of any State or political subdivision thereof, or any agency or instrumentality of any of the foregoing.

(2) EXCEPTION.—Paragraph (1) shall not apply to—

(A) any organization described in section 501(c)(1) of the Internal Revenue Code of 1986 and exempt from tax under section 501(a) of such Code, or

(B) any entity described in paragraph (1) if —

(i) such entity is a college or university, or

(ii) the principal purpose or function of such entity is providing medical or hospital care.

In the case of any entity described in subparagraph (B), such entity shall be treated as satisfying the requirements of subsection (c)(2)(A)(i).

(g) ELECTION TO NOT TAKE CERTAIN WAGES INTO ACCOUNT.—

(1) IN GENERAL.—This section shall not apply to so much of the qualified wages paid by an eligible employer as such employer elects (at such time and in such manner as the Secretary may prescribe) to not take into account for purposes of this section.

(2) COORDINATION WITH PAYCHECK PROTECTION PROGRAM.—The Secretary, in consultation with the Administrator of the Small Business Administration, shall issue guidance providing that payroll costs paid during the covered period shall not fail to be treated as qualified wages under this section by reason of an election under paragraph (1) to the extent that a covered loan of the eligible employer is not forgiven by reason of a decision under section 7A(g) of the Small Business Act or the application of section 7(a)(37)(J) of the Small Business Act. Terms used in the preceding sentence which are also used in section 7A(g) or 7(a)(37)(J) of the Small Business Act shall, when applied in connection with either such section, have the same meaning as when used in such section, respectively.

(h) SPECIAL RULES.—

(1) DENIAL OF DOUBLE BENEFIT.—Any wages taken into account in determining the credit allowed under this section shall not be taken into account as wages for purposes of sections 41, 45A, 45P, 45S, 51, and 1396 of the Internal Revenue Code of 1986.

(2) THIRD PARTY PAYORS.—Any credit allowed under this section shall be treated as a credit described in section 3511(d)(2) of such Code.

* * *

(j) ADVANCE PAYMENTS.—

(1) IN GENERAL.—Except as provided in paragraph (2), no advance payment of the credit under subsection (a) shall be allowed.

(2) ADVANCE PAYMENTS TO SMALL EMPLOYERS.—

(A) IN GENERAL.—Under rules provided by the Secretary, an eligible employer for which the average number of full-time employees (within the meaning of section 4980H of the Internal Revenue Code of 1986) employed by such eligible employer during 2019 was not greater than 500 may elect for any calendar quarter to receive an advance payment of the credit under subsection (a) for such quarter in an amount not to exceed 70 percent of the average quarterly wages paid by the employer in calendar year 2019.

(B) SPECIAL RULE FOR SEASONAL EMPLOYERS.—In the case of any employer who employs seasonal workers (as defined in section 45R(d)(5)(B) of the Internal Revenue Code of 1986), the employer may elect to substitute "the wages for the calendar quarter in 2019 which corresponds to the calendar quarter to which the election relates" for "the average quarterly wages paid by the employer in calendar year 2019".

(C) SPECIAL RULE FOR EMPLOYERS NOT IN EXISTENCE IN 2019.—In the case of any employer that was not in existence in 2019, subparagraphs (A) and (B) shall each be applied by substituting "2020" for "2019" each place it appears.

(3) RECONCILIATION OF CREDIT WITH ADVANCE PAYMENTS.—

(A) IN GENERAL.—The amount of credit which would (but for this subsection) be allowed under this section shall be reduced (but not below zero) by the aggregate payment allowed to the taxpayer under paragraph (2). Any failure to so reduce the credit shall be treated as arising out of a mathematical or clerical error and assessed according to section 6213(b)(1) of the Internal Revenue Code of 1986.

(B) EXCESS ADVANCE PAYMENTS.—If the advance payments to a taxpayer under paragraph (2) for a calendar quarter exceed the credit allowed by this section (determined without regard to subparagraph (A)), the tax imposed by chapter 21 or 22 of the Internal Revenue Code of 1986 (whichever is applicable) for the calendar quarter shall be increased by the amount of such excess.

(k) TREATMENT OF DEPOSITS.—The Secretary shall waive any penalty under section 6656 of the Internal Revenue Code of 1986 for any failure to make a deposit of any applicable employment taxes if the Secretary determines that such failure was due to the reasonable anticipation of the credit allowed under this section.

(l) REGULATIONS AND GUIDANCE.—The Secretary shall issue such forms, instructions, regulations, and guidance as are necessary—

(1) to allow the advance payment of the credit under subsection (a) as provided in paragraph (j)(2), subject to the limitations provided in this section, based on such information as the Secretary shall require,

(2) with respect to the application of the credit under subsection (a) to third party payors (including professional employer organizations, certified professional employer organizations, or agents under section 3504 of the Internal Revenue Code of 1986), including regulations or guidance allowing such payors to submit documentation necessary to substantiate the eligible employer status of employers that use such payors, and

(3) to prevent the avoidance of the purposes of the limitations under this section, including through the leaseback of employees.

Any forms, instructions, regulations, or guidance described in paragraph (2) shall require the customer to be responsible for the accounting of the credit and for any liability for improperly claimed credits and shall require the certified professional employer organization or other third party payor to accurately report such tax credits based on the information provided by the customer.

(m) APPLICATION.—This section shall only apply to wages paid after March 12, 2020, and before July 1, 2021.

* * *

P.L. 116-136, § 2302, provides:
SEC. 2302. DELAY OF PAYMENT OF EMPLOYER PAYROLL TAXES.

(a) IN GENERAL.—

(1) TAXES.—Notwithstanding any other provision of law, the payment for applicable employment taxes for the payroll tax deferral period shall not be due before the applicable date.

(2) DEPOSITS.—Notwithstanding section 6302 of the Internal Revenue Code of 1986, an employer shall be treated as having timely made all deposits of applicable employment taxes that are required to be made (without regard to this section) for such taxes during the payroll tax deferral period if all such deposits are made not later than the applicable date.

(3) EXCEPTION.—This subsection shall not apply to any taxpayer if such taxpayer has had indebtedness forgiven under section 1106 of this Act with respect to a loan under paragraph (36) of section 7(a) of the Small Business Act (15 U.S.C. 636(a)), as added by section 1102 of this Act, or indebtedness forgiven under section 1109 of this Act. [Stricken by P.L. 116-142, § 4(a), **effective** as if included in the CARES Act (P.L. 116-136) and applicable to any loan made pursuant to section 7(a)(36) of the Small Business Act (15 U.S.C. 636(a)(36)) or section 1109 of the CARES Act.]

(b) SECA.—

(1) IN GENERAL.—Notwithstanding any other provision of law, the payment for 50 percent of the taxes imposed under section 1401(a) of the Internal Revenue Code of 1986 for the payroll tax deferral period shall not be due before the applicable date.

(2) ESTIMATED TAXES.—For purposes of applying section 6654 of the Internal Revenue Code of 1986 to any taxable year which includes any part of the payroll tax deferral period, 50 percent of the taxes imposed under section 1401(a) of such Code for the payroll tax deferral period shall not be treated as taxes to which such section 6654 applies.

RAILROAD RETIREMENT TAX—EMPLOYERS

(c) LIABILITY OF THIRD PARTIES.—

(1) ACTS TO BE PERFORMED BY AGENTS.—For purposes of section 3504 of the Internal Revenue Code of 1986, in the case of any person designated pursuant to such section (and any regulations or other guidance issued by the Secretary with respect to such section) to perform acts otherwise required to be performed by an employer under such Code, if such employer directs such person to defer payment of any applicable employment taxes during the payroll tax deferral period under this section, such employer shall be solely liable for the payment of such applicable employment taxes before the applicable date for any wages paid by such person on behalf of such employer during such period.

(2) CERTIFIED PROFESSIONAL EMPLOYER ORGANIZATIONS.—For purposes of section 3511, in the case of a certified professional employer organization (as defined in subsection (a) of section 7705 of the Internal Revenue Code of 1986) that has entered into a service contract described in subsection (e)(2) of such section with a customer, if such customer directs such organization to defer payment of any applicable employment taxes during the payroll tax deferral period under this section, such customer shall, notwithstanding subsections (a) and (c) of section 3511, be solely liable for the payment of such applicable employment taxes before the applicable date for any wages paid by such organization to any work site employee performing services for such customer during such period.

(d) DEFINITIONS.—For purposes of this section—

(1) APPLICABLE EMPLOYMENT TAXES.—The term "applicable employment taxes" means the following:

(A) The taxes imposed under section 3111(a) of the Internal Revenue Code of 1986.

(B) So much of the taxes imposed under section 3211(a) of such Code as are attributable to the rate in effect under section 3111(a) of such Code.

(C) So much of the taxes imposed under section 3221(a) of such Code as are attributable to the rate in effect under section 3111(a) of such Code.

(2) PAYROLL TAX DEFERRAL PERIOD.—The term "payroll tax deferral period" means the period beginning on the date of the enactment of this Act and ending before January 1, 2021.

(3) APPLICABLE DATE.—The term "applicable date" means—

(A) December 31, 2021, with respect to 50 percent of the amounts to which subsection (a) or (b), as the case may be, apply, and

(B) December 31, 2022, with respect to the remaining such amounts.

(4) SECRETARY.—The term "Secretary" means the Secretary of the Treasury (or the Secretary's delegate).

* * *

(f) REGULATORY AUTHORITY.—The Secretary shall issue such regulations or other guidance as necessary to carry out the purposes of this section, including rules for the administration and enforcement of subsection (c).

• 2020, Families First Coronavirus Response Act (P.L. 116-127)

P.L. 116-127, §7001 (as amended by P.L. 116-136, §3606(a)(1)-(3); P.L. 116-260, §286(a) and (b)(1), Div. N, §288(a)(1)-(2), and (b)-(c), Div. N, and §303(d)(3)(C)(i), Div. EE), provides:

SEC. 7001. PAYROLL CREDIT FOR REQUIRED PAID SICK LEAVE.

(a) IN GENERAL.—In the case of an employer, there shall be allowed as a credit against the tax imposed by section 3111(a) or 3221(a) of the Internal Revenue Code of 1986 for each calendar quarter an amount equal to 100 percent of the qualified sick leave wages paid by such employer with respect to such calendar quarter.

(b) LIMITATIONS AND REFUNDABILITY.—

(1) WAGES TAKEN INTO ACCOUNT.—The amount of qualified sick leave wages taken into account under subsection (a) with respect to any individual shall not exceed $200 ($511 in the case of any day any portion of which is paid sick time described in paragraph (1), (2), or (3) of section 5102(a) of the Emergency Paid Sick Leave Act) for any day (or portion thereof) for which the individual is paid qualified sick leave wages.

(2) OVERALL LIMITATION ON NUMBER OF DAYS TAKEN INTO ACCOUNT.—The aggregate number of days taken into account under paragraph (1) for any calendar quarter shall not exceed the excess (if any) of—

(A) 10, over

(B) the aggregate number of days so taken into account for all preceding calendar quarters.

(3) CREDIT LIMITED TO CERTAIN EMPLOYMENT TAXES.—The credit allowed by subsection (a) with respect to any calendar quarter shall not exceed the tax imposed by section 3111(a) or 3221(a) of such Code for such calendar quarter (reduced by any credits allowed under subsections (e) and (f) of section 3111 of such Code, and section 303(d) of the Taxpayer Certainty and Disaster Tax Relief Act of 2020, for such quarter) on the wages paid with respect to the employment of all employees of the employer.

(4) REFUNDABILITY OF EXCESS CREDIT.—

(A)(i) CREDIT IS REFUNDABLE.—If the amount of the credit under subsection (a) exceeds the limitation of paragraph (3) for any calendar quarter, such excess shall be treated as an overpayment that shall be refunded under sections 6402(a) and 6413(b) of such Code.

(ii) ADVANCING CREDIT.—In anticipation of the credit, including the refundable portion under clause (i), the credit may be advanced, according to forms and instructions provided by the Secretary, up to an amount calculated under subsection (a), subject to the limits under subsection (b), both calculated through the end of the most recent payroll period in the quarter.

(B) TREATMENT OF PAYMENTS.—For purposes of section 1324 of title 31, United States Code, any amounts due to an employer under this paragraph shall be treated in the same manner as a refund due from a credit provision referred to in subsection (b)(2) of such section.

(c) QUALIFIED SICK LEAVE WAGES.—For purposes of this section, the term "qualified sick leave wages" means wages (as defined in section 3121(a) of the Internal Revenue Code of 1986, determined without regard to paragraphs (1) through (22) of section 3121(b) of such Code and section 7005(a) of this Act, [sic]) and compensation (as defined in section 3231(e) of the Internal Revenue Code, determined without regard to the sentence in paragraph (1) thereof which begins "Such term does not include remuneration" and without regard to section 7005(a) of this Act) paid by an employer—

(1) which are required to be paid by reason of the Emergency Paid Sick Leave Act, or

(2) both—

(A) which would be so required to be paid if such Act were applied—

(i) by substituting "March 31, 2021" for "December 31, 2020" in section 5109 thereof, and

(ii) without regard to section 5102(b)(3) thereof, and

(B) with respect to which all requirements of such Act (other than subsections (a) and (b) of section 5105 thereof, and determined by substituting "To be compliant with section 5102, an employer may not" for "It shall be unlawful for any employer to" in section 5104 thereof) which would apply if so required are satisfied.

(d) ALLOWANCE OF CREDIT FOR CERTAIN HEALTH PLAN EXPENSES.—

(1) IN GENERAL.—The amount of the credit allowed under subsection (a) shall be increased by so much of the employer's qualified health plan expenses as are properly allocable to the qualified sick leave wages for which such credit is so allowed.

(2) QUALIFIED HEALTH PLAN EXPENSES.—For purposes of this subsection, the term "qualified health plan expenses" means amounts paid or incurred by the employer to provide and maintain a group health plan (as defined in section 5000(b)(1) of the Internal Revenue Code of 1986), but only to the extent that such amounts are excluded from the gross income of employees by reason of section 106(a) of such Code.

(3) ALLOCATION RULES.—For purposes of this section, qualified health plan expenses shall be allocated to qualified sick leave wages in such manner as the Secretary of the Treasury (or the Secretary's delegate) may prescribe. Except as otherwise provided by the Secretary, such allocation shall be treated as properly made if made on the basis of being pro rata among covered employees and pro rata on the basis of periods of coverage (relative to the time periods of leave to which such wages relate).

(e) SPECIAL RULES.—

(1) DENIAL OF DOUBLE BENEFIT.—For purposes of chapter 1 of such Code, the gross income of the employer, for the taxable year which includes the last day of any calendar quarter with respect to which a credit is allowed under this section, shall be increased by the amount of such credit. Any wages taken into account in determining the credit allowed under this section shall not be taken into account for purposes of determining the credit allowed under section 45S of such Code.

(2) ELECTION NOT TO HAVE SECTION APPLY.—This section shall not apply with respect to any employer for any calendar quarter if such employer elects (at such time and in such manner as the Secretary of the Treasury (or the Secretary's delegate) may prescribe) not to have this section apply.

(3) CERTAIN TERMS.—Except as otherwise provided in this section, any term used in this section which is also used in chapter 21 of such Code shall have the same meaning as when used in such chapter.

(4) CERTAIN GOVERNMENTAL EMPLOYERS.—This credit shall not apply to the Government of the United States, the government of any State or political subdivision thereof, or any agency or instrumentality of any of the foregoing.

(4) [(5)] REFERENCES TO RAILROAD RETIREMENT TAX.—Any reference in this section to the tax imposed by section 3221(a) of the Internal Revenue Code of 1986 shall be treated as a reference to so much of such tax as is attributable to the rate in effect under section 3111(a) of such Code.

(f) REGULATIONS.—The Secretary of the Treasury (or the Secretary's delegate) shall prescribe such regulations or other guidance as may be necessary to carry out the purposes of this section, including—

(1) regulations or other guidance to prevent the avoidance of the purposes of the limitations under this section,

(2) regulations or other guidance to minimize compliance and record-keeping burdens under this section,

(3) regulations or other guidance providing for waiver of penalties for failure to deposit amounts in anticipation of the allowance of the credit allowed under this section,

(4) regulations or other guidance for recapturing the benefit of credits determined under this section in cases where there is a subsequent adjustment to the credit determined under subsection (a),

(5) regulations or other guidance to ensure that the wages taken into account under this section conform with the paid sick time required to be provided under the Emergency Paid Sick Leave Act, and

(6) regulations or other guidance to permit the advancement of the credit determined under subsection (a).

(g) APPLICATION OF SECTION.—This section shall apply only to wages paid with respect to the period beginning on a date selected by the Secretary of the Treasury (or the Secretary's delegate) which is during the 15-day period beginning on the date of the enactment of this Act, and ending on March 31, 2021.

* * *

(i) TREATMENT OF DEPOSITS.—The Secretary of the Treasury (or the Secretary's delegate) shall waive any penalty under section 6656 of the Internal Revenue Code of 1986 for any failure to make a deposit of the tax imposed by section 3111(a) or 3221(a) of such Code if the Secretary determines that such failure was due to the anticipation of the credit allowed under this section.

P.L. 116-127, §7003 (as amended by P.L. 116-136, §3606(b)-(c); P.L. 116-260, §286(a) and (b)(3), Div. N, §288(a)(1)-(2), and (b)-(c), Div. N, and §303(d)(3)(C)(ii), Div. EE), provides:

SEC. 7003. PAYROLL CREDIT FOR REQUIRED PAID FAMILY LEAVE.

(a) IN GENERAL.—In the case of an employer, there shall be allowed as a credit against the tax imposed by section 3111(a) or 3221(a) of the Internal Revenue Code of 1986 for each calendar quarter an amount equal to 100 percent of the qualified family leave wages paid by such employer with respect to such calendar quarter.

Sec. 3221(a)

(b) LIMITATIONS AND REFUNDABILITY.—

(1) WAGES TAKEN INTO ACCOUNT.—The amount of qualified family leave wages taken into account under subsection (a) with respect to any individual shall not exceed—

(A) for any day (or portion thereof) for which the individual is paid qualified family leave wages, $200, and

(B) in the aggregate with respect to all calendar quarters, $10,000.

(2) CREDIT LIMITED TO CERTAIN EMPLOYMENT TAXES.—The credit allowed by subsection (a) with respect to any calendar quarter shall not exceed the tax imposed by section 3111(a) or 3221(a) of such Code for such calendar quarter (reduced by any credits allowed under subsections (e) and (f) of section 3111 of such Code, section 7001 of this Act, and section 303(d) of the Taxpayer Certainty and Disaster Tax Relief Act of 2020, for such quarter) on the wages paid with respect to the employment of all employees of the employer.

(3) REFUNDABILITY OF EXCESS CREDIT.—

(A) CREDIT IS REFUNDABLE.—If the amount of the credit under subsection (a) exceeds the limitation of paragraph (2) for any calendar quarter, such excess shall be treated as an overpayment that shall be refunded under sections 6402(a) and 6413(b) of such Code.

(B) ADVANCING CREDIT.—In anticipation of the credit, including the refundable portion under subparagraph (A), the credit may be advanced, according to forms and instructions provided by the Secretary, up to an amount calculated under subsection (a), subject to the limits under subsection (b), both calculated through the end of the most recent payroll period in the quarter.

(c) QUALIFIED FAMILY LEAVE WAGES.—For purposes of this section, the term "qualified family leave wages" means wages (as defined in section 3121(a) of such Code) and compensation (as defined in section 3231(e) of the Internal Revenue Code, determined without regard to the sentence in paragraph (1) thereof which begins "Such term does not include remuneration" and without regard to section 7005(a) of this Act) paid by an employer—[P.L. 116-260, § 288(a)(1)(A) and (b)(1), Div. N, amendments cannot be made because the text "as defined in section 3121(a) of the Internal Revenue Code of 1986" does not exist.—CCH]

(1) which are required to be paid by reason of the Emergency Family and Medical Leave Expansion Act (including the amendments made by such Act), or

(2) both—

(A) which would be so required to be paid if section 102(a)(1)(F) of the Family and Medical Leave Act of 1993, as amended by the Emergency Family and Medical Leave Expansion Act, were applied by substituting "March 31, 2021" for "December 31, 2020", and

(B) with respect to which all requirements of the Family and Medical Leave Act of 1993 (other than section 107 thereof, and determined by substituting "To be compliant with section 102(a)(1)(F), an employer may not" for "It shall be unlawful for any employer to" each place it appears in subsection (a) of section 105 thereof, by substituting "made unlawful in this title or described in this section" for "made unlawful by this title" in paragraph (2) of such subsection, and by substituting "To be compliant with section 102(a)(1)(F), an employer may not" for "It shall be unlawful for any person to" in subsection (b) of such section) which relate to such section 102(a)(1)(F), and which would apply if so required, are satisfied.

(d) ALLOWANCE OF CREDIT FOR CERTAIN HEALTH PLAN EXPENSES.—

(1) IN GENERAL.—The amount of the credit allowed under subsection (a) shall be increased by so much of the employer's qualified health plan expenses as are properly allocable to the qualified family leave wages for which such credit is so allowed.

(2) QUALIFIED HEALTH PLAN EXPENSES.—For purposes of this subsection, the term "qualified health plan expenses" means amounts paid or incurred by the employer to provide and maintain a group health plan (as defined in section 5000(b)(1) of the Internal Revenue Code of 1986), but only to the extent that such amounts are excluded from the gross income of employees by reason of section 106(a) of such Code.

(3) ALLOCATION RULES.—For purposes of this section, qualified health plan expenses shall be allocated to qualified family leave wages in such manner as the Secretary of the Treasury (or the Secretary's delegate) may prescribe. Except as otherwise provided by the Secretary, such allocation shall be treated as properly made if made on the basis of being pro rata among covered employees and pro rata on the basis of periods of coverage (relative to the time periods of leave to which such wages relate).

(e) SPECIAL RULES.—

(1) DENIAL OF DOUBLE BENEFIT.—For purposes of chapter 1 of such Code, the gross income of the employer, for the taxable year which includes the last day of any calendar quarter with respect to which a credit is allowed under this section, shall be increased by the amount of such credit. Any wages taken into account in determining the credit allowed under this section shall not be taken into account for purposes of determining the credit allowed under section 45S of such Code.

(2) ELECTION NOT TO HAVE SECTION APPLY.—This section shall not apply with respect to any employer for any calendar quarter if such employer elects (at such time and in such manner as the Secretary of the Treasury (or the Secretary's delegate) may prescribe) not to have this section apply.

(3) CERTAIN TERMS.—Except as otherwise provided in this section, any term used in this section which is also used in chapter 21 of such Code shall have the same meaning as when used in such chapter.

(4) CERTAIN GOVERNMENTAL EMPLOYERS.—This credit shall not apply to the Government of the United States, the government of any State or political subdivision thereof, or any agency or instrumentality of any of the foregoing.

(4) [(5)] REFERENCES TO RAILROAD RETIREMENT TAX.—Any reference in this section to the tax imposed by section 3221(a) of the Internal Revenue Code of 1986 shall be treated as a reference to so much of such tax as is attributable to the rate in effect under section 3111(a) of such Code.

(f) REGULATIONS.—The Secretary of the Treasury (or the Secretary's delegate) shall prescribe such regulations or other guidance as may be necessary to carry out the purposes of this section, including—

(1) regulations or other guidance to prevent the avoidance of the purposes of the limitations under this section,

(2) regulations or other guidance to minimize compliance and record-keeping burdens under this section,

(3) regulations or other guidance providing for waiver of penalties for failure to deposit amounts in anticipation of the allowance of the credit allowed under this section,

(4) regulations or other guidance for recapturing the benefit of credits determined under this section in cases where there is a subsequent adjustment to the credit determined under subsection (a),

(5) regulations or other guidance to ensure that the wages taken into account under this section conform with the paid leave required to be provided under the Emergency Family and Medical Leave Expansion Act (including the amendments made by such Act), and

(6) regulations or other guidance to permit the advancement of the credit determined under subsection (a).

(g) APPLICATION OF SECTION.—This section shall apply only to wages paid with respect to the period beginning on a date selected by the Secretary of the Treasury (or the Secretary's delegate) which is during the 15-day period beginning on the date of the enactment of this Act, and ending on March 31, 2021.

* * *

(i) TREATMENT OF DEPOSITS.—The Secretary of the Treasury (or the Secretary's delegate) shall waive any penalty under section 6656 of the Internal Revenue Code of 1986 for any failure to make a deposit of the tax imposed by section 3111(a) or 3221(a) of such Code if the Secretary determines that such failure was due to the anticipation of the credit allowed under this section.

P.L. 116-127, § 7005(a)-(b) (as amended by P.L. 116-260, § 286(b)(5), Div. N, and § 288(d)-(e), Div. N) provides:

SEC. 7005. SPECIAL RULE RELATED TO TAX ON EMPLOYERS.

(a) IN GENERAL.—Any wages required to be paid by reason of the Emergency Paid Sick Leave Act and the Emergency Family and Medical Leave Expansion Act (or, in the case of wages paid after December 31, 2020, and before April 1, 2021, with respect to which a credit is allowed under section 7001 or 7003) shall not be considered wages for purposes of section 3111(a) of the Internal Revenue Code of 1986 or compensation for purposes of section 3221(a) of such Code. Any reference in this subsection to the tax imposed by section 3221(a) of such Code shall be treated as a reference to so much of the tax as is attributable to the rate in effect under section 3111(a) of such Code.

(b) ALLOWANCE OF CREDIT FOR HOSPITAL INSURANCE TAXES.—

(1) IN GENERAL.—The credit allowed by section 7001 and the credit allowed by section 7003 shall each be increased by the amount of the tax imposed by section 3111(b) of the Internal Revenue Code of 1986 and so much of the taxes imposed under section 3221(a) of such Code as are attributable to the rate in effect under section 3111(b) of such Code on qualified sick leave wages, or qualified family leave wages, for which credit is allowed under such section 7001 or 7003 (respectively).

(2) DENIAL OF DOUBLE BENEFIT.—For denial of double benefit with respect to the credit increase under paragraph (1), see sections 7001(e)(1) and 7003(e)(1).

- **1990, Omnibus Budget Reconciliation Act of 1990 (P.L. 101-508)**

P.L. 101-508, § 5125(c)(1)-(2):

Amended Code Sec. 3221(a) by striking "following" and inserting "applicable", and by striking "employer:" and all that follows and inserting "employer. For purposes of the preceding sentence, the term `applicable percentage' means the percentage equal to the sum of the rates of tax in effect under subsections (a) and (b) of section 3111 for the calendar year." **Effective** on 11-5-90. Prior to amendment, Code Sec. 3221(a) read as follows:

(a) TIER 1 TAX.—In addition to other taxes, there is hereby imposed on every employer an excise tax, with respect to having individuals in his employ, equal to the following percentage of compensation paid during any calendar year by such employer for services rendered to such employer:

In the case of compensation received during:	The rate shall be:
1985	7.05
1986 or 1987	7.15
1988 or 1989	7.51
1990 or thereafter	7.65

- **1983, Railroad Retirement Solvency Act of 1983 (P.L. 98-76)**

P.L. 98-76, § 211(b):

Amended Code Sec. 3221(a). **Effective** for compensation paid for services rendered after 12-31-83, and before 1-1-85. Prior to amendment, Code Sec. 3221(a) read as follows:

(a) In addition to other taxes, there is hereby imposed on every employer an excise tax, with respect to having individuals in his employ, equal to 11.75 percent of so much of the compensation paid in any calendar month by such employer for services rendered to him as is, with respect to any employee for any calendar month, not in excess of an amount equal to one-twelfth of the current maximum annual taxable "wages" as defined in section 3121 for any month, except that if an employee is paid compensation by more than one employer for services rendered during any calendar month, the tax imposed by this section shall apply to not more than an amount equal to one-twelfth of the current maximum annual taxable "wages" as defined in section 3121 for any month of the aggregate compensation paid to such employee by all such employers for services rendered during such month, and each employer other than a subordinate unit of a national railway-labor-organization employer shall be liable for that proportion of the tax with respect to such compensation paid by all such employers which the compensation paid by him to the employee for services rendered during such month bears to the total compensation paid by all such employers to such employee for services rendered during such month; and in the event that the

RAILROAD RETIREMENT TAX—EMPLOYERS

compensation so paid by such employers to the employee for services rendered during such month is less than an amount equal to one-twelfth of the current maximum annual taxable "wages" as defined in section 3121 for any month each subordinate unit of a national railway-labor-organization employer shall be liable for such proportion of any additional tax as the compensation paid by such employer to such employee for services rendered during such month bears to the total compensation paid by all such employers to such employee for services rendered during such month. Where compensation for services rendered in a month is paid an employee by two or more employers, one of the employers who has knowledge of such joint employment may, by proper notice to the Secretary, and by agreement with such other employer or employers as to settlement of their respective liabilities under this section and section 3202, elect for the tax imposed by section 3201 and this section to apply to all of the compensation paid by such employer for such month as does not exceed the maximum amount of compensation in respect to which taxes are imposed by such section 3201 and this section; and in such case the liability of such other employer or employers under this section and section 3202 shall be limited to the difference, if any, between the compensation paid by the electing employer and the maximum amount of compensation to which section 3201 and this section apply.

P.L. 98-76, §222(a):

Amended Code Sec. 3221. **Effective** for remuneration paid after 12-31-84. Prior to amendment, Code Sec. 3221(a) read as follows:

(a) In addition to other taxes, there is hereby imposed on every employer an excise tax, with respect to having individuals in his employ, equal to 12.75 percent of so much of the compensation paid in any calendar month by such employer for services rendered to him as is, with respect to any employee for any calendar month, not in excess of an amount equal to one-twelfth of the current maximum annual taxable "wages" as defined in section 3121 for any month, except that if an employee is paid compensation by more than one employer for services rendered during any calendar month, the tax imposed by this section shall apply to not more than an amount equal to one-twelfth of the current maximum annual taxable "wages" as defined in section 3121 for any month of the aggregate compensation paid to such employee by all such employers for services rendered during such month, and each employer other than a subordinate unit of a national railway-labor-organization employer shall be liable for that proportion of the tax with respect to such compensation paid by all such employers which the compensation paid by him to the employee for services rendered during such month bears to the total compensation paid by all such employers to such employee for services rendered during such month; and in the event that the compensation so paid by such employers to the employee for services rendered during such month is less than an amount equal to one-twelfth of the current maximum annual taxable "wages" as defined in section 3121 for any month each subordinate unit of a national railway-labor-organization employer shall be liable for such proportion of any additional tax as the compensation paid by such employer to such employee for services rendered during such month bears to the total compensation paid by all such employers to such employee for services rendered during such month. Where compensation for services rendered in a month is paid an employee by two or more employers, one of the employers who has knowledge of such joint employment may, by proper notice to the Secretary, and by agreement with such other employer or employers as to settlement of their respective liabilities under this section and section 3202, elect for the tax imposed by section 3201 and this section to apply to all of the compensation paid by such employer for such month as does not exceed the maximum amount of compensation in respect to which taxes are imposed by such section 3201 and this section; and in such case the liability of such other employer or employers under this section and section 3202 shall be limited to the difference, if any, between the compensation paid by the electing employer and the maximum amount of compensation to which section 3201 and this section apply.

• 1981, Economic Recovery Tax Act of 1981 (P.L. 97-34)

P.L. 97-34, §741(c):

Amended Code Sec. 3221(a) by striking out "9.5" and inserting "11.75". **Effective** for compensation paid for services rendered after 9-30-81.

• 1976, Tax Reform Act of 1976 (P.L. 94-455)

P.L. 94-455, §1903(a)(9)(A), (d):

Amended the first sentence of Code Sec. 3221(a) by deleting "after September 30, 1973," each place it appeared; by substituting ", except that" for "after September 30, 1973; except that"; by substituting "of the aggregate" for "after September 30, 1973 of the aggregate"; by deleting "of the Internal Revenue Code of 1954" each place it appeared; and by inserting a comma before "the tax imposed." **Effective** with respect to compensation paid for services rendered after 12-31-76.

P.L. 94-455, §1906(b)(13)(G):

Deleted "of the Treasury" in the second sentence of Code Sec. 3221(a). **Effective** 2-1-77.

• 1975 (P.L. 94-93)

P.L. 94-93, §§203 and 207:

Amended Code Sec. 3221(a) by striking out "compensation paid by such employer" and inserting in lieu thereof "compensation paid in any calendar month by such employer". **Effective** for tax years ending on or after 8-9-75, and for tax years ending before 8-9-75, as to which the period for assessment and collection of tax or the filing of a claim for credit or refund has not expired on 8-9-75.

• 1973 (P.L. 93-69)

P.L. 93-69, §102(d), (e):

Amended Code Sec. 3221(a). (The **effective** date is the same as that for Code Sec. 3201. See the historical comment for P.L. 93-69 under Code Sec. 3201.) Prior to amendment, Code Sec. 3221(a) read as follows:

"(a) In addition to other taxes, there is hereby imposed on every employer an excise tax, with respect to having individuals in his employ, equal to—

"(1) $6\frac{1}{4}$ percent of so much of the compensation paid by such employer for services rendered to him after September 30, 1965,

"(2) $6\frac{1}{2}$ percent of so much of the compensation paid by such employer for services rendered to him after December 31, 1965,

"(3) 7 percent of so much of the compensation paid by such employer for services rendered to him after December 31, 1966,

"(4) $7\frac{1}{4}$ percent of so much of the compensation paid by such employer for services rendered to him after December 31, 1967, and

"(5) $7\frac{1}{2}$ percent of so much of the compensation paid by such employer for services rendered to him after December 31, 1968,

as is, with respect to any employee for any calendar month, not in excess of (i) $450, or (ii) an amount equal to one-twelfth of the current maximum annual taxable 'wages' as defined in section 3121 of the Internal Revenue Code of 1954, whichever is greater, for any month after September 30, 1965; except that if an employee is paid compensation after September 30, 1965, by more than one employer for services rendered during any calendar month after September 30, 1965, the tax imposed by this section shall apply to not more than (i) $450, or (ii) an amount equal to one-twelfth of the current maximum annual taxable 'wages' as defined in section 3121 of the Internal Revenue Code of 1954, whichever is greater, for any month after September 30, 1965 of the aggregate compensation paid to such employee by all such employers after September 30, 1965, for services rendered during such month, and each employer other than a subordinate unit of a national railway-labor-organization employer shall be liable for that proportion of the tax with respect to such compensation paid by all such employers which the compensation paid by him after September 30, 1965, to the employee for services rendered during such month bears to the total compensation paid by all such employers after September 30, 1965, to such employee for services rendered during such month; and in the event that the compensation so paid by such employers to the employee for services rendered during such month is less than (i) $450, or (ii) an amount equal to one-twelfth of the current maximum annual taxable 'wages' as defined in section 3121 of the Internal Revenue Code of 1954, whichever is greater, for any month after September 30, 1965, each subordinate unit of a national railway-labor-organization employer shall be liable for such proportion of any additional tax as the compensation paid by such employer after September 30, 1965, to such employee for services rendered during such month bears to the total compensation paid by all such employers after September 30, 1965, to such employee for services rendered during such month. Where compensation for services rendered in a month is paid an employee by two or more employers, one of the employers who has knowledge of such joint employment may, by proper notice to the Secretary of the Treasury, and by agreement with such other employer or employers as to settlement of their respective liabilities under this section and section 3202, elect for the tax imposed by section 3201 and this section to apply to all of the compensation paid by such employer for such month as does not exceed the maximum amount of compensation in respect to which taxes are imposed by such section 3201 and this section; and in such case the liability of such other employer or employers under this section and section 3202 shall be limited to the difference, if any, between the compensation paid by the electing employer and the maximum amount of compensation to which section 3201 and this section apply."

• 1966 (P.L. 89-700)

P.L. 89-700, §302:

Added the last sentence of Code Sec. 3221(a).

P.L. 89-700, §301(v):

Amended Code Sec. 3221(a) by deleting "$400 for any calendar month before the calendar month next following the month in which this provision was amended in 1963, or $450 for any calendar month after the month in which this provision was so amended and before the calendar month next following the calendar month in which this provision was amended in 1965," each place it appears and by substituting "September 30, 1965" for "the month in which this provision was so amended" in (ii) each place it appears. **Effective** 11-1-66.

P.L. 89-700, §301(iii):

Amended Code Sec. 3221(a) by substituting "after September 30, 1965" for "after the month in which this provision was amended in 1959" each place it appears. **Effective** 11-1-66.

• 1966 (P.L. 89-699)

P.L. 89-699, §301(c):

Amended Code Sec. 3221(a) by substituting "7 percent" for "$6\frac{3}{4}$ percent" in subdivision (3), by substituting "$7\frac{1}{4}$ percent" for "7 percent" in subdivision (4), and by substituting "$7\frac{1}{2}$ percent" for "$7\frac{1}{4}$ percent" in subdivision (5). **Effective** 11-1-66.

• 1965 (P.L. 89-212)

P.L. 89-212, §4:

Amended Code Sec. 3221(a) by inserting "and before the calendar month next following the calendar month in which this provision was amended in 1965, or (i) $450, or (ii) an amount equal to one-twelfth of the current maximum annual taxable 'wages' as defined in section 3121 of the Internal Revenue Code of 1954, whichever is greater, for any month after the month in which this provision was so amended" immediately after "or $450 for any calendar month after the month in which this provision was so amended" each place it appears. **Effective** only with respect to calendar months after September 1965.

P.L. 89-212, §5:

Amended Code Sec. 3221(a) by substituting paragraphs (1)-(5) for paragraphs (1) and (2). **Effective** only with respect to compensation paid for services rendered after 9-30-65. Prior to amendment, paragraphs (1) and (2) read as follows:

"(1) $6\frac{3}{4}$ percent of so much of the compensation paid by such employer for services rendered to him after the month in which this provision was amended in 1959, and before January 1, 1962, and

"(2) $7\frac{1}{4}$ percent of so much of the compensation paid by such employer for services rendered to him after December 31, 1961,".

• 1963 (P.L. 88-133)

P.L. 88-133, §202:

Amended Sec. 3221(a) by inserting the following immediately after "$400" each place it appears: "for any calendar month before the calendar month next following

Sec. 3221(a)

the month in which this provision was amended in 1963, or $450 for any calendar month after the month in which this provision was so amended." **Effective** 11-1-63.

- **1958 (P.L. 86-28)**

P.L. 86-28, §201(d):

Changed Sec. 3221 to Sec. 3221(a) and amended it. **Effective**, except as otherwise provided, as of the first day of the calendar month next following the month in which this Act was enacted [May, 1959], and shall apply only with respect to compensation paid after the month of such enactment, for services rendered after such month of enactment. Prior to amendment Sec. 3221 read as follows:

"In addition to other taxes, there is hereby imposed on every employer an excise tax, with respect to having individuals in his employ, equal to 6¼ percent of so much of the compensation paid by such employer after December 31, 1954, for services rendered to him after December 31, 1954, as is, with respect to any employee for any calendar month, not in excess of $350; except that if an employee is paid compensation after December 31, 1954, by more than one employer for services rendered during any calendar month after 1954, the tax imposed by this section shall apply to not more than $350 of the aggregate compensation paid to such employee by all such employers after December 31, 1954, for services rendered during such month, and each employer other than a subordinate unit of a national railway-labor-organization employer shall be liable for that proportion of the tax with respect to such compensation paid by all such employers which the compensation paid by him after December 31, 1954, to the employee for services rendered during such month bears to the total compensation paid by all such employers after December 31, 1954, to such employee for services rendered during such month; and, in the event that the compensation so paid by such employers to the employee for services rendered during such month is less than $350, each subordinate unit of a national railway-labor-organization employer shall be liable for such proportion of any additional tax as the compensation paid by such employer after December 31, 1954, to such employee for services rendered during such month bears to the total compensation paid by all such employers after December 31, 1954, to such employee for services rendered during such month."

- **1954 (P.L. 746, 83rd Cong.)**

P.L. 746, 83rd Cong., §§206(a), 407:

Amended Code § 3221 by substituting $350 for $300 in each place where the former amount now appears. **Effective** 1-1-55.

[Sec. 3221(b)]

(b) TIER 2 TAX.—In addition to other taxes, there is hereby imposed on every employer an excise tax, with respect to having individuals in his employ, equal to the percentage determined under section 3241 for any calendar year of the compensation paid during such calendar year by such employer for services rendered to such employer.

Amendments

- **2014, Tax Technical Corrections Act of 2014 (P.L. 113-295)**

P.L. 113-295, §221(a)(100)(C), Division A:

Amended Code Sec. 3221(b). **Effective** generally 12-19-2014. For a special rule, see Act Sec. 221(b)(2), Division A, below. Prior to amendment, Code Sec. 3221(b) read as follows:

(b) TIER 2 TAX.—

(1) IN GENERAL.—In addition to other taxes, there is hereby imposed on every employer an excise tax, with respect to having individuals in his employ, equal to the applicable percentage of the compensation paid during any calendar year by such employer for services rendered to such employer.

(2) APPLICABLE PERCENTAGE.—For purposes of paragraph (1), the term "applicable percentage" means—

(A) 15.6 percent in the case of compensation paid during 2002,

(B) 14.2 percent in the case of compensation paid during 2003, and

(C) in the case of compensation paid during any calendar year after 2003, the percentage determined under section 3241 for such calendar year.

P.L. 113-295, §221(b)(2), Division A, provides:

(2) SAVINGS PROVISION.—If—

(A) any provision amended or repealed by the amendments made by this section applied to—

(i) any transaction occurring before the date of the enactment of this Act,

(ii) any property acquired before such date of enactment, or

(iii) any item of income, loss, deduction, or credit taken into account before such date of enactment, and

(B) the treatment of such transaction, property, or item under such provision would (without regard to the amendments or repeals made by this section) affect the liability for tax for periods ending after date of enactment, nothing in the amendments or repeals made by this section shall be construed to affect the treatment of such transaction, property, or item for purposes of determining liability for tax for periods ending after such date of enactment.

- **2001, Railroad Retirement and Survivors' Improvement Act of 2001 (P.L. 107-90)**

P.L. 107-90, §204(a):

Amended Code Sec. 3221(b). **Effective** for calendar years beginning after 12-31-2001. Prior to amendment, Code Sec. 3221(b) read as follows:

(b) TIER 2 TAX.—In addition to other taxes, there is hereby imposed on every employer an excise tax, with respect to having individuals in his employ, equal to 16.10 percent of the compensation paid during any calendar year by such employer for services rendered to such employer.

- **1987, Revenue Act of 1987 (P.L. 100-203)**

P.L. 100-203, §9032(a):

Amended Code Sec. 3221(b). **Effective** with respect to compensation paid after 12-31-87. Prior to amendment, Code Sec. 3221(b) read as follows:

(b) TIER 2 TAX.—In addition to other taxes, there is hereby imposed on every employer an excise tax, with respect to having individuals in his employ, equal to the following percentage of compensation paid during any calendar year by such employer for services rendered to such employer:

In the case of compensation paid during:	The rate shall be:
1985	13.75
1986 or thereafter	14.75

- **1983, Railroad Retirement Solvency Act of 1983 (P.L. 98-76)**

P.L. 98-76, §222(a):

Amended Code Sec. 3221(b). **Effective** for remuneration paid after 1984. Prior to amendment, Code Sec. 3221(b) read as follows:

(b) The rate of tax imposed by subsection (a) shall be increased by the rate of tax imposed with respect to wages by section 3111(a) plus the rate imposed by section 3111(b).

- **1976, Tax Reform Act of 1976 (P.L. 94-455)**

P.L. 94-455, §1903(a)(9)(B), (d):

Amended Code Sec. 3221(b). **Effective** with respect to compensation paid for services rendered after 12-31-76. Prior to amendment, Code Sec. 3221(b) read as follows:

(b) The rate of tax imposed by subsection (a) shall be increased, with respect to compensation paid for services rendered after September 30, 1973, by the rate of tax imposed with respect to wages by section 3111(a), of the Internal Revenue Code of 1954 plus the rate imposed by section 3111(b) of such Code.

- **1973 (P.L. 93-69)**

P.L. 93-69, §102(f):

Amended Code Sec. 3221(b). (The **effective** date is the same as that for Code Sec. 3201. See the historical comment for P.L. 93-69 under Code Sec. 3201.) Prior to amendment, Code Sec. 3221(b) read as follows:

"(b) The rate of tax imposed by subsection (a) shall be increased, with respect to compensation paid for services rendered after September 30, 1965, by a number of percentage points (including fractional points) equal at any given time to the number of percentage points (including fractional points) by which the rate of the tax imposed with respect to wages by section 3111(a) plus the rate imposed by section 3111(b) at such time exceeds 2¾ percent (the rate provided by paragraph (2) of section 3111 as amended by the Social Security Amendments of 1956)."

- **1966 (P.L. 89-700)**

P.L. 89-700, §301(vi):

Amended Code Sec. 3221(b) by substituting "after September 30, 1965" for "after December 31, 1964". **Effective** 11-1-66.

- **1965, Social Security Amendments of 1965 (P.L. 89-97)**

P.L. 89-97, §§105(b), 111(c):

Amended Sec. 3221(b) by striking out "the rate of the tax imposed with respect to wages by section 3111 at such time exceeds the rate provided by paragraph (2) of such section 3111 as amended by the Social Security Amendments of 1956" and inserting in lieu thereof "the rate of the tax imposed with respect to wages by section 3111(a) plus the rate imposed by section 3111(b) at such time exceeds 2¾ percent (the rate provided by paragraph (2) of section 3111 as amended by the Social Security Amendments of 1956)." **Effective** with respect to compensation paid for services rendered after 12-31-65.

- **1959 (P.L. 86-28)**

P.L. 86-28, §201(d):

Added Sec. 3221(b). **Effective**, except as otherwise provided, as of the first day of the calendar month next following the month in which this Act was enacted [May, 1959], and shall apply only with respect to compensation paid after the month of such enactment, for services rendered after such month of enactment.

RAILROAD RETIREMENT TAX—EMPLOYERS

Amendments

• **2018, Tax Technical Corrections Act of 2018 (P.L. 115-141)**

P.L. 115-141, §401(b)(36), Div. U:

Amended Code Sec. 3221 by striking subsection (c) and by redesignating subsection (d) as subsection (c). **Effective** 3-23-2018. For a special rule, see Act Sec. 401(e), Div. U, below. Prior to being stricken, Code Sec. 3221(c) read as follows:

(c) SPECIAL RATE FOR CERTAIN INDIVIDUALS HIRED IN 2010.—

(1) IN GENERAL.—In the case of compensation paid by a qualified employer during the period beginning on the day after the date of the enactment of this subsection and ending on December 31, 2010, with respect to having a qualified individual in the employer's employ for services rendered to such qualified employer, the applicable percentage under subsection (a) shall be equal to the rate of tax in effect under section 3111(b) for the calendar year.

(2) QUALIFIED EMPLOYER.—The term "qualified employer" means any employer other than the United States, any State, or any political subdivision thereof, or any instrumentality of the foregoing.

(3) QUALIFIED INDIVIDUAL.—For purposes of this subsection, the term "qualified individual" means any individual who—

(A) begins employment with a qualified employer after February 3, 2010, and before January 1, 2011,

(B) certifies by signed affidavit, under penalties of perjury, that such individual has not been employed for more than 40 hours during the 60-day period ending on the date such individual begins such employment,

(C) is not employed by the qualified employer to replace another employee of such employer unless such other employee separated from employment voluntarily or for cause, and

(D) is not an individual described in section 51(i)(1) (applied by substituting "qualified employer" for "taxpayer" each place it appears).

(4) ELECTION.—A qualified employer may elect to have this subsection not apply. Such election shall be made in such manner as the Secretary may require.

[Sec. 3221(c)]

(c) CROSS REFERENCE.—

For application of different contribution bases with respect to the taxes imposed by subsections (a) and (b), see section 3231(e)(2).

Amendments

• **2018, Tax Technical Corrections Act of 2018 (P.L. 115-141)**

P.L. 115-141, §401(b)(36), Div. U:

Amended Code Sec. 3221 by redesignating subsection (d) as subsection (c). **Effective** 3-23-2018. For a special rule, see Act Sec. 401(e), Div. U, below.

P.L. 115-141, §401(e), Div. U, provides:

(e) GENERAL SAVINGS PROVISION WITH RESPECT TO DEADWOOD PROVISIONS.—If—

(1) any provision amended or repealed by the amendments made by subsection (b) or (d) applied to—

(A) any transaction occurring before the date of the enactment of this Act,

(B) any property acquired before such date of enactment, or

(C) any item of income, loss, deduction, or credit taken into account before such date of enactment, and

(2) the treatment of such transaction, property, or item under such provision would (without regard to the amendments or repeals made by such subsection) affect the liability for tax for periods ending after such date of enactment,

nothing in the amendments or repeals made by this section shall be construed to affect the treatment of such transaction, property, or item for purposes of determining liability for tax for periods ending after such date of enactment.

[Sec. 3221(c)—Stricken]

Amendments

• **2001, Railroad Retirement and Survivors' Improvement Act of 2001 (P.L. 107-90)**

P.L. 107-90, §203(b):

Amended Code Sec. 3221 by striking subsection (c). **Effective** for calendar years beginning after 12-31-2001. Prior to being stricken, Code Sec. 3221(c) read as follows:

(c) In addition to other taxes, there is hereby imposed on every employer an excise tax, with respect to having individuals in his employ, for each man-hour for which compensation is paid by such employer for services rendered to him during any calendar quarter, at such rate as will make available sufficient funds to meet the obligation to pay supplemental annuities at the level provided under section 3(j) of the Railroad Retirement Act of 1937 as in effect on December 31, 1974 and administrative expenses in connection therewith. For the purpose of this subsection, the Railroad Retirement Board is directed to determine what rate is required for each calendar quarter. The Railroad Retirement Board shall make the determinations provided for not later than fifteen days before each calendar quarter. As soon as practicable after each determination of the rate, as provided in this subsection, the Railroad Retirement Board shall publish a notice in the Federal Register, and shall advise all employers, employee representatives, and the Secretary, of the rate so determined. With respect to daily, weekly, or monthly rates of compensation such tax shall apply to the number of hours comprehended in the rate together with the number of overtime hours for which compensation in addition to the daily, weekly, or monthly rate is paid. With respect to compensation paid on a mileage or piecework basis such tax shall apply to the number of hours constituting the hourly equivalent of the compensation paid.

Each employer of employees whose supplemental annuities are reduced pursuant to section 3(j)(2) of the Railroad Retirement Act of 1937 or section 2(h)(2) of the Railroad Retirement Act of 1974 shall be allowed as a credit against the tax imposed by this subsection an amount equivalent in each month to the aggregate amount of reductions in supplemental annuities accruing in such month to employees of such

[Sec. 3221(c)—Stricken]

(5) SPECIAL RULE FOR FIRST CALENDAR QUARTER OF 2010.—

(A) NONAPPLICATION OF EXEMPTION DURING FIRST QUARTER.—Paragraph (1) shall not apply with respect to compensation paid during the first calendar quarter of 2010.

(B) CREDITING OF FIRST QUARTER EXEMPTION DURING SECOND QUARTER.—The amount by which the tax imposed under subsection (a) would (but for subparagraph (A)) have been reduced with respect to compensation paid by a qualified employer during the first calendar quarter of 2010 shall be treated as a payment against the tax imposed under subsection (a) with respect to the qualified employer for the second calendar quarter of 2010 which is made on the date that such tax is due.

P.L. 115-141, §401(e), Div. U, provides:

(e) GENERAL SAVINGS PROVISION WITH RESPECT TO DEADWOOD PROVISIONS.—If—

(1) any provision amended or repealed by the amendments made by subsection (b) or (d) applied to—

(A) any transaction occurring before the date of the enactment of this Act,

(B) any property acquired before such date of enactment, or

(C) any item of income, loss, deduction, or credit taken into account before such date of enactment, and

(2) the treatment of such transaction, property, or item under such provision would (without regard to the amendments or repeals made by such subsection) affect the liability for tax for periods ending after such date of enactment,

nothing in the amendments or repeals made by this section shall be construed to affect the treatment of such transaction, property, or item for purposes of determining liability for tax for periods ending after such date of enactment.

• **2010, Hiring Incentives to Restore Employment Act (P.L. 111-147)**

P.L. 111-147, §101(d)(1):

Amended Code Sec. 3221 by redesignating subsection (c) as subsection (d) and by inserting after subsection (b) a new subsection (c). **Effective** for compensation paid after 3-18-2010.

• **2010, Hiring Incentives to Restore Employment Act (P.L. 111-147)**

P.L. 111-147, §101(d)(1):

Amended Code Sec. 3221 by redesignating subsection (c) as subsection (d). **Effective** for compensation paid after 3-18-2010.

• **2001, Railroad Retirement and Survivors' Improvement Act of 2001 (P.L. 107-90)**

P.L. 107-90, §203(b):

Amended Code Sec. 3221 by striking subsections (c) and (d) and by redesignating subsection (e) as subsection (c). **Effective** for calendar years beginning after 12-31-2001.

• **1983, Railroad Retirement Solvency Act of 1983 (P.L. 98-76)**

P.L. 98-76, §222(b):

Added Code Sec. 3221(e). **Effective** for remuneration paid after 12-31-84.

employer. If the credit so allowed to such an employer for any month exceeds the tax liability of such employer accruing under this subsection in such month, the excess may be carried forward for credit against such taxes accruing in subsequent months but the total credit allowed by this paragraph to an employer shall not exceed the total of the taxes on such employer imposed by this subsection. At the end of each calendar quarter the Railroad Retirement Board shall certify to the Secretary with respect to each such employer the amount of credit accruing to such employer under this paragraph during such quarter and shall notify such employer as to the amount so certified.

• **1976, Tax Reform Act of 1976 (P.L. 94-455)**

P.L. 94-455, §§1903(a)(9)(C), (d), 1906(b)(13)(G), (d):

Amended Code Sec. 3221(c) by deleting "(1) at the rate of 2 cents for the period beginning November 1, 1966, and ending March 31, 1970, and (2) commencing April 1, 1970,"; and by deleting "commencing with the quarter beginning April 1, 1970." **Effective** with respect to compensation paid for services rendered after 12-31-76.

P.L. 94-455, §1906(b)(13)(G):

Deleted "of the Treasury" each place it appeared in Code Sec. 3221(c). **Effective** 2-1-77.

• **1974 (P.L. 93-445)**

P.L. 93-445, §501(a):

Amended Code Sec. 3221(c) by amending the first sentence of the first paragraph and by adding "or section 2(h)(2) of the Railroad Retirement Act of 1974" in the first sentence of the second paragraph. **Effective** 1-1-75, and only with respect to compensation paid for services rendered on or after that date. Prior to amendment, the first sentence of the first paragraph of Code Sec. 3221(c) read as follows:

In addition to other taxes, there is hereby imposed on every employer an excise tax, with respect to having individuals in his employ, for each man-hour for which

RAILROAD RETIREMENT TAX—GENERAL PROVISIONS

compensation is paid by such employer for services rendered to him during any calendar quarter, (1) at the rate of 2 cents for the period beginning November 1, 1966, and ending March 31, 1970, and (2) commencing April 1, 1970, at such rate as will make available for appropriation to the Railroad Retirement Supplemental Account provided for in section 15(b) of the Railroad Retirement Act of 1937 sufficient funds to meet the obligation to pay supplemental annuities under section 3(j) of such Act and administrative expenses in connection therewith.

In addition to other taxes, there is hereby imposed on every employer an excise tax, with respect to having individuals in his employ, equal to 2 cents for each man-hour, for which compensation is paid.

- **1966 (P.L. 89-699)**

P.L. 89-699, §301(e):

Added Code Sec. 3221(c). **Effective** with respect to man-hours, for sixty months beginning with November 1966, for which compensation is paid.

- **1969 (P.L. 91-215)**

P.L. 91-215, §5(a):

Amended the first sentence of Code Sec. 3221(c). **Effective** 3-18-70. Prior to amendment, the first sentence read as follows:

[Sec. 3221(d)—Stricken]

Amendments

- **2001, Railroad Retirement and Survivors' Improvement Act of 2001 (P.L. 107-90)**

P.L. 107-90, §203(b):

Amended Code Sec. 3221 by striking subsection (d). **Effective** for calendar years beginning after 12-31-2001. Prior to being stricken, Code Sec. 3221(d) read as follows:

(d) Notwithstanding the provisions of subsection (c) of this section, the tax imposed by such subsection (c) shall not apply to an employer with respect to employees who are covered by a supplemental pension plan which is established pursuant to an agreement reached through collective bargaining between the employer and employees. There is hereby imposed on every such employer an excise tax equal to the amount of the supplemental annuity paid to each such employee under section 2(b) of the Railroad Retirement Act of 1974, plus a percentage thereof determined by the Railroad Retirement Board to be sufficient to cover the administrative costs attributable to such payments under section 2(b) of such Act.

- **1974 (P.L. 93-445)**

P.L. 93-445, §501(b):

Amended Code Sec. 3221(d) by substituting "section 2(b) of the Railroad Retirement Act of 1974" for "section 3(j) of the Railroad Retirement Act of 1937" and by substituting "section 2(b) of such Act" for "section 3(j) of such Act". **Effective** 1-1-75, and only with respect to compensation paid for services rendered on or after that date.

- **1969 (P.L. 91-215)**

P.L. 91-215, §5(b):

Added Code Sec. 3221(d). **Effective** for (1) supplemental annuities paid on or after 4-1-70, and (2) man-hours with respect to which compensation is paid for services rendered to such employer on or after 4-1-70. Also added Code Sec. 3221(c). **Effective** with respect to man-hours, for sixty months beginning with November 1966, for which compensation is paid.

Subchapter D—General Provisions

Sec. 3231.   Definitions.
Sec. 3232.   Court jurisdiction.
Sec. 3233.   Short title.

[Sec. 3231]

SEC. 3231. DEFINITIONS.

[Sec. 3231(a)]

(a) EMPLOYER.—For purposes of this chapter, the term "employer" means any carrier (as defined in subsection (g)), and any company which is directly or indirectly owned or controlled by one or more such carriers or under common control therewith, and which operates any equipment or facility or performs any service (except trucking service, casual service, and the casual operation of equipment or facilities) in connection with the transportation of passengers or property by railroad, or the receipt, delivery, elevation, transfer in transit, refrigeration or icing, storage, or handling of property transported by railroad, and any receiver, trustee, or other individual or body, judicial or otherwise, when in the possession of the property or operating all or any part of the business of any such employer; except that the term "employer" shall not include any street, interurban, or suburban electric railway, unless such railway is operating as a part of a general steamrailroad system of transportation, but shall not exclude any part of the general steamrailroad system of transportation now or hereafter operated by any other motive power. The Surface Transportation Board is hereby authorized and directed upon request of the Secretary, or upon complaint of any party interested, to determine after hearing whether any line operated by electric power falls within the terms of this exception. The term "employer" shall also include railroad associations, traffic associations, tariff bureaus, demurrage bureaus, weighing and inspection bureaus, collection agencies and other associations, bureaus, agencies, or organizations controlled and maintained wholly or principally by two or more employers as hereinbefore defined and engaged in the performance of services in connection with or incidental to railroad transportation; and railway labor organizations, national in scope, which have been or may be organized in accordance with the provisions of the Railway Labor Act, as amended (45 U. S. C., chapter 8), and their State and National legislative committees and their general committees and their insurance departments and their local lodges and divisions, established pursuant to the constitutions and bylaws of such organizations. The term "employer" shall not include any company by reason of its being engaged in the mining of coal, the supplying of coal to an employer where delivery is not beyond the mine tipple, and the operation of equipment or facilities therefor, or in any of such activities.

Amendments

- **1996, Small Business Job Protection Act of 1996 (P.L. 104-188)**

P.L. 104-88, §304(d)(1):

Amended Code Sec. 3231(a) by striking "Interstate Commerce Commission" and inserting in lieu thereof "Surface Transportation Board". **Effective** 1-1-96.

- **1976, Tax Reform Act of 1976 (P.L. 94-455)**

P.L. 94-455, §1903(a)(10)(A):

Deleted "44 Stat. 577;" in Code Sec. 3231(a). **Effective** with respect to compensation paid for services rendered after 12-31-76.

P.L. 94-455, §1906(b)(13)(A):

Amended 1954 Code by substituting "Secretary" for "Secretary or his delegate" each place it appeared. **Effective** 2-1-77.

[Sec. 3231(b)]

(b) EMPLOYEE.—For purposes of this chapter, the term "employee" means any individual in the service of one or more employers for compensation. The term "employee" includes an officer of an employer. The term "employee" shall not include any individual while such individual is engaged in the physical operations consisting of the mining of coal, the preparation of coal, the handling (other than movement by rail with standard railroad locomotives) of coal not beyond the mine tipple, or the loading of coal at the tipple.

Amendments

- **2014, Tax Technical Corrections Act of 2014 (P.L. 113-295)**

P.L. 113-295, §221(a)(100)(D)(i)-(ii), Division A:

Amended Code Sec. 3231(b) by striking "compensation; except" and all that follows in the first sentence and inserting "compensation.", and by striking the second sentence. **Effective** generally 12-19-2014. For a special rule, see Act Sec. 221(b)(2), Division A, below. Prior to amendment, Code Sec. 3231(b) read as follows:

(b) EMPLOYEE.—For purposes of this chapter, the term "employee" means any individual in the service of one or more employers for compensation; except that the term "employee" shall include an employee of a local lodge or division defined as an employer in subsection (a) only if he was in the service of or in the employment relation to a carrier on or after August 29, 1935. An individual shall be deemed to have been in the employment relation to a carrier on August 29, 1935, if—

(1) he was on that date on leave of absence from his employment, expressly granted to him by the carrier by whom he was employed, or by a duly authorized representative of such carrier, and the grant of such leave of absence was established to the satisfaction of the Railroad Retirement Board before July 1947; or

(2) he was in the service of a carrier after August 29, 1935, and before January 1946 in each of 6 calendar months, whether or not consecutive; or

(3) before August 29, 1935, he did not retire and was not retired or discharged from the service of the last carrier by whom he was employed or its corporate or operating successor, but—

RAILROAD RETIREMENT TAX—GENERAL PROVISIONS

(A) solely by reason of his physical or mental disability he ceased before August 29, 1935, to be in the service of such carrier and thereafter remained continuously disabled until he attained age 65 or until August 1945, or

(B) solely for such last stated reason a carrier by whom he was employed before August 29, 1935, or a carrier who is its successor did not on or after August 29, 1935, and before August 1945 call him to return to service, or

(C) if he was so called he was solely for such reason unable to render service in 6 calendar months as provided in paragraph (2); or

(4) he was on August 29, 1935, absent from the service of a carrier by reason of a discharge which, within 1 year after the effective date thereof, was protested, to an appropriate labor representative or to the carrier, as wrongful, and which was followed within 10 years of the effective date thereof by his reinstatement in good faith to his former service with all his seniority rights;

except that an individual shall not be deemed to have been on August 29, 1935, in the employment relation to a carrier if before that date he was granted a pension or gratuity on the basis of which a pension was awarded to him pursuant to section 6 of the Railroad Retirement Act of 1937 (45 U. S. C. 228(f), or if during the last payroll period before August 29, 1935, in which he rendered service to a carrier he was not in the service of an employer, in accordance with subsection (d), with respect to any service in such payroll period, or if he could have been in the employment relation to an employer only by reason of his having been, either before or after August 29, 1935, in the service of a local lodge or division defined as an employer in subsection (a). The term "employee" includes an officer of an employer. The term "employee" shall not include any individual while such individual is engaged in the physical operations consisting of the mining of coal, the preparation of coal, the handling (other than movement by rail with standard railroad locomotives) of coal not beyond the mine tipple, or the loading of coal at the tipple.

P.L. 113-295, §221(b)(2), Division A, provides:

(2) SAVINGS PROVISION.—If—

(A) any provision amended or repealed by the amendments made by this section applied to—

(i) any transaction occurring before the date of the enactment of this Act,

(ii) any property acquired before such date of enactment, or

(iii) any item of income, loss, deduction, or credit taken into account before such date of enactment, and

(B) the treatment of such transaction, property, or item under such provision would (without regard to the amendments or repeals made by this section) affect the liability for tax for periods ending after date of enactment, nothing in the amendments or repeals made by this section shall be construed to affect the treatment of such transaction, property, or item for purposes of determining liability for tax for periods ending after such date of enactment.

• **1976, Tax Reform Act of 1976 (P.L. 94-455)**

P.L. 94-455, §1903(a)(10)(B), (d):

Deleted "50 Stat. 312;" in Code Sec. 3231(b). **Effective** with respect to compensation paid for services rendered after 12-31-76.

[Sec. 3231(c)]

(c) EMPLOYEE REPRESENTATIVE.—For purposes of this chapter, the term "employee representative" means any officer or official representative of a railway labor organization other than a labor organization included in the term "employer" as defined in subsection (a), who before or after June 29, 1937, was in the service of an employer as defined in subsection (a) and who is duly authorized and designated to represent employees in accordance with the Railway Labor Act (45 U. S. C., chapter 8), as amended, and any individual who is regularly assigned to or regularly employed by such officer or official representative in connection with the duties of his office.

Amendments

• **1976, Tax Reform Act of 1976 (P.L. 94-455)**

P.L. 94-455, §1903(a)(10)(C), (d):

Deleted "44 Stat. 577;" in Code Sec. 3231(c). **Effective** with respect to compensation paid for services rendered after 12-31-76.

[Sec. 3231(d)]

(d) SERVICE.—For purposes of this chapter, an individual is in the service of an employer whether his service is rendered within or without the United States, if—

(1) he is subject to the continuing authority of the employer to supervise and direct the manner of rendition of his service, or he is rendering professional or technical services and is integrated into the staff of the employer, or he is rendering, on the property used in the employer's operations, other personal services the rendition of which is integrated into the employer's operations, and

(2) he renders such service for compensation;

except that an individual shall be deemed to be in the service of an employer, other than a local lodge or division or a general committee of a railway-labor-organization employer, not conducting the principal part of its business in the United States, only when he is rendering service to it in the United States; and an individual shall be deemed to be in the service of such a local lodge or division only if—

(3) all, or substantially all, the individuals constituting its membership are employees of an employer conducting the principal part of its business in the United States; or

(4) the headquarters of such local lodge or division is located in the United States;

and an individual shall be deemed to be in the service of such a general committee only if—

(5) he is representing a local lodge or division described in paragraph (3) or (4) immediately above; or

(6) all, or substantially all, the individuals represented by it are employees of an employer conducting the principal part of its business in the United States; or

(7) he acts in the capacity of a general chairman or an assistant general chairman of a general committee which represents individuals rendering service in the United States to an employer, but in such case if his office or headquarters is not located in the United States and the individuals represented by such general committee are employees of an employer not conducting the principal part of its business in the United States, only such proportion of the remuneration for such service shall be regarded as compensation as the proportion which the mileage in the United States under the jurisdiction of such general committee bears to the total mileage under its jurisdiction, unless such mileage formula is inapplicable, in which case such other formula as the Railroad Retirement Board may have prescribed pursuant to section 1(c) of the Railroad Retirement Act of 1937 (45 U. S. C. 228(a) shall be applicable, and if the application of such mileage formula, or such other formula as the Board may prescribe, would result in the compensation of the individual being less than 10 percent of his remuneration for such service, no part of such remuneration shall be regarded as compensation;

Provided however, that an individual not a citizen or resident of the United States shall not be deemed to be in the service of an employer when rendering service outside the United States to an employer who is required under the laws applicable in the place where the service is rendered to employ therein, in whole or in part, citizens or residents thereof; and the laws applicable on August 29, 1935, in the place where the service is rendered shall be deemed to have been applicable there at all times prior to that date.

Amendments

• **1976, Tax Reform Act of 1976 (P.L. 94-455)**

P.L. 94-455, §1903(a)(10)(D), (d):

Deleted "50 Stat. 308;" in Code Sec. 3231(d)(7). **Effective** with respect to compensation paid for services rendered after 12-31-76.

[Sec. 3231(e)]

(e) COMPENSATION.—For purposes of this chapter—

(1) The term "compensation" means any form of money remuneration paid to an individual for services rendered as an employee to one or more employers. Such term does not include (i) the amount of any payment (including any amount paid by an employer for insurance or annuities, or into a fund, to provide for any such payment) made to, or on behalf of, an employee or any of his dependents under a plan or system established by an employer which makes provision for his employees generally (or for his employees generally and their dependents) or for a class or classes of his employees (or for a class or classes of his employees and their dependents), on account of sickness or accident

disability or medical or hospitalization expenses in connection with sickness or accident disability or death, except that this clause does not apply to a payment for group-term life insurance to the extent that such payment is includible in the gross income of the employee, (ii) tips (except as is provided under paragraph (3)), (iii) an amount paid specifically—either as an advance, as reimbursement or allowance—for traveling or other bona fide and necessary expenses incurred or reasonably expected to be incurred in the business of the employer provided any such payment is identified by the employer either by a separate payment or by specifically indicating the separate amounts where both wages and expense reimbursement or allowance are combined in a single payment. Such term does not include remuneration for service which is performed by a nonresident alien individual for the period he is temporarily present in the United States as a nonimmigrant under subparagraph (F), (J), (M), or (Q) of section 101(a)(15) of the Immigration and Nationality Act, as amended, and which is performed to carry out the purpose specified in subparagraph (F), (J), (M), or (Q), as the case may be. For the purpose of determining the amount of taxes under sections 3201 and 3221, compensation earned in the service of a local lodge or division of a railway-labor-organization employer shall be disregarded with respect to any calendar month if the amount thereof is less than $25. Compensation for service as a delegate to a national or international convention of a railway labor organization defined as an "employer" in subsection (a) of this section shall be disregarded for purposes of determining the amount of taxes due pursuant to this chapter if the individual rendering such service has not previously rendered service, other than as such a delegate, which may be included in his "years of service" for purposes of the Railroad Retirement Act, or (iv) any remuneration which would not (if chapter 21 applied to such remuneration) be treated as wages (as defined in section 3121(a)) by reason of section 3121(a)(5). Nothing in the regulations prescribed for purposes of chapter 24 (relating to wage withholding) which provides an exclusion from "wages" as used in such chapter shall be construed to require a similar exclusion from "compensation" in regulations prescribed for purposes of this chapter.

(2) APPLICATION OF CONTRIBUTION BASES.—

(A) COMPENSATION IN EXCESS OF APPLICABLE BASE EXCLUDED.—

(i) IN GENERAL.—The term "compensation" does not include that part of remuneration paid during any calendar year to an individual by an employer after remuneration equal to the applicable base has been paid during such calendar year to such individual by such employer for services rendered as an employee to such employer.

(ii) REMUNERATION NOT TREATED AS COMPENSATION EXCLUDED.—There shall not be taken into account under clause (i) remuneration which (without regard to clause (i)) is not treated as compensation under this subsection.

(iii) HOSPITAL INSURANCE TAXES.—Clause (i) shall not apply to—

(I) so much of the rate applicable under section 3201(a) or 3221(a) as does not exceed the rate of tax in effect under section 3101(b), and

(II) so much of the rate applicable under section 3211(a) as does not exceed the rate of tax in effect under section 1401(b).

(B) APPLICABLE BASE.—

(i) TIER 1 TAXES.—Except as provided in clause (ii), the term "applicable base" means for any calendar year the contribution and benefit base determined under section 230 of the Social Security Act for such calendar year.

(ii) TIER 2 TAXES, ETC.—For purposes of—

(I) the taxes imposed by sections 3201(b), 3211(b), and 3221(b), and

(II) computing average monthly compensation under section 3(j) of the Railroad Retirement Act of 1974 (except with respect to annuity amounts determined under subsection (a) or (f)(3) of section 3 of such Act),

clause (2) of the first sentence, and the second sentence, of subsection (c) of section 230 of the Social Security Act shall be disregarded.

(C) SUCCESSOR EMPLOYERS.—For purposes of this paragraph, the second sentence of section 3121(a)(1) (relating to successor employers) shall apply, except that—

(i) the term "services" shall be substituted for "employment" each place it appears,

(ii) the term "compensation" shall be substituted for "remuneration (other than remuneration referred to in the succeeding paragraphs of this subsection)" each place it appears, and

(iii) the terms "employer", "services", and "compensation" shall have the meanings given such terms by this section.

(3) Solely for purposes of the taxes imposed by section 3201 and other provisions of this chapter insofar as they relate to such taxes, the term "compensation" also includes cash tips received by an employee in any calendar month in the course of his employment by an employer unless the amount of such cash tips is less than $20.

(4)(A) For purposes of applying sections 3201(a), 3211(a), and 3221(a), in the case of payments made to an employee or any of his dependents on account of sickness or accident disability, clause (i) of the second sentence of paragraph (1) shall exclude from the term "compensation" only—

(i) payments which are received under a workmen's compensation law, and

(ii) benefits received under the Railroad Retirement Act of 1974.

(B) Notwithstanding any other provision of law, for purposes of the sections specified in subparagraph (A), the term "compensation" shall include benefits paid under section 2(a) of the Railroad Unemployment Insurance Act for days of sickness, except to the extent that such sickness (as determined in accordance with standards prescribed by the Railroad Retirement Board) is the result of on-the-job injury.

(C) Under regulations prescribed by the Secretary, subparagraphs (A) and (B) shall not apply to payments made after the expiration of a 6-month period comparable to the 6-month period described in section 3121(a)(4).

(D) Except as otherwise provided in regulations prescribed by the Secretary, any third party which makes a payment included in compensation solely by reason of subparagraph (A) or (B) shall be treated for purposes of this chapter as the employer with respect to such compensation.

(5) The term "compensation" shall not include any benefit provided to or on behalf of an employee if at the time such benefit is provided it is reasonable to believe that the employee will be able to exclude such benefit from income under section 74(c), 108(f)(4), 117, or 132.

(6) The term "compensation" shall not include any payment made, or benefit furnished, to or for the benefit of an employee if at the time of such payment or such furnishing it is reasonable to believe that the employee will be able to exclude such payment or benefit from income under section 127.

(7) [Stricken.]

(8) TREATMENT OF CERTAIN DEFERRED COMPENSATION AND SALARY REDUCTION ARRANGEMENTS.—

(A) CERTAIN EMPLOYER CONTRIBUTIONS TREATED AS COMPENSATION.—Nothing in any paragraph of this subsection (other than paragraph (2)) shall exclude from the term "compensation" any amount described in subparagraph (A) or (B) of section 3121(v)(1).

(B) TREATMENT OF CERTAIN NONQUALIFIED DEFERRED COMPENSATION.—The rules of section 3121(v)(2) which apply for purposes of chapter 21 shall also apply for purposes of this chapter.

RAILROAD RETIREMENT TAX—GENERAL PROVISIONS

(9) MEALS AND LODGING.—The term "compensation" shall not include the value of meals or lodging furnished by or on behalf of the employer if at the time of such furnishing it is reasonable to believe that the employee will be able to exclude such items from income under section 119.

(10) ARCHER MSA CONTRIBUTIONS.—The term "compensation" shall not include any payment made to or for the benefit of an employee if at the time of such payment it is reasonable to believe that the employee will be able to exclude such payment from income under section 106(b).

(11) HEALTH SAVINGS ACCOUNT CONTRIBUTIONS.—The term "compensation" shall not include any payment made to or for the benefit of an employee if at the time of such payment it is reasonable to believe that the employee will be able to exclude such payment from income under section 106(d).

(12) QUALIFIED STOCK OPTIONS.—The term "compensation" shall not include any remuneration on account of—

(A) a transfer of a share of stock to any individual pursuant to an exercise of an incentive stock option (as defined in section 422(b)) or under an employee stock purchase plan (as defined in section 423(b)), or

(B) any disposition by the individual of such stock.

Amendments

• **2014, Tax Technical Corrections Act of 2014 (P.L. 113-295)**

P.L. 113-295, § 221(a)(19)(B)(v), Division A:

Amended Code Sec. 3231(e) by striking paragraph (7). **Effective** generally 12-19-2014. For a special rule, see Act Sec. 221(b)(2), Division A, below. Prior to being stricken, Code Sec. 3231(e)(7) read as follows:

(7) The term "compensation" shall not include any contribution, payment, or service provided by an employer which may be excluded from the gross income of an employee, his spouse, or his dependents, under the provisions of section 120 (relating to amounts received under qualified group legal services plans).

P.L. 113-295, § 221(b)(2), Division A, provides:

(2) SAVINGS PROVISION.—If—

(A) any provision amended or repealed by the amendments made by this section applied to—

(i) any transaction occurring before the date of the enactment of this Act,

(ii) any property acquired before such date of enactment, or

(iii) any item of income, loss, deduction, or credit taken into account before such date of enactment, and

(B) the treatment of such transaction, property, or item under such provision would (without regard to the amendments or repeals made by this section) affect the liability for tax for periods ending after date of enactment, nothing in the amendments or repeals made by this section shall be construed to affect the treatment of such transaction, property, or item for purposes of determining liability for tax for periods ending after such date of enactment.

• **2004, American Jobs Creation Act of 2004 (P.L. 108-357)**

P.L. 108-357, § 251(a)(2):

Amended Code Sec. 3231(e) by adding at the end a new paragraph (12). **Effective** for stock acquired pursuant to options exercised after 10-22-2004.

P.L. 108-357, § 320(b)(2):

Amended Code Sec. 3231(e)(5) by inserting "108(f)(4)," after "74(c),". **Effective** for amounts received by an individual in tax years beginning after 12-31-2003.

• **2003, Medicare Prescription Drug, Improvement, and Modernization Act of 2003 (P.L. 108-173)**

P.L. 108-173, § 1201(d)(2)(A):

Amended Code Sec. 3231(e) by adding at the end a new paragraph (11). **Effective** for tax years beginning after 12-31-2003.

• **2001, Railroad Retirement and Survivors' Improvement Act of 2001 (P.L. 107-90)**

P.L. 107-90, § 204(e)(3):

Amended Code Sec. 3231(e)(2)(A)(iii)(II) and (4)(A) by striking "3211(a)(1)" and inserting "3211(a)". **Effective** for calendar years beginning after 12-31-2001.

P.L. 107-90, § 204(e)(4):

Amended Code Sec. 3231(e)(2)(B)(ii)(I) by striking "3211(a)(2)" and inserting "3211(b)". **Effective** for calendar years beginning after 12-31-2001.

• **2000, Community Renewal Tax Relief Act of 2000 (P.L. 106-554)**

P.L. 106-554, § 202(b)(5):

Amended the heading for Code Sec. 3231(e)(10) by striking "MEDICAL SAVINGS ACCOUNT" and inserting "ARCHER MSA". **Effective** 12-21-2000.

• **1996, Health Insurance Portability and Accountability Act of 1996 (P.L. 104-191)**

P.L. 104-191, § 301(c)(2)(A):

Amended Code Sec. 3231(e) by adding at the end a new paragraph (10). **Effective** for tax years beginning after 12-31-96.

• **1994, Social Security Independence and Program Improvements Act of 1994 (P.L. 103-296)**

P.L. 103-296, § 320(a)(1)(D):

Amended Code Sec. 3231(e)(1) by striking "(J), or (M)" each place it appears and inserting "(J), (M), or (Q)". **Effective** with the calendar quarter following 8-15-94.

• **1993, Omnibus Budget Reconciliation Act of 1993 (P.L. 103-66)**

P.L. 103-66, § 13207(c)(1):

Amended Code Sec. 3231(e)(2)(A) by adding at the end thereof new clause (iii). **Effective** for 1994 and later calendar years.

P.L. 103-66, § 13207(c)(2):

Amended Code Sec. 3231(e)(2)(B)(i). **Effective** for 1994 and later calendar years. Prior to amendment, Code Sec. 3231(e)(2)(B)(i) read as follows:

(i) TIER 1 TAXES.—

(I) IN GENERAL.—Except as provided in subclause (II) of this clause and in clause (ii), the term "applicable base" means for any calendar year the contribution and benefit base determined under section 230 of the Social Security Act for such calendar year.

(II) HOSPITAL INSURANCE TAXES.—For purposes of applying so much of the rate applicable under section 3201(a) or 3221(a) (as the case may be) as does not exceed the rate of tax in effect under section 3101(b), and for purposes of applying so much of the rate of tax applicable under section 3211(a)(1) as does not exceed the rate of tax in effect under section 1401(b), the term "applicable base" means for any calendar year the applicable contribution base determined under section 3121(x)(2) for such calendar year.

• **1990, Omnibus Budget Reconciliation Act of 1990 (P.L. 101-508)**

P.L. 101-508, § 11331(c):

Amended Code Sec. 3231(e)(2)(B)(i). **Effective** for 1991 and later calendar years. Prior to amendment, Code Sec. 3231(e)(2)(B)(i) read as follows:

(i) TIER 1 TAXES.—Except as provided in clause (ii), the term "applicable base" means for any calendar year the contribution and benefit base determined under section 230 of the Social Security Act for such calendar year.

P.L. 101-508, § 11704(a)(19):

Amended Code Sec. 3231(e) by redesignating paragraphs (9) and (10) as paragraphs (8) and (9), respectively. **Effective** 11-5-90.

• **1989, Omnibus Budget Reconciliation Act of 1989 (P.L. 101-239)**

P.L. 101-239, § 10205(a):

Amended Code Sec. 3231(e)(1) by striking ", (ii) tips" and inserting "or death, except that this clause does not apply to a payment for group-term life insurance to the extent that such payment is includible in the gross income of the employee, (ii) tips". **Effective** for group-term life insurance coverage in effect after 12-31-89, and remuneration paid before 1-1-90 which the employer treated as compensation when paid. For an exception, see Act Sec. 10205(b)(2)-(3), below.

P.L. 101-239, § 10205(b)(2)-(3), provides:

(2) EXCEPTION.—The amendment made by subsection (a) shall not apply with respect to payments by the employer (or a successor of such employer) for group-term life insurance for such employer's former employees who separated from employment with the employer on or before December 12, 1989, to the extent that such payments are not for coverage for any such employee for any period for which such employee is employed by such employer (or a successor of such employer) after the date of such separation.

(3) BENEFIT DETERMINATIONS TO TAKE INTO ACCOUNT REMUNERATION ON WHICH TAX PAID.—The term "compensation" as defined in section 1(h) of the Railroad Retirement Act of 1974 includes any remuneration which is included in the term "compensation" as defined in section 3231(e)(1) of the Internal Revenue Code of 1986 by reason of the amendment made by subsection (a).

P.L. 101-239, § 10206(a):

Amended Code Sec. 3231(e)(1) by striking "or (iii)" and inserting "(iii)" and by inserting ", (iv) any remuneration which would not (if chapter 21 applied to such remuneration) be treated as wages (as defined in section 3121(a)) by reason of section 3121(a)(5)" before the period. **Effective** for remuneration paid after 12-31-89.

P.L. 101-239, § 10206(b):

Amended Code Sec. 3231(e) by adding at the end thereof a new paragraph (9)[8]. For the effective date, see Act Sec. 10206(c)(2)-(5), below.

P.L. 101-239, § 10206(c)(2)-(5), provides:

(2) SUBSECTION (b).—Except as otherwise provided in this subsection—

(A) IN GENERAL.—The amendment made by subsection (b) shall apply to—

(i) remuneration paid after December 31, 1989, and

(ii) remuneration paid before January 1, 1990, which the employer treated as compensation when paid.

(B) BENEFIT DETERMINATIONS TO TAKE INTO ACCOUNT REMUNERATION ON WHICH TAX PAID.—The term "compensation" as defined in section 1(h) of the Railroad Retirement Act of 1974 includes any remuneration which is included in the term "compensation" as defined in section 3231(e)(1) of the Internal Revenue Code of 1986 by reason of the amendment made by subsection (b).

(3) SPECIAL RULE FOR CERTAIN PAYMENTS.—For purposes of applying the amendment made by subsection (b) to remuneration paid after December 31, 1989, which would have been taken into account before January 1, 1990, if such amendments had applied to periods before January 1, 1990, such remuneration shall be taken into account

Sec. 3231(e)(9)

RAILROAD RETIREMENT TAX—GENERAL PROVISIONS

when paid (or, at the election of the payor, at the time which would be appropriate if such amendments had applied).

(4) EXCEPTION FOR CERTAIN 401(k) CONTRIBUTIONS.—The amendment made by subsection (b) shall not apply to employer contributions made during 1990 and attributable to services performed during 1989 under a qualified cash or deferred arrangement (as defined in section 401(k) of the Internal Revenue Code of 1986) if, under the terms of the arrangement as in effect on June 15, 1989—

(A) the employee makes an election with respect to such contributions before January 1, 1990, and

(B) the employer identifies the amount of such contribution before January 1, 1990.

(5) SPECIAL RULE WITH RESPECT TO NONQUALIFIED DEFERRED COMPENSATION PLANS.—In the case of an agreement in existence on June 15, 1989, between a nonqualified deferred compensation plan (as defined in section 3121(v)(2)(C) of such Code) and an individual, the amendment made by subsection (b) shall apply with respect to services performed by the individual after December 31, 1989. The preceding sentence shall not apply in the case of a plan to which section 457(a) of such Code applies.

P.L. 101-239, § 10207(a):

Amended Code Sec. 3231(e) by adding at the end thereof a new paragraph (10)[9]. **Effective** for remuneration paid after 12-31-89.

P.L. 101-239, § 10207(b):

Amended Code Sec. 3231(e)(1) by adding at the end thereof a new sentence. **Effective** for remuneration paid after 12-31-89.

• **1989 (P.L. 101-140)**

P.L. 101-140, § 203(a)(2), provides:

(2) Each provision of law amended by paragraph (22), (27), or (31) of section 1011B(a) of the Technical and Miscellaneous Revenue Act of 1988 is amended to read as if the amendments made by such paragraph had not been enacted.

• **1989 (P.L. 101-136)**

P.L. 101-136, § 528, provides:

SEC. 528. No monies appropriated by this Act may be used to implement or enforce section 1151 of the Tax Reform Act of 1986 or the amendments made by such section.

• **1988, Technical and Miscellaneous Revenue Act of 1988 (P.L. 100-647)**

P.L. 100-647, § 1001(d)(2)(C)(ii):

Amended Code Sec. 3231(e)(1) by striking out "(F) or (J)" each place it appears and inserting in lieu thereof "(F), (J), or (M)". **Effective** as if included in the provision of P.L. 99-514 to which it relates.

P.L. 100-647, § 1011B(a)(22)(B):

Amended Code Sec. 3231(e) by adding at the end thereof new paragraph (8). Not **effective** for any individual who separated from service with the employer before 1-1-89 [but see P.L. 101-140, § 203(a)(2), above.—CCH].

• **1986, Tax Reform Act of 1986 (P.L. 99-514)**

P.L. 99-514, § 121(e)(2):

Amended Code Sec. 3231(e)(5) by striking out "117 or" and inserting in lieu thereof "74(c), 117, or". **Effective** for amounts received after 12-31-86, in tax years ending after such date.

P.L. 99-514, § 1899A(41):

Amended Code Sec. 3231(e) by redesignating the paragraph (6) added by P.L. 98-612 as paragraph (7). **Effective** 10-22-86.

• **1984 (P.L. 98-612)**

P.L. 98-612, § 1(c):

Amended Code Sec. 3231(e) by adding at the end thereof new paragraph (6)[7]. **Effective** for remuneration paid after 12-31-84.

• **1984 (P.L. 98-611)**

P.L. 98-611, § 1(f):

Amended Code Sec. 3231(e) by adding at the end thereof new paragraph (6). **Effective** for remuneration paid after 12-31-84.

• **1984, Deficit Reduction Act of 1984 (P.L. 98-369)**

P.L. 98-369, § 531(d)(2):

Amended Code Sec. 3231(e) by adding at the end thereof a new paragraph (5). **Effective** 1-1-85.

• **1983, Railroad Retirement Solvency Act of 1983 (P.L. 98-76)**

P.L. 98-76, § 225(a)(1), (2), (c)(1)(C), (6), (7):

Amended Code Sec. 3231(e). **Effective** for remuneration paid after 12-31-84. Prior to amendment, Code Sec. 3231(e) read as follows:

(e) COMPENSATION.—For purposes of this chapter—

(1) The term "compensation" means any form of money remuneration paid to an individual for services rendered as an employee to one or more employers. Such term does not include (i) the amount of any payment (including any amount paid by an employer for insurance or annuities, or into a fund, to provide for any such payment) made to, or on behalf of, an employee or any of his dependents under a plan or system established by an employer which makes provision for his employees generally (or for his employees generally and their dependents) or for a class or classes of his employees (or for a class or classes of his employees and their dependents), on account of sickness or accident disability or medical or hospitalization expenses in connection with sickness or accident disability, (ii) tips (except as is provided under paragraph (3)), or (iii) an amount paid specifically—either as an advance, as reimbursement or allowance—for traveling or other bona fide and necessary expenses incurred or reasonably expected to be incurred in the business of the employer provided any such payment is identified by the employer either by a separate payment or by specifically indicating the separate amounts where both wages and expense reimbursement or allowance are combined in a single payment. Such term does not include remuneration for service which is performed by a nonresident alien individual for the period he is temporarily present in the United States as a nonimmigrant under subparagraph (F) or (J) of section 101(a)(15) of the Immigration and Nationality Act, as amended, and which is performed to carry out the purpose specified in subparagraph (F) or (J), as the case may be. Compensation which is paid in one calendar month but which would be payable in a prior or subsequent taxable month but for the fact that prescribed date of payment would fall on a Saturday, Sunday or legal holiday shall be deemed to have been paid in such prior or subsequent taxable month. Compensation which is earned during the period for which the Secretary shall require a return of taxes under this chapter to be made and which is payable during the calendar month following such period shall be deemed to have been paid during such period only. For the purpose of determining the amount of taxes under sections 3201 and 3221, compensation earned in the service of a local lodge or division of a railway-labor-organization employer shall be disregarded with respect to any calendar month if the amount thereof is less than $25. Compensation for service as a delegate to a national or international convention of a railway labor organization defined as an "employer" in subsection (a) of this section shall be disregarded for purposes of determining the amount of taxes due pursuant to this chapter if the individual rendering such service has not previously rendered service, other than as such a delegate, which may be included in his "years of service" for purposes of the Railroad Retirement Act.

(2) A payment made by an employer to an individual through the employer's payroll shall be presumed, in the absence of evidence to the contrary, to be compensation for service rendered by such individual as an employee of the employer in the period with respect to which the payment is made. An employee receiving retroactive wage payments shall be deemed to be paid compensation in the period during which such compensation is earned only upon a written request by such employee, made within six months following the payment, and a showing that such compensation was earned during a period other than the period in which it was paid. An employee shall be deemed to be paid "for time lost" the amount he is paid by an employer with respect to an identifiable period of absence from the active service of the employer, including absence on account of personal injury, and the amount he is paid by the employer for loss of earnings resulting from his displacement to a less remunerative position or occupation. If a payment is made by an employer with respect to a personal injury and includes pay for time lost, the total payment shall be deemed to be paid for time lost unless, at the time of payment, a part of such payment is specifically apportioned to factors other than time lost, in which event only such part of the payment as is not so apportioned shall be deemed to be paid for time lost.

(3) Solely for purposes of the tax imposed by section 3201 and other provisions of this chapter insofar as they relate to such tax, the term "compensation" also includes cash tips received by an employee in any calendar month in the course of his employment by an employer unless the amount of such cash tips is less than $20.

(4)(A) For purposes of applying sections 3201(b) and 3221(b) (and so much of section 3211(a) as relates to the rates of the taxes imposed by sections 3101 and 3111), in the case of payments made to an employee or any of his dependents on account of sickness or accident disability, clause (i) of the second sentence of paragraph (1) shall exclude from the term "compensation" only—

(i) payments which are received under a workmen's compensation law, and

(ii) benefits received under the Railroad Retirement Act of 1974.

(B) Notwithstanding any other provision of law, for purposes of the sections specified in subparagraph (A), the term "compensation" shall include benefits paid under section 2(a) of the Railroad Unemployment Insurance Act for days of sickness, except to the extent that such sickness (as determined in accordance with standards prescribed by the Railroad Retirement Board) is the result of on-the-job injury.

(C) Under regulations prescribed by the Secretary, subparagraphs (A) and (B) shall not apply to payments made after the expiration of a 6-month period comparable to the 6-month period described in section 3121(a)(4).

(D) Except as otherwise provided in regulations prescribed by the Secretary, any third party which makes a payment included in compensation solely by reason of subparagraph (A) or (B) shall be treated for purposes of this chapter as the employer with respect to such compensation.

• **1981 (P.L. 97-123)**

P.L. 97-123, § 3(c):

Amended Code Sec. 3231(e) by adding at the end thereof paragraph (4). **Effective** with respect to remuneration paid after 12-31-81.

P.L. 97-123, § 3(g)(2), provides:

(2) This section (and the amendments made by this section) shall not apply with respect to any payment made by a third party to an employee pursuant to a contractual relationship of an employer with such third party entered into before December 14, 1981, if—

(A) coverage by such third party for the group in which such employee falls ceases before March 1, 1982, and

(B) no payment by such third party is made to such employee under such relationship after February 28, 1982.

See the historical comment for P.L. 97-123, § 3(d)-(f), following Code Sec. 3121(a) for provisions related to the issuance of regulations providing procedures under which the employer rather than a third party will be liable for the employer's portion of taxes involved and for meeting the Code Sec. 6051 requirements with respect to wages or compensation involved.

• **1981, Economic Recovery Tax Act of 1981 (P.L. 97-34)**

P.L. 97-34, § 714(d)(2):

Amended Code Sec. 3231(e)(1) by striking out "(iii) the voluntary payment by an employer, without deduction from the remuneration of the employee, of the tax imposed on such employee by section 3201, or (iv)" and inserting "or (iii)". **Effective** for compensation paid for services rendered after 9-30-81.

Internal Revenue Code   Sec. 3231(e)(12)(B)

RAILROAD RETIREMENT TAX—GENERAL PROVISIONS

P.L. 97-34, §743(a):

Amended Code Sec. 3231(e)(1) by adding a new fourth sentence. **Effective** for tax years ending after 12-31-81.

P.L. 97-34, §743(b):

Amended Code Sec. 3231(e)(2) by adding a new first sentence. **Effective** for tax years beginning after 12-31-81.

P.L. 97-34, §743(c):

Amended Code Sec. 3231(e)(2) by striking from the second sentence "An employee" and inserting "An employee receiving retroactive wage payments". **Effective** for tax years beginning after 12-31-81.

- **1976 (P.L. 94-457)**

P.L. 94-547, §4(b):

Substituted the second sentence of Code Sec. 3231(e). **Effective** for compensation paid for services rendered after 12-31-76. Prior to amendment, such second sentence read as follows:

Such term does not include tips (except as is provided under paragraph (3)), or the voluntary payment by an employer, without deduction from the remuneration of the employee, of the tax imposed on such employee by section 3201.

P.L. 94-547, §4(c)(2), provides:

The amendments made by subsection (b) of this section shall apply with respect to taxable years ending after December 31, 1953: *Provided, however,* That any taxes paid under the Railroad Retirement Tax Act prior to the date on which this Act is enacted shall not be affected or adjusted by reason of the amendments made by such subsection (b) except to the extent that the applicable period of limitation for the assessment of tax and the filing of a claim for credit or refund has not expired prior to the date on which this Act is enacted. If the applicable period of limitation for the filing of a claim for credit or refund would expire within the six-month period following the date on which this Act is enacted, the applicable period for the filing of such a claim for credit or refund shall be extended to include such six-month period.

- **1976, Tax Reform Act of 1976 (P.L. 94-455)**

P.L. 94-455, §1906(b)(13)(A):

Amended 1954 Code by substituting "Secretary" for "Secretary or his delegate" each place it appeared. **Effective** 2-1-77.

- **1975 (P.L. 94-93)**

P.L. 94-93, §§204, 207:

Amended the first sentence of Code Sec. 3231(e)(1). **Effective** for tax years ending on or after 8-9-75, and for tax years ending 8-9-75, as to which the period for assessment and collection of tax or the filing of a claim for credit or refund has not expired on 8-9-75. Prior to amendment the first sentence of Code Sec. 3231(e)(1) read as follows:

"The term `compensation' means any form of money remuneration earned by an individual for services rendered as an employee to one or more employers, or as an employee representative, including remuneration paid for the time lost as an employee, but remuneration paid for time lost shall be deemed earned in the month in which such time is lost."

P.L. 94-93, §§205, 206, 207:

Amended Code Sec. 3231(e)(2) by changing the first sentence thereof. **Effective** for tax years beginning on or after 8-9-75 provided however, that with respect to payment made prior to 8-9-75, the employee may file a written request under section 206 of P.L. 94-93 within six months after the enactment of such Act. Prior to amendment, the first sentence of 3231(e)(2) read as follows:

"A payment made by an employer to an individual through the employer's payroll shall be presumed, in the absence of evidence to the contrary, to be compensation for service rendered by such individual as an employee of the employer in the period with respect to which the payment is made."

- **1975 (P.L. 94-92)**

P.L. 94-92, §203(b)-(c):

Amended the fifth sentence of paragraph (1) of Code Sec. 3231(e) by striking out "$3" and inserting in lieu thereof "$25". **Effective** 1-1-75, and applicable only with respect to compensation paid for services rendered on or after that date.

- **1968 (P.L. 90-624)**

P.L. 90-624, §1:

Amended Code Sec. 3231(e)(1) by adding the third sentence therein. **Effective** for service performed after 12-31-61.

P.L. 90-624, §4(a), provides:

(a)(1) The amendments made by the first two sections of this Act shall apply with respect to service performed after December 31, 1961.

(2) Notwithstanding the expiration before the date of the enactment of this Act or within 6 months after such date of the period for filing claim for credit or refund, claim for credit or refund of any overpayment of any tax imposed by chapter 22 of the Internal Revenue Code of 1954 attributable to the amendment made by the first section of this Act may be filed at any time within one year after such date of enactment.

(3) Any credit or refund of an overpayment of the tax imposed by section 3201 or 3211 of the Internal Revenue Code of 1954 which is attributable to the amendment made by the first section of this Act shall be appropriately adjusted for any lump-sum payment which has been made under section 5(f)(2) of the Railroad Retirement Act of 1937 before the date of the allowance of such credit or the making of such refund.

- **1965 (P.L. 89-212)**

P.L. 89-212, §2(b):

Amended Code Sec. 3231(e)(1) by inserting "(except as is provided under paragraph (3))" immediately after "tips" in the second sentence and by adding paragraph (3). **Effective** with respect to tips received after 1965.

- **1954 (P.L. 746, 83rd Cong.)**

P.L. 746, 83rd Cong., §§206(b), 407:

Amended Code §3231(e)(1) by adding the last sentence thereof. **Effective** as if enacted as a part of the 1954 Code, that is, with respect to remuneration paid after 12-31-54, which is for services rendered after such date.

[Sec. 3231(f)]

(f) COMPANY.—For purposes of this chapter, the term "company" includes corporations, associations, and joint-stock companies.

[Sec. 3231(g)]

(g) CARRIER.—For purposes of this chapter, the term "carrier" means a rail carrier subject to part A of subtitle IV of title 49.

Amendments

- **1995, ICC Termination Act of 1995 (P.L. 104-88)**

P.L. 104-88, §304(d)(2):

Amended Code Sec. 3231(g) by striking "an express carrier, sleeping car carrier, or rail carrier providing transportation subject to subchapter I of chapter 105" and inserting in lieu thereof "a rail carrier subject to part A of subtitle IV". **Effective** 1-1-96.

- **1978 (P.L. 95-473)**

P.L. 95-473, §2(a)(2)(G):

Amended Code Section 3231(g) by striking out "express company, sleeping-car company, or carrier by railroad, subject to part I of the Interstate Commerce Act (49 U.S.C., chapter 1)" and substituting "express carrier, sleeping car carrier, or rail carrier providing transportation subject to subchapter I of chapter 105 of title 49". **Effective** 10-17-78.

[Sec. 3231(h)]

(h) TIPS CONSTITUTING COMPENSATION, TIME DEEMED PAID.—For purposes of this chapter, tips which constitute compensation for purposes of the taxes imposed under section 3201 shall be deemed to be paid at the time a written statement including such tips is furnished to the employer pursuant to section 6053(a) or (if no statement including such tips is so furnished) at the time received.

Amendments

- **1983, Railroad Retirement Solvency Act of 1983 (P.L. 98-76)**

P.L. 98-76, §225(c)(8):

Amended Code Sec. 3231(h). **Effective** for remuneration paid after 1984. Prior to amendment, Code Sec. 3231(h) read as follows:

(h) TIPS CONSTITUTING COMPENSATION, TIME DEEMED PAID.—For purposes of this chapter, tips which constitute compensation for purposes of the tax imposed under section 3201 shall be deemed to be paid at the time a written statement including such tips is furnished to the employer pursuant to section 6053(a) or (if no statement including such tips is so furnished) at the time received; and tips so deemed to be paid in any month shall be deemed paid for services rendered in such month.

- **1965 (P.L. 89-212)**

P.L. 89-212, §2(b)(3):

Added Code Sec. 3231(h). **Effective** with respect to tips received after 1965.

[Sec. 3231(i)]

(i) CONCURRENT EMPLOYMENT BY 2 OR MORE EMPLOYERS.—For purposes of this chapter, if 2 or more related corporations which are employers concurrently employ the same individual and compensate such individual through a common paymaster which is 1 of such corporations, each such corporation shall be considered to have paid as remuneration to such individual only the amounts actually disbursed by it to such individual and shall not be considered to have paid as remuneration to such individual amounts actually disbursed to such individual by another of such corporations.

Sec. 3231(f)

Amendments

• 1983, Railroad Retirement Solvency Act of 1983 (P.L. 98-76)

P.L. 98-76, § 225(b):

Added Code Sec. 3231(i). **Effective** for remuneration paid after 1984.

[Sec. 3232]

SEC. 3232. COURT JURISDICTION.

The several district courts of the United States shall have jurisdiction to entertain an application by the Attorney General on behalf of the Secretary to compel an employee or other person residing within the jurisdiction of the court or an employer subject to service of process within its jurisdiction to comply with any obligations imposed on such employee, employer, or other person under the provisions of this chapter. The jurisdiction herein specifically conferred upon such Federal courts shall not be held exclusive of any jurisdiction otherwise possessed by such courts to entertain civil actions, whether legal or equitable in nature, in aid of the enforcement of rights or obligations arising under the provisions of this chapter.

Amendments

• 1976, Tax Reform Act of 1976 (P.L. 94-455)

P.L. 94-455, § 1906(b)(13)(A):

Amended 1954 Code by substituting "Secretary" for "Secretary or his delegate" each place it appeared. **Effective** 2-1-77.

[Sec. 3233]

SEC. 3233. SHORT TITLE.

This chapter may be cited as the "Railroad Retirement Tax Act."

Subchapter E—Tier 2 Tax Rate Determination

Sec. 3241.   Determination of tier 2 tax rate based on average account benefits ratio.

[Sec. 3241]

SEC. 3241. DETERMINATION OF TIER 2 TAX RATE BASED ON AVERAGE ACCOUNT BENEFITS RATIO.

[Sec. 3241(a)]

(a) IN GENERAL.—For purposes of sections 3201(b), 3211(b), and 3221(b), the applicable percentage for any calendar year is the percentage determined in accordance with the table in subsection (b).

[Sec. 3241(b)]

(b) TAX RATE SCHEDULE.—

Average account benefits ratio		Applicable percentage for sections 3211(b) and 3221(b)	Applicable percentage for section 3201(b)
At least	But less than		
	2.5	22.1	4.9
2.5	3.0	18.1	4.9
3.0	3.5	15.1	4.9
3.5	4.0	14.1	4.9
4.0	6.1	13.1	4.9
6.1	6.5	12.6	4.4
6.5	7.0	12.1	3.9
7.0	7.5	11.6	3.4
7.5	8.0	11.1	2.9
8.0	8.5	10.1	1.9
8.5	9.0	9.1	0.9
9.0		8.2	0

[Sec. 3241(c)]

(c) DEFINITIONS RELATED TO DETERMINATION OF RATES OF TAX.—

    (1) AVERAGE ACCOUNT BENEFITS RATIO.—For purposes of this section, the term "average account benefits ratio" means, with respect to any calendar year, the average determined by the Secretary of the account benefits ratios for the 10 most recent fiscal years ending before such calendar year. If the amount determined under the preceding sentence is not a multiple of 0.1, such amount shall be increased to the next highest multiple of 0.1.

    (2) ACCOUNT BENEFITS RATIO.—For purposes of this section, the term "account benefits ratio" means, with respect to any fiscal year, the amount determined by the Railroad Retirement Board by dividing the fair market value of the assets in the Railroad Retirement Account and of the National Railroad Retirement Investment Trust (and for years before 2002, the Social Security Equivalent Benefits Account) as of the close of such fiscal year by the total benefits and administrative expenses paid from the Railroad Retirement Account and the National Railroad Retirement Investment Trust during such fiscal year.

[Sec. 3241(d)]

(d) NOTICE.—No later than December 1 of each calendar year, the Secretary shall publish a notice in the Federal Register of the rates of tax determined under this section which are applicable for the following calendar year.

Amendments

• 2001, Railroad Retirement and Survivors' Improvement Act of 2001 (P.L. 107-90)

P.L. 107-90, § 204(d):

Amended chapter 22 by adding at the end a new subchapter E (Code Sec. 3241). **Effective** for calendar years beginning after 12-31-2001.

UNEMPLOYMENT TAX

CHAPTER 23—FEDERAL UNEMPLOYMENT TAX ACT

Sec. 3301. Rate of tax.
Sec. 3302. Credits against tax.
Sec. 3303. Conditions of additional credit allowance.
Sec. 3304. Approval of State laws.
Sec. 3305. Applicability of State law.
Sec. 3306. Definitions.
Sec. 3307. Deductions as constructive payments.
Sec. 3308. Instrumentalities of the United States.
Sec. 3309. State law coverage of services performed for nonprofit organizations or governmental entities.
Sec. 3310. Judicial review.
Sec. 3311. Short title.

[Sec. 3301]

SEC. 3301. RATE OF TAX.

There is hereby imposed on every employer (as defined in section 3306(a)) for each calendar year an excise tax, with respect to having individuals in his employ, equal to 6 percent of the total wages (as defined in section 3306(b)) paid by such employer during the calendar year with respect to employment (as defined in section 3306(c)).

Amendments

• **2018, Tax Technical Corrections Act of 2018 (P.L. 115-141)**

P.L. 115-141, §401(b)(37), Div. U:

Amended Code Sec. 3301 by striking "equal to—"and all that follows and inserting "equal to 6 percent of the total wages (as defined in section 3306(b)) paid by such employer during the calendar year with respect to employment (as defined in section 3306(c)).". **Effective** 3-23-2018. For a special rule, see Act Sec. 401(e), Div. U, below. Prior to being stricken, "equal to—"and all that follows in Code Sec. 3301 read as follows:

equal to—

(1) 6.2 percent in the case of calendar years 1988 through 2010 and the first 6 months of calendar year 2011; or

(2) 6.0 percent in the case of the remainder of calendar year 2011 and each calendar year thereafter;

of the total wages (as defined in section 3306(b)) paid by him during the calendar year (or portion of the calendar year) with respect to employment (as defined in section 3306(c)).

P.L. 115-141, §401(e), Div. U, provides:

(e) GENERAL SAVINGS PROVISION WITH RESPECT TO DEADWOOD PROVISIONS.—If—

(1) any provision amended or repealed by the amendments made by subsection (b) or (d) applied to—

(A) any transaction occurring before the date of the enactment of this Act,

(B) any property acquired before such date of enactment, or

(C) any item of income, loss, deduction, or credit taken into account before such date of enactment, and

(2) the treatment of such transaction, property, or item under such provision would (without regard to the amendments or repeals made by such subsection) affect the liability for tax for periods ending after such date of enactment,

nothing in the amendments or repeals made by this section shall be construed to affect the treatment of such transaction, property, or item for purposes of determining liability for tax for periods ending after such date of enactment.

• **2009, Worker, Homeownership, and Business Assistance Act of 2009 (P.L. 111-92)**

P.L. 111-92, §10(a)(1)-(3):

Amended Code Sec. 3301 by striking "through 2009" in paragraph (1) and inserting "through 2010 and the first 6 months of calendar year 2011", by striking "calendar year 2010" in paragraph (2) and inserting "the remainder of calendar year 2011", and by inserting "(or portion of the calendar year)" after "during the calendar year". **Effective** for wages paid after 12-31-2009.

• **2008, Energy Improvement and Extension Act of 2008 (P.L. 110-343)**

P.L. 110-343, Division B, §404(a)(1)-(2):

Amended Code Sec. 3301 by striking "through 2008" in paragraph (1) and inserting "through 2009", and by striking "calendar year 2009" in paragraph (2) and inserting "calendar year 2010". **Effective** for wages paid after 12-31-2008.

• **2007, Energy Independence and Security Act of 2007 (P.L. 110-140)**

P.L. 110-140, §1501(a)(1)-(2):

Amended Code Sec. 3301 by striking "2007" in paragraph (1) and inserting "2008", and by striking "2008" in paragraph (2) and inserting "2009". **Effective** for wages paid after 12-31-2007.

• **1997, Taxpayer Relief Act of 1997 (P.L. 105-34)**

P.L. 105-34, §1035(1)-(2):

Amended Code Sec. 3301 by striking "1998" in paragraph (1) and inserting "2007", and by striking "1999" in paragraph (2) and inserting "2008". **Effective** 8-5-97.

• **1993, Omnibus Budget Reconciliation Act of 1993 (P.L. 103-66)**

P.L. 103-66, §13751(1)-(2):

Amended Code Sec. 3301 by striking "1996" in paragraph (1) and inserting "1998", and by striking "1997" in paragraph (2) and inserting "1999". **Effective** 8-10-93.

• **1991, Emergency Unemployment Compensation Act of 1991 (P.L. 102-164)**

P.L. 102-164, §402(1)-(2):

Amended Code Sec. 3301 by striking "1995" in paragraph (1) and inserting "1996", and by striking "1996" in paragraph (2) and inserting "1997". **Effective** 11-15-91.

• **1990, Omnibus Budget Reconciliation Act of 1990 (P.L. 101-508)**

P.L. 101-508, §11333(a)(1)-(2):

Amended Code Sec. 3301 by striking "1988, 1989, and 1990" in paragraph (1) and inserting "1988 through 1995" and by striking "1991" in paragraph (2) and inserting "1996". **Effective** for wages paid after 12-31-90.

• **1987, Revenue Act of 1987 (P.L. 100-203)**

P.L. 100-203, §9153(a):

Amended Code Sec. 3301(1) and (2). **Effective** for wages paid on or after 1-1-88. Prior to amendment Code Sec. 3301(1) and (2) read as follows:

(1) 6.2 percent, in the case of a calendar year beginning before the first calendar year after 1976, as of January 1 of which there is not a balance of repayable advances made to the extended unemployment compensation account (established by section 905(a) of the Social Security Act); or

(2) 6.0 percent, in the case of such first calendar year and each calendar year thereafter;

• **1986, Tax Reform Act of 1986 (P.L. 99-514)**

P.L. 99-514, §1899A(42):

Amended Code Sec. 3301(1) by striking out "unemployed" and inserting in lieu thereof "unemployment". **Effective** 10-22-86.

• **1982, Tax Equity and Fiscal Responsibility Act of 1982 (P.L. 97-248)**

P.L. 97-248, §271(b)(1):

Amended Code Sec. 3301(1) by striking out "3.4 percent" and inserting in lieu thereof "3.5 percent". **Effective** for remuneration paid after 12-31-82.

P.L. 97-248, §271(c)(1):

Amended Code Sec. 3301 by striking out in paragraph (1) "3.5 percent" and inserting "6.2 percent" and by striking out in paragraph (2) "3.2 percent" and inserting "6.0 percent". **Effective** for remuneration paid after 12-31-84.

• **1976, Unemployment Compensation Amendments of 1976 (P.L. 94-566)**

P.L. 94-566, §211(b), (d)(2):

Amended Code Sec. 3301. **Effective** for remuneration paid after 12-31-76. Prior to amendment, Code Sec. 3301 read as follows:

SEC. 3301. RATE OF TAX.

There is hereby imposed on every employer (as defined in section 3306(a)) for each calendar year an excise tax, with respect to having individuals in his employ, equal to 3.2 percent of the total wages (as defined in section 3306(b)) paid by him during the calendar year with respect to employment (as defined in section 3306(c)).

• **1976, Tax Reform Act of 1976 (P.L. 94-455)**

P.L. 94-455, §1903(a)(11)(A), (B), (d):

Substituted "each calendar year" for "the calendar year 1970 and each calendar year thereafter" and deleted the last sentence of Code Sec. 3301. **Effective** for wages paid after 12-31-76. Prior to amendment, the last sentence of Code Sec. 3301 read as follows:

In the case of wages paid during the calendar year 1973, the rate of such tax shall be 3.28 percent in lieu of 3.2 percent.

• **1972 (P.L. 92-329)**

P.L. 92-329, §2(a):

Added the last sentence in Code Sec. 3301.

UNEMPLOYMENT TAX

• **1970, Employment Security Amendments of 1970 (P.L. 91-373)**

P.L. 91-373, § 301(a):

Amended Code Sec. 3301. **Effective** with respect to remuneration paid after 12-31-69. Prior to amendment, Code Sec. 3301 read as follows:

"There is hereby imposed on every employer (as defined in section 3306(a)) for the calendar year 1961 and for each calendar year thereafter an excise tax, with respect to having individuals in his employ, equal to 3.1 percent of the total wages (as defined in section 3306(b)) paid by him during the calendar year with respect to employment (as defined in section 3306(c)) after December 31, 1938. In the case of wages paid during the calendar year 1962, the rate of such tax shall be 3.5 percent in lieu of 3.1 percent. In the case of wages paid during the calendar year 1963, the rate of such tax shall be 3.35 percent in lieu of 3.1 percent."

• **1963 (P.L. 88-31)**

P.L. 88-31, § 2(a):

Amended Code Sec. 3301 by striking out the last sentence and inserting the last two new sentences. **Effective** for calendar year 1963. Prior to amendment, the last sentence read as follows:

In the case of wages paid during the calendar years 1962 and 1963, the rate of such tax shall be 3.5 percent in lieu of 3.1 percent.

• **1961, Temporary Extended Unemployment Compensation Act of 1961 (P.L. 87-6)**

P.L. 87-6, § 14(a):

Added the next to last sentence in Code Sec. 3301.

• **1960, Social Security Amendments of 1960 (P.L. 86-778)**

P.L. 86-778, § 523(a):

Amended Code Sec. 3301 by substituting "1961" for "1955" and "3.1 percent" for "3 percent". **Effective** for the calendar year 1961 and calendar years thereafter.

[Sec. 3302]

SEC. 3302. CREDITS AGAINST TAX.

[Sec. 3302(a)]

(a) CONTRIBUTIONS TO STATE UNEMPLOYMENT FUNDS.—

(1) The taxpayer may, to the extent provided in this subsection and subsection (c), credit against the tax imposed by section 3301 the amount of contributions paid by him into an unemployment fund maintained during the taxable year under the unemployment compensation law of a State which is certified as provided in section 3304 for the 12-month period ending on October 31 of such year.

(2) The credit shall be permitted against the tax for the taxable year only for the amount of contributions paid with respect to such taxable year.

(3) The credit against the tax for any taxable year shall be permitted only for contributions paid on or before the last day upon which the taxpayer is required under section 6071 to file a return for such year; except that credit shall be permitted for contributions paid after such last day, but such credit shall not exceed 90 percent of the amount which would have been allowable as credit on account of such contributions had they been paid on or before such last day.

(4) Upon the payment of contributions into the unemployment fund of a State which are required under the unemployment compensation law of that State with respect to remuneration on the basis of which, prior to such payment into the proper fund, the taxpayer erroneously paid an amount as contributions under another unemployment compensation law, the payment into the proper fund shall, for purposes of credit against the tax, be deemed to have been made at the time of the erroneous payment. If, by reason of such other law, the taxpayer was entitled to cease paying contributions with respect to services subject to such other law, the payment into the proper fund shall, for purposes of credit against the tax, be deemed to have been made on the date the return for the taxable year was filed under section 6071.

(5) In the case of wages paid by the trustee of an estate under title 11 of the United States Code, if the failure to pay contributions on time was without fault by the trustee, paragraph (3) shall be applied by substituting "100 percent" for "90 percent".

Amendments

• **1980, Bankruptcy Tax Act of 1980 (P.L. 96-589)**

P.L. 96-589, § 6(f):

Amended Code Sec. 3302(a) by adding a new paragraph (5). **Effective** 10-1-79, but inapplicable to any proceeding under the Bankruptcy Act commenced before that date.

• **1976, Tax Reform Act of 1976 (P.L. 94-455)**

P.L. 94-455, § 1903(a)(12)(A), (d):

Deleted "(10-month period in the case of October 31, 1972)" in Code Sec. 3302(a). **Effective** for compensation paid for services rendered after 12-31-76.

• **1970, Employment Security Amendments of 1970 (P.L. 91-373)**

P.L. 91-373, § 142(a):

Amended Code Sec. 3302(a). **Effective** with respect to tax year 1972 and tax years thereafter. Prior to amendment, Code Sec. 3302(a) read as follows:

"(1) The taxpayer may, to the extent provided in this subsection and subsection (c), credit against the tax imposed by section 3301 the amount of contributions paid by him into an unemployment fund maintained during the taxable year under the unemployment compensation law of a State which is certified for the taxable year as provided in section 3304."

[Sec. 3302(b)]

(b) ADDITIONAL CREDIT.—In addition to the credit allowed under subsection (a), a taxpayer may credit against the tax imposed by section 3301 for any taxable year an amount, with respect to the unemployment compensation law of each State certified as provided in section 3303 for the 12-month period ending on October 31, of such year, or with respect to any provisions thereof so certified, equal to the amount, if any, by which the contributions required to be paid by him with respect to the taxable year were less than the contributions such taxpayer would have been required to pay if throughout such 12-month period he had been subject under such State law to the highest rate applied thereunder in the taxable year to any person having individuals in his employ, or to a rate of 5.4%, whichever rate is lower.

Amendments

• **1982, Tax Equity and Fiscal Responsibility Act of 1982 (P.L. 97-248)**

P.L. 97-248, § 271(c)(2)(A):

Amended Code Sec. 3302(b) by striking out "2.7%" and inserting "5.4%". **Effective** for remuneration paid after 12-31-84.

P.L. 97-248, § 271(d)(3) (as redesignated by P.L. 98-601) and (d)(4) (as added by P.L. 98-601), provides:

(3) TRANSITIONAL RULE FOR CERTAIN EMPLOYEES.—

(A) IN GENERAL.—Notwithstanding section 3303 of the Internal Revenue Code of 1954, in the case of taxable years beginning after December 31, 1984, and before January 1, 1989, a taxpayer shall be allowed the additional credit under section 3302(b) of such Code with respect to any employee covered by a qualified specific industry provision if the requirements of subparagraph (B) are met with respect to such employee.

(B) REQUIREMENTS.—The requirements of this subparagraph are met for any taxable year with respect to any employee covered by a specific industry provision if the amount of contributions required to be paid for the taxable year to the unemployment fund of the State with respect to such employee are not less than the product of the required rate multiplied by the wages paid by the employer during the taxable year.

(C) REQUIRED RATE.—For purposes of subparagraph (B), the required rate for any taxable year is the sum of—

(i) the rate at which contributions were required to be made under the specific industry provision as in effect on August 10, 1982, and

(ii) the applicable percentage of the excess of 5.4 percent over the rate described in clause (i).

(D) APPLICABLE PERCENTAGE.—For purposes of subparagraph (C), the term "applicable percentage" means—

(i) 20 percent in the case of taxable year 1985,

(ii) 40 percent in the case of taxable year 1986,

(iii) 60 percent in the case of taxable year 1987, and

(iv) 80 percent in the case of taxable year 1988.

(E) QUALIFIED SPECIFIC INDUSTRY PROVISION.—For purposes of this paragraph, the term, "qualified specific industry provision" means a provision contained in a State unemployment compensation law (as in effect on August 10, 1982)—

(i) which applies to employees in a specific industry or to an otherwise defined type of employees, and

(ii) under which employers may elect to make contributions at a specified rate (without experience rating) which exceeds 2.7 percent.

(4) TRANSITIONAL RULE FOR CERTAIN SMALL BUSINESSES.—

(A) IN GENERAL.—Notwithstanding section 3303 of the Internal Revenue Code of 1954, in the case of taxable years beginning after December 31, 1984, and before January 1, 1989, a taxpayer shall be allowed the additional credit under section 3302(b) of such Code with respect to any employee covered by a qualified small

UNEMPLOYMENT TAX

business provision if the requirements of subparagraph (B) are met with respect to such employee.

(B) REQUIREMENTS.—The requirements of this subparagraph are met for any taxable year with respect to any employee covered by a qualified small business provision if the amount of contributions required to be paid for the taxable year to the unemployment fund of the State with respect to such employee are not less than the product of the required rate multiplied by the wages paid by the employer during the taxable year.

(C) REQUIRED RATE.—For purposes of subparagraph (B), the required rate for any taxable year is the sum of—

(i) 3.1 percent, plus

(ii) the applicable percentage (as defined in paragraph (3)(D)) of the excess of 5.4 percent over the rate described in clause (i).

(D) QUALIFIED SMALL BUSINESS PROVISION.—For purposes of this paragraph, the term "qualified small business provision" means a provision contained in a State unemployment compensation law (as in effect on the date of the enactment of this paragraph) which provides a maximum rate at which an employer is subject to contribution for wages paid during a calendar quarter if the total wages paid by such employer during such calendar quarter are less than $50,000.

(E) DEFINITION.—For purposes of this paragraph, the term "wages" means the remuneration subject to contributions under the State unemployment compensation law, except that for purposes of subparagraph (D) the amount of total wages paid by an employer shall be determined without regard to any limitation on the amount subject to contribution.

[Sec. 3302(c)]

(c) LIMIT ON TOTAL CREDITS.—

(1) The total credits allowed to a taxpayer under this section shall not exceed 90 percent of the tax against which such credits are allowable.

(2) If an advance or advances have been made to the unemployment account of a State under title XII of the Social Security Act, then the total credits (after applying subsections (a) and (b) and paragraph (1) of this subsection) otherwise allowable under this section for the taxable year in the case of a taxpayer subject to the unemployment compensation law of such State shall be reduced—

(A)(i) in the case of a taxable year beginning with the second consecutive January 1 as of the beginning of which there is a balance of such advances, by 5 percent of the tax imposed by section 3301 with respect to the wages paid by such taxpayer during such taxable year which are attributable to such State; and

(ii) in the case of any succeeding taxable year beginning with a consecutive January 1 as of the beginning of which there is a balance of such advances, by an additional 5 percent, for each succeeding taxable year, of the tax imposed by section 3301 with respect to the wages paid by such taxpayer during such taxable year which are attributable to such State;

(B) in the case of a taxable year beginning with the third or fourth consecutive January 1 as of the beginning of which there is a balance of such advances, by the amount determined by multiplying the wages paid by such taxpayer during such taxable year which are attributable to such State by the percentage (if any), multiplied by a fraction, the numerator of which is the State's average annual wage in covered employment for the calendar year in which the determination is made and the denominator of which is the wage base under this chapter, by which—

(i) 2.7 percent, multiplied by a fraction, the numerator of which is the wage base under this chapter and the denominator of which is the estimated United States average annual wage in covered employment for the calendar year in which the determination is to be made, exceeds

(ii) the average employer contribution rate for such State for the calendar year preceding such taxable year; and

(C) in the case of a taxable year beginning with the fifth or any succeeding consecutive January 1 as of the beginning of which there is a balance of such advances, by the amount determined by multiplying the wages paid by such taxpayer during such taxable year which are attributable to such State by the percentage (if any) by which—

(i) the 5-year benefit cost rate applicable to such State for such taxable year or (if higher) 2.7 percent, exceeds

(ii) the average employer contribution rate for such State for the calendar year preceding such taxable year.

Subparagraph (C) shall not apply with respect to any taxable year to which it would otherwise apply (but subparagraph (B) shall apply to such taxable year) if the Secretary of Labor determines (on or before November 10 of such taxable year) that the State meets the requirements of subsection (f)(2)(B) for such taxable year.

(3) If the Secretary of Labor determines that a State, or State agency, has not—

(A) entered into the agreement described in section 239 of the Trade Act of 1974, with the Secretary of Labor before July 15, 1975, or

(B) fulfilled its commitments under an agreement with the Secretary of Labor as described in section 239 of the Trade Act of 1974,

then, in the case of a taxpayer subject to the unemployment compensation law of such State, the total credits (after applying subsections (a) and (b) and paragraphs (1) and (2) of this section) otherwise allowable under this section for a year during which such State or agency does not enter into or fulfill such an agreement shall be reduced by $7^{1}/_{2}$ percent percent of the tax imposed with respect to wages paid by such taxpayer during such year which are attributable to such State.

Amendments

• **2018, Tax Technical Corrections Act of 2018 (P.L. 115-141)**

P.L. 115-141, § 401(b)(38), Div. U:

Amended Code Sec. 3302(c)(2) by striking the next to last sentence. **Effective** 3-23-2018. For a special rule, see Act Sec. 401(e), Div. U, below. Prior to being stricken, the next to last sentence of Code Sec. 3302(c)(2) read as follows:

The provisions of the preceding sentence shall not be applicable with respect to the taxable year beginning January 1, 1975, or any succeeding taxable year which begins before January 1, 1980; and, for purposes of such sentence, January 1, 1980, shall be deemed to be the first January 1 occurring after January 1, 1974, and consecutive taxable years in the period commencing January 1, 1980, shall be determined as if the taxable year which begins on January 1, 1980, were the taxable year immediately succeeding the taxable year which began on January 1, 1974.

P.L. 115-141, § 401(e), Div. U, provides:

(e) GENERAL SAVINGS PROVISION WITH RESPECT TO DEADWOOD PROVISIONS.—If—

(1) any provision amended or repealed by the amendments made by subsection (b) or (d) applied to—

(A) any transaction occurring before the date of the enactment of this Act,

• **1976, Tax Reform Act of 1976 (P.L. 94-455)**

P.L. 94-455, § 1903(a)(12)(B), (d):

Deleted "(10-month period in the case of October 31, 1972)" and substituted "12-month period" for "12 or 10-month period, as the case may be," in Code Sec. 3302(b). **Effective** for wages paid after 12-31-76.

• **1970, Employment Security Amendments of 1970 (P.L. 91-373)**

P.L. 91-373, § 142(b):

Amended Code Sec. 3302(b). **Effective** with respect to tax year 1972 and tax years thereafter. Prior to amendment, Code Sec. 3302(b) read as follows:

(b) Additional Credit.—In addition to the credit allowed under subsection (a), a taxpayer may credit against the tax imposed by section 3301 for any taxable year an amount, with respect to the unemployment compensation law of each State certified for the taxable year as provided in section 3303 (or with respect to any provisions thereof so certified), equal to the amount, if any, by which the contributions required to be paid by him with respect to the taxable year were less than the contributions such taxpayer would have been required to pay if throughout the taxable year he had been subject under such State law to the highest rate applied thereunder in the taxable year to any person having individuals in his employ, or to a rate of 2.7 percent, whichever rate is lower.

(B) any property acquired before such date of enactment, or

(C) any item of income, loss, deduction, or credit taken into account before such date of enactment, and

(2) the treatment of such transaction, property, or item under such provision would (without regard to the amendments or repeals made by such subsection) affect the liability for tax for periods ending after such date of enactment,

nothing in the amendments or repeals made by this section shall be construed to affect the treatment of such transaction, property, or item for purposes of determining liability for tax for periods ending after such date of enactment.

• **1992, Unemployment Compensation Awards of 1992 (P.L. 102-318)**

P.L. 102-318, § 304, provides:

SEC. 304. EXTENSION OF PERIOD FOR REPAYMENT OF FEDERAL LOANS TO STATE UNEMPLOYMENT FUNDS.

(a) GENERAL RULE.—If the Secretary of Labor determines that a State meets the requirements of subsection (b), paragraph (2) of section 3302(c) of the Internal Revenue Code of 1986 shall be applied with respect to such State for taxable years after 1991—

(1) by substituting "third" for "second" in subparagraph (A)(i),

(2) by substituting "fourth or fifth" for "third or fourth" in subparagraph (B), and

(3) by substituting "sixth" for "fifth" in subparagraph (C).

(b) REQUIREMENTS.—A State meets the requirements of this subsection if, during calendar year 1992 or 1993, the State amended its unemployment compensation law to increase estimated contributions required under such law by at least 25 percent.

(c) SPECIAL RULE.—This section shall not apply to any taxable year after 1994 unless—

(1) such taxable year is in a series of consecutive taxable years as of the beginning of each of which there was a balance referred to in section 3302(c)(2) of such Code, and

(2) such series includes a taxable year beginning in 1992, 1993, or 1994.

- **1986, Tax Reform Act of 1986 (P.L. 99-514)**

P.L. 99-514, §1884(1)(A) and (B)(i) and (ii):

Amended Code Sec. 3302(c)(2)(B) by striking out "determination" the second place it appears in the material preceding clause (i) and inserting in lieu thereof "denominator", by striking out "percent" immediately preceding the comma at the end of clause (i), and by inserting "percent" after "2.7" in clause (i). **Effective** 10-22-86.

- **1983, Social Security Act of 1983 (P.L. 98-21)**

P.L. 98-21, §513(b), (c):

Amended Code Sec. 3302(c)(2)(B). **Effective** for tax year 1983 and tax years thereafter. Prior to amendment, Code Sec. 3302(c)(2)(B) read as follows:

(B) in the case of a taxable year beginning with the third or fourth consecutive January 1 as of the beginning of which there is a balance of such advances, by the amount determined by multiplying the wages paid by such taxpayer during such taxable year which are attributable to such State by the percentage (if any) by which—

(i) 2.7 percent, exceeds

(ii) the average employer contribution rate for such State for the calendar year preceding such taxable year; and

- **1982, Tax Equity and Fiscal Responsibility Act of 1982 (P.L. 97-248)**

P.L. 97-248, §271(c)(3)(A):

Amended Code Sec. 3302(c)(2) by striking out "10 percent" each place it appeared and inserting in lieu thereof "5 percent". **Effective** for remuneration paid after 12-31-84.

P.L. 97-248, §271(c)(3)(B):

Amended Code Sec. 3302(c)(3) by striking out "15 percent" and inserting in lieu thereof "7 1/2 percent". **Effective** for remuneration paid after 12-31-84.

P.L. 97-248, §273(a):

Amended Code Sec. 3302(c)(2) by adding a new sentence at the end thereof. **Effective** for tax years beginning after 12-31-82.

- **1977, Emergency Unemployment Compensation Act of 1977 (P.L. 95-19)**

P.L. 95-19, §201:

Substituted "January 1, 1980" for "January 1, 1978" each place it appeared in the last sentence of Code Sec. 3302(c)(2). Not **effective** for any State unless the Secretary of Labor finds that such State meets the requirements of Sec. 110(b) of the Emergency Compensation and Special Unemployment Assistance Extension Act of 1975.

- **1976, Tax Reform Act of 1976 (P.L. 94-455)**

P.L. 94-455, §1903(a)(12)(C)(i):

Deleted paragraph (2) and the unnumbered paragraph immediately following such paragraph in Code Sec. 3302(c); and redesignated paragraphs (3) and (4) as paragraphs (2) and (3), respectively. **Effective** for compensation paid for services rendered after 12-31-76. Prior to amendment, such paragraphs read as follows:

(2) If an advance or advances have been made to the unemployment account of a State under title XII of the Social Security Act before the date of the enactment of the Employment Security Act of 1960, then the total credits (after applying subsections (a) and (b) and paragraph (1) of this subsection) otherwise allowable under this section for the taxable year in the case of a taxpayer subject to the unemployment compensation law of such State shall be reduced—

(A) in the case of a taxable year beginning on January 1, 1963 (and in the case of any succeeding taxable year beginning before January 1, 1968), as of the beginning of which there is a balance of such advances, by 5 percent of the tax imposed by section 3301 with respect to the wages paid by such taxpayer during such taxable year which are attributable to such State; and

(B) in the case of any succeeding taxable year beginning on or after January 1, 1968, as of the beginning of which there is a balance of such advances, by an additional 5 percent, for each such succeeding taxable year, of the tax imposed by section 3301 with respect to the wages paid by such taxpayer during such taxable year which are attributable to such State.

At the request (made before November 1 of the taxable year) of the Governor of any State, the Secretary of Labor shall, as soon as practicable after June 30 or (if later) the date of the receipt of such request, certify to such Governor and to the Secretary of the Treasury the amount he estimates equals .15 percent (plus an additional .15 percent for each additional 5-percent reduction, provided by subparagraph (B)) of the total of the remuneration which would have been subject to contributions under the State unemployment compensation law with respect to the calendar year preceding such certification if the dollar limit on remuneration subject to contributions under such law were equal to the dollar limit under section 3306(b)(1) for such calendar year. If, after receiving such certification and before November 10 of the taxable year, the State pays into the Federal unemployment account the amount so certified (and designates such payment as being made for purposes of this sentence), the reduction provided by the first sentence of this paragraph shall not apply for such taxable year.

P.L. 94-455, §1903(a)(12)(C)(ii):

Deleted "on or after the date of the enactment of the Employment Security Act of 1960" and substituted "paragraph (1)" for "paragraphs (1) and (2)" in Code Sec. 3302(c)(2), as redesignated by clause (i). **Effective** for compensation paid for services rendered after 12-31-76.

P.L. 94-455, §1903(a)(12)(C)(iii):

Substituted "paragraphs (1) and (2)" for "paragraphs (1), (2), and (3)" in Code Sec. 3302(c)(3), as redesignated by clause (i). **Effective** for compensation paid for services rendered after 12-31-76.

- **1975, Emergency Compensation and Special Unemployment Assistance Extension Act of 1975 (P.L. 94-45)**

P.L. 94-45, §110(a):

Amended Code Sec. 3302(c)(3) by adding the last sentence. **Effective** 6-30-75.

- **1975 (P.L. 93-618)**

P.L. 93-618, §239(e):

Amended Code Sec. 3302(c) by adding subparagraph (4). **Effective** 1-3-75.

- **1963 (P.L. 88-173)**

P.L. 88-173, §[1]:

Amended Code Sec. 3302(c)(2). **Effective** for tax years beginning on or after 1-1-63. Prior to amendment, Code Sec. 3302(c)(2) read as follows:

"(2) If an advance or advances have been made to the unemployment account of a State under title XII of the Social Security Act before the date of the enactment of the Employment Security Act of 1960, then the total credits (after applying subsections (a) and (b) and paragraph (1) of this subsection) otherwise allowable under this section for the taxable year in the case of a taxpayer subject to the unemployment compensation law of such State shall be reduced—

"(A) in the case of a taxable year beginning with the fourth consecutive January 1 as of the beginning of which there is a balance of such advances, by 5 percent of the tax imposed by section 3301 with respect to the wages paid by such taxpayer during such taxable year which are attributable to such State; and

"(B) in the case of any succeeding taxable year beginning with a consecutive January 1 as of the beginning of which there is a balance of such advances, by an additional 5 percent, for each such succeeding taxable year, of the tax imposed by section 3301 with respect to the wages paid by such taxpayer during such taxable year which are attributable to such State."

- **1960, Social Security Amendments of 1960 (P.L. 86-778)**

P.L. 86-778, §523(b):

Amended Code Sec. 3302(c). **Effective** 9-13-60. Prior to amendment, Code Sec. 3302(c) read as follows:

(c) LIMIT ON TOTAL CREDITS.—

(1) The total credits allowed to a taxpayer under this section shall not exceed 90 percent of the tax against which such credits are allowable.

(2) If an advance or advances have been made to the unemployment account of a State under title XII of the Social Security Act, and if any balance of such advance or advances has not been returned to the Federal unemployment account as provided in that title before December 1 of the taxable year, then the total credits (after other reductions under this section) otherwise allowable under this section for such taxable year in the case of a taxpayer subject to the unemployment compensation law of such State shall be reduced—

(A) in the case of a taxable year beginning with the fourth consecutive January 1 on which such a balance of unreturned advances existed, by 5 percent of the tax imposed by section 3301 with respect to the wages paid by such taxpayer during such taxable year which are attributable to such State; and

(B) in the case of any succeeding taxable year beginning with a consecutive January 1 on which such a balance of unreturned advances existed, by an additional 5 percent, for each such succeeding taxable year, of the tax imposed by section 3301 with respect to the wages paid by such taxpayer during such taxable year which are attributable to such State.

For purposes of this paragraph, wages shall be attributable to a particular State if they are subject to the unemployment compensation law of the State, or (if not subject to the unemployment compensation law of any State) if they are determined (under rules or regulations prescribed by the Secretary or his delegate) to be attributable to such State.

[Sec. 3302(d)]

(d) DEFINITIONS AND SPECIAL RULES RELATING TO SUBSECTION (c).—

(1) RATE OF TAX DEEMED TO BE 6 PERCENT.—In applying subsection (c), the tax imposed by section 3301 shall be computed at the rate of 6 percent in lieu of the rate provided by such section.

(2) WAGES ATTRIBUTABLE TO A PARTICULAR STATE.—For purposes of subsection (c), wages shall be attributable to a particular State if they are subject to the unemployment compensation law of the State, or (if not subject to the unemployment compensation law of any State) if they are determined (under rules or regulations prescribed by the the Secretary) to be attributable to such State.

UNEMPLOYMENT TAX

(3) ADDITIONAL TAXES INAPPLICABLE WHERE ADVANCES ARE REPAID BEFORE NOVEMBER 10 OF TAXABLE YEAR.—Paragraph (2) of subsection (c) shall not apply with respect to any State for the taxable year if (as of the beginning of November 10 of such year) there is no balance of advances referred to in such paragraph.

(4) AVERAGE EMPLOYER CONTRIBUTION RATE.—For purposes of subparagraphs (B) and (C) of subsection (c)(2), the average employer contribution rate for any State for any calendar year is that percentage obtained by dividing—

(A) the total of the contributions paid into the State unemployment fund with respect to such calendar year, by

(B)(i) for purposes of subparagraph (B) of subsection (c)(2), the total of the wages (as determined without any limitation on amount) attributable to such State subject to contributions under this chapter with respect to such calendar year, and

(ii) for purposes of subparagraph (C) of subsection (c)(2), the total of the remuneration subject to contributions under the State unemployment compensation law with respect to such calendar year.

For purposes of subparagraph (C) of subsection (c)(2), if the average employer contribution rate for any State for any calendar year (determined without regard to this sentence) equals or exceeds 2.7 percent, such rate shall be determined by increasing the amount taken into account under subparagraph (A) of the preceding sentence by the aggregate amount of employee payments (if any) into the unemployment fund of such State with respect to such calendar year which are to be used solely in the payment of unemployment compensation.

(5) 5-YEAR BENEFIT COST RATE.—For purposes of subparagraph (C) of subsection (c)(2), the 5-year benefit cost rate applicable to any State for any taxable year is that percentage obtained by dividing—

(A) one-fifth of the total of the compensation paid under the State unemployment compensation law during the 5-year period ending at the close of the second calendar year preceding such taxable year, by

(B) the total of the remuneration subject to contributions under the State unemployment compensation law with respect to the first calendar year preceding such taxable year.

(6) ROUNDING.—If any percentage referred to in either subparagraph (B) or (C) of subsection (c)(2) is not a multiple of .1 percent, it shall be rounded to the nearest multiple of .1 percent.

(7) DETERMINATION AND CERTIFICATION OF PERCENTAGES.—The percentage referred to in subsection (c)(2)(B) or (C) for any taxable year for any State having a balance referred to therein shall be determined by the Secretary of Labor, and shall be certified by him to the Secretary of the Treasury before June 1 of such year, on the basis of a report furnished by such State to the Secretary of Labor before May 1 of such year. Any such State report shall be made as of the close of March 31 of the taxable year, and shall be made on such forms, and shall contain such information, as the Secretary of Labor deems necessary to the performance of his duties under this section.

Amendments

- **1983, Social Security Act of 1983 (P.L. 98-21)**

P.L. 98-21, § 513(a):

Amended Code Sec. 3302(d)(4)(B). **Effective** for tax year 1983 and tax years thereafter. Prior to amendment, Code Sec. 3302(d)(4)(B) read as follows:

(B) the total of the remuneration subject to contributions under the State unemployment compensation law with respect to such calendar year.

- **1982, Tax Equity and Fiscal Responsibility Act of 1982 (P.L. 97-248)**

P.L. 97-248, § 271(c)(2)(B):

Amended Code Sec. 3302(d)(1) by striking out "3 percent" each place it appeared and inserting "6 percent". **Effective** for remuneration paid after 12-31-84.

- **1976, Tax Reform Act of 1976 (P.L. 94-455)**

P.L. 94-455, § 1903(a)(12)(C)(iv):

Deleted "or (3)" in Code Sec. 3302(d)(3). **Effective** for wages paid after 12-31-76.

P.L. 94-455, § 1903(a)(12)(C)(v):

Substituted "subsection (c)(2)" for "subsection (c)(3)" each place it appeared in Code Sec. 3302(d)(4), (5), and (6). **Effective** for wages paid after 12-31-76.

P.L. 94-455, § 1903(a)(12)(C)(vi):

Substituted "subsection (c)(2)(B) or (C)" for "subsection (c)(3)(B) or (C)" in Code Sec. 3302(d)(7). **Effective** for wages paid after 12-31-76.

P.L. 94-455, § 1903(a)(12)(D):

Deleted paragraph (8) of Code Sec. 3302(d). **Effective** for wages paid after 12-31-76. Prior to amendment, paragraph (8) read as follows:

(8) CROSS REFERENCES.—

For reduction of total credits allowable under subsection (c), see section 104 of the Temporary Unemployment Compensation Act of 1958.

P.L. 94-455, § 1906(b)(13)(A):

Amended 1954 Code by substituting "Secretary" for "Secretary or his delegate" each place it appeared. **Effective** 2-1-77.

- **1963 (P.L. 88-31)**

P.L. 88-31, § 2(b):

Amended Code Sec. 3302(d)(1). **Effective** for calendar year 1963 and subsequent years. Prior to amendment, Sec. 3302(d)(1) read as follows:

(1) RATE OF TAX DEEMED TO BE 3 PERCENT.—In applying subsection (c), the tax imposed by section 3301 shall be computed at the rate of 3 percent in lieu of 3.1 percent (or, in the case of the tax imposed with respect to the calendar years 1962 and 1963, in lieu of 3.5 percent).

- **1961, Temporary Extended Unemployment Compensation Act of 1961 (P.L. 87-6)**

P.L. 87-6, § 14(b):

Added the parenthetical phrase in Code Sec. 3302(d)(1).

- **1960, Social Security Amendments of 1960 (P.L. 86-778)**

P.L. 86-778, § 523(b):

Added subsection (d). **Effective** 9-13-60.

[Sec. 3302(e)]

(e) SUCCESSOR EMPLOYER.—Subject to the limits provided by subsection (c), if—

(1) an employer acquires during any calendar year substantially all the property used in the trade or business of another person, or used in a separate unit of a trade or business of such other person, and immediately after the acquisition employs in his trade or business one or more individuals who immediately prior to the acquisition were employed in the trade or business of such other person, and

(2) such other person is not an employer for the calendar year in which the acquisition takes place,

then, for the calendar year in which the acquisition takes place, in addition to the credits allowed under subsections (a) and (b), such employer may credit against the tax imposed by section 3301 for such year an amount equal to the credits which (without regard to subsection (c)) would have been allowable to such other person under subsections (a) and (b) and this subsection for such year, if such other person had been an employer, with respect to remuneration subject to contributions under the unemployment compensation law of a State paid by such other person to the individual or individuals described in paragraph (1).

Amendments

- **1961 (P.L. 87-321)**

P.L. 87-321, § 1:

Added Code Sec. 3302(e). **Effective** for calendar year 1961 and for each calendar year thereafter.

[Sec. 3302(f)]

(f) LIMITATION ON CREDIT REDUCTION.—

(1) LIMITATION.—In the case of any State which meets the requirements of paragraph (2) with respect to any taxable year, the reduction under subsection (c)(2) in credits otherwise applicable to taxpayers subject to the unemployment compensation law of such State shall not exceed the greater of—

(A) the reduction which was in effect with respect to such State under subsection (c)(2) for the preceding taxable year, or

(B) 0.6 percent of the wages paid by the taxpayer during such taxable year which are attributable to such State.

(2) REQUIREMENTS.—The requirements of this paragraph are met by any State with respect to any taxable year if the Secretary of Labor determines (on or before November 10 of such taxable year) that—

(A) no State action was taken during the 12-month period ending on September 30 of such taxable year (excluding any action required under State law as in effect prior to the date of the enactment of this subsection) which has resulted or will result in a reduction in such State's unemployment tax effort (as defined by the Secretary of Labor in regulations),

(B) no State action was taken during the 12-month period ending on September 30 of such taxable year (excluding any action required under State law as in effect prior to the date of the enactment of this subsection) which has resulted or will result in a net decrease in the solvency of the State unemployment compensation system (as defined by the Secretary of Labor in regulations),

(C) the State unemployment tax rate for the taxable year equals or exceeds the average benefit cost ratio for calendar years in the 5-calendar year period ending with the last calendar year before the taxable year, and

(D) the outstanding balance for such State of advances under title XII of the Social Security Act on September 30 of such taxable year was not greater than the outstanding balance for such State of such advances on September 30 of the third preceding taxable year.

(3) CREDIT REDUCTIONS FOR SUBSEQUENT YEARS.—If the credit reduction under subsection (c)(2) is limited by reason of paragraph (1) of this subsection for any taxable year, for purposes of applying subsection (c)(2) to subsequent taxable years (including years after 1987), the taxable year for which the credit reduction was so limited (and January 1 thereof) shall not be taken into account.

(4) STATE UNEMPLOYMENT TAX RATE.—For purposes of this subsection, the State unemployment tax rate for any taxable year is the percentage obtained by dividing—

(A) the total amount of contributions paid into the State unemployment fund with respect to such taxable year, by

(B) the total amount of the remuneration subject to contributions under the State unemployment compensation law with respect to such taxable year (determined without regard to any limitation on the amount of wages subject to contribution under the State law).

(5) BENEFIT COST RATIO.—For purposes of this subsection—

(A) IN GENERAL.—The benefit cost ratio for any calendar year is the percentage determined by dividing—

(i) the sum of the total of the compensation paid under the State unemployment compensation law during such calendar year and any interest paid during such calendar year on advances made to the State under title XII of the Social Security Act, by

(ii) the total amount of the remuneration subject to contributions under the State unemployment compensation law with respect to such calendar year (determined without regard to any limitation on the amount of remuneration subject to contribution under the State law).

(B) REIMBURSABLE BENEFITS NOT TAKEN INTO ACCOUNT.—For purposes of subparagraph (A), compensation shall not be taken into account to the extent—

(i) the State is entitled to reimbursement for such compensation under the provisions of any Federal law, or

(ii) such compensation is attributable to services performed for a reimbursing employer.

(C) REIMBURSING EMPLOYER.—The term "reimbursing employer" means any governmental entity or other organization (or group of governmental entities or any other organizations) which makes reimbursements in lieu of contributions to the State unemployment fund.

(D) ROUNDING.—If any percentage determined under subparagraph (A) is not a multiple of .1 percent, such percentage shall be reduced to the nearest multiple of .1 percent.

(6) REPORTS.—The Secretary of Labor may, by regulations, require a State to furnish such information at such time and in such manner as may be necessary for purposes of this subsection.

(7) DEFINITIONS AND SPECIAL RULES.—The definitions and special rules set forth in subsection (d) shall apply to this subsection in the same manner as they apply to subsection (c).

(8) PARTIAL LIMITATION.—

(A) In the case of a State which would meet the requirements of this subsection for a taxable year prior to 1986 but for its failure to meet one of the requirements contained in subparagraph (C) or (D) of paragraph (2), the reduction under subsection (c)(2) in credits otherwise applicable to taxpayers in such State for such taxable year and each subsequent year (in a period of consecutive years for each of which a credit reduction is in effect for taxpayers in such State) shall be reduced by 0.1 percentage point.

(B) In the case of a State which does not meet the requirements of paragraph (2) but meets the requirements of subparagraphs (A) and (B) of paragraph (2) and which also meets the requirements of section 1202(b)(8)(B) of the Social Security Act with respect to such taxable year, the reduction under subsection (c)(2) in credits otherwise applicable to taxpayers in such State for such taxable year and each subsequent year (in a period of consecutive years for each of which a credit reduction is in effect for taxpayers in such State) shall be further reduced by an additional 0.1 percentage point.

(C) In no case shall the application of subparagraphs (A) and (B) reduce the credit reduction otherwise applicable under subsection (c)(2) below the limitation under paragraph (1).

Amendments

• **2018, Tax Technical Corrections Act of 2018 (P.L. 115-141)**

P.L. 115-141, §401(b)(39)(A)-(B), Div. U:

Amended Code Sec. 3302(f)(2) by striking "(or, for purposes of applying this subparagraph to taxable year 1983, September 30, 1981)" following "the third preceding taxable year" in subparagraph (D), and by striking the last sentence. **Effective** 3-23-2018. For a special rule, see Act Sec. 401(e), Div. U, below. Prior to being stricken, the last sentence of Code Sec. 3302(f)(2) read as follows:

The requirements of subparagraphs (C) and (D) shall not apply to taxable years 1981 and 1982.

P.L. 115-141, §401(e), Div. U, provides:

(e) GENERAL SAVINGS PROVISION WITH RESPECT TO DEADWOOD PROVISIONS.—If—

(1) any provision amended or repealed by the amendments made by subsection (b) or (d) applied to—

(A) any transaction occurring before the date of the enactment of this Act,

(B) any property acquired before such date of enactment, or

(C) any item of income, loss, deduction, or credit taken into account before such date of enactment, and

(2) the treatment of such transaction, property, or item under such provision would (without regard to the amendments or repeals made by such subsection) affect the liability for tax for periods ending after such date of enactment,

nothing in the amendments or repeals made by this section shall be construed to affect the treatment of such transaction, property, or item for purposes of determining liability for tax for periods ending after such date of enactment.

• **2014, Tax Technical Corrections Act of 2014 (P.L. 113-295)**

P.L. 113-295, §221(a)(101)(A)(i)-(iv), Division A:

Amended Code Sec. 3302(f)(4) by striking "subsection—"and all that follows through "(A) IN GENERAL.—The" and inserting "subsection, the", by striking subparagraph (B), by redesignating clauses (i) and (ii) as subparagraphs (A) and (B), respectively, and by moving the text of such subparagraphs (as so redesignated) 2 ems to the left. **Effective** generally 12-19-2014. For a special rule, see Act Sec. 221(b)(2), below. Prior to being stricken, Code Sec. 3302(f)(4)(B) read as follows:

(B) TREATMENT OF ADDITIONAL TAX UNDER THIS CHAPTER.—

(i) TAXABLE YEAR 1983.—In the case of taxable year 1983, any additional tax imposed under this chapter with respect to any State by reason of subsection (c)(2) shall be treated as contributions paid into the State unemployment fund with respect to such taxable year.

(ii) TAXABLE YEAR 1984.—In the case of taxable year 1984, any additional tax imposed under this chapter with respect to any State by reason of subsection (c)(2) shall (to the extent such additional tax is attributable to a credit reduction in excess of 0.6 of wages attributable to such State) be treated as contributions paid into the State unemployment fund with respect to such taxable year.

UNEMPLOYMENT TAX

P.L. 113-295, § 221(a)(101)(B), Division A:

Amended Code Sec. 3302(f)(5) by striking subparagraph (D) and by redesignating subparagraph (E) as subparagraph (D). **Effective** generally 12-19-2014. For a special rule, see Act Sec. 221(b)(2), below. Prior to being stricken, Code Sec. 3302(f)(5)(B) read as follows:

(D) SPECIAL RULES FOR YEARS BEFORE 1985.—

(i) TAXABLE YEAR 1983.—For purposes of determining whether a State meets the requirements of paragraph (2)(C) for taxable year 1983, only regular compensation (as defined in section 205 of the Federal-State Extended Unemployment Compensation Act of 1970) shall be taken into account for purposes of determining the benefit ratio for any preceding calendar year before 1982.

(ii) TAXABLE YEAR 1984.—For purposes of determining whether a State meets the requirements of paragraph (2)(C) for taxable year 1984, only regular compensation (as so defined) shall be taken into account for purposes of determining the benefit ratio for any preceding calendar year before 1981.

P.L. 113-295, § 221(b)(2), Division A, provides:

(2) SAVINGS PROVISION.—If—

(A) any provision amended or repealed by the amendments made by this section applied to—

(i) any transaction occurring before the date of the enactment of this Act,

(ii) any property acquired before such date of enactment, or

(iii) any item of income, loss, deduction, or credit taken into account before such date of enactment, and

(B) the treatment of such transaction, property, or item under such provision would (without regard to the amendments or repeals made by this section) affect the liability for tax for periods ending after date of enactment, nothing in the amendments or repeals made by this section shall be construed to affect the treatment of such transaction, property, or item for purposes of determining liability for tax for periods ending after such date of enactment.

- **1986, Tax Reform Act of 1986 (P.L. 99-514)**

P.L. 99-514, § 1884(2):

Amended Code Sec. 3302(f)(8)(A) by striking out "1987" and inserting in lieu thereof "1986". **Effective** 10-22-86.

- **1983, Social Security Act of 1983 (P.L. 98-21)**

P.L. 98-21, § 512(a)(1):

Amended Code Sec. 3302(f) by adding paragraph (8). **Effective** with respect to tax year 1983 and thereafter.

P.L. 98-21, § 512(b):

Amended Code Sec. 3302(f)(1). **Effective** 4-20-83. Prior to amendment, Code Sec. 3302(f)(1) read as follows:

"(1) LIMITATION.—In the case of any State which meets the requirements of paragraph (2) with respect to any taxable year beginning before January 1, 1988, the reduction under subsection (c)(2) in credits otherwise applicable to taxpayers subject to the unemployment compensation law of such State shall not exceed the greater of—

(A) the reduction which was in effect with respect to such State under subsection (c)(2) for the preceding taxable year, or

(B) 0.6 percent of the wages paid by the taxpayer during such taxable year which are attributable to such State."

- **1981, Omnibus Budget Reconciliation Act of 1981 (P.L. 97-35)**

P.L. 97-35, § 2406(a):

Amended Code Sec. 3302 by adding at the end thereof new subsection (f). **Effective** for tax years beginning after 12-31-80.

[Sec. 3302(g)]

(g) CREDIT REDUCTION NOT TO APPLY WHEN STATE MAKES CERTAIN REPAYMENTS.—

(1) IN GENERAL.—In the case of any State which meets requirements of paragraph (2) with respect to any taxable year, subsection (c)(2) shall not apply to such taxable year; except that such taxable year (and January 1 of such taxable year) shall (except as provided in subsection (f)(3)) be taken into account for purposes of applying subsection (c)(2) to succeeding taxable years.

(2) REQUIREMENTS.—The requirements of this paragraph are met by any State with respect to any taxable year if the Secretary of Labor determines that—

(A) the repayments during the 1-year period ending on November 9 of such taxable year made by such State of advances under title XII of the Social Security Act are not less than the sum of—

(i) the potential additional taxes for such taxable year, and

(ii) any advances made to such State during such 1-year period under such title XII,

(B) there will be sufficient amounts in the State unemployment fund to pay all compensation during the 3-month period beginning on November 1 of such taxable year without receiving any advance under title XII of the Social Security Act, and

(C) there is a net increase in the solvency of the State unemployment compensation system for the taxable year attributable to changes made in the State law after the date on which the first advance taken into account in determining the amount of the potential additional taxes was made (or, if later, after the date of the enactment of this subsection) and such net increase equals or exceeds the potential additional taxes for such taxable year.

(3) DEFINITIONS.—For purposes of paragraph (2)—

(A) POTENTIAL ADDITIONAL TAXES.—The term "potential additional taxes" means, with respect to any State for any taxable year, the aggregate amount of the additional tax which would be payable under this chapter for such taxable year by all taxpayers subject to the unemployment compensation law of such State for such taxable year if paragraph (2) of subsection (c) had applied to such taxable year and any preceding taxable year without regard to this subsection but with regard to subsection (f).

(B) TREATMENT OF CERTAIN REDUCTIONS.—Any reduction in the State's balance under section 901(d)(1) of the Social Security Act shall not be treated as a repayment made by such State.

(4) REPORTS.—The Secretary of Labor may require a State to furnish such information at such time and in such manner as may be necessary for purposes of paragraph (2).

Amendments

- **1982, Tax Equity and Fiscal Responsibility Act of 1982 (P.L. 97-248)**

P.L. 97-248, § 272(a):

Added Code Sec. 3302(g). **Effective** for tax years beginning after 12-31-82.

[Sec. 3302(h)]

(h) TREATMENT OF CERTIFIED PROFESSIONAL EMPLOYER ORGANIZATIONS.—If a certified professional employer organization (as defined in section 7705), or a customer of such organization, makes a contribution to the State's unemployment fund with respect to wages paid to a work site employee, such certified professional employer organization shall be eligible for the credits available under this section with respect to such contribution.

Amendments

- **2014, Stephen Beck, Jr., Achieving a Better Life Experience Act of 2014 (P.L. 113-295)**

P.L. 113-295, § 206(c)(1), Division B:

Amended Code Sec. 3302 by adding at the end a new subsection (h). **Effective** generally for wages for services performed on or after January 1 of the first calendar year beginning more than 12 months after 12-19-2014. For a special rule, see Act Sec. 206(h), below.

P.L. 113-295, § 206(h), Division B, provides:

(h) NO INFERENCE.—Nothing contained in this section or the amendments made by this section shall be construed to create any inference with respect to the determination of who is an employee or employer—

(1) for Federal tax purposes (other than the purposes set forth in the amendments made by this section), or

(2) for purposes of any other provision of law.

UNEMPLOYMENT TAX

[Sec. 3303]

SEC. 3303. CONDITIONS OF ADDITIONAL CREDIT ALLOWANCE.

[Sec. 3303(a)]

(a) STATE STANDARDS.—A taxpayer shall be allowed an additional credit under section 3302(b) with respect to any reduced rate of contributions permitted by a State law, only if the Secretary of Labor finds that under such law—

(1) no reduced rate of contributions to a pooled fund or to a partially pooled account is permitted to a person (or group of persons) having individuals in his (or their) employ except on the basis of his (or their) experience with respect to unemployment or other factors bearing a direct relation to unemployment risk during not less than the 3 consecutive years immediately preceding the computation date;

(2) no reduced rate of contributions to a guaranteed employment account is permitted to a person (or a group of persons) having individuals in his (or their) employ unless—

(A) the guaranty of remuneration was fulfilled in the year preceding the computation date; and

(B) the balance of such account amounts to not less than $2^{1}/_{2}$ percent of that part of the payroll or payrolls for the 3 years preceding the computation date by which contributions to such account were measured; and

(C) such contributions were payable to such account with respect to 3 years preceding the computation date;

(3) no reduced rate of contributions to a reserve account is permitted to a person (or group of persons) having individuals in his (or their) employ unless—

(A) compensation has been payable from such account throughout the year preceding the computation date, and

(B) the balance of such account amounts to not less than five times the largest amount of compensation paid from such account within any 1 of the 3 years preceding such date, and

(C) the balance of such account amounts to not less than $2^{1}/_{2}$ percent of that part of the payroll or payrolls for the 3 years preceding such date by which contributions to such account were measured, and

(D) such contributions were payable to such account with respect to the 3 years preceding the computation date; and

(4) if the taxpayer is a certified professional employer organization (as defined in section 7705) that is treated as the employer under section 3511, such certified professional employer organization is permitted to collect and remit, in accordance with paragraphs (1), (2), and (3), contributions during the taxable year to the State unemployment fund with respect to a work site employee.

For any person (or group of persons) who has (or have) not been subject to the State law for a period of time sufficient to compute the reduced rates permitted by paragraphs (1), (2), (3), and (4) of this subsection on a 3-year basis (i) the period of time required may be reduced to the amount of time the person (or group of persons) has (or have) had experience under or has (or have) been subject to the State law, whichever is appropriate, but in no case less than 1 year immediately preceding the computation date, or (ii) a reduced rate (not less than 1 percent) may be permitted by the State law on a reasonable basis other than as permitted by paragraph (1), (2), (3), or (4).

Amendments

• **2020, Coronavirus Aid, Relief, and Economic Security (CARES) Act (P.L. 116-136)**

P.L. 116-136, § 2109(b)(3), provides:

(3) EMPLOYER PAYMENT OF COSTS.—Any short-time compensation plan entered into by an employer must provide that the employer will pay the State an amount equal to one-half of the amount of short-time compensation paid under such plan. Such amount shall be deposited in the State's unemployment fund and shall not be used for purposes of calculating an employer's contribution rate under section 3303(a)(1) of the Internal Revenue Code of 1986.

• **2014, Stephen Beck, Jr., Achieving a Better Life Experience Act of 2014 (P.L. 113-295)**

P.L. 113-295, § 206(c)(2)(A)-(B), Division B:

Amended Code Sec. 3303(a) by striking the period at the end of paragraph (3) and inserting "; and" and by inserting after paragraph (3) a new paragraph (4), and in the last sentence by striking "paragraphs (1), (2), and (3)" and inserting "paragraphs (1), (2), (3), and (4)", and by striking "paragraph (1), (2), or (3)" and inserting "paragraph (1), (2), (3), or (4)". **Effective** generally for wages for services performed on or after January 1 of the first calendar year beginning more than 12 months after 12-19-2014. For a special rule, see Act Sec. 206(h), below.

P.L. 113-295, § 206(h), Division B, provides:

(h) NO INFERENCE.—Nothing contained in this section or the amendments made by this section shall be construed to create any inference with respect to the determination of who is an employee or employer—

(1) for Federal tax purposes (other than the purposes set forth in the amendments made by this section), or

(2) for purposes of any other provision of law.

• **1970, Employment Security Amendments of 1970 (P.L. 91-373)**

P.L. 91-373, § 122(a):

Amended Code Sec. 3303(a) in the sentence following paragraph (3) by adding "(i)" in place of the comma following "3-year basis" and adding the material following "computation date". **Effective** with respect to tax years beginning after 12-31-71.

• **1954 (P.L. 767, 83rd Cong.)**

P.L. 767, 83rd Cong., § 2:

Amended Code Sec. 3303(a) by adding the unnumbered paragraph following paragraph (3)(D). **Effective** with respect to rates of contributions for periods after 12-31-54.

[Sec. 3303(b)]

(b) CERTIFICATION BY THE SECRETARY OF LABOR WITH RESPECT TO ADDITIONAL CREDIT ALLOWANCE.—

(1) On October 31 of each calendar year, the Secretary of Labor shall certify to the Secretary the law of each State (certified by the Secretary of Labor as provided in section 3304 for the 12-month period ending on such October 31), with respect to which he finds that reduced rates of contributions were allowable with respect to such 12-month period only in accordance with the provisions of subsection (a).

(2) If the Secretary of Labor finds that under the law of a single State (certified by the Secretary of Labor as provided in section 3304) more than one type of fund or account is maintained, and reduced rates of contributions to more than one type of fund or account were allowable with respect to any 12-month period ending on October 31, and one or more of such reduced rates were allowable under conditions not fulfilling the requirements of subsection (a), the Secretary of Labor shall, on such October 31, certify to the Secretary of the Treasury only those provisions of the State law pursuant to which reduced rates of contributions were allowable with respect to such 12-month period under conditions fulfilling the requirements of subsection (a), and shall, in connection therewith, designate the kind of fund or account, as defined in subsection (c), established by the provisions so certified. If the Secretary of Labor finds that a part of any reduced rate of contributions payable under such law or under such provisions is required to be paid into one fund or account and a part into another fund or account, the Secretary of Labor shall make such certification pursuant to this paragraph as he finds will assure the allowance of additional credits only with respect to that part of the reduced rate of contributions which is allowed under provisions which do fulfill the requirements of subsection (a).

(3) The Secretary of Labor shall, within 30 days after any State law is submitted to him for such purpose, certify to the State agency his findings with respect to reduced rates of contributions to a type of fund or account, as defined in subsection (c), which are allowable under such State law only in accordance with the provisions of subsection (a). After making such findings, the Secretary of Labor shall not withhold his certification to the Secretary of the Treasury of such State law, or of the provisions thereof with respect to which such findings were made, for any 12-month period ending on October 31 pursuant to paragraph (1) or (2) unless, after reasonable notice and opportunity for hearing to the State agency, the Secretary of Labor finds the State law no longer contains the provisions specified in subsection (a) or the State has, with respect to such 12-month period, failed to comply substantially with any such provision.

UNEMPLOYMENT TAX

Amendments

• **1976, Tax Reform Act of 1976 (P.L. 94-455)**

P.L. 94-455, § 1903(a)(13):

Deleted "(10-month period in the case of October 31, 1972)" each place it appeared in Code Sec. 3303(b), substituted "12-month period" for "12 or 10-month period, as the case may be," each place it appeared in paragraphs (1) and (2) of Code Sec. 3303(b), and substituted "12-month period," for "12 or 10-month period, as the case may be," in paragraph (3) of Code Sec. 3303(b). **Effective** for wages paid after 12-31-76.

P.L. 94-455, § 1906(b)(13)(C):

Substituted "to the Secretary of the Treasury" for "to the Secretary" each place it appeared in Code Sec. 3303(b). **Effective** 2-1-77.

• **1970, Employment Security Amendments of 1970 (P.L. 91-373)**

P.L. 91-373, § 142(c), (d):

Amended Code Sec. 3303(b). **Effective** with respect to tax year 1972 and tax years thereafter. Prior to amendment, Code Sec. 3303(b) read as follows:

(1) On December 31 in each taxable year, the Secretary of Labor shall certify to the Secretary the law of each State (certified with respect to such year by the Secretary of Labor as provided in section 3304) with respect to which he finds that reduced rates of contributions were allowable with respect to such taxable year only in accordance with the provisions of subsection (a).

(2) If the Secretary of Labor finds that under the law of a single State (certified by the Secretary of Labor as provided in section 3304) more than one type of fund or account is maintained, and reduced rates of contributions to more than one type of fund or account were allowable with respect to any taxable year, and one or more of such reduced rates were allowable under conditions not fulfilling the requirements of subsection (a), the Secretary of Labor shall, on December 31 of such taxable year, certify to the Secretary only those provisions of the State law pursuant to which reduced rates of contributions were allowable with respect to such taxable year under conditions fulfilling the requirements of subsection (a), and shall, in connection therewith, designate the kind of fund or account, as defined in subsection (c), established by the provisions so certified. If the Secretary of Labor finds that a part of any reduced rate of contributions payable under such law or under such provisions is required to be paid into one fund or account and a part into another fund or account, the Secretary of Labor shall make such certification pursuant to this paragraph as he finds will assure the allowance of additional credits only with respect to that part of the reduced rate of contributions which is allowed under provisions which do fulfill the requirements of subsection (a).

(3) The Secretary of Labor shall, within 30 days after any State law is submitted to him for such purpose, certify to the State agency his findings with respect to reduced rates of contributions to a type of fund or account, as defined in subsection (c), which are allowable under such State law only in accordance with the provisions of subsection (a). After making such findings, the Secretary of Labor shall not withhold his certification to the Secretary of such State law, or of the provisions thereof with respect to which such findings were made, for any taxable year pursuant to paragraph (1) or (2) unless, after reasonable notice and opportunity for hearing to the State agency, the Secretary of Labor finds the State law no longer contains the provisions specified in subsection (a) or the State has, with respect to such taxable year, failed to comply substantially with any such provision.

[Sec. 3303(c)]

(c) DEFINITIONS.—As used in this section—

(1) RESERVE ACCOUNT.—The term "reserve account" means a separate account in an unemployment fund, maintained with respect to a person (or group of persons) having individuals in his (or their) employ, from which account, unless such account is exhausted, is paid all and only compensation payable on the basis of services performed for such person (or for one or more of the persons comprising the group).

(2) POOLED FUND.—The term "pooled fund" means an unemployment fund or any part thereof (other than a reserve account or a guaranteed employment account) into which the total contributions of persons contributing thereto are payable, in which all contributions are mingled and undivided, and from which compensation is payable to all individuals eligible for compensation from such fund.

(3) PARTIALLY POOLED ACCOUNT.—The term "partially pooled account" means a part of an unemployment fund in which part of the fund all contributions thereto are mingled and undivided, and from which part of the fund compensation is payable only to individuals to whom compensation would be payable from a reserve account or from a guaranteed employment account but for the exhaustion or termination of such reserve account or of such guaranteed employment account. Payments from a reserve account or guaranteed employment account into a partially pooled account shall not be construed to be inconsistent with the provisions of paragraph (1) or (4).

(4) GUARANTEED EMPLOYMENT ACCOUNT.—The term "guaranteed employment account" means a separate account, in an unemployment fund, maintained with respect to a person (or group of persons) having individuals in his (or their) employ who, in accordance with the provisions of the State law or of a plan thereunder approved by the State agency,

(A) guarantees in advance at least 30 hours of work, for which remuneration will be paid at not less than stated rates, for each of 40 weeks (or if more, 1 weekly hour may be deducted for each added week guaranteed) in a year, to all the individuals who are in his (or their) employ in, and who continue to be available for suitable work in, one or more distinct establishments, except that any such individual's guaranty may commence after a probationary period (included within the 11 or less consecutive weeks immediately following the first week in which the individual renders services), and

(B) gives security or assurance, satisfactory to the State agency, for the fulfillment of such guaranties, from which account, unless such account is exhausted or terminated, is paid all and only compensation, payable on the basis of services performed for such person (or for one or more of the persons comprising the group), to any such individual whose guaranteed remuneration has not been paid (either pursuant to the guaranty or from the security or assurance provided for the fulfillment of the guaranty), or whose guaranty is not renewed and who is otherwise eligible for compensation under the State law.

(5) YEAR.—The term "year" means any 12 consecutive calendar months.

(6) BALANCE.—The term "balance", with respect to a reserve account or a guaranteed employment account, means the amount standing to the credit of the account as of the computation date; except that, if subsequent to January 1, 1940, any moneys have been paid into or credited to such account other than payments thereto by persons having individuals in their employ, such term shall mean the amount in such account as of the computation date less the total of such other moneys paid into or credited to such account subsequent to January 1, 1940.

(7) COMPUTATION DATE.—The term "computation date" means the date, occurring at least once in each calendar year and within 27 weeks prior to the effective date of new rates of contributions, as of which such rates are computed.

(8) REDUCED RATE.—The term "reduced rate" means a rate of contributions lower than the standard rate applicable under the State law, and the term "standard rate" means the rate on the basis of which variations therefrom are computed.

[Sec. 3303(d)]

(d) VOLUNTARY CONTRIBUTIONS.—A State law may, without being deemed to violate the standards set forth in subsection (a), permit voluntary contributions to be used in the computation of reduced rates if such contributions are paid prior to the expiration of 120 days after the beginning of the year for which such rates are effective.

[Sec. 3303(e)]

(e) PAYMENTS BY CERTAIN NONPROFIT ORGANIZATIONS.—A State may, without being deemed to violate the standards set forth in subsection (a), permit an organization (or group of organizations) described in section 501(c)(3) which is exempt from income tax under section 501(a) to elect (in lieu of paying contributions) to pay into the State unemployment fund amounts equal to the amounts of compensation attributable under the State law to service performed in the employ of such organization (or group).

Amendments

• **1970, Employment Security Amendments of 1970 (P.L. 91-373)**

P.L. 91-373, § 104(c):

Added Code Sec. 3303(e). **Effective** 1-1-70.

UNEMPLOYMENT TAX

[Sec. 3303(f)—Stricken]

Amendments

• **2011, Trade Adjustment Assistance Extension Act of 2011 (P.L. 112-40)**

P.L. 112-40, §252(a)(1):

Amended Code Sec. 3303 by striking subsection (f). For the **effective** date, see Act Sec. 252(b)(1)-(2), below. Prior to being stricken, Code Sec. 3303(f) read as follows:

(f) TRANSITION.—To facilitate the orderly transition to coverage of service to which section 3309(a)(1)(A) applies, a State law may provide that an organization (or group of organizations) which elects before April 1, 1972, to make payments (in lieu of contributions) into the State unemployment fund as provided in section 3309(a)(2), and which had paid contributions into such fund under the State law with respect to such service performed in its employ before January 1, 1969, is not required to make any such payment (in lieu of contributions) on account of compensation paid after its election as heretofore described which is attributable under the State law to service performed in its employ, until the total of such compensation equals the amount—

(1) by which the contributions paid by such organization (or group) with respect to a period before the election provided by section 3309(a)(2), exceed

(2) the unemployment compensation for the same period which was charged to the experience-rating account of such organization (or group) or paid under the State law on the basis of wages paid by it or service performed in its employ, whichever is appropriate.

P.L. 112-40, §252(b)(1)-(2), provides:

(b)EFFECTIVE DATE.—

(1) IN GENERAL.—Except as provided in paragraph (2), the amendments made by this section shall apply to erroneous payments established after the end of the 2-year period beginning on the date of the enactment of this Act [10-21-2011.—CCH].

(2) AUTHORITY.—A State may amend its State law to apply such amendments to erroneous payments established prior to the end of the period described in paragraph (1).

• **1983, Social Security Act of 1983 (P.L. 98-21)**

P.L. 98-21, §524, provides:

SEC. 524. If—

(1) an organization did not make an election to make payments (in lieu of contributions) as provided in section 3309(a)(2) of the Internal Revenue Code of 1954 before April 1, 1972, because such organization, as of such date, was treated as an organization described in section 501(c)(4) of such Code,

(2) the Internal Revenue Service subsequently determined that such organization was described in section 501(c)(3) of such Code, and

(3) such organization made such an election before the earlier of—

(A) the date 18 months after such election was first available to it under the State law, or

(B) January 1, 1984,

then section 3303(f) of such Code shall be applied with respect to such organization as if it did not contain the requirement that the election be made before April 1, 1972, and by substituting "January 1, 1982" for "January 1, 1969".

• **1976, Unemployment Compensation Amendments of 1976 (P.L. 94-566)**

P.L. 94-566, §122(b), (c):

Substituted "which elects before April 1, 1972" for "which elects, when such election first becomes available under the State law" in Code Sec. 3303(f). **Effective** 1-1-70.

• **1970, Employment Security Amendments of 1970 (P.L. 91-373)**

P.L. 91-373, §104(c):

Added Code Sec. 3303(f). **Effective** 1-1-70.

[Sec. 3303(f)]

(f) PROHIBITION ON NONCHARGING DUE TO EMPLOYER FAULT.—

(1) IN GENERAL.—A State law shall be treated as meeting the requirements of subsection (a)(1) only if such law provides that an employer's account shall not be relieved of charges relating to a payment from the State unemployment fund if the State agency determines that—

(A) the payment was made because the employer, or an agent of the employer, was at fault for failing to respond timely or adequately to the request of the agency for information relating to the claim for compensation; and

(B) the employer or agent has established a pattern of failing to respond timely or adequately to such requests.

(2) STATE AUTHORITY TO IMPOSE STRICTER STANDARDS.—Nothing in paragraph (1) shall limit the authority of a State to provide that an employer's account not be relieved of charges relating to a payment from the State unemployment fund for reasons other than the reasons described in subparagraphs (A) and (B) of such paragraph, such as after the first instance of a failure to respond timely or adequately to requests described in paragraph (1)(A).

Amendments

• **2011, Trade Adjustment Assistance Extension Act of 2011 (P.L. 112-40)**

P.L. 112-40, §252(a)(1)-(2):

Amended Code Sec. 3303 by striking subsections (f) and (g) and by inserting after subsection (e) a new subsection (f). For the **effective** date, see Act Sec. 252(b)(1)-(2), below.

P.L. 112-40, §252(b)(1)-(2), provides:

(b)EFFECTIVE DATE.—

(1) IN GENERAL.—Except as provided in paragraph (2), the amendments made by this section shall apply to erroneous payments established after the end of the 2-year period beginning on the date of the enactment of this Act [10-21-2011.—CCH].

(2) AUTHORITY.—A State may amend its State law to apply such amendments to erroneous payments established prior to the end of the period described in paragraph (1).

[Sec. 3303(g)—Stricken]

Amendments

• **2011, Trade Adjustment Assistance Extension Act of 2011 (P.L. 112-40)**

P.L. 112-40, §252(a)(1):

Amended Code Sec. 3303 by striking subsection (g). For the **effective** date, see Act Sec. 252(b)(1)-(2), below. Prior to being stricken, Code Sec. 3303(g) read as follows:

(g) TRANSITIONAL RULE FOR UNEMPLOYMENT COMPENSATION AMENDMENTS OF 1976.—To facilitate the orderly transition to coverage of service to which section 3309(a)(1)(A) applies by reason of the enactment of the Unemployment Compensation Amendments of 1976, a State law may provide that an organization (or group of organizations) which elects, when such election first becomes available under the State law with respect to such service, to make payments (in lieu of contributions) into the State unemployment fund as provided in section 3309(a)(2), and which had paid contributions into such fund under the State law with respect to such service performed in its employ before the date of the enactment of this subsection, is not required to make any such payment (in lieu of contributions) on account of compensation paid after its election as heretofore described which is attributable under the State law to such service performed in its employ, until the total of such compensation equals the amount—

(1) by which the contributions paid by such organization (or group) on the basis of wages for such service with respect to a period before the election provided by section 3309(a)(2), exceed

(2) the unemployment compensation for the same period which was charged to the experience-rating account of such organization (or group) or paid under the State law on the basis of such service performed in its employ or wages paid for such service, whichever is appropriate.

P.L. 112-40, §252(b)(1)-(2), provides:

(b)EFFECTIVE DATE.—

(1) IN GENERAL.—Except as provided in paragraph (2), the amendments made by this section shall apply to erroneous payments established after the end of the 2-year period beginning on the date of the enactment of this Act [10-21-2011.—CCH].

(2) AUTHORITY.—A State may amend its State law to apply such amendments to erroneous payments established prior to the end of the period described in paragraph (1).

• **1976, Unemployment Compensation Amendments of 1976 (P.L. 94-566)**

P.L. 94-566, §122(a), (c):

Added Code Sec. 3303(g). **Effective** 10-20-76.

[Sec. 3304]

SEC. 3304. APPROVAL OF STATE LAWS.

[Sec. 3304(a)]

(a) REQUIREMENTS.—The Secretary of Labor shall approve any State law submitted to him, within 30 days of such submission, which he finds provides that—

(1) all compensation is to be paid through public employment offices or such other agencies as the Secretary of Labor may approve;

(2) no compensation shall be payable with respect to any day of unemployment occurring within 2 years after the first day of the first period with respect to which contributions are required;

UNEMPLOYMENT TAX

(3) all money received in the unemployment fund shall (except for refunds of sums erroneously paid into such fund and except for refunds paid in accordance with the provisions of section 3305 (b)) immediately upon such receipt be paid over to the Secretary of the Treasury to the credit of the Unemployment Trust Fund established by section 904 of the Social Security Act (42 U. S. C. 1104);

(4) all money withdrawn from the unemployment fund of the State shall be used solely in the payment of unemployment compensation, exclusive of expenses of administration, and for refunds of sums erroneously paid into such fund and refunds paid in accordance with the provisions of section 3305(b); except that—

(A) an amount equal to the amount of employee payments into the unemployment fund of a State may be used in the payment of cash benefits to individuals with respect to their disability, exclusive of expenses of administration;

(B) the amounts specified by section 903(c)(2) or 903(d)(4) of the Social Security Act may, subject to the conditions prescribed in such section, be used for expenses incurred by the State for administration of its unemployment compensation law and public employment offices;

(C) nothing in this paragraph shall be construed to prohibit deducting an amount from unemployment compensation otherwise payable to an individual and using the amount so deducted to pay for health insurance, or the withholding of Federal, State, or local individual income tax, if the individual elected to have such deduction made and such deduction was made under a program approved by the Secretary of Labor;

(D) amounts shall be deducted from unemployment benefits and used to repay overpayments as provided in section 303(g) of the Social Security Act;

(E) amounts may be withdrawn for the payment of short-time compensation under a short-time compensation program (as defined under section 3306(v));

(F) amounts may be withdrawn for the payment of allowances under a self-employed assistance program (as defined in section 3306(t)); and

(G) with respect to amounts of covered unemployment compensation debt (as defined in section 6402(f)(4)) collected under section 6402(f)(4)—

(i) amounts may be deducted to pay any fees authorized under such section; and

(ii) the penalties and interest described in section 6402(f)(4)(C) may be transferred to the appropriate State fund into which the State would have deposited such amounts had the person owing the debt paid such amounts directly to the State;

(5) compensation shall not be denied in such State to any otherwise eligible individual for refusing to accept new work under any of the following conditions:

(A) if the position offered is vacant due directly to a strike, lockout, or other labor dispute;

(B) if the wages, hours, or other conditions of the work offered are substantially less favorable to the individual than those prevailing for similar work in the locality;

(C) if as a condition of being employed the individual would be required to join a company union or to resign from or refrain from joining any bona fide labor organization;

(6)(A) compensation is payable on the basis of service to which section 3309(a)(1) applies, in the same amount, on the same terms, and subject to the same conditions as compensation payable on the basis of other service subject to such law except that—

(i) with respect to services in an instructional, research, or principal administrative capacity for an educational institution to which section 3309(a)(1) applies, compensation shall not be payable based on such services for any week commencing during the period between two successive academic years or terms (or, when an agreement provides instead for a similar period between two regular but not successive terms, during such period) to any individual if such individual performs such services in the first of such academic years (or terms) and if there is a contract or reasonable assurance that such individual will perform services in any such capacity for any educational institution in the second of such academic years or terms,

(ii) with respect to services in any other capacity for an educational institution to which section 3309(a)(1) applies—

(I) compensation payable on the basis of such services may be denied to any individual for any week which commences during a period between 2 successive academic years or terms if such individual performs such services in the first of such academic years or terms and there is a reasonable assurance that such individual will perform such services in the second of such academic years or terms, except that

(II) if compensation is denied to any individual for any week under subclause (I) and such individual was not offered an opportunity to perform such services for the educational institution for the second of such academic years or terms, such individual shall be entitled to a retroactive payment of the compensation for each week for which the individual filed a timely claim for compensation and for which compensation was denied solely by reason of subclause (I),

(iii) with respect to any services described in clause (i) or (ii), compensation payable on the basis of such services may be denied [shall be denied (generally effective in the case of compensation paid for weeks beginning on or after April 1, 1984)] to any individual for any week which commences during an established and customary vacation period or holiday recess if such individual performs such services in the period immediately before such vacation period or holiday recess, and there is a reasonable assurance that such individual will perform such services in the period immediately following such vacation period or holiday recess,

(iv) with respect to any services described in clause (i) or (ii), compensation payable on the basis of services in any such capacity may be denied [shall be denied (generally effective in the case of compensation paid for weeks beginning on or after April 1, 1984)] as specified in clauses (i), (ii), and (iii) to any individual who performed such services in an educational institution while in the employ of an educational service agency, and for this purpose the term "educational service agency" means a governmental agency or governmental entity which is established and operated exclusively for the purpose of providing such services to one or more educational institutions,

(v) with respect to services to which section 3309(a)(1) applies, if such services are provided to or on behalf of an educational institution, compensation may be denied under the same circumstances as described in clauses (i) through (iv), and

(vi) with respect to services described in clause (ii), clauses (iii) and (iv) shall be applied by substituting "may be denied" for "shall be denied", and

(B) payments (in lieu of contributions) with respect to service to which section 3309(a)(1) applies may be made into the State unemployment fund on the basis set forth in section 3309(a)(2);

(7) an individual who has received compensation during his benefit year is required to have had work since the beginning of such year in order to qualify for compensation in his next benefit year;

(8) compensation shall not be denied to an individual for any week because he is in training with the approval of the State agency (or because of the application, to any such week in training, of State law provisions relating to availability for work, active search for work, or refusal to accept work);

Sec. 3304(a)(3)

(9)(A) compensation shall not be denied or reduced to an individual solely because he files a claim in another State (or a contiguous country with which the United States has an agreement with respect to unemployment compensation) or because he resides in another State (or such a contiguous country) at the time he files a claim for unemployment compensation;

(B) the State shall participate in any arrangements for the payment of compensation on the basis of combining an individual's wages and employment covered under the State law with his wages and employment covered under the unemployment compensation law of other States which are approved by the Secretary of Labor in consultation with the State unemployment compensation agencies as reasonably calculated to assure the prompt and full payment of compensation in such situations. Any such arrangement shall include provisions for (i) applying the base period of a single State law to a claim involving the combining of an individual's wages and employment covered under two or more State laws, and (ii) avoiding duplicate use of wages and employment by reason of such combining;

(10) compensation shall not be denied to any individual by reason of cancellation of wage credits or total reduction of his benefit rights for any cause other than discharge for misconduct connected with his work, fraud in connection with a claim for compensation, or receipt of disqualifying income;

(11) extended compensation shall be payable as provided by the Federal-State Extended Unemployment Compensation Act of 1970;

(12) no person shall be denied compensation under such State law solely on the basis of pregnancy or termination of pregnancy;

(13) compensation shall not be payable to any individual on the basis of any services, substantially all of which consist of participating in sports or athletic events or training or preparing to so participate, for any week which commences during the period between two successive sport seasons (or similar periods) if such individual performed such services in the first of such seasons (or similar periods) and there is a reasonable assurance that such individual will perform such services in the later of such seasons (or similar periods);

(14)(A) compensation shall not be payable on the basis of services performed by an alien unless such alien is an individual who was lawfully admitted for permanent residence at the time such services were performed, was lawfully present for purposes of performing such services, or was permanently residing in the United States under color of law at the time such services were performed (including an alien who was lawfully present in the United States as a result of the application of the provisions of section 212(d)(5) of the Immigration and Nationality Act),

(B) any data or information required of individuals applying for compensation to determine whether compensation is not payable to them because of their alien status shall be uniformly required from all applicants for compensation, and

(C) in the case of an individual whose application for compensation would otherwise be approved, no determination by the State agency that compensation to such individual is not payable because of his alien status shall be made except upon a preponderance of the evidence;

(15)(A) subject to subparagraph (B), the amount of compensation payable to an individual for any week which begins after March 31, 1980, and which begins in a period with respect to which such individual is receiving a governmental or other pension, retirement or retired pay, annuity, or any other similar periodic payment which is based on the previous work of such individual shall be reduced (but not below zero) by an amount equal to the amount of such pension, retirement or retired pay, annuity, or other payment, which is reasonably attributable to such week except that—

(i) the requirements of this paragraph shall apply to any pension, retirement or retired pay, annuity, or other similar periodic payment only if—

(I) such pension, retirement or retired pay, annuity, or similar payment is under a plan maintained (or contributed to) by a base period employer or chargeable employer (as determined under applicable law), and

(II) in the case of such a payment not made under the Social Security Act or the Railroad Retirement Act of 1974 (or the corresponding provisions of prior law), services performed for such employer by the individual after the beginning of the base period (or remuneration for such services) affect eligibility for, or increase the amount of, such pension, retirement or retired pay, annuity, or similar payment, and

(ii) the State law may provide for limitations on the amount of any such a reduction to take into account contributions made by the individual for the pension, retirement or retired pay, annuity, or other similar periodic payment, and

(B) the amount of compensation shall not be reduced on account of any payments of governmental or other pensions, retirement or retired pay, annuity, or other similar payments which are not includible in the gross income of the individual for the taxable year in which it was paid because it was part of a rollover distribution;

(16)(A) wage information contained in the records of the agency administering the State law which is necessary (as determined by the Secretary of Health and Human Services in regulations) for purposes of determining an individual's eligibility for assistance, or the amount of such assistance, under a State program funded under part A of title IV of the Social Security Act, shall be made available to a State or political subdivision thereof when such information is specifically requested by such State or political subdivision for such purposes,

(B) wage and unemployment compensation information contained in the records of such agency shall be furnished to the Secretary of Health and Human Services (in accordance with regulations promulgated by such Secretary) as necessary for the purposes of the National Directory of New Hires established under section 453(i) of the Social Security Act, and

(C) such safeguards are established as are necessary (as determined by the Secretary of Health and Human Services in regulations) to insure that information furnished under subparagraph (A) or (B) is used only for the purposes authorized under such subparagraph;

(17) any interest required to be paid on advances under title XII of the Social Security Act shall be paid in a timely manner and shall not be paid, directly or indirectly (by an equivalent reduction in State unemployment taxes or otherwise) by such State from amounts in such State's unemployment fund;

(18) Federal individual income tax from unemployment compensation is to be deducted and withheld if an individual receiving such compensation voluntarily requests such deduction and withholding; and

(19) all the rights, privileges, or immunities conferred by such law or by acts done pursuant thereto shall exist subject to the power of the legislature to amend or repeal such law at any time.

Amendments

• **2021, American Rescue Plan Act of 2021 (P.L. 117-2)**

P.L. 117-2, §9015, provides:

SEC. 9015. EXTENSION OF EMERGENCY STATE STAFFING FLEXIBILITY.

If a State modifies its unemployment compensation law and policies, subject to the succeeding sentence, with respect to personnel standards on a merit basis on an emergency temporary basis as needed to respond to the spread of COVID–19, such modifications shall be disregarded for the purposes of applying section 303 of the Social Security Act and section 3304 of the Internal Revenue Code of 1986 to such State law. Such modifications shall only apply through September 6, 2021, and shall be limited to engaging of temporary staff, rehiring of retirees or former employees on a non-competitive basis, and other temporary actions to quickly process applications and claims.

• **2020, Families First Coronavirus Response Act (P.L. 116-127)**

P.L. 116-127, §4102(b) (as amended by P.L. 116-136, §2106; P.L. 116-260, §205, Div. N), provides:

(b) EMERGENCY FLEXIBILITY.—Notwithstanding any other law, if a State modifies its unemployment compensation law and policies with respect to work search, waiting week, good cause, employer experience rating, or, subject to the succeeding sentence, personnel standards on a merit basis on an emergency temporary basis as needed to respond to the spread of COVID–19, such modifications shall be disregarded for the purposes of applying section 303 of the Social Security Act and section 3304 of the Internal Revenue Code of 1986 to such State law. The emergency flexibility for personnel standards on a merit basis shall only apply through March 14, 2021, and is limited to engaging of temporary staff, rehiring of retirees or former employees on a

UNEMPLOYMENT TAX

non-competitive basis, and other temporary actions to quickly process applications and claims.

- **2018, Tax Technical Corrections Act of 2018 (P.L. 115-141)**

P.L. 115-141, §401(a)(211), Div. U:

Amended Code Sec. 3304(a)(4)(G)(ii) by striking "section 6402(f)(4)(B)" and inserting "section 6402(f)(4)(C)". **Effective** 3-23-2018.

- **2012, Middle Class Tax Relief and Job Creation Act of 2012 (P.L. 112-96)**

P.L. 112-96, §2103(a):

Amended Code Sec. 3304(a)(4)(D) by striking "may" and inserting "shall". **Effective** for weeks beginning after the end of the first session of the State legislature which begins after 2-22-2012.

P.L. 112-96, §2161(b)(1)(A):

Amended Code Sec. 3304(a)(4)(E). **Effective** 2-22-2012. Prior to amendment, Code Sec. 3304(a)(4)(E) read as follows:

(E) amounts may be withdrawn for the payment of short-time compensation under a plan approved by the Secretary of Labor;

- **2008, Worker, Retiree, and Employer Recovery Act of 2008 (P.L. 110-458)**

P.L. 110-458, §111(b)(1)-(2):

Amended Code Sec. 3304(a) in paragraph (15), by redesignating clauses (i) and (ii) of subparagraph (A) as subclauses (I) and (II), by redesignating subparagraphs (A) and (B) as clauses (i) and (ii), by striking the semicolon at the end of clause (ii) (as so redesignated) and inserting ", and", by striking "(15)" and inserting "(15)(A) subject to subparagraph (B)", and by adding at the end a new subparagraph (B), and by striking the last sentence [of Code Sec. 3304(a)]. **Effective** as if included in the provision of the 2006 Act to which the amendment relates [effective for weeks beginning on or after 8-17-2006.—CCH]. Prior to being stricken, the last sentence of Code Sec. 3304(a) read as follows:

Compensation shall not be reduced under paragraph (15) for any pension, retirement or retired pay, annuity, or similar payment which is not includible in gross income of the individual for the taxable year in which paid because it was part of a rollover distribution.

- **2008, SSI Extension for Elderly and Disabled Refugees Act (P.L. 110-328)**

P.L. 110-328, §3(c)(1)-(3):

Amended Code Sec. 3304(a)(4) in subparagraph (E), by striking "and" after the semicolon; in subparagraph (F), by inserting "and" after the semicolon; and by adding at the end a new subparagraph (G). **Effective** for refunds payable under Code Sec. 6402 on or after 9-30-2008.

- **2006, Pension Protection Act of 2006 (P.L. 109-280)**

P.L. 109-280, §1105(a):

Amended Code Sec. 3304(a) by adding at the end a new flush sentence. **Effective** for weeks beginning on or after 8-17-2006.

- **2002, Job Creation and Worker Assistance Act of 2002 (P.L. 107-147)**

P.L. 107-147, §209(d)(1):

Amended Code Sec. 3304(a)(4)(B) by inserting "or 903(d)(4)" before "of the Social Security Act". **Effective** 3-9-2002. For a special rule, see Act Sec. 209(e), below.

P.L. 107-147, §209(e), provides:

(e) REGULATIONS.—The Secretary of Labor may prescribe any operating instructions or regulations necessary to carry out this section and the amendments made by this section.

- **1996, Personal Responsibility and Work Opportunity Reconciliation Act of 1996 (P.L. 104-193)**

P.L. 104-193, §110(l)(2):

Amended Code Sec. 3304(a)(16)[A] by striking "eligibility for aid or services," and all that follows through "children approved" and inserting "eligibility for assistance, or the amount of such assistance, under a State program funded". **Effective** 7-1-97. Prior to amendment, Code Sec. 3304(a)(16)(A) read as follows:

(16)(A) wage information contained in the records of the agency administering the State law which is necessary (as determined by the Secretary of Health and Human Services in regulations) for purposes of determining an individual's eligibility for aid or services, or the amount of such aid or services, under a State plan for aid and services to needy families with children approved under part A of title IV of the Social Security Act, shall be made available to a State or political subdivision thereof when such information is specifically requested by such State or political subdivision for such purposes, and

P.L. 104-193, §316(g)(2)(A)-(E):

Amended Code Sec. 3304(a)(16) by striking "Secretary of Health, Education, and Welfare" each place it appears and inserting "Secretary of Health and Human Services"; in subparagraph (B), by striking "such information" and all that follows and inserting "information furnished under subparagraph (A) or (B) is used only for the purposes authorized under such subparagraph", by striking "and" at the end of subparagraph (A), by redesignating subparagraph (B) as subparagraph (C), and by inserting after subparagraph (A) a new subparagraph (B). **Effective** 8-22-96. Prior to amendment, Code Sec. 3304(a)(16)(B) [prior to redesignation as subparagraph (C)]read as follows:

(B) such safeguards are established as are necessary (as determined by the Secretary of Health, Education, and Welfare in regulations) to insure that such information is used only for the purposes authorized under subparagraph (A);

- **1994, Uruguay Round Agreements Act (P.L. 103-465)**

P.L. 103-465, §702(b):

Amended Code Sec. 3304(a) by striking "and" at the end of paragraph (17), by redesignating paragraph (18) as paragraph (19), and by inserting after paragraph (17) a new paragraph (18). **Effective** for payments made after 12-31-96.

P.L. 103-465, §702(c)(1):

Amended Code Sec. 3304(a)(4)(C) by inserting ", or the withholding of Federal, State, or local individual income tax," after "health insurance". **Effective** for payments made after 12-31-96.

- **1993, North America Free Trade Agreement Implementation Act (P.L. 103-182)**

P.L. 103-182, §507(b)(1)(A)-(C):

Amended Code Sec. 3304(a)(4) by striking "; and" in subparagraph (D) and inserting a semicolon; by striking the semicolon in subparagraph (E) and inserting "; and"; and by adding at the end thereof new subparagraph (F). **Effective** 12-8-93.

P.L. 103-182, §507(e)(2), prior to repeal by P.L. 105-306, §3(a), provided:

(2) SUNSET.—The authority provided by this section, and the amendments made by this section, shall terminate 5 years after the date of the enactment of this Act.

- **1992, Unemployment Compensation Amendments of 1992 (P.L. 102-318)**

P.L. 102-318, §401(a)(1):

Amended Code Sec. 3304(a)(4)(C) by striking "and" at the end of subparagraph (C), by inserting "and" at the end of subparagraph (D) and by adding at the end thereof new paragraph (E). **Effective** 7-3-92.

- **1991, Emergency Unemployment Compensation Act of 1992 (P.L. 102-164)**

P.L. 102-164, §302(a)(1):

Amended Code Sec. 3304(a)(6)(A)(ii)(I) by striking "shall be denied" and inserting "may be denied". **Effective** in the case of compensation paid for weeks beginning on or after 11-15-91.

P.L. 102-164, §302(a)(2):

Amended Code Sec. 3304(a)(6)(A) by striking "and" at the end of clauses (iii) and (iv) and by inserting after clause (v) new clause (vi). **Effective** in the case of compensation paid for weeks beginning on or after 11-15-91.

- **1991, Emergency Unemployment Compensation Act of 1991 (P.L. 102-107)**

P.L. 102-107, §§1-7 and 10, provide:

SECTION 1. SHORT TITLE.

This Act may be cited as the "Emergency Unemployment Compensation Act of 1991".

SEC. 2. FEDERAL-STATE AGREEMENTS.

(a) IN GENERAL.—Any State which desires to do so may enter into and participate in an agreement under this Act with the Secretary of Labor (hereafter in this Act referred to as the "Secretary"). Any State which is a party to an agreement under this Act may, upon providing 30 days written notice to the Secretary, terminate such agreement.

(b) PROVISIONS OF AGREEMENT.—Any agreement under subsection (a) shall provide that the State agency of the State will make payments of emergency unemployment compensation—

(1) to individuals who—

(A) have exhausted all rights to regular compensation under the State law;

(B) have no rights to compensation (including both regular compensation and extended compensation) with respect to a week under such law or any other State unemployment compensation law or to compensation under any other Federal law (and are not paid or entitled to be paid any additional compensation under any State or Federal law); and

(C) are not receiving compensation with respect to such week under the unemployment compensation law of Canada; and

(2) for any week of unemployment which begins in the individual's period of eligibility (as defined in section 7(2)).

(c) EXHAUSTION OF BENEFITS.—For purposes of subsection (b)(1)(A), an individual shall be deemed to have exhausted such individual's rights to regular compensation under a State law when—

(1) no payments of regular compensation can be made under such law because such individual has received all regular compensation available to such individual based on employment or wages during such individual's base period; or

(2) such individual's rights to such compensation have been terminated by reason of the expiration of the benefit year with respect to which such rights existed.

(d) WEEKLY BENEFIT AMOUNT.—For purposes of any agreement under this Act—

(1) the amount of emergency unemployment compensation which shall be payable to any individual for any week of total unemployment shall be equal to the amount of the regular compensation (including dependent's allowances) payable to such individual during such individual's benefit year under the State law for a week of total unemployment;

(2) the terms and conditions of the State law which apply to claims for extended compensation and to the payment thereof shall apply to claims for emergency unemployment compensation and the payment thereof, except where inconsistent with the provisions of this Act, or with the regulations or operating instructions of the Secretary promulgated to carry out this Act; and

(3) the maximum amount of emergency unemployment compensation payable to any individual for whom an account is established under section 3 shall not exceed the amount established in such account for such individual.

(e) ELECTION.—Notwithstanding any other provision of Federal law (and if State law permits), the Governor of a State in a 7-percent period or an 8-percent period, as defined in section 3(c), is authorized to and may elect to trigger off an extended compensation period in order to provide payment of emergency unemployment compensation to individuals who have exhausted their rights to regular compensation under State law.

SEC. 3. EMERGENCY UNEMPLOYMENT COMPENSATION ACCOUNT.

(a) IN GENERAL.—Any agreement under this Act shall provide that the State will establish, for each eligible individual who files an application for emergency unemployment compensation, an emergency unemployment compensation account with respect to such individual's benefit year.

(b) AMOUNT IN ACCOUNT.—

(1) IN GENERAL.—The amount established in an account under subsection (a) shall be equal to the lesser of—

(A) 100 percent of the total amount of regular compensation (including dependents' allowances) payable to the individual with respect to the benefit year (as determined under the State law) on the basis of which the individual most recently received regular compensation, or

(B) the applicable limit times the individual's average weekly benefit amount for the benefit year.

(2) APPLICABLE LIMIT.—For purposes of this section—

(A) IN GENERAL.—Except as provided in this paragraph, the applicable limit shall be determined under the following table:

In the case of weeks beginning during a:	The applicable limit is:
8-percent period	20
7-percent period	13
6-percent period	7
Other period	4

(B) APPLICABLE LIMIT NOT REDUCED.—An individual's applicable limit for any week shall in no event be less than the highest applicable limit in effect for any prior week for which emergency unemployment compensation was payable to the individual from the account involved.

(C) INCREASE IN APPLICABLE LIMIT.—If the applicable limit in effect for any week is higher than the applicable limit for any prior week, the applicable limit shall be the higher applicable limit, reduced (but not below zero) by the number of prior weeks for which emergency unemployment compensation was paid to the individual from the account involved.

(3) REDUCTION FOR EXTENDED BENEFITS.—The amount in an account under paragraph (1) shall be reduced (but not below zero) by the aggregate amount of extended compensation (if any) received by such individual relating to the same benefit year under the Federal-State Extended Unemployment Compensation Act of 1970.

(4) WEEKLY BENEFIT AMOUNT.—For purposes of this subsection, an individual's weekly benefit amount for any week is the amount of regular compensation (including dependents' allowances) under the State law payable to such individual for such week for total unemployment.

(c) DETERMINATION OF PERIODS.—

(1) IN GENERAL.—For purposes of this section, the terms "8-percent period", "7-percent period", "6-percent period", and "other period" mean, with respect to any State, the period which—

(A) begins with the second Sunday of the month after the first month during which the applicable trigger for such period is on, and

(B) ends with the Saturday immediately preceding the second Sunday of the month after the first month during which the applicable trigger for such period is off.

(2) APPLICABLE TRIGGER.—In the case of an 8-percent period, 7-percent period, 6-percent period, or other period, as the case may be, the applicable trigger is on for any week with respect to any such period if the average rate of total unemployment in the State for the period consisting of the most recent 6-calendar month period for which data are available—

(A) equals or exceeds 6 percent, and

(B) falls within the applicable range (as defined in paragraph (3)).

Subparagraph (A) shall only apply in the case of an 8-percent period, 7-percent period, or 6-percent period.

(3) APPLICABLE RANGE.—For purposes of this subsection, the applicable range is as follows:

In the case of a:	The applicable range is:
8-percent period	A rate equal to or exceeding 8 percent.
7-percent period	A rate equal to or exceeding 7 percent but less than 8 percent.
6-percent period	A rate equal to or exceeding 6 percent but less than 7 percent.
Other period	A rate less than 6 percent.

(4) SPECIAL RULES FOR DETERMINING PERIODS.—

(A) MINIMUM PERIOD.—Except as provided in subparagraph (B), if for any week beginning after August 31, 1991, an 8-percent period, 7-percent period, 6-percent period, or other period, as the case may be, is triggered on with respect to such State, such period shall last for not less than 13 weeks.

(B) EXCEPTION IF APPLICABLE RANGE INCREASES.—If, but for subparagraph (A), another period with a higher applicable range would be in effect for such State, such other period shall take effect without regard to subparagraph (A).

(5) NOTIFICATION BY SECRETARY.—When a determination has been made that an 8-percent period, 7-percent period, 6-percent period, or other period is beginning or ending with respect to a State, the Secretary shall cause notice of such determination to be published in the Federal Register.

(d) EFFECTIVE DATE.—

(1) IN GENERAL.—Except as provided in paragraphs (2) and (3), no emergency unemployment compensation shall be payable to any individual under this Act for any week—

(A) beginning before the later of—

(i) September 1, 1991, or

(ii) the first week following the week in which an agreement under this Act is entered into, or

(B) beginning after July 4, 1992.

(2) TRANSITION.—In the case of an individual who is receiving emergency unemployment compensation for a week which includes July 4, 1992, such compensation shall continue to be payable to such individual in accordance with subsection (b) for any week beginning in a period of consecutive weeks for each of which the individual meets the eligibility requirements of this Act.

(3) REACHBACK PROVISIONS.—(A) IN GENERAL.—If—

(i) any individual exhausted such individual's rights to regular compensation (or extended compensation) under the State law after March 31, 1991, and before the first week following August 31, 1991 (or, if later, the week following the week in which the agreement under this Act is entered into), and

(ii) a period described in subsection (c)(2)(A) is in effect with respect to the State for the first week following August 31, 1991,

such individual shall be entitled to emergency unemployment compensation under this Act in the same manner as if such individual's benefit year ended no earlier than the last day of such following week.

(B) LIMITATION OF BENEFITS.—In the case of an individual who has exhausted such individual's rights to both regular and extended compensation, any emergency unemployment compensation payable under subparagraph (A) shall be reduced in accordance with subsection (b)(3).

SEC. 4. PAYMENTS TO STATES HAVING AGREEMENTS FOR THE PAYMENT OF EMERGENCY UNEMPLOYMENT COMPENSATION.

(a) GENERAL RULE.—There shall be paid to each State which has entered into an agreement under this Act an amount equal to 100 percent of the emergency unemployment compensation paid to individuals by the State pursuant to such agreement.

(b) TREATMENT OF REIMBURSABLE COMPENSATION.—No payment shall be made to any State under this section in respect of compensation to the extent the State is entitled to reimbursement in respect of such compensation under the provisions of any Federal law other than this Act or chapter 85 of title 5, United States Code. A State shall not be entitled to any reimbursement under such chapter 85 in respect of any compensation to the extent the State is entitled to reimbursement under this Act in respect of such compensation.

(c) DETERMINATION OF AMOUNT.—Sums payable to any State by reason of such State having an agreement under this Act shall be payable, either in advance or by way of reimbursement (as may be determined by the Secretary), in such amounts as the Secretary estimates the State will be entitled to receive under this Act for each calendar month, reduced or increased, as the case may be, by any amount by which the Secretary finds that his estimates for any prior calendar month were greater or less than the amounts which should have been paid to the State. Such estimates may be made on the basis of such statistical, sampling, or other method as may be agreed upon by the Secretary and the State agency of the State involved.

SEC. 5 FINANCING PROVISIONS.

(a) IN GENERAL.—Funds in the extended unemployment compensation account (as established by section 905 of the Social Security Act) of the Unemployment Trust Fund shall be used for the making of payments to States having agreements entered into under this Act.

(b) CERTIFICATION.—The Secretary shall from time to time certify to the Secretary of the Treasury for payment to each State the sums payable to such State under this Act. The Secretary of the Treasury, prior to audit or settlement by the General Accounting Office, shall make payments to the State in accordance with such certification, by transfers from the extended unemployment compensation account (as established by section 905 of the Social Security Act) to the account of such State in the Unemployment Trust Fund.

(c) ASSISTANCE TO STATES.—There are hereby authorized to be appropriated without fiscal year limitation, such funds as may be necessary for purposes of assisting States (as provided in title III of the Social Security Act) in meeting the costs of administration of agreements under this Act.

SEC. 6. FRAUD AND OVERPAYMENTS.

(a) IN GENERAL.—If an individual knowingly has made, or caused to be made by another, a false statement or representation of a material fact, or knowingly has failed, or caused another to fail, to disclose a material fact, and as a result of such false statement or representation or of such nondisclosure such individual has received an amount of emergency unemployment compensation under this Act to which he was not entitled, such individual—

(1) shall be ineligible for further emergency unemployment compensation under this Act in accordance with the provisions of the applicable State unemployment compensation law relating to fraud in connection with a claim for unemployment compensation; and

(2) shall be subject to prosecution under section 1001 of title 18, United States Code.

(b) REPAYMENT.—In the case of individuals who have received amounts of emergency unemployment compensation under this Act to which they were not entitled, the State shall require such individuals to repay the amounts of such emergency

UNEMPLOYMENT TAX

unemployment compensation to the State agency, except that the State agency may waive such repayment if it determines that—

(1) the payment of such emergency unemployment compensation was without fault on the part of any such individual, and

(2) such repayment would be contrary to equity and good conscience.

(c) RECOVERY BY STATE AGENCY.—

(1) IN GENERAL.—The State agency may recover the amount to be repaid, or any part thereof, by deductions from any emergency unemployment compensation payable to such individual under this Act or from any unemployment compensation payable to such individual under any Federal unemployment compensation law administered by the State agency or under any other Federal law administered by the State agency which provides for the payment of any assistance or allowance with respect to any week of unemployment, during the 3-year period after the date such individuals received the payment of the emergency unemployment compensation to which they were not entitled, except that no single deduction may exceed 50 percent of the weekly benefit amount from which such deduction is made.

(2) OPPORTUNITY FOR HEARING.—No repayment shall be required, and no deduction shall be made, until a determination has been made, notice thereof and an opportunity for a fair hearing has been given to the individual, and the determination has become final.

(d) REVIEW.—Any determination by a State agency under this section shall be subject to review in the same manner and to the same extent as determinations under the State unemployment compensation law, and only in that manner and to that extent.

SEC. 7. DEFINITIONS.

For purposes of this Act:

(1) IN GENERAL.—The terms "compensation", "regular compensation", "extended compensation", "additional compensation", "benefit year", "base period", "State", "State agency", "State law", and "week" have the meanings given such terms under section 205 of the Federal-State Extended Unemployment Compensation Act of 1970.

(2) ELIGIBILITY PERIOD.—An individual's eligibility period shall consist of the weeks in the individual's benefit year which begin in an 8-percent period, 7-percent period, 6-percent period, or other period under this Act and, if the individual's benefit year ends on or after August 31, 1991, any weeks thereafter which begin in any such period. In no event shall an individual's period of eligibility include any weeks after the 39th week after the end of the benefit year for which the indiviudal exhausted his rights to regular compensation or extended compensation.

(3) RATE OF TOTAL UNEMPLOYMENT.—The term "rate of total unemployment" means the average unadjusted total rate of unemployment (as determined by the Secretary) for a State for the period consisting of the most recent 6-calendar month period for which data are available.

***

SEC. 10. EMERGENCY DESIGNATION.

(a) EMERGENCY DESIGNATION.—Pursuant to sections 251(b)(2)(D)(i) and 252(e) of the Balanced Budget and Emergency Deficit Control Act of 1985, the Congress hereby designates all direct spending amounts provided by this Act (for all fiscal years) and all appropriations authorized by this Act (for all fiscal years) as emergency requirements within the meaning of part C of the Balanced Budget and Emergency Deficit Control Act of 1985.

(b) EFFECTIVENESS.—Notwithstanding any other provision of law or any other provision of this Act, none of the preceding sections of this Act shall take effect unless, not later than the date of the enactment of this Act, the President submits to the Congress a written designation of all direct spending amounts provided by this Act (for all fiscal years) and all appropriations authorized by this Act (for all fiscal years) as emergency requirements within the meaning of part C of the Balanced Budget and Emergency Deficit Control Act of 1985.

• **1990, Immigration Act of 1990 (P.L. 101-649)**

P.L. 101-649, §162(e)(4):

Amended Code Sec. 3304(a)(14)(A) by striking "section 203(a)(7) or" after "the provisions of". **Effective** 11-29-90.

• **1986, Consolidated Omnibus Budget Reconciliation Act of 1985 (P.L. 99-272)**

P.L. 99-272, §12401(b)(1)(A)-(C):

Amended Code Sec. 3304(a)(4) by striking out "and" at the end of subparagraph (B); by adding "and" at the end of subparagraph (C); and by adding at the end thereof new subparagraph (D). **Effective** for recoveries made on or after 4-7-86 and shall apply with respect to overpayments made before, on, or after such date.

• **1983, Social Security Act of 1983 (P.L. 98-21)**

P.L. 98-21, §515(b):

Amended Code Sec. 3304(a) by redesignating paragraph (17) as paragraph (18) and by inserting after paragraph (16) a new paragraph (17). **Effective** 4-20-83.

P.L. 98-21, §521(a)(1), (2):

Amended Code Sec. 3304(a)(6)(A) by adding clause (v). Amended Code Sec. 3304(a)(6)(A)(ii)(I), (iii), and (iv) by striking out "may be denied" and inserting in lieu thereof "shall be denied". **Effective** in the case of compensation paid for weeks beginning on or after 4-1-84. In the case of a State with respect to which the Secretary of Labor has determined that State legislation is required in order to comply with the amendment made by this section, the amendment made by this section shall apply in the case of compensation paid for weeks which begin on or after 4-1-84, and after the end of the first session of the State legislature which begins after the date of the enactment of this Act, or which began prior to the date of the enactment of this Act, and remained in session for at least twenty-five calendar days after such date of enactment. For purposes of the preceding sentence, the term "session" means a regular, special, budget, or other session of a State legislature.

P.L. 98-21, §523(a):

Amended Code Sec. 3304(a)(4) by adding subparagraph (C). **Effective** 4-20-83.

• **1982, Tax Equity and Fiscal Responsibility Act of 1982 (P.L. 97-248)**

P.L. 97-248, §193(a):

Amended Code Sec. 3304(a)(6)(A)(ii). **Effective** for weeks of unemployment beginning after the date of enactment. Insofar as it requires retroactive payments of compensation to employees of educational institutions other than institutions of higher education (as defined in Code Sec. 3304(f)), the amendment shall not be a requirement for any State law before 1-1-84. Prior to amendment, Code Sec. 3304(a)(6)(A)(ii) read as follows:

(ii) with respect to services in any other capacity for an educational institution (other than an institution of higher education) to which section 3309(a)(1) applies, compensation payable on the basis of such services may be denied to any individual for any week which commences during a period between two successive academic years or terms if such individual performs such services in the first of such academic years or terms and there is a reasonable assurance that such individual will perform such services in the second of such academic years or terms.

• **1980, Multiemployer Pension Plan Amendments Act of 1980 (P.L. 96-364)**

P.L. 96-364, §414(a):

Amended Code Sec. 3304(a) by striking out the semicolon at the end of paragraph (15) and adding the language following "attributable to such week". **Effective** for certifications of states for 1981 and subsequent years.

• **1977 (P.L. 95-216)**

P.L. 95-216, §403(b):

Amended Code Sec. 3304 by redesignating former paragraph (16) as paragraph (17) and by inserting a new paragraph (16).

• **1977 (P.L. 95-171)**

P.L. 95-171, §2(a):

Amended Code Sec. 3304(a)(6)(A) by deleting "and" at the end of clause (ii) and by adding clause (iv). **Effective** for weeks of unemployment which begin after 1977.

• **1977, Emergency Unemployment Compensation Act of 1977 (P.L. 95-19)**

P.L. 95-19, §302(a):

Amended Code Sec. 3304(a)(14)(A). **Effective** as if included in the amendment made by Sec. 314 of P.L. 94-566. Prior to amendment, Code Sec. 3304(a)(14)(A) read as follows:

(14)(A) compensation shall not be payable on the basis of services performed by an alien unless such alien is an individual who has been lawfully admitted for permanent residence or otherwise is permanently residing in the United States under color of law (including an alien who is lawfully present in the United States as a result of the application of the provisions of section 203(a)(7) or section 212(d)(5) of the Immigration and Nationality Act).

P.L. 95-19, §302(c):

Amended Code Sec. 3304(a)(6)(A)(i) by substituting "instructional, research" for "instructional research"; by substituting "two successive academic years or terms" for "two successive academic years"; by striking out "and" at the end of clause (i); and by adding clause (iii). **Effective** as if included in the amendments made by Sec. 115(c) of P.L. 94-566.

P.L. 95-19, §302(e):

Amended Code Sec. 3304(a)(15) by substituting "March 31, 1980" for "September 30, 1979". **Effective** 4-12-77.

• **1976, Unemployment Compensation Amendments of 1976 (P.L. 94-566)**

P.L. 94-566, §115(c)(1):

Amended Code Sec. 3304(a)(6)(A), by striking out after "such law" the following: "; except that, with respect to service in an instructional, research, or principal administrative capacity for an institution of higher education to which section 3309(a)(1) applies, compensation shall not be payable based on such service for any week commencing during the period between two successive academic years (or, when the contract provides instead for a similar period between two regular but not successive terms, during such period) to any individual who has a contract to perform services in any such capacity for any institution or institutions of higher education for both of such academic years or both of such terms, and" and in inserting in lieu thereof new material. **Effective** with respect to certifications of States for 1978 and subsequent years, but only with respect to services performed after 12-31-77.

P.L. 94-566, §312(a):

Amended Code Sec. 3304(a)(12). **Effective** with respect to certifications of States for 1978 and subsequent years. Prior to amendment, Code Sec. 3304(a)(12) read as follows:

(12) each political subdivision of the State shall have the right to elect to have compensation payable to employees thereof (whose services are not otherwise subject to such law) based on service performed by such employees in the hospitals and institutions of higher education (as defined in section 3309(d)) operated by such political subdivision; and, if any such political subdivision does elect to have compensation payable to such employees thereof (A) the political subdivision shall pay into the State unemployment fund, with respect to the service of such employees, payments (in lieu of contributions), and (B) such employees will be entitled to receive, on the basis of such service, compensation payable on the same conditions as compensation which is payable on the basis of similar service for the State which is subject to such law.

P.L. 94-566, §314(a):

Redesignated paragraph (13) as paragraph (16) and inserted after paragraph (12) new paragraphs (13), (14), and (15). **Effective** with respect to certifications of States

UNEMPLOYMENT TAX

for 1978 and subsequent years, or for 1979 and subsequent years in the case of States the legislatures of which do not meet in a regular session which closes in the calendar year 1977.

P.L. 94-566, § 506(b):

Substituted "section 3309(a)(1)" for "section 3309(a)(1)(A)" in Code Sec. 3304(a)(6)(B). **Effective** with respect to certifications of States for 1978 and subsequent years, but only with respect to services performed after 12-31-77.

• **1976, Tax Reform Act of 1976 (P.L. 94-455)**

P.L. 94-455, § 1903(a)(14)(A):

Deleted "49 Stat. 640; 52 Stat. 1104, 1105;" in Code Sec. 3304(a)(3). **Effective** for compensation paid for services rendered after 12-31-76.

P.L. 94-455, § 1906(b)(13)(C):

Substituted "to the Secretary of the Treasury" for "to the Secretary" in Code Sec. 3304(a)(3). **Effective** 2-1-77.

• **1970, Employment Security Amendments of 1970 (P.L. 91-373)**

P.L. 91-373, § 104(a):

Amended Code Sec. 3304(a) by redesignating paragraph (6) as paragraph (13) and by adding new paragraph (6). **Effective** with respect to certifications of State laws for 1972 and subsequent years but only with respect to service performed after 12-31-71. Further, Code Sec. 3304(a)(6) is not to be a requirement for the State law of any State prior to 7-1-72, if the legislature of such State does not meet in a regular session which closes during the calendar year 1971.

P.L. 91-373, § 108(a):

Amended Code Sec. 3304(a) by adding paragraph (12). **Effective** with respect to certifications of State laws for 1972 and subsequent years, except that Code Sec. 3304(a)(12) shall not be a requirement for the State law of any State prior to 7-1-72, if the legislature of such State does not meet in a regular session which closes during the calendar year 1971, or prior to 1-1-75, if compliance with such requirement would necessitate a change in the constitution of such State.

P.L. 91-373, § 121(a):

Amended Code Sec. 3304(a) by adding paragraphs (7) through (10). **Effective** 1-1-72, and apply to the tax year 1972 and tax years thereafter. However, paragraphs (7) through (10) of Code Sec. 3304(a) shall not be requirements for the State law of any State prior to 7-1-72, if the legislature of such State does not meet in a regular session which closes during the calendar year 1971.

P.L. 91-373, § 206:

Amended Code Sec. 3304(a) by adding paragraph (11). § 206(c), P.L. 91-373, further provides that paragraph (11) shall not be a requirement for the State law of any State (1) in the case of any State the legislature of which does not meet in a regular session which closes during the calendar year 1971, with respect to any week of unemployment which begins prior to 7-1-72, or (2) in the case of any other State, with respect to any week of unemployment which begins prior to 1-1-72.

P.L. 91-373, § 207(b)(1), provides:

In the case of a State law approved under Code Sec. 3304(a)(11), such State law may also provide that an extended benefit period may begin with a week established pursuant to such law which begins earlier than January 1, 1972, but not earlier than 60 days after August 10, 1970, the date of the enactment of P.L. 91-373.

[Sec. 3304(b)]

(b) NOTIFICATION.—The Secretary of Labor shall, upon approving such law, notify the governor of the State of his approval.

[Sec. 3304(c)]

(c) CERTIFICATION.—On October 31 of each taxable year the Secretary of Labor shall certify to the Secretary of the Treasury each State whose law he has previously approved, except that he shall not certify any State which, after reasonable notice and opportunity for hearing to the State agency, the Secretary of Labor finds has amended its law so that it no longer contains the provisions specified in subsection (a) or has with respect to the 12-month period ending on such October 31 failed to comply substantially with any such provision in such subsection. No finding of a failure to comply substantially with any provision in paragraph (5) of subsection (a) shall be based on an application or interpretation of State law (1) until all administrative review provided for under the laws of the State has been exhausted, or (2) with respect to which the time for judicial review provided by the laws of the State has not expired, or (3) with respect to which any judicial review is pending. On October 31 of any taxable year, the Secretary of Labor shall not certify any State which, after reasonable notice and opportunity for hearing to the State agency, the Secretary of Labor finds has failed to amend its law so that it contains each of the provisions required by law to be included therein (including provisions relating to the Federal-State Extended Unemployment Compensation Act of 1970 (or any amendments thereto) as required under subsection (a)(11)), or has, with respect to the twelve-month period ending on such October 31, failed to comply substantially with any such provision.

Amendments

• **1981, Omnibus Budget Reconciliation Act of 1981 (P.L. 97-35)**

P.L. 97-35, § 2408(a):

Amended Code Sec. 3304(c) by striking out the last two sentences and adding the last two sentences. **Effective** 8-13-81. Prior to amendment, the last two sentences of Code Sec. 3304(c) read as follows:

On October 31 of any taxable year after 1971, the Secretary of Labor shall not certify any State which, after reasonable notice and opportunity for hearing to the State agency, the Secretary of Labor finds has failed to amend its law so that it contains each of the provisions required by reason of the enactment of the Employment Security Amendments of 1970 to be included therein, or has with respect to the 12-month period ending on such October 31, failed to comply substantially with any such provision. On October 31 of any taxable year after 1977, the Secretary shall not certify any State which, after reasonable notice and opportunity for a hearing to the State agency, the Secretary of Labor finds has failed to amend its law so that it contains each of the provisions required by reason of the enactment of the Unemployment Compensation Amendments of 1976 to be included therein, or has with respect to the 12-month period ending on such October 31, failed to comply substantially with any such provision.

• **1976, Unemployment Compensation Amendments of 1976 (P.L. 94-566)**

P.L. 94-566, § 312(b), (c):

Added a new sentence at the end of Code Sec. 3304(c). **Effective** with respect to certifications of States for 1978 and subsequent years.

• **1976, Tax Reform Act of 1976 (P.L. 94-455)**

P.L. 94-455, § 1903(a)(14)(B):

Deleted "(10-month period in the case of October 31, 1972)" in Code Sec. 3304(c). **Effective** for compensation for services rendered after 12-31-76.

P.L. 94-455, § 1906(b)(13)(C):

Substituted "to the Secretary of the Treasury" for "to the Secretary" each place it appeared in Code Sec. 3304(c). **Effective** 2-1-77.

P.L. 94-455, § 1906(b)(13)(E):

Substituted "the Secretary of Labor shall" for "the Secretary shall" in the last sentence of Code Sec. 3304(c). **Effective** 2-1-77.

• **1970, Employment Security Amendments of 1970 (P.L. 91-373)**

P.L. 91-373, § 131(b)(2):

Amended Code Sec. 3304(c). **Effective** 8-10-70. Prior to amendment, Code Sec. 3304(c) read as follows:

(c) CERTIFICATION.—On December 31 of each taxable year the Secretary of Labor shall certify to the Secretary each State whose law he has previously approved, except that he shall not certify any State which, after reasonable notice and opportunity for hearing to the State agency, the Secretary of Labor finds has amended its law so that it no longer contains the provisions specified in subsection (a) or has with respect to such taxable year failed to comply substantially with any such provision and such finding has become effective. Such finding shall become effective on the 90th day after the governor of the State has been notified thereof, unless the State has before such 90th day so amended its law that it will comply substantially with the Secretary of Labor's interpretation of the provision of subsection (a), in which event such finding shall not become effective. No finding of a failure to comply substantially with the provision in State law specified in paragraph (5) of subsection (a) shall be based on an application or interpretation of State law with respect to which further administrative or judicial review is provided for under the laws of the State.

P.L. 91-373, § 142(f):

Amended Code Sec. 3304(c). **Effective** for the tax year 1972 and later tax years.

[Sec. 3304(d)]

(d) NOTICE OF NONCERTIFICATION.—If at any time the Secretary of Labor has reason to believe that a State whose law he has previously approved may not be certified under subsection (c), he shall promptly so notify the governor of such State.

Amendments

• **1970, Employment Security Amendments of 1970 (P.L. 91-373)**

P.L. 91-373, § 142(g):

Amended Code Sec. 3304(d) by substituting "If at any time" for "If, at any time during the taxable year,". **Effective** with respect to tax year 1972 and tax years thereafter.

[Sec. 3304(e)]

(e) CHANGE OF LAW DURING 12-MONTH PERIOD.—Whenever—

(1) any provision of this section, section 3302, or section 3303 refers to a 12-month period ending on October 31 of a year, and

UNEMPLOYMENT TAX

(2) the law applicable to one portion of such period differs from the law applicable to another portion of such period, then such provision shall be applied by taking into account for each such portion the law applicable to such portion.

Amendments

• 1970, Employment Security Amendments of 1970 (P.L. 91-373)

P.L. 91-373, § 142(h):

Added Code Sec. 3304(e). **Effective** with respect to the tax year 1972 and tax years thereafter.

[Sec. 3304(f)]

(f) DEFINITION OF INSTITUTION OF HIGHER EDUCATION.—For purposes of subsection (a)(6), the term "institution of higher education" means an educational institution in any State which—

(1) admits as regular students only individuals having a certificate of graduation from a high school, or the recognized equivalent of such a certificate;

(2) is legally authorized within such State to provide a program of education beyond high school;

(3) provides an educational program for it which awards a bachelor's or higher degree, or provides a program which is acceptable for full credit toward such a degree, or offers a program of training to prepare students for gainful employment in a recognized occupation; and

(4) is a public or other nonprofit institution.

Amendments

• 1976, Unemployment Compensation Amendments of 1976 (P.L. 94-566)

P.L. 94-566, § 115(c)(5), (d):

Added Code Sec. 3304(f). **Effective** with respect to certifications of States for 1978 and subsequent years, but only with respect to services performed after 12-31-77.

[Sec. 3305]

SEC. 3305. APPLICABILITY OF STATE LAW.

[Sec. 3305(a)]

(a) INTERSTATE AND FOREIGN COMMERCE.—No person required under a State law to make payments to an unemployment fund shall be relieved from compliance therewith on the ground that he is engaged in interstate or foreign commerce, or that the State law does not distinguish between employees engaged in interstate or foreign commerce and those engaged in intrastate commerce.

[Sec. 3305(b)]

(b) FEDERAL INSTRUMENTALITIES IN GENERAL.—The legislature of any State may require any instrumentality of the United States (other than an instrumentality to which section 3306(c)(6) applies), and the individuals in its employ, to make contributions to an unemployment fund under a State unemployment compensation law approved by the Secretary of Labor under section 3304 and (except as provided in section 5240 of the Revised Statutes, as amended (12 U.S.C., sec. 484), and as modified by subsection (c)), to comply otherwise with such law. The permission granted in this subsection shall apply (A) only to the extent that no discrimination is made against such instrumentality, so that if the rate of contribution is uniform upon all other persons subject to such law on account of having individuals in their employ, and upon all employees of such persons, respectively, the contributions required of such instrumentality or the individuals in its employ shall not be at a greater rate than is required of such other persons and such employees, and if the rates are determined separately for different persons or classes of persons having individuals in their employ or for different classes of employees, the determination shall be based solely upon unemployment experience and other factors bearing a direct relation to unemployment risk; (B) only if such State law makes provision for the refund of any contributions required under such law from an instrumentality of the United States or its employees for any year in the event such State is not certified by the Secretary of Labor under section 3304 with respect to such year; and (C) only if such State law makes provision for the payment of unemployment compensation to any employee of any such instrumentality of the United States in the same amount, on the same terms, and subject to the same conditions as unemployment compensation is payable to employees of other employers under the State unemployment compensation law.

Amendments

• 1960, Social Security Amendments of 1960 (P.L. 86-778)

P.L. 86-778, § 531(a):

Amended Code Sec. 3305(b). **Effective** 1-1-62. Prior to amendment, Code Sec. 3305(b) read as follows:

(b) FEDERAL INSTRUMENTALITIES IN GENERAL.—The legislature of any State may require any instrumentality of the United States (except such as are (1) wholly owned by the United States, or (2) exempt from the tax imposed by section 3301 by virtue of any other provision of law), and the individuals in its employ, to make contributions to an unemployment fund under a State unemployment compensation law approved by the Secretary of Labor under section 3304 and (except as provided in section 5240 of the Revised Statutes, as amended (12 U.S.C. 484), and as modified by subsection (c)), to comply otherwise with such law. The permission granted in this subsection shall apply (A) only to the extent that no discrimination is made against such instrumentality, so that if the rate of contribution is uniform upon all other persons subject to such law on account of having individuals in their employ, and upon all employees of such persons, respectively, the contributions required of such instrumentality or the individuals in its employ shall not be at a greater rate than is required of such other persons and such employees, and if the rates are determined separately for different persons or classes of persons having individuals in their employ or for different classes of employees, the determination shall be based solely upon unemployment experience and other factors bearing a direct relation to unemployment risk, and (B) only if such State law makes provision for the refund of any contributions required under such law from an instrumentality of the United States or its employees for any year in the event said State is not certified by the Secretary of Labor under section 3304 with respect to such year.

[Sec. 3305(c)]

(c) NATIONAL BANKS.—Nothing contained in section 5240 of the Revised Statutes, as amended (12 U. S. C. 484), shall prevent any State from requiring any national banking association to render returns and reports relative to the association's employees, their remuneration and services, to the same extent that other persons are required to render like returns and reports under a State law requiring contributions to an unemployment fund. The Comptroller of the Currency shall, upon receipt of a copy of any such return or report of a national banking association from, and upon request of, any duly authorized official, body, or commission of a State, cause an examination of the correctness of such return or report to be made at the time of the next succeeding examination of such association, and shall thereupon transmit to such official, body, or commission a complete statement of his findings respecting the accuracy of such returns or reports.

[Sec. 3305(d)]

(d) FEDERAL PROPERTY.—No person shall be relieved from compliance with a State unemployment compensation law on the ground that services were performed on land or premises owned, held, or possessed by the United States, and any State shall have full jurisdiction and power to enforce the provisions of such law to the same extent and with the same effect as though such place were not owned, held, or possessed by the United States.

UNEMPLOYMENT TAX

[Sec. 3305(e)—Repealed]

Amendments

• **1954 (P.L. 767, 83rd Cong.)**

P.L. 767, 83rd Cong., §4(c):

Repealed Sec. 3305(e). **Effective** with respect to services performed after 12-31-54. Prior to repeal, Code Sec. 3305(e) read as follows:

"(e) BONNEVILLE POWER ADMINISTRATOR.—The legislature of any State may, with respect to service performed after December 31, 1945, by a laborer, mechanic, or workman, in connection with construction work or the operation and maintenance of electrical facilities, as an employee performing service for the Bonneville Power Administrator, require the Administrator, who for purposes of this subsection is designated an instrumentality of the United States, and any such employee, to make contributions to an unemployment fund under a State unemployment compensation law approved by the Secretary of Labor under section 3304 and to comply otherwise with such law. Such permission is subject to the conditions imposed by subsection (b) of this section upon permission to State legislatures to require contributions from instrumentalities of the United States. The Bonneville Power Administrator is authorized and directed to comply with the provisions of any applicable State unemployment compensation law on behalf of the United States as the employer of individuals whose service constitutes employment under such law by reason of this subsection."

[Note: Sec. 1606(e), 1939 Code, was substantially the same provision as the repealed Sec. 3305(e). At the time Sec. 3305(e) was repealed by P.L. 767, 83rd Cong., Sec. 4(c), Sec. 4(b) of P.L. 767 amended the 1939 Code provision by inserting after "December 31, 1945," the following: "and before January 1, 1955,". The amendment was effective 9-1-54. Thus, the amendment of the 1939 Code provision had the same effect as the repeal of the 1954 Code provision.—CCH.]

[Sec. 3305(f)]

(f) AMERICAN VESSELS.—The legislature of any State in which a person maintains the operating office, from which the operations of an American vessel operating on navigable waters within or within and without the United States are ordinarily and regularly supervised, managed, directed and controlled, may require such person and the officers and members of the crew of such vessel to make contributions to its unemployment fund under its State unemployment compensation law approved by the Secretary of Labor under section 3304 and otherwise to comply with its unemployment compensation law with respect to the service performed by an officer or member of the crew on or in connection with such vessel to the same extent and with the same effect as though such service was performed entirely within such State. Such person and the officers and members of the crew of such vessel shall not be required to make contributions, with respect to such service, to the unemployment fund of any other State. The permission granted by this subsection is subject to the condition that such service shall be treated, for purposes of wage credits given employees, like other service subject to such State unemployment compensation law performed for such person in such State, and also subject to the same limitation, with respect to contributions required from such person and from the officers and members of the crew of such vessel, as is imposed by the second sentence (other than clause (B) thereof) of subsection (b) with respect to contributions required from instrumentalities of the United States and from individuals in their employ.

[Sec. 3305(g)]

(g) VESSELS OPERATED BY GENERAL AGENTS OF UNITED STATES.—The permission granted by subsection (f) shall apply in the same manner and under the same conditions (including the obligation to comply with all requirements of State unemployment compensation laws) to general agents of the Secretary of Transportation with respect to service performed by officers and members of the crew on or in connection with American vessels—

(1) owned by or bareboat chartered to the United States, and

(2) whose business is conducted by such general agents.

As to any such vessel, the State permitted to require contributions on account of such service shall be the State to which the general agent would make contributions if the vessel were operated for his own account. Such general agents are designated, for this purpose, instrumentalities of the United States neither wholly nor partially owned by it and shall not be exempt from the tax imposed by section 3301. The permission granted by this subsection is subject to the same conditions and limitations as are imposed in subsection (f), except that clause (B) of the second sentence of subsection (b) shall apply.

Amendments

• **2015, National Defense Authorization Act for Fiscal Year 2016 (P.L. 114-92)**

P.L. 114-92, §3503:

Amended Code Sec. 3305 by striking "Secretary of Commerce" each place that it appears and inserting "Secretary of Transportation". **Effective** 11-25-2015.

• **1976, Tax Reform Act of 1976 (P.L. 94-455)**

P.L. 94-455, §1903(a)(15)(A), (d):

Deleted "on or after July 1, 1953," in Code Sec. 3305(g). **Effective** for compensation paid for services rendered after 12-31-76.

• **1960, Social Security Amendments of 1960 (P.L. 86-778)**

P.L. 86-778, §531(b):

Amended Code Sec. 3305(g) by striking out "not wholly" in the third sentence and by substituting "neither wholly nor partially". **Effective** 1-1-62.

[Sec. 3305(h)]

(h) REQUIREMENT BY STATE OF CONTRIBUTIONS.—Any State may, as to service performed on account of which contributions are made pursuant to subsection (g)—

(1) require contributions from persons performing such service under its unemployment compensation law or temporary disability insurance law administered in connection therewith, and

(2) require general agents of the Secretary of Transportation to make contributions under such temporary disability insurance law and to make such deductions from wages or remuneration as are required by such unemployment compensation or temporary disability insurance law.

Amendments

• **2015, National Defense Authorization Act for Fiscal Year 2016 (P.L. 114-92)**

P.L. 114-92, §3503:

Amended Code Sec. 3305 by striking "Secretary of Commerce" each place that it appears and inserting "Secretary of Transportation". **Effective** 11-25-2015.

• **1976, Tax Reform Act of 1976 (P.L. 94-455)**

P.L. 94-455, §1903(a)(15)(B), (d):

Deleted "on or after July 1, 1953, and" in Code Sec. 3305(h). **Effective** for compensation paid for services rendered after 12-31-76.

[Sec. 3305(i)]

(i) GENERAL AGENT AS LEGAL ENTITY.—Each general agent of the Secretary of Transportation making contributions pursuant to subsection (g) or (h) shall, for purposes of such subsections, be considered a legal entity in his capacity as an instrumentality of the United States, separate and distinct from his identity as a person employing individuals on his own account.

Amendments

• **2015, National Defense Authorization Act for Fiscal Year 2016 (P.L. 114-92)**

P.L. 114-92, §3503:

Amended Code Sec. 3305 by striking "Secretary of Commerce" each place that it appears and inserting "Secretary of Transportation". **Effective** 11-25-2015.

UNEMPLOYMENT TAX

[Sec. 3305(j)]

(j) DENIAL OF CREDITS IN CERTAIN CASES.—Any person required, pursuant to the permission granted by this section, to make contributions to an unemployment fund under a State unemployment compensation law approved by the Secretary of Labor under section 3304 shall not be entitled to the credits permitted, with respect to the unemployment compensation law of a State, by subsections (a) and (b) of section 3302 against the tax imposed by section 3301 for any taxable year if, on October 31 of such taxable year, the Secretary of Labor certifies to the Secretary of the Treasury his finding, after reasonable notice and opportunity for hearing to the State agency, that the unemployment compensation law of such State is inconsistent with any one or more of the conditions on the basis of which such permission is granted or that, in the application of the State law with respect to the 12-month period ending on such October 31, there has been a substantial failure to comply with any one or more of such conditions. For purposes of section 3310, a finding of the Secretary of Labor under this subsection shall be treated as a finding under section 3304(c).

Amendments

- **1976, Tax Reform Act of 1976 (P.L. 94-455)**

P.L. 94-455, §1903(a)(15)(C):

Deleted "after December 31, 1971," in Code Sec. 3305(j). **Effective** for compensation paid for services rendered after 12-31-76.

P.L. 94-455, §1906(b)(13)(C):

Substituted "to the Secretary of the Treasury" for "to the Secretary" each place it appeared in Code Sec. 3305(j). **Effective** 2-1-77.

- **1970, Employment Security Amendments of 1970 (P.L. 91-373)**

P.L. 91-373, §123:

Added Code Sec. 3305(j). **Effective** 8-10-70.

[Sec. 3306]

SEC. 3306. DEFINITIONS.

[Sec. 3306(a)]

(a) EMPLOYER.—For purposes of this chapter—

(1) IN GENERAL.—The term "employer" means, with respect to any calendar year, any person who—

(A) during any calendar quarter in the calendar year or the preceding calendar year paid wages of $1,500 or more, or

(B) on each of some 20 days during the calendar year or during the preceding calendar year, each day being in a different calendar week, employed at least one individual in employment for some portion of the day.

For purposes of this paragraph, there shall not be taken into account any wages paid to, or employment of, an employee performing domestic services referred to in paragraph (3).

(2) AGRICULTURAL LABOR.—In the case of agricultural labor, the term "employer" means, with respect to any calendar year, any person who—

(A) during any calendar quarter in the calendar year or the preceding calendar year paid wages of $20,000 or more for agricultural labor, or

(B) on each of some 20 days during the calendar year or during the preceding calendar year, each day being in a different calendar week, employed at least 10 individuals in employment in agricultural labor for some portion of the day.

(3) DOMESTIC SERVICE.—In the case of domestic service in a private home, local college club, or local chapter of a college fraternity or sorority, the term "employer" means, with respect to any calendar year, any person who during any calendar quarter in the calendar year or the preceding calendar year paid wages in cash of $1,000 or more for such service.

(4) SPECIAL RULE.—A person treated as an employer under paragraph (3) shall not be treated as an employer with respect to wages paid for any service other than domestic service referred to in paragraph (3) unless such person is treated as an employer under paragraph (1) or (2) with respect to such other service.

Amendments

- **1976, Unemployment Compensation Amendments of 1976 (P.L. 94-566)**

P.L. 94-566, §114(a):

Amended Code Sec. 3306(a). **Effective** with respect to remuneration paid after 12-31-77, for services performed after such date. Prior to amendment, Code Sec. 3306(a) read as follows:

(a) EMPLOYER.—For purposes of this chapter, the term "employer" means, with respect to any calendar year, any person who—

(1) during any calendar quarter in the calendar year or the preceding calendar year paid wages of $1,500 or more, or

(2) on each of some 20 days during the calendar year or during the preceding calendar year, each day being in a different calendar week, employed at least one individual in employment for some portion of the day.

- **1970, Employment Security Amendments of 1970 (P.L. 91-373)**

P.L. 91-373, §101(a):

Amended Code Sec. 3306(a). **Effective** for calendar years beginning after 12-31-71. Prior to amendment, Code Sec. 3306(a) read as follows:

(a) Employer.—For purposes of this chapter, the term "employer" does not include any person unless on each of some 20 days during the taxable year or during the preceding taxable year, each day being in a different calendar week, the total number of individuals who were employed by him in employment for some portion of the day (whether or not at the same moment of time) was 4 or more.

- **1969 (P.L. 91-53)**

P.L. 91-53, §1:

Amended Code Sec. 3306(a) by adding "or during the preceding taxable year" beginning in the second line thereof. **Effective** for calendar years beginning after 12-31-69.

- **1954 (P.L. 767, 83rd Cong.)**

P.L. 767, 83rd Cong., [§1]:

Amended Sec. 3306(a) by striking out "eight or more" and inserting in lieu thereof "4 or more". **Effective** for services performed after 12-31-55.

[Sec. 3306(b)]

(b) WAGES.—For purposes of this chapter, the term "wages" means all remuneration for employment, including the cash value of all remuneration (including benefits) paid in any medium other than cash; except that such term shall not include—

(1) that part of the remuneration which, after remuneration (other than remuneration referred to in the succeeding paragraphs of this subsection) equal to $7,000 with respect to employment has been paid to an individual by an employer during any calendar year, is paid to such individual by such employer during such calendar year. If an employer (hereinafter referred to as successor employer) during any calendar year acquires substantially all the property used in a trade or business of another employer (hereinafter referred to as a predecessor), or used in a separate unit of a trade or business of a predecessor, and immediately after the acquisition employs in his trade or business an individual who immediately prior to the acquisition was employed in the trade or business of such predecessor, then, for the purpose of determining whether the successor employer has paid remuneration (other than remuneration referred to in the succeeding paragraphs of this subsection) with respect to employment equal to $7,000 to such individual during such calendar year, any remuneration (other than remuneration referred to in the succeeding paragraphs of this subsection) with respect to employment paid (or considered under this paragraph as having been paid) to such individual by such predecessor during such calendar year and prior to such acquisition shall be considered as having been paid by such successor employer;

(2) the amount of any payment (including any amount paid by an employer for insurance or annuities, or into a fund, to provide for any such payment) made to, or on behalf of, an employee or any of his dependents under a plan or system established by an employer which

UNEMPLOYMENT TAX

makes provision for his employees generally (or for his employees generally and their dependents) or for a class or classes of his employees (or for a class or classes of his employees and their dependents), on account of—

    (A) sickness or accident disability (but, in the case of payments made to an employee or any of his dependents, this subparagraph shall exclude from the term "wages" only payments which are received under a workmen's compensation law), or

    (B) medical or hospitalization expenses in connection with sickness or accident disability, or

    (C) death;

(3) [Stricken.]

(4) any payment on account of sickness or accident disability, or medical or hospitalization expenses in connection with sickness or accident disability, made by an employer to, or on behalf of, an employee after the expiration of 6 calendar months following the last calendar month in which the employee worked for such employer;

(5) any payment made to, or on behalf of, an employee or his beneficiary—

    (A) from or to a trust described in section 401(a) which is exempt from tax under section 501(a) at the time of such payment unless such payment is made to an employee of the trust as remuneration for services rendered as such employee and not as a beneficiary of the trust, or

    (B) under or to an annuity plan which, at the time of such payment, is a plan described in section 403(a),

    (C) under a simplified employee pension (as defined in section 408(k)(1)), other than any contributions described in section 408(k)(6),

    (D) under or to an annuity contract described in section 403(b), other than a payment for the purchase of such contract which is made by reason of a salary reduction agreement (whether evidenced by a written instrument or otherwise),

    (E) under or to an exempt governmental deferred compensation plan (as defined in section 3121(v)(3)),

    (F) to supplement pension benefits under a plan or trust described in any of the foregoing provisions of this paragraph to take into account some portion or all of the increase in the cost of living (as determined by the Secretary of Labor) since retirement but only if such supplemental payments are under a plan which is treated as a welfare plan under section 3(2)(B)(ii) of the Employee Retirement Income Security Act of 1974,

    (G) under a cafeteria plan (within the meaning of section 125) if such payment would not be treated as wages without regard to such plan and it is reasonable to believe that (if section 125 applied for purposes of this section) section 125 would not treat any wages as constructively received, or

    (H) under an arrangement to which section 408(p) applies, other than any elective contributions under paragraph (2)(A)(i) thereof,

(6) the payment by an employer (without deduction from the remuneration of the employee)—

    (A) of the tax imposed upon an employee under section 3101, or

    (B) of any payment required from an employee under a State unemployment compensation law,

with respect to remuneration paid to an employee for domestic service in a private home of the employer or for agricultural labor;

(7) remuneration paid in any medium other than cash to an employee for service not in the course of the employer's trade or business;

(8) [Stricken.]

(9) remuneration paid to or on behalf of an employee if (and to the extent that) at the time of the payment of such remuneration it is reasonable to believe that a corresponding deduction is allowable under section 217 (determined without regard to section 274(n));

(10) any payment or series of payments by an employer to an employee or any of his dependents which is paid—

    (A) upon or after the termination of an employee's employment relationship because of (i) death, or (ii) retirement for disability, and

    (B) under a plan established by the employer which makes provision for his employees generally or a class or classes of his employees (or for such employees or class or classes of employees and their dependents),

other than any such payment or series of payments which would have been paid if the employee's employment relationship had not been so terminated;

(11) remuneration for agricultural labor paid in any medium other than cash;

(12) [Stricken.]

(13) any payment made, or benefit furnished, to or for the benefit of an employee if at the time of such payment or such furnishing it is reasonable to believe that the employee will be able to exclude such payment or benefit from income under section 127, 129, 134(b)(4), or 134(b)(5);

(14) the value of any meals or lodging furnished by or on behalf of the employer if at the time of such furnishing it is reasonable to believe that the employee will be able to exclude such items from income under section 119;

(15) any payment made by an employer to a survivor or the estate of a former employee after the calendar year in which such employee died;

(16) any benefit provided to or on behalf of an employee if at the time such benefit is provided it is reasonable to believe that the employee will be able to exclude such benefit from income under section 74(c), 108(f)(4), 117 or 132;

(17) any payment made to or for the benefit of an employee if at the time of such payment it is reasonable to believe that the employee will be able to exclude such payment from income under section 106(b);

(18) any payment made to or for the benefit of an employee if at the time of such payment it is reasonable to believe that the employee will be able to exclude such payment from income under section 106(d);

(19) remuneration on account of—

    (A) a transfer of a share of stock to any individual pursuant to an exercise of an incentive stock option (as defined in section 422(b)) or under an employee stock purchase plan (as defined in section 423(b)), or

    (B) any disposition by the individual of such stock; or

(20) any benefit or payment which is excludable from the gross income of the employee under section 139B(b).

Except as otherwise provided in regulations prescribed by the Secretary, any third party which makes a payment included in wages solely by reason of the parenthetical matter contained in subparagraph (A) of paragraph (2) shall be treated for purposes of this chapter and chapter 22 as the employer with respect to such wages. Nothing in the regulations prescribed for purposes of chapter 24 (relating to income tax withholding) which provides an exclusion from "wages" as used in such chapter shall be construed to require a similar exclusion from "wages" in the regulations prescribed for purposes of this chapter.

Amendments

- **2018, Tax Technical Corrections Act of 2018 (P.L. 115-141)**

P.L. 115-141, §401(a)(212), Div. U:

Amended Code Sec. 3306(b)(5)(F) by striking the semicolon at the end and inserting a comma. **Effective** 3-23-2018.

- **2014, Tax Technical Corrections Act of 2014 (P.L. 113-295)**

P.L. 113-295, §221(a)(19)(B)(vi), Division A:

Amended Code Sec. 3306(b) by striking paragraph (12). **Effective** generally 12-19-2014. For a special rule, see Act Sec. 221(b)(2), Division A, below. Prior to being stricken, Code Sec. 3306(b)(12) read as follows:

UNEMPLOYMENT TAX

(12) any contribution, payment, or service, provided by an employer which may be excluded from the gross income of an employee, his spouse, or his dependents, under the provisions of section 120 (relating to amounts received under qualified group legal services plans);

P.L. 113-295, §221(b)(2), Division A, provides:

(2) SAVINGS PROVISION.—If—

(A) any provision amended or repealed by the amendments made by this section applied to—

(i) any transaction occurring before the date of the enactment of this Act,

(ii) any property acquired before such date of enactment, or

(iii) any item of income, loss, deduction, or credit taken into account before such date of enactment, and

(B) the treatment of such transaction, property, or item under such provision would (without regard to the amendments or repeals made by this section) affect the liability for tax for periods ending after date of enactment, nothing in the amendments or repeals made by this section shall be construed to affect the treatment of such transaction, property, or item for purposes of determining liability for tax for periods ending after such date of enactment.

- **2008, Heroes Earnings Assistance and Relief Tax Act of 2008 (P.L. 110-245)**

P.L. 110-245, §115(b):

Amended Code Sec. 3306(b) by striking "or" at the end of paragraph (18), by striking the period at the end of paragraph (19) and inserting "; or", and by inserting after paragraph (19) a new paragraph (20). **Effective** as if included in section 5 of the Mortgage Forgiveness Debt Relief Act of 2007 (P.L. 110-142) [effective for tax years beginning after 12-31-2007.—CCH].

- **2004, Ronald W. Reagan National Defense Authorization Act for Fiscal Year 2005 (P.L. 108-375)**

P.L. 108-375, §585(b)(2)(C):

Amended Code Sec. 3306(b)(13) by striking "or 134(b)(4)" and inserting "134(b)(4), or 134(b)(5)". **Effective** for travel benefits provided after 10-28-2004.

- **2004, American Jobs Creation Act of 2004 (P.L. 108-357)**

P.L. 108-357, §251(a)(3):

Amended Code Sec. 3306(b) by striking "or" at the end of paragraph (17), by striking the period at the end of paragraph (18) and inserting "; or", and by inserting after paragraph (18) a new paragraph (19). **Effective** for stock acquired pursuant to options exercised after 10-22-2004.

P.L. 108-357, §320(b)(3):

Amended Code Sec. 3306(b)(16) by inserting "108(f)(4)," after "74(c),". **Effective** for amounts received by an individual in tax years beginning after 12-31-2003.

- **2003, Medicare Prescription Drug, Improvement, and Modernization Act of 2003 (P.L. 108-173)**

P.L. 108-173, §1201(d)(2)(B):

Amended Code Sec. 3306(b) by striking "or" at the end of paragraph (16), by striking the period at the end of paragraph (17) and inserting "; or", and by inserting after paragraph (17) a new paragraph (18). **Effective** for tax years beginning after 12-31-2003.

- **2003, Military Family Tax Relief Act of 2003 (P.L. 108-121)**

P.L. 108-121, §106(b)(3):

Amended Code Sec. 3306(b)(13) by striking "or 129" and inserting ", 129, or 134(b)(4)". **Effective** for tax years beginning after 12-31-2002. For a special rule, see Act Sec. 106(d), below.

P.L. 108-121, §106(d), provides:

(d) NO INFERENCE.—No inference may be drawn from the amendments made by this section with respect to the tax treatment of any amounts under the program described in section 134(b)(4) of the Internal Revenue Code of 1986 (as added by this section) for any taxable year beginning before January 1, 2003.

- **1996, Health Insurance Portability and Accountability Act of 1996 (P.L. 104-191)**

P.L. 104-191, §301(c)(2)(B):

Amended Code Sec. 3306(b) by striking "or" at the end of paragraph (15), by striking the period at the end of paragraph (16) and inserting "; or", and by inserting after paragraph (16) a new paragraph (17). **Effective** for tax years beginning after 12-31-96.

- **1996, Small Business Job Protection Act of 1996 (P.L. 104-188)**

P.L. 104-188, §1421(b)(8)(C):

Amended Code Sec. 3306(b)(5) by striking "or" at the end of subparagraph (F), by inserting "or" at the end of subparagraph (G), and by adding at the end a new subparagraph (H). **Effective** for tax years beginning after 12-31-96.

- **1989, Omnibus Budget Reconciliation Act of 1989 (P.L. 101-239)**

P.L. 101-239, §10202(c)(1), provides:

(1) FEDERAL UNEMPLOYMENT TAX.—For purposes of chapter 23 of the Internal Revenue Code of 1986, the term "wages" shall not include the amount of any refund required under section 421 of the Medicare Catastrophic Coverage Act of 1988.

- **1989 (P.L. 101-136)**

P.L. 101-136, §528, provides:

SEC. 528. No monies appropriated by this Act may be used to implement or enforce section 1151 of the Tax Reform Act of 1986 or the amendments made by such section.

- **1988, Technical and Miscellaneous Revenue Act of 1988 (P.L. 100-647)**

P.L. 100-647, §1001(g)(4)(B)(ii):

Amended Code Sec. 3306(b)(9) by striking out "section 217" and inserting in lieu thereof "section 217 (determined without regard to section 274(n))". **Effective** as if included in the provision of P.L. 99-514 to which it relates.

P.L. 100-647, §1011B(a)(23)(A):

Amended Code Sec. 3306(b)(5)(G) by inserting "if such payment would not be treated as wages without regard to such plan and it is reasonable to believe that (if section 125 applied for purposes of this section) section 125 would not treat any wages as constructively received" after "section 125)". **Effective** as if included in the provision of P.L. 99-514 to which it relates.

- **1986, Tax Reform Act of 1986 (P.L. 99-514)**

P.L. 99-514, §122(e)(3):

Amended Code Sec. 3306(b)(16) by striking out "117 or" and inserting in lieu thereof "74(c), 117, or". **Effective** for prizes and awards granted after 12-31-86.

P.L. 99-514, §1108(g)(8):

Amended Code Sec. 3306(b)(5) by striking out subparagraph (C) and inserting in lieu thereof new subparagraph (C). **Effective** for years beginning after 12-31-86. Prior to amendment, Code Sec. 3306(b)(5)(C) read as follows:

(C) under a simplified employee pension if, at the time of the payment, it is reasonable to believe that the employee will be entitled to a deduction under section 219 [section 219(B)(2) (effective with respect to remuneration paid after December 31, 1984)] for such payment,

P.L. 99-514, §1151(d)(2)(B):

Amended Code Sec. 3306(b)(5)(E)-(G) by striking out "or" at the end of subparagraph (E), by inserting "or" at the end of subparagraph (F), and by inserting after subparagraph (F) new subparagraph (G). **Effective** for tax years beginning after 12-31-83.

P.L. 99-514, §1899A(44):

Amended Code Sec. 3306(b)(2)(A) by striking out "workman's compensation" and inserting in lieu thereof "workmen's compensation". **Effective** 10-22-86.

P.L. 99-514, §1899A(45):

Amended Code Sec. 3306(b)(13) by striking out the comma at the end thereof and inserting in lieu thereof a semicolon. **Effective** 10-22-86.

- **1984, Deficit Reduction Act of 1984 (P.L. 98-369)**

P.L. 98-369, §491(d)(37):

Amended Code Sec. 3306(b)(5) by striking out subparagraph (C) and by redesignating subparagraphs (D) through (G) as subparagraphs (C) through (F), respectively. **Effective** for obligations issued after 12-31-83. Prior to amendment, subparagraph (C) read as follows:

(C) under or to a bond purchase plan which, at the time of such payment, is a qualified bond purchase plan described in section 405(a),

P.L. 98-369, §531(d)(3):

Amended Code Sec. 3306(b) by striking out "all remuneration paid in any medium" in the material preceding paragraph (1) and inserting in lieu thereof "all remuneration (including benefits) paid in any medium", and by striking out "or" at the end of paragraph (14), by striking out the period at the end of paragraph (15) and inserting in lieu thereof "; or"; and by inserting after paragraph (15) new paragraph (16). **Effective** 1-1-85.

- **1983, Federal Supplemental Compensation Amendments of 1983 (P.L. 98-135)**

P.L. 98-135, §201(a):

Amended Code Sec. 3306(b) by striking out "or" at the end of paragraph (13), by striking out the period at the end of paragraph (14) and inserting in lieu thereof "; or", and by inserting after paragraph (14) new paragraph (15). **Effective** for remuneration paid after 10-24-83.

- **1983, Social Security Amendments of 1983 (P.L. 98-21)**

P.L. 98-21, §324(b)(2):

Amended Code Sec. 3306(b)(5) by adding subparagraphs (E)-(G). For the **effective** date, see Act Sec. 324(d)(2)-(4), below.

P.L. 98-21, §324(b)(3):

Amended Code Sec. 3306(b) by striking out subparagraph (A) in paragraph (2) and redesignating subparagraphs (B), (C), and (D) as subparagraphs (A), (B), and (C), respectively; by striking out paragraphs (3) and (8); and by amending paragraph (10)(A). For the **effective** date, see Act Sec. 324(d)(2)-(4), below. Prior to amendment, Code Sec. 3306(b)(2)(A), (b)(3), (b)(8), and (b)(10)(A) read as follows:

(A) retirement, or

***

(3) any payment made to an employee (including any amount paid by an employer for insurance or annuities, or into a fund, to provide for any such payment) on account of retirement;

***

(8) any payment (other than vacation or sick pay) made to an employee after the month in which he attains the age of 65, if he did not work for the employer in the period for which such payment is made;

***

(A) upon or after the termination of an employee's employment relationship because of (i) death, (ii) retirement for disability, or (iii) retirement after attaining an age specified in the plan referred to in subparagraph (B) or in a pension plan of the employer, and

UNEMPLOYMENT TAX

P.L. 98-21, §324(b)(4)(A):

Amended Code Sec. 3306(b)(2)(A), as redesignated by §324(b)(3) of P.L. 98-21. For the **effective** date, see Act Sec. 324(d)(2)-(4), below.

P.L. 98-21, §324(b)(4)(B):

Amended Code Sec. 3306(b) by adding at the end thereof the last flush sentence. For the **effective** date, see Act Sec. 324(d)(2)-(4), below.

P.L. 98-21, §324(d)(2)-(4), as amended by P.L. 98-369, §2662(f)(2)(B)-(C), provides:

(2) Except as otherwise provided in this subsection, the amendments made by subsection (b) shall apply to remuneration paid after December 31, 1984. For purposes of applying such amendments to remuneration paid after December 31, 1984, which would have been taken into account before January 1, 1985, if such amendments had applied to periods before January 1, 1985, such remuneration shall be taken into account when paid (or, at the election of the payor, at the time which would be appropriate if such amendments had applied). [Last sentence added by P.L. 98-369, §2662(f)(2)(B).]

(3) The amendments made by this section shall not apply to employer contributions made during 1984 and attributable to services performed during 1983 under a qualified cash or deferred arrangement (as defined in section 401(k) of the Internal Revenue Code of 1954) if, under the terms of such arrangement as in effect on March 24, 1983—

(A) the employee makes an election with respect to such contribution before January 1, 1984, and

(B) the employer identifies the amount of such contribution before January 1, 1984.

In the case of the amendments made by subsection (b), the preceding sentence shall be applied by substituting "1985" for "1984" each place it appears and by substituting "during 1984" for "during 1983".

(4) In the case of an agreement in existence on March 24, 1983, between a nonqualified deferred compensation plan (as defined in section 3121(v)(2)(C) of the Internal Revenue Code of 1954, as added by this section) and an individual—

(A) the amendments made by this section (other than subsection (b)) shall apply with respect to services performed by such individual after December 31, 1984, and

(B) the amendments made by subsection (b) shall apply with respect to services performed by such individual after December 31, 1984.

The preceding sentence shall not apply in the case of a plan to which section 457(a) of such Code applies. For purposes of this paragraph, any plan or agreement to make payments described in paragraph (2), (3), or (13)(A)(iii) of section 3121(a) of such Code (as in effect on the day before the date of the enactment of this Act) shall be treated as a nonqualified deferred compensation plan. [Last sentence added by P.L. 98-369, §2662(f)(2)(C).]

P.L. 98-21, §327(c)(1)-(3):

Amended Code Sec. 3306(b) by striking out "or" at the end of paragraph (12), by striking out the period at the end of paragraph (13) and inserting in lieu thereof ",or", by adding immediately after paragraph (13) new paragraph (14). **Effective** for remuneration paid after 12-31-84.

P.L. 98-21, §327(c)(4):

Amended Code Sec. 3306(b) by adding the flush sentence at the end thereof. **Effective** for remuneration (other than amounts excluded under Code Sec. 119) paid after 3-4-83, and for any such remuneration paid on or before such date which the employer treated as wages when paid. [**Effective** date changed by P.L. 98-369, §2662(g).]

P.L. 98-21, §328(c):

Amended Code Sec. 3306(b)(5)(D) by striking out "section 219" and inserting in lieu thereof "section 219(b)(2)". **Effective** for remuneration paid after 12-31-84.

• **1982, Tax Equity and Fiscal Responsibility Act of 1982 (P.L. 97-248)**

P.L. 97-248, §271(a):

Amended Code Sec. 3306(b)(1) by striking out "$6,000" each place it appears and inserting "$7,000". **Effective** for remuneration paid after 12-31-82.

• **1981, Economic Recovery Tax Act of 1981 (P.L. 97-34)**

P.L. 97-34, §124(e)(2):

Amended Code Sec. 3306(b)(13) by striking out "section 127" and inserting in lieu thereof "section 127 or 129". **Effective** for remuneration paid after 12-31-81.

• **1980, Omnibus Reconciliation Act of 1980 (P.L. 96-499)**

P.L. 96-499, §1141(b):

Amended Code Sec. 3306(b)(6). **Effective**, generally, for remuneration paid after 12-31-80. However, in the case of state and local governments, see Act Sec. 1141(c)(2), below. Prior to amendment, Code Sec. 3306(b)(6) read as follows:

(6) the payment by an employer (without deduction from the remuneration of the employee)—

(A) of the tax imposed upon an employee under section 3101 (or the corresponding section of prior law), or

(B) of any payment required from an employee under a State unemployment compensation law;

P.L. 96-499, §1141(c)(2), provides:

(2) EXCEPTION FOR STATE AND LOCAL GOVERNMENTS.—

(A) the amendments made by this section (insofar as they affect the application of section 218 of the Social Security Act) shall not apply to any payment made before January 1, 1984, by any governmental unit for positions of a kind for which all or a substantial portion of the social security employee taxes were paid by such governmental unit (without deduction from the remuneration of the employee) under the practices of such governmental unit in effect on October 1, 1980.

(B) For purposes of subparagraph (A), the term `social security employee taxes' means the amount required to be paid under section 218 of the Social Security Act as the equivalent of the taxes imposed by section 3101 of the Internal Revenue Code of 1954.

(C) For purposes of subparagraph (A), the term `governmental unit' means a State or political subdivision thereof within the meaning of section 218 of the Social Security Act.

• **1980, Technical Corrections Act of 1979 (P.L. 96-222)**

P.L. 96-222, §101(a)(10)(B)(ii):

Amended Code Sec. 3306(b)(5) by adding paragraph (D). **Effective** for payments made on or after 1-1-79.

• **1978, Revenue Act of 1978 (P.L. 95-600)**

P.L. 95-600, §164(b)(2)(A)-(C):

Amended Code Sec. 3306(b) by (A) striking out "or" at the end of paragraph (11); (B) striking out the period at the end of paragraph (12) and inserting in place thereof "; or"; and (C) adding paragraph (13). **Effective** for tax years beginning after 12-31-78

• **1978 (P.L. 95-472)**

P.L. 95-472, §3(a), (d):

Added Code Sec. 3306(b)(12). **Effective** for tax years beginning after 1976.

• **1976, Unemployment Compensation Amendments of 1976 (P.L. 94-566)**

P.L. 94-566, §111(a):

Amended Code Sec. 3306(b) by striking out "or" at the end of paragraph (9); by striking out the period at the end of paragraph (10) and inserting in lieu thereof "; or"; and by adding after paragraph (10) a new paragraph (11). **Effective** for remuneration paid after 12-31-77, for services performed after such date.

P.L. 94-566, §211(a):

Substituted "$6,000" for "$4,200" each place it appeared in Code Sec. 3306(b)(1). **Effective** for remuneration paid after 12-31-77.

• **1970, Employment Security Amendments of 1970 (P.L. 91-373)**

P.L. 91-373, §302:

Amended Code Sec. 3306(b)(1) by substituting "$4,200" for "$3,000" in the 3rd and 4th lines thereof. **Effective** for remuneration paid after 12-31-71.

• **1968, Social Security Amendments of 1967 (P.L. 90-248)**

P.L. 90-248, §504(b):

Amended Code Sec. 3306(b) by deleting "or" at the end of paragraph (8), by substituting "; or" for the period at the end of paragraph (9), and by adding new paragraph (10). **Effective** for remuneration paid after 1-2-68.

• **1964 (P.L. 88-650)**

P.L. 88-650, §4(c):

Added Code Sec. 3306(b)(9). **Effective** with respect to remuneration paid on or after the first day of the first calendar month which begins more than 10 days after 10-13-64, the date of enactment.

• **1962, Self-Employed Individuals Tax Retirement Act of 1962 (P.L. 87-792)**

P.L. 87-792, §7:

Amended Code Sec. 3306(b)(5) by striking out subparagraph (B) and inserting in lieu thereof new paragraphs (B) and (C). **Effective** 1-1-63. Prior to amendment, subparagraph (B) read as follows:

(B) under or to an annuity plan which, at the time of such payment, meets the requirements of section 401(a)(3), (4), (5), and (6);

[Sec. 3306(c)]

(c) EMPLOYMENT.—For purposes of this chapter, the term "employment" means any service performed prior to 1955, which was employment for purposes of subchapter C of chapter 9 of the Internal Revenue Code of 1939 under the law applicable to the period in which such service was performed, and (A) any service, of whatever nature, performed after 1954 by an employee for the person employing him, irrespective of the citizenship or residence of either, (i) within the United States, or (ii) on or in connection with an American vessel or American aircraft under a contract of service which is entered into within the United States or during the performance of which and while the employee is employed on the vessel or aircraft it touches at a port in the United States, if the employee is employed on and in connection with such vessel or aircraft when outside the United States, and (B) any service, of whatever nature, performed after 1971 outside the United States (except in a contiguous country with which the United States has an agreement relating to unemployment compensation) by a citizen of the United States as an employee of an American employer (as defined in subsection (j)(3)), except—

    (1) agricultural labor (as defined in subsection (k)) unless—

        (A) such labor is performed for a person who—

UNEMPLOYMENT TAX

(i) during any calendar quarter in the calendar year or the preceding calendar year paid remuneration in cash of $20,000 or more to individuals employed in agricultural labor (including labor performed by an alien referred to in subparagraph (B)), or

(ii) on each of some 20 days during the calendar year or the preceding calendar year, each day being in a different calendar week, employed in agricultural labor (including labor performed by an alien referred to in subparagraph (B)) for some portion of the day (whether or not at the same moment of time) 10 or more individuals; and

(B) such labor is not agricultural labor performed by an individual who is an alien admitted to the United States to perform agricultural labor pursuant to sections 214(c) and 101(a)(15)(H) of the Immigration and Nationality Act;

(2) domestic service in a private home, local college club, or local chapter of a college fraternity or sorority unless performed for a person who paid cash remuneration of $1,000 or more to individuals employed in such domestic service in any calendar quarter in the calendar year or the preceding calendar year;

(3) service not in the course of the employer's trade or business performed in any calendar quarter by an employee, unless the cash remuneration paid for such service is $50 or more and such service is performed by an individual who is regularly employed by such employer to perform such service. For purposes of this paragraph, an individual shall be deemed to be regularly employed by an employer during a calendar quarter only if—

(A) on each of some 24 days during such quarter such individual performs for such employer for some portion of the day service not in the course of the employer's trade or business, or

(B) such individual was regularly employed (as determined under subparagraph (A)) by such employer in the performance of such service during the preceding calendar quarter;

(4) service performed on or in connection with a vessel or aircraft not an American vessel or American aircraft, if the employee is employed on and in connection with such vessel or aircraft when outside the United States;

(5) service performed by an individual in the employ of his son, daughter, or spouse, and service performed by a child under the age of 21 in the employ of his father or mother;

(6) service performed in the employ of the United States Government or of an instrumentality of the United States which is—

(A) wholly or partially owned by the United States, or

(B) exempt from the tax imposed by section 3301 by virtue of any provision of law which specifically refers to such section (or the corresponding section of prior law) in granting such exemption;

(7) service performed in the employ of a State, or any political subdivision thereof, or in the employ of an Indian tribe, or any instrumentality of any one or more of the foregoing which is wholly owned by one or more States or political subdivisions or Indian tribes; and any service performed in the employ of any instrumentality of one or more States or political subdivisions to the extent that the instrumentality is, with respect to such service, immune under the Constitution of the United States from the tax imposed by section 3301;

(8) service performed in the employ of a religious, charitable, educational, or other organization described in section 501(c)(3) which is exempt from income tax under section 501(a);

(9) service performed by an individual as an employee or employee representative as defined in section 1 of the Railroad Unemployment Insurance Act (45 U.S.C. 351);

(10)(A) service performed in any calendar quarter in the employ of any organization exempt from income tax under section 501(a) (other than an organization described in section 401(a)) or under section 521, if the remuneration for such service is less than $50, or

(B) service performed in the employ of a school, college, or university, if such service is performed (i) by a student who is enrolled and is regularly attending classes at such school, college, or university, or (ii) by the spouse of such a student, if such spouse is advised, at the time such spouse commences to perform such service, that (I) the employment of such spouse to perform such service is provided under a program to provide financial assistance to such student by such school, college, or university, and (II) such employment will not be covered by any program of unemployment insurance, or

(C) service performed by an individual who is enrolled at a nonprofit or public educational institution which normally maintains a regular faculty and curriculum and normally has a regularly organized body of students in attendance at the place where its educational activities are carried on as a student in a full-time program, taken for credit at such institution, which combines academic instruction with work experience, if such service is an integral part of such program, and such institution has so certified to the employer, except that this subparagraph shall not apply to service performed in a program established for or on behalf of an employer or group of employers, or

(D) service performed in the employ of a hospital, if such service is performed by a patient of such hospital;

(11) service performed in the employ of a foreign government (including service as a consular or other officer or employee or a nondiplomatic representative);

(12) service performed in the employ of an instrumentality wholly owned by a foreign government—

(A) if the service is of a character similar to that performed in foreign countries by employees of the United States Government or of an instrumentality thereof; and

(B) if the Secretary of State shall certify to the Secretary of the Treasury that the foreign government, with respect to whose instrumentality exemption is claimed, grants an equivalent exemption with respect to similar service performed in the foreign country by employees of the United States Government and of instrumentalities thereof;

(13) service performed as a student nurse in the employ of a hospital or a nurses' training school by an individual who is enrolled and is regularly attending classes in a nurses' training school chartered or approved pursuant to State law; and service performed as an intern in the employ of a hospital by an individual who has completed a 4 years' course in a medical school chartered or approved pursuant to State law;

(14) service performed by an individual for a person as an insurance agent or as an insurance solicitor, if all such service performed by such individual for such person is performed for remuneration solely by way of commission;

(15)(A) service performed by an individual under the age of 18 in the delivery or distribution of newspapers or shopping news, not including delivery or distribution to any point for subsequent delivery or distribution;

(B) service performed by an individual in, and at the time of, the sale of newspapers or magazines to ultimate consumers, under an arrangement under which the newspapers or magazines are sold by him at a fixed price, his compensation being based on the retention of the excess of such price over the amount at which the newspapers or magazines are charged to him, whether or not he is guaranteed a minimum amount of compensation for such service, or is entitled to be credited with the unsold newspapers or magazines turned back;

(16) service performed in the employ of an international organization;

(17) service performed by an individual in (or as an officer or member of the crew of a vessel while it is engaged in) the catching, taking, harvesting, cultivating, or farming of any kind of fish, shellfish, crustacea, sponges, seaweeds, or other aquatic forms of animal and vegetable life (including service performed by any such individual as an ordinary incident to any such activity), except—

(A) service performed in connection with the catching or taking of salmon or halibut, for commercial purposes, and

(B) service performed on or in connection with a vessel of more than 10 net tons (determined in the manner provided for determining the register tonnage of merchant vessels under the laws of the United States);

Sec. 3306(c)(1)(A)(i)

UNEMPLOYMENT TAX

(18) service described in section 3121(b)(20);

(19) service which is performed by a nonresident alien individual for the period he is temporarily present in the United States as a nonimmigrant under subparagraph (F), (J), (M), or (Q) of section 101(a)(15) of the Immigration and Nationality Act, as amended (8 U.S.C. 1101(a)(15)(F), (J), (M), or (Q)), and which is performed to carry out the purpose specified in subparagraph (F), (J), (M), or (Q), as the case may be;

(20) service performed by a full time student (as defined in subsection (q)) in the employ of an organized camp—

(A) if such camp—

(i) did not operate for more than 7 months in the calendar year and did not operate for more than 7 months in the preceding calendar year, or

(ii) had average gross receipts for any 6 months in the preceding calendar year which were not more than $33^{1}/_{3}$ percent of its average gross receipts for the other 6 months in the preceding calendar year; and

(B) if such full time student performed services in the employ of such camp for less than 13 calendar weeks in such calendar year; or

(21) service performed by a person committed to a penal institution.

Amendments

• **2018, Tax Technical Corrections Act of 2018 (P.L. 115-141)**

P.L. 115-141, §401(a)(213), Div. U:

Amended Code Sec. 3306(c)(19) by striking "Service" and inserting "service". **Effective** 3-23-2018.

• **2000, Community Renewal Tax Relief Act of 2000 (P.L. 106-554)**

P.L. 106-554, §166(a)(1)-(2):

Amended Code Sec. 3306(c)(7) by inserting "or in the employ of an Indian tribe," after "service performed in the employ of a State, or any political subdivision thereof,"; and by inserting "or Indian tribes" after "wholly owned by one or more States or political subdivisions". **Effective** for service performed on or after 12-21-2000. For a transition rule, see Act Sec. 166(e)(2), below.

P.L. 106-554, §166(e)(2), provides:

(2) TRANSITION RULE.—For purposes of the Federal Unemployment Tax Act, service performed in the employ of an Indian tribe (as defined in section 3306(u) of the Internal Revenue Code of 1986 (as added by this section)) shall not be treated as employment (within the meaning of section 3306 of such Code) if—

(A) it is service which is performed before the date of the enactment of this Act and with respect to which the tax imposed under the Federal Unemployment Tax Act has not been paid, and

(B) such Indian tribe reimburses a State unemployment fund for unemployment benefits paid for service attributable to such tribe for such period.

• **1997, Balanced Budget Act of 1997 (P.L. 105-33)**

P.L. 105-33, §5406(a)(1)-(3):

Amended Code Sec. 3306(c) by striking "or" at the end of paragraph (19), by striking the period at the end of paragraph (20) and inserting "; or", and by adding at the end a new paragraph (21). **Effective** for service performed after 1-1-94.

• **1996, Small Business Job Protection Act of 1996 (P.L. 104-188)**

P.L. 104-188, §1203(a):

Amended Code Sec. 3306(c)(1)(B) by striking "before January 1, 1995," after "performed". **Effective** for services performed after 12-31-94.

• **1994, Social Security Independence and Program Improvements Act of 1994 (P.L. 103-296)**

P.L. 103-296, §320(a)(1)(E):

Amended Code Sec. 3306(c)(19) by striking "(J), or (M)" each place it appears and inserting "(J), (M), or (Q)". **Effective** with the calendar quarter following 8-15-94.

• **1992, Unemployment Compensation Amendments of 1992 (P.L. 102-318)**

P.L. 102-318, §303(a):

Amended Code Sec. 3306(c)(1)(B) by striking "January 1, 1993" and inserting "January 1, 1995". **Effective** 7-3-92.

• **1988, Technical and Miscellaneous Revenue Act of 1988 (P.L. 100-647)**

P.L. 100-647, §1001(d)(2)(C)(iii):

Amended Code Sec. 3306(c)(19) by striking out "(F) or (J)" each place it appears and inserting in lieu thereof "(F), (J), or (M)". **Effective** as if included in the provision of P.L. 99-514 to which it relates.

• **1986 (P.L. 99-595)**

P.L. 99-595, §111:

Amended Code Sec. 3306(c)(1)(B) by striking out "before January 1, 1988," and inserting in lieu thereof "before January 1, 1993,". **Effective** 10-31-86.

• **1986, Consolidated Omnibus Budget Reconciliation Act of 1985 (P.L. 99-272)**

P.L. 99-272, §13303(a):

Amended Code Sec. 3306(c)(1)(B) by striking out "January 1, 1986" and inserting in lieu thereof "January 1, 1988,". **Effective** 4-7-86.

• **1983, Federal Supplemental Compensation Amendments of 1983 (P.L. 98-135)**

P.L. 98-135, §202:

Amended Code Sec. 3306(c)(1)(B) by striking out "January 1, 1984" and inserting in lieu thereof "January 1, 1986". **Effective** 10-24-83.

• **1982, Tax Equity and Fiscal Responsibility Act of 1982 (P.L. 97-248)**

P.L. 97-248, §276(a)(1):

Amended Code Sec. 3306(c)(10)(C) by striking out "under the age of 22" immediately following "individual". **Effective** with respect to services performed after 9-3-82.

P.L. 97-248, §276(b)(1):

Amended Code Sec. 3306(c) by striking out "or" at the end of paragraph (18); by striking out the period at the end of paragraph (19) and inserting in lieu thereof "or", and by adding at the end thereof new paragraph (20). **Effective** for remuneration paid after 9-19-85 (**effective** date changed by P.L. 99-272, §13303(b)).

P.L. 97-248, §277:

Amended Code Sec. 3306(c)(1)(B) by striking out "January 1, 1982" and inserting "January 1, 1984". **Effective** with respect to services performed after 9-3-82.

• **1981, Economic Recovery Tax Act of 1981 (P.L. 97-34)**

P.L. 97-34, §822(a), as amended by P.L. 97-362, §203 and P.L. 99-272, §13303:

Amended Code Sec. 3306(c) by striking out "or" at the end of paragraph (17), by redesignating paragraph (18) as paragraph (19), and by adding a new paragraph (18). **Effective** with respect to remuneration paid after 12-31-80 ("after December 31, 1980 and before January 1, 1985", prior to P.L. 99-272, and "during 1981", prior to P.L. 97-362).

• **1979 (P.L. 96-84)**

P.L. 96-84, §4(a), (b):

Amended Code Sec. 3306(c)(1)(B) by changing "January 1, 1980" to "January 1, 1982", and Code Sec. 3306(c)(1)(A) by changing "not taking into account labor performed before January 1, 1980" each place it appears to "including labor performed by". **Effective** for remuneration paid after 12-31-79, for services performed after that date.

• **1976, Unemployment Compensation Amendments of 1976 (P.L. 94-566)**

P.L. 94-566, §111(b):

Amended Code Sec. 3306(c)(1). **Effective** with respect to remuneration paid after 12-31-77, for services performed after such date. Prior to amendment, paragraph (1) read as follows:

(1) agricultural labor (as defined in subsection (k));

P.L. 94-566, §113(a):

Amended Code Sec. 3306(c)(2). **Effective** with respect to remuneration paid after 12-31-77, for services performed after such date. Prior to amendment, paragraph (2) read as follows:

(2) domestic service in a private home, local college club, or local chapter of a college fraternity or sorority;

P.L. 94-566, §116(b)(1):

Deleted "or in the Virgin Islands" in the portion of Code Sec. 3306(c) which precedes paragraph (1) thereof. **Effective** with respect to remuneration paid after December 31 of the year in which the Secretary of Labor approves for the first time an unemployment compensation law submitted to him by the Virgin Islands for approval, for services performed after such December 31.

• **1976, Tax Reform Act of 1976 (P.L. 94-455)**

P.L. 94-455, §1903(a)(16)(A):

Deleted "52 Stat. 1094, 1095;" in Code Sec. 3306(c)(9). **Effective** for compensation paid for services rendered after 12-31-76.

P.L. 94-455, §1903(a)(16)(B):

Added after "Immigration and Nationality Act, as amended" in Code Sec. 3306(c)(18) the following: "(8 U.S.C. 1101(a)(15)(F) or (J))." **Effective** for compensation paid for services rendered after 12-31-76.

P.L. 94-455, §1906(b)(13)(C):

Substituted "to the Secretary of the Treasury" for "to the Secretary" each place it appeared in Code Sec. 3306(c)(12)(B). **Effective** 2-1-77.

• **1970, Employment Security Amendments of 1970 (P.L. 91-373)**

P.L. 91-373, §105(a):

Amended that portion of Code Sec. 3306(c) which precedes paragraph (1). **Effective** with respect to service performed after 12-31-71. Prior to amendment, that portion of Code Sec. 3306(c) which precedes paragraph (1) read as follows:

UNEMPLOYMENT TAX

(c) Employment.—For purposes of this chapter, the term "employment" means any service performed prior to 1955, which was employment for purposes of subchapter C of chapter 9 of the Internal Revenue Code of 1939 under the law applicable to the period in which such service was performed, and any service, of whatever nature, performed after 1954 by an employee for the person employing him, irrespective of the citizenship or residence of either, (A) within the United States, or (B) on or in connection with an American vessel or American aircraft under a contract of service which is entered into within the United States or during the performance of which and while the employee is employed on the vessel or aircraft it touches at a port in the United States, if the employee is employed on and in connection with such vessel or aircraft when outside the United States, except—

P.L. 91-373, § 106(a):

Amended Code Sec. 3306(c)(10) by substituting subparagraphs (B), (C) and (D) for subparagraph (B). **Effective** for remuneration paid after 12-31-69. Prior to amendment, Code Sec. 3306(c)(1)(B) read as follows:

(B) service performed in the employ of a school, college, or university, if such service is performed by a student who is enrolled and is regularly attending classes at such school, college, or university;

• **1961, Mutual Educational and Cultural Exchange Act of 1961 (P.L. 87-256)**

P.L. 87-256, § 110(f):

Struck out the "or" at the end of paragraph (16); struck out the period at the end of paragraph (17) and substituted "; or"; and added a new paragraph (18). **Effective** for services performed after 1961.

• **1960, Social Security Amendments of 1960 (P.L. 86-778)**

P.L. 86-778, § 531(c):

Amended Code Sec. 3306(c)(6). **Effective** with respect to remuneration paid after 1961 for services performed after 1961. Prior to amendment, Code Sec. 3306(c)(6) read as follows:

(6) service performed in the employ of the United States Government or of an instrumentality of the United States which is—

(A) wholly owned by the United States, or

(B) exempt from the tax imposed by section 3301 by virtue of any other provision of law;

P.L. 86-778, § 532(a):

Amended so much of section 3306(c) as precedes paragraph (1) by striking out "or (B) on or in connection with an American vessel under a contract of service which is entered into within the United States or during the performance of which the vessel touches at a port in the United States, if the employee is employed on and in connection with such vessel when outside the United States," and by substituting therefor "or (B) on or in connection with an American vessel or an American aircraft under a contract of service which is entered into within the United States or during the performance of which and while the employee is employed on the vessel or aircraft it touches at a port in the United States, if the employee is employed on and in connection with such vessel or aircraft when outside the United States". **Effective** with respect to remuneration paid after 1961 for services performed after 1961.

P.L. 86-778, § 532(b):

Amended Code Sec. 3306(c)(4). **Effective** with respect to remuneration paid after 1961 for services performed after 1961. Prior to amendment, Code Sec. 3306(c)(4) read as follows:

(4) service performed on or in connection with a vessel not an American vessel by an employee, if the employee is employed on and in connection with such vessel when outside the United States;

P.L. 86-778, § 533:

Amended Code Sec. 3306(c)(8). **Effective** with respect to remuneration paid after 1961 for services performed after 1961. Prior to amendment, Code Sec. 3306(c)(8) read as follows:

(8) service performed in the employ of a corporation, community chest, fund, or foundation, organized and operated exclusively for religious, charitable, scientific, testing for public safety, literary, or educational purposes, or for the prevention of cruelty to children or animals, no part of the net earnings of which inures to the benefit of any private shareholder or individual, and no substantial part of the activities of which is carrying on propaganda, or otherwise attempting, to influence legislation;

P.L. 86-778, § 534:

Amended Code Sec. 3306(c)(10). **Effective** with respect to remuneration paid after 1961 for services performed after 1961. Prior to amendment, Code Sec. 3306(c)(10) read as follows:

(10)(A) service performed in any calendar quarter in the employ of any organization exempt from income tax under section 501(a) (other than an organization described in section 401(a)) or under section 521, if—

(i) the remuneration for such service is less than $50, or

(ii) such service is in connection with the collection of dues or premiums for a fraternal beneficiary society, order, or association, and is performed away from the home office, or is ritualistic service in connection with any such society, order or association, or

(iii) such service is performed by a student who is enrolled and is regularly attending classes at a school, college, or university;

(B) service performed in the employ of an agricultural or horticultural organization described in section 501(c)(5) which is exempt from tax under section 501(a);

(C) service performed in the employ of a voluntary employees' beneficiary association providing for the payment of life, sick, accident, or other benefits to the members of such association or their dependents, if—

(i) no part of its net earnings inures (other than through such payments) to the benefit of any private shareholder or individual, and

(ii) 85 percent or more of the income consists of amounts collected from members for the sole purpose of making such payments and meeting expenses;

(D) service performed in the employ of a voluntary employees' beneficiary association providing for the payment of life, sick, accident, or other benefits to the members of such association or their dependents or their designated beneficiaries, if—

(i) admission to membership in such association is limited to individuals who are officers or employees of the United States Government, and

(ii) no part of the net earnings of such association inures (other than through such payments) to the benefit of any private shareholder or individual;

(E) service performed in the employ of a school, college, or university, not exempt from income tax under section 501(a), if such service is performed by a student who is enrolled and is regularly attending classes at such school, college, or university;

[Sec. 3306(d)]

(d) INCLUDED AND EXCLUDED SERVICE.—For purposes of this chapter, if the services performed during one-half or more of any pay period by an employee for the person employing him constitute employment, all the services of such employee for such period shall be deemed to be employment; but if the services performed during more than one-half of any such pay period by an employee for the person employing him do not constitute employment, then none of the services of such employee for such period shall be deemed to be employment. As used in this subsection, the term "pay period" means a period (of not more than 31 consecutive days) for which a payment of remuneration is ordinarily made to the employee by the person employing him. This subsection shall not be applicable with respect to services performed in a pay period by an employee for the person employing him, where any of such service is excepted by subsection (c)(9).

[Sec. 3306(e)]

(e) STATE AGENCY.—For purposes of this chapter, the term "State agency" means any State officer, board, or other authority, designated under a State law to administer the unemployment fund in such State.

[Sec. 3306(f)]

(f) UNEMPLOYMENT FUND.—For purposes of this chapter, the term "unemployment fund" means a special fund, established under a State law and administered by a State agency, for the payment of compensation. Any sums standing to the account of the State agency in the Unemployment Trust Fund established by section 904 of the Social Security Act, as amended (42 U. S. C. 1104), shall be deemed to be a part of the unemployment fund of the State, and no sums paid out of the Unemployment Trust Fund to such State agency shall cease to be a part of the unemployment fund of the State until expended by such State agency. An unemployment fund shall be deemed to be maintained during a taxable year only if throughout such year, or such portion of the year as the unemployment fund was in existence, no part of the moneys of such fund was expended for any purpose other than the payment of compensation (exclusive of expenses of administration) and for refunds of sums erroneously paid into such fund and refunds paid in accordance with the provisions of section 3305(b); except that—

(1) an amount equal to the amount of employee payments into the unemployment fund of a State may be used in the payment of cash benefits to individuals with respect to their disability, exclusive of expenses of administration;

(2) the amounts specified by section 903(c)(2) or 903(d)(4) of the Social Security Act may, subject to the conditions prescribed in such section, be used for expenses incurred by the State for administration of its unemployment compensation law and public employment offices;

(3) nothing in this subsection shall be construed to prohibit deducting any amount from unemployment compensation otherwise payable to an individual and using the amount so deducted to pay for health insurance, or the withholding of Federal, State, or local individual income tax, if the individual elected to have such deduction made and such deduction was made under a program approved by the Secretary of Labor;

(4) amounts may be deducted from unemployment benefits and used to repay overpayments as provided in section 303(g) of the Social Security Act;

UNEMPLOYMENT TAX

(5) amounts may be withdrawn for the payment of short-time compensation under a short-time compensation program (as defined in subsection (v)); and

(6) amounts may be withdrawn for the payment of allowances under a self-employment assistance program (as defined in subsection (t)).

Amendments

• **2012, Middle Class Tax Relief and Job Creation Act of 2012 (P.L. 112-96)**

P.L. 112-96, §2161(b)(1)(B)(i)-(ii):

Amended Code Sec. 3306(f) by striking paragraph (5) (relating to short-time compensation) and inserting a new paragraph (5); and by redesignating paragraph (5) (relating to self-employment assistance program) as paragraph (6). **Effective** 2-22-2012. Prior to being stricken, Code Sec. 3306(f)(5) read as follows:

(5) amounts may be withdrawn for the payment of short-time compensation under a plan approved by the Secretary of Labor; and

• **2002, Job Creation and Worker Assistance Act of 2002 (P.L. 107-147)**

P.L. 107-147, §209(d)(1):

Amended Code Sec. 3306(f)(2) by inserting "or 903(d)(4)" before "of the Social Security Act". **Effective** 3-9-2002. For a special rule, see Act Sec. 209(e), below.

P.L. 107-147, §209(e), provides:

(e) REGULATIONS.—The Secretary of Labor may prescribe any operating instructions or regulations necessary to carry out this section and the amendments made by this section.

• **1994, Uruguay Round Agreements Act (P.L. 103-465)**

P.L. 103-465, §702(c)(2):

Amended Code Sec. 3306(f) by redesignating paragraphs (3) and (4) [and (5)] as paragraphs (4) and (5) [and (6)], respectively, and by inserting after paragraph (2) a new paragraph (3). **Effective** for payments made after 12-31-96.

• **1983, North American Free Trade Agreement Implementation Act (P.L. 103-182)**

P.L. 103-182, §507(b)(2)(A)-(C):

Amended Code Sec. 3306(f) by striking "; and" in paragraph (3) and inserting a semicolon, by striking the period in paragraph (4) and inserting "; and", and by adding at the end thereof new paragraph (5). **Effective** 12-8-93.

P.L. 103-182, §507(e)(2), prior to repeal by P.L. 105-306, §3(a), provided:

(2) SUNSET.—The authority provided by this section, and the amendments made by this section, shall terminate 5 years after the date of the enactment of this Act.

• **1992, Unemployment Compensation Amendments of 1992 (P.L. 102-318)**

P.L. 102-318, §401(a)(2):

Amended Code Sec. 3306(f) by striking "and" at the end of paragraph (2), by striking the period at the end of paragraph (3) and inserting "; and", and by adding at the end thereof new paragraph (4). **Effective** 7-3-92.

• **1986, Consolidated Omnibus Budget Reconciliation Act of 1985 (P.L. 99-272)**

P.L. 99-272, §12401(b)(2)(A)-(C):

Amended Code Sec. 3306(f) by striking out "and" at the end of paragraph (1), by striking out the period at the end of paragraph (2) and inserting in lieu thereof "and", and by adding at the end thereof new paragraph (3). **Effective** for recoveries made on or after 4-7-86 and with respect to overpayments made before, on, or after such date.

• **1976, Tax Reform Act of 1976 (P.L. 94-455)**

P.L. 94-455, §1903(a)(16)(C):

Deleted "49 Stat. 640; 52 Stat. 1104, 1105;" in Code Sec. 3306(f). **Effective** for compensation paid for services rendered after 12-31-76.

[Sec. 3306(g)]

(g) CONTRIBUTIONS.—For purposes of this chapter, the term "contributions" means payments required by a State law to be made into an unemployment fund by any person on account of having individuals in his employ, to the extent that such payments are made by him without being deducted or deductible from the remuneration of individuals in his employ.

[Sec. 3306(h)]

(h) COMPENSATION.—For purposes of this chapter, the term "compensation" means cash benefits payable to individuals with respect to their unemployment.

[Sec. 3306(i)]

(i) EMPLOYEE.—For purposes of this chapter, the term "employee" has the meaning assigned to such term by section 3121(d), except that paragraph (4) and subparagraphs (B) and (C) of paragraph (3) shall not apply.

Amendments

• **1988, Technical and Miscellaneous Revenue Act of 1988 (P.L. 100-647)**

P.L. 100-647, §8016(a)(3)(B):

Amended Code Sec. 3306(i) by striking "paragraph (3) and subparagraphs (B) and (C) of paragraph (4)" and inserting "paragraph (4) and subparagraphs (B) and (C) of paragraph (3)". For the **effective** date, see Act Sec. 8016(b), below.

P.L. 100-647, §8016(b), provides:

(b) EFFECTIVE DATE.—(1) Except as provided in paragraph (2), the amendments made by this section shall be effective on the date of the enactment of this Act.

(2) Any amendment made by this section to a provision of a particular Public Law which is referred to by its number, or to a provision of the Social Security Act or the Internal Revenue Code of 1986 as added or amended by a provision of a particular Public Law which is so referred to, shall be effective as though it had been included or reflected in the relevant provisions of that Public Law at the time of its enactment.

• **1986, Omnibus Budget Reconciliation Act of 1986 (P.L. 99-509)**

P.L. 99-509, §9002(b)(2)(B):

Amended Code Sec. 3306(i) by striking out "subparagraphs (B) and (C) of paragraph (3)" and inserting in lieu thereof "paragraph (3) and subparagraphs (B) and (C) of paragraph (4)". For the **effective** date, see Act Sec. 9002(d), below.

P.L. 99-509, §9002(d), provides:

(d) EFFECTIVE DATE.—The amendments made by this section are effective with respect to payments due with respect to wages paid after December 31, 1986, including wages paid after such date by a State (or political subdivision thereof) that modified its agreement pursuant to the provisions of section 218(e)(2) of the Social Security Act prior to the date of the enactment of this Act; except that in cases where, in accordance with the currently applicable schedule, deposits of taxes due under an agreement entered into pursuant to section 218 of the Social Security Act would be required within 3 days after the close of an eighth-monthly period, such 3-day requirement shall be changed to a 7-day requirement for wages paid prior to October 1, 1987, and to a 5-day requirement for wages paid after September 30, 1987, and prior to October 1, 1988. For wages paid prior to October 1, 1988, the deposit schedule for taxes imposed under sections 3101 and 3111 shall be determined separately from the deposit schedule for taxes withheld under section 3402 if the taxes imposed under sections 3101 and 3111 are due with respect to service included under an agreement entered into pursuant to section 218 of the Social Security Act.

• **1970, Employment Security Amendments of 1970 (P.L. 91-373)**

P.L. 91-373, §102(a):

Amended Code Sec. 3306(i). **Effective** with respect to remuneration paid after 12-31-71, for services performed after such date. Prior to amendment, Code Sec. 3306(i) read as follows:

(i) EMPLOYEE.—For purposes of this chapter, the term "employee" includes an officer of a corporation, but such term does not include—

(1) any individual who, under the usual common law rules applicable in determining the employer-employee relationship, has the status of an independent contractor, or

(2) any individual (except an officer of a corporation) who is not an employee under such common law rules.

[Sec. 3306(j)]

(j) STATE, UNITED STATES, AND AMERICAN EMPLOYER.—For purposes of this chapter—

(1) STATE.—The term "State" includes the District of Columbia, the Commonwealth of Puerto Rico, and the Virgin Islands.

(2) UNITED STATES.—The term "United States" when used in a geographical sense includes the States, the District of Columbia, the Commonwealth of Puerto Rico, and the Virgin Islands.

(3) AMERICAN EMPLOYER.—The term "American employer" means a person who is—

(A) an individual who is a resident of the United States,

(B) a partnership, if two-thirds or more of the partners are residents of the United States,

(C) a trust, if all of the trustees are residents of the United States, or

(D) a corporation organized under the laws of the United States or of any State.

UNEMPLOYMENT TAX

An individual who is a citizen of the Commonwealth of Puerto Rico or the Virgin Islands (but not otherwise a citizen of the United States) shall be considered, for purposes of this section, as a citizen of the United States.

Amendments

- **1976, Unemployment Compensation Amendments of 1976 (P.L. 94-566)**

P.L. 94-566, §116(b)(2), (f)(2):

Amended Code Sec. 3306(j). **Effective** for remuneration paid after December 31 of the year in which the Secretary of Labor approves for the first time an unemployment compensation law submitted to him by the Virgin Islands for approval, for services performed after such December 31. Prior to amendment, Code Sec. 3306(j) read as follows:

(j) STATE, UNITED STATES, AND CITIZEN.—For purposes of this chapter—

(1) STATE.—The term "State" includes the District of Columbia and the Commonwealth of Puerto Rico.

(2) UNITED STATES.—The term "United States" when used in a geographical sense includes the States, the District of Columbia, and the Commonwealth of Puerto Rico.

(3) AMERICAN EMPLOYER.—The term "American employer" means a person who is—

(A) an individual who is a resident of the United States,

(B) a partnership, if two-thirds or more of the partners are residents of the United States,

(C) a trust, if all of the trustees are residents of the United States, or

(D) a corporation organized under the laws of the United States or of any State.

An individual who is a citizen of the Commonwealth of Puerto Rico (but not otherwise a citizen of the United States) shall be considered for purposes of this section, as a citizen of the United States.

- **1970, Employment Security Amendments of 1970 (P.L. 91-373)**

P.L. 91-373, §105(b):

Added paragraph (3) to Code Sec. 3306(j). **Effective** with respect to service performed after 12-31-71.

- **1960, Social Security Amendments of 1960 (P.L. 86-778)**

P.L. 86-778, §543(a):

Amended Code Sec. 3306(j). **Effective** 1-1-61. Prior to amendment, it read as follows:

(j) STATE.—For purposes of this chapter, the term "state" includes the District of Columbia.

- **1960, Hawaii Omnibus Act (P.L. 86-624)**

P.L. 86-624, §18(d):

Amended 1954 Code Sec. 3306(j) by striking out "Hawaii and" where it appeared following "includes". **Effective** 8-21-59.

- **1959, Alaska Omnibus Bill (P.L. 86-70)**

P.L. 86-70, §22(a):

Amended 1954 Code Sec. 3306(j) by striking out "Alaska," where it appeared following "includes." **Effective** 1-3-59.

[Sec. 3306(k)]

(k) AGRICULTURAL LABOR.—For purposes of this chapter, the term "agricultural labor" has the meaning assigned to such term by subsection (g) of section 3121, except that for purposes of this chapter subparagraph (B) of paragraph (4) of such subsection (g) shall be treated as reading:

"(B) in the employ of a group of operators of farms (or a cooperative organization of which such operators are members) in the performance of service described in subparagraph (A), but only if such operators produced more than one-half of the commodity with respect to which such service is performed;".

Amendments

- **1996, Small Business Job Protection Act of 1996 (P.L. 104-188)**

P.L. 104-188, §1704(t)(10):

Amended Code Sec. 3306(k) by inserting a period at the end thereof. **Effective** 8-20-96.

- **1970, Employment Security Amendments of 1970 (P.L. 91-373)**

P.L. 91-373, §103(a):

Amended Code Sec. 3306(k). **Effective** with respect to remuneration paid after 12-31-71, for services performed after such date. Prior to amendment, Code Sec. 3306(k) read as follows:

(k) AGRICULTURAL LABOR.—For purposes of this chapter, the term `agricultural labor' includes all service performed—

(1) on a farm, in the employ of any person, in connection with cultivating the soil, or in connection with raising or harvesting any agricultural or horticultural commodity, including the raising, shearing, feeding, caring for, training, and management of livestock, bees, poultry, and fur-bearing animals and wildlife;

(2) in the employ of the owner or tenant or other operator of a farm, in connection with the operation, management, conservation, improvement, or maintenance of such farm and its tools and equipment, or in salvaging timber or clearing land of brush and other debris left by a hurricane, if the major part of such service is performed on a farm;

(3) in connection with the production or harvesting of maple sirup or maple sugar or any commodity defined as an agricultural commodity in section 15(g) of the Agricultural Marketing Act, as amended (46 Stat. 1550, §3; 12 U. S. C. 1141j), or in connection with the raising or harvesting of mushrooms, or in connection with the hatching of poultry, or in connection with the ginning of cotton, or in connection with the operation or maintenance of ditches, canals, reservoirs, or waterways used exclusively for supplying and storing water for farming purposes; or

(4) in handling, planting, drying, packing, packaging, processing, freezing, grading, storing, or delivering to storage or to market or to a carrier for transportation to market, any agricultural or horticultural commodity; but only if such service is performed as an incident to ordinary farming operations or, in the case of fruits and vegetables, as an incident to the preparation of such fruits or vegetables for market. The provisions of this paragraph shall not be deemed to be applicable with respect to service performed in connection with commercial canning or commercial freezing or in connection with any agricultural or horticultural commodity after its delivery to a terminal market for distribution for consumption.

As used in this subsection, the term `farm' includes stock, dairy, poultry, fruit, fur-bearing animal, and truck farms, plantations, ranches, nurseries, ranges, greenhouses or other similar structures used primarily for the raising of agricultural or horticultural commodities, and orchards.

[Sec. 3306(l)—Repealed]

Amendments

- **1954 (P.L. 767, 83rd Cong.)**

P.L. 767, 83rd Cong., §4(c):

Repealed Sec. 3306(l). **Effective** with respect to services performed after 12-31-54. Prior to repeal, Code Sec. 3306(l) read as follows:

(l) CERTAIN EMPLOYEES OF BONNEVILLE POWER ADMINISTRATOR.—For purposes of this chapter—

(1) The term "employment" shall include such service as is determined by the Bonneville Power Administrator to be performed after December 31, 1945, by a laborer, mechanic, or workman, in connection with construction work or the operation and maintenance of electrical facilities, as an employee performing service for the Administrator.

(2) The term "wages" means, with respect to service which constitutes employment by reason of this subsection, such amount of remuneration as is determined (subject to the provisions of this section) by the Administrator to be paid for such service.

The Administrator is authorized and directed to comply with the provisions of the internal revenue laws on behalf of the United States as the employer of individuals whose service constitutes employment by reason of this subsection.

[**Note:** Sec. 1607(m), 1939 Code, was substantially the same provision as the repealed Sec. 3306(l). At the time Sec. 3306(l) was repealed by P.L. 767, 83rd Cong., Sec. 4(c), Sec. 4(b) of P.L. 767 amended the 1939 Code provision by inserting after "December 31, 1945," the following: "and before January 1, 1955,". The amendment was effective September 1, 1954. Thus, the amendment of the 1939 Code provision had the same effect as the repeal of the 1954 Code provision.—CCH.]

[Sec. 3306(m)]

(m) AMERICAN VESSEL AND AIRCRAFT.—For purposes of this chapter, the term "American vessel" means any vessel documented or numbered under the laws of the United States; and includes any vessel which is neither documented or numbered under the laws of the United States nor documented under the laws of any foreign country, if its crew is employed solely by one or more citizens or residents of the United States or corporations organized under the laws of the United States or of any State; and the term "American aircraft" means an aircraft registered under the laws of the United States.

Amendments

- **1960, Social Security Amendments of 1960 (P.L. 86-778)**

P.L. 86-778, §532(c):

Amended Code Sec. 3306(m) by adding "AND AIRCRAFT" in the heading, by striking out the period at the end of the paragraph, by inserting a semicolon in lieu of that period, and by adding the material following that semicolon. **Effective** 1-1-62.

Sec. 3306(k)

UNEMPLOYMENT TAX

[Sec. 3306(n)]

(n) VESSELS OPERATED BY GENERAL AGENTS OF UNITED STATES.—Notwithstanding the provisions of subsection (c)(6), service performed by officers and members of the crew of a vessel which would otherwise be included as employment under subsection (c) shall not be excluded by reason of the fact that it is performed on or in connection with an American vessel—

(1) owned by or bareboat chartered to the United States and

(2) whose business is conducted by a general agent of the Secretary of Transportation.

For purposes of this chapter, each such general agent shall be considered a legal entity in his capacity as such general agent, separate and distinct from his identity as a person employing individuals on his own account, and the officers and members of the crew of such an American vessel whose business is conducted by a general agent of the Secretary of Transportation shall be deemed to be performing services for such general agent rather than the United States. Each such general agent who in his capacity as such is an employer within the meaning of subsection (a) shall be subject to all the requirements imposed upon an employer under this chapter with respect to service which constitutes employment by reason of this subsection.

Amendments

• **2015, National Defense Authorization Act for Fiscal Year 2016 (P.L. 114-92)**

P.L. 114-92, §3503:

Amended Code Sec. 3306 by striking "Secretary of Commerce" each place that it appears and inserting "Secretary of Transportation". **Effective** 11-25-2015.

• **1976, Tax Reform Act of 1976 (P.L. 94-455)**

P.L. 94-455, §1903(a)(16)(D):

Deleted "on or after July 1, 1953," in Code Sec. 3306(n). **Effective** for compensation paid for services rendered after 12-31-76.

[Sec. 3306(o)]

(o) SPECIAL RULE IN CASE OF CERTAIN AGRICULTURAL WORKERS.—

(1) CREW LEADERS WHO ARE REGISTERED OR PROVIDE SPECIALIZED AGRICULTURAL LABOR.—For purposes of this chapter, any individual who is a member of a crew furnished by a crew leader to perform agricultural labor for any other person shall be treated as an employee of such crew leader—

(A) if—

(i) such crew leader holds a valid certificate of registration under the Migrant and Seasonal Agricultural Worker Protection Act; or

(ii) substantially all the menbers of such crew operate or maintain tractors, mechanized harvesting or cropdusting equipment, or any other mechanized equipment, which is provided by such crew leader; and

(B) if such individual is not an employee of such other person within the meaning of subsection (i).

(2) OTHER CREW LEADERS.—For purposes of this chapter, in the case of any individual who is furnished by a crew leader to perform agricultural labor for any other person and who is not treated as an employee of such crew leader under paragraph (1)—

(A) such other person and not the crew leader shall be treated as the employer of such individual; and

(B) such other person shall be treated as having paid cash remuneration to such individual in an amount equal to the amount of cash remuneration paid to such individual by the crew leader (either on his behalf or on behalf of such other person) for the agricultural labor performed for such other person.

(3) CREW LEADER.—For purposes of this subsection, the term "crew leader" means an individual who—

(A) furnishes individuals to perform agricultural labor for any other person,

(B) pays (either on his behalf or on behalf of such other person) the individuals so furnished by him for the agricultural labor performed by them, and

(C) has not entered into a written agreement with such other person under which such individual is designated as an employee of such other person.

Amendments

• **1986, Tax Reform Act of 1986 (P.L. 99-514)**

P.L. 99-514, §1884(3):

Amended Code Sec. 3306(o)(1)(A)(i) by striking out "Farm Labor Contractor Registration Act of 1963" and inserting in lieu thereof "Migrant and Seasonal Agricultural Worker Protection Act". **Effective** 10-22-86.

• **1976, Unemployment Compensation Amendments of 1976 (P.L. 94-566)**

P.L. 94-566, §112(a), (b):

Added Code Sec. 3306(o). **Effective** for remuneration paid after 12-31-77, for services performed after such date.

[Sec. 3306(p)]

(p) CONCURRENT EMPLOYMENT BY TWO OR MORE EMPLOYERS.—For purposes of sections 3301, 3302, and 3306(b)(1), if two or more related corporations concurrently employ the same individual and compensate such individual through a common paymaster which is one of such corporations, each such corporation shall be considered to have paid as remuneration to such individual only the amounts actually disbursed by it to such individual and shall not be considered to have paid as remuneration to such individual amounts actually disbursed to such individual by another of such corporations.

Amendments

• **1977 (P.L. 95-216)**

P.L. 95-216, §314(b), (c):

Added Code Sec. 3306(p). **Effective** for wages paid after 12-31-78.

[Sec. 3306(q)]

(q) FULL TIME STUDENT.—For purposes of subsection (c)(20), an individual shall be treated as a full time student for any period—

(1) during which the individual is enrolled as a full time student at an educational institution, or

(2) which is between academic years or terms if—

(A) the individual was enrolled as a full time student at an educational institution for the immediately preceding academic year or term, and

(B) there is a reasonable assurance that the individual will be so enrolled for the immediately succeeding academic year or term after the period described in subparagraph (A).

Amendments

• **1982, Tax Equity and Fiscal Responsibility Act of 1982 (P.L. 97-248)**

P.L. 97-248, §276(b)(2):

Added Code Sec. 3306(q). **Effective** for remuneration paid after 9-19-85. [**Effective** date changed by P.L. 99-272, §13303(b).]

Internal Revenue Code

Sec. 3306(q)(2)(B)

UNEMPLOYMENT TAX

[Sec. 3306(r)]

(r) TREATMENT OF CERTAIN DEFERRED COMPENSATION AND SALARY REDUCTION ARRANGEMENTS.—

(1) CERTAIN EMPLOYER CONTRIBUTIONS TREATED AS WAGES.—Nothing in any paragraph of subsection (b) (other than paragraph (1)) shall exclude from the term "wages"—

(A) any employer contribution under a qualified cash or deferred arrangement (as defined in section 401(k)) to the extent not included in gross income by reason of section 402(e)(3), or

(B) any amount treated as an employer contribution under section 414(h)(2) where the pickup referred to in such section is pursuant to a salary reduction agreement (whether evidenced by a written instrument or otherwise).

(2) TREATMENT OF CERTAIN NONQUALIFIED DEFERRED COMPENSATION PLANS.—

(A) IN GENERAL.—Any amount deferred under a nonqualified deferred compensation plan shall be taken into account for purposes of this chapter as of the later of—

(i) when the services are performed, or

(ii) when there is no substantial risk of forfeiture of the rights to such amount.

(B) TAXED ONLY ONCE.—Any amount taken into account as wages by reason of subparagraph (A) (and the income attributable thereto) shall not thereafter be treated as wages for purposes of this chapter.

(C) NONQUALIFIED DEFERRED COMPENSATION PLAN.—For purposes of this paragraph, the term "nonqualified deferred compensation plan" means any plan or other arrangement for deferral of compensation other than a plan described in subsection (b)(5).

Amendments

• **1992, Unemployment Compensation Amendments of 1992 (P.L. 102-318)**

P.L. 102-318, § 521(b)(35):

Amended Code Sec. 3306(r)(1)(A) by striking "section 402(a)(8)" and inserting "section 402(e)(3)". **Effective** for distributions after 12-31-92.

• **1984, Deficit Reduction Act of 1984 (P.L. 98-369)**

P.L. 98-369, § 2661(o)(4):

Amended Code Sec. 3306(r)(1)(B). **Effective** 1-1-85. Prior to amendment, Code Sec. 3306(r)(1)(B) read as follows:

(B) any amount treated as an employer contribution under section 414(h)(2).

• **1983, Social Security Amendments of 1983 (P.L. 98-21)**

P.L. 98-21, § 324(b)(1):

Added Code Sec. 3306(r). For the **effective** date, see Act Sec. 324(d)(2)-(4) in the amendments notes following Code Sec. 3306(b).

[Sec. 3306(s)]

(s) TIPS TREATED AS WAGES.—For purposes of this chapter, the term "wages" includes tips which are—

(1) received while performing services which constitute employment, and

(2) included in a written statement furnished to the employer pursuant to section 6053(a).

Amendments

• **1984, Deficit Reduction Act of 1984 (P.L. 98-369)**

P.L. 98-369, § 1073(a):

Amended Code Sec. 3306 by adding at the end thereof a new subsection (s). **Effective** 1-1-86. For an exception, see Act Sec. 1073(b)(2), below.

P.L. 98-369, § 1073(b)(2), provides:

(2) Exception for Certain States.—In the case of any State the legislature of which—

(A) did not meet in a regular session which begins during 1984 and after the date of the enactment of this Act, and

(B) did not meet in a session which began before the date of the enactment of this Act and remained in session for at least 25 calendar days after such date of enactment,

the amendment made by subsection (a) shall take effect on January 1, 1987.

[Sec. 3306(t)]

(t) SELF-EMPLOYMENT ASSISTANCE PROGRAM.—For the purposes of this chapter, the term "self-employment assistance program" means a program under which—

(1) individuals who meet the requirements described in paragraph (3) are eligible to receive an allowance in lieu of regular unemployment compensation under the State law for the purpose of assisting such individuals in establishing a business and becoming self-employed;

(2) the allowance payable to individuals pursuant to paragraph (1) is payable in the same amount, at the same interval, on the same terms, and subject to the same conditions, as regular unemployment compensation under the State law, except that—

(A) State requirements relating to availability for work, active search for work, and refusal to accept work are not applicable to such individuals;

(B) State requirements relating to disqualifying income are not applicable to income earned from self-employment by such individuals; and

(C) such individuals are considered to be unemployed for the purposes of Federal and State laws applicable to unemployment compensation,

as long as such individuals meet the requirements applicable under this subsection;

(3) individuals may receive the allowance described in paragraph (1) if such individuals—

(A) are eligible to receive regular unemployment compensation under the State law, or would be eligible to receive such compensation except for the requirements described in subparagraph (A) or (B) of paragraph (2);

(B) are identified pursuant to a State worker profiling system as individuals likely to exhaust regular unemployment compensation; and

(C) are participating in self-employment assistance activities which—

(i) include entrepreneurial training, business counseling, and technical assistance; and

(ii) are approved by the State agency; and

(D) are actively engaged on a full-time basis in activities (which may include training) relating to the establishment of a business and becoming self-employed;

(4) the aggregate number of individuals receiving the allowances under the program does not at any time exceed 5 percent of the number of individuals receiving regular unemployment compensation under the State law at such time;

(5) the program does not result in any cost to the Unemployment Trust Fund (established by section 904(a) of the Social Security Act) in excess of the cost that would be incurred by such State and charged to such fund if the State had not participated in such program; and

(6) the program meets such other requirements as the Secretary of Labor determines to be appropriate.

UNEMPLOYMENT TAX

Amendments

• 1993, North America Free Trade Agreement Implementation Act (P.L. 103-182)

P.L. 103-182, §507(a):

Amended Code Sec. 3306 by adding at the end thereof new subsection (t). Effective 12-8-93.

P.L. 103-182, §507(e)(2), prior to repeal by P.L. 105-306, §3(a), provided:

(2) SUNSET.—The authority provided by this section, and the amendments made by this section, shall terminate 5 years after the date of the enactment of this Act.

• 1989 (P.L. 101-140)

P.L. 101-140, §203(a)(2), provides:

(2) Each provision of law amended by paragraph (22), (27), or (31) or section 1011B(a) of the Technical and Miscellaneous Revenue Act of 1988 is amended to read as if the amendments made by such paragraph had not been enacted.

Effective as if included in section 1151 of P.L. 99-514. Code Sec. 3306(t), as added by P.L. 100-647, §1011B(a)(22)(C), read as follows:

(t) BENEFITS PROVIDED UNDER CERTAIN EMPLOYEE BENEFIT PLANS.—Notwithstanding any paragraph of subsection (b) (other than paragraph (1)), the term "wages" shall include any amount which is includible in gross income by reason of section 89.

• 1988, Technical and Miscellaneous Revenue Act of 1988 (P.L. 100-647)

P.L. 100-647, §1011B(a)(22)(C):

Amended Code Sec. 3306 by adding at the end thereof new subsection (t). Not effective for any individual who separated from service with the employer before 1-1-89.

• 1986, Tax Reform Act of 1986 (P.L. 99-514)

P.L. 99-514, §1705, provides:

SEC. 1705. APPLICABILITY OF UNEMPLOYMENT COMPENSATION TAX TO CERTAIN SERVICES PERFORMED FOR CERTAIN INDIAN TRIBAL GOVERNMENTS.

(a) IN GENERAL.—For purposes of the Federal Unemployment Tax Act, service performed in the employ of a qualified Indian tribal government shall not be treated as employment (within the meaning of section 3306 of such Act) if it is service—

(1) which is performed—

(A) before, on, or after the date of the enactment of this Act, but before January 1, 1988, and

(B) during a period in which the Indian tribal government is not covered by a State unemployment compensation program, and

(2) with respect to which the tax imposed under the Federal Unemployment Tax Act has not been paid.

(b) DEFINITION.—For purposes of this section, the term "qualified Indian tribal government" means an Indian tribal government the service for which is not covered by a State unemployment compensation program on June 11, 1986.

[Sec. 3306(u)]

(u) INDIAN TRIBE.—For purposes of this chapter, the term "Indian tribe" has the meaning given to such term by section 4(e) of the Indian Self-Determination and Education Assistance Act (25 U.S.C. 5304(e)), and includes any subdivision, subsidiary, or business enterprise wholly owned by such an Indian tribe.

Amendments

• 2018, Tax Technical Corrections Act of 2018 (P.L. 115-141)

P.L. 115-141, §401(a)(214), Div. U:

Amended Code Sec. 3306(u) by striking "25 U.S.C. 450b(e)" and inserting "25 U.S.C. 5304(e)". Effective 3-23-2018.

• 2000, Community Renewal Tax Relief Act of 2000 (P.L. 106-554)

P.L. 106-554, §166(d):

Amended Code Sec. 3306 by adding at the end a new subsection (u). Effective for service performed on or after 12-21-2000. For a transition rule, see Act Sec. 166(e)(2) in the amendment notes following Code Sec. 3306(c).

[Sec. 3306(v)]

(v) SHORT-TIME COMPENSATION PROGRAM.—For purposes of this section, the term "short-time compensation program" means a program under which—

(1) the participation of an employer is voluntary;

(2) an employer reduces the number of hours worked by employees in lieu of layoffs;

(3) such employees whose workweeks have been reduced by at least 10 percent, and by not more than the percentage, if any, that is determined by the State to be appropriate (but in no case more than 60 percent), are not disqualified from unemployment compensation;

(4) the amount of unemployment compensation payable to any such employee is a pro rata portion of the unemployment compensation which would otherwise be payable to the employee if such employee were unemployed;

(5) such employees meet the availability for work and work search test requirements while collecting short-time compensation benefits, by being available for their workweek as required by the State agency;

(6) eligible employees may participate, as appropriate, in training (including employer-sponsored training or worker training funded under the Workforce Innovation and Opportunity Act) to enhance job skills if such program has been approved by the State agency;

(7) the State agency shall require employers to certify that if the employer provides health benefits and retirement benefits under a defined benefit plan (as defined in section 414(j)) or contributions under a defined contribution plan (as defined in section 414(i)) to any employee whose workweek is reduced under the program that such benefits will continue to be provided to employees participating in the short-time compensation program under the same terms and conditions as though the workweek of such employee had not been reduced or to the same extent as other employees not participating in the short-time compensation program;

(8) the State agency shall require an employer to submit a written plan describing the manner in which the requirements of this subsection will be implemented (including a plan for giving advance notice, where feasible, to an employee whose workweek is to be reduced) together with an estimate of the number of layoffs that would have occurred absent the ability to participate in short-time compensation and such other information as the Secretary of Labor determines is appropriate;

(9) the terms of the employer's written plan and implementation shall be consistent with employer obligations under applicable Federal and State laws; and

(10) upon request by the State and approval by the Secretary of Labor, only such other provisions are included in the State law that are determined to be appropriate for purposes of a short-time compensation program.

Amendments

• 2020, Coronavirus Aid, Relief, and Economic Security (CARES) Act (P.L. 116-136)

P.L. 116-136, §2108(f):

Amended Code Sec. 3306(v)(6) by striking "Workforce Investment Act of 1998" and inserting "Workforce Innovation and Opportunity Act". Effective 3-27-2020.

• 2018, Tax Technical Corrections Act of 2018 (P.L. 115-141)

P.L. 115-141, §401(a)(215), Div. U:

Amended Code Sec. 3306(v) by striking "this part" and inserting "this section". Effective 3-23-2018.

• 2012, Middle Class Tax Relief and Job Creation Act of 2012 (P.L. 112-96)

P.L. 112-96, §2161(a)(1):

Amended Code Sec. 3306 by adding at the end a new subsection (v). Effective 2-22-2012. For a transitional rule, see Act Sec. 2161(a)(3), below.

P.L. 112-96, §2161(a)(3), provides:

(3) TRANSITION PERIOD FOR EXISTING PROGRAMS.—In the case of a State that is administering a short-time compensation program as of the date of the enactment of this Act and the State law cannot be administered consistent with the amendment made by paragraph (1), such amendment shall take effect on the earlier of—

(A) the date the State changes its State law in order to be consistent with such amendment; or

(B) the date that is 2 years and 6 months after the date of the enactment of this Act.

[Sec. 3307]

SEC. 3307. DEDUCTIONS AS CONSTRUCTIVE PAYMENTS.

Whenever under this chapter or any act of Congress, or under the law of any State, an employer is required or permitted to deduct any amount from the remuneration of an employee and to pay the amount deducted to the United States, a State, or any political subdivision thereof, then for purposes of this chapter the amount so deducted shall be considered to have been paid to the employee at the time of such deduction.

Internal Revenue Code

UNEMPLOYMENT TAX

[Sec. 3308]

SEC. 3308. INSTRUMENTALITIES OF THE UNITED STATES.

Notwithstanding any other provision of law (whether enacted before or after the enactment of this section) which grants to any instrumentality of the United States an exemption from taxation, such instrumentality shall not be exempt from the tax imposed by section 3301 unless such other provision of law grants a specific exemption, by reference to section 3301 (or the corresponding section of prior law), from the tax imposed by such section.

Amendments

- 1960, Social Security Amendments of 1960 (P.L. 86-778)

P.L. 86-778, §531(d):

Redesignated Code Sec. 3308 as 3309 and added a new section 3308. **Effective** 1-1-62.

[Sec. 3309]

SEC. 3309. STATE LAW COVERAGE OF SERVICES PERFORMED FOR NONPROFIT ORGANIZATIONS OR GOVERNMENTAL ENTITIES.

[Sec. 3309(a)]

(a) STATE LAW REQUIREMENTS.—For purposes of section 3304(a)(6)—

(1) except as otherwise provided in subsections (b) and (c), the services to which this paragraph applies are—

(A) service excluded from the term "employment" solely by reason of paragraph (8) of section 3306(c), and

(B) service excluded from the term "employment" solely by reason of paragraph (7) of section 3306(c); and

(2) the State law shall provide that a governmental entity, including an Indian tribe, or any other organization (or group of governmental entities or other organizations) which, but for the requirements of this paragraph, would be liable for contributions with respect to service to which paragraph (1) applies may elect, for such minimum period and at such time as may be provided by State law, to pay (in lieu of such contributions) into the State unemployment fund amounts equal to the amounts of compensation attributable under the State law to such service. The State law may provide safeguards to ensure that governmental entities or other organizations so electing will make the payments required under such elections.

Amendments

- 2000, Community Renewal Tax Relief Act of 2000 (P.L. 106-554)

P.L. 106-554, §166(b)(1):

Amended Code Sec. 3309(a)(2) by inserting ", including an Indian tribe," after "the State law shall provide that a governmental entity". **Effective** for service performed on or after 12-21-2000. For a transition rule, see Act Sec. 166(e)(2) in the amendment notes following Code Sec. 3306(c).

- 1977, Emergency Unemployment Compensation Act of 1977 (P.L. 95-19)

P.L. 95-19, §302(b):

Amended Code Sec. 3309(a)(2) by substituting "or group of governmental entities or other organizations" for "or group of organizations". **Effective** as if included in the amendments made by Sec. 506 of P.L. 94-566.

- 1976, Unemployment Compensation Amendments of 1976 (P.L. 94-566)

P.L. 94-566, §115(a):

Amended subparagraph (B) of Code Sec. 3309(a)(1). **Effective** with respect to certifications of States for 1978 and subsequent years, but only with respect to services performed after 12-31-77. Prior to amendment, subparagraph (B) read as follows:

(B) service performed in the employ of the State, or any instrumentality of the State or of the State and one or more other States, for a hospital or institution of higher education located in the State, if such service is excluded from the term "employment" solely by reason of paragraph (7) of section 3306(c); and

P.L. 94-566, §115(c)(3):

Amended the heading of Code Sec. 3309. **Effective** with respect to certifications of States for 1978 and subsequent years, but only with respect to services performed after 12-31-77. Prior to amendment, such heading read as follows:

SEC. 3309. STATE LAW COVERAGE OF CERTAIN SERVICES PERFORMED FOR NONPROFIT ORGANIZATIONS AND FOR STATE HOSPITALS AND INSTITUTIONS OF HIGHER EDUCATION.

P.L. 94-566, §506(a):

Amended paragraph (2) of Code Sec. 3309(a) by (1) substituting "a governmental entity or any other organization" for "an organization"; (2) substituting "paragraph (1)" for "paragraph (1)(A)"; and (3) substituting "that governmental entities or other organizations" for "that organizations." **Effective** with respect to certifications of States for 1978 and subsequent years, but only with respect to services performed after 12-31-77.

[Sec. 3309(b)]

(b) SECTION NOT TO APPLY TO CERTAIN SERVICE.—This section shall not apply to service performed—

(1) in the employ of (A) a church or convention or association of churches, (B) an organization which is operated primarily for religious purposes and which is operated, supervised, controlled, or principally supported by a church or convention or association of churches, or (C) an elementary or secondary school which is operated primarily for religious purposes, which is described in section 501(c)(3), and which is exempt from tax under section 501(a);

(2) by a duly ordained, commissioned, or licensed minister of a church in the exercise of his ministry or by a member of a religious order in the exercise of duties required by such order;

(3) in the employ of a governmental entity referred to in paragraph (7) of section 3306(c), if such service is performed by an individual in the exercise of his duties—

(A) as an elected official;

(B) as a member of a legislative body, or a member of the judiciary, of a State or political subdivision thereof, or of an Indian tribe;

(C) as a member of the State National Guard or Air National Guard;

(D) as an employee serving on a temporary basis in case of fire, storm, snow, earthquake, flood, or similar emergency;

(E) in a position which, under or pursuant to the State or tribal law, is designated as (i) a major nontenured policymaking or advisory position, or (ii) a policymaking or advisory position the performance of the duties of which ordinarily does not require more than 8 hours per week; or

(F) as an election official or election worker if the amount of remuneration received by the individual during the calendar year for services as an election official or election worker is less than $1,000;

(4) in a facility conducted for the purpose of carrying out a program of—

(A) rehabilitation for individuals whose earnings capacity is impaired by age or physical or mental deficiency or injury, or

(B) providing remunerative work for individuals who because of their impaired physical or mental capacity cannot be readily absorbed in the competitive labor market,

by an individual receiving such rehabilitation or remunerative work;

(5) as part of an unemployment work-relief or work-training program assisted or financed in whole or in part by any Federal agency or an agency of a State or political subdivision thereof or of an Indian tribe, by an individual receiving such work relief or work training; and

(6) by an inmate of a custodial or penal institution.

UNEMPLOYMENT TAX

Amendments

• **2000, Community Renewal Tax Relief Act of 2000 (P.L. 106-554)**

P.L. 106-554, §166(b)(2):

Amended Code Sec. 3309(b)(3)(B) by inserting ", or of an Indian tribe" after "of a State or political subdivision thereof". **Effective** for service performed on or after 12-21-2000. For a transition rule, see Act Sec. 166(e)(2) in the amendment notes following Code Sec. 3306(c).

P.L. 106-554, §166(b)(3):

Amended Code Sec. 3309(b)(3)(E) by inserting "or tribal" after "the State". **Effective** for service performed on or after 12-21-2000. For a transition rule, see Act Sec. 166(e)(2) in the amendment notes following Code Sec. 3306(c).

P.L. 106-554, §166(b)(4):

Amended Code Sec. 3309(b)(5) by inserting "or of an Indian tribe" after "an agency of a State or political subdivision thereof". **Effective** for service performed on or after 12-21-2000. For a transition rule, see Act Sec. 166(e)(2) in the amendment notes following Code Sec. 3306(c).

• **1997, Balanced Budget Act of 1997 (P.L. 105-33)**

P.L. 105-33, §5405(a)(1)-(3):

Amended Code Sec. 3309(b)(3) by striking "or" at the end of subparagraph (D), by adding "or" at the end of subparagraph (E), and by inserting after subparagraph (E) a new subparagraph (F). **Effective** with respect to service performed after 8-5-97.

P.L. 105-33, §5407(a)(1)-(2):

Amended Code Sec. 3309(b)(1) by striking "or" at the end of subparagraph (A), and by inserting before the semicolon at the end ", or (C) an elementary or secondary school which is operated primarily for religious purposes, which is described in section 501(c)(3), and which is exempt from tax under section 501(a)". **Effective** with respect to service performed after 8-5-97.

• **1976, Unemployment Compensation Amendments of 1976 (P.L. 94-566)**

P.L. 94-566, §115(b)(1):

Amended paragraph (3) of Code Sec. 3309(b). **Effective** with respect to certifications of States for 1978 and subsequent years, but only with respect to services performed after 12-31-77. Prior to amendment, paragraph (3) read as follows:

(3) in the employ of a school which is not an institution of higher education;

P.L. 94-566, §115(b)(2):

Amended paragraph (6) of Code Sec. 3309(b). **Effective** with respect to certifications of States for 1978 and subsequent years, but only with respect to services performed after 12-31-77. Prior to amendment, paragraph (6) read as follows:

(6) for a hospital in a State prison or other State correctional institution by an inmate of the prison or correctional institution.

[Sec. 3309(c)]

(c) NONPROFIT ORGANIZATIONS MUST EMPLOY 4 OR MORE.—This section shall not apply to service performed during any calendar year in the employ of any organization unless on each of some 20 days during such calendar year or the preceding calendar year, each day being in a different calendar week, the total number of individuals who were employed by such organization in employment (determined without regard to section 3306(c)(8) and by excluding service to which this section does not apply by reason of subsection (b)) for some portion of the day (whether or not at the same moment of time) was 4 or more.

Amendments

• **1970, Employment Security Amendments of 1970 (P.L. 91-373)**

P.L. 91-373, §104(b):

Added Code Sec. 3309. **Effective** with respect to certifications of State laws for 1972 and subsequent years, but only with respect to service performed after 12-31-71.

[Sec. 3309(d)]

(d) ELECTION BY INDIAN TRIBE.—The State law shall provide that an Indian tribe may make contributions for employment as if the employment is within the meaning of section 3306 or make payments in lieu of contributions under this section, and shall provide that an Indian tribe may make separate elections for itself and each subdivision, subsidiary, or business enterprise wholly owned by such Indian tribe. State law may require a tribe to post a payment bond or take other reasonable measures to assure the making of payments in lieu of contributions under this section. Notwithstanding the requirements of section 3306(a)(6), if, within 90 days of having received a notice of delinquency, a tribe fails to make contributions, payments in lieu of contributions, or payment of penalties or interest (at amounts or rates comparable to those applied to all other employers covered under the State law) assessed with respect to such failure, or if the tribe fails to post a required payment bond, then service for the tribe shall not be excepted from employment under section 3306(c)(7) until any such failure is corrected. This subsection shall apply to an Indian tribe within the meaning of section 4(e) of the Indian Self-Determination and Education Assistance Act (25 U.S.C. 5304(e)).

Amendments

• **2018, Tax Technical Corrections Act of 2018 (P.L. 115-141)**

P.L. 115-141, §401(a)(216), Div. U:

Amended Code Sec. 3309(d) by striking "25 U.S.C. 450b(e)" and inserting "25 U.S.C. 5304(e)". **Effective** 3-23-2018.

• **2000, Community Renewal Tax Relief Act of 2000 (P.L. 106-554)**

P.L. 106-554, §166(c):

Amended Code Sec. 3309 by adding at the end a new subsection (d). **Effective** for service performed on or after 12-21-2000. For a transition rule, see Act Sec. 166(e)(2) in the amendment notes following Code Sec. 3306(c).

• **1976, Unemployment Compensation Amendments of 1976 (P.L. 94-566)**

P.L. 94-566, §115(c)(2), (d):

Repealed Code Sec. 3309(d). **Effective** with respect to certifications of States for 1978 and subsequent years, but only with respect to services performed after 12-31-77. Prior to repeal, Code Sec. 3309(d) read as follows:

(d) DEFINITION OF INSTITUTION OF HIGHER EDUCATION.—For purposes of this section, the term "institution of higher education" means an educational institution in any State which—

(1) admits as regular students only individuals having a certificate of graduation from a high school, or the recognized equivalent of such a certificate;

(2) is legally authorized within such State to provide a program of education beyond high school;

(3) provides an educational program for which it awards a bachelor's or higher degree, or provides a program which is acceptable for full credit toward such a degree, or offers a program of training to prepare students for gainful employment in a recognized occupation; and

(4) is a public or other nonprofit institution.

[Sec. 3310]

SEC. 3310. JUDICIAL REVIEW.

[Sec. 3310(a)]

(a) IN GENERAL.—Whenever under section 3303(b) or section 3304(c) the Secretary of Labor makes a finding pursuant to which he is required to withhold a certification with respect to a State under such section, such State may, within 60 days after the Governor of the State has been notified of such action, file with the United States court of appeals for the circuit in which such State is located or with the United States Court of Appeals for the District of Columbia, a petition for review of such action. A copy of the petition shall be forthwith transmitted by the clerk of the court to the Secretary of Labor. The Secretary of Labor thereupon shall file in the court the record of the proceedings on which he based his action as provided in section 2112 of title 28 of the United States Code.

[Sec. 3310(b)]

(b) FINDINGS OF FACT.—The findings of fact by the Secretary of Labor, if supported by substantial evidence, shall be conclusive; but the court, for good cause shown, may remand the case to the Secretary of Labor to take further evidence, and the Secretary of Labor may thereupon make new or modified findings of fact and may modify his previous action, and shall certify to the court the record of the further proceedings. Such new or modified findings of fact shall likewise be conclusive if supported by substantial evidence.

RAILROAD UNEMPLOYMENT REPAYMENT TAX

[Sec. 3310(c)]

(c) JURISDICTION OF COURT; REVIEW.—The court shall have jurisdiction to affirm the action of the Secretary of Labor or to set it aside, in whole or in part. The judgment of the court shall be subject to review by the Supreme Court of the United States upon certiorari or certification as provided in section 1254 of title 28 of the United States Code.

[Sec. 3310(d)]

(d) STAY OF SECRETARY OF LABOR'S ACTION.—

(1) The Secretary of Labor shall not withhold any certification under section 3303(b) or section 3304(c) until the expiration of 60 days after the Governor of the State has been notified of the action referred to in subsection (a) or until the State has filed a petition for review of such action, whichever is earlier.

(2) The commencement of judicial proceedings under this section shall stay the Secretary of Labor's action for a period of 30 days, and the court may thereafter grant interim relief if warranted, including a further stay of the Secretary of Labor's action and including such other relief as may be necessary to preserve status or rights.

Amendments

• 1976, Tax Reform Act of 1976 (P.L. 94-455)

P.L. 94-455, §1906(b)(13)(F), (d):

Substituted "the Secretary of Labor's action" for "the Secretary's action" each place it appeared in Code Sec. 3310(d)(2). **Effective** 2-1-77.

• 1970, Employment Security Amendments of 1970 (P.L. 91-373)

P.L. 91-373, §131(b)(1):

Added Code Sec. 3310. **Effective** 8-10-70.

[Sec. 3310(e)—Repealed]

Amendments

• 1984 (P.L. 98-620)

P.L. 98-620, §402(28)(A):

Repealed Code Sec. 3310(e). Not **effective** for cases pending on 11-8-84. Prior to repeal, Code Sec. 3310(e) read as follows:

(e) PREFERENCE.—Any judicial proceedings under this section shall be entitled to, and, upon request of the Secretary of Labor or the State, shall receive a preference and shall be heard and determined as expeditiously as possible.

• 1976, Tax Reform Act of 1976 (P.L. 94-455)

P.L. 94-455, §1906(b)(13)(H), (d):

Substituted "of the Secretary of Labor" for "of the Secretary" in Code Sec. 3310(e). **Effective** 2-1-77.

[Sec. 3311]

SEC. 3311. SHORT TITLE.

This chapter may be cited as the "Federal Unemployment Tax Act."

Amendments

• 1970, Employment Security Amendments of 1970 (P.L. 91-373)

P.L. 91-373, §104(b)(1):

Redesignated Code Sec. 3309 as Code Sec. 3311. **Effective** with respect to certifications of State laws for 1972 and subsequent years, but only with respect to services performed after 12-31-71.

• 1960, Social Security Amendments of 1960 (P.L. 86-778)

P.L. 86-778, §531(d):

Redesignated Code Sec. 3308 as 3309. **Effective** 1-1-62.

CHAPTER 23A—RAILROAD UNEMPLOYMENT REPAYMENT TAX

Sec. 3321.   Imposition of tax.
Sec. 3322.   Definitions.

[Sec. 3321]

SEC. 3321. IMPOSITION OF TAX.

[Sec. 3321(a)]

(a) GENERAL RULE.—There is hereby imposed on every rail employer for each calendar month an excise tax, with respect to having individuals in his employ, equal to 4 percent of the total rail wages paid by him during such month.

[Sec. 3321(b)]

(b) TAX ON EMPLOYEE REPRESENTATIVES.—

(1) IN GENERAL.—There is hereby imposed on the income of each employee representative a tax equal to 4 percent of the rail wages paid to him during the calendar month.

(2) DETERMINATION OF WAGES.—The rail wages of an employee representative for purposes of paragraph (1) shall be determined in the same manner and with the same effect as if the employee organization by which such employee representative is employed were a rail employer.

[Sec. 3321(c)]

(c) TERMINATION IF LOANS TO RAILROAD UNEMPLOYMENT FUND REPAID.—The tax imposed by this section shall not apply to rail wages paid on or after the 1st day of any calendar month if, as of such 1st day, there is—

(1) no balance of transfers made before October 1, 1985, to the railroad unemployment insurance account under section 10(d) of the Railroad Unemployment Insurance Act, and

(2) no unpaid interest on such transfers.

Amendments

• 1988, Technical and Miscellaneous Revenue Act of 1988 (P.L. 100-647)

P.L. 100-647, §1018(u)(17):

Amended Code Sec. 3321(c)(4) (prior to amendment by Act Sec. 7106(a)) by adding a period at the end thereof. **Effective** as if included in the provision of P.L. 99-514 to which it relates.

P.L. 100-647, §7106(a):

Amended chapter 23A by adding Code Sec. 3321. **Effective** for remuneration paid after 12-31-88. For a special rule, see Act Sec. 7106(b), below. Prior to amendment, chapter 23A read as follows:

CHAPTER 23A—RAILROAD UNEMPLOYMENT REPAYMENT TAX

Sec. 3321.   Imposition of tax.
Sec. 3322.   Taxable period.
Sec. 3323.   Other definitions.

SEC. 3321. IMPOSITION OF TAX.

[Sec. 3321(a)]

(a) GENERAL RULE.—There is hereby imposed on every rail employer for each taxable period an excise tax, with respect to having individuals in his employ, equal to the applicable percentage of the total rail wages paid by him during the taxable period.

RAILROAD UNEMPLOYMENT REPAYMENT TAX

[Sec. 3321(b)]

(b) TAX ON EMPLOYEE REPRESENTATIVES.—

(1) IN GENERAL.—There is hereby imposed on the income of each employee representative a tax equal to the applicable percentage of the rail wages paid to him during the taxable period.

(2) DETERMINATION OF WAGES.—The rail wages of an employee representative for purposes of paragraph (1) shall be determined in the same manner and with the same effect as if the employee organization by which such employee representative is employed were a rail employer.

[Sec. 3321(c)]

(c) RATE OF TAX.—For purposes of this section—

(1) IN GENERAL.—The applicable percentage for any taxable period shall be the sum of—

(A) the basic rate for such period, and

(B) the surtax rate (if any) for such period.

(2) BASIC RATE.—For purposes of paragraph (1)—

(A) FOR PERIODS BEFORE 1989.—The basic rate shall be—

(i) 4.3 percent for the taxable period beginning on July 1, 1986, and ending on December 31, 1986,

(ii) 4.7 percent for the 1987 taxable period, and

(iii) 6 percent for the 1988 taxable period.

(B) FOR PERIODS AFTER 1988.—For any taxable period beginning after December 31, 1988, the basic rate shall be the sum of—

(i) 2.9 percent, plus

(ii) 0.3 percent for each preceding taxable period after 1988.

In no event shall the basic rate under this subparagraph exceed 5 percent.

(3) SURTAX RATE.—For purposes of paragraph (1), the surtax rate shall be—

(A) 3.5 percent for any taxable period if, as of September 30 of the preceding calendar year, there was a balance of transfers (or unpaid interest thereon) made after September 30, 1985, to the railroad unemployment insurance account under section 10(d) of the Railroad Unemployment Insurance Act, and

(B) zero for any other taxable period.

(4) BASIC RATE NOT TO APPLY TO RAIL WAGES PAID AFTER SEPTEMBER 30, 1990.—The basic rate under paragraph (1)(A) shall not apply to rail wages paid after September 30, 1990.

Amendments

• **1986, Consolidated Omnibus Budget Reconciliation Act of 1985 (P.L. 99-272)**

P.L. 99-272, §13301(a):

Amended Code Sec. 3321(c). **Effective** 4-7-86. Prior to amendment, Code Sec. 3321(c) read as follows:

(c) RATE OF TAX.—For purposes of this section—

(1) FOR TAXABLE PERIOD JULY 1 THROUGH DECEMBER 31, 1986.—The applicable percentage for the taxable period beginning on July 1, 1986, and ending on December 31, 1986, shall be 2 percent.

(2) SUBSEQUENT TAXABLE PERIODS.—The applicable percentage for any taxable period beginning after 1986 shall be the sum of—

(A) 2 percent, plus

(B) 0.3 percent for each preceding taxable period.

In no event shall the applicable percentage exceed 5 percent.

• **1983, Railroad Retirement Solvency Act of 1983 (P.L. 98-76)**

P.L. 98-76, §231(a):

Added Code Sec. 3321. **Effective** for remuneration paid after 6-30-86.

SEC. 3322. TAXABLE PERIOD.

[Sec. 3322(a)]

(a) GENERAL RULE.—For purposes of this chapter, except as provided in subsection (b), the term "taxable period" means—

(1) the period beginning on July 1, 1986, and ending on December 31, 1986, and

(2) each calendar year after 1986.

Amendments

• **1986, Consolidated Omnibus Budget Reconciliation Act of 1985 (P.L. 99-272)**

P.L. 99-272, §13301(d)(1)(A) and (B):

Amended Code Sec. 3322(a) by adding "and" at the end of paragraph (1), and by striking out paragraphs (2) and (3) and inserting in lieu thereof new paragraph (2). **Effective** 4-7-86. Prior to amendment, Code Sec. 3322(a)(2) and (3) read as follows:

(2) each calendar year after 1986 and before 1990, and

(3) the period beginning on January 1, 1990, and ending on September 30, 1990.

[Sec. 3322(b)]

(b) EARLIER TERMINATION IF LOANS TO RAIL UNEMPLOYMENT FUND REPAID.—The basic rate under section 3321(c)(1)(A) of the tax imposed by section 3321 shall not apply to any rail wages paid on or after the first January 1 after 1986 as of which there is—

(1) no balance of transfers made before October 1, 1985, to the railroad unemployment insurance account under section 10(d) of the Railroad Unemployment Insurance Act, and

(2) no unpaid interest on such transfers.

Amendments

• **1986, Consolidated Omnibus Budget Reconciliation Act of 1985 (P.L. 99-272)**

P.L. 99-272, §13301(d)(2)(A) and (B):

Amended Code Sec. 3322(b) by striking out "The tax imposed by this chapter shall not apply" and inserting in lieu thereof "The basic rate under section 3321(c)(1)(A) of the tax imposed by section 3321 shall not apply", and by inserting "made before October 1, 1985," after "no balance of transfers" in paragraph (1) thereof. **Effective** 4-7-86.

• **1983, Railroad Retirement Solvency Act of 1983 (P.L. 98-76)**

P.L. 98-76, §231(a):

Added Code Sec. 3322. **Effective** for remuneration paid after 6-30-86.

SEC. 3323. OTHER DEFINITIONS.

[Sec. 3323(a)]

(a) RAIL EMPLOYER.—For purposes of this chapter, the term "rail employer" means any person who is an employer as defined in section 1 of the Railroad Unemployment Insurance Act.

[Sec. 3323(b)]

(b) RAIL WAGES.—

(1) IN GENERAL.—For purposes of this chapter, the term "rail wages" means compensation (as defined in section 3231(e) for purposes of the tax imposed by section 3201(a)) with the modifications specified in paragraph (2).

(2) MODIFICATIONS.—In applying subsection (e) of section 3231 for purposes of paragraph (1)—

(A) ONLY EMPLOYMENT COVERED BY RAILROAD UNEMPLOYMENT INSURANCE ACT TAKEN INTO ACCOUNT.—Such subsection (e) shall be applied—

(i) by substituting "rail employment" for "services" each place it appears,

(ii) by substituting "rail employer" for "employer" each place it appears, and

(iii) by substituting "rail employee" for "employee" each place it appears.

(B) $7,000 WAGE BASE.—Such subsection (e) shall be applied by substituting for "the applicable base" in paragraph (2)(A)(i) thereof—

(i) except as provided in clauses (ii) and (iii), "$7,000",

(ii) "$3,500" for the taxable period beginning on July 1, 1986, and ending on December 31, 1986, and

(iii) for purposes of applying the basic rate under section 3321(c)(1)(A), "$5,250" for the taxable period beginning on January 1, 1990.

(C) SUCCESSOR EMPLOYERS.—For purposes of this subsection, rules similar to the rules applicable under section 3231(e)(2)(C) shall apply.

Amendments

• **1986, Consolidated Omnibus Budget Reconciliation Act of 1985 (P.L. 99-272)**

P.L. 99-272, §13301(b):

Amended Code Sec. 3323(b). **Effective** 4-7-86. Prior to amendment, Code Sec. 3323(b) read as follows:

(b) RAIL WAGES.—

(1) IN GENERAL.—For purposes of this chapter, the term "rail wages" means wages as defined in section 3306(b) with the modifications specified in paragraph (2).

(2) MODIFICATIONS.—In applying subsection (b) of section 3306 for purposes of paragraph (1)—

(A) ONLY RAILROAD EMPLOYMENT TAKEN INTO ACCOUNT.—Such subsection (b) shall be applied—

(i) by substituting "rail employment" for "employment" each place it appears, and

(ii) by substituting "rail employer" for "employer" each place it appears.

(B) WAGE BASE FOR FIRST TAXABLE PERIOD.—In the case of the taxable period beginning on July 1, 1986, and ending on December 31, 1986, such subsection (b) shall be applied by substituting "$3,500" for "$7,000" each place it appears in paragraph (1) thereof.

(C) WAGE BASE FOR LAST TAXABLE PERIOD.—In the case of the taxable period beginning on January 1, 1990, and ending on September 30, 1990, such subsection (b) shall be applied by substituting "$5,250" for "$7,000" each place it appears in paragraph (1) thereof.

[Sec. 3323(c)]

(c) RAIL EMPLOYMENT.—For purposes of this chapter, the term "rail employment" means services performed by an individual as a rail employee or employee representative.

[Sec. 3323(d)]

(d) RAIL EMPLOYEE AND EMPLOYEE REPRESENTATIVE.—For purposes of this chapter—

(1) RAIL EMPLOYEE.—The term "rail employee" means any person who is an employee as defined in section 1 of the Railroad Unemployment Insurance Act.

(2) EMPLOYEE REPRESENTATIVE.—The term "employee representative" has the meaning given such term by section 1 of the Railroad Unemployment Insurance Act.

[Sec. 3323(e)]

(e) CONCURRENT EMPLOYMENT BY 2 OR MORE RAIL EMPLOYERS.—For purposes of this chapter, if 2 or more related corporations which are rail employers concurrently employ the same individual and compensate such individual through a common paymaster which is 1 of such corporations, each such corporation shall be considered to have paid as remuneration to such individual only the amounts actually disbursed

WITHHOLDING FROM WAGES

by it to such individual and shall not be considered to have paid as remuneration to such individual amounts actually disbursed to such individual by another of such corporations.

[Sec. 3323(f)]

(f) CERTAIN RULES MADE APPLICABLE.—For purposes of this chapter, rules similar to the rules of sections 3307 and 3308 shall apply.

Amendments

• **1983, Railroad Retirement Solvency Act of 1983 (P.L. 98-76)**

P.L. 98-76, § 231(a):

Added Code Sec. 3323. **Effective** for remuneration paid after 6-30-86.

P.L. 100-647, § 7106(b), provides:

(b) CONTINUATION OF SURTAX RATE THROUGH 1990.—

(1) IN GENERAL.—In the case of any calendar month beginning before January 1, 1991—

(A) there shall be substituted for "4 percent" in subsections (a) and (b) of section 3321 of the 1986 Code the percentage equal to the sum of—

(i) 4 percent, plus

(ii) the surtax rate (if any) for such calendar month, and

(B) subsection (c) of such section shall not apply to so much of the tax imposed by such section as is attributable to the surtax rate.

(2) SURTAX RATE.—For purposes of paragraph (1), the surtax rate shall be—

(A) 3.5 percent for each month during a calendar year if, as of September 30, of the preceding calendar year, there was a balance of transfers (or unpaid interest thereon) made after September 30, 1985, to the railroad unemployment insurance account under section 10(d) of the Railroad Unemployment Insurance Act, and

(B) zero for any other calendar month.

[Sec. 3322]

SEC. 3322. DEFINITIONS.

[Sec. 3322(a)]

(a) RAIL EMPLOYER.—For purposes of this chapter, the term "rail employer" means any person who is an employer as defined in section 1 of the Railroad Unemployment Insurance Act.

[Sec. 3322(b)]

(b) RAIL WAGES.—For purposes of this chapter, the term "rail wages" means, with respect to any calendar month, so much of the remuneration paid during such month which is subject to contributions under section 8(a) of the Railroad Unemployment Insurance Act.

Amendments

• **1989, Omnibus Budget Reconciliation Act of 1989 (P.L. 101-239)**

P.L. 101-239, § 10202(c)(3), provides:

(3) RAILROAD UNEMPLOYMENT REPAYMENT TAX.—For purposes of chapter 23A of the Internal Revenue Code of 1986, the term "rail wages" shall not include the amount of any refund required under section 421 of the Medicare Catastrophic Coverage Act of 1988.

[Sec. 3322(c)]

(c) EMPLOYEE REPRESENTATIVE.—For purposes of this chapter, the term "employee representative" has the meaning given such term by section 1 of the Railroad Unemployment Insurance Act.

[Sec. 3322(d)]

(d) CERTAIN RULES MADE APPLICABLE.—For purposes of this chapter, rules similar to the rules of section 3307 and 3308 shall apply.

Amendments

• **1988, Technical and Miscellaneous Revenue Act of 1988 (P.L. 100-647)**

P.L. 100-647, § 7106(a):

Amended chapter 23A by adding Code Sec. 3322. **Effective** for remuneration paid after 12-31-88. For the text of chapter 23A prior to amendment, see the amendment notes following Code Sec. 3321.

CHAPTER 24—COLLECTION OF INCOME TAX AT SOURCE ON WAGES

SUBCHAPTER A.   Withholding from wages.

Subchapter A—Withholding from Wages

Sec. 3401.	Definitions.
Sec. 3402.	Income tax collected at source.
Sec. 3403.	Liability for tax.
Sec. 3404.	Return and payment by governmental employer.
Sec. 3405.	Special rules for pensions, annuities, and certain other deferred income.
Sec. 3406.	Backup withholding.

[Sec. 3401]

SEC. 3401. DEFINITIONS.

[Sec. 3401(a)]

(a) WAGES.—For purposes of this chapter, the term "wages" means all remuneration (other than fees paid to a public official) for services performed by an employee for his employer, including the cash value of all remuneration (including benefits) paid in any medium other than cash; except that such term shall not include remuneration paid—

(1) for active service performed in a month for which such employee is entitled to the benefits of section 112 (relating to certain combat zone compensation of members of the Armed Forces of the United States) to the extent remuneration for such service is excludable from gross income under such section,

(2) for agricultural labor (as defined in section 3121(g)) unless the remuneration paid for such labor is wages (as defined in section 3121(a)),

(3) for domestic service in a private home, local college club, or local chapter of a college fraternity or sorority,

(4) for service not in the course of the employer's trade or business performed in any calendar quarter by an employee, unless the cash remuneration paid for such service is $50 or more and such service is performed by an individual who is regularly employed by such employer to perform such service. For purposes of this paragraph, an individual shall be deemed to be regularly employed by an employer during a calendar quarter only if—

(A) on each of some 24 days during such quarter such individual performs for such employer for some portion of the day service not in the course of the employer's trade or business, or

(B) such individual was regularly employed (as determined under subparagraph (A)) by such employer in the performance of such service during the preceding calendar quarter,

(5) for services by a citizen or resident of the United States for a foreign government or an international organization,

(6) for such services, performed by a nonresident alien individual, as may be designated by regulations prescribed by the Secretary,

(7) [Repealed.]

(8)(A) for services for an employer (other than the United States or any agency thereof)—

(i) performed by a citizen of the United States if, at the time of the payment of such remuneration, it is reasonable to believe that such remuneration will be excluded from gross income under section 911, or

(ii) performed in a foreign country or in a possession of the United States by such a citizen if, at the time of the payment of such remuneration, the employer is required by the law of any foreign country or possession of the United States to withhold income tax upon such remuneration,

(B) for services for an employer (other than the United States or any agency thereof) performed by a citizen of the United States within a possession of the United States (other than Puerto Rico), if it is reasonable to believe that at least 80 percent of the remuneration to be paid to the employee by such employer during the calendar year will be for such services,

(C) for services for an employer (other than the United States or any agency thereof) performed by a citizen of the United States within Puerto Rico, if it is reasonable to believe that during the entire calendar year the employee will be a bona fide resident of Puerto Rico, or

(D) for services for the United States (or any agency thereof) performed by a citizen of the United States within a possession of the United States to the extent the United States (or such agency) withholds taxes on such remuneration pursuant to an agreement with such possession,

(9) for services performed by a duly ordained, commissioned, or licensed minister of a church in the exercise of his ministry or by a member of a religious order in the exercise of duties required by such order,

(10)(A) for services performed by an individual under the age of 18 in the delivery or distribution of newspapers or shopping news, not including delivery or distribution to any point for subsequent delivery or distribution, or

(B) for services performed by an individual in, and at the time of, the sale of newspapers or magazines to ultimate consumers, under an arrangement under which the newspapers or magazines are to be sold by him at a fixed price, his compensation being based on the retention of the excess of such price over the amount at which the newspapers or magazines are charged to him, whether or not he is guaranteed a minimum amount of compensation for such services, or is entitled to be credited with the unsold newspapers or magazines turned back,

(11) for services not in the course of the employer's trade or business, to the extent paid in any medium other than cash,

(12) to, or on behalf of, an employee or his beneficiary—

(A) from or to a trust described in section 401(a) which is exempt from tax under section 501(a) at the time of such payment unless such payment is made to an employee of the trust as remuneration for services rendered as such employee and not as a beneficiary of the trust,

(B) under or to an annuity plan which, at the time of such payment, is a plan described in section 403(a),

(C) for a payment described in section 402(h)(1) and (2) if, at the time of such payment, it is reasonable to believe that the employee will be entitled to an exclusion under such section for payment,

(D) under an arrangement to which section 408(p) applies, or

(E) under or to an eligible deferred compensation plan which, at the time of such payment, is a plan described in section 457(b) which is maintained by an eligible employer described in section 457(e)(1)(A),

(13) pursuant to any provision of law other than section 5(c) or 6(1) of the Peace Corps Act, for service performed as a volunteer or volunteer leader within the meaning of such Act,

(14) in the form of group-term life insurance on the life of an employee,

(15) to or on behalf of an employee if (and to the extent that) at the time of the payment of such remuneration it is reasonable to believe that a corresponding deduction is allowable under section 217 (determined without regard to section 274(n)),

(16)(A) as tips in any medium other than cash,

(B) as cash tips to an employee in any calendar month in the course of his employment by an employer unless the amount of such cash tips is $20 or more,

(17) for service described in section 3121(b)(20),

(18) for any payment made, or benefit furnished, to or for the benefit of an employee if at the time of such payment or such furnishing it is reasonable to believe that the employee will be able to exclude such payment or benefit from income under section 127, 129, 134(b)(4), or 134(b)(5),

(19) for any benefit provided to or on behalf of an employee if at the time such benefit is provided it is reasonable to believe that the employee will be able to exclude such benefit from income under section 74(c), 108(f)(4), 117 or 132,

(20) for any medical care reimbursement made to or for the benefit of an employee under a self-insured medical reimbursement plan (within the meaning of section 105(h)(6)),

(21) for any payment made to or for the benefit of an employee if at the time of such payment it is reasonable to believe that the employee will be able to exclude such payment from income under section 106(b),

(22) any payment made to or for the benefit of an employee if at the time of such payment it is reasonable to believe that the employee will be able to exclude such payment from income under section 106(d), or

(23) for any benefit or payment which is excludable from the gross income of the employee under section 139B(b).

The term "wages" includes any amount includible in gross income of an employee under section 409A and payment of such amount shall be treated as having been made in the taxable year in which the amount is so includible.

Amendments

- **2018, Tax Technical Corrections Act of 2018 (P.L. 115-141)**

P.L. 115-141, §401(a)(217)(A), Div. U:

Amended Code Sec. 3401(a)(1), (2), (3), (4)(B), (5), (6), (8)(A)(ii), (8)(B), (8)(D), (9), (10)(B), (11), (12)(A), (12)(B), (12)(C), (13), (14), and (15) by striking "; or" at the end and inserting a comma. **Effective** 3-23-2018.

P.L. 115-141, §401(a)(217)(B), Div. U:

Amended Code Sec. 3401(a)(4)(A), (8)(A)(i), (8)(C), (10)(A), (12)(D), and (22) by striking "; or" at the end and inserting ", or". **Effective** 3-23-2018.

P.L. 115-141, §401(a)(217)(C), Div. U:

Amended Code Sec. 3401(a)(12)(E) by striking ", or" at the end and inserting a comma. **Effective** 3-23-2018.

P.L. 115-141, §401(a)(217)(D), Div. U:

Amended Code Sec. 3401(a)(16)(A), (16)(B), (17), (18), (19), (20), and (21) by striking the semicolon at the end and inserting a comma. **Effective** 3-23-2018.

WITHHOLDING FROM WAGES

- **2017, Tax Cuts and Jobs Act (P.L. 115-97)**

P.L. 115-97, §11026, provides:

SEC. 11026. TREATMENT OF CERTAIN INDIVIDUALS PERFORMING SERVICES IN THE SINAI PENINSULA OF EGYPT.

(a) IN GENERAL.—For purposes of the following provisions of the Internal Revenue Code of 1986, with respect to the applicable period, a qualified hazardous duty area shall be treated in the same manner as if it were a combat zone (as determined under section 112 of such Code):

(1) Section 2(a)(3) (relating to special rule where deceased spouse was in missing status).

(2) Section 112 (relating to the exclusion of certain combat pay of members of the Armed Forces).

(3) Section 692 (relating to income taxes of members of Armed Forces on death).

(4) Section 2201 (relating to members of the Armed Forces dying in combat zone or by reason of combat-zone-incurred wounds, etc.).

(5) Section 3401(a)(1) (defining wages relating to combat pay for members of the Armed Forces).

(6) Section 4253(d) (relating to the taxation of phone service originating from a combat zone from members of the Armed Forces).

(7) Section 6013(f)(1) (relating to joint return where individual is in missing status).

(8) Section 7508 (relating to time for performing certain acts postponed by reason of service in combat zone).

(b) QUALIFIED HAZARDOUS DUTY AREA.—For purposes of this section, the term "qualified hazardous duty area" means the Sinai Peninsula of Egypt, if as of the date of the enactment of this section any member of the Armed Forces of the United States is entitled to special pay under section 310 of title 37, United States Code (relating to special pay; duty subject to hostile fire or imminent danger), for services performed in such location. Such term includes such location only during the period such entitlement is in effect.

(c) APPLICABLE PERIOD.—

(1) IN GENERAL.—Except as provided in paragraph (2), the applicable period is—

(A) the portion of the first taxable year ending after June 9, 2015, which begins on such date, and

(B) any subsequent taxable year beginning before January 1, 2026.

(2) WITHHOLDING.—In the case of subsection (a)(5), the applicable period is—

(A) the portion of the first taxable year ending after the date of the enactment of this Act which begins on such date, and

(B) any subsequent taxable year beginning before January 1, 2026.

(d) EFFECTIVE DATE.—

(1) IN GENERAL.—Except as provided in paragraph (2), the provisions of this section shall take effect on June 9, 2015.

(2) WITHHOLDING.—Subsection (a)(5) shall apply to remuneration paid after the date of the enactment of this Act.

- **2008, Heroes Earnings Assistance and Relief Tax Act of 2008 (P.L. 110-245)**

P.L. 110-245, §115(c):

Amended Code Sec. 3401(a) by striking "or" at the end of paragraph (21), by striking the period at the end of paragraph (22) and inserting "; or", and by inserting after paragraph (22) a new paragraph (23). **Effective** as if included in section 5 of the Mortgage Forgiveness Debt Relief Act of 2007 (P.L. 110-142) [**effective** for tax years beginning after 12-31-2007.—CCH].

- **2006, Pension Protection Act of 2006 (P.L. 109-280)**

P.L. 109-280, §811, provides:

SEC. 811. PENSIONS AND INDIVIDUAL RETIREMENT ARRANGEMENT PROVISIONS OF ECONOMIC GROWTH AND TAX RELIEF RECONCILIATION ACT OF 2001 MADE PERMANENT.

Title IX of the Economic Growth and Tax Relief Reconciliation Act of 2001 [P.L. 107-16] shall not apply to the provisions of, and amendments made by, subtitles A through F of title VI [§§601-666]of such Act (relating to pension and individual retirement arrangement provisions).

- **2004, Ronald W. Reagan National Defense Authorization Act for Fiscal Year 2005 (P.L. 108-375)**

P.L. 108-375, §585(b)(2)(B):

Amended Code Sec. 3401(a)(18) by striking "or 134(b)(4)" and inserting "134(b)(4), or 134(b)(5)". **Effective** for travel benefits provided after 10-28-2004.

- **2004, American Jobs Creation Act of 2004 (P.L. 108-357)**

P.L. 108-357, §320(b)(4):

Amended Code Sec. 3401(a)(19) by inserting "108(f)(4)," after "74(c),". **Effective** for amounts received by an individual in tax years beginning after 12-31-2003.

P.L. 108-357, §885(b)(2):

Amended Code Sec. 3401(a) by adding at the end a new flush sentence. **Effective** generally for amounts deferred after 12-31-2004. For special rules, see Act Sec. 885(d)(2)-(3) and (f), below.

P.L. 108-357, §885(d)(2)-(3), provides:

(2) SPECIAL RULES.—

(A) EARNINGS.—The amendments made by this section shall apply to earnings on deferred compensation only to the extent that such amendments apply to such compensation.

(B) MATERIAL MODIFICATIONS.—For purposes of this subsection, amounts deferred in taxable years beginning before January 1, 2005, shall be treated as amounts deferred in a taxable year beginning on or after such date if the plan under which the deferral is made is materially modified after October 3, 2004, unless such modification is pursuant to the guidance issued under subsection (f).

(3) EXCEPTION FOR NONELECTIVE DEFERRED COMPENSATION.—The amendments made by this section shall not apply to any nonelective deferred compensation to which section 457 of the Internal Revenue Code of 1986 does not apply by reason of section 457(e)(12) of such Code, but only if such compensation is provided under a nonqualified deferred compensation plan—

(A) which was in existence on May 1, 2004,

(B) which was providing nonelective deferred compensation described in such section 457(e)(12) on such date, and

(C) which is established or maintained by an organization incorporated on July 2, 1974.

If, after May 1, 2004, a plan described in the preceding sentence adopts a plan amendment which provides a material change in the classes of individuals eligible to participate in the plan, this paragraph shall not apply to any nonelective deferred compensation provided under the plan on or after the date of the adoption of the amendment.

P.L. 108-357, §885(f), provides:

(f) GUIDANCE RELATING TO TERMINATION OF CERTAIN EXISTING ARRANGEMENTS.—Not later than 60 days after the date of the enactment of this Act, the Secretary of the Treasury shall issue guidance providing a limited period during which a nonqualified deferred compensation plan adopted before December 31, 2004, may, without violating the requirements of paragraphs (2), (3), and (4) of section 409A(a) of the Internal Revenue Code of 1986 (as added by this section), be amended—

(1) to provide that a participant may terminate participation in the plan, or cancel an outstanding deferral election with regard to amounts deferred after December 31, 2004, but only if amounts subject to the termination or cancellation are includible in income of the participant as earned (or, if later, when no longer subject to substantial risk of forfeiture), and

(2) to conform to the requirements of such section 409A with regard to amounts deferred after December 31, 2004.

- **2003, Medicare Prescription Drug, Improvement, and Modernization Act of 2003 (P.L. 108-173)**

P.L. 108-173, §1201(d)(2)(C):

Amended Code Sec. 3401(a) by striking "or" at the end of paragraph (20), by striking the period at the end of paragraph (21) and inserting "; or", and by inserting after paragraph (21) a new paragraph (22). **Effective** for tax years beginning after 12-31-2003.

- **2003, Military Family Tax Relief Act of 2003 (P.L. 108-121)**

P.L. 108-121, §106(b)(4):

Amended Code Sec. 3401(a)(18) by striking "or 129" and inserting ", 129, or 134(b)(4)". **Effective** for tax years beginning after 12-31-2002. For a special rule, see Act Sec. 106(d), below.

P.L. 108-121, §106(d), provides:

(d) NO INFERENCE.—No inference may be drawn from the amendments made by this section with respect to the tax treatment of any amounts under the program described in section 134(b)(4) of the Internal Revenue Code of 1986 (as added by this section) for any taxable year beginning before January 1, 2003.

- **2001, Economic Growth and Tax Relief Reconciliation Act of 2001 (P.L. 107-16)**

P.L. 107-16, §641(a)(1)(D)(i):

Amended Code Sec. 3401(a)(12) by adding at the end a new subparagraph (E). **Effective**, generally, for distributions after 12-31-2001. For a special rule, see Act Sec. 641(f)(3), below.

P.L. 107-16, §641(f)(3), provides:

(3) SPECIAL RULE.—Notwithstanding any other provision of law, subsections (h)(3) and (h)(5) of section 1122 of the Tax Reform Act of 1986 shall not apply to any distribution from an eligible retirement plan (as defined in clause (iii) or (iv) of section 402(c)(8)(B) of the Internal Revenue Code of 1986) on behalf of an individual if there was a rollover to such plan on behalf of such individual which is permitted solely by reason of any amendment made by this section.

P.L. 107-16, §901(a)-(b), as amended by P.L. 111-312, §101(a)(1), provides [but see P.L. 109-280, §811, above]:

SEC. 901. SUNSET OF PROVISIONS OF ACT.

(a) IN GENERAL.—All provisions of, and amendments made by, this Act shall not apply—

(1) to taxable, plan, or limitation years beginning after December 31, 2012, or

(2) in the case of title V, to estates of decedents dying, gifts made, or generation skipping transfers, after December 31, 2012.

(b) APPLICATION OF CERTAIN LAWS.—The Internal Revenue Code of 1986 and the Employee Retirement Income Security Act of 1974 shall be applied and administered to years, estates, gifts, and transfers described in subsection (a) as if the provisions and amendments described in subsection (a) had never been enacted.

- **1999 (P.L. 106-21)**

P.L. 106-21, §1(a)(5), (b) and (d)(2), provides:

SECTION 1. AVAILABILITY OF CERTAIN TAX BENEFITS FOR SERVICES AS PART OF OPERATION ALLIED FORCE.

(a) GENERAL RULE.—For purposes of the following provisions of the Internal Revenue Code of 1986, a qualified hazardous duty area shall be treated in the same manner as if it were a combat zone (as determined under section 112 of such Code):

* * *

(5) Section 3401(a)(1) (defining wages relating to combat pay for members of the Armed Forces).

* * *

(b) QUALIFIED HAZARDOUS DUTY AREA.—For purposes of this section, the term "qualified hazardous duty area" means any area of the Federal Republic of Yugoslavia (Serbia/Montenegro), Albania, the Adriatic Sea, and the northern Ionian Sea (above the 39th parallel) during the period (which includes the date of the enactment of this Act) that any member of the Armed Forces of the United States is entitled to special pay under section 310 of title 37, United States Code (relating to special pay: duty subject to hostile fire or imminent danger) for services performed in such area.

* * *

(d) EFFECTIVE DATES.—

* * *

(2) WITHHOLDING.—Subsection (a)(5) shall apply to remuneration paid after the date of the enactment of this Act [April 19, 1999].

- **1998, IRS Restructuring and Reform Act of 1998 (P.L. 105-206)**

P.L. 105-206, § 6023(14):

Amended Code Sec. 3401(a)(19) by inserting "for" before "any benefit provided to". **Effective** 7-22-98.

P.L. 105-206, § 6023(15):

Amended Code Sec. 3401(a)(21) by inserting "for" before "any payment made". **Effective** 7-22-98.

- **1996, Health Insurance Portability and Accountability Act of 1996 (P.L. 104-191)**

P.L. 104-191, § 301(c)(2)(C):

Amended Code Sec. 3401(a) by striking "or" at the end of paragraph (19), by striking the period at the end of paragraph (20) and inserting "; or", and by inserting after paragraph (20) a new paragraph (21). **Effective** for tax years beginning after 12-31-96.

- **1996, Small Business Job Protection Act of 1996 (P.L. 104-188)**

P.L. 104-188, § 1421(b)(8)(D):

Amended Code Sec. 3401(a)(12) by adding at the end a new subparagraph (D). **Effective** for tax years beginning after 12-31-96.

P.L. 104-188, § 1704(t)(4)(C):

Amended Code Sec. 3401(a)(1) by striking "combat pay" and inserting "combat zone compensation". **Effective** 8-20-96.

- **1996 (P.L. 104-117)**

P.L. 104-117, § 1(a)(5), (b) and (e)(2), provides:

SECTION 1. TREATMENT OF CERTAIN INDIVIDUALS PERFORMING SERVICES IN CERTAIN HAZARDOUS DUTY AREAS.

(a) GENERAL RULE.—For purposes of the following provisions of the Internal Revenue Code of 1986, a qualified hazardous duty area shall be treated in the same manner as if it were a combat zone (as determined under section 112 of such Code):

* * *

(5) Section 3401(a)(1) (defining wages relating to combat pay for members of the Armed Forces).

* * *

(b) QUALIFIED HAZARDOUS DUTY AREA.—For purposes of this section, the term "qualified hazardous duty area" means Bosnia and Herzegovina, Croatia, or Macedonia, if as of the date of the enactment of this section any member of the Armed Forces of the United States is entitled to special pay under section 310 of title 37, United States Code (relating to special pay; duty subject to hostile fire or imminent danger) for services performed in such country. Such term includes any such country only during the period such entitlement is in effect. Solely for purposes of applying section 7508 of the Internal Revenue Code of 1986, in the case of an individual who is performing services as part of Operation Joint Endeavor outside the United States while deployed away from such individual's permanent duty station, the term "qualified hazardous duty area" includes, during the period for which such entitlement is in effect, any area in which such services are performed.

* * *

(e) EFFECTIVE DATE.—

* * *

(2) WITHHOLDING.—Subsection (a)(5) and the amendments made by subsection (c) shall apply to remuneration paid after the date of the enactment of this Act [March 20, 1996].

P.L. 104-117, § 1(c):

Amended Code Sec. 3401(a)(1) by inserting before the semicolon the following: "to the extent remuneration for such service is excludable from gross income under such section". **Effective** for remuneration paid after 3-20-96.

- **1990, Omnibus Budget Reconciliation Act of 1990 (P.L. 101-508)**

P.L. 101-508, § 11703(f)(1):

Amended Code Sec. 3401(a) by striking "or" at the end of paragraph (18), by striking the period at the end of paragraph (19) and inserting "; or", and by adding at the end thereof a new paragraph (20). **Effective** as if included in the amendments made by section 1151 of P.L. 99-514, but shall not apply to any amount paid before 11-5-90 which the employer treated as wages for purposes of chapter 24 of the Internal Revenue Code of 1986 when paid.

- **1989, Omnibus Budget Reconciliation Act of 1989 (P.L. 101-239)**

P.L. 101-239, § 7631(a):

Amended Code Sec. 3401(a)(2). **Effective** for remuneration paid after 12-31-89. Prior to amendment, Code Sec. 3401(a)(2) read as follows:

(2) for agricultural labor (as defined in section 3121(g)); or

- **1988, Technical and Miscellaneous Revenue Act of 1988 (P.L. 100-647)**

P.L. 100-647, § 1001(g)(4)(B)(iii):

Amended Code Sec. 3401(a)(15) by striking out "section 217" and inserting in lieu thereof "section 217 (determined without regard to section 274(n))". **Effective** as if included in the provision of P.L. 99-514 to which it relates.

P.L. 100-647, § 1011(f)(9)(A)-(B):

Amended Code Sec. 3401(a)(12)(C) by striking out "section 219" and inserting in lieu thereof "section 402(h)(1) and (2)", and by striking out "a deduction" and inserting in lieu thereof "an exclusion". **Effective** as if included in the provision of P.L. 99-514 to which it relates.

P.L. 100-647, § 1011B(a)(33):

Amended Code Sec. 3401(a) by inserting "or" at the end of paragraph (18), by striking out paragraph (19), and by redesignating paragraph (20) as paragraph (19). **Effective** as if included in the provision of P.L. 99-514 to which it relates. Prior to amendment, Code Sec. 3401(a)(19) read as follows:

(19) for any medical care reimbursement made to or for the benefit of an employee under a self-insured medical reimbursement plan (within the meaning of section 105(h)(6)); or

- **1986, Tax Reform Act of 1986 (P.L. 99-514)**

P.L. 99-514, § 122(e)(4):

Amended Code Sec. 3401(a)(20) by striking out "117 or" inserting in lieu thereof "74(c), 117, or". **Effective** for prizes and awards granted after 12-31-86.

P.L. 99-514, § 1272(c):

Amended Code Sec. 3401(a)(8) by adding at the end thereof new subparagraph (D). **Effective**, generally, for tax years beginning after 12-31-86. However, for special rules and exceptions, see Act Sec. 1277(b)-(e) under the amendment notes to Code Sec. 48.

- **1984, Deficit Reduction Act of 1984 (P.L. 98-369)**

P.L. 98-369, § 491(d)(38):

Amended Code Sec. 3401(a)(12) by striking out subparagraph (C) and by redesignating subparagraph (D) as subparagraph (C). **Effective** for obligations issued after 12-31-83. Prior to amendment, subparagraph (C) read:

(C) under or to a bond purchase plan which, at the time of such payment, is a qualified bond purchase plan described in section 405(a); or

P.L. 98-369, § 531(d)(4):

Amended Code Sec. 3401(a) by striking out "all remuneration paid in any medium" in the material preceding paragraph (1) and inserting in lieu thereof "all remuneration (including benefits) paid in any medium", and by striking out "or" at the end of paragraph (18), by striking out the period at the end of pararaph (19) and inserting in lieu thereof "; or", and by adding at the end thereof new paragraph (20). **Effective** 1-1-85.

- **1983, Technical Corrections Act of 1982 (P.L. 97-448)**

P.L. 97-448, § 103(c)(12)(B):

Amended Code Sec. 3401(a)(12)(D) by striking out "section 219(a)" and inserting in lieu thereof "section 219". **Effective** as if included in the provision of P.L. 97-34 to which it relates.

- **1981, Economic Recovery Tax Act of 1981 (P.L. 97-34)**

P.L. 97-34, § 112(b)(5):

Amended Code Sec. 3401(a) by striking out paragraph (18) and redesignating paragraphs (19) and (20) as paragraphs (18) and (19), respectively. **Effective** with respect to tax years beginning after 12-31-81. Prior to repeal, Code Sec. 3401(a)(18) read as follows:

(18) to or on behalf of an employee if (and to the extent that) at the time of the payment of such remuneration it is reasonable to believe that a corresponding deduction is allowable under section 913 (relating to deduction for certain expenses of living abroad);

P.L. 97-34, § 124(e)(2)(A):

Amended Code Sec. 3401(a)(19), redesignated as (18) by P.L. 97-34, § 112(b)(5), by striking out "section 127" and inserting in lieu thereof "section 127 or 129". **Effective** with respect to remuneration paid after 12-31-81.

P.L. 97-34, § 311(h)(6):

Amended Code Sec. 3401(a)(12)(D) by striking out "section 219(a) or 220(a)" and inserting in lieu thereof "section 219(a)". **Effective** with respect to tax years beginning after 12-31-81.

P.L. 97-34, § 311(i)(2), provides:

(2) Transitional rule.—For purposes of the Internal Revenue Code of 1954, any amount allowed as a deduction under section 220 of such Code (as in effect before its repeal by this Act) shall be treated as if it were allowed by section 219 of such Code.

- **1980, Technical Corrections Act of 1979 (P.L. 96-222)**

P.L. 96-222, § 103(a)(13)(A)(i):

Amended Code Sec. 3401(a)(17) by striking out "or" at the end of the paragraph. **Effective** with respect to amounts reimbursed after 12-31-79.

P.L. 96-222, § 103(a)(13)(A)(ii):

Amended Code Sec. 3401(a)(18), as added by P.L. 95-615, by striking out the period at the end of the paragraph and inserting ";". **Effective** with respect to amounts reimbursed after 12-31-79.

P.L. 96-222, § 103(a)(13)(A)(iii):

Amended Code Sec. 3401(a)(18), as added by P.L. 95-600, by redesignating the paragraph as (19). **Effective** with respect to amounts reimbursed after 12-31-79.

WITHHOLDING FROM WAGES

P.L. 96-222, §103(a)(13)(A)(iv):

Amended redesignated Code Sec. 3401(a)(19) by striking out "section 124" and inserting "section 127; or". **Effective** with respect to amounts reimbursed after 12-31-79.

P.L. 96-222, §103(a)(13)(A)(v):

Amended Code Sec. 3401(a) by adding paragraph (20). **Effective** with respect to amounts reimbursed after 12-31-79.

- **1978, Tax Treatment Extension Act of 1978 (P.L. 95-615)**

P.L. 95-615, §§207(a), 209(b), (c):

Added Code Sec. 3401(a)(18). **Effective**, generally, for remuneration paid after 11-8-78, except for a special election provided in Act Sec. 209(c), below.

P.L. 95-615, §209(c), provides:

(c) ELECTION OF PRIOR LAW.—

(1) A taxpayer may elect not to have the amendments made by this title apply with respect to any taxable year beginning after December 31, 1977, and before January 1, 1979.

(2) An election under this subsection shall be filed with a taxpayer's timely filed return for the first taxable year beginning after December 31, 1977."

- **1978, Revenue Act of 1978 (P.L. 95-600)**

P.L. 95-600, §§164(b)(1)(A), (B), (C), (d):

Added Code Sec. 3401(a)(18) [designated as (a)(19) by CCH]. **Effective** for tax years beginning after 12-31-78.

P.L. 95-600, §530, as amended by P.L. 96-167, P.L. 96-541, P.L. 97-248, P.L. 99-514, P.L. 104-188, and P.L. 109-280, provides:

(a) TERMINATION OF CERTAIN EMPLOYMENT TAX LIABILITY.—

(1) IN GENERAL.—If—

(A) for purposes of employment taxes, the taxpayer did not treat an individual as an employee for any period, and

(B) in the case of periods after December 31, 1978, all Federal tax returns (including information returns) required to be filed by the taxpayer with respect to such individual for such period are filed on a basis consistent with the taxpayer's treatment of such individual as not being an employee,

then, for purposes of applying such taxes for such period with respect to the taxpayer, the individual shall be deemed not to be an employee unless the taxpayer had no reasonable basis for not treating such individual as an employee.

(2) STATUTORY STANDARDS PROVIDING ONE METHOD OF SATISFYING THE REQUIREMENTS OF PARAGRAPH (1).—For purposes of paragraph (1), a taxpayer shall in any case be treated as having a reasonable basis for not treating an individual as an employee for a period if the taxpayer's treatment of such individual for such period was in reasonable reliance on any of the following:

(A) judicial precedent, published rulings, technical advice with respect to the taxpayer, or a letter ruling to the taxpayer;

(B) a past Internal Revenue Service audit of the taxpayer in which there was no assessment attributable to the treatment (for employment tax purposes) of the individuals holding positions substantially similar to the position held by this individual; or

(C) long-standing recognized practice of a significant segment of the industry in which such individual was engaged.

(3) CONSISTENCY REQUIRED IN THE CASE OF PRIOR TAX TREATMENT.—Paragraph (1) shall not apply with respect to the treatment of any individual for employment tax purposes for any period ending after December 31, 1978, if the taxpayer (or a predecessor) has treated any individual holding a substantially similar position as an employee for purposes of the employment taxes for any period beginning after December 31, 1977.

(4) REFUND OR CREDIT OF OVERPAYMENT.—If refund or credit of any overpayment of an employment tax resulting from the application of paragraph (1) is not barred on the date of the enactment of this Act by any law or rule of law, the period for filing a claim for refund or credit of such overpayment (to the extent attributable to the application of paragraph (1)) shall not expire before the date 1 year after the date of the enactment of this Act.

(b) PROHIBITION AGAINST REGULATIONS AND RULINGS ON EMPLOYMENT STATUS.—No regulation or Revenue Ruling shall be published on or after the date of the enactment of this Act and before the effective date of any law hereafter enacted clarifying the employment status of individuals for purposes of the employment taxes by the Department of the Treasury (including the Internal Revenue Service) with respect to the employment status of any individual for purposes of the employment taxes.

(c) DEFINITIONS.—For purposes of this section—

(1) EMPLOYMENT TAX.—The term "employment tax" means any tax imposed by subtitle C of the Internal Revenue Code of 1954.

(2) EMPLOYMENT STATUS.—The term "employment status" means the status of an individual, under the usual common law rules applicable in determining the employer-employee relationship, as an employee or as an independent contractor (or other individual who is not an employee).

(d) EXCEPTION.—This section shall not apply in the case of an individual who, pursuant to an arrangement between the taxpayer and another person, provides services for such other person as an engineer, designer, drafter, computer programmer, systems analyst, or other similarly skilled worker engaged in a similar line of work.

(e) SPECIAL RULES FOR APPLICATION OF SECTION.—

(1) NOTICE OF AVAILABILITY OF SECTION.—An officer or employee of the Internal Revenue Service shall, before or at the commencement of any audit inquiry relating to the employment status of one or more individuals who perform services for the taxpayer, provide the taxpayer with a written notice of the provisions of this section.

(2) RULES RELATING TO STATUTORY STANDARDS.—For purposes of subsection (a)(2)—

(A) a taxpayer may not rely on an audit commenced after December 31, 1996, for purposes of subparagraph (B) thereof unless such audit included an examination for employment tax purposes of whether the individual involved (or any individual holding a position substantially similar to the position held by the individual involved) should be treated as an employee of the taxpayer,

(B) in no event shall the significant segment requirement of subparagraph (C) thereof be construed to require a reasonable showing of the practice of more than 25 percent of the industry (determined by not taking into account the taxpayer), and

(C) in applying the long-standing recognized practice requirement of subparagraph (C) thereof—

(i) such requirement shall not be construed as requiring the practice to have continued for more than 10 years, and

(ii) a practice shall not fail to be treated as longstaing merely because such practice began after 1978.

(3) AVAILABILITY OF SAFE HARBORS.—Nothing in this section shall be construed to provide that subsection (a) only applies where the individual involved is otherwise an employee of the taxpayer.

(4) BURDEN OF PROOF.—

(A) IN GENERAL.—If—

(i) a taxpayer establishes a prima facie case that it was reasonable not to treat an individual as an employee for purposes of this section, and

(ii) the taxpayer has fully cooperated with reasonable requests from the Secretary of the Treasury or his delegate,

then the burden of proof with respect to such treatment shall be on the Secretary.

(B) EXCEPTION FOR OTHER REASONABLE BASIS.—In the case of any issue involving whether the taxpayer had a reasonable basis not to treat an individual as an employee for purposes of this section, subparagraph (A) shall only apply for purposes of determining whether the taxpayer meets the requirements of subparagraph (A), (B), or (C) of subsection (a)(2).

(5) PRESERVATION OF PRIOR PERIOD SAFE HARBOR.—If—

(A) an individual would (but for the treatment referred to in subparagraph (B)) be deemed not to be an employee of the taxpayer under subsection (a) for any prior period, and

(B) such individual is treated by the taxpayer as an employee for employment tax purposes for any subsequent period,

then, for purposes of applying such taxes for such prior period with respect to the taxpayer, the individual shall be deemed not to be an employee.

(6) SUBSTANTIALLY SIMILAR POSITION.—For purposes of this section, the determination as to whether an individual holds a position substantially similar to a position held by another individual shall include consideration of the relationship between the taxpayer and such individuals.

(f) TREATMENT OF TEST ROOM SUPERVISORS AND PROCTORS WHO ASSIST IN THE ADMINISTRATION OF COLLEGE ENTRANCE AND PLACEMENT EXAMS.—

(1) IN GENERAL.—In the case of an individual described in paragraph (2) who is providing services as a test proctor or room supervisor by assisting in the administration of college entrance or placement examinations, this section shall be applied to such services performed after December 31, 2006 (and remuneration paid for such services) without regard to subsection (a)(3) thereof.

(2) APPLICABILITY.—An individual is described in this paragraph if the individual—

(A) is providing the services described in subsection (a) to an organization described in section 501(c), and exempt from tax under section 501(a), of the Internal Revenue Code of 1986, and

(B) is not otherwise treated as an employee of such organization for purposes of subtitle C of such Code (relating to employment taxes).

- **1976, Tax Reform Act of 1976 (P.L. 94-455)**

P.L. 94-455, §1207(e)(1)(C):

Amended Code Sec. 3401(a) by striking out the period at the end of paragraph (16) and inserting in lieu thereof "; or"; and by adding after paragraph (16) a new paragraph. **Effective** for tax years ending after 12-31-54 [Act Sec. 1207(f)(4), as amended by P.L. 95-600, Act Sec. 701(z)(1), (2), **effective** 10-4-76].

P.L. 94-455, §1501(b)(7):

Added "or 220(a)" after "219(a)" in Code Sec. 3401(a)(12). **Effective** for tax years beginning after 12-31-76.

P.L. 94-455, §1906(b)(13)(A):

Amended Code Sec. 3401(a)(6), by striking out "Secretary or his delegate" and inserting in place thereof "Secretary". **Effective** 2-1-77.

- **1974, Employee Retirement Income Security Act of 1974 (P.L. 93-406)**

P.L. 93-406, §2002(g)(7):

Amended Code Sec. 3401(a)(12) by adding new subparagraph (D). **Effective** 1-1-75.

- **1972 (P.L. 92-279)**

P.L. 92-279, §2:

Amended Code Sec. 3401(a)(1). **Effective** for wages paid on or after 6-1-72. Prior to amendment, Code Sec. 3401(a)(1) read as follows:

(1) for active service as a member of the Armed Forces of the United States performed in a month for which such member is entitled to the benefits of section 112; or

- **1966, Foreign Investors Tax Act of 1966 (P.L. 89-809)**

P.L. 89-809, §103(k):

Amended Code Sec. 3401(a) by deleting paragraphs (6) and (7) and adding a new paragraph (6). **Effective** with respect to remuneration paid after 12-31-66. Prior to amendment, Sec. 3401(a)(6) and (7) read as follows:

(6) for services performed by a nonresident alien individual, other than—

(A) a resident of a contiguous country who enters and leaves the United States at frequent intervals; or

Sec. 3401(a)(23)

WITHHOLDING FROM WAGES

(B) a resident of Puerto Rico if such services are performed as an employee of the United States or any agency thereof; or

(C) an individual who is temporarily present in the United States as a nonimmigrant under subparagraph (F) or (J) of section 101(a)(15) of the Immigration and Nationality Act, as amended, if such remuneration is exempt, under section 1441(c)(4)(B), from deduction and withholding under section 1441(a), and is not exempt from taxation under section 872(b)(3); or

(7) for such services, performed by a nonresident alien individual who is a resident of a contiguous country and who enters and leaves the United States at frequent intervals, as may be designated by regulations prescribed by the Secretary or his delegate; or

• **1965, Social Security Amendments of 1965 (P.L. 89-97)**

P.L. 89-97, §313(d):

Amended Sec. 3401(a) by adding paragraph (16). **Effective** with respect to tips received by employees after 1965.

• **1964, Revenue Act of 1964 (P.L. 88-272)**

P.L. 88-272, §204(b):

Amended subsection (a) to add paragraph (14).

P.L. 88-272, §213(c):

Amended subsection (a) to add paragraph (15). **Effective** with respect to remuneration paid after the seventh day following 2-26-64.

• **1962, Self-Employed Individuals Tax Retirement Act of 1962 (P.L. 87-792)**

P.L. 87-792, §7:

Amended Code Sec. 3401(a)(12) by striking out subparagraph (B) and inserting in lieu thereof new subparagraphs (B) and (C). **Effective** 1-1-63. Prior to amendment, subparagraph (B) read as follows:

(B) under or to an annuity plan which, at the time of such payment, meets the requirements of section 401(a)(3), (4), (5), and (6); or

• **1961, Mutual Educational and Cultural Exchange Act of 1961 (P.L. 87-256)**

P.L. 87-256, §110(g)(1):

Added subparagraph (C) to Code Sec. 3401(a)(6). **Effective** for wages paid after 1961.

• **1961, Peace Corps Act (P.L. 87-293)**

P.L. 87-293, §201(c):

Added paragraph (13). **Effective** for remuneration paid after 9-22-61.

• **1955 (P.L. 321, 84th Cong.)**

P.L. 321, 84th Cong., [§1]:

Amended paragraphs (8)(A)(ii) and (10)(B). **Effective** 8-9-55. Prior to amendment, paragraph (8)(A)(ii) read as follows:

(ii) performed in a foreign country by such a citizen if, at the time of the payment of such remuneration, the employer is required by the law of any foreign country to withhold income tax upon such remuneration, or

Paragraph (10)(B) was amended by substituting the word "services" for the word "service" where it appeared in the phrase "compensation for such service".

[Sec. 3401(b)]

(b) PAYROLL PERIOD.—For purposes of this chapter, the term "payroll period" means a period for which a payment of wages is ordinarily made to the employee by his employer, and the term "miscellaneous payroll period" means a payroll period other than a daily, weekly, biweekly, semimonthly, monthly, quarterly, semiannual, or annual payroll period.

[Sec. 3401(c)]

(c) EMPLOYEE.—For purposes of this chapter, the term "employee" includes an officer, employee, or elected official of the United States, a State, or any political subdivision thereof, or the District of Columbia, or any agency or instrumentality of any one or more of the foregoing. The term "employee" also includes an officer of a corporation.

Amendments

• **1976, Tax Reform Act of 1976 (P.L. 94-455)**

P.L. 94-455, §1903(c), (d):

Deleted "Territory," in Code Sec. 3401(c). **Effective** for wages paid after 12-31-76.

[Sec. 3401(d)]

(d) EMPLOYER.—For purposes of this chapter, the term "employer" means the person for whom an individual performs or performed any service, of whatever nature, as the employee of such person, except that—

(1) if the person for whom the individual performs or performed the services does not have control of the payment of the wages for such services, the term "employer" (except for purposes of subsection (a)) means the person having control of the payment of such wages, and

(2) in the case of a person paying wages on behalf of a nonresident alien individual, foreign partnership, or foreign corporation, not engaged in trade or business within the United States, the term "employer" (except for purposes of subsection (a)) means such person.

[Sec. 3401(e)—Stricken]

Amendments

• **2017, Tax Cuts and Jobs Act (P.L. 115-97)**

P.L. 115-97, §11041(c)(2)(A):

Amended Code Sec. 3401 by striking subsection (e). **Effective** generally for tax years beginning after 12-31-2017. For a special rule, see Act Sec. 11041(f)(2), below. Prior to being stricken, Code Sec. 3401(e) read as follows:

(e) NUMBER OF WITHHOLDING EXEMPTIONS CLAIMED.—For purposes of this chapter, the term "number of withholding exemptions claimed" means the number of withholding exemptions claimed in a withholding exemption certificate in effect under section 3402(f), or in effect under the corresponding section of prior law, except that if no such certificate is in effect, the number of withholding exemptions claimed shall be considered to be zero.

P.L. 115-97, §11041(f)(2), provides:

(2) WAGE WITHHOLDING.—The Secretary of the Treasury may administer section 3402 for taxable years beginning before January 1, 2019, without regard to the amendments made by subsections (a) and (c).

[Sec. 3401(f)]

(f) TIPS.—For purposes of subsection (a), the term "wages" includes tips received by an employee in the course of his employment. Such wages shall be deemed to be paid at the time a written statement including such tips is furnished to the employer pursuant to section 6053(a) or (if no statement including such tips is so furnished) at the time received.

• **1965, Social Security Amendments of 1965 (P.L. 89-97)**

P.L. 89-97, §313(d):

Added Code Sec. 3401(f). **Effective** with respect to tips received by employees after 1965.

[Sec. 3401(g)—Repealed]

Amendments

• **1989 (P.L. 101-140)**

P.L. 101-140, §203(a)(2), provides:

Code Sec. 3401(g) as added by Section 1011B(a)(22)(D) of P.L. 100-647 shall be applied as if the amendment made by such section had not been enacted. **Effective** as if included in section 1151 of P.L. 99-514. Code Sec. 3401(g) as added by Act Sec. 1011B(a)(22)(D) of P.L. 100-647 read as follows:

(g) BENEFITS PROVIDED UNDER CERTAIN EMPLOYEE BENEFIT PLANS.—Notwithstanding any paragraph of subsection (a), the term "wages" shall include any amount which is includible in gross income by reason of section 89.

• **1989 (P.L. 101-136)**

P.L. 101-136, §528, provides:

SEC. 528. No monies appropriated by this Act may be used to implement or enforce section 1151 of the Tax Reform Act of 1986 or the amendments made by such section.

• **1988, Technical and Miscellaneous Revenue Act of 1988 (P.L. 100-647)**

P.L. 100-647, §1011B(a)(22)(D):

Amended Code Sec. 3401 by adding at the end thereof new subsection (g). Not **effective** for any individual who separated from service with the employer before 1-1-89.

WITHHOLDING FROM WAGES

[Sec. 3401(g)]

(g) CREW LEADER RULES TO APPLY.—Rules similar to the rules of section 3121(o) shall apply for purposes of this chapter.

Amendments

• **2005, Gulf Opportunity Zone Act of 2005 (P.L. 109-135)**

P.L. 109-135, § 412(tt):

Amended Code Sec. 3401 by redesignating subsection (h) as subsection (g). **Effective** 12-21-2005.

• **1989, Omnibus Budget Reconciliation Act of 1989 (P.L. 101-239)**

P.L. 101-239, § 7631(b):

Amended Code Sec. 3401 by adding at the end thereof a new subsection (h). **Effective** for remuneration paid after 12-31-89.

[Sec. 3401(h)]

(h) DIFFERENTIAL WAGE PAYMENTS TO ACTIVE DUTY MEMBERS OF THE UNIFORMED SERVICES.—

(1) IN GENERAL.—For purposes of subsection (a), any differential wage payment shall be treated as a payment of wages by the employer to the employee.

(2) DIFFERENTIAL WAGE PAYMENT.—For purposes of paragraph (1), the term "differential wage payment" means any payment which—

(A) is made by an employer to an individual with respect to any period during which the individual is performing service in the uniformed services (as defined in chapter 43 of title 38, United States Code) while on active duty for a period of more than 30 days, and

(B) represents all or a portion of the wages the individual would have received from the employer if the individual were performing service for the employer.

Amendments

• **2008, Heroes Earnings Assistance and Relief Tax Act of 2008 (P.L. 110-245)**

P.L. 110-245, § 105(a)(1):

Amended Code Sec. 3401 by adding at the end a new subsection (h). **Effective** for remuneration paid after 12-31-2008.

[Sec. 3401(i)]

(i) QUALIFIED STOCK FOR WHICH AN ELECTION IS IN EFFECT UNDER SECTION 83(I).—For purposes of subsection (a), qualified stock (as defined in section 83(i)) with respect to which an election is made under section 83(i) shall be treated as wages—

(1) received on the earliest date described in section 83(i)(1)(B), and

(2) in an amount equal to the amount included in income under section 83 for the taxable year which includes such date.

Amendments

• **2017, Tax Cuts and Jobs Act (P.L. 115-97)**

P.L. 115-97, § 13603(b)(1):

Amended Code Sec. 3401 by adding at the end a new subsection (i). **Effective** generally for stock attributable to options exercised, or restricted stock units settled, after 12-31-2017. For a transition rule, see Act Sec. 13603(g), below.

P.L. 115-97, § 13603(g), provides:

(g) TRANSITION RULE.—Until such time as the Secretary (or the Secretary's delegate) issues regulations or other guidance for purposes of implementing the requirements of paragraph (2)(C)(i)(II) of section 83(i) of the Internal Revenue Code of 1986 (as added by this section), or the requirements of paragraph (6) of such section, a corporation shall be treated as being in compliance with such requirements (respectively) if such corporation complies with a reasonable good faith interpretation of such requirements.

[Sec. 3402]

SEC. 3402. INCOME TAX COLLECTED AT SOURCE.

[Sec. 3402(a)]

(a) REQUIREMENT OF WITHHOLDING.—

(1) IN GENERAL.—Except as otherwise provided in this section, every employer making payment of wages shall deduct and withhold upon such wages a tax determined in accordance with tables or computational procedures prescribed by the Secretary. Any tables or procedures prescribed under this paragraph shall—

(A) apply with respect to the amount of wages paid during such periods as the Secretary may prescribe, and

(B) be in such form, and provide for such amounts to be deducted and withheld, as the Secretary determines to be most appropriate to carry out the purposes of this chapter and to reflect the provisions of chapter 1 applicable to such periods.

(2) AMOUNT OF WAGES.—For purposes of applying tables or procedures prescribed under paragraph (1), the term "the amount of wages" means the amount by which the wages exceed the taxpayer's withholding allowance, prorated to the payroll period.

Amendments

• **2017, Tax Cuts and Jobs Act (P.L. 115-97)**

P.L. 115-97, § 11041(c)(1):

Amended Code Sec. 3402(a)(2) by striking "means the amount" and all that follows and inserting "means the amount by which the wages exceed the taxpayer's withholding allowance, prorated to the payroll period.". **Effective** generally for tax years beginning after 12-31-2017. For special rule, see Act Sec. 11041(f)(2), below. Prior to striking "means the amount" and all that follows, Code Sec. 3402(a)(2) read as follows:

(2) AMOUNT OF WAGES.—For purposes of applying tables or procedures prescribed under paragraph (1), the term "the amount of wages" means the amount by which the wages exceed the number of withholding exemptions claimed multiplied by the amount of one such exemption. The amount of each withholding exemption shall be equal to the amount of one personal exemption provided in section 151(b), prorated to the payroll period. The maximum number of withholding exemptions permitted shall be calculated in accordance with regulations prescribed by the Secretary under this section, taking into account any reduction in withholding to which an employee is entitled under this section.

P.L. 115-97, § 11041(f)(2), provides:

(2) WAGE WITHHOLDING.—The Secretary of the Treasury may administer section 3402 for taxable years beginning before January 1, 2019, without regard to the amendments made by subsections (a) and (c).

• **2004, American Jobs Creation Act of 2004 (P.L. 108-357)**

P.L. 108-357, § 904(a)-(b) and (d), provides:

SEC. 904. INCREASE IN WITHHOLDING FROM SUPPLEMENTAL WAGE PAYMENTS IN EXCESS OF $1,000,000.

(a) IN GENERAL.—If an employer elects under Treasury Regulation 31.3402(g)-1 to determine the amount to be deducted and withheld from any supplemental wage payment by using a flat percentage rate, the rate to be used in determining the amount to be so deducted and withheld shall not be less than 28 percent (or the corresponding rate in effect under section 1(i)(2) of the Internal Revenue Code of 1986 for taxable years beginning in the calendar year in which the payment is made).

(b) SPECIAL RULE FOR LARGE PAYMENTS.—

(1) IN GENERAL.—Notwithstanding subsection (a), if the supplemental wage payment, when added to all such payments previously made by the employer to the employee during the calendar year, exceeds $1,000,000, the rate used with respect to such excess shall be equal to the maximum rate of tax in effect under section 1 of such Code for taxable years beginning in such calendar year.

(2) AGGREGATION.—All persons treated as a single employer under subsection (a) or (b) of section 52 of the Internal Revenue Code of 1986 shall be treated as a single employer for purposes of this subsection.

(d) EFFECTIVE DATE.—The provisions of, and the amendment made by, this section shall apply to payments made after December 31, 2004.

• **1993, Omnibus Budget Reconciliation Act of 1993 (P.L. 103-66)**

P.L. 103-66, § 13273, as amended by P.L. 107-16, § 101(c)(11), provides [P.L. 103-66, § 13273, was repealed by P.L. 108-357, § 904(c), effective for payments made after 12-31-2004]:

SEC. 13273. INCREASE IN WITHHOLDING FROM SUPPLEMENTAL WAGE PAYMENTS.

If an employer elects under Treasury Regulation 31.3402(g)-1 to determine the amount to be deducted and withheld from any supplemental wage payment by using a flat percentage rate, the rate to be used in determining the amount to be so deducted and withheld shall not be less than the third lowest rate of tax applicable under section 1(c) of the Internal Revenue Code of 1986. The preceding sentence shall apply to payments made after December 31, 1993.

WITHHOLDING FROM WAGES

• **1990, Omnibus Budget Reconciliation Act of 1990 (P.L. 101-508)**

P.L. 101-508, §11801(a)(41):

Repealed Code Sec. 3402(a)(3). **Effective** 11-5-90. Prior to repeal, Code Sec. 3402(a)(3) read as follows:

(3) CHANGES MADE BY SECTION 101 OF THE ECONOMIC RECOVERY TAX ACT OF 1981.—Notwithstanding the provisions of this subsection, the Secretary shall modify the tables and procedures under paragraph (1) to reflect—

(A) the amendments made by section 101(b) of the Economic Recovery Tax Act of 1981, and such modification shall take effect on October 1, 1981, as if such amendments made a 5-percent reduction effective on such date, and

(B) the amendments made by section 101(a) of such Act, and such modifications shall take effect—

(i) on July 1, 1982, as if the reductions in the rate of tax under section 1 (as amended by such section) were attributable to a 10-percent reduction effective on such date, and

(ii) on July 1, 1983, as if such reductions were attributable to a 10-percent reduction effective on such date.

P.L. 101-508, §11821(b), provides:

(b) SAVINGS PROVISION.—If—

(1) any provision amended or repealed by this part applied to—

(A) any transaction occurring before the date of the enactment of this Act,

(B) any property acquired before such date of enactment, or

(C) any item of income, loss, deduction, or credit taken into account before such date of enactment, and

(2) the treatment of such transaction, property, or item under such provision would (without regard to the amendments made by this part) affect liability for tax for periods ending after such date of enactment,

nothing in the amendments made by this part shall be construed to affect the treatment of such transaction, property, or item for purposes of determining liability for tax for periods ending after such date of enactment.

• **1981, Economic Recovery Tax Act of 1981 (P.L. 97-34)**

P.L. 97-34, §101(e)(1):

Amended Code Sec. 3402(a). **Effective** with respect to remuneration paid after 9-30-81. Prior to amendment, Code Sec. 3402(a) read as follows:

(a) REQUIREMENT OF WITHHOLDING.—Except as otherwise provided in this section, every employer making payment of wages shall deduct and withhold upon such wages a tax determined in accordance with tables prescribed by the Secretary. With respect to wages paid after December 31, 1978, the tables so prescribed shall be the same as the tables prescribed under this subsection which were in effect on January 1, 1975, except that such tables shall be modified to the extent necessary to reflect the amendments made by sections 101 and 102 of the Tax Reduction and Simplification Act of 1977 and the amendments made by section 101 of the Revenue Act of 1978. For purposes of applying such tables, the term "the amount of wages" means the amount by which the wages exceed the number of withholding exemptions claimed, multiplied by the amount of one such exemption as shown in the table prescribed under subsection (b)(1).

• **1978, Revenue Act of 1978 (P.L. 95-600)**

P.L. 95-600, §101(e)(1), (f)(2):

Amended Code Sec. 3402(a). **Effective** for remuneration paid after 12-31-78. Prior to amendment, Code Sec. 3402(a) read as follows:

(a) REQUIREMENT OF WITHHOLDING.—Except as otherwise provided in this section, every employer making payment of wages shall deduct and withhold upon such wages a tax determined in accordance with tables prescribed by the Secretary. With respect to wages paid after May 31, 1977, and before January 1, 1979, the tables so prescribed shall be the same as the tables prescribed under this subsection which were in effect on January 1, 1976; except that such tables shall be modified to the extent necessary so that, had they been in effect for all of 1977, they would reflect the full year effect of the amendments made by sections 101 and 102 of the Tax Reduction and Simplification Act of 1977. With respect to wages paid after December 31, 1978, the tables so prescribed shall be the same as the tables prescribed under this subsection which were in effect on January 1, 1975, except that such tables shall be modified to the extent necessary to reflect the amendments made by sections 101 and 102 of the Tax Reduction and Simplification Act of 1977. For purposes of applying such tables, the term "the amount of wages" means the amount by which the wages exceed the number of withholding exemptions claimed, multiplied by the amount of one such exemption as shown in the table prescribed under subsection (b)(1).

• **1977, Tax Reduction and Simplification Act of 1977 (P.L. 95-30)**

P.L. 95-30, §105(a):

Amended Code Sec. 3402(a). **Effective** for wages paid after 4-30-77. Prior to amendment, Code Sec. 3402(a) read as follows:

(a) REQUIREMENT OF WITHHOLDING.—Except as otherwise provided in this section, every employer making payment of wages shall deduct and withhold upon such wages a tax determined in accordance with tables prescribed by the Secretary. With respect to wages paid prior to January 1, 1978, the tables so prescribed shall be the same as the tables prescribed under this section which were in effect on January 1, 1976. With respect to wages paid after December 31, 1977, the Secretary shall prescribe new tables which shall be the same as the tables prescribed under this subsection which were in effect on January 1, 1975, except that such tables shall be modified to the extent necessary to reflect the amendments made to subsections (b) and (c) of section 141 by the Tax Reform Act of 1976. For purposes of applying such tables, the term "the amount of wages" means the amount by which the wages exceed the number of withholding exemptions claimed, multiplied by the amount of one such exemption as shown in the table in subsection (b)(1).

P.L. 95-30, §304, provides:

SEC. 304. UNDERWITHHOLDING.

No person shall be liable in respect of any failure to deduct and withhold under section 3402 of the Internal Revenue Code of 1954 (relating to income tax collected at source) on remuneration paid before January 1, 1977, to the extent that the duty to deduct and withhold was created or increased by any provision of the Tax Reform Act of 1976.

• **1976, Tax Reform Act of 1976 (P.L. 94-455)**

P.L. 94-455, §401(d)(1), (e):

Amended Code Sec. 3402(a). **Effective** for wages paid after 9-14-76. Prior to amendment, Code Sec. 3402(a) read as follows:

(a) REQUIREMENT OF WITHHOLDING.—Except as otherwise provided in this section, every employer making payment of wages shall deduct and withhold upon such wages a tax determined in accordance with tables prescribed by the Secretary or his delegate. The tables so prescribed shall be the same as the tables contained in this subsection as in effect on January 1, 1975, except that the amounts set forth as amounts of income tax to be withheld with respect to wages paid after April 30, 1975, and before Janaury 1, 1976, shall reflect the full calendar year effect for 1975 of the amendments made by sections 201, 202, 203, and 204 of the Tax Reduction Act of 1975. The tables so prescribed with respect to wages paid after December 31, 1975, and before October 1, 1976, shall be the same as the tables prescribed under this subsection which were in effect on December 10, 1975. For purposes of applying such tables, the term "the amount of wages" means the amount by which the wages exceed the number of withholding exemptions claimed, multiplied by the amount of one such exemption as shown in the table in subsection (b)(1).

• **1976 (P.L. 94-414)**

P.L. 94-414, §3(a)(1):

Amended Code Sec. 3402(a) by substituting "October 1, 1976" for "September 15, 1976" in the third sentence. **Effective** 9-14-76.

• **1976 (P.L. 94-396)**

P.L. 94-396, §2(a)(1):

Amended Code Sec. 3402(a) by substituting "September 15, 1976" for "September 1, 1976" in the third sentence. **Effective** 8-31-76.

• **1976 (P.L. 94-331)**

P.L. 94-331, §3(a)(1):

Amended Code Sec. 3402(a) by substituting "September 1, 1976" for "July 1, 1976" in the third sentence. **Effective** 6-30-76.

• **1975, Revenue Adjustment Act of 1975 (P.L. 94-164)**

P.L. 94-164, §5(a):

Amended Code Sec. 3402(a) by adding the third sentence to read: "The tables so prescribed with respect to wages paid after December 31, 1975, and before July 1, 1976, shall be the same as the tables prescribed under this subsection which were in effect on December 10, 1975."

• **1975, Tax Reduction Act of 1975 (P.L. 94-12)**

P.L. 94-12, §205(a):

Amended Code Sec. 3402(a) to read as follows:

(a) REQUIREMENT OF WITHHOLDING.—Except as otherwise provided in this section, every employer making payment of wages shall deduct and withhold upon such wages a tax determined in accordance with tables prescribed by the Secretary or his delegate. The tables so prescribed shall be the same as the tables contained in this subsection as in effect on January 1, 1975, except that the amounts set forth as amounts of income tax to be withheld with respect to wages paid after April 30, 1975, and before January 1, 1976, shall reflect the full calendar year effect for 1975 of the amendments made by sections 201, 202, 203, and 204 of the Tax Reduction Act of 1975. For purposes of applying such tables, the term "the amount of wages" means the amount by which the wages exceed the number of withholding exemptions claimed, multiplied by the amount of one such exemption as shown in the table in subsection (b)(1).

Effective only for wages paid after 4-30-75 and before 1976. Prior to amendment, except for the tables which are not reproduced herein, Code Sec. 3402(a) read as follows:

(a) REQUIREMENT OF WITHHOLDING.—Every employer making payment of wages shall deduct and withhold upon such wages (except as otherwise provided in this section) a tax determined in accordance with the following tables. For purposes of applying such tables, the term "the amount of wages" means the amount by which the wages exceed the number of withholding exemptions claimed, multiplied by the amount of one such exemption as shown in the table in subsection (b)(1):

• **1971, Revenue Act of 1971 (P.L. 92-178)**

P.L. 92-178, §208(a):

Amended Code Sec. 3402(a). **Effective** with respect to wages paid after 1-15-72. Prior to amendment, except for the tables which are not reproduced herein, Code Sec. 3402(a) read as follows:

(a) Requirement of Withholding.—Every employer making payment of wages shall deduct and withhold upon such wages (except as otherwise provided in this section) a tax determined in accordance with the following tables. For purposes of applying such tables, the term "the amount of wages" means the amount by which the wages exceed the number of withholding exemptions claimed, multiplied by the amount of one such exemption as shown in the table in subsection (b)(1):

(1) In the case of wages paid after December 31, 1969, and before July 1, 1970:

WITHHOLDING FROM WAGES

[Withholding tables for the period January 1, 1970 through June 30, 1970, are not reproduced.—CCH.]

(2) In the case of wages paid after June 30, 1970, and before January 1, 1971:
[Withholding tables for the period July 1, 1970 through December 31, 1970, are not reproduced.—CCH.]

(3) In the case of wages paid after December 31, 1970, and before January 1, 1972 [extended to January 16, 1972, under P.L. 92-178, § 208(h)(1)]:
[Withholding tables for the period January 1, 1971, through January 15, 1972, are not reproduced.—CCH.]

(4) In the case of wages paid after December 31, 1971, and before January 1, 1973:
[The withholding tables prescribed by former Code Sec. 3402(a)(4) for the period January 1, 1972, through December 31, 1972, never took effect.—CCH.]

(5) In the case of wages paid after December 31, 1972:
[The withholding tables prescribed by former Code Sec. 3402(a)(5) for the period after December 31, 1972, never took effect.—CCH.]

• **1969, Tax Reform Act of 1969 (P.L. 91-172)**

P.L. 91-172, § 805(a):

Amended Sec. 3402(a) by inserting paragraphs (1)-(5) in lieu of paragraphs (1) and (2). **Effective** as to remuneration paid after 12-31-69. Prior to amendment, paragraphs (1) and (2), except for the tables which are not reproduced herein, read as follows:

(1) In the case of wages paid on or before the 15th day after the date of the enactment of the Revenue and Expenditure Control Act of 1968 or after December 31, 1969:

* * *

[Withholding tables for years prior to 1970 are not reproduced.—CCH.]

(2) In the case of wages paid after the 15th day after the date of the enactment of the Revenue and Expenditures Control Act of 1968 and before January 1, 1970:

* * *

[Withholding tables for years prior to 1970 are not reproduced.—CCH.]

[Sec. 3402(b)]

(b) PERCENTAGE METHOD OF WITHHOLDING.—

(1) If wages are paid with respect to a period which is not a payroll period, the withholding allowance allowable with respect to each payment of such wages shall be the allowance allowed for a miscellaneous payroll period containing a number of days (including Sundays and holidays) equal to the number of days in the period with respect to which such wages are paid.

(2) In any case in which wages are paid by an employer without regard to any payroll period or other period, the withholding allowance allowable with respect to each payment of such wages shall be the allowance allowed for a miscellaneous payroll period containing a number of days equal to the number of days (including Sundays and holidays) which have elapsed since the date of the last payment of such wages by such employer during the calendar year, or the date of commencement of employment with such employer during such year, or January 1 of such year, whichever is the later.

(3) In any case in which the period, or the time described in paragraph (2), in respect of any wages is less than one week, the Secretary, under regulations prescribed by him, may authorize an employer to compute the tax to be deducted and withheld as if the aggregate of the wages paid to the employee during the calendar week were paid for a weekly payroll period.

(4) In determining the amount to be deducted and withheld under this subsection, the wages may, at the election of the employer, be computed to the nearest dollar.

Amendments

• **2017, Tax Cuts and Jobs Act (P.L. 115-97)**

P.L. 115-97, § 11041(c)(2)(C):

Amended Code Sec. 3402(b)(1) and (2) by striking "exemption" each place it appears and inserting "allowance". **Effective** generally for tax years beginning after 12-31-2017. For a special rule, see Act Sec. 11041(f)(2), below.

P.L. 115-97, § 11041(f)(2), provides:

(2) WAGE WITHHOLDING.—The Secretary of the Treasury may administer section 3402 for taxable years beginning before January 1, 2019, without regard to the amendments made by subsections (a) and (c).

• **1981, Economic Recovery Tax Act of 1981 (P.L. 97-34)**

P.L. 97-34, § 101(e)(2):

Amended Code Sec. 3402(b) by striking out paragraph (1) and redesignating paragraphs (2) through (5) as paragraphs (1) through (4), respectively, and by striking out paragraph (3), as redesignated and inserting in lieu thereof the text of paragraph (3). **Effective** with respect to remuneration paid after 9-30-81. Prior to amendment, Code Sec. 3402(b) read as follows:

(b) PERCENTAGE METHOD OF WITHHOLDING.—

(1) The table referred to in subsection (a) is as follows:

PERCENTAGE METHOD WITHHOLDING TABLE

Payroll period	Amount of one withholding exemption
Weekly	$19.23
Biweekly	38.46
Semimonthly	41.66
Monthly	83.33
Quarterly	250.00
Semiannual	500.00
Annual	1,000.00
Daily or miscellaneous (per day of such period)	2.74

(2) If wages are paid with respect to a period which is not a payroll period, the withholding exemption allowable with respect to each payment of such wages shall be the exemption allowed for a miscellaneous payroll period containing a number of days (including Sundays and holidays) equal to the number of days in the period with respect to which such wages are paid.

(3) In any case in which wages are paid by an employer without regard to any payroll period or other period, the withholding exemption allowable with respect to each payment of such wages shall be the exemption allowed for a miscellaneous payroll period containing a number of days equal to the number of days (including Sundays and holidays) which have elapsed since the date of the last payment of such wages by such employer during the calendar year, or the date of commencement of employment with such employer during such year, or January 1 of such year, whichever is the later.

(4) In any case in which the period, or the time described in paragraph (3), in respect of any wages is less than one week, the Secretary, under regulations prescribed by him, may authorize an employer, in computing the tax required to be deducted and withheld, to use the excess of the aggregate of the wages paid to the employee during the calendar week over the withholding exemption allowed by this subsection for a weekly payroll period.

(5) In determining the amount to be deducted and withheld under this subsection, the wages may, at the election of the employer, be computed to the nearest dollar.

• **1978, Revenue Act of 1978 (P.L. 95-600)**

P.L. 95-600, § § 102(c)(1), (d)(2):

Amended Code Sec. 3402(b)(1) by striking out the old table and inserting the new table. **Effective** for remuneration paid after 12-31-78. Prior to amendment, the table in Code Sec. 3402(b)(1) read as follows:

Percentage Method Withholding Table

Payroll period	Amount of one withholding exemption
Weekly	$14.40
Biweekly	28.80
Semimonthly	31.30
Monthly	62.50
Quarterly	187.50
Semiannual	375.00
Annual	750.00
Daily or miscellaneous (per day of such period)	2.10

• **1976, Tax Reform Act of 1976 (P.L. 94-455)**

P.L. 94-455, § 1906(b)(13)(A):

Amended 1954 Code by substituting "Secretary" for "Secretary or his delegate" each place it appeared. **Effective** 2-1-77.

• **1971, Revenue Act of 1971 (P.L. 92-178)**

P.L. 92-178, § 208(b):

Amended the withholding table (as shown in Code Sec. 3402(b)(1)). **Effective** for wages paid after 1-15-72. The withholding table in effect prior to such amendment is not reproduced here.

• **1969, Tax Reform Act of 1969 (P.L. 91-172)**

P.L. 91-172, § 805(b):

Amended the withholding table in Code Sec. 3402(b)(1). **Effective** with respect to wages paid after 12-31-69. The withholding table in effect prior to such amendment is not reproduced here.

WITHHOLDING FROM WAGES

[Sec. 3402(c)]

(c) WAGE BRACKET WITHHOLDING.—

(1) At the election of the employer with respect to any employee, the employer shall deduct and withhold upon the wages paid to such employee a tax (in lieu of the tax required to be deducted and withheld under subsection (a)) determined in accordance with tables prescribed by the Secretary in accordance with paragraph (6).

(2) If wages are paid with respect to a period which is not a payroll period, the amount to be deducted and withheld shall be that applicable in the case of a miscellaneous payroll period containing a number of days (including Sundays and holidays) equal to the number of days in the period with respect to which such wages are paid.

(3) In any case in which wages are paid by an employer without regard to any payroll period or other period, the amount to be deducted and withheld shall be that applicable in the case of a miscellaneous payroll period containing a number of days equal to the number of days (including Sundays and holidays) which have elapsed since the date of the last payment of such wages by such employer during the calendar year, or the date of commencement of employment with such employer during such year, or January 1 of such year, whichever is the later.

(4) In any case in which the period, or the time described in paragraph (3), in respect of any wages is less than one week, the Secretary, under regulations prescribed by him, may authorize an employer to determine the amount to be deducted and withheld under the tables applicable in the case of a weekly payroll period, in which case the aggregate of the wages paid to the employee during the calendar week shall be considered the weekly wages.

(5) If the wages exceed the highest wage bracket, in determining the amount to be deducted and withheld under this subsection, the wages may, at the election of the employer, be computed to the nearest dollar.

(6) In the case of wages paid after December 31, 1969, the amount deducted and withheld under paragraph (1) shall be determined in accordance with tables prescribed by the Secretary. In the tables so prescribed, the amounts set forth as amounts of wages and amounts of income tax to be deducted and withheld shall be computed on the basis of the table for an annual payroll period prescribed pursuant to subsection (a).

Amendments

• **1976, Tax Reform Act of 1976 (P.L. 94-455)**

P.L. 94-455, §401(d)(2):

Amended paragraph (6) of Code Sec. 3402(c), as it was in effect on the day before the date of enactment of P.L. 94-12, by substituting "the table for an annual payroll period prescribed pursuant to subsection (a)" for table 7 contained in subsection (a). **Effective** for wages paid after 9-14-76.

P.L. 94-455, §1906(b)(13)(A):

Amended 1954 Code by substituting "Secretary" for "Secretary or his delegate" each place it appeared. **Effective** 2-1-77.

• **1976 (P.L. 94-414)**

P.L. 94-414, §3(a)(2):

Substituted "October 1, 1976" for "September 15, 1976" in section 209(c) of P.L. 94-12.

• **1976 (P.L. 94-396)**

P.L. 94-396, §2(a)(1):

Substituted "September 15, 1976" for "September 1, 1976" in section 209(c) of P.L. 94-12. **Effective** 8-31-76.

• **1976 (P.L. 94-331)**

P.L. 94-331, §3(a)(2):

Substituted "September 1, 1976" for "July 1, 1976" in section 209(c) of P.L. 94-12. **Effective** 6-30-76.

• **1975, Revenue Adjustment Act of 1975 (P.L. 94-164)**

P.L. 94-164, §5(a)(2):

Substituted "July 1, 1976" for "January 1, 1976" in section 209(c) of P.L. 94-12.

• **1975, Tax Reduction Act of 1975 (P.L. 94-12)**

P.L. 94-12, §205(b):

Amended Code Sec. 3402(b) by striking out "table 7 contained in subsection (a)" and inserting in lieu thereof "the table for an annual payroll period prescribed pursuant to subsection (a)". **Effective** only for wages paid after 4-30-75 and before 1-1-76.

• **1971, Revenue Act of 1971 (P.L. 92-178)**

P.L. 92-178, §208(g):

Amended the last sentence in Code Sec. 3402(c)(6). **Effective** with respect to wages paid after 1-15-72. Prior to amendment, such last sentence read as follows:

"In the tables so prescribed, the amounts set forth as amounts of wages and amounts of income tax to be deducted and withheld shall be computed on the basis of table 7 contained in paragraph (1), (2), (3), (4), or (5) (whichever is applicable) of subsection (a)."

• **1969, Tax Reform Act of 1969 (P.L. 91-172)**

P.L. 91-172, §805(c):

Amended paragraphs (c)(1) and (c)(6). **Effective** with respect to remuneration paid after 12-31-69. Prior to amendment, paragraphs (c)(1) and (c)(6) read as follows:

(1) At the election of the employer with respect to any employee, the employer shall deduct and withhold upon the wages paid to such employee a tax determined in accordance with the following tables, which shall be in lieu of the tax required to be deducted and withheld under subsection (a).

* * *

(6) In case of wages paid after the 15th day after the date of the enactment of the Revenue and Expenditure Control Act of 1968, and before January 1, 1970, the amount deducted and withheld under paragraph (1) shall be determined in accordance with tables prescribed by the Secretary or his delegate in lieu of the tables contained in paragraph (1). The tables so prescribed shall be the same as the tables contained in paragraph (1), except that amounts and rates set forth as amounts and rates of tax to be deducted and withheld shall be computed on the basis of table 7 contained in subsection (a)(2).

The wage bracket withholding tables, which were part of paragraph (c)(1) before amendment by Act Sec. 805(c), were for years prior to 1970 and are not reproduced here.

• **1969 (P.L. 91-53)**

P.L. 91-53, §6(a):

Amended paragraph (6) in Code Sec. 3402(c) by substituting "January 1, 1970" for "August 1, 1969." **Effective** with respect to wages paid after 7-31-69, and before 1-1-70.

• **1969 (P.L. 91-36)**

P.L. 91-36, §2(a):

Amended paragraph (6) in Code Sec. 3402(c) by substituting "August 1, 1969" for "July 1, 1969." **Effective** with respect to wages paid after 6-30-69.

• **1968, Revenue and Expenditure Control Act of 1968 (P.L. 90-364)**

P.L. 90-364, §102(c)(2):

Added paragraph (6) in Code Sec. 3402(c). **Effective** with respect to wages paid on and after 7-14-68.

[Sec. 3402(d)]

(d) TAX PAID BY RECIPIENT.—If the employer, in violation of the provisions of this chapter, fails to deduct and withhold the tax under this chapter, and thereafter the tax against which such tax may be credited is paid, the tax so required to be deducted and withheld shall not be collected from the employer; but this subsection shall in no case relieve the employer from liability for any penalties or additions to the tax otherwise applicable in respect of such failure to deduct and withhold.

[Sec. 3402(e)]

(e) INCLUDED AND EXCLUDED WAGES.—If the remuneration paid by an employer to an employee for services performed during one-half or more of any payroll period of not more than 31 consecutive days constitutes wages, all the remuneration paid by such employer to such employee for such period shall be deemed to be wages; but if the remuneration paid by an employer to an employee for services performed during more than one-half of any such payroll period does not constitute wages, then none of the remuneration paid by such employer to such employee for such period shall be deemed to be wages.

[Sec. 3402(f)]

(f) WITHHOLDING ALLOWANCE.—

(1) IN GENERAL.—Under rules determined by the Secretary, an employee receiving wages shall on any day be entitled to a withholding allowance determined based on—

WITHHOLDING FROM WAGES

(A) whether the employee is an individual for whom a deduction is allowable with respect to another taxpayer under section 151;

(B) if the employee is married, whether the employee's spouse is entitled to an allowance, or would be so entitled if such spouse were an employee receiving wages, under subparagraph (A) or (D), but only if such spouse does not have in effect a withholding allowance certificate claiming such allowance;

(C) the number of individuals with respect to whom, on the basis of facts existing at the beginning of such day, there may reasonably be expected to be allowable a credit under section 24 (determined after application of subsection (j) thereof) for the taxable year under subtitle A in respect of which amounts deducted and withheld under this chapter in the calendar year in which such day falls are allowed as a credit;

(D) any additional amounts to which the employee elects to take into account under subsection (m), but only if the employee's spouse does not have in effect a withholding allowance certificate making such an election;

(E) the standard deduction allowable to such employee (one-half of such standard deduction in the case of an employee who is married (as determined under section 7703) and whose spouse is an employee receiving wages subject to withholding); and

(F) whether the employee has withholding allowance certificates in effect with respect to more than 1 employer.

(2) ALLOWANCE CERTIFICATES.—

(A) ON COMMENCEMENT OF EMPLOYMENT.—On or before the date of the commencement of employment with an employer, the employee shall furnish the employer with a signed withholding allowance certificate relating to the withholding allowance claimed by the employee, which shall in no event exceed the amount to which the employee is entitled.

(B) CHANGE OF STATUS.—If, on any day during the calendar year, an employee's withholding allowance is in excess of the withholding allowance to which the employee would be entitled had the employee submitted a true and accurate withholding allowance certificate to the employer on that day, the employee shall within 10 days thereafter furnish the employer with a new withholding allowance certificate. If, on any day during the calendar year, an employee's withholding allowance is greater than the withholding allowance claimed, the employee may furnish the employer with a new withholding allowance certificate relating to the withholding allowance to which the employee is so entitled, which shall in no event exceed the amount to which the employee is entitled on such day.

(C) CHANGE OF STATUS WHICH AFFECTS NEXT CALENDAR YEAR.—If on any day during the calendar year the withholding allowance to which the employee will be, or may reasonably be expected to be, entitled at the beginning of the employee's next taxable year under subtitle A is different from the allowance to which the employee is entitled on such day, the employee shall, in such cases and at such times as the Secretary shall by regulations prescribe, furnish the employer with a withholding allowance certificate relating to the withholding allowance which the employee claims with respect to such next taxable year, which shall in no event exceed the withholding allowance to which the employee will be, or may reasonably be expected to be, so entitled.

(3) WHEN CERTIFICATE TAKES EFFECT.—

(A) FIRST CERTIFICATE FURNISHED.—A withholding allowance certificate furnished the employer in cases in which no previous such certificate is in effect shall take effect as of the beginning of the first payroll period ending, or the first payment of wages made without regard to a payroll period, on or after the date on which such certificate is so furnished.

(B) FURNISHED TO TAKE PLACE OF EXISTING CERTIFICATE.—

(i) IN GENERAL.—Except as provided in clauses (ii) and (iii), a withholding allowance certificate furnished to the employer in cases in which a previous such certificate is in effect shall take effect as of the beginning of the 1st payroll period ending (or the 1st payment of wages made without regard to a payroll period) on or after the 30th day after the day on which such certificate is so furnished.

(ii) EMPLOYER MAY ELECT EARLIER EFFECTIVE DATE.—At the election of the employer, a certificate described in clause (i) may be made effective beginning with any payment of wages made on or after the day on which the certificate is so furnished and before the 30th day referred to in clause (i).

(iii) CHANGE OF STATUS WHICH AFFECTS NEXT YEAR.—Any certificate furnished pursuant to paragraph (2)(C) shall not take effect, and may not be made effective, with respect to any payment of wages made in the calendar year in which the certificate is furnished.

(4) PERIOD DURING WHICH CERTIFICATE REMAINS IN EFFECT.—A withholding allowance certificate which takes effect under this subsection, or which on December 31, 1954, was in effect under the corresponding subsection of prior law, shall continue in effect with respect to the employer until another such certificate takes effect under this subsection.

(5) FORM AND CONTENTS OF CERTIFICATE.—Withholding allowance certificates shall be in such form and contain such information as the Secretary may by regulations prescribe.

(6) EXEMPTION OF CERTAIN NONRESIDENT ALIENS.—Notwithstanding the provisions of paragraph (1), a nonresident alien individual (other than an individual described in section 3401(a)(6)(A) or (B)) shall be entitled to only one withholding exemption.

(7) ALLOWANCE WHERE CERTIFICATE WITH ANOTHER EMPLOYER IS IN EFFECT.—If a withholding allowance certificate is in effect with respect to one employer, an employee shall not be entitled under a certificate in effect with any other employer to any withholding allowance which he has claimed under such first certificate.

Amendments

- **2021, American Rescue Plan Act of 2021 (P.L. 117-2)**

P.L. 117-2, § 9611(b)(3):

Amended Code Sec. 3402(f)(1)(C) by striking "section 24(a)" and inserting "section 24 (determined after application of subsection (j) there of)". **Effective** for tax years beginning after 12-31-2020.

- **2017, Tax Cuts and Jobs Act (P.L. 115-97)**

P.L. 115-97, § 11041(c)(2)(B):

Amended Code Sec. 3402(f)(1) and (2). **Effective** generally for tax years beginning after 12-31-2017. For a special rule, see Act Sec. 11041(f)(2), below. Prior to amendment, Code Sec. 3402(f)(1)-(2) read as follows:

(1) IN GENERAL.—An employee receiving wages shall on any day be entitled to the following withholding exemptions:

(A) an exemption for himself unless he is an individual described in section 151(d)(2);

(B) if the employee is married, any exemption to which his spouse is entitled, or would be entitled if such spouse were an employee receiving wages, under subparagraph (A) or (D) but only if such spouse does not have in effect a withholding exemption certificate claiming such exemption;

(C) an exemption for each individual with respect to whom, on the basis of facts existing at the beginning of such day, there may reasonably be expected to be allowable an exemption under section 151(c) for the taxable year under subtitle A in respect of which amounts deducted and withheld under this chapter in the calendar year in which such day falls are allowed as a credit;

(D) any allowance to which he is entitled under subsection (m), but only if his spouse does not have in effect a withholding exemption certificate claiming such allowance; and

(E) a standard deduction allowance which shall be an amount equal to one exemption (or more than one exemption if so prescribed by the Secretary) unless (i) he is married (as determined under section 7703) and his spouse is an employee receiving wages subject to withholding or (ii) he has withholding exemption certificates in effect with respect to more than one employer.

For purposes of this title, any standard deduction allowance under subparagraph (E) shall be treated as if it were denominated a withholding exemption.

(2) EXEMPTION CERTIFICATES.—

(A) ON COMMENCEMENT OF EMPLOYMENT.—On or before the date of the commencement of employment with an employer, the employee shall furnish the employer with a signed withholding exemption certificate relating to the number of withholding exemptions which he claims, which shall in no event exceed the number to which he is entitled.

(B) CHANGE OF STATUS.—If, on any day during the calendar year, the number of withholding exemptions to which the employee is entitled is less than the number of withholding exemptions claimed by the employee on the withholding exemption certificate then in effect with respect to him, the employee shall within 10 days thereafter furnish the employer with a new withholding exemption certificate relating to the number of withholding exemptions which the employee then claims, which shall in no event exceed the number to which he is entitled on such day. If, on any day during the calendar year, the number of withholding exemptions to which the employee is entitled is greater than the number of withholding exemptions claimed, the employee may furnish the employer with a new withholding exemption

WITHHOLDING FROM WAGES

certificate relating to the number of withholding exemptions which the employee then claims, which shall in no event exceed the number to which he is entitled on such day.

(C) CHANGE OF STATUS WHICH AFFECTS NEXT CALENDAR YEAR.—If on any day during the calendar year the number of withholding exemptions to which the employee will be, or may reasonably be expected to be, entitled at the beginning of his next taxable year under subtitle A is different from the number to which the employee is entitled on such day, the employee shall, in such cases and at such times as the Secretary may by regulations prescribe, furnish the employer with a withholding exemption certificate relating to the number of withholding exemptions which he claims with respect to such next taxable year, which shall in no event exceed the number to which he will be, or may reasonably be expected to be, so entitled.

P.L. 115-97, §11041(c)(2)(C):

Amended Code Sec. 3402(f)(3), (4), (5), and (7) (including the heading thereof) by striking "exemption" each place it appears and inserting "allowance". **Effective** generally for tax years beginning after 12-31-2017. For a special rule, see Act Sec. 11041(f)(2), below.

P.L. 115-97, §11041(c)(2)(D):

Amended the heading for Code Sec. 3402(f) by striking "EXEMPTIONS" and inserting "ALLOWANCE". **Effective** generally for tax years beginning after 12-31-2017. For a special rule, see Act Sec. 11041(f)(2), below.

P.L. 115-97, §11041(f)(2), provides:

(2) WAGE WITHHOLDING.—The Secretary of the Treasury may administer section 3402 for taxable years beginning before January 1, 2019, without regard to the amendments made by subsections (a) and (c).

• **1987, Revenue Act of 1987 (P.L. 100-203)**

P.L. 100-203, §10302(a):

Amended Code Sec. 3402(f)(3)(B). **Effective** for certificates furnished after the day 30 days after 12-22-87. Prior to amendment, Code Sec. 3402(f)(3)(B) read as follows:

(B) FURNISHED TO TAKE PLACE OF EXISTING CERTIFICATE.—A withholding exemption certificate furnished the employer in cases in which a previous such certificate is in effect shall take effect with respect to the first payment of wages made on or after the first status determination date which occurs at least 30 days from the date on which such certificate is so furnished, except that at the election of the employer such certificate may be made effective with respect to any payment of wages made on or after the date on which such certificate is so furnished; but a certificate furnished pursuant to paragraph (2)(C) shall not take effect, and may not be made effective, with respect to any payment of wages made in the calendar year in which the certificate is furnished. For purposes of this subparagraph, the term "status determination date" means January 1, May 1, July 1, and October 1 of each year.

• **1986, Tax Reform Act of 1986 (P.L. 99-514)**

P.L. 99-514, §104(b)(15)(A):

Amended Code Sec. 3402(f)(1) by striking out subparagraphs (B) and (C) and by redesignating subparagraphs (D), (E), (F), and (G) as subparagraphs (B), (C), (D), and (E), respectively. **Effective** for tax years beginning after 12-31-86. Prior to amendment, Code Sec. 3402(f)(1)(B) and (C) read as follows:

(B) one additional exemption for himself if, on the basis of facts existing at the beginning of such day, there may reasonably be expected to be allowable an exemption under section 151(c)(1) (relating to old age) for the taxable year under subtitle A in respect of which amounts deducted and withheld under this chapter in the calendar year in which such day falls are allowed as a credit;

(C) one additional exemption for himself if, on the basis of facts existing at the beginning of such day, there may reasonably be expected to be allowable an exemption under section 151(d)(1) (relating to the blind) for the taxable year under subtitle A in respect of which amounts deducted and withheld under this chapter in the calendar year in which such day falls are allowed as a credit;

P.L. 99-514, §104(b)(15)(B):

Amended Code Sec. 3402(f)(1)(A) by inserting "unless he is an individual described in section 151(d)(2)" after "himself". **Effective** for tax years beginning after 12-31-86.

P.L. 99-514, §104(b)(15)(C):

Amended Code Sec. 3402(f)(1)(B) as redesignated by Act Sec. 104(b)(15)(A), by striking out "subparagraph (A), (B), (C), or (F)" and inserting in lieu thereof "subparagraph (A) or (D)". **Effective** for tax years beginning after 12-31-86.

P.L. 99-514, §104(b)(15)(D):

Amended Code Sec. 3402(f)(1)(C), as redesignated by Act Sec. 104(b)(15)(A), by striking out "section 151(e)" and inserting in lieu thereof "section 151(c)". **Effective** for tax years beginning after 12-31-86.

P.L. 99-514, §104(b)(15)(E):

Amended Code Sec. 3402(f)(1)(E), as redesignated by Act Sec. 104(b)(15)(A), by striking out "zero bracket" and inserting in lieu thereof "standard deduction". **Effective** for tax years beginning after 12-31-86.

P.L. 99-514, §104(b)(15)(F)(i) and (ii):

Amended Code Sec. 3402(f)(1) by striking out "subparagraph (G)" and inserting in lieu thereof "subparagraph (E)", and by striking out "zero bracket" and inserting in lieu thereof "standard deduction" in the last sentence. **Effective** for tax years beginning after 12-31-86.

P.L. 99-514, §1301(j)(8):

Amended Code Sec. 3402(f) by striking out "section 143" each place it appears and inserting in lieu thereof "section 7703". **Effective** for bonds issued after 8-15-86.

• **1981, Economic Recovery Tax Act of 1981 (P.L. 97-34)**

P.L. 97-34, §101(e)(3):

Amended Code Sec. 3402(f)(1)(G) by inserting "(or more than one exemption if so prescribed by the Secretary)" after "one exemption". **Effective** with respect to remuneration paid after 9-30-81.

• **1977, Tax Reduction and Simplification Act of 1977 (P.L. 95-30)**

P.L. 95-30, §105(b)(1):

Amended Code Sec. 3402(f) by striking out "a standard deduction" in subparagraph (G) and inserting in lieu thereof "zero bracket" and by striking out "standard deduction" in the sentence following subparagraph (G) and inserting in lieu thereof "zero bracket". **Effective** with respect to wages paid after 4-30-77.

• **1976, Tax Reform Act of 1976 (P.L. 94-455)**

P.L. 94-455, §1906(b)(13)(A):

Amended 1954 Code by substituting "Secretary" for "Secretary or his delegate" each place it appeared. **Effective** 2-1-77.

• **1971, Revenue Act of 1971 (P.L. 92-178)**

P.L. 92-178, §208(c):

Amended Code Sec. 3402(f)(1) by deleting "and" at the end of subparagraph (E), substituting "; and" for the period at the end of subparagraph (F) and adding subparagraph (G). **Effective** with respect to wages paid after 1-15-72.

P.L. 92-178, §208(d):

Amended Code Sec. 3402(f) by adding paragraph (7). **Effective** with respect to wages paid after 1-15-72.

• **1966, Tax Adjustment Act of 1966 (P.L. 89-368)**

P.L. 89-368, §101(e)(1):

Amended Code Sec. 3402(f)(1) by striking out "and" at the end of subparagraph (D), by substituting "; and" for the period at the end of subparagraph (E), and by adding new subparagraph (F). **Effective** with respect to remuneration paid after 12-31-66, but only with respect to withholding exemptions based on estimation years beginning after such date.

P.L. 89-368, §101(e)(3):

Amended the last sentence of Code Sec. 3402(f)(3)(B). **Effective** with respect to remuneration paid after 4-30-66. Prior to amendment, the last sentence read as follows:

"For purposes of this subparagraph, the term `status determination date' means January 1 and July 1 of each year."

• **1961, Mutual Educational and Cultural Exchange Act of 1961 (P.L. 87-256)**

P.L. 87-256, §110(g)(2):

Added paragraph (6) to Code Sec. 3402(f). **Effective** for wages paid after 1961.

[Sec. 3402(g)]

(g) OVERLAPPING PAY PERIODS, AND PAYMENT BY AGENT OR FIDUCIARY.—If a payment of wages is made to an employee by an employer—

(1) with respect to a payroll period or other period, any part of which is included in a payroll period or other period with respect to which wages are also paid to such employee by such employer, or

(2) without regard to any payroll period or other period, but on or prior to the expiration of a payroll period or other period with respect to which wages are also paid to such employee by such employer, or

(3) with respect to a period beginning in one and ending in another calendar year, or

(4) through an agent, fiduciary, or other person who also has the control, receipt, custody, or disposal of, or pays, the wages payable by another employer to such employee,

the manner of withholding and the amount to be deducted and withheld under this chapter shall be determined in accordance with regulations prescribed by the Secretary under which the withholding allowance allowed to the employee in any calendar year shall approximate the withholding allowance allowable with respect to an annual payroll period.

Amendments

• **2017, Tax Cuts and Jobs Act (P.L. 115-97)**

P.L. 115-97, §11041(c)(2)(C):

Amended Code Sec. 3402(g)(4) by striking "exemption" each place it appears and inserting "allowance". **Effective** generally for tax years beginning after 12-31-2017. For a special rule, see Act Sec. 11041(f)(2), below.

P.L. 115-97, §11041(f)(2), provides:

(2) WAGE WITHHOLDING.—The Secretary of the Treasury may administer section 3402 for taxable years beginning before January 1, 2019, without regard to the amendments made by subsections (a) and (c).

WITHHOLDING FROM WAGES

- **1976, Tax Reform Act of 1976 (P.L. 94-455)**

P.L. 94-455, §1906(b)(13)(A):

Amended 1954 Code by substituting "Secretary" for "Secretary or his delegate" each place it appeared. **Effective** 2-1-77.

[Sec. 3402(h)]

(h) ALTERNATIVE METHODS OF COMPUTING AMOUNT TO BE WITHHELD.—The Secretary may, under regulations prescribed by him, authorize—

(1) WITHHOLDING ON BASIS OF AVERAGE WAGES.—An employer—

(A) to estimate the wages which will be paid to any employee in any quarter of the calendar year,

(B) to determine the amount to be deducted and withheld upon each payment of wages to such employee during such quarter as if the appropriate average of the wages so estimated constituted the actual wages paid, and

(C) to deduct and withhold upon any payment of wages to such employee during such quarter (and, in the case of tips referred to in subsection (k), within 30 days thereafter) such amount as may be necessary to adjust the amount actually deducted and withheld upon the wages of such employee during such quarter to the amount required to be deducted and withheld during such quarter without regard to this subsection.

(2) WITHHOLDING ON BASIS OF ANNUALIZED WAGES.—An employer to determine the amount of tax to be deducted and withheld upon a payment of wages to an employee for a payroll period by—

(A) multiplying the amount of an employee's wages for a payroll period by the number of such payroll periods in the calendar year,

(B) determining the amount of tax which would be required to be deducted and withheld upon the amount determined under subparagraph (A) if such amount constituted the actual wages for the calendar year and the payroll period of the employee were an annual payroll period, and

(C) dividing the amount of tax determined under subparagraph (B) by the number of payroll periods (described in subparagraph (A)) in the calendar year.

(3) WITHHOLDING ON BASIS OF CUMULATIVE WAGES.—An employer, in the case of any employee who requests to have the amount of tax to be withheld from his wages computed on the basis of his cumulative wages, to—

(A) add the amount of the wages to be paid to the employee for the payroll period to the total amount of wages paid by the employer to the employee during the calendar year,

(B) divide the aggregate amount of wages computed under subparagraph (A) by the number of payroll periods to which such aggregate amount of wages relates,

(C) compute the total amount of tax that would have been required to be deducted and withheld under subsection (a) if the average amount of wages (as computed under subparagraph (B)) had been paid to the employee for the number of payroll periods to which the aggregate amount of wages (computed under subparagraph (A)) relates,

(D) determine the excess, if any, of the amount of tax computed under subparagraph (C) over the total amount of tax deducted and withheld by the employer from wages paid to the employee during the calendar year, and

(E) deduct and withhold upon the payment of wages (referred to in subparagraph (A)) to the employee an amount equal to the excess (if any) computed under subparagraph (D).

(4) OTHER METHODS.—An employer to determine the amount of tax to be deducted and withheld upon the wages paid to an employee by any other method which will require the employer to deduct and withhold upon such wages substantially the same amount as would be required to be deducted and withheld by applying subsection (a) or (c), either with respect to a payroll period or with respect to the entire taxable year.

Amendments

- **1976, Tax Reform Act of 1976 (P.L. 94-455)**

P.L. 94-455, §1906(b)(13)(A):

Amended 1954 Code by substituting "Secretary" for "Secretary or his delegate" each place it appeared. **Effective** 2-1-77.

- **1969, Tax Reform Act of 1969 (P.L. 91-172)**

P.L. 91-172, §805(d):

Amended Code Sec. 3402(h). **Effective** for remuneration paid after 12-31-69. Prior to amendment, Code Sec. 3402(h) read as follows:

(h) Withholding on Basis of Average Wages.—The Secretary or his delegate may, under regulations prescribed by him, authorize employers—

(1) to estimate the wages which will be paid to any employee in any quarter of the calendar year,

(2) to determine the amount to be deducted and withheld upon each payment of wages to such employee during such quarter as if the appropriate average of the wages so estimated constituted the actual wages paid, and

(3) to deduct and withhold upon any payment of wages to such employee during such quarter (and, in the case of tips referred to in subsection (k), within 30 days thereafter) such amount as may be necessary to adjust the amount actually deducted and withheld upon the wages of such employee during such quarter to the amount required to be deducted and withheld during such quarter without regard to this subsection.

- **1965, Social Security Amendments of 1965 (P.L. 89-97)**

P.L. 89-97, §313(d):

Amended Sec. 3402(h)(3) by adding "(and, in the case of tips referred to in subsection (k), within 30 days thereafter)" after "quarter" in the second line. **Effective** with respect to tips received by employees after 1965.

[Sec. 3402(i)]

(i) CHANGES IN WITHHOLDING.—

(1) IN GENERAL.—The Secretary may by regulations provide for increases in the amount of withholding otherwise required under this section in cases where the employee requests such changes.

(2) TREATMENT AS TAX.—Any increased withholding under paragraph (1) shall for all purposes be considered tax required to be deducted and withheld under this chapter.

Amendments

- **1986, Tax Reform Act of 1986 (P.L. 99-514)**

P.L. 99-514, §1581(b):

Amended Code Sec. 3402(i) by striking out "or decreases". **Effective** 10-22-86. Prior to amendment, Code Sec. 3402(i) read as follows:

(i) CHANGES IN WITHHOLDING.—

(1) IN GENERAL.—The Secretary may by regulations provide for increases or decreases in the amount of withholding otherwise required under this section in cases where the employee requests such changes.

(2) TREATMENT AS TAX.—Any increased withholding under paragraph (1) shall for all purposes be considered tax required to be deducted and withheld under this chapter.

P.L. 99-514, §1581(a) and (c), as amended by P.L. 100-647, §1015(p), provides:

(a) IN GENERAL.—The Secretary of the Treasury or his delegate shall modify the withholding schedules and withholding exemption certificates under section 3402 of the Internal Revenue Code of 1954 to better approximate actual tax liability under the amendments made by this Act.

* * *

(c) EMPLOYER'S RESPONSIBILITY.—If an employee has not filed a revised withholding allowance certificate before October 1, 1987, the employer shall withhold income taxes from the employee's wages—

(1) as if the employee claimed 1 withholding allowance, if the employee checked the "single" box on the employee's previous withholding allowance certificate, or

(2) as if the employee claimed 2 withholding allowances, if the employee checked the "married" box on the employee's previous withholding allowance certificate.

The preceding sentence shall not apply if its application would result in an increase in the number of withholding allowances for the employees.

- **1981, Economic Recovery Tax Act of 1981 (P.L. 97-34)**

P.L. 97-34, §101(e)(4):

Amended Code Sec. 3402(i). **Effective** with respect to remuneration paid after 9-30-81. Prior to amendment, Code Sec. 3402(i) read as follows:

WITHHOLDING FROM WAGES

(i) ADDITIONAL WITHHOLDING.—The Secretary is authorized by regulations to provide, under such conditions and to such extent as he deems proper, for withholding in addition to that otherwise required under this section in cases in which the employer and the employee agree (in such form as the Secretary may by regulations prescribe) to such additional withholding. Such additional withholding shall for all purposes be considered tax required to be deducted and withheld under this chapter.

[Sec. 3402(j)]

(j) NONCASH REMUNERATION TO RETAIL COMMISSION SALESMAN.—In the case of remuneration paid in any medium other than cash for services performed by an individual as a retail salesman for a person, where the service performed by such individual for such person is ordinarily performed for remuneration solely by way of cash commission an employer shall not be required to deduct or withhold any tax under this subchapter with respect to such remuneration, provided that such employer files with the Secretary such information with respect to such remuneration as the Secretary may by regulation prescribe.

Amendments

• **1976, Tax Reform Act of 1976 (P.L. 94-455)**

P.L. 94-455, §1906(b)(13)(A):

Amended 1954 Code by substituting "Secretary" for "Secretary or his delegate" each place it appeared. **Effective** 2-1-77.

• **1955 (P.L. 306, 84th Cong.)**

P.L. 306, 84th Cong., §2(b):

Added subsection (j). **Effective** 8-10-58.

[Sec. 3402(k)]

(k) TIPS.—In the case of tips which constitute wages, subsection (a) shall be applicable only to such tips as are included in a written statement furnished to the employer pursuant to section 6053(a), and only to the extent that the tax can be deducted and withheld by the employer, at or after the time such statement is so furnished and before the close of the calendar year in which such statement is furnished, from such wages of the employee (excluding tips, but including funds turned over by the employee to the employer for the purpose of such deduction and withholding) as are under the control of the employer; and an employer who is furnished by an employee a written statement of tips (received in a calendar month) pursuant to section 6053(a) to which paragraph (16)(B) of section 3401(a) is applicable may deduct and withhold the tax with respect to such tips from any wages of the employee (excluding tips) under his control, even though at the time such statement is furnished the total amount of the tips included in statements furnished to the employer as having been received by the employee in such calendar month in the course of his employment by such employer is less than $20. Such tax shall not at any time be deducted and withheld in an amount which exceeds the aggregate of such wages and funds (including funds turned over under section 3102(c)(2) or section 3202(c)(2)) minus any tax required by section 3102(a) or section 3202(a) to be collected from such wages and funds.

Amendments

• **1965 (P.L. 89-212)**

P.L. 89-212, §2(c):

Amended Code Sec. 3402(k) by inserting "or section 3202(c)(2)" immediately after "section 3102(c)(2)" and "or section 3202(a)" immediately after "section 3102(a)" in the last sentence. **Effective** with respect to tips received after 1965.

• **1965, Social Security Amendments of 1965 (P.L. 89-97)**

P.L. 89-97, §313(d):

Added Code Sec. 3402(k). **Effective** with respect to tips received by employees after 1965.

[Sec. 3402(l)]

(l) DETERMINATION AND DISCLOSURE OF MARITAL STATUS.—

(1) DETERMINATION OF STATUS BY EMPLOYER.—For purposes of applying the tables in subsections (a) and (c) to a payment of wages, the employer shall treat the employee as a single person unless there is in effect with respect to such payment of wages a withholding allowance certificate furnished to the employer by the employee after the date of the enactment of this subsection indicating that the employee is married.

(2) DISCLOSURE OF STATUS BY EMPLOYEE.—An employee shall be entitled to furnish the employer with a withholding allowance certificate indicating he is married only if, on the day of such furnishing, he is married (determined with the application of the rules in paragraph (3)). An employee whose marital status changes from married to single shall, at such time as the Secretary may by regulations prescribe, furnish the employer with a new withholding allowance certificate.

(3) DETERMINATION OF MARITAL STATUS.—For purposes of paragraph (2), an employee shall on any day be considered—

(A) as not married, if (i) he is legally separated from his spouse under a decree of divorce or separate maintenance, or (ii) either he or his spouse is, or on any preceding day within the calendar year was, a nonresident alien; or

(B) as married, if (i) his spouse (other than a spouse referred to in subparagraph (A)) died within the portion of his taxable year which precedes such day, or (ii) his spouse died during one of the two taxable years immediately preceding the current taxable year and, on the basis of facts existing at the beginning of such day, the employee reasonably expects, at the close of his taxable year, to be a surviving spouse (as defined in section 2(a)).

Amendments

• **2017, Tax Cuts and Jobs Act (P.L. 115-97)**

P.L. 115-97, §11041(c)(2)(C):

Amended Code Sec. 3402(l)(1) and (2) by striking "exemption" each place it appears and inserting "allowance". **Effective** generally for tax years beginning after 12-31-2017. For a special rule, see Act Sec. 11041(f)(2), below.

P.L. 115-97, §11041(f)(2), provides:

(2) WAGE WITHHOLDING.—The Secretary of the Treasury may administer section 3402 for taxable years beginning before January 1, 2019, without regard to the amendments made by subsections (a) and (c).

• **1976, Tax Reform Act of 1976 (P.L. 94-455)**

P.L. 94-455, §1903(a)(17):

Substituted "section 2(a)" for "section 2(b)" in Code Sec. 3402(l)(3)(B). **Effective** for wages paid after 12-31-76.

P.L. 94-455, §1906(b)(13)(A):

Amended 1954 Code by substituting "Secretary" for "Secretary or his delegate" each place it appeared. **Effective** 2-1-77.

• **1966, Tax Adjustment Act of 1966 (P.L. 89-368)**

P.L. 89-368, §101(d):

Added Code Sec. 3402(l). **Effective** with respect to remuneration paid after 4-30-66.

[Sec. 3402(m)]

(m) WITHHOLDING ALLOWANCES.—Under regulations prescribed by the Secretary, an employee shall be entitled to an additional withholding allowance or additional reductions in withholding under this subsection. In determining the additional withholding allowance or the amount of additional reductions in withholding under this subsection, the employee may take into account (to the extent and in the manner provided by such regulations)—

(1) estimated itemized deductions allowable under chapter 1 and the estimated deduction allowed under section 199A (other than the deductions referred to in section 151 and other than the deductions required to be taken into account in determining adjusted gross income under section 62(a),

(2) estimated tax credits allowable under chapter 1, and

(3) such additional deductions (including the additional standard deduction under section 63(c)(3) for the aged and blind) and other items as may be specified by the Secretary in regulations.

WITHHOLDING FROM WAGES

Amendments

- **2017, Tax Cuts and Jobs Act (P.L. 115-97)**

P.L. 115-97, §11011(b)(4):

Amended Code Sec. 3402(m)(1) by inserting "and the estimated deduction allowed under section 199A" after "chapter 1". **Effective** for tax years beginning after 12-31-2017.

P.L. 115-97, §11041(c)(2)(E):

Amended Code Sec. 3402(m) by striking "additional withholding allowances or additional reductions in withholding under this subsection. In determining the number of additional withholding allowances" and inserting "an additional withholding allowance or additional reductions in withholding under this subsection. In determining the additional withholding allowance". **Effective** generally for tax years beginning after 12-31-2017. For a special rule, see Act Sec. 11041(f)(2), below.

P.L. 115-97, §11041(f)(2), provides:

(2) WAGE WITHHOLDING.—The Secretary of the Treasury may administer section 3402 for taxable years beginning before January 1, 2019, without regard to the amendments made by subsections (a) and (c).

P.L. 115-97, §11051(b)(2)(B), provides:

Amended Code Sec. 3402(m)(1) by striking "(other than paragraph (10) thereof)" following "under section 62(a)". For the **effective** date, see Act Sec. 11051(c)(1)-(2), below.

P.L. 115-97, §11051(c)(1)-(2), provides:

(c) EFFECTIVE DATE.—The amendments made by this section shall apply to—

(1) any divorce or separation instrument (as defined in section 71(b)(2) of the Internal Revenue Code of 1986 as in effect before the date of the enactment of this Act) executed after December 31, 2018, and

(2) any divorce or separation instrument (as so defined) executed on or before such date and modified after such date if the modification expressly provides that the amendments made by this section apply to such modification.

- **1988, Technical and Miscellaneous Revenue Act of 1988 (P.L. 100-647)**

P.L. 100-647, §1003(a)(2):

Amended Code Sec. 3402(m)(1) by striking out "section 62) (other than paragraph (13) thereof)" and inserting in lieu thereof "section 62(a) (other than paragraph (10) thereof)". **Effective** as if included in the provision of P.L. 99-514 to which it relates.

- **1986, Tax Reform Act of 1986 (P.L. 99-514)**

P.L. 99-514, §104(b)(15)(G):

Amended Code Sec. 3402(m)(3) by inserting "(including the additional standard deduction under section 63(c)(3) for the aged and blind)" after "deductions". **Effective** for tax years beginning after 12-31-86.

- **1981, Economic Recovery Tax Act of 1981 (P.L. 97-34)**

P.L. 97-34, §101(e)(5):

Amended Code Sec. 3402(m). **Effective** with respect to remuneration paid after 12-31-81. Prior to amendment, Code Sec. 3402(m) read as follows:

(m) WITHHOLDING ALLOWANCES BASED ON ITEMIZED DEDUCTIONS.—

(1) GENERAL RULE.—An employee shall be entitled to withholding allowances under this subsection with respect to a payment of wages in a number equal to the number determined by dividing by $1,000 the excess of—

(A) his estimated itemized deductions, over

(B) an amount equal to $3,400, $2,300 in the case of an individual who is not married (within the meaning of section 143) and who is not a surviving spouse (as defined in section 2(a)).

For purposes of this subsection, a fractional number shall not be taken into account unless it amounts to one-half or more, in which case it shall be increased to 1.

(2) DEFINITIONS.—For purposes of this subsection—

(A) ESTIMATED ITEMIZED DEDUCTIONS.—The term "estimated itemized deductions" means the aggregate amount which he reasonably expects will be allowable as deductions under chapter 1 (other than the deductions referred to in section 151 and other than the deductions required to be taken into account in determining adjusted gross income under section 62) (other than paragraph (13) thereof) for the estimation year. In no case shall such aggregate amount be greater than the sum of (i) the amount of such deductions (or the zero bracket amount (within the meaning of section 63(d))) reflected in his return of tax under subtitle A for the taxable year preceding the estimation year or (if such a return has not been filed for such preceding taxable year at the time the withholding exemption certificate is furnished the employer) the second taxable year preceding the estimation year and (ii) the amount of his determinable additional deductions for the estimation year.

(B) ESTIMATED WAGES.—The term "estimated wages" means the aggregate amount which he reasonably expects will constitute wages for the estimation year.

(C) DETERMINABLE ADDITIONAL DEDUCTIONS.—The term "determinable additional deductions" means those estimated itemized deductions which (i) are in excess of the deductions referred to in subparagraph (A) (or the zero bracket amount) reflected on his return of tax under subtitle A for the taxable year preceding the estimation year or the preceding taxable year which can reasonably be expected to cause an increase in the amount of such deductions on the return of tax under subtitle A for the estimation year.

(D) ESTIMATION YEAR.—In the case of an employee who files his return on the basis of a calendar year, the term "estimation year" means the calendar year in which the wages are paid. In the case of an employee who files his return on a basis other than the calendar year, his estimation year, and the amounts deducted and withheld to be governed by such estimation year, shall be determined under regulations prescribed by the Secretary.

(3) SPECIAL RULES.—

(A) MARRIED INDIVIDUALS.—The number of withholding allowances to which a husband and wife are entitled under this subsection shall be determined on the basis of their combined wages and deductions. This subparagraph shall not apply to a husband and wife who filed separate returns for the taxable year preceding the estimation year and who reasonably expect to file separate returns for the estimation year.

(B) LIMITATION.—In the case of employees whose estimated wages are at levels at which the amounts deducted and withheld under this chapter generally are insufficient (taking into account a reasonable allowance for deductions and exemptions) to offset the liability for tax under chapter 1 with respect to the wages from which such amounts are deducted and withheld, the Secretary may by regulation reduce the withholding allowances to which such employees would, but for this subparagraph, be entitled under this subsection.

(C) TREATMENT OF ALLOWANCES.—For purposes of this title, any withholding allowance under this subsection shall be treated as if it were denominated a withholding exemption.

(4) AUTHORITY TO PRESCRIBE TABLES.—The Secretary may prescribe tables pursuant to which employees shall determine the number of withholding allowances to which they are entitled under this subsection (in lieu of making such determination under paragraphs (1) and (3)). Such tables shall be consistent with the provisions of paragraphs (1) and (3), except that such tables—

(A) shall provide for entitlement to withholding allowances based on reasonable wage and itemized deduction brackets,

(B) may increase or decrease the number of withholding allowances to which employees in the various wage and itemized deduction brackets would, but for this subparagraph, be entitled to the end that, to the extent practicable, amounts deducted and withheld under this chapter (i) generally do not exceed the liability for tax under chapter 1 with respect to the wages from which such amounts are deducted and withheld, and (ii) generally are sufficient to offset such liability for tax, and

(C) may take into account tax credits to which employees are entitled.

- **1978, Revenue Act of 1978 (P.L. 95-600)**

P.L. 95-600, §101(e)(2)(A):

Amended Code Sec. 3402(m)(1) by striking out "$3,200" and inserting in place thereof "$3,400". **Effective** for remuneration paid after 12-31-78.

P.L. 95-600, §101(e)(2)(B):

Amended Code Sec. 3402(m)(1) by striking out "$2,200" and inserting in place thereof "$2,300". **Effective** for remuneration paid after 12-31-78.

P.L. 95-600, §102(c)(2):

Amended Code Sec. 3402(m)(1) by striking out "$750" and inserting in place thereof "$1,000". **Effective** for remuneration paid after 12-31-78.

- **1977, Tax Reduction and Simplification Act of 1977 (P.L. 95-30)**

P.L. 95-30, §105(b)(2)-(3):

Amended Code Sec. 3402(m)(1) and (2). **Effective** for wages paid after 4-30-77. Prior to amendment, Code Sec. 3402(m)(1) and (2) read as follows:

(m) WITHHOLDING ALLOWANCES BASED ON ITEMIZED DEDUCTIONS.—

(1) GENERAL RULE.—An employee shall be entitled to withholding allowances under this subsection with respect to a payment of wages in a number equal to the number determined by dividing by $750 the excess of—

(A) his estimated itemized deductions, over

(B) an amount equal to the lesser of (i) 16 percent of his estimated wages, or (ii) $2,800 ($2,400 in the case of an individual who is not married (within the meaning of section 143) and who is not a surviving spouse (as defined in section 2(a)).

For purposes of this subsection, a fractional number shall not be taken into account unless it amounts to one-half or more, in which case it shall be increased to 1.

(2) DEFINITIONS.—For purposes of this subsection—

(A) ESTIMATED ITEMIZED DEDUCTIONS.—The term "estimated itemized deductions" means the aggregate amount which he reasonably expects will be allowable as deductions under chapter 1 (other than the deductions referred to in sections 141 and 151 and other than the deductions required to be taken into account in determining adjusted gross income under section 62) (other than paragraph (13) thereof) for the estimation year. In no case shall such aggregate amount be greater than the sum of (i) the amount of such deductions (or the amount of the standard deduction) reflected in his return of tax under subtitle A for the taxable year preceding the estimation year or (if such a return has not been filed for such preceding taxable year at the time the withholding exemption certificate is furnished the employer) the second taxable year preceding the estimation year and (ii) the amount of his determinable additional deductions for the estimation year.

(B) ESTIMATED WAGES.—The term "estimated wages" means the aggregate amount which he reasonably expects will constitute wages for the estimation year.

(C) DETERMINABLE ADDITIONAL DEDUCTIONS.—The term "determinable additional deductions" means those estimated itemized deductions which (i) are in excess of the deductions referred to in subparagraph (A) (or the standard deduction) reflected on his return of tax under subtitle A for the taxable year preceding the estimation year, and (ii) are demonstrably attributable to an identifiable event during the estimation year or the preceding taxable year which can reasonably be expected to cause an increase in the amount of such deductions on the return of tax under subtitle A for the estimation year.

(D) ESTIMATION YEAR.—In the case of an employee who files his return on the basis of a calendar year, the term "estimation year" means the calendar year in which the wages are paid. In the case of an employee who files his return on a basis other than the calendar year, his estimation year, and the amounts deducted and withheld to be governed by such estimation year, shall be determined under regulations prescribed by the Secretary.

- **1976, Tax Reform Act of 1976 (P.L. 94-455)**

P.L. 94-455, §401(d)(3):

Made permanent the amendment made to Code Sec. 3402(m)(1)(B) by P.L. 94-164. **Effective** for wages paid after 9-14-76.

WITHHOLDING FROM WAGES

P.L. 94-455, § 502(b):

Substituted "under section 62 (other than paragraph (13) thereof)" for "under section 62" in Code Sec. 3402(m)(2)(A). **Effective** for tax years beginning after 12-31-76.

P.L. 94-455, § 504(c)(3):

Amended paragraph (4) of Code Sec. 3402(m) by striking out "and" at the end of subparagraph (A), by striking out the period at the end of subparagraph (B) and inserting in lieu thereof ", and", and by adding a new subparagraph (C). **Effective** for tax years beginning after 12-31-75.

P.L. 94-455, § 1906(b)(13)(A):

Amended 1954 Code by substituting "Secretary" for "Secretary or his delegate" each place it appeared. **Effective** 2-1-77.

• **1976 (P.L. 94-414)**

P.L. 94-414, § 3(b)(2):

Substituted "October 1, 1976" for "September 15, 1976" in section 209(c) of P.L. 94-12.

• **1976 (P.L. 94-396)**

P.L. 94-396, § 2(b):

Substituted "September 15, 1976" for "September 1, 1976" in section 209(c) of P.L. 94-12.

• **1976 (P.L. 94-331)**

P.L. 94-331, § 3(a)(2):

Substituted "September 1, 1976" for "July 1, 1976" in section 209(c) of P.L. 94-12. **Effective** 6-30-76.

• **1975, Revenue Adjustment Act of 1975 (P.L. 94-164)**

P.L. 94-164, § 2(b)(2):

Substituted "$2,800" for "$2,600" and "$2,400" for "$2,300" in Code Sec. 3402(m)(1)(B). **Effective** for tax years ending after 12-31-75, and before 1-1-77.

P.L. 94-164, § 5(a)(2):

Substituted "July 1, 1976" for "January 1, 1976" in section 209(c) of P.L. 94-12.

• **1975, Tax Reduction Act of 1975 (P.L. 94-12)**

P.L. 94-12, §§ 202(b), 209(c):

Amended Code Sec. 3402(m)(1)(B) to read as follows:

(B) an amount equal to the lesser of (i) 16 percent of his estimated wages, or (ii) $2,600 ($2,300 in the case of an individual who is not married (within the meaning of section 143) and who is not a surviving spouse (as defined in section 2(a)).

Effective for wages paid after 4-30-75, and before 1-1-76. Prior to amendment, Code Sec. 3402(m)(1)(B) read as follows:

(B) an amount equal to the lesser of (i) $2,000 or (ii) 15 percent of his estimated wages.

• **1971, Revenue Act of 1971 (P.L. 92-178)**

P.L. 92-178, § 208(e):

Amended Code Sec. 3402(m)(1)(B). **Effective** for wages paid after 1-15-72. Prior to amendment, such section read as follows:

(B) an amount equal to 15 percent of his estimated wages.

P.L. 92-178, § 208(f)(1):

Amended the second sentence of Code Sec. 3402(m)(2)(A) by adding "or (if such return has not been filed for such preceding taxable year at the time the withholding exemption certificate is furnished the employer) the second taxable year preceding the estimation year" after "for the taxable year preceding the estimation year". **Effective** with respect to wages paid after 1-15-72.

P.L. 92-178, § 208(f)(2):

Amended Code Sec. 3402(m)(2)(D). **Effective** with respect to wages paid after 1-15-72. Prior to amendment, such section read as follows:

(D) Estimation year.—In the case of an employee who files his return on the basis of a calendar year, the term `estimation year' means—

(i) with respect to payments of wages after April 30 and on or before December 31 of any calendar year, such calendar year, and

(ii) with respect to payments of wages on or after January 1 and before May 1 of any calendar year, the preceding calendar year (except that with respect to an exemption certificate furnished by an employee after he has filed his return for the preceding calendar year, such term means the current calendar year).

In the case of an employee who files his return on a basis other than the calendar year, his estimation year, and the amounts deducted and withheld to be governed by such estimation year, shall be determined under regulations prescribed by the Secretary or his delegate.

P.L. 92-178, § 208(f)(3):

Amended Code Sec. 3402(m)(3) by repealing subparagraphs (B) and (C) and by redesignating former subparagraphs (D) and (E) as (B) and (C). **Effective** with respect to wages paid after 1-15-72. Prior to repeal, subparagraphs (B) and (C) read as follows:

(B) Only one certificate to be in effect.—In the case of any employee, withholding allowances under this subsection may not be claimed with more than one employer at any one time.

(C) Termination of effectiveness.—In the case of an employee who files his return on the basis of a calendar year, that portion of a withholding exemption certificate which relates to allowances under this subsection shall not be effective with respect to payments of wages after the first April 30 following the close of the estimation year on which it is based.

• **1969, Tax Reform Act of 1969 (P.L. 91-172)**

P.L. 91-172, § 805(e):

Amended Code Sec. 3402(m) by redesignating old subparagraph (2)(C) as (2)(D), and by inserting that portion of subsection (m) as precedes redesignated subparagraph (2)(D) in lieu of the following:

(m) Withholding Allowances Based on Itemized Deductions.—

(1) General rule.—An employee shall be entitled to withholding allowances under this subsection with respect to a payment of wages in a number equal to the number determined by dividing by $700 the excess of—

(A) his estimated itemized deductions, over

(B) an amount equal to the sum of 10 percent of the first $7,500 of his estimated wages and 17 percent of the remainder of his estimated wages.

For purposes of this subsection, fractional numbers shall not be taken into account.

(2) Definitions.—For purposes of this subsection—

(A) Estimated itemized deductions.—The term "estimated itemized deductions" means the aggregate amount which he reasonably expects will be allowable as deductions under chapter 1 (other than the deductions referred to in sections 141 and 151 and other than the deductions required to be taken into account in determining adjusted gross income under section 62) for the estimation year. In no case shall such aggregate amount be greater than (i) the amount of such deductions shown on his return of tax under subtitle A for the taxable year preceding the estimation year, or (ii) in the case of an employee who did not show such deductions on his return for such preceding taxable year, an amount equal to the lesser of $1,000 or 10 percent of the wages shown on his return for such preceding taxable year.

(B) Estimated wages.—The term "estimated wages" means the aggregate amount which he reasonably expects will constitute wages for the estimation year. In no case shall such aggregate amount be less than the amount of wages shown on his return for the taxable year preceding the estimation year.

Effective with respect to remuneration paid after 12-31-69.

• **1966, Tax Adjustment Act of 1966 (P.L. 89-368)**

P.L. 89-368, § 101(e):

Added Code Sec. 3402(m). **Effective** with respect to remuneration paid after 12-31-66, but only with respect to withholding exemptions based on estimation years beginning after such date.

[Sec. 3402(n)]

(n) EMPLOYEES INCURRING NO INCOME TAX LIABILITY.—Notwithstanding any other provision of this section, an employer shall not be required to deduct and withhold any tax under this chapter upon a payment of wages to an employee if there is in effect with respect to such payment a withholding allowance certificate (in such form and containing such other information as the Secretary may prescribe) furnished to the employer by the employee certifying that the employee—

(1) incurred no liability for income tax imposed under subtitle A for his preceding taxable year, and

(2) anticipates that he will incur no liability for income tax imposed under subtitle A for his current taxable year.

The Secretary shall by regulations provide for the coordination of the provisions of this subsection with the provisions of subsection (f).

Amendments

• **2017, Tax Cuts and Jobs Act (P.L. 115-97)**

P.L. 115-97, § 11041(c)(2)(C):

Amended Code Sec. 3402(n) by striking "exemption" each place it appears and inserting "allowance". **Effective** generally for tax years beginning after 12-31-2017. For a special rule, see Act Sec. 11041(f)(2), below.

P.L. 115-97, § 11041(f)(2), provides:

(2) WAGE WITHHOLDING.—The Secretary of the Treasury may administer section 3402 for taxable years beginning before January 1, 2019, without regard to the amendments made by subsections (a) and (c).

• **1976, Tax Reform Act of 1976 (P.L. 94-455)**

P.L. 94-455, § 1906(b)(13)(A):

Amended 1954 Code by substituting "Secretary" for "Secretary or his delegate" each place it appeared. **Effective** 2-1-77.

• **1969, Tax Reform Act of 1969 (P.L. 91-172)**

P.L. 91-172, § 805(f)(1):

Added Code Sec. 3402(n). **Effective** for wages paid after 4-30-70.

[Sec. 3402(o)]

(o) EXTENSION OF WITHHOLDING TO CERTAIN PAYMENTS OTHER THAN WAGES.—

(1) GENERAL RULE.—For purposes of this chapter (and so much of subtitle F as relates to this chapter)—

WITHHOLDING FROM WAGES

(A) any supplemental unemployment compensation benefit paid to an individual,

(B) any payment of an annuity to an individual, if at the time the payment is made a request that such annuity be subject to withholding under this chapter is in effect, and

(C) any payment to an individual of sick pay which does not constitute wages (determined without regard to this subsection), if at the time the payment is made a request that such sick pay be subject to withholding under this chapter is in effect,

shall be treated as if it were a payment of wages by an employer to an employee for a payroll period.

(2) DEFINITIONS.—

(A) SUPPLEMENTAL UNEMPLOYMENT COMPENSATION BENEFITS.—For purposes of paragraph (1), the term "supplemental unemployment compensation benefit" means amounts which are paid to an employee, pursuant to a plan to which the employer is a party, because of an employee's involuntary separation from employment (whether or not such separation is temporary), resulting directly from a reduction in force, the discontinuance of a plant or operation, or other similar conditions, but only to the extent such benefits are includible in the employee's gross income.

(B) ANNUITY.—For purposes of this subsection, the term "annuity" means any amount paid to an individual as a pension or annuity.

(C) SICK PAY.—For purposes of this subsection, the term "sick pay" means any amount which—

(i) is paid to an employee pursuant to a plan to which the employer is a party, and

(ii) constitutes remuneration or a payment in lieu of remuneration for any period during which the employee is temporarily absent from work on account of sickness or personal injuries.

(3) AMOUNT WITHHELD FROM ANNUITY PAYMENTS OR SICK PAY.—If a payee makes a request that an annuity or any sick pay be subject to withholding under this chapter, the amount to be deducted and withheld under this chapter from any payment to which such request applies shall be an amount (not less than a minimum amount determined under regulations prescribed by the Secretary) specified by the payee in such request. The amount deducted and withheld with respect to a payment which is greater or less than a full payment shall bear the same relation to the specified amount as such payment bears to a full payment.

(4) REQUEST FOR WITHHOLDING.—A request that an annuity or any sick pay be subject to withholding under this chapter—

(A) shall be made by the payee in writing to the person making the payments and shall contain the social security number of the payee,

(B) shall specify the amount to be deducted and withheld from each full payment, and

(C) shall take effect—

(i) in the case of sick pay, with respect to payments made more than 7 days after the date on which such request is furnished to the payor, or

(ii) in the case of an annuity, at such time (after the date on which such request is furnished to the payor) as the Secretary shall by regulations prescribe.

Such a request may be changed or terminated by furnishing to the person making the payments a written statement of change or termination which shall take effect in the same manner as provided in subparagraph (C). At the election of the payor, any such request (or statement of change or revocation) may take effect earlier than as provided in subparagraph (C).

(5) SPECIAL RULE FOR SICK PAY PAID PURSUANT TO CERTAIN COLLECTIVE-BARGAINING AGREEMENTS.—In the case of any sick pay paid pursuant to a collective-bargaining agreement between employee representatives and one or more employers which contains a provision specifying that this paragraph is to apply to sick pay paid pursuant to such agreement and contains a provision for determining the amount to be deducted and withheld from each payment of such sick pay—

(A) the requirement of paragraph (1)(C) that a request for withholding be in effect shall not apply, and

(B) except as provided in subsection (n), the amounts to be deducted and withheld under this chapter shall be determined in accordance with such agreement.

The preceding sentence shall not apply with respect to sick pay paid pursuant to any agreement to any individual unless the social security number of such individual is furnished to the payor and the payor is furnished with such information as is necessary to determine whether the payment is pursuant to the agreement and to determine the amount to be deducted and withheld.

(6) COORDINATION WITH WITHHOLDING ON DESIGNATED DISTRIBUTIONS UNDER SECTION 3405.—This subsection shall not apply to any amount which is a designated distribution (within the meaning of section 3405(e)(1)).

Amendments

- **1992, Unemployment Compensation Amendments of 1992 (P.L. 102-318)**

P.L. 102-318, § 522(b)(2)(D):

Amended Code Sec. 3402(o)(6) by striking "section 3405(d)(1)" and inserting "section 3405(e)(1)". **Effective** for distributions after 12-31-92.

- **1982, Tax Equity and Fiscal Responsibility Act of 1982 (P.L. 97-248)**

P.L. 97-248, § 334(d):

Added new paragraph (6) of Code Sec. 3402(o). **Effective**, generally, for designated distributions made after 12-31-82. However, for applying the rules to periodic payments which commence prior to 1-1-83, see the amendment note for P.L. 97-248, under Code Sec. 3405.

- **1980 (P.L. 96-601)**

P.L. 96-601, § 4(a):

Amended Code Sec. 3402(o)(1) by striking out "and" at the end of subparagraph (A), by adding "and" at the end of subparagraph (B), and by adding a new subparagraph (C). **Effective** for payments made on or after 5-1-81.

P.L. 96-601, § 4(b):

Amended Code Sec. 3402(o) by striking out paragraph (3) and inserting in lieu thereof new paragraphs (3), (4) and (5). **Effective** for payments made on or after 5-1-81. Prior to amendment, Code Sec. 3402(o)(3) provided:

(3) REQUEST FOR WITHHOLDING.—A request that an annuity be subject to withholding under this chapter shall be made by the payee in writing to the person making the annuity payments, shall be accompanied by a withholding exemption certificate, executed in accordance with the provisions of subsection (f)(2), and shall take effect as provided in subsection (f)(3). Such a request may, notwithstanding the provisions of subsection (f)(4), be terminated by furnishing to the person making the payments a written statement of termination which shall be treated as a withholding exemption certificate for purposes of subsection (f)(3)(B).

P.L. 96-601, § 4(c):

Amended Code Sec. 3402(o)(2) by adding at the end thereof a new subparagraph (C). **Effective** for payments made on or after 5-1-81.

P.L. 96-601, § 4(d):

Amended Code Sec. 3402(o)(2)(B) by striking out ", but only to the extent that the amount is includible in the gross income of such individual" after "pension or annuity". **Effective** for payments made on or after 5-1-81.

- **1969, Tax Reform Act of 1969 (P.L. 91-172)**

P.L. 91-172, § 805(g):

Added Code Sec. 3402(o). **Effective** for payments made after 12-31-70.

[Sec. 3402(p)]

(p) VOLUNTARY WITHHOLDING AGREEMENTS.—

(1) CERTAIN FEDERAL PAYMENTS.—

(A) IN GENERAL.—If, at the time a specified Federal payment is made to any person, a request by such person is in effect that such payment be subject to withholding under this chapter, then for purposes of this chapter and so much of subtitle F as relates to this chapter, such payment shall be treated as if it were a payment of wages by an employer to an employee.

WITHHOLDING FROM WAGES

(B) AMOUNT WITHHELD.—The amount to be deducted and withheld under this chapter from any payment to which any request under subparagraph (A) applies shall be an amount equal to the percentage of such payment specified in such request. Such a request shall apply to any payment only if the percentage specified is 7 percent, any percentage applicable to any of the 3 lowest income brackets in the table under section 1(c), or such other percentage as is permitted under regulations prescribed by the Secretary.

(C) SPECIFIED FEDERAL PAYMENTS.—For purposes of this paragraph, the term "specified Federal payment" means—

(i) any payment of a social security benefit (as defined in section 86(d)),

(ii) any payment referred to in the second sentence of section 451(d) which is treated as insurance proceeds,

(iii) any amount which is includible in gross income under section 77(a), and

(iv) any other payment made pursuant to Federal law which is specified by the Secretary for purposes of this paragraph.

(D) REQUESTS FOR WITHHOLDING.—Rules similar to the rules that apply to annuities under subsection (o)(4) shall apply to requests under this paragraph and paragraph (2).

(2) VOLUNTARY WITHHOLDING ON UNEMPLOYMENT BENEFITS.—If, at the time a payment of unemployment compensation (as defined in section 85(b)) is made to any person, a request by such person is in effect that such payment be subject to withholding under this chapter, then for purposes of this chapter and so much of subtitle F as relates to this chapter, such payment shall be treated as if it were a payment of wages by an employer to an employee. The amount to be deducted and withheld under this chapter from any payment to which any request under this paragraph applies shall be an amount equal to 10 percent of such payment.

(3) AUTHORITY FOR OTHER VOLUNTARY WITHHOLDING.—The Secretary is authorized by regulations to provide for withholding—

(A) from remuneration for services performed by an employee for the employee's employer which (without regard to this paragraph) does not constitute wages, and

(B) from any other type of payment with respect to which the Secretary finds that withholding would be appropriate under the provisions of this chapter,

if the employer and employee, or the person making and the person receiving such other type of payment, agree to such withholding. Such agreement shall be in such form and manner as the Secretary may by regulations prescribe. For purposes of this chapter (and so much of subtitle F as relates to this chapter), remuneration or other payments with respect to which such agreement is made shall be treated as if they were wages paid by an employer to an employee to the extent that such remuneration is paid or other payments are made during the period for which the agreement is in effect.

Amendments

• **2013, American Taxpayer Relief Act of 2012 (P.L. 112-240)**

P.L. 112-240, §101(a)(1) and (3), provides:

SEC. 101. PERMANENT EXTENSION AND MODIFICATION OF 2001 TAX RELIEF.

(a) PERMANENT EXTENSION.—

(1) IN GENERAL.—The Economic Growth and Tax Relief Reconciliation Act of 2001 is amended by striking title IX.

* * *

(3) EFFECTIVE DATE.—The amendments made by this subsection shall apply to taxable, plan, or limitation years beginning after December 31, 2012, and estates of decedents dying, gifts made, or generation skipping transfers after December 31, 2012.

• **2001, Economic Growth and Tax Relief Reconciliation Act of 2001 (P.L. 107-16)**

P.L. 107-16, §101(c)(6):

Amended Code Sec. 3402(p)(1)(B) by striking "7, 15, 28, or 31 percent" and inserting "7 percent, any percentage applicable to any of the 3 lowest income brackets in the table under section 1(c),". For the **effective** date of the above amendment, see Act Sec. 101(d)(2), below.

P.L. 107-16, §101(c)(7):

Amended Code Sec. 3402(p)(2) by striking "15 percent" and inserting "10 percent". For the **effective** date of the above amendment, see Act Sec. 101(d)(2), below.

P.L. 107-16, §101(d)(2), provides:

(2) AMENDMENTS TO WITHHOLDING PROVISIONS.—The amendments made by paragraphs (6), (7), (8), (9), (10), and (11) of subsection (c) shall apply to amounts paid after the 60th day after the date of the enactment of this Act. References to income brackets and rates of tax in such paragraphs shall be applied without regard to section 1(i)(1)(D) of the Internal Revenue Code of 1986.

P.L. 107-16, §901(a)-(b), as amended by P.L. 111-312, §101(a)(1), provides [but see P.L. 112-240, §101(a)(1) and (3), above]:

SEC. 901. SUNSET OF PROVISIONS OF ACT.

(a) IN GENERAL.—All provisions of, and amendments made by, this Act shall not apply—

(1) to taxable, plan, or limitation years beginning after December 31, 2012, or

(2) in the case of title V, to estates of decedents dying, gifts made, or generation skipping transfers, after December 31, 2012.

(b) APPLICATION OF CERTAIN LAWS.—The Internal Revenue Code of 1986 and the Employee Retirement Income Security Act of 1974 shall be applied and administered to years, estates, gifts, and transfers described in subsection (a) as if the provisions and amendments described in subsection (a) had never been enacted.

• **1994, Uruguay Round Agreements Act (P.L. 103-465)**

P.L. 103-465, §702(a):

Amended Code Sec. 3402(p). **Effective** for payments made after 12-31-96. Prior to amendment, Code Sec. 3402(p) read as follows:

(p) VOLUNTARY WITHHOLDING AGREEMENTS.—The Secretary is authorized by regulations to provide for withholding—

(1) from remuneration for services performed by an employee for his employer which (without regard to this subsection) does not constitute wages, and

(2) from any other type of payment with respect to which the Secretary finds that withholding would be appropriate under the provisions of this chapter,

if the employer and the employee, or in the case of any other type of payment the person making and the person receiving the payment, agree to such withholding. Such agreement shall be made in such form and manner as the Secretary may by regulations provide. For purposes of this chapter (and so much of subtitle F as relates to this chapter) remuneration or other payments with respect to which such agreement is made shall be treated as if they were wages paid by an employer to an employee to the extent that such remuneration is paid or other payments are made during the period for which the agreement is in effect.

• **1976, Tax Reform Act of 1976 (P.L. 94-455)**

P.L. 94-455, §1906(b)(13)(A):

Amended 1954 Code by substituting "Secretary" for "Secretary or his delegate" each place it appeared. **Effective** 2-1-77.

• **1969, Tax Reform Act of 1969 (P.L. 91-172)**

P.L. 91-172, §805(g):

Added Code Sec. 3402(p). **Effective** for payments made after 6-30-70.

[Sec. 3402(q)]

(q) EXTENSION OF WITHHOLDING TO CERTAIN GAMBLING WINNINGS.—

(1) GENERAL RULE.—Every person, including the Government of the United States, a State, or a political subdivision thereof, or any instrumentalities of the foregoing, making any payment of winnings which are subject to withholding shall deduct and withhold from such payment a tax in an amount equal to the product of the third lowest rate of tax applicable under section 1(c) and such payment.

(2) EXEMPTION WHERE TAX OTHERWISE WITHHELD.—In the case of any payment of winnings which are subject to withholding made to a nonresident alien individual or a foreign corporation, the tax imposed under paragraph (1) shall not apply to any such payment subject to tax under section 1441(a) (relating to withholding on nonresident aliens) or tax under section 1442(a) (relating to withholding on foreign corporations).

(3) WINNINGS WHICH ARE SUBJECT TO WITHHOLDING.—For purposes of this subsection, the term "winnings which are subject to withholding" means proceeds from a wager determined in accordance with the following:

(A) IN GENERAL.—Except as provided in subparagraphs (B) and (C), proceeds of more than $5,000 from a wagering transaction, if the amount of such proceeds is at least 300 times as large as the amount wagered.

WITHHOLDING FROM WAGES

(B) STATE-CONDUCTED LOTTERIES.—Proceeds of more than $5,000 from a wager placed in a lottery conducted by an agency of a State acting under authority of State law, but only if such wager is placed with the State agency conducting such lottery, or with its authorized employees or agents.

(C) SWEEPSTAKES, WAGERING POOLS, CERTAIN PARIMUTUEL POOLS, JAI ALAI, AND LOTTERIES.—Proceeds of more than $5,000 from—

(i) a wager placed in a sweepstakes, wagering pool, or lottery (other than a wager described in subparagraph (B)), or

(ii) a wagering transaction in a parimutuel pool with respect to horse races, dog races, or jai alai if the amount of such proceeds is at least 300 times as large as the amount wagered.

(4) RULES FOR DETERMINING PROCEEDS FROM A WAGER.—For purposes of this subsection—

(A) proceeds from a wager shall be determined by reducing the amount received by the amount of the wager, and

(B) proceeds which are not money shall be taken into account at their fair market value.

(5) EXEMPTION FOR BINGO, KENO, AND SLOT MACHINES.—The tax imposed under paragraph (1) shall not apply to winnings from a slot machine, keno, and bingo.

(6) STATEMENT BY RECIPIENT.—Every person who is to receive a payment of winnings which are subject to withholding shall furnish the person making such payment a statement, made under the penalties of perjury, containing the name, address, and taxpayer identification number of the person receiving the payment and of each person entitled to any portion of such payment.

(7) COORDINATION WITH OTHER SECTIONS.—For purposes of sections 3403 and 3404 and for purposes of so much of subtitle F (except section 7205) as relates to this chapter, payments to any person of winnings which are subject to withholding shall be treated as if they were wages paid by an employer to an employee.

Amendments

• **2013, American Taxpayer Relief Act of 2012 (P.L. 112-240)**

P.L. 112-240, § 101(a)(1) and (3), provides:

SEC. 101. PERMANENT EXTENSION AND MODIFICATION OF 2001 TAX RELIEF.

(a) PERMANENT EXTENSION.—

(1) IN GENERAL.—The Economic Growth and Tax Relief Reconciliation Act of 2001 is amended by striking title IX.

* * *

(3) EFFECTIVE DATE.—The amendments made by this subsection shall apply to taxable, plan, or limitation years beginning after December 31, 2012, and estates of decedents dying, gifts made, or generation skipping transfers after December 31, 2012.

• **2001, Economic Growth and Tax Relief Reconciliation Act of 2001 (P.L. 107-16)**

P.L. 107-16, § 101(c)(8):

Amended Code Sec. 3402(q)(1) by striking "equal to 28 percent of such payment" and inserting "equal to the product of the third lowest rate of tax applicable under section 1(c) and such payment". For the **effective** date of the above amendment, see Act Sec. 101(d)(2) in the amendment notes to Code Sec. 3402(p).

P.L. 107-16, § 901(a)-(b), as amended by P.L. 111-312, § 101(a)(1), provides [but see P.L. 112-240, § 101(a)(1) and (3), above]:

SEC. 901. SUNSET OF PROVISIONS OF ACT.

(a) IN GENERAL.—All provisions of, and amendments made by, this Act shall not apply—

(1) to taxable, plan, or limitation years beginning after December 31, 2012, or

(2) in the case of title V, to estates of decedents dying, gifts made, or generation skipping transfers, after December 31, 2012.

(b) APPLICATION OF CERTAIN LAWS.—The Internal Revenue Code of 1986 and the Employee Retirement Income Security Act of 1974 shall be applied and administered to years, estates, gifts, and transfers described in subsection (a) as if the provisions and amendments described in subsection (a) had never been enacted.

• **1992, Energy Policy Act of 1992 (P.L. 102-486)**

P.L. 102-486, § 1934(a):

Amended Code Sec. 3402(q)(1) by striking "20 percent" and inserting "28 percent". **Effective** for payments received after 12-31-92.

P.L. 102-486, § 1942(a):

Amended Code Sec. 3402(q)(3)(A) and (C) by striking "$1,000" and inserting "$5,000". **Effective** for payments of winnings after 12-31-92.

• **1977, Tax Reduction and Simplification Act of 1977 (P.L. 95-30)**

P.L. 95-30, § 405(a):

Amended Code Sec. 3402(q)(3)(C). **Effective** for payments made after 4-30-77. Prior to amendment, Code Sec. 3402(q)(3)(C) read as follows:

(C) SWEEPSTAKES, WAGERING POOLS, AND OTHER LOTTERIES.—Proceeds of more than $1,000 from a wager placed in a sweepstake, wagering pool, or lottery (other than a wager described in subparagraph (B)).

• **1976, Tax Reform Act of 1976 (P.L. 94-455)**

P.L. 94-455, § 1207(d), (f)(3):

Added Code Sec. 3402(q). **Effective** for payments of winnings made after the 90th day after 10-4-76.

[Sec. 3402(r)]

(r) EXTENSION OF WITHHOLDING TO CERTAIN TAXABLE PAYMENTS OF INDIAN CASINO PROFITS.—

(1) IN GENERAL.—Every person, including an Indian tribe, making a payment to a member of an Indian tribe from the net revenues of any class II or class III gaming activity conducted or licensed by such tribe shall deduct and withhold from such payment a tax in an amount equal to such payment's proportionate share of the annualized tax.

(2) EXCEPTION.—The tax imposed by paragraph (1) shall not apply to any payment to the extent that the payment, when annualized, does not exceed an amount equal to the sum of—

(A) the basic standard deduction (as defined in section 63(c)) for an individual to whom section 63(c)(2)(C) applies, and

(B) the exemption amount (as defined in section 151(d)).

(3) ANNUALIZED TAX.—For purposes of paragraph (1), the term "annualized tax" means, with respect to any payment, the amount of tax which would be imposed by section 1(c) (determined without regard to any rate of tax in excess of the fourth lowest rate of tax applicable under section 1(c)) on an amount of taxable income equal to the excess of—

(A) the annualized amount of such payment, over

(B) the amount determined under paragraph (2).

(4) CLASSES OF GAMING ACTIVITIES, ETC.—For purposes of this subsection, terms used in paragraph (1) which are defined in section 4 of the Indian Gaming Regulatory Act (25 U.S.C. 2701 et seq.), as in effect on the date of the enactment of this subsection, shall have the respective meanings given such terms by such section.

(5) ANNUALIZATION.—Payments shall be placed on an annualized basis under regulations prescribed by the Secretary.

(6) ALTERNATE WITHHOLDING PROCEDURES.—At the election of an Indian tribe, the tax imposed by this subsection on any payment made by such tribe shall be determined in accordance with such tables or computational procedures as may be specified in regulations prescribed by the Secretary (in lieu of in accordance with paragraphs (2) and (3)).

(7) COORDINATION WITH OTHER SECTIONS.—For purposes of this chapter and so much of subtitle F as relates to this chapter, payments to any person which are subject to withholding under this subsection shall be treated as if they were wages paid by an employer to an employee.

Amendments

• **2013, American Taxpayer Relief Act of 2012 (P.L. 112-240)**

P.L. 112-240, § 101(a)(1) and (3), provides:

SEC. 101. PERMANENT EXTENSION AND MODIFICATION OF 2001 TAX RELIEF.

(a) PERMANENT EXTENSION.—

(1) IN GENERAL.—The Economic Growth and Tax Relief Reconciliation Act of 2001 is amended by striking title IX.

* * *

(3) EFFECTIVE DATE.—The amendments made by this subsection shall apply to taxable, plan, or limitation years beginning after December 31, 2012, and estates of

WITHHOLDING FROM WAGES

decedents dying, gifts made, or generation skipping transfers after December 31, 2012.

- **2001, Economic Growth and Tax Relief Reconciliation Act of 2001 (P.L. 107-16)**

P.L. 107-16, §101(c)(9):

Amended Code Sec. 3402(r)(3) by striking "31 percent" and inserting "the fourth lowest rate of tax applicable under section 1(c)". For the **effective** date of the above amendment, see Act Sec. 101(d)(2) in the amendment notes to Code Sec. 3402(p).

P.L. 107-16, §901(a)-(b), as amended by P.L. 111-312, §101(a)(1), provides [but see P.L. 112-240, §101(a)(1) and (3), above]:

SEC. 901. SUNSET OF PROVISIONS OF ACT.

(a) IN GENERAL.—All provisions of, and amendments made by, this Act shall not apply—

(1) to taxable, plan, or limitation years beginning after December 31, 2012, or

(2) in the case of title V, to estates of decedents dying, gifts made, or generation skipping transfers, after December 31, 2012.

(b) APPLICATION OF CERTAIN LAWS.—The Internal Revenue Code of 1986 and the Employee Retirement Income Security Act of 1974 shall be applied and administered to years, estates, gifts, and transfers described in subsection (a) as if the provisions and amendments described in subsection (a) had never been enacted.

- **1994, Uruguay Round Agreements Act (P.L. 103-465)**

P.L. 103-465, §701(a):

Amended Code Sec. 3402 by inserting after subsection (q) a new subsection (r). **Effective** for payments made after 12-31-94.

- **1986, Tax Reform Act of 1986 (P.L. 99-514)**

P.L. 99-514, §1303(b)(4):

Repealed Code Sec. 3402(r). **Effective** 10-22-86. Prior to repeal, Code Sec. 3402(r) read as follows:

(r) EXTENSION OF WITHHOLDING OF GSOC DISTRIBUTIONS.—

(1) GENERAL RULE.—An electing GSOC making any distribution to its shareholders shall deduct and withhold from such payment a tax in an amount equal to 25 percent of such payment.

(2) COORDNATION WITH OTHER SECTIONS.—For purposes of section 3403 and 3404 and for purposes of so much of subtitle F (except section 7205) as relates to this chapter, distributions of an electing GSOC to any shareholder which are subject to withholding shall be treated as if they were wages paid by an employer to an employee.

- **1978, Revenue Act of 1978 (P.L. 95-600)**

P.L. 95-600, §601(b)(2), (d):

Added Code Sec. 3402(r). **Effective** for corporations chartered after 12-31-78, and before 1-1-84.

[Sec. 3402(s)]

(s) EXEMPTION FROM WITHHOLDING FOR ANY VEHICLE FRINGE BENEFIT.—

(1) EMPLOYER ELECTION NOT TO WITHHOLD.—The employer may elect not to deduct and withhold any tax under this chapter with respect to any vehicle fringe benefit provided to any employee if such employee is notified by the employer of such election (at such time and in such manner as the Secretary shall by regulations prescribe). The preceding sentence shall not apply to any vehicle fringe benefit unless the amount of such benefit is included by the employer on a statement timely furnished under section 6051.

(2) EMPLOYER MUST FURNISH W-2.—Any vehicle fringe benefit shall be treated as wages from which amounts are required to be deducted and withheld under this chapter for purposes of section 6051.

(3) VEHICLE FRINGE BENEFIT.—For purposes of this subsection, the term "vehicle fringe benefit" means any fringe benefit—

(A) which constitutes wages (as defined in section 3401), and

(B) which consists of providing a highway motor vehicle for the use of the employee.

Amendments

- **1985 (P.L. 99-44)**

P.L. 99-44, §3:

Amended Code Sec. 3402 by adding at the end thereof new subsection (s). **Effective** 1-1-85.

P.L. 99-44, §5, provides:

Not later than October 1, 1985, the Secretary of the Treasury or his delegate shall prescribe regulations to carry out the provisions of this Act which shall fully reflect such provisions.

- **1983, Interest and Dividend Tax Compliance Act of 1983 (P.L. 98-67)**

P.L. 98-67, §104(d)(3):

Repealed Code Sec. 3402(s), which was added by P.L. 97-248. **Effective** with respect to payments made after 12-31-83. Prior to repeal, Code Sec. 3402(s) read as follows:

(s) EXTENSION OF WITHHOLDING TO CERTAIN PAYMENTS WHERE IDENTIFYING NUMBER NOT FURNISHED OR INACCURATE.—

(1) IN GENERAL.—If, in the case of any backup withholding payment—

(A) the payee fails to furnish his taxpayer identification number to the payor, or

(B) the Secretary notifies the payor that the number furnished by the payee is incorrect, then the payor shall deduct and withhold from such payment a tax equal to 15 percent of such payment.

(2) PERIOD FOR WHICH WITHHOLDING IS IN EFFECT.—

(A) FAILURE TO FURNISH NUMBER.—In the case of any failure described in subparagraph (A) of paragraph (1), paragraph (1) shall apply to any backup withholding payment made during the period during which the taxpayer identification number has not been furnished.

(B) NOTIFICATION OF INCORRECT NUMBER.—In any case where there is a notification described in subparagraph (B) of paragraph (1), paragraph (1) shall apply to any backup withholding payment made—

(i) after the close of the 15th day after the day on which the payor was so notified, and

(ii) before the payee furnishes another taxpayer identification number.

(C) 15-DAY GRACE PERIODS.—

(i) AFTER CORRECTION.—Unless the payor otherwise elects, paragraph (1) shall also apply to any backup withholding payment made after the close of the period described in subparagraph (A) or (B) (as the case may be) and before the 16th day after the close of such period.

(ii) AFTER NOTIFICATION.—If the payor so elects, paragraph (1) shall also apply to any backup withholding payment made during the 15-day period described in clause (i) of subparagraph (B).

(3) BACKUP WITHHOLDING PAYMENTS.—

(A) IN GENERAL.—For purposes of this subsection, the term "backup withholding payment" means any payment of a kind, and to a payee, required to be shown on a return required under—

(i) section 6041 (a) or (b) (relating to certain information at source),

(ii) section 6041A(a) (relating to returns regarding payments to nonemployees),

(iii) section 6042(a) (relating to payments of dividends),

(iv) section 6044 (relating to returns regarding patronage dividends) but only to the extent of payments of money,

(v) section 6045 (relating to returns of brokers),

(vi) section 6049(a) (relating to payments of interest), or

(vii) section 6050A (relating to reporting requirements of certain fishing boat operators), but only to the extent of payments of the proceeds of the catch.

(B) SPECIAL RULE.—For purposes of this subsection, the determination of whether any payment is of a kind required to be shown on a return described in subparagraph (A) shall be made without regard to any minimum amount which must be paid before a return is required.

(4) PAYMENTS MUST AGGREGATE $600 BEFORE WITHHOLDING REQUIRED FROM PAYMENTS DESCRIBED IN SECTION 6041(a) OR 6041 a.—In the case of any payment which is of a kind required to be shown on a return required under section 6041(a) or 6041A(a) and which is made during any calendar year, no amount shall be deducted and withheld with respect to such payment unless—

(A) the aggregate amount of such payment and all previous such payments to the payee involved during such calendar year equals or exceeds $600,

(B) the payor was required under section 6041(a) or 6041A(a) to file a return for the preceding calendar year with respect to payments to the payee involved, or

(C) during the preceding calendar year the payor made backup withholding payments to the payee with respect to which amounts were required to be deducted and withheld under paragraph (1).

(5) DEFINITIONS AND SPECIAL RULES.—For purposes of this subsection—

(A) OBVIOUSLY INCORRECT NUMBER.—A payee shall be treated as failing to furnish his taxpayer identification number if the number furnished does not contain the proper number of digits.

(B) PAYEE FURNISHES 2 INCORRECT NUMBERS.—If the payee furnishes a payor 2 incorrect numbers, the payor shall, after receiving notice of the second incorrect number, treat the payee as not having furnished another taxpayer identification number under paragraph (2)(B)(ii) until the day on which the payor receives notification from the Secretary that a correct taxpayer identification number has been furnished.

(C) EXCEPTION FOR PAYMENTS TO CERTAIN PAYEES.—Paragraph (1) shall not apply to any payment made to—

(i) the United States (as defined in section 3455(a)(3)),

(ii) any State (as defined in section 3455(a)(2)),

(iii) an organization which is exempt from taxation under section 501(a),

(iv) any foreign government (as defined in section 3455(a)(4)) or international organization (as defined in section 3455(a)(5)), or

(v) any other person specified in regulations.

(D) TAXPAYER IDENTIFICATION NUMBER.—The term "taxpayer identification number" means the identifying number assigned to a person under section 6109.

(E) AMOUNTS FOR WHICH WITHHOLDING OTHERWISE REQUIRED.—No tax shall be deducted or withheld under this subsection with respect to any amount for which withholding is otherwise required by this title.

(F) EXEMPTION WHILE WAITING FOR NUMBER.—The Secretary shall prescribe regulations for exemptions from the tax imposed by paragraph (1) during periods during which a person is waiting for receipt of a taxpayer identification number.

WITHHOLDING FROM WAGES

(G) NOMINEES.—In the case of a backup withholding payment described in clause (i) or (v) of paragraph (3)(A) to a nominee, in the manner provided in regulations, both the nominee and the ultimate payee shall be treated as the payee.

(H) REQUIREMENT OF NOTICE TO PAYEE.—Whenever the Secretary notifies a payor under paragraph (1)(B) that the taxpayer identification number furnished by any payee is incorrect, the Secretary shall at the same time furnish a copy of such notice to the payor, and the payor shall promptly furnish such copy to the payee.

(I) REQUIREMENT OF NOTICE TO SECRETARY.—If the Secretary notifies a payor under paragraph (1)(B) that the taxpayer identification number furnished by any payee is incorrect and such payee subsequently furnishes another taxpayer identification number to the payor, the payor shall promptly notify the Secretary of the other taxpayer identification number so furnished.

(J) COORDINATION WITH OTHER SECTIONS.—For purposes of section 31, this chapter (other than subsection (n) of this section), and so much of subtitle F (other than section 7205) as relates to this chapter, payments which are subject to withholding under this subsection shall be treated as if they were wages paid by an employer to an employee.

• 1982, Tax Equity and Fiscal Responsibility Act of 1982 (P.L. 97-248)

P.L. 97-248, §317(a):

Added Code Sec. 3402(s). **Effective** for amounts paid after 12-31-83.

[Sec. 3402(t)]

(t) RATE OF WITHHOLDING FOR CERTAIN STOCK.—In the case of any qualified stock (as defined in section 83(i)(2)) with respect to which an election is made under section 83(i)—

(1) the rate of tax under subsection (a) shall not be less than the maximum rate of tax in effect under section 1, and

(2) such stock shall be treated for purposes of section 3501(b) in the same manner as a non-cash fringe benefit.

Amendments

• 2017, Tax Cuts and Jobs Act (P.L. 115-97)

P.L. 115-97, §13603(b)(2):

Amended Code Sec. 3402 by adding at the end a new subsection (t). **Effective** generally for stock attributable to options exercised, or restricted stock units settled, after 12-31-2017. For a transition rule, see Act Sec. 13603(g), below.

Amendments

• 2011, 3% Withholding Repeal and Job Creation Act (P.L. 112-56)

P.L. 112-56, §102(a):

Amended Code Sec. 3402 by striking subsection (t). **Effective** for payments made after 12-31-2011. Prior to being stricken, Code Sec. 3402(t) read as follows:

(t) EXTENSION OF WITHHOLDING TO CERTAIN PAYMENTS MADE BY GOVERNMENT ENTITIES.—

(1) GENERAL RULE.—The Government of the United States, every State, every political subdivision thereof, and every instrumentality of the foregoing (including multi-State agencies) making any payment to any person providing any property or services (including any payment made in connection with a government voucher or certificate program which functions as a payment for property or services) shall deduct and withhold from such payment a tax in an amount equal to 3 percent of such payment.

(2) PROPERTY AND SERVICES SUBJECT TO WITHHOLDING.—Paragraph (1) shall not apply to any payment—

(A) except as provided in subparagraph (B), which is subject to withholding under any other provision of this chapter or chapter 3,

(B) which is subject to withholding under section 3406 and from which amounts are being withheld under such section,

(C) of interest,

(D) for real property,

P.L. 115-97, §13603(g), provides:

(g) TRANSITION RULE.—Until such time as the Secretary (or the Secretary's delegate) issues regulations or other guidance for purposes of implementing the requirements of paragraph (2)(C)(i)(II) of section 83(i) of the Internal Revenue Code of 1986 (as added by this section), or the requirements of paragraph (6) of such section, a corporation shall be treated as being in compliance with such requirements (respectively) if such corporation complies with a reasonable good faith interpretation of such requirements.

[Sec. 3402(t)—Stricken]

(E) to any governmental entity subject to the requirements of paragraph (1), any tax-exempt entity, or any foreign government,

(F) made pursuant to a classified or confidential contract described in section 6050M(e)(3),

(G) made by a political subdivision of a State (or any instrumentality thereof) which makes less than $100,000,000 of such payments annually,

(H) which is in connection with a public assistance or public welfare program for which eligibility is determined by a needs or income test, and

(I) to any government employee not otherwise excludable with respect to their services as an employee.

(3) COORDINATION WITH OTHER SECTIONS.—For purposes of sections 3403 and 3404 and for purposes of so much of subtitle F (except section 7205) as relates to this chapter, payments to any person for property or services which are subject to withholding shall be treated as if such payments were wages paid by an employer to an employee.

• 2006, Tax Increase Prevention and Reconciliation Act of 2005 (P.L. 109-222)

P.L. 109-222, §511(a):

Amended Code Sec. 3402 by adding at the end a new subsection (t). **Effective** for payments made after 12-31-2011 [**effective** date amended by P.L. 111-5, §1511.—CCH.].

[Sec. 3403]

SEC. 3403. LIABILITY FOR TAX.

The employer shall be liable for the payment of the tax required to be deducted and withheld under this chapter, and shall not be liable to any person for the amount of any such payment.

Amendments

• 1983, Interest and Dividend Tax Compliance Act of 1983 (P.L. 98-67)

P.L. 98-67, §102(a):

Repealed the amendment made to Code Sec. 3403 by P.L. 97-248 as though it had not been enacted. **Effective** as of the close of 6-30-83.

• 1982, Tax Equity and Fiscal Responsibility Act of 1982 (P.L. 97-248)

P.L. 97-248, §307(a)(2):

Amended Code Sec. 3403 by striking out "this chapter" and inserting "this subchapter". **Effective** 7-1-83.

[Sec. 3404]

SEC. 3404. RETURN AND PAYMENT BY GOVERNMENTAL EMPLOYER.

If the employer is the United States, or a State, or political subdivision thereof, or the District of Columbia, or any agency or instrumentality of any one or more of the foregoing, the return of the amount deducted and withheld upon any wages may be made by any officer or employee of the United States, or of such State, or political subdivision, or of the District of Columbia, or of such agency or instrumentality, as the case may be, having control of the payment of such wages, or appropriately designated for that purpose.

Amendments

• 1976, Tax Reform Act of 1976 (P.L. 94-455)

P.L. 94-455, §1903(c), (d):

Deleted "Territory," each place it appeared in Code Sec. 3404. **Effective** for wages paid after 12-31-76.

[Sec. 3405]

SEC. 3405. SPECIAL RULES FOR PENSIONS, ANNUITIES, AND CERTAIN OTHER DEFERRED INCOME.

[Sec. 3405(a)]

(a) PERIODIC PAYMENTS.—

(1) WITHHOLDING AS IF PAYMENT WERE WAGES.—The payor of any periodic payment (as defined in subsection (e)(2)) shall withhold from such payment the amount which would be required to be withheld from such payment if such payment were a payment of wages by an employer to an employee for the appropriate payroll period.

WITHHOLDING FROM WAGES

(2) ELECTION OF NO WITHHOLDING.—An individual may elect to have paragraph (1) not apply with respect to periodic payments made to such individual. Such an election shall remain in effect until revoked by such individual.

(3) WHEN ELECTION TAKES EFFECT.—Any election under this subsection (and any revocation of such an election) shall take effect as provided by subsection (f)(3) of section 3402 for withholding allowance certificates.

(4) AMOUNT WITHHELD WHERE NO WITHHOLDING ALLOWANCE CERTIFICATE IN EFFECT.—In the case of any payment with respect to which a withholding allowance certificate is not in effect, the amount withheld under paragraph (1) shall be determined under rules prescribed by the Secretary.

Amendments

- **2017, Tax Cuts and Jobs Act (P.L. 115-97)**

P.L. 115-97, §11041(c)(2)(F):

Amended Code Sec. 3405(a)(3) and (4) (and the heading for paragraph (4)) by striking "exemption" each place it appears and inserting "allowance". **Effective** generally for tax years beginning after 12-31-2017. For a special rule, see Act Sec. 11041(f)(2), below.

P.L. 115-97, §11041(c)(2)(G):

Amended Code Sec. 3405(a)(4) by striking "shall be determined" and all that follows through "3 withholding exemptions" and inserting "shall be determined under rules prescribed by the Secretary". **Effective** generally for tax years beginning after 12-31-2017. For a special rule, see Act Sec. 11041(f)(2), below. Prior to striking "shall be determined" and all that follows through "3 withholding exemptions", Code Sec. 3405(a)(4) read as follows:

(4) AMOUNT WITHHELD WHERE NO WITHHOLDING EXEMPTION CERTIFICATE IN EFFECT.—In the case of any payment with respect to which a withholding exemption certificate is not in effect, the amount withheld under paragraph (1) shall be determined by treating the payee as a married individual claiming 3 withholding exemptions.

P.L. 115-97, §11041(f)(2), provides:

EFFECTIVE DATE.—

(1) IN GENERAL.—Except as provided in paragraph (2), the amendments made by this section shall apply to taxable years beginning after December 31, 2017.

(2) WAGE WITHHOLDING.—The Secretary of the Treasury may administer section 3402 for taxable years beginning before January 1, 2019, without regard to the amendments made by subsections (a) and (c).

- **1992, Unemployment Compensation Amendments of 1992 (P.L. 102-318)**

P.L. 102-318, §521(b)(36):

Amended Code Sec. 3405(a) by striking "PENSIONS, ANNUITIES, ETC.—" from the heading thereof and inserting "PERIODIC PAYMENTS". **Effective** for distributions after 12-31-92.

P.L. 102-318, §522(b)(2)(A):

Amended Code Sec. 3405(a)(1) by striking "subsection (d)(2)" and inserting "subsection (e)(2)". **Effective** for distributions after 12-31-92.

[Sec. 3405(b)]

(b) NONPERIODIC DISTRIBUTION.—

(1) WITHHOLDING.—The payor of any nonperiodic distribution (as defined in subsection (e)(3)) shall withhold from such distribution an amount equal to 10 percent of such distribution.

(2) ELECTION OF NO WITHHOLDING.—

(A) IN GENERAL.—An individual may elect not to have paragraph (1) apply with respect to any nonperiodic distribution.

(B) SCOPE OF ELECTION.—An election under subparagraph (A)—

(i) except as provided in clause (ii), shall be on a distribution-by-distribution basis, or

(ii) to the extent provided in regulations, may apply to subsequent nonperiodic distributions made by the payor to the payee under the same arrangement.

Amendments

- **1992, Unemployment Compensation Amendments of 1992 (P.L. 102-318)**

P.L. 102-318, §521(b)(37)(A)-(B):

Amended Code Sec. 3405(b) by striking "the amount determined under paragraph (2)" from paragraph (1) thereof and inserting "an amount equal to 10 percent of such distribution", and by striking paragraph (2) and redesignating paragraph (3) as paragraph (2). **Effective** for distributions after 12-31-92. Prior to amendment, paragraph (2) read as follows:

(2) AMOUNT OF WITHHOLDING.—

(A) DISTRIBUTIONS WHICH ARE NOT QUALIFIED TOTAL DISTRIBUTIONS.—In the case of any nonperiodic distribution which is not a qualified total distribution, the amount withheld under paragraph (1) shall be the amount determined by multiplying such distribution by 10 percent.

(B) QUALIFIED TOTAL DISTRIBUTIONS.—In the case of any nonperiodic distribution which is a qualified total distribution, the amount withheld under paragraph (1) shall be determined under tables (or other computational procedures) prescribed by the Secretary which are based on the amount of tax which would be imposed on such distribution under section 402(e) if the recipient elected to treat such distribution as a lumpsum distribution (within the meaning of section 402(e)(4)(A)).

(C) SPECIAL RULE FOR DISTRIBUTIONS BY REASON OF DEATH.—In the case of any nonperiodic distribution from or under any plan or contract described in section 401(a), 403(a), or 403(b)—

(i) which is made by reason of a participant's death, and

(ii) with respect to which the requirements of clauses (ii) and (iv) of subsection (d)(4)(A) are met,

subparagraph (A) or (B) (as the case may be) shall be applied by taking into account the exclusion from gross income provided by section 101(b) (whether or not allowable).

P.L. 102-318, §522(b)(2)(B):

Amended Code Sec. 3405(b)(1) by striking "subsection (d)(3)" and inserting "subsection (e)(3)". **Effective** for distributions after 12-31-92.

- **1984, Deficit Reduction Act of 1984 (P.L. 98-369)**

P.L. 98-369, §714(j)(1):

Amended Code Sec. 3405(b)(2)(C). **Effective** as if included in the provision of P.L. 97-248 to which it relates. Prior to amendment, subparagraph (C) read as follows:

(C) Special Rule for Distributions by Reasons of Death.—In the case of any distribution described in subparagraph (B) from or under any plan or contract described in section 401(a), 403(a), or 403(b) which is made by reason of a participant's death, the Secretary, in prescribing tables or procedures under paragraph (1), shall take into account the exclusion from gross income provided by section 101(b) (whether or not allowable).

[Sec. 3405(c)]

(c) ELIGIBLE ROLLOVER DISTRIBUTIONS.—

(1) IN GENERAL.—In the case of any designated distribution which is an eligible rollover distribution—

(A) subsections (a) and (b) shall not apply, and

(B) the payor of such distribution shall withhold from such distribution an amount equal to 20 percent of such distribution.

(2) EXCEPTION.—Paragraph (1)(B) shall not apply to any distribution if the distributee elects under section 401(a)(31)(A) to have such distribution paid directly to an eligible retirement plan.

(3) ELIGIBLE ROLLOVER DISTRIBUTION.—For purposes of this subsection, the term "eligible rollover distribution" has the meaning given such term by section 402(f)(2)(A).

Amendments

- **2020, Taxpayer Certainty and Disaster Tax Relief Act of 2020 (P.L. 116-260)**

P.L. 116-260, §302(a)-(b), Div. EE, provides:

For a special rule, see Act Sec. 302(a)-(b), Div. EE, in the amendment notes for Code Sec. 72(t).

- **2020, Coronavirus Aid, Relief, and Economic Security (CARES) Act (P.L. 116-136)**

P.L. 116-136, §2202(a), provides:

For a special rule, see Act Sec. 2202(a) in the amendment notes for Code Sec. 72(t).

- **2019, Taxpayer Certainty and Disaster Tax Relief Act of 2019 (P.L. 116-94)**

P.L. 116-94, §202(a), Div. Q, provides:

For a special rule, see Act Sec. 202(a), Div. Q, in the amendment notes for Code Sec. 1400Q.

- **2018, Bipartisan Budget Act of 2018 (P.L. 115-123)**

P.L. 115-123, §20102(a), Div. B, provides:

For a special rule, see Act Sec. 20102(a), Div. B, in the amendment notes for Code Sec. 1400Q(a).

Internal Revenue Code

WITHHOLDING FROM WAGES

- **2017, Tax Cuts and Jobs Act (P.L. 115-97)**

P.L. 115-97, §11028(a) and (b)(1), provides:

For a special rule, see Act Sec. 11028(a) and (b)(1) in the amendment notes for Code Sec. 1400Q(a).

- **2017, Disaster Tax Relief and Airport and Airway Extension Act of 2017 (P.L. 115-63)**

P.L. 115-63, §502(a), provides:

For a special rule, see Act Sec. 502(a) in the amendment notes for Code Sec. 1400Q(a).

- **2006, Pension Protection Act of 2006 (P.L. 109-280)**

P.L. 109-280, §811, provides:

SEC. 811. PENSIONS AND INDIVIDUAL RETIREMENT ARRANGEMENT PROVISIONS OF ECONOMIC GROWTH AND TAX RELIEF RECONCILIATION ACT OF 2001 MADE PERMANENT.

Title IX of the Economic Growth and Tax Relief Reconciliation Act of 2001 [P.L. 107-16] shall not apply to the provisions of, and amendments made by, subtitles A through F of title VI [§§601-666]of such Act (relating to pension and individual retirement arrangement provisions).

- **2005, Katrina Emergency Tax Relief Act of 2005 (P.L. 109-73)**

P.L. 109-73, §101(f)(1) [repealed by P.L. 109-135, §201(b)(4)(A)], provides:

(1) EXEMPTION OF DISTRIBUTIONS FROM TRUSTEE TO TRUSTEE TRANSFER AND WITHHOLDING RULES.—For purposes of sections 401(a)(31), 402(f), and 3405 of such Code, qualified Hurricane Katrina distributions shall not be treated as eligible rollover distributions.

- **2001, Economic Growth and Tax Relief Reconciliation Act of 2001 (P.L. 107-16)**

P.L. 107-16, §641(a)(1)(D)(ii):

Amended Code Sec. 3405(c)(3). **Effective** for distributions after 12-31-2001. For a special rule, see Act Sec. 641(f)(3), below. Prior to amendment, Code Sec. 3405(c)(3) read as follows:

(3) ELIGIBLE ROLLOVER DISTRIBUTION.—For purposes of this subsection, the term "eligible rollover distribution" has the meaning given such term by section 402(f)(2)(A) (or in the case of an annuity contract under section 403(b), a distribution from such contract described in section 402(f)(2)(A)).

P.L. 107-16, §641(f)(3), provides:

(3) SPECIAL RULE.—Notwithstanding any other provision of law, subsections (h)(3) and (h)(5) of section 1122 of the Tax Reform Act of 1986 shall not apply to any distribution from an eligible retirement plan (as defined in clause (iii) or (iv) of section 402(c)(8)(B) of the Internal Revenue Code of 1986) on behalf of an individual if there was a rollover to such plan on behalf of such individual which is permitted solely by reason of any amendment made by this section.

P.L. 107-16, §901(a)-(b), as amended by P.L. 111-312, §101(a)(1), provides [but see P.L. 109-280, §811, above]:

SEC. 901. SUNSET OF PROVISIONS OF ACT.

(a) IN GENERAL.—All provisions of, and amendments made by, this Act shall not apply—

(1) to taxable, plan, or limitation years beginning after December 31, 2012, or

(2) in the case of title V, to estates of decedents dying, gifts made, or generation skipping transfers, after December 31, 2012.

(b) APPLICATION OF CERTAIN LAWS.—The Internal Revenue Code of 1986 and the Employee Retirement Income Security Act of 1974 shall be applied and administered to years, estates, gifts, and transfers described in subsection (a) as if the provisions and amendments described in subsection (a) had never been enacted.

- **1992, Unemployment Compensation Amendments of 1992 (P.L. 102-318)**

P.L. 102-318, §522(b)(1):

Amended Code Sec. 3405 by redesignating subsections (c), (d), and (e) as subsections (d), (e), and (f) and by inserting after subsection (b) new subsection (c). **Effective** for distributions after 12-31-92.

[Sec. 3405(d)]

(d) LIABILITY FOR WITHHOLDING.—

(1) IN GENERAL.—Except as provided in paragraph (2), the payor of a designated distribution (as defined in subsection (e)(1)) shall withhold, and be liable for, payment of the tax required to be withheld under this section.

(2) PLAN ADMINISTRATOR LIABLE IN CERTAIN CASES.—

(A) IN GENERAL.—In the case of any plan to which this paragraph applies, paragraph (1) shall not apply and the plan administrator shall withhold, and be liable for, payment of the tax unless the plan administrator—

(i) directs the payor to withhold such tax, and

(ii) provides the payor with such information as the Secretary may require by regulations.

(B) PLANS TO WHICH PARAGRAPH APPLIES.—This paragraph applies to any plan described in, or which at any time has been determined to be described in—

(i) section 401(a),

(ii) section 403(a),

(iii) section 301(d) of the Tax Reduction Act of 1975, or

(iv) section 457(b) and which is maintained by an eligible employer described in section 457(e)(1)(A).

Amendments

- **2006, Pension Protection Act of 2006 (P.L. 109-280)**

P.L. 109-280, §811, provides:

SEC. 811. PENSIONS AND INDIVIDUAL RETIREMENT ARRANGEMENT PROVISIONS OF ECONOMIC GROWTH AND TAX RELIEF RECONCILIATION ACT OF 2001 MADE PERMANENT.

Title IX of the Economic Growth and Tax Relief Reconciliation Act of 2001 [P.L. 107-16] shall not apply to the provisions of, and amendments made by, subtitles A through F of title VI [§§601-666]of such Act (relating to pension and individual retirement arrangement provisions).

- **2001, Economic Growth and Tax Relief Reconciliation Act of 2001 (P.L. 107-16)**

P.L. 107-16, §641(a)(1)(D)(iii):

Amended Code Sec. 3405(d)(2)(B) by striking "or" at the end of clause (ii), by striking the period at the end of clause (iii) and inserting ", or", and by adding at the end a new clause (iv). **Effective**, generally, for distributions after 12-31-2001. For a special rule, see Act Sec. 641(f)(3) in the amendment notes to Code Sec. 3405(c).

P.L. 107-16, §901(a)-(b), as amended by P.L. 111-312, §101(a)(1), provides [but see P.L. 109-280, §811, above]:

SEC. 901. SUNSET OF PROVISIONS OF ACT.

(a) IN GENERAL.—All provisions of, and amendments made by, this Act shall not apply—

(1) to taxable, plan, or limitation years beginning after December 31, 2012, or

(2) in the case of title V, to estates of decedents dying, gifts made, or generation skipping transfers, after December 31, 2012.

(b) APPLICATION OF CERTAIN LAWS.—The Internal Revenue Code of 1986 and the Employee Retirement Income Security Act of 1974 shall be applied and administered to years, estates, gifts, and transfers described in subsection (a) as if the provisions and amendments described in subsection (a) had never been enacted.

- **1992, Unemployment Compensation Amendments of 1992 (P.L. 102-318)**

P.L. 102-318, §522(b)(1):

Amended Code Sec. 3405 by redesignating subsection (c) as subsection (d). **Effective** for distributions after 12-31-92.

P.L. 102-318, §522(b)(2)(C):

Amended Code Sec. 3405(d)(1) (as redesignated by Act Sec. 522(b)(1)) by striking "subsection (d)(1)" and inserting "subsection (e)(1)". **Effective** for distributions after 12-31-92.

[Sec. 3405(e)]

(e) DEFINITIONS AND SPECIAL RULES.—For purposes of this section—

(1) DESIGNATED DISTRIBUTION.—

(A) IN GENERAL.—Except as provided in subparagraph (B), the term "designated distribution" means any distribution or payment from or under—

(i) an employer deferred compensation plan,

(ii) an individual retirement plan (as defined in section 7701(a)(37)), or

(iii) a commercial annuity.

(B) EXCEPTIONS.—The term "designated distribution" shall not include—

WITHHOLDING FROM WAGES

(i) any amount which is wages without regard to this section,

(ii) the portion of a distribution or payment which it is reasonable to believe is not includible in gross income,

(iii) any amount which is subject to withholding under subchapter A of chapter 3 (relating to withholding of tax on nonresident aliens and foreign corporations) by the person paying such amount or which would be so subject but for a tax treaty, or

(iv) any distribution described in section 404(k)(2).

For purposes of clause (ii), any distribution or payment from or under an individual retirement plan (other than a Roth IRA) shall be treated as includible in gross income.

(2) PERIODIC PAYMENT.—The term "periodic payment" means a designated distribution which is an annuity or similar periodic payment.

(3) NONPERIODIC DISTRIBUTION.—The term "nonperiodic distribution" means any designated distribution which is not a periodic payment.

(4) [Repealed.]

(5) EMPLOYER DEFERRED COMPENSATION PLAN.—The term "employer deferred compensation plan" means any pension, annuity, profit-sharing, or stock bonus plan or other plan deferring the receipt of compensation.

(6) COMMERCIAL ANNUITY.—The term "commercial annuity" means an annuity, endowment, or life insurance contract issued by an insurance company licensed to do business under the laws of any State.

(7) PLAN ADMINISTRATOR.—The term "plan administrator" has the meaning given such term by section 414(g).

(8) MAXIMUM AMOUNT WITHHELD.—The maximum amount to be withheld under this section on any designated distribution shall not exceed the sum of the amount of money and the fair market value of other property (other than securities of the employer corporation) received in the distribution. No amount shall be required to be withheld under this section in the case of any designated distribution which consists only of securities of the employer corporation and cash (not in excess of $200) in lieu of fractional shares. For purposes of this paragraph, the term "securities of the employer corporation" has the meaning given such term by section 402(e)(4)(E).

(9) SEPARATE ARRANGEMENTS TO BE TREATED SEPARATELY.—If the payor has more than 1 arrangement under which designated distributions may be made to any individual, each such arrangement shall be treated separately.

(10) TIME AND MANNER OF ELECTION.—

(A) IN GENERAL.—Any election and any revocation under this section shall be made at such time and in such manner as the Secretary shall prescribe.

(B) PAYOR REQUIRED TO NOTIFY PAYEE OF RIGHTS TO ELECT.—

(i) PERIODIC PAYMENTS.—The payor of any periodic payment—

(I) shall transmit to the payee notice of the right to make an election under subsection (a) not earlier than 6 months before the first of such payments and not later than when making the first of such payments,

(II) is [if] such a notice is not transmitted under subclause (I) when making such first payment, shall transmit such a notice when making such first payment, and

(III) shall transmit to payees, not less frequently than once each calendar year, notice of their rights to make elections under subsection (a) and to revoke such elections.

(ii) NONPERIODIC DISTRIBUTIONS.—The payor of any nonperiodic distribution shall transmit to the payee notice of the right to make any election provided in subsection (b) at the time of the distribution (or at such earlier time as may be provided in regulations).

(iii) NOTICE.—Any notice transmitted pursuant to this subparagraph shall be in such form and contain such information as the Secretary shall prescribe.

(11) WITHHOLDING INCLUDES DEDUCTION.—The terms "withholding", "withhold", and "withheld" include "deducting", "deduct", and "deducted".

(12) FAILURE TO PROVIDE CORRECT TIN.—If—

(A) a payee fails to furnish his TIN to the payor in the manner required by the Secretary, or

(B) the Secretary notifies the payor before any payment or distribution that the TIN furnished by the payee is incorrect,

no election under subsection (a)(2) or (b)(2) shall be treated as in effect and subsection (a)(4) shall not apply to such payee.

(13) ELECTION MAY NOT BE MADE WITH RESPECT TO CERTAIN PAYMENTS OUTSIDE THE UNITED STATES OR ITS POSSESSIONS.—

(A) IN GENERAL.—Except as provided in subparagraph (B), in the case of any periodic payment or nonperiodic distribution which is to be delivered outside of the United States and any possession of the United States, no election may be made under subsection (a)(2) or (b)(2) with respect to such payment.

(B) EXCEPTION.—Subparagraph (A) shall not apply if the recipient certifies to the payor, in such manner as the Secretary may prescribe, that such person is not—

(i) a United States citizen or a resident alien of the United States, or

(ii) an individual to whom section 877 applies.

Amendments

- **2000, Community Renewal Tax Relief Act of 2000 (P.L. 106-554)**

P.L. 106-554, § 314(b):

Amended Code Sec. 3405(e)(1)(B) by inserting "(other than a Roth IRA)" after "individual retirement plan" in the last sentence. **Effective** as if included in the provision of P.L. 105-34 to which it relates [**effective** for tax years beginning after 12-31-97.—CCH].

- **1996, Small Business Job Protection Act of 1996 (P.L. 104-188)**

P.L. 104-188, § 1704(t)(71):

Amended Code Sec. 3405(e)(12) by striking "(b)(3)" and inserting "(b)(2)". **Effective** 8-20-96.

- **1992, Unemployment Compensation Amendments of 1992 (P.L. 102-318)**

P.L. 102-318, § 521(b)(38):

Repealed Code Sec. 3405(d)(4). **Effective** for distributions after 12-31-92. Prior to repeal, Code Sec. 3405(d)(4) read as follows:

(4) QUALIFIED TOTAL DISTRIBUTION.—

(A) IN GENERAL.—The term "qualified total distribution" means any distribution which—

(i) is a designated distribution,

(ii) it is reasonable to believe is made within 1 taxable year of the recipient,

(iii) is made under a plan described in section 401(a), or 403(a), and

(iv) consists of the balance to the credit of the employee under such plan.

(B) SPECIAL RULE FOR ACCUMULATED DEDUCTIBLE EMPLOYEE CONTRIBUTIONS.—For purposes of subparagraph (A), accumulated deductible employee contributions (within the meaning of section 72(o)(5)(B)) shall be treated separately in determining if there has been a qualified total distribution.

P.L. 102-318, § 521(b)(39):

Amended Code Sec. 3405(d)(8). **Effective** for distributions after 12-31-92. Prior to amendment, Code Sec. 3405(d)(8) read as follows:

(8) MAXIMUM AMOUNT WITHHELD.—The maximum amount to be withheld under this section on any designated distribution shall not exceed the sum of the amount of money and the fair market value of other property (other than employer securities of the employer corporation (within the meaning of section 402(a)(3))) received in the distribution. No amount shall be required to be withheld under this section in the case of any designated distribution which consists only of employer securities of the employer corporation (within the meaning of section 402(a)(3)) and cash (not in excess of $200) in lieu of fractional shares.

P.L. 102-318, § 521(b)(40):

Amended Code Sec. 3405(d)(13)(A) by striking "(b)(3)" and inserting "(b)(2)". **Effective** for distributions after 12-31-92.

BACKUP WITHHOLDING

P.L. 102-318, § 522(b)(1):

Amended Code Sec. 3405 by redesignating subsection (d) as subsection (e). **Effective** for distributions after 12-31-92.

- **1988, Technical and Miscellaneous Revenue Act of 1988 (P.L. 100-647)**

P.L. 100-647, § 1012(bb)(2)(A):

Amended Code Sec. 3405(d)(13)(A) by striking out "the United States" and inserting in lieu thereof "the United States and any possession of the United States". **Effective** for distributions made after 11-10-88.

P.L. 100-647, § 1012(bb)(2)(B):

Amended Code Sec. 3405(d)(13)(B)(i). **Effective** for distributions made after 11-10-88. Prior to amendment, Code Sec. 3405(d)(13)(B)(i) read as follows:

(i) a United States citizen who is a bona fide resident of a foreign country, or

P.L. 100-647, § 1012(bb)(2)(C):

Amended Code Sec. 3405(d) by striking out "United States" in the heading of paragraph (13) and inserting in lieu thereof "United States or its possessions". **Effective** for distributions made after 11-10-88.

- **1986, Tax Reform Act of 1986 (P.L. 99-514)**

P.L. 99-514, § 1102(e)(1):

Amended Code Sec. 3405(d)(1)(B) by adding at the end thereof the flush sentence. **Effective** for contributions and distributions for tax years beginning after 12-31-86.

P.L. 99-514, § 1234(b)(1):

Amended Code Sec. 3405(d) by adding at the end thereof new paragraph (13). **Effective** for payments after 12-31-86.

P.L. 99-514, § 1875(c)(10):

Amended Code Sec. 3405(d)(1)(B) by striking out "or" at the end of clause (ii), and by striking out the material following clause (ii) and inserting in lieu thereof new clauses (iii) and (iv). **Effective** as if included in the provision of P.L. 98-369 to which it relates. Prior to amendment, Code Sec. 3405(d)(1)(B) read as follows:

(B) EXCEPTIONS.—The term "designated distribution" shall not include—

(i) any amount which is wages without regard to this section,

(ii) the portion of a distribution or payment which it is reasonable to believe is not includible in gross income, or

(iii) any amount which is subject to withholding under subchapter A of chapter 3 (relating to withholding of tax on nonresident aliens and foreign corporations) by the person paying such amount or which would be so subject but for a tax treaty.

(iii)[iv] any distribution described in section 404(k)(2).

- **1984, Deficit Reduction Act of 1984 (P.L. 98-369)**

P.L. 98-369, § 542(c):

Amended Code Sec. 3405(d)(1)(B) by striking out "and " at the end of clause (i), by striking out the period at the end of clause (ii) and inserting in lieu thereof ", or", and by adding a new clause (iii). **Effective** for tax years beginning after 7-18-84.

P.L. 98-369, § 714(j)(4):

Amended Code Sec. 3405(d)(1)(B) by striking out "and" at the end of clause (i), by striking out the period at the end of clause (ii) and inserting in lieu thereof ", and", and by adding at the end thereof a new clause (iii). **Effective** as if included in the provision of P.L. 97-248 to which it relates.

P.L. 98-369, § 714(j)(5):

Amended Code Sec. 3405(d)(8) by adding at the end thereof a new sentence. **Effective** as if included in the provision of P.L. 97-248 to which it relates.

P.L. 98-369, § 722(h)(4)(A):

Amended Code Sec. 3405(d) by adding new paragraph (12). **Effective** for distributions after 12-31-84, unless the payor elects to have such amendment apply to payments or distributions before 1-1-85.

[Sec. 3405(f)]

(f) WITHHOLDING TO BE TREATED AS WAGE WITHHOLDING UNDER SECTION 3402 FOR OTHER PURPOSES.—For purposes of this chapter (and so much of subtitle F as relates to this chapter)—

(1) any designated distribution (whether or not an election under this section applies to such distribution) shall be treated as if it were wages paid by an employer to an employee with respect to which there has been withholding under section 3402, and

(2) in the case of any designated distribution not subject to withholding under this section by reason of an election under this section, the amount withheld shall be treated as zero.

Amendments

- **1992, Unemployment Compensation Amendments of 1992 (P.L. 102-318)**

P.L. 102-318, § 522(b)(1):

Amended Code Sec. 3405 by redesignating subsection (e) as subsection (f). **Effective** for distributions after 12-31-92.

- **1982, Tax Equity and Fiscal Responsibility Act of 1982 (P.L. 97-248)**

P.L. 97-248, § 334(a):

Added new Code Sec. 3405. **Effective** for designated distributions made after 12-31-82. However, for purposes of applying the rules to periodic payments which commence prior to 1-1-83, the first periodic payment made after 12-31-82, is considered the first periodic payment made.

P.L. 97-248, § 334(d)(5), provides:

The Secretary of the Treasury shall prescribe such regulations which delay (but not beyond June 30, 1983) the application of some or all of the amendments made by this section with respect to any payor until such time as such payor is able to comply without undue hardship with the requirements of such provisions.

P.L. 97-248, § 334(e)(6), provides:

(6) Waiver of penalty.—No penalty shall be assessed under section 6672 with respect to any failure to withhold as required by the amendments made by this section if such failure was before July 1, 1983, and if the person made a good faith effort to comply with such withholding requirements.

[Sec. 3406]

SEC. 3406. BACKUP WITHHOLDING.

[Sec. 3406(a)]

(a) REQUIREMENT TO DEDUCT AND WITHHOLD.—

(1) IN GENERAL.—In the case of any reportable payment, if—

(A) the payee fails to furnish his TIN to the payor in the manner required,

(B) the Secretary notifies the payor that the TIN furnished by the payee is incorrect,

(C) there has been a notified payee underreporting described in subsection (c), or

(D) there has been a payee certification failure described in subsection (d),

then the payor shall deduct and withhold from such payment a tax equal to the product of the fourth lowest rate of tax applicable under section 1(c) and such payment.

(2) SUBPARAGRAPHS (C) AND (D) OF PARAGRAPH (1) APPLY ONLY TO INTEREST AND DIVIDEND PAYMENTS.—Subparagraphs (C) and (D) of paragraph (1) shall apply only to reportable interest or dividend payments.

Amendments

- **2013, American Taxpayer Relief Act of 2012 (P.L. 112-240)**

P.L. 112-240, § 101(a)(1) and (3), provides:

SEC. 101. PERMANENT EXTENSION AND MODIFICATION OF 2001 TAX RELIEF.

(a) PERMANENT EXTENSION.—

(1) IN GENERAL.—The Economic Growth and Tax Relief Reconciliation Act of 2001 is amended by striking title IX.

* * *

(3) EFFECTIVE DATE.—The amendments made by this subsection shall apply to taxable, plan, or limitation years beginning after December 31, 2012, and estates of decedents dying, gifts made, or generation skipping transfers after December 31, 2012.

- **2001, Economic Growth and Tax Relief Reconciliation Act of 2001 (P.L. 107-16)**

P.L. 107-16, § 101(c)(10):

Amended Code Sec. 3406(a)(1) by striking "equal to 31 percent of such payment" and inserting "equal to the product of the fourth lowest rate of tax applicable under section 1(c) and such payment". **Effective**, generally, for amounts paid after 6-7-2001. For special rules, see Act Sec. 101(d)(2), below.

P.L. 107-16, § 101(d)(2), provides:

(2) AMENDMENTS TO WITHHOLDING PROVISIONS.—The amendments made by paragraphs (6), (7), (8), (9), (10), and (11) of subsection (c) shall apply to amounts paid after the 60th day after the date of the enactment of this Act. References to income brackets and rates of tax in such paragraphs shall be applied without regard to section 1(i)(1)(D) of the Internal Revenue Code of 1986.

BACKUP WITHHOLDING

P.L. 107-16, §901(a)-(b), as amended by P.L. 111-312, §101(a)(1), provides [but see P.L. 112-240, §101(a)(1) and (3), above]:

SEC. 901. SUNSET OF PROVISIONS OF ACT.

(a) IN GENERAL.—All provisions of, and amendments made by, this Act shall not apply—

(1) to taxable, plan, or limitation years beginning after December 31, 2012, or

(2) in the case of title V, to estates of decedents dying, gifts made, or generation skipping transfers, after December 31, 2012.

(b) APPLICATION OF CERTAIN LAWS.—The Internal Revenue Code of 1986 and the Employee Retirement Income Security Act of 1974 shall be applied and administered to years, estates, gifts, and transfers described in subsection (a) as if the provisions and amendments described in subsection (a) had never been enacted.

• **1992, Energy Policy Act of 1992 (P.L. 102-486)**

P.L. 102-486, §1935(a):

Amended Code Sec. 3406(a)(1) by striking "20 percent" and inserting "31 percent". **Effective** for amounts paid after 12-31-92.

[Sec. 3406(b)]

(b) REPORTABLE PAYMENT, ETC.—For purposes of this section—

(1) REPORTABLE PAYMENT.—The term "reportable payment" means—

(A) any reportable interest or dividend payment, and

(B) any other reportable payment.

(2) REPORTABLE INTEREST OR DIVIDEND PAYMENT.—

(A) IN GENERAL.—The term "reportable interest or dividend payment" means any payment of a kind, and to a payee, required to be shown on a return required under—

(i) section 6049(a) (relating to payments of interest),

(ii) section 6042(a) (relating to payments of dividends), or

(iii) section 6044 (relating to payments of patronage dividends) but only to the extent such payment is in money.

(B) SPECIAL RULE FOR PATRONAGE DIVIDENDS.—For purposes of subparagraphs (C) and (D) of subsection (a)(1), the term "reportable interest or dividend payment" shall not include any payment to which section 6044 (relating to patronage dividends) applies unless 50 percent or more of such payment is in money.

(3) OTHER REPORTABLE PAYMENT.—The term "other reportable payment" means any payment of a kind, and to a payee, required to be shown on a return required under—

(A) section 6041 (relating to certain information at source),

(B) section 6041A(a) (relating to payments of remuneration for services),

(C) section 6045 (relating to returns of brokers),

(D) section 6050A (relating to reporting requirements of certain fishing boat operators), but only to the extent such payment is in money and represents a share of the proceeds of the catch,

(E) section 6050N (relating to payments of royalties), or

(F) section 6050W (relating to returns relating to payments made in settlement of payment card transactions).

(4) WHETHER PAYMENT IS OF REPORTABLE KIND DETERMINED WITHOUT REGARD TO MINIMUM AMOUNT.—The determination of whether any payment is of a kind required to be shown on a return described in paragraph (2) or (3) shall be made without regard to any minimum amount which must be paid before a return is required.

(5) EXCEPTION FOR CERTAIN SMALL PAYMENTS.—To the extent provided in regulations, the term "reportable payment" shall not include any payment which—

(A) does not exceed $10, and

(B) if determined for a 1-year period, would not exceed $10.

(6) OTHER REPORTABLE PAYMENTS INCLUDE PAYMENTS DESCRIBED IN SECTION 6041(a) OR 6041A(a) ONLY WHERE AGGREGATE FOR CALENDAR YEAR IS $600 OR MORE.—Any payment of a kind required to be shown on a return required under section 6041(a) or 6041A(a) which is made during any calendar year shall be treated as a reportable payment only if—

(A) the aggregate amount of such payment and all previous payments described in such sections by the payor to the payee during such calendar year equals or exceeds $600,

(B) the payor was required under section 6041(a) or 6041A(a) to file a return for the preceding calendar year with respect to payments to the payee, or

(C) during the preceding calendar year, the payor made reportable payments to the payee with respect to which amounts were required to be deducted and withheld under subsection (a).

(7) EXCEPTION FOR CERTAIN WINDOW PAYMENTS OF INTEREST, ETC.—For purposes of subparagraphs (C) and (D) of subsection (a)(1), the term "reportable interest or dividend payment" shall not include any payment—

(A) in redemption of a coupon on a bearer instrument or in redemption of a United States savings bond, or

(B) to the extent provided in regulations, of interest on instruments similar to those described in subparagraph (A).

The preceding sentence shall not apply for purposes of determining whether there is payee underreporting described in subsection (c).

Amendments

• **2008, Housing Assistance Tax Act of 2008 (P.L. 110-289)**

P.L. 110-289, §3091(c):

Amended Code Sec. 3406(b)(3) by striking "or" at the end of subparagraph (D), by striking the period at the end of subparagraph (E) and inserting ", or", and by adding at the end a new subparagraph (F). **Effective** generally for amounts paid after 12-31-2011. For a special rule, see Act Sec. 3091(e)(2)(B), below.

P.L. 110-289, §3091(e)(2)(B), provides:

(B) ELIGIBILITY FOR TIN MATCHING PROGRAM.—Solely for purposes of carrying out any TIN matching program established by the Secretary under section 3406(i) of the Internal Revenue Code of 1986—

(i) the amendments made [by] this section shall be treated as taking effect on the date of the enactment of this Act [7-30-2008.—CCH], and

(ii) each person responsible for setting the standards and mechanisms referred to in section 6050W(d)(2)(C) of such Code, as added by this section, for settling transactions involving payment cards shall be treated in the same manner as a payment settlement entity.

• **1986, Tax Reform Act of 1986 (P.L. 99-514)**

P.L. 99-514, §1523(b)(1)(A)-(C):

Amended Code Sec. 3406(b)(3) by striking out "or" at the end of subparagraph (C), by striking out the period at the end of subparagraph (D) and inserting in lieu thereof ", or", and by adding at the end thereof new subparagraph (E). **Effective** with respect to payments made after 12-31-86.

P.L. 99-514, §1899A(46):

Amended Code Sec. 3406(b)(6) by striking out "6041(A)(a)" in the heading and inserting in lieu thereof "6041A(a)". **Effective** 10-22-86.

[Sec. 3406(c)]

(c) NOTIFIED PAYEE UNDERREPORTING WITH RESPECT TO INTEREST AND DIVIDENDS.—

(1) NOTIFIED PAYEE UNDERREPORTING.—If—

(A) the Secretary determines with respect to any payee that there has been payee underreporting,

BACKUP WITHHOLDING

(B) at least 4 notices have been mailed by the Secretary to the payee (over a period of at least 120 days) with respect to the underreporting, and

(C) in the case of any payee who has filed a return for the taxable year, any deficiency of tax attributable to such failure has been assessed,

the Secretary may notify payors of reportable interest or dividend payments with respect to such payee of the requirement to deduct and withhold under subsection (a)(1)(C) (but not the reasons for the withholding under subsection (a)(1)(C)).

(2) PAYEE UNDERREPORTING DEFINED.—For purposes of this section, there has been payee underreporting if for any taxable year the Secretary determines that—

(A) the payee failed to include in his return of tax under chapter 1 for such year any portion of a reportable interest or dividend payment required to be shown on such return, or

(B) the payee may be required to file a return for such year and to include a reportable interest or dividend payment in such return, but failed to file such return.

(3) DETERMINATION BY SECRETARY TO STOP (OR NOT TO START) WITHHOLDING.—

(A) IN GENERAL.—If the Secretary determines that—

(i) there was no payee underreporting,

(ii) any payee underreporting has been corrected (and any tax, penalty, or interest with respect to the payee underreporting has been paid),

(iii) withholding under subsection (a)(1)(C) has caused (or would cause) undue hardship to the payee and it is unlikely that any payee underreporting by such payee will occur again, or

(iv) there is a bona fide dispute as to whether there has been any payee underreporting,

then the Secretary shall take the action described in subparagraph (B).

(B) SECRETARY TO TAKE ACTION TO STOP (OR NOT TO START) WITHHOLDING.—For purposes of subparagraph (A), if at the time of the Secretary's determination under subparagraph (A)—

(i) no notice has been given under paragraph (1) to any payor with respect to the underreporting, the Secretary shall not give any such notice, or

(ii) if such notice has been given, the Secretary shall—

(I) provide the payee with a written certification that withholding under subsection (a)(1)(C) is to stop, and

(II) notify the applicable payors (and brokers) that such withholding is to stop.

(C) TIME FOR TAKING ACTION WHERE NOTICE TO PAYOR HAS BEEN GIVEN.—In any case where notice has been given under paragraph (1) to any payor with respect to any underreporting, if the Secretary makes a determination under subparagraph (A) during the 12-month period ending on October 15 of any calendar year—

(i) except as provided in clause (ii), the Secretary shall take the action described in subparagraph (B)(ii) to bring about the stopping of withholding no later than December 1 of such calendar year, or

(ii) in the case of—

(I) a no payee underreporting determination under clause (i) of subparagraph (A), or

(II) a hardship determination under clause (iii) of subparagraph (A),

such action shall be taken no later than the 45th day after the day on which the Secretary made the determination.

(D) OPPORTUNITY TO REQUEST DETERMINATION.—The Secretary shall prescribe procedures under which—

(i) a payee may request a determination under subparagraph (A), and

(ii) the payee may provide information with respect to such request.

(4) PAYOR NOTIFIES PAYEE OF WITHHOLDING BECAUSE OF PAYEE UNDERREPORTING.—Any payor required to withhold any tax under subsection (a)(1)(C) shall, at the time such withholding begins, notify the payee of such withholding.

(5) PAYEE MAY BE REQUIRED TO NOTIFY SECRETARY WHO HIS PAYORS AND BROKERS ARE.—For purposes of this section, the Secretary may require any payee of reportable interest or dividend payments who is subject to withholding under subsection (a)(1)(C) to notify the Secretary of—

(A) all payors from whom the payee receives reportable interest or dividend payments, and

(B) all brokers with whom the payee has accounts which may involve reportable interest or dividend payments.

The Secretary may notify any such broker that such payee is subject to withholding under subsection (a)(1)(C).

Amendments

• **1984, Deficit Reduction Act of 1984 (P.L. 98-369)**

P.L. 98-369, §722(h)(2):

Amended Code Sec. 3406 (c)(1) by striking out "(but not the reasons therefor)" and inserting in lieu thereof "(but not the reasons for the withholding under subsection (a)(1)(C))". **Effective** as if included in the amendments made by P.L. 98-67.

[Sec. 3406(d)]

(d) INTEREST AND DIVIDEND BACKUP WITHHOLDING APPLIES TO NEW ACCOUNTS AND INSTRUMENTS UNLESS PAYEE CERTIFIES THAT HE IS NOT SUBJECT TO SUCH WITHHOLDING.—

(1) IN GENERAL.—There is a payee certification failure unless the payee has certified to the payor, under penalty of perjury, that such payee is not subject to withholding under subsection (a)(1)(C).

(2) SPECIAL RULES FOR READILY TRADABLE INSTRUMENTS.—

(A) IN GENERAL.—Subsection (a)(1)(D) shall apply to any reportable interest or dividend payment to any payee on any readily tradable instrument if (and only if) the payor was notified by a broker under subparagraph (B) or no certification was provided to the payor by the payee under paragraph (1) and—

(i) such instrument was acquired directly by the payee from the payor, or

(ii) such instrument is held by the payor as nominee for the payee.

(B) BROKER NOTIFIES PAYOR.—If—

(i) a payee acquires any readily tradable instrument through a broker, and

(ii) with respect to such acquisition—

(I) the payee fails to furnish his TIN to the broker in the manner required under subsection (a)(1)(A),

(II) the Secretary notifies such broker before such acquisition that the TIN furnished by the payee is incorrect,

(III) the Secretary notifies such broker before such acquisition that such payee is subject to withholding under subsection (a)(1)(C), or

(IV) the payee does not provide a certification to such broker under subparagraph (C),

such broker shall, within such period as the Secretary may prescribe by regulations (but not later than 15 days after such acquisition), notify the payor that such payee is subject to withholding under subparagraph (A), (B), (C), or (D) of subsection (a)(1), respectively.

(C) TIME FOR PAYEE TO PROVIDE CERTIFICATION TO BROKER.—In the case of any readily tradable instrument acquired by a payee through a broker, the certification described in paragraph (1) may be provided by the payee to such broker—

(i) at any time after the payee's account with the broker was established and before the acquisition of such instrument, or

(ii) in connection with the acquisition of such instrument.

(3) EXCEPTION FOR EXISTING ACCOUNTS, ETC.—This subsection and subsection (a)(1)(D) shall not apply to any reportable interest or dividend payment which is paid or credited—

(A) in the case of interest or any other amount of a kind reportable under section 6049, with respect to any account (whatever called) established before January 1, 1984, or with respect to any instrument acquired before January 1, 1984,

(B) in the case of dividends or any other amount reportable under section 6042, on any stock or other instrument acquired before January 1, 1984, or

(C) in the case of patronage dividends or other amounts of a kind reportable under section 6044, with respect to any membership acquired, or contract entered into, before January 1, 1984.

(4) EXCEPTION FOR READILY TRADABLE INSTRUMENTS ACQUIRED THROUGH EXISTING BROKERAGE ACCOUNTS.—Subparagraph (B) of paragraph (2) shall not apply with respect to a readily tradable instrument which was acquired through an account with a broker if—

(A) such account was established before January 1, 1984, and

(B) during 1983, such broker bought or sold instruments for the payee (or acted as a nominee for the payee) through such account.

The preceding sentence shall not apply with respect to any readily tradable instrument acquired through such account after the broker was notified by the Secretary that the payee is subject to withholding under subsection (a)(1)(C).

Amendments

• **1984, Deficit Reduction Act of 1984 (P.L. 98-369)**

P.L. 98-369, §722(h)(1)(A):

Amended Code Sec. 3406(d)(2)(A) by inserting "the payor was notified by a broker under subparagraph (B) or" after "if (and only if)", and by striking out clause (i) and redesignating clauses (ii) and (iii) as clauses (i) and (ii). **Effective** as if included in the amendments made by P.L. 98-67. Prior to amendment, Code Sec. 3406(d)(2)(A)(i) read as follows:

(i) the payor was notified by a broker under subparagraph (B),

P.L. 98-369, §722(h)(1)(B):

Amended Code Sec. 3406(d)(2)(B). **Effective** as if included in the amendments made by P.L. 98-67. Prior to amendment, Code Sec. 3406(d)(2)(B) read as follows:

(B) Broker Notifies Payor.—If—

(i) a payee acquires any readily tradable instrument through a broker, and

(ii)(I) the payee does not provide a certification to such broker under subparagraph (C), or (II) such broker is notified by the Secretary before such acquisition that such payee is subject to withholding under subsection (a)(1)(C), such broker shall, within 15 days after the date of the acquisition, notify the payor that such payee is subject to withholding under subsection (a)(1)(D) (or subsection (a)(1)(C) in the case of a notification described in clause (ii)(II)).

[Sec. 3406(e)]

(e) PERIOD FOR WHICH WITHHOLDING IS IN EFFECT.—

(1) FAILURE TO FURNISH TIN.—In the case of any failure by a payee to furnish his TIN to a payor in the manner required, subsection (a) shall apply to any reportable payment made by such payor during the period during which the TIN has not been furnished in the manner required. The Secretary may require that a TIN required to be furnished under subsection (a)(1)(A) be provided under penalties of perjury only with respect to interest, dividends, patronage dividends, and amounts subject to broker reporting.

(2) NOTIFICATION OF INCORRECT NUMBER.—In any case in which the Secretary notifies the payor that the TIN furnished by the payee is incorrect, subsection (a) shall apply to any reportable payment made by such payor—

(A) after the close of the 30th day after the day on which the payor received such notification, and

(B) before the payee furnishes another TIN in the manner required.

(3) NOTIFIED PAYEE UNDERREPORTING DESCRIBED IN SUBSECTION (c).—

(A) IN GENERAL.—In the case of any notified payee underreporting described in subsection (c), subsection (a) shall apply to any reportable interest or dividend payment made—

(i) after the close of the 30th day after the day on which the payor received notification from the Secretary of such underreporting, and

(ii) before the stop date.

(B) STOP DATE.—For purposes of this subsection, the term "stop date" means the determination effective date or, if later, the earlier of—

(i) the day on which the payor received notification from the Secretary under subsection (c)(3)(B) to stop withholding, or

(ii) the day on which the payor receives from the payee a cetification provided by the Secretary under subsection (c)(3)(B).

(C) DETERMINATION EFFECTIVE DATE.—For purposes of this subsection—

(i) IN GENERAL.—Except as provided in clause (ii), the determination effective date of any determination under subsection (c)(3)(A) which is made during the 12-month period ending on October 15 of any calendar year shall be the first January 1 following such October 15.

(ii) DETERMINATION THAT THERE WAS NO UNDERREPORTING; HARDSHIP.—In the case of any determination under clause (i) or (iii) of subsection (c)(3)(A), the determination effective date shall be the date on which the Secretary's determination is made.

(4) FAILURE TO PROVIDE CERTIFICATION THAT PAYEE IS NOT SUBJECT TO WITHHOLDING.—

(A) IN GENERAL.—In the case of any payee certification failure described in subsection (d)(1), subsection (a) shall apply to any reportable interest or dividend payment made during the period during which the certification described in subsection (d)(1) has not been furnished to the payor.

(B) SPECIAL RULE FOR READILY TRADABLE INSTRUMENTS ACQUIRED THROUGH BROKER WHERE NOTIFICATION.—In the case of any readily tradable instrument acquired by the payee through a broker, the period described in subparagraph (A) shall start with payments to the payee made after the close of the 30th day after the payor receives notification from a broker under subsection (d)(2)(B).

(5) 30-DAY GRACE PERIODS.—

(A) START-UP.—If the payor elects the application of this subparagraph with respect to the payee, subsection (a) shall also apply to any reportable payment made during the 30-day period described in paragraph (2)(A), (3)(A), or (4)(B).

(B) STOPPING.—Unless the payor elects not to have this subparagraph apply with respect to the payee, subsection (a) shall also apply to any reportable payment made after the close of the period described in paragraph (1), (2), or (4) (as the case may be) and before the 30th

BACKUP WITHHOLDING

day after the close of such period. A similar rule shall also apply with respect to the period described in paragraph (3)(A) where the stop date is determined under clause (i) or (ii) of paragraph (3)(B).

(C) ELECTION OF SHORTER GRACE PERIOD.—The payor may elect a period shorter than the grace period set forth in subparagraph (A) or (B), as the case may be.

Amendments

• **1984, Deficit Reduction Act of 1984 (P.L. 98-369)**

P.L. 98-369, § 152(a):

Amended Code Sec. 3406(e)(1) by adding the sentence at the end thereof. **Effective** 7-18-84.

[Sec. 3406(f)]

(f) CONFIDENTIALITY OF INFORMATION.—

(1) IN GENERAL.—No person may use any information obtained under this section (including any failure to certify under subsection (d)) except for purposes of meeting any requirement under this section or (subject to the safeguards set forth in section 6103) for purposes permitted under section 6103.

(2) CROSS REFERENCE.—

For provision providing for civil damages for violation of paragraph (1), see section 7431.

[Sec. 3406(g)]

(g) EXCEPTIONS.—

(1) PAYMENTS TO CERTAIN PAYEES.—Subsection (a) shall not apply to any payment made to—

(A) any organization or governmental unit described in subparagraph (B), (C), (D), (E), or (F) of section 6049(b)(4), or

(B) any other person specified in regulations.

(2) AMOUNTS FOR WHICH WITHHOLDING OTHERWISE REQUIRED.—Subsection (a) shall not apply to any amount for which withholding is otherwise required by this title.

(3) EXEMPTION WHILE WAITING FOR TIN.—The Secretary shall prescribe regulations for exemptions from the tax imposed by subsection (a) during the period during which a person is waiting for receipt of a TIN.

[Sec. 3406(h)]

(h) OTHER DEFINITIONS AND SPECIAL RULES.—For purposes of this section—

(1) OBVIOUSLY INCORRECT NUMBER.—A person shall be treated as failing to furnish his TIN if the TIN furnished does not contain the proper number of digits.

(2) PAYEE FURNISHES 2 INCORRECT TINS.—If the payee furnishes the payor 2 incorrect TINs in any 3-year period, the payor shall, after receiving notice of the second incorrect TIN, treat the payee as not having furnished another TIN under subsection (e)(2)(B) until the day on which the payor receives notification from the Secretary that a correct TIN has been furnished.

(3) JOINT PAYEES.—Except to the extent otherwise provided in regulations, any payment to joint payees shall be treated as if all the payment were made to the first person listed in the payment.

(4) PAYOR DEFINED.—The term "payor" means, with respect to any reportable payment, a person required to file a return described in paragraph (2) or (3) of subsection (b) with respect to such payment.

(5) BROKER.—

(A) IN GENERAL.—The term "broker" has the meaning given to such term by section 6045(c)(1).

(B) ONLY 1 BROKER PER ACQUISITION.—If, but for this subparagraph, there would be more than 1 broker with respect to any acquisition, only the broker having the closest contact with the payee shall be treated as the broker.

(C) PAYOR NOT TREATED AS BROKER.—In the case of any instrument, such term shall not include any person who is the payor with respect to such instrument.

(D) REAL ESTATE BROKER NOT TREATED AS A BROKER.—Except as provided by regulations, such term shall not include any real estate broker (as defined in section 6045(e)(2)).

(6) READILY TRADABLE INSTRUMENT—The term "readily tradable instrument" means—

(A) any instrument which is part of an issue any portion of which is traded on an established securities market (within the meaning of section 453(f)(5)), and

(B) except as otherwise provided in regulations prescribed by the Secretary, any instrument which is regularly quoted by brokers or dealers making a market.

(7) ORIGINAL ISSUE DISCOUNT.—To the extent provided in regulations, rules similar to the rules of paragraph (6) of section 6049(d) shall apply.

(8) REQUIREMENT OF NOTICE TO PAYEE.—Whenever the Secretary notifies a payor under paragraph (1)(B) of subsection (a) that the TIN furnished by any payee is incorrect, the Secretary shall at the same time furnish a copy of such notice to the payor, and the payor shall promptly furnish such copy to the payee.

(9) REQUIREMENT OF NOTICE TO SECRETARY.—If the Secretary notifies a payor under paragraph (1)(B) of subsection (a) that the TIN furnished by any payee is incorrect and such payee subsequently furnishes another TIN to the payor, the payor shall promptly notify the Secretary of the other TIN so furnished.

(10) COORDINATION WITH OTHER SECTIONS.—For purposes of section 31, this chapter (other than section 3402(n)), and so much of subtitle F (other than section 7205) as relates to this chapter, payments which are subject to withholding under this section shall be treated as if they were wages paid by an employer to an employee (and amounts deducted and withheld under this section shall be treated as if deducted and withheld under section 3402).

Amendments

• **1988, Technical and Miscellaneous Revenue Act of 1988 (P.L. 100-647)**

P.L. 100-647, § 1018(u)(44):

Amended Code Sec. 3406(h)(5)(D) by adding a period at the end thereof. **Effective** as if included in the provision of P.L. 99-514 to which it relates.

• **1986, Tax Reform Act of 1986 (P.L. 99-514)**

P.L. 99-514, § 1521(b):

Amended Code Sec. 3406(h)(5) by adding at the end thereof new subparagraph (D). **Effective** for real estate transactions closing after 12-31-86.

[Sec. 3406(i)]

(i) REGULATIONS.—The Secretary shall prescribe such regulations as may be necessary or appropriate to carry out the purposes of this section.

WITHHOLDING FROM INTEREST AND DIVIDENDS

Amendments

• **1983, Interest and Dividend Tax Compliance Act of 1983 (P.L. 98-67)**

P.L. 98-67, §104(a):

Added Code Sec. 3406. **Effective** with respect to payments made after 12-31-83.

P.L. 98-67, §103, provides:

SEC. 103. SENSE OF THE CONGRESS WITH RESPECT TO INCREASED APPROPRIATIONS.

It is the sense of the Congress—

(1) that additional amounts should be appropriated for purposes of collecting tax due with respect to reportable payments (as defined in section 3406(b) of the Internal Revenue Code of 1954), and

(2) that—

(A) such additional amounts should not be less than—

(i) $15,000,000 for fiscal year 1984, and

(ii) $300,000,000 for the period consisting of fiscal years 1984 through 1988, and

(B) it would be preferable that such additional amounts for such period be at least $600,000,000.

Subchapter B—Withholding From Interest and Dividends—[Repealed]

[Sec. 3451—Repealed]

Amendments

• **1983, Interest and Dividend Tax Compliance Act of 1983 (P.L. 98-67)**

P.L. 98-67, §102(a):

Repealed Code Sec. 3451 as though it had not been enacted (see P.L. 97-248, below). **Effective** as of the close of 6-30-83. Prior to repeal, Code Sec. 3451 read as follows:

SEC. 3451. INCOME TAX COLLECTED AT SOURCE ON INTEREST, DIVIDENDS, AND PATRONAGE DIVIDENDS.

(a) REQUIREMENT OF WITHHOLDING.—Except as otherwise provided in this subchapter, the payor of any interest, dividend, or patronage dividend shall withhold a tax equal to 10 percent of the amount of the payment.

(b) SPECIAL RULES.—

(1) TIME OF WITHHOLDING.—Except as otherwise provided in this subchapter, for purposes of this subchapter—

(A) any payment of interest, dividend, or patronage dividend shall be treated as made, and

(B) the tax imposed by this section shall be withheld, at the time such interest, dividend, or patronage dividend is paid or credited.

(2) PAYEE UNKNOWN.—If a payor is unable to determine the person to whom any interest, dividend, or patronage dividend is payable or creditable, the tax under this section shall be withheld at the time withholding would be required under paragraph (1) if the payee were known and were an individual.

(3) AMOUNT OF DIVIDEND, ETC., UNKNOWN.—

(A) IN GENERAL.—If the payor is unable to determine the portion of a distribution which is a dividend, the tax under this section shall be computed on the gross amount of the distribution. To the extent provided in regulations, a similar rule shall apply in the case of interest and patronage dividends.

(B) DISTRIBUTIONS WHICH ARE NOT DIVIDENDS.—To the extent provided in regulations, this section shall not apply to the extent that the portion of a distribution which is not a dividend may reasonably be estimated.

(4) WITHHOLDING FROM ALTERNATIVE SOURCE.—The Secretary shall prescribe regulations setting forth the circumstances under which the tax imposed by this section may be paid from an account or source other than the payment which gives rise to the liability for tax.

(c) LIABILITY FOR PAYMENT.—

(1) PAYOR LIABLE.—Except as otherwise provided in this subchapter, the payor—

(A) shall be liable for the payment of the tax imposed by this section which such payor is required to withhold under this section, and

(B) shall not be liable to any person (other than the United States) for the amount of any such payment.

(2) RELIANCE ON EXEMPTION CERTIFICATES.—The payor shall not be liable for the payment of tax imposed by this section which such payor is required to withhold under this section if—

(A) such payor fails to withhold such tax, and

(B) such failure is due to reasonable reliance on an exemption certificate delivered to such payor under section 3452(f) which is in effect with respect to the payee at the time such tax is required to be withheld under this section.

§102(a)-(d), P.L. 98-67, contained the following non-Code provisions:

(a) IN GENERAL.—Subtitle A of title III of the Tax Equity and Fiscal Responsibility Act of 1982 (relating to withholding of tax from interest and dividends) is hereby repealed as of the close of June 30, 1983.

(b) CONFORMING AMENDMENT.—Except as provided in this section, the Internal Revenue Code of 1954 shall be applied and administered as if such subtitle A (and the amendments made by such subtitle A) had not been enacted.

(c) REPEAL NOT TO APPLY TO AMOUNTS DEDUCTED AND WITHHELD BEFORE SEPTEMBER 2, 1983.—

(1) IN GENERAL.—If, notwithstanding the repeal made by subsection (a) (and the provisions of subsection (b)), an amount is deducted and withheld before September 2, 1983, under subchapter B of chapter 24 of the Internal Revenue Code of 1954 (as in effect before its repeal by subsection (a)), the repeal made by subsection (a) (and the provisions of subsection (b)) shall not apply to the amount so deducted and withheld.

(2) ELECTION TO HAVE PARAGRAPH (1) NOT APPLY.—Paragraph (1) shall not apply with respect to any payor who elects (at the time and in the manner prescribed by the Secretary of the Treasury or his delegte) to have paragraph (1) not apply.

(d) ESTIMATED TAX PAYMENTS.—For purposes of determining the amount of any addition to tax under section 6654 of the Internal Revenue Code of 1954 with respect to any installment required to be paid before July 1, 1983, the amount of the credit allowed by section 31 of such Code for any taxable year which includes any portion of the period beginning July 1, 1983, and ending December 31, 1983, shall be increased by an amount equal to 10 percent of the aggregate amount of payments—

(1) which are received during the portion of such taxable year after June 30, 1983, and before January 1, 1984, and

(2) which (but for the repeal made by subsection (a)) would have been subject to withholding under subchapter B of chapter 24 of such Code (determined without regard to any exemption described in section 3452 of such subchapter B).

• **1982, Tax Equity and Fiscal Responsibility Act of 1982 (P.L. 97-248)**

P.L. 97-248, §301:

Added Code Sec. 3451. **Effective**, generally, for interest, dividends and patronage dividends paid or credited after 6-30-83.

[Sec. 3452—Repealed]

Amendments

• **1983, Interest and Dividend Tax Compliance Act of 1983 (P.L. 98-67)**

P.L. 98-67, §102(a):

Repealed Code Sec. 3452 as though it had not been enacted (see P.L. 97-248, below). **Effective** as of the close of 6-30-83. For special provisions governing the repeal, see the historical comment for P.L. 98-67 under repealed Code Sec. 3451. Prior to repeal, Code Sec. 3452 read as follows:

SEC. 3452. EXEMPTIONS FROM WITHHOLDING.

(a) IN GENERAL.—Section 3451 shall not apply with respect to—

(1) any payment to an exempt individual,

(2) any payment to an exempt recipient,

(3) any minimal interest payment, or

(4) any qualified consumer cooperative payment.

(b) EXEMPT INDIVIDUALS.—

(1) IN GENERAL.—For purposes of this section, the term "exempt individual" means any individual—

(A) who is described in paragraph (2), and

(B) with respect to whom an exemption certificate is in effect.

(2) INDIVIDUALS DESCRIBED IN THIS PARAGRAPH.—An individual is described in this paragraph if—

(A) such individual's income tax liability for the preceding taxable year did not exceed $600 ($1,000 in the case of a joint return under section 6013), or

(B)(i) such individual is 65 or older, and

(ii) such individual's income tax liability for the preceding taxable year did not exceed $1,500 ($2,500 in the case of a joint return under section 6013).

(3) SPECIAL RULE FOR MARRIED PERSONS.—A husband and wife shall each be treated as satisfying the requirements of paragraph (2)(B)(i) if—

(A) either spouse is 65 or older, and

(B) such husband and wife made a joint return under section 6013 for the preceding taxable year.

(4) SPECIAL RULE FOR CERTAIN TRUSTS DISTRIBUTING CURRENTLY.—Under regulations, a trust—

(A) the terms of which provide that all of its income is required to be distributed currently, and

(B) all the beneficiaries of which are individuals described in paragraph (2) or organizations described in subsection (c)(2)(B),

shall be treated as an individual described in paragraph (2).

(5) INCOME TAX LIABILITY.—For purposes of this subsection, the term "income tax liability" means the amount of the tax imposed by subtitle A for the taxable year, reduced by the sum of the credits allowable against such tax (other than credits allowable by sections 31, 39, and 43).

(c) EXEMPT RECIPIENTS.—

(1) IN GENERAL.—For purposes of this section, the term "exempt recipient" means any person described in paragraph (2)—

(A) with respect to whom an exemption certificate is in effect, or

(B) who is described in regulations prescribed by the Secretary which permit exemption from withholding without certification.

(2) PERSONS DESCRIBED IN THIS PARAGRAPH.—A person is described in this paragraph if such person is—

(A) a corporation,

(B) an organization exempt from taxation under section 501(a) or an individual retirement plan,

(C) the United States or a State,

(D) a foreign government or international organization,

WITHHOLDING FROM INTEREST AND DIVIDENDS

(E) a foreign central bank of issue,

(F) a dealer in securities or commodities required to register as such under the laws of the United States or a State,

(G) a real estate investment trust (as defined in section 856),

(H) an entity registered at all times during the taxable year under the Investment Company Act of 1940,

(I) a common trust fund (as defined in section 584(a)),

(J) a nominee or custodian (except as otherwise provided in regulations),

(K) to the extent provided in regulations—

(i) a financial institution,

(ii) a broker, or

(iii) any other person specified in such regulations, who collects any interest, dividend, or patronage dividend for the payee or otherwise acts as a middleman between the payor and payee, or

(L) any trust which—

(i) is exempt from tax under section 664(c), or

(ii) is described in section 4947(a)(1).

(3) PAYOR MAY REQUIRE CERTIFICATION.—A person described in paragraph (1)(B) shall not be treated as an exempt recipient for purposes of this section with respect to any payment of such payor if—

(A) an exemption certificate is not in effect with respect to such person, and

(B) the payor does not treat such person as an exempt recipient.

(d) MINIMAL INTEREST PAYMENTS.—

(1) IN GENERAL.—For purposes of this section, the term "minimal interest payment" means any payment of interest—

(A) with respect to which an election by the payor made under paragraph (3) is in effect, and

(B) which—

(i) does not exceed $150, and

(ii) if determined for a 1-year period would not exceed $150.

(2) AGGREGATION OF PAYMENTS TO SAME PAYEE.—To the extent provided in regulations prescribed by the Secretary, payments of interest by a payor to the same payee shall be aggregated for purposes of applying paragraph (1)(B).

(3) ELECTION.—

(A) IN GENERAL.—Any payor may make an election under this paragraph with respect to any type of interest payments.

Amendments

• **1983, Interest and Dividend Tax Compliance Act of 1983 (P.L. 98-67)**

P.L. 98-67, §102(a):

Repealed Code Sec. 3453 as though it had not been enacted (see P.L. 97-248, below). **Effective** as of the close of 6-30-83. For special provisions governing the repeal, see the historical comment for P.L. 98-67 under repealed Code Sec. 3451. Prior to repeal, Code Sec. 3453 read as follows:

SEC. 3453. PAYOR DEFINED.

(a) GENERAL RULE.—Except as otherwise provided in this subchapter, for purposes of this subchapter, the term "payor" means the person paying or crediting the interest, dividend, or patronage dividend.

(b) CERTAIN MIDDLEMEN TREATED AS PAYORS.—For purposes of this subchapter—

(1) IN GENERAL.—To the extent provided in regulations—

(A) any custodian for, or nominee of, the payee,

(B) any corporate trustee of a trust which is the payee,

(C) any person which collects the payment for the payee or otherwise acts as a middleman between the payor and the payee, or

(D) any S corporation which receives any payment,

shall be treated as a payor with respect to the payment.

(2) RECEIPT TREATED AS PAYMENT.—To the extent provided in regulations, any person treated as a payor under paragraph (1) shall be treated as having paid the interest, dividend, or patronage dividend when such person received such amount.

(c) AGENTS, ETC.—In the case of—

(1) a fiduciary or agent with respect to the payment or crediting of any interest, dividend, or patronage dividend, or

(2) any other person who has the control, receipt, custody, or disposal of, or pays or credits any interest, dividend, or patronage dividend for any payor,

the Secretary, under regulations prescribed by him, may designate such fiduciary, agent, or other person as a payor with respect to such payment or crediting for purposes of this subchapter.

[Sec. 3454—Repealed]

Amendments

• **1983, Interest and Dividend Tax Compliance Act of 1983 (P.L. 98-67)**

P.L. 98-67, §102(a):

Repealed Code Sec. 3454 as though it had not been enacted. **Effective** as of the close of 6-30-83. For special provisions governing the repeal, see the historical comment for P.L. 98-67 under repealed Code Sec. 3451. Prior to repeal, Code Sec. 3454 read as follows:

SEC. 3454. DEFINITIONS OF INTEREST, DIVIDEND, AND PATRONAGE DIVIDEND.

(a) INTEREST DEFINED.—For purposes of this subchapter—

(1) GENERAL RULE.—The term "interest" means—

(A) interest on any obligation in registered form or of a type offered to the public,

(B) interest on deposits with persons carrying on the banking business,

(B) EFFECTIVE UNTIL REVOKED.—Except as provided in regulations prescribed by the Secretary, an election made by any person under this paragraph shall remain in effect until revoked by such person.

(C) TIME AND MANNER.—Any election or revocation of an election made under this paragraph shall be made at such time and in such manner as the Secretary shall prescribe by regulations.

(e) QUALIFIED CONSUMER COOPERATIVE PAYMENT.—For purposes of this section, the term "qualified consumer cooperative payment" means any payment by a cooperative which is exempt from reporting requirements under section 6044(a) by reason of section 6044(c).

(f) EXEMPTION CERTIFICATES.—

(1) IN GENERAL.—

(A) DELIVERY.—An exempt individual or exempt recipient may deliver an exemption certificate to a payor at any time. Such certificate shall be in such form and contain such information as the Secretary shall prescribe.

(B) CHANGE OF STATUS.—Any person who ceases to be an exempt individual or exempt recipient shall, not later than the close of the 10th day after the date of such cessation, notify each payor with whom such person has an exemption certificate of such change in status. No notice shall be required under the preceding sentence with respect to any payor if it reasonably appears that the person will not thereafter receive a payment of interest, dividends, or patronage dividends from such payor.

(2) EFFECTIVENESS OF CERTIFICATES.—

(A) GENERAL RULE.—Except as otherwise provided in regulations prescribed by the Secretary, an exemption certificate shall be effective until—

(i) revoked, or

(ii) notice of change in status is provided pursuant to paragraph (1)(B).

(B) WHEN CERTIFICATE TAKES EFFECT.—The Secretary shall prescribe regulations setting forth—

(i) the day on which a filed exemption certificate shall be considered effective, and

(ii) the circumstances under which a payor shall treat an exemption certificate as having ceased to be effective where the Secretary has determined that the person described therein is not an exempt individual or exempt recipient.

• **1982, Tax Equity and Fiscal Responsibility Act of 1982 (P.L. 97-248)**

P.L. 97-248, §301:

Added Code Sec. 3452. **Effective**, generally, for interest, dividends and patronage dividends paid or credited after 6-30-83.

[Sec. 3453—Repealed]

(d) TREATMENT OF PERSONS TO WHOM SUBSECTION (b) OR (c) APPLIES.—Any person treated as a payor under subsection (b) or (c)—

(1) shall perform such acts as are required of a payor (within the meaning of subsection (a)) and as may be specified by the Secretary, and

(2) shall be treated as a payor for all provisions of law (including penalties) applicable in respect to a payor (within the meaning of subsection (a)).

(e) RELIEF FROM DOUBLE WITHHOLDING.—The Secretary may by regulations provide that where any person is treated as a payor under subsection (b) or (c) with respect to any payment, any other person who (but for this subsection) would be treated as a payor with respect to such payment shall be relieved from the requirements of this subchapter to the extent provided in such regulations.

(f) LIABILITY OF THIRD PARTIES PAYING OR PROVIDING INTEREST, DIVIDENDS, OR PATRONAGE DIVIDENDS.—To the extent provided in regulations prescribed by the Secretary, rules similar to the rules of section 3505 (relating to liability of third parties paying or providing for wages) shall apply for purposes of this subchapter. For purposes of the preceding sentence, the last sentence of subsection (b) of section 3505 shall be applied by substituting "10 percent" for "25 percent".

• **1982, Subchapter S Revision Act of 1982 (P.L. 97-354)**

P.L. 97-354, §3(i)(1):

Amended Code Sec. 3453(b)(1) by striking out "or" at the end of subparagraph (B), by inserting "or" at the end of subparagraph (C), and by adding new subparagraph (D). **Effective** for tax years beginning after 1982.

• **1982, Tax Equity and Fiscal Responsibility Act of 1982 (P.L. 97-248)**

P.L. 97-248, §301:

Added Code Sec. 3453. **Effective**, generally, for interest, dividends and patronage dividends paid or credited after 6-30-83.

(C) amounts (whether or not designated as interest) paid by a mutual savings bank, savings and loan association, building and loan association, cooperative bank, homestead association, credit union, industrial loan association or bank, or similar organization, in respect of deposits, investment certificates, or withdrawable or repurchasable shares,

(D) interest on amounts held by an insurance company under an agreement to pay interest thereon,

(E) interest on deposits with brokers (as defined in section 6045(c)), and

(F) interest paid on amounts held by investment companies (as defined in section 3 of the Investment Company Act of 1940 (15 U.S.C. 80a-3)) and on amounts invested in other pooled funds or trusts,

(2) EXCEPTIONS.—The term "interest" does not include—

(A) interest on any obligation issued by a natural person,

Sec. 3453—Repealed

(B) interest on any obligation if such interest is exempt from taxation under section 103(a) or if such interest is exempt from tax (without regard to the identity of the holder) under any other provision of this title,

(C) any amount paid on a depository institution taxexempt certificate (as defined in section 128(c)(1) (as in effect for taxable years beginning before January 1, 1985)),

(D) any amount which is subject to withholding under subchapter A of chapter 3 (relating to withholding of tax on nonresident aliens and foreign corporations) by the person paying such amount,

(E) any amount which would be subject to withholding under subchapter A of chapter 3 by the person paying such amount but for the fact that—

(i) such amount is income from sources outside the United States,

(ii) the payor thereof is excepted from the application of section 1441(a) by reason of section 1441(c) or a tax treaty, or

(iii) such amount is original issue discount (within the meaning of section 1232(b)(1)),

(F) any amount which is exempt from tax under—

(i) section 892 (relating to income of foreign governments and of international organizations), or

(ii) section 895 (relating to income derived by a foreign central bank of issue from obligations of the United States or from bank deposits),

(G) except to the extent otherwise provided in regulations, any amount paid by—

(i) a foreign government or international organization or any agency or instrumentality thereof,

(ii) a foreign central bank of issue,

(iii) a foreign corporation not engaged in trade or business in the United States,

(iv) a foreign corporation, the interest payments of which would be exempt from withholding under subchapter A of chapter 3 if paid to a person who is not a United States person, or

(v) a partnership not engaged in a trade or business in the United States and composed in whole of nonresident aliens, individuals and persons described in clause (i), (ii), or (iii),

(H) any amount on which the person making payment is required to withhold a tax under section 1451 (relating to tax-free covenant bonds), or would be so required but for section 1451(d) (relating to benefit of personal exemptions), and

(I) except to the extent otherwise provided in regulations, any amount not described in the foregoing provisions of this paragraph which is paid outside the United States and is income from sources outside the United States.

(3) ADJUSTMENT FOR PENALTY BECAUSE OF PREMATURE WITHDRAWAL OF FUNDS FROM TIME SAVINGS ACCOUNTS OR DEPOSITS.—To the extent provided in regulations, the amount of any interest on a time savings account, certificate of deposit, or similar class of deposits shall be appropriately reduced for purposes of this subchapter by the amount of any penalty imposed for the premature withdrawal of funds.

(b) DIVIDEND DEFINED.—For purposes of this subchapter—

(1) GENERAL RULE.—The term "dividend" means—

(A) any distribution by a corporation which is a dividend (as defined in section 316), or

(B) any payment made by a stockbroker to any person as a substitute for a dividend (as so defined).

(2) EXCEPTIONS.—The term "dividend" shall not include—

(A) any amount paid as a distribution of stock described in section 305(e)(2)(A) (relating to reinvestment of dividends in stock of public utilities),

(B) any amount which is treated as a taxable dividend by reason of section 302 (relating to redemptions of stock), 306 (relating to disposition of certain stock), 356 (relating to receipt of additional consideration in connection with certain reorganizations), or 1081(e)(2) (relating to certain distributions pursuant to order of the Securities and Exchange Commission),

(C) any amount described in subparagraph (D), (E), or (F) of subsection (a)(2),

(D) to the extent provided in regulations, any amount paid by a foreign corporation not engaged in a trade or business in the United States,

(E) any amount which is a capital gain dividend distributed by—

(i) a regulated investment company (as defined in section 852(b)(3)(C)), or

(ii) a real estate investment trust (as defined in section 857(b)(3)(C)),

(F) any amount which is an exempt-interest dividend of a regulated investment company (as defined in section 852(b)(5)(A)), and

[Sec. 3455—Repealed]

Amendments

• 1983, Interest and Dividend Tax Compliance Act of 1983 (P.L. 98-67)

P.L. 98-67, §102(a):

Repealed Code Sec. 3455 as though it had not been enacted (see P.L. 97-248). Effective as of the close of 6-30-83. For special provisions governing the repeal, see the historical comment for P.L. 98-67 under repealed Code Sec. 3451. Prior to repeal, Code Sec. 3455 read as follows:

SEC. 3455. OTHER DEFINITIONS AND SPECIAL RULES.

(a) DEFINITIONS.—For purposes of this subchapter—

(1) PERSON.—The term "person" includes any governmental unit and any agency or instrumentality thereof and any international organization.

(2) STATE.—The term "State" means a State, the District of Columbia, a possession of the United States, any political subdivision of any of the foregoing, and any wholly owned agency or instrumentality of any one or more of the foregoing.

(3) UNITED STATES.—The term "United States" means the United States and any wholly owned agency or instrumentality thereof.

(4) FOREIGN GOVERNMENT.—The term "foreign government" means a foreign government, a political subdivision of a foreign government, and any wholly owned agency or instrumentality of any one or more of the foregoing.

(G) any amount paid or treated as paid by a regulated investment company during a year if, under regulations prescribed by the Secretary, it is anticipated that at least 95 percent of the dividends paid or treated as paid during such year (not including capital gain distributions) will be exempt-interest dividends.

(c) PATRONAGE DIVIDEND.—For purposes of this subchapter—

(1) IN GENERAL.—The term "patronage dividend" means—

(A) the amount of any patronage dividend (as defined in section 1388(a)) which is paid in money, qualified written notice of allocation, or other property (except a nonqualified written notice of allocation),

(B) any amount, described in section 1382(c)(2)(A) (relating to certain nonpatronage distributions), which is paid in money, qualified written notice of allocation, or other property (except nonqualified written notice of allocation) by an organization exempt from tax under section 521 (relating to exemption of farmers' cooperatives from tax), and

(C) any amount paid in money or other property (except written notice of allocation) in redemption of a nonqualified written notice of allocation attributable to any source described in subparagraph (A) or (B).

(2) EXCEPTIONS.—The term "patronage dividend" shall not include any amount described in subparagraph (D), (E), or (F) of subsection (a)(2).

(3) SPECIAL RULES.—In determining the amount of any patronage dividend—

(A) property (other than a written notice of allocation) shall be taken into account at its fair market value,

(B) a qualified written notice of allocation described in section 1388(c)(1)(A) shall be taken into account at its stated dollar amount, and

(C) a patronage dividend part of which is a qualified written notice of allocation described in section 1388(c)(1)(B) (and not in section 1388(c)(1)(A)) shall be taken into account only if 50 percent or more of such dividend is paid in money or by a qualified check, and any such qualified written notice of allocation which is taken into account after the application of this subparagraph shall be taken into account at its stated dollar amount.

(4) DEFINITIONS.—For purposes of this subsection—

(A) QUALIFIED WRITTEN NOTICE OF ALLOCATION.—The term "qualified written notice of allocation" has the meaning given to such term by section 1388(c).

(B) NONQUALIFIED WRITTEN NOTICE OF ALLOCATION.—The term "nonqualified written notice of allocation" has the meaning given to such term by section 1388(d).

(C) QUALIFIED CHECK.—The term "qualified check" has the meaning given to such term by section 1388(c)(4).

• 1983, Surface Transportation Act of 1982 (P.L. 97-424)

P.L. 97-424, §547(b)(3):

Amended Code Sec. 3454(a)(2)(B) by striking out "law" and inserting in lieu thereof "this title".

• 1982, Subchapter S Revision Act of 1982 (P.L. 97-354)

P.L. 97-354, §3(i)(2):

Amended Code Sec. 3454(b) by striking out paragraph (2) and by redesignating paragraph (3) as paragraph (2). Effective for tax years beginning after 12-31-82. Prior to being striken, paragraph (2) read:

"(2) SUBCHAPTER S DISTRIBUTIONS AFTER CLOSE OF YEAR.—The term `dividend' includes any distribution described in section 1375(f) (relating to distributions by electing small business corporations after the close of the taxable year)."

P.L. 97-354, §3(i)(3):

Amended Code Sec. 3454(b)(2) (as redesignated by Act Sec. 3(i)(2)) by inserting "and" at the end of subparagraph (F), by striking out ", and " at the end of subparagraph (G) and inserting in lieu thereof a period, and by striking subparagraph (H). Effective for tax years beginning after 12-31-82. Prior to being striken, subparagraph (H) read:

"(H) any amount described in section 1373 (relating to undistributed taxable income of electing small business corporations)."

• 1982, Tax Equity and Fiscal Responsibility Act of 1982 (P.L. 97-248)

P.L. 97-248, §301:

Added Code Sec. 3454. Effective, generally, for interest, dividends and patronage dividends paid or credited after 6-30-83.

(5) INTERNATIONAL ORGANIZATION.—The term "international organization" means an international organization and any wholly owned agency or instrumentality thereof.

(6) NONRESIDENT ALIEN.—The term "nonresident alien individual" includes an alien resident of Puerto Rico.

(7) WITHHOLD, ETC., INCLUDE DEDUCT.—The terms "withhold", "withholding", and "withheld" include deduct, deducting, and deducted.

(b) TREATMENT OF ORIGINAL ISSUE DISCOUNT.—

(1) IN GENERAL.—Except as provided in paragraphs (2) and (3) the tax imposed by section 3451 shall apply to the amount of original issue discount on any obligation which is includible in the gross income of the holder during the calendar year. Any such amount shall be treated as a payment for purposes of this subchapter.

(2) TRANSFERRED OBLIGATIONS.—

(A) IN GENERAL.—In the case of original issue discount on any obligation which has been transferred from the original holder, the tax imposed by section 3451 shall apply to such original issue discount as if the subsequent holder were the original holder.

(B) SPECIAL RULE FOR SHORT-TERM OBLIGATIONS.—In the case of any obligation with a fixed maturity date not exceeding 1 year from the date of issue which has been transferred from the original holder, if any subsequent purchaser establishes the date on which, and the purchase price at which, he acquired such obligation, the amount

EMPLOYMENT TAXES—GENERAL PROVISIONS

of original issue discount on such obligation shall be determined (subject to such regulations as the Secretary may prescribe) as if it were issued on the date such subsequent purchaser acquired such obligation for an issue price equal to the purchase price at which such subsequent purchaser acquired such obligation.

(3) LIMITATION ON AMOUNT WITHHELD.—

(A) IN GENERAL.—The amount of tax imposed by section 3451 on the original issue discount on any obligation which is required to be withheld under section 3451(a) in any calendar year shall not exceed the amount of cash paid with respect to such obligation during such calendar year.

(B) AUTHORITY OF SECRETARY TO ELIMINATE LIMITATION IN CERTAIN CASES.—If the Secretary determines by regulation that a type of obligation is frequently used to avoid the purposes of this subchapter, subparagraph (A) shall not apply with respect to original issue discount on any obligation of such type which is issued more than 30 days after the first date on which such regulations are published in the Federal Register.

Amendments

• **1983, Interest and Dividend Tax Compliance Act of 1983 (P.L. 98-67)**

P.L. 98-67, § 102(a):

Repealed Code Sec. 3456 as though it had not been enacted (see P.L. 97-248). **Effective** as of the close of 6-30-83. For special provisions governing the repeal, see the historical comment for P.L. 98-67 under repealed Code Sec. 3451. Prior to repeal, Code Sec. 3456 read as follows:

SEC. 3456. ADMINISTRATIVE PROVISIONS.

(a) RETURN AND PAYMENT BY GOVERNMENTAL UNITS.—If the payor of any payment subject to withholding under section 3451 is the United States or a State, or an agency or instrumentality thereof, the return of the tax withheld under this subchapter shall be made by the officer or employee having control of the payment of the amount subject to withholding or by any officer or employee appropriately designated to make such withholding.

(b) ANNUAL WITHHOLDING BY FINANCIAL INSTITUTIONS.—

(1) IN GENERAL.—Under regulations prescribed by the Secretary, a financial institution described in subparagraph (B) or (C) of section 3454(a)(1) may elect to defer withholding of the tax imposed by section 3451 during any calendar year on interest paid on savings accounts, interest-bearing checking accounts, and similar accounts until a date which is not later than the last day of such year.

(2) CONDITION FOR ELECTION.—The regulations prescribed under paragraph (1) shall provide that an election under such paragraph is conditional on agreement by the person making the election—

(C) PAYMENTS FROM WHICH WITHHOLDING IS TO BE MADE.—Except to the extent otherwise provided in regulations, the tax imposed by section 3451 with respect to original issue discount for any calendar year shall be withheld from each cash payment made with respect to such obligation during such calendar year in the proportion which the amount of such payment bears to the aggregate of such payments.

(4) ORIGINAL ISSUE DISCOUNT DEFINED.—For purposes of this subsection, the term "original issue discount" has the meaning given such term by section 1232(b)(1).

• **1982, Tax Equity and Fiscal Responsibility Act of 1982 (P.L. 97-248)**

P.L. 97-248, § 301:

Added Code Sec. 3455. **Effective**, generally, for interest, dividends and patronage dividends paid or credited after 6-30-83.

[Sec. 3456—Repealed]

(A) that the balance in any account subject to such election shall at no time be less than an amount equal to the tax under section 3451 which would have been withheld as of such time if such election were not in effect, and

(B) that if an account subject to such election is closed before the date on which the tax under section 3451 would (but for this subparagraph) be withheld as a result of such an election, the tax shall be withheld before the time of closing such account.

(c) TAX PAID BY RECIPIENT.—If a payor, in violation of the provisions of this subchapter, fails to withhold the tax imposed under section 3451, and thereafter the tax against which such tax may be credited is paid, the tax so required to be withheld shall not be collected from the payor; but this subsection shall in no case relieve the payor from liability for any penalties or additions to the tax otherwise applicable in respect of such failure to withhold.

(d) REGULATIONS.—The Secretary shall prescribe such regulations as may be necessary or appropriate to carry out the purposes of this subchapter.

• **1982, Tax Equity and Fiscal Responsibility Act of 1982 (P.L. 97-248)**

P.L. 97-248, § 301:

Added Code Sec. 3456. **Effective**, generally, for interest, dividends and patronage dividends paid or credited after 6-30-83.

CHAPTER 25—GENERAL PROVISIONS RELATING TO EMPLOYMENT TAXES

Sec. 3501.	Collection and payment of taxes.
Sec. 3502.	Nondeductibility of taxes in computing taxable income.
Sec. 3503.	Erroneous payments.
Sec. 3504.	Acts to be performed by agents.
Sec. 3505.	Liability of third parties paying or providing for wages.
Sec. 3506.	Individuals providing companion sitting placement services.
Sec. 3508.	Treatment of real estate agents and direct sellers.
Sec. 3509.	Determination of employer's liability for certain employment taxes.
Sec. 3510.	Coordination of collection of domestic service employment taxes with collection of income taxes.
Sec. 3511.	Certified professional employer organizations.
Sec. 3512.	Treatment of certain persons as employers with respect to motion picture projects.

[Sec. 3501]

SEC. 3501. COLLECTION AND PAYMENT OF TAXES.

[Sec. 3501(a)]

(a) GENERAL RULE.—The taxes imposed by this subtitle shall be collected by the Secretary and shall be paid into the Treasury of the United States as internal-revenue collections.

[Sec. 3501(b)]

(b) TAXES WITH RESPECT TO NON-CASH FRINGE BENEFITS.—The taxes imposed by this subtitle with respect to non-cash fringe benefits shall be collected (or paid) by the employer at the time and in the manner prescribed by the Secretary by regulations.

Amendments

• **1984, Deficit Reduction Act of 1984 (P.L. 98-369)**

P.L. 98-369, § 531(d)(5):

Amended Code Sec. 3501 by striking out "The taxes" and inserting in lieu thereof: "(a) GENERAL RULE.—The taxes", and by adding at the end thereof new subsection (b) above. **Effective** 1-1-85.

• **1976, Tax Reform Act of 1976 (P.L. 94-455)**

P.L. 94-455, § 1906(b)(13)(A):

Amended 1954 Code by substituting "Secretary" for "Secretary or his delegate" each place it appeared. **Effective** 2-1-77.

[Sec. 3502]

SEC. 3502. NONDEDUCTIBILITY OF TAXES IN COMPUTING TAXABLE INCOME.

[Sec. 3502(a)]

(a) The taxes imposed by section 3101 of chapter 21, and by sections 3201 and 3211 of chapter 22 shall not be allowed as a deduction to the taxpayer in computing taxable income under subtitle A.

Sec. 3456—Repealed

EMPLOYMENT TAXES—GENERAL PROVISIONS

[Sec. 3502(b)]

(b) The tax deducted and withheld under chapter 24 shall not be allowed as a deduction either to the employer or to the recipient of the income in computing taxable income under subtitle A.

Amendments

• **1983, Interest and Dividend Tax Compliance Act of 1983 (P.L. 98-67)**

P.L. 98-67, §102(a):

Repealed the amendment to Code Sec. 3502(b) made by P.L. 97-248 as though it had not been enacted. **Effective** as of the close of 6-30-83.

• **1982, Tax Equity and Fiscal Responsibility Act of 1982 (P.L. 97-248)**

P.L. 97-248, §305(b)(1):

Amended Code Sec. 3502(b) by striking out "under chapter 24" and inserting in lieu thereof "under subchapter A of chapter 24". **Effective** 7-1-83.

[Sec. 3502(c)—Repealed]

Amendments

• **1983, Interest and Dividend Tax Compliance Act of 1983 (P.L. 98-67)**

P.L. 98-67, 102(a):

Repealed Code Sec. 3502(c) as added by P.L. 97-248 as though such section had not been enacted. **Effective** as of the close of 6-30-83. Prior to repeal, Code Sec. 3502(c) read as follows:

(c) The tax withheld under subchapter B of chapter 24 shall not be allowed as a deduction in computing taxable income under subtitle A either to the person withholding the tax or to the recipient of the amounts subject to withholding.

• **1982, Tax Equity and Fiscal Responsibility Act of 1982 (P.L. 97-248)**

P.L. 97-248, §305(b)(2):

Added Code Sec. 3502(c). **Effective** 7-1-83.

[Sec. 3503]

SEC. 3503. ERRONEOUS PAYMENTS.

Any tax paid under chapter 21 or 22 by a taxpayer with respect to any period with respect to which he is not liable to tax under such chapter shall be credited against the tax, if any, imposed by such other chapter upon the taxpayer, and the balance, if any, shall be refunded.

[Sec. 3504]

SEC. 3504. ACTS TO BE PERFORMED BY AGENTS.

In case a fiduciary, agent, or other person has the control, receipt, custody, or disposal of, or pays the wages of an employee or group of employees, employed by one or more employers, the Secretary, under regulations prescribed by him, is authorized to designate such fiduciary, agent, or other person to perform such acts as are required of employers under this title and as the Secretary may specify. Except as may be otherwise prescribed by the Secretary, all provisions of law (including penalties) applicable in respect of an employer shall be applicable to a fiduciary, agent, or other person so designated but, except as so provided, the employer for whom such fiduciary, agent, or other person acts shall remain subject to the provisions of law (including penalties) applicable in respect of employers.

Amendments

• **2020, Coronavirus Aid, Relief, and Economic Security (CARES) Act (P.L. 116-136)**

P.L. 116-136, §2302(a), (c)(1), (d), and (f), provides:

(a) IN GENERAL.—

(1) TAXES.—Notwithstanding any other provision of law, the payment for applicable employment taxes for the payroll tax deferral period shall not be due before the applicable date.

(2) DEPOSITS.—Notwithstanding section 6302 of the Internal Revenue Code of 1986, an employer shall be treated as having timely made all deposits of applicable employment taxes that are required to be made (without regard to this section) for such taxes during the payroll tax deferral period if all such deposits are made not later than the applicable date.

(3) EXCEPTION.—This subsection shall not apply to any taxpayer if such taxpayer has had indebtedness forgiven under section 1106 of this Act with respect to a loan under paragraph (36) of section 7(a) of the Small Business Act (15 U.S.C. 636(a)), as added by section 1102 of this Act, or indebtedness forgiven under section 1109 of this Act. [Stricken by P.L. 116-142, §4(a), **effective** as if included in the CARES Act (P.L. 116-136) and applicable to any loan made pursuant to section 7(a)(36) of the Small Business Act (15 U.S.C. 636(a)(36)) or section 1109 of the CARES Act.]

* * *

(c) LIABILITY OF THIRD PARTIES.—

(1) ACTS TO BE PERFORMED BY AGENTS.—For purposes of section 3504 of the Internal Revenue Code of 1986, in the case of any person designated pursuant to such section (and any regulations or other guidance issued by the Secretary with respect to such section) to perform acts otherwise required to be performed by an employer under such Code, if such employer directs such person to defer payment of any applicable employment taxes during the payroll tax deferral period under this section, such employer shall be solely liable for the payment of such applicable employment taxes before the applicable date for any wages paid by such person on behalf of such employer during such period.

* * *

(d) DEFINITIONS.—For purposes of this section—

(1) APPLICABLE EMPLOYMENT TAXES.—The term "applicable employment taxes" means the following:

(A) The taxes imposed under section 3111(a) of the Internal Revenue Code of 1986.

(B) So much of the taxes imposed under section 3211(a) of such Code as are attributable to the rate in effect under section 3111(a) of such Code.

(C) So much of the taxes imposed under section 3221(a) of such Code as are attributable to the rate in effect under section 3111(a) of such Code.

(2) PAYROLL TAX DEFERRAL PERIOD.—The term "payroll tax deferral period" means the period beginning on the date of the enactment of this Act and ending before January 1, 2021.

(3) APPLICABLE DATE.—The term "applicable date" means—

(A) December 31, 2021, with respect to 50 percent of the amounts to which subsection (a) or (b), as the case may be, apply, and

(B) December 31, 2022, with respect to the remaining such amounts.

(4) SECRETARY.—The term "Secretary" means the Secretary of the Treasury (or the Secretary's delegate).

* * *

(f) REGULATORY AUTHORITY.—The Secretary shall issue such regulations or other guidance as necessary to carry out the purposes of this section, including rules for the administration and enforcement of subsection (c).

• **1976, Tax Reform Act of 1976 (P.L. 94-455)**

P.L. 94-455, §1906(b)(13)(A):

Amended 1954 Code by substituting "Secretary" for "Secretary or his delegate" each place it appeared. **Effective** 2-1-77.

• **1958, Technical Amendments Act of 1958 (P.L. 85-866)**

P.L. 85-866, §71:

Substituted "title" for "subtitle" in the 5th line of Sec. 3504 above. **Effective** for remuneration paid after 12-31-54.

[Sec. 3505]

SEC. 3505. LIABILITY OF THIRD PARTIES PAYING OR PROVIDING FOR WAGES.

[Sec. 3505(a)]

(a) DIRECT PAYMENT BY THIRD PARTIES.—For purposes of sections 3102, 3202, 3402, and 3403, if a lender, surety, or other person, who is not an employer under such sections with respect to an employee or group of employees, pays wages directly to such an employee or group of employees, employed by one or more employers, or to an agent on behalf of such employee or employees, such lender, surety, or other person shall be liable in his own person and estate to the United States in a sum equal to the taxes (together with interest) required to be deducted and withheld from such wages by such employer.

[Sec. 3505(b)]

(b) PERSONAL LIABILITY WHERE FUNDS ARE SUPPLIED.—If a lender, surety, or other person supplies funds to or for the account of an employer for the specific purpose of paying wages of the employees of such employer, with actual notice or knowledge (within the meaning of section 6323(i)(1)) that such employer does not intend to or will not be able to make timely payment or deposit of the amounts of tax required by this subtitle to be deducted and withheld by such employer from such wages, such lender, surety, or other person shall be liable in his own person and estate to the United States in a sum equal to the taxes (together with interest) which are not paid over to the United States by such employer with respect to such

EMPLOYMENT TAXES—GENERAL PROVISIONS

wages. However, the liability of such lender, surety, or other person shall be limited to an amount equal to 25 percent of the amount so supplied to or for the account of such employer for such purpose.

[Sec. 3505(c)]

(c) EFFECT OF PAYMENT.—Any amounts paid to the United States pursuant to this section shall be credited against the liability of the employer.

Amendments

• 1966, Federal Tax Lien Act of 1966 (P.L. 89-719)

P.L. 89-719, §105(a):

Added Code Sec. 3505. **Effective**, generally, after 11-2-66, the date of enactment. However, see the amendment note for Code Sec. 6323 for exceptions to this effective date.

[Sec. 3506]

SEC. 3506. INDIVIDUALS PROVIDING COMPANION SITTING PLACEMENT SERVICES.

[Sec. 3506(a)]

(a) IN GENERAL.—For purposes of this subtitle, a person engaged in the trade or business of putting sitters in touch with individuals who wish to employ them shall not be treated as the employer of such sitters (and such sitters shall not be treated as employees of such person) if such person does not pay or receive the salary or wages of the sitters and is compensated by the sitters or the persons who employ them on a fee basis.

[Sec. 3506(b)]

(b) DEFINITION.—For purposes of this section, the term "sitters" means individuals who furnish personal attendance, companionship, or household care services to children or to individuals who are elderly or disabled.

[Sec. 3506(c)]

(c) REGULATIONS.—The Secretary shall prescribe such regulations as may be necessary to carry out the purpose of this section.

Amendments

• 1977 (P.L. 95-171)

P.L. 95-171, §10(a):

Added Code Sec. 3506. **Effective** for tax years beginning after 1974. However, this section is not to be construed as affecting any individual's right to receive unemployment compensation based on services performed before the date of enactment (11-12-77) or any individual's eligibility for social security benefits to the extent based on services performed before that date.

[Sec. 3507—Repealed]

Amendments

• 2010, (P.L. 111-226)

P.L. 111-226, §219(a)(1):

Repealed Code Sec. 3507. **Effective** for tax years beginning after 12-31-2010. Prior to repeal, Code Sec. 3507 read as follows:

SEC. 3507. ADVANCE PAYMENT OF EARNED INCOME CREDIT.

[Sec. 3507(a)]

(a) GENERAL RULE.—Except as otherwise provided in this section, every employer making payment of wages to an employee with respect to whom an earned income eligibility certificate is in effect shall, at the time of paying such wages, make an additional payment to such employee equal to such employee's earned income advance amount.

[Sec. 3507(b)]

(b) EARNED INCOME ELIGIBILITY CERTIFICATE.—For purposes of this title, an earned income eligibility certificate is a statement furnished by an employee to the employer which—

(1) certifies that the employee will be eligible to receive the credit provided by section 32 for the taxable year,

(2) certifies that the employee has 1 or more qualifying children (within the meaning of section 32(c)(3)) for such taxable year,

(3) certifies that the employee does not have an earned income eligibility certificate in effect for the calendar year with respect to the payment of wages by another employer, and

(4) states whether or not the employee's spouse has an earned income eligibility certificate in effect.

For purposes of this section, a certificate shall be treated as being in effect with respect to a spouse if such a certificate will be in effect on the first status determination date following the date on which the employee furnishes the statement in question.

Amendments

• 1993, Omnibus Budget Reconciliation Act of 1993 (P.L. 103-66)

P.L. 103-66, §13131(d)(4):

Amended Code Sec. 3507(b)(2)-(4) by redesignating paragraphs (2) and (3) as paragraphs (3) and (4), respectively, and by inserting after paragraph (1) a new paragraph (2). **Effective** for tax years beginning after 12-31-93.

• 1984, Deficit Reduction Act of 1984 (P.L. 98-369)

P.L. 98-369, §474(r)(30):

Amended Code Sec. 3507(b) by striking out "section 43" and inserting in lieu thereof "section 32". **Effective** for tax years beginning after 12-31-83, and to carrybacks from such years.

[Sec. 3507(c)]

(c) EARNED INCOME ADVANCE AMOUNT.—

(1) IN GENERAL.—For purposes of this title, the term "earned income advance amount" means, with respect to any payroll period, the amount determined—

(A) on the basis of the employee's wages from the employer for such period, and

(B) in accordance with tables prescribed by the Secretary.

In the case of an employee who is a member of the Armed Forces of the United States, the earned income advance amount shall be determined by taking into account such employee's earned income as determined for purposes of section 32.

(2) ADVANCE AMOUNT TABLES.—The tables referred to in paragraph (1)(B)—

(A) shall be similar in form to the tables prescribed under section 3402 and, to the maximum extent feasible, shall be coordinated with such tables, and

(B) if the employee is not married, or if no earned income eligibility certificate is in effect with respect to the spouse of the employee, shall treat the credit provided by section 32 as if it were a credit—

(i) of not more than 60 percent of the credit percentage in effect under section 32(b)(1) for an eligible individual with 1 qualifying child and with earned income not in excess of the earned income amount in effect under section 32(b)(2) for such an eligible individual, which

(ii) phases out at 60 percent of the phaseout percentage in effect under section 32(b)(1) for such an eligible individual between the phaseout amount in effect under section 32(b)(2) for such an eligible individual and the amount of earned income at which the credit under section 32(a) phases out for such an eligible individual, or

(C) if an earned income eligibility certificate is in effect with respect to the spouse of the employee, shall treat the credit as if it were a credit determined under subparagraph (B) by substituting ½ of the amounts of earned income described in such subparagraph for such amounts.

Amendments

• 1994, Uruguay Round Agreements Act (P.L. 103-465)

P.L. 103-465, §721(c):

Amended Code Sec. 3507(c)(1) by adding at the end a new sentence. **Effective** for remuneration paid after 12-31-94.

• 1993, Omnibus Budget Reconciliation Act of 1993 (P.L. 103-66)

P.L. 103-66, §13131(d)(5):

Amended Code Sec. 3507(c)(2)(B) by striking clauses (i) and (ii) and inserting new clauses (i) and (ii). **Effective** for tax years beginning after 12-31-93. Prior to amendment, Code Sec. 3507(c)(2)(B)(i)-(ii) read as follows:

(i) of not more than the credit percentage under section 32(b)(1) (without regard to subparagraph (D) thereof) for an eligible individual with 1 qualifying child and with earned income not in excess of the amount of earned income taken into account under section 32(a)(1), which

(ii) phases out between the amount of earned income at which the phaseout begins under section 32(b)(1)(B)(ii) and the amount of income at which the credit under section 32(a)(1) phases out for an eligible individual with 1 qualifying child, or

• 1990, Omnibus Budget Reconciliation Act of 1990 (P.L. 101-508)

P.L. 101-508, §11111(c):

Amended Code Sec. 3507(c)(2)(B) and (C). **Effective** for tax years beginning after 12-31-90. Prior to amendment, Code Sec. 3507(c)(2)(B) and (C) read as follows:

(B) if the employee is not married, or if no earned income eligibility certificate is in effect with respect to the spouse of the employee, shall treat the credit provided by section 32 as if it were a credit—

(i) of not more than 14 percent of earned income not in excess of the amount of earned income taken into account under section 32(a), which

(ii) phases out between the amount of earned income at which the phaseout begins under subsection (b) of section 32 and the amount of earned income at which the credit under section 32 is phased out under subsection, or

(C) if an earned income eligibility certificate is in effect with respect to the spouse of the employee, shall treat the credit provided by section 32 as if it were a credit—

(i) of not more than 14 percent of earned income not in excess of $1/2$ of the amount of earned income taken into account under section 32(a), which

(ii) phases out between amounts of earned income which are $1/2$ of the amounts of earned income described in subparagraph (B)(ii).

- **1986, Tax Reform Act of 1986 (P.L. 99-514)**

P.L. 99-514, § 111(d)(2):

Amended Code Sec. 3507(c)(2)(B) by striking out clauses (i) and (ii) and inserting in lieu thereof new clauses (i) and (ii). **Effective** for tax years beginning after 12-31-86. Prior to amendment, Code Sec. 3507(c)(2)(B)(i) and (ii) read as follows:

(i) of not more than 11 percent of the first $5,000 of earned income, which

(ii) phases out between $6,500 and $11,000 of earned income, or

P.L. 99-514, § 111(d)(3):

Amended Code Sec. 3507(c)(2)(C) by striking out clauses (i) and (ii) and inserting in lieu thereof new clauses (i) and (ii). **Effective** for tax years beginning after 12-31-86. Prior to amendment, Code Sec. 3507(c)(2)(C)(i) and (ii) read as follows:

(i) of not more than 11 percent of the first $2,500 of earned income, which

(ii) phases out between $3,250 and $5,500 of earned income.

- **1984, Deficit Reduction Act of 1984 (P.L. 98-369)**

P.L. 98-369, § 474(r)(30):

Amended Code Sec. 3507(c) by striking out "section 43" each place it appeared and inserting in lieu thereof "section 32". **Effective** for tax years beginning after 12-31-83, and to carrybacks from such years.

P.L. 98-369, § 1042(d)(3):

Amended Code Sec. 3507(c)(2)(B)(i) and (ii). **Effective** for tax years beginning after 12-31-84. Prior to amendment, clauses (i) and (ii) read as follows:

(i) of not more than 10 percent of the first $5,000 of earned income which

(ii) phases out between $6,000 and $10,000 of earned income, or

P.L. 98-369, § 1042(d)(4):

Amended Code Sec. 3507(c)(2)(C)(i) and (ii). **Effective** for tax years beginning after 12-31-84. Prior to amendment, clauses (i) and (ii) read as follows:

(i) of not more than 10 percent of the first $2,500 of earned income, which

(ii) phases out between $3,000 and $5,000 of earned income.

[Sec. 3507(d)]

(d) PAYMENTS TO BE TREATED AS PAYMENTS OF WITHHOLDING AND FICA TAXES.—

(1) IN GENERAL.—For purposes of this title, payments made by an employer under subsection (a) to his employees for any payroll period—

(A) shall not be treated as the payment of compensation, and

(B) shall be treated as made out of—

(i) amounts required to be deducted and withheld for the payroll period under section 3401 (relating to wage withholding), and

(ii) amounts required to be deducted for the payroll period under section 3102 (relating to FICA employee taxes), and

(iii) amounts of the taxes imposed for the payroll period under section 3111 (relating to FICA employer taxes),

as if the employer had paid to the Secretary, on the day on which the wages are paid to the employees, an amount equal to such payments.

(2) ADVANCE PAYMENTS EXCEED TAXES DUE.—In the case of any employer, if for any payroll period the aggregate amount of earned income advance payments exceeds the sum of the amounts referred to in paragraph (1)(B), each such advance payment shall be reduced by an amount which bears the same ratio to such excess as such advance payment bears to the aggregate amount of all such advance payments.

(3) EMPLOYER MAY MAKE FULL ADVANCE PAYMENTS.—The Secretary shall prescribe regulations under which an employer may elect (in lieu of any application of paragraph (2))—

(A) to pay in full all earned income advance amounts, and

(B) to have additional amounts paid by reason of this paragraph treated as the advance payment of taxes imposed by this title.

(4) FAILURE TO MAKE ADVANCE PAYMENTS.—For purposes of this title (including penalties), failure to make any advance payment under this section at the time provided therefor shall be treated as the failure at such time to deduct and withhold under chapter 24 an amount equal to the amount of such advance payment.

Amendments

- **1983, Interest and Dividend Tax Compliance Act of 1983 (P.L. 98-67)**

P.L. 98-67, § 102(a):

Repealed the amendment made to Code Sec. 3507(d)(4) by P.L. 97-248 as though it had not been enacted. **Effective** as of the close of 6-30-83.

- **1982, Tax Equity and Fiscal Responsibility Act of 1982 (P.L. 97-248)**

P.L. 97-248, § 307(a)(3):

Amended Code Sec. 3507(d)(4) by adding "subchapter A of" immediately preceding "chapter 24". **Effective** 7-1-83.

[Sec. 3507(e)]

(e) FURNISHING AND TAKING EFFECT OF CERTIFICATES.—For purposes of this section—

(1) WHEN CERTIFICATE TAKES EFFECT.—

(A) FIRST CERTIFICATE FURNISHED.—An earned income eligibility certificate furnished the employer in cases in which no previous such certificate had been in effect for the calendar year shall take effect as of the beginning of the first payroll period ending, or the first payment of wages made without regard to a payroll period, on or after the date on which such certificate is so furnished (or if later, the first day of the calendar year for which furnished).

(B) LATER CERTIFICATE.—An earned income eligibility certificate furnished the employer in cases in which a previous such certificate had been in effect for the calendar year shall take effect with respect to the first payment of wages made on or after the first status determination date which occurs at least 30 days after the date on which such certificate is so furnished, except that at the election of the employer such certificate may be made effective with respect to any payment of wages made on or after the date on which such certificate is so furnished. For purposes of this section, the term "status determination date" means January 1, May 1, July 1, and October 1 of each year.

(2) PERIOD DURING WHICH CERTIFICATE REMAINS IN EFFECT.—An earned income eligibility certificate which takes effect under this section for any calendar year shall continue in effect with respect to the employee during such calendar year until revoked by the employee or until another such certificate takes effect under this section.

(3) CHANGE OF STATUS.—

(A) REQUIREMENT TO REVOKE OR FURNISH NEW CERTIFICATE.—If, after an employee has furnished an earned income eligibility certificate under this section, there has been a change of circumstances which has the effect of—

(i) making the employee ineligible for the credit provided by section 32 for the taxable year, or

(ii) causing an earned income eligibility certificate to be in effect with respect to the spouse of the employee,

the employee shall, within 10 days after such change in circumstances, furnish the employer with a revocation of such certificate or with a new certificate (as the case may be). Such a revocation (or such a new certificate) shall take effect under the rules provided by paragraph (1)(B) for a later certificate and shall be made in such form as the Secretary shall by regulations prescribe.

(B) CERTIFICATE NO LONGER IN EFFECT.—If, after an employee has furnished an earned income eligibility certificate under this section which certifies that such a certificate is in effect with respect to the spouse of the employee, such a certificate is no longer in effect with respect to such spouse, then the employee may furnish the employer with a new earned income eligibility certificate.

(4) FORM AND CONTENTS OF CERTIFICATE.—Earned income eligibility certificates shall be in such form and contain such other information as the Secretary may by regulations prescribe.

(5) TAXABLE YEAR DEFINED.—The term "taxable year" means the last taxable year of the employee under subtitle A beginning in the calendar year in which the wages are paid.

Amendments

- **1984, Deficit Reduction Act of 1984 (P.L. 98-369)**

P.L. 98-369, § 474(r)(30):

Amended Code Sec. 3507(e) by striking out "section 43" and inserting in lieu thereof "section 32". **Effective** for tax years beginning after 12-31-83, and to carrybacks from such years.

- **1978, Revenue Act of 1978 (P.L. 95-600)**

P.L. 95-600, § 105(b)(1):

Added Code Sec. 3507. **Effective** for remuneration paid after 6-30-79. [Effective date amended by P.L. 96-222, § 101(a)(2)(D).]

[Sec. 3507(f)]

(f) INTERNAL REVENUE SERVICE NOTIFICATION.—The Internal Revenue Service shall take such steps as may be appropriate to ensure that taxpayers who have 1 or more qualifying children and who receive a refund of the credit under section 32 are aware of the availability of earned income advance amounts under this section.

Amendments

- **1993, Omnibus Budget Reconciliation Act of 1993 (P.L. 103-66)**

P.L. 103-66, § 13131(d)(6):

Amended Code Sec. 3507 by adding at the end thereof new subsection (f). **Effective** for tax years beginning after 12-31-93.

[Sec. 3508]

SEC. 3508. TREATMENT OF REAL ESTATE AGENTS AND DIRECT SELLERS.

[Sec. 3508(a)]

(a) GENERAL RULE.—For purposes of this title, in the case of services performed as a qualified real estate agent or as a direct seller—

(1) the individual performing such services shall not be treated as an employee, and

(2) the person for whom such services are performed shall not be treated as an employer.

EMPLOYMENT TAXES—GENERAL PROVISIONS

[Sec. 3508(b)]

(b) DEFINITIONS.—For purposes of this section—

(1) QUALIFIED REAL ESTATE AGENT.—The term "qualified real estate agent" means any individual who is a sales person if—

(A) such individual is a licensed real estate agent,

(B) substantially all of the remuneration (whether or not paid in cash) for the services performed by such individual as a real estate agent is directly related to sales or other output (including the performance of services) rather than to the number of hours worked, and

(C) the services performed by the individual are performed pursuant to a written contract between such individual and the person for whom the services are performed and such contract provides that the individual will not be treated as an employee with respect to such services for Federal tax purposes.

(2) DIRECT SELLER.—The term "direct seller" means any person if—

(A) such person—

(i) is engaged in the trade or business of selling (or soliciting the sale of) consumer products to any buyer on a buy-sell basis, a deposit-commission basis, or any similar basis which the Secretary prescribes by regulations, for resale (by the buyer or any other person) in the home or otherwise than in a permanent retail establishment,

(ii) is engaged in the trade or business of selling (or soliciting the sale of) consumer products in the home or otherwise than in a permanent retail establishment, or

(iii) is engaged in the trade or business of the delivering or distribution of newspapers or shopping news (including any services directly related to such trade or business),

(B) substantially all the remuneration (whether or not paid in cash) for the performance of the services described in subparagraph (A) is directly related to sales or other output (including the performance of services) rather than to the number of hours worked, and

(C) the services performed by the person are performed pursuant to a written contract between such person and the person for whom the services are performed and such contract provides that the person will not be treated as an employee with respect to such services for Federal tax purposes.

(3) COORDINATION WITH RETIREMENT PLANS FOR SELF-EMPLOYED.—This section shall not apply for purposes of subtitle A to the extent that the individual is treated as an employee under section 401(c)(1) (relating to self-employed individuals).

Amendments

- **1996, Small Business Job Protection Act of 1996 (P.L. 104-188)**

P.L. 104-188, § 1118(a):

Amended Code Sec. 3508(b)(2)(A) by striking "or" at the end of clause (i), by inserting "or" at the end of clause (ii), and by inserting after clause (ii) a new clause (iii). **Effective** for services performed after 12-31-95.

- **1982, Tax Equity and Fiscal Responsibility Act of 1982 (P.L. 97-248)**

P.L. 97-248, § 269(a):

Added Code Sec. 3508. **Effective** for services performed after 12-31-82.

[Sec. 3509]

SEC. 3509. DETERMINATION OF EMPLOYER'S LIABILITY FOR CERTAIN EMPLOYMENT TAXES.

[Sec. 3509(a)]

(a) IN GENERAL.—If any employer fails to deduct and withhold any tax under chapter 24 or subchapter A of chapter 21 with respect to any employee by reason of treating such employee as not being an employee for purposes of such chapter or subchapter, the amount of the employer's liability for—

(1) WITHHOLDING TAXES.—Tax under chapter 24 for such year with respect to such employee shall be determined as if the amount required to be deducted and withheld were equal to 1.5 percent of the wages (as defined in section 3401) paid to such employee.

(2) EMPLOYEE SOCIAL SECURITY TAX.—Taxes under subchapter A of chapter 21 with respect to such employee shall be determined as if the taxes imposed under such subchapter were 20 percent of the amount imposed under such subchapter without regard to this subparagraph.

[Sec. 3509(b)]

(b) EMPLOYER'S LIABILITY INCREASED WHERE EMPLOYER DISREGARDS REPORTING REQUIREMENTS.—

(1) IN GENERAL.—In the case of an employer who fails to meet the applicable requirements of section 6041(a), 6041A, or 6051 with respect to any employee, unless such failure is due to reasonable cause and not willful neglect, subsection (a) shall be applied with respect to such employee—

(A) by substituting "3 percent" for "1.5 percent" in paragraph (1); and

(B) by substituting "40 percent" for "20 percent" in paragraph (2).

(2) APPLICABLE REQUIREMENTS.—For purposes of paragraph (1), the term "applicable requirements" means the requirements described in paragraph (1) which would be applicable consistent with the employer's treatment of the employee as not being an employee for purposes of chapter 24 or subchapter A of chapter 21.

[Sec. 3509(c)]

(c) SECTION NOT TO APPLY IN CASES OF INTENTIONAL DISREGARD.—This section shall not apply to determination of the employer's liability for tax under chapter 24 or subchapter A of chapter 21 if such liability is due to the employer's intentional disregard of the requirement to deduct and withhold such tax.

[Sec. 3509(d)]

(d) SPECIAL RULES.—For purposes of this section—

(1) DETERMINATION OF LIABILITY.—If the amount of any liability for tax is determined under this section—

(A) the employee's liability for tax shall not be affected by the assessment or collection of the tax so determined,

(B) the employer shall not be entitled to recover from the employee any tax so determined, and

(C) section 3402(d) and section 6521 shall not apply.

(2) SECTION NOT TO APPLY WHERE EMPLOYER DEDUCTS WAGE BUT NOT SOCIAL SECURITY TAXES.—This section shall not apply to any employer with respect to any wages if—

(A) the employer deducted and withheld any amount of the tax imposed by chapter 24 on such wages, but

(B) failed to deduct and withhold the amount of the tax imposed by subchapter A of chapter 21 with respect to such wages.

(3) SECTION NOT TO APPLY TO CERTAIN STATUTORY EMPLOYEES.—This section shall not apply to any tax under subchapter A of chapter 21 with respect to an individual described in subsection (d)(3) of section 3121 (without regard to whether such individual is described in paragraph (1) or (2) of such subsection).

Amendments

• **2018, Tax Technical Corrections Act of 2018 (P.L. 115-141)**

P.L. 115-141, §401(a)(218), Div. U:

Amended Code Sec. 3509(d)(1)(C) by striking "sections" and inserting "section". **Effective** 3-23-2018.

• **1990, Omnibus Budget Reconciliation Act of 1990 (P.L. 101-508)**

P.L. 101-508, §5130(a)(4):

Amended Code Sec. 3509(d)(3) by striking "subsection (d)(4)" and inserting "subsection (d)(3)". **Effective** as if included in the enactment of the provision to which it relates [effective 11-10-88.—CCH].

• **1988, Technical and Miscellaneous Revenue Act of 1988 (P.L. 100-647)**

P.L. 100-647, §2003(d):

Amended Code Sec. 3509(d)(3) by striking out "subsection (d)(3)" and inserting in lieu thereof "subsection (d)(4)". **Effective** 11-10-88.

• **1982, Tax Equity and Fiscal Responsibility Act of 1982 (P.L. 97-248)**

P.L. 97-248, §270(a):

Added Code Sec. 3509. **Effective** 9-3-82, except that its provisions will not apply to any assessment made before 1-1-83.

[Sec. 3510]

SEC. 3510. COORDINATION OF COLLECTION OF DOMESTIC SERVICE EMPLOYMENT TAXES WITH COLLECTION OF INCOME TAXES.

[Sec. 3510(a)]

(a) GENERAL RULE.—Except as otherwise provided in this section—

(1) returns with respect to domestic service employment taxes shall be made on a calendar year basis,

(2) any such return for any calendar year shall be filed on or before the 15th day of the fourth month following the close of the employer's taxable year which begins in such calendar year, and

(3) no requirement to make deposits (or to pay installments under section 6157) shall apply with respect to such taxes.

[Sec. 3510(b)]

(b) DOMESTIC SERVICE EMPLOYMENT TAXES SUBJECT TO ESTIMATED TAX PROVISIONS.—

(1) IN GENERAL.—Solely for purposes of section 6654, domestic service employment taxes imposed with respect to any calendar year shall be treated as a tax imposed by chapter 2 for the taxable year of the employer which begins in such calendar year.

(2) EMPLOYERS NOT OTHERWISE REQUIRED TO MAKE ESTIMATED PAYMENTS.—Paragraph (1) shall not apply to any employer for any calendar year if—

(A) no credit for wage withholding is allowed under section 31 to such employer for the taxable year of the employer which begins in such calendar year, and

(B) no addition to tax would (but for this section) be imposed under section 6654 for such taxable year by reason of section 6654(e).

(3) ANNUALIZATION.—Under regulations prescribed by the Secretary, appropriate adjustments shall be made in the application of section 6654(d)(2) in respect of the amount treated as tax under paragraph (1).

Amendments

• **2014, Tax Technical Corrections Act of 2014 (P.L. 113-295)**

P.L. 113-295, §221(a)(102), Division A:

Amended Code Sec. 3510(b) by striking paragraph (4). **Effective** generally 12-19-2014. For a special rule, see Act Sec. 221(b)(2), Division A, below. Prior to being stricken, Code Sec. 3510(b)(4) read as follows.

(4) TRANSITIONAL RULE.—In the case of any taxable year beginning before January 1, 1998, no addition to tax shall be made under section 6654 with respect to any underpayment to the extent such underpayment was created or increased by this section.

P.L. 113-295, §221(b)(2), Division A, provides:

(2) SAVINGS PROVISION.—If—

(A) any provision amended or repealed by the amendments made by this section applied to—

(i) any transaction occurring before the date of the enactment of this Act,

(ii) any property acquired before such date of enactment, or

(iii) any item of income, loss, deduction, or credit taken into account before such date of enactment, and

(B) the treatment of such transaction, property, or item under such provision would (without regard to the amendments or repeals made by this section) affect the liability for tax for periods ending after date of enactment, nothing in the amendments or repeals made by this section shall be construed to affect the treatment of such transaction, property, or item for purposes of determining liability for tax for periods ending after such date of enactment.

[Sec. 3510(c)]

(c) DOMESTIC SERVICE EMPLOYMENT TAXES.—For purposes of this section, the term "domestic service employment taxes" means—

(1) any taxes imposed by chapter 21 or 23 on remuneration paid for domestic service in a private home of the employer, and

(2) any amount withheld from such remuneration pursuant to an agreement under section 3402(p).

For purposes of this subsection, the term "domestic service in a private home of the employer" includes domestic service described in section 3121(g)(5).

[Sec. 3510(d)]

(d) EXCEPTION WHERE EMPLOYER LIABLE FOR OTHER EMPLOYMENT TAXES.—To the extent provided in regulations prescribed by the Secretary, this section shall not apply to any employer for any calendar year if such employer is liable for any tax under this subtitle with respect to remuneration for services other than domestic service in a private home of the employer.

[Sec. 3510(e)]

(e) GENERAL REGULATORY AUTHORITY.—The Secretary shall prescribe such regulations as may be necessary or appropriate to carry out the purposes of this section. Such regulations may treat domestic service employment taxes as taxes imposed by chapter 1 for purposes of coordinating the assessment and collection of such employment taxes with the assessment and collection of domestic employers' income taxes.

[Sec. 3510(f)]

(f) AUTHORITY TO ENTER INTO AGREEMENTS TO COLLECT STATE UNEMPLOYMENT TAXES.—

(1) IN GENERAL.—The Secretary is hereby authorized to enter into an agreement with any State to collect, as the agent of such State, such State's unemployment taxes imposed on remuneration paid for domestic service in a private home of the employer. Any taxes to be collected by the Secretary pursuant to such an agreement shall be treated as domestic service employment taxes for purposes of this section.

(2) TRANSFERS TO STATE ACCOUNT.—Any amount collected under an agreement referred to in paragraph (1) shall be transferred by the Secretary to the account of the State in the Unemployment Trust Fund.

(3) SUBTITLE F MADE APPLICABLE.—For purposes of subtitle F, any amount required to be collected under an agreement under paragraph (1) shall be treated as a tax imposed by chapter 23.

(4) STATE.—For purposes of this subsection, the term "State" has the meaning given such term by section 3306(j)(1).

EMPLOYMENT TAXES—GENERAL PROVISIONS

Amendments

• 1994, Social Security Domestic Employment Reform Act of 1994 (P.L. 103-387)

P.L. 103-387, §2(b)(1):

Amended Chapter 25 by adding at the end thereof a new section 3510. **Effective** for remuneration paid in calendar years beginning after 12-31-94.

Amendments

• 1990, Omnibus Budget Reconciliation Act of 1990 (P.L. 101-508)

P.L. 101-508, §11801(a)(42):

Repealed Code Sec. 3510. **Effective** 11-5-90. Prior to repeal, Code Sec. 3510 read as follows:

SEC. 3510. CREDIT FOR INCREASED SOCIAL SECURITY EMPLOYEE TAXES AND RAILROAD RETIREMENT TIER 1 EMPLOYEE TAXES IMPOSED DURING 1984.

(a) GENERAL RULE.—There shall be allowed as a credit against the tax imposed by section 3101(a) on wages received during 1984 an amount equal to $^3/_{10}$ of 1 percent of the wages so received.

(b) TIME CREDIT ALLOWED.—The credit under subsection (a) shall be taken into account in determining the amount of the tax deducted under section 3102(a).

(c) WAGES.—For purposes of this section, the term "wages" has the meaning given to such term by section 3121(a).

(d) APPLICATION TO AGREEMENTS UNDER SECTION 218 OF THE SOCIAL SECURITY ACT.—For purposes of determining amounts equivalent to the tax imposed by section 3101(a) with respect to remuneration which—

(1) is covered by an agreement under section 218 of the Social Security Act, and

(2) is paid during 1984,

the credit allowed by subsection (a) shall be taken into account. A similar rule shall also apply in the case of an agreement under section 3121(l).

(e) CREDIT AGAINST RAILROAD RETIREMENT EMPLOYEE AND EMPLOYEE REPRESENTATIVE TAXES.—

(1) IN GENERAL.—There shall be allowed as a credit against the taxes imposed by sections 3201(a) and 3211(a) on compensation paid during 1984 and subject to such taxes at rates determined by reference to section 3101 an amount equal to $^3/_{10}$ of 1 percent of such compensation.

[Sec. 3510—Repealed]

P.L. 103-387, §2(b)(4), provides:

(4) EXPANDED INFORMATION TO EMPLOYERS.—The Secretary of the Treasury or the Secretary's delegate shall prepare and make available information on the Federal tax obligations of employers with respect to employees performing domestic service in a private home of the employer. Such information shall also include a statement that such employers may have obligations with respect to such employees under State laws relating to unemployment insurance and workers compensation.

(2) TIME CREDIT ALLOWED.—The credit under paragraph (1) shall be taken into account in determining the amount of the tax deducted under section 3202(a) (or the amount of the tax under section 3211(a)).

(3) COMPENSATION.—For purposes of this subsection, the term "compensation" has the meaning given to such term by section 3231(e).

(f) COORDINATION WITH SECTION 6413(c).—For purposes of subsection (c) of section 6413, in determining the amount of the tax imposed by section 3101 or 3201, any credit allowed by this section shall be taken into account.

P.L. 101-508, §11821(b), provides:

(b) SAVINGS PROVISION.—If—

(1) any provision amended or repealed by this part applied to—

(A) any transaction occurring before the date of the enactment of this Act,

(B) any property acquired before such date of enactment, or

(C) any item of income, loss, deduction, or credit taken into account before such date of enactment, and

(2) the treatment of such transaction, property, or item under such provision would (without regard to the amendments made by this part) affect liability for tax for periods ending after such date of enactment,

nothing in the amendments made by this part shall be construed to affect the treatment of such transaction, property, or item for purposes of determining liability for tax for periods ending after such date of enactment.

• 1983, Social Security Act of 1983 (P.L. 98-21)

P.L. 98-21, §123(b)(1):

Added Code Sec. 3510. **Effective** for remuneration paid during 1984.

[Sec. 3511]

SEC. 3511. CERTIFIED PROFESSIONAL EMPLOYER ORGANIZATIONS.

[Sec. 3511(a)]

(a) GENERAL RULES.—For purposes of the taxes, and other obligations, imposed by this subtitle—

(1) a certified professional employer organization shall be treated as the employer (and no other person shall be treated as the employer) of any work site employee performing services for any customer of such organization, but only with respect to remuneration remitted by such organization to such work site employee, and

(2) the exemptions, exclusions, definitions, and other rules which are based on type of employer and which would (but for paragraph (1)) apply shall apply with respect to such taxes imposed on such remuneration.

[Sec. 3511(b)]

(b) SUCCESSOR EMPLOYER STATUS.—For purposes of sections 3121(a)(1), 3231(e)(2)(C), and 3306(b)(1)—

(1) a certified professional employer organization entering into a service contract with a customer with respect to a work site employee shall be treated as a successor employer and the customer shall be treated as a predecessor employer during the term of such service contract, and

(2) a customer whose service contract with a certified professional employer organization is terminated with respect to a work site employee shall be treated as a successor employer and the certified professional employer organization shall be treated as a predecessor employer.

[Sec. 3511(c)]

(c) LIABILITY OF CERTIFIED PROFESSIONAL EMPLOYER ORGANIZATION.—Solely for purposes of its liability for the taxes and other obligations imposed by this subtitle—

(1) a certified professional employer organization shall be treated as the employer of any individual (other than a work site employee or a person described in subsection (f)) who is performing services covered by a contract meeting the requirements of section 7705(e)(2), but only with respect to remuneration remitted by such organization to such individual, and

(2) the exemptions, exclusions, definitions, and other rules which are based on type of employer and which would (but for paragraph (1)) apply shall apply with respect to such taxes imposed on such remuneration.

Amendments

• 2020, Coronavirus Aid, Relief, and Economic Security (CARES) Act (P.L. 116-136)

P.L. 116-136, §2302(a), (c)(2), (d), and (f), provides:

(a) IN GENERAL.—

(1) TAXES.—Notwithstanding any other provision of law, the payment for applicable employment taxes for the payroll tax deferral period shall not be due before the applicable date.

(2) DEPOSITS.—Notwithstanding section 6302 of the Internal Revenue Code of 1986, an employer shall be treated as having timely made all deposits of applicable employment taxes that are required to be made (without regard to this section) for such taxes during the payroll tax deferral period if all such deposits are made not later than the applicable date.

(3) EXCEPTION.—This subsection shall not apply to any taxpayer if such taxpayer has had indebtedness forgiven under section 1106 of this Act with respect to a loan under paragraph (36) of section 7(a) of the Small Business Act (15 U.S.C. 636(a)), as added by section 1102 of this Act, or indebtedness forgiven under section 1109 of this

Act. [Stricken by P.L. 116-142, §4(a), **effective** as if included in the CARES Act (P.L. 116-136) and applicable to any loan made pursuant to section 7(a)(36) of the Small Business Act (15 U.S.C. 636(a)(36)) or section 1109 of the CARES Act.]

* * *

(c) LIABILITY OF THIRD PARTIES.—

* * *

(2) CERTIFIED PROFESSIONAL EMPLOYER ORGANIZATIONS.—For purposes of section 3511, in the case of a certified professional employer organization (as defined in subsection (a) of section 7705 of the Internal Revenue Code of 1986) that has entered into a service contract described in subsection (e)(2) of such section with a customer, if such customer directs such organization to defer payment of any applicable employment taxes during the payroll tax deferral period under this section, such customer shall, notwithstanding subsections (a) and (c) of section 3511, be solely liable for the payment of such applicable employment taxes before the applicable date for any wages paid by such organization to any work site employee performing services for such customer during such period.

(d) DEFINITIONS.—For purposes of this section—

(1) APPLICABLE EMPLOYMENT TAXES.—The term "applicable employment taxes" means the following:

(A) The taxes imposed under section 3111(a) of the Internal Revenue Code of 1986.

(B) So much of the taxes imposed under section 3211(a) of such Code as are attributable to the rate in effect under section 3111(a) of such Code.

(C) So much of the taxes imposed under section 3221(a) of such Code as are attributable to the rate in effect under section 3111(a) of such Code.

(2) PAYROLL TAX DEFERRAL PERIOD.—The term "payroll tax deferral period" means the period beginning on the date of the enactment of this Act and ending before January 1, 2021.

(3) APPLICABLE DATE.—The term "applicable date" means—

(A) December 31, 2021, with respect to 50 percent of the amounts to which subsection (a) or (b), as the case may be, apply, and

(B) December 31, 2022, with respect to the remaining such amounts.

(4) SECRETARY.—The term "Secretary" means the Secretary of the Treasury (or the Secretary's delegate).

***

(f) REGULATORY AUTHORITY.—The Secretary shall issue such regulations or other guidance as necessary to carry out the purposes of this section, including rules for the administration and enforcement of subsection (c).

[Sec. 3511(d)]

(d) TREATMENT OF CREDITS.—

(1) IN GENERAL.—For purposes of any credit specified in paragraph (2)—

(A) such credit with respect to a work site employee performing services for the customer applies to the customer, not the certified professional employer organization,

(B) the customer, and not the certified professional employer organization, shall take into account wages and employment taxes—

(i) paid by the certified professional employer organization with respect to the work site employee, and

(ii) for which the certified professional employer organization receives payment from the customer, and

(C) the certified professional employer organization shall furnish the customer and the Secretary with any information necessary for the customer to claim such credit.

(2) CREDITS SPECIFIED.—A credit is specified in this paragraph if such credit is allowed under—

(A) section 41 (credit for increasing research activity),

(B) section 45A (Indian employment credit),

(C) section 45B (credit for portion of employer social security taxes paid with respect to employee cash tips),

(D) section 45C (clinical testing expenses for certain drugs for rare diseases or conditions),

(E) section 45R (employee health insurance expenses of small employers),

(F) section 45AA (military spouse retirement plan eligibility credit),

(G) section 51 (work opportunity credit),

(H) section 1396 (empowerment zone employment credit), and

(I) any other section as provided by the Secretary.

- 2022, SECURE 2.0 Act of 2022 (P.L. 117-328)

P.L. 117-328, § 112(c):

Amended Code Sec. 3511(d)(2) by redesignating subparagraphs (F), (G), and (H) as subparagraphs (G), (H), and (I), respectively, and by inserting after subparagraph (E) a new subparagraph (F). **Effective** for tax years beginning after 12-29-2022.

[Sec. 3511(e)]

(e) SPECIAL RULE FOR RELATED PARTY.—This section shall not apply in the case of a customer which bears a relationship to a certified professional employer organization described in section 267(b) or 707(b). For purposes of the preceding sentence, such sections shall be applied by substituting "10 percent" for "50 percent".

[Sec. 3511(f)]

(f) SPECIAL RULE FOR CERTAIN INDIVIDUALS.—For purposes of the taxes imposed under this subtitle, an individual with net earnings from self-employment derived from the customer's trade or business (including a partner in a partnership that is a customer) is not a work site employee with respect to remuneration paid by a certified professional employer organization.

[Sec. 3511(g)]

(g) REPORTING REQUIREMENTS AND OBLIGATIONS.—The Secretary shall develop such reporting and recordkeeping rules, regulations, and procedures as the Secretary determines necessary or appropriate to ensure compliance with this title by certified professional employer organizations or persons that have been so certified. Such rules shall include—

(1) notification of the Secretary in such manner as the Secretary shall prescribe in the case of the commencement or termination of a service contract described in section 7705(e)(2) between such a person and a customer, and the employer identification number of such customer,

(2) such information as the Secretary determines necessary for the customer to claim the credits identified in subsection (d) and the manner in which such information is to be provided, as prescribed by the Secretary, and

(3) such other information as the Secretary determines is essential to promote compliance with respect to the credits identified in subsection (d) and section 3302, and

shall be designed in a manner which streamlines, to the extent possible, the application of requirements of this section and section 7705, the exchange of information between a certified professional employer organization and its customers, and the reporting and recordkeeping obligations of the certified professional employer organization.

[Sec. 3511(h)]

(h) REGULATIONS.—The Secretary shall prescribe such regulations as may be necessary or appropriate to carry out the purposes of this section.

Amendments

- 2014, Stephen Beck, Jr., Achieving a Better Life Experience Act of 2014 (P.L. 113-295)

P.L. 113-295, § 206(a), Division B:

Amended Chapter 25 by adding at the end a new Code Sec. 3511. **Effective** generally for wages for services performed on or after January 1 of the first calendar year beginning more than 12 months after 12-19-2014. For a special rule, see Act Sec. 206(h), below:

P.L. 113-295, § 206(h), Division B, provides:

(h) NO INFERENCE.—Nothing contained in this section or the amendments made by this section shall be construed to create any inference with respect to the determination of who is an employee or employer—

(1) for Federal tax purposes (other than the purposes set forth in the amendments made by this section), or

(2) for purposes of any other provision of law.

EMPLOYMENT TAXES—GENERAL PROVISIONS

[Sec. 3512]

SEC. 3512. TREATMENT OF CERTAIN PERSONS AS EMPLOYERS WITH RESPECT TO MOTION PICTURE PROJECTS.

[Sec. 3512(a)]

(a) IN GENERAL.—For purposes of sections 3121(a)(1) and 3306(b)(1), remuneration paid to a motion picture project worker by a motion picture project employer during a calendar year shall be treated as remuneration paid with respect to employment of such worker by such employer during the calendar year. The identity of such employer for such purposes shall be determined as set forth in this section and without regard to the usual common law rules applicable in determining the employer-employee relationship.

[Sec. 3512(b)]

(b) DEFINITIONS.—For purposes of this section—

(1) MOTION PICTURE PROJECT EMPLOYER.—The term "motion picture project employer" means any person if—

(A) such person (directly or through affiliates)—

(i) is a party to a written contract covering the services of motion picture project workers with respect to motion picture projects in the course of a client's trade or business,

(ii) is contractually obligated to pay remuneration to the motion picture project workers without regard to payment or reimbursement by any other person,

(iii) controls the payment (within the meaning of section 3401(d)(1)) of remuneration to the motion picture project workers and pays such remuneration from its own account or accounts,

(iv) is a signatory to one or more collective bargaining agreements with a labor organization (as defined in 29 U.S.C. 152(5)) that represents motion picture project workers, and

(v) has treated substantially all motion picture project workers that such person pays as employees and not as independent contractors during such calendar year for purposes of determining employment taxes under this subtitle, and

(B) at least 80 percent of all remuneration (to which section 3121 applies) paid by such person in such calendar year is paid to motion picture project workers.

(2) MOTION PICTURE PROJECT WORKER.—The term "motion picture project worker" means any individual who provides services on motion picture projects for clients who are not affiliated with the motion picture project employer.

(3) MOTION PICTURE PROJECT.—The term "motion picture project" means the production of any property described in section 168(f)(3). Such term does not include property with respect to which records are required to be maintained under section 2257 of title 18, United States Code.

(4) AFFILIATE; AFFILIATED.—A person shall be treated as an affiliate of, or affiliated with, another person if such persons are treated as a single employer under subsection (b) or (c) of section 414.

Amendments

- **2015, Protecting Americans from Tax Hikes Act of 2015 (P.L. 114-113)**

P.L. 114-113, §346(a), Div. Q:

Amended chapter 25 by adding at the end a new Code Sec. 3512. **Effective** for remuneration paid after 12-31-2015. For a special rule, see Act Sec. 346(d), below.

P.L. 114-113, §346(d), Div. Q, provides:

(d) NO INFERENCE.—Nothing in the amendments made by this section shall be construed to create any inference on the law before the date of the enactment of this Act.

[The next page is 3701.]

Subtitle D—Miscellaneous Excise Taxes

CHAPTER 31.	Retail excise taxes.
CHAPTER 32.	Manufacturers excise taxes.
CHAPTER 33.	Facilities and services.
CHAPTER 34.	Taxes on certain insurance policies.
CHAPTER 35.	Taxes on wagering.
CHAPTER 36.	Certain other excise taxes.
CHAPTER 37.	Repurchase of corporate stock.
CHAPTER 37.	[Repealed.]
CHAPTER 38.	Environmental taxes.
CHAPTER 39.	Registration-required obligations.
CHAPTER 40.	General provisions relating to occupational taxes.
CHAPTER 41.	Public charities.
CHAPTER 42.	Private foundations and certain other tax-exempt organizations.
CHAPTER 43.	Qualified pension, etc., plans.
CHAPTER 44.	Qualified investment entities.
CHAPTER 45.	Provisions relating to expatriated entities.
CHAPTER 46.	Golden parachute payments.
CHAPTER 47.	Certain group health plans.
CHAPTER 48.	Maintenance of Minimum Essential Coverage.
CHAPTER 49.	Cosmetic Services
CHAPTER 50.	Foreign Procurement
CHAPTER 50A.	Designated drugs

CHAPTER 31—RETAIL EXCISE TAXES

SUBCHAPTER A.	Luxury passenger automobiles. [Stricken]
SUBCHAPTER B.	Special fuels.
SUBCHAPTER C.	Heavy trucks and trailers.

Subchapter A—Luxury Passenger Automobiles—[Stricken]

[Sec. 4001—Stricken]

Amendments

• 2014, Tax Technical Corrections Act of 2014 (P.L. 113-295)

P.L. 113-295, §221(a)(103)(A), Division A:

Amended chapter 31 by striking subchapter A (Code Secs. 4001-4003). **Effective** generally 12-19-2014. For a special rule, see Act Sec. 221(b)(2), Division A, below.

P.L. 113-295, §221(b)(2), Division A, provides:

(2) SAVINGS PROVISION.—If—

(A) any provision amended or repealed by the amendments made by this section applied to—

(i) any transaction occurring before the date of the enactment of this Act,

(ii) any property acquired before such date of enactment, or

(iii) any item of income, loss, deduction, or credit taken into account before such date of enactment, and

(B) the treatment of such transaction, property, or item under such provision would (without regard to the amendments or repeals made by this section) affect the liability for tax for periods ending after date of enactment, nothing in the amendments or repeals made by this section shall be construed to affect the treatment of such transaction, property, or item for purposes of determining liability for tax for periods ending after such date of enactment.

Prior to being stricken, Code Sec. 4001 read as follows:

SEC. 4001. IMPOSITION OF TAX.

[Sec. 4001(a)]

(a) IMPOSITION OF TAX.—

(1) IN GENERAL.—There is hereby imposed on the 1st retail sale of any passenger vehicle a tax equal to 10 percent of the price for which so sold to the extent such price exceeds the applicable amount.

(2) APPLICABLE AMOUNT.—

(A) IN GENERAL.—Except as provided in subparagraphs (B) and (C), the applicable amount is $30,000.

(B) QUALIFIED CLEAN-FUEL VEHICLE PROPERTY.—In the case of a passenger vehicle which is propelled by a fuel which is not a clean-burning fuel and to which is installed qualified clean-fuel vehicle property (as defined in section 179A(c)(1)(A)) for purposes of permitting such vehicle to be propelled by a clean-burning fuel, the applicable amount is equal to the sum of—

(i) the dollar amount in effect under subparagraph (A), plus

(ii) the increase in the price for which the passenger vehicle was sold (within the meaning of section 4002) due to the installation of such property.

(C) PURPOSE BUILT PASSENGER VEHICLE.—

(i) IN GENERAL.—In the case of a purpose built passenger vehicle, the applicable amount is equal to 150 percent of the dollar amount in effect under subparagraph (A).

(ii) PURPOSE BUILT PASSENGER VEHICLE.—For purposes of clause (i), the term "purpose built passenger vehicle" means a passenger vehicle produced by an original equipment manufacturer and designed so that the vehicle may be propelled primarily by electricity.

Amendments

• 1997, Taxpayer Relief Act of 1997 (P.L. 105-34)

P.L. 105-34, §906(a):

Amended Code Sec. 4001(a). **Effective** for sales and installations occurring after 8-5-97. Prior to amendment, Code Sec. 4001(a) read as follows:

(a) IMPOSITION OF TAX.—There is hereby imposed on the 1st retail sale of any passenger vehicle a tax equal to 10 percent of the price for which so sold to the extent such price exceeds $30,000.

[Sec. 4001(b)]

(b) PASSENGER VEHICLE.—

(1) IN GENERAL.—For purposes of this subchapter, the "passenger vehicle" means any 4-wheeled vehicle—

(A) which is manufactured primarily for use on public streets, roads, and highways, and

(B) which is rated at 6,000 pounds unloaded gross vehicle weight or less.

(2) SPECIAL RULES.—

(A) TRUCKS AND VANS.—In the case of a truck or van, paragraph (1)(B) shall be applied by substituting "gross vehicle weight" for "unloaded gross vehicle weight".

(B) LIMOUSINES.—In the case of a limousine, paragraph (1) shall be applied without regard to subparagraph (B) thereof.

[Sec. 4001(c)]

(c) EXCEPTIONS FOR TAXICABS, ETC.—The tax imposed by this section shall not apply to the sale of any passenger vehicle for use by the purchaser exclusively in the active conduct of a trade or business of transporting persons or property for compensation or hire.

[Sec. 4001(d)]

(d) EXEMPTION FOR LAW ENFORCEMENT USES, ETC.—No tax shall be imposed by this section on the sale of any passenger vehicle—

(1) to the Federal Government, or a State or local government, for use exclusively in police, firefighting, search and rescue, or other law enforcement or public safety activities, or in public works activities, or

(2) to any person for use exclusively in providing emergency medical services.

d [Sec. 4001(e)]

(e) INFLATION ADJUSTMENT.—

(1) IN GENERAL.—The $30,000 amount in subsection (a) shall be increased by an amount equal to—

(A) $30,000, multiplied by

EXCISE TAXES—RETAIL EXCISE TAXES

(B) the cost-of-living adjustment under section 1(f)(3) for the calendar year in which the vehicle is sold, determined by substituting "calendar year 1990" for "calendar year 1992" in subparagraph (B) thereof.

(2) ROUNDING.—If any amount as adjusted under paragraph (1) is not a multiple of $2,000, such amount shall be rounded to the next lowest multiple of $2,000.

Amendments

• **1997, Taxpayer Relief Act of 1997 (P.L. 105-34)**

P.L. 105-34, §906(b)(1):

Amended Code Sec. 4001(e) by striking "and section 4003(a)" after "in subsection (a)". **Effective** for sales and installations occurring after 8-5-97.

• **1996, Small Business Job Protection Act of 1996 (P.L. 104-188)**

P.L. 104-188, §1703(c)(1):

Amended Code Sec. 4001(e). **Effective** 8-20-96. Prior to amendment, Code Sec. 4001(e) read as follows:

(e) INFLATION ADJUSTMENT.—

(1) IN GENERAL.—If, for any calendar year, the excess (if any) of—

(A) $30,000, increased by the cost-of-living adjustment for the calendar year, over

(B) the dollar amount in effect under subsection (a) for the calendar year,

is equal to or greater than $2,000, then the $30,000 amount in subsection (a) and section 4003(a) (as previously adjusted under this subsection) for any subsequent calendar year shall be increased by the amount of such excess rounded to the next lowest multiple of $2,000.

(2) COST-OF-LIVING ADJUSTMENT.—For purposes of paragraph (1), the cost-of-living adjustment for any calendar year shall be the cost-of-living adjustment under section 1(f)(3) for such calendar year, determined by substituting "calendar year 1990" for "calendar year 1992" in subparagraph (B) thereof.

[Sec. 4001(f)]

(f) PHASEDOWN.—For sales occurring in calendar years after 1995 and before 2003, subsection (a)(1) and section 4003(a) shall be applied by substituting for "10 percent", each place it appears, the percentage determined in accordance with the following table:

If the calendar year is:	The percentage is:
1996	9 percent
1997	8 percent
1998	7 percent
1999	6 percent
2000	5 percent
2001	4 percent
2002	3 percent

Amendments

• **1997, Taxpayer Relief Act of 1997 (P.L. 105-34)**

P.L. 105-34, §906(b)(2):

Amended Code Sec. 4001(f) by striking "subsection (a)" and inserting "subsection (a)(1)". **Effective** for sales and installations occurring after 8-5-97.

P.L. 105-34, §1601(f)(3)(A)(i)-(ii):

Amended Code Sec. 4001(f) by inserting "and section 4003(a)" after "subsection (a)", and by inserting ", each place it appears," before "the percentage". **Effective** for sales after 8-5-97.

• **1996, Small Business Job Protection Act of 1996 (P.L. 104-188)**

P.L. 104-188, §1607(b):

Amended Code Sec. 4001 by redesignating subsection (f) (as amended by Act Sec. 1607(a)) as subsection (g) and inserting after subsection (e) a new subsection (f). **Effective** with respect to sales occurring after the date which is 7 days after 8-20-96.

[Sec. 4001(g)]

(g) TERMINATION.—The taxes imposed by this section and section 4003 shall not apply to any sale, use, or installation after December 31, 2002.

Amendments

• **2014, Tax Technical Corrections Act of 2014 (P.L. 113-295)**

P.L. 113-295, §221(a)(103)(A), Division A:

Amended chapter 31 by striking subchapter A (Code Secs. 4001-4003). **Effective** generally 12-19-2014. For a special rule, see Act Sec. 221(b)(2), Division A, below.

P.L. 113-295, §221(b)(2), Division A, provides:

(2) SAVINGS PROVISION.—If—

(A) any provision amended or repealed by the amendments made by this section applied to—

(i) any transaction occurring before the date of the enactment of this Act,

(ii) any property acquired before such date of enactment, or

(iii) any item of income, loss, deduction, or credit taken into account before such date of enactment, and

Sec. 4002—Stricken

Amendments

• **1997, Taxpayer Relief Act of 1997 (P.L. 105-34)**

P.L. 105-34, §1601(f)(3)(B):

Amended Code Sec. 4001(g) by striking "tax imposed by this section" and inserting "taxes imposed by this section and section 4003" and by striking "or use" and inserting ", use, or installation". **Effective** for sales after 8-5-97.

• **1996, Small Business Job Protection Act of 1996 (P.L. 104-188)**

P.L. 104-188, §1607(a):

Amended Code Sec. 4001(f) by striking "1999" and inserting "2002". **Effective** with respect to sales occurring after the date which is 7 days after 8-20-96.

P.L. 104-188, §1607(b):

Amended Code Sec. 4001 by redesignating subsection (f) (as amended by Act Sec. 1607(a)) as subsection (g). **Effective** with respect to sales occurring after the date which is 7 days after 8-20-96.

• **1993, Omnibus Budget Reconciliation Act of 1993 (P.L. 103-66)**

P.L. 103-66, §13161(a):

Amended Subchapter A by adding Code Secs. 4001-4003, and removing Code Secs. 4001-4004, 4006-4007 and 4011-4012. **Effective** 1-1-93. Prior to amendment, the table of contents for Subchapter A and Code Sec. 4001 read as follows:

Subchapter A—Certain Luxury Items

Part I. Imposition of taxes.
Part II. Rules of general applicability.

PART I. IMPOSITION OF TAXES

Subpart A. Passenger vehicles, boats, and aircraft.
Subpart B. Jewelry and furs.

Subpart A—Passenger Vehicles, Boats, and Aircraft

Sec. 4001. Passenger vehicles.
Sec. 4002. Boats.
Sec. 4003. Aircraft.
Sec. 4004. Rules applicable to subpart A.

SEC. 4001. PASSENGER VEHICLES.

(a) IMPOSITION OF TAX.—There is hereby imposed on the 1st retail sale of any passenger vehicle a tax equal to 10 percent of the price for which so sold to the extent such price exceeds $30,000.

(b) PASSENGER VEHICLE.—

(1) IN GENERAL.—For purposes of subsection (a), the term "passenger vehicle" means any 4-wheeled vehicle—

(A) which is manufactured primarily for use on public streets, roads, and highways, and

(B) which is rated at 6,000 pounds unloaded gross vehicle weight or less.

(2) SPECIAL RULES.—

(A) TRUCKS AND VANS.—In the case of a truck or van, paragraph (1)(B) shall be applied by substituting "gross vehicle weight" for "unloaded gross vehicle weight".

(B) LIMOUSINES.—In the case of a limousine, paragraph (1) shall be applied without regard to subparagraph (B) thereof.

(c) EXCEPTIONS FOR TAXICABS, ETC.—The tax imposed by this section shall not apply to the sale of any passenger vehicle for use by the purchaser exclusively in the active conduct of a trade or business of transporting persons or property for compensation or hire.

• **1990, Omnibus Budget Reconciliation Act of 1990 (P.L. 101-508)**

P.L. 101-508, §11221(a):

Amended chapter 31 by adding new Code Sec. 4001. For the **effective** date, see Act Sec. 11221(f)(1)-(2) below.

P.L. 101-508, §11221(f)(1)-(2), provides:

(f) EFFECTIVE DATE.—

(1) IN GENERAL.—The amendments made by this section shall take effect on January 1, 1991.

(2) EXCEPTION FOR BINDING CONTRACTS.—In determining whether any tax imposed by subchapter A of chapter 31 of the Internal Revenue Code of 1986, as added by this section, applies to any sale after December 31, 1990, there shall not be taken into account the amount paid for any article (or any part or accessory therefor) if the purchaser held on September 30, 1990, a contract (which was binding on such date and at all times thereafter before the purchase) for the purchase of such article (or such part or accessory).

[Sec. 4002—Stricken]

(B) the treatment of such transaction, property, or item under such provision would (without regard to the amendments or repeals made by this section) affect the liability for tax for periods ending after date of enactment, nothing in the amendments or repeals made by this section shall be construed to affect the treatment of such transaction, property, or item for purposes of determining liability for tax for periods ending after such date of enactment.

Prior to being stricken, Code Sec. 4002 read as follows:

SEC. 4002. 1ST RETAIL SALE; USES, ETC. TREATED AS SALES; DETERMINATION OF PRICE.

[Sec. 4002(a)]

(a) 1ST RETAIL SALE.—For purposes of this subchapter, the term "1st retail sale" means the 1st sale, for a purpose other than resale, after manufacture, production, or importation.

EXCISE TAXES—RETAIL EXCISE TAXES

[Sec. 4002(b)]

(b) USE TREATED AS SALE.—

(1) IN GENERAL.—If any person uses a passenger vehicle (including any use after importation) before the 1st retail sale of such vehicle, then such person shall be liable for tax under this subchapter in the same manner as if such vehicle were sold at retail by him.

(2) EXEMPTION FOR FURTHER MANUFACTURE.—Paragraph (1) shall not apply to use of a vehicle as material in the manufacture or production of, or as a component part of, another vehicle taxable under this subchapter to be manufactured or produced by him.

(3) EXEMPTION FOR DEMONSTRATION USE.—Paragraph (1) shall not apply to any use of a passenger vehicle as a demonstrator.

(4) EXCEPTION FOR USE AFTER IMPORTATION OF CERTAIN VEHICLES.—Paragraph (1) shall not apply to the use of a vehicle after importation if the user or importer establishes to the satisfaction of the Secretary that the 1st use of the vehicle occurred before January 1, 1991, outside the United States.

(5) COMPUTATION OF TAX.—In the case of any person made liable for tax by paragraph (1), the tax shall be computed on the price at which similar vehicles are sold at retail in the ordinary course of trade, as determined by the Secretary.

[Sec. 4002(c)]

(c) LEASES CONSIDERED AS SALES.—For purposes of this subchapter—

(1) IN GENERAL.—Except as otherwise provided in this subsection, the lease of a vehicle (including any renewal or any extension of a lease or any subsequent lease of such vehicle) by any person shall be considered a sale of such vehicle at retail.

(2) SPECIAL RULES FOR LONG-TERM LEASES.—

(A) TAX NOT IMPOSED ON SALE FOR LEASING IN A QUALIFIED LEASE.—The sale of a passenger vehicle to a person engaged in a passenger vehicle leasing or rental trade or business for leasing by such person in a long-term lease shall not be treated as the 1st retail sale of such vehicle.

(B) LONG-TERM LEASE.—For purposes of subparagraph (A), the term "long-term lease" means any long-term lease (as defined in section 4052).

(C) SPECIAL RULES.—In the case of a long-term lease of a vehicle which is treated as the 1st retail sale of such vehicle—

(i) DETERMINATION OF PRICE.—The tax under this subchapter shall be computed on the lowest price for which the vehicle is sold by retailers in the ordinary course of trade.

(ii) PAYMENT OF TAX.—Rules similar to the rules of section 4217(e)(2) shall apply.

(iii) NO TAX WHERE EXEMPT USE BY LESSEE.—No tax shall be imposed on any lease payment under a long-term lease if the lessee's lease of the vehicle under such lease is an exempt use (as defined in section 4003(b)) of such vehicle.

[Sec. 4002(d)]

(d) DETERMINATION OF PRICE.—

(1) IN GENERAL.—In determining price for purposes of this subchapter—

(A) there shall be included any charge incident to placing the passenger vehicle in condition ready for use,

(B) there shall be excluded—

(i) the amount of the tax imposed by this subchapter,

(ii) if stated as a separate charge, the amount of any retail sales tax imposed by any State or political subdivision thereof or the District of Columbia, whether the liability for such tax is imposed on the vendor or vendee, and

(iii) the value of any component of such passenger vehicle if—

(I) such component is furnished by the 1st user of such passenger vehicle, and

(II) such component has been used before such furnishing, and

(C) the price shall be determined without regard to any trade-in.

(2) OTHER RULES.—Rules similar to the rules of paragraphs (2) and (4) of section 4052(b) shall apply for purposes of this subchapter.

Amendments

• **1993, Omnibus Budget Reconciliation Act of 1993 (P.L. 103-66)**

P.L. 103-66, §13161(a):

Amended subchapter A of chapter 31 by adding new Code Sec. 4002. **Effective** 1-1-93. Prior to amendment, Code Sec. 4002 read as follows:

SEC. 4002. BOATS.

(a) IMPOSITION OF TAX.—There is hereby imposed on the 1st retail sale of any boat a tax equal to 10 percent of the price for which so sold to the extent such price exceeds $100,000.

(b) EXCEPTIONS.—The tax imposed by this section shall not apply to the sale of any boat for use by the purchaser exclusively in the active conduct of—

(1) a trade or business of commercial fishing or transporting persons or property for compensation or hire, or

(2) any other trade or business unless the boat is to be used predominantly in any activity which is of a type generally considered to constitute entertainment, amusement, or recreation.

• **1990, Omnibus Budget Reconciliation Act of 1990 (P.L. 101-508)**

P.L. 101-508, §11221(a):

Amended chapter 31 by adding new Code Sec. 4002. For the **effective** date, see Act Sec. 11221(f)(1)-(2) below.

P.L. 101-508, §11221(f)(1)-(2), provides:

(f) EFFECTIVE DATE.—

(1) IN GENERAL.—The amendments made by this section shall take effect on January 1, 1991.

(2) EXCEPTION FOR BINDING CONTRACTS.—In determining whether any tax imposed by subchapter A of chapter 31 of the Internal Revenue Code of 1986, as added by this section, applies to any sale after December 31, 1990, there shall not be taken into account the amount paid for any article (or any part or accessory therefore) if the purchaser held on September 30, 1990, a contract (which was binding on such date and at all times thereafter before the purchase) for the purchase of such article (or such part or accessory).

[Sec. 4003—Stricken]

Amendments

• **2014, Tax Technical Corrections Act of 2014 (P.L. 113-295)**

P.L. 113-295, §221(a)(103)(A), Division A:

Amended chapter 31 by striking subchapter A (Code Sec. 4003). **Effective** generally 12-19-2014. For a special rule, see Act Sec. 221(b)(2), Division A, below.

P.L. 113-295, §221(b)(2), Division A, provides:

(2) SAVINGS PROVISION.—If—

(A) any provision amended or repealed by the amendments made by this section applied to—

(i) any transaction occurring before the date of the enactment of this Act,

(ii) any property acquired before such date of enactment, or

(iii) any item of income, loss, deduction, or credit taken into account before such date of enactment, and

(B) the treatment of such transaction, property, or item under such provision would (without regard to the amendments or repeals made by this section) affect the liability for tax for periods ending after date of enactment, nothing in the amendments or repeals made by this section shall be construed to affect the treatment of such transaction, property, or item for purposes of determining liability for tax for periods ending after such date of enactment.

Prior to being stricken, Code Sec. 4003 read as follows:

SEC. 4003. SPECIAL RULES.

[Sec. 4003(a)]

(a) SEPARATE PURCHASE OF VEHICLE AND PARTS AND ACCESSORIES THEREFOR.—Under regulations prescribed by the Secretary—

(1) IN GENERAL.—Except as provided in paragraph (2), if—

(A) the owner, lessee, or operator of any passenger vehicle installs (or causes to be installed) any part or accessory (other than property described in section 4001(a)(2)(B)) on such vehicle, and

(B) such installation is not later than the date 6 months after the date the vehicle was 1st placed in service,

then there is hereby imposed on such installation a tax equal to 10 percent of the price of such part or accessory and its installation.

(2) LIMITATION.—The tax imposed by paragraph (1) on the installation of any part or accessory shall not exceed 10 percent of the excess (if any) of—

(A) the sum of—

(i) the price of such part or accessory and its installation,

(ii) the aggregate price of the parts and accessories (and their installation) installed before such part or accessory, plus

(iii) the price for which the passenger vehicle was sold, over

(B) the appropriate applicable amount as determined under section 4001(a)(2).

(3) EXCEPTIONS.—Paragraph (1) shall not apply if—

(A) the part or accessory installed is a replacement part or accessory,

(B) the part or accessory is installed to enable or assist an individual with a disability to operate the vehicle, or to enter or exit the vehicle, by compensating for the effect of such disability, or

(C) the aggregate price of the parts and accessories (and their installation) described in paragraph (1) with respect to the vehicle does not exceed $1,000 (or such other amount or amounts as the Secretary may by regulation prescribe).

The price of any part or accessory (and its installation) to which paragraph (1) does not apply by reason of this paragraph shall not be taken into account under paragraph (2)(A).

(4) INSTALLERS SECONDARILY LIABLE FOR TAX.—The owners of the trade or business installing the parts or accessories shall be secondarily liable for the tax imposed by this subsection.

Amendments

• **1997, Taxpayer Relief Act of 1997 (P.L. 105-34)**

P.L. 105-34, §906(b)(3):

Amended Code Sec. 4003(a)(1)(A) by inserting "(other than property described in section 4001(a)(2)(B))" after "part or accessory". **Effective** for sales and installations occurring after 8-5-97.

P.L. 105-34, §906(b)(4):

Amended Code Sec. 4003(a)(2)(B). **Effective** for sales and installations occurring after 8-5-97. Prior to amendment, Code Sec. 4003(a)(2)(B) read as follows:

(B) $30,000.

P.L. 105-34, §1401(a):

Amended Code Sec. 4003(a)(3)(C) by striking "$200" and inserting "$1,000". **Effective** for installations on vehicles sold after 8-5-97.

[Sec. 4003(b)]

(b) IMPOSITION OF TAX ON SALES, ETC., WITHIN 2 YEARS OF VEHICLES PURCHASED TAX-FREE.—

(1) IN GENERAL.—If—

EXCISE TAXES—RETAIL EXCISE TAXES

(A) no tax was imposed under this subchapter on the 1st retail sale of any passenger vehicle by reason of its exempt use, and

(B) within 2 years after the date of such 1st retail sale, such vehicle is resold by the purchaser or such purchaser makes a substantial nonexempt use of such vehicle,

then such sale or use of such vehicle by such purchaser shall be treated as the 1st retail sale of such vehicle for a price equal to its fair market value at the time of such sale or use.

(2) EXEMPT USE.—For purposes of this subsection, the term "exempt use" means any use of a vehicle if the 1st retail sale of such vehicle is not taxable under this subchapter by reason of such use.

[Sec. 4003(c)]

(c) PARTS AND ACCESSORIES SOLD WITH TAXABLE PASSENGER VEHICLE.—Parts and accessories sold on, in connection with, or with the sale of any passenger vehicle shall be treated as part of the vehicle.

[Sec. 4003(d)]

(d) PARTIAL PAYMENTS, ETC.—In the case of a contract, sale, or arrangement described in paragraph (2), (3), or (4) of section 4216(c), rules similar to the rules of section 4217(e)(2) shall apply for purposes of this subchapter.

Amendments

• **1993, Omnibus Budget Reconciliation Act of 1993 (P.L. 103-66)**

P.L. 103-66, § 13161(a):

Amended subchapter A of chapter 31 by adding new Code Sec. 4003. **Effective** 1-1-93. Prior to amendment, Code Sec. 4003 read as follows:

SEC. 4003. AIRCRAFT.

(a) IMPOSITION OF TAX.—There is hereby imposed on the 1st retail sale of any aircraft a tax equal to 10 percent of the price for which so sold to the extent such price exceeds $250,000.

(b) AIRCRAFT.—For purposes of this section, the term "aircraft" means any aircraft—

(1) which is propelled by a motor, and

(2) which is capable of carrying 1 or more individuals.

(c) 80 PERCENT GENERAL BUSINESS USE.—

(1) IN GENERAL.—The tax imposed by this section shall not apply to the sale of any aircraft if 80 percent of the use by the purchaser is in any trade or business.

(2) PROOF OF BUSINESS USE.—On the income tax return for each of the 1st 2 taxable years ending after the date an aircraft on which no tax was imposed by this section by reason of paragraph (1) was placed in service, the taxpayer filing such return shall demonstrate to the satisfaction of the Secretary that the use of such aircraft during each such year met the requirement of paragraph (1).

(3) IMPOSITION OF LUXURY TAX WHERE FAILURE OF PROOF.—If the requirement of paragraph (2) is not met for either of the taxable years referred to therein, the taxpayer filing such returns shall pay the tax which would (but for paragraph (1)) have been imposed on such aircraft plus interest determined under subchapter C of chapter 67 during the period beginning on the date such tax would otherwise have been imposed. If such taxpayer fails to pay the tax imposed pursuant to the preceding sentence, no deduction shall be allowed under section 168 for any taxable year with respect to the aircraft involved.

(d) OTHER EXCEPTIONS.—The tax imposed by this section shall not apply to the sale of any aircraft for use by the purchaser exclusively—

(1) in the aerial application of fertilizers or other substances,

(2) in the case of a helicopter, in a use described in paragraph (1) or (2) of section 4261(e),

(3) in a trade or business of providing flight training, or

(4) in a trade or business of transporting persons or property for compensation or hire.

Amendments

• **1990, Omnibus Budget Reconciliation Act of 1990 (P.L. 101-508)**

P.L. 101-508, § 11221(a):

Amended chapter 31 by adding new Code Sec. 4003. For the **effective** date, see Act Sec. 11221(f)(1)-(2) below.

P.L. 101-508, § 11221(f)(1)-(2), provides:

(f) EFFECTIVE DATE.—

(1) IN GENERAL.—The amendments made by this section shall take effect on January 1, 1991.

(2) EXCEPTION FOR BINDING CONTRACTS.—In determining whether any tax imposed by subchapter A of chapter 31 of the Internal Revenue Code of 1986, as added by this section, applies to any sale after December 31, 1990, there shall not be taken into account the amount paid for any article (or any part or accessory therefor) if the purchaser held on September 30, 1990, a contract (which was binding on such date and at all times thereafter before the purchase) for the purchase of such article (or such part or accessory).

[Sec. 4004—Repealed]

Amendments

• **1993, Omnibus Budget Reconciliation Act of 1993 (P.L. 103-66)**

P.L. 103-66, § 13161(a):

Amended subchapter A of chapter 31 and removed former Code Sec. 4004. **Effective** 1-1-93. Prior to amendment, Code Sec. 4004 read as follows:

SEC. 4004. RULES APPLICABLE TO SUBPART A.

[Sec. 4004(a)]

(a) EXEMPTION FOR LAW ENFORCEMENT USES, ETC.—No tax shall be imposed under this subpart on the sale of any article—

(1) to the Federal Government, or a State or local government, for use exclusively in police, firefighting, search and rescue, or other law enforcement or public safety activities, or in public works activities, or

(2) to any person for use exclusively in providing emergency medical services.

[Sec. 4004(b)]

(b) SEPARATE PURCHASE OF ARTICLE AND PARTS AND ACCESSORIES THEREFOR.—Under regulations prescribed by the Secretary—

(1) IN GENERAL.—Except as provided in paragraph (2), if—

(A) the owner, lessee, or operator of any article taxable under this subpart (determined without regard to price) installs (or causes to be installed) any part or accessory on such article, and

(B) such installation is not later than the date 6 months after the date the article was 1st placed in service,

then there is hereby imposed on such installation a tax equal to 10 percent of the price of such part or accessory and its installation.

(2) LIMITATION.—The tax imposed by paragraph (1) on the installation of any part or accessory shall not exceed 10 percent of the excess (if any) of—

(A) the sum of—

(i) the price of such part or accessory and its installation,

(ii) the aggregate price of the parts and accessories (and their installation) installed before such part or accessory, plus

(iii) the price for which the passenger vehicle, boat, or aircraft was sold, over

(B) $30,000 in the case of a passenger vehicle, $100,000 in the case of a boat, and $250,000 in the case of an aircraft.

(3) EXCEPTIONS.—Paragraph (1) shall not apply if—

(A) the part or accessory installed is a replacement part or accessory,

(B) the part or accessory is installed on a passenger vehicle to enable or assist an individual with a disability to operate the vehicle, or to enter or exit the vehicle, by compensating for the effect of such disability, or

(C) the aggregate price of the parts and accessories (and their installation) described in paragraph (1) with respect to the taxable article does not exceed $200 (or such other amount or amounts as the Secretary may by regulation prescribe).

The price of any part or accessory (and its installation) to which paragraph (1) does not apply by reason of this paragraph shall not be taken into account under paragraph (2)(A).

Sec. 4004—Repealed

(4) INSTALLERS SECONDARILY LIABLE FOR TAX.—The owners of the trade or business installing the parts or accessories shall be secondarily liable for the tax imposed by this subsection.

Amendments

• **1993, Omnibus Budget Reconciliation Act of 1993 (P.L. 103-66)**

P.L. 103-66, § 13162(a)(1)-(4):

Amended Code Sec. 4004(b)(3)(A)-(C) by striking "or" at the end of subparagraph (A), by redesignating subparagraph (B) as subparagraph (C), by inserting after subparagraph (A) a new subparagraph (B), and by inserting after subparagraph (C) a new flush sentence. **Effective** as if included in the amendments made by section 11221(a) of P.L. 101-508.

[Sec. 4004(c)]

(c) IMPOSITION OF TAX ON SALES, ETC., WITHIN 2 YEARS OF ARTICLES PURCHASED TAX-FREE.—

(1) IN GENERAL.—If—

(A) no tax was imposed under this subchapter on the 1st retail sale of any article by reason of its exempt use, and

(B) within 2 years after the date of such 1st retail sale, such article is resold by the purchaser or such purchaser makes a substantial non-exempt use of such article,

then such sale or use of such article by such purchaser shall be treated as the 1st retail sale of such article for a price equal to its fair market value at the time of such sale or use.

(2) EXEMPT USE.—For purposes of this subsection, the term "exempt use" means any use of an article if the 1st retail sale of such article is not taxable under this subchapter by reason of such use.

Amendments

• **1990, Omnibus Budget Reconciliation Act of 1990 (P.L. 101-508)**

P.L. 101-508, § 11221(a):

Amended chapter 31 by adding new Code Sec. 4004. For the **effective** date, see Act Sec. 11221(f)(1)-(2) below.

P.L. 101-508, § 11221(f)(1)-(2), provides:

(f) EFFECTIVE DATE.—

(1) IN GENERAL.—The amendments made by this section shall take effect on January 1, 1991.

(2) EXCEPTION FOR BINDING CONTRACTS.—In determining whether any tax imposed by subchapter A of chapter 31 of the Internal Revenue Code of 1986, as added by this section, applies to any sale after December 31, 1990, there shall not be taken into account the amount paid for any article (or any part or accessory therefor) if the purchaser held on September 30, 1990, a contract (which was binding on such date and at all times thereafter before the purchase) for the purchase of such article (or such part or accessory).

EXCISE TAXES—RETAIL EXCISE TAXES

[Sec. 4006—Repealed]

Amendments

• **1993, Omnibus Budget Reconciliation Act of 1993 (P.L. 103-66)**

P.L. 103-66, §13161(a):

Amended subchapter A of chapter 31 and removed former Supart B and Code Sec. 4006. **Effective** 1-1-93. Prior to amendment, the table of contents for Subpart B and Code Sec. 4006 read as follows:

Subpart B—Jewelry and Furs

Sec. 4006. Jewelry.

Sec. 4007. Furs.

SEC. 4006. JEWELRY.

(a) IMPOSITION OF TAX.—There is hereby imposed on the 1st retail sale of any jewelry a tax equal to 10 percent of the price for which so sold to the extent such price exceeds $10,000.

(b) JEWELRY.—For purposes of subsection (a), the term "jewelry" means all articles commonly or commercially known as jewelry, whether real or imitation, including watches.

(c) MANUFACTURE FROM CUSTOMER'S MATERIAL.—If—

(1) a person, in the course of a trade or business, produces jewelry from material furnished directly or indirectly by a customer, and

(2) the jewelry is for the use of, and not for resale by, such customer,

the delivery of such jewelry to such customer shall be treated as the 1st retail sale of such jewelry for a price equal to its fair market value at the time of such delivery.

• **1990, Omnibus Budget Reconciliation Act of 1990 (P.L. 101-508)**

P.L. 101-508, §11221(a):

Amended chapter 31 by adding new Code Sec. 4006. For the **effective** date, see Act Sec. 11221(f)(1)-(2) below.

P.L. 101-508, §11221(f)(1)-(2), provides:

(f) EFFECTIVE DATE.—

(1) IN GENERAL.—The amendments made by this section shall take effect on Janaury 1, 1991.

(2) EXCEPTION FOR BINDING CONTRACTS.—In determining whether any tax imposed by subchapter A of chapter 31 of the Internal Revenue Code of 1986, as added by this section, applies to any sale after December 31, 1990, there shall not be taken into account the amount paid for any article (or any part or accessory therefor) if the purchaser held on September 30, 1990, a contract (which was binding on such date and at all times thereafter before the purchase) for the purchase of such article (or such part or accessory).

[Sec. 4007—Repealed]

Amendments

• **1993, Omnibus Budget Reconciliation Act of 1993 (P.L. 103-66)**

P.L. 103-66, §13161(a):

Amended subchapter A of chapter 31 and removed former Code Sec. 4007. **Effective** 1-1-93. Prior to amendment, Code Sec. 4007 read as follows:

SEC. 4007. FURS.

(a) IMPOSITION OF TAX.—There is hereby imposed on the 1st retail sale of the following articles a tax equal to 10 percent of the price for which so sold to the extent such price exceeds $10,000:

(1) Articles made of fur on the hide or pelt.

(2) Articles of which such fur is a major component.

(b) MANUFACTURE FROM CUSTOMER'S MATERIAL.—If—

(1) a person, in the course of a trade or business, produces an article of the kind described in subsection (a) from fur on the hide or pelt furnished, directly or indirectly, by a customer, and

(2) the article is for the use of, and not for resale by, such customer,

the delivery of such article to such customer shall be treated as the 1st retail sale of such article for a price equal to its fair market value at the time of such delivery.

• **1990, Omnibus Budget Reconciliation Act of 1990 (P.L. 101-508)**

P.L. 101-508, §11221(a):

Amended chapter 31 by adding new Code Sec. 4007. For the **effective** date, see Act Sec. 11221(f)(1)-(2) below.

P.L. 101-508, §11221(f)(1)-(2), provides:

(f) EFFECTIVE DATE.—

(1) IN GENERAL.—The amendments made by this section shall take effect on January 1, 1991.

(2) EXCEPTION FOR BINDING CONTRACTS.—In determining whether any tax imposed by subchapter A of chapter 31 of the Internal Revenue Code of 1986, as added by this section, applies to any sale after December 31, 1990, there shall not be taken into account the amount paid for any article (or any part or accessory therefor) if the purchaser held on September 30, 1990, a contract (which was binding on such date and at all times thereafter before the purchase) for the purchase of such article (or such part or accessory).

[Sec. 4011—Repealed]

Amendments

• **1993, Omnibus Budget Reconciliation Act of 1993 (P.L. 103-66)**

P.L. 103-66, §13161(a):

Amended subchapter A of chapter 31 and removed former Part II and Code Sec. 4011. **Effective** 1-1-93. Prior to amendment, the table of contents for Part II and Code Sec. 4011 read as follows:

PART II—RULES OF GENERAL APPLICABILITY

Sec. 4011. Definitions and special rules.

Sec. 4012. Termination.

SEC. 4011. DEFINITIONS AND SPECIAL RULES.

(a) 1ST RETAIL SALE.—For purposes of this subchapter, the term "1st retail sale" means the 1st sale, for a purpose other than resale, after manufacture, production, or importation.

(b) USE TREATED AS SALE.—

(1) IN GENERAL.—If any person uses an article taxable under this subchapter (including any use after importation) before the 1st retail sale of such article, then such person shall be liable for tax under this subchapter in the same manner as if such article were sold at retail by him.

(2) EXEMPTION FOR FURTHER MANUFACTURE.—Paragraph (1) shall not apply to use of an article as material in the manufacture or production of, or as a component part of, another article taxable under this subchapter to be manufactured or produced by him.

(3) EXEMPTION FOR DEMONSTRATION USE OF PASSENGER VEHICLES.—Paragraph (1) shall not apply to any use of a passenger vehicle as a demonstrator for a potential customer while the potential customer is in the vehicle.

(4) EXCEPTION FOR USE AFTER IMPORTATION OF CERTAIN ARTICLES.—Paragraph (1) shall not apply to the use of an article after importation if the user or importer establishes to the satisfaction of the Secretary that the 1st use of the article occurred before January 1, 1991, outside the United States.

(5) COMPUTATION OF TAX.—In the case of any person made liable for tax by paragraph (1), the tax shall be computed on the price at which similar articles are sold at retail in the ordinary course of trade, as determined by the Secretary.

(c) LEASES CONSIDERED AS SALES.—For purposes of this subchapter—

(1) IN GENERAL.—Except as otherwise provided in this subsection, the lease of an article (including any renewal or any extension of a lease or any subsequent lease of such article) by any person shall be considered a sale of such article at retail.

(2) SPECIAL RULES FOR CERTAIN LEASES OF PASSENGER VEHICLES, BOATS, AND AIRCRAFT.—

(A) TAX NOT IMPOSED ON SALE FOR LEASING IN A QUALIFIED LEASE.—The sale of a passenger vehicle, boat, or aircraft to a person engaged in a leasing or rental trade or business of the article involved for leasing by such person in a qualified lease shall not be treated as the 1st retail sale of such article.

(B) QUALIFIED LEASE.—For purposes of subparagraph (A), the term "qualified lease" means—

(i) any lease in the case of a boat or an aircraft, and

(ii) any long-term lease (as defined in section 4052) in the case of any passenger vehicle.

(C) SPECIAL RULES.—In the case of a qualified lease of an article which is treated as the 1st retail sale of such article—

(i) DETERMINATION OF PRICE.—The tax under this subchapter shall be computed on the lowest price for which the article is sold by retailers in the ordinary course of trade.

(ii) PAYMENT OF TAX.—Rules similar to the rules of section 4217(e)(2) shall apply.

(iii) NO TAX WHERE EXEMPT USE BY LESSEE.—No tax shall be imposed on any lease payment under a qualified lease if the lessee's use of the article under such lease is an exempt use (as defined in section 4004(c)) of such article.

(d) DETERMINATION OF PRICE.—

(1) IN GENERAL.—In determining price for purposes of this subchapter—

(A) there shall be included any charge incident to placing the article in condition ready for use,

(B) there shall be excluded—

(i) the amount of the tax imposed by this subchapter,

(ii) if stated as a separate charge, the amount of any retail sales tax imposed by any State or political subdivision thereof or the District of Columbia, whether the liability for such tax is imposed on the vendor or vendee, and

(iii) the value of any component of such article if—

(I) such component is furnished by the 1st user of such article, and

(II) such component has been used before such furnishing, and

(C) the price shall be determined without regard to any trade-in.

Subparagraph (B)(iii) shall not apply for purposes of the taxes imposed by sections 4006 and 4007.

(2) OTHER RULES.—Rules similar to the rules of paragraphs (2) and (4) of section 4052(b) shall apply for purposes of this subchapter.

(e) PARTS AND ACCESSORIES SOLD WITH TAXABLE ARTICLE.—Parts and accessories sold on, in connection with, or with the sale of any article taxable under this subchapter shall be treated as part of the article.

(f) PARTIAL PAYMENTS, ETC.—In the case of a contract, sale, or arrangement described in paragraph (2), (3), or (4) of section 4216(c), rules similar to the rules of section 4217(e)(2) shall apply for purposes of this subchapter.

EXCISE TAXES—RETAIL EXCISE TAXES

• **1990, Omnibus Budget Reconciliation Act of 1990 (P.L. 101-508)**

P.L. 101-508, § 11221(a):

Amended chapter 31 by adding new Code Sec. 4011. For the **effective** date, see Act Sec. 11221(f)(1)-(2) below.

P.L. 101-508, § 11221(f)(1)-(2), provides:

(f) EFFECTIVE DATE.—

(1) IN GENERAL.—The amendments made by this section shall take effect on January 1, 1991.

Amendments

• **1993, Omnibus Budget Reconciliation Act of 1993 (P.L. 103-66)**

P.L. 103-66, § 13161(a):

Amended subchapter A of chapter 31 and removed former Code Sec. 4012. **Effective** 1-1-93. Prior to amendment, Code Sec. 4012 read as follows:

SEC. 4012. TERMINATION.

The taxes imposed by this subchapter shall not apply to any sale or use after December 31, 1999.

• **1990, Omnibus Budget Reconciliation Act of 1990 (P.L. 101-508)**

P.L. 101-508, § 11221(a):

Amended chapter 31 by adding new Code Sec. 4012. For the **effective** date, see Act Sec. 11221(f)(1)-(2) below.

(2) EXCEPTION FOR BINDING CONTRACTS.—In determining whether any tax imposed by subchapter A of chapter 31 of the Internal Revenue Code of 1986, as added by this section, applies to any sale after December 31, 1990, there shall not be taken into account the amount paid for any article (or any part or accessory therefor) if the purchaser held on September 30, 1990, a contract (which was binding on such date and at all times thereafter before the purchase) for the purchase of such article (or such part or accessory).

[Sec. 4012—Repealed]

P.L. 101-508, § 11221(f)(1)-(2), provides:

(f) EFFECTIVE DATE.—

(1) IN GENERAL.—The amendments made by this section shall take effect on January 1, 1991.

(2) EXCEPTION FOR BINDING CONTRACTS.—In determining whether any tax imposed by subchapter A of chapter 31 of the Internal Revenue Code of 1986, as added by this section, applies to any sale after December 31, 1990, there shall not be taken into account the amount paid for any article (or any part or accessory therefor) if the purchaser held on September 30, 1990, a contract (which was binding on such date and at all times thereafter before the purchase) for the purchase of such article (or such part or accessory).

Subchapter B—Special Fuels

Sec. 4041.   Imposition of tax.
Sec. 4042.   Tax on fuel used in commercial transportation on inland waterways.
Sec. 4043.   Surtax on fuel used in aircraft part of a fractional ownership program.

[Sec. 4041]

SEC. 4041. IMPOSITION OF TAX.

[Sec. 4041(a)]

(a) DIESEL FUEL AND SPECIAL MOTOR FUELS.—

(1) TAX ON DIESEL FUEL AND KEROSENE IN CERTAIN CASES.—

(A) IN GENERAL.—There is hereby imposed a tax on any liquid other than gasoline (as defined in section 4083)—

(i) sold by any person to an owner, lessee, or other operator of a diesel-powered highway vehicle or a diesel-powered train for use as a fuel in such vehicle or train, or

(ii) used by any person as a fuel in a diesel-powered highway vehicle or a diesel-powered train unless there was a taxable sale of such fuel under clause (i).

(B) EXEMPTION FOR PREVIOUSLY TAXED FUEL.—No tax shall be imposed by this paragraph on the sale or use of any liquid if tax was imposed on such liquid under section 4081 (other than such tax at the Leaking Underground Storage Tank Trust Fund financing rate) and the tax thereon was not credited or refunded.

(C) RATE OF TAX.—

(i) IN GENERAL.—Except as otherwise provided in this subparagraph, the rate of the tax imposed by this paragraph shall be the rate of tax specified in section 4081(a)(2)(A) on diesel fuel which is in effect at the time of such sale or use.

(ii) RATE OF TAX ON TRAINS.—In the case of any sale for use, or use, of diesel fuel in a train, the rate of tax imposed by this paragraph shall be—

(I) 3.3 cents per gallon after December 31, 2004, and before July 1, 2005,

(II) 2.3 cents per gallon after June 30, 2005, and before January 1, 2007, and

(III) 0 after December 31, 2006.

(iii) RATE OF TAX ON CERTAIN BUSES.—

(I) IN GENERAL.—Except as provided in subclause (II), in the case of fuel sold for use or used in a use described in section 6427(b)(1) (after the application of section 6427(b)(3)), the rate of tax imposed by this paragraph shall be 7.3 cents per gallon (4.3 cents per gallon after September 30, 2028).

(II) SCHOOL BUS AND INTRACITY TRANSPORTATION.—No tax shall be imposed by this paragraph on any sale for use, or use, described in subparagraph (B) or (C) of section 6427(b)(2).

(2) ALTERNATIVE FUELS.—

(A) IN GENERAL.—There is hereby imposed a tax on any liquid (other than gas oil, fuel oil, or any product taxable under section 4081 (other than such tax at the Leaking Underground Storage Tank Trust Fund financing rate))—

(i) sold by any person to an owner, lessee, or other operator of a motor vehicle or motorboat for use as a fuel in such motor vehicle or motorboat, or

(ii) used by any person as a fuel in a motor vehicle or motorboat unless there was a taxable sale of such liquid under clause (i).

(B) RATE OF TAX.—The rate of the tax imposed by this paragraph shall be—

(i) except as otherwise provided in this subparagraph, the rate of tax specified in section 4081(a)(2)(A)(i) which is in effect at the time of such sale or use,

(ii) in the case of liquefied petroleum gas, 18.3 cents per energy equivalent of a gallon of gasoline,

(iii) in the case of any liquid fuel (other than ethanol and methanol) derived from coal (including peat) and liquid hydrocarbons derived from biomass (as defined in section 45K(c)(3)), 24.3 cents per gallon, and

(iv) in the case of liquefied natural gas, 24.3 cents per energy equivalent of a gallon of diesel.

(C) ENERGY EQUIVALENT OF A GALLON OF GASOLINE.—For purposes of this paragraph, the term "energy equivalent of a gallon of gasoline" means, with respect to a liquefied petroleum gas fuel, the amount of such fuel having a Btu content of 115,400 (lower heating value). For purposes of the preceding sentence, a Btu content of 115,400 (lower heating value) is equal to 5.75 pounds of liquefied petroleum gas.

Sec. 4012—Repealed

EXCISE TAXES—RETAIL EXCISE TAXES

(D) ENERGY EQUIVALENT OF A GALLON OF DIESEL.—For purposes of this paragraph, the term "energy equivalent of a gallon of diesel" means, with respect to a liquefied natural gas fuel, the amount of such fuel having a Btu content of 128,700 (lower heating value). For purposes of the preceding sentence, a Btu content of 128,700 (lower heating value) is equal to 6.06 pounds of liquefied natural gas.

(3) COMPRESSED NATURAL GAS.—

(A) IN GENERAL.—There is hereby imposed a tax on compressed natural gas—

(i) sold by any person to an owner, lessee, or other operator of a motor vehicle or motorboat for use as a fuel in such motor vehicle or motorboat, or

(ii) used by any person as a fuel in a motor vehicle or motorboat unless there was a taxable sale of such gas under clause (i).

The rate of the tax imposed by this paragraph shall be 18.3 cents per energy equivalent of a gallon of gasoline.

(B) BUS USES.—No tax shall be imposed by this paragraph on any sale for use, or use, described in subparagraph (B) or (C) of section 6427(b)(2) (relating to school bus and intracity transportation).

(C) ADMINISTRATIVE PROVISIONS.—For purposes of applying this title with respect to the taxes imposed by this subsection, references to any liquid subject to tax under this subsection shall be treated as including references to compressed natural gas subject to tax under this paragraph, and references to gallons shall be treated as including references to energy equivalent of a gallon of gasoline with respect to such gas.

(D) ENERGY EQUIVALENT OF A GALLON OF GASOLINE.—For purposes of this paragraph, the term "energy equivalent of a gallon of gasoline" means 5.66 pounds of compressed natural gas.

Amendments

- **2021, Infrastructure Investment and Jobs Act (P.L. 117-58)**

P.L. 117-58, §80102(a)(1)(A), Div. H:

Amended Code Sec. 4041(a)(1)(C)(iii)(I) by striking "September 30, 2022" and inserting "September 30, 2028". **Effective** 10-1-2021.

- **2015, Fixing America's Surface Transportation Act (P.L. 114-94)**

P.L. 114-94, §31102(a)(1)(A):

Amended Code Sec. 4041(a)(1)(C)(iii)(I) by striking "September 30, 2016" and inserting "September 30, 2022". **Effective** 10-1-2016.

- **2015, Surface Transportation and Veterans Health Care Choice Improvement Act of 2015 (P.L. 114-41)**

P.L. 114-41, §2008(a)(1):

Amended Code Sec. 4041(a)(2)(B) by striking "and" at the end of clause (i), by redesignating clause (ii) as clause (iii), and by inserting after clause (i) a new clause (ii). **Effective** for any sale or use of fuel after 12-31-2015.

P.L. 114-41, §2008(a)(2):

Amended Code Sec. 4041(a)(2) by adding at the end a new subparagraph (C). **Effective** for any sale or use of fuel after 12-31-2015.

P.L. 114-41, §2008(b)(1):

Amended Code Sec. 4041(a)(2)(B), as amended by Act Sec. 2008(a)(1), by striking "and" at the end of clause (ii), by striking the period at the end of clause (iii) and inserting ", and" and by inserting after clause (iii) a new clause (iv). **Effective** for any sale or use of fuel after 12-31-2015.

P.L. 114-41, §2008(b)(2):

Amended Code Sec. 4041(a)(2), as amended by Act Sec. 2008(a)(2), by adding at the end a new subparagraph (D). **Effective** for any sale or use of fuel after 12-31-2015.

P.L. 114-41, §2008(b)(3)(A)-(B):

Amended Code Sec. 4041(a)(2)(B)(iii), as redesignated by Act Sec. 2008(a)(1), by striking "liquefied natural gas," following "case of", and by striking "peat), and" and inserting "peat) and". **Effective** for any sale or use of fuel after 12-31-2015.

P.L. 114-41, §2008(c):

Amended Code Sec. 4041(a)(3) by adding at the end a new subparagraph (D). **Effective** for any sale or use of fuel after 12-31-2015.

- **2012, Highway Investment, Job Creation, and Economic Growth Act of 2012 (P.L. 112-141)**

P.L. 112-141, §40102(a)(1)(A):

Amended Code Sec. 4041(a)(1)(C)(iii)(I) by striking "June 30, 2012" and inserting "September 30, 2016". **Effective** 7-1-2012.

- **2012, Temporary Surface Transportation Extension Act of 2012 (P.L. 112-140)**

P.L. 112-140, §1(c), provides:

(c) SPECIAL RULE FOR EXECUTION OF AMENDMENTS IN MAP–21.—On the date of enactment of the MAP–21 [P.L. 112-141]—

(1) this Act and the amendments made by this Act shall cease to be effective;

(2) the text of the laws amended by this Act shall revert back so as to read as the text read on the day before the date of enactment of this Act; and

(3) the amendments made by the MAP–21 shall be executed as if this Act had not been enacted.

P.L. 112-140, §402(a)(1)(A):

Amended Code Sec. 4041(a)(1)(C)(iii)(I) by striking "June 30, 2012" and inserting "July 6, 2012". **Effective** 7-1-2012. For a special rule, see Act Sec. 1(c), above.

- **2012, Surface Transportation Extension Act of 2012 (P.L. 112-102)**

P.L. 112-102, §402(a)(1)(A):

Amended Code Sec. 4041(a)(1)(C)(iii)(I) by striking "March 31, 2012" and inserting "June 30, 2012". **Effective** 4-1-2012.

- **2011, Surface Transportation Extension Act of 2011, Part II (P.L. 112-30)**

P.L. 112-30, §142(a)(1)(A):

Amended Code Sec. 4041(a)(1)(C)(iii)(I) by striking "September 30, 2011" and inserting "March 31, 2012". **Effective** 10-1-2011.

- **2005, Safe, Accountable, Flexible, Efficient Transportation Equity Act: A Legacy for Users (P.L. 109-59)**

P.L. 109-59, §11101(a)(1)(A):

Amended Code Sec. 4041(a)(1)(C)(iii)(I) by striking "2005" and inserting "2011". **Effective** 8-10-2005.

P.L. 109-59, §11101(a)(1)(B):

Amended Code Sec. 4041(a)(2)(B) by striking "2005" and inserting "2011". **Effective** 8-10-2005.

P.L. 109-59, §11113(a)(1)(A)-(D):

Amended Code Sec. 4041(a)(2)(B) by adding "and" at the end of clause (i), by striking clauses (ii) and (iii), by striking the last sentence, and by adding after clause (i) a new clause (ii). **Effective** for any sale or use for any period after 9-30-2006. Prior to amendment, Code Sec. 4041(a)(2)(B) read as follows:

(B) RATE OF TAX.—The rate of the tax imposed by this paragraph shall be—

(i) except as otherwise provided in this subparagraph, the rate of tax specified in section 4081(a)(2)(A)(i) which is in effect at the time of such sale or use,

(ii) 13.6 cents per gallon in the case of liquefied petroleum gas, and

(iii) 11.9 cents per gallon in the case of liquefied natural gas.

In the case of any sale or use after September 30, 2011, clause (ii) shall be applied by substituting "3.2 cents" for "13.6 cents", and clause (iii) shall be applied by substituting "2.8 cents" for "11.9 cents".

P.L. 109-59, §11113(a)(2)(A)-(B):

Amended Code Sec. 4041(a)(3) by striking "48.54 cents per MCF (determined at standard temperature and pressure)" in subparagraph (A) and inserting "18.3 cents per energy equivalent of a gallon of gasoline", and by striking "MCF" in subparagraph (C) and inserting "energy equivalent of a gallon of gasoline". **Effective** for any sale or use for any period after 9-30-2006.

P.L. 109-59, §11113(a)(3):

Amended the heading for Code Sec. 4041(a)(2) by striking "SPECIAL MOTOR FUELS" and inserting "ALTERNATIVE FUELS". **Effective** for any sale or use for any period after 9-30-2006.

P.L. 109-59, §11151(e)(2):

Amended Code Sec. 4041(a)(2)(B)(ii), as amended by Act Sec. 11113, by striking "section 29(c)(3)" and inserting "section 45K(c)(3)". **Effective** as if included in the provision of the Energy Tax Incentives Act of 2005 to which it relates [effective for credits determined for tax years ending after 12-31-2005.—CCH].

P.L. 109-59, §11161(b)(3)(A):

Amended Code Sec. 4041(a)(1)(B) by striking the last sentence. **Effective** for fuels or liquids removed, entered, or sold after 9-30-2005. Prior to being stricken, the last sentence of Code Sec. 4041(a)(1)(B) read as follows:

This subparagraph shall not apply to aviation-grade kerosene.

- **2005, Energy Tax Incentives Act of 2005 (P.L. 109-58)**

P.L. 109-58, §1362(b)(2)(A):

Amended Code Sec. 4041(a)(1)(B) and (2)(A) by inserting "(other than such tax at the Leaking Underground Storage Tank Trust Fund financing rate)" after "section 4081". **Effective** for fuel entered, removed, or sold after 9-30-2005.

- **2004, American Jobs Creation Act of 2004 (P.L. 108-357)**

P.L. 108-357, §241(a)(1):

Amended Code Sec. 4041(a)(1)(C)(ii) by striking subclauses (I), (II), and (III) and inserting new subclauses (I), (II) and (III). **Effective** 1-1-2005. Prior to amendment, Code Sec. 4041(a)(1)(C)(ii)(I)-(III) read as follows:

(I) 6.8 cents per gallon after September 30, 1993, and before October 1, 1995,

EXCISE TAXES—RETAIL EXCISE TAXES

(II) 5.55 cents per gallon after September 30, 1995, and before November 1, 1998, and

(III) 4.3 cents per gallon after October 31, 1998.

P.L. 108-357, §853(a)(6)(A):

Amended Code Sec. 4041(a)(1)(B) by adding at the end a new sentence. **Effective** for aviation-grade kerosene removed, entered, or sold after 12-31-2004. For special rules, see Act Sec. 853(f) in the amendments for Code Sec. 4041(c).

P.L. 108-357, §853(a)(6)(B):

Amended the heading for Code Sec. 4041(a)(1) by inserting "AND KEROSENE" after "DIESEL FUEL". **Effective** for aviation-grade kerosene removed, entered, or sold after 12-31-2004. For special rules, see Act Sec. 853(f) in the amendments for Code Sec. 4041(c).

- **1998, Transportation Equity Act for the 21st Century (P.L. 105-178)**

P.L. 105-178, §9002(a)(1)(A):

Amended Code Sec. 4041(a)(1)(C)(iii)(I) by striking "1999" and inserting "2005". **Effective** 6-9-98.

P.L. 105-178, §9002(a)(1)(B):

Amended Code Sec. 4041(a)(2)(B) by striking "1999" and inserting "2005". **Effective** 6-9-98.

P.L. 105-178, §9006(a)(1)-(2):

Amended Code Sec. 4041(a)(1)(C)(ii) by striking "October 1, 1999" in subclause (II) and inserting "November 1, 1998", and by striking "September 30, 1999" in subclause (III) and inserting "October 31, 1998". **Effective** 6-9-98.

- **1997, Taxpayer Relief Act of 1997 (P.L. 105-34)**

P.L. 105-34, §901(e), provides:

(e) DELAYED DEPOSITS OF HIGHWAY MOTOR FUEL TAX REVENUES.—Notwithstanding section 6302 of the Internal Revenue Code of 1986, in the case of deposits of taxes imposed by sections 4041 and 4081 (other than subsection (a)(2)(A)(ii)) of the Internal Revenue Code of 1986, the due date for any deposit which would (but for this subsection) be required to be made after July 31, 1998, and before October 1, 1998, shall be October 5, 1998.

P.L. 105-34, §902(b)(1)(A)-(B):

Amended Code Sec. 4041(a)(1)(A) by striking ", a diesel-powered train, or a diesel-powered boat" each place it appears and inserting "or a diesel-powered train", and by striking "vehicle, train, or boat" and inserting "vehicle or train". **Effective** 1-1-98.

P.L. 105-34, §902(b)(2):

Amended Code Sec. 4041(a)(1) by striking subparagraph (D). **Effective** 1-1-98. Prior to being stricken, Code Sec. 4041(a)(1)(D) read as follows:

(D) DIESEL FUEL USED IN MOTORBOATS.—In the case of any sale for use, or use, of fuel in a diesel-powered motorboat—

(i) no tax shall be imposed by subsection (a) or (d)(1) during the period beginning on the date which is 7 days after the date of the enactment of the Small Business Job Protection Act of 1996 and ending on December 31, 1997,

(ii) effective during the period after September 30, 1999, and before January 1, 2000, the rate of tax imposed by this paragraph is 24.3 cents per gallon, and

(iii) the termination of the tax under subsection (d) shall not occur before January 1, 2000.

P.L. 105-34, §907(a)(1):

Amended Code Sec. 4041(a)(2). **Effective** 10-1-97. Prior to amendment, Code Sec. 4041(a)(2) read as follows:

(2) SPECIAL MOTOR FUELS.—There is hereby imposed a tax on benzol, benzene, naphtha, liquefied petroleum gas, casing head and natural gasoline, or any other liquid (other than a Kerosene, gas oil, or fuel oil, or any product taxable under section 4081)—

(A) sold by any person to an owner, lessee, or other operator of a motor vehicle or motorboat for use as a fuel in such motor vehicle or motorboat, or

(B) used by any person as a fuel in a motor vehicle or motorboat unless there was a taxable sale of such liquid under subparagraph (A).

The rate of the tax imposed by this paragraph shall be the rate of tax specified in section 4081(a)(2)(A)(i) on gasoline which is in effect at the time of such sale or use.

P.L. 105-34, §1032(e)(1):

Amended Code Sec. 4041(a)(2) by striking "kerosene" after "(other than)". **Effective** 7-1-98.

P.L. 105-34, §1601(f)(4)(B):

Amended Code Sec. 4041(a)(2) by striking "section 4081(a)(2)(A)" in the last sentence and inserting "section 4081(a)(2)(A)(i)". **Effective**, generally, as if included in the provision of P.L. 104-188 to which it relates [**effective** 8-27-96.—CCH].

- **1996, Small Business Job Protection Act of 1996 (P.L. 104-188)**

P.L. 104-188, §1208:

Amended Code Sec. 4041(a)(1)(D) by redesignating clauses (i) and (ii) as clauses (ii) and (iii), respectively, and by inserting before clause (ii) (as redesignated) a new clause (i). **Effective** 8-20-96.

- **1993, Omnibus Budget Reconciliation Act of 1993 (P.L. 103-66)**

P.L. 103-66, §13163(a)(2)(A)-(B):

Amended Code Sec. 4041(a)(1) by striking "diesel-powered highway vehicle" each place it appears and inserting "diesel-powered highway vehicle or diesel-powered boat", and by striking "such vehicle" and inserting "such vehicle or boat". **Effective** 1-1-94.

P.L. 103-66, §13241(e)(1):

Amended Code Sec. 4041(a) by adding new paragraph (3). **Effective** 10-1-93.

P.L. 103-66, §13242(d)(3):

Amended Code Sec. 4041(a)(1) (as amended by subchapter A (Act Sec. 13163(a)(2)(A)-(B)). **Effective** 1-1-94. Prior to amendment, Code Sec. 4041(a)(1) read as follows:

(1) TAX ON DIESEL FUEL WHERE NO TAX IMPOSED UNDER SECTION 4091.—There is hereby imposed a tax on any liquid (other than any product taxable under section 4081)—

(A) sold by any person to an owner, lessee, or other operator of a diesel-powered highway vehicle or diesel-powered boat for use as a fuel in such vehicle or boat; or

(B) used by any person as a fuel in a diesel-powered highway vehicle or diesel-powered boat unless there was a taxable sale of such liquid under paragraph (A).

The rate of the tax imposed by this paragraph shall be the sum of the Highway Trust Fund financing rate and the diesel fuel deficit reduction rate in effect under section 4091 at the time of such sale or use. No tax shall be imposed by this paragraph on the sale or use of any liquid if there was a taxable sale of such liquid under section 4091.

P.L. 103-66, §13242(d)(4)(A)-(B):

Amended Code Sec. 4041(a)(2) by striking "or paragraph (1) of this subsection" following "section 4081" and by striking the last sentence and inserting a new last sentence. **Effective** 1-1-94. Prior to amendment, the last sentence read as follows:

The rate of the tax imposed by this paragraph shall be the sum of the Highway Trust Fund financing rate and the deficit reduction rate in effect under section 4081 at the time of such sale or use.

- **1990, Omnibus Budget Reconciliation Act of 1990 (P.L. 101-508)**

P.L. 101-508, §11211(b)(3):

Amended Code Sec. 4041(a)(2) by striking "of 9 cents a gallon" after "a tax" and by inserting at the end thereof a new sentence. **Effective** 12-1-90.

P.L. 101-508, §11211(b)(6)(C)(i):

Amended Code Sec. 4041(a)(1) by striking "of 15 cents a gallon" after "a tax" and by inserting before the last sentence a new sentence. **Effective** 12-1-90.

P.L. 101-508, §11211(b)(6)(C)(ii):

Amended Code Sec. 4041(a) by striking paragraph (3). **Effective** 12-1-90. Prior to being stricken, Code Sec. 4041(a)(3) read as follows:

(3) TERMINATION.—On and after October 1, 1993, the taxes imposed by this subsection shall not apply.

- **1987, Revenue Act of 1987 (P.L. 100-203)**

P.L. 100-203, §10502(b)(1)(A)-(B):

Amended Code Sec. 4041(a)(1) by striking out "Diesel fuel" in the heading and inserting in lieu thereof "Tax on diesel fuel where no tax imposed on fuel under section 4091", and by adding at the end thereof a new sentence. **Effective** for sales after 3-31-88.

- **1987, Surface Transportation and Uniform Relocation Assistance Act of 1987 (P.L. 100-17)**

P.L. 100-17, §502(a)(1):

Amended Code Sec. 4041(a)(3) by striking out "1988" and inserting in lieu thereof "1993". **Effective** 4-2-87.

- **1984, Deficit Reduction Act of 1984 (P.L. 98-369)**

P.L. 98-369, §911(a):

Amended Code Sec. 4041(a)(1) by striking out "9 cents" and inserting in lieu thereof "15 cents". **Effective** 8-1-84.

- **1983, Surface Transportation Act of 1982 (P.L. 97-424)**

P.L. 97-424, §511(a)(2):

Struck out Code Sec. 4041(a) and inserted new subsection (a). **Effective** 4-1-83. Prior to being stricken, subsection (a) read as follows:

(a) DIESEL FUEL.—There is hereby imposed a tax of 4 cents a gallon upon any liquid (other than any product taxable under section 4081)—

(1) sold by any person to an owner, lessee, or other operator of a diesel-powered highway vehicle, for use as a fuel in such vehicle; or

(2) used by any person as a fuel in a diesel-powered highway vehicle unless there was a taxable sale of such liquid under paragraph (1).

In the case of a liquid taxable under this subsection sold for use or used as a fuel in a diesel-powered highway vehicle (A) which (at the time of such sale or use) is not registered, and is not required to be registered, for highway use under the laws of any State or foreign country, or (B) which, in the case of a diesel-powered highway vehicle owned by the United States, is not used on the highway, the tax imposed by paragraph (1) or by paragraph (2) shall be 2 cents a gallon. If a liquid on which tax was imposed by paragraph (1) at the rate of 2 cents a gallon by reason of the preceding sentence is used as a fuel in a diesel-powered highway vehicle (A) which (at the time of such use) is registered, or is required to be registered, for highway use under the laws of any State or foreign country, or (B) which, in the case of a diesel-powered highway vehicle owned by the United States, is used on the highway, a tax of 2 cents a gallon shall be imposed under paragraph (2).

P.L. 97-424, §516(a)(1)(A):

Added Code Sec. 4041(a)(3). **Effective** 1-6-83.

- **1961, Federal-Aid Highway Act of 1961 (P.L. 87-61)**

P.L. 87-61, §201(a):

Amended Sec. 4041(a) by substituting "4 cents" for "3 cents"; and by substituting "2 cents" for "1 cent." **Effective** 7-1-61.

EXCISE TAXES—RETAIL EXCISE TAXES

• **1959, Federal-Aid Highway Act of 1959 (P.L. 86-342)**

P.L. 86-342, § 201(b)(2):

Amended Sec. 4041(a) by striking out "in lieu of 3 cents a gallon" where it appeared following the phrase "2 cents a gallon" in the second sentence.

• **1956 (P.L. 627, 84th Cong.)**

P.L. 627, 84th Cong., 2d Sess., § 202(a):

Amended subsection (a) by striking out "2 cents a gallon" and inserting in lieu thereof "3 cents a gallon", and by adding the provisions following paragraph (2). **Effective** 7-1-56.

[Sec. 4041(b)]

(b) EXEMPTION FOR OFF-HIGHWAY BUSINESS USE; REDUCTION IN TAX FOR QUALIFIED METHANOL AND ETHANOL FUEL.—

(1) EXEMPTION FOR OFF-HIGHWAY BUSINESS USE.—

(A) IN GENERAL.—No tax shall be imposed by subsection (a) on liquids sold for use or used in an off-highway business use.

(B) TAX WHERE OTHER USE.—If a liquid on which no tax was imposed by reason of subparagraph (A) is used otherwise than in an off-highway business use, a tax shall be imposed by paragraph (1)(B), (2)(B), or (3)(A)(ii) of subsection (a) (whichever is appropriate) and by the corresponding provision of subsection (d)(1) (if any).

(C) OFF-HIGHWAY BUSINESS USE DEFINED.—For purposes of this subsection, the term "off-highway business use" has the meaning given to such term by section 6421(e)(2); except that such term shall not, for purposes of subsection (a)(1), include use in a diesel-powered train.

(2) QUALIFIED METHANOL AND ETHANOL FUEL.—

(A) IN GENERAL.—In the case of any qualified methanol or ethanol fuel—

(i) the rate applicable under subsection (a)(2) shall be the applicable blender rate per gallon less than the otherwise applicable rate (6 cents per gallon in the case of a mixture none of the alcohol in which consists of ethanol), and

(ii) subsection (d)(1) shall be applied by substituting "0.05 cent" for "0.1 cent" with respect to the sales and uses to which clause (i) applies.

(B) QUALIFIED METHANOL AND ETHANOL FUEL PRODUCED FROM COAL.—The term "qualified methanol or ethanol fuel" means any liquid at least 85 percent of which consists of methanol, ethanol, or other alcohol produced from coal (including peat).

(C) APPLICABLE BLENDER RATE.—For purposes of subparagraph (A)(i), the applicable blender rate is—

(i) except as provided in clause (ii), 5.4 cents, and

(ii) for sales or uses during calendar years 2001 through 2008, $1/10$ of the blender amount applicable under section 40(h)(2) for the calendar year in which the sale or use occurs.

(D) TERMINATION.—On and after January 1, 2009, subparagraph (A) shall not apply.

Amendments

• **2006, Tax Relief and Health Care Act of 2006 (P.L. 109-432)**

P.L. 109-432, Division A, § 208(a):

Amended Code Sec. 4041(b)(2)(D) by striking "October 1, 2007" and inserting "January 1, 2009". **Effective** 12-20-2006.

P.L. 109-432, Division A, § 208(b):

Amended Code Sec. 4041(b)(2)(C)(ii) by striking "2007" and inserting "2008". **Effective** 12-20-2006.

P.L. 109-432, Division A, § 208(c):

Amended the heading for Code Sec. 4041(b)(2)(B). **Effective** 12-20-2006. Prior to amendment, the heading for Code Sec. 4041(b)(2)(B) read as follows:

QUALIFIED METHANOL OR ETHANOL FUEL.

• **2005, Energy Tax Incentives Act of 2005 (P.L. 109-58)**

P.L. 109-58, § 1362(b)(2)(B):

Amended Code Sec. 4041(b)(1)(A) by striking "or (d)(1))" after "subsection (a)". [Note: The second parenthesis does not appear in the text.—CCH] **Effective** for fuel entered, removed, or sold after 9-30-2005.

• **2004, American Jobs Creation Act of 2004 (P.L. 108-357)**

P.L. 108-357, § 301(c)(5):

Amended Code Sec. 4041(b)(2)(B) by striking "a substance other than petroleum or natural gas" and inserting "coal (including peat)". **Effective** for fuel sold or used after 12-31-2004.

• **1998, Transportation Equity Act for the 21st Century (P.L. 105-178)**

P.L. 105-178, § 9003(a)(1)(A):

Amended Code Sec. 4041(b)(2)(C) by striking "2000" and inserting "2007". **Effective** 6-9-98.

P.L. 105-178, § 9003(b)(2)(A)(i):

Amended Code Sec. 4041(b)(2)(A)(i) by striking "5.4 cents" and inserting "the applicable blender rate". **Effective** 1-1-2001.

P.L. 105-178, § 9003(b)(2)(A)(ii):

Amended Code Sec. 4041(b)(2) by redesignating subparagraph (C), as amended by Act Sec. 9003(a)(1)(A), as subparagraph (D) and inserting after subparagraph (B) a new subparagraph (C). **Effective** 1-1-2001.

• **1993, Omnibus Budget Reconciliation Act of 1993 (P.L. 103-66)**

P.L. 103-66, § 13242(d)(5)(A):

Amended Code Sec. 4041(b)(1)(B) by striking "paragraph (1)(B) or (2)(B)" and inserting "paragraph (1)(B), (2)(B), or (3)(A)(ii)" and by inserting before the period "(if any)". **Effective** 1-1-94.

P.L. 103-66, § 13242(d)(5)(B):

Amended Code Sec. 4041(b)(1)(C) by inserting before the period "; except that such term shall not, for purposes of subsection (a)(1), include use in a diesel-powered train". **Effective** 1-1-94.

P.L. 103-66, § 13242(d)(5)(C):

Amended Code Sec. 4041(b)(2)(A)(i) by striking "Highway Trust Fund financing" preceding "rate applicable". **Effective** 1-1-94.

• **1990, Omnibus Budget Reconciliation Act of 1990 (P.L. 101-508)**

P.L. 101-508, § 11211(b)(6)(D):

Amended Code Sec. 4041(b)(2)(A)(i). **Effective** 12-1-90. Prior to amendment, Code Sec. 4041(b)(2)(A)(i) read as follows:

(i) subsection (a)(2) shall be applied by substituting "3 cents" for "9 cents", and

P.L. 101-508, § 11211(e)(1):

Amended Code Sec. 4041(b)(2)(C) by striking "1993" each place it appears and inserting "2000". **Effective** 11-5-90.

• **1988, Technical and Miscellaneous Revenue Act of 1988 (P.L. 100-647)**

P.L. 100-647, § 1017(c)(3):

Amended Code Sec. 4041(b)(1)(C) by striking out "section 6421(d)(2)" and inserting in lieu thereof "section 6421(e)(2)". **Effective** as if included in the provision of P.L. 99-514 to which it relates.

P.L. 100-647, § 2001(d)(3)(A):

Amended Code Sec. 4041(b)(1)(A) by striking out "subsection (a)" and inserting in lieu thereof "subsection (a) or (d)(1)". **Effective** as if included in the provision of P.L. 99-499 to which it relates.

P.L. 100-647, § 2001(d)(3)(B):

Amended Code Sec. 4041(b)(1)(B) by inserting before the period "and by the corresponding provision of subsection (d)(1)". **Effective** as if included in the provision of P.L. 99-499 to which it relates.

P.L. 100-647, § 2001(d)(3)(C):

Amended Code Sec. 4041(b) by striking out paragraph (3). **Effective** as if included in the provision of P.L. 99-499 to which it relates. Prior to amendment, Code Sec. 4041(b)(3) read as follows:

(3) COORDINATION WITH TAXES IMPOSED BY SUBSECTION (d).—

(A) OFF-HIGHWAY BUSINESS USE.—

(i) IN GENERAL.—Except as provided in clause (ii), rules similar to the rules of paragraph (1) shall apply with respect to the taxes imposed by subsection (d).

(ii) LIMITATION ON EXEMPTION FOR OFF-HIGHWAY BUSINESS USE.—For purposes of subparagraph (A), paragraph (1) shall apply only with respect to off-highway business use in a vessel employed in the fisheries or in the whaling business.

(B) QUALIFIED METHANOL AND ETHANOL FUEL.—In the case of qualified methanol or ethanol fuel, subsection (d) shall be applied by substituting "0.05 cents" for "0.1 cents" in paragraph (1) thereof.

P.L. 100-647, § 2001(d)(3)(D):

Amended Code Sec. 4041(b)(2)(A). **Effective** as if included in the provision of P.L. 99-499 to which it relates. Prior to amendment, Code Sec. 4041(b)(2)(A) read as follows:

(A) IN GENERAL.—In the case of any qualified methanol or ethanol fuel, subsection (a)(2) shall be applied by substituting "3 cents" for "9 cents".

• **1987, Surface Transportation and Uniform Relocation Assistance Act of 1987 (P.L. 100-17)**

P.L. 100-17, § 502(b)(1):

Amended Code Sec. 4041(b)(2)(C) by striking out "1988" and inserting in lieu thereof "1993". **Effective** 4-2-87.

EXCISE TAXES—RETAIL EXCISE TAXES

- **1986, Tax Reform Act of 1986 (P.L. 99-514)**

P.L. 99-514, § 422(a)(1):

Amended Code Sec. 4041(b)(2)(A). **Effective** 1-1-87. Prior to amendment, Code Sec. 4041(b)(2)(A) read as follows:

(A) IN GENERAL.—No tax shall be imposed by subsection (a) on any qualified methanol or ethanol fuel.

P.L. 99-514, § 422(a)(2):

Amended Code Sec. 4041(b) by striking out "EXEMPTION" the second place it appears in the heading and inserting in lieu thereof "REDUCTION IN TAX". **Effective** 1-1-87.

- **1986, Superfund Amendments and Reauthorization Act of 1986 (P.L. 99-499)**

P.L. 99-499, § 521(d)(1):

Amended Code Sec. 4041(b) by adding at the end thereof new paragraph (3). **Effective** 1-1-87.

- **1983, Surface Transportation Act of 1982 (P.L. 97-424)**

P.L. 97-424, § 511(a)(2):

Struck out Code Sec. 4041(b). **Effective** 4-1-83. Prior to being stricken, subsection (b) read as follows:

(b) SPECIAL MOTOR FUELS.—There is hereby imposed a tax of 4 cents a gallon upon benzol, benezene, naphtha, liquefied petroleum gas, casing head and natural gasoline, or any other liquid (other than kerosene, gas oil, or fuel oil, or any product taxable under section 4081 or subsection (a) of this section)—

(1) sold by any person to an owner, lessee, or other operator of a motor vehicle or motorboat for use as a fuel in such motor vehicle or motorboat; or

(2) used by any person as a fuel in a motor vehicle or motorboat unless there was a taxable sale of such liquid under paragraph (1).

In the case of a liquid taxable under this subsection sold for use, or used, in a qualified business use, the tax imposed by paragraph (1) or by paragraph (2) shall be 2 cents a gallon. If a liquid on which tax was imposed by paragraph (1) at the rate of 2 cents a gallon by reason of the preceding sentence is used otherwise than in a qualified business use, a tax of 2 cents a gallon shall be imposed under paragraph (2). For purposes of this subsection, the term "qualified business use" has the meaning given to such term by section 6421(d)(2).

P.L. 97-424, § 511(b)(1):

Added Code Sec. 4041(b)(2). **Effective** 4-1-83.

P.L. 97-424, § 511(c)(2):

Added Code Sec. 4041(b)(1). **Effective** 4-1-83.

- **1978, Energy Tax Act of 1978 (P.L. 95-618)**

P.L. 95-618, § 233(a)(3)(B), (d):

Amended the last sentence of Code Sec. 4041(b), as added by Act Sec. 222(a)(2) by inserting "6421(d)(2)" in place of "6421(d)(3)". **Effective** 12-1-78.

P.L. 95-618, § 222(a)(2), (b):

Amended Code Sec. 4041(b) by striking out the second and third sentences and inserting in place thereof the following:

"In the case of a liquid taxable under this subsection sold for use, or used, in a qualified business use, the tax imposed by paragraph (1) or by paragraph (2) shall be 2 cents a gallon. If a liquid on which tax was imposed by paragraph (1) at the rate of 2 cents a gallon by reason of the preceding sentence is used otherwise than in a qualified business use, a tax of 2 cents a gallon shall be imposed under paragraph (2). For purposes of this subsection, the term `qualified business use' has the meaning given to such term by section 6421(d)(3)." **Effective** 11-10-78, but applicable to uses after 12-31-78. Prior to being stricken, the second and third sentences of Code Sec. 4041(b) read:

In the case of a liquid taxable under this subsection sold for use or used otherwise than as a fuel in a highway vehicle (A) which (at the time of such sale or use) is registered, or is required to be registered, for highway use under the laws of any State or foreign country, or (B) which, in the case of a highway vehicle owned by the United States, is used on the highway, the tax imposed by paragraph (1) or by paragraph (2) shall be 2 cents a gallon. If a liquid on which tax was imposed by paragraph (1) at the rate of 2 cents a gallon by reason of the preceding sentence is used as a fuel in a highway vehicle (A) which (at the time of such use) is registered, or is required to be registered, for highway use under the laws of any State or foreign country, or (B) which, in the case of a highway vehicle owned by the United States, is used on the highway, a tax of 2 cents a gallon shall be imposed under paragraph (2).

- **1970 (P.L. 91-258)**

P.L. 91-258, § 202(b):

Amended Code Sec. 4041(b). **Effective** 7-1-70. Prior to amendment, Code Sec. 4041(b) read as follows:

(b) SPECIAL MOTOR FUELS.—There is hereby imposed a tax of 4 cents a gallon upon benzol, benezene, naphtha, liquefied petroleum gas, casing head and natural gasoline, or any other liquid (other than kerosene, gas oil, or fuel oil, or any product taxable under section 4081 or subsection (a) of this section)—

(1) sold by any person to an owner, lessee, or other operator of a motor vehicle, motorboat, or airplane for use as a fuel for the propulsion of such motor vehicle, motorboat, or airplane; or

(2) used by any person as a fuel for the propulsion of a motor vehicle, motorboat, or airplane unless there was a taxable sale of such liquid under paragraph (1).

In the case of a liquid taxable under this subsection sold for use or used otherwise than as a fuel for the propulsion of a highway vehicle (A) which (at the time of such sale or use) is registered, or is required to be registered, for highway use under the laws of any State or foreign country, or (B) which, in the case of a highway vehicle owned by the United States, is used on the highway, the tax imposed by paragraph (1) or by paragraph (2) shall be 2 cents a gallon. If a liquid on which tax was imposed by paragraph (1) at the rate of 2 cents a gallon by reason of the preceding sentence is used as a fuel for the propulsion of a highway vehicle (A) which (at the time of such use) is registered, or is required to be registered, for highway use under the laws of any State or foreign country, or (B) which, in the case of a highway vehicle owned by the United States, is used on the highway, a tax of 2 cents a gallon shall be imposed under paragraph (2).

- **1965, Excise Tax Reduction Act of 1965 (P.L. 89-44)**

P.L. 89-44, § 802(a)(2):

Amended Sec. 4041(b) by adding the words "casing head and natural gasoline," in the material preceding paragraph (1). **Effective** 7-1-65.

- **1961, Federal-Aid Highway Act of 1961 (P.L. 87-61)**

P.L. 87-61, § 201(a):

Amended Sec. 4041(b) by substituting "4 cents" for "3 cents"; and by substituting "2 cents" for "1 cent." **Effective** 7-1-61.

- **1959, Federal-Aid Highway Act of 1959 (P.L. 86-342)**

P.L. 86-342, § 201(b)(2):

Amended Sec. 4041(b) by striking out "in lieu of 3 cents a gallon" where it appeared following the phrase "2 cents a gallon" in the second sentence.

- **1956 (P.L. 627, 84th Cong.)**

P.L. 627, 84th Cong., 2d Sess., § 202(b):

Amended subsection (b) by striking out "2 cents a gallon" and inserting in lieu thereof "3 cents a gallon", and by adding the provisions following paragraph (2). **Effective** 7-1-56.

[Sec. 4041(c)]

(c) CERTAIN LIQUIDS USED AS A FUEL IN AVIATION.—

(1) IN GENERAL.—There is hereby imposed a tax upon any liquid for use as a fuel other than aviation gasoline—

(A) sold by any person to an owner, lessee, or other operator of an aircraft for use in such aircraft, or

(B) used by any person in an aircraft unless there was a taxable sale of such fuel under subparagraph (A).

(2) EXEMPTION FOR PREVIOUSLY TAXED FUEL.—No tax shall be imposed by this subsection on the sale or use of any liquid for use as a fuel other than aviation gasoline if tax was imposed on such liquid under section 4081 (other than such tax at the Leaking Underground Storage Tank Trust Fund financing rate) and the tax thereon was not credited or refunded.

(3) RATE OF TAX.—The rate of tax imposed by this subsection shall be 21.8 cents per gallon (4.3 cents per gallon with respect to any sale or use for commercial aviation).

Amendments

- **2020, Coronavirus Aid, Relief, and Economic Security (CARES) Act (P.L. 116-136)**

P.L. 116-136, § 4007(b)-(c), provides:

(b) USE OF KEROSENE IN COMMERCIAL AVIATION.—In the case of kerosene used in commercial aviation (as defined in section 4083 of the Internal Revenue Code of 1986) during the excise tax holiday period—

(1) no tax shall be imposed on such kerosene under—

(A) section 4041(c) of the Internal Revenue Code of 1986, or

(B) section 4081 of such Code (other than at the rate provided in subsection (a)(2)(B) thereof), and

(2) section 6427(l) of such Code shall be applied—

(A) by treating such use as a nontaxable use, and

(B) without regard to paragraph (4)(A)(ii) thereof.

(c) EXCISE TAX HOLIDAY PERIOD.—For purposes of this section, the term "excise tax holiday period" means the period beginning after the date of the enactment of this section and ending before January 1, 2021.

- **2005, Safe, Accountable, Flexible, Efficient Transportation Equity Act: A Legacy for Users (P.L. 109-59)**

P.L. 109-59, § 11161(b)(1)(A)-(D):

Amended Code Sec. 4041(c) by striking "aviation-grade kerosene" in paragraph (1) and inserting "any liquid for use as a fuel other than aviation gasoline", by striking "aviation-grade kerosene" in paragraph (2) and inserting "liquid for use as a fuel other than aviation gasoline", by striking paragraph (3) and inserting a new paragraph (3), and by striking "AVIATION-GRADE KEROSENE" in the heading and inserting "CERTAIN LIQUIDS USED AS A FUEL IN AVIATION". **Effective** for fuels or liquids removed, entered, or sold after 9-30-2005. Prior to being stricken, Code Sec. 4041(c)(3) read as follows:

(3) RATE OF TAX.—The rate of tax imposed by this subsection shall be the rate of tax applicable under section 4081(a)(2)(A)(iv) which is in effect at the time of such sale or use.

• **2005, Energy Tax Incentives Act of 2005 (P.L. 109-58)**

P.L. 109-58, § 1362(b)(2)(A):

Amended Code Sec. 4041(c)(2) by inserting "(other than such tax at the Leaking Underground Storage Tank Trust Fund financing rate)" after "section 4081". **Effective** for fuel entered, removed, or sold after 9-30-2005.

• **2004, American Jobs Creation Act of 2004 (P.L. 108-357)**

P.L. 108-357, § 853(d)(2)(A):

Amended Code Sec. 4041(c). **Effective** for aviation-grade kerosene removed, entered, or sold after 12-31-2004. For special rules, see Act Sec. 853(f), below. Prior to amendment, Code Sec. 4041(c) read as follows:

(c) NONCOMMERCIAL AVIATION.—

(1) TAX ON NONGASOLINE FUELS WHERE NO TAX IMPOSED ON FUEL UNDER SECTION 4091.—There is hereby imposed a tax upon kerosene and any other liquid (other than any product taxable under section 4081)—

(A) sold by any person to an owner, lessee, or other operator of an aircraft, for use as a fuel in such aircraft in noncommercial aviation; or

(B) used by any person as a fuel in an aircraft in noncommercial aviation, unless there was a taxable sale of such liquid under this section.

The rate of the tax imposed by this paragraph shall be the rate of tax specified in section 4091(b)(1) which is in effect at the time of such sale or use. No tax shall be imposed by this paragraph on the sale or use of kerosene and any other liquid if there was a taxable sale of such liquid under section 4091.

(2) DEFINITION OF NONCOMMERCIAL AVIATION.—For purposes of this chapter, the term "noncommercial aviation" means any use of an aircraft, other than use in a business of transporting persons or property for compensation or hire by air. The term also includes any use of an aircraft, in a business described in the preceding sentence, which is properly allocable to any transportation exempt from the taxes imposed by sections 4261 and 4271 by reason of section 4281 or 4282 or by reason of section 4261(h).

(3) TERMINATION.—The rate of the taxes imposed by paragraph (1) shall be 4.3 cents per gallon—

(A) after December 31, 1996, and before the date which is 7 days after the date of the enactment of the Airport and Airway Trust Fund Tax Reinstatement Act of 1997, and

(B) after September 30, 2007.

P.L. 108-357, § 853(f), provides:

(f) FLOOR STOCKS TAX.—

(1) IN GENERAL.—There is hereby imposed on aviation-grade kerosene held on January 1, 2005, by any person a tax equal to—

(A) the tax which would have been imposed before such date on such kerosene had the amendments made by this section been in effect at all times before such date, reduced by

(B) the sum of—

(i) the tax imposed before such date on such kerosene under section 4091 of the Internal Revenue Code of 1986, as in effect on such date, and

(ii) in the case of kerosene held exclusively for such person's own use, the amount which such person would (but for this clause) reasonably expect (as of such date) to be paid as a refund under section 6427(l) of such Code with respect to such kerosene.

(2) EXCEPTION FOR FUEL HELD IN AIRCRAFT FUEL TANK.—Paragraph (1) shall not apply to kerosene held in the fuel tank of an aircraft on January 1, 2005.

(3) LIABILITY FOR TAX AND METHOD OF PAYMENT.—

(A) LIABILITY FOR TAX.—The person holding the kerosene on January 1, 2005, to which the tax imposed by paragraph (1) applies shall be liable for such tax.

(B) METHOD AND TIME FOR PAYMENT.—The tax imposed by paragraph (1) shall be paid at such time and in such manner as the Secretary of the Treasury (or the Secretary's delegate) shall prescribe, including the nonapplication of such tax on de minimis amounts of kerosene.

(4) TRANSFER OF FLOOR STOCK TAX REVENUES TO TRUST FUNDS.—For purposes of determining the amount transferred to any trust fund, the tax imposed by this subsection shall be treated as imposed by section 4081 of the Internal Revenue Code of 1986—

(A) in any case in which tax was not imposed by section 4091 of such Code, at the Leaking Underground Storage Tank Trust Fund financing rate under such section to the extent of 0.1 cents per gallon, and

(B) at the rate under section 4081(a)(2)(A)(iv) of such Code to the extent of the remainder.

(5) HELD BY A PERSON.—For purposes of this subsection, kerosene shall be considered as held by a person if title thereto has passed to such person (whether or not delivery to the person has been made).

(6) OTHER LAWS APPLICABLE.—All provisions of law, including penalties, applicable with respect to the tax imposed by section 4081 of such Code shall, insofar as applicable and not inconsistent with the provisions of this subsection, apply with respect to the floor stock tax imposed by paragraph (1) to the same extent as if such tax were imposed by such section.

• **1997, Taxpayer Relief Act of 1997 (P.L. 105-34)**

P.L. 105-34, § 1031(a)(3):

Amended Code Sec. 4041(c)(3)(B) by striking "September 30, 1997" and inserting "September 30, 2007". **Effective** 10-1-97.

P.L. 105-34, § 1032(e)(2):

Amended Code Sec. 4041(c)(1) by striking "any liquid" and inserting "kerosene and any other liquid". **Effective** 7-1-98.

P.L. 105-34, § 1435(b):

Amended Code Sec. 4041(c)(2) by inserting before the period "or by reason of section 4261(h)" in the last sentence. **Effective** 10-1-97.

• **1997, Airport and Airway Trust Fund Tax Reinstatement Act of 1997 (P.L. 105-2)**

P.L. 105-2, § 2(a)(3):

Amended Code Sec. 4041(c)(3). **Effective** for periods beginning on or after 3-7-97. Prior to amendment, Code Sec. 4041(c)(3) read as follows:

(3) TERMINATION.—The taxes imposed by paragraph (1) shall apply during the period beginning on September 1, 1982, and ending on December 31, 1995, and during the period beginning on the date which is 7 calendar days after the date of the enactment of the Small Business Job Protection Act of 1996 and ending on December 31, 1996. The termination under the preceding sentence shall not apply to so much of the tax imposed by paragraph (1) as does not exceed 4.3 cents per gallon.

P.L. 105-2, § 2(f):

For the text of Act Sec. 2(f), concerning the application of the look-back safe harbor for deposits, see Code Sec. 9502(b).

• **1996, Small Business Job Protection Act of 1996 (P.L. 104-188)**

P.L. 104-188, § 1609(a)(3):

Amended Code Sec. 4041(c)(5) by inserting ", and during the period beginning on the date which is 7 calendar days after the date of the enactment of the Small Business Job Protection Act of 1996 and ending on December 31, 1996" after "December 31, 1995". **Effective** 8-27-96.

P.L. 104-188, § 1609(g)(3)(A):

Amended Code Sec. 4041(c) by striking paragraphs (2) and (3) and by redesignating paragraphs (4) and (5) as paragraphs (2) and (3), respectively. **Effective** 8-27-96. Prior to amendment, Code Sec. 4041(c)(2)-(3) read as follows:

(2) GASOLINE.—There is hereby imposed a tax (at the rate specified in paragraph (3)) upon gasoline (as defined in section 4083)—

(A) sold by any person to an owner, lessee, or other operator of an aircraft, for use as a fuel in such aircraft in noncommercial aviation; or

(B) used by any person as a fuel in an aircraft in noncommercial aviation, unless there was a taxable sale of such product under subparagraph (A).

The tax imposed by this paragraph shall be in addition to any tax imposed under section 4081.

(3) RATE OF TAX.—The rate of tax imposed by paragraph (2) on any gasoline is 1 cent per gallon.

P.L. 104-188, § 1609(g)(3)(B):

Amended Code Sec. 4041(c)(3), as redesignated by Act Sec. 1609(g)(1) [(3)(A)], by striking "paragraphs (1) and (2)" and inserting "paragraph (1)". **Effective** 8-27-96.

• **1993, Omnibus Budget Reconciliation Act of 1993 (P.L. 103-66)**

P.L. 103-66, § 13241(b)(2)(A):

Amended Code Sec. 4041(c)(3). **Effective** 10-1-93. Prior to amendment, Code Sec. 4041(c)(3) read as follows:

(3) RATE OF TAX.—The rate of tax imposed by paragraph (2) on any gasoline is the excess of 15 cents a gallon over the sum of the Highway Trust Fund financing rate plus the deficit reduction rate at which tax was imposed on such gasoline under section 4081.

P.L. 103-66, § 13241(b)(2)(B)(iii)(I)-(II):

Amended Code Sec. 4041(c)(1) by striking "of 17.5 cents a gallon", following "imposed a tax" and by inserting before the last sentence a new sentence. **Effective** 10-1-93.

P.L. 103-66, § 13242(d)(6):

Amended Code Sec. 4041(c)(1), as amended by subpart A (Act Sec. 13241(b)(2)(B)(iii)(I)-(II)), by striking the next to last sentence and inserting a new sentence. **Effective** 1-1-94. Prior to amendment, the next to last sentence read as follows:

The rate of the tax imposed by this paragraph shall be the sum of the Airport and Airway Trust Fund financing rate and the aviation fuel deficit reduction rate in effect under section 4091 at the time of such sale or use.

P.L. 103-66, § 13242(d)(7):

Amended Code Sec. 4041(c)(2) by striking "any product taxable under section 4081" and inserting "gasoline (as defined in section 4083)". **Effective** 1-1-94.

P.L. 103-66, § 13242(d)(8):

Amended Code Sec. 4041(c)(5) by adding at the end thereof the new sentence. **Effective** 1-1-94.

• **1990, Omnibus Budget Reconciliation Act of 1990 (P.L. 101-508)**

P.L. 101-508, § 11211(a)(4)(A)-(B):

Amended Code Sec. 4041(c)(3) by striking "12 cents" and inserting "15 cents", and by striking "the Highway Trust Fund financing rate" and inserting "the sum of the Highway Trust Fund financing rate plus the deficit reduction rate". **Effective** for gasoline removed (as defined in section 4082 of the Internal Revenue Code of 1986) after 11-30-90.

P.L. 101-508, § 11213(b)(2)(A):

Amended Code Sec. 4041(c)(1) by striking "14 cents" and inserting "17.5 cents". **Effective** 12-1-90. However, see the provisions of Act Sec. 11213(b)(5) reproduced below.

EXCISE TAXES—RETAIL EXCISE TAXES

P.L. 101-508, §11213(d)(2)(B):

Amended Code Sec. 4041(c)(5) by striking "December 31, 1990" and inserting "December 31, 1995". **Effective** 11-5-90. However, see the provisions of Act Sec. 11213(f) reproduced below.

P.L. 101-508, §11213(e)(3):

Amended Code Sec. 4041(c) by striking paragraph (6). **Effective** 11-5-90. However, see the provisions of Act Sec. 11213(f) reproduced below. Prior to being stricken, Code Sec. 4041(c)(6) read as follows:

(6) REDUCTION IN RATES OF TAX IN CERTAIN CIRCUMSTANCES.—For reduction of rates of taxes imposed by paragraphs (1) and (2) in certain circumstances, see section 4283.

P.L. 101-508, §11213(b)(5), provides:

(5) FLOOR STOCK TAXES.—

(A) IMPOSITION OF TAX.—In the case of aviation fuel on which tax was imposed under section 4041(c)(1) or 4091 of the Internal Revenue Code of 1986 before December 1, 1990, and which is held on such date by any person, there is hereby imposed a floor stocks tax on such fuel.

(B) RATE OF TAX.—The rate of the tax imposed by subparagraph (A) shall be 3.5 cents per gallon.

(C) LIABILITY FOR TAX AND METHOD OF PAYMENT.—

(i) LIABILITY FOR TAX.—A person holding fuel on December 1, 1990, to which the tax imposed by this paragraph applies shall be liable for such tax.

(ii) METHOD OF PAYMENT.—The tax imposed by this paragraph shall be paid in such manner as the Secretary shall prescribe.

(iii) TIME FOR PAYMENT.—The tax imposed by this paragraph shall be paid on or before May 31, 1991.

(D) DEFINITIONS.—For purposes of this paragraph—

(i) HELD BY A PERSON.—Fuel shall be considered as "held by a person" if title thereto has passed to such person (whether or not delivery to the person has been made).

(ii) AVIATION FUEL.—The term "aviation fuel" has the meaning given such term by section 4092(a) of such Code.

(iii) SECRETARY.—The term "Secretary" means the Secretary of the Treasury or his delegate.

(E) EXCEPTION FOR EXEMPT USES.—The tax imposed by this paragraph shall not apply to fuel held by any person exclusively for any use which is a nontaxable use (as defined in section 6427(l) of such Code).

(F) OTHER LAWS APPLICABLE.—All provisions of law, including penalties, applicable with respect to the taxes imposed by section 4091 of such Code shall, insofar as applicable and not inconsistent with the provisions of this paragraph, apply with respect to the floor stock taxes imposed by this paragraph to the same extent as if such taxes were imposed by such section 4091.

P.L. 101-508, §11213(f), provides:

(f) COORDINATION WITH OTHER PROVISIONS.—No amendment or any other provision of this section shall take effect unless the Airport Noise and Capacity Act of 1990, the Aviation Safety and Capacity Expansion Act of 1990, and the Federal Aviation Administration Research, Engineering, and Development Authorization Act of 1990 are enacted as part of this Act and are identical to the provisions of such Acts as included in the conference report on H.R. 5835 of the 101st Congress.

- **1988, Technical and Miscellaneous Revenue Act of 1988 (P.L. 100-647)**

P.L. 100-647, §2001(d)(2):

Amended Code Sec. 4041(c)(3) by striking out "the rate at which" and inserting in lieu thereof "the Highway Trust Fund financing rate at which". **Effective** as if included in P.L. 99-499 to which it relates.

- **1987, Airport and Airway Revenue Act of 1987 (P.L. 100-223)**

P.L. 100-223, §402(b):

Amended Code Sec. 4041(c)(5) by striking out "December 31, 1987" and inserting in lieu thereof "December 31, 1990". **Effective** 12-30-87.

P.L. 100-223, §405(b)(3):

Amended Code Sec. 4041(c) by adding at the end thereof a new paragraph (6). **Effective** 12-30-87.

- **1987, Revenue Act of 1987 (P.L. 100-203)**

P.L. 100-203, §10502(b)(2)(A)-(B):

Amended Code Sec. 4041(c)(1) by striking out "IN GENERAL" in the heading and inserting in lieu thereof "TAX ON NONGASOLINE FUELS WHERE NO TAX IMPOSED ON FUEL UNDER SECTION 4091", and by adding at the end thereof a new sentence. **Effective** for sales after 3-31-88.

- **1983, Surface Transportation Act of 1982 (P.L. 97-424)**

P.L. 97-424, §511(g)(1):

Amended Code Sec. 4041(c)(3). **Effective** 4-1-83. Prior to amendment, Code Sec. 4041(c)(3) read as follows:

(3) RATE OF TAX.—The rate of tax imposed by paragraph (2) is 8 cents a gallon ($10^{1}/_{2}$ cents a gallon in the case of any gasoline with respect to which a tax is imposed under section 4081 at the rate set forth in subsection (b) thereof).

- **1982, Tax Equity and Fiscal Responsibility Act of 1982 (P.L. 97-248)**

P.L. 97-248, §279(a)(1):

Amended Code Sec. 4041(c)(3) by striking out "3 cents a gallon" and inserting in lieu thereof "8 cents a gallon ($10^{1}/_{2}$ cents a gallon in the case of any gasoline with respect to which a tax is imposed under section 4081 at the rate set forth in subsection (b) thereof)". **Effective** 9-1-82.

P.L. 97-248, §279(a)(2):

Amended Code Sec. 4041(c)(1) by striking out "7 cents" and inserting in lieu thereof "14 cents". **Effective** 9-1-82.

P.L. 97-248, §279(a)(3):

Amended Code Sec. 4041(c)(5). **Effective** 9-1-82. Prior to amendment, paragraph (5) read as follows:

(5) TERMINATION.—On and after October 1, 1980, the taxes imposed by paragraphs (1) and (2) shall not apply.

- **1980 (P.L. 96-298)**

P.L. 96-298, §1(a):

Substituted "October 1, 1980" for "July 1, 1980" in Code Sec. 4041(c)(5).

- **1978, Surface Transportation Assistance Act of 1978 (P.L. 95-599)**

P.L. 95-599, §502(b):

Amended Code Sec. 4041(c)(3). **Effective** 11-7-78. Prior to amendment, Code Sec. 4041(c)(3) read:

(3) RATE OF TAX.—The rate of tax imposed by paragraph (2) is as follows:

3 cents a gallon for the period ending September 30, 1979; and

$5^{1}/_{2}$ cents a gallon for the period after September 30, 1979.

- **1976 (P.L. 94-280)**

P.L. 94-280, §303(a)(1):

Substituted "1979" for "1977" in Code Sec. 4041(c)(3).

- **1970, Federal-Aid Highway Act of 1970 (P.L. 91-605)**

P.L. 91-605, §303(a)(1):

Substituted "1977" for "1972" in Code Sec. 4041(c)(3).

- **1970 (P.L. 91-258)**

P.L. 91-258, §202(a):

Amended Code Sec. 4041(c). **Effective** 7-1-70. Prior to amendment, Code Sec. 4041(c) read as follows:

(c) RATE REDUCTION.—On and after October 1, 1972—

(1) the taxes imposed by this section shall be $1^{1}/_{2}$ cents a gallon; and

(2) the second and third sentences of subsections (a) and (b) shall not apply.

- **1961, Federal-Aid Highway Act of 1961 (P.L. 87-61)**

P.L. 87-61, §201(c):

Amended Sec. 4041(c) by substituting "October 1" for "July 1." **Effective** 7-1-61.

- **1956 (P.L. 627, 84th Cong.)**

P.L. 627, 84th Cong., 2d Sess., §202(c):

Amended subsection (c). Prior to amendment, Code Sec. 4041(c) read:

(c) RATE REDUCTION.—On and after April 1, 1957, the taxes imposed by this section shall be $1^{1}/_{2}$ cents a gallon in lieu of 2 cents a gallon.

- **1956, Tax Rate Extension Act of 1956 (P.L. 458, 84th Cong.)**

P.L. 458, 84th Cong., 2d Sess., §3(a)(1):

Substituted "1957" for "1956" in Sec. 4041(c).

- **1955, Tax Rate Extension Act of 1955 (P.L. 18, 84th Cong.)**

P.L. 18, 84th Cong., 2d Sess., §3(a)(1):

Substituted "1956" for "1955" in Sec. 4041(c). **Effective** 3-30-55.

[Sec. 4041(d)]

(d) ADDITIONAL TAXES TO FUND LEAKING UNDERGROUND STORAGE TANK TRUST FUND.—

(1) TAX ON SALES AND USES SUBJECT TO TAX UNDER SUBSECTION (a).—In addition to the taxes imposed by subsection (a), there is hereby imposed a tax of 0.1 cent a gallon on the sale or use of any liquid (other than liquefied petroleum gas and other than liquefied natural gas) if tax is imposed by subsection (a)(1) or (2) on such sale or use. No tax shall be imposed under the preceding sentence on the sale or use of any liquid if tax was imposed with respect to such liquid under section 4081 at the Leaking Underground Storage Tank Trust Fund financing rate.

(2) LIQUIDS USED IN AVIATION.—In addition to the taxes imposed by subsection (c), there is hereby imposed a tax of 0.1 cent a gallon on any liquid (other than gasoline (as defined in section 4083))—

(A) sold by any person to an owner, lessee, or other operator of an aircraft for use as a fuel in such aircraft, or

(B) used by any person as a fuel in an aircraft unless there was a taxable sale of such liquid under subparagraph (A).

No tax shall be imposed by this paragraph on the sale or use of any liquid if there was a taxable sale of such liquid under section 4081.

(3) DIESEL FUEL USED IN TRAINS.—In the case of any sale for use or use after December 31, 2006, there is hereby imposed a tax of 0.1 cent per gallon on any liquid other than gasoline (as defined in section 4083)—

(A) sold by any person to an owner, lessee, or other operator of a diesel-powered train for use as a fuel in such train, or

(B) used by any person as a fuel in a diesel-powered train unless there was a taxable sale of such fuel under subparagraph (A). No tax shall be imposed by this paragraph on the sale or use of any liquid if tax was imposed on such liquid under section 4081.

(4) TERMINATION.—The taxes imposed by this subsection shall not apply during any period during which the Leaking Underground Storage Tank Trust Fund financing rate under section 4081 does not apply.

(5) NONAPPLICATION OF EXEMPTIONS OTHER THAN FOR EXPORTS.—For purposes of this section, the tax imposed under this subsection shall be determined without regard to subsections (b)(1)(A), (f), (g), (h), and (l). The preceding sentence shall not apply with respect to subsection (g)(3) and so much of subsection (g)(1) as relates to vessels (within the meaning of section 4221(d)(3)) employed in foreign trade or trade between the United States and any of its possessions.

Amendments

• **2007, Tax Technical Corrections Act of 2007 (P.L. 110-172)**

P.L. 110-172, §6(d)(1)(A):

Amended Code Sec. 4041(d)(1) by adding at the end a new sentence. **Effective** as if included in the provision of the Energy Tax Incentives Act of 2005 (P.L. 109-58) to which it relates [**effective** for fuel entered, removed, or sold after 9-30-2005.—CCH].

P.L. 110-172, §6(d)(1)(C), provides:

(C) Notwithstanding section 6430 of the Internal Revenue Code of 1986, a refund, credit, or payment may be made under subchapter B of chapter 65 of such Code for taxes imposed with respect to any liquid after September 30, 2005, and before the date of the enactment of this Act under section 4041(d)(1) or 4042 of such Code at the Leaking Underground Storage Tank Trust Fund financing rate to the extent that tax was imposed with respect to such liquid under section 4081 at the Leaking Underground Storage Tank Trust Fund financing rate.

P.L. 110-172, §6(d)(2)(A)(i)-(ii):

Amended Code Sec. 4041(d)(5) by striking "(other than with respect to any sale for export under paragraph (3) thereof)" following "subsections (f), (g)", and by adding at the end a new sentence. **Effective** as if included in the provision of the Energy Tax Incentives Act of 2005 (P.L. 109-58) to which it relates [**effective** for fuel entered, removed, or sold after 9-30-2005.—CCH].

P.L. 110-172, §6(d)(3):

Amended Code Sec. 4041(d)(5) by inserting "(b)(1)(A)," after "subsections". **Effective** for fuel sold for use or used after 12-29-2007.

• **2005, Energy Tax Incentives Act of 2005 (P.L. 109-58)**

P.L. 109-58, §1362(b)(2)(C):

Amended Code Sec. 4041(d) by adding at the end a new paragraph (5). **Effective** for fuel entered, removed, or sold after 9-30-2005.

• **2004, American Jobs Creation Act of 2004 (P.L. 108-357)**

P.L. 108-357, §241(a)(2)(A):

Amended Code Sec. 4041(d) by redesignating paragraph (3) as paragraph (4) and by inserting after paragraph (2) a new paragraph (3). **Effective** 1-1-2005.

P.L. 108-357, §853(d)(2)(B):

Amended Code Sec. 4041(d)(2) by striking "section 4091" and inserting "section 4081". **Effective** for aviation-grade kerosene removed, entered, or sold after 12-31-2004. For special rules, see Act Sec. 853(f) in the amendments for Code Sec. 4041(c).

• **1997, Taxpayer Relief Act of 1997 (P.L. 105-34)**

P.L. 105-34, §907(a)(2):

Amended Code Sec. 4041(d)(1) by inserting "and other than liquefied natural gas" after "liquefied petroleum gas". **Effective** 10-1-97.

• **1993, Omnibus Budget Reconciliation Act of 1993 (P.L. 103-66)**

P.L. 103-66, §13241(e)(2):

Amended Code Sec. 4041(d)(1) by striking "subsection (a)" the second place it appears and inserting "subsection (a)(1) or (2)". **Effective** 10-1-93.

P.L. 103-66, §13242(d)(9):

Amended Code Sec. 4041(d) by striking paragraph (2) and by redesignating paragraphs (3) and (4) as paragraphs (2) and (3), respectively. **Effective** 1-1-94. Prior to amendment, Code Sec. 4041(d)(2) read as follows:

(2) TAX ON DIESEL FUEL USED IN TRAINS.—There is hereby imposed a tax of 0.1 cent a gallon on any liquid (other than a product taxable under section 4081)—

(A) sold by any person to an owner, lessee, or other operator of a diesel-powered train for use as a fuel in such train, or

(B) used by any person as a fuel in a diesel-powered train unless there was a taxable sale of such liquid under subparagraph (A).

No tax shall be imposed by this paragraph on the sale or use of any liquid if there was a taxable sale of such liquid under section 4091.

P.L. 103-66, §13242(d)(10):

Amended Code Sec. 4041(d)(2), as redesignated by Act Sec. 13242(d)(9), by striking "(other than any product taxable under section 4081)" and inserting "(other than gasoline (as defined in section 4083))". **Effective** 1-1-94.

• **1987, Revenue Act of 1987 (P.L. 100-203)**

P.L. 100-203, §10502(b)(3):

Amended Code Sec. 4041(d) by redesignating paragraph (3) as paragraph (4) and by striking out paragraphs (1) and (2) and inserting in lieu thereof new paragraphs (1)-(3). **Effective** for sales after 3-31-88. Prior to amendment, paragraphs (1) and (2) read as follows:

(1) LIQUIDS OTHER THAN GASOLINE, ETC., USED IN MOTOR VEHICLES, MOTORBOATS, OR TRAINS.—In addition to the taxes imposed by subsection (a), there is hereby imposed a tax of 0.1 cents a gallon on benzol, benzene, naphtha, casing head and natural gasoline, or any other liquid (other than kerosene, gas oil, liquefied petroleum gas, or fuel oil, or any product taxable under section 4081)—

(A) sold by any person to an owner, lessee, or other operator of a motor vehicle, motorboat, or train for use as a fuel in such motor vehicle, motorboat, or train, or

(B) used by any person as a fuel in a motor vehicle, motorboat, or train unless there was a taxable sale of such liquid under subparagraph (A).

(2) LIQUIDS USED IN AVIATION.—In addition to the taxes imposed by subsection (c) and section 4081, there is hereby imposed a tax of 0.1 cents a gallon on any liquid—

(A) sold by any person to an owner, lessee, or other operator of an aircraft for use as a fuel in such aircraft, or

(B) used by any person as a fuel in an aircraft unless there was a taxable sale of such liquid under subparagraph (A).

The tax imposed by this paragraph shall not apply to any product taxable under section 4081 which is used as a fuel in an aircraft other than in noncommercial aviation.

• **1986, Superfund Amendments and Reauthorization Act of 1986 (P.L. 99-499)**

P.L. 99-499, §521(A)(2):

Amended Code Sec. 4041 by redesignating subsection (d) as subsection (e) and by inserting after subsection (c) new subsection (d). **Effective** 1-1-87.

[Sec. 4041(e)—Stricken]

Amendments

• **2004, American Jobs Creation Act of 2004 (P.L. 108-357)**

P.L. 108-357, §853(d)(2)(C):

Amended Code Sec. 4041 by striking subsection (e). **Effective** for aviation-grade kerosene removed, entered, or sold after 12-31-2004. For special rules, see Act Sec. 853(f) in the amendments for Code Sec. 4041(c). Prior to being stricken, Code Sec. 4041(e) read as follows:

(e) ADDITIONAL TAX.—If a liquid on which tax was imposed on the sale thereof is taxable at a higher rate under subsection (c)(1) of this section on the use thereof, there is hereby imposed a tax equal to the difference between the tax so imposed and the tax payable at such higher rate.

• **1986, Superfund Amendments and Reauthorization Act of 1986 (P.L. 99-499)**

P.L. 99-499, §521(a)(2):

Amended Code Sec. 4041 by redesignating subsection (d) as subsection (e). **Effective** 1-1-87.

[Sec. 4041(e)—Repealed]

Amendments

• **1983, Surface Transportation Act of 1982 (P.L. 97-424)**

P.L. 97-424, §516(a)(1)(B):

Repealed Code Sec. 4041(e). **Effective** 1-6-83. Prior to its repeal, Code Sec. 4041(e) read as follows:

(e) Rate Reduction.—On and after October 1, 1984—

• **1970 (P.L. 91-258)**

P.L. 91-258, §202(a):

Amended Code Sec. 4041(d). **Effective** 7-1-70. Prior to amendment, Code Sec. 4041(d) read as follows:

(d) Exemption for Farm Use.—

(1) Exemption.—Under regulations prescribed by the Secretary or his delegate—

(A) no tax shall be imposed under subsection (a)(1) or (b)(1) on the sale of any liquid sold for use on a farm for farming purposes, and

"(B) no tax shall be imposed under subsection (a)(2) or (b)(2) on the use of any liquid used on a farm for farming purposes.

(2) Use on a farm for farming purposes.—For purposes of paragraph (1) of this subsection, use on a farm for farming purposes shall be determined in accordance with paragraphs (1), (2), and (3) of section 6420(c).

• **1956 (P.L. 466, 84th Cong.)**

P.L. 466, 84th Cong., §2(a):

Added subsection (d) to Code Sec. 4041. **Effective** 4-3-56.

(1) the taxes imposed by subsections (a) and (b) shall be 1½ cents a gallon, and

(2) the second and third sentences of subsections (a) and (b) shall not apply.

• **1978, Surface Transportation Assistance Act of 1978 (P.L. 95-599)**

P.L. 95-599, §502(a)(1):

Substituted "1984" for "1979" in Code Sec. 4041(e). **Effective** 11-7-78.

EXCISE TAXES—RETAIL EXCISE TAXES

• 1976 (P.L. 94-280)

P.L. 94-280, § 303(a)(2):

Substituted "1979" for "1977" in Code Sec. 4041(e).

• 1970, Federal-Aid Highway Act of 1970 (P.L. 91-605)

P.L. 91-605, § 303(a)(2):

Amended Code Sec. 4041(e) by substituting "1977" for "1972."

• 1970 (P.L. 91-258)

P.L. 91-258, § 202(a):

Amended Code Sec. 4041(e). **Effective** 7-1-70. Prior to amendment, Code Sec. 4041(e) read as follows:

"(e) Exemption for Use as Supplies for Vessels.—Under regulations prescribed by the Secretary or his delegate, no tax shall be imposed under subsection (b) in the case of any fuel sold for use or used as supplies for vessels or aircraft (within the meaning of section 4221(d)(3))."

• 1958, Excise Tax Technical Changes Act of 1958 (P.L. 85-859)

P.L. 85-859, § 119(b):

Added new subsection (e) to Sec. 4041. **Effective** 1-1-59.

[Sec. 4041(f)]

(f) EXEMPTION FOR FARM USE.—

(1) EXEMPTION.—Under regulations prescribed by the Secretary, no tax shall be imposed under this section on any liquid sold for use or used on a farm for farming purposes.

(2) USE ON A FARM FOR FARMING PURPOSES.—For purposes of paragraph (1) of this subsection, use on a farm for farming purposes shall be determined in accordance with paragraphs (1), (2), and (3) of section 6420(c).

Amendments

• 1993, Omnibus Budget Reconciliation Act of 1993 (P.L. 103-66)

P.L. 103-66, § 13241(f)(1):

Amended Code Sec. 4041(f) by repealing paragraph (3). **Effective** 10-1-93. Prior to repeal, Code Sec. 4041(f)(3) read as follows:

(3) TERMINATION.—Except with respect to the taxes imposed by subsection (d), paragraph (1) shall not apply on and after October 1, 1999.

• 1991, Intermodal Surface Transportation Efficiency Act of 1991 (P.L. 102-240)

P.L. 102-240, § 8002(b)(1):

Amended Code Sec. 4041(f)(3) by striking "1995" each place it appears and inserting "1999". **Effective** 12-18-96.

• 1990, Omnibus Budget Reconciliation Act of 1990 (P.L. 101-508)

P.L. 101-508, § 11211(d)(1):

Amended Code Sec. 4041(f)(3) by striking out "1993" each place it appears and inserting "1995". **Effective** 11-5-90.

• 1988, Technical and Miscellaneous Revenue Act of 1988 (P.L. 100-647)

P.L. 100-647, § 1017(c)(4):

Amended Code Sec. 4041(f)(3). **Effective** as if included in the provision of P.L. 99-514 to which it relates. Prior to amendment, Code Sec. 4041(f)(3) read as follows:

(3) TERMINATION.—Except with respect to the taxes imposed by subsection (d) on and after October 1, 1993, paragraph (1) shall not apply.

• 1987, Surface Transportation and Uniform Relocation Assistance Act of 1987 (P.L. 100-17)

P.L. 100-17, § 502(b)(2):

Amended Code Sec. 4041(f)(3) by striking out "1988" and inserting in lieu thereof "1993". **Effective** 4-2-87.

• 1986, Superfund Amendments and Reauthorization Act of 1986 (P.L. 99-499)

P.L. 99-499, § 521(d)(2):

Amended Code Sec. 4041(f)(3) by striking out "On and after" and inserting in lieu thereof "Except with respect to the taxes imposed by subsection (d) on and after". **Effective** 1-1-87.

• 1983, Surface Transportation Act of 1982 (P.L. 97-424)

P.L. 97-424, § 516(b)(1)(A):

Added Code Sec. 4041(f)(3). **Effective** 1-6-83.

• 1976, Tax Reform Act of 1976 (P.L. 94-455)

P.L. 94-455, § 1906(b)(13)(A):

Amended 1954 Code by substituting "Secretary" for "Secretary or his delegate" each place it appeared. **Effective** 2-1-77.

• 1970 (P.L. 91-258)

P.L. 91-258, § 202(a):

Added Code Sec. 4041(f). **Effective** 7-1-70.

• 1961, Federal-Aid Highway Act of 1961 (P.L. 87-61)

P.L. 87-61, § 201(d):

Repealed Sec. 4041(f). **Effective** as of 7-1-61. Prior to repeal, Sec. 4041(f) read as follows:

(f) Temporary Increases in Tax.—On and after October 1, 1959, and before July 1, 1961—

(1) if (without regard to this subsection) the tax imposed by subsection (a) or (b) is 3 cents a gallon, the tax imposed by such subsection shall be 4 cents a gallon, and

(2) if (without regard to this subsection) the tax imposed under paragraph (2) of subsection (a) or (b) is 1 cent a gallon, the tax imposed under such paragraph shall be 2 cents a gallon.

• 1959, Federal-Aid Highway Act of 1959 (P.L. 86-342)

P.L. 86-342, § 201(b)(1):

Added new subsection (f) to Sec. 4041.

[Sec. 4041(g)]

(g) OTHER EXEMPTIONS.—Under regulations prescribed by the Secretary, no tax shall be imposed under this section—

(1) on any liquid sold for use or used as supplies for vessels or aircraft (within the meaning of section 4221(d)(3));

(2) with respect to the sale of any liquid for the exclusive use of any State, any political subdivision of a State, or the District of Columbia, or with respect to the use by any of the foregoing of any liquid as a fuel;

(3) upon the sale of any liquid for export, or for shipment to a possession of the United States, and in due course so exported or shipped;

(4) with respect to the sale of any liquid to a nonprofit educational organization for its exclusive use, or with respect to the use by a nonprofit educational organization of any liquid as a fuel; and

(5) with respect to the sale of any liquid to a qualified blood collector organization (as defined in section 7701(a)(49)) for such organization's exclusive use in the collection, storage, or transportation of blood.

For purposes of paragraph (4), the term "nonprofit educational organization" means an educational organization described in section 170(b)(1)(A)(ii) which is exempt from income tax under section 501(a). The term also includes a school operated as an activity of an organization described in section 501(c)(3) which is exempt from income tax under section 501(a), if such school normally maintains a regular faculty and curriculum and normally has a regularly enrolled body of pupils or students in attendance at the place where its educational activities are regularly carried on.

Amendments

• 2006, Pension Protection Act of 2006 (P.L. 109-280)

P.L. 109-280, § 1207(a):

Amended Code Sec. 4041(g) by striking "and" at the end of paragraph (3), by striking the period in paragraph (4) and inserting "; and", and by inserting after paragraph (4) a new paragraph (5). **Effective** 1-1-2007.

• 1993, Omnibus Budget Reconciliation Act of 1993 (P.L. 103-66)

P.L. 103-66, § 13241(f)(2):

Amended Code Sec. 4041(g) by striking the last sentence. **Effective** 10-1-93. Prior to amendment, the last sentence read as follows:

Except with respect to the taxes imposed by subsection (d), paragraphs (2) and (4) shall not apply on and after October 1, 1999.

• 1991, Intermodal Surface Transportation Efficiency Act of 1991 (P.L. 102-240)

P.L. 102-240, § 8002(b)(2):

Amended Code Sec. 4041(g) by striking "1995" each place it appears and inserting "1999". **Effective** 12-18-91.

EXCISE TAXES—RETAIL EXCISE TAXES

• **1990, Omnibus Budget Reconciliation Act of 1990 (P.L. 101-508)**

P.L. 101-508, § 11211(d)(2):

Amended Code Sec. 4041(g) by striking out "1993" each place it appears and inserting "1995". **Effective** 11-5-90.

• **1987, Surface Transportation and Uniform Relocation Assistance Act of 1987 (P.L. 100-17)**

P.L. 100-17, § 502(b)(3):

Amended Code Sec. 4041(g) by striking out "1988" and inserting in lieu thereof "1993". **Effective** 4-2-87.

• **1986, Superfund Amendments and Reauthorization Act of 1986 (P.L. 99-499)**

P.L. 99-499, § 521(d)(3):

Amended the last sentence of Code Sec. 4041(g) by striking out "Paragraphs" and inserting in lieu thereof "Except with respect to the taxes imposed by subsection (d), paragraphs". **Effective** 1-1-87.

• **1983, Surface Transportation Act of 1982 (P.L. 97-424)**

P.L. 97-424, § 516(b)(1)(B):

Added the sentence at the end of Code Sec. 4041(g). **Effective** 1-6-83.

• **1976, Tax Reform Act of 1976 (P.L. 94-455)**

P.L. 94-455, § 1904(a)(1)(B):

Amended Code Sec. 4041(g). **Effective** 2-1-77. Prior to amendment, Code Sec. 4041(g) read as follows:

(g) EXEMPTION FOR USE AS SUPPLIES FOR VESSELS.—Under regulations prescribed by the Secretary or his delegate, no tax shall be imposed under this section on any liquid sold for use or used as supplies for vessels or aircraft (within the meaning of section 4221(d)(3)).

• **1970 (P.L. 91-258)**

P.L. 91-258, § 202(a):

Added Code Sec. 4041(g). **Effective** 7-1-70.

[Sec. 4041(h)]

(h) EXEMPTION FOR USE BY CERTAIN AIRCRAFT MUSEUMS.—

(1) EXEMPTION.—Under regulations prescribed by the Secretary or his delegate, no tax shall be imposed under this section on any liquid sold for use or used by an aircraft museum in an aircraft or vehicle owned by such museum and used exclusively for purposes set forth in paragraph (2)(C).

(2) DEFINITION OF AIRCRAFT MUSEUM.—For purposes of this subsection, the term "aircraft museum" means an organization—

(A) described in section 501(c)(3) which is exempt from income tax under section 501(a),

(B) operated as a museum under charter by a State or the District of Columbia, and

(C) operated exclusively for the procurement, care, and exhibition of aircraft of the type used for combat or transport in World War II.

Amendments

• **1978, Revenue Act of 1978 (P.L. 95-600)**

P.L. 95-600, § 703(l)(1), (r):

Amended Code Sec. 4041(h)(2) by striking out "term `aircraft' means" and inserting "term `aircraft museum' means" in place thereof. **Effective** 10-4-76.

• **1976 (P.L. 94-530)**

P.L. 94-530, § [1](a):

Redesignated former Code Sec. 4041(h) as Code Sec. 4041(i) and added new Code Sec. 4041(h). **Effective** 10-1-76.

[Sec. 4041(i)—Stricken]

Amendments

• **2004, American Jobs Creation Act of 2004 (P.L. 108-357)**

P.L. 108-357, § 853(d)(2)(D):

Amended Code Sec. 4041 by striking subsection (i). **Effective** for aviation-grade kerosene removed, entered, or sold after 12-31-2004. For special rules, see Act Sec 853(f) in the amendments for Code Sec. 4041(c). Prior to being stricken, Code Sec. 4041(i) read as follows:

(i) REGISTRATION.—If any liquid is sold by any person for use as a fuel in an aircraft, it shall be presumed for purposes of this section that a tax imposed by this section applies to the sale of such liquid unless the purchaser is registered in such manner (and furnishes such information in respect of the use of the liquid) as the Secretary shall by regulations provide.

• **1976 (P.L. 94-530)**

P.L. 94-530, § [1](a):

Redesignated former Code Sec. 4041(h) as Code Sec. 4041(i). **Effective** 10-1-76.

• **1976, Tax Reform Act of 1976 (P.L. 94-455)**

P.L. 94-455, § 1906(b)(13)(A):

Amended 1954 Code by substituting "Secretary" for "Secretary or his delegate" each place it appeared. **Effective** 2-1-77.

• **1970 (P.L. 91-258)**

P.L. 91-258, § 202(a):

Added Code Sec. 4041(h). **Effective** 7-1-70.

[Sec. 4041(j)]

(j) SALES BY UNITED STATES, ETC.—The taxes imposed by this section shall apply with respect to liquids sold at retail by the United States, or by any agency or instrumentality of the United States, unless sales by such agency or instrumentality are by statute specifically exempted from such taxes.

Amendments

• **1978, Revenue Act of 1978 (P.L. 95-600)**

P.L. 95-600, § 703(l)(2), (r):

Redesignated Code Sec. 4041(i), as added by P.L. 95-455, Sec. 1904(a)(1)(C), as Code Sec. 4041(j). **Effective** 10-4-76.

• **1976, Tax Reform Act of 1976 (P.L. 94-455)**

P.L. 94-455, § 1904(a)(1)(C):

Added Code Sec. 4041(i). The redesignation of former Code Sec. 4041(h) as Code Sec. 4041(i) by P.L. 94-530, § [1](a), required that Code Sec. 4041(i) (as added by P.L. 94-455) be redesignated Code Sec. 4041(j). **Effective** 2-1-77.

[Sec. 4041(k)—Stricken]

Amendments

• **2004, American Jobs Creation Act of 2004 (P.L. 108-357)**

P.L. 108-357, § 301(c)(6):

Amended Code Sec. 4041 by striking subsection (k). **Effective** for fuel sold or used after 12-31-2004. Prior to being stricken, Code Sec. 4041(k) read as follows:

(k) FUELS CONTAINING ALCOHOL.—

(1) IN GENERAL.—Under regulations prescribed by the Secretary, in the case of the sale or use of any liquid at least 10 percent of which consists of alcohol (as defined in section 4081(c)(3))—

(A) the rates under paragraphs (1) and (2) of subsection (a) shall be the comparable rates under section 4081(c), and

(B) the rate of the tax imposed by subsection (c)(1) shall be the comparable rate under section 4091(c).

(2) LATER SEPARATION.—If any person separates the liquid fuel from a mixture of the liquid fuel and alcohol to which paragraph (1) applied, such separation shall be treated as a sale of the liquid fuel. Any tax imposed on such sale shall be reduced by the amount (if any) of the tax imposed on the sale of such mixture.

(3) TERMINATION.—Paragraph (1) shall not apply to any sale or use after September 30, 2007.

• **1998, Transportation Equity Act for the 21st Century (P.L. 105-178)**

P.L. 105-178, § 9003(a)(1)(B):

Amended Code Sec. 4041(k)(3) by striking "2000" and inserting "2007". **Effective** 6-9-98.

• **1996, Small Business Job Protection Act of 1996 (P.L. 104-188)**

P.L. 104-188, § 1609(g)(4)(A):

Amended Code Sec. 4041(k)(1) by adding "and" at the end of subparagraph (A), by striking ", and" at the end of subparagraph (B) and inserting a period, and striking subparagraph (C). **Effective** on the 7th calendar day after 8-20-96. Prior to amendment, Code Sec. 4041(k)(1)(C) read as follows:

(C) no tax shall be imposed by subsection (c)(2).

• **1993, Omnibus Budget Reconciliation Act of 1993 (P.L. 103-66)**

P.L. 103-66, § 13242(d)(11)(A)-(B):

Amended Code Sec. 4041(k)(1)(A) by striking "Highway Trust Fund financing" preceding "rates under", and by striking "sections 4081(c) and 4091(c), as the case may be" and inserting "section 4081(c)". **Effective** 1-1-94.

P.L. 103-66, § 13242(d)(12):

Amended Code Sec. 4041(k)(1)(B) by striking "4091(d)" and inserting "4091(c)". **Effective** 1-1-94.

• **1990, Omnibus Budget Reconciliation Act of 1990 (P.L. 101-508)**

P.L. 101-508, § 11211(b)(6)(E)(i):

Amended Code Sec. 4041(k)(1) by striking subparagraphs (A), (B), and (C) and inserting new subparagraphs (A)-(C). **Effective** 12-1-90. Prior to amendment, Code Sec. 4041(k)(1)(A)-(C) read as follows:

(A) subsection (a)(1) shall be applied by substituting "9 cents" for "15 cents", and

EXCISE TAXES—RETAIL EXCISE TAXES

(B) subsection (a)(2) shall be applied by substituting "3 cents" for "9 cents", and

(C) no tax shall be imposed by subsection (c).

P.L. 101-508, § 11211(e)(2):

Amended Code Sec. 4041(k)(3) by striking "1993" each place it appears and inserting "2000". **Effective** 11-5-90.

P.L. 101-508, § 11213(b)(2)(B)(i):

Amended Code Sec. 4041(k)(1)(B), as amended by Act Sec. 11211. **Effective** 12-1-90. However, see Act Sec. 11213(f) reproduced under the amendment notes for Code Sec. 4041(c). Prior to amendment, Code Sec. 4041(k)(1)(B) read as follows:

(B) no tax shall be imposed by subsection (c)(1), and

• **1987, Surface Transportation and Uniform Relocation Assistance Act of 1987 (P.L. 100-17)**

P.L. 100-17, § 502(c)(1):

Amended Code Sec. 4041(k)(3) by striking out "December 31, 1992" and inserting in lieu thereof "September 30, 1993". **Effective** 4-2-87.

• **1984, Deficit Reduction Act of 1984 (P.L. 98-369)**

P.L. 98-369, § 912(a):

Amended Code Sec. 4041(k)(1). **Effective** 1-1-85. Prior to amendment, it read as follows:

(1) IN GENERAL.—Under regulations prescribed by the Secretary, in the case of the sale or use of any liquid fuel at least 10 percent of which consists of alcohol (as defined in section 4081(c)(3))—

(A) subsection (a) shall be applied by substituting "4 cents" for "9 cents" each place it appears, and

(B) no tax shall be imposed by subsection (c).

• **1982, Surface Transportation Act of 1982 (P.L. 97-424)**

P.L. 97-424, § 511(d)(2):

Amended Code Sec. 4041(k). **Effective** 4-1-83. Prior to amendment, it read as follows:

(k) FUELS CONTAINING ALCOHOL.—

(1) IN GENERAL.—Under regulations prescribed by the Secretary, no tax shall be imposed by this section on the sale or use of any liquid fuel at least 10 percent of which consists of alcohol (as defined by section 4081(c)(3)).

(2) LATER SEPARATION.—If any person separates the liquid fuel from a mixture of the liquid fuel and alcohol on which tax was not imposed by reason of this subsection, such separation shall be treated as a sale of the liquid fuel.

(3) TERMINATION.—Paragraph (1) shall not apply to any sale or use after December 31, 1992.

• **1980, Crude Oil Windfall Profit Tax Act of 1980 (P.L. 96-223)**

P.L. 96-223, § 232(a)(2):

Amended Code Sec. 4041(k) by adding paragraph (3). **Effective** 4-3-80.

• **1978, Energy Tax Act of 1978 (P.L. 95-618)**

P.L. 95-618, § 221(b):

Added Code Sec. 4041(k). **Effective** for sales or use after 12-31-78, and before 10-1-84.

[Sec. 4041(l)]

(l) EXEMPTION FOR CERTAIN USES.—No tax shall be imposed under this section on any liquid sold for use in, or used in, a helicopter or a fixed-wing aircraft for purposes of providing transportation with respect to which the requirements of subsection (f) or (g) of section 4261 are met, but only if the helicopter does not take off from, or land at a facility eligible for assistance under the Airport and Airway Development Act of 1970, or otherwise use services provided pursuant to the Airport and Airway System Improvement Act of 1982 during such use.

Amendments

• **1998, IRS Restructuring and Reform Act of 1998 (P.L. 105-206)**

P.L. 105-206, § 6010(g)(1):

Amended Code Sec. 4041(l) by striking "subsection (e) or (f)" and inserting "subsection (f) or (g)". **Effective** as if included in the provision of P.L. 105-34 to which it relates [**effective** 10-1-97.—CCH].

• **1997, Taxpayer Relief Act of 1997 (P.L. 105-34)**

P.L. 105-34, § 1601(f)(4)(A)(i)-(ii):

Amended Code Sec. 4041(l) by inserting "or a fixed-wing aircraft" after "helicopter", and by striking "HELICOPTER" in the heading before "USES". **Effective** as if included in the provision of P.L. 104-188 to which it relates [**effective** 8-27-96.—CCH].

• **1987, Airport and Airway Revenue Act of 1987 (P.L. 100-223)**

P.L. 100-223, § 404(b):

Amended Code Sec. 4041(l). **Effective** 10-1-88. Prior to amendment, Code Sec. 4041(l) read as follows:

(l) EXEMPTION FOR CERTAIN HELICOPTER USES.—No tax shall be imposed under this section on any liquid sold for use in, or used in, a helicopter for the purpose of—

(1) transporting individuals, equipment, or supplies in the exploration for, or the development or removal of, hard minerals, oil, or gas, or

(2) The planting, cultivation, cutting or transportation of, or caring for, trees (including logging operation),

• **1986, Tax Reform Act of 1986 (P.L. 99-514)**

P.L. 99-514, § 1878(c)(1):

Amended Code Sec. 4041(l)(1). **Effective** as if included in the provision of P.L. 98-369 to which it relates. Prior to amendment, Code Sec. 4041(l)(1) read as follows:

(1) transporting individuals, equipment, or supplies in—

(A) the exploration for, or the development or removal of, hard minerals, or

(B) the exploration for oil or gas, or

• **1984, Deficit Reduction Act of 1984 (P.L. 98-369)**

P.L. 98-369, § 1018(a):

Amended Code Sec. 4041(l)(1). Prior to amendment, it read as follows:

(1) transporting individuals, equipment, or supplies in the exploration for, or the development or removal of, hard minerals, or

• **1982, Tax Equity and Fiscal Responsibility Act of 1982 (P.L. 97-248)**

P.L. 97-248, § 279(b)(1):

Amended Code Sec. 4041 by adding at the end thereof new subsection (l). **Effective** 9-1-82.

[Sec. 4041(m)]

(m) CERTAIN ALCOHOL FUELS.—

(1) IN GENERAL.—In the case of the sale or use of any partially exempt methanol or ethanol fuel the rate of the tax imposed by subsection (a)(2) shall be—

(A) after September 30, 1997, and before October 1, 2028—

(i) in the case of fuel none of the alcohol in which consists of ethanol, 9.15 cents per gallon, and

(ii) in any other case, 11.3 cents per gallon, and

(B) after September 30, 2028—

(i) in the case of fuel none of the alcohol in which consists of ethanol, 2.15 cents per gallon, and

(ii) in any other case, 4.3 cents per gallon.

(2) PARTIALLY EXEMPT METHANOL OR ETHANOL FUEL.—The term "partially exempt methanol or ethanol fuel" means any liquid at least 85 percent of which consists of methanol, ethanol, or other alcohol produced from natural gas.

Amendments

• **2021, Infrastructure Investment and Jobs Act (P.L. 117-58)**

P.L. 117-58, § 80102(a)(1)(B), Div. H:

Amended Code Sec. 4041(m)(1)(B) by striking "September 30, 2022" and inserting "September 30, 2028". **Effective** 10-1-2021.

P.L. 117-58, § 80102(a)(2)(A), Div. H:

Amended Code Sec. 4041(m)(1)(A) by striking "October 1, 2022" and inserting "October 1, 2028". **Effective** 10-1-2021.

• **2015, Fixing America's Surface Transportation Act (P.L. 114-94)**

P.L. 114-94, § 31102(a)(1)(B):

Amended Code Sec. 4041(m)(1)(B) by striking "September 30, 2016" and inserting "September 30, 2022". **Effective** 10-1-2016.

P.L. 114-94, § 31102(a)(2)(A):

Amended Code Sec. 4041(m)(1)(A) by striking "October 1, 2016" and inserting "October 1, 2022". **Effective** 10-1-2016.

• **2012, Highway Investment, Job Creation, and Economic Growth Act of 2012 (P.L. 112-141)**

P.L. 112-141, § 40102(a)(1)(B):

Amended Code Sec. 4041(m)(1)(B) by striking "June 30, 2012" and inserting "September 30, 2016". **Effective** 7-1-2012.

P.L. 112-141, § 40102(a)(2)(A):

Amended Code Sec. 4041(m)(1)(A) by striking "July 1, 2012" and inserting "October 1, 2016". **Effective** 7-1-2012.

EXCISE TAXES—RETAIL EXCISE TAXES

• **2012, Temporary Surface Transportation Extension Act of 2012 (P.L. 112-140)**

P.L. 112-140, §1(c), provides:

(c) SPECIAL RULE FOR EXECUTION OF AMENDMENTS IN MAP–21.—On the date of enactment of the MAP–21 [P.L. 112-141]—

(1) this Act and the amendments made by this Act shall cease to be effective;

(2) the text of the laws amended by this Act shall revert back so as to read as the text read on the day before the date of enactment of this Act; and

(3) the amendments made by the MAP–21 shall be executed as if this Act had not been enacted.

P.L. 112-140, §402(a)(1)(B):

Amended Code Sec. 4041(m)(1)(B) by striking "June 30, 2012" and inserting "July 6, 2012". **Effective** 7-1-2012. For a special rule, see Act Sec. 1(c), above.

P.L. 112-140, §402(a)(2)(A):

Amended Code Sec. 4041(m)(1)(A) by striking "July 1, 2012" and inserting "July 7, 2012". **Effective** 7-1-2012. For a special rule, see Act Sec. 1(c), above.

• **2012, Surface Transportation Extension Act of 2012 (P.L. 112-102)**

P.L. 112-102, §402(a)(1)(B):

Amended Code Sec. 4041(m)(1)(B) by striking "March 31, 2012" and inserting "June 30, 2012". **Effective** 4-1-2012.

P.L. 112-102, §402(a)(2)(A):

Amended Code Sec. 4041(m)(1)(A) by striking "April 1, 2012" and inserting "July 1, 2012". **Effective** 4-1-2012.

• **2011, Surface Transportation Extension Act of 2011, Part II (P.L. 112-30)**

P.L. 112-30, §142(a)(1)(B):

Amended Code Sec. 4041(m)(1)(B) by striking "September 30, 2011" and inserting "March 31, 2012". **Effective** 10-1-2011.

P.L. 112-30, §142(a)(2)(A):

Amended Code Sec. 4041(m)(1)(A) by striking "October 1, 2011" and inserting "April 1, 2012". **Effective** 10-1-2011.

• **2005, Safe, Accountable, Flexible, Efficient Transportation Equity Act: A Legacy for Users (P.L. 109-59)**

P.L. 109-59, §11101(a)(1)(C):

Amended Code Sec. 4041(m)(1) by striking "2005" each place it appears and inserting "2011". **Effective** 8-10-2005.

• **2004, American Jobs Creation Act of 2004 (P.L. 108-357)**

P.L. 108-357, §853(d)(2)(E):

Amended Code Sec. 4041(m)(1). **Effective** for aviation-grade kerosene removed, entered, or sold after 12-31-2004. For special rules, see Act Sec 853(f) in the amendments for Code Sec. 4041(c). Prior to amendment, Code Sec. 4041(m)(1) read as follows:

(1) IN GENERAL.—In the case of the sale or use of any partially exempt methanol or ethanol fuel—

(A) the rate of the tax imposed by subsection (a)(2) shall be—

(i) after September 30, 1997, and before October 1, 2005—

(I) in the case of fuel none of the alcohol in which consists of ethanol, 9.15 cents per gallon, and

(II) in any other case, 11.3 cents per gallon, and

(ii) after September 30, 2005—

(I) in the case of fuel none of the alcohol in which consists of ethanol, 2.15 cents per gallon, and

(II) in any other case, 4.3 cents per gallon, and

(B) the rate of the tax imposed by subsection (c)(1) shall be the comparable rate under section 4091(c)(1).

• **1998, Transportation Equity Act for the 21st Century (P.L. 105-178)**

P.L. 105-178, §9002(a)(1)(C):

Amended Code Sec. 4041(m)(1)(A) by striking "1999" each place it appears and inserting "2005". **Effective** 6-9-98.

• **1997, Taxpayer Relief Act of 1997 (P.L. 105-34)**

P.L. 105-34, §907(b):

Amended Code Sec. 4041(m)(1)(A). **Effective** 10-1-97. Prior to amendment, Code Sec. 4041(m)(1)(A) read as follows:

(A) the rate of the tax imposed by subsection (a)(2) shall be—

(i) 11.3 cents per gallon after September 30, 1993, and before October 1, 1999, and

(ii) 4.3 cents per gallon after September 30, 1999, and

• **1993, Omnibus Budget Reconciliation Act of 1993 (P.L. 103-66)**

P.L. 103-66, §13242(d)(13):

Amended Code Sec. 4041(m)(1)(A)-(B). **Effective** 1-1-94. Prior to amendment, Code Sec. 4041(m)(1)(A)-(B) read as follows:

(A) under subsection (a)(2)—

(i) the Highway Trust Fund financing rate shall be 5.75 cents per gallon, and

(ii) the deficit reduction rate shall be 5.55 cents per gallon.

(B) the rate of the tax imposed by subsection (c)(1) shall be the comparable rate under section 4091(d)(1).

P.L. 103-66, §13241(c):

Amended Code Sec. 4041(m)(1)(A). **Effective** 10-1-93. Prior to amendment, Code Sec. 4041(m)(1)(A) read as follows:

(A) under subsection (a)(2) the Highway Trust Fund financing rate shall be 5.75 cents per gallon and the deficit reduction rate shall be 1.25 cents per gallon, and

• **1990, Omnibus Budget Reconciliation Act of 1990 (P.L. 101-508)**

P.L. 101-508, §11211(b)(6)(F):

Amended Code Sec. 4041(m)(1)(A). **Effective** 12-1-90. Prior to amendment, Code Sec. 4041(m)(1)(A) read as follows:

(A) subsection (a)(2) shall be applied by substituting "4^1/$_2$ cents" for "9 cents", and

P.L. 101-508, §11213(b)(2)(B)(ii):

Amended Code Sec. 4041(m)(1)(B). **Effective** 12-1-90. However, see Act Sec. 11213(f) reproduced under the amendment notes for Code Sec. 4041(c). Prior to amendment, Code Sec. 4041(m)(1)(B) read as follows:

(B) no tax shall be imposed by subsection (c).

• **1984, Deficit Reduction Act of 1984 (P.L. 98-369)**

P.L. 98-369, §913(a):

Amended Code Sec. 4041 by adding at the end thereof new subsection (m). **Effective** 8-1-84.

[Sec. 4041(n)—Repealed]

Amendments

• **1987, Revenue Act of 1987 (P.L. 100-203)**

P.L. 100-203, §10502(b)(4):

Repealed Code Sec. 4041(n). **Effective** for sales after 3-31-88. Prior to repeal, Code Sec. 4041(n) read as follows:

(n) TAX ON DIESEL FUEL FOR HIGHWAY VEHICLE USE MAY BE IMPOSED ON SALE TO RETAILER.—Under regulations prescribed by the Secretary—

(1) IN GENERAL.—Upon the written consent of the seller, the tax imposed by subsection (a)(1)—

(A) shall apply to the sale of diesel fuel to a qualified retailer (and such sale shall be treated as described in subsection (a)(1)(A)), and

(B) shall not apply to the sale of diesel fuel by such retailer or the use of diesel fuel described in subsection (a)(1)(B) if tax was imposed on such fuel under subparagraph (A) of this paragraph.

(2) LIABILITY FOR VIOLATION OF CERTIFICATION.—Notwithstanding paragraph (1), a qualified retailer shall be liable for the tax on liquid described in paragraph (3)(C)(ii) if such liquid is used as fuel in a diesel-powered highway vehicle.

(3) DEFINITIONS.—For purposes of this subsection—

(A) QUALIFIED RETAILER.—The term "qualified retailer" means any retailer—

(i) who elects (under such terms and conditions as may be prescribed by the Secretary) to have paragraph (1) apply to all sales of diesel fuel to such retailer by any person, and

(ii) who agrees to provide a written notice to such person that paragraph (1) applies to all sales of diesel fuel by such person to such retailer.

Such election and notice shall be effective for such period or periods as may be prescribed by the Secretary.

(B) RETAILER.—The term "retailer" means any person who sells diesel fuel for use as a fuel in a diesel-powered highway vehicle. Such term does not include any person who sells diesel fuel primarily for resale.

(C) DIESEL FUEL.—

(i) IN GENERAL.—The term "diesel fuel" means any liquid on which tax would be imposed by subsection (a)(1) if sold to a person, and for a use, described in subsection (a)(1)(A).

(ii) EXCEPTION.—A liquid shall not be treated as diesel fuel for purposes of this subsection if the retailer certifies in writing to the seller of such liquid that such liquid will not be sold for use as a fuel in a diesel-powered highway vehicle.

(4) FAILURE TO NOTIFY SELLER.—

(A) IN GENERAL.—If a qualified retailer fails to provide the notice described in paragraph (3)(A)(ii) to any seller of diesel fuel to such retailer—

(i) paragraph (1) shall not apply to sales of diesel fuel by such seller to such retailer during the period for which such failure continues, and

(ii) any diesel fuel sold by such seller to such retailer during such period shall be treated as sold by such retailer (in a sale described in subsection (a)(1)(A)) on the date such fuel was sold to such retailer.

(B) PENALTY.—For penalty for failing to notify seller, see section 6652(j).

(5) EXEMPTIONS NOT TO APPLY.—

(A) IN GENERAL.—No exemption from the tax imposed by subsection (a)(1) shall apply to a sale to which paragraph (1) or (4)(A) of this subsection applies.

(B) CROSS REFERENCE.—

For provisions allowing a credit or refund for certain sales and uses of fuel, see sections 6416 and 6427.

• **1986, Tax Reform Act of 1986 (P.L. 99-514)**

P.L. 99-514, §1702(a):

Amended Code Sec. 4041 by adding at the end thereof new subsection (n). **Effective** for sales after the first calendar quarter beginning more than 60 days after 10-22-86.

EXCISE TAXES—RETAIL EXCISE TAXES

[Sec. 4042]

SEC. 4042. TAX ON FUEL USED IN COMMERCIAL TRANSPORTATION ON INLAND WATERWAYS.

[Sec. 4042(a)]

(a) IN GENERAL.—There is hereby imposed a tax on any liquid used during any calendar quarter by any person as a fuel in a vessel in commercial waterway transportation.

[Sec. 4042(b)]

(b) AMOUNT OF TAX.—

(1) IN GENERAL.—The rate of the tax imposed by subsection (a) is the sum of—

(A) the Inland Waterways Trust Fund financing rate, and

(B) the Leaking Underground Storage Tank Trust Fund financing rate.

(2) RATES.—For purposes of paragraph (1)—

(A) The Inland Waterways Trust Fund financing rate is 29 cents per gallon.

(B) The Leaking Underground Storage Tank Trust Fund financing rate is 0.1 cent per gallon.

(3) EXCEPTION FOR FUEL ON WHICH LEAKING UNDERGROUND STORAGE TANK TRUST FUND FINANCING RATE SEPARATELY IMPOSED.—The Leaking Underground Storage Tank Trust Fund financing rate under paragraph (2)(B) shall not apply to the use of any fuel if tax was imposed with respect to such fuel under section 4041(d) or 4081 at the Leaking Underground Storage Tank Trust Fund financing rate.

(4) TERMINATION OF LEAKING UNDERGROUND STORAGE TANK TRUST FUND FINANCING RATE.—The Leaking Underground Storage Tank Trust Fund financing rate under paragraph (2)(B) shall not apply during any period during which the Leaking Underground Storage Tank Trust Fund financing rate under section 4081 does not apply.

Amendments

• **2018, Tax Technical Corrections Act of 2018 (P.L. 115-141)**

P.L. 115-141, §401(b)(40), Div. U:

Amended Code Sec. 4042(b)(1) by adding "and" at the end of subparagraph (A), by striking ", and" at the end of subparagraph (B) and inserting a period, and by striking subparagraph (C). **Effective** 3-23-2018. For a special rule, see Act Sec. 401(e), Div. U, below. Prior to being stricken, Code Sec. 4042(b)(1)(C) read as follows:

(C) the deficit reduction rate.

P.L. 115-141, §401(b)(41), Div. U:

Amended Code Sec. 4042(b)(2) by striking subparagraph (C). **Effective** 3-23-2018. For a special rule, see Act Sec. 401(e), Div. U, below. Prior to being stricken, Code Sec. 4042(b)(2)(C) read as follows:

(C) The deficit reduction rate is—

(i) 3.3 cents per gallon after December 31, 2004, and before July 1, 2005,

(ii) 2.3 cents per gallon after June 30, 2005, and before January 1, 2007, and

(iii) 0 after December 31, 2006.

P.L. 115-141, §401(e), Div. U, provides:

(e) GENERAL SAVINGS PROVISION WITH RESPECT TO DEADWOOD PROVISIONS.—If—

(1) any provision amended or repealed by the amendments made by subsection (b) or (d) applied to—

(A) any transaction occurring before the date of the enactment of this Act,

(B) any property acquired before such date of enactment, or

(C) any item of income, loss, deduction, or credit taken into account before such date of enactment, and

(2) the treatment of such transaction, property, or item under such provision would (without regard to the amendments or repeals made by such subsection) affect the liability for tax for periods ending after such date of enactment,

nothing in the amendments or repeals made by this section shall be construed to affect the treatment of such transaction, property, or item for purposes of determining liability for tax for periods ending after such date of enactment.

• **2014, Stephen Beck, Jr., Achieving a Better Life Experience Act of 2014 (P.L. 113-295)**

P.L. 113-295, §205(a), Division B:

Amended Code Sec. 4042(b)(2)(A). **Effective** for fuel used after 3-31-2015. Prior to amendment, Code Sec. 4042(b)(2)(A) read as follows:

(A) The Inland Waterways Trust Fund financing rate is the rate determined in accordance with the following table:

If the use occurs:	The tax per gallon is:
Before 1990	10 cents
During 1990	11 cents
During 1991	13 cents
During 1992	15 cents
During 1993	17 cents
During 1994	19 cents
After 1994	20 cents

• **2007, Tax Technical Corrections Act of 2007 (P.L. 110-172)**

P.L. 110-172, §6(d)(1)(B):

Amended Code Sec. 4042(b)(3). **Effective** as if included in the provision of the Energy Tax Incentives Act of 2005 (P.L. 109-58) to which it relates [effective for fuel entered, removed, or sold after 9-30-2005.—CCH]. Prior to amendment, Code Sec. 4042(b)(3) read as follows:

(3) EXCEPTION FOR FUEL TAXED UNDER SECTION 4041(d).—The Leaking Underground Storage Tank Trust Fund financing rate under paragraph (2)(B) shall not apply to the use of any fuel if tax under section 4041(d) was imposed on the sale of such fuel or is imposed on such use.

P.L. 110-172, §6(d)(1)(C), provides:

(C) Notwithstanding section 6430 of the Internal Revenue Code of 1986, a refund, credit, or payment may be made under subchapter B of chapter 65 of such Code for taxes imposed with respect to any liquid after September 30, 2005, and before the date of the enactment of this Act under section 4041(d)(1) or 4042 of such Code at the Leaking Underground Storage Tank Trust Fund financing rate to the extent that tax was imposed with respect to such liquid under section 4081 at the Leaking Underground Storage Tank Trust Fund financing rate.

• **2004, American Jobs Creation Act of 2004 (P.L. 108-357)**

P.L. 108-357, §241(b):

Amended Code Sec. 4042(b)(2)(C). **Effective** 1-1-2005. Prior to amendment, Code Sec. 4042(b)(2)(C) read as follows:

(C) The deficit reduction rate is 4.3 cents per gallon.

• **1993, Omnibus Budget Reconciliation Act of 1993 (P.L. 103-66)**

P.L. 103-66, §13241(d)(1)(A)–(C):

Amended Code Sec. 4042(b)(1) by striking "and" at the end of subparagraph (A), by striking the period at the end of subparagraph (B) and inserting ", and", and by adding at the end thereof new subparagraph (C). **Effective** 10-1-93.

P.L. 103-66, §13241(d)(2):

Amended Code Sec. 4042(b)(2) by adding at the end thereof new subparagraph (C). **Effective** 10-1-93.

• **1988, Technical and Miscellaneous Revenue Act of 1988 (P.L. 100-647)**

P.L. 100-647, §2002(a)(2):

Amended Code Sec. 4042(b)(2). **Effective** as if included in the amendments made by section 521(a)(3) of P.L. 99-499. [effective date amended by P.L. 101-239, §7812(b).—CCH.] Prior to amendment, Code Sec. 4042(b) read as follows:

(2) RATES.—For purposes of paragraph (1)—

(A) the Inland Waterways Trust Fund financing rate is 10 cents a gallon, and

(B) the Leaking Underground Storage Tank Trust Fund financing rate is 0.1 cents a gallon.

• **1986, Water Resources Development Act of 1986 (P.L. 99-662)**

P.L. 99-662, §1404(a):

Amended Code Sec. 4042(b). **Effective** 1-1-87.

• **1986, Superfund Amendments and Reauthorization Act of 1986 (P.L. 99-499)**

P.L. 99-499, §521(a)(3):

Amended Code Sec. 4042(b). **Effective** 1-1-87. Prior to amendment, Code Sec. 4042(b) read as follows:

(b) AMOUNT OF TAX.—The tax imposed by subsection (a) shall be determined from the following table:

If the use occurs	The tax is—
After September 30, 1980 and before October 1, 1981	4 cents a gallon
After September 30, 1981 and before October 1, 1983	6 cents a gallon
After September 30, 1983 and before October 1, 1985	8 cents a gallon
After September 30, 1985	10 cents a gallon

EXCISE TAXES—RETAIL EXCISE TAXES

[Sec. 4042(c)]

(c) EXEMPTIONS.—

(1) DEEP-DRAFT OCEAN-GOING VESSELS.—The tax imposed by subsection (a) shall not apply with respect to any vessel designed primarily for use on the high seas which has a draft of more than 12 feet.

(2) PASSENGER VESSELS.—The tax imposed by subsection (a) shall not apply with respect to any vessel used primarily for the transportation of persons.

(3) USE BY STATE OR LOCAL GOVERNMENT IN TRANSPORTING PROPERTY IN A STATE OR LOCAL BUSINESS.—Subparagraph (B) of subsection (d)(1) shall not apply with respect to use by a State or political subdivision thereof.

(4) USE IN MOVING LASH AND SEABEE OCEAN-GOING BARGES.—The tax imposed by subsection (a) shall not apply with respect to use for movement by tug of exclusively LASH (Lighter-aboard-ship) and SEABEE ocean-going barges released by their ocean-going carriers solely to pick up or deliver international cargoes.

[Sec. 4042(d)]

(d) DEFINITIONS.—For purposes of this section—

(1) COMMERCIAL WATERWAY TRANSPORTATION.—The term "commercial waterway transportation" means any use of a vessel on any inland or intracoastal waterway of the United States—

(A) in the business of transporting property for compensation or hire, or

(B) in transporting property in the business of the owner, lessee, or operator of the vessel (other than fish or other aquatic animal life caught on the voyage).

(2) INLAND OR INTRACOASTAL WATERWAY OF THE UNITED STATES.—The term "inland or intracoastal waterway of the United States" means any inland or intracoastal waterway of the United States which is described in section 206 of the Inland Waterways Revenue Act of 1978.

(3) PERSON.—The term "person" includes the United States, a State, a political subdivision of a State, or any agency or instrumentality of any of the foregoing.

[Sec. 4042(e)]

(e) DATE FOR FILING RETURN.—The date for filing the return of the tax imposed by this section for any calendar quarter shall be the last day of the first month following such quarter.

Amendments

- 1978 (P.L. 95-502)

P.L. 95-502, § 202(a), (d):

Added Code Sec. 4042. **Effective** 10-1-80.

[Sec. 4043]

SEC. 4043. SURTAX ON FUEL USED IN AIRCRAFT PART OF A FRACTIONAL OWNERSHIP PROGRAM.

[Sec. 4043(a)]

(a) IN GENERAL.—There is hereby imposed a tax on any liquid used (during any calendar quarter by any person) in a fractional program aircraft as fuel—

(1) for the transportation of a qualified fractional owner with respect to the fractional ownership aircraft program of which such aircraft is a part, or

(2) with respect to the use of such aircraft on account of such a qualified fractional owner, including use in deadhead service.

[Sec. 4043(b)]

(b) AMOUNT OF TAX.—The rate of tax imposed by subsection (a) is 14.1 cents per gallon.

[Sec. 4043(c)]

(c) DEFINITIONS AND SPECIAL RULES.—For purposes of this section—

(1) FRACTIONAL PROGRAM AIRCRAFT.—The term "fractional program aircraft" means, with respect to any fractional ownership aircraft program, any aircraft which—

(A) is listed as a fractional program aircraft in the management specifications issued to the manager of such program by the Federal Aviation Administration under subpart K of part 91 of title 14, Code of Federal Regulations, and

(B) is registered in the United States.

(2) FRACTIONAL OWNERSHIP AIRCRAFT PROGRAM.—The term "fractional ownership aircraft program" means a program under which—

(A) a single fractional ownership program manager provides fractional ownership program management services on behalf of the fractional owners,

(B) there are 1 or more fractional owners per fractional program aircraft, with at least 1 fractional program aircraft having more than 1 owner,

(C) with respect to at least 2 fractional program aircraft, none of the ownership interests in such aircraft are—

(i) less than the minimum fractional ownership interest, or

(ii) held by the program manager referred to in subparagraph (A),

(D) there exists a dry-lease aircraft exchange arrangement among all of the fractional owners, and

(E) there are multi-year program agreements covering the fractional ownership, fractional ownership program management services, and dry-lease aircraft exchange aspects of the program.

(3) DEFINITIONS RELATED TO FRACTIONAL OWNERSHIP INTERESTS.—

(A) QUALIFIED FRACTIONAL OWNER.—The term "qualified fractional owner" means any fractional owner which has a minimum fractional ownership interest in at least one fractional program aircraft.

(B) MINIMUM FRACTIONAL OWNERSHIP INTEREST.—The term "minimum fractional ownership interest" means, with respect to each type of aircraft—

(i) a fractional ownership interest equal to or greater than 1/16 of at least 1 subsonic, fixed wing, or powered lift aircraft, or

(ii) a fractional ownership interest equal to or greater than 1/32 of at least 1 rotorcraft aircraft.

(C) FRACTIONAL OWNERSHIP INTEREST.—The term "fractional ownership interest" means—

(i) the ownership of an interest in a fractional program aircraft,

EXCISE TAXES—RETAIL EXCISE TAXES

(ii) the holding of a multi-year leasehold interest in a fractional program aircraft, or

(iii) the holding of a multi-year leasehold interest which is convertible into an ownership interest in a fractional program aircraft.

(D) FRACTIONAL OWNER.—The term "fractional owner" means any person owning any interest (including the entire interest) in a fractional program aircraft.

(4) DRY-LEASE AIRCRAFT EXCHANGE.—The term "dry-lease aircraft exchange" means an agreement, documented by the written program agreements, under which the fractional program aircraft are available, on an as needed basis without crew, to each fractional owner.

(5) SPECIAL RULE RELATING TO USE OF FRACTIONAL PROGRAM AIRCRAFT FOR FLIGHT DEMONSTRATION, MAINTENANCE, OR TRAINING.—For purposes of subsection (a), a fractional program aircraft shall not be considered to be used for the transportation of a qualified fractional owner, or on account of such qualified fractional owner, when it is used for flight demonstration, maintenance, or crew training.

(6) SPECIAL RULE RELATING TO DEADHEAD SERVICE.—A fractional program aircraft shall not be considered to be used on account of a qualified fractional owner when it is used in deadhead service and a person other than a qualified fractional owner is separately charged for such service.

[Sec. 4043(d)]

(d) TERMINATION.—This section shall not apply to liquids used as a fuel in an aircraft after September 30, 2028.

Amendments

• **2024, FAA Reauthorization Act of 2024 (P.L. 118-63)**

P.L. 118-63, §1302(c)(1):

Amended Code Sec. 4043(d) by striking "May 10, 2024" and inserting "September 30, 2028". **Effective** 5-16-2024.

• **2024, Airport and Airway Extension Act of 2024, Part II (P.L. 118-60)**

P.L. 118-60, §202(a), provides:

SEC. 202. EXTENSION OF TAXES FUNDING AIRPORT AND AIRWAY TRUST FUND

(a) Sections 4043(d), 4081(d)(2)(B), 4261(j), 4261(k)(1)(A)(ii), and 4271(d)(1)(A)(ii) of the Internal Revenue Code of 1986 shall be applied by substituting "May 17, 2024" for "May 10, 2024".

• **2024, Airport and Airway Extension Act of 2024 (P.L. 118-41)**

P.L. 118-41, §202(c)(1):

Amended Code Sec. 4043(d) by striking "March 8, 2024" and inserting "May 10, 2024". **Effective** 3-8-2024.

• **2023, Airport and Airway Extension Act of 2023, Part II (P.L. 118-34)**

P.L. 118-34, §202(c)(1):

Amended Code Sec. 4043(d) by striking "December 31, 2023" and inserting "March 8, 2024". **Effective** 12-26-2023.

• **2023, Continuing Appropriations Act, 2024 and Other Extensions Act (P.L. 118-15)**

P.L. 118-15, §2212(c)(1):

Amended Code Sec. 4043(d) by striking "September 30, 2023" and inserting "December 31, 2023". **Effective** 9-30-2023.

• **2018, FAA Reauthorization Act of 2018 (P.L. 115-254)**

P.L. 115-254, §802(c)(1):

Amended Code Sec. 4043(d) by striking "September 30, 2021" and inserting "September 30, 2023". **Effective** 10-5-2018.

• **2012, FAA Modernization and Reform Act of 2012 (P.L. 112-95)**

P.L. 112-95, §1103(a)(1):

Amended subchapter B of chapter 31 by adding at the end a new Code Sec. 4043. **Effective** for fuel used after 3-31-2012.

Subchapter C—Heavy Trucks and Trailers

Sec. 4051. Imposition of tax on heavy trucks and trailers sold at retail.
Sec. 4052. Definitions and special rules.
Sec. 4053. Exemptions.

[Sec. 4051]

SEC. 4051. IMPOSITION OF TAX ON HEAVY TRUCKS AND TRAILERS SOLD AT RETAIL.

[Sec. 4051(a)]

(a) IMPOSITION OF TAX.—

(1) IN GENERAL.—There is hereby imposed on the first retail sale of the following articles (including in each case parts or accessories sold on or in connection therewith or with the sale thereof) a tax of 12 percent of the amount for which the article is so sold:

(A) Automobile truck chassis.

(B) Automobile truck bodies.

(C) Truck trailer and semitrailer chassis.

(D) Truck trailer and semitrailer bodies.

(E) Tractors of the kind chiefly used for highway transportation in combination with a trailer or semitrailer.

(2) EXCLUSION FOR TRUCKS WEIGHING 33,000 POUNDS OR LESS.—The tax imposed by paragraph (1) shall not apply to automobile truck chassis and automobile truck bodies, suitable for use with a vehicle which has a gross vehicle weight of 33,000 pounds or less (as determined under regulations prescribed by the Secretary).

(3) EXCLUSION FOR TRAILERS WEIGHING 26,000 POUNDS OR LESS.—The tax imposed by paragraph (1) shall not apply to truck trailer and semitrailer chassis and bodies, suitable for use with a trailer or semitrailer which has a gross vehicle weight of 26,000 pounds or less (as determined under regulations prescribed by the Secretary).

(4) EXCLUSION FOR TRACTORS WEIGHING 19,500 POUNDS OR LESS.—The tax imposed by paragraph (1) shall not apply to tractors of the kind chiefly used for highway transportation in combination with a trailer or semitrailer if—

(A) such tractor has a gross vehicle weight of 19,500 pounds or less (as determined by the Secretary), and

(B) such tractor, in combination with a trailer or semitrailer, has a gross combined weight of 33,000 pounds or less (as determined by the Secretary).

(5) SALE OF TRUCKS, ETC., TREATED AS SALE OF CHASSIS AND BODY.—For purposes of this subsection, a sale of an automobile truck or truck trailer or semitrailer shall be considered to be a sale of a chassis and of a body described in paragraph (1).

Amendments

• **2018, Tax Technical Corrections Act of 2018 (P.L. 115-141)**

P.L. 115-141, §401(a)(219), Div. U:

Amended Code Sec. 4051(a)(3) by striking "Secretary." and inserting "Secretary)". **Effective** 3-23-2018.

• **2005, Safe, Accountable,Flexible, Efficient Transportation Equity Act: A Legacy for Users (P.L. 109-59)**

P.L. 109-59, §11112(a):

Amended Code Sec. 4051(a) by redesignating paragraph (4) as paragraph (5) and by inserting after paragraph (3) a new paragraph (4). **Effective** for sales after 9-30-2005.

[Sec. 4051(b)]

(b) SEPARATE PURCHASE OF TRUCK OR TRAILER AND PARTS AND ACCESSORIES THEREFOR.—Under regulations prescribed by the Secretary—

EXCISE TAXES—RETAIL EXCISE TAXES

(1) IN GENERAL.—If—

(A) the owner, lessee, or operator of any vehicle which contains an article taxable under subsection (a) installs (or causes to be installed) any part or accessory on such vehicle, and

(B) such installation is not later than the date 6 months after the date such vehicle (as it contains such article) was first placed in service,

then there is hereby imposed on such installation a tax equal to 12 percent of the price of such part or accessory and its installation.

(2) EXCEPTIONS.—Paragraph (1) shall not apply if—

(A) the part or accessory installed is a replacement part or accessory, or

(B) the aggregate price of the parts and accessories (and their installation) described in paragraph (1) with respect to any vehicle does not exceed $1,000 (or such other amount or amounts as the Secretary may by regulations prescribe).

(3) INSTALLERS SECONDARILY LIABLE FOR TAX.—The owners of the trade or business installing the parts or accessories shall be secondarily liable for the tax imposed by paragraph (1).

Amendments

• **1997, Taxpayer Relief Act of 1997 (P.L. 105-34)**

P.L. 105-34, §1401(a):

Amended Code Sec. 4051(b)(2)(B) by striking "$200" and inserting "$1,000". **Effective** for installations on vehicles sold after 8-5-97.

• **1984, Deficit Reduction Act of 1984 (P.L. 98-369)**

P.L. 98-369, §734(g):

Amended the text of Code Sec. 4051(b)(3). **Effective** as if included in the provision of the Highway Revenue Act of 1982 to which it relates. Prior to amendment, it read as follows:

In addition to the owner, lessee, or operator of the vehicle, the owner of the trade or business installing the part or accessory shall be liable for the tax imposed by paragraph (1).

[Sec. 4051(c)]

(c) TERMINATION.—On and after October 1, 2028, the taxes imposed by this section shall not apply.

Amendments

• **2021, Infrastructure Investment and Jobs Act (P.L. 117-58)**

P.L. 117-58, §80102(a)(2)(B), Div. H:

Amended Code Sec. 4051(c) by striking "October 1, 2022" and inserting "October 1, 2028". **Effective** 10-1-2021.

• **2015, Fixing America's Surface Transportation Act (P.L. 114-94)**

P.L. 114-94, §31102(a)(2)(B):

Amended Code Sec. 4051(c) by striking "October 1, 2016" and inserting "October 1, 2022". **Effective** 10-1-2016.

• **2012, Highway Investment, Job Creation, and Economic Growth Act of 2012 (P.L. 112-141)**

P.L. 112-141, §40102(a)(2)(B):

Amended Code Sec. 4051(c) by striking "July 1, 2012" and inserting "October 1, 2016". **Effective** 7-1-2012.

• **2012, Temporary Surface Transportation Extension Act of 2012 (P.L. 112-140)**

P.L. 112-140, §1(c), provides:

(c) SPECIAL RULE FOR EXECUTION OF AMENDMENTS IN MAP–21.—On the date of enactment of the MAP–21 [P.L. 112-141]—

(1) this Act and the amendments made by this Act shall cease to be effective;

(2) the text of the laws amended by this Act shall revert back so as to read as the text read on the day before the date of enactment of this Act; and

(3) the amendments made by the MAP–21 shall be executed as if this Act had not been enacted.

P.L. 112-140, §402(a)(2)(B):

Amended Code Sec. 4051(c) by striking "July 1, 2012" and inserting "July 7, 2012". **Effective** 7-1-2012. For a special rule, see Act Sec. 1(c), above.

• **2012, Surface Transportation Extension Act of 2012 (P.L. 112-102)**

P.L. 112-102, §402(a)(2)(B):

Amended Code Sec. 4051(c) by striking "April 1, 2012" and inserting "July 1, 2012". **Effective** 4-1-2012.

• **2011, Surface Transportation Extension Act of 2011, Part II (P.L. 112-30)**

P.L. 112-30, §142(a)(2)(B):

Amended Code Sec. 4051(c) by striking "October 1, 2011" and inserting "April 1, 2012". **Effective** 10-1-2011.

• **2005, Safe, Accountable, Flexible, Efficient Transportation Equity Act: A Legacy for Users (P.L. 109-59)**

P.L. 109-59, §11101(a)(1)(D):

Amended Code Sec. 4051(c) by striking "2005" and inserting "2011". **Effective** 8-10-2005.

• **1998, Transportation Equity Act for the 21st Century (P.L. 105-178)**

P.L. 105-178, §9002(a)(1)(D):

Amended Code Sec. 4051(c) by striking "1999" and inserting "2005". **Effective** 6-9-98.

• **1991, Intermodal Surface Transportation Efficiency Act of 1991 (P.L. 102-240)**

P.L. 102-240, §8002(a)(1):

Amended Code Sec. 4051(c) by striking "1995" each place it appears and inserting "1999". **Effective** 12-18-91.

• **1990, Omnibus Budget Reconciliation Act of 1990 (P.L. 101-508)**

P.L. 101-508, §11211(c)(1):

Amended Code Sec. 4051(c) by striking "1993" each place it appears and inserting "1995". **Effective** 11-5-90.

• **1987, Surface Transportation and Uniform Relocation Assistance Act of 1987 (P.L. 100-17)**

P.L. 100-17, §502(a)(2):

Amended Code Sec. 4051(c) by striking out "1988" and inserting in lieu thereof "1993". **Effective** 4-2-87.

[Sec. 4051(d)—Stricken]

Amendments

• **1997, Taxpayer Relief Act of 1997 (P.L. 105-34)**

P.L. 105-34, §1432(a):

Amended Code Sec. 4051 by striking subsection (d) and by redesignating subsection (e) as subsection (d). **Effective** 8-5-97. Prior to being stricken, Code Sec. 4051(d) read as follows:

(d) TEMPORARY REDUCTION IN TAX ON CERTAIN PIGGYBACK TRAILERS.—

(1) IN GENERAL.—In the case of piggyback trailers or semitrailers sold within the 1-year period beginning on July 18, 1984, subsection (a) shall be applied by substituting "6 percent" for "12 percent".

(2) PIGGYBACK TRAILERS OR SEMITRAILERS.—For purposes of this subsection, the term "piggyback trailers or semitrailers" means any trailer or semitrailer—

(A) which is designed for use principally in connection with trailer-on-flatcar service by rail, and

(B)(i) both the seller and the purchaser of which are registered in a manner similar to registration under section 4222, and

(ii) with respect to which the purchaser certifies (at such time and in such form and manner as the Secretary prescribes by regulations) to the seller that such trailer or semitrailer—

(I) will be used, or resold for use, principally in connection with such service, or

(II) will be incorporated into an article which will be so used or resold.

(3) ADDITIONAL TAX WHERE NONQUALIFIED USE.—If any piggyback trailer or semitrailer was subject to tax under subsection (a) at the 6 percent rate and such trailer or semitrailer is used or resold for use other than for a use described in paragraph (2)—

(A) such use or resale shall be treated as a sale to which subsection (a) applies,

(B) the amount of the tax imposed under subsection (a) on such sale shall be equal to the amount of the tax which was imposed on the first retail sale, and

(C) the person so using or reselling such trailer or semitrailer shall be liable for the tax imposed by subsection (a).

No tax shall be imposed by reason of this paragraph on any use or resale which occurs more than 6 years after the date of the first retail sale.

• **1986, Tax Reform Act of 1986 (P.L. 99-514)**

P.L. 99-514, §1877(c):

Amended Code Sec. 4051(d)(3) by adding the last sentence. **Effective** as if included in the provision of P.L. 98-369 to which it relates.

P.L. 99-514, §1899A(47):

Amended Code Sec. 4051(d)(1) by striking out "the date of the enactment of the Tax Reform Act of 1984" and inserting in lieu thereof "July 18, 1984". **Effective** 10-22-86.

EXCISE TAXES—RETAIL EXCISE TAXES

• **1984, Deficit Reduction Act of 1984 (P.L. 98-369)**

P.L. 98-369, § 921:

Amended Code Sec. 4051 by redesignating subsection (d) as subsection (e) and inserting after subsection (c) the following new subsection (d). **Effective** 7-18-84.

• **1983, Surface Transportation Act of 1982 (P.L. 97-424)**

P.L. 97-424, § 512(b)(1):

Added Code Sec. 4051 as part of new Subchapter B. **Effective** 4-1-83.

[Sec. 4051(d)]

(d) CREDIT AGAINST TAX FOR TIRE TAX.—If—

(1) tires are sold on or in connection with the sale of any article, and

(2) tax is imposed by this subchapter on the sale of such tires,

there shall be allowed as a credit against the tax imposed by this subchapter an amount equal to the tax (if any) imposed by section 4071 on such tires.

Amendments

• **1997, Taxpayer Relief Act of 1997 (P.L. 105-34)**

P.L. 105-34, § 1402(a):

Amended Code Sec. 4051(e). **Effective** 1-1-98. Prior to amendment, Code Sec. 4051(e) read as follows:

(e) TRANSITIONAL RULE.—In the case of any article taxable under subsection (a) on which tax was imposed under section 4061(a), subsection (a) shall be applied by substituting "2 percent" for "12 percent".

P.L. 105-34, § 1432(a):

Amended Code Sec. 4051 by redesignating subsection (e) as subsection (d). **Effective** 8-5-97.

[Sec. 4052]

SEC. 4052. DEFINITIONS AND SPECIAL RULES.

[Sec. 4052(a)]

(a) FIRST RETAIL SALE.—For purposes of this subchapter—

(1) IN GENERAL.—The term "first retail sale" means the first sale, for a purpose other than for resale or leasing in a long-term lease, after production, manufacture, or importation.

(2) LEASES CONSIDERED AS SALES.—Rules similar to the rules of section 4217 shall apply.

(3) USE TREATED AS SALE.—

(A) IN GENERAL.—If any person uses an article taxable under section 4051 before the first retail sale of such article, then such person shall be liable for tax under section 4051 in the same manner as if such article were sold at retail by him.

(B) EXEMPTION FOR USE IN FURTHER MANUFACTURE.—Subparagraph (A) shall not apply to use of an article as material in the manufacture or production of, or as a component part of, another article to be manufactured or produced by him.

(C) COMPUTATION OF TAX.—In the case of any person made liable for tax by subparagraph (A), the tax shall be computed on the price at which similar articles are sold at retail in the ordinary course of trade, as determined by the Secretary.

Amendments

• **1988, Technical and Miscellaneous Revenue Act of 1988 (P.L. 100-647)**

P.L. 100-647, § 6111(a):

Amended Code Sec. 4052(a)(1) by striking out "manufacture, production" and inserting in lieu thereof "production, manufacture". **Effective** 1-1-88.

• **1987, Surface Transportation and Uniform Relocation Assistance Act of 1987 (P.L. 100-17)**

P.L. 100-17, § 505(a):

Amended Code Sec. 4052(a)(1) by striking out "other than for resale" and inserting in lieu thereof "other than for resale or leasing in a long-term lease". **Effective** with respect to articles sold by the manufacturer, producer, or importer on or after the 1st day of the 1st calendar quarter which begins more than 90 days after 4-2-87.

[Sec. 4052(b)]

(b) DETERMINATION OF PRICE.—

(1) IN GENERAL.—In determining price for purposes of this subchapter—

(A) there shall be included any charge incident to placing the article in condition ready for use,

(B) there shall be excluded—

(i) the amount of the tax imposed by this subchapter,

(ii) if stated as a separate charge, the amount of any retail sales tax imposed by any State or political subdivision thereof or the District of Columbia, whether the liability for such tax is imposed on the vendor or vendee, and

(iii) the value of any component of such article if—

(I) such component is furnished by the first user of such article, and

(II) such component has been used before such furnishing, and

(C) the price shall be determined without regard to any trade-in.

(2) SALES NOT AT ARM'S LENGTH.—In the case of any article sold (otherwise than through an arm's-length transaction) at less than the fair market price, the tax under this subchapter shall be computed on the price for which similar articles are sold at retail in the ordinary course of trade, as determined by the Secretary.

(3) LONG-TERM LEASE.—

(A) IN GENERAL.—In the case of any long-term lease of an article which is treated as the first retail sale of such article, the tax under this subchapter shall be computed on a price equal to—

(i) the sum of—

(I) the price (determined under this subchapter but without regard to paragraph (4)) at which such article was sold to the lessor, and

(II) the cost of any parts and accessories installed by the lessor on such article before the first use by the lessee or leased in connection with such long-term lease, plus

(ii) an amount equal to the presumed markup percentage of the sum described in clause (i).

(B) PRESUMED MARKUP PERCENTAGE.—For purposes of subparagraph (A), the term "presumed markup percentage" means the average markup percentage of retailers of articles of the type involved, as determined by the Secretary.

(C) EXCEPTIONS UNDER REGULATIONS.—To the extent provided in regulations prescribed by the Secretary, subparagraph (A) shall not apply to specified types of leases where its application is not necessary to carry out the purposes of this subsection.

(4) SPECIAL RULE WHERE TAX PAID BY MANUFACTURER, PRODUCER, OR IMPORTER.—

(A) IN GENERAL.—In any case where the manufacturer, producer, or importer of any article (or a related person) is liable for tax imposed by this subchapter with respect to such article, the tax under this subchapter shall be computed on a price equal to the sum of—

EXCISE TAXES—RETAIL EXCISE TAXES

(i) the price which would (but for this paragraph) be determined under this subchapter, plus

(ii) the product of the price referred to in clause (i) and the presumed markup percentage determined under paragraph (3)(B).

(B) RELATED PERSON.—For purposes of this paragraph—

(i) IN GENERAL.—Except as provided in clause (ii), the term "related person" means any person who is a member of the same controlled group (within the meaning of section 5061(e)(3)) as the manufacturer, producer, or importer.

(ii) EXCEPTION FOR RETAIL ESTABLISHMENT.—To the extent provided in regulations prescribed by the Secretary, a person shall not be treated as a related person with respect to the sale of any article if such article is sold through a permanent retail establishment in the normal course of the trade or business of being a retailer.

Amendments

• **1997, Taxpayer Relief Act of 1997 (P.L. 105-34)**

P.L. 105-34, §1402(b):

Amended Code Sec. 4052(b)(1)(B) by striking clause (iii), by adding "and" at the end of clause (ii), and by redesignating clause (iv) as clause (iii). **Effective** 1-1-98. Prior to amendment, Code Sec. 4052(b)(1)(B)(iii) read as follows:

(iii) the fair market value (including any tax imposed by section 4071) at retail of any tires (not including any metal rim or rim base), and

• **1987, Surface Transportation and Uniform Relocation Assistance Act of 1987 (P.L. 100-17)**

P.L. 100-17, §505(b):

Amended Code Sec. 4052(b) by adding at the end thereof new paragraph (3). **Effective** with respect to articles sold by the manufacturer, producer, or importer on or after the 1st day of the 1st calendar quarter which begins more than 90 days after 4-2-87.

P.L. 100-17, §506(a):

Amended Code Sec. 4052(b) by adding at the end thereof new paragraph (4). **Effective** with respect to articles sold by the manufacturer, producer, or importer on or after the 1st day of the 1st calendar quarter which begins more than 90 days after 4-2-87.

• **1984, Deficit Reduction Act of 1984 (P.L. 98-369)**

P.L. 98-369, §731:

Amended Code Sec. 4052(b)(1)(B) by striking out "and" at the end of clause (ii) and by inserting after clause (iii) new clause (iv). **Effective** as if included in the provision of the Highway Revenue Act of 1982 to which it relates.

[Sec. 4052(c)]

(c) CERTAIN COMBINATIONS NOT TREATED AS MANUFACTURE.—

(1) IN GENERAL.—For purposes of this subchapter (other than subsection (a)(3)(B)), a person shall not be treated as engaged in the manufacture of any article by reason of merely combining such article with any item listed in paragraph (2).

(2) ITEMS.—The items listed in this paragraph are any coupling device (including any fifth wheel), wrecker crane, loading and unloading equipment (including any crane, hoist, winch, or power liftgate), aerial ladder or tower, snow and ice control equipment, earthmoving, excavation and construction equipment, spreader, sleeper cab, cab shield, or wood or metal floor.

Amendments

• **1984, Deficit Reduction Act of 1984 (P.L. 98-369)**

P.L. 98-369, §735(b)(2):

Amended Code Sec. 4052(c). **Effective** as if included in the provision of the Highway Revenue Act of 1982 to which it relates. Prior to amendment, it read as follows:

(c) Certain Combinations Not Treated as Manufacture.—For purposes of this subchapter (other than subsection (a)(3)(B)), a person shall not be treated as engaged in the manufacture of any article by reason of merely combining such article with any equipment or other item listed in section 4063(d).

[Sec. 4052(d)]

(d) CERTAIN OTHER RULES MADE APPLICABLE.—Under regulations prescribed by the Secretary, rules similar to the rules of subsections (c) and (d) of section 4216 (relating to partial payments) shall apply for purposes of this subchapter.

Amendments

• **1997, Taxpayer Relief Act of 1997 (P.L. 105-34)**

P.L. 105-34, §1434(b)(1):

Amended Code Sec. 4052(d) by striking "rules of—" and all that follows through "shall apply" and inserting "rules of subsections (c) and (d) of section 4216 (relating to partial payments) shall apply". **Effective** 1-1-98. Prior to amendment, Code Sec. 4052(d) read as follows:

(d) CERTAIN OTHER RULES MADE APPLICABLE.—Under regulations prescribed by the Secretary, rules similar to the rules of—

(1) subsections (c) and (d) of section 4216 (relating to partial payments), and

(2) section 4222 (relating to registration),

shall apply for purposes of this subchapter.

• **1983, Surface Transportation Act of 1982 (P.L. 97-424)**

P.L. 97-424, §512(b)(1):

Added Code Sec. 4052 as part of new Subchapter B. **Effective** 4-1-83.

[Sec. 4052(e)]

(e) LONG-TERM LEASE.—For purposes of this section, the term "long-term lease" means any lease with a term of 1 year or more. In determining a lease term for purposes of the preceding sentence, the rules of section 168(i)(3)(A) shall apply.

Amendments

• **1997, Taxpayer Relief Act of 1997 (P.L. 105-34)**

P.L. 105-34, §1434(a):

Amended Code Sec. 4052 by redesignating the subsection defining a long-term lease as subsection (e). **Effective** 1-1-98.

• **1987, Surface Transportation and Uniform Relocation Assistance Act of 1987 (P.L. 100-17)**

P.L. 100-17, §505(c):

Amended Code Sec. 4052 by adding at the end thereof new subsection (f)[e]. **Effective** with respect to articles sold by the manufacturer, producer, or importer on or after the 1st day of the 1st calendar quarter which begins more than 90 days after 4-2-87.

[Sec. 4052(f)]

(f) CERTAIN REPAIRS AND MODIFICATIONS NOT TREATED AS MANUFACTURE.—

(1) IN GENERAL.—An article described in section 4051(a)(1) shall not be treated as manufactured or produced solely by reason of repairs or modifications to the article (including any modification which changes the transportation function of the article or restores a wrecked article to a functional condition) if the cost of such repairs and modifications does not exceed 75 percent of the retail price of a comparable new article.

(2) EXCEPTION.—Paragraph (1) shall not apply if the article (as repaired or modified) would, if new, be taxable under section 4051 and the article when new was not taxable under such section or the corresponding provision of prior law.

Amendments

• **1998, IRS Restructuring and Reform Act of 1998 (P.L. 105-206)**

P.L. 105-206, §6014(c):

Amended Code Sec. 4052(f)(2) by striking "this section" and inserting "such section". **Effective** as if included in the provision of P.L. 105-34 to which it relates [effective 1-1-98.—CCH].

• **1997, Taxpayer Relief Act of 1997 (P.L. 105-34)**

P.L. 105-34, §1434(a):

Amended Code Sec. 4052 by adding at the end a new subsection (f). **Effective** 1-1-98.

[Sec. 4052(g)]

(g) REGULATIONS.—The Secretary shall prescribe regulations which permit, in lieu of any other certification, persons who are purchasing articles taxable under this subchapter for resale or leasing in a long-term lease to execute a statement (made under penalties of perjury) on the sale invoice that such sale is for resale. The Secretary shall not impose any registration requirement as a condition of using such procedure.

EXCISE TAXES—RETAIL EXCISE TAXES

Amendments

• **1997, Taxpayer Relief Act of 1997 (P.L. 105-34)**

P.L. 105-34, §1434(b)(2):

Amended Code Sec. 4052 by adding at the end a new subsection (g). **Effective** 1-1-98.

[Sec. 4053]

SEC. 4053. EXEMPTIONS.

No tax shall be imposed by section 4051 on any of the following articles:

(1) CAMPER COACHES BODIES FOR SELF-PROPELLED MOBILE HOMES.—Any article designed—

    (A) to be mounted or placed on automobile trucks, automobile truck chassis, or automobile chassis, and

    (B) to be used primarily as living quarters or camping accommodations.

(2) FEED, SEED, AND FERTILIZER EQUIPMENT.—Any body primarily designed—

    (A) to process or prepare seed, feed, or fertilizer for use on farms,

    (B) to haul feed, seed, or fertilizer to and on farms,

    (C) to spread feed, seed, or fertilizer on farms,

    (D) to load or unload feed, seed, or fertilizer on farms, or

    (E) for any combination of the foregoing.

(3) HOUSE TRAILERS.—Any house trailer.

(4) AMBULANCES, HEARSES, ETC.—Any ambulance, hearse, or combination ambulance-hearse.

(5) CONCRETE MIXERS.—Any article designed—

    (A) to be placed or mounted on an automobile truck chassis or truck trailer or semitrailer chassis, and

    (B) to be used to process or prepare concrete.

(6) TRASH CONTAINERS, ETC.—Any box, container, receptacle, bin or other similar article—

    (A) which is designed to be used as a trash container and is not designed for the transportation of freight other than trash, and

    (B) which is not designed to be permanently mounted on or permanently affixed to an automobile truck chassis or body.

(7) RAIL TRAILERS AND RAIL VANS.—Any chassis or body of a trailer or semitrailer which is designed for use both as a highway vehicle and a railroad car. For purposes of the preceding sentence, piggy-back trailer or semitrailer shall not be treated as designed for use as a railroad car.

(8) MOBILE MACHINERY.—Any vehicle which consists of a chassis—

    (A) to which there has been permanently mounted (by welding, bolting, riveting, or other means) machinery or equipment to perform a construction, manufacturing, processing, farming, mining, drilling, timbering, or similar operation if the operation of the machinery or equipment is unrelated to transportation on or off the public highways,

    (B) which has been specially designed to serve only as a mobile carriage and mount (and a power source, where applicable) for the particular machinery or equipment involved, whether or not such machinery or equipment is in operation, and

    (C) which, by reason of such special design, could not, without substantial structural modification, be used as a component of a vehicle designed to perform a function of transporting any load other than that particular machinery or equipment or similar machinery or equipment requiring such a specially designed chassis.

(9) IDLING REDUCTION DEVICE.—Any device or system of devices which—

    (A) is designed to provide to a vehicle those services (such as heat, air conditioning, or electricity) that would otherwise require the operation of the main drive engine while the vehicle is temporarily parked or remains stationary using one or more devices affixed to a tractor, and

    (B) is determined by the Administrator of the Environmental Protection Agency, in consultation with the Secretary of Energy and the Secretary of Transportation, to reduce idling of such vehicle at a motor vehicle rest stop or other location where such vehicles are temporarily parked or remain stationary.

(10) ADVANCED INSULATION.—Any insulation that has an R value of not less than R35 per inch.

Amendments

• **2008, Energy Improvement and Extension Act of 2008 (P.L. 110-343)**

P.L. 110-343, Division B, §206(a):

Amended Code Sec. 4053 by adding at the end new paragraphs (9)-(10). **Effective** for sales or installations after 10-3-2008.

• **2004, American Jobs Creation Act of 2004 (P.L. 108-357)**

P.L. 108-357, §851(a)(1):

Amended Code Sec. 4053 by adding at the end a new paragraph (8). **Effective** 10-23-2004.

• **1984, Deficit Reduction Act of 1984 (P.L. 98-369)**

P.L. 98-369, §735(b)(1):

Amended Code Sec. 4053. **Effective** as if included in the provision of the Highway Revenue Act of 1982 to which it relates. Prior to amendment, it read as follows:

SEC. 4053. EXEMPTIONS.

(a) Exemption of Specified Articles.—No tax shall be imposed under section 4051 on any article specified in subsection (a) of section 4063.

(b) Certain Exemptions Made Applicable.—The exemptions provided by section 4221(a) are hereby extended to the tax imposed by section 4051.

• **1983, Surface Transportation Act of 1982 (P.L. 97-424)**

P.L. 97-424, §512(b)(1):

Added Code Sec. 4053 as part of new Subchapter B. **Effective** 4-1-83.

CHAPTER 32—MANUFACTURERS EXCISE TAXES

SUBCHAPTER A.	Automotive and related items.
SUBCHAPTER B.	Coal.
SUBCHAPTER C.	Certain vaccines.
SUBCHAPTER D.	Recreational equipment.
SUBCHAPTER F.	Special provisions applicable to manufacturers tax.
SUBCHAPTER G.	Exemptions, registration, etc.

Subchapter A—Automotive and Related Items

Part I.	Gas guzzlers.
Part II.	Tires.
Part III.	Petroleum products.

MANUFACTURERS TAXES—GAS GUZZLERS

PART I—GAS GUZZLERS

Sec. 4064.   Gas guzzler[s] tax.

[Sec. 4061—Stricken]

Amendments

• **1984, Deficit Reduction Act of 1984 (P.L. 98-369)**

P.L. 98-369, §735(a):

Struck out Code Sec. 4061. **Effective** as if included in the provision of the Highway Revenue Act of 1982 to which such amendment relates. Prior to being stricken, Code Sec. 4061 read as follows:

SEC. 4061. IMPOSITION OF TAX.

[Sec. 4061(a)]

(a) TRUCKS, BUSES, TRACTORS, ETC.—

(1) TAX IMPOSED.—There is hereby imposed upon the following articles (including in each case parts or accessories therefor sold on or in connection therewith or with the sale thereof) sold by the manufacturer, producer, or importer a tax of 10 percent of the price for which so sold, except that on and after October 1, 1984, the rate shall be 5 percent—

Automobile truck chassis.
Automobile truck bodies.
Automobile bus chassis.
Automobile bus bodies.
Truck and bus trailer and semitrailer chassis.
Truck and bus trailer and semitrailer and bus trailer and semitrailer chassis.
Truck and bus trailer and semitrailer bodies.
Tractors of the kind chiefly used for highway transportation in combination with a trailer or semitrailer.

A sale of an automobile truck, bus, truck or bus trailer or semitrailer shall, for the purposes of this subsection, be considered to be a sale of a chassis and of a body enumerated in this subsection.

(2) EXCLUSION FOR TRUCKS WITH GROSS VEHICLE WEIGHT OF 33,000 POUNDS OR LESS, AND CERTAIN TRAILERS.—

(A) The tax imposed by paragraph (1) shall not apply to automobile truck chassis and automobile truck bodies, suitable for use with a vehicle which has a gross vehicle weight of 33,000 pounds or less (as determined under regulations prescribed by the Secretary).

(B) The tax imposed by paragraph (1) shall not apply to truck trailer and semi-trailer chassis and bodies, suitable for use with a trailer or semitrailer which has a gross vehicle weight of 26,000 pounds or less (as determined under regulations prescribed by the Secretary).

Amendments

• **1983, Surface Transportation Act of 1982 (P.L. 97-424)**

P.L. 97-424, §512(a)(1):

Amended Code Sec. 4061(a)(2). **Effective** 1-7-83. Prior to amendment, Code Sec. 4061(a)(2) read as follows:

"(2) Exclusion for light-duty trucks, etc.—The tax imposed by paragraph (1) shall not apply to a sale by the manufacturer, producer, or importer of the following articles suitable for use with a vehicle having a gross vehicle weight of 10,000 pounds or less (as determined under regulations prescribed by the Secretary)—

Automobile truck chassis.
Automobile truck bodies.
Automobile bus chassis.
Automobile bus bodies.

Truck trailer and semitrailer chassis and bodies, suitable for use with a trailer or semitrailer having a gross vehicle weight of 10,000 pounds or less (as so determined)."

• **1978, Surface Transportation Assistance Act of 1978 (P.L. 95-599)**

P.L. 95-599, §502(a)(2):

Substituted "1984" for "1979" in Code Sec. 4061(a)(1). **Effective** 11-7-78.

• **1976, Tax Reform Act of 1976 (P.L. 94-455)**

P.L. 94-455, §1906(b)(13)(A):

Amended 1954 Code by substituting "Secretary" for "Secretary or his delegate" each place it appeared. **Effective** 2-1-77.

• **1971, Revenue Act of 1971 (P.L. 92-178)**

P.L. 92-178, §401(a):

Amended Code Sec. 4061(a). **Effective** as noted in Act Sec. 401(h) following former Code Sec. 4061(b). Prior to amendment, Code Sec. 4061(a) read as follows:

"(a) Automobiles.—There is hereby imposed upon the following articles (including in each case parts or accessories therefor sold on or in connection therewith or with the sale thereof) sold by the manufacturer, producer, or importer a tax equivalent to the specified percent of the price for which so sold:

"(1) Articles taxable at 10 percent, except that on and after October 1, 1977, the rate shall be 5 percent—

"Automobile truck chassis.
"Automobile truck bodies.
"Automobile bus chassis.
"Automobile bus bodies.
"Truck and bus trailer and semitrailer chassis.
"Truck and bus trailer and semitrailer bodies.
"Tractors of the kind chiefly used for highway transportation in combination with a trailer or semitrailer.

A sale of an automobile truck, bus, truck or bus trailer or semitrailer shall, for the purposes of this paragraph, be considered to be a sale of a chassis and of a body enumerated in this paragraph.

"(2)(A) Articles enumerated in subparagraph (B) are taxable at whichever of the following rates is applicable:

"If the article is sold—	The tax rate is—
"Before January 1, 1973	7 percent.
"During 1973	6 percent.
"During 1974, 1975, 1976, or 1977	5 percent.
"During 1978	4 percent.
"During 1979	3 percent.
"During 1980	2 percent.
"During 1981	1 percent.

The tax imposed by this subsection shall not apply with respect to articles enumerated in subparagraph (B) which are sold by the manufacturer, producer, or importer after December 31, 1981.

"(B) The articles to which subparagraph (A) applies are:

"Automobile chassis and bodies other than those taxable under paragraph (1).

"Chassis and bodies for trailers and semitrailers (other than house trailers) suitable for use in connection with passenger automobiles.

A sale of an automobile, or of a trailer or semitrailer suitable for use in connection with a passenger automobile, shall, for the purposes of this paragraph, be considered to be a sale of a chassis and of a body enumerated in this subparagraph."

• **1970, Excise, Estate, and Gift Tax Adjustment Act of 1970 (P.L. 91-614)**

P.L. 91-614, §201(a)(1):

Amended the rate table in Code Sec. 4061(a)(2)(A). Prior to amendment, the table read as follows:

"Before January 1, 1971	7 percent.
During 1971	5 percent.
During 1972	3 percent.
During 1973	1 percent."

• **1969, Tax Reform Act of 1969 (P.L. 91-172)**

P.L. 91-172, §702(a)(1):

Amended Code Sec. 4061(a)(2)(A). Prior to amendment, Code Sec. 4061(a)(2)(A) read as follows:

"(2)(A) Articles enumerated in subparagraph (B) are taxable at whichever of the following rates is applicable:

If the article is sold—	The tax rate is—
Before January 1, 1970	7 percent
During 1970	5 percent
During 1971	3 percent
During 1972	1 percent.

The tax imposed by this subsection shall not apply with respect to articles enumerated in subparagraph (B) which are sold by the manufacturer, producer, or importer after December 31, 1972."

• **1968, Revenue and Expenditure Control Act of 1968 (P.L. 90-364)**

P.L. 90-364, §105(a)(1):

Amended Code Sec. 4061(a)(2)(A). **Effective** 4-30-68. Prior to amendment, Sec. 4061(a)(2)(A) read as follows:

"(2)(A) Articles enumerated in subparagraph (B) are taxable at whichever of the following rates is applicable:

"7 percent for the period beginning with the day after the date of the enactment of the Tax Adjustment Act of 1966 through Apirl 30, 1968.

"2 percent for the period May 1, 1968, through December 31, 1968.

"1 percent for the period after December 31, 1968."

• **1968 (P.L. 90-285)**

P.L. 90-285:

Amended Code Sec. 4061(a)(2)(A) by substituting "April 30, 1968" for "March 31, 1968" and by substituting "May 1, 1968" for "April 1, 1968". **Effective** 3-31-68.

MANUFACTURERS TAXES—GAS GUZZLERS

- **1966, Tax Adjustment Act of 1966 (P.L. 89-368)**

P.L. 89-368, §201(a):

Amended Code Sec. 4061(a)(2)(A). **Effective** with respect to articles sold after 3-15-66, the date of enactment. Prior to amendment, Sec. 4061(a)(2)(A) read as follows:

"(2)(A) Articles enumerated in subparagraph (B) are taxable at whichever of the following rates is applicable:

10 percent for the period ending on the date of the enactment of the Excise Tax Reduction Act of 1965.

7 percent for the period beginning with the day after the date of the enactment of the Excise Tax Reduction Act of 1965 through December 31, 1965.

6 percent for the period January 1, 1966, through December 31, 1966.

4 percent for the period January 1, 1967, through December 31, 1967.

2 percent for the period January 1, 1968, through December 31, 1968.

1 percent for the period after December 31, 1968."

- **1965, Excise Tax Reduction Act of 1965 (P.L. 89-44)**

P.L. 89-44, §201(a):

Amended the last sentence of subsection (a)(1) of Sec. 4061. **Effective** 6-22-65. Prior to the amendment, the last sentence of subsection (a)(1) of Sec. 4061 read as follows:

"A sale of an automobile truck, bus, truck or bus trailer or semitrailer shall, for the purposes of this paragraph, be considered to be a sale of the chassis and of the body."

Amended subsection (a)(2) of Sec. 4061. Prior to the amendment, subsection (a)(2) read as follows:

"(2) Articles taxable at 10 percent except that on and after July 1, 1965, the rate shall be 7 percent—

"Automobile chassis and bodies other than those taxable under paragraph (1).

"Chassis and bodies for trailers and semitrailers (other than house trailers) suitable for use in connection with passenger automobiles.

"A sale of an automobile, trailer, or semitrailer shall, for the purposes of this paragraph, be considered to be a sale of the chassis and of the body."

- **1961, Federal-Aid Highway Act of 1961 (P.L. 87-61)**

P.L. 87-61, §204:

Amended Sec. 4061(a)(1) by substituting "October 1, 1972" for "July 1, 1972". **Effective** 7-1-61.

- **1956 (P.L. 627, 84th Cong.)**

P.L. 627, 84th Cong., 2d Sess., §203:

Amended subsection (a)(1) by substituting "10 percent" for "8 percent" and "July 1, 1972" for "April 1, 1957". **Effective** 7-1-56.

- **1955 (P.L. 379, 84th Cong.)**

P.L. 379, 84th Cong., §[1]:

Amended subsection (a)(2) to delete the word "motorcycles". **Effective** for articles sold on or after 9-1-55.

[Sec. 4061(b)]

(b) PARTS AND ACCESSORIES.—

(1) Except as provided in paragraph (2), there is hereby imposed upon parts or accessories (other than tires and inner tubes) for any of the articles enumerated in subsection (a)(1) sold by the manufacturer, producer, or importer a tax equivalent to 8 percent of the price for which so sold, except that on and after October 1, 1984, the rate shall be 5 percent.

(2) No tax shall be imposed under this subsection upon any part or accessory which is suitable for use (and ordinarily is used) on or in connection with, or as a component part of, any chassis or body for a passenger automobile, any chassis or body for a trailer or semitrailer suitable for use in connection with a passenger automobile, or a house trailer.

Amendments

- **1978, Surface Transportation Assistance Act of 1978 (P.L. 95-599)**

P.L. 95-599, §502(a)(3):

Substituted "1984" for "1979" in Code Sec. 4061(b)(1). **Effective** 11-7-78.

- **1976 (P.L. 94-280)**

P.L. 94-280, §303(a)(3) and (4):

Amended Code Sec. 4061(a)(1) and (b)(1) by substituting "1979" for "1977".

- **1971, Revenue Act of 1971 (P.L. 92-178)**

P.L. 92-178, §401(g)(1):

Amended Code Sec. 4061(b)(2) by substituting "any chassis or body for a passenger automobile, any chassis or body for a trailer or semitrailer suitable for use in connection with a passenger automobile, or a house trailer" for "any article enumerated in subsection (a)(2) or a house trailer". **Effective** as noted under Act Sec. 401(h), below.

P.L. 92-178, §401(b)-(e) and §401(h), provide:

"(b) Floor Stocks Refunds.—

"(1) In general.—Where, before the day after the date of the enactment [December 10, 1971] of this Act, any tax-repealed article (as defined in subsection (e)) has been sold by the manufacturer, producer, or importer and on such day is held by a dealer and has not been used and is intended for sale, there shall be credited or refunded (without interest) to the manufacturer, producer, or importer an amount equal to the tax paid by such manufacturer, producer, or importer on his sale of the article, if—

"(A) claim for such credit or refund is filed with the Secretary of the Treasury or his delegate before the first day of the 10th calendar month beginning after the day after the date of the enactment [December 10, 1971] of this Act based upon a request submitted to the manufacturer, producer, or importer before the first day of the 7th calendar month beginning after the day after the date of the enactment of this Act by the dealer who held the article in respect of which the credit or refund is claimed; and

"(B) on or before the first day of such 10th calendar month reimbursement has been made to the dealer by the manufacturer, producer, or importer in an amount equal to the tax paid on the article or written consent has been obtained from the dealer to allowance of the credit or refund.

"(2) Limitation on eligibility for credit or refund.—No manufacturer, producer, or importer shall be entitled to credit or refund under paragraph (1) unless he has in his possession such evidence of the inventories with respect to which the credit or refund is claimed as may be required by regulations prescribed by the Secretary of the Treasury or his delegate under this subsection.

"(3) Other laws applicable.—All provisions of law, including penalties, applicable with respect to the taxes imposed by sections 4061(a) of the Internal Revenue Code of 1954 shall, insofar as applicable and not inconsistent with paragraphs (1) and (2) of this subsection, apply in respect of the credits and refunds provided for in paragraph (1) to the same extent as if the credits or refunds constituted overpayments of the tax.

"(c) Refunds With Respect to Certain Consumer Purchases.—

"(1) In general.—Except as otherwise provided in paragraph (2), where—

"(A) after August 15, 1971, with respect to any article which was subject to the tax imposed by section 4061(a)(2) of the Internal Revenue Code of 1954 (as in effect on the day before the date of the enactment [December 10, 1971] of this Act), or

"(B) after September 22, 1971, with respect to any article which was subject to the tax imposed by section 4061(a)(1) of such Code (as in effect on the day before the date of the enactment [December 10, 1971] of this Act),

and on or before such date of enactment [December 10, 1971], a tax-repealed article (as defined in subsection (e)) has been sold to an ultimate purchaser, there shall be credited or refunded (without interest) to the manufacturer, producer, or importer of such article an amount equal to the tax paid by such manufacturer, producer, or importer on his sale of the article.

"(2) Limitation on eligibility for credit or refund.—No manufacturer, producer, or importer shall be entitled to a credit or refund under paragraph (1) with respect to an article unless—

"(A) he has in his possession such evidence of the sale of the article to an ultimate purchaser, and of the reimbursement of the tax to such purchaser, as may be required by regulations prescribed by the Secretary of the Treasury or his delegate under this subsection;

"(B) claim for such credit or refund is filed with the Secretary of the Treasury or his delegate before the first day of the 10th calendar month beginning after the date of the enactment [December 10, 1971] of this Act based upon information submitted to the manufacturer, producer, or importer before the first day of the 7th calendar month beginning after the day after the date of the enactment [December 10, 1971] of this Act by the person who sold the article (in respect of which the credit or refund is claimed) to the ultimate purchaser; and

"(C) on or before the first day of such 10th calendar month reimbursement has been made to the ultimate purchaser in an amount equal to the tax paid on the article.

"(3) Other laws applicable.—All provisions of law, including penalties, applicable with respect to the taxes imposed by section 4061(a) of the Internal Revenue Code of 1954 shall, insofar as applicable and not inconsistent with paragraph (1) or (2) of this subsection, apply in respect of the credits and refunds provided for in paragraph (1) to the same extent as if the credits or refunds constituted overpayments of the tax.

"(d) Certain Uses by Manufacturer, Etc.—Any tax paid by reason of section 4218(a) of the Internal Revenue Code of 1954 (relating to use by manufacturer or importer considered sale) shall be deemed an overpayment of such tax with respect to—

"(1) any article which was subject to the tax imposed by section 4061(a)(2) of such Code as in effect on the day before the date of the enactment [December 10, 1971] of this Act if tax was imposed on such article by reason of such section 4218(a) after August 15, 1971, and

"(2) any article which was subject to the tax imposed by section 4061(a)(1) of such Code as in effect on the day before the date of the enactment [December 10, 1971] of this Act and on which such tax is no longer imposed (by reason of subsection (a) of this section) if tax was imposed on such article by reason of such section 4218(a) after September 22, 1971.

"(e) Definitions.—For purposes of this section—

"(1) The term `dealer' includes a wholesaler, jobber, distributor, or retailer.

"(2) An article shall be considered as `held by a dealer' if title thereto has passed to such dealer (whether or not delivery to him has been made) and if for purposes of consumption title to such article or possession thereof has not at any time been transferred to any person other than a dealer.

"(3) The term `tax-repealed article' means an article on which a tax was imposed by section 4061(a) of the Internal Revenue Code of 1954 as in effect on the day before the date of the enactment of this Act and is not imposed (without regard to the amendment made by paragraph (2) of subsection (a) of this section) under such section 4061(a) as in effect on the day after the date of the enactment of this Act.

"(h) Effective Date.—

"(1) Except as otherwise provided in this section, the amendments made by subsections (a), (f), and (g) of this section shall apply with respect to articles sold on or after the day after the date of the enactment [December 10, 1971] of this Act.

"(2) For purposes of paragraph (1), an article shall not be considered sold before the day after the date of the enactment [December 10, 1971] of this Act unless possession or right to possession passes to the purchaser before such day.

"(3) In the case of—

"(A) a lease,

"(B) a contract for the sale of an article where it is provided that the price shall be paid by installments and title to the article sold does not pass until a future date notwithstanding partial payment by installments,

"(C) a conditional sale, or

"(D) a chattel mortgage arrangement wherein it is provided that the sale price shall be paid in installments,

Sec. 4061—Stricken

entered into on or before the date of the enactment [December 10, 1971] of this Act, payments made after such date with respect to the article leased or sold shall, for purposes of this subsection, be considered as payments made with respect to an article sold after such date, if the lessor or vendor establishes that the amount of payments payable after such date with respect to such article has been reduced by an amount equal to that portion of the tax applicable with respect to the lease or sale of such article which is due and payable after such date. If the lessor or vendor does not establish that the payments have been so reduced, they shall be treated as payments made in respect of an article sold before the day after the date of the enactment [December 10, 1971] of this Act."

P.L. 92-178, §401(g)(7)(A):

Repealed Sec. 304 of P.L. 91-614. **Effective** for acts or failures to act after 12-10-71. Prior to repeal, Sec. 304 of P.L. 91-614 read as follows:

"Sec. 304. New Car Labels to Show Rate of Applicable Federal Manufacturers Excise Tax.

"(a) General Rule.—In the case of any new automobile distributed in commerce after March 31, 1971, on the sale of which by the manufacturer, producer, or importer tax was imposed by section 4061(a) of the Internal Revenue Code of 1954, any person required by section 3 of the Automobile Information Disclosure Act (15 U. S. C., sec. 1232) to affix a label to such new automobile shall include in such label a clear, distinct, and legible endorsement stating—

"(1) that Federal excise tax was imposed on such sale, and

"(2) the percentage rate at which such tax was imposed.

"(b) Penalty.—Any person required by subsection (a) of this section to endorse any label who willfully fails to endorse clearly, distinctly, and legibly such label as required by subsection (a), or who makes a false endorsement of such label, shall be fined not more than $1,000. Such failure or false endorsement with respect to each automobile shall constitute a separate offense."

- **1970, Federal-Aid Highway Act of 1970 (P.L. 91-605)**

P.L. 91-605, §303(a)(3), (4):

Amended Code Sec. 4061(a)(1) and (b)(1) by substituting "1977" for "1972."

- **1965, Excise Tax Reduction Act of 1965 (P.L. 89-44)**

P.L. 89-44, §201(b)(1):

Amended Sec. 4061(b). **Effective** 6-22-65. Prior to amendment, Sec. 4061(b) read as follows:

"(b) Parts and Accessories.—There is hereby imposed upon parts or accessories (other than tires and inner tubes and other than automobile radio and television receiving sets) for any of the articles enumerated in subsection (a) sold by the manufacturer, producer, or importer a tax equivalent to 8 percent of the price for which so sold, except that on and after July 1, 1965, the rate shall be 5 percent."

P.L. 89-44, §201(b)(2):

Amended Sec. 4061(b). **Effective** 1-1-66. Prior to amendment, Sec. 4061(b) read as follows:

"(b) Parts and Accessories.—There is hereby imposed upon parts or accessories (other than tires and inner tubes) for any of the articles enumerated in subsection (a) sold by the manufacturer, producer, or importer a tax equivalent to 8 percent of the price for which so sold."

- **1964, Excise Tax Rate Extension Act of 1964 (P.L. 88-348)**

P.L. 88-348, §2(a)(1):

Amended Sec. 4061 by substituting "July 1, 1965" for "July 1, 1964" wherever it appeared.

- **1963, Tax Rate Extension Act of 1963 (P.L. 88-52)**

P.L. 88-52, §3(a)(1):

Amended Sec. 4061 by substituting "July 1, 1964" for "July 1, 1963" wherever it appeared.

- **1962, Tax Rate Extension Act of 1962 (P.L. 87-508)**

P.L. 87-508, §3(a)(1):

Amended Sec. 4061 by substituting "July 1, 1963" for "July 1, 1962" wherever it appeared.

- **1961, Tax Rate Extension Act of 1961 (P.L. 87-72)**

P.L. 87-72, §3(a)(1):

Amended Sec. 4061 by substituting "July 1, 1962" for "July 1, 1961" wherever it appeared.

- **1960, Public Debt and Tax Rate Extension Act of 1960 (P.L. 86-564)**

P.L. 86-564, §202(a):

Amended 1954 Code Sec. 4061 by striking out "1960" wherever it appeared and by substituting "1961".

- **1959, Tax Rate Extension Act of 1959 (P.L. 86-75)**

P.L. 86-75, §3(a):

Amended 1954 Code Sec. 4061 by striking out "1959" wherever it appeared, and by substituting "1960".

- **1958, Tax Rate Extension Act of 1958 (P.L. 85-475)**

P.L. 85-475, §3(a):

Substituted "July 1, 1959" for "July 1, 1958" in Sec. 4061.

- **1957, Tax Rate Extension Act of 1957 (P.L. 85-12)**

P.L. 85-12, §3(a):

Substituted "July 1, 1958" for "April 1, 1957" wherever it appeared in Sec. 4061.

- **1956, Tax Rate Extension Act of 1956 (P.L. 458, 84th Cong.)**

P.L. 458, 84th Cong., 2d Sess., §3(a)(2):

Substituted "1957" for "1956" in Sec. 4061. **Effective** 3-30-55.

- **1955, Tax Rate Extension Act of 1955 (P.L. 18, 84th Cong.)**

P.L. 18, 84th Cong., §3(a)(2):

Substituted "1956" for "1955" wherever it appeared in Sec. 4061. **Effective** 3-30-55.

[Sec. 4061(c)]

(c) TERMINATION.—

(1) TAX ON PARTS AND ACCESSORIES.—On and after the day after the date of the enactment of this subsection, the tax imposed by subsection (b) shall not apply.

(2) TAX ON TRUCKS.—On and after April 1, 1983, the tax imposed by subsection (a) shall not apply.

Amendments

- **1983, Surface Transportation Act of 1982 (P.L. 97-424)**

P.L. 97-424, §512(a)(2):

Added Code Sec. 4061(c). **Effective** 1-7-83.

[Sec. 4062—Stricken]

Amendments

- **1984, Deficit Reduction Act of 1984 (P.L. 98-369)**

P.L. 98-369, §735(a):

Struck out Code Sec. 4062. **Effective** as if included in the provision of the Highway Revenue Act of 1982 to which it relates. Prior to being stricken, Code Sec. 4062 read as follows:

SEC. 4062. ARTICLES CLASSIFIED AS PARTS.

For the purposes of section 4061, spark plugs, storage batteries, leaf springs, coils, timers, and tire chains, which are suitable for use on or in connection with, or as component parts of, any of the articles enumerated in section 4061(a), shall be considered parts or accessories for such articles, whether or not primarily adapted for such use.

- **1971, Revenue Act of 1971 (P.L. 92-178)**

P.L. 92-178, §401(g)(2):

Amended Code Sec. 4062. For **effective** date, see the amendatory note for §401(h) under former Code Sec. 4061(b). Prior to amendment, Code Sec. 4062 read as follows:

"SEC. 4062. DEFINITIONS.

"(a) Certain Articles Considered as Parts.—For the purposes of section 4061, spark plugs, storage batteries, leaf springs, coils, timers, and tire chains, which are suitable for use on or in connection with, or as component parts of, any of the articles enumerated in section 4061(a), shall be considered parts or accessories for such articles, whether or not primarily adapted for such use.

"(b) Ambulances, Hearses, Etc.—For purposes of section 4061(a), a sale of an ambulance, hearse, or combination ambulance-hearse shall be considered to be a sale of an automobile chassis and an automobile body enumerated in subparagraph (B) of section 4061(a)(2)."

- **1966, Foreign Investors Tax Act of 1966 (P.L. 89-809)**

P.L. 89-809, §212(a):

Added Code Sec. 4062(b). **Effective** with respect to articles sold after 11-13-66.

- **1964 (P.L. 88-653)**

P.L. 88-653, §5(b):

Amended Code Sec. 4062 by deleting paragraph (b). **Effective** with respect to articles sold or after the first day of the first calendar quarter which begins after the date of the enactment of this Act. Prior to deletion, paragraph (b) read as follows:

"(b) SALE PRICE OF REBUILT PARTS.—In determining the sale price of a rebuilt automobile part or accessory there shall be excluded from the price, in accordance with regulations prescribed by the Secretary or his delegate, the value of a like part or accessory accepted in exchange."

[Sec. 4063—Stricken]

(1) CAMPER COACHES BODIES FOR SELF-PROPELLED MOBILE HOMES.—The tax imposed under section 4061 shall not apply in the case of articles designed (A) to be mounted or placed on automobile trucks, automobile truck chassis, or automobile chassis, and (B) to be used primarily as living quarters or camping accommodations.

(2) FEED, SEED, AND FERTILIZER EQUIPMENT.—The tax imposed under section 4061 shall not apply in the case of any body, part or accessory primarily designed—

(A) to process or prepare seed, feed, or fertilizer for use on farms;

(B) to haul feed, seed, or fertilizer to and on farms;

(C) to spread feed, seed, or fertilizer on farms;

Amendments

- **1984, Deficit Reduction Act of 1984 (P.L. 98-369)**

P.L. 98-369, §735(a):

Struck out Code Sec. 4063. **Effective** as if included in the provision of the Highway Revenue Act of 1982 to which it relates. Prior to being stricken, Code Sec. 4063 read as follows:

SEC. 4063. EXEMPTIONS.

[Sec. 4063(a)]

(a) SPECIFIED ARTICLES.—

MANUFACTURERS TAXES—GAS GUZZLERS

(D) to load or unload feed, seed, or fertilizer on farms; or

(E) for any combination of the foregoing.

(3) HOUSE TRAILERS.—The tax imposed under section 4061(a) shall not apply in the case of house trailers.

(4) AMBULANCES, HEARSES, ETC.—The tax imposed by section 4061(a) shall not apply in the case of an ambulance, hearse, or combination ambulance-hearse.

(5) CONCRETE MIXERS.—The tax imposed under section 4061 shall not apply in the case of—

(A) any article designed (i) to be placed or mounted on an automobile truck chassis or truck trailer or semitrailer chassis and (ii) to be used to process or prepare concrete, and

(B) parts or accessories designed primarily for use on or in connection with an article described in subparagraph (A).

(6) BUSES.—The tax imposed under section 4061(a) shall not apply in the case of any automobile bus chassis or automobile bus body.

(7) TRASH CONTAINERS, ETC.—The tax imposed under section 4061(a) shall not apply in the case of any box, container, receptacle, bin, or other similar article which is to be used as a trash container and is not designed for the transportation of freight other than trash, and which is not designed to be permanently mounted on or permanently affixed to an automobile truck chassis or body, or in the case of parts or accessories designed primarily for use on, in connection with, or as a component part of any such article.

(8) RAIL TRAILERS AND RAIL VANS.—The tax imposed under section 4061 shall not apply in the case of—

(A) any chassis or body of a trailer or semitrailer which is designed for use both as a highway vehicle and a railroad car, and

(B) any parts or accessories designed primarily for use on or in connection with an article described in subparagraph (A).

For purposes of this paragraph, a piggy-back trailer or semitrailer shall not be treated as designed for use as a railroad car.

Amendments

• **1983, Surface Transportation Act of 1982 (P.L. 97-424)**

P.L. 97-424, § 512(a)(3):

Added Code Sec. 4063. Effective 1-7-83.

• **1982, Tax Equity and Fiscal Responsibility Act of 1982 (P.L. 97-248)**

P.L. 97-248, § 294:

Amended P.L. 95-618, § 231(c)(2)(C) by striking out "the first day of such 10th calendar month" and inserting "December 31, 1982" and amended subparagraph (A) of § 231(c) (2) by inserting before the semicolon ", or, in lieu of evidence of reimbursement, he makes such reimbursement simultaneously with the receipt of such a refund under an arrangement satisfactory to such Secretary which assures such simultaneous reimbursement".

• **1978, Energy Tax Act of 1978 (P.L. 95-618)**

P.L. 95-618, § 231(a):

Amended Code Sec. 4063(a)(6). **Effective** with respect to articles sold after the date of enactment of the Act. Prior to amendment Code Sec. 4063(a)(6) read as follows:

"(6) LOCAL TRANSIT BUSES.—The tax imposed under section 4061(a) shall not apply in the case of automobile bus chassis or automobile bus bodies which are to be used predominately by the purchaser in mass transportation service in urban areas."

P.L. 95-618, § 231(b)-(e), provides:

(b) FLOOR STOCKS REFUNDS.—

(1) IN GENERAL.—Where, before the day after the date of the enactment of this Act, any tax-repealed article (as defined in subsection (e)) has been sold by the manufacturer, producer, or importer and on such day is held by a dealer and has not been used and is intended for sale, there shall be credited or refunded (without interest) to the manufacturer, producer, or importer an amount equal to the tax paid by such manufacturer, producer, or importer on his sale of the article, if—

(A) claim for such credit or refund is filed with the Secretary of the Treasury before the first day of the 10th calendar month beginning after the day after the date of the enactment of this Act based upon a request submitted to the manufacturer, producer, or importer before the first day of the 7th calendar month beginning after the day after the date of the enactment of this Act by the dealer who held the article in respect of which the credit or refunds is claimed; and

(B) on or before the first day of such 10th calendar month reimbursement has been made to the dealer by the manufacturer, producer, or importer in an amount equal to the tax paid on the article or written consent has been obtained from the dealer to allowance of the credit or refund.

(2) LIMITATION ON ELIGIBILITY FOR CREDIT OR REFUND.—No manufacturer, producer, or importer shall be entitled to credit or refund under paragraph (1) unless he has in his possession such evidence of the inventories with respect to which the credit or refund is claimed as may be required by regulations prescribed by the Secretary of the Treasury under this subsection.

(3) OTHER LAWS APPLICABLE.—All provisions of law, including penalties, applicable with respect to the taxes imposed by section 4061(a) of the Internal Revenue Code of 1954 shall, insofar as applicable and not inconsistent with paragraphs (1) and (2) of this subsection, apply in respect of the credits and refunds provided for in paragraph (1) to the same extent as if the credits or refunds constituted overpayments of the tax.

(c) REFUNDS WITH RESPECT TO CERTAIN CONSUMER PURCHASES.—

(1) IN GENERAL.—Except as otherwise provided in paragraph (2), where on or after April 20, 1977, and on or before the date of the enactment of this Act, a tax-repealed article (as defined in subsection (e)) has been sold to an ultimate purchaser, there shall be credited or refunded (without interest) to the manufacturer, producer, or importer of such article an amount equal to the tax paid by such manufacturer, producer, or importer on his sale of the article.

(2) LIMITATION ON ELIGIBILITY FOR CREDIT OR REFUND.—No manufacturer, producer, or importer shall be entitled to a credit or refund under paragraph (1) with respect to an article unless—

(A) he has in his possession such evidence of the sale of the article to an ultimate purchaser, and of the reimbursement of the tax to such purchaser, as may be required by regulations prescribed by the Secretary of the Treasury under this subsection, or, in lieu of evidence of reimbursement, he makes such reimbursement simultaneously with the receipt of such a refund under an arrangement satisfactory to such Secretary which assures such simultaneous reimbursement;

(B) claim for such credit or refund is filed with the Secretary of the Treasury before the first day of the 10th calendar month beginning after the day after the date of the enactment of this Act based upon information submitted to the manufacturer, producer, or importer before the first day of the 7th calendar month beginning after the day after the date of the enactment of this Act by the person who sold the article (in respect of which the credit or refund is claimed) to the ultimate purchaser; and

(C) on or before December 31, 1982 reimbursement has been made to the ultimate purchaser in an amount equal to the tax paid on the article.

(3) OTHER LAWS APPLICABLE.—All provisions of laws, including penalties, applicable with respect to the taxes imposed by section 4061(a) of such Code shall, insofar as applicable and not inconsistent with paragraph (1) or (2) of this subsection, apply with respect to the credits and refunds provided for in paragraph (1) to the same extent as if the credits or refunds constituted overpayment of the tax.

(d) CERTAIN USES BY MANUFACTURER, ETC.—Any tax paid by reason of section 4218(a) of such Code (relating to use by manufacturer or importer considered sale) on any tax-repealed article shall be deemed an overpayment of such tax if the tax was imposed on such article by reason of such section 4218(a) on or after April 20, 1977.

(e) DEFINITIONS.—For purposes of this section—

(1) The term "dealer" includes a wholesaler, jobber, distributor, or retailer.

(2) An article shall be considered as "held by a dealer" if title thereto has passed to such dealer (whether or not delivery to him has been made) and if, for purposes of consumption, title to such article or possession thereof has not at any time been transferred to any person other than a dealer.

(3) The term "tax-repealed article" means an article on which a tax was imposed by section 4061(a) of such Code (as in effect on the day before the date of the enactment of this Act) and which is exempted from such tax by paragraph (6) of section 4063(a) of such Code (as amended by subsection (a) of this section).

• **1971, Revenue Act of 1971 (P.L. 92-178)**

P.L. 92-178, § 401(a)(2):

Added Code Secs. 4063(a)(6) and 4063(a)(7). For **effective** date, see Act Sec. 401(h), under former Code Sec. 4061(b).

P.L. 92-178, § 401(g)(3):

Amended Code Sec. 4063(a)(4). For **effective** date, see Act Sec. 401(h), under former Code Sec. 4061. Prior to amendment, Code Sec. 4063(a)(4) read as follows:

(4) Small 3-wheeled trucks.—The tax imposed under section 4061(a) shall not apply in the case of—

(A) an automobile truck chassis which—

(i) has only 3 wheels,

(ii) is powered by a motor which does not exceed 18 brake horsepower (rated at 4,000 revolutions per minute), and

(iii) does not exceed 1,000 pounds gross weight; or

(B) a body designed primarily to be mounted on a chassis described in subparagraph (A).

• **1970, Excise, Estate, and Gift Tax Adjustment Act of 1970 (P.L. 91-614)**

P.L. 91-614, § 303(a):

Amended Code Sec. 4063(a)(1) by adding "or camping accommodations" at the end thereof. Effective with respect to sales made on or after 12-31-70.

• **1969, Tax Reform Act of 1969 (P.L. 91-172)**

P.L. 91-172, § 931(a):

Added paragraph (a)(5). **Effective** for articles sold after 12-31-69.

• **1965, Excise Tax Reduction Act of 1965 (P.L. 89-44)**

P.L. 89-44, § 801(a):

Amended Sec. 4063(a). **Effective** 6-22-65. Prior to amendment, Sec. 4063(a) read as follows:

(a) Specific Articles Exempt From Tax on Automobiles.—The tax imposed under section 4061(a)(2) shall not apply in the case of house trailers or tractors.

[Sec. 4063(b)]

(b) SALES TO MANUFACTURERS.—Under regulations prescribed by the Secretary, the tax under section 4061 shall not apply in the case of sales of bodies by the manufacturer, producer, or importer to a manufacturer or producer of automobile trucks or other automobiles to be sold by such vendee. For the purposes of section 4061, such vendee shall be considered the manufacturer or producer of such bodies.

Amendments

• **1976, Tax Reform Act of 1976 (P.L. 94-455)**

P.L. 94-455, § 1906(b)(13)(A):

Amended 1954 Code by substituting "Secretary" for "Secretary or his delegate" each place it appeared. Effective 2-1-77.

• **1955 (P.L. 367, 84th Cong.)**

P.L. 367, 84th Cong., 1st Sess., § [1](g):

Amended Code Sec. 4063(b) by deleting the words "or parts or accessories" where they appeared following the word "bodies" in the first sentence, and by deleting the

Sec. 4063—Stricken

MANUFACTURERS TAXES—GAS GUZZLERS

phrase ", or parts or accessories" where the phrase appeared at the end of the second sentence. **Effective** 9-1-55.

[Sec. 4063(c)]

(c) REBUILT PARTS AND ACCESSORIES.—Under regulations prescribed by the Secretary, the tax imposed under section 4061(b) shall not apply in the case of rebuilt parts or accessories.

Amendments

• **1976, Tax Reform Act of 1976 (P.L. 94-455)**

P.L. 94-455, §1906(b)(13)(A):

Amended 1954 Code by substituting "Secretary" for "Secretary or his delegate" each place it appeared. **Effective** 2-1-77.

• **1964 (P.L. 88-653)**

P.L. 88-653, §5(a):

Added Code Sec. 4063(c). **Effective** with respect to articles sold on or after the first day of the first calendar quarter which begins after 10-13-64.

[Sec. 4063(d)]

(d) RESALE AFTER CERTAIN MODIFICATIONS.—Under regulations prescribed by the Secretary, the tax imposed by section 4061 shall not apply to the resale of any article described in section 4061(a)(1) if before such resale such article was merely combined with any coupling device (including any fifth wheel), wrecker crane, loading and unloading equipment (including any crane, hoist, winch, or power liftgate), aerial ladder or tower, snow and ice control equipment, earthmoving, excavation and construction equipment, spreader, sleeper cab, cab shield, or wood or metal floor.

Amendments

• **1976, Tax Reform Act of 1976 (P.L. 94-455)**

P.L. 94-455, §2109(a):

Added Code Sec. 4063(d). **Effective** 10-4-76.

[Sec. 4063(e)]

(e) PARTS FOR LIGHT-DUTY TRUCKS.—The tax imposed by section 4061(b) shall not apply to the sale by the manufacturer, producer, or importer of any article which is to be resold by the purchaser on or in connection with the first retail sale of a light-duty truck, as described in section 4061(a)(2), or which is to be resold by the purchaser to a second purchaser for resale by such second purchaser on or in connection with the first retail sale of a light-duty truck.

Amendments

• **1978, Revenue Act of 1978 (P.L. 95-600)**

P.L. 95-600, §701(ff)(1):

Added Code Sec. 4063(e). **Effective** 12-1-78.

[Sec. 4064]

SEC. 4064. GAS GUZZLER[S] TAX.

[Sec. 4064(a)]

(a) IMPOSITION OF TAX.—There is hereby imposed on the sale by the manufacturer of each automobile a tax determined in accordance with the following table:

If the fuel economy of the model type in which the automobile falls is:	The tax is:
At least 22.5	$ 0
At least 21.5 but less than 22.5	1,000
At least 20.5 but less than 21.5	1,300
At least 19.5 but less than 20.5	1,700
At least 18.5 but less than 19.5	2,100
At least 17.5 but less than 18.5	2,600
At least 16.5 but less than 17.5	3,000
At least 15.5 but less than 16.5	3,700
At least 14.5 but less than 15.5	4,500
At least 13.5 but less than 14.5	5,400
At least 12.5 but less than 13.5	6,400
Less than 12.5	7,700

Amendments

• **1990, Omnibus Budget Reconciliation Act of 1990 (P.L. 101-508)**

P.L. 101-508, §11216(a):

Amended Code Sec. 4064(a). **Effective** for sales after 12-31-90. Prior to amendment, Code Sec. 4064(a) read as follows:

(a) IMPOSITION OF TAX.—There is hereby imposed on the sale by the manufacturer of each automobile a tax determined in accordance with the following tables:

(1) In the case of a 1980 model year automobile:

If the fuel economy of the model type in which the automobile falls is:	The tax is:
At least 15	$ 0
At least 14 but less than 15	200
At least 13 but less than 14	300
Less than 13	550

(2) In the case of a 1981 model year automobile:

If the fuel economy of the model type in which the automobile falls is:	The tax is:
At least 17	$ 0
At least 16 but less than 17	200
At least 15 but less than 16	350
At least 14 but less than 15	450
At least 13 but less than 14	550
Less than 13	650

(3) In the case of a 1982 model year automobile:

If the fuel economy of the model type in which the automobile falls is:	The tax is:
At least 18.5	$ 0
At least 17.5 but less than 18.5	200
At least 16.5 but less than 17.5	350
At least 15.5 but less than 16.5	450
At least 14.5 but less than 15.5	600
At least 13.5 but less than 14.5	750
At least 12.5 but less than 13.5	950
Less than 12.5	1,200

(4) In the case of a 1983 model year automobile:

If the fuel economy of the model type in which the automobile falls is:	The tax is:
At least 19	$ 0
At least 18 but less than 19	350
At least 17 but less than 18	500
At least 16 but less than 17	650
At least 15 but less than 16	800
At least 14 but less than 15	1,000
At least 13 but less than 14	1,250
Less than 13	1,550

(5) In the case of a 1984 model year automobile:

If the fuel economy of the model type in which the automobile falls is:	The tax is:
At least 19.5	$ 0
At least 18.5 but less than 19.5	450
At least 17.5 but less than 18.5	600
At least 16.5 but less than 17.5	750
At least 15.5 but less than 16.5	950
At least 14.5 but less than 15.5	1,150
At least 13.5 but less than 14.5	1,450
At least 12.5 but less than 13.5	1,750
Less than 12.5	2,150

(6) In the case of a 1985 model year automobile:

MANUFACTURERS TAXES—GAS GUZZLERS

If the fuel economy of the model type in which the automobile falls is:	The tax is:
At least 21	$ 0
At least 20 but less than 21	500
At least 19 but less than 20	600
At least 18 but less than 19	800
At least 17 but less than 18	1,000
At least 16 but less than 17	1,200
At least 15 but less than 16	1,500
At least 14 but less than 15	1,800
At least 13 but less than 14	2,200
Less than 13	2,650

(7) In the case of a 1986 or later model year automobile:

If the fuel economy of the model type in which the automobile falls is:	The tax is:
At least 22.5	$ 0
At least 21.5 but less than 22.5	500
At least 20.5 but less than 21.5	650
At least 19.5 but less than 20.5	850
At least 18.5 but less than 19.5	1,050
At least 17.5 but less than 18.5	1,300
At least 16.5 but less than 17.5	1,500
At least 15.5 but less than 16.5	1,850
At least 14.5 but less than 15.5	2,250
At least 13.5 but less than 14.5	2,700
At least 12.5 but less than 13.5	3,200
Less than 12.5	3,850

[Sec. 4064(b)]

(b) DEFINITIONS.—For purposes of this section—

(1) AUTOMOBILE.—

(A) IN GENERAL.—The term "automobile" means any 4-wheeled vehicle propelled by fuel—

(i) which is manufactured primarily for use on public streets, roads, and highways (except any vehicle operated exclusively on a rail or rails), and

(ii) which is rated at 6,000 pounds unloaded gross vehicle weight or less.

(B) EXCEPTION FOR CERTAIN VEHICLES.—The term "automobile" does not include any vehicle which is treated as a non-passenger automobile under the rules which were prescribed by the Secretary of Transportation for purposes of section 32901 of title 49, United States Code, and which were in effect on the date of the enactment of this section.

(C) EXCEPTION FOR EMERGENCY VEHICLES.—The term "automobile" does not include any vehicle sold for use and used—

(i) as an ambulance or combination ambulance-hearse,

(ii) by the United States or by a State or local government for police or other law enforcement purposes, or

(iii) for other emergency uses prescribed by the Secretary by regulations.

(2) FUEL ECONOMY.—The term "fuel economy" means the average number of miles traveled by an automobile per gallon of gasoline (or equivalent amount of other fuel) consumed, as determined by the EPA Administrator in accordance with procedures established under subsection (c).

(3) MODEL TYPE.—The term "model type" means a particular class of automobile as determined by regulation by the EPA Administrator.

(4) MODEL YEAR.—The term "model year", with reference to any specific calendar year, means a manufacturer's annual production period (as determined by the EPA Administrator) which includes January 1 of such calendar year. If a manufacturer has no annual production period, the term "model year" means the calendar year.

(5) MANUFACTURER.—

(A) IN GENERAL.—The term "manufacturer" includes a producer or importer.

(B) LENGTHENING TREATED AS MANUFACTURE.—For purposes of this section, subchapter G of this chapter, and section 6416(b)(3), the lengthening of an automobile by any person shall be treated as the manufacture of an automobile by such person.

(6) EPA ADMINISTRATOR.—The term "EPA Administrator" means the Administrator of the Environmental Protection Agency.

(7) FUEL.—The term "fuel" means gasoline and diesel fuel. The Secretary (after consultation with the Secretary of Transportation) may, by regulation, include any product of petroleum or natural gas within the meaning of such term if he determines that such inclusion is consistent with the need of the Nation to conserve energy.

Amendments

• **2005, Safe, Accountable, Flexible, Efficient Transportation Equity Act: A Legacy for Users (P.L. 109-59)**

P.L. 109-59, §11111(a):

Amended Code Sec. 4064(b)(1)(A) by striking the second sentence. **Effective** 10-1-2005. Prior to being stricken, the second sentence of Code Sec. 4064(b)(1)(A) read as follows:

In the case of a limousine, the preceding sentence shall be applied without regard to clause (ii).

• **1994 (P.L. 103-272)**

P.L. 103-272, §5(g)(1):

Amended Code Sec. 4064(b)(1)(B) by striking "section 501 of the Motor Vehicle Information and Cost Savings Act (15 U.S.C. 2001)" and substituting "section 32901 of title 49, United States Code,". **Effective** 7-5-94.

• **1990, Omnibus Budget Reconciliation Act of 1990 (P.L. 101-508)**

P.L. 101-508, §11216(b):

Amended Code Sec. 4064(b)(1)(A) by adding at the end thereof a new sentence. **Effective** for sales after 12-31-90.

P.L. 101-508, §11216(c):

Amended Code Sec. 4064(b)(5)(B). **Effective** 1-1-91. Prior to amendment, Code Sec. 4064(b)(5)(B) read as follows:

(B) EXCEPTION FOR CERTAIN SMALL MANUFACTURERS.—A person shall not be treated as the manufacturer of any automobile if—

(i) such person would (but for this subparagraph) be so treated solely by reason of lengthening an existing automobile, and

(ii) such person is a small manufacturer (as defined in subsection (d)(4)) for the model year in which such lengthening occurs.

• **1986, Tax Reform Act of 1986 (P.L. 99-514)**

P.L. 99-514, §1812(e)(1)(B)(i):

Amended Code Sec. 4064(b)(1)(A)(ii) by striking out "gross vehicle weight" and inserting in lieu thereof "unloaded gross vehicle weight". **Effective** as indicated in Act Sec. 1812(e)(1)(B)(iii), below.

P.L. 99-514, §1812(e)(1)(B)(ii):

Amended Code Sec. 4064(b)(5). **Effective** as if included in the amendments made by section 201 of P.L. 95-618. But, see Act Sec. 1812(e)(1)(B)(iii), below. Prior to amendment, Code Sec. 4064(b)(5) read as follows:

(5) MANUFACTURER.—The term "manufacturer" includes a producer or importer.

P.L. 99-514, §1812(e)(1)(B)(iii), provides:

(iii) The amendments made by clauses (i) and (ii) shall take effect as if included in the amendments made by section 201 of Public Law 95-618; except that the amendment made by clause (i) shall not apply to any station wagon if—

(I) such station wagon is originally equipped with more than 6 seat belts,

(II) such station wagon was manufactured before November 1, 1985, and

(III) such station wagon is of the 1985 or 1986 model year.

[Sec. 4064(c)]

(c) DETERMINATION OF FUEL ECONOMY.—For purposes of this section—

MANUFACTURERS TAXES—TIRES

(1) IN GENERAL.—Fuel economy for any model type shall be measured in accordance with testing and calculation procedures established by the EPA Administrator by regulation. Procedures so established shall be the procedures utilized by the EPA Administrator for model year 1975 (weighted 55 percent urban cycle, and 45 percent highway cycle), or procedures which yield comparable results. Procedures under this subsection, to the extent practicable, shall require that fuel economy tests be conducted in conjunction with emissions tests conducted under section 206 of the Clean Air Act. The EPA Administrator shall report any measurements of fuel economy to the Secretary.

(2) SPECIAL RULE FOR FUELS OTHER THAN GASOLINE.—The EPA Administrator shall by regulation determine that quantity of any other fuel which is the equivalent of one gallon of gasoline.

(3) TIME BY WHICH REGULATIONS MUST BE ISSUED.—Testing and calculation procedures applicable to a model year, and any amendment to such procedures (other than a technical or clerical amendment), shall be promulgated not less than 12 months before the model year to which such procedures apply.

[Sec. 4064(d)—Stricken]

Amendments

• **1990, Omnibus Budget Reconciliation Act of 1990 (P.L. 101-508)**

P.L. 101-508, §11216(d):

Amended Code Sec. 4064 by striking subsection (d). **Effective** 11-5-90. Prior to being stricken, Code Sec. 4064(d) read as follows:

(d) SPECIAL RULES FOR SMALL MANUFACTURERS.—

(1) IN GENERAL.—If, on the application of a small manufacturer, the Secretary determines that it is not feasible for such manufacturer to meet the tax-free fuel economy level for the model year with respect to all automobiles produced by such manufacturer or with respect to a model type produced by such manufacturer, the Secretary may by regulation prescribe an alternate rate schedule for such model year for all automobiles produced by such manufacturer or for such model type, as the case may be. The alternate rate schedule shall be based on the maximum feasible fuel economy level which such manufacturer can meet for such model year with respect to all automobiles or with respect to such model type, as the case may be.

(2) APPLICATION TO INCLUDE NECESSARY INFORMATION.—An application under this subsection for any model year shall contain such information as the Secretary may by regulations prescribe.

(3) DETERMINATIONS TO BE MADE ONLY AFTER CONSULTATION.—Determinations under paragraph (1) shall be made by the Secretary only after consultation with the Secretary of Energy, the Secretary of Transportation, and other appropriate Federal officers.

(4) SMALL MANUFACTURER DEFINED.—

(A) IN GENERAL.—For purposes of this subsection, the term "small manufacturer" means any manufacturer—

(i) who manufactured (whether or not in the United States) fewer than 10,000 automobiles in the second model year preceding the model year for which the determination under paragraph (1) is being made, and

(ii) who can reasonably be expected to manufacture (whether or not in the United States) fewer than 10,000 automobiles in the model year for which the determination under paragraph (1) is being made.

(B) SPECIAL RULES.—For purposes of subparagraph (A)—

(i) MANUFACTURER OF AUTOMOBILES PRODUCED ABROAD DETERMINED WITHOUT REGARD TO IMPORTATION.—The meaning of the term "manufacturer" shall be determined without regard to subsection (b)(5).

(ii) CONTROLLED GROUPS.—Persons who are members of the same controlled group of corporations shall be treated as one manufacturer. For purposes of the preceding sentence, the term "controlled group of corporations" has the meaning given to such term by section 1563(a); except that "more than 50 percent" shall be substituted for "at least 80 percent" each place it appears in section 1563(a).

• **1978, Energy Tax Act of 1978 (P.L. 95-618)**

P.L. 95-618, §201(a):

Added Code Sec. 4064. **Effective** with respect to 1980 and later model year automobiles (as defined in section 4064(b)).

PART II—TIRES

Sec. 4071. Imposition of tax.
Sec. 4072. Definitions.
Sec. 4073. Exemptions.

[Sec. 4071]

SEC. 4071. IMPOSITION OF TAX.

[Sec. 4071(a)]

(a) IMPOSITION AND RATE OF TAX.—There is hereby imposed on taxable tires sold by the manufacturer, producer, or importer thereof a tax at the rate of 9.45 cents (4.725 cents in the case of a biasply tire or super single tire) for each 10 pounds so much of the maximum rated load capacity thereof as exceeds 3,500 pounds.

Amendments

• **2004, American Jobs Creation Act of 2004 (P.L. 108-357)**

P.L. 108-357, §869(a):

Amended Code Sec. 4071(a). **Effective** for sales in calendar years beginning more than 30 days after 10-22-2004. Prior to amendment, Code Sec. 4071(a) read as follows:

(a) IMPOSITION AND RATE OF TAX.—There is hereby imposed on tires of the type used on highway vehicles, if wholly or in part made of rubber, sold by the manufacturer, producer, or importer a tax at the following rates:

If the tire weighs:	The rate of tax is:
Not more than 40 lbs.	No tax.
More than 40 lbs. but not more than 70 lbs.	15 cents per lb. in excess of 40 lbs.
More than 70 lbs. but not more than 90 lbs.	$4.50 plus 30 cents per lb. in excess of 70 lbs.
More than 90 lbs.	$10.50 plus 50 cents per lb. in excess of 90 lbs.

• **1983, Surface Transportation Act of 1982 (P.L. 97-424)**

P.L. 97-424, §514(a):

Amended Code Sec. 4071(a). **Effective** for articles sold on or after 1-1-84. Prior to amendment, Code Sec. 4071(a) read as follows:

(a) IMPOSITION AND RATE OF TAX.—There is hereby imposed upon the following articles, if wholly or in part of rubber, sold by the manufacturer, producer, or importer, a tax at the following rates:

(1) Tires of the type used on highway vehicles, 9.75 cents a pound.

(2) Other tires (other than laminated tires to which paragraph (5) applies), 4.875 cents a pound.

(3) Inner tubes for tires, 10 cents a pound.

(4) Tread rubber, 5 cents a pound.

(5) Laminated tires (not of the type used on highway vehicles) which consist wholly of scrap rubber from used tire casings with an internal metal fastening agent, 1 cent a pound.

P.L. 97-424, §§521(b) and (d)(2), provides:

SEC. 521. FLOOR STOCKS TAXES.

* * *

(b) 1984 TAX ON TIRES.—On any article which would be subject to tax under section 4071(a) if sold by the manufacturer, producer, or importer on or after January 1, 1984, which on January 1, 1984, is held by a dealer and has not been used and is intended for sale, there shall be imposed a floor stocks tax equal to the excess of the amount of tax which would be imposed on such article if it were sold by the manufacturer, producer, or importer after January 1, 1984, over the amount of tax imposed under section 4071(a) on the sale of such article by the manufacturer, producer, or importer.

* * *

(d) DUE DATE OF TAXES.—The taxes imposed by this section shall be paid at such time after—

* * *

(2) February 15, 1984, in the case of the tax imposed by subsection (b),

as may be prescribed by the Secretary of the Treasury or his delegate.

* * *

For additional floor stock provisions relating to the overpayment of floor stocks taxes, the transfer of such taxes to the Highway Trust Fund, floor stock refunds, and definitions and special rules, see the amendment notes for Act Sec. 521(c) following Code Sec. 6416 and for Act Secs. 521(e), 522 and 523 following Code Sec. 6412.

• **1980 (P.L. 96-596)**

P.L. 96-596, §4(a):

Amended Code Sec. 4071(a)(1) by striking out "10 cents" and inserting in lieu thereof "9.75 cents" and amended Code Sec. 4071(a)(2) by striking out "5 cents" and inserting in lieu thereof "4.875 cents". **Effective** 1-1-81.

P.L. 96-596, §4(b), provides:

(b) DETERMINATION OF OVERPAYMENT.—

(1) IN GENERAL.—The determination of the extent to which any overpayment of tax imposed by section 4071(a)(1) or (2) or section 4071(b) has arisen by reason of an adjustment of a tire after the original sale pursuant to a warranty or guarantee, and

MANUFACTURERS TAXES—TIRES

the allowance of a credit or refund of any such overpayment, shall be determined in accordance with the principles set forth in regulations and rulings relating thereto to the extent in effect on March 31, 1978.

This provision is effective with respect to adjustments of tires after 3-31-78, and prior to 1-1-83.

- **1961, Federal-Aid Highway Act of 1961 (P.L. 87-61)**

P.L. 87-61, § 202(a):

Amended Sec. 4071(a)(1) by substituting "10 cents" for "8 cents." **Effective** 7-1-61.

P.L. 87-61, § 202(b):

Amended Sec. 4071(a)(3) by substituting "10 cents" for "9 cents." **Effective** 7-1-61.

P.L. 87-61, § 202(c):

Amended Sec. 4071(a)(4) by substituting "5 cents" for "3 cents." **Effective** 7-1-61.

- **1960 (P.L. 86-440)**

P.L. 86-440, § [1](a):

Amended Code Sec. 4071(a) by adding the phrase "(other than laminated tires to which paragraph (5) applies)" to paragraph (2) and by adding a new paragraph (5). **Effective** 6-1-60.

[Sec. 4071(b)]

(b) SPECIAL RULE FOR MANUFACTURERS WHO SELL AT RETAIL.—Under regulations prescribed by the Secretary, if the manufacturer, producer, or importer of any tire delivers such tire to a retail store or retail outlet of such manufacturer, producer, or importer, he shall be liable for tax under subsection (a) in respect of such tire in the same manner as if it had been sold at the time it was delivered to such retail store or outlet. This subsection shall not apply to an article in respect to which tax has been imposed by subsection (a). Subsection (a) shall not apply to an article in respect of which tax has been imposed by this subsection.

Amendments

- **1984, Deficit Reduction Act of 1984 (P.L. 98-369)**

P.L. 98-369, § 735(c)(2)(A):

Amended Code Sec. 4071(b) by striking out "or inner tube" and by striking out "or tube" each place it appeared. **Effective** as if included in the provisions of the Highway Revenue Act of 1982 to which it relates. Prior to amendment, subsection (b) read as follows:

(b) SPECIAL RULE FOR MANUFACTURERS WHO SELL AT RETAIL.—Under regulations prescribed by the Secretary, if the manufacturer, producer, or importer of any tire or inner tube delivers such tire or tube to a retail store or retail outlet of such manufacturer, producer, or importer, he shall be liable for tax under subsection (a) in respect of such tire or tube in the same manner as if it had been sold at the time it was delivered to such retail store or outlet. This subsection shall not apply to an article in respect to which tax has been imposed by subsection (a). Subsection (a) shall not apply to an article in respect of which tax has been imposed by this subsection.

- **1976, Tax Reform Act of 1976 (P.L. 94-455)**

P.L. 94-455, § 1906(b)(13)(A):

Amended 1954 Code by substituting "Secretary" for "Secretary or his delegate" each place it appeared. **Effective** 2-1-77.

- **1966 (P.L. 89-523)**

P.L. 89-523, § [1](a):

Redesignated Code Sec. 4071(b) and (c) as (c) and (d), and added new Code Sec. 4071(b). **Effective** on the first day of the first calendar quarter which begins more than 20 days after the date of enactment, 8-1-66.

[Sec. 4071(c)]

(c) TIRES ON IMPORTED ARTICLES.—For the purposes of subsection (a), if an article imported into the United States is equipped with tires—

(1) the importer of the article shall be treated as the importer of the tires with which such article is equipped, and

(2) the sale of the article by the importer thereof shall be treated as the sale of the tires with which such article is equipped.

This subsection shall not apply with respect to the sale of an automobile bus chassis or an automobile bus body.

Amendments

- **2004, American Jobs Creation Act of 2004 (P.L. 108-357)**

P.L. 108-357, § 869(d)(1)[(e)(1)]:

Amended Code Sec. 4071 by striking subsection (c) and by moving subsection (e) after subsection (b) and redesignating subsection (e) as subsection (c). **Effective** for sales in calendar years beginning more than 30 days after 10-22-2004.

- **1984, Deficit Reduction Act of 1984 (P.L. 98-369)**

P.L. 98-369, § 735(c)(2)(C):

Amended Code Sec. 4071(e) by striking out "or inner tubes (other than bicycle tires and inner tubes)", by striking out "and inner tubes" in paragraphs (1) and (2), and by striking out the last sentence and inserting in lieu thereof a new sentence. **Effective** as if included in the provisions of the Highway Revenue Act of 1982 to which it relates. Prior to amendment, subsection (e) read as follows:

(e) Tires on Imported Articles.—For the purposes of subsection (a), if an article imported into the United States is equipped with tires or inner tubes (other than bicycle tires and inner tubes)—

(1) the importer of the article shall be treated as the importer of the tires and inner tubes with which such article is equipped, and

(2) the sale of the article by the importer thereof shall be treated as the sale of the tires and inner tubes with which such article is equipped.

This subsection shall not apply with respect to the sale of an article if a tax on such sale is imposed under section 4061 or if such article is an automobile bus chassis or an automobile bus body.

- **1980, Technical Corrections Act of 1979 (P.L. 96-222)**

P.L. 96-222, § 108(c)(3)(C):

Amended Code Sec. 4071(e) by changing "under section 4061" to "under section 4061 or if such article is an automobile bus chassis or an automobile bus body". **Effective** with respect to articles sold after 11-9-78.

- **1971, Revenue Act of 1971 (P.L. 92-178)**

P.L. 92-178, § 401(f):

Added Code Sec. 4071(e). For **effective** date, see Act Sec. 401(h) under Code Sec. 4061(b).

[Sec. 4071(c)—Stricken]

(c) Determination of Weight.—For purposes of this section, weight shall be based on total weight, except that in the case of tires such total weight shall be exclusive of metal rims or rim bases. Total weight of the articles shall be determined under regulations prescribed by the Secretary.

Amendments

- **2004, American Jobs Creation Act of 2004 (P.L. 108-357)**

P.L. 108-357, § 869(d)(1)[(e)(1)]:

Amended Code Sec. 4071 by striking subsection (c) and by moving subsection (e) after subsection (b) and redesignating subsection (e) as subsection (c). **Effective** for sales in calendar years beginning more than 30 days after 10-22-2004. Prior to being stricken, Code Sec. 4071(c) read as follows:

(c) DETERMINATION OF WEIGHT.—For purposes of this section, weight shall be based on total weight exclusive of metal rims or rim bases. Total weight of the articles shall be determined under regulations prescribed by the Secretary.

- **1984, Deficit Reduction Act of 1984 (P.L. 98-369)**

P.L. 98-369, § 735(c)(2)(B):

Amended Code Sec. 4071(c) by striking out "on total weight," and all that followed and inserting in lieu thereof "on total weight exclusive of metal rims or rim bases." **Effective** as if included in the provisions of the Highway Revenue Act of 1982 to which it relates. Prior to amendment, subsection (c) read as follows:

- **1976, Tax Reform Act of 1976 (P.L. 94-455)**

P.L. 94-455, § 1906(b)(13)(A):

Amended 1954 Code by substituting "Secretary" for "Secretary or his delegate" each place it appeared. **Effective** 2-1-77.

- **1966 (P.L. 89-523)**

P.L. 89-523, § [1](a):

Redesignated Code Sec. 4071(b) as 4071(c). **Effective** on the first day of the first calendar quarter which begins more than 20 days after 8-1-66.

[Sec. 4071(d)]

(d) TERMINATION.—On and after October 1, 2028, the taxes imposed by subsection (a) shall not apply.

Amendments

- **2021, Infrastructure Investment and Jobs Act (P.L. 117-58)**

P.L. 117-58, § 80102(a)(2)(C), Div. H:

Amended Code Sec. 4071(d) by striking "October 1, 2022" and inserting "October 1, 2028". **Effective** 10-1-2021.

- **2015, Fixing America's Surface Transportation Act (P.L. 114-94)**

P.L. 114-94, § 31102(a)(2)(C):

Amended Code Sec. 4071(d) by striking "October 1, 2016" and inserting "October 1, 2022". **Effective** 10-1-2016.

MANUFACTURERS TAXES—TIRES

• **2012, Highway Investment, Job Creation, and Economic Growth Act of 2012 (P.L. 112-141)**

P.L. 112-141, §40102(a)(2)(C):

Amended Code Sec. 4071(d) by striking "July 1, 2012" and inserting "October 1, 2016". **Effective** 7-1-2012.

• **2012, Temporary Surface Transportation Extension Act of 2012 (P.L. 112-140)**

P.L. 112-140, §1(c), provides:

(c) SPECIAL RULE FOR EXECUTION OF AMENDMENTS IN MAP–21.—On the date of enactment of the MAP–21 [P.L. 112-141]—

(1) this Act and the amendments made by this Act shall cease to be effective;

(2) the text of the laws amended by this Act shall revert back so as to read as the text read on the day before the date of enactment of this Act; and

(3) the amendments made by the MAP–21 shall be executed as if this Act had not been enacted.

P.L. 112-140, §402(a)(2)(C):

Amended Code Sec. 4071(d) by striking "July 1, 2012" and inserting "July 7, 2012". **Effective** 7-1-2012. For a special rule, see Act Sec. 1(c), above.

• **2012, Surface Transportation Extension Act of 2012 (P.L. 112-102)**

P.L. 112-102, §402(a)(2)(C):

Amended Code Sec. 4071(d) by striking "April 1, 2012" and inserting "July 1, 2012". **Effective** 4-1-2012.

• **2011, Surface Transportation Extension Act of 2011, Part II (P.L. 112-30)**

P.L. 112-30, §142(a)(2)(B):

Amended Code Sec. 4071(d) by striking "October 1, 2011" and inserting "April 1, 2012". **Effective** 10-1-2011.

• **2005, Safe, Accountable, Flexible, Efficient Transportation Equity Act: A Legacy for Users (P.L. 109-59)**

P.L. 109-59, §11101(a)(1)(E):

Amended Code Sec. 4071(d) by striking "2005" and inserting "2011". **Effective** 8-10-2005.

• **1998, Transportation Equity Act for the 21st Century (P.L. 105-178)**

P.L. 105-178, §9002(a)(1)(E):

Amended Code Sec. 4071(d) by striking "1999" and inserting "2005". **Effective** 6-9-98.

• **1991, Intermodal Surface Transportation Efficiency Act of 1991 (P.L. 102-240)**

P.L. 102-240, §8002(a)(2):

Amended Code Sec. 4071(d) by striking "1995" each place it appears and inserting "1999". **Effective** 12-18-91.

• **1990, Omnibus Budget Reconciliation Act of 1990 (P.L. 101-508)**

P.L. 101-508, §11211(c)(2):

Amended Code Sec. 4071(d) by striking "1993" each place it appears and inserting "1995". **Effective** 11-5-90.

• **1987, Surface Transportation and Uniform Relocation Assistance Act of 1987 (P.L. 100-17)**

P.L. 100-17, §502(a)(3):

Amended Code Sec. 4071(d) by striking out "1988" and inserting in lieu thereof "1993". **Effective** 4-2-87.

Amendments

• **1984, Deficit Reduction Act of 1984 (P.L. 98-369)**

P.L. 98-369, §735(c)(2)(D):

Amended Code Sec. 4071 by repealing subsection (f). **Effective** as if included in the provisions of the Highway Revenue Act of 1982 to which it relates. Prior to amendment, subsection (f) read as follows:

(f) IMPORTED RECAPPED OR RETREADED UNITED STATES TIRES.—

(1) IN GENERAL.—For purposes of subsection (a)(4), in the case of a tire which has been exported from the United States, recapped or retreaded (other than from bead to bead) outside the United States, and imported into the United States—

(A) the person importing such tire shall be treated as importing the tread rubber used in such recapping or retreading (determined as of the completion of the recapping or retreading), and

• **1983, Surface Transportation Act of 1982 (P.L. 97-424)**

P.L. 97-424, §516(a)(2):

Amended Code Sec. 4071(d). **Effective** 1-6-83. Prior to amendment, Code Sec. 4071(d) read as follows:

"(d) RATE REDUCTION.—On and after October 1, 1984—

(1) the tax imposed by paragraph (1) of subsection (a) shall be 4.875 cents a pound;

(2) the tax imposed by paragraph (3) of subsection (a) shall be 9 cents a pound; and

(3) paragraph (4) of subsection (a) shall not apply."

• **1980 (P.L. 96-596)**

P.L. 96-596, §4(a):

Amended Code Sec. 4071(d)(1) by striking out "5 cents" and inserting "4.875 cents". **Effective** 1-1-81.

• **1978, Surface Transportation Assistance Act of 1978 (P.L. 95-599)**

P.L. 95-599, §502(a)(4):

Substituted "1984" for "1979" in Code Sec. 4071(d). **Effective** 11-7-78.

• **1976 (P.L. 94-280)**

P.L. 94-280, §303(a)(5):

Amended Code Sec. 4071(d) by substituting "1979" for "1977".

• **1970, Federal-Aid Highway Act of 1970 (P.L. 91-605)**

P.L. 91-605, §303(a)(5):

Amended Code Sec. 4071(d) by substituting "1977" for "1972."

• **1966 (P.L. 89-523)**

P.L. 89-523, §[1](a):

Redesignated Code Sec. 4071(c) as 4071(d). **Effective** on the first day of the first calendar quarter which begins more than 20 days after 8-1-66.

• **1961, Federal-Aid Highway Act of 1961 (P.L. 87-61)**

P.L. 87-61, §202(d):

Amended Sec. 4071(c). **Effective** 7-1-61. Prior to amendment, Sec. 4071(c) read:

"(c) Rate Reduction.—On and after July 1, 1972—

"(1) the tax imposed by paragraph (1) of subsection (a) shall be 5 cents a pound; and

"(2) paragraph (4) of subsection (a) shall not apply."

• **1956 (P.L. 627, 84th Cong.)**

P.L. 627, 84th Cong., §204(a):

Amended Sec. 4071. **Effective** 7-1-56. Prior to amendment Section 4071 read as follows:

"There is hereby imposed upon the following articles sold by the manufacturer, producer, or importer a tax at the following rates:

"(1) Tires wholly or in part of rubber, 5 cents a pound on total weight (exclusive of metal rims or rim bases);

"(2) Inner tubes (for tires) wholly or in part of rubber, 9 cents a pound on total weight.

The total weight of the foregoing articles is to be determined under regulations prescribed by the Secretary or his delegate."

[Sec. 4071(f)—Repealed]

(B) the sale of such tire by the importer thereof shall be treated as the sale of such tread rubber.

(2) EXCEPTION FOR CERTAIN TAXABLE SALES.—Paragraph (1) shall not apply with respect to the sale of any tire if such tire is sold on or in connection with the sale of an article on which tax is imposed under section 4061.

• **1980 (P.L. 96-598)**

P.L. 96-598, §1(d):

Amended Code Sec. 4071 by adding at the end thereof subsection (f). **Effective** 2-1-80.

[Sec. 4072]

SEC. 4072. DEFINITIONS.

[Sec. 4072(a)]

(a) TAXABLE TIRE.—For purposes of this chapter, the term "taxable tire" means any tire of the type used on highway vehicles if wholly or in part made of rubber and if marked pursuant to Federal regulations for highway use.

Amendments

• **2004, American Jobs Creation Act of 2004 (P.L. 108-357)**

P.L. 108-357, §869(b)[(c)]:

Amended Code Sec. 4072, as amended by Act Sec. 869(a) [Act Sec. 869(b)], by redesignating subsections (a), (b), (c), and (d) as subsections (b), (c), (d), and (e), respectively, and by inserting before subsection (b) (as so redesignated) a new subsection (a). **Effective** for sales in calendar years beginning more than 30 days after 10-22-2004.

MANUFACTURERS TAXES—TIRES

[Sec. 4072(b)]

(b) RUBBER.—For purposes of this chapter, the term "rubber" includes synthetic and substitute rubber.

Amendments

• **2004, American Jobs Creation Act of 2004 (P.L. 108-357)**

P.L. 108-357, § 869(b)[(c)]:

Amended Code Sec. 4072 by redesignating subsection (a) as subsection (b). **Effective** for sales in calendar years beginning more than 30 days after 10-22-2004.

[Sec. 4072(c)]

(c) TIRES OF THE TYPE USED ON HIGHWAY VEHICLES.—For purposes of this part, the term "tires of the type used on highway vehicles" means tires of the type used on—

(1) motor vehicles which are highway vehicles, or

(2) vehicles of the type used in connection with motor vehicles which are highway vehicles.

Such term shall not include tires of a type used exclusively on vehicles described in section 4053(8).

Amendments

• **2004, American Jobs Creation Act of 2004 (P.L. 108-357)**

P.L. 108-357, § 851(c)(1):

Amended Code Sec. 4072(b)(2) by adding at the end a flush sentence. **Effective** on the day after 10-22-2004.

P.L. 108-357, § 869(b)[(c)]:

Amended Code Sec. 4072 by redesignating subsection (b) as subsection (c). **Effective** for sales in calendar years beginning more than 30 days after 10-22-2004.

• **1984, Deficit Reduction Act of 1984 (P.L. 98-369)**

P.L. 98-369, § 735(c)(3):

Amended Code Sec. 4072 by striking out subsection (b) and redesignating subsection (c) as subsection (b). **Effective** as if included in the provisions of the Highway Revenue Act of 1982 to which it relates. Prior to amendment, subsection (b) read as follows:

(b) Tread Rubber.—For purposes of this chapter, the term "tread rubber" means any material—

(1) which is commonly or commercially known as tread rubber or camelback; or

(2) which is a substitute for a material described in paragraph (1) and is of a type used in recapping or retreading tires.

• **1956 (P.L. 627, 84th Cong.)**

P.L. 627, 84th Cong., § 204(b):

Amended Sec. 4072. **Effective** 7-1-56. Prior to amendment, Section 4072 read as follows:

SEC. 4072. DEFINITION OF RUBBER.

For the purposes of this chapter, the term "rubber" includes synthetic and substitute rubber.

[Sec. 4072(d)]

(d) BIASPLY.—For purposes of this part, the term "biasply tire" means a pneumatic tire on which the ply cords that extend to the beads are laid at alternate angles substantially less than 90 degrees to the centerline of the tread.

Amendments

• **2004, American Jobs Creation Act of 2004 (P.L. 108-357)**

P.L. 108-357, § 869(b):

Amended Code Sec. 4072 by adding at the end a new subsection (c). **Effective** for sales in calendar years beginning more than 30 days after 10-22-2004.

P.L. 108-357, § 869(b)[(c)]:

Amended Code Sec. 4072, as amended by Act Sec. 869(a) [Act Sec. 869(b)], by redesignating subsection (c) as subsection (d). **Effective** for sales in calendar years beginning more than 30 days after 10-22-2004.

[Sec. 4072(e)]

(e) SUPER SINGLE TIRE.—For purposes of this part, the term "super single tire" means a single tire greater than 13 inches in cross section width designed to replace 2 tires in a dual fitment. Such term shall not include any tire designed for steering.

Amendments

• **2005, Energy Tax Incentives Act of 2005 (P.L. 109-58)**

P.L. 109-58, § 1364(a):

Amended Code Sec. 4072(e) by adding at the end a new sentence. **Effective** as if included in section 869 of P.L. 108-357 [effective for sales in calendar years beginning more than 30 days after 10-22-2004.—CCH].

• **2004, American Jobs Creation Act of 2004 (P.L. 108-357)**

P.L. 108-357, § 869(b):

Amended Code Sec. 4072 by adding at the end a new subsection (d). **Effective** for sales in calendar years beginning more than 30 days after 10-22-2004.

P.L. 108-357, § 869(b)[(c)]:

Amended Code Sec. 4072, as amended by Act Sec. 869(a) [Act Sec. 869(b)], by redesignating subsection (d) as subsection (e). **Effective** for sales in calendar years beginning more than 30 days after 10-22-2004.

[Sec. 4073]

SEC. 4073. EXEMPTIONS.

The tax imposed by section 4071 shall not apply to tires sold for the exclusive use of the Department of Defense or the Coast Guard.

Amendments

• **2004, American Jobs Creation Act of 2004 (P.L. 108-357)**

P.L. 108-357, § 869(c)[(d)]:

Amended Code Sec. 4073. **Effective** for sales in calendar years beginning more than 30 days after 10-22-2004. Prior to amendment, Code Sec. 4073 read as follows:

SEC. 4073. EXEMPTION FOR TIRES WITH INTERNAL WIRE FASTENING.

The tax imposed by section 4071 shall not apply to tires of extruded tiring with an internal wire fastening agent.

Amendments

• **1984, Deficit Reduction Act of 1984 (P.L. 98-369)**

P.L. 98-369, § 735(c)(4):

Amended Code Sec. 4073. **Effective** as if included in the provisions of the Highway Revenue Act of 1982 to which it relates. Prior to amendment, it read as follows:

SEC. 4073. EXEMPTIONS.

(a) TIRES OF CERTAIN SIZES.—The tax imposed by section 4071 shall not apply to tires which are not more than 20 inches in diameter and not more than 1 3/4 inches in cross section, if such tires are of all-rubber construction (whether hollow center or solid) without fabric or metal reinforcement.

(b) TIRES WITH INTERNAL WIRE FASTENING.—The tax imposed by section 4071 shall not apply to tires of extruded tiring with an internal wire fastening agent.

(c) EXEMPTION FROM TAX ON TREAD RUBBER IN CERTAIN CASES.—Under regulations prescribed by the Secretary, the tax imposed by section 4071(a)(4) shall not apply to tread rubber sold by the manufacturer, producer, or importer, to any person for use by such person otherwise than in the recapping or retreading of tires of the type used on highway vehicles.

• **1976, Tax Reform Act of 1976 (P.L. 94-455)**

P.L. 94-455, § 1906(b)(13)(A):

Amended 1954 Code by substituting "Secretary" for "Secretary or his delegate" each place it appeared. **Effective** 2-1-77.

• **1956 (P.L. 627, 84th Cong.)**

P.L. 627, 84th Cong., 2d Sess., § 204(c):

Amended Sec. 4073 by the adding subsection (c). **Effective** 7-1-56.

MANUFACTURERS TAXES—MOTOR AND AVIATION FUELS

PART III—PETROLEUM PRODUCTS

Subpart A.   Motor and aviation fuels.
Subpart B.   Special provisions applicable to fuels tax.

Subpart A—Motor and Aviation Fuels

Sec. 4081.   Imposition of tax.
Sec. 4082.   Exemptions for diesel fuel and kerosene.
Sec. 4083.   Definitions; special rule; administrative authority.
Sec. 4084.   Cross references.

[Sec. 4081]

SEC. 4081. IMPOSITION OF TAX.

[Sec. 4081(a)]

(a) TAX IMPOSED.—

(1) TAX ON REMOVAL, ENTRY, OR SALE.—

(A) IN GENERAL.—There is hereby imposed a tax at the rate specified in paragraph (2) on—

(i) the removal of a taxable fuel from any refinery,

(ii) the removal of a taxable fuel from any terminal,

(iii) the entry into the United States of any taxable fuel for consumption, use, or warehousing, and

(iv) the sale of a taxable fuel to any person who is not registered under section 4101 unless there was a prior taxable removal or entry of such fuel under clause (i), (ii), or (iii).

(B) EXEMPTION FOR BULK TRANSFERS TO REGISTERED TERMINALS OR REFINERIES.—

(i) IN GENERAL.—The tax imposed by this paragraph shall not apply to any removal or entry of a taxable fuel transferred in bulk by pipeline or vessel to a terminal or refinery if the person removing or entering the taxable fuel, the operator of such pipeline or vessel (except as provided in clause (ii)), and the operator of such terminal or refinery are registered under section 4101.

(ii) NONAPPLICATION OF REGISTRATION TO VESSEL OPERATORS ENTERING BY DEEP-DRAFT VESSEL.—For purposes of clause (i), a vessel operator is not required to be registered with respect to the entry of a taxable fuel transferred in bulk by a vessel described in section 4042(c)(1).

(2) RATES OF TAX.—

(A) IN GENERAL.—The rate of the tax imposed by this section is—

(i) in the case of gasoline other than aviation gasoline, 18.3 cents per gallon,

(ii) in the case of aviation gasoline, 19.3 cents per gallon, and

(iii) in the case of diesel fuel or kerosene, 24.3 cents per gallon.

(B) LEAKING UNDERGROUND STORAGE TANK TRUST FUND TAX.—The rates of tax specified in subparagraph (A) shall each be increased by 0.1 cent per gallon. The increase in tax under this subparagraph shall in this title be referred to as the Leaking Underground Storage Tank Trust Fund financing rate.

(C) TAXES IMPOSED ON FUEL USED IN AVIATION.—In the case of kerosene which is removed from any refinery or terminal directly into the fuel tank of an aircraft for use in aviation, the rate of tax under subparagraph (A)(iii) shall be—

(i) in the case of use for commercial aviation by a person registered for such use under section 4101, 4.3 cents per gallon, and

(ii) in the case of use for aviation not described in clause (i), 21.8 cents per gallon.

(D) DIESEL-WATER FUEL EMULSION.—In the case of diesel-water fuel emulsion at least 14 percent of which is water and with respect to which the emulsion additive is registered by a United States manufacturer with the Environmental Protection Agency pursuant to section 211 of the Clean Air Act (as in effect on March 31, 2003), subparagraph (A)(iii) shall be applied by substituting "19.7 cents" for "24.3 cents". The preceding sentence shall not apply to the removal, sale, or use of diesel-water fuel emulsion unless the person so removing, selling, or using such fuel is registered under section 4101.

(3) CERTAIN REFUELER TRUCKS, TANKERS, AND TANK WAGONS TREATED AS TERMINAL.—

(A) IN GENERAL.—For purposes of paragraph (2)(C), a refueler truck, tanker, or tank wagon shall be treated as part of a terminal if—

(i) such terminal is located within an airport,

(ii) any kerosene which is loaded in such truck, tanker, or wagon at such terminal is for delivery only into aircraft at the airport in which such terminal is located,

(iii) such truck, tanker, or wagon meets the requirements of subparagraph (B) with respect to such terminal, and

(iv) except in the case of exigent circumstances identified by the Secretary in regulations, no vehicle registered for highway use is loaded with kerosene at such terminal.

(B) REQUIREMENTS.—A refueler truck, tanker, or tank wagon meets the requirements of this subparagraph with respect to a terminal if such truck, tanker, or wagon—

(i) has storage tanks, hose, and coupling equipment designed and used for the purposes of fueling aircraft,

(ii) is not registered for highway use, and

(iii) is operated by—

(I) the terminal operator of such terminal, or

(II) a person that makes a daily accounting to such terminal operator of each delivery of fuel from such truck, tanker, or wagon.

(C) REPORTING.—The Secretary shall require under section 4101(d) reporting by such terminal operator of—

(i) any information obtained under subparagraph (B)(iii)(II), and

(ii) any similar information maintained by such terminal operator with respect to deliveries of fuel made by trucks, tankers, or wagons operated by such terminal operator.

(D) APPLICABLE RATE.—For purposes of paragraph (2)(C), in the case of any kerosene treated as removed from a terminal by reason of this paragraph—

(i) the rate of tax specified in paragraph (2)(C)(i) in the case of use described in such paragraph shall apply if such terminal is located within a secured area of an airport, and

(ii) the rate of tax specified in paragraph (2)(C)(ii) shall apply in all other cases.

MANUFACTURERS TAXES—MOTOR AND AVIATION FUELS

(4) LIABILITY FOR TAX ON KEROSENE USED IN COMMERCIAL AVIATION.—For purposes of paragraph (2(C)(i), the person who uses the fuel for commercial aviation shall pay the tax imposed under such paragraph. For purposes of the preceding sentence, fuel shall be treated as used when such fuel is removed into the fuel tank.

Amendments

• **2020, Coronavirus Aid, Relief, and Economic Security (CARES) Act (P.L. 116-136)**

P.L. 116-136, §4007(b)-(c), provides:

(b) USE OF KEROSENE IN COMMERCIAL AVIATION.—In the case of kerosene used in commercial aviation (as defined in section 4083 of the Internal Revenue Code of 1986) during the excise tax holiday period—

(1) no tax shall be imposed on such kerosene under—

(A) section 4041(c) of the Internal Revenue Code of 1986, or

(B) section 4081 of such Code (other than at the rate provided in subsection (a)(2)(B) thereof), and

(2) section 6427(l) of such Code shall be applied—

(A) by treating such use as a nontaxable use, and

(B) without regard to paragraph (4)(A)(ii) thereof.

(c) EXCISE TAX HOLIDAY PERIOD.—For purposes of this section, the term "excise tax holiday period" means the period beginning after the date of the enactment of this section and ending before January 1, 2021.

• **2005, Safe, Accountable, Flexible, Efficient Transportation Equity Act: A Legacy for Users (P.L. 109-59)**

P.L. 109-59, §11151(b)(1):

Amended Code Sec. 4081(a)(2)(C) by striking "for use in commercial aviation" and inserting "for use in commercial aviation by a person registered for such use under section 4101". **Effective** as if included in the provision of P.L. 108-357 to which it relates [**effective** for aviation-grade kerosene removed, entered, or sold after 12-31-2004.—CCH].

P.L. 109-59, §11161(a)(1):

Amended Code Sec. 4081(a)(2)(A) by adding "and" at the end of clause (ii), by striking ", and" at the end of clause (iii) and inserting a period, and by striking clause (iv). **Effective** for fuels or liquids removed, entered, or sold after 9-30-2005. Prior to being stricken, Code Sec. 4081(a)(2)(A)(iv) read as follows:

(iv) in the case of aviation-grade kerosene, 21.8 cents per gallon.

P.L. 109-59, §11161(a)(2):

Amended Code Sec. 4081(a)(2)(C). **Effective** for fuels or liquids removed, entered, or sold after 9-30-2005. Prior to amendment, Code Sec. 4081(a)(2)(C) read as follows:

(C) TAXES IMPOSED ON FUEL USED IN COMMERCIAL AVIATION.—In the case of aviation-grade kerosene which is removed from any refinery or terminal directly into the fuel tank of an aircraft for use in commercial aviation by a person registered for such use under section 4101, the rate of tax under subparagraph (A)(iv) shall be 4.3 cents per gallon.

P.L. 109-59, §11161(a)(3)(A)-(B):

Amended Code Sec. 4081(a)(3) by striking "a secured area of" before "an airport" in subparagraph (A)(i), and by adding at the end a new subparagraph (D). **Effective** for fuels or liquids removed, entered, or sold after 9-30-2005.

P.L. 109-59, §11161(a)(4)(A):

Amended Code Sec. 4081(a)(3)(A) by striking "aviation-grade" each place it appears. **Effective** for fuels or liquids removed, entered, or sold after 9-30-2005. Prior to amendment, Code Sec. 4081(a)(3)(A) read as follows:

(A) IN GENERAL.—For purposes of paragraph (2)(C), a refueler truck, tanker, or tank wagon shall be treated as part of a terminal if—

(i) such terminal is located within an airport,

(ii) any aviation-grade kerosene which is loaded in such truck, tanker, or wagon at such terminal is for delivery only into aircraft at the airport in which such terminal is located,

(iii) such truck, tanker, or wagon meets the requirements of subparagraph (B) with respect to such terminal, and

(iv) except in the case of exigent circumstances identified by the Secretary in regulations, no vehicle registered for highway use is loaded with aviation-grade kerosene at such terminal.

P.L. 109-59, §11161(a)(4)(B):

Amended Code Sec. 4081(a)(4) by striking "paragraph (2)(C)" and inserting "paragraph (2)(C)(i)". **Effective** for fuels or liquids removed, entered, or sold after 9-30-2005.

P.L. 109-59, §11161(a)(4)(C):

Amended the heading for Code Sec. 4081(a)(4) by striking "AVIATION-GRADE" before "KEROSENE". **Effective** for fuels or liquids removed, entered, or sold after 9-30-2005.

P.L. 109-59, §11166(b)(1):

Amended Code Sec. 4081(a)(1)(B). **Effective** 8-10-2005. Prior to amendment, Code Sec. 4081(a)(1)(B) read as follows:

(B) EXEMPTION FOR BULK TRANSFERS TO REGISTERED TERMINALS OR REFINERIES.—The tax imposed by this paragraph shall not apply to any removal or entry of a taxable fuel transferred in bulk by pipeline or vessel to a terminal or refinery if the person removing or entering the taxable fuel, the operator of such pipeline or vessel, and the operator of such terminal or refinery are registered under section 4101.

• **2005, Energy Tax Incentives Act of 2005 (P.L. 109-58)**

P.L. 109-58, §1343(a):

Amended Code Sec. 4081(a)(2) by adding at the end a new subparagraph (D). **Effective** 1-1-2006.

• **2004, American Jobs Creation Act of 2004 (P.L. 108-357)**

P.L. 108-357, §853(a)(1):

Amended Code Sec. 4081(a)(2)(A) by striking "and" at the end of clause (ii), by striking the period at the end of clause (iii) and inserting ", and", and by adding at the end a new clause (iv). **Effective** for aviation-grade kerosene removed, entered, or sold after 12-31-2004. For special rules, see Act Sec. 853(f), below.

P.L. 108-357, §853(a)(2):

Amended Code Sec. 4081(a)(2) by adding at the end a new subparagraph (C). **Effective** for aviation-grade kerosene removed, entered, or sold after 12-31-2004. For special rules, see Act Sec. 853(f), below.

P.L. 108-357, §853(a)(3)(A):

Amended Code Sec. 4081(a) by adding at the end a new paragraph (3). **Effective** for aviation-grade kerosene removed, entered, or sold after 12-31-2004. For special rules, see Act Sec. 853(f), below.

P.L. 108-357, §853(a)(3)(B), provides:

(B) LIST OF AIRPORTS WITH SECURED TERMINALS.—Not later than December 15, 2004, the Secretary of the Treasury shall publish and maintain a list of airports which include a secured area in which a terminal is located (within the meaning of section 4081(a)(3)(A)(i) of the Internal Revenue Code of 1986, as added by this paragraph).

P.L. 108-357, §853(a)(4):

Amended Code Sec. 4081(a) by adding at the end a new paragraph (4). **Effective** for aviation-grade kerosene removed, entered, or sold after 12-31-2004. For special rules, see Act Sec. 853(f), below.

P.L. 108-357, §853(f), provides:

(f) FLOOR STOCKS TAX.—

(1) IN GENERAL.—There is hereby imposed on aviation-grade kerosene held on January 1, 2005, by any person a tax equal to—

(A) the tax which would have been imposed before such date on such kerosene had the amendments made by this section been in effect at all times before such date, reduced by

(B) the sum of—

(i) the tax imposed before such date on such kerosene under section 4091 of the Internal Revenue Code of 1986, as in effect on such date, and

(ii) in the case of kerosene held exclusively for such person's own use, the amount which such person would (but for this clause) reasonably expect (as of such date) to be paid as a refund under section 6427(l) of such Code with respect to such kerosene.

(2) EXCEPTION FOR FUEL HELD IN AIRCRAFT FUEL TANK.—Paragraph (1) shall not apply to kerosene held in the fuel tank of an aircraft on January 1, 2005.

(3) LIABILITY FOR TAX AND METHOD OF PAYMENT.—

(A) LIABILITY FOR TAX.—The person holding the kerosene on January 1, 2005, to which the tax imposed by paragraph (1) applies shall be liable for such tax.

(B) METHOD AND TIME FOR PAYMENT.—The tax imposed by paragraph (1) shall be paid at such time and in such manner as the Secretary of the Treasury (or the Secretary's delegate) shall prescribe, including the nonapplication of such tax on de minimis amounts of kerosene.

(4) TRANSFER OF FLOOR STOCK TAX REVENUES TO TRUST FUNDS.—For purposes of determining the amount transferred to any trust fund, the tax imposed by this subsection shall be treated as imposed by section 4081 of the Internal Revenue Code of 1986—

(A) in any case in which tax was not imposed by section 4091 of such Code, at the Leaking Underground Storage Tank Trust Fund financing rate under such section to the extent of 0.1 cents per gallon, and

(B) at the rate under section 4081(a)(2)(A)(iv) of such Code to the extent of the remainder.

(5) HELD BY A PERSON.—For purposes of this subsection, kerosene shall be considered as held by a person if title thereto has passed to such person (whether or not delivery to the person has been made).

(6) OTHER LAWS APPLICABLE.—All provisions of law, including penalties, applicable with respect to the tax imposed by section 4081 of such Code shall, insofar as applicable and not inconsistent with the provisions of this subsection, apply with respect to the floor stock tax imposed by paragraph (1) to the same extent as if such tax were imposed by such section.

P.L. 108-357, §860(a)(1)-(2):

Amended Code Sec. 4081(a)(1)(B) by inserting "by pipeline or vessel" after "transferred in bulk", and by inserting ", the operator of such pipeline or vessel," after "the taxable fuel". **Effective** 3-1-2005.

• **1997, Taxpayer Relief Act of 1997 (P.L. 105-34)**

P.L. 105-34, §901(e), provides:

(e) DELAYED DEPOSITS OF HIGHWAY MOTOR FUEL TAX REVENUES.—Notwithstanding section 6302 of the Internal Revenue Code of 1986, in the case of deposits of taxes imposed by sections 4041 and 4081 (other than subsection (a)(2)(A)(ii)) of the Internal Revenue Code of 1986, the due date for any deposit which would (but for this subsection) be required to be made after July 31, 1998, and before October 1, 1998, shall be October 5, 1998.

P.L. 105-34, §1031(g)[(f)](3), provides:

(g)[(f)] DELAYED DEPOSITS OF AIRPORT TRUST FUND TAX REVENUES.—Notwithstanding section 6302 of the Internal Revenue Code of 1986—

* * *

MANUFACTURERS TAXES—MOTOR AND AVIATION FUELS

(3) in the case of deposits of taxes imposed by sections 4081(a)(2)(A)(ii), 4091, and 4271 of such Code, the due date for any such deposit which would (but for this subsection) be required to be made after July 31, 1998, and before October 1, 1998, shall be October 5, 1998.

P.L. 105-34, § 1032(b):

Amended Code Sec. 4081(a)(2)(A)(iii) by inserting "or kerosene" after "diesel fuel". **Effective** 7-1-98.

P.L. 105-34, § 1032(g), provides:

(g) FLOOR STOCK TAXES.—

(1) IMPOSITION OF TAX.—In the case of kerosene which is held on July 1, 1998, by any person, there is hereby imposed a floor stocks tax of 24.4 cents per gallon.

(2) LIABILITY FOR TAX AND METHOD OF PAYMENT.—

(A) LIABILITY FOR TAX.—A person holding kerosene on July 1, 1998, to which the tax imposed by paragraph (1) applies shall be liable for such tax.

(B) METHOD OF PAYMENT.—The tax imposed by paragraph (1) shall be paid in such manner as the Secretary shall prescribe.

(C) TIME FOR PAYMENT.—The tax imposed by paragraph (1) shall be paid on or before August 31, 1998.

(3) DEFINITIONS.—For purposes of this subsection—

(A) HELD BY A PERSON.—Kerosene shall be considered as "held by a person" if title thereto has passed to such person (whether or not delivery to the person has been made).

(B) SECRETARY.—The term "Secretary" means the Secretary of the Treasury or his delegate.

(4) EXCEPTION FOR EXEMPT USES.—The tax imposed by paragraph (1) shall not apply to kerosene held by any person exclusively for any use to the extent a credit or refund of the tax imposed by section 4081 of the Internal Revenue Code of 1986 is allowable for such use.

(5) EXCEPTION FOR FUEL HELD IN VEHICLE TANK.—No tax shall be imposed by paragraph (1) on kerosene held in the tank of a motor vehicle or motorboat.

(6) EXCEPTION FOR CERTAIN AMOUNTS OF FUEL.—

(A) IN GENERAL.—No tax shall be imposed by paragraph (1) on kerosene held on July 1, 1998, by any person if the aggregate amount of kerosene held by such person on such date does not exceed 2,000 gallons. The preceding sentence shall apply only if such person submits to the Secretary (at the time and in the manner required by the Secretary) such information as the Secretary shall require for purposes of this paragraph.

(B) EXEMPT FUEL.—For purposes of subparagraph (A), there shall not be taken into account fuel held by any person which is exempt from the tax imposed by paragraph (1) by reason of paragraph (4) or (5).

(C) CONTROLLED GROUPS.—For purposes of this paragraph—

(i) CORPORATIONS.—

(I) IN GENERAL.—All persons treated as a controlled group shall be treated as 1 person.

(II) CONTROLLED GROUP.—The term "controlled group" has the meaning given to such term by subsection (a) of section 1563 of such Code; except that for such purposes the phrase "more than 50 percent" shall be substituted for the phrase "at least 80 percent" each place it appears in such subsection.

(ii) NONINCORPORATED PERSONS UNDER COMMON CONTROL.—Under regulations prescribed by the Secretary, principles similar to the principles of clause (i) shall apply to a group of persons under common control where 1 or more of such persons is not a corporation.

(7) COORDINATION WITH SECTION 4081.—No tax shall be imposed by paragraph (1) on kerosene to the extent that tax has been (or will be) imposed on such kerosene under section 4081 or 4091 of such Code.

(8) OTHER LAWS APPLICABLE.—All provisions of law, including penalties, applicable with respect to the taxes imposed by section 4081 of such Code shall, insofar as applicable and not inconsistent with the provisions of this subsection, apply with respect to the floor stock taxes imposed by paragraph (1) to the same extent as if such taxes were imposed by such section 4081.

• **1996, Small Business Job Protection Act of 1996 (P.L. 104-188)**

P.L. 104-188, § 1609(g)(1):

Amended Code Sec. 4081(a)(2)(A) by redesignating clause (ii) as clause (iii) and by striking clause (i) and inserting new clauses (i) and (ii). **Effective** on the 7th calendar day after 8-20-96. Prior to amendment, Code Sec. 4081(a)(2)(A)(i) read as follows:

(i) in the case of gasoline, 18.3 cents per gallon, and

[Sec. 4081(b)]

(b) TREATMENT OF REMOVAL OR SUBSEQUENT SALE BY BLENDER.—

(1) IN GENERAL.—There is hereby imposed a tax at the rate determined under subsection (a) on taxable fuel removed or sold by the blender thereof.

(2) CREDIT FOR TAX PREVIOUSLY PAID.—If—

(A) tax is imposed on the removal or sale of a taxable fuel by reason of paragraph (1), and

(B) the blender establishes the amount of the tax paid with respect to such fuel by reason of subsection (a),

the amount of the tax so paid shall be allowed as a credit against the tax imposed by reason of paragraph (1).

[Sec. 4081(c)—Stricken]

Amendments

• **2004, American Jobs Creation Act of 2004 (P.L. 108-357)**

P.L. 108-357, § 301(c)(7):

Amended Code Sec. 4081 by striking subsection (c). **Effective** for fuel sold or used after 12-31-2004. Prior to being stricken, Code Sec. 4081(c) read as follows:

(c) TAXABLE FUELS MIXED WITH ALCOHOL.—Under regulations prescribed by the Secretary—

(1) IN GENERAL.—The rate of tax under subsection (a) shall be the alcohol mixture rate in the case of the removal or entry of any qualified alcohol mixture.

(2) TAX PRIOR TO MIXING.—

(A) IN GENERAL.—In the case of the removal or entry of any taxable fuel for use in producing at the time of such removal or entry a qualified alcohol mixture, the rate of tax under subsection (a) shall be the applicable fraction of the alcohol mixture rate. Subject to such terms and conditions as the Secretary may prescribe (including the application of section 4101), the treatment under the preceding sentence also shall apply to sue in producing a qualified alcohol mixture after the time of such removal or entry.

(B) APPLICABLE FRACTION.—For purposes of subparagraph (A), the applicable fraction is—

(i) in the case of a qualified alcohol mixture which contains gasoline, the fraction the numerator of which is 10 and the denominator of which is—

(I) 9 in the case of 10 percent gasohol,

(II) 9.23 in the case of 7.7 percent gasohol, and

(III) 9.43 in the case of 5.7 percent gasohol, and

(ii) in the case of a qualified alcohol mixture which does not contain gasoline, 10/9.

(3) ALCOHOL; QUALIFIED ALCOHOL MIXTURE.—For purposes of this subsection—

(A) ALCOHOL.—The term "alcohol" includes methanol and ethanol but does not include alcohol produced from petroleum, natural gas, or coal (including peat). Such term does not include alcohol with a proof of less than 190 (determined without regard to any added denaturants).

(B) QUALIFIED ALCOHOL MIXTURE.—The term "qualified alcohol mixture" means—

(i) any mixture of gasoline with alcohol if at least 5.7 percent of such mixture is alcohol, and

(ii) any mixture of diesel fuel with alcohol if at least 10 percent of such mixture is alcohol.

(4) ALCOHOL MIXTURE RATES FOR GASOLINE MIXTURES.—For purposes of this subsection—

(A) GENERAL RULES.—

(i) MIXTURES CONTAINING ETHANOL.—Except as provided in clause (ii), in the case of a qualified alcohol mixture which contains gasoline, the alcohol mixture rate is the excess of the rate which would (but for this paragraph) be determined under subsection (a) over—

(I) in the case of 10 percent gasohol, the applicable blender rate (as defined in section 4041(b)(2)(C)) per gallon,

(II) in the case of 7.7 percent gasohol, the number of cents per gallon equal to 77 percent of such applicable blender rate, and

(III) in the case of 5.7 percent gasohol, the number of cents per gallon equal to 57 percent of such applicable blender rate.

(ii) MIXTURES NOT CONTAINING ETHANOL.—In the case of a qualified alcohol mixture which contains gasoline and none of the alcohol in which consists of ethanol, the alcohol mixture rate is the excess of the rate which would (but for this paragraph) be determined under subsection (a) over—

(I) in the case of 10 percent gasohol, 6 cents per gallon,

(II) in the case of 7.7 percent gasohol, 4.62 cents per gallon, and

(III) in the case of 5.7 percent gasohol, 3.42 cents per gallon.

(B) 10 PERCENT GASOHOL.—The term "10 percent gasohol" means any mixture of gasoline with alcohol if at least 10 percent of such mixture is alcohol.

(C) 7.7 PERCENT GASOHOL.—The term "7.7 percent gasohol" means any mixture of gasoline with alcohol if at least 7.7 percent, but not 10 percent or more, of such mixture is alcohol.

(D) 5.7 PERCENT GASOHOL.—The term "5.7 percent gasohol" means any mixture of gasoline with alcohol if at least 5.7 percent, but not 7.7 percent or more, of such mixture is alcohol.

(5) ALCOHOL MIXTURE RATE FOR DIESEL FUEL MIXTURES.—The alcohol mixture rate for a qualified alcohol mixture which does not contain gasoline is the excess of the rate which would (but for this paragraph) be determined under subsection (a) over the applicable blender rate (as defined in section 4041(b)(2)(C)) per gallon (6 cents per gallon in the case of a qualified alcohol mixture none of the alcohol in which consists of ethanol).

(6) LIMITATION.—In no event shall any alcohol mixture rate determined under this subsection be less than 4.3 cents per gallon.

(7) LATER SEPARATION OF FUEL FROM QUALIFIED ALCOHOL MIXTURE.—If any person separates the taxable fuel from a qualified alcohol mixture on which tax was imposed under subsection (a) at a rate determined under paragraph (1) or (2) (or with respect to which a credit or payment was allowed or made by reason of section 6427(f)(1)),

MANUFACTURERS TAXES—MOTOR AND AVIATION FUELS

such person shall be treated as the refiner of such taxable fuel. The amount of tax imposed on any removal of such fuel by such person shall be reduced by the amount of tax imposed (and not credited or refunded) on any prior removal or entry of such fuel.

(8) TERMINATION.—Paragraphs (1) and (2) shall not apply to any removal, entry, or sale after September 30, 2007.

- **1998, Transportation Equity Act for the 21st Century (P.L. 105-178)**

P.L. 105-178, § 9003(a)(1)(C):

Amended Code Sec. 4081(c)(8) by striking "2000" and inserting "2007". **Effective** 6-9-98.

P.L. 105-178, § 9003(b)(2)(B):

Amended Code Sec. 4081(c)(4)(A). **Effective** 1-1-2001. Prior to amendment, Code Sec. 4081(c)(4)(A) read as follows:

[Sec. 4081(c)]

(c) LATER SEPARATION OF FUEL FROM DIESEL-WATER FUEL EMULSION.—If any person separates the taxable fuel from a diesel-water fuel emulsion on which tax was imposed under subsection (a) at a rate determined under subsection (a)(2)(D) (or with respect to which a credit or payment was allowed or made by reason of section 6427), such person shall be treated as the refiner of such taxable fuel. The amount of tax imposed on any removal of such fuel by such person shall be reduced by the amount of tax imposed (and not credited or refunded) on any prior removal or entry of such fuel.

Amendments

- **2005, Energy Tax Incentives Act of 2005 (P.L. 109-58)**

P.L. 109-58, § 1343(b)(2):

Amended Code Sec. 4081 by inserting after subsection (b) a new subsection (c). **Effective** 1-1-2006.

(A) IN GENERAL.—The alcohol mixture rate for a qualified alcohol mixture which contains gasoline is the excess of the rate which would (but for this paragraph) be determined under subsection (a) over—

(i) 5.4 cents per gallon for 10 percent gasohol,

(ii) 4.158 cents per gallon for 7.7 percent gasohol, and

(iii) 3.078 cents per gallon for 5.7 percent gasohol.

In the case of a mixture none of the alcohol in which consists of ethanol, clauses (i), (ii), and (iii) shall be applied by substituting "6 cents" for "5.4 cents", "4.62 cents" for "4.158 cents", and "3.42 cents" for "3.078 cents".

P.L. 105-178, § 9003(b)(2)(C):

Amended Code Sec. 4081(c)(5) by striking "5.4 cents" and inserting "the applicable blender rate (as defined in section 4041(b)(2)(C))". **Effective** 1-1-2001.

[Sec. 4081(d)]

(d) TERMINATION.—

(1) IN GENERAL.—The rates of tax specified in clauses (i) and (iii) of subsection (a)(2)(A) shall be 4.3 cents per gallon after September 30, 2028.

(2) AVIATION FUELS.—The rates of tax specified in subsections (a)(2)(A)(ii) and (a)(2)(C)(ii) shall be 4.3 cents per gallon—

(A) after December 31, 1996, and before the date which is 7 days after the date of the enactment of the Airport and Airway Trust Fund Tax Reinstatement Act of 1997, and

(B) after September 30, 2028.

(3) LEAKING UNDERGROUND STORAGE TANK TRUST FUND FINANCING RATE.—The Leaking Underground Storage Tank Trust Fund financing rate under subsection (a)(2) shall apply after September 30, 1997, and before October 1, 2028.

Amendments

- **2024, FAA Reauthorization Act of 2024 (P.L. 118-63)**

P.L. 118-63, § 1302(a):

Amended Code Sec. 4081(d)(2)(B) by striking "May 10, 2024" and inserting "September 30, 2028". **Effective** 5-16-2024.

- **2024, Airport and Airway Extension Act of 2024, Part II (P.L. 118-60)**

P.L. 118-60, § 202(a), provides:

SEC. 202. EXTENSION OF TAXES FUNDING AIRPORT AND AIRWAY TRUST FUND.

(a) Sections 4043(d), 4081(d)(2)(B), 4261(j), 4261(k)(1)(A)(ii), and 4271(d)(1)(A)(ii) of the Internal Revenue Code of 1986 shall be applied by substituting "May 17, 2024" for "May 10, 2024".

- **2024, Airport and Airway Extension Act of 2024 (P.L. 118-41)**

P.L. 118-41, § 202(a):

Amended Code Sec. 4081(d)(2)(B) by striking "March 8, 2024" and inserting "May 10, 2024". **Effective** 3-8-2024.

- **2023, Airport and Airway Extension Act of 2023, Part II (P.L. 118-34)**

P.L. 118-34, § 202(a):

Amended Code Sec. 4081(d)(2)(B) by striking "December 31, 2023" and inserting "March 8, 2024". **Effective** 12-26-2023.

- **2023, Continuing Appropriations Act, 2024 and Other Extensions Act (P.L. 118-15)**

P.L. 118-15, § 2212(a):

Amended Code Sec. 4081(d)(2)(B) by striking "September 30, 2023" and inserting "December 31, 2023". **Effective** 9-30-2023.

- **2021, Infrastructure Investment and Jobs Act (P.L. 117-58)**

P.L. 117-58, § 80102(a)(1)(C), Div. H:

Amended Code Sec. 4081(d)(1) by striking "September 30, 2022" and inserting "September 30, 2028". **Effective** 10-1-2021.

P.L. 117-58, § 80102(a)(2)(D), Div. H:

Amended Code Sec. 4081(d)(3) by striking "October 1, 2022" and inserting "October 1, 2028". **Effective** 10-1-2021.

- **2018, FAA Reauthorization Act of 2018 (P.L. 115-254)**

P.L. 115-254, § 802(a):

Amended Code Sec. 4081(d)(2)(B) by striking "September 30, 2018" and inserting "September 30, 2023". **Effective** 10-5-2018.

- **2018, Airport and Airway Extension Act of 2018, Part II (P.L. 115-250)**

P.L. 115-250, § 5(a), provides:

(a) Sections 4081(d)(2)(B), 4261(j), 4261(k)(1)(A)(ii), and 4271(d)(1)(A)(ii) of the Internal Revenue Code of 1986 shall be applied by substituting "October 7, 2018" for "September 30, 2018".

- **2018, Airport and Airway Extension Act of 2018 (P.L. 115-141)**

P.L. 115-141, § 202(a), Div. M:

Amended Code Sec. 4081(d)(2)(B) by striking "March 31, 2018" and inserting "September 30, 2018". **Effective** 3-23-2018.

- **2017, Disaster Tax Relief and Airport and Airway Extension Act of 2017 (P.L. 115-63)**

P.L. 115-63, § 202(a):

Amended Code Sec. 4081(d)(2)(B) by striking "September 30, 2017" and inserting "March 31, 2018". **Effective** 9-29-2017.

- **2016, FAA Extension, Safety, and Security Act of 2016 (P.L. 114-190)**

P.L. 114-190, § 1202(a):

Amended Code Sec. 4081(d)(2)(B) by striking "July 15, 2016" and inserting "September 30, 2017". **Effective** 7-15-2016.

- **2016, Airport and Airway Extension Act of 2016 (P.L. 114-141)**

P.L. 114-141, § 202(a):

Amended Code Sec. 4081(d)(2)(B) by striking "March 31, 2016" and inserting "July 15, 2016". **Effective** 3-30-2016.

- **2015, Fixing America's Surface Transportation Act (P.L. 114-94)**

P.L. 114-94, § 31102(a)(1)(C):

Amended Code Sec. 4081(d)(1) by striking "September 30, 2016" and inserting "September 30, 2022". **Effective** 10-1-2016.

P.L. 114-94, § 31102(a)(2)(D):

Amended Code Sec. 4081(d)(3) by striking "October 1, 2016" and inserting "October 1, 2022". **Effective** 10-1-2016.

- **2015, Airport and Airway Extension Act of 2015 (P.L. 114-55)**

P.L. 114-55, § 202(a):

Amended Code Sec. 4081(d)(2)(B) by striking "September 30, 2015" and inserting "March 31, 2016". **Effective** 9-30-2015.

MANUFACTURERS TAXES—MOTOR AND AVIATION FUELS

• 2012, Highway Investment, Job Creation, and Economic Growth Act of 2012 (P.L. 112-141)

P.L. 112-141, §40102(a)(1)(C):

Amended Code Sec. 4081(d)(1) by striking "June 30, 2012" and inserting "September 30, 2016". **Effective** 7-1-2012.

P.L. 112-141, §40102(a)(2)(D):

Amended Code Sec. 4081(d)(3) by striking "July 1, 2012" and inserting "October 1, 2016". **Effective** 7-1-2012.

• 2012, Temporary Surface Transportation Extension Act of 2012 (P.L. 112-140)

P.L. 112-140, §1(c), provides:

(c) SPECIAL RULE FOR EXECUTION OF AMENDMENTS IN MAP–21.—On the date of enactment of the MAP–21 [P.L. 112-141]—

(1) this Act and the amendments made by this Act shall cease to be effective;

(2) the text of the laws amended by this Act shall revert back so as to read as the text read on the day before the date of enactment of this Act; and

(3) the amendments made by the MAP–21 shall be executed as if this Act had not been enacted.

P.L. 112-140, §402(a)(1)(C):

Amended Code Sec. 4081(d)(1) by striking "June 30, 2012" and inserting "July 6, 2012". **Effective** 7-1-2012. For a special rule, see Act Sec. 1(c), above.

P.L. 112-140, §402(a)(2)(D):

Amended Code Sec. 4081(d)(3) by striking "July 1, 2012" and inserting "July 7, 2012". **Effective** 7-1-2012. For a special rule, see Act Sec. 1(c), above.

• 2012, Surface Transportation Extension Act of 2012 (P.L. 112-102)

P.L. 112-102, §402(a)(1)(C):

Amended Code Sec. 4081(d)(1) by striking "March 31, 2012" and inserting "June 30, 2012". **Effective** 4-1-2012.

P.L. 112-102, §402(a)(2)(D):

Amended Code Sec. 4081(d)(3) by striking "April 1, 2012" and inserting "July 1, 2012". **Effective** 4-1-2012.

• 2012, FAA Modernization and Reform Act of 2012 (P.L. 112-95)

P.L. 112-95, §1101(a):

Amended Code Sec. 4081(d)(2)(B) by striking "February 17, 2012" and inserting "September 30, 2015". **Effective** 2-18-2012.

• 2012, Airport and Airway Extension Act of 2012 (P.L. 112-91)

P.L. 112-91, §2(a):

Amended Code Sec. 4081(d)(2)(B) by striking "January 31, 2012" and inserting "February 17, 2012". **Effective** 2-1-2012.

• 2011, Surface Transportation Extension Act of 2011, Part II (P.L. 112-30)

P.L. 112-30, §142(a)(1)(C):

Amended Code Sec. 4081(d)(1) by striking "September 30, 2011" and inserting "March 31, 2012". **Effective** 10-1-2011.

P.L. 112-30, §142(a)(2)(D):

Amended Code Sec. 4081(d)(3) by striking "October 1, 2011" and inserting "April 1, 2012". **Effective** 10-1-2011.

• 2011, Airport and Airway Extension Act of 2011, Part V (P.L. 112-30)

P.L. 112-30, §202(a):

Amended Code Sec. 4081(d)(2)(B) by striking "September 16, 2011" and inserting "January 31, 2012". **Effective** 9-17-2011.

• 2011, Airport and Airway Extension Act of 2011, Part IV (P.L. 112-27)

P.L. 112-27, §2(a):

Amended Code Sec. 4081(d)(2)(B) by striking "July 22, 2011" and inserting "September 16, 2011". **Effective** 7-23-2011.

• 2011, Airport and Airway Extension Act of 2011, Part III (P.L. 112-21)

P.L. 112-21, §2(a):

Amended Code Sec. 4081(d)(2)(B) by striking "June 30, 2011" and inserting "July 22, 2011". **Effective** 7-1-2011.

• 2011, Airport and Airway Extension Act of 2011, Part II (P.L. 112-16)

P.L. 112-16, §2(a):

Amended Code Sec. 4081(d)(2)(B) by striking "May 31, 2011" and inserting "June 30, 2011". **Effective** 6-1-2011.

• 2011, Airport and Airway Extension Act of 2011 (P.L. 112-7)

P.L. 112-7, §2(a):

Amended Code Sec. 4081(d)(2)(B) by striking "March 31, 2011" and inserting "May 31, 2011". **Effective** 4-1-2011.

• 2010, Airport and Airway Extension Act of 2010, Part IV (P.L. 111-329)

P.L. 111-329, §2(a):

Amended Code Sec. 4081(d)(2)(B) by striking "December 31, 2010" and inserting "March 31, 2011". **Effective** 1-1-2011.

• 2010, Airport and Airway Extension Act of 2010, Part III (P.L. 111-249)

P.L. 111-249, §2(a):

Amended Code Sec. 4081(d)(2)(B) by striking "September 30, 2010" and inserting "December 31, 2010". **Effective** 10-1-2010.

• 2010, Airline Safety and Federal Aviation Administration Extension Act of 2010 (P.L. 111-216)

P.L. 111-216, §101(a):

Amended Code Sec. 4081(d)(2)(B) by striking "August 1, 2010" and inserting "September 30, 2010". **Effective** 8-2-2010.

• 2010, Airport and Airway Extension Act of 2010, Part II (P.L. 111-197)

P.L. 111-197, §2(a):

Amended Code Sec. 4081(d)(2)(B) by striking "July 3, 2010" and inserting "August 1, 2010". **Effective** 7-4-2010.

• 2010, Airport and Airway Extension Act of 2010 (P.L. 111-161)

P.L. 111-161, §2(a):

Amended Code Sec. 4081(d)(2)(B) by striking "April 30, 2010" and inserting "July 3, 2010". **Effective** 5-1-2010.

• 2010, Federal Aviation Administration Extension Act of 2010 (P.L. 111-153)

P.L. 111-153, §2(a):

Amended Code Sec. 4081(d)(2)(B) by striking "March 31, 2010" and inserting "April 30, 2010". **Effective** 4-1-2010.

• 2009, Fiscal Year 2010 Federal Aviation Administration Extension Act, Part II (P.L. 111-116)

P.L. 111-116, §2(a):

Amended Code Sec. 4081(d)(2)(B) by striking "December 31, 2009" and inserting "March 31, 2010". **Effective** 1-1-2010.

• 2009, Fiscal Year 2010 Federal Aviation Administration Extension Act (P.L. 111-69)

P.L. 111-69, §2(a):

Amended Code Sec. 4081(d)(2)(B) by striking "September 30, 2009" and inserting "December 31, 2009". **Effective** 10-1-2009.

• 2009, (P.L. 111-68)

P.L. 111-68, §156(a), provides:

(a) Sections 4081(d)(2)(B), 4261(j)(1)(A)(ii), and 4271(d)(1)(A)(ii) of the Internal Revenue Code of 1986 shall each be applied by substituting the date specified in section 106(3) [October 31, 2009] of this joint resolution for "September 30, 2009".

• 2009, Federal Aviation Administration Extension Act of 2009 (P.L. 111-12)

P.L. 111-12, §2(a):

Amended Code Sec. 4081(d)(2)(B) by striking "March 31, 2009" and inserting "September 30, 2009". **Effective** 4-1-2009.

• 2008, Federal Aviation Administration Extension Act of 2008, Part II (P.L. 110-330)

P.L. 110-330, §2(a):

Amended Code Sec. 4081(d)(2)(B) by striking "September 30, 2008" and inserting "March 31, 2009". **Effective** 10-1-2008.

• 2008, Federal Aviation Administration Extension Act of 2008 (P.L. 110-253)

P.L. 110-253, §2(a):

Amended Code Sec. 4081(d)(2)(B) by striking "June 30, 2008" and inserting "September 30, 2008". **Effective** 7-1-2008.

• 2008, Airport and Airway Extension Act of 2008 (P.L. 110-190)

P.L. 110-190, §2(a):

Amended Code Sec. 4081(d)(2)(B) by striking "February 29, 2008" and inserting "June 30, 2008". **Effective** 3-1-2008.

• 2007, Department of Transportation Appropriations Act, 2008 (P.L. 110-161)

P.L. 110-161, §116(a):

Amended Code Sec. 4081(d)(2)(B) by striking "September 30, 2007" and inserting "February 29, 2008". **Effective** 10-1-2007.

• 2007 (P.L. 110-92)

P.L. 110-92, §149(a), provides:

SEC. 149. (a) Sections 4081(d)(2)(B), 4261(j)(1)(A)(ii), 4271(d)(1)(A)(ii), 9502(d)(1), and 9502(f)(2) of the Internal Revenue Code of 1986 shall each be applied by substituting the date specified in section 106(3) of this joint resolution [November 16, 2007.—CCH] for "September 30, 2007" or "October 1, 2007", as the case may be.

MANUFACTURERS TAXES—MOTOR AND AVIATION FUELS

- **2005, Safe, Accountable, Flexible, Efficient Transportation Equity Act: A Legacy for Users (P.L. 109-59)**

P.L. 109-59, §11101(a)(1)(F):

Amended Code Sec. 4081(d)(1) by striking "2005" and inserting "2011". **Effective** 8-10-2005.

P.L. 109-59, §11151(b)(2):

Amended so much of Code Sec. 4081(d)(2) as precedes subparagraph (A). **Effective** as if included in the provision of P.L. 108-357 to which it relates [effective for aviation-grade kerosene removed, entered, or sold after 12-31-2004.—CCH]. Prior to amendment, the matter preceding Code Sec. 4081(d)(2)(A) read as follows:

(2) AVIATION GASOLINE.—The rate of tax specified in subsection (a)(2)(A)(ii) shall be 4.3 cents per gallon—

P.L. 109-59, §11161(a)(4)(D):

Amended Code Sec. 4081(d)(2) by striking so much as precedes subparagraph (A) and inserting new text beginning with "(2)". **Effective** for fuels or liquids removed, entered, or sold after 9-30-2005. Prior to being stricken, so much of Code Sec. 4081(d)(2) as precedes subparagraph (A) read as follows:

(2) AVIATION FUELS.—The rates of tax specified in clauses (ii) and (iv) of subsection (a)(2)(A) shall be 4.3 cents per gallon—

- **2005, Energy Tax Incentives Act of 2005 (P.L. 109-58)**

P.L. 109-58, §1362(a):

Amended Code Sec. 4081(d)(3) by striking "2005" and inserting "2011". **Effective** 10-1-2005.

- **2005 (P.L. 109-6)**

P.L. 109-6, §1(a):

Amended Code Sec. 4081(d)(3) by striking "April 1, 2005" and inserting "October 1, 2005". **Effective** 3-31-2005.

- **1998, Transportation Equity Act for the 21st Century (P.L. 105-178)**

P.L. 105-178, §9002(a)(1)(F):

Amended Code Sec. 4081(d)(1) by striking "1999" and inserting "2005". **Effective** 6-9-98.

- **1997, Taxpayer Relief Act of 1997 (P.L. 105-34)**

P.L. 105-34, §1031(a)(2):

Amended Code Sec. 4081(d)(2)(B) by striking "September 30, 1997" and inserting "September 30, 2007". **Effective** 10-1-97.

P.L. 105-34, §1033:

Amended Code Sec. 4081(d)(3) by striking "shall not apply after December 31, 1995" and inserting "shall apply after September 30, 1997, and before April 1, 2005". **Effective** 8-5-97.

- **1997, Airport and Airway Trust Fund Tax Reinstatement Act of 1997 (P.L. 105-2)**

P.L. 105-2, §2(a)(2):

Amended Code Sec. 4081(d) by striking the paragraph (3) added by P.L. 104-188, §1609(a), and by striking paragraphs (1) and (2) and inserting new paragraphs (1) and (2). **Effective** for periods beginning on or after 3-7-97. Prior to being stricken, Code Sec. 4081(d)(1)-(3) read as follows

(1) IN GENERAL.—On and after October 1, 1999, the rates of tax specified in clauses (i) and (iii) of subsection (a)(2)(A) (other than the tax on aviation gasoline) shall be 4.3 cents per gallon.

(2) AVIATION GASOLINE.—On and after January 1, 1997, the rate specified in subsection (a)(2)(A)(ii) shall be 4.3 cents per gallon.

(3) AVIATION GASOLINE.—After December 31, 1996, the rate of tax specified in subsection (a)(2)(A)(i)[ii]on aviation gasoline shall be 4.3 cents per gallon.

P.L. 105-2, §2(d), provides:

(d) FLOOR STOCKS TAXES ON AVIATION GASOLINE AND AVIATION FUEL.—

(1) IMPOSITION OF TAX.—In the case of any aviation liquid on which tax was imposed under section 4081 or 4091 of the Internal Revenue Code of 1986 before the tax effective date and which is held on such date by any person, there is hereby imposed a floor stocks tax of—

(A) 15 cents per gallon in the case of aviation gasoline, and

(B) 17.5 cents per gallon in the case of aviation fuel.

(2) LIABILITY FOR TAX AND METHOD OF PAYMENT.—

(A) LIABILITY FOR TAX.—A person holding, on the tax effective date, any aviation liquid to which the tax imposed by paragraph (1) applies shall be liable for such tax.

(B) METHOD OF PAYMENT.—The tax imposed by paragraph (1) shall be paid in such manner as the Secretary shall prescribe.

(C) TIME FOR PAYMENT.—The tax imposed by paragraph (1) shall be paid on or before the first day of the 5th month beginning after the tax effective date.

(3) DEFINITIONS.—For purposes of this subsection—

(A) TAX EFFECTIVE DATE.—The term "tax effective date" means the date which is 7 days after the date of the enactment of this Act.

(B) AVIATION LIQUID.—The term "aviation liquid" means aviation gasoline and aviation fuel.

(C) AVIATION GASOLINE.—The term "aviation gasoline" has the meaning given such term in section 4081 of such Code.

(D) AVIATION FUEL.—The term "aviation fuel" has the meaning given such term by section 4093 of such Code.

(E) HELD BY A PERSON.—Aviation liquid shall be considered as "held by a person" if title thereto has passed to such person (whether or not delivery to the person has been made).

(F) SECRETARY.—The term "Secretary" means the Secretary of the Treasury or the Secretary's delegate.

(4) EXCEPTION FOR EXEMPT USES.—The tax imposed by paragraph (1) shall not apply to—

(A) aviation liquid held by any person on the tax effective date exclusively for any use for which a credit or refund of the entire tax imposed by section 4081 or 4091 of such Code (as the case may be) is allowable for such liquid purchased on or after such tax effective date for such use, or

(B) aviation fuel held by any person on the tax effective date exclusively for any use described in section 4092(b) of such Code.

(5) EXCEPTION FOR CERTAIN AMOUNTS OF FUEL.—

(A) IN GENERAL.—No tax shall be imposed by paragraph (1) on any aviation liquid held on the tax effective date by any person if the aggregate amount of such liquid (determined separately for aviation gasoline and aviation fuel) held by such person on such date does not exceed 2,000 gallons. The preceding sentence shall apply only if such person submits to the Secretary (at the time and in the manner required by the Secretary) such information as the Secretary shall require for purposes of this paragraph.

(B) EXEMPT FUEL.—Any liquid to which the tax imposed by paragraph (1) does not apply by reason of paragraph (4) shall not be taken into account under subparagraph (A).

(C) CONTROLLED GROUPS.—For purposes of this paragraph—

(i) CORPORATIONS.—

(I) IN GENERAL.—All persons treated as a controlled group shall be treated as 1 person.

(II) CONTROLLED GROUP.—The term "controlled group" has the meaning given such term by subsection (a) of section 1563 of such Code; except that for such purposes, the phrase "more than 50 percent" shall be substituted for the phrase "at least 80 percent" each place it appears in such subsection.

(ii) NONINCORPORATED PERSONS UNDER COMMON CONTROL.—Under regulations prescribed by the Secretary, principles similar to the principles of clause (i) shall apply to a group of persons under common control where 1 or more of such persons is not a corporation.

(6) OTHER LAWS APPLICABLE.—All provisions of law, including penalties, applicable with respect to the taxes imposed by section 4081 or 4091 of such Code shall, insofar as applicable and not inconsistent with the provisions of this subsection, apply with respect to the floor stocks taxes imposed by paragraph (1) to the same extent as if such taxes were imposed by such section 4081 or 4091, as the case may be.

P.L. 105-2, §2(f):

For the text of Act Sec. 2(f), concerning the application of the look-back safe harbor for deposits, see the amendment notes following Code Sec. 9502(b).

- **1996, Small Business Job Protection Act of 1996 (P.L. 104-188)**

P.L. 104-188, §1609(a)(2)(A)-(B):

Amended Code Sec. 4081(d) by adding at the end [sic] a new paragraph (3) and inserting "(other than the tax on aviation gasoline)" after "subsection (a)(2)(A)" [in paragraph (1)]. **Effective** 8-27-96.

P.L. 104-188, §1609(g):

Amended Code Sec. 4081(d) by redesignating paragraph (2) as paragraph (3) and inserting after paragraph (1) a new paragraph (2). **Effective** 8-27-96.

P.L. 104-188, §1609(g)(4)(B):

Amended Code Sec. 4081(d)(1) by striking "each rate of tax specified in subsection (a)(2)(A)" and inserting "the rates of tax specified in clauses (i) and (iii) of subsection (a)(2)(A)". **Effective** 8-27-96.

[Sec. 4081(e)]

(e) REFUNDS IN CERTAIN CASES.—Under regulations prescribed by the Secretary, if any person who paid the tax imposed by this section with respect to any taxable fuel establishes to the satisfaction of the Secretary that a prior tax was paid (and not credited or refunded) with respect to such taxable fuel, then an amount equal to the tax paid by such person shall be allowed as a refund (without interest) to such person in the same manner as if it were an overpayment of tax imposed by this section.

Amendments

- **1993, Omnibus Budget Reconciliation Act of 1993 (P.L. 103-66)**

P.L. 103-66, §13242(a):

Amended subparts A and B of part III of subchapter A of chapter 32 (Code Secs. 4081-4093), as amended by subpart A (Act Sec. 13241(a)). **Effective** 1-1-94.

P.L. 103-66, §13243, provides:

SEC. 13243. FLOOR STOCKS TAX.

(a) IN GENERAL.—There is hereby imposed a floor stocks tax on diesel fuel held by any person on January 1, 1994, if—

(1) no tax was imposed on such fuel under section 4041(a) or 4091 of the Internal Revenue Code of 1986 as in effect on December 31, 1993, and

(2) tax would have been imposed by section 4081 of such Code, as amended by this Act, on any prior removal, entry, or sale of such fuel had such section 4081 applied to such fuel for periods before January 1, 1994.

(b) RATE OF TAX.—The rate of the tax imposed by subsection (a) shall be the amount of tax which would be imposed under section 4081 of the Internal Revenue Code of 1986 if there were a taxable sale of such fuel on such date.

(c) LIABILITY AND PAYMENT OF TAX.—

MANUFACTURERS TAXES—MOTOR AND AVIATION FUELS

(1) LIABILITY FOR TAX.—A person holding the diesel fuel on January 1, 1994, to which the tax imposed by this section applies shall be liable for such tax.

(2) METHOD OF PAYMENT.—The tax imposed by this section shall be paid in such manner as the Secretary shall prescribe.

(3) TIME FOR PAYMENT.—The tax imposed by this section shall be paid on or before July 31, 1994.

(d) DEFINITIONS.—For purposes of this section—

(1) DIESEL FUEL.—The term "diesel fuel" has the meaning given such term by section 4083(a) of such Code.

(2) SECRETARY.—The term "Secretary" means the Secretary of the Treasury or his delegate.

(e) EXCEPTIONS.—

(1) PERSONS ENTITLED TO CREDIT OR REFUND.—The tax imposed by this section shall not apply to fuel held by any person exclusively for any use to the extent a credit or refund of the tax imposed by section 4081 is allowable for such use.

(2) COMPLIANCE WITH DYEING REQUIRED.—Paragraph (1) shall not apply to the holder of any fuel if the holder of such fuel fails to comply with any requirement imposed by the Secretary with respect to dyeing and marking such fuel.

(f) OTHER LAWS APPLICABLE.—All provisions of law, including penalties, applicable with respect to the taxes imposed by section 4081 of such Code shall, insofar as applicable and not inconsistent with the provisions of this section, apply with respect to the floor stock taxes imposed by this section to the same extent as if such taxes were imposed by such section 4081.

Prior to amendment by P.L. 103-66, Code Sec. 4081 read as follows:

SEC. 4081. IMPOSITION OF TAX.

[Sec. 4081(a)]

(a) TAX IMPOSED.—

(1) TAX ON REMOVAL, ENTRY, OR SALE.—

(A) IN GENERAL.—There is hereby imposed a tax at the rate specified in paragraph (2) on—

(i) the removal of gasoline from any refinery,

(ii) the removal of gasoline from any terminal,

(iii) the entry into the United States of gasoline for consumption, use, or warehousing, and

(iv) the sale of gasoline to any person who is not registered under section 4101 unless there was a prior taxable removal or entry of such gasoline under clause (i), (ii), or (iii).

(B) EXCEPTION FOR BULK TRANSFERS TO REGISTERED TERMINALS.—The tax imposed by this paragraph shall not apply to any removal or entry of gasoline transferred in bulk to a terminal if the person removing or entering the gasoline and the operator of such terminal are registered under section 4101.

(2) RATES OF TAX.—

(A) IN GENERAL.—The rate of the tax imposed by this section is the sum of—

(i) the Highway Trust Fund financing rate,

(ii) the Leaking Underground Storage Tank Trust Fund financing rate, and

(iii) the deficit reduction rate.

(B) RATES.—For purposes of subparagraph (A)—

(i) the Highway Trust Fund financing rate is 11.5 cents a gallon,

(ii) the Leaking Underground Storage Tank Trust Fund financing rate is 0.1 cent a gallon, and

(iii) the deficit reduction rate is 6.8 cents a gallon.

Amendments

• **1993, Omnibus Budget Reconciliation Act of 1993 (P.L. 103-66)**

P.L. 103-66, §13241(a):

Amended Code Sec. 4081(a)(2)(B)(iii). **Effective** 10-1-93. However, see Act Sec. 13241(h), below. Prior to amendment, Code Sec. 4081(a)(2)(B)(iii) read as follows:

(iii) the deficit reduction rate is 2.5 cents a gallon.

P.L. 103-66, §13241(h), provides:

(h) FLOOR STOCKS TAXES.—

(1) IMPOSITION OF TAX.—In the case of gasoline, diesel fuel, and aviation fuel on which tax was imposed under section 4081 or 4091 of the Internal Revenue Code of 1986 before October 1, 1993, and which is held on such date by any person, there is hereby imposed a floor stocks tax of 4.3 cents per gallon on such gasoline, diesel fuel, and aviation fuel.

(2) LIABILITY FOR TAX AND METHOD OF PAYMENT.—

(A) LIABILITY FOR TAX.—A person holding gasoline, diesel fuel, or aviation fuel on October 1, 1993, to which the tax imposed by paragraph (1) applies shall be liable for such tax.

(B) METHOD OF PAYMENT.—The tax imposed by paragraph (1) shall be paid in such manner as the Secretary shall prescribe.

(C) TIME FOR PAYMENT.—The tax imposed by paragraph (1) shall be paid on or before November 30, 1993.

(3) DEFINITIONS.—For purposes of this subsection—

(A) HELD BY A PERSON.—Gasoline, diesel fuel, and aviation fuel shall be considered as "held by a person" if title thereto has passed to such person (whether or not delivery to the person has been made).

(B) GASOLINE.—The term "gasoline" has the meaning given such term by section 4082 of such Code.

(C) DIESEL FUEL.—The term "diesel fuel" has the meaning given such term by section 4092 of such Code.

(D) AVIATION FUEL.—The term "aviation fuel" has the meaning given such term by section 4092 of such Code.

(E) SECRETARY.—The term "Secretary" means the Secretary of the Treasury or his delegate.

(4) EXCEPTION FOR EXEMPT USES.—The tax imposed by paragraph (1) shall not apply to gasoline, diesel fuel, or aviation fuel held by any person exclusively for any use to the extent a credit or refund of the tax imposed by section 4081 or 4091 of such Code, as the case may be, is allowable for such use.

(5) EXCEPTION FOR FUEL HELD IN VEHICLE TANK.—No tax shall be imposed by paragraph (1) on gasoline or diesel fuel held in the tank of a motor vehicle or motorboat.

(6) EXCEPTION FOR CERTAIN AMOUNTS OF FUEL.—

(A) IN GENERAL.—No tax shall be imposed by paragraph (1)—

(i) on gasoline held on October 1, 1993, by any person if the aggregate amount of gasoline held by such person on such date does not exceed 4,000 gallons, and

(ii) on diesel fuel or aviation fuel held on October 1, 1993, by any person if the aggregate amount of diesel fuel or aviation fuel held by such person on such date does not exceed 2,000 gallons.

The preceding sentence shall apply only if such person submits to the Secretary (at the time and in the manner required by the Secretary) such information as the Secretary shall require for purposes of this paragraph.

(B) EXEMPT FUEL.—For purposes of subparagraph (A), there shall not be taken into account fuel held by any person which is exempt from the tax imposed by paragraph (1) by reason of paragraph (4) or (5).

(C) CONTROLLED GROUPS.—For purposes of this paragraph—

(i) CORPORATIONS.—

(I) IN GENERAL.—All persons treated as a controlled group shall be treated as 1 person.

(II) CONTROLLED GROUP.—The term "controlled group" has the meaning given to such term by subsection (a) of section 1563 of such Code; except that for such purposes the phrase "more that 50 percent" shall be substituted for the phrase "at least 80 percent" each place it appears in such subsection.

(ii) NONINCORPORATED PERSONS UNDER COMMON CONTROL.—Under regulations prescribed by the Secretary, principles similar to the principles of clause (i) shall apply to a group of persons under common control where 1 or more of such persons is not a corporation.

(7) OTHER LAW APPLICABLE.—All provisions of law, including penalties, applicable with respect to the taxes imposed by section 4081 of such Code in the case of gasoline and section 4091 of such Code in the case of diesel fuel and aviation fuel shall, insofar as applicable and not inconsistent with the provisions of this subsection, apply with respect to the floor stock taxes imposed by paragraph (1) to the same extent as if such taxes were imposed by such section 4081 or 4091.

• **1990, Omnibus Budget Reconciliation Act of 1990 (P.L. 101-508)**

P.L. 101-508, §11211(a)(1)(A):

Amended Code Sec. 4081(a)(2)(A)(i) by striking "and" at the end thereof. **Effective** for gasoline removed (as defined in section 4082 of the Internal Revenue Code of 1986) after 11-30-90.

P.L. 101-508, §11211(a)(1)(B):

Amended Code Sec. 4081(a)(2)(A)(ii) by striking the period at the end and inserting ", and". **Effective** for gasoline removed (as defined in section 4082 of the Internal Revenue Code of 1986) after 11-30-90.

P.L. 101-508, §11211(a)(1)(C):

Amended Code Sec. 4081(a)(2)(A) by adding at the end thereof a new clause (iii). **Effective** for gasoline removed (as defined in section 4082 of the Internal Revenue Code of 1986) after 11-30-90.

P.L. 101-508, §11211(a)(2)(A):

Amended Code Sec. 4081(a)(2)(B) by striking "9 cents a gallon," and inserting "11.5 cents a gallon,". **Effective** for gasoline removed (as defined in section 4082 of the Internal Revenue Code of 1986) after 11-30-90.

P.L. 101-508, §11211(a)(2)(B):

Amended Code Sec. 4081(a)(2)(B)(ii) by striking the period at the end and inserting ", and". **Effective** for gasoline removed (as defined in section 4082 of the Internal Revenue Code of 1986) after 11-30-90.

P.L. 101-508, §11211(a)(2)(C):

Amended Code Sec. 4081(a)(2)(B) by adding at the end thereof a new clause (iii). **Effective** for gasoline removed (as defined in section 4082 of the Internal Revenue Code of 1986) after 11-30-90.

P.L. 101-508, §11212(a):

Amended Code Sec. 4081(a)(1). **Effective** 7-1-91. Prior to amendment, Code Sec. 4081(a)(1) read as follows:

(1) IN GENERAL.—There is hereby imposed a tax at the rate specified in paragraph (2) on the earlier of—

(A) the removal, or

(B) the sale,

of gasoline by the refiner or importer thereof or the terminal operator.

P.L. 101-508, §11212(e)(2):

Amended Code Sec. 4081(a) by striking paragraph (3). **Effective** 7-1-91. Prior to amendment, Code Sec. 4081(a)(3) read as follows:

(3) BULK TRANSFER TO TERMINAL OPERATOR.—For purposes of paragraph (1), the bulk transfer of gasoline to a terminal operator by a refiner or importer shall not be considered a removal or sale of gasoline by such refiner or importer.

• **1988, Technical and Miscellaneous Revenue Act of 1988 (P.L. 100-647)**

P.L. 100-647, §1017(c)(1)(A):

Amended Code Sec. 4081(a), as amended by P.L. 99-514, §1703, by redesignating paragraph (2) as paragraph (3) and by striking out paragraph (1) and inserting in lieu thereof new paragraphs (1) and (2). **Effective** as if included in the provision of P.L. 99-514 to which it relates. Prior to amendment, Code Sec. 4081(a)(1) read as follows:

MANUFACTURERS TAXES—MOTOR AND AVIATION FUELS

(1) IN GENERAL.—There is hereby imposed a tax at the rate specified in subsection (d) on the earlier of—

(A) the removal, or

(B) the sale,

of gasoline by the refiner or importer thereof or the terminal operator.

- **1986, Superfund Amendments and Reauthorization Act of 1986 (P.L. 99-499)**

P.L. 99-499, §521(a)(1)(B)(i):

Amended Code Sec. 4081(a), as amended by the Tax Reform Act of 1986, by striking out "of 9 cents a gallon" and inserting in lieu thereof "at the rate specified in subsection (d)". **Effective** 1-1-87.

[Sec. 4081(b)]

(b) TREATMENT OF REMOVAL OR SUBSEQUENT SALE BY BLENDER OR COMPOUNDER.—

(1) IN GENERAL.—There is hereby imposed a tax at the rate specified in subsection (a) on gasoline removed or sold by the blender or compounder thereof.

(2) CREDIT FOR TAX PREVIOUSLY PAID.—If—

(A) tax is imposed on the removal or sale of gasoline by reason of paragraph (1), and

(B) the blender or compounder establishes the amount of the tax paid with respect to such gasoline by reason of subsection (a),

the amount of the tax so paid shall be allowed as a credit against the tax imposed by reason of paragraph (1).

Amendments

- **1988, Technical and Miscellaneous Revenue Act of 1988 (P.L. 100-647)**

P.L. 100-647, §1017(c)(1)(B):

Amended Code Sec. 4081(b), as amended by P.L. 99-514, §1703, by striking out "subsection (d)" and inserting in lieu thereof "subsection (a)". **Effective** as if included in the provision of P.L. 99-514 to which it relates.

- **1986, Superfund Amendments and Reauthorization Act of 1986 (P.L. 99-499)**

P.L. 99-499, §521(a)(1)(B)(i):

Amended Code Sec. 4081(b), as amended by the Tax Reform Act of 1986, by striking out "of 9 cents a gallon" and inserting in lieu thereof "at the rate specified in subsection (d)". **Effective** 1-1-87.

[Sec. 4081(c)]

(c) GASOLINE MIXED WITH ALCOHOL AT REFINERY, ETC.—

(1) IN GENERAL.—Under regulations prescribed by the Secretary, subsection (a) shall be applied by multiplying the otherwise applicable rate by a fraction the numerator of which is 10 and the denominator of which is—

(A) 9 in the case of 10 percent gasohol,

(B) 9.23 in the case of 7.7 percent gasohol, and

(C) 9.43 in the case of 5.7 percent gasohol,

in the case of the removal or entry of any gasoline for use in producing gasohol at the time of such removal or entry. Subject to such terms and conditions as the Secretary may prescribe (including the application of section 4101), the treatment under the preceding sentence also shall apply to use in producing gasohol after the time of such removal or entry.

(2) LATER SEPARATION OF GASOLINE FROM GASOHOL.—If any person separates the gasoline from a mixture of gasoline and alcohol on which tax was imposed under subsection (a) at a Highway Trust Fund financing rate equivalent to an otherwise applicable rate by reason of this subsection (or with respect to which a credit or payment was allowed or made by reason of section 6427(f)(1)), such person shall be treated as the refiner of such gasoline. The amount of tax imposed on any sale of such gasoline by such person shall be reduced by the amount of tax imposed (and not credited or refunded) on any prior removal or sale of such fuel.

(3) ALCOHOL DEFINED.—For purposes of this subsection, the term "alcohol" includes methanol and ethanol but does not include alcohol produced from petroleum, natural gas, or coal (including peat). Such term does not include alcohol with a proof of less than 190 (determined without regard to any added denaturants).

(4) OTHERWISE APPLICABLE RATE.—For purposes of this subsection—

(A) IN GENERAL.—In the case of the Highway Trust Fund financing rate, the term "otherwise applicable rate" means—

(i) 6.1 cents a gallon for 10 percent gasohol,

(ii) 7.342 cents a gallon for 7.7 percent gasohol, and

(iii) 8.422 cents a gallon for 5.7 percent gasohol.

In the case of gasohol none of the alcohol in which consists of ethanol, clauses (i), (ii), and (iii) shall be applied by substituting "5.5 cents" for "6.1 cents", "6.88 cents" for "7.342 cents", and "8.08 cents" for "8.422 cents".

(B) 10 PERCENT GASOHOL.—The term "10 percent gasohol" means any mixture of gasoline with alcohol if at least 10 percent of such mixture is alcohol.

(C) 7.7 PERCENT GASOHOL.—The term "7.7 percent gasohol" means any mixture of gasoline with alcohol if at least 7.7 percent, but not 10 percent or more, of such mixture is alcohol.

(D) 5.7 PERCENT GASOHOL.—The term "5.7 percent gasohol" means any mixture of gasoline with alcohol if at least 5.7 percent, but not 7.7 percent or more, of such mixture is alcohol.

(5) TERMINATION.—Paragraph (1) shall not apply to any removal or sale after September 30, 2000.

Amendments

- **1992, Energy Policy Act of 1992 (P.L. 102-486)**

P.L. 102-486, §1920(a):

Amended Code Sec. 4081(c)(1). **Effective** for gasoline removed (as defined in section 4082 of the Internal Revenue Code of 1986) or entered after 12-31-92. Prior to amendment, Code Sec. 4081(c)(1) read as follows:

(1) IN GENERAL.—Under regulations prescribed by the Secretary, subsection (a) shall be applied by substituting rates which are 10/9th of the otherwise applicable rates in the case of the removal or sale of any gasoline for use in producing gasohol at the time of such removal or sale. Subject to such terms and conditions as the Secretary may prescribe (including the application of section 4101), the treatment under the preceding sentence also shall apply to use in producing gasohol after the time of such removal or sale. For purposes of this paragraph, the term "gasohol" means any mixture of gasoline if at least 10 percent of such mixture is alcohol. For purposes of this subsection, in the case of the Highway Trust Fund financing rate, the otherwise applicable rate is 6.1 cents a gallon.

P.L. 102-486, §1920(b)(1)-(2):

Amended Code Sec. 4081(c) by striking "6.1 cents a gallon" in paragraph (2) and inserting "an otherwise applicable rate", and by striking paragraph (4) and inserting new paragraph (4). **Effective** for gasoline removed (as defined in section 4082 of the Internal Revenue Code of 1986) or entered after 12-31-92. Prior to amendment, Code Sec. 4081(c)(4) read as follows:

(4) LOWER RATE ON GASOHOL MADE OTHER THAN FROM ETHANOL.—In the case of gasohol none of the alcohol in which consists of ethanol, paragraphs (1) and (2) shall be applied by substituting "5.5 cents" for "6.1 cents".

- **1990, Omnibus Budget Reconciliation Act of 1990 (P.L. 101-508)**

P.L. 101-508, §11211(a)(5)(A)(i)-(ii):

Amended Code Sec. 4081(c)(1) by striking "applied by" and all that follows through "in the case" and inserting "applied by substituting rates which are 10/9th of the otherwise applicable rates in the case", and by adding at the end thereof a new sentence. **Effective** for gasoline removed (as defined in section 4082 of the Internal Revenue Code of 1986) after 11-30-90. Prior to amendment, Code Sec. 4081(c)(1) read as follows:

(1) IN GENERAL.—Under regulations prescribed by the Secretary, subsection (a) shall be applied by substituting "3$1/3$ cents" for "9 cents" and by substituting "$1/9$ cent" for "0.1 cent" in the case of the removal or sale of any gasoline for use in producing gasohol at the time of such removal or sale. Subject to such terms and conditions as the Secretary may prescribe (including the application of section 4101), the treatment under the preceding sentence also shall apply to use in producing gasohol after the time of such removal or sale. For purposes of this paragraph, the term "gasohol" means any mixture of gasoline if at least 10 percent of such mixture is alcohol.

P.L. 101-508, §11211(a)(5)(B):

Amended Code Sec. 4081(c)(2) by striking "at a rate equivalent to 3 cents", and inserting "at a Highway Trust Fund financing rate equivalent to 6.1 cents". **Effective** for gasoline removed (as defined in section 4082 of the Internal Revenue Code of 1986) after 11-30-90.

P.L. 101-508, §11211(a)(5)(C):

Amended Code Sec. 4081(c) by redesignating paragraph (4) as paragraph (5) and by inserting after paragraph (3) a new paragraph (4). **Effective** for gasoline removed (as defined in section 4082 of the Internal Revenue Code of 1986) after 11-30-90.

P.L. 101-508, §11211(e)(3):

Amended Code Sec. 4081(c)(5) (as redesignated by Act Sec. 11211(a)(5)(C)) by striking "1993" each place it appears and inserting "2000". **Effective** 11-5-90.

- **1988, Technical and Miscellaneous Revenue Act of 1988 (P.L. 100-647)**

P.L. 100-647, §1017(c)(1)(B):

Amended Code Sec. 4081(c), as amended by P.L. 99-514, §1703, by striking out "subsection (d)" and inserting in lieu thereof "subsection (a)". **Effective** as if included in the provision of P.L. 99-514 to which it relates.

P.L. 100-647, §1017(c)(14):

Amended Code Sec. 4081(c)(1), as amended by P.L. 99-514, §1703, by striking out "3 cents" and inserting in lieu thereof "3$1/3$ cents". **Effective** as if included in the provision of P.L. 99-514 to which it relates.

P.L. 100-647, §2001(d)(5)(A):

Amended Code Sec. 4081(c)(1), as amended by §1703 of P.L. 99-514, by inserting "and by substituting '$1/9$ cent' for '0.1 cent'" before "in the case of the removal". **Effective** as if included in the provision of P.L. 99-499 to which it relates.

P.L. 100-647, §2001(d)(5)(B):

Amended Code Sec. 4081(c)(2) by striking out "5$2/3$ cents a gallon" and inserting in lieu thereof "reduced by the amount of tax imposed (and not credited or refunded) on any prior removal or sale of such fuel" in the last sentence. **Effective** as if included in the provision of P.L. 99-499 to which it relates.

P.L. 100-647, §6104(a):

Amended Code Sec. 4081(c)(1) by adding after the first sentence a new sentence. **Effective** 10-1-89.

Sec. 4081(e)

MANUFACTURERS TAXES—MOTOR AND AVIATION FUELS

• **1987, Surface Transportation and Uniform Relocation Assistance Act of 1987 (P.L. 100-17)**

P.L. 100-17, §502(c)(2):

Amended Code Sec. 4081(c)(4), as amended by P.L. 99-514, by striking out "December 31, 1992" and inserting in lieu thereof "September 30, 1993". **Effective** 4-2-87.

[Sec. 4081(d)]

(d) TERMINATION.—

(1) HIGHWAY TRUST FUND FINANCING RATE.—On and after October 1, 1999, the Highway Trust Fund financing rate under subsection (a)(2) shall not apply.

(2) LEAKING UNDERGROUND STORAGE TANK TRUST FUND FINANCING RATE.—The Leaking Underground Storage Tank Trust Fund financing rate under subsection (a)(2) shall not apply after December 31, 1995.

(3) DEFICIT REDUCTION RATE.—On and after October 1, 1995, the deficit reduction rate under subsection (a)(2) shall not apply.

Amendments

• **1991, Intermodal Surface Transportation Efficiency Act of 1991 (P.L. 102-240)**

P.L. 102-240, §8002(a)(3):

Amended Code Sec. 4081(d)(1) by striking "1995" and inserting "1999". **Effective** 12-18-91.

• **1990, Omnibus Budget Reconciliation Act of 1990 (P.L. 101-508)**

P.L. 101-508, §11211(a)(3):

Amended Code Sec. 4081(d) by adding at the end thereof a new paragraph (3). **Effective** for gasoline removed (as defined in section 4082 of the Internal Revenue Code of 1986) after 11-30-90.

P.L. 101-508, §11211(c)(3):

Amended Code Sec. 4081(d)(1) by striking "1993" each place it appears and inserting "1995". **Effective** 11-5-90.

P.L. 101-508, §11215(a):

Amended Code Sec. 4081(d)(2). **Effective** 12-1-90. Prior to amendment, Code Sec. 4081(d)(2) read as follows:

(2) LEAKING UNDERGROUND STORAGE TANK TRUST FUND FINANCING RATE.—

(A) IN GENERAL.—The Leaking Underground Storage Tank Trust Fund financing rate under subsection (a)(2) shall not apply after the earlier of—

(i) December 31, 1991, or

(ii) the last day of the termination month.

(B) TERMINATION MONTH.—For purposes of subparagraph (A), the termination month is the 1st month as of the close of which the Secretary estimates that the net revenues are at least $500,000,000 from taxes imposed by section 4041(d) and taxes attributable to Leaking Underground Storage Tank Trust financing rate imposed under this section and sections 4042 and 4091.

(C) NET REVENUES.—For purposes of subparagraph (B), the term "net revenues" means the excess of gross revenues over amounts payable by reason of section 9508(c)(2) (relating to transfer from Leaking Underground Storage Tank Trust Fund for certain repayments and credits).

• **1988, Technical and Miscellaneous Revenue Act of 1988 (P.L. 100-647)**

P.L. 100-647, §1017(c)(1)(C)(i)-(ii):

Amended Code Sec. 4081(e), as amended by P.L. 99-514, §1703, by striking out "subsection (d)(2)(A)" in paragraph (1) and inserting in lieu thereof "subsection (a)(2)", and by striking out "subsection (d)(2)(B)" each place it appears in paragraph (2) and inserting in lieu thereof "subsection (a)(2)". **Effective** as if included in the provision of P.L. 99-514 to which it relates.

P.L. 100-647, §1017(c)(1)(D):

Amended Code Sec. 4081, as amended by P.L. 99-514, §1703, by striking out subsection (d) and by redesignating subsection (e) as subsection (d). **Effective** as if included in the provision of P.L. 99-514 to which it relates. Prior to amendment, Code Sec. 4081(d) read as follows:

(d) RATE OF TAX.—

(1) IN GENERAL.—The rate of the tax imposed by this section is the sum of—

(A) the Highway Trust Fund financing rate, and

(B) the Leaking Underground Storage Tank Trust Fund financing rate.

(2) RATES.—For purposes of paragraph (1)—

(A) the Highway Trust Fund financing rate is 9 cents a gallon, and

(B) the Leaking Underground Storage Tank Trust Fund financing rate is 0.1 cents a gallon.

• **1987, Revenue Act of 1987 (P.L. 100-203)**

P.L. 100-203, §10502(d)(2):

Amended Code Sec. 4081(e)(2)(B), as amended by section 1703 of the Tax Reform Act of 1986, by striking out "net revenues" and all that follows and inserting in lieu thereof "net revenues are at least $500,000,000 from taxes imposed by section 4041(d) and taxes attributable to Leaking Underground Storage Tank Trust Fund financing rate imposed under this section and sections 4042 and 4091." **Effective** for sales after 3-31-88. Prior to amendment, all that followed "net revenues" read as follows:

from the taxes imposed by this section (to the extent attributable to the Leaking Underground Storage Tank Trust Fund financing rate under subsection (d)(2)(B)), section 4041(d), and section 4042 (to the extent attributable to the Leaking Underground Storage Tank Trust Fund financing rate under section 4042(b)) are at least $500,000,000.

• **1987, Surface Transportation and Uniform Relocation Assistance Act of 1987 (P.L. 100-17)**

P.L. 100-17, §502(a)(4):

Amended Code Sec. 4081(e)(1) (as amended by P.L. 99-514 and P.L. 99-499, §521(a)(1)(B)) by striking out "1988" and inserting in lieu thereof "1993". **Effective** 4-2-87.

• **1986, Superfund Amendments and Reauthorization Act of 1986 (P.L. 99-499)**

P.L. 99-499, §521(a)(1)(B)(ii):

Amended Code Sec. 4081, as amended by the Tax Reform Act of 1986, by striking out subsection (d) and inserting in lieu thereof new subsections (d) and (e). **Effective** 1-1-87. Prior to amendment, Code Sec. 4081(d) read as follows:

(d) TERMINATION.—On and after October 1, 1988, the taxes imposed by this section shall not apply.

[Sec. 4081(e)]

(e) REFUNDS IN CERTAIN CASES.—Under regulations prescribed by the Secretary, if any person who paid the tax imposed by this section with respect to any gasoline establishes to the satisfaction of the Secretary that a prior tax was paid (and not credited or refunded) with respect to such gasoline, then an amount equal to the tax paid by such person shall be allowed as a refund (without interest) to such person in the same manner as if it were an overpayment of tax imposed by this section.

Amendments

• **1990, Omnibus Budget Reconciliation Act of 1990 (P.L. 101-508)**

P.L. 101-508, §11211(j), provides:

(j) FLOOR STOCKS TAXES.—

(1) IMPOSITION OF TAX.—In the case of—

(A) gasoline and diesel fuel on which tax was imposed under section 4081 or 4091 of such Code before December 1, 1990, and which is held on such date by any person, or

(B) diesel fuel on which no tax was imposed under section 4091 of such Code at the Highway Trust Fund financing rate before December 1, 1990, and which is held on such date by any person for use as a fuel in a train,

there is hereby imposed a floor stocks tax on such gasoline and diesel fuel.

(2) RATE OF TAX.—The rate of the tax imposed by paragraph (1) shall be—

(A) 5 cents per gallon in the case of fuel described in paragraph (1)(A), and

(B) 2.5 cents per gallon in the case of fuel described in paragraph (1)(B).

In the case of any fuel held for use in producing a mixture described in section 4081(c)(1) or section 4091(c)(1)(A) of such Code, subparagraph (A) shall be applied by substituting "6.22 cents" for "5 cents". If no alcohol in such mixture is ethanol, the preceding sentence shall be applied by substituting "5.56 cents" for "6.22 cents".

(3) LIABILITY FOR TAX AND METHOD OF PAYMENT.—

(A) LIABILITY FOR TAX.—A person holding gasoline or diesel fuel on December 1, 1990, to which the tax imposed by paragraph (1) applies shall be liable for such tax.

(B) METHOD OF PAYMENT.—The tax imposed by paragraph (1) shall be paid in such manner as the Secretary shall prescribe.

(C) TIME FOR PAYMENT.—The tax imposed by paragraph (1) shall be paid on or before May 31, 1991.

(4) DEFINITIONS.—For purposes of this subsection—

(A) HELD BY A PERSON.—Gasoline and diesel fuel shall be considered as "held by a person" if title thereto has passed to such person (whether or not delivery to the person has been made).

(B) GASOLINE.—The term "gasoline" has the meaning given such term by section 4082 of such Code.

(C) DIESEL FUEL.—The term "diesel fuel" has the meaning given such term by section 4092 of such Code.

(D) SECRETARY.—The term "Secretary" means the Secretary of the Treasury of his delegate.

(5) EXCEPTION FOR EXEMPT USES.—The tax imposed by paragraph (1) shall not apply to gasoline or diesel fuel held by any person exclusively for any use to the extent a credit or refund of the tax imposed by section 4081 or 4091 of such Code, as the case may be, is allowable for such use.

(6) EXCEPTION FOR FUEL HELD IN VEHICLE TANK.—No tax shall be imposed by paragraph (1) on gasoline or diesel fuel held in the tank of a motor vehicle or motorboat.

(7) EXCEPTION FOR CERTAIN AMOUNTS OF FUEL.—

(A) IN GENERAL.—No tax shall be imposed by paragraph (1)—

(i) on gasoline held on December 1, 1990, by any person if the aggregate amount of gasoline held by such person on such date does not exceed 4,000 gallons, and

(ii) on diesel fuel held on December 1, 1990, by any person if the aggregate amount of diesel fuel held by such person on such date does not exceed 2,000 gallons.

The preceding sentence shall apply only if such person submits to the Secretary (at the time and in the manner required by the Secretary) such information as the Secretary shall require for purposes of this paragraph.

(B) EXEMPT FUEL.—For purposes of subparagraph (A), there shall not be taken into account fuel held by any person which is exempt from the tax imposed by paragraph (1) by reason of paragraph (5) or (6).

(C) CONTROLLED GROUPS.—For purposes of this paragraph, rules similar to the rules of paragraph (6) of section 11201(e) of this Act shall apply.

(8) OTHER LAWS APPLICABLE.—All provisions of law, including penalties, applicable with respect to the taxes imposed by section 4081 of such Code in the case of gasoline and section 4091 of such Code in the case of diesel fuel shall, insofar as applicable

MANUFACTURERS TAXES—MOTOR AND AVIATION FUELS

and not inconsistent with the provisions of this subsection, apply with respect to the floor stock taxes imposed by paragraph (1) to the same extent as if such taxes were imposed by such section 4081 or 4091.

(9) TRANSFER OF PORTION OF FLOOR STOCKS REVENUE TO HIGHWAY TRUST FUND.—For purposes of determining the amount transferred to the Highway Trust Fund, the tax imposed by paragraph (1) on fuel described in subparagraph (A) thereof shall be treated as imposed at a Highway Trust Fund financing rate to the extent of 2.5 cents per gallon.

P.L. 101-508, §11212(d)(1):

Amended Code Sec. 4081 by adding at the end thereof a new subsection (e). **Effective** 7-1-91.

- **1986, Tax Reform Act of 1986 (P.L. 99-514)**

P.L. 99-514, §1703(a):

Amended Code Sec. 4081. **Effective** for gasoline removed, as defined in Code Sec. 4082, as amended by Act Sec. 1703(a), after 12-31-87. For special rules regarding floor stock taxes, see Act Sec. 1703(f), below.

P.L. 99-514, §1703(f), as amended by P.L. 100-647, §§1017(c)(13) and 2001(d)(4), provides:

(f) FLOOR STOCK TAXES.—

(1) IN GENERAL.—On gasoline subject to tax under section 4081 of the Internal Revenue Code of 1986 which, on January 1, 1988, is held by a dealer for sale, and with respect to which no tax has been imposed under such section, there is hereby imposed a floor stocks tax at the rate of 9.1 cents a gallon.

(2) OVERPAYMENT OF FLOOR STOCKS TAXES.—Section 6416 of such Code shall apply in respect of the floor stocks taxes imposed by this section, so as to entitle, subject to all provisions of such section, any person paying such floor stocks taxes to a credit or refund thereof for any reasons specified in such section. All other provisions of law, including penalties, applicable with respect to the taxes imposed by section 4081 of the Internal Revenue Code of 1986 shall apply to the floor stocks taxes imposed by this section.

(3) DUE DATE OF TAXES.—The taxes imposed by this subsection shall be paid before February 16, 1988.

(4) TRANSFER OF FLOOR STOCK TAX REVENUES TO TRUST FUNDS.—For purposes of determining the amount transferred to any trust fund, the tax imposed by this section shall be treated as imposed by section 4081 of the Internal Revenue Code of 1986—

(A) at the Highway Trust Fund financing rate under such section to the extent of 9 cents per gallon, and

(B) at the Leaking Underground Storage Tank Trust Fund financing rate under such section to the extent of 0.1 cent per gallon.

(5) DEFINITIONS AND SPECIAL RULE.—For purposes of this subsection—

(A) DEALER.—The term "dealer" includes a wholesaler, jobber, distributor, or retailer.

(B) HELD BY A DEALER.—Gasoline shall be considered as "held by a dealer" if title thereto has passed to such dealer (whether or not delivery to him has been made) and if for purposes of consumption title to such gasoline or possession thereof has not at any time been transferred to any person other than a dealer.

(C) GASOLINE.—The term "gasoline" has the same meaning given to such term by section 4082(a) of the Internal Revenue Code of 1986.

Prior to amendment by P.L. 99-514, Code Sec. 4081 read as follows:

SEC. 4081. IMPOSITION OF TAX.

[Sec. 4081(a)]

(a) IN GENERAL.—There is hereby imposed on gasoline sold by the producer or importer thereof, or by any producer of gasoline, a tax at the rate specified in subsection (b).

Amendments

- **1986, Superfund Amendments and Reauthorization Act of 1986 (P.L. 99-499)**

P.L. 99-499, §521(a)(1)(A)(i):

Amended Code Sec. 4081(a), as in effect on the day before the date of the enactment of the P.L. 99-514. **Effective** 1-1-87. Prior to amendment, Code Sec. 4081(a) read as follows:

(a) IN GENERAL.—There is hereby imposed on gasoline sold by the producer or importer thereof, or by any producer of gasoline, a tax of 9 cents a gallon.

- **1983, Surface Transportation Assistance Act of 1982 (P.L. 97-424)**

P.L. 97-424, §511(a)(1):

Amended Code Sec. 4081(a) by striking out "4 cents a gallon" and inserting "9 cents a gallon". **Effective** 4-1-83.

[Sec. 4081(b)]

(b) RATE OF TAX.—

(1) IN GENERAL.—The rate of the tax imposed by this section is the sum of—

(A) the Highway Trust Fund financing rate, and

(B) the Leaking Underground Storage Tank Trust Fund financing rate.

(2) RATES.—For purposes of paragraph (1)—

(A) the Highway Trust Fund financing rate is 9 cents a gallon, and

(B) the Leaking Underground Storage Tank Trust Fund financing rate is 0.1 cents a gallon.

Sec. 4081(e)

Amendments

- **1986, Superfund Amendments and Reauthorization Act of 1986 (P.L. 99-499)**

P.L. 99-499, §521(a)(1)(A)(i):

Amended Code Sec. 4081(b), as in effect on the day before the date of the enactment of P.L. 99-514. **Effective** 1-1-87. Prior to amendment, Code Sec. 4081(b) read as follows:

(b) TERMINATION.—On and after October 1, 1988, the taxes imposed by this section shall not apply.

- **1983, Surface Transportation Assistance Act of 1982 (P.L. 97-424)**

P.L. 97-424, §516(a)(3):

Amended Code Sec. 4081(b). **Effective** 1-6-83. Prior to amendment, Code Sec. 4081(b) read as follows:

"(b) RATE REDUCTION.—On and after October 1, 1984, the tax imposed by this section shall be 1½ cents a gallon."

P.L. 97-424, §521(a), as amended by P.L. 98-369, §732(b), and (d)(1), provides:

SEC. 521. FLOOR STOCKS TAXES.

(a) 1983 Tax on Gasoline.—On gasoline subject to tax under section 4081 which, on April 1, 1983, is held by a dealer for sale, there is hereby imposed a floor stocks tax at the rate of 5 cents a gallon (4 cents a gallon in the case of a gallon of gasohol, as defined in section 4081(c)).

* * *

(d) Due Date of Taxes.—The taxes imposed by this section shall be paid at such time after—

(1) May 15, 1983, in the case of the tax imposed by subsection (a), or

* * *

as may be prescribed by the Secretary of the Treasury or his delegate.

For additional floor stock provisions, relating to the overpayment of floor stock taxes, the transfer of such taxes to the Highway Trust Fund, floor stock refunds, and definitions and special rules, see the amendment notes for Act Sec. 521(c) following Code Sec. 6416 and Act Secs. 521(e), 522 and 523 following Code Sec. 6412.

Also, an extension of time for paying certain fuel taxes is contained in Act Sec. 518, below.

P.L. 97-424, §518, as amended by P.L. 98-369, §734, provides:

(a) 14-Day Extension.—The Secretary shall prescribe regulations which permit any qualified person whose liability for tax under section 4081 of the Internal Revenue Code of 1954 is payable with respect to semi-monthly periods to pay such tax on or before the day which is 14 days after the close of such semi-monthly period if such payment is made by wire transfer to, except as provided in regulations prescribed by the Secretary of the Treasury or his delegate, any Federal Reserve Bank.

(b) Qualified Person Defined.—For purposes of this section—

(1) In general.—The term "qualified person" means—

(A) any person other than any person whose average daily production of crude oil for the preceding calendar quarter exceeds 1,000 barrels, and

(B) any independent refiner (within the meaning of section 4995(b)(4) of such Code).

(2) Aggregation rules.—For purposes of paragraph (1), in determining whether any person's production exceeds 1,000 barrels per day, rules similar to the rules of section 4992(e) of the Internal Revenue Code of 1954 shall apply.

(c) Special Rule Where 14th Day Falls on Saturday, Sunday or Holiday.—If, but for this subsection, the due date under subsection (a) would fall on a Saturday, Sunday, or a holiday in the District of Columbia, such due date shall be deemed to be the immediately preceding day which is not a Saturday, Sunday, or such a holiday.

- **1978, Surface Transportation Asssistance Act of 1978 (P.L. 95-599)**

P.L. 95-599, §502(a)(5):

Substituted "1984" for "1979" in Code Sec. 4081(b). **Effective** 11-7-78.

- **1976 (P.L. 94-280)**

P.L. 94-280, §303(a)(6):

Amended Code Sec. 4081(b) by substituting "1979" for "1977."

- **1970, Federal-Aid Highway Act of 1970 (P.L. 91-605)**

P.L. 91-605, §303(a)(6):

Amended Code Sec. 4081(b) by substituting "1977" for "1972."

- **1961, Federal-Aid Highway Act of 1961 (P.L. 87-61)**

P.L. 87-61, §201(b):

Amended Sec. 4081(a) by substituting "4 cents" for "3 cents." **Effective** 7-1-61.

P.L. 87-61, §201(c):

Amended Sec. 4081(b) by substituting "October 1, 1972" for "July 1, 1972." **Effective** 7-1-61.

P.L. 87-61, §201(d):

Repealed Sec. 4081(c). **Effective** 7-1-61. Prior to repeal, Sec. 4081(c) read:

(c) TEMPORARY INCREASE IN TAX.—On and after October 1, 1959, and before July 1, 1961, the tax imposed by this section shall be 4 cents a gallon.

MANUFACTURERS TAXES—MOTOR AND AVIATION FUELS

- **1959, Federal-Aid Highway Act of 1959 (P.L. 86-342)**

P.L. 86-342, §201(a):

Added subsection (c) to Sec. 4081.

- **1956 (P.L. 627, 84th Cong.)**

P.L. 627, 84th Cong., 2d Sess., §205:

Amended Sec. 4081 by substituting "3 cents a gallon" for "2 cents a gallon" and "July 1, 1972" for "April 1, 1957". **Effective** 7-1-56.

- **1956, Tax Rate Extension Act of 1956 (P.L. 458, 84th Cong.)**

P.L. 458, 84th Cong., 2d Sess., §3(a)(3):

Substituted "1957" for "1956" in Sec. 4081.

- **1955, Tax Rate Extension Act of 1955 (P.L. 18, 84th Cong.)**

P.L. 18, 84th Cong., §3(a)(3):

Substituted "1956" for "1955" in Sec. 4081.

[Sec. 4081(c)]

(c) GASOLINE MIXED WITH ALCOHOL.—

(1) IN GENERAL.—Under regulations prescribed by the Secretary, subsection (b) shall be applied—

(A) by substituting "3 cents" for "9 cents" in the case of the sale of any gasohol (the gasoline in which was not taxed under subparagraph (B)), and

(B) by substituting "$3^{1}/_{3}$ cents" for "9 cents" in the case of the sale of any gasoline for use in producing gasohol.

For purposes of this paragraph, the term "gasohol" means any mixture of gasoline if at least 10 percent of such mixture is alcohol.

(2) Later separation of gasoline.—If any person separates the gasoline from a mixture of gasoline and alcohol on which tax was imposed under subsection (a) at a Highway Trust Fund financing rate equivalent to 3 cents a gallon by reason of this subsection (or with respect to which a credit or payment was allowed or made by reason of section 6427(f)(1)), such person shall be treated as the producer of such gasoline. The amount of tax imposed on any sale of such gasoline by such person shall be $5^{2}/_{3}$ cents a gallon.

(3) ALCOHOL DEFINED.—For purposes of this subsection, the term "alcohol" includes methanol and ethanol but does not include alcohol produced from petroleum, natural gas, or coal (including peat). Such term does not include alcohol with a proof of less than 190 (determined without regard to any added denaturants).

(4) TERMINATION.—Paragraph (1) shall not apply to any sale after December 31, 1992.

Amendments

- **1986, Superfund Amendments and Reauthorization Act of 1986 (P.L. 99-499)**

P.L. 99-499, §521(a)(1)(A)(iii)(I)-(II):

Amended Sec. 4081(c) by striking out "subsection (a)" in paragraph (1) and inserting in lieu thereof "subsection (b)", and by striking out "a rate" in paragraph (2) and inserting in lieu thereof "a Highway Trust Fund financing rate". **Effective** 1-1-87.

- **1984, Deficit Reduction Act of 1984 (P.L. 98-369)**

P.L. 98-369, §732(a)(1):

Amended Code Sec. 4081(c)(1). **Effective** as if included in the provision of the Highway Revenue Act of 1982 to which it relates. Prior to amendment, paragraph (1) read as follows:

(1) In General.—Under regulations prescribed by the Secretary, subsection (a) shall be applied by substituting "4 cents" for "9 cents" in the case of the sale of any gasoline—

(A) in a mixture with alcohol, if at least 10 percent of the mixture is alcohol, or

(B) for use in producing a mixture at least 10 percent of which is alcohol.

P.L. 98-369, §732(a)(2):

Amended Code Sec. 4081(c)(2) by striking out "at the rate of 4 cents a gallon" and inserting in lieu thereof "at a rate equivalent to 4 cents a gallon", and by striking out "5 cents a gallon" and inserting in lieu thereof "$4^{5}/_{9}$ cents a gallon". **Effective** as if included in the provision of the Highway Revenue Act of 1982 to which it relates.

P.L. 98-369, §912(b):

Amended Code Sec. 4081(c), as amended by this Act, by striking out "4 cents" each place it appears and inserting in lieu thereof "3 cents", by striking out "$4^{4}/_{9}$ cents" and inserting in lieu thereof "$3^{1}/_{3}$ cents", and by striking out "$4^{5}/_{9}$ cents" and inserting in lieu thereof "$5^{2}/_{3}$ cents". **Effective** 1-1-85.

P.L. 98-369, §912(f):

Amended Sec. 4081(c)(3) by striking out "coal" and inserting in lieu thereof "coal (including peat)". **Effective** 1-1-85.

- **1983, Surface Transportation Assistance Act of 1982 (P.L. 97-424)**

P.L. 97-424, §511(d)(1)(A):

Amended Code Sec. 4081(c)(1) by striking out "no tax shall be imposed by this section on the sale of any gasoline" and inserting "subsection (a) shall be applied by substituting '4 cents' for '9 cents' in the case of the sale of any gasoline." **Effective** 4-1-83.

P.L. 97-424, §511(d)(1)(B):

Amended Code Sec. 4081(c)(2) by striking out "tax was not imposed by reason of this subsection" and inserting "tax was imposed under subsection (a) at the rate of 4 cents a gallon by reason of this subsection" and by adding a new last sentence. **Effective** 4-1-83.

- **1980, Crude Oil Windfall Profit Tax Act of 1980 (P.L. 96-223)**

P.L. 96-223, §232(a)(1):

Amended Code Sec. 4081(c) by adding paragraph (4). **Effective** 4-3-80.

P.L. 96-223, §232(b)(3)(A):

Amended Code Sec. 4081(c)(3) by adding the last sentence. **Effective** for sales and uses after 9-30-80, in tax years ending after such date.

P.L. 96-223, §232(d)(3):

Amended Code Sec. 4081(c)(2) by inserting "(or with respect to which a credit or payment was allowed or made by reason of section 6427(f)(1))" after "this subsection". **Effective** 1-1-79.

- **1978, Energy Tax Act of 1978 (P.L. 95-618)**

P.L. 95-618, §221(a):

Added Code Sec. 4081(c). **Effective** for sales after 12-31-78, and before 10-1-84.

[Sec. 4081(d)]

(d) TERMINATION.—

(1) HIGHWAY TRUST FUND FINANCING RATE.—On and after October 1, 1988, the Highway Trust Fund financing rate under subsection (b)(2)(A) shall not apply.

(2) LEAKING UNDERGROUND STORAGE TANK TRUST FUND FINANCING RATE.—

(A) IN GENERAL.—The Leaking Underground Storage Tank Trust Fund financing rate under subsection (b)(2)(B) shall not apply after the earlier of—

(i) December 31, 1991, or

(ii) the last day of the termination month.

(B) TERMINATION MONTH.—For purposes of subparagraph (A), the termination month is the 1st month as of the close of which the Secretary estimates that the net revenues from the taxes imposed by this section (to the extent attributable to the Leaking Underground Storage Tank Trust Fund financing rate under subsection (b)(2)(B)), section 4041(d), and section 4042 (to the extent attributable to the Leaking Underground Storage Tank Trust Fund financing rate under section 4042(b)) are at least $500,000,000.

(C) NET REVENUES.—For purposes of subparagraph (B), the term "net revenues" means the excess of gross revenues over amounts payable by reason of section 9508(c)(2) (relating to transfer from Leaking Underground Storage Tank Trust Fund for certain repayments and credits).

Amendments

- **1986, Superfund Amendments and Reauthorization Act of 1986 (P.L. 99-499)**

P.L. 99-499, §521(a)(1)(A)(ii):

Amended Sec. 4081 by adding at the end thereof new subsection (d). **Effective** 1-1-87.

[Sec. 4082]

SEC. 4082. EXEMPTIONS FOR DIESEL FUEL AND KEROSENE.

[Sec. 4082(a)]

(a) IN GENERAL.—The tax imposed by section 4081 shall not apply to diesel fuel and kerosene—

(1) which the Secretary determines is destined for a nontaxable use,

(2) which is indelibly dyed by mechanical injection in accordance with regulations which the Secretary shall prescribe, and

(3) which meets such marking requirements (if any) as may be prescribed by the Secretary in regulations.

Such regulations shall allow an individual choice of dye color approved by the Secretary or chosen from any list of approved dye colors that the Secretary may publish.

Amendments

- **2007, Tax Technical Corrections Act of 2007 (P.L. 110-172)**

P.L. 110-172, §6(d)(2)(B)(i):

Amended Code Sec. 4082(a) by striking "(other than such tax at the Leaking Underground Storage Tank Trust Fund financing rate imposed in all cases other than for export)" following "by section 4081". **Effective** as if included in the provision of the Energy Tax Incentives Act of 2005 (P.L. 109-58) to which it relates [effective for fuel entered, removed, or sold after 9-30-2005.—CCH].

- **2005, Energy Tax Incentives Act of 2005 (P.L. 109-58)**

P.L. 109-58, §1362(b)(1):

Amended Code Sec. 4082(a) by inserting "(other than such tax at the Leaking Underground Storage Tank Trust Fund financing rate imposed in all cases other than for export)" after "section 4081". **Effective** for fuel entered, removed, or sold after 9-30-2005.

Internal Revenue Code

MANUFACTURERS TAXES—MOTOR AND AVIATION FUELS

- **2004, American Jobs Creation Act of 2004 (P.L. 108-357)**

P.L. 108-357, §854(a):

Amended Code Sec. 4082(a)(2) by inserting "by mechanical injection" after "indelibly dyed". **Effective** on the 180th day after the date on which the Secretary issues the regulations described in Act Sec. 854(b), below.

P.L. 108-357, §854(b), provides:

(b) DYE INJECTOR SECURITY.—Not later than 180 days after the date of the enactment of this Act, the Secretary of the Treasury shall issue regulations regarding mechanical dye injection systems described in the amendment made by subsection (a), and such regulations shall include standards for making such systems tamper resistant.

- **1997, Taxpayer Relief Act of 1997 (P.L. 105-34)**

P.L. 105-34, §1032(c)(1):

Amended Code Sec. 4082(a) by striking "diesel fuel" each place it appears and inserting "diesel fuel and kerosene". **Effective** 7-1-98.

P.L. 105-34, §1032(e)(3)(A):

Amended Code Sec. 4082 by inserting "AND KEROSENE" in the heading after "DIESEL FUEL". **Effective** 7-1-98.

[Sec. 4082(b)]

(b) NONTAXABLE USE.—For purposes of this section, the term "nontaxable use" means—

(1) any use which is exempt from the tax imposed by section 4041(a)(1) other than by reason of a prior imposition of tax,

(2) any use in a train, and

(3) any use described in section 4041(a)(1)(C)(iii)(II).

The term "nontaxable use" does not include the use of kerosene in an aircraft and such term shall not include any use described in section 6421(e)(2)(C).

Amendments

- **2007, Tax Technical Corrections Act of 2007 (P.L. 110-172)**

P.L. 110-172, §11(a)(28):

Amended Code Sec. 4082(b). **Effective** 12-29-2007. Prior to amendment, Code Sec. 4082(b) read as follows:

(b) NONTAXABLE USE.—For purposes of this section, the term "nontaxable use" means—

(1) any use which is exempt from the tax imposed by section 4041(a)(1) other than by reason of a prior imposition of tax,

(2) any use in a train, and

(3) any use described in section 4041(a)(1)(C)(iii)(II).

The term "nontaxable use" does not include the use of kerosene in an aircraft and such term shall not include any use described in section 6421(e)(2)(C).

[Sec. 4082(c)]

(c) EXCEPTION TO DYEING REQUIREMENTS.—Paragraph (2) of subsection (a) shall not apply with respect to any diesel fuel and kerosene—

(1) removed, entered, or sold in a State for ultimate sale or use in an area of such State during the period such area is exempted from the fuel dyeing requirements under subsection (i) of section 211 of the Clean Air Act (as in effect on the date of the enactment of this subsection) by the Administrator of the Environmental Protection Agency under paragraph (4) of such subsection (i) (as so in effect), and

(2) the use of which is certified pursuant to regulations issued by the Secretary.

Amendments

- **1997, Taxpayer Relief Act of 1997 (P.L. 105-34)**

P.L. 105-34, §1032(c)(1):

Amended Code Sec. 4082(c) by striking "diesel fuel" each place it appears and inserting "diesel fuel and kerosene". **Effective** 7-1-98.

- **1996, Small Business Job Protection Act of 1996 (P.L. 104-188)**

P.L. 104-188, §1801(a):

Amended Code Sec. 4082 by redesignating subsections (c) and (d) as subsections (d) and (e), respectively, and by inserting after subsection (b) a new subsection (c). **Effective** for fuel removed, entered, or sold on or after the first day of the first calendar quarter beginning after 8-20-96.

[Sec. 4082(d)]

(d) ADDITIONAL EXCEPTIONS TO DYEING REQUIREMENTS FOR KEROSENE.—

(1) USE FOR NON-FUEL FEEDSTOCK PURPOSES.—Subsection (a)(2) shall not apply to kerosene—

(A) received by pipeline or vessel for use by the person receiving the kerosene in the manufacture or production of any substance (other than gasoline, diesel fuel, or special fuels referred to in section 4041), or

(B) to the extent provided in regulations, removed or entered—

(i) for such a use by the person removing or entering the kerosene, or

(ii) for resale by such person for such a use by the purchaser, but only if the person receiving, removing, or entering the kerosene and such purchaser (if any) are registered under section 4101 with respect to the tax imposed by section 4081.

(2) WHOLESALE DISTRIBUTORS.—To the extent provided in regulations, subsection (a)(2) shall not apply to kerosene received by a wholesale distributor of kerosene if such distributor—

(A) is registered under section 4101 with respect to the tax imposed by section 4081 on kerosene, and

(B) sells kerosene exclusively to ultimate vendors described in section 6427(l)(5)(B) with respect to kerosene.

Amendments

- **2006, Tax Relief and Health Care Act of 2006 (P.L. 109-432)**

P.L. 109-432, Division A, §420(b)(2):

Amended Code Sec. 4082(d)(2)(B) by striking "section 6427(l)(6)(B)" and inserting "section 6427(l)(5)(B)". **Effective** generally for kerosene sold after 9-30-2005. For special rules, see Act Sec. 420(c)(2) and (d) in the amendment notes following Code Sec. 6427(l).

- **2005, Safe, Accountable, Flexible, Efficient Transportation Equity Act: A Legacy for Users (P.L. 109-59)**

P.L. 109-59, §11161(b)(3)(C):

Amended Code Sec. 4082(d)(2)(B) by striking "section 6427(l)(5)(B)" and inserting "section 6427(l)(6)(B)". **Effective** for fuels or liquids removed, entered, or sold after 9-30-2005.

- **2004, American Jobs Creation Act of 2004 (P.L. 108-357)**

P.L. 108-357, §853(a)(5)(B)(ii):

Amended Code Sec. 4082(d) by striking paragraph (1) and by redesignating paragraphs (2) and (3) as paragraphs (1) and (2), respectively. **Effective** for aviation-grade kerosene removed, entered, or sold after 12-31-2004. For special rules, see Act Sec. 853(f) in the amendments to Code Sec. 4082(e). Prior to being stricken, Code Sec. 4082(d)(1) read as follows:

(1) AVIATION-GRADE KEROSENE.—Subsection (a)(2) shall not apply to aviation-grade kerosene (as determined under regulations prescribed by the Secretary) which the Secretary determines is destined for use as a fuel in an aircraft.

- **1998, IRS Restructuring and Reform Act of 1998 (P.L. 105-206)**

P.L. 105-206, §6010(h)(3):

Amended Code Sec. 4082(d)(1). **Effective** as if included in the provision of P.L. 105-34 to which it relates [**effective** 7-1-98.—CCH]. Prior to amendment, Code Sec. 4082(d)(1) read as follows:

(1) AVIATION-GRADE KEROSENE.—Subsection (a)(2) shall not apply to a removal, entry, or sale of aviation-grade kerosene (as determined under regulations prescribed by the Secretary) if the person receiving the kerosene is registered under section 4101 with respect to the tax imposed by section 4091.

P.L. 105-206, §6010(h)(4):

Amended Code Sec. 4082(d)(3) by striking "a removal, entry, or sale of kerosene to" and inserting "kerosene received by". **Effective** as if included in the provision of P.L. 105-34 to which it relates [**effective** 7-1-98.—CCH].

- **1997, Taxpayer Relief Act of 1997 (P.L. 105-34)**

P.L. 105-34, §1032(c)(2):

Amended Code Sec. 4082 by redesignating subsections (d) and (e) as subsections (e) and (f), respectively, and by inserting after subsection (c) a new subsection (d). **Effective** 7-1-98.

MANUFACTURERS TAXES—MOTOR AND AVIATION FUELS

[Sec. 4082(e)]

(e) KEROSENE REMOVED INTO AN AIRCRAFT.—In the case of kerosene (other than kerosene with respect to which tax is imposed under section 4043) which is exempt from the tax imposed by section 4041(c) (other than by reason of a prior imposition of tax) and which is removed from any refinery or terminal directly into the fuel tank of an aircraft—

(1) the rate of tax under section 4081(a)(2)(A)(iii) shall be zero, and

(2) if such aircraft is employed in foreign trade or trade between the United States and any of its possessions, the increase in such rate under section 4081(a)(2)(B) shall be zero.

For purposes of this subsection, any removal described in section 4081(a)(3)(A) shall be treated as a removal from a terminal but only if such terminal is located within a secure area of an airport.

Amendments

• **2012, FAA Modernization and Reform Act of 2012 (P.L. 112-95)**

P.L. 112-95, §1103(a)(2):

Amended Code Sec. 4082(e) by inserting "(other than kerosene with respect to which tax is imposed under section 4043)" after "In the case of kerosene". **Effective** for fuel used after 3-31-2012.

• **2007, Tax Technical Corrections Act of 2007 (P.L. 110-172)**

P.L. 110-172, §6(d)(2)(C)(i):

Amended Code Sec. 4082(e) by striking "an aircraft, the rate of tax under section 4081(a)(2)(A)(iii) shall be zero" and inserting "an aircraft—" and new paragraphs (1) and (2). **Effective** as if included in the provision of the Energy Tax Incentives Act of 2005 (P.L. 109-58) to which it relates [**effective** for fuel entered, removed, or sold after 9-30-2005.—CCH].

P.L. 110-172, §6(d)(2)(C)(ii):

Amended Code Sec. 4082(e) by moving the last sentence flush with the margin of such subsection (following the paragraph (2) added by Act Sec. 6(d)(2)(C)(i)). **Effective** as if included in section 11161 of the Safe, Accountable, Flexible, Efficient Transportation Equity Act: A Legacy for Users (P.L. 109-59) [**effective** for fuels or liquids removed, entered, or sold after 9-30-2005.—CCH].

• **2005, Safe, Accountable, Flexible, Efficient Transportation Equity Act: A Legacy for Users (P.L. 109-59)**

P.L. 109-59, §11161(a)(4)(E)(i)-(iv):

Amended Code Sec. 4082(e) by striking "aviation-grade" following "case of", by striking "section 4081(a)(2)(A)(iv)" and inserting "section 4081(a)(2)(A)(iii)", by adding at the end a new sentence, and by striking "AVIATION-GRADE KEROSENE" in the heading and inserting "KEROSENE REMOVED INTO AN AIRCRAFT". **Effective** for fuels or liquids removed, entered, or sold after 9-30-2005. Prior to amendment, Code Sec. 4082(e) read as follows:

(e) AVIATION-GRADE KEROSENE.—In the case of aviation-grade kerosene which is exempt from the tax imposed by section 4041(c) (other than by reason of a prior imposition of tax) and which is removed from any refinery or terminal directly into the fuel tank of an aircraft, the rate of tax under section 4081(a)(2)(A)(iv) shall be zero.

• **2004, American Jobs Creation Act of 2004 (P.L. 108-357)**

P.L. 108-357, §853(a)(5)(A):

Amended Code Sec. 4082 by redesignating subsections (e) and (f) as subsections (f) and (g), respectively, and by inserting after subsection (d) a new subsection (e). **Effective** for aviation-grade kerosene removed, entered, or sold after 12-31-2004. For special rules, see Act Sec. 853(f), below.

P.L. 108-357, §853(f), provides:

(f) FLOOR STOCKS TAX.—

(1) IN GENERAL.—There is hereby imposed on aviation-grade kerosene held on January 1, 2005, by any person a tax equal to—

(A) the tax which would have been imposed before such date on such kerosene had the amendments made by this section been in effect at all times before such date, reduced by

(B) the sum of—

(i) the tax imposed before such date on such kerosene under section 4091 of the Internal Revenue Code of 1986, as in effect on such date, and

(ii) in the case of kerosene held exclusively for such person's own use, the amount which such person would (but for this clause) reasonably expect (as of such date) to be paid as a refund under section 6427(l) of such Code with respect to such kerosene.

(2) EXCEPTION FOR FUEL HELD IN AIRCRAFT FUEL TANK.—Paragraph (1) shall not apply to kerosene held in the fuel tank of an aircraft on January 1, 2005.

(3) LIABILITY FOR TAX AND METHOD OF PAYMENT.—

(A) LIABILITY FOR TAX.—The person holding the kerosene on January 1, 2005, to which the tax imposed by paragraph (1) applies shall be liable for such tax.

(B) METHOD AND TIME FOR PAYMENT.—The tax imposed by paragraph (1) shall be paid at such time and in such manner as the Secretary of the Treasury (or the Secretary's delegate) shall prescribe, including the nonapplication of such tax on de minimis amounts of kerosene.

(4) TRANSFER OF FLOOR STOCK TAX REVENUES TO TRUST FUNDS.—For purposes of determining the amount transferred to any trust fund, the tax imposed by this subsection shall be treated as imposed by section 4081 of the Internal Revenue Code of 1986—

(A) in any case in which tax was not imposed by section 4091 of such Code, at the Leaking Underground Storage Tank Trust Fund financing rate under such section to the extent of 0.1 cents per gallon, and

(B) at the rate under section 4081(a)(2)(A)(iv) of such Code to the extent of the remainder.

(5) HELD BY A PERSON.—For purposes of this subsection, kerosene shall be considered as held by a person if title thereto has passed to such person (whether or not delivery to the person has been made).

(6) OTHER LAWS APPLICABLE.—All provisions of law, including penalties, applicable with respect to the tax imposed by section 4081 of such Code shall, insofar as applicable and not inconsistent with the provisions of this subsection, apply with respect to the floor stock tax imposed by paragraph (1) to the same extent as if such tax were imposed by such section.

[Sec. 4082(f)]

(f) EXCEPTION FOR LEAKING UNDERGROUND STORAGE TANK TRUST FUND FINANCING RATE.—

(1) IN GENERAL.—Subsection (a) shall not apply to the tax imposed under section 4081 at the Leaking Underground Storage Tank Trust Fund financing rate.

(2) EXCEPTION FOR EXPORT, ETC.—Paragraph (1) shall not apply with respect to any fuel if the Secretary determines that such fuel is destined for export or for use by the purchaser as supplies for vessels (within the meaning of section 4221(d)(3)) employed in foreign trade or trade between the United States and any of its possessions.

Amendments

• **2007, Tax Technical Corrections Act of 2007 (P.L. 110-172)**

P.L. 110-172, §6(d)(2)(B)(ii):

Amended Code Sec. 4082 by redesignating subsections (f) and (g) as subsections (g) and (h), respectively, and by inserting after subsection (e) a new subsection (f). **Effective** as if included in the provision of the Energy Tax Incentives Act of 2005 (P.L. 109-58) to which it relates [**effective** for fuel entered, removed, or sold after 9-30-2005.—CCH].

[Sec. 4082(g)]

(g) REGULATIONS.—The Secretary shall prescribe such regulations as may be necessary to carry out this section, including regulations requiring the conspicuous labeling of retail diesel fuel and kerosene pumps and other delivery facilities to assure that persons are aware of which fuel is available only for nontaxable uses.

Amendments

• **2007, Tax Technical Corrections Act of 2007 (P.L. 110-172)**

P.L. 110-172, §6(d)(2)(B)(ii):

Amended Code Sec. 4082 by redesignating subsection (f) as subsection (g). **Effective** as if included in the provision of the Energy Tax Incentives Act of 2005 (P.L. 109-58) to which it relates [**effective** for fuel entered, removed, or sold after 9-30-2005.—CCH].

• **2004, American Jobs Creation Act of 2004 (P.L. 108-357)**

P.L. 108-357, §853(a)(5)(A):

Amended Code Sec. 4082 by redesignating subsection (e) as subsection (f). **Effective** for aviation-grade kerosene removed, entered, or sold after 12-31-2004.

• **1997, Taxpayer Relief Act of 1997 (P.L. 105-34)**

P.L. 105-34, §1032(c)(1):

Amended Code Sec. 4082(d) by striking "diesel fuel" each place it appears and inserting "diesel fuel and kerosene". **Effective** 7-1-98.

P.L. 105-34, §1032(c)(2):

Amended Code Sec. 4082 by redesignating subsection (d) as subsection (e). **Effective** 7-1-98.

• **1996, Small Business Job Protection Act of 1996 (P.L. 104-188)**

P.L. 104-188, §1801(a):

Amended Code Sec. 4082 by redesignating subsection (c) as subsection (d). **Effective** with respect to fuel removed, entered, or sold on or after the first day of the first calendar quarter beginning after 8-20-96.

MANUFACTURERS TAXES—MOTOR AND AVIATION FUELS

[Sec. 4082(h)]

(h) CROSS REFERENCE.—

For tax on train and certain bus uses of fuel purchased tax-free, see subsections (a)(1) and (d)(3) of section 4041.

Amendments

- **2007, Tax Technical Corrections Act of 2007 (P.L. 110-172)**

P.L. 110-172, § 6(d)(2)(B)(ii):

Amended Code Sec. 4082 by redesignating subsection (g) as subsection (h). **Effective** as if included in the provision of the Energy Tax Incentives Act of 2005 (P.L. 109-58) to which it relates [**effective** for fuel entered, removed, or sold after 9-30-2005.—CCH].

- **2004, American Jobs Creation Act of 2004 (P.L. 108-357)**

P.L. 108-357, § 241(a)(2)(B):

Amended Code Sec. 4082(f) by striking "section 4041(a)(1)" and inserting "subsections (a)(1) and (d)(3) of section 4041". **Effective** 1-1-2005.

P.L. 108-357, § 853(a)(5)(A):

Amended Code Sec. 4082 by redesignating subsection (f) as subsection (g). **Effective** for aviation-grade kerosene removed, entered, or sold after 12-31-2004.

- **1997, Taxpayer Relief Act of 1997 (P.L. 105-34)**

P.L. 105-34, § 1032(c)(2):

Amended Code Sec. 4082 by redesignating subsection (e) as subsection (f). **Effective** 7-1-98.

- **1996, Small Business Job Protection Act of 1996 (P.L. 104-188)**

P.L. 104-188, § 1801(a):

Amended Code Sec. 4082 by redesignating subsection (d) as subsection (e). **Effective** for fuel removed, entered, or sold on or after the first day of the first calendar quarter beginning after 8-20-96.

- **1993, Omnibus Budget Reconciliation Act of 1993 (P.L. 103-66)**

P.L. 103-66, § 13242(a):

Amended subparts A and B of part III of subchapter A of chapter 32 (Code Secs. 4081-4093). **Effective** 1-1-94. Prior to amendment, Code Sec. 4082 read as follows:

[Sec. 4082]

SEC. 4082. DEFINITIONS.

[Sec. 4082(a)]

(a) GASOLINE.—For purposes of this subpart, the term "gasoline" includes, to the extent prescribed in regulations—

(1) gasoline blend stocks, and

(2) products commonly used as additives in gasoline.

For purposes of paragraph (1), the term "gasoline blend stocks" means any petroleum product component of gasoline.

[Sec. 4082(b)]

(b) CERTAIN USES DEFINED AS REMOVAL.—If a refiner, importer, terminal operator, blender, or compounder uses (other than in the production of gasoline or special fuels referred to in section 4041) gasoline refined, imported, blended, or compounded by him, such use shall for the purposes of this chapter be considered a removal.

Amendments

- **1986, Tax Reform Act of 1986 (P.L. 99-514)**

P.L. 99-514, § 1703(a):

Amended Code Sec. 4082. **Effective** for gasoline removed as defined in Code Sec. 4082, as amended by Act Sec. 1703(a), after 12-31-87. Prior to amendment, Code Sec. 4082 read as follows:

[Sec. 4082]

SEC. 4082. DEFINITIONS.

[Sec. 4082(a)]

(a) PRODUCER.—As used in this subpart, the term "producer" includes a refiner, compounder, blender, or wholesale distributor, and a dealer selling gasoline exclusively to producers of gasoline, as well as a producer. Any person to whom gasoline is sold tax-under this subpart shall be considered the producer of such gasoline.

Amendments

- **1959, Federal-Aid Highway Act of 1959 (P.L. 86-342)**

P.L. 86-342, § 201(e)(1):

Amended the first sentence of Code Sec. 4082(a). **Effective** 1-1-60. Prior to amendment, the first sentence read as follows: "As used in this subpart, the term "producer" includes a refiner, compounder, or blender, and a dealer selling gasoline exclusively to producers of gasoline, as well as a producer."

[Sec. 4082(b)]

(b) GASOLINE.—As used in this subpart, the term "gasoline" means all products commonly or commerically known or sold as gasoline which are suitable for use as a motor fuel.

Amendments

- **1965, Excise Tax Reduction Act of 1965 (P.L. 89-44)**

P.L. 89-44, § 802(a):

Amended Sec. 4082(b) by substituting the words "which are suitable for use as a motor fuel" for "(including casinghead and natural gasoline)" therein; amended Sec. 4082(d)(2). **Effective** 7-1-65. Prior to amendment, Sec. 4082(d)(2) read as follows: "(2) elects to register and give a bond with respect to the tax imposed by section 4081."

[Sec. 4082(c)]

(c) CERTAIN USES DEFINED AS SALES.—If a producer or importer uses (otherwise than in the production of gasoline or of special fuels referred to in section 4041) gasoline sold to him free of tax, or produced or imported by him, such use shall for the purposes of this chapter be considered a sale.

[Sec. 4082(d)]

(d) WHOLESALE DISTRIBUTOR.—As used in subsection (a), the term "wholesale distributor" includes—

(1) any person who—

(A) sells gasoline to producers, retailers, or to users who purchase in bulk quantities and deliver into bulk storage tanks, or

(B) purchases gasoline from a producer and distributes such gasoline to 10 or more retail gasoline stations under common managment with such person,

(2) but only if such person elects to register with respect to the tax imposed by section 4081.

Such term does not include any person who (excluding the term "wholesale distributor" from subsection (a)) is a producer or importer.

Amendments

- **1984, Deficit Reduction Act of 1984 (P.L. 98-369)**

P.L. 98-369, § 733(a):

Amended Code Sec. 4082(d). **Effective** on the first day of the first calendar quarter beginning after 7-18-84. Prior to amendment, Code Sec. 4082(d) read as follows:

(d) Wholesale Distributor.—As used in subsection (a), the term "wholesale distributor" includes any person who—

(1) sells gasoline to producers, to retailers, or to users who purchase in bulk quantities for delivery into bulk storage tanks, and

(2) elects to register with respect to the tax imposed by section 4081.

Such term does not include any person who (excluding the term "wholesale distributor" from subsection (a)) is a producer or importer.

- **1970 (P.L. 91-258)**

P.L. 91-258, § 205(c)(6):

Amended Code Sec. 4082(c) by substituting "special fuels referred to in section 4041" for "special motor fuels referred to in section 4041(b)". **Effective** 7-1-70.

- **1965, Excise Tax Reduction Act of 1965 (P.L. 89-44)**

P.L. 89-44, § 802(b)(1):

Amended Sec. 4082(d)(2) by deleting "and give a bond" after "register". **Effective** 7-1-65.

- **1959, Federal-Aid Highway Act of 1959 (P.L. 86-342)**

P.L. 86-342, § 201(e)(2):

Amended Code Sec. 4082 by adding subsection (d). **Effective** 1-1-60.

[Sec. 4082(e)]

(e) CERTAIN SELLERS OF GASOLINE FOR USE IN NONCOMMERCIAL AVIATION TREATED AS PRODUCERS.—For purposes of this subpart, the term "producer" includes any person who regularly sells gasoline to owners, lessees, or operators of aircraft for use as fuel in such aircraft in noncommercial aviation (as defined in section 4041(c)(4)).

Amendments

- **1984, Deficit Reduction Act of 1984 (P.L. 98-369)**

P.L. 98-369, § 734(c)(1):

Amended Code Sec. 4082 by adding new subsection (e). **Effective** on the first day of the first calendar quarter beginning after 7-18-84.

[Sec. 4083]

SEC. 4083. DEFINITIONS; SPECIAL RULE; ADMINISTRATIVE AUTHORITY.

[Sec. 4083(a)]

(a) TAXABLE FUEL.—For purposes of this subpart—

(1) IN GENERAL.—The term "taxable fuel" means—

(A) gasoline,

(B) diesel fuel, and

(C) kerosene.

(2) GASOLINE.—The term "gasoline"—

MANUFACTURERS TAXES—MOTOR AND AVIATION FUELS

(A) includes any gasoline blend, other than qualified methanol or ethanol fuel (as defined in section 4041(b)(2)(B)), partially exempt methanol or ethanol fuel (as defined in section 4041(m)(2)), or a denatured alcohol, and

(B) includes, to the extent prescribed in regulations—

(i) any gasoline blend stock, and

(ii) any product commonly used as an additive in gasoline (other than alcohol).

For purposes of subparagraph (B)(i), the term "gasoline blend stock" means any petroleum product component of gasoline.

(3) DIESEL FUEL.—

(A) IN GENERAL.—The term "diesel fuel" means—

(i) any liquid (other than gasoline) which is suitable for use as a fuel in a diesel-powered highway vehicle, or a diesel-powered train,

(ii) transmix, and

(iii) diesel fuel blend stocks identified by the Secretary.

(B) TRANSMIX.—For purposes of subparagraph (A), the term "transmix" means a byproduct of refined products pipeline operations created by the mixing of different specification products during pipeline transportation.

Amendments

• **2004, American Jobs Creation Act of 2004 (P.L. 108-357)**

P.L. 108-357, §301(c)(8):

Amended Code Sec. 4083(a)(2). **Effective** for fuel sold or used after 12-31-2004. Prior to amendment, Code Sec. 4083(a)(2) read as follows:

(2) GASOLINE.—The term "gasoline" includes, to the extent prescribed in regulations—

(A) gasoline blend stocks, and

(B) products commonly used as additives in gasoline.

For purposes of subparagraph (A), the term "gasoline blend stock" means any petroleum product component of gasoline.

P.L. 108-357, §870(a):

Amended Code Sec. 4083(a)(3). **Effective** for fuel removed, sold, or used after 12-31-2004. Prior to amendment, Code Sec. 4083(a)(3) read as follows:

(3) DIESEL FUEL.—The term "diesel fuel" means any liquid (other than gasoline) which is suitable for use as a fuel in a diesel-powered highway vehicle or a diesel-powered train.

• **1997, Taxpayer Relief Act of 1997 (P.L. 105-34)**

P.L. 105-34, §902(b)(3):

Amended Code Sec. 4083(a)(3) by striking ", a diesel-powered train, or a diesel-powered boat" and inserting "or a diesel-powered train". **Effective** 1-1-98.

P.L. 105-34, §1032(a) (as amended by P.L. 105-206, §6010(h)(1)):

Amended Code Sec. 4083(a)(1) by striking "and" at the end of subparagraph (A), by striking the period at the end of subparagraph (B) and inserting ", and", and by adding a new subparagraph (C). **Effective** 7-1-98. For the provision on floor stocks taxes on kerosene, see Act Sec. 1032(g) in the amendment notes following Code Sec. 4081(a).

[Sec. 4083(b)]

(b) COMMERCIAL AVIATION.—For purposes of this subpart, the term "commercial aviation" means any use of an aircraft in a business of transporting persons or property for compensation or hire by air, unless properly allocable to any transportation exempt from the taxes imposed by sections 4261 and 4271 by reason of section 4281 or 4282 or by reason of subsection (h) or (i) of section 4261. Such term shall not include the use of any aircraft before October 1, 2028, if tax is imposed under section 4043 with respect to the fuel consumed in such use or if no tax is imposed on such use under section 4043 by reason of subsection (c)(5) thereof.

Amendments

• **2024, FAA Reauthorization Act of 2024 (P.L. 118-63)**

P.L. 118-63, §1302(c)(2):

Amended Code Sec. 4083(b) by striking "May 11, 2024" and inserting "October 1, 2028". **Effective** 5-16-2024.

• **2024, Airport and Airway Extension Act of 2024, Part II (P.L. 118-60)**

P.L. 118-60, §202(b), provides:

SEC. 202. EXTENSION OF TAXES FUNDING AIRPORT AND AIRWAY TRUST FUND.

(b) Section 4083(b) of such Code shall be applied by substituting "May 18, 2024" for "May 11, 2024".

• **2024, Airport and Airway Extension Act of 2024 (P.L. 118-41)**

P.L. 118-41, §202(c)(2):

Amended Code Sec. 4083(b) by striking "March 9, 2024" and inserting "May 11, 2024". **Effective** 3-8-2024.

• **2023, Airport and Airway Extension Act of 2023, Part II (P.L. 118-34)**

P.L. 118-34, §202(c)(2):

Amended Code Sec. 4083(b) by striking "January 1, 2024" and inserting "March 9, 2024". **Effective** 12-26-2023.

• **2023, Continuing Appropriations Act, 2024 and Other Extensions Act (P.L. 118-15)**

P.L. 118-15, §2212(c)(2):

Amended Code Sec. 4083(b) by striking "October 1, 2023" and inserting "January 1, 2024". **Effective** 9-30-2023.

• **2018, FAA Reauthorization Act of 2018 (P.L. 115-254)**

P.L. 115-254, §802(c)(2):

Amended Code Sec. 4083(b) by striking "October 1, 2018" and inserting "October 1, 2023". **Effective** 10-5-2018.

• **2018, Airport and Airway Extension Act of 2018, Part II (P.L. 115-250)**

P.L. 115-250, §5(b), provides:

(b) Section 4083(b) of such Code shall be applied by substituting "October 8, 2018" for "October 1, 2018".

• **2018, Airport and Airway Extension Act of 2018 (P.L. 115-141)**

P.L. 115-141, §202(c)(1), Div. M:

Amended Code Sec. 4083(b) by striking "April 1, 2018" and inserting "October 1, 2018". **Effective** 3-23-2018.

• **2017, Disaster Tax Relief and Airport and Airway Extension Act of 2017 (P.L. 115-63)**

P.L. 115-63, §202(c)(1):

Amended Code Sec. 4083(b) by striking "October 1, 2017" and inserting "April 1, 2018". **Effective** 9-29-2017.

• **2016, FAA Extension, Safety, and Security Act of 2016 (P.L. 114-190)**

P.L. 114-190, §1202(c)(1):

Amended Code Sec. 4083(b) by striking "July 16, 2016" and inserting "October 1, 2017". **Effective** 7-15-2016.

• **2016, Airport and Airway Extension Act of 2016 (P.L. 114-141)**

P.L. 114-141, §202(c)(1):

Amended Code Sec. 4083(b) by striking "April 1, 2016" and inserting "July 16, 2016". **Effective** 3-30-2016.

• **2015, Airport and Airway Extension Act of 2015 (P.L. 114-55)**

P.L. 114-55, §202(c)(1):

Amended Code Sec. 4083(b) by striking "October 1, 2015" and inserting "April 1, 2016". **Effective** 9-30-2015.

• **2012, FAA Modernization and Reform Act of 2012 (P.L. 112-95)**

P.L. 112-95, §1103(b):

Amended Code Sec. 4083(b) by adding at the end a new sentence. **Effective** for uses of aircraft after 3-31-2012.

• **2005, Safe, Accountable, Flexible, Efficient Transportation Equity Act: A Legacy for Users (P.L. 109-59)**

P.L. 109-59, §11123(b):

Amended Code Sec. 4083(b) by striking "section 4261(h)" and inserting "subsection (h) or (i) of section 4261". **Effective** for transportation beginning after 9-30-2005.

• **2004, American Jobs Creation Act of 2004 (P.L. 108-357)**

P.L. 108-357, §853(b):

Amended Code Sec. 4083 by redesignating subsections (b) and (c) as subsections (c) and (d), respectively, and by inserting after subsection (a) a new subsection (b). **Effective** for aviation-grade kerosene removed, entered, or sold after 12-31-2004. For special rules, see Act Sec. 853(f), below.

P.L. 108-357, §853(f), provides:

(f) FLOOR STOCKS TAX.—

(1) IN GENERAL.—There is hereby imposed on aviation-grade kerosene held on January 1, 2005, by any person a tax equal to—

MANUFACTURERS TAXES—MOTOR AND AVIATION FUELS

(A) the tax which would have been imposed before such date on such kerosene had the amendments made by this section been in effect at all times before such date, reduced by

(B) the sum of—

(i) the tax imposed before such date on such kerosene under section 4091 of the Internal Revenue Code of 1986, as in effect on such date, and

(ii) in the case of kerosene held exclusively for such person's own use, the amount which such person would (but for this clause) reasonably expect (as of such date) to be paid as a refund under section 6427(l) of such Code with respect to such kerosene.

(2) EXCEPTION FOR FUEL HELD IN AIRCRAFT FUEL TANK.—Paragraph (1) shall not apply to kerosene held in the fuel tank of an aircraft on January 1, 2005.

(3) LIABILITY FOR TAX AND METHOD OF PAYMENT.—

(A) LIABILITY FOR TAX.—The person holding the kerosene on January 1, 2005, to which the tax imposed by paragraph (1) applies shall be liable for such tax.

(B) METHOD AND TIME FOR PAYMENT.—The tax imposed by paragraph (1) shall be paid at such time and in such manner as the Secretary of the Treasury (or the Secretary's delegate) shall prescribe, including the nonapplication of such tax on de minimis amounts of kerosene.

(4) TRANSFER OF FLOOR STOCK TAX REVENUES TO TRUST FUNDS.—For purposes of determining the amount transferred to any trust fund, the tax imposed by this subsection shall be treated as imposed by section 4081 of the Internal Revenue Code of 1986—

(A) in any case in which tax was not imposed by section 4091 of such Code, at the Leaking Underground Storage Tank Trust Fund financing rate under such section to the extent of 0.1 cents per gallon, and

(B) at the rate under section 4081(a)(2)(A)(iv) of such Code to the extent of the remainder.

(5) HELD BY A PERSON.—For purposes of this subsection, kerosene shall be considered as held by a person if title thereto has passed to such person (whether or not delivery to the person has been made).

(6) OTHER LAWS APPLICABLE.—All provisions of law, including penalties, applicable with respect to the tax imposed by section 4081 of such Code shall, insofar as applicable and not inconsistent with the provisions of this subsection, apply with respect to the floor stock tax imposed by paragraph (1) to the same extent as if such tax were imposed by such section.

[Sec. 4083(c)]

(c) CERTAIN USES DEFINED AS REMOVAL.—If any person uses taxable fuel (other than in the production of taxable fuels or special fuels referred to in section 4041), such use shall for the purposes of this chapter be considered a removal.

Amendments

• **2004, American Jobs Creation Act of 2004 (P.L. 108-357)**

P.L. 108-357, §853(b):

Amended Code Sec. 4083 by redesignating subsection (b) as subsection (c). **Effective** for aviation-grade kerosene removed, entered, or sold after 12-31-2004.

• **1997, Taxpayer Relief Act of 1997 (P.L. 105-34)**

P.L. 105-34, §1032(e)(4):

Amended Code Sec. 4083(b) by striking "gasoline, diesel fuel," and inserting "taxable fuels". **Effective** 7-1-98.

[Sec. 4083(d)]

(d) ADMINISTRATIVE AUTHORITY.—

(1) IN GENERAL.—In addition to the authority otherwise granted by this title, the Secretary may in administering compliance with this subpart, section 4041, and penalties and other administrative provisions related thereto—

(A) enter any place at which taxable fuel is produced or is stored (or may be stored) for purposes of—

(i) examining the equipment used to determine the amount or composition of such fuel and the equipment used to store such fuel,

(ii) taking and removing samples of such fuel, and

(iii) inspecting any books and records and any shipping papers pertaining to such fuel, and

(B) detain, for the purposes referred in subparagraph (A), any container which contains or may contain any taxable fuel.

(2) INSPECTION SITES.—The Secretary may establish inspection sites for purposes of carrying out the Secretary's authority under paragraph (1)(B).

(3) PENALTY FOR REFUSAL OF ENTRY.—

(A) FORFEITURE.— The penalty provided by section 7342 shall apply to any refusal to admit entry or other refusal to permit an action by the Secretary authorized by paragraph (1), except that section 7342 shall be applied by substitution "$1,000" for "$500" for each such refusal.

(B) ASSESSABLE PENALTY.—For additional assessable penalty for the refusal to admit entry or other refusal to permit an action by the Secretary authorized by paragraph (1), see section 6717.

Amendments

• **2004, American Jobs Creation Act of 2004 (P.L. 108-357)**

P.L. 108-357, §853(b):

Amended Code Sec. 4083 by redesignating subsection (c) as subsection (d). **Effective** for aviation-grade kerosene removed, entered, or sold after 12-31-2004.

P.L. 108-357, §858(a):

Amended Code Sec. 4083(d)(1)(A), as amended by Act Sec. 853(b), by striking "and" at the end of clause (i) and by inserting after clause (ii) a new clause (iii). **Effective** 10-22-2004.

P.L. 108-357, §859(b)(1)(A)-(B):

Amended Code Sec. 4083(d)(3), as amended by Act Sec. 853(b), by striking "ENTRY.—The penalty" and inserting: "ENTRY.—(A) FORFEITURE.—The penalty", and by adding at the end a new subparagraph (B). **Effective** 1-1-2005.

• **1993, Omnibus Budget Reconciliation Act of 1993 (P.L. 103-66)**

P.L. 103-66, §13242(a):

Amended subparts A and B of part III of subchapter A of chapter 32 (Code Secs. 4081-4093). **Effective** 1-1-94. Prior to amendment, Code Sec. 4083 read as follows:

[Sec. 4083]

SEC. 4083. CROSS REFERENCES.

(1) For provisions to relieve farmers from excise tax in the case of gasoline used on the farm for farming purposes, see section 6420.

(2) For provisions to relieve purchasers of gasoline from excise tax in the case of gasoline used for certain nonhighway purposes, used by local transit systems, or sold for certain exempt purposes, see section 6421.

(3) For provisions to relieve purchasers of gasoline from excise tax in the case of gasoline not used for taxable purposes, see section 6427.

Amendments

• **1986, Tax Reform Act of 1986 (P.L. 99-514)**

P.L. 99-514, §1703(a):

Amended Code Sec. 4083. **Effective** for gasoline removed, as defined in Code Sec. 4082, as amended by Act Sec. 1703(a), after 12-31-87. Prior to amendment, Code Sec. 4083 read as follows:

SEC. 4083. EXEMPTION OF SALES TO PRODUCER.

Under regulations prescribed by the Secretary the tax imposed by section 4081 shall not apply in the case of sales of gasoline to a producer of gasoline.

• **1976, Tax Reform Act of 1976 (P.L. 94-455)**

P.L. 94-455, §1906(b)(13)(A):

Amended 1954 Code by substituting "Secretary" for "Secretary or his delegate" each place it appeared. **Effective** 2-1-77.

[Sec. 4084]

SEC. 4084. CROSS REFERENCES.

(1) For provisions to relieve farmers from excise tax in the case of gasoline used on the farm for farming purposes, see section 6420.

(2) For provisions to relieve purchasers of gasoline from excise tax in the case of gasoline used for certain nonhighway purposes, used by local transit systems, or sold for certain exempt purposes, see section 6421.

(3) For provisions to relieve purchasers from excise tax in the case of taxable fuel not used for taxable purposes, see section 6427.

Amendments

• **1993, Omnibus Budget Reconciliation Act of 1993 (P.L. 103-66)**

P.L. 103-66, §13242(a):

Added Code Sec. 4084. **Effective** 1-1-94.

• **1986, Tax Reform Act of 1986 (P.L. 99-514)**

P.L. 99-514, §1703(a):

Amended subpart A of part III of subchapter A of chapter 32 by replacing Code Secs. 4081-4084 with Code Secs. 4081-4083. **Effective** for gasoline removed, as defined

MANUFACTURERS TAXES—DIESEL FUEL

in Code Sec. 4082, as amended by Act Sec. 1703(a), after 12-31-87. Prior to amendment, Code Sec. 4084 read as follows:

SEC. 4084. CROSS REFERENCES.

(1) For provisions to relieve farmers from excise tax in the case of gasoline used on the farm for farming purposes, see section 6420.

(2) For provisions to relieve purchasers of gasoline from excise tax in the case of gasoline used for certain nonhighway purposes or by local transit systems, see section 6421.

• **1956 (P.L. 627, 84th Cong.)**

P.L. 627, 84th Cong., 2d Sess., § 208(e)(1):

Amended Sec. 4084. **Effective** 7-1-56. Prior to amendment, Section 4084 read as follows:

SEC. 4084. RELIEF OF FARMERS FROM TAX IN CASE OF GASOLINE USED ON THE FARM.

For provisions to relieve farmers from excise tax in the case of gasoline used on the farm for farming purposes, see section 6420.

• **1956 (P.L. 466, 84th Cong.)**

P.L. 466, 84th Cong., 2d Sess., § 4(a):

Added Code Sec. 4084.

Subpart B—Diesel Fuel and Aviation Fuel—[Stricken]

[Sec. 4091—Stricken]

Amendments

• **2004, American Jobs Creation Act of 2004 (P.L. 108-357)**

P.L. 108-357, § 853(d)(1):

Amended part III of subchapter A of chapter 32 by striking subpart B (Code Secs. 4091-4093) and by redesignating subpart C as subpart B. **Effective** for aviation-grade kerosene removed, entered, or sold after 12-31-2004. Prior to being stricken, Code Sec. 4091 read as follows:

SEC. 4091. IMPOSITION OF TAX.

[Sec. 4091(a)]

(a) TAX ON SALE.—

(1) IN GENERAL.—There is hereby imposed a tax on the sale of aviation fuel by the producer or the importer thereof or by any producer of aviation fuel.

(2) USE TREATED AS SALE.—For purposes of paragraph (1), if any producer uses aviation fuel (other than for a nontaxable use as defined in section 6427(l)(2)(B)) on which no tax has been imposed under such paragraph or on which tax has been credited or refunded, then such use shall be considered a sale.

Amendments

• **1998, IRS Restructuring and Reform Act of 1998 (P.L. 105-206)**

P.L. 105-206, § 6014(d):

Amended Code Sec. 4091(a)(2) by inserting "or on which tax has been credited or refunded" after "such paragraph". **Effective** as if included in the provision of P.L. 105-34 to which it relates [**effective** for fuel acquired by the producer after 9-30-97.—CCH].

[Sec. 4091(b)]

(b) RATE OF TAX.—

(1) IN GENERAL.—The rate of the tax imposed by subsection (a) shall be 21.8 cents per gallon.

(2) LEAKING UNDERGROUND STORAGE TANK TRUST FUND TAX.—The rate of tax specified in paragraph (1) shall be increased by 0.1 cent per gallon. The increase in tax under this paragraph shall in this title be referred to as the Leaking Underground Storage Tank Trust Fund financing rate.

(3) TERMINATION.—

(A) The rate of tax specified in paragraph (1) shall be 4.3 cents per gallon—

(i) after December 31, 1996, and before the date which is 7 days after the date of the enactment of the Airport and Airway Trust Fund Tax Reinstatement Act of 1997, and

(ii) after September 30, 2007.

(B) The Leaking Underground Storage Tank Fund financing rate shall not apply during any period during which the Leaking Underground Storage Tank Trust Fund financing rate under section 4081 does not apply.

Amendments

• **1997, Taxpayer Relief Act of 1997 (P.L. 105-34)**

P.L. 105-34, § 1031(a)(1):

Amended Code Sec. 4091(b)(3)(A)(ii) by striking "September 30, 1997" and inserting "September 30, 2007". **Effective** 10-1-97.

P.L. 105-34, § 1031(g)[(f)](3), provides:

(g)[(f)] DELAYED DEPOSITS OF AIRPORT TRUST FUND TAX REVENUES.—Notwithstanding section 6302 of the Internal Revenue Code of 1986—

* * *

(3) in the case of deposits of taxes imposed by sections 4081(a)(2)(A)(ii), 4091, and 4271 of such Code, the due date for any such deposit which would (but for this subsection) be required to be made after July 31, 1998, and before October 1, 1998, shall be October 5, 1998.

• **1997, Airport and Airway Trust Fund Tax Reinstatement Act of 1997 (P.L. 105-2)**

P.L. 105-2, § 2(a)(1):

Amended Code Sec. 4091(b)(3)(A). **Effective** for periods beginning on or after 3-7-97. Prior to amendment, Code Sec. 4091(b)(3)(A) read as follows:

(A) The rate of tax specified in paragraph (1) shall be 4.3 cents per gallon—

(i) after December 31, 1995, and before the date which is 7 calendar days after the date of the enactment of the Small Business Job Protection Act of 1996, and

(ii) after December 31, 1996.

P.L. 105-2, § 2(d):

For the text of P.L. 105-2, § 2(d), concerning floor stocks taxes on aviation gasoline and aviation fuel, see the amendment notes under Code Sec. 4081(a).

P.L. 105-2, § 2(f):

For the text of P.L. 105-2, § 2(f), concerning the application of the look-back safe harbor for deposits, see the amendment notes under Code Sec. 9502(b).

• **1996, Small Business Job Protection Act of 1996 (P.L. 104-188)**

P.L. 104-188, § 1609(a)(1):

Amended Code Sec. 4091(b)(3)(A). **Effective** 8-27-96. For special rules, see Act Sec. 1609(h), below. Prior to amendment, Code Sec. 4091(b)(3)(A) read as follows:

(A) On and after January 1, 1996, the rate of tax specified in paragraph (1) shall be 4.3 cents per gallon.

P.L. 104-188, § 1609(h), as amended by P.L. 105-34, § 1601(f)(4)(F), and P.L. 105-206, § 6018(e), provides:

(h) FLOOR STOCKS TAXES ON AVIATION FUEL.—

(1) IMPOSITION OF TAX.—In the case of aviation fuel on which tax was imposed under section 4091 of the Internal Revenue Code of 1986 before the tax-increase date described in paragraph (3)(A) and which is held on such date by any person, there is hereby imposed a floor stocks tax of 17.5 cents per gallon.

(2) LIABILITY FOR TAX AND METHOD OF PAYMENT.—

(A) LIABILITY FOR TAX.—A person holding aviation fuel on a tax-increase date to which the tax imposed by paragraph (1) applies shall be liable for such tax.

(B) METHOD OF PAYMENT.—The tax imposed by paragraph (1) shall be paid in such manner as the Secretary shall prescribe.

(C) TIME FOR PAYMENT.—The tax imposed by paragraph (1) with respect to any tax-increase date shall be paid on or before the first day of the 7th month beginning after such tax-increase date.

(3) DEFINITIONS.—For purposes of this subsection—

(A) TAX INCREASE DATE.—The term "tax-increase date" means the date which is 7 calendar days after the date of the enactment of this Act.

(B) AVIATION FUEL.—The term "aviation fuel" has the meaning given such term by section 4093 of such Code.

(C) HELD BY A PERSON.—Aviation fuel shall be considered as "held by a person" if title thereto has passed to such person (whether or not delivery to the person has been made).

(D) SECRETARY.—The term "Secretary" means the Secretary of the Treasury or his delegate.

(4) EXCEPTION FOR EXEMPT USES.—The tax imposed by paragraph (1) shall not apply to aviation fuel held by any person on such tax-increase date exclusively for any use for which a credit or refund of the entire tax imposed by section 4091 of such Code is allowable for aviation fuel purchased on or after such tax-increase date for such use or exclusively for the use described in section 4092(b) of such Code.

(5) EXCEPTION FOR CERTAIN AMOUNTS OF FUEL.—

(A) IN GENERAL.—No tax shall be imposed by paragraph (1) on aviation fuel held on any tax-increase date by any person if the aggregate amount of aviation fuel held by such person on such date does not exceed 2,000 gallons. The preceding sentence shall apply only if such person submits to the Secretary (at the time and in the manner required by the Secretary) such information as the Secretary shall require for purposes of this paragraph.

(B) EXEMPT FUEL.—For purposes of subparagraph (A), there shall not be taken into account fuel held by any person which is exempt from the tax imposed by paragraph (1) by reason of paragraph (4).

(C) CONTROLLED GROUPS.—For purposes of this paragraph—

(i) CORPORATIONS.—

(I) IN GENERAL.—All persons treated as a controlled group shall be treated as 1 person.

(II) CONTROLLED GROUP.—The term "controlled group" has the meaning given to such term by subsection (a) of section 1563 of such Code; except that for such purposes the phrase "more than 50 percent" shall be substituted for the phrase "at least 80 percent" each place it appears in such subsection.

(ii) NONINCORPORATED PERSONS UNDER COMMON CONTROL.—Under regulations prescribed by the Secretary, principles similar to the principles of clause (i) shall apply to a group of persons under common control where 1 or more of such persons is not a corporation.

(6) OTHER LAW APPLICABLE.—All provisions of law, including penalties, applicable with respect to the taxes imposed by section 4091 of such Code shall, insofar as

MANUFACTURERS TAXES—DIESEL FUEL

applicable and not inconsistent with the provisions of this subsection, apply with respect to the floor stock taxes imposed by paragraph (1) to the same extent as if such taxes were imposed by such section 4091.

[Sec. 4091(c)]

(c) REDUCED RATE OF TAX FOR AVIATION FUEL IN ALCOHOL MIXTURE, ETC.—Under regulations prescribed by the Secretary—

(1) IN GENERAL.—The rate of tax under subsection (a) shall be reduced by the applicable blender amount per gallon in the case of the sale of any mixture of aviation fuel if—

(A) at least 10 percent of such mixture consists of alcohol (as defined in section 4081(c)(3)), and

(B) the aviation fuel in such mixture was not taxed under paragraph (2).

In the case of such a mixture none of the alcohol in which is ethanol, the preceding sentence shall be applied by substituting "14 cents" for "the applicable blender amount". For purposes of this paragraph, the term "applicable blender amount" means 13.3 cents in the case of any sale or use during 2001 or 2002, 13.2 cents in the case of any sale or use during 2003 or 2004, 13.1 cents in the case of any sale or use during 2005, 2006, or 2007, and 13.4 cents in the case of any sale or use during 2008 or thereafter.

(2) TAX PRIOR TO MIXING.—In the case of the sale of aviation fuel for use (at the time of such sale) in producing a mixture described in paragraph (1), the rate of tax under subsection (a) shall be $^{10}/_9$ of the rate which would (but for this paragraph) have been applicable to such mixture had such mixture been created prior to such sale.

(3) LATER SEPARATION.—If any person separates the aviation fuel from a mixture of the aviation fuel and alcohol on which tax was imposed under subsection (a) at a rate determined under paragraph (1) or (2) (or with respect to which a credit or payment was allowed or made by reason of section 6427(f)(1)), such person shall be treated as the producer of such aviation fuel. The amount of tax imposed on any sale of such aviation fuel by such person shall be reduced by the amount of tax imposed (and not credited or refunded) on any prior sale of such fuel.

(4) LIMITATION.—In no event shall any rate determined under paragraph (1) be less than 4.3 cents per gallon.

(5) TERMINATION.—Paragraphs (1) and (2) shall not apply to any sale after September 30, 2007.

Amendments

• **1998, Transportation Equity Act for the 21st Century (P.L. 105-178)**

P.L. 105-178, § 9003(a)(1)(D):

Amended Code Sec. 4091(c)(5) by striking "2000" and inserting "2007". **Effective** 6-9-98.

P.L. 105-178, § 9003(b)(2)(D):

Amended Code Sec. 4091(c)(1) by striking "13.4 cents" each place it appears and inserting "the applicable blender amount" and by adding a new last sentence. **Effective** 1-1-2001.

• **1993, Omnibus Budget Reconciliation Act of 1993 (P.L. 103-66)**

P.L. 103-66, § 13241(b)(1):

Amended Code Sec. 4091(b)(4) by striking "2.5 cents" and inserting "6.8 cents". **Effective** 10-1-93. However, see Act Secs. 13241(h), 13243, 13245, and 13421(c), below.

P.L. 103-66, § 13241(b)(2)(B)(i):

Amended Code Sec. 4091(b)(1)(A)(ii) by inserting "and the aviation fuel deficit reduction rate" after "financing rate". **Effective** 10-1-93. However, see Act Secs. 13241(h), 13243, 13245, and 13421(c), below.

P.L. 103-66, § 13241(b)(2)(B)(ii):

Amended Code Sec. 4091(b) by redesignating paragraph (6) as paragraph (7) and by inserting after paragraph (5) a new paragraph (6). **Effective** 10-1-93. However, see Act Secs. 13241(h), 13243, 13245, and 13421(c), below.

P.L. 103-66, § 13241(h), provides:

(h) FLOOR STOCKS TAXES.—

(1) IMPOSITION OF TAX.—In the case of gasoline, diesel fuel, and aviation fuel on which tax was imposed under section 4081 or 4091 of the Internal Revenue Code of 1986 before October 1, 1993, and which is held on such date by any person, there is hereby imposed a floor stocks tax of 4.3 cents per gallon on such gasoline, diesel fuel, and aviation fuel.

(2) LIABILITY FOR TAX AND METHOD OF PAYMENT.—

(A) LIABILITY FOR TAX.—A person holding gasoline, diesel fuel, or aviation fuel on October 1, 1993, to which the tax imposed by paragraph (1) applies shall be liable for such tax.

(B) METHOD OF PAYMENT.—The tax imposed by paragraph (1) shall be paid in such manner as the Secretary shall prescribe.

(C) TIME FOR PAYMENT.—The tax imposed by paragraph (1) shall be paid on or before November 30, 1993.

(3) DEFINITIONS.—For purposes of this subsection—

(A) HELD BY A PERSON.—Gasoline, diesel fuel, and aviation fuel shall be considered as "held by a person" if title thereto has passed to such person (whether or not delivery to the person has been made).

(B) GASOLINE.—The term "gasoline" has the meaning given such term by section 4082 of such Code.

(C) DIESEL FUEL.—The term "diesel fuel" has the meaning given such term by section 4092 of such Code.

(D) AVIATION FUEL.—The term "aviation fuel" has the meaning given such term by section 4092 of such Code.

(E) SECRETARY.—The term "Secretary" means the Secretary of the Treasury or his delegate.

(4) EXCEPTION FOR EXEMPT USES.—The tax imposed by paragraph (1) shall not apply to gasoline, diesel fuel, or aviation fuel held by any person exclusively for any use to

the extent a credit or refund of the tax imposed by section 4081 or 4091 of such Code, as the case may be, is allowable for such use.

(5) EXCEPTION FOR FUEL HELD IN VEHICLE TANK.—No tax shall be imposed by paragraph (1) on gasoline or diesel fuel held in the tank of a motor vehicle or motorboat.

(6) EXCEPTION FOR CERTAIN AMOUNTS OF FUEL.—

(A) IN GENERAL.—No tax shall be imposed by paragraph (1)—

(i) on gasoline held on October 1, 1993, by any person if the aggregate amount of gasoline held by such person on such date does not exceed 4,000 gallons, and

(ii) on diesel fuel or aviation fuel held on October 1, 1993, by any person if the aggregate amount of diesel fuel or aviation fuel held by such person on such date does not exceed 2,000 gallons.

The preceding sentence shall apply only if such person submits to the Secretary (at the time and in the manner required by the Secretary) such information as the Secretary shall require for purposes of this paragraph.

(B) EXEMPT FUEL.—For purposes of subparagraph (A), there shall not be taken into account fuel held by any person which is exempt from the tax imposed by paragraph (1) by reason of paragraph (4) or (5).

(C) CONTROLLED GROUPS.—For purposes of this paragraph—

(i) CORPORATIONS.—

(I) IN GENERAL.—All persons treated as a controlled group shall be treated as 1 person.

(II) CONTROLLED GROUP.—The term "controlled group" has the meaning given to such term by subsection (a) of section 1563 of such Code; except that for such purposes the phrase "more than 50 percent" shall be substituted for the phrase "at least 80 percent" each place it appears in such subsection.

(ii) NONINCORPORATED PERSONS UNDER COMMON CONTROL.—Under regulations prescribed by the Secretary, principles similar to the principles of clause (i) shall apply to a group of persons under common control where 1 or more of such persons is not a corporation.

(7) OTHER LAW APPLICABLE.—All provisions of law, including penalties, applicable with respect to the taxes imposed by section 4081 of such Code in the case of gasoline and section 4091 of such Code in the case of diesel fuel and aviation fuel shall, insofar as applicable and not inconsistent with the provisions of this subsection, apply with respect to the floor stock taxes imposed by paragraph (1) to the same extent as if such taxes were imposed by such section 4081 or 4091.

P.L. 103-66, § 13243, provides:

SEC. 13243. FLOOR STOCKS TAX.

(a) IN GENERAL.—There is hereby imposed a floor stocks tax on diesel fuel held by any person on January 1, 1994, if—

(1) no tax was imposed on such fuel under section 4041(a) or 4091 of the Internal Revenue Code of 1986 as in effect on December 31, 1993, and

(2) tax would have been imposed by section 4081 of such Code, as amended by this Act, on any prior removal, entry, or sale of such fuel had such section 4081 applied to such fuel for periods before January 1, 1994.

(b) RATE OF TAX.—The rate of the tax imposed by subsection (a) shall be the amount of tax which would be imposed under section 4081 of the Internal Revenue Code of 1986 if there were a taxable sale of such fuel on such date.

(c) LIABILITY AND PAYMENT OF TAX.—

(1) LIABILITY FOR TAX.—A person holding the diesel fuel on January 1, 1994, to which the tax imposed by this section applies shall be liable for such tax.

(2) METHOD OF PAYMENT.—The tax imposed by this section shall be paid in such manner as the Secretary shall prescribe.

(3) TIME FOR PAYMENT.—The tax imposed by this section shall be paid on or before July 31, 1994.

(d) DEFINITIONS.—For purposes of this section—

(1) DIESEL FUEL.—The term "diesel fuel" has the meaning given such term by section 4083(a) of such Code.

(2) SECRETARY.—The term "Secretary" means the Secretary of the Treasury or his delegate.

(e) EXCEPTIONS.—

(1) PERSONS ENTITLED TO CREDIT OR REFUND.—The tax imposed by this section shall not apply to fuel held by any person exclusively for any use to the extent a credit or refund of the tax imposed by section 4081 is allowable for such use.

(2) COMPLIANCE WITH DYEING REQUIRED.—Paragraph (1) shall not apply to the holder of any fuel if the holder of such fuel fails to comply with any requirement imposed by the Secretary with respect to dyeing and marking such fuel.

(f) OTHER LAWS APPLICABLE.—All provisions of law, including penalties, applicable with respect to the taxes imposed by section 4081 of such Code shall, insofar as applicable and not inconsistent with the provisions of this section, apply with respect to the floor stock taxes imposed by this section to the same extent as if such taxes were imposed by such section 4081.

P.L. 103-66, § 13245, provides:

SEC. 13245. FLOOR STOCKS TAX ON COMMERCIAL AVIATION FUEL HELD ON OCTOBER 1, 1995.

(a) IMPOSITION OF TAX.—In the case of commercial aviation fuel on which tax was imposed under section 4091 of the Internal Revenue Code of 1986 before October 1, 1995, and which is held on such date by any person, there is hereby imposed a floor stocks tax of 4.3 cents per gallon.

(b) LIABILITY FOR TAX AND METHOD OF PAYMENT.—

(1) LIABILITY FOR TAX.—A person holding aviation fuel on October 1, 1995, to which the tax imposed by subsection (a) applies shall be liable for such tax.

(2) METHOD OF PAYMENT.—The tax imposed by subsection (a) shall be paid in such manner as the Secretary shall prescribe.

(3) TIME FOR PAYMENT.—The tax imposed by subsection (a) shall be paid on or before April 30, 1996.

(c) DEFINITIONS.—For purposes of this subsection—

Sec. 4091—Stricken

MANUFACTURERS TAXES—DIESEL FUEL

(1) HELD BY A PERSON.—Aviation fuel shall be considered as "held by a person" if title thereto has passed to such person (whether or not delivery to the person has been made).

(2) COMMERCIAL AVIATION FUEL.—The term "commercial aviation fuel" means aviation fuel (as defined in section 4093 of such Code) which is held on October 1, 1995, for sale or use in commercial aviation (as defined in section 4092(b) of such Code).

(3) SECRETARY.—The term "Secretary" means the Secretary of the Treasury or his delegate.

(d) EXCEPTION FOR EXEMPT USES.—The tax imposed by subsection (a) shall not apply to aviation fuel held by any person exclusively for any use for which a credit or refund of the entire tax imposed by section 4091 of such Code is allowable for aviation fuel purchased after September 30, 1995, for such use.

(e) EXCEPTION FOR CERTAIN AMOUNTS OF FUEL.—

(1) IN GENERAL.—No tax shall be imposed by subsection (a) on aviation fuel held on October 1, 1995, by any person if the aggregate amount of commercial aviation fuel held by such person on such date does not exceed 2,000 gallons. The preceding sentence shall apply only if such person submits to the Secretary (at the time and in the manner required by the Secretary) such information as the Secretary shall require for purposes of this paragraph.

(2) EXEMPT FUEL.—For purposes of paragraph (1), there shall not be taken into account fuel held by any person which is exempt from the tax imposed by subsection (a) by reason of subsection (d).

(3) CONTROLLED GROUPS.—For purposes of this subsection—

(A) CORPORATIONS.—

(i) IN GENERAL.—All persons treated as a controlled group shall be treated as 1 person.

(ii) CONTROLLED GROUP.—The term "controlled group" has the meaning given to such term by subsection (a) of section 1563 of such Code; except that for such purposes the phrase "more than 50 percent" shall be substituted for the phrase "at least 80 percent" each place it appears in such subsection.

(B) NONINCORPORATED PERSONS UNDER COMMON CONTROL.—Under regulations prescribed by the Secretary, principles similar to the principles of subparagraph (A) shall apply to a group of persons under common control where 1 or more of such persons is not a corporation.

(f) OTHER LAW APPLICABLE.—All provisions of law, including penalties, applicable with respect to the taxes imposed by section 4091 of such Code shall, insofar as applicable and not inconsistent with the provisions of this section, apply with respect to the floor stock taxes imposed by subsection (a) to the same extent as if such taxes were imposed by such section 4091.

P.L. 103-66, §13421(c), provides:

(c) FLOOR STOCKS TAX.—

(1) IMPOSITION OF TAX.—On any taxable vaccine—

(A) which was sold by the manufacturer, producer, or importer on or before the date of the enactment of this Act,

(B) on which no tax was imposed by section 4131 of the Internal Revenue Code of 1986 (or, if such tax was imposed, was credited or refunded), and

(C) which is held on such date by any person for sale or use,

there is hereby imposed a tax in the amount determined under section 4131(b) of such Code.

(2) LIABILITY FOR TAX AND METHOD OF PAYMENT.—

(A) LIABILITY FOR TAX.—The person holding any taxable vaccine to which the tax imposed by paragraph (1) applies shall be liable for such tax.

(B) METHOD OF PAYMENT.—The tax imposed by paragraph (1) shall be paid in such manner as the Secretary shall prescribe by regulations.

(C) TIME FOR PAYMENT.—The tax imposed by paragraph (1) shall be paid on or before the last day of the 6th month beginning after the date of the enactment of this Act.

(3) DEFINITIONS.—For purposes of this subsection, terms used in this subsection which are also used in section 4131 of such Code shall have the respective meanings such terms have in such section.

(4) OTHER LAWS APPLICABLE.—All provisions of law, including penalties, applicable with respect to the taxes imposed by section 4131 of such Code shall, insofar as applicable and not inconsistent with the provisions of this subsection, apply to the floor stocks taxes imposed by paragraph (1), to the same extent as if such taxes were imposed by such section 4131.

P.L. 103-66, §13242(a):

Amended subparts A and B of part III of subchapter A of chapter 32 (Code Secs. 4081–4093), as amended by subpart A (Act Sec. 13241(b)). **Effective** 1-1-94. Prior to amendment, Code Sec. 4091 read as follows:

SEC. 4091. IMPOSITION OF TAX.

[Sec. 4091(a)]

(a) IN GENERAL.—There is hereby imposed a tax on the sale of any taxable fuel by the producer or the importer thereof or by any producer of a taxable fuel.

[Sec. 4091(b)]

(b) RATE OF TAX.—

(1) IN GENERAL.—The rate of the tax imposed by subsection (a) shall be the sum of—

(A)(i) the Highway Trust Fund financing rate and the diesel fuel deficit reduction rate in the case of diesel fuel, and

(ii) the Airport and Airway Trust Fund financing rate and the aviation fuel deficit reduction rate in the case of aviation fuel, and

(B) the Leaking Underground Storage Tank Trust Fund financing rate in the case of any taxable fuel.

(2) HIGHWAY TRUST FUND FINANCING RATE.—For purposes of paragraph (1), except as provided in subsection (c), the Highway Trust Fund financing rate is 17.5 cents per gallon.

(3) AIRPORT AND AIRWAY TRUST FUND FINANCING RATE.—For purposes of paragraph (1) except as provided in subsection (d), the Airport and Airway Trust Fund financing rate is 17.5 cents per gallon.

(4) DIESEL FUEL DEFICIT REDUCTION RATE.—For purposes of paragraph (1), except as provided in subsection (c), the diesel fuel deficit reduction rate is 6.8 cents per gallon.

(5) LEAKING UNDERGROUND STORAGE TANK TRUST FUND FINANCING RATE.—For purposes of paragraph (1), except as provided in subsection (c), the Leaking Underground Storage Tank Trust Fund financing rate is 0.1 cent per gallon.

(6) AVIATION FUEL DEFICIT REDUCTION RATE.—For purposes of paragraph (1), the aviation fuel deficit reduction rate is 4.3 cents per gallon.

(7) TERMINATION OF RATES.—

(A) The Highway Trust Fund financing rate shall not apply on and after October 1, 1999.

(B) The Airport and Airway Trust Fund financing rate shall not apply on and after January 1, 1996.

(C) The Leaking Underground Storage Tank Trust Fund financing rate shall not apply during any period during which the Leaking Underground Storage Tank Trust Fund financing rate under section 4081 does not apply.

(D) The diesel fuel deficit reduction rate shall not apply on and after October 1, 1995.

Amendments

• **1991, Intermodal Surface Transportation Efficiency Act of 1991 (P.L. 102-240)**

P.L. 102-240, §8002(a)(4):

Amended Code Sec. 4091(b)(6)(A) by striking "1995" each place it appears and inserting "1999". **Effective** 12-18-91.

• **1990, Omnibus Budget Reconciliation Act of 1990 (P.L. 101-508)**

P.L. 101-508, §11211(b)(1)(A):

Amended Code Sec. 4091(b)(1)(A)(i) by inserting "and the diesel fuel deficit reduction rate" after "financing rate". **Effective** 12-1-90.

P.L. 101-508, §11211(b)(1)(B):

Amended Code Sec. 4091(b) by redesignating paragraphs (4) and (5) as paragraphs (5) and (6), respectively, and by inserting after paragraph (3) a new paragraph (4). **Effective** 12-1-90.

P.L. 101-508, §11211(b)(1)(C):

Amended Code Sec. 4091(b)(6), as redesignated by Act Sec. 11211(b)(1)(B), by adding at the end thereof a new subparagraph (D). **Effective** 12-1-90.

P.L. 101-508, §11211(b)(2):

Amended Code Sec. 4091(b)(2) by striking "15 cents" and inserting "17.5 cents". **Effective** 12-1-90.

P.L. 101-508, §11211(c)(4):

Amended Code Sec. 4091(b)(6)(A), as redesignated by Act Sec. 11211(b)(1)(B), by striking "1993" each place it appears and inserting "1995". **Effective** 11-5-90.

P.L. 101-508, §11211(j), provides:

(j) FLOOR STOCKS TAXES.—

(1) IMPOSITION OF TAX.—In the case of—

(A) gasoline and diesel fuel on which tax was imposed under section 4081 or 4091 of such Code before December 1, 1990, and which is held on such date by any person, or

(B) diesel fuel on which no tax was imposed under section 4091 of such Code at the Highway Trust Fund financing rate before December 1, 1990, and which is held on such date by any person for use as a fuel in a train,

there is hereby imposed a floor stocks tax on such gasoline and diesel fuel.

(2) RATE OF TAX.—The rate of the tax imposed by paragraph (1) shall be—

(A) 5 cents per gallon in the case of fuel described in paragraph (1)(A), and

(B) 2.5 cents per gallon in the case of fuel described in paragraph (1)(B).

In the case of any fuel held for use in producing a mixture described in section 4081(c)(1) or section 4091(c)(1)(A) of such Code, subparagraph (A) shall be applied by substituting "6.22 cents" for "5 cents". If no alcohol in such mixture is ethanol, the preceding sentence shall be applied by substituting "5.56 cents" for "6.22 cents".

(3) LIABILITY FOR TAX AND METHOD OF PAYMENT.—

(A) LIABILITY FOR TAX.—A person holding gasoline or diesel fuel on December 1, 1990, to which the tax imposed by paragraph (1) applies shall be liable for such tax.

(B) METHOD OF PAYMENT.—The tax imposed by paragraph (1) shall be paid in such manner as the Secretary shall prescribe.

(C) TIME FOR PAYMENT.—The tax imposed by paragraph (1) shall be paid on or before May 31, 1991.

(4) DEFINITIONS.—For purposes of this subsection—

(A) HELD BY A PERSON.—Gasoline and diesel fuel shall be considered as "held by a person" if title thereto has passed to such person (whether or not delivery to the person has been made).

(B) GASOLINE.—The term "gasoline" has the meaning given such term by section 4082 of such Code.

(C) DIESEL FUEL.—The term "diesel fuel" has the meaning given such term by section 4092 of such Code.

(D) SECRETARY.—The term "Secretary" means the Secretary of the Treasury or his delegate.

(5) EXCEPTION FOR EXEMPT USES.—The tax imposed by paragraph (1) shall not apply to gasoline or diesel fuel held by any person exclusively for any use to the extent a credit or refund of the tax imposed by section 4081 or 4091 of such Code, as the case may be, is allowable for such use.

Sec. 4091—Stricken

MANUFACTURERS TAXES—DIESEL FUEL

(6) EXCEPTION FOR FUEL HELD IN VEHICLE TANK.—No tax shall be imposed by paragraph (1) on gasoline or diesel fuel held in the tank of a motor vehicle or motorboat.

(7) EXCEPTION FOR CERTAIN AMOUNTS OF FUEL.—

(A) IN GENERAL.—No tax shall be imposed by paragraph (1)—

(i) on gasoline held on December 1, 1990, by any person if the aggregate amount of gasoline held by such person on such date does not exceed 4,000 gallons, and

(ii) on diesel fuel held on December 1, 1990, by any person if the aggregate amount of diesel fuel held by such person on such date does not exceed 2,000 gallons.

The preceding sentence shall apply only if such person submits to the Secretary (at the time and in the manner required by the Secretary) such information as the Secretary shall require for purposes of this paragraph.

(B) EXEMPT FUEL.—For purposes of subparagraph (A), there shall not be taken into account fuel held by any person which is exempt from the tax imposed by paragraph (1) by reason of paragraph (5) or (6).

(C) CONTROLLED GROUPS.—For purposes of this paragraph, rules similar to the rules of paragraph (6) of section 11201(e) of this Act shall apply.

(8) OTHER LAWS APPLICABLE.—All provisions of law, including penalties, applicable with respect to the taxes imposed by section 4081 of such Code in the case of gasoline and section 4091 of such Code in the case of diesel fuel shall, insofar as applicable and not inconsistent with the provisions of this subsection, apply with respect to the floor stock taxes imposed by paragraph (1) to the same extent as if such taxes were imposed by such section 4081 or 4091.

(9) TRANSFER OF PORTION OF FLOOR STOCKS REVENUE TO HIGHWAY TRUST FUND.—For purposes of determining the amount transferred to the Highway Trust Fund, the tax imposed by paragraph (1) on fuel described in subparagraph (A) thereof shall be treated as imposed at a Highway Trust Fund financing rate to the extent of 2.5 cents per gallon.

P.L. 101-508, § 11213(b)(1)(A)-(B):

Amended Code Sec. 4091(b)(3) by striking "14 cents" and inserting "17.5 cents", and by inserting "except as provided in subsection (d)," after "paragraph (1),". **Effective** 12-1-90. However, see Act Sec. 11213(f) in the amendment notes following Code Sec. 4041(c).

P.L. 101-508, § 11213(d)(2)(A):

Amended Code Sec. 4091(b)(6)(B), as redesignated by Act Sec. 11211, by striking "January 1, 1991" and inserting "January 1, 1996". **Effective** 11-5-90. However, see Act Sec. 11213(f) in the amendment notes following Code Sec. 4041(c).

- **1988, Technical and Miscellaneous Revenue Act of 1988 (P.L. 100-647)**

P.L. 100-647, § 2001(d)(6)(B):

Amended Code Sec. 4091(b)(4) by inserting "except as provided in subsection (c)," after "paragraph (1),". **Effective** as if included in the amendments made by section 10502 of P.L. 100-203.

P.L. 100-647, § 1017(c)(5), provides:

(5) The amendment made by section 10502(d)(4) of the Revenue Act of 1987 shall be treated as if included in the amendments made by section 1703 of the Reform Act except that the reference to section 4091 of the Internal Revenue Code of 1986 shall not apply to sales before April 1, 1988.

[Sec. 4091(c)]

(c) REDUCED RATE OF TAX FOR DIESEL FUEL IN ALCOHOL MIXTURE, ETC.—Under regulations prescribed by the Secretary—

(1) IN GENERAL.—The Highway Trust Fund financing rate shall be—

(A) 12.1 cents per gallon in the case of the sale of any mixture of diesel fuel if—

(i) at least 10 percent of such mixture consists of alcohol (as defined in section 4081(c)(3)), and

(ii) the diesel fuel in such mixture was not taxed under subparagraph (B) and

(B) 13.44 cents per gallon in the case of the sale of diesel fuel for use (at the time of such sale) in producing a mixture described in subparagraph (A).

In the case of a sale described in subparagraph (B), the Leaking Underground Storage Tank Trust Fund financing rate and the diesel fuel deficit reduction rate shall be 10/9th of the otherwise applicable such rates.

(2) LATER SEPARATION.—If any person separates the diesel fuel from a mixture of the diesel fuel and alcohol on which tax was imposed under subsection (a) at a Highway Trust Fund financing rate equivalent to 12.1 cents a gallon by reason of this subsection (or with respect to which a credit or payment was allowed or made by reason of section 6427(f)(1)), such person shall be treated as the producer of such diesel fuel. The amount of tax imposed on any sale of such diesel fuel by such person shall be reduced by the amount of tax imposed (and not credited or refunded) on any prior sale of such fuel.

(3) TERMINATION.—Paragraph (1) shall not apply to any sale after September 30, 2000.

Amendments

- **1990, Omnibus Budget Reconciliation Act of 1990 (P.L. 101-508)**

P.L. 101-508, § 11211(b)(6)(A)(i)-(ii):

Amended Code Sec. 4091(c)(1) by striking "9 cents" and inserting "12.1 cents" and by striking "10 cents" and inserting "13.44 cents", and by striking "shall be 1/9 cent per gallon" and inserting "and the diesel fuel deficit reduction rate shall be 10/9th of the otherwise applicable such rates". **Effective** 12-1-90.

P.L. 101-508, § 11211(b)(6)(B):

Amended Code Sec. 4091(c)(2) by striking "9 cents" and inserting "12.1 cents". **Effective** 12-1-90.

P.L. 101-508, § 11211(e)(4):

Amended Code Sec. 4091(c)(3) by striking "1993" each place it appears and inserting "2000". **Effective** 11-5-90.

- **1988, Technical and Miscellaneous Revenue Act of 1988 (P.L. 100-647)**

P.L. 100-647, § 2001(d)(6)(A):

Amended Code Sec. 4091(c)(1) by adding at the end thereof a new sentence. **Effective** as if included in section 10502 of P.L. 100-203.

P.L. 100-647, § 2001(d)(6)(C):

Amended Code Sec. 4091(c)(2) by striking out "5 cents a [per] gallon" and inserting in lieu thereof "reduced by the amount of tax imposed (and not credited or refunded) on any prior sale of such fuel" in the last sentence. **Effective** as if included in section 10502 of P.L. 100-203.

P.L. 100-647, § 1017(c)(5), provides:

(5) The amendment made by section 10502(d)(4) of the Revenue Act of 1987 shall be treated as if included in the amendments made by section 1703 of the Reform Act except that the reference to section 4091 of the Internal Revenue Code of 1986 shall not apply to sales before April 1, 1988.

[Sec. 4091(d)]

(d) REDUCED RATE OF TAX FOR AVIATION FUEL IN ALCOHOL MIXTURE, ETC.—

(1) IN GENERAL.—The Airport and Airway Trust Fund financing rate shall be—

(A) 4.1 cents per gallon in the case of the sale of any mixture of aviation fuel if—

(i) at least 10 percent of such mixture consists of alcohol (as defined in section 4081(c)(3)), and

(ii) the aviation fuel in such mixture was not taxed under subparagraph (B), and

(B) 4.56 cents per gallon in the case of the sale of aviation fuel for use (at the time of such sale) in producing a mixture described in subparagraph (A).

In the case of a sale described in subparagraph (B), the Leaking Underground Storage Tank Trust Fund financing rate shall be 1/9 cent per gallon.

(2) LATER SEPARATION.—If any person separates the aviation fuel from a mixture of the aviation fuel and alcohol on which tax was imposed under subsection (a) at the Airport and Airway Trust Fund financing rate equivalent to 4.1 cents per gallon by reason of this subsection (or with respect to which a credit or payment was allowed or made by reason of section 6427(f)(1)), such person shall be treated as the producer of such aviation fuel. The amount of tax imposed on any sale of such aviation fuel by such person shall be reduced by the amount of tax imposed (and not credited or refunded) on any prior sale of such fuel.

(3) TERMINATION.—Paragraph (1) shall not apply to any sale after September 30, 2000.

Amendments

- **1990, Omnibus Budget Reconciliation Act of 1990 (P.L. 101-508)**

P.L. 101-508, § 11211(e)(4):

Amended Code Sec. 4091(d)(3) by striking "1993" each place it appears and inserting "2000". **Effective** 11-5-90.

P.L. 101-508, § 11213(b)(2)(C)(1):

Amended Code Sec. 4091(d)(1). **Effective** 12-1-90. Prior to amendment, Code Sec. 4091(d)(1) read as follows:

(d) EXEMPTION FROM TAX FOR AVIATION FUEL IN ALCOHOL MIXTURE, ETC.—

(1) IN GENERAL.—The Airport and Airway Trust Fund financing rate shall not apply to the sale of—

(A) any mixture of aviation fuel at least 10 percent of which consists of alcohol (as defined in section 4081(c)(3)), or

(B) any aviation fuel for use (at the time of such sale) in producing a mixture described in subparagraph (A).

P.L. 101-508, § 11213(b)(2)(C)(i):

Amended Code Sec. 4091(d)(2). **Effective** 12-1-90. Prior to amendment, Code Sec. 4091(d)(2) read as follows:

(2) LATER SEPARATION.—If any person separates the aviation fuel from a mixture of the aviation fuel and alcohol on which the Airport and Airway Trust Fund financing rate did not apply by reason of this subsection (or with respect to which a credit or payment was allowed or made by reason of section 6427(f)(2)), such person shall be treated as the producer of such aviation fuel.

P.L. 101-508, § 11213(b)(2)(C)(ii):

Amended the heading of Code Sec. 4091(d) by striking "EXEMPTION FROM" and inserting "REDUCED RATE OF". **Effective** 12-1-90.

- **1987, Revenue Act of 1987 (P.L. 100-203)**

P.L. 100-203, § 10502(a):

Amended part III of subchapter 32 by inserting after subpart A a new subpart B. **Effective** for sales after 3-31-88.

P.L. 100-203, § 10502(f), provides:

(f) FLOOR STOCKS TAX.—

(1) IMPOSITION OF TAX.—On any taxable fuel which on April 1, 1988, is held by a taxable person, there is hereby imposed a floor stocks tax at the rate of tax which would be imposed if such fuel were sold on such date in a sale subject to tax under section 4091 of the Internal Revenue Code of 1986 (as added by this section).

(2) OVERPAYMENT OF FLOOR STOCKS TAXES, ETC.—Sections 6416 and 6427 of such Code shall apply in respect of the floor stocks taxes imposed by this subsection so as to entitle, subject to all provisions of such sections, any person paying such floor stocks taxes to a credit or refund thereof for any reason specified in such sections. All provisions of law, including penalties, applicable with respect to the taxes imposed by section 4091 of such Code (as so added) shall apply to the floor stocks taxes imposed by this subsection.

(3) DUE DATE OF TAX.—The taxes imposed by this subsection shall be paid before June 16, 1988.

Sec. 4091—Stricken

MANUFACTURERS TAXES—DIESEL FUEL

(4) DEFINITIONS.—For purposes of this subsection—

(A) TAXABLE FUEL.—

(i) IN GENERAL.—The term "taxable fuel" means any taxable fuel (as defined in section 4092 of such Code, as added by this section) on which no tax has been imposed under section 4041 of such Code.

(ii) EXCEPTION FOR FUEL HELD FOR NONTAXABLE USES.—The term "taxable fuel" shall not include fuel held exclusively for any use which is a nontaxable use (as defined in section 6427(l) of such Code, as added by this section).

(B) TAXABLE PERSON.—The term "taxable person" means any person other than a producer (as defined in section 4092 of such Code, as so added) or importer of taxable fuel.

(C) HELD BY A TAXABLE PERSON.—An article shall be treated as held by a person if title thereto has passed to such person (whether or not delivery to such person had been made).

(5) SPECIAL RULE FOR FUEL HELD FOR USE IN TRAINS AND COMMERCIAL AIRCRAFT.—Only the Leaking Underground Storage Tank Trust Fund financing rate under section 4091 of such Code shall apply for purposes of this subsection with respect to—

(A) diesel fuel held exclusively for use as a fuel in a diesel-powered train, and

(B) aviation fuel held exclusively for use as a fuel in an aircraft not in noncommercial aviation (as defined in section 4041(c)(4) of such Code).

(6) TRANSFER OF FLOOR STOCK REVENUES TO TRUST FUNDS.—For purposes of determining the amount transferred to any trust fund, the tax imposed by this subsection shall be treated as imposed by section 4091 of such Code (as so added).

(g) COORDINATION WITH AIRPORT AND AIRWAY SAFETY AND CAPACITY EXPANSION ACT OF 1987.—If the Airport and Airway Safety and Capacity Expansion Act of 1987 is enacted, effective on December 31, 1987, sections 4091(b)(5)(B) and 9502(b)(3) of such Code (as added by this section) are each amended by striking out "January 1, 1988" and inserting in lieu thereof "January 1, 1991", and.

[Sec. 4091(e)]

(e) LOWER RATES OF TAX ON ALCOHOL MIXTURES NOT MADE FROM ETHANOL.—In the case of a mixture described in subsection (c)(1)(A)(i) or (d)(1)(A)(i) none of the alcohol in which is ethanol—

(1) subsections (c)(1)(A) and (c)(2), and subsections (d)(A)(1) and (d)(2), shall each be applied by substituting rates which are 0.6 cents less than the rates contained therein, and

(2) subsections (c)(1)(B) and (d)(1)(B) shall be applied by substituting rates which are $^{10}/_9$ of the rates determined under paragraph (1).

Amendments

• **1990, Omnibus Budget Reconciliation Act of 1990 (P.L. 101-508)**

P.L. 101-508, §11213(b)(2)(D):

Amended Code Sec. 4091 by adding at the end thereof a new subsection (e). **Effective** 12-1-90.

[Sec. 4092—Stricken]

Amendments

• **2004, American Jobs Creation Act of 2004 (P.L. 108-357)**

P.L. 108-357, §853(d)(1):

Amended part III of subchapter A of chapter 32 by striking subpart B (Code Secs. 4091-4093) and by redesignating subpart C as subpart B. **Effective** for aviation-grade kerosene removed, entered, or sold after 12-31-2004. Prior to being stricken, Code Sec. 4092 read as follows:

SEC. 4092. EXEMPTIONS.

[Sec. 4092(a)]

(a) NONTAXABLE USES.—No tax shall be imposed by section 4091 on aviation fuel sold by a producer or importer for use by the purchaser in a nontaxable use (as defined in section 6427(l)(2)(B)).

[Sec. 4092(b)]

(b) NO EXEMPTION FROM CERTAIN TAXES ON FUEL USED IN COMMERCIAL AVIATION.—In the case of fuel sold for use in commercial aviation (other than supplies for vessels or aircraft within the meaning of section 4221(d)(3)), subsection (a) shall not apply to so much of the tax imposed by section 4091 as is attributable to—

(1) the Leaking Underground Storage Tank Trust Fund financing rate imposed by such section, and

(2) in the case of fuel sold after September 30, 1995, 4.3 cents per gallon of the rate specified in section 4091(b)(1).

For purposes of the preceding sentence, the term "commercial aviation" means any use of an aircraft other than in noncommercial aviation (as defined in section 4041(c)(2)).

Amendments

• **1998, IRS Restructuring and Reform Act of 1998 (P.L. 105-206)**

P.L. 105-206, §6023(16):

Amended Code Sec. 4092(b) by striking "section 4041(c)(4)" and inserting "section 4041(c)(2)". **Effective** 7-22-98. [This amendment was previously made by P.L. 105-34, §1601(f)(4)(c), **effective** 8-27-96. Therefore, the language "section 4041(c)(4)" no longer appears, and the amendment by P.L. 105-206, §6023(16), cannot be made.—CCH.]

[Sec. 4091—Repealed]

Amendments

• **1983, Surface Transportation Assistance Act of 1982 (P.L. 97-424)**

P.L. 97-424, §515(a):

Repealed Code Sec. 4091. **Effective** with respect to articles sold after 1-6-83. Prior to its repeal, Code Sec. 4091 read as follows:

SEC. 4091. IMPOSITION OF TAX.

There is hereby imposed tax on lubricating oil (other than cutting oils) which is sold in the United States by the manufacturer or producer a tax of 6 cents a gallon, to be paid by the manufacturer or producer.

• **1965, Excise Tax Reduction Act of 1965 (P.L. 89-44)**

P.L. 89-44, §202(a):

Amended Sec. 4091. **Effective** 1-1-66. Prior to amendment, Sec. 4091 read as follows:

"There is hereby imposed upon the following articles sold in the United States by the manufacturer or producer a tax at the following rates, to be paid by the manufacturer or producer:

"(1) cutting oils, 3 cents a gallon; and

"(2) other lubricating oils, 6 cents a gallon."

• **1955 (P.L. 355, 84th Cong., 1st Sess.)**

P.L. 355, 84th Cong., 1st Sess., §[1](a):

Amended the section. **Effective** 10-1-55. Prior to amendment, Section 4091 read as follows:

"There is hereby imposed upon lubricating oils sold in the United States by the manufacturer or producer at the rate of 6 cents a gallon (except that, in the case of cutting oils, the tax shall not exceed 10 percent of the price for which so sold), to be paid by the manufacturer or producer. For purposes of this section, the term `cutting oils' means oils used primarily in cutting and machining operations (including forging, drawing, rolling, shearing, punching, and stamping) on metals and known commercially as cutting oils."

[Sec. 4091(d)]

(d) REFUND OF TAX-PAID AVIATION FUEL TO REGISTERED PRODUCER OF FUEL.—If—

(1) a producer of aviation fuel is registered under section 4101, and

(2) such producer establishes to the satisfaction of the Secretary that a prior tax was paid (and not credited or refunded) on aviation fuel held by such producer,

then an amount equal to the tax so paid shall be allowed as a refund (without interest) to such producer in the same manner as if it were an overpayment of tax imposed by this section.

Amendments

• **1997, Taxpayer Relief Act of 1997 (P.L. 105-34)**

P.L. 105-34, §1436(a):

Amended Code Sec. 4091 by adding at the end a new subsection (d). **Effective** for fuel acquired by the producer after 9-30-97.

• **1997, Taxpayer Relief Act of 1997 (P.L. 105-34)**

P.L. 105-34, §1601(f)(4)(C):

Amended Code Sec. 4092(b) by striking "section 4041(c)(4)" and inserting "section 4041(c)(2)". **Effective** as if included in the provision of P.L. 104-188 to which it relates [effective 8-27-96.—CCH].

[Sec. 4092(c)]

(c) SALES TO PRODUCER.—Under regulations prescribed by the Secretary, the tax imposed by section 4091 shall not apply to aviation fuel sold to a producer of such fuel.

Amendments

• **1993, Omnibus Budget Reconciliation Act of 1993 (P.L. 103-66)**

P.L. 103-66, §13163(a)(1):

Amended Code Sec. 4092(a)(2) by striking "or a diesel-powered train" and inserting ", a diesel-powered train, or a diesel-powered boat". **Effective** 1-1-94.

P.L. 103-66, §13163(a)(3):

Amended Code Sec. 4092(b)(1)(B) by striking "commercial and noncommercial vessels" each place it appears and inserting "vessels for use in an off-highway business use (as defined in section 6421(e)(2)(B))". **Effective** 1-1-94.

P.L. 103-66, §13242(a):

Amended subparts A and B of part III of subchapter A of chapter 32 (Code Secs. 4081-4093), as amended by subpart A. **Effective** 1-1-94. Prior to amendment, Code Sec. 4092 read as follows:

SEC. 4092. DEFINITIONS.

[Sec. 4092(a)]

(a) TAXABLE FUEL.—For purposes of this subpart—

(1) IN GENERAL.—The term "taxable fuel" means—

(A) diesel fuel, and

(B) aviation fuel.

(2) DIESEL FUEL.—The term "diesel fuel" means any liquid (other than any product taxable under section 4081) which is suitable for use as a fuel in a diesel-powered highway vehicle, a diesel-powered train, or a diesel-powered boat.

MANUFACTURERS TAXES—DIESEL FUEL

(3) AVIATION FUEL.—The term "aviation fuel" means any liquid (other than any product taxable under section 4081) which is suitable for use as a fuel in an aircraft.

[Sec. 4092(b)]

(b) PRODUCER.—For purposes of this subpart—

(1) CERTAIN PERSONS TREATED AS PRODUCERS.—

(A) IN GENERAL.—The term "producer" includes any person described in subparagraph (B) who elects to register under section 4101 with respect to the tax imposed by section 4091.

(B) PERSONS DESCRIBED.—A person is described in this subparagraph if such person is—

(i) a refiner, compounder, blender, or wholesale distributor of a taxable fuel, or

(ii) a dealer selling any taxable fuel exclusively to producers of such taxable fuel, or

(iii) a retailer selling diesel fuel exclusively to purchasers as supplies for vessels for use in an off-highway business use (as defined in section 6421(e)(2)(B)).

To the extent provided in regulations, a retailer shall not be treated as not described in clause (iii) by reason of selling de minimis amounts of diesel fuel other than as supplies for vessels for use in an off-highway business use (as defined in section 6421(e)(2)(B)).

(C) TAX-FREE PURCHASERS TREATED AS PRODUCERS.—Any person to whom any taxable fuel is sold tax-free under this subpart shall be treated as the producer of such fuel.

(2) WHOLESALE DISTRIBUTOR.—For purposes of paragraph (1), the term "wholesale distributor" includes any person who sells a taxable fuel to producers, retailers, or to users who purchase in bulk quantities and deliver into bulk storage tanks. Such term does not include any person who (excluding the term "wholesale distributor" from paragraph (1)) is a producer or importer.

Amendments

• **1988, Technical and Miscellaneous Revenue Act of 1988 (P.L. 100-647)**

P.L. 100-647, § 3003(a):

Amended Code Sec. 4092(b)(1)(B) by striking out the period at the end of clause (ii) and inserting in lieu thereof ", or" and by adding at the end thereof a new clause (iii) and flush sentence. **Effective** for sales after 12-31-88.

Amendments

• **2004, American Jobs Creation Act of 2004 (P.L. 108-357)**

P.L. 108-357, § 853(d)(1):

Amended part III of subchapter A of chapter 32 by striking subpart B (Code Secs. 4091-4093) and by redesignating subpart C as subpart B. **Effective** for aviation-grade kerosene removed, entered, or sold after 12-31-2004. Prior to being stricken, Code Sec. 4093 read as follows:

SEC. 4093. DEFINITIONS.

[Sec. 4093(a)]

(a) AVIATION FUEL.—For purposes of this subpart, the term "aviation fuel" means kerosene and any other liquid (other than any product taxable under section 4081) which is suitable for use as a fuel in an aircraft.

Amendments

• **1997, Taxpayer Relief Act of 1997 (P.L. 105-34)**

P.L. 105-34, § 1032(e)(5):

Amended Code Sec. 4093(a) by striking "any liquid" and inserting "kerosene and any other liquid". **Effective** 7-1-98.

[Sec. 4093(b)]

(b) PRODUCER.—For purposes of this subpart—

(1) CERTAIN PERSONS TREATED AS PRODUCERS.—

(A) IN GENERAL.—The term "producer" includes any person described in subparagraph (B) and registered under section 4101 with respect to the tax imposed by section 4091.

(B) PERSONS DESCRIBED.—A person is described in this subparagraph if such person is—

(i) a refiner, blender, or wholesale distributor of aviation fuel, or

(ii) a dealer selling aviation fuel exclusively to producers of aviation fuel.

(C) REDUCED RATE PURCHASERS TREATED AS PRODUCERS.—Any person to whom aviation fuel is sold at a reduced rate under this subpart shall be treated as the producer of such fuel.

(2) WHOLESALE DISTRIBUTOR.—For purposes of paragraph (1), the term "wholesale distributor" includes any person who sells aviation fuel to producers, retailers, or to users who purchase in bulk quantities and accept delivery into bulk storage tanks. Such term does not include any person who (excluding the term "wholesale distributor" from paragraph (1)) is a producer or importer.

Amendments

• **1993, Omnibus Budget Reconciliation Act of 1993 (P.L. 103-66)**

P.L. 103-66, § 13241(f)(3):

Amended Code Sec. 4093(c)(2)(A) and (B). **Effective** 10-31-93. Prior to amendment, Code Sec. 4093(c)(2)(A) and (B) read as follows:

(A) CERTAIN LEAKING UNDERGROUND STORAGE TANK TRUST FUND TAXES.—In the case of fuel sold for use in—

(i) a diesel-powered train, and

(ii) an aircraft,

paragraph (1) shall not apply to so much of the tax imposed by section 4091 as is attributable to the Leaking Underground Storage Tank Trust Fund financing rate imposed by such section.

• **1987, Revenue Act of 1987 (P.L. 100-203)**

P.L. 100-203, § 10502(a):

Amended part III of subchapter 32 by adding new Code Sec. 4092. **Effective** for sales after 3-31-88. For special rules, see Act Sec. 10502(f) in the amendment notes following Code Sec. 4091.

[Sec. 4092—Repealed]

Amendments

• **1983, Surface Transportation Assistance Act of 1982 (P.L. 97-424)**

P.L. 97-424, § 515(a):

Repealed Code Sec. 4092. **Effective** with respect to articles sold after 1-6-83. Prior to its repeal, Code Sec. 4092 read as follows:

SEC. 4092. DEFINITIONS.

(a) CERTAIN VENDEES CONSIDERED AS MANUFACTURERS.—For purposes of this subpart, a vendee who has purchased lubricating oils free of tax under section 4093(a) shall be considered the manufacturer or producer of such lubricating oils.

(b) CUTTING OILS.—For purposes of this subpart, the term "cutting oils" means oils sold for the use in cutting and machining operation (including forging, drawing, rolling, shearing, punching, and stamping) on metals.

• **1978, Energy Tax Act of 1978 (P.L. 95-618)**

P.L. 95-618, § 404(b):

Amended Code Sec. 4092(a) by striking out "4093" and inserting in lieu thereof "4093(a)". **Effective** for sales on or after 12-1-78.

• **1955 (P.L. 355, 84th Cong.)**

P.L. 355, 84th Cong., 1st Sess., § [1](b):

Amended Code Sec. 4092. **Effective** 10-1-55. Prior to amendment, Section 4092 read as follows:

"For the purposes of this subpart a vendee who has purchased lubricating oils free of tax under section 4093 shall be considered the manufacturer or producer of such lubricating oils."

[Sec. 4093—Stricken]

(B) DEFICIT REDUCTION TAX ON FUEL USED IN TRAINS.—In the case of fuel sold for use in a diesel-powered train, paragraph (1) also shall not apply to so much of the tax imposed by section 4091 as is attributable to the diesel fuel deficit reduction rate imposed by such section.

P.L. 103-66, § 13241(f)(4):

Amended Code Sec. 4093(d) by inserting "and the aviation fuel deficit reduction rate" after "rate". **Effective** 10-31-93.

P.L. 103-66, § 13242(a):

Amended subparts A and B of part III of subchapter A of chapter 32 (Code Secs. 4081-4093), as amended by subpart A (Act Sec. 13241(f)(3)-(4)). **Effective** 1-1-94. Prior to amendment, Code Sec. 4093 read as follows:

SEC. 4093. EXEMPTIONS: SPECIAL RULE.

[Sec. 4093(a)]

(a) HEATING OIL.—The tax imposed by section 4091 shall not apply in the case of sales of any taxable fuel which the Secretary determines is destined for use as heating oil.

[Sec. 4093(b)]

(b) SALES TO PRODUCER.—Under regulations prescribed by the Secretary, the tax imposed by section 4091 shall not apply in the case of sales of a taxable fuel to a producer of such fuel.

[Sec. 4093(c)]

(c) EXEMPTION FOR NONTAXABLE USES AND BUS USES.—

(1) IN GENERAL.—No tax shall be imposed by section 4091 on fuel sold by a producer or importer for use by the purchaser in a nontaxable use (as defined in section 6427(l)(2)) or a use described in section 6427(b)(1).

(2) EXCEPTIONS.—

(A) NO EXEMPTION FROM CERTAIN TAXES ON FUEL USED IN DIESEL-POWERED TRAINS.—In the case of fuel sold for use in a diesel-powered train, paragraph (1) shall not apply to so much of the tax imposed by section 4091 as is attributable to the Leaking Underground Storage Tank Trust Fund financing rate and the diesel fuel deficit reduction rate imposed under such section. The preceding sentence shall not apply in the case of fuel sold for exclusive use by a State or any political subdivision thereof.

(B) NO EXEMPTION FROM LEAKING UNDERGROUND STORAGE TANK TRUST FUND TAXES ON FUEL USED IN COMMERCIAL AVIATION.—In the case of fuel sold for use in commercial aviation (other than supplies for vessels or aircraft within the meaning of section 4221(d)(3)), paragraph (1) also shall not apply to so much of the tax imposed by section 4091 as is attributable to the Leaking Underground Storage Tank Trust Fund financing rate imposed by such section. For purposes of the preceding sentence, the term "commercial aviation" means any use of an aircraft other than in noncommercial aviation (as defined in section 4041(c)(4)) unless such fuel is sold for exclusive use by a State or any political subdivision thereof.

(C) CERTAIN BUS USES.—Paragraph (1) shall not apply to so much of the tax imposed by section 4091 as is not refundable by reason of the application of section 6427(b)(2)(A).

(3) REGISTRATION REQUIRED.—Except to the extent provided by the Secretary paragraph (1) shall not apply to any sale unless—

(A) both the seller and the purchaser are registered under section 4101, and

(B) the purchaser's name, address, and registration number under such section are provided to the seller.

(4) INFORMATION REPORTING.—

MANUFACTURERS TAXES—DIESEL FUEL

(A) RETURNS BY PRODUCERS AND IMPORTERS.—Each producer or importer who makes a reduced-tax sale during the calendar year shall make a return (at such time and in such form as the Secretary may by regulations prescribe) showing with respect to each such sale—

(i) the name, address, and registration number under section 4101 of the purchaser,

(ii) the amount of fuel sold, and

(iii) such other information as the Secretary may require.

(B) STATEMENTS TO PURCHASERS.—Every person required to make a return under subparagraph (A) shall furnish to each purchaser whose name is required to be set forth on such return a written statement showing the name and address of the person required to make such return, the registration number under section 4101 of such person, and the information required to be shown on the return with respect to such purchaser. The written statement required under the preceding sentence shall be furnished to the purchaser on or before January 31 of the year following the calendar year for which the return under subparagraph (A) is required to be made.

(C) RETURNS BY PURCHASERS.—Each person who uses during the calendar year fuel purchased in a reduced-tax sale shall make a return (at such time and in such form as the Secretary may by regulations prescribe) showing—

(i) whether such use was a nontaxable use (as defined in section 6427(l)(2)) or a use described in section 6427(b)(1) and the amount of fuel so used,

(ii) the date of the sale of the fuel so used,

(iii) the name, address, and registration number under section 4101 of the seller, and

(iv) such other information as the Secretary may require.

(D) REDUCED-TAX SALE.—For purposes of this paragraph, the term "reduced-tax sale" means any sale of taxable fuel on which the amount of tax otherwise required to be paid under section 4091 is reduced by reason of paragraph (1) (other than sales described in subsections (a) and (b) of this section).

Amendments

• **1996, Small Business Job Protection Act of 1996 (P.L. 104-188)**

P.L. 104-188, §1702(b)(2)(A):

Amended Code Sec. 4093(c)(2)(B), as in effect before the amendments made by P.L. 103-66, by inserting before the period "unless such fuel is sold for exclusive use by a State or any political subdivision thereof". **Effective** as if included in the provision of P.L. 101-508 to which it relates.

• **1990, Omnibus Budget Reconciliation Act of 1990 (P.L. 101-508)**

P.L. 101-508, §11211(b)(4)(A):

Amended Code Sec. 4093(c)(2) by redesignating subparagraph (B) as subparagraph (C) and inserting after subparagraph (A) a new subparagraph (B). **Effective** 12-1-90.

P.L. 101-508, §11704(a)(20):

Amended Code Sec. 4093(c)(4)(D) by striking "reduced tax sale" and inserting "reduced-tax sale". **Effective** 11-5-90.

• **1988, Technical and Miscellaneous Revenue Act of 1988 (P.L. 100-647)**

P.L. 100-647, §3001(a):

Amended Code Sec. 4093(c). **Effective** 1-1-89. For a special rule see Act Sec. 3001(c)(2), below. Prior to amendment Code Sec. 4093(c) read as follows:

(c) AUTHORITY TO EXEMPT CERTAIN OTHER USES.—Subject to such terms and conditions as the Secretary may provide (including the application of section 4101), the Secretary may by regulation provide that—

(1) the Highway Trust Fund financing rate under section 4091 shall not apply to diesel fuel sold for use by any purchaser as a fuel in a diesel-powered train,

(2) the Airport and Airway Trust Fund financing rate under section 4091 shall not apply to aviation fuel sold for use by any purchaser as a fuel in an aircraft used in noncommercial aviation (as defined in section 4041(c)(4)),

(3) the tax imposed by section 4091 shall not apply to taxable fuel sold for use by any purchaser other than as a motor fuel, and

(4) the tax imposed by section 4091 shall not apply to taxable fuel sold for the exclusive use of any State, any political subdivision of a State, or the District of Columbia.

P.L. 100-647, §3001(c)(2), provides:

(2) REFUNDS WITH INTEREST FOR PRE-EFFECTIVE DATE PURCHASES.—

(A) IN GENERAL.—In the case of fuel—

(i) which is purchased from a producer or importer during the period beginning on April 1, 1988, and ending on December 31, 1988,

(ii) which is used (before the claim under this subparagraph is filed) by any person in a nontaxable use (as defined in section 6427(l)(2) of the 1988 Code), and

(iii) with respect to which a claim is not permitted to be filed for any quarter under section 6427(i) of the 1986 Code,

the Secretary of the Treasury or the Secretary's delegate shall pay (with interest) to such person the amount of tax imposed on such fuel under section 4091 of the 1986 Code (to the extent not attributable to amounts described in section 6427(l)(3) of the 1986 Code) if claim therefor is filed not later than June 30, 1989. Not more than 1 claim may be filed under the preceding sentence and such claim shall not be taken into account under section 6427(i) of the 1986 Code. Any claim for refund filed under this paragraph shall be considered a claim for refund under section 6427(l) of the 1986 Code.

(B) INTEREST.—The amount of interest payable under subparagraph (A) shall be determined under section 6611 of the 1986 Code except that the date of the overpayment with respect to fuel purchased during any month shall be treated as being the 1st day of the succeeding month. No interest shall be paid under this paragraph with respect to fuel used by any agency of the United States.

(C) REGISTRATION PROCEDURES REQUIRED TO BE SPECIFIED.—Not later than the 30th day after the date of the enactment of this Act, the Secretary of the Treasury or the Secretary's delegate shall prescribe the procedures for complying with the requirements of section 4093(c)(3) of the 1986 Code (as added by this section).

[Sec. 4093(d)]

(d) CERTAIN AVIATION FUEL SALES.—Under regulations prescribed by the Secretary, the Leaking Underground Storage Tank Trust Fund financing rate and the aviation fuel deficit reduction rate under section 4091 shall not apply to aviation fuel sold for use or used as supplies for vessels or aircraft (within the meaning of section 4221(d)(3)).

Amendments

• **1988, Technical and Miscellaneous Revenue Act of 1988 (P.L. 100-647)**

P.L. 100-647, §2004(s)(1):

Amended Code Sec. 4093 by redesignating subsections (d) and (e) as subsections (e) and (f), respectively, and by inserting after subsection (c) a new subsection (d). **Effective** as if included in the provision of P.L. 100-203 to which it relates.

[Sec. 4093(e)—Stricken]

Amendments

• **1990, Omnibus Budget Reconciliation Act of 1990 (P.L. 101-508)**

P.L. 101-508, §11212(b)(4):

Amended Code Sec. 4093 by striking subsection (e) and redesignating subsection (f) as subsection (e). **Effective** 12-1-90. Prior to amendment, Code Sec. 4093(e) read as follows:

(e) SPECIAL ADMINISTRATIVE RULES.—The Secretary may require—

(1) information reporting by each remitter of the tax imposed by section 4091, and

(2) information reporting by, and registration of, such other person as the Secretary deems necessary to carry out this subpart.

• **1988, Technical and Miscellaneous Revenue Act of 1988 (P.L. 100-647)**

P.L. 100-647, §2004(s)(1):

Amended Code Sec. 4093 by redesignating subsections (d) and (e) as subsections (e) and (f), respectively, and by inserting after subsection (c) a new subsection (d). **Effective** as if included in the provision of P.L. 100-203 to which it relates.

[Sec. 4093(e)]

(e) CROSS REFERENCES.—

(1) For imposition of tax where certain uses of diesel fuel or aviation fuel occur before imposition of tax by section 4091, see subsections (a)(1) and (c)(1) of section 4041.

(2) For provisions allowing a credit or refund for fuel not used for certain taxable purposes, see section 6427.

Amendments

• **1990, Omnibus Budget Reconciliation Act of 1990 (P.L. 101-508)**

P.L. 101-508, §11212(b)(4):

Amended Code Sec. 4093 by redesignating subsection (f) as subsection (e). **Effective** 12-1-90.

• **1988, Technical and Miscellaneous Revenue Act of 1988 (P.L. 100-647)**

P.L. 100-647, §2004(s)(1):

Amended Code Sec. 4093 by redesignating subsections (d) and (e) as subsections (e) and (f), respectively, and by inserting after subsection (c) a new subsection (d). **Effective** as if included in the provision of P.L. 100-203 to which it relates.

• **1987, Revenue Act of 1987 (P.L. 100-203)**

P.L. 100-203, §10502(a):

Amended part III of subchapter 32 by adding new Code Sec. 4093. **Effective** for sales after 3-31-88. For special rules, see Act Sec. 10502(f) in the amendment notes following Code Sec. 4091.

[Sec. 4093—Repealed]

Amendments

• **1983, Surface Transportation Assistance Act of 1982 (P.L. 97-424)**

P.L. 97-424, §515(a):

Repealed Code Sec. 4093. **Effective** with respect to articles sold after 1-6-83. Prior to repeal, Code Sec. 4093 read as follows:

SEC. 4093. EXEMPTIONS.

(a) SALES TO MANUFACTURERS OR PRODUCERS FOR RESALE.—Under regulations prescribed by the Secretary, no tax shall be imposed by section 4091 on lubricating oils sold to a manufacturer or producer of lubricating oils for resale by him.

(b) USE IN PRODUCING REREFINED OIL.—

(1) Sales to rerefiners.—Under regulations prescribed by the Secretary, no tax shall be imposed by section 4091 on lubricating oil sold for use in mixing with used or waste lubricating oil which has been cleaned, renovated, or rerefined. Any person to whom lubricating oil is sold tax-free under this paragraph shall be treated as the producer of such lubricating oil.

(2) USE IN PRODUCING REREFINED OIL.—Under regulations prescribed by the Secretary, no tax shall be imposed by section 4091 on lubricating oil used in producing rerefined oil to the extent that the amount of such lubricating oil does not exceed 55 percent of such rerefined oil.

(3) REREFINED OIL DEFINED.—For purposes of this subsection, the term "rerefined oil" means oil 25 percent or more of which is used or waste lubricating oil which has been cleaned, renovated, or rerefined.

• **1978, Energy Tax Act of 1978 (P.L. 95-618)**

P.L. 95-618, §404(a):

Amended Code Sec. 4093. **Effective** for sales on or after 12-1-78. Prior to amendment, Code Sec. 4093 read as follows:

MANUFACTURERS TAXES—FUELS TAX

SEC. 4093. EXEMPTION OF SALES TO PRODUCERS.

Under regulations prescribed by the Secretary, no tax shall be imposed under this subpart upon lubricating oils sold to a manufacturer or producer of lubricating oils for resale by him.

Amendments

• **1983, Surface Transportation Assistance Act of 1982 (P.L. 97-424)**

P.L. 97-424, § 515(a):

Repealed Code Sec. 4094. **Effective** with respect to articles sold after 1-6-83. Prior to repeal, Code Sec. 4094 read as follows:

SEC. 4094. CROSS REFERENCE.

For provisions to relieve purchasers of lubricating oil from excise tax in the case of lubricating oil used otherwise than in a highway motor vehicle, see sections 39 and 6424.

[Sec. 4094—Repealed]

• **1976, Tax Reform Act of 1976 (P.L. 94-455)**

P.L. 94-455, § 1906(b)(13)(A):

Amended 1954 Code by substituting "Secretary" for "Secretary or his delegate" each place it appeared. **Effective** 2-1-77.

• **1965, Excise Tax Reduction Act of 1965 (P.L. 89-44)**

P.L. 89-44, § 202(c)(1)(A):

Added Sec. 4094 to chapter 32 of the 1954 Code. **Effective** 1-1-66.

Subpart B—Special Provisions Applicable to Fuels Tax

Sec. 4101.	Registration and bond.
Sec. 4102.	Inspection of records by local officers.
Sec. 4103.	Certain additional persons liable for tax where willful failure to pay.
Sec. 4104.	Information reporting for persons claiming certain tax benefits.
Sec. 4105.	Two-party exchanges.

[Sec. 4101]

SEC. 4101. REGISTRATION AND BOND.

[Sec. 4101(a)]

(a) REGISTRATION.—

(1) IN GENERAL.—Every person required by the Secretary to register under this section with respect to the tax imposed by section 4041(a) or 4081, every person producing or importing biodiesel (as defined in section 40A(d)(1)) or alcohol (as defined in section 6426(b)(4)(A)), every person producing or importing sustainable aviation fuel (as defined in section 40B), and every person producing second generation biofuel (as defined in section 40(b)(6)(E)) shall register with the Secretary at such time, in such form and manner, and subject to such terms and conditions, as the Secretary may by regulations prescribe. A registration under this section may be used only in accordance with regulations prescribed under this section.

(2) REGISTRATION OF PERSONS WITHIN FOREIGN TRADE ZONES, ETC.—The Secretary shall require registration by any person which—

(A) operates a terminal or refinery within a foreign trade zone or within a customs bonded storage facility, or

(B) holds an inventory position with respect to a taxable fuel in such a terminal.

(3) DISPLAY OF REGISTRATION.—Every operator of a vessel required by the Secretary to register under this section shall display proof of registration through an identification device prescribed by the Secretary on each vessel used by such operator to transport any taxable fuel.

(4) REGISTRATION OF PERSONS EXTENDING CREDIT ON CERTAIN EXEMPT SALES OF FUEL.—The Secretary shall require registration by any person which—

(A) extends credit by credit card to any ultimate purchaser described in subparagraph (C) or (D) of section 6416(b)(2) for the purchase of taxable fuel upon which tax has been imposed under section 4041 or 4081, and

(B) does not collect the amount of such tax from such ultimate purchaser.

(5) REREGISTRATION IN EVENT OF CHANGE IN OWNERSHIP.—Under regulations prescribed by the Secretary, a person (other than a corporation the stock of which is regularly traded on an established securities market) shall be required to reregister under this section if after a transaction (or series of related transactions) more than 50 percent of ownership interests in, or assets of, such person are held by persons other than persons (or persons related thereto) who held more than 50 percent of such interests or assets before the transaction (or series of related transactions).

Amendments

• **2022, Inflation Reduction Act of 2022 (P.L. 117-169)**

P.L. 117-169, § 13203(d)(2)(C):

Amended Code Sec. 4101(a)(1) by inserting "every person producing or importing sustainable aviation fuel (as defined in section 40B)," before "and every person producing second generation biofuel". **Effective** for fuel sold or used after 12-31-2022.

P.L. 117-169, § 13704(b)(5):

Amended Code Sec. 4101(a)(1), as amended by the preceding provisions of this Act, by inserting "every person producing a fuel eligible for the clean fuel production credit (pursuant to section 45Z)," after "section 6426(k)(3)),". [Note: Code Sec. 4101(a)(1) does not contain the text "section 6426(k)(3)),". Therefore, this amendment cannot be made.—CCH] **Effective** for transportation fuel produced after 12-31-2024.

• **2013, American Taxpayer Relief Act of 2012 (P.L. 112-240)**

P.L. 112-240, § 404(b)(3)(C):

Amended Code Sec. 4101(a)(1) by striking "cellulosic biofuel" and inserting "second generation biofuel". **Effective** for fuels sold or used after 1-2-2013.

• **2008, Heartland, Habitat, Harvest, and Horticulture Act of 2008 (P.L. 110-246)**

P.L. 110-246, § 15321(b)(3)(A)(i)-(ii):

Amended Code Sec. 4101(a)(1) by striking "and every person" and inserting ", every person", and by inserting ", and every person producing cellulosic biofuel (as defined in section 40(b)(6)(E))" after "section 6426(b)(4)(A))". **Effective** for fuel produced after 12-31-2008.

• **2007, Tax Technical Corrections Act of 2007 (P.L. 110-172)**

P.L. 110-172, § 11(a)(29):

Amended Code Sec. 4101(a) by redesignating paragraph (4) as paragraph (5). **Effective** 12-29-2007.

• **2005, Safe, Accountable, Flexible, Efficient Transportation Equity Act: A Legacy for Users (P.L. 109-59)**

P.L. 109-59, § 11113(c):

Amended Code Sec. 4101(a)(1) by striking "4041(a)(1)" and inserting "4041(a)". **Effective** for any sale or use for any period after 9-30-2006.

P.L. 109-59, § 11163(a):

Amended Code Sec. 4101(a) by adding at the end a new paragraph (4). **Effective** for sales after 12-31-2005.

P.L. 109-59, § 11164(a):

Amended Code Sec. 4101(a) by adding at the end a new paragraph (4)[(5)]. **Effective** for actions, or failures to act, after 8-10-2005.

P.L. 109-59, § 11166(a), provides:

(a) IN GENERAL.—On and after the date of the enactment of this Act, the Secretary of the Treasury shall require that a vessel described in section 4042(c)(1) of the Internal Revenue Code of 1986 be considered a vessel for purposes of the registration of the operator of such vessel under section 4101 of such Code, unless such operator uses such vessel exclusively for purposes of the entry of taxable fuel.

MANUFACTURERS TAXES—FUELS TAX

• **2004, American Jobs Creation Act of 2004 (P.L. 108-357)**

P.L. 108-357, § 301(b):

Amended Code Sec. 4101(a)(1), as amended by Act Sec. 861, by inserting "and every person producing or importing biodiesel (as defined in section 40A(d)(1)) or alcohol (as defined in section 6426(b)(4)(A))" before "shall register with the Secretary". **Effective** 4-1-2005.

P.L. 108-357, § 853(d)(2)(F):

Amended Code Sec. 4101(a) by striking ", 4081, or 4091" and inserting "or 4081". **Effective** for aviation-grade kerosene removed, entered, or sold after 12-31-2004. For special rules, see Act Sec. 853(f), below.

P.L. 108-357, § 853(f), provides:

(f) FLOOR STOCKS TAX.—

(1) IN GENERAL.—There is hereby imposed on aviation-grade kerosene held on January 1, 2005, by any person a tax equal to—

(A) the tax which would have been imposed before such date on such kerosene had the amendments made by this section been in effect at all times before such date, reduced by

(B) the sum of—

(i) the tax imposed before such date on such kerosene under section 4091 of the Internal Revenue Code of 1986, as in effect on such date, and

(ii) in the case of kerosene held exclusively for such person's own use, the amount which such person would (but for this clause) reasonably expect (as of such date) to be paid as a refund under section 6427(l) of such Code with respect to such kerosene.

(2) EXCEPTION FOR FUEL HELD IN AIRCRAFT FUEL TANK.—Paragraph (1) shall not apply to kerosene held in the fuel tank of an aircraft on January 1, 2005.

(3) LIABILITY FOR TAX AND METHOD OF PAYMENT.—

(A) LIABILITY FOR TAX.—The person holding the kerosene on January 1, 2005, to which the tax imposed by paragraph (1) applies shall be liable for such tax.

(B) METHOD AND TIME FOR PAYMENT.—The tax imposed by paragraph (1) shall be paid at such time and in such manner as the Secretary of the Treasury (or the Secretary's delegate) shall prescribe, including the nonapplication of such tax on de minimis amounts of kerosene.

(4) TRANSFER OF FLOOR STOCK TAX REVENUES TO TRUST FUNDS.—For purposes of determining the amount transferred to any trust fund, the tax imposed by this subsection shall be treated as imposed by section 4081 of the Internal Revenue Code of 1986—

(A) in any case in which tax was not imposed by section 4091 of such Code, at the Leaking Underground Storage Tank Trust Fund financing rate under such section to the extent of 0.1 cents per gallon, and

(B) at the rate under section 4081(a)(2)(A)(iv) of such Code to the extent of the remainder.

(5) HELD BY A PERSON.—For purposes of this subsection, kerosene shall be considered as held by a person if title thereto has passed to such person (whether or not delivery to the person has been made).

(6) OTHER LAWS APPLICABLE.—All provisions of law, including penalties, applicable with respect to the tax imposed by section 4081 of such Code shall, insofar as applicable and not inconsistent with the provisions of this subsection, apply with respect to the floor stock tax imposed by paragraph (1) to the same extent as if such tax were imposed by such section.

P.L. 108-357, § 861(a)(1)-(2):

Amended Code Sec. 4101(a) by striking "Every" and inserting "(1) IN GENERAL.—Every", and by adding at the end a new paragraph (2). **Effective** 1-1-2005.

P.L. 108-357, § 862(a):

Amended Code Sec. 4101(a), as amended by this Act, by redesignating paragraph (2) as paragraph (3), and by inserting after paragraph (1) a new paragraph (2). **Effective** 1-1-2005.

• **1993, Omnibus Budget Reconciliation Act of 1993 (P.L. 103-66)**

P.L. 103-66, § 13242(d)(1):

Amended Code Sec. 4101(a) by striking "4081" and inserting "4041(a)(1), 4081,". **Effective** 1-1-94.

[Sec. 4101(b)]

(b) BONDS AND LIENS.—

(1) IN GENERAL.—Under regulations prescribed by the Secretary, the Secretary may require, as a condition of permitting any person to be registered under subsection (a), that such person—

(A) give a bond in such sum as the Secretary determines appropriate, and

(B) agree to the imposition of a lien—

(i) on such property (or rights to property) of such person used in the trade or business for which the registration is sought, or

(ii) with the consent of such person, on any other property (or rights to property) of such person as the Secretary determines appropriate.

Rules similar to the rules of section 6323 shall apply to the lien imposed pursuant to this paragraph.

(2) RELEASE OR DISCHARGE OF LIEN.—If a lien is imposed pursuant to paragraph (1), the Secretary shall issue a certificate of discharge or a release of such lien in connection with a transfer of the property if there is furnished to the Secretary (and accepted by him) a bond in such sum as the Secretary determines appropriate or the transferor agrees to the imposition of a substitute lien under paragraph (1)(B) in such sum as the Secretary determines appropriate. The Secretary shall respond to any request to discharge or release a lien imposed pursuant to paragraph (1) in connection with a transfer of property not later than 90 days after the date the request for such a discharge or release is made.

[Sec. 4101(c)]

(c) DENIAL, REVOCATION, OR SUSPENSION OF REGISTRATION.—Rules similar to the rules of section 4222(c) shall apply to registration under this section.

[Sec. 4101(d)]

(d) INFORMATION REPORTING.—The Secretary may require—

(1) information reporting by any person registered under this section, and

(2) information reporting by such other persons as the Secretary deems necessary to carry out this part.

Any person who is required to report under this subsection and who has 25 or more reportable transactions in a month shall file such report in electronic format.

Amendments

• **2004, American Jobs Creation Act of 2004 (P.L. 108-357)**

P.L. 108-357, § 864(a):

Amended Code Sec. 4101(d) by adding at the end a new flush sentence. **Effective** 1-1-2006.

• **1990, Omnibus Budget Reconciliation Act of 1990 (P.L. 101-508)**

P.L. 101-508, § 11212(b)(1):

Amended Code Sec. 4101. **Effective** 12-1-90. Prior to amendment, Code Sec. 4101 read as follows:

SEC. 4101. REGISTRATION AND BOND.

[Sec. 4101(a)]

(a) REGISTRATION.—Every person subject to tax under section 4081 or 4091 shall, before incurring any liability for tax under such section, register with the Secretary.

• **1987, Revenue Act of 1987 (P.L. 100-203)**

P.L. 100-203, § 10502(d)(3):

Amended Code Sec. 4101(a), as amended by section 1703 of the Tax Reform Act of 1986, by inserting "or 4091" after "section 4081". **Effective** for sales after 3-31-88. For special rules, see Act Sec. 10502(f) in the amendment notes following Code Sec. 4091.

[Sec. 4101(b)]

(b) BOND.—Under regulations prescribed by the Secretary, every person who registers under subsection (a) may be required to give a bond in such sum as the Secretary determines.

Amendments

• **1986, Tax Reform Act of 1986 (P.L. 99-514)**

P.L. 99-514, § 1703(b)(1):

Amended Code Sec. 4101. **Effective** for gasoline removed (as defined in Code Sec. 4082, as amended) after 12-31-87. Prior to amendment, Code Sec. 4101 read as follows:

SEC. 4101. REGISTRATION.

Every person subject to tax under section 4081 shall, before incurring any liability for tax under such section, register with the Secretary.

• **1983, Surface Transportation Assistance Act of 1982 (P.L. 97-424)**

P.L. 97-424, § 515(b)(8):

Amended Code Sec. 4101 by striking out "or section 4091" after "section 4081". **Effective** with respect to articles sold after 1-6-83.

MANUFACTURERS TAXES—FUELS TAX

• **1976, Tax Reform Act of 1976 (P.L. 94-455)**

P.L. 94-455, § 1906(b)(13)(A):

Amended 1954 Code by substituting "Secretary" for "Secretary or his delegate" each place it appeared. **Effective** 2-1-77.

• **1965, Excise Tax Reduction Act of 1965 (P.L. 89-44)**

P.L. 89-44, § 802(b)(2):

Amended Sec. 4101. **Effective** 7-1-65. Prior to amendment, Sec. 4101 read as follows:

Sec. 4101. Registration and Bond.

Every person subject to tax under section 4081 or section 4091 shall, before incurring any liability for tax under such sections, register with the Secretary or his delegate and shall give a bond, to be approved by the Secretary or his delegate, conditioned that he shall not engage in any attempt, by himself or by collusion with others, to defraud the United States of any tax under such sections; that he shall render truly and completely all returns, statements, and inventories required by law or regulations in pursuance thereof and shall pay all taxes due under such sections; and that he shall comply with all requirements of law and regulations in pursuance thereof with respect to tax under such sections. Such bond shall be in such sum as the Secretary or his delegate may require in accordance with regulations prescribed by him, but not less than $2,000. The Secretary or his delegate may from time to time require a new or additional bond in accordance with this section.

[Sec. 4101(e)—Repealed]

Amendments

• **2002, Job Creation and Worker Assistance Act of 2002 (P.L. 107-147)**

P.L. 107-147, § 615(a):

Repealed Code Sec. 4101(e). **Effective** 1-1-2002. Prior to repeal, Code Sec. 4101(e) read as follows:

(e) CERTAIN APPROVED TERMINALS OF REGISTERED PERSONS REQUIRED TO OFFER DYED DIESEL FUEL AND KEROSENE FOR NONTAXABLE PURPOSES.—

(1) IN GENERAL.—A terminal for kerosene or diesel fuel may not be an approved facility for storage of non-tax-paid diesel fuel or kerosene under this section unless the operator of such terminal offers such fuel in a dyed form for removal for nontaxable use in accordance with section 4082(a).

(2) EXCEPTION.—Paragraph (1) shall not apply to any terminal exclusively providing aviation-grade kerosene by pipeline to an airport.

• **1998, IRS Restructuring and Reform Act of 1998 (P.L. 105-206)**

P.L. 105-206, § 6010(h)(5):

Amended Code Sec. 4101(e)(1) by striking "dyed diesel fuel and kerosene" and inserting "such fuel in a dyed form." **Effective** as if included in the provision of P.L. 105-34 to which it relates [effective 1-1-2002.—CCH].

• **1997, Taxpayer Relief Act of 1997 (P.L. 105-34)**

P.L. 105-34, § 1032(d):

Amended Code Sec. 4101 by adding at the end a new subsection (e). **Effective** 1-1-2002. [Effective date amended by P.L. 105-178, § 9008, and P.L. 106-170, § 524.]

[Sec. 4102]

SEC. 4102. INSPECTION OF RECORDS BY LOCAL OFFICERS.

Under regulations prescribed by the Secretary, records required to be kept with respect to taxes under this part shall be open to inspection by such officers of a State, or a political subdivision of any such State, as shall be charged with the enforcement or collection of any tax on any taxable fuel (as defined in section 4083).

Amendments

• **1993, Omnibus Budget Reconciliation Act of 1993 (P.L. 103-66)**

P.L. 103-66, § 13242(d)(2):

Amended Code Sec. 4102 by striking "gasoline" and inserting "any taxable fuel (as defined in section 4083)". **Effective** 1-1-94.

• **1983, Surface Transportation Assistance Act of 1982 (P.L. 97-424)**

P.L. 97-424, § 515(b)(9):

Amended Code Sec. 4102 by striking out "or lubricating oils" after "any tax on gasoline". **Effective** with respect to articles sold after 1-6-83.

• **1976, Tax Reform Act of 1976 (P.L. 94-455)**

P.L. 94-455, § 1202(c)(1):

Amended Code Sec. 4102. **Effective** 1-1-77. Prior to amendment, Code Sec. 4102 read as follows:

SEC. 4102. INSPECTION OF RECORDS, RETURNS, ETC., BY LOCAL OFFICERS.

Under regulations prescribed by the Secretary or his delegate, records required to be kept with respect to taxes under this part, and returns, reports, and statements with respect to such taxes filed with the Secretary or his delegate, shall be open to inspection by such officers of any State or Territory or political subdivision thereof or the District of Columbia as shall be charged with the enforcement or collection of any tax on gasoline or lubricating oils. The Secretary or his delegate shall furnish to any of such officers, upon written request, certified copies of any such statements, reports, or returns filed in his office, upon the payment of a fee of $1 for each 100 words or fraction thereof in the copy or copies requested.

[Sec. 4103]

SEC. 4103. CERTAIN ADDITIONAL PERSONS LIABLE FOR TAX WHERE WILLFUL FAILURE TO PAY.

In any case in which there is a willful failure to pay the tax imposed by section 4041(a)(1) or 4081, each person—

(1) who is an officer, employee, or agent of the taxpayer who is under a duty to assure the payment of such tax and who willfully fails to perform such duty, or

(2) who willfully causes the taxpayer to fail to pay such tax,

shall be jointly and severally liable with the taxpayer for the tax to which such failure relates.

Amendments

• **2004, American Jobs Creation Act of 2004 (P.L. 108-357)**

P.L. 108-357, § 853(d)(2)(F):

Amended Code Sec. 4103 by striking ", 4081, or 4091" and inserting "or 4081". **Effective** for aviation-grade kerosene removed, entered, or sold after 12-31-2004.

• **1993, Omnibus Budget Reconciliation Act of 1993 (P.L. 103-66)**

P.L. 103-66, § 13242(d)(1):

Amended Code Sec. 4103 by striking "4081" and inserting "4041(a)(1), 4081,". **Effective** 1-1-94.

• **1990, Omnibus Budget Reconciliation Act of 1990 (P.L. 101-508)**

P.L. 101-508, § 11212(c):

Amended subpart C of part III of subchapter A of chapter 32 by adding at the end thereof a new Code Sec. 4103. **Effective** 12-1-90.

[Sec. 4104]

SEC. 4104. INFORMATION REPORTING FOR PERSONS CLAIMING CERTAIN TAX BENEFITS.

[Sec. 4104(a)]

(a) IN GENERAL.—The Secretary shall require any person claiming tax benefits—

(1) under the provisions of sections 34, 40, and 40A, to file a return at the time such person claims such benefits (in such manner as the Secretary may prescribe), and

(2) under the provisions of section 4041(b)(2), 6426, or 6427(e) to file a quarterly return (in such manner as the Secretary may prescribe).

Amendments

• **2018, Tax Technical Corrections Act of 2018 (P.L. 115-141)**

P.L. 115-141, § 401(a)(220), Div. U:

Amended Code Sec. 4104(a)(1) by striking "section" and inserting "sections". **Effective** 3-23-2018.

Sec. 4101(e)—Repealed

MANUFACTURERS TAXES—COAL

[Sec. 4104(b)]

(b) CONTENTS OF RETURN.—Any return filed under this section shall provide such information relating to such benefits and the coordination of such benefits as the Secretary may require to ensure the proper administration and use of such benefits.

[Sec. 4104(c)]

(c) ENFORCEMENT.—With respect to any person described in subsection (a) and subject to registration requirements under this title, rules similar to rules of section 4222(c) shall apply with respect to any requirement under this section.

- **2004, American Jobs Creation Act of 2004 (P.L. 108-357)**

P.L. 108-357, § 303(a):

Amended subpart C of part III of subchapter A of chapter 32 by adding at the end a new Code Sec. 4104. **Effective** 1-1-2005.

[Sec. 4105]

SEC. 4105. TWO-PARTY EXCHANGES.

[Sec. 4105(a)]

(a) IN GENERAL.—In a two-party exchange, the delivering person shall not be liable for the tax imposed under section 4081(a)(1)(A)(ii).

[Sec. 4105(b)]

(b) TWO-PARTY EXCHANGE.—The term "two-party exchange" means a transaction, other than a sale, in which taxable fuel is transferred from a delivering person registered under section 4101 as a taxable fuel registrant to a receiving person who is so registered where all of the following occur:

(1) The transaction includes a transfer from the delivering person, who holds the inventory position for taxable fuel in the terminal as reflected in the records of the terminal operator.

(2) The exchange transaction occurs before or contemporaneous with completion of removal across the rack from the terminal by the receiving person.

(3) The terminal operator in its books and records treats the receiving person as the person that removes the product across the terminal rack for purposes of reporting the transaction to the Secretary.

(4) The transaction is the subject of a written contract.

Amendments

- **2004, American Jobs Creation Act of 2004 (P.L. 108-357)**

P.L. 108-357, § 866(a):

Amended subpart C of part III of subchapter A of chapter 32, as amended by this Act, by inserting after Code Sec. 4104 a new Code Sec. 4105. **Effective** 10-22-2004.

Subchapter B—Coal

Sec. 4121.   Imposition of tax.

[Sec. 4121]

SEC. 4121. IMPOSITION OF TAX.

[Sec. 4121(a)]

(a) TAX IMPOSED.—

(1) IN GENERAL.—There is hereby imposed on coal from mines located in the United States sold by the producer, a tax equal to the rate per ton determined under subsection (b).

(2) LIMITATION ON TAX.—The amount of the tax imposed by paragraph (1) with respect to a ton of coal shall not exceed the applicable percentage (determined under subsection (b)) of the price at which such ton of coal is sold by the producer.

Amendments

- **1986, Consolidated Omnibus Budget Reconciliation Act of 1985 (P.L. 99-272)**

P.L. 99-272, § 13203(a):

Amended Code Sec. 4121(a). **Effective** for sales after 3-31-86. Prior to amendment, Code Sec. 4121(a) read as follows:

TAX IMPOSED.—There is hereby imposed on coal sold by the producer a tax at the rates of—

(1) 50 cents per ton in the case of coal from underground mines located in the United States, and

(2) 25 cents per ton in the case of coal from surface mines located in the United States.

[Sec. 4121(b)]

(b) DETERMINATION OF RATES AND LIMITATION ON TAX.—For purposes of subsection (a)—

(1) the rate of tax on coal from underground mines shall be $1.10,

(2) the rate of tax on coal from surface mines shall be $.55, and

(3) the applicable percentage shall be 4.4 percent.

Amendments

- **1986, Tax Reform Act of 1986 (P.L. 99-514)**

P.L. 99-514, § 1897(a):

Amended Code Sec. 4121(b) by striking out ", in the case of sales during any calendar year beginning after December 31, 1985". **Effective** as if included in the amendment made by section 13203 of P.L. 99-272.

- **1986, Consolidated Omnibus Budget Reconciliation Act of 1985, (P.L. 99-272)**

P.L. 99-272, § 13203(a):

Amended Code Sec. 4121(b). **Effective** for sales after 3-31-86. Prior to amendment, Code Sec. 4121(b) read as follows:

(b) LIMITATION ON TAX.—The amount of the tax imposed by subsection (a) with respect to a ton of coal shall not exceed 2 percent of the price at which such ton of coal is sold by the producer.

[Sec. 4121(c)]

(c) TAX NOT TO APPLY TO LIGNITE.—The tax imposed by subsection (a) shall not apply in the case of lignite.

[Sec. 4121(d)]

(d) DEFINITIONS.—For purposes of this subchapter—

(1) COAL FROM SURFACE MINES.—Coal shall be treated as produced from a surface mine if all of the geological matter above the coal being mined is removed before the coal is extracted from the earth. Coal extracted by auger shall be treated as coal from a surface mine.

MANUFACTURERS TAXES—COAL

(2) COAL FROM UNDERGROUND MINES.—Coal shall be treated as produced from an underground mine if it is not produced from a surface mine.

(3) UNITED STATES.—The term "United States" has the meaning given to it by paragraph (1) of section 638.

(4) TON.—The term "ton" means 2,000 pounds.

[Sec. 4121(e)]—Stricken

Amendments

• **2022, Inflation Reduction Act of 2022 (P.L. 117-169)**

P.L. 117-169, § 13901(a):

Amended Code Sec. 4121 by striking subsection (e). **Effective** for sales in calendar quarters beginning after the date which is 1 day after 8-16-2022. Prior to being stricken, Code Sec. 4121(e) read as follows:

(e) REDUCTION IN AMOUNT OF TAX.—

(1) IN GENERAL.—Effective with respect to sales after the temporary increase termination date, subsection (b) shall be applied—

(A) by substituting "$.50" for "$1.10",

(B) by substituting "$.25" for "$.55", and

(C) by substituting "2 percent" for "4.4 percent".

(2) TEMPORARY INCREASE TERMINATION DATE.—For purposes of paragraph (1), the temporary increase termination date is the earlier of—

(A) December 31, 2021 or

(B) the first December 31 after 2007 as of which there is—

(i) no balance of repayable advances made to the Black Lung Disability Trust Fund, and

(ii) no unpaid interest on such advances.

• **2020, Taxpayer Certainty and Disaster Tax Relief Act of 2020 (P.L. 116-260)**

P.L. 116-260, § 149(a), Div. EE:

Amended Code Sec. 4121(e)(2)(A) by striking "December 31, 2020" and inserting "December 31, 2021". **Effective** for sales after 12-31-2020.

• **2019, Taxpayer Certainty and Disaster Tax Relief Act of 2019 (P.L. 116-94)**

P.L. 116-94, § 105(a), Div. Q:

Amended Code Sec. 4121(e)(2)(A) by striking "December 31, 2018" and inserting "December 31, 2020". **Effective** on and after the first day of the first calendar month beginning after 12-20-2019.

• **2008, Energy Improvement and Extension Act of 2008 (P.L. 110-343)**

P.L. 110-343, Division B, § 113(a)(1)-(2):

Amended Code Sec. 4121(e)(2) by striking "January 1, 2014" in subparagraph (A) and inserting "December 31, 2018", and by striking "January 1 after 1981" in subparagraph (B) and inserting "December 31 after 2007". **Effective** 10-3-2008.

P.L. 110-343, Division B, § 114, provides:

SEC. 114. SPECIAL RULES FOR REFUND OF THE COAL EXCISE TAX TO CERTAIN COAL PRODUCERS AND EXPORTERS.

(a) REFUND.—

(1) COAL PRODUCERS.—

(A) IN GENERAL.—Notwithstanding subsections (a)(1) and (c) of section 6416 and section 6511 of the Internal Revenue Code of 1986, if—

(i) a coal producer establishes that such coal producer, or a party related to such coal producer, exported coal produced by such coal producer to a foreign country or shipped coal produced by such coal producer to a possession of the United States, or caused such coal to be exported or shipped, the export or shipment of which was other than through an exporter who meets the requirements of paragraph (2),

(ii) such coal producer filed an excise tax return on or after October 1, 1990, and on or before the date of the enactment of this Act [10-3-2008.—CCH], and

(iii) such coal producer files a claim for refund with the Secretary not later than the close of the 30-day period beginning on the date of the enactment of this Act,

then the Secretary shall pay to such coal producer an amount equal to the tax paid under section 4121 of such Code on such coal exported or shipped by the coal producer or a party related to such coal producer, or caused by the coal producer or a party related to such coal producer to be exported or shipped.

(B) SPECIAL RULES FOR CERTAIN TAXPAYERS.—For purposes of this section—

(i) IN GENERAL.—If a coal producer or a party related to a coal producer has received a judgment described in clause (iii), such coal producer shall be deemed to have established the export of coal to a foreign country or shipment of coal to a possession of the United States under subparagraph (A)(i).

(ii) AMOUNT OF PAYMENT.—If a taxpayer described in clause (i) is entitled to a payment under subparagraph (A), the amount of such payment shall be reduced by any amount paid pursuant to the judgment described in clause (iii).

(iii) JUDGMENT DESCRIBED.—A judgment is described in this subparagraph if such judgment—

(I) is made by a court of competent jurisdiction within the United States,

(II) relates to the constitutionality of any tax paid on exported coal under section 4121 of the Internal Revenue Code of 1986, and

(III) is in favor of the coal producer or the party related to the coal producer.

(2) EXPORTERS.—Notwithstanding subsections (a)(1) and (c) of section 6416 and section 6511 of the Internal Revenue Code of 1986, and a judgment described in paragraph (1)(B)(iii) of this subsection, if—

(A) an exporter establishes that such exporter exported coal to a foreign country or shipped coal to a possession of the United States, or caused such coal to be so exported or shipped,

(B) such exporter filed a tax return on or after October 1, 1990, and on or before the date of the enactment of this Act, and

(C) such exporter files a claim for refund with the Secretary not later than the close of the 30-day period beginning on the date of the enactment of this Act,

then the Secretary shall pay to such exporter an amount equal to $0.825 per ton of such coal exported by the exporter or caused to be exported or shipped, or caused to be exported or shipped, by the exporter.

(b) LIMITATIONS.—Subsection (a) shall not apply with respect to exported coal if a settlement with the Federal Government has been made with and accepted by, the coal producer, a party related to such coal producer, or the exporter, of such coal, as of the date that the claim is filed under this section with respect to such exported coal. For purposes of this subsection, the term "settlement with the Federal Government" shall not include any settlement or stipulation entered into as of the date of the enactment of this Act, the terms of which contemplate a judgment concerning which any party has reserved the right to file an appeal, or has filed an appeal.

(c) SUBSEQUENT REFUND PROHIBITED.—No refund shall be made under this section to the extent that a credit or refund of such tax on such exported or shipped coal has been paid to any person.

(d) DEFINITIONS.—For purposes of this section—

(1) COAL PRODUCER.—The term "coal producer" means the person in whom is vested ownership of the coal immediately after the coal is severed from the ground, without regard to the existence of any contractual arrangement for the sale or other disposition of the coal or the payment of any royalties between the producer and third parties. The term includes any person who extracts coal from coal waste refuse piles or from the silt waste product which results from the wet washing (or similar processing) of coal.

(2) EXPORTER.—The term "exporter" means a person, other than a coal producer, who does not have a contract, fee arrangement, or any other agreement with a producer or seller of such coal to export or ship such coal to a third party on behalf of the producer or seller of such coal and—

(A) is indicated in the shipper's export declaration or other documentation as the exporter of record, or

(B) actually exported such coal to a foreign country or shipped such coal to a possession of the United States, or caused such coal to be so exported or shipped.

(3) RELATED PARTY.—The term "a party related to such coal producer" means a person who—

(A) is related to such coal producer through any degree of common management, stock ownership, or voting control,

(B) is related (within the meaning of section 144(a)(3) of the Internal Revenue Code of 1986) to such coal producer, or

(C) has a contract, fee arrangement, or any other agreement with such coal producer to sell such coal to a third party on behalf of such coal producer.

(4) SECRETARY.—The term "Secretary" means the Secretary of Treasury or the Secretary's designee.

(e) TIMING OF REFUND.—With respect to any claim for refund filed pursuant to this section, the Secretary shall determine whether the requirements of this section are met not later than 180 days after such claim is filed. If the Secretary determines that the requirements of this section are met, the claim for refund shall be paid not later than 180 days after the Secretary makes such determination.

(f) INTEREST.—Any refund paid pursuant to this section shall be paid by the Secretary with interest from the date of overpayment determined by using the overpayment rate and method under section 6621 of the Internal Revenue Code of 1986.

(g) DENIAL OF DOUBLE BENEFIT.—The payment under subsection (a) with respect to any coal shall not exceed—

(1) in the case of a payment to a coal producer, the amount of tax paid under section 4121 of the Internal Revenue Code of 1986 with respect to such coal by such coal producer or a party related to such coal producer, and

(2) in the case of a payment to an exporter, an amount equal to $0.825 per ton with respect to such coal exported by the exporter or caused to be exported by the exporter.

(h) APPLICATION OF SECTION.—This section applies only to claims on coal exported or shipped on or after October 1, 1990, through the date of the enactment of this Act [10-3-2008.—CCH].

(i) STANDING NOT CONFERRED.—

(1) EXPORTERS.—With respect to exporters, this section shall not confer standing upon an exporter to commence, or intervene in, any judicial or administrative proceeding concerning a claim for refund by a coal producer of any Federal or State tax, fee, or royalty paid by the coal producer.

(2) COAL PRODUCERS.—With respect to coal producers, this section shall not confer standing upon a coal producer to commence, or intervene in, any judicial or administrative proceeding concerning a claim for refund by an exporter of any Federal or State tax, fee, or royalty paid by the producer and alleged to have been passed on to an exporter.

• **1987, Revenue Act of 1987 (P.L. 100-203)**

P.L. 100-203, § 10503:

Amended Code Sec. 4121(e)(2)(A) by striking out "January 1, 1996" and inserting in lieu thereof "January 1, 2014". **Effective** 12-22-87.

MANUFACTURERS TAXES—CERTAIN VACCINES

• **1986, Consolidated Omnibus Budget Reconciliation Act of 1985, (P.L. 99-272)**

P.L. 99-272, §13203(c):

Amended so much of Code Sec. 4121(e) as precedes paragraph (2). **Effective** for sales after 3-31-86. Prior to amendment, so much of Code, Sec. 4121(e) as precedes paragraph (2) read as follows:

(e) TEMPORARY INCREASE IN AMOUNT OF TAX.—

IN GENERAL.—Effective with respect to sales after December 31, 1981, and before the temporary increase termination date—

(A) Subsection (a) shall be applied—

(i) by substituting "$1" for "50 cents", and

(ii) by substituting "50 cents" for "25 cents", and

(B) subsection (b) shall be applied by substituting "4 percent" for "2 percent".

• **1981, Black Lung Benefits Revenue Act of 1981 (P.L. 97-119)**

P.L. 97-119, §102(a):

Amended Code Sec. 4121 by adding at the end thereof subsection (e). **Effective** with respect to sales after 12-31-81.

• **1978, Black Lung Benefits Revenue Act of 1977 (P.L. 95-227)**

P.L. 95-227, §2(a):

Added Code Sec. 4121. **Effective** with respect to sales after 3-31-78. However, this **effective** date was contingent upon enactment of the Black Lung Benefits Reform Act (P.L. 109-280544), which was enacted as P.L. 95-239 on 3-1-78.

Subchapter C—Certain Vaccines

Sec. 4131.   Imposition of tax.
Sec. 4132.   Definitions and special rules.

[Sec. 4131]

SEC. 4131. IMPOSITION OF TAX.

[Sec. 4131(a)]

(a) GENERAL RULE.—There is hereby imposed a tax on any taxable vaccine sold by the manufacturer, producer, or importer thereof.

[Sec. 4131(b)]

(b) AMOUNT OF TAX.—

(1) IN GENERAL.—The amount of the tax imposed by subsection (a) shall be 75 cents per dose of any taxable vaccine.

(2) COMBINATIONS OF VACCINES.—If any taxable vaccine is described in more than 1 subparagraph of section 4132(a)(1), the amount of the tax imposed by subsection (a) on such vaccine shall be the sum of the amounts for the vaccines which are so included.

Amendments

• **1997, Taxpayer Relief Act of 1997 (P.L. 105-34)**

P.L. 105-34, §904(a):

Amended Code Sec. 4131(b). **Effective** 8-5-97. Prior to amendment, Code Sec. 4131(b) read as follows:

(b) AMOUNT OF TAX.—

(1) IN GENERAL.—The amount of the tax imposed by subsection (a) shall be determined in accordance with the following table:

If the taxable vaccine is:	The tax per dose is:
DPT vaccine	$4.56
DT vaccine	0.06
MMR vaccine	4.44
Polio vaccine	0.29

(2) COMBINATIONS OF VACCINES.—If any taxable vaccine is included in more than 1 category of vaccines in the table contained in paragraph (1), the amount of the tax imposed by subsection (a) on such vaccine shall be the sum of the amounts determined under such table for each category in which such vaccine is so included.

[Sec. 4131(c)]

(c) APPLICATION OF SECTION.—The tax imposed by this section shall apply—

(1) after December 31, 1987, and before January 1, 1993, and

(2) during periods after the date of the enactment of the Revenue Reconciliation Act of 1993.

Amendments

• **1993, Omnibus Budget Reconciliation Act of 1993 (P.L. 103-66)**

P.L. 103-66, §13421(a):

Amended Code Sec. 4131(c). **Effective** 8-10-93. Prior to amendment, Code Sec. 4131(c) read as follows:

(c) TERMINATION OF TAX IF AMOUNTS COLLECTED EXCEED PROJECTED FUND LIABILITY.—

(1) IN GENERAL.—If the Secretary estimates under paragraph (3) that the Vaccine Injury Compensation Trust Fund would not have a negative projected balance were the tax imposed by this section to terminate as of the close of any applicable date, no tax shall be imposed by this section after such date.

(2) APPLICABLE DATE.—For purposes of paragraph (1), the term "applicable date" means—

(A) the close of any calendar quarter ending on or after December 31, 1992, and

(B) the 1st date on which petitions may not be filed under section 2111 and 2111(a) of the Public Health Service Act by reason of section 2134 of such Act and each date thereafter.

(3) ESTIMATES BY SECRETARY.—

(A) IN GENERAL.—The Secretary shall estimate the projected balance of the Vaccine Injury Compensation Trust Fund as of—

(i) the close of each calendar quarter ending on or after December 31, 1992, and

(ii) such other times as are appropriate in the case of applicable dates described in paragraph (2)(B).

(B) DETERMINATION OF PROJECTED BALANCE.—In determining the projected balance of the Fund as of any date, the Secretary shall assume that—

(i) the tax imposed by this section will not apply after such date, and

(ii) there shall be paid from such Trust Fund all claims made or to be made against such Trust Fund—

(I) with respect to vaccines administered before October 1, 1992, in the case of an applicable date described in paragraph (2)(A), or

(II) with respect to petitions filed under section 2111 or section 2111(a) of the Public Health Service Act, in the case of an applicable date described in paragraph (2)(B).

P.L. 103-66, §13421(c), provides:

(c) FLOOR STOCKS TAX.—

(1) IMPOSITION OF TAX.—On any taxable vaccine—

(A) which was sold by the manufacturer, producer, or importer on or before the date of the enactment of this Act,

(B) on which no tax was imposed by section 4131 of the Internal Revenue Code of 1986 (or, if such tax was imposed, was credited or refunded), and

(C) which is held on such date by any person for sale or use,

there is hereby imposed a tax in the amount determined under section 4131(b) of such Code.

(2) LIABILITY FOR TAX AND METHOD OF PAYMENT.—

(A) LIABILITY FOR TAX.—The person holding any taxable vaccine to which the tax imposed by paragraph (1) applies shall be liable for such tax.

(B) METHOD OF PAYMENT.—The tax imposed by paragraph (1) shall be paid in such manner as the Secretary shall prescribe by regulations.

(C) TIME FOR PAYMENT.—The tax imposed by paragraph (1) shall be paid on or before the last day of the 6th month beginning after the date of the enactment of this Act.

(3) DEFINITIONS.—For purposes of this subsection, terms used in this subsection which are also used in section 4131 of such Code shall have the respective meanings such terms have in such section.

(4) OTHER LAWS APPLICABLE.—All provisions of law, including penalties, applicable with respect to the taxes imposed by section 4131 of such Code shall, insofar as applicable and not inconsistent with the provisions of this subsection, apply to the floor stocks taxes imposed by paragraph (1), to the same extent as if such taxes were imposed by such section 4131.

• **1987, Revenue Act of 1987 (P.L. 100-203)**

P.L. 100-203, §9201(a):

Amended chapter 32 by adding after subchapter B a new subchapter C. **Effective** 1-1-88.

MANUFACTURERS TAXES—CERTAIN VACCINES

[Sec. 4132]

SEC. 4132. DEFINITIONS AND SPECIAL RULES.

[Sec. 4132(a)]

(a) DEFINITIONS RELATING TO TAXABLE VACCINES.—For purposes of this subchapter—

(1) TAXABLE VACCINE.—The term "taxable vaccine" means any of the following vaccines which are manufactured or produced in the United States or entered into the United States for consumption, use, or warehousing:

(A) Any vaccine containing diphtheria toxoid.

(B) Any vaccine containing tetanus toxoid.

(C) Any vaccine containing pertussis bacteria, extracted or partial cell bacteria, or specific pertussis antigens.

(D) Any vaccine against measles.

(E) Any vaccine against mumps.

(F) Any vaccine against rubella.

(G) Any vaccine containing polio virus.

(H) Any HIB vaccine.

(I) Any vaccine against hepatitis A.

(J) Any vaccine against hepatitis B.

(K) Any vaccine against chicken pox.

(L) Any vaccine against rotavirus gastroenteritis.

(M) Any conjugate vaccine against streptococcus pneumoniae.

(N) Any trivalent vaccine against influenza or any other vaccine against seasonal influenza.

(O) Any meningococcal vaccine.

(P) Any vaccine against the human papillomavirus.

(2) VACCINE.—The term "vaccine" means any substance designed to be administered to a human being for the prevention of 1 or more diseases.

(3) UNITED STATES.—The term "United States" has the meaning given such term by section 4612(a)(4).

(4) IMPORTER.—The term "importer" means the person entering the vaccine for consumption, use, or warehousing.

Amendments

• 2013, (P.L. 113-15)

P.L. 113-15, §1(a):

Amended Code Sec. 4132(a)(1)(N) by inserting "or any other vaccine against seasonal influenza" before the period. For the **effective** date, see Act Sec. 1(b)(1)-(2), below.

P.L. 113-15, §1(b)(1)-(2), provides:

(b) EFFECTIVE DATE.—

(1) SALES, ETC.—The amendment made by this section shall apply to sales and uses on or after the later of—

(A) the first day of the first month which begins more than 4 weeks after the date of the enactment of this Act, or

(B) the date on which the Secretary of Health and Human Services lists any vaccine against seasonal influenza (other than any vaccine against seasonal influenza listed by the Secretary prior to the date of the enactment of this Act) for purposes of compensation for any vaccine-related injury or death through the Vaccine Injury Compensation Trust Fund.

(2) DELIVERIES.—For purposes of paragraph (1) and section 4131 of the Internal Revenue Code of 1986, in the case of sales on or before the effective date described in such paragraph for which delivery is made after such date, the delivery date shall be considered the sale date.

• 2006, Tax Relief and Health Care Act of 2006 (P.L. 109-432)

P.L. 109-432, Division A, §408(a):

Amended Code Sec. 4132(a)(1) by adding at the end a new subparagraph (O). For the **effective** date, see Act Sec. 408(c), below.

P.L. 109-432, Division A, §408(b):

Amended Code Sec. 4132(a)(1), as amended by Act Sec. 408(a), by adding at the end a new subparagraph (P). For the **effective** date, see Act Sec. 408(c), below.

P.L. 109-432, Division A, §408(c), provides:

(c) EFFECTIVE DATE.—

(1) SALES, ETC.—The amendments made by this section shall apply to sales and uses on or after the first day of the first month which begins more than 4 weeks after the date of the enactment of this Act.

(2) DELIVERIES.—For purposes of paragraph (1) and section 4131 of the Internal Revenue Code of 1986, in the case of sales on or before the effective date described in such paragraph for which delivery is made after such date, the delivery date shall be considered the sale date.

• 2004, American Jobs Creation Act of 2004 (P.L. 108-357)

P.L. 108-357, §889(a):

Amended Code Sec. 4132(a)(1) by redesignating subparagraphs (I), (J), (K), and (L) as subparagraphs (J), (K), (L), and (M), respectively, and by inserting after subparagraph (H) a new subparagraph (I). For the **effective** date, see Act Sec. 889(b)(1)-(2), below.

P.L. 108-357, §889(b)(1)-(2), provides:

(b) EFFECTIVE DATE.—

(1) SALES, ETC.—The amendment made by subsection (a) shall apply to sales and uses on or after the first day of the first month which begins more than 4 weeks after the date of the enactment of this Act.

(2) DELIVERIES.—For purposes of paragraph (1) and section 4131 of the Internal Revenue Code of 1986, in the case of sales on or before the effective date described in such paragraph for which delivery is made after such date, the delivery date shall be considered the sale date.

P.L. 108-357, §890(a):

Amended Code Sec. 4132(a)(1), as amended by Act Sec. 889(a), by adding at the end a new subparagraph (N). For the **effective** date, see Act Sec. 890(b)(1)-(2), below.

P.L. 108-357, §890(b)(1)-(2), provides:

(b) EFFECTIVE DATE.—

(1) SALES, ETC.—The amendment made by this section shall apply to sales and uses on or after the later of—

(A) the first day of the first month which begins more than 4 weeks after the date of the enactment of this Act, or

(B) the date on which the Secretary of Health and Human Services lists any vaccine against influenza for purposes of compensation for any vaccine-related injury or death through the Vaccine Injury Compensation Trust Fund.

(2) DELIVERIES.—For purposes of paragraph (1) and section 4131 of the Internal Revenue Code of 1986, in the case of sales on or before the effective date described in such paragraph for which delivery is made after such date, the delivery date shall be considered the sale date.

• 1999, Tax Relief Extension Act of 1999 (P.L. 106-170)

P.L. 106-170, §523(a)(1):

Amended Code Sec. 4132(a)(1) by adding at the end a new subparagraph (L). For the **effective** date, see Act Sec. 523(a)(2), below.

P.L. 106-170, §523(a)(2), provides:

(2) EFFECTIVE DATE.—

(A) SALES.—The amendment made by this subsection shall apply to vaccine sales after the date of the enactment of this Act, but shall not take effect if subsection (b) does not take effect.

(B) DELIVERIES.—For purposes of subparagraph (A), in the case of sales on or before the date described in such subparagraph for which delivery is made after such date, the delivery date shall be considered the sale date.

P.L. 106-170, §523(b)(1):

Retroactively repealed section 1503 of the Vaccine Injury Compensation Program Modification Act and it never took effect.

• 1998, Vaccine Injury Compensation Program Modification Act (P.L. 105-277)

P.L. 105-277, Div. C, §1503(a) (repealed by P.L. 106-170, §523(b)(1)):

Amended Code Sec. 4132[(a)](1) by adding at the end a new subparagraph (K). **Effective** for sales after 10-21-98. For a special rule, see Act Sec. 1503(b)(2), below.

P.L. 105-277, Div. C, §1503(b)(2), provides:

(2) DELIVERIES.—For purposes of paragraph (1), in the case of sales on or before the date of the enactment of this Act for which delivery is made after such date, the delivery date shall be considered the sale date.

MANUFACTURERS TAXES—SPORTING GOODS

- **1998, Tax and Trade Relief Extension Act of 1998 (P.L. 105-277)**

P.L. 105-277, § 3002(a):

Amended Code Sec. 4132(a)(1) by adding at the end a new subparagraph (K). [Note: The amendments made by Div. C, Act Sec. 1503(a), and Div. J, Act Sec. 3002(a), of P.L. 105-277 are identical.—CCH.] **Effective** for sales after 10-21-98. For a special rule, see Act Sec. 3002(b)(2), below.

P.L. 105-277, § 3002(b)(2), provides:

(2) DELIVERIES.—For purposes of paragraph (1), in the case of sales on or before the date of the enactment of this Act for which delivery is made after such date, the delivery date shall be considered the sale date.

- **1997, Taxpayer Relief Act of 1997 (P.L. 105-34)**

P.L. 105-34, § 904(b):

Amended Code Sec. 4132(a)(1). **Effective** 8-6-97. For a special rule, see Act Sec. 904(e), below. Prior to amendment, Code Sec. 4132(a)(1) read as follows:

(1) TAXABLE VACCINE.—The term "taxable vaccine" means any vaccine—

(A) which is listed in the table contained in section 4131(b)(1), and

(B) which is manufactured or produced in the United States or entered into the United States for consumption, use, or warehousing.

P.L. 105-34, § 904(c):

Amended Code Sec. 4132(a) by striking paragraphs (2), (3), (4), and (5) and by redesignating paragraphs (6) through (8) as paragraphs (2) through (4), respectively. **Effective** 8-6-97. For a special rule, see Act Sec. 904(e), below. Prior to amendment, Code Sec. 4132(a)(2)-(5) read as follows:

(2) DPT VACCINE.—The term "DPT vaccine" means any vaccine containing pertussis bacteria, extracted or partial cell bacteria, or specific pertussis antigens.

(3) DT VACCINE.—The term "DT vaccine" means any vaccine (other than a DPT vaccine) containing diphtheria toxoid or tetanus toxoid.

(4) MMR VACCINE.—The term "MMR vaccine" means any vaccine against measles, mumps, or rubella. Not more than 1 tax shall be imposed by section 4131 on any MMR vaccine by reason of being a vaccine against more than 1 of measles, mumps, or rubella.

(5) POLIO VACCINE.—The term "polio vaccine" means any vaccine containing polio virus.

P.L. 105-34, § 904(e), provides:

(e) LIMITATION ON CERTAIN CREDITS OR REFUNDS.—For purposes of applying section 4132(b) of the Internal Revenue Code of 1986 with respect to any claim for credit or refund filed before January 1, 1999, the amount of tax taken into account shall not exceed the tax computed under the rate in effect on the day after the date of the enactment of this Act.

[Sec. 4132(b)]

(b) CREDIT OR REFUND WHERE VACCINE RETURNED TO MANUFACTURER, ETC., OR DESTROYED.—

(1) IN GENERAL.—Under regulations prescribed by the Secretary, whenever any vaccine on which tax was imposed by section 4131 is—

(A) returned (other than for resale) to the person who paid such tax, or

(B) destroyed,

the Secretary shall abate such tax or allow a credit, or pay a refund (without interest), to such person equal to the tax paid under section 4131 with respect to such vaccine.

(2) CLAIM MUST BE FILED WITHIN 6 MONTHS.—Paragraph (1) shall apply to any returned or destroyed vaccine only with respect to claims filed within 6 months after the date the vaccine is returned or destroyed.

(3) CONDITION OF ALLOWANCE OF CREDIT OR REFUND.—No credit or refund shall be allowed or made under paragraph (1) with respect to any vaccine unless the person who paid the tax establishes that he—

(A) has repaid or agreed to repay the amount of the tax to the ultimate purchaser of the vaccine, or

(B) has obtained the written consent of such purchaser to the allowance of the credit or the making of the refund.

(4) TAX IMPOSED ONLY ONCE.—No tax shall be imposed by section 4131 on the sale of any vaccine if tax was imposed by section 4131 on any prior sale of such vaccine and such tax is not abated, credited, or refunded.

[Sec. 4132(c)]

(c) OTHER SPECIAL RULES.—

(1) CERTAIN USES TREATED AS SALES.—Any manufacturer, producer, or importer of a vaccine which uses such vaccine before it is sold shall be liable for the tax imposed by section 4131 in the same manner as if such vaccine were sold by such manufacturer, producer, or importer.

(2) TREATMENT OF VACCINES SHIPPED TO UNITED STATES POSSESSIONS.—Section 4221(a)(2) shall not apply to any vaccine shipped to a possession of the United States.

(3) FRACTIONAL PART OF A DOSE.—In the case of a fraction of a dose, the tax imposed by section 4131 shall be the same fraction of the amount of such tax imposed by a whole dose.

(4) DISPOSITION OF REVENUES FROM PUERTO RICO AND THE VIRGIN ISLANDS.—The provisions of subsections (a)(3) and (b)(3) of section 7652 shall not apply to any tax imposed by section 4131.

Amendments

- **1988, Technical and Miscellaneous Revenue Act of 1988 (P.L. 100-647)**

P.L. 100-647, § 2006(a):

Amended Code Sec. 4132(c) by redesignating paragraphs (1) and (2) as paragraphs (3) and (4), respectively, and by inserting before paragraph (3) new paragraphs (1) and (2). **Effective** as if included in the amendment made by P.L. 100-203, § 9201.

- **1987, Revenue Act of 1987 (P.L. 100-203)**

P.L. 100-203, § 9201(a):

Added Code Sec. 4132. **Effective** 1-1-88.

Subchapter D—Recreational Equipment

Part I.   Sporting goods.
Part III.   Firearms.

PART I—SPORTING GOODS

Sec. 4161.   Imposition of tax.
Sec. 4162.   Definitions; treatment of certain resales.

[Sec. 4161]

SEC. 4161. IMPOSITION OF TAX.

[Sec. 4161(a)]

(a) SPORT FISHING EQUIPMENT.—

(1) IMPOSITION OF TAX.—

(A) IN GENERAL.—There is hereby imposed on the sale of any article of sport fishing equipment by the manufacturer, producer, or importer a tax equal to 10 percent of the price for which so sold.

(B) LIMITATION ON TAX IMPOSED ON FISHING RODS AND POLES.—The tax imposed by subparagraph (A) on any fishing rod or pole shall not exceed $10.

(2) 3 PERCENT RATE OF TAX FOR ELECTRIC OUTBOARD MOTORS.—In the case of an electric outboard motor, paragraph (1) shall be applied by substituting "3 percent" for "10 percent".

MANUFACTURERS TAXES—SPORTING GOODS

(3) 3 PERCENT RATE OF TAX FOR TACKLE BOXES.—In the case of fishing tackle boxes, paragraph (1) shall be applied by substituting "3 percent" for "10 percent".

(4) PARTS OR ACCESSORIES SOLD IN CONNECTION WITH TAXABLE SALE.—In the case of any sale by the manufacturer, producer, or importer of any article of sport fishing equipment, such article shall be treated as including any parts or accessories of such article sold on or in connection therewith or with the sale thereof.

Amendments

• **2005, Gulf Opportunity Zone Act of 2005 (P.L. 109-135)**

P.L. 109-135, §412(uu):

Amended Code Sec. 4161(a)(2). **Effective** 12-21-2005. Prior to amendment, Code Sec. 4161(a)(2) read as follows:

(2) 3 PERCENT RATE OF TAX FOR ELECTRIC OUTBOARD MOTORS AND SONAR DEVICES SUITABLE FOR FINDING FISH.—

(A) IN GENERAL.—In the case of an electric outboard motor or a sonar device suitable for finding fish, paragraph (1)(A) shall be applied by substituting "3 percent" for "10 percent".

(B) $30 LIMITATION ON TAX IMPOSED ON SONAR DEVICES SUITABLE FOR FINDING FISH.—The tax imposed by paragraph (1)(A) on any sonar device suitable for finding fish shall not exceed $30.

• **2005, Safe, Accountable, Flexible, Efficient Transportation Equity Act: A Legacy for Users (P.L. 109-59)**

P.L. 109-59, §11117(a):

Amended Code Sec. 4161(a)(1). **Effective** for articles sold by the manufacturer, producer, or importer after 9-30-2005. Prior to amendment, Code Sec. 4161(a)(1) read as follows:

(1) IMPOSITION OF TAX.—There is hereby imposed on the sale of any article of sport fishing equipment by the manufacturer, producer, or importer a tax equal to 10 percent of the price for which so sold.

P.L. 109-59, §11117(b):

Amended Code Sec. 4161(a)(2) by striking "paragraph (1)" both places it appears and inserting "paragraph (1)(A)". **Effective** for articles sold by the manufacturer, producer, or importer after 9-30-2005.

• **2004, American Jobs Creation Act of 2004 (P.L. 108-357)**

P.L. 108-357, §333(a):

Amended Code Sec. 4161(a) by redesignating paragraph (3) as paragraph (4) and by inserting after paragraph (2) a new paragraph (3). **Effective** for articles sold by the manufacturer, producer, or importer after 12-31-2004.

• **1984, Deficit Reduction Act of 1984 (P.L. 98-369)**

P.L. 98-369, §1015(a):

Amended Code Sec. 4161(a). **Effective** for articles sold by the manufacturer, producer, or importer after 9-30-84. Prior to amendment, Code Sec. 4161 read as follows:

SEC. 4161. IMPOSITION OF TAX.

(a) Rods, Creels, Etc.—There is hereby imposed upon the sale of fishing rods, creels, reels, and artificial lures, baits, and flies (including parts or accessories of such articles sold on or in connection therewith, or with the sale thereof) by the manufacturer, producer, or importer a tax equivalent to 10 percent of the price for which so sold.

[Sec. 4161(b)]

(b) BOWS AND ARROWS, ETC.—

(1) BOWS.—

(A) IN GENERAL.—There is hereby imposed on the sale by the manufacturer, producer, or importer of any bow which has a peak draw weight of 30 pounds or more, a tax equal to 11 percent of the price for which so sold.

(B) ARCHERY EQUIPMENT.—There is hereby imposed on the sale by the manufacturer, producer, or importer—

(i) of any part or accessory suitable for inclusion in or attachment to a bow described in subparagraph (A), and

(ii) of any quiver, broadhead, or point suitable for use with an arrow described in paragraph (2),

a tax equal to 11 percent of the price for which so sold.

(2) ARROWS.—

(A) IN GENERAL.—There is hereby imposed on the first sale by the manufacturer, producer, or importer of any shaft (whether sold separately or incorporated as part of a finished or unfinished product) of a type used in the manufacture of any arrow which after its assembly—

(i) measures 18 inches overall or more in length, or

(ii) measures less than 18 inches overall in length but is suitable for use with a bow described in paragraph (1)(A),

a tax equal to 39 cents per shaft.

(B) EXEMPTION FOR CERTAIN WOODEN ARROW SHAFTS.—Subparagraph (A) shall not apply to any shaft consisting of all natural wood with no laminations or artificial means of enhancing the spine of such shaft (whether sold separately or incorporated as part of a finished or unfinished product) of a type used in the manufacture of any arrow which after its assembly—

(i) measures $5/16$ of an inch or less in diameter, and

(ii) is not suitable for use with a bow described in paragraph (1)(A).

(C) ADJUSTMENT FOR INFLATION.—

(i) IN GENERAL.—In the case of any calendar year beginning after 2005, the 39-cent amount specified in subparagraph (A) shall be increased by an amount equal to the product of—

(I) such amount, multiplied by

(II) the cost-of-living adjustment determined under section 1(f)(3) for such calendar year, determined by substituting "2004" for "2016" in subparagraph (A)(ii) thereof.

(ii) ROUNDING.—If any increase determined under clause (i) is not a multiple of 1 cent, such increase shall be rounded to the nearest multiple of 1 cent.

(3) COORDINATION WITH SUBSECTION (a).—No tax shall be imposed under this subsection with respect to any article taxable under subsection (a).

Amendments

• **2017, Tax Cuts and Jobs Act (P.L. 115-97)**

P.L. 115-97, §11002(d)(11):

Amended Code Sec. 4161(b)(2)(C)(i)(II) by striking "for '1992' in subparagraph (B)" and inserting "for '2016' in subparagraph (A)(ii)". **Effective** for tax years beginning after 12-31-2017.

• **2008, Tax Extenders and Alternative Minimum Tax Relief Act of 2008 (P.L. 110-343)**

P.L. 110-343, Division C, §503(a):

Amended Code Sec. 4161(b)(2) by redesignating subparagraph (B) as subparagraph (C) and by inserting after subparagraph (A) a new subparagraph (B). **Effective** for shafts first sold after 10-3-2008.

• **2004 (P.L. 108-493)**

P.L. 108-493, §1(a), provides:

(a) REPEAL.—Subsection (b) of section 332 of the American Jobs Creation Act of 2004 [P.L. 108-357], and the amendments made by such subsection, are hereby repealed; and the Internal Revenue Code of 1986 shall be applied as if such subsection and amendments had never been enacted.

P.L. 108-493, §1(b):

Amended Code Sec. 4161(b)(2). **Effective** for articles sold by the manufacturer, producer, or importer after 3-31-2005. Prior to amendment, Code Sec. 4161(b)(2) read as follows:

(2) ARROW COMPONENTS.—There is hereby imposed on the sale by the manufacturer, producer, or importer of any shaft, point (other than broadheads), nock, or vane of a type used in the manufacture of any arrow which after its assembly—

MANUFACTURERS TAXES—SPORTING GOODS

(A) measures 18 inches overall or more in length, or

(B) measures less than 18 inches overall in length but is suitable for use with a bow described in paragraph (1)(A),

a tax equal to 12.4 percent of the price for which so sold.

P.L. 108-493, §1(c):

Amended Code Sec. 4161(b)(1)(B)(ii) by striking "quiver or broadhead" and inserting "quiver, broadhead, or point". **Effective** for articles sold by the manufacturer, producer, or importer after 3-31-2005.

- **2004, American Jobs Creation Act of 2004 (P.L. 108-357)**

P.L. 108-357, §332(a):

Amended Code Sec. 4161(b)(1). **Effective** for articles sold by the manufacturer, producer, or importer after the date which is 30 days after 10-22-2004. Prior to amendment, Code Sec. 4161(b)(1) read as follows:

(1) Bows.—

(A) In general.—There is hereby imposed on the sale by the manufacturer, producer, or importer of any bow which has a draw weight of 10 pounds or more, a tax equal to 11 percent of the price for which so sold.

(B) Parts and accessories.—There is hereby imposed upon the sale by the manufacturer, producer, or importer—

(i) of any part of accessory suitable for inclusion in or attachment to a bow described in subparagraph (A), and

(ii) of any quiver suitable for use with arrows described in paragraph (2), a tax equivalent to 11 percent of the price for which so sold.

P.L. 108-357, §332(b) (repealed by P.L. 108-493, §1(a)):

Amended Code Sec. 4161(b) by redesignating paragraph (3) as paragraph (4) and inserting after paragraph (2) a new paragraph (3). **Effective** for articles sold by the manufacturer, producer, or importer after the date which is 30 days after 10-22-2004.

P.L. 108-357, §332(c)(1)-(2):

Amended Code Sec. 4161(b)(2) by inserting "(other than broadheads)" after "point", and by striking "Arrows.—"in the heading and inserting "Arrow components.—". **Effective** for articles sold by the manufacturer, producer, or importer after the date which is 30 days after 10-22-2004.

- **1997, Taxpayer Relief Act of 1997 (P.L. 105-34)**

P.L. 105-34, §1433(a):

Amended Code Sec. 4161(b). **Effective** for articles sold by the manufacturer, producer, or importer after 9-30-97. Prior to amendment, Code Sec. 4161(b) read as follows:

(b) Bows and Arrows, Etc.—

(1) Bows and arrows.—There is hereby imposed on the sale by the manufacturer, producer, or importer—

(A) of any bow which has a draw weight of 10 pounds or more, and

(B) of any arrow which—

(i) measures 18 inches overall or more in length, or

(ii) measures less than 18 inches overall in length but is suitable for use with a bow described in subparagraph (A),

a tax equal to 11 percent of the price for which so sold.

(2) Parts and accessories.—There is hereby imposed upon the sale by the manufacturer, producer, or importer—

(A) of any part or accessory suitable for inclusion in or attachment to a bow or arrow described in paragraph (1), and

(B) of any quiver suitable for use with arrows described in paragraph (1),

a tax equivalent to 11 percent of the price for which so sold.

(3) Coordination with subsection (a).—No tax shall be imposed under this subsection with respect to any article taxable under subsection (a).

- **1986, Tax Reform Act of 1986 (P.L. 99-514)**

P.L. 99-514, §1899A(48):

Amended Code Sec. 4161(b)(1)(B)(ii) by striking out the period at the end thereof and inserting in lieu thereof a comma. **Effective** 10-22-86.

- **1984, Deficit Reduction Act of 1984 (P.L. 98-369)**

P.L. 98-369, §1017(a):

Amended Code Sec. 4161(b)(1). **Effective** for articles sold by the manufacturer, producer, or importer after 9-30-84. Prior to amendment, Code Sec. 4161(b)(1) read as follows:

(1) Bows and Arrows.—There is hereby imposed upon the sale by the manufacturer, producer, or importer—

(A) of any bow which has a draw weight of 10 pounds or more, and

(B) of any arrow which measures 18 inches overall or more in length, a tax equivalent to 11 percent of the price for which so sold.

P.L. 98-369, §1017(b)(1):

Added Code Sec. 4161(b)(3). **Effective** for articles sold by the manufacturer, producer, or importer after 9-30-84.

P.L. 98-369, §1017(b)(2):

Amended Code Sec. 4161(b)(2) by striking out "(other than a fishing reel)" after "accessory". **Effective** for articles sold by the manufacturer, producer, or importer after 9-30-84.

- **1972 (P.L. 92-558)**

P.L. 92-558, §201:

Amended Code Sec. 4161. **Effective** with respect to bows, arrows, quivers, etc., sold by a manufacturer, producer, or importer on or after 1-1-75. (**Effective** date changed by P.L. 93-313.) Prior to amendment, Code Sec. 4161 read as follows:

There is hereby imposed upon the sale of fishing rods, creels, reels, and artificial lures, baits, and flies (including parts or accessories of such articles sold on or in connection therewith, or with the sale thereof) by the manufacturer, producer, or importer a tax equivalent to 10 percent of the price for which so sold.

- **1965, Excise Tax Reduction Act of 1965 (P.L. 89-44)**

P.L. 89-44, §205(a):

Amended Sec. 4161. **Effective** 6-22-65. Prior to amendment Code Sec. 4161 read as follows:

There is hereby imposed upon the sale by the manufacturer, producer, or importer of the following articles (including in each case parts or accessories of such articles sold on or in connection therewith, or with the sale thereof) a tax equivalent to 10 percent of the price for which so sold:

Badminton nets, rackets and racket frames (measuring 22 inches overall or more in length), racket string, shuttlecocks, and standards.

Billiard and pool tables (measuring 45 inches overall or more in length) and balls and cues for such tables.

Bowling balls and pins.

Clay pigeons and traps for throwing clay pigeons.

Cricket balls and bats.

Croquet balls and mallets.

Curling stones.

Deck tennis rings, nets and posts.

Fishing rods, creels, reels and artificial lures, baits and flies.

Golf bags (measuring 26 inches or more in length), balls and clubs (measuring 30 inches or more in length).

Lacrosse balls and sticks.

Polo balls and mallets.

Skis, ski poles, snowshoes, and snow toboggans and sleds (measuring more than 60 inches overall in length).

Squash balls, rackets and racket frames (measuring 22 inches overall or more in length), and racket string.

Table tennis tables, balls, nets and paddles.

Tennis balls, nets, rackets and racket frames (measuring 22 inches overall or more in length) and racket string.

[Sec. 4162]

SEC. 4162. DEFINITIONS; TREATMENT OF CERTAIN RESALES.

[Sec. 4162(a)]

(a) Sport Fishing Equipment Defined.—For purposes of this part, the term "sport fishing equipment" means—

(1) fishing rods and poles (and component parts therefor),

(2) fishing reels,

(3) fly fishing lines, and other fishing lines not over 130 pounds test,

(4) fishing spears, spear guns, and spear tips,

(5) items of terminal tackle, including—

(A) leaders,

(B) artificial lures,

(C) artificial baits,

(D) artificial flies,

(E) fishing hooks,

(F) bobbers,

(G) sinkers,

(H) snaps,

(I) drayles, and

(J) swivels,

Internal Revenue Code   Sec. 4162(a)(5)(J)

MANUFACTURERS TAXES—SPORTING GOODS

but not including natural bait or any item of terminal tackle designed for use and ordinarily used on fishing lines not described in paragraph (3), and

    (6) the following items of fishing supplies and accessories—

        (A) fish stringers,

        (B) creels,

        (C) tackle boxes,

        (D) bags, baskets, and other containers designed to hold fish,

        (E) portable bait containers,

        (F) fishing vests,

        (G) landing nets,

        (H) gaff hooks,

        (I) fishing hook disgorgers, and

        (J) dressing for fishing lines and artificial flies,

    (7) fishing tip-ups and tilts,

    (8) fishing rod belts, fishing rodholders, fishing harnesses, fish fighting chairs, fishing outriggers, and fishing downriggers, and

    (9) electric outboard boat motors.

Amendments

• **2004, American Jobs Creation Act of 2004 (P.L. 108-357)**

P.L. 108-357, § 334(a):

Amended Code Sec. 4162(a) by inserting "and" at the end of paragraph (8), by striking ", and" at the end of paragraph (9) and inserting a period, and by striking paragraph (10). **Effective** for articles sold by the manufacturer, producer, or importer after 12-31-2004. Prior to being stricken, Code Sec. 4162(a)(10) read as follows:

(10) sonar devices suitable for finding fish.

Amendments

• **2004, American Jobs Creation Act of 2004 (P.L. 108-357)**

P.L. 108-357, § 334(b):

Amended Code Sec. 4162 by striking subsection (b). **Effective** for articles sold by the manufacturer, producer, or importer after 12-31-2004. Prior to being stricken, Code Sec. 4162(b) read as follows:

• **1986, Tax Reform Act of 1986 (P.L. 99-514)**

P.L. 99-514, § 1878(b):

Amended Code Sec. 4162(a)(6)(I). **Effective** as if included in the provision of P.L. 98-369 to which it relates. Prior to amendment, Code Sec. 4162(a)(6)(I) read as follows:

(I) fishing hood disgorgers, and

[Sec. 4162(b)—Stricken]

(b) SONAR DEVICE SUITABLE FOR FINDING FISH.—For purposes of this part, the term "sonar device suitable for finding fish" shall not include any sonar device which is—

(1) a graph recorder,

(2) a digital type,

(3) a meter readout, or

(4) a combination graph recorder or combination meter readout.

[Sec. 4162(b)]

(b) TREATMENT OF CERTAIN RESALES.—

    (1) IN GENERAL.—If—

        (A) the manufacturer, producer, or importer sells any article taxable under section 4161(a) to any person,

        (B) the constructive sale price rules of section 4216(b) do not apply to such sale, and

        (C) such person (or any other person) sells such article to a related person with respect to the manufacturer, producer, or importer,

then such related person shall be liable for tax under section 4161 in the same manner as if such related person were the manufacturer of the article.

    (2) CREDIT FOR TAX PREVIOUSLY PAID.—If—

        (A) tax is imposed on the sale of any article by reason of paragraph (1), and

        (B) the related person establishes the amount of the tax which was paid on the sale described in paragraph (1)(A),

the amount of the tax so paid shall be allowed as a credit against the tax imposed by reason of paragraph (1).

    (3) RELATED PERSON.—For purposes of this subsection, the term "related person" has the meaning given such term by section 465(b)(3)(C).

    (4) REGULATIONS.—Except to the extent provided in regulations, rules similar to the rules of this subsection shall also apply in cases (not described in paragraph (1)) in which intermediaries or other devices are used for purposes of reducing the amount of the tax imposed by section 4161(a).

Amendments

• **2004, American Jobs Creation Act of 2004 (P.L. 108-357)**

P.L. 108-357, § 334(b):

Amended Code Sec. 4162 by striking subsection (b) and by redesignating subsection (c) as subsection (b). **Effective** for articles sold by the manufacturer, producer, or importer after 12-31-2004.

• **1986, Tax Reform Act of 1986 (P.L. 99-514)**

P.L. 99-514, § 201(d)(7)(C):

Amended Code Sec. 4162(b)(3) by striking out "section 168(e)(4)(D)" and inserting in lieu thereof "section 465(b)(3)(C)". **Effective**, generally, for property placed in service after 12-31-86, in tax years ending after such date. However, for an election, see Act Sec. 203(a)(1)(B), below.

P.L. 99-514, § 201(d)(12):

Amended Code Sec. 4162(b)(3) by striking out "section 168(e)(4)(D)" and inserting in lieu thereof "section 465(b)(3)(C)". **Effective**, generally, for property placed in service after 12-31-86, in tax years ending after such date. However, for an election, see Act Sec. 203(a)(1)(B), below.

P.L. 99-514, § 203(a)(1)(B), provides:

(B) ELECTION TO HAVE AMENDMENTS MADE BY SECTION 201 APPLY.—A taxpayer may elect (at such time and in such manner as the Secretary of the Treasury or his delegate may prescribe) to have the amendments made by section 201 apply to any property placed in service after July 31, 1986, and before January 1, 1987.

• **1984, Deficit Reduction Act of 1984 (P.L. 98-369)**

P.L. 98-369, § 1015(b):

Added Code Sec. 4162. **Effective** with respect to articles sold by the manufacturer, producer, or importer after 9-30-84. For a special rule, see P.L. 98-369, § 1015(e)(2), below.

P.L. 98-369, § 1015(e)(2), provides:

(2) Treatment of Certain Resales.—Subsection (c) of section 4162 of the Internal Revenue Code of 1954 (relating to treatment of certain resales), as added by this section, shall apply to sales by related persons (as defined in such subsection) after the date of the enactment of this Act.

PART III—FIREARMS

Sec. 4181.   Imposition of tax.

Sec. 4182.   Exemptions.

MANUFACTURERS TAXES—FIREARMS

[Sec. 4181]

SEC. 4181. IMPOSITION OF TAX.

There is hereby imposed upon the sale by the manufacturer, producer, or importer of the following articles a tax equivalent to the specified percent of the price for which so sold:

ARTICLES TAXABLE AT 10 PERCENT—
  Pistols.
  Revolvers.
ARTICLES TAXABLE AT 11 PERCENT—
  Firearms (other than pistols and revolvers).
  Shells, and cartridges.

Amendments

• 1982 (P.L. 97-257)

P.L. 97-257, Chap. XIII:

P.L. 97-257, which authorized supplemental appropriations for the fiscal year ended 9-30-82, allocated additional funds for salaries and expenses of the IRS, provided that "none of the funds appropriated by this Act shall be used to impose or assess any tax due on custom-made firearms under subchapter D of chapter 32 of the Internal Revenue Code of 1954, as amended, sections 4161 and 4181, in all cases where less than fifty items are manufactured or produced per annum."

[Sec. 4182]

SEC. 4182. EXEMPTIONS.

[Sec. 4182(a)]

(a) MACHINE GUNS AND SHORT BARRELLED FIREARMS.—The tax imposed by section 4181 shall not apply to any firearm on which the tax provided by section 5811 has been paid.

[Sec. 4182(b)]

(b) SALES TO DEFENSE DEPARTMENT.—No firearms, pistols, revolvers, shells, and cartridges purchased with funds appropriated for the military department shall be subject to any tax imposed on the sale or transfer of such articles.

[Sec. 4182(c)]

(c) SMALL MANUFACTURERS, ETC.—

(1) IN GENERAL.—The tax imposed by section 4181 shall not apply to any pistol, revolver, or firearm described in such section if manufactured, produced, or imported by a person who manufactures, produces, and imports less than an aggregate of 50 of such articles during the calendar year.

(2) CONTROLLED GROUPS.—All persons treated as a single employer for purposes of subsection (a) or (b) of section 52 shall be treated as one person for purposes of paragraph (1).

Amendments

• 2005, Safe, Accountable, Flexible, Efficient Transportation Equity Act: A Legacy for Users (P.L. 109-59)

P.L. 109-59, §11131(a):

Amended Code Sec. 4182 by redesignating subsection (c) as subsection (d) and by inserting after subsection (b) a new subsection (c). **Effective** for articles sold by the manufacturer, producer, or importer after 9-30-2005. For a special rule, see Act Sec. 11131(b)(2), below.

P.L. 109-59, §11131(b)(2), provides:

(2) NO INFERENCE.—Nothing in the amendments made by this section shall be construed to create any inference with respect to the proper tax treatment of any sales before the effective date of such amendments.

[Sec. 4182(d)]

(d) RECORDS.—Notwithstanding the provisions of sections 922(b)(5) and 923(g) of title 18, United States Code, no person holding a Federal license under chapter 44 of title 18, United States Code, shall be required to record the name, address, or other information about the purchaser of shotgun ammunition, ammunition suitable for use only in rifles generally available in commerce, or component parts for the aforesaid types of ammunition.

Amendments

• 2005, Safe, Accountable, Flexible, Efficient Transportation Equity Act: A Legacy for Users (P.L. 109-59)

P.L. 109-59, §11131(a):

Amended Code Sec. 4182 by redesignating subsection (c) as subsection (d). **Effective** for articles sold by the manufacturer, producer, or importer after 9-30-2005. For a special rule, see Act Sec. 11131(b)(2), below.

P.L. 109-59, §11131(b)(2), provides:

(2) NO INFERENCE.—Nothing in the amendments made by this section shall be construed to create any inference with respect to the proper tax treatment of any sales before the effective date of such amendments.

• 1969, Interest Equalization Tax Extension Act of 1969 (P.L. 91-128)

P.L. 91-128, §5:

Added Code Sec. 4182(c). **Effective** 11-26-69.

Subchapter E—Medical Devices—[Stricken]

[Sec. 4191—Stricken]

Amendments

• 2019, Further Consolidated Appropriations Act, 2020 (P.L. 116-94)

P.L. 116-94, §501(a), Div. N:

Amended chapter 32 by striking subchapter E (Code Sec. 4191). **Effective** for sales after 12-31-2019. Prior to being stricken, Code Sec. 4191 read as follows:

SEC. 4191. MEDICAL DEVICES.

[Sec. 4191(a)]

(a) IN GENERAL.—There is hereby imposed on the sale of any taxable medical device by the manufacturer, producer, or importer a tax equal to 2.3 percent of the price for which so sold.

[Sec. 4191(b)]

(b) TAXABLE MEDICAL DEVICE.—For purposes of this section—

(1) IN GENERAL.—The term "taxable medical device" means any device (as defined in section 201(h) of the Federal Food, Drug, and Cosmetic Act) intended for humans.

(2) EXEMPTIONS.—Such term shall not include—
(A) eyeglasses,
(B) contact lenses,
(C) hearing aids, and
(D) any other medical device determined by the Secretary to be of a type which is generally purchased by the general public at retail for individual use.

• 2010, Health Care and Education Reconciliation Act of 2010 (P.L. 111-152)

P.L. 111-152, §1405(a)(1):

Amended chapter 32 by inserting after subchapter D a new subchapter E (Code Sec. 4191). **Effective** for sales after 12-31-2012.

[Sec. 4191(c)]

(c) MORATORIUM.—The tax imposed under subsection (a) shall not apply to sales during the period beginning on January 1, 2016, and ending on December 31, 2019.

Amendments

• 2018 (P.L. 115-120)

P.L. 115-120, §4001(a), Div. D:

Amended Code Sec. 4191(c) by striking "December 31, 2017" and inserting "December 31, 2019". **Effective** for sales after 12-31-2017.

• 2015, Protecting Americans from Tax Hikes Act of 2015 (P.L. 114-113)

P.L. 114-113, §174(a), Div. Q:

Amended Code Sec. 4191 by adding at the end a new subsection (c). **Effective** for sales after 12-31-2015.

MANUFACTURERS TAXES—SPECIAL PROVISIONS

Subchapter F—Special Provisions Applicable to Manufacturers Tax

Sec. 4216. Definition of price.
Sec. 4217. Leases.
Sec. 4218. Use by manufacturer or importer considered sale.
Sec. 4219. Application of tax in case of sales by other than manufacturer or importer.

[Sec. 4216]

SEC. 4216. DEFINITION OF PRICE.

[Sec. 4216(a)]

(a) CONTAINERS, PACKING AND TRANSPORTATION CHARGES.—In determining, for the purposes of this chapter, the price for which an article is sold, there shall be included any charge for coverings and containers of whatever nature, and any charge incident to placing the article in condition packed ready for shipment, but there shall be excluded the amount of tax imposed by this chapter, whether or not stated as a separate charge. A transportation, delivery, insurance, installation, or other charge (not required by the foregoing sentence to be included) shall be excluded from the price only if the amount thereof is established to the satisfaction of the Secretary in accordance with the regulations.

Amendments
• 1976, Tax Reform Act of 1976 (P.L. 94-455)

P.L. 94-455, §1906(b)(13)(A):

Amended 1954 Code by substituting "Secretary" for "Secretary or his delegate" each place it appeared. **Effective** 2-1-77.

[Sec. 4216(b)]

(b) CONSTRUCTIVE SALE PRICE.—

(1) IN GENERAL.—If an article is—

(A) sold at retail,

(B) sold on consignment, or

(C) sold (otherwise than through an arm's length transaction) at less than the fair market price,

the tax under this chapter shall (if based on the price for which the article is sold) be computed on the price for which such articles are sold, in the ordinary course of trade, by manufacturers or producers thereof, as determined by the Secretary. In the case of an article sold at retail, the computation under the preceding sentence shall be on whichever of the following prices is the lower: (i) the price for which such article is sold, or (ii) the highest price for which such articles are sold to wholesale distributors, in the ordinary course of trade, by manufacturers or producers thereof, as determined by the Secretary. This paragraph shall not apply if paragraph (2) applies.

(2) SPECIAL RULE.—If an article is sold at retail or to a retailer, and if—

(A) the manufacturer, producer, or importer of such article regularly sells such articles at retail or to retailers, as the case may be,

(B) the manufacturer, producer, or importer of such article regularly sells such articles to one or more wholesale distributors in arm's length transactions and he establishes that his prices in such cases are determined without regard to any tax benefit under this paragraph, and

(C) the transaction is an arm's-length transaction,

the tax under this chapter shall (if based on the price for which the article is sold) be computed on whichever of the following prices is the lower: (i) the price for which such article is sold, or (ii) the highest price for which such articles are sold by such manufacturer, producer, or importer to wholesale distributors.

(3) CONSTRUCTIVE SALE PRICE IN CASE OF CERTAIN ARTICLES.—Except as provided in paragraph (4), for purposes of paragraph (1), if—

(A) the manufacturer, producer, or importer of an article regularly sells such article to a distributor which is a member of the same affiliated group of corporations (as defined in section 1504(a)) as the manufacturer, producer, or importer, and

(B) such distributor regularly sells such article to one or more independent retailers, but does not regularly sell to wholesale distributors,

the constructive sale price of such article shall be 90 percent of the lowest price for which such distributor regularly sells such article in arm's-length transactions to such independent retailers. The price determined under this paragraph shall not be adjusted for any exclusion (except for the tax imposed on such article) or readjustments under subsections (a) and (e) and under section 6416(b)(1). If both this paragraph and paragraph (4) apply with respect to an article, the constructive sale price for such article shall be the lower of the fair market price determined under this paragraph or paragraph (4).

(4) CONSTRUCTIVE SALE PRICE IN CASE OF CERTAIN OTHER ARTICLES.—For purposes of paragraph (1), if—

(A) the manufacturer, producer, or importer of an article regularly sells (except for tax-free sales) only to a distributor which is a member of the same affiliated group of corporations (as defined in section 1504(a)) as the manufacturer, producer, or importer,

(B) the distributor regularly sells (except for tax-free sales) such article only to retailers, and

(C) the normal method of sales for such articles within the industry by manufacturers, producers, or importers is to sell such articles in arm's-length transactions to distributors,

the constructive sale price for such article shall be the price at which such article is sold to retailers by the distributor, reduced by a percentage of such price equal to the percentage which (i) the difference between the price for which comparable articles are sold to wholesale distributors, in the ordinary course of trade, by manufacturers or producers thereof, and the price at which such wholesale distributors in arm's-length transactions sell such comparable articles to retailers, is of (ii) the price at which such wholesale distributors in arm's-length transactions sell such comparable articles to retailers. The price determined under this paragraph shall not be adjusted for any exclusion (except for the tax imposed on such article) or readjustment under subsections (a) and (e) and under section 6416(b)(1).

(5) DEFINITION OF LOWEST PRICE.—For purposes of paragraphs (1) and (3) the lowest price shall be determined—

(A) without requiring that any given percentage of sales be made at that price, and

(B) without including any fixed amount to which the purchaser has a right as a result of contractual arrangements existing at the time of the sale.

Amendments
• 1984, Deficit Reduction Act of 1984 (P.L. 98-369)

P.L. 98-369, §735(c)(6)(A):

Amended Code Sec. 4216(b)(1) by striking out "(other than an article the sale of which is taxable under section 4061(a))" in the second sentence, and by striking out the third sentence. **Effective** as if included in the provisions of the Highway Revenue Act of 1982 to which it relates. Prior to amendment, the third sentence of Code Sec. 4216(b)(1) read as follows:

In the case of an article the sale of which is taxable under section 4061(a) and which is sold at retail, the computation under the first sentence of this paragraph shall be a

MANUFACTURERS TAXES—SPECIAL PROVISIONS

percentage (not greater than 100 percent) of the actual selling price based on the highest price for which such articles are sold by manufacturers and producers in the ordinary course of trade (determined without regard to any individual manufacturer's or producer's cost).

P.L. 98-369, §735(c)(6)(B):

Amended Code Sec. 4216(b)(2) by striking out subparagraph (C), by adding "and" at the end of subparagraph (B), and by redesignating subparagraph (D) as subparagraph (C). **Effective** as if included in the provision of the Highway Revenue Act of 1982 to which it relates. Prior to amendment, subparagraph (C) read as follows:

(C) in the case of articles upon which tax is imposed under section 4061(a) (relating to trucks, buses, tractors, etc.), the normal method of sale for such articles within the industry is not to sell such articles at retail or to retailers, or combination thereof, and

P.L. 98-369, §735(c)(6)(C):

Amended Code Sec. 4216(b) by striking out paragraph (5). **Effective** as if included in the provision of the Highway Revenue Act of 1982 to which it relates. Prior to amendment, paragraph (5) read as follows:

(5) Constructive Sale Price in the Case of Automobiles, Trucks, Etc.—In the case of articles the sale of which is taxable under section 4061(a) (relating to trucks, buses, tractors, etc.), for purposes of paragraph (1), if—

(A) the manufacturer, producer, or importer of the article regularly sells such article to a distributor which is a member of the same affiliated group of corporations (as defined in section 1504(a)) as the manufacturer, producer, or importer, and

(B) such distributor regularly sells such article to one or more independent retailers,

the constructive sale price of such article shall be $98\frac{1}{2}$ percent of the lowest price for which such distributor regularly sells such article in arm's-length transactions to such independent retailers. The price determined under this paragraph shall not be adjusted for any exclusion (except for the tax imposed on such article) or readjustments under subsections (a) and (e) and under section 6416(b)(1).

P.L. 98-369, §735(c)(6)(D):

Amended Code Sec. 4216(b)(3) by striking out "paragraphs (4) and (5)" and inserting in lieu thereof "paragraph (4)". **Effective** as if included in the provision of the Highway Revenue Act of 1982 to which it relates.

P.L. 98-369, §735(c)(6)(E):

Amended Code Sec. 4216(b) by redesignating paragraph (6) as paragraph (5) and by striking out "(1), (3), and (5)" and inserting in lieu thereof "(1) and (3)". **Effective** as if included in the provision of the Highway Revenue Act of 1982 to which it relates.

• **1978 (P.L. 95-458)**

P.L. 95-458, §1(a), (c):

Amended Code Sec. 4216(b)(1) by adding the third sentence. **Effective** for articles sold by the manufacturer or producer on or after 1-1-79.

P.L. 95-458, §1(b), (c):

Amended the second sentence of Code Sec. 4216(b)(1) by inserting "(other than an article the sale of which is taxable under section 4061(a))" after "sold at retail". **Effective** for articles sold by the manufacturer or producer on or after 1-1-79.

• **1976, Tax Reform Act of 1976 (P.L. 94-455)**

P.L. 94-455, §1904(a)(2)(B):

Amended Code Sec. 4216(b) by substituting "subsections (a) and (e)" for "subsections (a) and (f)" in paragraphs (3), (4), and (5). **Effective** 2-1-77.

P.L. 94-455, §1906(b)(13)(A):

Amended 1954 Code by substituting "Secretary" for "Secretary or his delegate" each place it appeared. **Effective** 2-1-77.

• **1971, Revenue Act of 1971 (P.L. 92-178)**

P.L. 92-178, §401(g)(4)(A):

Amended Code Sec. 4216(b)(2)(C) and 4216(b)(5) by substituting "(relating to trucks, buses, tractors, etc.)" for "(relating to automobiles, trucks, etc.)".

• **1970, Excise, Estate, and Gift Tax Adjustment Act of 1970 (P.L. 91-614)**

P.L. 91-614, §301(a):

Amended Code Sec. 4216(b) by adding (5) and (6). For the **effective** date, see Act Sec. 301(c), below.

P.L. 91-614, §301(b):

Amended the heading of paragraph (3). Prior to amendment, the heading read as follows:

(3) Fair market price in case of certain articles.—Except as provided in paragraph (4), for purposes of paragraph (1)(C), if—

Amended the text of that portion of paragraph (3) which follows subparagraph (B) by substituting "constructive sale price" for "fair market price" in the two places such term appears.

Amended the heading of paragraph (4). Prior to amendment the heading read as follows:

(4) Fair market price in case of certain other articles.—For purposes of paragraph (1)(C), if—

Amended the text of that portion of paragraph (4) which follows subparagraph (C) by substituting "constructive sale price" for "fair market price."

P.L. 91-614, §301(c), provides:

The amendments made by this section shall apply with respect to articles sold after December 31, 1970; except that section 4216(b)(6) of the Internal Revenue Code of 1954 (as added by subsection (a)) shall also apply to (1) the application of paragraph (1) of such section 4216(b) to articles sold after June 30, 1962, and before January 1, 1971, and (2) the application of paragraph (3) of such section 4216(b) to articles sold after December 31 1969, and before January 1, 1971.

• **1969, Tax Reform Act of 1969 (P.L. 91-172)**

P.L. 91-172, §932(a):

Amended Code Sec. 4216(b) by adding paragraphs (3) and (4). **Effective** for articles sold after 12-31-69.

• **1965, Excise Tax Reduction Act of 1965 (P.L. 89-44)**

P.L. 89-44, §208(a):

Amended Code Sec. 4216(b)(2). **Effective** 6-22-65. Prior to amendment, Code Sec. 4216(b)(2) read as follows:

(2) Special rule.—If an article is sold at retail, to a retailer, or to a special dealer (as defined in paragraph (3)), and if—

(A) the manufacturer, producer, or importer of such article regularly sells such articles at retail, to retailers, or to special dealers, as the case may be,

(B) the manufacturer, producer, or importer of such article regularly sells such articles to one or more wholesale distributors (other than special dealers) in arm's length transactions and he establishes that his prices in such cases are determined without regard to any tax benefit under this paragraph,

(C) in the case of articles upon which tax is imposed under section 4061(a) (relating to automobiles, trucks, etc.), 4191 (relating to business machines), or 4211 (relating to matches), the normal method of sales for such articles within the industry is not to sell such articles at retail or to retailers, or combinations thereof, and

(D) the transaction is an arm's length transaction.

the tax under this chapter shall (if based on the price for which the article is sold) be computed on whichever of the following prices is the lower: (i) the price for which such article is sold, or (ii) the highest price for which such articles are sold by such manufacturer, producer, or importer to wholesale distributors (other than special dealers).

P.L. 89-44, §208(b):

Repealed subsection (b)(3) of Code Sec. 4216. Prior to repeal, Code Sec. 4216(b)(3) read as follows:

(3) Special dealer.—For purposes of paragraph (2), the term "special dealer" means a distributor of articles taxable under section 4121 who does not maintain a sales force to resell the article whose constructive price is established under paragraph (2) but relies on salesmen of the manufacturer, producer, or importer of the article for resale of the article to retailers.

• **1962 (P.L. 87-858)**

P.L. 87-858, §1(a):

Amended Code Sec. 4216(b)(2)(C). **Effective** with respect to articles sold by the manufacturer, producer, or importer on or after 10-1-62. Prior to amendment, Code Sec. 4216(b)(2)(C) read as follows:

(C) the normal method of sales for such articles within the industry is not to sell such articles at retail or to retailers, or combinations thereof, and

• **1958, Excise Tax Technical Changes Act of 1958 (P.L. 85-859)**

P.L. 85-859, §115:

Amended Code Sec. 4216(b). **Effective** 1-1-59. Prior to amendment, Code Sec. 4216(b) read as follows:

(b) Constructive Sale Price.—If an article is—

(1) sold at retail,

(2) sold on consignment, or

(3) sold (otherwise than through an arm's length transaction) at less than the fair market price.

the tax under this chapter shall (if based on the price for which the article is sold) be computed on the price for which such articles are sold, in the ordinary course of trade, by manufacturers or producers thereof, as determined by the Secretary or his delegate.

[Sec. 4216(c)]

(c) PARTIAL PAYMENTS.—In the case of—

(1) a lease (other than a lease to which section 4217(b) applies),

(2) a contract for the sale of an article wherein it is provided that the price shall be paid by installments and title to the article sold does not pass until a future date notwithstanding partial payment by installments,

(3) a conditional sale, or

(4) a chattel mortgage arrangement wherein it is provided that the sales price shall be paid in installments,

there shall be paid upon each payment with respect to the article a percentage of such payment equal to the rate of tax in effect on the date such payment is due.

MANUFACTURERS TAXES—SPECIAL PROVISIONS

Amendments

• **1965, Excise Tax Reduction Act of 1965 (P.L. 89-44)**

P.L. 89-44, §207(a):

Amended Code Sec. 4216(c). **Effective** 6-22-65. Prior to amendment, the material after Code Sec. 4216(c)(4) read as follows: "there shall be paid upon each payment with respect to the article that portion of the total tax which is proportionate to the portion of the total amount to be paid represented by such payment."

• **1958, Excise Tax Technical Changes Act of 1958 (P.L. 85-859)**

P.L. 85-859, §117(b):

Amended Code Sec. 4216(c)(1). Not **effective** for any lease of an article if Code Sec. 4216(d) applied to any lease of such article before 1-1-59. Prior to amendment, Code Sec. 4216(c)(1) read as follows:

(1) a lease (other than a lease to which subsection (d) applies),

• **1955 (P.L. 317, 84th Cong.)**

P.L. 317, 84th Cong., §[1]:

Amended Code Sec. 4216(c)(1). For the **effective** date, see Act Sec. 4, in the amendment notes following Code Sec. 4216(d). Prior to amendment Code Sec. 4216(c)(1) read as follows:

(1) a lease,

[Sec. 4216(d)]

(d) SALES OF INSTALLMENT ACCOUNTS.—If installment accounts, with respect to payments on which tax is being computed as provided in subsection (c), are sold or otherwise disposed of, then subsection (c) shall not apply with respect to any subsequent payments on such accounts (other than subsequent payments on returned accounts with respect to which credit or refund is allowable by reason of section 6416(b)(5)), but instead—

(1) there shall be paid an amount equal to the difference between (A) the tax previously paid on the payments on such installment accounts, and (B) the total tax which would be payable if such installment accounts had not been sold or otherwise disposed of (computed as provided in subsection (c)); except that

(2) if any such sale is pursuant to the order of, or subject to the approval of, a court of competent jurisdiction in a bankruptcy or insolvency proceeding, the amount computed under paragraph (1) shall not exceed the sum of the amounts computed by multiplying (A) the proportionate share of the amount for which such accounts are sold which is allocable to each unpaid installment payment by (B) the rate of tax under this chapter in effect on the date such unpaid installment payment is or was due.

The sum of the amounts payable under this subsection and subsection (c) in respect of the sale of any article shall not exceed the total tax.

Amendments

• **1976, Tax Reform Act of 1976 (P.L. 94-455)**

P.L. 94-455, §1904(a)(2)(A):

Redesignated Code Sec. 4216(e) as Code Sec. 4216(d). **Effective** 2-1-77.

• **1965, Excise Tax Reduction Act of 1965 (P.L. 89-44)**

P.L. 89-44, §207(b):

Amended Code Sec. 4216(e). **Effective** 6-22-65. Prior to amendment, Code Sec. 4216(e)(1)-(2) read as follows:

(1) there shall be paid an amount equal to the difference between (A) the tax previously paid on the payments on such installment accounts, and (B) the total tax; except that

(2) if any such sale is pursuant to the order of, or subject to the approval of, a court of competent jurisdiction in a bankruptcy or insolvency proceeding, the amount computed under paragraph (1) shall not exceed the amount computed by multiplying (A) the amount for which such accounts are sold, by (B) the rate of tax under this chapter which applied on the day on which the transaction giving rise to such installment accounts took place.

• **1958, Excise Tax Technical Changes Act of 1958 (P.L. 85-859)**

P.L. 85-859, §116:

Added Code Sec. 4216(e). **Effective** 1-1-59.

P.L. 85-859, §117(b):

Repealed Code Sec. 4216(d). Not **effective** for any lease of an article if Code Sec. 4216(d) applied to any lease of such article before 1-1-59. Prior to repeal, Code Sec. 4216(d) read as follows:

(d) Leases of Certain Trailers.—In the case of any lease of a trailer or semitrailer taxable under section 4061(a) and suitable for use in connection with passenger automobiles, there shall be paid, at the election of the taxpayer—

(1) upon the initial lease a tax at the applicable rate specified in section 4061(a) based upon the fair market value on the date of such lease, or

(2) upon each lease payment with respect to such trailer or semitrailer, a percentage of such payment equal to the rate of tax which would be imposed upon the sale of such trailer or semitrailer, until the total of the tax payments under such lease and any prior lease equals the total tax. In any case where a trailer or semitrailer which has been leased is sold before the total tax has been paid, the tax payable on such sale shall be the difference between the tax paid on the lease payments and the total tax. For purposes of this paragraph, the term "total tax" means the tax computed, at the rate in effect on the date of the initial lease, on the fair market value on the date of such lease. However, in the case where a trailer or semitrailer which has been leased is sold before the total tax has been paid, the total tax shall not exceed a tax computed, at the rate in effect on the date of the initial lease, on the amount received on such sale (determined without regard to section 4216(b)) plus the total of the payments received by the lessor under any lease of such trailer or a semitrailer.

• **1955 (P.L. 317, 84th Cong.)**

P.L. 317, 84th Cong., 1st Sess., §2:

Amended Code Sec. 4216 by adding subsection (d). For the **effective** date, see Act Sec. 4, below.

P.L. 317, 84th Cong., 1st Sess., §4, provides:

SEC. 4. The amendments made by subsection (a) [sic] shall take effect on the first day of the first month which begins more than 10 days after the date of the enactment of this Act [8-9-55]. In the application of section 4216(d) of the Internal Revenue Code of 1954 (as added by this Act) to any article which has been leased before the effective date specified in the preceding sentence [9-1-55], under regulations prescribed by the Secretary of the Treasury or his delegate—

(1) the fair market value of such article shall be the fair market value determined as of such effective date;

(2) only payments under a lease received on or after such effective date shall be considered in determining when the total tax (as defined in such section 4216(d)) has been paid;

(3) any lease existing on such effective date, or if there is none, the first lease entered into after such effective date, shall be considered an initial lease (except that fair market value shall be determined as provided in paragraph (1) of this sentence); and

(4) any lease existing on such effective date [9-1-55] shall be considered as having been entered into on such date.

[Sec. 4216(e)]

(e) EXCLUSION OF LOCAL ADVERTISING CHARGE FROM SALE PRICE.—

(1) EXCLUSION.—In determining, for purposes of this chapter, the price for which an article is sold, there shall be excluded a charge for local advertising (as defined in paragraph (4)) to the extent that such charge—

(A) does not exceed 5 percent of the price for which the article is sold (as determined under this section by excluding any charge for local advertising),

(B) is a separate charge made when the article is sold, and

(C) is intended to be refunded to the purchaser or any subsequent vendee in reimbursement of costs incurred for local advertising.

In the case of any such charge (or portion thereof) which is not so refunded before the first day of the fifth calendar month following the calendar year during which the article was sold, the exclusion provided by the preceding sentence shall cease to apply as of such first day.

(2) AGGREGATE AMOUNT WHICH MAY BE EXCLUDED.—In the case of articles upon the sale of which tax was imposed under the same section of this chapter—

(A) The sum of (i) the aggregate of the charges for local advertising excluded under paragraph (1), plus (ii) the aggregate of the readjustments for local advertising under section 6416(b)(1) (relating to credits or refunds for price readjustments), shall not exceed

(B) 5 percent of the aggregate of the prices (determined under this section by excluding all charges for local advertising) at which such articles were sold in sales on which tax was imposed by such section of this chapter.

The preceding sentence shall be applied to each manufacturer, producer, and importer as of the close of each calendar quarter, taking into account the items specified in subparagraphs (A) and (B) for such calendar quarter and preceding calendar quarters in the same calendar year.

Sec. 4216(d)

MANUFACTURERS TAXES—SPECIAL PROVISIONS

(3) NO ADJUSTMENT FOR OTHER ADVERTISING CHARGES.—Except to the extent provided by paragraphs (1) and (2), no charge or expenditure for advertising shall serve, for purposes of this section or section 6416(b)(1), as the basis for an exclusion from, or as a readjustment of, the price of any article.

(4) LOCAL ADVERTISING DEFINED.—For purposes of this section and section 6416(b)(1), the term "local advertising" means only advertising which—

(A) is initiated or obtained by the purchaser or any subsequent vendee,

(B) names the article for which the price is determinable under this section and states the location at which such article may be purchased at retail, and

(C) is broadcast over a radio station or television station or appears in a newspaper or magazine, or is displayed by means of an outdoor advertising sign or poster.

Amendments

- **1976, Tax Reform Act of 1976 (P.L. 94-455)**

P.L. 94-455, §1904(a)(2)(A):
Redesignated Code Sec. 4216(f) as Code Sec. 4216(e). **Effective** 2-1-77.

- **1962 (P.L. 87-770)**

P.L. 87-770, §2(a):
Amended Code Sec. 4216(f)(4)(C) by inserting "or magazine, or is displayed by means of an outdoor advertising sign or poster." immediately after "newspaper".

Amendments

- **1984, Deficit Reduction Act of 1984 (P.L. 98-369)**

P.L. 98-369, §735(c)(6)(F):
Amended Code Sec. 4216 by repealing subsection (f). **Effective** as if included in the provision of the Highway Revenue Act of 1982 to which it relates. Prior to amendment, Code Sec. 4216(f) read as follows:

(f) CERTAIN TRUCKS INCORPORATING USED COMPONENTS.—For purposes of the tax imposed by section 4061(a)(1) (relating to trucks, buses, tractors, etc.), in determining the price for which an article is sold, the value of any component of such article shall be excluded from the price, if—

(1) such component is furnished by the first user of such article, and

(2) such component has been used prior to such furnishing.

Effective for articles sold on or after the first day of the first calendar quarter beginning more than 20 days after 10-9-62.

- **1960 (P.L. 86-781)**

P.L. 86-781, §[1]:
Amended Code Sec. 4216 by adding a new subsection (f). **Effective** for articles sold on or after 1-1-61.

[Sec. 4216(f)—Repealed]

- **1976, Tax Reform Act of 1976 (P.L. 94-455)**

P.L. 94-455, §1904(a)(2)(A):
Redesignated Code Sec. 4216(g) as Code Sec. 4216(f).

- **1971, Revenue Act of 1971 (P.L. 92-178)**

P.L. 92-178, §401(g)(4)(B):
Added "tractors," in the second line of Code Sec. 4216(g).

- **1965, Excise Tax Reduction Act of 1965 (P.L. 89-44)**

P.L. 89-44, §801(b):
Amended Code Sec. 4216 by adding subsection (g).

[Sec. 4217]

SEC. 4217. LEASES.

[Sec. 4217(a)]

(a) LEASE CONSIDERED AS SALE.—For purposes of this chapter, the lease of an article (including any renewal or any extension of a lease or any subsequent lease of such article) by the manufacturer, producer, or importer shall be considered a sale of such article.

[Sec. 4217(b)]

(b) LIMITATION ON TAX.—In the case of any lease described in subsection (a) of an article taxable under this chapter, if the tax under this chapter is based on the price for which such articles are sold, there shall be paid on each lease payment with respect to such article a percentage of such payment equal to the rate of tax in effect on the date of such payment, until the total of the tax payments under such lease and any prior lease to which this subsection applies equals the total tax.

[Sec. 4217(c)]

(c) DEFINITION OF TOTAL TAX.—For purposes of this section, the term "total tax" means—

(1) except as provided in paragraph (2), the tax computed on the constructive sale price for such article which would be determined under section 4216(b) if such article were sold at retail on the date of the first lease to which subsection (b) applies; or

(2) if the first lease to which subsection (b) applies is not the first lease of the article, the tax computed on the fair market value of such article on the date of the first lease to which subsection (b) applies.

Any such computation of tax shall be made at the applicable rate specified in this chapter in effect on the date of the first lease to which subsection (b) applies.

[Sec. 4217(d)]

(d) SPECIAL RULES.—

(1) LESSOR MUST ALSO BE ENGAGED IN SELLING.—Subsection (b) shall not apply to any lease of an article unless at the time of making the lease, or any prior lease of such article to which subsection (b) applies, the person making the lease or prior lease was also engaged in the business of selling in arm's length transactions the same type and model of article.

(2) SALE BEFORE TOTAL TAX BECOMES PAYABLE.—If the taxpayer sells an article before the total tax has become payable, then the tax payable on such sale shall be whichever of the following is the smaller:

(A) the difference between (i) the tax imposed on lease payments under leases of such article to which subsection (b) applies, and (ii) the total tax, or

(B) a tax computed, at the rate in effect on the date of the sale, on the price for which the article is sold.

For purposes of subparagraph (B), if the sale is at arm's length, section 4216(b) shall not apply.

(3) SALE AFTER TOTAL TAX HAS BECOME PAYABLE.—If the taxpayer sells an article after the total tax has become payable, no tax shall be imposed under this chapter on such sale.

[Sec. 4217(e)]

(e) LEASES OF AUTOMOBILES SUBJECT TO GAS GUZZLER TAX.—

(1) IN GENERAL.—In the case of the lease of an automobile the sale of which by the manufacturer would be taxable under section 4064, the foregoing provisions of this section shall not apply, but, for purposes of this chapter—

(A) the first lease of such automobile by the manufacturer shall be considered to be a sale, and

(B) any lease of such automobile by the manufacturer after the first lease of such automobile shall not be considered to be a sale.

(2) PAYMENT OF TAX.—In the case of a lease described in paragraph (1)(A)—

MANUFACTURERS TAXES—SPECIAL PROVISIONS

(A) there shall be paid by the manufacturer on each lease payment that portion of the total gas guzzler tax which bears the same ratio to such total gas guzzler tax as such payment bears to the total amount to be paid under such lease,

(B) if such lease is canceled, or the automobile is sold or otherwise disposed of, before the total gas guzzler tax is payable, there shall be paid by the manufacturer on such cancellation, sale, or disposition the difference between the tax imposed under subparagraph (A) on the lease payments and the total gas guzzler tax, and

(C) if the automobile is sold or otherwise disposed of after the total gas guzzler tax is payable, no tax shall be imposed under section 4064 on such sale or disposition.

(3) DEFINITIONS.—For purposes of this subsection—

(A) MANUFACTURER.—The term "manufacturer" includes a producer or importer.

(B) TOTAL GAS GUZZLER TAX.—The term "total gas guzzler tax" means the tax imposed by section 4064, computed at the rate in effect on the date of the first lease.

Amendments

• **1978, Energy Tax Act of 1978 (P.L. 95-618)**

P.L. 95-618, §201(d):

Added Code Sec. 4217(e). For **effective** date, see historical comment for P.L. 95-618 under Code Sec. 4064.

• **1976, Tax Reform Act of 1976 (P.L. 94-455)**

P.L. 94-455, §1904(a)(3):

Struck out Code Sec. 4217(d)(4). **Effective** 2-1-77. Before being struck, Code Sec. 4217(d)(4) read as follows:

(4) TRANSITIONAL RULES.—For purposes of this subsection and subsections (b) and (c), in the case of any lease entered into before the effective date of subsection (b) and existing on such date—

(A) such lease shall be considered as having been entered into on such date;

(B) the total tax shall be computed on the fair market value of the article on such date; and

(C) the lease payments under such lease shall include only payments attributable to periods on and after such date.

• **1958, Excise Tax Technical Changes Act of 1958 (P.L. 85-859)**

P.L. 85-859, §117:

Amended Sec. 4217 to read as prior to amendment by P.L. 94-455. **Effective** 1-1-59. Prior to amendment Sec. 4217 read as follows:

Sec. 4217. Lease Considered As Sale.

For the purposes of this chapter, the lease of an article (including any renewal or any extension of a lease or any subsequent lease of such article) by the manufacturer, producer, or importer shall be considered a taxable sale of such article. This section shall not apply to the lease of an article upon which the tax has been paid in the manner provided in section 4216(d)(1) or the total tax has been paid in the manner provided in section 4216(d)(2).

• **1955 (P.L. 317, 84th Cong.)**

P.L. 317, 84th Cong., 1st Sess., §3:

Amended Sec. 4217 by adding at the end a new sentence. For the **effective** date, see Act Sec. 4, in the amendment notes following Code Sec. 4216(d).

[Sec. 4218]
SEC. 4218. USE BY MANUFACTURER OR IMPORTER CONSIDERED SALE.

[Sec. 4218(a)]

(a) GENERAL RULE.—If any person manufactures, produces, or imports an article (other than a tire taxable under section 4071) and uses it (otherwise than as material in the manufacture or production of, or as a component part of, another article taxable under this chapter to be manufactured or produced by him), then he shall be liable for tax under this chapter in the same manner as if such article were sold by him. This subsection shall not apply in the case of gasoline used by any person, for nonfuel purposes, as a material in the manufacture or production of another article to be manufactured or produced by him. For the purpose of applying the first sentence of this subsection to coal taxable under section 4121, the words "(otherwise than as material in the manufacture or production of, or as a component part of, another article taxable under this chapter to be manufactured or produced by him)" shall be disregarded.

Amendments

• **1984, Deficit Reduction Act of 1984 (P.L. 98-369)**

P.L. 98-369, §735(c)(7)(D):

Amended Code Sec. 4218(a) by striking out "(other than an article specified in subsection (b), (c), or (d))" and inserting in lieu thereof "(other than a tire taxable under section 4071)". **Effective** as if included in the provision of the Highway Revenue Act of 1982 to which it relates.

• **1978, Black Lung Benefits Revenue Act of 1977 (P.L. 95-227)**

P.L. 95-227, §2(b)(1):

Added the last sentence in Code Sec. 4218(a). For **effective** date, see the historical comment for P.L. 95-227 under Code Sec. 4121.

• **1961, Federal-Aid Highway Act of 1961 (P.L. 87-61)**

P.L. 87-61, §205(b):

Added the last sentence of Code Sec. 4218(a). **Effective** only in the case of gasoline used on or after 10-1-61.

• **1960 (P.L. 86-418)**

P.L. 86-418, §2(a):

Substituted "subsection (b), (c), or (d)" for "subsection (b) or (c)" in Code Sec. 4218(a). **Effective** 5-1-60.

• **1958, Excise Tax Technical Changes Act of 1958 (P.L. 85-859)**

P.L. 85-859, §118:

Amended Code Sec. 4218(a). **Effective** 1-1-59. Prior to amendment, Code Sec. 4218(a) read as follows:

(a) General Rule.—If—

(1) any person manufactures, produces, or imports an article (other than a tire, inner tube, or automobile radio or television receiving set taxable under section 4141 and other than an automobile part or accessory taxable under section 4061(b), a refrigerator component taxable under section 4111, a radio or television component taxable under section 4141, or a camera lens taxable under section 4171) and uses it (otherwise than as material in the manufacture or production of, or as a component part of, another article to be manufactured or produced by him which will be taxable under this chapter or sold free of tax by virtue of section 4220 or 4224, relating to tax-free sales), or

(2) any person manufactures, produces, or imports a tire, inner tube, or automobile radio or television receiving set taxable under section 4141 and sells it on or in connection with, or with the sale of, an article taxable under section 4061, relating to the tax on automobiles, or uses it, he shall be liable for tax under this chapter in the same manner as if such article was sold by him, and the tax (if based on the price for which the article is sold) shall be computed on the price at which such or similar articles are sold, in the ordinary course of trade, by manufacturers, producers, or importers thereof, as determined by the Secretary or his delegate.

• **1955 (P.L. 367, 84th Cong.)**

P.L. 367, 84th Cong., 1st Sess., §[1](a):

Amended Code Sec. 4218(a)(1). **Effective** 9-1-55. Prior to amendment, Code Sec. 4218(a)(1) read as follows:

(1) any person manufactures, produces, or imports an article (other than a tire, inner tube, or automobile radio or television receiving set taxable under section 4141) and uses it (otherwise than as material in the manufacture or production of, or as a component part of, another article to be manufactured or produced by him which will be taxable under this chapter or sold free of tax by virtue of section 4220 or 4224, relating to tax-free sales), or.

[Sec. 4218(b)]

(b) TIRES.—If any person manufactures, produces, or imports a tire taxable under section 4071, and sells it on or in connection with the sale of any article, or uses it, then he shall be liable for tax under this chapter in the same manner as if such article were sold by him.

Amendments

• **1984, Deficit Reduction Act of 1984 (P.L. 98-369)**

P.L. 98-369, §735(c)(7)(A):

Amended Code Sec. 4218(b) by striking out "or inner tube", and by striking out "Except as provided in subsection (d), if" and inserting in lieu thereof "If". **Effective** as if included in the provision of the Highway Revenue Act of 1982 to which it relates. Prior to amendment, Code Sec. 4218(b) read as follows:

(b) Tires and Tubes.—Except as provided in subsection (d), if any person manufactures, produces, or imports a tire or inner tube taxable under section 4071, and sells it on or in connection with the sale of any article, or uses it, then he shall be liable for tax under this chapter in the same manner as if such article were sold by him.

Sec. 4217(e)(2)(A)

MANUFACTURERS TAXES—EXEMPTIONS

P.L. 98-369, §735(c)(7)(B):

Amended the heading of Code Sec. 4218(b) by striking out "and Tubes". **Effective** as if included in the provision of the Highway Revenue Act of 1982 to which it relates.

- **1965, Excise Tax Reduction Act of 1965 (P.L. 89-44)**

P.L. 89-44, §208(c):

Substituted "TIRES AND TUBES" for "TIRES, TUBES, AND AUTOMOTIVE RECEIVING SETS" in the heading for Code Sec. 4218(b) and deleted "or an automobile radio or television receiving set taxable under section 4141," after "section 4071," in Code Sec. 4218(b). **Effective** 6-22-65.

- **1960 (P.L. 86-418)**

P.L. 86-418, §2(a):

Substituted "except as provided in subsection (d), if any" for "If any" in Code Sec. 4218(b). **Effective** 5-1-60.

- **1958, Excise Tax Technical Changes Act of 1958 (P.L. 85-859)**

P.L. 85-859, §118:

Amended Code Sec. 4218(b). **Effective** 1-1-59. Prior to amendment, Code Sec. 4218(b) read as follows:

(b) Exception.—This section shall not apply with respect to the use by the manufacturer, producer, or importer of an automobile part or accessory taxable under section 4061(b), a refrigerator component taxable under section 4111, a radio or television component taxable under section 4141, or a camera lens taxable under section 4171, if such part, accessory, component, or lens is used by him as material in the manufacture or production of, or as a component part of, any article.

- **1955 (P.L. 367, 84th Cong.)**

P.L. 367, 84th Cong., 1st Sess., §[1](b):

Amended Code Sec. 4218(b). **Effective** 9-1-55. Prior to amendment, Code Sec. 4218(b) read as follows:

(b) Exception.—This section shall not apply with respect to the use by the manufacturer, producer, or importer of articles described in section 4141 if such articles are used by him as material in the manufacture or production of, or as a component part of, communication, detection, or navigation receivers of the type used in commercial, military, or marine installations if such receivers are to be sold to the United States for its exclusive use.

[Sec. 4218(c)]

(c) COMPUTATION OF TAX.—Except as provided in section 4223(b), in any case in which a person is made liable for tax by the preceding provisions of this section, the tax (if based on the price for which the article is sold) shall be computed on the price at which such or similar articles are sold, in the ordinary course of trade, by manufacturers, producers, or importers, thereof, as determined by the Secretary.

Amendments

- **1984, Deficit Reduction Act of 1984 (P.L. 98-369)**

P.L. 98-369, §735(c)(7)(C):

Amended Code Sec. 4218 by striking out subsections (c) and (d) and by redesignating subsection (e) as subsection (c). **Effective** as if included in the provision of the Highway Revenue Act of 1982 to which it relates. Prior to amendment, subsections (c) and (d) read as follows:

(c) Automotive Parts and Accessories.—If any person manufactures, produces, or imports a part or accessory taxable under section 4061(b), and uses it (otherwise than as material in the manufacture or production of, or as a component part of, any other article to be manufactured or produced by him), then he shall be liable for tax under this chapter in the same manner as if such article were sold by him.

(d) Bicycle Tires and Tubes.—If any person manufactures, produces, or imports a bicycle tire (as defined in section 4221(e)(4)(B)) or an inner tube for such a tire, and uses it (otherwise than as material in the manufacture or production of, or as a component part of, a bicycle, other than a rebuilt or reconditioned bicycle, to be manufactured or produced by him), then he shall be liable for tax under this chapter in the same manner as if such article were sold by him.

- **1976, Tax Reform Act of 1976 (P.L. 94-455)**

P.L. 94-455, §1906(b)(13)(A):

Amended 1954 Code by substituting "Secretary" for "Secretary or his delegate" each place it appeared. **Effective** 2-1-77.

- **1965, Excise Tax Reduction Act of 1965 (P.L. 89-44)**

P.L. 89-44, §208(c):

Amended the heading of Code Sec. 4218(c) and deleted "a radio or television component taxable under section 4141, or a camera lens taxable under section 4171," after "section 4061(b)" in Code Sec. 4218(c). **Effective** 6-22-65. Prior to amendment, the heading of Code Sec. 4218(c) read as follows: "AUTOMOBILE PARTS, RADIO COMPONENTS, CAMERA LENSES, ETC."

- **1960 (P.L. 86-418)**

P.L. 86-418, §2(a):

Redesignated former Code Sec. 4218(d) as Code Sec. 4218(e) and added new subsection (d). **Effective** 5-1-60.

- **1958, Excise Tax Technical Changes Act of 1958 (P.L. 85-859)**

P.L. 85-859, §118:

Added Code Sec. 4218(c) and (d) (redesignated as Code Sec. 4218(e)) to read as prior to amendment by P.L. 94-455. **Effective** 1-1-59.

[Sec. 4219]

SEC. 4219. APPLICATION OF TAX IN CASE OF SALES BY OTHER THAN MANUFACTURER OR IMPORTER.

In case any person acquires from the manufacturer, producer, or importer of an article, by operation of law or as a result of any transaction not taxable under this chapter, the right to sell such article, the sale of such article by such person shall be taxable under this chapter as if made by the manufacturer, producer, or importer, and such person shall be liable for the tax.

Subchapter G—Exemptions, Registration, Etc.

Sec. 4221.	Certain tax-free sales.
Sec. 4222.	Registration.
Sec. 4223.	Special rules relating to further manufacture.
Sec. 4225.	Exemption of articles manufactured or produced by Indians.
Sec. 4227.	Cross references.

[Sec. 4221]

SEC. 4221. CERTAIN TAX-FREE SALES.

[Sec. 4221(a)]

(a) GENERAL RULE.—Under regulations prescribed by the Secretary, no tax shall be imposed under this chapter (other than under section 4121 or 4081) on the sale by the manufacturer (or under subchapter C of chapter 31 on the first retail sale) of an article—

(1) for use by the purchaser for further manufacture, or for resale by the purchaser to a second purchaser for use by such second purchaser in further manufacture,

(2) for export, or for resale by the purchaser to a second purchaser for export,

(3) for use by the purchaser as supplies for vessels or aircraft,

(4) to a State or local government for the exclusive use of a State or local government,

(5) to a nonprofit educational organization for its exclusive use, or

(6) to a qualified blood collector organization (as defined in section 7701(a)(49)) for such organization's exclusive use in the collection, storage, or transportation of blood,

but only if such exportation or use is to occur before any other use. Paragraphs (4), (5), and (6) shall not apply to the tax imposed by section 4064. In the case of taxes imposed by section 4051 or 4071, paragraphs (4) and (5) shall not apply on and after October 1, 2028. In the case of the tax imposed

MANUFACTURERS TAXES—EXEMPTIONS

by section 4131, paragraphs (3), (4), and (5) shall not apply and paragraph (2) shall apply only if the use of the exported vaccine meets such requirements as the Secretary may by regulations prescribe. In the case of taxes imposed by subchapter C or D, paragraph (6) shall not apply.

Amendments

- **2021, Infrastructure Investment and Jobs Act (P.L. 117-58)**

P.L. 117-58, §80102(d)(1), Div. H:

Amended Code Sec. 4221(a) by striking "October 1, 2022" and inserting "October 1, 2028". **Effective** 10-1-2021.

- **2019, Further Consolidated Appropriations Act, 2020 (P.L. 116-94)**

P.L. 116-94, §501(b)(1), Div. N:

Amended Code Sec. 4221(a) by striking the last sentence. **Effective** for sales after 12-31-2019. Prior to being stricken, the last sentence of Code Sec. 4221(a) read as follows:

In the case of the tax imposed by section 4191, paragraphs (3), (4), (5), and (6) shall not apply.

- **2018, Tax Technical Corrections Act of 2018 (P.L. 115-141)**

P.L. 115-141, §401(a)(221), Div. U:

Amended Code Sec. 4221(a) by striking "section 4051," and inserting "section 4051". **Effective** 3-23-2018.

- **2015, Fixing America's Surface Transportation Act (P.L. 114-94)**

P.L. 114-94, §31102(d)(1):

Amended Code Sec. 4221(a) by striking "October 1, 2016" and inserting "October 1, 2022". **Effective** 10-1-2016.

- **2014, Tax Technical Corrections Act of 2014 (P.L. 113-295)**

P.L. 113-295, §221(a)(103)(B)(i)(I)-(II), Division A:

Amended Code Sec. 4221(a) by striking "subchapter A or" and inserting "subchapter" and by striking "In the case of taxes imposed by subchapter A of chapter 31, paragraphs (1), (3), (4), and (5) shall not apply." following "the Secretary may by regulations prescribe.". **Effective** generally 12-19-2014. For a special rule, see Act Sec. 221(b)(2), Division A, below.

P.L. 113-295, §221(b)(2), Division A, provides:

(2) SAVINGS PROVISION.—If—

(A) any provision amended or repealed by the amendments made by this section applied to—

(i) any transaction occurring before the date of the enactment of this Act,

(ii) any property acquired before such date of enactment, or

(iii) any item of income, loss, deduction, or credit taken into account before such date of enactment, and

(B) the treatment of such transaction, property, or item under such provision would (without regard to the amendments or repeals made by this section) affect the liability for tax for periods ending after date of enactment, nothing in the amendments or repeals made by this section shall be construed to affect the treatment of such transaction, property, or item for purposes of determining liability for tax for periods ending after such date of enactment.

- **2012, Highway Investment, Job Creation, and Economic Growth Act of 2012 (P.L. 112-141)**

P.L. 112-141, §40102(d)(1):

Amended Code Sec. 4221(a) by striking "July 1, 2012" and inserting "October 1, 2016". **Effective** 7-1-2012.

- **2012, Temporary Surface Transportation Extension Act of 2012 (P.L. 112-140)**

P.L. 112-140, §1(c), provides:

(c) SPECIAL RULE FOR EXECUTION OF AMENDMENTS IN MAP–21.—On the date of enactment of the MAP–21 [P.L. 112-141]—

(1) this Act and the amendments made by this Act shall cease to be effective;

(2) the text of the laws amended by this Act shall revert back so as to read as the text read on the day before the date of enactment of this Act; and

(3) the amendments made by the MAP–21 shall be executed as if this Act had not been enacted.

P.L. 112-140, §402(c):

Amended Code Sec. 4221(a) by striking "July 1, 2012" and inserting "July 7, 2012". **Effective** 7-1-2012. For a special rule, see Act Sec. 1(c), above.

- **2012, Surface Transportation Extension Act of 2012 (P.L. 112-102)**

P.L. 112-102, §402(d):

Amended Code Sec. 4221(a) by striking "April 1, 2012" and inserting "July 1, 2012". **Effective** 4-1-2012.

- **2011, Surface Transportation Extension Act of 2011, Part II (P.L. 112-30)**

P.L. 112-30, §142(d):

Amended Code Sec. 4221(a) by striking "October 1, 2011" and inserting "April 1, 2012". **Effective** 10-1-2011.

- **2010, Health Care and Education Reconciliation Act of 2010 (P.L. 111-152)**

P.L. 111-152, §1405(b)(1):

Amended Code Sec. 4221(a) by adding at the end a new sentence. **Effective** for sales after 12-31-2012.

- **2006, Pension Protection Act of 2006 (P.L. 109-280)**

P.L. 109-280, §1207(b)(1):

Amended Code Sec. 4221(a) by striking "or" at the end of paragraph (4), by adding "or" at the end of paragraph (5), and by inserting after paragraph (5) a new paragraph (6). **Effective** 1-1-2007.

P.L. 109-280, §1207(b)(2):

Amended Code Sec. 4221(a) by adding at the end a new sentence. **Effective** 1-1-2007.

P.L. 109-280, §1207(b)(3)(A):

Amended the second sentence of Code Sec. 4221(a) by striking "Paragraphs (4) and (5)" and inserting "Paragraphs (4), (5), and (6)". **Effective** 1-1-2007.

- **2005, Safe, Accountable, Flexible, Efficient Transportation Equity Act: A Legacy for Users (P.L. 109-59)**

P.L. 109-59, §11101(b)(1):

Amended Code Sec. 4221(a) by striking "2005" and inserting "2011". **Effective** 8-10-2005.

- **2004, American Jobs Creation Act of 2004 (P.L. 108-357)**

P.L. 108-357, §853(d)(2)(F):

Amended Code Sec. 4221(a) by striking ", 4081, or 4091" and inserting "or 4081". **Effective** for aviation-grade kerosene removed, entered, or sold after 12-31-2004.

- **1998, Transportation Equity Act for the 21st Century (P.L. 105-178)**

P.L. 105-178, §9002(b)(1):

Amended Code Sec. 4221(a) by striking "1999" and inserting "2005". **Effective** 6-9-98.

- **1991, Intermodal Surface Transportation Efficiency Act of 1991 (P.L. 102-240)**

P.L. 102-240, §8002(b)(3):

Amended Code Sec. 4221(a) by striking "1995" each place it appears and inserting "1999". **Effective** 12-18-91.

- **1990, Omnibus Budget Reconciliation Act of 1990 (P.L. 101-508)**

P.L. 101-508, §11211(d)(3):

Amended Code Sec. 4221(a) by striking "1993" each place it appears and inserting "1995". **Effective** 11-5-90.

P.L. 101-508, §11221(b)(1):

Amended the material preceding Code Sec. 4221(a)(1) by striking "section 4051" and inserting "subchapter A or C of chapter 31". **Effective**, generally, 1-1-91. For an exception, see Act Sec. 11221(f)(2), below.

P.L. 101-508, §11221(b)(2):

Amended Code Sec. 4221(a) by adding at the end thereof a new sentence. **Effective**, generally, 1-1-91. For an exception, see Act Sec. 11221(f)(2), below.

P.L. 101-508, §11221(f)(2), provides:

(2) EXCEPTION FOR BINDING CONTRACTS.—In determining whether any tax imposed by subchapter A of chapter 31 of the Internal Revenue Code of 1986, as added by this section, applies to any sale after December 31, 1990, there shall not be taken into account the amount paid for any article (or any part or accessory therefor) if the purchaser held on September 30, 1990, a contract (which was binding on such date and at all times thereafter before the purchase) for the purchase of such article (or such part or accessory).

- **1987, Revenue Act of 1987 (P.L. 100-203)**

P.L. 100-203, §9201(b)(1):

Amended Code Sec. 4221(a) by adding at the end thereof a new sentence. **Effective** 1-1-88.

P.L. 100-203, §10502(d)(4):

Amended Code Sec. 4221(a) by striking out "(other than" and all that follows through "sale by the manufacturer" and inserting in lieu thereof "(other than under section 4121, 4081, or 4091) on the sale by the manufacturer". **Effective** for sales after 3-31-88. For special rules, see Act Sec. 10502(f) in the amendment notes following Code Sec. 4091. Prior to amendment, "(other than" and all that follows through "sale by the manufacturer" read as follows:

(other than under section 4121 on the sale by the manufacturer

- **1987, Surface Transportation and Uniform Relocation Assistance Act of 1987 (P.L. 100-17)**

P.L. 100-17, §502(b)(4):

Amended Code Sec. 4221(a) by striking out "1988" each place it appears and inserting in lieu thereof "1993". **Effective** 4-2-87.

- **1986, Tax Reform Act of 1986 (P.L. 99-514)**

P.L. 99-514, §1703(c)(2)(C)(i)-(ii) (as amended by H.R. 2005):

Amended Code Sec. 4221(a) (as amended by P.L. 108-27005) by inserting "or section 4081 (at the Highway Trust Fund financing rate)" before [after] "section 4121" in the 1st sentence and by striking out "4071, or 4081 (at the Highway Trust Fund financing rate)" in the last sentence and inserting in lieu thereof "or 4071". **Effective** for gasoline removed (as defined in Code Sec. 4082, as amended) after 12-31-87.

MANUFACTURERS TAXES—EXEMPTIONS

- **1986, Superfund Amendments and Reauthorization Act of 1986 (P.L. 99-499)**

P.L. 99-499, § 521(d)(4)(A):

Amended the last sentence of Code Sec. 4221(a) by striking out "4081" and inserting in lieu thereof "4081 (at the Highway Trust Fund financing rate)". **Effective** 1-1-87.

- **1984, Deficit Reduction Act of 1984 (P.L. 98-369)**

P.L. 98-369, § 735(c)(8)(A):

Amended Code Sec. 4221(a) by inserting "(or under section 4051 on the first retail sale)" after "manufacturer". **Effective** as if included in the provision of the Highway Revenue Act of 1982 to which it relates.

- **1983, Surface Transportation Act of 1983 (P.L. 97-424)**

P.L. 97-424, § 516(b)(2):

Added the last sentence of Code Sec. 4221(a). **Effective** 1-6-83.

- **1978, Energy Tax Act of 1978 (P.L. 95-618)**

P.L. 95-618, § 201(c)(1):

Added "Paragraphs (4) and (5) shall not apply to the tax imposed by section 4064." to the end of Code Sec. 4221(a). For **effective** date, see historical comment for P.L. 95-618, § 201(a), under Code Sec. 4064.

- **1978, Black Lung Benefits Revenue Act of 1977 (P.L. 95-227)**

P.L. 95-227, § 2(b)(2):

Added "(other than under section 4121)" in the second line of Code Sec. 4221. For **effective** date, see the historical comment for P.L. 95-227 under Code Sec. 4121.

- **1976, Tax Reform Act of 1976 (P.L. 94-455)**

P.L. 94-455, § 1906(b)(13)(A):

Amended 1954 Code by substituting "Secretary" for "Secretary or his delegate" each place it appeared. **Effective** 2-1-77.

[Sec. 4221(b)]

(b) PROOF OF RESALE FOR FURTHER MANUFACTURE; PROOF OF EXPORT.—Where an article has been sold free of tax under subsection (a)—

(1) for resale by the purchaser to a second purchaser for use by such second purchaser in further manufacture, or

(2) for export, or for resale by the purchaser to a second purchaser for export,

subsection (a) shall cease to apply in respect of such sale of such article unless, within the 6-month period which begins on the date of the sale by the manufacturer (or, if earlier, on the date of shipment by the manufacturer), the manufacturer receives proof that the article has been exported or resold for use in further manufacture.

[Sec. 4221(c)]

(c) MANUFACTURER RELIEVED FROM LIABILITY IN CERTAIN CASES.—In the case of any article sold free of tax under this section (other than a sale to which subsection (b) applies), and in the case of any article sold free of tax under section 4053(6), if the manufacturer in good faith accepts a certification by the purchaser that the article will be used in accordance with the applicable provisions of law, no tax shall thereafter be imposed under this chapter in respect of such sale by such manufacturer.

Amendments

- **2014, Tax Technical Corrections Act of 2014 (P.L. 113-295)**

P.L. 113-295, § 221(a)(103)(B)(i)(III), Division A:

Amended Code Sec. 4221(c) by striking "4001(c), 4001(d), or" following "free of tax under section". **Effective** generally 12-19-2014. For a special rule, see Act Sec. 221(b)(2), Division A, below.

P.L. 113-295, § 221(b)(2), Division A, provides:

(2) SAVINGS PROVISION.—If—

(A) any provision amended or repealed by the amendments made by this section applied to—

(i) any transaction occurring before the date of the enactment of this Act,

(ii) any property acquired before such date of enactment, or

(iii) any item of income, loss, deduction, or credit taken into account before such date of enactment, and

(B) the treatment of such transaction, property, or item under such provision would (without regard to the amendments or repeals made by this section) affect the liability for tax for periods ending after date of enactment, nothing in the amendments or repeals made by this section shall be construed to affect the treatment of such transaction, property, or item for purposes of determining liability for tax for periods ending after such date of enactment.

- **1998, IRS Restructuring and Reform Act of 1998 (P.L. 105-206)**

P.L. 105-206, § 6023(17):

Amended Code Sec. 4221(c) by striking "4053(a)(6)" and inserting "4053(6)". **Effective** 7-22-98.

- **1993, Omnibus Budget Reconciliation Act of 1993 (P.L. 103-66)**

P.L. 103-66, § 13161(b)(1):

Amended Code Sec. 4221(c) by striking "4002(b), 4003(c), 4004(a)" and inserting "4001(d)". **Effective** 1-1-93.

- **1990, Omnibus Budget Reconciliation Act of 1990 (P.L. 101-508)**

P.L. 101-508, § 11221(d)(1):

Amended Code Sec. 4221(c) by striking "section 4053(a)(6)" and inserting "section 4001(c), 4002(b), 4003(c), 4004(a), or 4053(a)(6)". **Effective**, generally, 1-1-91. For an exception, see Act Sec. 11221(f)(2) in the amendment notes following Code Sec. 4221(a).

- **1989, Omnibus Budget Reconciliation Act of 1989 (P.L. 101-239)**

P.L. 101-239, § 7841(d)(17):

Amended Code Sec. 4221(c) by striking "or 4083" after "4053(a)(6)". **Effective** 12-19-89.

- **1984, Deficit Reduction Act of 1984 (P.L. 98-369)**

P.L. 98-369, § 735(c)(8)(B):

Amended Code Sec. 4221(c) by striking out "section 4063(a)(6) or (7), 4063(b), 4063(e)," and inserting in lieu thereof "section 4053(a)(6)". **Effective** as if included in the provision of the Highway Revenue Act of 1982 to which it relates.

- **1983, Surface Transportation Act of 1983 (P.L. 97-424)**

P.L. 97-424, § 515(b)(1):

Amended Code Sec. 4221(c) by striking out "4083, or 4093" and inserting "or 4083". **Effective** with respect to articles sold after 1-6-83.

- **1978, Revenue Act of 1978 (P.L. 95-600)**

P.L. 95-600, § 701(ff)(2)(A):

Amended Code Sec. 4221(c) by inserting "4063(e)," after "4063(b)". **Effective** 12-1-78.

- **1971, Revenue Act of 1971 (P.L. 92-178)**

P.L. 92-178, § 401(a)(3)(A):

Added "4063(a)(6) or (7)," in Code Sec. 4221(c). For **effective** date, see the amendatory note for P.L. 92-178, § 401(h), under Code Sec. 4061.

[Sec. 4221(d)]

(d) DEFINITIONS.—For purposes of this section—

(1) MANUFACTURER.—The term "manufacturer" includes a producer or importer of an article, and, in the case of the taxes imposed by subchapter C of chapter 31, includes the retailer with respect to the first retail sale.

(2) EXPORT.—The term "export" includes shipment to a possession of the United States; and the term "exported" includes shipped to a possession of the United States.

(3) SUPPLIES FOR VESSELS OR AIRCRAFT.—The term "supplies for vessels or aircraft" means fuel supplies, ships' stores, sea stores, or legitimate equipment on vessels of war of the United States or of any foreign nation, vessels employed in the fisheries or in the whaling business, or vessels actually engaged in foreign trade or trade between the Atlantic and Pacific ports of the United States or between the United States and any of its possessions. For purposes of the preceding sentence, the term "vessels" includes civil aircraft employed in foreign trade or trade between the United States and any of its possessions, and the term "vessels of war of the United States or of any foreign nation" includes aircraft owned by the United States or by any foreign nation and constituting a part of the armed forces thereof.

(4) STATE OR LOCAL GOVERNMENT.—The term "State or local government" means any State, any political subdivision thereof, or the District of Columbia.

(5) NONPROFIT EDUCATIONAL ORGANIZATION.—The term "nonprofit educational organization" means an educational organization described in section 170(b)(1)(A)(ii) which is exempt from income tax under section 501(a). The term also includes a school operated as an activity of an organization described in section 501(c)(3) which is exempt from income tax under section 501(a), if such school normally maintains a regular faculty and curriculum and normally has a regularly enrolled body of pupils or students in attendance at the place where its educational activities are regularly carried on.

Internal Revenue Code

Sec. 4221(d)(5)

MANUFACTURERS TAXES—EXEMPTIONS

(6) USE IN FURTHER MANUFACTURE.—An article shall be treated as sold for use in further manufacture if—

(A) such article is sold for use by the purchaser as material in the manufacture or production of, or as a component part of, another article taxable under this chapter to be manufactured or produced by him; or

(B) in the case of gasoline taxable under section 4081, such gasoline is sold for use by the purchaser, for nonfuel purposes, as a material in the manufacture or production of another article to be manufactured or produced by him.

(7) QUALIFIED BUS.—

(A) IN GENERAL.—The term "qualified bus" means—

(i) an intercity or local bus, and

(ii) a school bus.

(B) INTERCITY OR LOCAL BUS.—The term "intercity or local bus" means any automobile bus which is used predominantly in furnishing (for compensation) passenger land transportation available to the general public if—

(i) such transportation is scheduled and along regular routes, or

(ii) the seating capacity of such bus is at least 20 adults (not including the driver).

(C) SCHOOL BUS.—The term "school bus" means any automobile bus substantially all the use of which is in transporting students and employees of schools. For purposes of the preceding sentence, the term "school" means an educational organization which normally maintains a regular faculty and curriculum and normally has a regularly enrolled body of pupils or students in attendance at the place where its educational activities are carried on.

Amendments

• **2014, Tax Technical Corrections Act of 2014 (P.L. 113-295)**

P.L. 113-295, § 221(a)(103)(B)(i)(I), Division A:

Amended Code Sec. 4221(d)(1) by striking "subchapter A or" and inserting "subchapter". **Effective** generally 12-19-2014. For a special rule, see Act Sec. 221(b)(2), Division A, below.

P.L. 113-295, § 221(b)(2), Division A, provides:

(2) SAVINGS PROVISION.—If—

(A) any provision amended or repealed by the amendments made by this section applied to—

(i) any transaction occurring before the date of the enactment of this Act,

(ii) any property acquired before such date of enactment, or

(iii) any item of income, loss, deduction, or credit taken into account before such date of enactment, and

(B) the treatment of such transaction, property, or item under such provision would (without regard to the amendments or repeals made by this section) affect the liability for tax for periods ending after date of enactment, nothing in the amendments or repeals made by this section shall be construed to affect the treatment of such transaction, property, or item for purposes of determining liability for tax for periods ending after such date of enactment.

• **1990, Omnibus Budget Reconciliation Act of 1990 (P.L. 101-508)**

P.L. 101-508, § 11221(d)(2):

Amended Code Sec. 4221(d)(1) by striking "the tax imposed by section 4051" and inserting "taxes imposed by subchapter A or C of chapter 31". **Effective**, generally, 1-1-91. For an exception, see Act Sec. 11221(f)(2) in the amendment notes following Code Sec. 4221(a).

• **1984, Deficit Reduction Act of 1984 (P.L. 98-369)**

P.L. 98-369, § 735(c)(8)(C):

Amended Code Sec. 4221(d)(1) by inserting before the period ", and, in the case of the tax imposed by section 4051, includes the retailer with respect to the first retail sale". **Effective** as if included in Act Sec. 513 of the Highway Revenue Act of 1982.

P.L. 98-369, § 735(c)(8)(D):

Amended Code Sec. 4221(d)(6) by striking out subparagraph (B) and the last sentence, by striking out "(other than an article referred to in subparagraph (B))" in subparagraph (A), by redesignating subparagraph (C) as subparagraph (B), and by adding "or" at the end of subparagraph (A). **Effective** as if included in Act Sec. 513 of the Highway Revenue Act of 1982. Prior to amendment, subparagraph (B) and the last sentence read as follows:

(B) in the case of a part or accessory taxable under section 4061(b), such article is sold for use by the purchaser as material in the manufacture or production of, or as a component part of, another article to be manufactured or produced by him; or

* * *

For purposes of subparagraph (B), the rebuilding of a part or accessory which is exempt from tax under section 4063(c) shall not constitute the manufacture or production of such part or accessory.

• **1978, Energy Tax Act of 1978 (P.L. 95-618)**

P.L. 95-618, § 233(c)(2):

Added Code Sec. 4221(d)(7). **Effective** 12-1-78.

• **1969, Tax Reform Act of 1969 (P.L. 91-172)**

P.L. 91-172, § 101(j)(26):

Amended Code Sec. 4221(d)(5) by substituting "section 170(b)(1)(A)(ii)" for "section 503(b)(2)". **Effective** 1-1-70.

• **1965, Excise Tax Reduction Act of 1965 (P.L. 89-44)**

P.L. 89-44, § 208(d)(1):

Amended Code Sec. 4221(d)(6)(B) by deleting "a radio or television component taxable under section 4141, or a camera lens taxable under section 4171," after "section 4061(b),". **Effective** 6-22-65.

P.L. 89-44, § 801(c):

Amended Code Sec. 4221(d)(6) by adding the last sentence. **Effective** 1-1-65.

• **1961, Federal-Aid Highway Act of 1961 (P.L. 87-61)**

P.L. 87-61, § 205(a):

Amended Code Sec. 4221(d)(6) by striking "or" at the end of subparagraph (A), by substituting "; or" for a period at the end of subparagraph (B), and by adding subparagraph (C). **Effective** only in the case of gasoline sold on or after 10-1-61.

• **1960, Hawaii Omnibus Act (P.L. 86-624)**

P.L. 86-624, § 18(e):

Amended 1954 Code Sec. 4221(d)(4). **Effective** 8-21-59. Prior to amendment, Code Sec. 4221(d)(4) read as follows:

(4) State or Local Government.—The term "State or local government" means any State, Hawaii, the District of Columbia, or any political subdivision of any of the foregoing.

• **1959 (P.L. 86-344)**

P.L. 86-344, § 2(b):

Added the second sentence to Code Sec. 4221(d)(5). **Effective** 1-1-59.

• **1959, Alaska Omnibus Bill (P.L. 86-70)**

P.L. 86-70, § 22(a):

Amended 1954 Code Sec. 4221(d)(4) by striking out "Alaska," where it appeared following "means any State,". **Effective** 1-1-59.

[Sec. 4221(e)]

(e) SPECIAL RULES.—

(1) RECIPROCITY REQUIRED IN CASE OF CIVIL AIRCRAFT.—In the case of articles sold for use as supplies for aircraft, the privileges granted under subsection (a)(3) in respect of civil aircraft employed in foreign trade or trade between the United States and any of its possessions, in respect of aircraft registered in a foreign country, shall be allowed only if the Secretary of the Treasury has been advised by the Secretary of Commerce that he has found that such foreign country allows, or will allow, substantially reciprocal privileges in respect of aircraft registered in the United States. If the Secretary of the Treasury is advised by the Secretary of Commerce that he has found that a foreign country has discontinued or will discontinue the allowance of such privileges, the privileges granted under subsection (a)(3) shall not apply thereafter in respect of civil aircraft registered in that foreign country and employed in foreign trade or trade between the United States and any of its possessions.

(2) TIRES.—

(A) TAX-FREE SALES.—Under regulations prescribed by the Secretary, no tax shall be imposed under section 4071 on the sale by the manufacturer of a tire if—

(i) such tire is sold for use by the purchaser for sale on or in connection with the sale of another article manufactured or produced by such purchaser; and

MANUFACTURERS TAXES—EXEMPTIONS

(ii) such other article is to be sold by such purchaser in a sale which either will satisfy the requirements of paragraph (2), (3), (4), or (5) of subsection (a) for a tax-free sale, or would satisfy such requirements but for the fact that such other article is not subject to tax under this chapter.

(B) PROOF.—Where a tire has been sold free of tax under this paragraph, this paragraph shall cease to apply unless, within the 6-month period which begins on the date of the sale by him (or, if earlier, on the date of the shipment by him), the manufacturer of such tire receives proof that the other article referred to in clause (ii) of subparagraph (A) has been sold in a manner which satisfies the requirements of such clause (ii) (including in the case of a sale for export, proof of export of such other article).

(C) SUBSECTION (a)(1) DOES NOT APPLY.—Paragraph (1) of subsection (a) shall not apply with respect to the tax imposed under section 4071 on the sale of a tire.

(3) TIRES USED ON INTERCITY, LOCAL, AND SCHOOL BUSES.—Under regulations prescribed by the Secretary, the tax imposed by section 4071 shall not apply in the case of tires sold for use by the purchaser on or in connection with a qualified bus.

Amendments

• **1984, Deficit Reduction Act of 1984 (P.L. 98-369)**

P.L. 98-369, §735(c)(8)(E):

Amended Code Sec. 4221(e)(2) by striking out "or inner tube" each place it appeared and by striking out "or tube" each place it appeared. **Effective** as if included in the provision of the Highway Revenue Act of 1982 to which it relates. Prior to amendment, paragraph (2) read as follows:

(2) Tires and Tubes.

(A) Tax-Free Sales.—Under regulations prescribed by the Secretary, no tax shall be imposed under section 4071 on the sale by the manufacturer of a tire or inner tube if—

(i) such tire or tube is sold for use by the purchaser for sale on or in connection with the sale of another article manufactured or produced by such purchaser; and

(ii) such other article is to be sold by such purchaser in a sale which either will satisfy the requirements of paragraph (2), (3), (4), or (5) of subsection (a) for a tax-free sale, or would satisfy such requirements but for the fact that such other article is not subject to tax under this chapter.

(B) Proof.—Where a tire or tube has been sold free of tax under this paragraph, this paragraph shall cease to apply unless, within the 6-month period which begins on the date of the sale by him (or, if earlier, on the date of the shipment by him), the manufacturer of such tire or tube receives proof that the other article referred to in clause (ii) of subparagraph (A) has been sold in a manner which satisfies the requirements of such clause (ii) (including in the case of a sale for export, proof of export of such other article).

(C) Subsection (a)(1) Does Not Apply.—Paragraph (1) of subsection (a) shall not apply with respect to the tax imposed under section 4071 on the sale of a tire or inner tube.

P.L. 98-369, §735(c)(8)(F):

Amended Code Sec. 4221(e) by striking out "AND TUBES" in the heading of paragraph (2). **Effective** as if included in the provision of the Highway Revenue Act of 1982 to which it relates.

P.L. 98-369, §735(c)(8)(G):

Amended Code Sec. 4221(e) by striking out paragraphs (4), (5), and (6) and inserting in lieu thereof new paragraph (3). **Effective** as if included in the provision of the Highway Revenue Act of 1982 to which it relates. Prior to amendment, paragraphs (4), (5), and (6) read as follows:

(4) Bicycle Tires or Tubes Sold to Bicycle Manufacturer.—

(A) In General.—Under regulations prescribed by the Secretary, no tax shall be imposed under section 4071 on the sale of a bicycle tire (or an inner tube for such a tire) by the manufacturer thereof if such tire or tube is sold for use by the purchaser as material in the manufacture or production of, or as a component part of, a bicycle (other than a rebuilt or reconditioned bicycle).

(B) Bicycle Tire Defined.—As used in this paragraph the term "bicycle tire" means a tire, composed of rubber in combination with fabric or other reinforcing element, which is not more than 28 inches in outer diameter and not more than $2\frac{1}{4}$ inches in cross section and which is primarily designed or adapted for use on bicycles.

(C) Proof.—Where a bicycle tire or tube has been sold free of tax under this paragraph, this paragraph shall cease to apply unless, within the 6-month period which begins on the date of the sale by him (or, if earlier, on the date of shipment by him), the manufacturer of such bicycle tire or tube receives proof that the tire or tube has been used in the manner described in subparagraph (A).

(5) Tires, Tubes, and Tread Rubber Used on Intercity, Local and School Buses.—Under regulations prescribed by the Secretary—

(A) the taxes imposed by paragraphs (1) and (3) of section 4071(a) shall not apply in the case of tires or inner tubes for tires sold for use by the purchaser on or in connection with a qualified bus, and

(B) the tax imposed by paragraph (4) of section 4071(a) shall not apply in the case of tread rubber sold for use by the purchaser in the recapping or retreading of any tire to be used by the purchaser on or in connection with a qualified bus.

Amendments

• **1965, Excise Tax Reduction Act of 1965 (P.L. 89-44)**

P.L. 89-44, §208(d)(7):

Repealed Code Sec. 4221(f). **Effective** 6-22-65. Prior to repeal, Code Sec. 4221(f) read as follows:

(6) Bus Parts and Accessories.—Under regulations prescribed by the Secretary, the tax imposed by section 4061(b) shall not apply to any part or accessory which is sold for use by the purchaser on or in connection with an automobile bus, or is to be resold by the purchaser or a second purchaser for such use.

• **1980, Technical Corrections Act of 1979 (P.L. 96-222)**

P.L. 96-222, §108(c)(5):

Amended Code Sec. 4221(e)(6). **Effective** for sales by the manufacturer, producer, or importer on or after 5-1-80. Prior to amendment, Code Sec. 4221(e)(6) read as follows:

(6) BUS PARTS AND ACCESSORIES.—Under regulations prescribed by the Secretary, the tax imposed by section 4061(b) shall not apply to any part or accessory which is sold for use by the purchaser on or in connection with an automobile bus.

• **1978, Energy Tax Act of 1978 (P.L. 95-618)**

P.L. 95-618, §232(a):

Added subsection (6) to Code Sec. 4221(e). **Effective** for sales on or after 12-1-78.

P.L. 95-618, §233(c)(1):

Amended Code Sec. 4221(e)(5). **Effective** 12-1-78. Prior to amendment, Code Sec. 4221(e)(5) read as follows:

(5) SCHOOL BUSES.—Under regulations prescribed by the Secretary, the tax imposed by section 4061(a) shall not apply to a bus sold to any person for use exclusively in transporting students and employees of schools operated by State or local governments or by nonprofit educational organizations. For purposes of this paragraph, incidental use of a bus in providing transportation for a State or local government or a nonprofit organization described in section 501(c) which is exempt from tax under section 501(a) shall be disregarded.

• **1976, Tax Reform Act of 1976 (P.L. 94-455)**

P.L. 94-455, §1906(b)(13)(A):

Amended 1954 Code by substituting "Secretary" for "Secretary or his delegate" each place it appeared. **Effective** 2-1-77.

• **1965, Excise Tax Reduction Act of 1965 (P.L. 89-44)**

P.L. 89-44, §208(d):

Amended Code Sec. 4221(e)(2) by changing the heading to "TIRES AND TUBES" from "TIRES, TUBES, AND AUTOMOBILE RECEIVING SETS", by deleting "or 4141" after "4071" in Code Sec. 4221(e)(2)(A), by inserting "tire or tube" in lieu of "tire, tube, or receiving set" wherever it appeared, by inserting "tire or inner tube" in lieu of "tire, inner tube, or automobile radio or television receiving set" wherever it appeared, and by repealing Code Sec. 4221(e)(3). **Effective** 6-22-65. Prior to repeal, Code Sec. 4221(e)(3) read as follows:

(3) Musical instruments sold for religious use.—Under regulations prescribed by the Secretary or his delegate, the tax imposed by section 4151 shall not apply to musical instruments sold to a religious institution for exclusively religious purposes.

P.L. 89-44, §801(d)(1):

Amended Code Sec. 4221(e) by adding paragraph (5). **Effective** 6-22-65.

• **1960 (P.L. 86-418)**

P.L. 86-418, §1:

Added paragraph (4) of Code Sec. 4221(e). **Effective** 5-1-60.

• **1958, Excise Tax Technical Changes Act of 1958 (P.L. 85-859)**

P.L. 85-859, §119(a):

Struck out Code Secs. 4220 to 4225 and added subchapter G, of which Code Sec. 4221 is a part. **Effective** 1-1-59.

[Sec. 4221(f)—Repealed]

(f) SALES OF MECHANICAL PENCILS AND PENS FOR EXPORT.—Under regulations prescribed by the Secretary or his delegate, mechanical pencils, fountain pens, and ball point pens subject to the tax imposed by section 4201 may be sold by the manufacturer free of tax for export or for resale for export upon receipt by him of notice of intent to export or to resell for export.

[Sec. 4222]

SEC. 4222. REGISTRATION.

[Sec. 4222(a)]

(a) GENERAL RULE.—Except as provided in subsection (b), section 4221 shall not apply with respect to the sale of any article unless the manufacturer, the first purchaser, and the second purchaser (if any) are all registered under this section. Registration under this section shall be

MANUFACTURERS TAXES—EXEMPTIONS

made at such time, in such manner and form, and subject to such terms and conditions, as the Secretary may by regulations prescribe. A registration under this section may be used only in accordance with regulations prescribed under this section.

Amendments

• **1976, Tax Reform Act of 1976 (P.L. 94-455)**

P.L. 94-455, § 1906(b)(13)(A):

Amended 1954 Code by substituting "Secretary" for "Secretary or his delegate" each place it appeared. **Effective** 2-1-77.

[Sec. 4222(b)]

(b) EXCEPTIONS.—

(1) PURCHASES BY STATE AND LOCAL GOVERNMENTS.—Subsection (a) shall not apply to any State or local government in connection with the purchase by it of any article if such State or local government complies with such regulations relating to the use of exemption certificates in lieu of registration as the Secretary shall prescribe to carry out the purpose of this paragraph.

(2) UNDER REGULATIONS.—Subject to such regulations as the Secretary may prescribe for the purpose of this paragraph, the Secretary may relieve the purchaser or the second purchaser, or both, from the requirement of registering under this section.

(3) CERTAIN PURCHASES AND SALES BY THE UNITED STATES.—Subsection (a) shall apply to purchases and sales by the United States only to the extent provided by regulations prescribed by the Secretary.

(4) [Repealed.]

(5) SUPPLIES FOR VESSELS OR AIRCRAFT.—Subsection (a) shall not apply to a sale of an article for use by the purchaser as supplies for any vessel or aircraft if such purchaser complies with such regulations relating to the use of exemption certificates in lieu of registration as the Secretary shall prescribe to carry out the purpose of this paragraph.

Amendments

• **1997, Taxpayer Relief Act of 1997 (P.L. 105-34)**

P.L. 105-34, § 1431(a)(1)-(2):

Amended Code Sec. 4222(b)(2) by striking "in the case of any sale or resale for export," after "paragraph," and by striking "EXPORT" and inserting "UNDER REGULATIONS" in the heading. **Effective** 8-5-97.

• **1976, Tax Reform Act of 1976 (P.L. 94-455)**

P.L. 94-455, § 1906(b)(13)(A):

Amended 1954 Code by substituting "Secretary" for "Secretary or his delegate" each place it appeared. **Effective** 2-1-77.

• **1965, Excise Tax Reduction Act of 1965 (P.L. 89-44)**

P.L. 89-44, § 208(e):

Repealed Code Sec. 4222(b)(4) (but did not renumber (5)). **Effective** 6-22-65. Prior to repeal, Code Sec. 4222(b)(4) read as follows:

(4) Mechanical pencils, fountain pens, and ball point pens.—Subsection (a) shall not apply in the case of mechanical pencils, fountain pens, and ball point pens subject to the tax imposed by section 4201 sold by the manufacturer for export or for resale for export.

P.L. 89-44, § 802(c):

Added Code Sec. 4222(b)(5). **Effective** 7-1-65.

[Sec. 4222(c)]

(c) DENIAL, REVOCATION, OR SUSPENSION OF REGISTRATION.—Under regulations prescribed by the Secretary, the registration of any person under this section may be denied, revoked, or suspended if the Secretary determines—

(1) that such person has used such registration to avoid the payment of any tax imposed by this chapter, or to postpone or in any manner to interfere with the collection of any such tax, or

(2) that such denial, revocation, or suspension is necessary to protect the revenue.

The denial, revocation, or suspension under this subsection shall be in addition to any penalty provided by law for any act or failure to act.

Amendments

• **1990, Omnibus Budget Reconciliation Act of 1990 (P.L. 101-508)**

P.L. 101-508, § 11212(b)(2)(A)-(C):

Amended Code Sec. 4222(c) by striking "revoked or suspended" in the material preceding paragraph (1) and inserting "denied, revoked, or suspended", by striking "revocation or suspension" each place it appears and inserting "denial, revocation, or suspension" and by striking "REVOCATION OR SUSPENSION" in the heading and inserting "DENIAL, REVOCATION, OR SUSPENSION". **Effective** 12-1-90.

• **1976, Tax Reform Act of 1976 (P.L. 94-455)**

P.L. 94-455, § 1906(b)(13)(A):

Amended 1954 Code by substituting "Secretary" for "Secretary or his delegate" each place it appeared. **Effective** 2-1-77.

[Sec. 4222(d)]

(d) REGISTRATION IN THE CASE OF CERTAIN OTHER EXEMPTIONS.—The provisions of this section may be extended to, and made applicable with respect to, the exemptions provided by sections 4053(6), 4064(b)(1)(C), 4101, and 4182(b), and the exemptions authorized under section 4293 in respect of the taxes imposed by this chapter, to the extent provided by regulations prescribed by the Secretary.

Amendments

• **2014, Tax Technical Corrections Act of 2014 (P.L. 113-295)**

P.L. 113-295, § 221(a)(103)(B)(ii), Division A:

Amended Code Sec. 4222[(d)] by striking "4001(c), 4001(d)," following "provided by sections". **Effective** generally 12-19-2014. For a special rule, see Act Sec. 221(b)(2), Division A, below.

P.L. 113-295, § 221(b)(2), Division A, provides:

(2) SAVINGS PROVISION.—If—

(A) any provision amended or repealed by the amendments made by this section applied to—

(i) any transaction occurring before the date of the enactment of this Act,

(ii) any property acquired before such date of enactment, or

(iii) any item of income, loss, deduction, or credit taken into account before such date of enactment, and

(B) the treatment of such transaction, property, or item under such provision would (without regard to the amendments or repeals made by this section) affect the liability for tax for periods ending after date of enactment, nothing in the amendments or repeals made by this section shall be construed to affect the treatment of such transaction, property, or item for purposes of determining liability for tax for periods ending after such date of enactment.

• **1998, IRS Restructuring and Reform Act of 1998 (P.L. 105-206)**

P.L. 105-206, § 6023(17):

Amended Code Sec. 4222(d) by striking "4053(a)(6)" and inserting "4053(6)". **Effective** 7-22-98.

• **1993, Omnibus Budget Reconciliation Act of 1993 (P.L. 103-66)**

P.L. 103-66, § 13161(b)(2):

Amended Code Sec. 4222(d) by striking "4002(b), 4003(c), 4004(a)" and inserting "4001(d)". **Effective** 1-1-93.

• **1990, Omnibus Budget Reconciliation Act of 1990 (P.L. 101-508)**

P.L. 101-508, § 11221(d)(3):

Amended Code Sec. 4222(d) by striking "sections 4053(a)(6)" and inserting "sections 4001(c), 4002(b), 4003(c), 4004(a), 4053(a)(6)". **Effective**, generally, 1-1-91. For an exception, see Act Sec. 11221(f)(2), below.

P.L. 101-508, § 11221(f)(2), provides:

(2) EXCEPTION FOR BINDING CONTRACTS.—In determining whether any tax imposed by subchapter A of chapter 31 of the Internal Revenue Code of 1986, as added by this section, applies to any sale after December 31, 1990, there shall not be taken into account the amount paid for any article (or any part or accessory therefor) if the purchaser held on September 30, 1990, a contract (which was binding on such date and at all times thereafter before the purchase) for the purchase of such article (or such part or accessory).

• **1988, Technical and Miscellaneous Revenue Act of 1988 (P.L. 100-647)**

P.L. 100-647, § 1017(c)(16):

Amended Code Sec. 4222(d) by striking out "4083" and inserting in lieu thereof "4101". **Effective** as if included in the provision of P.L. 99-514 to which it relates.

MANUFACTURERS TAXES—EXEMPTIONS

• **1984, Deficit Reduction Act of 1984 (P.L. 98-369)**

P.L. 98-369, §735(c)(9):

Amended Code Sec. 4222(d) by striking out "4063(a)(7), 4063(b), 4063(e)," and inserting in lieu thereof "4053(a)(6),". **Effective** as if included in the provision of the Highway Revenue Act of 1982 to which it relates.

• **1983, Surface Transportation Act of 1983 (P.L. 97-424)**

P.L. 97-424, §515(b)(2):

Amended Code Sec. 4222(d) by striking out "4093,". **Effective** with respect to articles sold after 1-6-83.

• **1978, Energy Tax Act of 1978 (P.L. 95-618)**

P.L. 95-618, §201(e):

Inserted "4064(b)(1)(C)" before "4083" in Code Sec. 4222(d). For **effective** date, see historical comment for P.L. 95-618, §201(a), under Code Sec. 4064.

P.L. 95-618, §231(f)(2):

Amended Code Sec. 4222(d) by striking out "4063(a)(6) or (7)" and inserting in lieu thereof "4063(a)(7)". **Effective** with respect to articles sold after 11-10-78.

• **1958, Excise Tax Technical Changes Act of 1958 (P.L. 85-859)**

P.L. 85-859, §119(a):

Struck out sections 4220 to 4225 of subchapter F of chapter 32 and added subchapter G, of which Code Sec. 4222 is a part. **Effective** 1-1-59.

• **1978, Revenue Act of 1978 (P.L. 95-600)**

P.L. 95-600, §701(ff)(2)(B):

Amended Code Sec. 4222(d) by inserting "4063(e)," after "4063(b),". **Effective** 12-1-78.

• **1976, Tax Reform Act of 1976 (P.L. 94-455)**

P.L. 94-455, §1906(b)(13)(A):

Amended 1954 Code by substituting "Secretary" for "Secretary or his delegate" each place it appeared. **Effective** 2-1-77.

• **1971, Revenue Act of 1971 (P.L. 92-178)**

P.L. 92-178, §401(a)(3)(B):

Added "4063(a)(6) or (7)," in Code Sec. 4222(d). For **effective** date, see the amendatory note for P.L. 92-178, §401(h), under Code Sec. 4061.

[Sec. 4222(e)]

(e) DEFINITIONS.—Terms used in this section which are defined in section 4221(d) shall have the meaning given to them by section 4221(d).

[Sec. 4223]

SEC. 4223. SPECIAL RULES RELATING TO FURTHER MANUFACTURE.

[Sec. 4223(a)]

(a) PURCHASING MANUFACTURER TO BE TREATED AS THE MANUFACTURER.—For purposes of this chapter, a manufacturer or producer to whom an article is sold or resold free of tax under section 4221(a)(1) for use by him in further manufacture shall be treated as the manufacturer or producer of such article.

[Sec. 4223(b)]

(b) COMPUTATION OF TAX.—If the manufacturer or producer referred to in subsection (a) incurs liability for tax under this chapter on his sale or use of an article referred to in subsection (a) and the tax is based on the price for which the article is sold, the article shall be treated as having been sold by him—

(1) at the price for which the article was sold by him (or, where the tax is on his use of the article, at the price referred to in section 4218(c)); or

(2) if he so elects and establishes such price to the satisfaction of the Secretary—

(A) at the price for which the article was sold to him; or

(B) at the price for which the article was sold by the person who (without regard to subsection (a)) is the manufacturer, producer, or importer of such article.

For purposes of this subsection, the price for which the article was sold shall be determined as provided in section 4216. For purposes of paragraph (2) no adjustment or readjustment shall be made in such price by reason of any discount, rebate, allowance, return or repossession of a container or covering, or otherwise. An election under paragraph (2) shall be made in the return reporting the tax applicable to the sale or use of the article, and may not be revoked.

Amendments

• **1984, Deficit Reduction Act of 1984 (P.L. 98-369)**

P.L. 98-369, §735(c)(10):

Amended Code Sec. 4223(b)(1) by striking out "section 4218(e)" and inserting in lieu thereof "section 4218(c)". **Effective** as if included in the provision of the Highway Revenue Act of 1982 to which it relates.

• **1976, Tax Reform Act of 1976 (P.L. 94-455)**

P.L. 94-455, §1906(b)(13)(A):

Amended 1954 Code by substituting "Secretary" for "Secretary or his delegate" each place it appeared. **Effective** 2-1-77.

• **1960 (P.L. 86-418)**

P.L. 86-418, §2(b):

Amended Code Sec. 4223(b)(1) by striking out "section 4218(d)" and substituting "section 4218(e)". **Effective** 5-1-60.

• **1958, Excise Tax Technical Changes Act of 1958 (P.L. 85-859)**

P.L. 85-859, §119(a):

Struck out sections 4220 to 4225 of subchapter F of chapter 32 and added subchapter G, of which Code Sec. 4223 is a part. **Effective** 1-1-59.

[Sec. 4225]

SEC. 4225. EXEMPTION OF ARTICLES MANUFACTURED OR PRODUCED BY INDIANS.

No tax shall be imposed under this chapter on any article of native Indian handicraft manufactured or produced by Indians on Indian reservations, or in Indian schools, or by Indians under the jurisdiction of the United States Government in Alaska.

Amendments

• **1958, Excise Tax Technical Changes Act of 1958 (P.L. 85-859)**

P.L. 85-859, §119(a):

Struck out sections 4220 to 4225 of subchapter F of chapter 32 and added a new subchapter G, of which Code Sec. 4225 is a part. **Effective** 1-1-59.

[Sec. 4227]

SEC. 4227. CROSS REFERENCES.

For exception for a sale to an Indian tribal government (or its subdivision) for the exclusive use of an Indian tribal government (or its subdivision), see section 7871.

Amendments

• **1986, Tax Reform Act of 1986 (P.L. 99-514)**

P.L. 99-514, §1899A(49):

Amended Code Sec. 4227. **Effective** 10-22-86. Prior to amendment, Code Sec. 4227 read as follows:

SEC. 4227. CROSS REFERENCES.

(1) For exception for a sale to an Indian tribal government (or its subdivision) for the exclusive use of an Indian tribal governmnent (or its subdivision), see section 7871.

(2) For credit for taxes on tires, see section 6416(c).

EXCISE TAXES—COMMUNICATIONS

• **1984, Deficit Reduction Act of 1984 (P.L. 98-369)**

P.L. 98-369, §735(c)(11):

Amended Code Sec. 4227(2) by striking out "and tubes". **Effective** as if included in the provision of the Highway Revenue Act of 1982 to which it relates.

• **1983 (P.L. 97-473)**

P.L. 97-473, §202(b)(8):

Amended Code Sec. 4227. For the **effective** date, see Act Sec. 204 in the amendment notes following Code Sec. 7871(d).

• **1976, Tax Reform Act of 1976 (P.L. 94-455)**

P.L. 94-455, §1904(a)(5):

Amended Code Sec. 4227. **Effective** 2-1-77. Prior to amendment, Code Sec. 4227 read as follows:

SEC. 4227. CROSS REFERENCES.

(1) For exemption from tax in case of certain sales to the United States, see section 4293.

(2) For credit for taxes on tires and inner tubes, see section 6416(c).

(3) For administrative provisions of general application to the taxes imposed under this chapter, see subtitle F.

• **1965, Excise Tax Reduction Act of 1965 (P.L. 89-44)**

P.L. 89-44, §208(f):

Amended Code Sec. 4227(2) by deleting "and automobile radio and television receiving sets," after "inner tubes,". **Effective** 6-22-65.

• **1958, Excise Tax Technical Changes Act of 1958 (P.L. 85-859)**

P.L. 85-859, §119(a):

Redesignated Code Sec. 4227 of subchapter F of chapter 32 as Code Sec. 4227 of subchapter G of chapter 32. **Effective** 1-1-59.

• **1956 (P.L. 627, 84th Cong.)**

P.L. 627, 84th Cong., 2d Sess., §207(a):

Amended subchapter F of chapter 32 of the 1954 Code by renumbering Code Sec. 4226 as Code Sec. 4227. **Effective** 7-1-56.

CHAPTER 33—FACILITIES AND SERVICES

SUBCHAPTER B.	Communications.
SUBCHAPTER C.	Transportation by air.
SUBCHAPTER E.	Special provisions applicable to services and facilities taxes.

Subchapter B—Communications

Sec. 4251.	Imposition of tax.
Sec. 4252.	Definitions.
Sec. 4253.	Exemptions.
Sec. 4254.	Computation of tax.

[Sec. 4251]

SEC. 4251. IMPOSITION OF TAX.

[Sec. 4251(a)]

(a) TAX IMPOSED.—

(1) IN GENERAL.—There is hereby imposed on amounts paid for communications services a tax equal to the applicable percentage of amounts so paid.

(2) PAYMENT OF TAX.—The tax imposed by this section shall be paid by the person paying for such services.

Amendments

• **1982, Tax Equity and Fiscal Responsibility Act of 1982 (P.L. 97-248)**

P.L. 97-248, §282(a):

Amended Code Sec. 4251(a). **Effective** for amounts paid for communications services pursuant to bills first rendered after 12-31-82. Prior to amendment, Code Sec. 4251(a) read as follows:

(a) IN GENERAL.—

(1) Except as provided in subsection (b), there is hereby imposed on amounts paid for the following communication services a tax equal to the percent of the amount so paid specified in paragraph (2):

Local telephone service.

Toll telephone service.

Teletypewriter exchange service.

The taxes imposed by this section shall be paid by the person paying for the services.

(2) The rate of tax referred to in paragraph (1) is as follows:

Amounts paid pursuant to bills first rendered—	Percent—
Before January 1, 1973	10
During 1973	9
During 1974	8
During 1975	7
During 1976	6
During 1977	5
During 1978	4
During 1979	3
During 1980 or 1981	2
During 1982, 1983, or 1984	1

• **1981, Economic Recovery Tax Act of 1981 (P.L. 97-34)**

P.L. 97-34, §821(a):

Amended the table in Code Sec. 4251(a)(2) by striking out "During 1982" and inserting "During 1982, 1983, or 1984". **Effective** 8-13-81.

• **1980, Omnibus Reconciliation Act of 1980 (P.L. 96-499)**

P.L. 96-499, §1151(a):

Amended the rate table in Code Sec. 4251(a)(2) by striking out the last two lines and inserting two new lines. Prior to amendment, the last two lines of the table provided:

During 1980	2
During 1981	1.

• **1970, Excise, Estate, and Gift Tax Adjustment Act of 1970 (P.L. 91-614)**

P.L. 91-614, §201(b)(1):

Amended the rate table in Code Sec. 4251(a)(2). Prior to amendment, the table read as follows:

Before January 1, 1971	10
During 1971	5
During 1972	3
During 1973	1.

• **1969, Tax Reform Act of 1969 (P.L. 91-172)**

P.L. 91-172, §702(b)(1):

Amended Code Sec. 4251(a)(2) by amending the rate table. Prior to amendment, the table in Code Sec. 4251(a)(2) read as follows:

Amounts paid pursuant to bills first rendered	Percent
Before January 1, 1970	10
During 1970	5
During 1971	3
During 1972	1.

EXCISE TAXES—COMMUNICATIONS

• **1968, Revenue and Expenditure Control Act of 1968 (P.L. 90-364)**

P.L. 90-364, §105(b)(1):

Amended Sec. 4251(a)(2). **Effective** 4-30-68. Prior to amendment, Sec. 4251(a)(2) read as follows:

(2) The rate of tax referred to in paragraph (1) is as follows:

Amounts paid pursuant to bills first rendered	Percent
Before May 1, 1968	10
After April 30, and before January 1, 1969	1

P.L. 90-364, §105(b)(3), as amended by P.L. 91-172, §702(b)(3), and P.L. 91-614, §201(b)(3), provides:

(3) Repeal of Subchapter B of Chapter 33.—Effective with respect to amounts paid pursuant to bills first rendered on or after January 1, 1982, subchapter B of chapter 33 (relating to the tax on communications) is repealed. For purposes of the preceding sentence, in the case of communications services rendered before November 1, 1981, for which a bill has not been rendered before January 1, 1982, a bill shall be treated as having been first rendered on December 31, 1981. Effective January 1, 1982, the table of subchapters for chapter 33 is amended by striking out the item relating to such subchapter B.

[Note: The communications excise tax was subsequently extended by various tax acts during the 1980's and made permanent by P.L. 101-508. Thus, its repeal, as noted above, never took effect.—CCH.]

• **1968 (P.L. 90-285)**

P.L. 90-285:

Amended Code Sec. 4251(a)(2) by substituting "May 1, 1968" for "April 1, 1968" and by substituting "April 30, 1968" for "March 31, 1968". **Effective** 3-31-68.

• **1966, Tax Adjustment Act of 1966 (P.L. 89-368)**

P.L. 89-368, §202(a)(1):

Amended Code Sec. 4251(a)(2). **Effective** for amounts paid pursuant to bills first rendered on or after 4-1-66, for services rendered on or after such date. In the case of amounts paid pursuant to bills rendered on or after such date for services which were rendered before such date and for which no previous bill was rendered, such amendments shall apply except with respect to such services as were rendered more than 2 months before such date. In the case of services rendered more than 2 months before such date, the provisions of subchapter B of chapter 33 of the Code in effect at the time such services were rendered, subject to the provision of section 701(b)(2) of the Excise Tax Reduction Act of 1965, shall apply to the amounts paid for such services. Prior to amendment, Code Sec. 4251(a)(2) read as follows:

(2) The rate of tax referred to in paragraph (1) is as follows:

Amounts paid pursuant to bills first rendered	Percent
During 1966	3
During 1967	2
During 1968	1

• **1965, Excise Tax Reduction Act of 1965 (P.L. 89-44)**

P.L. 89-44, §302:

Amended Code Sec. 4251(a). **Effective** for amounts paid pursuant to bills rendered on or after 1-1-66, for services rendered on or after such date. In the case of amounts paid pursuant to bills rendered on or after 1-1-66, for services which were rendered before such date and for which no previous bill was rendered, such amendments shall apply except with respect to such services as were rendered more than 2 months before such date. In the case of services rendered more than 2 months before such date, the provisions of subchapter B of chapter 33 of the Code in effect at the time such services were rendered shall apply to the amounts paid for such services. Prior to amendment, Code Sec. 4251(a) read as follows:

(a) In General.—There is hereby imposed on amounts paid for the communication services enumerated in the following table a tax equal to the percent of the amount so paid as is specified in such table:

Taxable service	Rate of tax Percent
General telephone service	10
Toll telephone service	10
Telegraph service	10
Teletypewriter exchange service	10
Wire mileage service	10
Wire and equipment service	8

The taxes imposed by this section shall be paid by the person paying for the services.

• **1959, Tax Rate Extension Act of 1959 (P.L. 86-75)**

P.L. 86-75, §5:

Amended 1954 Code Sec. 4251 by inserting "(a) IN GENERAL.—" at the beginning of the text of such section.

• **1958, Excise Tax Technical Changes Act of 1958 (P.L. 85-859)**

P.L. 85-859, §133(a):

Amended Code Sec. 4251. For the **effective** date, see Act Sec. 133(b), below. Prior to amendment, Code Sec. 4251 read as follows:

SEC. 4251. IMPOSITION OF TAX.

There is hereby imposed on amounts paid for the communication services or facilities enumerated in the following table a tax equal to the percent of the amount so paid as is specified in such table:

Taxable service	Rate of tax Percent
Local telephone service	10
Long distance telephone service	10
Telegraph service	10
Leased wire, teletypewriter or talking circuit special service	10
Wire and equipment service	8

The taxes imposed by this section shall be paid by the person paying for the services or facilities.

P.L. 85-159, §133(b), provides:

(b) Effective Date.—

(1) Subject to the provisions of paragraph (2), the amendment made by subsection (a) shall apply with respect to amounts paid on or after the effective date prescribed in section 1(c) of this Act [1-1-59] for services rendered on or after such date.

(2) The amendment made by subsection (a) shall not apply with respect to amounts paid pursuant to bills rendered before the effective date prescribed in section 1(c) of this Act [1-1-59]. In the case of amounts paid pursuant to bills rendered on or after such date for services for which no previous bill was rendered, such amendments shall apply except with respect to such services as were rendered more than 2 months before such date. In the case of services rendered more than 2 months before such date the provisions of subchapter B of chapter 33 of the Internal Revenue Code of 1954 in effect at the time such services were rendered shall apply to the amounts paid for such services.

[Sec. 4251(b)]

(b) DEFINITIONS.—For purposes of subsection (a)—

(1) COMMUNICATIONS SERVICES.—The term "communications services" means—

(A) local telephone service;

(B) toll telephone service; and

(C) teletypewriter exchange service.

(2) APPLICABLE PERCENTAGE.—The term "applicable percentage" means 3 percent.

Amendments

• **1990, Omnibus Budget Reconciliation Act of 1990 (P.L. 101-508)**

P.L. 101-508, §11217(a):

Amended Code Sec. 4251(b)(2) by striking "percent;" and all that follows and inserting "percent." **Effective** 11-5-90. Prior to amendment, Code Sec. 4251(b)(2) read as follows:

(2) APPLICABLE PERCENTAGE.—The term "applicable percentage" means 3 percent; except that, with respect to amounts paid pursuant to bills first rendered after 1990, the applicable percentage shall be zero.

• **1987, Revenue Act of 1987 (P.L. 100-203)**

P.L. 100-203, §10501:

Amended Code Sec. 4251(b)(2). **Effective** 12-22-87. Prior to amendment, Code Sec. 4251(b)(2) read as follows:

(2) APPLICABLE PERCENTAGE.—The term "applicable percentage" means—

With respect to amounts paid pursuant to bills first rendered:	The applicable percentage is:
During 1983, 1984, 1985, 1986, or 1987	3
During 1988 or thereafter	0

• **1986, Tax Reform Act of 1986 (P.L. 99-514)**

P.L. 99-514, §1801(b):

Amended Code Sec. 4251(b)(2) by inserting "1985," after "1984," in the table contained in such section. **Effective** as if included in the provision of P.L. 98-369 to which it relates.

EXCISE TAXES—COMMUNICATIONS

- **1984, Deficit Reduction Act of 1984 (P.L. 98-369)**

P.L. 98-369, § 26:

Amended Code Sec. 4251(b)(2) by striking out the table therein and inserting a new table. **Effective** 7-18-84. Prior to amendment, the table read as follows:

With respect to amounts paid pursuant to bills first rendered:	The percentage is
During 1983, 1984, or 1985	3
During 1986 or thereafter	0

- **1982, Tax Equity and Fiscal Responsibility Act of 1982 (P.L. 97-248)**

P.L. 97-248, § 282(a):

Amended Code Sec. 4251(b). **Effective** with respect to amounts paid for communications services pursuant to bills first rendered after 12-31-82. Prior to amendment, Code Sec. 4251(b) read as follows:

(b) TERMINATION OF TAX.—The tax imposed by subsection (a) shall not apply to amounts paid pursuant to bills first rendered on or after January 1, 1985.

- **1981, Economic Recovery Tax Act of 1981 (P.L. 97-34)**

P.L. 97-34, § 821(b):

Amended Code Sec. 4251(b) by striking out "January 1, 1983" and inserting "January 1, 1985". **Effective** 8-13-81.

- **1980, Omnibus Reconciliation Act of 1980 (P.L. 96-499)**

P.L. 96-499, § 1151(b):

Amended Code Sec. 4251(b) by striking out "January 1, 1982" and inserting in lieu thereof "January 1, 1983".

- **1970, Excise, Estate, and Gift Tax Adjustment Act of 1970 (P.L. 91-614)**

P.L. 91-614, § 201(b)(2):

Amended Code Sec. 4251(b) by substituting "January 1, 1982" for "January 1, 1974".

- **1969, Tax Reform Act of 1969 (P.L. 91-172)**

P.L. 91-172, § 702(b)(3):

Amended Code Sec. 4251(b) by substituting "January 1, 1974" for "January 1, 1973".

- **1968, Revenue and Expenditure Control Act of 1968 (P.L. 90-364)**

P.L. 90-364, § 105(b)(2):

Amended Code Sec. 4251(b) by substituting "January 1, 1973" for "January 1, 1969." **Effective** 4-30-68.

- **1965, Excise Tax Reduction Act of 1965 (P.L. 89-44)**

P.L. 89-44, § 302:

Amended Code Sec. 4251(b). Prior to amendment, Code Sec. 4251(b) read as follows:

(b) Termination of Tax on General Telephone Service.—

(1) In General.—Effective as provided in paragraph (2), the tax imposed by this section on amounts paid for general telephone service shall cease to apply.

(2) Effective date.—

(A) Subject to the provisions of subparagraph (B), paragraph (1) shall apply with respect to amounts paid on or after July 1, 1965, for services rendered on or after such date.

(B) Paragraph (1) shall not apply with respect to amounts paid pursuant to bills rendered before July 1, 1965. In the case of amounts paid pursuant to bills rendered on or after such date for services for which no previous bill was rendered, paragraph (1) shall apply except with respect to such services as were rendered more than 2 months before such date. Paragraph (1) shall not apply with respect to amounts paid for services rendered more than 2 months before such date.

The amendment applies to amounts paid pursuant to bills rendered on or after January 1, 1966, for services rendered on or after such date. In the case of amounts paid pursuant to bills rendered on or after January 1, 1966, for services which were rendered before such date and for which no previous bill was rendered, such amendments shall apply except with respect to such services as were rendered more than 2 months before such date. In the case of services rendered more than 2 months before such date, the provisions of subchapter B of chapter 33 of the Code in effect at the time such services were rendered shall apply to the amounts paid for such services.

- **1964, Excise Tax Rate Extension Act of 1964 (P.L. 88-348)**

P.L. 88-348, § 2(a)(2):

Amended Code Sec. 4251(b)(2) by substituting "1965" for "1964" wherever it appeared.

- **1963, Tax Rate Extension Act of 1963 (P.L. 88-52)**

P.L. 88-52, § 3(a)(2):

Amended Code Sec. 4251(b)(2) by substituting "1964" for "1963" wherever it appeared.

- **1962, Tax Rate Extension Act of 1962 (P.L. 87-508)**

P.L. 87-508, § 3(a)(2):

Amended Code Sec. 4251(b)(2) by substituting "1963" for "1962" wherever it appeared.

- **1961, Tax Rate Extension Act of 1961 (P.L. 87-72)**

P.L. 87-72, § 3(a)(2):

Amended Code Sec. 4251(b)(2) by substituting "1962" for "1961" wherever it appeared.

- **1960, Public Debt and Tax Rate Extension Act of 1960 (P.L. 86-564)**

P.L. 86-564, § 202(a):

Amended 1954 Code Sec. 4251(b)(2) by striking out "1960" wherever it appeared and by substituting "1961".

- **1959, Tax Rate Extension Act of 1959 (P.L. 86-75)**

P.L. 86-75, § 5:

Amended 1954 Code Sec. 4251 by adding subsection (b).

[Sec. 4251(c)]

(c) SPECIAL RULE.—For purposes of subsections (a) and (b), in the case of communications services rendered before November 1 of a calendar year for which a bill has not been rendered before the close of such year, a bill shall be treated as having been first rendered on December 31 of such year.

Amendments

- **1968, Revenue and Expenditure Control Act of 1968 (P.L. 90-364)**

P.L. 90-364, § 105(b)(2):

Amended Code Sec. 4251(c). **Effective** 4-30-68. Prior to amendment, Sec. 4251(c) read as follows:

(c) Special Rule.—For purposes of subsection (a), in the case of communications services rendered before March 1, 1968, for which a bill has not been rendered before May 1, 1968, a bill shall be treated as having been first rendered on April 30, 1968. For purposes of subsections (a) and (b), in the case of communications services rendered after February 29, 1968, and before November 1, 1968, for which a bill has not been rendered before January 1, 1969, a bill shall be treated as having been first rendered on December 31, 1968.

- **1968 (P.L. 90-285)**

P.L. 90-285:

Amended Code Sec. 4251(c) by substituting "March 1, 1968" for "February 1, 1968", "May 1, 1968" for "April 1, 1968", "April 30, 1968" for "March 31, 1968", and "February 29, 1968" for "January 31, 1968". **Effective** as of 3-31-68.

- **1966, Tax Adjustment Act of 1966 (P.L. 89-368)**

P.L. 89-368, § 202(a)(2):

Amended Code Sec. 4251(c). For **effective** date, see amendment note for Code Sec. 4251(a). Prior to amendment, Code Sec. 4251(c) read as follows:

(c) Special Rule.—For purposes of subsections (a) and (b), in the case of communication services rendered before November 1 of any calendar year for which a bill has not been rendered before the close of such year, a bill shall be treated as having been first rendered during such year.

- **1965, Excise Tax Reduction Act of 1965 (P.L. 89-44)**

P.L. 89-44, § 302:

Added subsection (c) of Sec. 4251. **Effective** 1-1-66.

[Sec. 4251(d)]

(d) TREATMENT OF PREPAID TELEPHONE CARDS.—

(1) IN GENERAL.—For purposes of this subchapter, in the case of communications services acquired by means of a prepaid telephone card—

(A) the face amount of such card shall be treated as the amount paid for such communications services, and

(B) that amount shall be treated as paid when the card is transferred by any telecommunications carrier to any person who is not such a carrier.

(2) DETERMINATION OF FACE AMOUNT IN ABSENCE OF SPECIFIED DOLLAR AMOUNT.—In the case of any prepaid telephone card which entitles the user other than to a specified dollar amount of use, the face amount shall be determined under regulations prescribed by the Secretary.

(3) PREPAID TELEPHONE CARD.—For purposes of this subsection, the term "prepaid telephone card" means any card or any other similar arrangement which permits its holder to obtain communications services and pay for such services in advance.

EXCISE TAXES—COMMUNICATIONS

Amendments

• **1998, IRS Restructuring and Reform Act of 1998 (P.L. 105-206)**

P.L. 105-206, §6010(i):

Amended Code Sec. 4251(d)(3) by striking "other similar arrangement" and inserting "any other similar arrangement". **Effective** as if included in the provision of P.L. 105-34 to which it relates [**effective** for amounts paid in calendar months beginning after 10-4-97.—CCH].

• **1997, Taxpayer Relief Act of 1997 (P.L. 105-34)**

P.L. 105-34, §1034(a):

Amended Code Sec. 4251 by adding at the end a new subsection (d). **Effective** for amounts paid in calendar months beginning more than 60 days after 8-5-97.

[Sec. 4252]

SEC. 4252. DEFINITIONS.

[Sec. 4252(a)]

(a) LOCAL TELEPHONE SERVICE.—For purposes of this subchapter, the term "local telephone service" means—

(1) the access to a local telephone system, and the privilege of telephonic quality communication with substantially all persons having telephone or radio telephone stations constituting a part of such local telephone system, and

(2) any facility or service provided in connection with a service described in paragraph (1).

The term "local telephone service" does not include any service which is a "toll telephone service" or a "private communication service" as defined in subsections (b) and (d).

[Sec. 4252(b)]

(b) TOLL TELEPHONE SERVICE.—For purposes of this subchapter, the term "toll telephone service" means—

(1) a telephonic quality communication for which (A) there is a toll charge which varies in amount with the distance and elapsed transmission time of each individual communication and (B) the charge is paid within the United States, and

(2) a service which entitles the subscriber, upon payment of a periodic charge (determined as a flat amount or upon the basis of total elapsed transmission time), to the privilege of an unlimited number of telephonic communications to or from all or a substantial portion of the persons having telephone or radio telephone stations in a specified area which is outside the local telephone system area in which the station provided with this service is located.

[Sec. 4252(c)]

(c) TELETYPEWRITER EXCHANGE SERVICE.—For purposes of this subchapter, the term "teletypewriter exchange service" means the access from a teletypewriter or other data station to the teletypewriter exchange system of which such station is a part, and the privilege of intercommunication by such station with substantially all persons having teletypewriter or other data stations constituting a part of the same teletypewriter exchange system, to which the subscriber is entitled upon payment of a charge or charges (whether such charge or charges are determined as a flat periodic amount, on the basis of distance and elapsed transmission time, or in some other manner). The term "teletypewriter exchange service" does not include any service which is "local telephone service" as defined in subsection (a).

[Sec. 4252(d)]

(d) PRIVATE COMMUNICATION SERVICE.—For purposes of this subchapter, the term "private communication service" means—

(1) the communication service furnished to a subscriber which entitles the subscriber—

(A) to exclusive or priority use of any communication channel or groups of channels, or

(B) to the use of an intercommunication system for the subscriber's stations,

regardless of whether such channel, groups of channels, or intercommunication system may be connected through switching with a service described in subsection (a), (b), or (c),

(2) switching capacity, extension lines and stations, or other associated services which are provided in connection with, and are necessary or unique to the use of, channels or systems described in paragraph (1), and

(3) the channel mileage which connects a telephone station located outside a local telephone system area with a central office in such local telephone system,

except that such term does not include any communication service unless a separate charge is made for such service.

Amendments

• **1968, Revenue and Expenditure Control Act of 1968 (P.L. 90-364)**

P.L. 90-364, §105(b)(3), as amended by P.L. 91-172, §702(b)(3), and by P.L. 91-614, §201(b)(3):

Repealed Subchapter B of Chapter 33. **Effective** 1-1-82. See amendment note for §105(b)(3) following Code Sec. 4251(a).

[Note: The communications excise tax was subsequently extended by various tax acts during the 1980's and made permanent by P.L. 101-508. Thus, its repeal, as noted above, never took effect.—CCH.]

• **1965, Excise Tax Reduction Act of 1965 (P.L. 89-44)**

P.L. 89-44, §302:

Amended Code Sec. 4252. For the **effective** date, see Act Sec. 701(a)(2)(A), below. Prior to amendment, Code Sec. 4252 read as follows:

SEC. 4252. DEFINITIONS.

(a) General Telephone Service.—For purposes of this subchapter, the term "general telephone service" means any telephone or radio telephone service furnished in connection with any fixed or mobile telephone or radio telephone station which may be connected (directly or indirectly) to an exchange operated by a person engaged in the business of furnishing communication service, if by means of such connection communication may be established with any other fixed or mobile telephone or radio telephone station. Without limiting the preceding sentence, any service described therein shall be treated as including the use of—

(1) any private branch exchange (and any fixed or mobile telephone or radio telephone station connected, directly or indirectly, with such an exchange), and

(2) any tie line or extension line.

The term "general telephone service" does not include any service which is toll telephone service or wire and equipment service.

(b) Toll Telephone Service.—For purposes of this subchapter, the term "toll telephone service" means a telephone or radio telephone message or conversation for which (1) there is a toll charge, and (2) the charge is paid within the United States.

(c) Telegraph Service.—For purposes of this subchapter, the term "telegraph service" means a telegram, cable, or radio dispatch or message for which the charge is paid within the United States.

(d) Teletypewriter Exchange Service.—For purposes of this subchapter, the term "teletypewriter exchange service" means any service where a teletypewriter (or similar device) may be connected (directly or indirectly) to an exchange operated by a person engaged in the business of furnishing communication service, if by means of such connection communication may be established with any other teletypewriter (or similar device).

(e) Wire Mileage Service.—For purposes of this subchapter, the term "wire mileage service" means—

(1) any telephone or radiotelephone service not used in the conduct of a trade or business, and

(2) any other wire or radio circuit service not used in the conduct of a trade or business,

not included in any other subsection of this section; except that such term does not include service used exclusively in furnishing wire and equipment service.

(f) Wire and Equipment Service.—For purposes of this subchapter, the term "wire and equipment service" includes stock quotation and information services, burglar alarm or fire alarm service, and all other similar services (whether or not oral transmission is involved). Such term does not include teletypewriter exchange service.

P.L. 89-44, §701(a)(2)(A), provides:

(A) The amendments made by section 302 shall apply to amounts paid pursuant to bills rendered on or after January 1, 1966, for services rendered on or after such date. In the case of amounts paid pursuant to bills rendered on or after January 1, 1966, for services which were rendered before such date and for which no previous bill was rendered, such amendments shall apply except with respect to such services as were rendered more than 2 months before such date. In the case of services rendered more than 2 months before such date, the provisions of subchapter B of chapter 33 of the Code in effect at the time such services were rendered shall apply to the amounts paid for such services.

EXCISE TAXES—COMMUNICATIONS

• **1962, Tax Rate Extension Act of 1962 (P.L. 87-508)**

P.L. 87-508, §4(a):

Amended Code Sec. 4252(e). **Effective** 1-1-63. Prior to amendment, Code Sec. 4252(e) read as follows:

(e) Wire Mileage Service.—For purposes of this subchapter, the term "wire mileage service" means—

(1) any telephone or radio telephone service, and

(2) any other wire or radio circuit service,

not included in any other subsection of this section; except that such term does not include service used exclusively in furnishing wire and equipment service.

• **1958, Excise Tax Technical Changes Act of 1958 (P.L. 85-859)**

P.L. 85-859, §133(a):

Amended Code Sec. 4252. For the **effective** date, see Act Sec. 133(b), below. Prior to amendment, Code Sec. 4252 read as follows:

SEC. 4252. DEFINITIONS.

(a) LOCAL TELEPHONE SERVICE.—As used in section 4251 the term, "local telephone service" means any telephone service not taxable as long distance telephone service; leased wire, teletypewriter or talking circuit special service; or wire and equipment service. Amounts paid for the installation of instruments, wires, poles, switchboards, apparatus, and equipment shall not be considered amounts paid for service. This subsection shall not be construed as defining as local telephone service, amounts paid for services and facilities which are exempted from other communication taxes by section 4253(b).

(b) LONG DISTANCE TELEPHONE SERVICE.—As used in section 4251 the term "long distance telephone service" means a telephone or radio telephone message or conversation for which the toll charge is more than 24 cents and for which the charge is paid within the United States.

(c) Telegraph Service.—As used in section 4251 the term "telegraph service" means a telegraph, cable, or radio dispatch or message for which the charge is paid within the United States.

(d) Leased Wire, Teletypewriter or Talking Circuit Special Service.—As used in section 4251 the term "leased wire, teletypewriter or talking circuit special service" does not include any service used exclusively in rendering a service taxable as wire and equipment service. The tax imposed by section 4251 with respect to a leased wire, teletypewriter or talking circuit special service shall apply whether or not the wires or services are within a local exchange area.

(e) Wire and Equipment Service.—As used in section 4251 the term "wire and equipment service" shall include stock quotation and information services, burglar alarm or fire alarm service, and all other similar services, but not including service described in subsection (d) of this section. The tax imposed by section 4251 with respect to wire and equipment service shall apply whether or not the wires or services are within a local exchange area.

P.L. 85-859, §133(b), provides:

(b) Effective Date.—

(1) Subject to the provisions of paragraph (2), the amendment made by subsection (a) shall apply with respect to amounts paid on or after the effective date prescribed in section 1(c) of this Act [1-1-59] for services rendered on or after such date.

(2) The amendment made by subsection (a) shall not apply with respect to amounts paid pursuant to bills rendered before the effective date prescribed in section 1(c) of this Act [1-1-59]. In the case of amounts paid pursuant to bills rendered on or after such date for services for which no previous bill was rendered, such amendments shall apply except with respect to such services as were rendered more than 2 months before such date. In the case of services rendered more than 2 months before such date the provisions of subchapter B of chapter 33 of the Internal Revenue Code of 1954 in effect at the time such services were rendered shall apply to the amounts paid for such services.

[Sec. 4253]

SEC. 4253. EXEMPTIONS.

[Sec. 4253(a)]

(a) CERTAIN COIN-OPERATED SERVICE.—Services paid for by inserting coins in coin-operated telephones available to the public shall not be subject to the tax imposed by section 4251 with respect to local telephone service, or with respect to toll telephone service if the charge for such toll telephone service is less than 25 cents; except that where such coin-operated telephone service is furnished for a guaranteed amount, the amounts paid under such guarantee plus any fixed monthly or other periodic charge shall be subject to the tax.

[Sec. 4253(b)]

(b) NEWS SERVICES.—No tax shall be imposed under section 4251, except with respect to local telephone service, on any payment received from any person for services used in the collection of news for the public press, or a news ticker service furnishing a general news service similar to that of the public press, or radio broadcasting, or in the dissemination of news through the public press, or a news ticker service furnishing a general news service similar to that of the public press, or by means of radio broadcasting, if the charge for such service is billed in writing to such person.

[Sec. 4253(c)]

(c) INTERNATIONAL, ETC., ORGANIZATIONS.—No tax shall be imposed under section 4251 on any payment received for services furnished to an international organization, or to the American National Red Cross.

[Sec. 4253(d)]

(d) SERVICEMEN IN COMBAT ZONE.—No tax shall be imposed under section 4251 on any payment received for any toll telephone service which originates within a combat zone, as defined in section 112, from a member of the Armed Forces of the United States performing service in such combat zone, as determined under such section, provided a certificate, setting forth such facts as the Secretary or his delegate may by regulations prescribe, is furnished to the person receiving such payment.

Amendments

• **2017, Tax Cuts and Jobs Act (P.L. 115-97)**

P.L. 115-97, §11026, provides:

For a special rule, see Act Sec. 11026 in the amendment notes for Code Sec. 112(c).

• **1999 (P.L. 106-21)**

P.L. 106-21, §1(a)(6), (b) and (d)(1), provide:

SECTION 1. AVAILABILITY OF CERTAIN TAX BENEFITS FOR SERVICES AS PART OF OPERATION ALLIED FORCE.

(a) GENERAL RULE.—For purposes of the following provisions of the Internal Revenue Code of 1986, a qualified hazardous duty area shall be treated in the same manner as if it were a combat zone (as determined under section 112 of such Code):

* * *

(6) Section 4253(d) (relating to the taxation of phone service originating from a combat zone from members of the Armed Forces).

* * *

(b) QUALIFIED HAZARDOUS DUTY AREA.—For purposes of this section, the term "qualified hazardous duty area" means any area of the Federal Republic of Yugoslavia (Serbia/Montenegro), Albania, the Adriatic Sea, and the northern Ionian Sea (above the 39th parallel) during the period (which includes the date of the enactment of this Act) that any member of the Armed Forces of the United States is entitled to special pay under section 310 of title 37, United States Code (relating to special pay: duty subject to hostile fire or imminent danger) for services performed in such area.

* * *

(d) EFFECTIVE DATES.—

(1) IN GENERAL.—Except as provided in paragraph (2), this section shall take effect on March 24, 1999.

• **1996 (P.L. 104-117)**

P.L. 104-117, §1(a)(6), (b) and (e)(1), provide:

SECTION 1. TREATMENT OF CERTAIN INDIVIDUALS PERFORMING SERVICES IN CERTAIN HAZARDOUS DUTY AREAS.

(a) GENERAL RULE.—For purposes of the following provisions of the Internal Revenue Code of 1986, a qualified hazardous duty area shall be treated in the same manner as if it were a combat zone (as determined under section 112 of such Code):

* * *

(6) Section 4253(d) (relating to the taxation of phone service originating from a combat zone from members of the Armed Forces).

* * *

(b) QUALIFIED HAZARDOUS DUTY AREA.—For purposes of this section, the term "qualified hazardous duty area" means Bosnia and Herzegovina, Croatia, or Macedonia, if as of the date of the enactment of this section any member of the Armed Forces of the United States is entitled to special pay under section 310 of title 37, United States Code (relating to special pay; duty subject to hostile fire or imminent danger) for services performed in such country. Such term includes any such country only during the period such entitlement is in effect. Solely for purposes of applying section 7508 of the Internal Revenue Code of 1986, in the case of an individual who is performing services as part of Operation Joint Endeavor outside the United States while deployed away from such individual's permanent duty station, the term "qualified hazardous duty area" includes, during the period for which such entitlement is in effect, any area in which such services are performed.

* * *

(e) EFFECTIVE DATE.—

(1) IN GENERAL.—Except as provided in paragraph (2), the provisions of and amendments made by this section shall take effect on November 21, 1995.

EXCISE TAXES—COMMUNICATIONS

[Sec. 4253(e)]

(e) ITEMS OTHERWISE TAXED.—Only one payment of tax under section 4251 shall be required with respect to the tax on any service, notwithstanding the lines or stations of one or more persons are used in furnishing such service.

[Sec. 4253(f)]

(f) COMMON CARRIERS AND COMMUNICATIONS COMPANIES.—No tax shall be imposed under section 4251 on the amount paid for any toll telephone service described in section 4252(b)(2) to the extent that the amount so paid is for use by a common carrier, telephone or telegraph company, or radio broadcasting station or network in the conduct of its business as such.

Amendments

- **1965, Excise Tax Reduction Act of 1965 (P.L. 89-44)**

P.L. 89-44, §302:

Amended Code Sec. 4253, including Code Sec. 4253(f). See amendment note for §302 following Code Sec. 4253(g).

- **1959 (P.L. 86-344)**

P.L. 86-344, §4(a):

Amended Code Sec. 4253(f). **Effective** 1-1-59. Prior to amendment, Code Sec. 4253(f) read as follows:

(f) Special Wire Service in Company Business.—No tax shall be imposed under section 4251 on the amount paid for so much of any wire mileage service or wire and equipment service as is used in the conduct, by a common carrier or a telephone or telegraph company or radio broadcasting station or network, of its business as such.

P.L. 86-344, §4(b), provides:

(b) Effective Date.—

(1) Subject to the provisions of paragraph (2), the amendment made by subsection (a) shall apply with respect to amounts paid on or after January 1, 1959, for services rendered on or after such date.

(2) The amendment made by subsection (a) shall not apply with respect to amounts paid pursuant to bills rendered before January 1, 1959. In the case of amounts paid pursuant to bills rendered on or after such date for services for which no bill was rendered before such date, such amendment shall apply except with respect to such services as were rendered more than 2 months before such date. In the case of services rendered more than 2 months before such date, the provisions of subchapter B of chapter 33 of the Internal Revenue Code of 1954 in effect at the time such services were rendered shall apply to the amounts paid for such services.

[Sec. 4253(g)]

(g) INSTALLATION CHARGES.—No tax shall be imposed under section 4251 on so much of any amount paid for the installation of any instrument, wire, pole, switchboard, apparatus, or equipment as is properly attributable to such installation.

Amendments

- **1965, Excise Tax Reduction Act of 1965 (P.L. 89-44)**

P.L. 89-44, §302:

Amended Sec. 4253. **Effective** for amounts paid pursuant to bills rendered on or after 1-1-66, for services rendered on or after such date. In the case of amounts paid pursuant to bills rendered on or after 1-1-66, for services which were rendered before such date and for which no previous bill was rendered, such amendments shall apply except with respect to such services as were rendered more than 2 months before such date. In the case of services rendered more than 2 months before such date, the provisions of subchapter B of chapter 33 of the Code in effect at the time such services were rendered shall apply to the amounts paid for such services. Prior to amendment, Sec. 4253 read as follows:

SEC. 4253. EXEMPTIONS.

(a) Certain Coin-Operated Service.—Services paid for by inserting coins in coin-operated telephones available to the public shall not be subject to the tax imposed by section 4251 with respect to general telephone service, or with respect to toll telephone service or telegraph service if the charge for such toll telephone service or telegraph service is less than 25 cents; except that where such coin-operated telephone service is furnished for a guaranteed amount, the amounts paid under such guarantee plus any fixed monthly or other periodic charge shall be subject to the tax.

(b) News Services.—No tax shall be imposed under section 4251, except with respect to general telephone service, on any payment received from any person for services used in the collection of news for the public press, or a news ticker service furnishing a general news service similar to that of the public press, or radio broadcasting, or in the dissemination of news through the public press, or a news ticker service furnishing a general news service similar to that of the public press, or by means of radio broadcasting, if the charge for such services is billed in writing to such person.

(c) Certain Organizations.—No tax shall be imposed under section 4251 on any payment received for services furnished to an international organization, or to the American National Red Cross.

(d) Servicemen in Combat Zone.—No tax shall be imposed under section 4251 on any payment received for any toll telephone service which originates within a combat zone, as defined in section 112, from a member of the Armed Forces of the United States performing service in such combat zone, as determined under such section, provided a certificate, setting forth such facts as the Secretary or his delegate may by regulations prescribe, is furnished to the person receiving such payment.

(e) For Items Otherwise Taxed.—Only one payment of tax under section 4251 shall be required with respect to the tax on toll telephone service, telegraph service, or teletypewriter exchange service, notwithstanding the lines or stations of one or more persons are used in furnishing such service.

(f) Common Carriers and Communications Companies.—No tax shall be imposed under section 4251 on the amount paid for—

(1) any wire mileage service or wire and equipment service; or

(2) the use of any telephone or radio telephone line or channel which constitutes general telephone service (within the meaning of section 4252(a)), but only if such line or channel connects stations between any two of which there would otherwise be a toll charge,

to the extent that the amount so paid is for use by a common carrier, telephone or telegraph company, or radio broadcasting station or network in the conduct of its business as such.

(g) Installation Charges.—No tax shall be imposed under section 4251 on so much of any amount paid for the installation of any instrument, wire, pole, switchboard, apparatus, or equipment as is properly attributable to such installation.

(h) Terminal Facilities in Case of Wire Mileage Service.—No tax shall be imposed under section 4251 on so much of any amount paid for wire mileage service as is paid for, and properly attributable to, the use of any sending or receiving set or device which is station terminal equipment.

(i) Certain Interior Communication Systems.—No tax shall be imposed under section 4251 on any amount paid for wire mileage service or wire and equipment service, if such service is rendered through the use of an interior communication system. For purposes of the preceding sentence, the term 'interior communication system' means any system—

(1) no part of which is situated off the premises of the subscriber, and which may not be connected (directly or indirectly) with any communication system any part of which is situated off the premises of the subscriber, or

(2) which is situated exclusively in a vehicle of the subscriber.

(j) Certain Private Communications Services.—No tax shall be imposed under section 4251 on any amount paid for the use of any telephone or radio-telephone line or channel which constitutes general telephone service (within the meaning of section 4252(a)), if—

(1) such line or channel is furnished between specified locations in different States or between specified locations in different counties, municipalities, or similar political subdivisions of a State, and

(2) such use is in the conduct of a trade or business.

- **1962, Tax Rate Extension Act of 1962 (P.L. 87-508)**

P.L. 87-508, §4(b):

Added Code Sec. 4253(j). **Effective** 1-1-63.

- **1958, Excise Tax Technical Changes Act of 1958 (P.L. 85-859)**

P.L. 85-859, §133(a):

Amended Code Sec. 4253. For the **effective** date, see Act Sec. 133(b), below. Prior to amendment, Code Sec. 4253 read as follows:

SEC. 4253. EXEMPTIONS.

(a) Certain Coin-Operated Service.—Services paid for by inserting coins in coin-operated telephones available to the public shall not be subject to the tax imposed by section 4251 with respect to local telephone service, except that where such coin-operated telephone service is furnished for a guaranteed amount, the amounts paid under such guarantee plus any fixed monthly or other periodic charge shall be subject to the tax.

(b) News Services.—No tax shall be imposed under section 4251, except with respect to local telephone service, upon any payment received from any person for services or facilities utilized in the collection of news for the public press, or a news ticker service furnishing a general news service similar to that of the public press, or radio broadcasting, or in the dissemination of news through the public press, or a news ticker service furnishing a general news service similar to that of the public press, or by means of radio broadcasting, if the charge for such services or facilities is billed in writing to such person.

(c) Certain Organizations.—No tax shall be imposed under section 4251 upon any payment received for services or facilities furnished to an international organization, or any organization created by act of Congress to act in matters of relief under the treaty of Geneva of August 22, 1864.

(d) Servicemen in Combat Zone.—No tax shall be imposed under section 4251 with respect to long distance telephone service upon any payment received for any telephone or radio telephone message which originates within a combat zone, as defined in section 112, from a member of the Armed Forces of the United States performing service in such combat zone, as determined under such section, provided a certificate, setting forth such facts as the Secretary or his delegate may by regulations prescribe, is furnished to the person receiving such payment.

(e) For Items Otherwise Taxed.—Only one payment of tax under section 4251 shall be required with respect to the tax on long distance telephone service or telegraph service notwithstanding the lines or stations of one or more persons are used in the transmission of such dispatch, message or conversation.

(f) Special Wire Service in Company Business.—No tax shall be imposed under section 4251 on the amount paid for so much of the service described in sections 4252(d) and (e) as is utilized in the conduct, by a common carrier or a telephone or telegraph company or radio broadcasting station or network, of its business as such.

P.L. 85-859, §133(b), provides:

(b) Effective Date.—

EXCISE TAXES—COMMUNICATIONS

(1) Subject to the provisions of paragraph (2), the amendment made by subsection (a) shall apply with respect to amounts paid on or after the effective date prescribed in section 1(c) of this Act [1-1-59] for services rendered on or after such date.

(2) The amendment made by subsection (a) shall not apply with respect to amounts paid pursuant to bills rendered before the effective date prescribed in section 1(c) of this Act [1-1-59]. In the case of amounts paid pursuant to bills rendered on or after such date for services for which no previous bill was rendered, such amendments shall apply except with respect to such services as were rendered more than 2 months before such date. In the case of services rendered more than 2 months before such date the provisions of subchapter B of chapter 33 of the Internal Revenue Code of 1954 in effect at the time such services were rendered shall apply to the amounts paid for such services.

[Sec. 4253(h)]

(h) NONPROFIT HOSPITALS.—No tax shall be imposed under section 4251 on any amount paid by a nonprofit hospital for services furnished to such organization. For purposes of this subsection, the term "nonprofit hospital" means a hospital referred to in section 170(b)(1)(A)(iii) which is exempt from income tax under section 501(a).

Amendments

• **1969, Tax Reform Act of 1969 (P.L. 91-172)**

P.L. 91-172, §101(j)(27):

Amended Code Sec. 4253(h) by substituting "section 170(b)(1)(A)(iii)" for "section 503(b)(5)". **Effective** 1-1-70.

• **1966, Tax Adjustment Act of 1966 (P.L. 89-368)**

P.L. 89-368, §202(b):

Added Code Sec. 4253(h). **Effective** with respect to amounts paid pursuant to bills first rendered on or after 4-1-66, for services rendered on or after such date. In the case of amounts paid pursuant to bills rendered on or after such date for services which were rendered before such date and for which no previous bill was rendered, the provision shall apply except with respect to such services as were rendered more than 2 months before such date. In the case of services rendered more than 2 months before such date, the provisions of subchapter B of chapter 33 of the Code in effect at the time such services were rendered, subject to the provision of section 701(b)(2) of the Excise Tax Reduction Act of 1965, shall apply to amounts paid for such services.

[Sec. 4253(i)]

(i) STATE AND LOCAL GOVERNMENTAL EXEMPTION.—Under regulations prescribed by the Secretary, no tax shall be imposed under section 4251 upon any payment received for services or facilities furnished to the government of any State, or any political subdivision thereof, or the District of Columbia.

Amendments

• **1976, Tax Reform Act of 1976 (P.L. 94-455)**

P.L. 94-455, §1904(a)(6):

Added Code Sec. 4253(i). **Effective** 2-1-77.

[Sec. 4253(j)]

(j) EXEMPTION FOR NONPROFIT EDUCATIONAL ORGANIZATIONS.—Under regulations prescribed by the Secretary, no tax shall be imposed under section 4251 on any amount paid by a nonprofit educational organization for services or facilities furnished to such organization. For purposes of this subsection, the term "nonprofit educational organization" means an educational organization described in section 170(b)(1)(A)(ii) which is exempt from income tax under section 501(a). The term also includes a school operated as an activity of an organization described in section 501(c)(3) which is exempt from income tax under section 501(a), if such school normally maintains a regular faculty and curriculum and normally has a regularly enrolled body of pupils or students in attendance at the place where its educational activities are regularly carried on.

Amendments

• **1976, Tax Reform Act of 1976 (P.L. 94-455)**

P.L. 94-455, §1904(a)(6):

Added Code Sec. 4253(j). **Effective** 2-1-77.

• **1968, Revenue and Expenditure Control Act of 1968 (P.L. 90-364)**

P.L. 90-364, §105(b)(3), as amended by P.L. 91-172, §702(b)(3), and by P.L. 91-614, §201(b)(3):

Repealed subchapter B of chapter 33. **Effective** 1-1-82. See amendment note for Act Sec. 105(b)(3) following Code Sec. 4251(a).

[Note: The communications excise tax was subsequently extended by various tax acts during the 1980's and made permanent by P.L. 101-508. Thus, its repeal, as noted above, never took effect.—CCH.]

[Sec. 4253(k)]

(k) EXEMPTION FOR QUALIFIED BLOOD COLLECTOR ORGANIZATIONS.—Under regulations provided by the Secretary, no tax shall be imposed under section 4251 on any amount paid by a qualified blood collector organization (as defined in section 7701(a)(49)) for services or facilities furnished to such organization.

Amendments

• **2006, Pension Protection Act of 2006 (P.L. 109-280)**

P.L. 109-280, §1207(c)(1):

Amended Code Sec. 4253 by redesignating subsection (k) as subsection (l) and inserting after subsection (j) a new subsection (k). **Effective** 1-1-2007.

[Sec. 4253(l)]

(l) FILING OF EXEMPTION CERTIFICATES.—

(1) IN GENERAL.—In order to claim an exemption under subsection (c), (h), (i), (j), or (k), a person shall provide to the provider of communications services a statement (in such form and manner as the Secretary may provide) certifying that such person is entitled to such exemption.

(2) DURATION OF CERTIFICATE.—Any statement provided under paragraph (1) shall remain in effect until—

(A) the provider of communications services has actual knowledge that the information provided in such statement is false, or

(B) such provider is notified by the Secretary that the provider of the statement is no longer entitled to an exemption described in paragraph (1).

If any information provided in such statement is no longer accurate, the person providing such statement shall inform the provider of communications services within 30 days of any change of information.

Amendments

• **2006, Pension Protection Act of 2006 (P.L. 109-280)**

P.L. 109-280, §1207(c)(1):

Amended Code Sec. 4253 by redesignating subsection (k) as subsection (l). **Effective** 1-1-2007.

P.L. 109-280, §1207(c)(2):

Amended Code Sec. 4253(l), as redesignated by Act Sec. 1207(c)(1), by striking "or (j)" and inserting "(j), or (k)". **Effective** 1-1-2007.

• **1990, Omnibus Budget Reconciliation Act of 1990 (P.L. 101-508)**

P.L. 101-508, §11217(c)(1):

Amended Code Sec. 4253 by adding at the end thereof a new subsection (k). **Effective** for any claim for exemption made after 11-5-90. For a special rule, see Act Sec. 11217(c)(2)(B), below.

P.L. 101-508, §11217(c)(2)(B), provides:

(B) DURATION OF EXISTING CERTIFICATES.—Any annual certificate of exemption effective on the date of the enactment of this Act shall remain effective until the end of the annual period.

Sec. 4253(h)

EXCISE TAXES—TRANSPORTATION OF PERSONS

[Sec. 4254]

SEC. 4254. COMPUTATION OF TAX.

[Sec. 4254(a)]

(a) GENERAL RULE.—If a bill is rendered the taxpayer for local telephone service or toll telephone service—

(1) the amount on which the tax with respect to such services shall be based shall be the sum of all charges for such services included in the bill; except that

(2) if the person who renders the bill groups individual items for purposes of rendering the bill and computing the tax, then (A) the amount on which the tax with respect to each such group shall be based shall be the sum of all items within that group, and (B) the tax on the remaining items not included in any such group shall be based on the charge for each item separately.

[Sec. 4254(b)]

(b) WHERE PAYMENT IS MADE FOR TOLL TELEPHONE SERVICE IN COIN-OPERATED TELEPHONES.—If the tax imposed by section 4251 with respect to toll telephone service is paid by inserting coins in coin-operated telephones, tax shall be computed to the nearest multiple of 5 cents, except that, where the tax is midway between multiples of 5 cents, the next higher multiple shall apply.

Amendments

• **1968, Revenue and Expenditure Control Act of 1968 (P.L. 90-364)**

P.L. 90-364, §105(b)(3), as amended by P.L. 91-172, §702(b)(3), and by P.L. 91-614, §201(b)(3):

Repealed Subchapter B of Chapter 33. **Effective** 1-1-82. See amendment note for §105(b)(3) following Code Sec. 4251(a).

[Note: The communications excise tax was subsequently extended by various tax acts during the 1980's and made permanent by P.L. 101-508. Thus, its repeal, as noted above, never took effect.—CCH.]

• **1965, Excise Tax Reduction Act of 1965 (P.L. 89-44)**

P.L. 89-44, §302:

Amended Code Sec. 4254. For the **effective** date, see Act Sec. 701(a)(2)(A), below. Prior to amendment, Code Sec. 4254 read as follows:

SEC. 4254. COMPUTATION OF TAX.

(a) General Rule.—If a bill is rendered the taxpayer for general telephone service, toll telephone service, or telegraph service—

(1) the amount on which the tax with respect to such services shall be based shall be the sum of all charges for such services included in the bill; except that

(2) if the person who renders the bill groups individual items for purposes of rendering the bill and computing the tax, then (A) the amount on which the tax with respect to each such group shall be based shall be the sum of all items within that group, and (B) the tax on the remaining items not included in any such group shall be based on the charge for each item separately.

(b) Where Payment Is Made for Toll Telephone Service or Telegraph Service in Coin-Operated Telephones.—If the tax imposed by section 4251 with respect to toll telephone service or telegraph service is paid by inserting coins in coin-operated telephones, tax shall be computed to the nearest multiple of 5 cents, except that where the tax is midway between multiples of 5 cents, the next higher multiple shall apply.

P.L. 89-44, §701(a)(2)(A), provides:

(A) The amendments made by section 302 shall apply to amounts paid pursuant to bills rendered on or after January 1, 1966, for services rendered on or after such date. In the case of amounts paid pursuant to bills rendered on or after January 1, 1966, for services which were rendered before such date and for which no previous bill was rendered, such amendments shall apply except with respect to such services as were rendered more than 2 months before such date. In the case of services rendered more than 2 months before such date, the provisions of subchapter B of chapter 33 of the Code in effect at the time such services were rendered shall apply to the amounts paid for such services.

• **1958, Excise Tax Technical Changes Act of 1958 (P.L. 85-859)**

P.L. 85-859, §133(a):

Amended Code Sec. 4254. For the **effective** date, see Act Sec. 133(b), below. Prior to amendment, Code Sec. 4254 read as follows:

SEC. 4254. COMPUTATION OF TAX.

(a) In General.—If a bill is rendered the taxpayer for telephone services or telegraph services with respect to which a tax is imposed by section 4251, the amount upon which the tax shall be based shall be the sum of all such charges included in the bill, and the tax shall not be based upon the charge for each item, separately, included in the bill.

(b) Where Payment Is Made for Long Distance Telephone Service or Telegraph Service in Coin-Operated Telephones.—If the tax imposed by section 4251 with respect to long distance telephone service or telegraph service is paid by inserting coins in coin-operated telephones, tax shall be computed to the nearest multiple of 5 cents, except that where the tax is midway between multiples of 5 cents, the next higher multiple shall apply.

P.L. 85-859, §133(b), provides:

(b) Effective Date.—

(1) Subject to the provisions of paragraph (2), the amendment made by subsection (a) shall apply with respect to amounts paid on or after the effective date prescribed in section 1(c) of this Act [1-1-59] for services rendered on or after such date.

(2) The amendment made by subsection (a) shall not apply with respect to amounts paid pursuant to bills rendered before the effective date prescribed in section 1(c) of this Act [1-1-59]. In the case of amounts paid pursuant to bills rendered on or after such date for services for which no previous bill was rendered, such amendments shall apply except with respect to such services as were rendered more than 2 months before such date. In the case of services rendered more than 2 months before such date the provisions of subchapter B of chapter 33 of the Internal Revenue Code of 1954 in effect at the time such services were rendered shall apply to the amounts paid for such services.

[Sec. 4254(c)]

(c) CERTAIN STATE AND LOCAL TAXES NOT INCLUDED.—For purposes of this subchapter, in determining the amounts paid for communications services, there shall not be included the amount of any State or local tax imposed on the furnishing or sale of such services, if the amount of such tax is separately stated in the bill.

Amendments

• **1977 (P.L. 95-172)**

P.L. 95-172, §2:

Added Code Sec. 4254(c). **Effective** with respect to amounts paid pursuant to bills first rendered on or after 1-1-78. For purposes of the preceding sentence, in the case of communications services rendered more than two months before 12-1-77, no bill shall be treated as having been first rendered on or after 1-1-78.

Subchapter C—Transportation by Air

Part I.   Persons.
Part II.   Property.
Part III.   Special provisions applicable to taxes on transportation by air.

PART I—PERSONS

Sec. 4261.   Imposition of tax.
Sec. 4262.   Definition of taxable transportation.
Sec. 4263.   Special rules.

[Sec. 4261]

SEC. 4261. IMPOSITION OF TAX.

[Sec. 4261(a)]

(a) IN GENERAL.—There is hereby imposed on the amount paid for taxable transportation of any person a tax equal to 7.5 percent of the amount so paid.

EXCISE TAXES—TRANSPORTATION OF PERSONS

Amendments

• **2020, Coronavirus Aid, Relief, and Economic Security (CARES) Act (P.L. 116-136)**

P.L. 116-136, § 4007(a) and (c), provides:

(a) TRANSPORTATION BY AIR.—In the case of any amount paid for transportation by air (including any amount treated as paid for transportation by air by reason of section 4261(e)(3) of the Internal Revenue Code of 1986) during the excise tax holiday period, no tax shall be imposed under section 4261 or 4271 of such Code. The preceding sentence shall not apply to amounts paid on or before the date of the enactment of this Act.

* * *

(c) EXCISE TAX HOLIDAY PERIOD.—For purposes of this section, the term "excise tax holiday period" means the period beginning after the date of the enactment of this section and ending before January 1, 2021.

• **1997, Taxpayer Relief Act of 1997 (P.L. 105-34)**

P.L. 105-34, § 1031(c)(1):

Amended Code Sec. 4261 by striking subsection (a) and inserting a new subsection (a). **Effective**, generally, for transportation beginning on or after 10-1-97. For special rules, see Act Sec. 1031(e)(2)(B) and (g)[(f)], below. Prior to being stricken, Code Sec. 4261(a) read as follows:

(a) IN GENERAL.—There is hereby imposed upon the amount paid for taxable transportation (as defined in section 4262) of any person a tax equal to 10 percent of the amount so paid. In the case of amounts paid outside of the United States for taxable transportation, the tax imposed by this subsection shall apply only if such transportation begins and ends in the United States.

P.L. 105-34, § 1031(e)(2)(B), provides:

(B) TREATMENT OF AMOUNTS PAID FOR TICKETS PURCHASED BEFORE OCTOBER 1, 1997.—The amendments made by subsection (c) shall not apply to amounts paid before October 1, 1997; except that—

(i) the amendment made to section 4261(c) of the Internal Revenue Code of 1986 shall apply to amounts paid more than 7 days after the date of the enactment of this Act for transportation beginning on or after October 1, 1997, and

(ii) the amendment made to section 4263(c) of such Code shall apply to the extent related to taxes imposed under the amendment made to such section 4261(c) on the amounts described in clause (i).

P.L. 105-34, § 1031(g)[(f)], provides:

(g)[(f)] DELAYED DEPOSITS OF AIRPORT TRUST FUND TAX REVENUES.—Notwithstanding section 6302 of the Internal Revenue Code of 1986—

(1) in the case of deposits of taxes imposed by section 4261 of such Code, the due date for any such deposit which would (but for this subsection) be required to be made after August 14, 1997, and before October 1, 1997, shall be October 10, 1997,

(2) in the case of deposits of taxes imposed by section 4261 of such Code, the due date for any such deposit which would (but for this subsection) be required to be made after August 14, 1998, and before October 1, 1998, shall be October 5, 1998, and

(3) in the case of deposits of taxes imposed by sections 4081(a)(2)(A)(ii), 4091, and 4271 of such Code, the due date for any such deposit which would (but for this subsection) be required to be made after July 31, 1998, and before October 1, 1998, shall be October 5, 1998.

• **1990, Omnibus Budget Reconciliation Act of 1990 (P.L. 101-508)**

P.L. 101-508, § 11213(a)(1):

Amended Code Sec. 4261(a) by striking "8 percent" and inserting "10 percent". **Effective** for transportation beginning after 11-30-90, but not for amounts paid on or before such date. However, see Act Sec. 11213(f) in the amendment notes following Code Sec. 4041(c).

• **1976, Tax Reform Act of 1976 (P.L. 94-455)**

P.L. 94-455, § 1904(a)(7)(A):

Struck out "which begins after June 30, 1970," after "of any person" in Code Sec. 4261(a). **Effective** 2-1-77.

[Sec. 4261(b)]

(b) DOMESTIC SEGMENTS OF TAXABLE TRANSPORTATION.—

(1) IN GENERAL.—There is hereby imposed on the amount paid for each domestic segment of taxable transportation by air a tax in the amount of $3.00.

(2) DOMESTIC SEGMENT.—For purposes of this section, the term "domestic segment" means any segment consisting of 1 takeoff and 1 landing and which is taxable transportation described in section 4262(a)(1).

(3) CHANGES IN SEGMENTS BY REASON OF REROUTING.—If—

(A) transportation is purchased between 2 locations on specified flights, and

(B) there is a change in the route taken between such 2 locations which changes the number of domestic segments, but there is no change in the amount charged for such transportation,

the tax imposed by paragraph (1) shall be determined without regard to such change in route.

Amendments

• **2018, Tax Technical Corrections Act of 2018 (P.L. 115-141)**

P.L. 115-141, § 401(b)(42), Div. U:

Amended Code Sec. 4261(b)(1) by striking "a tax in the amount" and all that follows and inserting "a tax in the amount of $3.00.". **Effective** 3-23-2018. For a special rule, see Act Sec. 401(e), Div. U, below. Prior to being stricken, "a tax in the amount" and all that follows in Code Sec. 4261(b)(1) read as follows:

a tax in the amount determined in accordance with the following table for the period in which the segment begins:

In the case of segments beginning:	The tax is:
After September 30, 1997, and before October 1, 1998	$1.00
After September 30, 1998, and before October 1, 1999	$2.00
After September 30, 1999, and before January 1, 2000	$2.25
During 2000	$2.50
During 2001	$2.75
During 2002 or thereafter	$3.00

P.L. 115-141, § 401(e), Div. U, provides:

(e) GENERAL SAVINGS PROVISION WITH RESPECT TO DEADWOOD PROVISIONS.—If—

(1) any provision amended or repealed by the amendments made by subsection (b) or (d) applied to—

(A) any transaction occurring before the date of the enactment of this Act,

(B) any property acquired before such date of enactment, or

(C) any item of income, loss, deduction, or credit taken into account before such date of enactment, and

(2) the treatment of such transaction, property, or item under such provision would (without regard to the amendments or repeals made by such subsection) affect the liability for tax for periods ending after such date of enactment,

nothing in the amendments or repeals made by this section shall be construed to affect the treatment of such transaction, property, or item for purposes of determining liability for tax for periods ending after such date of enactment.

• **1997, Taxpayer Relief Act of 1997 (P.L. 105-34)**

P.L. 105-34, § 1031(c)(1):

Amended Code Sec. 4261 by striking subsection (b) and inserting a new subsection (b). **Effective**, generally, for transportation beginning on or after 10-1-97. For special rules, see Act Sec. 1031(e)(2)(B), below, and Act Sec. 1031(g)[(f)] in the amendment notes following Code Sec. 4261(a). Prior to being stricken, Code Sec. 4261(b) read as follows:

(b) SEATS, BERTHS, ETC.—There is hereby imposed upon the amount paid for seating or sleeping accommodations in connection with transportation and with respect to which a tax is imposed by subsection (a), a tax equal to 10 percent of the amount so paid.

P.L. 105-34, § 1031(e)(2)(B), provides:

(B) TREATMENT OF AMOUNTS PAID FOR TICKETS PURCHASED BEFORE OCTOBER 1, 1997.—The amendments made by subsection (c) shall not apply to amounts paid before October 1, 1997; except that—

(i) the amendment made to section 4261(c) of the Internal Revenue Code of 1986 shall apply to amounts paid more than 7 days after the date of the enactment of this Act for transportation beginning on or after October 1, 1997, and

(ii) the amendment made to section 4263(c) of such Code shall apply to the extent related to taxes imposed under the amendment made to such section 4261(c) on the amounts described in clause (i).

• **1990, Omnibus Budget Reconciliation Act of 1990 (P.L. 101-508)**

P.L. 101-508, § 11213(a)(1):

Amended Code Sec. 4261(b) by striking "8 percent" and inserting "10 percent". **Effective** for transportation beginning after 11-30-90, but not for amounts paid on or before such date. However, see Act Sec. 11213(f) in the amendment notes following Code Sec. 4041(c).

• **1976, Tax Reform Act of 1976 (P.L. 94-455)**

P.L. 94-455, § 1904(a)(7)(A):

Struck out "which begins after June 30, 1970," after "transportation" in Code Sec. 4261(b). **Effective** 2-1-77.

[Sec. 4261(c)]

(c) USE OF INTERNATIONAL TRAVEL FACILITIES.—

(1) IN GENERAL.—There is hereby imposed a tax of $12.00 on any amount paid (whether within or without the United States) for any transportation of any person by air, if such transportation begins or ends in the United States.

(2) EXCEPTION FOR TRANSPORTATION ENTIRELY TAXABLE UNDER SUBSECTION (a).—This subsection shall not apply to any transportation all of which is taxable under subsection (a) (determined without regard to sections 4281 and 4282).

Sec. 4261(b)

EXCISE TAXES—TRANSPORTATION OF PERSONS

(3) SPECIAL RULE FOR ALASKA AND HAWAII.—In any case in which the tax imposed by paragraph (1) applies to a domestic segment beginning or ending in Alaska or Hawaii, such tax shall apply only to departures and shall be at the rate of $6.

Amendments

• **1997, Taxpayer Relief Act of 1997 (P.L. 105-34)**

P.L. 105-34, § 1031(c)(1):

Amended Code Sec. 4261 by striking subsection (c) and inserting a new subsection (c). **Effective**, generally, for transportation beginning on or after 10-1-97. For special rules, see Act Sec. 1031(e)(2)(B), below, and Act Sec. 1031(g)[(f)] in the amendment notes following Code Sec. 4261(a). Prior to being stricken, Code Sec. 4261(c) read as follows:

(c) USE OF INTERNATIONAL TRAVEL FACILITIES.—There is hereby imposed a tax of $6 upon any amount paid (whether within or without the United States) for any transportation of any person by air, if such transportation begins in the United States. This subsection shall not apply to any transportation all of which is taxable under subsection (a) (determined without regard to sections 4281 and 4282).

P.L. 105-34, § 1031(e)(2)(B), provides:

(B) TREATMENT OF AMOUNTS PAID FOR TICKETS PURCHASED BEFORE OCTOBER 1, 1997.—The amendments made by subsection (c) shall not apply to amounts paid before October 1, 1997; except that—

(i) the amendment made to section 4261(c) of the Internal Revenue Code of 1986 shall apply to amounts paid more than 7 days after the date of the enactment of this Act for transportation beginning on or after October 1, 1997, and

(ii) the amendment made to section 4263(c) of such Code shall apply to the extent related to taxes imposed under the amendment made to such section 4261(c) on the amounts described in clause (i).

• **1989, Omnibus Budget Reconciliation Act of 1989 (P.L. 101-239)**

P.L. 101-239, § 7503(a):

Amended Code Sec. 4261(c) by striking "$3" and inserting "$6". **Effective** for transportation beginning after 12-31-89, which was not paid for before such date.

• **1976, Tax Reform Act of 1976 (P.L. 94-455)**

P.L. 94-455, § 1904(a)(7)(B):

Struck out "and begins after June 30, 1970" at the end of the first sentence of Code Sec. 4261(c). **Effective** 2-1-77.

[Sec. 4261(d)]

(d) BY WHOM PAID.—Except as provided in section 4263(a), the taxes imposed by this section shall be paid by the person making the payment subject to the tax.

[Sec. 4261(e)]

(e) SPECIAL RULES.—

(1) SEGMENTS TO AND FROM RURAL AIRPORTS.—

(A) EXCEPTION FROM SEGMENT TAX.—The tax imposed by subsection (b)(1) shall not apply to any domestic segment beginning or ending at an airport which is a rural airport for the calendar year in which such segment begins or ends (as the case may be).

(B) RURAL AIRPORT.—For purposes of this paragraph, the term "rural airport" means, with respect to any calendar year, any airport if—

(i) there were fewer than 100,000 commercial passengers departing by air (in the case of any airport described in clause (ii)(III), on flight segments of at least 100 miles) during the second preceding calendar year from such airport, and

(ii) such airport—

(I) is not located within 75 miles of another airport which is not described in clause (i),

(II) is receiving essential air service subsidies as of the date of the enactment of this paragraph, or

(III) is not connected by paved roads to another airport.

(2) AMOUNTS PAID OUTSIDE THE UNITED STATES.—In the case of amounts paid outside the United States for taxable transportation, the taxes imposed by subsections (a) and (b) shall apply only if such transportation begins and ends in the United States.

(3) AMOUNTS PAID FOR RIGHT TO AWARD FREE OR REDUCED RATE AIR TRANSPORTATION.—

(A) IN GENERAL.—Any amount paid (and the value of any other benefit provided) to an air carrier (or any related person) for the right to provide mileage awards for (or other reductions in the cost of) any transportation of persons by air shall be treated for purposes of subsection (a) as an amount paid for taxable transportation, and such amount shall be taxable under subsection (a) without regard to any other provision of this subchapter.

(B) CONTROLLED GROUP.—For purposes of subparagraph (A), a corporation and all wholly owned subsidiaries of such corporation shall be treated as 1 corporation.

(C) REGULATIONS.—The Secretary shall prescribe rules which reallocate items of income, deduction, credit, exclusion, or other allowance to the extent necessary to prevent the avoidance of tax imposed by reason of this paragraph. The Secretary may prescribe rules which exclude from the tax imposed by subsection (a) amounts attributable to mileage awards which are used other than for transportation of persons by air.

(4) INFLATION ADJUSTMENT OF DOLLAR RATES OF TAX.—

(A) IN GENERAL.—In the case of taxable events in a calendar year after the last nonindexed year, the $3.00 amount contained in subsection (b) and each dollar amount contained in subsection (c) shall be increased by an amount equal to—

(i) such dollar amount, multiplied by

(ii) the cost-of-living adjustment determined under section 1(f)(3) for such calendar year by substituting the year before the last nonindexed year for "calendar year 2016" in subparagraph (A)(ii) thereof.

If any increase determined under the preceding sentence is not a multiple of 10 cents, such increase shall be rounded to the nearest multiple of 10 cents.

(B) LAST NONINDEXED YEAR.—For purposes of subparagraph (A), the last nonindexed year is—

(i) 2002 in the case of the $3.00 amount contained in subsection (b), and

(ii) 1998 in the case of the dollar amounts contained in subsection (c).

(C) TAXABLE EVENT.—For purposes of subparagraph (A), in the case of the tax imposed by subsection (b), the beginning of the domestic segment shall be treated as the taxable event.

(D) SPECIAL RULE FOR AMOUNTS PAID FOR DOMESTIC SEGMENTS BEGINNING AFTER 2002.—If an amount is paid during a calendar year for a domestic segment beginning in a later calendar year, then the rate of tax under subsection (b) on such amount shall be the rate in effect for the calendar year in which such amount is paid.

(5) AMOUNTS PAID FOR AIRCRAFT MANAGEMENT SERVICES.—

(A) IN GENERAL.—No tax shall be imposed by this section or section 4271 on any amounts paid by an aircraft owner for aircraft management services related to—

(i) maintenance and support of the aircraft owner's aircraft, or

(ii) flights on the aircraft owner's aircraft.

(B) AIRCRAFT MANAGEMENT SERVICES.—For purposes of subparagraph (A), the term "aircraft management services" includes—

(i) assisting an aircraft owner with administrative and support services, such as scheduling, flight planning, and weather forecasting,

EXCISE TAXES—TRANSPORTATION OF PERSONS

      (ii) obtaining insurance,

      (iii) maintenance, storage and fueling of aircraft,

      (iv) hiring, training, and provision of pilots and crew,

      (v) establishing and complying with safety standards, and

      (vi) such other services as are necessary to support flights operated by an aircraft owner.

    (C) LESSEE TREATED AS AIRCRAFT OWNER.—

      (i) IN GENERAL.—For purposes of this paragraph, the term "aircraft owner" includes a person who leases the aircraft other than under a disqualified lease.

      (ii) DISQUALIFIED LEASE.—For purposes of clause (i), the term "disqualified lease" means a lease from a person providing aircraft management services with respect to such aircraft (or a related person (within the meaning of section 465(b)(3)(C)) to the person providing such services), if such lease is for a term of 31 days or less.

    (D) PRO RATA ALLOCATION.—In the case of amounts paid to any person which (but for this subsection) are subject to the tax imposed by subsection (a), a portion of which consists of amounts described in subparagraph (A), this paragraph shall apply on a pro rata basis only to the portion which consists of amounts described in such subparagraph.

Amendments

• **2017, Tax Cuts and Jobs Act (P.L. 115-97)**

P.L. 115-97, §11002(d)(1)(FF):

Amended Code Sec. 4261(e)(4)(A)(ii) by striking "for 'calendar year 1992' in subparagraph (B)" and inserting "for 'calendar year 2016' in subparagraph (A)(ii)". **Effective** for tax years beginning after 12-31-2017.

P.L. 115-97, §13822(a):

Amended Code Sec. 4261(e) by adding at the end a new paragraph (5). **Effective** for amounts paid after 12-22-2017.

• **2014, Tax Technical Corrections Act of 2014 (P.L. 113-295)**

P.L. 113-295, §221(a)(104)(A)-(B), Division A:

Amended Code Sec. 4261(e) by striking subparagraph (C) in paragraph (1), and by striking paragraph (5). **Effective** generally 12-19-2014. For a special rule, see Act Sec. 221(b)(2), Division A, below. Prior to being stricken, Code Sec. 4261(e)(1)(C) and (5) read as follows:

(C) NO PHASEIN OF REDUCED TICKET TAX.—In the case of transportation beginning before October 1, 1999—

(i) IN GENERAL.—Paragraph (5) shall not apply to any domestic segment beginning or ending at an airport which is a rural airport for the calendar year in which such segment begins or ends (as the case may be).

(ii) TRANSPORTATION INVOLVING MULTIPLE SEGMENTS.—In the case of transportation involving more than 1 domestic segment at least 1 of which does not begin at or end at a rural airport, the 7.5 percent rate applicable by reason of clause (i) shall be applied by taking into account only an amount which bears the same ratio to the amount paid for such transportation as the number of specified miles in domestic segments which begin or end at a rural airport bears to the total number of specified miles in such transportation.

* * *

(5) RATES OF TICKET TAX FOR TRANSPORTATION BEGINNING BEFORE OCTOBER 1, 1999.—Subsection (a) shall be applied by substituting for "7.5 percent"—

(A) "9 percent" in the case of transportation beginning after September 30, 1997, and before October 1, 1998, and

(B) "8 percent" in the case of transportation beginning after September 30, 1998, and before October 1, 1999.

P.L. 113-295, §221(b)(2), Division A, provides:

(2) SAVINGS PROVISION.—If—

(A) any provision amended or repealed by the amendments made by this section applied to—

(i) any transaction occurring before the date of the enactment of this Act,

(ii) any property acquired before such date of enactment, or

(iii) any item of income, loss, deduction, or credit taken into account before such date of enactment, and

(B) the treatment of such transaction, property, or item under such provision would (without regard to the amendments or repeals made by this section) affect the liability for tax for periods ending after date of enactment, nothing in the amendments or repeals made by this section shall be construed to affect the treatment of such transaction, property, or item for purposes of determining liability for tax for periods ending after such date of enactment.

• **2005, Gulf Opportunity Zone Act of 2005 (P.L. 109-135)**

P.L. 109-135, §412(vv):

Amended Code Sec. 4261(e)(4)(C) by striking "imposed subsection (b)" and inserting "imposed by subsection (b)". **Effective** 12-21-2005.

• **2005, Safe, Accountable, Flexible, Efficient Transportation Equity Act: A Legacy for Users (P.L. 109-59)**

P.L. 109-59, §11122(a)(1)-(2):

Amended Code Sec. 4261(e)(1)(B) by inserting "(in the case of any airport described in clause (ii)(III), on flight segments of at least 100 miles)" after "by air" in clause (i), and by striking "or" at the end of subclause (I) of clause (ii), by striking the period at the end of subclause (II) of clause (ii) and inserting ", or", and by adding at the end of clause (ii) a new subclause (III). **Effective** 10-1-2005.

• **2003, Vision 100—Century of Aviation Reauthorization Act (P.L. 108-176)**

P.L. 108-176, §902(a):

Amended Code Sec. 4261(e)(4) by adding at the end a new subparagraph (D). **Effective** as if included in the provisions of P.L. 105-34 to which it relates [**effective** for transportation beginning on or after 10-1-97.—CCH].

• **1997, Taxpayer Relief Act of 1997 (P.L. 105-34)**

P.L. 105-34, §1031(c)(2):

Amended Code Sec. 4261 by redesignating subsections (e), (f), and (g) as subsections (f), (g), and (h), respectively, and by inserting after subsection (d) a new subsection (e). **Effective**, generally, for transportation beginning on or after 10-1-97. For special rules, see Act Sec. 1031(e)(2)(B)-(C).

P.L. 105-34, §1031(e)(2)(B)-(C), provides:

(B) TREATMENT OF AMOUNTS PAID FOR TICKETS PURCHASED BEFORE OCTOBER 1, 1997.—The amendments made by subsection (c) shall not apply to amounts paid before October 1, 1997; except that—

(i) the amendment made to section 4261(c) of the Internal Revenue Code of 1986 shall apply to amounts paid more than 7 days after the date of the enactment of this Act for transportation beginning on or after October 1, 1997, and

(ii) the amendment made to section 4263(c) of such Code shall apply to the extent related to taxes imposed under the amendment made to such section 4261(c) on the amounts described in clause (i).

(C) AMOUNTS PAID FOR RIGHT TO AWARD MILEAGE AWARDS.—

(i) IN GENERAL.—Paragraph (3) of section 4261(e) of the Internal Revenue Code of 1986 (as added by the amendment made by subsection (c)) shall apply to amounts paid (and other benefits provided) after September 30, 1997.

(ii) PAYMENTS WITHIN CONTROLLED GROUP.—For purposes of clause (i), any amount paid after June 11, 1997, and before October 1, 1997, by 1 member of a controlled group for a right which is described in such section 4261(e)(3) and is furnished by another member of such group after September 30, 1997, shall be treated as paid after September 30, 1997. For purposes of the preceding sentence, all persons treated as a single employer under subsection (a) or (b) of section 52 of such Code shall be treated as members of a controlled group.

[Sec. 4261(f)]

(f) EXEMPTION FOR CERTAIN USES.—No tax shall be imposed under subsection (a) or (b) on air transportation—

    (1) by helicopter for the purpose of transporting individuals, equipment, or supplies in the exploration for, or the development or removal of, hard minerals, oil, or gas, or

    (2) by helicopter or by fixed-wing aircraft for the purpose of the planting, cultivation, cutting, or transportation of, or caring for, trees (including logging operations),

but only if the helicopter or fixed-wing aircraft does not take off from, or land at, a facility eligible for assistance under the Airport and Airway Development Act of 1970, or otherwise use services provided pursuant to section 44509 or 44913(b) or subchapter I of chapter 471 of title 49, United States Code, during such use. In the case of helicopter transportation described in paragraph (1), this subsection shall be applied by treating each flight segment as a distinct flight.

Amendments

• **2005, Safe, Accountable, Flexible, Efficient Transportation Equity Act: A Legacy for Users (P.L. 109-59)**

P.L. 109-59, §11121(c):

Amended Code Sec. 4261(f). **Effective** for fuel use or air transportation after 9-30-2005. Prior to amendment, Code Sec. 4261(f) read as follows:

(f) EXEMPTION FOR CERTAIN HELICOPTER USES.—No tax shall be imposed under subsection (a) or (b) on air transportation by helicopter for the purpose of—

(1) transporting individuals, equipment, or supplies in the exploration for, or the development or removal of, hard minerals, oil, or gas, or

(2) the planting, cultivation, cutting, or transportation of, or caring for, trees (including logging operations),

EXCISE TAXES—TRANSPORTATION OF PERSONS

but only if the helicopter does not take off from, or land at, a facility eligible for assistance under the Airport and Airway Development Act of 1970, or otherwise use services provided pursuant to section 44509 or 44913(b) or subchapter I of chapter 471 of title 49, United States Code, during such use. In the case of helicopter transportation described in paragraph (1), this subsection shall be applied by treating each flight segment as a distinct flight.

• **1997, Taxpayer Relief Act of 1997 (P.L. 105-34)**

P.L. 105-34, §1031(c)(2):

Amended Code Sec. 4261 by redesignating subsection (e) as subsection (f). **Effective**, generally, for transportation beginning on or after 10-1-97. For a special rule, see Act Sec. 1031(c)(2)(B)-(C) in the amendment notes following Code Sec. 4261(e).

• **1996, Small Business Job Protection Act of 1996 (P.L. 104-188)**

P.L. 104-188, §1609(e):

Amended Code Sec. 4261(e) by adding at the end a new sentence. **Effective** 8-27-96.

• **1994 (P.L. 103-272)**

P.L. 103-272, §5(g)(2):

Amended Code Sec. 4261(e) by striking "the Airport and Airway Improvement Act of 1982" and substituting "section 44509 or 44913(b) or subchapter I of chapter 471 of title 49, United States Code,". **Effective** 7-5-94.

• **1987, Airport and Airway Revenue Act of 1987 (P.L. 100-223)**

P.L. 100-223, §404(c):

Amended Code Sec. 4261(e) by striking out "System Improvement Act" and inserting in lieu thereof "Improvement Act". **Effective** 12-30-87.

• **1986, Tax Reform Act of 1986 (P.L. 99-514)**

P.L. 99-514, §1878(c)(2):

Amended Code Sec. 4261(e)(1). **Effective** as if included in the provision of P.L. 98-369 to which it relates. Prior to amendment, Code Sec. 4261(e)(1) read as follows:

(1) transporting individuals, equipment, or supplies in—

(A) the exploration for, or the development or removal of, hard minerals, or

(B) the exploration for oil or gas, or

• **1984, Deficit Reduction Act of 1984 (P.L. 98-369)**

P.L. 98-369, §1018(b):

Amended Code Sec. 4261(e)(1). **Effective** for transportation beginning after 3-31-84, but not for any amount paid on or before such date. Prior to amendment, Code Sec. 4261(e)(1) read as follows:

(1) transporting individuals, equipment, or supplies in the exploration for, or the development or removal of, hard minerals, or

• **1982, Tax Equity and Fiscal Responsibility Act of 1982 (P.L. 97-248)**

P.L. 97-248, §280(a):

Amended Code Sec. 4261(e). **Effective** with respect to transportation beginning after 8-31-82, except that such amendment will not apply to any amount paid on or before that date. Prior to amendment, Code Sec. 4261(e) read as follows:

(e) REDUCTION, ETC., OF RATES.—Effective with respect to transportation beginning after September 30, 1980—

(1) the rate of the taxes imposed by subsections (a) and (b) shall be 5 percent, and

(2) the tax imposed by subsection (c) shall not apply.

[Sec. 4261(g)]

(g) EXEMPTION FOR AIR AMBULANCES PROVIDING CERTAIN EMERGENCY MEDICAL TRANSPORTATION.—No tax shall be imposed under this section or section 4271 on any air transportation for the purpose of providing emergency medical services—

(1) by helicopter, or

(2) by a fixed-wing aircraft equipped for and exclusively dedicated on that flight to acute care emergency medical services.

Amendments

• **1997, Taxpayer Relief Act of 1997 (P.L. 105-34)**

P.L. 105-34, §1031(c)(2):

Amended Code Sec. 4261 by redesignating subsection (f) as subsection (g). **Effective**, generally, for transportation beginning on or after 10-1-97. For special rules, see Act Sec. 1031(e)(2)(B)-(C) in the amendment notes following Code Sec. 4261(e).

P.L. 105-34, §1601(f)(4)(D):

Amended Code Sec. 4261(g), as redesignated by Act Sec. 1031(c)(2), by inserting "on that flight" after "dedicated". **Effective** as if included in the provision of P.L. 104-188 to which it relates [effective 8-27-96.—CCH].

• **1996, Small Business Job Protection Act of 1996 (P.L. 104-188)**

P.L. 104-188, §1609(d):

Amended Code Sec. 4261(f). **Effective** 8-27-96. Prior to amendment, Code Sec. 4261(f) read as follows:

(f) EXEMPTION FOR CERTAIN EMERGENCY MEDICAL TRANSPORTATION.—No tax shall be imposed under this section or section 4271 on any air transportation by helicopter for the purpose of providing emergency medical services if such helicopter—

(1) does not take off from, or land at, a facility eligible for assistance under the Airport and Airway Development Act of 1970 during such transportation, and

(2) does not otherwise use services provided pursuant to section 44509 or 44913(b) or subchapter I of chapter 471 of title 49, United States Code, during such transportation.

• **1994 (P.L. 103-272)**

P.L. 103-272, §5(g)(2):

Amended Code Sec. 4261(f)(2) by striking "the Airport and Airway Improvement Act of 1982" and substituting "section 44509 or 44913(b) or subchapter I of chapter 471 of title 49, United States Code,". **Effective** 7-5-94.

• **1987, Airport and Airway Revenue Act of 1987 (P.L. 100-223)**

P.L. 100-223, §404(a):

Amended Code Sec. 4261 by redesignating subsection (f) as subsection (g) and by inserting after subsection (e) a new subsection (f). **Effective** for transportation beginning after 9-30-88, but not for amounts paid on or before such date.

[Sec. 4261(h)]

(h) EXEMPTION FOR SKYDIVING USES.—No tax shall be imposed by this section or section 4271 on any air transportation exclusively for the purpose of skydiving.

Amendments

• **1997, Taxpayer Relief Act of 1997 (P.L. 105-34)**

P.L. 105-34, §1435(a):

Amended Code Sec. 4261, as amended by Act Sec. 1031(c)(2), by redesignating subsection (h) as subsection (i) and by inserting after subsection (g) a new subsection (h). **Effective** for amounts paid after 9-30-97.

[Sec. 4261(i)]

(i) EXEMPTION FOR SEAPLANES.—No tax shall be imposed by this section or section 4271 on any air transportation by a seaplane with respect to any segment consisting of a takeoff from, and a landing on, water, but only if the places at which such takeoff and landing occur have not received and are not receiving financial assistance from the Airport and Airways Trust Fund.

Amendments

• **2005, Safe, Accountable, Flexible, Efficient Transportation Equity Act: A Legacy for Users (P.L. 109-59)**

P.L. 109-59, §11123(a):

Amended Code Sec. 4261 by redesignating subsection (i) as subsection (j) and by inserting after subsection (h) a new subsection (i). **Effective** for transportation beginning after 9-30-2005.

[Sec. 4261(j)]

(j) EXEMPTION FOR AIRCRAFT IN FRACTIONAL OWNERSHIP AIRCRAFT PROGRAMS.—No tax shall be imposed by this section or section 4271 on any air transportation if tax is imposed under section 4043 with respect to the fuel used in such transportation. This subsection shall not apply after September 30, 2028.

EXCISE TAXES—TRANSPORTATION OF PERSONS

Amendments

• **2024, FAA Reauthorization Act of 2024 (P.L. 118-63)**

P.L. 118-63, §1302(c)(3):

Amended Code Sec. 4261(j) by striking "May 10, 2024" and inserting "September 30, 2028". **Effective** 5-16-2024.

• **2024, Airport and Airway Extension Act of 2024, Part II (P.L. 118-60)**

P.L. 118-60, §202(a), provides:

SEC. 202. EXTENSION OF TAXES FUNDING AIRPORT AND AIRWAY TRUST FUND.

(a) Sections 4043(d), 4081(d)(2)(B), 4261(j), 4261(k)(1)(A)(ii), and 4271(d)(1)(A)(ii) of the Internal Revenue Code of 1986 shall be applied by substituting "May 17, 2024" for "May 10, 2024".

• **2024, Airport and Airway Extension Act of 2024 (P.L. 118-41)**

P.L. 118-41, §202(c)(3):

Amended Code Sec. 4261(j) by striking "March 8, 2024" and inserting "May 10, 2024". **Effective** 3-8-2024.

• **2023, Airport and Airway Extension Act of 2023, Part II (P.L. 118-34)**

P.L. 118-34, §202(c)(3):

Amended Code Sec. 4261(j) by striking "December 31, 2023" and inserting "March 8, 2024". **Effective** 12-26-2023.

• **2023, Continuing Appropriations Act, 2024 and Other Extensions Act (P.L. 118-15)**

P.L. 118-15, §2212(c)(3):

Amended Code Sec. 4261(j) by striking "September 30, 2023" and inserting "December 31, 2023". **Effective** 9-30-2023.

• **2018, FAA Reauthorization Act of 2018 (P.L. 115-254)**

P.L. 115-254, §802(c)(3):

Amended Code Sec. 4261(j) by striking "September 30, 2018" and inserting "September 30, 2023". **Effective** 10-5-2018.

• **2018, Airport and Airway Extension Act of 2018, Part II (P.L. 115-250)**

P.L. 115-250, §5(a), provides:

(a) Sections 4081(d)(2)(B), 4261(j), 4261(k)(1)(A)(ii), and 4271(d)(1)(A)(ii) of the Internal Revenue Code of 1986 shall be applied by substituting "October 7, 2018" for "September 30, 2018".

• **2018, Airport and Airway Extension Act of 2018 (P.L. 115-141)**

P.L. 115-141, §202(c)(2), Div. M:

Amended Code Sec. 4261(j) by striking "March 31, 2018" and inserting "September 30, 2018". **Effective** 3-23-2018.

• **2017, Disaster Tax Relief and Airport and Airway Extension Act of 2017 (P.L. 115-63)**

P.L. 115-63, §202(c)(2):

Amended Code Sec. 4261(j) by striking "September 30, 2017" and inserting "March 31, 2018". **Effective** 9-29-2017.

• **2016, FAA Extension, Safety, and Security Act of 2016 (P.L. 114-190)**

P.L. 114-190, §1202(c)(2):

Amended Code Sec. 4261(j) by striking "July 15, 2016" and inserting "September 30, 2017". **Effective** 7-15-2016.

• **2016, Airport and Airway Extension Act of 2016 (P.L. 114-141)**

P.L. 114-141, §202(c)(2):

Amended Code Sec. 4261(j) by striking "March 31, 2016" and inserting "July 15, 2016". **Effective** 3-30-2016.

• **2015, Airport and Airway Extension Act of 2015 (P.L. 114-55)**

P.L. 114-55, §202(c)(2):

Amended Code Sec. 4261(j) by striking "September 30, 2015" and inserting "March 31, 2016". **Effective** 9-30-2015.

• **2012, FAA Modernization and Reform Act of 2012 (P.L. 112-95)**

P.L. 112-95, §1103(c):

Amended Code Sec. 4261, as amended by this Act, by redesignating subsection (j) as subsection (k) and by inserting after subsection (i) a new subsection (j). **Effective** for taxable transportation provided after 3-31-2012.

[Sec. 4261(k)]

(k) APPLICATION OF TAXES.—

(1) IN GENERAL.—The taxes imposed by this section shall apply to—

(A) transportation beginning during the period—

(i) beginning on the 7th day after the date of the enactment of the Airport and Airway Trust Fund Tax Reinstatement Act of 1997, and

(ii) ending on September 30, 2028, and

(B) amounts paid during such period for transportation beginning after such period.

(2) REFUNDS.—If, as of the date any transportation begins, the taxes imposed by this section would not have applied to such transportation if paid for on such date, any tax paid under paragraph (1)(B) with respect to such transportation shall be treated as an overpayment.

Amendments

• **2024, FAA Reauthorization Act of 2024 (P.L. 118-63)**

P.L. 118-63, §1302(b)(1):

Amended Code Sec. 4261(k)(1)(A)(ii) by striking "May 10, 2024" and inserting "September 30, 2028". **Effective** 5-16-2024.

• **2024, Airport and Airway Extension Act of 2024, Part II (P.L. 118-60)**

P.L. 118-60, §202(a), provides:

SEC. 202. EXTENSION OF TAXES FUNDING AIRPORT AND AIRWAY TRUST FUND.

(a) Sections 4043(d), 4081(d)(2)(B), 4261(j), 4261(k)(1)(A)(ii), and 4271(d)(1)(A)(ii) of the Internal Revenue Code of 1986 shall be applied by substituting "May 17, 2024" for "May 10, 2024".

• **2024, Airport and Airway Extension Act of 2024 (P.L. 118-41)**

P.L. 118-41, §202(b)(1):

Amended Code Sec. 4261(k)(1)(A)(ii) by striking "March 8, 2024" and inserting "May 10, 2024". **Effective** 3-8-2024.

• **2023, Airport and Airway Extension Act of 2023, Part II (P.L. 118-34)**

P.L. 118-34, §202(b)(1):

Amended Code Sec. 4261(k)(1)(A)(ii) by striking "December 31, 2023" and inserting "March 8, 2024". **Effective** 12-26-2023.

• **2023, Continuing Appropriations Act, 2024 and Other Extensions Act (P.L. 118-15)**

P.L. 118-15, §2212(b)(1):

Amended Code Sec. 4261(k)(1)(A)(ii) by striking "September 30, 2023" and inserting "December 31, 2023". **Effective** 9-30-2023.

• **2018, FAA Reauthorization Act of 2018 (P.L. 115-254)**

P.L. 115-254, §802(b)(1):

Amended Code Sec. 4261(k)(1)(A)(ii) by striking "September 30, 2018" and inserting "September 30, 2023". **Effective** 10-5-2018.

• **2018, Airport and Airway Extension Act of 2018, Part II (P.L. 115-250)**

P.L. 115-250, §5(a), provides:

(a) Sections 4081(d)(2)(B), 4261(j), 4261(k)(1)(A)(ii), and 4271(d)(1)(A)(ii) of the Internal Revenue Code of 1986 shall be applied by substituting "October 7, 2018" for "September 30, 2018".

• **2018, Airport and Airway Extension Act of 2018 (P.L. 115-141)**

P.L. 115-141, §202(b)(1), Div. M:

Amended Code Sec. 4261(k)(1)(A)(ii) by striking "March 31, 2018" and inserting "September 30, 2018". **Effective** 3-23-2018.

• **2017, Disaster Tax Relief and Airport and Airway Extension Act of 2017 (P.L. 115-63)**

P.L. 115-63, §202(b)(1):

Amended Code Sec. 4261(k)(1)(A)(ii) by striking "September 30, 2017" and inserting "March 31, 2018". **Effective** 9-29-2017.

• **2016, FAA Extension, Safety, and Security Act of 2016 (P.L. 114-190)**

P.L. 114-190, §1202(b)(1):

Amended Code Sec. 4261(k)(1)(A)(ii) by striking "July 15, 2016" and inserting "September 30, 2017". **Effective** 7-15-2016.

EXCISE TAXES—TRANSPORTATION OF PERSONS

- **2016, Airport and Airway Extension Act of 2016 (P.L. 114-141)**

P.L. 114-141, §202(b)(1):

Amended Code Sec. 4261(k)(1)(A)(ii) by striking "March 31, 2016" and inserting "July 15, 2016". **Effective** 3-30-2016.

- **2015, Airport and Airway Extension Act of 2015 (P.L. 114-55)**

P.L. 114-55, §202(b)(1):

Amended Code Sec. 4261(k)(1)(A)(ii) by striking "September 30, 2015" and inserting "March 31, 2016". **Effective** 9-30-2015.

- **2012, FAA Modernization and Reform Act of 2012 (P.L. 112-95)**

P.L. 112-95, §1101(b)(1):

Amended Code Sec. 4261(j)(1)(A)(ii) by striking "February 17, 2012" and inserting "September 30, 2015". **Effective** 2-18-2012.

P.L. 112-95, §1103(c):

Amended Code Sec. 4261, as amended by this Act, by redesignating subsection (j) as subsection (k). **Effective** for taxable transportation provided after 3-31-2012.

- **2012, Airport and Airway Extension Act of 2012 (P.L. 112-91)**

P.L. 112-91, §2(b)(1):

Amended Code Sec. 4261(j)(1)(A)(ii) by striking "January 31, 2012" and inserting "February 17, 2012". **Effective** 2-1-2012.

- **2011, Airport and Airway Extension Act of 2011, Part V (P.L. 112-30)**

P.L. 112-30, §202(b)(1):

Amended Code Sec. 4261(j)(1)(A)(ii) by striking "September 16, 2011" and inserting "January 31, 2012". **Effective** 9-17-2011.

- **2011, Airport and Airway Extension Act of 2011, Part IV (P.L. 112-27)**

P.L. 112-27, §2(b)(1):

Amended Code Sec. 4261(j)(1)(A)(ii) by striking "July 22, 2011" and inserting "September 16, 2011". **Effective** 7-23-2011.

- **2011, Airport and Airway Extension Act of 2011, Part III (P.L. 112-21)**

P.L. 112-21, §2(b)(1):

Amended Code Sec. 4261(j)(1)(A)(ii) by striking "June 30, 2011" and inserting "July 22, 2011". **Effective** 7-1-2011.

- **2011, Airport and Airway Extension Act of 2011, Part II (P.L. 112-16)**

P.L. 112-16, §2(b)(1):

Amended Code Sec. 4261(j)(1)(A)(ii) by striking "May 31, 2011" and inserting "June 30, 2011". **Effective** 6-1-2011.

- **2011, Airport and Airway Extension Act of 2011 (P.L. 112-7)**

P.L. 112-7, §2(b)(1):

Amended Code Sec. 4261(j)(1)(A)(ii) by striking "March 31, 2011" and inserting "May 31, 2011". **Effective** 4-1-2011.

- **2010, Airport and Airway Extension Act of 2010, Part IV (P.L. 111-329)**

P.L. 111-329, §2(b)(1):

Amended Code Sec. 4261(j)(1)(A)(ii) by striking "December 31, 2010" and inserting "March 31, 2011". **Effective** 1-1-2011.

- **2010, Airport and Airway Extension Act of 2010, Part III (P.L. 111-249)**

P.L. 111-249, §2(b)(1):

Amended Code Sec. 4261(j)(1)(A)(ii) by striking "September 30, 2010" and inserting "December 31, 2010". **Effective** 10-1-2010.

- **2010, Airline Safety and Federal Aviation Administration Extension Act of 2010 (P.L. 111-216)**

P.L. 111-216, §101(b)(1):

Amended Code Sec. 4261(j)(1)(A)(ii) by striking "August 1, 2010" and inserting "September 30, 2010". **Effective** 8-2-2010.

- **2010, Airport and Airway Extension Act of 2010, Part II (P.L. 111-197)**

P.L. 111-197, §2(b)(1):

Amended Code Sec. 4261(j)(1)(A)(ii) by striking "July 3, 2010" and inserting "August 1, 2010". **Effective** 7-4-2010.

- **2010, Airport and Airway Extension Act of 2010 (P.L. 111-161)**

P.L. 111-161, §2(b)(1):

Amended Code Sec. 4261(j)(1)(A)(ii) by striking "April 30, 2010" and inserting "July 3, 2010". **Effective** 5-1-2010.

- **2010, Federal Aviation Administration Extension Act of 2010 (P.L. 111-153)**

P.L. 111-153, §2(b)(1):

Amended Code Sec. 4261(j)(1)(A)(ii) by striking "March 31, 2010" and inserting "April 30, 2010". **Effective** 4-1-2010.

- **2009, Fiscal Year 2010 Federal Aviation Administration Extension Act, Part II (P.L. 111-116)**

P.L. 111-116, §2(b)(1):

Amended Code Sec. 4261(j)(1)(A)(ii) by striking "December 31, 2009" and inserting "March 31, 2010". **Effective** 1-1-2010.

- **2009, Fiscal Year 2010 Federal Aviation Administration Extension Act (P.L. 111-69)**

P.L. 111-69, §2(b)(1):

Amended Code Sec. 4261(j)(1)(A)(ii) by striking "September 30, 2009" and inserting "December 31, 2009". **Effective** 10-1-2009.

- **2009, (P.L. 111-68)**

P.L. 111-68, §156(a), provides:

(a) Sections 4081(d)(2)(B), 4261(j)(1)(A)(ii), and 4271(d)(1)(A)(ii) of the Internal Revenue Code of 1986 shall each be applied by substituting the date specified in section 106(3) [October 31, 2009] of this joint resolution for "September 30, 2009".

- **2009, Federal Aviation Administration Extension Act of 2009 (P.L. 111-12)**

P.L. 111-12, §2(b)(1):

Amended Code Sec. 4261(j)(1)(A)(ii) by striking "March 31, 2009" and inserting "September 30, 2009". **Effective** 4-1-2009.

- **2008, Federal Aviation Administration Extension Act of 2008, Part II (P.L. 110-330)**

P.L. 110-330, §2(b)(1):

Amended Code Sec. 4261(j)(1)(A)(ii) by striking "September 30, 2008" and inserting "March 31, 2009". **Effective** 10-1-2008.

- **2008, Federal Aviation Administration Extension Act of 2008 (P.L. 110-253)**

P.L. 110-253, §2(b)(1):

Amended Code Sec. 4261(j)(1)(A)(ii) by striking "June 30, 2008" and inserting "September 30, 2008". **Effective** 7-1-2008.

- **2008, Airport and Airway Extension Act of 2008 (P.L. 110-190)**

P.L. 110-190, §2(b)(1):

Amended Code Sec. 4261(j)(1)(A)(ii) by striking "February 29, 2008" and inserting "June 30, 2008". **Effective** 3-1-2008.

- **2007, Department of Transportation Appropriations Act, 2008 (P.L. 110-161)**

P.L. 110-161, §116(b)(1):

Amended Code Sec. 4261(j)(1)(A)(ii) by striking "September 30, 2007" and inserting "February 29, 2008". **Effective** 10-1-2007.

- **2007 (P.L. 110-92)**

P.L. 110-92, §149(a), provides:

SEC. 149. (a) Sections 4081(d)(2)(B), 4261(j)(1)(A)(ii), 4271(d)(1)(A)(ii), 9502(d)(1), and 9502(f)(2) of the Internal Revenue Code of 1986 shall each be applied by substituting the date specified in section 106(3) of this joint resolution [November 16, 2007.—CCH] for "September 30, 2007" or "October 1, 2007", as the case may be.

- **2005, Safe, Accountable, Flexible, Efficient Transportation Equity Act: A Legacy for Users (P.L. 109-59)**

P.L. 109-59, §11123(a):

Amended Code Sec. 4261 by redesignating subsection (i) as subsection (j). **Effective** for transportation beginning after 9-30-2005.

- **1997, Taxpayer Relief Act of 1997 (P.L. 105-34)**

P.L. 105-34, §1031(b)(1):

Amended Code Sec. 4261(g)(1)(A)(ii) by striking "September 30, 1997" and inserting "September 30, 2007". **Effective**, generally, for transportation beginning on or after 10-1-97. For a special rule, see Act Sec. 1031(e)(2)(B)-(C) in the amendment notes following Code Sec. 4261(e).

P.L. 105-34, §1031(c)(2):

Amended Code Sec. 4261 by redesignating subsection (g) as subsection (h). **Effective**, generally, for transportation beginning on or after 10-1-97. For special rules, see Act Sec. 1031(e)(2)(B)-(C) in the amendment notes following Code Sec. 4261(e).

P.L. 105-34, §1435(a):

Amended Code Sec. 4261, as amended by Act Sec. 1031(c)(2), by redesignating subsection (h) as subsection (i). **Effective** for amounts paid after 9-30-97.

- **1997, Airport and Airway Trust Fund Reinstatement Act of 1997 (P.L. 105-2)**

P.L. 105-2, §2(b)(1):

Amended Code Sec. 4261(g). **Effective** for transportation beginning on or after 3-7-97. For a special rule, see Act Sec. 2(e)(2)(A)-(C), below. Prior to amendment, Code Sec. 4261(g) read as follows:

(g) TERMINATION.—The taxes imposed by this section shall apply with respect to transportation beginning after August 31, 1982, and before January 1, 1996, and to transportation beginning on or after the date which is 7 calendar days after the date of the enactment of the Small Business Job Protection Act of 1996 and before January 1, 1997.

P.L. 105-2, §2(e)(2)(A)-(C), provides:

(2) TICKET TAXES.—

(A) IN GENERAL.—The amendments made by subsection (b) shall apply to transportation beginning on or after such 7th day.

EXCISE TAXES—TRANSPORTATION OF PERSONS

(B) EXCEPTION FOR CERTAIN PAYMENTS.—Except as provided in subparagraph (C), the amendments made by subsection (b) shall not apply to any amount paid before such 7th day.

(C) PAYMENTS OF PROPERTY TRANSPORTATION TAX WITHIN CONTROLLED GROUP.—In the case of the tax imposed by section 4271 of the Internal Revenue Code of 1986, subparagraph (B) shall not apply to any amount paid by 1 member of a controlled group for transportation furnished by another member of such group. For purposes of the preceding sentence, all persons treated as a single employer under subsection (a) or (b) of section 52 of the Internal Revenue Code of 1986 shall be treated as members of a controlled group.

P.L. 105-2, §2(f):

For the text of Act Sec. 2(f), concerning the application of the look-back safe harbor for deposits, see Code Sec. 9502(b).

- **1996, Small Business Job Protection Act of 1996 (P.L. 104-188)**

P.L. 104-188, §1609(b):

Amended Code Sec. 4261(g) by striking "January 1, 1996" and inserting "January 1, 1996, and to transportation beginning on or after the date which is 7 calendar days after the date of the enactment of the Small Business Job Protection Act of 1996 and before January 1, 1997". **Effective** 8-27-96, but does not apply to any amount paid before such date.

- **1990, Omnibus Budget Reconciliation Act of 1990 (P.L. 101-508)**

P.L. 101-508, §11213(d)(1):

Amended Code Sec. 4261(g) by striking "January 1, 1991" and inserting "January 1, 1996". **Effective** 11-5-90. However, see Act Sec. 11213(f) in the amendment notes following Code Sec. 4041(c).

- **1987, Airport and Airway Revenue Act of 1987 (P.L. 100-223)**

P.L. 100-223, §402(a)(1):

Amended Code Sec. 4261(f) by striking out "January 1, 1988" each place it appears and inserting in lieu thereof "January 1, 1991". **Effective** 12-30-87.

P.L. 100-223, §404(a):

Amended Code Sec. 4261 by redesignating subsection (f) as subsection (g). **Effective** for transportation beginning after 9-30-88, but not for amounts paid on or before such date.

- **1982, Tax Equity and Fiscal Responsibility Act of 1982 (P.L. 97-248)**

P.L. 97-248, §280(a):

Added Code Sec. 4261(f). **Effective** with respect to transportation beginning after 8-31-82, except that such amendment will not apply to any amount paid on or before that date.

- **1980 (P.L. 96-298)**

P.L. 96-298, §1(b):

Substituted September 30, 1980 for June 30, 1980 in Code Sec. 4261(e).

- **1970 (P.L. 91-258)**

P.L. 91-258, §203(a):

Amended Code Sec. 4261. **Effective** for transportation beginning after 6-30-70. Prior to amendment, Code Sec. 4261 read as follows:

SEC. 4261. IMPOSITION OF TAX.

(a) Amounts Paid Within the United States.—There is hereby imposed upon the amount paid within the United States for taxable transportation (as defined in section 4262) of any person by air a tax equal to 5 percent of the amount so paid for transportation which begins after November 15, 1962.

(b) Amounts Paid Outside the United States.—There is hereby imposed upon the amount paid without the United States for taxable transportation (as defined in section 4262) of any person by air, but only if such transportation begins and ends in the United States, a tax equal to 5 percent of the amount so paid for transportation which begins after November 15, 1962.

(c) Seats, Berths, etc.—There is hereby imposed upon the amount paid for seating or sleeping accommodations in connection with transportation with respect to which a tax is imposed by subsection (a) or (b) a tax equivalent to 5 percent of the amount so paid in connection with transportation which begins after November 15, 1962.

(d) By Whom Paid.—Except as provided in section 4264, the taxes imposed by this section shall be paid by the person making the payment subject to the tax.

- **1965, Excise Tax Reduction Act of 1965 (P.L. 89-44)**

P.L. 89-44, §303:

Amended Sec. 4261 by inserting "November 15, 1962" in lieu of "November 15, 1962, and before July 1, 1965" wherever it appeared. **Effective** 7-1-65.

- **1964, Excise Tax Rate Extension Act of 1964 (P.L. 88-348)**

P.L. 88-348, §2(a)(3):

Amended Sec. 4261 by substituting "1965" for "1964" wherever it appeared.

- **1963, Tax Rate Extension Act of 1963 (P.L. 88-52)**

P.L. 88-52, §3(a)(3):

Amended Sec. 4261 by substituting "1964" for "1963" wherever it appeared.

- **1962, Tax Rate Extension Act of 1962 (P.L. 87-508)**

P.L. 87-508, §5(a):

Amended Code Sec. 4261(a)-(c). Prior to amendment, Code Sec. 4261(a)-(c) read as follows:

(a) Amounts Paid Within the United States.—There is hereby imposed upon the amount paid within the United States for taxable transportation (as defined in section 4262) of any person by rail, motor vehicle, water, or air a tax equal to—

(1) 10 percent of the amount so paid before July 1, 1962; or

(2) 5 percent of the amount so paid on or after July 1, 1962.

(b) Amounts Paid Outside the United States.—There is hereby imposed upon the amount paid without the United States for taxable transportation (as defined in section 4262) of any person by rail, motor vehicle, water, or air, but only if such transportation begins and ends in the United States, a tax equal to—

(1) 10 percent of the amount so paid before July 1, 1962; or

(2) 5 percent of the amount so paid on or after July 1, 1962.

(c) Seats, Berths, etc.—There is hereby imposed upon the amount paid for seating or sleeping accommodations in connection with transportation with respect to which a tax is imposed by subsection (a) or (b) a tax equivalent to—

(1) 10 percent of the amount so paid before July 1, 1962; or

(2) 5 percent of the amount so paid on or after July 1, 1962.

P.L. 87-508, §5(b):

Amended Code Sec. 4261. **Effective** for periods beginning after 11-15-62. Prior to amendment, Code Sec. 4261 read as follows:

SEC. 4261. IMPOSITION OF TAX.

(a) Amounts Paid Within the United States.—There is hereby imposed upon the amount paid within the United States for taxable transportation (as defined in section 4262) of any person by rail, motor vehicle, water, or air a tax equal to 10 percent of the amount so paid for transportation which begins before November 16, 1962.

(b) Amounts Paid Outside the United States.—There is hereby imposed upon the amount paid without the United States for taxable transportation (as defined in section 4262) of any person by rail, motor vehicle, water, or air, but only if such transportation begins and ends in the United States, a tax equal to 10 percent of the amount so paid for transportation which begins before November 16, 1962.

(c) Seats, Berths, etc.—There is hereby imposed upon the amount paid for seating or sleeping accommodations in connection with transportation with respect to which a tax is imposed by subsection (a) or (b) a tax equivalent to 10 percent of the amount so paid in connection with transportation which begins before November 16, 1962.

(d) By Whom Paid.—Except as provided in section 4264, the taxes imposed by this section shall be paid by the person making the payment subject to the tax.

- **1961, Tax Rate Extension Act of 1961 (P.L. 87-72)**

P.L. 87-72, §3(a)(3):

Amended Sec. 4261 by substituting "1962" for "1961" wherever it appeared.

- **1960, Public Debt and Tax Rate Extension Act of 1960 (P.L. 86-564)**

P.L. 86-564, §202(a):

Amended Sec. 4261 by substituting "1961" for "1960" wherever it appeared.

- **1959, Tax Rate Extension Act of 1959 (P.L. 86-75)**

P.L. 86-75, §4:

Amended Code Sec. 4261(a)-(c) by striking out "10 percent of the amount so paid" where it appeared at the end of each such section and by adding paragraphs (1) and (2) thereof.

- **1956 (P.L. 796, 84th Cong.)**

P.L. 796, 84th Cong., 2d Sess., §[1]:

Amended Code Sec. 4261(a), (b) and (d). **Effective** 10-1-56. Prior to amendment, these sections read as follows:

(a) Amounts Paid Within the United States.—There is hereby imposed upon the amount paid within the United States for the transportation of persons by rail, motor vehicle, water, or air within or without the United States a tax equal to 10 percent of the amount so paid.

(b) Amounts Paid Without the United States.—There is hereby imposed upon the amount paid without the United States for the transportation of persons by rail, motor vehicle, water, or air which begins and ends in the United States a tax equal to 10 percent of the amount so paid.

* * *

(d) By Whom Paid.—The taxes imposed by this section shall be paid by the person making the payment subject to the tax.

[Sec. 4262]

SEC. 4262. DEFINITION OF TAXABLE TRANSPORTATION.

[Sec. 4262(a)]

(a) TAXABLE TRANSPORTATION; IN GENERAL.—For purposes of this part, except as provided in subsection (b), the term "taxable transportation" means—

(1) transportation by air which begins in the United States or in the 225-mile zone and ends in the United States or in the 225-mile zone; and

EXCISE TAXES—TRANSPORTATION OF PERSONS

(2) in the case of transportation by air other than transportation described in paragraph (1), that portion of such transportation which is directly or indirectly from one port or station in the United States to another port or station in the United States, but only if such portion is not a part of uninterrupted international air transportation (within the meaning of subsection (c)(3)).

[Sec. 4262(b)]

(b) EXCLUSION OF CERTAIN TRAVEL.—For purposes of this part, the term "taxable transportation" does not include that portion of any transportation by air which meets all 4 of the following requirements:

(1) such portion is outside the United States;

(2) neither such portion nor any segment thereof is directly or indirectly—

(A) between (i) a point where the route of the transportation leaves or enters the continental United States, or (ii) a port or station in the 225-mile zone, and

(B) a port or station in the 225-mile zone;

(3) such portion—

(A) begins at either (i) the point where the route of the transportation leaves the United States, or (ii) a port or station in the 225-mile zone, and

(B) ends at either (i) the point where the route of the transportation enters the United States, or (ii) a port or station in the 225-mile zone; and

(4) a direct line from the point (or the port or station) specified in paragraph (3)(A), to the point (or the port or station) specified in paragraph (3)(B), passes through or over a point which is not within 225 miles of the United States.

[Sec. 4262(c)]

(c) DEFINITIONS.—For purposes of this section—

(1) CONTINENTAL UNITED STATES.—The term "continental United States" means the District of Columbia and the States other than Alaska and Hawaii.

(2) 225-MILE ZONE.—The term "225-mile zone" means that portion of Canada and Mexico which is not more than 225 miles from the nearest point in the continental United States.

(3) UNINTERRUPTED INTERNATIONAL AIR TRANSPORTATION.—The term "uninterrupted international air transportation" means any transportation by air which is not transportation described in subsection (a)(1) and in which—

(A) the scheduled interval between (i) the beginning or end of the portion of such transportation which is directly or indirectly from one port or station in the United States to another port or station in the United States and (ii) the end or beginning of the other portion of such transportation is not more than 12 hours, and

(B) the scheduled interval between the beginning or end and the end or beginning of any two segments of the portion of such transportation referred to in subparagraph (A)(i) is not more than 12 hours.

For purposes of this paragraph, in the case of personnel of the United States Army, Air Force, Navy, Marine Corps, and Coast Guard traveling in uniform at their own expense when on official leave, furlough, or pass, the scheduled interval described in subparagraph (A) shall be deemed to be not more than 12 hours if a ticket for the subsequent portion of such transportation is purchased within 12 hours after the end of the earlier portion of such transportation and the purchaser accepts and utilizes the first accommodations actually available to him for such subsequent portion.

Amendments

• **1982, Tax Equity and Fiscal Responsibility Act of 1982 (P.L. 97-248)**

P.L. 97-248, §281A(a)(1):

Amended Code Sec. 4262(c)(3) by striking out "6 hours" each place it appeared and inserting "12 hours". **Effective** for transportation beginning after 8-31-82.

[Sec. 4262(d)]

(d) TRANSPORTATION.—For purposes of this part, the term "transportation" includes layover or waiting time and movement of the aircraft in deadhead service.

Amendments

• **1970 (P.L. 91-258)**

P.L. 91-258, §203(b):

Amended the first line of Code Sec. 4262(a) and 4262(b) by substituting "part" for "subchapter.", amended Code Sec. 4262(a)(1) and (a)(2) by substituting "transportation by air" for "transportation.", amended Code Sec. 4262(b) by substituting "transportation by air" for "transportation.", and added new Code Sec. 4262(d). **Effective** for transportation beginning after 6-30-70.

• **1965, Excise Tax Reduction Act of 1965 (P.L. 89-44)**

P. L. 89-44, §803(a):

Amended Sec. 4262(c) by adding the last sentence. **Effective** 7-1-65.

• **1962, Tax Rate Extension Act of 1962 (P.L. 87-508)**

P. L. 87-508, §5(b):

Added Code Sec. 4262. **Effective** for transportation of persons by air beginning after 11-15-62.

[Sec. 4262(e)]

(e) AUTHORITY TO WAIVE 225-MILE ZONE PROVISIONS.—

(1) IN GENERAL.—If the Secretary of the Treasury determines that Canada or Mexico has entered into a qualified agreement—

(A) the Secretary shall publish a notice of such determination in the Federal Register, and

(B) effective with respect to transportation beginning after the date specified in such notice, to the extent provided in the agreement, the term "225-mile zone" shall not include part or all of the country with respect to which such determination is made.

(2) TERMINATION OF WAIVER.—If a determination was made under paragraph (1) with respect to any country and the Secretary of the Treasury subsequently determines that the agreement is no longer in effect or that the agreement is no longer a qualified agreement—

(A) the Secretary shall publish a notice of such determination in the Federal Register, and

(B) subparagraph (B) of paragraph (1) shall cease to apply with respect to transportation beginning after the date specified in such notice.

(3) QUALIFIED AGREEMENT.—For purposes of this subsection, the term "qualified agreement" means an agreement between the United States and Canada or Mexico (as the case may be)—

(A) setting forth that portion of such country which is not to be treated as within the 225-mile zone, and

(B) providing that the tax imposed by such country on transportation described in subparagraphs (A) will be at a level which the Secretary of the Treasury determines to be appropriate.

EXCISE TAXES—TRANSPORTATION OF PERSONS

(4) REQUIREMENT THAT AGREEMENT BE SUBMITTED TO CONGRESS.—No notice may be published under paragraph (1)(A) with respect to any qualified agreement before the date 90 days after the date on which a copy of such agreement was furnished to the Committee on Ways and Means of the House of Representatives and the Committee on Finance of the Senate.

Amendments

• **1982, Tax Equity and Fiscal Responsibility Act of 1982 (P.L. 97-248)**

P.L. 97-248, §281A(a)(2):

Added Code Sec. 4262(e). **Effective** for transportation beginning after 8-31-82.

[Sec. 4263]

SEC. 4263. SPECIAL RULES.

[Sec. 4263(a)]

(a) PAYMENTS MADE OUTSIDE THE UNITED STATES FOR PREPAID ORDERS.—If the payment upon which tax is imposed by section 4261 is made outside the United States for a prepaid order, exchange order, or similar order, the person furnishing the initial transportation pursuant to such order shall collect the amount of the tax.

[Sec. 4263(b)]

(b) TAX DEDUCTED UPON REFUNDS.—Every person who refunds any amount with respect to a ticket or order which was purchased without payment of the tax imposed by section 4261 shall deduct from the amount refundable, to the extent available, any tax due under such section as a result of the use of a portion of the transportation purchased in connection with such ticket or order, and shall report to the Secretary the amount of any such tax remaining uncollected.

Amendments

• **1976, Tax Reform Act of 1976 (P.L. 94-455)**

P.L. 94-455, §1906(b)(13)(A):

Amended 1954 Code by substituting "Secretary" for "Secretary or his delegate" each place it appeared. **Effective** 2-1-77.

[Sec. 4263(c)]

(c) PAYMENT OF TAX.—Where any tax imposed by section 4261 is not paid at the time payment for transportation is made, then, under regulations prescribed by the Secretary, to the extent that such tax is not collected under any other provision of this subchapter, such tax shall be paid by the carrier providing the initial segment of such transportation which begins or ends in the United States.

Amendments

• **1997, Taxpayer Relief Act of 1997 (P.L. 105-34)**

P.L. 105-34, §1031(c)(3):

Amended Code Sec. 4263(c) by striking "subchapter—" and all that follows and inserting "subchapter, such tax shall be paid by the carrier providing the initial segment of such transportation which begins or ends in the United States." **Effective**, generally, for transportation beginning on or after 10-1-97. For a special rule, see Act Sec. 1031(e)(2)(B). Prior to amendment, Code Sec. 4263(c) read as follows:

(c) PAYMENT OF TAX.—Where any tax imposed by section 4261 is not paid at the time payment for transportation is made, then, under regulations prescribed by the Secretary, to the extent that such tax is not collected under any other provision of this subchapter—

(1) such tax shall be paid by the person paying for the transportation or by the person using the transportation;

(2) such tax shall be paid within such time as the Secretary shall prescribe by regulations after whichever of the following first occurs:

(A) the rights to the transportation expire; or

(B) the time when the transportation becomes subject to tax; and

(3) payment of such tax shall be made to the Secretary, to the person to whom the payment for transportation was made, or, in the case of transportation other than transportation described in section 4262(a)(1), to any person furnishing any portion of such transportation.

P.L. 105-34, §1031(e)(2)(B), provides:

(B) TREATMENT OF AMOUNTS PAID FOR TICKETS PURCHASED BEFORE OCTOBER 1, 1997.—The amendments made by subsection (c) shall not apply to amounts paid before October 1, 1997; except that—

(i) the amendment made to section 4261(c) of the Internal Revenue Code of 1986 shall apply to amounts paid more than 7 days after the date of the enactment of this Act for transportation beginning on or after October 1, 1997, and

(ii) the amendment made to section 4263(c) of such Code shall apply to the extent related to taxes imposed under the amendment made to such section 4261(c) on the amounts described in clause (i).

• **1976, Tax Reform Act of 1976 (P.L. 94-455)**

P.L. 94-455, §1906(b)(13)(A):

Amended 1954 Code by substituting "Secretary" for "Secretary or his delegate" each place it appeared. **Effective** 2-1-77.

[Sec. 4263(d)]

(d) APPLICATION OF TAX.—The tax imposed by section 4261 shall apply to any amount paid within the United States for transportation of any person by air unless the taxpayer establishes, pursuant to regulations prescribed by the Secretary, at the time of payment for the transportation, that the transportation is not transportation in respect of which tax is imposed by section 4261.

Amendments

• **1976, Tax Reform Act of 1976 (P.L. 94-455)**

P.L. 94-455, §1906(b)(13)(A):

Amended 1954 Code by substituting "Secretary" for "Secretary or his delegate" each place it appeared. **Effective** 2-1-77.

[Sec. 4263(e)]

(e) ROUND TRIPS.—In applying this subchapter to a round trip, such round trip shall be considered to consist of transportation from the point of departure to the destination, and of separate transportation thereafter.

[Sec. 4263(f)]

(f) TRANSPORTATION OUTSIDE THE NORTHERN PORTION OF THE WESTERN HEMISPHERE.—In applying this subchapter to transportation any part of which is outside the northern portion of the Western Hemisphere, if the route of such transportation leaves and reenters the northern portion of the Western Hemisphere, such transportation shall be considered to consist of transportation to a point outside such northern portion, and of separate transportation thereafter. For purposes of this subsection, the term "northern portion of the Western Hemisphere" means the area lying west of the 30th meridian west of Greenwich, east of the international dateline, and north of the Equator, but not including any country of South America.

Amendments

• **1970 (P.L. 91-258)**

P.L. 91-258, §205(c)(1)-(2):

Repealed former Code Sec. 4263 and redesignated former Code Sec. 4264 as Code Sec. 4263. **Effective** 7-1-70.

• **1962, Tax Rate Extension Act of 1962 (P.L. 87-508)**

P.L. 87-508, §5(b):

Amended Code Sec. 4264. **Effective** for transportation beginning after 11-15-62. Prior to amendment, Code Sec. 4264 read as follows:

Sec. 4262(e)(4)

EXCISE TAXES—TRANSPORTATION OF PROPERTY

"SEC. 4264. SPECIAL RULES.

"(a) Payments Made Outside the United States for Prepaid Orders.—If the payment upon which tax is imposed by section 4261 is made outside the United States for a prepaid order, exchange order, or similar order, the person furnishing the initial transportation pursuant to such order shall collect the amount of the tax.

"(b) Tax Deducted Upon Refunds.—Every person who refunds any amount with respect to a ticket or order which was purchased without payment of the tax imposed by section 4261, shall deduct from the amount refundable, to the extent available, any tax due under such section as a result of the use of a portion of the transportation purchased in connection with such ticket or order, and shall report to the Secretary or his delegate the amount of any such tax remaining uncollected.

"(c) Payment of Tax.—Where any tax imposed by section 4261 is not paid at the time payment for transportation is made, then, under regulations prescribed by the Secretary or his delegate, to the extent that such tax is not collected under any other provision of this subchapter—

"(1) such tax shall be paid by the person paying for the transportation or by the person using the transportation;

"(2) such tax shall be paid within such time as the Secretary or his delegate shall prescribe by regulations after whichever of the following first occurs:

"(A) the rights to the transportation expire; or

"(B) the time when the transportation becomes subject to tax; and

"(3) payment of such tax shall be made to the person to whom the payment for transportation was made or to the Secretary or his delegate.

"(d) Application of Tax.—The tax imposed by section 4261 shall apply to any amount paid within the United States for transportation of any person unless the taxpayer establishes, pursuant to regulations prescribed by the Secretary or his delegate, at the time of payment for the transportation, that the transportation is not transportation in respect of which tax is imposed by section 4261.

"(e) Round Trips.—In applying this part to a round trip, such round trip shall be considered to consist of transportation from the point of departure to the destination, and of separate transportation thereafter.

"(f) Transportation Outside the Northern Portion of the Western Hemisphere.—In applying this part to transportation any part of which is outside the northern portion of the Western Hemisphere—

"(1) If the route of such transportation leaves and reenters the northern portion of the Western Hemisphere, such transportation shall be considered to consist of transportation to a point outside such northern portion, and of separate transportation thereafter.

"(2) If such transportation is transportation by water on a vessel which makes one or more intermediate stops at ports within the United Sates on a voyage which begins or ends in the United States and ends or begins outside the northern portion of the Western Hemisphere, a stop at an intermediate port within the United States at which such vessel is not authorized both to discharge and to take on passengers shall not be considered to be a stop at a port within the United States.

"For purposes of this subsection, the term `northern portion of the Western Hemisphere' means the area lying west of the 30th meridian west of Greenwich, east of the International Date Line, and north of the equator, but not including any country of South America."

PART II—PROPERTY

Sec. 4271.   Imposition of tax.
Sec. 4272.   Definition of taxable transportation, etc.

[Sec. 4271]

SEC. 4271. IMPOSITION OF TAX.

[Sec. 4271(a)]

(a) In General.—There is hereby imposed upon the amount paid within or without the United States for the taxable transportation (as defined in section 4272) of property a tax equal to 6.25 percent of the amount so paid for such transportation. The tax imposed by this subsection shall apply only to amounts paid to a person engaged in the business of transporting property by air for hire.

Amendments

• **2020, Coronavirus Aid, Relief, and Economic Security (CARES) Act (P.L. 116-136)**

P.L. 116-136, §4007(a) and (c), provides:

(a) Transportation by Air.—In the case of any amount paid for transportation by air (including any amount treated as paid for transportation by air by reason of section 4261(e)(3) of the Internal Revenue Code of 1986) during the excise tax holiday period, no tax shall be imposed under section 4261 or 4271 of such Code. The preceding sentence shall not apply to amounts paid on or before the date of the enactment of this Act.

***

(c) Excise Tax Holiday Period.—For purposes of this section, the term "excise tax holiday period" means the period beginning after the date of the enactment of this section and ending before January 1, 2021.

• **1990, Omnibus Budget Reconciliation Act of 1990 (P.L. 101-508)**

P.L. 101-508, §11213(a)(2):

Amended Code Sec. 4271(a) by striking "5 percent" and inserting "6.25 percent". **Effective** for transportation beginning after 11-30-90, but shall not apply to amounts paid on or before such date. However, see Act Sec. 11213(f) in the amendment notes following Code Sec. 4041(c).

• **1976, Tax Reform Act of 1976 (P.L. 94-455)**

P.L. 94-455, §1904(a)(8):

Struck out "which begins after June 30, 1970," after "of property" in Code Sec. 4271(a). **Effective** 2-1-77.

[Sec. 4271(b)]

(b) By Whom Paid.—

(1) In general.—Except as provided by paragraph (2), the tax imposed by subsection (a) shall be paid by the person making the payment subject to tax.

(2) Payments made outside the United States.—If a payment subject to tax under subsection (a) is made outside the United States and the person making such payment does not pay such tax, such tax—

(A) shall be paid by the person to whom the property is delivered in the United States by the person furnishing the last segment of the taxable transportation in respect of which such tax is imposed, and

(B) shall be collected by the person furnishing the last segment of such taxable transportation.

[Sec. 4271(c)]

(c) Determination of Amounts Paid in Certain Cases.—For purposes of this section, in any case in which a person engaged in the business of transporting property by air for hire and one or more other persons not so engaged jointly provide services which include taxable transportation of property, and the person so engaged receives, for the furnishing of such taxable transportation, a portion of the receipts from the joint providing of such services, the amount paid for the taxable transportation shall be treated as being the sum of (1) the portion of the receipts so received, and (2) any expenses incurred by any of the persons not so engaged which are properly attributable to such taxable transportation and which are taken into account in determining the portion of the receipts so received.

[Sec. 4271(d)]

(d) Application of Tax.—

(1) In general.—The tax imposed by subsection (a) shall apply to—

(A) transportation beginning during the period—

(i) beginning on the 7th day after the date of the enactment of the Airport and Airway Trust Fund Tax Reinstatement Act of 1997, and

(ii) ending on September 30, 2028, and

(B) amounts paid during such period for transportation beginning after such period.

EXCISE TAXES—TRANSPORTATION OF PROPERTY

(2) REFUNDS.—If, as of the date any transportation begins, the taxes imposed by this section would not have applied to such transportation if paid for on such date, any tax paid under paragraph (1)(B) with respect to such transportation shall be treated as an overpayment.

Amendments

• **2024, FAA Reauthorization Act of 2024 (P.L. 118-63)**

P.L. 118-63, §1302(b)(2):

Amended Code Sec. 4271(d)(1)(A)(ii) by striking "May 10, 2024" and inserting "September 30, 2028". **Effective** 5-16-2024.

• **2024, Airport and Airway Extension Act of 2024, Part II (P.L. 118-60)**

P.L. 118-60, §202(a), provides:
SEC. 202. EXTENSION OF TAXES FUNDING AIRPORT AND AIRWAY TRUST FUND.

(a) Sections 4043(d), 4081(d)(2)(B), 4261(j), 4261(k)(1)(A)(ii), and 4271(d)(1)(A)(ii) of the Internal Revenue Code of 1986 shall be applied by substituting "May 17, 2024" for "May 10, 2024".

• **2024, Airport and Airway Extension Act of 2024 (P.L. 118-41)**

P.L. 118-41, §202(b)(2):

Amended Code Sec. 4271(d)(1)(A)(ii) by striking "March 8, 2024" and inserting "May 10, 2024". **Effective** 3-8-2024.

• **2023, Airport and Airway Extension Act of 2023, Part II (P.L. 118-34)**

P.L. 118-34, §202(b)(2):

Amended Code Sec. 4271(d)(1)(A)(ii) by striking "December 31, 2023" and inserting "March 8, 2024". **Effective** 12-26-2023.

• **2023, Continuing Appropriations Act, 2024 and Other Extensions Act (P.L. 118-15)**

P.L. 118-15, §2212(b)(2):

Amended Code Sec. 4271(d)(1)(A)(ii) by striking "September 30, 2023" and inserting "December 31, 2023". **Effective** 9-30-2023.

• **2018, FAA Reauthorization Act of 2018 (P.L. 115-254)**

P.L. 115-254, §802(b)(2):

Amended Code Sec. 4271(d)(1)(A)(ii) by striking "September 30, 2018" and inserting "September 30, 2023". **Effective** 10-5-2018.

• **2018, Airport and Airway Extension Act of 2018, Part II (P.L. 115-250)**

P.L. 115-250, §5(a), provides:

(a) Sections 4081(d)(2)(B), 4261(j), 4261(k)(1)(A)(ii), and 4271(d)(1)(A)(ii) of the Internal Revenue Code of 1986 shall be applied by substituting "October 7, 2018" for "September 30, 2018".

• **2018, Airport and Airway Extension Act of 2018 (P.L. 115-141)**

P.L. 115-141, §202(b)(2), Div. M:

Amended Code Sec. 4271(d)(1)(A)(ii) by striking "March 31, 2018" and inserting "September 30, 2018". **Effective** 3-23-2018.

• **2017, Disaster Tax Relief and Airport and Airway Extension Act of 2017 (P.L. 115-63)**

H.R. P.L. 115-63, §202(b)(2):

Amended Code Sec. 4271(d)(1)(A)(ii) by striking "September 30, 2017" and inserting "March 31, 2018". **Effective** 9-29-2017.

• **2016, FAA Extension, Safety, and Security Act of 2016 (P.L. 114-190)**

P.L. 114-190, §1202(b)(2):

Amended Code Sec. 4271(d)(1)(A)(ii) by striking "July 15, 2016" and inserting "September 30, 2017". **Effective** 7-15-2016.

• **2016, Airport and Airway Extension Act of 2016 (P.L. 114-121)**

P.L. 114-121, §202(b)(2):

Amended Code Sec. 4271(d)(1)(A)(ii) by striking "March 31, 2016" and inserting "July 15, 2016". **Effective** 3-30-2016.

• **2015, Airport and Airway Extension Act of 2015 (P.L. 114-55)**

P.L. 114-55, §202(b)(2):

Amended Code Sec. 4271(d)(1)(A)(ii) by striking "September 30, 2015" and inserting "March 31, 2016". **Effective** 9-30-2015.

• **2012, FAA Modernization and Reform Act of 2012 (P.L. 112-95)**

P.L. 112-95, §1101(b)(2):

Amended Code Sec. 4271(d)(1)(A)(ii) by striking "February 17, 2012" and inserting "September 30, 2015". **Effective** 2-18-2012.

• **2012, Airport and Airway Extension Act of 2012 (P.L. 112-91)**

P.L. 112-91, §2(b)(2):

Amended Code Sec. 4271(d)(1)(A)(ii) by striking "January 31, 2012" and inserting "February 17, 2012". **Effective** 2-1-2012.

• **2011, Airport and Airway Extension Act of 2011, Part V (P.L. 112-30)**

P.L. 112-30, §202(b)(2):

Amended Code Sec. 4271(d)(1)(A)(ii) by striking "September 16, 2011" and inserting "January 31, 2012". **Effective** 9-17-2011.

• **2011, Airport and Airway Extension Act of 2011, Part IV (P.L. 112-27)**

P.L. 112-27, §2(b)(2):

Amended Code Sec. 4271(d)(1)(A)(ii) by striking "July 22, 2011" and inserting "September 16, 2011". **Effective** 7-23-2011.

• **2011, Airport and Airway Extension Act of 2011, Part III (P.L. 112-21)**

P.L. 112-21, §2(b)(2):

Amended Code Sec. 4271(d)(1)(A)(ii) by striking "June 30, 2011" and inserting "July 22, 2011". **Effective** 7-1-2011.

• **2011, Airport and Airway Extension Act of 2011, Part II (P.L. 112-16)**

P.L. 112-16, §2(b)(2):

Amended Code Sec. 4271(d)(1)(A)(ii) by striking "May 31, 2011" and inserting "June 30, 2011". **Effective** 6-1-2011.

• **2011, Airport and Airway Extension Act of 2011 (P.L. 112-7)**

P.L. 112-7, §2(b)(2):

Amended Code Sec. 4271(d)(1)(A)(ii) by striking "March 31, 2011" and inserting "May 31, 2011". **Effective** 4-1-2011.

• **2010, Airport and Airway Extension Act of 2010, Part IV (P.L. 111-329)**

P.L. 111-329, §2(b)(2):

Amended Code Sec. 4271(d)(1)(A)(ii) by striking "December 31, 2010" and inserting "March 31, 2011". **Effective** 1-1-2011.

• **2010, Airport and Airway Extension Act of 2010, Part III (P.L. 111-249)**

P.L. 111-249, §2(b)(2):

Amended Code Sec. 4271(d)(1)(A)(ii) by striking "September 30, 2010" and inserting "December 31, 2010". **Effective** 10-1-2010.

• **2010, Airline Safety and Federal Aviation Administration Extension Act of 2010 (P.L. 111-216)**

P.L. 111-216, §101(b)(2):

Amended Code Sec. 4271(d)(1)(A)(ii) by striking "August 1, 2010" and inserting "September 30, 2010". **Effective** 8-2-2010.

• **2010, Airport and Airway Extension Act of 2010, Part II (P.L. 111-197)**

P.L. 111-197, §2(b)(2):

Amended Code Sec. 4271(d)(1)(A)(ii) by striking "July 3, 2010" and inserting "August 1, 2010". **Effective** 7-4-2010.

• **2010, Airport and Airway Extension Act of 2010 (P.L. 111-161)**

P.L. 111-161, §2(b)(2):

Amended Code Sec. 4271(d)(1)(A)(ii) by striking "April 30, 2010" and inserting "July 3, 2010". **Effective** 5-1-2010.

• **2010, Federal Aviation Administration Extension Act of 2010 (P.L. 111-153)**

P.L. 111-153, §2(b)(2):

Amended Code Sec. 4271(d)(1)(A)(ii) by striking "March 31, 2010" and inserting "April 30, 2010". **Effective** 4-1-2010.

• **2009, Fiscal Year 2010 Federal Aviation Administration Extension Act, Part II (P.L. 111-116)**

P.L. 111-116, §2(b)(2):

Amended Code Sec. 4271(d)(1)(A)(ii) by striking "December 31, 2009" and inserting "March 31, 2010". **Effective** 1-1-2010.

• **2009, Fiscal Year 2010 Federal Aviation Administration Extension Act (P.L. 111-69)**

P.L. 111-69, §2(b)(2):

Amended Code Sec. 4271(d)(1)(A)(ii) by striking "September 30, 2009" and inserting "December 31, 2009". **Effective** 10-1-2009.

• **2009, (P.L. 111-68)**

P.L. 111-68, §156(a), provides:

(a) Sections 4081(d)(2)(B), 4261(j)(1)(A)(ii), and 4271(d)(1)(A)(ii) of the Internal Revenue Code of 1986 shall each be applied by substituting the date specified in section 106(3) [October 31, 2009] of this joint resolution for "September 30, 2009".

• **2009, Federal Aviation Administration Extension Act of 2009 (P.L. 111-12)**

P.L. 111-12, §2(b)(2):

Amended Code Sec. 4271(d)(1)(A)(ii) by striking "March 31, 2009" and inserting "September 30, 2009". **Effective** 4-1-2009.

EXCISE TAXES—TRANSPORTATION OF PROPERTY

• **2008, Federal Aviation Administration Extension Act of 2008, Part II (P.L. 110-330)**

P.L. 110-330, §2(b)(2):

Amended Code Sec. 4271(d)(1)(A)(ii) by striking "September 30, 2008" and inserting "March 31, 2009". **Effective** 10-1-2008.

• **2008, Federal Aviation Administration Extension Act of 2008 (P.L. 110-253)**

P.L. 110-253, §2(b)(2):

Amended Code Sec. 4271(d)(1)(A)(ii) by striking "June 30, 2008" and inserting "September 30, 2008". **Effective** 7-1-2008.

• **2008, Airport and Airway Extension Act of 2008 (P.L. 110-190)**

P.L. 110-190, §2(b)(2):

Amended Code Sec. 4271(d)(1)(A)(ii) by striking "February 29, 2008" and inserting "June 30, 2008". **Effective** 3-1-2008.

• **2007, Department of Transportation Appropriations Act, 2008 (P.L. 110-161)**

P.L. 110-161, §116(b)(2):

Amended Code Sec. 4271(d)(1)(A)(ii) by striking "September 30, 2007" and inserting "February 29, 2008". **Effective** 10-1-2007.

• **2007 (P.L. 110-92)**

P.L. 110-92, §149(a), provides:

SEC. 149. (a) Sections 4081(d)(2)(B), 4261(j)(1)(A)(ii), 4271(d)(1)(A)(ii), 9502(d)(1), and 9502(f)(2) of the Internal Revenue Code of 1986 shall each be applied by substituting the date specified in section 106(3) of this joint resolution [November 16, 2007.—CCH] for "September 30, 2007" or "October 1, 2007", as the case may be.

• **1997, Taxpayer Relief Act of 1997 (P.L. 105-34)**

P.L. 105-34, §1031(b)(2):

Amended Code Sec. 4271(d)(1)(A)(ii) by striking "September 30, 1997" and inserting "September 30, 2007". **Effective**, generally, for transportation beginning on or after 10-1-97.

P.L. 105-34, §1031(g)[(f)](3), provides:

(g) [(f)] DELAYED DEPOSITS OF AIRPORT TRUST FUND TAX REVENUES.—Notwithstanding section 6302 of the Internal Revenue Code of 1986—

* * *

(3) in the case of deposits of taxes imposed by sections 4081(a)(2)(A)(ii), 4091, and 4271 of such Code, the due date for any such deposit which would (but for this subsection) be required to be made after July 31, 1998, and before October 1, 1998, shall be October 5, 1998.

• **1997, Airport and Airway Trust Fund Reinstatement Act of 1997 (P.L. 105-2)**

P.L. 105-2, §2(b)(2):

Amended Code Sec. 4271(d). **Effective** for transportation beginning on or after 3-7-97. For a special rule, see P.L. 105-2, §2(e)(2)(A)-(C). Prior to amendment, Code Sec. 4271(d) read as follows:

(d) TERMINATION.—The tax imposed by subsection (a) shall apply with respect to transportation beginning after August 31, 1982, and before January 1, 1996, and to transportation beginning on or after the date which is 7 calendar days after the date of the enactment of the Small Business Job Protection Act of 1996 and before January 1, 1997.

P.L. 105-2, §2(e)(2)(A)-(C), provides:

(2) TICKET TAXES.—

(A) IN GENERAL.—The amendments made by subsection (b) shall apply to transportation beginning on or after such 7th day.

(B) EXCEPTION FOR CERTAIN PAYMENTS.—Except as provided in subparagraph (C), the amendments made by subsection (b) shall not apply to any amount paid before such 7th day.

(C) PAYMENTS OF PROPERTY TRANSPORTATION TAX WITHIN CONTROLLED GROUP.—In the case of the tax imposed by section 4271 of the Internal Revenue Code of 1986, subparagraph (B) shall not apply to any amount paid by 1 member of a controlled group for transportation furnished by another member of such group. For purposes of the preceding sentence, all persons treated as a single employer under subsection (a) or (b) of section 52 of the Internal Revenue Code of 1986 shall be treated as members of a controlled group.

P.L. 105-2, §2(f):

For the text of Act Sec. 2(f), concerning the application of the look-back safe harbor for deposits, see Code Sec. 9502(b).

• **1996, Small Business Job Protection Act of 1996 (P.L. 104-188)**

P.L. 104-188, §1609(b):

Amended Code Sec. 4271(d) by striking "January 1, 1996" and inserting "January 1, 1996, and to transportation beginning on or after the date which is 7 calendar days after the date of the enactment of the Small Business Job Protection Act of 1996 and before January 1, 1997". **Effective** 8-27-96, but does not apply to any amount paid before such date.

• **1990, Omnibus Budget Reconciliation Act of 1990 (P.L. 101-508)**

P.L. 101-508, §11213(d)(1):

Amended Code Sec. 4271(d) by striking "January 1, 1991" and inserting "January 1, 1996". **Effective** 11-5-90. However, see Act Sec. 11213(f) in the amendment notes following Code Sec. 4041(c).

• **1987, Airport and Airway Revenue Act of 1987 (P.L. 100-223)**

P.L. 100-223, §402(a)(2):

Amended Code Sec. 4271(d) by striking out "January 1, 1988" each place it appears and inserting in lieu thereof "January 1, 1991". **Effective** 12-30-87.

• **1982, Tax Equity and Fiscal Responsibility Act of 1982 (P.L. 97-248)**

P.L. 97-248, §280(b):

Amended Code Sec. 4271(d). **Effective** for transportation beginning after 8-31-82, except that such amendment will not apply to any amount paid on or before that date. Prior to amendment, Code Sec. 4271(d) read as follows:

(d) TERMINATION.—Effective with respect to transportation beginning after September 30, 1980, the tax imposed by subsection (a) shall not apply.

• **1980 (P.L. 96-298)**

P.L. 96-298, §1(b):

Substituted September 30, 1980 for June 30, 1980 in Code Sec. 4271(d).

• **1970 (P.L. 91-258)**

P.L. 91-258, §204:

Added Code Sec. 4271. **Effective** for transportation beginning after 6-30-70.

[Sec. 4272]

SEC. 4272. DEFINITION OF TAXABLE TRANSPORTATION, ETC.

[Sec. 4272(a)]

(a) IN GENERAL.—For purposes of this part, except as provided in subsection (b), the term "taxable transportation" means transportation by air which begins and ends in the United States.

[Sec. 4272(b)]

(b) EXCEPTIONS.—For purposes of this part, the term "taxable transportation" does not include—

(1) that portion of any transportation which meets the requirements of paragraphs (1), (2), (3), and (4) of section 4262(b), or

(2) under regulations prescribed by the Secretary, transportation of property in the course of exportation (including shipment to a possession of the United States) by continuous movement, and in due course so exported.

Amendments

• **1976, Tax Reform Act of 1976 (P.L. 94-455)**

P.L. 94-455, §1906(b)(13)(A):

Amended 1954 Code by substituting "Secretary" for "Secretary or his delegate" each place it appeared. **Effective** 2-1-77.

[Sec. 4272(c)]

(c) EXCESS BAGGAGE OF PASSENGERS.—For purposes of this part, the term "property" does not include excess baggage accompanying a passenger traveling on an aircraft operated on an established line.

[Sec. 4272(d)]

(d) TRANSPORTATION.—For purposes of this part, the term "transportation" includes layover or waiting time and movement of the aircraft in deadhead service.

EXCISE TAXES—TRANSPORTATION BY AIR

Amendments

- 1970 (P.L. 91-258)

P.L. 91-258, § 204:

Added Code Sec. 4272. **Effective** for transportation beginning after 6-30-70.

PART III—SPECIAL PROVISIONS APPLICABLE TO TAXES ON TRANSPORTATION BY AIR

Sec. 4281. Small aircraft on nonestablished lines.
Sec. 4282. Transportation by air for other members of affiliated group.

[Sec. 4281]

SEC. 4281. SMALL AIRCRAFT ON NONESTABLISHED LINES.

[Sec. 4281(a)]

(a) IN GENERAL.—The taxes imposed by sections 4261 and 4271 shall not apply to transportation by an aircraft having a maximum certificated takeoff weight of 6,000 pounds or less, except when such aircraft is operated on an established line or when such aircraft is a jet aircraft.

[Sec. 4281(b)]

(b) MAXIMUM CERTIFICATED TAKEOFF WEIGHT.—For purposes of this section, the term "maximum certificated takeoff weight" means the maximum such weight contained in the type certificate or airworthiness certificate.

[Sec. 4281(c)]

(c) SIGHTSEEING.—For purposes of this section, an aircraft shall not be considered as operated on an established line at any time during which such aircraft is being operated on a flight the sole purpose of which is sightseeing.

[Sec. 4281(d)]

(d) JET AIRCRAFT.—For purposes of this section, the term "jet aircraft" shall not include any aircraft which is a rotorcraft or propeller aircraft.

Amendments

- 2014, Tax Technical Corrections Act of 2014 (P.L. 113-295)

P.L. 113-295, § 204(a), Division A:

Amended Code Sec. 4281. **Effective** as if included in section 1107 of the FAA Modernization and Reform Act of 2012 (P.L. 112-95) to which it relates [effective for taxable transportation provided after 3-31-2012.—CCH]. Prior to amendment, Code Sec. 4281 read as follows:

SEC. 4281. SMALL AIRCRAFT ON NONESTABLISHED LINES.

The taxes imposed by sections 4261 and 4271 shall not apply to transportation by an aircraft having a maximum certificated takeoff weight of 6,000 pounds or less, except when such aircraft is operated on an established line or when such aircraft is a jet aircraft. For purposes of the preceding sentence, the term "maximum certificated takeoff weight" means the maximum such weight contained in the type certificate or airworthiness certificate. For purposes of this section, an aircraft shall not be considered as operated on an established line at any time during which such aircraft is being operated on a flight the sole purpose of which is sightseeing.

Amendments

- 2012, FAA Modernization and Reform Act of 2012 (P.L. 112-95)

P.L. 112-95, § 1107(a):

Amended Code Sec. 4281 by inserting "or when such aircraft is a jet aircraft" after "an established line" in the first sentence. **Effective** for taxable transportation provided after 3-31-2012.

- 2005, Safe, Accountable, Flexible, Efficient Transportation Equity Act: A Legacy for Users (P.L. 109-59)

P.L. 109-59, § 11124(a):

Amended Code Sec. 4281 by adding at the end a new sentence. **Effective** with respect to transportation beginning after 9-30-2005, but shall not apply to any amount paid before such date for such transportation.

- 1982, Tax Equity and Fiscal Responsibility Act of 1982 (P.L. 97-248)

P.L. 97-248, § 280(c)(2)(B):

Amended Code Sec. 4281 by striking out "(as defined in section 4492(b))" and by adding at the end a new sentence. **Effective** with respect to transportation beginning after 8-31-82, except that the amendment will not apply to any amount paid on or before that date.

- 1970 (P.L. 91-258)

P.L. 91-258, § 205(a)(1):

Added Code Sec. 4281. **Effective** 7-1-70.

[Sec. 4282]

SEC. 4282. TRANSPORTATION BY AIR FOR OTHER MEMBERS OF AFFILIATED GROUP.

[Sec. 4282(a)]

(a) GENERAL RULE.—Under regulations prescribed by the Secretary, if—

(1) one member of an affiliated group is the owner or lessee of an aircraft, and

(2) such aircraft is not available for hire by persons who are not members of such group,

no tax shall be imposed under section 4261 or 4271 upon any payment received by one member of the affiliated group from another member of such group for services furnished to such other member in connection with the use of such aircraft.

Amendments

- 1976, Tax Reform Act of 1976 (P.L. 94-455)

P.L. 94-455, § 1906(b)(13)(A):

Amended 1954 Code by substituting "Secretary" for "Secretary or his delegate" each place it appeared. **Effective** 2-1-77.

[Sec. 4282(b)]

(b) AVAILABILITY FOR HIRE.—For purposes of subsection (a), the determination of whether an aircraft is available for hire by persons who are not members of an affiliated group shall be made on a flight-by-flight basis.

Amendments

- 1996, Small Business Job Protection Act of 1996 (P.L. 104-188)

P.L. 104-188, § 1609(f):

Amended Code Sec. 4282 by redesignating subsection (b) as subsection (c) and by inserting after subsection (a) a new subsection (b). **Effective** 8-27-96.

[Sec. 4282(c)]

(c) AFFILIATED GROUP.—For purposes of subsection (a), the term "affiliated group" has the meaning assigned to such term by section 1504(a), except that all corporations shall be treated as includible corporations (without any exclusion under section 1504(b)).

EXCISE TAXES—SPECIAL PROVISIONS

Amendments

• **1996, Small Business Job Protection Act of 1996 (P.L. 104-188)**

P.L. 104-188, §1609(f):

Amended Code Sec. 4282 by redesignating subsection (b) as subsection (c). **Effective** on the 7th calendar day after 8-20-96.

Amendments

• **1990, Omnibus Budget Reconciliation Act of 1990 (P.L. 101-508)**

P.L. 101-508, §11213(e)(1):

Repealed Code Sec. 4283. **Effective** 11-5-90. However, see Act Sec. 11213(f) in the amendment notes following Code Sec. 4041(c). Prior to repeal, Code Sec. 4283 read as follows:

SEC. 4283. REDUCTION IN AVIATION-RELATED TAXES IN CERTAIN CASES.

[Sec. 4283(a)]

(a) REDUCTION IN RATES.—If the funding percentage is less than 85 percent, with respect to any taxable event occurring during 1991—

(1) subsections (a) and (b) of section 4261 (relating to tax on transportation of persons by air) shall each be applied by substituting "4 percent" for "8 percent",

(2) subsection (a) of section 4271 (relating to tax on transportation of property by air) shall be applied by substituting "2.5 percent" for "5 percent",

(3) paragraph (1) of section 4041(c) (relating to tax on certain fuels used in noncommercial aviation) shall be applied by substituting "7 cents" for "14 cents", and

(4) paragraph (2) of section 4041(c) (relating to tax on gasoline used in noncommercial aviation) shall not apply.

Amendments

• **1989, Omnibus Budget Reconciliation Act of 1989 (P.L. 101-239)**

P.L. 101-239, §7501(a):

Amended Code Sec. 4283(a) by striking "1990" and inserting "1991". **Effective** 12-17-89.

[Sec. 4283(b)]

(b) FUNDING PERCENTAGE.—

(1) IN GENERAL.—For purposes of this section, the funding percentage is the percentage (determined by the Secretary) which—

(A) the sum of—

(i) the aggregate amounts obligated under section 505 of the Airport and Airway Improvement Act of 1982 for fiscal years 1989 and 1990, and

(ii) the aggregate amounts appropriated under subsections (a) and (b) of section 506 of such Act for such fiscal years, is of

(B) the sum of—

(i) the aggregate amounts authorized to be obligated under such section 505 for such fiscal years, and

(ii) the aggregate amounts authorized to be appropriated under subsections (a) and (b) of such section 506 for such fiscal years.

• **1970 (P.L. 91-258)**

P.L. 91-258, §205(a)(1):

Added Code Sec. 4282. **Effective** 7-1-70.

[Sec. 4283—Repealed]

(2) RULES FOR APPLYING PARAGRAPH (1).—

(A) TREATMENT OF PRIOR YEAR AMOUNTS.—For purposes of paragraph (1), an amount shall be treated as authorized, obligated, or appropriated only for the 1st fiscal year for which it is authorized, obligated, or appropriated, as the case may be.

(B) TREATMENT OF SEQUESTERED AMOUNTS.—The determination under paragraph (1)(A) shall be made without regard to the sequestration of any amount described therein pursuant to an order under part C of title II of the Balanced Budget and Emergency Deficit Control Act of 1985 (for any successor law).

(3) DETERMINATION OF FUNDING PERCENTAGE.—

(A) IN GENERAL.—Not later than December 1, 1990, the Secretary shall determine—

(i) the funding percentage, and

(ii) whether the rate reductions under this section shall apply to taxable events occurring during 1991.

(B) DETERMINATIONS TO BE PUBLISHED IN FEDERAL REGISTER.—As soon as practicable after making the determinations under subparagraph (A), the Secretary shall publish such determinations in the Federal Register.

Amendments

• **1989, Omnibus Budget Reconciliation Act of 1989 (P.L. 101-239)**

P.L. 101-239, §7501(b)(1):

Amended Code Sec. 4283(b)(1)(A)(i) by striking "1988 and 1989" and inserting "1989 and 1990". **Effective** 12-19-89.

P.L. 101-239, §7501(b)(2)(A)-(B):

Amended Code Sec. 4283(b)(3) by striking "1990" and inserting "1991", and by striking "1989" and inserting "1990". **Effective** 12-19-89.

[Sec. 4283(c)]

(c) TAXABLE EVENT.—For purposes of this section—

(1) TAXABLE TRANSPORTATION BY AIR.—In the case of the taxes imposed by sections 4261 and 4271, the taxable event shall be treated as occurring when the payment for the taxable transportation is made.

(2) SALE OR USE OF FUEL.—In the case of the taxes imposed by section 4041(c), the taxable event shall be the sale or use on which tax is imposed.

Amendments

• **1987, Airport and Airway Revenue Act of 1987 (P.L. 100-223)**

P.L. 100-223, §405(a):

Amended part III of subchapter C of chapter 33 by adding at the end thereof a new section 4283. **Effective** 12-30-87.

Subchapter E—Special Provisions Applicable to Services and Facilities Taxes

Sec. 4291.   Cases where persons receiving payment must collect tax.
Sec. 4293.   Exemption for United States and possessions.

[Sec. 4291]

SEC. 4291. CASES WHERE PERSONS RECEIVING PAYMENT MUST COLLECT TAX.

Except as otherwise provided in section 4263(a), every person receiving any payment for facilities or services on which a tax is imposed upon the payor thereof under this chapter shall collect the amount of the tax from the person making such payment.

Amendments

• **1970 (P.L. 91-258)**

P.L. 91-258, §205(c)(3):

Amended Code Sec. 4291 by substituting "section 4263(a)" for "section 4264(a)". **Effective** 7-1-70.

• **1965, Excise Tax Reduction Act of 1965 (P.L. 89-44)**

P.L. 89-44, §305(a):

Amended Sec. 4291. **Effective** 1-1-66. Prior to amendment, Sec. 4291 read as follows:

"Except as otherwise provided in sections 4231 and 4264(a), every person receiving any payment for facilities or services on which a tax is imposed upon the payor thereof under this chapter shall collect the amount of the tax from the person making such payment. For the purpose of this section every club or organization having life members shall collect the tax imposed on life memberships by section 4241."

• **1958, Excise Tax Technical Changes Act of 1958 (P.L. 85-859)**

P.L. 85-859, §131(g):

Amended Code Sec. 4291 by substituting the words "Except as otherwise provided in sections 4231 and 4264(a)," for the words "Except as provided in section 4264(a),". **Effective** 1-1-59.

• **1956 (P.L. 796, 84th Cong.)**

P.L. 796, 84th Cong., §2:

Amended the first sentence of Code Sec. 4291. **Effective** for amounts paid on or after 10-1-56 for transportation commencing on or after that date. Prior to amendment, the first sentence of Code §4291 read:

Every person receiving any payment for facilities or services on which a tax is imposed upon the payor thereof under this chapter, shall collect the amount of the tax from the person making such payment, except that if the payment specified in section 4261 is made outside the United States for a prepaid order, exchange order, or similar order, the person furnishing the initial transportation pursuant to such order shall collect the amount of the tax.

[Sec. 4293]

SEC. 4293. EXEMPTION FOR UNITED STATES AND POSSESSIONS.

The Secretary of the Treasury may authorize exemption from the taxes imposed by section 4041, section 4051, chapter 32 (other than the taxes imposed by sections 4064 and 4121) and subchapter B of chapter 33, as to any particular article, or service or class of articles or services, to be purchased for the exclusive use of the United States, if he determines that the imposition of such taxes with respect to such articles or services, or class of articles or services will cause substantial burden or expense which can be avoided by granting tax exemption and that full benefit of such exemption, if granted, will accrue to the United States.

EXCISE TAXES—POLICIES OF FOREIGN INSURERS

Amendments

• **2014, Tax Technical Corrections Act of 2014 (P.L. 113-295)**

P.L. 113-295, §221(a)(103)(B)(iii), Division A:

Amended Code Sec. 4293 by striking "subchapter A of chapter 31," before "section 4041,". **Effective** generally 12-19-2014. For a special rule, see Act Sec. 221(b)(2), Division A, below.

P.L. 113-295, §221(b)(2), Division A, provides:

(2) SAVINGS PROVISION.—If—

(A) any provision amended or repealed by the amendments made by this section applied to—

(i) any transaction occurring before the date of the enactment of this Act,

(ii) any property acquired before such date of enactment, or

(iii) any item of income, loss, deduction, or credit taken into account before such date of enactment, and

(B) the treatment of such transaction, property, or item under such provision would (without regard to the amendments or repeals made by this section) affect the liability for tax for periods ending after date of enactment, nothing in the amendments or repeals made by this section shall be construed to affect the treatment of such transaction, property, or item for purposes of determining liability for tax for periods ending after such date of enactment.

• **1990, Omnibus Budget Reconciliation Act of 1990 (P.L. 101-508)**

P.L. 101-508, §11221(c):

Amended Code Sec. 4293 by inserting "subchapter A of chapter 31," before "section 4041". **Effective** 1-1-91. For an exception, see Act Sec. 11221(f)(2), below.

P.L. 101-508, §11221(f)(2), provides:

(2) EXCEPTION FOR BINDING CONTRACTS.—In determining whether any tax imposed by subchapter A of chapter 31 of the Internal Revenue Code of 1986, as added by this section, applies to any sale after December 31, 1990, there shall not be taken into account the amount paid for any article (or any part or accessory therefor) if the purchaser held on September 30, 1990, a contract (which was binding on such date and at all times thereafter before the purchase) for the purchase of such article (or such part or accessory).

• **1988, Technical and Miscellaneous Revenue Act of 1988 (P.L. 100-647)**

P.L. 100-647, §6103(a):

Amended Code Sec. 4293 by inserting "section 4051," after "section 4041". **Effective** 11-11-88.

• **1978, Energy Tax Act of 1978 (P.L. 95-618)**

P.L. 95-618, §201(c)(2):

Amended Code Sec. 4293 by substituting "taxes imposed by sections 4064 and 4121" for "tax imposed by section 4121". For **effective** date, see historical comment for P.L. 95-618, §201 under Code Sec. 4064.

• **1978 (P.L. 95-502)**

P.L. 95-502, §202(b), (d):

Amended Code Sec. 4293 by striking out "chapters 31 and 32" and inserting in place thereof "section 4041, chapter 32". **Effective** 10-1-80.

• **1978, Black Lung Benefits Revenue Act of 1977 (P.L. 95-227)**

P.L. 95-227, §2(b)(3):

Added "(other than the tax imposed by section 4121)" in the second line of Code Sec. 4293. For **effective** date, see the historical comment for P.L. 95-227 under Code Sec. 4121.

• **1976, Tax Reform Act of 1976 (P.L. 94-455)**

P.L. 94-455, §1906(b)(13)(B):

Substituted "Secretary of the Treasury" for "Secretary" in Code Sec. 4293. **Effective** 2-1-77.

• **1970 (P.L. 91-258)**

P.L. 91-258, §205(a)(3):

Amended Code Sec. 4293 by substituting "subchapter B" for "subchapters B and C." **Effective** 7-1-70.

CHAPTER 34—TAXES ON CERTAIN INSURANCE POLICIES

SUBCHAPTER A.   Policies issued by foreign insurers.
SUBCHAPTER B.   Insured and self-insured health plans.

Subchapter A—Policies Issued by Foreign Insurers

Sec. 4371.   Imposition of tax.
Sec. 4372.   Definitions.
Sec. 4373.   Exemptions.
Sec. 4374.   Liability for tax.

[Sec. 4371]

SEC. 4371. IMPOSITION OF TAX.

There is hereby imposed, on each policy of insurance, indemnity bond, annuity contract, or policy of reinsurance issued by any foreign insurer or reinsurer, a tax at the following rates:

(1) CASUALTY INSURANCE AND INDEMNITY BONDS.—4 cents on each dollar, or fractional part thereof, of the premium paid on the policy of casualty insurance or the indemnity bond, if issued to or for, or in the name of, an insured as defined in section 4372(d);

(2) LIFE INSURANCE, SICKNESS AND ACCIDENT POLICIES, AND ANNUITY CONTRACTS.—1 cent on each dollar, or fractional part thereof, of the premium paid on the policy of life, sickness, or accident insurance, or annuity contract; and

(3) REINSURANCE.—1 cent on each dollar, or fractional part thereof, of the premium paid on the policy of reinsurance covering any of the contracts taxable under paragraph (1) or (2).

Amendments

• **1989, Omnibus Budget Reconciliation Act of 1989 (P.L. 101-239)**

P.L. 101-239, §7811(i)(11):

Amended Code Sec. 4371(2) by striking ", unless the insurer is subject to tax under section 842(b)" after "annuity contract,". **Effective** as if included in the provision of P.L. 100-647 to which it relates.

• **1987, Revenue Act of 1987 (P.L. 100-203)**

P.L. 100-203, §10242(c)(3):

Amended Code Sec. 4371(2) by striking out "section 813" and inserting in lieu thereof "section 842(b)". **Effective** for tax years beginning after 12-31-87.

• **1984, Deficit Reduction Act of 1984 (P.L. 98-369)**

P.L. 98-369, §211(b)(23):

Amended Code Sec. 4371(2) by striking out "section 819" and inserting in lieu thereof "section 813". **Effective** for tax years beginning after 12-31-83.

• **1976, Tax Reform Act of 1976 (P.L. 94-455)**

P.L. 94-455, §1904(a)(12):

Amended Chapter 34 to include only amended Code Secs. 4371 through 4374. **Effective** 2-1-77. Prior to amendment, Code Sec. 4371 read as follows:

There is hereby imposed, on each policy of insurance, indemnity bond, annuity contract, or policy of reinsurance issued by any foreign insurer or reinsurer, a tax at the following rates:

(1) CASUALTY INSURANCE AND INDEMNITY BONDS.—Four cents on each dollar, or fractional part thereof, of the premium charged on the policy of casualty insurance or the indemnity bond, if issued to or for, or in the name of, an insured as defined in section 4372(d);

(2) LIFE INSURANCE, SICKNESS, AND ACCIDENT POLICIES, AND ANNUITY CONTRACTS.—One cent on each dollar, or fractional part thereof, of the premium charged on the policy of life, sickness, or accident insurance, or annuity contract, unless the insurer is subject to tax under section 819;

(3) REINSURANCE.—One cent on each dollar, or fractional part thereof, of the premium charged on the policy of reinsurance covering any of the contracts taxable under paragraph (1) or (2).

If the tax imposed by this section is paid on the basis of a return under regulations prescribed under section 4374, the tax under paragraphs (1), (2), and (3) shall be computed on the premium paid in lieu of the premium charged.

• **1965, Excise Tax Reduction Act of 1965 (P.L. 89-44)**

P.L. 89-44, §804(b):

Amended Sec. 4371 by adding the last sentence following subparagraph (3). **Effective** 7-1-65.

• **1959, Life Insurance Company Income Tax Act of 1959 (P.L. 86-69)**

P.L. 86-69, §3(f)(3):

Amended Sec. 4371(2) by striking out "816" and by inserting in lieu thereof "819". **Effective** for tax years beginning after 12-31-57.

EXCISE TAXES—POLICIES OF FOREIGN INSURERS

• **1958, Excise Tax Technical Changes Act of 1958 (P.L. 85-859)**

P.L. 85-859, §141(a):

Amended Sec. 4371 by changing the material preceding paragraph (1). **Effective** 1-1-59. Prior to amendment, that material read as follows:

"There shall be imposed a tax on each policy of insurance, indemnity bond, annuity contract, or policy of reinsurance issued by any foreign insurer or reinsurer at the following rates:".

• **1956, Life Insurance Company Tax Act for 1955 (P.L. 429, 84th Cong.)**

P.L. 429, 84th Cong., §5(9):

Amended Sec. 4371(2) by substituting "816" in lieu of "807". **Effective** for tax years beginning after 12-31-54.

[Sec. 4372]

SEC. 4372. DEFINITIONS.

[Sec. 4372(a)]

(a) FOREIGN INSURER OR REINSURER.—For purposes of section 4371, the term "foreign insurer or reinsurer" means an insurer or reinsurer who is a nonresident alien individual, or a foreign partnership, or a foreign corporation. The term includes a nonresident alien individual, foreign partnership, or foreign corporation which shall become bound by an obligation of the nature of an indemnity bond. The term does not include a foreign government, or municipal or other corporation exercising the taxing power.

Amendments

• **1976, Tax Reform Act of 1976 (P.L. 94-455)**

P.L. 94-455, §1904(a)(12):

Amended Chapter 34 to include only amended Code Secs. 4371 through 4374. **Effective** 2-1-77. Prior to amendment, Code Sec. 4372(a) read as follows:

(a) FOREIGN INSURER OR REINSURER.—For purposes of this subchapter, the term "foreign insurer or reinsurer" means an insurer or reinsurer who is a nonresident alien individual, foreign partnership, or a foreign corporation. The term includes a nonresident alien individual, foreign partnership, or foreign corporation which shall become bound by an obligation of the nature of an indemnity bond.

[Sec. 4372(b)]

(b) POLICY OF CASUALTY INSURANCE.—For purposes of section 4371(1), the term "policy of casualty insurance" means any policy (other than life) or other instrument by whatever name called whereby a contract of insurance is made, continued, or renewed.

Amendments

• **1976, Tax Reform Act of 1976 (P.L. 94-455)**

P.L. 94-455, §1904(a)(12):

Amended Chapter 34 to include only amended Code Secs. 4371 through 4374. The amendment did not alter Code Sec. 4372(b). **Effective** 2-1-77.

[Sec. 4372(c)]

(c) INDEMNITY BOND.—For purposes of this chapter, the term "indemnity bond" means any instrument by whatever name called whereby an obligation of the nature of an indemnity, fidelity, or surety bond is made, continued, or renewed. The term includes any bond for indemnifying any person who shall have become bound or engaged as surety, and any bond for the due execution or performance of any contract, obligation, or requirement, or the duties of any office or position, and to account for money received by virtue thereof, where a premium is charged for the execution of such bond.

Amendments

• **1976, Tax Reform Act of 1976 (P.L. 94-455)**

P.L. 94-455, §1904(a)(12):

Amended Chapter 34 to include only amended Code Secs. 4371 through 4374, and also substituted "chapter" for "subchapter" in the first sentence of Code Sec. 4372(c). **Effective** 2-1-77.

[Sec. 4372(d)]

(d) INSURED.—For purposes of section 4371(1), the term "insured" means—

(1) a domestic corporation or partnership, or an individual resident of the United States, against, or with respect to, hazards, risks, losses, or liabilities wholly or partly within the United States, or

(2) a foreign corporation, foreign partnership, or nonresident individual, engaged in a trade or business within the United States, against, or with respect to, hazards, risks, losses, or liabilities within the United States.

Amendments

• **1976, Tax Reform Act of 1976 (P.L. 94-455)**

P.L. 94-455, §1904(a)(12)

Amended Chapter 34 to include only amended Code Secs. 4371 through 4374, and also added "against" and "or with respect to" in Code Sec. 4372(d)(2). **Effective** 2-1-77.

[Sec. 4372(e)]

(e) POLICY OF LIFE, SICKNESS, OR ACCIDENT INSURANCE, OR ANNUITY CONTRACT.—For purposes of section 4371(2), the term "policy of life, sickness, or accident insurance, or annuity contract" means any policy or other instrument by whatever name called whereby a contract of insurance or an annuity contract is made, continued, or renewed with respect to the life or hazards to the person of a citizen or resident of the United States.

[Sec. 4372(f)]

(f) POLICY OF REINSURANCE.—For purposes of section 4371(3), the term "policy of reinsurance" means any policy or other instrument by whatever name called whereby a contract of reinsurance is made, continued, or renewed against, or with respect to, any of the hazards, risks, losses, or liabilities covered by contracts taxable under paragraph (1) or (2) of section 4371.

Amendments

• **1958, Excise Tax Technical Changes Act of 1958 (P.L. 85-859)**

P.L. 85-859, §141(a):

Amended Sec. 4372 by deleting the phrase "For the purpose" and substituting the phrase "For purposes" in each of the subsections (a) through (f), and amended paragraph (2) by inserting after the phrase "trade or business within the United States," the phrase "against or" and by inserting "losses," immediately following "risks,". **Effective** 1-1-59.

[Sec. 4373]

SEC. 4373. EXEMPTIONS.

The tax imposed by section 4371 shall not apply to—

(1) EFFECTIVELY CONNECTED ITEMS.—Any amount which is effectively connected with the conduct of a trade or business within the United States unless such amount is exempt from the application of section 882(a) pursuant to a treaty obligation of the United States.

EXCISE TAXES—POLICIES OF FOREIGN INSURERS

(2) INDEMNITY BOND.—Any indemnity bond required to be filed by any person to secure payment of any pension, allowance, allotment, relief, or insurance by the United States, or to secure a duplicate for, or the payment of, any bond, note, certificate of indebtedness, war-saving certificate, warrant, or check, issued by the United States.

Amendments

• **1988, Technical and Miscellaneous Revenue Act of 1988 (P.L. 100-647)**

P.L. 100-647, § 1012(q)(13)(A):

Amended Code Sec. 4373(1). **Effective** with respect to premiums amendment, Code Sec. 4373(1) read as follows:

(1) DOMESTIC AGENT.—Any policy, indemnity bond, or annuity contract signed or countersigned by an officer or agent of the insurer in a State, or in the District of Columbia, within which such insurer is authorized to do business; or

• **1976, Tax Reform Act of 1976 (P.L. 94-455)**

P.L. 94-455, § 1904(a)(12):

Amended Chapter 34 to include only amended Code Secs. 4371 through 4374, and also altered Code Sec. 4373(1) by: (1) substituting "or in the District of Columbia," for "Territory, or District of the United States"; and (2) substituting "; or" for the period at the end of Code Sec. 4373(1). **Effective** 2-1-77.

• **1958, Excise Tax Technical Changes Act of 1958 (P.L. 85-859)**

P.L. 85-859, § 141(a):

Amended Sec. 4373 by deleting "; or" at the end of paragraph (1) and substituting a period. **Effective** 1-1-59.

[Sec. 4374]

SEC. 4374. LIABILITY FOR TAX.

The tax imposed by this chapter shall be paid, on the basis of a return, by any person who makes, signs, issues, or sells any of the documents and instruments subject to the tax, or for whose use or benefit the same are made, signed, issued, or sold. The United States or any agency or instrumentality thereof shall not be liable for the tax.

Amendments

• **1976, Tax Reform Act of 1976 (P.L. 94-455)**

P.L. 94-455, § 1904(a)(12):

Amended Chapter 34 to include only amended Code Secs. 4371 through 4374, and also altered Code Sec. 4374. **Effective** 2-1-77. Prior to amendment, Code Sec. 4374 read as follows:

SEC. 4374. PAYMENT OF TAX.

Any person to or for whom or in whose name any policy, indemnity bond, or annuity contract referred to in section 4371 is issued, or any solicitor or broker acting for or on behalf of such person in the procurement of any such instrument, shall affix the proper stamps to such instrument. Notwithstanding the preceding sentence, the Secretary or his delegate may, by regulations, provide that the tax imposed by section 4371 shall be paid on the basis of a return.

• **1965, Excise Tax Reduction Act of 1965 (P.L. 89-44)**

P.L. 89-44, § 804(a):

Amended Sec. 4374 by adding the last sentence, and also amended the heading of Sec. 4374. Prior to amendment, the heading read: "SEC. 4374. AFFIXING OF STAMPS." **Effective** 7-1-65.

Subchapter B—Insured and Self-Insured Health Plans

Sec. 4375.   Health insurance.
Sec. 4376.   Self-insured health plans.
Sec. 4377.   Definitions and special rules.

[Sec. 4375]

SEC. 4375. HEALTH INSURANCE.

[Sec. 4375(a)]

(a) IMPOSITION OF FEE.—There is hereby imposed on each specified health insurance policy for each policy year ending after September 30, 2012, a fee equal to the product of $2 ($1 in the case of policy years ending during fiscal year 2013) multiplied by the average number of lives covered under the policy.

[Sec. 4375(b)]

(b) LIABILITY FOR FEE.—The fee imposed by subsection (a) shall be paid by the issuer of the policy.

[Sec. 4375(c)]

(c) SPECIFIED HEALTH INSURANCE POLICY.—For purposes of this section:

(1) IN GENERAL.—Except as otherwise provided in this section, the term "specified health insurance policy" means any accident or health insurance policy (including a policy under a group health plan) issued with respect to individuals residing in the United States.

(2) EXEMPTION FOR CERTAIN POLICIES.—The term "specified health insurance policy" does not include any insurance if substantially all of its coverage is of excepted benefits described in section 9832(c).

(3) TREATMENT OF PREPAID HEALTH COVERAGE ARRANGEMENTS.—

(A) IN GENERAL.—In the case of any arrangement described in subparagraph (B), such arrangement shall be treated as a specified health insurance policy, and the person referred to in such subparagraph shall be treated as the issuer.

(B) DESCRIPTION OF ARRANGEMENTS.—An arrangement is described in this subparagraph if under such arrangement fixed payments or premiums are received as consideration for any person's agreement to provide or arrange for the provision of accident or health coverage to residents of the United States, regardless of how such coverage is provided or arranged to be provided.

[Sec. 4375(d)]

(d) ADJUSTMENTS FOR INCREASES IN HEALTH CARE SPENDING.—In the case of any policy year ending in any fiscal year beginning after September 30, 2014, the dollar amount in effect under subsection (a) for such policy year shall be equal to the sum of such dollar amount for policy years ending in the previous fiscal year (determined after the application of this subsection), plus an amount equal to the product of—

(1) such dollar amount for policy years ending in the previous fiscal year, multiplied by

(2) the percentage increase in the projected per capita amount of National Health Expenditures, as most recently published by the Secretary before the beginning of the fiscal year.

[Sec. 4375(e)]

(e) TERMINATION.—This section shall not apply to policy years ending after September 30, 2029.

Amendments

• **2019, Further Consolidated Appropriations Act, 2020 (P.L. 116-94)**

P.L. 116-94, § 104(b), Div. N:

Amended Code Sec. 4375(e) by striking "2019" and inserting "2029". **Effective** 12-20-2019.

• **2010, Patient Protection and Affordable Care Act (P.L. 111-148)**

P.L. 111-148, § 6301(e)(2)(A):

Amended chapter 34 by adding at the end a new subchapter B [sic] (Code Secs. 4375-4377). **Effective** 3-23-2010.

EXCISE TAXES—POLICIES OF FOREIGN INSURERS

[Sec. 4376]

SEC. 4376. SELF-INSURED HEALTH PLANS.

[Sec. 4376(a)]

(a) IMPOSITION OF FEE.—In the case of any applicable self-insured health plan for each plan year ending after September 30, 2012, there is hereby imposed a fee equal to $2 ($1 in the case of plan years ending during fiscal year 2013) multiplied by the average number of lives covered under the plan.

[Sec. 4376(b)]

(b) LIABILITY FOR FEE.—

(1) IN GENERAL.—The fee imposed by subsection (a) shall be paid by the plan sponsor.

(2) PLAN SPONSOR.—For purposes of paragraph (1) the term "plan sponsor" means—

(A) the employer in the case of a plan established or maintained by a single employer,

(B) the employee organization in the case of a plan established or maintained by an employee organization,

(C) in the case of—

(i) a plan established or maintained by 2 or more employers or jointly by 1 or more employers and 1 or more employee organizations,

(ii) a multiple employer welfare arrangement, or

(iii) a voluntary employees' beneficiary association described in section 501(c)(9), the association, committee, joint board of trustees, or other similar group of representatives of the parties who establish or maintain the plan, or

(D) the cooperative or association described in subsection (c)(2)(F) in the case of a plan established or maintained by such a cooperative or association.

[Sec. 4376(c)]

(c) APPLICABLE SELF-INSURED HEALTH PLAN.—For purposes of this section, the term "applicable self-insured health plan" means any plan for providing accident or health coverage if—

(1) any portion of such coverage is provided other than through an insurance policy, and

(2) such plan is established or maintained—

(A) by 1 or more employers for the benefit of their employees or former employees,

(B) by 1 or more employee organizations for the benefit of their members or former members,

(C) jointly by 1 or more employers and 1 or more employee organizations for the benefit of employees or former employees,

(D) by a voluntary employees' beneficiary association described in section 501(c)(9),

(E) by any organization described in section 501(c)(6), or

(F) in the case of a plan not described in the preceding subparagraphs, by a multiple employer welfare arrangement (as defined in section 3(40) of [the] Employee Retirement Income Security Act of 1974), a rural electric cooperative (as defined in section 3(40)(B)(iv) of such Act), or a rural telephone cooperative association (as defined in section 3(40)(B)(v) of such Act).

[Sec. 4376(d)]

(d) ADJUSTMENTS FOR INCREASES IN HEALTH CARE SPENDING.—In the case of any plan year ending in any fiscal year beginning after September 30, 2014, the dollar amount in effect under subsection (a) for such plan year shall be equal to the sum of such dollar amount for plan years ending in the previous fiscal year (determined after the application of this subsection), plus an amount equal to the product of—

(1) such dollar amount for plan years ending in the previous fiscal year, multiplied by

(2) the percentage increase in the projected per capita amount of National Health Expenditures, as most recently published by the Secretary before the beginning of the fiscal year.

[Sec. 4376(e)]

(e) TERMINATION.—This section shall not apply to plan years ending after September 30, 2029.

Amendments

• **2019, Further Consolidated Appropriations Act, 2020 (P.L. 116-94)**

P.L. 116-94, §104(c), Div. N:

Amended Code Sec. 4376(e) by striking "2019" and inserting "2029". **Effective** 12-20-2019.

• **2010, Patient Protection and Affordable Care Act (P.L. 111-148)**

P.L. 111-148, §6301(e)(2)(A):

Amended chapter 34 by adding at the end a new subchapter B [sic] (Code Secs. 4375-4377). **Effective** 3-23-2010.

[Sec. 4377]

SEC. 4377. DEFINITIONS AND SPECIAL RULES.

[Sec. 4377(a)]

(a) DEFINITIONS.—For purposes of this subchapter—

(1) ACCIDENT AND HEALTH COVERAGE.—The term "accident and health coverage" means any coverage which, if provided by an insurance policy, would cause such policy to be a specified health insurance policy (as defined in section 4375(c)).

(2) INSURANCE POLICY.—The term "insurance policy" means any policy or other instrument whereby a contract of insurance is issued, renewed, or extended.

(3) UNITED STATES.—The term "United States" includes any possession of the United States.

[Sec. 4377(b)]

(b) TREATMENT OF GOVERNMENTAL ENTITIES.—

(1) IN GENERAL.—For purposes of this subchapter—

(A) the term "person" includes any governmental entity, and

(B) notwithstanding any other law or rule of law, governmental entities shall not be exempt from the fees imposed by this subchapter except as provided in paragraph (2).

(2) TREATMENT OF EXEMPT GOVERNMENTAL PROGRAMS.—In the case of an exempt governmental program, no fee shall be imposed under section 4375 or section 4376 on any covered life under such program.

(3) EXEMPT GOVERNMENTAL PROGRAM DEFINED.—For purposes of this subchapter, the term "exempt governmental program" means—

EXCISE TAXES—WAGERS

(A) any insurance program established under title XVIII of the Social Security Act,
(B) the medical assistance program established by title XIX or XXI of the Social Security Act,
(C) any program established by Federal law for providing medical care (other than through insurance policies) to individuals (or the spouses and dependents thereof) by reason of such individuals being members of the Armed Forces of the United States or veterans, and
(D) any program established by Federal law for providing medical care (other than through insurance policies) to members of Indian tribes (as defined in section 4(d) of the Indian Health Care Improvement Act).

[Sec. 4377(c)]

(c) TREATMENT AS TAX.—For purposes of subtitle F, the fees imposed by this subchapter shall be treated as if they were taxes.

[Sec. 4377(d)]

(d) NO COVER OVER TO POSSESSIONS.—Notwithstanding any other provision of law, no amount collected under this subchapter shall be covered over to any possession of the United States.

Amendments

• **2010, Patient Protection and Affordable Care Act (P.L. 111-148)**

P.L. 111-148, §6301(e)(2)(A):

Amended chapter 34 by adding at the end a new subchapter B (Code Secs. 4375-4377). **Effective** 3-23-2010.

CHAPTER 35—TAXES ON WAGERING

SUBCHAPTER A.	Tax on wagers.
SUBCHAPTER B.	Occupational tax.
SUBCHAPTER C.	Miscellaneous provisions.

Subchapter A—Tax on Wagers

Sec. 4401.	Imposition of tax.
Sec. 4402.	Exemptions.
Sec. 4403.	Record requirements.
Sec. 4404.	Territorial extent.
Sec. 4405.	Cross references.

[Sec. 4401]

SEC. 4401. IMPOSITION OF TAX.

[Sec. 4401(a)]

(a) WAGERS.—
(1) STATE AUTHORIZED WAGERS.—There shall be imposed on any wager authorized under the law of the State in which accepted an excise tax equal to 0.25 percent of the amount of such wager.
(2) UNAUTHORIZED WAGERS.—There shall be imposed on any wager not described in paragraph (1) an excise tax equal to 2 percent of the amount of such wager.

Amendments

• **1982, Miscellaneous Revenue Act of 1982 (P.L. 97-362)**

P.L. 97-362, §109(a):

Amended Code Sec. 4401(a). **Effective** 1-1-83. Prior to amendment, Code Sec. 4401(a) read as follows:

(a) WAGERS.—There shall be imposed on wagers, as defined in section 4421, an excise tax equal to 2 percent of the amount thereof.

• **1974 (P.L. 93-499)**

P.L. 93-499, §3(a):

Amended Code Sec. 4401(a) by substituting "2 percent" for "10 percent". **Effective** on 12-1-74, but applicable only with respect to wagers placed on or after such date.

[Sec. 4401(b)]

(b) AMOUNT OF WAGER.—In determining the amount of any wager for the purposes of this subchapter, all charges incident to the placing of such wager shall be included; except that if the taxpayer establishes, in accordance with regulations prescribed by the Secretary, that an amount equal to the tax imposed by this subchapter has been collected as a separate charge from the person placing such wager, the amount so collected shall be excluded.

Amendments

• **1976, Tax Reform Act of 1976 (P.L. 94-455)**

P.L. 94-455, §1906(b)(13)(A):

Amended 1954 Code by substituting "Secretary" for "Secretary or his delegate" each place it appeared. **Effective** 2-1-77.

[Sec. 4401(c)]

(c) PERSONS LIABLE FOR TAX.—Each person who is engaged in the business of accepting wagers shall be liable for and shall pay the tax under this subchapter on all wagers placed with him. Each person who conducts any wagering pool or lottery shall be liable for and shall pay the tax under this subchapter on all wagers placed in such pool or lottery. Any person required to register under section 4412 who receives wagers for or on behalf of another person without having registered under section 4412 the name and place of residence of such other person shall be liable for and shall pay the tax under this subchapter on all such wagers received by him.

Amendments

• **1958, Excise Tax Technical Changes Act of 1958 (P.L. 85-859)**

P.L. 85-859, §151(a):

Added the last sentence in Sec. 4401(c). **Effective** for wagers received after 9-2-58.

[Sec. 4402]

SEC. 4402. EXEMPTIONS.

No tax shall be imposed by this subchapter—

Sec. 4377(b)(3)(A)

EXCISE TAXES—WAGERS, OCCUPATIONAL TAX

(1) PARIMUTUELS.—On any wager placed with, or on any wager placed in a wagering pool conducted by, a parimutuel wagering enterprise licensed under State law,

(2) COIN-OPERATED DEVICES.—On any wager placed in a coin-operated device (as defined in section 4462 as in effect for years beginning before July 1, 1980), or on any amount paid, in lieu of inserting a coin, token, or similar object, to operate a device described in section 4462(a)(2) (as so in effect), or

(3) STATE-CONDUCTED LOTTERIES, ETC.—On any wager placed in a sweepstakes, wagering pool, or lottery which is conducted by an agency of a State acting under authority of State law, but only if such wager is placed with the State agency conducting such sweepstakes, wagering pool, or lottery, or with its authorized employees or agents.

Amendments

- **1978, Revenue Act of 1978 (P.L. 95-600)**

P.L. 95-600, §521(c)(1):

Amended Code Sec. 4402(2). **Effective** with respect to years beginning after 6-30-80. Prior to amendment, Code Sec. 4402(2) read as follows:

"(2) COIN-OPERATED DEVICES.—On any wager placed in a coin-operated device with respect to which an occupational tax is imposed by section 4461, or on any amount paid, in lieu of inserting a coin, token, or similar object, to operate a device described in section 4462(a)(2) if an occupational tax is imposed with respect to such device by section 4461, or".

- **1976, Tax Reform Act of 1976 (P.L. 94-455)**

P.L. 94-455, §1208(a):

Amended Code Sec. 4402(3). **Effective** with respect to wagers placed after 3-10-64. Prior to amendment, Code Sec. 4402(3) read as follows:

(3) STATE-CONDUCTED SWEEPSTAKES.—On any wager placed in a sweepstakes, wagering pool, or lottery—

(A) which is conducted by an agency of a State acting under authority of State law, and

(B) the ultimate winners in which are determined by the results of a horse race,

but only if such wager is placed with the State agent conducting such sweepstakes, wagering pool, or lottery, or with its authorized employees or agents.

- **1965, Excise Tax Reduction Act of 1965 (P.L. 89-44)**

P.L. 89-44, §405(a):

Amended subsection (2) of Sec. 4402 by inserting "section 4462(a)(2)" in lieu of "section 4462(a)(2)(B)". **Effective** 7-1-65.

P.L. 89-44, §813(a):

Amended Sec. 4402. **Effective** 3-11-64. Prior to amendment, Sec. 4402 read as follows:

"SEC. 4402 EXEMPTIONS.

"No tax shall be imposed by this subchapter—

"(1) Parimutuels.—On any wager placed with, or on any wager placed in a wagering pool conducted by, a parimutuel wagering enterprise licensed under State law, and

"(2) Coin-operated devices.—On any wager placed in a coin-operated device with respect to which an occupational tax is imposed by section 4461, or on any amount paid, in lieu of inserting a coin, token, or similar object, to operate a device described in section 4462(a)(2)(B), if an occupational tax is imposed with respect to such device by section 4461."

- **1958, Excise Tax Technical Changes Act of 1958 (P.L. 85-859)**

P.L. 85-859, §152(b):

Added the last sentence in Sec. 4402(2). **Effective** 1-1-59.

[Sec. 4403]

SEC. 4403. RECORD REQUIREMENTS.

Each person liable for tax under this subchapter shall keep a daily record showing the gross amount of all wagers on which he is so liable, in addition to all other records required pursuant to section 6001(a).

[Sec. 4404]

SEC. 4404. TERRITORIAL EXTENT.

The tax imposed by this subchapter shall apply only to wagers

(1) accepted in the United States, or

(2) placed by a person who is in the United States

(A) with a person who is a citizen or resident of the United States, or

(B) in a wagering pool or lottery conducted by a person who is a citizen or resident of the United States.

[Sec. 4405]

SEC. 4405. CROSS REFERENCES.

For penalties and other administrative provisions applicable to this subchapter, see sections 4421 to 4423, inclusive; and subtitle F.

Subchapter B—Occupational Tax

Sec. 4411.   Imposition of tax.
Sec. 4412.   Registration.
Sec. 4413.   Certain provisions made applicable.
Sec. 4414.   Cross references.

[Sec. 4411]

SEC. 4411. IMPOSITION OF TAX.

[Sec. 4411(a)]

(a) IN GENERAL.—There shall be imposed a special tax of $500 per year to be paid by each person who is liable for the tax imposed under section 4401 or who is engaged in receiving wagers for or on behalf of any person so liable.

[Sec. 4411(b)]

(b) AUTHORIZED PERSONS.—Subsection (a) shall be applied by substituting "$50" for "$500" in the case of—

(1) any person whose liability for tax under section 4401 is determined only under paragraph (1) of section 4401(a), and

(2) any person who is engaged in receiving wagers only for or on behalf of persons described in paragraph (1).

Amendments

- **1982, Miscellaneous Revenue Act of 1982 (P.L. 97-362)**

P.L. 97-362, §109(b):

Amended Code Sec. 4411. **Effective** 7-1-83. Prior to amendment, Code Sec. 4411 read as follows:

There shall be imposed a special tax of $500 per year to be paid by each person who is liable for tax under section 4401 or who is engaged in receiving wagers for or on behalf of any person so liable.

- **1974 (P.L. 93-499)**

P.L. 93-499, §3(b):

Amended Code Sec. 4411 by substituting "$500" for "$50".

P. L. 93-499, §3(d), provides:

"(d) Effective Date.—

"(1) In general.—The amendments made by this section take effect on December 1, 1974, and shall apply only with respect to wagers placed on or after such date.

"(2) Transitional rules.—

"(A) Any person who, on December 1, 1974, is engaged in an activity which makes him liable for payment of the tax imposed by section 4411 of the Internal Revenue Code of 1954 (as in effect on such date) shall be treated as commencing such activity on such date for purposes of such section and section 4901 of such Code.

"(B) Any person who, before December 1, 1974,—

EXCISE TAXES—WAGERS, MISCELLANEOUS PROVISIONS

"(i) became liable for and paid the tax imposed by section 4411 of the Internal Revenue Code of 1954 (as in effect on July 1, 1974) for the year ending June 30, 1975, shall not be liable for any additional tax under such section for such year, and

"(ii) registered under section 4412 of such Code (as in effect on July 1, 1974) for the year ending June 30, 1975, shall not be required to reregister under such section for such year."

[Sec. 4412]

SEC. 4412. REGISTRATION.

[Sec. 4412(a)]

(a) REQUIREMENT.—Each person required to pay a special tax under this subchapter shall register with the official in charge of the internal revenue district—

(1) his name and place of residence;

(2) if he is liable for tax under subchapter A, each place of business where the activity which makes him so liable is carried on, and the name and place of residence of each person who is engaged in receiving wagers for him or on his behalf; and

(3) if he is engaged in receiving wagers for or on behalf of any person liable for tax under subchapter A, the name and place of residence of each such person.

[Sec. 4412(b)]

(b) FIRM OR COMPANY.—Where subsection (a) requires the name and place of residence of a firm or company to be registered, the names and places of residence of the several persons constituting the firm or company shall be registered.

[Sec. 4412(c)]

(c) SUPPLEMENTAL INFORMATION.—In accordance with regulations prescribed by the Secretary, the Secretary may require from time to time such supplemental information from any person required to register under this section as may be needful to the enforcement of this chapter.

Amendments

• 1976, Tax Reform Act of 1976 (P.L. 94-455)

P.L. 94-455, § 1906(b)(13)(I):

Substituted "the Secretary" for "he or his delegate" in Code Sec. 4412(c). **Effective** 2-1-77.

[Sec. 4413]

SEC. 4413. CERTAIN PROVISIONS MADE APPLICABLE.

Sections 4901, 4902, 4904, 4905, and 4906 shall extend to and apply to the special tax imposed by this subchapter and to the persons upon whom it is imposed, and for that purpose any activity which makes a person liable for special tax under this subchapter shall be considered to be a business or occupation referred to in such sections. No other provision of sections 4901 to 4907, inclusive, shall so extend or apply.

[Sec. 4414]

SEC. 4414. CROSS REFERENCES.

For penalties and other general and administrative provisions applicable to this subchapter, see sections 4421 to 4423, inclusive; and subtitle F.

Subchapter C—Miscellaneous Provisions

Sec. 4421.	Definitions.
Sec. 4422.	Applicability of federal and state laws.
Sec. 4423.	Inspection of books.
Sec. 4424.	Disclosure of wagering tax information.

[Sec. 4421]

SEC. 4421. DEFINITIONS.

For purposes of this chapter—

(1) WAGER.—The term "wager" means—

(A) any wager with respect to a sports event or a contest placed with a person engaged in the business of accepting such wagers,

(B) any wager placed in a wagering pool with respect to a sports event or a contest, if such pool is conducted for profit, and

(C) any wager placed in a lottery conducted for profit.

(2) LOTTERY.—The term "lottery" includes the numbers game, policy, and similar types of wagering. The term does not include—

(A) any game of a type in which usually

(i) the wagers are placed,

(ii) the winners are determined, and

(iii) the distribution of prizes or other property is made, in the presence of all persons placing wagers in such game, and

(B) any drawing conducted by an organization exempt from tax under sections 501 and 521, if no part of the net proceeds derived from such drawing inures to the benefit of any private shareholder or individual.

[Sec. 4422]

SEC. 4422. APPLICABILITY OF FEDERAL AND STATE LAWS.

The payment of any tax imposed by this chapter with respect to any activity shall not exempt any person from any penalty provided by a law of the United States or of any State for engaging in the same activity, nor shall the payment of any such tax prohibit any State from placing a tax on the same activity for State or other purposes.

[Sec. 4423]

SEC. 4423. INSPECTION OF BOOKS.

Notwithstanding section 7605(b), the books of account of any person liable for tax under this chapter may be examined and inspected as frequently as may be needful to the enforcement of this chapter.

Sec. 4412

EXCISE TAXES—HARBOR MAINTENANCE TAX

[Sec. 4424]
SEC. 4424. DISCLOSURE OF WAGERING TAX INFORMATION.

[Sec. 4424(a)]

(a) GENERAL RULE.—Except as otherwise provided in this section, neither the Secretary nor any other officer or employee of the Treasury Department may divulge or make known in any manner whatever to any person—

(1) any original, copy, or abstract of any return, payment, or registration made pursuant to this chapter,

(2) any record required for making any such return, payment, or registration, which the Secretary is permitted by the taxpayer to examine or which is produced pursuant to section 7602, or

(3) any information come at by the exploitation of any such return, payment, registration, or record.

Amendments

• **1976, Tax Reform Act of 1976 (P.L. 94-455)**

P.L. 94-455, §1906(b)(13)(A):

Amended 1954 Code by substituting "Secretary" for "Secretary or his delegate" each place it appeared. **Effective** 2-1-77.

[Sec. 4424(b)]

(b) PERMISSIBLE DISCLOSURE.—A disclosure otherwise prohibited by subsection (a) may be made in connection with the administration or civil or criminal enforcement of any tax imposed by this title. However, any document or information so disclosed may not be—

(1) divulged or made known in any manner whatever by any officer or employee of the United States to any person except in connection with the administration or civil or criminal enforcement of this title, nor

(2) used, directly or indirectly, in any criminal prosecution for any offense occurring before the date of enactment of this section.

[Sec. 4424(c)]

(c) USE OF DOCUMENTS POSSESSED BY TAXPAYER.—Except in connection with the administration or civil or criminal enforcement of any tax imposed by this title—

(1) any stamp denoting payment of the special tax under this chapter,

(2) any original, copy, or abstract possessed by a taxpayer of any return, payment, or registration made by such taxpayer pursuant to this chapter, and

(3) any information come at by the exploitation of any such document, shall not be used against such taxpayer in any criminal proceeding.

[Sec. 4424(d)]

(d) INSPECTION BY COMMITTEES OF CONGRESS.—Section 6103(f) shall apply with respect to any return, payment, or registration made pursuant to this chapter.

Amendments

• **1976, Tax Reform Act of 1976 (P.L. 94-455)**

P.L. 94-455, §1202(h)(6):

Substituted "6103(f)" for "6103(d)" in Code Sec. 4424(d). **Effective** 1-1-77.

• **1974 (P.L. 93-499)**

P.L. 93-499, §3(c):

Added Code Sec. 4424. **Effective** 12-1-74 and only with respect to wagers placed on or after such date.

CHAPTER 36—CERTAIN OTHER EXCISE TAXES

SUBCHAPTER A.	Harbor maintenance tax.
SUBCHAPTER B.	Transportation by water.
SUBCHAPTER D.	Tax on use of certain vehicles.
SUBCHAPTER E.	[Repealed.]
SUBCHAPTER F.	[Repealed.]

Subchapter A—Harbor Maintenance Tax

Sec. 4461.	Imposition of tax.
Sec. 4462.	Definitions and special rules.

[Sec. 4461]
SEC. 4461. IMPOSITION OF TAX.

[Sec. 4461(a)]

(a) GENERAL RULE.—There is hereby imposed a tax on any port use.

[Sec. 4461(b)]

(b) AMOUNT OF TAX.—The amount of the tax imposed by subsection (a) on any port use shall be an amount equal to 0.125 percent of the value of the commercial cargo involved.

Amendments

• **1990, Omnibus Budget Reconciliation Act of 1990 (P.L. 101-508)**

P.L. 101-508, §11214(a):

Amended Code Sec. 4461(b) by striking "0.04 percent" and inserting "0.125 percent". **Effective** 1-1-91.

[Sec. 4461(c)]

(c) LIABILITY AND TIME OF IMPOSITION OF TAX.—

(1) LIABILITY.—The tax imposed by subsection (a) shall be paid by—

(A) in the case of cargo entering the United States, the importer, or

(B) in any other case, the shipper.

(2) TIME OF IMPOSITION.—Except as provided by regulations, the tax imposed by subsection (a) shall be imposed at the time of unloading.

EXCISE TAXES—HARBOR MAINTENANCE TAX

Amendments

• **2005, Safe, Accountable, Flexible, Efficient Transportation Equity Act: A Legacy for Users (P.L. 109-59)**

P.L. 109-59, § 11116(b)(1):

Amended Code Sec. 4461(c)(1) by adding "or" at the end of subparagraph (A), by striking subparagraph (B), and by redesignating subparagraph (C) as subparagraph (B). **Effective** before, on, and after 8-10-2005. Prior to being stricken, Code Sec. 4461(c)(1)(B) read as follows:

(B) in the case of cargo to be exported from the United States, the exporter, or

P.L. 109-59, § 11116(b)(2):

Amended Code Sec. 4461(c)(2) by striking "imposed—" and all that follows through "in any other case," and inserting "imposed". **Effective** before, on, and after 8-10-2005. Prior to amendment, Code Sec. 4461(c)(2) read as follows:

Amendments

• **1978, Revenue Act of 1978 (P.L. 95-600)**

P.L. 95-600, § 521(b):

Repealed Code Sec. 4461. **Effective** with respect to years beginning after 6-30-80. Prior to its repeal, Code Sec. 4461 read as follows:

SEC. 4461. IMPOSITION OF TAX.

(a) IN GENERAL.—There shall be imposed a special tax to be paid by every person who maintains for use or permits the use of, on any place or premises occupied by him, a coin-operated gaming device (as defined in section 4462) at the following rates:

(1) $250 a year; and

(2) $250 a year for each additional device so maintained or the use of which is so permitted. If one such device is replaced by another, such other device shall not be considered an additional device.

(b) EXCEPTION.—No tax shall be imposed on a device which is commonly known as a claw, crane, or digger machine if—

(1) the charge for each operation of such device is not more than 10 cents,

(2) such device never dispenses a prize other than merchandise of a maximum retail value of $1, and with respect to such device there is never a display or offer of any prize or merchandise other than merchandise dispensed by such machine,

(3) such device is actuated by a crank and operates solely by means of a nonelectrical mechanism, and

(4) such device is not operated other than in connection with and as part of carnivals or county or State fairs.

(2) TIME OF IMPOSITION.—Except as provided by regulations, the tax imposed by subsection (a) shall be imposed—

(A) in the case of cargo to be exported from the United States, at the time of loading, and

(B) in any other case, at the time of unloading.

• **1986, Water Resources Development Act of 1986 (P.L. 99-662)**

P.L. 99-662, § 1402(a):

Amended chapter 36 of the Internal Revenue Code of 1954 by inserting after the chapter heading new subchaper A, containing Code Sec. 4461. **Effective** 4-1-87.

[Sec. 4461—Repealed]

• **1965, Excise Tax Reduction Act of 1965 (P.L. 89-44)**

P.L. 89-44, § 403(a):

Amended subsection (a) and so much of subsection (b) as precedes paragraph (1). **Effective** 7-1-65. Prior to amendment, these provisions read as follows:

(a) In General.—There shall be imposed a special tax to be paid by every person who maintains for use or permits the use of, on any place or premises occupied by him, a coin-operated amusement or gaming device at the following rates:

(1) $10 a year, in the case of a device defined in paragraph (1) of section 4462(a);

(2) $250 a year, in the case of a device defined in paragraph (2) of section 4462(a); and

(3) $10 or $250 a year, as the case may be, for each additional device so maintained or the use of which is so permitted. If one such device is replaced by another, such other device shall not be considered an additional device.

(b) Reduced Rate.—In the case of a device which is defined in paragraph (2) of section 4462(a) and which is commonly known as a claw, crane, or digger machine, the tax imposed by subsection (a) shall be at the rate of $10 a year (in lieu of $250 a year) if—

• **1959 (P.L. 86-344)**

P.L. 86-344, § 6(a):

Amended Code Sec. 4461 by adding "(a) IN GENERAL.—" at the beginning thereof and by adding a new subsection (b). **Effective** 7-1-60.

[Sec. 4462]

SEC. 4462. DEFINITIONS AND SPECIAL RULES.

[Sec. 4462(a)]

(a) DEFINITIONS.—For purposes of this subchapter—

(1) PORT USE.—The term "port use" means—

(A) the loading of commercial cargo on, or

(B) the unloading of commercial cargo from, a commercial vessel at a port.

(2) PORT.—

(A) IN GENERAL.—The term "port" means any channel or harbor (or component thereof) in the United States, which—

(i) is not an inland waterway, and

(ii) is open to public navigation.

(B) EXCEPTION FOR CERTAIN FACILITIES.—The term "port" does not include any channel or harbor with respect to which no Federal funds have been used since 1977 for construction, maintenance, or operation, or which was deauthorized by Federal law before 1985.

(C) SPECIAL RULE FOR COLUMBIA RIVER.—The term "port" shall include the channels of the Columbia River in the States of Oregon and Washington only up to the down-stream side of Bonneville lock and dam.

(3) COMMERCIAL CARGO.—

(A) IN GENERAL.—The term "commercial cargo" means any cargo transported on a commercial vessel, including passengers transported for compensation or hire.

(B) CERTAIN ITEMS NOT INCLUDED.—The term "commercial cargo" does not include—

(i) bunker fuel, ship's stores, sea stores, or the legitimate equipment necessary to the operation of a vessel, or

(ii) fish or other aquatic animal life caught and not previously landed on shore.

(4) COMMERCIAL VESSEL.—

(A) IN GENERAL.—The term "commercial vessel" means any vessel used—

(i) in transporting cargo by water for compensation or hire, or

(ii) in transporting cargo by water in the business of the owner, lessee, or operator of the vessel.

(B) EXCLUSION OF FERRIES.—

(i) IN GENERAL.—The term "commercial vessel" does not include any ferry engaged primarily in the ferrying of passengers (including their vehicles) between points within the United States, or between the United States and contiguous countries.

(ii) FERRY.—The term "ferry" means any vessel which arrives in the United States on a regular schedule during its operating season at intervals of at least once each business day.

(5) VALUE.—

(A) IN GENERAL.—The term "value" means, except as provided in regulations, the value of any commercial cargo as determined by standard commercial documentation.

(B) TRANSPORTATION OF PASSENGERS.—In the case of the transportation of passengers for hire, the term "value" means the actual charge paid for such service or the prevailing charge for comparable service if no actual charge is paid.

Sec. 4461—Repealed

EXCISE TAXES—HARBOR MAINTENANCE TAX

[Sec. 4462(b)]

(b) SPECIAL RULE FOR ALASKA, HAWAII, AND POSSESSIONS.—

(1) IN GENERAL.—No tax shall be imposed under section 4461(a) with respect to—

(A) cargo loaded on a vessel in a port in the United States mainland for transportation to Alaska, Hawaii, or any possession of the United States for ultimate use or consumption in Alaska, Hawaii, or any possession of the United States,

(B) cargo loaded on a vessel in Alaska, Hawaii, or any possession of the United States for transportation to the United States mainland, Alaska, Hawaii, or such a possession for ultimate use or consumption in the United States mainland, Alaska, Hawaii, or such a possession,

(C) the unloading of cargo described in subparagraph (A) or (B) in Alaska, Hawaii, or any possession of the United States, or in the United States mainland, respectively, or

(D) cargo loaded on a vessel in Alaska, Hawaii, or a possession of the United States and unloaded in the State or possession in which loaded, or passengers transported on United States flag vessels operating solely within the State waters of Alaska or Hawaii and adjacent international waters.

(2) CARGO DOES NOT INCLUDE CRUDE OIL WITH RESPECT TO ALASKA.—For purposes of this subsection, the term "cargo" does not include crude oil with respect to Alaska.

(3) UNITED STATES MAINLAND.—For purposes of this subsection, the term "United States mainland" means the continental United States (not including Alaska).

Amendments

• **1996, Small Business Job Protection Act of 1996 (P.L. 104-188)**

P.L. 104-188, §1704(i)(1):

Amended Code Sec. 4462(b)(1)(D) by inserting before the period ", or passengers transported on United States flag vessels operating solely within the State waters of Alaska or Hawaii and adjacent international waters". **Effective** as if included in the amendments made by section 1402(a) of P.L. 99-662.

• **1988, Technical and Miscellaneous Revenue Act of 1988 (P.L. 100-647)**

P.L. 100-647, §2002(b):

Amended Code Sec. 4462(b)(1)(B). **Effective** as if included in the provision of P.L. 99-662 to which it relates. Prior to amendment, Code Sec. 4462(b)(1)(B) read as follows:

(B) cargo loaded on a vessel in Alaska, Hawaii, or any possession of the United States for transportation to the United States mainland for ultimate use or consumption in the United States mainland.

[Sec. 4462(c)]

(c) COORDINATION OF TAX WHERE TRANSPORTATION SUBJECT TO TAX IMPOSED BY SECTION 4042.—No tax shall be imposed under this subchapter with respect to the loading or unloading of any cargo on or from a vessel if any fuel of such vessel has been (or will be) subject to the tax imposed by section 4042 (relating to tax on fuel used in commercial transportation on inland waterways).

[Sec. 4462(d)]

(d) NONAPPLICABILITY OF TAX TO EXPORTS.—The tax imposed by section 4461(a) shall not apply to any port use with respect to any commercial cargo to be exported from the United States.

Amendments

• **2005, Safe, Accountable, Flexible, Efficient Transportation Equity Act: A Legacy for Users (P.L. 109-59)**

P.L. 109-59, §11116(a):

Amended Code Sec. 4462(d). **Effective** before, on, and after 8-10-2005. Prior to amendment, Code Sec. 4462(d) read as follows:

(d) NONAPPLICABILITY OF TAX TO CERTAIN CARGO.—

(1) IN GENERAL.—Subject to paragraph (2), the tax imposed by section 4461(a) shall not apply to bonded commercial cargo entering the United States for transportation and direct exportation to a foreign country.

(2) IMPOSITION OF CHARGES.—Paragraph (1) shall not apply to any cargo exported to Canada or Mexico—

(A) during the period—

(i) after the date on which the Secretary determines that the Government of Canada or Mexico (as the case may be) has imposed a substantially equivalent tax, fee, or charge on commercial vessels or commercial cargo utilizing ports of such country, and

(ii) subject to subparagraph (B), before the date on which the Secretary determines that such tax, fee, charge has been discontinued by such country, and

(B) with respect to a particular United States port (or to any transaction or class of transactions at any such port) to the extent that the study made pursuant to section 1407(a) of the Water Resources Development Act of 1986 (or a review thereof pursuant to section 1407(b) of such Act) finds that—

(i) the imposition of the tax imposed by this subchapter at such port (or to any transaction or class of transactions at such port) is not likely to divert a significant amount of cargo from such port to a port in a country contiguous to the United States, or that any such diversion is not likely to result in significant economic loss to such port, or

(ii) the nonapplicability of such tax at such port (or to any transaction or class of transactions at such port) is likely to result in significant economic loss to any other United States port.

[Sec. 4462(e)]

(e) EXEMPTION FOR UNITED STATES.—No tax shall be imposed under this subchapter on the United States or any agency or instrumentality thereof.

[Sec. 4462(f)]

(f) EXTENSION OF PROVISIONS OF LAW APPLICABLE TO CUSTOMS DUTY.—

(1) IN GENERAL.—Except to the extent otherwise provided in regulations, all administrative and enforcement provisions of customs laws and regulations shall apply in respect of the tax imposed by this subchapter (and in respect of persons liable therefor) as if such tax were a customs duty. For purposes of the preceding sentence, any penalty expressed in terms of a relationship to the amount of the duty shall be treated as not less than the amount which bears a similar relationship to the value of the cargo.

(2) JURISDICTION OF COURTS AND AGENCIES.—For purposes of determining the jurisdiction of any court of the United States or any agency of the United States, the tax imposed by this subchapter shall be treated as if such tax were a customs duty.

(3) ADMINISTRATIVE PROVISIONS APPLICABLE TO TAX LAW NOT TO APPLY.—The tax imposed by this subchapter shall not be treated as a tax for purposes of subtitle F or any other provision of law relating to the administration and enforcement of internal revenue taxes.

[Sec. 4462(g)]

(g) SPECIAL RULES.—Except as provided by regulations—

(1) TAX IMPOSED ONLY ONCE.—Only 1 tax shall be imposed under section 4461(a) with respect to the loading on and unloading from, or the unloading from and the loading on, the same vessel of the same cargo.

(2) EXCEPTION FOR INTRAPORT MOVEMENTS.—Under regulations, no tax shall be imposed under section 4461(a) on the mere movement of cargo within a port.

(3) RELAY CARGO.—Only 1 tax shall be imposed under section 4461(a) on cargo (moving under a single bill of lading) which is unloaded from one vessel and loaded onto another vessel at any port in the United States for relay to or from any port in Alaska, Hawaii, or any possession of the United States. For purposes of this paragraph, the term "cargo" does not include any item not treated as cargo under subsection (b)(2).

EXCISE TAXES—HARBOR MAINTENANCE TAX

Amendments
- **1988, Technical and Miscellaneous Revenue Act of 1988 (P.L. 100-647)**

P.L. 100-647, § 6110(a):

Amended Code Sec. 4462(g) by adding at the end thereof new paragraph (3). **Effective** on the date of enactment of this Act.

[Sec. 4462(h)]

(h) EXEMPTION FOR HUMANITARIAN AND DEVELOPMENT ASSISTANCE CARGOS.—No tax shall be imposed under this subchapter on any nonprofit organization or cooperative for cargo which is owned or financed by such nonprofit organization or cooperative and which is certified by the United States Customs Service as intended for use in humanitarian or development assistance overseas.

Amendments
- **1988, Technical and Miscellaneous Revenue Act of 1988 (P.L. 100-647)**

P.L. 100-647, § 6109(a):

Amended Code Sec. 4462 by redesignating subsection (h) as subsection (i) and by inserting after subsection (g) new subsection (h). **Effective** 4-1-87.

[Sec. 4462(i)]

(i) REGULATIONS.—The Secretary may prescribe such additional regulations as may be necessary to carry out the purposes of this subchapter including, but not limited to, regulations—

(1) providing for the manner and method of payment and collection of the tax imposed by this subchapter,

(2) providing for the posting of bonds to secure payment of such tax,

(3) exempting any transaction or class of transactions from such tax where the collection of such tax is not administratively practical, and

(4) providing for the remittance or mitigation of penalties and the settlement or compromise of claims.

Amendments
- **1988, Technical and Miscellaneous Revenue Act of 1988 (P.L. 100-647)**

P.L. 100-647, § 6109(a):

Amended Code Sec. 4462 by redesignating subsection (h) as subsection (i) and by inserting after subsection (g) new subsection (h). **Effective** 4-1-87.

Amendments
- **1986, Water Resources Development Act of 1986 (P.L. 99-662)**

P.L. 99-662, § 1402(a):

Amended chapter 36 of the Internal Revenue Code of 1954 by inserting after the chapter heading new subchapter A, containing Code Sec. 4462. **Effective** 4-1-87.

[Sec. 4462—Repealed]

Amendments
- **1978, Revenue Act of 1978 (P.L. 95-600)**

P.L. 95-600, § 521(b):

Repealed Code Sec. 4462. **Effective** with respect to years beginning after 6-30-80. Prior to its repeal, Code Sec. 4462 read as follows:

SEC. 4462. DEFINITION OF COIN-OPERATED GAMING DEVICE.

(a) IN GENERAL.—For purposes of this subchapter, the term "coin-operated gaming device" means any machine which is—

(1) a so-called "slot" machine which operates by means of the insertion of a coin, token, or similar object and which, by application of the element of chance, may deliver, or entitle the person playing or operating the machine to receive, cash, premiums, merchandise, or tokens, or

(2) a machine which is similar to machines described in paragraph (1) and is operated without the insertion of a coin, token, or similar object.

(b) EXCLUSIONS.—The term "coin-operated gaming device" does not include—

(1) a bona fide vending or amusement machine in which gaming features are not incorporated;

(2) a vending machine operated by means of the insertion of a one cent coin, which, when it dispenses a prize, never dispenses a prize of a retail value of, or entitles a person to receive a prize of a retail value of, more than 5 cents, and if the only prize dispensed is merchandise and not cash or tokens; or

(3) a vending machine which—

(A) dispenses tickets on a sweepstakes, wagering pool, or lottery which is conducted by an agency of a State acting under authority of State law, and

(B) is maintained by the state agency conducting such sweepstakes, wagering pool, or lottery, or by its authorized employees or agents.

- **1976, Tax Reform Act of 1976 (P.L. 94-455)**

P.L. 94-455, § 1208(b):

Struck out "or" at the end of Code Sec. 4462(b)(1), substituted "; or" for the period at the end of Code Sec. 4462(b)(2), and added Code Sec. 4462(b)(3). **Effective** with respect to periods after 3-10-64.

- **1965, Excise Tax Reduction Act of 1965 (P.L. 89-44)**

P.L. 89-44, § 403(b):

Amended Code Sec. 4462. **Effective** 7-1-65. Prior to amendment, Code Sec. 4462 read as follows:

(a) In General.—For purposes of this subchapter, the term "coin-operated amusement or gaming device" means—

(1) any machine which is—

(A) a music machine operated by means of the insertion of a coin, token, or similar object,

(B) a vending machine operated by means of the insertion of a one cent coin, which, when it dispenses a prize, never dispenses a prize of a retail value of, or entitles a person to receive a prize of a retail value of, more than 5 cents, and if the only prize dispensed is merchandise and not cash or tokens,

(C) an amusement machine operated by means of the insertion of a coin, token, or similar object, but not including any device defined in paragraph (2) of this subsection, or

(D) a machine which is similar to machines described in subparagraph (A), (B), or (C), and is operated without the insertion of a coin, token, or similar object; and

(2) any machine which is—

(A) a so-called "slot" machine which operates by means of the insertion of a coin, token, or similar object and which, by application of the element of chance, may deliver, or entitle the person playing or operating the machine to receive, cash, premiums, merchandise, or tokens, or

(B) a machine which is similar to machines described in subparagraph (A) and is operated without the insertion of a coin, token, or similar object.

(b) Exclusion.—The term "coin-operated amusement or gaming device" does not include bona fide vending machines in which are not incorporated gaming or amusement features.

- **1958, Excise Tax Technical Changes Act of 1958 (P.L. 85-859)**

P.L. 85-859, § 152(a):

Amended Code Sec. 4462. **Effective** 1-1-59. Prior to amendment, Code Sec. 4462 read as follows:

Sec. 4462. Definition of Coin-Operated Amusement or Gaming Device.

(a) In General.—As used in sections 4461 to 4463, inclusive, the term "coin-operated amusement or gaming device" means—

(1) any amusement or music machine operated by means of the insertion of a coin, token, or similar object, and

(2) so-called "slot" machines which operate by means of insertion of a coin, token, or similar object and which, by application of the element of chance, may deliver, or entitle the person playing or operating the machine to receive cash, premiums, merchandise, or tokens.

(b) Exclusion.—The term "coin-operated amusement or gaming device" does not include bona fide vending machines in which are not incorporated gaming or amusement features.

(c) 1-Cent Vending Machine.—For purposes of sections 4461 to 4463, inclusive, a vending machine operated by means of the insertion of a 1-cent coin, which, when it dispenses a prize, never dispenses a prize of a retail value of, or entitles a person to receive a prize of a retail value of, more than 5 cents, and if the only prize dispensed is merchandise and not cash or tokens, shall be classified under paragraph (1) and not under paragraph (2) of subsection (a).

P.L. 85-859, § 152(c), provides:

In the case of the year beginning July 1, 1958, where the trade or business on which the tax is imposed under section 4461 of the Internal Revenue Code of 1954 was commenced before the effective date specified in § 1(c) of this Act, the tax imposed for such year solely by reason of the amendment made by subsection (a)—

(1) shall be the amount reckoned proportionately from such effective date through 6-30-59, and

(2) shall be due on, and payable on or before, the last day of the month the first day of which is such effective date.

EXCISE TAXES—TRANSPORTATION BY WATER

[Sec. 4463—Repealed]

Amendments

• **1978, Revenue Act of 1978 (P.L. 95-600)**

P.L. 95-600, § 521(b):

Repealed Code Sec. 4463. **Effective** with respect to years beginning after 6-30-80. Prior to its repeal, Code Sec. 4463 read as follows:

SEC. 4463. ADMINISTRATIVE PROVISIONS.

(a) TRADE OR BUSINESS.—An operator of a place or premises who maintains for use or permits the use of any coin-operated device shall be considered, for purposes of chapter 40, to be engaged in a trade or business in respect of each such device.

(b) CROSS REFERENCE.—

For penalties and other administrative provisions applicable to this subchapter, see chapter 40 and subtitle F.

[Sec. 4464—Repealed]

Amendments

• **1978, Revenue Act of 1978 (P.L. 95-600)**

P.L. 95-600, § 521(a):

Amended Code Sec. 4464(b)(2) by striking out "80 percent" and inserting in lieu thereof "95 percent". **Effective** for years ending 6-30-79, and 6-30-80.

P.L. 95-600, § 521(b):

Repealed Code Sec. 4464. **Effective** with respect to years beginning after 6-30-80. Prior to its repeal, Code Sec. 4464 read as follows:

SEC. 4464. CREDIT FOR STATE-IMPOSED TAXES.

(a) IN GENERAL.—There shall be allowed as a credit against the tax imposed by section 4461 with respect to any coin-operated gaming device for any year an amount equal to the amount of State tax paid for such year with respect to such device by the person liable for the tax imposed by section 4461, if such State tax (1) is paid under a law of the State in which the place or premises on which such device is maintained or used is located, and (2) is similar to the tax imposed by section 4461 (including a tax, other than a general personal property tax, imposed on such device).

(b) LIMITATIONS.—

(1) DEVICES MUST BE LEGAL UNDER STATE LAW.—Credit shall be allowed under subsection (a) for a tax imposed by a State only if the maintenance of the coin-operated gaming device by the person liable for the tax imposed by section 4461 on the place or premises occupied by him does not violate any law of such State.

(2) CREDIT NOT TO EXCEED 95 PERCENT OF TAX.—The credit under subsection (a) with respect to any coin-operated gaming device shall not exceed 95 percent of the tax imposed by section 4461 with respect to such device.

(c) SPECIAL PROVISIONS FOR PAYMENT OF TAX.—Under regulations prescribed by the Secretary, a person who believes he will be entitled to a credit under subsection (a) with respect to any coin-operated gaming device for any year shall, for purposes of this subtitle and subtitle F, satisfy his liability for the tax imposed by section 4461 with respect to such device for such year if—

(1) on or before the date prescribed by law for payment of the tax imposed by section 4461 with respect to such device for such year, he has paid the amount of such tax reduced by the amount of the credit which he estimates will be allowable under subsection (a) with respect to such device for such year, and

(2) on or before the last day of such year, pays the amount (if any) by which the credit for such year is less than the credit estimated under paragraph (1).

• **1976, Tax Reform Act of 1976 (P.L. 94-455)**

P.L. 94-455, § 1906(b)(13)(A):

Amended 1954 Code by substituting "Secretary" for "Secretary or his delegate" each place it appeared. **Effective** 2-1-77.

• **1971, Revenue Act of 1971 (P.L. 92-178)**

P.L. 92-178, § 402(a):

Added Code Sec. 4464. **Effective** on and after 7-1-72.

Subchapter B—Transportation by Water

Sec. 4471. Imposition of tax.
Sec. 4472. Definitions.

[Sec. 4471]

SEC. 4471. IMPOSITION OF TAX.

[Sec. 4471(a)]

(a) IN GENERAL.—There is hereby imposed a tax of $3 per passenger on a covered voyage.

[Sec. 4471(b)]

(b) BY WHOM PAID.—The tax imposed by this section shall be paid by the person providing the covered voyage.

[Sec. 4471(c)]

(c) TIME OF IMPOSITION.—The tax imposed by this section shall be imposed only once for each passenger on a covered voyage, either at the time of first embarkation or disembarkation in the United States.

Amendments

• **1989, Omnibus Budget Reconciliation Act of 1989 (P.L. 101-239)**

P.L. 101-239, § 7504(a):

Amended chapter 36 by inserting after subchapter A a new subchapter B. For a special **effective** date, see Act Sec. 7504(c), below.

P.L. 101-239, § 7504(c), provides:

(c) EFFECTIVE DATE.—

(1) IN GENERAL.—The amendments made by this section shall apply to voyages beginning after December 31, 1989, which were not paid for before such date.

(2) NO DEPOSITS REQUIRED BEFORE APRIL 1, 1990.—No deposit of any tax imposed by subchapter B of chapter 36 of the Internal Revenue Code of 1986, as added by this section, shall be required to be made before April 1, 1990.

[Sec. 4472]

SEC. 4472. DEFINITIONS.

For purposes of this subchapter—

(1) COVERED VOYAGE.—

(A) IN GENERAL.—The term "covered voyage" means a voyage of—

(i) a commercial passenger vessel which extends over 1 or more nights, or

(ii) a commercial vessel transporting passengers engaged in gambling aboard the vessel beyond the territorial waters of the United States,

during which passengers embark or disembark the vessel in the United States. Such term shall not include any voyage on any vessel owned or operated by the United States, a State, or any agency or subdivision thereof.

(B) EXCEPTION FOR CERTAIN VOYAGES ON PASSENGER VESSELS.—The term "covered voyage" shall not include a voyage of a passenger vessel of less than 12 hours between 2 ports in the United States.

(2) PASSENGER VESSEL.—The term "passenger vessel" means any vessel having berth or stateroom accommodations for more than 16 passengers.

Amendments

• **1989, Omnibus Budget Reconciliation Act of 1989 (P.L. 101-239)**

P.L. 101-239, § 7504(a):

Amended chapter 36 by adding a new section 4472. For a special **effective** date, see Act Sec. 7504(c), below.

P.L. 101-239, § 7504(c), provides:

(c) EFFECTIVE DATE.—

(1) IN GENERAL.—The amendments made by this section shall apply to voyages beginning after December 31, 1989, which were not paid for before such date.

EXCISE TAX—CERTAIN VEHICLES

(2) NO DEPOSITS REQUIRED BEFORE APRIL 1, 1990.—No deposit of any tax imposed by subchapter B of chapter 36 of the Internal Revenue Code of 1986, as added by this section, shall be required to be made before April 1, 1990.

Subchapter D—Tax on Use of Certain Vehicles

Sec. 4481.   Imposition of tax.
Sec. 4482.   Definitions.
Sec. 4483.   Exemptions.
Sec. 4484.   Cross references.

[Sec. 4481]

SEC. 4481. IMPOSITION OF TAX.

[Sec. 4481(a)]

(a) IMPOSITION OF TAX.—A tax is hereby imposed on the use of any highway motor vehicle which (together with the semitrailers and trailers customarily used in connection with highway motor vehicles of the same type as such highway motor vehicle) has a taxable gross weight of at least 55,000 pounds at the rate specified in the following table:

Taxable gross weight:	Rate of tax:
At least 55,000 pounds, but not over 75,000 pounds.	$100 per year plus $22 for each 1,000 pounds (or fraction thereof) in excess of 55,000 pounds.
Over 75,000 pounds	$550.

Amendments

- **1984, Deficit Reduction Act of 1984 (P.L. 98-369)**

P.L. 98-369, § 734(f):

Amended Code Sec. 4481(a) by striking out the last sentence. **Effective** as if included in the provision of the Highway Revenue Act of 1982 to which it relates. Prior to amendment, the last sentence read as follows:

In the case of the taxable period beginning on July 1, 1984, and ending on September 30, 1984, the tax shall be at the rate of 75 cents for such period for each 1,000 pounds of taxable gross weight or fraction thereof.

P.L. 98-369, § 901(a):

Amended Code Sec. 4481(a), as amended by the Highway Revenue Act of 1982. **Effective** 7-1-84. Special rules appear below.

Prior to amendment, Code Sec. 4481(a) read as follows:

(a) IMPOSITION OF TAX.—A tax is hereby imposed on the use of any highway motor vehicle which (together with the semitrailers and trailers customarily used in connection with highway motor vehicles of the same type as such highway motor vehicle) has a taxable gross weight of more than 26,000 pounds, at the rate of $3.00 a year for each 1,000 pounds of taxable gross weight or fraction thereof.

P.L. 98-369, § 901(b) and (c), provide:

(b) Special Rules in the Case of Certain Owner-Operators.—

(1) Special rule for Taxable Period Beginning on July 1, 1984.—In the case of a small owner-operator, the amount of the tax imposed by section 4481 of the Internal Revenue Code of 1954 on the use of any highway motor vehicle subject to tax under section 4481(a) of such Code (as amended by subsection (a)) for the taxable period which begins on July 1, 1984, shall be the lesser of—

(A) $3 for each 1,000 pounds of taxable gross weight (or fraction thereof), or

(B) the amount of the tax which would be imposed under such section 4481(a) without regard to this paragraph.

(2) Exemption for Vehicles Used for Less Than 5,000 Miles (and Certain Other Amendments) to Take Effect on July 1, 1984.—In the case of a small owner-operator, notwithstanding subsection (f)(2) of section 513 of the Highway Revenue Act of 1982, the amendments made by subsections (b), (c) and (d) of such section shall take effect on July 1, 1984.

(3) Small Owner-Operator Defined.—For purposes of this subsection, the term "small owner-operator" has the meaning given such term by section 513(f)(2) of the Highway Revenue Act of 1982.

(4) Taxable Gross Weight.—For purposes of this subsection, the term "taxable gross weight" has the same meaning as when used in section 4481 of the Internal Revenue Code of 1954.

(c) Effective Date.—The amendment made by subsection (a) (and the provisions of subsection (b)) shall take effect on July 1, 1984.

- **1983, Surface Transportation Act of 1983 (P.L. 97-424)**

P.L. 97-424, § 513(a):

Amended Code Sec. 4481(a). **Effective** 7-1-84. However, Act Sec. 513(f)(2), below, provides a special rule in the case of certain owner-operators, and Act Sec. 513(g), below, provides that a study be undertaken to determine alternatives to the tax on use of heavy trucks.

(f) EFFECTIVE DATE.—

* * *

(2) SPECIAL RULE IN THE CASE OF CERTAIN OWNER-OPERATORS.—

(A) IN GENERAL.—In the case of a small owner-operator, paragraph (1) of this subsection and paragraph (2) of section 4481(a) of the Internal Revenue Code of 1954 (as added by this section) shall be applied by substituting for each date contained in such paragraphs a date which is 1 year after the date so contained.

(B) SMALL OWNER-OPERATOR.—For purposes of this paragraph, the term "small owner-operator" means any person who owns and operates at any time during the taxable period no more than 5 highway motor vehicles with respect to which a tax is imposed by section 4481 of such Code for such taxable period.

[There is no subparagraph (C).]

(D) AGGREGATION OF VEHICLE OWNERSHIPS.—For purposes of subparagraph (B), all highway motor vehicles with respect to which a tax is imposed by section 4481 of such Code which are owned by—

(i) any trade or business (whether or not incorporated) which is under common control with the taxpayer (within the meaning of section 52(b)), or

(ii) any member of any controlled groups of corporations of which the taxpayer is a member, for any taxable period shall be treated as being owned by the taxpayer during such period. The Secretary shall prescribe regulations which provide attribution rules that take into account, in addition to the persons and entities described in the preceding sentence, taxpayers who own highway motor vehicles through partnerships, joint ventures, and corporations.

(E) CONTROLLED GROUPS OF CORPORATIONS.—For purposes of this paragraph, the term "controlled group of corporations" has the meaning given to such term by section 1563(a), except that—

(i) "more than 50 percent" shall be substituted for "at least 80 percent" each place it appears in section 1563(a)(1), and

(ii) the determination shall be made without regard to subsections (a)(4) and (e)(3)(C) of section 1563.

(F) HIGHWAY MOTOR VEHICLES.—For purposes of this paragraph, the term "highway motor vehicle" has the meaning given to such term by section 4482(a) of such Code.

(g) STUDY OF ALTERNATIVES TO TAX ON USE OF HEAVY TRUCKS.—

(1) IN GENERAL.—The Secretary of Transportation (in consultation with the Secretary of the Treasury) shall conduct a study of—

(A) alternatives to the tax on heavy vehicles imposed by section 4481(a) of the Internal Revenue Code of 1954, and

(B) plans for improving the collecting and enforcement of such tax and alternatives to such tax.

(2) ALTERNATIVES INCLUDED.—The alternatives studied under paragraph (1) shall include taxes based either singly or in suitable combinations on vehicle size or configuration; vehicle weight, both registered and actual operating weight; and distance traveled. Plans for improving tax collection and enforcement shall, to the extent practical, provide for Federal and State cooperation in such activities.

(3) CONSULTATION WITH STATE OFFICIALS AND OTHER AFFECTED PARTIES.—The study required under subsection (a) shall be conducted in consultation with State officials, motor carriers, and other affected parties.

(4) REPORT.—Not later than January 1, 1985, the Secretary of Transportation shall submit to the Committee on Ways and Means of the House of Representatives and the Committee on Finance of the Senate a report on the study conducted under paragraph (1) together with such recommendations as he may deem advisable.

- **1978, Surface Transportation Assistance Act of 1978 (P.L. 95-599)**

P.L. 95-599, § 502(a)(6):

Substituted "1984" for "1979" in the two places in which the year appears in Code Sec. 4481(a). **Effective** 11-7-78.

- **1976 (P.L. 94-280)**

P.L. 94-280, § 303(a)(7):

Amended Code Sec. 4481(a) by substituting "1979" for "1977" in the two places in which the year appears.

- **1970, Federal-Aid Highway Act of 1970 (P.L. 91-605)**

P.L. 91-605, § 303(a)(7):

Amended Code Sec. 4481(a) by substituting "1977" for "1972" in the two places in which the year appears.

- **1961, Federal-Aid Highway Act of 1961 (P.L. 87-61)**

P.L. 87-61, § 203(a):

Amended Sec. 4481(a) by substituting "$3.00" for "$1.50." **Effective** 7-1-61.

P.L. 87-61, § 203(b)(2)(A):

Amended Sec. 4481(a) by adding the last sentence. **Effective** 7-1-61.

EXCISE TAX—CERTAIN VEHICLES

[Sec. 4481(b)]

(b) By Whom Paid.—The tax imposed by this section shall be paid by the person in whose name the highway motor vehicle is, or is required to be, registered under the law of the State or contiguous foreign country in which such vehicle is, or is required to be, registered, or, in case the highway motor vehicle is owned by the United States, by the agency or instrumentality of the United States operating such vehicle.

Amendment

• **1987, Surface Transportation and Uniform Relocation Assistance Act of 1987 (P.L. 100-17)**

P.L. 100-17, § 507(a):

Amended Code Sec. 4481(b) by inserting "or contiguous foreign country" after "State". **Effective** 7-1-87.

[Sec. 4481(c)]

(c) Proration of Tax.—

(1) Where first use occurs after first month.—If in any taxable period the first use of the highway motor vehicle is after the first month in such period, the tax shall be reckoned proportionately from the first day of the month in which such use occurs to and including the last day in such taxable period.

(2) Where vehicle sold, destroyed, or stolen.—

(A) In general.—If in any taxable period a highway motor vehicle is sold, destroyed, or stolen before the first day of the last month in such period and not subsequently used during such taxable period, the tax shall be reckoned proportionately from the first day of the month in such period in which the first use of such highway motor vehicle occurs to and including the last day of the month in which such highway motor vehicle was sold, destroyed, or stolen.

(B) Destroyed.—For purposes of subparagraph (A), a highway motor vehicle is destroyed if such vehicle is damaged by reason of an accident or other casualty to such an extent that it is not economic to rebuild.

Amendments

• **2004, American Jobs Creation Act of 2004 (P.L. 108-357)**

P.L. 108-357, § 867(a)(1):

Amended Code Sec. 4481(c)(2)(A) by striking "destroyed or stolen" both places it appears and inserting "sold, destroyed, or stolen". **Effective** for tax periods beginning after 10-22-2004.

P.L. 108-357, § 867(a)(2):

Amended the heading for Code Sec. 4481(c)(2) by striking "Destroyed or stolen" and inserting "Sold, destroyed, or stolen". **Effective** for tax periods beginning after 10-22-2004.

• **1983, Surface Transportation Act of 1983 (P.L. 97-424)**

P.L. 97-424, § 513(d):

Amended Code Sec. 4481(c). **Effective** 7-1-84. Prior to amendment, Code Sec. 4481(c) read as follows:

(c) Proration of Tax.—If in any taxable period the first use of the highway motor vehicle is after the first month in such period, the tax shall be reckoned proportionately from the first day of the month in which such use occurs to and including the last day in such taxable period.

• **1961, Federal-Aid Highway Act of 1961 (P.L. 87-61)**

P.L. 87-61, § 203(b)(2)(B):

Amended Sec. 4481(c). **Effective** 7-1-61. Prior to amendment, Sec. 4481(c) read:

(c) Proration of Tax.—If in any year the first use of the highway motor vehicle is after July 31, the tax shall be reckoned proportionately from the first day of the month in which such use occurs to and including the 30th day of June following.

[Sec. 4481(d)]

(d) One Tax Liability Per Period.—To the extent that the tax imposed by this section is paid with respect to any highway motor vehicle for any taxable period, no further tax shall be imposed by this section for such taxable period with respect to such vehicle.

Amendments

• **2018, Tax Technical Corrections Act of 2018 (P.L. 115-141)**

P.L. 115-141, § 401(b)(43), Div. U:

Amended Code Sec. 4481(d). **Effective** 3-23-2018. For a special rule, see Act Sec. 401(e), Div. U, below. Prior to amendment, Code Sec. 4481(d) read as follows:

(d) One Tax Liability Per Period.—

(1) In general.—To the extent that the tax imposed by this section is paid with respect to any highway motor vehicle for any taxable period, no further tax shall be imposed by this section for such taxable period with respect to such vehicle.

(2) Cross reference.—

For privilege of paying tax imposed by this section in installments, see section 6156.

P.L. 115-141, § 401(e), Div. U, provides:

(e) General Savings Provision With Respect to Deadwood Provisions.—If—

(1) any provision amended or repealed by the amendments made by subsection (b) or (d) applied to—

(A) any transaction occurring before the date of the enactment of this Act,

(B) any property acquired before such date of enactment, or

(C) any item of income, loss, deduction, or credit taken into account before such date of enactment, and

(2) the treatment of such transaction, property, or item under such provision would (without regard to the amendments or repeals made by such subsection) affect the liability for tax for periods ending after such date of enactment,

nothing in the amendments or repeals made by this section shall be construed to affect the treatment of such transaction, property, or item for purposes of determining liability for tax for periods ending after such date of enactment.

• **1961, Federal-Aid Highway Act of 1961 (P.L. 87-61)**

P.L. 87-61, § 203(b)(2)(B):

Amended Sec. 4481(d). **Effective** 7-1-61. Prior to amendment, Sec. 4481(d) read:

(d) One Payment Per Year.—If the tax imposed by this section is paid with respect to any highway motor vehicle for any year, no further tax shall be imposed by this section for such year with respect to such vehicle.

[Sec. 4481(e)]

(e) Electronic Filing.—Any taxpayer who files a return under this section with respect to 25 or more vehicles for any taxable period shall file such return electronically.

Amendments

• **2004, American Jobs Creation Act of 2004 (P.L. 108-357)**

P.L. 108-357, § 867(c):

Amended Code Sec. 4481 by redesignating subsection (e) as subsection (f) and by inserting after subsection (d) a new subsection (e). **Effective** for tax periods beginning after 10-22-2004.

[Sec. 4481(f)]

(f) Period Tax in Effect.—The tax imposed by this section shall apply only to use before October 1, 2029.

Amendments

• **2021, Infrastructure Investment and Jobs Act (P.L. 117-58)**

P.L. 117-58, § 80102(b)(1), Div. H:

Amended Code Sec. 4481(f) by striking "2023" each place it appears and inserting "2029". **Effective** 10-1-2021.

• **2015, Fixing America's Surface Transportation Act (P.L. 114-94)**

P.L. 114-94, § 31102(b)(1):

Amended Code Sec. 4481(f) by striking "2017" and inserting "2023". **Effective** 10-1-2016.

EXCISE TAX—CERTAIN VEHICLES

- **2012, Highway Investment, Job Creation, and Economic Growth Act of 2012 (P.L. 112-141)**

P.L. 112-141, §40102(b)(1)(A):

Amended Code Sec. 4481(f) by striking "2013" and inserting "2017". **Effective** 7-1-2012.

- **2012, Surface Transportation Extension Act of 2012 (P.L. 112-102)**

P.L. 112-102, §402(b)(1):

Amended Code Sec. 4481(f) by striking "2012" and inserting "2013". **Effective** 4-1-2012.

- **2011, Surface Transportation Extension Act of 2011, Part II (P.L. 112-30)**

P.L. 112-30, §142(b)(1):

Amended Code Sec. 4481(f) by striking "2011" and inserting "2012". **Effective** 10-1-2011.

- **2005, Safe, Accountable, Flexible, Efficient Transportation Equity Act: A Legacy for Users (P.L. 109-59)**

P.L. 109-59, §11101(a)(2)(A):

Amended Code Sec. 4481(f) by striking "2006" and inserting "2011". **Effective** 8-10-2005.

- **2005, Surface Transportation Extension Act of 2005 (P.L. 109-14)**

P.L. 109-14, §9(c)(1):

Amended Code Sec. 4481(f) by striking "2005" and inserting "2006". **Effective** 5-31-2005.

- **2004, American Jobs Creation Act of 2004 (P.L. 108-357)**

P.L. 108-357, §867(c):

Amended Code Sec. 4481 by redesignating subsection (e) as subsection (f). **Effective** for tax periods beginning after 10-22-2004.

- **1998, Transportation Equity Act for the 21st Century (P.L. 105-178)**

P.L. 105-178, §9002(a)(1)(G):

Amended Code Sec. 4481(e) by striking "1999" and inserting "2005". **Effective** 6-9-98.

- **1991, Intermodal Surface Transportation Efficiency Act of 1991 (P.L. 102-240)**

P.L. 102-240, §8002(a)(5) (as amended by P.L. 104-188, §1704(t)(57)):

Amended Code Sec. 4481(e) by striking "1995" each place it appears and inserting "1999". **Effective** 12-18-91.

- **1990, Omnibus Budget Reconciliation Act of 1990 (P.L. 101-508)**

P.L. 101-508, §11211(c)(5):

Amended Code Sec. 4481(e) by striking "1993" each place it appears and inserting "1995". **Effective** 11-5-90.

- **1987, Surface Transportation and Uniform Relocation Assistance Act of 1987 (P.L. 100-17)**

P.L. 100-17, §502(a)(5):

Amended Code Sec. 4481(e) by striking out "1988" and inserting in lieu thereof "1993". **Effective** 4-2-87.

P.L. 100-17, §507(c), provides:

(c) REGULATIONS REQUIRED WITHIN 120 DAYS.—The Secretary of the Treasury or the delegate of the Secretary shall within 120 days after the date of the enactment of this section prescribe regulations governing payment of the tax imposed by section 4481 of the Internal Revenue Code of 1986 on any highway motor vehicle operated by a motor carrier domiciled in any contiguous foreign country or owned or controlled by persons of any contiguous foreign country. Such regulations shall include a procedure by which the operator of such motor vehicle shall evidence that such operator has paid such tax at the time such motor vehicle enters the United States. In the event of the failure to provide evidence of payment, such regulations may provide for denial of entry of such motor vehicle into the United States.

- **1983, Surface Transportation Act of 1983 (P.L. 97-424)**

P.L. 97-424, §516(a)(4):

Amended Code Sec. 4481(e) by striking out "1984" and inserting in lieu thereof "1988". **Effective** 1-6-83.

- **1978, Surface Transportation Assistance Act of 1978 (P.L. 95-599)**

P.L. 95-599, §502(a)(7):

Substituted "1984" for "1979" in Code Sec. 4481(e). **Effective** 11-7-78.

- **1976 (P.L. 94-280)**

P.L. 94-280, §303(a)(7):

Amended Code Sec. 4481(e) by substituting "1979" for "1977."

- **1970, Federal-Aid Highway Act of 1970 (P.L. 91-605)**

P.L. 91-605, §303(a)(8):

Amended Code Sec. 4481(e) by substituting "1977" for "1972."

- **1961, Federal-Aid Highway Act of 1961 (P.L. 87-61)**

P.L. 87-61, §203(b)(1):

Amended Sec. 4481(e) by substituting "before October 1, 1972" for "after June 30, 1956, and before July 1, 1972." **Effective** 7-1-61.

P.L. 627, 84th Cong., §206(a):

Added Sec. 4481 to chapter 36 of the 1954 Code. **Effective** 7-1-56.

[Sec. 4482]

SEC. 4482. DEFINITIONS.

[Sec. 4482(a)]

(a) HIGHWAY MOTOR VEHICLE.—For purposes of this subchapter, the term "highway motor vehicle" means any motor vehicle which is a highway vehicle.

[Sec. 4482(b)]

(b) TAXABLE GROSS WEIGHT.—For purposes of this subchapter, the term "taxable gross weight", when used with respect to any highway motor vehicle, means the sum of—

(1) the actual unloaded weight of—

(A) such highway motor vehicle fully equipped for service, and

(B) the semitrailers and trailers (fully equipped for service) customarily used in connection with highway motor vehicles of the same type as such highway motor vehicle, and

(2) the weight of the maximum load customarily carried on highway motor vehicles of the same type as such highway motor vehicle and on the semitrailers and trailers referred to in paragraph (1)(B).

Taxable gross weight shall be determined under regulations prescribed by the Secretary (which regulations may include formulas or other methods for determining the taxable gross weight of vehicles by classes, specifications, or otherwise).

Amendments

- **1976, Tax Reform Act of 1976 (P.L. 94-455)**

P.L. 94-455, §1906(b)(13)(A):

Amended 1954 Code by substituting "Secretary" for "Secretary or his delegate" each place it appeared. **Effective** 2-1-77.

[Sec. 4482(c)]

(c) OTHER DEFINITIONS AND SPECIAL RULE.—For purposes of this subchapter—

(1) STATE.—The term "State" means a State and the District of Columbia.

(2) YEAR.—The term "year" means the one-year period beginning on July 1.

(3) USE.—The term "use" means use in the United States on the public highways.

(4) TAXABLE PERIOD.—The term "taxable period" means any year beginning before July 1, 2029, and the period which begins on July 1, 2029, and ends at the close of September 30, 2029.

(5) CUSTOMARY USE.—A semitrailer or trailer shall be treated as customarily used in connection with a highway motor vehicle if such vehicle is equipped to tow such semitrailer or trailer.

EXCISE TAX—CERTAIN VEHICLES

Amendments

• **2021, Infrastructure Investment and Jobs Act (P.L. 117-58)**

P.L. 117-58, §80102(b)(2), Div. H:

Amended Code Sec. 4482(c)(4) by striking "2023" each place it appears and inserting "2029". **Effective** 10-1-2021.

• **2015, Fixing America's Surface Transportation Act (P.L. 114-94)**

P.L. 114-94, §31102(b)(2):

Amended Code Sec. 4482(c)(4) by striking "2017" each place it appears and inserting "2023". **Effective** 10-1-2016.

• **2012, Highway Investment, Job Creation, and Economic Growth Act of 2012 (P.L. 112-141)**

P.L. 112-141, §40102(b)(2)(A):

Amended Code Sec. 4482(c)(4). **Effective** as if included in the amendments made by section 142 of the Surface Transportation Extension Act of 2011, Part II [effective 10-1-2011.—CCH]. Prior to amendment, Code Sec. 4482(c)(4) read as follows:

(4) TAXABLE PERIOD.—The term "taxable period" means any year beginning before July 1, 2013, and the period which begins on July 1, 2013, and ends at the close of September 30, 2013.

• **2012, Temporary Surface Transportation Extension Act of 2012 (P.L. 112-140)**

P.L. 112-140, §1(c), provides:

(c) SPECIAL RULE FOR EXECUTION OF AMENDMENTS IN MAP–21.—On the date of enactment of the MAP–21 [P.L. 112-141]—

(1) this Act and the amendments made by this Act shall cease to be effective;

(2) the text of the laws amended by this Act shall revert back so as to read as the text read on the day before the date of enactment of this Act; and

(3) the amendments made by the MAP–21 shall be executed as if this Act had not been enacted.

P.L. 112-140, §402(e):

Amended Code Sec. 4482(c)(4). **Effective** as if included in section 402 of the Surface Transportation Extension Act of 2012 [effective 4-1-2012.—CCH]. [Note: Code Sec. 4482(c)(4), as amended by Act Sec. 402(e), is identical to Code Sec. 4482(c)(4), prior to such amendment.—CCH.] For a special rule, see Act Sec. 1(c), above. Prior to amendment, Code Sec. 4482(c)(4) read as follows:

(4) TAXABLE PERIOD.—The term "taxable period" means any year beginning before July 1, 2013, and the period which begins on July 1, 2013, and ends at the close of September 30, 2013.

• **2012, Surface Transportation Extension Act of 2012 (P.L. 112-102)**

P.L. 112-102, §402(b)(2):

Amended Code Sec. 4482(c)(4) by striking "2012" [each place it appears] and inserting "2013". **Effective** 4-1-2012.

• **2011, Surface Transportation Extension Act of 2011, Part II (P.L. 112-30)**

P.L. 112-30, §142(b)(2):

Amended Code Sec. 4482(c)(4) by striking "2011" and inserting "2012". **Effective** 10-1-2011.

• **2005, Safe, Accountable, Flexible, Efficient Transportation Equity Act: A Legacy for Users (P.L. 109-59)**

P.L. 109-59, §11101(a)(2)(B):

Amended Code Sec. 4482(c)(4) by striking "2006" each place it appears and inserting "2011". **Effective** 8-10-2005.

• **2005, Surface Transportation Extension Act of 2005 (P.L. 109-14)**

P.L. 109-14, §9(c)(2):

Amended Code Sec. 4482(c)(4) by striking "2005" each place it appears and inserting "2006". **Effective** 5-31-2005.

• **1998, Transportation Equity Act for the 21st Century (P.L. 105-178)**

P.L. 105-178, §9002(a)(1)(H):

Amended Code Sec. 4482(c)(4) by striking "1999" each place it appears and inserting "2005". **Effective** 6-9-98.

• **1991, Intermodal Surface Transportation Efficiency Act of 1991 (P.L. 102-240)**

P.L. 102-240, §8002(a)(5):

Amended Code Sec. 4482(c)(4) by striking "1995" each place it appears and inserting "1999". **Effective** 12-18-91.

• **1990, Omnibus Budget Reconciliation Act of 1990 (P.L. 101-508)**

P.L. 101-508, §11211(c)(5):

Amended Code Sec. 4482(c)(4) by striking "1993" each place it appears and inserting "1995". **Effective** 11-5-90.

• **1987, Surface Transportation and Uniform Relocation Assistance Act of 1987 (P.L. 100-17)**

P.L. 100-17, §502(a)(5):

Amended Code Sec. 4482(c)(4) by striking out "1988" each place it appears and inserting in lieu thereof "1993". **Effective** 4-2-87.

• **1983, Surface Transportation Act of 1983 (P.L. 97-424)**

P.L. 97-424, §513(c)(1):

Added Code Sec. 4482(c)(5). **Effective** 7-1-84.

P.L. 97-424, §513(c)(2):

Amended Code Sec. 4482(c) by inserting "AND SPECIAL RULE" after "DEFINITIONS" in the subsection heading. **Effective** 7-1-84.

P.L. 97-424, §516(a)(4):

Amended Code Sec. 4482(c)(4) by striking out "1984" each place it appeared and inserting in lieu thereof "1988". **Effective** 1-6-83.

• **1978, Surface Transportation Assistance Act of 1978 (P.L. 95-599)**

P.L. 95-599, §502(a)(8):

Substituted "1984" for "1979" in the three places in which the year appears in Code Sec. 4482(c). **Effective** 11-7-78.

• **1976, Tax Reform Act of 1976 (P.L. 94-455)**

P.L. 94-455, §1904(c):

Struck out ", a Territory of the United States," after "means a State" in Code Sec. 4482(c)(1). **Effective** 2-1-77.

• **1976 (P.L. 94-280)**

P.L. 94-280, §303(a)(9):

Amended Code Sec. 4482(c)(4) by substituting "1979" for "1977" in the three places in which the year appears.

• **1970, Federal-Aid Highway Act of 1970 (P.L. 91-605)**

P.L. 91-605, §303(a)(9):

Amended Code Sec. 4482(c)(4) by substituting "1977" for "1972" in the three places in which the year appears.

• **1961, Federal-Aid Highway Act of 1961 (P.L. 87-61)**

P.L. 87-61, §203(b)(2)(C):

Added Sec. 4482(c)(4). **Effective** 7-1-61.

• **1956 (P.L. 627, 84th Cong.)**

P.L. 627, 84th Cong., 2d Sess., §206(a):

Added Sec. 4482 to chapter 36 of the 1954 Code. **Effective** 7-1-56.

[Sec. 4482(d)]

(d) SPECIAL RULE FOR TAXABLE PERIOD IN WHICH TERMINATION DATE OCCURS.—In the case of the taxable period which ends on September 30, 2029, the amount of the tax imposed by section 4481 with respect to any highway motor vehicle shall be determined by reducing each dollar amount in the table contained in section 4481(a) by 75 percent.

Amendments

• **2021, Infrastructure Investment and Jobs Act (P.L. 117-58)**

P.L. 117-58, §80102(b)(2), Div. H:

Amended Code Sec. 4482(d) by striking "2023" each place it appears and inserting "2029". **Effective** 10-1-2021.

• **2015, Fixing America's Surface Transportation Act (P.L. 114-94)**

P.L. 114-94, §31102(b)(2):

Amended Code Sec. 4482(d) by striking "2017" and inserting "2023". **Effective** 10-1-2016.

• **2012, Highway Investment, Job Creation, and Economic Growth Act of 2012 (P.L. 112-141)**

P.L. 112-141, §40102(b)(1)(B):

Amended Code Sec. 4482(d) by striking "2013" and inserting "2017". **Effective** 7-1-2012.

• **2012, Surface Transportation Extension Act of 2012 (P.L. 112-102)**

P.L. 112-102, §402(b)(2):

Amended Code Sec. 4482(d) by striking "2012" and inserting "2013". **Effective** 4-1-2012.

• **2011, Surface Transportation Extension Act of 2011, Part II (P.L. 112-30)**

P.L. 112-30, §142(b)(2):

Amended Code Sec. 4482(d) by striking "2011" and inserting "2012". **Effective** 10-1-2011.

• **2005, Safe, Accountable, Flexible, Efficient Transportation Equity Act: A Legacy for Users (P.L. 109-59)**

P.L. 109-59, §11101(a)(2)(C):

Amended Code Sec. 4482(d) by striking "2006" and inserting "2011". **Effective** 8-10-2005.

EXCISE TAX—CERTAIN VEHICLES

- **2005, Surface Transportation Extension Act of 2005 (P.L. 109-14)**

P.L. 109-14, §9(c)(3):

Amended Code Sec. 4482(d) by striking "2005" and inserting "2006". **Effective** 5-31-2005.

- **1998, Transportation Equity Act for the 21st Century (P.L. 105-178)**

P.L. 105-178, §9002(a)(1)(I):

Amended Code Sec. 4482(d) by striking "1999" and inserting "2005". **Effective** 6-9-98.

- **1991, Intermodal Surface Transportation Efficiency Act of 1991 (P.L. 102-240)**

P.L. 102-240, §8002(a)(5):

Amended Code Sec. 4482(d) by striking "1995" each place it appears and inserting "1999". **Effective** 12-18-91.

- **1990, Omnibus Budget Reconciliation Act of 1990 (P.L. 101-508)**

P.L. 101-508, §11211(c)(5):

Amended Code Sec. 4482(d) by striking "1993" each place it appears and inserting "1995". **Effective** 11-5-90.

- **1987, Surface Transportation and Uniform Relocation Assistance Act of 1987 (P.L. 100-17)**

P.L. 100-17, §502(a)(5):

Amended Code Sec. 4482(d) by striking out "1988" and inserting in lieu thereof "1993". **Effective** 4-2-87.

- **1983, Surface Transportation Act of 1983 (P.L. 97-424)**

P.L. 97-424, §513(e):

Added Code Sec. 4482(d). **Effective** 7-1-84.

[Sec. 4483]

SEC. 4483. EXEMPTIONS.

[Sec. 4483(a)]

(a) STATE AND LOCAL GOVERNMENTAL EXEMPTION.—Under regulations prescribed by the Secretary, no tax shall be imposed by section 4481 on the use of any highway motor vehicle by any State or any political subdivision of a State.

Amendments

- **1976, Tax Reform Act of 1976 (P.L. 94-455)**

P.L. 94-455, §1906(b)(13)(A):

Amended 1954 Code by substituting "Secretary" for "Secretary or his delegate" each place it appeared. **Effective** 2-1-77.

[Sec. 4483(b)]

(b) EXEMPTION FOR UNITED STATES.—The Secretary of the Treasury may authorize exemption from the tax imposed by section 4481 as to the use by the United States of any particular highway motor vehicle, or class of highway motor vehicles, if he determines that the imposition of such tax with respect to such use will cause substantial burden or expense which can be avoided by granting tax exemption and that full benefit of such exemption, if granted, will accrue to the United States.

Amendments

- **1976, Tax Reform Act of 1976 (P.L. 94-455)**

P.L. 94-455, §1906(b)(13)(B):

Substituted "Secretary of the Treasury" for "Secretary" in Code Sec. 4483(b). **Effective** 2-1-77.

[Sec. 4483(c)]

(c) CERTAIN TRANSIT-TYPE BUSES.—Under regulations prescribed by the Secretary, no tax shall be imposed by section 4481 on the use of any bus which is of the transit type (rather than of the intercity type) by a person who, for the last 3 months of the preceding year (or for such other period as the Secretary may by regulations prescribe for purposes of this subsection), met the 60-percent passenger fare revenue test set forth in section 6421(b)(2) (as in effect on the day before the date of the enactment of the Energy Tax Act of 1978) as applied to the period prescribed for the purposes of this subsection.

Amendments

- **1978, Energy Tax Act of 1978 (P.L. 95-618)**

P.L. 95-618, §233(a)(3)(C):

Amended Code Sec. 4483(c) by inserting "(as in effect on the day before the date of enactment of the Energy Tax Act of 1978)" after "section 6421(b)(2)". **Effective** on the first day of the first calendar month which begins more than 10 days after the date of the enactment of the Energy Tax Act of 1978.

- **1976, Tax Reform Act of 1976 (P.L. 94-455)**

P.L. 94-455, §1906(b)(13)(A):

Amended 1954 Code by substituting "Secretary" for "Secretary or his delegate" each place it appeared. **Effective** 2-1-77.

- **1956 (P.L. 627, 84th Cong.)**

P.L. 627, 84th Cong., 2d Sess., §206(a):

Added Sec. 4483 to chapter 36 of the 1954 Code. **Effective** 7-1-56.

[Sec. 4483(d)]

(d) EXEMPTION FOR TRUCKS USED FOR LESS THAN 5,000 MILES ON PUBLIC HIGHWAYS.—

(1) SUSPENSION OF TAX.—

(A) IN GENERAL.—If—

(i) it is reasonable to expect that the use of any highway motor vehicle on public highways during any taxable period will be less than 5,000 miles, and

(ii) the owner of such vehicle furnishes such information as the Secretary may by forms or regulations require with respect to the expected use of such vehicle,

then the collection of the tax imposed by section 4481 with respect to the use of such vehicle shall be suspended during the taxable period.

(B) SUSPENSION CEASES TO APPLY WHERE USE EXCEEDS 5,000 MILES.—Subparagraph (A) shall cease to apply with respect to any highway motor vehicle whenever the use of such vehicle on public highways during the taxable period exceeds 5,000 miles.

(2) EXEMPTION.—If—

(A) the collection of the tax imposed by section 4481 with respect to any highway motor vehicle is suspended under paragraph (1),

(B) such vehicle is not used during the taxable period on public highways for more than 5,000 miles, and

(C) except as otherwise provided in regulations, the owner of such vehicle furnishes such information as the Secretary may require with respect to the use of such vehicle during the taxable period,

then no tax shall be imposed by section 4481 on the use of such vehicle for the taxable period.

(3) REFUND WHERE TAX PAID AND VEHICLE NOT USED FOR MORE THAN 5,000 MILES.—If—

(A) the tax imposed by section 4481 is paid with respect to any highway motor vehicle for any taxable period, and

(B) the requirements of subparagraphs (B) and (C) of paragraph (2) are met with respect to such taxable period,

the amount of such tax shall be credited or refunded (without interest) to the person who paid such tax.

EXCISE TAX—CERTAIN VEHICLES

(4) RELIEF FROM LIABILITY FOR TAX UNDER CERTAIN CIRCUMSTANCES WHERE TRUCK IS TRANSFERRED.—Under regulations prescribed by the Secretary, the owner of a highway motor vehicle with respect to which the collection of the tax imposed by section 4481 is suspended under paragraph (1) shall not be liable for the tax imposed by section 4481 (and the new owner shall be liable for such tax) with respect to such vehicle if—

(A) such vehicle is transferred to a new owner,

(B) such suspension is in effect at the time of such transfer, and

(C) the old owner furnishes such information as the Secretary by forms and regulations requires with respect to the transfer of such vehicle.

(5) 7,500-MILES EXEMPTION FOR AGRICULTURAL VEHICLES.—

(A) IN GENERAL.—In the case of an agricultural vehicle, paragraphs (1) and (2) shall be applied by substituting "7,500" for "5,000" each place it appears.

(B) DEFINITIONS.—For purposes of this paragraph—

(i) AGRICULTURAL VEHICLE.—The term "agricultural vehicle" means any highway motor vehicle—

(I) used primarily for farming purposes, and

(II) registered (under the laws of the State in which such vehicle is required to be registered) as a highway motor vehicle used for farming purposes.

(ii) FARMING PURPOSES.—The term "farming purposes" means the transporting of any farm commodity to or from a farm or the use directly in agricultural production.

(iii) FARM COMMODITY.—The term "farm commodity" means any agricultural or horticultural commodity, feed, seed, fertilizer, livestock, bees, poultry, fur-bearing animals, or wildlife.

(6) OWNER DEFINED.—For purposes of this subsection, the term "owner" means, with respect to any highway motor vehicle, the person described in section 4481(b).

Amendments

• **1984, Deficit Reduction Act of 1984 (P.L. 98-369)**

P.L. 98-369, § 903(a):

Amended Code Sec. 4483(d) by redesignating paragraph (5) as paragraph (6) and by inserting after paragraph (4) new paragraph (5). **Effective** as if included in the amendments made by section 513 of the Highway Revenue Act of 1982.

• **1983, Surface Transportation Act of 1983 (P.L. 97-424)**

P.L. 97-424, § 513(b):

Added Code Sec. 4483(d). **Effective** 7-1-84.

[Sec. 4483(e)]

(e) REDUCTION IN TAX FOR TRUCKS USED IN LOGGING.—The tax imposed by section 4481 shall be reduced by 25 percent with respect to any highway motor vehicle if—

(1) the exclusive use of such vehicle during any taxable period is the transportation, to and from appoint located on a forested site, of products harvested from such forested site, and

(2) such vehicle is registered (under the laws of the State in which such vehicle is required to be registered) as a highway motor vehicle used in the transportation of harvested forest products.

Amendments

• **1984, Deficit Reduction Act of 1984 (P.L. 98-369)**

P.L. 98-369, § 902(a)

Amended Code Sec. 4483 by redesignating subsection (e) as subsection (f) and inserting new subsection (e). **Effective** 7-18-84.

[Sec. 4483(f)—Stricken]

Amendments

• **2004, American Jobs Creation Act of 2004 (P.L. 108-357)**

P.L. 108-357, § 867(d):

Amended Code Sec. 4483 by striking subsection (f). **Effective** for tax periods beginning after 10-22-2004. Prior to being stricken, Code Sec. 4483(f) read as follows:

(f) REDUCTION IN TAX FOR TRUCKS BASE-PLATED IN A CONTIGUOUS FOREIGN COUNTRY.—If the base for registration purposes of any highway motor vehicle is in a contiguous foreign country for any taxable period, the tax imposed by section 4481 for such period shall be 75 percent of the tax which would (but for this subsection) be imposed by section 4481 for such period.

• **1987, Surface Transportation and Uniform Relocation Assistance Act of 1987 (P.L. 100-17)**

P.L. 100-17, § 507(b):

Amended Code Sec. 4483 by redesignating subsection (f) as subsection (g) and by inserting after subsection (e) new subsection (f). **Effective** 7-1-87.

[Sec. 4483(g)]

(g) EXEMPTION FOR MOBILE MACHINERY.—No tax shall be imposed by section 4481 on the use of any vehicle described in section 4053(8).

Amendments

• **2004, American Jobs Creation Act of 2004 (P.L. 108-357)**

P.L. 108-357, § 851(b)(1):

Amended Code Sec. 4483 by redesignating subsection (g) as subsection (h) and by inserting after subsection (f) a new subsection (g). **Effective** 10-23-2004.

[Sec. 4483(h)]

(h) EXEMPTION FOR VEHICLES USED IN BLOOD COLLECTION.—

(1) IN GENERAL.—No tax shall be imposed by section 4481 on the use of any qualified blood collector vehicle by a qualified blood collector organization.

(2) QUALIFIED BLOOD COLLECTOR VEHICLE.—For purposes of this subsection, the term "qualified blood collector vehicle" means a vehicle at least 80 percent of the use of which during the prior taxable period was by a qualified blood collector organization in the collection, storage, or transportation of blood.

(3) SPECIAL RULE FOR VEHICLES FIRST PLACED IN SERVICE IN A TAXABLE PERIOD.—In the case of a vehicle first placed in service in a taxable period, a vehicle shall be treated as a qualified blood collector vehicle for such taxable period if such qualified blood collector organization certifies to the Secretary that the organization reasonably expects at least 80 percent of the use of such vehicle by the organization during such taxable period will be in the collection, storage, or transportation of blood.

(4) QUALIFIED BLOOD COLLECTOR ORGANIZATION.—The term "qualified blood collector organization" has the meaning given such term by section 7701(a)(49).

EXCISE TAXES—CIVIL AIRCRAFT

Amendments

- **2006, Pension Protection Act of 2006 (P.L. 109-280)**

P.L. 109-280, §1207(d):

Amended Code Sec. 4483 by redesignating subsection (h) as subsection (i) and by inserting after subsection (g) a new subsection (h). **Effective** for tax periods beginning on or after 7-1-2007.

[Sec. 4483(i)]

(i) TERMINATION OF EXEMPTIONS.—Subsections (a) and (c) shall not apply on and after October 1, 2029.

Amendments

- **2021, Infrastructure Investment and Jobs Act (P.L. 117-58)**

P.L. 117-58, §80102(d)(2), Div. H:

Amended Code Sec. 4483(i) by striking "October 1, 2023" and inserting "October 1, 2029". **Effective** 10-1-2021.

- **2015, Fixing America's Surface Transportation Act (P.L. 114-94)**

P.L. 114-94, §31102(d)(2):

Amended Code Sec. 4483(i) by striking "October 1, 2017" and inserting "October 1, 2023". **Effective** 10-1-2016.

- **2012, Highway Investment, Job Creation, and Economic Growth Act of 2012 (P.L. 112-141)**

P.L. 112-141, §40102(d)(2):

Amended Code Sec. 4483(i) by striking "July 1, 2012" and inserting "October 1, 2017". **Effective** 7-1-2012.

- **2012, Temporary Surface Transportation Extension Act of 2012 (P.L. 112-140)**

P.L. 112-140, §1(c), provides:

(c) SPECIAL RULE FOR EXECUTION OF AMENDMENTS IN MAP-21.—On the date of enactment of the MAP-21 [P.L. 112-141]—

(1) this Act and the amendments made by this Act shall cease to be effective;

(2) the text of the laws amended by this Act shall revert back so as to read as the text read on the day before the date of enactment of this Act; and

(3) the amendments made by the MAP-21 shall be executed as if this Act had not been enacted.

P.L. 112-140, §402(c):

Amended Code Sec. 4483(i) by striking "July 1, 2012" and inserting "July 7, 2012". **Effective** 7-1-2012. For a special rule, see Act Sec. 1(c), above.

- **2012, Surface Transportation Extension Act of 2012 (P.L. 112-102)**

P.L. 112-102, §402(d):

Amended Code Sec. 4483(i) by striking "April 1, 2012" and inserting "July 1, 2012". **Effective** 4-1-2012.

- **2011, Surface Transportation Extension Act of 2011, Part II (P.L. 112-30)**

P.L. 112-30, §142(d):

Amended Code Sec. 4483(i) by striking "October 1, 2011" and inserting "April 1, 2012". **Effective** 10-1-2011.

- **2006, Pension Protection Act of 2006 (P.L. 109-280)**

P.L. 109-280, §1207(d):

Amended Code Sec. 4483, by redesignating subsection (h) as subsection (i). **Effective** for tax periods beginning on or after 7-1-2007.

- **2005, Safe, Accountable, Flexible, Efficient Transportation Equity Act: A Legacy for Users (P.L. 109-59)**

P.L. 109-59, §11101(b)(2):

Amended Code Sec. 4483(i) by striking "2006" and inserting "2011". **Effective** 8-10-2005.

- **2005, Surface Transportation Extension Act of 2005 (P.L. 109-14)**

P.L. 109-14, §9(c)(4):

Amended Code Sec. 4483(i) by striking "2005" and inserting "2006". **Effective** 5-31-2005.

- **2004, American Jobs Creation Act of 2004 (P.L. 108-357)**

P.L. 108-357, §851(b)(1):

Amended Code Sec. 4483 by redesignating subsection (g) as subsection (h). **Effective** 10-23-2004.

- **1998, Transportation Equity Act for the 21st Century (P.L. 105-178)**

P.L. 105-178, §9002(b)(2):

Amended Code Sec. 4483(g) by striking "1999" and inserting "2005". **Effective** 6-9-98.

- **1991, Intermodal Surface Transportation Efficiency Act of 1991 (P.L. 102-240)**

P.L. 102-240, §8002(b)(4):

Amended Code Sec. 4483(g) by striking "1995" each place it appears and inserting "1999". **Effective** 12-18-91.

- **1990, Omnibus Budget Reconciliation Act of 1990 (P.L. 101-508)**

P.L. 101-508, §11211(d)(4):

Amended Code Sec. 4483(g) by striking out "1993" each place it appears and inserting "1995". **Effective** 11-5-90.

- **1987, Surface Transportation and Uniform Relocation Assistance Act of 1987 (P.L. 100-17)**

P.L. 100-17, §502(b)(5):

Amended Code Sec. 4483(f) by striking out "1988" and inserting in lieu thereof "1993". **Effective** 4-2-87.

P.L. 100-17, §507(b):

Redesignated subsection (f) as subsection (g). **Effective** 7-1-87.

- **1984, Deficit Reduction Act of 1984 (P.L. 98-369)**

P.L. 98-369, §902(a):

Amended Code Sec. 4483 by redesignating subsection (e) as subsection (f) and inserting new subsection (e). **Effective** 7-18-84.

- **1983, Surface Transportation Act of 1983 (P.L. 97-424)**

P.L. 97-424, §516(b)(3):

Added Code Sec. 4483(e). **Effective** 1-6-83.

[Sec. 4484]

SEC. 4484. CROSS REFERENCES.

(1) For penalties and administrative provisions applicable to this subchapter, see subtitle F.

(2) For exemption for uses by Indian tribal governments (or their subdivisions), see section 7871.

Amendments

- **1983 (P.L. 97-473)**

P.L. 97-473, §202(b)(10):

Amended Code Sec. 4484.

- **1956 (P.L. 627, 84th Cong.)**

P.L. 627, 84th Cong., §206(a):

Added Sec. 4484 to chapter 36 of the 1954 Code. **Effective** 7-1-56.

Subchapter E—Tax on Use of Civil Aircraft—[Repealed]

[Sec. 4491—Repealed]

Amendments

- **1982, Tax Equity and Fiscal Responsibility Act of 1982 (P.L. 97-248)**

P.L. 97-248, §280(c)(1):

Repealed Code Sec. 4491. **Effective** with respect to transportation beginning after 8-31-82, except that the amendment will not apply to any amount paid on or before that date. Prior to its repeal, Code Sec. 4491 read as follows:

SEC. 4491. IMPOSITION OF TAX.

(a) IMPOSITION OF TAX.—A tax is hereby imposed on the use of any taxable civil aircraft during any year at the rate of—

(1) $6.25, plus

(2)(A) in the case of an aircraft (other than a turbine-engine-powered aircraft), $1/2$ cent a pound for each pound of the maximum certificated takeoff weight in excess of 2,500 pounds, or

(B) in the case of any turbine-engine-powered aircraft, $7/8$ cent a pound for each pound of the maximum certificated takeoff weight.

(b) BY WHOM PAID.—Except as provided in section 4493(a), the tax imposed by this section shall be paid—

(1) in the case of a taxable civil aircraft described in section 4492(a)(1), by the person in whose name the aircraft is, or is required to be, registered, or

(2) in the case of a taxable civil aircraft described in section 4492(a)(2), by the United States person by or for whom the aircraft is owned.

(c) PRORATION OF TAX.—If in any year the first use of the taxable civil aircraft is after the first month in such year, that portion of the tax which is determined under subsection (a)(2) shall be reckoned proportionately from the first day of the month in which such use occurs to and including the last day in such year.

(d) ONE TAX LIABILITY PER YEAR.—

EXCISE TAXES—CIVIL AIRCRAFT

(1) IN GENERAL.—To the extent that the tax imposed by this section is paid with respect to any taxable civil aircraft for any year no further tax shall be imposed by this section for such year with respect to such aircraft.

(2) CROSS REFERENCE.—

For privilege of paying tax imposed by this section in installments, see section 6156.

(e) TERMINATION.—On and after October 1, 1980, the tax imposed by subsection (a) shall not apply.

• **1980 (P.L. 96-298)**

P.L. 96-298, § 1(c):

Substituted "October 1, 1980" for "July 1, 1980" in Code Sec. 4491(e). For the period July 1, 1980 to October 1, 1980, amended Code Sec. 4491(a)(1) by substituting "$6.25" for "$25"; amended Code Sec. 4491(a)(2)(A) by substituting "$1/2$" cent for "2 cents"; and, amended Code Sec. 4491(a)(2)(B) by substituting "$7/8$ cent" for "$3 1/2$ cents". The period July 1, 1980 to October 1, 1980 is treated as a year for purposes of these changes.

• **1970, Excise, Estate, and Gift Tax Adjustment Act of 1970 (P.L. 91-614)**

P.L. 91-614, § 305(a):

Amended Code Sec. 4491(a)(2)(A). **Effective** 7-1-71. Prior to amendment, subparagraph (2)(A) read as follows:

(2)(A) in the case of an aircraft (other than a turbine-engine-powered aircraft), having a maximum certificated takeoff weight of more than 2,500 pounds, 2 cents a pound for each pound of the maximum certificated takeoff weight, or

• **1970 (P.L. 91-258)**

P.L. 91-258, § 206(a):

Added Code Sec. 4491. **Effective** 7-1-70.

[Sec. 4492—Repealed]

Amendments

• **1982, Tax Equity and Fiscal Responsibility Act of 1982 (P.L. 97-248)**

P.L. 97-248, § 280(c)(1):

Repealed Code Sec. 4492. **Effective** for transportation beginning after 8-31-82, except that such amendment will not apply to any amount paid on or before that date. Prior to its appeal, Code Sec. 4492 read as follows:

SEC. 4492. DEFINITIONS.

(a) TAXABLE CIVIL AIRCRAFT.—For purposes of this subchapter, the term "taxable civil aircraft" means any engine driven aircraft—

(1) registered, or required to be registered, under section 501(a) of the Federal Aviation Act of 1958 (49 U.S.C., sec. 1401(a)), or

(2) which is not described in paragraph (1) but which is owned by or for a United States person.

Such term does not include any aircraft owned by an aircraft museum (as defined in section 4041(h)(2)) and used exclusively for purposes set forth in section 4041(h)(2)(C).

(b) WEIGHT.—For purposes of this subchapter, the term "maximum certificated takeoff weight" means the maximum such weight contained in the type certificate or airworthiness certificate.

(c) OTHER DEFINITIONS.—For purposes of this subchapter—

(1) YEAR.—The term "year" means the one-year period beginning on July 1.

(2) USE.—The term "use" means use in the navigable airspace of the United States.

(3) NAVIGABLE AIRSPACE OF THE UNITED STATES.—The term 'navigable airspace of the United States' has the definition given to such term by section 101(24) of the Federal Aviation Act of 1958 (49 U.S.C., sec. 1301(24)), except that such term does not include the navigable airspace of the Commonwealth of Puerto Rico or of any possession of the United States."

• **1976 (P.L. 94-530)**

P.L. 94-530, § 2(a):

Amended Code Sec. 4492(a) by adding at the end thereof a new sentence. **Effective** 10-1-76.

• **1970 (P.L. 91-258)**

P.L. 91-258, § 206(a):

Added Code Sec. 4492. **Effective** 7-1-70.

[Sec. 4493—Repealed]

Amendments

• **1982, Tax Equity and Fiscal Responsibility Act of 1982 (P.L. 97-248)**

P.L. 97-248, § 280(c)(1):

Repealed Code Sec. 4493. **Effective** for transportation beginning after 8-31-82, except that such amendment will not apply to any amount paid on or before that date. Prior to amendment, Code Sec. 4493 read as follows:

SEC. 4493. SPECIAL RULES.

(a) PAYMENT OF TAX BY LESSEE.—

(1) IN GENERAL.—Any person who is the lessee of any taxable civil aircraft on the day in any year on which occurs the first use which subjects such aircraft to the tax imposed by section 4491 for such year may, under regulations prescribed by the Secretary, elect to be liable for payment of such tax. Notwithstanding any such election, if such lessee does not pay such tax, the lessor shall also be liable for payment of such tax.

(2) EXCEPTION.—No election may be made under paragraph (1) with respect to any taxable civil aircraft which is leased from a person engaged in the business of transporting persons or property for compensation or hire by air.

(b) CERTAIN PERSONS ENGAGED IN FOREIGN AIR COMMERCE.—

(1) ELECTION TO PAY TENTATIVE TAX.—Any person who is a significant user of taxable civil aircraft in foreign air commerce may, with respect to that portion of the tax imposed by section 4491 which is determined under section 4491(a)(2) on any taxable civil aircraft for any year, elect to pay the tentative tax determined under paragraph (2). The payment of such tentative tax shall not relieve such person from payment of the net liability for the tax imposed by section 4491 on such taxable civil aircraft (determined as of the close of such year).

(2) TENTATIVE TAX.—For purposes of paragraph (1), the tentative tax with respect to any taxable civil aircraft for any year is an amount equal to that portion of the tax imposed by section 4491 on such aircraft for such year which is determined under section 4491(a)(2), reduced by a percentage of such amount equal to the percentage which the aggregate of the payments to which such person was entitled under section 6426 (determined without regard to section 6426(c)(2)) with respect to the preceding year is of the aggregate of the taxes imposed by section 4491 for which such person was liable for payment for the preceding year.

(3) SIGNIFICANT USERS OF AIRCRAFT IN FOREIGN AIR COMMERCE.—For purposes of paragraph (1), a person is a significant user of taxable civil aircraft in foreign air commerce for any year only if the aggregate of the payments to which such person was entitled under section 6426 (determined without regard to section 6426(c)(2)) with respect to the preceding year was at least 10 percent of the aggregate of the taxes imposed by section 4491 for which such person was liable for payment for the preceding year.

(4) NET LIABILITY FOR TAX.—For purposes of paragraph (1), the net liability for the tax imposed by section 4491 with respect to any taxable civil aircraft for any year is—

(A) the amount of the tax imposed by such section, reduced by

(B) the amount payable under section 6426 with respect to such aircraft for the year (determined without regard to section 6426(c)(2)).

• **1976, Tax Reform Act of 1976 (P.L. 94-455)**

P.L. 94-455, § 1904(a)(13):

Struck out "beginning on or after July 1, 1970" following "for any year" in Code Sec. 4493(b)(1); and struck out the last sentence in Code Sec. 4493(b)(2). **Effective** 2-1-77. Prior to being stricken, the last sentence of Code Sec. 4493(b)(2) read as follows:

In the case of the year beginning on July 1, 1970, this subsection shall apply only if the person electing to pay the tentative tax establishes what the tentative tax would have been for such year if section 4491 had taken effect on July 1, 1969.

P.L. 94-455, § 1906(b)(13)(A):

Amended the 1954 Code by substituting "Secretary" for "Secretary or his delegate" each place it appeared. **Effective** 2-1-77.

• **1970 (P.L. 91-258)**

P.L. 91-258, § 206(a):

Added Code Sec. 4493. **Effective** 7-1-70.

[Sec. 4494—Repealed]

Amendments

• **1982, Tax Equity and Fiscal Responsibility Act of 1982 (P.L. 97-248)**

P.L. 97-248, § 280(c)(1):

Repealed Code Sec. 4494. **Effective** for transportation beginning after 8-31-82, except that such amendment will not apply to amounts paid on or before that date. Prior to amendment, Code Sec. 4494 read as follows:

SEC. 4494. CROSS REFERENCE.

For penalties and administrative provisions applicable to this subchapter, see subtitle F.

• **1970 (P.L. 91-258)**

P.L. 91-258, § 206(a):

Added Code Sec. 4494. **Effective** 7-1-70.

EXCISE TAXES—MINERAL RESOURCES

Subchapter F—Tax on Removal of Hard Mineral Resources From Deep Seabed—[Repealed]

[Sec. 4495—Repealed]

Amendments

• **1997, Taxpayer Relief Act of 1997 (P.L. 105-34)**

P.L. 105-34, §1432(b)(1):

Repealed subchapter F of chapter 36 (Code Secs. 4495-4498). **Effective** 8-5-97. Prior to repeal, Code Sec. 4495 read as follows:

SEC. 4495. IMPOSITION OF TAX.

(a) GENERAL RULE.—There is hereby imposed a tax on any removal of a hard mineral resource from the deep seabed pursuant to a deep seabed permit.

(b) AMOUNT OF TAX.—The amount of the tax imposed by subsection (a) on any removal shall be 3.75 percent of the imputed value of the resource so removed.

(c) LIABILITY FOR TAX.—The tax imposed by subsection (a) shall be paid by the person to whom the deep seabed permit is issued.

(d) TIME FOR PAYING TAX.—The time for paying the tax imposed by subsection (a) shall be the time prescribed by the Secretary by regulations. The time so prescribed with respect to any removal shall be not earlier than the earlier of—

(1) the commercial use of, or the sale or disposition of, any portion of the resource so removed, or

(2) the day which is 12 months after the date of the removal of the resource.

• **1980, Deep Seabed Hard Mineral Resources Act (P.L. 96-283)**

P.L. 96-283, §402(a):

Added Code Sec. 4495. **Effective** 1-1-80.

[Sec. 4496—Repealed]

Amendments

• **1997, Taxpayer Relief Act of 1997 (P.L. 105-34)**

P.L. 105-34, §1432(b)(1):

Repealed Code Sec. 4496. **Effective** 8-5-97. Prior to repeal, Code Sec. 4496 read as follows:

SEC. 4496. DEFINITIONS.

(a) DEEP SEABED PERMIT.—For purposes of this subchapter, the term "deep seabed permit" means a permit issued under title I of the Deep Seabed Hard Minerals Resources Act.

(b) HARD MINERAL RESOURCE.—For purposes of this subchapter, the term "hard mineral resource" means any deposit or accretion on, or just below, the surface of the deep seabed of nodules which contain one or more minerals, at least one of which is manganese, nickel, cobalt, or copper.

(c) DEEP SEABED.—For purposes of this subchapter, the term "deep seabed" means the seabed, and the subsoil thereof to a depth of 10 meters, lying seaward of, and outside—

(1) the Continental Shelf of any nation; and

(2) any area of national resource jurisdiction of any foreign nation, if such area extends beyond the Continental Shelf of such nation and such jurisdiction is recognized by the United States.

(d) CONTINENTAL SHELF.—For purposes of this subchapter, the term "Continental Shelf" means—

(1) the seabed and subsoil of the submarine areas adjacent to the coast but outside the area of the territorial sea, to a depth of 200 meters or, beyond that limit, to where the depth of the superjacent waters admits of the exploitation of the natural resources of such areas; and

(2) the seabed and subsoil of similar submarine areas adjacent to the coasts of islands.

• **1980, Deep Seabed Hard Mineral Resources Act (P.L. 96-283)**

P.L. 96-283, §402(a):

Added Code Sec. 4496. **Effective** 1-1-80.

[Sec. 4497—Repealed]

Amendments

• **1964, Revenue Act of 1964 (P.L. 88-272)**

P.L. 105-34, §1432(b)(1):

Repealed Code Sec. 4497. **Effective** 8-5-97. Prior to repeal, Code Sec. 4497 read as follows:

SEC. 4497. IMPUTED VALUE.

(a) IN GENERAL.—For purposes of this subchapter, the term "imputed value" means, with respect to any hard mineral resource, 20 percent of the fair market value of the commercially recoverable metals and minerals contained in such resource. Such fair market value shall be determined—

(1) as of the date of the removal of the hard mineral resource from the deep seabed; and

(2) as if the metals and minerals contained in such resource were separated from such resource and were in the most basic form for which there is a readily ascertainable market price.

(b) COMMERCIAL RECOVERABILITY.—

(1) MANGANESE, NICKEL, COBALT, AND COPPER.—For purposes of subsection (a), manganese, nickel, cobalt, and copper shall be treated as commercially recoverable.

(2) MINIMUM QUANTITIES AND PERCENTAGES.—The Secretary may by regulations prescribe for each metal or mineral quantities or percentages below which the metal or mineral shall be treated as not commercially recoverable.

(c) SUSPENSION OF TAX WITH RESPECT TO CERTAIN METALS AND MINERALS HELD FOR LATER PROCESSING.—

(1) ELECTION.—The permittee may, in such manner and at such time as may be prescribed by regulations, elect to have the application of the tax suspended with respect to one or more commercially recoverable metals or minerals in the resource which the permittee does not intend to process within one year of the date of extraction. Any metal or mineral affected by such election shall not be taken into account in determining the imputed value of the resource at the time of its removal from the deep seabed. Any suspension under this paragraph with respect to a metal or mineral shall be permanent unless there is a redetermination affecting such metal or mineral under paragraph (2).

(2) LATER COMPUTATION OF TAX.—If the permittee processes any metal or mineral affected by the election under paragraph (1), or if he sells any portion of the resource containing such a metal or mineral, then the amount of the tax under section 4495 shall be redetermined as if there had been no suspension under paragraph (1) with respect to such metal or mineral. In any such case there shall be added to the increase in tax determined under the preceding sentence an amount equal to the interest (at the underpayment rate determined under section 6621) on such increase for the period from the date prescribed for paying the tax on the resources (determined under section 4495(d)) to the date of the processing or sale.

(d) DETERMINATIONS OF VALUE.—All determinations of value necessary for the application of this subchapter shall be made by the Secretary (after consultation with other appropriate Federal officials) on the basis of the best available information. Such determinations shall be made under procedures established by the Secretary by regulations.

• **1986, Tax Reform Act of 1986 (P.L. 99-514)**

P.L. 99-514, §1511(c)(7):

Amended Code Sec. 4497(c)(2) by striking out "at rates determined under section 6621" and inserting in lieu thereof "at the underpayment rate established under section 6621". **Effective** for purposes of determining interest for periods after 12-31-86.

• **1980, Deep Seabed Hard Mineral Resources Act (P.L. 96-283)**

P.L. 96-283, §402(a):

Added Code Sec. 4497. **Effective** 1-1-80.

[Sec. 4498—Repealed]

Amendments

• **1997, Taxpayer Relief Act of 1997 (P.L. 105-34)**

P.L. 105-34, §1432(b)(1):

Repealed Code Sec. 4498. **Effective** 8-5-97. Prior to repeal, Code Sec. 4498 read as follows:

SEC. 4498. TERMINATION.

(a) GENERAL RULE.—The tax imposed by section 4495 shall not apply to any removal from the deep seabed after the earlier of—

(1) the date on which an international deep seabed treaty takes effect with respect to the United States, or

(2) the date 10 years after the date of the enactment of this subchapter.

(b) INTERNATIONAL DEEP SEABED TREATY.—For purposes of subsection (a), the term "international deep seabed treaty" means any treaty which—

(1) is adopted by a United Nations Conference on the Law of the Sea, and

(2) requires contributions to an international fund for the sharing of revenues from deep seabed mining.

• **1980, Deep Seabed Hard Mineral Resources Act (P.L. 96-283)**

P.L. 96-283, §402(a):

Added Code Sec. 4498. **Effective** 1-1-80.

CHAPTER 37—REPURCHASE OF CORPORATE STOCK

Sec. 4501. Repurchase of corporate stock.

SEC. 4501. REPURCHASE OF CORPORATE STOCK.

(a) GENERAL RULE.—There is hereby imposed on each covered corporation a tax equal to 1 percent of the fair market value of any stock of the corporation which is repurchased by such corporation during the taxable year.

(b) COVERED CORPORATION.—For purposes of this section, the term "covered corporation" means any domestic corporation the stock of which is traded on an established securities market (within the meaning of section 7704(b)(1)).

(c) REPURCHASE.—For purposes of this section—

   (1) IN GENERAL.—The term "repurchase" means—
      (A) a redemption within the meaning of section 317(b) with regard to the stock of a covered corporation, and
      (B) any transaction determined by the Secretary to be economically similar to a transaction described in subparagraph (A).

   (2) TREATMENT OF PURCHASES BY SPECIFIED AFFILIATES.—
      (A) IN GENERAL.—The acquisition of stock of a covered corporation by a specified affiliate of such covered corporation, from a person who is not the covered corporation or a specified affiliate of such covered corporation, shall be treated as a repurchase of the stock of the covered corporation by such covered corporation.
      (B) SPECIFIED AFFILIATE.—For purposes of this section, the term "specified affiliate" means, with respect to any corporation—
         (i) any corporation more than 50 percent of the stock of which is owned (by vote or by value), directly or indirectly, by such corporation, and
         (ii) any partnership more than 50 percent of the capital interests or profits interests of which is held, directly or indirectly, by such corporation.

   (3) ADJUSTMENT.—The amount taken into account under subsection (a) with respect to any stock repurchased by a covered corporation shall be reduced by the fair market value of any stock issued by the covered corporation during the taxable year, including the fair market value of any stock issued or provided to employees of such covered corporation or employees of a specified affiliate of such covered corporation during the taxable year, whether or not such stock is issued or provided in response to the exercise of an option to purchase such stock.

(d) SPECIAL RULES FOR ACQUISITION OF STOCK OF CERTAIN FOREIGN CORPORATIONS.—

   (1) IN GENERAL.—In the case of an acquisition of stock of an applicable foreign corporation by a specified affiliate of such corporation (other than a foreign corporation or a foreign partnership (unless such partnership has a domestic entity as a direct or indirect partner)) from a person who is not the applicable foreign corporation or a specified affiliate of such applicable foreign corporation, for purposes of this section—
      (A) such specified affiliate shall be treated as a covered corporation with respect to such acquisition,
      (B) such acquisition shall be treated as a repurchase of stock of a covered corporation by such covered corporation, and
      (C) the adjustment under subsection (c)(3) shall be determined only with respect to stock issued or provided by such specified affiliate to employees of the specified affiliate.

   (2) SURROGATE FOREIGN CORPORATIONS.—In the case of a repurchase of stock of a covered surrogate foreign corporation by such covered surrogate foreign corporation, or an acquisition of stock of a covered surrogate foreign corporation by a specified affiliate of such corporation, for purposes of this section—
      (A) the expatriated entity with respect to such covered surrogate foreign corporation shall be treated as a covered corporation with respect to such repurchase or acquisition,
      (B) such repurchase or acquisition shall be treated as a repurchase of stock of a covered corporation by such covered corporation, and
      (C) the adjustment under subsection (c)(3) shall be determined only with respect to stock issued or provided by such expatriated entity to employees of the expatriated entity.

   (3) DEFINITIONS.—For purposes of this subsection—
      (A) APPLICABLE FOREIGN CORPORATION.—The term "applicable foreign corporation" means any foreign corporation the stock of which is traded on an established securities market (within the meaning of section 7704(b)(1)).
      (B) COVERED SURROGATE FOREIGN CORPORATION.—The term "covered surrogate foreign corporation" means any surrogate foreign corporation (as determined under section 7874(a)(2)(B) by substituting "September 20, 2021" for "March 4, 2003" each place it appears) the stock of which is traded on an established securities market (within the meaning of section 7704(b)(1)), but only with respect to taxable years which include any portion of the applicable period with respect to such corporation under section 7874(d)(1).
      (C) EXPATRIATED ENTITY.—The term "expatriated entity" has the meaning given such term by section 7874(a)(2)(A).

(e) EXCEPTIONS.—Subsection (a) shall not apply—

   (1) to the extent that the repurchase is part of a reorganization (within the meaning of section 368(a)) and no gain or loss is recognized on such repurchase by the shareholder under chapter 1 by reason of such reorganization,

   (2) in any case in which the stock repurchased is, or an amount of stock equal to the value of the stock repurchased is, contributed to an employer-sponsored retirement plan, employee stock ownership plan, or similar plan,

   (3) in any case in which the total value of the stock repurchased during the taxable year does not exceed $1,000,000,

   (4) under regulations prescribed by the Secretary, in cases in which the repurchase is by a dealer in securities in the ordinary course of business,

   (5) to repurchases by a regulated investment company (as defined in section 851) or a real estate investment trust, or

   (6) to the extent that the repurchase is treated as a dividend for purposes of this title.

(f) REGULATIONS AND GUIDANCE.—The Secretary shall prescribe such regulations and other guidance as are necessary or appropriate to carry out, and to prevent the avoidance of, the purposes of this section, including regulations and other guidance—

EXCISE TAXES—SUGAR

(1) to prevent the abuse of the exceptions provided by subsection (e),
(2) to address special classes of stock and preferred stock, and
(3) for the application of the rules under subsection (d).

Amendments

• **2022, Inflation Reduction Act of 2022 (P.L. 117-169)**

P.L. 117-169, § 10201(a):

Amended subtitle D by inserting after chapter 36 a new chapter 37 (Code Sec. 4501). **Effective** for repurchases (within the meaning Code Sec. 4501(c), as added by Act Sec. 10201) of stock after 12-31-2022.

CHAPTER 37—SUGAR—[Repealed]

[Sec. 4501—Repealed]

Amendments

• **1990, Omnibus Budget Reconciliation Act of 1990 (P.L. 101-508)**

P.L. 101-508, § 11801(a)(48):

Repealed Code Sec. 4501. **Effective** 11-5-90.

P.L. 101-508, § 11821(b), provides:

(b) SAVINGS PROVISION.—If—

(1) any provision amended or repealed by this part applied to—

(A) any transaction occurring before the date of the enactment of this Act,

(B) any property acquired before such date of enactment, or

(C) any item of income, loss, deduction, or credit taken into account before such date of enactment, and

(2) the treatment of such transaction, property, or item under such provision would (without regard to the amendments made by this part) affect liability for tax for periods ending after such date of enactment,

nothing in the amendments made by this part shall be construed to affect the treatment of such transaction, property, or item for purposes of determining liability for tax for periods ending after such date of enactment.

Prior to repeal, Code Sec. 4501 read as follows:

SEC. 4501. IMPOSITION OF TAX.

[Sec. 4501(a)]

(a) GENERAL.—There is hereby imposed upon manufactured sugar manufactured in the United States, a tax, to be paid by the manufacturer at the rate of 0.53 cent per pound of the total sugars therein. The manufacturer shall pay the tax with respect to manufactured sugar (1) which has been sold, or used in the production of other articles, by the manufacturer during the preceding month (if the tax has not already been paid) and (2) which has not been so sold or used within 12 months ending during the preceding calendar month, after it was manufactured (if the tax has not already been paid). For the purpose of determining whether sugar has been sold or used within 12 months after it was manufactured, sugar shall be considered to have been sold or used in the order in which it was manufactured.

Amendments

• **1976, Tax Reform Act of 1976 (P.L. 94-455)**

P.L. 94-455, § 1904(a)(14):

Amended the title of Chapter 37 by striking out ", COCONUT AND PALM OIL" following "SUGAR", struck out the table of subchapters of Chapter 27, and amended the table of sections for Subchapter A of Chapter 37 by deleting the heading and "Sec. 4504. Import tax imposed as tariff duty." **Effective** 2-1-77. Prior to striking, the table of subchapters of Chapter 37 read as follows:

Subchapter A. Sugar.

Subchapter B. Coconut and palm oil.

• **1962, Tariff Classification Act of 1962 (P.L. 87-456)**

P.L. 87-456, § 302(A):

Amended the first sentence of Code Sec. 4501(a). **Effective** 8-31-63. Prior to amendment, the first sentence of Sec. 4501(a) read as follows:

There is hereby imposed upon manufactured sugar manufactured in the United States, a tax, to be paid by the manufacturer at the following rates:

(1) on all manufactured sugar testing by the polariscope 92 sugar degrees, 0.465 cent per pound, and, for each additional sugar degree shown by the polariscopic test, 0.00875 cent per pound additional, and fractions of a degree in proportion;

(2) on all manufactured sugar testing by the polariscope less than 92 sugar degrees, 0.5144 cent per pound of the total sugars therein.

[Sec. 4501(b)]

(b) TERMINATION OF TAX.—No tax shall be imposed under this subchapter on the manufacture or use of sugar or articles composed in chief value of sugar after June 30, 1975, or June 30 of the first year commencing after the effective date of any law limiting payments under title III of the Sugar Act of 1948, as amended, whichever is the earlier date. Notwithstanding the provisions of subsection (a), no tax shall be imposed under this subchapter with respect to unsold sugar held by a manufacturer on June 30, 1975, or June 30 of the first year commencing after the effective date of any law limiting payments under title III of the Sugar Act of 1948, as amended, whichever is the earlier date, or with respect to sugar or articles composed in chief value of sugar held in customs custody or control on such date.

Amendments

• **1990, Omnibus Budget Reconciliation Act of 1990 (P.L. 101-508)**

P.L. 101-508, § 11801(a)(48):

Repealed Code Sec. 4502. **Effective** 11-5-90.

Amendments

• **1971, Sugar Act Amendments of 1971 (P.L. 92-138)**

P.L. 92-138, § 18:

Amended Code Sec. 4501(b) by deleting "June 30, 1972" in the two places it appeared and substituting "June 30, 1975, or June 30 of the first year commencing after the effective date of any law limiting payments under title III of the Sugar Act of 1948, as amended, whichever is the earlier date". **Effective** 1-1-72.

• **1965, Sugar Act Amendments of 1965 (P.L. 89-331)**

P.L. 89-331, § 13:

Amended Code Sec. 4501(b) by substituting "1972" for "1967" each place it appears. **Effective** 1-1-65.

• **1962, Tariff Classification Act of 1962 (P.L. 87-456)**

P.L. 87-456, § 302(b):

Repealed former Code Sec. 4501(b) and redesignated Code Sec. 4501(c) as 4501(b). Amended new Code Sec. 4501(b) by substituting "manufacture or use" for "manufacture, use, or importation" in the first sentence and by substituting "subsection (a)" for "subsection (a) or (b)" in the second sentence. **Effective** 8-31-63.

P.L. 87-456, § 302(b):

Repealed Code Sec. 4501(b). Prior to repeal, Code Sec. 4501 read as follows:

(b) IMPORT TAX.—In addition to any other tax or duty imposed by law, there is hereby imposed, under such regulations as the Secretary or his delegate shall prescribe, a tax upon articles imported or brought into the United States as follows:

(1) on all manufactured sugar testing by the polariscope 92 sugar degrees, 0.465 cent per pound, and, for each additional sugar degree shown by the polariscopic test, 0.00875 cent per pound additional, and fractions of a degree in proportion;

(2) on all manufactured sugar testing by the polariscope less than 92 sugar degrees, 0.5144 cent per pound of the total sugars therein;

(3) on all articles composed in chief value of manufactured sugar, 0.5144 cent per pound of the total sugars therein.

• **1962, Sugar Act Amendments of 1962 (P.L. 87-535)**

P.L. 87-535, § 18(a):

Amended Code Sec. 4501(c) by striking out "December 31, 1962" in each place it appeared and by substituting "June 30, 1967" therefor.

• **1961 (P.L. 87-15)**

P.L. 87-15, § 2(a):

Amended Code Sec. 4501(c) by striking out "September 30, 1961" in each place it appeared and by substituting "December 31, 1962" therefor.

• **1960 (P.L. 86-592)**

P.L. 86-592, § 2:

Amended Code Sec. 4501(c) by striking out "June 30, 1961" in each place it appeared and by substituting "September 30, 1961" therefor.

• **1958, Excise Tax Technical Changes Act of 1958 (P.L. 85-859)**

P.L. 85-859, § 162(b):

Deleted the last sentence in Sec. 4501(c). That sentence, prior to deletion, read as follows: "With respect to any sugar or articles composed in chief value of sugar upon which tax imposed under subsection (b) has been paid and which, on June 30, 1961, are held by the importer and intended for sale or other disposition, there shall be refunded (without interest) to such importer, subject to such regulations as may be prescribed by the Secretary or his delegate, an amount equal to the tax paid with respect to such sugar or articles composed in chief value of sugar."

• **1956 (P.L. 545, 84th Cong.)**

P.L. 545, 84th Cong., § 19:

Deleted "1957" wherever it appeared in Sec. 4501(c) and substituted "1961". **Effective** 1-1-56.

[Sec. 4502—Repealed]

P.L. 101-508, § 11821(b), provides:

(b) SAVINGS PROVISION.—If—

(1) any provision amended or repealed by this part applied to—

(A) any transaction occurring before the date of the enactment of this Act,

Sec. 4501(f)(1)

(B) any property acquired before such date of enactment, or

(C) any item of income, loss, deduction, or credit taken into account before such date of enactment, and

(2) the treatment of such transaction, property, or item under such provision would (without regard to the amendments made by this part) affect liability for tax for periods ending after such date of enactment,

nothing in the amendments made by this part shall be construed to affect the treatment of such transaction, property, or item for purposes of determining liability for tax for periods ending after such date of enactment.

Prior to repeal, Code Sec. 4502 read as follows:

SEC. 4502. DEFINITIONS.

For the purposes of this subchapter—

(1) MANUFACTURER.—Any person who acquires any sugar which is to be manufactured into manufactured sugar but who, without further refining or otherwise improving it in quality, sells such sugar as manufactured sugar or uses such sugar as manufactured sugar in the production of other articles for sale shall be considered, for the purposes of section 4501(a), the manufacturer of manufactured sugar and, as such, liable for the tax under section 4501(a) with respect thereto.

(2) PERSON.—The term "person" means an individual, partnership, corporation, or association.

(3) MANUFACTURED SUGAR.—The term "manufactured sugar" means any sugar derived from sugar beets or sugarcane, which is not to be, and which shall not be, further refined or otherwise improved in quality; except sugar in liquid form which contains nonsugar solids (excluding any foreign substance that may have been added or developed in the product) equal to more than 6 per centum of the total soluble solids and except also sirup of cane juice produced from sugarcane grown in continental United States. The grades or types of sugar within the meaning of this definition shall include, but shall not be limited to, granulated sugar, lump sugar, cube sugar, powdered sugar, sugar in the form of blocks, cones, or molded shapes, confectioners' sugar, washed sugar, centrifugal sugar, clarified sugar, turbinado sugar, plantation white sugar, muscovado sugar, refiners' soft sugar, invert sugar mush, raw sugar, sirups, molasses, and sugar mixtures.

(4) TOTAL SUGARS.—The term "total sugars" means the total amount of the sucrose and of the reducing or invert sugars.

(5) UNITED STATES.—The term "United States" shall be deemed to include the States, the District of Columbia, and Puerto Rico.

Amendments

• **1960, Hawaii Omnibus Act (P.L. 86-624)**

P.L. 86-624, §18(f):

Amended 1954 Code Sec. 4502(5) by striking out "the Territory of Hawaii," immediately after the word "States,". **Effective** 8-21-59.

• **1959, Alaska Omnibus Bill (P.L. 86-70)**

P.L. 86-70, §22(a):

Amended 1954 Code Sec. 4502(5) by striking out "Territories of Hawaii and Alaska", and by substituting "Territory of Hawaii". **Effective** 1-3-59.

• **1956 (P.L. 545, 84th Cong.)**

P.L. 545, 84th Cong., §20:

Deleted the parenthetical word "(Clerget)" which immediately followed the term "sucrose" in the first sentence of Sec. 4502(4) and deleted the second sentence from Sec. 4502(4). **Effective** 1-1-56. Prior to deletion, that sentence read as follows: "The total sugars contained in any grade or type of manufactured sugar shall be ascertained in the manner prescribed in paragraphs 758, 759, 762, and 763 of the United States Customs Regulations (1931 edition)."

[Sec. 4503—Repealed]

Amendments

• **1990, Omnibus Budget Reconciliation Act of 1990 (P.L. 101-508)**

P.L. 101-508, §11801(a)(48):

Repealed Code Sec. 4503. **Effective** 11-5-90.

P.L. 101-508, §11821(b), provides:

(b) SAVINGS PROVISION.—If—

(1) any provision amended or repealed by this part applied to—

(A) any transaction occurring before the date of the enactment of this Act,

(B) any property acquired before such date of enactment, or

(C) any item of income, loss, deduction, or credit taken into account before such date of enactment, and

(2) the treatment of such transaction, property, or item under such provision would (without regard to the amendments made by this part) affect liability for tax for periods ending after such date of enactment,

nothing in the amendments made by this part shall be construed to affect the treatment of such transaction, property, or item for purposes of determining liability for tax for periods ending after such date of enactment.

Prior to repeal, Code Sec. 4503 read as follows:

SEC. 4503. EXEMPTIONS FOR SUGAR MANUFACTURED FOR HOME CONSUMPTION.

No tax shall be required to be paid under section 4501(a) upon the manufacture of manufactured sugar by or for the producer of the sugar beets or sugarcane from which such manufactured sugar was derived, for consumption by the producer's own family, employees, or household.

CHAPTER 38—ENVIRONMENTAL TAXES

SUBCHAPTER A.	Tax on petroleum.
SUBCHAPTER B.	Tax on certain chemicals.
SUBCHAPTER C.	Tax on certain imported substances.
SUBCHAPTER D.	Ozone depleting chemicals, etc.

Subchapter A—Tax on Petroleum

Sec. 4611.	Imposition of tax.
Sec. 4612.	Definitions and special rules.

[Sec. 4611]

SEC. 4611. IMPOSITION OF TAX.

[Sec. 4611(a)]

(a) GENERAL RULE.—There is hereby imposed a tax at the rate specified in subsection (c) on—

(1) crude oil received at a United States refinery, and

(2) petroleum products entered into the United States for consumption, use, or warehousing.

Amendments

• **1986, Omnibus Budget Reconciliation Act of 1986 (P.L. 99-509)**

P.L. 99-509, §8031(a):

Provided for the following amendment that was to become **effective** only if P.L. 99-499 was not enacted.

Amended Code Sec. 4611(a) by striking out "of 0.79 cent a barrel" and inserting in lieu thereof "at the rate specified in subsection (c)".

• **1986, Superfund Amendments and Reauthorization Act of 1986 (P.L. 99-499)**

P.L. 99-499, §512(a):

Amended Code Sec 4611(a) by striking out "of 0.79 cent a barrel" and inserting in lieu thereof "at the rate specified in subsection (c)". **Effective** 1-1-87.

[Sec. 4611(b)]

(b) TAX ON CERTAIN USES AND EXPORTATION.—

(1) IN GENERAL.—If—

(A) any domestic crude oil is used in or exported from the United States, and

(B) before such use or exportation, no tax was imposed on such crude oil under subsection (a),

then a tax at the rate specified in subsection (c) is hereby imposed on such crude oil.

(2) EXCEPTION FOR USE ON PREMISES WHERE PRODUCED.—Paragraph (1) shall not apply to any use of crude oil for extracting oil or natural gas on the premises where such crude oil was produced.

EXCISE TAXES—TAX ON PETROLEUM

Amendments

• **1986, Omnibus Budget Reconciliation Act of 1986 (P.L. 99-509)**

P.L. 99-509, § 8031(a):

Provided for the following amendment that was to become **effective** only if P.L. 99-499 was not enacted.

Amended Code Sec. 4611(b) by striking out "of 0.79 cent a barrel" and inserting in lieu thereof "at the rate specified in subsection (c)".

• **1986, Superfund Amendments and Reauthorization Act of 1986 (P.L. 99-499)**

P.L. 99-499, § 512(a):

Amended Code Sec. 4611(b) by striking out "of 0.79 cent a barrel" and inserting in lieu thereof "at the rate specified in subsection (c)". **Effective** 1-1-87.

[Sec. 4611(c)]

(c) RATE OF TAX.—

(1) IN GENERAL.—The rate of the taxes imposed by this section is the sum of—

(A) the Hazardous Substance Superfund financing rate, and

(B) the Oil Spill Liability Trust Fund financing rate.

(2) RATES.—For purposes of paragraph (1)—

(A) the Hazardous Substance Superfund financing rate is 16.4 cents a barrel, and

(B) the Oil Spill Liability Trust Fund financing rate is—

(i) in the case of crude oil received or petroleum products entered before January 1, 2017, 8 cents a barrel, and

(ii) in the case of crude oil received or petroleum products entered after December 31, 2016, 9 cents a barrel.

(3) ADJUSTMENT FOR INFLATION.—

(A) IN GENERAL.—In the case of a year beginning after 2023, the amount in paragraph (2)(A) shall be increased by an amount equal to—

(i) such amount, multiplied by

(ii) the cost-of-living adjustment determined under section 1(f)(3) for the calendar year, determined by substituting "calendar year 2022" for "calendar year 2016" in subparagraph (A)(ii) thereof.

(B) ROUNDING.—If any amount as adjusted under subparagraph (A) is not a multiple of $0.01, such amount shall be rounded to the next lowest multiple of $0.01.

Amendments

• **2022, Inflation Reduction Act of 2022 (P.L. 117-169)**

P.L. 117-169, § 13601(a)(2)(A):

Amended Code Sec. 4611(c)(2)(A) by striking "9.7 cents" and inserting "16.4 cents". **Effective** 1-1-2023.

P.L. 117-169, § 13601(a)(2)(B):

Amended Code Sec. 4611(c) by adding at the end a new paragraph (3). **Effective** 1-1-2023.

• **2008, Energy Improvement and Extension Act of 2008 (P.L. 110-343)**

P.L. 110-343, Division B, § 405(a)(1):

Amended Code Sec. 4611(c)(2)(B) by striking "is 5 cents a barrel." and inserting "is—" and new clauses (i)-(ii). **Effective** on and after the first day of the first calendar quarter beginning more than 60 days after 10-3-2008.

• **1989, Omnibus Budget Reconciliation Act of 1989 (P.L. 101-239)**

P.L. 101-239, § 7505(b):

Amended Code Sec. 4611(c)(2)(B) by striking "1.3 cents" and inserting "5 cents". **Effective** 12-19-89.

P.L. 101-239, § 7505(d)(1), provides:

(d) OIL SPILL LIABILITY TRUST FUND TO BE OPERATING FUND.—

(1) IN GENERAL.—For purposes of sections 8032(d) and 8033(c) of the Omnibus Budget Reconciliation Act of 1986, the commencement date is January 1, 1990.

• **1989, Steel Trade Liberalization Program Implementation Act (P.L. 101-221)**

P.L. 101-221, § 8(a):

Amended Code Sec. 4611(c)(2)(A). **Effective** 12-12-89. Prior to amendment, Code Sec. 4611(c)(2)(A) read as follows:

(A) the Hazardous Substance Superfund financing rate is—

(i) except as provided in clause (ii), 8.2 cents a barrel, and

(ii) 11.7 cents a barrel in the case of the tax imposed by subsection (a)(2), and

• **1986, Omnibus Budget Reconciliation Act of 1986 (P.L. 99-509)**

P.L. 99-509, § 8031(b):

Provided for the following amendment that was to become **effective** only if P.L. 99-499 was not enacted.

Amended Code Sec. 4611 by redesignating subsections (c) and (d) as subsections (d) and (e), respectively, and by inserting after subsection (b) new subsection (c) to read as follows:

(c) RATE OF TAX.—

(1) IN GENERAL.—The rate of the taxes imposed by this section is the sum of—

(A) the Hazardous Substance Superfund financing rate, and

(B) the Oil Spill Liability Trust Fund financing rate.

(2) RATES.—For purposes of paragraph (1)—

(A) the Hazardous Substance Superfund financing rate is 0.79 cent a barrel, and

(B) the Oil Spill Liability Trust Fund financing rate is 1.3 cents a barrel.

P.L. 99-509, § 8032(a):

Amended Code Sec. 4611(c), as added by P.L. 99-499, § 512(b). For the **effective** date, see Act Sec. 8032(d), below. Prior to amendment, Code Sec. 4611(c) read as follows:

(c) RATE OF TAX.—

(1) IN GENERAL.—Except as provided in paragraph (2), the rate of taxes imposed by this section is 8.2 cents a barrel.

(2) IMPORTED PETROLEUM PRODUCTS.—The rate of the tax imposed by subsection (a)(2) shall be 11.7 cents a barrel.

P.L. 99-509, § 8032(d), provides:

(d) EFFECTIVE DATE.—

(1) IN GENERAL.—Except as provided in paragraph (2), the amendments made by this section shall take effect on the commencement date (as defined in section 4611(f)(2) of the Internal Revenue Code of 1954, as added by this section).

(2) COORDINATION WITH SUPERFUND REAUTHORIZATION.—The amendments made by this section shall take effect only if the Superfund Amendments and Reauthorization Act of 1986 is enacted.

• **1986, Superfund Amendments and Reauthorization Act of 1986 (P.L. 99-499)**

P.L. 99-499, § 512(b):

Amended Code Sec. 4611 by redesignating subsections (c) and (d) as subsections (d) and (e), respectively, and by inserting after subsection (b) new subsection (c). **Effective** 1-1-87.

[Sec. 4611(d)]

(d) PERSONS LIABLE FOR TAX.—

(1) CRUDE OIL RECEIVED AT REFINERY.—The tax imposed by subsection (a)(1) shall be paid by the operator of the United States refinery.

(2) IMPORTED PETROLEUM PRODUCT.—The tax imposed by subsection (a)(2) shall be paid by the person entering the product for consumption, use, or warehousing.

(3) TAX ON CERTAIN USES OR EXPORTS.—The tax imposed by subsection (b) shall be paid by the person using or exporting the crude oil, as the case may be.

Amendments

• **1986, Omnibus Budget Reconciliation Act of 1986 (P.L. 99-509)**

P.L. 99-509, § 8031(b):

Provided for the following amendment that was to become **effective** only if P.L. 99-499 was not enacted.

Amended Code Sec. 4611 by redesignating subsections (c) and (d) as subsections (d) and (e), respectively.

• **1986, Superfund Amendments and Reauthorization Act of 1986 (P.L. 99-499)**

P.L. 99-499, § 512(b):

Amended Code Sec. 4611 by redesignating subsections (c) and (d) as subsections (d) and (e), respectively. **Effective** 1-1-87.

Sec. 4611(c)

EXCISE TAXES—TAX ON PETROLEUM

[Sec. 4611(e)—Stricken]

Amendments

• **2022, Inflation Reduction Act of 2022 (P.L. 117-169)**

P.L. 117-169, §13601(a)(1):

Amended Code Sec. 4611 by striking subsection (e). **Effective** 1-1-2023. Prior to being stricken, Code Sec. 4611(e) read as follows:

(e) APPLICATION OF HAZARDOUS SUBSTANCE SUPERFUND FINANCING RATE.—

(1) IN GENERAL.—Except as provided in paragraphs (2) and (3), the Hazardous Substance Superfund financing rate under this section shall apply after December 31, 1986, and before January 1, 1996.

(2) NO TAX IF UNOBLIGATED BALANCE IN FUND EXCEEDS $3,500,000,000.—If on December 31, 1993, or December 31, 1994—

(A) the unobligated balance in the Hazardous Substance Superfund exceeds $3,500,000,000 and

(B) the Secretary, after consultation with the Administrator of the Environmental Protection Agency, determines that the unobligated balance in the Hazardous Substance Superfund will exceed $3,500,000,000 on December 31 of 1994 or 1995, respectively, if no tax is imposed under this section and sections 4661 and 4671,

then no tax shall be imposed under this section (to the extent attributable to the Hazardous Substance Superfund financing rate) during 1994 or 1995, as the case may be.

(3) NO TAX IF AMOUNTS COLLECTED EXCEED $11,970,000,000.—

(A) ESTIMATES BY SECRETARY.—The Secretary as of the close of each calendar quarter (and at such other times as the Secretary determines appropriate) shall make an estimate of the amount of taxes which will be collected under this section (to the extent attributable to the Hazardous Substance Superfund financing rate) and sections 4661 and 4671 and credited to the Hazardous Substance Superfund during the period beginning January 1, 1987, and ending December 31, 1995.

(B) TERMINATION IF $11,970,000,000 CREDITED BEFORE JANUARY 1, 1996.—If the Secretary estimates under subparagraph (A) that more than $11,970,000,000 will be credited to the Fund before January 1, 1996, the Hazardous Substance Superfund financing rate under this section shall not apply after the date on which (as estimated by the Secretary) $11,970,000,000 will be so credited to the Fund.

• **2014, Tax Technical Corrections Act of 2014 (P.L. 113-295)**

P.L. 113-295, §221(a)(12)(I)(i)-(ii), Division A:

Amended Code Sec. 4611(e) by striking "section 59A, this section," in paragraph (2)(B) and inserting "this section", and in paragraph (3)(A) by striking "section 59A," following "which will be collected under", and by striking the comma after "rate)". **Effective** generally 12-19-2014. For a special rule, see Act Sec. 221(b)(2), Division A, below.

P.L. 113-295, §221(b)(2), Division A, provides:

(2) SAVINGS PROVISION.—If—

(A) any provision amended or repealed by the amendments made by this section applied to—

(i) any transaction occurring before the date of the enactment of this Act,

(ii) any property acquired before such date of enactment, or

(iii) any item of income, loss, deduction, or credit taken into account before such date of enactment, and

(B) the treatment of such transaction, property, or item under such provision would (without regard to the amendments or repeals made by this section) affect the liability for tax for periods ending after date of enactment, nothing in the amendments or repeals made by this section shall be construed to affect the treatment of such transaction, property, or item for purposes of determining liability for tax for periods ending after such date of enactment.

• **1990, Omnibus Budget Reconciliation Act of 1990 (P.L. 101-508)**

P.L. 101-508, §11231(a)(1)(B):

Amended Code Sec. 4611(e)(1) by striking "January 1, 1992" and inserting "January 1, 1996". **Effective** 11-5-90.

P.L. 101-508, §11231(a)(1)(B):

Amended Code Sec. 4611(e)(3) by striking "January 1, 1992" and inserting "January 1, 1996". **Effective** 11-5-90.

P.L. 101-508, §11231(a)(2)(A)-(C):

Amended Code Sec. 4611(e)(2) by striking "1989" and inserting "1993", by striking "1990" each place it appears and inserting "1994", and by striking "1991" each place it appears and inserting "1995". **Effective** 11-5-90.

P.L. 101-508, §11231(b):

Amended Code Sec. 4611(e)(3) by striking "$6,650,000,000" each place it appears and inserting "$11,970,000,000" and by striking "December 31, 1991" and inserting "December 31, 1995". **Effective** 11-5-90.

• **1989, Omnibus Budget Reconciliation Act of 1989 (P.L. 101-239)**

P.L. 101-239, §7505(d)(1), provides:

(d) OIL SPILL LIABILITY TRUST FUND TO BE OPERATING FUND.—

(1) IN GENERAL.—For purposes of sections 8032(d) and 8033(c) of the Omnibus Budget Reconciliation Act of 1986, the commencement date is January 1, 1990.

• **1986, Omnibus Budget Reconciliation Act of 1986 (P.L. 99-509)**

P.L. 99-509, §8031(b):

Provided for the following amendment that was to become **effective** only if P.L. 99-499 was not enacted.

Amended Code Sec. 4611 by redesignating subsections (c) and (d) as subsections (d) and (e), respectively.

P.L. 99-509, §8031(d)(1):

Provided for the following amendment that was to become **effective** only if P.L. 99-499 was not enacted.

Amended Code Sec. 4611(e), (as redesignated by Act Sec. 8031(b)) to read as follows:

(e) APPLICATION OF TAXES.—

(1) SUPERFUND RATE.—The Hazardous Substance Superfund financing rate under subsection (c) shall not apply after September 30, 1985.

(2) OIL SPILL RATE.—

(A) IN GENERAL.—Except as provided in subparagraph (C), the Oil Spill Liability Trust Fund financing rate under subsection (c) shall apply on and after the commencement date and before January 1, 1992.

(B) COMMENCEMENT DATE.—

(i) IN GENERAL.—For purposes of this paragraph, the term "commencement date" means the later of—

(I) February 1, 1987, or

(II) the 1st day of the 1st calendar month beginning more than 30 days after the date of the enactment of qualified authorizing legislation.

(ii) QUALIFIED AUTHORIZING LEGISLATION.—For purposes of clause (i), the term "qualified authorizing legislation" means any law enacted before September 1, 1987, which is substantially identical to subtitle E of title VI, or subtitle D of title VIII, of H.R. 5300 of the 99th Congress as passed the House of Representatives.

(c) NO TAX IF AMOUNTS COLLECTED EXCEED $300,000,000.—

(i) ESTIMATES BY SECRETARY.—The Secretary as of the close of each calendar quarter (and at such other times as the Secretary determines appropriate) shall make an estimate of the amount of taxes which will be collected under this section (to the extent attributable to the Oil Spill Liability Trust Fund financing rate) during the period beginning on the commencement date and ending on December 31, 1991.

(ii) TERMINATION IF $300,000,000 CREDITED BEFORE JANUARY 1, 1992.—If the Secretary estimates under clause (i) that more than $300,000,000 will be credited to the Fund before January 1, 1992, the Oil Spill Liability Trust Fund financing rate shall not apply after the date on which (as estimated by the Secretary) $300,000,000 will be so credited to the Fund.

P.L. 99-509, §8032(c)(1)(A)-(D):

Amended Code Sec. 4611(e) in the subsection heading by striking out "Taxes" and inserting in lieu thereof "Hazardous Substance Superfund Financing Rate", in paragraph (1) by striking out "the taxes imposed by this section" and inserting in lieu thereof "the Hazardous Substance Superfund financing rate under this section", in paragraphs (2) and (3)(A) after "this section" by inserting "(to the extent attributable to the Hazardous Substance Superfund (financing rate)", and in paragraph (3)(B) by striking out "no tax shall be imposed under this section" and inserting in lieu thereof "the Hazardous Substance Superfund financing rate under this section shall not apply". For the **effective** date, see Act Sec. 8032(d), below.

P.L. 99-509, §8032(d), provides:

(d) EFFECTIVE DATE.—

(1) IN GENERAL.—Except as provided in paragraph (2), the amendments made by this section shall take effect on the commencement date (as defined in section 4611(f)(2) of the Internal Revenue Code of 1954, as added by this section).

(2) COORDINATION WITH SUPERFUND REAUTHORIZATION.—The amendments made by this section shall take effect only if the Superfund Amendments and Reauthorization Act of 1986 is enacted.

• **1986, Superfund Amendments and Reauthorization Act of 1986 (P.L. 99-499)**

P.L. 99-499, §511(a):

Amended Code Sec. 4611(d). **Effective** 1-1-87. Prior to amendment, Code Sec. 4611(d) read as follows:

(d) TERMINATION.—The taxes imposed by this section shall not apply after September 30, 1985, except that if on September 30, 1983, or September 30, 1984—

(1) the unobligated balance in the Hazardous Substance Response Trust Fund as of such date exceeds $900,000,000, and

(2) the Secretary, after consultation with the Administrator of the Environmental Protection Agency, determines that such unobligated balance will exceed $500,000,000 on September 30 of the following year if no tax is imposed under section 4611 or 4661 during the calendar year following the date referred to above,

then no tax shall be imposed by this section during the first calendar year beginning after the date referred to in paragraph (1).

P.L. 99-499, §512(b):

Amended Code Sec. 4611 by redesignating subsections (c) and (d) as subsections (d) and (e), respectively. **Effective** 1-1-87.

• **1980, Comprehensive Environmental Response, Compensation, and Liability Act of 1980 (P.L. 96-510)**

P.L. 96-510, §211(a):

Added Code Sec. 4611. **Effective** 4-1-81.

EXCISE TAXES—TAX ON PETROLEUM

[Sec. 4611(f)]

(f) APPLICATION OF OIL SPILL LIABILITY TRUST FUND FINANCING RATE.—

(1) IN GENERAL.—Except as provided in paragraph (2), the Oil Spill Liability Trust Fund financing rate under subsection (c) shall apply on and after April 1, 2006, or if later, the date which is 30 days after the last day of any calendar quarter for which the Secretary estimates that, as of the close of that quarter, the unobligated balance in the Oil Spill Liability Trust Fund is less than $2,000,000,000.

(2) TERMINATION.—The Oil Spill Liability Trust Fund financing rate shall not apply after December 31, 2025.

Amendments

• **2020, Taxpayer Certainty and Disaster Tax Relief Act of 2020 (P.L. 116-260)**

P.L. 116-260, §117(a), Div. EE:

Amended Code Sec. 4611(f)(2) by striking "December 31, 2020" and inserting "December 31, 2025". **Effective** on and after 1-1-2021.

• **2019, Taxpayer Certainty and Disaster Tax Relief Act of 2019 (P.L. 116-94)**

P.L. 116-94, §134(a), Div. Q:

Amended Code Sec. 4611(f)(2) by striking "December 31, 2018" and inserting "December 31, 2020". **Effective** on and after the first day of the first calendar month beginning after 12-20-2019.

• **2018, Bipartisan Budget Act of 2018 (P.L. 115-123)**

P.L. 115-123, §40416(a), Div. D:

Amended Code Sec. 4611(f)(2) by striking "December 31, 2017" and inserting "December 31, 2018". **Effective** on and after the first day of the first calendar month beginning after 2-9-2018.

• **2008, Energy Improvement and Extension Act of 2008 (P.L. 110-343)**

P.L. 110-343, Division B, §405(b)(1):

Amended Code Sec. 4611(f) by striking paragraphs (2) and (3) and inserting a new paragraph (2). **Effective** 10-3-2008. Prior to being stricken, Code Sec. 4611(f)(2)-(3) read as follows:

(2) FUND BALANCE.—The Oil Spill Liability Trust Fund financing rate shall not apply during a calendar quarter if the Secretary estimates that, as of the close of the preceding calendar quarter, the unobligated balance in the Oil Spill Liability Trust Fund exceeds $2,700,000,000.

(3) TERMINATION.—The Oil Spill Liability Trust Fund financing rate shall not apply after December 31, 2014.

P.L. 110-343, Division B, §405(b)(2):

Amended Code Sec. 4611(f)(1) by striking "paragraphs (2) and (3)" and inserting "paragraph (2)". **Effective** 10-3-2008.

• **2005, Energy Tax Incentives Act of 2005 (P.L. 109-58)**

P.L. 109-58, §1361:

Amended Code Sec. 4611(f). **Effective** 8-8-2005. Prior to amendment, Code Sec. 4611(f) read as follows:

(f) APPLICATION OF OIL SPILL LIABILITY TRUST FUND FINANCING RATE.—

(1) IN GENERAL.—Except as provided in paragraph (2), the Oil Spill Liability Trust Fund financing rate under subsection (c) shall apply after December 31, 1989, and before January 1, 1995.

(2) NO TAX IF UNOBLIGATED BALANCE IN FUND EXCEEDS $1,000,000,000.—The Oil Spill Liability Trust Fund financing rate shall not apply during any calendar quarter if the Secretary estimates that as of the close of the preceding calendar quarter the unobligated balance in the Oil Spill Liability Trust Fund exceeds $1,000,000,000.

• **1989, Omnibus Budget Reconciliation Act of 1989 (P.L. 101-239)**

P.L. 101-239, §7505(a)(1):

Amended Code Sec. 4611(f). **Effective** 12-19-89. Prior to amendment, Code Sec. 4611(f) read as follows:

(f) APPLICATION OF OIL SPILL LIABILITY TRUST FUND FINANCING RATE.—

(1) IN GENERAL.—Except as provided in paragraph (3), the Oil Spill Liability Trust Fund financing rate under subsection (c) shall apply on and after the commencement date and before January 1, 1992.

(2) COMMENCEMENT DATE.—

(A) IN GENERAL.—For purposes of this subsection, the term "commencement date" means the later of—

(i) February 1, 1987, or

(ii) the 1st day of the 1st calendar month beginning more than 30 days after the date of the enactment of qualified authorizing legislation.

(B) QUALIFIED AUTHORIZING LEGISLATION.—For purposes of subparagraph (A), the term "qualified authorizing legislation" means any law enacted before December 31, 1990, which is substantially identical to subtitle E of title VI, or subtitle D of title VIII, of H.R. 5300 of the 99th Congress as passed by the House of Representatives.

(3) NO TAX IF AMOUNTS COLLECTED EXCEED $300,000,000.—

(A) ESTIMATES BY SECRETARY.—The Secretary as of the close of each calendar quarter (and at such other times as the Secretary determines appropriate) shall make an estimate of the amount of taxes which will be collected under this section (to the extent attributable to the Oil Spill Liability Trust Fund financing rate) during the period beginning on the commencement date and ending on December 31, 1991.

(B) TERMINATION IF $300,000,000 CREDITED BEFORE JANUARY 1, 1992.—If the Secretary estimates under subparagraph (A) that more than $300,000,000 will be credited to the Fund before January 1, 1992, the Oil Spill Liability Trust Fund financing rate shall not apply after the date on which (as estimated by the Secretary) $300,000,000 will be so credited to the Fund.

P.L. 101-239, §7505(d)(1), provides:

(d) OIL SPILL LIABILITY TRUST FUND TO BE OPERATING FUND.—

(1) IN GENERAL.—For purposes of sections 8032(d) and 8033(c) of the Omnibus Budget Reconciliation Act of 1986, the commencement date is January 1, 1990.

• **1988, Technical and Miscellaneous Revenue Act of 1988 (P.L. 100-647)**

P.L. 100-647, §6108:

Amended Code Sec. 4611(f)(2)(B) by striking out "September 1, 1987" and inserting in lieu thereof "December 31, 1990". **Effective** 11-10-88.

• **1986, Omnibus Budget Reconciliation Act of 1986 (P.L. 99-509)**

P.L. 99-509, §8032(c)(2):

Amended Code Sec. 4611 by adding at the end new subsection (f), For the **effective date**, see Act Sec. 8032(d), below.

P.L. 99-509, §8032(d), provides:

(d) EFFECTIVE DATE.—

(1) IN GENERAL.—Except as provided in paragraph (2), the amendments made by this section shall take effect on the commencement date (as defined in section 4611(f)(2) of the Internal Revenue Code of 1954, as added by this section).

(2) COORDINATION WITH SUPERFUND REAUTHORIZATION.—The amendments made by this section shall take effect only if the Superfund Amendments and Reauthorization Act of 1986 is enacted.

[Sec. 4612]

SEC. 4612. DEFINITIONS AND SPECIAL RULES.

[Sec. 4612(a)]

(a) DEFINITIONS.—For purposes of this subchapter—

(1) CRUDE OIL.—The term "crude oil" includes crude oil condensates and natural gasoline.

(2) DOMESTIC CRUDE OIL.—The term "domestic crude oil" means any crude oil produced from a well located in the United States.

(3) PETROLEUM PRODUCT.—The term "petroleum product" includes crude oil.

(4) UNITED STATES.—

(A) IN GENERAL.—The term "United States" means the 50 States, the District of Columbia, the Commonwealth of Puerto Rico, any possession of the United States, the Commonwealth of the Northern Mariana Islands, and the Trust Territory of the Pacific Islands.

(B) UNITED STATES INCLUDES CONTINENTAL SHELF AREAS.—The principles of section 638 shall apply for purposes of the term "United States".

(C) UNITED STATES INCLUDES FOREIGN TRADE ZONES.—The term "United States" includes any foreign trade zone of the United States.

(5) UNITED STATES REFINERY.—The term "United States refinery" means any facility in the United States at which crude oil is refined.

(6) REFINERIES WHICH PRODUCE NATURAL GASOLINE.—In the case of any United States refinery which produces natural gasoline from natural gas, the gasoline so produced shall be treated as received at such refinery at the time so produced.

(7) PREMISES.—The term "premises" has the same meaning as when used for purposes of determining gross income from the property under section 613.

(8) BARREL.—The term "barrel" means 42 United States gallons.

EXCISE TAXES—TAX ON PETROLEUM

(9) FRACTIONAL PART OF BARREL.—In the case of a fraction of a barrel, the tax imposed by section 4611 shall be the same fraction of the amount of such tax imposed on a whole barrel.

[Sec. 4612(b)]

(b) ONLY 1 TAX IMPOSED WITH RESPECT TO ANY PRODUCT.—No tax shall be imposed by section 4611 with respect to any petroleum product if the person who would be liable for such tax establishes that a prior tax imposed by such section has been imposed with respect to such product.

[Sec. 4612(c)]

(c) CREDIT WHERE CRUDE OIL RETURNED TO PIPELINE.—Under regulations prescribed by the Secretary, if an operator of a United States refinery—

(1) removes crude oil from a pipeline, and

(2) returns a portion of such crude oil into a stream of other crude oil in the same pipeline,

there shall be allowed as a credit against the tax imposed by section 4611 to such operator an amount equal to the product of the rate of tax imposed by section 4611 on the crude oil so removed by such operator and the number of barrels of crude oil returned by such operator to such pipeline. Any crude oil so returned shall be treated for purposes of this subchapter as crude oil on which no tax has been imposed by section 4611.

Amendments

• **1986, Omnibus Budget Reconciliation Act of 1986 (P.L. 99-509)**

P.L. 99-509, § 8031(c):

Provided for the following amendment that was to become **effective** only if P.L. 99-499 was not enacted.

Amended Code Sec. 4612 by redesignating subsection (c) as subsection (d) and by inserting after subsection (b) new subsection (c) to read as follows:

(c) CREDIT AGAINST PORTION OF TAX ATTRIBUTABLE TO OIL SPILL RATE.—There shall be allowed as a credit against so much of the tax imposed by section 4611 as is attributable to the Oil Spill Liability Trust Fund financing rate of any period an amount equal to the excess of—

(1) the sum of—

(A) the aggregate amounts paid by the taxpayer before January 1, 1987, into the Deepwater Port Liability Trust Fund and the Offshore Oil Pollution Compensation Fund, and

(B) the interest accrued on such amounts before such date, over

(2) the amount of such payments taken into account under this subsection for all prior periods.

• **1986, Superfund Amendments and Reauthorization Act of 1986 (P.L. 99-499)**

P.L. 99-499, § 512(c):

Amended Code Sec. 4612 by redesignating subsection (c) as subsection (d) and by inserting after subsection (b) new subsection (c). **Effective** 1-1-87.

[Sec. 4612(d)]

(d) CREDIT AGAINST PORTION OF TAX ATTRIBUTABLE TO OIL SPILL RATE.—There shall be allowed as a credit against so much of the tax imposed by section 4611 as is attributable to the Oil Spill Liability Trust Fund financing rate for any period an amount equal to the excess of—

(1) the sum of—

(A) the aggregate amounts paid by the taxpayer before January 1, 1987, into the Deepwater Port Liability Trust fund and the Offshore Oil Pollution Compensation Fund, and

(B) the interest accrued on such amounts before such date, over

(2) the amount of such payments taken into account under this subsection for all prior periods.

The preceding sentence shall also apply to amounts paid by the taxpayer into the Trans-Alaska Pipeline Liability Fund to the extent of amounts transferred from such Fund into the Oil Spill Liability Trust Fund. For purposes of this subsection, all taxpayers which would be members of the same affiliated group (as defined in section 1504(a)) if section 1504(a)(2) were applied by substituting "100 percent" for "80 percent" shall be treated as 1 taxpayer.

Amendments

• **1990, Oil Pollution Act of 1990 (P.L. 101-380)**

P.L. 101-380, § 9002(a):

Amended Code Sec. 4612(d) by striking out the last sentence. **Effective** 8-18-90. Prior to amendment, the last sentence read as follows:

Amounts may be transferred from the Trans-Alaska Pipeline Liability Fund into the Oil Spill Liability Trust Fund only to the extent the administrators of the Trans-Alaska Pipeline Liability Fund determine that such amounts are not needed to satisfy claims against such Fund.

P.L. 101-380, § 9002(b):

Amended Code Sec. 4612(d) by adding at the end thereof a new sentence. **Effective** 8-18-90.

• **1989, Omnibus Budget Reconciliation Act of 1989 (P.L. 101-239)**

P.L. 101-239, § 7505(c):

Amended Code Sec. 4612(d) by adding at the end thereof a new sentence. **Effective** 12-19-89.

P.L. 101-239, § 7505(d)(1), provides:

(d) OIL SPILL LIABILITY TRUST FUND TO BE OPERATING FUND.—

(1) IN GENERAL.—For purposes of sections 8032(d) and 8033(c) of the Omnibus Budget Reconciliation Act of 1986, the commencement date is January 1, 1990.

• **1986, Omnibus Budget Reconciliation Act of 1986 (P.L. 99-509)**

P.L. 99-509, § 8032(b):

Amended Code Sec. 4612 by redesignating subsection (d) as subsection (e) and by inserting after subsection (c) new subsection (d). For the **effective** date, see Act Sec. 8032(d), below.

P.L. 99-509, § 8032(d), provides:

(d) EFFECTIVE DATE.—

(1) IN GENERAL.—Except as provided in paragraph (2), the amendments made by this section shall take effect on the commencement date (as defined in section 4611(f)(2) of the Internal Revenue Code of 1954, as added by this section).

(2) COORDINATION WITH SUPERFUND REAUTHORIZATION.—The amendments made by this section shall take effect only of the Superfund Amendments and Reauthorization Act of 1986 is enacted.

[Sec. 4612(e)]

(e) INCOME TAX CREDIT FOR UNUSED PAYMENTS INTO TRANS-ALASKA PIPELINE LIABILITY FUND.—

(1) IN GENERAL.—For purposes of section 38, the current year business credit shall include the credit determined under this subsection.

(2) DETERMINATION OF CREDIT.—

(A) IN GENERAL.—The credit determined under this subsection for any taxable year is an amount equal to the aggregate credit which would be allowed to the taxpayer under subsection (d) for amounts paid into the Trans-Alaska Pipeline Liability Fund had the Oil Spill Liability Trust Fund financing rate not ceased to apply.

(B) LIMITATION.—

(i) IN GENERAL.—The amount of the credit determined under this subsection for any taxable year with respect to any taxpayer shall not exceed the excess of—

(I) the amount determined under clause (ii), over

(II) the aggregate amount of the credit determined under this subsection for prior taxable years with respect to such taxpayer.

(ii) OVERALL LIMITATION.—The amount determined under this clause with respect to any taxpayer is the excess of—

(I) the aggregate amount of credit which would have been allowed under subsection (d) to the taxpayer for periods before the termination date specified in section 4611(f)(1), if amounts in the Trans-Alaska Pipeline Liability Fund which are actually transferred into the Oil Spill Liability Fund were transferred on January 1, 1990, and the Oil Spill Liability Trust Fund financing rate did not terminate before such termination date, over

EXCISE TAXES—TAX ON CHEMICALS

(II) the aggregate amount of the credit allowed under subsection (d) to the taxpayer.

(3) COST OF INCOME TAX CREDIT BORNE BY TRUST FUND.—

(A) IN GENERAL.—The Secretary shall from time to time transfer from the Oil Spill Liability Trust Fund to the general fund of the Treasury amounts equal to the credits allowed by reason of this subsection.

(B) TRUST FUND BALANCE MAY NOT BE REDUCED BELOW $1,000,000,000.—Transfers may be made under subparagraph (A) only to the extent that the unobligated balance of the Oil Spill Liability Trust Fund exceeds $1,000,000,000. If any transfer is not made by reason of the preceding sentence, such transfer shall be made as soon as permitted under such sentence.

(4) NO CARRYBACK.—No portion of the unused business credit for any taxable year which is attributable to the credit determined under this subsection may be carried to a taxable year beginning on or before the date of the enactment of this paragraph.

Amendments

• **2018, Tax Technical Corrections Act of 2018 (P.L. 115-141)**

P.L. 115-141, §401(a)(223), Div. U:

Amended Code Sec. 4612(e)(2)(B)(ii)(I) by striking "tranferred" and inserting "transferred". **Effective** 3-23-2018.

• **1992, Energy Policy Act of 1992 (P.L. 102-486)**

P.L. 102-486, §1922(a):

Amended Code Sec. 4612 by redesignating subsection (e) as subsection (f) and by inserting after subsection (d) new subsection (e). **Effective** for tax years beginning after the date of the enactment of this Act [10-24-92.—CCH].

[Sec. 4612(f)]

(f) DISPOSITION OF REVENUES FROM PUERTO RICO AND THE VIRGIN ISLANDS.—The provisions of subsections (a)(3) and (b)(3) of section 7652 shall not apply to any tax imposed by section 4611.

Amendments

• **1992, Energy Policy Act of 1992 (P.L. 102-486)**

P.L. 102-486, §1922(a):

Amended Code Sec. 4612 by redesignating subsection (e) as subsection (f). **Effective** for tax years beginning after the date of the enactment of this Act [10-24-92.—CCH].

• **1989, Omnibus Budget Reconciliation Act of 1989 (P.L. 101-239)**

P.L. 101-239, §7505(d)(1), provides:

(d) OIL SPILL LIABILITY TRUST FUND TO BE OPERATING FUND.—

(1) IN GENERAL.—For purposes of sections 8032(d) and 8033(c) of the Omnibus Budget Reconciliation Act of 1986, the commencement date is January 1, 1990.

• **1986, Omnibus Budget Reconciliation Act of 1986 (P.L. 99-509)**

P.L. 99-509, §8031(c):

Provided for the following amendment that was to become **effective** only if P.L. 99-499 was not enacted.

Amended Code Sec. 4612 by redesignating subsection (c) as subsection (d).

P.L. 99-509, §8032(b):

Amended Code Sec. 4612 by redesignating subsection (d) as subsection (e). For the **effective** date, see Act Sec. 8032(d), below.

P.L. 99-509, §8032(d), provides:

(d) EFFECTIVE DATE.—

(1) IN GENERAL.—Except as provided in paragraph (2), the amendments made by this section shall take effect on the commencement date (as defined in section 4611(f)(2) of the Internal Revenue Code of 1954, as added by this section).

(2) COORDINATION WITH SUPERFUND REAUTHORIZATION.—The amendments made by this section shall take effect only if the Superfund Amendments and Reauthorization Act of 1986 is enacted.

• **1986, Superfund Amendments and Reauthorization Act of 1986 (P.L. 99-499)**

P.L. 99-499, §512(c):

Amended Code Sec. 4612 by redesignating subsection (c) as subsection (d). **Effective** 1-1-87.

• **1980, Comprehensive Environmental Response, Compensation, and Liability Act of 1980 (P.L. 96-510)**

P.L. 96-510, §211(a):

Added Code Sec. 4612. **Effective** 4-1-81.

Subchapter B—Tax on Certain Chemicals

Sec. 4661. Imposition of tax.
Sec. 4662. Definitions and special rules.

[Sec. 4661]

SEC. 4661. IMPOSITION OF TAX.

[Sec. 4661(a)]

(a) GENERAL RULE.—There is hereby imposed a tax on any taxable chemical sold by the manufacturer, producer, or importer thereof.

[Sec. 4661(b)]

(b) AMOUNT OF TAX.—The amount of tax imposed by subsection (a) shall be determined in accordance with the following table:

In the case of:	The tax is the following amount per ton:
Acetylene	$9.74
Benzene	9.74
Butane	9.74
Butylene	9.74
Butadiene	9.74
Ethylene	9.74
Methane	6.88
Napthalene	9.74
Propylene	9.74
Toluene	9.74
Xylene	9.74
Ammonia	5.28
Antimony	8.90
Antimony trioxide	7.50
Arsenic	8.90
Arsenic trioxide	6.82
Barium sulfide	4.60
Bromine	8.90
Cadmium	8.90
Chlorine	5.40

EXCISE TAXES—TAX ON CHEMICALS

In the case of:	The tax is the following amount per ton:
Chromium	8.90
Chromite	3.04
Potassium dichromate	3.38
Sodium dichromate	3.74
Cobalt	8.90
Cupric sulfate	3.74
Cupric oxide	7.18
Cuprous oxide	7.94
Hydrochloric acid	0.58
Hydrogen fluoride	8.46
Lead oxide	8.28
Mercury	8.90
Nickel	8.90
Phosphorus	8.90
Stannous chloride	5.70
Stannic chloride	4.24
Zinc chloride	4.44
Zinc sulfate	3.80
Potassium hydroxide	0.44
Sodium hydroxide	0.56
Sulfuric acid	0.52
Nitric acid	0.48

Amendments

• **2021, Infrastructure Investment and Jobs Act (P.L. 117-58)**

P.L. 117-58, § 80201(b)(1), Div. H:

Amended Code Sec. 4661(b). **Effective** 7-1-2022. Prior to amendment, Code Sec. 4661(b) reads as follows:

(b) AMOUNT OF TAX.—The amount of the tax imposed by subsection (a) shall be determined in accordance with the following table:

In the case of:	The tax is the following amount per ton
Acetylene	$4.87
Benzene	4.87
Butane	4.87
Butylene	4.87
Butadiene	4.87
Ethylene	4.87
Methane	3.44
Naphthalene	4.87
Propylene	4.87
Toluene	4.87
Xylene	4.87
Ammonia	2.64
Antimony	4.45
Antimony trioxide	3.75
Arsenic	4.45
Arsenic trioxide	3.41
Barium sulfide	2.30
Bromine	4.45
Cadmium	4.45
Chlorine	2.70
Chromium	4.45
Chromite	1.52
Potassium dichromate	1.69
Sodium dichromate	1.87
Cobalt	4.45
Cupric sulfate	1.87
Cupric oxide	3.59
Cuprous oxide	3.97
Hydrochloric acid	0.29
Hydrogen fluoride	4.23
Lead oxide	4.14
Mercury	4.45
Nickel	4.45
Phosphorus	4.45
Stannous chloride	2.85
Stannic chloride	2.12
Zinc chloride	2.22
Zinc sulfate	1.90
Potassium hydroxide	0.22
Sodium hydroxide	0.28
Sulfuric acid	0.26
Nitric acid	0.24

For periods before 1992, the item relating to xylene in the preceding table shall be applied by substituting "10.13" for "4.87".

• **1986, Superfund Amendments and Reauthorization Act of 1986 (P.L. 99-499)**

P.L. 99-499, § 513(a):

Amended the table contained in Code Sec. 4661(b) by adding at the end thereof a new sentence. **Effective** 1-1-87. However, see Act Sec. 513(h)(2)-(5).

P.L. 99-499, § 513(h)(2)-(5), provides:

(2) REPEAL OF TAX ON XYLENE FOR PERIODS BEFORE OCTOBER 1, 1985.—

(A) REFUND OF TAX PREVIOUSLY IMPOSED.—

(i) IN GENERAL.—In the case of any tax imposed by section 4661 of the Internal Revenue Code of 1954 on the sale or use of xylene before October 1, 1985, such tax (including interest, additions to tax, and additional amounts) shall not be assessed, and if assessed, the assessment shall be abated, and if collected shall be credited or refunded (with interest) as an overpayment.

(ii) CONDITION TO ALLOWANCE.—Clause (i) shall not apply to a sale of xylene unless the person who (but for clause (i)) would be liable for the tax imposed by section 4661 on such sale meets requirements similar to the requirements of paragraph (1) of section 6416(a) of such Code. For purposes of the preceding sentence, subparagraph (A) of section 6416(a)(1) of such Code shall be applied without regard to the material preceding "has not collected".

(B) WAIVER OF STATUTE OF LIMITATIONS.—If on the date of the enactment of this Act (or at any time within 1 year after such date of enactment) refund or credit of any overpayment of tax resulting from the application of subparagraph (A) is barred by any law or rule of law, refund or credit of such overpayment shall, nevertheless, be made or allowed if claim therefor is filed before the date 1 year after the date of the enactment of this Act.

(C) XYLENE TO INCLUDE ISOMERS.—For purposes of this paragraph, the term "xylene" shall include any isomer of xylene whether or not separated.

(3) INVENTORY EXCHANGES.—

(A) IN GENERAL.—Except as otherwise provided in this paragraph, the amendment made by subsection (f) shall apply as if included in the amendments made by section 211 of the Hazardous Substance Response Revenue Act of 1980.

(B) RECIPIENT MUST AGREE TO TREATMENT AS MANUFACTURER.—In the case of any inventory exchange before January 1, 1987, the amendment made by subsection (f) shall apply only if the person receiving the chemical from the manufacturer, producer, or importer in the exchange agrees to be treated as the manufacturer, producer, or importer of such chemical for purposes of subchapter B of chapter 38 of the Internal Revenue Code of 1954.

EXCISE TAXES—TAX ON CHEMICALS

(C) EXCEPTION WHERE MANUFACTURER PAID TAX.—In the case of any inventory exchange before January 1, 1987, the amendment made by subsection (f) shall not apply if the manufacturer, producer, or importer treated such exchange as a sale for purposes of section 4661 of such Code and paid the tax imposed by such section.

(D) REGISTRATION REQUIREMENTS.—Section 4662(c)(2)(B) of such Code (as added by subsection (f)) shall apply to exchanges made after December 31, 1986.

(4) EXPORTS OF TAXABLE SUBSTANCES.—Subclause (II) of section 4662(e)(2)(A)(ii) of such Code (as added by this section) shall not apply to the export of any taxable substance (as defined in section 4672(a) of such Code) before January 1, 1989.

(5) SALES OF INTERMEDIATE HYDROCARBON STREAMS.—

(A) IN GENERAL.—Except as otherwise provided in this paragraph, the amendment made by subsection (g) shall apply as if included in the amendments made by section 211 of the Hazardous Substances Response Revenue Act of 1980.

(B) Purchaser must agree to treatment as manufacturer.—In the case of any sale before January 1, 1987, of any intermediate hydrocarbon stream, the amendment made by subsection (g) shall apply only if the purchaser agrees to be treated as the manufacturer, producer, or importer for purposes of subchapter B of chapter 38 of such Code.

(C) EXCEPTION WHERE MANUFACTURER PAID TAX.—In the case of any sale before January 1, 1987, of any intermediate hydrocarbon stream, the amendment made by subsection (g) shall not apply if the manufacturer, producer, or importer of such stream paid the tax imposed by section 4661 with respect to such sale on all taxable chemicals contained in such stream.

(D) REGISTRATION REQUIREMENTS.—Section 4662(b)(10)(C) of such Code (as added by subsection (g)) shall apply to exchanges made after December 31, 1986.

[Sec. 4661(c)]

(c) TERMINATION.—No tax shall be imposed by this section after December 31, 2031.

Amendments

• **2021, Infrastructure Investment and Jobs Act (P.L. 117-58)**

P.L. 117-58, §80201(a)(1), Div. H:

Amended Code Sec. 4661(c). **Effective** 7-1-2022. Prior to amendment, Code Sec. 4661(c) reads as follows:

(c) TERMINATION.—No tax shall be imposed under this section during any period during which the Hazardous Substance Superfund financing rate under section 4611 does not apply.

• **1986, Omnibus Budget Reconciliation Act of 1986 (P.L. 99-509)**

P.L. 99-509, §8031(d)(2):

Provided for the following amendment that was to become **effective** only if P.L. 99-499 was not enacted.

Amended Code Sec. 4661(c) to read as follows:

(c) TERMINATION.—The tax imposed by this section shall not apply after September 30, 1985.

P.L. 99-509, §8032(c)(3):

Amended Code Sec. 4661(c) by striking out "no tax is imposed under section 4611(a)" and inserting in lieu thereof "the Hazardous Substance Superfund financing rate under section 4611 does not apply". For the **effective** date, see Act Sec. 8032(d), below.

P.L. 99-509, §8032(d), provides:

(d) EFFECTIVE DATE.—

(1) IN GENERAL.—Except as provided in paragraph (2), the amendments made by this section shall take effect on the commencement date (as defined in section 4611(f)(2) of the Internal Revenue Code of 1954, as added by this section).

(2) COORDINATION WITH SUPERFUND REAUTHORIZATION.—The amendments made by this section shall take effect only if the Superfund Amendments and Reauthorization Act of 1986 is enacted.

• **1980, Comprehensive Environmental Response, Compensation, and Liability Act of 1980 (P.L. 96-510)**

P.L. 96-510, §211(a):

Added Code Sec. 4661. **Effective** 4-1-81.

[Sec. 4662]

SEC. 4662. DEFINITIONS AND SPECIAL RULES.

[Sec. 4662(a)]

(a) DEFINITIONS.—For purposes of this subchapter—

(1) TAXABLE CHEMICAL.—Except as provided in subsection (b), the term "taxable chemical" means any substance—

(A) which is listed in the table under section 4661(b), and

(B) which is manufactured or produced in the United States or entered into the United States for consumption, use, or warehousing.

(2) UNITED STATES.—The term "United States" has the meaning given such term by section 4612(a)(4).

(3) IMPORTER.—The term "importer" means the person entering the taxable chemical for consumption, use, or warehousing.

(4) TON.—The term "ton" means 2,000 pounds. In the case of any taxable chemical which is a gas, the term "ton" menas the amount of such gas in cubic feet which is the equivalent of 2,000 pounds on a molecular weight basis.

(5) FRACTIONAL PART OF TON.—In the case of a fraction of a ton, the tax imposed by section 4661 shall be the same fraction of the amount of such tax imposed on a whole ton.

[Sec. 4662(b)]

(b) EXCEPTIONS; OTHER SPECIAL RULES.—For purposes of this subchapter—

(1) METHANE OR BUTANE USED AS A FUEL.—Under regulations prescribed by the Secretary, methane or butane shall be treated as a taxable chemical only if it is used otherwise than as a fuel or in the manufacture or production of any motor fuel, diesel fuel, aviation fuel, or jet fuel (and, for purposes of section 4661(a), the person so using it shall be treated as the manufacturer thereof).

(2) SUBSTANCES USED IN THE PRODUCTION OF FERTILIZER.—

(A) IN GENERAL.—In the case of nitric acid, sulfuric acid, ammonia, or methane used to produce ammonia which is a qualified fertilizer substance, no tax shall be imposed under section 4661(a).

(B) QUALIFIED FERTILIZER SUBSTANCE.—For purposes of this section, the term "qualified fertilizer substance" means any substance—

(i) used in a qualified fertilizer use by the manufacturer, producer, or importer,

(ii) sold for use by any purchaser in a qualified fertilizer use, or

(iii) sold for resale by any purchaser for use, or resale for ultimate use, in a qualified fertilizer use.

(C) QUALIFIED FERTILIZER USE.—The term "qualified fertilizer use" means any use in the manufacture or production of fertilizer or for direct application as a fertilizer.

(D) TAXATION OF NONQUALIFIED SALE OR USE.—For purposes of section 4661(a), if no tax was imposed by such section on the sale or use of any chemical by reason of subparagraph (A), the first person who sells or uses such chemical other than in a sale or use described in subparagraph (A) shall be treated as the manufacturer of such chemical.

(3) SULFURIC ACID PRODUCED AS A BYPRODUCT OF AIR POLLUTION CONTROL.—In the case of sulfuric acid produced solely as a byproduct of and on the same site as air pollution control equipment, no tax shall be imposed under section 4661.

(4) SUBSTANCES DERIVED FROM COAL.—For purposes of this subchapter, the term "taxable chemical" shall not include any substance to the extent derived from coal.

(5) SUBSTANCES USED IN THE PRODUCTION OF MOTOR FUEL, ETC.—

(A) IN GENERAL.—In the case of any chemical described in subparagraph (D) which is a qualified fuel substance, no tax shall be imposed under section 4661(a).

(B) QUALIFIED FUEL SUBSTANCE.—For purposes of this section, the term "qualified fuel substance" means any substance—

(i) used in a qualified fuel use by the manufacturer, producer, or importer,

(ii) sold for use by any purchaser in a qualified fuel use, or

(iii) sold for resale by any purchaser for use, or resale for ultimate use, in a qualified fuel use.

(C) QUALIFIED FUEL USE.—For purposes of this subsection, the term "qualified fuel use" means—

(i) any use in the manufacture or production of any motor fuel, diesel fuel, aviation fuel, or jet fuel, or

(ii) any use as such a fuel.

(D) CHEMICALS TO WHICH PARAGRAPH APPLIES.—For purposes of this subsection, the chemicals described in this subparagraph are acetylene, benzene, butylene, butadiene, ethylene, naphthalene, propylene, toluene, and xylene.

(E) TAXATION OF NONQUALIFIED SALE OR USE.—For purposes of section 4661(a), if no tax was imposed by such section on the sale or use of any chemical by reason of subparagraph (A), the first person who sells or uses such chemical other than in a sale or use described in subparagraph (A) shall be treated as the manufacturer of such chemical.

(6) SUBSTANCE HAVING TRANSITORY PRESENCE DURING REFINING PROCESS, ETC.—

(A) IN GENERAL.—No tax shall be imposed under section 4661(a) on any taxable chemical described in subparagraph (B) by reason of the transitory presence of such chemical during any process of smelting, refining, or otherwise extracting any substance not subject to tax under section 4661(a).

(B) CHEMICALS TO WHICH SUBPARAGRAPH (A) APPLIES.—The chemicals described in this subparagraph are—

(i) barium sulfide, cupric sulfate, cupric oxide, cuprous oxide, lead oxide, zinc chloride, and zinc sulfate, and

(ii) any solution or mixture containing any chemical described in clause (i).

(C) REMOVAL TREATED AS USE.—Nothing in subparagraph (A) shall be construed to apply to any chemical which is removed from or ceases to be part of any smelting, refining, or other extraction process.

(7) SPECIAL RULE FOR XYLENE.—Except in the case of any substance imported into the United States or exported from the United States, the term "xylene" does not include any separated isomer of xylene.

(8) RECYCLED CHROMIUM, COBALT, AND NICKEL.—

(A) IN GENERAL.—No tax shall be imposed under section 4661(a) on any chromium, cobalt, or nickel which is diverted or recovered in the United States from any solid waste as part of a recycling process (and not as part of the original manufacturing or production process).

(B) EXEMPTION NOT TO APPLY WHILE CORRECTIVE ACTION UNCOMPLETED.—Subparagraph (A) shall not apply during any period that required corrective action by the taxpayer at the unit at which the recycling occurs is uncompleted.

(C) REQUIRED CORRECTIVE ACTION.—For purposes of subparagraph (B), required corrective action shall be treated as uncompleted during the period—

(i) beginning on the date that the corrective action is required by the Administrator or an authorized State pursuant to—

(I) a final permit under section 3005 of the Solid Waste Disposal Act or a final order under section 3004 or 3008 of such Act, or

(II) a final order under section 106 of the Comprehensive Environmental Response, Compensation, and Liability Act of 1980, and

(ii) ending on the date the Administrator or such State (as the case may be) certifies to the Secretary that such corrective action has been completed.

(D) SPECIAL RULE FOR GROUNDWATER TREATMENT.—In the case of corrective action requiring groundwater treatment, such action shall be treated as completed as of the close of the 10-year period beginning on the date such action is required if such treatment complies with the permit or order applicable under subparagraph (C)(i) throughout such period. The preceding sentence shall cease to apply beginning on the date such treatment ceases to comply with such permit or order.

(E) SOLID WASTE.—For purposes of this paragraph, the term "solid waste" has the meaning given such term by section 1004 of the Solid Waste Disposal Act, except that such term shall not include any byproduct, coproduct, or other waste from any process of smelting, refining, or otherwise extracting any metal.

(9) SUBSTANCES USED IN THE PRODUCTION OF ANIMAL FEED.—

(A) IN GENERAL.—In the case of—

(i) nitric acid,

(ii) sulfuric acid,

(iii) ammonia, or

(iv) methane used to produce ammonia,

which is a qualified animal feed substance, no tax shall be imposed under section 4661(a).

(B) QUALIFIED ANIMAL FEED SUBSTANCE.—For purposes of this section, the term "qualified animal feed substance" means any substance—

(i) used in a qualified animal feed use by the manufacturer, producer, or importer,

(ii) sold for use by any purchaser in a qualified animal feed use, or

(iii) sold for resale by any purchaser for use, or resale for ultimate use, in a qualified animal feed use.

(C) QUALIFIED ANIMAL FEED USE.—The term "qualified animal feed use" means any use in the manufacture or production of animal feed or animal feed supplements, or of ingredients used in animal feed or animal feed supplements.

(D) TAXATION OF NONQUALIFIED SALE OR USE.—For purposes of section 4661(a), if no tax was imposed by such section on the sale or use of any chemical by reason of subparagraph (A), the 1st person who sells or uses such chemical other than in a sale or use described in subparagraph (A) shall be treated as the manufacturer of such chemical.

(10) HYDROCARBON STREAMS CONTAINING MIXTURES OF ORGANIC TAXABLE CHEMICALS.—

(A) IN GENERAL.—No tax shall be imposed under section 4661(a) on any organic taxable chemical while such chemical is part of an intermediate hydrocarbon stream containing one or more organic taxable chemicals.

(B) REMOVAL, ETC., TREATED AS USE.—For purposes of this part, if any organic taxable chemical on which no tax was imposed by reason of subparagraph (A) is isolated, extracted, or otherwise removed from, or ceases to be part of, an intermediate hydrocarbon stream—

(i) such isolation, extraction, removal, or cessation shall be treated as use by the person causing such event, and

(ii) such person shall be treated as the manufacturer of such chemical.

(C) REGISTRATION REQUIREMENT.—Subparagraph (A) shall not apply to any sale of any intermediate hydrocarbon stream unless the registration requirements of clauses (i) and (ii) of subsection (c)(2)(B) are satisfied.

(D) ORGANIC TAXABLE CHEMICAL.—For purposes of this paragraph, the term "organic taxable chemical" means any taxable chemical which is an organic substance.

EXCISE TAXES—TAX ON CHEMICALS

Amendments

• **1988, Technical and Miscellaneous Revenue Act of 1988 (P.L. 100-647)**

P.L. 100-647, §2001(a)(2):

Amended Code Sec. 4662(b)(10)(A) by striking out "a mixture of" and inserting in lieu thereof "one or more". **Effective** as if included in the provision of P.L. 99-499 to which it relates.

• **1986, Superfund Amendments and Reauthorization Act of 1986 (P.L. 99-499)**

P.L. 99-499, §513(c):

Amended Code Sec. 4662(b) by adding after paragraph (6) new paragraph (7). **Effective** 1-1-87. However, see Act Sec. 513(h)(2)-(5) reproduced under the amendment notes for Code Sec. 4661(b).

P.L. 99-499, §513(d):

Amended Code Sec. 4662(b) by adding after paragraph (7) new paragraph (8). **Effective** 1-1-87. However, see Act Sec. 513(h)(2)-(5) reproduced under the amendment notes for Code Sec. 4661(b).

P.L. 99-499, §513(e)(1):

Amended Code Sec. 4662(b) by adding after paragraph (8) new paragraph (9). **Effective** 1-1-87. However, see Act Sec. 513(h)(2)-(5) reproduced under the amendment notes for Code Sec. 4661(b).

P.L. 99-499, §513(g):

Amended Code Sec. 4662(b) by adding after paragraph (9) new paragraph (10). **Effective** 1-1-87. However, see Act Sec. 513(h)(2)-(5) reproduced under the amendment notes for Code Sec. 4661(b).

• **1984, Deficit Reduction Act of 1984 (P.L. 98-369)**

P.L. 98-369, §1019(a)(1):

Amended Code Sec. 4662(b) by adding paragraphs (5) and (6). **Effective** as if included in the amendments made by section 211(a) of the Hazardous Substance Response Revenue Act of 1980. For a special rule, see Act Sec. 1019(d)(2), below.

P.L. 98-369, §1019(a)(3):

Amended Code Sec. 4662(b)(1) by inserting "or in the manufacture or production of any motor fuel, diesel fuel, aviation fuel, or jet fuel" after "than as a fuel".

Effective as if included in the amendments made by section 211(a) of the Hazardous Substance Response Revenue Act of 1980. For a special rule, see Act Sec. 1019(d)(2), below.

P.L. 98-369, §1019(b)(1):

Amended Code Sec. 4662(b)(2) by striking out subparagraphs (B) and (C) and inserting subparagraphs (B), (C), and (D) in lieu thereof. **Effective** as if included in the amendments made by section 211(a) of the Hazardous Substance Response Revenue Act of 1980. For a special rule, see Act Sec. 1019(d)(2), below. Prior to amendment, Code Sec. 4662(b)(2) read as follows:

(2) Substances Used in the Production of Fertilizer.—

(A) In General.—In the case of nitric acid, sulfuric acid, ammonia, or methane used to produce ammonia which is a qualified substance, no tax shall be imposed under section 4661(a).

(B) Qualified Substance.—For purposes of this section, the term "qualified substance" means any substance—

(i) used in a qualified use by the manufacturer, producer, or importer,

(ii) sold for use by the purchaser in a qualified use, or

(iii) sold for resale by the purchaser to a second purchaser for use by such second purchaser in a qualified use.

(C) Qualified Use.—For purposes of this subsection, the term "qualified use" means any use in the manufacture or production of a fertilizer.

P.L. 98-369, §1019(b)(2)(A):

Amended Code Sec. 4662(b)(2)(A) by striking out "qualified substance" and inserting in lieu thereof "qualified fertilizer substance". **Effective** as if included in the amendments made by section 211(a) of the Hazardous Substance Response Revenue Act of 1980. For a special rule, see Act Sec. 1019(d)(2), below.

P.L. 98-369, §1019(d)(2), provides:

(2) Waiver of Limitation.—If refund or credit of any overpayment of tax resulting from the application of the amendments made by this section is prevented at any time before the date which for one year after the date of the enactment of this Act by the operation of any law or rule of law (including res judicata), refund or credit of such overpayment (to the extent attributable to the application of such amendments) may, nevertheless, be made or allowed if claim therefor is filed on or before the date which for one year after the date of the enactment of this Act [sic].

[Sec. 4662(c)]

(c) USE AND CERTAIN EXCHANGES BY MANUFACTURER, ETC.—

(1) USE TREATED AS SALE.—Except as provided in subsections (b) and (e), if any person manufactures, produces, or imports any taxable chemical and uses such chemical, then such person shall be liable for tax under section 4661 in the same manner as if such chemical were sold by such person.

(2) SPECIAL RULES FOR INVENTORY EXCHANGES.—

(A) IN GENERAL.—Except as provided in this paragraph, in any case in which a manufacturer, producer, or importer of a taxable chemical exchanges such chemical as part of an inventory exchange with another person—

(i) such exchange shall not be treated as a sale, and

(ii) such other person shall, for purposes of section 4661, be treated as the manufacturer, producer, or importer of such chemical.

(B) REGISTRATION REQUIREMENT.—Subparagraph (A) shall not apply to any inventory exchange unless—

(i) both parties are registered with the Secretary as manufacturers, producers, or importers of taxable chemicals, and

(ii) the person receiving the taxable chemical has, at such time as the Secretary may prescribe, notified the manufacturer, producer, or importer of such person's registration number and the internal revenue district in which such person is registered.

(C) INVENTORY EXCHANGE.—For purposes of this paragraph, the term "inventory exchange" means any exchange in which 2 persons exchange property which is, in the hands of each person, property described in section 1221(a)(1).

Amendments

• **1999, Tax Relief Extension Act of 1999 (P.L. 106-170)**

P.L. 106-170, §532(c)(2)(U):

Amended Code Sec. 4662(c)(2)(C) by striking "section 1221(1)" and inserting "section 1221(a)(1)". **Effective** for any instrument held, acquired, or entered into, any transaction entered into, and supplies held or acquired on or after 12-17-99.

• **1986, Superfund Amendments and Reauthorization Act of 1986 (P.L. 99-499)**

P.L. 99-499, §513(f):

Amended Code Sec. 4662(c). **Effective** 1-1-87. However, see Act Sec. 513(h)(2)-(5), reproduced in the amendment notes for Code Sec. 4661(b). Prior to amendment, Code Sec. 4662(c) read as follows:

(c) USE BY MANUFACTURER, ETC., CONSIDERED SALE.—Except as provided in subsection (b), if any person manufactures, produces, or imports a taxable chemical and uses such chemical, then such person shall be liable for tax under section 4661 in the same manner as if such chemical were sold by such person.

• **1984, Deficit Reduction Act of 1984 (P.L. 98-369)**

P.L. 98-369, §1019(c):

Amended Code Sec. 4662(c) by striking out "If" and inserting in lieu thereof "Except as provided in subsection (b), if". **Effective** as if included in the amendments made by section 211(a) of the Hazardous Substance Response Revenue Act of 1980. For a special rule, see Act Sec. 1019(d)(2), below.

P.L. 98-369, §1019(d)(2), provides:

(2) Waiver of Limitation.—If refund or credit of any overpayment of tax resulting from the application of the amendments made by this section is prevented at any time before the date which for one year after the date of the enactment of this Act by the operation of any law or rule of law (including res judicata), refund or credit of such overpayment (to the extent attributable to the application of such amendments) may, nevertheless, be made or allowed if claim therefor is filed on or before the date which for one year after the date of the enactment of this Act [sic].

[Sec. 4662(d)]

(d) REFUND OR CREDIT FOR CERTAIN USES.—

(1) IN GENERAL.—Under regulations prescribed by the Secretary, if—

(A) a tax under section 4661 was paid with respect to any taxable chemical, and

(B) such chemical was used by any person in the manufacture or production of any other substance which is a taxable chemical,

then an amount equal to the tax so paid shall be allowed as a credit or refund (without interest) to such person in the same manner as if it were an overpayment of tax imposed by such section. In any case to which this paragraph applies, the amount of any such credit or refund shall not exceed the amount of tax imposed by such section on the other substance manufactured or produced (or which would have been imposed by such section on such other substance but for subsection (b) or (e) of this section).

(2) USE AS FERTILIZER.—Under regulations prescribed by the Secretary, if—

EXCISE TAXES—TAX ON CHEMICALS

(A) a tax under section 4661 was paid with respect to nitric acid, sulfuric acid, ammonia, or methane used to make ammonia without regard to subsection (b)(2), and

(B) any person uses such substance as a qualified fertilizer substance,

then an amount equal to the excess of the tax so paid over the tax determined with regard to subsection (b)(2) shall be allowed as a credit or refund (without interest) to such person in the same manner as if it were an overpayment of tax imposed by this section.

(3) USE AS QUALIFIED FUEL.—Under regulations prescribed by the Secretary, if—

(A) a tax under section 4661 was paid with respect to any chemical described in subparagraph (D) of subsection (b)(5) without regard to subsection (b)(5), and

(B) any person uses such chemical as a qualified fuel substance,

then an amount equal to the excess of the tax so paid over the tax determined with regard to subsection (b)(5) shall be allowed as a credit or refund (without interest) to such person in the same manner as if it were an overpayment of tax imposed by this section.

(4) USE IN THE PRODUCTION OF ANIMAL FEED.—Under regulations prescribed by the Secretary, if—

(A) a tax under section 4661 was paid with respect to nitric acid, sulfuric acid, ammonia, or methane used to produce ammonia, without regard to subsection (b)(9), and

(B) any person uses such substance as a qualified animal feed substance,

then an amount equal to the excess of the tax so paid over the tax determined with regard to subsection (b)(9) shall be allowed as a credit or refund (without interest) to such person in the same manner as if it were an overpayment of tax imposed by this section.

Amendments

• **1986, Superfund Amendments and Reauthorization Act of 1986 (P.L. 99-499)**

P.L. 99-499, § 513(b)(2)(A)-(B):

Amended Code Sec. 4662(d)(1) by striking out "the sale of which by such person would be taxable under such section" and inserting in lieu thereof "which is a taxable chemical", and by striking out "imposed by such section on the other substance manufactured or produced" and inserting in lieu thereof "imposed by such section on the other substance manufactured or produced (or which would have been imposed by such section on such other substance but for subsection (b) or (e) of this section)". **Effective** 1-1-87. However, see Act Sec. 513(h)(2)-(5), reproduced in the amendment notes for Code Sec. 4661(b). Prior to amendment, Code Sec. 4662(d)(1) read as follows:

(d) REFUND OR CREDIT FOR CERTAIN USES.—

(1) IN GENERAL.—Under regulations prescribed by the Secretary, if—

(A) a tax under section 4661 was paid with respect to any taxable chemical, and

(B) such chemical was used by any person in the manufacture or production of any other substance the sale of which by such person would be taxable under such section,

then an amount equal to the tax so paid shall be allowed as a credit or refund (without interest) to such person in the same manner as if it were an overpayment of tax imposed by such section. In any case to which this paragraph applies, the amount of any such credit or refund shall not exceed the amount of tax imposed by such section on the other substance manufactured or produced.

P.L. 99-499, § 513(e)(2):

Amended Code Sec. 4662(d) by adding at the end thereof new paragraph (4). **Effective** 1-1-87. However, see Act Sec. 513(h)(2)-(5), reproduced in the amendment notes for Code Sec. 4661(b).

• **1984, Deficit Reduction Act of 1984 (P.L. 98-369)**

P.L. 98-369, § 1019(a)(2):

Amended Code Sec. 4662(d) by adding paragraph (3). **Effective** as if included in the amendments made by section 211(a) of the Hazardous Substance Response Revenue Act of 1980. For a special rule, see Act Sec. 1019(d)(2), below.

P.L. 98-369, § 1019(b)(2)(B):

Amended Code Sec. 4662(d)(2)(B). **Effective** as if included in the amendments made by section 211(a) of the Hazardous Substance Response Revenue Act of 1980. See the special rule, below. Prior to amendment, it read as follows:

(B) any person uses such substance, or sells such substance for use, as a qualified substance,

P.L. 98-369, § 1019(d)(2), provides:

(2) Waiver of Limitation.—If refund or credit of any overpayment of tax resulting from the application of the amendments made by this section is prevented at any time before the date which for one year after the date of the enactment of this Act by the operation of any law or rule of law (including res judicata), refund or credit of such overpayment (to the extent attributable to the application of such amendments) may, nevertheless, be made or allowed if claim therefor is filed on or before the date which for one year after the date of the enactment of this Act [sic].

[Sec. 4662(e)]

(e) EXEMPTION FOR EXPORTS OF TAXABLE CHEMICALS.—

(1) TAX-FREE SALES.—

(A) IN GENERAL.—No tax shall be imposed under section 4661 on the sale by the manufacturer or producer of any taxable chemical for export, or for resale by the purchaser to a second purchaser for export.

(B) PROOF OF EXPORT REQUIRED.—Rules similar to the rules of section 4221(b) shall apply for purposes of subparagraph (A).

(2) CREDIT OR REFUND WHERE TAX PAID.—

(A) IN GENERAL.—Except as provided in subparagraph (B), if—

(i) tax under section 4661 was paid with respect to any taxable chemical, and

(ii)(I) such chemical was exported by any person, or

(II) such chemical was used as a material in the manufacture or production of a substance which was exported by any person and which, at the time of export, was a taxable substance (as defined in section 4672(a)),

credit or refund (without interest) of such tax shall be allowed or made to the person who paid such tax.

(B) CONDITION TO ALLOWANCE.—No credit or refund shall be allowed or made under subparagraph (A) unless the person who paid the tax establishes that he—

(i) has repaid or agreed to repay the amount of the tax to the person who exported the taxable chemical or taxable substance (as so defined), or

(ii) has obtained the written consent of such exporter to the allowance of the credit or the making of the refund.

(3) REFUNDS DIRECTLY TO EXPORTER.—The Secretary shall provide, in regulations, the circumstances under which a credit or refund (without interest) of the tax under section 4661 shall be allowed or made to the person who exported the taxable chemical or taxable substance, where—

(A) the person who paid the tax waives his claim to the amount of such credit or refund, and

(B) the person exporting the taxable chemical or taxable substance provides such information as the Secretary may require in such regulations.

(4) REGULATIONS.—The Secretary shall prescribe such regulations as may be necessary to carry out the purposes of this subsection.

Amendments

• **1988, Technical and Miscellaneous Revenue Act of 1988 (P.L. 100-647)**

P.L. 100-647, § 2001(a)(1):

Amended Code Sec. 4662(e) by redesignating paragraph (3) as paragraph (4) and inserting after paragraph (2) new paragraph (3). **Effective** as if included in the provision of P.L. 99-499 to which it relates.

• **1986, Superfund Amendments and Reauthorization Act of 1986 (P.L. 99-499)**

P.L. 99-499, § 513(b)(1):

Amended Code Sec. 4662 by redesignating subsection (e) as subsection (f) and by inserting after subsection (d) new subsection (e). **Effective** 1-1-87. However, see Act Sec. 513(h)(2)-(5), reproduced in the amendment notes for Code Sec. 4661(b).

[Sec. 4662(f)]

(f) DISPOSITION OF REVENUES FROM PUERTO RICO AND THE VIRGIN ISLANDS.—The provisions of subsections (a)(3) and (b)(3) of section 7652 shall not apply to any tax imposed by section 4661.

EXCISE TAXES—IMPORTED SUBSTANCES

Amendments

• **1986, Superfund Amendments and Reauthorization Act of 1986 (P.L. 99-499)**

P.L. 99-499, §513(b)(1):

Amended Code Sec. 4662 by redesignating subsection (e) as subsection (f). **Effective** 1-1-87. However, see Act Sec. 513(h)(2)-(5), reproduced in the amendment notes for Code Sec. 4661(b).

• **1980, Comprehensive Environmental Response, Compensation, and Liability Act of 1980 (P.L. 96-510)**

P.L. 96-510, §211(a):

Added Code Sec. 4662. **Effective** 4-1-81.

Subchapter C—Tax on Certain Imported Substances

Sec. 4671. Imposition of tax.
Sec. 4672. Definitions and special rules.

[Sec. 4671]

SEC. 4671. IMPOSITION OF TAX.

[Sec. 4671(a)]

(a) GENERAL RULE.—There is hereby imposed a tax on any taxable substance sold or used by the importer thereof.

[Sec. 4671(b)]

(b) AMOUNT OF TAX.—

(1) IN GENERAL.—Except as provided in paragraph (2), the amount of the tax imposed by subsection (a) with respect to any taxable substance shall be the amount of the tax which would have been imposed by section 4661 on the taxable chemicals used as materials in the manufacture or production of such substance if such taxable chemicals had been sold in the United States for use in the manufacture or production of such taxable substance.

(2) RATE WHERE IMPORTER DOES NOT FURNISH INFORMATION TO SECRETARY.—If the importer does not furnish to the Secretary (at such time and in such manner as the Secretary shall prescribe) sufficient information to determine under paragraph (1) the amount of the tax imposed by subsection (a) on any taxable substance, the amount of the tax imposed on such taxable substance shall be 10 percent of the appraised value of such substance as of the time such substance was entered into the United States for consumption, use, or warehousing.

(3) AUTHORITY TO PRESCRIBE RATE IN LIEU OF PARAGRAPH (2) RATE.—The Secretary may prescribe for each taxable substance a tax which, if prescribed, shall apply in lieu of the tax specified in paragraph (2) with respect to such substance. The tax prescribed by the Secretary shall be equal to the amount of tax which would be imposed by subsection (a) with respect to the taxable substance if such substance were produced using the predominant method of production of such substance.

Amendments

• **2021, Infrastructure Investment and Jobs Act (P.L. 117-58)**

P.L. 117-58, §80201(b)(2), Div. H:

Amended Code Sec. 4671(b)(2) by striking "5 percent" and inserting "10 percent". **Effective** 7-1-2022.

[Sec. 4671(c)]

(c) EXEMPTIONS FOR SUBSTANCES TAXED UNDER SECTIONS 4611 AND 4661.—No tax shall be imposed by this section on the sale or use of any substance if tax is imposed on such sale or use under section 4611 or 4661.

[Sec. 4671(d)]

(d) TAX-FREE SALES, ETC. FOR SUBSTANCES USED AS CERTAIN FUELS OR IN THE PRODUCTION OF FERTILIZER OR ANIMAL FEED.—Rules similar to the following rules shall apply for purposes of applying this section with respect to taxable substances used or sold for use as described in such rules:

(1) Paragraphs (2), (5), and (9) of section 4662(b) (relating to tax-free sales of chemicals used as fuel or in the production of fertilizer or animal feed).

(2) Paragraphs (2), (3), and (4) of section 4662(d) (relating to refund or credit of tax on certain chemicals used as fuel or in the production of fertilizer or animal feed).

[Sec. 4671(e)]

(e) TERMINATION.—No tax shall be imposed by this section after December 31, 2031.

Amendments

• **2021, Infrastructure Investment and Jobs Act (P.L. 117-58)**

P.L. 117-58, §80201(a)(2), Div. H:

Amended Code Sec. 4671(e). **Effective** 7-1-2022. Prior to amendment, Code Sec. 4671(e) reads as follows:

(e) TERMINATION.—No tax shall be imposed under this section during any period during which the Hazardous Substance Superfund financing rate under section 4611 does not apply.

• **1986, Omnibus Budget Reconciliation Act of 1986 (P.L. 99-509)**

P.L. 99-509, §8032(c)(3):

Amended Code Sec. 4671(e) by striking out "no tax is imposed under section 4611(a)" and inserting in lieu thereof "the Hazardous Substance Superfund financing rate under section 4611 does not apply". For the **effective** date, see Act Sec. 8032(d), below.

P.L. 99-509, §8032(d), provides:

(d) EFFECTIVE DATE.—

(1) IN GENERAL.—Except as provided in paragraph (2), the amendments made by this section shall take effect on the commencement date (as defined in section 4611(f)(2) of the Internal Revenue Code of 1954, as added by this section).

(2) COORDINATION WITH SUPERFUND REAUTHORIZATION.—The amendments made by this section shall take effect only if the Superfund Amendments and Reauthorization Act of 1986 is enacted.

• **1986, Superfund Amendments and Reauthorization Act of 1986 (P.L. 99-499)**

P.L. 99-499, §515(a):

Amended chapter 38 of the Internal Revenue Code of 1986 by adding after subchapter B new subchapter C, containing new Code Sec. 4671. **Effective** 1-1-89.

[Sec. 4672]

SEC. 4672. DEFINITIONS AND SPECIAL RULES.

[Sec. 4672(a)]

(a) TAXABLE SUBSTANCE.—For purposes of this subchapter—

(1) IN GENERAL.—The term "taxable substance" means any substance which, at the time of sale or use by the importer, is listed as a taxable substance by the Secretary for purposes of this subchapter.

(2) DETERMINATION OF SUBSTANCES ON LIST.—A substance shall be listed under paragraph (1) if—

(A) the substance is contained in the list under paragraph (3), or

EXCISE TAXES—IMPORTED SUBSTANCES

(B) the Secretary determines, in consultation with the Administrator of the Environmental Protection Agency and the Commissioner of Customs, that taxable chemicals constitute more than 20 percent of the weight (or more than 20 percent of the value) of the materials used to produce such substance (determined on the basis of the predominant method of production).

If an importer or exporter of any substance requests that the Secretary determine whether such substance be listed as a taxable substance under paragraph (1) or be removed from such listing, the Secretary shall make such determination within 180 days after the date the request was filed.

(3) INITIAL LIST OF TAXABLE SUBSTANCES.—

Cumene	Phenolic resins
Styrene	Polyvinylchloride resins
Ammonium nitrate	Polystyrene resins and copolymers
Nickel oxide	Ethyl alcohol for nonbeverage use
Isopropyl alcohol	Ethylbenzene
Methylene chloride	Acrylonitrile
Polypropylene	Methanol
Propylene glycol	Propylene oxide
Formaldehyde	Polypropylene resins
Acetone	Ethylene oxide
Ethylene glycol	Ethylene dichloride
Vinyl chloride	Cyclohexane
Polyethylene resins, total	Isophthalic acid
Polybutadiene	Maleic anhydride
Styrene-butadiene, latex	Phthalic anhydride
Styrene-butadiene, snpf	Ethyl methyl ketone
Synthetic rubber, not containing fillers	Chloroform
Urea	Carbon tetrachloride
Ferronickel	Chromic acid
Ferrochromium nov 3 pct.	Hydrogen peroxide
Ferrochrome ov 3 pct. carbon	Polystyrene homopolymer resins
Unwrought nickel	Melamine
Nickel waste and scrap	Acrylic and methacrylic acid resins
Wrought nickel rods and wire	Vinyl resins
Nickel powders	Vinyl resins, NSPF.

(4) MODIFICATIONS TO LIST.—The Secretary shall add to the list under paragraph (3) substances which meet either the weight or value tests of paragraph (2)(B) and may remove from such list only substances which meet neither of such tests.

Amendments

• **2021, Infrastructure Investment and Jobs Act (P.L. 117-58)**

P.L. 117-58, §80201(c)(1), Div. H:

Amended Code Sec. 4672(a)(2)(B) by striking "50 percent" each place it appears and inserting "20 percent". **Effective** 7-1-2022.

• **1988, Technical and Miscellaneous Revenue Act of 1988 (P.L. 100-647)**

P.L. 100-647, §2001(b)(1):

Amended Code Sec. 4672(a)(2)(B) by inserting "(or more than 50 percent of the value)" after "more than 50 percent of the weight". **Effective** as if included in the provision of P.L. 99-499 to which it relates.

P.L. 100-647, §2001(b)(2):

Amended Code Sec. 4672(a)(2) by adding at the end thereof a new sentence. **Effective** as if included in the provision of P.L. 99-499 to which it relates.

P.L. 100-647, §2001(b)(3):

Amended Code Sec. 4672(a)(4). **Effective** as if included in the provision of P.L. 99-499 to which it relates. Prior to amendment, Code Sec. 4672(a)(4) read as follows:

(4) MODIFICATIONS TO LIST.—

(A) IN GENERAL.—The Secretary may add substances to or remove substances from the list under paragraph (3) (including items listed by reason of paragraph (2)) as necessary to carry out the purposes of this subchapter.

(B) AUTHORITY TO ADD SUBSTANCES TO LIST BASED ON VALUE.—The Secretary may, to the extent necessary to carry out the purposes of this subchapter, add any substance to the list under paragraph (3) if such substance would be described in paragraph (2)(B) if "value" were substituted for "weight" therein.

[Sec. 4672(b)]

(b) OTHER DEFINITIONS.—For purposes of this subchapter—

(1) IMPORTER.—The term "importer" means the person entering the taxable substance for consumption, use, or warehousing.

(2) TAXABLE CHEMICALS; UNITED STATES.—The terms "taxable chemical" and "United States" have the respective meanings given such terms by section 4662(a).

[Sec. 4672(c)]

(c) DISPOSITION OF REVENUES FROM PUERTO RICO AND THE VIRGIN ISLANDS.—The provisions of subsection (a)(3) and (b)(3) of section 7652 shall not apply to any tax imposed by section 4671.

Amendments

• **1986, Superfund Amendments and Reauthorization Act of 1986 (P.L. 99-499)**

P.L. 99-499, §515(a):

Amended chapter 38 of the Internal Revenue Code of 1986 by adding after subchapter B new subchapter C, containing new Code Sec. 4672. **Effective** 1-1-89.

EXCISE TAXES—HAZARDOUS WASTES

Subchapter C—Tax on Hazardous Wastes—[Repealed]

[Sec. 4681—Repealed]

Amendments

• **1986, Superfund Amendments and Reauthorization Act of 1986 (P.L. 99-499)**

P.L. 99-499, §514(a)(1):

Repealed subchapter C of chapter 38 of the Internal Revenue Code of 1986 (Code Secs. 4681-4682). **Effective** 10-1-83. However, see P.L. 96-510, Act Sec. 514(c)(2), below. Prior to repeal, Code Sec. 4681 read as follows:

SEC 4681. IMPOSITION OF TAX.

(a) GENERAL RULE.—There is hereby imposed a tax on the receipt of hazardous waste at a qualified hazardous waste disposal facility.

(b) AMOUNT OF TAX.—The amount of the tax imposed by subsection (a) shall be equal to $2.13 per dry weight ton of hazardous waste.

Amendments

• **1986, Superfund Amendments and Reauthorization Act of 1986 (P.L. 99-499)**

P.L. 99-499, §514(a)(1):

Repealed subchapter C of chapter 38 of the Internal Revenue Code of 1986 (Code Secs. 4681-4682). **Effective** 10-1-83. However, see P.L. 96-510, Act Sec. 514(c)(2), below. Prior to repeal, Code Sec. 4682 read as follows:

P.L. 96-510, §514(c)(2), provides:

(2) WAIVER OF STATUTE OF LIMITATIONS.—If on the date of the enactment of this Act (or at any time within 1 year after such date of enactment) refund or credit of any overpayment of tax resulting from the application of this section is barred by any law or rule of law, refund or credit of such overpayment shall, nevertheless, be made or allowed if claim therefor is filed before the date 1 year after the date of the enactment of this Act.

SEC. 4682. DEFINITIONS AND SPECIAL RULES.

(a) DEFINITIONS.—For purposes of this subchapter—

(1) HAZARDOUS WASTE.—The term "hazardous waste" means any waste—

(A) having the characteristics identified under section 3001 of the Solid Waste Disposal Act, as in effect on the date of the enactment of this Act (other than waste the regulation of which under such Act has been suspended by Act of Congress on that date), or

(B) subject to the reporting or recordkeeping requirements of sections 3002 and 3004 of such Act, as so in effect.

• **1980, Comprehensive Environmental Response, Compensation, and Liability Act of 1980 (P.L. 96-510)**

P.L. 96-510, §231(a):

Added Code Sec. 4681. **Effective** 12-11-80.

P.L. 96-510, §514(c)(2), provides:

(2) WAIVER OF STATUTE OF LIMITATIONS.—If on the date of the enactment of this Act (or at any time within 1 year after such date of enactment) refund or credit of any overpayment of tax resulting from the application of this section is barred by any law or rule of law, refund or credit of such overpayment shall, nevertheless, be made or allowed if claim therefor is filed before the date 1 year after the date of the enactment of this Act.

[Sec. 4682—Repealed]

(2) QUALIFIED HAZARDOUS WASTE DISPOSAL FACILITY.—The term "qualified hazardous waste disposal facility" means any facility which has received a permit or is accorded interim status under section 3005 of the Solid Waste Disposal Act.

(b) TAX IMPOSED ON OWNER OR OPERATOR.—The tax imposed by section 4681 shall be imposed on the owner or operator of the qualified hazardous waste disposal facility.

(c) TAX NOT TO APPLY TO CERTAIN WASTES.—The tax imposed by section 4681 shall not apply to any hazardous waste which will not remain at the qualified hazardous waste disposal facility after the facility is closed.

(d) APPLICABILITY OF SECTION.—The tax imposed by section 4681 shall apply to the receipt of hazardous waste after September 30, 1983, except that if, as of September 30 of any subsequent calendar year, the unobligated balance of the Post-closure Liability Trust Fund exceeds $200,000,000, no tax shall be imposed under such section during the following calendar year.

• **1980, Comprehensive Environmental Response, Compensation, and Liability Act of 1980 (P.L. 96-510)**

P.L. 96-510, §231(a):

Added Code Sec. 4682. **Effective** 12-11-80.

P.L. 96-510, §514(c)(2), provides:

(2) WAIVER OF STATUTE OF LIMITATIONS.—If on the date of the enactment of this Act (or at any time within 1 year after such date of enactment) refund or credit of any overpayment of tax resulting from the application of this section is barred by any law or rule of law, refund or credit of such overpayment shall, nevertheless, be made or allowed if claim therefor is filed before the date 1 year after the date of the enactment of this Act.

Subchapter D—Ozone Depleting Chemicals, Etc.

Sec. 4681. Imposition of tax.
Sec. 4682. Definitions and special rules.

[Sec. 4681]

SEC. 4681. IMPOSITION OF TAX.

[Sec. 4681(a)]

(a) GENERAL RULE.—There is hereby imposed a tax on—

(1) any ozone-depleting chemical sold or used by the manufacturer, producer, or importer thereof, and

(2) any imported taxable product sold or used by the importer thereof.

[Sec. 4681(b)]

(b) AMOUNT OF TAX.—

(1) OZONE-DEPLETING CHEMICALS.—

(A) IN GENERAL.—The amount of the tax imposed by subsection (a) on each pound of ozone-depleting chemical shall be an amount equal to—

(i) the base tax amount, multiplied by

(ii) the ozone-depletion factor for such chemical.

(B) BASE TAX AMOUNT.—The base tax amount for purposes of subparagraph (A) with respect to any sale or use during any calendar year after 1995 shall be $5.35 increased by 45 cents for each year after 1995.

(2) IMPORTED TAXABLE PRODUCT.—

(A) IN GENERAL.—The amount of the tax imposed by subsection (a) on any imported taxable product shall be the amount of tax which would have been imposed by subsection (a) on the ozone-depleting chemicals used as materials in the manufacture or production of such product if such ozone-depleting chemicals had been sold in the United States on the date of the sale of such imported taxable product.

(B) CERTAIN RULES TO APPLY.—Rules similar to the rules of paragraphs (2) and (3) of section 4671(b) shall apply.

Amendments

• **1997, Taxpayer Relief Act of 1997 (P.L. 105-34)**

P.L. 105-34, §1432(c)(1):

Amended Code Sec. 4681(b)(1) by striking subparagraphs (B) and (C) and inserting a new subparagraph (B). **Effective** 8-5-97. Prior to being stricken, Code Sec. 4681(b)(1)(B)-(C) read as follows:

(B) BASE TAX AMOUNT.—The base tax amount for purposes of subparagraph (A) with respect to any sale or use during a calendar year before 1996 with respect to any ozone-depleting chemical is the amount determined under the following table for such calendar year:

Calendar year:	Base tax amount:
1993	3.35
1994	4.35
1995	5.35

(C) BASE TAX AMOUNT FOR LATER YEARS.—The base tax amount for purposes of subparagraph (A) with respect to any sale or use of an ozone-depleting chemical

Sec. 4681—Repealed

EXCISE TAXES—OZONE DEPLETING CHEMICALS

during a calendar year after the last year specified in the table under subparagraph (B) applicable to such chemical shall be the base tax amount for such last year increased by 45 cents for each year after such last year.

- **1992, Energy Policy Act of 1992 (P.L. 102-486)**

P.L. 102-486, § 1931(a):

Amended Code Sec. 4681(b)(1)(B). **Effective** for taxable chemicals sold or used on or after 1-1-93. Prior to amendment, Code Sec. 4681(b)(1)(B) read as follows:

(B) BASE TAX AMOUNT.—

(i) INITIALLY LISTED CHEMICALS.—The base tax amount for purposes of subparagraph (A) with respect to any sale or use during a calendar year before 1995 with respect to any ozone-depleting chemical other than a newly listed chemical (as defined in section 4682(d)(3)(C)) is the amount determined under the following table for such calendar year:

Calendar Year	Base Tax Amount
1990 or 1991	$1.37
1992	1.67
1993 or 1994	2.65

(ii) NEWLY LISTED CHEMICALS.—The base tax amount for purposes of subparagraph (A) with respect to any sale or use during a calendar year before 1996 with respect to any ozone-depleting chemical which is a newly listed chemical (as so defined) is the amount determined under the following table for such calendar year:

Calendar Year	Base Tax Amount
1991 or 1992	$1.37
1993	1.67
1994	3.00
1995	3.10

- **1990, Omnibus Budget Reconciliation Act of 1990 (P.L. 101-508)**

P.L. 101-508, § 11203(c):

Amended Code Sec. 4681(b)(1)(B)-(C). **Effective** 1-1-91. Prior to amendment, Code Sec. 4681(b)(1)(B)-(C) read as follows:

(B) BASE TAX AMOUNT FOR YEARS BEFORE 1995.—The base tax amount for purposes of subparagraph (A) with respect to any sale or use during a calendar year before 1995 is the amount determined under the following table for such calendar year:

Calendar year	Base tax amount
1990 or 1991	$1.37
1992	1.67
1993 or 1994	2.65

(C) BASE TAX AMOUNT FOR YEARS AFTER 1994.—The base tax amount for purposes of subparagraph (A) with respect to any sale or use during a calendar year after 1994 shall be the base tax amount for 1994 increased by 45 cents for each year after 1994.

- **1989, Omnibus Budget Reconciliation Act of 1989 (P.L. 101-239)**

P.L. 101-239, § 7506(a):

Amended chapter 38 by adding at the end thereof a new subchapter D (Code Secs. 4681 and 4682). **Effective** 1-1-90. However, see Act Sec. 7506(c)(2), below, for a special rule.

P.L. 101-239, § 7506(c)(2), provides:

(2) NO DEPOSITS REQUIRED BEFORE APRIL 1, 1990.—No deposit of any tax imposed by subchapter D of chapter 38 of the Internal Revenue Code of 1986, as added by this section, shall be required to be made before April 1, 1990.

[Sec. 4682]

SEC. 4682. DEFINITIONS AND SPECIAL RULES.

[Sec. 4682(a)]

(a) OZONE-DEPLETING CHEMICAL.—For purposes of this subchapter—

(1) IN GENERAL.—The term "ozone-depleting chemical" means any substance—

(A) which, at the time of the sale or use by the manufacturer, producer, or importer, is listed as an ozone-depleting chemical in the table contained in paragraph (2), and

(B) which is manufactured or produced in the United States or entered into the United States for consumption, use, or warehousing.

(2) OZONE-DEPLETING CHEMICALS.—

Common name:	Chemical nomenclature:
CFC-11	trichlorofluoromethane
CFC-12	dichlorodifluoromethane
CFC-113	trichlorotrifluoroethane
CFC-114	1,2-dichloro-1,1,2,2-tetra-fluoroethane
CFC-115	chloropentafluoroethane
Halon-1211	bromochlorodifluoromethane
Halon-1301	bromotrifluoromethane
Halon-2402	dibromotetrafluoroethane
Carbon tetrachloride	tetrachloromethane
Methyl chloroform	1,1,1-trichloroethane
CFC-13	CF3C1
CFC-111	C2FC15
CFC-112	C2F2C14
CFC-211	C3FC17
CFC-212	C3F2C16
CFC-213	C3F3C15
CFC-214	C3F4C14
CFC-215	C3F5C13
CFC-216	C3F6C12
CFC-217	C3F7C1

Amendments

- **1990, Omnibus Budget Reconciliation Act of 1990 (P.L. 101-508)**

P.L. 101-508, § 11203(a)(1):

Amended the table set forth in Code Sec. 4682(a)(2) by striking the period after the last item of the table and by adding at the end thereof new items. **Effective** 1-1-91.

[Sec. 4682(b)]

(b) OZONE-DEPLETION FACTOR.—For purposes of this subchapter, the term "ozone-depletion factor" means, with respect to an ozone-depleting chemical, the factor assigned to such chemical under the following table:

EXCISE TAXES—OZONE DEPLETING CHEMICALS

Ozone-depleting chemical:	Ozone-depletion factor:
CFC-11	1.0
CFC-12	1.0
CFC-113	0.8
CFC-114	1.0
CFC-115	0.6
Halon-1211	3.0
Halon-1301	10.0
Halon-2402	6.0
Carbon tetrachloride	1.1
Methyl chloroform	0.1
CFC-13	1.0
CFC-111	1.0
CFC-112	1.0
CFC-211	1.0
CFC-212	1.0
CFC-213	1.0
CFC-214	1.0
CFC-215	1.0
CFC-216	1.0
CFC-217	1.0.

Amendments

• **1990, Omnibus Budget Reconciliation Act of 1990 (P.L. 101-508)**
P.L. 101-508, §11203(a)(2):
Amended the table set forth in Code Sec. 4682(b) by striking the period after the last item of the table and by adding at the end thereof new items. **Effective** 1-1-91.

[Sec. 4682(c)]

(c) IMPORTED TAXABLE PRODUCT.—For purposes of this subchapter—

(1) IN GENERAL.—The term "imported taxable product" means any product (other than an ozone-depleting chemical) entered into the United States for consumption, use, or warehousing if any ozone-depleting chemical was used as material in the manufacture or production of such product.

(2) DE MINIMIS EXCEPTION.—The term "imported taxable product" shall not include any product specified in regulations prescribed by the Secretary as using a de minimis amount of ozone-depleting chemicals as materials in the manufacture or production thereof. The preceding sentence shall not apply to any product in which any ozone-depleting chemical (other than methyl chloroform) is used for purposes of refrigeration or air conditioning, creating an aerosol or foam, or manufacturing electronic components.

Amendments

• **1990, Omnibus Budget Reconciliation Act of 1990 (P.L. 101-508)**
P.L. 101-508, §11203(d)(1):
Amended the last sentence of Code Sec. 4682(c)(2) by inserting "(other than methyl chloroform)" after "ozone-depleting chemical". **Effective** 1-1-91.

[Sec. 4682(d)]

(d) EXCEPTIONS.—

(1) RECYCLING.—No tax shall be imposed by section 4681 on any ozone-depleting chemical which is diverted or recovered in the United States as part of a recycling process (and not as part of the original manufacturing or production process), or on any recycled Halon-1301 or recycled Halon-2402 imported from any country which is a signatory to the Montreal Protocol on Substances that Deplete the Ozone Layer.

(2) USE IN FURTHER MANUFACTURE.—

(A) IN GENERAL.—No tax shall be imposed by section 4681—

(i) on the use of any ozone-depleting chemical in the manufacture or production of any other chemical if the ozone-depleting chemical is entirely consumed in such use,

(ii) on the sale by the manufacturer, producer, or importer of any ozone-depleting chemical—

(I) for a use by the purchaser which meets the requirements of clause (i), or

(II) for resale by the purchaser to a second purchaser for a use by the second purchaser which meets the requirements of clause (i).

Clause (ii) shall apply only if the manufacturer, producer, and importer, and the 1st and 2d purchasers (if any), meet such registration requirements as may be prescribed by the Secretary.

(B) CREDIT OR REFUND.—Under regulations prescribed by the Secretary, if—

(i) a tax under this subchapter was paid with respect to any ozone-depleting chemical, and

(ii) such chemical was used (and entirely consumed) by any person in the manufacture or production of any other chemical,

then an amount equal to the tax so paid shall be allowed as a credit or refund (without interest) to such person in the same manner as if it were an overpayment of tax imposed by section 4681.

(3) EXPORTS.—

(A) IN GENERAL.—Except as provided in subparagraph (B), rules similar to the rules of section 4662(e) (other than section 4662(e)(2)(A)(ii)(II)) shall apply for purposes of this subchapter.

(B) LIMIT ON BENEFIT.—

(i) IN GENERAL.—The aggregate tax benefit allowable under subparagraph (A) with respect to ozone-depleting chemicals manufactured, produced, or imported by any person during a calendar year shall not exceed the sum of—

(I) the amount equal to the 1986 export percentage of the aggregate tax which would (but for this subsection and subsection (g)) be imposed by this subchapter with respect to the maximum quantity of ozone-depleting chemicals permitted to be manufactured or produced by such person during such calendar year under regulations prescribed by the Environmental Protection Agency (other than chemicals with respect to which subclause (II) applies),

EXCISE TAXES—OZONE DEPLETING CHEMICALS

(II) the aggregate tax which would (but for this subsection and subsection (g)) be imposed by this subchapter with respect to any additional production allowance granted to such person with respect to ozone-depleting chemicals manufactured or produced by such person during such calendar year by the Environmental Protection Agency under 40 CFR Part 82 (as in effect on September 14, 1989), and

(III) the aggregate tax which was imposed by this subchapter with respect to ozone-depleting chemicals imported by such person during the calendar year.

(ii) 1986 EXPORT PERCENTAGE.—A person's 1986 export percentage is the percentage equal to the ozone-depletion factor adjusted pounds of ozone-depleting chemicals manufactured or produced by such person during 1986 which were exported during 1986, divided by the ozone-depletion factor adjusted pounds of all ozone-depleting chemicals manufactured or produced by such person during 1986. The percentage determined under the preceding sentence shall be computed by taking into account the sum of such person's direct 1986 exports (as determined by the Environmental Protection Agency) and such person's indirect 1986 exports (as allocated to such person by such Agency in determining such person's consumption and production rights for ozone-depleting chemicals).

(C) SEPARATE APPLICATION OF LIMIT FOR NEWLY LISTED CHEMICALS.—

(i) IN GENERAL.—Subparagraph (B) shall be applied separately with respect to newly listed chemicals and other chemicals.

(ii) APPLICATION TO NEWLY LISTED CHEMICALS.—In applying subparagraph (B) to newly listed chemicals—

(I) subparagraph (B) shall be applied by substituting "1989" for "1986" each place it appears, and

(II) clause (i)(II) thereof shall be applied by substituting for the regulations referred to therein any regulations (whether or not prescribed by the Secretary) which the Secretary determines are comparable to the regulations referred to in such clause with respect to newly listed chemicals.

(iii) NEWLY LISTED CHEMICAL.—For purposes of this subparagraph, the term "newly listed chemical" means any substance which appears in the table contained in subsection (a)(2) below Halon-2402.

Amendments

• **1997, Taxpayer Relief Act of 1997 (P.L. 105-34)**

P.L. 105-34, § 903(a):

Amended Code Sec. 4682(d)(1) by striking "recycled halon" and inserting "recycled Halon-1301 or recycled Halon-2402. **Effective** 8-5-97.

• **1996, Small Business Job Protection Act of 1996 (P.L. 104-188)**

P.L. 104-188, § 1803(a)(1):

Amended Code Sec. 4682(d)(1) by inserting ", or on any recycled halon imported from any country which is a signatory to the Montreal Protocol on Substances that Deplete the Ozone Layer" before the period at the end. **Effective**, generally, 1-1-97. For an exception, see Act Sec. 1803(c)(1)(B), below.

P.L. 104-188, § 1803(a)(2), provides:

(2) CERTIFICATION SYSTEM.—The Secretary of the Treasury, after consultation with the Administrator of the Environmental Protection Agency, shall develop a certification system to ensure compliance with the recycling requirement for imported halon under section 4682(d)(1) of the Internal Revenue Code of 1986, as amended by paragraph (1).

P.L. 104-188, § 1803(c)(1)(B), provides:

(B) HALON-1211.—In the case of Halon-1211, the amendment made by subsection (a)(1) shall take effect on January 1, 1998.

• **1990, Omnibus Budget Reconciliation Act of 1990 (P.L. 101-508)**

P.L. 101-508, § 11203(b):

Amended Code Sec. 4682(d)(3) by adding at the end thereof a new subparagraph (C). **Effective** 1-1-91.

P.L. 101-508, § 11701(g)(1):

Amended Code Sec. 4682(d)(3)(B)(i) by striking "or produced" in the material preceding subclause (I) and inserting ", produced, or imported". **Effective** as if included in the provision of P.L. 101-239 to which it relates.

P.L. 101-508, § 11701(g)(2):

Amended Code Sec. 4682(d)(3)(B)(i)(I). **Effective** as if included in the provision of P.L. 101-239 to which it relates. Prior to amendment, subclause (I) read as follows:

(I) the amount equal to the 1986 export percentage of the aggregate tax imposed by this subchapter with respect to ozone-depleting chemicals manufactured or produced by such person during such calendar year (other than chemicals with respect to which subclause (II) applies), and

P.L. 101-508, § 11701(g)(3):

Amended Code Sec. 4682(d)(3)(B)(i)(II) by striking "tax imposed" and inserting "tax which would (but for this subsection and subsection (g)) be imposed". **Effective** as if included in the provision of P.L. 101-239 to which it relates.

P.L. 101-508, § 11701(g)(4):

Amended Code Sec. 4682(d)(3)(B)(i) by striking the period at the end of subclause (II) and inserting ", and" and by adding at the end thereof a new subclause (III). **Effective** as if included in the provision of P.L. 101-239 to which it relates.

P.L. 101-508, § 11701(g)(5):

Amended Code Sec. 4682(d)(3)(B)(ii) by amending the last sentence. **Effective** as if included in the provision of P.L. 101-239 to which it relates. Prior to amendment, the sentence read as follows:

The percentage determined under the preceding sentence shall be based on data published by the Environmental Protection Agency.

[Sec. 4682(e)]

(e) OTHER DEFINITIONS.—For purposes of this subchapter—

(1) IMPORTER.—The term "importer" means the person entering the article for consumption, use, or warehousing.

(2) UNITED STATES.—The term "United States" has the meaning given such term by section 4612(a)(4).

[Sec. 4682(f)]

(f) SPECIAL RULES.—

(1) FRACTIONAL PARTS OF A POUND.—In the case of a fraction of a pound, the tax imposed by this subchapter shall be the same fraction of the amount of such tax imposed on a whole pound.

(2) DISPOSITION OF REVENUES FROM PUERTO RICO AND THE VIRGIN ISLANDS.—The provisions of subsections (a)(3) and (b)(3) of section 7652 shall not apply to any tax imposed by this subchapter.

[Sec. 4682(g)]

(g) CHEMICALS USED AS PROPELLANTS IN METERED-DOSE INHALERS.—

(1) EXEMPTION FROM TAX.—

(A) IN GENERAL.—No tax shall be imposed by section 4681 on—

(i) any use of any substance as a propellant in metered-dose inhalers, or

(ii) any qualified sale by the manufacturer, producer, or importer of any substance.

(B) QUALIFIED SALE.—For purposes of subparagraph (A), the term "qualified sale" means any sale by the manufacturer, producer, or importer of any substance—

(i) for use by the purchaser as a propellant in metered dose inhalers, or

(ii) for resale by the purchaser to a 2d purchaser for such use by the 2d purchaser.

The preceding sentence shall apply only if the manufacturer, producer, and importer, and the 1st and 2d purchasers (if any) meet such registration requirements as may be prescribed by the Secretary.

(2) OVERPAYMENTS.—If any substance on which tax was paid under this subchapter is used by any person as a propellant in metered-dose inhalers, credit or refund without interest shall be allowed to such person in an amount equal to the tax so paid. Amounts payable under the

EXCISE TAXES—OZONE DEPLETING CHEMICALS

preceding sentence with respect to uses during the taxable year shall be treated as described in section 34(a) for such year unless claim thereof has been timely filed under this paragraph.

Amendments

• **1997, Taxpayer Relief Act of 1997 (P.L. 105-34)**

P.L. 105-34, §1432(c)(2):

Amended Code Sec. 4682(g). **Effective** 8-5-97. Prior to amendment, Code Sec. 4682(g) read as follows:

(g) PHASE-IN OF TAX ON CERTAIN SUBSTANCES.—

(1) TREATMENT FOR 1990.—

(A) HALONS.—The term "ozone-depleting chemical" shall not include halon-1211, halon-1301, or halon-2402 with respect to any sale or use during 1990.

(B) CHEMICALS USED IN RIGID FOAM INSULATION.—No tax shall be imposed by section 4681—

(i) on the use during 1990 of any substance in the manufacture of rigid foam insulation,

(ii) on the sale during 1990 by the manufacturer, producer, or importer of any substance—

(I) for use by the purchaser in the manufacture of rigid foam insulation, or

(II) for resale by the purchaser to a second purchaser for such use by the second purchaser, or

(iii) on the sale or use during 1990 by the importer of any rigid foam insulation.

Clause (ii) shall apply only if the manufacturer, producer, and importer, and the 1st and 2d purchasers (if any) meet such registration requirements as may be prescribed by the Secretary.

(2) TREATMENT FOR 1991, 1992, AND 1993.—

(A) HALONS.—The tax imposed by section 4681 during 1991, 1992, or 1993 by reason of the treatment of halon-1211, halon-1301, and halon-2402 as ozone-depleting chemicals shall be the applicable percentage (determined under the following table) of the amount of such tax which would (but for this subparagraph) be imposed.

In the case of:	The applicable percentage in the case of sales or use during 1993 is:
Halon-1211	2.49
Halon-1301	0.75
Halon-2402	1.24

(B) CHEMICALS USED IN RIGID FOAM INSULATION.—In the case of a sale or use during 1991, 1992, or 1993 on which no tax would have been imposed by reason of paragraph (1)(B) had such sale or use occurred during 1990, the tax imposed by section 4681 shall be the applicable percentage (determined in accordance with the following table) of the amount of such tax which would (but for this subparagraph) be imposed.

In the case of sales or use during:	The applicable percentage is:
1991	18
1992	15
1993	7.46

(3) OVERPAYMENTS WITH RESPECT TO CHEMICALS USED IN RIGID FOAM INSULATION.—If any substance on which tax was paid under this subchapter is used during 1990, 1991, 1992, or 1993 by any person in the manufacture of rigid foam insulation, credit or refund (without interest) shall be allowed to such person an amount equal to the excess of—

(A) the tax paid under this subchapter on such substance, over

(B) the tax (if any) which would be imposed by section 4681 if such substance were used for such use by the manufacturer, producer, or importer thereof on the date of its use by such person.

Amounts payable under the preceding sentence with respect to uses during the taxable year shall be treated as described in section 34(a) for such year unless claim therefor has been timely filed under this paragraph.

(4) CHEMICALS USED AS PROPELLANTS IN METERED-DOSE INHALERS.—

(A) TAX-EXEMPT.—

(i) IN GENERAL.—No tax shall be imposed by section 4681 on—

(I) any use of any substance as a propellant in metered-dose inhalers, or

(II) any qualified sale by the manufacturer, producer, or importer of any substance.

(ii) QUALIFIED SALE.—For purposes of clause (i), the term "qualified sale" means any sale by the manufacturer, producer, or importer of any substance—

(I) for use by the purchaser as a propellant in metered-dose inhalers, or

(II) for resale by the purchaser to a 2d purchaser for such use by the 2d purchaser.

The preceding sentence shall apply only if the manufacturer, producer, and importer, and the 1st and 2d purchasers (if any) meet such registration requirements as may be prescribed by the Secretary.

(B) OVERPAYMENTS.—If any substance on which tax was paid under this subchapter is used by any person as a propellant in metered-dose inhalers, credit or refund without interest shall be allowed to such person in an amount equal to the tax so paid. Amounts payable under the preceding sentence with respect to uses during the taxable year shall be treated as described in section 34(a) for such year unless claim thereof has been timely filed under this subparagraph.

(5) TREATMENT OF METHYL CHLOROFORM.—The tax imposed by section 4681 during 1993 by reason of the treatment of methyl chloroform as an ozone-depleting chemical shall be 63.02 percent of the amount of such tax which would (but for this paragraph) be imposed.

• **1996, Small Business Job Protection Act of 1996 (P.L. 104-188)**

P.L. 104-188, §1803(b):

Amended Code Sec. 4682(g)(4). **Effective** on the 7th day after 8-20-96. Prior to amendment, Code Sec. 4682(g)(4) read as follows:

(4) CHEMICALS USED FOR STERILIZING MEDICAL INSTRUMENTS AND AS PROPELLANTS IN METERED-DOSE INHALERS.—

(A) RATE OF TAX.—

(i) IN GENERAL.—In the case of—

(I) any use during the applicable period of any substance to sterilize medical instruments or as propellants in metered-dose inhalers, or

(II) any qualified sale during such period by the manufacturer, producer, or importer of any substance,

the tax imposed by section 4681 shall be equal to $1.67 per pound.

(ii) QUALIFIED SALE.—For purposes of clause (i), the term "qualified sale" means any sale by the manufacturer, producer, or importer of any substance—

(I) for use by the purchaser to sterilize medical instruments or as propellants in metered-dose inhalers, or

(II) for resale by the purchaser to a 2d purchaser for such use by the 2d purchaser.

The preceding sentence shall apply only if the manufacturer, producer, and importer, and the 1st and 2d purchasers (if any) meet such registration requirements as may be prescribed by the Secretary.

(B) OVERPAYMENTS.—If any substance on which tax was paid under this subchapter is used during the applicable period by any person to sterilize medical instruments or as propellants in metered-dose inhalers, credit or refund without interest shall be allowed to such person in an amount equal to the excess of—

(i) the tax paid under this subchapter on such substance, or

(ii) the tax (if any) which would be imposed by section 4681 if such substance were used for such use by the manufacture[r], producer, or importer thereof on the date of its use by such person.

Amounts payable under the preceding sentence with respect to uses during the taxable year shall be treated as described in section 34(a) for such year unless claim thereof has been timely filed under this subparagraph.

(C) APPLICABLE PERIOD.—For purposes of this paragraph, the term "applicable period" means—

(i) 1993 in the case of substances to sterilize medical instruments, and

(ii) any period after 1992 in the case of propellants in metered-dose inhalers.

• **1992, Energy Policy Act of 1992 (P.L. 102-486)**

P.L. 102-486, §1931(b):

Amended Code Sec. 4682(g)(2)(B) by striking "10" and inserting "7.46". **Effective** for taxable chemicals sold or used on or after 1-1-93.

P.L. 102-486, §1932(a):

Amended Code Sec. 4682(g)(2)(A). **Effective** for sales and uses on or after 1-1-93. Prior to amendment, Code Sec. 4682(g)(2)(A) read as follows:

(A) HALONS.—The tax imposed by section 4681 during 1991, 1992, or 1993 by reason of the treatment of halon-1211, halon-1301, and halon-2402 as ozone-depleting chemicals shall be the applicable percentage (determined under the following table) of the amount of such tax which would (but for this subparagraph) be imposed.

	The applicable percentage is		
In the case of:	For sales or use during 1991	For sales or use during 1992	For sales or use during 1993
Halon-1211	6.0	5.0	3.3
Halon-1301	1.8	1.5	1.0
Halon-2402	3.0	2.5	1.6

P.L. 102-486, §1932(b):

Amended Code Sec. 4682(g) by adding at the end thereof new paragraph (4). **Effective** for sales and uses on or after 1-1-93.

P.L. 102-486, §1932(c):

Amended Code Sec. 4682(g) (as amended by this Act) by adding at the end thereof new paragraph (5). **Effective** for sales and uses on or after 1-1-93.

[Sec. 4682(h)]

(h) IMPOSITION OF FLOOR STOCKS TAXES.—

(1) IN GENERAL.—

(A) IN GENERAL.—If, on any tax-increase date, any ozone-depleting chemical is held by any person (other than the manufacturer, producer, or importer thereof) for sale or for use in further manufacture, there is hereby imposed a floor stocks tax.

EXCISE TAXES—REGISTRATION-REQUIRED OBLIGATIONS

(B) AMOUNT OF TAX.—The amount of the tax imposed by subparagraph (A) shall be the excess (if any) of—

(i) the tax which would be imposed under section 4681 on such substance if the sale of such chemical by the manufacturer, producer, or importer thereof had occurred on the tax-increase date, over

(ii) the prior tax (if any) imposed by this subchapter on such substance.

(C) TAX-INCREASE DATE.—For purposes of this paragraph, the term "tax-increase date" means January 1 of any calendar year.

(2) DUE DATE.—The taxes imposed by this subsection on January 1 of any calendar year shall be paid on or before June 30 of such year.

(3) APPLICATION OF OTHER LAWS.—All other provisions of law, including penalties, applicable with respect to the taxes imposed by section 4681 shall apply to the floor stocks taxes imposed by this subsection.

Amendments

• **2014, Tax Technical Corrections Act of 2014 (P.L. 113-295)**

P.L. 113-295, §221(a)(107)(A), Division A:

Amended Code Sec. 4682(h) by striking paragraph (1) and redesignating paragraphs (2), (3), and (4) as paragraphs (1), (2), and (3), respectively. **Effective** generally 12-19-2014. For a special rule, see Act Sec. 221(b)(2), Division A, below. Prior to being stricken, Code Sec. 4682(h)(1) read as follows:

(1) JANUARY 1, 1990, TAX.—On any ozone-depleting chemical which on January 1, 1990, is held by any person (other than the manufacturer, producer, or importer thereof) for sale or for use in further manufacture, there is hereby imposed a floor stocks tax in an amount equal to the tax which would be imposed by section 4681 on such chemical if the sale of such chemical by the manufacturer, producer, or importer thereof had occurred during 1990.

P.L. 113-295, §221(a)(107)(B), Division A:

Amended Code Sec. 4682(h) by striking the heading in paragraph (1) (as redesignated by Act Sec. 221(a)(107)(A)) and inserting "IN GENERAL", and by striking "after 1991" following "January 1 of any calendar year" in subparagraph (C). **Effective** generally 12-19-2014. For a special rule, see Act Sec. 221(b)(2), Division A, below. Prior to being stricken, the heading for Code Sec. 4682(h)(1) (as redesignated) read as follows:

OTHER TAX-INCREASE DATES.—

P.L. 113-295, §221(b)(2), Division A, provides:

(2) SAVINGS PROVISION.—If—

(A) any provision amended or repealed by the amendments made by this section applied to—

(i) any transaction occurring before the date of the enactment of this Act,

(ii) any property acquired before such date of enactment, or

(iii) any item of income, loss, deduction, or credit taken into account before such date of enactment, and

(B) the treatment of such transaction, property, or item under such provision would (without regard to the amendments or repeals made by this section) affect the liability for tax for periods ending after date of enactment, nothing in the amendments or repeals made by this section shall be construed to affect the treatment of such transaction, property, or item for purposes of determining liability for tax for periods ending after such date of enactment.

• **1992, Energy Policy Act of 1992 (P.L. 102-486)**

P.L. 102-486, §1931(c):

Amended Code Sec. 4682(h)(2)(C) by striking "of 1991, 1992, 1993, and 1994" and inserting "of any calendar year after 1991". **Effective** for taxable chemicals sold or used on or after 1-1-93.

• **1990, Omnibus Budget Reconciliation Act of 1990 (P.L. 101-508)**

P.L. 101-508, §11203(d)(2):

Amended Code Sec. 4682(h)(3) by striking "April 1" and inserting "June 30". **Effective** 1-1-91.

P.L. 101-508, §11203(f), provides:

No deposit of any tax imposed by subchapter D of chapter 38 of the Internal Revenue Code of 1986 on any substance treated as an ozone-depleting chemical by reason of the amendment made by subsection (a)(1) shall be required to be made before April 1, 1991.

• **1989, Omnibus Budget Reconciliation Act of 1989 (P.L. 101-239)**

P.L. 101-239, §7506(a):

Amended chapter 38 by adding a new section 4682. **Effective** 1-1-90. However, for a special rule see Act Sec. 7506(c)(2), below.

P.L. 101-239, §7506(c)(2), provides:

(2) NO DEPOSITS REQUIRED BEFORE APRIL 1, 1990.—No deposit of any tax imposed by subchapter D of chapter 38 of the Internal Revenue Code of 1986, as added by this section, shall be required to be made before April 1, 1990.

CHAPTER 39—REGISTRATION-REQUIRED OBLIGATIONS

Sec. 4701.   Tax on issuer of registration-required obligation not in registered form.

[Sec. 4701]

SEC. 4701. TAX ON ISSUER OF REGISTRATION-REQUIRED OBLIGATION NOT IN REGISTERED FORM.

[Sec. 4701(a)]

(a) IMPOSITION OF TAX.—In the case of any person who issues a registration-required obligation which is not in registered form, there is hereby imposed on such person on the issuance of such obligation a tax in an amount equal to the product of—

(1) 1 percent of the principal amount of such obligation, multiplied by

(2) the number of calendar years (or portions thereof) during the period beginning on the date of issuance of such obligation and ending on the date of maturity.

[Sec. 4701(b)]

(b) DEFINITIONS.—For purposes of this section—

(1) REGISTRATION-REQUIRED OBLIGATION.—

(A) IN GENERAL.—The term "registration-required obligation" has the same meaning as when used in section 163(f), except that such term shall not include any obligation which—

(i) is required to be registered under section 149(a), or

(ii) is described in subparagraph (B).

(B) CERTAIN OBLIGATIONS NOT INCLUDED.—An obligation is described in this subparagraph if—

(i) there are arrangements reasonably designed to ensure that such obligation will be sold (or resold in connection with the original issue) only to a person who is not a United States person,

(ii) interest on such obligation is payable only outside the United States and its possessions, and

(iii) on the face of such obligation there is a statement that any United States person who holds such obligation will be subject to limitations under the United States income tax laws.

(2) REGISTERED FORM.—The term "registered form" has the same meaning as when used in section 163(f).

Amendments

• **2010, Hiring Incentives to Restore Employment Act (P.L. 111-147)**

P.L. 111-147, §502(e):

Amended Code Sec. 4701(b)(1). **Effective** for obligations issued after the date which is 2 years after 3-18-2010. Prior to amendment, Code Sec. 4701(b)(1) read as follows:

(1) REGISTRATION-REQUIRED OBLIGATION.—The term "registration-required obligation" has the same meaning as when used in section 163(f), except that such term shall not include any obligation required to be registered under section 149(a).

• **1986, Tax Reform Act of 1986 (P.L. 99-514)**

P.L. 99-514, §1301(j)(5):

Amended Code Sec. 4701(b)(1) by striking out "section 103(j)" and inserting in lieu thereof "section 149(a)". **Effective** for bonds issued after 8-15-86. For special transitional rules, see Act Secs. 1312-1318, reproduced in the amendment notes for Code Sec. 103.

EXCISE TAXES—OCCUPATIONAL TAXES

- **1982, Tax Equity and Fiscal Responsibility Act of 1982 (P.L. 97-248)**

P.L. 97-248, § 310(b)(4)(A):

Added Code Sec. 4701. **Effective**, generally, for obligations issued after 12-31-82. However, the provisions of Code Sec. 4701 will not apply to any obligations issued after 12-31-82, on the exercise of a warrant or the conversion of a convertible obligation if such warrant or obligation was offered or sold outside the United States without registration under the Securities Act of 1933 and was issued before 8-10-82. A rule similar to this rule will also apply in the case of any regulations that are issued under Code Sec. 163(f)(2)(C), as added by P.L. 97-248, except that the date on which such regulations take effect will be substituted for "August 10, 1982."

CHAPTER 40—GENERAL PROVISIONS RELATING TO OCCUPATIONAL TAXES

Sec. 4901.	Payment of tax.
Sec. 4902.	Liability of partners.
Sec. 4903.	Liability in case of business in more than one location.
Sec. 4904.	Liability in case of different businesses of same ownership and location.
Sec. 4905.	Liability in case of death or change of location.
Sec. 4906.	Application of state laws.
Sec. 4907.	Federal agencies or instrumentalities.

[Sec. 4901]

SEC. 4901. PAYMENT OF TAX.

[Sec. 4901(a)]

(a) CONDITION PRECEDENT TO CARRYING ON CERTAIN BUSINESS.—No person shall be engaged in or carry on any trade or business subject to the tax imposed by section 4411 (wagering) until he has paid the special tax therefor.

Amendments

- **1978, Revenue Act of 1978 (P.L. 95-600)**

P.L. 95-600, § 521(c)(2):

Amended Code Sec. 4901(a) by striking "or 4461(a)(1) (coin-operated gaming devices)" after "section 4411 (wagering)". **Effective** with respect to years beginning after 6-30-80.

- **1970 (P.L. 91-513)**

P.L. 91-513, § 1102(a):

Amended Code Sec. 4901(a) by adding "or" after "(wagering)" and by deleting ", 4721 (narcotic drugs), or 4751 (marihuana)" which previously followed "coin-operated gaming devices)". **Effective** 5-1-71.

- **1965, Excise Tax Reduction Act of 1965 (P.L. 89-44)**

P.L. 89-44, § 405(b):

Amended subsection (a) of Section 4901 by inserting "4461(a)(1)" in lieu of "4461(2)". **Effective** 7-1-65.

[Sec. 4901(b)]

(b) COMPUTATION.—All special taxes shall be imposed as of on the first day of July in each year, or on commencing any trade or business on which such tax is imposed. In the former case the tax shall be reckoned for 1 year, and in the latter case it shall be reckoned proportionately, from the first day of the month in which the liability to a special tax commenced, to and including the 30th day of June following.

[Sec. 4901(c)—Repealed]

Amendments

- **1976, Tax Reform Act of 1976 (P.L. 94-455)**

P.L. 94-455, § 1904(a)(19):

Struck out Code Sec. 4901(c). **Effective** 2-1-77. Prior to being stricken, Code Sec. 4901(c) read as follows:

(c) HOW PAID.—

(1) STAMP.—All special taxes imposed by law shall be paid by stamps denoting the tax.

(2) ASSESSMENT.—

For authority of the Secretary or his delegate to make assessments where the special taxes have not been duly paid by stamp at the time and in the manner provided by law, see subtitle F.

[Sec. 4902]

SEC. 4902. LIABILITY OF PARTNERS.

Any number of persons doing business in copartnership at any one place shall be required to pay but one special tax.

[Sec. 4903]

SEC. 4903. LIABILITY IN CASE OF BUSINESS IN MORE THAN ONE LOCATION.

The payment of the special tax imposed, other than the tax imposed by section 4411, shall not exempt from an additional special tax the person carrying on a trade or business in any other place than that stated in the register kept in the office of the official in charge of the internal revenue district; but nothing herein contained shall require a special tax for the storage of goods, wares, or merchandise in other places than the place of business, nor, except as provided in this subtitle, for the sale by manufacturers or producers of their own goods, wares, and merchandise, at the place of production or manufacture, and at their principal office or place of business, provided no goods, wares, or merchandise shall be kept except as samples at said office or place of business.

[Sec. 4904]

SEC. 4904. LIABILITY IN CASE OF DIFFERENT BUSINESSES OF SAME OWNERSHIP AND LOCATION.

Whenever more than one of the pursuits or occupations described in this subtitle are carried on in the same place by the same person at the same time, except as otherwise provided in this subtitle, the tax shall be paid for each according to the rates severally prescribed.

[Sec. 4905]

SEC. 4905. LIABILITY IN CASE OF DEATH OR CHANGE OF LOCATION.

[Sec. 4905(a)]

(a) REQUIREMENTS.—When any person who has paid the special tax for any trade or business dies, his spouse or child, or executors or administrators or other legal representatives, may occupy the house or premises, and in like manner carry on, for the residue of the term for which the tax is paid, the same trade or business as the deceased before carried on, in the same house and upon the same premises, without the payment of any additional tax. When any person removes from the house or premises for which any trade or business was taxed to any other place, he may carry on the trade or business specified in the register kept in the office of the official in charge of the internal revenue district at the place to which he removes, without the payment of any additional tax: *Provided*, That all cases of death, change, or removal, as aforesaid, with the name of the successor to any person deceased, or of the person making such change or removal, shall be registered with the Secretary, under regulations to be prescribed by the Secretary.

Amendments

• **1976, Tax Reform Act of 1976 (P.L. 94-455)**

P.L. 94-455, §1904(a)(20):

Substituted "spouse" for "wife" in Code Sec. 4905(a). **Effective** 2-1-77.

[Sec. 4905(b)]

(b) REGISTRATION.—For registration in case of wagering, see section 4412.

Amendments

• **1976, Tax Reform Act of 1976 (P.L. 94-455)**

P.L. 94-455, §1904(b)(8)(A):

Amended Code Sec. 4905(b). **Effective** 2-1-77. Prior to amendment, Code Sec. 4905(b) read as follows:

(b) REGISTRATION.—(1) For registration in case of wagering and white phosphorus matches, see sections 4412 and 4804(d), respectively.

(2) For other provisions relating to registration, see subtitle F.

P.L. 94-455, §1906(b)(13)(A):

Amended 1954 Code by substituting "Secretary" for "Secretary or his delegate" each place it appeared. **Effective** 2-1-77.

• **1970 (P.L. 91-513)**

P.L. 91-513, §1102(b):

Amended Code Sec. 4905(b)(1) by deleting ", narcotics, marihuana," after "wagering" and by deleting ", 4722, 4753," after "4412". **Effective** 5-1-71.

• **1965, Excise Tax Reduction Act of 1965 (P.L. 89-44)**

P.L. 89-44, §405(c):

Amended subsection (b)(1) of Section 4905 by deleting "playing cards," after "wagering," and by deleting "4455," after "4412,". **Effective** 6-22-65.

[Sec. 4906]

SEC. 4906. APPLICATION OF STATE LAWS.

The payment of any special tax imposed by this subtitle for carrying on any trade or business shall not be held to exempt any person from any penalty or punishment provided by the laws of any State for carrying on the same within such State, or in any manner to authorize the commencement or continuance of such trade or business contrary to the laws of such State or in places prohibited by municipal law; nor shall the payment of any such tax be held to prohibit any State from placing a duty or tax on the same trade or business, for State or other purposes.

[Sec. 4907]

SEC. 4907. FEDERAL AGENCIES OR INSTRUMENTALITIES.

Any special tax imposed by this subtitle, except the tax imposed by section 4411, shall apply to any agency or instrumentality of the United States unless such agency or instrumentality is granted by statute a specific exemption from such tax.

CHAPTER 41—PUBLIC CHARITIES

Sec. 4911.   Tax on excess expenditures to influence legislation.
Sec. 4912.   Tax on disqualifying lobbying expenditures of certain organizations.

[Sec. 4911]

SEC. 4911. TAX ON EXCESS EXPENDITURES TO INFLUENCE LEGISLATION.

[Sec. 4911(a)]

(a) TAX IMPOSED.—

(1) IN GENERAL.—There is hereby imposed on the excess lobbying expenditures of any organization to which this section applies a tax equal to 25 percent of the amount of the excess lobbying expenditures for the taxable year.

(2) ORGANIZATIONS TO WHICH THIS SECTION APPLIES.—This section applies to any organization with respect to which an election under section 501(h)[(i)] (relating to lobbying expenditures by public charities) is in effect for the taxable year.

[Sec. 4911(b)]

(b) EXCESS LOBBYING EXPENDITURES.—For purposes of this section, the term "excess lobbying expenditures" means, for a taxable year, the greater of—

(1) the amount by which the lobbying expenditures made by the organization during the taxable year exceed the lobbying nontaxable amount for such organization for such taxable year, or

(2) the amount by which the grass roots expenditures made by the organization during the taxable year exceed the grass roots nontaxable amount for such organization for such taxable year.

[Sec. 4911(c)]

(c) DEFINITIONS.—For purposes of this section—

(1) LOBBYING EXPENDITURES.—The term "lobbying expenditures" means expenditures for the purpose of influencing legislation (as defined in subsection (d)).

(2) LOBBYING NONTAXABLE AMOUNT.—The lobbying nontaxable amount for any organization for any taxable year is the lesser of (A) $1,000,000 or (B) the amount determined under the following table:

If the exempt purpose expenditures are—	The lobbying nontaxable amount is—
Not over $500,000	20 percent of the exempt purpose expenditures.
Over $500,000 but not over $1,000,000	$100,000 plus 15 percent of the excess of the exempt purpose expenditures over $500,000.
Over $1,000,000 but not over $1,500,000	$175,000 plus 10 percent of the excess of the exempt purpose expenditures over $1,000,000.
Over $1,500,000	$225,000 plus 5 percent of the excess of the exempt purpose expenditures over $1,500,000.

(3) GRASS ROOTS EXPENDITURES.—The term "grass roots expenditures" means expenditures for the purpose of influencing legislation (as defined in subsection (d) without regard to paragraph (1)(B) thereof).

(4) GRASS ROOTS NONTAXABLE AMOUNT.—The grass roots nontaxable amount for any organization for any taxable year is 25 percent of the lobbying nontaxable amount (determined under paragraph (2)) for such organization for such taxable year.

EXCISE TAXES—PUBLIC CHARITIES

Amendments

- 1978, Revenue Act of 1978 (P.L. 95-600)

P.L. 95-600, § 703(g)(1):

Amended Code Sec. 4911(c)(2) by striking out "proposed expenditures" in the heading of the table contained in this paragraph and inserting in place thereof "exempt purpose expenditures". **Effective** as if included in the provision of P.L. 94-568 to which it relates [**effective** 10-22-76.—CCH].

[Sec. 4911(d)]

(d) INFLUENCING LEGISLATION.—

(1) GENERAL RULE.—Except as otherwise provided in paragraph (2), for purposes of this section, the term "influencing legislation" means—

(A) any attempt to influence any legislation through an attempt to affect the opinions of the general public or any segment thereof, and

(B) any attempt to influence any legislation through communication with any member or employee of a legislative body, or with any government official or employee who may participate in the formulation of the legislation.

(2) EXCEPTIONS.—For purposes of this section, the term "influencing legislation", with respect to an organization, does not include—

(A) making available the results of nonpartisan analysis, study, or research;

(B) providing of technical advice or assistance (where such advice would otherwise constitute the influencing of legislation) to a governmental body or to a committee or other subdivision thereof in response to a written request by such body or subdivision, as the case may be;

(C) appearances before, or communications to, any legislative body with respect to a possible decision of such body which might affect the existence of the organization, its powers and duties, tax-exempt status, or the deduction of contributions to the organization;

(D) communications between the organization and its bona fide members with respect to legislation or proposed legislation of direct interest to the organization and such members, other than communications described in paragraph (3); and

(E) any communication with a government official or employee, other than—

(i) a communication with a member or employee of a legislative body (where such communication would otherwise constitute the influencing of legislation), or

(ii) a communication the principal purpose of which is to influence legislation.

(3) COMMUNICATIONS WITH MEMBERS.—

(A) A communication between an organization and any bona fide member of such organization to directly encourage such member to communicate as provided in paragraph (1)(B) shall be treated as a communication described in paragraph (1)(B).

(B) A communication between an organization and any bona fide member of such organization to directly encourage such member to urge persons other than members to communicate as provided in either subparagraph (A) or subparagraph (B) of paragraph (1) shall be treated as a communication described in paragraph (1)(A).

[Sec. 4911(e)]

(e) OTHER DEFINITIONS AND SPECIAL RULES.—For purposes of this section—

(1) EXEMPT PURPOSE EXPENDITURES.—

(A) IN GENERAL.—The term "exempt purpose expenditures" means, with respect to any organization for any taxable year, the total of the amounts paid or incurred by such organization to accomplish purposes described in section 170(c)(2)(B) (relating to religious, charitable, educational, etc., purposes).

(B) CERTAIN AMOUNTS INCLUDED.—The term "exempt purpose expenditures" includes—

(i) administrative expenses paid or incurred for purposes described in section 170(c)(2)(B), and

(ii) amounts paid or incurred for the purpose of influencing legislation (whether or not for purposes described in section 170(c)(2)(B)).

(C) CERTAIN AMOUNTS EXCLUDED.—The term "exempt purpose expenditures" does not include amounts paid or incurred to or for—

(i) a separate fundraising unit of such organization, or

(ii) one or more other organizations, if such amounts are paid or incurred primarily for fundraising.

(2) LEGISLATION.—The term "legislation" includes action with respect to Acts, bills, resolutions, or similar items by the Congress, any State legislature, any local council, or similar governing body, or by the public in a referendum, initiative, constitutional amendment, or similar procedure.

(3) ACTION.—The term "action" is limited to the introduction, amendment, enactment, defeat, or repeal of Acts, bills, resolutions, or similar items.

(4) DEPRECIATION, ETC., TREATED AS EXPENDITURES.—In computing expenditures paid or incurred for the purpose of influencing legislation (within the meaning of subsection (b)(1) or (b)(2)) or exempt purpose expenditures (as defined in paragraph (1)), amounts properly chargeable to capital account shall not be taken into account. There shall be taken into account a reasonable allowance for exhaustion, wear and tear, obsolescence, or amortization. Such allowance shall be computed only on the basis of the straight-line method of depreciation. For purposes of this section, a determination of whether an amount is properly chargeable to capital account shall be made on the basis of the principles that apply under subtitle A to amounts which are paid or incurred in a trade or business.

[Sec. 4911(f)]

(f) AFFILIATED ORGANIZATIONS.—

(1) IN GENERAL.—Except as otherwise provided in paragraph (4), if for a taxable year two or more organizations described in section 501(c)(3) are members of an affiliated group of organizations as defined in paragraph (2), and an election under section 501(h) is effective for at least one such organization for such year, then—

(A) the determination as to whether excess lobbying expenditures have been made and the determination as to whether the expenditure limits of section 501(h)(1) have been exceeded shall be made as though such affiliated group is one organization,

(B) if such group has excess lobbying expenditures, each such organization as to which an election under section 501(h) is effective for such year shall be treated as an organization which has excess lobbying expenditures in an amount which equals such organization's proportionate share of such group's excess lobbying expenditures,

(C) if the expenditure limits of section 501(h)(1) are exceeded, each such organization as to which an election under section 501(h) is effective for such year shall be treated as an organization which is not described in section 501(c)(3) by reason of the application of 501(h), and

(D) subparagraphs (C) and (D) of subsection (d)(2), paragraph (3) of subsection (d), and clause (i) of subsection (e)(1)(C) shall be applied as if such affiliated group were one organization.

EXCISE TAXES—PUBLIC CHARITIES

(2) DEFINITION OF AFFILIATION.—For purposes of paragraph (1), two organizations are members of an affiliated group of organizations but only if—

(A) the governing instrument of one such organization requires it to be bound by decisions of the other organization on legislative issues, or

(B) the governing board of one such organization includes persons who—

(i) are specifically designated representatives of another such organization or are members of the governing board, officers, or paid executive staff members of such other organization, and

(ii) by aggregating their votes, have sufficient voting power to cause or prevent action on legislative issues by the first such organization.

(3) DIFFERENT TAXABLE YEARS.—If members of an affiliated group of organizations have different taxable years, their expenditures shall be computed for purposes of this section in a manner to be prescribed by regulations promulgated by the Secretary.

(4) LIMITED CONTROL.—If two or more organizations are members of an affiliated group of organizations (as defined in paragraph (2) without regard to subparagraph (B) thereof), no two members of such affiliated group are affiliated (as defined in paragraph (2) without regard to subparagraph (A) thereof), and the governing instrument of no such organization requires it to be bound by decisions of any of the other such organizations on legislative issues other than as to action with respect to Acts, bills, resolutions, or similar items by the Congress, then—

(A) in the case of any organization whose decisions bind one or more members of such affiliated group, directly or indirectly, the determination as to whether such organization has paid or incurred excess lobbying expenditures and the determination as to whether such organization has exceeded the expenditure limits of section 501(h)(1) shall be made as though such organization has paid or incurred those amounts paid or incurred by such members of such affiliated group to influence legislation with respect to Acts, bills, resolutions, or similar items by the Congress, and

(B) in the case of any organization to which subparagraph (A) does not apply, but which is a member of such affiliated group, the determination as to whether such organization has paid or incurred excess lobbying expenditures and the determination as to whether such organization has exceeded the expenditure limits of section 501(h)(1) shall be made as though such organization is not a member of such affiliated group.

Amendments

• 1976, Tax Reform Act of 1976 (P.L. 94-455)

P.L. 94-455, §1307(b):

Added a new Chapter 41, which includes Code Sec. 4911. **Effective** for tax years beginning after 12-31-76.

[Sec. 4912]

SEC. 4912. TAX ON DISQUALIFYING LOBBYING EXPENDITURES OF CERTAIN ORGANIZATIONS.

[Sec. 4912(a)]

(a) TAX ON ORGANIZATION.—If an organization to which this section applies is not described in section 501(c)(3) for any taxable year by reason of making lobbying expenditures, there is hereby imposed a tax on the lobbying expenditures of such organization for such taxable year equal to 5 percent of the amount of such expenditures. The tax imposed by this subsection shall be paid by the organization.

[Sec. 4912(b)]

(b) ON MANAGEMENT.—If tax is imposed under subsection (a) on the lobbying expenditures of any organization, there is hereby imposed on the agreement of any organization manager to the making of any such expenditures, knowing that such expenditures are likely to result in the organization not being described in section 501(c)(3), a tax equal to 5 percent of the amount of such expenditures, unless such agreement is not willful and is due to reasonable cause. The tax imposed by this subsection shall be paid by any manager who agreed to the making of the expenditures.

[Sec. 4912(c)]

(c) ORGANIZATIONS TO WHICH SECTION APPLIES.—

(1) IN GENERAL.—Except as provided in paragraph (2), this section shall apply to any organization which was exempt (or was determined by the Secretary to be exempt) from taxation under section 501(a) by reason of being an organization described in section 501(c)(3).

(2) EXCEPTIONS.—This section shall not apply to any organization—

(A) to which an election under section 501(h) applies,

(B) which is a disqualified organization (within the meaning of section 501(h)(5)), or

(C) which is a private foundation.

[Sec. 4912(d)]

(d) DEFINITIONS.—

(1) LOBBYING EXPENDITURES.—The term "lobbying expenditure" means any amount paid or incurred by the organization in carrying on propaganda, or otherwise attempting to influence legislation.

(2) ORGANIZATION MANAGER.—The term "organization manager" has the meaning given to such term by section 4955(f)(2).

(3) JOINT AND SEVERAL LIABILITY.—If more than 1 person is liable under subsection (b), all such persons shall be jointly and severally liable under such subsection.

Amendments

• 1981, Economic Recovery Tax Act of 1981 (P.L. 97-34)

P.L. 100-203, §10714(a):

Amended chapter 41 by adding at the end thereof a new section 4912. **Effective** for tax years beginning after 12-22-87.

CHAPTER 42—PRIVATE FOUNDATIONS AND CERTAIN OTHER TAX-EXEMPT ORGANIZATIONS

SUBCHAPTER A.	Private foundations.
SUBCHAPTER B.	Black lung benefit trusts.
SUBCHAPTER C.	Political expenditures of section 501(c)(3) organizations.
SUBCHAPTER D.	Failure by certain charitable organizations to meet certain qualification requirements.

EXCISE TAXES—PRIVATE FOUNDATIONS

Subchapter E.	Abatement of first and second tier taxes in certain cases.
Subchapter F.	Tax shelter transactions.
Subchapter G.	Donor advised funds.
Subchapter H.	Excise tax based on investment income of private colleges and universities.

Subchapter A—Private Foundations

Sec. 4940.	Excise tax based on investment income.
Sec. 4941.	Taxes on self-dealing.
Sec. 4942.	Taxes on failure to distribute income.
Sec. 4943.	Taxes on excess business holdings.
Sec. 4944.	Taxes on investments which jeopardize charitable purpose.
Sec. 4945.	Taxes on taxable expenditures.
Sec. 4946.	Definitions and special rules.
Sec. 4947.	Application of taxes to certain nonexempt trusts.
Sec. 4948.	Application of taxes and denial of exemption with respect to certain foreign organizations.

[Sec. 4940]

SEC. 4940. EXCISE TAX BASED ON INVESTMENT INCOME.

[Sec. 4940(a)]

(a) Tax-Exempt Foundations.—There is hereby imposed on each private foundation which is exempt from taxation under section 501(a) for the taxable year, with respect to the carrying on of its activities, a tax equal to 1.39 percent of the net investment income of such foundation for the taxable year.

Amendments

• **2019, Taxpayer Certainty and Disaster Tax Relief Act of 2019 (P.L. 116-94)**

P.L. 116-94, § 206(a), Div. Q:

Amended Code Sec. 4940(a) by striking "2 percent" and inserting "1.39 percent". **Effective** for tax years beginning after 12-20-2019.

• **1978, Revenue Act of 1978 (P.L. 95-600)**

P.L. 95-600, § 520(a):

Amended Code Sec. 4940(a) by changing "4 percent" to "2 percent". **Effective** for tax years beginning after 9-30-77.

[Sec. 4940(b)]

(b) Taxable Foundations.—There is hereby imposed on each private foundation which is not exempt from taxation under section 501(a) for the taxable year, with respect to the carrying on of its activities, a tax equal to—

(1) the amount (if any) by which the sum of (A) the tax imposed under subsection (a) (computed as if such subsection applied to such private foundation for the taxable year), plus (B) the amount of the tax which would have been imposed under section 511 for the taxable year if such private foundation had been exempt from taxation under section 501(a), exceeds

(2) the tax imposed under subtitle A on such private foundation for the taxable year.

[Sec. 4940(c)]

(c) Net Investment Income Defined.—

(1) In general.—For purposes of subsection (a), the net investment income is the amount by which (A) the sum of the gross investment income and the capital gain net income exceeds (B) the deductions allowed by paragraph (3). Except to the extent inconsistent with the provisions of this section, net investment income shall be determined under the principles of subtitle A.

(2) Gross investment income.—For purposes of paragraph (1), the term "gross investment income" means the gross amount of income from interest, dividends, rents, payments with respect to securities loans (as defined in section 512(a)(5)), and royalties, but not including any such income to the extent included in computing the tax imposed by section 511. Such term shall also include income from sources similar to those in the preceding sentence.

(3) Deductions.—

(A) In general.—For purposes of paragraph (1), there shall be allowed as a deduction all the ordinary and necessary expenses paid or incurred for the production or collection of gross investment income or for the management, conservation, or maintenance of property held for the production of such income, determined with the modifications set forth in subparagraph (B).

(B) Modifications.—For purposes of subparagraph (A)—

(i) The deduction provided by section 167 shall be allowed, but only on the basis of the straight line method of depreciation.

(ii) The deduction for depletion provided by section 611 shall be allowed, but such deduction shall be determined without regard to section 613 (relating to percentage depletion).

(4) Capital gains and losses.—For purposes of paragraph (1) in determining capital gain net income—

(A) There shall not be taken into account any gain or loss from the sale or other disposition of property to the extent that such gain or loss is taken into account for purposes of computing the tax imposed by section 511.

(B) The basis for determining gain in the case of property held by the private foundation on December 31, 1969, and continuously thereafter to the date of its disposition shall be deemed to be not less than the fair market value of such property on December 31, 1969.

(C) Losses from sales or other dispositions of property shall be allowed only to the extent of gains from such sales or other dispositions, and there shall be no capital loss carryovers or carrybacks.

(D) Except to the extent provided by regulation, under rules similar to the rules of section 1031 (including the exception under subsection (a)(2) thereof), no gain or loss shall be taken into account with respect to any portion of property used for a period of not less than 1 year for a purpose or function constituting the basis of the private foundation's exemption if the entire property is exchanged immediately following such period solely for property of like kind which is to be used primarily for a purpose or function constituting the basis for such foundation's exemption.

(5) Tax-exempt income.—For purposes of this section, net investment income shall be determined by applying section 103 (relating to State and local bonds) and section 265 (relating to expenses and interest relating to tax-exempt income).

EXCISE TAXES—PRIVATE FOUNDATIONS

Amendments

• **2007, Tax Technical Corrections Act of 2007 (P.L. 110-172)**

P.L. 110-172, §3(f):

Amended Code Sec. 4940(c)(4)(A). **Effective** as if included in the provision of the Pension Protection Act of 2006 (P.L. 109-280) to which it relates [**effective** for tax years beginning after 8-17-2006.—CCH]. Prior to amendment, Code Sec. 4940(c)(4)(A) read as follows:

(A) There shall be taken into account only gains and losses from the sale or other disposition of property used for the production of gross investment income (as defined in paragraph (2)), and property used for the production of income included in computing the tax imposed by section 511 (except to the extent gain or loss from the sale or other disposition of such property is taken into account for purposes of such tax).

• **2006, Pension Protection Act of 2006 (P.L. 109-280)**

P.L. 109-280, §1221(a)(1):

Amended Code Sec. 4940(c)(2) by adding at the end a new sentence. **Effective** for tax years beginning after 8-17-2006.

P.L. 109-280, §1221(b)(1)-(3):

Amended Code Sec. 4940(c)(4) by striking "used for the production of interest, dividends, rents, and royalties" and inserting "used for the production of gross investment income (as defined in paragraph (2))" in subparagraph (A), by inserting "or carrybacks" after "carryovers" in subparagraph (C), and by adding at the end a new subparagraph (D). **Effective** for tax years beginning after 8-17-2006.

• **1986, Tax Reform Act of 1986 (P.L. 99-514)**

P.L. 99-514, §1301(j)(6):

Amended Code Sec. 4940(c)(5) by striking out "(relating to interest on certain governmental obligations)" and inserting in lieu thereof "(relating to State and local bonds)". **Effective**, generally, for bonds issued after 8-15-86.

• **1978 (P.L. 95-345)**

P.L. 95-345, §2(a)(4):

Amended Code Sec. 4940(c)(2) by adding "payments with respect to securities loans (as defined in section 512(a)(5))," after "rents". **Effective** with respect to (1) amounts received after 12-31-76 as payments with respect to securities loans (as defined in Code Sec. 512(a)(5), and (2) transfers of securities under agreements described in Code Sec. 1058 occurring after such date.

• **1976, Tax Reform Act of 1976 (P.L. 94-455)**

P.L. 94-455, §1901(b)(33)(N):

Substituted "capital gain net income" for "net capital gain" in Code Secs. 4940(c)(1) and 4940(c)(4). **Effective** for tax years beginning after 12-31-76.

• **1969, Tax Reform Act of 1969 (P.L. 91-172)**

P.L. 91-172, §101(b):

Added Code Sec. 4940. **Effective** for tax years beginning after 12-31-69.

P.L. 91-172, §101(l)(8), provides:

(8) Certain redemptions.—For purposes of applying section 302(b)(1) to the determination of the amount of gross investment income under sections 4940 and 4948(a), any distribution made to a private foundation in redemption of stock held by such private foundation in a business enterprise shall be treated as not essentially equivalent to a dividend, if such redemption is described in paragraph (2)(B) of this subsection.

[Sec. 4940(d)]

(d) EXEMPTION FOR CERTAIN OPERATING FOUNDATIONS.—

(1) IN GENERAL.—No tax shall be imposed by this section on any private foundation which is an exempt operating foundation for the taxable year.

(2) EXEMPT OPERATING FOUNDATION.—For purposes of this subsection, the term "exempt operating foundation" means, with respect to any taxable year, any private foundation if—

(A) such foundation is an operating foundation (as defined in section 4942(j)(3)),

(B) such foundation has been publicly supported for at least 10 taxable years,

(C) at all times during the taxable year, the governing body of such foundation—

(i) consists of individuals at least 75 percent of whom are not disqualified individuals, and

(ii) is broadly representative of the general public, and

(D) at no time during the taxable year does such foundation have an officer who is a disqualified individual.

(3) DEFINITIONS.—For purposes of this subsection—

(A) PUBLICLY SUPPORTED.—A private foundation is publicly supported for a taxable year if it meets the requirements of section 170(b)(1)(A)(vi) or 509(a)(2) for such taxable year.

(B) DISQUALIFIED INDIVIDUAL.—The term "disqualified individual" means, with respect to any private foundation, an individual who is—

(i) a substantial contributor to the foundation,

(ii) an owner of more than 20 percent of—

(I) the total combined voting power of a corporation,

(II) the profits interest of a partnership, or

(III) the beneficial interest of a trust or unincorporated enterprise,

which is a substantial contributor to the foundation, or

(iii) a member of the family of any individual described in clause (i) or (ii).

(C) SUBSTANTIAL CONTRIBUTOR.—The term "substantial contributor" means a person who is described in section 507(d)(2).

(D) FAMILY.—The term "family" has the meaning given to such term by section 4946(d).

(E) CONSTRUCTIVE OWNERSHIP.—The rules of paragraphs (3) and (4) of section 4946(a) shall apply for purposes of subparagraph (B)(ii).

Amendments

• **1988, Technical and Miscellaneous Revenue Act of 1988 (P.L. 100-647)**

P.L. 100-647, §6204, provides:

For purposes of section 302(c)(3) of the Deficit Reduction Act of 1984 [P.L. 98-369], a private foundation which constituted an operating foundation (as defined in section 4942(j)(3) of the Internal Revenue Code of 1986) for its last taxable year ending before January 1, 1983, shall be treated as constituting an operating foundation as of January 1, 1983.

• **1984, Deficit Reduction Act of 1984 (P.L. 98-369)**

P.L. 98-369, §302(a):

Added Code Sec. 4940(d). **Effective** for tax years beginning after 12-31-84. However, for a special rule, see Act Sec. 302(c)(3), below.

P.L. 98-369, §302(c)(3), provides:

(3) Certain Existing Foundations.—A foundation which was an operating foundation (as defined in section 4942(j)(3) of the Internal Revenue Code of 1954) as of January 1, 1983, shall be treated as meeting the requirements of section 4940(d)(2)(B) of such Code (as added by subsection (a)).

[Sec. 4940(e)—Stricken]

(e) REDUCTION IN TAX WHERE PRIVATE FOUNDATION MEETS CERTAIN DISTRIBUTION REQUIREMENTS.—

Amendments

• **2019, Taxpayer Certainty and Disaster Tax Relief Act of 2019 (P.L. 116-94)**

P.L. 116-94, §206(b), Div. Q:

Amended Code Sec. 4940 by striking subsection (e). **Effective** for tax years beginning after 12-20-2019. Prior to being stricken, Code Sec. 4940(e) read as follows:

(1) IN GENERAL.—In the case of any private foundation which meets the requirements of paragraph (2) for any taxable year, subsection (a) shall be applied with respect to such taxable year by substituting "1 percent" for "2 percent".

EXCISE TAXES—PRIVATE FOUNDATIONS

(2) REQUIREMENTS.—A private foundation meets the requirements of this paragraph for any taxable year if—

(A) the amount of the qualifying distributions made by the private foundation during such taxable year equals or exceeds the sum of—

(i) an amount equal to the assets of such foundation for such taxable year multiplied by the average percentage payout for the base period, plus

(ii) 1 percent of the net investment income of such foundation for such taxable year, and

(B) such private foundation was not liable for tax under section 4942 with respect to any year in the base period.

(3) AVERAGE PERCENTAGE PAYOUT FOR BASE PERIOD.—For purposes of this subsection—

(A) IN GENERAL.—The average percentage payout for the base period is the average of the percentage payouts for taxable years in the base period.

(B) PERCENTAGE PAYOUT.—The term "percentage payout" means, with respect to any taxable year, the percentage determined by dividing—

(i) the amount of the qualifying distributions made by the private foundation during the taxable year, by

(ii) the assets of the private foundation for the taxable year.

(C) SPECIAL RULE WHERE TAX REDUCED UNDER THIS SUBSECTION.—For purposes of this paragraph, if the amount of the tax imposed by this section for any taxable year in the base period is reduced by reason of this subsection, the amount of the qualifying distributions made by the private foundation during such year shall be reduced by the amount of such reduction in tax.

(4) BASE PERIOD.—For purposes of this subsection—

(A) IN GENERAL.—The term "base period" means, with respect to any taxable year, the 5 taxable years preceding such taxable year.

(B) NEW PRIVATE FOUNDATIONS, ETC.—If an organization has not been a private foundation throughout the base period referred to in subparagraph (A), the base period shall consist of the taxable years during which such foundation has been in existence.

(5) OTHER DEFINITIONS.—For purposes of this subsection—

(A) QUALIFYING DISTRIBUTION.—The term "qualifying distribution" has the meaning given such term by section 4942(g).

(B) ASSETS.—The assets of a private foundation for any taxable year shall be treated as equal to the excess determined under section 4942(e)(1).

(6) TREATMENT OF SUCCESSOR ORGANIZATIONS, ETC.—In the case of—

(A) a private foundation which is a successor to another private foundation, this subsection shall be applied with respect to such successor by taking into account the experience of such other foundation, and

(B) a merger, reorganization, or division of a private foundation, this subsection shall be applied under regulations prescribed by the Secretary.

[Sec. 4941]

SEC. 4941. TAXES ON SELF-DEALING.

[Sec. 4941(a)]

(a) INITIAL TAXES.—

(1) ON SELF-DEALER.—There is hereby imposed a tax on each act of self-dealing between a disqualified person and a private foundation. The rate of tax shall be equal to 10 percent of the amount involved with respect to the act of self-dealing for each year (or part thereof) in the taxable period. The tax imposed by this paragraph shall be paid by any disqualified person (other than a foundation manager acting only as such) who participates in the act of self-dealing. In the case of a government official (as defined in section 4946(c)), a tax shall be imposed by this paragraph only if such disqualified person participates in the act of self-dealing knowing that it is such an act.

(2) ON FOUNDATION MANAGER.—In any case in which a tax is imposed by paragraph (1), there is hereby imposed on the participation of any foundation manager in an act of self-dealing between a disqualified person and a private foundation, knowing that it is such an act, a tax equal to 5 percent of the amount involved with respect to the act of self-dealing for each year (or part thereof) in the taxable period, unless such participation is not willful and is due to reasonable cause. The tax imposed by this paragraph shall be paid by any foundation manager who participated in the act of self-dealing.

Amendments

• **2006, Pension Protection Act of 2006 (P.L. 109-280)**

P.L. 109-280, § 1212(a)(1)(A)-(B):

Amended Code Sec. 4941(a) by striking "5 percent" and inserting "10 percent" in paragraph (1), and by striking "2½ percent" and inserting "5 percent" in paragraph (2). **Effective** for tax years beginning after 8-17-2006.

• **1984, Deficit Reduction Act of 1984 (P.L. 98-369)**

P.L. 98-369, § 312, provides:

SEC. 312. TAX ON SELF-DEALING NOT TO APPLY TO CERTAIN STOCK PURCHASES.

(a) GENERAL RULE.—Section 4941 of the Internal Revenue Code of 1954 (relating to taxes on self-dealing) shall not apply to the purchase during 1978 of stock from a private foundation (and to any note issued in connection with such purchase) if—

(1) consideration for such purchase equaled or exceeded the fair market value of such stock,

(2) the purchaser of such stock did not make any contribution to such foundation at any time during the 5-year period ending on the date of such purchase,

(3) the aggregate contributions to such foundation by the purchaser before such date were less than $10,000 and less than 2 percent of the total contributions received by the foundation as of such date, and

(4) such purchase was pursuant to the settlement of litigation involving the purchaser.

(b) STATUTE OF LIMITATIONS.—If credit or refund of any overpayment of tax resulting from subsection (a) is prevented at any time before the close of the 1-year period beginning on the date of the enactment of this Act by the operation of any law or rule of law, refund or credit of such overpayment may, nevertheless, be made or allowed if claim therefor is filed before the close of such 1-year period.

[Sec. 4941(b)]

(b) ADDITIONAL TAXES.—

(1) ON SELF-DEALER.—In any case in which an initial tax is imposed by subsection (a)(1) on an act of self-dealing by a disqualified person with a private foundation and the act is not corrected within the taxable period, there is hereby imposed a tax equal to 200 percent of the amount involved. The tax imposed by this paragraph shall be paid by any disqualified person (other than a foundation manager acting only as such) who participated in the act of self-dealing.

(2) ON FOUNDATION MANAGER.—In any case in which an additional tax is imposed by paragraph (1), if a foundation manager refused to agree to part or all of the correction, there is hereby imposed a tax equal to 50 percent of the amount involved. The tax imposed by this paragraph shall be paid by any foundation manager who refused to agree to part or all of the correction.

Amendments

• **1980 (P.L. 96-596)**

P.L. 96-596, § 2(a)(1):

Amended Code Sec. 4941(b)(1) by striking out "correction period" and inserting in lieu thereof "taxable period". **Effective** with respect to second-tier taxes assessed after 12-24-80 (except in cases where there is a court decision with regard to which res judicata applies on that date).

[Sec. 4941(c)]

(c) SPECIAL RULES.—For purposes of subsections (a) and (b)—

(1) JOINT AND SEVERAL LIABILITY.—If more than one person is liable under any paragraph of subsection (a) or (b) with respect to any one act of self-dealing, all such persons shall be jointly and severally liable under such paragraph with respect to such act.

(2) $20,000 LIMIT FOR MANAGEMENT.—With respect to any one act of self-dealing, the maximum amount of the tax imposed by subsection (a)(2) shall not exceed $20,000, and the maximum amount of the tax imposed by subsection (b)(2) shall not exceed $20,000.

Amendments

• **2006, Pension Protection Act of 2006 (P.L. 109-280)**

P.L. 109-280, § 1212(a)(2):

Amended Code Sec. 4941(c)(2) by striking "$10,000" each place it appears in the text and heading thereof and inserting "$20,000". **Effective** for tax years beginning after 8-17-2006.

EXCISE TAXES—PRIVATE FOUNDATIONS

[Sec. 4941(d)]

(d) SELF-DEALING.—

(1) IN GENERAL.—For purposes of this section, the term "self-dealing" means any direct or indirect—

(A) sale or exchange, or leasing, of property between a private foundation and a disqualified person;

(B) lending of money or other extension of credit between a private foundation and a disqualified person;

(C) furnishing of goods, services, or facilities between a private foundation and a disqualified person;

(D) payment of compensation (or payment or reimbursement of expenses) by a private foundation to a disqualified person;

(E) transfer to, or use by or for the benefit of, a disqualified person of the income or assets of a private foundation; and

(F) agreement by a private foundation to make any payment of money or other property to a government official (as defined in section 4946(c)), other than an agreement to employ such individual for any period after the termination of his government service if such individual is terminating his government service within a 90-day period.

(2) SPECIAL RULES.—For purposes of paragraph (1)—

(A) the transfer of real or personal property by a disqualified person to a private foundation shall be treated as a sale or exchange if the property is subject to a mortgage or similar lien which the foundation assumes or if it is subject to a mortgage or similar lien which a disqualified person placed on the property within the 10-year period ending on the date of the transfer;

(B) the lending of money by a disqualified person to a private foundation shall not be an act of self-dealing if the loan is without interest or other charge (determined without regard to section 7872) and if the proceeds of the loan are used exclusively for purposes specified in section 501(c)(3);

(C) the furnishing of goods, services, or facilities by a disqualified person to a private foundation shall not be an act of self-dealing if the furnishing is without charge and if the goods, services, or facilities so furnished are used exclusively for purposes specified in section 501(c)(3);

(D) the furnishing of goods, services, or facilities by a private foundation to a disqualified person shall not be an act of self-dealing if such furnishing is made on a basis no more favorable than that on which such goods, services, or facilities are made available to the general public;

(E) except in the case of a government official (as defined in section 4946(c)), the payment of compensation (and the payment or reimbursement of expenses) by a private foundation to a disqualified person for personal services which are reasonable and necessary to carrying out the exempt purpose of the private foundation shall not be an act of self-dealing if the compensation (or payment or reimbursement) is not excessive;

(F) any transaction between a private foundation and a corporation which is a disqualified person (as defined in section 4946(a)), pursuant to any liquidation, merger, redemption, recapitalization, or other corporate adjustment, organization, or reorganization, shall not be an act of self-dealing if all of the securities of the same class as that held by the foundation are subject to the same terms and such terms provide for receipt by the foundation of no less than fair market value;

(G) in the case of a government official (as defined in section 4946(c)), paragraph (1) shall in addition not apply to—

(i) prizes and awards which are subject to the provisions of section 74(b) (determined without regard to paragraph (3) thereof), if the recipients of such prizes and awards are selected from the general public,

(ii) scholarships and fellowship grants which would be subject to the provisions of section 117(a) (as in effect on the day before the date of the enactment of the Tax Reform Act of 1986) and are to be used for study at an educational organization described in section 170(b)(1)(A)(ii),

(iii) any annuity or other payment (forming part of a stock-bonus, pension, or profit-sharing plan) by a trust which is a qualified trust under section 401,

(iv) any annuity or other payment under a plan which meets the requirements of section 404(a)(2),

(v) any contribution or gift (other than a contribution or gift of money) to, or services or facilities made available to, any such individual, if the aggregate value of such contributions, gifts, services, and facilities to, or made available to, such individual during any calendar year does not exceed $25,

(vi) any payment made under chapter 41 of title 5, United States Code, or

(vii) any payment or reimbursement of traveling expenses for travel solely from one point in the United States to another point in the United States, but only if such payment or reimbursement does not exceed the actual cost of the transportation involved plus an amount for all other traveling expenses not in excess of 125 percent of the maximum amount payable under section 5702 of title 5, United States Code, for like travel by employees of the United States; and

(H) the leasing by a disqualified person to a private foundation of office space for use by the foundation in a building with other tenants who are not disqualified persons shall not be treated as an act of self-dealing if—

(i) such leasing of office space is pursuant to a binding lease which was in effect on October 9, 1969, or pursuant to renewals of such a lease;

(ii) the execution of such lease was not a prohibited transaction (within the meaning of section 503(b) or any corresponding provision of prior law) at the time of such execution; and

(iii) the terms of the lease (or any renewal) reflect an arm's-length transaction.

Amendments

• **1988, Technical and Miscellaneous Revenue Act of 1988 (P.L. 100-647)**

P.L. 100-647, §1001(d)(1)(A):

Amended Code Sec. 4941(d)(2)(G)(ii). **Effective** as if included in the provision of P.L. 99-514 to which it relates. Prior to amendment, Code Sec. 4941(d)(2)(G)(ii) read as follows:

(ii) scholarships and fellowship grants which are subject to the provisions of section 117(a) and are to be used for study at an educational organization described in section 170(b)(1)(A)(ii).

• **1986, Tax Reform Act of 1986 (P.L. 99-514)**

P.L. 99-514, §122(a)(2)(A):

Amended Code Sec. 4941(d)(2)(G)(i) by striking out "section 74(b)" and inserting in lieu thereof "section 74(b) (without regard to paragraph (3) thereof)" **Effective** for prizes and awards granted after 12-31-86.

P.L. 99-514, §1812(b)(1):

Amended Code Sec. 4941(d)(2)(B) by striking out "without interest or other charge" and inserting in lieu thereof "without interest or other charge (determined without regard to section 7872)". **Effective** as if included in the provision of P.L. 98-369 to which it relates.

• **1980 (P.L. 96-608)**

P.L. 96-608, §5:

Amended Code Sec. 4941(d)(2) by: (1) striking out "and" at the end of subparagraph (F); (2) striking out the period at the end of subparagraph (G) and inserting "; and"; and (3) adding at the end thereof subparagraph (H). **Effective** 12-28-80.

• **1976, Tax Reform Act of 1976 (P.L. 94-455)**

P.L. 94-455, §1901(b)(8)(H):

Substituted "educational organization described in section 170(b)(1)(A)(ii)" for "educational institution described in section 151(e)(4)" in Code Sec. 4941(d)(2)(G)(ii). **Effective** for tax years beginning after 12-31-76.

EXCISE TAXES—PRIVATE FOUNDATIONS

[Sec. 4941(e)]

(e) OTHER DEFINITIONS.—For purposes of this section—

(1) TAXABLE PERIOD.—The term "taxable period" means, with respect to any act of self-dealing, the period beginning with the date on which the act of self-dealing occurs and ending on the earliest of—

(A) the date of mailing a notice of deficiency with respect to the tax imposed by subsection (a)(1) under section 6212,

(B) the date on which the tax imposed by subsection (a)(1) is assessed, or

(C) the date on which correction of the act of self-dealing is completed.

(2) AMOUNT INVOLVED.—The term "amount involved" means, with respect to any act of self-dealing, the greater of the amount of money and the fair market value of the other property given or the amount of money and the fair market value of the other property received; except that, in the case of services described in subsection (d)(2)(E), the amount involved shall be only the excess compensation. For purposes of the preceding sentence, the fair market value—

(A) in the case of the taxes imposed by subsection (a), shall be determined as of the date on which the act of self-dealing occurs; and

(B) in the case of the taxes imposed by subsection (b), shall be the highest fair market value during the taxable period.

(3) CORRECTION.—The terms "correction" and "correct" mean, with respect to any act of self-dealing, undoing the transaction to the extent possible, but in any case placing the private foundation in a financial position not worse than that in which it would be if the disqualified person were dealing under the highest fiduciary standards.

Amendments

- **1980 (P.L. 96-596)**

P.L. 96-596, § 2(a)(1):

Amended Code Sec. 4941(e)(2)(B) by striking out "correction period" and inserting in lieu thereof "taxable period". **Effective** with respect to second-tier taxes assessed after 12-24-80 (except in cases where there is a court decision with regard to which res judicata applies on that date).

P.L. 96-596, § 2(a)(2):

Amended Code Sec. 4941(e)(1). **Effective** with respect to second-tier taxes assessed after 12-24-80 (except in cases where there is a court decision with regard to which res judicata applies on that date). Prior to amendment, Code Sec. 4941(e)(1) read:

(1) TAXABLE PERIOD.—The term "taxable period" means, with respect to any act of self-dealing, the period beginning with the date on which the act of self-dealing occurs and ending on whichever of the following is the earlier: (A) the date of mailing of a notice of deficiency with respect to the tax imposed by subsection (a)(1) under section 6212, or (B) the date on which correction of the act of self-dealing is completed.

P.L. 96-596, § 2(a)(3):

Amended Code Sec. 4941(e) by striking out paragraph 4. **Effective** 12-24-80. Prior to amendment, Code Sec. 4941(e)(4) read:

(4) CORRECTION PERIOD.—The term "correction period" means, with respect to any act of self-dealing, the period beginning with the date on which the act of self-dealing occurs and ending 90 days after the date of mailing of a notice of deficiency with respect to the tax imposed by subsection (b)(1) under section 6212, extended by—

(A) any period in which a deficiency cannot be assessed under section 6213(a), and

(B) any other period which the Secretary determines is reasonable and necessary to bring about correction of the act of self-dealing.

- **1976, Tax Reform Act of 1976 (P.L. 94-455)**

P.L. 94-455, § 1906(b)(13)(A):

Amended 1954 Code by substituting "Secretary" for "Secretary or his delegate" each place it appeared. **Effective** 2-1-77.

- **1969, Tax Reform Act of 1969 (P.L. 91-172)**

P.L. 91-172, § 101(b):

Added Code Sec. 4941. **Effective** 1-1-70. For exceptions, see Act Sec. 101(l)(2), below.

P.L. 91-172, § 101(l)(2), as amended by P.L. 94-455, §§ 1301(a) and 1309(a), and P.L. 95-600, § 703(f), provides:

Section 4941 shall not apply to—

(A) any transaction between a private foundation and a corporation which is a disqualified person (as defined in section 4946), pursuant to the terms of securities of such corporation in existence at the time acquired by the foundation, if such securities were acquired by the foundation before May 27, 1969;

(B) the sale, exchange, or other disposition of property which is owned by a private foundation on May 26, 1969 (or which is acquired by a private foundation under the terms of a trust which was irrevocable on May 26, 1969, or under the terms of a will executed on or before such date, which are in effect on such date and at all times thereafter), to a disqualified person, if such foundation is required to dispose of such property in order not to be liable for tax under section 4943 (relating to taxes on excess business holdings) applied, in the case of a disposition before January 1, 1977, without taking section 4943(c)(4) into account and it receives in return an amount which equals or exceeds the fair market value of such property at the time of such disposition or at the time a contract for such disposition was previously executed in a transaction which would not constitute a prohibited transaction (within the meaning of section 503(b) or the corresponding provisions of prior law);

(C) the leasing of property or the lending of money or other extension of credit between a disqualified person and a private foundation pursuant to a binding contract in effect on October 9, 1969 (or pursuant to renewals of such a contract), until taxable years beginning after December 31, 1979, if such leasing or lending (or other extension of credit) remains at least as favorable as an arm's-length transaction with an unrelated party and if the execution of such contract was not at the time of such execution a prohibited transaction (within the meaning of section 503(b) or the corresponding provisions of prior law);

(D) the use of goods, services, or facilities which are shared by a private foundation and a disqualified person until taxable years beginning after December 31, 1979, if such use is pursuant to an arrangement in effect before October 9, 1969, and such arrangement was not a prohibited transaction (within the meaning of section 503(b) or the corresponding provisions of prior law) at the time it was made and would not be a prohibited transaction if such section continued to apply;

(E) the use of property in which a private foundation and a disqualified person have a joint or common interest, if the interests of both in such property were acquired before October 9, 1969; and

(F) the sale, exchange, or other disposition (other than by lease) of property which is owned by a private foundation to a disqualified person if—

(i) such foundation is leasing substantially all of such property under a lease to which subparagraph (C) applies,

(ii) the disposition to such disqualified person occurs before January 1, 1978, and

(iii) such foundation receives in return for the disposition to such disqualified person an amount which equals or exceeds the fair market value of such property at the time of the disposition or at the time (after June 30, 1976) a contract for the disposition was previously executed in a transaction which would not constitute a prohibited transaction (within the meaning of section 503(b) or any corresponding provision of prior law).

[Sec. 4942]

SEC. 4942. TAXES ON FAILURE TO DISTRIBUTE INCOME.

[Sec. 4942(a)]

(a) INITIAL TAX.—There is hereby imposed on the undistributed income of a private foundation for any taxable year, which has not been distributed before the first day of the second (or any succeeding) taxable year following such taxable year (if such first day falls within the taxable period), a tax equal to 30 percent of the amount of such income remaining undistributed at the beginning of such second (or succeeding) taxable year. The tax imposed by this subsection shall not apply to the undistributed income of a private foundation—

(1) for any taxable year for which it is an operating foundation (as defined in subsection (j)(3)), or

(2) to the extent that the foundation failed to distribute any amount solely because of an incorrect valuation of assets under subsection (e), if—

(A) the failure to value the assets properly was not willful and was due to reasonable cause,

(B) such amount is distributed as qualifying distributions (within the meaning of subsection (g)) by the foundation during the allowable distribution period (as defined in subsection (j)(2)),

(C) the foundation notifies the Secretary that such amount has been distributed (within the meaning of subparagraph (B)) to correct such failure, and

(D) such distribution is treated under subsection (h)(2) as made out of the undistributed income for the taxable year for which a tax would (except for this paragraph) have been imposed under this subsection.

EXCISE TAXES—PRIVATE FOUNDATIONS

Amendments

- **2006, Pension Protection Act of 2006 (P.L. 109-280)**

P.L. 109-280, §1212(b):

Amended Code Sec. 4942(a) by striking "15 percent" and inserting "30 percent". **Effective** for tax years beginning after 8-17-2006.

- **1984, Deficit Reduction Act of 1984 (P.L. 98-369)**

P.L. 98-369, §314(a)(1):

Amended Code Sec. 4942(a)(2)(B) by striking out "subsection (j)(4)" and inserting in lieu thereof "subsection (j)(2)". **Effective** 7-18-84.

- **1976, Tax Reform Act of 1976 (P.L. 94-455)**

P.L. 94-455, §1906(b)(13)(A):

Amended 1954 Code by substituting "Secretary" for "Secretary or his delegate" each place it appeared. **Effective** 2-1-77.

[Sec. 4942(b)]

(b) ADDITIONAL TAX.—In any case in which an initial tax is imposed under subsection (a) on the undistributed income of a private foundation for any taxable year, if any portion of such income remains undistributed at the close of the taxable period, there is hereby imposed a tax equal to 100 percent of the amount remaining undistributed at such time.

Amendments

- **1980 (P.L. 96-596)**

P.L. 96-596, §2(a)(1):

Amended Code Sec. 4942(b) by striking out "correction period" and inserting in lieu thereof "taxable period". **Effective** with respect to second-tier taxes assessed after 12-24-80 (except in cases where there is a court decision with regard to which res judicata applies on that date).

[Sec. 4942(c)]

(c) UNDISTRIBUTED INCOME.—For purposes of this section, the term "undistributed income" means, with respect to any private foundation for any taxable year as of any time, the amount by which—

(1) the distributable amount for such taxable year, exceeds

(2) the qualifying distributions made before such time out of such distributable amount.

[Sec. 4942(d)]

(d) DISTRIBUTABLE AMOUNT.—For purposes of this section, the term "distributable amount" means, with respect to any foundation for any taxable year, an amount equal to—

(1) the sum of the minimum investment return plus the amounts described in subsection (f)(2)(C), reduced by

(2) the sum of the taxes imposed on such private foundation for the taxable year under subtitle A and section 4940.

Amendments

- **1984, Deficit Reduction Act of 1984 (P.L. 98-369)**

P.L. 98-369, §304(b):

Amended Code Sec. 4942(d)(1). **Effective** for tax years beginning after 12-31-84. Prior to amendment, it read as follows:

(1) the minimum investment return, reduced by

- **1981, Economic Recovery Tax Act of 1981 (P.L. 97-34)**

P.L. 97-34, §823(a)(1):

Amended Code Sec. 4942(d)(1) by striking out "or the adjusted net income (whichever is higher)". **Effective** for tax years beginning after 12-31-81.

[Sec. 4942(e)]

(e) MINIMUM INVESTMENT RETURN.—

(1) IN GENERAL.—For purposes of subsection (d), the minimum investment return for any private foundation for any taxable year is 5 percent of the excess of—

(A) the aggregate fair market value of all assets of the foundation other than those which are used (or held for use) directly in carrying out the foundation's exempt purpose, over

(B) the acquisition indebtedness with respect to such assets (determined under section 514(c)(1) without regard to the taxable year in which the indebtedness was incurred).

(2) VALUATION.—

(A) IN GENERAL.—For purposes of paragraph (1)(A), the fair market value of securities for which market quotations are readily available shall be determined on a monthly basis. For all other assets, the fair market value shall be determined at such times and in such manner as the Secretary shall by regulations prescribe.

(B) REDUCTIONS IN VALUE FOR BLOCKAGE OR SIMILAR FACTORS.—In determining the value of any securities under this paragraph, the fair market value of such securities (determined without regard to any reduction in value) shall not be reduced unless, and only to the extent that, the private foundation establishes that as a result of—

(i) the size of the block of such securities,

(ii) the fact that the securities held are securities in a closely held corporation, or

(iii) the fact that the sale of such securities would result in a forced or distress sale,

the securities could not be liquidated within a reasonable period of time except at a price less than such fair market value. Any reduction in value allowable under this subparagraph shall not exceed 10 percent of such fair market value.

Amendments

- **1976, Tax Reform Act of 1976 (P.L. 94-455)**

P.L. 94-455, §1303(a):

Amended Code Sec. 4942(e). **Effective** for tax years beginning after 12-31-75. Prior to amendment, Code Sec. 4942(e) read as follows:

(e) MINIMUM INVESTMENT RETURN.—

(1) IN GENERAL.—For purposes of subsection (d), the minimum investment return for any private foundation for any taxable year is the amount determined by multiplying—

(A) the excess of (i) the aggregate fair market value of all assets of the foundation other than those being used (or held for use) directly in carrying out the foundation's exempt purpose over (ii) the acquisition indebtedness with respect to such assets (determined under section 514(c)(1), but without regard to the taxable year in which the indebtedness was incurred), by

(B) the applicable percentage for such year, determined under paragraph (3).

(2) VALUATION.—For purposes of paragraph (1)(A), the fair market value of securities for which market quotations are readily available shall be determined on a monthly basis. For all other assets, the fair market value shall be determined at such times and in such manner as the Secretary or his delegate shall by regulations prescribe.

(3) APPLICABLE PERCENTAGE.—For purposes of paragraph (1)(B), the applicable percentage for taxable years beginning in 1970 is 6 percent. The applicable percentage for any taxable year beginning after 1970 shall be determined and published by the Secretary or his delegate and shall bear a relationship to 6 percent which the Secretary or his delegate determines to be comparable to the relationship which the money rates and investment yields for the calendar year immediately preceding the beginning of the taxable year bear to the money rates and investment yields for the calendar year 1969.

(4) TRANSITIONAL RULES.—For special rules applicable to organizations created before May 27, 1969, see section 101(1)(3) of the Tax Reform Act of 1969.

EXCISE TAXES—PRIVATE FUNDATIONS

[Sec. 4942(f)]

(f) ADJUSTED NET INCOME.—

(1) DEFINED.—For purposes of subsection (j), the term "adjusted net income" means the excess (if any) of—

(A) the gross income for the taxable year (determined with the income modifications provided by paragraph (2)), over

(B) the sum of the deductions (determined with the deduction modifications provided by paragraph (3)) which would be allowed to a corporation subject to the tax imposed by section 11 for the taxable year.

(2) INCOME MODIFICATIONS.—The income modifications referred to in paragraph (1)(A) are as follows:

(A) section 103 (relating to state and local bonds) shall not apply,

(B) capital gains and losses from the sale or other disposition of property shall be taken into account only in an amount equal to any net short-term capital gain for the taxable year;

(C) there shall be taken into account—

(i) amounts received or accrued as repayments of amounts which were taken into account as a qualifying distribution within the meaning of subsection (g)(1)(A) for any taxable year;

(ii) notwithstanding subparagraph (B), amounts received or accrued from the sale or other disposition of property to the extent that the acquisition of such property was taken into account as a qualifying distribution (within the meaning of subsection (g)(1)(B)) for any taxable year; and

(iii) any amount set aside under subsection (g)(2) to the extent it is determined that such amount is not necessary for the purposes for which it was set aside; and

(D) section 483 (relating to imputed interest) shall not apply in the case of a binding contract made in a taxable year beginning before January 1, 1970.

(3) DEDUCTION MODIFICATIONS.—The deduction modifications referred to in paragraph (1)(B) are as follows:

(A) no deduction shall be allowed other than all the ordinary and necessary expenses paid or incurred for the production or collection of gross income or for the management, conservation, or maintenance of property held for the production of such income and the allowances for depreciation and depletion determined under section 4940(c)(3)(B), and

(B) section 265 (relating to expenses and interest relating to tax-exempt interest) shall not apply.

(4) TRANSITIONAL RULE.—For purposes of paragraph (2)(B), the basis (for purposes of determining gain) of property held by a private foundation on December 31, 1969, and continuously thereafter to the date of its disposition, shall be deemed to be not less than the fair market value of such property on December 31, 1969.

Amendments

• **1986, Tax Reform Act of 1986 (P.L. 99-514)**

P.L. 99-514, §1301(j)(6):

Amended Code Sec. 4942(f)(2)(A) by striking out "(relating to interest on certain governmental obligations)" and inserting in lieu thereof "(relating to State and local bonds)". **Effective**, generally, for bonds issued after 8-15-86.

• **1984, Deficit Reduction Act of 1984 (P.L. 98-369)**

P.L. 98-369, §314(a)(2):

Amended Code Sec. 4942(f)(1) by striking out "subsection (d)" and inserting in lieu thereof "subsection (j)". **Effective** 7-18-84.

• **1976, Tax Reform Act of 1976 (P.L. 94-455)**

P.L. 94-455, §1310(a):

Struck out "and" at the end of Code Sec. 4942(f)(2)(B), substituted "; and" for the period at the end of Code Sec. 4942(f)(2)(C), and added Code Sec. 4942(f)(2)(D). **Effective** for tax years ending after 10-4-76.

[Sec. 4942(g)]

(g) QUALIFYING DISTRIBUTIONS DEFINED.—

(1) IN GENERAL.—For purposes of this section, the term "qualifying distribution" means—

(A) any amount (including that portion of reasonable and necessary administrative expenses) paid to accomplish one or more purposes described in section 170(c)(2)(B), other than any contribution to (i) an organization controlled (directly or indirectly) by the foundation or one or more disqualified persons (as defined in section 4946) with respect to the foundation, except as provided in paragraph (3), or (ii) a private foundation which is not an operating foundation (as defined in subsection (j)(3)), except as provided in paragraph (3), or

(B) any amount paid to acquire an asset used (or held for use) directly in carrying out one or more purposes described in section 170(c)(2)(B).

(2) CERTAIN SET-ASIDES.—

(A) IN GENERAL.—Subject to such terms and conditions as may be prescribed by the Secretary, an amount set aside for a specific project which comes within one or more purposes described in section 170(c)(2)(B) may be treated as a qualifying distribution if it meets the requirements of subparagraph (B).

(B) REQUIREMENTS.—An amount set aside for a specific project shall meet the requirements of this subparagraph if at the time of the set-aside the foundation establishes to the satisfaction of the Secretary that the amount will be paid for the specific project within 5 years, and either—

(i) at the time of the set-aside the private foundation establishes to the satisfaction of the Secretary that the project is one which can better be accomplished by such set-aside than by immediate payment of funds, or

(ii)(I) the project will not be completed before the end of the taxable year of the foundation in which the set-aside is made,

(II) the private foundation in each taxable year beginning after December 31, 1975 (or after the end of the fourth taxable year following the year of its creation, whichever is later), distributes amounts, in cash or its equivalent, equal to not less than the distributable amount determined under subsection (d) (without regard to subsection (i)) for purposes described in section 170(c)(2)(B) (including but not limited to payments with respect to set-asides which were treated as qualifying distributions in one or more prior years), and

(III) the private foundation has distributed (including but not limited to payments with respect to set-asides which were treated as qualifying distributions in one or more prior years) during the four taxable years immediately preceding its first taxable year beginning after December 31, 1975, or the fifth taxable year following the year of its creation, whichever is later, an aggregate amount, in cash or its equivalent, of not less than the sum of the following: 80 percent of the first preceding taxable year's distributable amount; 60 percent of the second preceding taxable year's distributable amount; 40 percent of the third preceding taxable year's distributable amount; and 20 percent of the fourth preceding taxable year's distributable amount.

(C) CERTAIN FAILURES TO DISTRIBUTE.—If, for any taxable year to which clause (ii)(II) of subparagraph (B) applies, the private foundation fails to distribute in cash or its equivalent amounts not less than those required by such clause and—

(i) the failure to distribute such amounts was not willful and was due to reasonable cause, and

EXCISE TAXES—PRIVATE FOUNDATIONS

(ii) the foundation distributes an amount in cash or its equivalent which is not less than the difference between the amounts required to be distributed under clause (ii)(II) of subparagraph (B) and the amounts actually distributed in cash or its equivalent during that taxable year within the correction period (as defined in section 4963(e)),

such distribution in cash or its equivalent shall be treated for the purposes of this subparagraph as made during such year.

(D) REDUCTION IN DISTRIBUTION AMOUNT.—If, during the taxable years in the adjustment period for which the organization is a private foundation, the foundation distributes amounts in cash or its equivalent which exceed the amount required to be distributed under clause (ii)(II) of subparagraph (B) (including but not limited to payments with respect to set-asides which were treated as qualifying distributions in prior years), then for purposes of this subsection the distribution required under clause (ii)(II) of subparagraph (B) for the taxable year shall be reduced by an amount equal to such excess.

(E) ADJUSTMENT PERIOD.—For purposes of subparagraph (D), with respect to any taxable year of a private foundation, the taxable years in the adjustment period are the taxable years (not exceeding 5) beginning after December 31, 1975, and immediately preceding the taxable year.

In the case of a set-aside which satisfies the requirements of clause (i) of subparagraph (B), for good cause shown, the period for paying the amount set aside may be extended by the Secretary.

(3) CERTAIN CONTRIBUTIONS TO SECTION 501(c)(3) ORGANIZATIONS.—For purposes of this section, the term "qualifying distribution" includes a contribution to a section 501(c)(3) organization described in paragraph (1)(A)(i) or (ii) if—

(A) not later than the close of the first taxable year after its taxable year in which such contribution is received, such organization makes a distribution equal to the amount of such contribution and such distribution is a qualifying distribution (within the meaning of paragraph (1) or (2), without regard to this paragraph) which is treated under subsection (h) as a distribution out of corpus (or would be so treated if such section 501(c)(3) organization were a private foundation which is not an operating foundation), and

(B) the private foundation making the contribution obtains adequate records or other sufficient evidence from such organization showing that the qualifying distribution described in subparagraph (A) has been made by such organization.

(4) LIMITATION ON DISTRIBUTIONS BY NONOPERATING PRIVATE FOUNDATIONS TO SUPPORTING ORGANIZATIONS.—

(A) IN GENERAL.—For purposes of this section, the term "qualifying distribution" shall not include any amount paid by a private foundation which is not an operating foundation to—

(i) any type III supporting organization (as defined in section 4943(f)(5)(A)) which is not a functionally integrated type III supporting organization (as defined in section 4943(f)(5)(B)), and

(ii) any organization which is described in subparagraph (B) or (C) if—

(I) a disqualified person of the private foundation directly or indirectly controls such organization or a supported organization (as defined in section 509(f)(3)) of such organization, or

(II) the Secretary determines by regulations that a distribution to such organization otherwise is inappropriate.

(B) TYPE I AND TYPE II SUPPORTING ORGANIZATIONS.—An organization is described in this subparagraph if the organization meets the requirements of subparagraphs (A) and (C) of section 509(a)(3) and is—

(i) operated, supervised, or controlled by one or more organizations described in paragraph (1) or (2) of section 509(a), or

(ii) supervised or controlled in connection with one or more such organizations.

(C) FUNCTIONALLY INTEGRATED TYPE III SUPPORTING ORGANIZATIONS.—An organization is described in this subparagraph if the organization is a functionally integrated type III supporting organization (as defined under section 4943(f)(5)(B)).

Amendments

- **2014, Tax Technical Corrections Act of 2014 (P.L. 113-295)**

P.L. 113-295, §221(a)(105)(A), Division A:

Amended Code Sec. 4942(g) by striking "For all taxable years beginning on or after January 1, 1975, subject" in paragraph (2)(A) and inserting "Subject". **Effective** generally 12-19-2014. For a special rule, see Act Sec. 221(b)(2), Division A, below.

P.L. 113-295, §221(b)(2), Division A, provides:

(2) SAVINGS PROVISION.—If—

(A) any provision amended or repealed by the amendments made by this section applied to—

(i) any transaction occurring before the date of the enactment of this Act,

(ii) any property acquired before such date of enactment, or

(iii) any item of income, loss, deduction, or credit taken into account before such date of enactment, and

(B) the treatment of such transaction, property, or item under such provision would (without regard to the amendments or repeals made by this section) affect the liability for tax for periods ending after date of enactment, nothing in the amendments or repeals made by this section shall be construed to affect the treatment of such transaction, property, or item for purposes of determining liability for tax for periods ending after such date of enactment.

- **2006, Pension Protection Act of 2006 (P.L. 109-280)**

P.L. 109-280, §1244(a):

Amended Code Sec. 4942(g)(4). **Effective** for distributions and expenditures after 8-17-2006. Prior to amendment, Code Sec. 4942(g)(4) read as follows:

(4) LIMITATION ON ADMINISTRATIVE EXPENSES ALLOCABLE TO MAKING OF CONTRIBUTIONS, GIFTS, AND GRANTS.—

(A) IN GENERAL.—The amount of the grant administrative expenses paid during any taxable year which may be taken into account as qualifying distributions shall not exceed the excess (if any) of—

(i) .65 percent of the sum of the net assets of the private foundation for such taxable year and the immediately preceding 2 taxable years, over

(ii) the aggregate amount of grant administrative expenses paid during the 2 preceding taxable years which were taken into account as qualifying distributions.

(B) GRANT ADMINISTRATIVE EXPENSES.—For purposes of this paragraph, the term "grant administrative expenses" means any administrative expenses which are allocable to the making of qualified grants.

(C) QUALIFIED GRANTS.—For purposes of this paragraph, the term "qualified grant" means any contribution, gift, or grant which is a qualifying distribution.

(D) NET ASSET.—For purposes of this paragraph, the term "net assets" means, with respect to any taxable year, the excess determined under subsection (e)(1) for such taxable year.

(E) TRANSITIONAL RULE.—In the case of any preceding taxable year which begins before January 1, 1985, the amount of the grant administrative expenses taken into account under subparagraph (A)(ii) shall not exceed .65 percent of the net assets of the private foundation for such taxable year.

(F) TERMINATION.—This paragraph shall not apply to taxable years beginning after December 31, 1990.

- **1984, Deficit Reduction Act of 1984 (P.L. 98-369)**

P.L. 98-369, §304(a)(1):

Amended Code Sec. 4942(g) by adding at the end thereof new paragraph (4). **Effective** for tax years beginning after 12-31-84.

P.L. 98-369, §304(a)(2):

Amended Code Sec. 4942(g)(1)(A) by striking out "including administrative expenses" and inserting in lieu thereof "including that portion of reasonable and necessary administrative expenses". **Effective** for tax years beginning after 12-31-84.

P.L. 98-369, §305(b)(4):

Amended Code Sec. 4942(g)(2)(C) by striking out "section 4962(e)" and inserting in lieu thereof "section 4963(e)". **Effective** for tax events occurring after 12-31-84.

- **1980 (P.L. 96-596)**

P.L. 96-596, §2(a)(3):

Amended Code Sec. 4942(g)(2)(C)(ii) by striking out "the initial correction period provided in subsection (j)(2)" and inserting in lieu thereof "the correction period (as defined in section 4962(e))". **Effective** 12-24-80.

- **1976, Tax Reform Act of 1976 (P.L. 94-455)**

P.L. 94-455, §1302(a):

Amended Code Sec. 4942(g)(2). **Effective** for tax years beginning after 12-31-74. Prior to amendment, Code Sec. 4942(g)(2) read as follows:

(2) CERTAIN SET-ASIDES.—Subject to such terms and conditions as may be prescribed by the Secretary or his delegate, an amount set aside for a specific project which comes within one or more purposes described in section 170(c)(2)(B) may be treated as a qualifying distribution, but only if, at the time of the set-aside, the private foundation establishes to the satisfaction of the Secretary or his delegate that—

(A) the amount will be paid for the specific project within 5 years, and

(B) the project is one which can be better accomplished by such set-aside than by immediate payment of funds.

For good cause shown, the period for paying the amount set aside may be extended by the Secretary or his delegate.

EXCISE TAXES—PRIVATE FOUNDATIONS

[Sec. 4942(h)]

(h) TREATMENT OF QUALIFYING DISTRIBUTIONS.—

(1) IN GENERAL.—Except as provided in paragraph (2), any qualifying distribution made during a taxable year shall be treated as made—

(A) first out of the undistributed income of the immediately preceding taxable year (if the private foundation was subject to the tax imposed by this section for such preceding taxable year) to the extent thereof,

(B) second out of the undistributed income for the taxable year to the extent thereof, and

(C) then out of corpus.

For purposes of this paragraph, distributions shall be taken into account in the order of time in which made.

(2) CORRECTION OF DEFICIENT DISTRIBUTIONS FOR PRIOR TAXABLE YEARS, ETC.—In the case of any qualifying distribution which (under paragraph (1)) is not treated as made out of the undistributed income of the immediately preceding taxable year, the foundation may elect to treat any portion of such distribution as made out of the undistributed income of a designated prior taxable year or out of corpus. The election shall be made by the foundation at such time and in such manner as the Secretary shall by regulations prescribe.

Amendments

• **1976, Tax Reform Act of 1976 (P.L. 94-455)**

P.L. 94-455, § 1906(b)(13)(A):

Amended 1954 Code by substituting "Secretary" for "Secretary or his delegate" each place it appeared. **Effective** 2-1-77.

[Sec. 4942(i)]

(i) ADJUSTMENT OF DISTRIBUTABLE AMOUNT WHERE DISTRIBUTIONS DURING PRIOR YEARS HAVE EXCEEDED INCOME.—

(1) IN GENERAL.—If, for the taxable years in the adjustment period for which an organization is a private foundation—

(A) the aggregate qualifying distributions treated (under subsection (h)) as made out of the undistributed income for such taxable year or as made out of corpus (except to the extent subsection (g)(3) with respect to the recipient private foundation or section 170(b)(1)(F)(ii) applies) during such taxable years, exceed

(B) the distributable amounts for such taxable years (determined without regard to this subsection),

then, for purposes of this section (other than subsection (h)), the distributable amount for the taxable year shall be reduced by an amount equal to such excess.

(2) TAXABLE YEARS IN ADJUSTMENT PERIOD.—For purposes of paragraph (1), with respect to any taxable year of a private foundation the taxable years in the adjustment period are the taxable years (not exceeding 5) immediately preceding the taxable year.

Amendments

• **2014, Tax Technical Corrections Act of 2014 (P.L. 113-295)**

P.L. 113-295, § 221(a)(105)(B), Division A:

Amended Code Sec. 4942(i)(2) by striking "beginning after December 31, 1969, and" following "(not exceeding 5)". **Effective** generally 12-19-2014. For a special rule, see Act Sec. 221(b)(2), Division A, below.

P.L. 113-295, § 221(b)(2), Division A, provides:

(2) SAVINGS PROVISION.—If—

(A) any provision amended or repealed by the amendments made by this section applied to—

(i) any transaction occurring before the date of the enactment of this Act,

(ii) any property acquired before such date of enactment, or

(iii) any item of income, loss, deduction, or credit taken into account before such date of enactment, and

(B) the treatment of such transaction, property, or item under such provision would (without regard to the amendments or repeals made by this section) affect the liability for tax for periods ending after date of enactment, nothing in the amendments or repeals made by this section shall be construed to affect the treatment of such transaction, property, or item for purposes of determining liability for tax for periods ending after such date of enactment.

• **2007, Tax Technical Corrections Act of 2007 (P.L. 110-172)**

P.L. 110-172, § 11(a)(14)(D):

Amended Code Sec. 4942(i)(1)(A) by striking "section 170(b)(1)(E)(ii)" and inserting "section 170(b)(1)(F)(ii)". **Effective** 12-29-2007.

[Sec. 4942(j)]

(j) OTHER DEFINITIONS.—For purposes of this section—

(1) TAXABLE PERIOD.—The term "taxable period" means, with respect to the undistributed income for any taxable year, the period beginning with the first day of the taxable year and ending on the earlier of—

(A) the date of mailing of a notice of deficiency with respect to the tax imposed by subsection (a) under section 6212, or

(B) the date on which the tax imposed by subsection (a) is assessed.

(2) ALLOWABLE DISTRIBUTION PERIOD.—The term "allowable distribution period" means, with respect to any private foundation, the period beginning with the first day of the first taxable year following the taxable year in which the incorrect valuation (described in subsection (a)(2)) occurred and ending 90 days after the date of mailing of a notice of deficiency (with respect to the tax imposed by subsection (a)) under section 6212 extended by—

(A) any period in which a deficiency cannot be assessed under section 6213(a), and

(B) any other period which the Secretary determines is reasonable and necessary to permit a distribution of undistributed income under this section.

(3) OPERATING FOUNDATION.—For purposes of this section, the term "operating foundation" means any organization—

(A) which makes qualifying distributions (within the meaning of paragraph (1) or (2) of subsection (g)) directly for the active conduct of the activities constituting the purpose or function for which it is organized and operated equal to substantially all of the lesser of—

(i) its adjusted net income (as defined in subsection (f)), or

(ii) its minimum investment return; and

(B)(i) substantially more than half of the assets of which are devoted directly to such activities or to functionally related businesses (as defined in paragraph (4)), or to both, or are stock of a corporation which is controlled by the foundation and substantially all of the assets of which are so devoted,

(ii) which normally makes qualifying distributions (within the meaning of paragraph (1) or (2) of subsection (g)) directly for the active conduct of the activities constituting the purpose or function for which it is organized and operated in an amount not less than two-thirds of its minimum investment return (as defined in subsection (e)), or

(iii) substantially all of the support (other than gross investment income as defined in section 509(e)) of which is normally received from the general public and from 5 or more exempt organizations which are not described in section 4946(a)(1)(H) with respect to each other or the recipient foundation; not more than 25 percent of the support (other than gross investment income) of which is normally received from any one such exempt organization; and not more than half of the support of which is normally received from gross investment income.

Notwithstanding the provisions of subparagraph (A), if the qualifying distributions (within the meaning of paragraph (1) or (2) of subsection (g)) of an organization for the taxable year exceed the minimum investment return for the taxable year, clause (ii) of subparagraph (A) shall not

EXCISE TAXES—PRIVATE FOUNDATIONS

apply unless substantially all of such qualifying distributions are made directly for the active conduct of the activities constituting the purpose or function for which it is organized and operated.

(4) FUNCTIONALLY RELATED BUSINESS.—The term "functionally related business" means—

(A) a trade or business which is not an unrelated trade or business (as defined in section 513), or

(B) an activity which is carried on within a larger aggregate of similar activities or within a larger complex of other endeavors which is related (aside from the need of the organization for income or funds or the use it makes of the profits derived) to the exempt purposes of the organization.

(5) CERTAIN ELDERLY CARE FACILITIES.—For purposes of this section (but no other provisions of this title), the term "operating foundation" includes any organization which, on May 26, 1969, and at all times thereafter before the close of the taxable year, operated and maintained as its principal functional purpose facilities for the long-term care, comfort, maintenance, or education of permanently and totally disabled persons, elderly persons, needy widows, or children but only if such organization meets the requirements of paragraph (3)(B)(ii).

Amendments

- **1983, Technical Corrections Act of 1982 (P.L. 97-448)**

P.L. 97-448, §108(b):

Amended Code Sec. 4942(j)(3)(A) by striking out "and" at the end of clause (i) and inserting in lieu thereof "or". **Effective** as if included in the provision of P.L. 97-34 to which it relates.

- **1981, Economic Recovery Tax Act of 1981 (P.L. 97-34)**

P.L. 97-34, §823(a)(2):

Amended Code Sec. 4942(j)(3)(A). **Effective** for tax years beginning after 12-31-81. Prior to amendment, Code Sec. 4942(j)(3)(A) read as follows:

(A) which makes qualifying distributions (within the meaning of paragraph (1) or (2) of subsection (g)) directly for the active conduct of the activities constituting the purpose or function for which it is organized and operated equal to substantially all of its adjusted net income (as defined in subsection (f)); and

P.L. 97-34, §823(a)(3):

Amended Code Sec. 4942(j)(3) by adding the last sentence. **Effective** for tax years beginning after 12-31-81.

- **1980 (P.L. 96-596)**

P.L. 96-596, §2(a)(2):

Amended Code Sec. 4942(j)(1). **Effective** with respect to second-tier taxes assessed after 12-24-80 (except in cases where there is a court decision with regard to which res judicata applies on that date). Prior to amendment, Code Sec. 4942(j)(1) read:

"(1) TAXABLE PERIOD.—The term `taxable period' means, with respect to the undistributed income for any taxable year, the period beginning with the first day of the taxable year and ending on the date of mailing of a notice of deficiency with respect to the tax imposed by subsection (a) under section 6212."

P.L. 96-596, §2(a)(3):

Amended Code Sec. 4942(j) by: (1) striking out paragraph (2), (2) striking out "paragraph (5)" in paragraph (3)(B)(i) and inserting in lieu thereof "paragraph (4)", (3) redesignating paragraph (4) as paragraph (2), and (4) redesignating paragraphs (5) and (6) as paragraphs (4) and (5), respectively. **Effective** 12-24-80. Prior to amendment, Code Sec. 4942(j)(2) read:

"(2) CORRECTION PERIOD.—The term `correction period' means, with respect to any private foundation for any taxable year, the period beginning with the first day of the taxable year and ending 90 days after the date of mailing of a notice of deficiency (with respect to the tax imposed by subsection (b)) under section 6212, extended by—

"(A) any period in which a deficiency cannot be assessed under section 6213(a), and

"(B) any other period which the Secretary determines is reasonable and necessary to permit a distribution of undistributed income under this section."

- **1978, Revenue Act of 1978 (P.L. 95-600)**

P.L. 95-600, §522(a):

Amended Code Sec. 4942(j) by adding new paragraph (6). **Effective** for tax years beginning after 12-31-69.

- **1976, Tax Reform Act of 1976 (P.L. 94-455)**

P.L. 94-455, §1906(b)(13)(A):

Amended 1954 Code by substituting "Secretary" for "Secretary or his delegate" each place it appeared. **Effective** 2-1-77.

- **1969, Tax Reform Act of 1969 (P.L. 91-172)**

P.L. 91-172, §101(b):

Added Code Sec. 4942. **Effective** for tax years beginning after 12-31-69, except as noted below.

P.L. 91-172, §101(1)(3) [as amended by P.L. 93-490, §4], provides:

"In the case of organizations organized before May 27, 1969, section 4942 shall—

"(A) for all purposes other than the determination of the minimum investment return under section 4942(j)(3)(B)(ii), for taxable years beginning before January 1, 1972, apply without regard to section 4942(e) (relating to minimum investment return), and for taxable years beginning in 1972, 1973, and 1974, apply with an applicable percentage (as prescribed in section 4942(e)(3)) which does not exceed 4½ percent, 5 percent, and 5½ percent, respectively;

"(B) not apply to an organization to the extent its income is required to be accumulated pursuant to the mandatory terms (as in effect on May 26, 1969, and at all times thereafter) of an instrument executed before May 27, 1969, with respect to the transfer of income producing property to such organization, except that section 4942 shall apply to such organization if the organization would have been denied exemption if section 504(a) had not been repealed by this Act, or would have had its deductions under section 642(c) limited if section 681(c) had not been repealed by this Act. In applying the preceding sentence, in addition to the limitations contained in section 504(a) or 681(c) before its repeal, section 504(a)(1) or 681(c)(1) shall be treated as not applying to an organization to the extent its income is required to be accumulated pursuant to the mandatory terms (as in effect on January 1, 1951, and at all times thereafter) of an instrument executed before January 1, 1951, with respect to the transfer of income producing property to such organization before such date, if such transfer was irrevocable on such date;

"(C) apply to a grant to a private foundation described in section 4942(g)(1)(A)(ii) which is not described in section 4942(g)(1)(A)(i), pursuant to a written commitment which was binding on May 26, 1969, and at all times thereafter, as if such grant is a grant to an operating foundation (as defined in section 4942(j)(3)), if such grant is made for one or more of the purposes described in section 170(c)(2)(B) and is to be paid out to such private foundation on or before December 31, 1974;

"(D) apply, for purposes of section 4942(f), in such a manner as to treat any distribution made to a private foundation in redemption of stock held by such private foundation in a business enterprise as not essentially equivalent to a dividend under section 302(b)(1) if such redemption is described in paragraph (2)(B) of this subsection;

"(E) not apply to an organization which is prohibited by its governing instrument or other instrument from distributing capital or corpus to the extent the requirements of section 4942 are inconsistent with such prohibition; and

"(F) apply, in the case of an organization described in paragraph (4)(A) of this subsection,

"(i) by applying section 4942(e) without regard to the stock to which paragraph (4)(A)(ii) of this subsection applies,

"(ii) by applying section 4942(f) without regard to dividend income for [from] such stock, and

"(iii) by defining the distributable amount as the sum of the amount determined under section 4942(d) (after the application of clauses (i) and (ii)), and the amount of the dividend income from such stock.

With respect to taxable years beginning after December 31, 1971, subparagraphs (B) and (E) shall apply only during the pendency of any judicial proceeding by the private foundation which is necessary to reform, or to excuse such foundation from compliance with, its governing instrument or any other instrument (as in effect on May 26, 1969) in order to comply with the provisions of section 4942, and in the case of subparagraph (B) for all periods after the termination of such judicial proceeding during which the governing instrument or any other instrument does not permit compliance with such provisions."

[Sec. 4943]

SEC. 4943. TAXES ON EXCESS BUSINESS HOLDINGS.

[Sec. 4943(a)]

(a) INITIAL TAX.—

(1) IMPOSITION.—There is hereby imposed on the excess business holdings of any private foundation in a business enterprise during any taxable year which ends during the taxable period a tax equal to 10 percent of the value of such holdings.

(2) SPECIAL RULES.—The tax imposed by paragraph (1)—

(A) shall be imposed on the last day of the taxable year, but

(B) with respect to the private foundation's holdings in any business enterprise, shall be determined as of that day during the taxable year when the foundation's excess holdings in such enterprise were the greatest.

EXCISE TAXES—PRIVATE FOUNDATIONS

Amendments

• 2006, Pension Protection Act of 2006 (P.L. 109-280)

P.L. 109-280, § 1212(c):

Amended Code Sec. 4943(a)(1) by striking "5 percent" and inserting "10 percent".
Effective for tax years beginning after 8-17-2006.

[Sec. 4943(b)]

(b) ADDITIONAL TAX.—In any case in which an initial tax is imposed under subsection (a) with respect to the holdings of a private foundation in any business enterprise, if, at the close of the taxable period with respect to such holdings, the foundation still has excess business holdings in such enterprise, there is hereby imposed a tax equal to 200 percent of such excess business holdings.

Amendments

• 1980 (P.L. 96-596)

P.L. 96-596, § 2(a)(1):

Amended Code Sec. 4943(b) by striking out "correction period" and inserting in lieu thereof "taxable period". **Effective** with respect to second-tier taxes assessed after 12-24-80 (except in cases where there is a court decision with regard to which res judicata applies on that date).

[Sec. 4943(c)]

(c) EXCESS BUSINESS HOLDINGS.—For purposes of this section—

(1) IN GENERAL.—The term "excess business holdings" means, with respect to the holdings of any private foundation in any business enterprise, the amount of stock or other interest in the enterprise which the foundation would have to dispose of to a person other than a disqualified person in order for the remaining holdings of the foundation in such enterprise to be permitted holdings.

(2) PERMITTED HOLDINGS IN A CORPORATION.—

(A) IN GENERAL.—The permitted holdings of any private foundation in an incorporated business enterprise are—

(i) 20 percent of the voting stock, reduced by

(ii) the percentage of the voting stock owned by all disqualified persons.

In any case in which all disqualified persons together do not own more than 20 percent of the voting stock of an incorporated business enterprise, nonvoting stock held by the private foundation shall also be treated as permitted holdings.

(B) 35 PERCENT RULE WHERE THIRD PERSON HAS EFFECTIVE CONTROL OF ENTERPRISE.—If—

(i) the private foundation and all disqualified persons together do not own more than 35 percent of the voting stock of an incorporated business enterprise, and

(ii) it is established to the satisfaction of the Secretary that effective control of the corporation is in one or more persons who are not disqualified persons with respect to the foundation,

then subparagraph (A) shall be applied by substituting 35 percent for 20 percent.

(C) 2 PERCENT DE MINIMIS RULE.—A private foundation shall not be treated as having excess business holdings in any corporation in which it (together with all other private foundations which are described in section 4946(a)(1)(H)) owns not more than 2 percent of the voting stock and not more than 2 percent in value of all outstanding shares of all classes of stock.

(3) PERMITTED HOLDINGS IN PARTNERSHIPS, ETC.—The permitted holdings of a private foundation in any business enterprise which is not incorporated shall be determined under regulations prescribed by the Secretary. Such regulations shall be consistent in principle with paragraphs (2) and (4), except that—

(A) in the case of a partnership or joint venture, "profits interest" shall be substituted for "voting stock", and "capital interest" shall be substituted for "nonvoting stock",

(B) in the case of a proprietorship, there shall be no permitted holdings, and

(C) in any other case, "beneficial interest" shall be substituted for "voting stock".

(4) PRESENT HOLDINGS.—

(A)(i) In applying this section with respect to the holdings of any private foundation in a business enterprise, if such foundation and all disqualified persons together have holdings in such enterprise in excess of 20 percent of the voting stock on May 26, 1969, the percentage of such holdings shall be substituted for "20 percent," and for "35 percent" (if the percentage of such holdings is greater than 35 percent), wherever it appears in paragraph (2), but in no event shall the percentage so substituted be more than 50 percent.

(ii) If the percentage of the holdings of any private foundation and all disqualified persons together in a business enterprise (or if the percentage of the holdings of the private foundation in such enterprise) decreases for any reason, clause (i) and subparagraph (D) shall, except as provided in the next sentence, be applied for all periods after such decrease by substituting such decreased percentage for the percentage held on May 26, 1969, but in no event shall the percentage substituted be less than 20 percent. For purposes of the preceding sentence, any decrease in percentage holdings attributable to issuances of stock (or to issuances of stock coupled with redemptions of stock) shall be disregarded so long as—

(I) the net percentage decrease disregarded under this sentence does not exceed 2 percent, and

(II) the number of shares held by the foundation is not affected by any such issuance or redemption.

(iii) The percentage substituted under clause (i), and any percentage substituted under subparagraph (D), shall be applied both with respect to the voting stock and, separately, with respect to the value of all outstanding shares of all classes of stock.

(iv) In the case of any merger, recapitalization, or other reorganization involving one or more business enterprises, the application of clauses (i), (ii), and (iii) shall be determined under regulations prescribed by the Secretary.

(B) Any interest in a business enterprise which a private foundation holds on May 26, 1969, if the private foundation on such date has excess business holdings, shall (while held by the foundation) be treated as held by a disqualified person (rather than by the private foundation)—

(i) during the 20-year period beginning on such date, if the private foundation and all disqualified persons have more than a 95 percent voting stock interest on such date,

(ii) except as provided in clause (i), during the 15-year period beginning on such date, if the foundation and all disqualified persons have more than a 75 percent voting stock interest (or more than a 75 percent profits or beneficial interest in the case of any unincorporated enterprise) on such date or more than a 75 percent interest in the value of all outstanding shares of all classes of stock (or more than a 75 percent capital interest in the case of a partnership or joint venture) on such date, or

(iii) during the 10-year period beginning on such date, in any other case.

(C) The 20-year, 15-year, and 10-year periods described in subparagraph (B) for the disposition of excess business holdings shall be suspended during the pendency of any judicial proceeding by the private foundation which is necessary to reform, or to excuse such foundation from compliance with, its governing instrument or any other instrument (as in effect on May 26, 1969) in order to allow disposition of such holdings.

(D)(i) If, at any time during the second phase, all disqualified persons together have holdings in a business enterprise, in excess of 2 percent of the voting stock of such enterprise, then subparagraph (A)(i) shall be applied by substituting for "50 percent" the following: "50 percent, of which not more than 25 percent shall be voting stock held by the private foundation".

(ii) If, immediately before the close of the second phase, clause (i) of this subparagraph did not apply with respect to a business enterprise, then for all periods after the close of the second phase subparagraph (A)(i) shall be applied by substituting for "50 percent" the following: "35 percent, or if at any time after the close of the second phase all disqualified persons together have had holdings in such enterprise which exceed 2 percent of the voting stock, 35 percent, of which not more than 25 percent shall be voting stock held by the private foundation".

(iii) For purposes of this subparagraph, the term "second phase" means the 15-year period immediately following the 20-year, 15-year, or 10-year period described in subparagraph (B), whichever applies, as modified by subparagraph (C).

(E) Clause (ii) of subparagraph (B) shall not apply with respect to any business enterprise if before January 1, 1971, one or more individuals who are substantial contributors (or members of the family (within the meaning of section 4946(d)) of one or more substantial contributors) to the private foundation and who on May 26, 1969, held more than 15 percent of the voting stock of the enterprise elect, in such manner as the Secretary may by regulations prescribe, not to have such clause (ii) apply with respect to such enterprise.

(5) HOLDINGS ACQUIRED BY TRUST OR WILL.—Paragraph (4) (other than subparagraph (B)(i)) shall apply to any interest in a business enterprise which a private foundation acquires under the terms of a trust which was irrevocable on May 26, 1969, or under the terms of a will executed on or before such date, which are in effect on such date and at all times thereafter, as if such interest were held on May 26, 1969, except that the 15-year and 10-year periods prescribed in clauses (ii) and (iii) of paragraph (4)(B) shall commence with respect to such interest on the date of distribution under the trust or will in lieu of May 26, 1969.

(6) 5-YEAR PERIOD TO DISPOSE OF GIFTS, BEQUESTS, ETC.—Except as provided in paragraph (5), if, after May 26, 1969, there is a change in the holdings in a business enterprise (other than by purchase by the private foundation or by a disqualified person) which causes the private foundation to have—

(A) excess business holdings in such enterprise, the interest of the foundation in such enterprise (immediately after such change) shall (while held by the foundation) be treated as held by a disqualified person (rather than by the foundation) during the 5-year period beginning on the date of such change in holdings; or

(B) an increase in excess business holdings in such enterprise (determined without regard to subparagraph (A)), subparagraph (A) shall apply, except that the excess holdings immediately preceding the increase therein shall not be treated, solely because of such increase, as held by a disqualified person (rather than by the foundation).

In any case where an acquisition by a disqualified person would result in a substitution under clause (i) or (ii) of subparagraph (D) of paragraph (4), the preceding sentence shall be applied with respect to such acquisition as if it did not contain the phrase "or by a disqualified person" in the material preceding subparagraph (A).

(7) 5-YEAR EXTENSION OF PERIOD TO DISPOSE OF CERTAIN LARGE GIFTS AND BEQUESTS.—The Secretary may extend for an additional 5-year period the period under paragraph (6) for disposing of excess business holdings in the case of an unusually large gift or bequest of diverse holdings or holdings with complex corporate structures if—

(A) the foundation establishes that—

(i) diligent efforts to dispose of such holdings have been made within the initial 5-year period, and

(ii) disposition within the initial 5-year period has not been possible (except at a price substantially below fair market value) by reason of such size and complexity or diversity of such holdings,

(B) before the close of the initial 5-year period—

(i) the private foundation submits to the Secretary a plan for disposing of all of the excess business holdings involved in the extension, and

(ii) the private foundation submits the plan described in clause (i) to the Attorney General (or other appropriate State official) having administrative or supervisory authority or responsibility with respect to the foundation's disposition of the excess business holdings involved and submits to the Secretary any response received by the private foundation from the Attorney General (or other appropriate State official) to such plan during such 5-year period, and

(C) the Secretary determines that such plan can reasonably be expected to be carried out before the close of the extension period.

Amendments

- **1984, Deficit Reduction Act of 1984 (P.L. 98-369)**

P.L. 98-369, §307(a):

Amended Code Sec. 4943(c) by adding new paragraph (7). **Effective** for business holdings with respect to which the 5-year period described in Code Sec. 4943(c)(6) ends on or after 11-1-83. Any plan submitted to the Secretary of the Treasury or his delegate on or before the 60th day after 7-18-84 shall be treated as submitted before the close of the initial 5-year period referred to in Code Sec. 4943(c)(7)(B) (as added by subsection (a)).

P.L. 98-369, §308(a):

Amended the second sentence of Code Sec. 4943(c)(4)(A)(ii). **Effective** for increases and decreases occurring after 7-18-84. Prior to amendment, the second sentence of Code Sec. 4943(c)(4)(A)(ii) read as follows:

For purposes of this clause, any decrease in percentage holdings attributable to issuances of stock (or to issuances of stock coupled with redemptions of stock) shall be determined only as of the close of each taxable year of the private foundation unless the aggregate of the percentage decreases attributable to the issuances of stock (or such issuances and redemptions) during such taxable year equals or exceeds 1 percent.

P.L. 98-369, §309(a):

Amended Code Sec. 4943(c)(4)(B)(i) by striking out "the private foundation has" and inserting in lieu thereof "the private foundation and all disqualified persons have". **Effective** as if included in Act Sec. 101(b) of P.L. 91-172.

P.L. 98-369, §310(a):

Amended Code Sec. 4943(c)(6) by adding at the end thereof a new sentence. **Effective** for acquisitions after 7-18-84.

- **1976, Tax Reform Act of 1976 (P.L. 94-455)**

P.L. 94-455, §1906(b)(13)(A):

Amended 1954 Code by substituting "Secretary" for "Secretary or his delegate" each place it appeared. **Effective** 2-1-77.

[Sec. 4943(d)]

(d) DEFINITIONS; SPECIAL RULES.—For purposes of this section—

(1) BUSINESS HOLDINGS.—In computing the holdings of a private foundation, or a disqualified person (as defined in section 4946) with respect thereto, in any business enterprise, any stock or other interest owned, directly or indirectly, by or for a corporation, partnership, estate, or trust shall be considered as being owned proportionately by or for its shareholders, partners, or beneficiaries. The preceding sentence shall not apply with respect to an income or remainder interest of a private foundation in a trust described in section 4947(a)(2), but only if, in the case of property transferred in trust after May 26, 1969, such foundation holds only an income interest or only a remainder interest in such trust.

(2) TAXABLE PERIOD.—The term "taxable period" means, with respect to any excess business holdings of a private foundation in a business enterprise, the period beginning on the first day on which there are such excess holdings and ending on the earlier of—

(A) the date of mailing of a notice of deficiency with respect to the tax imposed by subsection (a) under section 6212 in respect of such holdings, or

(B) the date on which the tax imposed by subsection (a) in respect of such holdings is assessed.

EXCISE TAXES—PRIVATE FOUNDATIONS

(3) BUSINESS ENTERPRISE.—The term "business enterprise" does not include—

(A) a functionally related business (as defined in section 4942(j)(4)), or

(B) a trade or business at least 95 percent of the gross income of which is derived from passive sources.

For purposes of subparagraph (B), gross income from passive sources includes the items excluded by section 512(b)(1), (2), (3), and (5), and income from the sale of goods (including charges or costs passed on at cost to purchasers of such goods or income received in settlement of a dispute concerning or in lieu of the exercise of the right to sell such goods) if the seller does not manufacture, produce, physically receive or deliver, negotiate sales of, or maintain inventories in such goods.

(4) DISQUALIFIED PERSON.—The term "disqualified person" (as defined in section 4946(a)) does not include a plan described in section 4975(e)(7) with respect to the holdings of a private foundation described in paragraphs (4) and (5) of subsection (c).

Amendments

• **1984, Deficit Reduction Act of 1984 (P.L. 98-369)**

P.L. 98-369, § 314(c)(1):

Amended Code Sec. 4943(d) by adding at the end thereof new paragraph (4). **Effective** with respect to tax years beginning after 7-18-84.

• **1980 (P.L. 96-596)**

P.L. 96-596, § 2(a)(2):

Amended Code Sec. 4943(d)(2). **Effective** with respect to second-tier taxes assessed after 12-24-80 (except in cases where there is a court decision with regard to which res judicata applies on that date). Prior to amendment, Code Sec. 4943(d)(2) read:

"(2) TAXABLE PERIOD.—The term 'taxable period' means, with respect to any excess business holdings of a private foundation in a business enterprise, the period beginning on the first day on which there are such excess holdings and ending on the date of mailing of a notice of deficiency with respect to the tax imposed by subsection (a) under section 6212 in respect of such holdings."

P.L. 96-596, § 2(a)(3):

Amended Code Sec. 4943(d) by: (1) striking out paragraph (3) and redesignating paragraph (4) as paragraph (3), and (2) by striking out "4942(j)(5)" and inserting in lieu thereof "4942(j)(4)" in Code Sec. 4943(d)(3)(A) (as redesignated). Prior to amendment, Code Sec. 4943(d)(3) read:

"(3) CORRECTION PERIOD.—The term 'correction period' means, with respect to excess business holdings of a private foundation in a business enterprise, the period ending 90 days after the date of mailing of a notice of deficiency (with respect to the tax imposed by subsection (b)) under section 6212, extended by—

"(A) any period in which a deficiency cannot be assessed under section 6213(a), and

"(B) any other period which the Secretary determines is reasonable and necessary to permit orderly disposition of such excess business holdings."

• **1976, Tax Reform Act of 1976 (P.L. 94-455)**

P.L. 94-455, § 1906(b)(13)(A):

Amended 1954 Code by substituting "Secretary" for "Secretary or his delegate" each place it appeared. **Effective** 2-1-77.

• **1969, Tax Reform Act of 1969 (P.L. 91-172)**

P.L. 91-172, § 101(b):

Added Code Sec. 4943. **Effective** for tax years beginning after 12-31-69, except as noted below.

P.L. 91-172, § 101(1)(4), as amended by P.L. 98-369, § 314(b), provides:

"(A) In the case of a private foundation—

"(i) which was incorporated before January 1, 1951;

"(ii) substantially all of the assets of which on May 26, 1969, consist of more than 90 percent of the stock of an incorporated business enterprise which is licensed and regulated, the sales or contracts of which are regulated, and the professional representatives of which are licensed, by State regulatory agencies in at least 10 States; and

"(iii) which acquired such stock solely by gift, devise, or bequest, section 4943(c)(4)(A)(i) shall be applied with respect to the holdings of such foundation in such incorporated business enterprise 'as if it did not contain the phrase ", but in no event shall the percentage so substituted be more than 50 percent"', and section 4943(c)(4)(D) shall not apply with respect to such holdings. For purposes of the preceding sentence, stock of such enterprise in a trust created before May 27, 1969, of which the foundation is the remainder beneficiary shall be deemed to be held by such foundation on May 26, 1969, if such foundation held (without regard to such trust) more than 20 percent of the stock of such enterprise on May 26, 1969.

"(B) Subparagraph (A) shall apply to a private foundation only if—

"(i) the foundation does not purchase any stock or other interest in the enterprise described in subparagraph (A) after May 26, 1969, and does not acquire any stock or other interest in any other business enterprise which constitutes excess business holdings under section 4943; and

"(ii) in the last 5 taxable years ending on or before December 31, 1970, the foundation expends substantially all of its adjusted net income (as defined in section 4942(f)) for the purpose or function for which it is organized and operated.

"(C) For purposes of section 4943(c)(6), the term "purchase" does not include an exchange which is described in paragraph (2)(B) of this subsection and which is pursuant to a plan for disposition of excess business holdings."

[Sec. 4943(e)]

(e) APPLICATION OF TAX TO DONOR ADVISED FUNDS.—

(1) IN GENERAL.—For purposes of this section, a donor advised fund (as defined in section 4966(d)(2)) shall be treated as a private foundation.

(2) DISQUALIFIED PERSON.—In applying this section to any donor advised fund (as so defined), the term "disqualified person" means, with respect to the donor advised fund, any person who is—

(A) described in section 4966(d)(2)(A)(iii),

(B) a member of the family of an individual described in subparagraph (A), or

(C) a 35-percent controlled entity (as defined in section 4958(f)(3) by substituting "persons described in subparagraph (A) or (B) of section 4943(e)(2)" for "persons described in subparagraph (A) or (B) of paragraph (1)" in subparagraph (A)(i) thereof).

(3) PRESENT HOLDINGS.—For purposes of this subsection, rules similar to the rules of paragraphs (4), (5), and (6) of subsection (c) shall apply to donor advised funds (as so defined), except that—

(A) "the date of the enactment of this subsection" shall be substituted for "May 26, 1969" each place it appears in paragraphs (4), (5), and (6), and

(B) "January 1, 2007" shall be substituted for "January 1, 1971" in paragraph (4)(E).

Amendments

• **2014, Tax Technical Corrections Act of 2014 (P.L. 113-295)**

P.L. 113-295, § 220(r), Division A:

Amended Code Sec. 4943(e)(3)(B) by striking "January 1, 1970" and inserting "January 1, 1971". **Effective** 12-19-2014.

• **2006, Pension Protection Act of 2006 (P.L. 109-280)**

P.L. 109-280, § 1233(a):

Amended Code Sec. 4943 by adding at the end a new subsection (e). **Effective** for tax years beginning after 8-17-2006.

[Sec. 4943(f)]

(f) APPLICATION OF TAX TO SUPPORTING ORGANIZATIONS.—

(1) IN GENERAL.—For purposes of this section, an organization which is described in paragraph (3) shall be treated as a private foundation.

(2) EXCEPTION.—The Secretary may exempt the excess business holdings of any organization from the application of this subsection if the Secretary determines that such holdings are consistent with the purpose or function constituting the basis for its exemption under section 501.

(3) ORGANIZATIONS DESCRIBED.—An organization is described in this paragraph if such organization is—

(A) a type III supporting organization (other than a functionally integrated type III supporting organization), or

(B) an organization which meets the requirements of subparagraphs (A) and (C) of section 509(a)(3) and which is supervised or controlled in connection with or one or more organizations described in paragraph (1) or (2) of section 509(a), but only if such organization accepts any gift or contribution from any person described in section 509(f)(2)(B).

(4) DISQUALIFIED PERSON.—

(A) IN GENERAL.—In applying this section to any organization described in paragraph (3), the term "disqualified person" means, with respect to the organization—

EXCISE TAXES—PRIVATE FOUNDATIONS

   (i) any person who was, at any time during the 5-year period ending on the date described in subsection (a)(2)(A), in a position to exercise substantial influence over the affairs of the organization,

   (ii) any member of the family (determined under section 4958(f)(4)) of an individual described in clause (i),

   (iii) any 35-percent controlled entity (as defined in section 4958(f)(3) by substituting "persons described in clause (i) or (ii) of section 4943(f)(4)(A)" for "persons described in subparagraph (A) or (B) of paragraph (1)" in subparagraph (A)(i) thereof),

   (iv) any person described in section 4958(c)(3)(B), and

   (v) any organization—

      (I) which is effectively controlled (directly or indirectly) by the same person or persons who control the organization in question, or

      (II) substantially all of the contributions to which were made (directly or indirectly) by the same person or persons described in subparagraph (B) or a member of the family (within the meaning of section 4946(d)) of such a person.

   (B) PERSONS DESCRIBED.—A person is described in this subparagraph if such person is—

      (i) a substantial contributor to the organization (as defined in section 4958(c)(3)(C)),

      (ii) an officer, director, or trustee of the organization (or an individual having powers or responsibilities similar to those of the officers, directors, or trustees of the organization), or

      (iii) an owner of more than 20 percent of—

         (I) the total combined voting power of a corporation,

         (II) the profits interest of a partnership, or

         (III) the beneficial interest of a trust or unincorporated enterprise,

      which is a substantial contributor (as so defined) to the organization.

(5) TYPE III SUPPORTING ORGANIZATION; FUNCTIONALLY INTEGRATED TYPE III SUPPORTING ORGANIZATION.—For purposes of this subsection—

   (A) TYPE III SUPPORTING ORGANIZATION.—The term "type III supporting organization" means an organization which meets the requirements of subparagraphs (A) and (C) of section 509(a)(3) and which is operated in connection with one or more organizations described in paragraph (1) or (2) of section 509(a).

   (B) FUNCTIONALLY INTEGRATED TYPE III SUPPORTING ORGANIZATION.—The term "functionally integrated type III supporting organization" means a type III supporting organization which is not required under regulations established by the Secretary to make payments to supported organizations (as defined under section 509(f)(3)) due to the activities of the organization related to performing the functions of, or carrying out the purposes of, such supported organizations.

(6) SPECIAL RULE FOR CERTAIN HOLDINGS OF TYPE III SUPPORTING ORGANIZATIONS.—For purposes of this subsection, the term "excess business holdings" shall not include any holdings of a type III supporting organization in any business enterprise if, as of November 18, 2005, the holdings were held (and at all times thereafter, are held) for the benefit of the community pursuant to the direction of a State attorney general or a State official with jurisdiction over such organization.

(7) PRESENT HOLDINGS.—For purposes of this subsection, rules similar to the rules of paragraphs (4), (5), and (6) of subsection (c) shall apply to organizations described in section 509(a)(3), except that—

   (A) "the date of the enactment of this subsection" shall be substituted for "May 26, 1969" each place it appears in paragraphs (4), (5), and (6), and

   (B) "January 1, 2007" shall be substituted for "January 1, 1971" in paragraph (4)(E).

Amendments

• **2014, Tax Technical Corrections Act of 2014 (P.L. 113-295)**

P.L. 113-295, § 220(r), Division A:

Amended Code Sec. 4943(f)(7)(B) by striking "January 1, 1970" and inserting "January 1, 1971". **Effective** 12-19-2014.

• **2006, Pension Protection Act of 2006 (P.L. 109-280)**

P.L. 109-280, § 1243(a):

Amended Code Sec. 4943, as amended by this Act, by adding at the end a new subsection (f). **Effective** for tax years beginning after 8-17-2006.

[Sec. 4943(g)]

(g) EXCEPTION FOR CERTAIN HOLDINGS LIMITED TO INDEPENDENTLY-OPERATED PHILANTHROPIC BUSINESS.—

   (1) IN GENERAL.—Subsection (a) shall not apply with respect to the holdings of a private foundation in any business enterprise which meets the requirements of paragraphs (2), (3), and (4) for the taxable year.

   (2) OWNERSHIP.—The requirements of this paragraph are met if—

      (A) 100 percent of the voting stock in the business enterprise is held by the private foundation at all times during the taxable year, and

      (B) all the private foundation's ownership interests in the business enterprise were acquired by means other than by purchase.

   (3) ALL PROFITS TO CHARITY.—

      (A) IN GENERAL.—The requirements of this paragraph are met if the business enterprise, not later than 120 days after the close of the taxable year, distributes an amount equal to its net operating income for such taxable year to the private foundation.

      (B) NET OPERATING INCOME.—For purposes of this paragraph, the net operating income of any business enterprise for any taxable year is an amount equal to the gross income of the business enterprise for the taxable year, reduced by the sum of—

         (i) the deductions allowed by chapter 1 for the taxable year which are directly connected with the production of such income,

         (ii) the tax imposed by chapter 1 on the business enterprise for the taxable year, and

         (iii) an amount for a reasonable reserve for working capital and other business needs of the business enterprise.

   (4) INDEPENDENT OPERATION.—The requirements of this paragraph are met if, at all times during the taxable year—

      (A) no substantial contributor (as defined in section 4958(c)(3)(C)) to the private foundation or family member (as determined under section 4958(f)(4)) of such a contributor is a director, officer, trustee, manager, employee, or contractor of the business enterprise (or an individual having powers or responsibilities similar to any of the foregoing),

      (B) at least a majority of the board of directors of the private foundation are persons who are not—

         (i) directors or officers of the business enterprise, or

         (ii) family members (as so determined) of a substantial contributor (as so defined) to the private foundation, and

      (C) there is no loan outstanding from the business enterprise to a substantial contributor (as so defined) to the private foundation or to any family member of such a contributor (as so determined).

   (5) CERTAIN DEEMED PRIVATE FOUNDATIONS EXCLUDED.—This subsection shall not apply to—

      (A) any fund or organization treated as a private foundation for purposes of this section by reason of subsection (e) or (f),

      (B) any trust described in section 4947(a)(1) (relating to charitable trusts), and

EXCISE TAXES—PRIVATE FOUNDATIONS

(C) any trust described in section 4947(a)(2) (relating to split-interest trusts).

Amendments

• **2018, Bipartisan Budget Act of 2018 (P.L. 115-123)**

P.L. 115-123, § 41110(a), Div. D:

Amended Code Sec. 4943 by adding at the end a new subsection (g). **Effective** for tax years beginning after 12-31-2017.

[Sec. 4944]

SEC. 4944. TAXES ON INVESTMENTS WHICH JEOPARDIZE CHARITABLE PURPOSE.

[Sec. 4944(a)]

(a) INITIAL TAXES.—

(1) ON THE PRIVATE FOUNDATION.—If a private foundation invests any amount in such a manner as to jeopardize the carrying out of any of its exempt purposes, there is hereby imposed on the making of such investment a tax equal to 10 percent of the amount so invested for each year (or part thereof) in the taxable period. The tax imposed by this paragraph shall be paid by the private foundation.

(2) ON THE MANAGEMENT.—In any case in which a tax is imposed by paragraph (1), there is hereby imposed on the participation of any foundation manager in the making of the investment, knowing that it is jeopardizing the carrying out of any of the foundation's exempt purposes, a tax equal to 10 percent of the amount so invested for each year (or part thereof) in the taxable period, unless such participation is not willful and is due to reasonable cause. The tax imposed by this paragraph shall be paid by any foundation manager who participated in the making of the investment.

Amendments

• **2006, Pension Protection Act of 2006 (P.L. 109-280)**

P.L. 109-280, § 1212(d)(1):

Amended Code Sec. 4944(a) by striking "5 percent" both places it appears and inserting "10 percent". **Effective** for tax years beginning after 8-17-2006.

[Sec. 4944(b)]

(b) ADDITIONAL TAXES.—

(1) ON THE FOUNDATION.—In any case in which an initial tax is imposed by subsection (a)(1) on the making of an investment and such investment is not removed from jeopardy within the taxable period, there is hereby imposed a tax equal to 25 percent of the amount of the investment. The tax imposed by this paragraph shall be paid by the private foundation.

(2) ON THE MANAGEMENT.—In any case in which an additional tax is imposed by paragraph (1), if a foundation manager refused to agree to part or all of the removal from jeopardy, there is hereby imposed a tax equal to 5 percent of the amount of the investment. The tax imposed by this paragraph shall be paid by any foundation manager who refused to agree to part or all of the removal from jeopardy.

Amendments

• **1980 (P.L. 96-596)**

P.L. 96-596, § 2(a)(1):

Amended Code Sec. 4944(b)(1) by striking out "correction period" and inserting in lieu thereof "taxable period". **Effective** with respect to second-tier taxes assessed after 12-24-80 (except in cases where there is a court decision with regard to which res judicata applies on that date).

[Sec. 4944(c)]

(c) EXCEPTION FOR PROGRAM-RELATED INVESTMENTS.—For purposes of this section, investments, the primary purpose of which is to accomplish one or more of the purposes described in section 170(c)(2)(B), and no significant purpose of which is the production of income or the appreciation of property, shall not be considered as investments which jeopardize the carrying out of exempt purposes.

[Sec. 4944(d)]

(d) SPECIAL RULES.—For purposes of subsections (a) and (b)—

(1) JOINT AND SEVERAL LIABILITY.—If more than one person is liable under subsection (a)(2) or (b)(2) with respect to any one investment, all such persons shall be jointly and severally liable under such paragraph with respect to such investment.

(2) LIMIT FOR MANAGEMENT.—With respect to any one investment, the maximum amount of the tax imposed by subsection (a)(2) shall not exceed $10,000, and the maximum amount of the tax imposed by subsection (b)(2) shall not exceed $20,000.

Amendments

• **2006, Pension Protection Act of 2006 (P.L. 109-280)**

P.L. 109-280, § 1212(d)(2)(A)-(B):

Amended Code Sec. 4944(d)(2) by striking "$5,000," and inserting "$10,000,", and by striking "$10,000." and inserting "$20,000.". **Effective** for tax years beginning after 8-17-2006.

[Sec. 4944(e)]

(e) DEFINITIONS.—For purposes of this section—

(1) TAXABLE PERIOD.—The term "taxable period" means, with respect to any investment which jeopardizes the carrying out of exempt purposes, the period beginning with the date on which the amount is so invested and ending on the earliest of—

(A) the date of mailing of a notice of deficiency with respect to the tax imposed by subsection (a)(1) under section 6212,

(B) the date on which the tax imposed by subsection (a)(1) is assessed, or

(C) the date on which the amount so invested is removed from jeopardy.

(2) REMOVAL FROM JEOPARDY.—An investment which jeopardizes the carrying out of exempt purposes shall be considered to be removed from jeopardy when such investment is sold or otherwise disposed of, and the proceeds of such sale or other disposition are not investments which jeopardize the carrying out of exempt purposes.

Amendments

• **1980 (P.L. 96-596)**

P.L. 96-596, § 2(a)(2):

Amended Code Sec. 4944(e)(1). **Effective** with respect to second-tier taxes assessed after 12-24-80 (except in cases where there is a court decision with regard to which res judicata applies on that date). Prior to amendment, Code Sec. 4944(e)(1) read:

"(1) TAXABLE PERIOD.—The term `taxable period' means, with respect to any investment which jeopardizes the carrying out of exempt purposes, the period beginning with the date on which the amount is so invested and ending on whichever of the following is the earlier: (A) the date of mailing of a notice of deficiency with respect to the tax imposed by subsection (a)(1) under section 6212, or (B) the date on which the amount so invested is removed from jeopardy."

P.L. 96-596, § 2(a)(3):

Amended Code Sec. 4944(e) by striking out paragraph (3). **Effective** 12-24-80. Prior to amendment, Code Sec. 4944(e)(3) read:

"(3) CORRECTION PERIOD.—The term `correction period' means, with respect to any investment which jeopardizes the carrying out of exempt purposes, the period beginning with the date on which such investment is entered into and ending 90 days after the date of mailing of a notice of deficiency with respect to the tax imposed by subsection (b)(1) under section 6212, extended by—

"(A) any period in which a deficiency cannot be assessed under section 6213(a), and

"(B) any other period which the Secretary determines is reasonable and necessary to bring about removal from jeopardy."

• **1976, Tax Reform Act of 1976 (P.L. 94-455)**

P.L. 94-455, §1906(b)(13)(A):

Amended 1954 Code by substituting "Secretary" for "Secretary or his delegate" each place it appeared. **Effective** 2-1-77.

• **1969, Tax Reform Act of 1969 (P.L. 91-172)**

P.L. 91-172, §101(b):

Added Code Sec. 4944. **Effective** 1-1-70.

[Sec. 4945]

SEC. 4945. TAXES ON TAXABLE EXPENDITURES.

[Sec. 4945(a)]

(a) INITIAL TAXES.—

(1) ON THE FOUNDATION.—There is hereby imposed on each taxable expenditure (as defined in subsection (d)) a tax equal to 20 percent of the amount thereof. The tax imposed by this paragraph shall be paid by the private foundation.

(2) ON THE MANAGEMENT.—There is hereby imposed on the agreement of any foundation manager to the making of an expenditure, knowing that it is a taxable expenditure, a tax equal to 5 percent of the amount thereof, unless such agreement is not willful and is due to reasonable cause. The tax imposed by this paragraph shall be paid by any foundation manager who agreed to the making of the expenditure.

Amendments

• **2006, Pension Protection Act of 2006 (P.L. 109-280)**

P.L. 109-280, §1212(e)(1)(A)-(B):

Amended Code Sec. 4945(a) by striking "10 percent" and inserting "20 percent" in paragraph (1), and by striking "2½ percent" and inserting "5 percent" in paragraph (2). **Effective** for tax years beginning after 8-17-2006.

[Sec. 4945(b)]

(b) ADDITIONAL TAXES.—

(1) ON THE FOUNDATION.—In any case in which an initial tax is imposed by subsection (a)(1) on a taxable expenditure and such expenditure is not corrected within the taxable period, there is hereby imposed a tax equal to 100 percent of the amount of the expenditure. The tax imposed by this paragraph shall be paid by the private foundation.

(2) ON THE MANAGEMENT.—In any case in which an additional tax is imposed by paragraph (1), if a foundation manager refused to agree to part or all of the correction, there is hereby imposed a tax equal to 50 percent of the amount of the taxable expenditure. The tax imposed by this paragraph shall be paid by any foundation manager who refused to agree to part or all of the correction.

Amendments

• **1980 (P.L. 96-596)**

P.L. 96-596, §2(a)(1):

Amended Code Sec. 4945(b)(1) by striking out "correction period" and inserting in lieu thereof "taxable period". **Effective** with respect to second-tier taxes assessed after 12-24-80 (except in cases where there is a court decision with regard to which res judicata applies on that date.)

[Sec. 4945(c)]

(c) SPECIAL RULES.—For purposes of subsections (a) and (b)—

(1) JOINT AND SEVERAL LIABILITY.—If more than one person is liable under subsection (a)(2) or (b)(2) with respect to the making of a taxable expenditure, all such persons shall be jointly and severally liable under such paragraph with respect to such expenditure.

(2) LIMIT FOR MANAGEMENT.—With respect to any one taxable expenditure, the maximum amount of the tax imposed by subsection (a)(2) shall not exceed $10,000, and the maximum amount of the tax imposed by subsection (b)(2) shall not exceed $20,000.

Amendments

• **2006, Pension Protection Act of 2006 (P.L. 109-280)**

P.L. 109-280, §1212(e)(2)(A)-(B):

Amended Code Sec. 4945(c)(2) by striking "$5,000," and inserting "$10,000,", and by striking "$10,000." and inserting "$20,000.". **Effective** for tax years beginning after 8-17-2006.

[Sec. 4945(d)]

(d) TAXABLE EXPENDITURE.—For purposes of this section, the term "taxable expenditure" means any amount paid or incurred by a private foundation—

(1) to carry on propaganda, or otherwise to attempt, to influence legislation, within the meaning of subsection (e),

(2) except as provided in subsection (f), to influence the outcome of any specific public election, or to carry on, directly or indirectly, any voter registration drive,

(3) as a grant to an individual for travel, study, or other similar purposes by such individual, unless such grant satisfies the requirements of subsection (g),

(4) as a grant to an organization unless—

(A) such organization—

(i) is described in paragraph (1) or (2) of section 509(a),

(ii) is an organization described in section 509(a)(3) (other than an organization described in clause (i) or (ii) of section 4942(g)(4)(A)), or

(iii) is an exempt operating foundation (as defined in section 4940(d)(2)), or

(B) the private foundation exercises expenditure responsibility with respect to such grant in accordance with subsection (h), or

(5) for any purpose other than one specified in section 170(c)(2)(B).

Amendments

• **2006, Pension Protection Act of 2006 (P.L. 109-280)**

P.L. 109-280, §1244(b):

Amended Code Sec. 4945(d)(4)(A). **Effective** for distributions and expenditures after 8-17-2006. Prior to amendment, Code Sec. 4945(d)(4)(A) read as follows:

(A) such organization is described in paragraph (1), (2), or (3) of section 509(a) or is an exempt operating foundation (as defined in section 4940(d)(2)), or

EXCISE TAXES—PRIVATE FOUNDATIONS

• **1984, Deficit Reduction Act of 1984 (P.L. 98-369)**

P.L. 98-369, §302(b):

Amended Code Sec. 4945(d)(4). **Effective** for grants made after 12-31-84, in tax years ending after such date, however a special rule appears below. Prior to amendment, Code Sec. 4945(d)(4) read as follows:

(4) as a grant to an organization (other than an organization described in paragraph (1), (2), or (3) of section 509(a)), unless the private foundation exercises expenditure responsibility with respect to such grant in accordance with subsection (h), or

P.L. 98-369, §302(c)(3), provides:

(3) Certain Existing Foundations.—A foundation which was an operating foundation (as defined in section 4942(j)(3) of the Internal Revenue Code of 1954) as of January 1, 1983, shall be treated as meeting the requirements of section 4940(d)(2)(B) of such Code (as added by subsection (a)).

[Sec. 4945(e)]

(e) ACTIVITIES WITHIN SUBSECTION (d)(1).—For purposes of subsection (d)(1), the term "taxable expenditure" means any amount paid or incurred by a private foundation for—

(1) any attempt to influence any legislation through an attempt to affect the opinion of the general public or any segment thereof, and

(2) any attempt to influence legislation through communication with any member or employee of a legislative body, or with any other government official or employee who may participate in the formulation of the legislation (except technical advice or assistance provided to a governmental body or to a committee or other subdivision thereof in response to a written request by such body or subdivision, as the case may be),

other than through making available the results of nonpartisan analysis, study, or research. Paragraph (2) of this subsection shall not apply to any amount paid or incurred in connection with an appearance before, or communication to, any legislative body with respect to a possible decision of such body which might affect the existence of the private foundation, its powers and duties, its tax-exempt status, or the deduction of contributions to such foundation.

[Sec. 4945(f)]

(f) NONPARTISAN ACTIVITIES CARRIED ON BY CERTAIN ORGANIZATIONS.—Subsection (d)(2) shall not apply to any amount paid or incurred by any organization—

(1) which is described in section 501(c)(3) and exempt from taxation under section 501(a),

(2) the activities of which are nonpartisan, are not confined to one specific election period, and are carried on in 5 or more States,

(3) substantially all of the income of which is expended directly for the active conduct of the activities constituting the purpose or function for which it is organized and operated,

(4) substantially all of the support (other than gross investment income as defined in section 509(e)) of which is received from exempt organizations, the general public, governmental units described in section 170(c)(1), or any combination of the foregoing; not more than 25 percent of such support is received from any one exempt organization (for this purpose treating private foundations which are described in section 4946(a)(1)(H) with respect to each other as one exempt organization); and not more than half of the support of which is received from gross investment income, and

(5) contributions to which for voter registration drives are not subject to conditions that they may be used only in specified States, possessions of the United States, or political subdivisions or other areas of any of the foregoing, or the District of Columbia, or that they may be used in only one specific election period.

In determining whether the organization meets the requirements of paragraph (4) for any taxable year of such organization, there shall be taken into account the support received by such organization during such taxable year and during the immediately preceding 4 taxable years of such organization. Subsection (d)(4) shall not apply to any grant to an organization which meets the requirements of this subsection.

Amendments

• **2014, Tax Technical Corrections Act of 2014 (P.L. 113-295)**

P.L. 113-295, §221(a)(106), Division A:

Amended Code Sec. 4945(f) by striking "(excluding therefrom any preceding taxable year which begins before January 1, 1970)" before the period at the end of the second sentence. **Effective** generally 12-19-2014. For a special rule, see Act Sec. 221(b)(2), Division A, below.

P.L. 113-295, §221(b)(2), Division A, provides:

(2) SAVINGS PROVISION.—If—

(A) any provision amended or repealed by the amendments made by this section applied to—

(i) any transaction occurring before the date of the enactment of this Act,

(ii) any property acquired before such date of enactment, or

(iii) any item of income, loss, deduction, or credit taken into account before such date of enactment, and

(B) the treatment of such transaction, property, or item under such provision would (without regard to the amendments or repeals made by this section) affect the liability for tax for periods ending after date of enactment, nothing in the amendments or repeals made by this section shall be construed to affect the treatment of such transaction, property, or item for purposes of determining liability for tax for periods ending after such date of enactment.

[Sec. 4945(g)]

(g) INDIVIDUAL GRANTS.—Subsection (d)(3) shall not apply to an individual grant awarded on an objective and nondiscriminatory basis pursuant to a procedure approved in advance by the Secretary, if it is demonstrated to the satisfaction of the Secretary that—

(1) the grant constitutes a scholarship or fellowship grant which would be subject to the provisions of section 117(a) (as in effect on the day before the date of the enactment of the Tax Reform Act of 1986) and is to be used for study at an educational organization described in section 170(b)(1)(A)(ii),

(2) the grant constitutes a prize or award which is subject to the provisions of section 74(b) (without regard to paragraph (3) thereof), if the recipient of such prize or award is selected from the general public, or

(3) the purpose of the grant is to achieve a specific objective, produce a report or other similar product, or improve or enhance a literary, artistic, musical, scientific, teaching, or other similar capacity, skill, or talent of the grantee.

Amendments

• **1988, Technical and Miscellaneous Revenue Act of 1988 (P.L. 100-647)**

P.L. 100-647, §1001(d)(1)(B):

Amended Code Sec. 4945(g)(1). **Effective** as if included in the provision of P.L. 99-514 to which it relates. Prior to amendment, Code Sec. 4945(g)(1) read as follows:

(1) the grant constitutes a scholarship or fellowship grant which is subject to the provisions of section 117(a) and is to be used for study at an educational organization described in section 170(b)(1)(A)(ii),

• **1986, Tax Reform Act of 1986 (P.L. 99-514)**

P.L. 99-514, §122(a)(2)(B):

Amended Code Sec. 4945(g)(2) by striking out "section 74(b)" and inserting in lieu thereof "section 74(b) (without regard to paragraph (3) thereof)". **Effective** for prizes and awards granted after 12-31-86.

• **1976, Tax Reform Act of 1976 (P.L. 94-455)**

P.L. 94-455, §1901(b)(8)(H):

Substituted "educational organization described in section 170(b)(1)(A)(ii)" for "educational institution described in section 151(e)(4)" in Code Sec. 4945(g)(1). **Effective** for tax years beginning after 12-31-76.

P.L. 94-455, §1906(b)(13)(A):

Amended 1954 Code by substituting "Secretary" for "Secretary or his delegate" each place it appeared. **Effective** 2-1-77.

EXCISE TAXES—PRIVATE FOUNDATIONS

[Sec. 4945(h)]

(h) EXPENDITURE RESPONSIBILITY.—The expenditure responsibility referred to in subsection (d)(4) means that the private foundation is responsible to exert all reasonable efforts and to establish adequate procedures—

(1) to see that the grant is spent solely for the purpose for which made,

(2) to obtain full and complete reports from the grantee on how the funds are spent, and

(3) to make full and detailed reports with respect to such expenditures to the Secretary.

Amendments

• **1976, Tax Reform Act of 1976 (P.L. 94-455)**

P.L. 94-455, §1906(b)(13)(A):

Amended 1954 Code by substituting "Secretary" for "Secretary or his delegate" each place it appeared. **Effective** 2-1-77.

[Sec. 4945(i)]

(i) OTHER DEFINITIONS.—For purposes of this section—

(1) CORRECTION.—The terms "correction" and "correct" mean, with respect to any taxable expenditure, (A) recovering part or all of the expenditure to the extent recovery is possible, and where full recovery is not possible such additional corrective action as is prescribed by the Secretary by regulations, or (B) in the case of a failure to comply with subsection (h)(2) or (h)(3), obtaining or making the report in question.

(2) TAXABLE PERIOD.—The term "taxable period" means, with respect to any taxable expenditure, the period beginning with the date on which the taxable expenditure occurs and ending on the earlier of—

(A) the date of mailing of a notice of deficiency with respect to the tax imposed by subsection (a)(1) under section 6212, or

(B) the date on which tax imposed by subsection (a)(1) is assessed.

Amendments

• **1980 (P.L. 96-596)**

P.L. 96-596, §2(a)(2):

Amended Code Sec. 4945(i)(2). **Effective** with respect to any second-tier tax assessed after 12-24-80. However, the assessment of a tax in a case to which the doctrine of res judicata applies on 12-24-80, will not be construed to be permitted by the preceding sentence. Prior to amendment, Code Sec. 4945(i)(2) read:

"(2) CORRECTION PERIOD.—The term 'correction period' means, with respect to any taxable expenditure, the period beginning with the date on which the taxable expenditure occurs and ending 90 days after the date of mailing of a notice of deficiency with respect to the tax imposed by subsection (b)(1) under section 6212, extended by—

"(A) any period in which a deficiency cannot be assessed under section 6213(a), and

"(B) any other period which the Secretary determines is reasonable and necessary to bring about correction of the taxable expenditure (except that such determination shall not be made with respect to any taxable expenditure within the meaning of paragraph (1), (2), (3), or (4) of subsection (d) because of any action by an appropriate State officer as defined in section 6104(c)(2))."

• **1976, Tax Reform Act of 1976 (P.L. 94-455)**

P.L. 94-455, §1906(b)(13)(A):

Amended 1954 Code by substituting "Secretary" for "Secretary or his delegate" each place it appeared. **Effective** 2-1-77.

• **1969, Tax Reform Act of 1969 (P.L. 91-172)**

P.L. 91-172, §101(b):

Added Code Sec. 4945. **Effective** 1-1-70.

P.L. 91-172, §101(1)(5), provides:

Code Sec. 4945(d)(4) and (h) shall not apply to a grant to a private foundation described in Code Sec. 4942(g)(1)(A)(ii) which is not described in Code Sec. 4942(g)(1)(A)(i), pursuant to a written commitment which was binding on May 26, 1969, and at all times thereafter, as if such grant is a grant to an operating foundation (as defined in Code Sec. 4942(j)(3)). If such grant is made for one or more of the purposes described in Code Sec. 170(c)(2)(B) and is to be paid out to such private foundation on or before December 31, 1974.

[Sec. 4946]

SEC. 4946. DEFINITIONS AND SPECIAL RULES.

[Sec. 4946(a)]

(a) DISQUALIFIED PERSON.—

(1) IN GENERAL.—For purposes of this subchapter, the term "disqualified person" means, with respect to a private foundation, a person who is—

(A) a substantial contributor to the foundation,

(B) a foundation manager (within the meaning of subsection (b)(1)),

(C) an owner of more than 20 percent of—

(i) the total combined voting power of a corporation,

(ii) the profits interest of a partnership, or

(iii) the beneficial interest of a trust or unincorporated enterprise,

which is a substantial contributor to the foundation,

(D) a member of the family (as defined in subsection (d)) of any individual described in subparagraph (A), (B), or (C),

(E) a corporation of which persons described in subparagraph (A), (B), (C), or (D) own more than 35 percent of the total combined voting power,

(F) a partnership in which persons described in subparagraph (A), (B), (C), or (D) own more than 35 percent of the profits interest,

(G) a trust or estate in which persons described in subparagraph (A), (B), (C), or (D) hold more than 35 percent of the beneficial interest,

(H) only for purposes of section 4943, a private foundation—

(i) which is effectively controlled (directly or indirectly) by the same person or persons who control the private foundation in question, or

(ii) substantially all of the contributions to which were made (directly or indirectly) by the same person or persons described in subparagraph (A), (B), or (C), or members of their families (within the meaning of subsection (d)), who made (directly or indirectly) substantially all of the contributions to the private foundation in question, and

(I) only for purposes of section 4941, a government official (as defined in subsection (c)).

(2) SUBSTANTIAL CONTRIBUTORS.—For purposes of paragraph (1), the term "substantial contributor" means a person who is described in section 507(d)(2).

(3) STOCKHOLDINGS.—For purposes of paragraphs (1)(C)(i) and (1)(E), there shall be taken into account indirect stockholdings which would be taken into account under section 267(c), except that, for purposes of this paragraph, section 267(c)(4) shall be treated as providing that the members of the family of an individual are the members within the meaning of subsection (d).

(4) PARTNERSHIPS; TRUSTS.—For purposes of paragraphs (1)(C)(ii) and (iii), (1)(F), and (1)(G), the ownership of profits or beneficial interests shall be determined in accordance with the rules for constructive ownership of stock provided in section 267(c) (other than paragraph (3)

EXCISE TAXES—PRIVATE FOUNDATIONS

thereof), except that section 267(c)(4) shall be treated as providing that the members of the family of an individual are the members within the meaning of subsection (d).

[Sec. 4946(b)]

(b) FOUNDATION MANAGER.—For purposes of this subchapter, the term "foundation manager" means, with respect to any private foundation—

(1) an officer, director, or trustee of a foundation (or an individual having powers or responsibilities similar to those of officers, directors, or trustees of the foundation), and

(2) with respect to any act (or failure to act), the employees of the foundation having authority or responsibility with respect to such act (or failure to act).

[Sec. 4946(c)]

(c) GOVERNMENT OFFICIAL.—For purposes of subsection (a)(1)(I) and section 4941, the term "government official" means, with respect to an act of self-dealing described in section 4941, an individual who, at the time of such act, holds any of the following offices or positions (other than as a "special Government employee", as defined in section 202(a) of title 18, United States Code):

(1) an elective public office in the executive or legislative branch of the Government of the United States,

(2) an office in the executive or judicial branch of the Government of the United States, appointment to which was made by the President,

(3) a position in the executive, legislative, or judicial branch of the Government of the United States—

(A) which is listed in schedule C of rule VI of the Civil Service Rules, or

(B) the compensation for which is equal to or greater than the lowest rate of basic pay for the Senior Executive Service under section 5382 of title 5, United States Code,

(4) a position under the House of Representatives or the Senate of the United States held by an individual receiving gross compensation at an annual rate of $15,000 or more,

(5) an elective or appointive public office in the executive, legislative, or judicial branch of the government of a State, possession of the United States, or political subdivision or other area of any of the foregoing, or of the District of Columbia, held by an individual receiving gross compensation at an annual rate of $20,000 or more,

(6) a position as personal or executive assistant or secretary to any of the foregoing, or

(7) a member of the Internal Revenue Service Oversight Board.

Amendments

• **2000, Community Renewal Tax Relief Act of 2000 (P.L. 106-554)**

P.L. 106-554, §319(16):

Amended Code Sec. 4946(c)(3)(B) by striking "the lowest rate of compensation prescribed for GS-16 of the General Schedule under section 5332" and inserting "the lowest rate of basic pay for the Senior Executive Service under section 5382". **Effective** 12-21-2000.

• **1998, IRS Restructuring and Reform Act of 1998 (P.L. 105-206)**

P.L. 105-206, §1101(c)(1):

Amended Code Sec. 4946(c) by striking "or" at the end of paragraph (5), by striking the period at the end of paragraph (6) and inserting ", or", and by adding at the end a new paragraph (7). **Effective** 7-22-98. For a special rule, see Act Sec. 1101(d)(2)-(3), below.

P.L. 105-206, §1101(d)(2)-(3), provides:

(2) INITIAL NOMINATIONS TO INTERNAL REVENUE SERVICE OVERSIGHT BOARD.—The President shall submit the initial nominations under section 7802 of the Internal Revenue Code of 1986, as added by this section, to the Senate not later than 6 months after the date of the enactment of this Act.

(3) EFFECT ON ACTIONS PRIOR TO APPOINTMENT OF OVERSIGHT BOARD.—Nothing in this section shall be construed to invalidate the actions and authority of the Internal Revenue Service prior to the appointment of the members of the Internal Revenue Service Oversight Board.

• **1986, Tax Reform Act of 1986 (P.L. 99-514)**

P.L. 99-514, §1606(a):

Amended Code Sec. 4946(c)(5) by striking out "$15,000" and inserting in lieu thereof "$20,000". **Effective** for compensation received after 12-31-85.

[Sec. 4946(d)]

(d) MEMBERS OF FAMILY.—For purposes of subsection (a)(1), the family of any individual shall include only his spouse, ancestors, children, grandchildren, great grandchildren, and the spouses of children, grandchildren, and great grandchildren.

Amendments

• **1984, Deficit Reduction Act of 1984 (P.L. 98-369)**

P.L. 98-369, §306(a):

Amended Code Sec. 4946(d). **Effective** 1-1-85. Prior to amendment, Code Sec. 4946(d) read as follows:

(d) MEMBERS OF FAMILY.—For purposes of subsection (a)(1), the family of any individual shall include only his spouse, ancestors, lineal descendants, and spouses of lineal descendants.

• **1978, Black Lung Benefits Revenue Act of 1977 (P.L. 95-227)**

P.L. 95-227, §4(c)(2)(B):

Amended Code Sec. 4946(a)(1) and (b) by changing "For purposes of this chapter" to "For purposes of this subchapter". **Effective** with respect to contributions, acts and expenditures made after 12-31-77, in and for tax years beginning after such date.

• **1969, Tax Reform Act of 1969 (P.L. 91-172)**

P.L. 91-172, §101(b):

Added Code Sec. 4946. **Effective** 1-1-70.

[Sec. 4947]

SEC. 4947. APPLICATION OF TAXES TO CERTAIN NONEXEMPT TRUSTS.

[Sec. 4947(a)]

(a) APPLICATION OF TAX.—

(1) CHARITABLE TRUSTS.—For purposes of part II of subchapter F of chapter 1 (other than section 508(a), (b), and (c)) and for purposes of this chapter, a trust which is not exempt from taxation under section 501(a), all of the unexpired interests in which are devoted to one or more of the purposes described in section 170(c)(2)(B), and for which a deduction was allowed under section 170, 545(b)(2), 642(c), 2055, 2106(a)(2), or 2522 (or the corresponding provisions of prior law), shall be treated as an organization described in section 501(c)(3). For purposes of section 509(a)(3)(A), such a trust shall be treated as if organized on the day on which it first becomes subject to this paragraph.

(2) SPLIT-INTEREST TRUSTS.—In the case of a trust which is not exempt from tax under section 501(a), not all of the unexpired interests in which are devoted to one or more of the purposes described in section 170(c)(2)(B), and which has amounts in trust for which a deduction was allowed under section 170, 545(b)(2), 642(c), 2055, 2106(a)(2), or 2522, section 507 (relating to termination of private foundation status), section 508(e) (relating to governing instruments) to the extent applicable to a trust described in this paragraph, section 4941 (relating to taxes on self-dealing), section 4943 (relating to taxes on excess business holdings) except as provided in subsection (b)(3), section 4944 (relating to investments which jeopardize charitable purpose) except as provided in subsection (b)(3), and section 4945 (relating to taxes on taxable expenditures) shall apply as if such trust were a private foundation. This paragraph shall not apply with respect to—

(A) any amounts payable under the terms of such trust to income beneficiaries, unless a deduction was allowed under section 170(f)(2)(B), 2055(e)(2)(B), or 2522(c)(2)(B),

(B) any amounts in trust other than amounts for which a deduction was allowed under section 170, 545(b)(2), 642(c), 2055, 2106(a)(2), or 2522, if such other amounts are segregated from amounts for which no deduction was allowable, or

(C) any amounts transferred in trust before May 27, 1969.

EXCISE TAXES—PRIVATE FOUNDATIONS

(3) SEGREGATED AMOUNTS.—For purposes of paragraph (2)(B), a trust with respect to which amounts are segregated shall separately account for the various income, deduction, and other items properly attributable to each of such segregated amounts.

Amendments

• **2013, American Taxpayer Relief Act of 2012 (P.L. 112-240)**

P.L. 112-240, § 101(a)(1)-(3), provides:

SEC. 101. PERMANENT EXTENSION AND MODIFICATION OF 2001 TAX RELIEF.

(a) PERMANENT EXTENSION.—

(1) IN GENERAL.—The Economic Growth and Tax Relief Reconciliation Act of 2001 is amended by striking title IX.

(2) CONFORMING AMENDMENT.—The Tax Relief, Unemployment Insurance Reauthorization, and Job Creation Act of 2010 is amended by striking section 304.

(3) EFFECTIVE DATE.—The amendments made by this subsection shall apply to taxable, plan, or limitation years beginning after December 31, 2012, and estates of decedents dying, gifts made, or generation skipping transfers after December 31, 2012.

• **2010, Tax Relief, Unemployment Insurance Reauthorization, and Job Creation Act of 2010 (P.L. 111-312)**

P.L. 111-312, § 301(a):

Amended Code Sec. 4947(a)(2)(A) to read as such provision would read if subtitle E of title V of the Economic Growth and Tax Relief Reconciliation Act of 2001 (P.L. 107-16) had never been enacted. **Effective** for estates of decedents dying, and transfers made, after 12-31-2009. For a special rule, see Act Sec. 301(c), below. Prior to amendment by P.L. 111-312, Code Sec. 4947(a)(2)(A) read as follows:

(A) any amounts payable under the terms of such trust to income beneficiaries, unless a deduction was allowed under section 170(f)(2)(B), 642(c), 2055(e)(2)(B), or 2522(c)(2)(B),

P.L. 111-312, § 301(c), provides:

(c) SPECIAL ELECTION WITH RESPECT TO ESTATES OF DECEDENTS DYING IN 2010.—Notwithstanding subsection (a), in the case of an estate of a decedent dying after December 31, 2009, and before January 1, 2011, the executor (within the meaning of section 2203 of the Internal Revenue Code of 1986) may elect to apply such Code as though the amendments made by subsection (a) do not apply with respect to chapter 11 of such Code and with respect to property acquired or passing from such decedent (within the meaning of section 1014(b) of such Code). Such election shall be made at such time and in such manner as the Secretary of the Treasury or the Secretary's delegate shall provide. Such an election once made shall be revocable only with the consent of the Secretary of the Treasury or the Secretary's delegate. For purposes of section 2652(a)(1) of such Code, the determination of whether any property is subject to the tax imposed by such chapter 11 shall be made without regard to any election made under this subsection.

P.L. 111-312, § 304, provides [but see P.L. 112-240, § 101(a)(2)-(3), above]:

SEC. 304. APPLICATION OF EGTRRA SUNSET TO THIS TITLE.

Section 901 of the Economic Growth and Tax Relief Reconciliation Act of 2001 shall apply to the amendments made by this title.

• **2004, American Jobs Creation Act of 2004 (P.L. 108-357)**

P.L. 108-357, § 413(c)(30):

Amended Code Sec. 4947 by striking "556(b)(2)," immediately preceding "642(c), 2055," each place it appears. **Effective** for tax years of foreign corporations beginning after 12-31-2004, and for tax years of United States shareholders with or within which such tax years of foreign corporations end.

• **2001, Economic Growth and Tax Relief Reconciliation Act of 2001 (P.L. 107-16)**

P.L. 107-16, § 542(e)(4):

Amended Code Sec. 4947(a)(2)(A) by inserting "642(c)," after "170(f)(2)(B),". **Effective** for deductions for tax years beginning after 12-31-2009.

P.L. 107-16, § 901(a)-(b), as amended by P.L. 111-312, § 101(a)(1), provides [but see P.L. 112-240, § 101(a)(1) and (3), above]:

SEC. 901. SUNSET OF PROVISIONS OF ACT.

(a) IN GENERAL.—All provisions of, and amendments made by, this Act shall not apply—

(1) to taxable, plan, or limitation years beginning after December 31, 2012, or

(2) in the case of title V, to estates of decedents dying, gifts made, or generation skipping transfers, after December 31, 2012.

(b) APPLICATION OF CERTAIN LAWS.—The Internal Revenue Code of 1986 and the Employee Retirement Income Security Act of 1974 shall be applied and administered to years, estates, gifts, and transfers described in subsection (a) as if the provisions and amendments described in subsection (a) had never been enacted.

[Sec. 4947(b)]

(b) SPECIAL RULES.—

(1) REGULATIONS.—The Secretary shall prescribe such regulations as may be necessary to carry out the purposes of this section.

(2) LIMIT TO SEGREGATED AMOUNTS.—If any amounts in the trust are segregated within the meaning of subsection (a)(2)(B) of this section, the value of the net assets for purposes of subsections (c)(2) and (g) of section 507 shall be limited to such segregated amounts.

(3) SECTIONS 4943 AND 4944.—Sections 4943 and 4944 shall not apply to a trust which is described in subsection (a)(2) if—

(A) all the income interest (and none of the remainder interest) of such trust is devoted solely to one or more of the purposes described in section 170(c)(2)(B), and all amounts in such trust for which a deduction was allowed under section 170, 545(b)(2), 642(c), 2055, 2106(a)(2), or 2522 have an aggregate value not more than 60 percent of the aggregate fair market value of all amounts in such trusts, or

(B) a deduction was allowed under section 170, 545(b)(2), 642(c), 2055, 2106(a)(2), or 2522 for amounts payable under the terms of such trust to every remainder beneficiary but not to any income beneficiary.

(4) SECTION 507.—The provisions of section 507(a) shall not apply to a trust which is described in subsection (a)(2) by reason of a distribution of qualified employer securities (as defined in section 664(g)(4)) to an employee stock ownership plan (as defined in section 4975(e)(7)) in a qualified gratuitous transfer (as defined by section 664(g)).

Amendments

• **2004, American Jobs Creation Act of 2004 (P.L. 108-357)**

P.L. 108-357, § 413(c)(30):

Amended Code Sec. 4947 by striking "556(b)(2)," immediately preceding "642(c), 2055," each place it appears. **Effective** for tax years of foreign corporations beginning after 12-31-2004, and for tax years of United States shareholders with or within which such tax years of foreign corporations end.

• **1997, Taxpayer Relief Act of 1997 (P.L. 105-34)**

P.L. 105-34, § 1530(c)(9):

Amended Code Sec. 4947(b) by inserting after paragraph (3) a new paragraph (4). **Effective** for transfers made by trusts to, or for the use of, an employee stock ownership plan after 8-5-97.

• **1976, Tax Reform Act of 1976 (P.L. 94-455)**

P.L. 94-455, § 1906(b)(13)(A):

Amended 1954 Code by substituting "Secretary" for "Secretary or his delegate" each place it appeared. **Effective** 2-1-77.

• **1969, Tax Reform Act of 1969 (P.L. 91-172)**

P.L. 91-172, § 101(b):

Added Code Sec. 4947. **Effective** 1-1-70.

[Sec. 4948]

SEC. 4948. APPLICATION OF TAXES AND DENIAL OF EXEMPTION WITH RESPECT TO CERTAIN FOREIGN ORGANIZATIONS.

[Sec. 4948(a)]

(a) TAX ON INCOME OF CERTAIN FOREIGN ORGANIZATIONS.—In lieu of the tax imposed by section 4940, there is hereby imposed for each taxable year on the gross investment income (within the meaning of section 4940(c)(2)) derived from sources within the United States (within the meaning of section 861) by every foreign organization which is a private foundation for the taxable year a tax equal to 4 percent of such income.

[Sec. 4948(b)]

(b) CERTAIN SECTIONS INAPPLICABLE.—Section 507 (relating to termination of private foundation status), section 508 (relating to special rules with respect to section 501(c)(3) organizations), and this chapter (other than this section) shall not apply to any foreign organization which has received substantially all of its support (other than gross investment income) from sources outside the United States.

Internal Revenue Code   Sec. 4948(b)

EXCISE TAXES—BLACK LUNG BENEFIT TRUSTS

[Sec. 4948(c)]

(c) DENIAL OF EXEMPTION TO FOREIGN ORGANIZATIONS ENGAGED IN PROHIBITED TRANSACTIONS.—

(1) GENERAL RULE.—A foreign organization described in subsection (b) shall not be exempt from taxation under section 501(a) if it has engaged in a prohibited transaction after December 31, 1969.

(2) PROHIBITED TRANSACTIONS.—For purposes of this subsection, the term "prohibited transaction" means any act or failure to act (other than with respect to section 4942(e)) which would subject a foreign organization described in subsection (b), or a disqualified person (as defined in section 4946) with respect thereto, to liability for a penalty under section 6684 or a tax under section 507 if such foreign organization were a domestic organization.

(3) TAXABLE YEARS AFFECTED.—

(A) Except as provided in subparagraph (B), a foreign organization described in subsection (b) shall be denied exemption from taxation under section 501(a) by reason of paragraph (1) for all taxable years beginning with the taxable year during which it is notified by the Secretary that it has engaged in a prohibited transaction. The Secretary shall publish such notice in the Federal Register on the day on which he so notifies such foreign organization.

(B) Under regulations prescribed by the Secretary, any foreign organization described in subsection (b) which is denied exemption from taxation under section 501(a) by reason of paragraph (1) may, with respect to the second taxable year following the taxable year in which notice is given under subparagraph (A) (or any taxable year thereafter), file claim for exemption from taxation under section 501(a). If the Secretary is satisfied that such organization will not knowingly again engage in a prohibited transaction, such organization shall not, with respect to taxable years beginning with the taxable year with respect to which such claim is filed, be denied exemption from taxation under section 501(a) by reason of any prohibited transaction which was engaged in before the date on which such notice was given under subparagraph (A).

(4) DISALLOWANCE OF CERTAIN CHARITABLE DEDUCTIONS.—No gift or bequest shall be allowed as a deduction under section 170, 545(b)(2), 642(c), 2055, 2106(a)(2), or 2522, if made—

(A) to a foreign organization described in subsection (b) after the date on which the Secretary publishes notice under paragraph (3)(A) that he has notified such organization that it has engaged in a prohibited transaction, and

(B) in a taxable year of such organization for which it is not exempt from taxation under section 501(a) by reason of paragraph (1).

Amendments

- 2004, American Jobs Creation Act of 2004 (P.L. 108-357)

P.L. 108-357, §413(c)(30):

Amended Code Sec. 4948(c)(4) by striking "556(b)(2)," immediately preceding "642(c), 2055,". **Effective** for tax years of foreign corporations beginning after 12-31-2004, and for tax years of United States shareholders with or within which such tax years of foreign corporations end.

- 1976, Tax Reform Act of 1976 (P.L. 94-455)

P.L. 94-455, §1906(b)(13)(A):

Amended 1954 Code by substituting "Secretary" for "Secretary or his delegate" each place it appeared. **Effective** 2-1-77.

- 1969, Tax Reform Act of 1969 (P.L. 91-172)

P.L. 91-172, §101(b):

Added Code Sec. 4948. **Effective** for tax years beginning after 12-31-69.

P. L. 91-172, §101(1)(8), provides:

"(8) Certain redemptions.—For purposes of applying section 302(b)(1) to the determination of the amount of gross investment income under sections 4940 and 4948(a), any distribution made to a private foundation in redemption of stock held by such private foundation in a business enterprise shall be treated as not essentially equivalent to a dividend, if such redemption is described in paragraph (2)(B) of this subsection."

Subchapter B—Black Lung Benefit Trusts

Sec. 4951.   Taxes on self-dealing.
Sec. 4952.   Taxes on taxable expenditures.
Sec. 4953.   Tax on excess contributions to black lung benefit trusts.

[Sec. 4951]

SEC. 4951. TAXES ON SELF-DEALING.

[Sec. 4951(a)]

(a) INITIAL TAXES.—

(1) ON SELF-DEALER.—There is hereby imposed a tax on each act of self-dealing between a disqualified person and a trust described in section 501(c)(21). The rate of tax shall be equal to 10 percent of the amount involved with respect to the act of self-dealing for each year (or part thereof) in the taxable period. The tax imposed by this paragraph shall be paid by any disqualified person (other than a trustee acting only as a trustee of the trust) who participates in the act of self-dealing.

(2) ON TRUSTEE.—In any case in which a tax is imposed by paragraph (1), there is hereby imposed on the participation of any trustee of such a trust in an act of self-dealing between a disqualified person and the trust, knowing that it is such an act, a tax equal to $2^{1}/_{2}$ percent of the amount involved with respect to the act of self-dealing for each year (or part thereof) in the taxable period, unless such participation is not willful and is due to reasonable cause. The tax imposed by this pargaraph shall be paid by any such trustee who participated in the act of self-dealing.

[Sec. 4951(b)]

(b) ADDITIONAL TAXES.—

(1) ON SELF-DEALER.—In any case in which an initial tax is imposed by subsection (a)(1) on an act of self-dealing by a disqualified person with a trust described in section 501(c)(21) and in which the act is not corrected within the taxable period, there is hereby imposed a tax equal to 100 percent of the amount involved. The tax imposed by this paragraph shall be paid by any disqualified person (other than a trustee acting only as a trustee of such a trust) who participated in the act of self-dealing.

(2) ON TRUSTEE.—In any case in which an additional tax is imposed by paragraph (1), if a trustee of such a trust refused to agree to part or all of the correction, there is hereby imposed a tax equal to 50 percent of the amount involved. The tax imposed by this paragraph shall be paid by any such trustee who refused to agree to part or all of the correction.

Amendments

- 1980 (P.L. 96-596)

P.L. 96-596, §2(a)(1):

Amended Code Sec. 4951(b)(1) by striking out "correction period" and inserting in lieu thereof "taxable period". **Effective** with respect to second-tier taxes assessed after 12-24-80 (except in cases where there is a court decision with regard to which res judicata applies on that date).

EXCISE TAXES—BLACK LUNG BENEFIT TRUSTS

[Sec. 4951(c)]

(c) JOINT AND SEVERAL LIABILITY.—If more than one person is liable under any paragraph of subsection (a) or (b) with respect to any one act of self-dealing, all such persons shall be jointly and severally liable under such paragraph with respect to such act.

[Sec. 4951(d)]

(d) SELF-DEALING.—

(1) IN GENERAL.—For purposes of this section, the term "self-dealing" means any direct or indirect—

(A) sale, exchange, or leasing of real or personal property between a trust described in section 501(c)(21) and a disqualified person;

(B) lending of money or other extension of credit between such a trust and a disqualified person;

(C) furnishing of goods, services, or facilities between such a trust and a disqualified person;

(D) payment of compensation (or payment or reimbursement of expenses) by such a trust to a disqualified person; and

(E) transfer to, or use by or for the benefit of, a disqualified person of the income or assets of such a trust.

(2) SPECIAL RULES.—For purposes of paragraph (1)—

(A) the transfer of personal property by a disqualified person to such a trust shall be treated as a sale or exchange if the property is subject to a mortgage or similar lien;

(B) the furnishing of goods, services, or facilities by a disqualified person to such a trust shall not be an act of self-dealing if the furnishing is without charge and if the goods, services, or facilities so furnished are used exclusively for the purposes specified in section 501(c)(21)(A); and

(C) the payment of compensation (and the payment or reimbursement of expenses) by such a trust to a disqualified person for personal services which are reasonable and necessary to carrying out the exempt purpose of the trust shall not be an act of self-dealing if the compensation (or payment or reimbursement) is not excessive.

[Sec. 4951(e)]

(e) DEFINITIONS.—For purposes of this section—

(1) TAXABLE PERIOD.—The term "taxable period" means, with respect to any act of self-dealing, the period beginning with the date on which the act of self-dealing occurs and ending on the earliest of—

(A) the date of mailing a notice of deficiency with respect to the tax imposed by subsection (a)(1) under section 6212,

(B) the date on which the tax imposed by subsection (a)(1) is assessed, or

(C) the date on which correction of the act of self-dealing is completed.

(2) AMOUNT INVOLVED.—The term "amount involved" means, with respect to any act of self-dealing, the greater of the amount of money and the fair market value of the other property given or the amount of money and the fair market value of the other property received; except that in the case of services described in subsection (d)(2)(C), the amount involved shall be only the excess compensation. For purposes of the preceding sentence, the fair market value—

(A) in the case of the taxes imposed by subsection (a), shall be determined as of the date on which the act of self-dealing occurs; and

(B) in the case of taxes imposed by subsection (b), shall be the highest fair market value during the taxable period.

(3) CORRECTION.—The terms "correction" and "correct" mean, with respect to any act of self-dealing, undoing the transaction to the extent possible, but in any case placing the trust in a financial position not worse than that in which it would be if the disqualified person were dealing under the highest fiduciary standards.

(4) DISQUALIFIED PERSON.—The term "disqualified person" means, with respect to a trust described in section 501(c)(21), a person who is—

(A) a contributor to the trust,

(B) a trustee of the trust,

(C) an owner of more than 10 percent of—

(i) the total combined voting power of a corporation,

(ii) the profits interest of a partnership, or

(iii) the beneficial interest of a trust or unincorporated enterprise,

which is a contributor to the trust,

(D) an officer, director, or employee of a person who is a contributor to the trust,

(E) the spouse, ancestor, lineal descendant, or spouse of a lineal descendant of an individual described in subparagraph (A), (B), (C), or (D),

(F) a corporation of which persons described in subparagraph (A), (B), (C), (D), or (E) own more than 35 percent of the total combined voting power,

(G) a partnership in which persons described in subparagraph (A), (B), (C), (D), or (E), own more than 35 percent of the profits interest, or

(H) a trust or estate in which persons described in subparagraph (A), (B), (C), (D), or (E), hold more than 35 percent of the beneficial interest.

For purposes of subparagraphs (C)(i) and (F), there shall be taken into account indirect stockholdings which would be taken into account under section 267(c), except that, for purposes of this paragraph, section 267(c)(4) shall be treated as providing that the members of the family of an individual are only those individuals described in subparagraph (E) of this paragraph. For purposes of subparagraphs (C)(ii) and (iii), (G), and (H), the ownership of profits or beneficial interest shall be determined in accordance with the rules for constructive ownership of stock provided in section 267(c) (other than paragraph (3) thereof), except that section 267(c)(4) shall be treated as providing that the members of the family of an individual are only those individuals described in subparagraph (E) of this paragraph.

Amendments

• **1980 (P.L. 96-596)**

P.L. 96-596 §2(a)(1):

Amended Code Sec. 4951(e)(2)(B) by striking out "correction period" and inserting in lieu thereof "taxable period". **Effective** with respect to second-tier taxes assessed after 12-24-80 (except in cases where there is a court decision with regard to which res judicata applies on that date).

P.L. 96-596 §2(a)(2):

Amended Code Sec. 4951(e)(1). **Effective** with respect to second-tier taxes assessed after 12-24-80 (except in cases where there is a court decision with regard to which res judicata applies on that date). Prior to amendment, Code Sec. 4951(e)(1) read:

"(1) TAXABLE PERIOD.—The term 'taxable period' means, with respect to any act of self-dealing, the period beginning with the date on which the act of self-dealing occurs and ending on the earlier of—

(A) the date of mailing of a notice of deficiency with respect to the tax imposed by subsection (a)(1) under section 6212, or

(B) the date on which correction of the act of self-dealing is completed."

P.L. 96-596, §2(a)(3):

Amended Code Sec. 4951(e) by striking out paragraph (4) and by redesignating paragraph (5) as paragraph (4). **Effective** 12-24-80. Prior to amendment, Code Sec. 4951(e)(4) read:

EXCISE TAXES—BLACK LUNG BENEFIT TRUSTS

"(4) CORRECTION PERIOD.—The term 'correction period' means, with respect to any act of self-dealing, the period beginning with the date on which the act of selfdealing occurs and ending 90 days after the date of mailing of a notice of deficiency under section 6212 with respect to the tax imposed by subsection (b)(1), extended by—

(A) any period in which a deficiency cannot be assessed under section 6213(a), and

(B) any other period which the Secretary determines is reasonable and necessary to bring about correction of the act of self-dealing."

[Sec. 4951(f)]

(f) PAYMENTS OF BENEFITS.—For purposes of this section, a payment, out of assets or income of a trust described in section 501(c)(21), for the purposes described in subclause (I) or (IV) of section 501(c)(21)(A)(i) shall not be considered an act of self-dealing.

Amendments

• **1992, Energy Policy Act of 1992 (P.L. 102-486)**

P.L. 102-486, §1940(b):

Amended Code Sec. 4951(f) by striking "clause (i) of section 501(c)(21)(A)" and inserting "subclause (I) or (IV) of section 501(c)(21)(A)(i)". **Effective** for tax years beginning after 12-31-91.

• **1978, Black Lung Benefits Revenue Act of 1977 (P.L. 95-227)**

P.L. 95-227, §4(c)(1):

Added Code Sec. 4951. **Effective** with respect to contributions, acts and expenditures made after 12-31-77, in and for tax years beginning after such date. However, this effective date was contingent upon enactment of P.L. 109-280544, which was enacted as P.L. 95-239, on 3-1-78.

[Sec. 4952]

SEC. 4952. TAXES ON TAXABLE EXPENDITURES.

[Sec. 4952(a)]

(a) TAX IMPOSED.—

(1) ON THE FUND.—There is hereby imposed on each taxable expenditure (as defined in subsection (d)) from the assets or income of a trust described in section 501(c)(21) a tax equal to 10 percent of the amount thereof. The tax imposed by this paragraph shall be paid by the trustee out of the assets of the trust.

(2) ON THE TRUSTEE.—There is hereby imposed on the agreement of any trustee of such a trust to the making of an expenditure, knowing that it is a taxable expenditure, a tax equal to $2^1/_2$ percent of the amount thereof, unless such agreement is not willful and is due to reasonable cause. The tax imposed by this paragraph shall be paid by the trustee who agreed to the making of the expenditure.

[Sec. 4952(b)]

(b) ADDITIONAL TAXES.—

(1) ON THE FUND.—In any case in which an initial tax is imposed by subsection (a)(1) on a taxable expenditure and such expenditure is not corrected within the taxable period, there is hereby imposed a tax equal to 100 percent of the amount of the expenditure. The tax imposed by this paragraph shall be paid by the trustee out of the assets of the trust.

(2) ON THE TRUSTEE.—In any case in which an additional tax is imposed by paragraph (1), if a trustee refused to agree to a part or all of the correction, there is hereby imposed a tax equal to 50 percent of the amount of the taxable expenditure. The tax imposed by this paragraph shall be paid by any trustee who refused to agree to part or all of the correction.

Amendments

• **1980 (P.L. 96-596)**

P.L. 96-596, §2(a)(1):

Amended Code Sec. 4952(b)(1) by striking out "correction period" and inserting in lieu thereof "taxable period". **Effective** with respect to second-tier taxes assessed after 12-24-80 (except in cases where there is a court decision with regard to res judicata which applies on that date).

[Sec. 4952(c)]

(c) JOINT AND SEVERAL LIABILITY.—For purposes of subsections (a) and (b), if more than one person is liable under subsection (a)(2) or (b)(2) with respect to the making of a taxable expenditure, all such persons shall be jointly and severally liable under such paragraph with respect to such expenditure.

[Sec. 4952(d)]

(d) TAXABLE EXPENDITURE.—For purposes of this section, the term "taxable expenditure" means any amount paid or incurred by a trust described in section 501(c)(21) other than for a purpose specified in such section.

[Sec. 4952(e)]

(e) DEFINITIONS.—

(1) CORRECTION.—The terms "correction" and "correct" mean, with respect to any taxable expenditure, recovering part or all of the expenditure to the extent recovery is possible, and where full recovery is not possible, contributions by the person or persons whose liabilities for black lung benefit claims (as defined in section 192(e)) are to be paid out of the trust to the extent necessary to place the trust in a financial position not worse than that in which it would be if the taxable expenditure had not been made.

(2) TAXABLE PERIOD.—The term "taxable period" means, with respect to any taxable expenditure, the period beginning with the date on which the taxable expenditure occurs and ending on the earlier of—

(A) the date of mailing a notice of deficiency with respect to the tax imposed by subsection (a)(1) under section 6212, or

(B) the date on which the tax imposed by subsection (a)(1) is assessed.

Amendments

• **1980 (P.L. 96-596)**

P.L. 96-596, §2(a)(2):

Amended Code Sec. 4952(e)(2). **Effective** with respect to second-tier taxes assessed after 12-24-80 (except in cases where there is a court decision with regard to which res judicata applies on that date). Prior to amendment, Code Sec. 4952(e)(2) read:

"(2) CORRECTION PERIOD.—The term 'correction period' means, with respect to any taxable expenditure, the period beginning with the date on which the taxable expenditure occurs and ending 90 days after the date of mailing of a notice of deficiency under section 6212 with respect to the tax imposed by subsection (b)(1), extended by—

(A) any period in which a deficiency cannot be assessed under section 6213(a), and

(B) any other period which the Secretary determines is reasonable and necessary to bring about correction of the taxable expenditure."

• **1978, Black Lung Benefits Revenue Act of 1977 (P.L. 95-227)**

P.L. 95-227, §4(c)(1):

Added Code Sec. 4952. **Effective** with respect to contributions, acts and expenditures made after 12-31-77, in and for tax years beginning after such date. However, see the historical comment for P.L. 95-227 under Code Sec. 4951.

[Sec. 4953]

SEC. 4953. TAX ON EXCESS CONTRIBUTIONS TO BLACK LUNG BENEFIT TRUSTS.

[Sec. 4953(a)]

(a) TAX IMPOSED.—There is hereby imposed for each taxable year a tax in an amount equal to 5 percent of the amount of the excess contributions made by a person to or under a trust or trusts described in section 501(c)(21). The tax imposed by this subsection shall be paid by the person making the excess contribution.

EXCISE TAXES—POLITICAL EXPENDITURES

[Sec. 4953(b)]

(b) EXCESS CONTRIBUTION.—For purposes of this section, the term "excess contribution" means the sum of—

(1) the amount by which the amount contributed for the taxable year to a trust or trusts described in section 501(c)(21) exceeds the amount of the deduction allowable to such person for such contributions for the taxable year under section 192, and

(2) the amount determined under this subsection for the preceding taxable year, reduced by the sum of—

(A) the excess of the maximum amount allowable as a deduction under section 192 for the taxable year over the amount contributed to the trust or trusts for the taxable year, and

(B) amounts distributed from the trust to the contributor which were excess contributions for the preceding taxable year.

[Sec. 4953(c)]

(c) TREATMENT OF WITHDRAWAL OF EXCESS CONTRIBUTIONS.—Amounts distributed during the taxable year from a trust described in section 501(c)(21) to the contributor thereof the sum of which does not exceed the amount of the excess contribution made by the contributor shall not be treated as—

(1) an act of self-dealing (within the meaning of section 4951),

(2) a taxable expenditure (within the meaning of section 4952), or

(3) an act contrary to the purposes for which the trust is exempt from taxation under section 501(a).

Amendments

- 1978, Black Lung Benefits Revenue Act of 1977 (P.L. 95-227)

P.L. 95-227, §4(c)(1):

Added Code Sec. 4953. **Effective** with respect to contributions, acts and expenditures made after 12-31-77, in and for tax years beginning after such date. However, see the historical comment for P.L. 95-227 under Code Sec. 4951.

Subchapter C—Political Expenditures of Section 501(c)(3) Organizations

Sec. 4955.   Taxes on political expenditures of section 501(c)(3) organizations.

[Sec. 4955]

SEC. 4955. TAXES ON POLITICAL EXPENDITURES OF SECTION 501(c)(3) ORGANIZATIONS.

[Sec. 4955(a)]

(a) INITIAL TAXES.—

(1) ON THE ORGANIZATION.—There is hereby imposed on each political expenditure by a section 501(c)(3) organization a tax equal to 10 percent of the amount thereof. The tax imposed by this paragraph shall be paid by the organization.

(2) ON THE MANAGEMENT.—There is hereby imposed on the agreement of any organization manager to the making of any expenditure, knowing that it is a political expenditure, a tax equal to $2^{1}/_{2}$ percent of the amount thereof, unless such agreement is not willful and is due to reasonable cause. The tax imposed by this paragraph shall be paid by any organization manager who agreed to the making of the expenditure.

[Sec. 4955(b)]

(b) ADDITIONAL TAXES.—

(1) ON THE ORGANIZATION.—In any case in which an initial tax is imposed by subsection (a)(1) on a political expenditure and such expenditure is not corrected within the taxable period, there is hereby imposed a tax equal to 100 percent of the amount of the expenditure. The tax imposed by this paragraph shall be paid by the organization.

(2) ON THE MANAGEMENT.—In any case in which an additional tax is imposed by paragraph (1), if an organization manager refused to agree to part or all of the correction, there is hereby imposed a tax equal to 50 percent of the amount of the political expenditure. The tax imposed by this paragraph shall be paid by any organization manager who refused to agree to part or all of the correction.

[Sec. 4955(c)]

(c) SPECIAL RULES.—For purposes of subsections (a) and (b)—

(1) JOINT AND SEVERAL LIABILITY.—If more than 1 person is liable under subsection (a)(2) or (b)(2) with respect to the making of a political expenditure, all such persons shall be jointly and severally liable under such subsection with respect to such expenditure.

(2) LIMIT FOR MANAGEMENT.—With respect to any 1 political expenditure, the maximum amount of the tax imposed by subsection (a)(2) shall not exceed $5,000, and the maximum amount of the tax imposed by subsection (b)(2) shall not exceed $10,000.

[Sec. 4955(d)]

(d) POLITICAL EXPENDITURE.—For purposes of this section—

(1) IN GENERAL.—The term "political expenditure" means any amount paid or incurred by a section 501(c)(3) organization in any participation in, or intervention in (including the publication or distribution of statements), any political campaign on behalf of (or in opposition to) any candidate for public office.

(2) CERTAIN OTHER EXPENDITURES INCLUDED.—In the case of an organization which is formed primarily for purposes of promoting the candidacy (or prospective candidacy) of an individual for public office (or which is effectively controlled by a candidate or prospective candidate and which is availed of primarily for such purposes), the term "political expenditure" includes any of the following amounts paid or incurred by the organization;

(A) Amounts paid or incurred to such individual for speeches or other services.

(B) Travel expenses of such individual.

(C) Expenses of conducting polls, surveys, or other studies, or preparing papers or other materials, for use by such individual.

(D) Expenses of advertising, publicity, and fundraising for such individual.

(E) Any other expense which has the primary effect of promoting public recognition, or otherwise primarily accruing to the benefit, of such individual.

[Sec. 4955(e)]

(e) COORDINATION WITH SECTIONS 4945 AND 4958.—If tax is imposed under this section with respect to any political expenditure, such expenditure shall not be treated as a taxable expenditure for purposes of section 4945 or an excess benefit for purposes of section 4958.

EXCISE TAXES—CERTAIN CHARITABLE ORGANIZATIONS

Amendments
- 1996, Taxpayer Bill of Rights 2 (P.L. 104-168)

P.L. 104-168, § 1311(c)(1)(A)-(B):

Amended Code Sec. 4955(e) by striking "SECTION 4945" in the heading and inserting "SECTIONS 4945 AND 4958", and by inserting before the period " or an excess benefit for purposes of section 4958". For the **effective** date, see Act Sec. 1311(d)(1)-(2), below.

P.L. 104-168, § 1311(d)(1)-(2), provides:

(1) IN GENERAL.—The amendments made by this section (other than subsection (b)) shall apply to excess benefit transactions occurring on or after September 14, 1995.

(2) BINDING CONTRACTS.—The amendments referred to in paragraph (1) shall not apply to any benefit arising from a transaction pursuant to any written contract which was binding on September 13, 1995, and at all times thereafter before such transaction occurred.

[Sec. 4955(f)]

(f) OTHER DEFINITIONS.—For purposes of this section—

(1) SECTION 501(C)(3) ORGANIZATION.—The term "section 501(c)(3) organization" means any organization which (without regard to any political expenditure) would be described in section 501(c)(3) and exempt from taxation under section 501(a).

(2) ORGANIZATION MANAGER.—The term "organization manager" means—

(A) any officer, director, or trustee of the organization (or individual having powers or responsibilities similar to those of officers, directors, or trustees of the organization), and

(B) with respect to any expenditure, any employee of the organization having authority or responsibility with respect to such expenditure.

(3) CORRECTION.—The terms "correction" and "correct" mean, with respect to any political expenditure, recovering part or all of the expenditure to the extent recovery is possible, establishment of safeguards to prevent future political expenditures, and where full recovery is not possible, such additional corrective action as is prescribed by the Secretary by regulations.

(4) TAXABLE PERIOD.—The term "taxable period" means, with respect to any political expenditure, the period beginning with the date on which the political expenditure occurs and ending on the earlier of—

(A) the date of mailing a notice of deficiency under section 6212 with respect to the tax imposed by subsection (a)(1), or

(B) the date on which tax imposed by subsection (a)(1) is assessed.

Amendments
- 1987, Revenue Act of 1987 (P.L. 100-203)

P.L. 100-203, § 10712(a):

Amended chapter 42 by redesignating subchapter C as subchapter D and by inserting after subchapter B a new subchapter C (Code Sec. 4955). **Effective** for tax years beginning after 12-22-87.

Subchapter D—Failure by Certain Charitable Organizations to Meet Certain Qualification Requirements

Sec. 4958.	Taxes on excess benefit transactions.
Sec. 4959.	Taxes on failures by hospital organizations.
Sec. 4960.	Tax on excess tax-exempt organization executive compensation.

[Sec. 4958]

SEC. 4958. TAXES ON EXCESS BENEFIT TRANSACTIONS.

[Sec. 4958(a)]

(a) INITIAL TAXES.—

(1) ON THE DISQUALIFIED PERSON.—There is hereby imposed on each excess benefit transaction a tax equal to 25 percent of the excess benefit. The tax imposed by this paragraph shall be paid by any disqualified person referred to in subsection (f)(1) with respect to such transaction.

(2) ON THE MANAGEMENT.—In any case in which a tax is imposed by paragraph (1), there is hereby imposed on the participation of any organization manager in the excess benefit transaction, knowing that it is such a transaction, a tax equal to 10 percent of the excess benefit, unless such participation is not willful and is due to reasonable cause. The tax imposed by this paragraph shall be paid by any organization manager who participated in the excess benefit transaction.

[Sec. 4958(b)]

(b) ADDITIONAL TAX ON THE DISQUALIFIED PERSON.—In any case in which an initial tax is imposed by subsection (a)(1) on an excess benefit transaction and the excess benefit involved in such transaction is not corrected within the taxable period, there is hereby imposed a tax equal to 200 percent of the excess benefit involved. The tax imposed by this subsection shall be paid by any disqualified person referred to in subsection (f)(1) with respect to such transaction.

[Sec. 4958(c)]

(c) EXCESS BENEFIT TRANSACTION; EXCESS BENEFIT.—For purposes of this section—

(1) EXCESS BENEFIT TRANSACTION.—

(A) IN GENERAL.—The term "excess benefit transaction" means any transaction in which an economic benefit is provided by an applicable tax-exempt organization directly or indirectly to or for the use of any disqualified person if the value of the economic benefit provided exceeds the value of the consideration (including the performance of services) received for providing such benefit. For purposes of the preceding sentence, an economic benefit shall not be treated as consideration for the performance of services unless such organization clearly indicated its intent to so treat such benefit.

(B) EXCESS BENEFIT.—The term "excess benefit" means the excess referred to in subparagraph (A).

(2) SPECIAL RULES FOR DONOR ADVISED FUNDS.—In the case of any donor advised fund (as defined in section 4966(d)(2))—

(A) the term "excess benefit transaction" includes any grant, loan, compensation, or other similar payment from such fund to a person described in subsection (f)(7) with respect to such fund, and

(B) the term "excess benefit" includes, with respect to any transaction described in subparagraph (A), the amount of any such grant, loan, compensation, or other similar payment.

(3) SPECIAL RULES FOR SUPPORTING ORGANIZATIONS.—

(A) IN GENERAL.—In the case of any organization described in section 509(a)(3)—

(i) the term "excess benefit transaction" includes—

EXCISE TAXES—CERTAIN CHARITABLE ORGANIZATIONS

(I) any grant, loan, compensation, or other similar payment provided by such organization to a person described in subparagraph (B), and

(II) any loan provided by such organization to a disqualified person (other than an organization described in subparagraph (C)(ii)), and

(ii) the term "excess benefit" includes, with respect to any transaction described in clause (i), the amount of any such grant, loan, compensation, or other similar payment.

(B) PERSON DESCRIBED.—A person is described in this subparagraph if such person is—

(i) a substantial contributor to such organization,

(ii) a member of the family (determined under section 4958(f)(4)) of an individual described in clause (i), or

(iii) a 35-percent controlled entity (as defined in section 4958(f)(3) by substituting "persons described in clause (i) or (ii) of section 4958(c)(3)(B)" for "persons described in subparagraph (A) or (B) of paragraph (1)" in subparagraph (A)(i) thereof).

(C) SUBSTANTIAL CONTRIBUTOR.—For purposes of this paragraph—

(i) IN GENERAL.—The term "substantial contributor" means any person who contributed or bequeathed an aggregate amount of more than $5,000 to the organization, if such amount is more than 2 percent of the total contributions and bequests received by the organization before the close of the taxable year of the organization in which the contribution or bequest is received by the organization from such person. In the case of a trust, such term also means the creator of the trust. Rules similar to the rules of subparagraphs (B) and (C) of section 507(d)(2) shall apply for purposes of this subparagraph.

(ii) EXCEPTION.—Such term shall not include—

(I) any organization described in paragraph (1), (2), or (4) of section 509(a), and

(II) any organization which is treated as described in such paragraph (2) by reason of the last sentence of section 509(a) and which is a supported organization (as defined in section 509(f)(3)) of the organization to which subparagraph (A) applies.

(4) AUTHORITY TO INCLUDE CERTAIN OTHER PRIVATE INUREMENT.—To the extent provided in regulations prescribed by the Secretary, the term "excess benefit transaction" includes any transaction in which the amount of any economic benefit provided to or for the use of a disqualified person is determined in whole or in part by the revenues of 1 or more activities of the organization but only if such transaction results in inurement not permitted under paragraph (3) or (4) of section 501(c), as the case may be. In the case of any such transaction, the excess benefit shall be the amount of the inurement not so permitted.

Amendments

• **2007, Tax Technical Corrections Act of 2007 (P.L. 110-172)**

P.L. 110-172, §3(i)(1):

Amended Code Sec. 4958(c)(3)(A)(i)(II) by striking "paragraph (1), (2), or (4) of section 509(a)" and inserting "subparagraph (C)(ii)". **Effective** as if included in the provision of the Pension Protection Act of 2006 (P.L. 109-280) to which it relates [effective for transactions occurring after 7-25-2006.—CCH].

P.L. 110-172, §3(i)(2):

Amended Code Sec. 4958(c)(3)(C)(ii). **Effective** as if included in the provision of the Pension Protection Act of 2006 (P.L. 109-280) to which it relates [effective for transactions occurring after 7-25-2006.—CCH]. Prior to amendment, Code Sec. 4958(c)(3)(C)(ii) read as follows:

(ii) EXCEPTION.—Such term shall not include any organization described in paragraph (1), (2), or (4) of section 509(a).

• **2006, Pension Protection Act of 2006 (P.L. 109-280)**

P.L. 109-280, §1232(b)(1):

Amended Code Sec. 4958(c) by redesignating paragraph (2) as paragraph (3) and by inserting after paragraph (1) a new paragraph (2). **Effective** for transactions occurring after 8-17-2006.

P.L. 109-280, §1242(b):

Amended Code Sec. 4958(c), as amended by this Act, by redesignating paragraph (3) as paragraph (4) and by inserting after paragraph (2) a new paragraph (3). **Effective** for transactions occurring after 7-25-2006.

[Sec. 4958(d)]

(d) SPECIAL RULES.—For purposes of this section—

(1) JOINT AND SEVERAL LIABILITY.—If more than 1 person is liable for any tax imposed by subsection (a) or subsection (b), all such persons shall be jointly and severally liable for such tax.

(2) LIMIT FOR MANAGEMENT.—With respect to any 1 excess benefit transaction, the maximum amount of the tax imposed by subsection (a)(2) shall not exceed $20,000.

Amendments

• **2006, Pension Protection Act of 2006 (P.L. 109-280)**

P.L. 109-280, §1212(a)(3):

Amended Code Sec. 4958(d)(2) by striking "$10,000" and inserting "$20,000". **Effective** for tax years beginning after 8-17-2006.

[Sec. 4958(e)]

(e) APPLICABLE TAX-EXEMPT ORGANIZATION.—For purposes of this subchapter, the term "applicable tax-exempt organization" means—

(1) any organization which (without regard to any excess benefit) would be described in paragraph (3), (4), or (29) of section 501(c) and exempt from tax under section 501(a), and

(2) any organization which was described in paragraph (1) at any time during the 5-year period ending on the date of the transaction.

Such term shall not include a private foundation (as defined in section 509(a)).

Amendments

• **2010, Patient Protection and Affordable Care Act (P.L. 111-148)**

P.L. 111-148, §1322(h)(3):

Amended Code Sec. 4958(e)(1) by striking "paragraph (3) or (4)" and inserting "paragraph (3), (4), or (29)". **Effective** 3-23-2010.

[Sec. 4958(f)]

(f) OTHER DEFINITIONS.—For purposes of this section—

(1) DISQUALIFIED PERSON.—The term "disqualified person" means, with respect to any transaction—

(A) any person who was, at any time during the 5-year period ending on the date of such transaction, in a position to exercise substantial influence over the affairs of the organization,

(B) a member of the family of an individual described in subparagraph (A),

(C) a 35-percent controlled entity,

(D) any person who is described in subparagraph (A), (B), or (C) with respect to an organization described in section 509(a)(3) and organized and operated exclusively for the benefit of, to perform the functions of, or to carry out the purposes of the applicable tax-exempt organization,

(E) which involves a donor advised fund (as defined in section 4966(d)(2)), any person who is described in paragraph (7) with respect to such donor advised fund (as so defined), and

EXCISE TAXES—CERTAIN CHARITABLE ORGANIZATIONS

(F) which involves a sponsoring organization (as defined in section 4966(d)(1)), any person who is described in paragraph (8) with respect to such sponsoring organization (as so defined).

(2) ORGANIZATION MANAGER.—The term "organization manager" means, with respect to any applicable tax-exempt organization, any officer, director, or trustee of such organization (or any individual having powers or responsibilities similar to those of officers, directors, or trustees of the organization).

(3) 35-PERCENT CONTROLLED ENTITY.—

(A) IN GENERAL.—The term "35-percent controlled entity" means—

(i) a corporation in which persons described in subparagraph (A) or (B) of paragraph (1) own more than 35 percent of the total combined voting power,

(ii) a partnership in which such persons own more than 35 percent of the profits interest, and

(iii) a trust or estate in which such persons own more than 35 percent of the beneficial interest.

(B) CONSTRUCTIVE OWNERSHIP RULES.—Rules similar to the rules of paragraphs (3) and (4) of section 4946(a) shall apply for purposes of this paragraph.

(4) FAMILY MEMBERS.—The members of an individual's family shall be determined under section 4946(d); except that such members also shall include the brothers and sisters (whether by the whole or half blood) of the individual and their spouses.

(5) TAXABLE PERIOD.—The term "taxable period" means, with respect to any excess benefit transaction, the period beginning with the date on which the transaction occurs and ending on the earliest of—

(A) the date of mailing a notice of deficiency under section 6212 with respect to the tax imposed by subsection (a)(1), or

(B) the date on which the tax imposed by subsection (a)(1) is assessed.

(6) CORRECTION.—The terms "correction" and "correct" mean, with respect to any excess benefit transaction, undoing the excess benefit to the extent possible, and taking any additional measures necessary to place the organization in a financial position not worse than that in which it would be if the disqualified person were dealing under the highest fiduciary standards, except that in the case of any correction of an excess benefit transaction described in subsection (c)(2), no amount repaid in a manner prescribed by the Secretary may be held in any donor advised fund.

(7) DONORS AND DONOR ADVISORS.—For purposes of paragraph (1)(E), a person is described in this paragraph if such person—

(A) is described in section 4966(d)(2)(A)(iii),

(B) is a member of the family of an individual described in subparagraph (A), or

(C) is a 35-percent controlled entity (as defined in paragraph (3) by substituting "persons described in subparagraph (A) or (B) of paragraph (7)" for "persons described in subparagraph (A) or (B) of paragraph (1)" in subparagraph (A)(i) thereof).

(8) INVESTMENT ADVISORS.—For purposes of paragraph (1)(F)—

(A) IN GENERAL.—A person is described in this paragraph if such person—

(i) is an investment advisor,

(ii) is a member of the family of an individual described in clause (i), or

(iii) is a 35-percent controlled entity (as defined in paragraph (3) by substituting "persons described in clause (i) or (ii) of paragraph (8)(A)" for "persons described in subparagraph (A) or (B) of paragraph (1)" in subparagraph (A)(i) thereof).

(B) INVESTMENT ADVISOR DEFINED.—For purposes of subparagraph (A), the term "investment advisor" means, with respect to any sponsoring organization (as defined in section 4966(d)(1)), any person (other than an employee of such organization) compensated by such organization for managing the investment of, or providing investment advice with respect to, assets maintained in donor advised funds (as defined in section 4966(d)(2)) owned by such organization.

Amendments

• **2018, Tax Technical Corrections Act of 2018 (P.L. 115-141)**

P.L. 115-141, § 401(a)(224), Div. U:

Amended Code Sec. 4958(f)(1)(D) by striking the period at the end and inserting a comma. **Effective** 3-23-2018.

• **2006, Pension Protection Act of 2006 (P.L. 109-280)**

P.L. 109-280, § 1232(a)(1):

Amended Code Sec. 4958(f)(1) by striking "and" at the end of subparagraph (B), by striking the period at the end of subparagraph (C) and inserting a comma, and by adding after subparagraph (C) new subparagraphs (D) and (E). **Effective** for transactions occurring after 8-17-2006.

P.L. 109-280, § 1232(a)(2):

Amended Code Sec. 4958(f) by adding at the end new paragraphs (7) and (8). **Effective** for transactions occurring after 8-17-2006.

P.L. 109-280, § 1232(b)(2):

Amended Code Sec. 4958(f)(6) by inserting ", except that in the case of any correction of an excess benefit transaction described in subsection (c)(2), no amount repaid in a manner prescribed by the Secretary may be held in any donor advised fund" after "standards". **Effective** for transactions occurring after 8-17-2006.

P.L. 109-280, § 1242(a):

Amended Code Sec. 4958(f)(1), as amended by this Act, by redesignating subparagraphs (D) and (E) as subparagraphs (E) and (F), respectively, and by adding after subparagraph (C) a new subparagraph (D). **Effective** for transactions occurring after 8-17-2006.

• **1996, Taxpayer Bill of Rights 2 (P.L. 104-168)**

P.L. 104-168, § 1311(a):

Amended chapter 42 by redesignating subchapter D (Code Secs. 4961-4963) as subchapter E and by inserting after subchapter C a new subchapter D (Code Sec. 4958). For the **effective** date, see Act Sec. 1311(d)(1)-(2), below.

P.L. 104-168, § 1311(d)(1)-(2), provides:

(1) IN GENERAL.—The amendments made by this section (other than subsection (b)) shall apply to excess benefit transactions occurring on or after September 14, 1995.

(2) BINDING CONTRACTS.—The amendments referred to in paragraph (1) shall not apply to any benefit arising from a transaction pursuant to any written contract which was binding on September 13, 1995, and at all times thereafter before such transaction occurred.

[Sec. 4959]

SEC. 4959. TAXES ON FAILURES BY HOSPITAL ORGANIZATIONS.

If a hospital organization to which section 501(r) applies fails to meet the requirement of section 501(r)(3) for any taxable year, there is imposed on the organization a tax equal to $50,000.

Amendments

• **2010, Patient Protection and Affordable Care Act (P.L. 111-148)**

P.L. 111-148, § 9007(b)(1):

Amended subchapter D of chapter 42 by adding at the end a new Code Sec. 4959. **Effective** for failures occurring after 3-23-2010.

[Sec. 4960]

SEC. 4960. TAX ON EXCESS TAX-EXEMPT ORGANIZATION EXECUTIVE COMPENSATION.

[Sec. 4960(a)]

(a) TAX IMPOSED.—There is hereby imposed a tax equal to the product of the rate of tax under section 11 and the sum of—

(1) so much of the remuneration paid (other than any excess parachute payment) by an applicable tax-exempt organization for the taxable year with respect to employment of any covered employee in excess of $1,000,000, plus

(2) any excess parachute payment paid by such an organization to any covered employee.

For purposes of the preceding sentence, remuneration shall be treated as paid when there is no substantial risk of forfeiture (within the meaning of section 457(f)(3)(B)) of the rights to such remuneration.

[Sec. 4960(b)]

(b) LIABILITY FOR TAX.—The employer shall be liable for the tax imposed under subsection (a).

[Sec. 4960(c)]

(c) DEFINITIONS AND SPECIAL RULES.—For purposes of this section—

(1) APPLICABLE TAX-EXEMPT ORGANIZATION.—The term "applicable tax-exempt organization" means any organization which for the taxable year—

(A) is exempt from taxation under section 501(a),

(B) is a farmers' cooperative organization described in section 521(b)(1),

(C) has income excluded from taxation under section 115(1), or

(D) is a political organization described in section 527(e)(1).

(2) COVERED EMPLOYEE.—For purposes of this section, the term "covered employee" means any employee (including any former employee) of an applicable tax-exempt organization if the employee—

(A) is one of the 5 highest compensated employees of the organization for the taxable year, or

(B) was a covered employee of the organization (or any predecessor) for any preceding taxable year beginning after December 31, 2016.

(3) REMUNERATION.—For purposes of this section:

(A) IN GENERAL.—The term "remuneration" means wages (as defined in section 3401(a)), except that such term shall not include any designated Roth contribution (as defined in section 402A(c)) and shall include amounts required to be included in gross income under section 457(f).

(B) EXCEPTION FOR REMUNERATION FOR MEDICAL SERVICES.—The term "remuneration" shall not include the portion of any remuneration paid to a licensed medical professional (including a veterinarian) which is for the performance of medical or veterinary services by such professional.

(4) REMUNERATION FROM RELATED ORGANIZATIONS.—

(A) IN GENERAL.—Remuneration of a covered employee by an applicable tax-exempt organization shall include any remuneration paid with respect to employment of such employee by any related person or governmental entity.

(B) RELATED ORGANIZATIONS.—A person or governmental entity shall be treated as related to an applicable tax-exempt organization if such person or governmental entity—

(i) controls, or is controlled by, the organization,

(ii) is controlled by one or more persons which control the organization,

(iii) is a supported organization (as defined in section 509(f)(3)) during the taxable year with respect to the organization,

(iv) is a supporting organization described in section 509(a)(3) during the taxable year with respect to the organization, or

(v) in the case of an organization which is a voluntary employees' beneficiary association described in section 501(c)(9), establishes, maintains, or makes contributions to such voluntary employees' beneficiary association.

(C) LIABILITY FOR TAX.—In any case in which remuneration from more than one employer is taken into account under this paragraph in determining the tax imposed by subsection (a), each such employer shall be liable for such tax in an amount which bears the same ratio to the total tax determined under subsection (a) with respect to such remuneration as—

(i) the amount of remuneration paid by such employer with respect to such employee, bears to

(ii) the amount of remuneration paid by all such employers to such employee.

(5) EXCESS PARACHUTE PAYMENT.—For purposes of determining the tax imposed by subsection (a)(2)—

(A) IN GENERAL.—The term "excess parachute payment" means an amount equal to the excess of any parachute payment over the portion of the base amount allocated to such payment.

(B) PARACHUTE PAYMENT.—The term "parachute payment" means any payment in the nature of compensation to (or for the benefit of) a covered employee if—

(i) such payment is contingent on such employee's separation from employment with the employer, and

(ii) the aggregate present value of the payments in the nature of compensation to (or for the benefit of) such individual which are contingent on such separation equals or exceeds an amount equal to 3 times the base amount.

(C) EXCEPTION.—Such term does not include any payment—

(i) described in section 280G(b)(6) (relating to exemption for payments under qualified plans),

(ii) made under or to an annuity contract described in section 403(b) or a plan described in section 457(b),

(iii) to a licensed medical professional (including a veterinarian) to the extent that such payment is for the performance of medical or veterinary services by such professional, or

(iv) to an individual who is not a highly compensated employee as defined in section 414(q).

(D) BASE AMOUNT.—Rules similar to the rules of 280G(b)(3) shall apply for purposes of determining the base amount.

(E) PROPERTY TRANSFERS; PRESENT VALUE.—Rules similar to the rules of paragraphs (3) and (4) of section 280G(d) shall apply.

(6) COORDINATION WITH DEDUCTION LIMITATION.—Remuneration the deduction for which is not allowed by reason of section 162(m) shall not be taken into account for purposes of this section.

[Sec. 4960(d)]

(d) REGULATIONS.—The Secretary shall prescribe such regulations as may be necessary to prevent avoidance of the tax under this section, including regulations to prevent avoidance of such tax through the performance of services other than as an employee or by providing compensation through a pass-through or other entity to avoid such tax.

EXCISE TAXES—FIRST AND SECOND TIER TAXES

Amendments

• **2017, Tax Cuts and Jobs Act (P.L. 115-97)**

P.L. 115-97, §13602(a):

Amended subchapter D of chapter 42 by adding at the end a new Code Sec. 4960. **Effective** for tax years beginning after 12-31-2017.

Subchapter E—Abatement of First and Second Tier Taxes in Certain Cases

Sec. 4961.	Abatement of second tier taxes where there is correction.
Sec. 4962.	Abatement of first tier taxes in certain cases.
Sec. 4963.	Definitions.

[Sec. 4961]

SEC. 4961. ABATEMENT OF SECOND TIER TAXES WHERE THERE IS CORRECTION.

[Sec. 4961(a)]

(a) GENERAL RULE.—If any taxable event is corrected during the correction period for such event, then any second tier tax imposed with respect to such event (including interest, additions to the tax, and additional amounts) shall not be assessed, and if assessed the assessment shall be abated, and if collected shall be credited or refunded as an overpayment.

[Sec. 4961(b)]

(b) SUPPLEMENTAL PROCEEDING.—If the determination by a court that the taxpayer is liable for a second-tier tax has become final, such court shall have jurisdiction to conduct any necessary supplemental proceeding to determine whether the taxable event was corrected during the correction period. Such a supplemental proceeding may be begun only during the period which ends on the 90th day after the last day of the correction period. Where such a supplemental proceeding has begun, the reference in the second sentence of section 6213(a) to a final decision of the Tax Court shall be treated as including a final decision in such supplemental proceeding.

[Sec. 4961(c)]

(c) SUSPENSION OF PERIOD OF COLLECTION FOR SECOND TIER TAX.—

(1) PROCEEDING IN DISTRICT COURT OR UNITED STATES COURT OF FEDERAL CLAIMS.—If, not later than 90 days after the day on which the second tier tax is assessed, the first tier tax is paid in full and a claim for refund of the amount so paid is filed, no levy or proceeding in court for the collection of the second tier tax shall be made, begun, or prosecuted until a final resolution of a proceeding begun as provided in paragraph (2) (and of any supplemental proceeding with respect thereto under subsection (b)). Notwithstanding section 7421(a), the collection by levy or proceeding may be enjoined during the time such prohibition is in force by a proceeding in the proper court.

(2) SUIT MUST BE BROUGHT TO DETERMINE LIABILITY.—If, within 90 days after the day on which his claim for refund is denied, the person against whom the second tier tax was assessed fails to begin a proceeding described in section 7422 for the determination of his liability for such tax, paragraph (1) shall cease to apply with respect to such tax, effective on the day following the close of the 90-day period referred to in this paragraph.

(3) SUSPENSION OF RUNNING OF PERIOD OF LIMITATIONS ON COLLECTION.—The running of the period of limitations provided in section 6502 on the collection by levy or by a proceeding in court with respect to any second tier tax described in paragraph (1) shall be suspended for the period during which the Secretary is prohibited from collecting by levy or a proceeding in court.

(4) JEOPARDY COLLECTION.—If the Secretary makes a finding that the collection of the second tier tax is in jeopardy, nothing in this subsection shall prevent the immediate collection of such tax.

Amendments

• **2018, Tax Technical Corrections Act of 2018 (P.L. 115-141)**

P.L. 115-141, §401(a)(325)(C), Div. U:

Amended the heading of Code Sec. 4961(c)(1) by striking "UNITED STATES CLAIMS COURT" and inserting "UNITED STATES COURT OF FEDERAL CLAIMS". **Effective** 3-23-2018.

• **1992, Court of Federal Claims Technical and Procedural Improvements Act of 1992 (P.L. 102-572)**

P.L. 102-572, §902(b)(1):

Amended the heading of Code Sec. 4961(c)(1) by striking "UNITED STATES CLAIMS COURT" and inserting "UNITED STATES COURT OF FEDERAL CLAIMS". **Effective** 10-29-92.

• **1986, Tax Reform Act of 1986 (P.L. 99-514)**

P.L. 99-514, §1899A(50):

Amended Code Sec. 4961(c) by striking out "COURT OF CLAIMS" in the heading for paragraph (1) and inserting in lieu thereof "UNITED STATES CLAIMS COURT". **Effective** 10-25-86.

• **1980 (P.L. 96-596)**

P.L. 96-596, §2(c)(1):

Added Code Sec. 4961. **Effective** with respect to second-tier taxes assessed after 12-24-80 (except in cases where there is a court decision with respect to which res judicata applies on that date).

[Sec. 4962]

SEC. 4962. ABATEMENT OF FIRST TIER TAXES IN CERTAIN CASES.

[Sec. 4962(a)]

(a) GENERAL RULE.—If it is established to the satisfaction of the Secretary that—

(1) a taxable event was due to reasonable cause and not to willful neglect, and

(2) such event was corrected within the correction period for such event,

then any qualified first tier tax imposed with respect to such event (including interest) shall not be assessed and, if assessed, the assessment shall be abated and, if collected, shall be credited or refunded as an overpayment.

• **1987, Revenue Act of 1987 (P.L. 100-203)**

P.L. 100-203, §10712(b)(2):

Amended Code Sec. 4962(a) by striking out "any private foundation first tier tax" and inserting in lieu thereof "any qualified first tier tax". **Effective** for tax years beginning after 12-22-87.

[Sec. 4962(b)]

(b) QUALIFIED FIRST TIER TAX.—For purposes of this section, the term "qualified first tier tax" means any first tier tax imposed by subchapter A, C, D, or G of this chapter, except that such term shall not include the tax imposed by section 4941(a) (relating to initial tax on self-dealing).

EXCISE TAXES—FIRST AND SECOND TIER TAXES

Amendments

• **2007, Tax Technical Corrections Act of 2007 (P.L. 110-172)**

P.L. 110-172, §3(h):

Amended Code Sec. 4962(b) by striking "or D" and inserting "D, or G". **Effective** as if included in the provision of the Pension Protection Act of 2006 (P.L. 109-280) to which it relates [**effective** for tax years beginning after 8-17-2006.—CCH].

• **1997, Taxpayer Relief Act of 1997 (P.L. 105-34)**

P.L. 105-34, §1603(a):

Amended Code Sec. 4962(b) by striking "subchapter A or C" and inserting "subchapter A, C, or D". **Effective** as if included in the provision of P.L. 104-168 to which it relates [**effective**, generally, for excess benefit transactions occurring on or after 9-14-95.—CCH].

[Sec. 4962(c)]

(c) SPECIAL RULE FOR TAX ON POLITICAL EXPENDITURES OF SECTION 501(c)(3) ORGANIZATIONS.—In the case of the tax imposed by section 4955(a), subsection (a)(1) shall be applied by substituting "not willful and flagrant" for "due to reasonable cause and not to willful neglect."

Amendments

• **1987, Revenue Act of 1987 (P.L. 100-203)**

P.L. 100-203, §10712(b)(1):

Amended Code Sec. 4962 by striking out subsection (b) and inserting in lieu thereof new subsections (b) and (c). **Effective** for tax years beginning after 12-22-87. Prior to amendment, Code Sec. 4962(b) read as follows:

(b) PRIVATE FOUNDATION FIRST TIER TAX.—For purposes of this section, the term "private foundation first tier tax" means any first tier tax imposed by subchapter A of chapter 42, except that such term shall not include the tax imposed by section 4941(a) (relating to initial tax on self-dealing).

P.L. 100-203, §10712(b)(4):

Amended Code Sec. 4962 by striking out "PRIVATE FOUNDATION" before "FIRST" in the section heading. **Effective** for tax years beginning after 12-22-87.

• **1984, Deficit Reduction Act of 1984 (P.L. 98-369)**

P.L. 98-369, §305(a):

Amended Subchapter C of chapter 42 by redesignating Code Sec. 4962 as Code Sec. 4963 and by inserting after Code Sec. 4961 new Code Sec. 4962. **Effective** for taxable events occurring after 12-31-84.

[Sec. 4963]

SEC. 4963. DEFINITIONS.

[Sec. 4963(a)]

(a) FIRST TIER TAX.—For purposes of this subchapter, the term "first tier tax" means any tax imposed by subsection (a) of section 4941, 4942, 4943, 4944, 4945, 4951, 4952, 4955, 4958, 4966, 4967, 4971, or 4975.

Amendments

• **2006, Pension Protection Act of 2006 (P.L. 109-280)**

P.L. 109-280, §1231(b)(1):

Amended Code Sec. 4963(a) by inserting "4966, 4967," after "4958,". **Effective** for tax years beginning after 8-17-2006.

• **1996, Taxpayer Bill of Rights 2 (P.L. 104-168)**

P.L. 104-168, §1311(c)(2):

Amended Code Sec. 4963(a) by inserting "4958," after "4955,". **Effective**, generally, for excess benefit transactions occurring on or after 9-14-95. For a special rule, see Act Sec. 1311(d)(2) in the amendment notes following Code Sec. 4963(c).

• **1987, Revenue Act of 1987 (P.L. 100-203)**

P.L. 100-203, §10712(b)(3):

Amended Code Sec. 4963(a) by striking out "4952," and inserting in lieu thereof "4952, 4955,". **Effective** for tax years beginning after 12-22-87.

[Sec. 4963(b)]

(b) SECOND TIER TAX.—For purposes of this subchapter, the term "second tier tax" means any tax imposed by subsection (b) of section 4941, 4942, 4943, 4944, 4945, 4951, 4952, 4955, 4958, 4971, or 4975.

Amendments

• **1996, Taxpayer Bill of Rights 2 (P.L. 104-168)**

P.L. 104-168, §1311(c)(2):

Amended Code Sec. 4963(b) by inserting "4958," after "4955,". **Effective**, generally, for excess benefit transactions occurring on or after 9-14-95. For a special rule, see Act Sec. 1311(d)(2) in the amendment notes following Code Sec. 4963(c).

• **1987, Revenue Act of 1987 (P.L. 100-203)**

P.L. 100-203, §10712(b)(3):

Amended Code Sec. 4963(b) by striking out "4952," and inserting in lieu thereof "4952, 4955,". **Effective** for tax years beginning after 12-22-87.

[Sec. 4963(c)]

(c) TAXABLE EVENT.—For purposes of this subchapter, the term "taxable event" means any act (or failure to act) giving rise to liability for tax under section 4941, 4942, 4943, 4944, 4945, 4951, 4952, 4955, 4958, 4966, 4967, 4971, or 4975.

Amendments

• **2006, Pension Protection Act of 2006 (P.L. 109-280)**

P.L. 109-280, §1231(b)(1):

Amended Code Sec. 4963(c) by inserting "4966, 4967," after "4958." **Effective** for tax years beginning after 8-17-2006.

• **1996, Taxpayer Bill of Rights 2 (P.L. 104-168)**

P.L. 104-168, §1311(c)(2):

Amended Code Sec. 4963(c) by inserting "4958," after "4955,". **Effective**, generally, for excess benefit transactions occurring on or after 9-14-95. For a special rule, see Act Sec. 1311(d)(2), below.

P.L. 104-168, §1311(d)(2), provides:

(2) BINDING CONTRACTS.—The amendments referred to in paragraph (1) shall not apply to any benefit arising from a transaction pursuant to any written contract which was binding on September 13, 1995, and at all times thereafter before such transaction occurred.

• **1987, Revenue Act of 1987 (P.L. 100-203)**

P.L. 100-203, §10712(b)(3):

Amended Code Sec. 4963(c) by striking out "4952," and inserting in lieu thereof "4952, 4955,". **Effective** for tax years beginning after 12-22-87.

[Sec. 4963(d)]

(d) CORRECT.—For purposes of this subchapter—

(1) IN GENERAL.—Except as provided in paragraph (2), the term "correct" has the same meaning as when used in the section which imposes the second tier tax.

(2) SPECIAL RULES.—The term "correct" means—

(A) in the case of the second tier tax imposed by section 4942(b), reducing the amount of the undistributed income to zero,

(B) in the case of the second tier tax imposed by section 4943(b), reducing the amount of the excess business holdings to zero, and

(C) in the case of the second tier tax imposed by section 4944, removing the investment from jeopardy.

[Sec. 4963(e)]

(e) CORRECTION PERIOD.—For purposes of this subchapter—

(1) IN GENERAL.—The term "correction period" means, with respect to any taxable event, the period beginning on the date on which such event occurs and ending 90 days after the date of mailing under section 6212 of a notice of deficiency with respect to the second tier tax imposed on such taxable event, extended by—

(A) any period in which a deficiency cannot be assessed under section 6213(a) (determined without regard to the last sentence of section 4961(b)), and

EXCISE TAXES—TAX SHELTER TRANSACTIONS

(B) any other period which the Secretary determines is reasonable and necessary to bring about correction of the taxable event.

(2) SPECIAL RULES FOR WHEN TAXABLE EVENT OCCURS.—For purposes of paragraph (1), the taxable event shall be treated as occurring—

(A) in the case of section 4942, on the first day of the taxable year for which there was a failure to distribute income,

(B) in the case of section 4943, on the first day on which there are excess business holdings,

(C) in the case of section 4971, on the last day of the plan year in which there is an accumulated funding deficiency, and

(D) in any other case, the date on which such event occurred.

Amendments

- **1984, Deficit Reduction Act of 1984 (P.L. 98-369)**

P.L. 98-369, §305(a):

Redesignated Code Sec. 4962 as Code Sec. 4963. **Effective** for taxable events occurring after 12-31-84.

- **1980 (P.L. 96-596)**

P.L. 96-596, §2(c)(1):

Added Code Sec. 4962(e). **Effective** with respect to any first tier tax as if included in the Internal Revenue Code of 1954 when such tax was first imposed and with respect to second-tier taxes assessed after 12-24-80 (except in cases where there is a court decision with regard to which res judicata applies on that date).

Subchapter F—Tax Shelter Transactions

Sec. 4965. Excise tax on certain tax-exempt entities entering into prohibited tax shelter transactions.

[Sec. 4965]

SEC. 4965. EXCISE TAX ON CERTAIN TAX-EXEMPT ENTITIES ENTERING INTO PROHIBITED TAX SHELTER TRANSACTIONS.

[Sec. 4965(a)]

(a) BEING A PARTY TO AND APPROVAL OF PROHIBITED TRANSACTIONS.—

(1) TAX-EXEMPT ENTITY.—

(A) IN GENERAL.—If a transaction is a prohibited tax shelter transaction at the time any tax-exempt entity described in paragraph (1), (2), or (3) of subsection (c) becomes a party to the transaction, such entity shall pay a tax for the taxable year in which the entity becomes such a party and any subsequent taxable year in the amount determined under subsection (b)(1).

(B) POST-TRANSACTION DETERMINATION.—If any tax-exempt entity described in paragraph (1), (2), or (3) of subsection (c) is a party to a subsequently listed transaction at any time during a taxable year, such entity shall pay a tax for such taxable year in the amount determined under subsection (b)(1).

(2) ENTITY MANAGER.—If any entity manager of a tax-exempt entity approves such entity as (or otherwise causes such entity to be) a party to a prohibited tax shelter transaction at any time during the taxable year and knows or has reason to know that the transaction is a prohibited tax shelter transaction, such manager shall pay a tax for such taxable year in the amount determined under subsection (b)(2).

[Sec. 4965(b)]

(b) AMOUNT OF TAX.—

(1) ENTITY.—In the case of a tax-exempt entity—

(A) IN GENERAL.—Except as provided in subparagraph (B), the amount of the tax imposed under subsection (a)(1) with respect to any transaction for a taxable year shall be an amount equal to the product of the highest rate of tax under section 11, and the greater of—

(i) the entity's net income (after taking into account any tax imposed by this subtitle (other than by this section) with respect to such transaction) for such taxable year which—

(I) in the case of a prohibited tax shelter transaction (other than a subsequently listed transaction), is attributable to such transaction, or

(II) in the case of a subsequently listed transaction, is attributable to such transaction and which is properly allocable to the period beginning on the later of the date such transaction is identified by guidance as a listed transaction by the Secretary or the first day of the taxable year, or

(ii) 75 percent of the proceeds received by the entity for the taxable year which—

(I) in the case of a prohibited tax shelter transaction (other than a subsequently listed transaction), are attributable to such transaction, or

(II) in the case of a subsequently listed transaction, are attributable to such transaction and which are properly allocable to the period beginning on the later of the date such transaction is identified by guidance as a listed transaction by the Secretary or the first day of the taxable year.

(B) INCREASE IN TAX FOR CERTAIN KNOWING TRANSACTIONS.—In the case of a tax-exempt entity which knew, or had reason to know, a transaction was a prohibited tax shelter transaction at the time the entity became a party to the transaction, the amount of the tax imposed under subsection (a)(1)(A) with respect to any transaction for a taxable year shall be the greater of—

(i) 100 percent of the entity's net income (after taking into account any tax imposed by this subtitle (other than by this section) with respect to the prohibited tax shelter transaction) for such taxable year which is attributable to the prohibited tax shelter transaction, or

(ii) 75 percent of the proceeds received by the entity for the taxable year which are attributable to the prohibited tax shelter transaction.

This subparagraph shall not apply to any prohibited tax shelter transaction to which a tax-exempt entity became a party on or before the date of the enactment of this section.

(2) ENTITY MANAGER.—In the case of each entity manager, the amount of the tax imposed under subsection (a)(2) shall be $20,000 for each approval (or other act causing participation) described in subsection (a)(2).

[Sec. 4965(c)]

(c) TAX-EXEMPT ENTITY.—For purposes of this section, the term "tax-exempt entity" means an entity which is—

(1) described in section 501(c) or 501(d),

(2) described in section 170(c) (other than the United States),

(3) an Indian tribal government (within the meaning of section 7701(a)(40)),

(4) described in paragraph (1), (2), or (3) of section 4979(e),

(5) a program described in section 529,

(6) an eligible deferred compensation plan described in section 457(b) which is maintained by an employer described in section 457(e)(1)(A),

(7) an arrangement described in section 4973(a), or

Sec. 4963(e)(1)(B)

EXCISE TAXES—DONOR ADVISED FUNDS

(8) a program described in section 529A.

Amendments

• 2014, Stephen Beck, Jr., Achieving a Better Life Experience Act of 2014 (P.L. 113-295)

P.L. 113-295, §102(e)(3), Division B:

Amended Code Sec. 4965(c) by striking "or" at the end of paragraph (6), by striking the period at the end of paragraph (7) and inserting ", or", and by inserting after paragraph (7) a new paragraph (8). **Effective** for tax years beginning after 12-31-2014.

• 2007, Tax Technical Corrections Act of 2007 (P.L. 110-172)

P.L. 110-172, §11(a)(30):

Amended Code Sec. 4965(c)(6) by striking "section 4457(e)(1)(A)" and inserting "section 457(e)(1)(A)". **Effective** 12-29-2007.

[Sec. 4965(d)]

(d) ENTITY MANAGER.—For purposes of this section, the term "entity manager" means—

(1) in the case of an entity described in paragraph (1), (2), or (3) of subsection (c)—

(A) the person with authority or responsibility similar to that exercised by an officer, director, or trustee of an organization, and

(B) with respect to any act, the person having authority or responsibility with respect to such act, and

(2) in the case of an entity described in paragraph (4), (5), (6), or (7) of subsection (c), the person who approves or otherwise causes the entity to be a party to the prohibited tax shelter transaction.

[Sec. 4965(e)]

(e) PROHIBITED TAX SHELTER TRANSACTION; SUBSEQUENTLY LISTED TRANSACTION.—For purposes of this section—

(1) PROHIBITED TAX SHELTER TRANSACTION.—

(A) IN GENERAL.—The term "prohibited tax shelter transaction" means—

(i) any listed transaction, and

(ii) any prohibited reportable transaction.

(B) LISTED TRANSACTION.—The term "listed transaction" has the meaning given such term by section 6707A(c)(2).

(C) PROHIBITED REPORTABLE TRANSACTION.—The term "prohibited reportable transaction" means any confidential transaction or any transaction with contractual protection (as defined under regulations prescribed by the Secretary) which is a reportable transaction (as defined in section 6707A(c)(1)).

(2) SUBSEQUENTLY LISTED TRANSACTION.—The term "subsequently listed transaction" means any transaction to which a tax-exempt entity is a party and which is determined by the Secretary to be a listed transaction at any time after the entity has become a party to the transaction. Such term shall not include a transaction which is a prohibited reportable transaction at the time the entity became a party to the transaction.

[Sec. 4965(f)]

(f) REGULATORY AUTHORITY.—The Secretary is authorized to promulgate regulations which provide guidance regarding the determination of the allocation of net income or proceeds of a tax-exempt entity attributable to a transaction to various periods, including before and after the listing of the transaction or the date which is 90 days after the date of the enactment of this section.

[Sec. 4965(g)]

(g) COORDINATION WITH OTHER TAXES AND PENALTIES.—The tax imposed by this section is in addition to any other tax, addition to tax, or penalty imposed under this title.

Amendments

• 2006, Tax Increase Prevention and Reconciliation Act of 2005 (P.L. 109-222)

P.L. 109-222, §516(a)(1):

Amended chapter 42 by adding at the end a new subchapter F (Code Sec. 4965). **Effective** for tax years ending after 5-17-2006, with respect to transactions before, on, or after such date, except that no tax under Code Sec. 4965(a), as added by Act Sec. 516, shall apply with respect to income or proceeds that are properly allocable to any period ending on or before the date which is 90 days after 5-17-2006.

Subchapter G—Donor Advised Funds

Sec. 4966.   Taxes on taxable distributions.
Sec. 4967.   Taxes on prohibited benefits.

[Sec. 4966]

SEC. 4966. TAXES ON TAXABLE DISTRIBUTIONS.

[Sec. 4966(a)]

(a) IMPOSITION OF TAXES.—

(1) ON THE SPONSORING ORGANIZATION.—There is hereby imposed on each taxable distribution a tax equal to 20 percent of the amount thereof. The tax imposed by this paragraph shall be paid by the sponsoring organization with respect to the donor advised fund.

(2) ON THE FUND MANAGEMENT.—There is hereby imposed on the agreement of any fund manager to the making of a distribution, knowing that it is a taxable distribution, a tax equal to 5 percent of the amount thereof. The tax imposed by this paragraph shall be paid by any fund manager who agreed to the making of the distribution.

[Sec. 4966(b)]

(b) SPECIAL RULES.—For purposes of subsection (a)—

(1) JOINT AND SEVERAL LIABILITY.—If more than one person is liable under subsection (a)(2) with respect to the making of a taxable distribution, all such persons shall be jointly and severally liable under such paragraph with respect to such distribution.

(2) LIMIT FOR MANAGEMENT.—With respect to any one taxable distribution, the maximum amount of the tax imposed by subsection (a)(2) shall not exceed $10,000.

[Sec. 4966(c)]

(c) TAXABLE DISTRIBUTION.—For purposes of this section—

(1) IN GENERAL.—The term "taxable distribution" means any distribution from a donor advised fund—

(A) to any natural person, or

(B) to any other person if—

EXCISE TAXES—DONOR ADVISED FUNDS

(i) such distribution is for any purpose other than one specified in section 170(c)(2)(B), or

(ii) the sponsoring organization does not exercise expenditure responsibility with respect to such distribution in accordance with section 4945(h).

(2) EXCEPTIONS.—Such term shall not include any distribution from a donor advised fund—

(A) to any organization described in section 170(b)(1)(A) (other than a disqualified supporting organization),

(B) to the sponsoring organization of such donor advised fund, or

(C) to any other donor advised fund.

[Sec. 4966(d)]

(d) DEFINITIONS.—For purposes of this subchapter—

(1) SPONSORING ORGANIZATION.—The term "sponsoring organization" means any organization which—

(A) is described in section 170(c) (other than in paragraph (1) thereof, and without regard to paragraph (2)(A) thereof),

(B) is not a private foundation (as defined in section 509(a)), and

(C) maintains 1 or more donor advised funds.

(2) DONOR ADVISED FUND.—

(A) IN GENERAL.—Except as provided in subparagraph (B) or (C), the term "donor advised fund" means a fund or account—

(i) which is separately identified by reference to contributions of a donor or donors,

(ii) which is owned and controlled by a sponsoring organization, and

(iii) with respect to which a donor (or any person appointed or designated by such donor) has, or reasonably expects to have, advisory privileges with respect to the distribution or investment of amounts held in such fund or account by reason of the donor's status as a donor.

(B) EXCEPTIONS.—The term "donor advised fund" shall not include any fund or account—

(i) which makes distributions only to a single identified organization or governmental entity, or

(ii) with respect to which a person described in subparagraph (A)(iii) advises as to which individuals receive grants for travel, study, or other similar purposes, if—

(I) such person's advisory privileges are performed exclusively by such person in the person's capacity as a member of a committee all of the members of which are appointed by the sponsoring organization,

(II) no combination of persons described in subparagraph (A)(iii) (or persons related to such persons) control, directly or indirectly, such committee, and

(III) all grants from such fund or account are awarded on an objective and nondiscriminatory basis pursuant to a procedure approved in advance by the board of directors of the sponsoring organization, and such procedure is designed to ensure that all such grants meet the requirements of paragraphs (1), (2), or (3) of section 4945(g).

(C) SECRETARIAL AUTHORITY.—The Secretary may exempt a fund or account not described in subparagraph (B) from treatment as a donor advised fund—

(i) if such fund or account is advised by a committee not directly or indirectly controlled by the donor or any person appointed or designated by the donor for the purpose of advising with respect to distributions from such fund (and any related parties), or

(ii) if such fund benefits a single identified charitable purpose.

(3) FUND MANAGER.—The term "fund manager" means, with respect to any sponsoring organization—

(A) an officer, director, or trustee of such sponsoring organization (or an individual having powers or responsibilities similar to those of officers, directors, or trustees of the sponsoring organization), and

(B) with respect to any act (or failure to act), the employees of the sponsoring organization having authority or responsibility with respect to such act (or failure to act).

(4) DISQUALIFIED SUPPORTING ORGANIZATION.—

(A) IN GENERAL.—The term "disqualified supporting organization" means, with respect to any distribution—

(i) any type III supporting organization (as defined in section 4943(f)(5)(A)) which is not a functionally integrated type III supporting organization (as defined in section 4943(f)(5)(B)), and

(ii) any organization which is described in subparagraph (B) or (C) if—

(I) the donor or any person designated by the donor for the purpose of advising with respect to distributions from a donor advised fund (and any related parties) directly or indirectly controls a supported organization (as defined in section 509(f)(3)) of such organization, or

(II) the Secretary determines by regulations that a distribution to such organization otherwise is inappropriate.

(B) TYPE I AND TYPE II SUPPORTING ORGANIZATIONS.—An organization is described in this subparagraph if the organization meets the requirements of subparagraphs (A) and (C) of section 509(a)(3) and is—

(i) operated, supervised, or controlled by one or more organizations described in paragraph (1) or (2) of section 509(a), or

(ii) supervised or controlled in connection with one or more such organizations.

(C) FUNCTIONALLY INTEGRATED TYPE III SUPPORTING ORGANIZATIONS.—An organization is described in this subparagraph if the organization is a functionally integrated type III supporting organization (as defined under section 4943(f)(5)(B)).

Amendments

• **2006, Pension Protection Act of 2006 (P.L. 109-280)**

P.L. 109-280, § 1231(a):

Amended chapter 42, as amended by the Tax Increase Prevention and Reconciliation Act of 2005 (P.L. 109-222), by adding at the end a new subchapter G (Code Secs. 4966-4967). **Effective** for tax years beginning after 8-17-2006.

[Sec. 4967]

SEC. 4967. TAXES ON PROHIBITED BENEFITS.

[Sec. 4967(a)]

(a) IMPOSITION OF TAXES.—

(1) ON THE DONOR, DONOR ADVISOR, OR RELATED PERSON.—There is hereby imposed on the advice of any person described in subsection (d) to have a sponsoring organization make a distribution from a donor advised fund which results in such person or any other person described in subsection (d) receiving, directly or indirectly, a more than incidental benefit as a result of such distribution, a tax equal to 125 percent of such

benefit. The tax imposed by this paragraph shall be paid by any person described in subsection (d) who advises as to the distribution or who receives such a benefit as a result of the distribution.

(2) ON THE FUND MANAGEMENT.—There is hereby imposed on the agreement of any fund manager to the making of a distribution, knowing that such distribution would confer a benefit described in paragraph (1), a tax equal to 10 percent of the amount of such benefit. The tax imposed by this paragraph shall be paid by any fund manager who agreed to the making of the distribution.

[Sec. 4967(b)]

(b) EXCEPTION.—No tax shall be imposed under this section with respect to any distribution if a tax has been imposed with respect to such distribution under section 4958.

[Sec. 4967(c)]

(c) SPECIAL RULES.—For purposes of subsection (a)—

(1) JOINT AND SEVERAL LIABILITY.—If more than one person is liable under paragraph (1) or (2) of subsection (a) with respect to a distribution described in subsection (a), all such persons shall be jointly and severally liable under such paragraph with respect to such distribution.

(2) LIMIT FOR MANAGEMENT.—With respect to any one distribution described in subsection (a), the maximum amount of the tax imposed by subsection (a)(2) shall not exceed $10,000.

[Sec. 4967(d)]

(d) PERSON DESCRIBED.—A person is described in this subsection if such person is described in section 4958(f)(7) with respect to a donor advised fund.

Amendments

- 2006, Pension Protection Act of 2006 (P.L. 109-280)

P.L. 109-280, §1231(a):

Amended chapter 42, as amended by the Tax Increase Prevention and Reconciliation Act of 2005 (P.L. 109-222), by adding at the end a new subchapter G (Code Secs. 4966-4967). **Effective** for tax years beginning after 8-17-2006.

Subchapter H—Excise Tax Based on Investment Income of Private Colleges and Universities

Sec. 4968. Excise tax based on investment income of private colleges and universities.

[Sec. 4968]

SEC. 4968. EXCISE TAX BASED ON INVESTMENT INCOME OF PRIVATE COLLEGES AND UNIVERSITIES.

[Sec. 4968(a)]

(a) TAX IMPOSED.—There is hereby imposed on each applicable educational institution for the taxable year a tax equal to 1.4 percent of the net investment income of such institution for the taxable year.

[Sec. 4968(b)]

(b) APPLICABLE EDUCATIONAL INSTITUTION.—For purposes of this subchapter—

(1) IN GENERAL.—The term "applicable educational institution" means an eligible educational institution (as defined in section 25A(f)(2))—

(A) which had at least 500 tuition-paying students during the preceding taxable year,

(B) more than 50 percent of the tuition-paying students of which are located in the United States,

(C) which is not described in the first sentence of section 511(a)(2)(B) (relating to State colleges and universities), and

(D) the aggregate fair market value of the assets of which at the end of the preceding taxable year (other than those assets which are used directly in carrying out the institution's exempt purpose) is at least $500,000 per student of the institution.

(2) STUDENTS.—For purposes of paragraph (1), the number of students of an institution (including for purposes of determining the number of students at a particular location) shall be based on the daily average number of full-time students attending such institution (with part-time students taken into account on a full-time student equivalent basis).

Amendments

- 2018, Bipartisan Budget Act of 2018 (P.L. 115-123)

P.L. 115-123, §41109(a)(1)-(2), Div. D:

Amended Code Sec. 4968(b)(1), as added by section 13701(a) of P.L. 115-97, by inserting "tuition-paying" after "500" in subparagraph (A), and by inserting "tuition-paying" after "50 percent of the" in subparagraph (B). **Effective** for tax years beginning after 12-31-2017.

[Sec. 4968(c)]

(c) NET INVESTMENT INCOME.—For purposes of this section, net investment income shall be determined under rules similar to the rules of section 4940(c).

[Sec. 4968(d)]

(d) ASSETS AND NET INVESTMENT INCOME OF RELATED ORGANIZATIONS.—

(1) IN GENERAL.—For purposes of subsections (b)(1)(C) and (c), assets and net investment income of any related organization with respect to an educational institution shall be treated as assets and net investment income, respectively, of the educational institution, except that—

(A) no such amount shall be taken into account with respect to more than 1 educational institution, and

(B) unless such organization is controlled by such institution or is described in section 509(a)(3) with respect to such institution for the taxable year, assets and net investment income which are not intended or available for the use or benefit of the educational institution shall not be taken into account.

(2) RELATED ORGANIZATION.—For purposes of this subsection, the term "related organization" means, with respect to an educational institution, any organization which—

(A) controls, or is controlled by, such institution,

(B) is controlled by 1 or more persons which also control such institution, or

(C) is a supported organization (as defined in section 509(f)(3)), or an organization described in section 509(a)(3), during the taxable year with respect to such institution.

EXCISE TAXES—QUALIFIED PENSION, ETC., PLANS

- **2017, Tax Cuts and Jobs Act (P.L. 115-97)**

P.L. 115-97, §13701(a):
Amended chapter 42 by adding at the end a new subchapter H (Code Sec. 4968). **Effective** for tax years beginning after 12-31-2017.

CHAPTER 43—QUALIFIED PENSION, ETC., PLANS

Sec. 4971.	Taxes on failure to meet minimum funding standards.
Sec. 4972.	Tax on nondeductible contributions to qualified employer plans.
Sec. 4973.	Tax on excess contributions to certain tax-favored accounts and annuities.
Sec. 4974.	Excise tax on certain accumulations in qualified retirement plans.
Sec. 4975.	Tax on prohibited transactions.
Sec. 4976.	Taxes with respect to funded welfare benefit plans.
Sec. 4977.	Tax on certain fringe benefits provided by an employer.
Sec. 4978.	Tax on certain dispositions by employee stock ownership plans and certain cooperatives.
Sec. 4978B.	Tax on disposition of employer securities to which section 133 applied.
Sec. 4979.	Tax on certain excess contributions.
Sec. 4979A.	Tax on certain prohibited allocations of qualified securities.
Sec. 4980.	Tax on reversion of qualified plan assets to employer.
Sec. 4980A.	Tax on excess distributions from qualified retirement plans.
Sec. 4980B.	Failure to satisfy continuation coverage requirements of group health plans.
Sec. 4980C.	Requirements for issuers of qualified long-term care insurance contracts.
Sec. 4980D.	Failure to meet certain group health plan requirements.
Sec. 4980E.	Failure of employer to make comparable Archer MSA contributions.
Sec. 4980F.	Failure of applicable plans reducing benefit accruals to satisfy notice requirements.
Sec. 4980G.	Failure of employer to make comparable health savings account contributions.
Sec. 4980H.	Shared responsibility for employers regarding health coverage.

[Sec. 4971]

SEC. 4971. TAXES ON FAILURE TO MEET MINIMUM FUNDING STANDARDS.

[Sec. 4971(a)]

(a) INITIAL TAX.—If at any time during any taxable year an employer maintains a plan to which section 412 applies, there is hereby imposed for the taxable year a tax equal to—

(1) in the case of a single-employer plan, 10 percent of the aggregate unpaid minimum required contributions for all plan years remaining unpaid as of the end of any plan year ending with or within the taxable year,

(2) in the case of a multiemployer plan, 5 percent of the accumulated funding deficiency determined under section 431 as of the end of any plan year ending with or within the taxable year, and

(3) in the case of a CSEC plan, 10 percent of the CSEC accumulated funding deficiency as of the end of the plan year ending with or within the taxable year.

Amendments

- **2014, Cooperative and Small Employer Charity Pension Flexibility Act (P.L. 113-97)**

P.L. 113-97, §202(c)(8)(A):
Amended Code Sec. 4971(a) by striking "and" at the end of paragraph (1), by striking the period at the end of paragraph (2) and inserting ", and", and by adding at the end a new paragraph (3). **Effective** for years beginning after 12-31-2013.

- **2006, Pension Protection Act of 2006 (P.L. 109-280)**

P.L. 109-280, §114(e)(1):
Amended Code Sec. 4971(a). **Effective** for tax years beginning after 2007, but only with respect to plan years described in paragraph (1) which end with or within any such tax year [effective date amended by P.L. 110-458, §101(d)(3).—CCH]. Prior to amendment, Code Sec. 4971(a) read as follows:

(a) INITIAL TAX.—For each taxable year of an employer who maintains a plan to which section 412 applies, there is hereby imposed a tax of 10 percent (5 percent in the case of a multiemployer plan) on the amount of the accumulated funding deficiency under the plan, determined as of the end of the plan year ending with or within such taxable year.

P.L. 109-280, §214, provides:

SEC. 214. EXEMPTION FROM EXCISE TAXES FOR CERTAIN MULTIEMPLOYER PENSION PLANS.

(a) IN GENERAL.—Notwithstanding any other provision of law, no tax shall be imposed under subsection (a) or (b) of section 4971 of the Internal Revenue Code of 1986 with respect to any accumulated funding deficiency of a plan described in subsection (b) of this section for any taxable year beginning before the earlier of—

(1) the taxable year in which the plan sponsor adopts a rehabilitation plan under section 305(e) of the Employee Retirement Income Security Act of 1974 and section 432(e) of such Code (as added by this Act); or

(2) the taxable year that contains January 1, 2009.

(b) PLAN DESCRIBED.—A plan described under this subsection is a multiemployer pension plan—

(1) with less than 100 participants;

(2) with respect to which the contributing employers participated in a Federal fishery capacity reduction program;

(3) with respect to which employers under the plan participated in the Northeast Fisheries Assistance Program; and

(4) with respect to which the annual normal cost is less than $100,000 and the plan is experiencing a funding deficiency on the date of enactment of this Act.

- **1987, Revenue Act of 1987 (P.L. 100-203)**

P.L. 100-203, §9304(c)(1):
Amended Code Sec. 4971(a) by striking out "5 percent" and inserting in lieu thereof "10 percent (5 percent in the case of a multiemployer plan)". **Effective** for plan years beginning after 1988.

P.L. 100-203, §9305(a)(2)(A):
Amended Code Sec. 4971(a) by striking out the last sentence. **Effective** with respect to plan years beginning after 12-31-87. Prior to amendment, the last sentence read as follows:

The tax imposed by this subsection shall be paid by the employer responsible for contributing to or under the plan the amount described in section 412(b)(3)(A).

[Sec. 4971(b)]

(b) ADDITIONAL TAX.—If—

(1) a tax is imposed under subsection (a)(1) on any unpaid minimum required contribution and such amount remains unpaid as of the close of the taxable period,

(2) a tax is imposed under subsection (a)(2) on any accumulated funding deficiency and the accumulated funding deficiency is not corrected within the taxable period, or

(3) a tax is imposed under subsection (a)(3) on any CSEC accumulated funding deficiency and the CSEC accumulated funding deficiency is not corrected within the taxable period,

there is hereby imposed a tax equal to 100 percent of the unpaid minimum required contribution, accumulated funding deficiency, or CSEC accumulated funding deficiency, whichever is applicable, to the extent not so paid or corrected.

Amendments

• **2018, Tax Technical Corrections Act of 2018 (P.L. 115-141)**

P.L. 115-141, § 401(a)(225), Div. U:

Amended Code Sec. 4971(b) by striking "minimum required contribution," in the flush left text and all that follows through "whichever is applicable" and inserting "minimum required contribution, accumulated funding deficiency, or CSEC accumulated funding deficiency, whichever is applicable". **Effective** 3-23-2018. [Note: This language was previously added to Code Sec. 4971(b) by P.L. 113-97, § 202(c)(8)(B)(iii).—CCH.] Prior to amendment, the flush left text in Code Sec. 4971(b) read as follows:

there is hereby imposed a tax equal to 100 percent of the unpaid minimum required contribution, accumulated funding deficiency, or CSEC accumulated funding deficiency, whichever is applicable, to the extent not so paid or corrected.

• **2014, Cooperative and Small Employer Charity Pension Flexibility Act (P.L. 113-97)**

P.L. 113-97, § 202(c)(8)(B)(i)-(ii):

Amended Code Sec. 4971(b) by striking "or" at the end of paragraph (1), by adding "or" at the end of paragraph (2), and by inserting immediately after paragraph (2) a new paragraph (3), and by striking "minimum required contributions or accumulated funding deficiency" and inserting "minimum required contribution, accumulated funding deficiency, or CSEC accumulated funding deficiency". **Effective** for years beginning after 12-31-2013.

• **2008, Worker, Retiree, and Employer Recovery Act of 2008 (P.L. 110-458)**

P.L. 110-458, § 101(d)(2)(F)(i):

Amended Code Sec. 4971(b)(1) by striking "required minimum" and inserting "minimum required". **Effective** as if included in the provision of the 2006 Act to which the amendment relates [effective for tax years beginning after 2007, but only with respect to plan years beginning after 2007 which end with or within any such tax year.—CCH].

• **2006, Pension Protection Act of 2006 (P.L. 109-280)**

P.L. 109-280, § 114(e)(1):

Amended Code Sec. 4971(b). **Effective** for tax years beginning after 2007, but only with respect to plan years described in paragraph (1) which end with or within any such tax year [effective date amended by P.L. 110-458, § 101(d)(3).—CCH]. Prior to amendment, Code Sec. 4971(b) read as follows:

(b) ADDITIONAL TAX.—In any case in which an initial tax is imposed by subsection (a) on an accumulated funding deficiency and such accumulated funding deficiency is not corrected within the taxable period, there is hereby imposed a tax equal to 100 percent of such accumulated funding deficiency to the extent not corrected.

P.L. 109-280, § 214, provides:

SEC. 214. EXEMPTION FROM EXCISE TAXES FOR CERTAIN MULTIEMPLOYER PENSION PLANS.

(a) IN GENERAL.—Notwithstanding any other provision of law, no tax shall be imposed under subsection (a) or (b) of section 4971 of the Internal Revenue Code of 1986 with respect to any accumulated funding deficiency of a plan described in subsection (b) of this section for any taxable year beginning before the earlier of—

(1) the taxable year in which the plan sponsor adopts a rehabilitation plan under section 305(e) of the Employee Retirement Income Security Act of 1974 and section 432(e) of such Code (as added by this Act); or

(2) the taxable year that contains January 1, 2009.

(b) PLAN DESCRIBED.—A plan described under this subsection is a multiemployer pension plan—

(1) with less than 100 participants;

(2) with respect to which the contributing employers participated in a Federal fishery capacity reduction program;

(3) with respect to which employers under the plan participated in the Northeast Fisheries Assistance Program; and

(4) with respect to which the annual normal cost is less than $100,000 and the plan is experiencing a funding deficiency on the date of enactment of this Act.

• **1987, Revenue Act of 1987 (P.L. 100-203)**

P.L. 100-203, § 9305(a)(2)(B):

Amended Code Sec. 4971(b) by striking out the last sentence. **Effective** with respect to plan years beginning after 12-31-87. Prior to amendment, the last sentence read as follows:

The tax imposed by this subsection shall be paid by the employer described in subsection (a).

• **1980 (P.L. 96-596)**

P.L. 96-596, § 2(a)(1):

Amended Code Sec. 4971(b) by striking out "correction period" and inserting in lieu thereof "taxable period". **Effective** with respect to second-tier taxes assessed after 12-24-80 (except in cases where there is a court decision with regard to res judicata which applies on that date).

[Sec. 4971(c)]

(c) DEFINITIONS.—For purposes of this section—

(1) ACCUMULATED FUNDING DEFICIENCY.—The term "accumulated funding deficiency" has the meaning given to such term by section 431.

(2) CORRECT.—The term "correct" means, with respect to an accumulated funding deficiency or CSEC accumulated funding deficiency, the contribution, to or under the plan, of the amount necessary to reduce such accumulated funding deficiency or CSEC accumulated funding deficiency as of the end of a plan year in which such deficiency arose to zero.

(3) TAXABLE PERIOD.—The term "taxable period" means, with respect to an accumulated funding deficiency, CSEC accumulated funding deficiency, or unpaid minimum required contribution, whichever is applicable, the period beginning with the end of a plan year in which there is an accumulated funding deficiency, CSEC accumulated funding deficiency, or unpaid minimum required contribution, whichever is applicable, and ending on the earlier of—

(A) the date of mailing of a notice of deficiency with respect to the tax imposed by subsection (a), or

(B) the date on which the tax imposed by subsection (a) is assessed.

(4) UNPAID MINIMUM REQUIRED CONTRIBUTION.—

(A) IN GENERAL.—The term "unpaid minimum required contribution" means, with respect to any plan year, any minimum required contribution under section 430 for the plan year which is not paid on or before the due date (as determined under section 430(j)(1)) for the plan year.

(B) ORDERING RULE.—Any payment to or under a plan for any plan year shall be allocated first to unpaid minimum required contributions for all preceding plan years on a first-in, first-out basis and then to the minimum required contribution under section 430 for the plan year.

(5) CSEC ACCUMULATED FUNDING DEFICIENCY.—The term "CSEC accumulated funding deficiency" means the accumulated funding deficiency determined under section 433.

Amendments

• **2018, Tax Technical Corrections Act of 2018 (P.L. 115-141)**

P.L. 115-141, § 401(a)(226), Div. U:

Amended Code Sec. 4971(c)(3) by striking "applicable and" and inserting "applicable, and". **Effective** 3-23-2018.

• **2014, Cooperative and Small Employer Charity Pension Flexibility Act (P.L. 113-97)**

P.L. 113-97, § 202(c)(8)(C)(i)-(iii):

Amended Code Sec. 4971(c) by striking "accumulated funding deficiency" each place it appears in paragraph (2) and inserting "accumulated funding deficiency or CSEC accumulated funding deficiency", by striking "accumulated funding deficiency or unpaid minimum required contribution" each place it appears in paragraph (3) and inserting "accumulated funding deficiency, CSEC accumulated funding deficiency, or unpaid minimum required contribution", and by adding at the end a new paragraph (5). **Effective** for years beginning after 12-31-2013.

• **2008, Worker, Retiree, and Employer Recovery Act of 2008 (P.L. 110-458)**

P.L. 110-458, § 101(d)(2)(F)(ii):

Amended Code Sec. 4971(c)(3) by inserting "or unpaid minimum required contribution, whichever is applicable" after "accumulated funding deficiency" each place it appears. **Effective** as if included in the provision of the 2006 Act to which the amendment relates [effective for tax years beginning after 2007, but only with respect to plan years beginning after 2007 which end with or within any such tax year.—CCH].

• **2006, Pension Protection Act of 2006 (P.L. 109-280)**

P.L. 109-280, § 114(e)(2)(A)-(B):

Amended Code Sec. 4971(c) by striking "the last two sentences of section 412(a)" in paragraph (1) and inserting "section 431", and by adding at the end a new paragraph (4). **Effective** for tax years beginning after 2007, but only with respect to plan years

EXCISE TAXES—QUALIFIED PENSION, ETC., PLANS

described in paragraph (1) which end with or within any such tax year [**effective** date amended by P.L. 110-458, §101(d)(3).—CCH].

• **1980 (P.L. 96-596)**

P.L. 96-596, §2(a)(2):

Amended Code Sec. 4971(c)(3). **Effective** with respect to second-tier taxes assessed after 12-24-80 (except in cases where there is a court decision with respect to which res judicata applies on that date). Prior to amendment, Code Sec. 4971(c)(3) read:

"(3) CORRECTION PERIOD.—The term `correction period' means, with respect to an accumulated funding deficiency, the period beginning with the end of a plan year in which there is an accumulated funding deficiency and ending 90 days after the date of mailing of a notice of deficiency under section 6212 with respect to the tax imposed by subsection (b), extended—

(A) by any period in which a deficiency cannot be assessed under section 6213(a), and

(B) by any other period which the Secretary determines is reasonable and necessary to permit a reduction of the accumulated funding deficiency to zero under this section."

• **1980, Multiemployer Pension Plan Amendments Act of 1980 (P.L. 96-364)**

P.L. 96-364, §204(1):

Amended Code Sec. 4971(c)(1) by striking out "last sentence" and inserting in lieu thereof "last two sentences." **Effective** 9-26-80.

• **1976, Tax Reform Act of 1976 (P.L. 94-455)**

P.L. 94-455, §1906(b)(13)(A):

Amended 1954 Code by substituting "Secretary" for "Secretary or his delegate" each place it appeared. **Effective** 2-1-77.

[Sec. 4971(d)]

(d) NOTIFICATION OF THE SECRETARY OF LABOR.—Before issuing a notice of deficiency with respect to the tax imposed by subsection (a) or (b), the Secretary shall notify the Secretary of Labor and provide him a reasonable opportunity (but not more than 60 days)—

(1) to require the employer responsible for contributing to or under the plan to eliminate the accumulated funding deficiency, CSEC accumulated funding deficiency, or unpaid minimum required contribution, whichever is applicable, or

(2) to comment on the imposition of such tax.

Amendments

• **2018, Tax Technical Corrections Act of 2018 (P.L. 115-141)**

P.L. 115-141, §401(b)(44), Div. U:

Amended Code Sec. 4971(d) by striking the last sentence. **Effective** 3-23-2018. For a special rule, see Act Sec. 401(e), Div. U, below. Prior to being stricken, the last sentence of Code Sec. 4971(d) read as follows:

In the case of a multiemployer plan which is in reorganization under section 418, the same notice and opportunity shall be provided to the Pension Benefit Guaranty Corporation.

P.L. 115-141, §401(e), Div. U, provides:

(e) GENERAL SAVINGS PROVISION WITH RESPECT TO DEADWOOD PROVISIONS.—If—

(1) any provision amended or repealed by the amendments made by subsection (b) or (d) applied to—

(A) any transaction occurring before the date of the enactment of this Act,

(B) any property acquired before such date of enactment, or

(C) any item of income, loss, deduction, or credit taken into account before such date of enactment, and

(2) the treatment of such transaction, property, or item under such provision would (without regard to the amendments or repeals made by such subsection) affect the liability for tax for periods ending after such date of enactment,

nothing in the amendments or repeals made by this section shall be construed to affect the treatment of such transaction, property, or item for purposes of determining liability for tax for periods ending after such date of enactment.

• **2014, Cooperative and Small Employer Charity Pension Flexibility Act (P.L. 113-97)**

P.L. 113-97, §202(c)(8)(D):

Amended Code Sec. 4971(d)(1) by striking "accumulated funding deficiency or unpaid minimum required contribution" and inserting "accumulated funding deficiency, CSEC accumulated funding deficiency, or unpaid minimum required contribution". **Effective** for years beginning after 12-31-2013.

• **2008, Worker, Retiree, and Employer Recovery Act of 2008 (P.L. 110-458)**

P.L. 110-458, §101(d)(2)(F)(ii):

Amended Code Sec. 4971(d)(1) by inserting "or unpaid minimum required contribution, whichever is applicable" after "accumulated funding deficiency". **Effective** as if included in the provision of the 2006 Act to which the amendment relates [**effective** for tax years beginning after 2007, but only with respect to plan years beginning after 2007 which end with or within any such tax year.—CCH].

• **1980, Multiemployer Pension Plan Amendments Act of 1980 (P.L. 96-364)**

P.L. 96-364, §204(2):

Amended Code Sec. 4971(d) by adding the last sentence. **Effective** 9-26-80.

• **1976, Tax Reform Act of 1976 (P.L. 94-455)**

P.L. 94-455, §1906(b)(13)(A):

Amended 1954 Code by substituting "Secretary" for "Secretary or his delegate" each place it appeared. **Effective** 2-1-77.

[Sec. 4971(e)]

(e) LIABILITY FOR TAX.—

(1) IN GENERAL.—Except as provided in paragraph (2), the tax imposed by subsection (a), (b), or (f) shall be paid by the employer responsible for contributing to or under the plan the amount described in section 412(a)(2).

(2) JOINT AND SEVERAL LIABILITY WHERE EMPLOYER MEMBER OF CONTROLLED GROUP.—

(A) IN GENERAL.—If an employer referred to in paragraph (1) is a member of a controlled group, each member of such group shall be jointly and severally liable for the tax imposed by subsection (a), (b), (f), or (g).

(B) CONTROLLED GROUP.—For purposes of subparagraph (A), the term "controlled group" means any group treated as a single employer under subsection (b), (c), (m), or (o) of section 414.

Amendments

• **2008, Worker, Retiree, and Employer Recovery Act of 2008 (P.L. 110-458)**

P.L. 110-458, §101(d)(2)(F)(iii):

Amended Code Sec. 4971(e)(1) by striking "section 412(a)(1)(A)" and inserting "section 412(a)(2)". **Effective** as if included in the provision of the 2006 Act to which the amendment relates [**effective** for tax years beginning after 2007, but only with respect to plan years beginning after 2007 which end with or within any such tax year.—CCH].

• **2006, Pension Protection Act of 2006 (P.L. 109-280)**

P.L. 109-280, §114(e)(3):

Amended Code Sec. 4971(e)(1) by striking "section 412(b)(3)(A)" and inserting "section 412(a)(1)(A)". **Effective** for tax years beginning after 2007, but only with respect to plan years described in paragraph (1) which end with or within any such tax year [**effective** date amended by P.L. 110-458, §101(d)(3).—CCH].

P.L. 109-280, §206, provides:

SEC. 206. SPECIAL RULE FOR CERTAIN BENEFITS FUNDED UNDER AN AGREEMENT APPROVED BY THE PENSION BENEFIT GUARANTY CORPORATION.

In the case of a multiemployer plan that is a party to an agreement that was approved by the Pension Benefit Guaranty Corporation prior to June 30, 2005, and that—

(1) increases benefits, and

(2) provides for special withdrawal liability rules under section 4203(f) of the Employee Retirement Income Security Act of 1974 (29 U.S.C. 1383),

the amendments made by sections 201, 202, 211, and 212 of this Act shall not apply to the benefit increases under any plan amendment adopted prior to June 30, 2005, that are funded pursuant to such agreement if the plan is funded in compliance with such agreement (and any amendments thereto).

P.L. 109-280, §212(b)(2)(A)-(B) [as amended by P.L. 110-458, §102(b)(3)(A)]:

Amended Code Sec. 4971(e)(2) by striking "In the case of a plan other than a multiemployer plan, if the" and inserting "If an", and by striking "or (f)" and inserting "(f), or (g)". **Effective** for tax years beginning after 2007, but only with respect to plan years beginning after 2007 which end with or within any such taxable year [**effective** date amended by P.L. 110-458, §102(b)(3)(B).—CCH]. For special rules, see Act Sec. 212(e)(2)-(3) in the amendment notes following Code Sec. 4971(g), below.

P.L. 109-280, §221(c) (repealed by P.L. 113-235, §101(a), Division O, effective 12-16-2014), provides:

(c) SUNSET.—

(1) IN GENERAL.—Except as provided in this subsection, notwithstanding any other provision of this Act, the provisions of, and the amendments made by, sections 201(b), 202, and 212 shall not apply to plan years beginning after December 31, 2014.

(2) FUNDING IMPROVEMENT AND REHABILITATION PLANS.—If a plan is operating under a funding improvement or rehabilitation plan under section 305 of such Act or 432 of such Code for its last year beginning before January 1, 2015, such plan shall continue to operate under such funding improvement or rehabilitation plan during any period after December 31, 2014, such funding improvement or rehabilitation plan is in effect and all provisions of such Act or Code relating to the operation of such funding improvement or rehabilitation plan shall continue in effect during such period.

EXCISE TAXES—QUALIFIED PENSION, ETC., PLANS

• **1994, Uruguay Round Agreements Act (P.L. 103-465)**

P.L. 103-465, §751(a)(9)(B)(i):

Amended Code Sec. 4971(e) by striking "(a) or (b)" wherever it appears and inserting "(a), (b), or (f)". **Effective** for plan years beginning after 12-31-94.

• **1987, Revenue Act of 1987 (P.L. 100-203)**

P.L. 100-203, §9305(a)(1):

Amended Code Sec. 4971 by redesignating subsection (e) as subsection (f) and inserting after subsection (d) new subsection (e). **Effective** with respect to plan years beginning after 12-31-87.

• **1974, Employee Retirement Income Security Act of 1974 (P.L. 93-406)**

P.L. 93-406, §1013(b):

Added Code Sec. 4971. For the **effective** date of Code Sec. 4971, see the amendment note for P.L. 93-406 under Code Sec. 410.

[Sec. 4971(f)]

(f) FAILURE TO PAY LIQUIDITY SHORTFALL.—

(1) IN GENERAL.—In the case of a plan to which section 430(j)(4) or 433(f) applies, there is hereby imposed a tax of 10 percent of the excess (if any) of—

(A) the amount of the liquidity shortfall for any quarter, over

(B) the amount of such shortfall which is paid by the required installment under section 430(j) or 433(f), whichever is applicable, for such quarter (but only if such installment is paid on or before the due date for such installment).

(2) ADDITIONAL TAX.—If the plan has a liquidity shortfall as of the close of any quarter and as of the close of each of the following 4 quarters, there is hereby imposed a tax equal to 100 percent of the amount on which tax was imposed by paragraph (1) for such first quarter.

(3) DEFINITIONS AND SPECIAL RULE.—

(A) LIQUIDITY SHORTFALL; QUARTER.—For purposes of this subsection, the terms "liquidity shortfall" and "quarter" have the respective meanings given such terms by section 430(j) or 433(f), whichever is applicable.

(B) SPECIAL RULE.—If the tax imposed by paragraph (2) is paid with respect to any liquidity shortfall for any quarter, no further tax shall be imposed by this subsection on such shortfall for such quarter.

(4) WAIVER BY SECRETARY.—If the taxpayer establishes to the satisfaction of the Secretary that—

(A) the liquidity shortfall described in paragraph (1) was due to reasonable cause and not willful neglect, and

(B) reasonable steps have been taken to remedy such liquidity shortfall,

the Secretary may waive all or part of the tax imposed by this subsection.

Amendments

• **2018, Tax Technical Corrections Act of 2018 (P.L. 115-141)**

P.L. 115-141, §401(a)(227), Div. U:

Amended Code Sec. 4971(f) by striking "applicable for" and inserting "applicable, for". **Effective** 3-23-2018.

• **2014, Cooperative and Small Employer Charity Pension Flexibility Act (P.L. 113-97)**

P.L. 113-97, §202(c)(8)(E)(i)-(iii):

Amended Code Sec. 4971(f) by striking "430(j)(4)" in paragraph (1) and inserting "430(j)(4) or 433(f)", by striking "430(j)" in paragraph (1)(B) and inserting "430(j) or 433(f), whichever is applicable", and by striking "412(m)(5)" in paragraph (3)(A) and inserting "430(j) or 433(f), whichever is applicable". **Effective** for years beginning after 12-31-2013.

• **2006, Pension Protection Act of 2006 (P.L. 109-280)**

P.L. 109-280, §114(e)(4)(A)-(B):

Amended Code Sec. 4971(f)(1) by striking "section 412(m)(5)" and inserting "section 430(j)(4)", and by striking "section 412(m)" and inserting "section 430(j)". **Effec**tive for tax years beginning after 2007, but only with respect to plan years described in paragraph (1) which end with or within any such tax year [**effective** date amended by P.L. 110-458, §101(d)(3).—CCH].

• **1996, Small Business Job Protection Act of 1996 (P.L. 104-188)**

P.L. 104-188, §1464(a):

Amended Code Sec. 4971(f) by adding at the end a new paragraph (4). **Effective** as if included in the amendment made by section 751(a)(9)(B)(ii) of the Retirement Protection Act of 1994 (108 Stat. 5020).

• **1994, Uruguay Round Agreements Act (P.L. 103-465)**

P.L. 103-465, §751(a)(9)(B)(ii):

Amended Code Sec. 4971 by redesignating subsection (f) as subsection (g) and adding a new subsection (f). **Effective** for plan years beginning after 12-31-94.

[Sec. 4971(g)]

(g) MULTIEMPLOYER PLANS IN ENDANGERED OR CRITICAL STATUS.—

(1) IN GENERAL.—Except as provided in this subsection—

(A) no tax shall be imposed under this section for a taxable year with respect to a multiemployer plan if, for the plan years ending with or within the taxable year, the plan is in critical status pursuant to section 432, and

(B) any tax imposed under this subsection for a taxable year with respect to a multiemployer plan if, for the plan years ending with or within the taxable year, the plan is in endangered status pursuant to section 432 shall be in addition to any other tax imposed by this section.

(2) FAILURE TO COMPLY WITH FUNDING IMPROVEMENT OR REHABILITATION PLAN.—

(A) IN GENERAL.—If any funding improvement plan or rehabilitation plan in effect under section 432 with respect to a multiemployer plan requires an employer to make a contribution to the plan, there is hereby imposed a tax on each failure of the employer to make the required contribution within the time required under such plan.

(B) AMOUNT OF TAX.—The amount of the tax imposed by subparagraph (A) shall be equal to the amount of the required contribution the employer failed to make in a timely manner.

(C) LIABILITY FOR TAX.—The tax imposed by subparagraph (A) shall be paid by the employer responsible for contributing to or under the rehabilitation plan which fails to make the contribution.

(3) FAILURE TO MEET REQUIREMENTS FOR PLANS IN ENDANGERED OR CRITICAL STATUS.—If—

(A) a plan which is in seriously endangered status fails to meet the applicable benchmarks by the end of the funding improvement period, or

(B) a plan which is in critical status either—

(i) fails to meet the requirements of section 432(e) by the end of the rehabilitation period, or

(ii) has received a certification under section 432(b)(3)(A)(ii) for 3 consecutive plan years that the plan is not making the scheduled progress in meeting its requirements under the rehabilitation plan,

the plan shall be treated as having an accumulated funding deficiency for purposes of this section for the last plan year in such funding improvement, rehabilitation, or 3-consecutive year period (and each succeeding plan year until such benchmarks or requirements are met) in an amount equal to the greater of the amount of the contributions necessary to meet such benchmarks or requirements or the amount of such accumulated funding deficiency without regard to this paragraph.

EXCISE TAXES—QUALIFIED PENSION, ETC., PLANS

(4) FAILURE TO ADOPT REHABILITATION PLAN.—

(A) IN GENERAL.—In the case of a multiemployer plan which is in critical status, there is hereby imposed a tax on the failure of such plan to adopt a rehabilitation plan within the time prescribed under section 432.

(B) AMOUNT OF TAX.—The amount of the tax imposed under subparagraph (A) with respect to any plan sponsor for any taxable year shall be the greater of—

(i) the amount of tax imposed under subsection (a) for the taxable year (determined without regard to this subsection), or

(ii) the amount equal to $1,100 multiplied by the number of days during the taxable year which are included in the period beginning on the day following the close of the 240-day period described in section 432(e)(1)(A) and ending on the day on which the rehabilitation plan is adopted.

(C) LIABILITY FOR TAX.—

(i) IN GENERAL.—The tax imposed by subparagraph (A) shall be paid by each plan sponsor.

(ii) PLAN SPONSOR.—For purposes of clause (i), the term "plan sponsor" has the meaning given such term by section 432(j)(9).

(5) WAIVER.—In the case of a failure described in paragraph (2) or (3) which is due to reasonable cause and not to willful neglect, the Secretary may waive part or all of the tax imposed by this subsection. For purposes of this paragraph, reasonable cause includes unanticipated and material market fluctuations, the loss of a significant contributing employer, or other factors to the extent that the payment of tax under this subsection with respect to the failure would be excessive or otherwise inequitable relative to the failure involved.

(6) TERMS USED IN SECTION 432.—For purposes of this subsection, any term used in this subsection which is also used in section 432 shall have the meaning given such term by section 432.

Amendments

- **2018, Tax Technical Corrections Act of 2018 (P.L. 115-141)**

P.L. 115-141, §401(a)(228), Div. U:

Amended Code Sec. 4971(g)(4)(C)(ii) by striking "section 432(i)(9)" and inserting "section 432(j)(9)". **Effective** 3-23-2018.

- **2008, Worker, Retiree, and Employer Recovery Act of 2008 (P.L. 110-458)**

P.L. 110-458, §102(b)(2)(I)(i)-(ii):

Amended Code Sec. 4971(g)(4) by striking "first day of" and inserting "day following the close of" in subparagraph (B)(ii), and by striking clause (ii) of subparagraph (C) and inserting a new clause (ii). **Effective** as if included in the provision of the 2006 Act to which the amendment relates [**effective** generally with respect to plan years beginning after 2007.—CCH]. Prior to being stricken, Code Sec. 4971(g)(4)(C)(ii) read as follows:

(ii) PLAN SPONSOR.—For purposes of clause (i), the term "plan sponsor" in the case of a multiemployer plan means the association, committee, joint board of trustees, or other similar group of representatives of the parties who establish or maintain the plan.

- **2006, Pension Protection Act of 2006 (P.L. 109-280)**

P.L. 109-280, §206, provides:

SEC. 206. SPECIAL RULE FOR CERTAIN BENEFITS FUNDED UNDER AN AGREEMENT APPROVED BY THE PENSION BENEFIT GUARANTY CORPORATION.

In the case of a multiemployer plan that is a party to an agreement that was approved by the Pension Benefit Guaranty Corporation prior to June 30, 2005, and that—

(1) increases benefits, and

(2) provides for special withdrawal liability rules under section 4203(f) of the Employee Retirement Income Security Act of 1974 (29 U.S.C. 1383),

the amendments made by sections 201, 202, 211, and 212 of this Act shall not apply to the benefit increases under any plan amendment adopted prior to June 30, 2005, that are funded pursuant to such agreement if the plan is funded in compliance with such agreement (and any amendments thereto).

P.L. 109-280, §212(b)(1):

Amended Code Sec. 4971 by redesignating subsection (g) as subsection (h) and by inserting after subsection (f) a new subsection (g). **Effective** for tax years beginning after 2007, but only with respect to plan years beginning after 2007 which end with or within any such taxable year [**effective** date amended by P.L. 110-458, §102(b)(3)(B).—CCH]. For special rules, see Act Sec. 212(e)(2)-(3), below.

P.L. 109-280, §212(e)(2)-(3) [as amended by P.L. 110-458, §102(b)(3)(C)], provides:

(2) SPECIAL RULE FOR CERTAIN NOTICES.—In any case in which a plan's actuary certifies that it is reasonably expected that a multiemployer plan will be in critical status under section 432(b) of the Internal Revenue Code of 1986, as added by this section, with respect to the first plan year beginning after 2007, the notice required under subparagraph (D) of such section may be provided at any time after the date of enactment, so long as it is provided on or before the last date for providing the notice under such subparagraph.

(3) SPECIAL RULE FOR CERTAIN RESTORED BENEFITS.—In the case of a multiemployer plan—

(A) with respect to which benefits were reduced pursuant to a plan amendment adopted on or after January 1, 2002, and before June 30, 2005, and

(B) which, pursuant to the plan document, the trust agreement, or a formal written communication from the plan sponsor to participants provided before June 30, 2005, provided for the restoration of such benefits,

the amendments made by this section shall not apply to such benefit restorations to the extent that any restriction on the providing or accrual of such benefits would otherwise apply by reason of such amendments.

P.L. 109-280, §221(c) (repealed by P.L. 113-235, §101(a), Division O, effective 12-16-2014), provides:

(c) SUNSET.—

(1) IN GENERAL.—Except as provided in this subsection, notwithstanding any other provision of this Act, the provisions of, and the amendments made by, sections 201(b), 202, and 212 shall not apply to plan years beginning after December 31, 2014.

(2) FUNDING IMPROVEMENT AND REHABILITATION PLANS.—If a plan is operating under a funding improvement or rehabilitation plan under section 305 of such Act or 432 of such Code for its last year beginning before January 1, 2015, such plan shall continue to operate under such funding improvement or rehabilitation plan during any period after December 31, 2014, such funding improvement or rehabilitation plan is in effect and all provisions of such Act or Code relating to the operation of such funding improvement or rehabilitation plan shall continue in effect during such period.

[Sec. 4971(h)]

(h) FAILURE OF A CSEC PLAN SPONSOR TO ADOPT FUNDING RESTORATION PLAN.—

(1) IN GENERAL.—In the case of a CSEC plan that is in funding restoration status (within the meaning of section 433(j)(5)(A)), there is hereby imposed a tax on the failure of such plan to adopt a funding restoration plan within the time prescribed under section 433(j)(3).

(2) AMOUNT OF TAX.—The amount of the tax imposed under paragraph (1) with respect to any plan sponsor for any taxable year shall be the amount equal to $100 multiplied by the number of days during the taxable year which are included in the period beginning on the day following the close of the 180-day period described in section 433(j)(3) and ending on the day on which the funding restoration plan is adopted.

(3) WAIVER BY SECRETARY.—In the case of a failure described in paragraph (1) which the Secretary determines is due to reasonable cause and not to willful neglect, the Secretary may waive a portion or all of the tax imposed by such paragraph.

(4) LIABILITY FOR TAX.—The tax imposed by paragraph (1) shall be paid by the plan sponsor (within the meaning of section 433(j)(5)(E)).

Amendments

- **2014, Cooperative and Small Employer Charity Pension Flexibility Act (P.L. 113-97)**

P.L. 113-97, §202(c)(9):

Amended Code Sec. 4971 by redesignating subsection (h) as subsection (i), and by inserting after subsection (g) a new subsection (h). **Effective** for years beginning after 12-31-2013.

[Sec. 4971(i)]

(i) CROSS REFERENCES.—

For disallowance of deductions for taxes paid under this section, see section 275.

EXCISE TAXES—QUALIFIED PENSION, ETC., PLANS

For liability for tax in case of an employer party to collective bargaining agreement, see section 413(b)(6).

For provisions concerning notification of Secretary of Labor of imposition of tax under this section, waiver of the tax imposed by subsection (b), and other coordination between Secretary of the Treasury and Secretary of Labor with respect to compliance with this section, see section 3002(b) of title III of the Employee Retirement Income Security Act of 1974.

Amendments

• **2014, Cooperative and Small Employer Charity Pension Flexibility Act (P.L. 113-97)**

P.L. 113-97, §202(c)(9):

Amended Code Sec. 4971 by redesignating subsection (h) as subsection (i). **Effective** for years beginning after 12-31-2013.

• **2006, Pension Protection Act of 2006 (P.L. 109-280)**

P.L. 109-280, §212(b)(1):

Amended Code Sec. 4971 by redesignating subsection (g) as subsection (h). **Effective** for tax years beginning after 2007, but only with respect to plan years beginning after 2007 which end with or within any such taxable year [effective date amended by P.L. 110-458, §102(b)(3)(B).—CCH]. For special rules, see Act Sec. 212(e)(2)-(3) in the amendment notes following Code Sec. 4971(g), above.

P.L. 109-280, §221(c) (repealed by P.L. 113-235, §101(a), Division O, effective 12-16-2014), provides:

(c) SUNSET.—

(1) IN GENERAL.—Except as provided in this subsection, notwithstanding any other provision of this Act, the provisions of, and the amendments made by, sections 201(b), 202, and 212 shall not apply to plan years beginning after December 31, 2014.

(2) FUNDING IMPROVEMENT AND REHABILITATION PLANS.—If a plan is operating under a funding improvement or rehabilitation plan under section 305 of such Act or 432 of such Code for its last year beginning before January 1, 2015, such plan shall continue to operate under such funding improvement or rehabilitation plan during any period after December 31, 2014, such funding improvement or rehabilitation plan is in effect and all provisions of such Act or Code relating to the operation of such funding improvement or rehabilitation plan shall continue in effect during such period.

• **1994, Uruguay Round Agreements Act (P.L. 103-465)**

P.L. 103-465, §751(a)(9)(B)(ii):

Amended Code Sec. 4971 by redesignating subsection (f) as subsection (g). **Effective** for plan years beginning after 12-31-94.

• **1987, Revenue Act of 1987 (P.L. 100-203)**

P.L. 100-203, §9305(a)(1):

Amended Code Sec. 4971 by redesignating subsection (e) as subsection (f). **Effective** with respect to plan years beginning after 12-31-87.

[Sec. 4972]

SEC. 4972. TAX ON NONDEDUCTIBLE CONTRIBUTIONS TO QUALIFIED EMPLOYER PLANS.

[Sec. 4972(a)]

(a) TAX IMPOSED.—In the case of any qualified employer plan, there is hereby imposed a tax equal to 10 percent of the nondeductible contributions under the plan (determined as of the close of the taxable year of the employer).

[Sec. 4972(b)]

(b) EMPLOYER LIABLE FOR TAX.—The tax imposed by this section shall be paid by the employer making the contributions.

[Sec. 4972(c)]

(c) NONDEDUCTIBLE CONTRIBUTIONS.—For purposes of this section—

(1) IN GENERAL.—The term "nondeductible contributions" means, with respect to any qualified employer plan, the sum of—

(A) the excess (if any) of—

(i) the amount contributed for the taxable year by the employer to or under such plan, over

(ii) the amount allowable as a deduction under section 404 for such contributions (determined without regard to subsection (e) thereof), and

(B) the amount determined under this subsection for the preceding taxable year reduced by the sum of—

(i) the portion of the amount so determined returned to the employer during the taxable year, and

(ii) the portion of the amount so determined deductible under section 404 for the taxable year (determined without regard to subsection (e) thereof).

(2) ORDERING RULE FOR SECTION 404.—For purposes of paragraph (1), the amount allowable as a deduction under section 404 for any taxable year shall be treated as—

(A) first from carryforwards to such taxable year from preceding taxable years (in order of time), and

(B) then from contributions made during such taxable year.

(3) CONTRIBUTIONS WHICH MAY BE RETURNED TO EMPLOYER.—In determining the amount of nondeductible contributions for any taxable year, there shall not be taken into account any contribution for such taxable year which is distributed to the employer in a distribution described in section 4980(c)(2)(B)(ii) if such distribution is made on or before the last day on which a contribution may be made for such taxable year under section 404(a)(6).

(4) SPECIAL RULE FOR SELF-EMPLOYED INDIVIDUALS.—For purposes of paragraph (1), if—

(A) the amount which is required to be contributed to a plan under section 412 on behalf of an individual who is an employee (within the meaning of section 401(c)(1)), exceeds

(B) the earned income (within the meaning of section 404(a)(8)) of such individual derived from the trade or business with respect to which such plan is established,

such excess shall be treated as an amount allowable as a deduction under section 404.

(5) PRE-1987 CONTRIBUTIONS.—The term "nondeductible contribution" shall not include any contribution made for a taxable year beginning before January 1, 1987.

(6) EXCEPTIONS.—In determining the amount of nondeductible contributions for any taxable year, there shall not be taken into account—

(A) so much of the contributions to 1 or more defined contribution plans which are not deductible when contributed solely because of section 404(a)(7) as does not exceed the amount of contributions described in section 401(m)(4)(A), or

(B) so much of the contributions to a simple retirement account (within the meaning of 408(p)), a simple plan (within the meaning of section 401(k)(11)), or a simplified employee pension (within the meaning of section 408(k)) which are not deductible when contributed solely because such contributions are not made in connection with a trade or business of the employer.

For purposes of subparagraph (A), the deductible limits under section 404(a)(7) shall first be applied to amounts contributed to a defined benefit plan and then to amounts described in subparagraph (A). Subparagraph (B) shall not apply to contributions made on behalf of the employer or a member of the employer's family (as defined in section 447(e)(1)).

(7) DEFINED BENEFIT PLAN EXCEPTION.—In determining the amount of nondeductible contributions for any taxable year, an employer may elect for such year not to take into account any contributions to a defined benefit plan except, in the case of a multiemployer plan, to the extent that such contributions exceed the full-funding limitation (as defined in section 431(c)(6)). For purposes of this paragraph, the deductible limits under section 404(a)(7) shall first be applied to amounts contributed to defined contribution plans and then to amounts described in this

EXCISE TAXES—QUALIFIED PENSION, ETC., PLANS

paragraph. If an employer makes an election under this paragraph for a taxable year, paragraph (6) shall not apply to such employer for such taxable year.

Amendments

• **2022, SECURE 2.0 Act of 2022 (P.L. 117-328)**

P.L. 117-328, §118(a)(1)-(2):

Amended Code Sec. 4972(c)(6)(B) by striking "408(p)) or" and inserting "408(p)),"; and by inserting ", or a simplified employee pension (within the meaning of section 408(k))" after "401(k)(11))". **Effective** for years beginning after 12-29-2022. For a special rule, see Act Sec. 118(b)(2), below.

P.L. 117-328, §118(b)(2), provides:

(2) NO INFERENCE.—Nothing in the amendments made by this section shall be construed to infer the proper treatment under section 4972(c)(6) of the Internal Revenue Code of 1986 of nondeductible contributions to which the amendments made by this section do not apply.

• **2006, Pension Protection Act of 2006 (P.L. 109-280)**

P.L. 109-280, §114(e)(5):

Amended Code Sec. 4972(c)(7) by striking "except to the extent that such contributions exceed the full-funding limitation (as defined in section 412(c)(7), determined without regard to subparagraph (A)(i)(I) thereof)" and inserting "except, in the case of a multiemployer plan, to the extent that such contributions exceed the full-funding limitation (as defined in section 431(c)(6))". **Effective** for tax years beginning after 2007, but only with respect to plan years described in paragraph (1) which end with or within any such tax year [effective date amended by H.R. 7327, §101(d)(3).—CCH].

P.L. 109-280, §803(c):

Amended Code Sec. 4972(c)(6)(A). **Effective** for contributions for tax years beginning after 12-31-2005. Prior to amendment, Code Sec. 4972(c)(6)(A) read as follows:

(A) so much of the contributions to 1 or more defined contribution plans which are not deductible when contributed solely because of section 404(a)(7) as does not exceed the greater of—

(i) the amount of contributions not in excess of 6 percent of compensation (within the meaning of section 404(a) and as adjusted under section 404(a)(12)) paid or accrued (during the taxable year for which the contributions were made) to beneficiaries under the plans, or

(ii) the amount of contributions described in section 401(m)(4)(A), plus

P.L. 109-280, §811, provides:

SEC. 811. PENSIONS AND INDIVIDUAL RETIREMENT ARRANGEMENT PROVISIONS OF ECONOMIC GROWTH AND TAX RELIEF RECONCILIATION ACT OF 2001 MADE PERMANENT.

Title IX of the Economic Growth and Tax Relief Reconciliation Act of 2001 [P.L. 107-16] shall not apply to the provisions of, and amendments made by, subtitles A through F of title VI [§§601-666]of such Act (relating to pension and individual retirement arrangement provisions).

• **2004, Working Families Tax Relief Act of 2004 (P.L. 108-311)**

P.L. 108-311, §404(c):

Amended Code Sec. 4972(c)(6)(A)(ii). **Effective** as if included in the provision of the Economic Growth and Tax Relief Reconciliation Act of 2001 (P.L. 107-16) to which it relates [effective for years beginning after 12-31-2001.—CCH]. Prior to amendment, Code Sec. 4972(c)(6)(A)(ii) read as follows:

(ii) the sum of—

(I) the amount of contributions described in section 401(m)(4)(A), plus

(II) the amount of contributions described in section 402(g)(3)(A), or

• **2001, Economic Growth and Tax Relief Reconciliation Act of 2001 (P.L. 107-16)**

P.L. 107-16, §616(b)(2)(B):

Amended Code Sec. 4972(c)(6)(B)(i) by striking "(within the meaning of section 404(a))" and inserting "(within the meaning of section 404(a) and as adjusted under section 404(a)(12))". **Effective** for years beginning after 12-31-2001.

P.L. 107-16, §637(a):

Amended Code Sec. 4972(c)(6), as amended by Act Sec. 616, by striking "and" at the end of subparagraph (A), by striking the period and inserting ", or" at the end of subparagraph (B), and by inserting after subparagraph (B) a new subparagraph (C). **Effective** for tax years beginning after 12-31-2001. For an exception, see Act Sec. 637(c), below.

P.L. 107-16, §637(b):

Amended Code Sec. 4972(c)(6), as amended by Act Sec. 637(a), by adding at the end a new sentence. **Effective** for tax years beginning after 12-31-2001. For an exception, see Act Sec. 637(c), below.

P.L. 107-16, §637(c), provides:

(c) NO INFERENCE.—Nothing in the amendments made by this section shall be construed to infer the proper treatment of nondeductible contributions under the laws in effect before such amendments.

P.L. 107-16, §652(b)(1)-(4), as amended by P.L. 108-311, §408(b)(9):

Amended Code Sec. 4972(c)(6), as amended by Act Secs. 616 and 637, by striking subparagraph (A) and redesignating subparagraphs (B) and (C) as subparagraphs (A) and (B), respectively; by striking the first sentence following subparagraph (B) as so redesignated; by striking "subparagraph (B)" each place it appears in the next to last sentence and inserting "subparagraph (A)"; and by striking "Subparagraph (C)" in the last sentence and inserting "Subparagraph (B)". **Effective** for plan years beginning after 12-31-2001. Prior to amendment, Code Sec. 4972(c)(6), as amended by Act Secs. 616 and 637, read as follows:

(6) EXCEPTIONS.—In determining the amount of nondeductible contributions for any taxable year, there shall not be taken into account—

(A) contributions that would be deductible under section 404(a)(1)(D) if the plan had more than 100 participants if—

(i) the plan is covered under section 4021 of the Employee Retirement Income Security Act of 1974,

(ii) the plan is terminated under section 4041(b) of such Act on or before the last day of the taxable year,

(B) so much of the contributions to 1 or more defined contribution plans which are not deductible when contributed solely because of section 404(a)(7) as does not exceed the greater of—

(i) the amount of contributions not in excess of 6 percent of compensation (within the meaning of section 404(a) and as adjusted under section 404(a)(12)) paid or accrued (during the taxable year for which the contributions were made) to beneficiaries under the plans, or

(ii) the sum of—

(I) the amount of contributions described in section 401(m)(4)(A), plus

(II) the amount of contributions described in section 402(g)(3)(A), or

(C) so much of the contributions to a simple retirement account (within the meaning of section 408(p)) or a simple plan (within the meaning of section 401(k)(11)) which are not deductible when contributed solely because such contributions are not made in connection with a trade or business of the employer.

If 1 or more defined benefit plans were taken into account in determining the amount allowable as a deduction under section 404 for contributions to any defined contribution plan, subparagraph (B) shall apply only if such defined benefit plans are described in section 404(a)(1)(D). For purposes of subparagraph (B), the deductible limits under section 404(a)(7) shall first be applied to amounts contributed to a defined benefit plan and then to amounts described in subparagraph (B). Subparagraph (C) shall not apply to contributions made on behalf of the employer or a member of the employer's family (as defined in section 447(e)(1)).

P.L. 107-16, §653(a):

Amended Code Sec. 4972(c) by adding at the end a new paragraph (7). **Effective** for years beginning after 12-31-2001.

P.L. 107-16, §901(a)-(b), provides [but see P.L. 109-280, §811, above]:

SEC. 901. SUNSET OF PROVISIONS OF ACT.

(a) IN GENERAL.—All provisions of, and amendments made by, this Act shall not apply—

(1) to taxable, plan, or limitation years beginning after December 31, 2010, or

(2) in the case of title V, to estates of decedents dying, gifts made, or generation skipping transfers, after December 31, 2010.

(b) APPLICATION OF CERTAIN LAWS.—The Internal Revenue Code of 1986 and the Employee Retirement Income Security Act of 1974 shall be applied and administered to years, estates, gifts, and transfers described in subsection (a) as if the provisions and amendments described in subsection (a) had never been enacted.

• **1997, Taxpayer Relief Act of 1997 (P.L. 105-34)**

P.L. 105-34, §1507(a):

Amended Code Sec. 4972(c)(6)(B). **Effective** for tax years beginning after 12-31-97. Prior to amendment, Code Sec. 4972(c)(6)(B) read as follows:

(B) contributions to 1 or more defined contribution plans which are not deductible when contributed solely because of section 404(a)(7), but only to the extent such contributions do not exceed 6 percent of compensation (within the meaning of section 404(a)) paid or accrued (during the taxable year for which the contributions were made) to beneficiaries under the plans.

• **1994, Uruguay Round Agreements Act (P.L. 103-465)**

P.L. 103-465, §755(a):

Amended Code Sec. 4972(c) by adding at the end a new paragraph (6). Code Sec. 4972(c)(6)(A) is **effective** for tax years ending on or after 12-8-94 and Code Sec. 4972(c)(6)(B) is **effective** for tax years ending on or after 12-31-92.

• **1988, Technical and Miscellaneous Revenue Act of 1988 (P.L. 100-647)**

P.L. 100-647, §1011A(e)(1):

Amended Code Sec. 4972(c). **Effective** as if included in the provision of P.L. 99-514 to which it relates. For a special rule, see Act Sec. 1011A(e)(5), below. Prior to amendment, Code Sec. 4972(c) read as follows:

(c) NONDEDUCTIBLE CONTRIBUTIONS.—For purposes of this section, the term "nondeductible contributions" means, with respect to any qualified employer plan, the sum of—

(1) the excess (if any) of—

(A) the amount contributed for the taxable year by the employer to or under such plan, over

(B) the amount allowable as a deduction under section 404 for such contributions, and

(2) the amount determined under this subsection for the preceding taxable year reduced by the sum of—

(A) the portion of the amount so determined returned to the employer during the taxable year, and

(B) the portion of the amount so determined deductible under section 404 for the taxable year.

P.L. 100-647, §1011A(e)(5), provides:

(5) In the case of any taxable year beginning in 1987, the amount under section 4972(c)(1)(A)(ii) of the 1986 Code for a plan to which title IV of the Employee Retirement Income Security Act of 1974 applies shall be increased by the amount (if any) by which, as of the close of the plan year with or within which such taxable year begins—

Sec. 4972(c)(7)

EXCISE TAXES—QUALIFIED PENSION, ETC., PLANS

(A) the liabilities of such plan (determined as if the plan had terminated as of such time), exceed

(B) the assets of such plan.

P.L. 100-647, §2005(a)(1):

Amended Code Sec. 4972(c) by redesignating paragraph (4) as paragraph (5) and inserting after paragraph (3) new paragraph (4). **Effective** as if included in the amendments made by section 1131(c) of P.L. 99-514 [**effective** date amended by P.L. 101-239, §7812(d).—CCH].

[Sec. 4972(d)]

(d) DEFINITIONS.—For purposes of this section—

(1) QUALIFIED EMPLOYER PLAN.—

(A) IN GENERAL.—The term "qualified employer plan" means—

(i) any plan meeting the requirements of section 401(a) which includes a trust exempt from tax under section 501(a).

(ii) an annuity plan described in section 403(a),

(iii) any simplified employee pension (within the meaning of section 408(k)), and

(iv) any simple retirement account (within the meaning of section 408(p)).

(B) EXEMPTION FOR GOVERNMENTAL AND TAX EXEMPT PLANS.—The term "qualified employer plan" does not include a plan described in subparagraph (A) or (B) of section 4980(c)(1).

(2) EMPLOYER.—In the case of a plan which provides contributions or benefits for employees some or all of whom are self-employed individuals within the meaning of section 401(c)(1), the term "employer" means the person treated as the employer under section 401(c)(4).

Amendments

- **1996, Small Business Job Protection Act of 1996 (P.L. 104-188)**

P.L. 104-188, §1421(b)(9)(D):

Amended Code Sec. 4972(d)(1)(A) by striking "and" at the end of clause (ii), by striking the period at the end of clause (iii) and inserting ", and", and by adding after clause (iii) a new clause (iv). **Effective** for tax years beginning after 12-31-96.

- **1988, Technical and Miscellaneous Revenue Act of 1988 (P.L. 100-647)**

P.L. 100-647, §1011A(e)(2):

Amended Code Sec. 4972(d)(1). **Effective** as if included in the provision of P.L. 99-514 to which it relates. Prior to amendment, Code Sec. 4972(d)(1) read as follows:

(1) QUALIFIED EMPLOYER PLAN.—The term "qualified employer plan" means—

(A) any plan meeting the requirements of section 401(a) which includes a trust exempt from the tax under section 501(a),

(B) an annuity plan described in section 403(a), and

(C) any simplified employee pension (within the meaning of section 408(k)).

- **1986, Tax Reform Act of 1986 (P.L. 99-514)**

P.L. 99-514, §1131(c)(1):

Amended Chapter 43 by inserting after Code Sec. 4971 new Code Sec. 4972. **Effective** for tax years beginning after 12-31-86. For a special rule, see Act Sec. 1131(d)(2), below. Prior to amendment, Code Sec. 4972 read as follows:

SEC. 4972. TAX ON EXCESS CONTRIBUTIONS FOR SELF-EMPLOYED INDIVIDUALS.

[Sec. 4972(a)]

(a) TAX IMPOSED.—In the case of a plan which provides contributions or benefits for employees some or all of whom are employees within the meaning of section 401(c)(1), there is imposed, for each taxable year of the employer who maintains such plan, a tax in an amount equal to 6 percent of the amount of the excess contributions under the plan (determined as of the close of the taxable year). The tax imposed by this subsection shall be paid by the employer who maintains the plan. This section applies only to plans which include a trust described in section 401(a) or which are described in section 403(a).

Amendments

- **1984, Deficit Reduction Act of 1984 (P.L. 98-369)**

P.L. 98-369, §497(d)(40):

Amended Code Sec. 4972(a) by striking out the last sentence and inserting a new one. **Effective** for obligations issued after 12-31-83. [This change would appear unnecessary since Code Sec. 4972 is repealed for tax years beginning after 1983.] Prior to amendment, the last sentence of Code Sec. 4972(a) read as follows:

This section applies only to plans which include a trust described in section 401(a), which are described in section 403(a), or which are described in section 405(a).

[Sec. 4972(b)]

(b) EXCESS CONTRIBUTIONS.—

(1) IN GENERAL.—For purposes of this section, the term "excess contributions" means the sum of the amounts (if any) determined under paragraphs (2), (3), and (4), reduced by the sum of the correcting distributions (as defined in paragraph (5)) made in all prior taxable years beginning after December 31, 1975. For purposes of this subsection the amount of any contribution which is allocable (determined under regulations prescribed by the Secretary) to the purchase of life, accident, health, or other insurance shall not be taken into account.

(2) CONTRIBUTIONS BY OWNER-EMPLOYEES.—The amount determined under this paragraph, in the case of a plan which provides contributions or benefits for employees some or all of whom are owner-employees (within the meaning of section 401(3)(3)), is the sum of—

(A) the excess (if any) of—

(i) the amount contributed under the plan by each owner-employee (as an employee) for the taxable year, over

(ii) the amount permitted to be contributed by each owner-employee (as an employee) for such year, and

(B) the amount determined under this paragraph for the preceding taxable year of the employer,

reduced by the excess (if any) of the amount described in subparagraph (A)(ii) over the amount described in subparagraph (A)(i). No contribution by an owner-employee which is a deductible employee contribution (as defined in section 72(o)(5)) shall be taken into account under this paragraph.

(3) DEFINED BENEFIT PLANS.—The amount determined under this paragraph, in the case of a defined benefit plan, is the amount contributed under the plan by the employer during the taxable year or any prior taxable year beginning after December 31, 1975, if—

(A) as of the close of the taxable year, the full funding limitation of the plan (determined under section 412(c)(7)) is zero, and

(B) such amount has not been deductible for the taxable year or any prior taxable year.

(4) DEFINED CONTRIBUTION PLANS.—The amount determined under this paragraph, in the case of a plan other than a defined benefit plan, is the portion of the amounts contributed under the plan by the employer during the taxable year and each prior taxable year beginning after December 31, 1975, which has not been deductible for the taxable year or any prior taxable year.

(5) CORRECTING DISTRIBUTION.—For purposes of this subsection the term "correcting distribution" means—

(A) in the case of a contribution made by an owner-employee as an employee, regardless of the type of plan, the amount determined under paragraph (2) distributed to the owner-employee who contributed such amount,

(B) in the case of a defined benefit plan, the amount determined under paragraph (3) which is distributed from the plan to the employer, and

(C) in the case of a defined contribution plan, the amount determined under paragraph (4) which is distributed from the plan to the employer or to the employee to the account of whom the amount described was contributed.

(6) EXCESS CONTRIBUTIONS RETURNED BEFORE DUE DATE.—For purposes of this subsection, any contribution which is distributed in a distribution to which section 72(m)(9) applies shall be treated as an amount not contributed.

Amendments

- **1983, Technical Corrections Act of 1982 (P.L. 97-448)**

P.L. 97-448, §103(c)(10)(B):

Amended Code Sec. 4972(b)(2) by adding the sentence at the end thereof. **Effective** as if included in the provision of P.L. 97-34 to which it relates.

- **1981, Economic Recovery Tax Act of 1981 (P.L. 97-34)**

P.L. 97-34, §312(e)(3):

Added Code Sec. 4972(b)(6). **Effective** for plans that include employees within the meaning of Code Sec. 401(c)(1) with respect to tax years beginning after 12-31-81.

- **1976, Tax Reform Act of 1976 (P.L. 94-455)**

P.L. 94-455, §1906(b)(13)(A):

Amended 1954 Code by substituting "Secretary" for "Secretary or his delegate" each place it appeared. **Effective** 2-1-77.

[Sec. 4972(c)]

(c) AMOUNT PERMITTED TO BE CONTRIBUTED BY OWNER-EMPLOYEE.—For purposes of subsection (b)(2), the amount permitted to be contributed under a plan by an owner-employee (as an employee) for any taxable year is the smallest of the following:

(1) $2,500,

(2) 10 percent of the earned income (as defined in section 401(c)(2)) for such taxable year derived by such owner-employee from the trade or business with respect to which the plan is established, or

(3) the amount of the contribution which would be contributed by the owner-employee (as an employee) if such contribution were made at the rate of contributions permitted to be made by employees other than owner-employees.

In any case in which there are no employees other than owner-employees, the amount determined under the preceding sentence shall be zero.

P.L. 99-514, §1131(d)(2), as added by P.L. 100-647, §1011A(e)(3), provides:

(2) SPECIAL RULES FOR COLLECTIVE BARGAINING AGREEMENTS.—In the case of a plan maintained pursuant to 1 or more collective bargaining agreements between em-

EXCISE TAXES—QUALIFIED PENSION, ETC., PLANS

ployee representatives and 1 or more employers ratified before March 1, 1986, the amendments made by this section shall not apply to contributions pursuant to any such agreement for taxable years beginning before the earlier of—

(A) January 1, 1989, or

(B) the date on which the last of such collective bargaining agreements terminates (determined without regard to any extension thereof after February 28, 1986).

• **1982, Tax Equity and Fiscal Responsibility Act of 1982 (P.L. 97-248)**

P.L. 97-248, § 237(c)(1):

Repealed Code Sec. 4972. **Effective** with respect to tax years beginning after 12-31-83.

[Sec. 4973]

SEC. 4973. TAX ON EXCESS CONTRIBUTIONS TO CERTAIN TAX-FAVORED ACCOUNTS AND ANNUITIES.

[Sec. 4973(a)]

(a) TAX IMPOSED.—In the case of—

(1) an individual retirement account (within the meaning of section 408(a)),

(2) an Archer MSA (within the meaning of section 220(d)),

(3) an individual retirement annuity (within the meaning of section 408(b)), a custodial account treated as an annuity contract under section 403(b)(7)(A) (relating to custodial accounts for regulated investment company stock),

(4) a Coverdell education savings account (as defined in section 530),

(5) a health savings account (within the meaning of section 223(d)), or

(6) an ABLE account (within the meaning of section 529A),

there is imposed for each taxable year a tax in an amount equal to 6 percent of the amount of the excess contributions to such individual's accounts or annuities (determined as of the close of the taxable year). The amount of such tax for any taxable year shall not exceed 6 percent of the value of the account or annuity (determined as of the close of the taxable year). In the case of an endowment contract described in section 408(b), the tax imposed by this section does not apply to any amount allocable to life, health, accident, or other insurance under such contract. The tax imposed by this subsection shall be paid by such individual.

Amendments

• **2014, Stephen Beck, Jr., Achieving a Better Life Experience Act of 2014 (P.L. 113-295)**

P.L. 113-295, § 102(b)(1), Division B:

Amended Code Sec. 4973(a) by striking "or" at the end of paragraph (4), by inserting "or" at the end of paragraph (5), and by inserting after paragraph (5) a new paragraph (6). **Effective** for tax years beginning after 12-31-2014.

• **2003, Medicare Prescription Drug, Improvement, and Modernization Act of 2003 (P.L. 108-173)**

P.L. 108-173, § 1201(e)(1):

Amended Code Sec. 4973 by striking "or" at the end of subsection (a)(3), by inserting "or" at the end of subsection (a)(4), and by inserting after subsection (a)(4) a new paragraph (5). **Effective** for tax years beginning after 12-31-2003.

• **2001 (P.L. 107-22)**

P.L. 107-22, § 1(b)(1)(C):

Amended Code Sec. 4973(a) by striking "an education individual retirement" and inserting "a Coverdell education savings". **Effective** 7-26-2001.

• **2000, Community Renewal Tax Relief Act of 2000 (P.L. 106-554)**

P.L. 106-554, § 202(a)(6):

Amended Code Sec. 4973(a)(2) by striking "medical savings account" and inserting "Archer MSA". **Effective** 12-21-2000.

P.L. 106-554, § 202(b)(10):

Amended Code Sec. 4973(a)(2) by striking "a Archer" and inserting "an Archer". **Effective** 12-21-2000.

• **1998, IRS Restructuring and Reform Act of 1998 (P.L. 105-206)**

P.L. 105-206, § 6023(18)(A):

Amended the heading of Code Sec. 4973. **Effective** 7-22-98. Prior to amendment, the heading of Code Sec. 4973 read as follows:

SEC. 4973. TAX ON EXCESS CONTRIBUTIONS TO INDIVIDUAL RETIREMENT ACCOUNTS, MEDICAL SAVINGS ACCOUNTS, CERTAIN SECTION 403(b) CONTRACTS, AND CERTAIN INDIVIDUAL RETIREMENT ANNUITIES.

• **1997, Taxpayer Relief Act of 1997 (P.L. 105-34)**

P.L. 105-34, § 213(d)(1):

Amended Code Sec. 4973(a) by striking "or" at the end of paragraph (2), by adding "or" at the end of paragraph (3), and by inserting a new paragraph (4). **Effective** for tax years beginning after 12-31-97.

• **1996, Health Insurance Portability and Accountability Act of 1996 (P.L. 104-191)**

P.L. 104-191, § 301(e)(1):

Amended Code Sec. 4973 by inserting "**MEDICAL SAVINGS ACCOUNTS,**" after "**ACCOUNTS,**" in the heading. **Effective** for tax years beginning after 12-31-96.

P.L. 104-191, § 301(e)(2)-(3):

Amended Code Sec. 4973(a) by striking "or" at the end of paragraph (1), and by redesignating paragraph (2) as paragraph (3) and inserting after paragraph (1) a new paragraph (2). **Effective** for tax years beginning after 12-31-96.

• **1974, Employee Retirement Income Security Act of 1974 (P.L. 93-406)**

P.L. 93-406, § 2001(f):

Added Code Sec. 4972. **Effective** for tax years beginning after 12-31-75.

• **1984, Deficit Reduction Act of 1984 (P.L. 98-369)**

P.L. 98-369, § 491(d)(41):

Amended Code Sec. 4973(a) by striking out paragraph (3), by striking out "or" at the end of paragraph (2), by adding "or" at the end of paragraph (1), by striking out ", annuities, or bonds" and inserting in lieu thereof "or annuities", and by striking out ", annuity, or bond" and inserting in lieu thereof "or annuity". **Effective** for obligations issued after 12-31-83. Prior to amendment, paragraph (3) read as follows:

(3) a retirement bond (within the meaning of section 409), established for the benefit of any individual,

P.L. 98-369, § 491(d)(55):

Amended the title of Code Sec. 4973 by striking out "CERTAIN INDIVIDUAL RETIREMENT ANNUITIES, AND CERTAIN RETIREMENT BONDS" and inserting in lieu thereof "AND CERTAIN INDIVIDUAL RETIREMENT ANNUITIES". **Effective** for obligations issued after 12-31-83.

• **1981, Economic Recovery Tax Act of 1981 (P.L. 97-34)**

P.L. 97-34, § 311(h)(9):

Amended Code Sec. 4973(a)(3) by striking out the last sentence and inserting a new sentence. **Effective** for tax years beginning after 12-31-81. The transitional rule provides, that, for purposes of the 1954 Code, any amount allowed as a deduction under section 220 of such Code (as in effect before its repeal by P.L. 97-34), shall be treated as if it were allowed by section 219 of the Code. Prior to amendment, the last sentence of paragraph (a)(3) read as follows:

"The tax imposed by this subsection shall be paid by the individual to whom a deduction is allowed for the taxable year under section 219 (determined without regard to subsection (b)(1) thereof) or section 220 (determined without regard to subsection (b)(1) thereof), whichever is appropriate."

• **1976, Tax Reform Act of 1976 (P.L. 94-455)**

P.L. 94-455, § 1501(b)(8)(A):

Substituted "the individual to whom a deduction is allowed for the taxable year under section 219 (determined without regard to subsection (b)(1) thereof) or section 220 (determined without regard to subsection (b)(1) thereof), whichever is appropriate" for "such individual" at the end of Code Sec. 4973(a)(3). **Effective** for tax years beginning after 12-31-76.

P.L. 94-455, § 1904(a)(22)(A):

Amended as much of Code Sec. 4973(a)(3) as followed "of any individual," to read as prior to amendment by P.L. 94-455, § 1501(b)(8)(A). **Effective** 2-1-77. Prior to amendment by § 1904(a)(22)(A), Code Sec. 4973(a)(3) read as follows:

(3) a retirement bond (within the meaning of section 409), established for the benefit of any individual, there is imposed for each taxable year a tax in an amount equal to 6 percent of the amount of the excess contributions to such individual's accounts, annuities, or bonds (determined as of the close of the taxable year). The amount of such tax for any taxable year shall not exceed 6 percent of the value of the account, annuity, or bond (determined as of the close of the taxable year). In the case of an endowment contract described in section 408(b), the tax imposed by this section does not apply to any amount allocable to life, health, accident, or other insurance under such contract. The tax imposed by this subsection shall be paid by such individual.

EXCISE TAXES—QUALIFIED PENSION, ETC., PLANS

[Sec. 4973(b)]

(b) EXCESS CONTRIBUTIONS.—For purposes of this section, in the case of individual retirement accounts, or individual retirement annuities the term "excess contributions" means the sum of—

(1) the excess (if any) of—

(A) the amount contributed for the taxable year to the accounts or for the annuities or bonds (other than a contribution to a Roth IRA or a rollover contribution described in section 402(c), 403(a)(4), 403(b)(8), 408(d)(3), or 457(e)(16)), over

(B) the amount allowable as a deduction under section 219 for such contributions, and

(2) the amount determined under this subsection for the preceding taxable year, reduced by the sum of—

(A) the distributions out of the account for the taxable year which were included in the gross income of the payee under section 408(d)(1),

(B) the distributions out of the account for the taxable year to which section 408(d)(5) applies, and

(C) the excess (if any) of the maximum amount allowable as a deduction under section 219 for the taxable year over the amount contributed (determined without regard to section 219(f)(6)) to the accounts or for the annuities (including the amount contributed to a Roth IRA) or bonds for the taxable year.

For purposes of this subsection, any contribution which is distributed from the individual retirement account or the individual retirement annuity in a distribution to which section 408(d)(4) applies shall be treated as an amount not contributed. For purposes of paragraphs (1)(B) and (2)(C), the amount allowable as a deduction under section 219 shall be computed without regard to section 219(g). Such term shall not include any designated nondeductible contribution (as defined in subparagraph (C) of section 408(o)(2)) which does not exceed the nondeductible limit under subparagraph (B) thereof by reason of an election under section 408(o)(5).

Amendments

• **2022, SECURE 2.0 Act of 2022 (P.L. 117-328)**

P.L. 117-328, §401(a)(3):

Amended Code Sec. 4973(b) by adding at the end of the flush matter the following "Such term shall not include any designated nondeductible contribution (as defined in subparagraph (C) of section 408(o)(2)) which does not exceed the nondeductible limit under subparagraph (B) thereof by reason of an election under section 408(o)(5).". **Effective** as if included in the section of the Setting Every Community Up for Retirement Enhancement Act of 2019 to which the amendment relates [**effective** for contributions after 12-20-2019.—CCH].

• **2006, Pension Protection Act of 2006 (P.L. 109-280)**

P.L. 109-280, §811, provides:

SEC. 811. PENSIONS AND INDIVIDUAL RETIREMENT ARRANGEMENT PROVISIONS OF ECONOMIC GROWTH AND TAX RELIEF RECONCILIATION ACT OF 2001 MADE PERMANENT.

Title IX of the Economic Growth and Tax Relief Reconciliation Act of 2001 [P.L. 107-16] shall not apply to the provisions of, and amendments made by, subtitles A through F of title VI [§§601-666]of such Act (relating to pension and individual retirement arrangement provisions).

• **2001, Economic Growth and Tax Relief Reconciliation Act of 2001 (P.L. 107-16)**

P.L. 107-16, §641(e)(11):

Amended Code Sec. 4973(b)(1)(A) by striking "or 408(d)(3)" and inserting "408(d)(3), or 457(e)(16)". **Effective** for distributions after 12-31-2001. For a special rule, see Act Sec. 641(f)(3), below.

P.L. 107-16, §641(f)(3), provides:

(3) SPECIAL RULE.—Notwithstanding any other provision of law, subsections (h)(3) and (h)(5) of section 1122 of the Tax Reform Act of 1986 shall not apply to any distribution from an eligible retirement plan (as defined in clause (iii) or (iv) of section 402(c)(8)(B) of the Internal Revenue Code of 1986) on behalf of an individual if there was a rollover to such plan on behalf of such individual which is permitted solely by reason of any amendment made by this section.

P.L. 107-16, §901(a)-(b), as amended by P.L. 111-312, §101(a)(1), provides [but see P.L. 109-280, §811, above]:

SEC. 901. SUNSET OF PROVISIONS OF ACT.

(a) IN GENERAL.—All provisions of, and amendments made by, this Act shall not apply—

(1) to taxable, plan, or limitation years beginning after December 31, 2012, or

(2) in the case of title V, to estates of decedents dying, gifts made, or generation skipping transfers, after December 31, 2012.

(b) APPLICATION OF CERTAIN LAWS.—The Internal Revenue Code of 1986 and the Employee Retirement Income Security Act of 1974 shall be applied and administered to years, estates, gifts, and transfers described in subsection (a) as if the provisions and amendments described in subsection (a) had never been enacted.

• **1998, IRS Restructuring and Reform Act of 1998 (P.L. 105-206)**

P.L. 105-206, §6005(b)(8)(B)(i)-(ii):

Amended Code Sec. 4973(b) by inserting "a contribution to a Roth IRA or" after "other than" in paragraph (1)(A), and by inserting "(including the amount contributed to a Roth IRA)" after "annuities" in paragraph (2)(C). **Effective** as if included in the provision of P.L. 105-34 to which it relates [**effective** for tax years beginning after 12-31-97.—CCH].

• **1996, Small Business Job Protection Act of 1996 (P.L. 104-188)**

P.L. 104-188, §1704(t)(70):

Amended Code Sec. 4973(b)(1)(A) by striking "sections 402(c)" and inserting "section 402(c)". **Effective** 8-20-96.

• **1992, Unemployment Compensation Amendments of 1992 (P.L. 102-318)**

P.L. 102-318, §521(b)(41) (as amended by P.L. 104-188, §1704(t)(72)):

Amended Code Sec. 4973(b)(1)(A) by striking "section 402(a)(5), 402(a)(7)" and inserting "sections 402(c)". **Effective** for distributions after 12-31-92.

• **1988, Technical and Miscellaneous Revenue Act of 1988 (P.L. 100-647)**

P.L. 100-647, §1011(b)(3):

Amended Code Sec. 4973(b) by striking out all that follows "section 219" in the last sentence therof and inserting in lieu thereof "shall be computed without regard to section 219(g).". **Effective** as if included in the provision of P.L. 99-514 to which it relates. Prior to amendment, the last sentence of Code Sec. 4973(b) read as follows:

For purposes of paragraphs (1)(B) and (2)(C), the amount allowable as a deduction under section 219 (after application of section 408(o)(2)(B)(ii)) shall be increased by the nondeductible limit under section 408(o)(2)(B).

• **1986, Tax Reform Act of 1986 (P.L. 99-514)**

P.L. 99-514, §1102(b)(1):

Amended Code Sec. 4973(b) by adding at the end thereof a new sentence. **Effective** for contributions and distributions for tax years beginning after 12-31-86.

P.L. 99-514, §1848(f)(1)-(3):

Amended Code Sec. 4973(b) by striking out ", individual retirement annuities, or bonds" in the material preceding paragraph (1) and inserting in lieu thereof "or individual retirement annuities", by striking out subparagraph (A) of paragraph (1) and inserting in lieu thereof new subparagraph (A), and by striking out "or bonds" in paragraph (2)(C) thereof. **Effective** as if included in the provision of P.L. 98-369 to which it relates. Prior to amendment, Code Sec. 4973(b) read as follows:

(b) EXCESS CONTRIBUTIONS.—For purposes of this section, in the case of individual retirement accounts, individual retirement annuities, or bonds, the term "excess contributions" means the sum of—

(1) the excess (if any) of—

(A) the amount contributed for the taxable year to the accounts or for the annuities or bonds (other than a rollover contribution described in sections 402(a)(5), 402(a)(7), 403(a)(4), 403(b)(8), and 408(b)(3)), over

(B) the amount allowable as a deduction under section 219 for such contributions, and

(2) the amount determined under this subsection for the preceding taxable year, reduced by the sum of—

(A) the distributions out of the account for the taxable year which were included in the gross income of the payee under section 408(d)(1),

(B) the distributions out of the account for the taxable year to which section 408(d)(5) applies, and

(C) the excess (if any) of the maximum amount allowable as a deduction under section 219 for the taxable year over the amount contributed (determined without regard to section 219(f)(6)) to the accounts or for the annuities or bonds for the taxable year.

For purposes of this subsection, any contribution which is distributed from the individual retirement account or the individual retirement annuity in a distribution to which section 408(d)(4) applies shall be treated as an amount not contributed.

• **1984, Deficit Reduction Act of 1984 (P.L. 98-369)**

P.L. 98-369, §491(d)(42):

Amended Code Sec. 4973(b)(1)(A) by striking out "408(d)(3), and 409(b)(3)(C)" and inserting in lieu thereof "and 408(d)(3)". **Effective** for obligations issued after 12-31-83.

EXCISE TAXES—QUALIFIED PENSION, ETC., PLANS

P.L. 98-369, §491(d)(43):

Amended the last sentence of Code Sec. 4973(b) by striking out ", individual retirement annuity, or bond" and inserting in lieu thereof "or the individual retirement annuity". **Effective** for obligations issued after 12-31-83.

• **1981, Economic Recovery Tax Act of 1981 (P.L. 97-34)**

P.L. 97-34, §311(h)(7):

Amended Code Sec. 4973(b) by striking out "section 219 or 220" each place it appeared and inserting "section 219". **Effective** for tax years beginning after 12-31-81. The transitional rule provides, that, for purposes of the 1954 Code, any amount allowed as a deduction under section 220 of the Code, (as in effect before its repeal by P.L. 97-34) shall be treated as if it were allowed by section 219 of the Code.

P.L. 97-34, §311(h)(10):

Amended Code Sec. 4973(b)(2) by striking out "sections 219(c)(5) and 220(c)(6)" and inserting "section 219(f)(6)". **Effective** for tax years beginning after 12-31-81. For the transitional rule, see amendment note at P.L. 97-34, §311(h)(7).

P.L. 97-34, §313(b)(2):

Amended Code Sec. 4973(b)(1)(A) by inserting "405(d)(3)" after "403(b)(8)". **Effective** for redemptions after 8-13-81, in tax years ending after such date.

• **1980, Technical Corrections Act of 1979 (P.L. 96-222)**

P.L. 96-222, §101(a)(13)(A):

Amended Act Sec. 156(d) of P.L. 95-600 to change the **effective** date of the amendment of Code Sec. 4973(b)(1)(A) made by Act Sec. 156(c)(3) of P.L. 95-600 from "distributions or transfers made after December 31, 1978, in taxable years beginning after that date" to "distributions or transfers made after December 31, 1977, in taxable years beginning after that date."

P.L. 96-222, §101(a)(14)(B):

Amended Code Sec. 4973(b)(1)(A) by adding "402(a)(7)" after "section 402(a)(5),". **Effective** for distributions or transfers made after 12-31-77, in tax years beginning after such date.

• **1978, Revenue Act of 1978 (P.L. 95-600)**

P.L. 95-600, §§156(c)(3), 157(b)(3), 157(j)(1):

Amended Code Sec. 4973(b). **Effective** for the determination of deductions for tax years beginning after 12-31-75. Prior to amendment, Code Sec. 4973(b) read as follows:

"(b) EXCESS CONTRIBUTIONS.—For purposes of this section, in the case of individual retirement accounts, individual retirement annuities, or bonds, the term "excess contributions" means the sum of—

"(1) the excess (if any) of—

"(A) the amount contributed for the taxable year to the accounts or for the annuities or bonds (other than a rollover contribution described in section 402(a)(5), 403(a)(4), 408(d)(3), or 409(b)(3)(C)), over

"(B) the amount allowable as a deduction under section 219 or 220 for such contributions, and

"(2) the amount determined under this subsection for the preceding taxable year, reduced by the excess (if any) of the maximum amount allowable as a deduction under section 219 or 220 for the taxable year over the amount contributed to the accounts or for the annuities or bonds for the taxable year and reduced by the sum of the distributions out of the account (for the taxable year and all prior taxable years) which were included in the gross income of the payee under section 408(d)(1).

For purposes of this subsection, any contribution which is distributed from the individual retirement account, individual retirement annuity, or bond in a distribution to which section 408(d)(4) applies shall be treated as an amount not contributed if such distribution consists of an excess contribution solely because of ineligibility under section 219(b)(2) or section 220(b)(3) or by reason of the application of section 219(b)(1) (without regard to the $1,500 limitation) or section 220(b)(1) (without regard to the $1,750 limitation) and only if such distribution does not exceed the excess of $1,500, or $1,750, if applicable over the amount described in paragraph (1)(B)."

P.L. 95-600, §701(aa)(1):

Amended Code Sec. 4973(b) by striking out "solely because of employer contributions to a plan or contract described in section 219(b)(2)" and inserting in place thereof "solely because of ineligibility under section 219(b)(2) or section 220(b)(3)". **Effective** as if included in section 1501 of P.L. 94-455 at the time of the enactment of such Act.

• **1976, Tax Reform Act of 1976 (P.L. 94-455)**

P.L. 94-455, §1501(b)(8)(B):

Inserted "or 220" after "219" in Code Sec. 4973(b)(1)(B). **Effective** for tax years beginning after 12-31-76.

P.L. 94-455, §1501(b)(8)(C):

Amended Code Sec. 4973(b)(2). **Effective** for tax years beginning after 12-31-76. Prior to amendment, Code Sec. 4973(b)(2) read as follows:

(2) the amount determined under this subsection for the preceding taxable year, reduced by the excess (if any) of the maximum amount allowable as a deduction under section 219 for the taxable year over the amount contributed to the accounts or for the annuities or bonds for the taxable year and reduced by the sum of the distributions out of the account (for all prior taxable years) which were included in the gross income of the payee under section 408(d)(1). For purposes of this paragraph, any contribution which is distributed out of the individual retirement account, individual retirement annuity, or bond in a distribution to which section 408(d)(4) applies shall be treated as an amount not contributed.

[Sec. 4973(c)]

(c) SECTION 403(b) CONTRACTS.—For purposes of this section, in the case of a custodial account referred to in subsection (a)(3), the term "excess contributions" means the sum of—

(1) the excess (if any) of the amount contributed for the taxable year to such account (other than a rollover contribution described in section 403(b)(8), or 408(d)(3)(A)(iii)), over the lesser of the amount excludable from gross income under section 403(b) or the amount permitted to be contributed under the limitations contained in section 415 (or under whichever such section is applicable, if only one is applicable), and

(2) the amount determined under this subsection for the preceding taxable year, reduced by—

(A) the excess (if any) of the lesser of (i) the amount excludable from gross income under section 403(b) or (ii) the amount permitted to be contributed under the limitations contained in section 415 over the amount contributed to the account for the taxable year (or under whichever such section is applicable, if only one is applicable), and

(B) the sum of the distributions out of the account (for all prior taxable years) which are included in gross income under section 72(e).

Amendments

• **2004, Working Families Tax Relief Act of 2004 (P.L. 108-311)**

P.L. 108-311, §408(a)(22):

Amended Code Sec. 4973(c) by striking "subsection (a)(2)" and inserting "subsection (a)(3)". **Effective** 10-4-2004.

• **1984, Deficit Reduction Act of 1984 (P.L. 98-369)**

P.L. 98-369, §491(d)(44):

Amended Code Sec. 4973(c)(1) by striking out ", 408(d)(3)(A)(iii), or 409(b)(3)(C)" and inserting in lieu thereof "or 408(d)(3)(A)(iii)". **Effective** for obligations issued after 12-31-83.

• **1980, Technical Corrections Act of 1979 (P.L. 96-222)**

P.L. 96-222, §101(a)(13)(A):

Amended Act Sec. 156(d) of P.L. 95-600 to change the **effective** date of the amendment of Code Sec. 4973(c)(1) made by Act Sec. 156(c)(5) of P.L. 95-600 from "distributions or transfers made after December 31, 1978, in taxable years beginning after that date" to "distributions or transfers made after December 31, 1977, in taxable years beginning after that date."

P.L. 96-222, §101(a)(13)(C):

Amended Code Sec. 4973(c)(1) by changing "409(d)(3)(C)" to "409(b)(3)(C)". **Effective** for distributions or transfers made after 12-31-78, in tax years beginning after such date.

• **1978, Revenue Act of 1978 (P.L. 95-600)**

P.L. 95-600, §156(c)(5):

Amended Code Sec. 4973(c)(1) by adding after "account" "(other than a rollover contribution described in section 403(b)(8), 408(d)(3)(A)(iii), or 409(b)(3)(C))". **Effective** for distributions or transfers made after 12-31-78, in tax years beginning after such date.

• **1976, Tax Reform Act of 1976 (P.L. 94-455)**

P.L. 94-455, §1904(a)(22)(B):

Substituted "subsection (a)(2)" for "subsection (a)(3)" in Code Sec. 4973(c). **Effective** 2-1-77.

• **1974, Employee Retirement Income Security Act of 1974 (P.L. 93-406)**

P.L. 93-406, §2002(d):

Added Code Sec. 4973. **Effective** 1-1-75.

[Sec. 4973(d)]

(d) EXCESS CONTRIBUTIONS TO ARCHER MSAs.—For purposes of this section, in the case of Archer MSAs (within the meaning of section 220(d)), the term "excess contributions" means the sum of—

(1) the aggregate amount contributed for the taxable year to the accounts (other than rollover contributions described in section 220(f)(5)) which is neither excludable from gross income under section 106(b) nor allowable as a deduction under section 220 for such year, and

(2) the amount determined under this subsection for the preceding taxable year, reduced by the sum of—

(A) the distributions out of the accounts which were included in gross income under section 220(f)(2), and

(B) the excess (if any) of—

EXCISE TAXES—QUALIFIED PENSION, ETC., PLANS

(i) the maximum amount allowable as a deduction under section 220(b)(1) (determined without regard to section 106(b)) for the taxable year, over

(ii) the amount contributed to the accounts for the taxable year.

For purposes of this subsection, any contribution which is distributed out of the Archer MSA in a distribution to which section 220(f)(3) or section 138(c)(3) applies shall be treated as an amount not contributed.

Amendments

• **2000, Community Renewal Tax Relief Act of 2000 (P.L. 106-554)**

P.L. 106-554, §202(a)(6):

Amended Code Sec. 4973(d) by striking "medical savings account" and inserting "Archer MSA". **Effective** 12-21-2000.

P.L. 106-554, §202(b)(2)(C):

Amended Code Sec. 4973(d) by striking "medical savings accounts" and inserting "Archer MSAs". **Effective** 12-21-2000.

P.L. 106-554, §202(b)(6):

Amended the heading for Code Sec. 4973(d) by striking "MEDICAL SAVINGS ACCOUNTS" and inserting "ARCHER MSAS". **Effective** 12-21-2000.

• **1997, Balanced Budget Act of 1997 (P.L. 105-33)**

P.L. 105-33, §4006(b)(1):

Amended the last sentence of Code Sec. 4973(d) by inserting "or section 138(c)(3)" after "section 220(f)(3)". **Effective** for tax years beginning after 12-31-98.

• **1996, Health Insurance Portability and Accountability Act of 1996 (P.L. 104-191)**

P.L. 104-191, §301(e)(4):

Amended Code Sec. 4973 by adding at the end a new subsection (d). **Effective** for tax years beginning after 12-31-96.

[Sec. 4973(e)]

(e) EXCESS CONTRIBUTIONS TO COVERDELL EDUCATION SAVINGS ACCOUNTS.—For purposes of this section—

(1) IN GENERAL.—In the case of Coverdell education savings accounts maintained for the benefit of any one beneficiary, the term "excess contributions" means the sum of—

(A) the amount by which the amount contributed for the taxable year to such accounts exceeds $2,000 (or, if less, the sum of the maximum amounts permitted to be contributed under section 530(c) by the contributors to such accounts for such year); and

(B) the amount determined under this subsection for the preceding taxable year, reduced by the sum of—

(i) the distributions out of the accounts for the taxable year (other than rollover distributions), and

(ii) the excess (if any) of the maximum amount which may be contributed to the accounts for the taxable year over the amount contributed to the accounts for the taxable year.

(2) SPECIAL RULES.—For purposes of paragraph (1), the following contributions shall not be taken into account:

(A) Any contribution which is distributed out of the Coverdell education savings account in a distribution to which section 530(d)(4)(C) applies.

(B) Any rollover contribution.

Amendments

• **2013, American Taxpayer Relief Act of 2012 (P.L. 112-240)**

P.L. 112-240, §101(a)(1) and (3), provides:

SEC. 101. PERMANENT EXTENSION AND MODIFICATION OF 2001 TAX RELIEF.

(a) PERMANENT EXTENSION.—

(1) IN GENERAL.—The Economic Growth and Tax Relief Reconciliation Act of 2001 is amended by striking title IX.

* * *

(3) EFFECTIVE DATE.—The amendments made by this subsection shall apply to taxable, plan, or limitation years beginning after December 31, 2012, and estates of decedents dying, gifts made, or generation skipping transfers after December 31, 2012.

• **2006, Pension Protection Act of 2006 (P.L. 109-280)**

P.L. 109-280, §1304(a), provides:

(a) PERMANENT EXTENSION OF MODIFICATIONS.—Section 901 of the Economic Growth and Tax Relief Reconciliation Act of 2001 [P.L. 107-16] (relating to sunset provisions) shall not apply to section 402 of such Act (relating to modifications to qualified tuition programs).

• **2001 (P.L. 107-22)**

P.L. 107-22, §1(b)(2)(B):

Amended Code Sec. 4973(e) by striking "education individual retirement" each place it appears in the text and inserting "Coverdell education savings". **Effective** 7-26-2001.

P.L. 107-22, §1(b)(4):

Amended the heading for Code Sec. 4973(e) by striking "EDUCATION INDIVIDUAL RETIREMENT" and inserting "COVERDELL EDUCATION SAVINGS". **Effective** 7-26-2001.

• **2001, Economic Growth and Tax Relief Reconciliation Act of 2001 (P.L. 107-16)**

P.L. 107-16, §401(a)(2):

Amended Code Sec. 4973(e)(1)(A) by striking "$500" and inserting "$2,000". **Effective** for tax years beginning after 12-31-2001.

P.L. 107-16, §401(g)(2)(D):

Amended Code Sec. 4973(e)(1) by adding "and" at the end of subparagraph (A), by striking subparagraph (B), and by redesignating subparagraph (C) as subparagraph (B). **Effective** for tax years beginning after 12-31-2001. Prior to being stricken, Code Sec. 4973(e)(1)(B) read as follows:

(B) if any amount is contributed (other than a contribution described in section 530(b)(2)(B)) during such year to a qualified State tuition program for the benefit of such beneficiary, any amount contributed to such accounts for such taxable year; and

P.L. 107-16, §402(a)(4)(A):

Amended Code Sec. 4973(e) by striking "qualified State tuition" each place it appears and inserting "qualified tuition". **Effective** for tax years beginning after 12-31-2001. [Note: The amendment made by Act Sec. 401(g)(2)(D) deleted the text to which this amendment applied. Thus, essentially it never took effect.—CCH.]

P.L. 107-16, §901(a)-(b), as amended by P.L. 111-312, §101(a)(1), provides [but see P.L. 109-280, §1304(a), and P.L. 112-240, §101(a)(1) and (3), above]:

SEC. 901. SUNSET OF PROVISIONS OF ACT.

(a) IN GENERAL.—All provisions of, and amendments made by, this Act shall not apply—

(1) to taxable, plan, or limitation years beginning after December 31, 2012, or

(2) in the case of title V, to estates of decedents dying, gifts made, or generation skipping transfers, after December 31, 2012.

(b) APPLICATION OF CERTAIN LAWS.—The Internal Revenue Code of 1986 and the Employee Retirement Income Security Act of 1974 shall be applied and administered to years, estates, gifts, and transfers described in subsection (a) as if the provisions and amendments described in subsection (a) had never been enacted.

• **1998, IRS Restructuring and Reform Act of 1998 (P.L. 105-206)**

P.L. 105-206, §6004(d)(10)(A):

Amended Code Sec. 4973(e)(1). **Effective** as if included in the provision of P.L. 105-34 to which it relates [effective for tax years beginning after 12-31-97.—CCH]. Prior to amendment, Code Sec. 4973(e)(1) read as follows:

(1) IN GENERAL.—In the case of education individual retirement accounts maintained for the benefit of any 1 beneficiary, the term "excess contributions" means—

(A) the amount by which the amount contributed for the taxable year to such accounts exceeds $500, and

(B) any amount contributed to such accounts for any taxable year if any amount is contributed during such year to a qualified State tuition program for the benefit of such beneficiary.

P.L. 105-206, §6004(d)(10)(B):

Amended Code Sec. 4973(e)(2) by striking subparagraph (B) and by redesignating subparagraph (C) as subparagraph (B). **Effective** as if included in the provision of P.L. 105-34 to which it relates [effective for tax years beginning after 12-31-97.—CCH]. Prior to amendment, Code Sec. 4973(e)(2)(B) read as follows:

(B) Any contribution described in section 530(b)(2)(B) to a qualified State tuition program.

• **1997, Taxpayer Relief Act of 1997 (P.L. 105-34)**

P.L. 105-34, §213(d)(2):

Amended Code Sec. 4973 by adding a new subsection (e). **Effective** for tax years beginning after 12-31-97.

[Sec. 4973(f)]

(f) EXCESS CONTRIBUTIONS TO ROTH IRAS.—For purposes of this section, in the case of contributions to a Roth IRA (within the meaning of section 408A(b)), the term "excess contributions" means the sum of—

(1) the excess (if any) of—

EXCISE TAXES—QUALIFIED PENSION, ETC., PLANS

    (A) the amount contributed for the taxable year to Roth IRAs (other than a qualified rollover contribution described in section 408A(e)), over

    (B) the amount allowable as a contribution under sections 408A (c)(2) and (c)(3), and

  (2) the amount determined under this subsection for the preceding taxable year, reduced by the sum of—

    (A) the distributions out of the accounts for the taxable year, and

    (B) the excess (if any) of the maximum amount allowable as a contribution under sections 408A(c)(2) and (c)(3) for the taxable year over the amount contributed by the individual to all individual retirement plans for the taxable year.

For purposes of this subsection, any contribution which is distributed from a Roth IRA in a distribution described in section 408(d)(4) shall be treated as an amount not contributed.

Amendments

• **1998, IRS Restructuring and Reform Act of 1998 (P.L. 105-206)**

P.L. 105-206, §6005(b)(8)(A)(i)-(ii):

Amended Code Sec. 4973(f) by striking "such accounts" in paragraph (1)(A) and inserting "Roth IRAs", and by striking "to the accounts" in paragraph (2)(B) and inserting "by the individual to all individual retirement plans". **Effective** as if included in the provision of P.L. 105-34 to which it relates [**effective** for tax years beginning after 12-31-97.—CCH].

• **1997, Taxpayer Relief Act of 1997 (P.L. 105-34)**

P.L. 105-34, §302(b) (as amended by P.L. 105-206, §6005(b)(8):

Amended Code Sec. 4973, as amended by Act Sec. 213(d)(2), by adding at the end new subsection (f). **Effective** for tax years beginning after 12-31-97.

[Sec. 4973(g)]

  (g) EXCESS CONTRIBUTIONS TO HEALTH SAVINGS ACCOUNTS.—For purposes of this section, in the case of health savings accounts (within the meaning of section 223(d)), the term "excess contributions" means the sum of—

  (1) the aggregate amount contributed for the taxable year to the accounts (other than a rollover contribution described in section 220(f)(5) or 223(f)(5)) which is neither excludable from gross income under section 106(d) nor allowable as a deduction under section 223 for such year, and

  (2) the amount determined under this subsection for the preceding taxable year, reduced by the sum of—

    (A) the distributions out of the accounts which were included in gross income under section 223(f)(2), and

    (B) the excess (if any) of—

     (i) the maximum amount allowable as a deduction under section 223(b) (determined without regard to section 106(d)) for the taxable year, over

     (ii) the amount contributed to the accounts for the taxable year.

For purposes of this subsection, any contribution which is distributed out of the health savings account in a distribution to which section 223(f)(3) applies shall be treated as an amount not contributed.

Amendments

• **2003, Medicare Prescription Drug, Improvement, and Modernization Act of 2003 (P.L. 108-173)**

P.L. 108-173, §1201(e)(2):

Amended Code Sec. 4973 by adding at the end a new subsection (g). **Effective** for tax years beginning after 12-31-2003.

[Sec. 4973(h)]

  (h) EXCESS CONTRIBUTIONS TO ABLE ACCOUNT.—For purposes of this section—

  (1) IN GENERAL.—In the case of an ABLE account (within the meaning of section 529A), the term "excess contributions" means the amount by which the amount contributed for the taxable year to such account (other than contributions under section 529A(c)(1)(C)) exceeds the contribution limit under section 529A(b)(2)(B).

  (2) SPECIAL RULE.—For purposes of this subsection, any contribution which is distributed out of the ABLE account in a distribution to which the last sentence of section 529A(b)(2) applies shall be treated as an amount not contributed.

Amendments

• **2014, Stephen Beck, Jr., Achieving a Better Life Experience Act of 2014 (P.L. 113-295)**

P.L. 113-295, §102(b)(2), Division B:

Amended Code Sec. 4973 by adding at the end a new subsection (h). **Effective** for tax years beginning after 12-31-2014.

[Sec. 4974]

SEC. 4974. EXCISE TAX ON CERTAIN ACCUMULATIONS IN QUALIFIED RETIREMENT PLANS.

[Sec. 4974(a)]

  (a) GENERAL RULE.—If the amount distributed during the taxable year of the payee under any qualified retirement plan or any eligible deferred compensation plan (as defined in section 457(b)) is less than the minimum required distribution for such taxable year, there is hereby imposed a tax equal to 25 percent of the amount by which such minimum required distribution exceeds the actual amount distributed during the taxable year. The tax imposed by this section shall be paid by the payee.

Amendments

• **2022, SECURE 2.0 Act of 2022 (P.L. 117-328)**

P.L. 117-328, §302(a):

Amended Code Sec. 4974(a) by striking "50 percent" and inserting "25 percent". **Effective** for tax years beginning after 12-29-2022.

• **1986, Tax Reform Act of 1986 (P.L. 99-514)**

P.L. 99-514, §1121(a)(1):

Amended Code Sec. 4974(a). **Effective**, generally, for years beginning after 12-31-88. However, see Act Sec. 1121(d)(3)-(5), below. Prior to amendment, Code Sec. 4974(a) read as follows:

SEC. 4974. EXCISE TAX ON CERTAIN ACCUMULATIONS IN INDIVIDUAL RETIREMENT ACCOUNTS OR ANNUITIES.

  (a) IMPOSITION OF TAX.—If, in the case of an individual retirement account or individual retirement annuity, the amount distributed during the taxable year of the payee is less than the minimum amount required to be distributed under section 408(a)(6) or 408(b)(3) during such year, there is imposed a tax equal to 50 percent of the amount by which the minimum amount required to be distributed during such year exceeds the amount actually distributed during the year. The tax imposed by this section shall be paid by such payee.

P.L. 99-514, §1121(d)(3)-(5), as amended by P.L. 100-647, §1011A(a)(3)-(4), provides:

(3) COLLECTIVE BARGAINING AGREEMENTS.—In the case of a plan maintained pursuant to 1 or more collective bargaining agreements between employee representatives and 1 or more employers ratified before March 1, 1986, the amendments made by this section shall not apply to distributions to individuals covered by such agreements in years beginning before the earlier of—

  (A) the later of—

    (i) the date on which the last of such collective bargaining agreements terminates (determined without regard to any extension thereof after February 28, 1986), or

    (ii) January 1, 1989, or

  (B) January 1, 1991.

(4) TRANSITION RULES.—

EXCISE TAXES—QUALIFIED PENSION, ETC., PLANS

(A) The amendments made by subsections (a) and (b) shall not apply with respect to any benefits with respect to which a designation is in effect under section 242(b)(2) of the Tax Equity and Fiscal Responsibility Act of 1982.

(B)(i) Except as provided in clause (ii), the amendment made by subsection (b) shall not apply in the case of any individual who has attained age 70½ before January 1, 1988.

(ii) Clause (i) shall not apply to any individual who is a 5-percent owner (as defined in section 416(i) of the Internal Revenue Code of 1986), at any time during—

(I) the plan year ending with or within the calendar year in which such owner attains age 66½, and

(II) any subsequent plan year.

(5) PLANS MAY INCORPORATE SECTION (401(a)(9) REQUIREMENTS BY REFERENCE.—Notwithstanding any other provisions of law, except as provided in regulations prescribed by the Secretary of the Treasury or his delegate, a plan may incorporate by reference the requirements of section 401(a)(9) of the Internal Revenue Code of 1986.

P.L. 99-514, § 1852(a)(7)(B):

Amended Code Sec. 4974(a) by striking out "section 408(a)(6) or (7), or 408(b)(3) or (4)" and inserting in lieu thereof "section 408(a)(6) or 408(b)(3)". **Effective** as if included in the provision of P.L. 98-369 to which it relates.

[Sec. 4974(b)]

(b) MINIMUM REQUIRED DISTRIBUTION.—For purposes of this section, the term "minimum required distribution" means the minimum amount required to be distributed during a taxable year under section 401(a)(9), 403(b)(10), 408(a)(6), 408(b)(3), or 457(d)(2), as the case may be, as determined under regulations prescribed by the Secretary.

Amendments

• **1986, Tax Reform Act of 1986 (P.L. 99-514)**

P.L. 99-514, § 1121(a)(1):

Amended Code Sec. 4974(b). **Effective**, generally, for years beginning after 12-31-88. However, for a special rule, see Act Sec. 1121(d)(3)-(5) in the amendments for Code Sec. 4974(a). Prior to amendment, Code Sec. 4974(b) read as follows:

(b) REGULATIONS.—For purposes of this section, the minimum amount required to be distributed during a taxable year under section 408(a)(6) or 408(b)(3) shall be determined under regulations prescribed by the Secretary.

P.L. 99-514, § 1852(a)(7)(C):

Amended Code Sec. 4974(b) by striking out "section 408(a)(6) or (7) or 408(b)(3) or (4)" and inserting in lieu thereof "section 408(a)(6) or 408(b)(3)". **Effective** as if included in the provision of P.L. 98-369 to which it relates.

• **1976, Tax Reform Act of 1976 (P.L. 94-455)**

P.L. 94-455, § 1906(b)(13)(A):

Amended 1954 Code by substituting "Secretary" for "Secretary or his delegate" each place it appeared. **Effective** 2-1-77.

• **1974, Employee Retirement Income Security Act of 1974 (P.L. 93-406)**

P.L. 93-406, § 2002(e):

Added Code Sec. 4974. **Effective** 1-1-75.

[Sec. 4974(c)]

(c) QUALIFIED RETIREMENT PLAN.—For purposes of this section, the term "qualified retirement plan" means—

(1) a plan described in section 401(a) which includes a trust exempt from tax under section 501(a),

(2) an annuity plan described in section 403(a),

(3) an annuity contract described in section 403(b),

(4) an individual retirement account described in section 408(a), or

(5) an individual retirement annuity described in section 408(b).

Such term includes any plan, contract, account, or annuity which, at any time, has been determined by the Secretary to be such a plan, contract, account, or annuity.

Amendments

• **1986, Tax Reform Act of 1986 (P.L. 99-514)**

P.L. 99-514, § 1121(a)(1):

Amended Code Sec. 4974(c). **Effective**, generally, for years beginning after 12-31-88. However, for a special rule, see Act Sec. 1121(d)(3)-(5) under Code Sec. 4974(a). Prior to amendment, Code Sec. 4974(c) read as follows:

(c) WAIVER OF TAX IN CERTAIN CASES.—If the taxpayer establishes to the satisfaction of the Secretary that—

(1) the shortfall described in subsection (a) in the amount distributed during any taxable year was due to reasonable error, and

(2) reasonable steps are being taken to remedy the shortfall,

the Secretary may waive the tax imposed by subsection (a) for the taxable year.

• **1978, Revenue Act of 1978 (P.L. 95-600)**

P.L. 95-600, § 157(i)(1):

Added subsection (c). **Effective** for tax years beginning after 12-31-75.

[Sec. 4974(d)]

(d) WAIVER OF TAX IN CERTAIN CASES.—If the taxpayer establishes to the satisfaction of the Secretary that—

(1) the shortfall described in subsection (a) in the amount distributed during any taxable year was due to reasonable error, and

(2) reasonable steps are being taken to remedy the shortfall, the Secretary may waive the tax imposed by subsection (a) for the taxable year.

Amendments

• **1986, Tax Reform Act of 1986 (P.L. 99-514)**

P.L. 99-514, § 1121(a)(1):

Added Code Sec. 4974(d). **Effective**, generally, for years beginning after 12-31-88. However, for a special rule, see Act Sec. 1121(d)(3)-(5) in the amendments for Code Sec. 4974(a).

[Sec. 4974(e)]

(e) REDUCTION OF TAX IN CERTAIN CASES.—

(1) REDUCTION.—In the case of a taxpayer who—

(A) receives a distribution, during the correction window, of the amount which resulted in imposition of a tax under subsection (a) from the same plan to which such tax relates, and

(B) submits a return, during the correction window, reflecting such tax (as modified by this subsection), the first sentence of subsection (a) shall be applied by substituting "10 percent" for "25 percent".

(2) CORRECTION WINDOW.—For purposes of this subsection, the term "correction window" means the period of time beginning on the date on which the tax under subsection (a) is imposed with respect to a shortfall of distributions from a plan described in subsection (a), and ending on the earliest of—

(A) the date of mailing a notice of deficiency with respect to the tax imposed by subsection (a) under section 6212,

(B) the date on which the tax imposed by subsection (a) is assessed, or

(C) the last day of the second taxable year that begins after the end of the taxable year in which the tax under subsection (a) is imposed.

Amendments

• **2022, SECURE 2.0 Act of 2022 (P.L. 117-328)**

P.L. 117-328, § 302(b):

Amended Code Sec. 4974 by adding at the end a new subsection (e). **Effective** for tax years beginning after 12-29-2022.

EXCISE TAXES—QUALIFIED PENSION, ETC., PLANS

[Sec. 4975]

SEC. 4975. TAX ON PROHIBITED TRANSACTIONS.

[Sec. 4975(a)]

(a) INITIAL TAXES ON DISQUALIFIED PERSON.—There is hereby imposed a tax on each prohibited transaction. The rate of tax shall be equal to 15 percent of the amount involved with respect to the prohibited transaction for each year (or part thereof) in the taxable period. The tax imposed by this subsection shall be paid by any disqualified person who participates in the prohibited transaction (other than a fiduciary acting only as such).

Amendments

• **1997, Taxpayer Relief Act of 1997 (P.L. 105-34)**

P.L. 105-34, § 1074(a):

Amended Code Sec. 4975(a) by striking "10 percent" and inserting "15 percent". **Effective** for prohibited transactions occurring after 8-5-97.

• **1996, Small Business Job Protection Act of 1996 (P.L. 104-188)**

P.L. 104-188, § 1453(a):

Amended Code Sec. 4975(a) by striking "5 percent" and inserting "10 percent". **Effective** for prohibited transactions occurring after 8-20-96.

[Sec. 4975(b)]

(b) ADDITIONAL TAXES ON DISQUALIFIED PERSON.—In any case in which an initial tax is imposed by subsection (a) on a prohibited transaction and the transaction is not corrected within the taxable period, there is hereby imposed a tax equal to 100 percent of the amount involved. The tax imposed by this subsection shall be paid by any disqualified person who participated in the prohibited transaction (other than a fiduciary acting only as such).

Amendments

• **1980 (P.L. 96-596)**

P.L. 96-596, § 2(a)(1):

Amended Code Sec. 4975(b) by striking out "correction period" and inserting in lieu thereof "taxable period". **Effective** with respect to second-tier taxes assessed after 12-24-80 (except in cases where there is a court decision with regard to which res judicata applies on that date).

[Sec. 4975(c)]

(c) PROHIBITED TRANSACTION.—

(1) GENERAL RULE.—For purposes of this section, the term "prohibited transaction" means any direct or indirect—

(A) sale or exchange, or leasing, of any property between a plan and a disqualified person;

(B) lending of money or other extension of credit between a plan and a disqualified person;

(C) furnishing of goods, services, or facilities between a plan and a disqualified person;

(D) transfer to, or use by or for the benefit of, a disqualified person of the income or assets of a plan;

(E) act by a disqualified person who is a fiduciary whereby he deals with the income or assets of a plan in his own interest or for his own account; or

(F) receipt of any consideration for his own personal account by any disqualified person who is a fiduciary from any party dealing with the plan in connection with a transaction involving the income or assets of the plan.

(2) SPECIAL EXEMPTION.—The Secretary shall establish an exemption procedure for purposes of this subsection. Pursuant to such procedure, he may grant a conditional or unconditional exemption of any disqualified person or transaction or class of disqualified persons or transactions, from all or part of the restrictions imposed by paragraph (1) of this subsection. Action under this subparagraph may be taken only after consultation and coordination with the Secretary of Labor. The Secretary may not grant an exemption under this paragraph unless he finds that such exemption is—

(A) administratively feasible,

(B) in the interests of the plan and of its participants and beneficiaries, and

(C) protective of the rights of participants and beneficiaries of the plan.

Before granting an exemption under this paragraph, the Secretary shall require adequate notice to be given to interested persons and shall publish notice in the Federal Register of the pendency of such exemption and shall afford interested persons an opportunity to present views. No exemption may be granted under this paragraph with respect to a transaction described in subparagraph (E) or (F) of paragraph (1) unless the Secretary affords an opportunity for a hearing and makes a determination on the record with respect to the findings required under subparagraphs (A), (B), and (C) of this paragraph, except that in lieu of such hearing the Secretary may accept any record made by the Secretary of Labor with respect to an application for exemption under section 408(a) of title I of the Employee Retirement Income Security Act of 1974.

(3) SPECIAL RULE FOR INDIVIDUAL RETIREMENT ACCOUNTS.—An individual for whose benefit an individual retirement account is established and his beneficiaries shall be exempt from the tax imposed by this section with respect to any transaction concerning such account (which would otherwise be taxable under this section) if, with respect to such transaction, the account ceases to be an individual retirement account by reason of the application of section 408(e)(2)(A) or if section 408(e)(4) applies to such account.

(4) SPECIAL RULE FOR ARCHER MSAS.—An individual for whose benefit an Archer MSA (within the meaning of section 220(d)) is established shall be exempt from the tax imposed by this section with respect to any transaction concerning such account (which would otherwise be taxable under this section) if section 220(e)(2) applies to such transaction.

(5) SPECIAL RULE FOR COVERDELL EDUCATION SAVINGS ACCOUNTS.—An individual for whose benefit a Coverdell education savings account is established and any contributor to such account shall be exempt from the tax imposed by this section with respect to any transaction concerning such account (which would otherwise be taxable under this section) if section 530(d) applies with respect to such transaction.

(6) SPECIAL RULE FOR HEALTH SAVINGS ACCOUNTS.—An individual for whose benefit a health savings account (within the meaning of section 223(d)) is established shall be exempt from the tax imposed by this section with respect to any transaction concerning such account (which would otherwise be taxable under this section) if, with respect to such transaction, the account ceases to be a health savings account by reason of the application of section 223(e)(2) to such account.

(7) SPECIAL RULE FOR PROVISION OF PHARMACY BENEFIT SERVICES.—Any party to an arrangement which satisfies the requirements of section 408(h) of the Employee Retirement Income Security Act of 1974 shall be exempt from the tax imposed by this section with respect to such arrangement.

Amendments

• **2019, Temporary Relief from Certain ERISA Requirements Act of 2020 (P.L. 116-94)**

P.L. 116-94, § 1302(b), Div. P:

Amended Code Sec. 4975(c) by adding at the end a new paragraph (7). **Effective** 12-20-2019. For a special rule, see Act Sec. 1302(c), Div. P.

P.L. 116-94, § 1302(c), Div. P, provides:

(c) APPLICABILITY.—With respect to a group health plan subject to subsection (h) of section 408 of the Employee Retirement Income Security Act of 1974 (29 U.S.C. 1108) (as amended by subsection (a)) and subsection (c) of section 4975 of the Internal Revenue Code of 1986 (as amended by subsection (b)), beginning at the end of the fifth plan year of such group health plan that begins after the date of enactment of

EXCISE TAXES—QUALIFIED PENSION, ETC., PLANS

• 2003, Medicare Prescription Drug, Improvement, and Modernization Act of 2003 (P.L. 108-173)

P.L. 108-173, §1201(f)(1):

Amended Code Sec. 4975(c) by adding at the end a new paragraph (6). **Effective** for tax years beginning after 12-31-2003.

• 2001 (P.L. 107-22)

P.L. 107-22, §1(b)(1)(D):

Amended Code Sec. 4975(c) by striking "an education individual retirement" and inserting "a Coverdell education savings". **Effective** 7-26-2001.

P.L. 107-22, §1(b)(3)(D):

Amended the heading for Code Sec. 4975(c)(5) by striking "EDUCATION INDIVIDUAL RETIREMENT" and inserting "COVERDELL EDUCATION SAVINGS". **Effective** 7-26-2001.

• 2000, Community Renewal Tax Relief Act of 2000 (P.L. 106-554)

P.L. 106-554, §202(a)(7):

Amended Code Sec. 4975(c)(4) by striking "medical savings account" and inserting "Archer MSA". **Effective** 12-21-2000.

P.L. 106-554, §202(b)(7):

Amended the heading for Code Sec. 4975(c)(4) by striking "MEDICAL SAVINGS ACCOUNTS" and inserting "ARCHER MSAS". **Effective** 12-21-2000.

P.L. 106-554, §202(b)(10):

Amended Code Sec. 4975(c)(4) by striking "a Archer" and inserting "an Archer". **Effective** 12-21-2000.

• 1998, IRS Restructuring and Reform Act of 1998 (P.L. 105-206)

P.L. 105-206, §6023(19)(A):

Amended Code Sec. 4975(c)(3) by striking "exempt for the tax" and inserting "exempt from the tax". **Effective** 7-22-98.

• 1997, Taxpayer Relief Act of 1997 (P.L. 105-34)

P.L. 105-34, §213(b)(2):

Amended Code Sec. 4975(c) by adding at the end a new paragraph (5). **Effective** for tax years beginning after 12-31-97.

P.L. 105-34, §1602(a)(5):

Amended Code Sec. 4975(c)(4) by striking "if, with respect to such transaction" and all that follows and inserting "if section 220(e)(2) applies to such transaction.". **Effective** as if included in the provision of P.L. 104-91 to which it relates [**effective** for tax years beginning after 12-31-96.—CCH]. Prior to amendment, Code Sec. 4975(c)(4) read as follows:

(4) SPECIAL RULE FOR MEDICAL SAVINGS ACCOUNTS.—An individual for whose benefit a medical savings account (within the meaning of section 220(d)) is established shall be exempt from the tax imposed by this section with respect to any transaction concerning such account (which would otherwise be taxable under this section) if, with respect to such transaction, the account ceases to be a medical savings account by reason of the application of section 220(e)(2) to such account.

• 1996, Health Insurance Portability and Accountability Act of 1996 (P.L. 104-191)

P.L. 104-191, §301(f)(1):

Amended Code Sec. 4975(c) by adding at the end a new paragraph (4). **Effective** for tax years beginning after 12-31-96.

• 1976, Tax Reform Act of 1976 (P.L. 94-455)

P.L. 94-455, §1906(b)(13)(A):

Amended 1954 Code by substituting "Secretary" for "Secretary or his delegate" each place it appeared. **Effective** 2-1-77.

[Sec. 4975(d)]

(d) EXEMPTIONS.—Except as provided in subsection (f)(6), the prohibitions provided in subsection (c) shall not apply to—

(1) any loan made by the plan to a disqualified person who is a participant or beneficiary of the plan if such loan—

(A) is available to all such participants or beneficiaries on a reasonably equivalent basis,

(B) is not made available to highly compensated employees (within the meaning of section 414(q) of the Internal Revenue Code of 1986) in an amount greater than the amount made available to other employees,

(C) is made in accordance with specific provisions regarding such loans set forth in the plan,

(D) bears a reasonable rate of interest, and

(E) is adequately secured;

(2) any contract, or reasonable arrangement, made with a disqualified person for office space, or legal, accounting, or other services necessary for the establishment or operation of the plan, if no more than reasonable compensation is paid therefor;

(3) any loan to a leveraged employee stock ownership plan (as defined in subsection (e)(7)), if—

(A) such loan is primarily for the benefit of participants and beneficiaries of the plan, and

(B) such loan is at a reasonable rate of interest, and any collateral which is given to a disqualified person by the plan consists only of qualifying employer securities (as defined in subsection (e)(8));

(4) the investment of all or part of a plan's assets in deposits which bear a reasonable interest rate in a bank or similar financial institution supervised by the United States or a State, if such bank or other institution is a fiduciary of such plan and if—

(A) the plan covers only employees of such bank or other institution and employees of affiliates of such bank or other institution, or

(B) such investment is expressly authorized by a provision of the plan or by a fiduciary (other than such bank or institution or affiliates thereof) who is expressly empowered by the plan to so instruct the trustee with respect to such investment;

(5) any contract for life insurance, health insurance, or annuities with one or more insurers which are qualified to do business in a State if the plan pays no more than adequate consideration, and if each such insurer or insurers is—

(A) the employer maintaining the plan, or

(B) a disqualified person which is wholly owned (directly or indirectly) by the employer establishing the plan, or by any person which is a disqualified person with respect to the plan, but only if the total premiums and annuity considerations written by such insurers for life insurance, health insurance, or annuities for all plans (and their employers) with respect to which such insurers are disqualified persons (not including premiums or annuity considerations written by the employer maintaining the plan) do not exceed 5 percent of the total premiums and annuity considerations written for all lines of insurance in that year by such insurers (not including premiums or annuity considerations written by the employer maintaining the plan);

(6) the provision of any ancillary service by a bank or similar financial institution supervised by the United States or a State, if such service is provided at not more than reasonable compensation, if such bank or other institution is a fiduciary of such plan, and if—

(A) such bank or similar financial institution has adopted adequate internal safeguards which assure that the provision of such ancillary service is consistent with sound banking and financial practice, as determined by Federal or State supervisory authority, and

(B) the extent to which such ancillary service is provided is subject to specific guidelines issued by such bank or similar financial institution (as determined by the Secretary after consultation with Federal and State supervisory authority), and under such guidelines the bank or similar financial institution does not provide such ancillary service—

(i) in an excessive or unreasonable manner, and

(ii) in a manner that would be inconsistent with the best interests of participants and beneficiaries of employee benefit plans;

(7) the exercise of a privilege to convert securities, to the extent provided in regulations of the Secretary, but only if the plan receives no less than adequate consideration pursuant to such conversion;

(8) any transaction between a plan and a common or collective trust fund or pooled investment fund maintained by a disqualified person which is a bank or trust company supervised by a State or Federal agency or between a plan and a pooled investment fund of an insurance company qualified to do business in a State if—

(A) the transaction is a sale or purchase of an interest in the fund,

EXCISE TAXES—QUALIFIED PENSION, ETC., PLANS

(B) the bank, trust company, or insurance company receives not more than reasonable compensation, and

(C) such transaction is expressly permitted by the instrument under which the plan is maintained, or by a fiduciary (other than the bank, trust company, or insurance company, or an affiliate thereof) who has authority to manage and control the assets of the plan;

(9) receipt by a disqualified person of any benefit to which he may be entitled as a participant or beneficiary in the plan, so long as the benefit is computed and paid on a basis which is consistent with the terms of the plan as applied to all other participants and beneficiaries;

(10) receipt by a disqualified person of any reasonable compensation for services rendered, or for the reimbursement of expenses properly and actually incurred, in the performance of his duties with the plan, but no person so serving who already receives full-time pay from an employer or an association of employers, whose employees are participants in the plan, or from an employee organization whose members are participants in such plan shall receive compensation from such fund, except for reimbursement of expenses properly and actually incurred;

(11) service by a disqualified person as a fiduciary in addition to being an officer, employee, agent, or other representative of a disqualified person;

(12) the making by a fiduciary of a distribution of the assets of the trust in accordance with the terms of the plan if such assets are distributed in the same manner as provided under section 4044 of title IV of the Employee Retirement Income Security Act of 1974 (relating to allocation of assets);

(13) any transaction which is exempt from section 406 of such Act by reason of section 408(e) of such Act (or which would be so exempt if such section 406 applied to such transaction) or which is exempt from section 406 of such Act by reason of section 408(b)(12) of such Act;

(14) any transaction required or permitted under part 1 of subtitle E of title IV or section 4223 of the Employee Retirement Income Security Act of 1974, but this paragraph shall not apply with respect to the application of subsection (c)(1)(E) or (F);

(15) a merger of multiemployer plans, or the transfer of assets or liabilities between multiemployer plans, determined by the Pension Benefit Guaranty Corporation to meet the requirements of section 4231 of such Act, but this paragraph shall not apply with respect to the application of subsection (c)(1)(E) or (F);

(16) a sale of stock held by a trust which constitutes an individual retirement account under section 408(a) to the individual for whose benefit such account is established if—

(A) such stock is in a bank (as defined in section 581) or a depository institution holding company (as defined in section 3(w)(1) of the Federal Deposit Insurance Act (12 U.S.C. 1813(w)(1))),

(B) such stock is held by such trust as of the date of the enactment of this paragraph,

(C) such sale is pursuant to an election under section 1362(a) by such bank or company,

(D) such sale is for fair market value at the time of sale (as established by an independent appraiser) and the terms of the sale are otherwise at least as favorable to such trust as the terms that would apply on a sale to an unrelated party,

(E) such trust does not pay any commissions, costs, or other expenses in connection with the sale, and

(F) the stock is sold in a single transaction for cash not later than 120 days after the S corporation election is made;

(17) any transaction in connection with the provision of investment advice described in subsection (e)(3)(B) to a participant or beneficiary in a plan that permits such participant or beneficiary to direct the investment of plan assets in an individual account, if—

(A) the transaction is—

(i) the provision of the investment advice to the participant or beneficiary of the plan with respect to a security or other property available as an investment under the plan,

(ii) the acquisition, holding, or sale of a security or other property available as an investment under the plan pursuant to the investment advice, or

(iii) the direct or indirect receipt of fees or other compensation by the fiduciary adviser or an affiliate thereof (or any employee, agent, or registered representative of the fiduciary adviser or affiliate) in connection with the provision of the advice or in connection with an acquisition, holding, or sale of a security or other property available as an investment under the plan pursuant to the investment advice; and

(B) the requirements of subsection (f)(8) are met,

(18) any transaction involving the purchase or sale of securities, or other property (as determined by the Secretary of Labor), between a plan and a disqualified person (other than a fiduciary described in subsection (e)(3)) with respect to a plan if—

(A) the transaction involves a block trade,

(B) at the time of the transaction, the interest of the plan (together with the interests of any other plans maintained by the same plan sponsor), does not exceed 10 percent of the aggregate size of the block trade,

(C) the terms of the transaction, including the price, are at least as favorable to the plan as an arm's length transaction, and

(D) the compensation associated with the purchase and sale is not greater than the compensation associated with an arm's length transaction with an unrelated party,

(19) any transaction involving the purchase or sale of securities, or other property (as determined by the Secretary of Labor), between a plan and a disqualified person if—

(A) the transaction is executed through an electronic communication network, alternative trading system, or similar execution system or trading venue subject to regulation and oversight by—

(i) the applicable Federal regulating entity, or

(ii) such foreign regulatory entity as the Secretary of Labor may determine by regulation,

(B) either—

(i) the transaction is effected pursuant to rules designed to match purchases and sales at the best price available through the execution system in accordance with applicable rules of the Securities and Exchange Commission or other relevant governmental authority, or

(ii) neither the execution system nor the parties to the transaction take into account the identity of the parties in the execution of trades,

(C) the price and compensation associated with the purchase and sale are not greater than the price and compensation associated with an arm's length transaction with an unrelated party,

(D) if the disqualified person has an ownership interest in the system or venue described in subparagraph (A), the system or venue has been authorized by the plan sponsor or other independent fiduciary for transactions described in this paragraph, and

(E) not less than 30 days prior to the initial transaction described in this paragraph executed through any system or venue described in subparagraph (A), a plan fiduciary is provided written or electronic notice of the execution of such transaction through such system or venue,

(20) transactions described in subparagraphs (A), (B), and (D) of subsection (c)(1) between a plan and a person that is a disqualified person other than a fiduciary (or an affiliate) who has or exercises any discretionary authority or control with respect to the investment of the

EXCISE TAXES—QUALIFIED PENSION, ETC., PLANS

plan assets involved in the transaction or renders investment advice (within the meaning of subsection (e)(3)(B)) with respect to those assets, solely by reason of providing services to the plan or solely by reason of a relationship to such a service provider described in subparagraph (F), (G), (H), or (I) of subsection (e)(2), or both, but only if in connection with such transaction the plan receives no less, nor pays no more, than adequate consideration,

(21) any foreign exchange transactions, between a bank or broker-dealer (or any affiliate of either) and a plan (as defined in this section) with respect to which such bank or broker-dealer (or affiliate) is a trustee, custodian, fiduciary, or other disqualified person, if—

(A) the transaction is in connection with the purchase, holding, or sale of securities or other investment assets (other than a foreign exchange transaction unrelated to any other investment in securities or other investment assets),

(B) at the time the foreign exchange transaction is entered into, the terms of the transaction are not less favorable to the plan than the terms generally available in comparable arm's length foreign exchange transactions between unrelated parties, or the terms afforded by the bank or broker-dealer (or any affiliate of either) in comparable arm's-length foreign exchange transactions involving unrelated parties,

(C) the exchange rate used by such bank or broker-dealer (or affiliate) for a particular foreign exchange transaction does not deviate by more than 3 percent from the interbank bid and asked rates for transactions of comparable size and maturity at the time of the transaction as displayed on an independent service that reports rates of exchange in the foreign currency market for such currency, and

(D) the bank or broker-dealer (or any affiliate of either) does not have investment discretion, or provide investment advice, with respect to the transaction,

(22) any transaction described in subsection (c)(1)(A) involving the purchase and sale of a security between a plan and any other account managed by the same investment manager, if—

(A) the transaction is a purchase or sale, for no consideration other than cash payment against prompt delivery of a security for which market quotations are readily available,

(B) the transaction is effected at the independent current market price of the security (within the meaning of section 270.17a-7(b) of title 17, Code of Federal Regulations),

(C) no brokerage commission, fee (except for customary transfer fees, the fact of which is disclosed pursuant to subparagraph (D)), or other remuneration is paid in connection with the transaction,

(D) a fiduciary (other than the investment manager engaging in the cross-trades or any affiliate) for each plan participating in the transaction authorizes in advance of any cross-trades (in a document that is separate from any other written agreement of the parties) the investment manager to engage in cross trades at the investment manager's discretion, after such fiduciary has received disclosure regarding the conditions under which cross trades may take place (but only if such disclosure is separate from any other agreement or disclosure involving the asset management relationship), including the written policies and procedures of the investment manager described in subparagraph (H),

(E) each plan participating in the transaction has assets of at least $100,000,000, except that if the assets of a plan are invested in a master trust containing the assets of plans maintained by employers in the same controlled group (as defined in section 407(d)(7) of the Employee Retirement Income Security Act of 1974), the master trust has assets of at least $100,000,000,

(F) the investment manager provides to the plan fiduciary who authorized cross trading under subparagraph (D) a quarterly report detailing all cross trades executed by the investment manager in which the plan participated during such quarter, including the following information, as applicable: (i) the identity of each security bought or sold; (ii) the number of shares or units traded; (iii) the parties involved in the cross-trade; and (iv) trade price and the method used to establish the trade price,

(G) the investment manager does not base its fee schedule on the plan's consent to cross trading, and no other service (other than the investment opportunities and cost savings available through a cross trade) is conditioned on the plan's consent to cross trading,

(H) the investment manager has adopted, and cross-trades are effected in accordance with, written cross-trading policies and procedures that are fair and equitable to all accounts participating in the cross-trading program, and that include a description of the manager's pricing policies and procedures, and the manager's policies and procedures for allocating cross trades in an objective manner among accounts participating in the cross-trading program, and

(I) the investment manager has designated an individual responsible for periodically reviewing such purchases and sales to ensure compliance with the written policies and procedures described in subparagraph (H), and following such review, the individual shall issue an annual written report no later than 90 days following the period to which it relates signed under penalty of perjury to the plan fiduciary who authorized cross trading under subparagraph (D) describing the steps performed during the course of the review, the level of compliance, and any specific instances of non-compliance.

The written report shall also notify the plan fiduciary of the plan's right to terminate participation in the investment manager's cross-trading program at any time,

(23) except as provided in subsection (f)(11), a transaction described in subparagraph (A), (B), (C), or (D) of subsection (c)(1) in connection with the acquisition, holding, or disposition of any security or commodity, if the transaction is corrected before the end of the correction period,

(24) the provision of a de minimis financial incentive described in section 401(k)(4)(A), or

(25) the receipt of fees and compensation by the automatic portability provider for services provided in connection with an automatic portability transaction.

Amendments

• **2022, SECURE 2.0 Act of 2022 (P.L. 117-328)**

P.L. 117-328, §113(c):

Amended Code Sec. 4975(d) by striking "or" at the end of paragraph (22), by striking the period at the end of paragraph (23) and inserting ", or", and by adding at the end a new paragraph (24). **Effective** for plan years beginning after 12-29-2022. For a special rule, see Act Sec. 120(c), below.

P.L. 117-328, §120(c), provides:

(c) REGULATORY AUTHORITY.—Not later than 12 months after the date of the enactment of this Act, the Secretary of Labor shall issue such guidance as may be necessary to carry out the purposes of the amendments made by this section, including regulations or other guidance which—

(1) require an automatic portability provider to provide a notice to individuals on whose behalf the individual retirement plan described in paragraph (12)(A)(i)(I) of section 4975(f) of the Internal Revenue Code of 1986, as added by this section, is established in advance of the notices specified in paragraph (12)(B)(v) of such section, as so added,

(2) require an automatic portability provider to disclose to plans described in paragraph (12)(A)(i)(II) of section 4975(f) of the Internal Revenue Code of 1986, as added by this section, information required to be provided by a covered service provider pursuant to section 2550.408b-2(c) of title 29, Code of Federal Regulations,

(3) require a plan described in such paragraph (12)(A)(i)(II), as so added, to fully disclose fees related to an automatic portability transaction in its summary plan description or summary of material modifications, as relevant,

(4) require a plan described in such paragraph, as so added, to invest amounts received on behalf of a participant pursuant to an automatic portability transaction in the participant's current investment election under the plan or, if no election is made or permitted, in the plan's qualified default investment alternative (within the meaning of section 2550.404c-5 of title 29, Code of Federal Regulations) or another investment selected by a fiduciary with respect to such plan,

(5) prohibit or restrict the receipt or payment of third party compensation (other than a direct fee paid by a plan sponsor which is in lieu of a fee imposed on an individual retirement plan owner) by an automatic portability provider in connection with an automatic portability transaction,

(6) prohibit exculpatory provisions in an automatic portability provider's contracts or communications with individuals disclaiming or limiting its liability in the event that an automatic portability transaction results in an improper transfer,

(7) require an automatic portability provider to take actions necessary to reasonably ensure that participant and beneficiary data is current and accurate,

(8) limit the use of data related to automatic portability transactions for any purpose other than the execution of such transactions or locating missing participants, except as permitted by the Secretary of Labor,

EXCISE TAXES—QUALIFIED PENSION, ETC., PLANS

(9) provide for corrections procedures in the event an auditor determines the automatic portability provider was not in compliance with this provision and related regulations as specified in paragraph (12)(B)(ix)(II) of section 4975(f) of such Code, as so added, including deadlines, supplemental audits, and corrective actions which may include a temporary prohibition from relying on the exemption provided by paragraph (25) of section 4975(d) of such Code, as added by this section,

(10) ensure that the appropriate participants and beneficiaries, in fact, receive all the required notices and disclosures, and

(11) make clear that the exemption provided by paragraph (25) of section 4975(d) of such Code, as added by this section, applies solely to the automatic portability transactions described therein, and, to the extent the Secretary deems necessary or advisable, specify how the application of the exemption relates to or coordinates with the application of other statutory provisions, regulations, administrative guidance, or exemptions.

Any term used in this subsection which is used in paragraph (12) of section 4975(f) of such Code, as added by this section, has the same meaning as when used in such paragraph.

P.L. 117-328, § 120(a):

Amended Code Sec. 4975(d), as amended by the preceding provisions of this Act, by striking "or" at the end of paragraph (23), by striking the period at the end of paragraph (24) and inserting ", or", and by adding at the end a new paragraph (25). **Effective** for transactions occurring on or after the date which is 12 months after 12-29-2022. For a special rule, see Act Sec. 120(d), below.

P.L. 117-328, § 120(d), provides:

(d) REPORT TO CONGRESS.—

(1) IN GENERAL.—Not later than 2 years after the date of the first audit report received by the Secretary of Labor from any automatic portability provider, and every 3 years thereafter, the Secretary of Labor shall report to the Committees on Health, Education, Labor and Pensions and Finance of the Senate and the Committees on Education and Labor and Ways and Means of the House of Representatives on—

(A) the effectiveness of automatic portability transactions under the exemption provided by paragraph (25) of section 4975(d) of the Internal Revenue Code of 1986, as added by this section, detailing—

(i) the number of automatic cash outs from qualified plans to individual retirement plans described in section 4975(f)(12)(A)(i)(I) of such Code,

(ii) the number of completed automatic portability transactions to employer-sponsored retirement plans described in section 4975(f)(12)(A)(i)(II) of such Code,

(iii) the number of individual retirement plans described in section 4975(f)(12)(A)(i)(I) of such Code which have been transferred to designated beneficiaries,

(iv) the number of individual retirement plans described in section 4975(f)(12)(A)(i)(I) of such Code for which the automatic portability provider is searching for next of kin due to a deceased account holder without a designated beneficiary, and

(v) the number of accounts that were reduced to a zero balance while in the automatic portability provider's custody;

(B) a summary of any consumer complaints submitted to the Employee Benefits Security Administration regarding automatic portability transactions;

(C) a summary of compliance issues found in the annual audit described in section 4975(f)(12)(B)(xiii)(II) of such Code, if any, and their corrections;

(D) a summary of the fees individuals are charged in connection with automatic portability transactions, including whether those fees have increased since the last report;

(E) recommendations of any necessary statutory changes to this exemption to improve the effectiveness of automatic portability transactions, including repeal of this provision in the event of a pattern of noncompliance; and

(F) any other information the Secretary of Labor deems important.

The report required by this subsection shall be made publicly available.

(2) REPORT ON NOTICES RELATING TO AUTOMATIC TRANSFERS.—Not later than 2 years after the date of the enactment of this Act, the Secretary of Treasury shall report to the Committee on Finance of the Senate and the Committee on Ways and Means on the adequacy of the notices relating to transfers under section 401(a)(31)(B)(i) of the Internal Revenue Code of 1986.

• **2018, Tax Technical Corrections Act of 2018 (P.L. 115-141)**

P.L. 115-141, § 401(a)(190), Div. U:

Amended Code Sec. 4975(d)(16)(A) by striking "1813(w)(1))," and inserting "1813(w)(1))),". **Effective** 3-23-2018.

P.L. 115-141, § 401(a)(229), Div. U:

Amended Code Sec. 4975(d)(3) by striking "an leveraged" and inserting "a leveraged". **Effective** 3-23-2018.

P.L. 115-141, § 401(a)(230), Div. U:

Amended Code Sec. 4975(d)(17) by striking "Any" and inserting "any". **Effective** 3-23-2018.

P.L. 115-141, § 401(a)(231), Div. U:

Amended Code Sec. 4975(d)(21) by striking "person person" and inserting "person". **Effective** 3-23-2018.

• **2008, Worker, Retiree, and Employer Recovery Act of 2008 (P.L. 110-458)**

P.L. 110-458, § 106(a)(2)(A):

Amended the matter preceding Code Sec. 4975(d)(17)(A) by striking "and that permits" and inserting "that permits". **Effective** as if included in the provision of the 2006 Act to which the amendment relates [**effective** with respect to advice referred to in Code Sec. 4975(e)(3)(B) provided after 12-31-2006.—CCH].

Sec. 4975(d)(25)

P.L. 110-458, § 106(b)(2)(A)-(C):

Amended Code Sec. 4975(d) in the matter preceding paragraph (18)(A) by striking "party in interest" and inserting "disqualified person", and by striking "subsection (e)(3)(B)" and inserting "subsection (e)(3)", in paragraphs (19), (20), and (21), by striking "party in interest" each place it appears and inserting "disqualified person", and in paragraph (21)(C), by striking "or less" before "than 3 percent". **Effective** as if included in the provision of the 2006 Act to which the amendment relates [**effective** for transactions occurring after 8-17-2006.—CCH]

• **2006, Pension Protection Act of 2006 (P.L. 109-280)**

P.L. 109-280, § 601(b)(1)(A)-(C):

Amended Code Sec. 4975(d) by striking "or" at the end of paragraph (15); by striking the period at the end of paragraph (16) and inserting ";or [sic]"; and by adding at the end a new paragraph (17). **Effective** with respect to advice referred to in Code Sec. 4975(e)(3)(B) provided after 12-31-2006 [**effective** date amended by P.L. 110-458, § 106(a)(3).—CCH].

P.L. 109-280, § 601(c), provides:

(c) COORDINATION WITH EXISTING EXEMPTIONS.—Any exemption under section 408(b) of the Employee Retirement Income Security Act of 1974 and section 4975(d) of the Internal Revenue Code of 1986 provided by the amendments made by this section shall not in any manner alter existing individual or class exemptions, provided by statute or administrative action.

P.L. 109-280, § 611(a)(2)(A):

Amended Code Sec. 4975(d), as amended by Act Sec. 611, by striking "or" at the end of paragraph (16), by striking the period at the end of paragraph (17) and inserting ", or", and by adding at the end a new paragraph (18). **Effective** for transactions occurring after 8-17-2006.

P.L. 109-280, § 611(c)(2):

Amended Code Sec. 4975(d), as amended by Act Sec. 611(a), by striking "or" at the end of paragraph (17), by striking the period at the end of paragraph (18) and inserting ", or", and by adding at the end a new paragraph (19). **Effective** for transactions occurring after 8-17-2006.

P.L. 109-280, § 611(d)(2)(A):

Amended Code Sec. 4975(d), as amended by Act Sec. 611(c), by striking "or" at the end of paragraph (18), by striking the period at the end of paragraph (19) and inserting ", or", and by adding at the end a new paragraph (20). **Effective** for transactions occurring after 8-17-2006.

P.L. 109-280, § 611(e)(2):

Amended Code Sec. 4975(d), as amended by Act Sec. 611(d), by striking "or" at the end of paragraph (19), by striking the period at the end of paragraph (20) and inserting ", or", and by adding at the end a new paragraph (21). **Effective** for transactions occurring after 8-17-2006.

P.L. 109-280, § 611(g)(2):

Amended Code Sec. 4975(d), as amended by Act Sec. 611(e), by striking "or" at the end of paragraph (20), by striking the period at the end of paragraph (21) and inserting ", or", and by adding at the end a new paragraph (22). **Effective** for transactions occurring after 8-17-2006.

P.L. 109-280, § 612(b)(1):

Amended Code Sec. 4975(d), as amended by Act Secs. 601 and 611, by striking "or" at the end of paragraph (21), by striking the period at the end of paragraph (22) and inserting ", or", and by adding at the end a new paragraph (23). **Effective** for any transaction which the fiduciary or disqualified person discovers, or reasonably should have discovered, after 8-17-2006 constitutes a prohibited transaction.

• **2005, Gulf Opportunity Zone Act of 2005 (P.L. 109-135)**

P.L. 109-135, § 413(a)(2)(A)-(B):

Amended Code Sec. 4975(d)(16) by inserting "or a depository institution holding company (as defined in section 3(w)(1) of the Federal Deposit Insurance Act (12 U.S.C. 1813(w)(1))" after "a bank (as defined in section 581)" in subparagraph (A), and by inserting "or company" after "such bank" in subparagraph (C). **Effective** as if included in the provision of the American Jobs Creation Act of 2004 (P.L. 108-357) to which it relates [**effective** 10-22-2004.—CCH].

• **2004, American Jobs Creation Act of 2004 (P.L. 108-357)**

P.L. 108-357, § 233(c):

Amended Code Sec. 4975(d) by striking "or" at the end of paragraph (14), by striking the period at the end of paragraph (15) and inserting "; or", and by adding at the end a new paragraph (16). **Effective** 10-22-2004.

• **1997, Taxpayer Relief Act of 1997 (P.L. 105-34)**

P.L. 105-34, § 1506(b)(1)(B)(i)-(ii):

Amended Code Sec. 4975(d) by striking "The prohibitions" and inserting "Except as provided in subsection (f)(6), the prohibitions", and by striking the last two sentences thereof. **Effective** for tax years beginning after 12-31-97. Prior to amendment, the last two sentences of Code Sec. 4975(d) read as follows:

The exemptions provided by this subsection (other than paragraphs (9) and (12)) shall not apply to any transaction with respect to a trust described in section 401(a) which is part of a plan providing contributions or benefits for employees some or all of whom are owner-employees (as defined in section 401(c)(3)) in which a plan directly or indirectly lends any part of the corpus or income of the plan to, pays any compensation for personal services rendered to the plan to, or acquires for the plan any property from or sells any property to, any such owner-employee, a member of the family (as defined in section 267(c)(4)) of any such owner-employee, or a corporation controlled by any such owner-employee through the ownership, directly or indirectly, of 50 percent or more of the total combined voting power of all classes of stock entitled to vote or 50 percent or more of the total value of shares of all classes of stock of the corporation. For purposes of the preceding sentence, a shareholder-

EXCISE TAXES—QUALIFIED PENSION, ETC., PLANS

employee (as defined in section 1379, as in effect on the day before the date of the enactment of the Subchapter S Revision Act of 1982, a participant or beneficiary of an individual retirement account or an individual retirement annuity (as defined in section 408), and an employer or association of employees which establishes such an account or annuity under section 408(c) shall be deemed to be an owner-employee.

• **1996, Small Business Job Protection Act of 1996 (P.L. 104-188)**

P.L. 104-188, §1702(g)(3):

Amended Code Sec. 4975(d)(13) by striking "section 408(b)" and inserting "section 408(b)(12)". **Effective** as if included in the provision of P.L. 101-508 to which it relates.

• **1990, Omnibus Budget Reconciliation Act of 1990 (P.L. 101-508)**

P.L. 101-508, §11701(m):

Amended Code Sec. 4975(d)(13) by inserting before the semicolon at the end thereof "or which is exempt from section 406 of such Act by reason of section 408(b) of such Act". **Effective** as if included in the provision of P.L. 101-239 to which it relates.

• **1986, Tax Reform Act of 1986 (P.L. 99-514)**

P.L. 99-514, §1114(b)(15)(A):

Amended Code Sec. 4975(d)(1)(B) by striking out "highly compensated employees, officers, or shareholders" and inserting in lieu thereof "highly compensated employees (within the meaning of section 414(q))". **Effective** for years beginning after 12-31-88.

P.L. 99-514, §1899A(51):

Amended Code Sec. 4975(d) by striking out "and (12) shall not" in the second sentence and inserting in lieu thereof "and (12)) shall not". **Effective** 10-22-86.

• **1984, Deficit Reduction Act of 1984 (P.L. 98-369)**

P.L. 98-369, §491(d)(45):

Amended the last sentence of Code Sec. 4975(d) by striking out ", individual retirement annuity, or an individual retirement bond (as defined in section 408 or 409)" and inserting in lieu thereof "or an individual retirement annuity (as defined in section 408)". **Effective** for obligations issued after 12-31-83.

• **1983, Technical Corrections Act of 1982 (P.L. 97-448)**

P.L. 97-448, §305(d)(5):

Amended Code Sec. 4975(d) by striking out "section 1379" in the last sentence and inserting in lieu thereof "section 1379, as in effect on the day before the date of the enactment of the Subchapter S Revision Act of 1982". **Effective** 10-19-82.

• **1980, Multiemployer Pension Plan Amendments Act of 1980 (P.L. 96-364)**

P.L. 96-364, §208(b):

Amended Code Sec. 4975(d) by striking out "or" at the end of paragraph (12), by striking out the period at the end of paragraph (13) and inserting in lieu thereof a semicolon, and by inserting after paragraph (13) new paragraphs (14) and (15). **Effective** 9-26-80.

• **1980, Technical Corrections Act of 1979 (P.L. 96-222)**

P.L. 96-222, §101(a)(7)(B):

Amended Act Sec. 141 of P.L. 95-600 by adding paragraph (h) to provide **effective** dates for the amendments of Code Secs. 4975(d)(3) and 4975(e)(7). Paragraph (h) reads as follows:

"(h) EFFECTIVE DATES FOR SECTION 4975 EMPLOYEE STOCK OWNERSHIP PLANS.—Paragraphs (5) and (6) of subsection (f) shall apply—

"(1) insofar as they make the requirements of subsections (e) and (h)(1)(B) of section 409A of the Internal Revenue Code of 1954 applicable to section 4975 of such Code, to stock acquired after December 31, 1979, and

(2) insofar as they make paragraphs (1)(A) and (2) of section 409A(h) of such Code applicable to such section 4975, to distributions after December 31, 1978."

• **1978, Revenue Act of 1978 (P.L. 95-600)**

P.L. 95-600, §141(f)(6):

Amended Code Sec. 4975(d)(3) by substituting "a leveraged employee stock ownership plan" for "an employee stock ownership plan". **Effective** with respect to qualified investment for tax years beginning after 1978.

• **1976, Tax Reform Act of 1976 (P.L. 94-455)**

P.L. 94-455, §1906(b)(13)(A):

Amended 1954 Code by substituting "Secretary" for "Secretary or his delegate" each place it appeared. **Effective** 2-1-77.

[Sec. 4975(e)]

(e) DEFINITIONS.—

(1) PLAN.—For purposes of this section, the term "plan" means—

(A) a trust described in section 401(a) which forms a part of a plan, or a plan described in section 403(a), which trust or plan is exempt from tax under section 501(a),

(B) an individual retirement account described in section 408(a),

(C) an individual retirement annuity described in section 408(b),

(D) an Archer MSA described in section 220(d),

(E) a health savings account described in section 223(d),

(F) a Coverdell education savings account described in section 530, or

(G) a trust, plan, account, or annuity which, at any time, has been determined by the Secretary to be described in any preceding subparagraph of this paragraph.

(2) DISQUALIFIED PERSON.—For purposes of this section, the term "disqualified person" means a person who is—

(A) a fiduciary;

(B) a person providing services to the plan;

(C) an employer any of whose employees are covered by the plan;

(D) an employee organization any of whose members are covered by the plan;

(E) an owner, direct or indirect, of 50 percent or more of—

(i) the combined voting power of all classes of stock entitled to vote or the total value of shares of all classes of stock of a corporation,

(ii) the capital interest or the profits interest of a partnership, or

(iii) the beneficial interest of a trust or unincorporated enterprise,

which is an employer or an employee organization described in subparagraph (C) or (D);

(F) a member of the family (as defined in paragraph (6)) of any individual described in subparagraph (A), (B), (C), or (E);

(G) a corporation, partnership, or trust or estate of which (or in which) 50 percent or more of—

(i) the combined voting power of all classes of stock entitled to vote or the total value of shares of all classes of stock of such corporation,

(ii) the capital interest or profits interest of such partnership, or

(iii) the beneficial interest of such trust or estate,

is owned directly or indirectly, or held by persons described in subparagraph (A), (B), (C), (D), or (E);

(H) an officer, director (or an individual having powers or responsibilities similar to those of officers or directors), a 10 percent or more shareholder, or a highly compensated employee (earning 10 percent or more of the yearly wages of an employer) of a person described in subparagraph (C), (D), (E), or (G); or

(I) a 10 percent or more (in capital or profits) partner or joint venturer of a person described in subparagraph (C), (D), (E), or (G).

The Secretary, after consultation and coordination with the Secretary of Labor or his delegate, may by regulation prescribe a percentage lower than 50 percent for subparagraphs (E) and (G) and lower than 10 percent for subparagraphs (H) and (I).

(3) FIDUCIARY.—For purposes of this section, the term "fiduciary" means any person who—

(A) exercises any discretionary authority or discretionary control respecting management of such plan or exercises any authority or control respecting management or disposition of its assets,

EXCISE TAXES—QUALIFIED PENSION, ETC., PLANS

(B) renders investment advice for a fee or other compensation, direct or indirect, with respect to any moneys or other property of such plan, or has any authority or responsibility to do so, or

(C) has any discretionary authority or discretionary responsibility in the administration of such plan.

Such term includes any person designated under section 405(c)(1)(B) of the Employee Retirement Income Security Act of 1974.

(4) STOCKHOLDINGS.—For purposes of paragraphs (2)(E)(i), and (G)(i) there shall be taken into account indirect stockholdings which would be taken into account under section 267(c), except that, for purposes of this paragraph, section 267(c)(4) shall be treated as providing that the members of the family of an individual are the members within the meaning of paragraph (6).

(5) PARTNERSHIPS; TRUSTS.—For purposes of paragraphs (2)(E)(ii) and (iii), (G)(ii) and (iii), and (I) the ownership of profits or beneficial interests shall be determined in accordance with the rules for constructive ownership of stock provided in section 267(c) (other than paragraph (3) thereof), except that section 267(c)(4) shall be treated as providing that the members of the family of an individual are the members within the meaning of paragraph (6).

(6) MEMBER OF FAMILY.—For purposes of paragraph (2)(F), the family of any individual shall include his spouse, ancestor, lineal descendant, and any spouse of a lineal descendant.

(7) EMPLOYEE STOCK OWNERSHIP PLAN.—The term "employee stock ownership plan" means a defined contribution plan—

(A) which is a stock bonus plan which is qualified, or a stock bonus and a money purchase plan both of which are qualified under section 401(a) and which are designed to invest primarily in qualifying employer securities; and

(B) which is otherwise defined in regulations prescribed by the Secretary.

A plan shall not be treated as an employee stock ownership plan unless it meets the requirements of section 409(h), section 409(o), and, if applicable, section 409(n), section 409(p), and section 664(g) and, if the employer has a registration-type class of securities (as defined in section 409(e)(4)), it meets the requirements of section 409(e).

(8) QUALIFYING EMPLOYER SECURITY.—The term "qualifying employer security" means an employer security within the meaning of section 409(l).

If any moneys or other property of a plan are invested in shares of an investment company registered under the Investment Company Act of 1940, the investment shall not cause that investment company or that investment company's investment adviser or principal underwriter to be treated as a fiduciary or a disqualified person for purposes of this section, except when an investment company or its investment adviser or principal underwriter acts in connection with a plan covering employees of the investment company, its investment adviser, or its principal underwriter.

(9) SECTION MADE APPLICABLE TO WITHDRAWAL LIABILITY PAYMENT FUNDS.—For purposes of this section—

(A) IN GENERAL.—The term "plan" includes a trust described in section 501(c)(22).

(B) DISQUALIFIED PERSON.—In the case of any trust to which this section applies by reason of subparagraph (A), the term "disqualified person" includes any person who is a disqualified person with respect to any plan to which such trust is permitted to make payments under section 4223 of the Employee Retirement Income Security Act of 1974.

Amendments

- **2006, Pension Protection Act of 2006 (P.L. 109-280)**

P.L. 109-280, § 811, provides:

SEC. 811. PENSIONS AND INDIVIDUAL RETIREMENT ARRANGEMENT PROVISIONS OF ECONOMIC GROWTH AND TAX RELIEF RECONCILIATION ACT OF 2001 MADE PERMANENT.

Title IX of the Economic Growth and Tax Relief Reconciliation Act of 2001 [P.L. 107-16] shall not apply to the provisions of, and amendments made by, subtitles A through F of title VI [§§ 601-666]of such Act (relating to pension and individual retirement arrangement provisions).

- **2003, Medicare Prescription Drug, Improvement, and Modernization Act of 2003 (P.L. 108-173)**

P.L. 108-173, § 1201(f)(2):

Amended Code Sec. 4975(e)(1) by redesignating subparagraphs (E) and (F) as subparagraphs (F) and (G), respectively, and by inserting after subparagraph (D) a new subparagraph (E). **Effective** for tax years beginning after 12-31-2003.

- **2001 (P.L. 107-22)**

P.L. 107-22, § 1(b)(1)(D):

Amended Code Sec. 4975(e) by striking "an education individual retirement" and inserting "a Coverdell education savings". **Effective** 7-26-2001.

- **2001, Economic Growth and Tax Relief Reconciliation Act of 2001 (P.L. 107-16)**

P.L. 107-16, § 656(b):

Amended the last sentence of Code Sec. 4975(e)(7) by inserting ", section 409(p)," after "409(n)". **Effective** for plan years beginning after 12-31-2004. For an exception, see Act Sec. 656(d)(2), below.

P.L. 107-16, § 656(d)(2), provides:

(2) EXCEPTION FOR CERTAIN PLANS.—In the case of any—

(A) employee stock ownership plan established after March 14, 2001, or

(B) employee stock ownership plan established on or before such date if employer securities held by the plan consist of stock in a corporation with respect to which an election under section 1362(a) of the Internal Revenue Code of 1986 is not in effect on such date,

the amendments made by this section shall apply to plan years ending after March 14, 2001.

P.L. 107-16, § 901(a)-(b), provides [but see P.L. 109-280, § 811, above]:

SEC. 901. SUNSET OF PROVISIONS OF ACT.

(a) IN GENERAL.—All provisions of, and amendments made by, this Act shall not apply—

(1) to taxable, plan, or limitation years beginning after December 31, 2010, or

(2) in the case of title V, to estates of decedents dying, gifts made, or generation skipping transfers, after December 31, 2010.

(b) APPLICATION OF CERTAIN LAWS.—The Internal Revenue Code of 1986 and the Employee Retirement Income Security Act of 1974 shall be applied and administered to years, estates, gifts, and transfers described in subsection (a) as if the provisions and amendments described in subsection (a) had never been enacted.

- **2000, Community Renewal Tax Relief Act of 2000 (P.L. 106-554)**

P.L. 106-554, § 202(a)(7):

Amended Code Sec. 4975(e)(1)(D) by striking "medical savings account" and inserting "Archer MSA". **Effective** 12-21-2000.

P.L. 106-554, § 202(b)(10):

Amended Code Sec. 4975(e)(1)(D) by striking "a Archer" and inserting "an Archer". **Effective** 12-21-2000.

- **1997, Taxpayer Relief Act of 1997 (P.L. 105-34)**

P.L. 105-34, § 213(b)(1):

Amended Code Sec. 4975(e)(1) by striking "or" at the end of subparagraph (D), by redesignating subparagraph (E) as subparagraph (F), and by inserting after subparagraph (D) a new subparagraph (E). **Effective** for tax years beginning after 12-31-97.

P.L. 105-34, § 1530(c)(10):

Amended Code Sec. 4975(e)(7) by inserting "and section 664(g)" after "section 409(n)" in the last sentence. **Effective** for transfers made by trusts to, or for the use of, an employee stock ownership plan after 8-5-97.

- **1996, Health Insurance Portability and Accountability Act of 1996 (P.L. 104-191)**

P.L. 104-191, § 301(f)(2):

Amended Code Sec. 4975(e)(1). **Effective** for tax years beginning after 12-31-96. Prior to amendment, Code Sec. 4975(e)(1) read as follows:

(1) PLAN.—For purposes of this section, the term "plan" means a trust described in section 401(a) which forms a part of a plan, or a plan described in section 403(a), which trust or plan is exempt from tax under section 501(a), an individual retirement account described in section 408(a) or an individual retirement annuity described in section 408(b) (or a trust, plan, account, or annuity which, at any time, has been determined by the Secretary to be such a trust, plan, or account).

- **1986, Tax Reform Act of 1986 (P.L. 99-514)**

P.L. 99-514, § 1854(f)(3)(A):

Amended Code Sec. 4975(e)(7) by inserting ", section 409(o), and, if applicable, section 409(n)" after "section 409(h)". **Effective** as if included in the provision of P.L. 98-369 to which it relates.

- **1984, Deficit Reduction Act of 1984 (P.L. 98-369)**

P.L. 98-369, § 491(d)(46):

Amended Code Sec. 4975(e)(1) by striking out "or 405(a)", by striking out "or a retirement bond described in section 409", by striking out "annuity, or bond" and inserting in lieu thereof "or annuity", and by striking out "account, or bond" and inserting in lieu thereof "or account". **Effective** for obligations issued after 12-31-83.

P.L. 98-369, § 491(e)(7):

Amended Code Sec. 4975(e)(7) by striking out "section 409A(h)" and inserting in lieu thereof "section 409(h)", by striking out "section 409A(e)(4)" and inserting in lieu thereof "section 409(e)(4)", and by striking out "section 409A(e)" and inserting in lieu thereof "section 409(e)". **Effective** 1-1-84.

P.L. 98-369, §491(e)(8):

Amended Code Sec. 4975(e)(8) by striking out "section 409A(1)" and inserting in lieu thereof "section 409(l)".

- **1980, Multiemployer Pension Plan Amendments Act of 1980 (P.L. 96-364)**

P.L. 96-364, §209(b):

Amended Code Sec. 4975(e) by adding at the end thereof paragraph (9). **Effective** for tax years ending after 9-26-80.

- **1980, Technical Corrections Act of 1979 (P.L. 96-222)**

P.L. 96-222, §101(a)(7)(B):

Amended Act Sec. 141 of P.L. 95-600 by adding paragraph (h) to provide **effective** dates for the amendments of Code Secs. 4975(d)(3) and 4975(e)(7). For the text of paragraph (h), see the amendment note for Code Sec. 4975(d).

P.L. 96-222, §101(a)(7)(C):

Amended Code Sec. 4975(e)(8) by changing the first sentence. **Effective** for stock acquired after 12-31-79. Prior to amendment, the first sentence of Code Sec. 4975(e)(8) read as follows:

(8) QUALIFYING EMPLOYER SECURITY.—The term "qualifying employer security" means an employer security which is—

(A) stock or otherwise an equity security, or

(B) a bond, debenture, note, or certificate or other evidence of indebtedness which is described in paragraphs (1), (2), and (3) of section 503(e)."

P.L. 96-222, §101(a)(7)(K):

Amended Code Sec. 4975(e) by striking out the last sentence and adding a new sentence. For the **effective** date, see the amendment note at §101(a)(7)(B), P.L. 96-222, following the text of Code Sec. 4975(e). Prior to amendment, the last sentence read as follows:

A plan shall not be treated as a leveraged employee stock ownership plan unless it meets the requirements of subsections (e) and (h) of section 409A.

P.L. 96-222, §101(a)(7)(L)(iv)(III):

Amended Code Sec. 4975(e)(7) (other than in the paragraph heading) by striking out "leveraged employee stock ownership plan" and inserting "employee stock ownership plan". **Effective** for tax years beginning after 12-31-78.

P.L. 96-222, §101(a)(7)(L)(v)(XI):

Amended the paragraph heading of Code Sec. 4975(e)(7) by striking out "LEVERAGED EMPLOYEE STOCK OWNERSHIP PLAN" and inserting "EMPLOYEE STOCK OWNERSHIP PLAN". **Effective** for tax years beginning after 12-31-78.

- **1978, Revenue Act of 1978 (P.L. 95-600)**

P.L. 95-600, §141(f)(5):

Amended Code Sec. 4975(e)(7). **Effective** with respect to qualified investment for tax years beginning after 12-31-78. Prior to amendment, Code Sec. 4975(e)(7) read as follows:

"(7) EMPLOYEE STOCK OWNERSHIP PLAN.—The term 'employee stock ownership plan' means a defined contribution plan—

"(A) which is a stock bonus plan which is qualified, or a stock bonus and a money purchase plan both of which are qualified under section 401(a) and which are designed to invest primarily in qualifying employer securities; and

"(B) which is otherwise defined in regulations prescribed by the Secretary."

- **1976, Tax Reform Act of 1976 (P.L. 94-455)**

P.L. 94-455, §1906(b)(13)(A):

Amended 1954 Code by substituting "Secretary" for "Secretary or his delegate" each place it appeared. **Effective** 2-1-77.

[Sec. 4975(f)]

(f) OTHER DEFINITIONS AND SPECIAL RULES.—For purposes of this section—

(1) JOINT AND SEVERAL LIABILITY.—If more than one person is liable under subsection (a) or (b) with respect to any one prohibited transaction, all such persons shall be jointly and severally liable under such subsection with respect to such transaction.

(2) TAXABLE PERIOD.—The term "taxable period" means, with respect to any prohibited transaction, the period beginning with the date on which the prohibited transaction occurs and ending on the earliest of—

(A) the date of mailing a notice of deficiency with respect to the tax imposed by subsection (a) under section 6212,

(B) the date on which the tax imposed by subsection (a) is assessed, or

(C) the date on which correction of the prohibited transaction is completed.

(3) SALE OR EXCHANGE; ENCUMBERED PROPERTY.—A transfer of real or personal property by a disqualified person to a plan shall be treated as a sale or exchange if the property is subject to a mortgage or similar lien which the plan assumes or if it is subject to a mortgage or similar lien which a disqualified person placed on the property within the 10-year period ending on the date of the transfer.

(4) AMOUNT INVOLVED.—The term "amount involved" means, with respect to a prohibited transaction, the greater of the amount of money and the fair market value of the other property given or the amount of money and the fair market value of the other property received; except that, in the case of services described in paragraphs (2) and (10) of subsection (d) the amount involved shall be only the excess compensation. For purposes of the preceding sentence, the fair market value—

(A) in the case of the tax imposed by subsection (a), shall be determined as of the date on which the prohibited transaction occurs; and

(B) in the case of the tax imposed by subsection (b), shall be the highest fair market value during the taxable period.

(5) CORRECTION.—The terms "correction" and "correct" mean, with respect to a prohibited transaction, undoing the transaction to the extent possible, but in any case placing the plan in a financial position not worse than that in which it would be if the disqualified person were acting under the highest fiduciary standards.

(6) EXEMPTIONS NOT TO APPLY TO CERTAIN TRANSACTIONS.—

(A) IN GENERAL.—In the case of a trust described in section 401(a) which is part of a plan providing contributions or benefits for employees some or all of whom are owner-employees (as defined in section 401(c)(3)), the exemptions provided by subsection (d) (other than paragraphs (9) and (12)) shall not apply to a transaction in which the plan directly or indirectly—

(i) lends any part of the corpus or income of the plan to,

(ii) pays any compensation for personal services rendered to the plan to, or

(iii) acquires for the plan any property from, or sells any property to,

any such owner-employee, a member of the family (as defined in section 267(c)(4)) of any such owner-employee, or a corporation in which any such owner-employee owns, directly or indirectly, 50 percent or more of the total combined voting power of all classes of stock entitled to vote or 50 percent or more of the total value of shares of all classes of stock of the corporation.

(B) SPECIAL RULES FOR SHAREHOLDER-EMPLOYEES, ETC.—

(i) IN GENERAL.—For purposes of subparagraph (A), the following shall be treated as owner-employees:

(I) A shareholder-employee.

(II) A participant or beneficiary of an individual retirement plan (as defined in section 7701(a)(37)).

(III) An employer or association of employees which establishes such an individual retirement plan under section 408(c).

(ii) EXCEPTION FOR CERTAIN TRANSACTIONS INVOLVING SHAREHOLDER-EMPLOYEES.—Subparagraph (A)(iii) shall not apply to a transaction which consists of a sale of employer securities to an employee stock ownership plan (as defined in subsection (e)(7)) by a shareholder-employee, a member of the family (as defined in section 267(c)(4)) of such shareholder-employee, or a corporation in which such a shareholder-employee owns stock representing a 50 percent or greater interest described in subparagraph (A).

(iii) LOAN EXCEPTION.—For purposes of subparagraph (A)(i), the term "owner-employee" shall only include a person described in subclause (II) or (III) of clause (i).

(C) SHAREHOLDER-EMPLOYEE.—For purposes of subparagraph (B), the term "shareholder-employee" means an employee or officer of an S corporation who owns (or is considered as owning within the meaning of section 318(a)(1)) more than 5 percent of the outstanding stock of the corporation on any day during the taxable year of such corporation.

EXCISE TAXES—QUALIFIED PENSION, ETC., PLANS

(7) S CORPORATION REPAYMENT OF LOANS FOR QUALIFYING EMPLOYER SECURITIES.—A plan shall not be treated as violating the requirements of section 401 or 409 or subsection (e)(7), or as engaging in a prohibited transaction for purposes of subsection (d)(3), merely by reason of any distribution (as described in section 1368(a)) with respect to S corporation stock that constitutes qualifying employer securities, which in accordance with the plan provisions is used to make payments on a loan described in subsection (d)(3) the proceeds of which were used to acquire such qualifying employer securities (whether or not allocated to participants). The preceding sentence shall not apply in the case of a distribution which is paid with respect to any employer security which is allocated to a participant unless the plan provides that employer securities with a fair market value of not less than the amount of such distribution are allocated to such participant for the year which (but for the preceding sentence) such distribution would have been allocated to such participant.

(8) PROVISION OF INVESTMENT ADVICE TO PARTICIPANT AND BENEFICIARIES.—

(A) IN GENERAL.—The prohibitions provided in subsection (c) shall not apply to transactions described in subsection (d)(17) if the investment advice provided by a fiduciary adviser is provided under an eligible investment advice arrangement.

(B) ELIGIBLE INVESTMENT ADVICE ARRANGEMENT.—For purposes of this paragraph, the term "eligible investment advice arrangement" means an arrangement—

(i) which either—

(I) provides that any fees (including any commission or other compensation) received by the fiduciary adviser for investment advice or with respect to the sale, holding, or acquisition of any security or other property for purposes of investment of plan assets do not vary depending on the basis of any investment option selected, or

(II) uses a computer model under an investment advice program meeting the requirements of subparagraph (C) in connection with the provision of investment advice by a fiduciary adviser to a participant or beneficiary, and

(ii) with respect to which the requirements of subparagraphs (D), (E), (F), (G), (H), and (I) are met.

(C) INVESTMENT ADVICE PROGRAM USING COMPUTER MODEL.—

(i) IN GENERAL.—An investment advice program meets the requirements of this subparagraph if the requirements of clauses (ii), (iii), and (iv) are met.

(ii) COMPUTER MODEL.—The requirements of this clause are met if the investment advice provided under the investment advice program is provided pursuant to a computer model that—

(I) applies generally accepted investment theories that take into account the historic returns of different asset classes over defined periods of time,

(II) utilizes relevant information about the participant, which may include age, life expectancy, retirement age, risk tolerance, other assets or sources of income, and preferences as to certain types of investments,

(III) utilizes prescribed objective criteria to provide asset allocation portfolios comprised of investment options available under the plan,

(IV) operates in a manner that is not biased in favor of investments offered by the fiduciary adviser or a person with a material affiliation or contractual relationship with the fiduciary adviser, and

(V) takes into account all investment options under the plan in specifying how a participant's account balance should be invested and is not inappropriately weighted with respect to any investment option.

(iii) CERTIFICATION.—

(I) IN GENERAL.—The requirements of this clause are met with respect to any investment advice program if an eligible investment expert certifies, prior to the utilization of the computer model and in accordance with rules prescribed by the Secretary of Labor, that the computer model meets the requirements of clause (ii).

(II) RENEWAL OF CERTIFICATIONS.—If, as determined under regulations prescribed by the Secretary of Labor, there are material modifications to a computer model, the requirements of this clause are met only if a certification described in subclause (I) is obtained with respect to the computer model as so modified.

(III) ELIGIBLE INVESTMENT EXPERT.—The term "eligible investment expert" means any person which meets such requirements as the Secretary of Labor may provide and which does not bear any material affiliation or contractual relationship with any investment adviser or a related person thereof (or any employee, agent, or registered representative of the investment adviser or related person).

(iv) EXCLUSIVITY OF RECOMMENDATION.—The requirements of this clause are met with respect to any investment advice program if—

(I) the only investment advice provided under the program is the advice generated by the computer model described in clause (ii), and

(II) any transaction described in subsection (d)(17)(A)(ii) occurs solely at the direction of the participant or beneficiary.

Nothing in the preceding sentence shall preclude the participant or beneficiary from requesting investment advice other than that described in clause (i), but only if such request has not been solicited by any person connected with carrying out the arrangement.

(D) EXPRESS AUTHORIZATION BY SEPARATE FIDUCIARY.—The requirements of this subparagraph are met with respect to an arrangement if the arrangement is expressly authorized by a plan fiduciary other than the person offering the investment advice program, any person providing investment options under the plan, or any affiliate of either.

(E) AUDITS.—

(i) IN GENERAL.—The requirements of this subparagraph are met if an independent auditor, who has appropriate technical training or experience and proficiency and so represents in writing—

(I) conducts an annual audit of the arrangement for compliance with the requirements of this paragraph, and

(II) following completion of the annual audit, issues a written report to the fiduciary who authorized use of the arrangement which presents its specific findings regarding compliance of the arrangement with the requirements of this paragraph.

(ii) SPECIAL RULE FOR INDIVIDUAL RETIREMENT AND SIMILAR PLANS.—In the case of a plan described in subparagraphs (B) through (F) (and so much of subparagraph (G) as relates to such subparagraphs) of subsection (e)(1), in lieu of the requirements of clause (i), audits of the arrangement shall be conducted at such times and in such manner as the Secretary of Labor may prescribe.

(iii) INDEPENDENT AUDITOR.—For purposes of this subparagraph, an auditor is considered independent if it is not related to the person offering the arrangement to the plan and is not related to any person providing investment options under the plan.

(F) DISCLOSURE.—The requirements of this subparagraph are met if—

(i) the fiduciary adviser provides to a participant or a beneficiary before the initial provision of the investment advice with regard to any security or other property offered as an investment option, a written notification (which may consist of notification by means of electronic communication)—

(I) of the role of any party that has a material affiliation or contractual relationship with the fiduciary adviser in the development of the investment advice program and in the selection of investment options available under the plan,

(II) of the past performance and historical rates of return of the investment options available under the plan,

(III) of all fees or other compensation relating to the advice that the fiduciary adviser or any affiliate thereof is to receive (including compensation provided by any third party) in connection with the provision of the advice or in connection with the sale, acquisition, or holding of the security or other property,

(IV) of any material affiliation or contractual relationship of the fiduciary adviser or affiliates thereof in the security or other property,

(V) of the manner, and under what circumstances, any participant or beneficiary information provided under the arrangement will be used or disclosed,

(VI) of the types of services provided by the fiduciary adviser in connection with the provision of investment advice by the fiduciary adviser,

(VII) that the adviser is acting as a fiduciary of the plan in connection with the provision of the advice, and

(VIII) that a recipient of the advice may separately arrange for the provision of advice by another adviser, that could have no material affiliation with and receive no fees or other compensation in connection with the security or other property, and

(ii) at all times during the provision of advisory services to the participant or beneficiary, the fiduciary adviser—

(I) maintains the information described in clause (i) in accurate form and in the manner described in subparagraph (H),

(II) provides, without charge, accurate information to the recipient of the advice no less frequently than annually,

(III) provides, without charge, accurate information to the recipient of the advice upon request of the recipient, and

(IV) provides, without charge, accurate information to the recipient of the advice concerning any material change to the information required to be provided to the recipient of the advice at a time reasonably contemporaneous to the change in information.

(G) OTHER CONDITIONS.—The requirements of this subparagraph are met if—

(i) the fiduciary adviser provides appropriate disclosure, in connection with the sale, acquisition, or holding of the security or other property, in accordance with all applicable securities laws,

(ii) the sale, acquisition, or holding occurs solely at the direction of the recipient of the advice,

(iii) the compensation received by the fiduciary adviser and affiliates thereof in connection with the sale, acquisition, or holding of the security or other property is reasonable, and

(iv) the terms of the sale, acquisition, or holding of the security or other property are at least as favorable to the plan as an arm's length transaction would be.

(H) STANDARDS FOR PRESENTATION OF INFORMATION.—

(i) IN GENERAL.—The requirements of this subparagraph are met if the notification required to be provided to participants and beneficiaries under subparagraph (F)(i) is written in a clear and conspicuous manner and in a manner calculated to be understood by the average plan participant and is sufficiently accurate and comprehensive to reasonably apprise such participants and beneficiaries of the information required to be provided in the notification.

(ii) MODEL FORM FOR DISCLOSURE OF FEES AND OTHER COMPENSATION.—The Secretary of Labor shall issue a model form for the disclosure of fees and other compensation required in subparagraph (F)(i)(III) which meets the requirements of clause (i).

(I) MAINTENANCE FOR 6 YEARS OF EVIDENCE OF COMPLIANCE.—The requirements of this subparagraph are met if a fiduciary adviser who has provided advice referred to in subparagraph (A) maintains, for a period of not less than 6 years after the provision of the advice, any records necessary for determining whether the requirements of the preceding provisions of this paragraph and of subsection (d)(17) have been met. A transaction prohibited under subsection (c) shall not be considered to have occurred solely because the records are lost or destroyed prior to the end of the 6-year period due to circumstances beyond the control of the fiduciary adviser.

(J) DEFINITIONS.—For purposes of this paragraph and subsection (d)(17)—

(i) FIDUCIARY ADVISER.—The term "fiduciary adviser" means, with respect to a plan, a person who is a fiduciary of the plan by reason of the provision of investment advice referred to in subsection (e)(3)(B) by the person to a participant or beneficiary of the plan and who is—

(I) registered as an investment adviser under the Investment Advisers Act of 1940 (15 U.S.C. 80b-1 et seq.) or under the laws of the State in which the fiduciary maintains its principal office and place of business,

(II) a bank or similar financial institution referred to in subsection (d)(4) or a savings association (as defined in section 3(b)(1) of the Federal Deposit Insurance Act (12 U.S.C. 1813(b)(1)), but only if the advice is provided through a trust department of the bank or similar financial institution or savings association which is subject to periodic examination and review by Federal or State banking authorities,

(III) an insurance company qualified to do business under the laws of a State,

(IV) a person registered as a broker or dealer under the Securities Exchange Act of 1934 (15 U.S.C. 78a et seq.),

(V) an affiliate of a person described in any of subclauses (I) through (IV), or

(VI) an employee, agent, or registered representative of a person described in subclauses (I) through (V) who satisfies the requirements of applicable insurance, banking, and securities laws relating to the provision of the advice.

For purposes of this title, a person who develops the computer model described in subparagraph (C)(ii) or markets the investment advice program or computer model shall be treated as a person who is a fiduciary of the plan by reason of the provision of investment advice referred to in subsection (e)(3)(B) to a participant or beneficiary and shall be treated as a fiduciary adviser for purposes of this paragraph and subsection (d)(17), except that the Secretary of Labor may prescribe rules under which only 1 fiduciary adviser may elect to be treated as a fiduciary with respect to the plan.

(ii) AFFILIATE.—The term "affiliate" of another entity means an affiliated person of the entity (as defined in section 2(a)(3) of the Investment Company Act of 1940 (15 U.S.C. 80a-2(a)(3))).

(iii) REGISTERED REPRESENTATIVE.—The term "registered representative" of another entity means a person described in section 3(a)(18) of the Securities Exchange Act of 1934 (15 U.S.C. 78c(a)(18)) (substituting the entity for the broker or dealer referred to in such section) or a person described in section 202(a)(17) of the Investment Advisers Act of 1940 (15 U.S.C. 80b-2(a)(17)) (substituting the entity for the investment adviser referred to in such section).

(9) BLOCK TRADE.—The term "block trade" means any trade of at least 10,000 shares or with a market value of at least $200,000 which will be allocated across two or more unrelated client accounts of a fiduciary.

(10) ADEQUATE CONSIDERATION.—The term "adequate consideration" means—

(A) in the case of a security for which there is a generally recognized market—

(i) the price of the security prevailing on a national securities exchange which is registered under section 6 of the Securities Exchange Act of 1934, taking into account factors such as the size of the transaction and marketability of the security, or

(ii) if the security is not traded on such a national securities exchange, a price not less favorable to the plan than the offering price for the security as established by the current bid and asked prices quoted by persons independent of the issuer and of the party in interest, taking into account factors such as the size of the transaction and marketability of the security, and

(B) in the case of an asset other than a security for which there is a generally recognized market, the fair market value of the asset as determined in good faith by a fiduciary or fiduciaries in accordance with regulations prescribed by the Secretary of Labor.

(11) CORRECTION PERIOD.—

(A) IN GENERAL.—For purposes of subsection (d)(23), the term "correction period" means the 14-day period beginning on the date on which the disqualified person discovers, or reasonably should have discovered, that the transaction would (without regard to this paragraph and subsection (d)(23)) constitute a prohibited transaction.

(B) EXCEPTIONS.—

(i) EMPLOYER SECURITIES.—Subsection (d)(23) does not apply to any transaction between a plan and a plan sponsor or its affiliates that involves the acquisition or sale of an employer security (as defined in section 407(d)(1) of the Employee Retirement Income Security Act of 1974) or the acquisition, sale, or lease of employer real property (as defined in section 407(d)(2) of such Act).

(ii) KNOWING PROHIBITED TRANSACTION.—In the case of any disqualified person, subsection (d)(23) does not apply to a transaction if, at the time the transaction is entered into, the disqualified person knew (or reasonably should have known) that the transaction would (without regard to this paragraph) constitute a prohibited transaction.

(C) ABATEMENT OF TAX WHERE THERE IS A CORRECTION.—If a transaction is not treated as a prohibited transaction by reason of subsection (d)(23), then no tax under subsection (a) and (b) shall be assessed with respect to such transaction, and if assessed the assessment shall be abated, and if collected shall be credited or refunded as an overpayment.

(D) DEFINITIONS.—For purposes of this paragraph and subsection (d)(23)—

(i) SECURITY.—The term "security" has the meaning given such term by section 475(c)(2) (without regard to subparagraph (F)(iii) and the last sentence thereof).

(ii) COMMODITY.—The term "commodity" has the meaning given such term by section 475(e)(2) (without regard to subparagraph (D)(iii) thereof).

(iii) CORRECT.—The term "correct" means, with respect to a transaction—

(I) to undo the transaction to the extent possible and in any case to make good to the plan or affected account any losses resulting from the transaction, and

(II) to restore to the plan or affected account any profits made through the use of assets of the plan.

(12) RULES RELATING TO AUTOMATIC PORTABILITY TRANSACTIONS.—

(A) IN GENERAL.—For purposes of subsection (d)(25)—

(i) AUTOMATIC PORTABILITY TRANSACTION.—An automatic portability transaction is a transfer of assets made—

(I) from an individual retirement plan which is established on behalf of an individual and to which amounts were transferred under section 401(a)(31)(B)(i),

(II) to an employer-sponsored retirement plan described in clause (iii), (iv), (v), or (vi) of section 402(c)(8)(B) (other than a defined benefit plan) in which such individual is an active participant, and

(III) after such individual has been given advance notice of the transfer and has not affirmatively opted out of such transfer.

(ii) AUTOMATIC PORTABILITY PROVIDER.—An automatic portability provider is a person, other than an individual, who executes transfers described in clause (i).

(B) CONDITIONS FOR AUTOMATIC PORTABILITY TRANSACTIONS.—Subsection (d)(25) shall not apply to an automatic portability transaction unless the following requirements are satisfied:

(i) ACKNOWLEDGMENT OF FIDUCIARY STATUS.—An automatic portability provider shall acknowledge in writing, at such time and format as specified by the Secretary of Labor, that the provider is a fiduciary with respect to the individual retirement plan described in subparagraph (A)(i)(I).

(ii) FEES.—The fees and compensation received, directly or indirectly, by the automatic portability provider for services provided in connection with the automatic portability transaction (including any increase in such fees or compensation and any fees or compensation in connection with, but received before, the transaction)—

(I) shall not exceed reasonable compensation, and

(II) shall be fully disclosed to and approved in writing in advance of the transaction by a plan fiduciary of the plan described in subparagraph (A)(i)(II) which is independent of the automatic portability provider.

An automatic portability provider shall not receive any fees or compensation in connection with an automatic portability transaction involving a plan which is sponsored or maintained by the automatic portability provider.

(iii) DATA USAGE.—The automatic portability provider shall not market or sell data relating to the individual retirement plan described in subparagraph (A)(i)(I) or to the participants of the plan described in subparagraph (A)(i)(II).

(iv) OPEN PARTICIPATION.—The automatic portability provider shall offer automatic portability transactions on the same terms to any plan described in subparagraph (A)(i)(II).

(v) PRE-TRANSACTION NOTICE.—At least 60 days in advance of an automatic portability transaction, the automatic portability provider shall provide notice to the individual on whose behalf the individual retirement plan described in subparagraph (A)(i)(I) is established which includes—

(I) a description of the automatic portability transaction and a complete and accurate statement of all fees which will be charged and all compensation which will be received in connection with the transaction,

(II) a clear and prominent description of the individual's right to affirmatively elect not to participate in the transaction as well as the other available distribution options, the deadline by which the individual must make an election, the procedures for such an election, and a telephone number for the automatic portability provider that the individual may call to make such election,

(III) a description of the individual's right to designate a beneficiary and the procedures to do so, and

(IV) such other disclosures as the Secretary of Labor may require by regulation.

(vi) POST-TRANSACTION NOTICE.—Not later than 3 business days after an automatic portability transaction, the automatic portability provider shall provide notice to the individual on whose behalf the individual retirement plan described in subparagraph (A)(i)(I) is established of—

EXCISE TAXES—QUALIFIED PENSION, ETC., PLANS

(I) the actions taken by the automatic portability provider with respect to the individual's account,

(II) all relevant information regarding the location and amount of any transferred assets,

(III) a statement of fees charged against the account by the automatic portability provider or its affiliates in connection with the transfer,

(IV) a telephone number at which the individual can contact the automatic portability provider, and

(V) such other disclosures as the Secretary of Labor may require by regulation.

(vii) NOTICE REQUIREMENTS.—The notices required under clauses (v) and (vi) shall be written in a manner calculated to be understood by the average person and shall not include inaccurate or misleading statements.

(viii) FREQUENCY OF SEARCHES.—The automatic portability provider shall query on at least a monthly basis whether any individual with an individual retirement plan described in subparagraph (A)(i)(I) has an account in a plan described in subparagraph (A)(i)(II).

(ix) TIMELINESS OF EXECUTION.—After liquidating the assets of an individual retirement plan described in subparagraph (A)(i)(I) to cash, an automatic portability provider shall transfer the account balance of such plan as soon as practicable to the plan described in subparagraph (A)(i)(II).

(x) LIMITATION ON EXERCISE OF DISCRETION.—The automatic portability provider shall neither have nor exercise discretion to affect the timing or amount of the transfer pursuant to an automatic portability transaction other than to deduct the appropriate fees as described in clause (ii).

(xi) RECORD RETENTION AND AUDITS.—

(I) IN GENERAL.—An automatic portability provider shall, for not less than 6 years after the automatic portability transaction has occurred, maintain the records sufficient to demonstrate the terms of this subparagraph have been met. The automatic portability provider shall make such records available to any authorized employee of the Department of the Treasury or the Department of Labor within 30 calendar days of the date of a written request for such records.

(II) AUDITS.—An automatic portability provider shall conduct an annual audit, in accordance with regulations promulgated by the Secretary of Labor, of automatic portability transactions occurring during the calendar year to demonstrate compliance with this paragraph and any regulations thereunder and identify any instances of noncompliance therewith, and shall submit such audit annually to the Secretary of Labor, in such form and manner as specified by such Secretary.

(xii) WEBSITE.—The automatic portability provider shall maintain a website which contains—

(I) a list of recordkeepers for each plan described in subparagraph (A)(i)(II) with respect to which the provider carries out automatic portability transactions, and

(II) a list of all fees described in clause (ii)(II) paid to the provider.

Amendments

- **2022, SECURE 2.0 Act of 2022 (P.L. 117-328)**

P.L. 117-328, §120(b):

Amended Code Sec. 4975(f) by adding at the end a new paragraph (12). **Effective** for transactions occurring on or after the date which is 12 months after 12-29-2022. For a special rule, see Act Sec. 120(c)-(d), below.

P.L. 117-328, §120(c)-(d), provides:

(c) REGULATORY AUTHORITY.—Not later than 12 months after the date of the enactment of this Act, the Secretary of Labor shall issue such guidance as may be necessary to carry out the purposes of the amendments made by this section, including regulations or other guidance which—

(1) require an automatic portability provider to provide a notice to individuals on whose behalf the individual retirement plan described in paragraph (12)(A)(i)(I) of section 4975(f) of the Internal Revenue Code of 1986, as added by this section, is established in advance of the notices specified in paragraph (12)(B)(v) of such section, as so added,

(2) require an automatic portability provider to disclose to plans described in paragraph (12)(A)(i)(II) of section 4975(f) of the Internal Revenue Code of 1986, as added by this section, information required to be provided by a covered service provider pursuant to section 2550.408b-2(c) of title 29, Code of Federal Regulations,

(3) require a plan described in such paragraph (12)(A)(i)(II), as so added, to fully disclose fees related to an automatic portability transaction in its summary plan description or summary of material modifications, as relevant,

(4) require a plan described in such paragraph, as so added, to invest amounts received on behalf of a participant pursuant to an automatic portability transaction in the participant's current investment election under the plan or, if no election is made or permitted, in the plan's qualified default investment alternative (within the meaning of section 2550.404c-5 of title 29, Code of Federal Regulations) or another investment selected by a fiduciary with respect to such plan,

(5) prohibit or restrict the receipt or payment of third party compensation (other than a direct fee paid by a plan sponsor which is in lieu of a fee imposed on an individual retirement plan owner) by an automatic portability provider in connection with an automatic portability transaction,

(6) prohibit exculpatory provisions in an automatic portability provider's contracts or communications with individuals disclaiming or limiting its liability in the event that an automatic portability transaction results in an improper transfer,

(7) require an automatic portability provider to take actions necessary to reasonably ensure that participant and beneficiary data is current and accurate,

(8) limit the use of data related to automatic portability transactions for any purpose other than the execution of such transactions or locating missing participants, except as permitted by the Secretary of Labor,

(9) provide for corrections procedures in the event an auditor determines the automatic portability provider was not in compliance with this provision and related regulations as specified in paragraph (12)(B)(ix)(II) of section 4975(f) of such Code, as so added, including deadlines, supplemental audits, and corrective actions which may include a temporary prohibition from relying on the exemption provided by paragraph (25) of section 4975(d) of such Code, as added by this section,

(10) ensure that the appropriate participants and beneficiaries, in fact, receive all the required notices and disclosures, and

(11) make clear that the exemption provided by paragraph (25) of section 4975(d) of such Code, as added by this section, applies solely to the automatic portability transactions described therein, and, to the extent the Secretary deems necessary or advisable, specify how the application of the exemption relates to or coordinates with the application of other statutory provisions, regulations, administrative guidance, or exemptions.

Any term used in this subsection which is used in paragraph (12) of section 4975(f) of such Code, as added by this section, has the same meaning as when used in such paragraph.

(d) REPORT TO CONGRESS.—

(1) IN GENERAL.—Not later than 2 years after the date of the first audit report received by the Secretary of Labor from any automatic portability provider, and every 3 years thereafter, the Secretary of Labor shall report to the Committees on Health, Education, Labor and Pensions and Finance of the Senate and the Committees on Education and Labor and Ways and Means of the House of Representatives on—

(A) the effectiveness of automatic portability transactions under the exemption provided by paragraph (25) of section 4975(d) of the Internal Revenue Code of 1986, as added by this section, detailing—

(i) the number of automatic cash outs from qualified plans to individual retirement plans described in section 4975(f)(12)(A)(i)(I) of such Code,

(ii) the number of completed automatic portability transactions to employer-sponsored retirement plans described in section 4975(f)(12)(A)(i)(II) of such Code,

(iii) the number of individual retirement plans described in section 4975(f)(12)(A)(i)(I) of such Code which have been transferred to designated beneficiaries,

(iv) the number of individual retirement plans described in section 4975(f)(12)(A)(i)(I) of such Code for which the automatic portability provider is searching for next of kin due to a deceased account holder without a designated beneficiary, and

(v) the number of accounts that were reduced to a zero balance while in the automatic portability provider's custody;

(B) a summary of any consumer complaints submitted to the Employee Benefits Security Administration regarding automatic portability transactions;

(C) a summary of compliance issues found in the annual audit described in section 4975(f)(12)(B)(xiii)(II) of such Code, if any, and their corrections;

(D) a summary of the fees individuals are charged in connection with automatic portability transactions, including whether those fees have increased since the last report;

(E) recommendations of any necessary statutory changes to this exemption to improve the effectiveness of automatic portability transactions, including repeal of this provision in the event of a pattern of noncompliance; and

(F) any other information the Secretary of Labor deems important.

The report required by this subsection shall be made publicly available.

(2) REPORT ON NOTICES RELATING TO AUTOMATIC TRANSFERS.—Not later than 2 years after the date of the enactment of this Act, the Secretary of Treasury shall report to the Committee on Finance of the Senate and the Committee on Ways and Means on the adequacy of the notices relating to transfers under section 401(a)(31)(B)(i) of the Internal Revenue Code of 1986.

- **2018, Tax Technical Corrections Act of 2018 (P.L. 115-141)**

P.L. 115-141, §401(a)(232), Div. U:

Amended Code Sec. 4975(f)(8)(C)(iv)(II) by inserting "subsection" before "(d)(17)(A)(ii)". **Effective** 3-23-2018.

EXCISE TAXES—QUALIFIED PENSION, ETC., PLANS

P.L. 115-141, § 401(a)(233), Div. U:

Amended Code Sec. 4975(f)(8)(F)(i)(I) by striking "adviser," and inserting "adviser". **Effective** 3-23-2018.

P.L. 115-141, § 401(a)(234), Div. U:

Amended Code Sec. 4975(f)(8)(F)(i)(V) by inserting "of" before "the manner". **Effective** 3-23-2018.

• **2008, Worker, Retiree, and Employer Recovery Act of 2008 (P.L. 110-458)**

P.L. 110-458, § 106(a)(2)(B)(i)-(v):

Amended Code Sec. 4975(f)(8) by striking "subsection (b)(14)" and inserting "subsection (d)(17)" in subparagraph (A), by striking "subsection (b)(14)(B)(ii)" and inserting "(d)(17)(A)(ii)" in subparagraph (C)(iv)(II), by striking "financial adviser" and inserting "fiduciary adviser," in subparagraph (F)(i)(I), by striking "section 406" and inserting "subsection (c)" in subparagraph (I), and by striking "the participant" each place it appears in subparagraph (J)(i) and inserting "a participant", by inserting "referred to in subsection (e)(3)(B)" after "investment advice" in the matter preceding subparagraph (J)(i)(I), and by striking "section 408(b)(4)" and inserting "subsection (d)(4)" in subparagraph (J)(i)(II). **Effective** as if included in the provision of the 2006 Act to which the amendment relates [**effective** with respect to advice referred to in Code Sec. 4975(e)(3)(B) provided after 12-31-2006.—CCH].

P.L. 110-458, § 106(c)(1)-(2):

Amended Code Sec. 4975(f)(11)(B)(i) by inserting "of the Employee Retirement Income Security Act of 1974" after "section 407(d)(1)", and inserting "of such Act" after "section 407(d)(2)". **Effective** as if included in the provision of the 2006 Act to which the amendment relates [**effective** for any transaction which the fiduciary or disqualified person discovers, or reasonably should have discovered, after 8-17-2006 constitutes a prohibited transaction.—CCH].

• **2006, Pension Protection Act of 2006 (P.L. 109-280)**

P.L. 109-280, § 601(b)(2):

Amended Code Sec. 4975(f) by adding at the end a new paragraph (8). **Effective** with respect to advice referred to in Code Sec. 4975(e)(3)(B) provided after 12-31-2006, [effective date amended by P.L. 110-458, § 106(a)(3).—CCH].

P.L. 109-280, § 601(b)(3), provides:

(3) DETERMINATION OF FEASIBILITY OF APPLICATION OF COMPUTER MODEL INVESTMENT ADVICE PROGRAMS FOR INDIVIDUAL RETIREMENT AND SIMILAR PLANS.—

(A) SOLICITATION OF INFORMATION.—As soon as practicable after the date of the enactment of this Act, the Secretary of Labor, in consultation with the Secretary of the Treasury, shall—

(i) solicit information as to the feasibility of the application of computer model investment advice programs for plans described in subparagraphs (B) through (F) (and so much of subparagraph (G) as relates to such subparagraphs) of section 4975(e)(1) of the Internal Revenue Code of 1986, including soliciting information from—

(I) at least the top 50 trustees of such plans, determined on the basis of assets held by such trustees, and

(II) other persons offering computer model investment advice programs based on nonproprietary products, and

(ii) shall on the basis of such information make the determination under subparagraph (B).

The information solicited by the Secretary of Labor under clause (i) from persons described in subclauses (I) and (II) of clause (i) shall include information on computer modeling capabilities of such persons with respect to the current year and preceding year, including such capabilities for investment accounts maintained by such persons.

(B) DETERMINATION OF FEASIBILITY.— The Secretary of Labor, in consultation with the Secretary of the Treasury, shall, on the basis of information received under subparagraph (A), determine whether there is any computer model investment advice program which may be utilized by a plan described in subparagraph (A)(i) to provide investment advice to the account beneficiary of the plan which—

(i) utilizes relevant information about the account beneficiary, which may include age, life expectancy, retirement age, risk tolerance, other assets or sources of income, and preferences as to certain types of investments,

(ii) takes into account the full range of investments, including equities and bonds, in determining the options for the investment portfolio of the account beneficiary, and

(iii) allows the account beneficiary, in directing the investment of assets, sufficient flexibility in obtaining advice to evaluate and select investment options.

The Secretary of Labor shall report the results of such determination to the committees of Congress referred to in subparagraph (D)(ii) not later than December 31, 2007.

(C) APPLICATION OF COMPUTER MODEL INVESTMENT ADVICE PROGRAM.—

(i) CERTIFICATION REQUIRED FOR USE OF COMPUTER MODEL.—

(I) RESTRICTION ON USE.—Subclause (II) of section 4975(f)(8)(B)(i) of the Internal Revenue Code of 1986 shall not apply to a plan described in subparagraph (A)(i).

(II) RESTRICTION LIFTED IF MODEL CERTIFIED.—If the Secretary of Labor determines under subparagraph (B) or (D) that there is a computer model investment advice program described in subparagraph (B), subclause (I) shall cease to apply as of the date of such determination.

(ii) CLASS EXEMPTION IF NO INITIAL CERTIFICATION BY SECRETARY.—If the Secretary of Labor determines under subparagraph (B) that there is no computer model investment advice program described in subparagraph (B), the Secretary of Labor shall grant a class exemption from treatment as a prohibited transaction under section 4975(c) of the Internal Revenue Code of 1986 to any transaction described in section 4975(d)(17)(A) of such Code with respect to plans described in subparagraph (A)(i), subject to such conditions as set forth in such exemption as are in the interests of the plan and its account beneficiary and protective of the rights of the account beneficiary and as are necessary to—

(I) ensure the requirements of sections 4975(d)(17) and 4975(f)(8) (other than subparagraph (C) thereof) of the Internal Revenue Code of 1986 are met, and

(II) ensure the investment advice provided under the investment advice program utilizes prescribed objective criteria to provide asset allocation portfolios comprised of securities or other property available as investments under the plan.

If the Secretary of Labor solicits any information under subparagraph (A) from a person and such person does not provide such information within 60 days after the solicitation, then, unless such failure was due to reasonable cause and not wilful neglect, such person shall not be entitled to utilize the class exemption under this clause.

(D) SUBSEQUENT DETERMINATION.—

(i) IN GENERAL.—If the Secretary of Labor initially makes a determination described in subparagraph (C)(ii), the Secretary may subsequently determine that there is a computer model investment advice program described in subparagraph (B). If the Secretary makes such subsequent determination, then the class exemption described in subparagraph (C)(ii) shall cease to apply after the later of—

(I) the date which is 2 years after such subsequent determination, or

(II) the date which is 3 years after the first date on which such exemption took effect.

(ii) REQUESTS FOR DETERMINATION.—Any person may request the Secretary of Labor to make a determination under this subparagraph with respect to any computer model investment advice program, and the Secretary of Labor shall make a determination with respect to such request within 90 days. If the Secretary of Labor makes a determination that such program is not described in subparagraph (B), the Secretary shall, within 10 days of such determination, notify the Committee on Ways and Means and the Committee on Education and the Workforce of the House of Representatives and the Committee on Finance and the Committee on Health, Education, Labor, and Pensions of the Senate of such determination and the reasons for such determination.

(E) EFFECTIVE DATE.—The provisions of this paragraph shall take effect on the date of the enactment of this Act.

P.L. 109-280, § 611(a)(2)(B):

Amended Code Sec. 4975(f), as amended by Act Sec. 601, by adding at the end a new paragraph (9). **Effective** for transactions occurring after 8-17-2006.

P.L. 109-280, § 611(d)(2)(B):

Amended Code Sec. 4975(f), as amended by Act Sec. 611(a), by adding at the end a new paragraph (10). **Effective** for transactions occurring after 8-17-2006.

P.L. 109-280, § 612(b)(2):

Amended Code Sec. 4975(f), as amended by Act Secs. 601 and 611, by adding at the end a new paragraph (11). **Effective** for any transaction which the fiduciary or disqualified person discovers, or reasonably should have discovered, after 8-17-2006 constitutes a prohibited transaction.

P.L. 109-280, § 811, provides:

SEC. 811. PENSIONS AND INDIVIDUAL RETIREMENT ARRANGEMENT PROVISIONS OF ECONOMIC GROWTH AND TAX RELIEF RECONCILIATION ACT OF 2001 MADE PERMANENT.

Title IX of the Economic Growth and Tax Relief Reconciliation Act of 2001 [P.L. 107-16] shall not apply to the provisions of, and amendments made by, subtitles A through F of title VI [§§ 601-666]of such Act (relating to pension and individual retirement arrangement provisions).

• **2004, American Jobs Creation Act of 2004 (P.L. 108-357)**

P.L. 108-357, § 240(a):

Amended Code Sec. 4975(f) by adding at the end a new paragraph (7). **Effective** for distributions with respect to S corporation stock made after 12-31-97.

• **2001, Economic Growth and Tax Relief Reconciliation Act of 2001 (P.L. 107-16)**

P.L. 107-16, § 612(a):

Amended Code Sec. 4975(f)(6)(B) by adding at the end a new clause (iii). **Effective** for years beginning after 12-31-2001.

P.L. 107-16, § 901(a)-(b), provides [but see P.L. 109-280, § 811, above]:

SEC. 901. SUNSET OF PROVISIONS OF ACT.

(a) IN GENERAL.—All provisions of, and amendments made by, this Act shall not apply—

(1) to taxable, plan, or limitation years beginning after December 31, 2010, or

(2) in the case of title V, to estates of decedents dying, gifts made, or generation skipping transfers, after December 31, 2010.

(b) APPLICATION OF CERTAIN LAWS.—The Internal Revenue Code of 1986 and the Employee Retirement Income Security Act of 1974 shall be applied and administered to years, estates, gifts, and transfers described in subsection (a) as if the provisions and amendments described in subsection (a) had never been enacted.

• **1997, Taxpayer Relief Act of 1997 (P.L. 105-34)**

P.L. 105-34, § 1506(b)(1)(A):

Amended Code Sec. 4975(f) by inserting at the end a new paragraph (6). **Effective** for tax years beginning after 12-31-97.

• **1980 (P.L. 96-596)**

P.L. 96-596, § 2(a)(1):

Amended Code Sec. 4975(f)(4)(B) by striking out "correction period" and inserting in lieu thereof "taxable period". **Effective** with respect to second-tier taxes assessed after 12-24-80 (except in cases where there is a court decision with regard to which res judicata applies on that date).

Sec. 4975(f)(12)(B)(xii)(II)

EXCISE TAXES—QUALIFIED PENSION, ETC., PLANS

P.L. 96-596, § 2(a)(2):

Amended Code Sec. 4975(f)(2). **Effective** with respect to second-tier taxes assessed after 12-24-80 (except in cases where there is a court decision with regard to which res judicata applies on that date). Before amendment, Code Sec. 4975(f)(2) read:

(2) "TAXABLE PERIOD.—the term `taxable period' means, with respect to any prohibited transaction, the period beginning with the date on which the prohibited transaction occurs and ending on the earlier of—

(A) the date of mailing of a notice of deficiency pursuant to section 6212, with respect to the tax imposed by subsection (a), or

(B) the date on which correction of the prohibited transaction is completed."

P.L. 96-596, § 2(a)(3):

Amended Code Sec. 4975(f) by striking out paragraph (6). **Effective** 12-24-80. Prior to amendment, Code Sec. 4975(f)(6) read:

"(6) CORRECTION PERIOD.—The term `correction period' means, with respect to a prohibited transaction, the period beginning with the date on which the prohibited transaction occurs and ending 90 days after the date of mailing of a notice of deficiency with respect to the tax imposed by subsection (b) under section 6212, extended by—

(A) any period in which a deficiency cannot be assessed under section 6213(a), and

(B) any other period which the Secretary determines is reasonable and necessary to bring about the correction of the prohibited transaction."

• **1976, Tax Reform Act of 1976 (P.L. 94-455)**

P.L. 94-455, § 1906(b)(13)(A):

Amended 1954 Code by substituting "Secretary" for "Secretary or his delegate" each place it appeared. **Effective** 2-1-77.

[Sec. 4975(g)]

(g) APPLICATION OF SECTION.—This section shall not apply—

(1) in the case of a plan to which a guaranteed benefit policy (as defined in section 401(b)(2)(B) of the Employee Retirement Income Security Act of 1974) is issued, to any assets of the insurance company, insurance service, or insurance organization merely because of its issuance of such policy;

(2) to a governmental plan (within the meaning of section 414(d)); or

(3) to a church plan (within the meaning of section 414(e)) with respect to which the election provided by section 410(d) has not been made.

In the case of a plan which invests in any security issued by an investment company registered under the Investment Company Act of 1940, the assets of such plan shall be deemed to include such security but shall not, by reason of such investment, be deemed to include any assets of such company.

[Sec. 4975(h)]

(h) NOTIFICATION OF SECRETARY OF LABOR.—Before sending a notice of deficiency with respect to the tax imposed by subsection (a) or (b), the Secretary shall notify the Secretary of Labor and provide him a reasonable opportunity to obtain a correction of the prohibited transaction or to comment on the imposition of such tax.

Amendments

• **1976, Tax Reform Act of 1976 (P.L. 94-455)**

P.L. 94-455, § 1906(b)(13)(A):

Amended 1954 Code by substituting "Secretary" for "Secretary or his delegate" each place it appeared. **Effective** 2-1-77.

[Sec. 4975(i)]

(i) CROSS REFERENCE.—

For provisions concerning coordination procedures between Secretary of Labor and Secretary of the Treasury with respect to application of tax imposed by this section and for authority to waive imposition of the tax imposed by subsection (b), see section 3003 of the Employee Retirement Income Security Act of 1974.

Amendments

• **1998, IRS Restructuring and Reform Act of 1998 (P.L. 105-206)**

P.L. 105-206, § 6023(19)(B):

Amended Code Sec. 4975(i) by striking "Secretary of Treasury" and inserting "Secretary of the Treasury". **Effective** 7-22-98.

• **1974, Employee Retirement Income Security Act of 1974 (P.L. 93-406)**

P.L. 93-406, § 2003(a):

Added Code Sec. 4975.

P.L. 93-406, § 2003(c), provides:

(c) Effective Date and Savings Provisions.—

(1)(A) The amendments made by this section shall take effect on January 1, 1975.

(B) If, before the amendments made by this section take effect, an organization described in section 401(a) of the Internal Revenue Code of 1954 is denied exemption under section 501(a) of such Code by reason of section 503 of such Code, the denial of such exemption shall not apply if the disqualified person elects (in such manner and at such time as the Secretary or his delegate shall by regulations prescribe) to pay, with respect to the prohibited transaction (within the meaning of section 503(b) or (g)) which resulted in such denial of exemption, a tax in the amount and in the manner provided with respect to the tax imposed under section 4975 of such Code. An election made under this subparagraph, once made, shall be irrevocable. The Secretary of the Treasury or his delegate shall prescribe such regulations as may be necessary to carry out the purposes of this subparagraph.

(2) Section 4975 of the Internal Revenue Code of 1954 (relating to tax on prohibited transactions) shall not apply to—

(A) a loan of money or other extension of credit between a plan and a disqualified person under a binding contract in effect on July 1, 1974 (or pursuant to renewals of such a contract), until June 30, 1984, if such loan or other extension of credit remains at least as favorable to the plan as an arm's-length transaction with an unrelated party would be, and if the execution of the contract, the making of the loan, or the extension of credit was not, at the time of such execution, making, or extension, a prohibited transaction (within the meaning of section 503(b) of such Code or the corresponding provisions of prior law);

(B) a lease or joint use of property involving the plan and a disqualified person pursuant to a binding contract in effect on July 1, 1974 (or pursuant to renewals of such a contract), until June 30, 1984, if such lease or joint use remains at least as favorable to the plan as an arm's-length transaction with an unrelated party would be and if the execution of the contract was not, at the time of such execution, a prohibited transaction (within the meaning of section 503(b) of such Code) or the corresponding provisions of prior law;

(C) the sale, exchange, or other disposition of property described in subparagraph (B) between a plan and a disqualified person before June 30, 1984, if—

(i) in the case of a sale, exchange, or other disposition of the property by the plan to the disqualified person, the plan receives an amount which is not less than the fair market value of the property at the time of such disposition; and

(ii) in the case of the acquisition of the property by the plan, the plan pays an amount which is not in excess of the fair market value of the property at the time of such acquisition;

(D) until June 30, 1977, the provision of services to which subparagraphs (A) (B), and (C) do not apply between a plan and a disqualified person (i) under a binding contract in effect on July 1, 1974 (or pursuant to renewals of such contract), or (ii) if the disqualified person ordinarily and customarily furnished such services on June 30, 1974, if such provision of services remains at least as favorable to the plan as an arm's-length transaction with an unrelated party would be and if the provision of services was not, at the time of such provision, a prohibited transaction (within the meaning of section 503(b) of such Code) or the corresponding provisions of prior law; or

(E) the sale, exchange, or other disposition of property which is owned by a plan on June 30, 1974, and all times thereafter, to a disqualified person, if such plan is required to dispose of such property in order to comply with the provisions of section 407(a)(2)(A) (relating to the prohibition against holding excess employer securities and employer real property) of the Employee Retirement Income Security Act of 1974, and if the plan receives not less than adequate consideration. "For the purposes of this paragraph, the term "disqualified person" has the meaning provided by section 4975(e)(2) of the Internal Revenue Code of 1954.

SEC. 4976. TAXES WITH RESPECT TO FUNDED WELFARE BENEFIT PLANS.

[Sec. 4976(a)]

(a) GENERAL RULE.—If—

(1) an employer maintains a welfare benefit fund, and

(2) there is a disqualified benefit provided during any taxable year,

EXCISE TAXES—QUALIFIED PENSION, ETC., PLANS

there is hereby imposed on such employer a tax equal to 100 percent of such disqualified benefit.

[Sec. 4976(b)]

(b) DISQUALIFIED BENEFIT.—For purposes of subsection (a)—

(1) IN GENERAL.—The term "disqualified benefit" means—

(A) any post-retirement medical benefit or life insurance benefit provided with respect to a key employee if a separate account is required to be established for such employee under section 419A(d) and such payment is not from such account,

(B) any post-retirement medical benefit or life insurance benefit provided with respect to an individual in whose favor discrimination is prohibited unless the plan meets the requirements of section 505(b) with respect to such benefit (whether or not such requirements apply to such plan), and

(C) any portion of a welfare benefit fund reverting to the benefit of the employer.

(2) EXCEPTION FOR COLLECTIVE BARGAINING PLANS.—Paragraph (1)(B) shall not apply to any plan maintained pursuant to an agreement between employee representatives and 1 or more employers if the Secretary finds that such agreement is a collective bargaining agreement and that the benefits referred to in paragraph (1)(B) were the subject of good faith bargaining between such employee representatives and such employer or employers.

(3) EXCEPTION FOR NONDEDUCTIBLE CONTRIBUTIONS.—Paragraph (1)(C) shall not apply to any amount attributable to a contribution to the fund which is not allowable as a deduction under section 419 for the taxable year or any prior taxable year (and such contribution shall not be included in any carryover under section 419(d)).

(4) EXCEPTION FOR CERTAIN AMOUNTS CHARGED AGAINST EXISTING RESERVE.—Subparagraphs (A) and (B) of paragraph (1) shall not apply to post-retirement benefits charged against an existing reserve for post-retirement medical or life insurance benefits (as defined in section 512(a)(3)(E)) or charged against the income on such reserve.

Amendments

- **1989 (P.L. 101-140)**

P.L. 101-140, §203(a)(2), provides:

Code Sec. 4976(b)(5) as added by Section 1011B(a)(27)(B) of P.L. 100-647 shall be applied as if the amendment made by such section had not been enacted. **Effective** as if included in section 1151 of P.L. 99-514. Code Sec. 4976(b)(5) as added by Act Sec. 1011B(a)(27)(B) of P.L. 100-647 read as follows:

(5) LIMITATION IN CASE OF BENEFITS TO WHICH SECTION 89 APPLIES.—If section 89 applies to any post-retirement medical benefit or life insurance benefit provided by a fund, the amount of the disqualified benefit under paragraph (1)(B) with respect to such benefit shall not exceed the aggregate excess benefits provided by the plan (as determined under section 89).

- **1988, Technical and Miscellaneous Revenue Act of 1988 (P.L. 100-647)**

P.L. 100-647, §1011B(a)(27)(B):

Amended Code Sec. 4976(b) by adding at the end thereof a new paragraph (5). **Effective** as if included in the provision of P.L. 99-514 to which it relates.

- **1986, Tax Reform Act of 1986 (P.L. 99-514)**

P.L. 99-514, §1851(a)(11):

Amended Code Sec. 4976(b). **Effective** as if included in the provision of P.L. 98-369 to which it relates. Prior to amendment, Code Sec. 4976(b) read as follows:

(b) DISQUALIFIED BENEFIT.—For purposes of subsection (a), the term "disqualified benefit" means—

(1) any medical benefit or life insurance benefit provided with respect to a key employee other than from a separate account established for such owner under section 419A(d), and

(2) any post-retirement medical or life insurance benefit unless the plan meets the requirements of section 505(b)(1) with respect to such benefit, and

(3) any portion of such fund reverting to the benefit of the employer.

[Sec. 4976(c)]

(c) DEFINITION.—For purposes of this section, the terms used in this section shall have the same respective meanings as when used in subpart D of part I of subchapter D of chapter 1.

Amendments

- **1989 (P.L. 101-140)**

P.L. 101-140, §203(a)(2), provides:

Code Sec. 4976(c)-(d) as amended by Section 1011B(a)(27)(A) of P.L. 100-647 shall be applied as if the amendment made by such section had not been enacted. **Effective** as if included in section 1151 of P.L. 99-514. Prior to amendment, Code Sec. 4976(c), as amended by Act Sec. 1011B(a)(27)(A) of P.L. 100-647, read as follows:

(c) TAX ON FUNDED WELFARE BENEFIT FUNDS WHICH INCLUDE DISCRIMINATORY EMPLOYEE BENEFIT PLAN.—

(1) IN GENERAL.—If—

(A) an employer maintains a welfare benefit fund, and

(B) a discriminatory employee benefit plan (within the meaning of section 89) is part of such fund for any testing year (as defined in section 89(j)(13)),

there is hereby imposed on such employer for the taxable year with or within which the plan year ends a tax in the amount determined under paragraph (2).

(2) AMOUNT OF TAX.—The amount of the tax under paragraph (1) shall be equal to the excess (if any) of—

(A) the product of the highest rate of tax imposed by section 11, multiplied by the lesser of—

(i) the aggregate excess benefits (as defined in section 89) for such testing year, or

(ii) the taxable income of the fund for such testing year, over

(B) the amount of tax imposed by chapter 1 on such fund for such plan year.

- **1989 (P.L. 101-136)**

P.L. 101-136, §528 provides:

SEC. 528. No monies appropriated by this Act may be used to implement or enforce section 1151 of the Tax Reform Act of 1986 or the amendments made by such section.

- **1988, Technical and Miscellaneous Revenue Act of 1988 (P.L. 100-647)**

P.L. 100-647, §1011B(a)(27)(A):

Amended Code Sec. 4976 by redesignating subsection (c) as subsection (d) and by inserting after subsection (b) a new subsection (c). **Effective** as if included in the provision of P.L. 99-514 to which it relates.

P.L. 100-647, §3021(a)(1)(C)(i)-(ii):

Amended Code Sec. 4976(c), as added by title I, by striking out "any plan year" in paragraph (1) and inserting in lieu thereof "any testing year (as defined in section 89(j)(13))", and by striking out "such plan year" each place it appears in paragraph (2)(A) and inserting in lieu thereof "such testing year". **Effective** as if included in the amendments made by section 1151 of P.L. 99-514.

- **1984, Deficit Reduction Act of 1984 (P.L. 98-369)**

P.L. 98-369, §511(c)(1):

Added Code Sec. 4976. **Effective** for contributions paid or accrued after 12-31-85, in tax years ending after such date. Special rules appear in Act Sec. 511(e)(2)-(5) following Code Sec. 419.

[Sec. 4977]

SEC. 4977. TAX ON CERTAIN FRINGE BENEFITS PROVIDED BY AN EMPLOYER.

[Sec. 4977(a)]

(a) IMPOSITION OF TAX.—In the case of an employer to whom an election under this section applies for any calendar year, there is hereby imposed a tax for such calendar year equal to 30 percent of the excess fringe benefits.

[Sec. 4977(b)]

(b) EXCESS FRINGE BENEFITS.—For purposes of subsection (a), the term "excess fringe benefits" means, with respect to any calendar year—

(1) the aggregate value of the fringe benefits provided by the employer during the calendar year which were not includible in gross income under paragraphs (1) and (2) of section 132(a), over

(2) 1 percent of the aggregate amount of compensation—

(A) which was paid by the employer during such calendar year to employees, and

(B) was includible in gross income for purposes of chapter 1.

Sec. 4976(b)

EXCISE TAXES—QUALIFIED PENSION, ETC., PLANS

[Sec. 4977(c)]

(c) EFFECT OF ELECTION ON SECTION 132(a).—If—

(1) an election under this section is in effect with respect to an employer for any calendar year, and

(2) at all times on or after January 1, 1984, and before the close of the calendar year involved, substantially all of the employees of the employer were entitled to employee discounts on goods or services provided by the employer in 1 line of business,

for purposes of paragraphs (1) and (2) of section 132(a) (but not for purposes of section 132(h)), all employees of any line of business of the employer which was in existence on January 1, 1984, shall be treated as employees of the line of business referred to in paragraph (2).

Amendments

• **1996, Small Business Job Protection Act of 1996 (P.L. 104-188)**

P.L. 104-188, §1704(t)(66):

Amended Code Sec. 4977(c) by striking "section 132(i)(2)" and inserting "section 132(h)". **Effective** 8-20-96.

• **1993, Omnibus Budget Reconciliation Act of 1993 (P.L. 103-66)**

P.L. 103-66, §13213(d)(3)(D):

Amended Code Sec. 4977(c) by striking "section 132(g)(2)" and inserting "section 132(i)(2)". **Effective** for reimbursements or other payments in respect of expenses incurred after 12-31-93.

• **1986, Tax Reform Act of 1986 (P.L. 99-514)**

P.L. 99-514, §1853(c)(1):

Amended Code Sec. 4977(c)(2). **Effective** as if included in the provision of P.L 98-369 to which it relates. Prior to amendment, Code Sec. 4977(c)(2) read as follows:

(2) as of January 1, 1984, substantially all of the employees of the employer were entitled to employee discounts or services provided by the employer in 1 line of business,

[Sec. 4977(d)]

(d) PERIOD OF ELECTION.—An election under this section shall apply to the calendar year for which made and all subsequent calendar years unless revoked by the employer.

[Sec. 4977(e)]

(e) TREATMENT OF CONTROLLED GROUPS.—All employees treated as employed by a single employer under subsection (b), (c), or (m) of section 414 shall be treated as employed by a single employer for purposes of this section.

Amendments

• **1984, Deficit Reduction Act of 1984 (P.L. 98-369)**

P.L. 98-369, §531(e)(1):

Added Code Sec. 4977. **Effective** 1-1-85.

[Sec. 4977(f)]

(f) SECTION TO APPLY ONLY TO EMPLOYMENT WITHIN THE UNITED STATES.—Except as otherwise provided in regulations, this section shall apply only with respect to employment within the United States.

Amendments

• **1986, Tax Reform Act of 1986 (P.L. 99-514)**

P.L. 99-514, §1853(c)(2):

Amended Code Sec. 4977 by adding at the end thereof new subsection (f). **Effective** as if included in the provision of P.L 98-369 to which it relates. For a special rule, see Act Sec. 1853(c)(3), below.

P.L. 99-514, §1853(c)(3), provides:

(3) For purposes of determining whether the requirements of section 4977(c) of the Internal Revenue Code of 1954 are met in the case of an agricultural cooperative incorporated in 1964, there shall not be taken into account employees of a member of the same controlled group as such cooperative which became a member during July 1980.

[Sec. 4978]

SEC. 4978. TAX ON CERTAIN DISPOSITIONS BY EMPLOYEE STOCK OWNERSHIP PLANS AND CERTAIN COOPERATIVES.

[Sec. 4978(a)]

(a) TAX ON DISPOSITIONS OF SECURITIES TO WHICH SECTION 1042 APPLIES BEFORE CLOSE OF MINIMUM HOLDING PERIOD.—If, during the 3-year period after the date on which the employee stock ownership plan or eligible worker-owned cooperative acquired any qualified securities in a sale to which section 1042 applied or acquired any qualified employer securities in a qualified gratuitous transfer to which section 664(g) applied, such plan or cooperative disposes of any qualified securities and—

(1) the total number of shares held by such plan or cooperative after such disposition is less than the total number of employer securities held immediately after such sale, or

(2) except to the extent provided in regulations, the value of qualified securities held by such plan or cooperative after such disposition is less than 30 percent of the total value of all employer securities as of such disposition (60 percent of the total value of all employer securities as of such disposition in the case of any qualified employer securities acquired in a qualified gratuitous transfer to which section 664(g) applied),

there is hereby imposed a tax on the disposition equal to the amount determined under subsection (b).

Amendments

• **2004, Working Families Tax Relief Act of 2004 (P.L. 108-311)**

P.L. 108-311, §408(a)(23):

Amended Code Sec. 4978(a)(2) by striking "60 percent" and inserting "(60 percent". **Effective** 10-4-2004.

• **1997, Taxpayer Relief Act of 1997 (P.L. 105-34)**

P.L. 105-34, §1530(c)(11)(A)-(B):

Amended Code Sec. 4978(a) by inserting "or acquired any qualified employer securities in a qualified gratuitous transfer to which section 664(g) applied" after "section 1042 applied", and by inserting before the comma at the end of paragraph (2) "60 percent of the total value of all employer securities as of such disposition in the case of any qualified employer securities acquired in a qualified gratuitous transfer to which section 664(g) applied)". **Effective** for transfers made by trusts to, or for the use of, an employee stock ownership plan after 8-5-97.

• **1986, Tax Reform Act of 1986 (P.L. 99-514)**

P.L. 99-514, §1854(e)(1):

Amended Code Sec. 4978(a)(1) by striking out "then" and inserting in lieu thereof "than". **Effective** as if included in the provision of P.L. 98-369 to which it relates.

[Sec. 4978(b)]

(b) AMOUNT OF TAX.—

(1) IN GENERAL.—The amount of the tax imposed by subsection (a) shall be equal to 10 percent of the amount realized on the disposition.

(2) LIMITATION.—The amount realized taken into account under paragraph (1) shall not exceed that portion allocable to qualified securities acquired in the sale to which section 1042 applied or acquired in the qualified gratuitous transfer to which section 664(g) applied determined as if such securities were disposed of—

(A) first from qualified securities to which section 1042 applied or to which section 664(g) applied acquired during the 3-year period ending on the date of the disposition, beginning with the securities first so acquired, and

(B) then from any other employer securities.

If subsection (d) applies to a disposition, the disposition shall be treated as made from employer securities in the opposite order of the preceding sentence.

EXCISE TAXES—QUALIFIED PENSION, ETC., PLANS

(3) DISTRIBUTIONS TO EMPLOYEES.—The amount realized on any distribution to an employee for less than fair market value shall be determined as if the qualified security had been sold to the employee at fair market value.

Amendments

• **1997, Taxpayer Relief Act of 1997 (P.L. 105-34)**

P.L. 105-34, §1530(c)(12)(A)-(B):

Amended Code Sec. 4978(b)(2) by inserting "or acquired in the qualified gratuitous transfer to which section 664(g) applied" after "section 1042 applied", and by inserting "or to which section 664(g) applied" after "section 1042 applied" in subparagraph (A) thereof. **Effective** for transfers made by trusts to, or for the use of, an employee stock ownership plan after 8-5-97.

• **1996, Small Business Job Protection Act of 1996 (P.L. 104-188)**

P.L. 104-188, §1602(b)(4):

Amended Code Sec. 4978(b)(2) by striking subparagraph (A) and all that follows and inserting new subparagraphs (A) and (B) and a flush sentence. For the **effective** date, see Act Sec. 1602(c), below. Prior to amendment, Code Sec. 4978(b)(2)(A)-(D) read as follows:

(A) first, from section 133 securities (as defined in section 4978B(e)(2)) acquired during the 3-year period ending on the date of such disposition, beginning with the securities first so acquired.

(B) second, from section 133 securities (as so defined) acquired before such 3-year period unless such securities (or proceeds from the disposition) have been allocated to accounts of participants or beneficiaries.

(C) third, from qualified securities to which section 1042 applied acquired during the 3-year period ending on the date of the disposition, beginning with the securities first so acquired, and

(D) then from any other employer securities.

If subsection (d) or section 4978B(d) applies to a disposition, the disposition shall be treated as made from employer securities in the opposite order of the preceding sentence.

P.L. 104-188, §1602(c), provides:

(c) EFFECTIVE DATE.—

(1) IN GENERAL.—The amendments made by this section shall apply to loans made after the date of the enactment of this Act.

(2) REFINANCINGS.—The amendments made by this section shall not apply to loans made after the date of the enactment of this Act to refinance securities acquisition loans (determined without regard to section 133(b)(1)(B) of the Internal Revenue Code of 1986, as in effect on the day before the date of the enactment of this Act) made on or before such date or to refinance loans described in this paragraph if—

(A) the refinancing loans meet the requirements of section 133 of such Code (as so in effect),

(B) immediately after the refinancing the principal amount of the loan resulting from the refinancing does not exceed the principal amount of the refinanced loan (immediately before the refinancing), and

(C) the term of such refinancing loan does not extend beyond the last day of the term of the original securities acquisition loan.

For purposes of this paragraph, the term "securities acquisition loan" includes a loan from a corporation to an employee stock ownership plan described in section 133(b)(3) of such Code (as so in effect).

(3) EXCEPTION.—Any loan made pursuant to a binding written contract in effect before June 10, 1996, and at all times thereafter before such loan is made, shall be treated for purposes of paragraphs (1) and (2) as a loan made on or before the date of the enactment of this Act.

• **1989, Omnibus Budget Reconciliation Act of 1989 (P.L. 101-239)**

P.L. 101-239, §7304(a)(2)(C)(ii):

Amended Code Sec. 4978(b)(2). **Effective** for the estates of decedents dying after 12-19-89. Prior to amendment, Code Sec. 4978(b)(2) read as follows:

(2) LIMITATION.—The amount realized taken into account under paragraph (1) shall not exceed that portion allocable to qualified securities acquired in the sale to which section 1042 applied (determined as if such securities were disposed of in the order described in section 4978A(e)).

• **1987, Revenue Act of 1987 (P.L. 100-203)**

P.L. 100-203, §10413(b)(1):

Amended Code Sec. 4978(b)(2) by striking out the parenthetical and inserting in lieu thereof "(determined as if such securities were disposed of in the order described in section 4978A(e))". **Effective** for taxable events (within the meaning of section 4978A(c) of the Internal Revenue Code of 1986) occurring after 2-26-87. Prior to amendment, the parenthetical read as follows:

(determined as if such securities were disposed of before any other securities)

• **1986, Tax Reform Act of 1986 (P.L. 99-514)**

P.L. 99-514, §1854(e)(2):

Amended Code Sec. 4978(b)(1) by striking out "paragraph (1)" and inserting in lieu thereof "subsection (a)". **Effective** as if included in the provision of P.L. 98-369 to which it relates.

[Sec. 4978(c)]

(c) LIABILITY FOR PAYMENT OF TAXES.—The tax imposed by this subsection shall be paid by—

(1) the employer, or

(2) the eligible worker-owned cooperative,

that made the written statement described in section 664(g)(1)(E) or in section 1042(b)(3) (as the case may be).

Amendments

• **1997, Taxpayer Relief Act of 1997 (P.L. 105-34)**

P.L. 105-34, §1530(c)(13):

Amended Code Sec. 4978(c) by striking "written statement" and all that follows and inserting "written statement described in section 664(g)(1)(E) or in section 1042(b)(3) (as the case may be)." **Effective** for transfers made by trusts to, or for the use of, an employee stock ownership plan after 8-5-97. Prior to amendment, Code Sec. 4978(c) read as follows:

(c) LIABILITY FOR PAYMENT OF TAXES.—The tax imposed by this subsection shall be paid by—

(1) the employer, or

(2) the eligible worker-owned cooperative,

that made the written statement described in section 1042(b)(3).

• **1986, Tax Reform Act of 1986 (P.L. 99-514)**

P.L. 99-514, §1854(e)(3):

Amended Code Sec. 4978(c) by striking out "section 1042(a)(2)(B)" and inserting in lieu thereof "section 1042(b)(3)". **Effective** as if included in the provision of P.L. 98-369 to which it relates.

[Sec. 4978(d)]

(d) SECTION NOT TO APPLY TO CERTAIN DISPOSITIONS.—

(1) CERTAIN DISTRIBUTIONS TO EMPLOYEES.—This section shall not apply with respect to any distribution of qualified securities (or sale of such securities) which is made by reason of—

(A) the death of the employee,

(B) the retirement of the employee after the employee has attained $59^{1}/_{2}$ years of age,

(C) the disability of the employee (within the meaning of section 72(m)(7)), or

(D) the separation of the employee from service for any period which results in a 1-year break in service (within the meaning of section 411(a)(6)(A)).

(2) CERTAIN REORGANIZATIONS.—In the case of any exchange of qualified securities in any reorganization described in section 368(a)(1) for stock of another corporation, such exchange shall not be treated as a disposition for purposes of this section.

(3) LIQUIDATION OF CORPORATION INTO COOPERATIVE.—In the case of any exchange of qualified securities pursuant to the liquidation of the corporation issuing qualified securities into the eligible worker-owned cooperative in a transaction which meets the requirements of section 332 (determined by substituting "100 percent" for "80 percent" each place it appears in section 332(b)(1)), such exchange shall not be treated as a disposition for purposes of this section.

(4) DISPOSITIONS TO MEET DIVERSIFICATION REQUIREMENTS.—This section shall not apply to any disposition of qualified securities which is required under section 401(a)(28).

Amendments

• **1988, Technical and Miscellaneous Revenue Act of 1988 (P.L. 100-647)**

P.L. 100-647, §1011B(j)(4):

Amended Code Sec. 4978(d) by adding at the end thereof new paragraph (4). **Effective** as if included in the provision of P.L. 99-514 to which it relates.

• **1986, Tax Reform Act of 1986 (P.L. 99-514)**

P.L. 99-514, §1854(e)(4):

Amended Code Sec. 4978(d)(1)(C) by striking out "section 72(m)(5)" and inserting in lieu thereof "section 72(m)(7)". **Effective** as if included in the provision of P.L. 98-369 to which it relates.

P.L. 99-514, §1854(e)(7):

Amended Code Sec. 4978(d) by adding at the end thereof new paragraph (3). **Effective** as if included in the provision of P.L. 98-369 to which it relates.

Sec. 4978(b)(3)

EXCISE TAXES—QUALIFIED PENSION, ETC., PLANS

[Sec. 4978(e)]

(e) DEFINITIONS AND SPECIAL RULES.—For purposes of this section—

(1) EMPLOYEE STOCK OWNERSHIP PLAN.—The term "employee stock ownership plan" has the meaning given to such term by section 4975(e)(7).

(2) QUALIFIED SECURITIES.—The term "qualified securities" has the meaning given to such term by section 1042(c)(1); except that such section shall be applied without regard to subparagraph (B) thereof for purposes of applying this section and section 4979A with respect to securities acquired in a qualified gratuitous transfer (as defined in section 664(g)(1)).

(3) ELIGIBLE WORKER-OWNED COOPERATIVE.—The term "eligible worker-owned cooperative" has the meaning given to such term by section 1042(c)(2).

(4) DISPOSITION.—The term "disposition" includes any distribution.

(5) EMPLOYER SECURITIES.—The term "employer securities" has the meaning given to such term by section 409(l).

Amendments

• **1997, Taxpayer Relief Act of 1997 (P.L. 105-34)**

P.L. 105-34, § 1530(c)(14):

Amended Code Sec. 4978(e)(2) by striking the period and inserting "; except that such section shall be applied without regard to subparagraph (B) thereof for purposes of applying this section and section 4979A with respect to securities acquired in a qualified gratuitous transfer (as defined in section 664(g)(1))." **Effective** for transfers made by trusts to, or for the use of, an employee stock ownership plan after 8-5-97.

• **1986, Tax Reform Act of 1986 (P.L. 99-514)**

P.L. 99-514, § 1854(e)(5):

Amended Code Sec. 4978(e)(2) by striking out "section 1042(b)(1)" and inserting in lieu thereof "section 1042(c)(1)". **Effective** as if included in the provision of P.L. 98-369 to which it relates.

P.L. 99-514, § 1854(e)(6):

Amended Code Sec. 4978(e)(3) by striking out "section 1042(b)(1)" and inserting in lieu thereof "section 1042(c)(2)". **Effective** as if included in the provision of P.L. 98-369 to which it relates.

• **1984, Deficit Reduction Act of 1984 (P.L. 98-369)**

P.L. 98-369, § 545(a):

Added Code Sec. 4978. **Effective** for tax years beginning after 7-18-84.

[Sec. 4978A—Repealed]

Amendments

• **1989, Omnibus Budget Reconciliation Act of 1989 (P.L. 101-239)**

P.L. 101-239, § 7304(a)(2)(C)(i):

Repealed Code Sec. 4978A. **Effective** for estates of decedents dying after 12-19-89. Prior to repeal, Code Sec. 4978A read as follows:

SEC. 4978A. TAX ON CERTAIN DISPOSITIONS OF EMPLOYER SECURITIES TO WHICH SECTION 2057 APPLIED.

[Sec. 4978A(a)]

(a) IMPOSITION OF TAX.—In the case of a taxable event involving qualified employer securities held by an employee stock ownership plan or eligible worker-owned cooperative, there is hereby imposed a tax equal to the amount determined under subsection (b).

[Sec. 4978A(b)]

(b) AMOUNT OF TAX.—

(1) IN GENERAL.—The amount of the tax imposed by subsection (a) shall be equal to 30 percent of—

(A) the amount realized on the disposition in the case of a taxable event described in paragraph (1) or (2) of subsection (c), or

(B) the amount repaid on the loan in the case of a taxable event described in paragraph (3) of subsection (c).

(2) DISPOSITIONS OTHER THAN SALES OR EXCHANGES.—For purposes of paragraph (1), in the case of a disposition of employer securities which is not a sale or exchange, the amount realized on such disposition shall be the fair market value of such employer securities at the time of disposition.

[Sec. 4978A(c)]

(c) TAXABLE EVENT.—For purposes of this section, the term "taxable event" means the following:

(1) DISPOSITION WITHIN 3 YEARS OF ACQUISITION.—Any disposition of employer securities by an employee stock ownership plan or eligible worker-owned cooperative within 3 years after such plan or cooperative acquired qualified employer securities.

(2) STOCKS DISPOSED OF BEFORE ALLOCATION.—Any disposition of qualified employer securities to which paragraph (1) does not apply if—

(A) such disposition occurs before such securities are allocated to accounts of participants or their beneficiaries, and

(B) the proceeds from such disposition are not so allocated.

(3) USE OF ASSETS TO REPAY ACQUISITION LOANS.—The payment by an employee stock ownership plan of any portion of any loan used to acquire employer securities from transferred assets (within the meaning of section 2057(c)(2)(B)).

[Sec. 4978A(d)]

(d) ORDERING RULES.—For purposes of this section and section 4978, any disposition of employer securities shall be treated as having been made in the following order:

(1) First, from qualified employer securities acquired during the 3-year period ending on the date of such disposition, beginning with the securities first so acquired.

(2) Second, from qualified employer securities acquired before such 3-year period unless such securities (or the proceeds from such disposition) have been allocated to accounts of participants or their beneficiaries.

(3) Third, from qualified securities (within the meaning of section 4978(e)(2)) to which section 1042 applied acquired during the 3-year period ending on the date of such disposition, beginning with the securities first so acquired.

(4) Finally, from any other employer securities. In the case of a disposition to which section 4978(d) or subsection (e) applies, the disposition of employer securities shall be treated as having been made in the opposite order of the preceding sentence.

[Sec. 4978A(e)]

(e) SECTION NOT TO APPLY TO CERTAIN DISPOSITIONS.—

(1) IN GENERAL.—This section shall not apply to any disposition described in paragraph (1) or (3) of section 4978(d).

(2) CERTAIN REORGANIZATIONS.—For purposes of this section, any exchange of qualified employer securities for employer securities of another corporation in any reorganization described in section 368(a)(1) shall not be treated as a disposition, but the employer securities which were received shall be treated—

(A) as qualified employer securities of the plan or cooperative, and

(B) as having been held by the plan or cooperative during the period the qualified employer securities were held.

(3) DISPOSITION TO MEET DIVERSIFICATION REQUIREMENTS.—Any disposition which is made to meet the requirements of section 401(a)(28) shall not be treated as a disposition.

(4) FORCED DISPOSITION OCCURRING BY OPERATION OF A STATE LAW.—Any forced disposition of qualified employer securities by the employee stock ownership plan of a corporation occurring by operation of a State law shall not be treated as a disposition. This paragraph shall only apply to securities which, at the time such securities were purchased by the employee stock ownership plan, were regularly traded on an established securities market.

Amendments

• **1988, Technical and Miscellaneous Revenue Act of 1988 (P.L. 100-647)**

P.L. 100-647, § 6060(a):

Amended Code Sec. 4978A(e) by adding at the end thereof new paragraph (4). **Effective** as if included in the amendments made by section 10413 of P.L. 100-203.

[Sec. 4978A(f)]

(f) DEFINITIONS AND SPECIAL RULES.—For purposes of this section—

(1) TERMS USED IN SECTION 2057.—Any term used in this section which is used in section 2057 shall have the meaning given such term by section 2057.

(2) QUALIFIED EMPLOYER SECURITIES.—The term "qualified employer securities" has the meaning given such term by section 2057, except that such term shall include employer securities sold before February 27, 1987, for which a deduction was allowed under section 2057.

(3) DISPOSITION.—The term "disposition" includes any distribution.

(4) LIABILITY FOR PAYMENT OF TAXES.—The tax imposed by this section shall be paid by—

(A) the employer, or

(B) the eligible worker-owned cooperative, which made the written statement described in section 2057(e).

Amendments

• **1987, Revenue Act of 1987 (P.L. 100-203)**

P.L. 100-203, § 10413(a):

Amended chapter 43 by adding after Code Sec. 4978 new Code Sec. 4978A. **Effective** for taxable events (within the meaning of section 4978A of the Internal Revenue Code of 1986) occurring after 2-26-87.

EXCISE TAXES—QUALIFIED PENSION, ETC., PLANS

[Sec. 4978B—Repealed]

Amendments

• **1996, Small Business Job Protection Act of 1996 (P.L. 104-188)**

P.L. 104-188, §1602(b)(5)(A):

Repealed Code Sec. 4978B. For the **effective** date, see Act Sec. 1602(c), below.

P.L. 104-188, §1602(c), provides:

(c) EFFECTIVE DATE.—

(1) IN GENERAL.—The amendments made by this section shall apply to loans made after the date of the enactment of this Act.

(2) REFINANCINGS.—The amendments made by this section shall not apply to loans made after the date of the enactment of this Act to refinance securities acquisition loans (determined without regard to section 133(b)(1)(B) of the Internal Revenue Code of 1986, as in effect on the day before the date of the enactment of this Act) made on or before such date or to refinance loans described in this paragraph if—

(A) the refinancing loans meet the requirements of section 133 of such Code (as so in effect),

(B) immediately after the refinancing the principal amount of the loan resulting from the refinancing does not exceed the principal amount of the refinanced loan (immediately before the refinancing), and

(C) the term of such refinancing loan does not extend beyond the last day of the term of the original securities acquisition loan.

For purposes of this paragraph, the term "securities acquisition loan" includes a loan from a corporation to an employee stock ownership plan described in section 133(b)(3) of such Code (as so in effect).

(3) EXCEPTION.—Any loan made pursuant to a binding written contract in effect before June 10, 1996, and at all times thereafter before such loan is made, shall be treated for purposes of paragraphs (1) and (2) as a loan made on or before the date of the enactment of this Act.

Prior to repeal, Code Sec. 4978B read as follows:

SEC. 4978B. TAX ON DISPOSITION OF EMPLOYER SECURITIES TO WHICH SECTION 133 APPLIED.

[Sec. 4978B(a)]

(a) IMPOSITION OF TAX.—In the case of an employee stock ownership plan which has acquired section 133 securities, there is hereby imposed a tax on each taxable event in an amount equal to the amount determined under subsection (b).

[Sec. 4978B(b)]

(b) AMOUNT OF TAX.—

(1) IN GENERAL.—The amount of the tax imposed by subsection (a) shall be equal to 10 percent of the amount realized on the disposition to the extent allocable to section 133 securities under section 4978(b)(2).

(2) DISPOSITIONS OTHER THAN SALES OR EXCHANGES.—For purposes of paragraph (1), in the case of a disposition of employer securities which is not a sale or exchange, the amount realized on such disposition shall be the fair market value of such securities at the time of disposition.

[Sec. 4978B(c)]

(c) TAXABLE EVENT.—For purposes of this section, the term "taxable event" means any of the following dispositions:

(1) DISPOSITIONS WITHIN 3 YEARS.—Any disposition of any employer securities by an employee stock ownership plan within 3 years after such plan acquired section 133 securities if—

(A) the total number of employer securities held by such plan after such disposition is less than the total number of employer securities held after such acquisition, or

(B) except to the extent provided in regulations, the value of employer securities held by such plan after the disposition is 50 percent or less of the total value of all employer securities as of the time of the disposition.

For purposes of subparagraph (B), the aggregation rule of section 133(b)(6)(D) shall apply.

(2) STOCK DISPOSED OF BEFORE ALLOCATION.—Any disposition of section 133 securities to which paragraph (1) does not apply if—

(A) such disposition occurs before such securities are allocated to accounts of participants or their beneficiaries, and

(B) the proceeds from such disposition are not so allocated.

[Sec. 4978B(d)]

(d) SECTION NOT TO APPLY TO CERTAIN DISPOSITIONS.—

(1) IN GENERAL.—This section shall not apply to any disposition described in paragraph (1), (3), or (4) of section 4978(d).

(2) CERTAIN REORGANIZATIONS.—For purposes of this section, any exchange of section 133 securities for employer securities of another corporation in any reorganization described in section 368(a)(1) shall not be treated as a disposition, but the employer securities received shall be treated as section 133 securities and as having been held by the plan during the period the securities which were exchanged were held.

(3) FORCED DISPOSITION OCCURRING BY OPERATION OF STATE LAW.—Any forced disposition of section 133 securities by an employee stock ownership plan occurring by operation of a State law shall not be treated as a disposition. This paragraph shall only apply to securities which, at the time the securities were acquired by the plan, were regularly traded on an established securities market.

(4) COORDINATION WITH OTHER TAXES.—This section shall not apply to any disposition which is subject to tax under section 4978 or section 4978A (as in effect on the day before the date of enactment of this section).

Amendments

• **1990, Omnibus Budget Reconciliation Act of 1990 (P.L. 101-508)**

P.L. 101-508, §11701(e)(2):

Amended Code Sec. 4978B(d) by adding at the end thereof a new paragraph (4). **Effective** as if included in the provision of P.L. 101-239 to which it relates.

[Sec. 4978B(e)]

(e) DEFINITIONS AND SPECIAL RULES.—For purposes of this section—

(1) LIABILITY FOR PAYMENT OF TAXES.—The tax imposed by this section shall be paid by the employer.

(2) SECTION 133 SECURITIES.—The term "section 133 securities" means employer securities acquired by an employee stock ownership plan in a transaction to which section 133 applied.

(3) DISPOSITION.—The term "disposition" includes any distribution.

(4) ORDERING RULES.—For ordering rules for dispositions of employer securities, see section 4978(b)(2).

Amendments

• **1990, Omnibus Budget Reconciliation Act of 1990 (P.L. 101-508)**

P.L. 101-508, §11701(e)(1):

Amended Code Sec. 4978B(e)(2). **Effective** as if included in the provision of P.L. 101-239 to which it relates. Prior to amendment, paragraph (2) read as follows:

(2) SECTION 133 SECURITIES.—The term "section 133 securities" means employer securities acquired by an employee stock ownership plan in a transaction to which section 133 applied, except that such term shall not include—

(A) qualified securities (as defined in section 4978(e)(2)), or

(B) qualified employer securities (as defined in section 4978A(f)(2), as in effect on the day before the date of the enactment of this section).

• **1989, Omnibus Budget Reconciliation Act of 1989 (P.L. 101-239)**

P.L. 101-239, §7301(d)(1):

Amended Chapter 43 by inserting after section 4978A a new section 4978B. **Effective**, generally, for loans made after 7-10-89. However, for exceptions, see Act Sec. 7301(f)(2)-(6) in the amendment notes following Code Sec. 133(b), above.

[Sec. 4979]

SEC. 4979. TAX ON CERTAIN EXCESS CONTRIBUTIONS.

[Sec. 4979(a)]

(a) GENERAL RULE.—In the case of any plan, there is hereby imposed a tax for the taxable year equal to 10 percent of the sum of—

(1) any excess contributions under such plan for the plan year ending in such taxable year, and

(2) any excess aggregate contributions under the plan for the plan year ending in such taxable year.

Amendments

• **1988, Technical and Miscellaneous Revenue Act of 1988 (P.L. 100-647)**

P.L. 100-647, §1011(l)(8):

Amended Code Sec. 4979(a)(1) by striking out "a cash or deferred arrangement which is part of" before "such plan". **Effective** as if included in the provision of P.L. 99-514 to which it relates.

[Sec. 4979(b)]

(b) LIABILITY FOR TAX.—The tax imposed by subsection (a) shall be paid by the employer.

[Sec. 4979(c)]

(c) EXCESS CONTRIBUTIONS.—For purposes of this section, the term "excess contributions" has the meaning given such term by sections 401(k)(8)(B), 408(k)(6)(C), and 501(c)(18).

EXCISE TAXES—QUALIFIED PENSION, ETC., PLANS

Amendments
- **1988, Technical and Miscellaneous Revenue Act of 1988 (P.L. 100-647)**

P.L. 100-647, § 1011(l)(9)(A)-(B):

Amended Code Sec. 4979(c) by striking out "403(b)," after "401(k)(8)(B)", and by striking out "408(k)(8)(B)" and inserting in lieu thereof "408(k)(6)(C)". **Effective** as if included in the provision of P.L. 99-514 to which it relates.

[Sec. 4979(d)]

(d) EXCESS AGGREGATE CONTRIBUTION.—For purposes of this section, the term "excess aggregate contribution" has the meaning given to such term by section 401(m)(6)(B). For purposes of determining excess aggregate contributions under an annuity contract described in section 403(b), such contract shall be treated as a plan described in subsection (e)(1).

Amendments
- **1988, Technical and Miscellaneous Revenue Act of 1988 (P.L. 100-647)**

P.L. 100-647, § 1011(l)(10):

Amended Code Sec. 4979(d) by adding at the end thereof a new sentence. **Effective** as if included in the provision of P.L. 99-514 to which it relates.

[Sec. 4979(e)]

(e) PLAN.—For purposes of this section, the term "plan" means—

(1) a plan described in section 401(a) which includes a trust exempt from tax under section 501(a),

(2) any annuity plan described in section 403(a),

(3) any annuity contract described in section 403(b),

(4) a simplified employee pension of an employer which satisfies the requirements of section 408(k), and

(5) a plan described in section 501(c)(18).

Such term includes any plan which, at any time, has been determined by the Secretary to be such a plan.

[Sec. 4979(f)]

(f) NO TAX WHERE EXCESS DISTRIBUTED WITHIN SPECIFIED PERIOD AFTER CLOSE OF YEAR.—

(1) IN GENERAL.—No tax shall be imposed under this section on any excess contribution or excess aggregate contribution, as the case may be, to the extent such contribution (together with any income allocable thereto through the end of the plan year for which the contribution was made) is distributed (or, if forfeitable, is forfeited) before the close of the first 2 $^1/_2$ months (6 months in the case of an excess contribution or excess aggregate contribution to an eligible automatic contribution arrangement (as defined in section 414(w)(3))) of the following plan year.

(2) YEAR OF INCLUSION.—Any amount distributed as provided in paragraph (1) shall be treated as earned and received by the recipient in the recipient's taxable year in which such distributions were made.

Amendments
- **2006, Pension Protection Act of 2006 (P.L. 109-280)**

P.L. 109-280, § 902(e)(1)(A)-(B):

Amended Code Sec. 4979(f) by inserting "(6 months in the case of an excess contribution or excess aggregate contribution to an eligible automatic contribution arrangement (as defined in section 414(w)(3)))" after "2$^1/_2$ months" in paragraph (1), and by striking "2$^1/_2$ MONTHS OF" in the heading and inserting "SPECIFIED PERIOD AFTER". **Effective** for plan years beginning after 12-31-2007.

P.L. 109-280, § 902(e)(2):

Amended Code Sec. 4979(f)(2). **Effective** for plan years beginning after 12-31-2007. Prior to amendment, Code Sec. 4979(f)(2) read as follows:

(2) YEAR OF INCLUSION.—

(A) IN GENERAL.—Except as provided in subparagraph (B), any amount distributed as provided in paragraph (1) shall be treated as received and earned by the recipient in his taxable year for which such contribution was made.

(B) DE MINIMIS DISTRIBUTIONS.—If the total excess contributions and excess aggregate contributions distributed to a recipient under a plan for any plan year are less than $100, such distributions (and any income allocable thereto) shall be treated as earned and received by the recipient in his taxable year in which such distributions were made.

P.L. 109-280, § 902(e)(3)(A):

Amended Code Sec. 4979(f)(1) by adding "through the end of the plan year for which the contribution was made" after "thereto". **Effective** for plan years beginning after 12-31-2007.

- **1988, Technical and Miscellaneous Revenue Act of 1988 (P.L. 100-647)**

P.L. 100-647, § 1011(l)(11):

Amended Code Sec. 4979(f)(2). **Effective** as if included in the provision of P.L. 99-514 to which it relates. Prior to amendment, Code Sec. 4979(f)(2) read as follows:

(2) INCLUDED IN PRIOR YEAR.—Any amount distributed as provided in paragraph (1) shall be treated as received and earned by the recipient in his taxable year for which such contribution was made.

- **1986, Tax Reform Act of 1986 (P.L. 99-514)**

P.L. 99-514, § 1117(b)(1):

Amended Chapter 43 by adding at the end thereof new Code Sec. 4979. **Effective**, generally, for plan years beginning after 12-31-86. However, see Act Sec. 1117(d)(2) and (3), below.

P.L. 99-514, § 1117(d)(2)-(3), provides:

(2) COLLECTIVE BARGAINING AGREEMENTS.—In the case of a plan maintained pursuant to 1 or more collective bargaining agreements between employee representatives and 1 or more employers ratified before March 1, 1986, the amendments made by this section shall not apply to plan years beginning before the earlier of—

(A) January 1, 1989, or

(B) the date on which the last of such collective bargaining agreements terminates (determined without regard to any extension thereof after February 28, 1986).

(3) ANNUITY CONTRACTS.—In the case of an annuity contract under section 403(b) of the Internal Revenue Code of 1986—

(A) the amendments made by this section shall apply to plan years beginning after December 31, 1988, and

(B) in the case of a collective bargaining agreement described in paragraph (2), the amendments made by this section shall not apply to years beginning before the earlier of—

(i) the later of—

(I) January 1, 1989, or

(II) the date determined under paragraph (2)(B), or

(ii) January 1, 1991.

[Sec. 4979A]

SEC. 4979A. TAX ON CERTAIN PROHIBITED ALLOCATIONS OF QUALIFIED SECURITIES.

[Sec. 4979A(a)]

(a) IMPOSITION OF TAX.—If—

(1) there is a prohibited allocation of qualified securities by any employee stock ownership plan or eligible worker-owned cooperative,

(2) there is an allocation described in section 664(g)(5)(A),

(3) there is any allocation of employer securities which violates the provisions of section 409(p), or a nonallocation year described in subsection (e)(2)(C) with respect to an employee stock ownership plan, or

(4) any synthetic equity is owned by a disqualified person in any nonallocation year,

there is hereby imposed a tax on such allocation or ownership equal to 50 percent of the amount involved.

EXCISE TAXES—QUALIFIED PENSION, ETC., PLANS

Amendments

• **2006, Pension Protection Act of 2006 (P.L. 109-280)**

P.L. 109-280, §811, provides:

SEC. 811. PENSIONS AND INDIVIDUAL RETIREMENT ARRANGEMENT PROVISIONS OF ECONOMIC GROWTH AND TAX RELIEF RECONCILIATION ACT OF 2001 MADE PERMANENT.

Title IX of the Economic Growth and Tax Relief Reconciliation Act of 2001 [P.L. 107-16] shall not apply to the provisions of, and amendments made by, subtitles A through F of title VI [§§601-666]of such Act (relating to pension and individual retirement arrangement provisions).

• **2001, Economic Growth and Tax Relief Reconciliation Act of 2001 (P.L. 107-16)**

P.L. 107-16, §656(c)(1)(A)-(B):

Amended Code Sec. 4979A(a) by striking "or" at the end of paragraph (1), and by striking all that follows paragraph (2) and inserting new text [which includes new paragraphs (3) and (4)]. **Effective** for plan years beginning after 12-31-2004. For an exception, see Act Sec. 656(d)(2), below. Prior to being stricken, the material that followed paragraph (2) read as follows:

there is hereby imposed a tax on such allocation equal to 50 percent of the amount involved.

P.L. 107-16, §656(d)(2), provides:

(2) EXCEPTION FOR CERTAIN PLANS.—In the case of any—

(A) employee stock ownership plan established after March 14, 2001, or

(B) employee stock ownership plan established on or before such date if employer securities held by the plan consist of stock in a corporation with respect to which an election under section 1362(a) of the Internal Revenue Code of 1986 is not in effect on such date,

the amendments made by this section shall apply to plan years ending after March 14, 2001.

P.L. 107-16, §901(a)-(b), provides [but see P.L. 109-280, §811, above]:

SEC. 901. SUNSET OF PROVISIONS OF ACT.

(a) IN GENERAL.—All provisions of, and amendments made by, this Act shall not apply—

(1) to taxable, plan, or limitation years beginning after December 31, 2010, or

(2) in the case of title V, to estates of decedents dying, gifts made, or generation skipping transfers, after December 31, 2010.

(b) APPLICATION OF CERTAIN LAWS.—The Internal Revenue Code of 1986 and the Employee Retirement Income Security Act of 1974 shall be applied and administered to years, estates, gifts, and transfers described in subsection (a) as if the provisions and amendments described in subsection (a) had never been enacted.

• **1997, Taxpayer Relief Act of 1997 (P.L. 105-34)**

P.L. 105-34, §1530(c)(15):

Amended Code Sec. 4979A(a). **Effective** for transfers made by trusts to, or for the use of, an employee stock ownership plan after 8-5-97. Prior to amendment, Code Sec. 4979A(a) read as follows:

(a) IMPOSITION OF TAX.—If there is a prohibited allocation of qualified securities by any employee stock ownership plan or eligible worker-owned cooperative, there is hereby imposed a tax on such allocation equal to 50 percent of the amount involved.

[Sec. 4979A(b)]

(b) PROHIBITED ALLOCATION.—For purposes of this section, the term "prohibited allocation" means—

(1) any allocation of qualified securities acquired in a sale to which section 1042 applies which violates the provisions of section 409(n), and

(2) any benefit which accrues to any person in violation of the provisions of section 409(n).

Amendments

• **1989, Omnibus Budget Reconciliation Act of 1989 (P.L. 101-239)**

P.L. 101-239, §7304(a)(2)(D)(i):

Amended Code Sec. 4979A(b)(1) by striking "or section 2057" after "section 1042". **Effective** for estates of decedents dying after 12-19-89.

[Sec. 4979A(c)]

(c) LIABILITY FOR TAX.—The tax imposed by this section shall be paid—

(1) in the case of an allocation referred to in paragraph (1) or (2) of subsection (a), by—

(A) the employer sponsoring such plan, or

(B) the eligible worker-owned cooperative,

which made the written statement described in section 664(g)(1)(E) or in section 1042(b)(3)(B) (as the case may be), and

(2) in the case of an allocation or ownership referred to in paragraph (3) or (4) of subsection (a), by the S corporation the stock in which was so allocated or owned.

Amendments

• **2006, Pension Protection Act of 2006 (P.L. 109-280)**

P.L. 109-280, §811, provides:

SEC. 811. PENSIONS AND INDIVIDUAL RETIREMENT ARRANGEMENT PROVISIONS OF ECONOMIC GROWTH AND TAX RELIEF RECONCILIATION ACT OF 2001 MADE PERMANENT.

Title IX of the Economic Growth and Tax Relief Reconciliation Act of 2001 [P.L. 107-16] shall not apply to the provisions of, and amendments made by, subtitles A through F of title VI [§§601-666]of such Act (relating to pension and individual retirement arrangement provisions).

• **2001, Economic Growth and Tax Relief Reconciliation Act of 2001 (P.L. 107-16)**

P.L. 107-16, §656(c)(2):

Amended Code Sec. 4979A(c). **Effective** for plan years beginning after 12-31-2004. For an exception, see Act Sec. 656(d)(2), in the amendment notes to Code Sec. 4979A(a). Prior to amendment, Code Sec. 4979A(c) read as follows:

(c) LIABILITY FOR TAX.—The tax imposed by this section shall be paid by—

(1) the employer sponsoring such plan, or

(2) the eligible worker-owned cooperative,

which made the written statement described in section 664(g)(1)(E) or in section 1042(b)(3)(B) (as the case may be).

P.L. 107-16, §901(a)-(b), provides [but see P.L. 109-280, §811, above]:

SEC. 901. SUNSET OF PROVISIONS OF ACT.

(a) IN GENERAL.—All provisions of, and amendments made by, this Act shall not apply—

(1) to taxable, plan, or limitation years beginning after December 31, 2010, or

(2) in the case of title V, to estates of decedents dying, gifts made, or generation skipping transfers, after December 31, 2010.

(b) APPLICATION OF CERTAIN LAWS.—The Internal Revenue Code of 1986 and the Employee Retirement Income Security Act of 1974 shall be applied and administered to years, estates, gifts, and transfers described in subsection (a) as if the provisions and amendments described in subsection (a) had never been enacted.

• **1997, Taxpayer Relief Act of 1997 (P.L. 105-34)**

P.L. 105-34, §1530(c)(16):

Amended Code Sec. 4979A(c). **Effective** for transfers made by trusts to, or for the use of, an employee stock ownership plan after 8-5-97. Prior to amendment, Code Sec. 4979A(c) read as follows:

(c) LIABILITY FOR TAX.—The tax imposed by this section shall be paid by—

(1) the employer sponsoring such plan, or

(2) the eligible worker-owned cooperative, which made the written statement described in section 1042(b)(3)(B).

• **1989, Omnibus Budget Reconciliation Act of 1989 (P.L. 101-239)**

P.L. 101-239, §7304(a)(2)(D)(ii) (as amended by P.L. 104-188, §1704(t)(22)):

Amended Code Sec. 4979A(c) by striking "or section 2057(d)" after "section 1042(b)(3)(B)". **Effective** for estates of decedents dying after 12-19-89.

[Sec. 4979A(d)]

(d) SPECIAL STATUTE OF LIMITATIONS FOR TAX ATTRIBUTABLE TO CERTAIN ALLOCATIONS.—The statutory period for the assessment of any tax imposed by this section on an allocation described in subsection (a)(2) of qualified employer securities shall not expire before the date which is 3 years from the later of—

(1) the 1st allocation of such securities in connection with a qualified gratuitous transfer (as defined in section 664(g)(1)), or

(2) the date on which the Secretary is notified of the allocation described in subsection (a)(2).

Sec. 4979A(b)

EXCISE TAXES—QUALIFIED PENSION, ETC., PLANS

Amendments

● **1997, Taxpayer Relief Act of 1997 (P.L. 105-34)**

P.L. 105-34, §1530(c)(17):

Amended Code Sec. 4979A by redesignating subsection (d) as subsection (e) and by inserting after subsection (c) a new subsection (d). **Effective** for transfers made by trusts to, or for the use of, an employee stock ownership plan after 8-5-97.

[Sec. 4979A(e)]

(e) DEFINITIONS AND SPECIAL RULES.—For purposes of this section—

(1) DEFINITIONS.—Except as provided in paragraph (2), terms used in this section have the same respective meanings as when used in sections 409 and 4978.

(2) SPECIAL RULES RELATING TO TAX IMPOSED BY REASON OF PARAGRAPH (3) OR (4) OF SUBSECTION(a).—

(A) PROHIBITED ALLOCATIONS.—The amount involved with respect to any tax imposed by reason of subsection (a)(3) is the amount allocated to the account of any person in violation of section 409(p)(1).

(B) SYNTHETIC EQUITY.—The amount involved with respect to any tax imposed by reason of subsection (a)(4) is the value of the shares on which the synthetic equity is based.

(C) SPECIAL RULE DURING FIRST NONALLOCATION YEAR.—For purposes of subparagraph (A), the amount involved for the first nonallocation year of any employee stock ownership plan shall be determined by taking into account the total value of all the deemed-owned shares of all disqualified persons with respect to such plan.

(D) STATUTE OF LIMITATIONS.—The statutory period for the assessment of any tax imposed by this section by reason of paragraph (3) or (4) of subsection (a) shall not expire before the date which is 3 years from the later of—

(i) the allocation or ownership referred to in such paragraph giving rise to such tax, or

(ii) the date on which the Secretary is notified of such allocation or ownership.

Amendments

● **2006, Pension Protection Act of 2006 (P.L. 109-280)**

P.L. 109-280, §811, provides:

SEC. 811. PENSIONS AND INDIVIDUAL RETIREMENT ARRANGEMENT PROVISIONS OF ECONOMIC GROWTH AND TAX RELIEF RECONCILIATION ACT OF 2001 MADE PERMANENT.

Title IX of the Economic Growth and Tax Relief Reconciliation Act of 2001 [P.L. 107-16] shall not apply to the provisions of, and amendments made by, subtitles A through F of title VI [§§601-666]of such Act (relating to pension and individual retirement arrangement provisions).

● **2001, Economic Growth and Tax Relief Reconciliation Act of 2001 (P.L. 107-16)**

P.L. 107-16, §656(c)(3):

Amended Code Sec. 4979A(e). **Effective** for plan years beginning after 12-31-2004. For an exception, see Act Sec. 656(d)(2) in the amendment notes to Code Sec. 4979A(a). Prior to amendment, Code Sec. 4979A(e) read as follows:

(e) DEFINITIONS.—Terms used in this section have the same respective meaning as when used in section 4978.

P.L. 107-16, §901(a)-(b), provides [but see P.L. 109-280, §811, above]:

SEC. 901. SUNSET OF PROVISIONS OF ACT.

(a) IN GENERAL.—All provisions of, and amendments made by, this Act shall not apply—

(1) to taxable, plan, or limitation years beginning after December 31, 2010, or

(2) in the case of title V, to estates of decedents dying, gifts made, or generation skipping transfers, after December 31, 2010.

(b) APPLICATION OF CERTAIN LAWS.—The Internal Revenue Code of 1986 and the Employee Retirement Income Security Act of 1974 shall be applied and administered to years, estates, gifts, and transfers described in subsection (a) as if the provisions and amendments described in subsection (a) had never been enacted.

● **1997, Taxpayer Relief Act of 1997 (P.L. 105-34)**

P.L. 105-34, §1530(c)(17):

Amended Code Sec. 4979A by redesignating subsection (d) as subsection (e). **Effective** for transfers made by trusts to, or for the use of, an employee stock ownership plan after 8-5-97.

● **1986, Tax Reform Act of 1986 (P.L. 99-514)**

P.L. 99-514, §1854(a)(9)(A):

Amended chapter 43 by adding at the end thereof new Code Sec. 4979A. **Effective** for sales of securities after 10-22-86.

P.L. 99-514, §1172(b)(2)(A)-(B):

Amended Code Sec. 4979A [as added by Act Sec. 1854(a)(9)(A)]by inserting "or section 2057" after "section 1042" in subsection (b)(1) thereof, and by inserting "or section 2057(d)" after "section 1042(b)(3)(B)" in subsection (c) thereof. **Effective** for sales after 10-22-86 with respect to which an election is made by the executor of an estate who is required to file the return of the tax imposed by the Internal Revenue Code of 1986 on a date (including extensions) after the date of the enactment of this Act.

[Sec. 4980]

SEC. 4980. TAX ON REVERSION OF QUALIFIED PLAN ASSETS TO EMPLOYER.

[Sec. 4980(a)]

(a) IMPOSITION OF TAX.—There is hereby imposed a tax of 20 percent of the amount of any employer reversion from a qualified plan.

Amendments

● **1990, Omnibus Budget Reconciliation Act of 1990 (P.L. 101-508)**

P.L. 101-508, §12001:

Amended Code Sec. 4980(a) by striking "15 percent" and inserting "20 percent". **Effective**, generally, for reversions occurring after 9-30-90. However, for exceptions see Act Sec. 12003(b).

P.L. 101-508, §12003(b), provides:

(b) EXCEPTION.—The amendments made by this subtitle shall not apply to any reversion after September 30, 1990, if—

(1) in the case of plans subject to title IV of the Employee Retirement Income Security Act of 1974, a notice of intent to terminate under such title was provided to participants (or if no participants, to the Pension Benefit Guaranty Corporation) before October 1, 1990,

(2) in the case of plans subject to title I (and not to title IV) of such Act, a notice of intent to reduce future accruals under section 204(h) of such Act was provided to participants in connection with the termination before October 1, 1990,

(3) in the case of plans not subject to title I or IV of such Act, a request for a determination letter with respect to the termination was filed with the Secretary of the Treasury or the Secretary's delegate before October 1, 1990, or

(4) in the case of plans not subject to title I or IV of such Act and having only 1 participant, a resolution terminating the plan was adopted by the employer before October 1, 1990.

● **1988, Technical and Miscellaneous Revenue Act of 1988 (P.L. 100-647)**

P.L. 100-647, §6069(a):

Amended Code Sec. 4980(a) by striking out "10 percent" and inserting in lieu thereof "15 percent". **Effective** for reversions occurring on or after 10-21-88. However, for an exception see Act Sec. 6069(b)(2).

P.L. 100-647, §6069(b)(2), provides:

(b)(2) EXCEPTION.—The amendment made by subsection (a) shall not apply to any reversion on or after October 21, 1988, pursuant to a plan termination if—

(A) with respect to plans subject to title IV of the Employee Retirement Income Security Act of 1974, a notice of intent to terminate required under such title was provided to participants (or if no participants, to the Pension Benefit Guaranty Corporation) before October 21, 1988,

(B) with respect to plans subject to title I of such Act, a notice of intent to reduce future accruals required under section 204(h) of such Act was provided to participants in connection with the termination before October 21, 1988,

(C) with respect to plans not subject to title I or IV of such Act, the Board of Directors of the employer approved the termination or the employer took other binding action before October 21, 1988, or

(D) such plan termination was directed by a final order of a court of competent jurisdiction entered before October 21, 1988, and notice of such order was provided to participants before such date.

[Sec. 4980(b)]

(b) LIABILITY FOR TAX.—The tax imposed by subsection (a) shall be paid by the employer maintaining the plan.

[Sec. 4980(c)]

(c) DEFINITIONS AND SPECIAL RULES.—For purposes of this section—

Internal Revenue Code

EXCISE TAXES—QUALIFIED PENSION, ETC., PLANS

(1) QUALIFIED PLAN.—The term "qualified plan" means any plan meeting the requirements of section 401(a) or 403(a), other than—

(A) a plan maintained by an employer if such employer has, at all times, been exempt from tax under subtitle A, or

(B) a governmental plan (within the meaning of section 414(d)).

Such term shall include any plan which, at any time, has been determined by the Secretary to be a qualified plan.

(2) EMPLOYER REVERSION.—

(A) IN GENERAL.—The term "employer reversion" means the amount of cash and the fair market value of other property received (directly or indirectly) by an employer from the qualified plan.

(B) EXCEPTIONS.—The term "employer reversion" shall not include—

(i) except as provided in regulations, any amount distributed to or on behalf of any employee (or his beneficiaries) if such amount could have been so distributed before termination of such plan without violating any provision of section 401,

(ii) any distribution to the employer which is allowable under section 401(a)(2)—

(I) in the case of a multiemployer plan, by reason of mistakes of law or fact or the return of any withdrawal liability payment,

(II) in the case of a plan other than a multiemployer plan, by reason of mistake of fact, or

(III) in the case of a plan, by reason of the failure of the plan to initially qualify or the failure of contributions to be deductible, or

(iii) any transfer described in section 420(f)(2)(B)(ii)(II).

(3) EXCEPTION FOR EMPLOYEE STOCK OWNERSHIP PLANS.—

(A) IN GENERAL.—If upon an employer reversion from a qualified plan, any applicable amount is transferred from such plan to an employee stock ownership plan described in section 4975(e)(7) or a tax credit employee stock ownership plan (as described in section 409), such amount shall not be treated as an employer reversion for purposes of this section (or includible in the gross income of the employer) if the requirements of subparagraphs (B), (C), and (D) are met.

(B) INVESTMENT IN EMPLOYER SECURITIES.—The requirements of this subparagraph are met if, within 90 days after the transfer (or such longer period as the Secretary may prescribe), the amount transferred is invested in employer securities (as defined in section 409(l)) or used to repay loans used to purchase such securities.

(C) ALLOCATION REQUIREMENTS.—The requirements of this subparagraph are met if the portion of the amount transferred which is not allocated under the plan to accounts of participants in the plan year in which the transfer occurs—

(i) is credited to a suspense account and allocated from such account to accounts of participants no less rapidly than ratably over a period not to exceed 7 years, and

(ii) when allocated to accounts of participants under the plan, is treated as an employer contribution for purposes of section 415(c), except that—

(I) the annual addition (as determined under section 415(c)) attributable to each such allocation shall not exceed the value of such securities as of the time such securities were credited to such suspense account, and

(II) no additional employer contributions shall be permitted to an employee stock ownership plan described in subparagraph (A) of the employer before the allocation of such amount.

The amount allocated in the year of transfer shall not be less than the lesser of the maximum amount allowable under section 415 or $1/8$ of the amount attributable to the securities acquired. In the case of dividends on securities held in the suspense account, the requirements of this subparagraph are met only if the dividends are allocated to accounts of participants or paid to participants in proportion to their accounts, or used to repay loans used to purchase employer securities.

(D) PARTICIPANTS.—The requirements of this subparagraph are met if at least half of the participants in the qualified plan are participants in the employee stock ownership plan (as of the close of the 1st plan year for which an allocation of the securities is required).

(E) APPLICABLE AMOUNT.—For purposes of this paragraph, the term "applicable amount" means any amount which—

(i) is transferred after March 31, 1985, and before January 1, 1989, or

(ii) is transferred after December 31, 1988, pursuant to a termination which occurs after March 31, 1985, and before January 1, 1989.

(F) NO CREDIT OR DEDUCTION ALLOWED.—No credit or deduction shall be allowed under chapter 1 for any amount transferred to an employee stock ownership plan in a transfer to which this paragraph applies.

(G) AMOUNT TRANSFERRED TO INCLUDE INCOME THEREON, ETC.—The amount transferred shall not be treated as meeting the requirements of subparagraphs (B) and (C) unless amounts attributable to such amount also meet such requirements.

(4) TIME FOR PAYMENT OF TAX.—For purposes of subtitle F, the time for payment of the tax imposed by subsection (a) shall be the last day of the month following the month in which the employer reversion occurs.

Amendments

- **2008, Worker, Retiree, and Employer Recovery Act of 2008 (P.L. 110-458)**

P.L. 110-458, § 108(i)(3):

Amended Code Sec. 4980(c)(2)(B) by striking "or" at the end of clause (i), by striking the period at the end of clause (ii) and inserting ", or", and by adding at the end a new clause (iii). **Effective** as if included in the provision of the 2006 Act to which the amendment relates [effective for transfers after 8-17-2006.—CCH].

- **2006, Pension Protection Act of 2006 (P.L. 109-280)**

P.L. 109-280, § 901(a)(2)(C):

Amended Code Sec. 4980(c)(3)(A) by striking "if—" and all that follows and inserting "if the requirements of subparagraphs (B), (C), and (D) are met.". For the **effective** date, see Act Sec. 901(c), below. Prior to being stricken, all that follows "if—" in Code Sec. 4980(c)(3)(A) read as follows:

(i) the requirements of subparagraphs (B), (C), and (D) are met, and

(ii) under the plan, employer securities to which subparagraph (B) applies must, except to the extent necessary to meet the requirements of section 401(a)(28), remain in the plan until distribution to participants in accordance with the provisions of such plan.

P.L. 109-280, § 901(c), provides:

(c) EFFECTIVE DATES.—

(1) IN GENERAL.—Except as provided in paragraphs (2) and (3), the amendments made by this section shall apply to plan years beginning after December 31, 2006.

(2) SPECIAL RULE FOR COLLECTIVELY BARGAINED AGREEMENTS.—In the case of a plan maintained pursuant to 1 or more collective bargaining agreements between employee representatives and 1 or more employers ratified on or before the date of the enactment of this Act, paragraph (1) shall be applied to benefits pursuant to, and individuals covered by, any such agreement by substituting for "December 31, 2006" the earlier of—

(A) the later of—

(i) December 31, 2007, or

(ii) the date on which the last of such collective bargaining agreements terminates (determined without regard to any extension thereof after such date of enactment), or

(B) December 31, 2008.

(3) SPECIAL RULE FOR CERTAIN EMPLOYER SECURITIES HELD IN AN ESOP.—

(A) IN GENERAL.—In the case of employer securities to which this paragraph applies, the amendments made by this section shall apply to plan years beginning after the earlier of—

(i) December 31, 2007, or

(ii) the first date on which the fair market value of such securities exceeds the guaranteed minimum value described in subparagraph (B)(ii).

(B) APPLICABLE SECURITIES.—This paragraph shall apply to employer securities which are attributable to employer contributions other than elective deferrals, and which, on September 17, 2003—

(i) consist of preferred stock, and

(ii) are within an employee stock ownership plan (as defined in section 4975(e)(7) of the Internal Revenue Code of 1986), the terms of which provide that the value of the securities cannot be less than the guaranteed minimum value specified by the plan on such date.

(C) COORDINATION WITH TRANSITION RULE.—In applying section 401(a)(35)(H) of the Internal Revenue Code of 1986 and section 204(j)(7) of the Employee Retirement Income Security Act of 1974 (as added by this section) to employer securities to which this paragraph applies, the applicable percentage shall be determined without regard to this paragraph.

- **1988, Technical and Miscellaneous Revenue Act of 1988 (P.L. 100-647)**

P.L. 100-647, §1011A(f)(1):

Amended Code Sec. 4980(c)(1)(A) by striking out "this subtitle" and inserting in lieu thereof "subtitle A". **Effective** as if included in the provision of P.L. 99-514 to which it relates.

P.L. 100-647, §1011A(f)(2)(A)-(B):

Amended Code Sec. 4980(c)(3)(A) by inserting "or a tax credit employee stock ownership plan (as described in section 409)" after "section 4975(e)(7)", and by inserting ", except to the extent necessary to meet the requirements of section 401(a)(28)," after "must". **Effective** as if included in the provision of P.L. 99-514 to which it relates.

P.L. 100-647, §1011A(f)(3)(A)-(B):

Amended Code Sec. 4980(c)(3)(C) by striking out "(by reason of the limitations of section 415)" after "not allocated", and by adding at the end thereof a new sentence. **Effective** as if included in the provision of P.L. 99-514 to which it relates.

P.L. 100-647, §1011A(f)(6):

Amended Code Sec. 4980(c)(3) by adding at the end thereof new subparagraphs (F)-(G). **Effective** as if included in the provision of P.L. 99-514 to which it relates.

P.L. 100-647, §1011A(f)(7):

Amended Code Sec. 4980(c)(3)(C) by adding at the end thereof a new sentence. **Effective** as if included in the provision of P.L. 99-514 to which it relates.

P.L. 100-647, §5072(a):

Amended Code Sec. 4980(c) by adding at the end thereof a new paragraph (4). **Effective** for reversions after 12-31-88.

- **1986, Tax Reform Act of 1986 (P.L. 99-514)**

P.L. 99-514, §1132(a):

Amended Chapter 43 by adding at the end thereof new Code Sec. 4980. **Effective**, generally, for reversions occurring after 12-31-85. For an exception and transitional rule, see Act Sec. 1132(c)(2)-(5).

P.L. 99-514, §1132(c)(2)-(5), as amended by P.L. 100-647, §1011A(f)(4)-(5), provides:

(2) EXCEPTION WHERE TERMINATION DATE OCCURRED BEFORE JANUARY 1, 1986.—

(A) IN GENERAL.—Except as provided in subparagraph (B), the amendments made by this section shall not apply to any reversion after December 31, 1985, which occurs pursuant to a plan termination where the termination date is before January 1, 1986.

(B) ELECTION TO HAVE AMENDMENTS APPLY.—A corporation may elect to have the amendments made by this section apply to any reversion after 1985 pursuant to a plan termination occurring before 1986 if such corporation was incorporated in the State of Delaware in March, 1978, and became a parent corporation of the consolidated group on September 19, 1978, pursuant to a merger agreement recorded in the State of Nevada on September 19, 1978.

(3) TERMINATION DATE.—For purposes of paragraph (2), the term "termination date" is the date of the termination (within the meaning of section 411(d)(3) of the Internal Revenue Code of 1986) of the plan.

(4) TRANSITION RULE FOR CERTAIN TERMINATIONS.—

(A) IN GENERAL.—In the case of a taxpayer to which this paragraph applies, the amendments made by this section shall not apply to any termination occurring before the date which is 1 year after the date of the enactment of this Act.

(B) TAXPAYERS TO WHOM PARAGRAPH APPLIES.—This paragraph shall apply to—

(i) a corporation incorporated on June 13, 1917, which has its principal place of business in Bartlesville, Oklahoma,

(ii) a corporation incorporated on January 17, 1917, which is located in Coatesville, Pennsylvania,

(iii) a corporation incorporated on January 23, 1928, which has its principal place of business in New York, New York,

(iv) a corporation incorporated on April 23, 1956, which has its principal place of business in Dallas, Texas, and

(v) a corporation incorporated in the State of Nevada, the principal place of business of which is in Denver, Colorado, and which filed for relief from creditors under the United States Bankruptcy Code on August 28, 1986.

(5) SPECIAL RULE FOR EMPLOYEE STOCK OWNERSHIP PLANS.—Section 4980(c)(3) of the Internal Revenue Code of 1986 (as added by subsection (a)) shall apply to reversions occurring after March 31, 1985.

[Sec. 4980(d)]

(d) INCREASE IN TAX FOR FAILURE TO ESTABLISH REPLACEMENT PLAN OR INCREASE BENEFITS.—

(1) IN GENERAL.—Subsection (a) shall be applied by substituting "50 percent" for "20 percent" with respect to any employer reversion from a qualified plan unless—

(A) the employer establishes or maintains a qualified replacement plan, or

(B) the plan provides benefit increases meeting the requirements of paragraph (3).

(2) QUALIFIED REPLACEMENT PLAN.—For purposes of this subsection, the term "qualified replacement plan" means a qualified plan established or maintained by the employer in connection with a qualified plan termination (hereinafter referred to as the "replacement plan") with respect to which the following requirements are met:

(A) PARTICIPATION REQUIREMENT.—At least 95 percent of the active participants in the terminated plan who remain as employees of the employer after the termination are active participants in the replacement plan.

(B) ASSET TRANSFER REQUIREMENT.—

(i) 25 PERCENT CUSHION.—A direct transfer from the terminated plan to the replacement plan is made before any employer reversion, and the transfer is in an amount equal to the excess (if any) of—

(I) 25 percent of the maximum amount which the employer could receive as an employer reversion without regard to this subsection, over

(II) the amount determined under clause (ii).

(ii) REDUCTION FOR INCREASE IN BENEFITS.—The amount determined under this clause is an amount equal to the present value of the aggregate increases in the accrued benefits under the terminated plan of any participants or beneficiaries pursuant to a plan amendment which—

(I) is adopted during the 60-day period ending on the date of termination of the qualified plan, and

(II) takes effect immediately on the termination date.

(iii) TREATMENT OF AMOUNT TRANSFERRED.—In the case of the transfer of any amount under clause (i)—

(I) such amount shall not be includible in the gross income of the employer,

(II) no deduction shall be allowable with respect to such transfer, and

(III) such transfer shall not be treated as an employer reversion for purposes of this section.

(C) ALLOCATION REQUIREMENTS.—

(i) IN GENERAL.—In the case of any defined contribution plan, the portion of the amount transferred to the replacement plan under subparagraph (B)(i) is—

(I) allocated under the plan to the accounts of participants in the plan year in which the transfer occurs, or

(II) credited to a suspense account and allocated from such account to accounts of participants no less rapidly than ratably over the 7-plan-year period beginning with the year of the transfer.

(ii) COORDINATION WITH SECTION 415 LIMITATION.—If, by reason of any limitation under section 415, any amount credited to a suspense account under clause (i)(II) may not be allocated to a participant before the close of the 7-year period under such clause—

(I) such amount shall be allocated to the accounts of other participants, and

(II) if any portion of such amount may not be allocated to other participants by reason of any such limitation, shall be allocated to the participant as provided in section 415.

EXCISE TAXES—QUALIFIED PENSION, ETC., PLANS

(iii) TREATMENT OF INCOME.—Any income on any amount credited to a suspense account under clause (i)(II) shall be allocated to accounts of participants no less rapidly than ratably over the remainder of the period determined under such clause (after application of clause (ii)).

(iv) UNALLOCATED AMOUNTS AT TERMINATION.—If any amount credited to a suspense account under clause (i)(II) is not allocated as of the termination date of the replacement plan—

(I) such amount shall be allocated to the accounts of participants as of such date, except that any amount which may not be allocated by reason of any limitation under section 415 shall be allocated to the accounts of other participants, and

(II) if any portion of such amount may not be allocated to other participants under subclause (I) by reason of such limitation, such portion shall be treated as an employer reversion to which this section applies.

(3) PRO RATA BENEFIT INCREASES.—

(A) IN GENERAL.—The requirements of this paragraph are met if a plan amendment to the terminated plan is adopted in connection with the termination of the plan which provides pro rata increases in the accrued benefits of all qualified participants which—

(i) have an aggregate present value not less than 20 percent of the maximum amount which the employer could receive as an employer reversion without regard to this subsection, and

(ii) take effect immediately on the termination date.

(B) PRO RATA INCREASE.—For purposes of subparagraph (A), a pro rata increase is an increase in the present value of the accrued benefit of each qualified participant in an amount which bears the same ratio to the aggregate amount determined under subparagraph (A)(i) as—

(i) the present value of such participant's accrued benefit (determined without regard to this subsection), bears to

(ii) the aggregate present value of accrued benefits of the terminated plan (as so determined).

Notwithstanding the preceding sentence, the aggregate increases in the present value of the accrued benefits of qualified participants who are not active participants shall not exceed 40 percent of the aggregate amount determined under subparagraph (A)(i) by substituting "equal to" for "not less than".

(4) COORDINATION WITH OTHER PROVISIONS.—

(A) LIMITATIONS.—A benefit may not be increased under paragraph (2)(B)(ii) or (3)(A), and an amount may not be allocated to a participant under paragraph (2)(C), if such increase or allocation would result in a failure to meet any requirement under section 401(a)(4) or 415.

(B) TREATMENT AS EMPLOYER CONTRIBUTIONS.—Any increase in benefits under paragraph (2)(B)(ii) or (3)(A), or any allocation of any amount (or income allocable thereto) to any account under paragraph (2)(C), shall be treated as an annual benefit or annual addition for purposes of section 415.

(C) 10-YEAR PARTICIPATION REQUIREMENT.—Except as provided by the Secretary, section 415(b)(5)(D) shall not apply to any increase in benefits by reason of this subsection to the extent that the application of this subparagraph does not discriminate in favor of highly compensated employees (as defined in section 414(q)).

(5) DEFINITIONS AND SPECIAL RULES.—For purposes of this subsection—

(A) QUALIFIED PARTICIPANT.—The term "qualified participant" means an individual who—

(i) is an active participant,

(ii) is a participant or beneficiary in pay status as of the termination date,

(iii) is a participant not described in clause (i) or (ii)—

(I) who has a nonforfeitable right to an accrued benefit under the terminated plan as of the termination date, and

(II) whose service, which was creditable under the terminated plan, terminated during the period beginning 3 years before the termination date and ending with the date on which the final distribution of assets occurs, or

(iv) is a beneficiary of a participant described in clause (iii)(II) and has a nonforfeitable right to an accrued benefit under the terminated plan as of the termination date.

(B) PRESENT VALUE.—Present value shall be determined as of the termination date and on the same basis as liabilities of the plan are determined on termination.

(C) REALLOCATION OF INCREASE.—Except as provided in paragraph (2)(C), if any benefit increase is reduced by reason of the last sentence of paragraph (3)(A)(ii) or paragraph (4), the amount of such reduction shall be allocated to the remaining participants on the same basis as other increases (and shall be treated as meeting any allocation requirement of this subsection).

(D) PLANS TAKEN INTO ACCOUNT.—For purposes of determining whether there is a qualified replacement plan under paragraph (2), the Secretary may provide that—

(i) 2 or more plans may be treated as 1 plan, or

(ii) a plan of a successor employer may be taken into account.

(E) SPECIAL RULE FOR PARTICIPATION REQUIREMENT.—For purposes of paragraph (2)(A), all employers treated as 1 employer under section 414(b), (c), (m), or (o) shall be treated as 1 employer.

(6) SUBSECTION NOT TO APPLY TO EMPLOYER IN BANKRUPTCY.—This subsection shall not apply to an employer who, as of the termination date of the qualified plan, is in bankruptcy liquidation under chapter 7 of title 11 of the United States Code or in similar proceedings under State law.

Amendments

• **1990, Omnibus Budget Reconciliation Act of 1990 (P.L. 101-508)**

P.L. 101-508, §12002(a):

Amended Code Sec. 4980 by adding a new subsection (d). **Effective**, generally, for reversions occurring after 9-30-90. However, for exceptions see Act Sec. 12003(b).

P.L. 101-508, §12003(b), provides:

(b) EXCEPTION.—The amendments made by this subtitle shall not apply to any reversion after September 30, 1990, if—

(1) in the case of plans subject to title IV of the Employee Retirement Income Security Act of 1974, a notice of intent to terminate under such title was provided to participants (or if no participants, to the Pension Benefit Guaranty Corporation) before October 1, 1990,

(2) in the case of plans subject to title I (and not to title IV) of such Act, a notice of intent to reduce future accruals under section 204(h) of such Act was provided to participants in connection with the termination before October 1, 1990,

(3) in the case of plans not subject to title I or IV of such Act, a request for a determination letter with respect to the termination was filed with the Secretary of the Treasury or the Secretary's delegate before October 1, 1990, or

(4) in the case of plans not subject to title I or IV of such Act and having only 1 participant, a resolution terminating the plan was adopted by the employer before October 1, 1990.

[Sec. 4980A—Repealed]

Amendments

• **1997, Taxpayer Relief Act of 1997 (P.L. 105-34)**

P.L. 105-34, §1073(a):

Repealed Code Sec. 4980A. **Effective**, generally, for excess distributions received after 12-31-96. For a special rule, see Act Sec. 1073(c)(2), below.

P.L. 105-34, §1073(c)(2), provides:

(2) EXCESS RETIREMENT ACCUMULATION TAX REPEAL.—The repeal made by subsection (a) with respect to section 4980A(d) of the Internal Revenue Code of 1986 and the amendments made by subsection (b) shall apply to estates of decedents dying after December 31, 1996.

EXCISE TAXES—QUALIFIED PENSION, ETC., PLANS

Prior to repeal, Code Sec. 4980A read as follows:

SEC. 4980A. TAX ON EXCESS DISTRIBUTIONS FROM QUALIFIED RETIREMENT PLANS.

[Sec. 4980A(a)]

(a) GENERAL RULE.—There is hereby imposed a tax equal to 15 percent of the excess distributions with respect to any individual during any calendar year.

[Sec. 4980A(b)]

(b) LIABILITY FOR TAX.—The individual with respect to whom the excess distributions are made shall be liable for the tax imposed by subsection (a). The amount of the tax imposed by subsection (a) shall be reduced by the amount (if any) of the tax imposed by section 72(t) to the extent attributable to such excess distributions.

[Sec. 4980A(c)]

(c) EXCESS DISTRIBUTIONS.—For purposes of this section—

(1) IN GENERAL.—The term "excess distributions" means the aggregate amount of the retirement distributions with respect to any individual during any calendar year to the extent such amount exceeds the greater of—

(A) $150,000, or

(B) $112,500 (adjusted at the same time and in the same manner as under section 415(d)).

(2) EXCLUSION OF CERTAIN DISTRIBUTIONS.—The following distributions shall not be taken into account under paragraph (1):

(A) Any retirement distribution with respect to an individual made after the death of such individual.

(B) Any retirement distribution with respect to an individual payable to an alternate payee pursuant to a qualified domestic relations order (within the meaning of section 414(p)) if includible in income of the alternate payee.

(C) Any retirement distribution with respect to an individual which is attributable to the individual's investment in the contract (as defined in section 72(f)).

(D) Any retirement distribution to the extent not included in gross income by reason of a rollover contribution.

(E) Any retirement distribution with respect to an individual of an annuity contract the value of which is not includible in gross income at the time of the distribution (other than distributions under, or proceeds from the sale or exchange of, such contract).

(F) Any retirement distribution with respect to an individual of—

(i) excess deferrals (and income allocable thereto) under section 402(g)(2)(A)(ii), or

(ii) excess contributions (and income allocable thereto) under section 401(k)(8) or 408(d)(4) or excess aggregate contributions (and income allocable thereto) under section 401(m)(6).

Any distribution described in subparagraph (B) shall be treated as a retirement distribution to the person to whom paid for purposes of this section.

(3) AGGREGATION OF PAYMENTS.—If retirement distributions with respect to any individual during any calendar year are received by the individual and 1 or more other persons, all such distributions shall be aggregated for purposes of determining the amount of the excess distributions for the calendar year.

(4) SPECIAL ONE-TIME ELECTION.—If the retirement distributions with respect to any individual during any calendar year include a lump sum distribution (as defined in section 402(e)(4)(D)) with respect to which the individual elects to have this paragraph apply—

(A) paragraph (1) shall be applied separately with respect to such lump sum distribution and other retirement distributions, and

(B) the limitation under paragraph (1) with respect to such lump sum distribution shall be equal to 5 times the amount of such limitation determined without regard to this subparagraph.

An individual may elect to have this paragraph apply to only one lump-sum distribution.

Amendments

- **1996, Small Business Job Protection Act of 1996 (P.L. 104-188)**

P.L. 104-188, §1401(b)(12)(A)-(C):

Amended Code Sec. 4980A(c)(4) by striking "to which an election under section 402(d)(4)(B) applies" and inserting "(as defined in section 402(e)(4)(D)) with respect to which the individual elects to have this paragraph apply", by adding at the end a new flush sentence, and by striking the heading and inserting a new heading. **Effective**, generally, for tax years beginning after 12-31-99. For a special transitional rule, see Act Sec. 1401(c)(2) in the amendment notes following Code Sec. 402(d). Prior to being stricken, the heading read as follows:

(4) SPECIAL RULE WHERE TAXPAYER ELECTS INCOME AVERAGING.—

- **1992, Unemployment Compensation Amendments of 1992 (P.L. 102-318)**

P.L. 102-318, §521(b)(42):

Amended Code Sec. 4980A(c)(4) by striking "section 402(e)(4)(B)" and inserting "section 402(d)(4)(B)". **Effective** for distributions after 12-31-92.

- **1988, Technical and Miscellaneous Revenue Act of 1988 (P.L. 100-647)**

P.L. 100-647, §1011A(g)(2):

Amended Code Sec. 4980A(c)(1) (as redesignated) by striking out "$112,500 (adjusted at the same time and in the same manner as under section 415(d))" and inserting in lieu thereof "the greater of—

"(A) $150,000, or

"(B) $112,500 (adjusted at the same time and in the same manner as under section 415(d))." **Effective** as if included in the provision of P.L. 99-514 to which it relates.

P.L. 100-647, §1011A(g)(3)(A)-(B):

Amended Code Sec. 4980A(c)(2) (as redesignated) by striking out "employee's" in subparagraph (C) and inserting in lieu thereof "individual's", and by adding after subparagraph (D) new subparagraph (E)-(F). **Effective** as if included in the provision of P.L. 99-514 to which it relates.

P.L. 100-647, §1011A(g)(4)(B):

Amended Code Sec. 4980A(c) (as redesignated) by striking out paragraph (5). **Effective** as if included in the provision of P.L. 99-514 to which it relates. Prior to amendment, Code Sec. 4980A(c)(5) read as follows:

(5) SPECIAL RULE FOR ACCRUED BENEFITS AS OF AUGUST 1, 1986.—

(A) IN GENERAL.—If the employee elects on a return filed for a taxable year ending before January 1, 1989 to have this paragraph apply, the portion of any retirement distribution which is attributable (as determined under rules prescribed by the Secretary) to the accrued benefit of an employee as of August 1, 1986, shall be taken into account for purposes of paragraph (1), but no tax shall be imposed under this section with respect to such portion of such distribution.

(B) LIMITATION.—An employee may not make an election under subparagraph (A) unless the accrued benefit of such employee as of August 1, 1986, exceeds $562,500.

(C) TAXPAYER NOT MAKING ELECTION.—If an employee does not elect the application of this paragraph, paragraph (1) shall be applied by substituting $150,000 for such dollar limitation unless such dollar limitation is greater than $150,000.

[Sec. 4980A(d)]

(d) INCREASE IN ESTATE TAX IF INDIVIDUAL DIES WITH EXCESS ACCUMULATION.—

(1) IN GENERAL.—The tax imposed by chapter 11 with respect to the estate of any individual shall be increased by an amount equal to 15 percent of the individual's excess retirement accumulation.

(2) NO CREDIT ALLOWABLE.—No credit shall be allowable under chapter 11 with respect to any portion of the tax imposed by chapter 11 attributable to the increase under paragraph (1).

(3) EXCESS RETIREMENT ACCUMULATION.—For purposes of paragraph (1), the term "excess retirement accumulation" means the excess (if any) of—

(A) the value of the individual's interests (other than as beneficiary, determined after application of paragraph (5)) in qualified employer plans and individual retirement plans as of the date of the decedent's death (or, in the case of an election under section 2032, the applicable valuation date prescribed by such section), over

(B) the present value (as determined under rules prescribed by the Secretary as of the valuation date prescribed in subparagraph (A)) of a single life annuity with annual payments equal to the limitation of subsection (c) (as in effect for the year in which death occurs and as if the individual had not died).

(4) RULES FOR COMPUTING EXCESS RETIREMENT ACCUMULATION.—The excess retirement accumulation of an indiviudal shall be computed without regard to—

(A) any community property law,

(B) the value of—

(i) amounts payable to an alternate payee pursuant to a qualified domestic relations order (within the meaning of section 414(p)) if includible in income of the alternate payee, and

(ii) the individual's investment in the contract (as defined in section 72(f)), and

(C) the excess (if any) of—

(i) any interests which are payable immediately after death, over

(ii) the value of such interests immediately before death.

(5) ELECTION BY SPOUSE TO HAVE EXCESS DISTRIBUTION RULE APPLY.—

(A) IN GENERAL.—If the spouse of an individual is the beneficiary of all of the interests described in paragraph (3)(A), the spouse may elect—

(i) not to have this subsection apply, and

(ii) to have this section apply to such interests and any retirement distribution attributable to such interests as if such interests were the spouse's.

(B) DE MINIMIS EXCEPTION.—If 1 or more persons other than the spouse are beneficiaries of a de minimis portion of the interests described in paragraph (3)(A)—

(i) the spouse shall not be treated as failing to meet the requirements of subparagraph (A), and

(ii) if the spouse makes the election under subparagraph (A), this section shall not apply to such portion or any retirement distribution attributable to such portion.

Amendments

- **1988, Technical and Miscellaneous Revenue Act of 1988 (P.L. 100-647)**

P.L. 100-647, §1011A(g)(5)(A)-(B):

Amended Code Sec. 4980A(d) (as redesignated) by striking out "section 2010" in paragraph (2) and inserting in lieu thereof "chapter 11", and by adding at the end thereof new paragraphs (4)-(5). **Effective** as if included in the provision of P.L. 99-514 to which it relates.

P.L. 100-647, §1011A(g)(6):

Amended Code Sec. 4980A(d)(3)(B) (as redesignated). **Effective** as if included in the provision of P.L. 99-514 to which it relates. Prior to amendment, Code Sec. 4980A(d)(3)(B) read as follows:

(B) the present value (as determined under rules prescribed by the Secretary as of the valuation date prescribed in subparagraph (A)) of an annuity for a term certain—

(i) with annual payments equal to the limitation of subsection (c) (as in effect for the year in which the death occurs), and

(ii) payable for a period equal to the life expectancy of the individual immediately before his death.

P.L. 100-647, §1011A(g)(9):

Amended Code Sec. 4980A(d)(3)(A) by inserting "(other than as beneficiary, determined after application of paragraph (5))" after "the individual's interests". **Effective** as if included in the provision of P.L. 99-514 to which it relates.

[Sec. 4980A(e)]

(e) RETIREMENT DISTRIBUTIONS.—For purposes of this section—

(1) IN GENERAL.—The term "retirement distribution" means, with respect to any individual, the amount distributed during the taxable year under—

EXCISE TAXES—QUALIFIED PENSION, ETC., PLANS

(A) any qualified employer plan with respect to which such individual is or was the employee, and

(B) any individual retirement plan.

(2) QUALIFIED EMPLOYER PLAN.—The term "qualified employer plan" means—

(A) any plan described in section 401(a) which includes a trust exempt from tax under section 501(a),

(B) an annuity plan described in section 403(a), or

(C) an annuity contract described in section 403(b).

Such term includes any plan or contract which, at any time, has been determined by the Secretary to be such a plan or contract.

Amendments

• **1986, Tax Reform Act of 1986 (P.L. 99-514)**

P.L. 99-514, §1133(a):

Amended Chapter 43 by adding at the end thereof new Code Sec. 4981A. **Effective**, generally, for distributions made after 12-31-86, other than a distribution with respect to a decedent dying before 1-1-87 [effective date changed by P.L. 100-647, §1011A(g)(8)]. For exceptions, see Act Sec. 1134(c)(2)-(3), below.

P.L. 99-514, §1134(c)(2)-(3), provides:

(2) ESTATE TAX.—Section 4981A(d) of the Internal Revenue Code of 1986 (as added by subsection (a)) shall apply to the estates of decedents dying after December 31, 1986.

(3) PLAN TERMINATIONS BEFORE 1987.—The amendments made by this section shall not apply to distributions before January 1, 1988, which are made on account of the termination of a qualified employer plan if such termination occurred before January 1, 1987.

[Sec. 4980A(f)]

(f) EXEMPTION OF ACCRUED BENEFITS IN EXCESS OF $562,500 ON AUGUST 1, 1986.—For purposes of this section—

(1) IN GENERAL.—If an election is made with respect to an eligible individual to have this subsection apply, the individual's excess distributions and excess retirement accumulation shall be computed without regard to any distributions or interests attributable to the accrued benefit of the individual as of August 1, 1986.

(2) REDUCTION IN AMOUNTS WHICH MAY BE RECEIVED WITHOUT TAX.—If this subsection applies to any individual—

(A) EXCESS DISTRIBUTIONS.—Subsection (c)(1) shall be applied—

(i) without regard to subparagraph (A), and

(ii) by reducing (but not below zero) the amount determined under subparagraph (B) thereof by retirement distributions attributable (as determined under rules prescribed by the Secretary) to the individual's accrued benefit as of August 1, 1986.

(B) EXCESS RETIREMENT ACCUMULATION.—The amount determined under subsection (d)(3)(B) (without regard to subsection (c)(1)(A)) with respect to such individual shall be reduced (but not below zero) by the present value of the individual's accrued benefit as of August 1, 1986, which has not been distributed as of the date of death.

(3) ELIGIBLE INDIVIDUAL.—For purposes of this subsection, the term "eligible individual" means any individual if, on August 1, 1986, the present value of such individual's interest in qualified employer plans and individual retirement plans exceeded $562,500.

(4) CERTAIN AMOUNTS EXCLUDED.—In determining an individual's accrued benefit for purposes of this subsection, there shall not be taken into account any portion of the accrued benefit—

(A) payable to an alternate payee pursuant to a qualified domestic relations order (within the meaning of section 414(p)) if includible in income of the alternate payee, or

(B) attributable to the individual's investment in the contract (as defined in section 72(f)).

(5) ELECTION.—An election under paragraph (1) shall be made on an individual's return of tax imposed by chapter 1 or 11 for a taxable year beginning before January 1, 1989.

Amendments

• **1988, Technical and Miscellaneous Revenue Act of 1988 (P.L. 100-647)**

P.L. 100-647, §1011A(g)(1)(A):

Redesignated Code Sec. 4981A, as added by P.L. 99-514, §1133, as Code Sec. 4980A. **Effective** as if included in the provision of P.L. 99-514 to which it relates.

P.L. 100-647, §1011A(g)(4)(A):

Amended Code Sec. 4980A (as redesignated) by adding at the end thereof new subsection (f). **Effective** as if included in the provision of P.L. 99-514 to which it relates.

[Sec. 4980A(g)]

(g) LIMITATION ON APPLICATION.—This section shall not apply to distributions during years beginning after December 31, 1996, and before January 1, 2000, and such distributions shall be treated as made first from amounts not described in subsection (f).

Amendments

• **1996, Small Business Job Protection Act of 1996 (P.L. 104-188)**

P.L. 104-188, §1452(b):

Amended Code Sec. 4980A by adding at the end a new subsection (g). **Effective** for years beginning after 12-31-96.

[Sec. 4980B]

SEC. 4980B. FAILURE TO SATISFY CONTINUATION COVERAGE REQUIREMENTS OF GROUP HEALTH PLANS.

[Sec. 4980B(a)]

(a) GENERAL RULE.—There is hereby imposed a tax on the failure of a group health plan to meet the requirements of subsection (f) with respect to any qualified beneficiary.

[Sec. 4980B(b)]

(b) AMOUNT OF TAX.—

(1) IN GENERAL.—The amount of the tax imposed by subsection (a) on any failure with respect to a qualified beneficiary shall be $100 for each day in the noncompliance period with respect to such failure.

(2) NONCOMPLIANCE PERIOD.—For purposes of this section, the term "noncompliance period" means, with respect to any failure, the period—

(A) beginning on the date such failure 1st occurs, and

(B) ending on the earlier of—

(i) the date such failure is corrected, or

(ii) the date which is 6 months after the last day in the period applicable to the qualified beneficiary under subsection (f)(2)(B) (determined without regard to clause (iii) thereof).

If a person is liable for tax under subsection (e)(1)(B) by reason of subsection (e)(2)(B) with respect to any failure, the noncompliance period for such person with respect to such failure shall not begin before the 45th day after the written request described in subsection (e)(2)(B) is provided to such person.

(3) MINIMUM TAX FOR NONCOMPLIANCE PERIOD WHERE FAILURE DISCOVERED AFTER NOTICE OF EXAMINATION.—Notwithstanding paragraphs (1) and (2) of subsection (c)—

(A) IN GENERAL.—In the case of 1 or more failures with respect to a qualified beneficiary—

(i) which are not corrected before the date a notice of examination of income tax liability is sent to the employer, and

(ii) which occurred or continued during the period under examination,

the amount of tax imposed by subsection (a) by reason of such failures with respect to such beneficiary shall not be less than the lesser of $2,500 or the amount of tax which would be imposed by subsection (a) without regard to such paragraphs.

(B) HIGHER MINIMUM TAX WHERE VIOLATIONS ARE MORE THAN DE MINIMIS.—To the extent violations by the employer (or the plan in the case of a multiemployer plan) for any year are more than de minimis, subparagraph (A) shall be applied by substituting "$15,000" for "$2,500" with respect to the employer (or such plan).

[Sec. 4980B(c)]

(c) LIMITATIONS ON AMOUNT OF TAX.—

(1) TAX NOT TO APPLY WHERE FAILURE NOT DISCOVERED EXERCISING REASONABLE DILIGENCE.—No tax shall be imposed by subsection (a) on any failure during any period for which it is established to the satisfaction of the Secretary that none of the persons referred to in subsection (e) knew, or exercising reasonable diligence would have known, that such failure existed.

(2) TAX NOT TO APPLY TO FAILURES CORRECTED WITHIN 30 DAYS.—No tax shall be imposed by subsection (a) on any failure if—

(A) such failure was due to reasonable cause and not to willful neglect, and

(B) such failure is corrected during the 30-day period beginning on the 1st date any of the persons referred to in subsection (e) knew, or exercising reasonable diligence would have known, that such failure existed.

(3) $100 LIMIT ON AMOUNT OF TAX FOR FAILURES ON ANY DAY WITH RESPECT TO A QUALIFIED BENEFICIARY.—

(A) IN GENERAL.—Except as provided in subparagraph (B), the maximum amount of tax imposed by subsection (a) on failures on any day during the noncompliance period with respect to a qualified beneficiary shall be $100.

(B) SPECIAL RULE WHERE MORE THAN 1 QUALIFIED BENEFICIARY.—If there is more than 1 qualified beneficiary with respect to the same qualifying event, the maximum amount of tax imposed by subsection (a) on all failures on any day during the noncompliance period with respect to such qualified beneficiaries shall be $200.

(4) OVERALL LIMITATION FOR UNINTENTIONAL FAILURES.—In the case of failures which are due to reasonable cause and not to willful neglect—

(A) SINGLE EMPLOYER PLANS.—

(i) IN GENERAL.—In the case of failures with respect to plans other than multiemployer plans, the tax imposed by subsection (a) for failures during the taxable year of the employer shall not exceed the amount equal to the lesser of—

(I) 10 percent of the aggregate amount paid or incurred by the employer (or predecessor employer) during the preceding taxable year for group health plans, or

(II) $500,000.

(ii) TAXABLE YEARS IN THE CASE OF CERTAIN CONTROLLED GROUPS.—For purposes of this subparagraph, if not all persons who are treated as a single employer for purposes of this section have the same taxable year, the taxable years taken into account shall be determined under principles similar to the principles of section 1561.

(B) MULTIEMPLOYER PLANS.—

(i) IN GENERAL.—In the case of failures with respect to a multiemployer plan, the tax imposed by subsection (a) for failures during the taxable year of the trust forming part of such plan shall not exceed the amount equal to the lesser of—

(I) 10 percent of the amount paid or incurred by such trust during such taxable year to provide medical care (as defined in section 213(d)) directly or through insurance, reimbursement, or otherwise, or

(II) $500,000.

For purposes of the preceding sentence, all plans of which the same trust forms a part shall be treated as 1 plan.

(ii) SPECIAL RULE FOR EMPLOYERS REQUIRED TO PAY TAX.—If an employer is assessed a tax imposed by subsection (a) by reason of a failure with respect to a multiemployer plan, the limit shall be determined under subparagraph (A) (and not under this subparagraph) and as if such plan were not a multiemployer plan.

(C) SPECIAL RULE FOR PERSONS PROVIDING BENEFITS.—In the case of a person described in subsection (e)(1)(B) (and not subsection (e)(1)(A)), the aggregate amount of tax imposed by subsection (a) for failures during a taxable year with respect to all plans shall not exceed $2,000,000.

(5) WAIVER BY SECRETARY.—In the case of a failure which is due to reasonable cause and not to willful neglect, the Secretary may waive part or all of the tax imposed by subsection (a) to the extent that the payment of such tax would be excessive relative to the failure involved.

[Sec. 4980B(d)]

(d) TAX NOT TO APPLY TO CERTAIN PLANS.—This section shall not apply to—

(1) any failure of a group health plan to meet the requirements of subsection (f) with respect to any qualified beneficiary if the qualifying event with respect to such beneficiary occurred during the calendar year immediately following a calendar year during which all employers maintaining such plan normally employed fewer than 20 employees on a typical business day,

(2) any governmental plan (within the meaning of section 414(d)), or

(3) any church plan (within the meaning of section 414(e)).

Amendments

• **1990, Omnibus Budget Reconciliation Act of 1990 (P.L. 101-508)**

P.L. 101-508, §11702(f):

Amended Code Sec. 4980B(d)(1). **Effective** as if included in the provision of P.L. 100-647 to which it relates. Prior to amendment, paragraph (1) read as follows:

(1) any failure of a group health plan to meet the requirements of subsection (f) if all employers maintaining such plan normally employed fewer than 20 employees on a typical business day during the preceding calendar year,

[Sec. 4980B(e)]

(e) LIABILITY FOR TAX.—

(1) IN GENERAL.—Except as otherwise provided in this subsection, the following shall be liable for the tax imposed by subsection (a) on a failure:

(A)(i) In the case of a plan other than a multiemployer plan, the employer.

(ii) In the case of a multiemployer plan, the plan.

(B) Each person who is responsible (other than in a capacity as an employee) for administering or providing benefits under the plan and whose act or failure to act caused (in whole or in part) the failure.

(2) SPECIAL RULES FOR PERSONS DESCRIBED IN PARAGRAPH (1)(B).—

(A) NO LIABILITY UNLESS WRITTEN AGREEMENT.—Except in the case of liability resulting from the application of subparagraph (B) of this paragraph, a person described in subparagraph (B) (and not in subparagraph (A)) of paragraph (1) shall be liable for the tax imposed by subsection (a) on any failure only if such person assumed (under a legally enforceable written agreement) responsibility for the performance of the act to which the failure relates.

(B) FAILURE TO COVER QUALIFIED BENEFICIARIES WHERE CURRENT EMPLOYEES ARE COVERED.—A person shall be treated as described in paragraph (1)(B) with respect to a qualified beneficiary if—

(i) such person provides coverage under a group health plan for any similarly situated beneficiary under the plan with respect to whom a qualifying event has not occurred, and

(ii) the—

(I) employer or plan administrator, or

(II) in the case of a qualifying event described in subparagraph (C) or (E) of subsection (f)(3) where the person described in clause (i) is the plan administrator, the qualified beneficiary,

submits to such person a written request that such person make available to such qualified beneficiary the same coverage which such person provides to the beneficiary referred to in clause (i).

EXCISE TAXES—QUALIFIED PENSION, ETC., PLANS

[Sec. 4980B(f)]

(f) CONTINUATION COVERAGE REQUIREMENTS OF GROUP HEALTH PLANS.—

(1) IN GENERAL.—A group health plan meets the requirements of this subsection only if the coverage of the costs of pediatric vaccines (as defined under section 1928(h)(6) of the Social Security Act (42 U.S.C. 1396s(h)(6))) is not reduced below the coverage provided by the plan as of May 1, 1993, and only if each qualified beneficiary who would lose coverage under the plan as a result of a qualifying event is entitled to elect, within the election period, continuation coverage under the plan.

(2) CONTINUATION COVERAGE.—For purposes of paragraph (1), the term "continuation coverage" means coverage under the plan which meets the following requirements:

(A) TYPE OF BENEFIT COVERAGE.—The coverage must consist of coverage which, as of the time the coverage is being provided, is identical to the coverage provided under the plan to similarly situated beneficiaries under the plan with respect to whom a qualifying event has not occurred. If coverage under the plan is modified for any group of similarly situated beneficiaries, the coverage shall also be modified in the same manner for all individuals who are qualified beneficiaries under the plan pursuant to this subsection in connection with such group.

(B) PERIOD OF COVERAGE.—The coverage must extend for at least the period beginning on the date of the qualifying event and ending not earlier than the earliest of the following:

(i) MAXIMUM REQUIRED PERIOD.—

(I) GENERAL RULE FOR TERMINATIONS AND REDUCED HOURS.—In the case of a qualifying event described in paragraph (3)(B), except as provided in subclause (II), the date which is 18 months after the date of the qualifying event.

(II) SPECIAL RULE FOR MULTIPLE QUALIFYING EVENTS.—If a qualifying event (other than a qualifying event described in paragraph (3)(F)) occurs during the 18 months after the date of a qualifying event described in paragraph (3)(B), the date which is 36 months after the date of the qualifying event described in paragraph (3)(B).

(III) SPECIAL RULE FOR CERTAIN BANKRUPTCY PROCEEDINGS.—In the case of a qualifying event described in paragraph (3)(F) (relating to bankruptcy proceedings), the date of the death of the covered employee or qualified beneficiary (described in subsection (g)(1)(D)(iii)), or in the case of the surviving spouse or dependent children of the covered employee, 36 months after the date of the death of the covered employee.

(IV) GENERAL RULE FOR OTHER QUALIFYING EVENTS.—In the case of a qualifying event not described in paragraph (3)(B) or (3)(F), the date which is 36 months after the date of the qualifying event.

(V) SPECIAL RULE FOR PBGC RECIPIENTS.—In the case of a qualifying event described in paragraph (3)(B) with respect to a covered employee who (as of such qualifying event) has a nonforfeitable right to a benefit any portion of which is to be paid by the Pension Benefit Guaranty Corporation under title IV of the Employee Retirement Income Security Act of 1974, notwithstanding subclause (I) or (II), the date of the death of the covered employee, or in the case of the surviving spouse or dependent children of the covered employee, 24 months after the date of the death of the covered employee. The preceding sentence shall not require any period of coverage to extend beyond January 1, 2014.

(VI) SPECIAL RULE FOR TAA-ELIGIBLE INDIVIDUALS.—In the case of a qualifying event described in paragraph (3)(B) with respect to a covered employee who is (as of the date that the period of coverage would, but for this subclause or subclause (VII), otherwise terminate under subclause (I) or (II)) a TAA-eligible individual (as defined in paragraph (5)(C)(iv)(II)), the period of coverage shall not terminate by reason of subclause (I) or (II), as the case may be, before the later of the date specified in such subclause or the date on which such individual ceases to be such a TAA-eligible individual. The preceding sentence shall not require any period of coverage to extend beyond January 1, 2014.

(VII) MEDICARE ENTITLEMENT FOLLOWED BY QUALIFIYING EVENT.—In the case of a qualifying event described in paragraph (3)(B) that occurs less than 18 months after the date the covered employee became entitled to benefits under title XVIII of the Social Security Act, the period of coverage for qualified beneficiaries other than the covered employee shall not terminate under this clause before the close of the 36-month period beginning on the date the covered employee became so entitled.

(VIII) SPECIAL RULE FOR DISABILITY.—In the case of a qualified beneficiary who is determined, under title II or XVI of the Social Security Act, to have been disabled at any time during the first 60 days of continuation coverage under this section, any reference in subclause (I) or (II) to 18 months is deemed a reference to 29 months (with respect to all qualified beneficiaries), but only if the qualified beneficiary has provided notice of such determination under paragraph (6)(C) before the end of such 18 months.

(ii) END OF PLAN.—The date on which the employer ceases to provide any group health plan to any employee.

(iii) FAILURE TO PAY PREMIUM.—The date on which coverage ceases under the plan by reason of a failure to make timely payment of any premium required under the plan with respect to the qualified beneficiary. The payment of any premium (other than any payment referred to in the last sentence of subparagraph (C)) shall be considered to be timely if made within 30 days after the date due or within such longer period as applies to or under the plan.

(iv) GROUP HEALTH PLAN COVERAGE OR MEDICARE ENTITLEMENT.—The date on which the qualified beneficiary first becomes, after the date of the election—

(I) covered under any other group health plan (as an employee or otherwise) which does not contain any exclusion or limitation with respect to any preexisting condition of such beneficiary (other than such an exclusion or limitation which does not apply to (or is satisfied by) such beneficiary by reason of chapter 100 of this title, part 7 of subtitle B of title I of the Employee Retirement Income Security Act of 1974, or title XXVII of the Public Health Service Act), or

(II) in the case of a qualified beneficiary other than a qualified beneficiary described in subsection (g)(1)(D) entitled to benefits under title XVIII of the Social Security Act.

(v) TERMINATION OF EXTENDED COVERAGE FOR DISABILITY.—In the case of a qualified beneficiary who is disabled at any time during the first 60 days of continuation coverage under this section, the month that begins more than 30 days after the date of the final determination under title II or XVI of the Social Security Act that the qualified beneficiary is no longer disabled.

(C) PREMIUM REQUIREMENTS.—The plan may require payment of a premium for any period of continuation coverage, except that such premium—

(i) shall not exceed 102 percent of the applicable premium for such period, and

(ii) may, at the election of the payor, be made in monthly installments.

In no event may the plan require the payment of any premium before the day which is 45 days after the day on which the qualified beneficiary made the initial election for continuation coverage. In the case of an individual described in the last sentence of subparagraph (B)(i), any reference in clause (i) of this subparagraph to "102 percent" is deemed a reference to "150 percent" for any month after the 18th month of continuation coverage described in subclause (I) or (II) of subparagraph (B)(i).

(D) NO REQUIREMENT OF INSURABILITY.—The coverage may not be conditioned upon, or discriminate on the basis of lack of, evidence of insurability.

(E) CONVERSION OPTION.—In the case of a qualified beneficiary whose period of continuation coverage expires under subparagraph (B)(i), the plan must, during the 180-day period ending on such expiration date, provide to the qualified beneficiary the option of enrollment under a conversion health plan otherwise generally available under the plan.

(3) QUALIFYING EVENT.—For purposes of this subsection, the term "qualifying event" means, with respect to any covered employee, any of the following events which, but for the continuation coverage required under this subsection, would result in the loss of coverage of a qualified beneficiary—

(A) The death of the covered employee.

(B) The termination (other than by reason of such employee's gross misconduct), or reduction of hours, of the covered employee's employment.

(C) The divorce or legal separation of the covered employee from the employee's spouse.

(D) The covered employee becoming entitled to benefits under title XVIII of the Social Security Act.

(E) A dependent child ceasing to be a dependent child under the generally applicable requirements of the plan.

(F) A proceeding in a case under title 11, United States Code, commencing on or after July 1, 1986, with respect to the employer from whose employment the covered employee retired at any time.

In the case of an event described in subparagraph (F), a loss of coverage includes a substantial elimination of coverage with respect to a qualified beneficiary described in subsection (g)(1)(D) within one year before or after the date of commencement of the proceeding.

(4) APPLICABLE PREMIUM.—For purposes of this subsection—

(A) IN GENERAL.—The term "applicable premium" means, with respect to any period of continuation coverage of qualified beneficiaries, the cost to the plan for such period of the coverage for similarly situated beneficiaries with respect to whom a qualifying event has not occurred (without regard to whether such cost is paid by the employer or employee).

(B) SPECIAL RULE FOR SELF-INSURED PLANS.—To the extent that a plan is a self-insured plan—

(i) IN GENERAL.—Except as provided in clause (ii), the applicable premium for any period of continuation coverage of qualified beneficiaries shall be equal to a reasonable estimate of the cost of providing coverage for such period for similarly situated beneficiaries which—

(I) is determined on an actuarial basis, and

(II) takes into account such factors as the Secretary may prescribe in regulations.

(ii) DETERMINATION ON BASIS OF PAST COST.—If a plan administrator elects to have this clause apply, the applicable premium for any period of continuation coverage of qualified beneficiaries shall be equal to—

(I) the cost to the plan for similarly situated beneficiaries for the same period occurring during the preceding determination period under subparagraph (C), adjusted by

(II) the percentage increase or decrease in the implicit price deflator of the gross national product (calculated by the Department of Commerce and published in the Survey of Current Business) for the 12-month period ending on the last day of the sixth month of such preceding determination period.

(iii) CLAUSE (ii) NOT TO APPLY WHERE SIGNIFICANT CHANGE.—A plan administrator may not elect to have clause (ii) apply in any case in which there is any significant difference between the determination period and the preceding determination period, in coverage under, or in employees covered by, the plan. The determination under the preceding sentence for any determination period shall be made at the same time as the determination under subparagraph (C).

(C) DETERMINATION PERIOD.—The determination of any applicable premium shall be made for a period of 12 months and shall be made before the beginning of such period.

(5) ELECTION.—For purposes of this subsection—

(A) ELECTION PERIOD.—The term "election period" means the period which—

(i) begins not later than the date on which coverage terminates under the plan by reason of a qualifying event,

(ii) is of at least 60 days' duration, and

(iii) ends not earlier than 60 days after the later of—

(I) the date described in clause (i), or

(II) in the case of any qualified beneficiary who receives notice under paragraph (6)(D), the date of such notice.

(B) EFFECT OF ELECTION ON OTHER BENEFICIARIES.—Except as otherwise specified in an election, any election of continuation coverage by a qualified beneficiary described in subparagraph (A)(i) or (B) of subsection (g)(1) shall be deemed to include an election of continuation coverage on behalf of any other qualified beneficiary who would lose coverage under the plan by reason of the qualifying event. If there is a choice among types of coverage under the plan, each qualified beneficiary is entitled to make a separate selection among such types of coverage.

(C) TEMPORARY EXTENSION OF COBRA ELECTION PERIOD FOR CERTAIN INDIVIDUALS.—

(i) IN GENERAL.—In the case of a nonelecting TAA-eligible individual and notwithstanding subparagraph (A), such individual may elect continuation coverage under this subsection during the 60-day period that begins on the first day of the month in which the individual becomes a TAA-eligible individual, but only if such election is made not later than 6 months after the date of the TAA-related loss of coverage.

(ii) COMMENCEMENT OF COVERAGE; NO REACH-BACK.—Any continuation coverage elected by a TAA-eligible individual under clause (i) shall commence at the beginning of the 60-day election period described in such paragraph and shall not include any period prior to such 60-day election period.

(iii) PREEXISTING CONDITIONS.—With respect to an individual who elects continuation coverage pursuant to clause (i), the period—

(I) beginning on the date of the TAA-related loss of coverage, and

(II) ending on the first day of the 60-day election period described in clause (i),

shall be disregarded for purposes of determining the 63-day periods referred to in section 9801(c)(2), section 701(c)(2) of the Employee Retirement Income Security Act of 1974, and section 2704(c)(2) of the Public Health Service Act.

(iv) DEFINITIONS.—For purposes of this subsection:

(I) NONELECTING TAA-ELIGIBLE INDIVIDUAL.—The term "nonelecting TAA-eligible individual" means a TAA-eligible individual who has a TAA-related loss of coverage and did not elect continuation coverage under this subsection during the TAA-related election period.

(II) TAA-ELIGIBLE INDIVIDUAL.—The term "TAA-eligible individual" means an eligible TAA recipient (as defined in paragraph (2) of section 35(c) and an eligible alternative TAA recipient (as defined in paragraph (3) of such section).

EXCISE TAXES—QUALIFIED PENSION, ETC., PLANS

(III) TAA-RELATED ELECTION PERIOD.—The term "TAA-related election period" means, with respect to a TAA-related loss of coverage, the 60-day election period under this subsection which is a direct consequence of such loss.

(IV) TAA-RELATED LOSS OF COVERAGE.—The term "TAA-related loss of coverage" means, with respect to an individual whose separation from employment gives rise to being an TAA-eligible individual, the loss of health benefits coverage associated with such separation.

(6) NOTICE REQUIREMENT.—In accordance with regulations prescribed by the Secretary—

(A) The group health plan shall provide, at the time of commencement of coverage under the plan, written notice to each covered employee and spouse of the employee (if any) of the rights provided under this subsection.

(B) The employer of an employee under a plan must notify the plan administrator of a qualifying event described in subparagraph (A), (B), (D), or (F) of paragraph (3) with respect to such employee within 30 days (or, in the case of a group health plan which is a multiemployer plan, such longer period of time as may be provided in terms of the plan) of the date of the qualifying event.

(C) Each covered employee or qualified beneficiary is responsible for notifying the plan administrator of the occurrence of any qualifying event described in subparagraph (C) or (E) of paragraph (3) within 60 days after the date of the qualifying event and each qualified beneficiary who is determined, under title II or XVI of the Social Security Act, to have been disabled at any time during the first 60 days of continuation coverage under this section is responsible for notifying the plan administrator of such determination within 60 days after the date of the determination and for notifying the plan administrator within 30 days of the date of any final determination under such title or titles that the qualified beneficiary is no longer disabled.

(D) The plan administrator shall notify—

(i) in the case of a qualifying event described in subparagraph (A), (B), (D), or (F) of paragraph (3), any qualified beneficiary with respect to such event, and

(ii) in the case of a qualifying event described in subparagraph (C) or (E) of paragraph (3) where the covered employee notifies the plan administrator under subparagraph (C), any qualified beneficiary with respect to such event,

of such beneficiary's rights under this subsection.

The requirements of subparagraph (B) shall be considered satisfied in the case of a multiemployer plan in connection with a qualifying event described in paragraph (3)(B) if the plan provides that the determination of the occurrence of such qualifying event will be made by the plan administrator. For purposes of subparagraph (D), any notification shall be made within 14 days (or, in the case of a group health plan which is a multiemployer plan, such longer period of time as may be provided in the terms of the plan) of the date on which the plan administrator is notified under subparagraph (B) or (C), whichever is applicable, and any such notification to an individual who is a qualified beneficiary as the spouse of the covered employee shall be treated as notification to all other qualified beneficiaries residing with such spouse at the time such notification is made.

(7) COVERED EMPLOYEE.—For purposes of this subsection, the term "covered employee" means an individual who is (or was) provided coverage under a group health plan by virtue of the performance of services by the individual for 1 or more persons maintaining the plan (including as an employee defined in section 401(c)(1)).

(8) OPTIONAL EXTENSION OF REQUIRED PERIODS.—A group health plan shall not be treated as failing to meet the requirements of this subsection solely because the plan provides both—

(A) that the period of extended coverage referred to in paragraph (2)(B) commences with the date of the loss of coverage, and

(B) that the applicable notice period provided under paragraph (6)(B) commences with the date of the loss of coverage.

Amendments

• 2021, American Rescue Plan Act of 2021 (P.L. 117-2)

P.L. 117-2, §9501, provides:

SEC. 9501. PRESERVING HEALTH BENEFITS FOR WORKERS.

(a) PREMIUM ASSISTANCE FOR COBRA CONTINUATION COVERAGE FOR INDIVIDUALS AND THEIR FAMILIES.—

(1) PROVISION OF PREMIUM ASSISTANCE.—

(A) REDUCTION OF PREMIUMS PAYABLE.—In the case of any premium for a period of coverage during the period beginning on the first day of the first month beginning after the date of the enactment of this Act, and ending on September 30, 2021, for COBRA continuation coverage with respect to any assistance eligible individual described in paragraph (3), such individual shall be treated for purposes of any COBRA continuation provision as having paid in full the amount of such premium.

(B) PLAN ENROLLMENT OPTION.—

(i) IN GENERAL.—Solely for purposes of this subsection, the COBRA continuation provisions shall be applied such that any assistance eligible individual who is enrolled in a group health plan offered by a plan sponsor may, not later than 90 days after the date of notice of the plan enrollment option described in this subparagraph, elect to enroll in coverage under a plan offered by such plan sponsor that is different than coverage under the plan in which such individual was enrolled at the time, in the case of any assistance eligible individual described in paragraph (3), the qualifying event specified in section 603(2) of the Employee Retirement Income Security Act of 1974, section 4980B(f)(3)(B) of the Internal Revenue Code of 1986, or section 2203(2) of the Public Health Service Act, except for the voluntary termination of such individual's employment by such individual, occurred, and such coverage shall be treated as COBRA continuation coverage for purposes of the applicable COBRA continuation coverage provision.

(ii) REQUIREMENTS.—Any assistance eligible individual may elect to enroll in different coverage as described in clause (i) only if—

(I) the employer involved has made a determination that such employer will permit such assistance eligible individual to enroll in different coverage as provided under this subparagraph;

(II) the premium for such different coverage does not exceed the premium for coverage in which such individual was enrolled at the time such qualifying event occurred;

(III) the different coverage in which the individual elects to enroll is coverage that is also offered to similarly situated active employees of the employer at the time at which such election is made; and

(IV) the different coverage in which the individual elects to enroll is not—

(aa) coverage that provides only excepted benefits as defined in section 9832(c) of the Internal Revenue Code of 1986, section 733(c) of the Employee Retirement Income Security Act of 1974, and section 2791(c) of the Public Health Service Act;

(bb) a qualified small employer health reimbursement arrangement (as defined in section 9831(d)(2) of the Internal Revenue Code of 1986); or

(cc) a flexible spending arrangement (as defined in section 106(c)(2) of the Internal Revenue Code of 1986).

(2) LIMITATION OF PERIOD OF PREMIUM ASSISTANCE.—

(A) ELIGIBILITY FOR ADDITIONAL COVERAGE.—Paragraph (1)(A) shall not apply with respect to any assistance eligible individual described in paragraph (3) for months of coverage beginning on or after the earlier of—

(i) the first date that such individual is eligible for coverage under any other group health plan (other than coverage consisting of only excepted benefits (as defined in section 9832(c) of the Internal Revenue Code of 1986, section 733(c) of the Employee Retirement Income Security Act of 1974, and section 2791(c) of the Public Health Service Act), coverage under a flexible spending arrangement (as defined in section 106(c)(2) of the Internal Revenue Code of 1986), coverage under a qualified small employer health reimbursement arrangement (as defined in section 9831(d)(2) of the Internal Revenue Code of 1986)), or eligible for benefits under the Medicare program under title XVIII of the Social Security Act; or

(ii) the earlier of—

(I) the date following the expiration of the maximum period of continuation coverage required under the applicable COBRA continuation coverage provision; or

(II) the date following the expiration of the period of continuation coverage allowed under paragraph (4)(B)(ii).

(B) NOTIFICATION REQUIREMENT.—Any assistance eligible individual shall notify the group health plan with respect to which paragraph (1)(A) applies if such paragraph ceases to apply by reason of clause (i) of subparagraph (A) (as applicable). Such notice shall be provided to the group health plan in such time and manner as may be specified by the Secretary of Labor.

(3) ASSISTANCE ELIGIBLE INDIVIDUAL.—For purposes of this section, the term "assistance eligible individual" means, with respect to a period of coverage during the period beginning on the first day of the first month beginning after the date of the enactment of this Act, and ending on September 30, 2021, any individual that is a qualified beneficiary who—

(A) is eligible for COBRA continuation coverage by reason of a qualifying event specified in section 603(2) of the Employee Retirement Income Security Act of 1974, section 4980B(f)(3)(B) of the Internal Revenue Code of 1986, or section 2203(2) of the Public Health Service Act, except for the voluntary termination of such individual's employment by such individual; and

(B) elects such coverage.

(4) EXTENSION OF ELECTION PERIOD AND EFFECT ON COVERAGE.—

(A) IN GENERAL.—For purposes of applying section 605(a) of the Employee Retirement Income Security Act of 1974, section 4980B(f)(5)(A) of the Internal Revenue Code of 1986, and section 2205(a) of the Public Health Service Act, in the case of—

(i) an individual who does not have an election of COBRA continuation coverage in effect on the first day of the first month beginning after the date of the enactment of this Act but who would be an assistance eligible individual described in paragraph (3) if such election were so in effect; or

(ii) an individual who elected COBRA continuation coverage and discontinued from such coverage before the first day of the first month beginning after the date of the enactment of this Act,

such individual may elect the COBRA continuation coverage under the COBRA continuation coverage provisions containing such provisions during the period beginning on the first day of the first month beginning after the date of the enactment of this Act and ending 60 days after the date on which the notification required under paragraph (5)(C) is provided to such individual.

(B) COMMENCEMENT OF COBRA CONTINUATION COVERAGE.—Any COBRA continuation coverage elected by a qualified beneficiary during an extended election period under subparagraph (A)—

(i) shall commence (including for purposes of applying the treatment of premium payments under paragraph (1)(A) and any cost-sharing requirements for items and services under a group health plan) with the first period of coverage beginning on or after the first day of the first month beginning after the date of the enactment of this Act, and

(ii) shall not extend beyond the period of COBRA continuation coverage that would have been required under the applicable COBRA continuation coverage provision if the coverage had been elected as required under such provision or had not been discontinued.

(5) NOTICES TO INDIVIDUALS.—

(A) GENERAL NOTICE.—

(i) IN GENERAL.—In the case of notices provided under section 606(a)(4) of the Employee Retirement Income Security Act of 1974 (29 U.S.C. 1166(4)), section 4980B(f)(6)(D) of the Internal Revenue Code of 1986, or section 2206(4) of the Public Health Service Act (42 U.S.C. 300bb–6(4)), with respect to individuals who, during the period described in paragraph (3), become entitled to elect COBRA continuation coverage, the requirements of such provisions shall not be treated as met unless such notices include an additional written notification to the recipient in clear and understandable language of—

(I) the availability of premium assistance with respect to such coverage under this subsection; and

(II) the option to enroll in different coverage if the employer permits assistance eligible individuals described in paragraph (3) to elect enrollment in different coverage (as described in paragraph (1)(B)).

(ii) ALTERNATIVE NOTICE.—In the case of COBRA continuation coverage to which the notice provision under such subsections does not apply, the Secretary of Labor, in consultation with the Secretary of the Treasury and the Secretary of Health and Human Services, shall, in consultation with administrators of the group health plans (or other entities) that provide or administer the COBRA continuation coverage involved, provide rules requiring the provision of such notice.

(iii) FORM.—The requirement of the additional notification under this subparagraph may be met by amendment of existing notice forms or by inclusion of a separate document with the notice otherwise required.

(B) SPECIFIC REQUIREMENTS.—Each additional notification under subparagraph (A) shall include—

(i) the forms necessary for establishing eligibility for premium assistance under this subsection;

(ii) the name, address, and telephone number necessary to contact the plan administrator and any other person maintaining relevant information in connection with such premium assistance;

(iii) a description of the extended election period provided for in paragraph (4)(A);

(iv) a description of the obligation of the qualified beneficiary under paragraph (2)(B) and the penalty provided under section 6720C of the Internal Revenue Code of 1986 for failure to carry out the obligation;

(v) a description, displayed in a prominent manner, of the qualified beneficiary's right to a subsidized premium and any conditions on entitlement to the subsidized premium; and

(vi) a description of the option of the qualified beneficiary to enroll in different coverage if the employer permits such beneficiary to elect to enroll in such different coverage under paragraph (1)(B).

(C) NOTICE IN CONNECTION WITH EXTENDED ELECTION PERIODS.—In the case of any assistance eligible individual described in paragraph (3) (or any individual described in paragraph (4)(A)) who became entitled to elect COBRA continuation coverage before the first day of the first month beginning after the date of the enactment of this Act, the administrator of the applicable group health plan (or other entity) shall provide (within 60 days after such first day of such first month) for the additional notification required to be provided under subparagraph (A) and failure to provide such notice shall be treated as a failure to meet the notice requirements under the applicable COBRA continuation provision.

(D) MODEL NOTICES.—Not later than 30 days after the date of enactment of this Act, with respect to any assistance eligible individual described in paragraph (3), the Secretary of Labor, in consultation with the Secretary of the Treasury and the Secretary of Health and Human Services, shall prescribe models for the additional notification required under this paragraph.

(6) NOTICE OF EXPIRATION OF PERIOD OF PREMIUM ASSISTANCE.—

(A) IN GENERAL.—With respect to any assistance eligible individual, subject to subparagraph (B), the requirements of section 606(a)(4) of the Employee Retirement Income Security Act of 1974 (29 U.S.C. 1166(4)), section 4980B(f)(6)(D) of the Internal Revenue Code of 1986, or section 2206(4) of the Public Health Service Act (42 U.S.C. 300bb–6(4)), shall not be treated as met unless the plan administrator of the individual, during the period specified under subparagraph (C), provides to such individual a written notice in clear and understandable language—

(i) that the premium assistance for such individual will expire soon and the prominent identification of the date of such expiration; and

(ii) that such individual may be eligible for coverage without any premium assistance through—

(I) COBRA continuation coverage; or

(II) coverage under a group health plan.

(B) EXCEPTION.—The requirement for the group health plan administrator to provide the written notice under subparagraph (A) shall be waived if the premium assistance for such individual expires pursuant to clause (i) of paragraph (2)(A).

(C) PERIOD SPECIFIED.—For purposes of subparagraph (A), the period specified in this subparagraph is, with respect to the date of expiration of premium assistance for any assistance eligible individual pursuant to a limitation requiring a notice under this paragraph, the period beginning on the day that is 45 days before the date of such expiration and ending on the day that is 15 days before the date of such expiration.

(D) MODEL NOTICES.—Not later than 45 days after the date of enactment of this Act, with respect to any assistance eligible individual, the Secretary of Labor, in consultation with the Secretary of the Treasury and the Secretary of Health and Human Services, shall prescribe models for the notification required under this paragraph.

(7) REGULATIONS.—The Secretary of the Treasury and the Secretary of Labor may jointly prescribe such regulations or other guidance as may be necessary or appropriate to carry out the provisions of this subsection, including the prevention of fraud and abuse under this subsection, except that the Secretary of Labor and the Secretary of Health and Human Services may prescribe such regulations (including interim final regulations) or other guidance as may be necessary or appropriate to carry out the provisions of paragraphs (5), (6), and (8).

* * *

(9) DEFINITIONS.—For purposes of this section:

(A) ADMINISTRATOR.—The term "administrator" has the meaning given such term in section 3(16)(A) of the Employee Retirement Income Security Act of 1974, and includes a COBRA administrator.

(B) COBRA CONTINUATION COVERAGE.—The term "COBRA continuation coverage" means continuation coverage provided pursuant to part 6 of subtitle B of title I of the Employee Retirement Income Security Act of 1974 (other than under section 609), title XXII of the Public Health Service Act, or section 4980B of the Internal Revenue Code of 1986 (other than subsection (f)(1) of such section insofar as it relates to pediatric vaccines), or under a State program that provides comparable continuation coverage. Such term does not include coverage under a health flexible spending arrangement under a cafeteria plan within the meaning of section 125 of the Internal Revenue Code of 1986.

(C) COBRA CONTINUATION PROVISION.—The term "COBRA continuation provision" means the provisions of law described in subparagraph (B).

(D) COVERED EMPLOYEE.—The term "covered employee" has the meaning given such term in section 607(2) of the Employee Retirement Income Security Act of 1974.

(E) QUALIFIED BENEFICIARY.—The term "qualified beneficiary" has the meaning given such term in section 607(3) of the Employee Retirement Income Security Act of 1974.

(F) GROUP HEALTH PLAN.—The term "group health plan" has the meaning given such term in section 607(1) of the Employee Retirement Income Security Act of 1974.

(G) STATE.—The term "State" includes the District of Columbia, the Commonwealth of Puerto Rico, the Virgin Islands, Guam, American Samoa, and the Commonwealth of the Northern Mariana Islands.

(H) PERIOD OF COVERAGE.—Any reference in this subsection to a period of coverage shall be treated as a reference to a monthly or shorter period of coverage with respect to which premiums are charged with respect to such coverage.

(I) PLAN SPONSOR.—The term "plan sponsor" has the meaning given such term in section 3(16)(B) of the Employee Retirement Income Security Act of 1974.

(J) PREMIUM.—The term "premium" includes, with respect to COBRA continuation coverage, any administrative fee.

* * *

• **2018, Tax Technical Corrections Act of 2018 (P.L. 115-141)**

P.L. 115-141, § 401(a)(235), Div. U:

Amended Code Sec. 4980B(f)(1) by striking "section 2162 of the Public Health Service Act" and inserting "section 1928(h)(6) of the Social Security Act (42 U.S.C. 1396s(h)(6))". **Effective** 3-23-2018.

P.L. 115-141, § 401(a)(236), Div. U:

Amended Code Sec. 4980B(f)(5)(C)(iii) by striking "section 2701(c)(2)" and inserting "section 2704(c)(2)". **Effective** 3-23-2018.

• **2011, Trade Adjustment Assistance Extension Act of 2011 (P.L. 112-40)**

P.L. 112-40, § 243(a)(3):

Amended Code Sec. 4980B(f)(2)(B)(i)(V) by striking "February 12, 2011" and inserting "January 1, 2014". **Effective** for periods of coverage which would (without regard to the amendments made by this section) end on or after the date which is 30 days after 10-21-2011.

P.L. 112-40, § 243(a)(4):

Amended Code Sec. 4980B(f)(2)(B)(i)(VI) by striking "February 12, 2011" and inserting "January 1, 2014". **Effective** for periods of coverage which would (without regard to the amendments made by this section) end on or after the date which is 30 days after 10-21-2011.

• **2010, Omnibus Trade Act of 2010 (P.L. 111-344)**

P.L. 111-344, § 116(b)(1):

Amended Code Sec. 4980B(f)(2)(B)(i)(V) by striking "December 31, 2010" and inserting "February 12, 2011". **Effective** for periods of coverage which would (without regard to the amendments made by this section) end on or after 12-31-2010.

EXCISE TAXES—QUALIFIED PENSION, ETC., PLANS

P.L. 111-344, §116(b)(2):

Amended Code Sec. 4980B(f)(2)(B)(i)(VI) by striking "December 31, 2010" and inserting "February 12, 2011". **Effective** for periods of coverage which would (without regard to the amendments made by this section) end on or after 12-31-2010.

• **2009, TAA Health Coverage Improvement Act of 2009 (P.L. 111-5)**

P.L. 111-5, §1899F(b)(1)-(2):

Amended Code Sec. 4980B(f)(2)(B)(i) by striking "In the case of a qualified beneficiary" and inserting "(VI) SPECIAL RULE FOR DISABILITY.—In the case of a qualified beneficiary", and by redesignating subclauses (V) and (VI), as amended by Act Sec. 1899F(b)(1), as subclauses (VII) and (VIII), respectively, and by inserting after clause (IV) new subclauses (V)-(VI). **Effective** for periods of coverage which would (without regard to the amendments made by this section) end on or after 2-17-2009.

• **2002, Trade Act of 2002 (P.L. 107-210)**

P.L. 107-210, §203(e)(3):

Amended Code Sec. 4980B(f)(5) by adding at the end a new subparagraph (C). **Effective** 8-6-2002.

P.L. 107-210, §203(f), provides:

(f) RULE OF CONSTRUCTION.—Nothing in this title (or the amendments made by this title), other than provisions relating to COBRA continuation coverage and reporting requirements, shall be construed as creating any new mandate on any party regarding health insurance coverage.

• **1996, Health Insurance Portability and Accountability Act of 1996 (P.L. 104-191)**

P.L. 104-191, §421(c)(1)(A)(i)-(iii):

Amended the last sentence of Code Sec. 4980B(f)(2)(B)(i) by striking "at the time of a qualifying event described in paragraph (3)(B)" and inserting "at any time during the first 60 days of continuation coverage under this section", by striking "with respect to such event", and by inserting "(with respect to all qualified beneficiaries)" after "29 months". **Effective** 1-1-97, regardless of whether the qualifying event occurred before, on, or after such date.

P.L. 104-191, §421(c)(1)(B):

Amended Code Sec. 4980B(f)(2)(B)(iv)(I) by inserting before ", or" the phrase "(other than such an exclusion or limitation which does not apply to (or is satisfied by) such beneficiary by reason of chapter 100 of this title, part 7 of subtitle B of title I of the Employee Retirement Income Security Act of 1974, or title XXVII of the Public Health Service Act)". **Effective** 1-1-97, regardless of whether the qualifying event occurred before, on, or after such date.

P.L. 104-191, §421(c)(1)(C):

Amended Code Sec. 4980B(f)(2)(B)(v) by striking "at the time of a qualifying event described in paragraph (3)(B)" and inserting "at any time during the first 60 days of continuation coverage under this section". **Effective** 1-1-97, regardless of whether the qualifying event occurred before, on, or after such date.

P.L. 104-191, §421(c)(2):

Amended Code Sec. 4980B(f)(6)(C) by striking "at the time of a qualifying event described in paragraph (3)(B)" and inserting "at any time during the first 60 days of continuation coverage under this section". **Effective** 1-1-97, regardless of whether the qualifying event occurred before, on, or after such date.

• **1996, Small Business Job Protection Act of 1996 (P.L. 104-188)**

P.L. 104-188, §1704(g)(1)(A):

Amended Code Sec. 4980B(f)(2)(B)(i)(V). **Effective** for plan years beginning after 12-31-89. Prior to amendment, Code Sec. 4980B(f)(2)(B)(i)(V) read as follows:

(V) QUALIFYING EVENT INVOLVING MEDICARE ENTITLEMENT.—In the case of an event described in paragraph (3)(D) (without regard to whether such event is a qualifying event), the period of coverage for qualified beneficiaries other than the covered employee for such event or any subsequent qualifying event shall not terminate before the close of the 36-month period beginning on the date the covered employee becomes entitled to benefits under title XVIII of the Social Security Act.

• **1993, Omnibus Budget Reconciliation Act of 1993 (P.L. 103-66)**

P.L. 103-66, §13422(a):

Amended Code Sec. 4980B(f)(1) by inserting "the coverage of the costs of pediatric vaccines (as defined under section 2162 of the Public Health Service Act) is not reduced below the coverage provided by the plan as of May 1, 1993, and only if" after "only if". **Effective** with respect to plan years beginning after 8-10-93.

• **1989, Omnibus Budget Reconciliation Act of 1989 (P.L. 101-239)**

P.L. 101-239, §6701(a)(1)-(2) (as amended by P.L. 104-188, §1704(t)(21)):

Amended Code Sec. 4980B(f)(2)(B) by adding after and below subclause (V) of clause (i) a new sentence, and by adding at the end a new clause (v). **Effective** for plan years beginning on or after 12-19-89, regardless of whether the qualifying event occurred before, on, or after such date.

P.L. 101-239, §6701(b):

Amended Code Sec. 4980B(f)(2)(C), after the amendment made by Act Sec. 7862(c)(4)(B), by adding at the end thereof a new sentence. **Effective** for plan years beginning on or after 12-19-89, regardless of whether the qualifying event occurred before, on, or after such date.

P.L. 101-239, §6701(c):

Amended Code Sec. 4980B(f)(6)(C) by inserting "and each qualified beneficiary who is determined, under title II or XVI of the Social Security Act, to have been disabled at the time of a qualifying event described in paragraph (3)(B) is responsible for notifying the plan administrator of such determination within 60 days of the date of the determination and for notifying the plan administrator within 30 days of the date of any final determination under such title or titles that the qualified beneficiary is no longer disabled" before the period at the end thereof. **Effective** for plan years beginning on or after 12-19-89, regardless of whether the qualifying event occurred before, on, or after such date.

P.L. 101-239, §7862(c)(2)(B):

Amended Code Sec. 4980B(f)(7) by striking "the individual's employment or previous employment with an employer" and inserting "the performance of services by the individual for 1 or more persons maintaining the plan (including as an employee defined in section 401(c)(1))". **Effective** for plan years beginning after 12-31-89.

P.L. 101-239, §7862(c)(3)(C)(i)-(ii):

Amended Code Sec. 4980B(f)(2)(B)(iv) by striking "eligibility" in the heading and inserting "entitlement", and by inserting "which does not contain any exclusion or limitation with respect to any preexisting condition of such beneficiary" after "or otherwise)" in subclause (I). For the **effective** date, see Act Sec. 7862(c)(3)(D), below.

P.L. 101-239, §7862(c)(3)(D), provides:

(D) The amendments made by this paragraph shall apply to—

(i) qualifying events occurring after December 31, 1989, and

(ii) in the case of qualified beneficiaries who elected continuation coverage after December 31, 1988, the period for which the required premium was paid (or was attempted to be paid but was rejected as such).

P.L. 101-239, §7862(c)(4)(B):

Amended the last sentence of Code Sec. 4980B(f)(2)(C), prior to amendment by Act Sec. 6701(b). **Effective** for plan years beginning after 12-31-89. Prior to amendment, the last sentence of Code Sec. 4980B(f)(2)(C) read as follows:

If an election is made after the qualifying event, the plan shall permit payment for continuation coverage during the period preceding the election to be made within 45 days of the date of the election.

P.L. 101-239, §7862(c)(5)(A):

Amended Code Sec. 4980B(f)(2)(B)(i) by adding at the end thereof a new subclause (V). **Effective** for plan years beginning after 12-31-89.

P.L. 101-239, §7891(d)(1)(B)(i)(I)-(II):

Amended Code Sec. 4980B(f)(6) by inserting "(or, in the case of a group health plan which is a multiemployer plan, such longer period of time as may be provided in the terms of the plan)" in subparagraph (B) after "30 days", and by inserting "(or, in the case of a group health plan which is a multiemployer plan, such longer period of time as may be provided in the terms of the plan)" in the first sentence following subparagraph (D) after "14 days". **Effective** with respect to plan years beginning on or after 1-1-90.

P.L. 101-239, §7891(d)(1)(B)(ii):

Amended Code Sec. 4980B(f)(6) by inserting after and below subparagraph (D) a new flush left sentence. **Effective** with respect to plan years beginning on or after 1-1-90.

P.L. 101-239, §7891(d)(2)(A):

Amended Code Sec. 4980B(f) by adding at the end a new paragraph (8). **Effective** with respect to plan years beginning on or after 1-1-90.

[Sec. 4980B(g)]

(g) DEFINITIONS.—For purposes of this section—

(1) QUALIFIED BENEFICIARY.—

(A) IN GENERAL.—The term "qualified beneficiary" means, with respect to a covered employee under a group health plan, any other individual who, on the day before the qualifying event for that employee, is a beneficiary under the plan—

(i) as the spouse of the covered employee, or

(ii) as the dependent child of the employee.

Such term shall also include a child who is born to or placed for adoption with the covered employee during the period of continuation coverage under this section.

(B) SPECIAL RULE FOR TERMINATIONS AND REDUCED EMPLOYMENT.—In the case of a qualifying event described in subsection (f)(3)(B), the term "qualified beneficiary" includes the covered employee.

(C) EXCEPTION FOR NONRESIDENT ALIENS.—Notwithstanding subparagraphs (A) and (B), the term "qualified beneficiary" does not include an individual whose status as a covered employee is attributable to a period in which such individual was a nonresident alien who received no earned income (within the meaning of section 911(d)(2)) from the employer which constituted income from sources within the United States (within the meaning of section 861(a)(3)). If an individual is not a qualified beneficiary pursuant to the previous

EXCISE TAXES—QUALIFIED PENSION, ETC., PLANS

sentence, a spouse or dependent child of such individual shall not be considered a qualified beneficiary by virtue of the relationship of the individual.

(D) SPECIAL RULE FOR RETIREES AND WIDOWS.—In the case of a qualifying event described in subsection (f)(3)(F), the term "qualified beneficiary" includes a covered employee who had retired on or before the date of substantial elimination of coverage and any other individual who, on the day before such qualifying event, is a beneficiary under the plan—

    (i) as the spouse of the covered employee,

    (ii) as the dependent child of the covered employee, or

    (iii) as the surviving spouse of the covered employee.

(2) GROUP HEALTH PLAN.—The term "group health plan" has the meaning given such term by section 5000(b)(1). Such term shall not include any plan substantially all of the coverage under which is for qualified long-term care services (as defined in section 7702B(c)).

(3) PLAN ADMINISTRATOR.—The term "plan administrator" has the meaning given the term "administrator" by section 3(16)(A) of the Employee Retirement Income Security Act of 1974.

(4) CORRECTION.—A failure of a group health plan to meet the requirements of subsection (f) with respect to any qualified beneficiary shall be treated as corrected if—

    (A) such failure is retroactively undone to the extent possible, and

    (B) the qualified beneficiary is placed in a financial position which is as good as such beneficiary would have been in had such failure not occurred.

For purposes of applying subparagraph (B), the qualified beneficiary shall be treated as if he had elected the most favorable coverage in light of the expenses he incurred since the failure first occurred.

Amendments

• **1996, Health Insurance Portability and Accountability Act of 1996 (P.L. 104-191)**

P.L. 104-191, § 321(d)(1):

Amended Code Sec. 4980B(g)(2) by adding at the end a new sentence. For the **effective** date and special rules, see Act Sec. 321(f)-(g), below.

P.L. 104-191, § 321(f)-(g), provides:

(f) EFFECTIVE DATES.—

(1) GENERAL EFFECTIVE DATES.—

(A) IN GENERAL.—Except as provided in subparagraph (B), the amendments made by this section shall apply to contracts issued after December 31, 1996.

(B) RESERVE METHOD.—The amendment made by subsection (b) shall apply to contracts issued after December 31, 1997.

(2) CONTINUATION OF EXISTING POLICIES.—In the case of any contract issued before January 1, 1997, which met the long-term care insurance requirements of the State in which the contract was sitused at the time the contract was issued—

(A) such contract shall be treated for purposes of the Internal Revenue Code of 1986 as a qualified long-term care insurance contract (as defined in section 7702B(b) of such Code), and

(B) services provided under, or reimbursed by, such contract shall be treated for such purposes as qualified long-term care services (as defined in section 7702B(c) of such Code).

In the case of an individual who is covered on December 31, 1996, under a State long-term care plan (as defined in section 7702B(f)(2) of such Code), the terms of such plan on such date shall be treated for purposes of the preceding sentence as a contract issued on such date which met the long-term care insurance requirements of such State.

(3) EXCHANGES OF EXISTING POLICIES.—If, after the date of enactment of this Act and before January 1, 1998, a contract providing for long-term care insurance coverage is exchanged solely for a qualified long-term care insurance contract (as defined in section 7702B(b) of such Code), no gain or loss shall be recognized on the exchange. If, in addition to a qualified long-term care insurance contract, money or other property is received in the exchange, then any gain shall be recognized to the extent of the sum of the money and the fair market value of the other property received. For purposes of this paragraph, the cancellation of a contract providing for long-term care insurance coverage and reinvestment of the cancellation proceeds in a qualified long-term care insurance contract within 60 days thereafter shall be treated as an exchange.

(4) ISSUANCE OF CERTAIN RIDERS PERMITTED.—For purposes of applying sections 101(f), 7702, and 7702A of the Internal Revenue Code of 1986 to any contract—

(A) the issuance of a rider which is treated as a qualified long-term care insurance contract under section 7702B, and

(B) the addition of any provision required to conform any other long-term care rider to be so treated,

shall not be treated as a modification or material change of such contract.

(5) APPLICATION OF PER DIEM LIMITATION TO EXISTING CONTRACTS.—The amount of per diem payments made under a contract issued on or before July 31, 1996, with respect to an insured which are excludable from gross income by reason of section 7702B of the Internal Revenue Code of 1986 (as added by this section) shall not be reduced under subsection (d)(2)(B) thereof by reason of reimbursements received under a contract issued on or before such date. The preceding sentence shall cease to apply as of the date (after July 31, 1996) such contract is exchanged or there is any contract modification which results in an increase in the amount of such per diem payments or the amount of such reimbursements.

(g) LONG-TERM CARE STUDY REQUEST.—The Chairman of the Committee on Ways and Means of the House of Representatives and the Chairman of the Committee on Finance of the Senate shall jointly request the National Association of Insurance Commissioners, in consultation with representatives of the insurance industry and consumer organizations, to formulate, develop, and conduct a study to determine the marketing and other effects of per diem limits on certain types of long-term care policies. If the National Association of Insurance Commissioners agrees to the study request, the National Association of Insurance Commissioners shall report the results of its study to such committees not later than 2 years after accepting the request.

P.L. 104-191, § 421(c)(3):

Amended Code Sec. 4980B(g)(1)(A) by adding at the end thereof a new sentence. **Effective** 1-1-97, regardless of whether the qualifying event occurred before, on, or after such date.

• **1989, Omnibus Budget Reconciliation Act of 1989 (P.L. 101-239)**

P.L. 101-239, § 6202(b)(3)(B):

Amended Code Sec. 4980B(g)(2) by striking "162(i)" and inserting "5000(b)(1)". **Effective** for items and services furnished after 12-19-89.

• **1988, Technical and Miscellaneous Revenue Act of 1988 (P.L. 100-647)**

P.L. 100-647, § 3011(a):

Amended Chapter 43 by adding at the end thereof a new section 4980B. **Effective** for tax years beginning after 12-31-88, but shall not apply to any plan for any plan year to which section 162(k) of the Internal Revenue Code of 1986 (as in effect on the day before the date of enactment of this Act) did not apply by reason of Section 10001(e)(2) of P.L. 99-272.

[Sec. 4980C]

SEC. 4980C. REQUIREMENTS FOR ISSUERS OF QUALIFIED LONG-TERM CARE INSURANCE CONTRACTS.

[Sec. 4980C(a)]

(a) GENERAL RULE.—There is hereby imposed on any person failing to meet the requirements of subsection (c) or (d) a tax in the amount determined under subsection (b).

[Sec. 4980C(b)]

(b) AMOUNT.—

(1) IN GENERAL.—The amount of the tax imposed by subsection (a) shall be $100 per insured for each day any requirement of subsection (c) or (d) is not met with respect to each qualified long-term care insurance contract.

(2) WAIVER.—In the case of a failure which is due to reasonable cause and not to willful neglect, the Secretary may waive part or all of the tax imposed by subsection (a) to the extent that payment of the tax would be excessive relative to the failure involved.

[Sec. 4980C(c)]

(c) RESPONSIBILITIES.—The requirements of this subsection are as follows:

(1) REQUIREMENTS OF MODEL PROVISIONS.—

(A) MODEL REGULATION.—The following requirements of the model regulation must be met:

(i) Section 13 (relating to application forms and replacement coverage).

EXCISE TAXES—QUALIFIED PENSION, ETC., PLANS

(ii) Section 14 (relating to reporting requirements), except that the issuer shall also report at least annually the number of claims denied during the reporting period for each class of business (expressed as a percentage of claims denied), other than claims denied for failure to meet the waiting period or because of any applicable preexisting condition.

(iii) Section 20 (relating to filing requirements for marketing).

(iv) Section 21 (relating to standards for marketing), including inaccurate completion of medical histories, other than sections 21C(1) and 21C(6) thereof, except that—

(I) in addition to such requirements, no person shall, in selling or offering to sell a qualified long-term care insurance contract, misrepresent a material fact; and

(II) no such requirements shall include a requirement to inquire or identify whether a prospective applicant or enrollee for long-term care insurance has accident and sickness insurance.

(v) Section 22 (relating to appropriateness of recommended purchase).

(vi) Section 24 (relating to standard format outline of coverage).

(vii) Section 25 (relating to requirement to deliver shopper's guide).

(B) MODEL ACT.—The following requirements of the model Act must be met:

(i) Section 6F (relating to right to return), except that such section shall also apply to denials of applications and any refund shall be made within 30 days of the return or denial.

(ii) Section 6G (relating to outline of coverage).

(iii) Section 6H (relating to requirements for certificates under group plans).

(iv) Section 6I (relating to policy summary).

(v) Section 6J (relating to monthly reports on accelerated death benefits).

(vi) Section 7 (relating to incontestability period).

(C) DEFINITIONS.—For purposes of this paragraph, the terms "model regulation" and "model Act" have the meanings given such terms by section 7702B(g)(2)(B).

(2) DELIVERY OF POLICY.—If an application for a qualified long-term care insurance contract (or for a certificate under such a contract for a group) is approved, the issuer shall deliver to the applicant (or policyholder or certificateholder) the contract (or certificate) of insurance not later than 30 days after the date of the approval.

(3) INFORMATION ON DENIALS OF CLAIMS.—If a claim under a qualified long-term care insurance contract is denied, the issuer shall, within 60 days of the date of a written request by the policyholder or certificateholder (or representative)—

(A) provide a written explanation of the reasons for the denial, and

(B) make available all information directly relating to such denial.

[Sec. 4980C(d)]

(d) DISCLOSURE.—The requirements of this subsection are met if the issuer of a long-term care insurance policy discloses in such policy and in the outline of coverage required under subsection (c)(1)(B)(ii) that the policy is intended to be a qualified long-term care insurance contract under section 7702B(b).

[Sec. 4980C(e)]

(e) QUALIFIED LONG-TERM CARE INSURANCE CONTRACT DEFINED.—For purposes of this section, the term "qualified long-term care insurance contract" has the meaning given such term by section 7702B.

[Sec. 4980C(f)]

(f) COORDINATION WITH STATE REQUIREMENTS.—If a State imposes any requirement which is more stringent than the analogous requirement imposed by this section or section 7702B(g), the requirement imposed by this section or section 7702B(g) shall be treated as met if the more stringent State requirement is met.

Amendments

• **1996, Health Insurance Portability and Accountability Act of 1996 (P.L. 104-191)**

P.L. 104-191, §326(a):

Amended Chapter 43 by adding at the end a new Code Sec. 4980C. **Effective** for actions taken after 12-31-96.

[Sec. 4980D]

SEC. 4980D. FAILURE TO MEET CERTAIN GROUP HEALTH PLAN REQUIREMENTS.

[Sec. 4980D(a)]

(a) GENERAL RULE.—There is hereby imposed a tax on any failure of a group health plan to meet the requirements of chapter 100 (relating to group health plan requirements).

Amendments

• **2005, Gulf Opportunity Zone Act of 2005 (P.L. 109-135)**

P.L. 109-135, §412(ww):

Amended Code Sec. 4980D(a) by striking "plans" and inserting "plan". **Effective** 12-21-2005.

• **1997, Taxpayer Relief Act of 1997 (P.L. 105-34)**

P.L. 105-34, §1531(b)(2)(A):

Amended Code Sec. 4980D(a) by striking "plan portability, access, and renewability" and inserting "plans". **Effective** with respect to group health plans for plan years beginning on or after 1-1-98.

[Sec. 4980D(b)]

(b) AMOUNT OF TAX.—

(1) IN GENERAL.—The amount of the tax imposed by subsection (a) on any failure shall be $100 for each day in the noncompliance period with respect to each individual to whom such failure relates.

(2) NONCOMPLIANCE PERIOD.—For purposes of this section, the term "noncompliance period" means, with respect to any failure, the period—

(A) beginning on the date such failure first occurs, and

(B) ending on the date such failure is corrected.

(3) MINIMUM TAX FOR NONCOMPLIANCE PERIOD WHERE FAILURE DISCOVERED AFTER NOTICE OF EXAMINATION.—Notwithstanding paragraphs (1) and (2) of subsection (c)—

(A) IN GENERAL.—In the case of 1 or more failures with respect to an individual—

EXCISE TAXES—QUALIFIED PENSION, ETC., PLANS

(i) which are not corrected before the date a notice of examination of income tax liability is sent to the employer, and

(ii) which occurred or continued during the period under examination,

the amount of tax imposed by subsection (a) by reason of such failures with respect to such individual shall not be less than the lesser of $2,500 or the amount of tax which would be imposed by subsection (a) without regard to such paragraphs.

(B) HIGHER MINIMUM TAX WHERE VIOLATIONS ARE MORE THAN DE MINIMIS.—To the extent violations for which any person is liable under subsection (e) for any year are more than de minimis, subparagraph (A) shall be applied by substituting "$15,000" for "$2,500" with respect to such person.

(C) EXCEPTION FOR CHURCH PLANS.—This paragraph shall not apply to any failure under a church plan (as defined in section 414(e)).

[Sec. 4980D(c)]

(c) LIMITATIONS ON AMOUNT OF TAX.—

(1) TAX NOT TO APPLY WHERE FAILURE NOT DISCOVERED EXERCISING REASONABLE DILIGENCE.—No tax shall be imposed by subsection (a) on any failure during any period for which it is established to the satisfaction of the Secretary that the person otherwise liable for such tax did not know, and exercising reasonable diligence would not have known, that such failure existed.

(2) TAX NOT TO APPLY TO FAILURES CORRECTED WITHIN CERTAIN PERIODS.—No tax shall be imposed by subsection (a) on any failure if—

(A) such failure was due to reasonable cause and not to willful neglect, and

(B) (i) in the case of a plan other than a church plan (as defined in section 414(e)), such failure is corrected during the 30-day period beginning on the 1st date the person otherwise liable for such tax knew, or exercising reasonable diligence would have known, that such failure existed, and

(ii) in the case of a church plan (as so defined), such failure is corrected before the close of the correction period (determined under the rules of section 414(e)(4)(C)).

(3) OVERALL LIMITATION FOR UNINTENTIONAL FAILURES.—In the case of failures which are due to reasonable cause and not to willful neglect—

(A) SINGLE EMPLOYER PLANS.—

(i) IN GENERAL.—In the case of failures with respect to plans other than specified multiple employer health plans, the tax imposed by subsection (a) for failures during the taxable year of the employer shall not exceed the amount equal to the lesser of—

(I) 10 percent of the aggregate amount paid or incurred by the employer (or predecessor employer) during the preceding taxable year for group health plans, or

(II) $500,000.

(ii) TAXABLE YEARS IN THE CASE OF CERTAIN CONTROLLED GROUPS.—For purposes of this subparagraph, if not all persons who are treated as a single employer for purposes of this section have the same taxable year, the taxable years taken into account shall be determined under principles similar to the principles of section 1561.

(B) SPECIFIED MULTIPLE EMPLOYER HEALTH PLANS.—

(i) IN GENERAL.—In the case of failures with respect to a specified multiple employer health plan, the tax imposed by subsection (a) for failures during the taxable year of the trust forming part of such plan shall not exceed the amount equal to the lesser of—

(I) 10 percent of the amount paid or incurred by such trust during such taxable year to provide medical care (as defined in section 9832(d)(3)) directly or through insurance, reimbursement, or otherwise, or

(II) $500,000.

For purposes of the preceding sentence, all plans of which the same trust forms a part shall be treated as 1 plan.

(ii) SPECIAL RULE FOR EMPLOYERS REQUIRED TO PAY TAX.—If an employer is assessed a tax imposed by subsection (a) by reason of a failure with respect to a specified multiple employer health plan, the limit shall be determined under subparagraph (A) (and not under this subparagraph) and as if such plan were not a specified multiple employer health plan.

(4) WAIVER BY SECRETARY.—In the case of a failure which is due to reasonable cause and not to willful neglect, the Secretary may waive part or all of the tax imposed by subsection (a) to the extent that the payment of such tax would be excessive relative to the failure involved.

Amendments

- **1997, Taxpayer Relief Act of 1997 (P.L. 105-34)**

P.L. 105-34, §1531(b)(2)(B):

Amended Code Sec. 4980D(c)(3)(B)(i)(I) by striking "9805(d)(3)" and inserting "9832(d)(3)". **Effective** with respect to group health plans for plan years beginning on or after 1-1-98.

[Sec. 4980D(d)]

(d) TAX NOT TO APPLY TO CERTAIN INSURED SMALL EMPLOYER PLANS.—

(1) IN GENERAL.—In the case of a group health plan of a small employer which provides health insurance coverage solely through a contract with a health insurance issuer, no tax shall be imposed by this section on the employer on any failure (other than a failure attributable to section 9811) which is solely because of the health insurance coverage offered by such issuer.

(2) SMALL EMPLOYER.—

(A) IN GENERAL.—For purposes of paragraph (1), the term "small employer" means, with respect to a calendar year and a plan year, an employer who employed an average of at least 2 but not more than 50 employees on business days during the preceding calendar year and who employs at least 2 employees on the first day of the plan year. For purposes of the preceding sentence, all persons treated as a single employer under subsection (b), (c), (m), or (o) of section 414 shall be treated as 1 employer.

(B) EMPLOYERS NOT IN EXISTENCE IN PRECEDING YEAR.—In the case of an employer which was not in existence throughout the preceding calendar year, the determination of whether such employer is a small employer shall be based on the average number of employees that it is reasonably expected such employer will employ on business days in the current calendar year.

(C) PREDECESSORS.—Any reference in this paragraph to an employer shall include a reference to any predecessor of such employer.

(3) HEALTH INSURANCE COVERAGE; HEALTH INSURANCE ISSUER.—For purposes of paragraph (1), the terms "health insurance coverage" and "health insurance issuer" have the respective meanings given such terms by section 9832.

Amendments

- **1997, Taxpayer Relief Act of 1997 (P.L. 105-34)**

P.L. 105-34, §1531(b)(2)(C):

Amended Code Sec. 4980D(d)(1) by inserting "(other than a failure attributable to section 9811)" after "on any failure". **Effective** with respect to group health plans for plan years beginning on or after 1-1-98.

P.L. 105-34, §1531(b)(2)(D):

Amended Code Sec. 4980D(d)(3) by striking "9805" and inserting "9832". **Effective** with respect to group health plans for plan years beginning on or after 1-1-98.

EXCISE TAXES—QUALIFIED PENSION, ETC., PLANS

[Sec. 4980D(e)]

(e) LIABILITY FOR TAX.—The following shall be liable for the tax imposed by subsection (a) on a failure:

(1) Except as otherwise provided in this subsection, the employer.

(2) In the case of a multiemployer plan, the plan.

(3) In the case of a failure under section 9803 (relating to guaranteed renewability) with respect to a plan described in subsection (f)(2)(B), the plan.

[Sec. 4980D(f)]

(f) DEFINITIONS.—For purposes of this section—

(1) GROUP HEALTH PLAN.—The term "group health plan" has the meaning given such term by section 9832(a).

(2) SPECIFIED MULTIPLE EMPLOYER HEALTH PLAN.—The term "specified multiple employer health plan" means a group health plan which is—

(A) any multiemployer plan, or

(B) any multiple employer welfare arrangement (as defined in section 3(40) of the Employee Retirement Income Security Act of 1974, as in effect on the date of the enactment of this section).

(3) CORRECTION.—A failure of a group health plan shall be treated as corrected if—

(A) such failure is retroactively undone to the extent possible, and

(B) the person to whom the failure relates is placed in a financial position which is as good as such person would have been in had such failure not occurred.

Amendments

• **1997, Taxpayer Relief Act of 1997 (P.L. 105-34)**

P.L. 105-34, §1531(b)(2)(E):

Amended Code Sec. 4980D(f)(1) by striking "9805(a)" and inserting "9832(a)". **Effective** with respect to group health plans for plan years beginning on or after 1-1-98.

• **1996, Health Insurance Portability and Accountability Act of 1996 (P.L. 104-191)**

P.L. 104-191, §402(a):

Amended chapter 43 by adding after Code Sec. 4980C a new Code Sec. 4980D. **Effective** for failures under chapter 100 of the Internal Revenue Code of 1986 (as added by section 401 of this Act).

[Sec. 4980E]

SEC. 4980E. FAILURE OF EMPLOYER TO MAKE COMPARABLE ARCHER MSA CONTRIBUTIONS.

[Sec. 4980E(a)]

(a) GENERAL RULE.—In the case of an employer who makes a contribution to the Archer MSA of any employee with respect to coverage under a high deductible health plan of the employer during a calendar year, there is hereby imposed a tax on the failure of such employer to meet the requirements of subsection (d) for such calendar year.

Amendments

• **2002, Job Creation and Worker Assistance Act of 2002 (P.L. 107-147)**

P.L. 107-147, §417(17)(A):

Amended the section heading for Code Sec. 4980E. **Effective** 3-9-2002. Prior to amendment, the section heading for Code Sec. 4980E read as follows:

SEC. 4980E. FAILURE OF EMPLOYER TO MAKE COMPARABLE MEDICAL SAVINGS ACCOUNT CONTRIBUTIONS.

• **2000, Community Renewal Tax Relief Act of 2000 (P.L. 106-554)**

P.L. 106-554, §202(a)(8):

Amended Code Sec. 4980E(a) by striking "medical savings account" and inserting "Archer MSA". **Effective** 12-21-2000.

[Sec. 4980E(b)]

(b) AMOUNT OF TAX.—The amount of the tax imposed by subsection (a) on any failure for any calendar year is the amount equal to 35 percent of the aggregate amount contributed by the employer to Archer MSAs of employees for taxable years of such employees ending with or within such calendar year.

Amendments

• **2000, Community Renewal Tax Relief Act of 2000 (P.L. 106-554)**

P.L. 106-554, §202(b)(2)(D):

Amended Code Sec. 4980E(b) by striking "medical savings accounts" and inserting "Archer MSAs". **Effective** 12-21-2000.

[Sec. 4980E(c)]

(c) WAIVER BY SECRETARY.—In the case of a failure which is due to reasonable cause and not to willful neglect, the Secretary may waive part or all of the tax imposed by subsection (a) to the extent that the payment of such tax would be excessive relative to the failure involved.

[Sec. 4980E(d)]

(d) EMPLOYER REQUIRED TO MAKE COMPARABLE MSA CONTRIBUTIONS FOR ALL PARTICIPATING EMPLOYEES.—

(1) IN GENERAL.—An employer meets the requirements of this subsection for any calendar year if the employer makes available comparable contributions to the Archer MSAs of all comparable participating employees for each coverage period during such calendar year.

(2) COMPARABLE CONTRIBUTIONS.—

(A) IN GENERAL.—For purposes of paragraph (1), the term "comparable contributions" means contributions—

(i) which are the same amount, or

(ii) which are the same percentage of the annual deductible limit under the high deductible health plan covering the employees.

(B) PART-YEAR EMPLOYEES.—In the case of an employee who is employed by the employer for only a portion of the calendar year, a contribution to the Archer MSA of such employee shall be treated as comparable if it is an amount which bears the same ratio to the comparable amount (determined without regard to this subparagraph) as such portion bears to the entire calendar year.

(3) COMPARABLE PARTICIPATING EMPLOYEES.—For purposes of paragraph (1), the term "comparable participating employees" means all employees—

(A) who are eligible individuals covered under any high deductible health plan of the employer, and

(B) who have the same category of coverage. For purposes of subparagraph (B), the categories of coverage are self-only and family coverage.

(4) PART-TIME EMPLOYEES.—

(A) IN GENERAL.—Paragraph (3) shall be applied separately with respect to part-time employees and other employees.

(B) PART-TIME EMPLOYEE.—For purposes of subparagraph (A), the term "part-time employee" means any employee who is customarily employed for fewer than 30 hours per week.

Amendments

• **2000, Community Renewal Tax Relief Act of 2000 (P.L. 106-554)**

P.L. 106-554, §202(a)(8):

Amended Code Sec. 4980E(d)(2)(B) by striking "medical savings account" and inserting "Archer MSA". **Effective** 12-21-2000.

P.L. 106-554, §202(b)(2)(D):

Amended Code Sec. 4980E(d)(1) by striking "medical savings accounts" and inserting "Archer MSAs". **Effective** 12-21-2000.

[Sec. 4980E(e)]

(e) CONTROLLED GROUPS.—For purposes of this section, all persons treated as a single employer under subsection (b), (c), (m), or (o) of section 414 shall be treated as 1 employer.

[Sec. 4980E(f)]

(f) DEFINITIONS.—Terms used in this section which are also used in section 220 have the respective meanings given such terms in section 220.

Amendments

• **1996, Health Insurance Portability and Accountability Act of 1996 (P.L. 104-191)**

P.L. 104-191, §301(c)(4)(A):

Amended Chapter 43 by adding after Code Sec. 4980D a new section 4980E. **Effective** for tax years beginning after 12-31-96.

[Sec. 4980F]

SEC. 4980F. FAILURE OF APPLICABLE PLANS REDUCING BENEFIT ACCRUALS TO SATISFY NOTICE REQUIREMENTS.

[Sec. 4980F(a)]

(a) IMPOSITION OF TAX.—There is hereby imposed a tax on the failure of any applicable pension plan to meet the requirements of subsection (e) with respect to any applicable individual.

[Sec. 4980F(b)]

(b) AMOUNT OF TAX.—

(1) IN GENERAL.—The amount of the tax imposed by subsection (a) on any failure with respect to any applicable individual shall be $100 for each day in the noncompliance period with respect to such failure.

(2) NONCOMPLIANCE PERIOD.—For purposes of this section, the term "noncompliance period" means, with respect to any failure, the period beginning on the date the failure first occurs and ending on the date the notice to which the failure relates is provided or the failure is otherwise corrected.

[Sec. 4980F(c)]

(c) LIMITATIONS ON AMOUNT OF TAX.—

(1) TAX NOT TO APPLY WHERE FAILURE NOT DISCOVERED AND REASONABLE DILIGENCE EXERCISED.—No tax shall be imposed by subsection (a) on any failure during any period for which it is established to the satisfaction of the Secretary that any person subject to liability for the tax under subsection (d) did not know that the failure existed and exercised reasonable diligence to meet the requirements of subsection (e).

(2) TAX NOT TO APPLY TO FAILURES CORRECTED WITHIN 30 DAYS.—No tax shall be imposed by subsection (a) on any failure if—

(A) any person subject to liability for the tax under subsection (d) exercised reasonable diligence to meet the requirements of subsection (e), and

(B) such person provides the notice described in subsection (e) during the 30-day period beginning on the first date such person knew, or exercising reasonable diligence would have known, that such failure existed.

(3) OVERALL LIMITATION FOR UNINTENTIONAL FAILURES.—

(A) IN GENERAL.—If the person subject to liability for tax under subsection (d) exercised reasonable diligence to meet the requirements of subsection (e), the tax imposed by subsection (a) for failures during the taxable year of the employer (or, in the case of a multiemployer plan, the taxable year of the trust forming part of the plan) shall not exceed $500,000. For purposes of the preceding sentence, all multiemployer plans of which the same trust forms a part shall be treated as 1 plan.

(B) TAXABLE YEARS IN THE CASE OF CERTAIN CONTROLLED GROUPS.—For purposes of this paragraph, if all persons who are treated as a single employer for purposes of this section do not have the same taxable year, the taxable years taken into account shall be determined under principles similar to the principles of section 1561.

(4) WAIVER BY SECRETARY.—In the case of a failure which is due to reasonable cause and not to willful neglect, the Secretary may waive part or all of the tax imposed by subsection (a) to the extent that the payment of such tax would be excessive or otherwise inequitable relative to the failure involved.

[Sec. 4980F(d)]

(d) LIABILITY FOR TAX.—The following shall be liable for the tax imposed by subsection (a):

(1) In the case of a plan other than a multiemployer plan, the employer.

(2) In the case of a multiemployer plan, the plan.

[Sec. 4980F(e)]

(e) NOTICE REQUIREMENTS FOR PLANS SIGNIFICANTLY REDUCING BENEFIT ACCRUALS.—

(1) IN GENERAL.—If an applicable pension plan is amended to provide for a significant reduction in the rate of future benefit accrual, the plan administrator shall provide the notice described in paragraph (2) to each applicable individual (and to each employee organization representing applicable individuals) and to each employer who has an obligation to contribute to the plan.

(2) NOTICE.—The notice required by paragraph (1) shall be written in a manner calculated to be understood by the average plan participant and shall provide sufficient information (as determined in accordance with regulations prescribed by the Secretary) to allow applicable individuals to understand the effect of the plan amendment. The Secretary may provide a simplified form of notice for, or exempt from any notice requirement, a plan—

(A) which has fewer than 100 participants who have accrued a benefit under the plan, or

(B) which offers participants the option to choose between the new benefit formula and the old benefit formula.

(3) TIMING OF NOTICE.—Except as provided in regulations, the notice required by paragraph (1) shall be provided within a reasonable time before the effective date of the plan amendment.

EXCISE TAXES—QUALIFIED PENSION, ETC., PLANS

(4) DESIGNEES.—Any notice under paragraph (1) may be provided to a person designated, in writing, by the person to which it would otherwise be provided.

(5) NOTICE BEFORE ADOPTION OF AMENDMENT.—A plan shall not be treated as failing to meet the requirements of paragraph (1) merely because notice is provided before the adoption of the plan amendment if no material modification of the amendment occurs before the amendment is adopted.

Amendments

• 2006, Pension Protection Act of 2006 (P.L. 109-280)

P.L. 109-280, § 502(c)(2):

Amended Code Sec. 4980F(e)(1) by adding at the end before the period the following: "and to each employer who has an obligation to contribute to the plan". Effective for plan years beginning after 12-31-2007.

P.L. 109-280, § 811, provides:

SEC. 811. PENSIONS AND INDIVIDUAL RETIREMENT ARRANGEMENT PROVISIONS OF ECONOMIC GROWTH AND TAX RELIEF RECONCILIATION ACT OF 2001 MADE PERMANENT.

Title IX of the Economic Growth and Tax Relief Reconciliation Act of 2001 [P.L. 107-16] shall not apply to the provisions of, and amendments made by, subtitles A through F of title VI [§§ 601-666]of such Act (relating to pension and individual retirement arrangement provisions).

• 2002, Job Creation and Worker Assistance Act of 2002 (P.L. 107-147)

P.L. 107-147, § 411(u)(1)(A):

Amended Code Sec. 4980F(e)(1) by striking "written notice" and inserting "the notice described in paragraph (2)". Effective as if included in the provision of P.L. 107-16 to which it relates [generally effective for plan amendments taking effect on or after 6-7-2001.—CCH].

• 2001, Economic Growth and Tax Relief Reconciliation Act of 2001 (P.L. 107-16)

P.L. 107-16, § 901(a)-(b), provides [but see P.L. 109-280, § 811, above]:

SEC. 901. SUNSET OF PROVISIONS OF ACT.

(a) IN GENERAL.—All provisions of, and amendments made by, this Act shall not apply—

(1) to taxable, plan, or limitation years beginning after December 31, 2010, or

(2) in the case of title V, to estates of decedents dying, gifts made, or generation skipping transfers, after December 31, 2010.

(b) APPLICATION OF CERTAIN LAWS.—The Internal Revenue Code of 1986 and the Employee Retirement Income Security Act of 1974 shall be applied and administered to years, estates, gifts, and transfers described in subsection (a) as if the provisions and amendments described in subsection (a) had never been enacted.

[Sec. 4980F(f)]

(f) DEFINITIONS AND SPECIAL RULES.—For purposes of this section—

(1) APPLICABLE INDIVIDUAL.—The term "applicable individual" means, with respect to any plan amendment—

(A) each participant in the plan, and

(B) any beneficiary who is an alternate payee (within the meaning of section 414(p)(8)) under an applicable qualified domestic relations order (within the meaning of section 414(p)(1)(A)),

whose rate of future benefit accrual under the plan may reasonably be expected to be significantly reduced by such plan amendment.

(2) APPLICABLE PENSION PLAN.—The term "applicable pension plan" means—

(A) any defined benefit plan described in section 401(a) which includes a trust exempt from tax under section 501(a), or

(B) an individual account plan which is subject to the funding standards of section 412.

Such term shall not include a governmental plan (within the meaning of section 414(d)) or a church plan (within the meaning of section 414(e)) with respect to which the election provided by section 410(d) has not been made.

(3) EARLY RETIREMENT.—A plan amendment which eliminates or reduces any early retirement benefit or retirement-type subsidy (within the meaning of section 411(d)(6)(B)(i)) shall be treated as having the effect of reducing the rate of future benefit accrual.

Amendments

• 2006, Pension Protection Act of 2006 (P.L. 109-280)

P.L. 109-280, § 811, provides:

SEC. 811. PENSIONS AND INDIVIDUAL RETIREMENT ARRANGEMENT PROVISIONS OF ECONOMIC GROWTH AND TAX RELIEF RECONCILIATION ACT OF 2001 MADE PERMANENT.

Title IX of the Economic Growth and Tax Relief Reconciliation Act of 2001 [P.L. 107-16] shall not apply to the provisions of, and amendments made by, subtitles A through F of title VI [§§ 601-666]of such Act (relating to pension and individual retirement arrangement provisions).

• 2002, Job Creation and Worker Assistance Act of 2002 (P.L. 107-147)

P.L. 107-147, § 411(u)(1)(B):

Amended Code Sec. 4980F(f)(2)(A). Effective as if included in the provision of P.L. 107-16 to which it relates [generally effective for plan amendments taking effect on or after 6-7-2001.—CCH]. Prior to amendment, Code Sec. 4980F(f)(2)(A) read as follows:

(A) any defined benefit plan, or

P.L. 107-147, § 411(u)(1)(C):

Amended Code Sec. 4980F(f)(3) by striking "significantly" preceding "reduces" and "reducing", respectively, both places it appears. Effective as if included in the provision of P.L. 107-16 to which it relates [generally effective for plan amendments taking effect on or after 6-7-2001.—CCH].

• 2001, Economic Growth and Tax Relief Reconciliation Act of 2001 (P.L. 107-16)

P.L. 107-16, § 901(a)-(b), provides [but see P.L. 109-280, § 811, above]:

SEC. 901. SUNSET OF PROVISIONS OF ACT.

(a) IN GENERAL.—All provisions of, and amendments made by, this Act shall not apply—

(1) to taxable, plan, or limitation years beginning after December 31, 2010, or

(2) in the case of title V, to estates of decedents dying, gifts made, or generation skipping transfers, after December 31, 2010.

(b) APPLICATION OF CERTAIN LAWS.—The Internal Revenue Code of 1986 and the Employee Retirement Income Security Act of 1974 shall be applied and administered to years, estates, gifts, and transfers described in subsection (a) as if the provisions and amendments described in subsection (a) had never been enacted.

[Sec. 4980F(g)]

(g) NEW TECHNOLOGIES.—The Secretary may by regulations allow any notice under subsection (e) to be provided by using new technologies.

Amendments

• 2006, Pension Protection Act of 2006 (P.L. 109-280)

P.L. 109-280, § 811, provides:

SEC. 811. PENSIONS AND INDIVIDUAL RETIREMENT ARRANGEMENT PROVISIONS OF ECONOMIC GROWTH AND TAX RELIEF RECONCILIATION ACT OF 2001 MADE PERMANENT.

Title IX of the Economic Growth and Tax Relief Reconciliation Act of 2001 [P.L. 107-16] shall not apply to the provisions of, and amendments made by, subtitles A through F of title VI [§§ 601-666]of such Act (relating to pension and individual retirement arrangement provisions).

• 2001, Economic Growth and Tax Relief Reconciliation Act of 2001 (P.L. 107-16)

P.L. 107-16, § 659(a)(1):

Amended chapter 43 by adding at the end a new Code Sec. 4980F. Effective, generally, for plan amendments taking effect on or after 6-7-2001. For transition and special rules, see Act Sec. 659(c)(2)-(3), below.

P.L. 107-16, § 659(c)(2)-(3) (as amended by P.L. 107-147, § 411(u)(3)), provides:

(2) TRANSITION.—Until such time as the Secretary of the Treasury issues regulations under sections 4980F(e)(2) and (3) of the Internal Revenue Code of 1986, and section 204(h) of the Employee Retirement Income Security Act of 1974, as added by the amendments made by this section, a plan shall be treated as meeting the requirements of such sections if it makes a good faith effort to comply with such requirements.

(3) SPECIAL NOTICE RULE.—

(A) IN GENERAL.—The period for providing any notice required by the amendments made by this section shall not end before the date which is 3 months after the date of the enactment of this Act.

(B) REASONABLE NOTICE.—The amendments made by this section shall not apply to any plan amendment taking effect on or after the date of the enactment of this Act if, before April 25, 2001, notice was provided to participants and beneficiaries adversely affected by the plan amendment (and their representatives) which was reasonably expected to notify them of the nature and effective date of the plan amendment.

P.L. 107-16, § 901(a)-(b), provides [but see P.L. 109-280, § 811, above]:

SEC. 901. SUNSET OF PROVISIONS OF ACT.

(a) IN GENERAL.—All provisions of, and amendments made by, this Act shall not apply—

(1) to taxable, plan, or limitation years beginning after December 31, 2010, or

(2) in the case of title V, to estates of decedents dying, gifts made, or generation skipping transfers, after December 31, 2010.

EXCISE TAXES—QUALIFIED PENSION, ETC., PLANS

(b) APPLICATION OF CERTAIN LAWS.—The Internal Revenue Code of 1986 and the Employee Retirement Income Security Act of 1974 shall be applied and administered to years, estates, gifts, and transfers described in subsection (a) as if the provisions and amendments described in subsection (a) had never been enacted.

[Sec. 4980G]
SEC. 4980G. FAILURE OF EMPLOYER TO MAKE COMPARABLE HEALTH SAVINGS ACCOUNT CONTRIBUTIONS.

[Sec. 4980G(a)]
(a) GENERAL RULE.—In the case of an employer who makes a contribution to the health savings account of any employee during a calendar year, there is hereby imposed a tax on the failure of such employer to meet the requirements of subsection (b) for such calendar year.

[Sec. 4980G(b)]
(b) RULES AND REQUIREMENTS.—Rules and requirements similar to the rules and requirements of section 4980E shall apply for purposes of this section.

[Sec. 4980G(c)]
(c) REGULATIONS.—The Secretary shall issue regulations to carry out the purposes of this section, including regulations providing special rules for employers who make contributions to Archer MSAs and health savings accounts during the calendar year.

[Sec. 4980G(d)]
(d) EXCEPTION.—For purposes of applying section 4980E to a contribution to a health savings account of an employee who is not a highly compensated employee (as defined in section 414(q)), highly compensated employees shall not be treated as comparable participating employees.

Amendments

• **2006, Tax Relief and Health Care Act of 2006 (P.L. 109-432)**

P.L. 109-432, Division A, § 306(a):

Amended Code Sec. 4980G by adding at the end a new subsection (d). **Effective** for tax years beginning after 12-31-2006.

• **2003, Medicare Prescription Drug, Improvement, and Modernization Act of 2003 (P.L. 108-173)**

P.L. 108-173, § 1201(d)(4)(A):

Amended chapter 43 by adding after Code Sec. 4980F a new Code Sec. 4980G. **Effective** for tax years beginning after 12-31-2003.

[Sec. 4980H]
SEC. 4980H. SHARED RESPONSIBILITY FOR EMPLOYERS REGARDING HEALTH COVERAGE.

[Sec. 4980H(a)]
(a) LARGE EMPLOYERS NOT OFFERING HEALTH COVERAGE.—If—

(1) any applicable large employer fails to offer to its full-time employees (and their dependents) the opportunity to enroll in minimum essential coverage under an eligible employer-sponsored plan (as defined in section 5000A(f)(2)) for any month, and

(2) at least one full-time employee of the applicable large employer has been certified to the employer under section 1411 of the Patient Protection and Affordable Care Act as having enrolled for such month in a qualified health plan with respect to which an applicable premium tax credit or cost-sharing reduction is allowed or paid with respect to the employee,

then there is hereby imposed on the employer an assessable payment equal to the product of the applicable payment amount and the number of individuals employed by the employer as full-time employees during such month.

[Sec. 4980H(b)—Stricken]

Amendments

• **2010, Health Care and Education Reconciliation Act of 2010 (P.L. 111-152)**

P.L. 111-152, § 1003(d):

Amended Code Sec. 4980H, as added by section 1513 of the Patient Protection and Affordable Care Act (P.L. 111-148) and amended by section 10106 of such Act, and as amended by Act Sec. 1003(a)-(c) of this Act, by striking subsection (b) and redesignating subsections (c), (d), and (e) as subsections (b), (c), and (d), respectively. **Effective** 3-30-2010. Prior to being stricken, Code Sec. 4980H(b) read as follows:

(b) LARGE EMPLOYERS WITH WAITING PERIODS EXCEEDING 60 DAYS.—

(1) IN GENERAL.—In the case of any applicable large employer which requires an extended waiting period to enroll in any minimum essential coverage under an employer-sponsored plan (as defined in section 5000A(f)(2)), there is hereby imposed on the employer an assessable payment of $600 for each full-time employee of the employer to whom the extended waiting period applies.

(2) EXTENDED WAITING PERIOD.—The term "extended waiting period" means any waiting period (as defined in section 2701(b)(4) of the Public Health Service Act) which exceeds 60 days.

• **2010, Patient Protection and Affordable Care Act (P.L. 111-148)**

P.L. 111-148, § 10106(e):

Amended Code Sec. 4980H(b), as added by Act Sec. 1513(a). **Effective** 3-23-2010. Prior to amendment, Code Sec. 4980H(b) read as follows:

(b) LARGE EMPLOYERS WITH WAITING PERIODS EXCEEDING 30 DAYS.—

(1) IN GENERAL.—In the case of any applicable large employer which requires an extended waiting period to enroll in any minimum essential coverage under an employer-sponsored plan (as defined in section 5000A(f)(2)), there is hereby imposed on the employer an assessable payment, in the amount specified in paragraph (2), for each full-time employee of the employer to whom the extended waiting period applies.

(2) AMOUNT.—For purposes of paragraph (1), the amount specified in this paragraph for a full-time employee is—

(A) in the case of an extended waiting period which exceeds 30 days but does not exceed 60 days, $400, and

(B) in the case of an extended waiting period which exceeds 60 days, $600.

(3) EXTENDED WAITING PERIOD.—The term "extended waiting period" means any waiting period (as defined in section 2701(b)(4) of the Public Health Service Act) which exceeds 30 days.

[Sec. 4980H(b)]
(b) LARGE EMPLOYERS OFFERING COVERAGE WITH EMPLOYEES WHO QUALIFY FOR PREMIUM TAX CREDITS OR COST-SHARING REDUCTIONS.—

(1) IN GENERAL.—If—

(A) an applicable large employer offers to its full-time employees (and their dependents) the opportunity to enroll in minimum essential coverage under an eligible employer-sponsored plan (as defined in section 5000A(f)(2)) for any month, and

(B) 1 or more full-time employees of the applicable large employer has been certified to the employer under section 1411 of the Patient Protection and Affordable Care Act as having enrolled for such month in a qualified health plan with respect to which an applicable premium tax credit or cost-sharing reduction is allowed or paid with respect to the employee,

then there is hereby imposed on the employer an assessable payment equal to the product of the number of full-time employees of the applicable large employer described in subparagraph (B) for such month and an amount equal to $1/12$ of $3,000.

(2) OVERALL LIMITATION.—The aggregate amount of tax determined under paragraph (1) with respect to all employees of an applicable large employer for any month shall not exceed the product of the applicable payment amount and the number of individuals employed by the employer as full-time employees during such month.

Amendments

• **2011, Department of Defense and Full-Year Continuing Appropriations Act, 2011 (P.L. 112-10)**

P.L. 112-10, § 1858(b)(4):

Amended Code Sec. 4980H(b) by striking paragraph (3). **Effective** as if included in the provision of, and the amendments made by, the provision of the Patient Protection and Affordable Care Act (P.L. 111-148) to which it relates [**effective** for months beginning after 12-31-2013.—CCH]. Prior to being stricken, Code Sec. 4980H(b)(3) read as follows:

(3) SPECIAL RULES FOR EMPLOYERS PROVIDING FREE CHOICE VOUCHERS.—No assessable payment shall be imposed under paragraph (1) for any month with respect to any employee to whom the employer provides a free choice voucher under section 10108 of the Patient Protection and Affordable Care Act for such month.

EXCISE TAXES—QUALIFIED PENSION, ETC., PLANS

- 2010, Health Care and Education Reconciliation Act of 2010 (P.L. 111-152)

P.L. 111-152, § 1003(b)(1):

Amended Code Sec. 4980H, as added by section 1513 of the Patient Protection and Affordable Care Act (P.L. 111-148) and amended by section 10106 of such Act, in the flush text following subsection (c)(1)(B), by striking "400 percent of the applicable payment amount" and inserting "an amount equal to $1/12$ of $3,000". **Effective** 3-30-2010.

P.L. 111-152, § 1003(d):

Amended Code Sec. 4980H, as added by section 1513 of the Patient Protection and Affordable Care Act (P.L. 111-148) and amended by section 10106 of such Act, and as amended by Act Sec. 1003(a)-(c) of this Act, by redesignating subsection (c) as subsection (b). **Effective** 3-30-2010.

- 2010, Patient Protection and Affordable Care Act (P.L. 111-148)

P.L. 111-148, § 10108(i)(1)(A):

Amended Code Sec. 4980H(c), as added by Act Sec. 1513, by adding at the end a new paragraph (3). **Effective** for months beginning after 12-31-2013.

[Sec. 4980H(c)]

(c) DEFINITIONS AND SPECIAL RULES.—For purposes of this section—

(1) APPLICABLE PAYMENT AMOUNT.—The term "applicable payment amount" means, with respect to any month, $1/12$ of $2,000.

(2) APPLICABLE LARGE EMPLOYER.—

(A) IN GENERAL.—The term "applicable large employer" means, with respect to a calendar year, an employer who employed an average of at least 50 full-time employees on business days during the preceding calendar year.

(B) EXEMPTION FOR CERTAIN EMPLOYERS.—

(i) IN GENERAL.—An employer shall not be considered to employ more than 50 full-time employees if—

(I) the employer's workforce exceeds 50 full-time employees for 120 days or fewer during the calendar year, and

(II) the employees in excess of 50 employed during such 120-day period were seasonal workers.

(ii) DEFINITION OF SEASONAL WORKERS.—The term "seasonal worker" means a worker who performs labor or services on a seasonal basis as defined by the Secretary of Labor, including workers covered by section 500.20(s)(1) of title 29, Code of Federal Regulations and retail workers employed exclusively during holiday seasons.

(C) RULES FOR DETERMINING EMPLOYER SIZE.—For purposes of this paragraph—

(i) APPLICATION OF AGGREGATION RULE FOR EMPLOYERS.—All persons treated as a single employer under subsection (b), (c), (m), or (o) of section 414 of the Internal Revenue Code of 1986 shall be treated as 1 employer.

(ii) EMPLOYERS NOT IN EXISTENCE IN PRECEDING YEAR.—In the case of an employer which was not in existence throughout the preceding calendar year, the determination of whether such employer is an applicable large employer shall be based on the average number of employees that it is reasonably expected such employer will employ on business days in the current calendar year.

(iii) PREDECESSORS.—Any reference in this subsection to an employer shall include a reference to any predecessor of such employer.

(D) APPLICATION OF EMPLOYER SIZE TO ASSESSABLE PENALTIES.—

(i) IN GENERAL.—The number of individuals employed by an applicable large employer as full-time employees during any month shall be reduced by 30 solely for purposes of calculating—

(I) the assessable payment under subsection (a), or

(II) the overall limitation under subsection (b)(2).

(ii) AGGREGATION.—In the case of persons treated as 1 employer under subparagraph (C)(i), only 1 reduction under subclause (I) or (II) shall be allowed with respect to such persons and such reduction shall be allocated among such persons ratably on the basis of the number of full-time employees employed by each such person.

(E) FULL-TIME EQUIVALENTS TREATED AS FULL-TIME EMPLOYEES.—Solely for purposes of determining whether an employer is an applicable large employer under this paragraph, an employer shall, in addition to the number of full-time employees for any month otherwise determined, include for such month a number of full-time employees determined by dividing the aggregate number of hours of service of employees who are not full-time employees for the month by 120.

(F) EXEMPTION FOR HEALTH COVERAGE UNDER TRICARE OR THE DEPARTMENT OF VETERANS AFFAIRS.—Solely for purposes of determining whether an employer is an applicable large employer under this paragraph for any month, an individual shall not be taken into account as an employee for such month if such individual has medical coverage for such month under—

(i) chapter 55 of title 10, United States Code, including coverage under the TRICARE program, or

(ii) under a health care program under chapter 17 or 18 of title 38, United States Code, as determined by the Secretary of Veterans Affairs, in coordination with the Secretary of Health and Human Services and the Secretary.

(3) APPLICABLE PREMIUM TAX CREDIT AND COST-SHARING REDUCTION.—The term "applicable premium tax credit and cost-sharing reduction" means—

(A) any premium tax credit allowed under section 36B,

(B) any cost-sharing reduction under section 1402 of the Patient Protection and Affordable Care Act, and

(C) any advance payment of such credit or reduction under section 1412 of such Act.

(4) FULL-TIME EMPLOYEE.—

(A) IN GENERAL.—The term "full-time employee" means, with respect to any month, an employee who is employed on average at least 30 hours of service per week.

(B) HOURS OF SERVICE.—The Secretary, in consultation with the Secretary of Labor, shall prescribe such regulations, rules, and guidance as may be necessary to determine the hours of service of an employee, including rules for the application of this paragraph to employees who are not compensated on an hourly basis.

(5) INFLATION ADJUSTMENT.—

(A) IN GENERAL.—In the case of any calendar year after 2014, each of the dollar amounts in subsection (b) and paragraph (1) shall be increased by an amount equal to the product of—

(i) such dollar amount, and

(ii) the premium adjustment percentage (as defined in section 1302(c)(4) of the Patient Protection and Affordable Care Act) for the calendar year.

(B) ROUNDING.—If the amount of any increase under subparagraph (A) is not a multiple of $10, such increase shall be rounded to the next lowest multiple of $10.

(6) OTHER DEFINITIONS.—Any term used in this section which is also used in the Patient Protection and Affordable Care Act shall have the same meaning as when used in such Act.

EXCISE TAXES—QUALIFIED PENSION, ETC., PLANS

(7) TAX NONDEDUCTIBLE.—For denial of deduction for the tax imposed by this section, see section 275(a)(6).

Amendments

- **2018, Tax Technical Corrections Act of 2018 (P.L. 115-141)**

P.L. 115-141, §401(a)(2)(B), Div. U:

Amended the heading of Code Sec. 4980H(c)(2)(F) by striking "VETERANS ADMINISTRATION" and inserting "DEPARTMENT OF VETERANS AFFAIRS". **Effective** 3-23-2018.

- **2015, Surface Transportation and Veterans Health Care Choice Improvement Act of 2015 (P.L. 114-41)**

P.L. 114-41, §4007(a)(1):

Amended Code Sec. 4980H(c)(2) by adding at the end a new subparagraph (F). **Effective** for months beginning after 12-31-2013.

- **2010, Health Care and Education Reconciliation Act of 2010 (P.L. 111-152)**

P.L. 111-152, §1003(a):

Amended subsection (d)(2)(D) of Code Sec. 4980H, as added by section 1513 of the Patient Protection and Affordable Care Act (P.L. 111-148) and amended by section 10106 of such Act. **Effective** 3-30-2010. Prior to amendment, Code Sec. 4980H(d)(2)(D) read as follows:

(D) APPLICATION TO CONSTRUCTION INDUSTRY EMPLOYERS.—In the case of any employer the substantial annual gross receipts of which are attributable to the construction industry—

(i) subparagraph (A) shall be applied by substituting "who employed an average of at least 5 full-time employees on business days during the preceding calendar year and whose annual payroll expenses exceed $250,000 for such preceding calendar year" for "who employed an average of at least 50 full-time employees on business days during the preceding calendar year", and

(ii) subparagraph (B) shall be applied by substituting "5" for "50".

P.L. 111-152, §1003(b)(2):

Amended Code Sec. 4980H, as added by section 1513 of the Patient Protection and Affordable Care Act (P.L. 111-148) and amended by section 10106 of such Act, in subsection (d)(1), by striking "$750" and inserting "$2,000". **Effective** 3-30-2010.

P.L. 111-152, §1003(b)(3):

Amended Code Sec. 4980H, as added by section 1513 of the Patient Protection and Affordable Care Act (P.L. 111-148) and amended by section 10106 of such Act, in the matter preceding clause (i) of subsection (d)(5)(A), by striking "subsection (b)(2) and (d)(1)" and inserting "subsection (b) and paragraph (1)". **Effective** 3-30-2010.

P.L. 111-152, §1003(c):

Amended Code Sec. 4980H(d)(2), as added by section 1513 of the Patient Protection and Affordable Care Act (P.L. 111-148) and amended by section 10106 of such Act and as amended by Act Sec. 1003(a) of this Act, by adding at the end a new subparagraph (E). **Effective** 3-30-2010.

P.L. 111-152, §1003(d):

Amended Code Sec. 4980H, as added by section 1513 of the Patient Protection and Affordable Care Act (P.L. 111-148) and amended by section 10106 of such Act, and as amended by Act Sec. 1003(a)-(c) of this Act, by redesignating subsection (d) as subsection (c). **Effective** 3-30-2010.

- **2010, Patient Protection and Affordable Care Act (P.L. 111-148)**

P.L. 111-148, §10106(f)(1):

Amended Code Sec. 4980H(d)(4)(A), as added by Act Sec. 1513(a), by inserting ", with respect to any month," after "means". **Effective** 3-23-2010.

P.L. 111-148, §10106(f)(2):

Amended Code Sec. 4980H(d)(2), as added by Act Sec. 1513(a), by adding at the end a new subparagraph (D). **Effective** for months beginning after 12-31-2013.

[Sec. 4980H(d)]

(d) ADMINISTRATION AND PROCEDURE.—

(1) IN GENERAL.—Any assessable payment provided by this section shall be paid upon notice and demand by the Secretary, and shall be assessed and collected in the same manner as an assessable penalty under subchapter B of chapter 68.

(2) TIME FOR PAYMENT.—The Secretary may provide for the payment of any assessable payment provided by this section on an annual, monthly, or other periodic basis as the Secretary may prescribe.

(3) COORDINATION WITH CREDITS, ETC.—The Secretary shall prescribe rules, regulations, or guidance for the repayment of any assessable payment (including interest) if such payment is based on the allowance or payment of an applicable premium tax credit or cost-sharing reduction with respect to an employee, such allowance or payment is subsequently disallowed, and the assessable payment would not have been required to be made but for such allowance or payment.

Amendments

- **2010, Health Care and Education Reconciliation Act of 2010 (P.L. 111-152)**

P.L. 111-152, §1003(d):

Amended Code Sec. 4980H, as added by section 1513 of the Patient Protection and Affordable Care Act (P.L. 111-148) and amended by section 10106 of such Act, and as amended by Act Sec. 1003(a)-(c) of this Act, by redesignating subsection (e) as subsection (d). **Effective** 3-30-2010.

- **2010, Patient Protection and Affordable Care Act (P.L. 111-148)**

P.L. 111-148, §1513(a):

Amended chapter 43 by adding at the end a new Code Sec. 4980H. **Effective** for months beginning after 12-31-2013.

[Sec. 4980I—Stricken]

Amendments

- **2019, Further Consolidated Appropriations Act, 2020 (P.L. 116-94)**

P.L. 116-94, §503(a), Div. N:

Amended chapter 43 by striking Code Sec. 4980I. **Effective** for tax years beginning after 12-31-2019. Prior to being stricken, Code Sec. 4980I read as follows:

SEC. 4980I. EXCISE TAX ON HIGH COST EMPLOYER-SPONSORED HEALTH COVERAGE.

[Sec. 4980I(a)]

(a) IMPOSITION OF TAX.—If—

(1) an employee is covered under any applicable employer-sponsored coverage of an employer at any time during a taxable period, and

(2) there is any excess benefit with respect to the coverage,

there is hereby imposed a tax equal to 40 percent of the excess benefit.

[Sec. 4980I(b)]

(b) EXCESS BENEFIT.—For purposes of this section—

(1) IN GENERAL.—The term "excess benefit" means, with respect to any applicable employer-sponsored coverage made available by an employer to an employee during any taxable period, the sum of the excess amounts determined under paragraph (2) for months during the taxable period.

(2) MONTHLY EXCESS AMOUNT.—The excess amount determined under this paragraph for any month is the excess (if any) of—

(A) the aggregate cost of the applicable employer-sponsored coverage of the employee for the month, over

(B) an amount equal to $1/12$ of the annual limitation under paragraph (3) for the calendar year in which the month occurs.

(3) ANNUAL LIMITATION.—For purposes of this subsection—

(A) IN GENERAL.—The annual limitation under this paragraph for any calendar year is the dollar limit determined under subparagraph (C) for the calendar year.

(B) APPLICABLE ANNUAL LIMITATION.—

(i) IN GENERAL.—Except as provided in clause (ii), the annual limitation which applies for any month shall be determined on the basis of the type of coverage (as determined under subsection (f)(1)) provided to the employee by the employer as of the beginning of the month.

(ii) MULTIEMPLOYER PLAN COVERAGE.—Any coverage provided under a multiemployer plan (as defined in section 414(f)) shall be treated as coverage other than self-only coverage.

(C) APPLICABLE DOLLAR LIMIT.—

(i) 2018.—In the case of 2018, the dollar limit under this subparagraph is—

(I) in the case of an employee with self-only coverage, $10,200 multiplied by the health cost adjustment percentage (determined by only taking into account self-only coverage), and

(II) in the case of an employee with coverage other than self-only coverage, $27,500 multiplied by the health cost adjustment percentage (determined by only taking into account coverage other than self-only coverage).

(ii) HEALTH COST ADJUSTMENT PERCENTAGE.—For purposes of clause (i), the health cost adjustment percentage is equal to 100 percent plus the excess (if any) of—

(I) the percentage by which the per employee cost for providing coverage under the Blue Cross/Blue Shield standard benefit option under the Federal Employees Health Benefits Plan for plan year 2018 (determined by using the benefit package for such coverage in 2010) exceeds such cost for plan year 2010, over

(II) 55 percent.

(iii) AGE AND GENDER ADJUSTMENT.—

(I) IN GENERAL.—The amount determined under subclause (I) or (II) of clause (i), whichever is applicable, for any taxable period shall be increased by the amount determined under subclause (II).

(II) AMOUNT DETERMINED.—The amount determined under this subclause is an amount equal to the excess (if any) of—

(aa) the premium cost of the Blue Cross/Blue Shield standard benefit option under the Federal Employees Health Benefits Plan for the type of coverage provided such individual in such taxable period if priced for the age and gender characteristics of all employees of the individual's employer, over

(bb) that premium cost for the provision of such coverage under such option in such taxable period if priced for the age and gender characteristics of the national workforce.

(iv) EXCEPTION FOR CERTAIN INDIVIDUALS.—In the case of an individual who is a qualified retiree or who participates in a plan sponsored by an employer the majority

EXCISE TAXES—QUALIFIED PENSION, ETC., PLANS

of whose employees covered by the plan are engaged in a high-risk profession or employed to repair or install electrical or telecommunications lines—

(I) the dollar amount in clause (i)(I) shall be increased by $1,650, and

(II) the dollar amount in clause (i)(II) shall be increased by $3,450.

(v) SUBSEQUENT YEARS.—In the case of any calendar year after 2018, each of the dollar amounts under clauses (i) (after the application of clause (ii)) and (iv) shall be increased to the amount equal to such amount as determined for the calendar year preceding such year, increased by an amount equal to the product of—

(I) such amount as so determined, multiplied by

(II) the cost-of-living adjustment determined under section 1(f)(3) for such year (determined by substituting the calendar year that is 2 years before such year for "2016" in subparagraph (A)(ii) thereof), increased by 1 percentage point in the case of determinations for calendar years beginning before 2020.

If any amount determined under this clause is not a multiple of $50, such amount shall be rounded to the nearest multiple of $50.

Amendments

- **2018, Tax Technical Corrections Act of 2018 (P.L. 115-141)**

P.L. 115-141, §401(a)(237), Div. U:

Amended Code Sec. 4980I(b)(3)(C)(iv) by striking the comma at the end and inserting a period. **Effective** 3-23-2018.

P.L. 115-141, §401(a)(238), Div. U:

Amended Code Sec. 4980I(b)(3)(C)(v) by striking "for for" and inserting "for". **Effective** 3-23-2018.

- **2017, Tax Cuts and Jobs Act (P.L. 115-97)**

P.L. 115-97, §11002(d)(12):

Amended Code Sec. 4980I(b)(3)(C)(v)(II) by striking "for '1992' in subparagraph (B)" and inserting "for '2016' in subparagraph (A)(ii)". **Effective** for tax years beginning after 12-31-2017.

- **2015, Consolidated Appropriations Act, 2016 (P.L. 114-113)**

P.L. 114-113, §101(b)(1)-(2), Div. P:

Amended Code Sec. 4980I(b)(3)(C)(v) by striking "as in effect" and inserting "as determined for", and by striking "as so in effect" and inserting "as so determined". **Effective** 12-18-2015.

- **2010, Health Care and Education Reconciliation Act of 2010 (P.L. 111-152)**

P.L. 111-152, §1401(a)(1)(A)-(B):

Amended Code Sec. 4980I, as added by section 9001 of the Patient Protection and Affordable Care Act (P.L. 111-148), and amended by section 10901 of such Act, by striking "The annual" in subsection (b)(3)(B) and inserting:

"(i) IN GENERAL.—Except as provided in clause (ii), the annual";

and by adding at the end a new clause (ii). **Effective** 3-30-2010.

P.L. 111-152, §1401(a)(2)(A)-(E):

Amended Code Sec. 4980I, as added by section 9001 of the Patient Protection and Affordable Care Act (P.L. 111-148), and amended by section 10901 of such Act, by striking "Except as provided in subparagraph (D)—" in subsection (b)(3)(C); by striking "2013" in clause (i) of subsection (b)(3)(C) each place it appears in the heading and the text and inserting "2018"; by striking "$8,500" in subclause (I) and inserting "$10,200 multiplied by the health cost adjustment percentage (determined by only taking into account self-only coverage)"; and by striking "$23,000" in subclause (II) and inserting "$27,500 multiplied by the health cost adjustment percentage (determined by only taking into account coverage other than self-only coverage)"; by redesignating clauses (ii) and (iii) of subsection (b)(3)(C) as clauses (iv) and (v), respectively, and by inserting after clause (i) new clauses (ii) and (iii); in clause (iv) of subsection (b)(3)(C), as redesignated by Act Sec. 1401(a)(2)(C), by inserting "covered by the plan" after "whose employees"; and by striking subclauses (I) and (II) and inserting new subclauses (I) and (II); in clause (v) of subsection (b)(3)(C), as redesignated by Act Sec. 1401(a)(2)(C), by striking "2013" and inserting "2018"; by striking "clauses (i) and (ii)" and inserting "clauses (i) (after the application of clause (ii)) and (iv)"; and by inserting "in the case of determinations for calendar years beginning before 2020" after "1 percentage point" in subclause (II) thereof. **Effective** 3-30-2010. Prior to amendment, Code Sec. 4980I(b)(3)(C) read as follows:

(C) APPLICABLE DOLLAR LIMIT.—Except as provided in subparagraph (D)—

(i) 2013.—In the case of 2013, the dollar limit under this subparagraph is—

(I) in the case of an employee with self-only coverage, $8,500, and

(II) in the case of an employee with coverage other than self-only coverage, $23,000.

(ii) EXCEPTION FOR CERTAIN INDIVIDUALS.—In the case of an individual who is a qualified retiree or who participates in a plan sponsored by an employer the majority of whose employees are engaged in a high-risk profession or employed to repair or install electrical or telecommunications lines—

(I) the dollar amount in clause (i)(I) (determined after the application of subparagraph (D)) shall be increased by $1,350, and

(II) the dollar amount in clause (i)(II) (determined after the application of subparagraph (D)) shall be increased by $3,000.

(iii) SUBSEQUENT YEARS.—In the case of any calendar year after 2013, each of the dollar amounts under clauses (i) and (ii) shall be increased to the amount equal to such amount as in effect for the calendar year preceding such year, increased by an amount equal to the product of—

(I) such amount as so in effect, multiplied by

(II) the cost-of-living adjustment determined under section 1(f)(3) for such year (determined by substituting the calendar year that is 2 years before such year for "1992" in subparagraph (B) thereof), increased by 1 percentage point.

If any amount determined under this clause is not a multiple of $50, such amount shall be rounded to the nearest multiple of $50.

P.L. 111-152, §1401(a)(3):

Amended Code Sec. 4980I, as added by section 9001 of the Patient Protection and Affordable Care Act (P.L. 111-148), and amended by section 10901 of such Act, by striking subparagraph (D) of subsection (b)(3). **Effective** 3-30-2010. Prior to being stricken, Code Sec. 4980I(b)(3)(D) read as follows:

(D) TRANSITION RULE FOR STATES WITH HIGHEST COVERAGE COSTS.—

(i) IN GENERAL.—If an employee is a resident of a high cost State on the first day of any month beginning in 2013, 2014, or 2015, the annual limitation under this paragraph for such month with respect to such employee shall be an amount equal to the applicable percentage of the annual limitation (determined without regard to this subparagraph or subparagraph (C)(ii)).

(ii) APPLICABLE PERCENTAGE.—The applicable percentage is 120 percent for 2013, 110 percent for 2014, and 105 percent for 2015.

(iii) HIGH COST STATE.—The term "high cost State" means each of the 17 States which the Secretary of Health and Human Services, in consultation with the Secretary, estimates had the highest average cost during 2012 for employer-sponsored coverage under health plans. The Secretary's estimate shall be made on the basis of aggregate premiums paid in the State for such health plans, determined using the most recent data available as of August 31, 2012.

[Sec. 4980I(c)]

(c) LIABILITY TO PAY TAX.—

(1) IN GENERAL.—Each coverage provider shall pay the tax imposed by subsection (a) on its applicable share of the excess benefit with respect to an employee for any taxable period.

(2) COVERAGE PROVIDER.—For purposes of this subsection, the term "coverage provider" means each of the following:

(A) HEALTH INSURANCE COVERAGE.—If the applicable employer-sponsored coverage consists of coverage under a group health plan which provides health insurance coverage, the health insurance issuer.

(B) HSA AND MSA CONTRIBUTIONS.—If the applicable employer-sponsored coverage consists of coverage under an arrangement under which the employer makes contributions described in subsection (b) or (d) of section 106, the employer.

(C) OTHER COVERAGE.—In the case of any other applicable employer-sponsored coverage, the person that administers the plan benefits.

(3) APPLICABLE SHARE.—For purposes of this subsection, a coverage provider's applicable share of an excess benefit for any taxable period is the amount which bears the same ratio to the amount of such excess benefit as—

(A) the cost of the applicable employer-sponsored coverage provided by the provider to the employee during such period, bears to

(B) the aggregate cost of all applicable employer-sponsored coverage provided to the employee by all coverage providers during such period.

(4) RESPONSIBILITY TO CALCULATE TAX AND APPLICABLE SHARES.—

(A) IN GENERAL.—Each employer shall—

(i) calculate for each taxable period the amount of the excess benefit subject to the tax imposed by subsection (a) and the applicable share of such excess benefit for each coverage provider, and

(ii) notify, at such time and in such manner as the Secretary may prescribe, the Secretary and each coverage provider of the amount so determined for the provider.

(B) SPECIAL RULE FOR MULTIEMPLOYER PLANS.—In the case of applicable employer-sponsored coverage made available to employees through a multiemployer plan (as defined in section 414(f)), the plan sponsor shall make the calculations, and provide the notice, required under subparagraph (A).

[Sec. 4980I(d)]

(d) APPLICABLE EMPLOYER-SPONSORED COVERAGE; COST.—For purposes of this section—

(1) APPLICABLE EMPLOYER-SPONSORED COVERAGE.—

(A) IN GENERAL.—The term "applicable employer-sponsored coverage" means, with respect to any employee, coverage under any group health plan made available to the employee by an employer which is excludable from the employee's gross income under section 106, or would be so excludable if it were employer-provided coverage (within the meaning of such section 106).

(B) EXCEPTIONS.—The term "applicable employer-sponsored coverage" shall not include—

(i) any coverage (whether through insurance or otherwise) described in section 9832(c)(1) (other than subparagraph (G) thereof) or for long-term care, or

(ii) any coverage under a separate policy, certificate, or contract of insurance which provides benefits substantially all of which are for treatment of the mouth (including any organ or structure within the mouth) or for treatment of the eye, or

(iii) any coverage described in section 9832(c)(3) the payment for which is not excludable from gross income and for which a deduction under section 162(l) is not allowable.

(C) COVERAGE INCLUDES EMPLOYEE PAID PORTION.—Coverage shall be treated as applicable employer-sponsored coverage without regard to whether the employer or employee pays for the coverage.

(D) SELF-EMPLOYED INDIVIDUAL.—In the case of an individual who is an employee within the meaning of section 401(c)(1), coverage under any group health plan providing health insurance coverage shall be treated as applicable employer-sponsored coverage if a deduction is allowable under section 162(l) with respect to all or any portion of the cost of the coverage.

(E) GOVERNMENTAL PLANS INCLUDED.—Applicable employer-sponsored coverage shall include coverage under any group health plan established and maintained primarily for its civilian employees by the Government of the United States, by the government of any State or political subdivision thereof, or by any agency or instrumentality of any such government.

Sec. 4980I—Stricken

(2) DETERMINATION OF COST.—

(A) IN GENERAL.—The cost of applicable employer-sponsored coverage shall be determined under rules similar to the rules of section 4980B(f)(4), except that in determining such cost, any portion of the cost of such coverage which is attributable to the tax imposed under this section shall not be taken into account and the amount of such cost shall be calculated separately for self-only coverage and other coverage. In the case of applicable employer-sponsored coverage which provides coverage to retired employees, the plan may elect to treat a retired employee who has not attained the age of 65 and a retired employee who has attained the age of 65 as similarly situated beneficiaries.

(B) HEALTH FSAS.—In the case of applicable employer-sponsored coverage consisting of coverage under a flexible spending arrangement (as defined in section 106(c)(2)), the cost of the coverage shall be equal to the sum of—

(i) the amount of employer contributions under any salary reduction election under the arrangement, plus

(ii) the amount determined under subparagraph (A) with respect to any reimbursement under the arrangement in excess of the contributions described in clause (i).

(C) ARCHER MSAS AND HSAS.—In the case of applicable employer-sponsored coverage consisting of coverage under an arrangement under which the employer makes contributions described in subsection (b) or (d) of section 106, the cost of the coverage shall be equal to the amount of employer contributions under the arrangement.

(D) QUALIFIED SMALL EMPLOYER HEALTH REIMBURSEMENT ARRANGEMENTS.—In the case of applicable employer-sponsored coverage consisting of coverage under any qualified small employer health reimbursement arrangement (as defined in section 9831(d)(2)), the cost of coverage shall be equal to the amount described in section 6051(a)(15).

(E) ALLOCATION ON A MONTHLY BASIS.—If cost is determined on other than a monthly basis, the cost shall be allocated to months in a taxable period on such basis as the Secretary may prescribe.

(3) EMPLOYEE.—The term "employee" includes any former employee, surviving spouse, or other primary insured individual.

Amendments

• **2016, 21st Century Cures Act (P.L. 114-255)**

P.L. 114-255, §18001(a)(4)(B):

Amended Code Sec. 4980I(d)(2) by redesignating subparagraph (D) as subparagraph (E) and by inserting after subparagraph (C) a new subparagraph (D). **Effective** for years beginning after 12-31-2016.

• **2010, Health Care and Education Reconciliation Act of 2010 (P.L. 111-152)**

P.L. 111-152, §1401(a)(4)-(5):

Amended Code Sec. 4980I, as added by section 9001 of the Patient Protection and Affordable Care Act (P.L. 111-148), and amended by section 10901 of such Act, by redesignating clause (ii) as clause (iii) in subsection (d)(1)(B), and by inserting after clause (i) a new clause (ii); and by adding at the end of subsection (d) a new paragraph (3). **Effective** 3-30-2010.

• **2010, Patient Protection and Affordable Care Act (P.L. 111-148)**

P.L. 111-148, §10901(b):

Amended Code Sec. 4980I(d)(1)(B)(i), as added by Act Sec. 9001, by striking "section 9832(c)(1)(A)" and inserting "section 9832(c)(1) (other than subparagraph (G) thereof)". **Effective** for tax years beginning after 12-31-2019 [**effective** date changed by P.L. 111-152, §1401(b)(2), and P.L. 114-113, §101(a), Div. P].

[Sec. 4980I(e)]

(e) PENALTY FOR FAILURE TO PROPERLY CALCULATE EXCESS BENEFIT.—

(1) IN GENERAL.—If, for any taxable period, the tax imposed by subsection (a) exceeds the tax determined under such subsection with respect to the total excess benefit calculated by the employer or plan sponsor under subsection (c)(4)—

(A) each coverage provider shall pay the tax on its applicable share (determined in the same manner as under subsection (c)(4)) of the excess, but no penalty shall be imposed on the provider with respect to such amount, and

(B) the employer or plan sponsor shall, in addition to any tax imposed by subsection (a), pay a penalty in an amount equal to such excess, plus interest at the underpayment rate determined under section 6621 for the period beginning on the due date for the payment of tax imposed by subsection (a) to which the excess relates and ending on the date of payment of the penalty.

(2) LIMITATIONS ON PENALTY.—

(A) PENALTY NOT TO APPLY WHERE FAILURE NOT DISCOVERED EXERCISING REASONABLE DILIGENCE.—No penalty shall be imposed by paragraph (1)(B) on any failure to properly calculate the excess benefit during any period for which it is established to the satisfaction of the Secretary that the employer or plan sponsor neither knew, nor exercising reasonable diligence would have known, that such failure existed.

(B) PENALTY NOT TO APPLY TO FAILURES CORRECTED WITHIN 30 DAYS.—No penalty shall be imposed by paragraph (1)(B) on any such failure if—

(i) such failure was due to reasonable cause and not to willful neglect, and

(ii) such failure is corrected during the 30-day period beginning on the 1st date that the employer knew, or exercising reasonable diligence would have known, that such failure existed.

(C) WAIVER BY SECRETARY.—In the case of any such failure which is due to reasonable cause and not to willful neglect, the Secretary may waive part or all of the penalty imposed by paragraph (1), to the extent that the payment of such penalty would be excessive or otherwise inequitable relative to the failure involved.

[Sec. 4980I(f)]

(f) OTHER DEFINITIONS AND SPECIAL RULES.—For purposes of this section—

(1) COVERAGE DETERMINATIONS.—

(A) IN GENERAL.—Except as provided in subparagraph (B), an employee shall be treated as having self-only coverage with respect to any applicable employer-sponsored coverage of an employer.

(B) MINIMUM ESSENTIAL COVERAGE.—An employee shall be treated as having coverage other than self-only coverage only if the employee is enrolled in coverage other than self-only coverage in a group health plan which provides minimum essential coverage (as defined in section 5000A(f)) to the employee and at least one other beneficiary, and the benefits provided under such minimum essential coverage do not vary based on whether any individual covered under such coverage is the employee or another beneficiary.

(2) QUALIFIED RETIREE.—The term "qualified retiree" means any individual who—

(A) is receiving coverage by reason of being a retiree,

(B) has attained age 55, and

(C) is not entitled to benefits or eligible for enrollment under the Medicare program under title XVIII of the Social Security Act.

(3) EMPLOYEES ENGAGED IN HIGH-RISK PROFESSION.—The term "employees engaged in a high-risk profession" means law enforcement officers (as such term is defined in section 1204 of the Omnibus Crime Control and Safe Streets Act of 1968), employees in fire protection activities (as such term is defined in section 3(y) of the Fair Labor Standards Act of 1938), individuals who provide out-of-hospital emergency medical care (including emergency medical technicians, paramedics, and first-responders), individuals whose primary work is longshore work (as defined in section 258(b) of the Immigration and Nationality Act (8 U.S.C. 1288(b)), determined without regard to paragraph (2) thereof), and individuals engaged in the construction, mining, agriculture (not including food processing), forestry, and fishing industries. Such term includes an employee who is retired from a high-risk profession described in the preceding sentence, if such employee satisfied the requirements of such sentence for a period of not less than 20 years during the employee's employment.

(4) GROUP HEALTH PLAN.—The term "group health plan" has the meaning given such term by section 5000(b)(1). Section 9831(d)(1) shall not apply for purposes of this section.

(5) HEALTH INSURANCE COVERAGE; HEALTH INSURANCE ISSUER.—

(A) HEALTH INSURANCE COVERAGE.—The term "health insurance coverage" has the meaning given such term by section 9832(b)(1) (applied without regard to subparagraph (B) thereof, except as provided by the Secretary in regulations).

(B) HEALTH INSURANCE ISSUER.—The term "health insurance issuer" has the meaning given such term by section 9832(b)(2).

(6) PERSON THAT ADMINISTERS THE PLAN BENEFITS.—The term "person that administers the plan benefits" shall include the plan sponsor if the plan sponsor administers benefits under the plan.

(7) PLAN SPONSOR.—The term "plan sponsor" has the meaning given such term in section 3(16)(B) of the Employee Retirement Income Security Act of 1974.

(8) TAXABLE PERIOD.—The term "taxable period" means the calendar year or such shorter period as the Secretary may prescribe. The Secretary may have different taxable periods for employers of varying sizes.

(9) AGGREGATION RULES.—All employers treated as a single employer under subsection (b), (c), (m), or (o) of section 414 shall be treated as a single employer.

(10) DEDUCTIBILITY OF TAX.—Section 275(a)(6) shall not apply to the tax imposed by subsection (a).

Amendments

• **2016, 21st Century Cures Act (P.L. 114-255)**

P.L. 114-255, §18001(a)(4)(A):

Amended Code Sec. 4980I(f)(4) by adding at the end a new sentence. **Effective** for years beginning after 12-31-2016.

• **2015, Consolidated Appropriations Act, 2016 (P.L. 114-113)**

P.L. 114-113, §102, Div. P:

Amended Code Sec. 4980I(f)(10). **Effective** 12-18-2015. Prior to amendment, Code Sec. 4980I(f)(10) read as follows:

(10) DENIAL OF DEDUCTION.—For denial of a deduction for the tax imposed by this section, see section 275(a)(6).

• **2010, Patient Protection and Affordable Care Act (P.L. 111-148)**

P.L. 111-148, §10901(a):

Amended Code Sec. 4980I(f)(3), as added by Act Sec. 9001, by inserting "individuals whose primary work is longshore work (as defined in section 258(b) of the Immigration and Nationality Act (8 U.S.C. 1288(b)), determined without regard to paragraph (2) thereof)," before "and individuals engaged in the construction, mining". **Effective** for tax years beginning after 12-31-2019 [**effective** date changed by P.L. 111-152, §1401(b)(2), and P.L. 114-113, §101(a), Div. P].

[Sec. 4980I(g)]

(g) REGULATIONS.—The Secretary shall prescribe such regulations as may be necessary to carry out this section.

Amendments

• **2010, Patient Protection and Affordable Care Act (P.L. 111-148)**

P.L. 111-148, §9001(a):

Amended chapter 43, as amended by Act Sec. 1513, by adding at the end a new Code Sec. 4980I. **Effective** for tax years beginning after 12-31-2021 [**effective** date changed by P.L. 111-152, §1401(b)(1), P.L. 114-113, §101(a), Div. P, and P.L. 115-120, §4002, Div. D].

EXCISE TAXES—QUALIFIED INVESTMENT ENTITIES

CHAPTER 44—QUALIFIED INVESTMENT ENTITIES

Sec. 4981.   Excise tax on undistributed income of real estate investment trusts.
Sec. 4982.   Excise tax on undistributed income of regulated investment companies.

[Sec. 4981]

SEC. 4981. EXCISE TAX ON UNDISTRIBUTED INCOME OF REAL ESTATE INVESTMENT TRUSTS.

[Sec. 4981(a)]

(a) IMPOSITION OF TAX.—There is hereby imposed a tax on every real estate investment trust for each calendar year equal to 4 percent of the excess (if any) of—
    (1) the required distribution for such calendar year, over
    (2) the distributed amount for such calendar year.

[Sec. 4981(b)]

(b) REQUIRED DISTRIBUTION.—For purposes of this section—
    (1) IN GENERAL.—The term "required distribution" means, with respect to any calendar year, the sum of—
        (A) 85 percent of the real estate investment trust's ordinary income for such calendar year, plus
        (B) 95 percent of the real estate investment trust's capital gain net income for such calendar year.
    (2) INCREASE BY PRIOR YEAR SHORTFALL.—The amount determined under paragraph (1) for any calendar year shall be increased by the excess (if any) of—
        (A) the grossed up required distribution for the preceding calendar year, over
        (B) the distributed amount for such preceding calendar year.
    (3) GROSSED UP REQUIRED DISTRIBUTION.—The grossed up required distribution for any calendar year is the required distribution for such year determined—
        (A) with the application of paragraph (2) to such taxable year, and
        (B) by substituting "100 percent" for each percentage set forth in paragraph (1).

[Sec. 4981(c)]

(c) DISTRIBUTED AMOUNT.—For purposes of this section—
    (1) IN GENERAL.—The term "distributed amount" means, with respect to any calendar year, the sum of—
        (A) the deduction for dividends paid (as defined in section 561) during such calendar year (but computed without regard to that portion of such deduction which is attributable to the amount excluded under section 857(b)(2)(D), and
        (B) any amount on which tax is imposed under subsection (b)(1) or (b)(3)(A) of section 857 for any taxable year ending in such calendar year.
    (2) INCREASE BY PRIOR YEAR OVERDISTRIBUTION.—The amount determined under paragraph (1) for any calendar year shall be increased by the excess (if any) of—
        (A) the distributed amount for the preceding calendar year (determined with the application of this paragraph to such preceding calendar year), over
        (B) the grossed up required distribution for such preceding calendar year.
    (3) DETERMINATION OF DIVIDENDS PAID.—The amount of the dividends paid during any calendar year shall be determined without regard to the provisions of section 858.

Amendments

• **1988, Technical and Miscellaneous Revenue Act of 1988 (P.L. 100-647)**

P.L. 100-647, § 1006(s)(3):

Amended Code Sec. 4981(c)(1)(A) by striking out "such calendar year" and inserting in lieu thereof "such calendar year (but computed without regard to that portion of such deduction which is attributable to the amount excluded under section 857(b)(2)(D))". **Effective** as if included in the provision of P.L. 99-514 to which it relates.

[Sec. 4981(d)]

(d) TIME FOR PAYMENT OF TAX.—The tax imposed by this section for any calendar year shall be paid on or before March 15 of the following calendar year.

[Sec. 4981(e)]

(e) DEFINITIONS AND SPECIAL RULES.—For purposes of this section—
    (1) ORDINARY INCOME.—The term "ordinary income" means the real estate investment trust taxable income (as defined in section 857(b)(2)) determined—
        (A) without regard to subparagraph (B) of section 857(b)(2),
        (B) by not taking into account any gain or loss from the sale or exchange of capital asset, and
        (C) by treating the calendar year as the trust's taxable year.
    (2) CAPITAL GAIN NET INCOME.—
        (A) IN GENERAL.—The term "capital gain net income" has the meaning given such term by section 1222(9) (determined by treating the calendar year as the trust's taxable year).
        (B) REDUCTION FOR NET ORDINARY LOSS.—The amount determined under subparagraph (A) shall be reduced by the amount of the trust's net ordinary loss for the taxable year.
        (C) NET ORDINARY LOSS.—For purposes of this paragraph, the net ordinary loss for the calendar year is the amount which would be net operating loss of the trust for the calendar year if the amount of such loss were determined in the same manner as ordinary income is determined under paragraph (1).
    (3) TREATMENT OF DEFICIENCY DISTRIBUTIONS.—In the case of any deficiency dividend (as defined in section 860(f))—
        (A) such dividend shall be taken into account when paid without regard to section 860, and
        (B) any income giving rise to the adjustment shall be treated as arising when the dividend is paid.

Amendments

• **1988, Technical and Miscellaneous Revenue Act of 1988 (P.L. 100-647)**

P.L. 100-647, § 1006(s)(1):

Amended Code Sec. 4981(e)(2). **Effective** as if included in the provision of P.L. 99-514 to which it relates. Prior to amendment, Code Sec. 4981(e)(2) read as follows:

(2) CAPITAL GAIN NET INCOME.—The term "capital gain net income" has the meaning given to such term by section 1222(9) (determined by treating the calendar year as the trust's taxable year).

EXCISE TAXES—QUALIFIED INVESTMENT ENTITIES

- **1986, Tax Reform Act of 1986 (P.L. 99-514)**

P.L. 99-514, §668(a):

Amended Code Sec. 4981. **Effective** for calendar years beginning after 12-31-86. Prior to amendment, Code Sec. 4981 read as follows:

SEC. 4981. EXCISE TAX BASED ON CERTAIN REAL ESTATE INVESTMENT TRUST TAXABLE INCOME NOT DISTRIBUTED DURING THE TAXABLE YEAR.

Effective with respect to taxable years beginning after December 31, 1979, there is hereby imposed on each real estate investment trust for the taxable year a tax equal to 3 percent of the amount (if any) by which 75 percent of the real estate investment trust taxable income (as defined in section 857(b)(2), but determined without regard to section 857(b)(2)(B), and by excluding any net capital gain for the taxable year) exceeds the amount of the dividends paid deduction (as defined in section 561, but computed without regard to capital gains dividends as defined in section 857(b)(3)(C) and without regard to any dividend paid after the close of the taxable year) for the taxable year. For purposes of the preceding sentence, the determination of the real estate investment trust taxable income shall be made by taking into account only the amount and character of the items of income and deduction as reported by such trust in its return for the taxable year.

- **1976, Tax Reform Act of 1976 (P.L. 94-455)**

P.L. 94-455, §1605(a):

Added Chapter 44.

P.L. 94-455, §1608(d), provides:

(d) OTHER AMENDMENTS.

(1) Except as provided in paragraphs (2) and (3), the amendments made by sections 1603, 1604, and 1605 shall apply to taxable years of real estate investment trusts beginning after the date of the enactment of this Act.

(2) If, as a result of a determination (as defined in section 859(c) of the Internal Revenue Code of 1954), occurring after the date of enactment of this Act, with respect to the real estate investment trust, such trust does not meet the requirement of section 856(a)(4) of the Internal Revenue Code of 1954 (as in effect before the amendment of such section by this Act) for any taxable year beginning on or before the date of the enactment of this Act, such trust may elect, within 60 days after such determination in the manner provided in regulations prescribed by the Secretary of the Treasury, to have the provisions of section 1603 (other than paragraphs (1), (2), (3), and (4) of section 1604(c)) apply with respect to such taxable year. Where the provisions of section 1603 apply to a real estate investment trust with respect to any taxable year beginning on or before the date of the enactment of this Act—

(A) credit or refund of any overpayment of tax which results from the application of section 1603 to such taxable year shall be made as if on the date of the determination (as defined in section 859(c) of the Internal Revenue Code of 1954) 2 years remained before the expiration of the period of limitation prescribed by section 6511 of such Code on the filing of claim for refund for the taxable year to which the overpayment relates,

(B) the running of the statute of limitations provided in section 6501 of such Code on the making of assessments, and the bringing of distraint or a proceeding in court for collection, in respect of any deficiency (as defined in section 6211 of such Code) established by such a determination, and all interest, additions to tax, additional amounts, or assessable penalties in respect thereof, shall be suspended for a period of 2 years after the date of such determination, and

(C) the collection of any deficiency (as defined in section 6211 of such Code) established by such determination and all interest, additions to tax, additional amounts, and assessable penalties in respect thereof shall, except in cases of jeopardy, be stayed until the expiration of 60 days after the date of such determination.

No distraint or proceeding in court shall be begun for the collection of an amount the collection of which is stayed under subparagraph (C) during the period for which the collection of such amount is stayed.

(3) Section 856(g)(3) of the Internal Revenue Code of 1954, as added by section 1604 of this Act, shall not apply with respect to a termination of an election, filed by a taxpayer under section 856(c)(1) of such Code on or before the date of the enactment of this Act, unless the provisions of part II of subchapter M of chapter 1 of subtitle A of such Code apply to such taxpayer for a taxable year ending after the date of the enactment of this Act for which such election is in effect.

[Sec. 4982]

SEC. 4982. EXCISE TAX ON UNDISTRIBUTED INCOME OF REGULATED INVESTMENT COMPANIES.

[Sec. 4982(a)]

(a) IMPOSITION OF TAX.—There is hereby imposed a tax on every regulated investment company for each calendar year equal to 4 percent of the excess (if any) of—

(1) the required distribution for such calendar year, over

(2) the distributed amount for such calendar year.

[Sec. 4982(b)]

(b) REQUIRED DISTRIBUTION.—For purposes of this section—

(1) IN GENERAL.—The term "required distribution" means, with respect to any calendar year, the sum of—

(A) 98 percent of the regulated investment company's ordinary income for such calendar year, plus

(B) 98.2 percent of the regulated investment company's capital gain net income for the 1-year period ending on October 31 of such calendar year.

(2) INCREASE BY PRIOR YEAR SHORTFALL.—The amount determined under paragraph (1) for any calendar year shall be increased by the excess (if any) of—

(A) the grossed up required distribution for the preceding calendar year, over

(B) the distributed amount for such preceding calendar year.

(3) GROSSED UP REQUIRED DISTRIBUTION.—The grossed up required distribution for any calendar year is the required distribution for such year determined—

(A) with the application of paragraph (2) to such taxable year, and

(B) by substituting "100 percent" for each percentage set forth in paragraph (1).

Amendments

- **2010, Regulated Investment Company Modernization Act of 2010 (P.L. 111-325)**

P.L. 111-325, §404(a):

Amended Code Sec. 4982(b)(1)(B) by striking "98 percent" and inserting "98.2 percent". **Effective** for calendar years beginning after 12-22-2010.

- **1989, Omnibus Budget Reconciliation Act of 1989 (P.L. 101-239)**

P.L. 101-239, §7204(a)(1):

Amended Code Sec. 4982(b)(1)(A) by striking "97 percent" and inserting "98 percent". **Effective** for calendar years ending after 7-10-89.

- **1987, Revenue Act of 1987 (P.L. 100-203)**

P.L. 100-203, §10104(b)(1):

Amended Code Sec. 4982(b)(1) by striking out "90 percent" in subparagraph (B) and inserting in lieu thereof "98 percent". **Effective** as if included in the amendments made by Act Sec. 651 of P.L. 99-514.

[Sec. 4982(c)]

(c) DISTRIBUTED AMOUNT.—For purposes of this section—

(1) IN GENERAL.—The term "distributed amount" means, with respect to any calendar year, the sum of—

(A) the deduction for dividends paid (as defined in section 561) during such calendar year, and

(B) any amount on which tax is imposed under subsection (b)(1) or (b)(3)(A) of section 852 for any taxable year ending in such calendar year.

(2) INCREASE BY PRIOR YEAR OVERDISTRIBUTION.—The amount determined under paragraph (1) for any calendar year shall be increased by the excess (if any) of—

(A) the distributed amount for the preceding calendar year (determined with the application of this paragraph to such preceding calendar year), over

(B) the grossed up required distribution for such preceding calendar year.

EXCISE TAXES—QUALIFIED INVESTMENT ENTITIES

(3) DETERMINATION OF DIVIDENDS PAID.—The amount of the dividends paid during any calendar year shall be determined without regard to—

(A) the provisions of section 855, and

(B) any exempt-interest dividend as defined in section 852(b)(5).

(4) SPECIAL RULE FOR ESTIMATED TAX PAYMENTS.—

(A) IN GENERAL.—In the case of a regulated investment company which elects the application of this paragraph for any calendar year—

(i) the distributed amount with respect to such company for such calendar year shall be increased by the amount on which qualified estimated tax payments are made by such company during such calendar year, and

(ii) the distributed amount with respect to such company for the following calendar year shall be reduced by the amount of such increase.

(B) QUALIFIED ESTIMATED TAX PAYMENTS.—For purposes of this paragraph, the term "qualified estimated tax payments" means, with respect to any calendar year, payments of estimated tax of a tax described in paragraph (1)(B) for any taxable year which begins (but does not end) in such calendar year.

Amendments

- **2010, Regulated Investment Company Modernization Act of 2010 (P.L. 111-325)**

P.L. 111-325, § 403(a):

Amended Code Sec. 4982(c) by adding at the end a new paragraph (4). **Effective** for calendar years beginning after 12-22-2010.

[Sec. 4982(d)]

(d) TIME FOR PAYMENT OF TAX.—The tax imposed by this section for any calendar year shall be paid on or before March 15 of the following calendar year.

[Sec. 4982(e)]

(e) DEFINITIONS AND SPECIAL RULES.—For purposes of this section—

(1) ORDINARY INCOME.—The term "ordinary income" means the investment company taxable income (as defined in section 852(b)(2)) determined—

(A) without regard to subparagraphs (A) and (D) of section 852(b)(2),

(B) by not taking into account any gain or loss from the sale or exchange of a capital asset, and

(C) by treating the calendar year as the company's taxable year.

(2) CAPITAL GAIN NET INCOME.—

(A) IN GENERAL.—Except as provided in subparagraph (B), the term "capital gain net income" has the meaning given such term by section 1222(9) (determined by treating the 1-year period ending on October 31 of any calendar year as the company's taxable year).

(B) REDUCTION BY NET ORDINARY LOSS FOR CALENDAR YEAR.—The amount determined under subparagraph (A) shall be reduced (but not below the net capital gain) by the amount of the company's net ordinary loss for the calendar year.

(C) DEFINITIONS.—For purposes of this paragraph—

(i) NET CAPITAL GAIN.—The term "net capital gain" has the meaning given such term by section 1222(11) (determined by treating the 1-year period ending on October 31 of the calendar year as the company's taxable year).

(ii) NET ORDINARY LOSS.—The net ordinary loss for the calendar year is the amount which would be the net operating loss of the company for the calendar year if the amount of such loss were determined in the same manner as ordinary income is determined under paragraph (1).

(3) TREATMENT OF DEFICIENCY DISTRIBUTIONS.—In the case of any deficiency dividend (as defined in section 860(f))—

(A) such dividend shall be taken into account when paid without regard to section 860, and

(B) any income giving rise to the adjustment shall be treated as arising when the dividend is paid.

(4) ELECTION TO USE TAXABLE YEAR IN CERTAIN CASES.—

(A) IN GENERAL.—If—

(i) the taxable year of the regulated investment company ends with the month of November or December, and

(ii) such company makes an election under this paragraph,

subsection (b)(1)(B) and paragraph (2) of this subsection shall be applied by taking into account the company's taxable year in lieu of the 1-year period ending on October 31 of the calendar year.

(B) ELECTION REVOCABLE ONLY WITH CONSENT.—An election under this paragraph, once made, may be revoked only with the consent of the Secretary.

(5) TREATMENT OF SPECIFIED GAINS AND LOSSES AFTER OCTOBER 31 OF CALENDAR YEAR.—

(A) IN GENERAL.—Any specified gain or specified loss which (but for this paragraph) would be properly taken into account for the portion of the calendar year after October 31 shall be treated as arising on January 1 of the following calendar year.

(B) SPECIFIED GAINS AND LOSSES.—For purposes of this paragraph—

(i) SPECIFIED GAIN.—The term "specified gain" means ordinary gain from the sale, exchange, or other disposition of property (including the termination of a position with respect to such property). Such term shall include any foreign currency gain attributable to a section 988 transaction (within the meaning of section 988) and any amount includible in gross income under section 1296(a)(1).

(ii) SPECIFIED LOSS.—The term "specified loss" means ordinary loss from the sale, exchange, or other disposition of property (including the termination of a position with respect to such property). Such term shall include any foreign currency loss attributable to a section 988 transaction (within the meaning of section 988) and any amount allowable as a deduction under section 1296(a)(2).

(C) SPECIAL RULE FOR COMPANIES ELECTING TO USE THE TAXABLE YEAR.—In the case of any company making an election under paragraph (4), subparagraph (A) shall be applied by substituting the last day of the company's taxable year for October 31.

(6) TREATMENT OF MARK TO MARKET GAIN.—

(A) IN GENERAL.—For purposes of determining a regulated investment company's ordinary income, notwithstanding paragraph (1)(C), each specified mark to market provision shall be applied as if such company's taxable year ended on October 31. In the case of a company making an election under paragraph (4), the preceding sentence shall be applied by substituting the last day of the company's taxable year for October 31.

EXCISE TAXES—EXPATRIATED ENTITIES

(B) SPECIFIED MARK TO MARKET PROVISION.—For purposes of this paragraph, the term "specified mark to market provision" means sections 1256 and 1296 and any other provision of this title (or regulations thereunder) which treats property as disposed of on the last day of the taxable year or which determines income by reference to the value of an item on the last day of the taxable year.

(7) ELECTIVE DEFERRAL OF CERTAIN ORDINARY LOSSES.—Except as provided in regulations prescribed by the Secretary, in the case of a regulated investment company which has a taxable year other than the calendar year—

(A) such company may elect to determine its ordinary income and net ordinary loss (as defined in paragraph (2)(C)(ii)) for the calendar year without regard to any portion of any net ordinary loss (determined without regard to specified gains and losses taken into account under paragraph (5)) which is attributable to the portion of such calendar year which is after the beginning of the taxable year which begins in such calendar year, and

(B) any amount of net ordinary loss not taken into account for a calendar year by reason of subparagraph (A) shall be treated as arising on the 1st day of the following calendar year.

Amendments

- **2014, Tax Technical Corrections Act of 2014 (P.L. 113-295)**

P.L. 113-295, §205(d)(1), Division A:

Amended Code Sec. 4982(e)(6)(B) by inserting before the period at the end the following: "or which determines income by reference to the value of an item on the last day of the taxable year". **Effective** as if included in the provision of the Regulated Investment Company Modernization Act of 2010 (P.L. 111-325) to which it relates [**effective** for calendar years beginning after 12-22-2010.—CCH].

P.L. 113-295, §205(d)(2), Division A:

Amended Code Sec. 4982(e)(7)(A) by striking "such company" and all that follows through "any net ordinary loss" and inserting "such company may elect to determine its ordinary income and net ordinary loss (as defined in paragraph (2)(C)(ii)) for the calendar year without regard to any portion of any net ordinary loss". **Effective** as if included in the provision of the Regulated Investment Company Modernization Act of 2010 (P.L. 111-325) to which it relates [**effective** for calendar years beginning after 12-22-2010.—CCH]. Prior amendment, Code Sec. 4982(e)(7)(A), read as follows:

(A) such company may elect to determine its ordinary income for the calendar year without regard to any net ordinary loss (determined without regard to specified gains and losses taken into account under paragraph (5)) which is attributable to the portion of such calendar year which is after the beginning of the taxable year which begins in such calendar year, and

- **2010, Regulated Investment Company Modernization Act of 2010 (P.L. 111-325)**

P.L. 111-325, §402(a):

Amended Code Sec. 4982(e) by striking paragraphs (5) and (6) and inserting new paragraphs (5), (6), and (7). **Effective** for calendar years beginning after 12-22-2010. Prior to being stricken, Code Sec. 4982(e)(5)-(6) read as follows:

(5) TREATMENT OF FOREIGN CURRENCY GAINS AND LOSSES AFTER OCTOBER 31 OF CALENDAR YEAR.—Any foreign currency gain or loss which is attributable to a section 988 transaction and which is properly taken into account for the portion of the calendar year after October 31 shall not be taken into account in determining the amount of the ordinary income of the regulated investment company for such calendar year but shall be taken into account in determining the ordinary income of the investment company for the following calendar year. In the case of any company making an election under paragraph (4), the preceding sentence shall be applied by substituting the last day of the company's taxable year for October 31.

(6) TREATMENT OF GAIN RECOGNIZED UNDER SECTION 1296.—For purposes of determining a regulated investment company's ordinary income—

(A) notwithstanding paragraph (1)(C), section 1296 shall be applied as if such company's taxable year ended on October 31, and

(B) any ordinary gain or loss from an actual disposition of stock in a passive foreign investment company during the portion of the calendar year after October 31 shall be taken into account in determining such regulated investment company's ordinary income for the following calendar year.

In the case of a company making an election under paragraph (4), the preceding sentence shall be applied by substituting the last day of the company's taxable year for October 31.

- **1997, Taxpayer Relief Act of 1997 (P.L. 105-34)**

P.L. 105-34, §1122(c)(1):

Amended Code Sec. 4982(e) by adding at the end thereof a new paragraph (6). **Effective** for tax years of United States persons beginning after 12-31-97, and tax years of foreign corporations ending with or within such tax years of United States persons.

- **1988, Technical and Miscellaneous Revenue Act of 1988 (P.L. 100-647)**

P.L. 100-647, §1006(l)(2):

Amended Code Sec. 4982(e)(2). **Effective** as if included in the provision of P.L. 99-514 to which it relates. Prior to amendment, Code Sec. 4982(e)(2) read as follows:

(2) CAPITAL GAIN NET INCOME.—The term "capital gain net income" has the meaning given to such term by section 1222(9) (determined by treating the 1-year period ending on October 31 of any calendar year as the company's taxable year).

P.L. 100-647, §1006(l)(5):

Amended Code Sec. 4982(e) by adding at the end thereof new paragraph (5). **Effective** as if included in the provision of P.L. 99-514 to which it relates.

- **1986, Tax Reform Act of 1986 (P.L. 99-514)**

P.L. 99-514, §651(a):

Amended Chapter 44 by adding at the end thereof new Code Sec. 4982. **Effective** for calendar years beginning after 12-31-86.

[Sec. 4982(f)]

(f) EXCEPTION FOR CERTAIN REGULATED INVESTMENT COMPANIES.—This section shall not apply to any regulated investment company for any calendar year if at all times during such calendar year each shareholder in such company was—

(1) a trust described in section 401(a) and exempt from tax under section 501(a),

(2) a segregated asset account of a life insurance company held in connection with variable contracts (as defined in section 817(d)),

(3) any other tax-exempt entity whose ownership of beneficial interests in the company would not preclude the application of section 817(h)(4), or

(4) another regulated investment company described in this subsection.

For purposes of the preceding sentence, any shares attributable to an investment in the regulated investment company (not exceeding $250,000) made in connection with the organization of such company shall not be taken into account.

Amendments

- **2014, Tax Technical Corrections Act of 2014 (P.L. 113-295)**

P.L. 113-295, §220(s), Division A:

Amended Code Sec. 4982(f)(2) by adding a comma at the end. **Effective** 12-19-2014.

- **2010, Regulated Investment Company Modernization Act of 2010 (P.L. 111-325)**

P.L. 111-325, §401(a)(1)-(4):

Amended Code Sec. 4982(f) by striking "either" in the matter preceding paragraph (1), by striking "or" at the end of paragraph (1), by striking the period [sic] at the end of paragraph (2), and by inserting after paragraph (2) the new paragraphs (3) and (4). **Effective** for calendar years beginning after 12-22-2010.

- **1988, Technical and Miscellaneous Revenue Act of 1988 (P.L. 100-647)**

P.L. 100-647, §1006(l)(6):

Amended Code Sec. 4982 by adding at the end thereof new subsection (f). **Effective** as if included in the provision of P.L. 99-514 to which it relates.

CHAPTER 45—PROVISIONS RELATING TO EXPATRIATED ENTITIES

Sec. 4985. Stock compensation of insiders in expatriated corporations.

[Sec. 4985]

SEC. 4985. STOCK COMPENSATION OF INSIDERS IN EXPATRIATED CORPORATIONS.

[Sec. 4985(a)]

(a) IMPOSITION OF TAX.—In the case of an individual who is a disqualified individual with respect to any expatriated corporation, there is hereby imposed on such person a tax equal to—

(1) the rate of tax specified in section 1(h)(1)(D), multiplied by

EXCISE TAXES—EXPATRIATED ENTITIES

(2) the value (determined under subsection (b)) of the specified stock compensation held (directly or indirectly) by or for the benefit of such individual or a member of such individual's family (as defined in section 267) at any time during the 12-month period beginning on the date which is 6 months before the expatriation date.

Amendments

• **2017, Tax Cuts and Jobs Act (P.L. 115-97)**

P.L. 115-97, §13604(a):

Amended Code Sec. 4985(a)(1) by striking "section 1(h)(1)(C)" and inserting "section 1(h)(1)(D)". **Effective** for corporations first becoming expatriated corporations (as defined in Code Sec. 4985) after 12-22-2017.

[Sec. 4985(b)]

(b) VALUE.—For purposes of subsection (a)—

(1) IN GENERAL.—The value of specified stock compensation shall be—

(A) in the case of a stock option (or other similar right) or a stock appreciation right, the fair value of such option or right, and

(B) in any other case, the fair market value of such compensation.

(2) DATE FOR DETERMINING VALUE.—The determination of value shall be made—

(A) in the case of specified stock compensation held on the expatriation date, on such date,

(B) in the case of such compensation which is canceled during the 6 months before the expatriation date, on the day before such cancellation, and

(C) in the case of such compensation which is granted after the expatriation date, on the date such compensation is granted.

[Sec. 4985(c)]

(c) TAX TO APPLY ONLY IF SHAREHOLDER GAIN RECOGNIZED.—Subsection (a) shall apply to any disqualified individual with respect to an expatriated corporation only if gain (if any) on any stock in such corporation is recognized in whole or part by any shareholder by reason of the acquisition referred to in section 7874(a)(2)(B)(i) with respect to such corporation.

[Sec. 4985(d)]

(d) EXCEPTION WHERE GAIN RECOGNIZED ON COMPENSATION.—Subsection (a) shall not apply to—

(1) any stock option which is exercised on the expatriation date or during the 6-month period before such date and to the stock acquired in such exercise, if income is recognized under section 83 on or before the expatriation date with respect to the stock acquired pursuant to such exercise, and

(2) any other specified stock compensation which is exercised, sold, exchanged, distributed, cashed-out, or otherwise paid during such period in a transaction in which income, gain, or loss is recognized in full.

[Sec. 4985(e)]

(e) DEFINITIONS.—For purposes of this section—

(1) DISQUALIFIED INDIVIDUAL.—The term "disqualified individual" means, with respect to a corporation, any individual who, at any time during the 12-month period beginning on the date which is 6 months before the expatriation date—

(A) is subject to the requirements of section 16(a) of the Securities Exchange Act of 1934 with respect to such corporation or any member of the expanded affiliated group which includes such corporation, or

(B) would be subject to such requirements if such corporation or member were an issuer of equity securities referred to in such section.

(2) EXPATRIATED CORPORATION; EXPATRIATION DATE.—

(A) EXPATRIATED CORPORATION.—The term "expatriated corporation" means any corporation which is an expatriated entity (as defined in section 7874(a)(2)). Such term includes any predecessor or successor of such a corporation.

(B) EXPATRIATION DATE.—The term "expatriation date" means, with respect to a corporation, the date on which the corporation first becomes an expatriated corporation.

(3) SPECIFIED STOCK COMPENSATION.—

(A) IN GENERAL.—The term "specified stock compensation" means payment (or right to payment) granted by the expatriated corporation (or by any member of the expanded affiliated group which includes such corporation) to any person in connection with the performance of services by a disqualified individual for such corporation or member if the value of such payment or right is based on (or determined by reference to) the value (or change in value) of stock in such corporation (or any such member).

(B) EXCEPTIONS.—Such term shall not include—

(i) any option to which part II of subchapter D of chapter 1 applies, or

(ii) any payment or right to payment from a plan referred to in section 280G(b)(6).

(4) EXPANDED AFFILIATED GROUP.—The term "expanded affiliated group" means an affiliated group (as defined in section 1504(a) without regard to section 1504(b)(3)); except that section 1504(a) shall be applied by substituting "more than 50 percent" for "at least 80 percent" each place it appears.

[Sec. 4985(f)]

(f) SPECIAL RULES.—For purposes of this section—

(1) CANCELLATION OF RESTRICTION.—The cancellation of a restriction which by its terms will never lapse shall be treated as a grant.

(2) PAYMENT OR REIMBURSEMENT OF TAX BY CORPORATION TREATED AS SPECIFIED STOCK COMPENSATION.—Any payment of the tax imposed by this section directly or indirectly by the expatriated corporation or by any member of the expanded affiliated group which includes such corporation—

(A) shall be treated as specified stock compensation, and

(B) shall not be allowed as a deduction under any provision of chapter 1.

(3) CERTAIN RESTRICTIONS IGNORED.—Whether there is specified stock compensation, and the value thereof, shall be determined without regard to any restriction other than a restriction which by its terms will never lapse.

(4) PROPERTY TRANSFERS.—Any transfer of property shall be treated as a payment and any right to a transfer of property shall be treated as a right to a payment.

(5) OTHER ADMINISTRATIVE PROVISIONS.—For purposes of subtitle F, any tax imposed by this section shall be treated as a tax imposed by subtitle A.

Sec. 4985(a)(2)

EXCISE TAXES—WINDFALL PROFIT TAX

[Sec. 4985(g)]

(g) REGULATIONS.—The Secretary shall prescribe such regulations as may be necessary or appropriate to carry out the purposes of this section.

Amendments

- **2004, American Jobs Creation Act of 2004 (P.L. 108-357)**

P.L. 108-357, §802(a):

Amended subtitle D by inserting after chapter 44 end [sic] a new chapter 45 (Code Sec. 4985). **Effective** 3-4-2003; except that periods before such date shall not be taken into account in applying the periods in Code Sec. 4985(a) and (e)(1), as added by Act Sec. 802.

CHAPTER 45—WINDFALL PROFIT TAX ON DOMESTIC CRUDE OIL—[Repealed]

[Sec. 4986—Repealed]

Amendments

- **1988, Omnibus Trade and Competitiveness Act of 1988 (P.L. 100-418)**

P.L. 100-418, §1941(a):

Repealed Chapter 45 (Code Secs. 4986-4998). **Effective** for crude oil removed from the premises on or after 8-23-88. Prior to repeal, Code Sec. 4986 read as follows:

SEC. 4986. IMPOSITION OF TAX.

(a) IMPOSITION OF TAX.—An excise tax is hereby imposed on the windfall profit from taxable crude oil removed from the premises during each taxable period.

(b) TAX PAID BY PRODUCER.—The tax imposed by this section shall be paid by the producer of the crude oil.

- **1984, Deficit Reduction Act of 1984 (P.L. 98-369)**

P.L. 98-369, §722(a)(7), provides:

(7)(A) If—

(i) there is an overpayment of tax imposed by section 4986 of the Internal Revenue Code of 1954 for any period before January 1, 1983, by reason of section 201(h)(1)(E) of the Technical Corrections Act of 1982.

(ii) refund of such overpayment is payable to the partners of a partnership, and

(iii) such partners are obligated to pay over any such refund to 1 or more organizations referred to in such section 201(h)(1)(E),

such partnership shall be treated as authorized to act for each person who was a partner at any time in such partnership in claiming and paying over such refund.

(B) Notwithstanding section 6511 of the Internal Revenue Code of 1954, the time for filing a claim for credit or refund of the overpayment referred to in subparagraph (A)(i) shall not expire before the date 1 year after the date of the enactment of this Act.

- **1980, Crude Oil Windfall Profit Tax Act of 1980 (P.L. 96-223)**

P.L. 96-223, §101(a)(1):

Added Code Sec. 4986. **Effective** as set forth in P.L. 96-223, §101(i).

P.L. 96-223, §101(i):

(i) EFFECTIVE DATE.—

(1) IN GENERAL.—The amendments made by this section shall apply to periods after February 29, 1980.

(2) TRANSITIONAL RULES.—For the period ending June 30, 1980, the Secretary of the Treasury or his delegate shall prescribe rules relating to the administration of chapter 45 of the Internal Revenue Code of 1954. To the extent provided in such rules, such rules shall supplement or supplant for such period the administrative provisions contained in chapter 45 of such Code (or in so much of subtitle F of such Code as relates to such chapter 45).

[Sec. 4987—Repealed]

Amendments

- **1988, Omnibus Trade and Competitiveness Act of 1988 (P.L. 100-418)**

P.L. 100-418, §1941(a):

Repealed Chapter 45 (Code Secs. 4986-4998). **Effective** for crude oil removed from the premises on or after 8-23-88. Prior to repeal, Code Sec. 4987 read as follows:

SEC. 4987. AMOUNT OF TAX.

[Sec. 4987(a)]

(a) IN GENERAL.—The amount of tax imposed by section 4986 with respect to any barrel of taxable crude oil shall be the applicable percentage of the windfall profit on such barrel.

[Sec. 4987(b)]

(b) APPLICABLE PERCENTAGE.—For purposes of subsection (a)—

(1) GENERAL RULE FOR TIERS 1 AND 2.—The applicable percentage for tier 1 oil and tier 2 oil which is not independent producer oil is—

Tier 1 70
Tier 2 60

(2) INDEPENDENT PRODUCER OIL.—The applicable percentage for independent producer oil which is tier 1 oil or tier 2 oil is—

Tier 1 50
Tier 2 30

(3) TIER 3 OIL.—

(A) IN GENERAL.—The applicable percentage for tier 3 oil which is is not newly discovered oil is 30 percent.

(B) NEWLY DISCOVERED OIL.—The applicable percentage for newly discovered oil shall be determined in accordance with the following table:

For taxable periods beginning in:	The applicable percentage is:
1984, 1985, 1986, or 1987	22 1/2
1988	20
1989 and thereafter	15

[Sec. 4988—Repealed]

Amendments

- **1988, Omnibus Trade and Competitiveness Act of 1988 (P.L. 100-418)**

P.L. 100-418, §1941(a):

Repealed Chapter 45 (Code Secs. 4986-4998). **Effective** for crude oil removed from the premises on or after 8-23-88. Prior to repeal, Code Sec. 4988 read as follows:

SEC. 4988. WINDFALL PROFIT; REMOVAL PRICE.

(a) GENERAL RULE.—For purposes of this chapter, the term "windfall profit" means the excess of the removal price of the barrel of crude oil over the sum of—

Amendments

- **1984, Deficit Reduction Act of 1984 (P.L. 98-369)**

P.L. 98-369, §25(a):

Amended Code Sec. 4987(b)(3)(B) by striking out the table contained therein and inserting in lieu thereof a new table. **Effective** for taxable periods beginning after 12-31-83. Prior to amendment, the table at Code Sec. 4987(b)(3)(B) read as follows:

For taxable periods beginning in:	The applicable percentage is:
1982	27 1/2
1983	25

For taxable periods beginning in:	The applicable percentage is:
1984	22 1/2
1985	20
1986 and thereafter	15

- **1981, Economic Recovery Tax Act of 1981 (P.L. 97-34)**

P.L. 97-34, §602(a):

Amended Code Sec. 4987(b)(3). **Effective** for taxable periods beginning after 12-31-81. Prior to amendment, Code Sec. 4987(b)(3) read as follows:

TIER 3 OIL.—The applicable percentage for tier 3 oil is 30 percent.

[Sec. 4987(c)]

(c) FRACTIONAL PART OF BARREL.—In the case of a fraction of a barrel, the tax imposed by section 4986 shall be the same fraction of the amount of such tax imposed on the whole barrel.

Amendments

- **1980, Crude Oil Windfall Profit Tax Act of 1980 (P.L. 96-223)**

P.L. 96-223, §101(a)(1):

Added Code Sec. 4987. For the **effective** date and transitional rules, see P.L. 96-223, §101(i) following Code Sec. 4986.

(1) the adjusted base price of such barrel, and

(2) the amount of the severance tax adjustment with respect to such barrel provided by section 4996(c).

(b) NET INCOME LIMITATION ON WINDFALL PROFIT.—

(1) IN GENERAL.—The windfall profit on any barrel of crude oil shall not exceed 90 percent of the net income attributable to such barrel.

(2) DETERMINATION OF NET INCOME.—For purposes of paragraph (1), the net income attributable to a barrel shall be determined by dividing—

EXCISE TAXES—WINDFALL PROFIT TAX

(A) the taxable income from the property for the taxable year attributable to taxable crude oil, by

(B) the number of barrels of taxable crude oil from such property taken into account for such taxable year.

(3) TAXABLE INCOME FROM THE PROPERTY.—For purposes of this subsection—

(A) IN GENERAL.—Except as otherwise provided in this paragraph, the taxable income from the property shall be determined under section 613(a).

(B) CERTAIN DEDUCTIONS NOT ALLOWED.—No deduction shall be allowed for—

(i) depletion,

(ii) the tax imposed by section 4986,

(iii) section 263(c) costs, or

(iv) qualified tertiary injectant expenses to which an election under subparagraph (E) applies.

(C) TAXABLE INCOME REDUCED BY COST DEPLETION.—Taxable income shall be reduced by the cost depletion which would have been allowable for the taxable year with respect to the property if—

(i) all—

(I) section 263(c) costs, and

(II) qualified tertiary injectant expenses to which an election under subparagraph (E) applies,

incurred by the taxpayer had been capitalized and taken into account in computing cost depletion, and

(ii) cost depletion had been used by the taxpayer with respect to such property for all taxable years.

(D) SECTION 263(c) COSTS.—For purposes of this paragraph, the term "section 263(c) costs" means intangible drilling and development costs incurred by the taxpayer which (by reason of an election under section 263(c)) may be deducted as expenses for purposes of this title (other than this paragraph). Such term shall not include costs incurred in drilling a nonproductive well.

(E) ELECTION TO CAPITALIZE QUALIFIED TERTIARY INJECTANT EXPENSES.—

(i) IN GENERAL.—Any taxpayer may elect, with respect to any property, to capitalize qualified tertiary injectant expenses for purposes of this paragraph. Any such election shall apply to all qualified tertiary injectant expenses allocable to the property for which the election is made, and may be revoked only with the consent of the Secretary. Any such election shall be made at such time and in such manner as the Secretary shall by regulations prescribe.

(ii) QUALIFIED TERTIARY INJECTANT EXPENSES.—The term "qualified tertiary injectant expenses" means any expense allowable as a deduction under section 193.

(4) SPECIAL RULE FOR APPLYING PARAGRAPH (3)(c) TO CERTAIN TRANSFERS OF PROVEN OIL OR GAS PROPERTIES.—

(A) IN GENERAL.—In the case of any proven oil or gas property transfer which (but for this subparagraph), would result in an increase in the amount determined under paragraph (3)(C) with respect to the transferee, paragraph (3)(C) shall be applied with respect to the transferee by taking into account only those amounts which would have been allowable with respect to the transferor under paragraph (3)(C) and those costs incurred during periods after such transfer.

(B) PROVEN OIL OR GAS PROPERTY TRANSFER.—For purposes of subparagraph (A), the term "proven oil or gas property transfer" means any transfer (including the subleasing of a lease or the creation of a production payment which gives the transferee an economic interest in the property) after 1978 of an interest (including an interest in a partnership or trust) in any proven oil or gas property (within the meaning of section 613A(c)(9)(A)).

(5) SPECIAL RULE WHERE THERE IS PRODUCTION PAYMENT.—For purposes of paragraph (2), if any portion of the taxable crude oil removed from the property is applied in discharge of a production payment, the gross income from such portion shall be included in the gross income from the property of both the person holding such production payment and the person holding the interest from which such production payment was created.

(6) COST RECOVERY OIL COVERED BY NET PROFITS AGREEMENT.—For purposes of paragraph (2), if any person is treated under section 4996(a)(1)(B) as the producer of any portion of the cost recovery oil covered by a net profits agreement (within the meaning of section 4996(h))—

(A) such person (and only such person) shall include in his gross income from the property the gross income from such portion, and

(B) the qualified costs allocable to such portion shall be treated as paid or incurred by such person (and only by such person).

(c) REMOVAL PRICE.—For purpose of this chapter—

(1) IN GENERAL.—Except as otherwise provided in this subsection, the term "removal price" means the amount for which the barrel is sold.

(2) SALES BETWEEN RELATED PERSONS.—In the case of a sale between related persons (within the meaning of section 144(a)(3)), the removal price shall not be less than the constructive sales price for purposes of determining gross income from the property under section 613.

(3) OIL REMOVED FROM PREMISES BEFORE SALE.—If crude oil is removed from the premises before it is sold, the removal price shall be the constructive sales price for purposes of determining gross income from the property under section 613.

(4) REFINING BEGUN ON PREMISES.—If the manufacture or conversion of crude oil into refined products begins before such oil is removed from the premises—

(A) such oil shall be treated as removed on the day such manufacture or conversion begins, and

(B) the removal price shall be the constructive sales price for purposes of determining gross income from the property under section 613.

(5) MEANING OF TERMS.—The terms "premises" and "refined product" have the same meaning as when used for purposes of determining gross income from the property under section 613.

- **1986, Tax Reform Act of 1986 (P.L. 99-514)**

P.L. 99-514, § 1301(j)(4):

Amended Code Sec. 4988(c)(2) by striking out "section 103(b)(6)(C)" and inserting in lieu thereof "section 144(a)(3)". **Effective** for bonds issued after 8-15-86.

- **1983, Technical Corrections Act of 1982 (P.L. 97-448)**

P.L. 97-448, § 201(a)(1):

Amended Code Sec. 4988(b)(3) by striking out "purposes of paragraph (2)" and inserting in lieu thereof "purposes of this subsection". **Effective** as if included in the provision of P.L. 96-223 to which it relates.

P.L. 97-448, § 201(a)(2):

Amended Code Sec. 4988(b)(3)(C)(ii) by striking out "all taxable periods" and inserting in lieu thereof "all taxable years". **Effective** as if included in the provision of P.L. 96-223 to which it relates.

P.L. 97-448, § 201(h)(1)(D):

Amended Code Sec. 4988(b) by adding at the end thereof new paragraph (6). **Effective** as if included in the provision of P.L. 96-223 to which it relates. See, however, the amendment notes following Code Sec. 4996 for a special rule.

- **1980, Crude Oil Windfall Profit Tax Act of 1980 (P.L. 96-223)**

P.L. 96-223, § 101(a)(1):

Added Code Sec. 4988. For the **effective** date and transitional rules, see P.L. 96-223, § 101(i) following Code Sec. 4986.

[Sec. 4989—Repealed]

Amendments

- **1988, Omnibus Trade and Competitiveness Act of 1988 (P.L. 100-418)**

P.L. 100-418, § 1941(a):

Repealed Chapter 45 (Code Secs. 4986-4998). **Effective** for crude oil removed from the premises on or after 8-23-88. Prior to repeal, Code Sec. 4989 read as follows:

SEC. 4989. ADJUSTED BASE PRICE.

(a) ADJUSTED BASE PRICE DEFINED.—For purposes of this chapter, the term "adjusted base price" means the base price for the barrel of crude oil plus an amount equal to—

(1) such base price, multiplied by

(2) the inflation adjustment for the calendar quarter in which the crude oil is removed from the premises.

The amount determined under the preceding sentence shall be rounded to the nearest cent.

(b) INFLATION ADJUSTMENT.—

(1) IN GENERAL.—For purposes of subsection (a), the inflation adjustment for any calendar quarter is the percentage by which—

(A) the implicit price deflator for the gross national product for the second preceding calendar quarter, exceeds

(B) such deflator for the calendar quarter ending June 30, 1979.

(2) ADDITIONAL ADJUSTMENT FOR TIER 3 OIL.—The adjusted base price for tier 3 oil shall be determined by substituting for the implicit price deflator referred to in paragraph (1)(A) an amount equal to such deflator multiplied by 1.005 to the nth power where "n" equals the number of calendar quarters beginning after September 1979 and before the calendar quarter in which the oil is removed from the premises.

(3) FIRST REVISION OF PRICE DEFLATOR USED.—For purposes of paragraphs (1)(A) and (2), the first revision of the price deflator shall be used. For purposes of applying paragraph (1)(B), the revision of the price deflator which is most consistent with the revision used for purposes of paragraph (1)(A) shall be used.

(c) BASE PRICE FOR TIER 1 OIL.—For purposes of this chapter, the base price for tier 1 oil is—

(1) the ceiling price which would have applied to such oil under the March 1979 energy regulations if it had been produced and sold in May 1979 as upper tier oil, reduced by

(2) 21 cents.

(d) BASE PRICES FOR TIER 2 OIL AND TIER 3 OIL.—For purposes of this chapter—

(1) GENERAL RULE.—Except as provided in paragraph (2), the base prices for tier 2 oil and tier 3 oil shall be prices determined pursuant to the method prescribed by the Secretary by regulations. Any method so prescribed shall be designed so as to yield, with respect to oil of any grade, quality, and field, a base price which approximates the price at which such oil would have sold in December 1979 if—

(A) all domestic crude oil were uncontrolled, and

(B) the average removal price for all domestic crude oil (other than Sadlerochit oil) were—

(i) $15.20 a barrel for purposes of determining base prices for tier 2 oil, and

(ii) $16.55 a barrel for purposes of determining base prices for tier 3 oil.

(2) INTERIM RULE.—For months beginning before October 1980 (or such earlier date as may be provided in regulations taking effect before such earlier date), the base prices for tier 2 oil and tier 3 oil, respectively, shall be the product of—

(A)(i) the highest posted price for December 31, 1979, for uncontrolled crude oil of the same grade, quality, and field, or

(ii) if there is no posted price described in clause (i), the highest posted price for such date for uncontrolled crude oil at the nearest domestic field for which prices for oil of the same grade and quality were posted for such date, multiplied by

(B) a fraction the denominator of which is $35, and the numerator of which is—

(i) $15.20 for purposes of determining base prices for tier 2 oil, and

(ii) $16.55 for purposes of determining base prices for tier 3 oil.

For purposes of the preceding sentence, no price which was posted after January 14, 1980, shall be taken into account.

(3) MINIMUM INTERIM BASE PRICE.—The base price determined under paragraph (2) for tier 2 oil or tier 3 oil shall not be less than the sum of—

(A) the ceiling price which would have applied to such oil under the March 1979 energy regulations if it had been produced and sold in May 1979 as upper tier oil, plus

(B)(i) $1 in the case of tier 2 oil, or

(ii) $2 in the case of tier 3 oil.

● **1983, Technical Corrections Act of 1982 (P.L. 97-448)**

P.L. 97-448, §201(b):

Amended Code Sec. 4989(b)(3) by striking out "paragraphs (1) and (2)" and inserting in lieu thereof "paragraphs (1)(A) and (2)", and by adding the sentence at the end thereof. **Effective** as if included in the provision of P.L. 96-223 to which it relates.

● **1980, Crude Oil Windfall Profit Tax Act of 1980 (P.L. 96-223)**

P.L. 96-223, §101(a)(1):

Added Code Sec. 4989. For the **effective** date and transitional rules, see P.L. 96-223, §101(i) following Code Sec. 4986.

[Sec. 4990—Repealed]

Amendments

● **1988, Omnibus Trade and Competitiveness Act of 1988 (P.L. 100-418)**

P.L. 100-418, §1941(a):

Repealed Chapter 45 (Code Secs. 4986-4998). **Effective** for crude oil removed from the premises on or after 8-23-88. Prior to repeal, Code Sec. 4990 read as follows:

SEC. 4990. PHASEOUT OF TAX.

(a) PHASEOUT.—Notwithstanding any other provision of this chapter, the tax imposed by this chapter with respect to any crude oil removed from the premises during any month during the phaseout period shall not exceed—

(1) the amount of tax which would have been imposed by this chapter with respect to such crude oil but for this subsection, multiplied by

(2) the phaseout percentage for such month.

(b) TERMINATION OF TAX.—Notwithstanding any other provision of this chapter, no tax shall be imposed by this chapter with respect to any crude oil removed from the premises after the phaseout period.

(c) DEFINITIONS.—For purposes of this section—

(1) PHASEOUT PERIOD.—The term "phaseout period" means the 33-month period beginning with the month following the target month.

(2) PHASEOUT PERCENTAGE.—The phaseout percentage for any month is 100 percent reduced by 3 percentage points for each month after the target month and before the month following the month for which the phaseout percentage is being determined.

(3) TARGET MONTH.—The term "target month" means the later of—

(A) December 1987, or

(B) the first month for which the Secretary publishes an estimate under subsection (d)(2).

In no event shall the target month be later than December 1990.

(d) DETERMINATION OF AGGREGATE NET WINDFALL REVENUE.—

(1) ESTIMATE BY THE SECRETARY.—For each month after 1986, the Secretary shall make an estimate of the aggregate net windfall revenue as of the close of such month. Any such estimate shall be made during the preceding month and shall be made on the basis of the best available data as of the date of making such estimate.

(2) PUBLICATION.—If the Secretary estimates under paragraph (1) that the aggregate net windfall revenue as of the close of any month will exceed $227,300,000,000, the Secretary shall (not later than the last day of the preceding month) publish notice in the Federal Register that he has made such an estimate for such month.

(3) AGGREGATE NET WINDFALL REVENUE DEFINED.—For purposes of this subsection, the term "aggregate net windfall revenue" means the amount which the Secretary estimates to be the excess of—

(A) the gross revenues from the tax imposed by section 4986 during the period beginning on March 1, 1980, and ending on the last day of the month for which the estimate is being made, over

(B) the sum of—

(i) the refunds of and other adjustments to such tax for such period, plus

(ii) the decrease in the income taxes imposed by chapter 1 resulting from the tax imposed by section 4986.

For purposes of subparagraph (A), there shall not be taken into account any revenue attributable to an economic interest in crude oil held by the United States.

● **1980, Crude Oil Windfall Profit Tax Act of 1980 (P.L. 96-223)**

P.L. 96-223, §101(a)(1):

Added Code Sec. 4990. For the **effective** date and transitional rules, see P.L. 96-223, §101(i) following Code Sec. 4986.

[Sec. 4991—Repealed]

Amendments

● **1988, Omnibus Trade and Competitiveness Act of 1988 (P.L. 100-418)**

P.L. 100-418, §1941(a):

Repealed Chapter 45 (Code Secs. 4986-4998). **Effective** for crude oil removed from the premises on or after 8-23-88. Prior to repeal, Code Sec. 4991 read as follows:

SEC. 4991. TAXABLE CRUDE OIL; CATEGORIES OF OIL.

[Sec. 4991(a)]

(a) TAXABLE CRUDE OIL.—For purposes of this chapter, the term "taxable crude oil" means all domestic crude oil other than exempt oil.

[Sec. 4991(b)]

(b) EXEMPT OIL.—For purposes of this chapter, the term "exempt oil" means—

(1) any crude oil from a qualified governmental interest or a qualified charitable interest,

(2) any exempt Indian oil,

(3) any exempt Alaskan oil,

(4) any exempt front-end oil,

(5) exempt royalty oil, and

(6) exempt stripper well oil.

Amendments

● **1981, Economic Recovery Tax Act of 1981 (P.L. 97-34)**

P.L. 97-34, §601(b)(1):

Amended Code Sec. 4991(b) by striking out "and" at the end of paragraph (3), by striking out the period at the end of paragraph (4), and inserting in lieu thereof, "and", and by adding at the end thereof paragraph (5). **Effective** for oil removed after 12-31-81.

P.L. 97-34, §603(a):

Amended Code Sec. 4991(b) (as amended by act section 601(b)) by striking out "and" at the end of paragraph (4), by striking out the period at the end of paragraph (5), and inserting in lieu thereof, "and", and by adding at the end thereof paragraph (6). **Effective** for oil removed from premises after 12-31-82.

[Sec. 4991(c)]

(c) TIER 1 OIL.—For purposes of this chapter, the term "tier 1 oil" means any taxable crude oil other than—

(1) tier 2 oil, and

(2) tier 3 oil.

[Sec. 4991(d)]

(d) TIER 2 OIL.—For purposes of this chapter—

(1) IN GENERAL.—Except as provided in paragraph (2), the term "tier 2 oil" means—

(A) any oil which is from a stripper well property within the meaning of the June 1979 energy regulations, and

(B) any oil from an economic interest in a Naval Petroleum Reserve held by the United States.

(2) EXCLUSION OF CERTAIN OIL.—The term "tier 2 oil" does not include tier 3 oil.

Amendments

● **1983, Technical Corrections Act of 1982 (P.L. 97-448)**

P.L. 97-448, §201(c):

Amended Code Sec. 4991(d)(1)(B) by striking out "National Petroleum Reserve" and inserting in lieu thereof "Naval Petroleum Reserve". **Effective** as if included in the provision of P.L. 96-223 to which it relates.

[Sec. 4991(e)]

(e) TIER 3 OIL.—For purposes of this chapter—

(1) IN GENERAL.—The term "tier 3 oil" means—

(A) newly discovered oil,

(B) heavy oil, and

(C) incremental tertiary oil.

(2) NEWLY DISCOVERED OIL.—The term "newly discovered oil" has the meaning given to such term by the June 1979 energy regulations. Such term includes any production from a property which did not produce oil in commercial quantities during calendar year 1978. For purposes of the preceding sentence, a property shall not be treated as producing oil in commercial quantities during calendar year 1978 if, during calendar year 1978 (A) the aggregate amount of oil produced from such property did not exceed 2,200 barrels (whether or not such oil was sold), and (B) no well on such property was in production for a total of more than 72 hours.

(3) HEAVY OIL.—The term "heavy oil" means all crude oil which is produced from a property if crude oil produced and sold from such property during—

(A) the last month before July 1979 in which crude oil was produced and sold from such property, or

(B) the taxable period,

had a weighted average gravity of 16 degrees API or less (corrected to 60 degrees Fahrenheit).

(4) INCREMENTAL TERTIARY OIL.—

For definition of incremental tertiary oil, see section 4993.

Amendments

● **1986, Tax Reform Act of 1986 (P.L. 99-514)**

P.L. 99-514, §1879(h)(1):

Amended Code Sec. 4991(e)(2) by adding at the end thereof two new sentences. **Effective** for oil removed after 2-29-80.

● **1980, Crude Oil Windfall Profit Tax Act of 1980 (P.L. 96-223)**

P.L. 96-223, §101(a)(1):

Added Code Sec. 4991. For the **effective** date and transitional rules, see P.L. 96-223, §101(i) following Code Sec. 4986.

EXCISE TAXES—WINDFALL PROFIT TAX

[Sec. 4992—Repealed]

Amendments

• **1988, Omnibus Trade and Competitiveness Act of 1988 (P.L. 100-418)**

P.L. 100-418, §1941(a):

Repealed Chapter 45 (Code Secs. 4986-4998). **Effective** for crude oil removed from the premises on or after 8-23-88. Prior to repeal, Code Sec. 4992 read as follows:

SEC. 4992. INDEPENDENT PRODUCER OIL.

[Sec. 4992(a)]

(a) GENERAL RULE.—For purposes of this chapter, the term "independent producer oil" means that portion of an independent producer's qualified production for the quarter which does not exceed such person's independent producer amount for such quarter.

[Sec. 4992(b)]

(b) INDEPENDENT PRODUCER DEFINED.—For purposes of this section—

(1) IN GENERAL.—The term "independent producer" means, with respect to any quarter in any calendar year, any person other than a person to whom subsection (c) of section 613A does not apply for such calendar year by reason of paragraph (2) (relating to certain retailers) or paragraph (4) (relating to certain refiners) of section 613A(d).

(2) RULES FOR APPLYING PARAGRAPHS (2) AND (4) OF SECTION 613A(d).—For purposes of paragraph (1), paragraphs (2) and (4) of section 613A(d) shall be applied by substituting "calendar year" for "taxable year" each place it appears in such paragraphs.

Amendments

• **1983, Technical Corrections Act of 1982 (P.L. 97-448)**

P.L. 97-448, §201(d)(1):

Amended Code Sec. 4992(b). **Effective** 1-1-83. Prior to amendment, Code Sec. 4992(b) read as follows:

(b) INDEPENDENT PRODUCER DEFINED.—For purposes of this section—

(1) IN GENERAL.—The term 'independent producer' means, with respect to any quarter, any person other than a person to whom subsection (c) of section 613A does not apply by reason of paragraph (2) (relating to certain retailers) or paragraph (4) (relating to certain refiners) of section 613A(d).

(2) RULES FOR APPLYING PARAGRAPHS (2) AND (4) OF SECTION 613A(d).—For purposes of paragraph (1), paragraphs (2) and (4) of section 613A(d) shall be applied—

(A) by substituting `quarter' for `taxable year' each place it appears in such paragraphs, and

(B) by substituting `$1,250,000' for `$5,000,000' in paragraph (2) of section 613A(d).

[Sec. 4992(c)]

(c) INDEPENDENT PRODUCER AMOUNT.—For purposes of this section—

(1) IN GENERAL.—A person's independent producer amount for any quarter is the product of—

(A) 1,000 barrels, multiplied by

(B) the number of days in such quarter (31 in the case of the first quarter of 1980).

(2) PRODUCTION EXCEEDS AMOUNT.—If a person's qualified production for any quarter exceeds such person's independent producer amount for such quarter, the independent producer amount shall be allocated—

(A) between tiers 1 and 2 in proportion to such person's qualified production of oil for such quarter in each such tier, and

(B) within any tier, on the basis of the removal prices for such person's qualified production of oil in such tier removed during such quarter, beginning with the highest of such prices.

Amendments

• **1983, Technical Corrections Act of 1982 (P.L. 97-448)**

P.L. 97-448, §201(d)(2):

Amended Code Sec. 4992(c)(2) by striking out "such person's production for such quarter of domestic crude oil" and inserting in lieu thereof "such person's qualified production of oil for such quarter", by striking out "such person's domestic crude oil" and inserting in lieu thereof "such person's qualified production of oil", and by striking out the last sentence. **Effective** as if included in the provision of P.L. 96-223 to which it relates. Prior to amendment, the last sentence of Code Sec. 4992(c)(2) read as follows:

"For purposes of the preceding sentence, tier 1 oil and tier 2 oil shall be treated as not including exempt stripper well oil."

• **1981, Economic Recovery Tax Act of 1981 (P.L. 97-34)**

P.L. 97-34, §603(c):

Added the last sentence to Code Sec. 4992(c)(2). **Effective** for oil removed from premises after 12-31-82.

[Sec. 4992(d)]

(d) QUALIFIED PRODUCTION OF OIL DEFINED.—For purposes of this section—

(1) IN GENERAL.—An independent producer's qualified production of oil for any quarter is the number of barrels of taxable crude oil—

(A) of which such person is the producer,

(B) which is removed during such quarter,

(C) which is tier 1 oil or tier 2 oil, and

(D) which is attributable to the independent producer's working interest in a property.

(2) WORKING INTEREST DEFINED.—

(A) IN GENERAL.—The term "working interest" means an operating mineral interest (within the meaning of section 614(d))—

(i) which was in existence as such an interest on January 1, 1980, or

(ii) which is attributable to a qualified overriding royalty interest.

(B) QUALIFIED OVERRIDING ROYALTY INTEREST.—For purposes of subparagraph (A)(ii), the term "qualified overriding royalty interest" means an overriding royalty interest in existence as such an interest on January 1, 1980, but only if on February 20, 1980, there was in existence a binding contract under which such interest was to be converted into an operating mineral interest (within the meaning of section 614(d)).

(3) PRODUCTION FROM TRANSFERRED PROPERTY.—

(A) IN GENERAL.—Except as otherwise provided in this paragraph, in the case of a transfer on or after January 1, 1980, of an interest in any property, the qualified production of the transferee shall not include any production attributable to such interest.

(B) SMALL PRODUCER TRANSFER EXEMPTION.—

(i) IN GENERAL.—Subparagraph (A) shall not apply to any transfer of an interest in property if the transferee establishes (in such manner as may be prescribed by the Secretary by regulations) that at no time after December 31, 1979, has the interest been held by a person who was a disqualified transferor for any quarter ending after September 30, 1979, and ending before the date such person transferred the interest.

(ii) DISQUALIFIED TRANSFEROR.—The term "disqualified transferor" means, with respect to any quarter, any person who—

(I) had qualified production for such quarter which exceeded such person's independent producer amount for such quarter, or

(II) was not an independent producer for such quarter.

(iii) SPECIAL RULES.—For purposes of this paragraph—

(I) PROPERTY HELD BY PARTNERSHIPS.—Property held by a partnership at any time shall be treated as owned proportionately by the partners of such partnership at such time.

(II) PROPERTY HELD BY TRUST OR ESTATE.—Property held by any trust or estate shall be treated as owned both by such trust or estate and proportionately by its beneficiaries.

(III) CONSTRUCTIVE APPLICATION.—This chapter shall be treated as having been in effect for periods after September 30, 1979, for purposes of making any determination under subclause (I) or (II) of clause (ii).

(C) OTHER EXCEPTIONS.—Subparagraph (A) shall not apply in the case of—

(i) a transfer of property at death,

(ii) a change of beneficiaries of a trust which qualifies under clause (iii) of section 613A(c)(9)(B) (determined without regard to the exception at the end of such clause), and

(iii) any transfer so long as the transferor and transferee are required by subsection (e) to share the 1,000 barrel amount contained in subsection (c)(1)(A).

The preceding sentence shall apply in the case of any property only if the production from the property was qualified production for the transferor.

(D) TRANSFERS INCLUDE SUBLEASES, ETC.—For purposes of this paragraph—

(i) a sublease shall be treated as a transfer, and

(ii) an interest in a partnership or trust shall be treated as an interest in property held by the partnership or trust.

Amendments

• **1983, Technical Corrections Act of 1982 (P.L. 97-448)**

P.L. 97-448, §201(d)(3):

Amended Code Sec. 4992(d)(3)(B)(i) by striking out "has the property" and inserting in lieu thereof "has the interest". **Effective** as if included in the provision of P.L. 96-223 to which it relates.

[Sec. 4992(e)]

(e) ALLOCATION WITHIN RELATED GROUP—

(1) IN GENERAL.—In the case of persons who are members of the same related group at any time during any quarter, the 1,000 barrel amount contained in subsection (c)(1)(A) for days during such quarter shall be reduced for each such person by allocating such amount among all such persons in proportion to their respective qualified production for such quarter.

(2) RELATED GROUP.—For purposes of this subsection, persons shall be treated as members of a related group if they are described in any of the following clauses:

(A) a family,

(B) a controlled group of corporations,

(C) a group of entities under common control; or

(D) if 50 percent or more of the beneficial interest in 1 or more corporations, trusts, or estates is owned by the same family, all such entities and such family.

(3) DEFINITIONS AND SPECIAL RULES.—For purposes of this subsection—

(A) CONTROLLED GROUP OF CORPORATIONS.—The term "controlled group of corporations" has the meaning given such term by section 613A(c)(8)(D)(i).

(B) GROUP OF ENTITIES UNDER COMMON CONTROL.—The term "group of entities under common control" means any group of corporations, trusts, or estates which (as determined under regulations prescribed by the Secretary) are under common control. Such regulations shall be based on principles similar to the principles which apply under subparagraph (A).

(C) FAMILY.—The term "family" means an individual and the spouse and minor children of such individual.

(D) CONSTRUCTIVE OWNERSHIP.—For purposes of paragraph (2)(D), an interest owned by or for a corporation, partnership, trust, or estate shall be considered as owned directly by the entity and proportionately by its shareholders, partners, or beneficiaries, as the case may be.

(E) MEMBERS OF MORE THAN 1 RELATED GROUP.—If a person is a member of more than 1 related group during any quarter, the determination of such person's allocation under paragraph (1) shall be made by reference to the related group which results in the smallest allocation for such person.

EXCISE TAXES—WINDFALL PROFIT TAX

Amendments
• **1980, Crude Oil Windfall Profit Tax Act of 1980 (P.L. 96-223)**

P.L. 96-223, §101(a)(1):

Added Code Sec. 4992. For the **effective** date and transitional rules, see P.L. 96-223, §101(i), following Code Sec. 4986.

[Sec. 4992(f)]

(f) S CORPORATION TREATED AS PARTNERSHIP.—For purposes of subsections (d) and (e)—

(1) an S corporation shall be treated as a partnership, and

(2) the shareholders of the S corporation shall be treated as partners of such partnership.

Amendments
• **1982, Subchapter S Revision Act of 1982 (P.L. 97-354)**

P.L. 97-354, §3(b)(2):

Added Code Sec. 4992(f). **Effective** for tax years beginning after 12-31-82.

[Sec. 4993—Repealed]

Amendments
• **1988, Omnibus Trade and Competitiveness Act of 1988 (P.L. 100-418)**

P.L. 100-418, §1941(a):

Repealed Chapter 45 (Code Secs. 4986-4998). **Effective** for crude oil removed from the premises on or after 8-23-88. Prior to repeal, Code Sec. 4993 read as follows:

SEC. 4993. INCREMENTAL TERTIARY OIL.

[Sec. 4993(a)]

(a) IN GENERAL.—For purposes of this chapter, the term "incremental tertiary oil" means the excess of—

(1) the amount of crude oil which is removed from a property during any month and which is produced on or after the project beginning date and during the period for which a qualified tertiary recovery project is in effect on the property, over

(2) the base level for such property for such month.

[Sec. 4993(b)]

(b) DETERMINATION OF AMOUNT.—For purposes of this section—

(1) BASE LEVEL.—The base level for any property for any month is the average monthly amount (determined under rules similar to rules used in determining the base production control level under the June 1979 energy regulations) of crude oil removed from such property during the 6-month period ending March 31, 1979, reduced (but not below zero) by the sum of—

(A) 1 percent of such amount for each month which begins after 1978 and before the first month beginning after the project beginning date, and

(B) 2½ percent of such amount for each month which begins after the project beginning date (or after 1978 if the project beginning date is before 1979) and before the month for which the base level is being determined.

(2) MINIMUM AMOUNT IN CASE OF PROJECTS CERTIFIED BY DOE.—In the case of a project described in subsection (c)(1)(A), for the period during which the project is in effect, the amount of the incremental tertiary oil shall not be less than the incremental production determined under the June 1979 energy regulations.

(3) ALLOCATION RULES.—The determination of which barrels of crude oil removed during any month are incremental tertiary oil shall be made—

(A) first by allocating the amount of incremental tertiary oil between—

(i) oil which (but for this subsection) would be tier 1 oil, and

(ii) oil which (but for this subsection) would be tier 2 oil,

in proportion to the respective amounts of each such oil removed from the property during such month, and

(B) then by taking into account barrels of crude oil so removed in the order of their respective removal prices, beginning with the highest of such prices.

[Sec. 4993(c)]

(c) QUALIFIED TERTIARY RECOVERY PROJECT.—For purposes of this section—

(1) IN GENERAL.—The term "qualified tertiary recovery project" means—

(A) a qualified tertiary enhanced recovery project with respect to which a certification as such has been approved and is in effect under the June 1979 energy regulations, or

(B) any project for enhancing recovery of crude oil which meets the requirements of paragraph (2).

(2) REQUIREMENTS.—A project meets the requirements of this paragraph if—

(A) the project involves the application (in accordance with sound engineering principles) of 1 or more tertiary recovery methods which can reasonably be expected to result in more than an insignificant increase in the amount of crude oil which will ultimately be recovered,

(B) the date on which the injection of liquids, gases, or other matter begins is after May 1979,

(C) the portion of the property to be affected by the project is adequately delineated,

(D) the operator submits (at such time and in such manner as the Secretary may by regulations prescribe) to the Secretary—

(i) a certification from a petroleum engineer that the project meets the requirements of subparagraphs (A), (B), and (C), or

(ii) a certification that a jurisdictional agency (within the meaning of subsection (d)(5)) has approved the project as meeting the requirements of subparagraphs (A), (B), and (C), and that such approval is still in effect, and

(E) the operator submits (at such time and such manner as the Secretary may by regulations prescribe) to the Secretary a certification from a petroleum engineer that the project continues to meet the requirements of subparagraphs (A), (B), and (C).

Amendments
• **1983, Technical Corrections Act of 1982 (P.L. 97-448)**

P.L. 97-448, §201(e):

Amended Code Sec. 4993(c)(2)(B). **Effective** as if included in the provision of P.L. 96-223 to which it relates. Prior to amendment, Code Sec. 4993(c)(2)(B) read as follows:

"(B) the project beginning date is after May 1979,".

[Sec. 4993(d)]

(d) DEFINITIONS AND SPECIAL RULES.—For purposes of this section—

(1) TERTIARY RECOVERY METHOD.—The term "tertiary recovery method" means—

(A) any method which is described in subparagraphs (1) through (9) of section 212.78(c) of the June 1979 energy regulations, or

(B) any other method to provide tertiary enhanced recovery which is approved by the Secretary for purposes of this chapter.

(2) PROJECT BEGINNING DATE.—The term "project beginning date" means the later of—

(A) the date on which the injection of liquids, gases, or other matter begins, or

(B) the date on which—

(i) in the case of a project described in subsection (c)(1)(A), the project is certified as a qualified tertiary enhanced recovery project under the June 1979 energy regulations, or

(ii) in the case of a project described in subsection (c)(1)(B), a petroleum engineer certifies, or a jurisdictional agency approves, the project as meeting the requirements of subparagraphs (A), (B), and (C) of subsection (c)(2).

(3) PROJECT ONLY AFFECTS PORTION OF PROPERTY.—If a qualified tertiary recovery project can reasonably be expected to increase the ultimate recovery of crude oil from only a portion of a property, such portion shall be treated as a separate property.

(4) SIGNIFICANT EXPANSION TREATED AS SEPARATE PROJECT.—A significant expansion of any project shall be treated as a separate project.

(5) JURISDICTIONAL AGENCY.—The term "jurisdictional agency" means—

(A) in the case of an application involving a tertiary recovery project on lands not under Federal jurisdiction—

(i) the appropriate State agency in the State in which such lands are located which is designated by the Governor of such State in a written notification submitted to the Secretary as the agency which will approve projects under this subsection, or

(ii) if the Governor of such State does not submit such written notification within 180 days after the date of the enactment of the Crude Oil Windfall Profit Tax Act of 1980, the United States Geological Survey (until such time as the Governor submits such notification), or

(B) in the case of an application involving a tertiary recovery project on lands under Federal jurisdiction, the United States Geological Survey.

(6) BASIS OF REVIEW OF CERTAIN QUALIFIED TERTIARY RECOVERY PROJECTS.—In the case of any project which is approved under subsection (c)(2)(D)(ii) and for which a certification is submitted to the Secretary, the project shall be considered as meeting the requirements of subparagraphs (A), (B), and (C) of subsection (c)(2) unless the Secretary determines that—

(A) the approval of the jurisdictional agency was not supported by substantial evidence on the record upon which such approval was based, or

(B) additional evidence not contained in the record upon which such approval was based demonstrates that such project does not meet the requirements of subparagraph (A), (B), or (C) of subsection (c)(2).

If the Secretary makes a determination described in subparagraph (A) or (B) of the preceding sentence, the determination of whether the project meets the requirements of subparagraphs (A), (B), and (C) of subsection (c)(2) shall be made without regard to the preceding sentence.

(7) RULINGS RELATING TO CERTAIN QUALIFIED TERTIARY RECOVERY PROJECTS.—In the case of any tertiary recovery project for which a certification is submitted to the Secretary under subsection (c)(2)(D)(ii), a taxpayer may request a ruling from the Secretary with respect to whether such project is a qualified tertiary recovery project. The Secretary shall issue such ruling within 180 days of the date after he receives the request and such information as may be necessary to make a determination.

Amendments
• **1980, Crude Oil Windfall Profit Tax Act of 1980 (P.L. 96-223)**

P.L. 96-223, §101(a)(1):

Added Code Sec. 4993. For the **effective** date and transitional rules, see P.L. 96-223, §101(i) following Code Sec. 4986.

[Sec. 4994—Repealed]

Amendments
• **1988, Omnibus Trade and Competitiveness Act of 1988 (P.L. 100-418)**

P.L. 100-418, §1941(a):

Repealed Chapter 45 (Code Secs. 4986-4998). **Effective** for crude oil removed from the premises on or after 8-23-88. Prior to repeal, Code Sec. 4994 read as follows:

SEC. 4994. DEFINITIONS AND SPECIAL RULES RELATING TO EXEMPTIONS.

[Sec. 4994(a)]

(a) QUALIFIED GOVERNMENTAL INTEREST.—For purposes of section 4991(b)—

(1) IN GENERAL.—The term "qualified governmental interest" means an economic interest in crude oil if—

(A) such interest is held by a State or political subdivision thereof or by an agency or instrumentality of a State or political subdivision thereof, and

EXCISE TAXES—WINDFALL PROFIT TAX

(B) under the applicable State or local law, all of the net income received pursuant to such interest is dedicated to a public purpose.

(2) NET INCOME.—For purposes of this paragraph, the term "net income" means gross income reduced by production costs, and severance taxes of general application, allocable to the interest.

(3) AMOUNTS PLACED IN CERTAIN PERMANENT FUNDS TREATED AS DEDICATED TO PUBLIC PURPOSE.—The requirements of paragraph (1)(B) shall be treated as met with respect to any net income which, under the applicable State or local law, is placed in a permanent fund the earnings on which are dedicated to a public purpose.

[Sec. 4994(b)]

(b) QUALIFIED CHARITABLE INTEREST.—For purposes of section 4991(b)—

(1) IN GENERAL.—The term "qualified charitable interest" means an economic interest in crude oil if—

(A) such interest is—

(i) held by an organization described in clause (ii), (iii), or (iv) of section 170(b)(1)(A) which is also described in section 170(c)(2),

(ii) held by an organization described in section 170(c)(2) which is organized and operated primarily for the residential placement, care, or treatment of delinquent, dependent, orphaned, neglected, or handicapped children,

(iii) held—

(I) by an organization described in clause (i) of section 170(b)(1)(A) which is also described in section 170(c)(2), and

(II) for the benefit of an organization described in clause (i) or (ii) of this subparagraph, or

(iv) held by an organization described in section 509(a)(3) which is operated exclusively for the benefit of an organization described in—

(I) clause (ii), or

(II) section 170(b)(1)(A)(ii) which is also described in section 170(c)(2), and

(B) such interest was held on January 21, 1980, and at all times thereafter before the last day of the taxable period, by the organization described in clause (i), (ii), or (iv) of subparagraph (A), or subclause (I) of subparagraph (A)(iii).

(2) SPECIAL RULE.—For purposes of clause (ii), (iii), or (iv) of paragraph (1)(A), an interest shall be treated as held for the benefit of an organization described in clause (i), (ii), or (iv) of paragraph (1)(A), whichever is applicable, only if all the proceeds from such interest were dedicated on January 21, 1980, and at all times thereafter before the last day of the taxable period, to the organization described in clause (i), (ii), or (iv) of paragraph (1)(A), whichever is applicable.

Amendments

• **1983, Technical Corrections Act of 1982 (P.L. 97-448)**

P.L. 97-448, § 201(f)(3)(A):

Amended Code Sec. 4994(b)(1)(A) by striking out "or" at the end of clause (ii), by striking out "and" at the end of clause (iii) and inserting in lieu thereof "or", and by adding at the end thereof new clause (iv). **Effective** as if included in the provision of P.L. 96-223 to which it relates.

P.L. 97-448, § 201(f)(3)(B):

Amended Code Sec. 4994(b)(1)(B) by striking out "or (ii)" and inserting in lieu thereof ", (ii), or (iv)". **Effective** as if included in the provision of P.L. 96-223 to which it relates.

P.L. 97-448, § 201(f)(3)(C):

Amended Code Sec. 4994(b)(2) by striking out "clause (ii) or (iii)" and inserting in lieu thereof "clause (ii), (iii), or (iv)", by striking out "clause (i) or (ii)" each place it appeared and inserting in lieu thereof "clause (i), (ii), or (iv)", and by inserting ", whichever is applicable," after "paragraph (1)(A)" each place it appeared. **Effective** as if included in the provision of P.L. 96-223 to which it relates.

• **1981, Economic Recovery Tax Act of 1981 (P.L. 97-34)**

P.L. 97-34, § 604(a):

Redesignated Code Sec. 4994(b)(1)(A)(ii) as Code Sec. 4994(b)(1)(A)(iii) and added a new clause (ii). **Effective** for taxable periods beginning after 12-31-80.

P.L. 97-34, § 604(b)(1):

Amended Code Sec. 4994(b)(1)(B). **Effective** for tax periods beginning after 12-31-80. Prior to amendment, Code Sec. 4994(b)(1)(B) read as follows:

(B) such interest was held by the organization described in clause (i) or subclause (I) of clause (ii) of subparagraph (A) on January 21, 1980, and at all times thereafter before the last day of the taxable period.

P.L. 97-34, § 604(b)(2):

Amended Code Sec. 4994(b)(2) by striking out "paragraph (1)(A)(ii)" and inserting "clause (i) or (iii) of paragraph (1)(A)", and by striking out "paragraph (1)(A)(i)" each place it appears and inserting "clause (i) or (ii) of paragraph (1)(A)". **Effective** for tax periods beginning after 12-31-80.

P.L. 97-34, § 604(c)(1):

Amended Code Sec. 4994(b)(1)(A) by striking out "or" at the end of clause (i). **Effective** for tax periods beginning after 12-31-80.

P.L. 97-34, § 604(c)(2):

Amended Code Sec. 4994(b)(1)(A)(ii)(II) by inserting "or (ii)" after "clause (i)". **Effective** for tax periods beginning after 12-31-80.

[Sec. 4994(c)]

(c) FRONT-END TERTIARY OIL.—

(1) EXEMPTION FOR TERTIARY PROJECTS OF INDEPENDENTS.—For purposes of this chapter, the term "exempt front-end oil" means any domestic crude oil—

(A) which is removed from the premises before October 1, 1981, and

(B) which is treated as front-end oil by reason of a front-end tertiary project on one or more properties each of which is a qualified property.

(2) REFUNDS FOR TERTIARY PROJECTS OF INTEGRATED PRODUCERS.—

(A) IN GENERAL.—In the case of any front-end tertiary project which does not meet the requirements of paragraph (1)(B), the excess of—

(i) the allowed expenses of the producer with respect to such project, over

(ii) the tertiary incentive revenue,

shall be treated as a payment by the producer with respect to the tax imposed by this chapter made on September 30, 1981.

(B) LIMITATION BASED ON AMOUNT OF TAX.—The amount of the payment determined under subparagraph (A) with respect to any producer shall not exceed the aggregate tax imposed by section 4986 with respect to front-end oil of that producer removed after February 1980 and before October 1981.

(C) TERTIARY INCENTIVE REVENUE.—For purposes of this paragraph, the term "tertiary incentive revenue" has the meaning given such term by the front-end tertiary provisions of the energy regulations.

(3) DEFINITION OF ALLOWED EXPENSES; PREPAID EXPENSES NOT TAKEN INTO ACCOUNT.—For purposes of this subsection (including the application of the front-end tertiary provisions for purposes of this subsection)—

(A) ALLOWED EXPENSES.—Except as provided in subparagraph (B), allowed expenses shall be determined under the front-end tertiary provisions of the energy regulations.

(B) PREPAID EXPENSES NOT TAKEN INTO ACCOUNT.—The term "allowed expenses" shall not include any amount attributable to periods after September 30, 1981.

(C) PERIOD TO WHICH ITEM IS ATTRIBUTABLE.—For purposes of subparagraph (B)—

(i) any injectant and any fuel shall be treated as attributable to periods before October 1, 1981, if the injectant is injected, or the fuel is used, before October 1, 1981, and

(ii) any other item shall be treated as attributable to periods before October 1, 1981, only to the extent that under chapter 1 deductions for such item (including depreciation in respect of such item) are properly allocable to periods before October 1, 1981.

For purposes of the preceding sentence, an act shall be treated as taken before a date if it would have been taken before such date but for an act of God, a severe mechanical breakdown, or an injunction.

(4) DEFINITIONS AND SPECIAL RULES.—For purposes of this subsection—

(A) FRONT-END TERTIARY PROVISIONS.—The term "front-end tertiary provisions" means—

(i) the provisions of section 212.78 of the energy regulations which exempt crude oil from ceiling price limitations to provide financing for tertiary projects (as such provisions took effect on October 1, 1979), and

(ii) any modification of such provisions, but only to the extent that such modification is for purposes of coordinating such provisions with the tax imposed by this chapter.

(B) FRONT-END OIL.—The term "front-end oil" means any domestic crude oil which is not subject to a first sale ceiling price under the energy regulations solely by reason of the front-end tertiary provisions of such regulations.

(C) QUALIFIED PROPERTY.—The term "qualified property" means any property if, on January 1, 1980, 50 percent or more of the operating mineral interest in such property is held by persons who were independent producers (within the meaning of section 4992(b)) for the last quarter of 1979.

(D) FRONT-END TERTIARY PROJECT.—The term "front-end tertiary project" means any project which qualifies under the front-end tertiary provisions of the energy regulations.

(E) ORDERING RULE.—Front-end oil of any taxpayer shall be treated as attributable first to projects which meet the requirements of paragraph (1)(B).

Amendments

• **1983, Technical Corrections Act of 1982 (P.L. 97-448)**

P.L. 97-448, § 201(f)(1):

Amended Code Sec. 4994(c)(2)(A) by striking out "the taxpayer" each place it appeared and inserting in lieu thereof "the producer". **Effective** as if included in the provision of P.L. 96-223 to which it relates.

[Sec. 4994(d)]

(d) EXEMPT INDIAN OIL.—For purposes of this chapter, the term "exempt Indian oil" means any domestic crude oil—

(1) the producer of which is an Indian tribe, an individual member of an Indian tribe, or an Indian tribal organization under an economic interest held by such a tribe, member, or organization on January 21, 1980, and which is produced from mineral interests which are—

(A) held in trust by the United States for the tribe, member, or organization, or

(B) held by the tribe, member, or organization subject to a restriction on alienation imposed by the United States because it is held by an Indian tribe, an individual member of an Indian tribe, or an Indian tribal organization,

(2) the producer of which is a native corporation organized pursuant to the Alaska Native Claims Settlement Act (as in effect on January 21, 1980), and which—

(A) is produced from mineral interests held by the corporation which were received under that Act, and

(B) is removed from the premises before 1992, or

(3) the proceeds from the sale of which are deposited in the Treasury of the United States to the credit of tribal or native trust funds pursuant to a provision of law in effect on January 21, 1980.

Amendments

• **1982, Tax Equity and Fiscal Responsibility Act of 1982 (P.L. 97-248)**

P.L. 97-248, § 291:

Amended Code Sec. 4994(d)(2) by striking out "under" the first time it appeared and inserting "pursuant to". **Effective** on the day after 9-3-82.

[Sec. 4994(e)]

(e) EXEMPT ALASKAN OIL.—For purposes of this chapter, the term "exempt Alaskan oil" means any crude oil (other than Sadlerochit oil) which is produced—

Sec. 4994—Repealed

EXCISE TAXES—WINDFALL PROFIT TAX

(1) from a well located north of the Arctic Circle or from a reservoir from which oil has been produced in commercial quantities through such a well, or

(2) from a well located on the northerly side of the divides of the Alaska and Aleutian ranges and at least 75 miles from the nearest point on the Trans-Alaska Pipeline System.

Amendments

• **1983, Technical Corrections Act of 1982 (P.L. 97-448)**

P.L. 97-448, § 201(f)(2)(A):

Amended Code Sec. 4994(e)(1). **Effective** as if included in the provision of P.L. 96-223 to which it relates. Prior to amendment, Code Sec. 4994(e)(1) read as follows:

"(1) from a reservoir from which oil has been produced in commercial quantities through a well located north of the Arctic Circle, or".

P.L. 97-448, § 201(f)(2)(B):

Amended Code Sec. 4994(e)(2) by striking out "the divide of the Alaskan-Aleutian range" and inserting in lieu thereof "the divides of the Alaska and Aleutian ranges". **Effective** as if included in the provision of P.L. 96-223 to which it relates.

• **1980, Crude Oil Windfall Profit Tax Act of 1980 (P.L. 96-223)**

P.L. 96-223, § 101(a)(1):

Added Code Sec. 4994. For the **effective** date and transitional rules, see P.L. 96-223, § 101(i) following Code Sec. 4986.

[Sec. 4994(f)]

(f) EXEMPT ROYALTY OIL.—

(1) IN GENERAL.—For purposes of this chapter, the term "exempt royalty oil" means that portion of the qualified royalty owner's qualified royalty production for the quarter which does not exceed the royalty limit for such quarter.

(2) ROYALTY LIMIT.—For purposes of this subsection—

(A) IN GENERAL.—Except as provided in subparagraph (C), a qualified royalty owner's royalty limit for any quarter is the product of—

(i) the number of days in such quarter, multiplied by

(ii) the limitation in barrels determined under the following table:

In the case of qualified royalty production during:	The limitation in barrels is:
1983	2
1983	2
1984	2
1985 and thereafter	3

(B) PRODUCTION EXCEEDS LIMITATION.—If a qualified royalty owner's qualified royalty production for any quarter exceeds the royalty limitation for such quarter, such royalty owner may allocate such limit to any qualified royalty production which he selects.

(C) ELECTION TO INCREASE SECTION 6430 ROYALTY CREDIT BY REDUCING EXEMPTION UNDER THIS SUBSECTION.—Any qualified royalty owner who is a qualified beneficiary (within the meaning of section 6430(d)(1)) for any quarter may elect (at such time and in such manner as the Secretary may prescribe by regulations) to reduce by any amount the qualified royalty owner's royalty limit determined under subparagraph (A) for such quarter (after the application of paragraph (3)(B)).

(3) DEFINITIONS.—

(A) IN GENERAL.—The terms "qualified royalty owner" and "qualified royalty production" have the meanings given to such terms by section 6429; except that the reference to qualified taxable crude oil in section 6429(d) shall be treated as a reference to oil which would have been taxable crude oil but for this section.

(B) ALLOCATION.—Rules similar to the rules of paragraphs (2), (3), and (4) of section 6429(c) shall apply to the limitation determined under paragraph (2)(A).

Amendments

• **1983, Technical Corrections Act of 1982 (P.L. 97-448)**

P.L. 97-448, § 106(a)(2):

Amended Code Sec. 4994(f)(3)(B) by striking out "subsection (b)(1)" and inserting in lieu thereof "paragraph (2)(A)". **Effective** as if included in the provision of P.L. 97-34 to which it relates.

P.L. 97-448, § 106(a)(4)(B):

Amended Code Sec. 4994(f)(2) by striking out "A qualified" in subparagraph (A) and inserting in lieu thereof "Except as provided in subparagraph (C), a qualified", and by adding at the end thereof new subparagraph (C). **Effective** with respect to calendar years beginning after 12-31-81.

• **1981, Economic Recovery Tax Act of 1981 (P.L. 97-34)**

P.L. 97-34, § 601(b)(2):

Added Code Sec. 4994(f). **Effective** for oil removed after 12-31-81.

[Sec. 4994(g)]

(g) EXEMPT STRIPPER WELL OIL.—

(1) IN GENERAL.—For purposes of this chapter, the term "exempt stripper well oil" means any oil—

(A) the producer of which is an independent producer (within the meaning of section 4992(b)(1)),

(B) which is from a stripper well property within the meaning of the June 1979 energy regulations, and

(C) which is attributable to the independent producer's working interest in the stripper well property.

(2) LIMITATION FOR CERTAIN TRANSFERRED PROPERTIES.—Exempt stripper well oil does not include production attributable to an interest in any property which at any time after July 22, 1981, was owned by any person (other than the producer) who during the period of ownership after such date was not an independent producer (within the meaning of section 4992(b)(1)). The preceding sentence shall not apply to property so owned by any person if, at the time of transfer of such property by such person, such property was not a proven property (within the meaning of section 613A(c)(9)(A)).

Amendments

• **1983, Technical Corrections Act of 1982 (P.L. 97-448)**

P.L. 97-448, § 106(b):

Amended Code Sec. 4994(g)(2) by striking out "owned by a person other than an indepof section 4992(b)(1))." and inserting in lieu thereof "owned by any person (other than the producer) who during the period of ownership after such date was not an independent producer (within the meaning of section 4992(b)(1)). The preceding sentence shall not apply to property so owned by any person if, at the time of transfer of such property by such person, such property was not a proven property (within the meaning of section 613A(c)(9)(A)).". **Effective** as if included in the provision of P.L. 97-34 to which it relates.

• **1981, Economic Recovery Tax Act of 1981 (P.L. 97-34)**

P.L. 97-34, § 603(b):

Added Code Sec. 4994(g). **Effective** for oil removed from premises after 12-31-82.

[Sec. 4995—Repealed]

Amendments

• **1988, Omnibus Trade and Competitiveness Act of 1988 (P.L. 100-418)**

P.L. 100-418, § 1941(a):

Repealed Chapter 45 (Code Secs. 4986-4998). **Effective** for crude oil removed from the premises on or after 8-23-88. Prior to repeal, Code Sec. 4995 read as follows:

SEC. 4995. WITHHOLDING; DEPOSITARY REQUIREMENTS

[Sec. 4995(a)]

(a) WITHHOLDING BY PURCHASER.—

(1) WITHHOLDING REQUIRED.—Except to the extent provided in regulations prescribed by the Secretary—

(A) the first purchaser of any domestic crude oil shall withhold a tax equal to the amount of the tax imposed by section 4986 with respect to such oil from amounts payable by such purchaser to the producer of such oil, and

(B) the first purchaser of such oil shall be liable for the payment of the tax required to be withheld under subparagraph (A) and shall not be liable to any person for the amount of any such payment.

(2) DETERMINATION OF AMOUNT TO BE WITHHELD.—

(A) IN GENERAL.—The purchaser shall determine the amount to be withheld under paragraph (1)—

(i) on the basis of the certification furnished to the purchaser under section 6050C, unless the purchaser has reason to believe that any information contained in such certification is not correct, or

(ii) if clause (i) does not apply, under regulations prescribed by the Secretary.

(B) NET INCOME LIMITATION NOT TO BE APPLIED.—For purposes of determining the amount to be withheld under paragraph (1), subsection (b) of section 4988 shall not apply.

(3) ADJUSTMENTS FOR WITHHOLDING ERRORS.—

(A) IN GENERAL.—To the extent provided in regulations prescribed by the Secretary, withholding errors made by a purchaser with respect to the crude oil of a producer shall be corrected by that purchaser by making proper adjustments in the amounts withheld from subsequent payments to such producer for crude oil.

(B) WITHHOLDING ERROR.—For purposes of subparagraph (A), there is a withholding error if the amount withheld by the purchaser under paragraph (1) with respect to any payment for any crude oil exceeds (or is less than) the tax imposed by section 4986 with respect to such oil (determined without regard to section 4988(b)).

(C) VOLUNTARY WITHHOLDING.—The Secretary may by regulations provide for withholding under this subsection of additional amounts from payments by any purchaser to any producer if the purchaser and producer agree to such withholding. For purposes of this title, any amount withheld pursuant to such an agreement shall be treated as an amount required to be withheld under paragraph (1).

(4) PRODUCER TREATED AS HAVING PAID WITHHELD AMOUNT.—

(A) IN GENERAL.—The producer of any domestic crude oil shall be treated as having paid any amount withheld with respect to such oil under this subsection.

(B) TIME PAYMENT DEEMED MADE.—For purposes of this chapter (and so much of subtitle F as relates to this chapter), the producer shall be treated as having made any payment described in subparagraph (A) on the last day of the first February after the calendar year in which the oil is removed from the premises.

(5) PRODUCER REQUIRED TO FILE RETURN ONLY TO EXTENT PROVIDED IN REGULATIONS.—Except to the extent provided in regulations, the producer of crude oil with respect to which withholding is required under paragraph (1) shall not be required to file a return of the tax imposed by section 4986 with respect to such oil.

(6) PURCHASER'S QUARTERLY RETURNS TO CONTAIN SUMMARY.—The purchaser's return of tax under this chapter for any calendar quarter of any calendar year shall contain such information (with respect to such quarter and the prior quarters of such calendar year) as may be necessary to facilitate the coordination of the withholding of tax by such purchaser with respect to each producer with the determination of the tax imposed by section 4986 with respect to such producer.

(7) ELECTION FOR PURCHASER AND OPERATOR TO HAVE OPERATOR TAKE PLACE OF PURCHASER.—

EXCISE TAXES—WINDFALL PROFIT TAX

(A) IN GENERAL.—If the purchaser of domestic crude oil and the operator of the property from which the crude oil was produced make a joint election under this paragraph with respect to such property (or portion thereof)—

(i) the operator shall be substituted for the purchaser for purposes of applying this subsection and subsection (b) (and so much of subtitle F as relates to such subsections), and

(ii) if the operator is not an integrated oil company, the operator shall be treated as having the same status as the purchaser for purposes of applying subsection (b) with respect to amounts withheld by the operator by reason of such election.

(B) REGULATIONS MAY LIMIT ELECTION.—The Secretary may by regulations limit the circumstances under which an election under this paragraph may be made to situations where substituting the operator for the purchaser is administratively more practicable.

(8) NO ASSESSMENTS OR REFUNDS BEFORE CLOSE OF THE YEAR.—Except to the extent provided in regulations prescribed by the Secretary, in the case of any oil subject to withholding under this subsection—

(A) no notice of any deficiency with respect to the tax imposed by section 4986 may be mailed under section 6212, and

(B) no proceeding in any court for the refund of the tax imposed by section 4986 may be begun,

before the last day of the first February after the calendar year in which such oil was removed from the premises.

(9) ADJUSTMENTS TO TAKE INTO ACCOUNT ROYALTY EXEMPTION.—The Secretary shall prescribe such regulations as may be necessary so that the withholding required under this subsection shall be reduced to take into account the exemption provided by section 4991(b)(5) (relating to exempt royalty oil), and he may prescribe such other regulations as may be necessary to administer such exemption.

Amendments

• **1983, Technical Corrections Act of 1982 (P.L. 97-448)**

P.L. 97-448, § 201(g)(1):

Amended Code Sec. 4995(a)(3)(A) by striking out "removed during any calendar year", and by striking out "removed during the same calendar year". **Effective** as if included in the provision of P.L. 96-223 to which it relates.

P.L. 97-448, § 201(g)(2):

Amended Code Sec. 4995(a)(3) by striking out subparagraph (C) and by redesignating subparagraph (D) as subparagraph (C). **Effective** as if included in the provision of P.L. 96-223 to which it relates. Prior to being stricken, subparagraph (C) read as follows:

"(C) LIMITATION ON AMOUNT OF ADJUSTMENTS.—No adjustment shall be required under subparagraph (A) with respect to any payment for any crude oil to the extent that such adjustment would result in amounts withheld from such payment in excess of the windfall profit from such crude oil."

P.L. 97-448, § 201(g)(3):

Amended Code Sec. 4995(a)(4)(B) by striking out "The producer" and inserting in lieu thereof "For purposes of this chapter (and so much of subtitle F as relates to this chapter), the producer". **Effective** as if included in the provision of P.L. 96-223 to which it relates.

Amendments

• **1988, Omnibus Trade and Competitiveness Act of 1988 (P.L. 100-418)**

P.L. 100-418, § 1941(a):

Repealed Chapter 45 (Code Secs. 4986-4998). **Effective** for crude oil removed from the premises on or after 8-23-88. Prior to repeal, Code Sec. 4996 read as follows:

SEC. 4996. OTHER DEFINITIONS AND SPECIAL RULES.

[Sec. 4996(a)]

(a) PRODUCER AND OPERATOR.—For purposes of this chapter—

(1) PRODUCER.—

(A) IN GENERAL.—Except as provided in subparagraphs (B) and (C), the term "producer" means the holder of the economic interest with respect to the crude oil.

(B) NET PROFITS INTERESTS.—

(i) IN GENERAL.—Except to the extent otherwise provided by regulations, in the case of any property, all cost recovery oil covered by a net profits agreement (within the meaning of subsection (h)) shall be treated as produced by the parties to such agreement in proportion to their respective shares (determined after reduction for such cost recovery oil) of the production of the crude oil covered by such agreement.

(ii) CLAUSE (i) NOT TO APPLY BEFORE PAYOUT.—In the case of any property, clause (i) shall only apply for—

(I) the first taxable period in which, under the agreement with respect to such property, one or more persons receives a share described in subsection (h)(1)(B), and

(II) all subsequent taxable periods to which such agreement applies.

(C) PARTNERSHIPS.—

(i) IN GENERAL.—If (but for this subparagraph) a partnership would be treated as the producer of any crude oil—

(I) such crude oil shall be allocated among the partners of such partnership, and

(II) any partner to whom such crude oil is allocated (and not the partnership) shall be treated as the producer of such crude oil.

(ii) ALLOCATION.—Except to the extent otherwise provided in regulations, any allocation under clause (i)(I) shall be determined on the basis of a person's proportionate share of the income of the partnership.

(C)[D] SUBCHAPTER S CORPORATIONS.—

(i) IN GENERAL.—If (but for this subparagraph) an S corporation would be treated as a producer of any crude oil—

(I) such crude oil shall be allocated among the shareholders of such corporation, and

• **1981, Economic Recovery Tax Act of 1981 (P.L. 97-34)**

P.L. 97-34, § 601(b)(3):

Added Code Sec. 4995(a)(9). **Effective** for oil removed after 12-31-81.

[Sec. 4995(b)]

(b) DEPOSITARY REQUIREMENTS.—

(1) INTEGRATED OIL COMPANIES.—In the case of an integrated oil company, deposit of the estimated amount of—

(A) withholding under subsection (a) by such company, and

(B) such company's liability for the tax imposed by section 4986 with respect to oil for which withholding is not required,

shall be made twice a month.

(2) PERSONS WHO ARE NOT INTEGRATED OIL COMPANIES.—In the case of a person, other than an integrated oil company—

(A) DEPOSITS OF WITHHELD AMOUNTS.—Deposit of the amounts required to be withheld under subsection (a) shall be made not later than—

(i) except as provided in clause (ii), 45 days after the close of the month in which the oil was removed, or

(ii) in the case of oil purchased under a contract therefor by an independent refiner under which no payment is required to be made before the 46th day after the close of the month in which the oil is purchased, before the first day of the 3rd month which begins after the close of the month in which such oil was removed.

(B) ESTIMATED SECTION 4986 TAX.—Deposits of the estimated amount of such person's liability for the tax imposed by section 4986 with respect to oil for which withholding is not required shall be made not later than 45 days after the close of the month in which the oil was removed from the premises.

(3) INTEGRATED OIL COMPANY DEFINED.—For purposes of this subsection, the term "integrated oil company" means a taxpayer described in paragraph (2) or (4) of section 613A(d) who is not an independent refiner.

(4) INDEPENDENT REFINER.—For purposes of this subsection, the term "independent refiner" has the same meaning as in paragraph (3) of section 3 of the Emergency Petroleum Allocation Act of 1973 (as in effect on January 1, 1980), except that "the preceding calendar quarter" shall be substituted for "November 27, 1973" in applying such paragraph for purposes of this paragraph.

[Sec. 4995(c)]

(c) CROSS REFERENCE.—

For provision authorizing the Secretary to establish by regulations the mode and time for collecting the tax imposed by section 4986 (to the extent not otherwise provided in this chapter), see section 6302(a).

Amendments

• **1980, Crude Oil Windfall Profit Tax Act of 1980 (P.L. 96-223)**

P.L. 96-223, § 101(a)(1):

Added Code Sec. 4995. For the **effective** date and transitional rules, see P.L. 96-223, § 101(i) following Code Sec. 4986.

[Sec. 4996—Repealed]

(II) any shareholder to whom such crude oil is allocated (and not the S corporation) shall be treated as the producer of such crude oil.

(ii) ALLOCATION.—Except to the extent otherwise provided in regulations, any allocation under clause (i)(I) shall be determined on the basis of the shareholder's pro rata share (as determined under section 1377(a)) of the income of the corporation.

(2) OPERATOR.—

(A) IN GENERAL.—Except as provided in subparagraph (B), the term "operator" means the person primarily responsible for the management and operation of crude oil production on a property.

(B) DESIGNATION OF OTHER PERSON.—Under regulations prescribed by the Secretary, the term "operator" means the person (or persons) designated with respect to a property (or portion thereof) as the operator for purposes of this chapter by persons holding operating mineral interests in the property.

Amendments

• **1983, Technical Corrections Act of 1982 (P.L. 97-448)**

P.L. 97-448, § 201(h)(1)(A):

Amended Code Sec. 4996(a)(1) by redesignating subparagraph (B) as subparagraph (C) and by inserting after subparagraph (A) new subparagraph (B). **Effective** as if included in the provision of P.L. 96-223 to which it relates. See, however, the special rule provided by Act Sec. 203(c), which appears in the amendment note for Act Sec. 201(h)(1)(C), following Code Sec. 4996(i).

P.L. 97-448, § 201(h)(1)(B):

Amended Code Sec. 4996(a)(1)(A) by striking out "subparagraph (B)" and inserting in lieu thereof "subparagraphs (B) and (C)". **Effective** as if included in the provision of P.L. 96-223 to which it relates. See, however, the special rule provided by Act Sec. 203(c), which appears in the amendment note for Act Sec. 201(h)(1)(C), following Code Sec. 4996(i).

• **1982, Subchapter S Revision Act of 1982 (P.L. 97-354)**

P.L. 97-354, § 3(b)(1):

Added Code Sec. 4996(a)(1)(C)[D]. **Effective** for tax years beginning after 12-31-82.

[Sec. 4996(b)]

(b) OTHER DEFINITIONS.—For purposes of this chapter—

(1) CRUDE OIL.—The term "crude oil" has the meaning given to such term by the June 1979 energy regulations. In the case of crude oil which is condensate recovered

off the premises by mechanical separation, such crude oil shall be treated as removed from the premises on the date on which it is so recovered.

(2) BARREL.—The term "barrel" means 42 United States gallons.

(3) DOMESTIC.—The term "domestic," when used with respect to crude oil, means crude oil produced from a well located in the United States or in a possession of the United States.

(4) UNITED STATES.—The term "United States" has the meaning given to such term by paragraph (1) of section 638 (relating to Continental Shelf areas).

(5) POSSESSION OF THE UNITED STATES.—The term "possession of the United States" has the meaning given to such term by paragraph (2) of section 638.

(6) INDIAN TRIBE.—The term "Indian tribe" has the meaning given to such term by section 106(b)(2)(C)(ii) of the Natural Gas Policy Act of 1978 (15 U.S.C. 3316(b)(2)(C)(ii)).

(7) TAXABLE PERIOD.—The term "taxable period" means—

(A) March 1980, and

(B) each calendar quarter beginning after March 1980.

(8) ENERGY REGULATIONS.—

(A) IN GENERAL.—The term "energy regulations" means regulations prescribed under section 4(a) of the Emergency Petroleum Allocation Act of 1973 (15 U.S.C. 753(a)).

(B) MARCH 1979 ENERGY REGULATIONS.—The March 1979 energy regulations shall be the terms of the energy regulations as such terms existed on March 1, 1979.

(C) JUNE 1979 ENERGY REGULATIONS.—The June 1979 energy regulations—

(i) shall be the terms of the energy regulations as such terms existed on June 1, 1979, and

(ii) shall be treated as including final action taken pursuant thereto before June 1, 1979, and as including action taken before, on, or after such date with respect to incremental production from qualified tertiary enhanced recovery projects.

(D) CONTINUED APPLICATION OF REGULATIONS AFTER DECONTROL.—Energy regulations shall be treated as continuing in effect without regard to decontrol of oil prices or any other termination of the application of such regulations.

Amendments

• **1983, Technical Corrections Act of 1982 (P.L. 97-448)**

P.L. 97-448, §201(h)(2)(A):

Amended Code Sec. 4996(b)(1) by adding the last sentence. **Effective** as if included in the provision of P.L. 96-223 to which it relates.

P.L. 97-448, §203(b)(4), provides:

(4) No withholding by reason of condensate provision.—No withholding of tax shall be required under section 4995 of the Internal Revenue Code of 1954 by reason of the amendment made by section 201(h)(2)(A) of this Act before the date on which regulations with respect to such amendment are published in the Federal Register.

P.L. 97-448, §201(h)(2)(B):

Amended Code Sec. 4996(b)(3) by striking out "an oil well" and inserting in lieu thereof "a well". **Effective** as if included in the provision of P.L. 96-223 to which it relates.

[Sec. 4996(c)]

(c) SEVERANCE TAX ADJUSTMENT.—For purposes of this chapter—

(1) IN GENERAL.—The severance tax adjustment with respect to any barrel of crude oil shall be the amount by which—

(A) any severance tax imposed with respect to such barrel, exceeds

(B) the severance tax which would have been imposed if the barrel had been valued at its adjusted base price.

(2) SEVERANCE TAX DEFINED.—For purposes of this subsection, the term "severance tax" means a tax—

(A) imposed by a State with respect to the extraction of oil, and

(B) determined on the basis of the gross value of the extracted oil.

(3) LIMITATIONS.—

(A) 15 PERCENT LIMITATION.—A severance tax shall not be taken into account to the extent that the rate thereof exceeds 15 percent.

(B) INCREASES AFTER MARCH 31, 1979, MUST APPLY EQUALLY.—The amount of the severance tax taken into account under paragraph (1) shall not exceed the amount which would have been imposed under a State severance tax in effect on March 31, 1979, unless such excess is attributable to an increase in the rate of the severance tax (or to the imposition of a severance tax) which applies equally to all portions of the gross value of each barrel of oil subject to such tax.

[Sec. 4996(d)]

(d) ALASKAN OIL FROM SADLEROCHIT RESERVOIR.—For purposes of this chapter—

(1) REMOVAL PRICE DETERMINED ON MONTHLY BASIS.—The removal price of Sadlerochit oil removed during any calendar month shall be the average of the producer's removal prices for such month.

(2) SADLEROCHIT OIL DEFINED.—The term "Sadlerochit oil" means crude oil produced from the Sadlerochit reservoir in the Prudhoe Bay oilfield.

Amendments

• **1982, Tax Equity and Fiscal Responsibility Act of 1982 (P.L. 97-248)**

P.L. 97-248, §284(a):

Amended Code Sec. 4996(d). **Effective** with respect to oil removed after 12-31-82. Prior to amendment, Code Sec. 4996(d) read as follows:

"(d) ALASKAN OIL FROM SADLEROCHIT RESERVOIR.—For purposes of this chapter—

(1) IN GENERAL.—In the case of Sadlerochit oil—

(A) ADJUSTED BASE PRICE INCREASED BY TAPS ADJUSTMENT.—The adjusted base price for any calendar quarter (determined without regard to this subsection) shall be increased by the TAPS adjustment (if any) for such quarter provided by paragraph (2).

(B) REMOVAL PRICE DETERMINED ON MONTHLY BASIS.—The removal price of such oil removed during any calendar month shall be the average of the producer's removal prices for such month.

(2) TAPS ADJUSTMENT.—

(A) IN GENERAL.—The TAPS adjustment for any calendar quarter is the excess (if any) of—

(i) $6.26, over

(ii) the TAPS tariff for the preceding calendar quarter.

(B) TAPS TARIFF.—For purposes of subparagraph (A), the TAPS tariff for the preceding calendar quarter is the average per barrel amount paid for all transportation (ending in such quarter) of crude oil through the TAPS.

(C) TAPS DEFINED.—For purposes of this paragraph, the term 'TAPS' means the Trans-Alaska Pipeline System.

(3) SADLEROCHIT OIL DEFINED.—The term 'Sadlerochit oil' means crude oil produced from the Sadlerochit reservoir in the Prudhoe Bay oilfield."

[Sec. 4996(e)]

(e) SPECIAL RULES FOR POST-1978 TRANSFERS OF PROPERTY.—In the case of a transfer after 1978 of any portion of a property, for purposes of this chapter (including the application of the June 1979 energy regulations for purposes of this chapter), after such transfer crude oil produced from any portion of such property shall not constitute oil from a stripper well property, newly discovered oil, or heavy oil, if such oil would not be so classified if the property had not been transferred.

[Sec. 4996(f)]

(f) ADJUSTMENT OF REMOVAL PRICE.—In determining the removal price of oil from a property in the case of any transaction, the Secretary may adjust the removal price to reflect clearly the fair market value of oil removed.

[Sec. 4996(g)]

(g) NO EXEMPTIONS FROM TAX.—No taxable crude oil, and no producer of such crude oil, shall be exempt from the tax imposed by this chapter except to the extent provided in this chapter or in any provision of law enacted after the date of the enactment of this chapter which grants a specific exemption, by reference to this chapter, from the tax imposed by this chapter.

[Sec. 4996(h)]

(h) TERMS USED IN SUBSECTION (a)(1)(B).—For purposes of subsection (a)(1)(B) and this subsection—

(1) NET PROFITS AGREEMENT.—The term "net profits agreement" means an agreement entered into (or renewed) after March 31, 1982, and providing for sharing part or all of the production of crude oil from a property where—

(A) 1 or more persons are to be reimbursed for qualified costs by the allocation of cost recovery oil, and

(B) 1 or more persons are to receive a share of any production of crude oil from the property remaining after reduction for the cost recovery oil referred to in subparagraph (A).

(2) COST RECOVERY OIL DEFINED.—The term "cost recovery oil" means crude oil produced from the property which is allocated to a person as reimbursement for qualified costs paid or incurred with respect to the property. The Secretary shall by regulation prescribe rules for allocating the cost recovery oil to the oil produced from the property.

(3) QUALIFIED COSTS.—The term "qualified costs" means any amount paid or incurred for exploring for, or developing or producing, 1 or more oil or gas wells on the property.

(4) SCOPE OF AGREEMENT.—A net profits agreement shall be treated as covering only shares of production of crude oil held by persons who hold economic interests in the property (determined without regard to subsection (a)(1)(B)).

Amendments

• **1983, Technical Corrections Act of 1982 (P.L. 94-448)**

P.L. 97-448, §201(h)(1)(E), provides:

(E) If 90 percent or more of the remaining production referred to in subparagraph (B) of section 4996(h)(1) of the Internal Revenue Code of 1954 is to be received by governmental entities, and organizations described in clause (i), (ii), or (iii) of section 4994(b)(1)(A) of such Code, which do not share in the costs referred to in subparagraph (A) of such section 4996(h)(1), then the requirement of paragraph (1) of section 4996(h) of such Code that the agreement be entered into (or renewed) after March 31, 1982, shall not apply.

[Sec. 4996(i)]

(i) CROSS REFERENCE.—

For the holder of the economic interest in the case of a production payment, see section 636.

Amendments

• **1983, Technical Corrections Act of 1982 (P.L. 97-448)**

P.L. 97-448, §201(h)(1)(C):

Amended Code Sec. 4996 by redesignating subsection (h) as subsection (i) and by inserting after subsection (g) new subsection (h). **Effective** as if included in the provision of P.L. 96-223 to which it relates.

P.L. 97-448, §203(c), provides:

(c) No Interest for Past Periods Resulting From Amendments Relating to Cost Recovery Oil.—No interest shall be paid or credited with respect to the credit or refund of any overpayment of tax imposed by the Internal Revenue Code of 1954, and no interest shall be assessed or collected with respect to any underpayment of tax imposed by such Code, for any period before the date which is 60 days after the date of the enactment of this Act, to the extent that such overpayment or underpayment is attributable to the amendments made by section 201(h)(1).

EXCISE TAXES—GOLDEN PARACHUTE PAYMENTS

- **1980, Crude Oil Windfall Profit Tax Act of 1980 (P.L. 96-223)**

P.L. 96-223, §101(a)(1):

Added Code Sec. 4996. For the **effective** date and transitional rules, see P.L. 96-223, §101(i) following Code Sec. 4986.

[Sec. 4997—Repealed]

Amendments

- **1988, Omnibus Trade and Competitiveness Act of 1988 (P.L. 100-418)**

P.L. 100-418, §1941(a):

Repealed Chapter 45 (Code Secs. 4986-4998). **Effective** for crude oil removed from the premises on or after 8-23-88. Prior to repeal, Code Sec. 4997 read as follows:

SEC. 4997. RECORDS AND INFORMATION; REGULATIONS.

[Sec. 4997(a)]

(a) RECORDS AND INFORMATION.—Each taxpayer liable for tax under section 4986, each partnership, trust, or estate producing domestic crude oil, each purchaser of domestic crude oil, and each operator of a well from which domestic crude oil was produced, shall keep such records, make such returns, and furnish such statements and other information (to the Secretary and to other persons having an interest in the oil) with respect to such oil as the Secretary may by regulations prescribe.

Amendments

- **1983, Technical Corrections Act of 1982 (P.L. 97-448)**

P.L. 97-448, §201(i)(1):

Amended Code Sec. 4997(a) by striking out "such information" and inserting in lieu thereof "such statements and other information". **Effective** with respect to returns and statements the due dates for which (without regard to extensions) are after 1-12-83.

[Sec. 4997(b)]

(b) REGULATIONS.—The Secretary shall prescribe such regulations as may be necessary or appropriate to carry out the purposes of this chapter, including such changes in the application of the energy regulations for purposes of this chapter as may be necessary or appropriate to carry out such purposes.

Amendments

- **1980, Crude Oil Windfall Profit Tax Act of 1980 (P.L. 96-223)**

P.L. 96-223, §101(a)(1):

Added Code Sec. 4997. For the **effective** date and transitional rules, see P.L. 96-223, §101(i), following Code Sec. 4986.

[Sec. 4998—Repealed]

Amendments

- **1988, Omnibus Trade and Competitiveness Act of 1988 (P.L. 100-418)**

P.L. 100-418, §1941(a):

Repealed Chapter 45 (Code Secs. 4986-4998). **Effective** for crude oil removed from the premises on or after 8-23-88. Prior to repeal, Code Sec. 4998 read as follows:

SEC. 4998. CROSS REFERENCES.

(1) For additions to the tax and additional amount for failure to file tax return or to pay tax, see section 6651.

(2) For additions to the tax and additional amounts for failure to file certain information returns, registration statements, etc., see section 6652.

(3) For additions to the tax and additional amounts for negligence and fraud, see section 6653.

(4) For additions to the tax and additional amounts for failure to make deposit of taxes, see section 6656.

(5) For additions to the tax and additional amounts for failure to collect and pay over tax, or attempt to evade or defeat tax, see section 6672.

(6) For criminal penalties for attempt to evade or defeat tax, willful failure to collect or pay over tax, willful failure to file return, supply information, or pay tax, and for fraud and false statements, see sections 7201, 7202, 7203, and 7206.

(7) For criminal penalties for failure to furnish certain information regarding windfall profit tax on domestic crude oil, see section 7241.

- **1980, Crude Oil Windfall Profit Tax Act of 1980 (P.L. 96-223)**

P.L. 96-223, §101(a)(1):

Added Code Sec. 4998. For the **effective** date and transitional rules, see P.L. 96-223, §101(i) following Code Sec. 4986.

CHAPTER 46—GOLDEN PARACHUTE PAYMENTS

Sec. 4999.　　Golden parachute payments

[Sec. 4999]

SEC. 4999. GOLDEN PARACHUTE PAYMENTS.

[Sec. 4999(a)]

(a) IMPOSITION OF TAX.—There is hereby imposed on any person who receives an excess parachute payment a tax equal to 20 percent of the amount of such payment.

[Sec. 4999(b)]

(b) EXCESS PARACHUTE PAYMENT DEFINED.—For purposes of this section, the term "Excess parachute payment" has the meaning given to such term by section 280G(b).

[Sec. 4999(c)]

(c) ADMINISTRATIVE PROVISIONS.—

(1) WITHHOLDING.—In the case of any excess parachute payment which is wages (within the meaning of section 3401) the amount deducted and withheld under section 3402 shall be increased by the amount of the tax imposed by this section on such payment.

(2) OTHER ADMINISTRATIVE PROVISIONS.—For purposes of subtitle F, any tax imposed by this section shall be treated as a tax imposed by subtitle A.

Amendments

- **1984, Deficit Reduction Act of 1984 (P.L. 98-369)**

P.L. 98-369, §67(b)(1):

Added Code Sec. 4999. **Effective** for payments under agreements entered into or renewed after 6-14-84, in tax years ending after such date. A special rule appears below.

P.L. 98-369, §67(e)(2), provides:

(2) Special rule for Contract Amendments.—Any contract entered into before June 15, 1984, which is amended after June 14, 1984, in any significant relevant aspect shall be treated as a contract entered into after June 14, 1984.

CHAPTER 47—CERTAIN GROUP HEALTH PLANS

Sec. 5000.　　Certain group health plans.

[Sec. 5000]

SEC. 5000. CERTAIN GROUP HEALTH PLANS.

[Sec. 5000(a)]

(a) IMPOSITION OF TAX.—There is hereby imposed on any employer (including a self-employed person) or employee organization that contributes to a nonconforming group health plan a tax equal to 25 percent of the employer's or employee organization's expenses incurred during the calendar year for each group health plan to which the employer (including a self-employed person) or employee organization contributes.

EXCISE TAXES—MINIMUM COVERAGE REQUIREMENT

Amendments

• **1993, Omnibus Budget Reconciliation Act of 1993 (P.L. 103-66)**

P.L. 103-66, §13561(e)(2)(A)(i):

Amended Code Sec. 5000(a) by inserting "(including a self-employed person)" after "employer" [each place it occurs]. **Effective** 8-10-93.

• **1989, Omnibus Budget Reconciliation Act of 1989 (P.L. 101-239)**

P.L. 101-239, §6202(b)(2)(A)-(B):

Amended Code Sec. 5000 by striking "LARGE" after "CERTAIN" in the heading, and by striking "large" before "group health" each place it appears in subsection (a). **Effective** for items and services furnished after 12-19-89.

[Sec. 5000(b)]

(b) GROUP HEALTH PLAN AND LARGE GROUP HEALTH PLAN.—For purposes of this section—

(1) GROUP HEALTH PLAN.—The term "group health plan" means a plan (including a self-insured plan) of, or contributed to by, an employer (including a self-employed person) or employee organization to provide health care (directly or otherwise) to the employees, former employees, the employer, others associated or formerly associated with the employer in a business relationship, or their families.

(2) LARGE GROUP HEALTH PLAN.—The term "large group health plan" means a plan of, or contributed to by, an employer or employee organization (including a self-insured plan) to provide health care (directly or otherwise) to the employees, former employees, the employer, others associated or formerly associated with the employer in a business relationship, or their families, that covers employees of at least one employer that normally employed at least 100 employees on a typical business day during the previous calendar year. For purposes of the preceding sentence—

(A) all employers treated as a single employer under subsection (a) or (b) of section 52 shall be treated as a single employer,

(B) all employees of the members of an affiliated service group (as defined in section 414(m)) shall be treated as employed by a single employer, and

(C) leased employees (as defined in section 414(n)(2)) shall be treated as employees of the person for whom they perform services to the extent they are so treated under section 414(n).

Amendments

• **1993, Omnibus Budget Reconciliation Act of 1993 (P.L. 103-66)**

P.L. 103-66, §13561(d)(2):

Amended Code Sec. 5000(b)(2) by adding a new sentence at the end thereof. **Effective** 90 days after 8-10-93.

P.L. 103-66, §13561(e)(2)(A)(ii):

Amended Code Sec. 5000(b)(1). **Effective** 8-10-93. Prior to amendment, Code Sec. 5000(b)(1) read as follows:

(1) GROUP HEALTH PLAN.—The term "group health plan" means any plan of, or contributed to by, an employer (including a self-insured plan) to provide health care (directly or otherwise) to the employer's employees, former employees, or the families of such employees or former employees.

• **1989, Omnibus Budget Reconciliation Act of 1989 (P.L. 101-239)**

P.L. 101-239, §6202(b)(2)(C):

Amended Code Sec. 5000(b). **Effective** for items and services furnished after 12-19-89. Prior to amendment, Code Sec. 5000(b) read as follows:

(b) LARGE GROUP HEALTH PLAN.—For purposes of this section, the term "large group health plan" means a plan of, or contributed to by, an employer or employee organization (including a self-insured plan) to provide health care (directly or otherwise) to the employees, former employees, the employer, others associated or formerly associated with the employer in a business relationship, or their families, that covers employees of at least one employer that normally employed at least 100 employees on a typical business day during the previous calendar year.

[Sec. 5000(c)]

(c) NONCONFORMING GROUP HEALTH PLAN.—For purposes of this section, the term "nonconforming group health plan" means a group health plan or large group health plan that at any time during a calendar year does not comply with the requirements of subparagraphs (A) and (C) or subparagraph (B) respectively, of paragraph (1) or with the requirements of paragraph (2), of section 1862(b) of the Social Security Act.

Amendments

• **1993, Omnibus Budget Reconciliation Act of 1993 (P.L. 103-66)**

P.L. 103-66, §13561(e)(2)(A)(iii):

Amended Code Sec. 5000(c) by striking "of section 1862(b)(1)" and inserting "of paragraph (1) or with the requirements of paragraph (2), of section 1862(b)". **Effective** 8-10-93.

• **1989, Omnibus Budget Reconciliation Act of 1989 (P.L. 101-239)**

P.L. 101-239, §6202(b)(2)(C):

Amended Code Sec. 5000(c). **Effective** for items and services furnished after 12-19-89. Prior to amendment, Code Sec. 5000(c) read as follows:

(c) NONCONFORMING LARGE GROUP HEALTH PLAN.—For purposes of this section, the term "nonconforming large group health plan" means a large group health plan that at any time during a calendar year does not comply with the requirements of section 1862(b)(4)(A)(i) of the Social Security Act.

[Sec. 5000(d)]

(d) GOVERNMENT ENTITIES.—For purposes of this section, the term "employer" does not include a Federal or other governmental entity.

Amendments

• **1986, Omnibus Budget Reconciliation Act of 1986 (P.L. 99-509)**

P.L. 99-509, §9319(d)(1):

Amended subtitle D of the Internal Revenue Code of 1954 by adding at the end new chapter 47, containing new Code Sec. 5000. **Effective** for items and services furnished on or after 1-1-87.

CHAPTER 48—MAINTENANCE OF MINIMUM ESSENTIAL COVERAGE

Sec. 5000A. Requirement to maintain minimum essential coverage.

[Sec. 5000A]

SEC. 5000A. REQUIREMENT TO MAINTAIN MINIMUM ESSENTIAL COVERAGE.

[Sec. 5000A(a)]

(a) REQUIREMENT TO MAINTAIN MINIMUM ESSENTIAL COVERAGE.—An applicable individual shall for each month beginning after 2013 ensure that the individual, and any dependent of the individual who is an applicable individual, is covered under minimum essential coverage for such month.

Amendments

• **2010, Patient Protection and Affordable Care Act (P.L. 111-148)**

P.L. 111-148, §1502(c), provides:

(c) NOTIFICATION OF NONENROLLMENT.—Not later than June 30 of each year, the Secretary of the Treasury, acting through the Internal Revenue Service and in consultation with the Secretary of Health and Human Services, shall send a notification to each individual who files an individual income tax return and who is not enrolled in minimum essential coverage (as defined in section 5000A of the Internal Revenue Code of 1986). Such notification shall contain information on the services available through the Exchange operating in the State in which such individual resides.

[Sec. 5000A(b)]

(b) SHARED RESPONSIBILITY PAYMENT.—

(1) IN GENERAL.—If a taxpayer who is an applicable individual, or an applicable individual for whom the taxpayer is liable under paragraph (3), fails to meet the requirement of subsection (a) for 1 or more months, then, except as provided in subsection (e), there is hereby imposed on the taxpayer a penalty with respect to such failures in the amount determined under subsection (c).

EXCISE TAXES—MINIMUM COVERAGE REQUIREMENT

(2) INCLUSION WITH RETURN.—Any penalty imposed by this section with respect to any month shall be included with a taxpayer's return under chapter 1 for the taxable year which includes such month.

(3) PAYMENT OF PENALTY.—If an individual with respect to whom a penalty is imposed by this section for any month—

(A) is a dependent (as defined in section 152) of another taxpayer for the other taxpayer's taxable year including such month, such other taxpayer shall be liable for such penalty, or

(B) files a joint return for the taxable year including such month, such individual and the spouse of such individual shall be jointly liable for such penalty.

Amendments

• **2010, Patient Protection and Affordable Care Act (P.L. 111-148)**

P.L. 111-148, §10106(b)(1):

Amended Code Sec. 5000A(b)(1), as added by Act Sec. 1501(b). **Effective** 3-23-2010. Prior to amendment, Code Sec. 5000A(b)(1) read as follows:

(1) IN GENERAL.—If an applicable individual fails to meet the requirement of subsection (a) for 1 or more months during any calendar year beginning after 2013, then, except as provided in subsection (d), there is hereby imposed a penalty with respect to the individual in the amount determined under subsection (c).

[Sec. 5000A(c)]

(c) AMOUNT OF PENALTY.—

(1) IN GENERAL.—The amount of the penalty imposed by this section on any taxpayer for any taxable year with respect to failures described in subsection (b)(1) shall be equal to the lesser of—

(A) the sum of the monthly penalty amounts determined under paragraph (2) for months in the taxable year during which 1 or more such failures occurred, or

(B) an amount equal to the national average premium for qualified health plans which have a bronze level of coverage, provide coverage for the applicable family size involved, and are offered through Exchanges for plan years beginning in the calendar year with or within which the taxable year ends.

(2) MONTHLY PENALTY AMOUNTS.—For purposes of paragraph (1)(A), the monthly penalty amount with respect to any taxpayer for any month during which any failure described in subsection (b)(1) occurred is an amount equal to $1/12$ of the greater of the following amounts:

(A) FLAT DOLLAR AMOUNT.—An amount equal to the lesser of—

(i) the sum of the applicable dollar amounts for all individuals with respect to whom such failure occurred during such month, or

(ii) 300 percent of the applicable dollar amount (determined without regard to paragraph (3)(C)) for the calendar year with or within which the taxable year ends.

(B) PERCENTAGE OF INCOME.—An amount equal to the following percentage of the excess of the taxpayer's household income for the taxable year over the amount of gross income specified in section 6012(a)(1) with respect to the taxpayer for the taxable year:

(i) 1.0 percent for taxable years beginning in 2014.

(ii) 2.0 percent for taxable years beginning in 2015.

(iii) Zero percent for taxable years beginning after 2015.

(3) APPLICABLE DOLLAR AMOUNT.—For purposes of paragraph (1)—

(A) IN GENERAL.—Except as provided in subparagraphs (B) and (C), the applicable dollar amount is $0.

(B) PHASE IN.—The applicable dollar amount is $95 for 2014 and $325 for 2015.

(C) SPECIAL RULE FOR INDIVIDUALS UNDER AGE 18.—If an applicable individual has not attained the age of 18 as of the beginning of a month, the applicable dollar amount with respect to such individual for the month shall be equal to one-half of the applicable dollar amount for the calendar year in which the month occurs.

(4) TERMS RELATING TO INCOME AND FAMILIES.—For purposes of this section—

(A) FAMILY SIZE.—The family size involved with respect to any taxpayer shall be equal to the number of individuals for whom the taxpayer is allowed a deduction under section 151 (relating to allowance of deduction for personal exemptions) for the taxable year.

(B) HOUSEHOLD INCOME.—The term "household income" means, with respect to any taxpayer for any taxable year, an amount equal to the sum of—

(i) the modified adjusted gross income of the taxpayer, plus

(ii) the aggregate modified adjusted gross incomes of all other individuals who—

(I) were taken into account in determining the taxpayer's family size under paragraph (1), and

(II) were required to file a return of tax imposed by section 1 for the taxable year.

(C) MODIFIED ADJUSTED GROSS INCOME.—The term "modified adjusted gross income" means adjusted gross income increased by—

(i) any amount excluded from gross income under section 911, and

(ii) any amount of interest received or accrued by the taxpayer during the taxable year which is exempt from tax.

Amendments

• **2017, Tax Cuts and Jobs Act (P.L. 115-97)**

P.L. 115-97, §11002(d)(1)(GG):

Amended Code Sec. 5000A(c)(3)(D)(ii) by striking "for 'calendar year 1992'" in subparagraph (B)" and inserting "for 'calendar year 2016'" in subparagraph (A)(ii)". **Effective** for tax years beginning after 12-31-2017.

P.L. 115-97, §11081(a)(1)-(2):

Amended Code Sec. 5000A(c) by striking "2.5 percent" in paragraph (2)(B)(iii) and inserting "Zero percent", and by striking "$695" in paragraph (3)(A) and inserting "$0", and by striking paragraph (3)(D). **Effective** for months beginning after 12-31-2018. Prior to being stricken, Code Sec. 5000A(c)(3)(D) read as follows:

(D) INDEXING OF AMOUNT.—In the case of any calendar year beginning after 2016, the applicable dollar amount shall be equal to $695, increased by an amount equal to—

(i) $695, multiplied by

(ii) the cost-of-living adjustment determined under section 1(f)(3) for the calendar year, determined by substituting "calendar year 2015" for "calendar year 1992" in subparagraph (B) thereof.

If the amount of any increase under clause (i) is not a multiple of $50, such increase shall be rounded to the next lowest multiple of $50.

• **2010, Health Care and Education Reconciliation Act of 2010 (P.L. 111-152)**

P.L. 111-152, §1002(a)(1)(A)-(D):

Amended Code Sec. 5000A(c), as added by section 1501(b) of the Patient Protection and Affordable Care Act (P.L. 111-148) and amended by section 10106, in the matter preceding clause (i) of paragraph (2)(B) by inserting "the excess of" before "the taxpayer's household income"; and inserting "for the taxable year over the amount of gross income specified in section 6012(a)(1) with respect to the taxpayer" before "for the taxable year"; by striking "0.5" and inserting "1.0" in clause (i) of paragraph (2)(B); by striking "1.0" and inserting "2.0" in clause (ii) of paragraph (2)(B); and by striking "2.0" and inserting "2.5" in clause (iii) of paragraph (2)(B). **Effective** 3-30-2010.

P.L. 111-152, §1002(a)(2)(A)-(C):

Amended Code Sec. 5000A(c), as added by section 1501(b) of the Patient Protection and Affordable Care Act (P.L. 111-148) and amended by section 10106, by striking "$750" and inserting "$695" in subparagraph (A) of paragraph (3); by striking "$495" and inserting "$325" in subparagraph (B) of paragraph (3); and in the matter preceding clause (i) of subparagraph (D) by striking "$750" and inserting "$695"; and by striking "$750" and inserting "$695" in clause (i) of subparagraph (D). **Effective** 3-30-2010.

EXCISE TAXES—MINIMUM COVERAGE REQUIREMENT

P.L. 111-152, § 1002(b)(1):

Amended Code Sec. 5000A, as added by section 1501(b) of the Patient Protection and Affordable Care Act (P.L. 111-148) and amended by section 10106, by striking subsection (c)(4)(D). **Effective** 3-30-2010. Prior to being stricken, Code Sec. 5000A(c)(4)(D) read as follows:

(D) POVERTY LINE.—

(i) IN GENERAL.—The term "poverty line" has the meaning given that term in section 2110(c)(5) of the Social Security Act (42 U.S.C. 1397jj(c)(5)).

(ii) POVERTY LINE USED.—In the case of any taxable year ending with or within a calendar year, the poverty line used shall be the most recently published poverty line as of the 1st day of such calendar year.

P.L. 111-152, § 1004(a)(1)(C):

Amended Code Sec. 5000A(c)(4)[(B)](i)-(ii), as added by section 1501(b) of the Patient Protection and Affordable Care Act (P.L. 111-148), by striking "modified gross" each place it appears and inserting "modified adjusted gross". **Effective** 3-30-2010.

P.L. 111-152, § 1004(a)(2)(B):

Amended Code Sec. 5000A(c)(4)(C), as added by section 1501(b) of the Patient Protection and Affordable Care Act (P.L. 111-148). **Effective** 3-30-2010. Prior to amendment, Code Sec. 5000A(c)(4)(C) read as follows:

(C) MODIFIED GROSS INCOME.—The term "modified gross income" means gross income—

(i) decreased by the amount of any deduction allowable under paragraph (1), (3), (4), or (10) of section 62(a),

(ii) increased by the amount of interest received or accrued during the taxable year which is exempt from tax imposed by this chapter, and

(iii) determined without regard to sections 911, 931, and 933.

• 2010, Patient Protection and Affordable Care Act (P.L. 111-148)

P.L. 111-148, § 10106(b)(2):

Amended Code Sec. 5000A(c)(1)-(2), as added by this Act. **Effective** 3-23-2010. Prior to amendment, Code Sec. 5000A(c)(1)-(2) read as follows:

(1) IN GENERAL.—The penalty determined under this subsection for any month with respect to any individual is an amount equal to $1/12$ of the applicable dollar amount for the calendar year.

(2) DOLLAR LIMITATION.—The amount of the penalty imposed by this section on any taxpayer for any taxable year with respect to all individuals for whom the taxpayer is liable under subsection (b)(3) shall not exceed an amount equal to 300 percent [of] the applicable dollar amount (determined without regard to paragraph (3)(C)) for the calendar year with or within which the taxable year ends.

P.L. 111-148, § 10106(b)(3):

Amended Code Sec. 5000A(c)(4)[(B)](i)-(iii), as added by Act Sec. 1501(b), by striking "$350" and inserting "$495". **Effective** 3-23-2010.

[Sec. 5000A(d)]

(d) APPLICABLE INDIVIDUAL.—For purposes of this section—

(1) IN GENERAL.—The term "applicable individual" means, with respect to any month, an individual other than an individual described in paragraph (2), (3), or (4).

(2) RELIGIOUS EXEMPTIONS.—

(A) RELIGIOUS CONSCIENCE EXEMPTIONS.—

(i) IN GENERAL.—Such term shall not include any individual for any month if such individual has in effect an exemption under section 1311(d)(4)(H) of the Patient Protection and Affordable Care Act which certifies that—

(I) such individual is a member of a recognized religious sect or division thereof which is described in section 1402(g)(1), and is adherent of established tenets or teachings of such sect or division as described in such section; or

(II) such individual is a member of a religious sect or division thereof which is not described in section 1402(g)(1), who relies solely on a religious method of healing, and for whom the acceptance of medical health services would be inconsistent with the religious beliefs of the individual.

(ii) SPECIAL RULES.—

(I) MEDICAL HEALTH SERVICES DEFINED.—For purposes of this subparagraph, the term "medical health services" does not include routine dental, vision and hearing services, midwifery services, vaccinations, necessary medical services provided to children, services required by law or by a third party, and such other services as the Secretary of Health and Human Services may provide in implementing section 1311(d)(4)(H) of the Patient Protection and Affordable Care Act.

(II) ATTESTATION REQUIRED.—Clause (i)(II) shall apply to an individual for months in a taxable year only if the information provided by the individual under section 1411(b)(5)(A) of such Act includes an attestation that the individual has not received medical health services during the preceding taxable year.

(B) HEALTH CARE SHARING MINISTRY.—

(i) IN GENERAL.—Such term shall not include any individual for any month if such individual is a member of a health care sharing ministry for the month.

(ii) HEALTH CARE SHARING MINISTRY.—The term "health care sharing ministry" means an organization—

(I) which is described in section 501(c)(3) and is exempt from taxation under section 501(a),

(II) members of which share a common set of ethical or religious beliefs and share medical expenses among members in accordance with those beliefs and without regard to the State in which a member resides or is employed,

(III) members of which retain membership even after they develop a medical condition,

(IV) which (or a predecessor of which) has been in existence at all times since December 31, 1999, and medical expenses of its members have been shared continuously and without interruption since at least December 31, 1999, and

(V) which conducts an annual audit which is performed by an independent certified public accounting firm in accordance with generally accepted accounting principles and which is made available to the public upon request.

(3) INDIVIDUALS NOT LAWFULLY PRESENT.—Such term shall not include an individual for any month if for the month the individual is not a citizen or national of the United States or an alien lawfully present in the United States.

(4) INCARCERATED INDIVIDUALS.—Such term shall not include an individual for any month if for the month the individual is incarcerated, other than incarceration pending the disposition of charges.

Amendments

• 2018, Substance Use–Disorder Prevention that Promotes Opioid Recovery and Treatment for Patients and Communities Act (P.L. 115-271)

P.L. 115-271, § 4003(a):

Amended Code Sec. 5000A(d)(2)(A). **Effective** for tax years beginning after 12-31-2018. For a special rule, see Act Sec. 4003(c), below. Prior to being amended, Code Sec. 5000A(d)(2)(A) read as follows:

(A) RELIGIOUS CONSCIENCE EXEMPTION.—Such term shall not include any individual for any month if such individual has in effect an exemption under section 1311(d)(4)(H) of the Patient Protection and Affordable Care Act which certifies that such individual is—

(i) a member of a recognized religious sect or division thereof which is described in section 1402(g)(1), and

(ii) an adherent of established tenets or teachings of such sect or division as described in such section.

P.L. 115-271, § 4003(c), provides:

(c) CONSTRUCTION.—Nothing in the amendment made by subsection (a) shall preempt any State law requiring the provision of medical treatment for children, especially those who are seriously ill.

• 2010, Patient Protection and Affordable Care Act (P.L. 111-148)

P.L. 111-148, § 10106(c):

Amended Code Sec. 5000A(d)(2)(A), as added by Act Sec. 1501(b). **Effective** 3-23-2010. Prior to amendment, Code Sec. 5000A(d)(2)(A) read as follows:

(A) RELIGIOUS CONSCIENCE EXEMPTION.—Such term shall not include any individual for any month if such individual has in effect an exemption under section 1311(d)(4)(H) of the Patient Protection and Affordable Care Act which certifies that such individual is a member of a recognized religious sect or division thereof described in section 1402(g)(1) and an adherent of established tenets or teachings of such sect or division as described in such section.

[Sec. 5000A(e)]

(e) EXEMPTIONS.—No penalty shall be imposed under subsection (a) with respect to—

EXCISE TAXES—MINIMUM COVERAGE REQUIREMENT

(1) INDIVIDUALS WHO CANNOT AFFORD COVERAGE.—

(A) IN GENERAL.—Any applicable individual for any month if the applicable individual's required contribution (determined on an annual basis) for coverage for the month exceeds 8 percent of such individual's household income for the taxable year described in section 1412(b)(1)(B) of the Patient Protection and Affordable Care Act. For purposes of applying this subparagraph, the taxpayer's household income shall be increased by any exclusion from gross income for any portion of the required contribution made through a salary reduction arrangement.

(B) REQUIRED CONTRIBUTION.—For purposes of this paragraph, the term "required contribution" means—

(i) in the case of an individual eligible to purchase minimum essential coverage consisting of coverage through an eligible-employer-sponsored plan, the portion of the annual premium which would be paid by the individual (without regard to whether paid through salary reduction or otherwise) for self-only coverage, or

(ii) in the case of an individual eligible only to purchase minimum essential coverage described in subsection (f)(1)(C), the annual premium for the lowest cost bronze plan available in the individual market through the Exchange in the State in the rating area in which the individual resides (without regard to whether the individual purchased a qualified health plan through the Exchange), reduced by the amount of the credit allowable under section 36B for the taxable year (determined as if the individual was covered by a qualified health plan offered through the Exchange for the entire taxable year).

(C) SPECIAL RULES FOR INDIVIDUALS RELATED TO EMPLOYEES.—For purposes of subparagraph (B)(i), if an applicable individual is eligible for minimum essential coverage through an employer by reason of a relationship to an employee, the determination under subparagraph (A) shall be made by reference to required contribution of the employee.

(D) INDEXING.—In the case of plan years beginning in any calendar year after 2014, subparagraph (A) shall be applied by substituting for "8 percent" the percentage the Secretary of Health and Human Services determines reflects the excess of the rate of premium growth between the preceding calendar year and 2013 over the rate of income growth for such period.

(2) TAXPAYERS WITH INCOME BELOW FILING THRESHOLD.—Any applicable individual for any month during a calendar year if the individual's household income for the taxable year described in section 1412(b)(1)(B) of the Patient Protection and Affordable Care Act is less than the amount of gross income specified in section 6012(a)(1) with respect to the taxpayer.

(3) MEMBERS OF INDIAN TRIBES.—Any applicable individual for any month during which the individual is a member of an Indian tribe (as defined in section 45A(c)(6)).

(4) MONTHS DURING SHORT COVERAGE GAPS.—

(A) IN GENERAL.—Any month the last day of which occurred during a period in which the applicable individual was not covered by minimum essential coverage for a continuous period of less than 3 months.

(B) SPECIAL RULES.—For purposes of applying this paragraph—

(i) the length of a continuous period shall be determined without regard to the calendar years in which months in such period occur,

(ii) if a continuous period is greater than the period allowed under subparagraph (A), no exception shall be provided under this paragraph for any month in the period, and

(iii) if there is more than 1 continuous period described in subparagraph (A) covering months in a calendar year, the exception provided by this paragraph shall only apply to months in the first of such periods.

The Secretary shall prescribe rules for the collection of the penalty imposed by this section in cases where continuous periods include months in more than 1 taxable year.

(5) HARDSHIPS.—Any applicable individual who for any month is determined by the Secretary of Health and Human Services under section 1311(d)(4)(H) to have suffered a hardship with respect to the capability to obtain coverage under a qualified health plan.

Amendments

• **2010, Health Care and Education Reconciliation Act of 2010 (P.L. 111-152)**

P.L. 111-152, § 1002(b)(2)(A)-(B):

Amended Code Sec. 5000A(e)(2), as added by section 1501(b) of the Patient Protection and Affordable Care Act (P.L. 111-148) and amended by section 10106, by striking "UNDER 100 PERCENT OF POVERTY LINE" and inserting "BELOW FILING THRESHOLD" [in the heading]; and by striking all that follows "less than" and inserting "the amount of gross income specified in section 6012(a)(1) with respect to the taxpayer.". **Effective** 3-30-2010. Prior to being stricken, all that followed "less than" in Code Sec. 5000A(e)(2) read as follows:

100 percent of the poverty line for the size of the family involved (determined in the same manner as under subsection (b)(4)).

• **2010, Patient Protection and Affordable Care Act (P.L. 111-148)**

P.L. 111-148, § 10106(d):

Amended Code Sec. 5000A(e)(1)(C), as added by Act Sec. 1501(b). **Effective** 3-23-2010. Prior to amendment, Code Sec. 5000A(e)(1)(C) read as follows:

(C) SPECIAL RULES FOR INDIVIDUALS RELATED TO EMPLOYEES.—For purposes of subparagraph (B)(i), if an applicable individual is eligible for minimum essential coverage through an employer by reason of a relationship to an employee, the determination shall be made by reference to the affordability of the coverage to the employee.

[Sec. 5000A(f)]

(f) MINIMUM ESSENTIAL COVERAGE.—For purposes of this section—

(1) IN GENERAL.—The term "minimum essential coverage" means any of the following:

(A) GOVERNMENT SPONSORED PROGRAMS.—Coverage under—

(i) the Medicare program under part A of title XVIII of the Social Security Act,

(ii) the Medicaid program under title XIX of the Social Security Act,

(iii) the CHIP program under title XXI of the Social Security Act or under a qualified CHIP look-alike program (as defined in section 2107(g) of the Social Security Act),

(iv) medical coverage under chapter 55 of title 10, United States Code, including coverage under the TRICARE program;

(v) a health care program under chapter 17 or 18 of title 38, United States Code, as determined by the Secretary of Veterans Affairs, in coordination with the Secretary of Health and Human Services and the Secretary [of the Treasury],

(vi) a health plan under section 2504(e) of title 22, United States Code (relating to Peace Corps volunteers); or

(vii) the Nonappropriated Fund Health Benefits Program of the Department of Defense, established under section 349 of the National Defense Authorization Act for Fiscal Year 1995 (Public Law 103–337; 10 U.S.C. 1587 note).

(B) EMPLOYER-SPONSORED PLAN.—Coverage under an eligible employer-sponsored plan.

(C) PLANS IN THE INDIVIDUAL MARKET.—Coverage under a health plan offered in the individual market within a State.

(D) GRANDFATHERED HEALTH PLAN.—Coverage under a grandfathered health plan.

(E) OTHER COVERAGE.—Such other health benefits coverage, such as a State health benefits risk pool, as the Secretary of Health and Human Services, in coordination with the Secretary, recognizes for purposes of this subsection.

(2) ELIGIBLE EMPLOYER-SPONSORED PLAN.—The term "eligible employer-sponsored plan" means, with respect to any employee, a group health plan or group health insurance coverage offered by an employer to the employee which is—

EXCISE TAXES—INDOOR TANNING SERVICES

(A) a governmental plan (within the meaning of section 2791(d)(8) of the Public Health Service Act), or

(B) any other plan or coverage offered in the small or large group market within a State.

Such term shall include a grandfathered health plan described in paragraph (1)(D) offered in a group market.

(3) EXCEPTED BENEFITS NOT TREATED AS MINIMUM ESSENTIAL COVERAGE.—The term "minimum essential coverage" shall not include health insurance coverage which consists of coverage of excepted benefits—

(A) described in paragraph (1) of subsection (c) of section 2791 of the Public Health Service Act; or

(B) described in paragraph (2), (3), or (4) of such subsection if the benefits are provided under a separate policy, certificate, or contract of insurance.

(4) INDIVIDUALS RESIDING OUTSIDE UNITED STATES OR RESIDENTS OF TERRITORIES.—Any applicable individual shall be treated as having minimum essential coverage for any month—

(A) if such month occurs during any period described in subparagraph (A) or (B) of section 911(d)(1) which is applicable to the individual, or

(B) if such individual is a bona fide resident of any possession of the United States (as determined under section 937(a)) for such month.

(5) INSURANCE-RELATED TERMS.—Any term used in this section which is also used in title I of the Patient Protection and Affordable Care Act shall have the same meaning as when used in such title.

Amendments

• **2018, HEALTHY KIDS Act (P.L. 115-120)**

P.L. 115-120, §3002(g)(2)(A), Div. C:

Amended Code Sec. 5000A(f)(1)(A)(iii) by inserting "or under a qualified CHIP look-alike program (as defined in section 2107(g) of the Social Security Act)" before the comma at the end. **Effective** with respect to tax years beginning after 12-31-2017.

• **2010 (P.L. 111-173)**

P.L. 111-173, §1(a):

Amended Code Sec. 5000A(f)(1)(A)(v), as added by section 1501(b) of the Patient Protection and Affordable Care Act (P.L. 111-148). **Effective** as if included in section 1501(b) of the Patient Protection and Affordable Care Act (P.L. 111-148) [**effective** for tax years ending after 12-31-2013.—CCH]. Prior to amendment, Code Sec. 5000A(f)(1)(A)(v) read as follows:

(v) the veteran's health care program under chapter 17 of title 38, United States Code,

• **2010, TRICARE Affirmation Act (P.L. 111-159)**

P.L. 111-159, §2(a):

Amended Code Sec. 5000A(f)(1)(A), as added by section 1501(b) of the Patient Protection and Affordable Care Act (P.L. 111-148), by striking clause (iv) and inserting a new clause (iv); by striking "or" at the end of clause (v); by striking the period at the end of clause (vi) and inserting "; or"; and by inserting after clause (vi) a new clause (vii). **Effective** as if included in section 1501(b) of the Patient Protection and Affordable Care Act (P.L. 111-148) [**effective** for tax years ending after 12-31-2013.—CCH]. Prior to being stricken, Code Sec. 5000A(f)(1)(A)(iv) read as follows:

(iv) the TRICARE for Life program,

[Sec. 5000A(g)]

(g) ADMINISTRATION AND PROCEDURE.—

(1) IN GENERAL.—The penalty provided by this section shall be paid upon notice and demand by the Secretary, and except as provided in paragraph (2), shall be assessed and collected in the same manner as an assessable penalty under subchapter B of chapter 68.

(2) SPECIAL RULES.—Notwithstanding any other provision of law—

(A) WAIVER OF CRIMINAL PENALTIES.—In the case of any failure by a taxpayer to timely pay any penalty imposed by this section, such taxpayer shall not be subject to any criminal prosecution or penalty with respect to such failure.

(B) LIMITATIONS ON LIENS AND LEVIES.—The Secretary shall not—

(i) file notice of lien with respect to any property of a taxpayer by reason of any failure to pay the penalty imposed by this section, or

(ii) levy on any such property with respect to such failure.

Amendments

• **2010, Patient Protection and Affordable Care Act (P.L. 111-148)**

P.L. 111-148, §1501(b):

Amended subtitle D by adding at the end a new chapter 48 (Code Sec. 5000A). **Effective** for tax years ending after 12-31-2013.

CHAPTER 49—COSMETIC SERVICES

Sec. 5000B.   Imposition of tax on indoor tanning services.

[Sec. 5000B]

SEC. 5000B. IMPOSITION OF TAX ON INDOOR TANNING SERVICES.

[Sec. 5000B(a)]

(a) IN GENERAL.—There is hereby imposed on any indoor tanning service a tax equal to 10 percent of the amount paid for such service (determined without regard to this section), whether paid by insurance or otherwise.

[Sec. 5000B(b)]

(b) INDOOR TANNING SERVICE.—For purposes of this section—

(1) IN GENERAL.—The term "indoor tanning service" means a service employing any electronic product designed to incorporate 1 or more ultraviolet lamps and intended for the irradiation of an individual by ultraviolet radiation, with wavelengths in air between 200 and 400 nanometers, to induce skin tanning.

(2) EXCLUSION OF PHOTOTHERAPY SERVICES.—Such term does not include any phototherapy service performed by a licensed medical professional.

[Sec. 5000B(c)]

(c) PAYMENT OF TAX.—

(1) IN GENERAL.—The tax imposed by this section shall be paid by the individual on whom the service is performed.

(2) COLLECTION.—Every person receiving a payment for services on which a tax is imposed under subsection (a) shall collect the amount of the tax from the individual on whom the service is performed and remit such tax quarterly to the Secretary at such time and in such manner as provided by the Secretary.

(3) SECONDARY LIABILITY.—Where any tax imposed by subsection (a) is not paid at the time payments for indoor tanning services are made, then to the extent that such tax is not collected, such tax shall be paid by the person who performs the service.

EXCISE TAXES—FOREIGN PROCUREMENT

Amendments

• 2010, Patient Protection and Affordable Care Act (P.L. 111-148)

P.L. 111-148, §10907(b):

Amended subtitle D, as amended by this Act, by adding at the end a new Chapter 49 (Code Sec. 5000B). **Effective** for services performed on or after 7-1-2010.

P.L. 111-148, §10907(a), provides:

(a) IN GENERAL.—The provisions of, and amendments made by, section 9017 of this Act are hereby deemed null, void, and of no effect.

P.L. 111-148, §9017(a), provided:

(a) IN GENERAL.—Subtitle D of the Internal Revenue Code of 1986, as amended by this Act, is amended by adding at the end the following new chapter [Chapter 49 (Code Sec. 5000B)]:

SEC. 5000B. IMPOSITION OF TAX ON ELECTIVE COSMETIC MEDICAL PROCEDURES.

(a) IN GENERAL.—There is hereby imposed on any cosmetic surgery and medical procedure a tax equal to 5 percent of the amount paid for such procedure (determined without regard to this section), whether paid by insurance or otherwise.

(b) COSMETIC SURGERY AND MEDICAL PROCEDURE.—For purposes of this section, the term "cosmetic surgery and medical procedure" means any cosmetic surgery (as defined in section 213(d)(9)(B)) or other similar procedure which—

(1) is performed by a licensed medical professional, and

(2) is not necessary to ameliorate a deformity arising from, or directly related to, a congenital abnormality, a personal injury resulting from an accident or trauma, or disfiguring disease.

(c) PAYMENT OF TAX.—

(1) IN GENERAL.—The tax imposed by this section shall be paid by the individual on whom the procedure is performed.

(2) COLLECTION.—Every person receiving a payment for procedures on which a tax is imposed under subsection (a) shall collect the amount of the tax from the individual on whom the procedure is performed and remit such tax quarterly to the Secretary at such time and in such manner as provided by the Secretary.

(3) SECONDARY LIABILITY.—Where any tax imposed by subsection (a) is not paid at the time payments for cosmetic surgery and medical procedures are made, then to the extent that such tax is not collected, such tax shall be paid by the person who performs the procedure.

CHAPTER 50—FOREIGN PROCUREMENT

Sec. 5000C. Imposition of tax on certain foreign procurement.

[Sec. 5000C]

SEC. 5000C. IMPOSITION OF TAX ON CERTAIN FOREIGN PROCUREMENT.

[Sec. 5000C(a)]

(a) IMPOSITION OF TAX.—There is hereby imposed on any foreign person that receives a specified Federal procurement payment a tax equal to 2 percent of the amount of such specified Federal procurement payment.

[Sec. 5000C(b)]

(b) SPECIFIED FEDERAL PROCUREMENT PAYMENT.—For purposes of this section, the term "specified Federal procurement payment" means any payment made pursuant to a contract with the Government of the United States for—

(1) the provision of goods, if such goods are manufactured or produced in any country which is not a party to an international procurement agreement with the United States, or

(2) the provision of services, if such services are provided in any country which is not a party to an international procurement agreement with the United States.

[Sec. 5000C(c)]

(c) FOREIGN PERSON.—For purposes of this section, the term "foreign person" means any person other than a United States person.

[Sec. 5000C(d)]

(d) ADMINISTRATIVE PROVISIONS.—

(1) WITHHOLDING.—The amount deducted and withheld under chapter 3 shall be increased by the amount of tax imposed by this section on such payment.

(2) OTHER ADMINISTRATIVE PROVISIONS.—For purposes of subtitle F, any tax imposed by this section shall be treated as a tax imposed by subtitle A.

Amendments

• 2011, James Zadroga 9/11 Health and Compensation Act of 2010 (P.L. 111-347)

P.L. 111-347, §301(a)(1):

Amended subtitle D by adding at the end a new Chapter 50 (Code Sec. 5000C). **Effective** for payments received pursuant to contracts entered into on and after 1-2-2011.

CHAPTER 50A—DESIGNATED DRUGS

Sec. 5000D. Designated drugs during noncompliance periods.

[Sec. 5000D]

SEC. 5000D. DESIGNATED DRUGS DURING NONCOMPLIANCE PERIODS.

[Sec. 5000D(a)]

(a) IN GENERAL.—There is hereby imposed on the sale by the manufacturer, producer, or importer of any designated drug during a day described in subsection (b) a tax in an amount such that the applicable percentage is equal to the ratio of—

(1) such tax, divided by

(2) the sum of such tax and the price for which so sold.

[Sec. 5000D(b)]

(b) NONCOMPLIANCE PERIODS.—A day is described in this subsection with respect to a designated drug if it is a day during one of the following periods:

(1) The period beginning on the March 1st (or, in the case of initial price applicability year 2026, the October 2nd) immediately following the date on which such drug is included on the list published under section 1192(a) of the Social Security Act and ending on the earlier of—

(A) the first date on which the manufacturer of such designated drug has in place an agreement described in section 1193(a) of such Act with respect to such drug, or

(B) the date that the Secretary of Health and Human Services has made a determination described in section 1192(c)(1) of such Act with respect to such designated drug.

(2) The period beginning on the November 2nd immediately following the March 1st described in paragraph (1) (or, in the case of initial price applicability year 2026, the August 2nd immediately following the October 2nd described in such paragraph) and ending on the earlier of—

(A) the first date on which the manufacturer of such designated drug and the Secretary of Health and Human Services have agreed to a maximum fair price under an agreement described in section 1193(a) of the Social Security Act, or

(B) the date that the Secretary of Health and Human Services has made a determination described in section 1192(c)(1) of such Act with respect to such designated drug.

(3) In the case of any designated drug which is a selected drug (as defined in section 1192(c) of the Social Security Act) that the Secretary of Health and Human Services has selected for renegotiation under section 1194(f) of such Act, the period beginning on the November 2nd of the year that begins 2 years prior to the first initial price applicability year of the price applicability period for which the maximum fair price established pursuant to such renegotiation applies and ending on the earlier of—

(A) the first date on which the manufacturer of such designated drug has agreed to a renegotiated maximum fair price under such agreement, or

(B) the date that the Secretary of Health and Human Services has made a determination described in section 1192(c)(1) of such Act with respect to such designated drug.

(4) With respect to information that is required to be submitted to the Secretary of Health and Human Services under an agreement described in section 1193(a) of the Social Security Act, the period beginning on the date on which such Secretary certifies that such information is overdue and ending on the date that such information is so submitted.

[Sec. 5000D(c)]

(c) SUSPENSION OF TAX.—

(1) IN GENERAL.—A day shall not be taken into account as a day during a period described in subsection (b) if such day is also a day during the period—

(A) beginning on the first date on which—

(i) the notice of terminations of all applicable agreements of the manufacturer have been received by the Secretary of Health and Human Services, and

(ii) none of the drugs of the manufacturer of the designated drug are covered by an agreement under section 1860D-14A or 1860D-14C of the Social Security Act, and

(B) ending on the last day of February following the earlier of—

(i) the first day after the date described in subparagraph (A) on which the manufacturer enters into any subsequent applicable agreement, or

(ii) the first date any drug of the manufacturer of the designated drug is covered by an agreement under section 1860D-14A or 1860D-14C of the Social Security Act.

(2) APPLICABLE AGREEMENT.—For purposes of this subsection, the term "applicable agreement" means the following:

(A) An agreement under—

(i) the Medicare coverage gap discount program under section 1860D-14A of the Social Security Act, or

(ii) the manufacturer discount program under section 1860D-14C of such Act.

(B) A rebate agreement described in section 1927(b) of such Act.

[Sec. 5000D(d)]

(d) APPLICABLE PERCENTAGE.—For purposes of this section, the term "applicable percentage" means—

(1) in the case of sales of a designated drug during the first 90 days described in subsection (b) with respect to such drug, 65 percent,

(2) in the case of sales of such drug during the 91st day through the 180th day described in subsection (b) with respect to such drug, 75 percent,

(3) in the case of sales of such drug during the 181st day through the 270th day described in subsection (b) with respect to such drug, 85 percent, and

(4) in the case of sales of such drug during any subsequent day, 95 percent.

[Sec. 5000D(e)]

(e) DEFINITIONS.—For purposes of this section—

(1) DESIGNATED DRUG.—The term "designated drug" means any negotiation-eligible drug (as defined in section 1192(d) of the Social Security Act) included on the list published under section 1192(a) of such Act which is manufactured or produced in the United States or entered into the United States for consumption, use, or warehousing.

(2) UNITED STATES.—The term "United States" has the meaning given such term by section 4612(a)(4).

(3) OTHER TERMS.—The terms "initial price applicability year", "price applicability period", and "maximum fair price" have the meaning given such terms in section 1191 of the Social Security Act.

[Sec. 5000D(f)]

(f) SPECIAL RULES.—

(1) COORDINATION WITH RULES FOR POSSESSIONS OF THE UNITED STATES.—Rules similar to the rules of paragraphs (2) and (4) of section 4132(c) shall apply for purposes of this section.

(2) ANTI-ABUSE RULE.—In the case of a sale which was timed for the purpose of avoiding the tax imposed by this section, the Secretary may treat such sale as occurring during a day described in subsection (b).

[Sec. 5000D(g)]

(g) EXPORTS.—Rules similar to the rules of section 4662(e) (other than section 4662(e)(2)(A)(ii)(II)) shall apply for purposes of this chapter.

[Sec. 5000D(h)]

(h) REGULATIONS.—The Secretary shall prescribe such regulations and other guidance as may be necessary to carry out this section.

Amendments

• **2022, Inflation Reduction Act of 2022 (P.L. 117-169)**
P.L. 117-169, § 11003(a):
Amended subtitle D by adding at the end a new chapter 50A (Code Sec. 5000D).
Effective for sales after 8-16-2022.

[The next page is 4101.]

Subtitle E—Alcohol, Tobacco, and Certain Other Excise Taxes

CHAPTER 51.	Distilled spirits, wines, and beer.
CHAPTER 52.	Tobacco products and cigarette papers and tubes.
CHAPTER 53.	Machine guns, destructive devices, and certain other firearms.
CHAPTER 54.	Greenmail.
CHAPTER 55.	Structured settlement factoring transactions.

CHAPTER 51—DISTILLED SPIRITS, WINES, AND BEER

SUBCHAPTER A.	Gallonage and occupational taxes.
SUBCHAPTER B.	Qualification requirements for distilled spirits plants.
SUBCHAPTER C.	Operation of distilled spirits plants.
SUBCHAPTER D.	Industrial use of distilled spirits.
SUBCHAPTER E.	General provisions relating to distilled spirits.
SUBCHAPTER F.	Bonded and taxpaid wine premises.
SUBCHAPTER G.	Breweries.
SUBCHAPTER H.	Miscellaneous plants and warehouses.
SUBCHAPTER I.	Miscellaneous general provisions.
SUBCHAPTER J.	Penalties, seizures, and forfeitures relating to liquors.

Subchapter A—Gallonage and Occupational Taxes

Part I.	Gallonage taxes.
Part II.	Occupational tax.

PART I—GALLONAGE TAXES

Subpart A.	Distilled spirits.
Subpart B.	[Repealed.]
Subpart C.	Wines.
Subpart D.	Beer.
Subpart E.	General provisions.

Subpart A—Distilled Spirits

Sec. 5001.	Imposition, rate, and attachment of tax.
Sec. 5002.	Definitions.
Sec. 5003.	Cross references to exemptions, etc.
Sec. 5004.	Lien for tax.
Sec. 5005.	Persons liable for tax.
Sec. 5006.	Determination of tax.
Sec. 5007.	Collection of tax on distilled spirits.
Sec. 5008.	Abatement, remission, refund, and allowance for loss or destruction of distilled spirits.
Sec. 5010.	Credit for wine content and for flavors content.
Sec. 5011.	Income tax credit for average cost of carrying excise tax.

[Sec. 5001]

SEC. 5001. IMPOSITION, RATE, AND ATTACHMENT OF TAX.

[Sec. 5001(a)]

(a) RATE OF TAX—

(1) IN GENERAL.—There is hereby imposed on all distilled spirits produced in or imported into the United States a tax at the rate of $13.50 on each proof gallon and a proportionate tax at the like rate on all fractional parts of a proof gallon.

(2) PRODUCTS CONTAINING DISTILLED SPIRITS.—All products of distillation, by whatever name known, which contain distilled spirits, on which the tax imposed by law has not been paid, and any alcoholic ingredient added to such products, shall be considered and taxed as distilled spirits.

(3) WINES CONTAINING MORE THAN 24 PERCENT ALCOHOL BY VOLUME.—Wines containing more than 24 percent of alcohol by volume shall be taxed as distilled spirits.

(4) DISTILLED SPIRITS WITHDRAWN FREE OF TAX.—Any person who removes, sells, transports, or uses distilled spirits, withdrawn free of tax under section 5214(a) or section 7510, in violation of laws or regulations now or hereafter in force pertaining thereto, and all such distilled spirits shall be subject to all provisions of law relating to distilled spirits subject to tax, including those requiring payment of the tax thereon; and the person so removing, selling, transporting, or using the distilled spirits shall be required to pay such tax.

(5) DENATURED DISTILLED SPIRITS OR ARTICLES.—Any person who produces, withdraws, sells, transports, or uses denatured distilled spirits or articles in violation of laws or regulations now or hereafter in force pertaining thereto, and all such denatured distilled spirits or articles shall be subject to all provisions of law pertaining to distilled spirits that are not denatured, including those requiring the payment of tax thereon; and the person so producing, withdrawing, selling, transporting, or using the denatured distilled spirits or articles shall be required to pay such tax.

(6) FRUIT-FLAVOR CONCENTRATES.—If any volatile fruit-flavor concentrate (or any fruit mash or juice from which such concentrate is produced) containing one-half of 1 percent or more of alcohol by volume, which is manufactured free from tax under section 5511, is sold, transported, or used by any person in violation of the provisions of this chapter or regulations promulgated thereunder, such person and such concentrate, mash, or juice shall be subject to all provisions of this chapter pertaining to distilled spirits and wines, including those requiring the payment of tax thereon; and the person so selling, transporting, or using such concentrate, mash, or juice shall be required to pay such tax.

ALCOHOL TAXES—GALLONAGE TAXES

(7) IMPORTED LIQUEURS AND CORDIALS.—Imported liqueurs and cordials, or similar compounds, containing distilled spirits, shall be taxed as distilled spirits.

(8) IMPORTED DISTILLED SPIRITS WITHDRAWN FOR BEVERAGE PURPOSES.—There is hereby imposed on all imported distilled spirits withdrawn from customs custody under section 5232 without payment of the internal revenue tax, and thereafter withdrawn from bonded premises for beverage purposes, an additional tax equal to the duty which would have been paid had such spirits been imported for beverage purposes, less the duty previously paid thereon.

(9) ALCOHOLIC COMPOUNDS FROM PUERTO RICO.—Except as provided in section 5314, upon bay rum, or any article containing distilled spirits, brought from Puerto Rico into the United States for consumption or sale there is hereby imposed a tax on the spirits contained therein at the rate imposed on distilled spirits produced in the United States.

Amendments

• **1994, Uruguay Round Agreements Act (P.L. 103-465)**

P.L. 103-465, §136(a):

Amended Code Sec. 5001(a) by striking paragraph (3) and redesignating the following paragraphs accordingly. **Effective** 1-1-95. Prior to amendment, Code Sec. 5001(a)(3) read as follows:

(3) IMPORTED PERFUMES CONTAINING DISTILLED SPIRITS.—There is hereby imposed on all perfumes imported into the United States containing distilled spirits a tax of $13.50 per wine gallon, and a proportionate tax at a like rate on all fractional parts of such wine gallon.

• **1990, Omnibus Budget Reconciliation Act of 1990 (P.L. 101-508)**

P.L. 101-508, §11201(a)(1):

Amended Code Sec. 5001(a)(1) by striking "$12.50" and inserting "$13.50". **Effective** 1-1-91.

P.L. 101-508, §11201(a)(1):

Amended Code Sec. 5001(a)(3) by striking "$12.50" and inserting "$13.50". **Effective** 1-1-91.

• **1984, Deficit Reduction Act of 1984 (P.L. 98-369)**

P.L. 98-369, §27(a)(1):

Amended Code Sec. 5001(a)(1) and (3) by striking out "$10.50" and inserting in lieu thereof $12.50. **Effective** 10-1-85.

• **1979, Trade Agreements Act of 1979 (P.L. 96-39)**

P.L. 96-39, §802:

Amended Code Sec. 5001(a)(1). **Effective** 1-1-80. Prior to amendment, Code Sec. 5001(a)(1) read as follows:

(a) RATE OF TAX—

(1) GENERAL.—There is hereby imposed on all distilled spirits in bond or produced in or imported into the United States an internal revenue tax at the rate of $10.50 on each proof gallon or wine gallon when below proof and a proportionate tax at a like rate on all fractional parts of such proof or wine gallon.

P.L. 96-39, §805(d):

Amended Code Sec. 5001(a)(2). **Effective** 1-1-80. Prior to amendment, Code Sec. 5001(a)(2) read as follows:

(2) PRODUCTS CONTAINING DISTILLED SPIRITS.—All products of distillation, by whatever name known, which contain distilled spirits, on which the tax imposed by law has not been paid, shall be considered and taxed as distilled spirits.

• **1965, Excise Tax Reduction Act of 1965 (P.L. 89-44)**

P.L. 89-44, §501(a):

Amended Code Sec. 5001(a)(1) and (3) by deleting the last sentences thereof. Prior to amendment, such sentences read: "On and after July 1, 1965, the rate of tax imposed by this paragraph shall be $9 in lieu of $10.50."

• **1964, Excise Tax Rate Extension Act of 1964 (P.L. 88-348)**

P.L. 88-348, §2(a)(4) and (5):

Substituted "1965" for "1964" wherever it appeared in Secs. 5001(a)(1) and (3).

• **1963, Tax Rate Extension Act of 1963 (P.L. 88-52)**

P.L. 88-52, §3(a)(4) and (5):

Substituted "1964" for "1963" wherever it appeared in Secs. 5001(a)(1) and (3).

• **1962, Tax Rate Extension Act of 1962 (P.L. 87-508)**

P.L. 87-508, §3(a)(3) and (4):

Substituted "1963" for "1962" wherever it appeared in Secs. 5001(a)(1) and (3).

• **1961, Tax Rate Extension Act of 1961 (P.L. 87-72)**

P.L. 87-72, §3(a)(4) and (5):

Substituted "1962" for "1961" wherever it appeared in Secs. 5001(a)(1) and (3).

• **1960, Public Debt and Tax Rate Extension Act of 1960 (P.L. 86-564)**

P.L. 86-564, §202(a):

Substituted "July 1, 1961" for "July 1, 1960" in Secs. 5001(a)(1) and (3).

• **1959, Tax Rate Extension Act of 1959 (P.L. 86-75)**

P.L. 86-75, §3(a):

Substituted "July 1, 1960" for "July 1, 1959" in Secs. 5001(a)(1) and (3).

[Sec. 5001(b)]

(b) TIME OF ATTACHMENT ON DISTILLED SPIRITS.—The tax shall attach to distilled spirits as soon as this substance is in existence as such, whether it be subsequently separated as pure or impure spirits, or be immediately, or at any subsequent time, transferred into any other substance, either in the process of original production or by any subsequent process.

[Sec. 5001(c)]

(c) REDUCED RATE.—

(1) IN GENERAL.—In the case of a distilled spirits operation, the otherwise applicable tax rate under subsection (a)(1) shall be—

(A) $2.70 per proof gallon on the first 100,000 proof gallons of distilled spirits, and

(B) $13.34 per proof gallon on the first 22,130,000 of proof gallons of distilled spirits to which subparagraph (A) does not apply,

which have been distilled or processed by such operation and removed during the calendar year for consumption or sale, or which have been imported by the importer into the United States during the calendar year but only if the importer is an electing importer under paragraph (3) and the proof gallons of distilled spirits have been assigned to the importer pursuant to such paragraph.

(2) CONTROLLED GROUPS.—

(A) IN GENERAL.—In the case of a controlled group, the proof gallon quantities specified under subparagraphs (A) and (B) of paragraph (1) shall be applied to such group and apportioned among the members of such group in such manner as the Secretary or their delegate shall by regulations prescribe.

(B) DEFINITION.—For purposes of subparagraph (A), the term "controlled group" shall have the meaning given such term by subsection (a) of section 1563, except that "more than 50 percent" shall be substituted for "at least 80 percent" each place it appears in such subsection.

(C) RULES FOR NON-CORPORATIONS.—Under regulations prescribed by the Secretary, principles similar to the principles of subparagraphs (A) and (B) shall be applied to a group under common control where one or more of the persons is not a corporation.

(D) SINGLE TAXPAYER.—Pursuant to rules issued by the Secretary, two or more entities (whether or not under common control) that produce or process distilled spirits under a license, franchise, or other arrangement shall be treated as a single taxpayer for purposes of the application of this subsection.

(3) REDUCED TAX RATE FOR FOREIGN MANUFACTURERS AND IMPORTERS.—

(A) IN GENERAL.—In the case of any proof gallons of distilled spirits which have been produced outside of the United States and imported into the United States, the rate of tax applicable under paragraph (1) (referred to in this paragraph as the "reduced tax rate") may be assigned by the distilled spirits operation (provided that such operation makes an election described in subparagraph (B)(ii)) to any electing importer of such proof gallons pursuant to the requirements established by the Secretary under subparagraph (B).

ALCOHOL TAXES—GALLONAGE TAXES

(B) ASSIGNMENT.—The Secretary of the Treasury, after consultation with the Secretary of the Department of Homeland Security, shall, through such rules, regulations, and procedures as are determined appropriate, establish procedures for assignment of the reduced tax rate provided under this paragraph, which shall include—

(i) a limitation to ensure that the number of proof gallons of distilled spirits for which the reduced tax rate has been assigned by a distilled spirits operation—

(I) to any importer does not exceed the number of proof gallons produced by such operation during the calendar year which were imported into the United States by such importer, and

(II) to all importers does not exceed the 22,230,000 proof gallons of distilled spirits to which the reduced tax rate applies,

(ii) procedures that allow the election of a distilled spirits operation to assign and an importer to receive the reduced tax rate provided under this paragraph,

(iii) requirements that the distilled spirits operation provide any information as the Secretary determines necessary and appropriate for purposes of carrying out this paragraph, and

(iv) procedures that allow for revocation of eligibility of the distilled spirits operation and the importer for the reduced tax rate provided under this paragraph in the case of any erroneous or fraudulent information provided under clause (iii) which the Secretary deems to be material to qualifying for such reduced rate.

(C) CONTROLLED GROUP.—

(i) IN GENERAL.—For purposes of this section, any importer making an election described in subparagraph (B)(ii) shall be deemed to be a member of the controlled group of the distilled spirits operation, as described under paragraph (2).

(ii) APPORTIONMENT.—For purposes of this paragraph, in the case of a controlled group, rules similar to section 5051(a)(5)(B) shall apply.

(4) REFUNDS IN LIEU OF REDUCED RATES FOR FOREIGN PRODUCTION REMOVED AFTER DECEMBER 31, 2022.—

(A) IN GENERAL.—In the case of any proof gallons of distilled spirits which have been produced outside the United States and imported into the United States, if such proof gallons of distilled spirits are removed after December 31, 2022—

(i) paragraph (1) shall not apply, and

(ii) the amount determined under subparagraph (B) shall be allowed as a refund, determined for periods not less frequently than quarterly, to the importer in the same manner as if such amount were an overpayment of tax imposed by this section.

(B) AMOUNT OF REFUND.—The amount determined under this subparagraph with respect to any importer for any period is an amount equal to the sum of—

(i) the excess (if any) of—

(I) the amount of tax imposed under this subpart on proof gallons of distilled spirits referred to in subparagraph (A) which were removed during such period, over

(II) the amount of tax which would have been imposed under this subpart on such proof gallons of distilled spirits if this section were applied without regard to this paragraph, plus

(ii) the amount of interest which would be allowed and paid on an overpayment of tax at the overpayment rate established under section 6621(a)(1) (without regard to the second sentence thereof) were such rate applied to the excess (if any) determined under clause (i) for the number of days in the filing period for which the refund under this paragraph is being determined.

(C) APPLICATION OF RULES RELATED TO ELECTIONS AND ASSIGNMENTS.—Subparagraph (A)(ii) shall apply only if the importer is an electing importer under paragraph (3) and the proof gallons of distilled spirits have been assigned to the importer pursuant to such paragraph.

(D) RULES FOR REFUNDS WITHIN 90 DAYS.—For purposes of refunds allowed under this paragraph, section 6611(e) shall be applied by substituting "90 days" for "45 days" each place it appears.

(5) PROCESSED DISTILLED SPIRITS.—A distilled spirit shall not be treated as processed for purposes of this subsection unless a process described in section 5002(a)(5)(A) (other than bottling) is performed with respect to such distilled spirit.

Amendments

• **2020, Taxpayer Certainty and Disaster Tax Relief Act of 2020 (P.L. 116-260)**

P.L. 116-260, §106(g)(1)(A)-(C), Div. EE:

Amended Code Sec. 5001(c) in the heading, by striking "TEMPORARY REDUCED RATE" and inserting "REDUCED RATE", in paragraph (3)(B), by striking "The Secretary" and inserting "The Secretary of the Treasury, after consultation with the Secretary of the Department of Homeland Security,", and by striking paragraph (4). **Effective** for distilled spirits removed after 12-31-2020. Prior to being stricken, Code Sec. 5001(c)(4) read as follows:

(4) TERMINATION.—This subsection shall not apply to distilled spirits removed after December 31, 2020.

P.L. 116-260, §107(a)(1), Div. EE:

Amended Code Sec. 5001(c), as amended by the preceding provisions of this Act, by adding at the end a new paragraph (4). **Effective** for distilled spirits brought into the United States and removed after 12-31-2022. For a special rule, see Act Sec. 107(e)-(g), Div. EE, below.

P.L. 116-260, §107(e)-(g), Div. EE, provides:

(e) ADMINISTRATION OF REFUNDS.—The Secretary of the Treasury (or the Secretary's delegate within the Department of the Treasury) shall implement and administer sections 5001(c)(4), 5041(c)(7), and 5051(a)(6) of the Internal Revenue Code of 1986, as added by this Act, in coordination with the United States Customs and Border Protection of the Department of Homeland Security.

(f) REGULATIONS.—The Secretary of the Treasury (or the Secretary's delegate within the Department of the Treasury) shall prescribe such regulations as may be necessary or appropriate to carry out the purposes of this section, including regulations to require foreign producers to provide information necessary to enforce the volume limitations under sections 5001(c), 5041(c), and 5051(a) of such Code.

(g) REPORT.—Not later than 180 days after the date of the enactment of this Act, the Secretary of the Treasury (or the Secretary's delegate within the Department of the Treasury) shall, in coordination with the United States Customs and Border Protection of the Department of Homeland Security, prepare, submit to Congress, and make publicly available a report detailing the plans for implementing and administering sections 5001(c)(4), 5041(c)(7), and 5051(a)(6) of such Code, as added by this Act.

P.L. 116-260, §109(a), Div. EE:

Amended Code Sec. 5001(c), as amended by the preceding provisions of this Act, by adding at the end a new paragraph (5). **Effective** for distilled spirits removed after 12-31-2021.

P.L. 116-260, §110(c)(1), Div. EE:

Amended Code Sec. 5001(c)(2)(D) by striking "marketed under a similar brand, license" and inserting "under a license". **Effective** for beer, wine, and distilled spirits removed after 12-31-2020.

P.L. 116-260, §110(c)(2), Div. EE:

Amended Code Sec. 5001(c)(2)(D) by inserting "or process" after "that produce". **Effective** for beer, wine, and distilled spirits removed after 12-31-2020.

• **2019, Taxpayer Certainty and Disaster Tax Relief Act of 2019 (P.L. 116-94)**

P.L. 116-94, §144(g)(1), Div. Q:

Amended Code Sec. 5001(c)(4) by striking "December 31, 2019" and inserting "December 31, 2020". **Effective** for distilled spirits removed after 12-31-2019.

P.L. 116-94, §144(g)(2), Div. Q:

Amended the heading for Code Sec. 5001(c) by striking "REDUCED RATE FOR 2018 AND 2019" and inserting "TEMPORARY REDUCED RATE". **Effective** for distilled spirits removed after 12-31-2019.

• **2017, Tax Cuts and Jobs Act (P.L. 115-97)**

P.L. 115-97, §13807(a):

Amended Code Sec. 5001 by redesignating subsection (c) as subsection (d) and by inserting after subsection (b) a new subsection (c). **Effective** for distilled spirits removed after 12-31-2017.

P.L. 115-97, §13807(c)(1)-(2):

Amended Code Sec. 5001(c), as added by Act Sec. 13807(a), by inserting "but only if the importer is an electing importer under paragraph (3) and the proof gallons of distilled spirits have been assigned to the importer pursuant to such paragraph" after "into the United States during the calendar year" in paragraph (1), and by redesignating paragraph (3) as paragraph (4) and by inserting after paragraph (2) a new paragraph (3). **Effective** for distilled spirits removed after 12-31-2017.

ALCOHOL TAXES—GALLONAGE TAXES

P.L. 115-97, § 13809 (as added by P.L. 115-123, § 41111, Div. D), provides:
SEC. 13809. RULE OF CONSTRUCTION.

Nothing in this subpart, the amendments made by this subpart, or any regulation promulgated under this subpart or the amendments made by this subpart, shall be construed to preempt, supersede, or otherwise limit or restrict any State, local, or tribal law that prohibits or regulates the production or sale of distilled spirits, wine, or malt beverages.

[Sec. 5001(d)]

(d) CROSS REFERENCE.—

For provisions relating to the tax on shipments to the United States of taxable articles from Puerto Rico and the Virgin Islands, see section 7652.

Amendments

• 2017, Tax Cuts and Jobs Act (P.L. 115-97)

P.L. 115-97, § 13807(a):

Amended Code Sec. 5001 by redesignating subsection (c) as subsection (d). **Effective** for distilled spirits removed after 12-31-2017.

[Sec. 5002]

SEC. 5002. DEFINITIONS.

[Sec. 5002(a)]

(a) IN GENERAL.—For purposes of this chapter—

(1) DISTILLED SPIRITS PLANT.—The term "distilled spirits plant" means an establishment which is qualified under subchapter B to perform any distilled spirits operation.

(2) DISTILLED SPIRITS OPERATION.—The term "distilled spirits operation" means any operation for which qualification is required under subchapter B.

(3) BONDED PREMISES.—The term "bonded premises", when used with respect to distilled spirits, means the premises of a distilled spirits plant, or part thereof, on which distilled spirits operations are authorized to be conducted.

(4) DISTILLER.—The term "distiller" includes any person who—

(A) produces distilled spirits from any source or substance,

(B) brews or makes mash, wort, or wash fit for distillation or for the production of distilled spirits (other than the making or using of mash, wort, or wash in the authorized production of wine or beer, or the production of vinegar by fermentation),

(C) by any process separates alcoholic spirits from any fermented substance, or

(D) making or keeping mash, wort, or wash, has a still in his possession or use.

(5) PROCESSOR.—

(A) IN GENERAL.—The term "processor", when used with respect to distilled spirits, means any person who—

(i) manufactures, mixes, or otherwise processes distilled spirits, or

(ii) manufactures any article.

(B) RECTIFIER, BOTTLER, ETC., INCLUDED.—The term "processor" includes (but is not limited to) a rectifier, bottler, and denaturer.

(6) CERTAIN OPERATIONS NOT TREATED AS PROCESSING.—In applying paragraph (5), there shall not be taken into account—

(A) OPERATIONS AS DISTILLER.—Any process which is the operation of a distiller.

(B) MIXING OF TAXPAID SPIRITS FOR IMMEDIATE CONSUMPTION.—Any mixing (after determination of tax) of distilled spirits for immediate consumption.

(C) USE BY APOTHECARIES.—Any process performed by an apothecary with respect to distilled spirits which such apothecary uses exclusively in the preparation or making up of medicines unfit for use for beverage purposes.

(7) WAREHOUSEMAN.—The term "warehouseman", when used with respect to distilled spirits, means any person who stores bulk distilled spirits.

(8) DISTILLED SPIRITS.—The terms "distilled spirits", "alcoholic spirits", and "spirits" mean that substance known as ethyl alcohol, ethanol, or spirits of wine in any form (including all dilutions and mixtures thereof from whatever source or by whatever process produced).

(9) BULK DISTILLED SPIRITS.—The term "bulk distilled spirits" means distilled spirits in a container having a capacity in excess of 1 wine gallon.

(10) PROOF SPIRITS.—The term "proof spirits" means that liquid which contains one-half its volume of ethyl alcohol of a specific gravity of 0.7939 at 60 degrees Fahrenheit (referring to water at 60 degrees Fahrenheit as unity).

(11) PROOF GALLON.—The term "proof gallon" means a United States gallon of proof spirits, or the alcoholic equivalent thereof.

(12) CONTAINER.—The term "container", when used with respect to distilled spirits, means any receptacle, vessel, or form of package, bottle, tank, or pipeline used, or capable of use, for holding, storing, transferring, or conveying distilled spirits.

(13) APPROVED CONTAINER.—The term "approved container", when used with respect to distilled spirits, means a container the use of which is authorized by regulations prescribed by the Secretary.

(14) ARTICLE.—Unless another meaning is distinctly expressed or manifestly intended, the term "article" means any substance in the manufacture of which denatured distilled spirits are used.

(15) EXPORT.—The terms "export", "exported", and "exportation" include shipments to a possession of the United States.

Amendments

• 1979, Trade Agreements Act of 1979 (P.L. 96-39)

P.L. 96-39, § 805(e):

Amended Code Sec. 5002(a). **Effective** 1-1-80. Prior to amendment, Code Sec. 5002(a) read as follows:

(a) DEFINITIONS.—When used in this chapter—

(1) DISTILLED SPIRITS PLANT.—The term "distilled spirits plant" means an establishment which is qualified under subchapter B to perform any operation, or any combination of operations, for which qualification is required under such subchapter.

(2) BONDED PREMISES.—The term "bonded premises", when used with reference to distilled spirits, means the premises of a distilled spirits plant, or part thereof, as described in the application required by section 5171(a), on which operations relating to production, storage, denaturation, or bottling of distilled spirits, prior to the payment or determination of the distilled spirits tax, are authorized to be conducted.

(3) BOTTLING PREMISES.—The term "bottling premises", when used with reference to distilled spirits plants, means the premises of a distilled spirits plant, or part thereof, as described in the application required by section 5171(a), on which operations relating to the rectification or bottling of distilled spirits or wines on which the tax has been paid or determined, are authorized to be conducted.

(4) BONDED WAREHOUSEMAN.—The term "bonded warehouseman" means the proprietor of a distilled spirits plant who is authorized to store distilled spirits after entry for deposit in storage and prior to payment or determination of the internal revenue tax or withdrawal as provided in section 5214 or 7510.

(5) DISTILLER.—The term "distiller" shall include every person—

(A) who produces distilled spirits from any source or substance; or

(B) who brews or makes mash, wort, or wash, fit for distillation or for the production of distilled spirits (except a person making or using such material in the authorized production of wine or beer, or the production of vinegar by fermentation); or

(C) who by any process separates alcoholic spirits from any fermented substance; or

(D) who, making or keeping mash, wort, or wash, has also in his possession or use a still.

(6) DISTILLED SPIRITS.—

(A) General Definition.—The terms "distilled spirits", "alcoholic spirits", and "spirits" mean that substance known as ethyl alcohol, ethanol, or spirits of wine, including all dilutions and mixtures thereof, from whatever source or by whatever process produced, and shall include whisky, brandy, rum, gin, and vodka.

(B) Products of Rectification.—As used in section 5291(a) the term "distilled spirits" includes products produced in such manner that the person producing them is a rectifier within the meaning of section 5082.

(7) PROOF SPIRITS.—The term "proof spirits" means that the liquid which contains one-half its volume of ethyl alcohol of a specific gravity of seven thousand nine hundred and thirty-nine ten-thousandths (.7939) at 60 degrees Fahrenheit referred to water at 60 degrees Fahrenheit as unity.

(8) PROOF GALLON.—The term "proof gallon" means a United States gallon of proof spirits, or the alcoholic equivalent thereof.

(9) CONTAINER.—The term "container", when used with respect to distilled spirits, means any receptacle, vessel, or form of package, bottle, tank, or pipeline used, or capable of use, for holding, storing, transferring, or conveying distilled spirits.

(10) APPROVED CONTAINER.—The term "approved container", when used with respect to distilled spirits, means a container the use of which is authorized by regulations prescribed by the Secretary.

(11) ARTICLES.—The term "articles" means any substance or preparation in the manufacture of which denatured distilled spirits are used, unless another meaning is distinctly expressed or manifestly intended.

(12) EXPORT.—The terms "export", "exported", and "exportation" shall include shipments to a possession of the United States.

• 1976, Tax Reform Act of 1976 (P.L. 94-455)

P.L. 94-455, § 1906(b)(13)(A):

Amended 1954 Code by substituting "Secretary" for "Secretary or his delegate" each place it appeared. **Effective** 2-1-77.

• 1965, Excise Tax Reduction Act of 1965 (P.L. 89-44)

P.L. 89-44, § 807(a):

Amended Sec. 5002(a) by adding paragraph (12) at the end thereof. **Effective** 7-1-65.

[Sec. 5002(b)]

(b) CROSS REFERENCES.—

(1) For definition of manufacturer of stills, see section 5102.

(2) For definition of dealer, see section 5121(c)(3).

(3) For definitions of wholesale dealers, see section 5121(c).

(4) For definitions of retail dealers, see section 5122(c).

(5) For definitions of general application to this title, see chapter 79.

Amendments

• 2005, Safe, Accountable, Flexible, Efficient Transportation Equity Act: A Legacy for Users (P.L. 109-59)

P.L. 109-59, § 11125(b)(13)(A)-(C):

Amended Code Sec. 5002(b) by striking "section 5112(a)" and inserting "section 5121(c)(3)", by striking "section 5112" and inserting "section 5121(c)", and by striking "section 5122" and inserting "section 5122(c)". **Effective** 7-1-2008, but not applicable to taxes imposed for periods before such date.

• 1994, Uruguay Round Agreements Act (P.L. 103-465)

P.L. 103-465, § 136(c)(1):

Amended Code Sec. 5002(b) by striking paragraph (1) and redesignating the following paragraphs accordingly. **Effective** 1-1-95. Prior to amendment, Code Sec. 5002(b)(1) read as follows:

(1) For definition of wine gallon, see section 5041(c).

• 1979, Trade Agreements Act of 1979 (P.L. 96-39)

P.L. 96-39, § 805(e):

Amended Code Sec. 5002(b). **Effective** 1-1-80. Prior to amendment, Code Sec. 5002(b) read as follows:

(b) CROSS REFERENCES.—

(1) For definition of wine gallon, see section 5041(c).

(2) For definition of rectifier, see section 5082.

(3) For definition of manufacturer of stills, see section 5102.

(4) For definition of dealer, see section 5112(a).

(5) For definitions of whosesale dealers, see section 5112.

(6) For definitions of retail dealers, see section 5122.

(7) For definitions of general application to this title, see chapter 79.

[Sec. 5003]

SEC. 5003. CROSS REFERENCES TO EXEMPTIONS, ETC.

(1) For provisions authorizing the withdrawal of distilled spirits free of tax for use by Federal or State agencies, see sections 5214(a)(2) and 5313.

(2) For provisions authorizing the withdrawal of distilled spirits free of tax by nonprofit educational organizations, scientific universities or colleges of learning, laboratories, hospitals, blood banks, sanitariums, and charitable clinics, see section 5214(a)(3).

(3) For provisions authorizing the withdrawal of certain imported distilled spirits from customs custody without payment of tax, see section 5232.

(4) For provisions authorizing the withdrawal of denatured distilled spirits free of tax, see section 5214(a)(1).

(5) For provisions exempting from tax distilled spirits for use in production of vinegar by the vaporizing process, see section 5505(j).

(6) For provisions relating to the withdrawal of wine spirits without payment of tax for use in the production of wine, see section 5373.

(7) For provisions exempting from tax volatile fruit-flavor concentrates, see section 5511.

(8) For provisions authorizing the withdrawal of distilled spirits from bonded premises without payment of tax for export, see section 5214(a)(4).

(9) For provisions authorizing withdrawal of distilled spirits without payment of tax to customs bonded warehouses for export, see section 5214(a)(9).

(10) For provisions relating to withdrawal of distilled spirits without payment of tax as supplies for certain vessels and aircraft, see 19 U. S. C 1309.

(11) For provisions authorizing regulations for withdrawal of distilled spirits for use of United States free of tax, see section 7510.

(12) For provisions relating to withdrawal of distilled spirits without payment of tax to foreign-trade zones, see 19 U. S. C. 81c.

(13) For provisions relating to exemption from tax of taxable articles going into the possessions of the United States, see section 7653(b).

(14) For provisions authorizing the withdrawal of distilled spirits without payment of tax for use in certain research, development, or testing, see section 5214(a)(10).

(15) For provisions authorizing the withdrawal of distilled spirits without payment of tax for transfer to manufacturing bonded warehouses for manufacturing for export, see section 5214(a)(6).

(16) For provisions authorizing the withdrawal of articles from the bonded premises of a distilled spirits plant free of tax when contained in an article, see section 5214(a)(11).

(17) For provisions relating to allowance for certain losses in bond, see section 5008(a).

ALCOHOL TAXES—GALLONAGE TAXES

Amendments

• **1979, Trade Agreements Act of 1979 (P.L. 96-39)**

P.L. 96-39, § 807(a)(1):

Amended Code Sec. 5003(9) by deleting "see section 5522(a) and", by adding paragraphs (15) and (16), and by redesignating former paragraph 15 as paragraph 17. **Effective** 1-1-80.

• **1977 (P.L. 95-176)**

P.L. 95-176, §§ 3(c), 4(f):

Amended Code Secs. 5003(9) and 5003(14). **Effective** 3-1-78. Prior sections read as follows:

"(9) For provisions authorizing withdrawal of distilled spirits without payment of tax to customs manufacturing bonded warehouses for export, see section 5522(a)."

"(14) For provisions authorizing the removal of samples free of tax for making tests or laboratory analyses, see section 5214(a)(9)."

[Sec. 5004]

SEC. 5004. LIEN FOR TAX.

[Sec. 5004(a)]

(a) DISTILLED SPIRITS SUBJECT TO LIEN.—

(1) GENERAL.—The tax imposed by section 5001(a)(1) shall be a first lien on the distilled spirits from the time the spirits are in existence as such until the tax is paid.

(2) EXCEPTIONS.—The lien imposed by paragraph (1), or any similar lien imposed on the spirits under prior provisions of internal revenue law, shall terminate in the case of distilled spirits produced on premises qualified under internal revenue law for the production of distilled spirits when such distilled spirits are—

(A) withdrawn from bonded premises on determination of tax; or

(B) withdrawn from bonded premises free of tax under provisions of section 5214(a)(1), (2), (3), (11), or (12), or section 7510; or

(C) exported, deposited in a foreign-trade zone, used in the production of wine, laden as supplies upon, or used in the maintenance or repair of, certain vessels or aircraft, deposited in a customs bonded warehouse, or used in certain research, development, or testing, as provided by law.

Amendments

• **1980, Crude Oil Windfall Profit Tax Act of 1980 (P.L. 96-223)**

P.L. 96-223, § 232(e)(2)(C):

Amended Code Sec. 5004(a)(2)(B) by striking out "or (11)" and inserting "(11), or (12)". **Effective** 7-1-80.

• **1979, Trade Agreements Act of 1979 (P.L. 96-39)**

P.L. 96-39, § 807(a)(2)(C):

Amended Code Sec. 5004(a)(2)(B) by changing "or (3)" to "(3), or (11)". **Effective** 1-1-80.

• **1977 (P.L. 95-176)**

P.L. 95-176, § 4(c):

Amended Code Sec. 5004(a)(2) by substituting "or (3)" for "(3), or (9)" in subparagraph (B) and by substituting subparagraph (C) for the following:

"(C) exported, deposited in a foreign-trade zone, used in the production of wine, deposited in customs manufacturing bonded warehouses, or laden as supplies upon, or used in the maintenance or repair of, certain vessels or aircraft, as provided by law." **Effective** 3-1-78.

[Sec. 5004(b)—Repealed]

Amendments

• **1979, Trade Agreements Act of 1979 (P.L. 96-39)**

P.L. 96-39, § 807:

Repealed Code Sec. 5004(b). **Effective** 1-1-80. Prior to repeal, Code Sec. 5004(b) read as follows:

(b) OTHER PROPERTY SUBJECT TO LIEN.—

(1) GENERAL.—The tax imposed by section 5001(a)(1) shall be a first lien on the distillery used for producing the distilled spirits, the stills, vessels, and fixtures therein, the lot or tract of land on which such distillery is situated, and on any building thereon, from the time such spirits are in existence as such until the tax is paid, or until the persons liable for the tax under section 5005(a) or (b) have been relieved of liability for such tax by reason of the provisions of section 5005 (c) (2), (c) (3), (d), or (e). In the case of a distilled spirits plant producing distilled spirits, the premises subject to lien shall comprise the bonded premises of such plant, any building containing any part of the bonded premises and the land on which such building is situated, as described in the application for registration of such plant. Any similar lien on the property described in this paragraph arising under prior provisions of internal revenue law shall not be assertable as to the tax on any distilled spirits in respect to which the persons liable for the tax have been relieved of liability therefor by reason of the provisions of section 5005(c)(2), (c)(3), (d), or (e).

(2) EXCEPTION DURING TERM OF BOND.—No lien shall attach to any lot or tract of land, distillery, building, or distilling apparatus, under this subsection, by reason of distilling done during any period included within the term of any bond given under section 5173(b)(1)(C).

(3) EXTINGUISHMENT OF LIEN.—Any lien under paragraph (1), or any similar lien imposed on the property described in paragraph (1) under prior provisions of internal revenue law, shall be held to be extinguished—

(A) if the property is no longer used for distilling and there is no outstanding liability against any person referred to in section 5005(a) or (b) for taxes or penalties imposed by law on the distilled spirits produced thereon, and no litigation is pending in respect of any such tax or penalty; or

(B) if an indemnity bond given under the provisions of section 5173(b)(1)(C), further conditioned to stand in lieu of such lien or liens and to indemnify the United States for the payment of all taxes and penalties which otherwise could be asserted against such property by reason of such lien or liens, is accepted and approved by the Secretary. Such bond shall not be accepted or approved if there is any pending litigation or outstanding assessment with respect to such taxes or penalties, or if the Secretary has knowledge of any circumstances indicating that such bond is tendered with intent to evade payment or defeat collection of any tax or penalty.

(4) CERTIFICATE OF DISCHARGE.—Any person claiming any interest in the property subject to lien under paragraph (1) may apply to the Secretary for a duly acknowledged certificate to the effect that such lien is discharged and, if the Secretary determines that such lien is extinguished, the Secretary shall issue such certificate, and any such certificate may be recorded.

• **1976, Tax Reform Act of 1976 (P.L. 94-455)**

P.L. 94-455, § 1906(b)(13)(A):

Amended 1954 Code by substituting "Secretary" for "Secretary or his delegate" each place it appeared. **Effective** 2-1-77.

[Sec. 5004(b)]

(b) CROSS REFERENCE.—

For provisions relating to extinguishing of lien in case of redistillation, see section 5223(e).

Amendments

• **1979, Trade Agreements Act of 1979 (P.L. 96-39)**

P.L. 96-39, § 807(a)(2)(B):

Redesignated Code Sec. 5004(c) as Code Sec. 5004(b). **Effective** 1-1-80.

• **1965, Excise Tax Reduction Act of 1965 (P.L. 89-44)**

P.L. 89-44, § 805(f)(1):

Amended subsection (c) of Section 5004 by inserting "5223(e)" in lieu of "5223(d)." **Effective** 10-1-65.

[Sec. 5005]

SEC. 5005. PERSONS LIABLE FOR TAX.

[Sec. 5005(a)]

(a) GENERAL.—The distiller or importer of distilled spirits shall be liable for the taxes imposed thereon by section 5001(a)(1).

ALCOHOL TAXES—GALLONAGE TAXES

[Sec. 5005(b)]

(b) DOMESTIC DISTILLED SPIRITS.—

(1) LIABILITY OF PERSONS INTERESTED IN DISTILLING.—Every proprietor or possessor of, and every person in any manner interested in the use of, any still, distilling apparatus, or distillery, shall be jointly and severally liable for the taxes imposed by law on the distilled spirits produced therefrom.

(2) EXCEPTION.—A person owning or having the right of control of not more than 10 percent of any class of stock of a corporate proprietor of a distilled spirits plant shall not be deemed to be a person liable for the tax for which such proprietor is liable under the provisions of paragraph (1). This exception shall not apply to an officer or director of such corporate proprietor.

[Sec. 5005(c)]

(c) PROPRIETORS OF DISTILLED SPIRITS PLANTS.—

(1) BONDED STORAGE.—Every person operating bonded premises of a distilled spirits plant shall be liable for the internal revenue tax on all distilled spirits while the distilled spirits are stored on such premises, and on all distilled spirits which are in transit to such premises (from the time of removal from the transferor's bonded premises) pursuant to application made by him. Such liability for the tax on distilled spirits shall continue until the distilled spirits are transferred or withdrawn from bonded premises as authorized by law, or until such liability for tax is relieved by reason of the provisions of section 5008(a). Nothing in this paragraph shall relieve any person from any liability imposed by subsection (a) or (b).

(2) TRANSFERS IN BOND.—When distilled spirits are transferred in bond in accordance with the provisions of section 5212, persons liable for the tax on such spirits under subsection (a) or (b), or under any similar prior provisions of internal revenue law, shall be relieved of such liability, if proprietors of transferring and receiving premises are independent of each other and neither has a proprietary interest, directly or indirectly, in the business of the other, and all persons liable for the tax under subsection (a) or (b), or under any similar prior provisions of internal revenue law, have divested themselves of all interest in the spirits so transferred. Such relief from liability shall be effective from the time of removal from the transferor's bonded premises, or from the time of divestment of interest, whichever is later.

Amendments

• **1979, Trade Agreements Act of 1979 (P.L. 96-39)**

P.L. 96-39, §807(a)(3)(A):

Amended Code Sec. 5005(c) by deleting paragraph (3). **Effective** 1-1-80. Prior to deletion, paragraph (3) read as follows:

(3) WITHDRAWALS ON DETERMINATION OF TAX.—

(A) Any person who withdraws distilled spirits from the bonded premises of a distilled spirits plant on determination of tax, upon giving of a withdrawal bond as provided for in section 5174, shall be liable for payment of the internal revenue tax on the distilled spirits so withdrawn, from the time of such withdrawal.

(B) All persons liable for the tax on distilled spirits under subsection (a) or (b), or under any similar prior provisions of internal revenue law, shall be relieved of liability with respect to the tax on any distilled spirits withdrawn on determination of tax under withdrawal bond (as provided for in section 5174) if the person withdrawing such spirits and the person, or persons, liable for the tax under subsection (a) or (b), or under any similar prior provisions of internal revenue law, are independent of each other and neither has a proprietary interest, directly or indirectly, in the business of the other, and all persons liable for the tax under subsection (a) or (b), or under any similar prior provisions of internal revenue law, have divested themselves of all interest in the spirits so withdrawn.

• **1976, Tax Reform Act of 1976 (P.L. 94-455)**

P.L. 94-455, §1905(a)(1):

Substituted the last sentence of Code Sec. 5005(c)(2) for the last two sentences of Code Sec. 5005(c)(2). **Effective** 2-1-77. Prior to amendment, the last two sentences of Code Sec. 5005(c)(2) read as follows:

Such relief from liability shall be effective from the time of removal from the transferor's bonded premises, from the time of such divestment of interest, or on July 1, 1959, whichever is later. The provisions of this paragraph shall be construed to apply to distilled spirits transferred in bond, whether such transfers occur prior to or on or after July 1, 1959, but shall not apply in any case in which the tax was paid or determined prior to such date.

[Sec. 5005(d)]

(d) WITHDRAWALS FREE OF TAX.—All persons liable for the tax under subsection (a) or (b), or under any similar prior provisions of internal revenue law, shall be relieved of such liability as to distilled spirits withdrawn free of tax under the provisions of section 5214(a)(1), (2), (3),(11), or (12), or under section 7510, at the time such spirits are so withdrawn from bonded premises.

Amendments

• **1980, Crude Oil Windfall Profit Tax Act of 1980 (P.L. 96-223)**

P.L. 96-223, §232(e)(2)(D):

Amended Code Sec. 5005(d) by striking out "or (11)" and inserting "(11), or (12)". **Effective** 7-1-80.

• **1979, Trade Agreements Act of 1979 (P.L. 96-39)**

P.L. 96-39, §807(a)(3)(B):

Amended Code Sec. 5005(d) by changing "or (3)" to "(3), or (11)". **Effective** 1-1-80.

• **1977 (P.L. 95-176)**

P.L. 95-176, §4(d):

Amended Code Sec. 5005(d) by substituting "or (3)" for "(3), or (9)". **Effective** 3-1-78.

[Sec. 5005(e)]

(e) WITHDRAWALS WITHOUT PAYMENT OF TAX.—

(1) LIABILITY FOR TAX.—Any person who withdraws distilled spirits from the bonded premises of a distilled spirits plant without payment of tax, as provided in section 5214(a)(4), (5), (6), (7), (8), (9), (10) or (13), shall be liable for the internal revenue tax on such distilled spirits, from the time of such withdrawal; and all persons liable for the tax on such distilled spirits under subsection (a) or (b), or under any similar prior provisions of internal revenue law, shall, at the time of such withdrawal, be relieved of any such liability on the distilled spirits so withdrawn if the person withdrawing such spirits and the person, or persons, liable for the tax under subsection (a) or (b), or under any similar prior provisions of internal revenue law, are independent of each other and neither has a proprietary interest, directly or indirectly, in the business of the other, and all persons liable for the tax under subsection (a) or (b), or under any similar prior provisions of internal revenue law, have divested themselves of all interest in the spirits so withdrawn.

(2) RELIEF FROM LIABILITY.—All persons liable for the tax on distilled spirits under paragraph (1) of this subsection, or under subsection (a) or (b), or under any similar prior provisions of internal revenue law, shall be relieved of any such liability at the time, as the case may be, the distilled spirits are exported, deposited in a foreign-trade zone, used in the production of wine, used in the production of nonbeverage wine or wine products, deposited in customs bonded warehouses, laden as supplies upon, or used in the maintenance or repair of, certain vessels or aircraft, or used in certain research, development, or testing, as provided by law.

Amendments

• **1984, Deficit Reduction Act of 1984 (P.L. 98-369)**

P.L. 98-369, §455(b)(1):

Amended Code Sec. 5005(e)(1) by striking out "or (10)" and inserting in lieu thereof "(10), or (13)". **Effective** 7-18-84.

P.L. 98-369, §455(b)(2):

Amended Code Sec. 5005(e)(2) by inserting "used in the production of nonbeverage wine or wine products," after "used in the production of wine,". **Effective** 7-18-84.

• **1977 (P.L. 95-176)**

P.L. 95-176, §4(b), (d):

Amended Code Sec. 5005(e)(1) by substituting "(8), (9), or (10)" for "or (8)" and amended Code Sec. 5005(e)(2). **Effective** 3-1-78. Prior to amendment, Code Sec. 5005(e)(2) read as follows:

"(2) RELIEF FROM LIABILITY.—All persons liable for the tax on distilled spirits under paragraph (1) of this subsection, or under subsection (a) or (b), or under any similar prior provisions of internal revenue law, shall be relieved of any such liability at the time, as the case may be, the distilled spirits are exported, deposited in a foreign-

ALCOHOL TAXES—GALLONAGE TAXES

trade zone, used in the production of wine, deposited in customs manufacturing bonded warehouses, or laden as supplies upon, or used in the maintenance or repair of, certain vessels or aircraft, as provided by law."

[Sec. 5005(f)]

(f) CROSS REFERENCES.—

(1) For provisions requiring bond covering operations at and withdrawals from, distilled spirits plants, see section 5173.

(2) For provisions relating to transfer of tax liability to redistiller in case of redistillation, see section 5223.

(3) For liability for tax on denatured distilled spirits, articles, and volatile fruit-flavor concentrates, see section 5001(a)(5) and (6).

(4) For liability for tax on distilled spirits withdrawn free of tax, see section 5001(a)(4).

(5) For liability of wine producer for unlawfully using wine spirits withdrawn for the production of wine, see section 5391.

(6) For provisions relating to transfer of tax liability for wine, see section 5043(a)(1)(A).

Amendments

• **1994, Uruguay Round Agreements Act (P.L. 103-465)**

P.L. 103-465, § 136(c)(2)(A)-(B):

Amended Code Sec. 5005(f) by striking "section 5001(a)(6) and (7)" in paragraph (3) and inserting "section 5001(a)(5) and (6)", and by striking "section 5001(a)(5)" in paragraph (4) and inserting "section 5001(a)(4)". **Effective** 1-1-95.

• **1979, Trade Agreements Act of 1979 (P.L. 96-39)**

P.L. 96-39, § 807(a)(3)(B), (C):

Amended Code Sec. 5005(f) by changing paragraph (1) and by adding paragraph (6). **Effective** 1-1-80. Prior to amendment, paragraph (1) read as follows:

(1) For provisions conditioning warehousing bonds on the payment of the tax, see section 5173(c).

[Sec. 5006]

SEC. 5006. DETERMINATION OF TAX.

[Sec. 5006(a)]

(a) REQUIREMENTS.—

(1) IN GENERAL.—Except as otherwise provided in this section, the tax on distilled spirits shall be determined when the spirits are withdrawn from bond. Such tax shall be determined by such means as the Secretary shall by regulations prescribe, and with the use of such devices and apparatus (including but not limited to tanks and pipelines) as the Secretary may require. The tax on distilled spirits withdrawn from the bonded premises of a distilled spirits plant shall be determined upon completion of the gauge for determination of tax and before withdrawal from bonded premises, under such regulations as the Secretary shall prescribe.

(2) DISTILLED SPIRITS NOT ACCOUNTED FOR.—If the Secretary finds that the distiller has not accounted for all the distilled spirits produced by him, he shall, from all the evidence he can obtain, determine what quantity of distilled spirits was actually produced by such distiller, and an assessment shall be made for the difference between the quantity reported and the quantity shown to have been actually produced at the rate of tax imposed by law for every proof gallon.

Amendments

• **1979, Trade Agreements Act of 1979 (P.L. 96-39)**

P.L. 96-39, § 804(a):

Amended Code Sec. 5006(a). **Effective** 1-1-80. Prior to amendment Code Sec. 5006(a) read as follows:

(a) REQUIREMENTS.—

(1) GENERAL.—Except as otherwise provided in this section, the internal revenue tax on distilled spirits shall be determined when the spirits are withdrawn from bond. Such tax shall be determined by such means as the Secretary shall by regulations prescribe, and with the use of such devices and apparatus (including but not limited to storage, gauging, and bottling tanks and pipelines) as the Secretary may require. The tax on distilled spirits withdrawn from the bonded premises of a distilled spirits plant shall be determined upon completion of the gauge for determination of tax and before withdrawal from bonded premises, under such regulations as the Secretary shall prescribe.

(2) DISTILLED SPIRITS ENTERED FOR STORAGE.—

(A) BONDING PERIOD LIMITATION.—Except as provided in subparagraph (B), the tax on distilled spirits entered for deposit in storage in internal revenue bond shall be determined within 20 years from the date of original entry for deposit in such storage.

(B) EXCEPTIONS.—Subparagraph (A) and section 5173(c)(1)(A) shall not apply in the case of—

(i) distilled spirits of 190 degrees or more of proof;

(ii) denatured distilled spirits; or

(iii) distilled spirits which on July 26, 1936, were 8 years of age or older and which were in bonded warehouses on that date.

(C) DISTILLED SPIRITS MINGLED IN INTERNAL REVENUE BOND.—In applying subparagraph (A) and section 5173(c)(1)(A) to distilled spirits entered for deposit in storage on different dates and lawfully mingled in internal revenue bond, the Secretary shall, by regulations, provide for the application of the 20-year period to such spirits in such manner that no more spirits will remain in bond than would have been the case had such mingling not occurred.

(3) DISTILLED SPIRITS NOT ACCOUNTED FOR.—If the Secretary finds that the distiller has not accounted for all the distilled spirits produced by him, he shall, from all the evidence he can obtain, determine what quantity of distilled spirits was actually produced by such distiller, and an assessment shall be made for the difference between the quantity reported and the quantity shown to have been actually produced, at the rate of tax imposed by law for every proof gallon.

• **1976, Tax Reform Act of 1976 (P.L. 94-455)**

P.L. 94-455, § 1906(b)(13)(A):

Amended 1954 Code by substituting "Secretary" for "Secretary or his delegate" each place it appeared. **Effective** 2-1-77.

[Sec. 5006(b)]

(b) TAXABLE LOSS.—

(1) ON ORIGINAL QUANTITY.—Where there is evidence satisfactory to the Secretary that there has been any loss of distilled spirits from any cask or other package deposited on bonded premises, other than a loss which by reason of section 5008(a) is not taxable, the Secretary may require the withdrawal from bonded premises of such distilled spirits, and direct the officer designated by him to collect the tax accrued on the original quantity of distilled spirits entered for deposit on bonded premises in such cask or package; except that, under regulations prescribed by the Secretary, when the extent of any loss from causes other than theft or unauthorized voluntary destruction can be established by the proprietor to the satisfaction of the Secretary, an allowance of the tax on the loss so established may be credited against the tax on the original quantity. If such tax is not paid on demand it shall be assessed and collected as other taxes are assessed and collected.

(2) ALTERNATIVE METHOD.—Where there is evidence satisfactory to the Secretary that there has been access, other than as authorized by law, to the contents of casks or packages stored on bonded premises, and the extent of such access is such as to evidence a lack of due diligence or a failure to employ necessary and effective controls on the part of the proprietor, the Secretary (in lieu of requiring the casks or packages to which such access has been had to be withdrawn and tax paid on the original quantity of distilled spirits entered for deposit on bonded premises in such casks or packages as provided in paragraph (1)) may assess an amount equal to the tax on 5 proof gallons of distilled spirits at the prevailing rate on each of the total number of such casks or packages as determined by him.

(3) APPLICATION OF SUBSECTION.—The provisions of this subsection shall apply to distilled spirits which are filled into casks or packages, as authorized by law, after entry and deposit on bonded premises, whether by recasking, filling from storage tanks, consolidation of packages, or otherwise; and the quantity filled into such casks or packages shall be deemed to be the original quantity for the purpose of this subsection, in the case of loss from such casks or packages.

ALCOHOL TAXES—GALLONAGE TAXES

Amendments
• **1979, Trade Agreements Act of 1979 (P.L. 96-39)**

P.L. 96-39, §807(a)(4)(A):

Amended Code Sec. 5006(b)(1) by changing ", notwithstanding that the time specified in any bond given for the withdrawal of the spirits entered in storage in such cask or package has not expired, except" to "; except". **Effective** 1-1-80.

P.L. 96-39, §807(a)(4)(B):

Amended Code Sec. 5006(b) by changing "in storage in internal revenue bond" each place it appeared to "on bonded premises". **Effective** 1-1-80.

• **1976, Tax Reform Act of 1976 (P.L. 94-455)**

P.L. 94-455, §1906(b)(13)(A):

Amended 1954 Code by substituting "Secretary" for "Secretary or his delegate" each place it appeared. **Effective** 2-1-77.

[Sec. 5006(c)]

(c) DISTILLED SPIRITS NOT BONDED.—

(1) GENERAL.—The tax on any distilled spirits, removed from the place where they were distilled and (except as otherwise provided by law) not deposited in storage on bonded premises of a distilled spirits plant, shall, at any time within the period of limitation provided in section 6501, when knowledge of such fact is obtained by the Secretary, be assessed on the distiller of such distilled spirits (or other person liable for the tax) and payment of such tax immediately demanded and, on the neglect or refusal of payment, the Secretary shall proceed to collect the same by distraint. This paragraph shall not exclude any other remedy or proceeding provided by law.

(2) PRODUCTION AT OTHER THAN QUALIFIED PLANTS.—Except as otherwise provided by law, the tax on any distilled spirits produced in the United States at any place other than a qualified distilled spirits plant shall be due and payable immediately upon production.

Amendments
• **1976, Tax Reform Act of 1976 (P.L. 94-455)**

P.L. 94-455, §1906(b)(13)(A):

Amended 1954 Code by substituting "Secretary" for "Secretary or his delegate" each place it appeared. **Effective** 2-1-77.

[Sec. 5006(d)]

(d) UNLAWFULLY IMPORTED DISTILLED SPIRITS.—Distilled spirits smuggled or brought into the United States unlawfully shall, for purposes of this chapter, be held to be imported into the United States, and the internal revenue tax shall be due and payable at the time of such importation.

[Sec. 5006(e)]

(e) CROSS REFERENCE.—

For provisions relating to removal of distilled spirits from bonded premises on determination of tax, see section 5213.

[Sec. 5007]

SEC. 5007. COLLECTION OF TAX ON DISTILLED SPIRITS.

[Sec. 5007(a)]

(a) TAX ON DISTILLED SPIRITS REMOVED FROM BONDED PREMISES.—The tax on domestic distilled spirits and on distilled spirits removed from customs custody under section 5232 shall be paid in accordance with section 5061.

Amendments
• **1979, Trade Agreements Act of 1979 (P.L. 96-39)**

P.L. 96-39, §807(a)(5):

Amended Code Sec. 5007(a). **Effective** 1-1-80. Prior to amendment, Code Sec. 5007(a) read as follows:

(a) TAX ON DISTILLED SPIRITS REMOVED FROM BONDED PREMISES.—

(1) GENERAL.—The tax on domestic distilled spirits and on distilled spirits removed from customs custody under section 5232 shall be paid in accordance with section 5061.

(2) DISTILLED SPIRITS WITHDRAWN TO BOTTLING PREMISES UNDER WITHDRAWAL BOND.—If distilled spirits are withdrawn from bonded premises under section 5213 and a withdrawal bond is posted under section 5174(a)(2), the Secretary shall, in fixing the time for filing the return and the time for payment of the tax under section 5061(a), make allowance for the period of transportation of the distilled spirits from the bonded premises to the bottling premises, not to exceed such maximum periods as he may by regulations prescribe.

• **1976, Tax Reform Act of 1976 (P.L. 94-455)**

P.L. 94-455, §1906(b)(13)(A):

Amended 1954 Code by substituting "Secretary" for "Secretary or his delegate" each place it appeared. **Effective** 2-1-77.

[Sec. 5007(b)]

(b) COLLECTION OF TAX ON IMPORTED DISTILLED SPIRITS.—The internal revenue tax imposed by section 5001(a)(1) and (2) upon imported distilled spirits shall be collected by the Secretary and deposited as internal revenue collections, under such regulations as the Secretary may prescribe. Section 5688 shall be applicable to the disposition of imported spirits.

Amendments
• **1994, Uruguay Round Agreements Act (P.L. 103-465)**

P.L. 103-465, §136(c)(3):

Amended Code Sec. 5007(b). **Effective** 1-1-95. Prior to amendment, Code Sec. 5007(b) read as follows:

(b) COLLECTION OF TAX ON IMPORTED DISTILLED SPIRITS AND PERFUMES CONTAINING DISTILLED SPIRITS.—

(1) DISTILLED SPIRITS.—The internal revenue tax imposed by section 5001(a)(1) and (2) upon imported distilled spirits shall be collected by the Secretary and deposited as internal revenue collections, under such regulations as the Secretary may prescribe. Section 5688 shall be applicable to the disposition of imported spirits.

(2) PERFUMES CONTAINING DISTILLED SPIRITS.—The internal revenue tax imposed by section 5001(a)(3) upon imported perfumes containing distilled spirits shall be collected by the Secretary and deposited as internal revenue collections, under such regulations as the Secretary may prescribe.

• **1976, Tax Reform Act of 1976 (P.L. 94-455)**

P.L. 94-455, §1905(b)(2)(A):

Struck out the second sentence of Code Sec. 5007(b)(1). **Effective** 2-1-77. Prior to striking, such sentence read as follows:

Such tax shall be in addition to any customs duty imposed under the Tariff Act of 1930 (46 Stat. 590; 19 U.S.C. chapter 4), or any subsequent act.

P.L. 94-455, §1906(b)(13)(A):

Amended 1954 Code by substituting "Secretary" for "Secretary or his delegate" each place it appeared. **Effective** 2-1-77.

[Sec. 5007(c)]

(c) CROSS REFERENCES.—

(1) For authority of the Secretary to make determinations and assessments of internal revenue taxes and penalties, see section 6201(a).

(2) For authority to assess tax on distilled spirits not bonded, see section 5006(c).

(3) For provisions relating to payment of tax, under certain conditions, on distilled spirits withdrawn free of tax, denatured distilled spirits, articles, and volatile fruit-flavor concentrates, see section 5001(a)(4), (5), and (6).

ALCOHOL TAXES—GALLONAGE TAXES

Amendments

• **1994, Uruguay Round Agreements Act (P.L. 103-465)**

P.L. 103-465, § 136(c)(4):

Amended Code Sec. 5007(c)(3) by striking "section 5001(a)(5), (6), and (7)" and inserting "section 5001(a)(4), (5) and (6)". **Effective** 1-1-95.

• **1976, Tax Reform Act of 1976 (P.L. 94-455)**

P.L. 94-455, § 1906(B)(13)(A):

Amended 1954 Code by substituting "Secretary" for "Secretary or his delegate" each place it appeared. **Effective** 2-1-77.

[Sec. 5008]

SEC. 5008. ABATEMENT, REMISSION, REFUND, AND ALLOWANCE FOR LOSS OR DESTRUCTION OF DISTILLED SPIRITS.

[Sec. 5008(a)]

(a) DISTILLED SPIRITS LOST OR DESTROYED IN BOND.—

(1) EXTENT OF LOSS ALLOWANCE.—No tax shall be collected in respect of distilled spirits lost or destroyed while in bond, except that such tax shall be collected—

(A) THEFT.—In the case of loss by theft, unless the Secretary finds that the theft occurred without connivance, collusion, fraud, or negligence on the part of the proprietor of the distilled spirits plant, owner, consignor, consignee, bailee, or carrier, or the employees or agents of any of them;

(B) VOLUNTARY DESTRUCTION.—In the case of voluntary destruction, unless such destruction is carried out as provided in subsection (b); and

(C) UNEXPLAINED SHORTAGE.—In the case of an unexplained shortage of bottled distilled spirits.

(2) PROOF OF LOSS.—In any case in which distilled spirits are lost or destroyed, whether by theft or otherwise, the Secretary may require the proprietor of the distilled spirits plant or other person liable for the tax to file a claim for relief from the tax and submit proof as to the cause of such loss. In every case where it appears that the loss was by theft, the burden shall be upon the proprietor of the distilled spirits plant or other person responsible for the distilled spirits tax to establish to the satisfaction of the Secretary that such loss did not occur as the result of connivance, collusion, fraud, or negligence on the part of the proprietor of the distilled spirits plant, owner, consignor, consignee, bailee, or carrier, or the employees or agents of any of them.

(3) REFUND OF TAX.—In any case where the tax would not be collectible by virtue of paragraph (1), but such tax has been paid, the Secretary shall refund such tax.

(4) LIMITATIONS.—Except as provided in paragraph (5), no tax shall be abated, remitted, credited, or refunded under this subsection where the loss occurred after the tax was determined (as provided in section 5006(a)). The abatement, remission, credit, or refund of taxes provided for by paragraphs (1) and (3) in the case of loss of distilled spirits by theft shall only be allowed to the extent that the claimant is not indemnified against or recompensed in respect of the tax for such loss.

(5) APPLICABILITY.—The provisions of this subsection shall extend to and apply in respect of distilled spirits lost after the tax was determined and before completion of the physical removal of the distilled spirits from the bonded premises.

Amendments

• **1979, Trade Agreements Act of 1979 (P.L. 96-39)**

P.L. 96-39, § 807(a)(6)(A), (B):

Amended Code Sec. 5008(a)(1) by adding subparagraph (3) and by changing Code Sec. 5008(a)(5). **Effective** 1-1-80. Prior to amendment, Code Sec. 5008(a)(5) read as follows:

(5) APPLICABILITY.—The provisions of this subsection shall extend to and apply in respect of distilled spirits lost after the tax was determined and prior to the completion of the physical removal of the distilled spirits from bonded premises, but shall not be applicable where the loss occurred after the time prescribed for the withdrawal of the distilled spirits from bonded premises under section 5006(a)(2) unless the loss occurred in the course of physical removal of the spirits immediately subsequent to such time. This paragraph shall not be applicable to any loss of distilled spirits for which abatement, remission, credit, or refund of tax is allowable under the provisions of subsection (c), or would be allowable except for the limitations established under subsection (c)(3).

• **1976, Tax Reform Act of 1976 (P.L. 94-455)**

P.L. 94-455, § 1906(b)(13)(A):

Amended 1954 Code by substituting "Secretary" for "Secretary or his delegate" each place it appeared. **Effective** 2-1-77.

[Sec. 5008(b)]

(b) VOLUNTARY DESTRUCTION.—The proprietor of the distilled spirits plant or other persons liable for the tax imposed by this chapter or by section 7652 with respect to any distilled spirits in bond may voluntarily destroy such spirits, but only if such destruction is under such supervision and under such regulations as the Secretary may prescribe.

Amendments

• **1979, Trade Agreements Act of 1979 (P.L. 96-39)**

P.L. 96-39, § 807(a)(6)(C):

Amended Code Sec. 5008(b). **Effective** 1-1-80. Prior to amendment, Code Sec. 5008(b) read as follows:

(b) VOLUNTARY DESTRUCTION.—

(1) DISTILLED SPIRITS IN BOND.—The proprietor of the distilled spirits plant or other persons liable for the tax imposed by this chapter or by section 7652 with respect to any distilled spirits in bond may voluntarily destroy such spirits, but only if such destruction is under such supervision, and under such regulations, as the Secretary may prescribe.

(2) DISTILLED SPIRITS WITHDRAWN FOR RECTIFICATION OR BOTTLING.—Any distilled spirits withdrawn from bond on payment or determination of tax for rectification or bottling may, before removal from the bottling premises of the distilled spirits plant to which removed from bond or after return to such bottling premises, on application to the Secretary, be destroyed after such gauge and under such supervision as the Secretary may by regulations prescribe. If a claim is filed within 6 months from the date of such destruction, the Secretary shall, under such regulations as he may prescribe, abate, remit, or, without interest, credit or refund the taxes imposed under section 5001(a)(1), under subpart B of this part, or under section 7652 on the spirits so destroyed, to the proprietor of the distilled spirits plant who withdrew the distilled spirits on payment or determination of tax.

• **1976, Tax Reform Act of 1976 (P.L. 94-455)**

P.L. 94-455, § 1905(a)(2)(A):

Added "or by section 7652" immediately following "the tax imposed by this chapter" in Code Sec. 5008(b)(1). **Effective** 2-1-77.

P.L. 94-455, § 1905(a)(2)(B):

Substituted ", under subpart B of this part, or under section 7652" for "or under subpart B of this part" in the last sentence of Code Sec. 5008(b)(2). **Effective** 2-1-77.

P.L. 94-455, § 1906(b)(13)(A):

Amended 1954 Code by substituting "Secretary" for "Secretary or his delegate" each place it appeared. **Effective** 2-1-77.

• **1971 (P.L. 91-659)**

P.L. 91-659, § 2(a):

Amended Code Sec. 5008(b)(2). **Effective** 5-1-71. Prior to amendment, paragraph (2) read as follows:

"(2) Distilled spirits withdrawn for rectification or bottling.—Whenever any distilled spirits withdrawn from bond on or after July 1, 1959, on payment or determination of tax for rectification or bottling are (before the completion of the bottling and casing or other packaging of such spirits for removal from the bottling premises of the distilled spirits plant to which removed from bond) found by the proprietor who withdrew such spirits to be unsuitable for the purpose for which intended to be used, such spirits may, on application to the Secretary or his delegate, be destroyed after such gauge and under such supervision as the Secretary or his delegate may by regulations prescribe. If a claim is filed within 6 months from the date of such destruction, the Secretary or his delegate shall, under such regulations as he may prescribe, abate, remit, or, without interest, credit or refund the tax imposed under section 5001(a)(1) on the spirits so destroyed, to the proprietor of the distilled spirits plant who withdrew the distilled spirits on payment or determination of tax."

ALCOHOL TAXES—GALLONAGE TAXES

[Sec. 5008(c)]

(c) DISTILLED SPIRITS RETURNED TO BONDED PREMISES.—

(1) IN GENERAL.—Whenever any distilled spirits on which tax has been determined or paid are returned to the bonded premises of a distilled spirits plant under section 5215(a), the Secretary shall abate or (without interest) credit or refund the tax imposed under section 5001(a)(1) (or the tax equal to such tax imposed under section 7652) on the spirits so returned.

(2) CLAIM MUST BE FILED WITHIN 6 MONTHS OF RETURN OF SPIRITS.—No allowance under paragraph (1) may be made unless claim therefor is filed within 6 months of the date of the return of the spirits. Such claim may be filed only by the proprietor of the distilled spirits plant to which the spirits were returned, and shall be filed in such form as the Secretary may by regulations prescribe.

Amendments

• **1997, Taxpayer Relief Act of 1997 (P.L. 105-34)**

P.L. 105-34, § 1411(a):

Amended Code Sec. 5008(c)(1) by striking "withdrawn from bonded premises on payment or determination of tax" and inserting "on which tax has been determined or paid". **Effective** on the 1st day of the 1st calendar quarter that begins at least 180 days after 8-5-97.

• **1979, Trade Agreements Act of 1979 (P.L. 96-39)**

P.L. 96-39, § 807(a)(6)(D):

Amended Code Sec. 5008(c). **Effective** 1-1-80. Prior to amendment Code Sec. 5008(c) read as follows:

(c) LOSS OF DISTILLED SPIRITS WITHDRAWN FROM BOND FOR RECTIFICATION OR BOTTLING.—

(1) GENERAL.—Whenever any distilled spirits withdrawn from bond on payment or determination of tax for rectification or bottling are lost before removal from the premises of the distilled spirits plant to which removed from bond, the Secretary shall, under such regulations as he may prescribe, abate, remit, or, without interest, credit or refund the tax imposed on such spirits under section 5001(a)(1) or under section 7652 to the proprietor of the distilled spirits plant who withdrew the distilled spirits on payment or determination of tax for removal to his bottling premises, if it is established to the satisfaction of the Secretary that—

(A) such loss occurred (i) by reason of accident while being removed from bond to bottling premises, or (ii) by reason of flood, fire, or other disaster, or (iii) by reason of accident while on the distilled spirits plant premises and amounts to 10 proof gallons or more in respect of any one accident; or

(B) such loss occurred (i) before the completion of the bottling and casing or other packaging of such spirits for removal from the bottling premises and (ii) by reason of, and was incident to, authorized rectifying, packaging, bottling, or casing operations (including losses by leakage or evaporation occurring during removal from bond to the bottling premises and during storage on bottling premises pending rectification or bottling).

(2) LIMITATION.—No abatement, remission, credit, or refund of taxes shall be made under this subsection—

(A) in any case where the claimant is indemnified or recompensed for the tax;

(B) in excess of the amount allowable under paragraph (3), in case of losses referred to in paragraph (1)(B); or

(C) unless a claim is filed, under such regulations as the Secretary may prescribe, by the proprietor of the distilled spirits plant who withdrew the distilled spirits on payment or determination of tax, (i) within 6 months from the date of the loss in case of losses referred to in paragraph (1)(A), or (ii) within 6 months from the close of the computation year in which the loss occurred in case of losses referred to in paragraph (1)(B).

The quantity of distilled spirits lost within the meaning of subparagraph (B) of paragraph (1) shall be determined at such times and by such means or methods as the Secretary shall by regulations prescribe.

(3) MAXIMUM LOSS ALLOWANCES.—

(A) If all the alcoholic ingredients used in distilled spirits products during the computation year were distilled spirits withdrawn from bond by the proprietor of the bottling premises on payment or determination of tax, for removal to such premises, the loss allowable in such computation year under paragraph (1)(B) shall not be greater than the excess of losses over gains, and shall not exceed the maximum amount of loss allowable as shown in the following schedule:

If total completions during the computation year in proof gallons are:	The maximum allowable loss in proof gallons is:
Not over 24,000	2 percent of completions.
Over 24,000 but not over 120,000	480 proof gallons plus 1% of excess over 24,000.
Over 120,000 but not over 600,000	1,440 proof gallons plus .6% of excess over 120,000.
Over 600,000 but not over 2,400,000	4,320 proof gallons plus .3% of excess over 600,000.
Over 2,400,000	9,720 proof gallons plus .2% of excess over 2,400,000.

The Secretary may, by regulations, reduce the amount of the maximum allowable losses in the preceding schedule when he finds that such adjustment is necessary for protection of the revenue, or increase the amount of such maximum allowable losses if he finds that such may be done without undue jeopardy to the revenue and is necessary to more nearly provide for the actual losses described in paragraph (1)(B). However, in no event shall allowable losses exceed 2 percent of total completions.

(B) If alcoholic ingredients other than distilled spirits withdrawn from bond by the proprietor of the bottling premises on payment or determination of tax, for removal to such premises, were used in distilled spirits products during the computation year, the loss allowable under paragraph (1)(B) shall be determined by first obtaining the amount that would have been allowable if all of the ingredients had been distilled spirits withdrawn from bond by the proprietor of the bottling premises on payment or determination of tax, for removal to such premises, and thereafter reducing this amount by an amount proportional to the percentage which the total proof gallons of such alcoholic ingredients bears to the total proof gallons of all alcoholic ingredients used in such distilled spirits products.

(C) As used in this subsection, the term "completions" means the distilled spirits products bottled and cased or otherwise packaged or placed in approved containers for removal from the bottling premises, and the term "computation year" means the period from July 1 of a calendar year through June 30 of the following year.

(D) The Secretary may, under such regulations and conditions as he may prescribe, make tentative allowances for losses provided for in paragraph (1)(B), for fractional parts of a year, which allowances shall be computed by the procedures prescribed in paragraphs (3)(A) and (3)(B), except that the numerical values for the completions and for the maximum allowable losses in proof gallons in the schedule in paragraph (3)(A) shall be divided by the number of such fractional parts within the computation year.

(E) The loss allowable to any proprietor qualifying for abatement, remission, credit, or refund of taxes under paragraph (1)(B) shall not exceed the quantity which would be allowed by a tentative estimates schedule constructed in accordance with paragraph (3)(D) for the portion of the computation year that such proprietor was qualified to operate the distilled spirits plant.

(F) Notwithstanding the limitations contained in the schedule in paragraph (3)(A) the Secretary may, under such regulations in addition to the losses allowable under paragraphs (1)(A) and (1)(B), allow actual determined losses incurred in the manufacture of gin and vodka where produced in closed systems in a manner similar to that authorized on bonded premises.

(4) ELIGIBLE PROPRIETORS.—

(A) The term "proprietor" as used in this subsection and in subsection (b)(2) shall, in the case of a corporation, include all affiliated or subsidiary corporations who are qualified during the computation year for successive operation of the same bottling premises and who make joint application to the Secretary to be treated as one proprietor for the purposes of this subsection and subsection (b)(2) and who comply with such conditions as the Secretary may by regulations prescribe.

(B) For the purposes of this subsection and subsection (b)(2) a proprietor of bottling premises of a distilled spirits plant who makes application to the Secretary for the withdrawal of distilled spirits from bond on payment of tax for removal to such bottling premises shall be deemed to be the proprietor who withdrew distilled spirits on payment of tax, and the distilled spirits withdrawn pursuant to such application shall be deemed to have been withdrawn by such proprietor on payment of tax, whether or not he was the person who paid the tax.

(5) DISTILLED SPIRITS RETURNED TO BOTTLING PREMISES.—Distilled spirits withdrawn from bond on payment or determination of tax for rectification or bottling which are removed from bottling premises and subsequently returned to the premises from which removed may be dumped and gauged after such return under such regulations as the Secretary may prescribe, and subsequent to such gauge shall be eligible for allowance of loss under this subsection as though they had not been removed from such bottling premises.

• **1976, Tax Reform Act of 1976 (P.L. 94-455)**

P.L. 94-455, § 1905(a)(2)(C):

Added "or under section 7652" immediately after "under section 5001(a)(1)" in Code Sec. 5008(c)(1). **Effective** 2-1-77.

P.L. 94-455, § 1906(b)(13)(A):

Amended 1954 Code by substituting "Secretary" for "Secretary or his delegate" each place it appeared. **Effective** 2-1-77.

• **1976, Fiscal Year Adjustment Act (P.L. 94-273)**

P.L. 94-273, § 47:

Amended Code Sec. 5008(c) by substituting "computation year" for "fiscal year" in paragraphs (2)(C), (3)(A), (B), (C), (D) and (E), and (4)(A). **Effective** 4-21-76.

• **1971 (P.L. 91-659)**

P.L. 91-659, §§ 1, 2(b):

Amended Code Sec. 5008(c)(1) by adding clause (iii). Also amended Code Sec. 5008(c)(5). **Effective** 5-1-71. Prior to amendment, Code Sec. 5008(c)(5) read as follows:

"(5) Applicability.—This subsection shall apply in respect of losses of distilled spirits withdrawn from bond on or after July 1, 1959. This subsection shall also apply in respect of losses, occurring on or after July 1, 1959, and after dumping for rectification or bottling, of distilled spirits withdrawn from bond prior to July 1, 1959, and such spirits shall be considered as having been withdrawn from bond on

ALCOHOL TAXES—GALLONAGE TAXES

payment or determination of tax by the proprietor of the bottling premises at which the spirits are dumped for rectification or bottling."

• **1968 (P.L. 90-630)**

P.L. 90-630, §1:

Amended paragraph (1) of Code Sec. 5008(c) by substituting "before removal from the premises" for "before the completion of the bottling and casing or other packaging of such spirits for removal from the bottling premises". Also amended subparagraph (1)(B) of Code Sec. 5008(c) by inserting after "such loss occurred" the following: "(i) before the completion of the bottling and casing or other packaging of such spirits for removal from the bottling premises and (ii)". **Effective** only for losses sustained on or after 2-1-69.

[Sec. 5008(d)—Repealed]

Amendments

• **1979, Trade Agreements Act of 1979 (P.L. 96-39)**

P.L. 96-39, §807(a)(6)(C):

Repealed Code Sec. 5008(d). **Effective** 1-1-80. Prior to repeal, Code Sec. 5008(d) read as follows:

(d) DISTILLED SPIRITS RETURNED TO BONDED PREMISES.—

(1) GENERAL.—Whenever any distilled spirits withdrawn from bonded premises on payment or determination of tax are returned to the bonded premises of a distilled spirits plant under section 5215(a), the Secretary shall abate, remit, or (without interest) credit or refund the tax imposed under section 5001(a)(1) (or the tax equal to such tax imposed under section 7652) on the spirits so returned.

(2) DISTILLED SPIRITS RETURNED TO BONDED PREMISES FOR STORAGE PENDING EXPORTATION.—Whenever any distilled spirits are returned under section 5215(b) to the bonded premises of a distilled spirits plant, the Secretary shall (without interest) credit or refund the internal revenue tax found to have been paid or determined with respect to such distilled spirits. Such amount of tax shall be the same amount which would be allowed as a drawback under section 5062(b) on the exportation of such distilled spirits.

(3) DISTILLED SPIRITS STAMPED AND LABELED AS BOTTLED IN BOND.—Whenever any distilled spirits are returned under section 5215(c) to the bonded premises of a distilled spirits plant, the Secretary shall (without interest) credit or refund the tax imposed under section 5001(a)(1) on the spirits so returned.

(4) LIMITATION.—No allowance under paragraph (1), (2), or (3) shall be made unless a claim is filed under such regulations as the Secretary may prescribe, by the proprietor of the distilled spirits plant to which the distilled spirits are returned within 6 months of the date of return.

• **1977 (P.L. 95-176)**

P.L. 95-176, §2(f):

Amended Code Sec. 5008(d). **Effective** 3-1-78. Prior to amendment, this section read as follows:

"(1) ALLOWANCE OF TAX.—Whenever any distilled spirits withdrawn from bonded premises on payment or determination of tax are returned under section 5215 to the bonded premises of a distilled spirits plant, the Secretary shall abate, remit, or (without interest) credit or refund the tax imposed under section 5001(a)(1) or under section 7652 on the spirits so returned.

"(2) LIMITATION.—No allowance under paragraph (1) shall be made unless a claim is filed, under such regulations as the Secretary may prescribe, by the proprietor of the distilled spirits plant to which the distilled spirits are returned, within 6 months of the date of return."

• **1976, Tax Reform Act of 1976 (P.L. 94-455)**

P.L. 94-455, §1905(a)(2)(C):

Added "or under section 7652" immediately after "under section 5001(a)(1)" in Code Sec. 5008(d)(1). **Effective** 2-1-77.

P.L. 94-455, §1905(a)(2)(D):

Struck out ", on or after July 1, 1959," following "withdrawn from bonded premises" in Code Sec. 5008(d)(1). **Effective** 2-1-77.

P.L. 94-455, §1906(b)(13)(A):

Amended 1954 Code by substituting "Secretary" for "Secretary or his delegate" each place it appeared. **Effective** 2-1-77.

• **1965, Excise Tax Reduction Act of 1965 (P.L. 89-44)**

P.L. 89-44, §805(a):

Amended subsection (d)(2) of Section 5008 by deleting "; and no claim shall be allowed in respect of any distilled spirits withdrawn from the bonded premises of a distilled spirits plant more than 6 months prior to the date of such return" from the end. **Effective** 7-1-65.

[Sec. 5008(d)]

(d) DISTILLED SPIRITS WITHDRAWN WITHOUT PAYMENT OF TAX.—The provisions of subsection (a) shall be applicable to loss of distilled spirits occurring during transportation from bonded premises of a distilled spirits plant to—

(1) the port of export, in case of withdrawal under section 5214(a)(4);

(2) the customs manufacturing bonded warehouse, in case of withdrawal under section 5214(a)(6);

(3) the vessel or aircraft, in case of withdrawal under section 5214(a)(7);

(4) the foreign-trade zone, in case of withdrawal under section 5214(a)(8); and

(5) the customs bonded warehouse in the case of withdrawal under sections 5066 and 5214(a)(9).

The provisions of subsection (a) shall be applicable to loss of distilled spirits withdrawn from bonded premises without payment of tax under section 5214(a)(10) for certain research, development, or testing, until such distilled spirits are used as provided by law.

Amendments

• **1979, Trade Agreements Act of 1979 (P.L. 96-39)**

P.L. 96-39, §807(a)(6)(D):

Redesignated Code Sec. 5008(f) as Code Sec. 5008(d). **Effective** 1-1-80.

• **1977 (P.L. 95-176)**

P.L. 95-176, §4(e):

Amended Code Sec. 5008(f) by deleting "and" at the end of paragraph (3), by substituting "; and" for the period at the end of paragraph (4), and by adding paragraph (5). **Effective** 3-1-78.

[Sec. 5008(e)—Repealed]

Amendments

• **1979, Trade Agreements Act of 1979 (P.L. 96-39)**

P.L. 96-39, §807(a)(6)(C):

Repealed Code Sec. 5008(e). **Effective** 1-1-80. Prior to repeal, Code Sec. 5008(e) read as follows:

(e) SAMPLES FOR USE BY THE UNITED STATES.—The Secretary shall, under such regulations as he may prescribe, without interest, credit or refund to the proprietor the tax on any samples of distilled spirits removed from the premises of a distilled spirits plant for analysis or testing by the United States.

• **1976, Tax Reform Act of 1976 (P.L. 94-455)**

P.L. 94-455, §1906(b)(13)(A):

Amended 1954 Code by substituting "Secretary" for "Secretary or his delegate" each place it appeared. **Effective** 2-1-77.

[Sec. 5008(e)]

(e) OTHER LAWS APPLICABLE.—All provisions of law, including penalties, applicable in respect of the internal revenue tax on distilled spirits, shall, insofar as applicable and not inconsistent with subsection (c), be applicable to the credits or refunds provided for under such subsection to the same extent as if such credits or refunds constituted credits or refunds of such tax.

Amendments

• **1979, Trade Agreements Act of 1979 (P.L. 96-39)**

P.L. 96-39, §807(a)(6)(D):

Redesignated Code Sec. 5008(g) as Code Sec. 5008(e). **Effective** 1-1-80.

P.L. 96-39, §807(a)(6)(E):

Amended Code Sec. 5008(e) by changing "subsections (b)(2), (c), and (d)," to "subsection (c)" and by changing "under such subsections" to "under such subsection". **Effective** 1-1-80.

[Sec. 5008(f)]

(f) CROSS REFERENCE.—

For provisions relating to allowance for loss in case of wine spirits withdrawn for use in wine production, see section 5373(b)(3).

Amendments

• **1979, Trade Agreements Act of 1979 (P.L. 96-39)**

P.L. 96-39, §807(a)(6)(D):

Redesignated Code Sec. 5008(h) as Code Sec. 5008(f). **Effective** 1-1-80.

Sec. 5008(d)—Repealed

ALCOHOL TAXES—GALLONAGE TAXES

[Sec. 5009—Repealed]

Amendments

• **1979, Trade Agreements Act of 1979 (P.L. 96-39)**

P.L. 96-39, §807(a)(7):

Repealed Code Sec. 5009. **Effective** 1-1-80. Prior to repeal, Code Sec. 5009 read as follows:

SEC. 5009. DRAWBACK.

[Sec. 5009(a)]

(a) DRAWBACK ON EXPORTATION OF DISTILLED SPIRITS IN CASKS OR PACKAGES.—On the exportation of distilled spirits in casks or packages containing not less than 20 wine gallons each, filled in internal revenue bond, drawback of the internal revenue tax paid or determined may be allowed, under such regulations, and on the filing of such bonds, reports, returns, and applications, and the keeping of such records, as the Secretary may prescribe. The drawback shall be paid or credited in an amount equal to such tax on the quantity of distilled spirits exported, as ascertained prior to exportation by such gauge as the Secretary may by regulations prescribe. The drawback shall be paid or credited only after all requirements of law and regulations have been complied with and on the filing, with the Secretary, of a proper claim and evidence satisfactory to the Secretary that the tax on such distilled spirits has been paid or determined and that the distilled spirits have been exported.

Amendments

• **1976, Tax Reform Act of 1976 (P.L. 94-455)**

P.L. 94-455, §1906(b)(13)(A):

Amended 1954 Code by substituting "Secretary" for "Secretary or his delegate" each place it appeared. **Effective** 2-1-77.

[Sec. 5009(b)]

(b) CROSS REFERENCES.—

(1) For provisions relating to drawback on distilled spirits packaged or bottled especially for export, see section 5062(b).

(2) For provisions relating to drawback on designated nonbeverage products, see sections 5131 through 5134.

(3) For drawback on distilled spirits used in flavoring extracts or medicinal or toilet preparations exported, see section 313(d) of the Tariff Act of 1930 (19 U. S. C. 1313).

(4) For drawback on articles removed to foreign-trade zones, see 19 U. S. C. 81c.

(5) For drawback on shipments from the United States to Puerto Rico, the Virgin Islands, Guam, or American Samoa, see section 7653(c).

Amendments

• **1976, Tax Reform Act of 1976 (P.L. 94-455)**

P.L. 94-455, §1905(a)(3):

Struck out "46 Stat. 694;" before "19 U.S.C. 1313" in Code Sec. 5009(b)(3). **Effective** 2-1-77.

[Sec. 5010]

SEC. 5010. CREDIT FOR WINE CONTENT AND FOR FLAVORS CONTENT.

[Sec. 5010(a)]

(a) ALLOWANCE OF CREDIT.—

(1) WINE CONTENT.—On each proof gallon of the wine content of distilled spirits, there shall be allowed a credit against the tax imposed by section 5001 (or 7652) equal to the excess of—

(A) $13.50, over

(B) the rate of tax which would be imposed on the wine under section 5041(b) but for its removal to bonded premises.

(2) FLAVORS CONTENT.—On each proof gallon of the flavors content of distilled spirits, there shall be allowed a credit against the tax imposed by section 5001 (or 7652) equal to $13.50.

(3) FRACTIONAL PART OF PROOF GALLON.—In the case of any fractional part of a proof gallon of the wine content, or of the flavors content, of distilled spirits, a proportionate credit shall be allowed.

Amendments

• **1990, Omnibus Budget Reconciliation Act of 1990 (P.L. 101-508)**

P.L. 101-508, §11201(a)(2):

Amended Code Sec. 5010(a)(1) by striking "$12.50" and inserting "$13.50". **Effective** 1-1-91.

P.L. 101-508, §11201(a)(2):

Amended Code Sec. 5010(a)(2) by striking "$12.50" and inserting "$13.50". **Effective** 1-1-91.

• **1984, Deficit Reduction Act of 1984 (P.L. 98-369)**

P.L. 98-369, §27(a)(2):

Amended Code Sec. 5010(a)(1) and (2) by striking out "$10.50" and inserting in lieu thereof "$12.50". **Effective** 10-1-85. However, see Act Sec. 27(b), below, for special rules.

P.L. 98-369, §27(b), provides:

(b) Floor Stocks Taxes on Distilled Spirits.—

(1) Imposition of Tax.—On distilled spirits on which tax was imposed under section 5001 or 7652 of the Internal Revenue Code of 1954 before October 1, 1985, and which were held on such date for sale by any person, there shall be imposed a tax at the rate of $2.00 for each proof gallon and a proportionate tax at the like rate on all fractional parts of a proof gallon.

(2) Exception for Certain Small Wholesale or Retail Dealers.—No tax shall be imposed by paragraph (1) on distilled spirits held on October 1, 1985, by any dealer if—

(a) the aggregate liquid volume of distilled spirits held by such dealer on such date does not exceed 500 wine gallons, and

(B) such dealer submits to the Secretary (at the time and in the manner required by the Secretary) such information as the Secretary shall require for purposes of this paragraph.

(3) Credit Against Tax.—Each dealer shall be allowed as a credit against the taxes imposed by paragraph (1) an amount equal to $800. Such credit shall not exceed the amount of taxes imposed by paragraph (1) for which the dealer is liable.

(4) Liability for Tax and Method of Payment.—

(A) Liability for Tax.—A person holding distilled spirits on October 1, 1985, to which the tax imposed by paragraph (1) applies shall be liable for such tax.

(B) Method of Payment.—The tax imposed by paragraph (1) shall be paid in such manner as the Secretary shall by regulations prescribe.

(C) Time for Payment.—

(i) In General.—Except as provided in clause (ii), the tax imposed by paragraph (1) shall be paid on or before April 1, 1986.

(ii) Installment Payment of Tax in Case of Small or Middle-Sized Dealers.—In the case of any small or middle-sized dealer, the tax imposed by paragraph (1) may be paid in 3 equal installments due as follows:

(I) The first installment shall be paid on or before April 1, 1986.

(II) The second installment shall be paid on or before July 1, 1986.

(III) The third installment shall be paid on or before October 1, 1986.

If the taxpayer does not pay any installment under this clause on or before the date prescribed for its payment, the whole of the unpaid tax shall be paid upon notice and demand from the Secretary.

(iii) Small or Middle-Sized Dealer.—For purposes of clause (ii), the term "small or middle-sized dealer" means any dealer if the aggregate gross sales receipts of such dealer for its most recent taxable year ending before October 1, 1985, does not exceed $500,000.

(5) Controlled Groups.—

(A) Controlled Groups of Corporations.—In the case of a controlled group—

(i) the 500 wine gallon amount specified in paragraph (2),

(ii) the $800 amount specified in paragraph (3), and

(iii) the $500,000 amount specified in paragraph (4)(C)(iii),

shall be apportioned among the dealers who are component members of such group in such manner as the Secretary shall by regulations prescribe. For purposes of the preceding sentence, the term "controlled group" has the meaning given to such term by subsection (a) of section 1563 of the Internal Revenue Code of 1954; except that for such purposes the phrase "more than 50 percent" shall be substituted for the phrase "at least 80 percent" each place it appears in such subsection.

(B) Nonincorporated Dealers Under Common Control.—Under regulations prescribed by the Secretary, principles similar to the principles of subparagraph (A) shall apply to a group of dealers under common control where 1 or more of such dealers is not a corporation.

(6) Other Laws Applicable.—All provisions of law, including penalties, applicable with respect to the taxes imposed by section 5001 of the Internal Revenue Code of 1954 shall, insofar as applicable and not inconsistent with the provisions of this subsection, apply in respect of the taxes imposed by paragraph (1) to the same extent as if such taxes were imposed by such section 5001.

(7) Definitions and Special Rules.—For purposes of this subsection—

(A) Dealer.—The term "dealer" means—

(i) any wholesale dealer in liquors (as defined in section 5112(b) of the Internal Revenue Code of 1954), and

(ii) any retail dealer in liquors (as defined in section 5122(a) of such Code).

(B) Distilled Spirits.—The term "distilled spirits" has the meaning given such term by section 5002(a)(8) of the Internal Revenue Code of 1954.

(C) Person.—The term "person" includes any State or political subdivision thereof, or any agency or instrumentality of a State or political subdivision thereof.

(D) Secretary.—The term "Secretary" means the Secretary of the Treasury or his delegate.

(E) Treatment of Imported Perfumes Containing Distilled Spirits.—Any article described in section 5001(a)(3) of such Code shall be treated as distilled spirits; except

ALCOHOL TAXES—GALLONAGE TAXES

that the tax imposed by paragraph (1) shall be imposed on a wine gallon basis in lieu of a proof gallon basis. To the extent provided in regulations prescribed by the Secretary, the preceding sentence shall not apply to any article held on October 1, 1985, on the premises of a retail establishment.

[Sec. 5010(b)]

(b) TIME FOR DETERMINING AND ALLOWING CREDIT.—

(1) IN GENERAL.—The credit allowable by subsection (a)—

(A) shall be determined at the same time the tax is determined under section 5006 (or 7652) on the distilled spirits containing the wine or flavors, and

(B) shall be allowable at the time the tax imposed by section 5001 (or 7652) on such distilled spirits is payable as if the credit allowable by this section constituted a reduction in the rate of tax.

(2) DETERMINATION OF CONTENT IN THE CASE OF IMPORTS.—For purposes of this section, the wine content, and the flavors content, of imported distilled spirits shall be established by such chemical analysis, certification, or other methods as may be set forth in regulations prescribed by the Secretary.

[Sec. 5010(c)]

(c) DEFINITIONS.—For purposes of this section—

(1) WINE CONTENT.—

(A) IN GENERAL.—The term "wine content" means alcohol derived from wine.

(B) WINE.—The term "wine"—

(i) means wine on which tax would be imposed by paragraph (1), (2), or (3) of section 5041(b) but for its removal to bonded premises, and

(ii) does not include any substance which has been subject to distillation at a distilled spirits plant after receipt in bond.

(2) FLAVORS CONTENT.—

(A) IN GENERAL.—Except as provided in subparagraph (B), the term "flavors content" means alcohol derived from flavors of a type for which drawback is allowable under section 5114.

(B) EXCEPTIONS.—The term "flavors content" does not include—

(i) alcohol derived from flavors made at a distilled spirits plant,

(ii) alcohol derived from flavors distilled at a distilled spirits plant, and

(iii) in the case of any distilled spirits product, alcohol derived from flavors to the extent such alcohol exceeds (on a proof gallon basis) $2^1/_2$ percent of the finished product.

Amendments

• 2005, Safe, Accountable, Flexible, Efficient Transportation Equity Act: A Legacy for Users (P.L. 109-59)

P.L. 109-59, § 11125(b)(14):

Amended Code Sec. 5010(c)(2)(A) by striking "section 5134" and inserting "section 5114". **Effective** 7-1-2008, but not applicable to taxes imposed for periods before such date.

• 1988, Technical and Miscellaneous Revenue Act of 1988 (P.L. 100-647)

P.L. 100-647, § 5063(a):

Amended Code Sec. 5010(c)(2)(B) by striking out the "and" at the end of clause (i), by redesignating clause (ii) as clause (iii) and by inserting after clause (i) a new clause (ii). **Effective** with respect to distilled spirits withdrawn from bond after the date of the enactment of this Act.

• 1980 (P.L. 96-598)

P.L. 96-598, § 6(a):

Added Code Sec. 5010. **Effective** 1-1-80.

[Sec. 5011]

SEC. 5011. INCOME TAX CREDIT FOR AVERAGE COST OF CARRYING EXCISE TAX.

[Sec. 5011(a)]

(a) IN GENERAL.—For purposes of section 38, the amount of the distilled spirits credit for any taxable year is the amount equal to the product of—

(1) in the case of—

(A) any eligible wholesaler, the number of cases of bottled distilled spirits—

(i) which were bottled in the United States, and

(ii) which are purchased by such wholesaler during the taxable year directly from the bottler of such spirits, or

(B) any person which is subject to section 5005 and which is not an eligible wholesaler, the number of cases of bottled distilled spirits which are stored in a warehouse operated by, or on behalf of, a State or political subdivision thereof, or an agency of either, on which title has not passed on an unconditional sale basis, and

(2) the average tax-financing cost per case for the most recent calendar year ending before the beginning of such taxable year.

[Sec. 5011(b)]

(b) ELIGIBLE WHOLESALER.—For purposes of this section, the term "eligible wholesaler" means any person which holds a permit under the Federal Alcohol Administration Act as a wholesaler of distilled spirits which is not a State or political subdivision thereof, or an agency of either.

[Sec. 5011(c)]

(c) AVERAGE TAX-FINANCING COST.—

(1) IN GENERAL.—For purposes of this section, the average tax-financing cost per case for any calendar year is the amount of interest which would accrue at the deemed financing rate during a 60-day period on an amount equal to the deemed Federal excise tax per case.

(2) DEEMED FINANCING RATE.—For purposes of paragraph (1), the deemed financing rate for any calendar year is the average of the corporate overpayment rates under paragraph (1) of section 6621(a) (determined without regard to the last sentence of such paragraph) for calendar quarters of such year.

(3) DEEMED FEDERAL EXCISE TAX PER CASE.—For purposes of paragraph (1), the deemed Federal excise tax per case is $25.68.

[Sec. 5011(d)]

(d) OTHER DEFINITIONS AND SPECIAL RULES.—For purposes of this section—

(1) CASE.—The term "case" means 12 80-proof 750-milliliter bottles.

(2) NUMBER OF CASES IN LOT.—The number of cases in any lot of distilled spirits shall be determined by dividing the number of liters in such lot by 9.

ALCOHOL TAXES—GALLONAGE TAXES

Amendments

• **2005, Safe, Accountable, Flexible, Efficient Transportation Equity Act: A Legacy for Users (P.L. 109-59)**

P.L. 109-59, §11126(a):

Amended subpart A of part I of subchapter A of chapter 51 by adding at the end a new Code Sec. 5011. **Effective** for tax years beginning after 9-30-2005.

Subpart B—Rectification—[Repealed]

[Sec. 5021—Repealed]

Amendments

• **1979, Trade Agreements Act of 1979 (P.L. 96-39)**

P.L. 96-39, §803(a):

Repealed Code Sec. 5021. **Effective** 1-1-80. Prior to repeal, Code Sec. 5021 read as follows:

SEC. 5021. IMPOSITION AND RATE OF TAX.

In addition to the tax imposed by this chapter on distilled spirits and wines, there is hereby imposed (except as otherwise provided in this chapter) a tax of 30 cents on each proof gallon and a proportionate tax at a like rate on all fractional parts of such proof gallon on all distilled spirits or wines rectified, purified, or refined in such manner, and on all mixtures produced in such manner, that the person so rectifying, purifying, refining, or mixing the same is a rectifier (as defined in section 5082). Spirits or wines shall not twice be subjected to tax under this section because of separate acts of rectification, pursuant to approved formula, between the time such spirits or wines are received on the bottling premises and the time they are removed therefrom.

[Sec. 5022—Repealed]

Amendments

• **1979, Trade Agreements Act of 1979 (P.L. 96-39)**

P.L. 96-39, §803(a):

Repealed Code Sec. 5022. **Effective** 1-1-80. Prior to amendment, Code Sec. 5022 read as follows:

SEC. 5022. TAX ON CORDIALS AND LIQUEURS CONTAINING WINE.

On all liqueurs, cordials, or similar compounds produced in the United States and not produced for sale as wine, wine specialties, or cocktails, which contain more than $2^1/_2$ percent by volume of wine of an alcoholic content in excess of 14 percent by volume, there shall be paid, in lieu of the tax imposed by section 5021, a tax at the rate of $1.92 per wine gallon and a proportionate tax at a like rate on all fractional parts of such wine gallon. The last sentence of section 5021 shall not be construed to limit the imposition of tax under this section. All other provisions of law applicable to rectification shall apply to the products subject to tax under this section.

• **1965, Excise Tax Reduction Act of 1965 (P.L. 89-44)**

P.L. 89-44, §501(b):

Amended Code Sec. 5022. **Effective** 7-1-65. Prior to amendment, Code Sec. 5022 read as follows:

"On all liqueurs, cordials or similar compounds produced in the United States and not produced for sale as wine, wine specialties, or cocktails, which contain more than $2^1/_2$ percent by volume of wine of an alcoholic content in excess of 14 percent by volume, there shall be paid, in lieu of the tax imposed by section 5021, a tax at the rate of $1.92 per wine gallon and a proportionate tax at a like rate on all fractional parts of such wine gallon until July 1, 1965, and on or after July 1, 1965, at the rate of $1.60 per wine gallon and a proportionate tax at a like rate on all fractional parts of such wine gallon. The last sentence of section 5021 shall not be construed to limit the imposition of tax under this section. All other provisions of law applicable to rectification shall apply to the products subject to tax under this section."

• **1964, Excise Tax Rate Extension Act of 1964 (P.L. 88-348)**

P.L. 88-348, §2(a)(6):

Substituted "1965" for "1964" wherever it appeared in Sec. 5022.

• **1963, Tax Rate Extension Act of 1963 (P.L. 88-52)**

P.L. 88-52, §3(a)(5):

Substituted "1964" for "1963" wherever it appeared in Sec. 5022.

• **1962, Tax Rate Extension Act of 1962 (P.L. 87-508)**

P.L. 87-508, §3(a)(5):

Substituted "1963" for "1962" wherever it appeared in Sec. 5022.

• **1961, Tax Rate Extension Act of 1961 (P.L. 87-72)**

P.L. 87-72, §3(a)(6):

Substituted "1962" for "1961" wherever it appeared in Sec. 5022.

• **1960, Public Debt and Tax Rate Extension Act of 1960 (P.L. 86-564)**

P.L. 86-564, §202(a):

Substituted "July 1, 1961" for "July 1, 1960" in Sec. 5022.

• **1959, Tax Rate Extension Act of 1959 (P.L. 86-75)**

P.L. 86-75, §3(a):

Substituted "July 1, 1960" for "July 1, 1959" in Sec. 5022.

[Sec. 5023—Repealed]

Amendments

• **1979, Trade Agreements Act of 1979 (P.L. 96-39)**

P.L. 96-39, §803(a):

Repealed Code Sec. 5023. **Effective** 1-1-80. Prior to repeal, Code Sec. 5023 read as follows:

SEC. 5023. TAX ON BLENDING OF BEVERAGE RUMS OR BRANDIES.

In the case of rums or fruit brandies mixed or blended pursuant to section 5234(c), in addition to the tax imposed by this chapter on the production of distilled spirits, there shall, except in the case of such rums or brandies which have been aged in wood at least 2 years at the time of their first blending or mixing, be paid a tax of 30 cents as to each proof gallon (and a proportionate tax at a like rate on all fractional parts of such proof gallon) of rums or brandies so mixed or blended and withdrawn from bonded premises, except when such rums or brandies are withdrawn under section 5214 or section 7510.

[Sec. 5024—Repealed]

Amendments

• **1979, Trade Agreements Act of 1979 (P.L. 96-39)**

P.L. 96-39, §803(a):

Repealed Code Sec. 5024. **Effective** 1-1-80. Prior to repeal, Code Sec. 5024 read as follows:

SEC. 5024. DEFINITIONS.

(1) For definition of "rectifier", see section 5082.

(2) For definition of "products of rectification" as "distilled spirits" for certain purposes, see section 5002(a)(6)(B).

(3) For other definitions relating to distilled spirits, see section 5002.

(4) For definitions of general application to this title, see chapter 79.

[Sec. 5025—Repealed]

Amendments

• **1979, Trade Agreements Act of 1979 (P.L. 96-39)**

P.L. 96-39, §803(a):

Repealed Code Sec. 5025. **Effective** 1-1-80. Prior to repeal, Code Sec. 5025 read as follows:

SEC. 5025. EXEMPTION FROM RECTIFICATION TAX.

[Sec. 5025(a)]

(a) ABSOLUTE ALCOHOL.—The process of extraction of water from high-proof distilled spirits for the production of absolute alcohol shall not be deemed to be rectification within the meaning of sections 5081 and 5082, and absolute alcohol shall not be subject to the tax imposed by section 5021, but the production of such absolute alcohol shall be under such regulations as the Secretary may prescribe.

Amendments

• **1976, Tax Reform Act of 1976 (P.L. 94-455)**

P.L. 94-455, §1906(b)(13)(A):

Amended 1954 Code by substituting "Secretary" for "Secretary or his delegate" each place it appeared. **Effective** 2-1-77.

[Sec. 5025(b)]

(b) PRODUCTION OF GIN AND VODKA.—The tax imposed by section 5021 shall not apply to gin produced on bottling premises of distilled spirits plants by the redistillation of a pure spirit over juniper berries and other natural aromatics, or the extraction of oils of such, or to vodka produced on bottling premises of distilled spirits plants from pure spirits in the manner authorized on bonded premises of distilled spirits plants.

ALCOHOL TAXES—GALLONAGE TAXES

Amendments

• **1977 (P.L. 95-176)**

P.L. 95-176, § 6:

Amended Code Sec. 5025(b) by adding ", or the extraction oils of such," after "natural aromatics". **Effective** 3-1-78.

[Sec. 5025(c)]

(c) REFINING SPIRITS IN COURSE OF ORIGINAL DISTILLATION.—The purifying or refining of distilled spirits, in the course of original and continuous distillation or other original and continuous processing, through any material which will not remain incorporated with such spirits when the production thereof is complete shall not be held to be rectification within the meaning of sections 5021, 5081, or 5082, nor shall these sections be held to prohibit such purifying or refining.

[Sec. 5025(d)]

(d) REDISTILLATION OF DISTILLED SPIRITS ON BONDED PREMISES.—Sections 5021, 5081, and 5082 shall not apply to the redistillation of distilled spirits under section 5223.

[Sec. 5025(e)]

(e) MINGLING OF DISTILLED SPIRITS.—Sections 5021, 5081, and 5082 shall not apply to—

(1) the mingling on bonded premises of spirits distilled at 190 degrees or more of proof; or

(2) the mingling of distilled spirits on bonded premises, or in the course of removal therefrom, for redistillation, storage, or any other purpose, incident to the requirements of the national defense; or

(3) the mingling in bulk gauging tanks on bonded premises of heterogeneous distilled spirits for immediate removal to bottling premises, exclusively for use in taxable rectification, or for blending under subsection (f), or for other mingling or treatment under subsection (k); or

(4) the blending on bonded premises of beverage brandies or rums, under the provisions of section 5234(c); or

(5) the mingling of homogeneous distilled spirits; or

(6) the mingling on bonded premises of distilled spirits for immediate redistillation, immediate denaturation, or immediate removal from such premises free of tax under section 5214(a)(1), (2), or (3), or section 7510; or

(7) the mingling on bonded premises of distilled spirits as authorized by section 5234(a)(2).

Amendments

• **1977 (P.L. 95-176)**

P.L. 95-176, § 5(b):

Amended Code Sec. 5025(e) by deleting "for further storage in bond" which formerly appeared after "distilled spirits". **Effective** 3-1-78.

• **1965, Excise Tax Reduction Act of 1965 (P.L. 89-44)**

P.L. 89-44, § 805(f)(2):

Amended subsection (e)(3) by inserting "for blending under subsection (f), or for other mingling or treatment under subsection (k)" in lieu of "in rectification under subsection (f)". **Effective** 10-1-65.

[Sec. 5025(f)]

(f) BLENDING STRAIGHT WHISKIES, RUMS, FRUIT BRANDIES, OR WINES.—The taxes imposed by this subpart shall not attach—

(1) to blends made exclusively of two or more pure straight whiskies, differing as to types, aged in wood for a period not less than 4 years and without the addition of coloring or flavoring matter or any other substance than pure water and if not reduced below 80 proof; or

(2) to blends made exclusively of two or more pure fruit brandies, differing as to types, distilled from the same kind of fruit, aged in wood for a period not less than 2 years and without the addition of coloring or flavoring matter (other than caramel) or any other substance than pure water and if not reduced below 80 proof; or

(3) to the mixing and blending of wines, where such blending is for the sole purpose of perfecting such wines according to commercial standards; or

(4) to blends made exclusively of two or more rums, differing as to types, aged in wood for a period not less than 2 years and without the addition of coloring or flavoring matter (other than caramel) or any other substance than pure water and if not reduced below 80 proof.

Such blended whiskies, blended rums, and blended fruit brandies shall be exempt from tax under this subpart only when blended in such tanks and under such conditions and supervision as the Secretary may by regulations prescribe.

Amendments

• **1976, Tax Reform Act of 1976 (P.L. 94-455)**

P.L. 94-455, § 1906(b)(13)(A):

Amended 1954 Code by substituting "Secretary" for "Secretary or his delegate" each place it appeared. **Effective** 2-1-77.

• **1965, Excise Tax Reduction Act of 1965 (P.L. 89-44)**

P.L. 89-44, § 805(f):

Amended subsection (f) of Section 5025 by inserting ", differing as to types," after "whiskies" in subsection (f)(1), after "brandies" in subsection (f)(2), and after "rums" in subsection (f)(4). **Effective** 10-1-65.

[Sec. 5025(g)]

(g) ADDITION OF CARAMEL TO BRANDY OR RUM.—The addition of caramel to commercial brandy or rum on the bonded premises of a distilled spirits plant, pursuant to regulations prescribed by the Secretary, shall not be deemed to be rectification within the meaning of sections 5021, 5081, and 5082.

Sec. 5025—Repealed

Amendments

• **1976, Tax Reform Act of 1976 (P.L. 94-455)**

P.L. 94-455, § 1906(b)(13)(A):

Amended 1954 Code by substituting "Secretary" for "Secretary or his delegate" each place it appeared. **Effective** 2-1-77.

[Sec. 5025(h)]

(h) APOTHECARIES.—The taxes imposed by this subpart and by part II of this subchapter shall not be imposed on apothecaries as to wines or distilled spirits which they use exclusively in the preparation or making up of medicines unfit for use for beverage purposes.

[Sec. 5025(i)]

(i) MANUFACTURER RECOVERING DISTILLED SPIRITS FOR REUSE IN PRODUCTS UNFIT FOR BEVERAGE PURPOSES.—The taxes imposed by this subpart and by part II of this subchapter shall not be imposed on any manufacturer for recovering distilled spirits, on which the tax has been paid or determined, from dregs or marc of percolation or extraction, or from medicines, medicinal preparations, food products, flavors, or flavoring extracts, which do not meet the manufacturer's standards, if such recovered distilled spirits are used by such manufacturer in the manufacture of medicines, medicinal preparations, food products, flavors, or flavoring extracts, which are unfit for use for beverage purposes.

[Sec. 5025(j)]

(j) STABILIZATION OF DISTILLED SPIRITS.—The removal, on the premises of a distilled spirits plant, of extraneous insoluble materials from distilled spirits, and minor changes in the soluble color or soluble solids of distilled spirits, which occur solely as a result of such filtrations or other physical treatments (which do not involve the addition of any substance which will remain incorporated in the completed product) at the time of, or preparatory to, the bottling of distilled spirits, or preparatory to exportation, as may be necessary or desirable to produce a stable product, shall not be deemed to be rectification within the meaning of sections 5021, 5081, and 5082, if such changes do not exceed maximum limitations which the Secretary may by regulations provide.

Amendments

• **1976, Tax Reform Act of 1976 (P.L. 94-455)**

P.L. 94-455, § 1905(a)(4):

Added "or preparatory to exportation," following "the bottling of distilled spirits," in Code Sec. 5025(j). **Effective** 2-1-77.

P.L. 94-455, § 1906(b)(13)(A):

Amended 1954 Code by substituting "Secretary" for "Secretary or his delegate" each place it appeared. **Effective** 2-1-77.

[Sec. 5025(k)]

(k) OTHER MINGLING OR TREATMENT OF DISTILLED SPIRITS.—The tax imposed by section 5021 shall not apply to the mingling of distilled spirits of the same class and type, or to the treatment of distilled spirits in such a manner as not to change the class and type of the distilled spirits, on bottling premises of a distilled spirits plant under such regulations as the Secretary may prescribe.

Amendments

• **1976, Tax Reform Act of 1976 (P.L. 94-455)**

P.L. 94-455, § 1906(b)(13)(A):

Amended 1954 Code by substituting "Secretary" for "Secretary or his delegate" each place it appeared. **Effective** 2-1-77.

• **1965, Excise Tax Reduction Act of 1965 (P.L. 89-44)**

P.L. 89-44, § 805(b):

Added new subsection (k) to Section 5025. **Effective** 10-1-65.

[Sec. 5025(l)]

(l) ADDITION OF TRACER ELEMENTS.—The authorized addition of tracer elements to distilled spirits under provisions of section 5201(d) shall not be deemed to be rectification within the meaning of sections 5021, 5081, and 5082.

Amendments

• **1965, Excise Tax Reduction Act of 1965 (P.L. 89-44)**

P.L. 89-44, § 805(b):

Redesignated former subsection (k) of Section 5025 as subsection (l) of Section 5025. **Effective** 10-1-65.

[Sec. 5025(m)]

(m) CROSS REFERENCES.—

(1) For provisions exempting distilled spirits and wines rectified in customs manufacturing bonded warehouses, see section 5523.

(2) For provisions exempting winemakers in the use or treatment of wines or wine spirits, see section 5391.

(3) For provisions exempting the manufacture of volatile fruit-flavor concentrates, see section 5511.

Amendments

• **1965, Excise Tax Reduction Act of 1965 (P.L. 89-44)**

P.L. 89-44, § 805(b):

Redesignated former subsection (l) of Section 5025 as subsection (m) of Section 5025. **Effective** 10-1-65.

ALCOHOL TAXES—GALLONAGE TAXES

[Sec. 5026—Repealed]

Amendments

• **1979, Trade Agreements Act of 1979 (P.L. 96-39)**

P.L. 96-39, §803(a):

Repealed Code Sec. 5026. **Effective** 1-1-80. Prior to repeal, Code Sec. 5026 read as follows:

SEC. 5026. DETERMINATION AND COLLECTION OF RECTIFICATION TAX.

[Sec. 5026(a)]

(a) DETERMINATION OF TAX.—

(1) GENERAL.—The taxes imposed by sections 5021 and 5022 shall be determined upon the completion of the process of rectification by such means as the Secretary shall by regulations prescribe and with the use of such devices and apparatus (including but not limited to storage, gauging, and bottling tanks, and pipelines) as the Secretary may by regulations prescribe.

(2) UNAUTHORIZED RECTIFICATION.—In the case of taxable rectification on premises other than premises on which rectification is authorized, the tax imposed by section 5021 or 5022 shall be due and payable at the time of such rectification.

Amendments

• **1976, Tax Reform Act of 1976 (P.L. 94-455)**

P.L. 94-455, §1906(b)(13)(A):

Amended 1954 Code by substituting "Secretary" for "Secretary or his delegate" each place it appeared. **Effective** 2-1-77.

[Sec. 5026(b)]

(b) PAYMENT OF TAX.—The taxes imposed by sections 5021, 5022, and 5023 shall be paid in accordance with section 5061.

Amendments

• **1976, Tax Reform Act of 1976 (P.L. 94-455)**

P.L. 94-455, §1905(b)(2)(B):

Substituted "The taxes" for "Except as provided in subsection (a)(3), the taxes" in Code Sec. 5026(b). **Effective** 2-1-77.

Subpart C—Wines

Sec. 5041. Imposition and rate of tax.
Sec. 5042. Exemption from tax.
Sec. 5043. Collection of taxes on wines.
Sec. 5044. Refund of tax on wine.
Sec. 5045. Cross references.

[Sec. 5041]

SEC. 5041. IMPOSITION AND RATE OF TAX.

[Sec. 5041(a)]

(a) IMPOSITION.—There is hereby imposed on all wines (including imitation, substandard, or artificial wine, and compounds sold as wine) having not in excess of 24 percent of alcohol by volume, in bond in, produced in, or imported into, the United States, taxes at the rates shown in subsection (b), such taxes to be determined as of the time of removal for consumption or sale. All wines containing more than 24 percent of alcohol by volume shall be classed as distilled spirits and taxed accordingly. Subject to subsection (h), still wines shall include those wines containing not more than 0.392 gram of carbon dioxide per hundred milliliters of wine; except that the Secretary may by regulations prescribe such tolerances to this maximum limitation as may be reasonably necessary in good commercial practice.

Amendments

• **2017, Tax Cuts and Jobs Act (P.L. 115-97)**

P.L. 115-97, §13806(a)(1):

Amended Code Sec. 5041(a) by striking "Still wines" and inserting "Subject to subsection (h), still wines". **Effective** for wine removed after 12-31-2017.

P.L. 115-97, §13809 (as added by P.L. 115-123, §41111, Div. D), provides:

SEC. 13809. RULE OF CONSTRUCTION.

Nothing in this subpart, the amendments made by this subpart, or any regulation promulgated under this subpart or the amendments made by this subpart, shall be construed to preempt, supersede, or otherwise limit or restrict any State, local, or tribal law that prohibits or regulates the production or sale of distilled spirits, wine, or malt beverages.

• **1976, Tax Reform Act of 1976 (P.L. 94-455)**

P.L. 94-455, §1906(b)(13)(A):

Amended 1954 Code by substituting "Secretary" for "Secretary or his delegate" each place it appeared. **Effective** 2-1-77.

• **1974 (P.L. 93-490)**

P.L. 93-490, §6:

Amended Code Sec. 5041(a) by substituting "0.392" for "0.277" in the last sentence thereof. **Effective** 2-1-75.

• **1965, Excise Tax Reduction Act of 1965 (P.L. 89-44)**

P.L. 89-44, §806(a):

Amended subsection (a) of Section 5041 by inserting "0.277" in lieu of "0.256." **Effective** 7-1-65.

[Sec. 5041(b)]

(b) RATES OF TAX.—

(1) On still wines containing not more than 16 percent of alcohol by volume, $1.07 per wine gallon;

(2) On still wines containing more than 16 percent and not exceeding 21 percent of alcohol by volume, $1.57 per wine gallon;

(3) On still wines containing more than 21 percent and not exceeding 24 percent of alcohol by volume, $3.15 per wine gallon;

(4) On champagne and other sparkling wines, $3.40 per wine gallon;

(5) On artificially carbonated wines, $3.30 per wine gallon; and

(6) On hard cider, 22.6 cents per wine gallon.

Amendments

• **2020, Taxpayer Certainty and Disaster Tax Relief Act of 2020 (P.L. 116-260)**

P.L. 116-260, §106(e)(1), Div. EE:

Amended Code Sec. 5041(b)(1) and (2) by striking "14 percent" and all that follows through "January 1, 2021" and inserting "16 percent". **Effective** for wine removed after 12-31-2020. Prior to being stricken, "14 percent" and all that follows through "January 1, 2021" in Code Sec. 5041(b)(1) and (2) read as follows:

14 percent (16 percent in the case of wine removed after December 31, 2017, and before January 1, 2021

• **2019, Taxpayer Certainty and Disaster Tax Relief Act of 2019 (P.L. 116-94)**

P.L. 116-94, §144(e)(1), Div. Q:

Amended Code Sec. 5041(b)(1) and (2) by striking "January 1, 2020" and inserting "January 1, 2021". **Effective** for wine removed after 12-31-2019.

• **2017, Tax Cuts and Jobs Act (P.L. 115-97)**

P.L. 115-97, §13805(a):

Amended Code Sec. 5041(b)(1) and (2) by inserting "(16 percent in the case of wine removed after December 31, 2017, and before January 1, 2020[)]" after "14 percent". **Effective** for wine removed after 12-31-2017.

P.L. 115-97, §13809 (as added by P.L. 115-123, §41111, Div. D), provides:

SEC. 13809. RULE OF CONSTRUCTION.

Nothing in this subpart, the amendments made by this subpart, or any regulation promulgated under this subpart or the amendments made by this subpart, shall be construed to preempt, supersede, or otherwise limit or restrict any State, local, or tribal law that prohibits or regulates the production or sale of distilled spirits, wine, or malt beverages.

ALCOHOL TAXES—GALLONAGE TAXES

- **2015, Protecting Americans from Tax Hikes Act of 2015 (P.L. 114-113)**

P.L. 114-113, §335(a)(1), Div. Q:

Amended Code Sec. 5041(b)(6) by striking "which is a still wine" and all that follows through "alcohol by volume". **Effective** for hard cider removed during calendar years beginning after 12-31-2016. Prior to being stricken, "which is a still wine" and all that follows through "alcohol by volume" in Code Sec. 5041(b)(6) read as follows:

which is a still wine derived primarily from apples or apple concentrate and water, containing no other fruit product, and containing at least one-half of 1 percent and less than 7 percent alcohol by volume

- **1998, IRS Restructuring and Reform Act of 1998 (P.L. 105-206)**

P.L. 105-206, §6009(a):

Amended Code Sec. 5041(b)(6) by inserting "which is a still wine" after "hard cider". **Effective** as if included in the provision of P.L. 105-34 to which it relates [effective 10-1-97.—CCH].

- **1997, Taxpayer Relief Act of 1997 (P.L. 105-34)**

P.L. 105-34, §908(a):

Amended Code Sec. 5041(b) by striking "and" at the end of paragraph (4), by striking the period at the end of paragraph (5) and inserting "; and", and by adding at the end a new paragraph (6). **Effective** 1-1-97.

- **1990, Omnibus Budget Reconciliation Act of 1990 (P.L. 101-508)**

P.L. 101-508, §11201(b)(1)(A):

Amended Code Sec. 5041(b)(1) by striking "17 cents" and inserting "$1.07". **Effective** 1-1-91.

P.L. 101-508, §11201(b)(1)(B):

Amended Code Sec. 5041(b)(2) by striking "67 cents" and inserting "$1.57". **Effective** 1-1-91.

P.L. 101-508, §11201(b)(1)(C):

Amended Code Sec. 5041(b)(3) by striking "$2.25" and inserting "$3.15". **Effective** 1-1-91.

P.L. 101-508, §11201(b)(1)(D):

Amended Code Sec. 5041(b)(5) by striking "$2.40" and inserting "$3.30". **Effective** 1-1-91.

- **1965, Excise Tax Reduction Act of 1965 (P.L. 89-44)**

P.L. 89-44, §501(c):

Amended Code Sec. 5041(b). **Effective** 7-1-65. Prior to amendment, Code Sec. 5041(b) read as below:

"(b) Rates of Tax.—

"(1) On still wines containing not more than 14 percent of alcohol by volume, 17 cents per wine gallon, except that on and after July 1, 1965, the rate shall be 15 cents per wine gallon;

"(2) On still wines containing more than 14 percent and not exceeding 21 percent of alcohol by volume, 67 cents per wine gallon, except that on and after July 1, 1965, the rate shall be 60 cents a wine gallon;

"(3) On still wines containing more than 21 percent and not exceeding 24 percent of alcohol by volume, $2.25 per wine gallon, except that on and after July 1, 1965, the rate shall be $2.00 per wine gallon;

"(4) On champagne and other sparkling wines, $3.40 per wine gallon, except that on and after July 1, 1965, the rate shall be $3.00 per wine gallon; and

"(5) On artificially carbonated wines, $2.40 per wine gallon, except that on and after July 1, 1965, the rate shall be $2.00 per wine gallon."

- **1964, Excise Tax Rate Extension Act of 1964 (P.L. 88-348)**

P.L. 88-348, §2(a)(7):

Substituted "1965" for "1964" wherever it appeared in Sec. 5041(b).

- **1963, Tax Rate Extension Act of 1963 (P.L. 88-52)**

P.L. 88-52, §3(a)(7):

Substituted "1964" for "1963" wherever it appeared in Sec. 5041(b).

- **1962, Tax Rate Extension Act of 1962 (P.L. 87-508)**

P.L. 87-508, §3(a)(6):

Substituted "1963" for "1962" wherever it appeared in Sec. 5041(b).

- **1961, Tax Rate Extension Act of 1961 (P.L. 87-72)**

P.L. 87-72, §3(a)(7):

Substituted "1962" for "1961" wherever it appeared in Sec. 5041(b).

- **1960, Public Debt and Tax Rate Extension Act of 1960 (P.L. 86-564)**

P.L. 86-564, §202(a):

Substituted "July 1, 1961" for "July 1, 1960" in Sec. 5041(b).

- **1959, Tax Rate Extension Act of 1959 (P.L. 86-75)**

P.L. 86-75, §3(a):

Substituted "July 1, 1960" for "July 1, 1959" in Sec. 5041(b).

[Sec. 5041(c)]

(c) CREDIT.—

(1) ALLOWANCE OF CREDIT.—

(A) IN GENERAL.—There shall be allowed as a credit against any tax imposed by this title (other than chapters 2, 21, and 22) an amount equal to the sum of—

(i) $1 per wine gallon on the first 30,000 wine gallons of wine, plus

(ii) 90 cents per wine gallon on the first 100,000 wine gallons of wine to which clause (i) does not apply, plus

(iii) 53.5 cents per wine gallon on the first 620,000 wine gallons of wine to which clauses (i) and (ii) do not apply,

which are produced by the producer and removed during the calendar year for consumption or sale, or which are imported by the importer into the United States during the calendar year but only if the importer is an electing importer under paragraph (6) and the wine gallons of wine have been assigned to the importer pursuant to such paragraph.

(B) ADJUSTMENT OF CREDIT FOR HARD CIDER.—In the case of wine described in subsection (b)(6), subparagraph (A) of this paragraph shall be applied—

(i) in clause (i) of such subparagraph, by substituting "6.2 cents" for "$1",

(ii) in clause (ii) of such subparagraph, by substituting "5.6 cents" for "90 cents", and

(iii) in clause (iii) of such subparagraph, by substituting "3.3 cents" for "53.5 cents".

(2) TIME FOR DETERMINING AND ALLOWING CREDIT.—The credit allowable by paragraph (1)—

(A) shall be determined at the same time the tax is determined under subsection (a) of this section, and

(B) shall be allowable at the time any tax described in paragraph (1) is payable as if the credit allowable by this subsection constituted a reduction in the rate of such tax.

(3) CONTROLLED GROUPS.—Rules similar to rules of section 5051(a)(5) shall apply for purposes of this subsection.

(4) DENIAL OF DEDUCTION.—Any deduction under subtitle A with respect to any tax against which a credit is allowed under this subsection shall only be for the amount of such tax as reduced by such credit.

(5) CREDIT FOR TRANSFEREE IN BOND.—If—

(A) wine produced by any person would be eligible for any credit under paragraph (1) if removed by such person during the calendar year,

(B) wine produced by such person is removed during such calendar year by any other person (hereafter in this paragraph referred to as the "transferee") to whom such wine was transferred in bond and who is liable for the tax imposed by this section with respect to such wine, and

(C) such producer holds title to such wine at the time of its removal and provides to the transferee such information as is necessary to properly determine the transferee's credit under this paragraph,

then, the transferee (and not the producer) shall be allowed the credit under paragraph (1) which would be allowed to the producer if the wine removed by the transferee had been removed by the producer on that date.

(6) ALLOWANCE OF CREDIT FOR FOREIGN MANUFACTURERS AND IMPORTERS.—

(A) IN GENERAL.—In the case of any wine gallons of wine which have been produced outside of the United States and imported into the United States, the credit allowable under paragraph (1) (referred to in this paragraph as the "tax credit") may be assigned by the

ALCOHOL TAXES—GALLONAGE TAXES

person who produced such wine (referred to in this paragraph as the "foreign producer"), provided that such person makes an election described in subparagraph (B)(ii), to any electing importer of such wine gallons pursuant to the requirements established by the Secretary under subparagraph (B).

(B) ASSIGNMENT.—The Secretary of the Treasury, after consultation with the Secretary of the Department of Homeland Security, shall, through such rules, regulations, and procedures as are determined appropriate, establish procedures for assignment of the tax credit provided under this paragraph, which shall include—

(i) a limitation to ensure that the number of wine gallons of wine for which the tax credit has been assigned by a foreign producer—

(I) to any importer does not exceed the number of wine gallons of wine produced by such foreign producer during the calendar year which were imported into the United States by such importer, and

(II) to all importers does not exceed the 750,000 wine gallons of wine to which the tax credit applies,

(ii) procedures that allow the election of a foreign producer to assign and an importer to receive the tax credit provided under this paragraph,

(iii) requirements that the foreign producer provide any information as the Secretary determines necessary and appropriate for purposes of carrying out this paragraph, and

(iv) procedures that allow for revocation of eligibility of the foreign producer and the importer for the tax credit provided under this paragraph in the case of any erroneous or fraudulent information provided under clause (iii) which the Secretary deems to be material to qualifying for such credit.

(C) CONTROLLED GROUP.—For purposes of this section, any importer making an election described in subparagraph (B)(ii) shall be deemed to be a member of the controlled group of the foreign producer, as described under paragraph (3).

(7) REFUNDS IN LIEU OF TAX CREDITS FOR FOREIGN PRODUCTION REMOVED AFTER DECEMBER 31, 2022.—

(A) IN GENERAL.—In the case of any wine gallons of wine which have been produced outside the United States and imported into the United States, if such wine gallons are removed after December 31, 2022—

(i) paragraph (1) shall not apply, and

(ii) the amount determined under subparagraph (B) shall be allowed as a refund, determined for periods not less frequently than quarterly, to the importer in the same manner as if such amount were an overpayment of tax imposed by this section.

(B) AMOUNT OF REFUND.—The amount determined under this subparagraph with respect to any importer for any period is an amount equal to the sum of—

(i) excess (if any) of—

(I) the amount of tax imposed under this section on wine gallons of wine referred to in subparagraph (A) which were removed during such period, over

(II) the amount of tax which would have been imposed under this section (including any allowable credits) on such gallons of wine if this section were applied without regard to this paragraph, plus

(ii) the amount of interest which would be allowed and paid on an overpayment of tax at the overpayment rate established under section 6621(a)(1) (without regard to the second sentence thereof) were such rate applied to the excess (if any) determined under clause (i) for the number of days in the filing period for which the refund under this paragraph is being determined.

(C) APPLICATION OF RULES RELATED TO ELECTIONS AND ASSIGNMENTS.—Subparagraph (A)(ii) shall apply only if the importer is an electing importer under paragraph (6) and the wine gallons of wine have been assigned to the importer pursuant to such paragraph.

(D) RULES FOR REFUNDS WITHIN 90 DAYS.—For purposes of refunds allowed under this paragraph, section 6611(e) shall be applied by substituting "90 days" for "45 days" each place it appears.

(8) REGULATIONS.—The Secretary may prescribe such regulations as may be necessary to carry out the purposes of this subsection, including regulations to ensure proper calculation of the credit provided in this subsection.

Amendments

• **2020, Taxpayer Certainty and Disaster Tax Relief Act of 2020 (P.L. 116-260)**

P.L. 116-260, § 106(d)(1)(A)-(F), Div. EE:

Amended Code Sec. 5041(c) by striking "FOR SMALL DOMESTIC PRODUCERS" following "CREDIT" in the heading, by amending paragraph (1), by striking paragraphs (2) and (8), by redesignating paragraphs (3) through (6) as paragraphs (2) through (5), respectively, by redesignating paragraph (9) as paragraph (6), and by amending paragraph (7). **Effective** for wine removed after 12-31-2020. Prior to amendment, Code Sec. 5041(c)(1) and (7) read as follows:

(1) ALLOWANCE OF CREDIT.—Except as provided in paragraph (2), in the case of a person who produces not more than 250,000 wine gallons of wine during the calendar year, there shall be allowed as a credit against any tax imposed by this title (other than chapters 2, 21, and 22) of 90 cents per wine gallon on the 1st 100,000 wine gallons of wine (other than wine described in subsection (b)(4)) which are removed during such year for consumption or sale and which have been produced at qualified facilities in the United States. In the case of wine described in subsection (b)(6), the preceding sentence shall be applied by substituting "5.6 cents" for "90 cents".

***

(7) REGULATIONS.—The Secretary may prescribe such regulations as may be necessary to carry out the purposes of this subsection, including regulations—

(A) to prevent the credit provided in this subsection from benefiting any person who produces more than 250,000 wine gallons of wine during a calendar year, and

(B) to assure proper reduction of such credit for persons producing more than 150,000 wine gallons of wine during a calendar year.

Prior to being stricken, Code Sec 5041(c)(2) and (8) read as follows:

(2) REDUCTION IN CREDIT.—The credit allowable by paragraph (1) shall be reduced (but not below zero) by 1 percent for each 1,000 wine gallons of wine produced in excess of 150,000 wine gallons of wine during the calendar year.

***

(8) TEMPORARY SPECIAL RULE.—

(A) IN GENERAL.—In the case of wine removed after December 31, 2017, and before January 1, 2021, paragraphs (1) and (2) shall not apply and there shall be allowed as a credit against any tax imposed by this title (other than chapters 2, 21, and 22) an amount equal to the sum of—

(i) $1 per wine gallon on the first 30,000 wine gallons of wine, plus

(ii) 90 cents per wine gallon on the first 100,000 wine gallons of wine to which clause (i) does not apply, plus

(iii) 53.5 cents per wine gallon on the first 620,000 wine gallons of wine to which clauses (i) and (ii) do not apply,

which are produced by the producer and removed during the calendar year for consumption or sale, or which are imported by the importer into the United States during the calendar year but only if the importer is an electing importer under paragraph (9) and the wine gallons of wine have been assigned to the importer pursuant to such paragraph.

(B) ADJUSTMENT OF CREDIT FOR HARD CIDER.—In the case of wine described in subsection (b)(6), subparagraph (A) of this paragraph shall be applied—

(i) in clause (i) of such subparagraph, by substituting "6.2 cents" for "$1",

(ii) in clause (ii) of such subparagraph, by substituting "5.6 cents" for "90 cents", and

(iii) in clause (iii) of such subparagraph, by substituting "3.3 cents" for "53.5 cents".

(C) APPLICATION OF CERTAIN RULES.—Paragraphs (3) and (6) shall be applied by substituting "paragraph (1) or (8)" for "paragraph (1)" each place it appears therein.

P.L. 116-260, § 106(d)(2)(A)-(B), Div. EE:

Amended Code Sec. 5041(c), as amended by Act Sec. 106(d)(1), by inserting "but only if the importer is an electing importer under paragraph (6) and the wine gallons of wine have been assigned to the importer pursuant to such paragraph" after "into the United States during the calendar year" in paragraph (1)(A), by striking "paragraph (8)" and inserting "paragraph (1)" in paragraph (6)(A), by striking "The Secretary" and inserting "The Secretary of the Treasury, after consultation with the Secretary of the Department of Homeland Security," in paragraph (6)(B), and by striking "paragraph (4)" and inserting "paragraph (3)" in paragraph (6)(C). **Effective** for wine removed after 12-31-2020.

P.L. 116-260, § 107(c)(1), Div. EE:

Amended Code Sec. 5041(c), as amended by the preceding provisions of this Act, by redesignating paragraph (7) as paragraph (8), and by inserting after paragraph (6) a new paragraph (7). **Effective** for wine removed after 12-31-2022. For a special rule, see Act Sec. 107(e)-(g), Div. EE, below.

P.L. 116-260, § 107(e)-(g), Div. EE, provides:

(e) ADMINISTRATION OF REFUNDS.—The Secretary of the Treasury (or the Secretary's delegate within the Department of the Treasury) shall implement and administer

ALCOHOL TAXES—GALLONAGE TAXES

sections 5001(c)(4), 5041(c)(7), and 5051(a)(6) of the Internal Revenue Code of 1986, as added by this Act, in coordination with the United States Customs and Border Protection of the Department of Homeland Security.

(f) REGULATIONS.—The Secretary of the Treasury (or the Secretary's delegate within the Department of the Treasury) shall prescribe such regulations as may be necessary or appropriate to carry out the purposes of this section, including regulations to require foreign producers to provide information necessary to enforce the volume limitations under sections 5001(c), 5041(c), and 5051(a) of such Code.

(g) REPORT.—Not later than 180 days after the date of the enactment of this Act, the Secretary of the Treasury (or the Secretary's delegate within the Department of the Treasury) shall, in coordination with the United States Customs and Border Protection of the Department of Homeland Security, prepare, submit to Congress, and make publicly available a report detailing the plans for implementing and administering sections 5001(c)(4), 5041(c)(7), and 5051(a)(6) of such Code, as added by this Act.

- **2019, Taxpayer Certainty and Disaster Tax Relief Act of 2019 (P.L. 116-94)**

P.L. 116-94, §144(d)(1), Div. Q.

Amended Code Sec. 5041(c)(8)(A) by striking "January 1, 2020" and inserting "January 1, 2021". **Effective** for wine removed after 12-31-2019.

P.L. 116-94, §144(d)(2), Div. Q.

Amended the heading for Code Sec. 5041(c)(8) by striking "SPECIAL RULE FOR 2018 AND 2019" and inserting "TEMPORARY SPECIAL RULE". **Effective** for wine removed after 12-31-2019.

P.L. 116-94, §144(j)(1), Div. Q.

Amended Code Sec. 5041(c)(8) by adding at the end a new subparagraph (C). **Effective** as if included in section 13804 of the Tax Cuts and Jobs Act (P.L. 115-97) [effective for wine removed after 12-31-2017.—CCH].

- **2017, Tax Cuts and Jobs Act (P.L. 115-97)**

P.L. 115-97, §13804(a):

Amended Code Sec. 5041(c) by adding at the end a new paragraph (8). **Effective** for wine removed after 12-31-2017.

P.L. 115-97, §13804(b):

Amended Code Sec. 5041(c)(4) by striking "section 5051(a)(2)(B)" and inserting "section 5051(a)(5)". **Effective** for wine removed after 12-31-2017.

P.L. 115-97, §13804(c)(1)-(2):

Amended Code Sec. 5041(c), as amended by Act Sec. 13804(a), by inserting "but only if the importer is an electing importer under paragraph (9) and the wine gallons of wine have been assigned to the importer pursuant to such paragraph" after "into the United States during the calendar year" in paragraph (8)(A), and by adding at the end a new paragraph (9). **Effective** for wine removed after 12-31-2017.

P.L. 115-97, §13809 (as added by P.L. 115-123, §41111, Div. D), provides:

SEC. 13809. RULE OF CONSTRUCTION.

Nothing in this subpart, the amendments made by this subpart, or any regulation promulgated under this subpart or the amendments made by this subpart, shall be construed to preempt, supersede, or otherwise limit or restrict any State, local, or tribal law that prohibits or regulates the production or sale of distilled spirits, wine, or malt beverages.

- **1997, Taxpayer Relief Act of 1997 (P.L. 105-34)**

P.L. 105-34, §908(b):

Amended Code Sec. 5041(c)(1) by adding at the end a new sentence. **Effective** 10-1-97.

- **1996, Small Business Job Protection Act of 1996 (P.L. 104-188)**

P.L. 104-188, §1702(b)(5):

Amended Code Sec. 5041(c) by striking paragraph (6) and by inserting new paragraphs (6) and (7). **Effective** as if included in the provision of P.L. 101-508 to which it relates. Prior to amendment, Code Sec. 5041(c)(6) read as follows:

(6) REGULATIONS.—The Secretary may prescribe such regulations as may be necessary to prevent the credit provided in this subsection from benefiting any person who produces more than 250,000 wine gallons of wine during a calendar year and to assure proper reduction of such credit for persons producing more than 150,000 wine gallons of wine during a calendar year.

- **1990, Omnibus Budget Reconciliation Act of 1990 (P.L. 101-508)**

P.L. 101-508, §11201(b)(2):

Amended Code Sec. 5041 by redesignating subsections (c), (d), and (e) as subsections (d), (e), and (f), respectively, and by inserting after subsection (b) a new subsection (c). **Effective** 1-1-91.

[Sec. 5041(d)]

(d) WINE GALLON.—For the purpose of this chapter, the term "wine gallon" means a United States gallon of liquid measure equivalent to the volume of 231 cubic inches. On lesser quantities the tax shall be paid proportionately (fractions of less than one-tenth gallon being converted to the nearest one-tenth gallon, and five-hundredths gallon being converted to the next full one-tenth gallon).

Amendments

- **1990, Omnibus Budget Reconciliation Act of 1990 (P.L. 101-508)**

P.L. 101-508, §11201(b)(2):

Amended Code Sec. 5041 by redesignating subsection (c) as subsection (d). **Effective** 1-1-91.

[Sec. 5041(e)]

(e) TOLERANCES.—Where the Secretary finds that the revenue will not be endangered thereby, he may by regulation prescribe tolerances (but not greater than $1/2$ of 1 percent) for bottles and other containers, and, if such tolerances are prescribed, no assessment shall be made and no tax shall be collected for any excess in any case where the contents of a bottle or other container are within the limit of the applicable tolerance prescribed.

Amendments

- **1990, Omnibus Budget Reconciliation Act of 1990 (P.L. 101-508)**

P.L. 101-508, §11201(b)(2):

Amended Code Sec. 5041 by redesignating subsection (d) as subsection (e). **Effective** 1-1-91.

- **1988, Technical and Miscellaneous Revenue Act of 1988 (P.L. 100-647)**

P.L. 100-647, §6101(a):

Amended Code Sec. 5041 by redesignating subsection (d) as subsection (e) and by inserting after subsection (c) new subsection (d). **Effective** for wine removed after 12-31-88.

[Sec. 5041(f)]

(f) ILLEGALLY PRODUCED WINE.—Notwithstanding subsection (a), any wine produced in the United States at any place other than the bonded premises provided for in this chapter shall (except as provided in section 5042 in the case of tax-free production) be subject to tax at the rate prescribed in subsection (b) at the time of production and whether or not removed for consumption or sale.

Amendments

- **1990, Omnibus Budget Reconciliation Act of 1990 (P.L. 101-508)**

P.L. 101-508, §11201(b)(2):

Amended Code Sec. 5041 by redesignating subsection (e) as subsection (f). **Effective** 1-1-91.

P.L. 101-508, §11201(e), provides:

(e) FLOOR STOCKS TAXES.—

(1) IMPOSITION OF TAX.—

(A) IN GENERAL.—In the case of any tax-increased article—

(i) on which tax was determined under part I of subchapter A of chapter 51 of the Internal Revenue Code of 1986 or section 7652 of such Code before January 1, 1991, and

(ii) which is held on such date for sale by any person,

there shall be imposed a tax at the applicable rate on each such article.

(B) APPLICABLE RATE.—For purposes of subparagraph (A), the applicable rate is—

(i) $1 per proof gallon in the case of distilled spirits,

(ii) $0.90 per wine gallon in the case of wine described in paragraph (1), (2), (3), or (5) of section 5041(b) of such Code, and

(iii) $9 per barrel in the case of beer.

In the case of a fraction of a gallon or barrel, the tax imposed by subparagraph (A) shall be the same fraction as the amount of such tax imposed on a whole gallon or barrel.

(C) TAX-INCREASED ARTICLE.—For purposes of this subsection, the term "tax-increased article" means distilled spirits, wine described in paragraph (1), (2), (3), or (5) of section 5041(b) of such Code, and beer.

(2) EXCEPTION FOR SMALL DOMESTIC PRODUCERS.—

(A) In the case of wine held by the producer thereof on January 1, 1991, if a credit would have been allowable under section 5041(c) of such Code (as added by this section) on such wine had the amendments made by subsection (b) applied to all wine removed during 1990 and had the wine so held been removed for consumption on December 31, 1990, the tax imposed by paragraph (1) on such wine shall be reduced by the credit which would have been so allowable.

(B) In the case of beer held by the producer thereof on January 1, 1991, if the rate of the tax imposed by section 5051 of such Code would have been determined under subsection (a)(2) thereof had the beer so held been removed for consumption on December 31, 1990, the tax imposed by paragraph (1) on such beer shall not apply.

(C) For purposes of this paragraph, an article shall not be treated as held by the producer if title thereto had at any time been transferred to any other person.

Sec. 5041(d)

(3) EXCEPTION FOR CERTAIN SMALL WHOLESALE OR RETAIL DEALERS.—No tax shall be imposed by paragraph (1) on tax-increased articles held on January 1, 1991, by any dealer if—

(A) the aggregate liquid volume of tax-increased articles held by such dealer on such date does not exceed 500 wine gallons, and

(B) such dealer submits to the Secretary (at the time and in the manner required by the Secretary) such information as the Secretary shall require for purposes of this paragraph.

(4) CREDIT AGAINST TAX.—Each dealer shall be allowed as a credit against the taxes imposed by paragraph (1) an amount equal to—

(A) $240 to the extent such taxes are attributable to distilled spirits,

(B) $270 to the extent such taxes are attributable to wine, and

(C) $87 to the extent such taxes are attributable to beer.

Such credit shall not exceed the amount of taxes imposed by paragraph (1) with respect to distilled spirits, wine, or beer, as the case may be, for which the dealer is liable.

(5) LIABILITY FOR TAX AND METHOD OF PAYMENT.—

(A) LIABILITY FOR TAX.—A person holding any tax-increased article on January 1, 1991, to which the tax imposed by paragraph (1) applies shall be liable for such tax.

(B) METHOD OF PAYMENT.—The tax imposed by paragraph (1) shall be paid in such manner as the Secretary shall prescribe by regulations.

(C) TIME FOR PAYMENT.—The tax imposed by paragraph (1) shall be paid on or before June 30, 1991.

(6) CONTROLLED GROUPS.—

(A) CORPORATIONS.—In the case of a controlled group—

(i) the 500 wine gallon amount specified in paragraph (3), and

(ii) the $240, $270, and $87 amounts specified in paragraph (4),

shall be apportioned among the dealers who are component members of such group in such manner as the Secretary shall by regulations prescribe. For purposes of the preceding sentence, the term "controlled group" has the meaning given to such term by subsection (a) of section 1563 of such Code; except that for such purposes the phrase "more than 50 percent" shall be substituted for the phrase "at least 80 percent" each place it appears in such subsection.

(B) NONINCORPORATED DEALERS UNDER COMMON CONTROL.—Under regulations prescribed by the Secretary, principles similar to the principles of subparagraph (A) shall apply to a group of dealers under common control where 1 or more of such dealers is not a corporation.

(7) OTHER LAWS APPLICABLE.—

(A) IN GENERAL.—All provisions of law, including penalties, applicable to the comparable excise tax with respect to any tax-increased article shall, insofar as applicable and not inconsistent with the provisions of this subsection, apply to the floor stocks taxes imposed by paragraph (1) to the same extent as if such taxes were imposed by the comparable excise tax.

(B) COMPARABLE EXCISE TAX.—For purposes of subparagraph (A), the term "comparable excise tax" means—

(i) the tax imposed by section 5001 of such Code in the case of distilled spirits,

(ii) the tax imposed by section 5041 of such Code in the case of wine, and

(iii) the tax imposed by section 5051 of such Code in the case of beer.

(8) DEFINITIONS.—For purposes of this subsection—

(A) IN GENERAL.—Terms used in this subsection which are also used in subchapter A of chapter 51 of such Code shall have the respective meanings such terms have in such part.

(B) PERSON.—The term "person" includes any State or political subdivision thereof, or any agency or instrumentality of a State or political subdivision thereof.

(C) SECRETARY.—The term "Secretary" means the Secretary of the Treasury or his delegate.

(9) TREATMENT OF IMPORTED PERFUMES CONTAINING DISTILLED SPIRITS.—For purposes of this subsection, any article described in section 5001(a)(3) of such Code shall be treated as distilled spirits; except that the tax imposed by paragraph (1) shall be imposed on a wine gallon basis in lieu of a proof gallon basis. To the extent provided by regulations prescribed by the Secretary, the preceding sentence shall not apply to any article held on January 1, 1991, on the premises of a retail establishment.

• **1988, Technical and Miscellaneous Revenue Act of 1988 (P.L. 100-647)**

P.L. 100-647, §6101(a):

Amended Code Sec. 5041 by redesignating subsection (d) as (e). **Effective** for wine removed after 12-31-88.

[Sec. 5041(g)]

(g) HARD CIDER.—For purposes of subsection (b)(6), the term "hard cider" means a wine—

(1) containing not more than 0.64 gram of carbon dioxide per hundred milliliters of wine, except that the Secretary may by regulations prescribe such tolerances to this limitation as may be reasonably necessary in good commercial practice,

(2) which is derived primarily—

(A) from apples or pears, or

(B) from—

(i) apple juice concentrate or pear juice concentrate, and

(ii) water,

(3) which contains no fruit product or fruit flavoring other than apple or pear, and

(4) which contains at least one-half of 1 percent and less than 8.5 percent alcohol by volume.

Amendments

• **2015, Protecting Americans from Tax Hikes Act of 2015 (P.L. 114-113)**

P.L. 114-113, §335(a)(2), Div. Q:

Amended Code Sec. 5041 by adding at the end a new subsection (g). **Effective** for hard cider removed during calendar years beginning after 12-31-2016.

[Sec. 5041(h)]

(h) MEAD AND LOW ALCOHOL BY VOLUME WINE.—

(1) IN GENERAL.—For purposes of subsections (a) and (b)(1), mead and low alcohol by volume wine shall be deemed to be still wines containing not more than 16 percent of alcohol by volume.

(2) DEFINITIONS.—

(A) MEAD.—For purposes of this section, the term "mead" means a wine—

(i) containing not more than 0.64 gram of carbon dioxide per hundred milliliters of wine, except that the Secretary may by regulations prescribe such tolerances to this limitation as may be reasonably necessary in good commercial practice,

(ii) which is derived solely from honey and water,

(iii) which contains no fruit product or fruit flavoring, and

(iv) which contains less than 8.5 percent alcohol by volume.

(B) LOW ALCOHOL BY VOLUME WINE.—For purposes of this section, the term "low alcohol by volume wine" means a wine—

(i) containing not more than 0.64 gram of carbon dioxide per hundred milliliters of wine, except that the Secretary may by regulations prescribe such tolerances to this limitation as may be reasonably necessary in good commercial practice,

(ii) which is derived—

(I) primarily from grapes, or

(II) from grape juice concentrate and water,

(iii) which contains no fruit product or fruit flavoring other than grape, and

(iv) which contains less than 8.5 percent alcohol by volume.

Amendments

• **2020, Taxpayer Certainty and Disaster Tax Relief Act of 2020 (P.L. 116-260)**

P.L. 116-260, §106(f)(1)(A)-(B), Div. EE:

Amended Code Sec. 5041(h) by striking "the Secretary shall" each place it appears in paragraph (2) and inserting "the Secretary may", and by striking paragraph (3).

Effective for wine removed after 12-31-2020. Prior to being stricken, Code Sec. 5041(h)(3) read as follows:

(3) TERMINATION.—This subsection shall not apply to wine removed after December 31, 2020.

ALCOHOL TAXES—GALLONAGE TAXES

- **2019, Taxpayer Certainty and Disaster Tax Relief Act of 2019 (P.L. 116-94)**

P.L. 116-94, §144(f)(1), Div. Q:

Amended Code Sec. 5041(h)(3) by striking "December 31, 2019" and inserting "December 31, 2020". **Effective** for wine removed after 12-31-2019.

- **2017, Tax Cuts and Jobs Act (P.L. 115-97)**

P.L. 115-97, §13806(a)(2):

Amended Code Sec. 5041 by adding at the end a new subsection (h). **Effective** for wine removed after 12-31-2017.

P.L. 115-97, §13809 (as added by P.L. 115-123, §41111, Div. D), provides:

SEC. 13809. RULE OF CONSTRUCTION.

Nothing in this subpart, the amendments made by this subpart, or any regulation promulgated under this subpart or the amendments made by this subpart, shall be construed to preempt, supersede, or otherwise limit or restrict any State, local, or tribal law that prohibits or regulates the production or sale of distilled spirits, wine, or malt beverages.

[Sec. 5042]

SEC. 5042. EXEMPTION FROM TAX.

[Sec. 5042(a)]

(a) TAX-FREE PRODUCTION.—

(1) CIDER.—Subject to regulations prescribed by the Secretary, the noneffervescent product of the normal alcoholic fermentation of apple juice only, which is produced at a place other than a bonded wine cellar and without the use of preservative methods or materials, and which is sold or offered for sale as cider and not as wine or as a substitute for wine, shall not be subject to tax as wine nor to the provisions of subchapter F.

(2) WINE FOR PERSONAL OR FAMILY USE.—Subject to regulations prescribed by the Secretary—

(A) EXEMPTION.—Any adult may, without payment of tax, produce wine for personal or family use and not for sale.

(B) LIMITATION.—The aggregate amount of wine exempt from tax under this paragraph with respect to any household shall not exceed—

(i) 200 gallons per calendar year if there are 2 or more adults in such household, or

(ii) 100 gallons per calendar year if there is only 1 adult in such household.

(C) ADULTS.—For purposes of this paragraph, the term "adult" means an individual who has attained 18 years of age, or the minimum age (if any) established by law applicable in the locality in which the household is situated at which wine may be sold to individuals, whichever is greater.

(3) EXPERIMENTAL WINE.—Subject to regulations prescribed by the Secretary, any scientific university, college of learning, or institution of scientific research may produce, receive, blend, treat, and store wine, without payment of tax, for experimental or research use but not for consumption (other than organoleptic tests) or sale, and may receive such wine spirits without payment of tax as may be necessary for such production.

Amendments

- **1978 (P.L. 95-458)**

P.L. 95-458, §2(a), (c):

Amended subsection (a)(2). **Effective** 2-1-79. Prior to amendment, subsection (a)(2) read as follows:

"(2) FAMILY WINE.—Subject to regulations prescribed by the Secretary, the duly registered head of any family may, without payment of tax, produce for family use and not for sale an amount of wine not exceeding 200 gallons per annum."

- **1976, Tax Reform Act of 1976 (P.L. 94-455)**

P.L. 94-455, §1906(b)(13)(A):

Amended 1954 Code by substituting "Secretary" for "Secretary or his delegate" each place it appeared. **Effective** 2-1-77.

[Sec. 5042(b)]

(b) CROSS REFERENCES.—

(1) For provisions relating to exemption of tax on losses of wine (including losses by theft or authorized destruction), see section 5370.

(2) For provisions exempting from tax samples of wine, see section 5372.

(3) For provisions authorizing withdrawals of wine free of tax or without payment of tax, see section 5362.

[Sec. 5043]

SEC. 5043. COLLECTION OF TAXES ON WINES.

[Sec. 5043(a)]

(a) PERSONS LIABLE FOR PAYMENT.—The taxes on wine provided for in this subpart shall be paid—

(1) BONDED WINE CELLARS.—In the case of wines removed from any bonded wine cellar, by the proprietor of such bonded wine cellar; except that—

(A) in the case of any transfer of wine in bond as authorized under the provisions of section 5362(b), the liability for payment of the tax shall become the liability of the transferee from the time of removal of the wine from the transferor's premises, and the transferor shall thereupon be relieved of such liability; and

(B) in the case of any wine withdrawn by a person other than such proprietor without payment of tax as authorized under the provisions of section 5362(c), the liability for payment of the tax shall become the liability of such person from the time of the removal of the wine from the bonded wine cellar, and such proprietor shall thereupon be relieved of such liability.

(2) FOREIGN WINE.—In the case of foreign wines which are not transferred to a bonded wine cellar free of tax under section 5364, by the importer thereof.

(3) OTHER WINES.—Immediately, in the case of any wine produced, imported, received, removed, or possessed otherwise than as authorized by law, by any person producing, importing, receiving, removing, or possessing such wine; and all such persons shall be jointly and severally liable for such tax with each other as well as with any proprietor, transferee, or importer who may be liable for the tax under this subsection.

Amendments

- **1998, IRS Restructuring and Reform Act of 1998 (P.L. 105-206)**

P.L. 105-206, §6014(b)(1):

Amended Code Sec. 5043(a)(2) by inserting "which are not transferred to a bonded wine cellar free of tax under section 5364" after "foreign wines". **Effective** as if included in the provision of P.L. 105-34 to which it relates [effective 4-1-98.—CCH].

[Sec. 5043(b)]

(b) PAYMENT OF TAX.—The taxes on wines shall be paid in accordance with section 5061.

ALCOHOL TAXES—GALLONAGE TAXES

Amendments

• **1979, Trade Agreements Act of 1979 (P.L. 96-39)**

P.L. 96-39, § 807(a)(8):

Amended Code Sec. 5043(a)(1)(A) by changing "in bond between bonded wine cellars" to "in bond". **Effective** 1-1-80.

• **1976, Tax Reform Act of 1976 (P.L. 94-455)**

P.L. 94-455, § 1905(b)(2)(C):

Substituted "The taxes" for "Except as provided in subsection (a)(3), the taxes" in Code Sec. 5043(b). **Effective** 2-1-77.

[Sec. 5044]

SEC. 5044. REFUND OF TAX ON WINE.

[Sec. 5044(a)]

(a) GENERAL.—In the case of any wine removed from a bonded wine cellar and returned to bond under section 5361—

(1) any tax imposed by section 5041 shall, if paid, be refunded or credited, without interest, to the proprietor of the bonded wine cellar to which such wine is delivered; or

(2) if any tax so imposed has not been paid, the person liable for the tax may be relieved of liability therefor,

under such regulations as the Secretary may prescribe. Such regulations may provide that claim for refund or credit under paragraph (1), or relief from liability under paragraph (2), may be made only with respect to minimum quantities specified in such regulations. The burden of proof in all such cases shall be on the applicant.

Amendments

• **1998, IRS Restructuring and Reform Act of 1998 (P.L. 105-206)**

P.L. 105-206, § 6014(b)(2):

Amended Code Sec. 5044(a) by striking "produced in the United States" and inserting "removed from a bonded wine cellar". **Effective** as if included in the provision of P.L. 105-34 to which it relates [effective 4-1-98.—CCH].

• **1997, Taxpayer Relief Act of 1997 (P.L. 105-34)**

P.L. 105-34, § 1416(a):

Amended Code Sec. 5044(a) by striking "as unmerchantable" after "returned to bond". **Effective** on the 1st day of the 1st calendar quarter that begins at least 180 days after 8-5-97.

P.L. 105-34, § 1416(b)(2):

Amended Code Sec. 5044 by striking "UNMERCHANTABLE" before "WINE" in the section heading. **Effective** on the 1st day of the 1st calendar quarter that begins at least 180 days after 8-5-97.

• **1976, Tax Reform Act of 1976 (P.L. 94-455)**

P.L. 94-455, § 1906(b)(13)(A):

Amended 1954 Code by substituting "Secretary" for "Secretary or his delegate" each place it appeared. **Effective** 2-1-77.

[Sec. 5044(b)]

(b) DATE OF FILING.—No claim under subsection (a) shall be allowed unless filed within 6 months after the date of the return of the wine to bond.

[Sec. 5044(c)]

(c) STATUS OF WINE RETURNED TO BOND.—All provisions of this chapter applicable to wine in bond on the premises of a bonded wine cellar and to removals thereof shall be applicable to wine returned to bond under the provisions of this section.

[Sec. 5045]

SEC. 5045. CROSS REFERENCES.

For provisions relating to the establishment and operation of wineries, see subchapter F, and for penalties pertaining to wine, see subchapter J.

Subpart D—Beer

Sec. 5051. Imposition and rate of tax.
Sec. 5052. Definitions.
Sec. 5053. Exemptions.
Sec. 5054. Determination and collection of tax on beer.
Sec. 5055. Drawback of tax.
Sec. 5056. Refund and credit of tax, or relief from liability.

[Sec. 5051]

SEC. 5051. IMPOSITION AND RATE OF TAX.

[Sec. 5051(a)]

(a) RATE OF TAX.—

(1) IN GENERAL.—

(A) IMPOSITION OF TAX.—A tax is hereby imposed on all beer brewed or produced, and removed for consumption or sale, within the United States, or imported into the United States. Except as provided in paragraph (2), the rate of such tax shall be—

(i) $16 on the first 6,000,000 barrels of beer—

(I) brewed by the brewer and removed during the calendar year for consumption or sale, or

(II) imported by the importer into the United States during the calendar year but only if the importer is an electing importer under paragraph (4) and the barrels have been assigned to the importer pursuant to such paragraph, and

(ii) $18 on any barrels of beer to which clause (i) does not apply.

(B) BARREL.—For purposes of this section, a barrel shall contain not more than 31 gallons of beer, and any tax imposed under this section shall be applied at a like rate for any other quantity or for fractional parts of a barrel.

(2) REDUCED RATE FOR CERTAIN DOMESTIC PRODUCTION.—

(A) $3.50 A BARREL RATE.—In the case of a brewer who produces not more than 2,000,000 barrels of beer during the calendar year, the per barrel rate of the tax imposed by this section shall be $3.50 on the first 60,000 barrels of beer which are removed in such year for consumption or sale and which have been brewed or produced by such brewer at qualified breweries in the United States.

(B) REGULATIONS.—The Secretary may prescribe such regulations as may be necessary to prevent the reduced rates provided in this paragraph from benefiting any person who produces more than 2,000,000 barrels of beer during a calendar year.

(3) TOLERANCES.—Where the Secretary finds that the revenue will not be endangered thereby, he may by regulations prescribe tolerances for barrels and fractional parts of barrels, and, if such tolerances are prescribed, no assessment shall be made and no tax shall be collected for any excess in any case where the contents of a barrel or a fractional part of a barrel are within the limit of the applicable tolerance prescribed.

Internal Revenue Code

ALCOHOL TAXES—GALLONAGE TAXES

(4) REDUCED TAX RATE FOR FOREIGN MANUFACTURERS AND IMPORTERS.—

(A) IN GENERAL.—In the case of any barrels of beer which have been brewed or produced outside of the United States and imported into the United States, the rate of tax applicable under clause (i) of paragraph (1)(A) (referred to in this paragraph as the "reduced tax rate") may be assigned by the brewer (provided that the brewer makes an election described in subparagraph (B)(ii)) to any electing importer of such barrels pursuant to the requirements established by the Secretary under subparagraph (B).

(B) ASSIGNMENT.—The Secretary, after consultation with the Secretary of the Department of Homeland Security, shall, through such rules, regulations, and procedures as are determined appropriate, establish procedures for assignment of the reduced tax rate provided under this paragraph, which shall include—

(i) a limitation to ensure that the number of barrels of beer for which the reduced tax rate has been assigned by a brewer—

(I) to any importer does not exceed the number of barrels of beer brewed or produced by such brewer during the calendar year which were imported into the United States by such importer, and

(II) to all importers does not exceed the 6,000,000 barrels to which the reduced tax rate applies,

(ii) procedures that allow the election of a brewer to assign and an importer to receive the reduced tax rate provided under this paragraph,

(iii) requirements that the brewer provide any information as the Secretary determines necessary and appropriate for purposes of carrying out this paragraph, and

(iv) procedures that allow for revocation of eligibility of the brewer and the importer for the reduced tax rate provided under this paragraph in the case of any erroneous or fraudulent information provided under clause (iii) which the Secretary deems to be material to qualifying for such reduced rate.

(C) CONTROLLED GROUP.—For purposes of this section, any importer making an election described in subparagraph (B)(ii) shall be deemed to be a member of the controlled group of the brewer, as described under paragraph (5).

(5) CONTROLLED GROUP AND SINGLE TAXPAYER RULES.—

(A) IN GENERAL.—Except as provided in subparagraph (B), in the case of a controlled group, the 6,000,000 barrel quantity specified in paragraph (1)(A)(i) and the 2,000,000 barrel quantity specified in paragraph (2)(A) shall be applied to the controlled group, and the 6,000,000 barrel quantity specified in paragraph (1)(A)(i) and the 60,000 barrel quantity specified in paragraph (2)(A) shall be apportioned among the brewers who are members of such group in such manner as the Secretary or their delegate shall by regulations prescribe. For purposes of the preceding sentence, the term "controlled group" has the meaning assigned to it by subsection (a) of section 1563, except that for such purposes the phrase "more than 50 percent" shall be substituted for the phrase "at least 80 percent" in each place it appears in such subsection. Under regulations prescribed by the Secretary, principles similar to the principles of the preceding two sentences shall be applied to a group of brewers under common control where one or more of the brewers is not a corporation.

(B) FOREIGN MANUFACTURERS AND IMPORTERS.—For purposes of paragraph (4), in the case of a controlled group, the 6,000,000 barrel quantity specified in paragraph (1)(A)(i) shall be applied to the controlled group and apportioned among the members of such group in such manner as the Secretary shall by regulations prescribe. For purposes of the preceding sentence, the term "controlled group" has the meaning given such term under subparagraph (A). Under regulations prescribed by the Secretary, principles similar to the principles of the preceding two sentences shall be applied to a group of brewers under common control where one or more of the brewers is not a corporation.

(C) SINGLE TAXPAYER.—Pursuant to rules issued by the Secretary, two or more entities (whether or not under common control) that produce beer under a license, franchise, or other arrangement shall be treated as a single taxpayer for purposes of the application of this subsection.

(6) REFUNDS IN LIEU OF REDUCED RATES FOR FOREIGN PRODUCTION REMOVED AFTER DECEMBER 31, 2022.—

(A) IN GENERAL.—In the case of any barrels of beer which have been produced outside the United States and imported into the United States, if such barrels of beer are removed after December 31, 2022—

(i) paragraph (1)(A)(i) shall not apply, and

(ii) the amount determined under subparagraph (B) shall be allowed as a refund, determined for periods not less frequently than quarterly, to the importer in the same manner as if such amount were an overpayment of tax imposed by this section.

(B) AMOUNT OF REFUND.—The amount determined under this subparagraph with respect to any importer for any period is an amount equal to the sum of—

(i) excess (if any) of—

(I) the amount of tax imposed under this section on barrels of beer referred to in subparagraph (A) which were removed during such period, over

(II) the amount of tax which would have been imposed under this section on such barrels of beer if this section were applied without regard to this paragraph, plus

(ii) the amount of interest which would be allowed and paid on an overpayment of tax at the overpayment rate established under section 6621(a)(1) (without regard to the second sentence thereof) were such rate applied to the excess (if any) determined under clause (i) for the number of days in the filing period for which the refund under this paragraph is being determined.

(C) APPLICATION OF RULES RELATED TO ELECTIONS AND ASSIGNMENTS.—Subparagraph (A)(ii) shall apply only if the importer is an electing importer under paragraph (4) and the barrels of beer have been assigned to the importer pursuant to such paragraph.

(D) RULES FOR REFUNDS WITHIN 90 DAYS.—For purposes of refunds allowed under this paragraph, section 6611(e) shall be applied by substituting "90 days" for "45 days" each place it appears.

Amendments

- 2020, Taxpayer Certainty and Disaster Tax Relief Act of 2020 (P.L. 116-260)

P.L. 116-260, §106(b)(1), Div. EE:

Amended Code Sec. 5051(a)(1). **Effective** for beer removed after 12-31-2020. Prior to amendment, Code Sec. 5051(a)(1) read as follows:

(1) IN GENERAL.—

(A) IMPOSITION OF TAX.—A tax is hereby imposed on all beer brewed or produced, and removed for consumption or sale, within the United States, or imported into the United States. Except as provided in paragraph (2), the rate of such tax shall be the amount determined under this paragraph.

(B) RATE.—Except as provided in subparagraph (C), the rate of tax shall be $18 for per barrel.

(C) SPECIAL RULE.—In the case of beer removed after December 31, 2017, and before January 1, 2021, the rate of tax shall be—

(i) $16 on the first 6,000,000 barrels of beer—

(I) brewed by the brewer and removed during the calendar year for consumption or sale, or

(II) imported by the importer into the United States during the calendar year but only if the importer is an electing importer under paragraph (4) and the barrels have been assigned to the importer pursuant to such paragraph, and

(ii) $18 on any barrels of beer to which clause (i) does not apply.

(D) BARREL.—For purposes of this section, a barrel shall contain not more than 31 gallons of beer, and any tax imposed under this section shall be applied at a like rate for any other quantity or for fractional parts of a barrel.

P.L. 116-260, §106(b)(2)(A)-(B), Div. EE:

Amended Code Sec. 5051(a)(2)(A) by inserting "$3.50 A BARREL" before "RATE" in the heading, and by striking "$7" and all that follows through "January 1, 2021)" and inserting "$3.50". **Effective** for beer removed after 12-31-2020. Prior to being stricken,

"$7" and all that follows through "January 1, 2021)" in Code Sec. 5051(a)(2)(A) read as follows:

$7 ($3.50 in the case of beer removed after December 31, 2017, and before January 1, 2021)

P.L. 116-260, §106(b)(3)(A)-(B), Div. EE:

Amended Code Sec. 5051(a) in paragraph (1)(A)(i)(II), as amended by Act Sec. 106(b)(1), by inserting "but only if the importer is an electing importer under paragraph (4) and the barrels have been assigned to the importer pursuant to such paragraph" after "during the calendar year", and in paragraph (4)(A), by striking "paragraph (1)(C)" and inserting "paragraph (1)(A)", and in subparagraph (B), by striking "The Secretary" and inserting "The Secretary, after consultation with the Secretary of the Department of Homeland Security,". **Effective** for beer removed after 12-31-2020.

P.L. 116-260, §106(b)(4), Div. EE:

Amended Code Sec. 5051(a)(5) by striking "paragraph (1)(C)(i)" each place it appears and inserting "paragraph (1)(A)(i)". **Effective** for beer removed after 12-31-2020.

P.L. 116-260, §107(b)(1), Div. EE:

Amended Code Sec. 5051(a) by adding at the end a new paragraph (6). **Effective** for beer removed after 12-31-2022. For a special rule, see Act Sec. 107(e)-(g), Div. EE, below.

P.L. 116-260, §107(e)-(g), Div. EE, provides:

(e) ADMINISTRATION OF REFUNDS.—The Secretary of the Treasury (or the Secretary's delegate within the Department of the Treasury) shall implement and administer sections 5001(c)(4), 5041(c)(7), and 5051(a)(6) of the Internal Revenue Code of 1986, as added by this Act, in coordination with the United States Customs and Border Protection of the Department of Homeland Security.

(f) REGULATIONS.—The Secretary of the Treasury (or the Secretary's delegate within the Department of the Treasury) shall prescribe such regulations as may be necessary or appropriate to carry out the purposes of this section, including regulations to require foreign producers to provide information necessary to enforce the volume limitations under sections 5001(c), 5041(c), and 5051(a) of such Code.

(g) REPORT.—Not later than 180 days after the date of the enactment of this Act, the Secretary of the Treasury (or the Secretary's delegate within the Department of the Treasury) shall, in coordination with the United States Customs and Border Protection of the Department of Homeland Security, prepare, submit to Congress, and make publicly available a report detailing the plans for implementing and administering sections 5001(c)(4), 5041(c)(7), and 5051(a)(6) of such Code, as added by this Act.

P.L. 116-260, §110(a), Div. EE:

Amended Code Sec. 5051(a)(5)(C) by striking "marketed under a similar brand, license" and inserting "under a license". **Effective** for beer, wine, and distilled spirits removed after 12-31-2020.

P.L. 116-260, §110(b), Div. EE, provides:

(b) WINE.—For single taxpayer rules relating to wine, see cross reference under section 5041(c)(3) of the Internal Revenue Code of 1986, as redesignated by this Act.

• **2019, Taxpayer Certainty and Disaster Tax Relief Act of 2019 (P.L. 116-94)**

P.L. 116-94, §144(b)(1), Div. Q:

Amended Code Sec. 5051(a)(1)(C) and (2)(A) by striking "January 1, 2020" and inserting "January 1, 2021". **Effective** for beer removed after 12-31-2019.

• **2017, Tax Cuts and Jobs Act (P.L. 115-97)**

P.L. 115-97, §13802(a):

Amended Code Sec. 5051(a)(1). **Effective** for beer removed after 12-31-2017. Prior to amendment, Code Sec. 5051(a)(1) read as follows:

(1) IN GENERAL.—A tax is hereby imposed on all beer brewed or produced, and removed for consumption or sale, within the United States, or imported into the United States. Except as provided in paragraph (2), the rate of such tax shall be $18 for every barrel containing not more than 31 gallons and at a like rate for any other quantity or for fractional parts of a barrel.

P.L. 115-97, §13802(b)(1)-(2):

Amended Code Sec. 5051(a)(2)(A) by striking "$7 A BARREL" before "RATE" in the heading, and by inserting "($3.50 in the case of beer removed after December 31, 2017, and before January 1, 2020)" after "$7". **Effective** for beer removed after 12-31-2017.

P.L. 115-97, §13802(c)(1)-(2):

Amended Code Sec. 5051(a) by inserting "but only if the importer is an electing importer under paragraph (4) and the barrels have been assigned to the importer pursuant to such paragraph" after "during the calendar year" in paragraph (1)(C)(i)(II), as amended by Act Sec. 13802(c), and by adding at the end a new paragraph (4). **Effective** for beer removed after 12-31-2017.

P.L. 115-97, §13802(d)(1)-(2):

Amended Code Sec. 5051(a), as amended by Act Sec. 13802, in paragraph (2) by striking subparagraph (B), and by redesignating subparagraph (C) as subparagraph (B), and by adding at the end a new paragraph (5). **Effective** for beer removed after 12-31-2017. Prior to being stricken, Code Sec. 5051(a)(2)(B) read as follows:

(B) CONTROLLED GROUPS.—In the case of a controlled group, the 2,000,000 barrel quantity specified in subparagraph (A) shall be applied to the controlled group, and the 60,000 barrel quantity specified in subparagraph (A) shall be apportioned among the brewers who are component members of such group in such manner as the Secretary shall by regulations prescribe. For purposes of the preceding sentence, the term "controlled group" has the meaning assigned to it by subsection (a) of section 1563, except that for such purposes the phrase "more than 50 percent" shall be substituted for the phrase "at least 80 percent" in each place it appears in such subsection. Under regulations prescribed by the Secretary, principles similar to the principles of the preceding two sentences shall be applied to a group of brewers under common control where one or more of the brewers is not a corporation.

P.L. 115-97, §13809 (as added by P.L. 115-123, §41111, Div. D), provides:

SEC. 13809. RULE OF CONSTRUCTION.

Nothing in this subpart, the amendments made by this subpart, or any regulation promulgated under this subpart or the amendments made by this subpart, shall be construed to preempt, supersede, or otherwise limit or restrict any State, local, or tribal law that prohibits or regulates the production or sale of distilled spirits, wine, or malt beverages.

• **1990, Omnibus Budget Reconciliation Act of 1990 (P.L. 101-508)**

P.L. 101-508, §11201(c)(1):

Amended Code Sec. 5051(a)(1) by striking "$9" and inserting "$18". **Effective** 1-1-91.

P.L. 101-508, §11201(c)(2):

Amended Code Sec. 5051(a)(2) by adding at the end thereof a new subparagraph (C). **Effective** 1-1-91.

• **1976 (P.L. 94-529)**

P.L. 94-529, §[1]:

Amended Code Sec. 5051(a). **Effective** 2-1-77. Prior to amendment, Code Sec. 5051(a) read as follows:

(a) RATE OF TAX.—There is hereby imposed on all beer, brewed or produced, and removed for consumption or sale, within the United States, or imported into the United States, a tax of $9 for every barrel containing not more than 31 gallons and at a like rate for any other quantity or for fractional parts of a barrel. Where the Secretary or his delegate finds that the revenue will not be endangered thereby, he may by regulations prescribe tolerances for barrels and fractional parts of barrels, and, if such tolerances are prescribed, no assessment shall be made and no tax shall be collected for any excess in any case where the contents of a barrel or a fractional part of a barrel are within the limit of the applicable tolerance prescribed.

• **1976, Tax Reform Act of 1976 (P.L. 94-455)**

P.L. 94-455, §1906(b)(13)(A):

Amended 1954 Code by substituting "Secretary" for "Secretary or his delegate" each place it appeared. **Effective** 2-1-77.

• **1965, Excise Tax Reduction Act of 1965 (P.L. 89-44)**

P.L. 89-44, §501(d):

Amended Code Sec. 5051(a) by deleting the second sentence thereof which formerly read: "On and after July 1, 1965, the tax imposed by this subsection shall be at the rate of $8 in lieu of $9."

• **1964, Excise Tax Rate Extension Act of 1964 (P.L. 88-348)**

P.L. 88-348, §2(a)(8):

Substituted "1965" for "1964" in Sec. 5051(a).

• **1963, Tax Rate Extension Act of 1963 (P.L. 88-52)**

P.L. 88-52, §3(a)(8):

Substituted "1964" for "1963" in Sec. 5051(a).

• **1962, Tax Rate Extension Act of 1962 (P.L. 87-508)**

P.L. 87-508, §3(a)(7):

Substituted "1963" for "1962" in Sec. 5051(a).

• **1961, Tax Rate Extension Act of 1961 (P.L. 87-72)**

P.L. 87-72, §3(a)(8):

Substituted "1962" for "1961" in Sec. 5051(a).

• **1960, Public Debt and Tax Rate Extension Act of 1960 (P.L. 86-564)**

P.L. 86-564, §202(a):

Substituted "July 1, 1961" for "July 1, 1960" in Sec. 5051(a).

• **1959, Tax Rate Extension Act of 1959 (P.L. 86-75)**

P.L. 86-75, §3(a):

Substituted "July 1, 1960" for "July 1, 1959" in Sec. 5051(a).

[Sec. 5051(b)]

(b) ASSESSMENT ON MATERIALS USED IN PRODUCTION IN CASE OF FRAUD.—Nothing contained in this subpart or subchapter G shall be construed to authorize an assessment on the quantity of materials used in producing or purchased for the purpose of producing beer, nor shall the quantity of materials so used or purchased be evidence, for the purpose of taxation, of the quantity of beer produced; but the tax on all beer shall be paid as provided in section 5054, and not otherwise; except that this subsection shall not apply to cases of fraud, and nothing in this subsection shall have the effect to change the rules of law respecting evidence in any prosecution or suit.

ALCOHOL TAXES—GALLONAGE TAXES

[Sec. 5051(c)]

(c) ILLEGALLY PRODUCED BEER.—The production of any beer at any place in the United States shall be subject to tax at the rate prescribed in subsection (a) and such tax shall be due and payable as provided in section 5054(a)(3) unless—

(1) such beer is produced in a brewery qualified under the provisions of subchapter G, or

(2) such production is exempt from tax under section 5053(e) (relating to beer for personal or family use).

Amendments

• 1978 (P.L. 95-458)

P.L. 95-458, § 2(b)(2)(A):

Added subsection (c). **Effective** 2-1-79.

[Sec. 5052]

SEC. 5052. DEFINITIONS.

[Sec. 5052(a)]

(a) BEER.—For purposes of this chapter (except when used with reference to distilling or distilling material) the term "beer" means beer, ale, porter, stout, and other similar fermented beverages (including saké or similar products) of any name or description containing one-half of 1 percent or more of alcohol by volume, brewed or produced from malt, wholly or in part, or from any substitute therefor.

[Sec. 5052(b)]

(b) GALLON.—For purposes of this subpart, the term "gallon" means the liquid measure containing 231 cubic inches.

[Sec. 5052(c)]

(c) REMOVED FOR CONSUMPTION OR SALE.—Except as provided for in the case of removal of beer without payment of tax, the term "removed for consumption or sale", for the purposes of this subpart, means—

(1) SALE OF BEER.—The sale and transfer of possession of beer for consumption at the brewery; or

(2) REMOVALS.—Any removal of beer from the brewery.

Amendments

• 1971 (P.L. 91-673)

P.L. 91-673, § 1(b):

Amended Code Sec. 5052(c)(2). **Effective** 5-1-71. Prior to amendment, subparagraph (2) read as follows:

"(2) Removals.—Any removal of beer from the brewery, except that such removal shall not include any beer returned to the brewery on the same day such beer is removed from the brewery."

[Sec. 5052(d)]

(d) BREWER.—For purposes of this chapter, the term "brewer" means any person who brews beer or produces beer for sale. Such term shall not include any person who produces only beer exempt from tax under section 5053(e).

Amendments

• 2005, Safe, Accountable, Flexible, Efficient Transportation Equity Act: A Legacy for Users (P.L. 109-59)

P.L. 109-59, § 11125(b)(15):

Amended Code Sec. 5052(d). **Effective** 7-1-2008, but not applicable to taxes imposed for periods before such date. Prior to amendment, Code Sec. 5052(d) read as follows:

(d) BREWER.—

For definition of brewer, see section 5092.

[Sec. 5053]

SEC. 5053. EXEMPTIONS.

[Sec. 5053(a)]

(a) REMOVALS FOR EXPORT.—Beer may be removed from the brewery, without payment of tax, for export, in such containers and under such regulations, and on the giving of such notices, entries, and bonds and other security, as the Secretary may by regulations prescribe.

Amendments

• 1976, Tax Reform Act of 1976 (P.L. 94-455)

P.L. 94-455, § 1906(b)(13)(A):

Amended 1954 Code by substituting "Secretary" for "Secretary or his delegate" each place it appeared. **Effective** 2-1-77.

• 1965, Excise Tax Reduction Act of 1965 (P.L. 89-44)

P.L. 89-44, § 807(b):

Amended Sec. 5053(a). **Effective** 7-1-65. Prior to amendment, Sec. 5053(a) read as follows:

"(a) Removals for Export.—Beer may be removed from the brewery, without payment of tax, for export to a foreign country, in such containers and under such regulations, and on the giving of such notices, entries, and bonds and other security, as the Secretary or his delegate may by regulations prescribe."

[Sec. 5053(b)]

(b) REMOVALS WHEN UNFIT FOR BEVERAGE USE.—When beer has become sour or damaged, so as to be incapable of use as such, a brewer may remove the same from his brewery without payment of tax, for manufacturing purposes, under such regulations as the Secretary may prescribe.

Amendments

• 1976, Tax Reform Act of 1976 (P.L. 94-455)

P.L. 94-455, § 1906(b)(13)(A):

Amended 1954 Code by substituting "Secretary" for "Secretary or his delegate" each place it appeared. **Effective** 2-1-77.

[Sec. 5053(c)]

(c) REMOVALS FOR LABORATORY ANALYSIS.—Beer may be removed from the brewery, without payment of tax, for laboratory analysis, subject to such limitations and under such regulations as the Secretary may prescribe.

Amendments

• 1976, Tax Reform Act of 1976 (P.L. 94-455)

P.L. 94-455, § 1906(b)(13)(A):

Amended 1954 Code by substituting "Secretary" for "Secretary or his delegate" each place it appeared. **Effective** 2-1-77.

ALCOHOL TAXES—GALLONAGE TAXES

[Sec. 5053(d)]

(d) REMOVALS FOR RESEARCH, DEVELOPMENT, OR TESTING.—Under such conditions and regulations as the Secretary may prescribe, beer may be removed from the brewery without payment of tax for use in research, development, or testing (other than consumer testing or other market analysis) of processes, systems, materials, or equipment relating to beer or brewery operations.

Amendments

• **1976, Tax Reform Act of 1976 (P.L. 94-455)**

P.L. 94-455, §1906(b)(13)(A):
Amended 1954 Code by substituting "Secretary" for "Secretary or his delegate" each place it appeared. **Effective** 2-1-77.

• **1971 (P.L. 91-673)**

P.L. 91-673, §2:
Added Code Sec. 5053(d). **Effective** 5-1-71.

[Sec. 5053(e)]

(e) BEER FOR PERSONAL OR FAMILY USE.—Subject to regulation prescribed by the Secretary, any adult may, without payment of tax, produce beer for personal or family use and not for sale. The aggregate amount of beer exempt from tax under this subsection with respect to any household shall not exceed—

(1) 200 gallons per calendar year if there are 2 or more adults in such household, or

(2) 100 gallons per calendar year if there is only 1 adult in such household.

For purposes of this subsection, the term "adult" means an individual who has attained 18 years of age, or the minimum age (if any) established by law applicable in the locality in which the household is situated at which beer may be sold to individuals, whichever is greater.

Amendments

• **1978 (P.L. 95-458)**

P.L. 95-458, §2(b)(1), (c):
Added subsection (e). **Effective** 2-1-79.

[Sec. 5053(f)]

(f) REMOVAL FOR USE AS DISTILLING MATERIAL.—Subject to such regulations as the Secretary may prescribe, beer may be removed from a brewery without payment of tax to any distilled spirits plant for use as distilling material.

Amendments

• **1997, Taxpayer Relief Act of 1997 (P.L. 105-34)**

P.L. 105-34, §1414(b):
Amended Code Sec. 5053 by redesignating subsection (f) as subsection (i) and by inserting after subsection (e) a new subsection (f). **Effective** on the 1st day of the 1st calendar quarter that begins at least 180 days after 8-5-97.

[Sec. 5053(g)]

(g) REMOVALS FOR USE OF FOREIGN EMBASSIES, LEGATIONS, ETC.—

(1) IN GENERAL.—Subject to such regulations as the Secretary may prescribe—

(A) beer may be withdrawn from the brewery without payment of tax for transfer to any customs bonded warehouse for entry pending withdrawal therefrom as provided in subparagraph (B), and

(B) beer entered into any customs bonded warehouse under subparagraph (A) may be withdrawn for consumption in the United States by, and for the official and family use of, such foreign governments, organizations, and individuals as are entitled to withdraw imported beer from such warehouses free of tax.

Beer transferred to any customs bonded warehouse under subparagraph (A) shall be entered, stored, and accounted for in such warehouse under such regulations and bonds as the Secretary may prescribe, and may be withdrawn therefrom by such governments, organizations, and individuals free of tax under the same conditions and procedures as imported beer.

(2) OTHER RULES TO APPLY.—Rules similar to the rules of paragraphs (2) and (3) of section 5362(e) shall apply for purposes of this subsection.

Amendments

• **1997, Taxpayer Relief Act of 1997 (P.L. 105-34)**

P.L. 105-34, §1418(a):
Amended Code Sec. 5053, as amended by Act Sec. 1414(b), by inserting after subsection (f) a new subsection (g). **Effective** on the 1st day of the 1st calendar quarter that begins at least 180 days after 8-5-97.

[Sec. 5053(h)]

(h) REMOVALS FOR DESTRUCTION.—Subject to such regulations as the Secretary may prescribe, beer may be removed from the brewery without payment of tax for destruction.

Amendments

• **1997, Taxpayer Relief Act of 1997 (P.L. 105-34)**

P.L. 105-34, §1419(a):
Amended Code Sec. 5053, as amended by Act Sec. 1418(a), by inserting after subsection (g) a new subsection (h). **Effective** on the 1st day of the 1st calendar quarter that begins at least 180 days after 8-5-97.

[Sec. 5053(i)]

(i) REMOVAL AS SUPPLIES FOR CERTAIN VESSELS AND AIRCRAFT.—

For exemption as to supplies for certain vessels and aircraft, see section 309 of the Tariff Act of 1930, as amended (19 U.S.C. 1309).

Amendments

• **1997, Taxpayer Relief Act of 1997 (P.L. 105-34)**

P.L. 105-34, §1414(b):
Amended Code Sec. 5053 by redesignating subsection (f) as subsection (i). **Effective** on the 1st day of the 1st calendar quarter that begins at least 180 days after 8-5-97.

• **1978 (P.L. 95-458)**

P.L. 95-458, §2(b)(1), (c):
Redesignated subsection (e) as subsection (f). **Effective** 2-1-79.

• **1971 (P.L. 91-673)**

P.L. 91-673, §2:
Redesignated former Code Sec. 5053(d) as Code Sec. 5053(e). **Effective** 5-1-71.

ALCOHOL TAXES—GALLONAGE TAXES

[Sec. 5054]
SEC. 5054. DETERMINATION AND COLLECTION OF TAX ON BEER.

[Sec. 5054(a)]

(a) TIME OF DETERMINATION.—

(1) BEER PRODUCED IN THE UNITED STATES; CERTAIN IMPORTED BEER.—Except as provided in paragraph (3), the tax imposed by section 5051 on beer produced in the United States, or imported into the United States and transferred to a brewery free of tax under section 5418, shall be determined at the time it is removed for consumption or sale, and shall be paid by the brewer thereof in accordance with section 5061.

(2) BEER IMPORTED INTO THE UNITED STATES.—Except as provided in paragraph (4), the tax imposed by section 5051 on beer imported into the United States and not transferred to a brewery free of tax under section 5418 shall be determined at the time of the importation thereof, or, if entered for warehousing, at the time of removal from the 1st such warehouse.

(3) ILLEGALLY PRODUCED BEER.—The tax on any beer produced in the United States shall be due and payable immediately upon production unless—

(A) such beer is produced in a brewery qualified under the provisions of subchapter G, or

(B) such production is exempt from tax under section 5053(e) (relating to beer for personal or family use).

(4) UNLAWFULLY IMPORTED BEER.—Beer smuggled or brought into the United States unlawfully shall, for purposes of this chapter, be held to be imported into the United States, and the internal revenue tax shall be due and payable at the time of such importation.

Amendments

• **2018, Tax Technical Corrections Act of 2018 (P.L. 115-141)**

P.L. 115-141, §401(a)(239), Div. U:

Amended Code Sec. 5054(a)(3)(B) by striking "sections" and inserting "section". **Effective** 3-23-2018.

• **1998, IRS Restructuring and Reform Act of 1998 (P.L. 105-206)**

P.L. 105-206, §6014(a)(1)(A)-(B):

Amended Code Sec. 5054(a)(1) by inserting ", or imported into the United States and transferred to a brewery free of tax under section 5418," after "produced in the United States," in the text, and by inserting "; CERTAIN IMPORTED BEER" after "PRODUCED IN THE UNITED STATES" in the heading. **Effective** as if included in the provision of P.L. 105-34 to which it relates [effective 4-1-98.—CCH].

P.L. 105-206, §6014(a)(2):

Amended Code Sec. 5054(a)(2) by inserting "and not transferred to a brewery free of tax under section 5418" after "United States". **Effective** as if included in the provision of P.L. 105-34 to which it relates [effective 4-1-98.—CCH].

• **1988, Technical and Miscellaneous Revenue Act of 1988 (P.L. 100-647)**

P.L. 100-647, §1018(u)(19):

Amended Code Sec. 5054(a)(2) by adding a period at the end thereof. **Effective** as if included in the provision of P.L. 99-514 to which it relates.

• **1986, Omnibus Budget Reconciliation Act of 1986 (P.L. 99-509)**

P.L. 99-509, §8011(b)(2):

Amended Code Sec. 5054(a)(2) by striking out all that follows "or," and inserting in lieu thereof "if entered for warehousing, at the time of removal from the 1st such warehouse". For the **effective** date, see Act Sec. 8011(c), below. Prior to amendment, Code Sec. 5054(a)(2) read as follows:

(2) BEER IMPORTED INTO THE UNITED STATES.—Except as provided in paragraph (4), the tax imposed by section 5051 on beer imported into the United States shall be determined at the time of the importation thereof, or, if entered into customs custody, at the time of removal from such custody, and shall be paid under such regulations as the Secretary shall prescribe.

P.L. 99-509, §8011(c), provides:

(c) EFFECTIVE DATES.—

(1) IN GENERAL.—Except as provided in paragraph (2), the amendments made by this section shall apply to removals during semimonthly periods ending on or after December 31, 1986.

(2) IMPORTED ARTICLES, ETC.—Subparagraphs (B) and (C) of section 5703(b)(2) of the Interal Revenue Code of 1954 (as added by this section), paragraphs (2) and (3) of section 5061(d) of such Code (as amended by this section), and the amendments made by subsections (a)(2) and (b)(2) shall apply to articles imported, entered for warehousing, or brought into the United States or a foreign trade zone after December 15, 1986.

(3) SPECIAL RULE FOR DISTILLED SPIRITS AND TOBACCO FOR SEMIMONTHLY PERIOD ENDING DECEMBER 15, 1986.—With respect to remittances of—

(A) taxes imposed on distilled spirits by section 5001 or 7652 of such Code, and

(B) taxes imposed on tobacco products and cigarette papers and tubes by section 5701 or 7652 of such Code,

for the semimonthly period ending December 15, 1986, the last day for payment of such remittances shall be January 14, 1987.

(4) TREATMENT OF SMOKELESS TOBACCO IN INVENTORY ON JUNE 30, 1986.—The tax imposed by section 5701(e) of the Internal Revenue Code of 1954 shall not apply to any smokeless tobacco which—

(A) on June 30, 1986, was in the inventory of the manufacturer or importer, and

(B) on such date was in a form ready for sale.

• **1978 (P.L. 95-458)**

P.L. 95-458, §2(b)(2)(B):

Amended Code Sec. 5054(a)(3). **Effective** 1-1-79. Prior to amendment, Code Sec. 5054(a)(3) read as follows:

(3) ILLEGALLY PRODUCED BEER.—The tax on any beer produced in the United States at any place other than a qualified brewery shall be due and payable immediately upon production.

• **1976, Tax Reform Act of 1976 (P.L. 94-455)**

P.L. 94-455, §1906(b)(13)(A):

Amended 1954 Code by substituting "Secretary" for "Secretary or his delegate" each place it appeared. **Effective** 2-1-77.

[Sec. 5054(b)]

(b) TAX ON RETURNED BEER.—Beer which has been removed for consumption or sale and is thereafter returned to the brewery shall be subject to all provisions of this chapter relating to beer prior to removal for consumption or sale, including the tax imposed by section 5051. The tax on any such returned beer which is again removed for consumption or sale shall be determined and paid without respect to the tax which was determined at the time of prior removal of the beer for consumption or sale.

[Sec. 5054(c)]

(c) APPLICABILITY OF OTHER PROVISIONS OF LAW.—All administrative and penal provisions of this title, insofar as applicable, shall apply to any tax imposed by section 5051.

Amendments

• **1976, Tax Reform Act of 1976 (P.L. 94-455)**

P.L. 94-455, §1905(a)(5):

Struck out former Code Sec. 5054(c) (see below) and redesignated former Code Sec. 5054(d) as Code Sec. 5054(c). **Effective** 2-1-77. Prior to striking, former Code Sec. 5054(c) read as follows:

(c) STAMPS OR OTHER DEVICES AS EVIDENCE OF PAYMENT OF TAX.—When the Secretary or his delegate finds it necessary for the protection of the revenue, he may require stamps, or other devices, evidencing the tax or indicating a compliance with the provisions of this chapter, to be affixed to hogsheads, barrels, or kegs of beer at the time of removal. The Secretary or his delegate shall by regulations prescribe the manner by which such stamps or other devices shall be supplied, affixed, and accounted for.

[Sec. 5055]
SEC. 5055. DRAWBACK OF TAX.

On the exportation of beer, brewed or produced in the United States, the brewer thereof shall be allowed a drawback equal in amount to the tax paid on such beer if there is such proof of exportation as the Secretary may by regulations require. For the purpose of this section, exportation shall include delivery for use as supplies on the vessels and aircraft described in section 309 of the Tariff Act of 1930, as amended (19 U. S. C. 1309).

Amendments

• **1997, Taxpayer Relief Act of 1997 (P.L. 105-34)**

P.L. 105-34, §1420(a):

Amended Code Sec. 5055 by striking "found to have been paid" and all that follows in the first sentence and inserting "paid on such beer if there is such proof of exportation as the Secretary may by regulations require.". **Effective** on the 1st day of the 1st calendar quarter that begins at least 180 days after 8-5-97. Prior to amendment, Code Sec. 5055 read as follows:

ALCOHOL TAXES—GALLONAGE TAXES

SEC. 5055. DRAWBACK OF TAX.
On the exportation of beer, brewed or produced in the United States, the brewer thereof shall be allowed a drawback equal in amount to the tax found to have been paid on such beer, to be paid on submission of such evidence, records and certificates indicating exportation, as the Secretary may by regulations prescribe. For the purpose of this section, exportation shall include delivery for use as supplies on the vessels and aircraft described in section 309 of the Tariff Act of 1930, as amended (19 U. S. C. 1309).

• **1976, Tax Reform Act of 1976 (P.L. 94-455)**

P.L. 94-455, § 1906(b)(13)(A):

Amended 1954 Code by substituting "Secretary" for "Secretary or his delegate" each place it appeared. **Effective** 2-1-77.

[Sec. 5056]
SEC. 5056. REFUND AND CREDIT OF TAX, OR RELIEF FROM LIABILITY.

[Sec. 5056(a)]

(a) BEER RETURNED OR VOLUNTARILY DESTROYED.—Any tax paid by any brewer on beer removed for consumption or sale may be refunded or credited to the brewer, without interest, or if the tax has not been paid, the brewer may be relieved of liability therefor, under such regulations as the Secretary may prescribe, if such beer is returned to any brewery of the brewer or is destroyed under the supervision required by such regulations. In determining the amount of tax due on beer removed on any day, the quantity of beer returned to the same brewery from which removed shall be allowed, under such regulations as the Secretary may prescribe, as an offset against or deduction from the total quantity of beer removed from that brewery on the day of such return.

Amendments
• **1998, IRS Restructuring and Reform Act of 1998 (P.L. 105-206)**

P.L. 105-206, § 6014(a)(3):

Amended Code Sec. 5056 by striking "produced in the United States" and inserting "removed for consumption or sale". **Effective** as if included in the provision of P.L. 105-34 to which it relates [**effective** 4-1-98.—CCH].

• **1976, Tax Reform Act of 1976 (P.L. 94-455)**

P.L. 94-455, § 1906(b)(13)(A):

Amended 1954 Code by substituting "Secretary" for "Secretary or his delegate" each place it appeared. **Effective** 2-1-77.

• **1971 (P.L. 91-673)**

P.L. 91-673, § 1(a):

Amended Code Sec. 5056(a). **Effective** 5-1-71. Prior to amendment, the section read as follows:

(a) BEER REMOVED FROM MARKET.—Any tax paid by any brewer on beer produced in the United States may be refunded or credited to the brewer, without interest, or if the tax has not been paid, the brewer may be relieved of liability therefor, under such regulations as the Secretary or his delegate may prescribe, if such beer is removed from the market and is returned to the brewery or is destroyed under the supervision required by such regulations.

[Sec. 5056(b)]

(b) BEER LOST BY FIRE, CASUALTY, OR ACT OF GOD.—Subject to regulations prescribed by the Secretary, the tax paid by any brewer on beer removed for consumption or sale may be refunded or credited to the brewer, without interest, or if the tax has not been paid, the brewer may be relieved of liability therefor, if such beer is lost, whether by theft or otherwise, or is destroyed or otherwise rendered unmerchantable by fire, casualty, or act of God before the transfer of title thereto to any other person. In any case in which beer is lost or destroyed, whether by theft or otherwise, the Secretary may require the brewer to file a claim for relief from the tax and submit proof as to the cause of such loss. In every case where it appears that the loss was by theft, the first sentence shall not apply unless the brewer establishes to the satisfaction of the Secretary that such theft occurred before removal from the brewery and occurred without connivance, collusion, fraud, or negligence on the part of the brewer, consignor, consignee, bailee, or carrier, or the employees or agents of any of them.

Amendments
• **1998, IRS Restructuring and Reform Act of 1998 (P.L. 105-206)**

P.L. 105-206, § 6014(a)(3):

Amended Code Sec. 5056 by striking "produced in the United States" and inserting "removed for consumption or sale". **Effective** as if included in the provision of P.L. 105-34 to which it relates [**effective** 4-1-98.—CCH].

• **1976, Tax Reform Act of 1976 (P.L. 94-455)**

P.L. 94-455, § 1906(b)(13)(A):

Amended 1954 Code by substituting "Secretary" for "Secretary or his delegate" each place it appeared. **Effective** 2-1-77.

• **1971 (P.L. 91-673)**

P.L. 91-673, § 1(a):

Amended Code Sec. 5056(b). **Effective** 5-1-71. Prior to amendment, the section read as follows:

(b) BEER LOST BY FIRE, CASUALTY, OR ACT OF GOD.—Subject to regulations prescribed by the Secretary or his delegate, the tax paid by any brewer on beer produced in the United States may be refunded or credited to the brewer, without interest, or if the tax has not been paid, the brewer may be relieved of liability therefor, if such beer is lost other than by theft, or is destroyed by fire, casualty, or act of God, before the transfer of title thereto to any other person.

[Sec. 5056(c)]

(c) BEER RECEIVED AT A DISTILLED SPIRITS PLANT.—Any tax paid by any brewer on beer removed for consumption or sale may be refunded or credited to the brewer, without interest, or if the tax has not been paid, the brewer may be relieved of liability therefor, under regulations as the Secretary may prescribe, if such beer is received on the bonded premises of a distilled spirits plant pursuant to the provisions of section 5222(b)(2), for use in the production of distilled spirits.

Amendments
• **1998, IRS Restructuring and Reform Act of 1998 (P.L. 105-206)**

P.L. 105-206, § 6014(a)(3):

Amended Code Sec. 5056 by striking "produced in the United States" and inserting "removed for consumption or sale". **Effective** as if included in the provision of P.L. 105-34 to which it relates [**effective** 4-1-98.—CCH].

• **1997, Taxpayer Relief Act of 1997 (P.L. 105-34)**

P.L. 105-34, § 1414(c)(1):

Amended Code Sec. 5056 by redesignating subsection (c) as subsection (d) and by inserting after subsection (b) a new subsection (c). **Effective** on the 1st day of the 1st calendar quarter that begins at least 180 days after 8-5-97.

[Sec. 5056(d)]

(d) LIMITATIONS.—No claim under this section shall be allowed (1) unless filed within 6 months after the date of the return, loss, destruction, rendering unmerchantable, or receipt on the bonded premises of a distilled spirits plant or (2) if the claimant was indemnified by insurance or otherwise in respect of the tax.

Amendments
• **1997, Taxpayer Relief Act of 1997 (P.L. 105-34)**

P.L. 105-34, § 1414(c)(1)-(2):

Amended Code Sec. 5056 by redesignating subsection (c) as subsection (d), and by striking "or rendering unmerchantable" in subsection (d) (as so redesignated) and inserting "rendering unmerchantable, or receipt on the bonded premises of a distilled spirits plant". **Effective** on the 1st day of the 1st calendar quarter that begins at least 180 days after 8-5-97.

• **1971 (P.L. 91-673)**

P.L. 91-673, § 1(a):

Amended Code Sec. 5056(c). **Effective** 5-1-71. Prior to amendment, the section read as follows:

(c) DATE OF FILING.—No claims under this section shall be allowed unless filed within 6 months after the date of such removal from the market, loss, or destruction, or if the claimant was indemnified by insurance or otherwise in respect of the tax.

Subpart E—General Provisions

Sec. 5061.	Method of collecting tax.
Sec. 5062.	Refund and drawback in case of exportation.
Sec. 5064.	Losses resulting from disaster, vandalism, or malicious mischief.

ALCOHOL TAXES—GALLONAGE TAXES

Sec. 5065. Territorial extent of law.
Sec. 5066. Distilled spirits for use of foreign embassies, legations, etc.
Sec. 5067. Reduced rates not allowed for smuggled or illegally produced beer, wine, or spirits.
Sec. 5068. Cross reference.

[Sec. 5061]

SEC. 5061. METHOD OF COLLECTING TAX.

[Sec. 5061(a)]

(a) COLLECTION BY RETURN.—The taxes on distilled spirits, wines, and beer shall be collected on the basis of a return. The Secretary shall, by regulation, prescribe the period or event for which such return shall be filed, the time for filing such return, the information to be shown in such return, and the time for payment of such tax.

Amendments

• **1979, Trade Agreements Act of 1979 (P.L. 96-39)**

P.L. 96-39, § 807(a)(9)(A):

Amended Code Sec. 5061(a) by changing the first sentence. **Effective** 1-1-80. Prior to amendment, the first sentence read as follows:

"The taxes on distilled spirits, wines, rectified distilled spirits and wines, and beer shall be collected on the basis of a return."

• **1976, Tax Reform Act of 1976 (P.L. 94-455)**

P.L. 94-455, § 1905(a)(6)(A):

Struck out the last sentence of Code Sec. 5061(a). **Effective** 2-1-77. Prior to striking, the last sentence of Code Sec. 5061(a) read as follows:

Notwithstanding the preceding sentences of this subsection, the taxes shall continue to be paid by stamp until the Secretary or his delegate shall by regulations provide for the collection of the taxes on the basis of a return.

P.L. 94-455, § 1906(b)(13)(A):

Amended 1954 Code by substituting "Secretary" for "Secretary or his delegate" each place it appeared. **Effective** 2-1-77.

[Sec. 5061(b)]

(b) EXCEPTIONS.—Notwithstanding the provisions of subsection (a), any taxes imposed on, or amounts to be paid or collected in respect of, distilled spirits, wines, rectified distilled spirits and wines, and beer under—

    (1) section 5001(a)(4), (5), or (6),
    (2) section 5006(c) or (d),
    (3) section 5041(f),
    (4) section 5043(a)(3),
    (5) section 5054(a)(3) or (4), or
    (6) section 5505(a),

shall be immediately due and payable at the time provided by such provisions (or if no specific time for payment is provided, at the time the event referred to in such provision occurs). Such taxes and amounts shall be assessed and collected by the Secretary on the basis of the information available to him in the same manner as taxes payable by return but with respect to which no return has been filed.

Amendments

• **1996, Small Business Job Protection Act of 1996 (P.L. 104-188)**

P.L. 104-188, § 1702(b)(6):

Amended Code Sec. 5061(b)(3). **Effective** as if included in the provision of P.L. 101-508 to which it relates. Prior to amendment, Code Sec. 5061(b)(3) read as follows:

(3) section 5041(e),

• **1994, Uruguay Round Agreements Act (P.L. 103-465)**

P.L. 103-465, § 136(c)(5):

Amended Code Sec. 5061(b)(1). **Effective** 1-1-95. Prior to amendment Code Sec. 5061(b)(1) read as follows:

(1) section 5001(a)(5), (6) or (7),

• **1990, Omnibus Budget Reconciliation Act of 1990 (P.L. 101-508)**

P.L. 101-508, § 11201(b)(3):

Amended Code Sec. 5061(b)(3). **Effective** 1-1-91. Prior to amendment, Code Sec. 5061(b)(3) read as follows:

(3) section 5041(e)

P.L. 101-508, § 11704(a)(21):

Amended Code Sec. 5061(b)(3). **Effective** 11-5-90. Prior to amendment, paragraph (3) read as follows:

(3) section 5041(d),

• **1979, Trade Agreements Act of 1979 (P.L. 96-39)**

P.L. 96-39, § 807(a)(9)(B):

Amended Code Sec. 5061(b) by deleting paragraph (3) and redesignating paragraphs (4), (5), (6), and (7) as paragraphs (3), (4), (5), and (6). **Effective** 1-1-80. Prior to deletion, paragraph (3) read as follows:

(3) section 5026(a)(2),

• **1976, Tax Reform Act of 1976 (P.L. 94-455)**

P.L. 94-455, § 1905(a)(6)(B):

Amended Code Sec. 5061(b). **Effective** 2-1-77. Prior to amendment, Code Sec. 5061(b) read as follows:

(b) DISCRETION[ARY] METHOD OF COLLECTION.—Whether or not the method of collecting any tax imposed by this part is specifically provided in this part, any such tax may, under regulations prescribed by the Secretary or his delegate, be collected by stamp, coupon, serially-numbered ticket, or the use of tax-stamp machines, or by such other reasonable device or method as may be necessary or helpful in securing collection of the tax.

[Sec. 5061(c)]

(c) IMPORT DUTIES.—The internal revenue taxes imposed by this part shall be in addition to any import duties unless such duties are specifically designated as being in lieu of internal revenue tax.

Amendments

• **1976, Tax Reform Act of 1976 (P.L. 94-455)**

P.L. 94-455, § 1905(a)(6)(C):

Amended Code Sec. 5061(c). **Effective** 2-1-77. Prior to amendment, Code Sec. 5061(c) read as follows:

(c) APPLICABILITY OF OTHER PROVISIONS OF LAW.—All administrative and penalty provisions of this title, insofar as applicable, shall apply to the collection of any tax which the Secretary or his delegate determines or prescribes shall be collected in any manner provided in this section.

[Sec. 5061(d)]

(d) TIME FOR COLLECTING TAX ON DISTILLED SPIRITS, WINES, AND BEER.—

    (1) IN GENERAL.—Except as otherwise provided in this subsection, in the case of distilled spirits, wines, and beer to which this part applies (other than subsection (b) of this section) which are withdrawn under bond for deferred payment of tax, the last day for payment of such tax shall be the 14th day after the last day of the semimonthly period during which the withdrawal occurs.

    (2) IMPORTED ARTICLES.—In the case of distilled spirits, wines, and beer which are imported into the United States (other than in bulk containers)—

        (A) IN GENERAL.—The last day for payment of tax shall be the 14th day after the last day of the semimonthly period during which the article is entered into the customs territory of the United States.

ALCOHOL TAXES—GALLONAGE TAXES

(B) SPECIAL RULE FOR ENTRY FOR WAREHOUSING.—Except as provided in subparagraph (D), in the case of an entry for warehousing, the last day for payment of tax shall not be later than the 14th day after the last day of the semimonthly period during which the article is removed from the 1st such warehouse.

(C) FOREIGN TRADE ZONES.—Except as provided in subparagraph (D) and in regulations prescribed by the Secretary, articles brought into a foreign zone shall, notwithstanding any other provision of law, be treated for purposes of this subsection as if such zone were a single customs warehouse.

(D) EXCEPTION FOR ARTICLES DESTINED FOR EXPORT.—Subparagraphs (B) and (C) shall not apply to any article which is shown to the satisfaction of the Secretary to be destined for export.

(3) DISTILLED SPIRITS, WINES, AND BEER BROUGHT INTO THE UNITED STATES FROM PUERTO RICO.—In the case of distilled spirits, wines, and beer which are brought into the United States (other than in bulk containers) from Puerto Rico, the last day for payment of tax shall be the 14th day after the last day of the semimonthly period during which the article is brought into the United States.

(4) TAXPAYERS LIABLE FOR TAXES OF NOT MORE THAN $50,000.—

(A) IN GENERAL.—

(i) MORE THAN $1,000 AND NOT MORE THAN $50,000 IN TAXES.—Except as provided in clause (ii), in the case of any taxpayer who reasonably expects to be liable for not more than $50,000 in taxes imposed with respect to distilled spirits, wines, and beer under subparts A, C, and D and section 7652 for the calendar year and who was liable for not more than $50,000 in such taxes in the preceding calendar year, the last day for the payment of tax on withdrawals, removals, and entries (and articles brought into the United States from Puerto Rico) shall be the 14th day after the last day of the calendar quarter during which the action giving rise to the imposition of such tax occurs.

(ii) NOT MORE THAN $1,000 IN TAXES.—In the case of any taxpayer who reasonably expects to be liable for not more than $1,000 in taxes imposed with respect to distilled spirits, wines, and beer under subparts A, C, and D and section 7652 for the calendar year and who was liable for not more than $1,000 in such taxes in the preceding calendar year, the last day for the payment of tax on withdrawals, removals, and entries (and articles brought into the United States from Puerto Rico) shall be the 14th day after the last day of the calendar year.

(B) NO APPLICATION AFTER LIMIT EXCEEDED.—

(i) EXCEEDS $50,000 LIMIT.—Subparagraph (A)(i) shall not apply to any taxpayer for any portion of the calendar year following the first date on which the aggregate amount of tax due under subparts A, C, and D and section 7652 from such taxpayer during such calendar year exceeds $50,000, and any tax under such subparts which has not been paid on such date shall be due on the 14th day after the last day of the semimonthly period in which such date occurs.

(ii) EXCEEDS $1,000 LIMIT.—Subparagraph (A)(ii) shall not apply to any taxpayer for any portion of the calendar year following the first date on which the aggregate amount of tax due under subparts A, C, and D and section 7652 from such taxpayer during such calendar year exceeds $1,000, and any tax under such subparts which has not been paid on such date shall be due on the 14th day after the last day of the calendar quarter in which such date occurs.

(C) CALENDAR QUARTER.—For purposes of this paragraph, the term "calendar quarter" means the three-month period ending on March 31, June 30, September 30, or December 31.

(5) SPECIAL RULE FOR TAX DUE IN SEPTEMBER.—

(A) IN GENERAL.—Notwithstanding the preceding provisions of this subsection, the taxes on distilled spirits, wines, and beer for the period beginning on September 16 and ending on September 26 shall be paid not later than September 29.

(B) SAFE HARBOR.—The requirement of subparagraph (A) shall be treated as met if the amount paid not later than September 29 is not less than $11/15$ of the taxes on distilled spirits, wines, and beer for the period beginning on September 1 and ending on September 15.

(C) TAXPAYERS NOT REQUIRED TO USE ELECTRONIC FUNDS TRANSFER.— In the case of payments not required to be made by electronic funds transfer, subparagraphs (A) and (B) shall be applied by substituting "September 25" for "September 26", September 28" for September 29", and "$2/3$" for "$11/15$".

(6) SPECIAL RULE WHERE DUE DATE FALLS ON SATURDAY, SUNDAY, OR HOLIDAY.—Notwithstanding section 7503, if, but for this paragraph, the due date under this subsection for payment of tax would fall on a Saturday, Sunday, or a legal holiday (within the meaning of section 7503), such due date shall be the immediately preceding day which is not a Saturday, Sunday, or such a holiday (or the immediately following day where the due date described in paragraph (5) falls on a Sunday).

Amendments

• **2015, Protecting Americans from Tax Hikes Act of 2015 (P.L. 114-113)**

P.L. 114-113, § 332(a)(1)-(2), Div. Q:

Amended Code Sec. 5061(d)(4) in subparagraph (A) by striking "In the case of" and inserting:

"(i) MORE THAN $1,000 AND NOT MORE THAN $50,000 IN TAXES.—Except as provided in clause (ii), in the case of",

by striking "under bond for deferred payment" following "Puerto Rico)", and by adding at the end a new clause (ii), and in subparagraph (B) by striking "Subparagraph (A)" and inserting:

"(i) EXCEEDS $50,000 LIMIT.—Subparagraph (A)(i)",

and by adding at the end a new clause (ii). **Effective** for any calendar quarters beginning more than 1 year after 12-18-2015.

• **2005, Safe, Accountable, Flexible, Efficient Transportation Equity Act: A Legacy for Users (P.L. 109-59)**

P.L. 109-59, § 11127(a):

Amended Code Sec. 5061(d) by redesignating paragraphs (4) and (5) as paragraphs (5) and (6), respectively, and by inserting after paragraph (3) a new paragraph (4). **Effective** with respect to quarterly periods beginning on and after 1-1-2006.

P.L. 109-59, § 11127(b):

Amended Code Sec. 5061(d)(6), as redesignated by Act Sec. 11127(a), by striking "paragraph (4)" and inserting "paragraph (5)". **Effective** with respect to quarterly periods beginning on and after 1-1-2006.

• **1994, Uruguay Round Agreements Act (P.L. 103-465)**

P.L. 103-465, § 712(b)(1):

Amended Code Sec. 5061(d) by redesignating paragraph (4) as paragraph (5) and by inserting after paragraph (3) a new paragraph (4). **Effective** 1-1-95.

P.L. 103-465, § 712(b)(2)(A)-(B):

Amended Code Sec. 5061(d)(5), as redesignated by Act Sec. 712(b)(1), by inserting "(or the immediately following day where the due date described in paragraph (4) falls on a Sunday)" before the period at the end, and by striking "14TH DAY" in the heading and inserting "DUE DATE". **Effective** 1-1-95.

• **1988, Technical and Miscellaneous Revenue Act of 1988 (P.L. 100-647)**

P.L. 100-647, § 2003(b)(1)(A):

Amended Code Sec. 5061(d)(2)(A) and (B) by striking out "the 14th day after the date on which" and inserting in lieu thereof "the 14th day after the last day of the semimonthly period during which". **Effective** as if included in the amendments made by Act Sec. 8011 of P.L. 99-509.

P.L. 100-647, § 2003(b)(1)(B):

Amended Code Sec. 5061(d)(3) by striking out "the 14th day after the date on which" and inserting in lieu thereof "the 14th day after the last day of the semimonthly period during which". **Effective** as if included in the amendments made by Act Sec. 8011 of P.L. 99-509.

• **1986, Omnibus Budget Reconciliation Act of 1986 (P.L. 99-509)**

P.L. 99-509, § 8011(b)(1):

Amended Code Sec. 5061(d). For the **effective** date, see Act Sec. 8011(c), below. Prior to amendment, Code Sec. 5061(d) read as follows:

(d) EXTENSION OF TIME FOR COLLECTING TAX ON DISTILLED SPIRITS.—In the case of distilled spirits to which subsection (a) applies which are withdrawn from the bonded premises of a distilled spirits plant under bond for deferred payment of tax, the last day for filing a return (with remittances) for each semimonthly return period shall be determined under the following table:

ALCOHOL TAXES—GALLONAGE TAXES

If the return period is in—	Such last day shall be—
1980	The last day of the first succeeding return period plus 5 days.
1981	The last day of the first succeeding return period plus 10 days.
1982 or any year thereafter	The last day of the second succeeding return period.

P.L. 99-509, § 8011(c), provides:

(c) EFFECTIVE DATES.—

(1) IN GENERAL.—Except as provided in paragraph (2), the amendments made by this section shall apply to removals during semimonthly periods ending on or after December 31, 1986.

(2) IMPORTED ARTICLES, ETC.—Subparagraphs (B) and (C) of section 5703(b)(2) of the Internal Revenue Code of 1954 (as added by this section), paragraphs (2) and (3) of section 5061(d) of such Code (as amended by this section), and the amendments made by subsections (a)(2) and (b)(2) shall apply to articles imported, entered for warehousing, or brought into the United States or a foreign trade zone after December 15, 1986.

(3) SPECIAL RULE FOR DISTILLED SPIRITS AND TOBACCO FOR SEMIMONTHLY PERIOD ENDING DECEMBER 15, 1986.—With respect to remittances of—

(A) taxes imposed on distilled spirits by section 5001 or 7652 of such Code, and

(B) taxes imposed on tobacco products and cigarette papers and tubes by section 5701 or 7652 of such Code,

for the semimonthly period ending December 15, 1986, the last day for payment of such remittances shall be January 14, 1987.

(4) TREATMENT OF SMOKELESS TOBACCO IN INVENTORY ON JUNE 30, 1986.—The tax imposed by section 5701(e) of the Internal Revenue Code of 1954 shall not apply to any smokeless tobacco which—

(A) on June 30, 1986, was in the inventory of the manufacturer or importer, and

(B) on such date was in a form ready for sale.

• **1979, Trade Agreements Act of 1979 (P.L. 96-39)**

P.L. 96-39, § 804(b):

Added Code Sec. 5061(d). **Effective** 1-1-80.

[Sec. 5061(d)—Repealed]

(d) CROSS REFERENCE.—

For penalty and forfeiture for tampering with a stamp machine, see section 5689.

Amendments

• **1976, Tax Reform Act of 1976 (P.L. 94-455)**

P.L. 94-455, § 1905(b)(2)(E)(iii):

Struck out Code Sec. 5061(d). **Effective** 2-1-77. Prior to striking, Code Sec. 5061(d) read as follows:

[Sec. 5061(e)]

(e) PAYMENT BY ELECTRONIC FUND TRANSFER.—

(1) IN GENERAL.—Any person who in any 12-month period ending December 31, was liable for a gross amount equal to or exceeding $5,000,000 in taxes imposed on distilled spirits, wines, or beer by sections 5001, 5041, and 5051 (or 7652), respectively, shall pay such taxes during the succeeding calendar year by electronic fund transfer to a Federal Reserve Bank.

(2) ELECTRONIC FUND TRANSFER.—The term "electronic fund transfer" means any transfer of funds, other than a transaction originated by check, draft, or similar paper instrument, which is initiated through an electronic terminal, telephonic instrument, or computer or magnetic tape so as to order, instruct, or authorize a financial institution to debit or credit an account.

(3) CONTROLLED GROUPS.—

(A) IN GENERAL.—In the case of a controlled group of corporations, all corporations which are component members of such group shall be treated as 1 taxpayer. For purposes of the preceding sentence, the term "controlled group of corporations" has the meaning given to such term by subsection (a) of section 1563, except that "more than 50 percent" shall be substituted for "at least 80 percent" each place it appears in such subsection.

(B) CONTROLLED GROUPS WHICH INCLUDE NONINCORPORATED PERSONS.—Under regulations prescribed by the Secretary, principles similar to the principles of subparagraph (A) shall apply to a group of persons under common control where 1 or more of such persons is not a corporation.

Amendments

• **1986, Tax Reform Act of 1986 (P.L. 99-514)**

P.L. 99-514, § 1801(c)(1):

Amended Code Sec. 5061(e) by adding at the end thereof new paragraph (3). **Effective** as if included in the provision of P.L. 98-369 to which it relates.

• **1984, Deficit Reduction Act of 1984 (P.L. 98-369)**

P.L. 98-369, § 27(c)(1):

Amended Code Sec. 5061 by adding at the end thereof new subsection (e). **Effective** for taxes required to be paid on or after 9-30-84.

[Sec. 5062]

SEC. 5062. REFUND AND DRAWBACK IN CASE OF EXPORTATION.

[Sec. 5062(a)]

(a) REFUND.—Under such regulations as the Secretary may prescribe, the amount of any internal revenue tax erroneously or illegally collected in respect to exported articles may be refunded to the exporter of the article, instead of to the manufacturer, if the manufacturer waives any claim for the amount so to be refunded.

Amendments

• **1976, Tax Reform Act of 1976 (P.L. 94-455)**

P.L. 94-455, § 1906(b)(13)(A):

Amended 1954 Code by substituting "Secretary" for "Secretary or his delegate" each place it appeared. **Effective** 2-1-77.

[Sec. 5062(b)]

(b) DRAWBACK.—On the exportation of distilled spirits or wines manufactured, produced, bottled, or packaged in casks or other bulk containers in the United States on which an internal revenue tax has been paid or determined, and which are contained in any cask or other bulk container, or in bottles packed in cases or other containers, there shall be allowed, under regulations prescribed by the Secretary, a drawback equal in amount to the tax found to have been paid or determined on such distilled spirits or wines. In the case of distilled spirits, the preceding sentence shall not apply unless the claim for drawback is filed by the bottler or packager of the spirits and unless such spirits have been marked, especially for export, under regulations prescribed by the Secretary. The Secretary is authorized to prescribe regulations governing the determination and payment or crediting of drawback of internal revenue tax on spirits and wines eligible for drawback under this subsection, including the requirements of such notices, bonds, bills of lading, and other evidence indicating payment or determination of tax and exportation as shall be deemed necessary.

Amendments

• **1984, Deficit Reduction Act of 1984 (P.L. 98-369)**

P.L. 98-369, § 454(c)(1):

Amended Code Sec. 5062(b) by striking out "stamped or restamped, and" in the second sentence preceding "marked". **Effective** 7-1-85.

• **1977 (P.L. 95-176)**

P.L. 95-176, § 1:

Amended Code Sec. 5062(b). **Effective** 3-1-78. Prior to amendment, Code Sec. 5062(b) read as follows:

Sec. 5061(d)—Repealed

ALCOHOL TAXES—GALLONAGE TAXES

"(b) DRAWBACK.—On the exportation of distilled spirits or wines manufactured or produced in the United States on which an internal revenue tax has been paid or determined, and which are contained in any cask or package, or in bottles packed in cases or other containers, there shall be allowed, under regulations prescribed by the Secretary, a drawback equal in amount to the tax found to have been paid or determined on such distilled spirits or wines. In the case of distilled spirits, the preceding sentence shall not apply unless the claim for drawback is filed by the bottler or packager of the spirits and unless such spirits have been stamped or restamped, and marked, especially for export, under regulations prescribed by the Secretary. The Secretary is authorized to prescribe regulations governing the determination and payment or crediting of drawback of internal revenue tax on domestic distilled spirits and wines, including the requirement of such notices, bonds, bills of lading, and other evidence indicating payment or determination of tax and exportation as shall be deemed necessary."

- **1976, Tax Reform Act of 1976 (P.L. 94-455)**

P.L. 94-455, §1906(b)(13)(A):

Amended 1954 Code by substituting "Secretary" for "Secretary or his delegate" each place it appeared. **Effective** 2-1-77.

[Sec. 5062(c)]

(c) EXPORTATION OF IMPORTED LIQUORS.—

(1) ALLOWANCE OF TAX.—Upon the exportation of imported distilled spirits, wines, and beer upon which the duties and internal revenue taxes have been paid or determined incident to their importation into the United States, and which have been found after entry to be unmerchantable or not to conform to sample or specifications, and which have been returned to customs custody, the Secretary shall, under such regulations as he shall prescribe, refund, remit, abate, or credit, without interest, to the importer thereof, the full amount of the internal revenue taxes paid or determined with respect to such distilled spirits, wines, or beer.

(2) DESTRUCTION IN LIEU OF EXPORTATION.—At the option of the importer, such imported distilled spirits, wines, and beer, after return to customs custody, may be destroyed under customs supervision and the importer thereof granted relief in the same manner and to the same extent as provided in this subsection upon exportation.

Amendments

- **1976, Tax Reform Act of 1976 (P.L. 94-455)**

P.L. 94-455, §1906(b)(13)(A):

Amended 1954 Code by substituting "Secretary" for "Secretary or his delegate" each place it appeared. **Effective** 2-1-77.

- **1968 (P.L. 90-630)**

P.L. 90-630, §2(a):

Amended subsection (b) of Code Sec. 5062 by substituting the second sentence therein for the following: "The preceding sentence shall not apply unless such distilled spirits have been packaged or bottled especially for export, or, in the case of distilled spirits originally bottled for domestic use, have been restamped and marked especially for export at the distilled spirits plant where originally bottled and before removal therefrom, under regulations prescribed by the Secretary or his delegate." **Effective** only for articles exported on or after 2-1-69.

- **1965, Excise Tax Reduction Act of 1965 (P.L. 89-44)**

P.L. 89-44, §805(f)(6):

Amended subsection (c) of Section 5062 by deleting "within six months of their release therefrom" after "custody". **Effective** 7-1-65.

- **1964 (P.L. 88-539)**

P.L. 88-539, §[1]:

Added Code Sec. 5062(c). **Effective** with respect to articles exported or destroyed after 8-31-64.

[Sec. 5064]

SEC. 5064. LOSSES RESULTING FROM DISASTER, VANDALISM, OR MALICIOUS MISCHIEF.

[Sec. 5064(a)]

(a) PAYMENTS.—The Secretary, under such regulations as he may prescribe, shall pay (without interest) an amount equal to the amount of the internal revenue taxes paid or determined and customs duties paid on distilled spirits, wines, and beer previously withdrawn, which were lost, rendered unmarketable, or condemned by a duly authorized official by reason of—

(1) fire, flood, casualty, or other disaster, or

(2) breakage, destruction, or other damage (but not including theft) resulting from vandalism or malicious mischief,

if such disaster or damage occurred in the United States and if such distilled spirits, wines, or beer were held and intended for sale at the time of such disaster or other damage. The payments provided for in this section shall be made to the person holding such distilled spirits, wines, or beer for sale at the time of such disaster or other damage.

Amendments

- **1978 (P.L. 95-423)**

P.L. 95-423, §1(a):

Amended Code Sec. 5064(a). **Effective** for disasters or other damage occurring on or after 2-1-79. Before amendment, subsection (a) read as follows:

"(a) AUTHORIZATION.—Where the President has determined under the Disaster Relief Act of 1974, that a 'major disaster' as defined in such Act has occurred in any part of the United States, the Secreatry shall pay (without interest) an amount equal to the amount of the internal revenue taxes paid or determined and customs duties paid on distilled spirits, wines, rectified products, and beer previously withdrawn, which were lost, rendered unmarketable, or condemned by a duly authorized official by reason of such disaster occurring in such part of the United States after June 30, 1959, if such distilled spirits, wines, rectified products, or beer were held and intended for sale at the time of such disaster. The payments authorized by this section shall be made to the person holding such distilled spirits, wines, rectified products, or beer for sale at the time of such disaster."

- **1976, Tax Reform Act of 1976 (P.L. 94-455)**

P.L. 94-455, §1906(b)(13)(A):

Amended 1954 Code by substituting "Secretary" for "Secretary or his delegate" each place it appeared. **Effective** 7-1-65.

- **1974, Disaster Relief Act of 1974 (P.L. 93-288)**

P.L. 93-288, §602(i):

Amended Code Sec. 5064(a) by substituting "Disaster Relief Act of 1974" for "Disaster Relief Act of 1970." **Effective** 4-1-73.

- **1970, Disaster Relief Act of 1970 (P.L. 91-606)**

P.L. 91-606, §301(i):

Amended Code Sec. 5064(a) by substituting "the Disaster Relief Act of 1970" for "the Act of September 30, 1950 (42 U. S. C., sec. 1855)". **Effective** 12-31-70.

[Sec. 5064(b)]

(b) CLAIMS.—

(1) PERIOD FOR MAKING CLAIM; PROOF.—No claim shall be allowed under this section unless—

(A) filed within 6 months after the date on which such distilled spirits, wines, or beer were lost, rendered unmarketable, or condemned by a duly authorized official, and

(B) the claimant furnishes proof satisfactory to the Secretary that the claimant—

(i) was not indemnified by any valid claim of insurance or otherwise in respect of the tax, or tax and duty, on the distilled spirits, wines, or beer covered by the claim; and

(ii) is entitled to payment under this section.

(2) MINIMUM CLAIM.—Except as provided in paragraph (3) (A), no claim of less than $250 shall be allowed under this section with respect to any disaster or other damage (as the case may be).

(3) SPECIAL RULES FOR MAJOR DISASTERS.—If the President has determined under the Robert T. Stafford Disaster Relief and Emergency Assistance Act that a "major disaster" (as defined in such Act) has occurred in any part of the United States, and if the disaster referred to in subsection (a)(1) occurs in such part of the United States by reason of such major disaster, then—

(A) paragraph (2) shall not apply, and

(B) the filing period set forth in paragraph (1)(A) shall not expire before the day which is 6 months after the date on which the President makes the determination that such major disaster has occurred.

ALCOHOL TAXES—GALLONAGE TAXES

(4) REGULATIONS.—Claims under this section shall be filed under such regulations as the Secretary shall prescribe.

Amendments

• **2004, Working Families Tax Relief Act of 2004 (P.L. 108-311)**

P.L. 108-311, §408(a)(7)(D):

Amended Code Sec. 5064(b)(3) by inserting "Robert T. Stafford" before "Disaster Relief and Emergency Assistance Act". **Effective** 10-4-2004.

• **1988, Disaster Relief and Emergency Assistance Amendments of 1988 (P.L. 100-707)**

P.L. 100-707, §109(l):

Amended Code Sec. 5064(b)(3) by striking out "Act of 1974" and inserting in lieu thereof "and Emergency Assistance Act". **Effective** 11-23-88.

• **1978 (P.L. 95-423)**

P.L. 95-423, §1(a):

Amended Code Sec. 5064(b). **Effective** for disasters or other damage occurring on or after 2-1-79. Before amendment, subsection (b) read as follows:

"(b) CLAIMS.—No claim shall be allowed under this section unless—

(1) filed within 6 months after the date on which the President makes the determination that the disaster referred to in subsection (a) has occurred; and

(2) the claimant furnishes proof to the satisfaction of the Secretary that—

(A) he was not indemnified by any valid claim of insurance or otherwise in respect of the tax, or tax and duty, on the distilled spirits, wines, rectified products, or beer covered by the claim; and

(B) he is entitled to payment under this section.

Claims under this section shall be filed under such regulations as the Secretary shall prescribe."

• **1976, Tax Reform Act of 1976 (P.L. 94-455)**

P.L. 94-455, §1906(b)(13)(A):

Amended 1954 Code by substituting "Secretary" for "Secretary or his delegate" each place it appeared. **Effective** 2-1-77.

[Sec. 5064(c)]

(c) DESTRUCTION OF DISTILLED SPIRITS, WINES, OR BEER.—When the Secretary has made payment under this section in respect of the tax, or tax and duty, on the distilled spirits, wines, or beer condemned by a duly authorized official or rendered unmarketable, such distilled spirits, wines, or beer shall be destroyed under such supervision as the Secretary may prescribe, unless such distilled spirits, wines, or beer were previously destroyed under supervision satisfactory to the Secretary.

Amendments

• **1979, Trade Agreements Act of 1979 (P.L. 96-39)**

P.L. 96-39, §807(a)(10):

Amended Code Sec. 5064(c) by deleting "Rectified Products," in the heading. **Effective** 1-1-80.

• **1976, Tax Reform Act of 1976 (P.L. 94-455)**

P.L. 94-455, §1906(b)(13)(A):

Amended 1954 Code by substituting "Secretary" for "Secretary or his delegate" each place it appeared. **Effective** 2-1-77.

[Sec. 5064(d)]

(d) PRODUCTS OF PUERTO RICO.—The provisions of this section shall not be applicable in respect of distilled spirits, wines, and beer of Puerto Rican manufacture brought into the United States and so lost or rendered unmarketable or condemned.

[Sec. 5064(e)]

(e) OTHER LAWS APPLICABLE.—All provisions of law, including penalties, applicable in respect of internal revenue taxes on distilled spirits, wines, and beer shall, insofar as applicable and not inconsistent with this section, be applied in respect of the payments provided for in this section to the same extent as if such payments constituted refunds of such taxes.

Amendments

• **1979, Trade Agreements Act of 1979 (P.L. 96-39)**

P.L. 96-39, §807(a)(10):

Amended Code Sec. 5064 by deleting "rectified products" each place it appeared. **Effective** 1-1-80.

[Sec. 5065]

SEC. 5065. TERRITORIAL EXTENT OF LAW.

The provisions of this part imposing taxes on distilled spirits, wines, and beer shall be held to extend to such articles produced anywhere within the exterior boundaries of the United States, whether the same be within an internal revenue district or not.

[Sec. 5066]

SEC. 5066. DISTILLED SPIRITS FOR USE OF FOREIGN EMBASSIES, LEGATIONS, ETC.

[Sec. 5066(a)]

(a) ENTRY INTO CUSTOMS BONDED WAREHOUSES.—

(1) BOTTLED DISTILLED SPIRITS WITHDRAWN FROM BONDED PREMISES.—Under such regulations as the Secretary may prescribe, bottled distilled spirits may be withdrawn from bonded premises as provided in section 5214(a)(4) for transfer to customs bonded warehouses in which imported distilled spirits are permitted to be stored in bond for entry therein pending withdrawal therefrom as provided in subsection (b).

(2) BOTTLED DISTILLED SPIRITS ELIGIBLE FOR EXPORT WITH BENEFIT OF DRAWBACK.—Under such regulations as the Secretary may prescribe, distilled spirits marked especially for export under the provisions of section 5062(b) may be shipped to a customs bonded warehouse in which imported distilled spirits are permitted to be stored, and entered in such warehouses pending withdrawal therefrom as provided in subsection (b), and the provisions of this chapter shall apply in respect of such distilled spirits as if such spirits were for exportation.

(3) TIME DEEMED EXPORTED.—For the purposes of this chapter, distilled spirits entered into a customs bonded warehouse as provided in this subsection shall be deemed exported at the time so entered.

Amendments

• **1984, Deficit Reduction Act of 1984 (P.L. 98-369)**

P.L. 98-369, §454(c)(2):

Amended Code Sec. 5066(a)(2) by striking out "stamped or restamped, and marked," and inserting in lieu thereof "marked". **Effective** 7-1-85.

• **1979, Trade Agreements Act of 1979 (P.L. 96-39)**

P.L. 96-39, §807(a)(11)(A):

Amended Code Sec. 5066(a) by changing "distilled spirits bottled in bond for export under the provisions of section 5233, or bottled distilled spirits returned to bonded premises under section 5215(b)," to "bottled distilled spirits". **Effective** 1-1-80.

• **1977 (P.L. 95-176)**

P.L. 95-176, §2(d):

Amended Code Sec. 5066(a)(1). **Effective** 3-1-78. Prior to amendment Code Sec. 5066(a)(1) read as follows:

"(1) DISTILLED SPIRITS BOTTLED IN BOND FOR EXPORT.—Under such regulations as the Secretary may prescribe, distilled spirits bottled in bond for export under the provisions of section 5233 may be withdrawn from bonded premises as provided in section 5214(a)(4) for transfer to customs bonded warehouses in which imported distilled spirits are permitted to be stored in bond for entry therein pending withdrawal therefrom as provided in subsection (b). For the purposes of this chapter, the withdrawal of distilled spirits from bonded premises under the provisions of this paragraph shall be treated as a withdrawal for exportation and all provisions of law applicable to distilled spirits withdrawn for exportation under the provisions of section 5214(a)(4) shall apply with respect to spirits withdrawn under this paragraph."

• **1976, Tax Reform Act of 1976 (P.L. 94-455)**

P.L. 94-455, §1906(b)(13)(A):

Amended 1954 Code by substituting "Secretary" for "Secretary or his delegate" each place it appeared. **Effective** 2-1-77.

ALCOHOL TAXES—MISCELLANEOUS PROVISIONS

[Sec. 5066(b)]

(b) WITHDRAWAL FROM CUSTOMS BONDED WAREHOUSES.—Notwithstanding any other provisions of law, distilled spirits entered into customs bonded warehouses under the provisions of subsection (a) may, under such regulations as the Secretary may prescribe, be withdrawn from such warehouses for consumption in the United States by and for the official or family use of such foreign governments, organizations, and individuals who are entitled to withdraw imported distilled spirits from such warehouses free of tax. Distilled spirits transferred to customs bonded warehouses under the provisions of this section shall be entered, stored, and accounted for in such warehouses under such regulations and bonds as the Secretary may prescribe, and may be withdrawn therefrom by such governments, organizations, and individuals free of tax under the same conditions and procedures as imported distilled spirits.

Amendments

• 1979, Trade Agreements Act of 1979 (P.L. 96-39)

P.L. 96-39, §807(a)(11)(B):

Amended Code Sec. 5066(b) by changing "under the provisions of subsection (a) or domestic distilled spirits transferred to customs bonded warehouses under section 5521(d)(2) may" to "under the provisions of subsection (a) may". **Effective** 1-1-80.

• 1976, Tax Reform Act of 1976 (P.L. 94-455)

P.L. 94-455, §1906(b)(13)(A):

Amended 1954 Code by substituting "Secretary" for "Secretary or his delegate" each place it appeared. **Effective** 2-1-77.

[Sec. 5066(c)]

(c) WITHDRAWAL FOR DOMESTIC USE.—Distilled spirits entered into customs bonded warehouses as authorized by this section may be withdrawn therefrom for domestic use, in which event they shall be treated as American goods exported and returned.

[Sec. 5066(d)]

(d) SALE OR UNAUTHORIZED USE PROHIBITED.—No distilled spirits withdrawn from customs bonded warehouses or otherwise brought into the United States free of tax for the official or family use of such foreign governments, organizations, or individuals as are authorized to obtain distilled spirits free of tax shall be sold, or shall be disposed of or possessed for any use other than an authorized use. The provisions of section 5001(a)(4) are hereby extended and made applicable to any person selling, disposing of, or possessing any distilled spirits in violation of the preceding sentence, and to the distilled spirits involved in any such violation.

Amendments

• 2018, Tax Technical Corrections Act of 2018 (P.L. 115-141)

P.L. 115-141, §401(a)(240), Div. U:

Amended Code Sec. 5066(d) by striking "section 5001(a)(5)" and inserting "section 5001(a)(4)". **Effective** 3-23-2018.

• 1971 (P.L. 91-659)

P.L. 91-659, §3(a):

Redesignated former Code Sec. 5066 as Code Sec. 5067 and added new Code Sec. 5066. **Effective** 5-1-71.

[Sec. 5067]

SEC. 5067. REDUCED RATES NOT ALLOWED FOR SMUGGLED OR ILLEGALLY PRODUCED BEER, WINE, OR SPIRITS.

In the case of beer, wine, or distilled spirits that are smuggled into the United States or produced other than as authorized by this chapter—

(1) the rates of tax under paragraphs (1)(A)(i) and (2) of section 5051(a) shall not apply in the case of any such beer,

(2) the credit under section 5041(c) shall not apply in the case of any such wine, and

(3) the rates of tax under section 5001(c) shall not apply in the case of any such distilled spirits.

Amendments

• 2020, Taxpayer Certainty and Disaster Tax Relief Act of 2020 (P.L. 116-260)

P.L. 116-260, §108(a), Div. EE:

Amended subpart E of part I of subchapter A of chapter 51 by redesignating Code Sec. 5067 as Code Sec. 5068 and by inserting after Code Sec. 5066 a new Code Sec. 5067. **Effective** for beer, wine, or distilled spirits, as the case may be, produced after 12-27-2020.

[Sec. 5068]

SEC. 5068. CROSS REFERENCE.

For general administrative provisions applicable to the assessment, collection, refund, etc., of taxes, see subtitle F.

Amendments

• 2020, Taxpayer Certainty and Disaster Tax Relief Act of 2020 (P.L. 116-260)

P.L. 116-260, §108(a), Div. EE:

Amended subpart E of part I of subchapter A of chapter 51 by redesignating Code Sec. 5067 as Code Sec. 5068. **Effective** for beer, wine, or distilled spirits, as the case may be, produced after 12-27-2020.

• 1971 (P.L. 91-659)

P.L. 91-659, §3(a):

Redesignated Code Sec. 5066 as Code Sec. 5067. **Effective** 5-1-71.

PART II—MISCELLANEOUS PROVISIONS

Subpart A.   Manufacturers of stills.
Subpart B.   Nonbeverage domestic drawback claimants.
Subpart C.   Recordkeeping by dealers.
Subpart D.   Other provisions.

Subpart A—Proprietors of Distilled Spirits Plants, Bonded Wine Cellars, etc.—[Repealed]

[Sec. 5081—Repealed]

Amendments

• 2005, Safe, Accountable, Flexible, Efficient Transportation Equity Act: A Legacy for Users (P.L. 109-59)

P.L. 109-59, §11125(a)(1)(A):

Repealed subpart A of part II of subchapter A of chapter 51 (Code Sec. 5081). **Effective** 7-1-2008, but not applicable to taxes imposed for periods before such date. Prior to repeal, Code Sec. 5081 read as follows:

SEC. 5081. SEC. 5081. IMPOSITION AND RATE OF TAX.

[Sec. 5081(a)]

(a) GENERAL RULE.—Every proprietor of—

(1) a distilled spirits plant,

(2) a bonded wine cellar,

(3) a bonded wine warehouse, or

(4) a taxpaid wine bottling house,

shall pay a tax of $1,000 per year in respect of each such premises.

[Sec. 5081(b)]

(b) REDUCED RATES FOR SMALL PROPRIETORS.—

(1) IN GENERAL.—Subsection (a) shall be applied by substituting "$500" for "$1,000" with respect to any taxpayer not described in subsection (c) the gross receipts of which (for the most recent taxable year ending before the 1st day of the taxable period to which the tax imposed by subsection (a) relates) are less than $500,000.

(2) CONTROLLED GROUP RULES.—All persons treated as 1 taxpayer under section 5061(e)(3) shall be treated as 1 taxpayer for purposes of paragraph (1).

ALCOHOL TAXES—MISCELLANEOUS PROVISIONS

(3) CERTAIN RULES TO APPLY.—For purposes of paragraph (1), rules similar to the rules of subparagraphs (B) and (C) of section 448(c)(3) shall apply.

Amendments

• **1988, Technical and Miscellaneous Revenue Act of 1988 (P.L. 100-647)**

P.L. 100-647, §6106(b):

Amended Code Sec. 5081(b)(1) by inserting "not described in subsection (c)" after "taxpayer". **Effective** 7-1-89.

• **1987, Revenue Act of 1987 (P.L. 100-203)**

P.L. 100-203, §10512(a)(1)(A):

Amended part II of subchapter A of chapter 51 by adding new Code Sec. 5081. For the **effective** date, see Act Sec. 10512(h), below.

P.L. 100-203, §10512(h), provides:

(h) EFFECTIVE DATE.—

(1) IN GENERAL.—The amendments made by this section shall take effect on January 1, 1988.

(2) ALL TAXPAYERS TREATED AS COMMENCING IN BUSINESS ON JANUARY 1, 1988.—

(A) IN GENERAL.—Any person engaged on January 1, 1988, in any trade or business which is subject to an occupational tax shall be treated for purposes of such tax as having 1st engaged in such trade or business on such date.

(B) LIMITATION ON AMOUNT OF TAX.—In the case of a taxpayer who paid an occupational tax in respect of any premises for any taxable period which began before January 1, 1988, and includes such date, the amount of the occupational tax imposed by reason of subparagraph (A) in respect of such premises shall not exceed an amount equal to $1/2$ the excess (if any) of—

(i) the rate of such tax as in effect on January 1, 1988, over

(ii) the rate of such tax as in effect on December 31, 1987.

(C) OCCUPATIONAL TAX.—For purposes of this paragraph, the term "occupational tax" means any tax imposed under part II of subchapter A of chapter 51, section 5276, section 5731, or section 5801 of the Internal Revenue Code of 1986 (as amended by this section).

(D) DUE DATE OF TAX.—The amount of any tax required to be paid by reason of this paragraph shall be due on April 1, 1988.

• **1979, Trade Agreements Act of 1979 (P.L. 96-39)**

P.L. 96-39, §803(b):

Repealed Code Sec. 5081. **Effective** 1-1-80.

[Sec. 5081(c)]

(c) EXEMPTION FOR SMALL PRODUCERS.—Subsection (a) shall not apply with respect to any taxpayer who is a proprietor of an eligible distilled spirits plant (as defined in section 5181(c)(4)).

Amendments

• **1988, Technical and Miscellaneous Revenue Act of 1988 (P.L. 100-647)**

P.L. 100-647, §6106(a):

Amended Code Sec. 5081 by adding at the end thereof new subsection (c). **Effective** 7-1-89.

[Sec. 5082—Repealed]

ous processing, from mash, wort, wash, or any other substance, through continuous closed vessels and pipes, until the production thereof is complete), and every person who, without rectifying, purifying, or refining distilled spirits, shall by mixing such spirits, wine, or other liquor with any material, manufacture any spurious, imitation, or compound liquors for sale, under the name of whisky, brandy, rum, gin, wine, spirits, cordials, or wine bitters, or any other name, shall be regarded as a rectifier, and as being engaged in the business of rectifying.

Amendments

• **1979, Trade Agreements Act of 1979 (P.L. 96-39)**

P.L. 96-39, §803(b):

Repealed Code Sec. 5082. **Effective** 1-1-80. Prior to repeal, Code Sec. 5082 read as follows:

SEC. 5082. DEFINITION OF RECTIFIER.

Every person who rectifies, purifies, or refines distilled spirits or wines by any process (other than by original and continuous distillation, or original and continu-

[Sec. 5083—Repealed]

Amendments

• **1979, Trade Agreements Act of 1979 (P.L. 96-39)**

P.L. 96-39, §803(b):

Repealed Code Sec. 5083. **Effective** 1-1-80. Prior to repeal, Code Sec. 5083 read as follows:

SEC. 5083. EXEMPTIONS.

For exemptions from tax under section 5021 or 5081 in case of—

(1) Absolute alcohol, see section 5025(a).

(2) Production of gin and vodka, see section 5025(b).

(3) Refining spirits in course of original distillation, see section 5025(c).

(4) Redistillation of spirits on bonded premises of a distilled spirits plant, see section 5025(d).

(5) Mingling of distilled spirits on bonded premises of a distilled spirits plant, see section 5025(e).

(6) Apothecaries, see section 5025(h).

(7) Manufacturers of chemicals and flavoring extracts, see section 5025(i).

(8) Distilled spirits and wines rectified in customs manufacturing bonded warehouses, see section 5523.

(9) Blending beverage brandies or rums on bonded premises of a distilled spirits plant, see section 5025(e)(4).

(10) Blending of straight whiskies, fruit brandies, rums or wines, see section 5025(f).

(11) Addition of caramel to brandy or rum, see section 5025(g).

(12) Winemakers' use or treatment of wines or wine spirits, see section 5391.

(13) Stabilization of distilled spirits, see section 5025(j).

(14) Other mingling or treatment of distilled spirits, see section 5025(k).

(15) Authorized addition of tracer elements, see section 5025(l).

• **1965, Excise Tax Reduction Act of 1965 (P.L. 89-44)**

P.L. 89-44, §805(f)(7):

Amended Section 5083 by inserting subsections (14) and (15) in lieu of subsection (14). **Effective** 10-1-65. Prior to amendment, subsection (14) read as follows:

"(14) Authorized addition of tracer elements, see section 5025(k)."

[Sec. 5084—Repealed]

Amendments

• **1979, Trade Agreements Act of 1979 (P.L. 96-39)**

P.L. 96-39, §803(b):

Repealed Code Sec. 5084. **Effective** 1-1-80. Prior to repeal, Code Sec. 5084 read as follows:

SEC. 5084. CROSS REFERENCES.

(1) For provisions relating to gallonage tax on rectification, see subpart B of part I of this subchapter.

(2) For provisions relating to qualifications of distilled spirits plants to engage in rectification, see subchapter B.

(3) For provisions relating to rectifying operations on the premises of distilled spirits plants, see subchapter C.

(4) For penalties, seizures, and forfeitures relating to rectifying and rectified products, see subchapter J and subtitle F.

Subpart B—Brewer—[Repealed]

[Sec. 5091—Repealed]

Amendments

• **2005, Safe, Accountable, Flexible, Efficient Transportation Equity Act: A Legacy for Users (P.L. 109-59)**

P.L. 109-59, §11125(a)(1)(B):

Repealed subpart B of part II of subchapter A of chapter 51 (Code Secs. 5091-5093). **Effective** 7-1-2008, but not applicable to taxes imposed for periods before such date. Prior to repeal, Code Sec. 5091 read as follows:

SEC. 5091. IMPOSITION AND RATE OF TAX.

[Sec. 5091(a)]

(a) GENERAL RULE.—Every brewer shall pay a tax of $1,000 per year in respect of each brewery.

[Sec. 5091(b)]

(b) REDUCED RATES FOR SMALL BREWERS.—Rules similar to the rules of section 5081(b) shall apply for purposes of subsection (a).

Amendments

• **1987, Revenue Act of 1987 (P.L. 100-203)**

P.L. 100-203, §10512(a)(2):

Amended Code Sec. 5091. For the **effective** date, see Act Sec. 10512(h), below. Prior to amendment, Code Sec. 5091 read as follows:

SEC. 5091. IMPOSITION AND RATE OF TAX.

Every brewer shall pay $110 a year in respect of each brewery; except that any brewer of less than 500 barrels a year shall pay the sum of $55 a year. Any beer procured by a brewer in his own hogsheads, barrels, or kegs under the provisions of section 5413 shall be included in calculating the liability to brewers' special tax of both the brewer who produces the same and the brewer who procures the same.

P.L. 100-203, §10512(h), provides:

(h) EFFECTIVE DATE.—

(1) IN GENERAL.—The amendments made by this section shall take effect on January 1, 1988.

(2) ALL TAXPAYERS TREATED AS COMMENCING IN BUSINESS ON JANUARY 1, 1988.—

(A) IN GENERAL.—Any person engaged on January 1, 1988, in any trade or business which is subject to an occupational tax shall be treated for purposes of such tax as having 1st engaged in such trade or business on such date.

(B) LIMITATION ON AMOUNT OF TAX.—In the case of a taxpayer who paid an occupational tax in respect of any premises for any taxable period which began before January 1, 1988, and includes such date, the amount of the occupational tax imposed by reason of subparagraph (A) in respect of such premises shall not exceed an amount equal to $1/2$ the excess (if any) of—

(i) the rate of such tax as in effect on January 1, 1988, over

(ii) the rate of such tax as in effect on December 31, 1987.

(C) OCCUPATIONAL TAX.—For purposes of this paragraph, the term "occupational tax" means any tax imposed under part II of subchapter A of chapter 51, section 5276, section 5731, or section 5801 of the Internal Revenue Code of 1986 (as amended by this section).

(D) DUE DATE OF TAX.—The amount of any tax required to be paid by reason of this paragraph shall be due on April 1, 1988.

[Sec. 5092—Repealed]

Amendments

• 2005, Safe, Accountable, Flexible, Efficient Transportation Equity Act: A Legacy for Users (P.L. 109-59)

P.L. 109-59, §11125(a)(1)(B):

Repealed subpart B of part II of subchapter A of chapter 51 (Code Secs. 5091-5093). **Effective** 7-1-2008, but not applicable to taxes imposed for periods before such date. Prior to repeal, Code Sec. 5092 read as follows:

SEC. 5092. DEFINITION OF BREWER.

Every person who brews beer (except a person who produces only beer exempt from tax under section 5053(e)) and every person who produces beer for sale shall be deemed to be a brewer.

Amendments

• 1978 (P.L. 95-458)

P.L. 95-458, §2(b)(3), (c):

Amended Code Sec. 5092. **Effective** 2-1-79. Prior to amendment, Code Sec. 5092 read as follows:

"Every person who brews or produces beer for sale shall be deemed a brewer."

[Sec. 5093—Repealed]

Amendments

• 2005, Safe, Accountable, Flexible, Efficient Transportation Equity Act: A Legacy for Users (P.L. 109-59)

P.L. 109-59, §11125(a)(1)(B):

Repealed subpart B of part II of subchapter A of chapter 51 (Code Secs. 5091-5093). **Effective** 7-1-2008, but not applicable to taxes imposed for periods before such date. Prior to repeal, Code Sec. 5093 read as follows:

SEC. 5093. CROSS REFERENCES.

(1) For exemption of brewer from special tax as wholesale and retail dealer, see section 5113(a).

(2) For provisions relating to liability for special tax for carrying on business in more than one location, see section 5143(c).

(3) For exemption from special tax in case of sales made on purchaser dealers' premises, see section 5113(d).

Subpart A—Manufacturers of Stills

Sec. 5101.   Notice of manufacture of still; notice of set up of still.
Sec. 5102.   Definition of manufacturer of stills.

[Sec. 5101]

SEC. 5101. NOTICE OF MANUFACTURE OF STILL; NOTICE OF SET UP OF STILL.

[Sec. 5101(a)]

(a) NOTICE REQUIREMENTS.—

(1) NOTICE OF MANUFACTURE OF STILL.—The Secretary may, pursuant to regulations, require any person who manufactures any still, boiler, or other vessel to be used for the purpose of distilling, to give written notice, before the still, boiler, or other vessel is removed from the place of manufacture, setting forth by whom it is to be used, its capacity, and the time of removal from the place of manufacture.

(2) NOTICE OF SET UP OF STILL.—The Secretary may, pursuant to regulations, require that no still, boiler, or other vessel be set up without the manufacturer of the still, boiler or other vessel first giving written notice to the Secretary of that purpose.

[Sec. 5101(b)]

(b) PENALTIES, ETC.—

(1) For penalty and forfeiture for failure to give notice of manufacture, or for setting up a still without first giving notice, when required by the Secretary, see sections 5615(2) and 5687.

(2) For penalty and forfeiture for failure to register still or distilling apparatus when set up, see section 5601(a)(1) and 5615(1).

Amendments

• 1984, Deficit Reduction Act of 1984 (P.L. 98-369)

P.L. 98-369, §451(a):

Amended Code Sec. 5101. **Effective** on the first day of the first calendar month which begins more than 90 days after 7-18-84. Prior to amendment, it read as follows:

SEC. 5101. IMPOSITION AND RATE OF TAX.

Every manufacturer of stills shall pay a special tax of $55 a year, and $22 for each still or condenser for distilling made by him.

[Sec. 5102]

SEC. 5102. DEFINITION OF MANUFACTURER OF STILLS.

Any person who manufactures any still or condenser to be used in distilling shall be deemed a manufacturer of stills.

Amendments

• 1984, Deficit Reduction Act of 1984 (P.L. 98-369)

P.L. 98-369, §451(a):

Amended Subpart C of part II of subchapter A of chapter 51 by amending Code Sec. 5102 to read as it formerly read. **Effective** 7-1-85.

[Sec. 5103—Repealed]

Amendments

• 1984, Deficit Reduction Act of 1984 (P.L. 98-369)

P.L. 98-369, §451(a):

Amended Subpart C of part II of subchapter A of chapter 51 by removing Code Secs. 5103-5106. **Effective** on the first day of the first calendar month which begins more than 90 days after 7-18-84. Prior to repeal, Code Sec. 5103 read as follows:

SEC. 5103. EXEMPTIONS.

The taxes imposed by section 5101 shall not apply in respect of stills or condensers manufactured by a proprietor of a distilled spirits plant exclusively for use in his plant or plants.

ALCOHOL TAXES—MISCELLANEOUS PROVISIONS

[Sec. 5105—Repealed]

Amendments

• **1984, Deficit Reduction Act of 1984 (P.L. 98-369)**

P.L. 98-369, § 451(a):

Amended Subpart C of part II of subchapter A of chapter 51 by amending Code Sec. 5101, by amending Code Sec. 5102 to read as it formerly read, and by removing Code Secs. 5103-5106. **Effective** on the first day of the first calendar month which begins more than 90 days after 7-18-84. Prior to repeal, Code Sec. 5105 read as follows:

SEC. 5105. NOTICE OF MANUFACTURE OF AND PERMIT TO SET UP STILL.

(a) REQUIREMENT.—Any person who manufactures any still, boiler, or other vessel to be used for the purpose of distilling shall, before the same is removed from the place of manufacture, notify the Secretary, setting forth in writing by whom it is to be used, its capacity, and the time when the same is to be removed from the place of manufacture; and no such still, boiler, or other vessel shall be set up without the permit in writing of the Secretary for that purpose. The notice required by this section shall be submitted in such form and manner as the Secretary may by regulations prescribe.

(b) PENALTY.—

(1) For penalty and forfeiture for failure to give notice of manufacture, or for setting up still without permit, see sections 5615(2) and 5687.

(2) For penalty and forfeiture for failure to register still or distilling apparatus when set up, see sections 5601(a)(1) and 5615(1).

• **1976, Tax Reform Act of 1976 (P.L. 94-455)**

P.L. 94-455, § 1905(b)(6)(A):

Struck out ", 5601(b)(1)," following "sections 5601(a)(1)" in Code Sec. 5105(b)(2). **Effective** 2-1-77.

P.L. 94-455, § 1906(b)(13)(A):

Amended 1954 Code by substituting "Secretary" for "Secretary or his delegate" each place it appeared. **Effective** 2-1-77.

[Sec. 5106—Repealed]

Amendments

• **1984, Deficit Reduction Act of 1984 (P.L. 98-369)**

P.L. 98-369, § 451(a):

Amended Subpart C of part II of subchapter A of chapter 51 by removing Code Sec. 5106. **Effective** on the first day of the first calendar month which begins more than 90 days after 7-18-84. Prior to repeal, Code Sec. 5106 read as follows:

SEC. 5106. EXPORT.

(a) WITHOUT PAYMENT OF TAX.—Under regulations prescribed by the Secretary, stills or condensers for distilling may be removed from the place of manufacture for export without payment of the tax imposed thereon by section 5101.

(b) DRAWBACK.—Stills and condensers on which the tax has been paid, and which have not been used, may be exported with the privilege of drawback, under such regulations as the Secretary may prescribe.

• **1976, Tax Reform Act of 1976 (P.L. 94-455)**

P.L. 94-455, § 1906(b)(13)(A):

Amended 1954 Code by substituting "Secretary" for "Secretary or his delegate" each place it appeared. **Effective** 2-1-77.

Subpart B—Nonbeverage Domestic Drawback Claimants

Sec. 5111.	Eligibility.
Sec. 5112.	Registration and regulation.
Sec. 5113.	Investigation of claims.
Sec. 5114.	Drawback.

[Sec. 5111]

SEC. 5111. ELIGIBILITY.

Any person using distilled spirits on which the tax has been determined, in the manufacture or production of medicines, medicinal preparations, food products, flavors, flavoring extracts, or perfume, which are unfit for beverage purposes shall be eligible for drawback at the time when such distilled spirits are used in the manufacture of such products as provided for in this subpart.

Amendments

• **2005, Safe, Accountable, Flexible, Efficient Transportation Equity Act: A Legacy for Users (P.L. 109-59)**

P.L. 109-59, § 11125(a)(2):

Amended Code Sec. 5131[(a)] by striking ", on payment of a special tax per annum," following "which are unfit for beverage purposes". **Effective** 7-1-2008, but not applicable to taxes imposed for periods before such date.

P.L. 109-59, § 11125(b)(3)(A):

Redesignated Code Secs. 5131-5134 as Code Secs. 5111-5114, respectively. **Effective** 7-1-2008, but not applicable to taxes imposed for periods before such date.

P.L. 109-59, § 11125(b)(3)(C)(i):

Amended Code Sec. 5111, as redesignated by Act Sec. 11125(b)(3)(A), by striking "AND RATE OF TAX" in the section heading. **Effective** 7-1-2008, but not applicable to taxes imposed for periods before such date. Prior to being stricken, the section heading for Code Sec. 5111 read as follows:

SEC. 5111. ELIGIBILITY AND RATE OF TAX.

[Sec. 5111(b)—Stricken]

Amendments

• **2005, Safe, Accountable, Flexible, Efficient Transportation Equity Act: A Legacy for Users (P.L. 109-59)**

P.L. 109-59, § 11125(b)(3)(C)(iii):

Amended Code Sec. 5111, as redesignated by Act Sec. 11125(b)(3)(A), by striking subsection (b). **Effective** 7-1-2008, but not applicable to taxes imposed for periods before such date. Prior to being stricken, Code Sec. 5111(b) read as follows:

(b) RATE OF TAX.—The special tax imposed by subsection (a) shall be $500 per year.

• **1987, Revenue Act of 1987 (P.L. 100-203)**

P.L. 100-203, § 10512(d):

Amended Code Sec. 5131(b). For the **effective** date, see Act Sec. 10512(h), below. Prior to amendment, Code Sec. 5131(b) read as follows:

(b) RATE OF TAX.—The special tax imposed by subsection (a) shall be graduated in amount as follows: (1) for total annual use not exceeding 25 proof gallons, $25 a year; (2) for total annual use not exceeding 50 proof gallons, $50 a year; (3) for total annual use of more than 50 proof gallons, $100 a year.

P.L. 100-203, § 10512(h), provides:

(h) EFFECTIVE DATE.—

P.L. 109-59, § 11125(b)(3)(C)(ii):

Amended Code Sec. 5111(a), as redesignated by Act Sec. 11125(b)(3)(A), by striking the subsection heading. **Effective** 7-1-2008, but not applicable to taxes imposed for periods before such date. Prior to being stricken, the heading for Code Sec. 5111(a) read as follows:

(a) ELIGIBILITY FOR DRAWBACK.—

• **1994, Uruguay Round Agreements Act (P.L. 103-465)**

P.L. 103-465, § 136(b):

Amended Code Sec. 5131(a) by striking "or flavoring extracts" and inserting "flavoring extracts, or perfume". **Effective** 1-1-95.

• **1976, Tax Reform Act of 1976 (P.L. 94-455)**

P.L. 94-455, § 1905(a)(11):

Struck out "produced in a domestic registered distillery or industrial alcohol plant and withdrawn from bond, or using distilled spirits withdrawn from the bonded premises of a distilled spirits plant," following "Any person using distilled spirits" in Code Sec. 5131(a). **Effective** 2-1-77.

(1) IN GENERAL.—The amendments made by this section shall take effect on January 1, 1988.

(2) ALL TAXPAYERS TREATED AS COMMENCING IN BUSINESS ON JANUARY 1, 1988.—

(A) IN GENERAL.—Any person engaged on January 1, 1988, in any trade or business which is subject to an occupational tax shall be treated for purposes of such tax as having 1st engaged in such trade or business on such date.

(B) LIMITATION ON AMOUNT OF TAX.—In the case of a taxpayer who paid an occupational tax in respect of any premises for any taxable period which began before January 1, 1988, and includes such date, the amount of the occupational tax imposed by reason of subparagraph (A) in respect of such premises shall not exceed an amount equal to $1/2$ the excess (if any) of—

(i) the rate of such tax as in effect on January 1, 1988, over

(ii) the rate of such tax as in effect on December 31, 1987.

(C) OCCUPATIONAL TAX.—For purposes of this paragraph, the term "occupational tax" means any tax imposed under part II of subchapter A of chapter 51, section 5276, section 5731, or section 5801 of the Internal Revenue Code of 1986 (as amended by this section).

(D) DUE DATE OF TAX.—The amount of any tax required to be paid by reason of this paragraph shall be due on April 1, 1988.

ALCOHOL TAXES—MISCELLANEOUS PROVISIONS

[Sec. 5111—Repealed]

Amendments

• **2005, Safe, Accountable, Flexible, Efficient Transportation Equity Act: A Legacy for Users (P.L. 109-59)**

P.L. 109-59, § 11125(a)(1)(C):

Repealed subpart D of part II of subchapter A of chapter 51 (other than Code Secs. 5114 and 5116) [Code Secs. 5111-5113, and Code Sec. 5117.—CCH]. **Effective** 7-1-2008, but not applicable to taxes imposed for periods before such date. Prior to repeal, Code Sec. 5111 read as follows:

SEC. 5111. IMPOSITION AND RATE OF TAX.

[Sec. 5111(a)]

(a) WHOLESALE DEALERS IN LIQUORS.—Every wholesale dealer in liquors shall pay a special tax of $500 a year.

Amendments

• **1987, Revenue Act of 1987 (P.L. 100-203)**

P.L. 100-203, § 10512(b)(1):

Amended Code Sec. 5111(a) by striking out "$255" and inserting in lieu thereof "$500". For the **effective** date, see Act Sec. 10512(h), below.

P.L. 100-203, § 10512(h), provides:

(h) EFFECTIVE DATE.—

(1) IN GENERAL.—The amendments made by this section shall take effect on January 1, 1988.

(2) ALL TAXPAYERS TREATED AS COMMENCING IN BUSINESS ON JANUARY 1, 1988.—

(A) IN GENERAL.—Any person engaged on January 1, 1988, in any trade or business which is subject to an occupational tax shall be treated for purposes of such tax as having 1st engaged in such trade or business on such date.

(B) LIMITATION ON AMOUNT OF TAX.—In the case of a taxpayer who paid an occupational tax in respect of any premises for any taxable period which began before January 1, 1988, and includes such date, the amount of the occupational tax imposed by reason of subparagraph (A) in respect of such premises shall not exceed an amount equal to $1/2$ the excess (if any) of—

(i) the rate of such tax as in effect on January 1, 1988, over

(ii) the rate of such tax as in effect on December 31, 1987.

(C) OCCUPATIONAL TAX.—For purposes of this paragraph, the term "occupational tax" means any tax imposed under part II of subchapter A of chapter 51, section 5276, section 5731, or section 5801 of the Internal Revenue Code of 1986 (as amended by this section).

(D) DUE DATE OF TAX.—The amount of any tax required to be paid by reason of this paragraph shall be due on April 1, 1988.

• **1976, Tax Reform Act of 1976 (P.L. 94-455)**

P.L. 94-455, § 1905(b)(3)(B):

Struck out the second sentence of Code Sec. 5111(a). **Effective** 2-1-77. Prior to striking, the second sentence of Code Sec. 5111(a) read as follows:

The Secretary or his delegate may by regulations provide for the issuance of a stamp denoting payment of such special tax as a "wholesale dealer in wines" or a "wholesale dealer in wines and beer" if, as the case may be, wines only, or wines and beer only, are sold by a wholesale dealer in liquors.

[Sec. 5111(b)]

(b) WHOLESALE DEALERS IN BEER.—Every wholesale dealer in beer shall pay a special tax of $500 a year.

Amendments

• **1987, Revenue Act of 1987 (P.L. 100-203)**

P.L. 100-203, § 10512(b)(2):

Amended Code Sec. 5111(b) by striking out "$123" and inserting in lieu thereof "$500". For the **effective** date, see Act Sec. 10512(h), below.

P.L. 100-203, § 10512(h), provides:

(h) EFFECTIVE DATE.—

(1) IN GENERAL.—The amendments made by this section shall take effect on January 1, 1988.

(2) ALL TAXPAYERS TREATED AS COMMENCING IN BUSINESS ON JANUARY 1, 1988.—

(A) IN GENERAL.—Any person engaged on January 1, 1988, in any trade or business which is subject to an occupational tax shall be treated for purposes of such tax as having 1st engaged in such trade or business on such date.

(B) LIMITATION ON AMOUNT OF TAX.—In the case of a taxpayer who paid an occupational tax in respect of any premises for any taxable period which began before January 1, 1988, and includes such date, the amount of the occupational tax imposed by reason of subparagraph (A) in respect of such premises shall not exceed an amount equal to $1/2$ the excess (if any) of—

(i) the rate of such tax as in effect on January 1, 1988, over

(ii) the rate of such tax as in effect on December 31, 1987.

(C) OCCUPATIONAL TAX.—For purposes of this paragraph, the term "occupational tax" means any tax imposed under part II of subchapter A of chapter 51, section 5276, section 5731, or section 5801 of the Internal Revenue Code of 1986 (as amended by this section).

(D) DUE DATE OF TAX.—The amount of any tax required to be paid by reason of this paragraph shall be due on April 1, 1988.

[Sec. 5112]

SEC. 5112. REGISTRATION AND REGULATION.

Every person claiming drawback under this subpart shall register annually with the Secretary; keep such books and records as may be necessary to establish the fact that distilled spirits received by him and on which the tax has been determined were used in the manufacture or production of medicines, medicinal preparations, food products, flavors, flavoring extracts, or perfume, which were unfit for use for beverage purposes; and be subject to such rules and regulations in relation thereto as the Secretary shall prescribe to secure the Treasury against frauds.

Amendments

• **2005, Safe, Accountable, Flexible, Efficient Transportation Equity Act: A Legacy for Users (P.L. 109-59)**

P.L. 109-59, § 11125(b)(3)(A):

Redesignated Code Secs. 5131-5134 as Code Secs. 5111-5114, respectively. **Effective** 7-1-2008, but not applicable to taxes imposed for periods before such date.

• **1994, Uruguay Round Agreements Act (P.L. 103-465)**

P.L. 103-465, § 136(b):

Amended Code Sec. 5132 by striking "or flavoring extracts" and inserting "flavoring extracts, or perfume". **Effective** 1-1-95.

• **1976, Tax Reform Act of 1976 (P.L. 94-455)**

P.L. 94-455, § 1906(b)(13)(A):

Amended 1954 Code by substituting "Secretary" for "Secretary or his delegate" each place it appeared. **Effective** 2-1-77.

[Sec. 5112—Repealed]

Amendments

• **2005, Safe, Accountable, Flexible, Efficient Transportation Equity Act: A Legacy for Users (P.L. 109-59)**

P.L. 109-59, § 11125(a)(1)(C):

Repealed subpart D of part II of subchapter A of chapter 51 (other than Code Secs. 5114 and 5116) [Code Secs. 5111-5113, and Code Sec. 5117.—CCH]. **Effective** 7-1-2008, but not applicable to taxes imposed for periods before such date. Prior to repeal, Code Sec. 5112 read as follows:

SEC. 5112. DEFINITIONS.

[Sec. 5112(a)]

(a) DEALER.—When used in this subpart, subpart E, or subpart G, the term "dealer" means any person who sells, or offers for sale, any distilled spirits, wines, or beer.

[Sec. 5112(b)]

(b) WHOLESALE DEALER IN LIQUORS.—When used in this chapter, the term "wholesale dealer in liquors" means any dealer, other than a wholesale dealer in beer, who sells, or offers for sale, distilled spirits, wines, or beer, to another dealer.

[Sec. 5112(c)]

(c) WHOLESALE DEALER IN BEER.—When used in this chapter, the term "wholesale dealer in beer" means a dealer who sells, or offers for sale, beer, but not distilled spirits or wines, to another dealer.

[Sec. 5113]

SEC. 5113. INVESTIGATION OF CLAIMS.

For the purpose of ascertaining the correctness of any claim filed under this subpart, the Secretary is authorized to examine any books, papers, records, or memoranda bearing upon the matters required to be alleged in the claim, to require the attendance of the person filing the claim or of any officer or employee of such person or the attendance of any other person having knowledge in the premises, to take testimony with reference to any matter covered by the claim, and to administer oaths to any person giving such testimony.

ALCOHOL TAXES—MISCELLANEOUS PROVISIONS

Amendments

• **2005, Safe, Accountable, Flexible, Efficient Transportation Equity Act: A Legacy for Users (P.L. 109-59)**

P.L. 109-59, §11125(b)(3)(A):

Redesignated Code Secs. 5131-5134 as Code Secs. 5111-5114, respectively. **Effective** 7-1-2008, but not applicable to taxes imposed for periods before such date.

Amendments

• **2005, Safe, Accountable, Flexible, Efficient Transportation Equity Act: A Legacy for Users (P.L. 109-59)**

P.L. 109-59, §11125(a)(1)(C):

Repealed subpart D of part II of subchapter A of chapter 51 (other than Code Secs. 5114 and 5116) [Code Secs. 5111-5113, and Code Sec. 5117.—CCH]. **Effective** 7-1-2008, but not applicable to taxes imposed for periods before such date. Prior to repeal, Code Sec. 5113 read as follows:

SEC. 5113. EXEMPTIONS.

[Sec. 5113(a)]

(a) SALES BY PROPRIETORS OF CONTROLLED PREMISES.—No proprietor of a distilled spirits plant, bonded wine cellar, taxpaid wine bottling house, or brewery, shall be required to pay special tax under section 5111 or section 5121 on account of the sale at his principal business office as designated in writing to the Secretary, or at his distilled spirits plant, bonded wine cellar, taxpaid wine bottling house, or brewery, as the case may be, of distilled spirits, wines, or beer, which, at the time of sale, are stored at his distilled spirits plant, bonded wine cellar, taxpaid wine bottling house, or brewery, as the case may be, or had been removed from such premises to a taxpaid storeroom operated in connection therewith and are stored therein. However, no such proprietor shall have more than one place of sale, as to each distilled spirits plant, bonded wine cellar, taxpaid wine bottling house, or brewery, that shall be exempt from special taxes by reason of the sale of distilled spirits, wines, or beer stored at such premises (or removed therefrom and stored as provided in this section), by reason of this subsection.

Amendments

• **1988, Technical and Miscellaneous Revenue Act of 1988 (P.L. 100-647)**

P.L. 100-647, §2004(t)(2)(A)-(B):

Amended Code Sec. 5113(a) by inserting "taxpaid wine bottling house," after "bonded wine cellar," each place it appears, and by striking out "Distilled Spirits Plants, Bonded Wine Cellars, or Breweries" in the heading and inserting in lieu thereof "Controlled Premises". **Effective** as if included in the provision of P.L. 100-203 to which it relates.

• **1976, Tax Reform Act of 1976 (P.L. 94-455)**

P.L. 94-455, §1906(b)(13)(A):

Amended 1954 Code by substituting "Secretary" for "Secretary or his delegate" each place it appeared. **Effective** 2-1-77.

[Sec. 5113(b)]

(b) SALES BY LIQUOR STORES OPERATED BY STATES, POLITICAL SUBDIVISIONS, ETC.—No liquor store engaged in the business of selling to persons other than dealers, which is operated by a State, by a political subdivision of a State or by the District of Columbia, shall be required to pay any special tax imposed under section 5111, by reason of selling distilled spirits, wines, or beer to dealers qualified to do business as such in such State, subdivision, or District, if such State, political subdivision, or District has paid the applicable special tax imposed under section 5121, and if such State, political subdivision, or District has paid special tax under section 5111 at its principal place of business.

Amendments

• **1962 (P.L. 87-863)**

P.L. 87-863, §4(b):

Amended Code Sec. 5113(b) by deleting "or Territory" in lines 3 and 4 and "Territory" in lines 6 and 8, and by substituting "if such State, political subdivision, or District" for "if such liquor store" in line 7. **Effective** 7-1-62.

[Sec. 5113(c)]

(c) CASUAL SALES.—

(1) SALES BY CREDITORS, FIDUCIARIES, AND OFFICERS OF COURT.—No person shall be deemed to be a dealer by reason of the sale of distilled spirits, wines, or beer which have been received by him as security for or in payment of a debt, or as an executor,

• **1976, Tax Reform Act of 1976 (P.L. 94-455)**

P.L. 94-455, §1906(b)(13)(A):

Amended 1954 Code by substituting "Secretary" for "Secretary or his delegate" each place it appeared. **Effective** 2-1-77.

[Sec. 5113—Repealed]

administrator, or other fiduciary, or which have been levied on by any officer under order or process of any court or magistrate, if such distilled spirits, wines, or beer are sold by such person in one parcel only or at public auction in parcels of not less than 20 wine gallons.

(2) SALES BY RETIRING PARTNERS OR REPRESENTATIVES OF DECEASED PARTNERS TO INCOMING OR REMAINING PARTNERS.—No person shall be deemed to be a dealer by reason of a sale of distilled spirits, wines, or beer made by such person as a retiring partner or the representative of a deceased partner to the incoming, remaining, or surviving partner or partners of a firm.

(3) RETURN OF LIQUORS FOR CREDIT, REFUND, OR EXCHANGE.—No person shall be deemed to be a dealer by reason of the bona fide return of distilled spirits, wines, or beer to the dealer from whom purchased (or to the successor of the vendor's business or line of merchandise) for credit, refund, or exchange, and the giving of such credit, refund, or exchange shall not be deemed to be a purchase within the meaning of section 5117.

[Sec. 5113(d)]

(d) DEALERS MAKING SALES ON PURCHASER DEALER'S PREMISES.—

(1) WHOLESALE DEALERS IN LIQUORS.—No wholesale dealer in liquors who has paid the special tax as such dealer shall again be required to pay special tax as such dealer on account of sales of wines or beer to wholesale or retail dealers in liquors, or to limited retail dealers, or of beer to wholesale or retail dealers in beer, consummated at the purchaser's place of business.

(2) WHOLESALE DEALERS IN BEER.—No wholesale dealer in beer who has paid the special tax as such a dealer shall again be required to pay special tax as such dealer on account of sales of beer to wholesale or retail dealers in liquors or beer, or to limited retail dealers, consummated at the purchaser's place of business.

[Sec. 5113(e)]

(e) SALES BY RETAIL DEALERS IN LIQUIDATION.—No retail dealer in liquors or retail dealer in beer, selling in liquidation his entire stock of liquors in one parcel or in parcels embracing not less than his entire stock of distilled spirits, of wines, or of beer to any other dealer, shall be deemed to be a wholesale dealer in liquors or a wholesale dealer in beer, as the case may be, by reason of such sale or sales.

[Sec. 5113(f)]

(f) SALES TO LIMITED RETAIL DEALERS.—

(1) RETAIL DEALERS IN LIQUORS.—No retail dealer in liquors who has paid special tax as such dealer under section 5121(a) shall be required to pay special tax under section 5111 on account of the sale at his place of business of distilled spirits, wines, or beer to limited retail dealers as defined in section 5122(c).

(2) RETAIL DEALERS IN BEER.—No retail dealer in beer who has paid special tax as such dealer under section 5121(b) shall be required to pay special tax under section 5111 on account of the sale at his place of business of beer to limited retail dealers as defined in section 5122(c).

Amendments

• **1976, Tax Reform Act of 1976 (P.L. 94-455)**

P.L. 94-455, §1905(a)(7):

Substituted "distilled spirits, wines, or beer" for "wines or beer" in Code Sec. 5113(f)(1). **Effective** 2-1-77.

[Sec. 5113(g)]

(g) COORDINATION OF TAXES UNDER SECTION 5111.—No tax shall be imposed by section 5111(a) with respect to a person's activities at any place during a year if such person has paid the tax imposed by section 5111(b) with respect to such place for such year.

Amendments

• **1988, Technical and Miscellaneous Revenue Act of 1988 (P.L. 100-647)**

P.L. 100-647, §2004(t)(4):

Amended Code Sec. 5113 by adding at the end thereof new subsection (g). **Effective** as if included in the provision of P.L. 100-203 to which it relates.

[Sec. 5114]

SEC. 5114. DRAWBACK.

[Sec. 5114(a)]

(a) RATE OF DRAWBACK.—In the case of distilled spirits on which the tax has been paid or determined, and which have been used as provided in this subpart, a drawback shall be allowed on each proof gallon at a rate of $1 less than the rate at which the distilled spirits tax has been paid or determined.

[Sec. 5114(b)]

(b) CLAIMS.—Such drawback shall be due and payable quarterly upon filing of a proper claim with the Secretary or his delegate; except that, where any person entitled to such drawback shall elect in writing to file monthly claims therefor, such drawback shall be due and payable monthly upon filing of a proper claim with the Secretary. The Secretary may require persons electing to file monthly drawback claims to file with him a bond or other security in such amount and with such conditions as he shall by regulations prescribe. Any such election may be revoked on filing of notice thereof with the Secretary. No claim under this subpart shall be allowed unless filed with the Secretary within the 6 months next succeeding the quarter in which the distilled spirits covered by the claim were used as provided in this subpart.

ALCOHOL TAXES—MISCELLANEOUS PROVISIONS

Amendments

• **1976, Tax Reform Act of 1976 (P.L. 94-455)**

P.L. 94-455, §1906(b)(13)(A):

Amended 1954 Code by substituting "Secretary" for "Secretary or his delegate" each place it appeared. **Effective** 2-1-77.

• **1968 (P.L. 90-615)**

P.L. 90-615, §2(a):

Amended the last sentence in subsection (b) of Section 5134 by substituting "6 months" for "3 months". **Effective** with respect to claims filed on or after 10-21-68.

[Sec. 5114(c)]

(c) ALLOWANCE OF DRAWBACK EVEN WHERE CERTAIN REQUIREMENTS NOT MET.—

(1) IN GENERAL.—No claim for drawback under this section shall be denied in the case of a failure to comply with any requirement imposed under this subpart or any rule or regulation issued thereunder upon the claimant's establishing to the satisfaction of the Secretary that distilled spirits on which the tax has been paid or determined were in fact used in the manufacture or production of medicines, medicinal preparations, food products, flavors, flavoring extracts, or perfume, which were unfit for beverage purposes.

(2) PENALTY.—

(A) IN GENERAL.—In the case of a failure to comply with any requirement imposed under this subpart or any rule or regulation issued thereunder, the claimant shall be liable for a penalty of $1,000 for each failure to comply unless it is shown that the failure to comply was due to reasonable cause.

(B) PENALTY MAY NOT EXCEED AMOUNT OF CLAIM.—The aggregate amount of the penalties imposed under subparagraph (A) for failures described in paragraph (1) in respect of any claim shall not exceed the amount of such claim (determined without regard to subparagraph (A)).

(3) PENALTY TREATED AS TAX.—The penalty imposed by paragraph (2) shall be assessed, collected, and paid in the same manner as taxes, as provided in section 6665(a).

Amendments

• **2005, Safe, Accountable, Flexible, Efficient Transportation Equity Act: A Legacy for Users (P.L. 109-59)**

P.L. 109-59, §11125(b)(3)(A):

Redesignated Code Secs. 5131-5134 as Code Secs. 5111-5114, respectively. **Effective** 7-1-2008, but not applicable to taxes imposed for periods before such date.

• **1996, Small Business Job Protection Act of 1996 (P.L. 104-188)**

P.L. 104-188, §1704(t)(12):

Amended Code Sec. 5134(c)(3) by striking "section 6662(a)" and inserting "section 6665(a)". **Effective** 8-20-96.

• **1994, Uruguay Round Agreements Act (P.L. 103-465)**

P.L. 103-465, §136(b):

Amended Code Sec. 5134(c)(1) by striking "or flavoring extracts" and inserting "flavoring extracts, or perfume". **Effective** 1-1-95.

• **1984, Deficit Reduction Act of 1984 (P.L. 98-369)**

P.L. 98-369, §452:

Amended Code Sec. 5134 by adding new subsection (c). **Effective** on the first day of the first calendar month which begins more than 90 days after 7-18-84.

[Sec. 5115—Repealed]

Amendments

• **1997, Taxpayer Relief Act of 1997 (P.L. 105-34)**

P.L. 105-34, §1415(a):

Repealed Code Sec. 5115. **Effective** 8-5-97. Prior to repeal, Code Sec. 5115 read as follows:

SEC. 5115. SIGN REQUIRED ON PREMISES.

[Sec. 5115(a)]

(a) REQUIREMENTS.—Every wholesale dealer in liquors who is required to pay special tax as such dealer shall, in the manner and form prescribed by regulations issued by the Secretary, place and keep conspicuously on the outside of the place of such business a sign, exhibiting, in plain and legible letters, the name or firm of the wholesale dealer, with the words: "wholesale liquor dealer". The requirements of this subsection will be met by the posting of a sign of the character prescribed herein, but with words conforming to the designation on the dealer's special tax stamp.

Amendments

• **1976, Tax Reform Act of 1976 (P.L. 94-455)**

P.L. 94-455, §1906(b)(13)(A):

Amended 1954 Code by substituting "Secretary" for "Secretary or his delegate" each place it appeared. **Effective** 2-1-77.

[Sec. 5115(b)]

(b) PENALTY.—

For penalty for failure to post sign, or for posting sign without paying the special tax, see section 5681.

[Sec. 5117—Repealed]

Amendments

• **2005, Safe, Accountable, Flexible, Efficient Transportation Equity Act: A Legacy for Users (P.L. 109-59)**

P.L. 109-59, §11125(a)(1)(C):

Repealed subpart D of part II of subchapter A of chapter 51 (other than Code Secs. 5114 and 5116) [Code Secs. 5111-5113, and Code Sec. 5117.—CCH]. **Effective** 7-1-2008, but not applicable to taxes imposed for periods before such date. Prior to repeal, Code Sec. 5117 read as follows:

SEC. 5117. PROHIBITED PURCHASES BY DEALERS.

[Sec. 5117(a)]

(a) GENERAL.—It shall be unlawful for any dealer to purchase distilled spirits for resale from any person other than—

(1) a wholesale dealer in liquors who has paid the special tax as such dealer to cover the place where such purchase is made; or

(2) a wholesale dealer in liquors who is exempt, at the place where such purchase is made, from payment of such tax under any provision of this chapter; or

(3) a person who is not required to pay special tax as a wholesale dealer in liquors.

[Sec. 5117(b)]

(b) LIMITED RETAIL DEALERS.—A limited retail dealer may lawfully purchase distilled spirits for resale from a retail dealer in liquors.

Amendments

• **1976, Tax Reform Act of 1976 (P.L. 94-455)**

P.L. 94-455, §1905(a)(8):

Redesignated former Code Sec. 5117(b) as Code Sec. 5117(c) and added Code Sec. 5117(b). **Effective** 2-1-77.

[Sec. 5117(c)]

(c) PENALTY AND FORFEITURE.—

For penalty and forfeiture provisions applicable to violation of subsection (a), see sections 5687 and 7302.

Amendments

• **1976, Tax Reform Act of 1976 (P.L. 94-455)**

P.L. 94-455, §1905(a)(8):

Redesignated former Code Sec. 5117(b) as Code Sec. 5117(c). **Effective** 2-1-77.

[Sec. 5117(d)]

(d) SPECIAL RULE DURING SUSPENSION PERIOD.—Except as provided in subsection (b) or by the Secretary, during the suspension period (as defined in section 5148) it shall be unlawful for any dealer to purchase distilled spirits for resale from any person other than a wholesale dealer in liquors who is required to keep records under section 5114.

Amendments

• **2004, American Jobs Creation Act of 2004 (P.L. 108-357)**

P.L. 108-357, §246(b):

Amended Code Sec. 5117 by adding at the end a new subsection (d). **Effective** 10-22-2004.

Subpart C—Recordkeeping and Registration by Dealers

Sec. 5121.	Recordkeeping by wholesale dealers.
Sec. 5122.	Recordkeeping by retail dealers.
Sec. 5123.	Preservation and inspection of records, and entry of premises for inspection.
Sec. 5124.	Registration by dealers.

ALCOHOL TAXES—MISCELLANEOUS PROVISIONS

[Sec. 5121]

SEC. 5121. RECORDKEEPING BY WHOLESALE DEALERS.

[Sec. 5121(a)]

(a) REQUIREMENTS.—

(1) DISTILLED SPIRITS.—Every wholesale dealer in liquors who sells distilled spirits to other dealers shall keep daily a record of distilled spirits received and disposed of by him, in such form and at such place and containing such information, and shall submit correct summaries of such records to the Secretary at such time and in such form and manner, as the Secretary shall by regulations prescribe. Such dealer shall also submit correct extracts from or copies of such records, at such time and in such form and manner as the Secretary may by regulations prescribe; however, the Secretary may on application by such dealer, in accordance with such regulations, relieve him from this requirement until further notice, whenever the Secretary deems that the submission of such extracts or copies serves no useful purpose in law enforcement or in protection of the revenue.

(2) WINES AND BEER.—Every wholesale dealer in liquors and every wholesale dealer in beer shall provide and keep, at such place as the Secretary shall by regulations prescribe, a record in book form of all wines and beer received, showing the quantities thereof and from whom and the dates received, or shall keep all invoices of, and bills for, all wines and beer received.

Amendments

• **2005, Safe, Accountable, Flexible, Efficient Transportation Equity Act: A Legacy for Users (P.L. 109-59)**

P.L. 109-59, § 11125(b)(5)(A) and (B)(i):

Amended Code Sec. 5114 by moving it to subpart C of part II of subchapter A of chapter 51, and inserting it after the table of sections for subchapter C, and by striking the section heading and inserting a new section heading. [Act Sec. 11125(b)(5)(A) of P.L. 109-59 moved Code Sec. 5114 to subpart C of part II of subchapter A of chapter 51, and inserted it after the table of sections for subchapter C, while Act Sec. 11125(b)(5)(B)(i) inserted a new section heading for Code Sec. 5432. Therefore, P.L. 109-59 has, in effect, redesignated Code Sec. 5114 as Code Sec. 5432.

However, the placement of such Code Sec. 5432 indicates that Code Sec. 5114 should have been redesignated as Code Sec. 5121.—CCH] **Effective** 7-1-2008, but not applicable to taxes imposed for periods before such date. Prior to being stricken, the section heading for Code Sec. 5114 read as follows:

SEC. 5114. RECORDS.

• **1976, Tax Reform Act of 1976 (P.L. 94-455)**

P.L. 94-455, § 1906(b)(13)(A):

Amended 1954 Code by substituting "Secretary" for "Secretary or his delegate" each place it appeared. **Effective** 2-1-77.

[Sec. 5121(b)]

(b) EXEMPTION OF STATES, POLITICAL SUBDIVISIONS, ETC.—The provisions of subsection (a) shall not apply to a State, to a political subdivision of a State, to the District of Columbia, or to liquor stores operated by any of them, if they maintain and make available for inspection by internal revenue officers such records as will enable such officers to trace all distilled spirits, wines, and beer received, and all distilled spirits disposed of by them. Such States, subdivisions, District, or liquor stores shall, upon the request of the Secretary, furnish him such transcripts, summaries and copies of their records with respect to distilled spirits as he shall require.

Amendments

• **1976, Tax Reform Act of 1976 (P.L. 94-455)**

P.L. 94-455, § 1905(c)(1):

Struck out "or Territory" following "State" each place it appeared in Code Sec. 5114(b), and struck out "Territories," following "States," in the last sentence of Code Sec. 5114(b). **Effective** 2-1-77.

P.L. 94-455, § 1906(b)(13)(A):

Amended 1954 Code by substituting "Secretary" for "Secretary or his delegate" each place it appeared. **Effective** 2-1-77.

[Sec. 5121(c)]

(c) WHOLESALE DEALERS.—For purposes of this part—

(1) WHOLESALE DEALER IN LIQUORS.—The term "wholesale dealer in liquors" means any dealer (other than a wholesale dealer in beer) who sells, or offers for sale, distilled spirits, wines, or beer, to another dealer.

(2) WHOLESALE DEALER IN BEER.—The term "wholesale dealer in beer" means any dealer who sells, or offers for sale, beer, but not distilled spirits or wines, to another dealer.

(3) DEALER.—The term "dealer" means any person who sells, or offers for sale, any distilled spirits, wines, or beer.

(4) PRESUMPTION IN CASE OF SALE OF 20 WINE GALLONS OR MORE.—The sale, or offer for sale, of distilled spirits, wines, or beer, in quantities of 20 wine gallons or more to the same person at the same time, shall be presumptive evidence that the person making such sale, or offer for sale, is engaged in or carrying on the business of a wholesale dealer in liquors or a wholesale dealer in beer, as the case may be. Such presumption may be overcome by evidence satisfactorily showing that such sale, or offer for sale, was made to a person other than a dealer.

Amendments

• **2005, Safe, Accountable, Flexible, Efficient Transportation Equity Act: A Legacy for Users (P.L. 109-59)**

P.L. 109-59, § 11125(b)(5)(B)(ii):

Amended Code Sec. 5114 [as redesignated as Code Sec. 5121] by redesignating subsection (c) as subsection (d) and by inserting after subsection (b) a new subsection (c). **Effective** 7-1-2008, but not applicable to taxes imposed for periods before such date.

[Sec. 5121(d)]

(d) CROSS REFERENCES.—

(1) For provisions requiring proprietors of distilled spirits plants to keep records and submit reports of receipts and dispositions of distilled spirits, see section 5207.

(2) For penalty for violation of subsection (a), see section 5603.

(3) For provisions relating to the preservation and inspection of records, and entry of premises for inspection, see section 5123.

Amendments

• **2007, Tax Technical Corrections Act of 2007 (P.L. 110-172)**

P.L. 110-172, § 11(a)(31):

Amended subpart C of part II of subchapter A of chapter 51 by redesignating Code Sec. 5432 as Code Sec. 5121. **Effective** 12-29-2007.

• **2005, Safe, Accountable, Flexible, Efficient Transportation Equity Act: A Legacy for Users (P.L. 109-59)**

P.L. 109-59, § 11125(b)(5)(B)(ii):

Amended Code Sec. 5114 [as redesignated as Code Sec. 5121] by redesignating subsection (c) as subsection (d). **Effective** 7-1-2008, but not applicable to taxes imposed for periods before such date.

P.L. 109-59, § 11125(b)(5)(C):

Amended Code Sec. 5121(d)(3), as redesignated, by striking "section 5146" and inserting "section 5123". **Effective** 7-1-2008, but not applicable to taxes imposed for periods before such date.

ALCOHOL TAXES—MISCELLANEOUS PROVISIONS

[Sec. 5121—Repealed]

Amendments

• **2005, Safe, Accountable, Flexible, Efficient Transportation Equity Act: A Legacy for Users (P.L. 109-59)**

P.L. 109-59, §11125(a)(1)(D):

Repealed subpart E of part II of subchapter A of chapter 51 (other than Code Sec. 5124) [Code Secs. 5121-5123 and Code Sec. 5125.—CCH]. **Effective** 7-1-2008, but not applicable to taxes imposed for periods before such date. Prior to repeal, Code Sec. 5121 read as follows:

SEC. 5121. IMPOSITION AND RATE OF TAX.

[Sec. 5121(a)]

(a) RETAIL DEALERS IN LIQUORS.—Every retail dealer in liquors shall pay a special tax of $250 a year.

Amendments

• **1987, Revenue Act of 1987 (P.L. 100-203)**

P.L. 100-203, §10512(c)(1):

Amended Code Sec. 5121(a) by striking out "$54" and inserting in lieu thereof "$250". For the **effective** date, see Act Sec. 10512(h), below.

P.L. 100-203, §10512(h), provides:

(h) EFFECTIVE DATE.—

(1) IN GENERAL.—The amendments made by this section shall take effect on January 1, 1988.

(2) ALL TAXPAYERS TREATED AS COMMENCING IN BUSINESS ON JANUARY 1, 1988.—

(A) IN GENERAL.—Any person engaged on January 1, 1988, in any trade or business which is subject to an occupational tax shall be treated for purposes of such tax as having 1st engaged in such trade or business on such date.

(B) LIMITATION ON AMOUNT OF TAX.—In the case of a taxpayer who paid an occupational tax in respect of any premises for any taxable period which began before January 1, 1988, and includes such date, the amount of the occupational tax imposed by reason of subparagraph (A) in respect of such premises shall not exceed an amount equal to $1/2$ the excess (if any) of—

(i) the rate of such tax as in effect on January 1, 1988, over

(ii) the rate of such tax as in effect on December 31, 1987.

(C) OCCUPATIONAL TAX.—For purposes of this paragraph, the term "occupational tax" means any tax imposed under part II of subchapter A of chapter 51, section 5276, section 5731, or section 5801 of the Internal Revenue Code of 1986 (as amended by this section).

(D) DUE DATE OF TAX.—The amount of any tax required to be paid by reason of this paragraph shall be due on April 1, 1988.

[Sec. 5121(c)—Repealed]

Amendments

• **1987, Revenue Act of 1987 (P.L. 100-203)**

P.L. 100-203, §10512(c)(3):

Repealed Code Sec. 5121(c). For the **effective** date, see Act Sec. 10512(h), below. Prior to amendment Code Sec. 5121(c) read as follows:

(c) LIMITED RETAIL DEALERS.—Every limited retail dealer shall pay a special tax of $4.50 for each calendar month in which sales are made as such dealer; except that the special tax shall be $2.20 for each calendar month in which only sales of beer or wine are made.

P.L. 100-203, §10512(h), provides:

(h) EFFECTIVE DATE.—

(1) IN GENERAL.—The amendments made by this section shall take effect on January 1, 1988.

(2) ALL TAXPAYERS TREATED AS COMMENCING IN BUSINESS ON JANUARY 1, 1988.—

(A) IN GENERAL.—Any person engaged on January 1, 1988, in any trade or business which is subject to an occupational tax shall be treated for purposes of such tax as having 1st engaged in such trade or business on such date.

(B) LIMITATION ON AMOUNT OF TAX.—In the case of a taxpayer who paid an occupational tax in respect of any premises for any taxable period which began before

• **1976, Tax Reform Act of 1976 (P.L. 94-455)**

P.L. 94-455, §1905(b)(3)(C):

Struck out the second sentence of Code Sec. 5121(a). **Effective** 2-1-77. Prior to being stricken, the second sentence of Code Sec. 5121(a) read as follows:

The Secretary or his delegate may by regulations provide for the issuance of a stamp denoting payment of such special tax as—

(1) a "retail dealer in wines" or a "retail dealer in wines and beer" if wines only, or wines and beer only, as the case may be, are sold by a retail dealer in liquors, or

(2) a "medicinal spirits dealer", in the case of a retail drug store or pharmacy making sales of liquors through a duly licensed pharmacist.

[Sec. 5121(b)]

(b) RETAIL DEALERS IN BEER.—Every retail dealer in beer shall pay a special tax of $250 a year.

Amendments

• **1987, Revenue Act of 1987 (P.L. 100-203)**

P.L. 100-203, §10512(c)(2):

Amended Code Sec. 5121(b) by striking out "$24" and inserting in lieu thereof "$250". For the **effective** date, see Act Sec. 10512(h), below.

P.L. 100-203, §10512(h), provides:

(h) EFFECTIVE DATE.—

(1) IN GENERAL.—The amendments made by this section shall take effect on January 1, 1988.

(2) ALL TAXPAYERS TREATED AS COMMENCING IN BUSINESS ON JANUARY 1, 1988.—

(A) IN GENERAL.—Any person engaged on January 1, 1988, in any trade or business which is subject to an occupational tax shall be treated for purposes of such tax as having 1st engaged in such trade or business on such date.

(B) LIMITATION ON AMOUNT OF TAX.—In the case of a taxpayer who paid an occupational tax in respect of any premises for any taxable period which began before January 1, 1988, and includes such date, the amount of the occupational tax imposed by reason of subparagraph (A) in respect of such premises shall not exceed an amount equal to $1/2$ the excess (if any) of—

(i) the rate of such tax as in effect on January 1, 1988, over

(ii) the rate of such tax as in effect on December 11, 1987.

(C) OCCUPATIONAL TAX.—For purposes of this paragraph, the term "occupational tax" means any tax imposed under part II of subchapter A of chapter 51, section 5267, section 5731, or section 5801 of the Internal Revenue Code of 1986 (as amended by this section).

(D) DUE DATE OF TAX.—The amount of any tax required to be paid by reason of this paragraph shall be due on April 1, 1988.

January 1, 1988, and includes such date, the amount of the occupational tax imposed by reason of subparagraph (A) in respect of such premises shall not exceed an amount equal to $1/2$ the excess (if any) of—

(i) the rate of such tax as in effect on January 1, 1988, over

(ii) the rate of such tax as in effect on December 31, 1987,

(C) OCCUPATIONAL TAX.—For purposes of this paragraph, the term "occupational tax" means any tax imposed under part II of subchapter A of chapter 51, section 5276, section 5731, or section 5801 of the Internal Revenue Code of 1986 (as amended by this section).

(D) DUE DATE OF TAX.—The amount of any tax required to be paid by reason of this paragraph shall be due on April 1, 1988.

• **1976, Tax Reform Act of 1976 (P.L. 94-455)**

P.L. 94-455, §1905(a)(9):

Amended Code Sec. 5121(c). **Effective** 2-1-77. Prior to amendment, Code Sec. 5121(c) read as follows:

(c) LIMITED RETAIL DEALERS.—Every limited retail dealer shall pay a special tax of $2.20 for each calendar month in which sales are made as such dealer.

[Sec. 5122]

SEC. 5122. RECORDKEEPING BY RETAIL DEALERS.

[Sec. 5122(a)]

(a) RECEIPTS.—Every retail dealer in liquors and every retail dealer in beer shall provide and keep in his place of business a record in book form of all distilled spirits, wines, and beer received showing the quantity thereof and from whom and the dates received, or shall keep all invoices of, and bills for, all distilled spirits, wines, and beer received.

Amendments

• **2005, Safe, Accountable, Flexible, Efficient Transportation Equity Act: A Legacy for Users (P.L. 109-59)**

P.L. 109-59, §11125(b)(6)(A) and (B)(i):

Amended Code Sec. 5124 by moving it to subpart C of part II of subchapter A of chapter 51 and inserting it after Code Sec. 5121, and by striking the section heading and inserting a new heading. [Act Sec. 11125(b)(6)(A) of P.L. 109-59 moved Code Sec. 5124 to subpart C of part II of subchapter A of chapter 51 and inserted it after Code Sec. 5121, while Act Sec. 11125(b)(6)(B)(i) inserted a new section number. Therefore, P.L. 109-59 has, in effect, redesignated Code Sec. 5124 as Code Sec. 5122.—CCH] **Effective** 7-1-2008, but not applicable to taxes imposed for periods before such date. Prior to being stricken, the section heading for Code Sec. 5124 read as follows:

SEC. 5124. RECORDS.

[Sec. 5122(b)]

(b) DISPOSITIONS.—When he deems it necessary for law enforcement purposes or the protection of the revenue, the Secretary may by regulations require retail dealers in liquors and retail dealers in beer to keep records of the disposition of distilled spirits, wines, or beer, in such form or manner and of such quantities as the Secretary may prescribe.

ALCOHOL TAXES—MISCELLANEOUS PROVISIONS

Amendments
- **1976, Tax Reform Act of 1976 (P.L. 94-455)**

P.L. 94-455, § 1906(b)(13)(A):

Amended 1954 Code by substituting "Secretary" for "Secretary or his delegate" each place it appeared. **Effective** 2-1-77.

[Sec. 5122(c)]

(c) RETAIL DEALERS.—For purposes of this section—

(1) RETAIL DEALER IN LIQUORS.—The term "retail dealer in liquors" means any dealer (other than a retail dealer in beer or a limited retail dealer) who sells, or offers for sale, distilled spirits, wines, or beer, to any person other than a dealer.

(2) RETAIL DEALER IN BEER.—The term "retail dealer in beer" means any dealer (other than a limited retail dealer) who sells, or offers for sale, beer, but not distilled spirits or wines, to any person other than a dealer.

(3) "LIMITED RETAIL DEALER.—The term "limited retail dealer" means any fraternal, civic, church, labor, charitable, benevolent, or ex-servicemen's organization making sales of distilled spirits, wine or beer on the occasion of any kind of entertainment, dance, picnic, bazaar, or festival held by it, or any person making sales of distilled spirits, wine or beer to the members, guests, or patrons of bona fide fairs, reunions, picnics, carnivals, or other similar outings, if such organization or person is not otherwise engaged in business as a dealer.

(4) DEALER.—The term "dealer" has the meaning given such term by section 5121(c)(3).

Amendments
- **2005, Safe, Accountable, Flexible, Efficient Transportation Equity Act: A Legacy for Users (P.L. 109-59)**

P.L. 109-59, § 11125(b)(6)(B)(iii):

Amended Code Sec. 5124 [as redesignated as Code Sec. 5122] by redesignating subsection (c) as subsection (d) and inserting after subsection (b) a new subsection (c). **Effective** 7-1-2008, but not applicable to taxes imposed for periods before such date.

[Sec. 5122(d)]

(d) CROSS REFERENCES.—

For provisions relating to the preservation and inspection of records, and entry of premises for inspection, see section 5123.

Amendments
- **2005, Safe, Accountable, Flexible, Efficient Transportation Equity Act: A Legacy for Users (P.L. 109-59)**

P.L. 109-59, § 11125(b)(6)(B)(ii):

Amended Code Sec. 5124(c) [as redesignated as Code Sec. 5122] by striking "section 5146" and inserting "section 5123". **Effective** 7-1-2008, but not applicable to taxes imposed for periods before such date.

P.L. 109-59, § 11125(b)(6)(B)(iii):

Amended Code Sec. 5124 [as redesignated as Code Sec. 5122] by redesignating subsection (c) as subsection (d). **Effective** 7-1-2008, but not applicable to taxes imposed for periods before such date.

[Sec. 5122—Repealed]

Amendments
- **2005, Safe, Accountable, Flexible, Efficient Transportation Equity Act: A Legacy for Users (P.L. 109-59)**

P.L. 109-59, § 11125(a)(1)(D):

Repealed subpart E of part II of subchapter A of chapter 51 (other than Code Sec. 5124) [Code Secs. 5121-5123 and Code Sec. 5125.—CCH]. **Effective** 7-1-2008, but not applicable to taxes imposed for periods before such date. Prior to repeal, Code Sec. 5122 read as follows:

SEC. 5122. DEFINITIONS.

[Sec. 5122(a)]

(a) RETAIL DEALER IN LIQUORS.—When used in this chapter, the term "retail dealer in liquors" means any dealer, other than a retail dealer in beer or a limited retail dealer, who sells, or offers for sale, any distilled spirits, wines, or beer, to any person other than a dealer.

[Sec. 5122(b)]

(b) RETAIL DEALER IN BEER.—When used in this chapter, the term "retail dealer in beer" means any dealer, other than a limited retail dealer, who sells, or offers for sale, beer, but not distilled spirits or wines, to any person other than a dealer.

[Sec. 5122(c)]

(c) LIMITED RETAIL DEALER.—When used in this chapter, the term "limited retail dealer" means any fraternal, civic, church, labor, charitable, benevolent, or ex-servicemen's organization making sales of distilled spirits, wine, or beer on the occasion of any kind of entertainment, dance, picnic, bazaar, or festival held by it, or any person making sales of distilled spirits, wine, or beer to the members, guests, or patrons of bona fide fairs, reunions, picnics, carnivals, or other similar outings, if such organization or person is not otherwise engaged in business as a dealer.

Amendments

- **1976, Tax Reform Act of 1976 (P.L. 94-455)**

P.L. 94-455, § 1905(a)(10):

Substituted "distilled spirits, wine, or beer" for "beer or wine" each place it appeared in Code Sec. 5122(c). **Effective** 2-1-77.

[Sec. 5123]

SEC. 5123. PRESERVATION AND INSPECTION OF RECORDS, AND ENTRY OF PREMISES FOR INSPECTION.

[Sec. 5123(a)]

(a) PRESERVATION AND INSPECTION OF RECORDS.—Any records or other documents required to be kept under this part or regulations issued pursuant thereto shall be preserved by the person required to keep such records or documents, as the Secretary may by regulations prescribe, and shall be kept available for inspection by any internal revenue officer during business hours.

Amendments
- **1976, Tax Reform Act of 1976 (P.L. 94-455)**

P.L. 94-455, § 1906(b)(13)(A):

Amended 1954 Code by substituting "Secretary" for "Secretary or his delegate" each place it appeared. **Effective** 2-1-77.

[Sec. 5123(b)]

(b) ENTRY OF PREMISES FOR INSPECTION.—The Secretary may enter during business hours the premises (including places of storage) of any dealer for the purpose of inspecting or examining any records or other documents required to be kept by such dealer under this chapter or regulations issued pursuant thereto and any distilled spirits, wines, or beer kept or stored by such dealer on such premises.

Sec. 5122(c)

ALCOHOL TAXES—MISCELLANEOUS PROVISIONS

Amendments

• **2005, Safe, Accountable, Flexible, Efficient Transportation Equity Act: A Legacy for Users (P.L. 109-59)**

P.L. 109-59, §11125(b)(7):

Amended Code Sec. 5146 by moving it to subpart C of part II of subchapter A of chapter 51, inserting it after Code Sec. 5122, and redesignating it as Code Sec. 5123. **Effective** 7-1-2008, but not applicable to taxes imposed for periods before such date.

Amendments

• **2005, Safe, Accountable, Flexible, Efficient Transportation Equity Act: A Legacy for Users (P.L. 109-59)**

P.L. 109-59, §11125(a)(1)(D):

Repealed subpart E of part II of subchapter A of chapter 51 (other than Code Sec. 5124) [Code Secs. 5121-5123 and Code Sec. 5125.—CCH]. **Effective** 7-1-2008, but not applicable to taxes imposed for periods before such date. Prior to repeal, Code Sec. 5123 read as follows:

SEC. 5123. EXEMPTIONS.

[Sec. 5123(a)]

(a) WHOLESALE DEALERS.—

(1) WHOLESALE DEALERS IN LIQUORS.—No special tax shall be imposed under section 5121(a) or (b) on any dealer by reason of the selling, or offering for sale, of distilled spirits, wines, or beer at any location where such dealer is required to pay special tax under section 5111(a).

(2) WHOLESALE DEALERS IN BEER.—No special tax shall be imposed under section 5121(b) on any dealer by reason of the selling, or offering for sale, of beer at any location where such dealer is required to pay special tax under section 5111(b).

[Sec. 5123(b)]

(b) BUSINESS CONDUCTED IN MORE THAN ONE LOCATION.—

(1) RETAIL DEALERS AT LARGE.—Any retail dealer in liquors or retail dealer in beer whose business is such as to require him to travel from place to place in different States of the United States may, under regulations prescribed by the Secretary, procure a special tax stamp "At Large" covering his activities throughout the United States with the payment of but one special tax as a retail dealer in liquors or as a retail dealer in beer, as the case may be.

(2) DEALERS ON TRAINS, AIRCRAFT, AND BOATS.—Nothing contained in this chapter shall prevent the issue, under such regulations as the Secretary may prescribe, of special tax stamps to—

(A) persons carrying on the business of retail dealers in liquors, or retail dealers in beer, on trains, aircraft, boats or other vessels, engaged in the business of carrying passengers; or

(B) persons carrying on the business of retail dealers in liquors or retail dealers in beer on boats or other vessels operated by them, when such persons operate from a fixed address in a port or harbor and supply exclusively boats or other vessels, or persons thereon, at such port or harbor.

(3) LIQUOR STORES OPERATED BY STATES, POLITICAL SUBDIVISIONS, ETC.—A State, a political subdivision of a State, or the District of Columbia shall not be required to pay more than one special tax as a retail dealer in liquors under section 5121(a) regardless of the number of locations at which such State, political subdivision, or District carries on business as a retail dealer in liquors.

[Sec. 5124]

SEC. 5124. REGISTRATION BY DEALERS.

Every dealer who is subject to the recordkeeping requirements under section 5121 or 5122 shall register with the Secretary such dealer's name or style, place of residence, trade or business, and the place where such trade or business is to be carried on. In the case of a firm or company, the names of the several persons constituting the same, and the places of residence, shall be so registered.

Amendments

• **2005, Safe, Accountable, Flexible, Efficient Transportation Equity Act: A Legacy for Users (P.L. 109-59)**

P.L. 109-59, §11125(b)(8):

Amended subpart C of part II of subchapter A of chapter 51, as amended by Act Sec. 11125(b)(7), by adding at the end a new Code Sec. 5124. **Effective** 7-1-2008, but not applicable to taxes imposed for periods before such date.

[Sec. 5125—Repealed]

Amendments

• **2005, Safe, Accountable, Flexible, Efficient Transportation Equity Act: A Legacy for Users (P.L. 109-59)**

P.L. 109-59, §11125(a)(1)(D):

Repealed subpart E of part II of subchapter A of chapter 51 (other than Code Sec. 5124) [Code Secs. 5121-5123 and Code Sec. 5125.—CCH]. **Effective** 7-1-2008, but not

• **1976, Tax Reform Act of 1976 (P.L. 94-455)**

P.L. 94-455, §1906(b)(13)(A):

Amended 1954 Code by substituting "Secretary" for "Secretary or his delegate" each place it appeared. **Effective** 2-1-77.

[Sec. 5123—Repealed]

Amendments

• **1976, Tax Reform Act of 1976 (P.L. 94-455)**

P.L. 94-455, §1906(b)(13)(A):

Amended 1954 Code by substituting "Secretary" for "Secretary or his delegate" each place it appeared. **Effective** 2-1-77.

• **1962 (P.L. 87-863)**

P.L. 87-863, §4(a):

Amended Code Sec. 5123(b) by adding paragraph (3). **Effective** 7-1-62.

[Sec. 5123(c)]

(c) COORDINATION OF TAXES UNDER SECTION 5121.—No tax shall be imposed by section 5121(a) with respect to a person's activities at any place during a year if such person has paid the tax imposed by section 5121(b) with respect to such place for such year.

Amendments

• **1988, Technical and Miscellaneous Revenue Act of 1988 (P.L. 100-647)**

P.L. 100-647, §2004(t)(3):

Amended Code Sec. 5123 by redesignating subsection (c) as subsection (d) and by inserting after subsection (b) new subsection (c). **Effective** as if included in the provision of P.L. 100-203 to which it relates.

[Sec. 5123(d)]

(d) CROSS REFERENCES.—

(1) For exemption of proprietors of distilled spirits plants, bonded wine cellars, and breweries from special tax as dealers, see section 5113(a).

(2) For provisions relating to sales by creditors, fiduciaries, and officers of courts, see section 5113(c)(1).

(3) For provisions relating to sales by retiring partners or representatives of deceased partners to incoming or remaining partners, see section 5113(c)(2).

(4) For provisions relating to return of liquors for credit, refund, or exchange, see section 5113(c)(3).

(5) For provisions relating to sales by retail dealers in liquidation, see section 5113(e).

Amendments

• **1988, Technical and Miscellaneous Revenue Act of 1988 (P.L. 100-647)**

P.L. 100-647, §2004(t)(3):

Amended Code Sec. 5123 by redesignating subsection (c) as (d). **Effective** as if included in the provision of P.L. 100-203 to which it relates.

applicable to taxes imposed for periods before such date. Prior to repeal, Code Sec. 5125 read as follows:

SEC. 5125. CROSS REFERENCES.

(1) For provisions relating to prohibited purchases by dealers, see section 5117.

(2) For provisions relating to presumptions of liability as wholesale dealer in case of sale of 20 wine gallons or more, see section 5691(b).

Subpart D—Other Provisions

Sec. 5131.   Packaging distilled spirits for industrial uses.
Sec. 5132.   Prohibited purchases by dealers.

ALCOHOL TAXES—MISCELLANEOUS PROVISIONS

[Sec. 5131]
SEC. 5131. PACKAGING DISTILLED SPIRITS FOR INDUSTRIAL USES.

[Sec. 5131(a)]

(a) GENERAL.—The Secretary may, at his discretion and under such regulations as he may prescribe, authorize a dealer (as defined in section 5121(c)) engaging in the business of supplying distilled spirits for industrial uses to package distilled spirits, on which the tax has been paid or determined, for such uses in containers of a capacity in excess of 1 wine gallon and not more than 5 wine gallons.

Amendments

• **2005, Safe, Accountable, Flexible, Efficient Transportation Equity Act: A Legacy for Users (P.L. 109-59)**

P.L. 109-59, § 11125(b)(11):

Amended Code Sec. 5131(a), as redesignated, by inserting "(as defined in section 5121(c))" after "dealer". **Effective** 7-1-2008, but not applicable to taxes imposed for periods before such date.

• **1976, Tax Reform Act of 1976 (P.L. 94-455)**

P.L. 94-455, § 1906(b)(13)(A):

Amended 1954 Code by substituting "Secretary" for "Secretary or his delegate" each place it appeared. **Effective** 2-1-77.

[Sec. 5131(b)]

(b) CROSS REFERENCE.—

For provisions relating to containers of distilled spirits, see section 5206.

Amendments

• **2005, Safe, Accountable, Flexible, Efficient Transportation Equity Act: A Legacy for Users (P.L. 109-59)**

P.L. 109-59, § 11125(b)(11):

Amended Code Sec. 5116 by moving it to subpart D of part II of subchapter A of chapter 51, inserting it after the table of sections, and redesignating it as Code Sec. 5131. **Effective** 7-1-2008, but not applicable to taxes imposed for periods before such date.

• **1984, Deficit Reduction Act of 1984 (P.L. 98-369)**

P.L. 98-369, § 454(c)(3):

Amended Code Sec. 5116(b). **Effective** 7-1-85. Prior to amendment, it read as follows:

(b) Cross References.—

(1) For provisions relating to stamps for immediate containers, see section 5205(a)(1).

(2) For provisions relating to containers of distilled spirits, see section 5206.

• **1979, Trade Agreements Act of 1979 (P.L. 96-39)**

P.L. 96-39, § 807(a)(12):

Amended Code Sec. 5116(b)(1) by changing "section 5205(a)(2)" to "section 5205(a)(1)". **Effective** 1-1-80.

[Sec. 5132]
SEC. 5132. PROHIBITED PURCHASES BY DEALERS.

[Sec. 5132(a)]

(a) IN GENERAL.—Except as provided in regulations prescribed by the Secretary, it shall be unlawful for a dealer to purchase distilled spirits for resale from any person other than a wholesale dealer in liquors who is required to keep the records prescribed by section 5121.

[Sec. 5132(b)]

(b) LIMITED RETAIL DEALERS.—A limited retail dealer may lawfully purchase distilled spirits for resale from a retail dealer in liquors.

[Sec. 5132(c)]

(c) PENALTY AND FORFEITURE.—

For penalty and forfeiture provisions applicable to violations of subsection (a), see sections 5687 and 7302.

Amendments

• **2005, Safe, Accountable, Flexible, Efficient Transportation Equity Act: A Legacy for Users (P.L. 109-59)**

P.L. 109-59, § 11125(b)(12):

Amended subpart D of part II of subchapter A of chapter 51 by adding at the end a new Code Sec. 5132. **Effective** 7-1-2008, but not applicable to taxes imposed for periods before such date.

Subpart G—General Provisions—[Repealed]

[Sec. 5141—Repealed]

Amendments

• **2005, Safe, Accountable, Flexible, Efficient Transportation Equity Act: A Legacy for Users (P.L. 109-59)**

P.L. 109-59, § 11125(a)(1)(E):

Repealed subpart G of part II of subchapter A of chapter 51 (other than Code Secs. 5142, 5143, 5145, and 5146) [Code Sec. 5141, and Code Secs. 5147-5149.—CCH].

Effective 7-1-2008, but not applicable to taxes imposed for periods before such date. Prior to repeal, Code Sec. 5141 read as follows:

SEC. 5141. REGISTRATION.

For provisions relating to registration in the case of persons engaged in any trade or business on which a special tax is imposed, see section 7011(a).

[Sec. 5147—Repealed]

Amendments

• **2005, Safe, Accountable, Flexible, Efficient Transportation Equity Act: A Legacy for Users (P.L. 109-59)**

P.L. 109-59, § 11125(a)(1)(E):

Repealed subpart G of part II of subchapter A of chapter 51 (other than Code Secs. 5142, 5143, 5145, and 5146) [Code Sec. 5141, and Code Secs. 5147-5149.—CCH].

Effective 7-1-2008, but not applicable to taxes imposed for periods before such date. Prior to repeal, Code Sec. 5147 read as follows:

SEC. 5147. APPLICATION OF SUBPART.

The provisions of this subpart shall extend to and apply to the special taxes imposed by the other subparts of this part and to the persons on whom such taxes are imposed.

[Sec. 5148—Repealed]

Amendments

• **2005, Safe, Accountable, Flexible, Efficient Transportation Equity Act: A Legacy for Users (P.L. 109-59)**

P.L. 109-59, § 11125(a)(1)(E):

Repealed subpart G of part II of subchapter A of chapter 51 (other than Code Secs. 5142, 5143, 5145, and 5146) [Code Sec. 5141, and Code Secs. 5147-5149.—CCH]. **Effective** 7-1-2008, but not applicable to taxes imposed for periods before such date. Prior to repeal, Code Sec. 5148 read as follows:

SEC. 5148. SUSPENSION OF OCCUPATIONAL TAX.

[Sec. 5148(a)]

(a) IN GENERAL.—Notwithstanding sections 5081, 5091, 5111, 5121, and 5131, the rate of tax imposed under such sections for the suspension period shall be zero. During such period, persons engaged in or carrying on a trade or business covered by such sections shall register under section 5141 and shall comply with the recordkeeping requirements under this part.

ALCOHOL TAXES—DISTILLED SPIRITS PLANTS

[Sec. 5148(b)]

(b) SUSPENSION PERIOD.—For purposes of subsection (a), the suspension period is the period beginning on July 1, 2005, and ending on June 30, 2008.

Amendments

• 2004, American Jobs Creation Act of 2004 (P.L. 108-357)

P.L. 108-357, §246(a):

Amended subpart G of part II of subchapter A of chapter 51 by redesignating Code Sec. 5148 as Code Sec. 5149 and by inserting after Code Sec. 5147 a new Code Sec. 5148. Effective 10-22-2004.

[Sec. 5149—Repealed]

Amendments

• 2005, Safe, Accountable, Flexible, Efficient Transportation Equity Act: A Legacy for Users (P.L. 109-59)

P.L. 109-59, §11125(a)(1)(E):

Repealed subpart G of part II of subchapter A of chapter 51 (other than Code Secs. 5142, 5143, 5145, and 5146) [Code Sec. 5141, and Code Secs. 5147-5149.—CCH]. Effective 7-1-2008, but not applicable to taxes imposed for periods before such date. Prior to repeal, Code Sec. 5149 read as follows:

SEC. 5149. CROSS REFERENCES.

(1) For penalties for willful nonpayment of special taxes, see section 5691.

(2) For penalties applicable to this part generally, see subchapter J.

(3) For penalties, authority for assessments, and other general and administrative provisions applicable to this part, see subtitle F.

Amendments

• 2004, American Jobs Creation Act of 2004 (P.L. 108-357)

P.L. 108-357, §246(a):

Amended subpart G of part II of subchapter A of chapter 51 by redesignating Code Sec. 5148 as Code Sec. 5149. Effective 10-22-2004.

• 1976, Tax Reform Act of 1976 (P.L. 94-455)

P.L. 94-455, §1905(b)(3)(E):

Added ", authority for assessments," following "penalties" in Code Sec. 5149(3). Effective 2-1-77.

Subchapter B—Qualification Requirements for Distilled Spirits Plants

Sec. 5171.	Establishment.
Sec. 5172.	Application.
Sec. 5173.	Bonds.
Sec. 5175.	Export bonds.
Sec. 5176.	New or renewed bonds.
Sec. 5177.	Other provisions relating to bonds.
Sec. 5178.	Premises of distilled spirits plants.
Sec. 5179.	Registration of stills.
Sec. 5180.	Signs.
Sec. 5181.	Distilled spirits for fuel use.
Sec. 5182.	Cross references.

[Sec. 5171]

SEC. 5171. ESTABLISHMENT.

[Sec. 5171(a)]

(a) CERTAIN OPERATIONS MAY BE CONDUCTED ONLY ON BONDED PREMISES.—Except as otherwise provided by law, operations as a distiller, warehouseman, or processor may be conducted only on the bonded premises of a distilled spirits plant by a person who is qualified under this subchapter.

[Sec. 5171(b)]

(b) ESTABLISHMENT OF DISTILLED SPIRITS PLANTS.—A distilled spirits plant may be established only by a person who intends to conduct at such plant operations as a distiller, as a warehouseman, or as both.

[Sec. 5171(c)]

(c) REGISTRATION.—

(1) IN GENERAL.—Each person shall, before commencing operations at a distilled spirits plant (and at such other times as the Secretary may by regulations prescribe), make application to the Secretary for, and receive notice of, the registration of such plant.

(2) APPLICATION REQUIRED WHERE NEW OPERATIONS ARE ADDED.—No operation in addition to those set forth in the application made pursuant to paragraph (1) may be conducted at a distilled spirits plant until the person has made application to the Secretary for, and received notice of, the registration of such additional operation.

(3) SECRETARY MAY ESTABLISH MINIMUM CAPACITY AND LEVEL OF ACTIVITY REQUIREMENTS.—The Secretary may by regulations prescribe for each type of operation minimum capacity and level of activity requirements for qualifying premises as a distilled spirits plant.

(4) APPLICANT MUST COMPLY WITH LAW AND REGULATIONS.—No plant (or additional operation) shall be registered under this section until the applicant has complied with the requirements of law and regulations in relation to the qualification of such plant (or additional operation).

[Sec. 5171(d)]

(d) PERMITS.—

(1) REQUIREMENTS.—Each person required to file an application for registration under subsection (c) whose distilled spirits operations (or any part thereof) are not required to be covered by a basic permit under the Federal Alcohol Administration Act (27 U.S.C. secs. 203 and 204) shall, before commencing the operations (or part thereof) not so covered, apply for and obtain a permit under this subsection from the Secretary to engage in such operations (or part thereof). Subsections (b), (c), (d), (e), (f), (g), and (h) of section 5271 are hereby made applicable to persons filing applications and permits required by or issued under this subsection.

(2) EXCEPTION FOR AGENCIES OF A STATE OR POLITICAL SUBDIVISION.—Paragraph (1) shall not apply to any agency of a State or political subdivision thereof or to any officer or employee of any such agency, and no such agency, officer, or employee shall be required to obtain a permit thereunder.

[Sec. 5171(e)]

(e) CROSS REFERENCES.—

(1) For penalty for failure of a distiller or processor to file application for registration as required by this section, see section 5601(a)(2).

(2) For penalty for the filing of a false application by a distiller, warehouseman, or processor of distilled spirits, see section 5601(a)(3).

ALCOHOL TAXES—DISTILLED SPIRITS PLANTS

Amendments
• **1979, Trade Agreements Act of 1979 (P.L. 96-39)**

P.L. 96-39, § 805(a):

Amended Code Sec. 5171. **Effective** 1-1-80. Prior to amendment, Code Sec. 5171 read as follows:

SEC. 5171. ESTABLISHMENT.

(a) GENERAL REQUIREMENTS.—Every person shall, before commencing or continuing the business of a distiller, bonded warehouseman, rectifier, or bottler of distilled spirits, and at such other times as the Secretary may by regulations prescribe, make application to the Secretary for and receive notice of the registration of his plant. No plant shall be registered under this section until the applicant has complied with the requirements of law and regulations in relation to the qualification of such business (or businesses).

(b) PERMITS.—

(1) REQUIREMENTS.—Every person required to file application for registration under subsection (a) whose distilling, warehousing, or bottling operations (or any part thereof) are not required to be covered by a basic permit under the Federal Alcohol Administration Act (27 U.S.C. 203, 204) shall, before commencing any such operations, apply for and obtain a permit under this subsection from the Secretary to engage in such operations. Section 5271(b), (c), (d), (e), (f), (g), and (h), and section 5274 are hereby made applicable to applications, to persons filing applications, and to permits required by or issued under this subsection.

(2) EXCEPTIONS FOR AGENCY OF A STATE OR POLITICAL SUBDIVISION.—Paragraph (1) shall not apply to any agency of a State or political subdivision thereof or to any officer or employee of any such agency, and no such agency or officer or employee shall be required to obtain a permit thereunder.

(c) CROSS REFERENCES.—

For penalty for failure of a distiller or rectifier to file application for registration as required by this section, see section 5601(a)(2), and for penalty for the filing of a false application by a distiller, bonded warehouseman, rectifier, or bottler of distilled spirits, see section 5601(a)(3).

• **1976, Tax Reform Act of 1976 (P.L. 94-455)**

P.L. 94-455, § 1905(a)(13):

Struck out "49 Stat. 978;" before "27 U.S.C. 203," in Code Sec. 5171(b)(1), and struck out Code Sec. 5171(b)(3). **Effective** 2-1-77. Prior to striking, Code Sec. 5171(b)(3) read as follows:

(3) CONTINUANCE OF BUSINESS.—Every person required by paragraph (1) to obtain a permit (covering operations not required to be covered by a basic permit under the Federal Alcohol Administration Act) who, on June 30, 1959, is qualified to perform such operations under the internal revenue laws, and who complies with the provisions of this chapter (other than this subsection) relating to qualification of such business or businesses, shall be entitled to continue such operations pending reasonable opportunity to make application for permit, and final action thereon.

P.L. 94-455, § 1906(b)(13)(A):

Amended 1954 Code by substituting "Secretary" for "Secretary or his delegate" each place it appeared. **Effective** 2-1-77.

[Sec. 5172]

SEC. 5172. APPLICATION.

The application for registration required by section 5171(c) shall, in such manner and form as the Secretary may by regulations prescribe, identify the applicant and persons interested in the business (or businesses) covered by the application, show the nature, location and extent of the premises, show the specific type or types of operations to be conducted on such premises, and show any other information which the Secretary may by regulations require for the purpose of carrying out the provisions of this chapter.

Amendments
• **1979, Trade Agreements Act of 1979 (P.L. 96-39)**

P.L. 96-39, § 807(a)(13):

Amended Code Sec. 5172 by changing "section 5171(a)" to "section 5171(c)". **Effective** 1-1-80.

• **1976, Tax Reform Act of 1976 (P.L. 94-455)**

P.L. 94-455, § 1906(b)(13)(A):

Amended 1954 Code by substituting "Secretary" for "Secretary or his delegate" each place it appeared. **Effective** 2-1-77.

[Sec. 5173]

SEC. 5173. BONDS.

[Sec. 5173(a)]

(a) OPERATIONS AT, AND WITHDRAWALS FROM, DISTILLED SPIRITS PLANT MUST BE COVERED BY BOND.—

(1) OPERATIONS.—Except as provided under section 5551(d), no person intending to establish a distilled spirits plant may commence operations at such plant unless such person has furnished bond covering operations at such plant.

(2) WITHDRAWALS.—Except as provided under section 5551(d), no distilled spirits (other than distilled spirits withdrawn under section 5214 or 7510) may be withdrawn from bonded premises except on payment of tax unless the proprietor of the bonded premises has furnished bond covering such withdrawal.

Amendments
• **2015, Protecting Americans from Tax Hikes Act of 2015 (P.L. 114-113)**

P.L. 114-113, § 332(b)(2)(A)(i)-(ii), Div. Q:

Amended Code Sec. 5173(a) in paragraph (1), by striking "No person" and inserting "Except as provided under section 5551(d), no person", and in paragraph (2), by striking "No distilled spirits" and inserting "Except as provided under section 5551(d), no distilled spirits". **Effective** for any calendar quarters beginning more than 1 year after 12-18-2015.

• **1976, Tax Reform Act of 1976 (P.L. 94-455)**

P.L. 94-455, § 1906(b)(13)(A):

Amended 1954 Code by substituting "Secretary" for "Secretary or his delegate" each place it appeared. **Effective** 2-1-77.

[Sec. 5173(b)]

(b) OPERATIONS BONDS.—The bond required by paragraph (1) of subsection (a) shall meet the requirements of paragraph (1), (2), or (3) of this subsection:

(1) ONE PLANT BOND.—The bond covers operations at a single distilled spirits plant.

(2) ADJACENT WINE CELLAR BOND.—The bond covers operations at a distilled spirits plant and at an adjacent bonded wine cellar.

(3) AREA BOND.—The bond covers operations at 2 or more distilled spirits plants (and adjacent bonded wine cellars) which—

(A) are located in the same geographical area (as designated in regulations prescribed by the Secretary), and

(B) are operated by the same person (or, in the case of a corporation, by such corporation and its controlled subsidiaries).

Amendments
• **1976, Tax Reform Act of 1976 (P.L. 94-455)**

P.L. 94-455, § 1906(b)(13)(A):

Amended 1954 Code by substituting "Secretary" for "Secretary or his delegate" each place it appeared. **Effective** 2-1-77.

• **1971 (P.L. 91-659)**

P.L. 91-659, § 4:

Amended Code Sec. 5173(b) by adding "or to any judgment or other lien covered by a bond given under paragraph (4)" in paragraph (1), by inserting "or (4)" in paragraph (2), and by adding paragraph (4). **Effective** 5-1-71.

[Sec. 5173(c)]

(c) WITHDRAWAL BONDS.—The bond required by paragraph (2) of subsection (a) shall cover withdrawals from 1 or more bonded premises the operations at which could be covered by the same operations bond under subsection (b).

Amendments
• **1976, Tax Reform Act of 1976 (P.L. 94-455)**

P.L. 94-455, § 1906(b)(13)(A):

Amended 1954 Code by substituting "Secretary" for "Secretary or his delegate" each place it appeared. **Effective** 2-1-77.

ALCOHOL TAXES—DISTILLED SPIRITS PLANTS

[Sec. 5173(d)]

(d) UNIT BONDS.—Under regulations prescribed by the Secretary, the requirements of paragraphs (1) and (2) of subsection (a) shall be treated as met by a unit bond which covers both operations at, and withdrawals from, 1 or more bonded premises which could be covered by the same operations bond under subsection (b).

[Sec. 5173(e)]

(e) TERMS AND CONDITIONS.—
(1) IN GENERAL.—Any bond furnished under this section shall be conditioned that the person furnishing the bond—
(A) will faithfully comply with all provisions of law and regulations relating to the activities covered by such bond, and
(B) will pay—
(i) all taxes imposed by this chapter, and
(ii) all penalties incurred by, or fines imposed on, such person for violation of any such provision.
(2) OTHER TERMS AND CONDITIONS.—Any bond furnished under this section shall contain such other terms and conditions as may be required by regulations prescribed by the Secretary.

[Sec. 5173(f)]

(f) AMOUNT.—
(1) IN GENERAL.—The penal sum of any bond shall be the amount determined under regulations prescribed by the Secretary.
(2) MAXIMUM AND MINIMUM AMOUNT.—The Secretary shall by regulations prescribe a minimum amount and a maximum amount for each type of bond which may be furnished under this section.

Amendments

• **1976, Tax Reform Act of 1976 (P.L. 94-455)**

P.L. 94-455, §1906(b)(13)(A):
Amended 1954 Code by substituting "Secretary" for "Secretary or his delegate" each place it appeared. **Effective** 2-1-77.

[Sec. 5173(g)]

(g) TOTAL AMOUNT AVAILABLE.—The total amount of any bond furnished under this section shall be available for the satisfaction of any liability incurred under the terms and conditions of such bond.

[Sec. 5173(h)]

(h) SPECIAL RULES.—For purposes of this section—
(1) WITHDRAWAL BONDS.—In the case of any bond furnished under this section which covers withdrawals but not operations—
(A) such bond shall be in addition to the operations bond, and
(B) if distilled spirits are withdrawn under such bond, the operations bond shall no longer cover liability for payment of the tax on the spirits withdrawn.
(2) ADJACENT WINE CELLARS.—
(A) REQUIREMENTS.—No wine cellar shall be treated as being adjacent to a distilled spirits plant unless—
(i) such distilled spirits plant is qualified under this subchapter for the production of distilled spirits, and
(ii) such wine cellar and the distilled spirits plant are operated by the same person (or, in the case of a corporation, by such corporation and its controlled subsidiaries).
(B) BOND IN LIEU OF WINE CELLAR BOND.—In the case of any adjacent wine cellar, a bond furnished under this section which covers operations at such wine cellar shall be in lieu of any bond which would otherwise be required under section 5354 with respect to such wine cellar (other than supplemental bonds required under the second sentence of section 5354).

Amendments

• **1979, Trade Agreements Act of 1979 (P.L. 96-39)**

P.L. 96-39, §805(c):
Amended Code Sec. 5173. **Effective** 1-1-80. Prior to amendment, Code Sec. 5173 read as follows:

SEC. 5173. QUALIFICATION BONDS.

(a) GENERAL PROVISIONS.—Every person intending to commence or to continue the business of a distiller, bonded warehouseman, or rectifier, on filing with the Secretary an application for registration of his plant, and before commencing or continuing such business, shall file bond in the form prescribed by the Secretary, conditioned that he shall faithfully comply with all the provisions of law and regulations relating to the duties and business of a distiller, bonded warehouseman, or rectifier, as the case may be (including the payment of taxes imposed by this chapter), and shall pay all penalties incurred or fines imposed on him for violation of any of the said provisions.

(b) DISTILLER'S BOND.—Every person intending to commence or continue the business of a distiller shall give bond in a penal sum not less than the amount of tax on spirits that will be produced in his distillery during a period of 15 days, except that such bond shall be in a sum of not less than $5,000 nor more than $100,000.

(1) CONDITIONS OF APPROVAL.—In addition to the requirements of subsection (a), the distiller's bond shall be conditioned that he shall not suffer the property, or any part thereof, subject to lien under section 5004(b)(1) to be encumbered by mortgage, judgment, or other lien during the time in which he shall carry on such business (except that this condition shall not apply during the term of any bond given under subparagraph (C) or to any judgment or other lien covered by a bond given under paragraph (4)), and no bond of a distiller shall be approved unless the Secretary is satisfied that the situation of the land and buildings which will constitute his bonded premises (as described in his application for registration) is not such as would enable the distiller to defraud the United States, and unless—

(A) the distiller is the owner in fee, unencumbered by any mortgage, judgment, or other lien, of the lot or tract of land subject to lien under section 5004(b)(1); or

(B) the distiller files with the officer designated for the purpose by the Secretary, in connection with his application for registration, the written consent of the owner of the fee, and of any mortgagee, judgment creditor, or other person having a lien thereon, duly acknowledged, that such premises may be used for the purpose of distilling spirits, subject to the provisions of law, and expressly stipulating that the lien of the United States, for taxes on distilled spirits produced thereon and penalties relating thereto, shall have priority of such mortgage, judgment, or other encumbrance, and that in the case of the forfeiture of such premises, or any part thereof, the title to the same shall vest in the United States, discharged from such mortgage, judgment, or other encumbrance; or

(C) the distiller files a bond, approved by the Secretary, in the penal sum equal to the appraised value of the property subject to lien under section 5004(b)(1), except that such bond shall not exceed the sum of $300,000. Such value shall be determined, and such bond shall be executed in such form and with such sureties and filed with the officer designated by the Secretary, under such regulations as the Secretary shall prescribe.

(2) CANCELLATION OF INDEMNITY BOND.—When the liability for which an indemnity bond given under paragraph (1)(C) or (4) ceases to exist, such bond may be cancelled upon application to the Secretary or his delegate.

(3) JUDICIAL SALE.—In the case of any distillery sold at judicial or other sale in favor of the United States, a bond in lieu of consent under paragraph (1)(B) may be taken at the discretion of the Secretary, and the person giving such bond may be allowed to operate such distillery during the existence of the right of redemption from such sale, on complying with all the other provisions of law.

(4) INVOLUNTARY LIEN.—In the case of a judgment or other lien imposed on the property subject to lien under section 5004(b)(1) without the consent of the distiller, the distiller may file bond, approved by the Secretary, in the amount of such judgment or other lien to indemnify the United States for any loss resulting from such encumbrance.

(c) BONDED WAREHOUSEMAN'S BONDS.—

(1) GENERAL REQUIREMENTS.—Every person intending to commence or continue the business of a bonded warehouseman shall give bond in a penal sum not less than the amount of tax on distilled spirits stored on such premises and in transit thereto, except that such bond shall not exceed the sum of $200,000. In addition to the requirements in subsection (a), such bond shall be conditioned—

(A) on the withdrawal of the spirits from storage on bonded premises within the time prescribed for the determination of tax under section 5006(a)(2), and

(B) on payment of the tax, except as otherwise provided by law, on all spirits withdrawn from storage on the bonded premises.

ALCOHOL TAXES—DISTILLED SPIRITS PLANTS

(2) EXCEPTION.—The Secretary may by regulations specify bonded warehousing operations, other than the storage of more than 500 casks or packages of distilled spirits in wooden containers, for which a bond in a maximum sum of less than $200,000 will be approved, and in such cases the Secretary shall by regulations prescribe the maximum penal sum of such bonds.

(d) RECTIFIER'S BOND.—Every person intending to commence or continue the business of a rectifier shall give bond in a penal sum not less than the amount of tax the rectifier will be liable to pay in a period of 30 days under sections 5021 and 5022, except that such bond shall not exceed the sum of $100,000, and shall not be less than $1,000.

(e) COMBINED OPERATIONS.—

(1) DISTILLED SPIRITS PLANTS.—Except as provided in paragraph (2), any person intending to commence or continue business as proprietor of a distilled spirits plant who would otherwise be required to give more than one bond under the provisions of subsections (b) (other than indemnity bonds), (c), and (d), shall, in lieu thereof, give bond in a penal sum equal to the combined penal sums which would have been required under such subsections; but in no case shall the combined operations bond be in a penal sum in excess of $200,000 if all operations are to be conducted on bonded premises, or in excess of $250,000 for the distilled spirits plant. Bonds given under this paragraph shall contain the terms and conditions of the bonds in lieu of which they are given.

(2) DISTILLED SPIRITS PLANTS AND ADJACENT BONDED WINE CELLARS.—Any person intending to commence or continue business as proprietor of a bonded wine cellar and an adjacent distilled spirits plant qualified for the production of distilled spirits shall, in lieu of the bonds which would otherwise be required under the provisions of subsection (b) (other than indemnity bonds), (c), and (d), and section 5354 (other than supplemental bonds to cover additional liability arising as a result of deferral of payment of tax), give bond in a penal sum equal to the combined penal sums which would have been required under such provisions; but in no case shall the combined operations bond be in a penal sum in excess of $150,000 if the distilled spirits plant is qualified solely for the production of distilled spirits, in excess of $250,000 if the distilled spirits plant is qualified only for production and bonded warehousing or for production and rectification and bottling, or in excess of $300,000 for the distilled spirits plant and bonded wine cellar. Bonds given under this paragraph shall contain the terms and conditions of the bonds in lieu of which they are given.

(f) BLANKET BONDS.—The Secretary may by regulations authorize any person (including, in the case of a corporation, controlled or wholly owned subsidiaries) operating more than one distilled spirits plant in a geographical area designated in regulations prescribed by the Secretary to give a blanket bond covering the operation of any two or more of such plants and any bonded wine cellars which are adjacent to such plants and which otherwise could be covered under a combined operations bond as provided for in subsection (e)(2). The penal sum of such blanket bond shall be calculated in accordance with the following table:

Total Penal Sums as Determined under Subsections (b), (c), (d), and (e)	Requirement for Penal Sum of Blanket Bond
First $300,000 or any part thereof	100%
Next $300,000 or any part thereof	70%
Next $400,000 or any part thereof	50%
Next $1,000,000 or any part thereof	35%
All over $2,000,000	25%

Bonds given under this subsection shall be in lieu of the bonds required under subsections (b) (other than indemnity bonds), (c), (d), and (e), as the case may be, and shall contain the terms and conditions of such bonds.

(g) LIABILITY UNDER COMBINED OPERATIONS AND BLANKET BONDS.—The total amount of any bond given under subsection (e) or (f) shall be available for the satisfaction of any liability incurred under the terms or conditions of such bond.

[Sec. 5174—Repealed]

Amendments

• **1979, Trade Agreements Act of 1979 (P.L. 96-39)**

P.L. 96-39, §807(a)(14):

Repealed Code Sec. 5174. **Effective** 1-1-80. Prior to repeal, Code Sec. 5174 read as follows:

SEC. 5174. WITHDRAWAL BONDS.

[Sec. 5174(a)]

(a) REQUIREMENTS.—No distilled spirits, other than distilled spirits withdrawn under section 5214 or section 7510, shall be withdrawn from bonded premises except on payment of tax unless—

(1) the proprietor of the bonded premises has furnished such bond (in addition to that required in section 5173) to secure payment of the tax on such spirits, under such regulations and conditions, and in such form and penal sum, as the Secretary may prescribe; or

(2) the proprietor of a distilled spirits plant authorized to rectify or bottle distilled spirits has—

(A) made application to the Secretary to withdraw distilled spirits from bond and has assumed liability at the receiving plant for payment of the tax thereon;

(B) furnished bond (in addition to any bond required by section 5173) to secure payment of the tax on such spirits, under such regulations and conditions, and in such form and penal sum, as the Secretary may prescribe; and

(C) complied with such other requirements as the Secretary may by regulations prescribe.

Amendments

• **1976, Tax Reform Act of 1976 (P.L. 94-455)**

P.L. 94-455, §1905(a)(14):

Substituted "distilled spirits from bond" for "such spirits" in Code Sec. 5174(a)(2)(A). **Effective** 2-1-77.

P.L. 94-455, §1906(b)(13)(A):

Amended 1954 Code by substituting "Secretary" for "Secretary or his delegate" each place it appeared. **Effective** 2-1-77.

[Sec. 5174(b)]

(b) RELEASE OF OTHER BONDS.—When a bond has been filed under subsection (a) and distilled spirits have been withdrawn from bonded premises thereunder, bonds of proprietors covering operations on bonded premises, and bonds given under prior provisions of internal revenue law to cover similar operations, shall no longer cover liability for payment of the tax on such spirits.

[Sec. 5175]

SEC. 5175. EXPORT BONDS.

[Sec. 5175(a)]

(a) REQUIREMENTS.—No distilled spirits shall be withdrawn from bonded premises for exportation, or for transfer to a customs bonded warehouse, without payment of tax unless the exporter has furnished bond to cover such withdrawal, under such regulations and conditions, and in such form and penal sum, as the Secretary may prescribe.

Amendments

• **1979, Trade Agreements Act of 1979 (P.L. 96-39)**

P.L. 96-39, §807(a)(15)(A):

Amended Code Sec. 5175(a) by changing "to a customs bonded warehouse for storage therein pending exportation" to "to a customs bonded warehouse". **Effective** 1-1-80.

• **1977 (P.L. 95-176)**

P.L. 95-176, §3(b):

Amended Code Sec. 5175(a) by adding ", or for transfer to a customs bonded warehouse for storage therein pending exportation,". **Effective** 3-1-78.

• **1976, Tax Reform Act of 1976 (P.L. 94-455)**

P.L. 94-455, §1906(b)(13)(A):

Amended 1954 Code by substituting "Secretary" for "Secretary or his delegate" each place it appeared. **Effective** 2-1-77.

[Sec. 5175(b)]

(b) EXCEPTION WHERE PROPRIETOR WITHDRAWS SPIRITS FOR EXPORTATION.—In the case of distilled spirits withdrawn from bonded premises by the proprietor for exportation without payment of tax, the bond of such proprietor required to be furnished under paragraph (1) of section 5173(a) covering such premises shall cover such exportation, and subsection (a) shall not apply.

Sec. 5174—Repealed

ALCOHOL TAXES—DISTILLED SPIRITS PLANTS

Amendments

• **1979, Trade Agreements Act of 1979 (P.L. 96-39)**

P.L. 96-39, § 807(a)(15)(B):

Amended Code Sec. 5175(b). **Effective** 1-1-80. Prior to amendment, Code Sec. 5175(b) read as follows:

(b) EXCEPTION.—In case of distilled spirits withdrawn for exportation without payment of tax on application of the proprietor of bonded premises, the bond of such proprietor covering such bonded premises shall cover such exportation and subsection (a) shall not be applicable.

[Sec. 5175(c)]

(c) CANCELLATION OR CREDIT OF EXPORT BONDS.—The bonds given under subsection (a) shall be cancelled or credited and the bonds liable under subsection (b) credited if there is such proof of exportation as the Secretary may by regulations require.

Amendments

• **1997, Taxpayer Relief Act of 1997 (P.L. 105-34)**

P.L. 105-34, § 1412(a):

Amended Code Sec. 5175(c) by striking "on the submission of" and all that follows and inserting "if there is such proof of exportation as the Secretary may by regulations require.". **Effective** on the 1st day of the 1st calendar quarter that begins at least 180 days after 8-5-97. Prior to amendment, Code Sec. 5175(c) read as follows:

(c) CANCELLATION OR CREDIT OF EXPORT BONDS.—The bonds given under subsection (a) shall be cancelled or credited and the bonds liable under subsection (b) credited on the submission of such evidence, records, and certification indicating exportation as the Secretary may by regulations prescribe.

• **1976, Tax Reform Act of 1976 (P.L. 94-455)**

P.L. 94-455, § 1906(b)(13)(A):

Amended 1954 Code by substituting "Secretary" for "Secretary or his delegate" each place it appeared. **Effective** 2-1-77.

[Sec. 5176]

SEC. 5176. NEW OR RENEWED BONDS.

[Sec. 5176(a)]

(a) GENERAL.—New bonds shall be required under sections 5173 and 5175 in case of insolvency or removal of any surety, and may, at the discretion of the Secretary, be required in any other contingency affecting the validity or impairing the efficiency of such bond.

Amendments

• **1979, Trade Agreements Act of 1979 (P.L. 96-39)**

P.L. 96-39, § 807(a)(16)(A):

Amended Code Sec. 5176(a) by changing "sections 5173, 5174, and 5175" to "sections 5173, and 5175". **Effective** 1-1-80.

• **1976, Tax Reform Act of 1976 (P.L. 94-455)**

P.L. 94-455, § 1906(b)(13)(A):

Amended 1954 Code by substituting "Secretary" for "Secretary or his delegate" each place it appeared. **Effective** 2-1-77.

[Sec. 5176(b)]

(b) BONDS.—If the proprietor of a distilled spirits plant fails or refuses to furnish a bond required under paragraph (1) of section 5173(a) or to renew the same, and neglects to immediately withdraw the spirits and pay the tax thereon, the Secretary shall proceed to collect the tax.

Amendments

• **1979, Trade Agreements Act of 1979 (P.L. 96-39)**

P.L. 96-39, § 807(a)(16)(B):

Amended Code Sec. 5176(b). **Effective** 1-1-80. Prior to amendment, Code Sec. 5176(b) read as follows:

(b) BONDED WAREHOUSEMAN'S BONDS.—In case the proprietor of a distilled spirits plant fails or refuses—

(1) to give a warehouseman's bond required under section 5173(c), or to renew the same, and neglects to immediately withdraw the spirits and pay the tax thereon; or

(2) to withdraw any spirits from storage on bonded premises before the expiration of the time limited in the bond and, except as otherwise provided by law, pay the tax thereon;

the Secretary shall proceed to collect the tax.

• **1976, Tax Reform Act of 1976 (P.L. 94-455)**

P.L. 94-455, § 1906(b)(13)(A):

Amended 1954 Code by substituting "Secretary" for "Secretary or his delegate" each place it appeared. **Effective** 2-1-77.

[Sec. 5177]

SEC. 5177. OTHER PROVISIONS RELATING TO BONDS.

[Sec. 5177(a)]

(a) GENERAL PROVISIONS RELATING TO BONDS.—The provisions of section 5551 shall be applicable to the bonds required by or given under sections 5173, and 5175.

Amendments

• **1979, Trade Agreements Act of 1979 (P.L. 96-39)**

P.L. 96-39, § 807(a)(17):

Amended Code Sec. 5177(a) by changing "sections 5173, 5174, and 5175" to "sections 5173, and 5175". **Effective** 1-1-80.

[Sec. 5177(b)]

(b) CROSS REFERENCES.—

(1) For deposit of United States bonds or notes in lieu of sureties, see section 9303 of title 31, United States Code.

(2) For penalty and forfeiture for failure or refusal to give bond, or for giving false, forged, or fraudulent bond, or for carrying on the business of a distiller without giving bond, see sections 5601(a)(4), 5601(a)(5), 5601(b), and 5615(3).

Amendments

• **1982 (P.L. 97-258)**

P.L. 97-258, § 3(f)(3):

Amended Code Sec. 5177(b)(1) by striking out "6 U.S.C. 15" and substituting "section 9303 of title 31, United States Code". **Effective** 9-13-82.

• **1976, Tax Reform Act of 1976 (P.L. 94-455)**

P.L. 94-455, § 1905(b)(6)(B):

Substituted "5601(b)," for "5601(b)(2)," in Code Sec. 5177(b)(2). **Effective** 2-1-77.

[Sec. 5178]

SEC. 5178. PREMISES OF DISTILLED SPIRITS PLANTS.

[Sec. 5178(a)]

(a) LOCATION, CONSTRUCTION, AND ARRANGEMENT.—

(1) GENERAL.—

(A) The premises of a distilled spirits plant shall be as described in the application required by section 5171(c). The Secretary shall prescribe such regulations relating to the location, construction, arrangement, and protection of distilled spirits plants as he deems necessary to facilitate inspection and afford adequate security to the revenue.

(B) No distilled spirits plant for the production of distilled spirits shall be located in any dwelling house, in any shed, yard, or inclosure connected with any dwelling house, or on board any vessel or boat, or on premises where beer or wine is made or produced, or

ALCOHOL TAXES—DISTILLED SPIRITS PLANTS

liquors of any description are retailed, or on premises where any other business is carried on (except when authorized under subsection (b)).

(C) Notwithstanding any other provision of this chapter relating to distilled spirits plants the Secretary may approve the location, construction, arrangement, and method of operation of any establishment which was qualified to operate on the date preceding the effective date of this section if he deems that such location, construction, arrangement, and method of operation will afford adequate security to the revenue.

(2) PRODUCTION OPERATIONS.—

(A) Any person establishing a distilled spirits plant may, as described in his application for registration, produce distilled spirits from any source or substance.

(B) The distilling system shall be continuous and shall be so designed and constructed and so connected as to prevent the unauthorized removal of distilled spirits before their production gauge.

(C) The Secretary is authorized to order and require—

(i) such identification of, changes of, and additions to, distilling apparatus, connecting pipes, pumps, tanks, and any machinery connected with or used in or on the premises, and

(ii) such fastenings, locks, and seals to be part of any of the stills, tubs, pipes, tanks, and other equipment,

as he may deem necessary to facilitate inspection and afford adequate security to the revenue.

(3) WAREHOUSING OPERATIONS.—

(A) Any person establishing a distilled spirits plant for the production of distilled spirits may, as described in the application for registration, warehouse bulk distilled spirits on the bonded premises of such plant.

(B) Distilled spirits plants for the bonded warehousing of bulk distilled spirits elsewhere than as described in subparagraph (A) may be established at the discretion of the Secretary by proprietors referred to in subparagraph (A) or by other persons under such regulations as the Secretary shall prescribe.

(4) PROCESSING OPERATIONS.—Any person establishing a distilled spirits plant may, as described in the application for registration, process distilled spirits on the bonded premises of such plant.

Amendments

• **1979, Trade Agreements Act of 1979 (P.L. 96-39)**

P.L. 96-39, § 805(b)(1):

Deleted paragraphs (2), (3), (4), and (5) of Code Sec. 5178(a) and added new paragraphs (2), (3), and (4). **Effective** 1-1-80. Prior to amendment, paragraphs (2), (3), (4), and (5) of Code Sec. 5178(a) read as follows:

(2) PRODUCTION FACILITIES.—

(A) Any person establishing a distilled spirits plant may, as described in his application for registration, provide facilities which may be used for the production of distilled spirits from any source or substance.

(B) The distilling system shall be continuous and closed at all points where potable or readily recoverable spirits are present and the distilling apparatus shall be so designed and constructed and so connected as to prevent the unauthorized removal of such spirits prior to their production gauge.

(C) The Secretary is authorized to order and require such identification of, changes of, or additions to, distilling apparatus, connecting pipes, pumps, tanks, or any machinery connected with or used in or on the bonded premises, or require to be put on any of the stills, tubs, pipes, tanks, or other equipment, such fastenings, locks or seals as he may deem necessary to facilitate inspection and afford adequate security to the revenue.

(3) BONDED WAREHOUSING FACILITIES.—

(A) Any person establishing a distilled spirits plant for the production of distilled spirits may, as described in his application for registration, establish warehousing facilities on the bonded premises of such plant.

(B) Distilled spirits plants for the bonded warehousing of distilled spirits elsewhere than as described in subparagraph (A) may be established at the discretion of the Secretary, by proprietors referred to in subparagraph (A) or by other persons, under such regulations as the Secretary shall prescribe.

(C) Facilities for the storage on bonded premises of distilled spirits in casks, packages, cases, or similar portable approved containers shall be established in a room or building used exclusively for the storage, bottling, or packaging of distilled spirits, and activities related thereto.

(D) A proprietor who has established facilities for the storage on bonded premises of distilled spirits under subparagraph (C) may establish a portion of such premises as an export storage facility for the storage of distilled spirits returned to bonded premises under section 5215(b).

(4) BOTTLING FACILITIES.—

(A) The proprietor of a distilled spirits plant authorized to store distilled spirits in casks, packages, cases, or similar portable approved containers on bonded premises—

(i) may establish a separate portion of such premises for the bottling in bond of distilled spirits under section 5233 prior to payment or determination of tax, or

(ii) may elect to use facilities on his bottling premises established under subparagraph (B) or (C) for bottling in accordance with the conditions and requirements of section 5233 and under the supervision provided for in section 5202(g), but after determination of tax.

Distilled spirits bottled after determination of the internal revenue tax under clause (ii) shall be stamped and labeled in the same manner as distilled spirits bottled before determination of tax under clause (i).

(B) Facilities for rectification of distilled spirits or wines upon which the tax has been paid or determined, may be established as a separate distilled spirits plant or as a part of a distilled spirits plant qualified for the production or bonded warehousing of distilled spirits. Such facilities, when qualified, may be used for the rectification of distilled spirits or wines, or the bottling or packaging of rectified or unrectified distilled spirits or wines on which the tax has been paid or determined.

(C) Facilities for bottling or packaging any distilled spirits upon which the tax has been paid or determined (other than bottling facilities established under subparagraph (B)), may be established and maintained only by a State or political subdivision thereof, or by the proprietor of a distilled spirits plant qualified for the production or bonded warehousing of distilled spirits, as a part of such plant or as a separate distilled spirits plant. Such facilities, when qualified, may be used for the bottling or packaging of rectified or unrectified distilled spirits or wines but may not be used for the rectification of distilled spirits or wines.

(D) Bottling premises established under subparagraphs (B) or (C) may not be located on bonded premises, and if the distilled spirits plant contains both bonded premises and bottling premises they shall be separated by such means or in such manner as the Secretary may by regulations prescribe.

(5) DENATURING FACILITIES.—The Secretary may by regulations require such arrangement and segregation of denaturing facilities as he deems necessary.

P.L. 96-39, § 807(a)(18):

Amended Code Sec. 5178(a) by changing "section 5171(a)" to "section 5171(c)". **Effective** 1-1-80.

• **1977 (P.L. 95-176)**

P.L. 95-176, § 2(b):

Amended Code Sec. 5178(a)(3) by adding subparagraph (D). **Effective** 3-1-78.

• **1976, Tax Reform Act of 1976 (P.L. 94-455)**

P.L. 94-455, § 1906(b)(13)(A):

Amended 1954 Code by substituting "Secretary" for "Secretary or his delegate" each place it appeared. **Effective** 2-1-77.

• **1971 (P.L. 91-659)**

P.L. 91-659, § 5:

Amended Code Sec. 5178(a)(4)(A). **Effective** 5-1-71. Prior to amendment, the subparagraph read as follows:

"(A) The proprietor of a distilled spirits plant authorized to store distilled spirits in casks, packages, cases, or similar portable approved containers on bonded premises may establish a separate portion of such premises for the bottling in bond of distilled spirits under section 5233 prior to payment or determination of the internal revenue tax."

[Sec. 5178(b)]

(b) USE OF PREMISES FOR OTHER BUSINESSES.—The Secretary may authorize the carrying on of such other businesses (not specifically prohibited by section 5601(a)(6)) on premises of distilled spirits plants, as he finds will not jeopardize the revenue. Such other businesses shall not be carried on until an application to carry on such business has been made to and approved by the Secretary.

Amendments

• **1976, Tax Reform Act of 1976 (P.L. 94-455)**

P.L. 94-455, § 1906(b)(13)(A):

Amended 1954 Code by substituting "Secretary" for "Secretary or his delegate" each place it appeared. **Effective** 2-1-77.

ALCOHOL TAXES—DISTILLED SPIRITS PLANTS

[Sec. 5178(c)]

(c) CROSS REFERENCES.—
(1) For provisions authorizing the Secretary to require installation of meters, tanks, and other apparatus, see section 5552.
(2) For penalty for distilling on prohibited premises, see section 5601(a)(6).
(3) For provisions relating to the bottling of distilled spirits labeled as alcohol, see section 5235.
(4) For provisions relating to the unauthorized use of distilled spirits in any manufacturing process, see section 5601(a)(9).

Amendments

• **1976, Tax Reform Act of 1976 (P.L. 94-455)**

P.L. 94-455, § 1906(b)(13)(A):
Amended 1954 Code by substituting "Secretary" for "Secretary or his delegate" each place it appeared. **Effective** 2-1-77.

[Sec. 5179]

SEC. 5179. REGISTRATION OF STILLS.

[Sec. 5179(a)]

(a) REQUIREMENTS.—Every person having in his possession or custody, or under his control, any still or distilling apparatus set up, shall register such still or apparatus with the Secretary immediately on its being set up, by subscribing and filing with the Secretary a statement, in writing, setting forth the particular place where such still or distilling apparatus is set up, the kind of still and its capacity, the owner thereof, his place of residence, and the purpose for which said still or distilling apparatus has been or is intended to be used (except that stills or distilling apparatus not used or intended to be used for the distillation, redistillation, or recovery of distilled spirits are not required to be registered under this section).

Amendments

• **1976, Tax Reform Act of 1976 (P.L. 94-455)**

P.L. 94-455, § 1906(b)(13)(A):
Amended 1954 Code by substituting "Secretary" for "Secretary or his delegate" each place it appeared. **Effective** 2-1-77.

[Sec. 5179(b)]

(b) CROSS REFERENCES.—
(1) For penalty and forfeiture provisions relating to unregistered stills, see sections 5601(a)(1) and 5615(1).
(2) For provisions requiring notification to set up a still, boiler, or other vessel for distilling, see section 5101(a)(2).

Amendments

• **1984, Deficit Reduction Act of 1984 (P.L. 98-369)**

P.L. 98-369, § 451(b)(1):
Amended Code Sec. 5179(b)(2). **Effective** on the first day of the first calendar month which begins more than 90 days after 7-18-84. Prior to amendment, it read as follows:
For provisions requiring permit to set up still, boiler or other vessel for distilling, see section 5105.

• **1976, Tax Reform Act of 1976 (P.L. 94-455)**

P.L. 94-455, § 1905(b)(6)(C):
Struck out ", 5601(b)(1)," following "5601(a)(1)" in Code Sec. 5179(b)(1). **Effective** 2-1-77.

[Sec. 5180]

SEC. 5180. SIGNS.

[Sec. 5180(a)]

(a) REQUIREMENTS.—Every person engaged in distilled spirits operations shall place and keep conspicuously on the outside of his place of business a sign showing the name of such person and denoting the business, or businesses, in which engaged. The sign required by this subsection shall be in such form and contain such information as the Secretary shall by regulations prescribe.

Amendments

• **1979, Trade Agreements Act of 1979 (P.L. 96-39)**

P.L. 96-39, § 807(a)(19):
Amended Code Sec. 5180(a) by changing the first sentence. **Effective** 1-1-80. Prior to amendment, the first sentence read as follows:
"Every person engaged in distilling, bonded warehousing, rectifying, or bottling of distilled spirits shall place and keep conspicuously on the outside of his place of business a sign showing the name of such person and denoting the business, or businesses, in which engaged".

• **1976, Tax Reform Act of 1976 (P.L. 94-455)**

P.L. 94-455, § 1906(b)(13)(A):
Amended 1954 Code by substituting "Secretary" for "Secretary or his delegate" each place it appeared. **Effective** 2-1-77.

[Sec. 5180(b)]

(b) PENALTY.—
For penalty and forfeiture relating to failure to post sign or improperly posting such sign, see section 5681.

[Sec. 5181]

SEC. 5181. DISTILLED SPIRITS FOR FUEL USE.

[Sec. 5181(a)]

(a) IN GENERAL.—
(1) PURPOSES FOR WHICH PLANT MAY BE ESTABLISHED.—On such application and bond and in such manner as the Secretary may prescribe by regulation, a person may establish a distilled spirits plant solely for the purpose of—
(A) producing, processing, and storing, and
(B) using or distributing,
distilled spirits to be used exclusively for fuel use.

(2) REGULATIONS.—In prescribing regulations under paragraph (1) and in carrying out the provisions of this section, the Secretary shall, to the greatest extent possible, take steps to—
(A) expedite all applications;
(B) establish a minimum bond; and
(C) generally encourage and promote (through regulation or otherwise) the production of alcohol for fuel purposes.

Internal Revenue Code — Sec. 5181(a)(2)(C)

ALCOHOL TAXES—DISTILLED SPIRITS PLANTS

[Sec. 5181(b)]

(b) AUTHORITY TO EXEMPT.—The Secretary may by regulation provide for the waiver of any provision of this chapter (other than this section or any provision requiring the payment of tax) for any distilled spirits plant described in subsection (a) if the Secretary finds it necessary to carry out the provisions of this section.

[Sec. 5181(c)]

(c) SPECIAL RULES FOR SMALL PLANT PRODUCTION.—

(1) APPLICATIONS.—

(A) IN GENERAL.—An application for an operating permit for an eligible distilled spirits plant shall be in such a form and manner, and contain such information, as the Secretary may by regulations prescribe; except that the Secretary shall, to the greatest extent possible, take steps to simplify the application so as to expedite the issuance of such permits.

(B) RECEIPT OF APPLICATION.—Within 15 days of receipt of an application under subparagraph (A), the Secretary shall send a written notice of receipt to the applicant, together with a statement as to whether the application meets the requirements of subparagraph (A). If such a notice is not sent and the applicant has a receipt indicating that the Secretary has received an application, paragraph (2) shall apply as if a written notice required by the preceding sentence, together with a statement that the application meets the requirements of subparagraph (A), had been sent on the 15th day after the date the Secretary received the application.

(C) MULTIPLE APPLICATIONS.—If more than one application is submitted with respect to any eligible distilled spirits plant in any calendar quarter, the provisions of this section shall apply only to the first application submitted with respect to such plant during such quarter. For purposes of the preceding sentence, if a corrected or amended first application is filed, such application shall not be considered as a separate application, and the 15-day period referred to in subparagraph (A) shall commence with receipt of the corrected or amended application.

(2) DETERMINATION.—

(A) IN GENERAL.—In any case in which the Secretary under paragraph (1)(B) has notified an applicant of receipt of an application which meets the requirements of paragraph (1)(A), the Secretary shall make a determination as to whether such operating permit is to be issued, and shall notify the applicant of such determination, within 45 days of the date on which notice was sent under paragraph (1)(B).

(B) FAILURE TO MAKE DETERMINATION.—If the Secretary has not notified an applicant within the time prescribed under subparagraph (A), the application shall be treated as approved.

(C) REJECTION OF APPLICATION.—If the Secretary determines under subparagraph (A) that a permit should not be issued—

(i) the Secretary shall include in the notice to the applicant of such determination under subparagraph (A) detailed reasons for such determination, and

(ii) such determination shall not prejudice any further application for such operating permit.

(3) BOND.—No bond shall be required for an eligible distilled spirit plant. For purposes of section 5212 and subsection (e)(2) of this section, the premises of an eligible distilled spirits plant shall be treated as bonded premises.

(4) ELIGIBLE DISTILLED SPIRITS PLANT.—The term "eligible distilled spirits plant" means a plant which is used to produce distilled spirits exclusively for fuel use and the production from which does not exceed 10,000 proof gallons per year.

[Sec. 5181(d)]

(d) WITHDRAWAL FREE OF TAX.—Distilled spirits produced under this section may be withdrawn free of tax from the bonded premises (and any premises which are not bonded by reason of subsection (c)(3)) of a distilled spirits plant exclusively for fuel use as provided in section 5214(a)(12).

[Sec. 5181(e)]

(e) PROHIBITED WITHDRAWAL, USE, SALE, OR DISPOSITION.—

(1) IN GENERAL.—Distilled spirits produced under this section shall not be withdrawn, used, sold, or disposed of for other than fuel use.

(2) RENDERING UNFIT FOR USE.—For protection of the revenue and under such regulations as the Secretary may prescribe, distilled spirits produced under this section shall, before withdrawal from the bonded premises of a distilled spirits plant, be rendered unfit for beverage use by the addition of substances which will not impair the quality of the spirits for fuel use.

[Sec. 5181(f)]

(f) DEFINITION OF DISTILLED SPIRITS.—For purposes of this section, the term "distilled spirits" does not include distilled spirits produced from petroleum, natural gas, or coal.

Amendments

- **1980, Crude Oil Windfall Profit Tax Act of 1980 (P.L. 96-223)**

P.L. 96-223, §232(e)(1):

Added Code Sec. 5181. **Effective** 7-1-80.

[Sec. 5182]

SEC. 5182. CROSS REFERENCES.

For provisions requiring recordkeeping by wholesale liquor dealers, see section 5121, and by retail liquor dealers, see section 5122.

Amendments

- **2018, Tax Technical Corrections Act of 2018 (P.L. 115-141)**

P.L. 115-141, §401(a)(243), Div. U:

Amended Code Sec. 5182 by striking "section 5112" and inserting "section 5121". **Effective** 3-23-2018.

- **2005, Safe, Accountable, Flexible, Efficient Transportation Equity Act: A Legacy for Users (P.L. 109-59)**

P.L. 109-59, §11125(b)(16):

Amended the text of Code Sec. 5182. **Effective** 7-1-2008, but not applicable to taxes imposed for periods before such date. Prior to amendment, the text of Code Sec. 5182 read as follows:

For provisions requiring payment of special (occupational) tax as wholesale liquor dealer, see section 5111, or as retail liquor dealer, see section 5121.

- **1980, Crude Oil Windfall Profit Tax Act of 1980 (P.L. 96-223)**

P.L. 96-223, §232(e)(1):

Redesignated Code Sec. 5181 as Code Sec. 5182. **Effective** 7-1-80.

- **1979, Trade Agreements Act of 1979 (P.L. 96-39)**

P.L. 96-39, §807(a)(20):

Amended Code Sec. 5181 by changing "tax as rectifier, see section 5081, or as wholesale liquor dealer" to "tax as wholesale liquor dealer". **Effective** 1-1-80.

Subchapter C—Operation of Distilled Spirits Plants

Part I.	General provisions.
Part II.	Operations on bonded premises.
Part III.	[Repealed.]

ALCOHOL TAXES—DISTILLED SPIRITS PLANTS

PART I—GENERAL PROVISIONS

Sec. 5201.   Regulation of operations.
Sec. 5202.   Supervision of operations.
Sec. 5203.   Entry and examination of premises.
Sec. 5204.   Gauging.
Sec. 5206.   Containers.
Sec. 5207.   Records and reports.

[Sec. 5201]

SEC. 5201. REGULATION OF OPERATIONS.

[Sec. 5201(a)]

(a) IN GENERAL.—Proprietors of distilled spirits plants shall conduct all operations authorized to be conducted on the premises of such plants under such regulations as the Secretary shall prescribe.

Amendments

• **1979, Trade Agreements Act of 1979 (P.L. 96-39)**

P.L. 96-39, §807(a)(21):

Amended Code Sec. 5201(a). **Effective** 1-1-80. Prior to amendment, Code Sec. 5201(a) read as follows:

(a) GENERAL.—Proprietors of distilled spirits plants shall conduct their operations relating to the production, storage, denaturing, rectification, and bottling of distilled spirits, and all other operations authorized to be conducted on the premises of such plants, under such regulations as the Secretary shall prescribe.

• **1976, Tax Reform Act of 1976 (P.L. 94-455)**

P.L. 94-455, §1906(b)(13)(A):

Amended 1954 Code by substituting "Secretary" for "Secretary or his delegate" each place it appeared. **Effective** 2-1-77.

[Sec. 5201(b)]

(b) DISTILLED SPIRITS FOR INDUSTRIAL USES.—The regulations of the Secretary under this chapter respecting the production, warehousing, denaturing, distribution, sale, export, and use of distilled spirits for industrial purposes shall be such as he deems necessary, advisable, or proper to secure the revenue, to prevent diversion to illegal uses, and to place the distilled spirits industry and other industries using such distilled spirits as a chemical raw material or for other lawful industrial purposes on the highest possible plane of scientific and commercial efficiency and development consistent with the provisions of this chapter. Where nonpotable chemical mixtures containing distilled spirits are produced for transfer to the bonded premises of a distilled spirits plant for completion of processing, the Secretary may waive any provision of this chapter with respect to the production of such mixtures, and the processing of such mixtures on the bonded premises shall be deemed to be production of distilled spirits for purposes of this chapter.

Amendments

• **1976, Tax Reform Act of 1976 (P.L. 94-455)**

P.L. 94-455, §1906(b)(13)(A):

Amended 1954 Code by substituting "Secretary" for "Secretary or his delegate" each place it appeared. **Effective** 2-1-77.

[Sec. 5201(c)]

(c) HOURS OF OPERATIONS.—The Secretary may prescribe regulations relating to hours for distillery operations and to hours for removal of distilled spirits from distilled spirits plants; however, such regulations shall not be more restrictive, as to any operation or function, than the provisions of internal revenue law and regulations relating to such operation or function in effect on the day preceding the effective date of this section.

Amendments

• **1976, Tax Reform Act of 1976 (P.L. 94-455)**

P.L. 94-455, §1906(b)(13)(A):

Amended 1954 Code by substituting "Secretary" for "Secretary or his delegate" each place it appeared. **Effective** 2-1-77.

[Sec. 5201(d)]

(d) IDENTIFICATION OF DISTILLED SPIRITS.—The Secretary may provide by regulations for the addition of tracer elements to distilled spirits to facilitate the enforcement of this chapter. Tracer elements to be added to distilled spirits at any distilled spirits plant under provisions of this subsection shall be of such character and in such quantity as the Secretary may authorize or require, and such as will not impair the quality of the distilled spirits for their intended use.

Amendments

• **1976, Tax Reform Act of 1976 (P.L. 94-455)**

P.L. 94-455, §1906(b)(13)(A):

Amended 1954 Code by substituting "Secretary" for "Secretary or his delegate" each place it appeared. **Effective** 2-1-77.

[Sec. 5202]

SEC. 5202. SUPERVISION OF OPERATIONS.

All operations on the premises of a distilled spirits plant shall be conducted under such supervision and controls (including the use of Government locks and seals) as the Secretary shall by regulations prescribe.

Amendments

• **1979, Trade Agreements Act of 1979 (P.L. 96-39)**

P.L. 96-39, §806(a):

Amended Code Sec. 5202. **Effective** 1-1-80. Prior to amendment, Code Sec. 5202 read as follows:

SEC. 5202. SUPERVISION OF OPERATIONS.

(a) GENERAL.—The operations on the premises of distilled spirits plants shall be conducted under such supervision as the Secretary shall by regulation prescribe. The Secretary shall assign such number of internal revenue officers to distilled spirits plants as he deems necessary to maintain supervision of the operations conducted on such premises.

(b) REMOVAL OF DISTILLED SPIRITS FROM DISTILLING SYSTEM.—The removal of distilled spirits from the closed distilling system shall be controlled by Government locks or seals, or by meters or other devices or methods as the Secretary may prescribe.

(c) STORAGE TANKS.—Approved containers for the storage of distilled spirits on bonded premises (other than containers required by subsection (d) to be in a locked room or building or those containing distilled spirits denatured as authorized by law) shall be kept securely closed, and the flow of distilled spirits into and out of such containers shall be controlled by Government locks or seals, or by meters or other devices or methods as the Secretary may prescribe.

(d) STORAGE ROOMS OR BUILDINGS.—Distilled spirits (other than denatured distilled spirits) on bonded premises in casks, packages, cases, or similar portable approved containers must be stored in a room or building provided as required by section

ALCOHOL TAXES—DISTILLED SPIRITS PLANTS

5178(a)(3)(C), which room or building shall be in the joint custody of the internal revenue officer assigned to such premises and the proprietor thereof, and shall be kept securely locked with Government locks and at no time be unlocked or opened, or remain open, except when such officer or person who may be designated to act for him is on the premises. Deposits of distilled spirits in, or removals of distilled spirits from, such room or building shall be under such supervision by internal revenue officers as the Secretary shall by regulations prescribe.

(e) DENATURATION OF DISTILLED SPIRITS.—The denaturation of distilled spirits on bonded premises shall be conducted under such supervision and controlled by such meters or other devices or methods as the Secretary shall prescribe.

(f) GAUGING.—The gauge of production of distilled spirits, gauge for determination of the tax imposed under section 5001(a)(1), and gauge for tax-free removal of other than denatured distilled spirits from bonded premises, shall be made or supervised by internal revenue officers, under such regulations as the Secretary shall prescribe.

(g) BOTTLING IN BOND.—The bottling of distilled spirits in bond shall be supervised by the internal revenue officer assigned to the premises in such manner as the Secretary shall by regulations prescribe.

- **1976, Tax Reform Act of 1976 (P.L. 94-455)**

P.L. 94-455, §1906(b)(13)(A):

Amended 1954 Code by substituting "Secretary" for "Secretary or his delegate" each place it appeared. **Effective** 2-1-77.

[Sec. 5203]

SEC. 5203. ENTRY AND EXAMINATION OF PREMISES.

[Sec. 5203(a)]

(a) KEEPING PREMISES ACCESSIBLE.—Every proprietor of a distilled spirits plant shall furnish the Secretary such keys as may be required for internal revenue officers to gain access to the premises and any structures thereon, and such premises shall always be kept accessible to any officer having such keys.

Amendments
- **1976, Tax Reform Act of 1976 (P.L. 94-455)**

P.L. 94-455, §1906(b)(13)(A):

Amended 1954 Code by substituting "Secretary" for "Secretary or his delegate" each place it appeared. **Effective** 2-1-77.

[Sec. 5203(b)]

(b) RIGHT OF ENTRY AND EXAMINATION.—It shall be lawful for any internal revenue officer at all times, as well by night as by day, to enter any distilled spirits plant, or any other premises where distilled spirits operations are carried on, or structure or place used in connection therewith for storage or other purposes; to make examination of the materials, equipment, and facilities thereon; and make such gauges and inventories as he deems necessary. Whenever any officer, having demanded admittance, and having declared his name and office, is not admitted into such premises by the proprietor or other person having charge thereof, it shall be lawful for such officer, at all times, as well by night as by day, to use such force as is necessary for him to gain entry to such premises.

Amendments
- **1979, Trade Agreements Act of 1979 (P.L. 96-39)**

P.L. 96-39, §807(a)(22)(A):

Amended Code Sec. 5203(b) by changing "where distilled spirits are produced or rectified" to "where distilled spirits operations are carried on". **Effective** 1-1-80.

[Sec. 5203(c)]

(c) FURNISHING FACILITIES AND ASSISTANCE.—On the demand of any internal revenue officer or agent, every proprietor of a distilled spirits plant shall furnish the necessary facilities and assistance to enable the officer or agent to gauge the spirits in any container or to examine any apparatus, equipment, containers, or materials on such premises. Such proprietor shall also, on demand of such officer or agent, open all doors, and open for examination all boxes, packages, and all casks, barrels, and other vessels on such premises.

Amendments
- **1979, Trade Agreements Act of 1979 (P.L. 96-39)**

P.L. 96-39, §807(a)(22)(B):

Amended Code Sec. 5203(c) by changing "not under the control of the internal revenue officer in charge" to "on such premises". **Effective** 1-1-80.

[Sec. 5203(d)]

(d) AUTHORITY TO BREAK UP GROUNDS OR WALLS.—It shall be lawful for any internal revenue officer, and any person acting in his aid, to break up the ground on any part of a distilled spirits plant or any other premises where distilled spirits operations are carried on, or any ground adjoining or near to such plant or premises, or any wall or partition thereof, or belonging thereto, or other place, to search for any pipe, cock, private conveyance, or utensil; and, upon finding any such pipe or conveyance leading therefrom or thereto, to break up any ground, house, wall, or other place through or into which such pipe or other conveyance leads, and to break or cut away such pipe or other conveyance, and turn any cock, or to examine whether such pipe or other conveyance conveys or conceals any distilled spirits, mash, wort, or beer, or other liquor, from the sight or view of the officer, so as to prevent or hinder him from taking a true account thereof.

Amendments
- **1979, Trade Agreements Act of 1979 (P.L. 96-39)**

P.L. 96-39, §807(a)(22)(C):

Amended Code Sec. 5203(d) by changing "where distilled spirits are produced or rectified" to "where distilled spirits operations are carried on". **Effective** 1-1-80.

[Sec. 5203(e)]

(e) PENALTY.—

For penalty for violation of this section, see section 5687.

[Sec. 5204]

SEC. 5204. GAUGING.

[Sec. 5204(a)]

(a) GENERAL.—The Secretary may by regulations require the gauging of distilled spirits for such purposes as he may deem necessary, and all required gauges shall be made at such times and under such conditions as he may by regulations prescribe.

Amendments
- **1979, Trade Agreements Act of 1979 (P.L. 96-39)**

P.L. 96-39, §807(a)(23):

Amended Code Sec. 5204(a) by changing "gauging of distilled spirits for such purposes, in addition to those specified in section 5202(f), as he may deem necessary" to "gauging of distilled spirits for such purposes as he may deem necessary". **Effective** 1-1-80.

- **1976, Tax Reform Act of 1976 (P.L. 94-455)**

P.L. 94-455, §1906(b)(13)(A):

Amended 1954 Code by substituting "Secretary" for "Secretary or his delegate" each place it appeared. **Effective** 2-1-77.

ALCOHOL TAXES—DISTILLED SPIRITS PLANTS

[Sec. 5204(b)]

(b) GAUGING INSTRUMENTS.—For the determination of tax and the prevention and detection of frauds, the Secretary may prescribe for use such hydrometers, saccharometers, weighing and gauging instruments, or other means or methods for ascertaining the quantity, gravity, and producing capacity of any mash, wort, or beer used, or to be used, in the production of distilled spirits, and the strength and quantity of spirits subject to tax, as he may deem necessary; and he may prescribe regulations to secure a uniform and correct system of inspection, weighing, marking, and gauging of spirits.

Amendments

• **1976, Tax Reform Act of 1976 (P.L. 94-455)**

P.L. 94-455, §1906(b)(13)(A):

Amended 1954 Code by substituting "Secretary" for "Secretary or his delegate" each place it appeared. **Effective** 2-1-77.

[Sec. 5204(c)]

(c) GAUGING, MARKING AND BRANDING BY PROPRIETORS.—The Secretary may by regulations require the proprietor of a distilled spirits plant, at the proprietor's expense and under such supervision as the Secretary may require, to do such gauging, marking, and branding and such mechanical labor pertaining thereto as the Secretary deems proper and determines may be done without danger to the revenue.

Amendments

• **1984, Deficit Reduction Act of 1984 (P.L. 98-369)**

P.L. 98-369, §454(c)(4):

Amended Code Sec. 5204(c) by striking out "Stamping" in the heading and "stamping," in the text. **Effective** 7-1-85.

• **1976, Tax Reform Act of 1976 (P.L. 94-455)**

P.L. 94-455, §1906(b)(13)(A):

Amended 1954 Code by substituting "Secretary" for "Secretary or his delegate" each place it appeared. **Effective** 2-1-77.

[Sec. 5205—Repealed]

Amendments

• **1984, Deficit Reduction Act of 1984 (P.L. 98-369)**

P.L. 98-369, §454(a):

Repealed Code Sec. 5205. **Effective** 7-1-85. Prior to repeal, Code Sec. 5205 read as follows:

SEC. 5205. STAMPS.

[Sec. 5205(a)]

(a) STAMPS FOR CONTAINERS OF DISTILLED SPIRITS.—

(1) CONTAINERS OF DISTILLED SPIRITS.—No person shall transport, possess, buy, sell, or transfer any distilled spirits, unless the immediate container thereof is stamped by a stamp evidencing the determination of the tax or indicating compliance with the provisions of this chapter. The provisions of this paragraph shall not apply to—

(A) distilled spirits, lawfully withdrawn from bond, placed in containers for immediate consumption on the premises or for preparation for such consumption;

(B) distilled spirits in bond or in customs custody;

(C) distilled spirits, lawfully withdrawn from bond, in immediate containers stamped under other provisions of internal revenue or customs law or regulations issued pursuant thereto;

(D) distilled spirits on which no internal revenue tax is required to be paid;

(E) distilled spirits lawfully withdrawn from bond and not intended for sale or for use in the manufacture or production of any article intended for sale; or

(F) any regularly established common carrier receiving, transporting, delivering, or holding for transportation or delivery distilled spirits in the ordinary course of its business as a common carrier.

(2) STAMP REGULATIONS.—The Secretary shall prescribe regulations with respect to the supplying or procuring of stamps required under this subsection or section 5235, the time and manner of applying for, issuing, affixing, and destroying such stamps, the form of such stamps and the information to be shown thereon, applications for the stamps, proof that applicants are entitled to such stamps, and the method of accounting for such stamps, and such other regulations as he may deem necessary for the enforcement of this subsection. In the case of a container of a capacity of 5 wine gallons or less, the stamp shall be affixed in such a manner as to be broken when the container is opened, unless the container is one that cannot again be used after opening.

Amendments

• **1979, Trade Agreements Act of 1979 (P.L. 96-39)**

P.L. 96-39, §807(a)(24)(A), (B):

Amended Code Sec. 5205(a). **Effective** 1-1-80. Prior to amendment, Code Sec. 5205(a) read as follows:

(a) STAMPS FOR CONTAINERS OF DISTILLED SPIRITS.—

(1) CONTAINERS OF DISTILLED SPIRITS BOTTLED IN BOND.—Every container of distilled spirits bottled in bond under section 5233 when filled shall be stamped by a stamp evidencing the bottling of such spirits in bond under the provisions of this paragraph and section 5233.

(2) CONTAINERS OF OTHER DISTILLED SPIRITS.—No person shall transport, possess, buy, sell, or transfer any distilled spirits, unless the immediate container thereof is stamped by a stamp evidencing the determination of the tax or indicating compliance with the provisions of this chapter. The provisions of this paragraph shall not apply to—

(A) distilled spirits, lawfully withdrawn from bond, placed in containers for immediate consumption on the premises or for preparation for such consumption;

(B) distilled spirits in bond or in customs custody;

(C) distilled spirits, lawfully withdrawn from bond, in immediate containers stamped under other provisions of internal revenue or customs law or regulations issued pursuant thereto;

(D) distilled spirits, lawfully withdrawn from bond, in actual process of rectification, blending, or bottling, or in actual use in processes of manufacture;

(E) distilled spirits on which no internal revenue tax is required to be paid;

(F) distilled spirits lawfully withdrawn from bond and not intended for sale or for use in the manufacture or production of any article intended for sale; or

(G) any regularly established common carrier receiving, transporting, delivering, or holding for transportation or delivery distilled spirits in the ordinary course of its business as a common carrier.

(3) STAMP REGULATIONS.—The Secretary shall prescribe regulations with respect to the supplying or procuring of stamps required under this subsection or section 5235, the time and manner of applying for, issuing, affixing, and destroying such stamps, the form of such stamps and the information to be shown thereon, applications for the stamps, proof that applicants are entitled to such stamps, and the method of accounting for such stamps, and such other regulations as he may deem necessary for the enforcement of this subsection. In the case of a container of a capacity of 5 wine gallons or less, the stamp shall be affixed in such a manner as to be broken when the container is opened, unless the container is one that cannot again be used after opening.

• **1976, Tax Reform Act of 1976 (P.L. 94-455)**

P.L. 94-455, §1906(b)(13)(A):

Amended 1954 Code by substituting "Secretary" for "Secretary or his delegate" each place it appeared. **Effective** 2-1-77.

[Sec. 5205(b)]

(b) STAMPS FOR CONTAINERS OF DISTILLED SPIRITS WITHDRAWN FROM BONDED PREMISES ON DETERMINATION OF TAX.—Containers of all distilled spirits withdrawn from bonded premises on determination of tax under section 5006(a) shall be stamped by a stamp under such regulations as the Secretary shall prescribe. This subsection shall not be construed to require stamps on cases of bottled distilled spirits filled and stamped on bonded premises.

Amendments

• **1976, Tax Reform Act of 1976 (P.L. 94-455)**

P.L. 94-455, §1906(b)(13)(A):

Amended 1954 Code by substituting "Secretary" for "Secretary or his delegate" each place it appeared. **Effective** 2-1-77.

[Sec. 5205(c)]

(c) STAMPS FOR CONTAINERS OF DISTILLED SPIRITS WITHDRAWN FOR EXPORTATION.—

(1) EXPORTATION WITHOUT PAYMENT OF TAX.—Every container of distilled spirits withdrawn for exportation under section 5214(a)(4) shall be stamped by a stamp under such regulations as the Secretary shall prescribe. This paragraph shall not be construed to require stamps on cases of bottled distilled spirits filled and stamped on bonded premises.

(2) EXPORTATION WITH BENEFIT OF DRAWBACK.—The Secretary may require any container of distilled spirits bottled or packaged especially for export with benefit of drawback to be stamped by a stamp under such regulations as he may prescribe.

Amendments

• **1979, Trade Agreements Act of 1979 (P.L. 96-39)**

P.L. 96-39, §807(a)(24)(C):

Amended Code Sec. 5205(c) by deleting the last sentence. **Effective** 1-1-80. Prior to deletion, the last sentence read as follows: "This paragraph shall also apply to every container of distilled spirits returned to the bonded premises under the provisions of section 5215(b)."

• **1977 (P.L. 95-176)**

P.L. 95-176, §2(c):

Amended Code Sec. 5205(c) by adding the last sentence thereof. **Effective** 3-1-78.

• **1976, Tax Reform Act of 1976 (P.L. 94-455)**

P.L. 94-455, §1906(b)(13)(A):

Amended 1954 Code by substituting "Secretary" for "Secretary or his delegate" each place it appeared. **Effective** 2-1-77.

[Sec. 5205(d)]

(d) ISSUE FOR RESTAMPING.—The Secretary, under regulations prescribed by him, may authorize restamping of containers of distilled spirits which have been duly

ALCOHOL TAXES—DISTILLED SPIRITS PLANTS

stamped but from which the stamps have been lost or destroyed by unavoidable accident.

Amendments

• **1979, Trade Agreements Act of 1979 (P.L. 96-39)**

P.L. 96-39, § 807(a)(24)(D):

Deleted Code Sec. 5205(d) and redesignated Code Sec. 5205(e) as Code Sec. 5205(d). **Effective** 1-1-80. Prior to deletion, Code Sec. 5205(d) read as follows:

(d) STAMPS FOR CONTAINERS OF 5 WINE GALLONS OR MORE OF DISTILLED SPIRITS FILLED ON BOTTLING PREMISES.—All containers of distilled spirits containing 5 wine gallons or more, which are filled on bottling premises of a distilled spirits plant for removal therefrom, shall be stamped by a stamp under such regulations as the Secretary shall prescribe.

• **1976, Tax Reform Act of 1976 (P.L. 94-455)**

P.L. 94-455, § 1906(b)(13)(A):

Amended 1954 Code by substituting "Secretary" for "Secretary or his delegate" each place it appeared. **Effective** 2-1-77.

[Sec. 5205(e)]

(e) ACCOUNTABILITY.—All stamps relating to distilled spirits shall be used and accounted for under such regulations as the Secretary may prescribe.

Amendments

• **1979, Trade Agreements Act of 1979 (P.L. 96-39)**

P.L. 96-39, § 807(a)(24)(D):

Redesignated Code Sec. 5205(f) as Code Sec. 5205(e). **Effective** 1-1-80.

• **1976, Tax Reform Act of 1976 (P.L. 94-455)**

P.L. 94-455, § 1906(b)(13)(A):

Amended 1954 Code by substituting "Secretary" for "Secretary or his delegate" each place it appeared. **Effective** 2-1-77.

[Sec. 5205(f)]

(f) EFFACEMENT OF STAMPS, MARKS, AND BRANDS ON EMPTIED CONTAINERS.—Every person who empties, or causes to be emptied, any immediate container of distilled spirits bearing any stamp, mark, or brand required by law or regulations prescribed pursuant thereto (other than containers stamped under subsection (a) or section 5235) shall at the time of emptying such container efface and obliterate such stamp, mark, or brand, except that the Secretary may, by regulations, waive any requirement of this subsection as to the effacement or obliteration of marks or brands (or portions thereof) where he determines that no jeopardy to the revenue will be involved.

Amendments

• **1979, Trade Agreements Act of 1979 (P.L. 96-39)**

P.L. 96-39, § 807(a)(24)(D):

Redesignated Code Sec. 5205(g) as Code Sec. 5205(f). **Effective** 1-1-80.

• **1976, Tax Reform Act of 1976 (P.L. 94-455)**

P.L. 94-455, § 1906(b)(13)(A):

Amended 1954 Code by substituting "Secretary" for "Secretary or his delegate" each place it appeared. **Effective** 2-1-77.

[Sec. 5205(g)]

(g) FORM OF STAMP.—Any stamp required by or prescribed pursuant to the provisions of this section or section 5235 may consist of such coupon, seriallynumbered ticket, imprint, design, other form of stamp, or other device as the Secretary shall by regulations prescribe.

Amendments

• **1979, Trade Agreements Act of 1979 (P.L. 96-39)**

P.L. 96-39, § 807(a)(24)(D):

Redesignated Code Sec. 5205(h) as Code Sec. 5205(g). **Effective** 1-1-80.

• **1977 (P.L. 94-569)**

P.L. 94-569, § [1]:

Amended Code Sec. 5205(h) by substituting "other form of stamp, or other device" for "or other form of stamp". **Effective** for months after October 1976.

• **1976, Tax Reform Act of 1976 (P.L. 94-455)**

P.L. 94-455, § 1906(b)(13)(A):

Amended 1954 Code by substituting "Secretary" for "Secretary or his delegate" each place it appeared. **Effective** 2-1-77.

[Sec. 5205(h)]

(h) CROSS REFERENCES.—

(1) For general provisions relating to stamps, see chapter 69.

(2) For provisions relating to the stamping, marking, and branding of containers of distilled spirits by proprietors, see section 5204(c).

(3) For provisions relating to the stamping of bottled alcohol, see section 5235.

(4) For penalties and forfeitures relating to stamps, marks, and brands, see sections 5604, 5613, 7208, and 7209.

Amendments

• **1979, Trade Agreements Act of 1979 (P.L. 96-39)**

P.L. 96-39, § 807(a)(24)(D):

Redesignated Code Sec. 5205(i) as Code Sec. 5205(h), deleted paragraph (4) and redesignated paragraph (5) as paragraph (4). **Effective** 1-1-80. Prior to deletion, former paragraph (4) read as follows:

(4) For authority of the Secretary to prescribe regulations regarding stamps for distilled spirits withdrawn to manufacturing bonded warehouses, see section 5522(a).

• **1976, Tax Reform Act of 1976 (P.L. 94-455)**

P.L. 94-455, § 1906(b)(13)(A):

Amended 1954 Code by substituting "Secretary" for "Secretary or his delegate" each place it appeared. **Effective** 2-1-77.

[Sec. 5206]

SEC. 5206. CONTAINERS.

[Sec. 5206(a)]

(a) AUTHORITY TO PRESCRIBE.—The Secretary shall by regulations prescribe the types or kinds of containers which may be used to contain, store, transfer, convey, remove, or withdraw distilled spirits.

Amendments

• **1976, Tax Reform Act of 1976 (P.L. 94-455)**

P.L. 94-455, § 1906(b)(13)(A):

Amended 1954 Code by substituting "Secretary" for "Secretary or his delegate" each place it appeared. **Effective** 2-1-77.

[Sec. 5206(b)]

(b) STANDARDS OF FILL.—The Secretary may by regulations prescribe the standards of fill for approved containers.

Amendments

• **1976, Tax Reform Act of 1976 (P.L. 94-455)**

P.L. 94-455, § 1906(b)(13)(A):

Amended 1954 Code by substituting "Secretary" for "Secretary or his delegate" each place it appeared. **Effective** 2-1-77.

[Sec. 5206(c)]

(c) MARKING, BRANDING, OR IDENTIFICATION.—Containers of distilled spirits (and cases containing bottles or other containers of such spirits) shall be marked, branded, or identified in such manner as the Secretary shall by regulations prescribe.

Amendments

• **1976, Tax Reform Act of 1976 (P.L. 94-455)**

P.L. 94-455, § 1906(b)(13)(A):

Amended 1954 Code by substituting "Secretary" for "Secretary or his delegate" each place it appeared. **Effective** 2-1-77.

[Sec. 5206(d)]

(d) EFFACEMENT OF MARKS AND BRANDS ON EMPTIED CONTAINERS.—Every person who empties, or causes to be emptied, any container of distilled spirits bearing any mark or brand required by law (or regulations pursuant thereto) shall at the time of emptying such container efface and

ALCOHOL TAXES—DISTILLED SPIRITS PLANTS

obliterate such mark or brand; except that the Secretary may, by regulations, waive any requirement of this subsection where he determines that no jeopardy to the revenue will be involved.

Amendments

• **1984, Deficit Reduction Act of 1984 (P.L. 98-369)**

P.L. 98-369, §454(c)(5)(A):

Amended Code Sec. 5206 by redesignating subsections (d) and (e) as subsections (e) and (f), respectively, and by inserting after subsection (c) new subsection (d). **Effective** 7-1-85.

[Sec. 5206(e)]

(e) APPLICABILITY.—This section shall be applicable exclusively with respect to containers of distilled spirits for industrial use, with respect to containers of distilled spirits of a capacity of more than one gallon for other than industrial use, and with respect to cases containing bottles or other containers of distilled spirits.

Amendments

• **1984, Deficit Reduction Act of 1984 (P.L. 98-369)**

P.L. 98-369, §454(c)(5)(A):

Amended Code Sec. 5206 by redesignating subsections (d) and (e) as subsections (e) and (f), respectively. **Effective** 7-1-85.

[Sec. 5206(f)]

(f) CROSS REFERENCES.—

(1) For other provisions relating to regulation of containers of distilled spirits, see section 5301.

(2) For provisions relating to labeling containers of distilled spirits of one gallon or less for nonindustrial uses, see section 105(e) of the Federal Alcohol Administration Act (27 U. S. C. 205(e)).

(3) For provisions relating to the marking and branding of containers of distilled spirits by proprietors, see section 5204(c).

(4) For penalties and forfeitures relating to marks and brands, see sections 5604 and 5613.

Amendments

• **1996, Small Business Job Protection Act of 1996 (P.L. 104-188)**

P.L. 104-188, §1704(t)(13):

Amended Code Sec. 5206(f)(2) by striking "section 5(e)" and inserting "section 105(e)". **Effective** 8-20-96.

• **1984, Deficit Reduction Act of 1984 (P.L. 98-369)**

P.L. 98-369, §454(c)(5)(A):

Amended Code Sec. 5206 by redesignating subsections (d) and (e) as subsections (e) and (f), respectively. **Effective** 7-1-85.

P.L. 98-369, §454(c)(5)(B):

Amended Code Sec. 5206(f), as redesignated by Act Sec. 454(c)(5)(A), by adding new subparagraphs (3) and (4). **Effective** 7-1-85.

[Sec. 5207]

SEC. 5207. RECORDS AND REPORTS.

[Sec. 5207(a)]

(a) RECORDS OF DISTILLED SPIRITS PLANT PROPRIETORS.—Every distilled spirits plant proprietor shall keep records in such form and manner as the Secretary shall by regulations prescribe of:

(1) The following production activities—
  (A) the receipt of materials intended for use in the production of distilled spirits, and the use thereof,
  (B) the receipt and use of distilled spirits received for redistillation, and
  (C) the kind and quantity of distilled spirits produced.

(2) The following storage activities—
  (A) the kind and quantity of distilled spirits, wines, and alcoholic ingredients entered into storage,
  (B) the kind and quantity of distilled spirits, wines, and alcoholic ingredients removed, and the purpose for which removed, and
  (C) the kind and quantity of distilled spirits returned to storage.

(3) The following denaturation activities—
  (A) the kind and quantity of denaturants received and used or otherwise disposed of,
  (B) the kind and quantity of distilled spirits denatured, and
  (C) the kind and quantity of denatured distilled spirits removed.

(4) The following processing activities—
  (A) all distilled spirits, wines, and alcoholic ingredients received or transferred,
  (B) the kind and quantity of distilled spirits packaged or bottled, and
  (C) the kind and quantity of distilled spirits removed from his premises.

(5) Such additional information with respect to activities described in paragraphs (1), (2), (3), and (4), and with respect to other activities, as may by regulations be required.

Amendments

• **1984, Deficit Reduction Act of 1984 (P.L. 98-369)**

P.L. 98-369, §454(c)(6):

Amended Code Sec. 5207(a)(4) by striking out subparagraph (D), by adding "and" at the end of subparagraph (B), and by striking out ", and" at the end of subparagraph (C) and inserting in lieu thereof a period. **Effective** 7-1-85. Prior to amendment, subparagraph (D) read as follows:

(D) the receipt, use, and balance on hand of all stamps required by law or regulations to be used by him.

• **1979, Trade Agreements Act of 1979 (P.L. 96-39)**

P.L. 96-39, §807(a)(25):

Amended Code Sec. 5207(a). **Effective** 1-1-80. Prior to amendment, Code Sec. 5207(a) read as follows:

(a) RECORDS OF DISTILLERS AND BONDED WAREHOUSEMEN.—Every distiller and every bonded warehouseman shall keep records in such form and manner as the Secretary shall by regulations prescribe of—

(1) the receipt of materials intended for use in the production of distilled spirits, and the use thereof,

(2) the receipt and use of distilled spirits received for redistillation,

(3) the kind and quantity of distilled spirits produced,

(4) the kind and quantity of distilled spirits entered into storage,

(5) the bottling of distilled spirits in bond,

(6) the kind and quantity of distilled spirits removed from bonded premises, and from any taxpaid storeroom operated in connection therewith, and the purpose for which removed,

(7) the kind and quantity of denaturants received and used or otherwise disposed of,

(8) the kind and quantity of distilled spirits denatured,

(9) the kind and quantity of denatured distilled spirits removed,

(10) the kind and quantity of distilled spirits returned to bonded premises, and

(11) such additional information as may by regulations be required.

ALCOHOL TAXES—DISTILLED SPIRITS PLANTS

- **1977 (P.L. 95-176)**

P.L. 95-176, § 2(e):

Amended Code Sec. 5207(a) by deleting "and" at the end of paragraph (9), by redesignating paragraph (10) and (11) and by adding a new paragraph (10). **Effective** 3-1-78.

- **1976, Tax Reform Act of 1976 (P.L. 94-455)**

P.L. 94-455, § 1906(b)(13)(A):

Amended 1954 Code by substituting "Secretary" for "Secretary or his delegate" each place it appeared. **Effective** 2-1-77.

[Sec. 5207(b)]

(b) REPORTS.—Every person required to keep records under subsection (a) shall render such reports covering his operations, at such times and in such form and manner and containing such information, as the Secretary shall by regulations prescribe.

Amendments

- **1979, Trade Agreements Act of 1979 (P.L. 96-39)**

P.L. 96-39, § 807(a)(25):

Deleted Code Sec. 5207(b) and (c) and added a new Code Sec. 5207(b). **Effective** 1-1-80. Prior to deletion, Code Sec. 5207(b) and (c) read as follows:

(b) RECORDS OF RECTIFIERS AND BOTTLERS.—Every rectifier and every bottler of distilled spirits shall keep records in such form and manner as the Secretary shall by regulations prescribe of—

(1) all distilled spirits and wines received,

(2) the kind and quantity of distilled spirits and wines rectified and packaged or bottled, or packaged or bottled without rectification,

(3) the kind and quantity of distilled spirits and wines removed from his premises,

(4) the receipt, use, and balance on hand of all stamps required by law or regulations to be used by him, and

(5) such additional information as may by regulations be required.

(c) REPORTS.—Every person required to keep records under subsection (a) or (b) shall render such reports covering his operations, at such times and in such form and manner and containing such information, as the Secretary shall by regulation prescribe.

- **1976, Tax Reform Act of 1976 (P.L. 94-455)**

P.L. 94-455, § 1906(b)(13)(A):

Amended 1954 Code by substituting "Secretary" for "Secretary or his delegate" each place it appeared. **Effective** 2-1-77.

[Sec. 5207(c)]

(c) PRESERVATION AND INSPECTION.—The records required by subsection (a) and a copy of each report required by subsection (b) shall be available for inspection by any internal revenue officer during business hours, and shall be preserved by the person required to keep such records and reports for such period as the Secretary shall by regulations prescribe.

Amendments

- **1997, Taxpayer Relief Act of 1997 (P.L. 105-34)**

P.L. 105-34, § 1413(a):

Amended Code Sec. 5207(c) by striking "shall be kept on the premises where the operations covered by the record are carried on and" after "subsection (b)". **Effective** on the 1st day of the 1st calendar quarter that begins at least 180 days after 8-5-97.

- **1979, Trade Agreements Act of 1979 (P.L. 96-39)**

P.L. 96-39, § 807(a)(25):

Deleted Code Sec. 5207(d) and added Code Sec. 5207(c). **Effective** 1-1-80. Prior to deletion, Code Sec. 5207(d) read as follows:

(d) PRESERVATION AND INSPECTION.—The records required by subsection (a) and (b), and a copy of each report required by subsection (c) shall be kept on the premises where the operations covered by the record are carried on and shall be available for inspection by any internal revenue officer during business hours, and shall be preserved by the person required to keep such records and reports for such period as the Secretary shall by regulations prescribe.

- **1976, Tax Reform Act of 1976 (P.L. 94-455)**

P.L. 94-455, § 1906(b)(13)(A):

Amended 1954 Code by substituting "Secretary" for "Secretary or his delegate" each place it appeared. **Effective** 2-1-77.

[Sec. 5207(d)]

(d) PENALTY.—

For penalty and forfeiture for refusal or neglect to keep records required under this section, or for false entries therein, see sections 5603 and 5615(5).

Amendments

- **1979, Trade Agreements Act of 1979 (P.L. 96-39)**

P.L. 96-39, § 807(a)(25):

Deleted Code Sec. 5207(e) and added Code Sec. 5207(d). **Effective** 1-1-80. Prior to deletion, Code Sec. 5207(e) read as follows:

(e) PENALTY.—

For penalty and forfeiture for refusal or neglect to keep records required under this section, or for false entries therein, see sections 5603 and 5615(5).

PART II—OPERATIONS ON BONDED PREMISES

Subpart A.	General.
Subpart B.	Production.
Subpart C.	Storage.
Subpart D.	Denaturation.

Subpart A—General

Sec. 5211.	Production and entry of distilled spirits.
Sec. 5212.	Transfer of distilled spirits between bonded premises.
Sec. 5213.	Withdrawal of distilled spirits from bonded premises on determination of tax.
Sec. 5214.	Withdrawal of distilled spirits from bonded premises free of tax or without payment of tax.
Sec. 5215.	Return of tax determined distilled spirits to bonded premises.
Sec. 5216.	Regulation of operations.

[Sec. 5211]

SEC. 5211. PRODUCTION AND ENTRY OF DISTILLED SPIRITS.

Distilled spirits in the process of production in a distilled spirits plant may be held prior to the production gauge only for so long as is reasonably necessary to complete the process of production. Under such regulations as the Secretary shall prescribe, all distilled spirits produced in a distilled spirits plant shall be gauged and a record made of such gauge within a reasonable time after the production thereof has been completed. The proprietor shall, pursuant to such production gauge and in accordance with such regulations as the Secretary shall prescribe, make appropriate entry for—

(1) deposit of such spirits on bonded premises for storage or processing;

(2) withdrawal upon determination of tax as authorized by law;

(3) withdrawal under the provisions of section 5214; and

(4) transfer for redistillation under the provisions of section 5223.

ALCOHOL TAXES—DISTILLED SPIRITS PLANTS

Amendments

• **1979, Trade Agreements Act of 1979 (P.L. 96-39)**

P.L. 96-39, § 807(a)(26):

Amended Code Sec. 5211 by changing paragraph (1), and by deleting paragraph (5). **Effective** 1-1-80. Prior to amendment and deletion, paragraphs (1) and (5) read as follows:

(1) deposit of such spirits in storage on bonded premises;

* * *

(5) immediate denaturation.

• **1976, Tax Reform Act of 1976 (P.L. 94-455)**

P.L. 94-455, § 1906(b)(13)(A):

Amended 1954 Code by substituting "Secretary" for "Secretary or his delegate" each place it appeared. **Effective** 2-1-77.

[Sec. 5212]

SEC. 5212. TRANSFER OF DISTILLED SPIRITS BETWEEN BONDED PREMISES.

Bulk distilled spirits on which the internal revenue tax has not been paid or determined as authorized by law may, under such regulations as the Secretary shall prescribe, be transferred in bond between bonded premises in any approved container. For the purposes of this chapter, the removal of bulk distilled spirits for transfer in bond between bonded premises shall not be construed to be a withdrawal from bonded premises. The provisions of this section restricting transfers to bulk distilled spirits shall not apply to alcohol bottled under the provisions of section 5235 which is to be withdrawn for industrial purposes. In the case of distilled spirits transferred in bond after December 31, 2017, between bonded premises belonging to the same person or members of the same controlled group (within the meaning of section 5001(c)(2)) this section shall be applied without regard to whether distilled spirits are bulk distilled spirits. In the case of distilled spirits transferred in bond from the person who distilled or processed such distilled spirits (hereinafter referred to as "transferor") to another person for bottling or storage of such distilled spirits, and returned to the transferor for removal, this section shall be applied without regard to whether distilled spirits are bulk distilled spirits, but only if the transferor retains title during the entire period between such distillation, or processing, and removal.

Amendments

• **2020, Taxpayer Certainty and Disaster Tax Relief Act of 2020 (P.L. 116-260)**

P.L. 116-260, § 106(h)(1), Div. EE:

Amended Code Sec. 5212 by striking "and before January 1, 2021," and inserting "between bonded premises belonging to the same person or members of the same controlled group (within the meaning of section 5001(c)(2))". **Effective** for distilled spirits transferred in bond after 12-31-2020.

P.L. 116-260, § 106(h)(2), Div. EE:

Amended Code Sec. 5212 by adding at the end a new sentence. **Effective** for distilled spirits transferred in bond after 12-31-2020.

• **2019, Taxpayer Certainty and Disaster Tax Relief Act of 2019 (P.L. 116-94)**

P.L. 116-94, § 144(h)(1), Div. Q:

Amended Code Sec. 5212 by striking "January 1, 2020" and inserting "January 1, 2021". **Effective** for distilled spirits transferred in bond after 12-31-2019.

• **2017, Tax Cuts and Jobs Act (P.L. 115-97)**

P.L. 115-97, § 13808(a):

Amended Code Sec. 5212 by adding at the end a new sentence. **Effective** for distilled spirits transferred in bond after 12-31-2017.

P.L. 115-97, § 13809 (as added by P.L. 115-123, § 41111, Div. D), provides:

SEC. 13809. RULE OF CONSTRUCTION.

Nothing in this subpart, the amendments made by this subpart, or any regulation promulgated under this subpart or the amendments made by this subpart, shall be construed to preempt, supersede, or otherwise limit or restrict any State, local, or tribal law that prohibits or regulates the production or sale of distilled spirits, wine, or malt beverages.

• **1980 (P.L. 96-598)**

P.L. 96-598, § 6(d):

Amended Code Sec. 5212 by adding the last sentence. **Effective** 12-24-80.

• **1979, Trade Agreements Act of 1979 (P.L. 96-39)**

P.L. 96-39, § 805(b)(2):

Amended Code Sec. 5212 by changing "Distilled spirits" to "Bulk distilled spirits" and by changing "distilled spirits" to "bulk distilled spirits". **Effective** 1-1-80.

• **1976, Tax Reform Act of 1976 (P.L. 94-455)**

P.L. 94-455, § 1906(b)(13)(A):

Amended 1954 Code by substituting "Secretary" for "Secretary or his delegate" each place it appeared. **Effective** 2-1-77.

[Sec. 5213]

SEC. 5213. WITHDRAWAL OF DISTILLED SPIRITS FROM BONDED PREMISES ON DETERMINATION OF TAX.

Subject to the provisions of section 5173, distilled spirits may be withdrawn from the bonded premises of a distilled spirits plant on payment or determination of tax thereon, in approved containers, under such regulations as the Secretary shall prescribe.

Amendments

• **1979, Trade Agreements Act of 1979 (P.L. 96-39)**

P.L. 96-39, § 807(a)(27):

Amended Code Sec. 5213. **Effective** 1-1-80. Prior to amendment Code Sec. 5213 read as follows:

On application to the Secretary and subject to the provisions of section 5174(a), distilled spirits may be withdrawn from the bonded premises of a distilled spirits plant on payment or determination of tax thereon, in approved containers, under such regulations as the Secretary shall prescribe.

• **1976, Tax Reform Act of 1976 (P.L. 94-455)**

P.L. 94-455, § 1906(b)(13)(A):

Amended 1954 Code by substituting "Secretary" for "Secretary or his delegate" each place it appeared. **Effective** 2-1-77.

[Sec. 5214]

SEC. 5214. WITHDRAWAL OF DISTILLED SPIRITS FROM BONDED PREMISES FREE OF TAX OR WITHOUT PAYMENT OF TAX.

[Sec. 5214(a)]

(a) PURPOSES.—Distilled spirits on which the internal revenue tax has not been paid or determined may, subject to such regulations as the Secretary shall prescribe, be withdrawn from the bonded premises of any distilled spirits plant in approved containers—

(1) free of tax after denaturation of such spirits in the manner prescribed by law for—

(A) exportation;

(B) use in the manufacture of ether, chloroform, or other definite chemical substance where such distilled spirits are changed into some other chemical substance and do not appear in the finished product; or

(C) any other use in the arts and industries (except for uses prohibited by section 5273(b) or (d)) and for fuel, light, and power; or

(2) free of tax by, and for the use of, the United States or any governmental agency thereof, any State, any political subdivision of a State, or the District of Columbia, for nonbeverage purposes; or

(3) free of tax for nonbeverage purposes and not for resale or use in the manufacture of any product for sale—

(A) for the use of any educational organization described in section 170(b)(1)(A)(ii) which is exempt from income tax under section 501(a), or for the use of any scientific university or college of learning;

(B) for any laboratory for use exclusively in scientific research;

(C) for use at any hospital, blood bank, or sanitarium (including use in making any analysis or test at such hospital, blood bank, or sanitarium), or at any pathological laboratory exclusively engaged in making analyses, or tests, for hospitals or sanitariums; or

(D) for the use of any clinic operated for charity and not for profit (including use in the compounding of bona fide medicines for treatment outside of such clinics of patients thereof); or

(4) without payment of tax for exportation, after making such application and entries, filing such bonds as are required by section 5175, and complying with such other requirements as may by regulations be prescribed; or

ALCOHOL TAXES—DISTILLED SPIRITS PLANTS

(5) without payment of tax for use in wine production, as authorized by section 5373; or

(6) without payment of tax for transfer to manufacturing bonded warehouses for manufacturing in such warehouses for export, as authorized by law; or

(7) without payment of tax for use of certain vessels and aircraft, as authorized by law; or

(8) without payment of tax for transfer to foreign-trade zones, as authorized by law; or

(9) without payment of tax, for transfer (for the purpose of storage pending exportation) to any customs bonded warehouse from which distilled spirits may be exported, and distilled spirits transferred to a customs bonded warehouse under this paragraph shall be entered, stored and accounted for under such regulations and bonds as the Secretary may prescribe; or

(10) without payment of tax by a proprietor of bonded premises for use in research, development, or testing (other than consumer testing or other market analysis) of processes, systems, materials, or equipment, relating to distilled spirits or distilled spirits operations, under such limitations and conditions as to quantities, use, and accountability as the Secretary may by regulations require for the protection of the revenue; or

(11) free of tax when contained in an article (within the meaning of section 5002(a)(14)); or

(12) free of tax in the case of distilled spirits produced under section 5181; or

(13) without payment of tax for use on bonded wine cellar premises in the production of wine or wine products which will be rendered unfit for beverage use and removed pursuant to section 5362(d); or

(14) with respect to distilled spirits removed after December 31, 2019, and before January 1, 2021, free of tax for use in or contained in hand sanitizer produced and distributed in a manner consistent with any guidance issued by the Food and Drug Administration that is related to the outbreak of virus SARS–CoV–2 or coronavirus disease 2019 (COVID–19).

Amendments

• **2020, Coronavirus Aid, Relief, and Economic Security (CARES) Act (P.L. 116-136)**

P.L. 116-136, § 2308(a)(1)-(2):

Amended Code Sec. 5214(a), in paragraph (13), by striking the period at the end and inserting "; or", and by adding at the end a new paragraph (14). **Effective** for distilled spirits removed after 12-31-2019. For a special rule, see Act Sec. 2308(c), below.

P.L. 116-136, § 2308(c), provides:

(c) APPLICATION OF OTHER LAWS.—Any distilled spirits or product described in paragraph (14) of section 5214(a) of the Internal Revenue Code of 1986 (as added by this section) shall not be subject to any requirements related to labeling or bulk sales under—

(1) section 105 or 106 of the Federal Alcohol Administration Act (27 U.S.C. 205, 206); or

(2) section 204 of the Alcoholic Beverage Labeling Act of 1988 (27 U.S.C. 215).

• **1984, Deficit Reduction Act of 1984 (P.L. 98-369)**

P.L. 98-369, § 455(a):

Amended Code Sec. 5214(a) by striking out the period at the end of paragraph (12) and inserting in lieu thereof "; or", and by adding at the end thereof new paragraph (13). **Effective** 7-14-84.

• **1980, Crude Oil Windfall Profit Tax Act of 1980 (P.L. 96-223)**

P.L. 96-223, § 232(e)(2)(B):

Amended Code Sec. 5214(a) by striking out the period at the end of paragraph (11) and inserting "; or" and by adding paragraph (12). **Effective** 7-1-80.

• **1979, Trade Agreements Act of 1979 (P.L. 96-39)**

P.L. 96-39, § 807(a)(28)(A)-(D):

Amended Code Sec. 5214(a) by changing paragraph (6), by changing "without payment of tax, in the case of distilled spirits bottled in bond for export under section 5233 or distilled spirits returned to bonded premises under section 5215(b), for transfer" to "without payment of tax, for transfer" in paragraph (9), by changing "distillery operations" to "distilled spirits operations" in paragraph (10) and by adding a new paragraph (11). **Effective** 1-1-80. Prior to amendment, paragraph (6) read as follows:

(6) without payment of tax for transfer to manufacturing bonded warehouses, as authorized by section 5522(a); or

• **1977 (P.L. 95-176)**

P.L. 95-176, §§ 3(a), 4(a):

Amended Code Sec. 5214(a) by revising paragraph (9) and by adding new paragraph (10). **Effective** 3-1-78. Prior to amendment, paragraph (9) read as follows:

"(9) free of tax for use as samples in making tests or laboratory analyses."

• **1976, Tax Reform Act of 1976 (P.L. 94-455)**

P.L. 94-455, § 1905(c)(2):

Struck out "or Territory" following "State" each place it appeared in Code Sec. 5214(a)(2). **Effective** 2-1-77.

P.L. 94-455, § 1906(b)(13)(A):

Amended 1954 Code by substituting "Secretary" for "Secretary or his delegate" each place it appeared. **Effective** 2-1-77.

• **1969, Tax Reform Act of 1969 (P.L. 91-172)**

P.L. 91-172, § 101(j)(29):

Amended Code Sec. 5214(a)(3)(A) by substituting "section 170(b)(1)(A)(ii)" for "section 503(b)(2)". **Effective** 1-1-70.

[Sec. 5214(b)]

(b) CROSS REFERENCES.—

(1) For provisions relating to denaturation, see sections 5241 and 5242.

(2) For provisions requiring permit for users of distilled spirits withdrawn free of tax and for users of specially denatured distilled spirits, see section 5271.

(3) For provisions relating to withdrawal of distilled spirits without payment of tax for use of certain vessels and aircraft, as authorized by law, see 19 U. S. C. 1309.

(4) For provisions relating to withdrawal of distilled spirits without payment of tax for manufacture in manufacturing bonded warehouse, see 19 U.S.C. 1311.

(5) For provisions relating to foreign-trade zones, see 19 U. S. C. 81c.

(6) For provisions authorizing regulations for withdrawal of distilled spirits free of tax for use of the United States, see section 7510.

(7) For provisions authorizing removal of distillates to bonded wine cellars for use in the production of distilling material, see section 5373(c).

(8) For provisions relating to distilled spirits for use of foreign embassies, legations, etc., see section 5066.

Amendments

• **1979, Trade Agreements Act of 1979 (P.L. 96-39)**

P.L. 96-39, § 807(a)(28)(E):

Amended Code Sec. 5214(b) by redesignating paragraphs (4), (5), (6), and (7) as paragraphs (5), (6), (7), and (8) and adding a new paragraph (4). **Effective** 1-1-80.

• **1977 (P.L. 95-176)**

P.L. 95-176, § 3(d):

Amended Code Sec. 5214(b) by adding paragraph (7). **Effective** 3-1-78.

[Sec. 5215]

SEC. 5215. RETURN OF TAX DETERMINED DISTILLED SPIRITS TO BONDED PREMISES.

[Sec. 5215(a)]

(a) GENERAL RULE.—Under such regulations as the Secretary may prescribe, distilled spirits on which tax has been determined or paid may be returned to the bonded premises of a distilled spirits plant but only for destruction, denaturation, redistillation, reconditioning, or rebottling.

ALCOHOL TAXES—DISTILLED SPIRITS PLANTS

Amendments

• **1979, Trade Agreements Act of 1979 (P.L. 96-39)**

P.L. 96-39, §807(a)(29):

Amended Code Sec. 5215(a). **Effective** 1-1-80. Prior to amendment, Code Sec. 5215(a) read as follows:

(a) GENERAL.—On such application and under such regulations as the Secretary may prescribe, distilled spirits withdrawn from bonded premises on payment or determination of tax (other than products to which any alcoholic ingredients other than such distilled spirits have been added) may be returned to the bonded premises of a distilled spirits plant. Such returned distilled spirits shall be destroyed, denatured, or redistilled, or shall be mingled as authorized in section 5234(a)(1) (other than subparagraph (C) thereof).

• **1977 (P.L. 95-176)**

P.L. 95-176, §2(a):

Amended Code Sec. 5215(a) by deleting the former last sentence which read as follows: "All provisions of this chapter applicable to distilled spirits in bond shall be applicable to distilled spirits returned to bonded premises under the provisions of this section on such return." **Effective** 3-1-78.

• **1976, Tax Reform Act of 1976 (P.L. 94-455)**

P.L. 94-455, §1906(b)(13)(A):

Amended 1954 Code by substituting "Secretary" for "Secretary or his delegate" each place it appeared. **Effective** 2-1-77.

• **1971 (P.L. 91-659)**

P.L. 91-659, §2(c):

Amended Code Sec. 5215(a) and repealed former Code Sec. 5215(b). **Effective** 5-1-71. Prior to amendment and repeal, those sections read as follows:

"(a) General.—On such application and under such regulations as the Secretary or his delegate may prescribe, distilled spirits withdrawn from bonded premises in bulk containers on or after July 1, 1959, on payment or determination of tax may be returned to the bonded premises of a distilled spirits plant, if such spirits have been found to be unsuitable for the purpose for which intended to be used before any processing thereof and before removal from the original container in which such distilled spirits were withdrawn from bonded premises. Such returned distilled spirits shall immediately be destroyed, redistilled, or denatured, or may, in lieu of destruction, redistillation, or denaturation, be mingled on bonded premises as authorized in section 5234(a)(1)(A), (a)(1)(D), or (a)(1)(E). All provisions of this chapter applicable to distilled spirits in bond shall be applicable to distilled spirits returned to bonded premises under the provisions of this section on such return.

"(b) Distilled Spirits Withdrawn by Pipeline.—In the case of distilled spirits removed by pipeline, 'original container in which such distilled spirits were withdrawn from bonded premises' as used in this section shall mean the bulk tank into which the distilled spirits were originally deposited from pipeline, and the permitted return of the spirits to bonded premises may be made by pipeline or by other approved containers."

• **1965, Excise Tax Reduction Act of 1965 (P.L. 89-44)**

P.L. 89-44, §805(c):

Amended subsection (a) of Section 5215 by inserting "destroyed, redistilled, or denatured" in lieu of "redistilled or denatured" and by inserting "destruction, redistillation, or denaturation" in lieu of "redistillation or denaturation" in the second sentence. **Effective** 7-1-65.

[Sec. 5215(b)]

(b) APPLICABILITY OF CHAPTER TO DISTILLED SPIRITS RETURNED TO A DISTILLED SPIRITS PLANT.—All provisions of this chapter applicable to distilled spirits in bond shall be applicable to distilled spirits returned to bonded premises under the provisions of this section on such return.

Amendments

• **1979, Trade Agreements Act of 1979 (P.L. 96-39)**

P.L. 96-39, §807(a)(29):

Amended Code Sec. 5215(b). **Effective** 1-1-80. Prior to amendment, Code Sec. 5215(b) read as follows:

(b) DISTILLED SPIRITS RETURNED TO BONDED PREMISES FOR STORAGE PENDING EXPORTATION.—On such application and under such conditions as the Secretary may by regulations prescribe, distilled spirits which would be eligible for allowance of drawback under section 5062(b) on exportation, may be returned by the bottler or packager of such distilled spirits to an export storage facility on the bonded premises of the distilled spirits plant where bottled or packaged, solely for the purpose of storage pending withdrawal without payment of tax under section 5214(a)(4), (7), (8), or (9), or free of tax under section 7510.

• **1977 (P.L. 95-176)**

P.L. 95-176, §2(a):

Amended Code Sec. 5215(b). **Effective** 3-1-78. Prior to amendment, the section read as follows:

"(b) CROSS REFERENCE.—

"For provisions relating to the remission, abatement, credit, or refund of tax on distilled spirits returned to bonded premises under provisions of this section, see section 5008(d)."

• **1971 (P.L. 91-659)**

P.L. 91-659, §2(c):

Redesignated former Code Sec. 5215(c) as Code Sec. 5215(b). **Effective** 5-1-71.

[Sec. 5215(c)]

(c) RETURN OF BOTTLED DISTILLED SPIRITS FOR RELABELING AND RECLOSING.—Under such regulations as the Secretary shall prescribe, bottled distilled spirits withdrawn from bonded premises may be returned to bonded premises for relabeling or reclosing, and the tax under section 5001 shall not again be collected on such spirits.

Amendments

• **1984, Deficit Reduction Act of 1984 (P.L. 98-369)**

P.L. 98-369, §454(c)(7):

Amended Code Sec. 5215(c) by striking out "Restamping" in the heading and inserting in lieu thereof "Reclosing", and by striking out "restamping" in the text and inserting in lieu thereof "reclosing". **Effective** 7-1-85.

• **1979, Trade Agreements Act of 1979 (P.L. 96-39)**

P.L. 96-39, §807(a)(29):

Amended Code Sec. 5215(c). **Effective** 1-1-80. Prior to amendment, Code Sec. 5215(c) read as follows:

(c) DISTILLED SPIRITS STAMPED AND LABELED AS BOTTLED IN BOND.—On such application and under such regulations as the Secretary may prescribe, a proprietor of bonded premises who has bottled distilled spirits under section 5178(a)(4)(A) (ii), which are stamped and labeled as bottled in bond for domestic consumption, may return cases of such bottled distilled spirits to appropriate storage facilities on the bonded premises of the distilled spirits plant where bottled for storage pending withdrawal for any purpose for which distilled spirits bottled under section 5178(a)(4)(A)(i) may be withdrawn from bonded premises.

• **1977 (P.L. 95-176)**

P.L. 95-176, §2(a):

Added Code Sec. 5215(c). **Effective** 3-1-78.

[Sec. 5215(d)]

(d) CROSS REFERENCE.—

For provisions relating to the abatement, credit, or refund of tax on distilled spirits returned to a distilled spirits plant under this section, see section 5008(c).

Amendments

• **1979, Trade Agreements Act of 1979 (P.L. 96-39)**

P.L. 96-39, §807(a)(29):

Amended Code Sec. 5215(d) and deleted Code Sec. 5215(e). **Effective** 1-1-80. Prior to amendment and deletion Code Secs. 5215(d) and 5215(e) read as follows:

(d) APPLICABILITY OF CHAPTER TO DISTILLED SPIRITS RETURNED TO BONDED PREMISES.—Except as otherwise provided in this section, all provisions of this chapter applicable to distilled spirits in bond shall be applicable to distilled spirits returned to bonded premises under the provisions of this section on such return.

(e) CROSS REFERENCES.—

(1) For provisions relating to the remission, abatement, credit, or refund of tax on distilled spirits returned to bonded premises under this section, see section 5008(d).

(2) For provisions relating to the establishment of an export storage facility on the bonded premises of a distilled spirits plant, see section 5178(a)(3)(D).

• **1977 (P.L. 95-176)**

P.L. 95-176, §2(a):

Added Code Secs. 5215(d) and 5215(e). **Effective** 3-1-78.

[Sec. 5216]

SEC. 5216. REGULATION OF OPERATIONS.

For general provisions relating to operations on bonded premises see part I of this subchapter.

Subpart B—Production

Sec. 5221.	Commencement, suspension, and resumption of operations.
Sec. 5222.	Production, receipt, removal, and use of distilling materials.
Sec. 5223.	Redistillation of spirits, articles, and residues.

ALCOHOL TAXES—DISTILLED SPIRITS PLANTS

[Sec. 5221]
SEC. 5221. COMMENCEMENT, SUSPENSION, AND RESUMPTION OF OPERATIONS.

[Sec. 5221(a)]

(a) COMMENCEMENT, SUSPENSION, AND RESUMPTION.—The proprietor of a distilled spirits plant authorized to produce distilled spirits shall not commence production operations until written notice has been given to the Secretary stating when operations will begin. Any proprietor of a distilled spirits plant desiring to suspend production of distilled spirits shall give notice in writing to the Secretary, stating when he will suspend such operations. Pursuant to such notice, an internal revenue officer shall take such action as the Secretary shall prescribe to prevent the production of distilled spirits. No proprietor, after having given such notice, shall, after the time stated therein, produce distilled spirits on such premises until he again gives notice in writing to the Secretary stating the time when he will resume operations. At the time stated in the notice for resuming such operations an internal revenue officer shall take such action as is necessary to permit operations to be resumed. The notices submitted under this section shall be in such form and submitted in such manner as the Secretary may by regulations require. Nothing in this section shall apply to suspensions caused by unavoidable accidents; and the Secretary shall prescribe regulations to govern such cases of involuntary suspension.

Amendments

• **1979, Trade Agreements Act of 1979 (P.L. 96-39)**

P.L. 96-39, § 806(b):

Amended Code Sec. 5221(a) by changing "until an internal revenue officer has been assigned to the premises" to "until written notice has been given to the Secretary stating when operations will begin". **Effective** 1-1-80.

• **1976, Tax Reform Act of 1976 (P.L. 94-455)**

P.L. 94-455, § 1906(b)(13)(A):

Amended 1954 Code by substituting "Secretary" for "Secretary or his delegate" each place it appeared. **Effective** 2-1-77.

[Sec. 5221(b)]

(b) PENALTY.—

For penalty and forfeiture for carrying on the business of distiller after having given notice of suspension, see sections 5601(a)(14) and 5615(3).

[Sec. 5222]
SEC. 5222. PRODUCTION, RECEIPT, REMOVAL, AND USE OF DISTILLING MATERIALS.

[Sec. 5222(a)]

(a) PRODUCTION, REMOVAL, AND USE.—

(1) No mash, wort, or wash fit for distillation or for the production of distilled spirits shall be made or fermented in any building or on any premises other than on the bonded premises of a distilled spirits plant duly authorized to produce distilled spirits according to law; and no mash, wort, or wash so made or fermented shall be removed from any such premises before being distilled, except as authorized by the Secretary; and no person other than an authorized distiller shall, by distillation or any other process, produce distilled spirits from any mash, wort, wash, or other material.

(2) Nothing in this subsection shall be construed to apply to—

(A) authorized operations performed on the premises of vinegar plants established under part I of subchapter H;

(B) authorized production and removal of fermented materials produced on authorized brewery or bonded wine cellar premises as provided by law;

(C) products exempt from tax under the provisions of section 5042 or 5053(e); or

(D) fermented materials used in the manufacture of vinegar by fermentation.

Amendments

• **1978 (P.L. 95-458)**

P.L. 95-458, § 2(b)(4), (c):

Amended Code Sec. 5222(a)(2)(C) by striking out "; or" and inserting in place thereof "or 5053(e); or". **Effective** 2-1-79.

• **1976, Tax Reform Act of 1976 (P.L. 94-455)**

P.L. 94-455, § 1906(b)(13)(A):

Amended 1954 Code by substituting "Secretary" for "Secretary or his delegate" each place it appeared. **Effective** 2-1-77.

[Sec. 5222(b)]

(b) RECEIPT.—Under such regulations as the Secretary may prescribe, fermented materials to be used in the production of distilled spirits may be received on the bonded premises of a distilled spirits plant authorized to produce distilled spirits as follows—

(1) from the premises of a bonded wine cellar authorized to remove such material by section 5362(c)(6);

(2) beer conveyed without payment of tax from brewery premises, beer which has been lawfully removed from brewery premises upon determination of tax, or

(3) cider exempt from tax under the provisions of section 5042(a)(1).

Amendments

• **1997, Taxpayer Relief Act of 1997 (P.L. 105-34)**

P.L. 105-34, § 1414(a):

Amended Code Sec. 5222(b)(2). **Effective** on the 1st day of the 1st calendar quarter that begins at least 180 days after 8-5-97. Prior to amendment, Code Sec. 5222(b)(2) read as follows:

(2) conveyed without payment of tax from contiguous brewery premises where produced; or

• **1976, Tax Reform Act of 1976 (P.L. 94-455)**

P.L. 94-455, § 1906(b)(13)(A):

Amended 1954 Code by substituting "Secretary" for "Secretary or his delegate" each place it appeared. **Effective** 2-1-77.

[Sec. 5222(c)]

(c) PROCESSING OF DISTILLED SPIRITS CONTAINING EXTRANEOUS SUBSTANCES.—The Secretary may by regulations provide for the removal from the distilling system, and the addition to the fermented or unfermented distilling material, of distilled spirits containing substantial quantities of fusel oil or aldehydes, or other extraneous substances.

Amendments

• **1979, Trade Agreements Act of 1979 (P.L. 96-39)**

P.L. 96-39, § 807(a)(30):

Amended Code Sec. 5222(c) by changing "or unfermented distilling material, in the production facilities of a distilled spirits plant, of distilled spirits" to "or unfermented distilling material, of distilled spirits". **Effective** 1-1-80.

• **1976, Tax Reform Act of 1976 (P.L. 94-455)**

P.L. 94-455, § 1906(b)(13)(A):

Amended 1954 Code by substituting "Secretary" for "Secretary or his delegate" each place it appeared. **Effective** 2-1-77.

ALCOHOL TAXES—DISTILLED SPIRITS PLANTS

[Sec. 5222(d)]

(d) PENALTY.—

For penalty and forfeiture for unlawful production, removal, or use of material fit for distillation or for the production of distilled spirits, and for penalty and forfeiture for unlawful production of distilled spirits, see sections 5601(a)(7), 5601(a)(8), and 5615(4).

Amendments

• **1976, Tax Reform Act of 1976 (P.L. 94-455)**

P.L. 94-455, § 1905(b)(6)(D):

Struck out "5601(b)(3), 5601(b)(4)," following "5601(a)(8)," in Code Sec. 5222(d). **Effective** 2-1-77.

[Sec. 5223]

SEC. 5223. REDISTILLATION OF SPIRITS, ARTICLES, AND RESIDUES.

[Sec. 5223(a)]

(a) SPIRITS ON BONDED PREMISES.—The proprietor of a distilled spirits plant authorized to produce distilled spirits may, under such regulations as the Secretary shall prescribe, redistill any distilled spirits which have not been withdrawn from bonded premises.

Amendments

• **1976, Tax Reform Act of 1976 (P.L. 94-455)**

P.L. 94-455, § 1906(b)(13)(A):

Amended 1954 Code by substituting "Secretary" for "Secretary or his delegate" each place it appeared. **Effective** 2-1-77.

[Sec. 5223(b)]

(b) DISTILLED SPIRITS RETURNED FOR REDISTILLATION.—Distilled spirits which have been lawfully removed from bonded premises free of tax or without payment of tax may, under such regulations as the Secretary may prescribe, be returned for redistillation to the bonded premises of a distilled spirits plant authorized to produce distilled spirits.

Amendments

• **1976, Tax Reform Act of 1976 (P.L. 94-455)**

P.L. 94-455, § 1906(b)(13)(A):

Amended 1954 Code by substituting "Secretary" for "Secretary or his delegate" each place it appeared. **Effective** 2-1-77.

[Sec. 5223(c)]

(c) REDISTILLATION OF ARTICLES AND RESIDUES.—Articles, containing denatured distilled spirits, which were manufactured under the provisions of subchapter D or on the bonded premises of a distilled spirits plant, and the spirits residues of manufacturing processes related thereto, may be received, and the distilled spirits therein recovered by redistillation, on the bonded premises of a distilled spirits plant authorized to produce distilled spirits, under such regulations as the Secretary may prescribe.

Amendments

• **1979, Trade Agreements Act of 1979 (P.L. 96-39)**

P.L. 96-39, § 807(a)(31)(A):

Amended Code Sec. 5223(c) by adding "or on the bonded premises of a distilled spirits plant". **Effective** 1-1-80.

• **1976, Tax Reform Act of 1976 (P.L. 94-455)**

P.L. 94-455, § 1906(b)(13)(A):

Amended 1954 Code by substituting "Secretary" for "Secretary or his delegate" each place it appeared. **Effective** 2-1-77.

• **1965, Excise Tax Reduction Act of 1965 (P.L. 89-44)**

P.L. 89-44, § 805(d):

Added new subsection (c) to Section 5223. **Effective** 10-1-65.

[Sec. 5223(d)]

(d) DENATURED DISTILLED SPIRITS, ARTICLES, AND RESIDUES.—Distilled spirits recovered by the redistillation of denatured distilled spirits, or by the redistillation of the articles or residues described in subsection (c), may not be withdrawn from bonded premises except for industrial use or after denaturation thereof in the manner prescribed by law.

Amendments

• **1965, Excise Tax Reduction Act of 1965 (P.L. 89-44)**

P.L. 89-44, § 805(d):

Redesignated former subsection (c) of Section 5223 as subsection (d) of Section 5223. **Effective** 10-1-65.

P.L. 89-44, § 805(f)(10):

Amended subsection (d) of Section 5223, as redesignated. **Effective** 10-1-65. Prior to amendment, subsection (d), as redesignated, read as follows:

"(d) Denatured Distilled Spirits.—Distilled spirits recovered by the redistillation of denatured distilled spirits may not be withdrawn from bonded premises except for industrial use or after denaturation thereof in the manner prescribed by law."

[Sec. 5223(e)]

(e) PRODUCTS OF REDISTILLATION.—All distilled spirits redistilled on bonded premises subsequent to production gauge shall be treated the same as if such spirits had been originally produced by the redistiller and all provisions of this chapter applicable to the original production of distilled spirits shall be applicable thereto. Any prior obligation as to taxes, liens, and bonds with respect to such distilled spirits shall be extinguished on redistillation. Nothing in this subsection shall be construed as affecting any provision of law relating to the labeling of distilled spirits or as limiting the authority of the Secretary to regulate the marking, branding, or identification of distilled spirits redistilled under this section.

Amendments

• **1979, Trade Agreements Act of 1979 (P.L. 96-39)**

P.L. 96-39, § 807(a)(31)(B):

Amended Code Sec. 5223(e) by deleting the last sentence. **Effective** 1-1-80. Prior to deletion, the last sentence of Code Sec. 5223(e) read as follows: "The processing of distilled spirits, subsequent to production gauge, in the manufacture of vodka in the production facilities of a distilled spirits plant shall be treated for the purposes of this subsection, subsection (a), and sections 5025(d) and 5215 as redistillation of the spirits."

• **1976, Tax Reform Act of 1976 (P.L. 94-455)**

P.L. 94-455, § 1906(b)(13)(A):

Amended 1954 Code by substituting "Secretary" for "Secretary or his delegate" each place it appeared. **Effective** 2-1-77.

• **1965, Excise Tax Reduction Act of 1965 (P.L. 89-44)**

P.L. 89-44, § 805(d):

Redesignated former subsection (d) of Section 5223 as subsection (e) of Section 5223. **Effective** 10-1-65.

P.L. 89-44, § 805(f)(8):

Amended the heading of Section 5223. **Effective** 10-1-65. Prior to amendment, the heading reads as follows:

"REDISTILLATION OF SPIRITS."

ALCOHOL TAXES—DISTILLED SPIRITS PLANTS

Subpart C—Storage

Sec. 5231.	Entry for deposit.
Sec. 5232.	Imported distilled spirits.
Sec. 5233.	Bottling of distilled spirits in bond [Repealed].
Sec. 5234.	Mingling and blending of distilled spirits [Repealed].
Sec. 5235.	Bottling of alcohol for industrial purposes.
Sec. 5236.	Discontinuance of storage facilities and transfer of distilled spirits.

[Sec. 5231]

SEC. 5231. ENTRY FOR DEPOSIT.

All distilled spirits entered for deposit on the bonded premises of a distilled spirits plant under section 5211 shall, under such regulations as the Secretary shall prescribe, be deposited in the facilities on the bonded premises designated in the entry for deposit.

Amendments

• **1979, Trade Agreements Act of 1979 (P.L. 96-39)**

P.L. 96-39, § 807(a)(32):

Amended Code Sec. 5231. **Effective** 1-1-80. Prior to amendment, Code Sec. 5231 read as follows:

(a) GENERAL.—All distilled spirits entered for deposit in storage under section 5211 shall, under such regulations as the Secretary shall prescribe, be deposited in storage facilities on the bonded premises designated in the entry for deposit.

(b) CROSS REFERENCE.—

For provisions requiring that all distilled spirits entered for deposit be withdrawn within 20 years from date of original entry for deposit, see section 5006(a)(2).

• **1976, Tax Reform Act of 1976 (P.L. 94-455)**

P.L. 94-455, § 1906(b)(13)(A):

Amended 1954 Code by substituting "Secretary" for "Secretary or his delegate" each place it appeared. **Effective** 2-1-77.

[Sec. 5232]

SEC. 5232. IMPORTED DISTILLED SPIRITS.

[Sec. 5232(a)]

(a) TRANSFER TO DISTILLED SPIRITS PLANT WITHOUT PAYMENT OF TAX.—Imported distilled spirits in bulk containers may, under such regulations as the Secretary shall prescribe, be withdrawn from customs custody and transferred in such bulk containers or by pipeline to the bonded premises of a distilled spirits plant without payment of the internal revenue tax imposed on imported distilled spirits by section 5001. The person operating the bonded premises of the distilled spirits plant to which such spirits are transferred shall become liable for the tax on distilled spirits withdrawn from customs custody under this section upon release of the spirits from customs custody, and the importer, or the person bringing such distilled spirits into the United States, shall thereupon be relieved of his liability for such tax.

Amendments

• **1976, Tax Reform Act of 1976 (P.L. 94-455)**

P.L. 94-455, § 1905(a)(15):

Substituted "and the importer, or the person bringing such distilled spirits into the United States," for "and the importer" in Code Sec. 5232(a). **Effective** 2-1-77.

P.L. 94-455, § 1906(b)(13)(A):

Amended 1954 Code by substituting "Secretary" for "Secretary or his delegate" each place it appeared. **Effective** 2-1-77.

[Sec. 5232(b)]

(b) WITHDRAWALS, ETC.—Imported distilled spirits transferred pursuant to subsection (a)—

(1) may be redistilled or denatured only if of 185 degrees or more of proof, and

(2) may be withdrawn for any purpose authorized by this chapter, in the same manner as domestic distilled spirits.

Amendments

• **1979, Trade Agreements Act of 1979 (P.L. 96-39)**

P.L. 96-39, § 807(a)(33):

Amended Code Sec. 5232(b) by deleting paragraph (1) and by redesignating paragraphs (2) and (3) as paragraphs (1) and (2). **Effective** 1-1-80. Prior to deletion paragraph (1) read as follows:

(1) may not be bottled in bond under section 5233,

• **1968 (P.L. 90-630)**

P.L. 90-630, § 3(a):

Amended Code Sec. 5232. **Effective** only for withdrawals from customs custody on or after 2-1-69. Prior to amendment, Code Sec. 5232 read as follows:

"Imported distilled spirits of 185 degrees or more of proof (or spirits of any proof imported for any purpose incident to the requirements of the national defense) may, under such regulations as the Secretary or his delegate shall prescribe, be withdrawn from customs custody, and transferred to the bonded premises of a distilled spirits plant, for nonbeverage use, without payment of the internal revenue tax imposed on imported distilled spirits by section 5001. Such spirits may be redistilled or denatured and may, without redistillation or denaturation, be withdrawn for any purpose authorized by this chapter, in the same manner as domestic distilled spirits."

[Sec. 5233—Repealed]

Amendments

• **1979, Trade Agreements Act of 1979 (P.L. 96-39)**

P.L. 96-39, § 807(a)(34):

Repealed Code Sec. 5233. **Effective** 1-1-80. Prior to repeal, Code Sec. 5233 read as follows:

SEC. 5233. BOTTLING OF DISTILLED SPIRITS IN BOND.

(a) GENERAL.—Distilled spirits stored on bonded premises which have been duly entered for bottling in bond before determination of tax or for bottling in bond for export, shall be dumped, gauged, bottled, packed, and cased in the manner which the Secretary shall by regulations prescribe. Such bottling, packing, and casing shall be conducted in the separate facilities provided therefor under section 5178(a)(4)(A).

(b) BOTTLING REQUIREMENTS.—

(1) The proprietor of a distilled spirits plant who has made entry for withdrawal of distilled spirits for bottling in bond may, under such regulations as the Secretary shall prescribe,

(A) remove extraneous insoluble materials, and effect minor changes in the soluble color or soluble solids solely by filtrations or other physical treatments (which do not involve the addition of any substance which will remain incorporated in the completed product), as may be necessary or desirable to produce a stable product, provided such changes shall not exceed maximum limitations prescribed under regulations issued by the Secretary, and

(B) reduce the proof of such spirits by the addition of pure water only to 100 proof for spirits for domestic use, or to not less than 80 proof for spirits for export purposes, and

(C) mingle, when dumped for bottling, distilled spirits of the same kind, differing only in proof, produced in the same distilling season by the same distiller at the same distillery.

(2) Nothing in this section shall authorize or permit any mingling of different products, or of the same products of different distilling seasons, or the addition or subtraction of any substance or material or the application of any method or process to alter or change in any way the original condition or character of the product except as authorized in this section.

(3) Distilled spirits (except gin and vodka for export) shall not be bottled in bond until they have remained in bond in wooden containers for at least 4 years.

(4) Nothing in this section shall authorize the labeling of spirits in bottles contrary to regulations issued pursuant to the Federal Alcohol Administration Act (27 U. S. C., chapter 8), or any amendment thereof.

(c) TRADEMARKS ON BOTTLES.—No trademarks shall be put on any bottle unless the real name of the actual bona fide distiller, or the name of the individual, firm, partnership, corporation, or association in whose name the spirits were produced and warehoused, shall also be placed conspicuously on such bottle.

(d) RETURN OF BOTTLED DISTILLED SPIRITS FOR REBOTTLING, RELABELING, OR RESTAMPING.—Under such regulations as the Secretary shall prescribe, distilled spirits which have been bottled under this section and removed from bonded premises may, on application to the Secretary, be returned to bonded premises for rebottling, relabeling, or restamping, and tax under section 5001(a)(1) shall not again be collected on such spirits.

(e) CROSS REFERENCES.—

(1) For provisions relating to stamps and stamping of distilled spirits bottled in bond, see section 5205.

(2) For provisions relating to marking or branding of cases of distilled spirits bottled in bond, see section 5206.

ALCOHOL TAXES—DISTILLED SPIRITS PLANTS

• **1976, Tax Reform Act of 1976 (P.L. 94-455)**

P.L. 94-455, § 1905(a)(16):

Struck out "49 Stat. 977;" before "27 U.S.C., chapter 8" in Code Sec. 5233(b)(4). **Effective** 2-1-77.

P.L. 94-455, § 1906(b)(13)(A):

Amended 1954 Code by substituting "Secretary" for "Secretary or his delegate" each place it appeared. **Effective** 2-1-77.

[Sec. 5234—Repealed]

Amendments

• **1979, Trade Agreements Act of 1979 (P.L. 96-39)**

P.L. 96-39, § 807(a)(35):

Repealed Code Sec. 5234. **Effective** 1-1-80. Prior to repeal, Code Sec. 5234 read as follows:

SEC. 5234. MINGLING AND BLENDING OF DISTILLED SPIRITS.

(a) MINGLING OF DISTILLED SPIRITS ON BONDED PREMISES.—

(1) IN GENERAL.—Under such regulations as the Secretary shall prescribe, distilled spirits may be mingled on bonded premises if such spirits—

(A) were distilled at 190 degrees or more of proof;

(B) are heterogeneous and are being dumped for gauging in bulk gauging tanks for immediate removal to bottling premises for use exclusively in taxable rectification, or for blending under section 5025(f), or for other mingling or treatment under section 5025(k);

(C) are homogeneous;

(D) are for immediate denaturation or immediate removal for an authorized taxfree purpose; or

(E) are for immediate redistillation.

(2) CONSOLIDATION OF PACKAGES.—Under such regulations as the Secretary shall prescribe, distilled spirits—

(A) of the same kind,

(B) distilled at the same distillery,

(C) distilled by the same proprietor (under his own or any trade name), and

(D) which have been stored in internal revenue bond in the same kind of cooperage for not less than 4 years (or 2 years in the case of rum or brandy),

may, within 20 years of the date of original entry for deposit of the spirits, be mingled on bonded premises.

(b) MINGLING OF DISTILLED SPIRITS FOR NATIONAL DEFENSE.—Under such regulations as the Secretary shall prescribe, distilled spirits may be mingled on bonded premises or in the course of removal therefrom, for any purpose incident to the national defense.

(c) BLENDING OF BEVERAGE RUMS OR BRANDIES.—Fruit brandies distilled from the same kind of fruit at not more than 170 degrees of proof may, for the sole purpose of perfecting such brandies according to commercial standards, be mixed or blended with each other, or with any such mixture or blend, on bonded premises. Rums may, for the sole purpose of perfecting them according to commercial standards, be mixed or blended with each other, or with any such mixture or blend, on bonded premises. Such rums or brandies so mixed or blended may be packaged, stored, transported, transferred in bond, withdrawn free of tax, withdrawn upon payment or determination of tax, or be otherwise disposed of, in the same manner as rums or brandies not so mixed or blended. The Secretary may make such rules or regulations as he may deem necessary to carry this subsection into effect.

(d) CROSS REFERENCE.—

For provisions imposing a tax on the blending of beverage rums or brandies under subsection (c), see section 5023.

• **1977 (P.L. 95-176)**

P.L. 95-176, § 5(a):

Amended Code Sec. 5234(a)(2). **Effective** 3-1-80. Prior to amendment, Code Sec. 5234(a)(2) read as follows:

(2) CONSOLIDATION OF PACKAGES FOR FURTHER STORAGE IN BOND.—Under such regulations as the Secretary shall prescribe, distilled spirits—

(A) of the same kind,

(B) distilled at the same distillery,

(C) distilled by the same proprietor (under his own or any trade name), and

(D) which have been stored in internal revenue bond in the same kind of cooperage for not less than 4 years (or 2 years in the case of rum or brandy),

may, within 20 years of the date of original entry for deposit of the spirits, be mingled on bonded premises for further storage in bond in as many as necessary of the same packages in which the spirits were stored before consolidation. Where distilled spirits produced in different distilling seasons are mingled under this paragraph, the mingled spirits shall consist of not less than 10 percent of spirits of each such season. No spirits mingled under the provisions of this paragraph shall be again mingled under the provisions thereof until at least one year has elapsed since the last prior mingling. For purposes of this chapter, the date of original entry for deposit of the spirits mingled under the provisions of this paragraph shall be the date of original entry for deposit of the youngest spirits contained in the mingled spirits, and the distilling season of such mingled spirits shall be the distilling season of the youngest spirits contained therein. Notwithstanding any other provisions of law, distilled spirits mingled under this paragraph may be bottled and labeled the same as if such spirits had not been so mingled. No statement claiming or implying age in excess of that of the youngest spirits contained in the mingled spirits shall be made on any stamp or label or in any advertisement.

• **1976, Tax Reform Act of 1976 (P.L. 94-455)**

P.L. 94-455, § 1905(a)(17):

Substituted "20 years" for "8 years" in the first sentence of Code Sec. 5234(a)(2). **Effective** 2-1-77.

P.L. 94-455, § 1906(b)(13)(A):

Amended 1954 Code by substituting "Secretary" for "Secretary or his delegate" each place it appeared. **Effective** 2-1-77.

• **1965, Excise Tax Reduction Act of 1965 (P.L. 89-44)**

P.L. 89-44, § 805(f)(11):

Amended subsection (a)(1)(B) of Section 5234 by inserting "rectification, or for blending under section 5025(f), or for other mingling or treatment under section 5025(k)" in lieu of "rectification or rectification under section 5025(f)". **Effective** 10-1-65.

[Sec. 5235]

SEC. 5235. BOTTLING OF ALCOHOL FOR INDUSTRIAL PURPOSES.

Alcohol for industrial purposes may be bottled, labeled, and cased on bonded premises of a distilled spirits plant prior to payment or determination of tax, under such regulations as the Secretary may prescribe.

Amendments

• **1984, Deficit Reduction Act of 1984 (P.L. 98-369)**

P.L. 98-369, § 454(c)(8):

Amended Code Sec. 5235 by striking out "stamped," in the first sentence and by striking out the second sentence. **Effective** 7-1-85. Prior to amendment, the second sentence read as follows:

The provisions of section 5205(a)(1) shall not apply to alcohol bottled, stamped, and labeled as such under this section.

• **1979, Trade Agreements Act of 1979 (P.L. 96-39)**

P.L. 96-39, § 807(a)(36):

Amended Code Sec. 5235 by changing the second sentence. **Effective** 1-1-80. Prior to amendment, the second sentence of Code Sec. 5235 read as follows: "The provisions of sections 5178(a)(4)(A), 5205(a)(1), and 5233 (relating to the bottling of distilled spirits in bond) shall not be applicable to alcohol bottled, stamped, and labeled as such under this section."

• **1976, Tax Reform Act of 1976 (P.L. 94-455)**

P.L. 94-455, § 1906(b)(13)(A):

Amended 1954 Code by substituting "Secretary" for "Secretary or his delegate" each place it appeared. **Effective** 2-1-77.

[Sec. 5236]

SEC. 5236. DISCONTINUANCE OF STORAGE FACILITIES AND TRANSFER OF DISTILLED SPIRITS.

When the Secretary finds any facilities for the storage of distilled spirits on bonded premises to be unsafe or unfit for use, or the spirits contained therein subject to great loss or wastage, he may require the discontinuance of the use of such facilities and require the spirits contained therein to be transferred to such other storage facilities as he may designate. Such transfer shall be made at such time and under such supervision as the Secretary may require and the expense of the transfer shall be paid by the owner or the warehouseman of the distilled spirits. Whenever the owner of such distilled spirits or the warehouseman fails to make such transfer within the time prescribed, or to pay the just and proper expense of such transfer, as ascertained and determined by the Secretary, such distilled spirits may be seized and sold by the Secretary in the same manner as goods are sold on distraint for taxes, and the proceeds of such sale shall be applied to the payment of the taxes due thereon and the cost and expenses of such sale and removal, and the balance paid over to the owner of such distilled spirits.

ALCOHOL TAXES—DISTILLED SPIRITS PLANTS

Amendments

- **1976, Tax Reform Act of 1976 (P.L. 94-455)**

P.L. 94-455, § 1906(b)(13)(A):

Amended 1954 Code by substituting "Secretary" for "Secretary or his delegate" each place it appeared. **Effective** 2-1-77.

Subpart D—Denaturation

Sec. 5241.	Authority to denature.
Sec. 5242.	Denaturing materials.
Sec. 5243.	Sale of abandoned spirits for denaturation without collection of tax.
Sec. 5244.	Cross references.

[Sec. 5241]

SEC. 5241. AUTHORITY TO DENATURE.

Under such regulations as the Secretary shall prescribe, distilled spirits may be denatured on the bonded premises of a distilled spirits plant qualified for the processing of distilled spirits. Distilled spirits to be denatured under this section shall be of such kind and such degree of proof as the Secretary shall by regulations prescribe. Distilled spirits denatured under this section may be used on the bonded premises of a distilled spirits plant in the manufacture of any article.

Amendments

- **1979, Trade Agreements Act of 1979 (P.L. 96-39)**

P.L. 96-39, § 807(a)(37):

Amended Code Sec. 5241. **Effective** 1-1-80. Prior to amendment, Code Sec. 5241 read as follows:

SEC. 5241. AUTHORITY TO DENATURE.

Under such regulations as the Secretary shall prescribe, distilled spirits may be denatured on the bonded premises of any distilled spirits plant operated by a proprietor who is authorized to produce distilled spirits at such plant or on other bonded premises. Any other person operating bonded premises may, at the discretion of the Secretary and under such regulations as he may prescribe, be authorized to denature distilled spirits on such bonded premises. Distilled spirits to be denatured under this section shall be of such kind and of such degree of proof as the Secretary shall by regulations prescribe.

- **1976, Tax Reform Act of 1976 (P.L. 94-455)**

P.L. 94-455, § 1906(b)(13)(A):

Amended 1954 Code by substituting "Secretary" for "Secretary or his delegate" each place it appeared. **Effective** 2-1-77.

[Sec. 5242]

SEC. 5242. DENATURING MATERIALS.

Methanol or other denaturing materials suitable to the use for which the denatured distilled spirits are intended to be withdrawn shall be used for the denaturation of distilled spirits. Denaturing materials shall be such as to render the spirits with which they are admixed unfit for beverage or internal human medicinal use. The character and the quantity of denaturing materials used shall be as prescribed by the Secretary by regulations.

Amendments

- **1976, Tax Reform Act of 1976 (P.L. 94-455)**

P.L. 94-455, § 1906(b)(13)(A):

Amended 1954 Code by substituting "Secretary" for "Secretary or his delegate" each place it appeared. **Effective** 2-1-77.

[Sec. 5243]

SEC. 5243. SALE OF ABANDONED SPIRITS FOR DENATURATION WITHOUT COLLECTION OF TAX.

Notwithstanding any other provision of law, any distilled spirits abandoned to the United States may be sold, in such cases as the Secretary may by regulation provide, to the proprietor of any distilled spirits plant for denaturation, or redistillation and denaturation, without the payment of the internal revenue tax thereon.

Amendments

- **1976, Tax Reform Act of 1976 (P.L. 94-455)**

P.L. 94-455, § 1906(b)(13)(A):

Amended 1954 Code by substituting "Secretary" for "Secretary or his delegate" each place it appeared. **Effective** 2-1-77.

[Sec. 5244]

SEC. 5244. CROSS REFERENCES.

(1) For provisions authorizing the withdrawal from the bonded premises of a distilled spirits plant of denatured distilled spirits, see section 5214(a)(1).

(2) For provisions requiring a permit to procure specially denatured distilled spirits, see section 5271.

PART III—OPERATIONS ON BOTTLING PREMISES—[Repealed]

[Sec. 5251—Repealed]

Amendments

- **1979, Trade Agreements Act of 1979 (P.L. 96-39)**

P.L. 96-39, § 807(a)(38):

Repealed Code Sec. 5251. **Effective** 1-1-80. Prior to repeal, Code Sec. 5251 read as follows:

SEC. 5251. NOTICE OF INTENTION TO RECTIFY.

The Secretary may by regulations require the proprietor of any distilled spirits plant authorized to rectify distilled spirits or wines to give notice of his intention to rectify or compound any distilled spirits or wines. Any notice so required shall be in such form, shall be submitted at such time, and shall contain such information as the Secretary may by regulations prescribe.

- **1976, Tax Reform Act of 1976 (P.L. 94-455)**

P.L. 94-455, § 1906(b)(13)(A):

Amended 1954 Code by substituting "Secretary" for "Secretary or his delegate" each place it appeared. **Effective** 2-1-77.

[Sec. 5252—Repealed]

Amendments

- **1979, Trade Agreements Act of 1979 (P.L. 96-39)**

P.L. 96-39, § 807(a)(38):

Repealed Code Sec. 5252. **Effective** 1-1-80. Prior to repeal, Code Sec. 5252 read as follows:

SEC. 5252. REGULATION OF OPERATIONS.

(1) For general provisions relating to operations on bottling premises, see part I of this subchapter.

(2) For provisions relating to bottling and packaging of wines on bottling premises, see section 5363.

Subchapter D—Industrial Use of Distilled Spirits

Sec. 5271.   Permits.
Sec. 5272.   Bonds.
Sec. 5273.   Sale, use, and recovery of denatured distilled spirits.
Sec. 5274.   Applicability of other laws.
Sec. 5275.   Records and reports.
Sec. 5276.   Occupational Tax.

[Sec. 5271]

SEC. 5271. PERMITS.

[Sec. 5271(a)]

(a) REQUIREMENTS.—No person shall—
  (1) procure or use distilled spirits free of tax under the provisions of section 5214(a)(2) or (3); or
  (2) procure, deal in, or use specially denatured distilled spirits; or
  (3) recover specially or completely denatured distilled spirits,
until he has filed an application with and received a permit to do so from the Secretary.

Amendments
• **1976, Tax Reform Act of 1976 (P.L. 94-455)**
P.L. 94-455, § 1906(b)(13)(A):
Amended 1954 Code by substituting "Secretary" for "Secretary or his delegate" each place it appeared. **Effective** 2-1-77.

[Sec. 5271(b)]

(b) FORM OF APPLICATION AND PERMIT.—
  (1) The application required by subsection (a) shall be in such form, shall be submitted at such times, and shall contain such information, as the Secretary shall by regulations prescribe.
  (2) Permits under this section shall, under such regulations as the Secretary shall prescribe, designate and limit the acts which are permitted, and the place where and time when such acts may be performed. Such permits shall be issued in such form and under such conditions as the Secretary may by regulations prescribe.

Amendments
• **1976, Tax Reform Act of 1976 (P.L. 94-455)**
P.L. 94-455, § 1906(b)(13)(A):
Amended 1954 Code by substituting "Secretary" for "Secretary or his delegate" each place it appeared. **Effective** 2-1-77.

[Sec. 5271(c)]

(c) DISAPPROVAL OF APPLICATION.—Any application submitted under this section may be disapproved and the permit denied if the Secretary, after notice and opportunity for hearing, finds that—
  (1) in case of an application to withdraw and use distilled spirits free of tax, the applicant is not authorized by law or regulations issued pursuant thereto to withdraw or use such distilled spirits; or
  (2) the applicant (including, in the case of a corporation, any officer, director, or principal stockholder, and, in the case of a partnership, a partner) is, by reason of his business experience, financial standing, or trade connections, not likely to maintain operations in compliance with this chapter; or
  (3) the applicant has failed to disclose any material information required, or made any false statement as to any material fact, in connection with his application; or
  (4) the premises on which it is proposed to conduct the business are not adequate to protect the revenue.

Amendments
• **1976, Tax Reform Act of 1976 (P.L. 94-455)**
P.L. 94-455, § 1906(b)(13)(A):
Amended 1954 Code by substituting "Secretary" for "Secretary or his delegate" each place it appeared. **Effective** 2-1-77.

[Sec. 5271(d)]

(d) CHANGES AFTER ISSUANCE OF PERMIT.—With respect to any change relating to the information contained in the application for a permit issued under this section, the Secretary may by regulations require the filing of written notice of such change and, where the change affects the terms of the permit, require the filing of an amended application.

Amendments
• **1976, Tax Reform Act of 1976 (P.L. 94-455)**
P.L. 94-455, § 1906(b)(13)(A):
Amended 1954 Code by substituting "Secretary" for "Secretary or his delegate" each place it appeared. **Effective** 2-1-77.

[Sec. 5271(e)]

(e) SUSPENSION OR REVOCATION.—If, after notice and hearing, the Secretary finds that any person holding a permit issued under this section—
  (1) has not in good faith complied with the provisions of this chapter or regulations issued thereunder; or
  (2) has violated the conditions of such permit; or
  (3) has made any false statement as to any material fact in his application therefor; or
  (4) has failed to disclose any material information required to be furnished; or
  (5) has violated or conspired to violate any law of the United States relating to intoxicating liquor, or has been convicted of any offense under this title punishable as a felony or of any conspiracy to commit such offense; or
  (6) is, in the case of any person who has a permit under subsection (a)(1) or (a)(2), by reason of his operations, no longer warranted in procuring or using the distilled spirits or specially denatured distilled spirits authorized by his permit; or

ALCOHOL TAXES—DISTILLED SPIRITS, INDUSTRIAL USE

(7) has, in the case of any person who has a permit under subsection (a)(2), manufactured articles which do not correspond to the descriptions and limitations prescribed by law and regulations; or

(8) has not engaged in any of the operations authorized by the permit for a period of more than 2 years;

such permit may, in whole or in part, be revoked or be suspended for such period as the Secretary deems proper.

Amendments
- **1976, Tax Reform Act of 1976 (P.L. 94-455)**

P.L. 94-455, § 1906(b)(13)(A):

Amended 1954 Code by substituting "Secretary" for "Secretary or his delegate" each place it appeared. **Effective** 2-1-77.

[Sec. 5271(f)]

(f) DURATION OF PERMITS.—Permits issued under this section, unless terminated by the terms of the permit, shall continue in effect until suspended or revoked as provided in this section, or until voluntarily surrendered.

[Sec. 5271(g)]

(g) POSTING OF PERMITS.—Permits issued under this section, to use distilled spirits free of tax, to deal in or use specially denatured distilled spirits, or to recover specially or completely denatured distilled spirits, shall be kept posted available for inspection on the premises covered by the permit.

[Sec. 5271(h)]

(h) REGULATIONS.—The Secretary shall prescribe all necessary regulations relating to issuance, denial, suspension, or revocation, of permits under this section, and for the disposition of distilled spirits (including specially denatured distilled spirits) procured under permit pursuant to this section which remain unused when such permit is no longer in effect.

Amendments
- **1976, Tax Reform Act of 1976 (P.L. 94-455)**

P.L. 94-455, § 1906(b)(13)(A):

Amended 1954 Code by substituting "Secretary" for "Secretary or his delegate" each place it appeared. **Effective** 2-1-77.

[Sec. 5272]

SEC. 5272. BONDS.

[Sec. 5272(a)]

(a) REQUIREMENTS.—Before any permit required by section 5271(a) is granted, the Secretary may require a bond, in such form and amount as he may prescribe, to insure compliance with the terms of the permit and the provisions of this chapter.

Amendments
- **1976, Tax Reform Act of 1976 (P.L. 94-455)**

P.L. 94-455, § 1906(b)(13)(A):

Amended 1954 Code by substituting "Secretary" for "Secretary or his delegate" each place it appeared. **Effective** 2-1-77.

[Sec. 5272(b)]

(b) EXCEPTIONS.—No bond shall be required in the case of permits issued to the United States or any governmental agency thereof, or to the several States or any political subdivision thereof, or to the District of Columbia.

Amendments
- **1976, Tax Reform Act of 1976 (P.L. 94-455)**

P.L. 94-455, § 1905(c)(3):

Struck out "and Territories" following "the several States" in Code Sec. 5272(b). **Effective** 2-1-77.

[Sec. 5273]

SEC. 5273. SALE, USE, AND RECOVERY OF DENATURED DISTILLED SPIRITS.

[Sec. 5273(a)]

(a) USE OF SPECIALLY DENATURED DISTILLED SPIRITS.—Any person using specially denatured distilled spirits in the manufacture of articles shall file such formulas and statements of process, submit such samples, and comply with such other requirements, as the Secretary shall by regulations prescribe, and no person shall use specially denatured distilled spirits in the manufacture or production of any article until approval of the article, formula, and process has been obtained from the Secretary.

Amendments
- **1976, Tax Reform Act of 1976 (P.L. 94-455)**

P.L. 94-455, § 1906(b)(13)(A):

Amended 1954 Code by substituting "Secretary" for "Secretary or his delegate" each place it appeared. **Effective** 2-1-77.

[Sec. 5273(b)]

(b) INTERNAL MEDICINAL PREPARATIONS AND FLAVORING EXTRACTS.—

(1) MANUFACTURE.—No person shall use denatured distilled spirits in the manufacture of medicinal preparations or flavoring extracts for internal human use where any of the spirits remains in the finished product.

(2) SALE.—No person shall sell or offer for sale for internal human use any medicinal preparations or flavoring extracts manufactured from denatured distilled spirits where any of the spirits remains in the finished product.

[Sec. 5273(c)]

(c) RECOVERY OF SPIRITS FOR REUSE IN MANUFACTURING.—Manufacturers employing processes in which denatured distilled spirits withdrawn under section 5214(a)(1) are expressed, evaporated, or otherwise removed, from the articles manufactured shall be permitted to recover such distilled spirits and to have such distilled spirits restored to a condition suitable solely for reuse in manufacturing processes under such regulations as the Secretary may prescribe.

ALCOHOL TAXES—DISTILLED SPIRITS, INDUSTRIAL USE

Amendments
- **1976, Tax Reform Act of 1976 (P.L. 94-455)**

P.L. 94-455, § 1906(b)(13)(A):

Amended 1954 Code by substituting "Secretary" for "Secretary or his delegate" each place it appeared. **Effective** 2-1-77.

[Sec. 5273(d)]

(d) PROHIBITED WITHDRAWAL OR SALE.—No person shall withdraw or sell denatured distilled spirits, or sell any article containing denatured distilled spirits for beverage purposes.

[Sec. 5273(e)]

(e) CROSS REFERENCES.—

(1) For penalty and forfeiture for unlawful use or concealment of denatured distilled spirits, see section 5607.

(2) For applicability of all provisions of law relating to distilled spirits that are not denatured, including those requiring payment of tax, to denatured distilled spirits or articles produced, withdrawn, sold, transported, or used in violation of law or regulations, see section 5001(a)(5).

(3) For definition of "articles", see section 5002(a)(14).

Amendments
- **2018, Tax Technical Corrections Act of 2018 (P.L. 115-141)**

P.L. 115-141, § 401(a)(244), Div. U:

Amended Code Sec. 5273(e)(2) by striking "section 5001(a)(6)" and inserting "section 5001(a)(5)". **Effective** 3-23-2018.

Amendments
- **1979, Trade Agreements Act of 1979 (P.L. 96-39)**

P.L. 96-39, § 807(a)(39):

Amended Code Sec. 5273(e)(3) by changing "section 5002(a)(11)" to "section 5002(a)(14)". **Effective** 1-1-80.

[Sec. 5274]

SEC. 5274. APPLICABILITY OF OTHER LAWS.

The provisions, including penalties, of sections 9 and 10 of the Federal Trade Commission Act (15 U. S. C., secs. 49, 50), as now or hereafter amended, shall apply to the jurisdiction, powers, and duties of the Secretary under this subtitle, and to any person (whether or not a corporation) subject to the provisions of this subtitle.

Amendments
- **1976, Tax Reform Act of 1976 (P.L. 94-455)**

P.L. 94-455, § 1906(b)(13)(A):

Amended 1954 Code by substituting "Secretary" for "Secretary or his delegate" each place it appeared. **Effective** 2-1-77.

[Sec. 5275]

SEC. 5275. RECORDS AND REPORTS.

Every person procuring or using distilled spirits withdrawn under section 5214(a)(2) or (3), or procuring, dealing in, or using specially denatured distilled spirits, or recovering specially denatured or completely denatured distilled spirits, shall keep such records and file such reports of the receipt and use of distilled spirits withdrawn free of tax, of the receipt, disposition, use, and recovery of denatured distilled spirits, the manufacture and disposition of articles, and such other information as the Secretary may by regulations require. The Secretary may require any person reprocessing, bottling, or repackaging articles, or dealing in completely denatured distilled spirits or articles, to keep such records, submit such reports, and comply with such other requirements as he may by regulations prescribe. Records required to be kept under this section and a copy of all reports required to be filed shall be preserved as regulations shall prescribe and shall be kept available for inspection by any internal revenue officer during business hours. Such officer may also inspect and take samples of distilled spirits, denatured distilled spirits, or articles (including any substances for use in the manufacture thereof), to which such records or reports relate.

Amendments
- **1976, Tax Reform Act of 1976 (P.L. 94-455)**

P.L. 94-455, § 1906(b)(13)(A):

Amended 1954 Code by substituting "Secretary" for "Secretary or his delegate" each place it appeared. **Effective** 2-1-77.

[Sec. 5276—Repealed]

Amendments
- **2005, Safe, Accountable, Flexible, Efficient Transportation Equity Act: A Legacy for Users (P.L. 109-59)**

P.L. 109-59, § 11125(a)(3):

Repealed Code Sec. 5276. **Effective** 7-1-2008, but not applicable to taxes imposed for periods before such date. Prior to repeal, Code Sec. 5276 read as follows:

SEC. 5276. OCCUPATIONAL TAX.

[Sec. 5276(a)]

(a) GENERAL RULE.—Except as otherwise provided in this section, a permit issued under section 5271 shall not be valid with respect to acts conducted at any place unless the person holding such permit pays a special tax of $250 with respect to such place.

Amendments
- **1989, Omnibus Budget Reconciliation Act of 1989 (P.L. 101-239)**

P.L. 101-239, § 7816(o)(2):

Amended Code Sec. 5276(a) by striking "Except as provided in subsection (c)," and inserting "Except as otherwise provided in this section,". **Effective** as if included in the provision of P.L. 100-647 to which it relates.

- **1988, Technical and Miscellaneous Revenue Act of 1988 (P.L. 100-647)**

P.L. 100-647, § 6105(b):

Amended Code Sec. 5276(a) by striking out "A permit" and inserting in lieu thereof "Except as provided in subsection (c), a permit". **Effective** 7-1-89.

[Sec. 5276(b)]

(b) CERTAIN OCCUPATIONAL TAX RULES TO APPLY.—Rules similar to the rules of subpart G of part II of subchapter A shall apply for purposes of this section.

Amendments
- **1987, Revenue Act of 1987 (P.L. 100-203)**

P.L. 100-203, § 10512(e)(1):

Amended subchapter D of chapter 51 by adding at the end thereof new Code Sec. 5276. For the **effective** date, see Act Sec. 10512(h), below.

P.L. 100-203, § 10512(h), provides:

(h) EFFECTIVE DATE.—

(1) IN GENERAL.—The amendments made by this section shall take effect on January 1, 1988.

(2) ALL TAXPAYERS TREATED AS COMMENCING IN BUSINESS ON JANUARY 1, 1988.—

(A) IN GENERAL.—Any person engaged on January 1, 1988, in any trade or business which is subject to an occupational tax shall be treated for purposes of such tax as having 1st engaged in such trade or business on such date.

(B) LIMITATION ON AMOUNT OF TAX.—In the case of a taxpayer who paid an occupational tax in respect of any premises for any taxable period which began before January 1, 1988, and includes such date, the amount of the occupational tax imposed by reason of subparagraph (A) in respect of such premises shall not exceed an amount equal to $1/2$ the excess (if any) of—

(i) the rate of such tax as in effect on January 1, 1988, over

(ii) the rate of such tax as in effect on December 31, 1987.

(C) OCCUPATIONAL TAX.—For purposes of this paragraph, the term "occupational tax" means any tax imposed under part II of subchapter A of chapter 51, section 5276, section 5731, or section 5801 of the Internal Revenue Code of 1986 (as amended by this section).

(D) DUE DATE OF TAX.—The amount of any tax required to be paid by reason of this paragraph shall be due on April 1, 1988.

ALCOHOL TAXES—DISTILLED SPIRITS, GENERAL

[Sec. 5276(c)]

(c) EXCEPTION FOR UNITED STATES.—Subsection (a) shall not apply to any permit issued to an agency or instrumentality of the United States.

Amendments

• 1988, Technical and Miscellaneous Revenue Act of 1988 (P.L. 100-647)

P.L. 100-647, § 2004(t)(1):

Amended Code Sec. 5276 by adding at the end thereof new subsection (c). **Effective** as if included in the provision of P.L. 100-203 to which it relates.

[Sec. 5276(d)]

(d) EXCEPTION FOR CERTAIN EDUCATIONAL INSTITUTIONS.—Subsection (a) shall not apply with respect to any scientific university, college of learning, or institution of scientific research which—

(1) is issued a permit order under section 5271, and

(2) with respect to any calendar year during which such permit is in effect, procures less than 25 gallons of distilled spirits free of tax for experimental or research use but not for consumption (other than organoleptic tests) or sale.

Amendments

• 1989, Omnibus Budget Reconciliation Act of 1989 (P.L. 101-239)

P.L. 101-239, § 7816(o)(1)(A)-(C):

Amended Code Sec. 5276(c), added by Act Sec. 6015 of P.L. 100-647, by striking "(c) Exemption" and inserting "(d) Exception", by striking "section 5271(a)(2)" in paragraph (1) and inserting "section 5271", and by striking "specially denatured distilled spirits" in paragraph (2) and inserting "distilled spirits free of tax". **Effective** as if included in the provision of P.L. 100-647 to which it relates.

• 1988, Technical and Miscellaneous Revenue Act of 1988 (P.L. 100-647)

P.L. 100-647, § 6105(a):

Amended Code Sec. 5276 by adding new subsection (c)[(d)]. **Effective** 7-1-89.

Subchapter E—General Provisions Relating to Distilled Spirits

Part I. Return of materials used in the manufacture or recovery of distilled spirits.
Part II. Regulation of traffic in containers of distilled spirits.
Part III. Miscellaneous provisions.

PART I—RETURN OF MATERIALS USED IN THE MANUFACTURE OR RECOVERY OF DISTILLED SPIRITS

Sec. 5291. General.

[Sec. 5291]

SEC. 5291. GENERAL.

[Sec. 5291(a)]

(a) REQUIREMENT.—Every person disposing of any substance of the character used in the manufacture of distilled spirits, or disposing of denatured distilled spirits or articles from which distilled spirits may be recovered, shall, when required by the Secretary, render a correct return, in such form and manner as the Secretary may by regulations prescribe, showing the name and address of the person to whom each disposition was made, with such details, as to the quantity so disposed of or other information which the Secretary may require as to each such disposition, as will enable the Secretary to determine whether all taxes due with respect to any distilled spirits manufactured or recovered from any such substance, denatured distilled spirits, or articles, have been paid. Every person required to render a return under this section shall keep such records as will enable such person to render a correct return. Such records shall be preserved for such period as the Secretary shall by regulations prescribe, and shall be kept available for inspection by any internal revenue officer during business hours.

Amendments

• 1976, Tax Reform Act of 1976 (P.L. 94-455)

P.L. 94-455, § 1906(b)(13)(A):

Amended 1954 Code by substituting "Secretary" for "Secretary or his delegate" each place it appeared. **Effective** 2-1-77.

[Sec. 5291(b)]

(b) CROSS REFERENCES.—

(1) For the definition of distilled spirits, see section 5002(a)(8).

(2) For the definition of articles, see section 5002(a)(14).

(3) For penalty for violation of subsection (a), see section 5605.

Amendments

• 1979, Trade Agreements Act of 1979 (P.L. 96-39)

P.L. 96-39, § 807(a)(40):

Amended Code Sec. 5291(b) by changing "section 5002(a)(6)" to "section 5002(a)(8)" in paragraph (1) and by changing "section 5002(a)(11)" to "section 5002(a)(14)" in paragraph (2). **Effective** 1-1-80.

PART II—REGULATION OF TRAFFIC IN CONTAINERS OF DISTILLED SPIRITS

Sec. 5301. General.

[Sec. 5301]

SEC. 5301. GENERAL.

[Sec. 5301(a)]

(a) REQUIREMENTS.—Whenever in his judgment such action is necessary to protect the revenue, the Secretary is authorized, by the regulations prescribed by him and permits issued thereunder if required by him—

(1) to regulate the kind, size, branding, marking, sale, resale, possession, use, and reuse of containers (of a capacity of not more than 5 wine gallons) designed or intended for use for the sale of distilled spirits (within the meaning of such term as it is used in section 5002(a)(8)) for other than industrial use; and

(2) to require, of persons manufacturing, dealing in, or using any such containers, the submission to such inspection, the keeping of such records, and the filing of such reports as may be deemed by him reasonably necessary in connection therewith.

Any requirements imposed under this section shall be in addition to any other requirements imposed by, or pursuant to, law and shall apply as well to persons not liable for tax under the internal revenue laws as to persons so liable.

ALCOHOL TAXES—DISTILLED SPIRITS, GENERAL

Amendments

• **1979, Trade Agreements Act of 1979 (P.L. 96-39)**

P.L. 96-39, §807(a)(41):

Amended Code Sec. 5301(a)(1) by changing "section 5002(a)(6)" to "section 5002(a)(8)". **Effective** 1-1-80.

• **1976, Tax Reform Act of 1976 (P.L. 94-455)**

P.L. 94-455, §1906(b)(13)(A):

Amended 1954 Code by substituting "Secretary" for "Secretary or his delegate" each place it appeared. **Effective** 2-1-77.

[Sec. 5301(b)]

(b) DISPOSITION.—Every person disposing of containers of the character used for the packaging of distilled spirits shall, when required by the Secretary, for protection of the revenue, render a correct return, in such form and manner as the Secretary may by regulations prescribe, showing the name and address of the person to whom each disposition was made, with such details as to the quantities so disposed of or other information which the Secretary may require as to each such disposition. Every person required to render a return under this section shall keep such records as will enable such person to render a correct return. Such records shall be preserved for such period as the Secretary shall by regulations prescribe, and shall be kept available for inspection by any internal revenue officer during business hours.

Amendments

• **1976, Tax Reform Act of 1976 (P.L. 94-455)**

P.L. 94-455, §1906(b)(13)(A):

Amended 1954 Code by substituting "Secretary" for "Secretary or his delegate" each place it appeared. **Effective** 2-1-77.

[Sec. 5301(c)]

(c) REFILLING OF LIQUOR BOTTLES.—No person who sells, or offers for sale, distilled spirits, or agent or employee of such person, shall—

(1) place in any liquor bottle any distilled spirits whatsoever other than those contained in such bottle at the time of tax determination under the provisions of this chapter; or

(2) possess any liquor bottle in which any distilled spirits have been placed in violation of the provisions of paragraph (1); or

(3) by the addition of any substance whatsoever to any liquor bottle, in any manner alter or increase any portion of the original contents contained in such bottle at the time of tax determination under the provisions of this chapter; or

(4) possess any liquor bottle, any portion of the contents of which has been altered or increased in violation of the provisions of paragraph (3);

except that the Secretary may by regulations authorize the reuse of liquor bottles, under such conditions as he may by regulations prescribe. When used in this subsection the term "liquor bottle" shall mean a liquor bottle or other container which has been used for the bottling or packaging of distilled spirits under regulations issued pursuant to subsection (a).

Amendments

• **1984, Deficit Reduction Act of 1984 (P.L. 98-369)**

P.L. 98-369, §454(c)(9):

Amended Code Sec. 5301(c) by striking out "stamping" in paragraphs (1) and (3) and inserting in lieu thereof "tax determination", and by striking out ", if the liquor bottles are to be again stamped under the provisions of this chapter". **Effective** 7-1-85.

[Sec. 5301(d)]

(d) CLOSURES.—The immediate container of distilled spirits withdrawn from bonded premises, or from customs custody, on determination of tax shall bear a closure or other device which is designed so as to require breaking in order to gain access to the contents of such container. The preceding sentence shall not apply to containers of bulk distilled spirits.

Amendments

• **1984, Deficit Reduction Act of 1984 (P.L. 98-369)**

P.L. 98-369, §454(b):

Amended Code Sec. 5301 by redesignating subsection (d) as subsection (e) and by inserting after subsection (c) new subsection (d). **Effective** 7-1-85.

• **1976, Tax Reform Act of 1976 (P.L. 94-455)**

P.L. 94-455, §1906(b)(13)(A):

Amended 1954 Code by substituting "Secretary" for "Secretary or his delegate" each place it appeared. **Effective** 2-1-77.

[Sec. 5301(e)]

(e) PENALTY.—

For penalty for violation of this section, see section 5606.

Amendments

• **1984, Deficit Reduction Act of 1984 (P.L. 98-369)**

P.L. 98-369, §454(b):

Amended Code Sec. 5301 by redesignating subsection (d) as subsection (e). **Effective** 7-1-85.

PART III—MISCELLANEOUS PROVISIONS

Sec. 5311.	Detention of containers.
Sec. 5312.	Production and use of distilled spirits for experimental research.
Sec. 5313.	Withdrawal of distilled spirits from customs custody free of tax for use of the United States.
Sec. 5314.	Special applicability of certain provisions.

[Sec. 5311]

SEC. 5311. DETENTION OF CONTAINERS.

It shall be lawful for any internal revenue officer to detain any container containing, or supposed to contain, distilled spirits, wines, or beer, when he has reason to believe that the tax imposed by law on such distilled spirits, wines, or beer has not been paid or determined as required by law, or that such container is being removed in violation of law; and every such container may be held by him at a safe place until it shall be determined whether the property so detained is liable by law to be proceeded against for forfeiture; but such summary detention shall not continue in any case longer than 72 hours without process of law or intervention of the officer to whom such detention is to be reported.

ALCOHOL TAXES—DISTILLED SPIRITS, GENERAL

[Sec. 5312]
SEC. 5312. PRODUCTION AND USE OF DISTILLED SPIRITS FOR EXPERIMENTAL RESEARCH.

[Sec. 5312(a)]

(a) SCIENTIFIC INSTITUTIONS AND COLLEGES OF LEARNING.—Under such regulations as the Secretary may prescribe and on the filing of such bonds and applications as he may require, any scientific university, college of learning, or institution of scientific research may produce, receive, blend, treat, test, and store distilled spirits, without payment of tax, for experimental or research use but not for consumption (other than organoleptic tests) or sale, in such quantities as may be reasonably necessary for such purposes.

Amendments
- **1976, Tax Reform Act of 1976 (P.L. 94-455)**

P.L. 94-455, § 1906(b)(13)(A):
Amended 1954 Code by substituting "Secretary" for "Secretary or his delegate" each place it appeared. **Effective** 2-1-77.

[Sec. 5312(b)]

(b) EXPERIMENTAL DISTILLED SPIRITS PLANTS.—Under such regulations as the Secretary may prescribe and on the filing of such bonds and applications as he may require, experimental distilled spirits plants may, at the discretion of the Secretary, be established and operated for specific and limited periods of time solely for experimentation in, or development of—

    (1) sources of materials from which distilled spirits may be produced;

    (2) processes by which distilled spirits may be produced or refined; or

    (3) industrial uses of distilled spirits.

Amendments
- **1976, Tax Reform Act of 1976 (P.L. 94-455)**

P.L. 94-455, § 1906(b)(13)(A):
Amended 1954 Code by substituting "Secretary" for "Secretary or his delegate" each place it appeared. **Effective** 2-1-77.

[Sec. 5312(c)]

(c) AUTHORITY TO EXEMPT.—The Secretary may by regulations provide for the waiver of any provision of this chapter (other than this section) to the extent he deems necessary to effectuate the purposes of this section, except that he may not waive the payment of any tax on distilled spirits removed from any such university, college, institution, or plant.

Amendments
- **1976, Tax Reform Act of 1976 (P.L. 94-455)**

P.L. 94-455, § 1906(b)(13)(A):
Amended 1954 Code by substituting "Secretary" for "Secretary or his delegate" each place it appeared. **Effective** 2-1-77.

[Sec. 5313]
SEC. 5313. WITHDRAWAL OF DISTILLED SPIRITS FROM CUSTOMS CUSTODY FREE OF TAX FOR USE OF THE UNITED STATES.

Distilled spirits may be withdrawn free of tax from customs custody by the United States or any governmental agency thereof for its own use for nonbeverage purposes, under such regulations as may be prescribed by the Secretary.

Amendments
- **1976, Tax Reform Act of 1976 (P.L. 94-455)**

P.L. 94-455, § 1906(b)(13)(A):
Amended 1954 Code by substituting "Secretary" for "Secretary or his delegate" each place it appeared. **Effective** 2-1-77.

[Sec. 5314]
SEC. 5314. SPECIAL APPLICABILITY OF CERTAIN PROVISIONS.

[Sec. 5314(a)]

(a) PUERTO RICO.—

    (1) APPLICABILITY.—The provisions of this subsection shall not apply to the Commonwealth of Puerto Rico unless the Legislative Assembly of the Commonwealth of Puerto Rico expressly consents thereto in the manner prescribed in the constitution of the Commonwealth of Puerto Rico for the enactment of a law. [Application of Sec. 5314(a) to Commonwealth of Puerto Rico consented to in Puerto Rican Act No. 3, approved May 6, 1959.]

    (2) IN GENERAL.—Distilled spirits for the purposes authorized in section 5214(a)(2) and (3), denatured distilled spirits, and articles, as described in this paragraph, produced or manufactured in Puerto Rico, may be brought into the United States free of any tax imposed by section 5001(a)(9) or 7652(a)(1) for disposal under the same conditions as like spirits, denatured spirits, and articles, produced or manufactured in the United States; and the provisions of this chapter and regulations promulgated thereunder (and all other provisions of the internal revenue laws applicable to the enforcement thereof, including the penalties of special application thereto) relating to the production, bonded warehousing, and denaturation of distilled spirits, to the withdrawal of distilled spirits or denatured distilled spirits, and to the manufacture of articles from denatured distilled spirits, shall, insofar as applicable, extend to and apply in Puerto Rico in respect of—

        (A) distilled spirits for shipment to the United States for the purposes authorized in section 5214(a)(2) and (3);

        (B) distilled spirits for denaturation;

        (C) denatured distilled spirits for shipment to the United States;

        (D) denatured distilled spirits for use in the manufacture of articles for shipment to the United States; and

        (E) articles, manufactured from denatured distilled spirits, for shipment to the United States.

    (3) WITHDRAWALS AUTHORIZED BY PUERTO RICO.—Distilled spirits (including denatured distilled spirits) may be withdrawn from the bonded premises of a distilled spirits plant in Puerto Rico pursuant to authorization issued under the laws of the Commonwealth of Puerto Rico; such spirits so withdrawn, and products containing such spirits so withdrawn, may not be brought into the United States free of tax.

    (4) COSTS OF ADMINISTRATION.—Any expenses incurred by the Treasury Department in connection with the enforcement in Puerto Rico of the provisions of this subtitle and section 7652(a), and regulations promulgated thereunder, shall be charged against and retained out of taxes collected under this title in respect of commodities of Puerto Rican manufacture brought into the United States. The funds so retained shall be deposited as a reimbursement to the appropriation to which such expenses were originally charged.

ALCOHOL TAXES—BONDED WINE PREMISES

Amendments

• **2018, Tax Technical Corrections Act of 2018 (P.L. 115-141)**

P.L. 115-141, §401(a)(245), Div. U:

Amended Code Sec. 5314(a)(2) by striking "section 5001(a)(10)" and inserting "section 5001(a)(9)". **Effective** 3-23-2018.

• **1976, Tax Reform Act of 1976 (P.L. 94-455)**

P.L. 94-455, §1905(a)(18):

Substituted "section 5001(a)(10)" for "section 5001(a)(4)" in Code Sec. 5314(a)(2). **Effective** 2-1-77.

[Sec. 5314(b)]

(b) VIRGIN ISLANDS.—

(1) IN GENERAL.—Distilled spirits for the purposes authorized in section 5214(a)(2) and (3), denatured distilled spirits, and articles, as described in this paragraph, produced, or manufactured in the Virgin Islands, may be brought into the United States free of any tax imposed by section 7652(b)(1) for disposal under the same conditions as like spirits, denatured spirits, and articles, produced or manufactured in the United States; and the provisions of this chapter and regulations promulgated thereunder (and all other provisions of the internal revenue laws applicable to the enforcement thereof, including the penalties of special application thereto) relating to the production, bonded warehousing, and denaturation of distilled spirits, to the withdrawal of distilled spirits or denatured distilled spirits, and to the manufacture of articles from denatured distilled spirits, shall, insofar as applicable, extend to and apply in the Virgin Islands in respect of—

    (A) distilled spirits for shipment to the United States for the purposes authorized in section 5214(a)(2) and (3);

    (B) distilled spirits for denaturation;

    (C) denatured distilled spirits for shipment to the United States;

    (D) denatured distilled spirits for use in the manufacture of articles for shipment to the United States; and

    (E) articles, manufactured from denatured distilled spirits, for shipment to the United States.

(2) ADVANCE OF FUNDS.—The insular government of the Virgin Islands shall advance to the Treasury of the United States such funds as may be required from time to time by the Secretary for the purpose of defraying all expenses incurred by the Treasury Department in connection with the enforcement in the Virgin Islands of paragraph (1) and regulations promulgated thereunder. The funds so advanced shall be deposited in a separate trust fund in the Treasury of the United States and shall be available to the Treasury Department for the purposes of this subsection.

(3) REGULATIONS ISSUED BY VIRGIN ISLANDS.—The Secretary may authorize the Governor of the Virgin Islands, or his duly authorized agents, to issue or adopt such regulations, to approve such bonds, and to issue, suspend, or revoke such permits, as are necessary to carry out the provisions of this subsection. When regulations have been issued or adopted under this paragraph with concurrence of the Secretary he may exempt the Virgin Islands from any provisions of law and regulations otherwise made applicable by the provisions of paragraph (1), except that denatured distilled spirits, articles, and distilled spirits for tax-free purposes which are brought into the United States from the Virgin Islands under the provisions of this subsection shall in all respects conform to the requirements of law and regulations imposed on like products of domestic manufacture.

Amendments

• **1976, Tax Reform Act of 1976 (P.L. 94-455)**

P.L. 94-455, §1906(b)(13)(A):

Amended 1954 Code by substituting "Secretary" for "Secretary or his delegate" each place it appeared. **Effective** 2-1-77.

Subchapter F—Bonded and Taxpaid Wine Premises

Part I.	Establishment.
Part II.	Operations.
Part III.	Cellar treatment and classification of wine.
Part IV.	General.

PART I—ESTABLISHMENT

Sec. 5351.	Bonded wine cellar.
Sec. 5352.	Taxpaid wine bottling house.
Sec. 5353.	Bonded wine warehouse.
Sec. 5354.	Bond.
Sec. 5355.	General provisions relating to bonds.
Sec. 5356.	Application.
Sec. 5357.	Premises.

[Sec. 5351]

SEC. 5351. BONDED WINE CELLAR.

[Sec. 5351(a)]

(a) IN GENERAL.—Any person establishing premises for the production, blending, cellar treatment, storage, bottling, packaging, or repackaging of untaxpaid wine (other than wine produced exempt from tax under section 5042), including the use of wine spirits in wine production, shall, before commencing operations, make application to the Secretary and, except as provided under section 5551(d), file bond and receive permission to operate.

[Sec. 5351(b)]

(b) DEFINITIONS.—For purposes of this chapter—

(1) BONDED WINE CELLAR.—The term "bonded wine cellar" means any premises described in subsection (a), including any such premises established by a taxpayer described in section 5551(d).

(2) BONDED WINERY.—At the discretion of the Secretary, any bonded wine cellar that engages in production operations may be designated as a "bonded winery".

Amendments

• **2015, Protecting Americans from Tax Hikes Act of 2015 (P.L. 114-113)**

P.L. 114-113, §332(b)(2)(B)(i)-(iv), Div. Q:

Amended Code Sec. 5351 by striking "Any person" and inserting "(a) IN GENERAL.—Any person", by inserting ", except as provided under section 5551(d)," before "file bond", by striking "Such premises shall" and all that follows through the period, and by adding at the end a new subsection (b). **Effective** for any calendar quarters beginning more

ALCOHOL TAXES—BONDED WINE PREMISES

than 1 year after 12-18-2015. Prior to amendment, "Such premises shall" and all that follows through the period in Code Sec. 5351 read as follows:

Such premises shall be known as "bonded wine cellars"; except that any such premises engaging in production operations may, in the discretion of the Secretary, be designated as a "bonded winery".

• **1976, Tax Reform Act of 1976 (P.L. 94-455)**

P.L. 94-455, § 1906(b)(13)(A):

Amended 1954 Code by substituting "Secretary" for "Secretary or his delegate" each place it appeared. **Effective** 2-1-77.

[Sec. 5352]

SEC. 5352. TAXPAID WINE BOTTLING HOUSE.

Any person bottling, packaging, or repackaging taxpaid wines shall, before commencing such operations, make application to the Secretary and receive permission to operate. Such premises shall be known as "taxpaid wine bottling houses".

Amendments

• **1979, Trade Agreements Act of 1979 (P.L. 96-39)**

P.L. 96-39, § 807(a)(42):

Amended Code Sec. 5352 by changing the first sentence. **Effective** 1-1-80. Prior to amendment, the first sentence of Code Sec. 5352 read as follows:

"Any person bottling, packaging, or repackaging taxpaid wines at premises other than the bottling premises of a distilled spirits plant shall, before commencing such operations, make application to the Secretary and receive permission to operate."

• **1976, Tax Reform Act of 1976 (P.L. 94-455)**

P.L. 94-455, § 1906(b)(13)(A):

Amended 1954 Code by substituting "Secretary" for "Secretary or his delegate" each place it appeared. **Effective** 2-1-77.

[Sec. 5353]

SEC. 5353. BONDED WINE WAREHOUSE.

Any responsible warehouse company or other responsible person may, upon filing application with the Secretary and consent of the proprietor and the surety on the bond of any bonded wine cellar, under regulations prescribed by the Secretary, establish on such premises facilities for the storage of wines and allied products for credit purposes, to be known as a "bonded wine warehouse". The proprietor of the bonded wine cellar shall remain responsible in all respects for operations in the warehouse and the tax on the wine or wine spirits stored therein.

Amendments

• **1976, Tax Reform Act of 1976 (P.L. 94-455)**

P.L. 94-455, § 1906(b)(13)(A):

Amended 1954 Code by substituting "Secretary" for "Secretary or his delegate" each place it appeared. **Effective** 2-1-77.

[Sec. 5354]

SEC. 5354. BOND.

The bond for a bonded wine cellar shall be in such form, on such conditions, and with such adequate surety, as regulations issued by the Secretary shall prescribe, and shall be in a penal sum not less than the tax on any wine or distilled spirits possessed or in transit at any one time (taking into account the appropriate amount of credit with respect to such wine under section 5041(c)), but not less than $1,000 nor more than $50,000; except that where the tax on such wine and on such distilled spirits exceeds $250,000, the penal sum of the bond shall be not more than $100,000. Where additional liability arises as a result of deferral of payment of tax payable on any return, the Secretary may require the proprietor to file a supplemental bond in such amount as may be necessary to protect the revenue. The liability of any person on any such bond shall apply whether the transaction or operation on which the liability of the proprietor is based occurred on or off the proprietor's premises.

Amendments

• **1996, Small Business Job Protection Act of 1996 (P.L. 104-188)**

P.L. 104-188, § 1702(b)(7):

Amended Code Sec. 5354 by inserting "(taking into account the appropriate amount of credit with respect to such wine under section 5041(c))" after "any one time". **Effective** as if included in the provision of P.L. 101-508 to which it relates.

• **1984, Deficit Reduction Act of 1984 (P.L. 98-369)**

P.L. 98-369, § 455(c):

Amended Code Sec. 5354 by striking out "wine spirits" each place it appeared and inserting in lieu thereof "distilled spirits". **Effective** 7-18-84.

• **1976, Tax Reform Act of 1976 (P.L. 94-455)**

P.L. 94-455, § 1906(b)(13)(A):

Amended 1954 Code by substituting "Secretary" for "Secretary or his delegate" each place it appeared. **Effective** 2-1-77.

[Sec. 5355]

SEC. 5355. GENERAL PROVISIONS RELATING TO BONDS.

The provisions of section 5551 (relating to bonds) shall be applicable to the bonds required under section 5354.

[Sec. 5356]

SEC. 5356. APPLICATION.

The application required by this part shall disclose, as regulations issued by the Secretary shall provide, such information as may be necessary to enable the Secretary to determine the location and extent of the premises, the type of operations to be conducted on such premises, and whether the operations will be in conformity with law and regulations.

Amendments

• **1976, Tax Reform Act of 1976 (P.L. 94-455)**

P.L. 94-455, § 1906(b)(13)(A):

Amended 1954 Code by substituting "Secretary" for "Secretary or his delegate" each place it appeared. **Effective** 2-1-77.

[Sec. 5357]

SEC. 5357. PREMISES.

Bonded wine cellar premises, including noncontiguous portions thereof, shall be so located, constructed, and equipped, as to afford adequate protection to the revenue, as regulations prescribed by the Secretary may provide.

Amendments

• **1976, Tax Reform Act of 1976 (P.L. 94-455)**

P.L. 94-455, § 1906(b)(13)(A):

Amended 1954 Code by substituting "Secretary" for "Secretary or his delegate" each place it appeared. **Effective** 2-1-77.

ALCOHOL TAXES—BONDED WINE PREMISES

PART II—OPERATIONS

Sec. 5361.	Bonded wine cellar operations.
Sec. 5362.	Removals of wine from bonded wine cellars.
Sec. 5363.	Taxpaid wine bottling house operations.
Sec. 5364.	Wine imported in bulk.
Sec. 5365.	Segregation of operations.
Sec. 5366.	Supervision.
Sec. 5367.	Records.
Sec. 5368.	Gauging and marking.
Sec. 5369.	Inventories.
Sec. 5370.	Losses.
Sec. 5371.	Insurance coverage, etc.
Sec. 5372.	Sampling.
Sec. 5373.	Wine spirits.

[Sec. 5361]

SEC. 5361. BONDED WINE CELLAR OPERATIONS.

In addition to the operations described in section 5351, the proprietor of a bonded wine cellar may, subject to regulations prescribed by the Secretary, on such premises receive taxpaid wine for return to bond, reconditioning, or destruction; prepare for market and store commercial fruit products and by-products not taxable as wines; produce or receive distilling material or vinegar stock; produce (with or without added wine spirits, and without added sugar) or receive on wine premises, subject to tax as wine but not for sale or consumption as beverage wine, (1) heavy bodied blending wines and Spanish-type blending sherries, and (2) other wine products made from natural wine for nonbeverage purposes; and such other operations as may be conducted in a manner that will not jeopardize the revenue or conflict with wine operations.

Amendments

• **1997, Taxpayer Relief Act of 1997 (P.L. 105-34)**

P.L. 105-34, §1416(b)(1):

Amended Code Sec. 5361 by striking "unmerchantable" after "on such premises receive". **Effective** on the 1st day of the 1st calendar quarter that begins at least 180 days after 8-5-97.

• **1979, Trade Agreements Act of 1979 (P.L. 96-39)**

P.L. 96-39, §807(a)(43):

Amended Code Sec. 5361 by changing "or receive on standard wine premises only" to "or receive on wine premises". **Effective** 1-1-80.

• **1976, Tax Reform Act of 1976 (P.L. 94-455)**

P.L. 94-455, §1906(b)(13)(A):

Amended 1954 Code by substituting "Secretary" for "Secretary or his delegate" each place it appeared. **Effective** 2-1-77.

[Sec. 5362]

SEC. 5362. REMOVALS OF WINE FROM BONDED WINE CELLARS.

[Sec. 5362(a)]

(a) WITHDRAWALS ON DETERMINATION OF TAX.—Wine may be withdrawn from bonded wine cellars on payment or determination of the tax thereon, under such regulations as the Secretary shall prescribe.

Amendments

• **1976, Tax Reform Act of 1976 (P.L. 94-455)**

P.L. 94-455, §1906(b)(13)(A):

Amended 1954 Code by substituting "Secretary" for "Secretary or his delegate" each place it appeared. **Effective** 2-1-77.

[Sec. 5362(b)]

(b) TRANSFERS OF WINE BETWEEN BONDED PREMISES.—

   (1) IN GENERAL.—Wine on which the tax has not been paid or determined may, under such regulations as the Secretary shall prescribe, be transferred in bond between bonded premises.

   (2) WINE TRANSFERRED TO A DISTILLED SPIRITS PLANT MAY NOT BE REMOVED FOR CONSUMPTION OR SALE AS WINE.—Any wine transferred to the bonded premises of a distilled spirits plant—

      (A) may be used in the manufacture of a distilled spirits product, and

      (B) may not be removed from such bonded premises for consumption or sale as wine.

   (3) CONTINUED LIABILITY FOR TAX.—The liability for tax on wine transferred to the bonded premises of a distilled spirits plant pursuant to paragraph (1) shall (except as otherwise provided by law) continue until the wine is used in a distilled spirits product.

   (4) TRANSFER IN BOND NOT TREATED AS REMOVAL FOR CONSUMPTION OR SALE.—For purposes of this chapter, the removal of wine for transfer in bond between bonded premises shall not be treated as a removal for consumption or sale.

   (5) BONDED PREMISES.—For purposes of this subsection, the term "bonded premises" means a bonded wine cellar or the bonded premises of a distilled spirits plant.

Amendments

• **1979, Trade Agreements Act of 1979 (P.L. 96-39)**

P.L. 96-39, §807(a)(44):

Amended Code Sec. 5362(b). **Effective** 1-1-80. Prior to amendment, Code Sec. 5362(b) read as follows:

(b) TRANSFERS OF WINE BETWEEN BONDED WINE CELLARS.—Wine on which the internal revenue tax has not been paid or determined may, under such regulations as the Secretary shall prescribe, be transferred in bond between bonded wine cellars. For the purposes of this chapter, the removal of wine for transfer in bond between bonded wine cellars shall not be construed to be a removal for consumption or sale.

• **1976, Tax Reform Act of 1976 (P.L. 94-455)**

P.L. 94-455, §1906(b)(13)(A):

Amended 1954 Code by substituting "Secretary" for "Secretary or his delegate" each place it appeared. **Effective** 2-1-77.

[Sec. 5362(c)]

(c) WITHDRAWALS OF WINE FREE OF TAX OR WITHOUT PAYMENT OF TAX.—Wine on which the tax has not been paid or determined may, under such regulations and bonds as the Secretary may deem necessary to protect the revenue, be withdrawn from bonded wine cellars—

ALCOHOL TAXES—BONDED WINE PREMISES

(1) without payment of tax for export by the proprietor or by any authorized exporter;

(2) without payment of tax for transfer to any foreign-trade zone;

(3) without payment of tax for use of certain vessels and aircraft as authorized by law;

(4) without payment of tax for transfer to any customs bonded warehouse;

(5) without payment of tax for use in the production of vinegar;

(6) without payment of tax for use in distillation in any distilled spirits plant authorized to produce distilled spirits;

(7) free of tax for experimental or research purposes by any scientific university, college of learning, or institution of scientific research;

(8) free of tax for use by or for the account of the proprietor or his agents for analysis or testing, organoleptic or otherwise; and

(9) free of tax for use by the United States or any agency thereof, and for use for analysis, testing, research, or experimentation by the governments of the several States and the District of Columbia or of any political subdivision thereof or by any agency of such governments. No bond shall be required of any such government or agency under this paragraph.

Amendments

• **1980 (P.L. 96-601)**

P.L. 96-601, §2(a):

Amended Code Sec. 5362(c)(4). **Effective** 4-1-81. Prior to amendment, Code Sec. 5362(c)(4) provided:

"(4) without payment of tax for transfer to any class 6 customs manufacturing warehouse;".

• **1976, Tax Reform Act of 1976 (P.L. 94-455)**

P.L. 94-455, §1905(c)(4):

Struck out "and Territories" following "of the several States" in Code Sec. 5362(c)(9). **Effective** 2-1-77.

P.L. 94-455, §1906(b)(13)(A):

Amended 1954 Code by substituting "Secretary" for "Secretary or his delegate" each place it appeared. **Effective** 2-1-77.

[Sec. 5362(d)]

(d) WITHDRAWAL FREE OF TAX OF WINE AND WINE PRODUCTS UNFIT FOR BEVERAGE USE.—Under such regulations as the Secretary may deem necessary to protect the revenue, wine, or wine products made from wine, when rendered unfit for beverage use, on which the tax has not been paid or determined, may be withdrawn from bonded wine cellars free of tax. The wine or wine products to be so withdrawn may be treated with methods or materials which render such wine or wine products suitable for their intended use. No wine or wine products so withdrawn shall contain more than 21 percent of alcohol by volume, or be used in the compounding of distilled spirits or wine for beverage use or in the manufacture of any product intended to be used in such compounding.

Amendments

• **1976, Tax Reform Act of 1976 (P.L. 94-455)**

P.L. 94-455, §1906(b)(13)(A):

Amended 1954 Code by substituting "Secretary" for "Secretary or his delegate" each place it appeared. **Effective** 2-1-77.

• **1967 (P.L. 90-73)**

P.L. 90-73:

Added Code Sec. 5362(d) to read as prior to amendment by P.L. 94-455. **Effective** the first day of the first month which begins 90 days or more after 8-29-67, the date of enactment.

[Sec. 5362(e)]

(e) WITHDRAWAL FROM CUSTOMS BONDED WAREHOUSES FOR USE OF FOREIGN EMBASSIES, LEGATIONS, ETC.—

(1) IN GENERAL.—Notwithstanding any other provision of law, wine entered into customs bonded warehouses under subsection (c)(4) may, under such regulations as the Secretary may prescribe, be withdrawn from such warehouses for consumption in the United States by and for the official or family use of such foreign governments, organizations, and individuals who are entitled to withdraw imported wines from such warehouses free of tax. Wines transferred to customs bonded warehouses under subsection (c)(4) shall be entered, stored, and accounted for in such warehouses under such regulations and bonds as the Secretary may prescribe, and may be withdrawn therefrom by such governments, organizations, and individuals free of tax under the same conditions and procedures as imported wines.

(2) WITHDRAWAL FOR DOMESTIC USE.—Wine entered into customs bonded warehouses under subsection (c)(4) for purposes of removal under paragraph (1) may be withdrawn therefrom for domestic use. Wines so withdrawn shall be treated as American goods exported and returned.

(3) SALE OR UNAUTHORIZED USE PROHIBITED.—Wine withdrawn from customs bonded warehouses or otherwise brought into the United States free of tax for the official or family use of foreign governments, organizations, or individuals authorized to obtain wine free of tax shall not be sold and shall not be disposed of or possessed for any use other than an authorized use. The provisions of paragraphs (1)(B) and (3) of section 5043(a) are hereby extended and made applicable to any person selling, disposing of, or possessing any wine in violation of the preceding sentence, and to the wine involved in any such violation.

Amendments

• **1980 (P.L. 96-601)**

P.L. 96-601, §2(b):

Added Code Sec. 5362(e). **Effective** 4-1-81.

[Sec. 5363]

SEC. 5363. TAXPAID WINE BOTTLING HOUSE OPERATIONS.

In addition to the operations described in section 5352, the proprietor of a taxpaid wine bottling house may, subject to regulations issued by the Secretary, on such premises mix wine of the same kind and taxable grade to facilitate handling; preserve, filter, or clarify wine; and conduct operations not involving wine where such operations will not jeopardize the revenue or conflict with wine operations.

Amendments

• **1979, Trade Agreements Act of 1979 (P.L. 96-39)**

P.L. 96-39, §807(a)(45):

Amended Code Sec. 5363 by deleting the last two sentences. **Effective** 1-1-80. Prior to deletion, the last two sentences read as follows:

"This subchapter shall apply to any wine received on the bottling premises of any distilled spirits plant for bottling, packaging, or repackaging, and to all operations relative thereto. Sections 5021, 5081, and 5082 shall not apply to the mixing or treatment of taxpaid wine under this section."

• **1976, Tax Reform Act of 1976 (P.L. 94-455)**

P.L. 94-455, §1906(b)(13)(A):

Amended 1954 Code by substituting "Secretary" for "Secretary or his delegate" each place it appeared. **Effective** 2-1-77.

[Sec. 5364]

SEC. 5364. WINE IMPORTED IN BULK.

Natural wine (as defined in section 5381) imported or brought into the United States in bulk containers may, under such regulations as the Secretary may prescribe, be withdrawn from customs custody and transferred in such bulk containers to the premises of a bonded wine cellar without payment of the internal revenue tax imposed on such wine. The proprietor of a bonded wine cellar to which such wine is transferred shall become liable for the tax on the wine withdrawn from customs custody under this section upon release of the wine from customs custody, and the importer, or the person bringing such wine into the United States, shall thereupon be relieved of the liability for such tax.

Sec. 5362(c)(1)

ALCOHOL TAXES—BONDED WINE PREMISES

Amendments

• **1998, IRS Restructuring and Reform Act of 1998 (P.L. 105-206)**

P.L. 105-206, §6014(b)(3):

Amended Code Sec. 5364 by striking "Wine imported or brought into" and inserting "Natural wine (as defined in section 5381) imported or brought into". **Effective** as if included in P.L. 105-34 to which it relates [effective 4-1-98.—CCH].

• **1997, Taxpayer Relief Act of 1997 (P.L. 105-34)**

P.L. 105-34, §1422(a):

Amended part II of subchapter F of chapter 51 by inserting after Code Sec. 5363 a new Code Sec. 5364. **Effective** on the 1st day of the 1st calendar quarter that begins at least 180 days after 8-5-97.

• **1979, Trade Agreements Act of 1979 (P.L. 96-39)**

P.L. 96-39, §807(a)(46):

Repealed Code Sec. 5364. **Effective** 1-1-80. Prior to repeal, Code Sec. 5364 read as follows:

SEC. 5364. STANDARD WINE PREMISES.

Except as otherwise specifically provided in this subchapter, no proprietor of a bonded wine cellar or taxpaid wine bottling house engaged in producing, receiving, storing or using any standard wine, shall produce, receive, store, or use any wine other than standard wine. The limitation contained in the preceding sentence shall not prohibit the production or receipt of high fermentation wines, distilling material, or vinegar stock in any bonded wine cellar.

[Sec. 5365]

SEC. 5365. SEGREGATION OF OPERATIONS.

The Secretary may require by regulations such segregation of operations within the premises, by partitions or otherwise, as may be necessary to prevent jeopardy to the revenue, to prevent confusion between untaxpaid wine operations and such other operations as are authorized in this subchapter, to prevent substitution with respect to the several methods of producing effervescent wines, and to prevent the commingling of standard wines with other than standard wines.

Amendments

• **1979, Trade Agreements Act of 1979 (P.L. 96-39)**

P.L. 96-39, §807(a)(47):

Amended Code Sec. 5365. **Effective** 1-1-80. Prior to amendment, Code Sec. 5365 read as follows:

SEC. 5365. SEGREGATION OF OPERATIONS.

The Secretary may require by regulations such segregation of operations within the premises, by partitions or otherwise, as may be necessary to prevent jeopardy to the revenue, to prevent confusion between untaxpaid wine operations and such other operations as are authorized in this subchapter, or to prevent substitution with respect to the several methods of producing effervescent wines.

• **1976, Tax Reform Act of 1976 (P.L. 94-455)**

P.L. 94-455, §1906(b)(13)(A):

Amended 1954 Code by substituting "Secretary" for "Secretary or his delegate" each place it appeared. **Effective** 2-1-77.

[Sec. 5366]

SEC. 5366. SUPERVISION.

The Secretary may by regulations require that operations at a bonded wine cellar or taxpaid wine bottling house be supervised by an internal revenue officer where necessary for the protection of the revenue or for the proper enforcement of this subchapter.

Amendments

• **1976, Tax Reform Act of 1976 (P.L. 94-455)**

P.L. 94-455, §1906(b)(13)(A):

Amended 1954 Code by substituting "Secretary" for "Secretary or his delegate" each place it appeared. **Effective** 2-1-77.

[Sec. 5367]

SEC. 5367. RECORDS.

The proprietor of a bonded wine cellar or a taxpaid wine bottling house shall keep such records and file such returns, in such form and containing such information, as the Secretary may by regulations provide.

Amendments

• **1976, Tax Reform Act of 1976 (P.L. 94-455)**

P.L. 94-455, §1906(b)(13)(A):

Amended 1954 Code by substituting "Secretary" for "Secretary or his delegate" each place it appeared. **Effective** 2-1-77.

[Sec. 5368]

SEC. 5368. GAUGING AND MARKING.

[Sec. 5368(a)]

(a) GAUGING AND MARKING.—All wine or wine spirits shall be locked, sealed, and gauged, and shall be marked, branded, labeled, or otherwise identified, in such manner as the Secretary may by regulations prescribe.

Amendments

• **1976, Tax Reform Act of 1976 (P.L. 94-455)**

P.L. 94-455, §1905(a)(20)(A):

Amended the heading of Code Sec. 5368. **Effective** 2-1-77. Prior to amendment, the heading of Code Sec. 5368 read as follows:

SEC. 5368. GAUGING, MARKING AND STAMPING.

P.L. 94-455, §1906(b)(13)(A):

Amended 1954 Code by substituting "Secretary" for "Secretary or his delegate" each place it appeared. **Effective** 2-1-77.

[Sec. 5368(b)]

(b) MARKING.—Wines shall be removed in such containers (including vessels, vehicles, and pipelines) bearing such marks and labels, evidencing compliance with this chapter, as the Secretary may by regulations prescribe.

Amendments

• **1976, Tax Reform Act of 1976 (P.L. 94-455)**

P.L. 94-455, §1905(a)(20)(B):

Amended Code Sec. 5368(b). **Effective** 2-1-77. Prior to amendment, Code Sec. 5368(b) read as follows:

(b) STAMPING.—Wines shall be removed in such containers (including vessels, vehicles, and pipelines) bearing such marks, labels, and stamps, evidencing compliance with this chapter, as the Secretary or his delegate may by regulations prescribe.

[Sec. 5369]

SEC. 5369. INVENTORIES.

Each proprietor of premises subject to the provisions of this subchapter shall take and report such inventories as the Secretary may by regulations prescribe.

Amendments

• **1976, Tax Reform Act of 1976 (P.L. 94-455)**

P.L. 94-455, §1906(b)(13)(A):

Amended 1954 Code by substituting "Secretary" for "Secretary or his delegate" each place it appeared. **Effective** 2-1-77.

ALCOHOL TAXES—BONDED WINE PREMISES

[Sec. 5370]

SEC. 5370. LOSSES.

[Sec. 5370(a)]

(a) GENERAL.—No tax shall be collected in respect of any wines lost or destroyed while in bond, except that tax shall be collected—

(1) THEFT.—In the case of loss by theft, unless the Secretary shall find that the theft occurred without connivance, collusion, fraud, or negligence on the part of the proprietor or other person responsible for the tax, or the owner, consignor, consignee, bailee, or carrier, or the agents or employees of any of them; and

(2) VOLUNTARY DESTRUCTION.—In the case of voluntary destruction, unless the wine was destroyed under Government supervision, or on such adequate notice to, and approval by, the Secretary as regulations shall provide.

Amendments

• **1976, Tax Reform Act of 1976 (P.L. 94-455)**

P.L. 94-455, § 1906(b)(13)(A):

Amended 1954 Code by substituting "Secretary" for "Secretary or his delegate" each place it appeared. **Effective** 2-1-77.

[Sec. 5370(b)]

(b) PROOF OF LOSS.—In any case in which the wine is lost or destroyed, whether by theft or otherwise, the Secretary may require by regulations the proprietor of the bonded wine cellar or other person liable for the tax to file a claim for relief from the tax and submit proof as to the cause of such loss. In every case where it appears that the loss was by theft, the burden shall be on the proprietor or other person liable for the tax to establish to the satisfaction of the Secretary, that such loss did not occur as the result of connivance, collusion, fraud, or negligence on the part of the proprietor, owner, consignor, consignee, bailee, or carrier, or the agents or employees of any of them.

Amendments

• **1976, Tax Reform Act of 1976 (P.L. 94-455)**

P.L. 94-455, § 1906(b)(13)(A):

Amended 1954 Code by substituting "Secretary" for "Secretary or his delegate" each place it appeared. **Effective** 2-1-77.

[Sec. 5371]

SEC. 5371. INSURANCE COVERAGE, ETC.

Any remission, abatement, refund, or credit of, or other relief from, taxes on wines or wine spirits authorized by law shall be allowed only to the extent that the claimant is not indemnified or recompensed for the tax.

[Sec. 5372]

SEC. 5372. SAMPLING.

Under regulations prescribed by the Secretary, wine may be utilized in any bonded wine cellar for testing, tasting, or sampling, free of tax.

Amendments

• **1976, Tax Reform Act of 1976 (P.L. 94-455)**

P.L. 94-455, § 1906(b)(13)(A):

Amended 1954 Code by substituting "Secretary" for "Secretary or his delegate" each place it appeared. **Effective** 2-1-77.

[Sec. 5373]

SEC. 5373. WINE SPIRITS.

[Sec. 5373(a)]

(a) IN GENERAL.—The wine spirits authorized to be used in wine production shall be brandy or wine spirits produced in a distilled spirits plant (with or without the use of water to facilitate extraction and distillation) exclusively from—

(1) fresh or dried fruit, or their residues,

(2) the wine or wine residues therefrom, or

(3) special natural wine under such conditions as the Secretary may by regulations prescribe;

except that where, in the production of natural wine or special natural wine, sugar has been used, the wine or the residuum thereof may not be used if the unfermented sugars therein have been refermented. Such wine spirits shall not be reduced with water from distillation proof, nor be distilled, unless regulations otherwise provide, at less than 140 degrees of proof (except that commercial brandy aged in wood for a period of not less than 2 years, and barreled at not less than 100 degrees of proof, shall be deemed wine spirits for the purpose of this subsection).

Amendments

• **1976, Tax Reform Act of 1976 (P.L. 94-455)**

P.L. 94-455, § 1906(b)(13)(A):

Amended 1954 Code by substituting "Secretary" for "Secretary or his delegate" each place it appeared. **Effective** 2-1-77.

• **1968 (P.L. 90-619)**

P.L. 90-619, § 1:

Amended the first sentence of Code Sec. 5373(a) to read as prior to amendment by P.L. 94-455. **Effective** 2-1-69. Prior to amendment, such sentence read as follows:

"The wine spirits authorized to be used in wine production shall be brandy or wine spirits produced in a distilled spirits plant (with or without the use of water to facilitate extraction and distillation) exclusively from fresh or dried fruit, or their residues, or the wine or wine residue therefrom (except that where, in the production of natural wine, sugar has been used, the wine or the residuum thereof may not be used, if the unfermented sugars therein have been refermented)."

[Sec. 5373(b)]

(b) WITHDRAWAL OF WINE SPIRITS.—

(1) The proprietor of any bonded wine cellar may withdraw and receive wine spirits without payment of tax from the bonded premises of any distilled spirits plant, or from any bonded wine cellar as provided in paragraph (2), for use in the production of natural wine, for addition to concentrated or unconcentrated juice for use in wine production, or for such other uses as may be authorized in this subchapter.

(2) Wine spirits so withdrawn, and not used in wine production or as otherwise authorized in this subchapter, may, as provided by regulations prescribed by the Secretary, be transferred to the bonded premises of any distilled spirits plant or bonded wine cellar, or may be taxpaid and removed as provided by law.

(3) On such use, transfer, or taxpayment, the Secretary shall credit the proprietor with the amount of wine spirits so used or transferred or taxpaid and, in addition, with such portion of wine spirits so withdrawn as may have been lost either in transit or on the bonded wine cellar premises, to the extent allowable under section 5008(a). Where the proprietor has used wine spirits in actual wine production but in violation

ALCOHOL TAXES—BONDED WINE PREMISES

of the requirements of this subchapter, the Secretary shall also extend such credit to the wine spirits so used if the proprietor satisfactorily shows that such wine spirits were not knowingly used in violation of law.

(4) Suitable samples of brandy or wine spirits may, under regulations prescribed by the Secretary, be withdrawn free of tax from the bonded premises of any distilled spirits plant, bonded wine cellar, or authorized experimental premises, for analysis or testing.

Amendments

• **1976, Tax Reform Act of 1976 (P.L. 94-455)**

P.L. 94-455, § 1906(b)(13)(A):

Amended 1954 Code by substituting "Secretary" for "Secretary or his delegate" each place it appeared. **Effective** 2-1-77.

[Sec. 5373(c)]

(c) DISTILLATES CONTAINING ALDEHYDES.—When the Secretary deems such removal and use will not jeopardize the revenue nor unduly increase administrative supervision, distillates containing aldehydes may, under such regulations as the Secretary may prescribe, be removed without payment of tax from the bonded premises of a distilled spirits plant to an adjacent bonded wine cellar and used therein in fermentation of wine to be used as distilling material at the distilled spirits plant from which such unfinished distilled spirits were removed.

Amendments

• **1976, Tax Reform Act of 1976 (P.L. 94-455)**

P.L. 94-455, § 1906(b)(13)(A):

Amended 1954 Code by substituting "Secretary" for "Secretary or his delegate" each place it appeared. **Effective** 2-1-77.

PART III—CELLAR TREATMENT AND CLASSIFICATION OF WINE

Sec. 5381.   Natural wine.
Sec. 5382.   Cellar treatment of natural wine.
Sec. 5383.   Amelioration and sweetening limitations for natural grape wines.
Sec. 5384.   Amelioration and sweetening limitations for natural fruit and berry wines.
Sec. 5385.   Specially sweetened natural wines.
Sec. 5386.   Special natural wines.
Sec. 5387.   Agricultural wines.
Sec. 5388.   Designation of wines.

[Sec. 5381]

SEC. 5381. NATURAL WINE.

Natural wine is the product of the juice or must of sound, ripe grapes or other sound, ripe fruit, made with such cellar treatment as may be authorized under section 5382 and containing not more than 21 percent by weight of total solids. Any wine conforming to such definition except for having become substandard by reason of its condition shall be deemed not to be natural wine, unless the condition is corrected.

Amendments

• **1979, Trade Agreements Act of 1979 (P.L. 96-39)**

P.L. 96-39, § 807(a)(48):

Amended Code Sec. 5381 by changing the last sentence. **Effective** 1-1-80. Prior to amendment, the last sentence of Code Sec. 5381 read as follows:

"Any wine conforming to such definition except for having become substandard by reason of its condition shall be deemed not to be natural wine and shall, unless the condition is corrected, be removed in due course for distillation, destroyed under Government supervision, or transferred to premises in which wines other than natural wine may be stored or used."

[Sec. 5382]

SEC. 5382. CELLAR TREATMENT OF NATURAL WINE.

[Sec. 5382(a)]

(a) PROPER CELLAR TREATMENT.—

  (1) IN GENERAL.—Proper cellar treatment of natural wine constitutes—

    (A) subject to paragraph (2), those practices and procedures in the United States, whether historical or newly developed, of using various methods and materials to correct or stabilize the wine, or the fruit juice from which it is made, so as to produce a finished product acceptable in good commercial practice in accordance with regulations prescribed by the Secretary; and

    (B) subject to paragraph (3), in the case of wine produced and imported subject to an international agreement or treaty, those practices and procedures acceptable to the United States under such agreement or treaty.

  (2) RECOGNITION OF CONTINUING TREATMENT.—For purposes of paragraph (1)(A), where a particular treatment has been used in customary commercial practice in the United States, it shall continue to be recognized as a proper cellar treatment in the absence of regulations prescribed by the Secretary finding such treatment not to be proper cellar treatment within the meaning of this subsection.

  (3) CERTIFICATION OF PRACTICES AND PROCEDURES FOR IMPORTED WINE.—

    (A) IN GENERAL.—In the case of imported wine produced after December 31, 2004, the Secretary shall accept the practices and procedures used to produce such wine, if, at the time of importation—

      (i) the Secretary has on file or is provided with a certification from the government of the producing country, accompanied by an affirmed laboratory analysis, that the practices and procedures used to produce the wine constitute proper cellar treatment under paragraph (1)(A),

      (ii) the Secretary has on file or is provided with such certification, if any, as may be required by an international agreement or treaty under paragraph (1)(B), or

      (iii) in the case of an importer that owns or controls or that has an affiliate that owns or controls a winery operating under a basic permit issued by the Secretary, the importer certifies that the practices and procedures used to produce the wine constitute proper cellar treatment under paragraph (1)(A).

    (B) AFFILIATE DEFINED.—For purposes of this paragraph, the term "affiliate" has the meaning given such term by section 117(a)(4) of the Federal Alcohol Administration Act (27 U.S.C. 211(a)(4)) and includes a winery's parent or subsidiary or any other entity in which the winery's parent or subsidiary has an ownership interest.

ALCOHOL TAXES—BONDED WINE PREMISES

Amendments

- **2006, Tax Relief and Health Care Act of 2006 (P.L. 109-432)**

P.L. 109-432, Division D, §3007:

Amended Code Sec. 5382(a)(1)(A) by striking "stabilize" and inserting "correct or stabilize". **Effective** 12-20-2006.

- **2004, Miscellaneous Trade and Technical Corrections Act of 2004 (P.L. 108-429)**

P.L. 108-429, §2002(a):

Amended Code Sec. 5382(a). **Effective** 1-1-2005. Prior to amendment, Code Sec. 5382(a) read as follows:

(a) GENERAL.—Proper cellar treatment of natural wine constitutes those practices and procedures in the United States and elsewhere, whether historical or newly developed, of using various methods and materials to correct or stabilize the wine, or the fruit juice from which it is made, so as to produce a finished product acceptable in good commercial practice. Where a particular treatment has been used in customary commercial practice, it shall continue to be recognized as a proper cellar treatment in the absence of regulations prescribed by the Secretary finding such treatment not to be a proper cellar treatment within the meaning of this subsection.

- **1976, Tax Reform Act of 1976 (P.L. 94-455)**

P.L. 94-455, §1906(b)(13)(A):

Amended 1954 Code by substituting "Secretary" for "Secretary or his delegate" each place it appeared. **Effective** 2-1-77.

[Sec. 5382(b)]

(b) SPECIFICALLY AUTHORIZED TREATMENTS.—The practices and procedures specifically enumerated in this subsection shall be deemed proper cellar treatment for natural wine:

(1) The preparation and use of pure concentrated or unconcentrated juice or must. Concentrated juice or must reduced with water to its original density or to not less than 22 degrees Brix or unconcentrated juice or must reduced with water to not less than 22 degrees Brix shall be deemed to be juice or must, and shall include such amounts of water to clear crushing equipment as regulations prescribed by the Secretary may provide.

(2) The addition to natural wine, or to concentrated or unconcentrated juice or must, from one kind of fruit, of wine spirits (whether or not taxpaid) distilled in the United States from the same kind of fruit; except that (A) the wine, juice, or concentrate shall not have an alcoholic content in excess of 24 percent by volume after the addition of wine spirits, and (B) in the case of still wines, wine spirits may be added in any State only to natural wines produced by fermentation in bonded wine cellars located within the same State.

(3) Amelioration and sweetening of natural grape wines in accordance with section 5383.

(4) Amelioration and sweetening of natural wines from fruits other than grapes in accordance with section 5384.

(5) In the case of effervescent wines, such preparations for refermentation and for dosage as may be acceptable in good commercial practice, but only if the alcoholic content of the finished product does not exceed 14 percent by volume.

(6) The natural darkening of the sugars or other elements in juice, must, or wine due to storage, concentration, heating processes, or natural oxidation.

(7) The blending of natural wines with each other or with heavy-bodied blending wine or with concentrated or unconcentrated juice, whether or not such juice contains wine spirits, if the wines, juice, or wine spirits are from the same kind of fruit.

(8) Such use of acids to correct natural deficiencies and stabilize the wine as may be acceptable in good commercial practice.

(9) The addition—

(A) to natural grape or berry wine of the winemaker's own production, of volatile fruit-flavor concentrate produced from the same kind and variety of grape or berry at a plant qualified under section 5511, or

(B) to natural fruit wine (other than grape or berry) of the winemaker's own production, of volatile fruit-flavor concentrate produced from the same kind of fruit at such a plant,

so long as the proportion of the volatile fruit-flavor concentrate to the wine does not exceed the proportion of the volatile fruit-flavor concentrate to the original juice or must from which it was produced. The transfer of volatile fruit-flavor concentrate from a plant qualified under section 5511 to a bonded wine cellar and its storage and use in such a cellar shall be under such applications and bonds, and under such other requirements, as may be provided in regulations prescribed by the Secretary.

Amendments

- **1976, Tax Reform Act of 1976 (P.L. 94-455)**

P.L. 94-455, §1906(b)(13)(A):

Amended 1954 Code by substituting "Secretary" for "Secretary or his delegate" each place it appeared. **Effective** 2-1-77.

- **1968 (P.L. 90-619)**

P.L. 90-619, §2:

Amended clause (B) of Code Sec. 5382(b)(2). **Effective** 2-1-69. Prior to amendment, such clause read as follows:

"(B) in the case of still wines, wine spirits may be added only to natural wines of the winemaker's own production."

- **1965, Excise Tax Reduction Act of 1965 (P.L. 89-44)**

P.L. 89-44, §806(c)(1):

Amended subsection (b)(2) of Section 5382 by deleting "made without added sugar or reserved as provided in sections 5383(b) and 5384(b)" from the end of subsection (b)(2). **Effective** 1-1-66.

- **1964 (P.L. 88-653)**

P.L. 88-653, §[1]:

Added Code Sec. 5382(b)(9). **Effective** on the first day of the second month which begins more than 10 days after 10-13-64.

[Sec. 5382(c)]

(c) OTHER AUTHORIZED TREATMENT.—The Secretary may by regulations prescribe limitations on the preparation and use of clarifying, stabilizing, preserving, fermenting, and corrective methods or materials, to the extent that such preparation or use is not acceptable in good commercial practice.

Amendments

- **1976, Tax Reform Act of 1976 (P.L. 94-455)**

P.L. 94-455, §1906(b)(13)(A):

Amended 1954 Code by substituting "Secretary" for "Secretary or his delegate" each place it appeared. **Effective** 2-1-77.

[Sec. 5382(d)]

(d) USE OF JUICE OR MUST FROM WHICH VOLATILE FRUIT FLAVOR HAS BEEN REMOVED.—For purposes of this part, juice, concentrated juice, or must processed at a plant qualified under section 5511 may be deemed to be pure juice, concentrated juice, or must even though volatile fruit flavor has been removed if, at a plant qualified under section 5511 or at the bonded wine cellar, there is added to such juice, concentrated juice, or must, or (in the case of a bonded wine cellar) to wine of the winemaker's own production made therefrom, either the identical volatile flavor removed or—

(1) in the case of natural grape or berry wine of the winemaker's own production, an equivalent quantity of volatile fruit-flavor concentrate produced at such a plant and derived from the same kind and variety of grape or berry, or

(2) in the case of natural fruit wine (other than grape or berry wine) of the winemaker's own production, an equivalent quantity of volatile fruit-flavored concentrate produced at such a plant and derived from the same kind of fruit.

ALCOHOL TAXES—BONDED WINE PREMISES

Amendments

• 1964 (P.L. 88-653)

P.L. 88-653, §2:

Added Code Sec. 5382(d). **Effective** on the first day of the second month which begins more than 10 days after 10-13-64.

[Sec. 5383]
SEC. 5383. AMELIORATION AND SWEETENING LIMITATIONS FOR NATURAL GRAPE WINES.

[Sec. 5383(a)]

(a) SWEETENING OF GRAPE WINES.—Any natural grape wine may be sweetened after fermentation and before taxpayment with pure dry sugar or liquid sugar if the total solids content of the finished wine does not exceed 12 percent of the weight of the wine and the alcoholic content of the finished wine after sweetening is not more than 14 percent by volume; except that the use under this subsection of liquid sugar shall be limited so that the resultant volume will not exceed the volume which could result from the maximum authorized use of pure dry sugar only.

Amendments

• 1968 (P.L. 90-619)

P.L. 90-619, §3(b):

Amended subsection (a) of Section 5383 by substituting "not more than 14 percent" for "less than 14 percent". **Effective** 2-1-69.

• 1965, Excise Tax Reduction Act of 1965 (P.L. 89-44)

P.L. 89-44, §806(b)(1):

Amended subsection (a) of Section 5383. **Effective** 1-1-66. Prior to amendment, subsection (a) read as follows:

"(a) Sweetening of Grape Wines.—Any natural grape wine made under this section may, if not in reserve inventory as hereinafter provided, be sweetened after fermentation and before taxpayment with pure dry sugar if the sugar solids content of the finished wine does not exceed 10 percent of the weight of the wine and the alcoholic content of the finished wine after sweetening is less than 14 percent by volume.

[Sec. 5383(b)]

(b) HIGH ACID WINES.—

(1) AMELIORATION.—Before, during, and after fermentation, ameliorating materials consisting of pure dry sugar or liquid sugar, water, or a combination of sugar and water, may be added to natural grape wines of a winemaker's own production when such wines are made from juice having a natural fixed acid content of more than five parts per thousand (calculated before fermentation and as tartaric acid). Ameliorating material so added shall not reduce the natural fixed acid content of the juice to less than five parts per thousand, nor exceed 35 percent of the volume of juice (calculated exclusive of pulp) and ameliorating material combined.

(2) SWEETENING.—Any wine produced under this subsection may be sweetened by the producer thereof, after amelioration and fermentation, with pure dry sugar or liquid sugar if the total solids content of the finished wine does not exceed (A) 17 percent by weight if the alcoholic content is more than 14 percent by volume, or (B) 21 percent by weight if the alcoholic content is not more than 14 percent by volume. The use under this paragraph of liquid sugar shall be limited to cases where the resultant volume does not exceed the volume which could result from the maximum authorized use of pure dry sugar only.

(3) WINE SPIRITS.—Wine spirits may be added (whether or not wine spirits were previously added) to wine produced under this subsection only if the wine contains not more than 14 percent of alcohol by volume derived from fermentation.

Amendments

• 1968 (P.L. 90-619)

P.L. 90-619, §3(a):

Amended subsection (b) of Section 5383. **Effective** 2-1-69. Prior to amendment, subsection (b) read as follows:

"(b) High Acid Wines.—

"(1) In general.—Before, during, and after fermentation, ameliorating material consisting of pure dry sugar or liquid sugar, water, or combination of sugar and water, may be added to natural grape wines of the winemaker's own production when such wines are made from juice having a natural fixed acid content of more than five parts per thousand (calculated before fermentation and as tartaric acid).

"(2) Limitations.—

"(A) Ameliorating material shall not reduce the natural fixed acid content of the juice to less than five parts per thousand.

"(B) The volume of authorized ameliorating material shall not exceed 35 percent of the volume of juice (calculated exclusive of pulp) and ameliorating material combined.

"(C) Sweetening material, consisting of pure dry sugar or liquid sugar, may be added to ameliorated wine in an amount which shall not increase its volume by more than 0.0675 gallon per gallon of juice and ameliorating material combined.

"(D) Wine spirits may be added only if the juice or wine contains less than 14 percent of alcohol by volume.

"(E) The total solids content of the finished wine shall not exceed 17 percent by weight if the alcoholic content is 14 percent or more by volume, nor more than 21 percent by weight if the alcoholic content is less than 14 percent by volume."

• 1965, Excise Tax Reduction Act of 1965 (P.L. 89-44)

P.L. 89-44, §806(b)(1):

Amended subsection (b) of Section 5383. **Effective** 1-1-66. Prior to amendment, subsection (b) read as follows:

"(b) High Acid Wines.—

"(1) Any natural grape wine of a winemaker's own production may, under this subsection, be ameliorated to correct high acid content, and, whether or not ameliorated, may be reserved as herein provided.

"(2) To wines produced under this subsection there may be added to the juice or to the wine, or both, before or during fermentation (including wines held pursuant to regulation in intermediate storage for completion of amelioration), ameliorating material consisting of either water, or pure dry sugar, or a combination of water and pure dry sugar, in such total volume as may be necessary to reduce the natural fixed acid content of the mixture of juice and such ameliorating material to a minimum of 5 parts per thousand (calculated before fermentation and as tartaric acid), but in no event shall the volume of such ameliorating material exceed 35 percent of the total volume of such ameliorated juice (calculated exclusive of pulp). The wine so made shall be transferred to a reserve inventory established as regulation issued by the Secretary or his delegate shall require; except that such wine containing less than 14 percent alcohol by volume after complete fermentation, or after complete fermentation and sweetening, need not be transferred into reserve inventory if all claim to further amelioration is waived.

"(3) The wines in the reserve inventory may be sweetened with dry sugar in an amount not exceeding, for the aggregate of the inventory—

"(A) the dry sugar equivalent of any volume of authorized ameliorating material not used for wine so transferred, plus

"(B) nine-tenths pound of dry sugar for each gallon of wine so transferred and such unused ameliorating material combined.

"(4) Wines so reserved may be blended together and sweetened with pure dry sugar to the extent provided in paragraph (3) or with concentrated or unconcentrated grape juice, and may have wine spirits added if such wine contains less than 14 percent of alcohol by volume at the time of such addition (unless wine spirits were previously added). Any wines withdrawn from reserve inventory shall have an alcoholic content of less than 14 percent by volume and a total solids content not exceeding 21 percent by weight, except that, if wine spirits have been added and the alcoholic content is 14 percent by volume or more, the sugar solids content shall not exceed 15 percent by weight.

"(5) The winemaker shall maintain and balance for his reserve inventory such accounts as regulations issued by the Secretary or his delegate shall prescribe."

[Sec. 5384]
SEC. 5384. AMELIORATION AND SWEETENING LIMITATIONS FOR NATURAL FRUIT AND BERRY WINES.

[Sec. 5384(a)]

(a) IN GENERAL.—To natural wine made from berries or fruit other than grapes, pure dry sugar or liquid sugar may be added to the juice in the fermenter, or to the wine after fermentation; but only if such wine has not more than 14 percent alcohol by volume after complete fermentation, or after complete fermentation and sweetening, and a total solids content not in excess of 21 percent by weight; and except that the use under this subsection of liquid sugar shall be limited so that the resultant volume will not exceed the volume which could result from the maximum authorized use of pure dry sugar only.

Internal Revenue Code   **Sec. 5384(a)**

ALCOHOL TAXES—BONDED WINE PREMISES

Amendments

• **1968 (P.L. 90-619)**

P.L. 90-619, §3(b):

Amended subsection (a) of Section 5384 by substituting "not more than 14 percent" for "less than 14 percent". **Effective** 2-1-69.

• **1965, Excise Tax Reduction Act of 1965 (P.L. 89-44)**

P.L. 89-44, §806(b)(2)(A):

Amended subsection (a) of Section 5384. **Effective** 1-1-66. Prior to amendment, subsection (a) read as follows:

"(a) In General.—To natural wine made from berries or fruit other than grapes, pure dry sugar may be added to the juice in the fermenter, or to the wine after fermentation; but only if such wine has less than 14 percent alcohol by volume after complete fermentation, or after complete fermentation and sweetening, and a total solids content not in excess of 21 percent by weight."

[Sec. 5384(b)]

(b) AMELIORATED FRUIT AND BERRY WINES.—

(1) Any natural fruit or berry wine (other than grape wine) of a winemaker's own production may, if not made under subsection (a) of this section, be ameliorated to correct high acid content. Ameliorating material calculations and accounting shall be separate for wines made from each different kind of fruit.

(2) Pure dry sugar or liquid sugar may be used in the production of wines under this subsection for the purpose of correcting natural deficiencies, but not to such an extent as would reduce the natural fixed acid in the corrected juice or wine to five parts per thousand. The quantity of sugar so used shall not exceed the quantity which would have been required to adjust the juice, prior to fermentation, to a total solids content of 25 degrees (Brix). Such sugar shall be added prior to the completion of fermentation of the wine. After such addition of the sugar, the wine or juice shall be treated and accounted for as provided in section 5383(b), covering the production of high acid grape wines, except that—

(A) Natural fixed acid shall be calculated as malic acid for apple wine and as citric acid for other fruit and berry wines, instead of tartaric acid;

(B) Juice adjusted with pure dry sugar or liquid sugar as provided in this paragraph shall be treated in the same manner as original natural juice under the provisions of section 5383(b); except that if liquid sugar is used, the volume of water contained therein must be deducted from the volume of ameliorating material authorized;

(C) Wines made under this subsection shall have a total solids content of not more than 21 percent by weight, whether or not wine spirits have been added; and

(D) Wines made exclusively from any fruit or berry with a natural fixed acid of 20 parts per thousand or more (before any correction of such fruit or berry) shall be entitled to a volume of ameliorating material not in excess of 60 percent (in lieu of 35 percent).

Amendments

• **1997, Taxpayer Relief Act of 1997 (P.L. 105-34)**

P.L. 105-34, §1417(a):

Amended Code Sec. 5384(b)(2)(D) by striking "loganberries, currants, or gooseberries," and inserting "any fruit or berry with a natural fixed acid of 20 parts per thousand or more (before any correction of such fruit or berry)". **Effective** on the 1st day of the 1st calendar quarter that begins at least 180 days after 8-5-97.

• **1965, Excise Tax Reduction Act of 1965 (P.L. 89-44)**

P.L. 89-44, §806(b)(2):

Amended subsection (b) of Section 5384. **Effective** 1-1-66. Prior to amendment, subsection (b) read as follows:

"(b) Reserve Fruit and Berry Wines.—

"(1) Any natural fruit or berry wine (other than grape wine) of a winemaker's own production may, if not made under subsection (a) of this section, be ameliorated to correct high acid content, and, whether or not ameliorated, may be reserved as herein provided. Separate reserve inventories shall be established for wines made from each different kind of fruit.

"(2) Pure dry sugar may be used in the production of wines under this subsection for the purpose of correcting natural deficiencies. The quantity of sugar so used shall not exceed the quantity which would have been required to adjust the juice, prior to fermentation, to a total solids content of 25 degrees (Brix). Such sugar shall be added prior to the completion of fermentation of the wine. After such addition of the sugar, the wine or juice shall be treated and accounted for as provided in section 5383(b), covering the production of reserved high acid grape wines, except that—

"(A) Natural fixed acid shall be calculated as malic acid for apple wine and as citric acid for other fruit and berry wines, instead of tartaric acid;

"(B) Juice adjusted with pure dry sugar as provided in this paragraph shall be treated in the same manner as original natural juice under the provisions of section 5383(b);

"(C) Wines made under this subsection may be withdrawn from reserve inventory with a total solids content of not more than 21 percent by weight, whether or not wine spirits have been added; and

"(D) Wines made exclusively from loganberries, currants, or gooseberries, shall be entitled to a volume of ameliorating material not in excess of 60 percent (in lieu of 35 percent)."

P.L. 89-44, §806(c):

Amended Section 5384 by inserting "AMELIORATED" in lieu of "RESERVE" in the heading of subsection (b) and by deleting "reserved" after "the production of" in the fourth sentence of subsection (b)(2). **Effective** 1-1-66.

[Sec. 5385]

SEC. 5385. SPECIALLY SWEETENED NATURAL WINES.

[Sec. 5385(a)]

(a) DEFINITION.—Specially sweetened natural wine is the product made by adding to natural wine of the winemaker's own production a sufficient quantity of pure dry sugar, or juice or concentrated juice from the same kind of fruit, separately or in combination, to produce a finished product having a total solids content in excess of 17 percent by weight and an alcoholic content of not more than 14 percent by volume, and shall include extra sweet kosher wine and similarly heavily sweetened wines.

Amendments

• **1968 (P.L. 90-619)**

P.L. 90-619, §3(b):

Amended subsection (a) of Section 5385 by substituting "not more than 14 percent" for "less than 14 percent". **Effective** 2-1-69.

• **1965, Excise Tax Reduction Act of 1965 (P.L. 89-44)**

P.L. 89-44, §806(c)(4):

Amended subsection (a) of Section 5385 by inserting "total solids content in excess of 17" in lieu of "sugar solids content in excess of 15." **Effective** 1-1-66.

[Sec. 5385(b)]

(b) CELLAR TREATMENT.—Specially sweetened natural wines may be blended with each other, or with natural wine or heavy bodied blending wine in the further production of specially sweetened natural wine only, if the wines so blended are made from the same kind of fruit. Wines produced under this section may be cellar treated under the provisions of section 5382(a) and (c). Wine spirits may not be added to specially sweetened natural wine.

Amendments

• **1968 (P.L. 90-619)**

P.L. 90-619, §4:

Amended subsection (b) of Section 5385. **Effective** 2-1-69. Prior to amendment, subsection (b) read as follows:

"(b) Blending, Etc.—The winemaker may blend specially sweetened natural wine from the same kind of fruit either before or after the special sweetening, or with additional natural wine or heavy bodied blending wine from the same kind of fruit in the further production of specially sweetened natural wine only, and may cellar treat any such wines as provided in section 5382(c). Wine spirits may not be added to specially sweetened natural wine, nor may such wine be blended except to produce a specially sweetened natural wine."

ALCOHOL TAXES—BONDED WINE PREMISES

[Sec. 5386]
SEC. 5386. SPECIAL NATURAL WINES.

[Sec. 5386(a)]

(a) IN GENERAL.—Special natural wines are the products made, pursuant to a formula approved under this section, from a base of natural wine (including heavy-bodied blending wine) exclusively, with the addition, before, during or after fermentation, of natural herbs, spices, fruit juices, aromatics, essences, and other natural flavorings in such quantities or proportions as to enable such products to be distinguished from any natural wine not so treated, and with or without carbon dioxide naturally or artificially added, and with or without the addition, separately or in combination, of pure dry sugar or a solution of pure dry sugar and water, or caramel. No added wine spirits or alcohol or other spirits shall be used in any wine under this section except as may be contained in the natural wine (including heavy-bodied blending wine) used as a base or except as may be necessary in the production of approved essences or similar approved flavorings. The Brix degree of any solution of pure dry sugar and water used may be limited by regulations prescribed by the Secretary or his delegate in accordance with good commercial practice.

[Sec. 5386(b)]

(b) CELLAR TREATMENT.—Special natural wines may be cellar treated under the provisions of section 5382(a) and (c).

Amendments

• 1968 (P.L. 90-619)

P.L. 90-619, §5:

Amended subsection (b) of Section 5386 by substituting "under the provisions of section 5382(a) and (c)" for "as provided in section 5382(c)". **Effective** 2-1-69.

[Sec. 5387]
SEC. 5387. AGRICULTURAL WINES.

[Sec. 5387(a)]

(a) IN GENERAL.—Wines made from agricultural products other than the juice of fruit shall be made in accordance with good commercial practice as may be prescribed by the Secretary by regulations. Wines made in accordance with such regulations shall be classed as "standard agricultural wines". Wines made under this section may be cellar treated under the provisions of section 5382(a) and (c).

Amendments

• 1976, Tax Reform Act of 1976 (P.L. 94-455)

P.L. 94-455, §1906(b)(13)(A):

Amended 1954 Code by substituting "Secretary" for "Secretary or his delegate" each place it appeared. **Effective** 2-1-77.

• 1968 (P.L. 90-619)

P.L. 90-619, §5:

Amended the first sentence in subsection (a) of Section 5387 by substituting "under the provisions of section 5382(a) and (c)" for "as provided in section 5382(c)". **Effective** 2-1-69.

[Sec. 5387(b)]

(b) LIMITATIONS.—No wine spirits may be added to wines produced under this section, nor shall any coloring material or herbs or other flavoring material (except hops in the case of honey wine) be used in their production.

[Sec. 5387(c)]

(c) RESTRICTION ON BLENDING.—Wines from different agricultural commodities shall not be blended together.

[Sec. 5388]
SEC. 5388. DESIGNATION OF WINES.

[Sec. 5388(a)]

(a) STANDARD WINES.—Standard wines may be removed from premises subject to the provisions of this subchapter and be marked, transported, and sold under their proper designation as to kind and origin, or, if there is no such designation known to the trade or consumers, then under a truthful and adequate statement of composition.

[Sec. 5388(b)]

(b) OTHER WINES.—Wines other than standard wines may be removed for consumption or sale and be marked, transported, or sold only under such designation as to kind and origin as adequately describes the true composition of such products and as adequately distinguish[es] them from standard wines, as regulations prescribed by the Secretary shall provide.

Amendments

• 1976, Tax Reform Act of 1976 (P.L. 94-455)

P.L. 94-455, §1906(b)(13)(A):

Amended 1954 Code by substituting "Secretary" for "Secretary or his delegate" each place it appeared. **Effective** 2-1-77.

[Sec. 5388(c)]

(c) USE OF SEMI-GENERIC DESIGNATIONS.—

(1) IN GENERAL.—Semi-generic designations may be used to designate wines of an origin other than that indicated by such name only if—

(A) there appears in direct conjunction therewith an appropriate appellation of origin disclosing the true place of origin of the wine, and

(B) the wine so designated conforms to the standard of identity, if any, for such wine contained in the regulations under this section or, if there is no such standard, to the trade understanding of such class or type.

(2) DETERMINATION OF WHETHER NAME IS SEMI-GENERIC.—

(A) IN GENERAL.—Except as provided in subparagraph (B), a name of geographic significance, which is also the designation of a class or type of wine, shall be deemed to have become semi-generic only if so found by the Secretary.

(B) CERTAIN NAMES TREATED AS SEMI-GENERIC.—The following names shall be treated as semi-generic: Angelica, Burgundy, Claret, Chablis, Champagne, Chianti, Malaga, Marsala, Madeira, Moselle, Port, Rhine Wine or Hock, Sauterne, Haut Sauterne, Sherry, Tokay.

(3) SPECIAL RULE FOR USE OF CERTAIN SEMIGENERIC DESIGNATIONS.—

(A) IN GENERAL.—In the case of any wine to which this paragraph applies—

(i) paragraph (1) shall not apply,

(ii) in the case of wine of the European Community, designations referred to in subparagraph (C)(i) may be used for such wine only if the requirement of subparagraph (B)(ii) is met, and

ALCOHOL TAXES—BONDED WINE PREMISES

(iii) in the case [of] any other wine bearing a brand name, or brand name and fanciful name, semi-generic designations may be used for such wine only if the requirements of clauses (i), (ii), and (iii) of subparagraph (B) are met.

(B) REQUIREMENTS.—

(i) The requirement of this clause is met if there appears in direct conjunction with the semi-generic designation an appropriate appellation of origin disclosing the origin of the wine.

(ii) The requirement of this clause is met if the wine conforms to the standard of identity, if any, for such wine contained in the regulations under this section or, if there is no such standard, to the trade understanding of such class or type.

(iii) The requirement of this clause is met if the person, or its successor in interest, using the semi-generic designation held a Certificate of Label Approval or Certificate of Exemption from Label Approval issued by the Secretary for a wine label bearing such brand name, or brand name and fanciful name, before March 10, 2006, on which such semi-generic designation appeared.

(C) WINES TO WHICH PARAGRAPH APPLIES.—

(i) IN GENERAL.—Except as provided in clause (ii), this paragraph shall apply to any grape wine which is designated as Burgundy, Claret, Chablis, Champagne, Chianti, Malaga, Marsala, Madeira, Moselle, Port, Retsina, Rhine Wine or Hock, Sauterne, Haut Sauterne, Sherry, or Tokay.

(ii) EXCEPTION.—This paragraph shall not apply to wine which—

(I) contains less than 7 percent or more than 24 percent alcohol by volume,

(II) is intended for sale outside the United States, or

(III) does not bear a brand name.

Amendments

• **2006, Tax Relief and Health Care Act of 2006 (P.L. 109-432)**

P.L. 109-432, Division A, §422(a):

Amended Code Sec. 5388(c) by adding at the end a new paragraph (3). **Effective** for wine imported or bottled in the United States on or after 12-20-2006.

• **1997, Taxpayer Relief Act of 1997 (P.L. 105-34)**

P.L. 105-34, §910(a):

Amended Code Sec. 5388 by adding at the end a new subsection (c). **Effective** 8-5-97.

PART IV—GENERAL

Sec. 5391.   Exemption from distilled spirits taxes.
Sec. 5392.   Definitions.

[Sec. 5391]

SEC. 5391. EXEMPTION FROM DISTILLED SPIRITS TAXES.

Notwithstanding any other provision of law, the tax imposed by section 5001 on distilled spirits shall not, except as provided in this subchapter, be assessed, levied, or collected from the proprietor of any bonded wine cellar with respect to his use of wine spirits in wine production, in such premises; except that, whenever wine or wine spirits are used in violation of this subchapter, the applicable tax imposed by section 5001 shall be collected unless the proprietor satisfactorily shows that such wine or wine spirits were not knowingly used in violation of law.

Amendments

• **1979, Trade Agreements Act of 1979 (P.L. 96-39)**

P.L. 96-39, §807(a)(49):

Amended Code Sec. 5391. **Effective** 1-1-80. Prior to amendment, Code Sec. 5391 read as follows:

SEC. 5391. EXEMPTION FROM RECTIFYING AND SPIRITS TAXES.

Notwithstanding any other provision of law, the taxes imposed by sections 5001 and 5021 on distilled spirits generally and on rectified spirits and wines shall not, except as provided in this subchapter, be assessed, levied, or collected from the proprietor of any bonded wine cellar with respect to his use or treatment of wine, or use of wine spirits in wine production, in such premises, nor shall such proprietor, by reason of such treatment or use, be deemed to be a rectifier within the meaning of section 5082; except that, whenever wine or wine spirits are used in violation of this subchapter, the applicable tax imposed by sections 5001 and 5021 shall be collected unless the proprietor satisfactorily shows that such wine or wine spirits were not knowingly used in violation of law.

[Sec. 5392]

SEC. 5392. DEFINITIONS.

[Sec. 5392(a)]

(a) STANDARD WINE.—For purposes of this subchapter the term "standard wine" means natural wine, specially sweetened natural wine, special natural wine, and standard agricultural wine, produced in accordance with the provisions of sections 5381, 5385, 5386, and 5387, respectively.

[Sec. 5392(b)]

(b) HEAVY BODIED BLENDING WINE.—For purposes of this subchapter the term "heavy bodied blending wine" means wine made from fruit without added sugar, and with or without added wine spirits, and conforming to the definition of natural wine in all respects except as to maximum total solids content.

[Sec. 5392(c)]

(c) PURE SUGAR.—For purposes of this subchapter the term "pure sugar" means pure refined sugar, suitable for human consumption, having a dextrose equivalent of not less than 95 percent on a dry basis, and produced from cane, beets, or fruit, or from grain or other sources of starch. Invert sugar syrup produced from such pure sugar by recognized methods of inversion may be used to prepare any sugar syrup, or solution of water and pure sugar, authorized in this subchapter.

Amendments

• **1965, Excise Tax Reduction Act of 1965 (P.L. 89-44)**

P.L. 89-44, §806(b)(3)(A):

Amended subsection (c) of Section 5392. **Effective** 1-1-66. Prior to amendment, subsection (c) read as follows:

"(c) Pure Sugar.—For purposes of this subchapter the term `pure sugar' means pure refined cane or beet sugar, or pure refined anhydrous or monohydrate dextrose sugar, of not less than 95 percent purity calculated on a dry basis. Invert sugar syrup produced from such pure sugar by recognized methods of inversion may be used to prepare any sugar syrup, or solution of water and pure sugar, authorized in this subchapter."

[Sec. 5392(d)]

(d) TOTAL SOLIDS.—For purposes of this subchapter the term "total solids", in the case of wine, means the degrees Brix of the dealcoholized wine.

[Sec. 5392(e)]

(e) SAME KIND OF FRUIT.—For purposes of this subchapter the term "same kind of fruit" includes, in the case of grapes, all of the several species and varieties of grapes. In the case of fruits other than grapes, this term includes all of the several species and varieties of any given kind; except that this shall not preclude a more precise identification of the composition of the product for the purpose of its designation.

ALCOHOL TAXES—BREWERIES

[Sec. 5392(f)]

(f) OWN PRODUCTION.—For purposes of this subchapter the term "own production", when used with reference to wine in a bonded wine cellar, means wine produced by fermentation in the same bonded wine cellar, whether or not produced by a predecessor in interest at such bonded wine cellar. This term may also include, under regulations, wine produced by fermentation in bonded wine cellars owned or controlled by the same or affiliated persons or firms when located within the same State; the term "affiliated" shall be deemed to include any one or more bonded wine cellar proprietors associated as members of any farm cooperative, or any one or more bonded wine cellar proprietors affiliated within the meaning of section 117(a)(5) of the Federal Alcohol Administration Act, as amended (27 U. S. C. 211).

Amendments

- **2018, Tax Technical Corrections Act of 2018 (P.L. 115-141)**

P.L. 115-141, §401(a)(246), Div. U:

Amended Code Sec. 5392(f) by striking "section 17(a)(5)" and inserting "section 117(a)(5)". **Effective** 3-23-2018.

- **1976, Tax Reform Act of 1976 (P.L. 94-455)**

P.L. 94-455, §1905(a)(21):

Struck out "49 Stat. 990;" before "27 U.S.C. 211" in Code Sec. 5392(f). **Effective** 2-1-77.

[Sec. 5392(g)]

(g) LIQUID SUGAR.—For purposes of this subchapter the term "liquid sugar" means a substantially colorless pure sugar and water solution containing not less than 60 percent pure sugar by weight (60 degrees Brix).

Amendments

- **1965, Excise Tax Reduction Act of 1965 (P.L. 89-44)**

P.L. 89-44, §806(b)(3)(B):

Added subsection (g) to Code Sec. 5392. **Effective** 1-1-66.

Subchapter G—Breweries

Part I.   Establishment.
Part II.   Operations.

PART I—ESTABLISHMENT

Sec. 5401.   Qualifying documents.
Sec. 5402.   Definitions.
Sec. 5403.   Cross references.

[Sec. 5401]

SEC. 5401. QUALIFYING DOCUMENTS.

[Sec. 5401(a)]

(a) NOTICE.—Every brewer shall, before commencing or continuing business, file with the officer designated for that purpose by the Secretary a notice in writing, in such form and containing such information as the Secretary shall by regulations prescribe as necessary to protect and insure collection of the revenue.

Amendments

- **1976, Tax Reform Act of 1976 (P.L. 94-455)**

P.L. 94-455, §1906(b)(13)(A):

Amended 1954 Code by substituting "Secretary" for "Secretary or his delegate" each place it appeared. **Effective** 2-1-77.

[Sec. 5401(b)]

(b) BONDS.—Every brewer, on filing notice as provided by subsection (a) of his intention to commence business, shall execute a bond to the United States in such reasonable penal sum as the Secretary shall by regulation prescribe as necessary to protect and insure collection of the revenue. The bond shall be conditioned (1) that the brewer shall pay, or cause to be paid, as herein provided, the tax required by law on all beer removed for transfer to the brewery from other breweries owned by him as provided in section 5414; (2) that he shall pay or cause to be paid the tax on all beer removed free of tax for export as provided in section 5053(a), which beer is not exported or returned to the brewery; and (3) that he shall in all respects faithfully comply, without fraud or evasion, with all requirements of law relating to the production and sale of any beer aforesaid. Once in every 4 years, or whenever required so to do by the Secretary, the brewer shall execute a new bond or a continuation certificate, in the penal sum prescribed in pursuance of this section, and conditioned as above provided, which bond or continuation certificate shall be in lieu of any former bond or bonds, or former continuation certificate or certificates, of such brewer in respect to all liabilities accruing after its approval. If the contract of surety between the brewer and the surety on an expiring bond or continuation certificate is continued in force between the parties for a succeeding period of not less than 4 years, the brewer may submit, in lieu of a new bond, a certificate executed, under penalties of perjury, by the brewer and the surety attesting to continuation of the bond, which certificate shall constitute a bond subject to all provisions of law applicable to bonds given pursuant to this section.

Amendments

- **1976, Tax Reform Act of 1976 (P.L. 94-455)**

P.L. 94-455, §1906(b)(13)(A):

Amended 1954 Code by substituting "Secretary" for "Secretary or his delegate" each place it appeared. **Effective** 2-1-77.

- **1971 (P.L. 91-673)**

P.L. 91-673, §3(a):

Substituted the last sentence in Code Sec. 5401(b) for the following: "Once in every 4 years, or whenever required so to do by the Secretary or his delegate, the brewer shall execute a new bond in the penal sum prescribed in pursuance of this section, and conditioned as above provided, which bond shall be in lieu of any former bond or bonds of such brewer in respect to all liabilities accruing after its approval." **Effective** 5-1-71.

[Sec. 5401(c)]

(c) EXCEPTION FROM BOND REQUIREMENTS FOR CERTAIN BREWERIES.—Subsection (b) shall not apply to any taxpayer for any period described in section 5551(d).

Amendments

- **2015, Protecting Americans from Tax Hikes Act of 2015 (P.L. 114-113)**

P.L. 114-113, §332(b)(2)(C), Div. Q:

Amended Code Sec. 5401 by adding at the end a new subsection (c). **Effective** for any calendar quarters beginning more than 1 year after 12-18-2015.

ALCOHOL TAXES—BREWERIES

[Sec. 5402]

SEC. 5402. DEFINITIONS.

[Sec. 5402(a)]

(a) BREWERY.—The brewery shall consist of the land and buildings described in the brewer's notice. The continuity of the brewery must be unbroken except where separated by public passageways, streets, highways, waterways, or carrier rights-of-way, or partitions; and if parts of the brewery are so separated they must abut on the dividing medium and be adjacent to each other. Notwithstanding the preceding sentence, facilities under the control of the brewer for case packing, loading, or storing which are located within reasonable proximity to the brewery packaging facilities may be approved by the Secretary or his delegate as a part of the brewery if the revenue will not be jeopardized thereby.

Amendments

• 1971 (P.L. 91-673)

P.L. 91-673, §3(b):

Amended Code Sec. 5402(a). Effective 5-1-71. Prior to amendment, the section read as follows:

"(a) Brewery.—The brewery shall consist of the land and buildings described in the brewer's notice."

[Sec. 5402(b)]

(b) BREWER.—

For definition of brewer, see section 5052(d).

Amendments

• 2005, Safe, Accountable, Flexible, Efficient Transportation Equity Act: A Legacy for Users (P.L. 109-59)

P.L. 109-59, §11125(b)(17):

Amended Code Sec. 5402(b) by striking "section 5092" and inserting "section 5052(d)". Effective 7-1-2008, but not applicable to taxes imposed for periods before such date.

[Sec. 5403]

SEC. 5403. CROSS REFERENCES.

(1) For authority of Secretary to disapprove brewers' bonds, see section 5551.

(2) For authority of Secretary to require the installation and use of meters, tanks, and other apparatus, see section 5552.

(3) For deposit of United States bonds or notes in lieu of sureties, see section 9303 of title 31, United States Code.

Amendments

• 1982 (P.L. 97-258)

P.L. 97-258, §3(f)(3):

Amended Code Sec. 5403(3) by striking out "6 U.S.C. 15" and substituting "section 9303 of title 31, United States Code". Effective 9-13-82.

• 1976, Tax Reform Act of 1976 (P.L. 94-455)

P.L. 94-455, §1906(b)(13)(A):

Amended 1954 Code by substituting "Secretary" for "Secretary or his delegate" each place it appeared. Effective 2-1-77.

PART II—OPERATIONS

Sec. 5411.	Use of brewery.
Sec. 5412.	Removal of beer in containers or by pipeline.
Sec. 5413.	Brewers procuring beer from other brewers.
Sec. 5414.	Removals from one brewery to another belonging to the same brewer.
Sec. 5415.	Records and returns.
Sec. 5416.	Definitions of packages and packaging.
Sec. 5417.	Pilot brewing plants.
Sec. 5418.	Beer imported in bulk.

[Sec. 5411]

SEC. 5411. USE OF BREWERY.

The brewery shall be used under regulations prescribed by the Secretary only for the purpose of producing, packaging, and storing beer, cereal beverages containing less than one-half of 1 percent of alcohol by volume, vitamins, ice, malt, malt sirup, and other byproducts and of soft drinks; for the purpose of processing spent grain, carbon dioxide, and yeast; and for such other purposes as the Secretary by regulation may find will not jeopardize the revenue.

Amendments

• 1976, Tax Reform Act of 1976 (P.L. 94-455)

P.L. 94-455, §1906(b)(13)(A):

Amended 1954 Code by substituting "Secretary" for "Secretary or his delegate" each place it appeared. Effective 2-1-77.

• 1971 (P.L. 91-673)

P.L. 91-673, §3(c):

Amended Code Sec. 5411. Effective 5-1-71. Prior to amendment, Code Sec. 5411 read as follows:

"The brewery shall be used under regulations prescribed by the Secretary or his delegate only for the purpose of producing beer, cereal beverages containing less than one-half of one percent of alcohol by volume, vitamins, ice, malt, malt sirup, and other by-products; of bottling beer and cereal beverages; of drying spent grain from the brewery; of recovering carbon dioxide and yeast; and of producing and bottling soft drinks; and for such other purposes as the Secretary or his delegate by regulation may find will not jeopardize the revenue. The bottling of beer and cereal beverages shall be conducted only in the brewery bottle house which shall consist of a separate portion of the brewery designated for that purpose."

[Sec. 5412]

SEC. 5412. REMOVAL OF BEER IN CONTAINERS OR BY PIPELINE.

Beer may be removed from the brewery for consumption or sale only in hogsheads, packages, and similar containers, marked, branded, or labeled in such manner as the Secretary may by regulation require, except that beer may be removed from the brewery pursuant to section 5414 or by pipeline to contiguous distilled spirits plants under section 5222.

Amendments

• 2017, Tax Cuts and Jobs Act (P.L. 115-97)

P.L. 115-97, §13803(b):

Amended Code Sec. 5412 by inserting "pursuant to section 5414 or" before "by pipeline". Effective for any calendar quarters beginning after 12-31-2017.

P.L. 115-97, §13809 (as added by P.L. 115-123, §41111, Div. D), provides:

SEC. 13809. RULE OF CONSTRUCTION.

Nothing in this subpart, the amendments made by this subpart, or any regulation promulgated under this subpart or the amendments made by this subpart, shall be construed to preempt, supersede, or otherwise limit or restrict any State, local, or

ALCOHOL TAXES—BREWERIES

tribal law that prohibits or regulates the production or sale of distilled spirits, wine, or malt beverages.

• **1976, Tax Reform Act of 1976 (P.L. 94-455)**

P.L. 94-455, §1906(b)(13)(A):

Amended 1954 Code by substituting "Secretary" for "Secretary or his delegate" each place it appeared. **Effective** 2-1-77.

• **1971 (P.L. 91-673)**

P.L. 91-673, §3(d):

Amended Code Sec. 5412 by substituting "packages" for "barrels, kegs, bottles". **Effective** 5-1-71.

[Sec. 5413]

SEC. 5413. BREWERS PROCURING BEER FROM OTHER BREWERS.

A brewer, under such regulations as the Secretary shall prescribe, may obtain beer in his own hogsheads, barrels, and kegs, marked with his name and address, from another brewer, with taxpayment thereof to be by the producer in the manner prescribed by section 5054.

Amendments

• **1976, Tax Reform Act of 1976 (P.L. 94-455)**

P.L. 94-455, §1906(b)(13)(A):

Amended 1954 Code by substituting "Secretary" for "Secretary or his delegate" each place it appeared. **Effective** 2-1-77.

[Sec. 5414]

SEC. 5414. TRANSFER OF BEER BETWEEN BONDED FACILITIES.

[Sec. 5414(a)]

(a) IN GENERAL.—Beer may be removed from one brewery to another brewery, without payment of tax, and may be mingled with beer at the receiving brewery, subject to such conditions, including payment of the tax, and in such containers, as the Secretary by regulations shall prescribe, which shall include—

(1) any removal from one brewery to another brewery belonging to the same brewer,

(2) any removal from a brewery owned by one corporation to a brewery owned by another corporation when—

(A) one such corporation owns the controlling interest in the other such corporation, or

(B) the controlling interest in each such corporation is owned by the same person or persons, and

(3) any removal from one brewery to another brewery when—

(A) the proprietors of transferring and receiving premises are independent of each other and neither has a proprietary interest, directly or indirectly, in the business of the other, and

(B) the transferor has divested itself of all interest in the beer so transferred and the transferee has accepted responsibility for payment of the tax.

[Sec. 5414(b)]

(b) TRANSFER OF LIABILITY FOR TAX.—For purposes of subsection (a)(3), such relief from liability shall be effective from the time of removal from the transferor's premises, or from the time of divestment of interest, whichever is later.

Amendments

• **2020, Taxpayer Certainty and Disaster Tax Relief Act of 2020 (P.L. 116-260)**

P.L. 116-260, §106(c)(1), Div. EE:

Amended Code Sec. 5414. **Effective** for any calendar quarters beginning after 12-31-2020. Prior to amendment, Code Sec. 5414 read as follows:

SEC. 5414. REMOVALS FROM ONE BREWERY TO ANOTHER BELONGING TO THE SAME BREWER.

[Sec. 5414(a)]

(a) IN GENERAL.—Beer may be removed from one brewery to another brewery belonging to the same brewer, without payment of tax, and may be mingled with beer at the receiving brewery, subject to such conditions, including payment of the tax, and in such containers, as the Secretary by regulations shall prescribe. The removal from one brewery to another brewery belonging to the same brewer shall be deemed to include any removal from a brewery owned by one corporation to a brewery owned by another corporation when (1) one such corporation owns the controlling interest in the other such corporation, or (2) the controlling interest in each such corporation is owned by the same person or persons.

Amendments

• **2017, Tax Cuts and Jobs Act (P.L. 115-97)**

P.L. 115-97, §13803(a)(1):

Amended Code Sec. 5414 by striking "Beer may be removed" and inserting "(a) IN GENERAL.—Beer may be removed". **Effective** for any calendar quarters beginning after 12-31-2017.

[Sec. 5414(b)]

(b) TRANSFER OF BEER BETWEEN BONDED FACILITIES.—

(1) IN GENERAL.—Beer may be removed from one bonded brewery to another bonded brewery, without payment of tax, and may be mingled with beer at the receiving brewery, subject to such conditions, including payment of the tax, and in such containers, as the Secretary by regulations shall prescribe, which shall include—

(A) any removal from one brewery to another brewery belonging to the same brewer,

(B) any removal from a brewery owned by one corporation to a brewery owned by another corporation when—

(i) one such corporation owns the controlling interest in the other such corporation, or

(ii) the controlling interest in each such corporation is owned by the same person or persons, and

(C) any removal from one brewery to another brewery when—

(i) the proprietors of transferring and receiving premises are independent of each other and neither has a proprietary interest, directly or indirectly, in the business of the other, and

(ii) the transferor has divested itself of all interest in the beer so transferred and the transferee has accepted responsibility for payment of the tax.

(2) TRANSFER OF LIABILITY FOR TAX.—For purposes of paragraph (1)(C), such relief from liability shall be effective from the time of removal from the transferor's bonded premises, or from the time of divestment of interest, whichever is later.

(3) TERMINATION.—This subsection shall not apply to any calendar quarter beginning after December 31, 2020.

Amendments

• **2019, Taxpayer Certainty and Disaster Tax Relief Act of 2019 (P.L. 116-94)**

P.L. 116-94, §144(c)(1), Div. Q:

Amended Code Sec. 5414(b)(3) by striking "December 31, 2019" and inserting "December 31, 2020". **Effective** for calendar quarters beginning after 12-31-2019.

• **2017, Tax Cuts and Jobs Act (P.L. 115-97)**

P.L. 115-97, §13803(a)(1)-(2):

Amended Code Sec. 5414 by striking "Beer may be removed" and inserting "(a) IN GENERAL.—Beer may be removed", and by adding at the end a new subsection (b). **Effective** for any calendar quarters beginning after 12-31-2017.

P.L. 115-97, §13809 (as added by P.L. 115-123, §41111, Div. D), provides:

SEC. 13809. RULE OF CONSTRUCTION.

Nothing in this subpart, the amendments made by this subpart, or any regulation promulgated under this subpart or the amendments made by this subpart, shall be construed to preempt, supersede, or otherwise limit or restrict any State, local, or tribal law that prohibits or regulates the production or sale of distilled spirits, wine, or malt beverages.

• **1976, Tax Reform Act of 1976 (P.L. 94-455)**

P.L. 94-455, §1906(b)(13)(A):

Amended 1954 Code by substituting "Secretary" for "Secretary or his delegate" each place it appeared. **Effective** 2-1-77.

ALCOHOL TAXES—MISCELLANEOUS PLANTS

[Sec. 5415]

SEC. 5415. RECORDS AND RETURNS.

[Sec. 5415(a)]

(a) RECORDS.—Every brewer shall keep records, in such form and containing such information as the Secretary shall prescribe by regulations as necessary for protection of the revenue. These records shall be preserved by the person required to keep such records for such period as the Secretary shall by regulations prescribe, and shall be available during business hours for examination and taking of abstracts therefrom by any internal revenue officer.

Amendments

• **1976, Tax Reform Act of 1976 (P.L. 94-455)**

P.L. 94-455, §1906(b)(13)(A):

Amended 1954 Code by substituting "Secretary" for "Secretary or his delegate" each place it appeared. **Effective** 2-1-77.

[Sec. 5415(b)]

(b) RETURNS.—Every brewer shall make true and accurate returns of his operations and transactions in the form, at the times, and for such periods as the Secretary shall by regulation prescribe.

Amendments

• **1976, Tax Reform Act of 1976 (P.L. 94-455)**

P.L. 94-455, §1906(b)(13)(A):

Amended 1954 Code by substituting "Secretary" for "Secretary or his delegate" each place it appeared. **Effective** 2-1-77.

[Sec. 5416]

SEC. 5416. DEFINITIONS OF PACKAGE AND PACKAGING.

For purposes of this subchapter, the term "package" means a bottle, can, keg, barrel, or other original consumer container, and the term "packaging" means the filling of any package.

Amendments

• **1971 (P.L. 91-673)**

P.L. 91-673, §3(e):

Amended Code Sec. 5416. **Effective** 5-1-71. Prior to amendment, the section read as follows:

SEC. 5416. DEFINITIONS OF BOTTLE AND BOTTLING.

For purposes of this subchapter, the word 'bottle' means a bottle, can, or similar container, and the word 'bottling' means the filling of bottles, cans, and similar containers.

[Sec. 5417]

SEC. 5417. PILOT BREWING PLANTS.

Under such regulations as the Secretary may prescribe, and on the filing of such bonds and applications as he may require, pilot brewing plants may, at the discretion of the Secretary, be established and operated off the brewery premises for research, analytical, experimental, or development purposes with regard to beer or brewery operations. Nothing in this section shall be construed as authority to waive the filing of any bond or the payment of any tax provided for in this chapter.

Amendments

• **1976, Tax Reform Act of 1976 (P.L. 94-455)**

P.L. 94-455, §1906(b)(13)(A):

Amended 1954 Code by substituting "Secretary" for "Secretary or his delegate" each place it appeared. **Effective** 2-1-77.

• **1971 (P.L. 91-673)**

P.L. 91-673, §4(a):

Added Code Sec. 5417. **Effective** 5-1-71.

[Sec. 5418]

SEC. 5418. BEER IMPORTED IN BULK.

Beer imported or brought into the United States in bulk containers may, under such regulations as the Secretary may prescribe, be withdrawn from customs custody and transferred in such bulk containers to the premises of a brewery without payment of the internal revenue tax imposed on such beer. The proprietor of a brewery to which such beer is transferred shall become liable for the tax on the beer withdrawn from customs custody under this section upon release of the beer from customs custody, and the importer, or the person bringing such beer into the United States, shall thereupon be relieved of the liability for such tax.

Amendments

• **1997, Taxpayer Relief Act of 1997 (P.L. 105-34)**

P.L. 105-34, §1421(a):

Amended part II of subchapter G of chapter 51 by adding at the end a new Code Sec. 5418. **Effective** on the 1st day of the 1st calendar quarter that begins at least 180 days after 8-5-97.

Subchapter H—Miscellaneous Plants and Warehouses

Part I.   Vinegar plants.
Part II.   Volatile fruit-flavor concentrate plants.
Part III.   [Repealed].

PART I—VINEGAR PLANTS

Sec. 5501.   Establishment.
Sec. 5502.   Qualification.
Sec. 5503.   Construction and equipment.
Sec. 5504.   Operation.
Sec. 5505.   Applicability of provisions of this chapter.

ALCOHOL TAXES—MISCELLANEOUS PLANTS

[Sec. 5501]

SEC. 5501. ESTABLISHMENT.

Plants for the production of vinegar by the vaporizing process, where distilled spirits of not more than 15 percent of alcohol by volume are to be produced exclusively for use in the manufacture of vinegar on the premises, may be established under this part.

[Sec. 5502]

SEC. 5502. QUALIFICATION.

[Sec. 5502(a)]

(a) REQUIREMENTS.—Every person, before commencing the business of manufacturing vinegar by the vaporizing process, and at such other times as the Secretary may by regulations prescribe, shall make application to the Secretary for the registration of his plant and receive permission to operate. No application required under this section shall be approved until the applicant has complied with all requirements of law, and regulations prescribed by the Secretary, in relation to such business. With respect to any change in such business after approval of an application, the Secretary may by regulations authorize the filing of written notice of such change or require the filing of an application to make such change.

Amendments

- 1976, Tax Reform Act of 1976 (P.L. 94-455)

P.L. 94-455, § 1906(b)(13)(A):

Amended 1954 Code by substituting "Secretary" for "Secretary or his delegate" each place it appeared. **Effective** 2-1-77.

[Sec. 5502(b)]

(b) FORM OF APPLICATION.—The application required by subsection (a) shall be in such form and contain such information as the Secretary shall by regulations prescribe to enable him to determine the identity of the applicant, the location and extent of the premises, the type of operations to be conducted on such premises, and whether the operations will be in conformity with law and regulations.

Amendments

- 1976, Tax Reform Act of 1976 (P.L. 94-455)

P.L. 94-455, § 1906(b)(13)(A):

Amended 1954 Code by substituting "Secretary" for "Secretary or his delegate" each place it appeared. **Effective** 2-1-77.

[Sec. 5503]

SEC. 5503. CONSTRUCTION AND EQUIPMENT.

Plants established under this part for the manufacture of vinegar by the vaporizing process shall be constructed and equipped in accordance with such regulations as the Secretary shall prescribe.

Amendments

- 1976, Tax Reform Act of 1976 (P.L. 94-455)

P.L. 94-455, § 1906(b)(13)(A):

Amended 1954 Code by substituting "Secretary" for "Secretary or his delegate" each place it appeared. **Effective** 2-1-77.

[Sec. 5504]

SEC. 5504. OPERATION.

[Sec. 5504(a)]

(a) IN GENERAL.—Any manufacturer of vinegar qualified under this part may, under such regulations as the Secretary shall prescribe, separate by a vaporizing process the distilled spirits from the mash produced by him, and condense the vapor by introducing it into the water or other liquid used in making vinegar in his plant.

Amendments

- 1976, Tax Reform Act of 1976 (P.L. 94-455)

P.L. 94-455, § 1906(b)(13)(A):

Amended 1954 Code by substituting "Secretary" for "Secretary or his delegate" each place it appeared. **Effective** 2-1-77.

[Sec. 5504(b)]

(b) REMOVALS.—No person shall remove, or cause to be removed, from any plant established under this part any vinegar or other fluid or material containing a greater proportion than 2 percent of proof spirits.

[Sec. 5504(c)]

(c) RECORDS.—Every person manufacturing vinegar by the vaporizing process shall keep such records and file such reports as the Secretary shall by regulations prescribe of the kind and quantity of materials received on his premises and fermented or mashed, the quantity of low wines produced, the quantity of such low wines used in the manufacture of vinegar, the quantity of vinegar produced, the quantity of vinegar removed from the premises, and such other information as may by regulations be required. Such records, and a copy of such reports, shall be preserved as regulations shall prescribe, and shall be kept available for inspection by any internal revenue officer during business hours.

Amendments

- 1976, Tax Reform Act of 1976 (P.L. 94-455)

P.L. 94-455, § 1906(b)(13)(A):

Amended 1954 Code by substituting "Secretary" for "Secretary or his delegate" each place it appeared. **Effective** 2-1-77.

[Sec. 5505]

SEC. 5505. APPLICABILITY OF PROVISIONS OF THIS CHAPTER.

[Sec. 5505(a)]

(a) TAX.—The taxes imposed by subchapter A shall be applicable to any distilled spirits produced in violation of section 5501 or removed in violation of section 5504(b).

ALCOHOL TAXES—MISCELLANEOUS PLANTS

[Sec. 5505(b)]

(b) PROHIBITED PREMISES.—Plants established under this part shall not be located on any premises where distilling is prohibited under section 5601(a)(6).

[Sec. 5505(c)]

(c) ENTRY AND EXAMINATION OF PREMISES.—The provisions of section 5203(b), (c), and (d), relating to right of entry and examination, furnishing facilities and assistance, and authority to break up grounds or walls, shall be applicable to all premises established under this part, and to all proprietors thereof, and their workmen or other persons employed by them.

[Sec. 5505(d)]

(d) REGISTRATION OF STILLS.—Stills on the premises of plants established under this part shall be registered as provided in section 5179.

[Sec. 5505(e)]

(e) INSTALLATION OF METERS, TANKS, AND OTHER APPARATUS.—The provisions of section 5552 relating to the installation of meters, tanks, and other apparatus shall be applicable to plants established under this part.

[Sec. 5505(f)]

(f) ASSIGNMENT OF INTERNAL REVENUE OFFICERS.—The provisions of section 5553(a) relating to the assignment of internal revenue officers shall be applicable to plants established under this part.

[Sec. 5505(g)]

(g) AUTHORITY TO WAIVE RECORDS, STATEMENTS, AND RETURNS.—The provisions of section 5555(b) relating to the authority of the Secretary to waive records, statements, and returns shall be applicable to records, statements, or returns required by this part.

[Sec. 5505(h)]

(h) REGULATIONS.—The provisions of section 5556 relating to the prescribing of regulations shall be applicable to this part.

[Sec. 5505(i)]

(i) PENALTIES.—The penalties and forfeitures provided in sections 5601(a)(1), (6), and (12), 5603, 5615(1) and (4), 5686, and 5687 shall be applicable to this part.

Amendments

• **1976, Tax Reform Act of 1976 (P.L. 94-455)**

P.L. 94-455, §1905(b)(6)(E):

Struck out "5601(b)(1)," before "5603," in Code Sec. 5505(i). **Effective** 2-1-77.

[Sec. 5505(j)]

(j) OTHER PROVISIONS.—This chapter (other than this part and the provisions referred to in subsections (a), (b), (c), (d), (e), (f), (g), (h), and (i)) shall not be applicable with respect to plants established or operations conducted under this part.

PART II—VOLATILE FRUIT-FLAVOR CONCENTRATE PLANTS

Sec. 5511. Establishment and operation.
Sec. 5512. Control of products after manufacture.

[Sec. 5511]

SEC. 5511. ESTABLISHMENT AND OPERATION.

This chapter (other than sections 5178(a)(2)(C), 5179, 5203(b), (c), and (d), and 5552) shall not be applicable with respect to the manufacture, by any process which includes evaporations from the mash or juice of any fruit, of any volatile fruit-flavor concentrate if—

(1) such concentrate, and the mash or juice from which it is produced, contains no more alcohol than is reasonably unavoidable in the manufacture of such concentrate; and

(2) such concentrate is rendered unfit for use as a beverage before removal from the place of manufacture, or (in the case of a concentrate which does not exceed 24 percent alcohol by volume) such concentrate is transferred to a bonded wine cellar for use in production of natural wine as provided in section 5382; and

(3) the manufacturer thereof makes such application, keeps such records, renders such reports, files such bonds, and complies with such other requirements with respect to the production, removal, sale, transportation, and use of such concentrate and of the mash or juice from which such concentrate is produced, as the Secretary may by regulations prescribe as necessary for the protection of the revenue.

Amendments

• **1976, Tax Reform Act of 1976 (P.L. 94-455)**

P.L. 94-455, §1906(b)(13)(A):

Amended 1954 Code by substituting "Secretary" for "Secretary or his delegate" each place it appeared. **Effective** 2-1-77.

• **1964 (P.L. 88-653)**

P.L. 88-653, §3:

Amended Code Sec. 5511(2). **Effective** on the first day of the second month which begins more than 10 days after October 13, 1964, the date on which this Act was enacted. Prior to amendment, Sec. 5511(2) read as follows:

"(2) such concentrate is rendered unfit for use as a beverage before removal from the place of manufacture; and".

[Sec. 5512]

SEC. 5512. CONTROL OF PRODUCTS AFTER MANUFACTURE.

For applicability of all provisions of this chapter pertaining to distilled spirits and wines, including those requiring payment of tax, to volatile fruit-flavor concentrates sold, transported, or used in violation of law or regulations, see section 5001(a)(6).

Amendments

• **2018, Tax Technical Corrections Act of 2018 (P.L. 115-141)**

P.L. 115-141, §401(a)(247), Div. U:

Amended Code Sec. 5512 by striking "section 5001(a)(7)" and inserting "section 5001(a)(6)". **Effective** 3-23-2018.

ALCOHOL TAXES—MISCELLANEOUS PROVISIONS

PART III—MANUFACTURING BONDED WAREHOUSES—[Repealed]

[Sec. 5521—Repealed]

Amendments

• **1979, Trade Agreements Act of 1979 (P.L. 96-39)**

P.L. 96-39, §807(a)(50):

Repealed Code Sec. 5521. **Effective** 1-1-80. Prior to repeal, Code Sec. 5521 read as follows:

SEC. 5521. ESTABLISHMENT AND OPERATION.

[Sec. 5521(a)]

(a) ESTABLISHMENT.—All medicines, preparations, compositions, perfumery, cosmetics, cordials, and other liquors manufactured wholly or in part of domestic spirits, intended for exportation, as provided by law, in order to be manufactured and sold or removed, without being charged with duty and without having a stamp affixed thereto, shall, under such regulations as the Secretary may prescribe, be made and manufactured in warehouses similarly constructed to those known and designated in Treasury regulations as bonded warehouses, class six. The manufacturer shall first give satisfactory bonds to the Secretary for the faithful observance of all the provisions of law and the regulations as aforesaid, in amount not less than half of that required by the regulations of the Secretary from persons allowed bonded warehouses.

Amendments

• **1976, Tax Reform Act of 1976 (P.L. 94-455)**

P.L. 94-455, §1906(b)(13)(A):

Amended 1954 Code by substituting "Secretary" for "Secretary or his delegate" each place it appeared. **Effective** 2-1-77.

[Sec. 5521(b)]

(b) SUPERVISION.—All labor performed and services rendered under this section shall be under the supervision of an officer of the customs, and at the expense of the manufacturer.

[Sec. 5521(c)]

(c) MATERIALS FOR MANUFACTURE.—

(1) EXPORTABLE FREE OF TAX.—Any manufacturer of the articles specified in subsection (a), or of any of them, having such bonded warehouse, shall be at liberty, under such regulations as the Secretary may prescribe, to convey therein any materials to be used in such manufacture which are allowed by the provisions of law to be exported free from tax or duty, as well as the necessary materials, implements, packages, vessels, brands, and labels for the preparation, putting up, and export of such manufactured articles; and every article so used shall be exempt from the payment of stamp and excise duty by such manufacturer. Articles and materials so to be used may be transferred from any bonded warehouse under such regulations as the Secretary may prescribe, into any bonded warehouse in which such manufacture may be conducted, and may be used in such manufacture, and when so used shall be exempt from stamp and excise duty; and the receipt of the officer in charge shall be received as a voucher for the manufacture of such articles.

(2) IMPORTED MATERIALS.—Any materials imported into the United States may, under such regulations as the Secretary may prescribe, and under the direction of the proper officer, be removed in original packages from on shipboard, or from the bonded warehouse in which the same may be, into the bonded warehouse in which such manufacture may be carried on, for the purpose of being used in such manufacture, without payment of duties thereon, and may there be used in such manufacture. No article so removed, nor any article manufactured in said bonded warehouse, shall be taken therefrom except for exportation, under the direction of the proper officer having charge thereof, whose certificate, describing the articles by their mark or otherwise, the quantity, the date of importation, and name of vessel, with such additional particulars as may from time to time be required, shall be received by the collector of customs in cancellation of the bond, or return of the amount of foreign import duties.

Amendments

• **1976, Tax Reform Act of 1976 (P.L. 94-455)**

P.L. 94-455, §1906(b)(13)(A):

Amended 1954 Code by substituting "Secretary" for "Secretary or his delegate" each place it appeared. **Effective** 2-1-77.

[Sec. 5521(d)]

(d) REMOVALS.—

(1) GENERAL.—Such goods, when manufactured in such warehouses, may be removed for exportation under the direction of the proper officer having charge thereof, who shall be designated by the Secretary, without being charged with duty and without having a stamp affixed thereto.

(2) TRANSPORTATION FOR EXPORT.—Any article manufactured in a bonded warehouse established under subsection (a) may be removed therefrom for transportation to a customs bonded warehouse at any port, for the purpose only of being exported therefrom, under such regulations and on the execution of such bonds or other security as the Secretary may prescribe.

Amendments

• **1976, Tax Reform Act of 1976 (P.L. 94-455)**

P.L. 94-455, §1906(b)(13)(A):

Amended 1954 Code by substituting "Secretary" for "Secretary or his delegate" each place it appeared. **Effective** 2-1-77.

[Sec. 5522—Repealed]

Amendments

• **1979, Trade Agreements Act of 1979 (P.L. 96-39)**

P.L. 96-39, §807(a)(50):

Repealed Code Sec. 5522. **Effective** 1-1-80. Prior to repeal, Code Sec. 5522 read as follows:

SEC. 5522. WITHDRAWAL OF DISTILLED SPIRITS TO MANUFACTURING BONDED WAREHOUSES.

[Sec. 5522(a)]

(a) AUTHORIZATION.—Under such regulations and requirement as to stamps, bonds, and other security as shall be prescribed by the Secretary, any manufacturer of medicines, preparations, compositions, perfumery, cosmetics, cordials, and other liquors, for export, manufacturing the same in a duly constituted manufacturing bonded warehouse, shall be authorized to withdraw, from the bonded premises of any distilled spirits plant, so much distilled spirits as he may require for such purpose, without the payment of the internal revenue tax thereon.

Amendments

• **1976, Tax Reform Act of 1976 (P.L. 94-455)**

P.L. 94-455, §1906(b)(13)(A):

Amended 1954 Code by substituting "Secretary" for "Secretary or his delegate" each place it appeared. **Effective** 2-1-77.

[Sec. 5522(b)]

(b) ALLOWANCE FOR LOSS OR LEAKAGE.—

For provisions relating to allowance for loss of distilled spirits withdrawn under subsection (a), see section 5008(f).

[Sec. 5523—Repealed]

Amendments

• **1979, Trade Agreements Act of 1979 (P.L. 96-39)**

P.L. 96-39, §807(a)(50):

Repealed Code Sec. 5523. **Effective** 1-1-80. Prior to repeal, Code Sec. 5523 read as follows:

SEC. 5523. SPECIAL PROVISIONS RELATING TO DISTILLED SPIRITS AND WINES RECTIFIED IN MANUFACTURING BONDED WAREHOUSES.

Distilled spirits and wines which are rectified in manufacturing bonded warehouses, class six, and distilled spirits which are reduced in proof and bottled or packaged in such warehouses, shall be deemed to have been manufactured within the meaning of section 311 of the Tariff Act of 1930 (19 U. S. C. 1311), and may be withdrawn as provided in such section, and likewise for shipment in bond to Puerto Rico, subject to the provisions of such section, and under such regulations as the Secretary may prescribe, there to be withdrawn for consumption or be rewarehoused and subsequently withdrawn for consumption. No internal revenue tax shall be imposed on distilled spirits and wines rectified in class six warehouses if such distilled spirits and wines are exported or shipped in accordance with such section 311. No person rectifying distilled spirits or wines in such warehouses shall be subject by reason of such rectification to the payment of special tax as a rectifier.

• **1976, Tax Reform Act of 1976 (P.L. 94-455)**

P.L. 94-455, §1906(b)(13)(A):

Amended 1954 Code by substituting "Secretary" for "Secretary or his delegate" each place it appeared. **Effective** 2-1-77.

Subchapter I—Miscellaneous General Provisions

Sec. 5551.	General provisions relating to bonds.
Sec. 5552.	Installation of meters, tanks, and other apparatus.
Sec. 5553.	Supervision of premises and operations.
Sec. 5554.	Pilot operations.
Sec. 5555.	Records, statements, and returns.
Sec. 5556.	Regulations.
Sec. 5557.	Officers and agents authorized to investigate, issue search warrants, and prosecute for violations.
Sec. 5558.	Authority of enforcement officers.

ALCOHOL TAXES—MISCELLANEOUS PROVISIONS

Sec. 5559.   Determinations.
Sec. 5560.   Other provisions applicable.
Sec. 5561.   Exemptions to meet the requirements of the national defense.
Sec. 5562.   Exemptions from certain requirements in cases of disaster.

[Sec. 5551]

SEC. 5551. GENERAL PROVISIONS RELATING TO BONDS.

[Sec. 5551(a)]

(a) APPROVAL AS CONDITION TO COMMENCING BUSINESS.—Except as provided under subsection (d), no individual, firm, partnership, corporation, or association, intending to commence or to continue the business of a distiller, warehouseman, processor, brewer, or winemaker, shall commence or continue the business of a distiller, warehouseman, processor, brewer, or winemaker until all bonds in respect of such a business, required by any provision of law, have been approved by the Secretary of the Treasury or the officer designated by him.

Amendments

• 2015, Protecting Americans from Tax Hikes Act of 2015 (P.L. 114-113)

P.L. 114-113, §332(b)(1)(A), Div. Q:

Amended Code Sec. 5551(a) by striking "No individual" and inserting "Except as provided under subsection (d), no individual". **Effective** for any calendar quarters beginning more than 1 year after 12-18-2015.

• 1979, Trade Agreements Act of 1979 (P.L. 96-39)

P.L. 96-39, §807(a)(51):

Amended Code Sec. 5551(a) by changing "bonded warehouseman, rectifier" to "warehouseman, processor" each place it appears. **Effective** 1-1-80.

• 1976, Tax Reform Act of 1976 (P.L. 94-455)

P.L. 94-455, §1906(b)(13)(B):

Substituted "Secretary of the Treasury" for "Secretary" in Code Sec. 5551(a). **Effective** 2-1-77.

[Sec. 5551(b)]

(b) DISAPPROVAL.—The Secretary of the Treasury or any officer designated by him may disapprove any such bond or bonds if the individual, firm, partnership, corporation, or association giving such bond or bonds, or owning, controlling, or actively participating in the management of the business of the individual, firm, partnership, corporation, or association giving such bond or bonds, shall have been previously convicted, in a court of competent jurisdiction, of—

(1) any fraudulent noncompliance with any provision of any law of the United States, if such provision related to internal revenue or customs taxation of distilled spirits, wines, or beer, or if such an offense shall have been compromised with the individual, firm, partnership, corporation, or association on payment of penalties or otherwise, or

(2) any felony under a law of any State, the District of Columbia, or the United States, prohibiting the manufacture, sale, importation, or transportation of distilled spirits, wine, beer, or other intoxicating liquor.

Amendments

• 1976, Tax Reform Act of 1976 (P.L. 94-455)

P.L. 94-455, §1905(c)(5):

Struck out "Territory, or" following "State," in Code Sec. 5551(b)(2). **Effective** 2-1-77.

P.L. 94-455, §1906(b)(13)(B):

Substituted "Secretary of the Treasury" for "Secretary" in Code Sec. 5551(b). **Effective** 2-1-77.

[Sec. 5551(c)]

(c) APPEAL FROM DISAPPROVAL.—In case the disapproval is by an officer designated by the Secretary of the Treasury to approve or disapprove such bonds, the individual, firm, partnership, corporation, or association giving the bond may appeal from such disapproval to the Secretary of the Treasury or an officer designated by him to hear such appeals, and the disapproval of the bond by the Secretary of the Treasury or officer designated to hear such appeals shall be final.

Amendments

• 1976, Tax Reform Act of 1976 (P.L. 94-455)

P.L. 94-455, §1906(b)(13)(B):

Substituted "Secretary of the Treasury" for "Secretary" each place it appeared in Code Sec. 5551(c). **Effective** 2-1-77.

[Sec. 5551(d)]

(d) REMOVAL OF BOND REQUIREMENTS.—

(1) IN GENERAL.—During any period to which subparagraph (A) of section 5061(d)(4) applies to a taxpayer (determined after application of subparagraph (B) thereof), such taxpayer shall not be required to furnish any bond covering operations or withdrawals of distilled spirits or wines for nonindustrial use or of beer.

(2) SATISFACTION OF BOND REQUIREMENTS.—Any taxpayer for any period described in paragraph (1) shall be treated as if sufficient bond has been furnished for purposes of covering operations and withdrawals of distilled spirits or wines for nonindustrial use or of beer for purposes of any requirements relating to bonds under this chapter.

Amendments

• 2015, Protecting Americans from Tax Hikes Act of 2015 (P.L. 114-113)

P.L. 114-113, §332(b)(1)(B), Div. Q:

Amended Code Sec. 5551 by adding at the end a new subsection (d). **Effective** for any calendar quarters beginning more than 1 year after 12-18-2015.

[Sec. 5552]

SEC. 5552. INSTALLATION OF METERS, TANKS, AND OTHER APPARATUS.

The Secretary is authorized to require at distilled spirits plants, breweries, and at any other premises established pursuant to this chapter as in his judgment may be deemed advisable, the installation of meters, tanks, pipes, or any other apparatus for the purpose of protecting the revenue, and such meters, tanks, and pipes and all necessary labor incident thereto shall be at the expense of the person on whose premises the installation is required. Any such person refusing or neglecting to install such apparatus when so required by the Secretary shall not be permitted to conduct business on such premises.

ALCOHOL TAXES—MISCELLANEOUS PROVISIONS

Amendments

• **1976, Tax Reform Act of 1976 (P.L. 94-455)**

P.L. 94-455, §1906(b)(13)(A):

Amended 1954 Code by substituting "Secretary" for "Secretary or his delegate" each place it appeared. **Effective** 2-1-77.

[Sec. 5553]

SEC. 5553. SUPERVISION OF PREMISES AND OPERATIONS.

[Sec. 5553(a)]

(a) ASSIGNMENT OF INTERNAL REVENUE OFFICERS.—The Secretary is authorized to assign to any premises established under the provisions of this chapter such number of internal revenue officers as may be deemed necessary.

Amendments

• **1976, Tax Reform Act of 1976 (P.L. 94-455)**

P.L. 94-455, §1906(b)(13)(A):

Amended 1954 Code by substituting "Secretary" for "Secretary or his delegate" each place it appeared. **Effective** 2-1-77.

[Sec. 5553(b)]

(b) FUNCTIONS OF INTERNAL REVENUE OFFICER.—When used in this chapter, the term "internal revenue officer assigned to the premises" means the internal revenue officer assigned by the Secretary to duties at premises established and operated under the provisions of this chapter.

Amendments

• **1976, Tax Reform Act of 1976 (P.L. 94-455)**

P.L. 94-455, §1906(b)(13)(A):

Amended 1954 Code by substituting "Secretary" for "Secretary or his delegate" each place it appeared. **Effective** 2-1-77.

[Sec. 5554]

SEC. 5554. PILOT OPERATIONS.

For the purpose of facilitating the development and testing of improved methods of governmental supervision (necessary for the protection of the revenue) over distilled spirits plants established under this chapter, the Secretary is authorized to waive any regulatory provisions of this chapter for temporary pilot or experimental operations. Nothing in this section shall be construed as authority to waive the filing of any bond or the payment of any tax provided for in this chapter.

Amendments

• **1976, Tax Reform Act of 1976 (P.L. 94-455)**

P.L. 94-455, §1906(b)(13)(A):

Amended 1954 Code by substituting "Secretary" for "Secretary or his delegate" each place it appeared. **Effective** 2-1-77.

[Sec. 5555]

SEC. 5555. RECORDS, STATEMENTS, AND RETURNS.

[Sec. 5555(a)]

(a) GENERAL.—Every person liable to any tax imposed by this chapter, or for the collection thereof, shall keep such records, render such statements, make such returns, and comply with such rules and regulations as the Secretary may prescribe. The Secretary shall permit a person to employ a unified system for any records, statements, and returns required to be kept, rendered, or made under this section for any beer produced in the brewery for which the tax imposed by section 5051 has been determined, including any beer which has been removed for consumption on the premises of the brewery.

Amendments

• **2020, Taxpayer Certainty and Disaster Tax Relief Act of 2020 (P.L. 116-260)**

P.L. 116-260, §106(i)(1), Div. EE:

Amended Code Sec. 5555(a) by striking "For calendar quarters beginning after the date of the enactment of this sentence, and before January 1, 2021, the Secretary" and inserting "The Secretary". **Effective** for calendar quarters beginning after 12-31-2020.

• **2019, Taxpayer Certainty and Disaster Tax Relief Act of 2019 (P.L. 116-94)**

P.L. 116-94, §144(i)(1), Div. Q:

Amended Code Sec. 5555(a) by striking "January 1, 2020" and inserting "January 1, 2021". **Effective** for calendar quarters beginning after 12-31-2019.

• **2018, Bipartisan Budget Act of 2018 (P.L. 115-123)**

P.L. 115-123, §41112(a), Div. D:

Amended Code Sec. 5555(a) by adding at the end a new sentence. **Effective** for calendar quarters beginning after 2-9-2018.

• **1984, Deficit Reduction Act of 1984 (P.L. 98-369)**

P.L. 98-369, §454(c)(10):

Amended Code Sec. 5555(a) by striking out "or for the affixing of any stamp required to be affixed by this chapter,". **Effective** 7-1-85.

• **1976, Tax Reform Act of 1976 (P.L. 94-455)**

P.L. 94-455, §1906(b)(13)(A):

Amended 1954 Code by substituting "Secretary" for "Secretary or his delegate" each place it appeared. **Effective** 2-1-77.

[Sec. 5555(b)]

(b) AUTHORITY TO WAIVE.—Whenever in this chapter any record is required to be made or kept, or statement or return is required to be made by any person, the Secretary may by regulation waive, in whole or in part, such requirement when he deems such requirement to no longer serve a necessary purpose. This subsection shall not be construed as authorizing the waiver of the payment of any tax.

Amendments

• **1976, Tax Reform Act of 1976 (P.L. 94-455)**

P.L. 94-455, §1906(b)(13)(A):

Amended 1954 Code by substituting "Secretary" for "Secretary or his delegate" each place it appeared. **Effective** 2-1-77.

[Sec. 5555(c)]

(c) PHOTOGRAPHIC COPIES.—Whenever in this chapter any record is required to be made and preserved by any person, the Secretary may by regulations authorize such person to record, copy, or reproduce by any photographic, photostatic, microfilm, microcard, miniature photographic, or other process, which accurately reproduces or forms a durable medium for so reproducing the original of such record and to retain such reproduction in lieu of the original. Every person who is authorized to retain such reproduction in lieu of the original shall, under such regulations as the Secretary may prescribe, preserve such reproduction in conveniently accessible files and make provision for examining, viewing, and using such reproduction the same as if it were the original. Such reproduction shall be treated and considered for all purposes as though it were the

ALCOHOL TAXES—MISCELLANEOUS PROVISIONS

original record and all provisions of law applicable to the original shall be applicable to such reproduction. Such reproduction, or enlargement or facsimile thereof, shall be admissible in evidence in the same manner and under the same conditions as provided for the admission of reproductions, enlargements, or facsimiles of records made in the regular course of business under section 1732(b) of title 28 of the United States Code.

Amendments

• **1976, Tax Reform Act of 1976 (P.L. 94-455)**

P.L. 94-455, §1906(b)(13)(A):

Amended 1954 Code by substituting "Secretary" for "Secretary or his delegate" each place it appeared. **Effective** 2-1-77.

[Sec. 5556]

SEC. 5556. REGULATIONS.

The regulations prescribed by the Secretary for enforcement of this chapter may make such distinctions in requirements relating to construction, equipment, or methods of operation as he deems necessary or desirable due to differences in materials or variations in methods used in production, processing, or storage of distilled spirits.

Amendments

• **1976, Tax Reform Act of 1976 (P.L. 94-455)**

P.L. 94-455, §1906(b)(13)(A):

Amended 1954 Code by substituting "Secretary" for "Secretary or his delegate" each place it appeared. **Effective** 2-1-77.

[Sec. 5557]

SEC. 5557. OFFICERS AND AGENTS AUTHORIZED TO INVESTIGATE, ISSUE SEARCH WARRANTS, AND PROSECUTE FOR VIOLATIONS.

[Sec. 5557(a)]

(a) GENERAL.—The Secretary shall investigate violations of this subtitle and in any case in which prosecution appears warranted the Secretary shall report the violation to the United States Attorney for the district in which such violation was committed, who is hereby charged with the duty of prosecuting the offenders, subject to the direction of the Attorney General, as in the case of other offenses against the laws of the United States; and the Secretary may swear out warrants before United States commissioners or other officers or courts authorized to issue warrants for the apprehension of such offenders, and may, subject to the control of such United States Attorney, conduct the prosecution at the committing trial for the purpose of having the offenders held for the action of a grand jury. Section 3041 of title 18 of the United States Code is hereby made applicable in the enforcement of this subtitle.

Amendments

• **1976, Tax Reform Act of 1976 (P.L. 94-455)**

P.L. 94-455, §1906(b)(13)(A):

Amended 1954 Code by substituting "Secretary" for "Secretary or his delegate" each place it appeared. **Effective** 2-1-77.

[Sec. 5557(b)]

(b) CROSS REFERENCE.—

For provisions relating to the issuance of search warrants, see the Federal Rules of Criminal Procedure.

[Sec. 5558]

SEC. 5558. AUTHORITY OF ENFORCEMENT OFFICERS.

For provisions relating to the authority of internal revenue enforcement officers, see section 7608.

[Sec. 5559]

SEC. 5559. DETERMINATIONS.

Whenever the Secretary is required or authorized, in this chapter, to make or verify any quantitative determination, such determination or verification may be made by actual count, weight, or measurement, or by the application of statistical methods, or by other means, under such regulations as the Secretary may prescribe.

Amendments

• **1976, Tax Reform Act of 1976 (P.L. 94-455)**

P.L. 94-455, §1906(b)(13)(A):

Amended 1954 Code by substituting "Secretary" for "Secretary or his delegate" each place it appeared. **Effective** 2-1-77.

[Sec. 5560]

SEC. 5560. OTHER PROVISIONS APPLICABLE.

All provisions of subtitle F, insofar as applicable and not inconsistent with the provisions of this subtitle, are hereby extended to and made a part of this subtitle.

[Sec. 5561]

SEC. 5561. EXEMPTIONS TO MEET THE REQUIREMENTS OF THE NATIONAL DEFENSE.

The Secretary may temporarily exempt proprietors of distilled spirits plants from any provision of the internal revenue laws relating to distilled spirits, except those requiring payment of the tax thereon, whenever in his judgment it may seem expedient to do so to meet the requirements of the national defense. Whenever the Secretary shall exercise the authority conferred by this section he may prescribe such regulations as may be necessary to accomplish the purpose which caused him to grant the exemption.

Amendments

• **1976, Tax Reform Act of 1976 (P.L. 94-455)**

P.L. 94-455, §1906(b)(13)(A):

Amended 1954 Code by substituting "Secretary" for "Secretary or his delegate" each place it appeared. **Effective** 2-1-77.

ALCOHOL TAXES—PENALTIES

[Sec. 5562]
SEC. 5562. EXEMPTIONS FROM CERTAIN REQUIREMENTS IN CASES OF DISASTER.
Whenever the Secretary finds that it is necessary or desirable, by reason of disaster, to waive provisions of internal revenue law with regard to distilled spirits, he may temporarily exempt proprietors of distilled spirits plants from any provision of the internal revenue laws relating to distilled spirits, except those requiring payment of the tax thereon, to the extent he may deem necessary or desirable.

Amendments

• 1976, Tax Reform Act of 1976 (P.L. 94-455)

P.L. 94-455, § 1906(b)(13)(A):
Amended 1954 Code by substituting "Secretary" for "Secretary or his delegate" each place it appeared. **Effective** 2-1-77.

Subchapter J—Penalties, Seizures, and Forfeitures Relating to Liquors

Part I.	Penalty, seizure, and forfeiture provisions applicable to distilling, rectifying, and distilled and rectified products.
Part II.	Penalty and forfeiture provisions applicable to wine and wine production.
Part III.	Penalty, seizure, and forfeiture provisions applicable to beer and brewing.
Part IV.	Penalty, seizure, and forfeiture provisions common to liquors.

PART I—PENALTY, SEIZURE, AND FORFEITURE PROVISIONS APPLICABLE TO DISTILLING, RECTIFYING, AND DISTILLED AND RECTIFIED PRODUCTS

Sec. 5601.	Criminal penalties.
Sec. 5602.	Penalty for tax fraud by distiller.
Sec. 5603.	Penalty relating to records, returns, and reports.
Sec. 5604.	Penalties relating to marks, brands, and containers.
Sec. 5605.	Penalty relating to return of materials used in the manufacture of distilled spirits, or from which distilled spirits may be recovered.
Sec. 5606.	Penalty relating to containers of distilled spirits.
Sec. 5607.	Penalty and forfeiture for unlawful use, recovery, or concealment of denatured distilled spirits, or articles.
Sec. 5608.	Penalty and forfeiture for fraudulent claims for export drawback or unlawful relanding.
Sec. 5609.	Destruction of unregistered stills, distilling apparatus, equipment, and materials.
Sec. 5610.	Disposal of forfeited equipment and material for distilling.
Sec. 5611.	Release of distillery before judgment.
Sec. 5612.	Forfeiture of taxpaid distilled spirits remaining on bonded premises.
Sec. 5613.	Forfeiture of distilled spirits not closed, marked, or branded as required by law.
Sec. 5614.	Burden of proof in cases of seizure of spirits.
Sec. 5615.	Property subject to forfeiture.

[Sec. 5601]
SEC. 5601. CRIMINAL PENALTIES.

[Sec. 5601(a)]
(a) OFFENSES.—Any person who—

(1) UNREGISTERED STILLS.—has in his possession or custody, or under his control, any still or distilling apparatus set up which is not registered, as required by section 5179(a); or

(2) FAILURE TO FILE APPLICATION.—engages in the business of a distiller or processor without having filed application for and received notice of registration, as required by section 5171(c); or

(3) FALSE OR FRAUDULENT APPLICATION.—engages, or intends to engage, in the business of distiller, warehouseman, or processor of distilled spirits, and files a false or fraudulent application under section 5171; or

(4) FAILURE OR REFUSAL OF DISTILLER, WAREHOUSEMAN, OR PROCESSOR TO GIVE BOND.—carries on the business of a distiller, warehouseman, or processor without having given bond as required by law; or

(5) FALSE, FORGED, OR FRAUDULENT BOND.—engages, or intends to engage, in the business of distiller, warehouseman, or processor of distilled spirits, and gives any false, forged, or fraudulent bond, under subchapter B; or

(6) DISTILLING ON PROHIBITED PREMISES.—uses, or possesses with intent to use, any still, boiler, or other utensil for the purpose of producing distilled spirits, or aids or assists therein, or causes or procures the same to be done, in any dwelling house, or in any shed, yard, or inclosure connected with such dwelling house (except as authorized under section 5178(a)(1)(C)), or on board any vessel or boat, or on any premises where beer or wine is made or produced, or where liquors of any description are retailed, or on premises where any other business is carried on (except when authorized under section 5178(b)); or

(7) UNLAWFUL PRODUCTION, REMOVAL, OR USE OF MATERIAL FIT FOR PRODUCTION OF DISTILLED SPIRITS.—except as otherwise provided in this chapter, makes or ferments mash, wort, or wash, fit for distillation or for the production of distilled spirits, in any building or on any premises other than the designated premises of a distilled spirits plant lawfully qualified to produce distilled spirits, or removes, without authorization by the Secretary, any mash, wort, or wash, so made or fermented, from the designated premises of such lawfully qualified plant before being distilled; or

(8) UNLAWFUL PRODUCTION OF DISTILLED SPIRITS.—not being a distiller authorized by law to produce distilled spirits, produces distilled spirits by distillation or any other process from any mash, wort, wash, or other material; or

(9) UNAUTHORIZED USE OF DISTILLED SPIRITS IN MANUFACTURING PROCESSES.—except as otherwise provided in this chapter, uses distilled spirits in any process of manufacture unless such spirits—

(A) have been produced in the United States by a distiller authorized by law to produce distilled spirits and withdrawn in compliance with law; or

(B) have been imported (or otherwise brought into the United States) and withdrawn in compliance with law; or

(10) UNLAWFUL PROCESSING.—engages in or carries on the business of a processor—

ALCOHOL TAXES—PENALTIES

(A) with intent to defraud the United States of any tax on the distilled spirits processed by him; or

(B) with intent to aid, abet, or assist any person or persons in defrauding the United States of the tax on any distilled spirits; or

(11) UNLAWFUL PURCHASE, RECEIPT, OR PROCESSING OF DISTILLED SPIRITS.—purchases, receives, or processes any distilled spirits, knowing or having reasonable grounds to believe that any tax due on such spirits has not been paid or determined as required by law; or

(12) UNLAWFUL REMOVAL OR CONCEALMENT OF DISTILLED SPIRITS.—removes, other than as authorized by law, any distilled spirits on which the tax has not been paid or determined, from the place of manufacture or storage, or from any instrument of transportation, or conceals spirits so removed; or

(13) CREATION OF FICTITIOUS PROOF.—adds, or causes to be added, any ingredient or substance (other than ingredients or substances authorized by law to be added) to any distilled spirits before the tax is paid thereon, or determined as provided by law, for the purpose of creating fictitious proof; or

(14) DISTILLING AFTER NOTICE OF SUSPENSION.—after the time fixed in the notice given under section 5221(a) to suspend operations as a distiller, carries on the business of a distiller on the premises covered by the notice of suspension, or has mash, wort, or beer on such premises, or on any premises connected therewith, or has in his possession or under his control any mash, wort, or beer, with intent to distill the same on such premises; or

(15) UNAUTHORIZED WITHDRAWAL, USE, SALE, OR DISTRIBUTION OF DISTILLED SPIRITS FOR FUEL USE.—withdraws, uses, sells, or otherwise disposes of distilled spirits produced under section 5181 for other than fuel use;

shall be fined not more than $10,000, or imprisoned not more than 5 years, or both, for each such offense.

Amendments

- **2018, Tax Technical Corrections Act of 2018 (P.L. 115-141)**

P.L. 115-141, §401(a)(248), Div. U:

Amended Code Sec. 5601(a)(15) by striking "Withdraws," and inserting "withdraws,". **Effective** 3-23-2018.

- **1980, Crude Oil Windfall Profit Tax Act of 1980 (P.L. 96-223)**

P.L. 96-223, §232(e)(2)(A):

Amended Code Sec. 5601(a) by adding "or" at the end of paragraph (14) and adding a new paragraph (15). **Effective** 7-1-80.

- **1979, Trade Agreements Act of 1979 (P.L. 96-39)**

P.L. 96-39, §807(a)(52):

Amended Code Sec. 5601(a) by changing paragraphs (2), (4), (10), and (11), and by changing "bonded warehouseman, rectifier, or bottler" to "warehouseman, or processor" in paragraphs (3) and (5). **Effective** 1-1-80. Prior to amendment, paragraphs (2), (4), (10), and (11) read as follows:

* * *

(2) FAILURE OF DISTILLER OR RECTIFIER TO FILE APPLICATION.—engages in the business of a distiller or rectifier without having filed application for and received notice of registration, as required by section 5171(a); or

* * *

(4) FAILURE OR REFUSAL OF DISTILLER OR RECTIFIER TO GIVE BOND.—carries on the business of a distiller or rectifier without having given bond as required by law; or

* * *

(10) UNLAWFUL RECTIFYING OR BOTTLING.—engages in or carries on the business of a rectifier, or a bottler of distilled spirits—

(A) with intent to defraud the United States of any tax on the distilled spirits rectified or bottled by him; or

(B) with intent to aid, abet, or assist any person or persons in defrauding the United States of the tax on any distilled spirits; or

(11) UNLAWFUL PURCHASE, RECEIPT, RECTIFICATION, OR BOTTLING OF DISTILLED SPIRITS.—purchases, receives, rectifies, or bottles any distilled spirits, knowing or having reasonable grounds to believe that any tax due on such spirits has not been paid or determined as required by law; or

- **1976, Tax Reform Act of 1976 (P.L. 94-455)**

P.L. 94-455, §1906(b)(13)(A):

Amended 1954 Code by substituting "Secretary" for "Secretary or his delegate" each place it appeared. **Effective** 2-1-77.

[Sec. 5601(b)]

(b) PRESUMPTION.—Whenever on trial for violation of subsection (a)(4) the defendant is shown to have been at the site or place where, and at the time when, the business of a distiller or processor was so engaged in or carried on, such presence of the defendant shall be deemed sufficient evidence to authorize conviction, unless the defendant explains such presence to the satisfaction of the jury (or of the court when tried without jury).

Amendments

- **1979, Trade Agreements Act of 1979 (P.L. 96-39)**

P.L. 96-39, §807(a)(52)(F):

Amended Code Sec. 5601(b) by changing "rectifier" to "processor". **Effective** 1-1-80.

- **1976, Tax Reform Act of 1976 (P.L. 94-455)**

P.L. 94-455, §1905(a)(22):

Amended Code Sec. 5601(b). **Effective** 2-1-77. Prior to amendment, Code Sec. 5601(b) read as follows:

(b) PRESUMPTIONS.—

(1) UNREGISTERED STILLS.—Whenever on trial for violation of subsection (a)(1) the defendant is shown to have been at the site or place where, and at the time when, a still or distilling apparatus was set up without having been registered, such presence of the defendant shall be deemed sufficient evidence to authorize conviction, unless the defendant explains such presence to the satisfaction of the jury (or of the court when tried without jury).

(2) FAILURE OR REFUSAL OF DISTILLER OR RECTIFIER TO GIVE BOND.—Whenever on trial for violation of subsection (a)(4) the defendant is shown to have been at the site or place where, and at the time when, the business of a distiller or rectifier was so engaged in or carried on, such presence of the defendant shall be deemed sufficient evidence to authorize conviction, unless the defendant explains such presence to the satisfaction of the jury (or of the court when tried without jury).

(3) UNLAWFUL PRODUCTION, REMOVAL, OR USE OF MATERIAL FIT FOR PRODUCTION OF DISTILLED SPIRITS.—Whenever on trial for violation of subsection (a) (7) the defendant is shown to have been at the place in the building or on the premises where such mash, wort, or wash fit for distillation or the production of distilled spirits, was made or fermented, and at the time such mash, wort, or wash was there possessed, such presence of the defendant shall be deemed sufficient evidence to authorize conviction, unless the defendant explains such presence to the satisfaction of the jury (or of the court when tried without jury).

(4) UNLAWFUL PRODUCTION OF DISTILLED SPIRITS.—Whenever on trial for violation of subsection (a)(8) the defendant is shown to have been at the site or place where, and at the time when, such distilled spirits were produced by distillation or any other process from mash, wort, wash, or other material, such presence of the defendant shall be deemed sufficient evidence to authorize conviction, unless the defendant explains such presence to the satisfaction of the jury (or of the court when tried without jury).

[Sec. 5602]

SEC. 5602. PENALTY FOR TAX FRAUD BY DISTILLER.

Whenever any person engaged in or carrying on the business of a distiller defrauds, attempts to defraud, or engages in such business with intent to defraud the United States of the tax on the spirits distilled by him, or of any part thereof, he shall be fined not more than $10,000, or imprisoned not more than 5 years, or both. No discontinuance or *nolle prosequi* of any prosecution under this section shall be allowed without the permission in writing of the Attorney General.

[Sec. 5603]

SEC. 5603. PENALTY RELATING TO RECORDS, RETURNS, AND REPORTS.

[Sec. 5603(a)]

(a) FRAUDULENT NONCOMPLIANCE.—Any person required by this chapter (other than subchapters F and G) or regulations issued pursuant thereto to keep or file any record, return, report, summary, transcript, or other document, who, with intent to defraud the United States, shall—

(1) fail to keep any such document or to make required entries therein; or

(2) make any false entry in such document; or

ALCOHOL TAXES—PENALTIES

(3) cancel, alter, or obliterate any part of such document or any entry therein, or destroy any part of such document or any entry therein; or

(4) hinder or obstruct any internal revenue officer from inspecting any such document or taking any abstracts therefrom; or

(5) fail or refuse to preserve or produce any such document, as required by this chapter or regulations issued pursuant thereto;

or who shall, with intent to defraud the United States, cause or procure the same to be done, shall be fined not more than $10,000, or imprisoned not more than 5 years, or both, for each such offense.

Amendments

• **2018, Tax Technical Corrections Act of 2018 (P.L. 115-141)**

P.L. 115-141, §401(a)(249), Div. U:

Amended the heading of Code Sec. 5603 by inserting a comma after "**RETURNS**". **Effective** 3-23-2018.

[Sec. 5603(b)]

(b) FAILURE TO COMPLY.—Any person required by this chapter (other than subchapters F and G) or regulations issued pursuant thereto to keep or file any record, return, report, summary, transcript, or other document, who, otherwise than with intent to defraud the United States, shall—

(1) fail to keep any such document or to make required entries therein; or

(2) make any false entry in such document; or

(3) cancel, alter, or obliterate any part of such document or any entry therein, or destroy any part of such document, or any entry therein, except as provided by this title or regulations issued pursuant thereto; or

(4) hinder or obstruct any internal revenue officer from inspecting any such document or taking any abstracts therefrom; or

(5) fail or refuse to preserve or produce any such document, as required by this chapter or regulations issued pursuant thereto;

or who shall, otherwise than with intent to defraud the United States, cause or procure the same to be done, shall be fined not more than $1,000, or imprisoned not more than 1 year, or both, for each such offense.

[Sec. 5604]

SEC. 5604. PENALTIES RELATING TO MARKS, BRANDS, AND CONTAINERS.

[Sec. 5604(a)]

(a) IN GENERAL.—Any person who shall—

(1) transport, possess, buy, sell, or transfer any distilled spirits unless the immediate container bears the type of closure or other device required by section 5301(d),

(2) with intent to defraud the United States, empty a container bearing the closure or other device required by section 5301(d) without breaking such closure or other device,

(3) empty, or cause to be emptied, any distilled spirits from an immediate container bearing any mark or brand required by law without effacing and obliterating such mark or brand as required by section 5206(d),

(4) place any distilled spirits in any bottle, or reuse any bottle for the purpose of containing distilled spirits, which has once been filled and fitted with a closure or other device under the provisions of this chapter, without removing and destroying such closure or other device,

(5) willfully and unlawfully remove, change, or deface any mark, brand, label, or seal affixed to any case of distilled spirits, or to any bottle contained therein,

(6) with intent to defraud the United States, purchase, sell, receive with intent to transport, or transport any empty cask or package having thereon any mark or brand required by law to be affixed to any cask or package containing distilled spirits, or

(7) change or alter any mark or brand on any cask or package containing distilled spirits, or put into any cask or package spirits of greater strength than is indicated by the inspection mark thereon, or fraudulently use any cask or package having any inspection mark thereon, for the purpose of selling other spirits, or spirits of quantity or quality different from the spirits previously inspected,

shall be fined not more than $10,000 or imprisoned not more than 5 years, or both, for each such offense.

[Sec. 5604(b)]

(b) CROSS REFERENCES.—

For provisions relating to the authority of internal revenue officers to enforce provisions of this section, see sections 5203, 5557, and 7608.

Amendments

• **1984, Deficit Reduction Act of 1984 (P.L. 98-369)**

P.L. 98-369, §454(c)(11)(A):

Amended Code Sec. 5604. **Effective** 7-1-85. Prior to amendment, it read as follows:

SEC. 5604. PENALTIES RELATING TO STAMPS, MARKS, BRANDS, AND CONTAINERS.

(a) In General.—Any person who shall—

(1) transport, possess, buy, sell, or transfer any distilled spirits, required to be stamped under the provisions of section 5205(a)(1), unless the immediate container thereof has affixed thereto a stamp as required by such section; or

(2) with intent to defraud the United States, empty a container stamped under the provisions of section 5205(a)(2) or section 5235 without destroying the stamp thereon as required by section 5205(a)(2) or regulations prescribed pursuant thereto; or

(3) empty, or cause to be emptied, any distilled spirits from any immediate container (other than a container stamped under section 5205(a) or section 5235) bearing any stamp, mark, or brand required by law without effacing and obliterating such stamp, mark, or brand as required by section 5205(f); or

(4) with intent to defraud the United States, falsely make, forge, alter, or counterfeit any stamp required under section 5205 or section 5235; or

(5) use, sell, or have in his possession any forged or fraudulently altered stamp, or counterfeit of any stamp, required under section 5205 or section 5235, or any plate or die used or which may be used in the manufacture thereof; or

(6) with intent to defraud the United States, use, reuse, sell, or have in his possession any stamp required to be destroyed by section 5205(a)(2) or regulations prescribed pursuant thereto; or

(7) remove any stamp required by law or regulations from any cask or package containing, or which had contained, distilled spirits, without defacing or destroying such stamp at the time of such removal; or

(8) have in his possession any undestroyed or undefaced stamp removed from any cask or package containing, or which had contained, distilled spirits; or

(9) have in his possession any cancelled stamp or any stamp which has been used, or which purports to have been used, upon any cask or package of distilled spirits; or

(10) make, use, sell, or have in his possession any paper in imitation of the paper used in the manufacture of any stamp required under section 5205 or section 5235; or

(11) reuse any stamp required under section 5205(a) or section 5235, after the same shall have once been affixed to a container as provided in such sections or regulations issued pursuant thereto; or

(12) place any distilled spirits in any bottle, or reuse any bottle for the purpose of containing distilled spirits, which has once been filled and stamped under the provisions of this chapter, without removing and destroying the stamp so previously affixed to such bottle; or

(13) affix any stamp issued pursuant to section 5205(a) to any container containing distilled spirits on which any tax due is unpaid or undetermined; or

(14) make any false statement in any application for stamps under section 5205; or

(15) possess any stamp prescribed under section 5205 or section 5235 obtained by him otherwise than as provided by such sections or regulations issued pursuant thereto; or

(16) willfully and unlawfully remove, change, or deface any stamp, mark, brand, label, or seal affixed to any case of distilled spirits, or to any bottle contained therein; or

(17) with intent to defraud the United States, purchase, sell, receive with intent to transport, or transport any empty cask or package having thereon any stamp, mark, or brand required by law to be affixed to any cask or package containing distilled spirits; or

(18) change or alter any stamp, mark, or brand on any cask or package containing distilled spirits, or put into any cask or package spirits of greater strength than is

ALCOHOL TAXES—PENALTIES

indicated by the inspection-mark thereon, or fraudulently use any cask or package having any inspection-mark or stamp thereon, for the purpose of selling other spirits, or spirits of quantity or quality different from the spirits previously inspected therein; or

(19) affix, or cause to be affixed, to or on any cask or package containing, or intended to contain, distilled spirits, any limitation stamp or other engraved, printed, stamped, or photographed label, device, or token, whether the same be designed as a trade mark, caution notice, caution, or otherwise, and which shall be in the similitude or likeness of, or shall have the resemblance or general appearance of, any internal revenue stamp required by law to be affixed to or upon any cask or package containing distilled spirits;

shall be fined not more than $10,000, or imprisoned not more than 5 years, or both, for each such offense.

(b) Officers Authorized To Enforce This Section.—Any officer authorized to enforce any provision of law relating to internal revenue stamps is authorized to enforce this section.

- 1979, Trade Agreements Act of 1979 (P.L. 96-39)

P.L. 96-39, § 807(a)(53):

Amended Code Sec. 5604(a) by changing "section 5205(a)(2)" to "section 5205(a)(1)" in paragraph (1), by changing "section 5205(a)(1) or (2)" to "section 5205(a)(2)" and "section 5205(a)(3)" to "section 5205(a)(2)" in paragraph (2), by changing "section 5205(g)" to "section 5205(f)" in paragraph (3), by changing "section 5205(a)(3)" to "section 5205(a)(2)" in paragraph (6), and by changing "section 5205(a)(2) and (3)" to "section 5205(a)" in paragraph (13). **Effective** 1-1-80.

[Sec. 5605]

SEC. 5605. PENALTY RELATING TO RETURN OF MATERIALS USED IN THE MANUFACTURE OF DISTILLED SPIRITS, OR FROM WHICH DISTILLED SPIRITS MAY BE RECOVERED.

Any person who willfully violates any provision of section 5291(a), or of any regulation issued pursuant thereto, and any officer, director, or agent of any such person who knowingly participates in such violation, shall be fined not more than $1,000, or imprisoned not more than 2 years, or both.

[Sec. 5606]

SEC. 5606. PENALTY RELATING TO CONTAINERS OF DISTILLED SPIRITS.

Whoever violates any provision of section 5301, or of any regulation issued pursuant thereto, or the terms or conditions of any permit issued pursuant to the authorization contained in such section, and any officer, director, or agent of any corporation who knowingly participates in such violation, shall, upon conviction, be fined not more than $1,000, or imprisoned not more than 1 year, or both, for each such offense.

[Sec. 5607]

SEC. 5607. PENALTY AND FORFEITURE FOR UNLAWFUL USE, RECOVERY, OR CONCEALMENT OF DENATURED DISTILLED SPIRITS, OR ARTICLES.

Any person who—

(1) uses denatured distilled spirits withdrawn free of tax under section 5214(a)(1) in the manufacture of any medicinal preparation or flavoring extract in violation of the provisions of section 5273(b)(1), or knowingly sells, or offers for sale, any such medicinal preparation or flavoring extract in violation of section 5273(b)(2); or

(2) knowingly withdraws any denatured distilled spirits free of tax under section 5214(a)(1) for beverage purposes; or

(3) knowingly sells any denatured distilled spirits withdrawn free of tax under section 5214(a)(1), or any articles containing such denatured distilled spirits, for beverage purposes; or

(4) recovers or attempts to recover by redistillation or by any other process or means (except as authorized in section 5223 or in section 5273(c)) any distilled spirits from any denatured distilled spirits withdrawn free of tax under section 5214(a)(1), or from any articles manufactured therefrom, or knowingly uses, sells, conceals, or otherwise disposes of distilled spirits so recovered or redistilled;

shall be fined not more than $10,000, or imprisoned not more than 5 years, or both, for each such offense; and all personal property used in connection with his business, together with the buildings and ground constituting the premises on which such unlawful acts are performed or permitted to be performed shall be forfeited to the United States.

[Sec. 5608]

SEC. 5608. PENALTY AND FORFEITURE FOR FRAUDULENT CLAIMS FOR EXPORT DRAWBACK OR UNLAWFUL RELANDING.

[Sec. 5608(a)]

(a) Fraudulent Claim for Drawback.—Every person who fraudulently claims, or seeks, or obtains an allowance of drawback on any distilled spirits, or fraudulently claims any greater allowance or drawback than the tax actually paid or determined thereon, shall forfeit and pay to the Government of the United States triple the amount wrongfully and fraudulently sought to be obtained, and shall be imprisoned not more than 5 years; and every owner, agent, or master of any vessel or other person who knowingly aids or abets in the fraudulent collection or fraudulent attempts to collect any drawback upon, or knowingly aids or permits any fraudulent change in the spirits so shipped, shall be fined not more than $5,000, or imprisoned not more than 3 years, or both, and the ship or vessel on board of which such shipment was made or pretended to be made shall be forfeited to the United States, whether a conviction of the master or owner be had or otherwise, and proceedings may be had in admiralty by libel for such forfeiture.

[Sec. 5608(b)]

(b) Unlawful Relanding.—Every person who, with intent to defraud the United States, relands within the jurisdiction of the United States any distilled spirits which have been shipped for exportation under the provisions of this chapter, or who receives such relanded distilled spirits, and every person who aids or abets in such relanding or receiving of such spirits, shall be fined not more than $5,000, or imprisoned not more than 3 years, or both; and all distilled spirits so relanded, together with the vessel from which the same were relanded within the jurisdiction of the United States, and all vessels, vehicles, or aircraft used in relanding and removing such distilled spirits, shall be forfeited to the United States.

Amendments

- 1965, Excise Tax Reduction Act of 1965 (P.L. 89-44)

P.L. 89-44, § 805(e):

Amended subsection (b) of Section 5608 by inserting ", with intent to defraud the United States," in lieu of "intentionally". **Effective** 7-1-65.

[Sec. 5609]

SEC. 5609. DESTRUCTION OF UNREGISTERED STILLS, DISTILLING APPARATUS, EQUIPMENT, AND MATERIALS.

[Sec. 5609(a)]

(a) General.—In the case of seizure elsewhere than on premises qualified under this chapter of any unregistered still, distilling or fermenting equipment or apparatus, or distilling or fermenting material, for any offense involving forfeiture of the same, where it shall be impracticable to remove the same to a place of safe storage from the place where seized, the seizing officer is authorized to destroy the same. In the case of seizure, other than on premises qualified under this chapter or in transit thereto or therefrom, of any distilled spirits on which the tax has not been paid or determined, for any offense involving forfeiture of the same, the seizing officer is authorized to destroy the distilled spirits forthwith. Any destruction under this subsection shall be in the presence of at least one credible witness. The seizing officer shall make such report of said seizure and destruction and take such samples as the Secretary may require.

ALCOHOL TAXES—PENALTIES

Amendments

• **1976, Tax Reform Act of 1976 (P.L. 94-455)**

P.L. 94-455, §1906(b)(13)(A):

Amended 1954 Code by substituting "Secretary" for "Secretary or his delegate" each place it appeared. **Effective** 2-1-77.

[Sec. 5609(b)]

(b) CLAIMS.—Within 1 year after destruction made pursuant to subsection (a) the owner of, including any person having an interest in, the property so destroyed may make application to the Secretary for reimbursement of the value of such property. If the claimant establishes to the satisfaction of the Secretary that—

   (1) such property had not been used in violation of law; or
   (2) any unlawful use of such property had been without his consent or knowledge,

the Secretary shall make an allowance to such claimant not exceeding the value of the property destroyed.

Amendments

• **1976, Tax Reform Act of 1976 (P.L. 94-455)**

P.L. 94-455, §1906(b)(13)(A):

Amended 1954 Code by substituting "Secretary" for "Secretary or his delegate" each place it appeared. **Effective** 2-1-77.

[Sec. 5610]

SEC. 5610. DISPOSAL OF FORFEITED EQUIPMENT AND MATERIAL FOR DISTILLING.

All boilers, stills, or other vessels, tools and implements, used in distilling or processing, and forfeited under any of the provisions of this chapter, and all condemned material, together with any engine or other machinery connected therewith, and all empty barrels, and all grain or other material suitable for fermentation or distillation, shall be sold at public auction or otherwise disposed of as the court in which such forfeiture was recovered shall in its discretion direct.

Amendments

• **1979, Trade Agreements Act of 1979 (P.L. 96-39)**

P.L. 96-39, §807(a)(54):

Amended Code Sec. 5610 by changing "or rectifying" to "or processing". **Effective** 1-1-80.

[Sec. 5611]

SEC. 5611. RELEASE OF DISTILLERY BEFORE JUDGMENT.

Any distillery or distilling apparatus seized on any premises qualified under this chapter, for any violation of law, may, in the discretion of the court, be released before final judgment to a receiver appointed by the court to operate such distillery or apparatus. Such receiver shall give bond, which shall be approved in open court, with corporate surety, for the full appraised value of all the property seized, to be ascertained by three competent appraisers designated and appointed by the court. Funds obtained from such operation shall be impounded as the court shall direct pending such final judgment.

[Sec. 5612]

SEC. 5612. FORFEITURE OF TAXPAID DISTILLED SPIRITS REMAINING ON BONDED PREMISES.

[Sec. 5612(a)]

(a) GENERAL.—No distilled spirits on which the tax has been paid or determined shall be stored or allowed to remain on the bonded premises of any distilled spirits plant, under the penalty of forfeiture of all spirits so found.

[Sec. 5612(b)]

(b) EXCEPTIONS.—Subsection (a) shall not apply in the case of—
   (1) distilled spirits in the process of prompt removal from bonded premises on payment or determination of the tax; or
   (2) distilled spirits returned to bonded premises in accordance with the provisions of section 5215.

Amendments

• **1979, Trade Agreements Act of 1979 (P.L. 96-39)**

P.L. 96-39, §807(a)(55):

Amended Code Sec. 5612(b). **Effective** 1-1-80. Prior to amendment, Code Sec. 5612(b) read as follows:

(b) EXCEPTIONS.—Subsection (a) shall not apply in the case of—
(1) distilled spirits which have been bottled in bond under section 5233, and which are returned to bonded premises for rebottling, relabeling, or restamping in accordance with the provisions of section 5233(d); or

(2) distilled spirits in the process of prompt removal from bonded premises on payment or determination of the tax; or

(3) distilled spirits returned to bonded premises in accordance with the provisions of section 5215; or

(4) distilled spirits, held on bonded premises, on which the tax has become payable by operation of law, but on which the tax has not been paid.

[Sec. 5613]

SEC. 5613. FORFEITURE OF DISTILLED SPIRITS NOT CLOSED, MARKED, OR BRANDED AS REQUIRED BY LAW.

[Sec. 5613(a)]

(a) UNMARKED OR UNBRANDED CASKS OR PACKAGES.—All distilled spirits found in any cask or package required by this chapter or any regulation issued pursuant thereto to bear a mark, brand, or identification, which cask or package is not marked, branded, or identified in compliance with this chapter and regulations issued pursuant thereto, shall be forfeited to the United States.

[Sec. 5613(b)]

(b) CONTAINERS WITHOUT CLOSURES.—All distilled spirits found in any container which is required by this chapter to bear a closure or other device and which does not bear a closure or other device in compliance with this chapter shall be forfeited to the United States.

Amendments

• **1984, Deficit Reduction Act of 1984 (P.L. 98-369)**

P.L. 98-369, §454(c)(12)(A):

Amended Code Sec. 5613(b). **Effective** 7-1-85. Prior to amendment, it read as follows:

(b) Unstamped Containers.—All distilled spirits found in any container required by this chapter or any regulations issued pursuant thereto to bear a stamp, which container is not stamped in compliance with this chapter and regulations issued pursuant therto, shall be forfeited to the United States.

P.L. 98-369, §454(c)(12)(B):

Amended Code Sec. 5613 by striking out "STAMPED" in the section heading and inserting in lieu thereof "CLOSED". **Effective** 7-1-85.

Internal Revenue Code   Sec. 5613(b)

ALCOHOL TAXES—PENALTIES

[Sec. 5614]

SEC. 5614. BURDEN OF PROOF IN CASES OF SEIZURE OF SPIRITS.

Whenever seizure is made of any distilled spirits found elsewhere than on the premises of a distilled spirits plant, or than in any warehouse authorized by law, or than in the store or place of business of a wholesale liquor dealer, or than in transit from any one of said places; or of any distilled spirits found in any one of the places aforesaid, or in transit therefrom, which have not been received into or sent out therefrom in conformity to law, or in regard to which any of the entries required by law, or regulations issued pursuant thereto, to be made in respect of such spirits, have not been made at the time or in the manner required, or in respect to which any owner or person having possession, control, or charge of said spirits, has omitted to do any act required to be done, or has done or committed any act prohibited in regard to said spirits, the burden of proof shall be upon the claimant of said spirits to show that no fraud has been committed, and that all the requirements of the law in relation to the payment of the tax have been complied with.

[Sec. 5615]

SEC. 5615. PROPERTY SUBJECT TO FORFEITURE.

The following property shall be forfeited to the United States:

(1) UNREGISTERED STILL OR DISTILLING APPARATUS.—Every still or distilling apparatus not registered as required by section 5179, together with all personal property in the possession or custody or under the control of the person required by section 5179 to register the still or distilling apparatus, and found in the building or in any yard or inclosure connected with the building in which such still or distilling apparatus is set up; and

(2) DISTILLING APPARATUS REMOVED WITHOUT NOTICE OR SET UP WITHOUT NOTICE.—Any still, boiler, or other vessel to be used for the purpose of distilling—

(A) which is removed without notice having been given when required by section 5101(a)(1), or

(B) which is set up without notice having been given when required by section 5101(a)(2); and

(3) DISTILLING WITHOUT GIVING BOND OR WITH INTENT TO DEFRAUD.—Whenever any person carries on the business of a distiller without having given bond as required by law or gives any false, forged, or fraudulent bond; or engages in or carries on the business of a distiller with intent to defraud the United States of the tax on the distilled spirits distilled by him, or any part thereof; or after the time fixed in the notice declaring his intention to suspend work, filed under section 5221(a), carries on the business of a distiller on the premises covered by such notice, or has mash, wort, or beer on such premises, or on any premises connected therewith, or has in his possession or under his control any mash, wort, or beer, with intent to distill the same on such premises—

(A) all distilled spirits or wines, and all stills or other apparatus fit or intended to be used for the distillation or rectification of spirits, or for the compounding of liquors, owned by such person, wherever found; and

(B) all distilled spirits, wines, raw materials for the production of distilled spirits, and personal property found in the distillery or in any building, room, yard, or inclosure connected therewith and used with or constituting a part of the premises; and

(C) all the right, title, and interest of such person in the lot or tract of land on which the distillery is situated; and

(D) all the right, title, and interest in the lot or tract of land on which the distillery is located of every person who knowingly has suffered or permitted the business of a distiller to be there carried on, or has connived at the same; and

(E) all personal property owned by or in possession of any person who has permitted or suffered any building, yard, or inclosure, or any part thereof, to be used for purposes of ingress or egress to or from the distillery, which shall be found in any such building, yard, or inclosure; and

(F) all the right, title, and interest of every person in any premises used for ingress or egress to or from the distillery who knowingly has suffered or permitted such premises to be used for such ingress or egress; and

(4) UNLAWFUL PRODUCTION AND REMOVALS FROM VINEGAR PLANTS.—

(A) all distilled spirits in excess of 15 percent of alcohol by volume produced on the premises of a vinegar plant; and

(B) all vinegar or other fluid or other material containing a greater proportion than 2 percent of proof spirits removed from any vinegar plant; and

(5) FALSE OR OMITTED ENTRIES IN RECORDS, RETURNS, AND REPORTS.—Whenever any person required by section 5207 to keep or file any record, return, report, summary, transcript, or other document, shall, with intent to defraud the United States—

(A) fail to keep any such document or to make required entries therein; or

(B) make any false entry in such document; or

(C) cancel, alter, or obliterate any part of such document, or any entry therein, or destroy any part of such document, or entry therein; or

(D) hinder or obstruct any internal revenue officer from inspecting any such document or taking any abstracts therefrom; or

(E) fail or refuse to preserve or produce any such document, as required by this chapter or regulations issued pursuant thereto; or

(F) permit any of the acts described in the preceding subparagraphs to be performed;

all interest of such person in the distillery, bonded warehouse, or rectifying or bottling establishment where such acts or omissions occur, and in the equipment thereon, and in the lot or tract of land on which such distilled spirits plant stands, and in all personal property on the premises of the distilled spirits plant where such acts or omissions occur, used in the business there carried on; and

(6) UNLAWFUL REMOVAL OF DISTILLED SPIRITS.—All distilled spirits on which the tax has not been paid or determined which have been removed, other than as authorized by law, from the place of manufacture, storage, or instrument of transportation; and

(7) CREATION OF FICTITIOUS PROOF.—All distilled spirits on which the tax has not been paid or determined as provided by law to which any ingredient or substance has been added for the purpose of creating fictitious proof.

Amendments

- **1984, Deficit Reduction Act of 1984 (P.L. 98-369)**

P.L. 98-369, § 451(b)(2):

Amended Code Sec. 5615(2). **Effective** on the first day of the first calendar month which begins more than 90 days after 7-18-84. Prior to amendment, it read as follows:

(2) Distilling Apparatus Removed Without Notice or Set Up Without Permit.—Any still, boiler, or other vessel to be used for the purpose of distilling which is removed without notice having been given as required by section 5105(a) or which is set up without permit first having been obtained as required by such section; and

- **1979, Trade Agreements Act of 1979 (P.L. 96-39)**

P.L. 96-39, § 807(a)(56):

Amended Code Sec. 5615(5) by changing "distillery, bonded warehouse, or rectifying or bottling establishment" to "distilled spirits plant" each place it appears. **Effective** 1-1-80.

ALCOHOL TAXES—PENALTIES

PART II—PENALTY AND FORFEITURE PROVISIONS APPLICABLE TO WINE AND WINE PRODUCTION

Sec. 5661.   Penalty and forfeiture for violation of laws and regulations relating to wine.
Sec. 5662.   Penalty for alteration of wine labels.
Sec. 5663.   Cross reference.

[Sec. 5661]

SEC. 5661. PENALTY AND FORFEITURE FOR VIOLATION OF LAWS AND REGULATIONS RELATING TO WINE.

[Sec. 5661(a)]

(a) FRAUDULENT OFFENSES.—Whoever, with intent to defraud the United States, fails to pay any tax imposed upon wine or violates, or fails to comply with, any provision of subchapter F or subpart C of part I of subchapter A, or regulations issued pursuant thereto, or recovers or attempts to recover any spirits from wine, shall be fined not more than $5,000, or imprisoned not more than 5 years, or both, for each such offense, and all products and materials used in any such violation shall be forfeited to the United States.

[Sec. 5661(b)]

(b) OTHER OFFENSES.—Any proprietor of premises subject to the provisions of subchapter F, or any employee or agent of such proprietor, or any other person, who otherwise than with intent to defraud the United States violates or fails to comply with any provision of subchapter F or subpart C of part I of subchapter A, or regulations issued pursuant thereto, or who aids or abets in any such violation, shall be fined not more than $1,000, or imprisoned not more than 1 year, or both, for each such offense.

[Sec. 5662]

SEC. 5662. PENALTY FOR ALTERATION OF WINE LABELS.

Any person who, without the permission of the Secretary, so alters as to materially change the meaning of any mark, brand, or label required to appear upon any wine upon its removal from premises subject to the provisions of subchapter F, or from customs custody, or who, after such removal, represents any wine, whether in its original containers or otherwise, to be of an identity or origin other than its proper identity or origin as shown by such mark, brand, or label, or who, directly or indirectly, and whether by manner of packaging or advertising or any other form of representation, represents any still wine to be an effervescent wine or a substitute for an effervescent wine, shall be fined not more than $1,000, or imprisoned not more than 1 year, or both, for each such offense.

Amendments

• **1976, Tax Reform Act of 1976 (P.L. 94-455)**

P.L. 94-455, §1905(b)(2)(D):
Struck out "stamp," before "mark" each place it appeared in Code Sec. 5662. **Effective** 2-1-77.

P.L. 94-455, §1906(b)(13)(A):
Amended 1954 Code by substituting "Secretary" for "Secretary or his delegate" each place it appeared. **Effective** 2-1-77.

[Sec. 5663]

SEC. 5663. CROSS REFERENCE.

For penalties of common application pertaining to liquors, including wines, see part IV.

Amendments

• **1979, Trade Agreements Act of 1979 (P.L. 96-39)**

P.L. 96-39, §807(a)(57):
Amended Code Sec. 5663. **Effective** 1-1-80. Prior to amendment Code Sec. 5663 read as follows:

SEC. 5663. CROSS REFERENCE.

For penalties of common application pertaining to liquors, including wines, see part IV, and for penalties for rectified products, see part I.

PART III—PENALTY, SEIZURE, AND FORFEITURE PROVISIONS APPLICABLE TO BEER AND BREWING

Sec. 5671.   Penalty and forfeiture for evasion of beer tax and fraudulent noncompliance with requirements.
Sec. 5672.   Penalty for failure of brewer to comply with requirements and to keep records and file returns.
Sec. 5673.   Forfeiture for flagrant and willful removal of beer without tax payment.
Sec. 5674.   Penalty for unlawful production or removal of beer.
Sec. 5675.   Penalty for intentional removal or defacement of brewer's marks and brands.

[Sec. 5671]

SEC. 5671. PENALTY AND FORFEITURE FOR EVASION OF BEER TAX AND FRAUDULENT NONCOMPLIANCE WITH REQUIREMENTS.

Whoever evades or attempts to evade any tax imposed by section 5051, or with intent to defraud the United States fails or refuses to keep and file true and accurate records and returns as required by section 5415 and regulations issued pursuant thereto, shall be fined not more than $5,000, or imprisoned not more than 5 years, or both, for each such offense, and shall forfeit all beer made by him or for him, and all the vessels, utensils, and apparatus used in making the same.

Amendments

• **2005, Safe, Accountable, Flexible, Efficient Transportation Equity Act: A Legacy for Users (P.L. 109-59)**

P.L. 109-59, §11125(b)(18):
Amended Code Sec. 5671 by striking "or 5091" following "section 5051". **Effective** 7-1-2008, but not applicable to taxes imposed for periods before such date.

[Sec. 5672]

SEC. 5672. PENALTY FOR FAILURE OF BREWER TO COMPLY WITH REQUIREMENTS AND TO KEEP RECORDS AND FILE RETURNS.

Every brewer who, otherwise than with intent to defraud the United States, fails or refuses to keep the records and file the returns required by section 5415 and regulations issued pursuant thereto, or refuses to permit any internal revenue officer to inspect his records in the manner provided, or violates any of the provisions of subchapter G or regulations issued pursuant thereto shall be fined not more than $1,000, or imprisoned not more than 1 year, or both, for each such offense.

[Sec. 5673]

SEC. 5673. FORFEITURE FOR FLAGRANT AND WILLFUL REMOVAL OF BEER WITHOUT TAX PAYMENT.

For flagrant and willful removal of taxable beer for consumption or sale, with intent to defraud the United States of the tax thereon, all the right, title, and interest of each person who knowingly has suffered or permitted such removal, or has connived at the same, in the lands and buildings constituting the brewery shall be forfeited by a proceeding in rem in the District Court of the United States having jurisdiction thereof.

Internal Revenue Code

Sec. 5673

ALCOHOL TAXES—PENALTIES

[Sec. 5674]
SEC. 5674. PENALTY FOR UNLAWFUL PRODUCTION OR REMOVAL OF BEER.

[Sec. 5674(a)]

(a) UNLAWFUL PRODUCTION.—Any person who brews beer or produces beer shall be fined not more than $1,000, or imprisoned not more than 1 year, or both, unless such beer is brewed or produced in a brewery qualified under subchapter G or such production is exempt from tax under section 5053(e) (relating to beer for personal or family use).

Amendments

• **1978 (P.L. 95-458)**

P.L. 95-458, §2(b)(5)(A), (c):

Amended Code Sec. 5674(a). **Effective** 2-1-79. Prior to amendment, Code Sec. 5674 read as follows:

SEC. 5674. PENALTY FOR UNLAWFUL REMOVAL OF BEER.

Any brewer or other person who removes or in any way aids in the removal from any brewery of beer without complying with the provisions of this chapter or regulations issued pursuant thereto shall be fined not more than $1,000, or imprisoned not more than 1 year, or both.

[Sec. 5674(b)]

(b) UNLAWFUL REMOVAL.—Any brewer or other person who removes or in any way aids in the removal from any brewery of beer without complying with the provisions of this chapter or regulations issued pursuant thereto shall be fined not more than $1,000, or imprisoned not more than 1 year, or both.

Amendments

• **1978 (P.L. 95-458)**

P.L. 95-458, §2(b)(5)(A), (c):

Added subsection (b). **Effective** 2-1-79.

[Sec. 5675]
SEC. 5675. PENALTY FOR INTENTIONAL REMOVAL OR DEFACEMENT OF BREWER'S MARKS AND BRANDS.

Every person other than the owner, or his agent authorized so to do, who intentionally removes or defaces any mark, brand, or label required by section 5412 and regulations issued pursuant thereto shall be liable to a penalty of $50 for each barrel or other container from which such mark, brand, or label is so removed or defaced.

PART IV—PENALTY, SEIZURE, AND FORFEITURE PROVISIONS COMMON TO LIQUORS

Sec.	Description
Sec. 5681.	Penalty relating to signs.
Sec. 5682.	Penalty for breaking locks or gaining access.
Sec. 5683.	Penalty and forfeiture for removal of liquors under improper brands.
Sec. 5684.	Penalties relating to the payment and collection of liquor taxes.
Sec. 5685.	Penalty and forfeiture relating to possession of devices for emitting gas, smoke, etc., explosives and firearms, when violating liquor laws.
Sec. 5686.	Penalty for having, possessing, or using liquor or property intended to be used in violating provisions of this chapter.
Sec. 5687.	Penalty for offenses not specifically covered.
Sec. 5688.	Disposition and release of seized property.
Sec. 5690.	Definition of the term "person".

[Sec. 5681]
SEC. 5681. PENALTY RELATING TO SIGNS.

[Sec. 5681(a)]

(a) FAILURE TO POST REQUIRED SIGN.—Every person engaged in distilled spirits operations who fails to post the sign required by section 5180(a) shall be fined not more than $1,000, or imprisoned not more than 1 year, or both.

Amendments

• **1997, Taxpayer Relief Act of 1997 (P.L. 105-34)**

P.L. 105-34, §1415(b)(1):

Amended Code Sec. 5681(a) by striking ", and every wholesale dealer in liquors," after "operations" and by striking "section 5115(a) or" after "required by". **Effective** 8-5-97.

• **1979, Trade Agreements Act of 1979 (P.L. 96-39)**

P.L. 96-39, §807(a)(58)(A):

Amended Code Sec. 5681(a) by changing "distilling, warehousing of distilled spirits, rectifying, or bottling of distilled spirits" to "distilled spirits operations". **Effective** 1-1-80.

[Sec. 5681(b)]

(b) POSTING OR DISPLAYING FALSE SIGN.—Every person, other than a distiller, warehouseman, or processor of distilled spirits who has received notice of registration of his plant under the provisions of section 5171(c), or other than a wholesale dealer in liquors who meets the requirements of section 5121(a) and section 5124 (or who is exempt from such requirements by reason of section 5121(b)), who puts up or keeps up any sign indicating that he may lawfully carry on the business of a distiller, warehouseman, or processor of distilled spirits, or wholesale dealer in liquors, as the case may be, shall be fined not more than $1,000, or imprisoned not more than 1 year, or both.

Amendments

• **2018, Tax Technical Corrections Act of 2018 (P.L. 115-141)**

P.L. 115-141, §108(a), Div. U:

Amended Code Sec. 5681(b) by striking "who has paid the special tax (or who is exempt from payment of such special tax by reason of the provisions of section 5113(a))" and inserting "who meets the requirements of section 5121(a) and section 5124 (or who is exempt from such requirements by reason of section 5121(b))". **Effective** as if included in section 11125 of the Safe, Accountable, Flexible, Efficient Transportation Equity Act: A Legacy for Users [**effective** 7-1-2008, but not applicable to taxes imposed for periods before such date.—CCH].

• **1979, Trade Agreements Act of 1979 (P.L. 96-39)**

P.L. 96-39, §807(a)(58)(B):

Amended Code Sec. 5681(b) by changing "distiller, warehouseman of distilled spirits, rectifier, or bottler of distilled spirits" to "distiller, warehouseman, or processor of distilled spirits", by changing "section 5171(a)" to "section 5171(c)", and by changing "distiller, bonded warehouseman, rectifier, bottler of distilled spirits" to "distiller, warehouseman, or processor of distilled spirits". **Effective** 1-1-80.

[Sec. 5681(c)]

(c) PREMISES WHERE NO SIGN IS PLACED OR KEPT.—Every person who works in any distilled spirits plant on which no sign required by section 5180(a) is placed or kept, and every person who knowingly receives at, or carries or conveys any distilled spirits to or from any such distilled spirits plant or who knowingly carries or delivers any grain, molasses, or other raw material to any distilled spirits plant on which such a sign is not placed and kept, shall forfeit all vehicles, aircraft, or vessels used in carrying or conveying such property and shall be fined not more than $1,000, or imprisoned not more than 1 year, or both.

ALCOHOL TAXES—PENALTIES

Amendments

• **1997, Taxpayer Relief Act of 1997 (P.L. 105-34)**

P.L. 105-34, §1415(b)(2)(A)-(B):

Amended Code Sec. 5681(c) by striking "or wholesale liquor establishment, on which no sign required by section 5115(a) or" and inserting "on which no sign required by", and by striking "or wholesale liquor establishment, or who" and inserting "or who". **Effective** 8-5-97.

• **1979, Trade Agreements Act of 1979 (P.L. 96-39)**

P.L. 96-39, §807(a)(58)(C):

Amended Code Sec. 5681(c). **Effective** 1-1-80. Prior to amendment, Code Sec. 5681(c) read as follows:

(c) PREMISES WHERE NO SIGN IS PLACED OR KEPT.—Every person who works in any distillery, or in any rectifying, distilled spirits bottling, or wholesale liquor establishment, on which no sign required by section 5115(a) or section 5180(a) is placed or kept, and every person who knowingly receives at, or carries or conveys any distilled spirits to or from any such distillery, or to or from any such rectifying, distilled spirits bottling, or wholesale liquor establishment, or who knowingly carries or delivers any grain, molasses, or other raw material to any distillery on which said sign is not placed and kept, shall forfeit all vehicles, aircraft, or vessels used in carrying or conveying such property and shall be fined not more than $1,000, or imprisoned not more than 1 year, or both.

[Sec. 5681(d)]

(d) PRESUMPTION.—Whenever on trial for violation of subsection (c) by working in a distilled spirits plant on which no sign required by section 5180(a) is placed or kept, the defendant is shown to have been present at such premises, such presence of the defendant shall be deemed sufficient evidence to authorize conviction, unless the defendant explains such presence to the satisfaction of the jury (or of the court when tried without jury).

Amendments

• **1979, Trade Agreements Act of 1979 (P.L. 96-39)**

P.L. 96-39, §807(a)(58)(C):

Amended Code Sec. 5681(d) by changing "distillery or rectifying establishment" to "distilled spirits plant". **Effective** 1-1-80.

[Sec. 5682]

SEC. 5682. PENALTY FOR BREAKING LOCKS OR GAINING ACCESS.

Every person, who destroys, breaks, injures, or tampers with any lock or seal which may be placed on any room, building, tank, vessel, or apparatus, by any authorized internal revenue officer or any approved lock or seal placed thereon by a distilled spirits plant proprietor, or who opens said lock, seal, room, building, tank, vessel, or apparatus, or in any manner gains access to the contents therein, in the absence of the proper officer, or otherwise than as authorized by law, shall be fined not more than $5,000, or imprisoned not more than 3 years, or both.

Amendments

• **1979, Trade Agreements Act of 1979 (P.L. 96-39)**

P.L. 96-39, §807(a)(59):

Amended Code Sec. 5682 by changing "duly authorized internal revenue officer, or" to "authorized internal revenue officer or any approved lock or seal placed thereon by a distilled spirits plant proprietor, or who". **Effective** 1-1-80.

[Sec. 5683]

SEC. 5683. PENALTY AND FORFEITURE FOR REMOVAL OF LIQUORS UNDER IMPROPER BRANDS.

Whenever any person ships, transports, or removes any distilled spirits, wines, or beer, under any other than the proper name or brand known to the trade as designating the kind and quality of the contents of the casks or packages containing the same, or causes such act to be done, he shall be fined not more than $1,000, or imprisoned not more than 1 year, or both, and shall forfeit such distilled spirits, wines, or beer, and casks or packages.

[Sec. 5684]

SEC. 5684. PENALTIES RELATING TO THE PAYMENT AND COLLECTION OF LIQUOR TAXES.

[Sec. 5684(a)]

(a) FAILURE TO PAY TAX.—Whoever fails to pay any tax imposed by part I of subchapter A at the time prescribed shall, in addition to any other penalty provided in this title, be liable to a penalty of 5 percent of the tax due but unpaid.

[Sec. 5684(b)]

(b) APPLICABILITY OF SECTION 6665.—The penalties imposed by subsection (a) shall be assessed, collected, and paid in the same manner as taxes, as provided in section 6665(a).

Amendments

• **1989, Omnibus Budget Reconciliation Act of 1989 (P.L. 101-239)**

P.L. 101-239, §7721(c)(3)(A)-(B):

Amended Code Sec. 5684(b) by striking "6662(a)" and inserting "6665(a)", and by striking "6662" in the subsection heading and inserting "6665". **Effective** for returns the due date for which (determined without regard to extensions) is after 12-31-89.

• **1984, Deficit Reduction Act of 1984 (P.L. 98-369)**

P.L. 98-369, §714(h)(1):

Amended Code Sec. 5684(b) by striking out "Section 6660" in the heading and inserting in lieu thereof "Section 6662", and by striking out "section 6660(a)" in the text and inserting in lieu thereof "section 6662(a)". **Effective** as if included in the provision of P.L. 97-248 to which it relates.

P.L. 98-369, §722(a)(5):

Amended Code Sec. 5684(b) by striking out "subsections (a) and (b)" and inserting in lieu thereof "subsection (a)". **Effective** as if included in the provision of P.L. 97-448 to which it relates.

[Sec. 5684(c)]

(c) CROSS REFERENCES.—

(1) For provisions relating to interest in the case of taxes not paid when due, see section 6601.

(2) For penalty for failure to file tax return or pay tax, see section 6651.

(3) For additional penalties for failure to pay tax, see section 6653.

(4) For penalty for failure to make deposits or for overstatement of deposits, see section 6656.

(5) For penalty for attempt to evade or defeat any tax imposed by this title, see section 7201.

(6) For penalty for willful failure to file return, supply information, or pay tax, see section 7203.

Amendments

• **1981, Economic Recovery Tax Act of 1981 (P.L. 97-34)**

P.L. 97-34, §722(a)(3):

Amended the heading and the text of Code Sec. 5684(c) by striking out "6659" and inserting "6660". **Effective** for returns filed after 12-31-81.

P.L. 97-34, §724(b)(4)(A):

Amended Code Sec. 5684 by striking out subsection (b) and by redesignating subsections (c) and (d) as subsections (b) and (c), respectively. **Effective** for returns filed after 12-31-81. Prior to amendment, Code Sec. 5684(b) read as follows:

ALCOHOL TAXES—PENALTIES

(b) FAILURE TO MAKE DEPOSIT OF TAXES.—Section 6656 relating to failure to make deposit of taxes shall apply to the failure to make any deposit of taxes imposed under part I of subchapter A on the date prescribed therefor, except that the penalty for such failure shall be 5 percent of the amount of the underpayment in lieu of the penalty provided by such section.

P.L. 97-34, § 724(b)(4)(B):

Amended Code Sec. 5684(c) by redesignating paragraphs (4) and (5) as paragraphs (5) and (6), respectively, and by inserting a new paragraph (4). **Effective** for returns filed after 12-31-81.

• **1969, Tax Reform Act of 1969 (P.L. 91-172)**

P.L. 91-172, § 943(c)(4):

Amended Sec. 5684(d)(2) by inserting "or pay tax" immediately following "tax return". **Effective** with respect to returns the date prescribed by law (without regard to any extension of time) for filing of which is after 12-31-69, and with respect to notices and demands for payment of tax made after 12-31-69.

[Sec. 5685]

SEC. 5685. PENALTY AND FORFEITURE RELATING TO POSSESSION OF DEVICES FOR EMITTING GAS, SMOKE, ETC., EXPLOSIVES AND FIREARMS, WHEN VIOLATING LIQUOR LAWS.

[Sec. 5685(a)]

(a) PENALTY FOR POSSESSION OF DEVICES FOR EMITTING GAS, SMOKE, ETC.—Whoever, when violating any law of the United States, or of any possession of the United States, or of the District of Columbia, in regard to the manufacture, taxation, or transportation of or traffic in distilled spirits, wines, or beer, or when aiding in any such violation, has in his possession or in his control any device capable of causing emission of gas, smoke, or fumes, and which may be used for the purpose of hindering, delaying, or preventing pursuit or capture, any explosive, or any firearm (as defined in section 5845), except a machine gun, or a shotgun having a barrel or barrels less than 18 inches in length, or a rifle having a barrel or barrels less than 16 inches in length, shall be fined not more than $5,000, or imprisoned not more than 10 years, or both, and all persons engaged in any such violation or in aiding in any such violation shall be held to be in possession or control of such device, firearm, or explosive.

Amendments

• **1976, Tax Reform Act of 1976 (P.L. 94-455)**

P.L. 94-455, § 1905(a)(23)(A):

Substituted "section 5845" for "section 5848" in Code Sec. 5685(a). **Effective** 2-1-77.

P.L. 94-455, § 1905(c)(6):

Struck out "Territory or" before "possession of the United States" in Code Sec. 5685(a). **Effective** 2-1-77.

• **1960 (P.L. 86-478)**

P.L. 86-478, § 4:

Amended Code Sec. 5685(a) by striking out "shotgun or rifle having a barrel or barrels less than 18 inches in length," and inserting in lieu thereof "shotgun having a barrel or barrels less than 18 inches in length, or a rifle having a barrel or barrels less than 16 inches in length,". **Effective** 7-1-60.

[Sec. 5685(b)]

(b) PENALTY FOR POSSESSION OF MACHINE GUN, ETC.—Whoever, when violating any such law, has in his possession or in his control a machine gun, or any shotgun having a barrel or barrels less than 18 inches in length, or a rifle having a barrel or barrels less than 16 inches in length, shall be imprisoned not more than 20 years; and all persons engaged in any such violation or in aiding in any such violation shall be held to be in possession and control of such machine gun, shotgun, or rifle.

Amendments

• **1960 (P.L. 86-478)**

P.L. 86-478, § 4:

Amended Code Sec. 5685(b) by striking out "shotgun or rifle having a barrel or barrels less than 18 inches in length," and inserting in lieu thereof "shotgun having a barrel or barrels less than 18 inches in length, or a rifle having a barrel or barrels less than 16 inches in length,". **Effective** 7-1-60.

[Sec. 5685(c)]

(c) FORFEITURE OF FIREARMS, DEVICES, ETC.—Every such firearm or device for emitting gas, smoke, or fumes, and every such explosive, machine gun, shotgun, or rifle, in the possession or control of any person when violating any such law, shall be seized and shall be forfeited and disposed of in the manner provided by section 5872.

Amendments

• **1976, Tax Reform Act of 1976 (P.L. 94-455)**

P.L. 94-455, § 1905(a)(23)(B):

Substituted "section 5872" for "section 5862" in Code Sec. 5685(c). **Effective** 2-1-77.

[Sec. 5685(d)]

(d) DEFINITION OF MACHINE GUN.—As used in this section, the term "machine gun" means a machine gun as defined in section 5845(b).

Amendments

• **1976, Tax Reform Act of 1976 (P.L. 94-455)**

P.L. 94-455, § 1905(a)(23)(C):

Amended Code Sec. 5685(d). **Effective** 2-1-77. Prior to amendment, Code Sec. 5685(d) read as follows:

(d) DEFINITION OF MACHINE GUN.—As used in this section the term "machine gun" means any weapon which shoots, or is designed to shoot, automatically or semiautomatically, more than one shot, without manual reloading, by a single function of the trigger.

[Sec. 5686]

SEC. 5686. PENALTY FOR HAVING, POSSESSING, OR USING LIQUOR OR PROPERTY INTENDED TO BE USED IN VIOLATING PROVISIONS OF THIS CHAPTER.

[Sec. 5686(a)]

(a) GENERAL.—It shall be unlawful to have or possess any liquor or property intended for use in violating any provision of this chapter or regulations issued pursuant thereto, or which has been so used, and every person so having or possessing or using such liquor or property, shall be fined not more than $5,000, or imprisoned not more than 1 year, or both.

[Sec. 5686(b)]

(b) CROSS REFERENCE.—

For seizure and forfeiture of liquor and property had, possessed, or used in violation of subsection (a), see section 7302.

[Sec. 5687]

SEC. 5687. PENALTY FOR OFFENSES NOT SPECIFICALLY COVERED.

Whoever violates any provision of this chapter or regulations issued pursuant thereto, for which a specific criminal penalty is not prescribed by this chapter, shall be fined not more than $1,000, or imprisoned not more than 1 year, or both, for each such offense.

OCCUPATIONAL TAXES—PENALTIES

[Sec. 5688]
SEC. 5688. DISPOSITION AND RELEASE OF SEIZED PROPERTY.

[Sec. 5688(a)]

(a) FORFEITURE.—

(1) DELIVERY.—All distilled spirits, wines, and beer forfeited, summarily or by order of court, under any law of the United States, shall be delivered to the Administrator of General Services to be disposed of as hereinafter provided.

(2) DISPOSAL.—The Administrator of General Services shall dispose of all distilled spirits, wines, and beer which have been delivered to him pursuant to paragraph (1)—

(A) by delivery to such Government agencies as, in his opinion, have a need for such distilled spirits, wines, or beer for medicinal, scientific, or mechanical purposes, or for any other official purpose for which appropriated funds may be expended by a Government agency; or

(B) by gifts to such eleemosynary institutions as, in his opinion, have a need for such distilled spirits, wines, or beer for medicinal purposes; or

(C) by destruction.

(3) LIMITATION ON DISPOSAL.—Except as otherwise provided by law, no distilled spirits, wines, or beer which have been seized under any law of the United States may be disposed of in any manner whatsoever except after forfeiture and as provided in this subsection.

(4) REGULATIONS.—The Administrator of General Services is authorized to make all rules and regulations necessary to carry out the provisions of this subsection.

(5) REMISSION OR MITIGATION OF FORFEITURES.—Nothing in this section shall affect the authority of the Secretary, under the customs or internal revenue laws, to remit or mitigate the forfeiture, or alleged forfeiture, or such distilled spirits, wines, or beer, or the authority of the Secretary, to compromise any civil or criminal case in respect of such distilled spirits, wines, or beer prior to commencement of suit thereon, or the authority of the Secretary to compromise any claim under the customs laws in respect to such distilled spirits, wines, or beer.

Amendments
- 1976, Tax Reform Act of 1976 (P.L. 94-455)

P.L. 94-455, §1906(b)(13)(A):

Amended 1954 Code by substituting "Secretary" for "Secretary or his delegate" each place it appeared. **Effective** 2-1-77.

[Sec. 5688(b)]

(b) DISTRAINT OR JUDICIAL PROCESS.—Except as provided in section 5243, all distilled spirits sold by order of court, or under process of distraint, shall be sold subject to tax; and the purchaser shall immediately, and before he takes possession of said spirits, pay the tax thereon, pursuant to the applicable provisions of this chapter and in accordance with regulations to be prescribed by the Secretary.

Amendments
- 1976, Tax Reform Act of 1976 (P.L. 94-455)

P.L. 94-455, §1906(b)(13)(A):

Amended 1954 Code by substituting "Secretary" for "Secretary or his delegate" each place it appeared. **Effective** 2-1-77.

[Sec. 5688(c)]

(c) RELEASE OF SEIZED VESSELS OR VEHICLES BY COURTS.—Notwithstanding any provisions of law relating to the return on bond of any vessel or vehicle seized for the violation of any law of the United States, the court having jurisdiction of the subject matter may, in its discretion and upon good cause shown by the United States, refuse to order such return of any such vessel or vehicle to the claimant thereof. As used in this subsection, the word "vessel" includes every description of watercraft used, or capable of being used, as a means of transportation in water or in water and air; and the word "vehicle" includes every animal and description of carriage or other contrivance used, or capable of being used, as a means of transportation on land or through the air.

[Sec. 5690]
SEC. 5690. DEFINITION OF THE TERM "PERSON".

The term "person", as used in this subchapter, includes an officer or employee of a corporation or a member or employee of a partnership, who as such officer, employee, or member is under a duty to perform the act in respect of which the violation occurs.

PART V—PENALTIES APPLICABLE TO OCCUPATIONAL TAXES—[Repealed]

[Sec. 5691—Repealed]

Amendments
- 2005, Safe, Accountable, Flexible, Efficient Transportation Equity Act: A Legacy for Users (P.L. 109-59)

P.L. 109-59, §11125(b)(19)(A):

Repealed part V of subchapter J of chapter 51 (Code Sec. 5691). **Effective** 7-1-2008, but not applicable to taxes imposed for periods before such date. Prior to repeal, Code Sec. 5691 read as follows:

SEC. 5691. PENALTIES FOR NONPAYMENT OF SPECIAL TAXES.

[Sec. 5691(a)]

(a) GENERAL.—Any person who shall carry on the business of a business subject to a special tax imposed by part II of subchapter A or section 5276 (relating to occupational taxes) fail to pay the special tax as required by law, shall be fined not more than $5,000, or imprisoned not more than 2 years, or both, for each such offense.

Amendments
- 1987, Revenue Act of 1987 (P.L. 100-203)

P.L. 100-203, §10512(a)(1)(B)(i):

Amended Code Sec. 5691(a) by striking out "the business of a brewer, wholesale dealer in liquors, retail dealer in liquors, wholesale dealer in beer, retail dealer in beer, or limited retail dealer," and inserting in lieu thereof "a business subject to a special tax imposed by part II of subchapter A or section 5276 (relating to occupational taxes)". For the **effective** date, see Act Sec. 10512(h), below.

P.L. 100-203, §10512(a)(1)(B)(ii):

Amended Code Sec. 5691 by striking out "RELATING TO LIQUORS" after "TAXES" in the section heading. For the **effective** date, see Act Sec. 10512(h), below.

P.L. 100-203, §10512(h), provides:

(h) EFFECTIVE DATE.—

(1) IN GENERAL.—The amendments made by this section shall take effect on January 1, 1988.

(2) ALL TAXPAYERS TREATED AS COMMENCING IN BUSINESS ON JANUARY 1, 1988.—

(A) IN GENERAL.—Any person engaged on January 1, 1988, in any trade or business which is subject to an occupational tax shall be treated for purposes of such tax as having 1st engaged in such trade or business on such date.

(B) LIMITATION ON AMOUNT OF TAX.—In the case of a taxpayer who paid an occupational tax in respect of any premises for any taxable period which began before January 1, 1988, and includes such date, the amount of the occupational tax imposed by reason of subparagraph (A) in respect of such premises shall not exceed an amount equal to $1/2$ the excess (if any) of—

(i) the rate of such tax as in effect on January 1, 1988, over

(ii) the rate of such tax as in effect on December 31, 1987.

(C) OCCUPATIONAL TAX.—For purposes of this paragraph, the term "occupational tax" means any tax imposed under part II of subchapter A of chapter 51, section 5276, section 5731, or section 5801 of the Internal Revenue Code of 1986 (as amended by this section).

TOBACCO TAXES—RATES

(D) DUE DATE OF TAX.—The amount of any tax required to be paid by reason of this paragraph shall be due on April 1, 1988.

- **1984, Deficit Reduction Act of 1984 (P.L. 98-369)**

P.L. 98-369, § 451(b)(3):

Amended Code Sec. 5691(a) by striking out "limited retail dealer, or manufacturer of stills" and inserting in lieu thereof "or limited retail dealer". **Effective** on the first day of the first calendar month which begins more than 90 days after 7-18-84.

- **1979, Trade Agreements Act of 1979 (P.L. 96-39)**

P.L. 96-39, § 807(a)(60):

Amended Code Sec. 5691(a) by changing "brewer, rectifier, wholesale dealer in liquors" to "brewer, wholesale dealer in liquors". **Effective** 1-1-80.

[Sec. 5691(b)]

(b) PRESUMPTION IN CASE OF THE SALE OF 20 WINE GALLONS OR MORE.—For the purposes of this chapter, the sale, or offer for sale, of distilled spirits, wines, or beer, in quantities of 20 wine gallons or more to the same person at the same time, shall be presumptive evidence that the person making such sale, or offer for sale, is engaged in or carrying on the business of a wholesale dealer in liquors or a wholesale dealer in beer, as the case may be. Such presumption may be overcome by evidence satisfactorily showing that such sale, or offer for sale, was made to a person other than a dealer, as defined in section 5112(a).

CHAPTER 52—TOBACCO PRODUCTS AND CIGARETTE PAPERS AND TUBES

SUBCHAPTER A.	Definitions; rate and payment of tax; exemption from tax; and refund and drawback of tax.
SUBCHAPTER B.	Qualification requirements for manufacturers and importers of tobacco products and cigarette papers and tubes, and export warehouse proprietors.
SUBCHAPTER C.	Operations by manufacturers and importers of tobacco products and cigarette papers and tubes and export warehouse proprietors.
SUBCHAPTER D.	Occupational tax.
SUBCHAPTER E.	Records of manufacturers and importers of tobacco products and cigarette papers and tubes, and export warehouse proprietors.
SUBCHAPTER F.	General provisions.
SUBCHAPTER G.	Penalties and forfeitures.

Subchapter A—Definitions; Rate and Payment of Tax; Exemption from Tax; and Refund and Drawback of Tax

Sec. 5701.	Rate of tax.
Sec. 5702.	Definitions.
Sec. 5703.	Liability for tax and method of payment.
Sec. 5704.	Exemption from tax.
Sec. 5705.	Credit, refund, or allowance of tax.
Sec. 5706.	Drawback of tax.
Sec. 5708.	Losses caused by disaster.

[Sec. 5701]

SEC. 5701. RATE OF TAX.

[Sec. 5701(a)]

(a) CIGARS.—On cigars, manufactured in or imported into the United States, there shall be imposed the following taxes:

(1) SMALL CIGARS.—On cigars, weighing not more than 3 pounds per thousand, $50.33 per thousand,

(2) LARGE CIGARS.—On cigars weighing more than 3 pounds per thousand, a tax equal to 52.75 percent of the price for which sold but not more than 40.26 cents per cigar.

Cigars not exempt from tax under this chapter which are removed but not intended for sale shall be taxed at the same rate as similar cigars removed for sale.

Amendments

- **2009, Children's Health Insurance Program Reauthorization Act of 2009 (P.L. 111-3)**

P.L. 111-3, § 701(a)(1)-(3):

Amended Code Sec. 5701(a) by striking "$1.828 cents per thousand ($1.594 cents per thousand on cigars removed during 2000 or 2001)" in paragraph (1) and inserting "$50.33 per thousand", by striking "20.719 percent (18.063 percent on cigars removed during 2000 or 2001)" in paragraph (2) and inserting "52.75 percent", and by striking "$48.75 per thousand ($42.50 per thousand on cigars removed during 2000 or 2001)" in paragraph (2) and inserting "40.26 cents per cigar". **Effective** for articles removed (as defined in Code Sec. 5702(j)) after 3-31-2009.

P.L. 111-3, § 701(h), provides:

(h) FLOOR STOCKS TAXES.—

(1) IMPOSITION OF TAX.—On tobacco products (other than cigars described in section 5701(a)(2) of the Internal Revenue Code of 1986) and cigarette papers and tubes manufactured in or imported into the United States which are removed before April 1, 2009, and held on such date for sale by any person, there is hereby imposed a tax in an amount equal to the excess of—

(A) the tax which would be imposed under section 5701 of such Code on the article if the article had been removed on such date, over

(B) the prior tax (if any) imposed under section 5701 of such Code on such article.

(2) CREDIT AGAINST TAX.—Each person shall be allowed as a credit against the taxes imposed by paragraph (1) an amount equal to $500. Such credit shall not exceed the amount of taxes imposed by paragraph (1) on April 1, 2009, for which such person is liable.

(3) LIABILITY FOR TAX AND METHOD OF PAYMENT.—

(A) LIABILITY FOR TAX.—A person holding tobacco products, cigarette papers, or cigarette tubes on April 1, 2009, to which any tax imposed by paragraph (1) applies shall be liable for such tax.

(B) METHOD OF PAYMENT.—The tax imposed by paragraph (1) shall be paid in such manner as the Secretary shall prescribe by regulations.

(C) TIME FOR PAYMENT.—The tax imposed by paragraph (1) shall be paid on or before August 1, 2009.

(4) ARTICLES IN FOREIGN TRADE ZONES.—Notwithstanding the Act of June 18, 1934 (commonly known as the Foreign Trade Zone Act, 48 Stat. 998, 19 U.S.C. 81a et seq.) or any other provision of law, any article which is located in a foreign trade zone on April 1, 2009, shall be subject to the tax imposed by paragraph (1) if—

(A) internal revenue taxes have been determined, or customs duties liquidated, with respect to such article before such date pursuant to a request made under the 1st proviso of section 3(a) of such Act, or

(B) such article is held on such date under the supervision of an officer of the United States Customs and Border Protection of the Department of Homeland Security pursuant to the 2d proviso of such section 3(a).

(5) DEFINITIONS.—For purposes of this subsection—

(A) IN GENERAL.—Any term used in this subsection which is also used in section 5702 of the Internal Revenue Code of 1986 shall have the same meaning as such term has in such section.

(B) SECRETARY.—The term "Secretary" means the Secretary of the Treasury or the Secretary's delegate.

(6) CONTROLLED GROUPS.—Rules similar to the rules of section 5061(e)(3) of such Code shall apply for purposes of this subsection.

(7) OTHER LAWS APPLICABLE.—All provisions of law, including penalties, applicable with respect to the taxes imposed by section 5701 of such Code shall, insofar as applicable and not inconsistent with the provisions of this subsection, apply to the floor stocks taxes imposed by paragraph (1), to the same extent as if such taxes were imposed by such section 5701. The Secretary may treat any person who bore the ultimate burden of the tax imposed by paragraph (1) as the person to whom a credit or refund under such provisions may be allowed or made.

- **1997, Balanced Budget Act of 1997 (P.L. 105-33)**

P.L. 105-33, § 9302(b)(1)-(2):

Amended Code Sec. 5701(a) by striking "$1.125 cents per thousand (93.75 cents per thousand on cigars removed during 1991 or 1992)" in paragraph (1) and inserting

TOBACCO TAXES—RATES

"$1.828 cents per thousand ($1.594 cents per thousand on cigars removed during 2000 or 2001)", and by striking "equal to" and all that follows in paragraph (2) and inserting "equal to 20.719 percent (18.063 percent on cigars removed during 2000 or 2001) of the price for which sold but not more than $48.75 per thousand ($42.50 per thousand on cigars removed during 2000 or 2001).". **Effective**, generally, for articles removed (as defined in Code Sec. 5702(k)) after 12-31-99. For a transitional rule, see Act Sec. 9302(i)(2), below. Prior to amendment, Code Sec. 5701(a)(2) read as follows:

(2) LARGE CIGARS.—On cigars weighing more than 3 pounds per thousand, a tax equal to—

(A) 10.625 percent of the price for which sold but not more than $25 per thousand on cigars removed during 1991 or 1992, and

(B) 12.75 percent of the price for which sold but not more than $30 per thousand on cigars removed after 1992.

P.L. 105-33, §9302(i)(2), provides:

(2) TRANSITIONAL RULE.—Any person who—

(A) on the date of the enactment of this Act is engaged in business as a manufacturer of roll-your-own tobacco or as an importer of tobacco products or cigarette papers and tubes, and

(B) before January 1, 2000, submits an application under subchapter B of chapter 52 of such Code to engage in such business,

may, notwithstanding such subchapter B, continue to engage in such business pending final action on such application. Pending such final action, all provisions of such chapter 52 shall apply to such applicant in the same manner and to the same extent as if such applicant were a holder of a permit under such chapter 52 to engage in such business.

P.L. 105-33, §9302(j), as amended by P.L. 106-554, §315(a)(1), provides:

(j) FLOOR STOCKS TAXES.—

(1) IMPOSITION OF TAX.—On tobacco products and cigarette papers and tubes manufactured in or imported into the United States which are removed before any tax increase date, and held on such date for sale by any person, there is hereby imposed a tax in an amount equal to the excess of—

(A) the tax which would be imposed under section 5701 of the Internal Revenue Code of 1986 on the article if the article had been removed on such date, over

(B) the prior tax (if any) imposed under section 5701 of such Code on such article.

(2) AUTHORITY TO EXEMPT CIGARETTES HELD IN VENDING MACHINES.—To the extent provided in regulations prescribed by the Secretary, no tax shall be imposed by paragraph (1) on cigarettes held for retail sale on any tax increase date, by any person in any vending machine. If the Secretary provides such a benefit with respect to any person, the Secretary may reduce the $500 amount in paragraph (3) with respect to such person.

(3) CREDIT AGAINST TAX.—Each person shall be allowed as a credit against the taxes imposed by paragraph (1) an amount equal to $500. Such credit shall not exceed the amount of taxes imposed by paragraph (1) on any tax increase date, for which such person is liable.

(4) LIABILITY FOR TAX AND METHOD OF PAYMENT.—

(A) LIABILITY FOR TAX.—A person holding cigarettes on any tax increase date, to which any tax imposed by paragraph (1) applies shall be liable for such tax.

(B) METHOD OF PAYMENT.—The tax imposed by paragraph (1) shall be paid in such manner as the Secretary shall prescribe by regulations.

(C) TIME FOR PAYMENT.—The tax imposed by paragraph (1) shall be paid on or before April 1 following any tax increase date.

(5) ARTICLES IN FOREIGN TRADE ZONES.—Notwithstanding the Act of June 18, 1934 (48 Stat. 998, 19 U.S.C. 81a) and any other provision of law, any article which is located in a foreign trade zone on any tax increase date, shall be subject to the tax imposed by paragraph (1) if—

(A) internal revenue taxes have been determined, or customs duties liquidated, with respect to such article before such date pursuant to a request made under the 1st proviso of section 3(a) of such Act, or

(B) such article is held on such date under the supervision of a customs officer pursuant to the 2d proviso of such section 3(a).

(6) DEFINITIONS.—For purposes of this subsection—

(A) IN GENERAL.—Terms used in this subsection which are also used in section 5702 of the Internal Revenue Code of 1986 shall have the respective meanings such terms have in such section, as amended by this Act.

(B) TAX INCREASE DATE.—The term "tax increase date" means January 1, 2000, and January 1, 2002.

(C) SECRETARY.—The term "Secretary" means the Secretary of the Treasury or the Secretary's delegate.

(7) CONTROLLED GROUPS.—Rules similar to the rules of section 5061(e)(3) of such Code shall apply for purposes of this subsection.

(8) OTHER LAWS APPLICABLE.—All provisions of law, including penalties, applicable with respect to the taxes imposed by section 5701 of such Code shall, insofar as applicable and not inconsistent with the provisions of this subsection, apply to the floor stocks taxes imposed by paragraph (1), to the same extent as if such taxes were imposed by such section 5701. The Secretary may treat any person who bore the ultimate burden of the tax imposed by paragraph (1) as the person to whom a credit or refund under such provisions may be allowed or made.

• **1990, Omnibus Budget Reconciliation Act of 1990 (P.L. 101-508)**

P.L. 101-508, §11202(a)(1):

Amended Code Sec. 5701(a)(1) by striking "75 cents per thousand" and inserting "$1.125 cents per thousand (93.75 cents per thousand on cigars removed during 1991 or 1992)". **Effective** with respect to articles removed after 12-31-90.

P.L. 101-508, §11202(a)(2):

Amended Code Sec. 5701(a)(2) by striking "equal to" and all that follows and inserting "equal to—

(A) 10.625 percent of the price for which sold but not more than $25 per thousand on cigars removed during 1991 or 1992, and

(B) 12.75 percent of the price for which sold but not more than $30 per thousand on cigars removed after 1992."

Prior to amendment, Code Sec. 5701(a)(2) read as follows:

(2) LARGE CIGARS.—On cigars weighing more than 3 pounds per thousand, a tax equal to $8^1/2$ percent of the wholesale price, but not more than $20 per thousand. **Effective** for articles removed after 12-31-90.

• **1976, Tax Reform Act of 1976 (P.L. 94-455)**

P.L. 94-455, §2128(a):

Amended so much of Code Sec. 5701(a) as follows paragraph (1). **Effective** 2-1-77. Prior to amendment, so much of Code Sec. 5701(a) as follows paragraph (1) read as follows:

(2) LARGE CIGARS.—On cigars, weighing more than 3 pounds per thousand;

(A) If removed to retail at not more than $2^1/2$ cents each, $2.50 per thousand;

(B) If removed to retail at more than $2^1/2$ cents each and not more than 4 cents each, $3 per thousand;

(C) If removed to retail at more than 4 cents each and not more than 6 cents each, $4 per thousand;

(D) If removed to retail at more than 6 cents each, and not more than 8 cents each, $7 per thousand;

(E) If removed to retail at more than 8 cents each and not more than 15 cents each, $10 per thousand;

(F) If removed to retail at more than 15 cents each and not more than 20 cents each, $15 per thousand;

(G) If removed to retail at more than 20 cents each, $20 per thousand.

In determining the retail price, for tax purposes, regard shall be had to the ordinary retail price of a single cigar in its principal market, exclusive of any State or local taxes imposed on cigars as a commodity. For purposes of the preceding sentence, the amount of State or local tax excluded from the retail price shall be the actual tax imposed; except that, if the combined taxes result in a numerical figure ending in a fraction of a cent, the amount so excluded shall be rounded to the next highest full cent unless such rounding would result in a tax lower than the tax which would be imposed in the absence of State or local tax. Cigars not exempt from tax under this chapter which are removed but not intended for sale shall be taxed at the same rate as similar cigars removed for sale.

• **1968 (P.L. 90-240)**

P.L. 90-240, §4:

Amended Code Sec. 5701(a) by adding the next to last sentence therein. **Effective** for the removal of cigars on or after the first day of the first calendar quarter which begins more than 30 days after 1-2-68.

• **1965, Excise Tax Reduction Act of 1965 (P.L. 89-44)**

P.L. 89-44, §502(a):

Repealed former Code Sec. 5701(a) and redesignated former Code Sec. 5701(b) as Code Sec. 5701(a). **Effective** 1-1-66. Prior to repeal, Code Sec. 5701(a) read as follows:

(a) TOBACCO.—On tobacco, manufactured in or imported into the United States, there shall be imposed a tax of 10 cents per pound.

• **1960 (P.L. 86-779)**

P.L. 86-779, §[1]:

Amended Code Sec. 5701(b) by striking out, in the next to the last sentence, the words "exclusive of any State or local taxes imposed on the retail sale of cigars" and by substituting the words "exclusive of any State or local taxes imposed on cigars as a commodity". **Effective** for cigars removed on or after 10-9-60.

• **1958, Excise Tax Technical Changes Act of 1958 (P.L. 85-859)**

P.L. 85-859, §202:

Amended Sec. 5701(b) by inserting at the end thereof the following: ", exclusive of any State or local taxes imposed on the retail sale of cigars. Cigars not exempt from tax under this chapter which are removed but not intended for sale shall be taxed at the same rate as similar cigars removed for sale". **Effective** 9-3-58.

[Sec. 5701(b)]

(b) CIGARETTES.—On cigarettes, manufactured in or imported into the United States, there shall be imposed the following taxes:

(1) SMALL CIGARETTES.—On cigarettes, weighing not more than 3 pounds per thousand, $50.33 per thousand;

(2) LARGE CIGARETTES.—On cigarettes, weighing more than 3 pounds per thousand, $105.69 per thousand; except that, if more than $6^1/2$ inches in length, they shall be taxable at the rate prescribed for cigarettes weighing not more than 3 pounds per thousand, counting each $2^3/4$ inches, or fraction thereof, of the length of each as one cigarette.

TOBACCO TAXES—RATES

Amendments

• **2009, Children's Health Insurance Program Reauthorization Act of 2009 (P.L. 111-3):**

P.L. 111-3, §701(b)(1)-(2):

Amended Code Sec. 5701(b) by striking "$19.50 per thousand ($17 per thousand on cigarettes removed during 2000 or 2001)" in paragraph (1) and inserting "$50.33 per thousand", and by striking "$40.95 per thousand ($35.70 per thousand on cigarettes removed during 2000 or 2001)" in paragraph (2) and inserting "$105.69 per thousand". **Effective** for articles removed (as defined in Code Sec. 5702(j)) after 3-31-2009.

• **1997, Balanced Budget Act of 1997 (P.L. 105-33):**

P.L. 105-33, §9302(a)(1)-(2):

Amended Code Sec. 5701(b) by striking "$12 per thousand ($10 per thousand on cigarettes removed during 1991 or 1992)" in paragraph (1) and inserting "$19.50 per thousand ($17 per thousand on cigarettes removed during 2000 or 2001)", and by striking "$25.20 per thousand ($21 per thousand on cigarettes removed during 1991 or 1992)" in paragraph (2) and inserting "$40.95 per thousand ($35.70 per thousand on cigarettes removed during 2000 or 2001)". **Effective**, generally, for articles removed (as defined in Code Sec. 5702(k)) after 12-31-99. For a transitional rule, see Act Sec. 9302(i)(2) in the amendment notes following Code Sec. 5701(a).

P.L. 105-33, §9302(k), as added by P.L. 105-34, §1604(f)(3), and subsequently repealed by P.L. 105-78, §519, effective 11-13-97, provides:

(k) COORDINATION WITH TOBACCO INDUSTRY SETTLEMENT AGREEMENT.—The increase in excise taxes collected as a result of the amendments made by subsections (a), (e), and (g) of this section shall be credited against the total payments made by parties pursuant to Federal legislation implementing the tobacco industry settlement agreement of June 20, 1997.

• **1990, Omnibus Budget Reconciliation Act of 1990 (P.L. 101-508):**

P.L. 101-508, §11202(b)(1):

Amended Code Sec. 5701(b)(1) by striking "$8 per thousand" and inserting "$12 per thousand ($10 per thousand on cigarettes removed during 1991 or 1992)". **Effective** with respect to articles removed after 12-31-90.

P.L. 101-508, §11202(b)(2):

Amended Code Sec. 5701(b)(2) by striking "$16.80 per thousand" and inserting "$25.20 per thousand ($21 per thousand on cigarettes removed during 1991 or 1992)". **Effective** with respect to articles removed after 12-31-90.

• **1982, Tax Equity and Fiscal Responsibility Act of 1982 (P.L. 97-248):**

P.L. 97-248, §283(a) (as amended by P.L. 99-107, §2, P.L. 99-155, §1, P.L. 99-181, §1, P.L. 99-189, §1, P.L. 99-201, §1 and P.L. 99-272, §13201(a)):

Amended subsection (b) of Code Sec. 5701 by striking out "$4" in paragraph (1) and inserting "$8", and by striking out "$8.40" in paragraph (2) and inserting "$16.80". **Effective** with respect to cigarettes removed after 12-31-82 [effective date changed by P.L. 99-107, P.L. 99-155, P.L. 99-181, P.L. 99-189, P.L. 99-201 and P.L. 99-272].

P.L. 97-248, §283(b), as amended by P.L. 97-448, §306(a)(14), provides:

(b) FLOOR STOCKS.—

(1) IMPOSITION OF TAX.—On cigarettes manufactured in or imported into the United States which are removed before January 1, 1983, and held on such date for sale by any person, there shall be imposed the following taxes:

(A) SMALL CIGARETTES.—On cigarettes, weighing not more than 3 pounds per thousand, $4 per thousand;

(B) LARGE CIGARETTES.—On cigarettes, weighing more than 3 pounds per thousand $8.40 per thousand; except that, if more than 6 1/2 inches in length, they shall be taxable at the rate prescribed for cigarettes weighing not more than 3 pounds per thousand, counting each 2 3/4 inches, or fraction thereof, of the length of each as one cigarette.

(2) LIABILITY FOR TAX AND METHOD OF PAYMENT.—

(A) LIABILITY FOR TAX.—A person holding cigarettes on January 1, 1983, to which any tax imposed by paragraph (1) applies shall be liable for such tax.

(B) METHOD OF PAYMENT.—The tax imposed by paragraph (1) shall be treated as a tax imposed under section 5701 and shall be due and payable on February 17, 1983 in the same manner as the tax imposed under such section is payable with respect to cigarettes removed on or after January 1, 1983.

(3) CIGARETTE.—For purposes of this subsection, the term "cigarette" shall have the meaning given to such term by subsection (b) of section 5702 of the Internal Revenue Code of 1954.

(4) EXCEPTION FOR RETAILERS.—The taxes imposed by paragraph (1) shall not apply to cigarettes in retail stocks held on January 1, 1983, at the place where intended to be sold at retail.

• **1965, Excise Tax Reduction Act of 1965 (P.L. 89-44):**

P.L. 89-44, §501(f):

Amended Code Sec. 5701(c)(1). Prior to amendment, Code Sec. 5701(c)(1) read as follows:

"(1) Small Cigarettes.—On cigarettes, weighing not more than 3 pounds per thousand, $4 per thousand until July 1, 1965, and $3.50 per thousand on and after July 1, 1965;".

P.L. 89-44, §502(a):

Redesignated Code Sec. 5701(c) as Sec. 5701(b). **Effective** for tax years beginning after 1-1-66.

• **1964, Excise Tax Reduction Act of 1964 (P.L. 88-348):**

P.L. 88-348, §2(a)(9):

Substituted "1965" for "1964" wherever it appeared in Sec. 5701(c)(1).

• **1963, Tax Rate Extension Act of 1963 (P.L. 88-52):**

P.L. 88-52, §3(a)(9):

Substituted "1964" for "1963" wherever it appeared in Sec. 5701(c)(1).

• **1962, Tax Rate Extension Act of 1962 (P.L. 87-508):**

P.L. 87-508, §3(a)(8):

Substituted "1963" for "1962" wherever it appeared in Sec. 5701(c)(1).

• **1961, Tax Rate Extension Act of 1961 (P.L. 87-72):**

P.L. 87-72, §3(a)(9):

Substituted "1962" for "1961" wherever it appeared in Sec. 5701(c)(1).

• **1960, Public Debt and Tax Rate Extension Act of 1960 (P.L. 86-564):**

P.L. 86-564, §202(a):

Amended 1954 Code Sec. 5701(c)(1) by substituting "1961" for "1960" wherever it appeared.

• **1959, Tax Rate Extension Act of 1959 (P.L. 86-75):**

P.L. 86-75, §3(a):

Amended 1954 Code Sec. 5701(c)(1) by striking out "1959" wherever it appeared, and by substituting "1960".

• **1958, Tax Rate Extension Act of 1958 (P.L. 85-475):**

P.L. 85-475, §3(a):

Substituted "July 1, 1959" for "July 1, 1958" in Sec. 5701(c)(1).

• **1957, Tax Rate Extension Act of 1957 (P.L. 85-12):**

P.L. 85-12, §3(a):

Substituted "July 1, 1958" for "April 1, 1957" in Sec. 5701(c)(1).

• **1956, Tax Rate Extension Act of 1956 (P.L. 458, 84th Cong.):**

P.L. 458, 84th Cong., 2nd Sess., §3(a)(9):

Substituted "1957" for "1956" wherever it appeared in Sec. 5701(c)(1).

• **1955, Tax Rate Extension Act of 1955 (P.L. 18, 84th Cong.):**

P.L. 18, 84th Cong., §3(a)(9):

Substituted "1956" for "1955" wherever it appeared in Sec. 5701(c)(1).

[Sec. 5701(c)]

(c) CIGARETTE PAPERS.—On cigarette papers, manufactured in or imported into the United States, there shall be imposed a tax of 3.15 cents for each 50 papers or fractional part thereof; except that, if cigarette papers measure more than 6 1/2 inches in length, they shall be taxable at the rate prescribed, counting each 2 3/4 inches, or fraction thereof, of the length of each as one cigarette paper.

Amendments

• **2009, Children's Health Insurance Program Reauthorization Act of 2009 (P.L. 111-3):**

P.L. 111-3, §701(c):

Amended Code Sec. 5701(c) by striking "1.22 cents (1.06 cents on cigarette papers removed during 2000 or 2001)" and inserting "3.15 cents". **Effective** for articles removed (as defined in Code Sec. 5702(j)) after 3-31-2009.

• **1997, Balanced Budget Act of 1997 (P.L. 105-33):**

P.L. 105-33, §9302(c):

Amended Code Sec. 5701(c) by striking "0.75 cent (0.625 cent on cigarette papers removed during 1991 or 1992)" and inserting "1.22 cents (1.06 cents on cigarette papers removed during 2000 or 2001)". **Effective**, generally, for articles removed (as defined in Code Sec. 5702(k)) after 12-31-99. For a transitional rule, see §9302(i)(2) in the amendment notes following Code Sec. 5701(a).

P.L. 105-33, §9302(h)(3):

Amended Code Sec. 5701(c) by striking "On each book or set of cigarette papers containing more than 25 papers," and inserting "On cigarette papers,". **Effective**, generally, for articles removed (as defined in Code Sec. 5702(k)) after 12-31-99. For a transitional rule, see §9302(i)(2) in the amendment notes following Code Sec. 5701(a).

• **1990, Omnibus Budget Reconciliation Act of 1990 (P.L. 101-508):**

P.L. 101-508, §11202(c):

Amended Code Sec. 5701(c) by striking "1/2 cent" and inserting "0.75 cent (0.625 cent on cigarette papers removed during 1991 or 1992)". **Effective** with respect to articles removed after 12-31-90.

• **1965, Excise Tax Reduction Act of 1965 (P.L. 89-44):**

P.L. 89-44, §502(a):

Redesignated Code Sec. 5701(d) as Sec. 5701(c). **Effective** for tax years beginning after 1-1-66.

• **1958, Excise Tax Technical Changes Act of 1958 (P.L. 85-859):**

P.L. 85-859, §202:

Amended Sec. 5701(d) by striking out "cigarette papers" where it followed the word "On" at the beginning of that section and substituting "each book or set of cigarette papers containing more than 25 papers" and by striking out ", on each

TOBACCO TAXES—RATES

package, book, or set containing more than 25 papers," where it followed "there shall be imposed". **Effective** 9-3-58.

[Sec. 5701(d)]

(d) CIGARETTE TUBES.—On cigarette tubes, manufactured in or imported into the United States, there shall be imposed a tax of 6.30 cents for each 50 tubes or fractional part thereof, except that if cigarette tubes measure more than $6^{1}/_{2}$ inches in length, they shall be taxable at the rate prescribed, counting each $2^{3}/_{4}$ inches, or fraction thereof, of the length of each as one cigarette tube.

Amendments

• **2009, Children's Health Insurance Program Reauthorization Act of 2009 (P.L. 111-3)**

P.L. 111-3, §701(d):

Amended Code Sec. 5701(d) by striking "2.44 cents (2.13 cents on cigarette tubes removed during 2000 or 2001)" and inserting "6.30 cents". **Effective** for articles removed (as defined in Code Sec. 5702(j)) after 3-31-2009.

• **1997, Balanced Budget Act of 1997 (P.L. 105-33)**

P.L. 105-33, §9302(d):

Amended Code Sec. 5701(d) by striking "1.5 cents (1.25 cents on cigarette tubes removed during 1991 or 1992" and inserting "2.44 cents (2.13 cents on cigarette tubes removed during 2000 or 2001)". **Effective**, generally, for articles removed (as defined in Code Sec. 5702(k)) after 12-31-99. For a transitional rule, see §9302(i)(2) in the amendment notes following Code Sec. 5701(a).

• **1990, Omnibus Budget Reconciliation Act of 1990 (P.L. 101-508)**

P.L. 101-508, §11202(d):

Amended Code Sec. 5701(d) by striking "1 cent" and inserting "1.5 cents (1.25 cents on cigarette tubes removed during 1991 or 1992)". **Effective** with respect to articles removed after 12-31-90.

• **1965, Excise Tax Reduction Act of 1965 (P.L. 89-44)**

P.L. 89-44, §502(a):

Redesignated Code Sec. 5701(e) as Sec. 5701(d). **Effective** for tax years beginning after 1-1-66.

[Sec. 5701(e)]

(e) SMOKELESS TOBACCO.—On smokeless tobacco, manufactured in or imported into the United States, there shall be imposed the following taxes:

(1) SNUFF.—On snuff, $1.51 per pound and a proportionate tax at the like rate on all fractional parts of a pound.

(2) CHEWING TOBACCO.—On chewing tobacco, 50.33 cents per pound and a proportionate tax at the like rate on all fractional parts of a pound.

Amendments

• **2018, Tax Technical Corrections Act of 2018 (P.L. 115-141)**

P.L. 115-141, §401(a)(250), Div. U:

Amended Code Sec. 5701(e) by striking "manufacturered" and inserting "manufactured". **Effective** 3-23-2018.

• **2009, Children's Health Insurance Program Reauthorization Act of 2009 (P.L. 111-3)**

P.L. 111-3, §701(e)(1)-(2):

Amended Code Sec. 5701(e) by striking "58.5 cents (51 cents on snuff removed during 2000 or 2001)" in paragraph (1) and inserting "$1.51", and by striking "19.5 cents (17 cents on chewing tobacco removed during 2000 or 2001)" in paragraph (2) and inserting "50.33 cents". **Effective** for articles removed (as defined in Code Sec. 5702(j)) after 3-31-2009.

• **1997, Balanced Budget Act of 1997 (P.L. 105-33)**

P.L. 105-33, §9302(e)(1)-(2):

Amended Code Sec. 5701(e) by striking "36 cents (30 cents on snuff removed during 1991 or 1992)" in paragraph (1) and inserting "58.5 cents (51 cents on snuff removed during 2000 or 2001)", and by striking "12 cents (10 cents on chewing tobacco removed during 1991 or 1992)" in paragraph (2) and inserting "19.5 cents (17 cents on chewing tobacco removed during 2000 or 2001)". **Effective**, generally, for articles removed (as defined in Code Sec. 5702(k)) after 12-31-99. For a transitional rule, see §9302(i)(2) in the amendment notes following Code Sec. 5701(a).

P.L. 105-33, §9302(k) (as added by P.L. 105-34, §1604(f)(3), and **subsequently repealed by P.L. 105-78, §519, effective 11-13-97**), provided:

(k) COORDINATION WITH TOBACCO INDUSTRY SETTLEMENT AGREEMENT.—The increase in excise taxes collected as a result of the amendments made by subsections (a), (e), and (g) of this section shall be credited against the total payments made by parties pursuant to Federal legislation implementing the tobacco industry settlement agreement of June 20, 1997.

• **1990, Omnibus Budget Reconciliation Act of 1990 (P.L. 101-508)**

P.L. 101-508, §11202(e)(1):

Amended Code Sec. 5701(e)(1) by striking "24 cents" and inserting "36 cents (30 cents on snuff removed during 1991 or 1992)". **Effective** with respect to articles removed after 12-31-90.

P.L. 101-508, §11202(e)(2):

Amended Code Sec. 5701(e)(2) by striking "8 cents" and inserting "12 cents (10 cents on chewing tobacco removed during 1991 or 1992)". **Effective** with respect to articles removed after 12-31-90.

• **1986, Consolidated Omnibus Budget Reconciliation Act of 1985 (P.L. 99-272)**

P.L. 99-272, §13202(a):

Amended Code Sec. 5701 by redesignating subsection (e) as subsection (f) and by inserting after subsection (d) new subsection (e). **Effective** for smokeless tobacco removed after 6-30-86. For a transitional rule, see Act Sec. 13202(c)(2), below.

P.L. 99-272, §13202(c)(2), provides:

(2) TRANSITIONAL RULE.—Any person who—

(A) on the date of the enactment of this Act, is engaged in business as a manufacturer of smokeless tobacco, and

(B) before July 1, 1986, submits an application under subchapter B of chapter 52 of the Internal Revenue Code of 1954 to engage in such business,

may, notwithstanding such subchapter B, continue to engage in such business pending final action on such application. Pending such final action, all provisions of chapter 52 of such Code shall apply to such applicant in the same manner and to the same extent as if such applicant were a holder of a permit to manufacture smokeless tobacco under such chapter 52.

[Sec. 5701(f)]

(f) PIPE TOBACCO.—On pipe tobacco, manufactured in or imported into the United States, there shall be imposed a tax of $2.8311 cents per pound (and a proportionate tax at the like rate on all fractional parts of a pound).

Amendments

• **2009, Children's Health Insurance Program Reauthorization Act of 2009 (P.L. 111-3)**

P.L. 111-3, §701(f):

Amended Code Sec. 5701(f) by striking "$1.0969 cents (95.67 cents on pipe tobacco removed during 2000 or 2001)" and inserting "$2.8311 cents". **Effective** for articles removed (as defined in Code Sec. 5702(j)) after 3-31-2009.

• **1997, Balanced Budget Act of 1997 (P.L. 105-33)**

P.L. 105-33, §9302(f):

Amended Code Sec. 5701(f) by striking "67.5 cents (56.25 cents on pipe tobacco removed during 1991 or 1992)" and inserting "$1.0969 cents (95.67 cents on pipe tobacco removed during 2000 or 2001)". **Effective**, generally, for articles removed (as defined in Code Sec. 5702(k)) after 12-31-99. For a transitional rule, see §9302(i)(2) in the amendment notes following Code Sec. 5701(a).

• **1990, Omnibus Budget Reconciliation Act of 1990 (P.L. 101-508)**

P.L. 101-508, §11202(f):

Amended Code Sec. 5701(f) by striking "45 cents" and inserting "67.5 cents (56.25 cents on pipe tobacco removed during 1991 or 1992)". **Effective** with respect to articles removed after 12-31-90.

P.L. 101-508, §11202(i), provides:

(i) FLOOR STOCKS TAXES ON CIGARETTES.—

(1) IMPOSITION OF TAX.—On cigarettes manufactured in or imported into the United States which are removed before any tax-increase date and held on such date for sale by any person, there shall be imposed the following taxes:

(A) SMALL CIGARETTES.—On cigarettes, weighing not more than 3 pounds per thousand, $2 per thousand.

(B) LARGE CIGARETTES.—On cigarettes weighing more than 3 pounds per thousand, $4.20 per thousand; except that, if more than $6^{1}/_{2}$ inches in length, they shall be taxable at the rate prescribed for cigarettes weighing not more than 3 pounds per thousand, counting each $2^{3}/_{4}$ inches, or fraction thereof, of the length of each as one cigarette.

(2) EXCEPTION FOR CERTAIN AMOUNTS OF CIGARETTES.—

(A) IN GENERAL.—No tax shall be imposed by paragraph (1) on cigarettes held on any tax-increase date by any person if—

(i) the aggregate number of cigarettes held by such person on such date does not exceed 30,000, and

(ii) such person submits to the Secretary (at the time and in the manner required by the Secretary) such information as the Secretary shall require for purposes of this subparagraph.

TOBACCO TAXES—RATES

For purposes of this subparagraph, in the case of cigarettes measuring more than $6^{1}/_{2}$ inches in length, each $2^{3}/_{4}$ inches (or fraction thereof) of the length of each shall be counted as one cigarette.

(B) AUTHORITY TO EXEMPT CIGARETTES HELD IN VENDING MACHINES.—To the extent provided in regulations prescribed by the Secretary, no tax shall be imposed by paragraph (1) on cigarettes held for retail sale on any tax-increase date by any person in any vending machine. If the Secretary provides such a benefit with respect to any person, the Secretary may reduce the 30,000 amount in subparagraph (A) and the $60 amount in paragraph (3) with respect to such person.

(3) CREDIT AGAINST TAX.—Each person shall be allowed as a credit against the taxes imposed by paragraph (1) an amount equal to $60. Such credit shall not exceed the amount of taxes imposed by paragraph (1) for which such person is liable.

(4) LIABILITY FOR TAX AND METHOD OF PAYMENT.—

(A) LIABILITY FOR TAX.—A person holding cigarettes on any tax-increase date to which any tax imposed by paragraph (1) applies shall be liable for such tax.

(B) METHOD OF PAYMENT.—The tax imposed by paragraph (1) shall be paid in such manner as the Secretary shall prescribe by regulations.

(C) TIME FOR PAYMENT.—The tax imposed by paragraph (1) shall be paid on or before the 1st June 30 following the tax-increase date.

(5) DEFINITIONS.—For purposes of this subsection—

(A) TAX-INCREASE DATE.—The term "tax-increase date" means January 1, 1991, and January 1, 1993.

(B) OTHER DEFINITIONS.—Terms used in this subsection which are also used in section 5702 of the Internal Revenue Code of 1986 shall have the respective meanings such terms have in such section.

(C) SECRETARY.—The term "Secretary" means the Secretary of the Treasury or his delegate.

(6) CONTROLLED GROUPS.—Rules similar to the rules of section 11201(e)(6) shall apply for purposes of this subsection.

(7) OTHER LAWS APPLICABLE.—All provisions of law, including penalties, applicable with respect to the taxes imposed by section 5701 of such Code shall, insofar as applicable and not inconsistent with the provisions of this subsection, apply to the floor stocks taxes imposed by paragraph (1), to the same extent as if such taxes were imposed by such section 5701.

- **1988, Technical and Miscellaneous Revenue Act of 1988 (P.L. 100-647)**

P.L. 100-647, § 5061(a):

Amended Code Sec. 5701 by redesignating subsection (f) as subsection (g) and by inserting after subsection (e) a new subsection (f). For the **effective** date, see Act Sec. 5061(d) and (e), below.

P.L. 100-647, § 5061(d) and (e), provides:

(d) EFFECTIVE DATE.—

(1) IN GENERAL.—The amendments made by this section shall apply to pipe tobacco removed (within the meaning of section 5702(k) of the 1986 Code) after December 31, 1988.

(2) TRANSITIONAL RULE.—Any person who—

(A) on the date of the enactment of this Act, is engaged in business as a manufacturer of pipe tobacco, and

(B) before January 1, 1989, submits an application under subchapter B of chapter 52 of the 1986 Code to engage in such business,

may, notwithstanding such subchapter B, continue to engage in such business pending final action on such application. Pending such final action, all provisions of chapter 52 of the 1986 Code shall apply to such applicant in the same manner and to the same extent as if such applicant were a holder of a permit to manufacture pipe tobacco under such chapter 52.

(e) FLOOR STOCKS TAX.—

(1) IMPOSITION OF TAX.—On pipe tobacco manufactured in or imported into the United States which is removed before January 1, 1989, and held on such date for sale by any person, there is hereby imposed a tax of 45 cents per pound (and a proportionate tax at the like rate on all fractional parts of a pound).

(2) LIABILITY FOR TAX AND METHOD OF PAYMENT.—

(A) LIABILITY FOR TAX.—A person holding pipe tobacco on January 1, 1989, to which the tax imposed by paragraph (1) applies shall be liable for such tax.

(B) METHOD OF PAYMENT.—The tax imposed by paragraph (1) shall be treated as a tax imposed by section 5701 of the 1986 Code and shall be due and payable on February 14, 1989, in the same manner as the tax imposed by such section is payable with respect to pipe tobacco removed on or after January 1, 1989.

(C) TREATMENT OF PIPE TOBACCO IN FOREIGN TRADE ZONES.—Notwithstanding the Act of June 18, 1934 (48 Stat. 998, 19 U.S.C. 81a) or any other provision of law, pipe tobacco which is located in a foreign trade zone on January 1, 1989, shall be subject to the tax imposed by paragraph (1) and shall be treated for purposes of this subsection as held on such date for sale if—

(i) internal revenue taxes have been determined, or customs duties liquidated, with respect to such pipe tobacco before such date pursuant to a request made under the first proviso of section 3(a) of such Act, or

(ii) such pipe tobacco is held on such date under the supervision of a customs officer pursuant to the second proviso of such section 3(a).

Under regulations prescribed by the Secretary of the Treasury or his delegate, provisions similar to sections 5706 and 5708 of the 1986 Code shall apply to pipe tobacco with respect to which tax is imposed by paragraph (1) by reason of this subparagraph.

(3) PIPE TOBACCO.—For purposes of this subsection, the term "pipe tobacco" shall have the meaning given to such term by subsection (o) of section 5702 of the 1986 Code.

(4) EXCEPTION WHERE LIABILITY DOES NOT EXCEED $1,000.—No tax shall be imposed by paragraph (1) on any person if the tax which would but for this paragraph be imposed on such person does not exceed $1,000. For purposes of the preceding sentence, all persons who are treated as a single taxpayer under section 5061(e)(3) of the 1986 Code shall be treated as 1 person.

[Sec. 5701(g)]

(g) ROLL-YOUR-OWN TOBACCO.—On roll-your-own tobacco, manufactured in or imported into the United States, there shall be imposed a tax of $24.78 per pound (and a proportionate tax at the like rate on all fractional parts of a pound).

Amendments

- **2009, Children's Health Insurance Program Reauthorization Act of 2009 (P.L. 111-3)**

P.L. 111-3, § 701(g):

Amended Code Sec. 5701(g) by striking "$1.0969 cents (95.67 cents on roll-your-own tobacco removed during 2000 or 2001)" and inserting "$24.78". **Effective** for articles removed (as defined in Code Sec. 5702(j)) after 3-31-2009.

- **1997, Balanced Budget Act of 1997 (P.L. 105-33)**

P.L. 105-33, § 9302(g)(1):

Amended Code Sec. 5701 by redesignating subsection (g) as subsection (h) and by inserting after subsection (f) a new subsection (g). **Effective**, generally, for articles removed (as defined in Code Sec. 5702(k)) after 12-31-99. For a transitional rule, see § 9302(i)(2) in the amendment notes following Code Sec. 5701(a).

P.L. 105-33, § 9302(k) (as added by P.L. 105-34, § 1604(f)(3), and subsequently repealed by P.L. 105-78, § 519, effective 11-13-97), provided:

(k) COORDINATION WITH TOBACCO INDUSTRY SETTLEMENT AGREEMENT.—The increase in excise taxes collected as a result of the amendments made by subsections (a), (e), and (g) of this section shall be credited against the total payments made by parties pursuant to Federal legislation implementing the tobacco industry settlement agreement of June 20, 1997.

[Sec. 5701(h)]

(h) IMPORTED TOBACCO PRODUCTS AND CIGARETTE PAPERS AND TUBES.—The taxes imposed by this section on tobacco products and cigarette papers and tubes imported into the United States shall be in addition to any import duties imposed on such articles, unless such import duties are imposed in lieu of internal revenue tax.

Amendments

- **1997, Balanced Budget Act of 1997 (P.L. 105-33)**

P.L. 105-33, § 9302(g)(1):

Amended Code Sec. 5701 by redesignating subsection (g) as subsection (h). **Effective**, generally, for articles removed (as defined in Code Sec. 5702(k)) after 12-31-99. For a transitional rule, see § 9302(i)(2) in the amendment notes following Code Sec. 5701(a).

P.L. 105-33, § 9302(k) (as added by P.L. 105-34, § 1604(f)(3), and subsequently repealed by P.L. 105-78, § 519, effective 11-13-97), provided:

(k) COORDINATION WITH TOBACCO INDUSTRY SETTLEMENT AGREEMENT.—The increase in excise taxes collected as a result of the amendments made by subsections (a), (e), and (g) of this section shall be credited against the total payments made by parties pursuant to Federal legislation implementing the tobacco industry settlement agreement of June 20, 1997.

- **1988, Technical and Miscellaneous Revenue Act of 1988 (P.L. 100-647)**

P.L. 100-647, § 5061(a):

Amended Code Sec. 5701 by redesignating subsection (f) as (e). For the **effective** date, see the amendment notes for Code Sec. 5701(f).

- **1986, Consolidated Omnibus Budget Reconciliation Act of 1985 (P.L. 99-272)**

P.L. 99-272, § 13202(a):

Redesignated Code Sec. 5701(e) as Code Sec. 5701(f). **Effective** for smokeless tobacco removed after 6-30-86. For a transitional rule, see Act Sec. 13202(c)(2) in the amendment notes following Code Sec. 5701(e).

- **1976, Tax Reform Act of 1976 (P.L. 94-455)**

P.L. 94-455, § 1905(a)(24):

Substituted ", unless such import duties are imposed in lieu of internal revenue tax." for the period at the end of Code Sec. 5701(e). **Effective** 2-1-77.

- **1965, Excise Tax Reduction Act of 1965 (P.L. 89-44)**

P.L. 89-44, § 502(a):

Redesignated Code Sec. 5701(f) as Sec. 5701(e). **Effective** for tax years beginning after 1-1-66.

Sec. 5701(g)

TOBACCO TAXES—DEFINITIONS

- **1958, Excise Tax Technical Changes Act of 1958 (P.L. 85-859)**

P.L. 85-859, §202:

Amended Sec. 5701(f). **Effective** 9-3-58. Prior to amendment, Sec. 5701(f) read as follows:

"(f) IMPORTED ARTICLES.—The taxes imposed on articles by this section shall be in addition to any import duties imposed on such articles."

[Sec. 5702]

SEC. 5702. DEFINITIONS.

When used in this chapter—

[Sec. 5702(a)]

(a) CIGAR.—"Cigar" means any roll of tobacco wrapped in leaf tobacco or in any substance containing tobacco (other than any roll of tobacco which is a cigarette within the meaning of subsection (b)(2)).

Amendments

- **1965, Excise Tax Reduction Act of 1965 (P.L. 89-44)**

P.L. 89-44, §502(b)(3):

Repealed former Code Sec. 5702(a) and redesignated former Code Sec. 5702(b) as Code Sec. 5702(a). **Effective** for tax years beginning after 1-1-66. Prior to repeal, Code Sec. 5702(a) read as follows:

(a) MANUFACTURED TOBACCO.—"Manufactured tobacco" means tobacco (other than cigars and cigarettes) prepared, processed, manipulated, or packaged, for removal, or merely removed, for consumption by smoking or for use in the mouth or nose, and any tobacco (other than cigars and cigarettes), not exempt from tax under this chapter, sold or delivered to any person contrary to this chapter or regulations prescribed thereunder.

[Sec. 5702(b)]

(b) CIGARETTE.—"Cigarette" means—

(1) any roll of tobacco wrapped in paper or in any substance not containing tobacco, and

(2) any roll of tobacco wrapped in any substance containing tobacco which, because of its appearance, the type of tobacco used in the filler, or its packaging and labeling, is likely to be offered to, or purchased by, consumers as a cigarette described in paragraph (1).

Amendments

- **1965, Excise Tax Reduction Act of 1965 (P.L. 89-44)**

P.L. 89-44, §502(b)(3):

Redesignated former Code Sec. 5702(c) as Code Sec. 5702(b). **Effective** for tax years beginning after 1-1-66.

P.L. 89-44, §808(a):

Amended Code Sec. 5702(b) (as redesignated). Prior to amendment, Code Sec. 5702(b) (as redesignated) read as follows:

(b) CIGARETTE.—"Cigarette" means any roll of tobacco, wrapped in paper or any substance other than tobacco.

[Sec. 5702(c)]

(c) TOBACCO PRODUCTS.—"Tobacco products" means cigars, cigarettes, smokeless tobacco, pipe tobacco, and roll-your-own tobacco.

Amendments

- **1997, Balanced Budget Act of 1997 (P.L. 105-33)**

P.L. 105-33, §9302(g)(3)(A):

Amended Code Sec. 5702(c) by striking "and pipe tobacco" and inserting "pipe tobacco, and roll-your-own tobacco". **Effective**, generally, for articles removed (as defined in Code Sec. 5702(k)) after 12-31-99. For a transitional rule, see Act Sec. 9302(i)(2) in the amendment notes following Code Sec. 5701(a).

P.L. 105-33, §9302(k) (as added by P.L. 105-34, §1604(f)(3), and subsequently repealed by P.L. 105-78, §519, effective 11-13-97), provided:

(k) COORDINATION WITH TOBACCO INDUSTRY SETTLEMENT AGREEMENT.—The increase in excise taxes collected as a result of the amendments made by subsections (a), (e), and (g) of this section shall be credited against the total payments made by parties pursuant to Federal legislation implementing the tobacco industry settlement agreement of June 20, 1997.

- **1988, Technical and Miscellaneous Revenue Act of 1988 (P.L. 100-647)**

P.L. 100-647, §5061(c)(1):

Amended Code Sec. 5702(c) by striking out "and smokeless tobacco" and inserting in lieu thereof "smokeless tobacco, and pipe tobacco". For the **effective** date, see Act Sec. 5061(d)-(e), below.

P.L. 100-647, §5061(d)-(e), provides:

(d) EFFECTIVE DATE.—

(1) IN GENERAL.— The amendments made by this section shall apply to pipe tobacco removed (within the meaning of section 5702(k) of the 1986 Code) after December 31, 1988.

(2) TRANSITIONAL RULE.—Any person who—

(A) on the date of the enactment of this Act, is engaged in business as a manufacturer of pipe tobacco, and

(B) before January 1, 1989, submits an application under subchapter B of chapter 52 of the 1986 Code to engage in such business,

may, notwithstanding such subchapter B, continue to engage in such business pending final action on such application. Pending such final action, all provisions of chapter 52 of the 1986 Code shall apply to such applicant in the same manner and to the same extent as if such applicant were a holder of a permit to manufacture pipe tobacco under such chapter 52.

(e) FLOOR STOCKS TAX.—

(1) IMPOSITION OF TAX.—On pipe tobacco manufactured in or imported into the United States which is removed before January 1, 1989, and held on such date for sale by any person, there is hereby imposed a tax of 45 cents per pound (and a proportionate tax at the like rate on all fractional parts of a pound).

(2) LIABILITY FOR TAX AND METHOD OF PAYMENT.—

(A) LIABILITY FOR TAX.—A person holding pipe tobacco on January 1, 1989, to which the tax imposed by paragraph (1) applies shall be liable for such tax.

(B) METHOD OF PAYMENT.—The tax imposed by paragraph (1) shall be treated as a tax imposed by section 5701 of the 1986 Code and shall be due and payable on February 14, 1989, in the same manner as the tax imposed by such section is payable with respect to pipe tobacco removed on or after January 1, 1989.

(C) TREATMENT OF PIPE TOBACCO IN FOREIGN TRADE ZONES.—Notwithstanding the Act of June 18, 1934 (48 Stat. 998, 19 U.S.C. 81a) or any other provision of law, pipe tobacco which is located in a foreign trade zone on January 1, 1989, shall be subject to the tax imposed by paragraph (1) and shall be treated for purposes of this subsection as held on such date for sale if—

(i) internal revenue taxes have been determined, or customs duties liquidated, with respect to such pipe tobacco before such date pursuant to a request made under the first proviso of section 3(a) of such Act, or

(ii) such pipe tobacco is held on such date under the supervision of a customs officer pursuant to the second proviso of such section 3(a).

Under regulations prescribed by the Secretary of the Treasury or his delegate, provisions similar to sections 5706 and 5708 of the 1986 Code shall apply to pipe tobacco with respect to which tax is imposed by paragraph (1) by reason of this subparagraph.

(3) PIPE TOBACCO.—For purposes of this subsection, the term "pipe tobacco" shall have the meaning given to such term by subsection (o) of section 5702 of the 1986 Code.

(4) EXCEPTION WHERE LIABILITY DOES NOT EXCEED $1,000.—No tax shall be imposed by paragraph (1) on any person if the tax which would but for this paragraph be imposed on such person does not exceed $1,000. For purposes of the preceding sentence, all persons who are treated as a single taxpayer under section 5061(e)(3) of the 1986 Code shall be treated as 1 person.

- **1986, Consolidated Omnibus Budget Reconciliation Act of 1985 (P.L. 99-272)**

P.L. 99-272, §13202(b)(2):

Amended Code Sec. 5702(c) by striking out "and cigarettes" and inserting in lieu thereof ", cigarettes, and smokeless tobacco". **Effective** for smokeless tobacco removed after 6-30-86. For a transitional rule, see Act Sec. 13202(c)(2) in the amendment notes following Code Sec. 5701(e).

- **1965, Excise Tax Reduction Act of 1965 (P.L. 89-44)**

P.L. 89-44, §502(b)(3):

Redesignated former Code Sec. 5702(d) as Code Sec. 5702(c) and amended Code Sec. 5702(c) (as redesignated). **Effective** for tax years beginning after 1-1-66. Prior to amendment, Code Sec. 5702(c) (as redesignated) read as follows:

(c) TOBACCO PRODUCTS.—"Tobacco products" means manufactured tobacco, cigars, and cigarettes.

[Sec. 5702(d)]

(d) MANUFACTURER OF TOBACCO PRODUCTS.—"Manufacturer of tobacco products" means any person who manufactures cigars, cigarettes, smokeless tobacco, pipe tobacco, or roll-your-own tobacco, except that such term shall not include—

(1) a person who produces cigars, cigarettes, smokeless tobacco, pipe tobacco, or roll-your-own tobacco solely for the person's own personal consumption or use, and

(2) a proprietor of a customs bonded manufacturing warehouse with respect to the operation of such warehouse.

TOBACCO TAXES—DEFINITIONS

Such term shall include any person who for commercial purposes makes available for consumer use (including such consumer's personal consumption or use under paragraph (1)) a machine capable of making cigarettes, cigars, or other tobacco products. A person making such a machine available for consumer use shall be deemed the person making the removal as defined by subsection (j) with respect to any tobacco products manufactured by such machine. A person who sells a machine directly to a consumer at retail for a consumer's personal home use is not making a machine available for commercial purposes if such machine is not used at a retail premises and is designed to produce tobacco products only in personal use quantities.

Amendments

• **2012, Moving Ahead for Progress in the 21st Century Act (P.L. 112-141)**

P.L. 112-141, §100122(a):

Amended Code Sec. 5702(d) by adding at the end a new flush sentence. **Effective** for articles removed after 7-6-2012.

• **1997, Balanced Budget Act of 1997 (P.L. 105-33)**

P.L. 105-33, §9302(g)(3)(B)(i)-(ii):

Amended Code Sec. 5702(d) by striking "or pipe tobacco" and inserting "pipe tobacco, or roll-your-own tobacco" in the material preceding paragraph (1), and by striking paragraph (1) and inserting a new paragraph (1). **Effective**, generally, for articles removed (as defined in Code Sec. 5702(k)) after 12-31-99. For a transitional rule, see Act Sec. 9302(i)(2) in the amendment notes following Code Sec. 5701(a). Prior to being stricken, Code Sec. 5702(d)(1) read as follows:

(1) a person who produces cigars or cigarettes solely for his own personal consumption or use; or

P.L. 105-33, §9302(k) (as added by P.L. 105-34, §1604(f)(3), and subsequently repealed by P.L. 105-78, §519, effective 11-13-97), provided:

(k) COORDINATION WITH TOBACCO INDUSTRY SETTLEMENT AGREEMENT.—The increase in excise taxes collected as a result of the amendments made by subsections (a), (e), and (g) of this section shall be credited against the total payments made by parties pursuant to Federal legislation implementing the tobacco industry settlement agreement of June 20, 1997.

• **1988, Technical and Miscellaneous Revenue Act of 1988 (P.L. 100-647)**

P.L. 100-647, §5061(c)(2):

Amended Code Sec. 5702(d) by striking out "or smokeless tobacco" and inserting in lieu thereof "smokeless tobacco, or pipe tobacco". **Effective**, generally, for pipe tobacco removed (within the meaning of section 5702(k)) after 12-31-88. However, see Act Sec. 5061(d)-(e), reproduced in the amendment notes following Code Sec. 5702(c) for transitional rules.

• **1986, Consolidated Omnibus Budget Reconciliation Act of 1985 (P.L. 99-272)**

P.L. 99-272, §13202(b)(3):

Amended Code Sec. 5702(d) by striking out "cigars or cigarettes" each place it appears and inserting in lieu thereof "cigars, cigarettes, or smokeless tobacco". **Effective** for smokeless tobacco removed after 6-30-86. For a transitional rule, see Act Sec. 13202(c)(2) in the amendment notes following Code Sec. 5701(e).

• **1965, Excise Tax Reduction Act of 1965 (P.L. 89-44)**

P.L. 89-44, §502(b)(3):

Redesignated former Code Sec. 5702(e) as Code Sec. 5702(d) and amended Code Sec. 5702(d) (as redesignated). **Effective** for tax years beginning after 1-1-66. Prior to amendment, Code Sec. 5702(d) (as redesignated) read as follows:

(d) MANUFACTURER OF TOBACCO PRODUCTS.—"Manufacturer of tobacco products" means any person who manufactures cigars or cigarettes, or who prepares, processes, manipulates, or packages, for removal, or merely removes, tobacco (other than cigars and cigarettes) for consumption by smoking or for use in the mouth or nose, or who sells or delivers any tobacco (other than cigars and cigarettes) contrary to this chapter or regulations prescribed thereunder. The term "manufacturer of tobacco products" shall not include—

(1) a person who in any manner prepares tobacco, or produces cigars or cigarettes, solely for his own personal consumption or use; or

(2) a proprietor of a customs bonded manufacturing warehouse with respect to the operation of such warehouse; or

(3) a farmer or grower of tobacco with respect to the sale of leaf tobacco of his own growth or raising, if it is in the condition as cured on the farm; or

(4) a bona fide association of farmers or growers of tobacco with respect to sales of leaf tobacco grown by farmer or grower members, if the tobacco so sold is in the condition as cured on the farm, and if the association maintains records of all leaf tobacco, acquired or received and sold or otherwise disposed of, in such manner as the Secretary or his delegate shall by regulations prescribe.

[Sec. 5702(e)]

(e) CIGARETTE PAPER.—"Cigarette paper" means paper, or any other material except tobacco, prepared for use as a cigarette wrapper.

Amendments

• **1965, Excise Tax Reduction Act of 1965 (P.L. 89-44)**

P.L. 89-44, §503(b)(3):

Redesignated former Code Sec. 5702(f) as Code Sec. 5702(e). **Effective** for tax years beginning after 1-1-66.

[Sec. 5702(f)—Stricken]

Amendments

• **2000, Community Renewal Tax Relief Act of 2000 (P.L. 106-554)**

P.L. 106-554, §315(a)(2)(B):

Amended Code Sec. 5702 by striking subsection (f) and by redesignating subsections (g) through (p) as subsections (f) through (o), respectively. **Effective** as if included in section 9302 of P.L. 105-33 [effective generally for articles removed after 12-31-99.—CCH]. Prior to being stricken, Code Sec. 5702(f) read as follows:

(f) CIGARETTE PAPERS.—"Cigarette papers" means taxable books or sets of cigarette papers.

• **1965, Excise Tax Reduction Act of 1965 (P.L. 89-44)**

P.L. 89-44, §502(b)(3):

Redesignated former Code Sec. 5702(g) as Code Sec. 5702(f). **Effective** for tax years beginning after 1-1-66.

[Sec. 5702(f)]

(f) CIGARETTE TUBE.—"Cigarette tube" means cigarette paper made into a hollow cylinder for use in making cigarettes.

Amendments

• **2000, Community Renewal Tax Relief Act of 2000 (P.L. 106-554)**

P.L. 106-554, §315(a)(2)(B):

Amended Code Sec. 5702 by striking subsection (f) and by redesignating subsection (g) as subsection (f). **Effective** as if included in section 9302 of P.L. 105-33 [effective generally for articles removed after 12-31-99.—CCH].

• **1965, Excise Tax Reduction Act of 1965 (P.L. 89-44)**

P.L. 89-44, §502(b)(3):

Redesignated former Code Sec. 5702(h) as Code Sec. 5702(g). **Effective** for tax years beginning after 1-1-66.

[Sec. 5702(g)]

(g) MANUFACTURER OF CIGARETTE PAPERS AND TUBES.—"Manufacturer of cigarette papers and tubes" means any person who makes up cigarette paper into books or sets containing more than 25 papers each, or into tubes, except for his own personal use or consumption.

Amendments

• **2000, Community Renewal Tax Relief Act of 2000 (P.L. 106-554)**

P.L. 106-554, §315(a)(2)(A):

Amended Code Sec. 5702(h), prior to redesignation by Act Sec. 315(a)(2)(B). **Effective** as if included in section 9302 of P.L. 105-33 [effective generally for articles removed after 12-31-99.—CCH]. Prior to amendment, Code Sec. 5702(h) read as follows:

(h) MANUFACTURER OF CIGARETTE PAPERS AND TUBES.—"Manufacturer of cigarette papers and tubes" means any person who makes up cigarette paper into books or sets containing more than 25 papers each, or into tubes, except for his own personal use or consumption.

P.L. 106-554, §315(a)(2)(B):

Amended Code Sec. 5702, as amended by Act Sec. 315(a)(2)(A), by redesignating subsection (h) as subsection (g). **Effective** as if included in section 9302 of P.L. 105-33 [effective generally for articles removed after 12-31-99.—CCH].

P.L. 89-44, §502(b)(3):

Redesignated former Code Sec. 5702(i) as Code Sec. 5702(h). **Effective** for tax years beginning after 1-1-66.

[Sec. 5702(h)]

(h) EXPORT WAREHOUSE.—"Export warehouse" means a bonded internal revenue warehouse for the storage of tobacco products or cigarette papers or tubes or any processed tobacco, upon which the internal revenue tax has not been paid, for subsequent shipment to a foreign country, Puerto Rico, the Virgin Islands, or a possession of the United States, or for consumption beyond the jurisdiction of the internal revenue laws of the United States.

TOBACCO TAXES—DEFINITIONS

Amendments

• **2009, Children's Health Insurance Program Reauthorization Act of 2009 (P.L. 111-3)**

P.L. 111-3, §702(a)(5)(A):

Amended Code Sec. 5702(h) by striking "tobacco products and cigarette papers and tubes" and inserting "tobacco products or cigarette papers or tubes or any processed tobacco". **Effective** 4-1-2009.

[Sec. 5702(i)]

(i) EXPORT WAREHOUSE PROPRIETOR.—"Export warehouse proprietor" means any person who operates an export warehouse.

Amendments

• **2000, Community Renewal Tax Relief Act of 2000 (P.L. 106-554)**

P.L. 106-554, §315(a)(2)(B):

Amended Code Sec. 5702 by redesignating subsection (j) as subsection (i). **Effective** as if included in section 9302 of P.L. 105-33 [**effective** generally for articles removed after 12-31-99.—CCH].

[Sec. 5702(j)]

(j) REMOVAL OR REMOVE.—"Removal" or "remove" means the removal of tobacco products or cigarette papers or tubes, or any processed tobacco, from the factory or from internal revenue bond under section 5704, as the Secretary shall by regulation prescribe, or release from customs custody, and shall also include the smuggling or other unlawful importation of such articles into the United States.

Amendments

• **2009, Children's Health Insurance Program Reauthorization Act of 2009 (P.L. 111-3)**

P.L. 111-3, §702(a)(5)(B):

Amended Code Sec. 5702(j) by inserting ", or any processed tobacco," after "tobacco products or cigarette papers or tubes". **Effective** 4-1-2009.

• **2000, Community Renewal Tax Relief Act of 2000 (P.L. 106-554)**

P.L. 106-554, §315(a)(2)(B):

Amended Code Sec. 5702 by redesignating subsection (k) as subsection (j). **Effective** as if included in section 9302 of P.L. 105-33 [**effective** generally for articles removed after 12-31-99.—CCH].

• **1997, Balanced Budget Act of 1997 (P.L. 105-33)**

P.L. 105-33, §9302(h)(4):

Amended Code Sec. 5702(k) by inserting "under section 5704" after "internal revenue bond". **Effective**, generally, for articles removed (as defined in Code Sec. 5702(k)) after 12-31-99. For a transitional rule, see Act Sec. 9302(i)(2) in the amendment notes following Code Sec. 5701(a).

• **1976, Tax Reform Act of 1976 (P.L. 94-455)**

P.L. 94-455, §1906(b)(13)(A):

Amended 1954 Code by substituting "Secretary" for "Secretary or his delegate" each place it appeared. **Effective** 9-3-58.

• **1965, Excise Tax Reduction Act of 1965 (P.L. 89-44)**

P.L. 89-44, §502(b)(3):

Repealed former Code Secs. 5702(l) and 5702(m) and redesignated former Code Sec. 5702(n) as Code Sec. 5702(k). **Effective** for tax years beginning after 1-1-66. Prior to repeal, Code Secs. 5702(l) and 5702(m) read as follows:

[Sec. 5702(k)]

(k) IMPORTER.—"Importer" means any person in the United States to whom nontaxpaid tobacco products or cigarette papers or tubes, or any processed tobacco, manufactured in a foreign country, Puerto Rico, the Virgin Islands, or a possession of the United States are shipped or consigned; any person who removes cigars or cigarettes for sale or consumption in the United States from a customs bonded manufacturing warehouse; and any person who smuggles or otherwise unlawfully brings tobacco products or cigarette papers or tubes, or any processed tobacco, into the United States.

Amendments

• **2009, Children's Health Insurance Program Reauthorization Act of 2009 (P.L. 111-3)**

P.L. 111-3, §702(a)(5)(B):

Amended Code Sec. 5702(k) by inserting ", or any processed tobacco," after "tobacco products or cigarette papers or tubes" [each place it appears]. **Effective** 4-1-2009.

• **2000, Community Renewal Tax Relief Act of 2000 (P.L. 106-554)**

P.L. 106-554, §315(a)(2)(B):

Amended Code Sec. 5702 by redesignating subsection (l) as subsection (k). **Effective** as if included in section 9302 of P.L. 105-33 [**effective** generally for articles removed after 12-31-99.—CCH].

• **1965, Excise Tax Reduction Act of 1965 (P.L. 89-44)**

P.L. 89-44, §502(b)(3):

Redesignated former Code Sec. 5702(o) as Code Sec. 5702(l). **Effective** for tax years beginning after 1-1-66.

• **1958, Excise Tax Technical Changes Act of 1958 (P.L. 85-859)**

P.L. 85-859, §202:

Amended Code Sec. 5702 to read as prior to amendment by P.L. 89-44. **Effective** 9-3-58. Prior to amendment, Code Sec. 5702 read as follows:

• **2000, Community Renewal Tax Relief Act of 2000 (P.L. 106-554)**

P.L. 106-554, §315(a)(2)(B):

Amended Code Sec. 5702 by redesignating subsection (i) as subsection (h). **Effective** as if included in section 9302 of P.L. 105-33 [**effective** generally for articles removed after 12-31-99.—CCH].

• **1965, Excise Tax Reduction Act of 1965 (P.L. 89-44)**

P.L. 89-44, §502(b)(3):

Redesignated former Code Sec. 5702(j) as Code Sec. 5702(i). **Effective** for tax years beginning after 1-1-66.

• **1965, Excise Tax Reduction Act of 1965 (P.L. 89-44)**

P.L. 89-44, §502(b)(3):

Redesignated former Code Sec. 5702(k) as Code Sec. 5702(j). **Effective** for tax years beginning after 1-1-66.

(l) TOBACCO MATERIALS.—"Tobacco materials" means tobacco other than manufactured tobacco, cigars, and cigarettes.

(m) DEALER IN TOBACCO MATERIALS.—"Dealer in tobacco materials" means any person who receives and handles tobacco materials for sale, shipment, or delivery to another dealer in such materials, to a manufacturer of tobacco products, or to a foreign country, Puerto Rico, the Virgin Islands, or a possession of the United States, or who receives tobacco materials, other than stems and waste, for use by him in the production of fertilizer, insecticide, or nicotine. The term "dealer in tobacco materials" shall not include—

(1) an operator of a warehouse who stores tobacco materials solely for a qualified dealer in tobacco materials, for a qualified manufacturer of tobacco products, for a farmer or grower of tobacco, or for a bona fide association of farmers or growers of tobacco; or

(2) a farmer or grower of tobacco with respect to the sale of leaf tobacco of his own growth or raising, or a bona fide association of farmers or growers of tobacco with respect to sales of leaf tobacco grown by farmer or grower members, if the tobacco so sold is in the condition as cured on the farm: *Provided*, That such association maintains records of all leaf tobacco acquired or received and sold or otherwise disposed of by the association, in such manner as the Secretary or his delegate shall by regulation prescribe; or

(3) a person who buys leaf tobacco on the floor of an auction warehouse, or who buys leaf tobacco from a farmer or grower, and places the tobacco on the floor of such a warehouse, or who purchases and sells warehouse receipts without taking physical possession of the tobacco covered thereby; or

(4) a qualified manufacturer of tobacco products with respect to tobacco materials received by him under his bond as such a manufacturer.

SEC. 5702. DEFINITIONS.

(a) Manufactured Tobacco.—'Manufactured tobacco' means all tobacco, other than cigars and cigarettes, prepared, processed, manipulated, or packaged for consumption by smoking or for use in the mouth or nose. Any other tobacco not exempt from tax under this chapter, which is sold or delivered to any person contrary to this chapter and regulations prescribed thereunder, shall be regarded as manufactured tobacco.

"(b) Manufacturer of Tobacco.—'Manufacturer of tobacco' means any person who manufactures tobacco by any method of preparing, processing, or manipulating, except for his own personal consumption or use; or who packages any tobacco for consumption by smoking or for use in the mouth or nose; or who sells or delivers any tobacco, not exempt from tax under this chapter, to any person, contrary to the provisions of this chapter and regulations prescribed thereunder. The term 'manufacturer of tobacco' shall not include—

(1) a farmer or grower of tobacco who sells leaf tobacco of his own growth or raising, or a bona fide association of farmers or growers of tobacco which sells only leaf tobacco grown by farmer or grower members, if the tobaccoo sold is in the condition as cured on the farm; or

(2) a dealer in tobacco materials who handles tobacco solely for sale, shipment, or delivery, in bulk, to another dealer in such materials or to a manufacturer of tobacco products, or to a foreign country, Puerto Rico, the Virgin Islands, or a possession of the United States.

(c) Cigar.—'Cigar' means any roll of tobacco wrapped in tobacco.

TOBACCO TAXES—DEFINITIONS

(d) Cigarette.—'Cigarette' means any roll of tobacco, wrapped in paper or any substance other than tobacco.

(e) Manufacturer of Cigars and Cigarettes.—'Manufacturer of cigars and cigarettes' means every person who produces cigars or cigarettes, except for his own personal consumption.

(f) Tobacco Products.—'Tobacco products' means manufactured tobacco, cigars, and cigarettes.

(g) Cigarette Paper.—'Cigarette paper' means paper, or any other material except tobacco, prepared for use as a cigarette wrapper.

(h) Cigarette Tube.—'Cigarette tube' means cigarette paper made into a hollow cylinder for use in making cigarettes.

(i) Manufacturer of Cigarette Papers and Tubes.—'Manufacturer of cigarette papers and tubes' means any person who makes up cigarette paper into packages, books, sets, or tubes, except for his own personal use or consumption.

(j) Articles.—'Articles' means manufactured tobacco, cigars, cigarettes, and cigarette papers and tubes.

(k) Tobacco Materials.—'Tobacco materials' means tobacco in process, leaf tobacco, and tobacco scraps, cuttings, clippings, siftings, dust, stems, and waste.

(l) Dealer in Tobacco Materials.—'Dealer in tobacco materials' means any person who handles tobacco materials for sale, shipment, or delivery solely to another dealer in such materials, to a manufacturer of tobacco products, or to a foreign country, Puerto Rico, the Virgin Islands, or a possession of the United States, but shall not include—

(1) an operator of a warehouse who stores tobacco materials solely for a dealer in tobacco materials, for a manufacturer of tobacco products, for a farmer or grower of tobacco, or for a bona fide association of farmers or growers of tobacco; or

(2) a farmer or grower of tobacco who sells leaf tobacco of his own growth or raising, or a bona fide association of farmers or growers of tobacco which sells only leaf tobacco grown by farmer or grower members, if the tobacco so sold is in the condition as cured on the farm.

(m) Removal or Remove.—'Removal' or 'remove' means removal of articles from the factory or from internal revenue bond, as the Secretary or his delegate shall, by regulation, prescribe, or from customs custody, and shall also include the smuggling or other unlawful importation of articles into the United States.

(n) Importer.—'Importer' means any person in the United States to whom nontaxpaid articles manufactured in a foreign country, Puerto Rico, the Virgin Islands, or a possession of the United States are shipped or consigned, and any person who smuggles or otherwise unlawfully brings such nontaxpaid articles into the United States.

[Sec. 5702(l)]

(l) DETERMINATION OF PRICE ON CIGARS.—In determining price for purposes of section 5701(a)(2)—

(1) there shall be included any charge incident to placing the article in condition ready for use,

(2) there shall be excluded—

(A) the amount of the tax imposed by this chapter or section 7652, and

(B) if stated as a separate charge, the amount of any retail sales tax imposed by any State or political subdivision thereof or the District of Columbia, whether the liability for such tax is imposed on the vendor or vendee, and

(3) rules similar to the rules of section 4216(b) shall apply.

Amendments

• **2000, Community Renewal Tax Relief Act of 2000 (P.L. 106-554)**

P.L. 106-554, § 315(a)(2)(B):

Amended Code Sec. 5702 by redesignating subsection (m) as subsection (l). **Effective** as if included in section 9302 of P.L. 105-33 [effective generally for articles removed after 12-31-99.—CCH].

• **1990, Omnibus Budget Reconciliation Act of 1990 (P.L. 101-508)**

P.L. 101-508, § 11202(g):

Amended Code Sec. 5702(m). **Effective** with respect to articles removed after 12-31-90. Prior to amendment, Code Sec. 5702(m) read as follows:

(m) WHOLESALE PRICE.—"Wholesale price" means the manufacturer's, or importer's, suggested delivered price at which the cigars are to be sold to retailers, inclusive of the tax imposed by this chapter or section 7652, but exclusive of any State or local taxes imposed on cigars as a commodity, and before any trade, cash, or other discounts, or any promotion, advertising, display, or similar allowances. Where the manufacturer's or importer's suggested delivered price to retailers is not adequately supported by bona fide arm's length sales, or where the manufacturer or importer has no suggested delivered price to retailers, the wholesale price shall be the price for which cigars of comparable retail price are sold to retailers in the ordinary course of trade as determined by the Secretary.

• **1976, Tax Reform Act of 1976 (P.L. 94-455)**

P.L. 94-455, § 2128(b):

Added Code Sec. 5702(m). **Effective** 2-1-77.

[Sec. 5702(m)]

(m) DEFINITIONS RELATING TO SMOKELESS TOBACCO.—

(1) SMOKELESS TOBACCO.—The term "smokeless tobacco" means any snuff or chewing tobacco.

(2) SNUFF.—The term "snuff" means any finely cut, ground, or powdered tobacco that is not intended to be smoked.

(3) CHEWING TOBACCO.—The term "chewing tobacco" means any leaf tobacco that is not intended to be smoked.

Amendments

• **2000, Community Renewal Tax Relief Act of 2000 (P.L. 106-554)**

P.L. 106-554, § 315(a)(2)(B):

Amended Code Sec. 5702 by redesignating subsection (n) as subsection (m). **Effective** as if included in section 9302 of P.L. 105-33 [effective generally for articles removed after 12-31-99.—CCH].

• **1986, Consolidated Omnibus Budget Reconciliation Act of 1985 (P.L. 99-272)**

P.L. 99-272, § 13202(b)(4):

Amended Code Sec. 5702 by adding at the end thereof new subsection (n). **Effective** for smokeless tobacco removed after 6-30-86. For a transitional rule, see Act Sec. 13202(c)(2) in the amendment notes following Code Sec. 5701(e).

[Sec. 5702(n)]

(n) PIPE TOBACCO.—The term "pipe tobacco" means any tobacco which, because of its appearance, type, packaging, or labeling, is suitable for use and likely to be offered to, or purchased by, consumers as tobacco to be smoked in a pipe.

Amendments

• **2000, Community Renewal Tax Relief Act of 2000 (P.L. 106-554)**

P.L. 106-554, § 315(a)(2)(B):

Amended Code Sec. 5702 by redesignating subsection (o) as subsection (n). **Effective** as if included in section 9302 of P.L. 105-33 [effective generally for articles removed after 12-31-99.—CCH].

• **1988, Technical and Miscellaneous Revenue Act of 1988 (P.L. 100-647)**

P.L. 100-647, § 5061(b):

Amended Code Sec. 5702 by adding at the end thereof a new subsection (o). **Effective**, generally, for pipe tobacco removed (within the meaning of section 5702(k)) after 12-31-88. However, for transitional rules, see Act Sec. 5061(d)-(e), reproduced in the amendment notes following Code Sec. 5702(c).

[Sec. 5702(o)]

(o) ROLL-YOUR-OWN TOBACCO.—The term "roll-your-own tobacco" means any tobacco which, because of its appearance, type, packaging, or labeling, is suitable for use and likely to be offered to, or purchased by, consumers as tobacco for making cigarettes or cigars, or for use as wrappers thereof.

Amendments

• **2009, Children's Health Insurance Program Reauthorization Act of 2009 (P.L. 111-3)**

P.L. 111-3, § 702(d)(1):

Amended Code Sec. 5702(o) by inserting "or cigars, or for use as wrappers thereof" before the period at the end. **Effective** for articles removed (as defined in Code Sec. 5702(j)) after 3-31-2009.

• **2000, Community Renewal Tax Relief Act of 2000 (P.L. 106-554)**

P.L. 106-554, § 315(a)(2)(B):

Amended Code Sec. 5702 by redesignating subsection (p) as subsection (o). **Effective** as if included in section 9302 of P.L. 105-33 [effective generally for articles removed after 12-31-99.—CCH].

TOBACCO TAXES—PAYMENT

• **1997, Balanced Budget Act of 1997 (P.L. 105-33)**

P.L. 105-33, §9302(g)(2):

Amended Code Sec. 5702 by adding at the end a new subsection (p). **Effective,** generally, for articles removed (as defined in Code Sec. 5702(k)) after 12-31-99. For a transitional rule, see §9302(i)(2) in the amendment notes following Code Sec. 5701(a), above.

P.L. 105-33, §9302(k) (as added by P.L. 105-34, §1604(f)(3), and subsequently repealed by P.L. 105-78, §519, effective 11-13-97), provided:

(k) COORDINATION WITH TOBACCO INDUSTRY SETTLEMENT AGREEMENT.—The increase in excise taxes collected as a result of the amendments made by subsections (a), (e), and (g) of this section shall be credited against the total payments made by parties pursuant to Federal legislation implementing the tobacco industry settlement agreement of June 20, 1997.

[Sec. 5702(p)]

(p) MANUFACTURER OF PROCESSED TOBACCO.—

(1) IN GENERAL.—The term "manufacturer of processed tobacco" means any person who processes any tobacco other than tobacco products.

(2) PROCESSED TOBACCO.—The processing of tobacco shall not include the farming or growing of tobacco or the handling of tobacco solely for sale, shipment, or delivery to a manufacturer of tobacco products or processed tobacco.

Amendments

• **2009, Children's Health Insurance Program Reauthorization Act of 2009 (P.L. 111-3)**

P.L. 111-3, §702(a)(4):

Amended Code Sec. 5702 by adding at the end a new subsection (p). **Effective** 4-1-2009.

[Sec. 5703]

SEC. 5703. LIABILITY FOR TAX AND METHOD OF PAYMENT.

[Sec. 5703(a)]

(a) LIABILITY FOR TAX.—

(1) ORIGINAL LIABILITY.—The manufacturer or importer of tobacco products and cigarette papers and tubes shall be liable for the taxes imposed thereon by section 5701.

(2) TRANSFER OF LIABILITY.—When tobacco products and cigarette papers and tubes are transferred, without payment of tax, pursuant to section 5704, the liability for tax shall be transferred in accordance with the provisions of this paragraph. When tobacco products and cigarette papers and tubes are transferred between the bonded premises of manufacturers and export warehouse proprietors, the transferee shall become liable for the tax upon receipt by him of such articles, and the transferor shall thereupon be relieved of his liability for such tax. When tobacco products and cigarette papers and tubes are released in bond from customs custody for transfer to the bonded premises of a manufacturer of tobacco products or cigarette papers and tubes, the transferee shall become liable for the tax on such articles upon release from customs custody, and the importer shall thereupon be relieved of his liability for such tax. All provisions of this chapter applicable to tobacco products and cigarette papers and tubes in bond shall be applicable to such articles returned to bond upon withdrawal from the market or returned to bond after previous removal for a tax-exempt purpose.

Amendments

• **1976, Tax Reform Act of 1976 (P.L. 94-455)**

P.L. 94-455, §1905(a)(25)(A):

Added the last sentence of Code Sec. 5703(a)(2). **Effective** 2-1-77.

[Sec. 5703(b)]

(b) METHOD OF PAYMENT OF TAX.—

(1) IN GENERAL.—The taxes imposed by section 5701 shall be determined at the time of removal of the tobacco products and cigarette papers and tubes. Such taxes shall be paid on the basis of [a] return. The Secretary shall, by regulations, prescribe the period or the event for which such return shall be made and the information to be furnished on such return. Any postponement under this subsection of the payment of taxes determined at the time of removal shall be conditioned upon the filing of such additional bonds, and upon compliance with such requirements, as the Secretary may prescribe for the protection of the revenue. The Secretary may, by regulations, require payment of tax on the basis of a return prior to removal of the tobacco products and cigarette papers and tubes where a person defaults in the postponed payment of tax on the basis of a return under this subsection or regulations prescribed thereunder. All administrative and penalty provisions of this title, insofar as applicable, shall apply to any tax imposed by section 5701.

(2) TIME FOR PAYMENT OF TAXES.—

(A) IN GENERAL.—Except as otherwise provided in this paragraph, in the case of taxes on tobacco products and cigarette papers and tubes removed during any semimonthly period under bond for deferred payment of tax, the last day for payment of such taxes shall be the 14th day after the last day of such semimonthly period.

(B) IMPORTED ARTICLES.—In the case of tobacco products and cigarette papers and tubes which are imported into the United States—

(i) IN GENERAL.—The last day for payment of tax shall be the 14th day after the last day of the semimonthly period during which the article is entered into the customs territory of the United States.

(ii) SPECIAL RULE FOR ENTRY FOR WAREHOUSING.—Except as provided in clause (iv), in the case of an entry for warehousing, the last day for payment of tax shall not be later than the 14th day after the last day of the semimonthly period during which the article is removed from the 1st such warehouse.

(iii) FOREIGN TRADE ZONES.—Except as provided in clause (iv) and in regulations prescribed by the Secretary, articles brought into a foreign trade zone shall, notwithstanding any other provision of law, be treated for purposes of this subsection as if such zone were a single customs warehouse.

(iv) EXCEPTION FOR ARTICLES DESTINED FOR EXPORT.—Clauses (ii) and (iii) shall not apply to any article which is shown to the satisfaction of the Secretary to be destined for export.

(C) TOBACCO PRODUCTS AND CIGARETTE PAPERS AND TUBES BROUGHT INTO THE UNITED STATES FROM PUERTO RICO.—In the case of tobacco products and cigarette papers and tubes which are brought into the United States from Puerto Rico, the last day for payment of tax shall be the 14th day after the last day of the semimonthly period during which the article is brought into the United States.

(D) SPECIAL RULE FOR TAX DUE IN SEPTEMBER.—

(i) IN GENERAL.—Notwithstanding the preceding provisions of this paragraph, the taxes on tobacco products and cigarette papers and tubes for the period beginning on September 16 and ending on September 26 shall be paid not later than September 29.

(ii) SAFE HARBOR.—The requirement of clause (i) shall be treated as met if the amount paid not later than September 29 is not less than $11/15$ of the taxes on tobacco products and cigarette papers and tubes for the period beginning on September 1 and ending on September 15.

TOBACCO TAXES—PAYMENT

(iii) TAXPAYERS NOT REQUIRED TO USE ELECTRONIC FUNDS TRANSFER.—In the case of payments not required to be made by electronic funds transfer, clauses (i) and (ii) shall be applied by substituting "September 25" for "September 26", "September 28" for "September 29", and "2/3" for "11/15".

(E) SPECIAL RULE WHERE DUE DATE FALLS ON SATURDAY, SUNDAY, OR HOLIDAY.—Notwithstanding section 7503, if, but for this subparagraph, the due date under this paragraph would fall on a Saturday, Sunday, or a legal holiday (as defined in section 7503), such due date shall be the immediately preceding day which is not a Saturday, Sunday, or such a holiday (or the immediately following day where the due date described in subparagraph (D) falls on a Sunday).

(F) SPECIAL RULE FOR UNLAWFULLY MANUFACTURED TOBACCO PRODUCTS.—In the case of any tobacco products, cigarette paper, or cigarette tubes manufactured in the United States at any place other than the premises of a manufacturer of tobacco products, cigarette paper, or cigarette tubes that has filed the bond and obtained the permit required under this chapter, tax shall be due and payable immediately upon manufacture.

(3) PAYMENT BY ELECTRONIC FUND TRANSFER.—Any person who in any 12-month period, ending December 31, was liable for a gross amount equal to or exceeding $5,000,000 in taxes imposed on tobacco products and cigarette papers and tubes by section 5701 (or 7652) shall pay such taxes during the succeeding calendar year by electronic fund transfer (as defined in section 5061(e)(2)) to a Federal Reserve Bank. Rules similar to the rules of section 5061(e)(3) shall apply to the $5,000,000 amount specified in the preceding sentence.

Amendments

• **2009, Children's Health Insurance Program Reauthorization Act of 2009 (P.L. 111-3)**

P.L. 111-3, §702(e)(1):

Amended Code Sec. 5703(b)(2) by adding at the end a new subparagraph (F). **Effective** 2-4-2009.

• **1994, Uruguay Round Agreements Act (P.L. 103-465)**

P.L. 103-465, §712(c)(1):

Amended Code Sec. 5703(b)(2) by redesignating subparagraph (D) as subparagraph (E) and by inserting after subparagraph (C) a new subparagraph (D). **Effective** 1-1-95.

P.L. 103-465, §712(c)(2)(A)-(B):

Amended Code Sec. 5703(b)(2)(E), as redesignated by Act Sec. 712(c)(1), by inserting "(or the immediately following day where the due date described in subparagraph (D) falls on a Sunday)" before the period at the end, and by striking "14TH DAY" in the heading and inserting "DUE DATE". **Effective** 1-1-95.

• **1988, Technical and Miscellaneous Revenue Act of 1988 (P.L. 100-647)**

P.L. 100-647, §2003(b)(1)(C):

Amended Code Sec. 5703(b)(2)(B)(i) and (ii) by striking out "the 14th day after the date on which" and inserting in lieu thereof "the 14th day after the last day of the semimonthly period during which". **Effective** as if included in the amendments made by section 8011 of P.L. 99-509.

P.L. 100-647, §2003(b)(1)(D):

Amended Code Sec. 5703(b)(2)(C) by striking out "the 14th day after the date on which" and inserting in lieu thereof "the 14th day after the last day of the semimonthly period during which". **Effective** as if included in the amendments made by section 8011 of P.L. 99-509.

• **1986, Tax Reform Act of 1986 (P.L. 99-514)**

P.L. 99-514, §1801(c)(2):

Amended Code Sec. 5703(b)(3) by adding at the end thereof a new sentence. **Effective** as if included in the provision of P.L. 98-369 to which it relates.

• **1986, Omnibus Budget Reconciliation Act of 1986 (P.L. 99-509)**

P.L. 99-509, §8011(a)(1):

Amended Code Sec. 5703(b)(2). For the **effective** date, see Act Sec. 8011(c), below. Prior to amendment, Code Sec. 5703(b)(2) read as follows:

(2) TIME FOR MAKING OF RETURN AND PAYMENT OF TAXES.—In the case of tobacco products and cigarette papers and tubes removed after December 31, 1982, under bond for deferred payment of tax, the last day for filing a return and paying any tax due for each return period shall be the last day of the first succeeding return period plus 10 days.

P.L. 99-509, §8011(c), provides:

(c) EFFECTIVE DATES.—

(1) IN GENERAL.—Except as provided in paragraph (2), the amendments made by this section shall apply to removals during semimonthly periods ending on or after December 31, 1986.

(2) IMPORTED ARTICLES, ETC.—Subparagraphs (B) and (C) of section 5703(b)(2) of the Internal Revenue Code of 1954 (as added by this section), paragraphs (2) and (3) of section 5061(d) of such Code (as amended by this section), and the amendments made by subsections (a)(2) and (b)(2) shall apply to articles imported, entered for warehousing, or brought into the United States or a foreign trade zone after December 15, 1986.

(3) SPECIAL RULE FOR DISTILLED SPIRITS AND TOBACCO FOR SEMIMONTHLY PERIOD ENDING DECEMBER 15, 1986.—With respect to remittances of—

(A) taxes imposed on distilled spirits by section 5001 or 7652 of such Code, and

(B) taxes imposed on tobacco products and cigarette papers and tubes by section 5701 or 7652 of such Code,

for the semimonthly period ending December 15, 1986, the last day for payment of such remittances shall be January 14, 1987.

(4) TREATMENT OF SMOKELESS TOBACCO IN INVENTORY ON JUNE 30, 1986.—The tax imposed by section 5701(e) of the Internal Revenue Code of 1954 shall not apply to any smokeless tobacco which—

(A) on June 30, 1986, was in the inventory of the manufacturer or importer, and

(B) on such date was in a form ready for sale.

• **1984, Deficit Reduction Act of 1984 (P.L. 98-369)**

P.L. 98-369, §27(c)(2):

Amended Code Sec. 5703(b) by adding new paragraph (3). **Effective** for taxes required to be paid on or after 9-30-84.

• **1983, Technical Corrections Act of 1982 (P.L. 97-448)**

P.L. 97-448, §308(a):

Amended Code Sec. 5703(b). **Effective** with respect to tobacco products and cigarette papers and tubes removed after 12-31-82. Prior to amendment, Code Sec. 5703(b) read as follows:

"(b) METHOD OF PAYMENT OF TAX.—The taxes imposed by section 5701 shall be determined at the time of removal of the tobacco products and cigarette papers and tubes. Such taxes shall be paid on the basis of a return. The Secretary shall, by regulations, prescribe the period or event for which such return shall be made, the information to be furnished on such return, the time for making such return, and the time for payment of such taxes. Any postponement under this subsection of the payment of taxes determined at the time of removal shall be conditioned upon the filing of such additional bonds, and upon compliance with such requirements, as the Secretary may, by regulations, prescribe for the protection of the revenue. The Secretary may, by regulations, require payment of tax on the basis of a return prior to removal of the tobacco products and cigarette papers and tubes where a person defaults in the postponed payment of tax on the basis of a return under this subsection or regulations prescribed thereunder. All administrative and penal provisions of this title, insofar as applicable, shall apply to any tax imposed by section 5701."

• **1976, Tax Reform Act of 1976 (P.L. 94-455)**

P.L. 94-455, §1905(a)(25)(B):

Struck out ", except that the taxes shall continue to be paid by stamp until the Secretary or his delegate provides, by regulations, for the payment of the taxes on the basis of a return" following "on the basis of a return" in the second sentence of Code Sec. 5703(b). **Effective** 2-1-77.

P.L. 94-455, §1906(b)(13)(A):

Amended 1954 Code by substituting "Secretary" for "Secretary or his delegate" each place it appeared. **Effective** 2-1-77.

[Sec. 5703(c)]

(c) USE OF GOVERNMENT DEPOSITARIES.—The Secretary may authorize Federal Reserve banks, and iancial agents of the United States, to receive any tax imposed by this chapter, in such manner, at such times, and under such con-ditions as he may prescribe; and he shall prescribe the manner, time, and condition under which the receipt of such tax by such banks and trust companies is to be treated as payment for tax purposes.

Amendments

• **1976, Tax Reform Act of 1976 (P.L. 94-455)**

P.L. 94-455, §1905(a)(25)(C):

Repealed former Code Sec. 5703(c) and redesignated former Code Sec. 5703(d) as Code Sec. 5703(c). **Effective** 2-1-77. Prior to repeal, Code Sec. 5703(c) read as follows:

(c) STAMPS TO EVIDENCE THE TAX.—If the Secretary or his delegate shall by regulation provide for the payment of tax by return and require the use of stamps to evidence the tax imposed by this chapter or to indicate compliance therewith, the Secretary or his delegate shall cause to be prepared suitable stamps to be issued to manufacturers and importers of tobacco products, to be used and accounted for, in accordance with such regulations as the Secretary or his delegate shall prescribe.

P.L. 94-455, §1906(b)(13)(A):

Amended 1954 Code by substituting "Secretary" for "Secretary or his delegate" each place it appeared. **Effective** 2-1-77.

[Sec. 5703(d)]

(d) ASSESSMENT.—Whenever any tax required to be paid by this chapter is not paid in full at the time required for such payment, it shall be the duty of the Secretary, subject to the limitations prescribed in section 6501, on proof satisfactory to him, to determine the amount of tax which has been omitted to be paid, and to make an assessment therefor against the person liable for the tax. The tax so assessed shall be in addition to the penalties imposed by law for failure to pay such tax when required. Except in cases where delay may jeopardize collection of the tax, or where the amount is nominal or the result of an evident mathematical error, no such assessment shall be made until and after the person liable for the tax has been afforded reasonable notice and opportunity to show cause, in writing, against such assessment.

Amendments

- **1976, Tax Reform Act of 1976 (P.L. 94-455)**

P.L. 94-455, § 1905(a)(25)(C):

Redesignated former Code Sec. 5703(e) as Code Sec. 5703(d). **Effective** 2-1-77.

P.L. 94-455, § 1906(b)(13)(A):

Amended 1954 Code by substituting "Secretary" for "Secretary or his delegate" each place it appeared. **Effective** 2-1-77.

- **1958, Excise Tax Technical Changes Act of 1958 (P.L. 85-859)**

P.L. 85-859, § 202:

Amended Code Sec. 5703 to read as prior to amendment by P.L. 94-455. **Effective** 9-3-58. Prior to amendment, Sec. 5703 read as follows:

SEC. 5703. LIABILITY FOR TAX AND METHOD OF PAYMENT.

(a) Persons Liable to Make Return and Pay Tax.—The taxes imposed by section 5701 shall be determined at the time of removal of the articles and shall be paid by the manufacturer or the importer thereof by return. The Secretary or his delegate shall, by regulation, prescribe the period for which the return shall be made, the information to be furnished on such return, the time for making such return, and the time for payment of such tax: *Provided, however,* That notwithstanding the provisions of this section the tax shall continue to be paid by stamp until the Secretary or his delegate shall, by regulation, provide for the payment of the tax by return. All administrative and penal provisions of this title, insofar as applicable, shall apply to any tax imposed by section 5701.

(b) Stamps to Evidence the Tax.—If the Secretary or his delegate shall, by regulation, require the use of stamps to evidence the tax or indicate compliance with this chapter, the Secretary or his delegate shall cause to be prepared suitable stamps to be issued to manufacturers and importers of articles, to be used and accounted for, in accordance with such regulations as the Secretary or his delegate shall prescribe.

(c) Use of Government Depositaries.—The Secretary or his delegate may authorize Federal Reserve banks, and incorporated banks or trust companies which are depositaries or financial agents of the United States, to receive any tax imposed by this chapter, in such manner, at such times, and under such conditions as he may prescribe; and he shall prescribe the manner, time, and condition under which the receipt of such tax by such banks and trust companies is to be treated as payment for tax purposes.

(d) Assessment.—Whenever any tax required to be paid by this chapter is not paid in full at the time required for such payment, it shall be the duty of the Secretary or his delegate, subject to the limitations prescribed in section 6501, on proof satisfactory to him, to determine the amount of tax which has been omitted to be paid, and to make an assessment therefor against the person liable for the tax. The tax so assessed shall be in addition to the penalties imposed by law for failure to pay such tax when required: *Provided, however,* That no such assessment shall be made until and after the person liable for the tax has been afforded reasonable notice and opportunity to show cause, in writing, against such assessment.

[Sec. 5704]

SEC. 5704. EXEMPTION FROM TAX.

[Sec. 5704(a)]

(a) TOBACCO PRODUCTS FURNISHED FOR EMPLOYEE USE OR EXPERIMENTAL PURPOSES.—Tobacco products may be furnished by a manufacturer of such products, without payment of tax, for use or consumption by employees or for experimental purposes, in such quantities, and in such manner as the Secretary shall by regulation prescribe.

Amendments

- **1976, Tax Reform Act of 1976 (P.L. 94-455)**

P.L. 94-455, § 1906(b)(13)(A):

Amended 1954 Code by substituting "Secretary" for "Secretary or his delegate" each place it appeared. **Effective** 2-1-77.

[Sec. 5704(b)]

(b) TOBACCO PRODUCTS AND CIGARETTE PAPERS AND TUBES TRANSFERRED OR REMOVED IN BOND FROM DOMESTIC FACTORIES AND EXPORT WAREHOUSES.—A manufacturer or export warehouse proprietor may transfer tobacco products and cigarette papers and tubes, without payment of tax, to the bonded premises of another manufacturer or export warehouse proprietor, or remove such articles, without payment of tax, for shipment to a foreign country, Puerto Rico, the Virgin Islands, or a possession of the United States, or for consumption beyond the jurisdiction of the internal revenue laws of the United States; and manufacturers may similarly remove such articles for use of the United States; in accordance with such regulations and under such bonds as the Secretary shall prescribe. Tobacco products and cigarette papers and tubes may not be transferred or removed under this subsection unless such products or papers and tubes bear such marks, labels, or notices as the Secretary shall by regulations prescribe.

Amendments

- **1997, Balanced Budget Act of 1997 (P.L. 105-33)**

P.L. 105-33, § 9302(h)(1)(A):

Amended Code Sec. 5704(b) by adding at the end a new sentence. **Effective,** generally, for articles removed (as defined in Code Sec. 5702(k)) after 12-31-99. For a transitional rule, see Act Sec. 9302(i)(2) in the amendment notes following Code Sec. 5701(a).

- **1976, Tax Reform Act of 1976 (P.L. 94-455)**

P.L. 94-455, § 1906(b)(13)(A):

Amended 1954 Code by substituting "Secretary" for "Secretary or his delegate" each place it appeared. **Effective** 2-1-77.

[Sec. 5704(c)]

(c) TOBACCO PRODUCTS AND CIGARETTE PAPERS AND TUBES RELEASED IN BOND FROM CUSTOMS CUSTODY.—Tobacco products and cigarette papers and tubes, imported or brought into the United States, may be released from customs custody, without payment of tax, for delivery to the proprietor of an export warehouse, or to a manufacturer of tobacco products or cigarette papers and tubes if such articles are not put up in packages, in accordance with such regulations and under such bond as the Secretary shall prescribe.

Amendments

- **1989, Omnibus Budget Reconciliation Act of 1989 (P.L. 101-239)**

P.L. 101-239, § 7508(a):

Amended Code Sec. 5704(c) by inserting "or to a manufacturer of tobacco products or cigarette papers and tubes if such articles are not put up in packages," after "export warehouse,". **Effective** for articles imported or brought into the United States after 12-19-89.

- **1986, Omnibus Budget Reconciliation Act of 1986 (P.L. 99-509)**

P.L. 99-509, § 8011(a)(2):

Amended Code Sec. 5704(c) by striking out "to a manufacturer of tobacco products or cigarette papers and tubes or". For the **effective** date, see Act Sec. 8011(c), below. Prior to amendment, Code Sec. 5704(c) read as follows:

(c) TOBACCO PRODUCTS AND CIGARETTE PAPERS AND TUBES RELEASED IN BOND FROM CUSTOMS CUSTODY.—Tobacco products and cigarette papers and tubes, imported or brought into the United States, may be released from customs custody, without payment of tax, for delivery to a manufacturer of tobacco products or cigarette papers and tubes or to the proprietor of an export warehouse, in accordance with such regulations and under such bond as the Secretary shall prescribe.

P.L. 99-509, § 8011(c), provides:

(c) EFFECTIVE DATES.—

(1) IN GENERAL.—Except as provided in paragraph (2), the amendments made by this section shall apply to removals during semimonthly periods ending on or after December 31, 1986.

(2) IMPORTED ARTICLES, ETC.—Subparagraphs (B) and (C) of section 5703(b)(2) of the Internal Revenue Code of 1954 (as added by this section), paragraphs (2) and (3) of section 5061(d) of such Code (as amended by this section), and the amendments made by subsections (a)(2) and (b)(2) shall apply to articles imported, entered for warehousing, or brought into the United States or a foreign trade zone after December 15, 1986.

(3) SPECIAL RULE FOR DISTILLED SPIRITS AND TOBACCO FOR SEMIMONTHLY PERIOD ENDING DECEMBER 15, 1986.—With respect to remittances of—

(A) taxes imposed on distilled spirits by section 5001 or 7652 of such Code, and

(B) taxes imposed on tobacco products and cigarette papers and tubes by section 5701 or 7652 of such Code,

for the semimonthly period ending December 15, 1986, the last day for payment of such remittances shall be January 14, 1987.

TOBACCO TAXES—REFUNDS

(4) TREATMENT OF SMOKELESS TOBACCO IN INVENTORY ON JUNE 30, 1986.—The tax imposed by section 5701(e) of the Internal Revenue Code of 1954 shall not apply to any smokeless tobacco which—

(A) on June 30, 1986, was in the inventory of the manufacturer or importer, and

(B) on such date was in a form ready for sale.

- **1976, Tax Reform Act of 1976 (P.L. 94-455)**

P.L. 94-455, §1905(a)(26):

Added "or to the proprietor of an export warehouse" following "to a manufacturer of tobacco products or cigarette papers and tubes" in Code Sec. 5704(c). **Effective** 2-1-77.

P.L. 94-455, §1906(b)(13)(A):

Amended 1954 Code by substituting "Secretary" for "Secretary or his delegate" each place it appeared. **Effective** 2-1-77.

- **1965, Excise Tax Reduction Act of 1965 (P.L. 89-44)**

P.L. 89-44, §502(b)(4):

Repealed former Code Sec. 5704(c), redesignated former Code Sec. 5704(d) as Code Sec. 5704(c), and amended Code Sec. 5704(c) (as redesignated). **Effective** for tax years beginning after 1-1-66. Prior to amendment, Code Sec. 5704(c) (as redesignated) read as follows:

(d) TOBACCO PRODUCTS, CIGARETTE PAPERS AND TUBES, AND TOBACCO MATERIALS RELEASED IN BOND FROM CUSTOMS CUSTODY.—Tobacco products, cigarette papers and tubes, and tobacco materials, imported or brought into the United States, may be released from customs custody, without payment of tax, for delivery to a manufacturer of tobacco products or cigarette papers and tubes and such tobacco materials may be similarly released for delivery to a dealer in tobacco materials, in accordance with such regulations and under such bond as the Secretary or his delegate shall prescribe.

Prior to repeal, Code Sec. 5704(c) read as follows:

(c) TOBACCO MATERIALS SHIPPED OR DELIVERED IN BOND.—A dealer in tobacco materials or a manufacturer of tobacco products may ship or deliver tobacco materials, without payment of tax, to another such dealer or manufacturer, or to a foreign country, Puerto Rico, the Virgin Islands, or a possession of the United States; or, in the case of tobacco stems and waste only, to any person for use by him as fertilizer or insecticide or in the production of fertilizer, insecticide, or nicotine; in accordance with such regulations and under such bonds as the Secretary or his delegate shall prescribe.

[Sec. 5704(d)]

(d) TOBACCO PRODUCTS AND CIGARETTE PAPERS AND TUBES EXPORTED AND RETURNED.—Tobacco products and cigarette papers and tubes classifiable under item 804.00 of title I of the Tariff Act of 1930 (relating to duty on certain articles previously exported and returned) may be released from customs custody, without payment of that part of the duty attributable to the internal revenue tax for delivery to the original manufacturer of such tobacco products or cigarette papers and tubes or to the proprietor of an export warehouse authorized by such manufacturer to receive such articles, in accordance with such regulations and under such bond as the Secretary shall prescribe. Upon such release such products, papers, and tubes shall be subject to this chapter as if they had not been exported or otherwise removed from internal-revenue bond.

Amendments

- **2000, Imported Cigarette Compliance Act of 2000 (P.L. 106-476)**

P.L. 106-476, §4002(b)(1)-(2):

Amended Code Sec. 5704(d) by striking "a manufacturer of" and inserting "the original manufacturer of such", and by inserting "authorized by such manufacturer to receive such articles" after "proprietor of an export warehouse". **Effective** 2-7-2001.

- **1976, Tax Reform Act of 1976 (P.L. 94-455)**

P.L. 94-455, §1905(a)(26):

Added "or to the proprietor of an export warehouse" following "to a manufacturer of tobacco products or cigarette papers and tubes" in Code Sec. 5704(d). **Effective** 2-1-77.

P.L. 94-455, §1906(b)(13)(A):

Amended 1954 Code by substituting "Secretary" for "Secretary or his delegate" each place it appeared. **Effective** 2-1-77.

- **1965, Excise Tax Reduction Act of 1965 (P.L. 89-44)**

P.L. 89-44, §502(b)(4):

Redesignated former Code Sec. 5704(e) as Code Sec. 5704(d). **Effective** for tax years beginning after 1-1-66.

- **1964 (P.L. 88-342)**

P.L. 88-342, §[1(b)]:

Added Code Sec. 5704(e). **Effective** with respect to articles entered, or withdrawn from warehouse, for consumption after 6-30-64.

- **1958, Excise Tax Technical Changes Act of 1958 (P.L. 85-859)**

P.L. 85-859, §202:

Amended Code Sec. 5704. **Effective** 9-3-58. Prior to amendment, Code Sec. 5704 read as follows:

SEC. 5704. EXEMPTION FROM TAX.

(a) Tobacco Products Furnished for Employee Use or Experimental Purposes.—Tobacco products may be furnished by a manufacturer of such products, without payment of tax, for use or consumption by employees or for experimental purposes, in such quantities, and in such manner as the Secretary or his delegate shall, by regulation, prescribe.

(b) Articles Transferred or Removed in Bond From Domestic Factories.—A manufacturer may transfer articles produced by him, without payment of tax, to the bonded premises of another manufacturer, or remove such articles, without payment of tax, for use of the United States, or for shipment to a foreign country, Puerto Rico, the Virgin Islands, or a possession of the United States, or for consumption beyond the jurisdiction of the internal revenue laws of the United States, or for consumption beyond the jurisdiction of the internal revenue laws of the United States, in accordance with such regulations and upon the filing of such bonds as the Secretary or his delegate shall prescribe.

(c) Tobacco Materials Shipped or Delivered in Bond.—A dealer in tobacco materials or a manufacturer of tobacco products may ship or deliver tobacco materials, without payment of tax, to another such dealer or manufacturer, or to a foreign country, Puerto Rico, the Virgin Islands, or a possession of the United States, in accordance with such regulations and upon the filing of such bonds as the Secretary or his delegate shall prescribe.

(d) Articles and Tobacco Materials Released in Bond From Customs Custody.—Articles and tobacco materials imported or brought into the United States may be released from customs custody, without payment of tax, for delivery to the bonded premises of a manufacturer of articles and such tobacco materials may be similarly released for delivery to the bonded premises of a dealer in tobacco materials, in accordance with such regulations and upon the filing of such bond as the Secretary or his delegate shall prescribe.

[Sec. 5705]

SEC. 5705. CREDIT, REFUND, OR ALLOWANCE OF TAX.

[Sec. 5705(a)]

(a) CREDIT OR REFUND.—Credit or refund of any tax imposed by this chapter or section 7652 shall be allowed or made (without interest) to the manufacturer, importer, or export warehouse proprietor, on proof satisfactory to the Secretary that the claimant manufacturer, importer, or export warehouse proprietor has paid the tax on tobacco products and cigarette papers and tubes withdrawn by him from the market; or on such articles lost (otherwise than by theft) or destroyed, by fire, casualty, or act of God, while in the possession or ownership of the claimant.

[Sec. 5705(b)]

(b) ALLOWANCE.—If the tax has not yet been paid on tobacco products and cigarette papers and tubes proved to have been withdrawn from the market or lost or destroyed as aforesaid, relief from the tax on such articles may be extended upon the filing of a claim for allowance therefor in accordance with such regulations as the Secretary shall prescribe.

[Sec. 5705(c)]

(c) LIMITATION.—Any claim for credit or refund of tax under this section shall be filed within 6 months after the date of the withdrawal from the market, loss, or destruction of the articles to which the claim relates, and shall be in such form and contain such information as the Secretary shall by regulations prescribe.

Amendments

- **1976, Tax Reform Act of 1976 (P.L. 94-455)**

P.L. 94-455, §1906(b)(13)(A):

Amended 1954 Code by substituting "Secretary" for "Secretary or his delegate" each place it appeared. **Effective** 2-1-77.

- **1965, Excise Tax Reduction Act of 1965 (P.L. 89-44)**

P.L. 89-44, §808(b)(1):

Amended Code Sec. 5705(a). **Effective** on 10-1-65. Prior to amendment, Code Sec. 5705(a) read as follows:

TOBACCO TAXES—DISASTER

"(a) Refund.—Refund of any tax imposed by this chapter shall be made (without interest) to the manufacturer, importer, or export warehouse proprietor, on proof satisfactory to the Secretary or his delegate that the claimant manufacturer, importer, or export warehouse proprietor has paid the tax on tobacco products and cigarette papers and tubes withdrawn by him from the market; or on such articles lost (otherwise than by theft) or destroyed, by fire, casualty, or act of God, while in the possession or ownership of the claimant."

P.L. 89-44, §808(b)(2):

Amended Code Sec. 5075(c). **Effective** on 10-1-65. Prior to amendment, Code Sec. 5705(c) read as follows:

(c) Limitation.—Any claim for refund of tax under this section shall be filed within 6 months after the date of the withdrawal from the market, loss, or destruction of the articles to which the claim relates, and shall be in such form and contain such information as the Secretary or his delegate shall by regulations prescribe.

P.L. 89-44, §808(c)(1):

Amended the heading of Code Sec. 5705. Prior to amendment, the heading read: "Refund or Allowance of Tax."

- **1958, Excise Tax Technical Changes Act of 1958 (P.L. 85-859)**

P.L. 85-859, §202:

Amended Sec. 5705. **Effective** 9-3-58. Prior to amendment, Sec. 5705 read as follows:

SEC. 5705. REFUND OR ALLOWANCE OF TAX.

(a) Refund.—Refund of any tax imposed by this chapter shall be made to the manufacturer or importer on proof satisfactory to the Secretary or his delegate that the claimant manufacturer or importer has paid the tax on articles withdrawn by him from the market; or on articles which are lost (otherwise than by theft) or destroyed, by fire, casualty, or act of God, while in the possession or ownership of the claimant; or where the tax has been paid in error.

(b) Allowance.—If the tax has not yet been paid on articles proved to have been lost or destroyed as aforesaid, relief from the tax on such articles may be extended upon the filing, with the return, of a claim for allowance of loss in the same manner as a claim for refund.

(c) Limitation.—Claims for refund of tax imposed by this chapter shall be filed within 3 years of the date of payment of tax, and shall be in such form and contain such information as the Secretary or his delegate shall by regulation prescribe.

[Sec. 5706]

SEC. 5706. DRAWBACK OF TAX.

There shall be an allowance of drawback of tax paid on tobacco products and cigarette papers and tubes, when shipped from the United States, in accordance with such regulations and upon the filing of such bond as the Secretary shall prescribe.

Amendments

- **1976, Tax Reform Act of 1976 (P.L. 94-455)**

P.L. 94-455, §1906(b)(13)(A):

Amended 1954 Code by substituting "Secretary" for "Secretary or his delegate" each place it appeared. **Effective** 2-1-77.

- **1958, Excise Tax Technical Changes Act of 1958 (P.L. 85-859)**

P.L. 85-859, §202:

Amended Code Sec. 5706 by striking out the word "articles" and substituting the phrase "tobacco products and cigarette papers and tubes". **Effective** 9-3-58.

[Sec. 5708]

SEC. 5708. LOSSES CAUSED BY DISASTER.

[Sec. 5708(a)]

(a) AUTHORIZATION.—Where the President has determined under the Robert T. Stafford Disaster Relief and Emergency Assistance Act, that a "major disaster" as defined in such Act has occurred in any part of the United States, the Secretary shall pay (without interest) an amount equal to the amount of the internal revenue taxes paid or determined and customs duties paid on tobacco products and cigarette papers and tubes removed, which were lost, rendered unmarketable, or condemned by a duly authorized official by reason of such disaster occurring in such part of the United States on and after the effective date of this section, if such tobacco products or cigarette papers or tubes were held and intended for sale at the time of such disaster. The payments authorized by this section shall be made to the person holding such tobacco products or cigarette papers or tubes for sale at the time of such disaster.

Amendments

- **2004, Working Families Tax Relief Act of 2004 (P.L. 108-311)**

P.L. 108-311, §408(a)(7)(E):

Amended Code Sec. 5708(a) by inserting "Robert T. Stafford" before "Disaster Relief and Emergency Assistance Act". **Effective** 10-4-2004.

- **1988, Disaster Relief and Emergency Assistance Amendments of 1988 (P.L. 100-707)**

P.L. 100-707, §109(l):

Amended Code Sec. 5708(a) by striking out "Act of 1974" and inserting in lieu thereof "and Emergency Assistance Act". **Effective** 11-23-88.

- **1976, Tax Reform Act of 1976 (P.L. 94-455)**

P.L. 94-455, §1906(b)(13)(A):

Amended 1954 Code by substituting "Secretary" for "Secretary or his delegate" each place it appeared. **Effective** 2-1-77.

- **1974, Disaster Relief Act of 1974 (P.L. 93-288)**

P.L. 93-288, §602(j):

Substituted "Disaster Relief Act of 1974" for "Disaster Relief Act of 1970" in Code Sec. 5708(a). **Effective** 4-1-73.

- **1970, Disaster Relief Act of 1970 (P.L. 91-606)**

P.L. 91-606, §301(j):

Substituted "Disaster Relief Act of 1970" for "Act of September 30, 1950 (42 U.S.C., sec. 1855)" in Code Sec. 5708(a). **Effective** 12-31-70.

[Sec. 5708(b)]

(b) CLAIMS.—No claim shall be allowed under this section unless—

(1) filed within 6 months after the date on which the President makes the determination that the disaster referred to in subsection (a) has occurred; and

(2) the claimant furnishes proof to the satisfaction of the Secretary that—

(A) he was not indemnified by any valid claim of insurance or otherwise in respect of the tax, or tax and duty, on the tobacco products or cigarette papers or tubes covered by the claim, and

(B) he is entitled to payment under this section.

Claims under this section shall be filed under such regulations as the Secretary shall prescribe.

Amendments

- **1976, Tax Reform Act of 1976 (P.L. 94-455)**

P.L. 94-455, §1906(b)(13)(A):

Amended 1954 Code by substituting "Secretary" for "Secretary or his delegate" each place it appeared. **Effective** 2-1-77.

[Sec. 5708(c)]

(c) DESTRUCTION OF TOBACCO PRODUCTS OR CIGARETTE PAPERS OR TUBES.—Before the Secretary makes payment under this section in respect of the tax, or tax and duty, on the tobacco products or cigarette papers or tubes condemned by a duly authorized official or rendered unmarketable, such tobacco products or cigarette papers or tubes shall be destroyed under such supervision as the Secretary may prescribe, unless such tobacco products or cigarette papers or tubes were previously destroyed under supervision satisfactory to the Secretary.

Internal Revenue Code

TOBACCO TAXES—BOND

Amendments

• **1976, Tax Reform Act of 1976 (P.L. 94-455)**

P.L. 94-455, § 1906(b)(13)(A):

Amended 1954 Code by substituting "Secretary" for "Secretary or his delegate" each place it appeared. **Effective** 2-1-77.

[Sec. 5708(d)]

(d) OTHER LAWS APPLICABLE.—All provisions of law, including penalties, applicable in respect of internal revenue taxes on tobacco products and cigarette papers and tubes shall, insofar as applicable and not inconsistent with this section, be applied in respect of the payments provided for in this section to the same extent as if such payments constituted refunds of such taxes.

Amendments

• **1958, Excise Tax Technical Changes Act of 1958 (P.L. 85-859)**

P.L. 85-859, § 202:

Added new Sec. 5708. **Effective** 9-3-58.

Subchapter B—Qualification Requirements for Manufacturers and Importers of Tobacco Products and Cigarette Papers and Tubes, and Export Warehouse Proprietors

Sec. 5711. Bond.
Sec. 5712. Application for permit.
Sec. 5713. Permit.

[Sec. 5711]

SEC. 5711. BOND.

[Sec. 5711(a)]

(a) WHEN REQUIRED.—Every person, before commencing business as a manufacturer of tobacco products or cigarette papers and tubes, or as an export warehouse proprietor shall file such bond, conditioned upon compliance with this chapter and regulations issued thereunder, in such form, amount, and manner as the Secretary shall by regulation prescribe. A new or additional bond may be required whenever the Secretary considers such action necessary for the protection of the revenue.

Amendments

• **1976, Tax Reform Act of 1976 (P.L. 94-455)**

P.L. 94-455, § 1906(b)(13)(A):

Amended 1954 Code by substituting "Secretary" for "Secretary or his delegate" each place it appeared. **Effective** 2-1-77.

• **1965, Excise Tax Reduction Act of 1965 (P.L. 89-44)**

P.L. 89-44, § 502(b)(6):

Amended the first sentence of Code Sec. 5711(a). **Effective** for tax years beginning after 1-1-66. Prior to amendment, the first sentence of Code Sec. 5711(a) read as follows: "Every person, before commencing business as a manufacturer of tobacco products or cigarette papers and tubes, as an export warehouse proprietor, or as a dealer in tobacco materials, shall file such bond, conditioned upon compliance with this chapter and regulations issued thereunder, in such form, amount, and manner as the Secretary or his delegate shall by regulation prescribe."

• **1958, Excise Tax Technical Changes Act of 1958 (P.L. 85-859)**

P.L. 85-859, § 202:

Amended Sec. 5711(a). **Effective** 9-3-58. Prior to amendment, Sec. 5711(a) read as follows:

SEC. 5711. BOND.

(a) When Required.—Every person, before commencing business as a manufacturer of articles or dealer in tobacco materials, shall file such bond, conditioned upon compliance with this chapter and regulations issued thereunder, in such form, amount, and manner as the Secretary or his delegate shall by regulation prescribe. A new or additional bond may be required whenever the Secretary or his delegate considers such action necessary for the protection of the revenue.

[Sec. 5711(b)]

(b) APPROVAL OR DISAPPROVAL.—No person shall engage in such business until he receives notice of approval of such bond. A bond may be disapproved, upon notice to the principal on the bond, if the Secretary determines that the bond is not adequate to protect the revenue.

Amendments

• **1976, Tax Reform Act of 1976 (P.L. 94-455)**

P.L. 94-455, § 1906(b)(13)(A):

Amended 1954 Code by substituting "Secretary" for "Secretary or his delegate" each place it appeared. **Effective** 2-1-77.

[Sec. 5711(c)]

(c) CANCELLATION.—Any bond filed hereunder may be canceled, upon notice to the principal on the bond, whenever the Secretary determines that the bond no longer adequately protects the revenue.

Amendments

• **1976, Tax Reform Act of 1976 (P.L. 94-455)**

P.L. 94-455, § 1906(b)(13)(A):

Amended 1954 Code by substituting "Secretary" for "Secretary or his delegate" each place it appeared. **Effective** 2-1-77.

[Sec. 5712]

SEC. 5712. APPLICATION FOR PERMIT.

Every person, before commencing business as a manufacturer or importer of tobacco products or processed tobacco or as an export warehouse proprietor, and at such other time as the Secretary shall by regulation prescribe, shall make application for the permit provided for in section 5713. The application shall be in such form as the Secretary shall prescribe and shall set forth, truthfully and accurately, the information called for on the form. Such application may be rejected and the permit denied if the Secretary, after notice and opportunity for hearing, finds that—

(1) the premises on which it is proposed to conduct the business are not adequate to protect the revenue;

(2) the activity proposed to be carried out at such premises does not meet such minimum capacity or activity requirements as the Secretary may prescribe, or

(3) such person (including, in the case of a corporation, any officer, director, or principal stockholder and, in the case of a partnership, a partner)—

(A) is, by reason of his business experience, financial standing, or trade connections or by reason of previous or current legal proceedings involving a felony violation of any other provision of Federal criminal law relating to tobacco products, processed tobacco, cigarette paper, or cigarette tubes, not likely to maintain operations in compliance with this chapter,

TOBACCO TAXES—PERMIT

(B) has been convicted of a felony violation of any provision of Federal or State criminal law relating to tobacco products, processed tobacco, cigarette paper, or cigarette tubes, or

(C) has failed to disclose any material information required or made any material false statement in the application therefor.

Amendments

• **2009, Children's Health Insurance Program Reauthorization Act of 2009 (P.L. 111-3)**

P.L. 111-3, §702(a)(1)(A):

Amended Code Sec. 5712 by inserting "or processed tobacco" after "tobacco products". **Effective** 4-1-2009. For a transitional rule, see Act Sec. 702(g), below.

P.L. 111-3, §702(b)(1):

Amended Code Sec. 5712(3). **Effective** 2-4-2009. For a transitional rule, see Act Sec. 702(g), below. Prior to amendment, Code Sec. 5712(3) read as follows:

(3) such person (including, in the case of a corporation, any officer, director, or principal stockholder and, in the case of a partnership, a partner) is, by reason of his business experience, financial standing, or trade connections, not likely to maintain operations in compliance with this chapter, or has failed to disclose any material information required or made any material false statement in the application therefor.

P.L. 111-3, §702(g), provides:

(g) TRANSITIONAL RULE.—Any person who—

(1) on April 1, 2009 is engaged in business as a manufacturer of processed tobacco or as an importer of processed tobacco, and

(2) before the end of the 90-day period beginning on such date, submits an application under subchapter B of chapter 52 of such Code to engage in such business, may, notwithstanding such subchapter B, continue to engage in such business pending final action on such application. Pending such final action, all provisions of such chapter 52 shall apply to such applicant in the same manner and to the same extent as if such applicant were a holder of a permit under such chapter 52 to engage in such business.

• **1997, Balanced Budget Act of 1997 (P.L. 105-33)**

P.L. 105-33, §9302(h)(2)(A):

Amended Code Sec. 5712 by inserting "or importer" after "manufacturer". **Effective**, generally, for articles removed (as defined in Code Sec. 5702(k)) after 12-31-99. For a transitional rule, see Act Sec. 9302(i)(2) in the amendment notes following Code Sec. 5701(a).

P.L. 105-33, §9302(h)(5):

Amended Code Sec. 5712 by striking "or" at the end of paragraph (1), by redesignating paragraph (2) as paragraph (3), and by inserting after paragraph (1) a new paragraph (2). **Effective**, generally, for articles removed (as defined in Code Sec. 5702(k)) after 12-31-99. For a transitional rule, see Act Sec. 9302(i)(2) in the amendment notes following Code Sec. 5701(a).

• **1976, Tax Reform Act of 1976 (P.L. 94-455)**

P.L. 94-455, §1905(a)(27):

Struck the last sentence of Code Sec. 5712. **Effective** 2-1-77. Prior to being stricken, the last sentence of Code Sec. 5712 read as follows:

No person subject to this section, who is lawfully engaged in business on the date of the enactment of the Excise Tax Technical Changes Act of 1958, shall be denied the right to carry on such business pending reasonable opportunity to make application for permit and final action thereon.

P.L. 94-455, §1906(b)(13)(A):

Amended 1954 Code by substituting "Secretary" for "Secretary or his delegate" each place it appeared. **Effective** 2-1-77.

• **1958, Excise Tax Technical Changes Act of 1958 (P.L. 85-859)**

P.L. 85-859, §202:

Amended Code Sec. 5712 by striking out, in the first sentence, "articles or dealer in tobacco materials," and substituting "tobacco products or as an export warehouse proprietor," and by amending the last sentence. **Effective** 9-3-58. Prior to amendment, the last sentence of Sec. 5712 read as follows:

"No person subject to this section, who is engaged in business on the effective date of this chapter, shall be denied the right to carry on such business pending reasonable opportunity to make application for permit and final action thereon."

[Sec. 5713]

SEC. 5713. PERMIT.

[Sec. 5713(a)]

(a) ISSUANCE.—A person shall not engage in business as a manufacturer or importer of tobacco products or processed tobacco or as an export warehouse proprietor without a permit to engage in such business. Such permit, conditioned upon compliance with this chapter and regulations issued thereunder, shall be issued in such form and in such manner as the Secretary shall by regulation prescribe, to every person properly qualified under sections 5711 and 5712. A new permit may be required at such other time as the Secretary shall by regulation prescribe.

Amendments

• **2009, Children's Health Insurance Program Reauthorization Act of 2009 (P.L. 111-3)**

P.L. 111-3, §702(a)(1)(B):

Amended Code Sec. 5713(a) by inserting "or processed tobacco" after "tobacco products". **Effective** 4-1-2009. For a transitional rule, see Act Sec. 702(g), below.

P.L. 111-3, §702(g), provides:

(g) TRANSITIONAL RULE.—Any person who—

(1) on April 1, 2009 is engaged in business as a manufacturer of processed tobacco or as an importer of processed tobacco, and

(2) before the end of the 90-day period beginning on such date, submits an application under subchapter B of chapter 52 of such Code to engage in such business, may, notwithstanding such subchapter B, continue to engage in such business pending final action on such application. Pending such final action, all provisions of such chapter 52 shall apply to such applicant in the same manner and to the same extent as if such applicant were a holder of a permit under such chapter 52 to engage in such business.

• **1997, Balanced Budget Act of 1997 (P.L. 105-33)**

P.L. 105-33, §9302(h)(2)(A):

Amended Code Sec. 5713(a) by inserting "or importer" after "manufacturer". **Effective**, generally, for articles removed (as defined in Code Sec. 5702(k)) after 12-31-99. For a transitional rule, see Act Sec. 9302(i)(2) in the amendment notes following Code Sec. 5701(a).

• **1976, Tax Reform Act of 1976 (P.L. 94-455)**

P.L. 94-455, §1906(b)(13)(A):

Amended 1954 Code by substituting "Secretary" for "Secretary or his delegate" each place it appeared. **Effective** 2-1-77.

• **1958, Excise Tax Technical Changes Act of 1958 (P.L. 85-859)**

P.L. 85-859, §202:

Amended Code Sec. 5713(a) by striking out "articles or dealer in tobacco materials" and substituting "tobacco products or as an export warehouse proprietor", and by striking out "or permits" where it preceded the phrase "to engage in such business."

[Sec. 5713(b)]

(b) SUSPENSION OR REVOCATION.—

(1) SHOW CAUSE HEARING.—If the Secretary has reason to believe that any person holding a permit—

(A) has not in good faith complied with this chapter, or with any other provision of this title involving intent to defraud,

(B) has violated the conditions of such permit,

(C) has failed to disclose any material information required or made any material false statement in the application for such permit,

(D) has failed to maintain his premises in such manner as to protect the revenue,

(E) is, by reason of previous or current legal proceedings involving a felony violation of any other provision of Federal criminal law relating to tobacco products, processed tobacco, cigarette paper, or cigarette tubes, not likely to maintain operations in compliance with this chapter, or

(F) has been convicted of a felony violation of any provision of Federal or State criminal law relating to tobacco products, processed tobacco, cigarette paper, or cigarette tubes,

the Secretary shall issue an order, stating the facts charged, citing such person to show cause why his permit should not be suspended or revoked.

(2) ACTION FOLLOWING HEARING.—If, after hearing, the Secretary finds that such person has not shown cause why his permit should not be suspended or revoked, such permit shall be suspended for such period as the Secretary deems proper or shall be revoked.

TOBACCO TAXES—INVENTORIES

Amendments

• **2009, Children's Health Insurance Program Reauthorization Act of 2009 (P.L. 111-3)**

P.L. 111-3, §702(b)(2):

Amended Code Sec. 5713(b). **Effective** 2-4-2009. For a transitional rule, see Act Sec. 702(g), below. Prior to amendment, Code Sec. 5713(b) read as follows:

(b) REVOCATION.—If the Secretary has reason to believe that any person holding a permit has not in good faith complied with this chapter, or with any other provision of this title involving intent to defraud, or has violated the conditions of such permit, or has failed to disclose any material information required or made any material false statement in the application for such permit, or has failed to maintain his premises in such manner as to protect the revenue, the Secretary shall issue an order, stating the facts charged, citing such person to show cause why his permit should not be suspended or revoked. If, after hearing, the Secretary finds that such person has not in good faith complied with this chapter or with any other provision of this title involving intent to defraud, has violated the conditions of such permit, has failed to disclose any material information required or made any material false statement in the application therefor, or has failed to maintain his premises in such manner as to protect the revenue, such permit shall be suspended for such period as the Secretary deems proper or shall be revoked.

P.L. 111-3, §702(g), provides:

(g) TRANSITIONAL RULE.—Any person who—

(1) on April 1, 2009 is engaged in business as a manufacturer of processed tobacco or as an importer of processed tobacco, and

(2) before the end of the 90-day period beginning on such date, submits an application under subchapter B of chapter 52 of such Code to engage in such business, may, notwithstanding such subchapter B, continue to engage in such business pending final action on such application. Pending such final action, all provisions of such chapter 52 shall apply to such applicant in the same manner and to the same extent as if such applicant were a holder of a permit under such chapter 52 to engage in such business.

• **1976, Tax Reform Act of 1976 (P.L. 94-455)**

P.L. 94-455, §1906(b)(13)(A):

Amended 1954 Code by substituting "Secretary" for "Secretary or his delegate" each place it appeared. **Effective** 2-1-77.

• **1958, Excise Tax Technical Changes Act of 1958 (P.L. 85-859)**

P.L. 85-859, §202:

Deleted subsection (b) and redesignated subsection (c) as subsection (b) with amendments and deleted subsection (d). **Effective** 9-3-58. Prior to deletion, old subsections (b)-(d) read as follows:

(b) Posting.—Such permit shall be posted in accordance with such regulations as the Secretary or his delegate shall prescribe.

(c) Revocation.—If the Secretary or his delegate has reason to believe that any person holding a permit has not in good faith complied with this chapter, or with any other provision of this title involving intent to defraud, or has violated the conditions of such permit, failed to disclose any material information required or made any material false statement in the application for such a permit, or has failed to maintain his premises in such manner as to protect the revenue, the Secretary or his delegate shall issue an order, stating the facts charged, citing such person to show cause why his permit should not be suspended or revoked. If, after hearing, the Secretary or his delegate finds that such person has not in good faith complied with this chapter, or with other provisions of this title involving intent to defraud, or has violated the conditions of such permit, failed to disclose any material information required or made any material false statement in the application therefor, or has failed to maintain his premises in such manner as to protect the revenue, such permit shall be revoked or suspended for such period as to the Secretary or his delegate may seem proper.

* * *

(d) Limitation.—No permit shall be issued to any person within 1 year after revocation of an existing permit or after rejection of an application.

Subchapter C—Operations by Manufacturers and Importers of Tobacco Products and Cigarette Papers and Tubes and Export Warehouse Proprietors

Sec. 5721.   Inventories.
Sec. 5722.   Reports.
Sec. 5723.   Packages, marks, labels, and notices.

[Sec. 5721]

SEC. 5721. INVENTORIES.

Every manufacturer or importer of tobacco products, processed tobacco, or cigarette papers and tubes, and every export warehouse proprietor, shall make a true and accurate inventory at the time of commencing business, at the time of concluding business, and at such other times, in such manner and form, and to include such items, as the Secretary shall by regulation prescribe. Such inventories shall be subject to verification by any revenue officer.

Amendments

• **2009, Children's Health Insurance Program Reauthorization Act of 2009 (P.L. 111-3)**

P.L. 111-3, §702(a)(2)(A):

Amended Code Sec. 5721 by inserting ", processed tobacco," after "tobacco products". **Effective** 4-1-2009.

• **1997, Balanced Budget Act of 1997 (P.L. 105-33)**

P.L. 105-33, §9302(h)(2)(A):

Amended Code Sec. 5721 by inserting "or importer" after "manufacturer". **Effective**, generally, for articles removed (as defined in Code Sec. 5702(k)) after 12-31-99. For a transitional rule, see Act Sec. 9302(i)(2) in the amendment notes following Code Sec. 5701(a).

• **1976, Tax Reform Act of 1976 (P.L. 94-455)**

P.L. 94-455, §1906(b)(13)(A):

Amended 1954 Code by substituting "Secretary" for "Secretary or his delegate" each place it appeared. **Effective** 2-1-77.

• **1958, Excise Tax Technical Changes Act of 1958 (P.L. 85-859)**

P.L. 85-859, §202:

Amended Sec. 5721 by striking out "articles" and substituting "tobacco products or cigarette papers and tubes, and every export warehouse proprietor,". **Effective** 9-3-58.

[Sec. 5722]

SEC. 5722. REPORTS.

Every manufacturer or importer of tobacco products, processed tobacco, or cigarette papers and tubes, and every export warehouse proprietor, shall make reports containing such information, in such form, at such times, and for such periods as the Secretary shall by regulation prescribe.

Amendments

• **2009, Children's Health Insurance Program Reauthorization Act of 2009 (P.L. 111-3)**

P.L. 111-3, §702(a)(2)(B):

Amended Code Sec. 5722 by inserting ", processed tobacco," after "tobacco products". **Effective** 4-1-2009.

• **1997, Balanced Budget Act of 1997 (P.L. 105-33)**

P.L. 105-33, §9302(h)(2)(A):

Amended Code Sec. 5722 by inserting "or importer" after "manufacturer". **Effective**, generally, for articles removed (as defined in Code Sec. 5702(k)) after 12-31-99. For a transitional rule, see Act Sec. 9302(i)(2) in the amendment notes following Code Sec. 5701(a).

• **1976, Tax Reform Act of 1976 (P.L. 94-455)**

P.L. 94-455, §1906(b)(13)(A):

Amended 1954 Code by substituting "Secretary" for "Secretary or his delegate" each place it appeared. **Effective** 2-1-77.

• **1958, Excise Tax Technical Changes Act of 1958 (P.L. 85-859)**

P.L. 85-859, §202:

Amended Sec. 5722 by striking out "articles" and substituting "tobacco products or cigarette papers and tubes, and every export warehouse proprietor,". **Effective** 9-3-58.

[Sec. 5723]

SEC. 5723. PACKAGES, MARKS, LABELS, AND NOTICES.

[Sec. 5723(a)]

(a) PACKAGES.—All tobacco products, processed tobacco, and cigarette papers and tubes shall, before removal, be put up in such packages as the Secretary shall by regulation prescribe.

TOBACCO TAXES—OCCUPATIONAL TAX

Amendments

• **2009, Children's Health Insurance Program Reauthorization Act of 2009 (P.L. 111-3)**

P.L. 111-3, §702(a)(2)(C):

Amended Code Sec. 5723 by inserting ", processed tobacco," after "tobacco products" each place it appears. **Effective** 4-1-2009.

• **1976, Tax Reform Act of 1976 (P.L. 94-455)**

P.L. 94-455, §1905(a)(28)(A):

Amended the heading of Code Sec. 5723 by substituting "AND NOTICES" for "NOTICES AND STAMPS". **Effective** 2-1-77.

P.L. 94-455, §1906(b)(13)(A):

Amended 1954 Code by substituting "Secretary" for "Secretary or his delegate" each place it appeared. **Effective** 2-1-77.

[Sec. 5723(b)]

(b) MARKS, LABELS, AND NOTICES.—Every package of tobacco products, processed tobacco, or cigarette papers or tubes shall, before removal, bear the marks, labels, and notices, if any, that the Secretary by regulation prescribes.

Amendments

• **2009, Children's Health Insurance Program Reauthorization Act of 2009 (P.L. 111-3)**

P.L. 111-3, §702(a)(2)(C):

Amended Code Sec. 5723 by inserting ", processed tobacco," after "tobacco products" each place it appears. **Effective** 4-1-2009.

• **1976, Tax Reform Act of 1976 (P.L. 94-455)**

P.L. 94-455, §1905(a)(28)(B):

Amended Code Sec. 5723(b). **Effective** 2-1-77. Prior to amendment, Code Sec. 5723(b) read as follows:

(b) MARKS, LABELS, NOTICES, AND STAMPS.—Every package of tobacco products or cigarette papers or tubes shall, before removal, bear the marks, labels, notices, and stamps, if any, that the Secretary or his delegate by regulation prescribes.

[Sec. 5723(c)]

(c) LOTTERY FEATURES.—No certificate, coupon, or other device purporting to be or to represent a ticket, chance, share, or an interest in, or dependent on, the event of a lottery shall be contained in, attached to, or stamped, marked, written, or printed on any package of tobacco products, processed tobacco, or cigarette papers or tubes.

Amendments

• **2009, Children's Health Insurance Program Reauthorization Act of 2009 (P.L. 111-3)**

P.L. 111-3, §702(a)(2)(C):

Amended Code Sec. 5723 by inserting ", processed tobacco," after "tobacco products" each place it appears. **Effective** 4-1-2009.

[Sec. 5723(d)]

(d) INDECENT OR IMMORAL MATERIAL PROHIBITED.—No indecent or immoral picture, print, or representation shall be contained in, attached to, or stamped, marked, written, or printed on any package of tobacco products, processed tobacco, or cigarette papers or tubes.

Amendments

• **2009, Children's Health Insurance Program Reauthorization Act of 2009 (P.L. 111-3)**

P.L. 111-3, §702(a)(2)(C):

Amended Code Sec. 5723 by inserting ", processed tobacco," after "tobacco products" each place it appears. **Effective** 4-1-2009.

[Sec. 5723(e)]

(e) EXCEPTIONS.—Tobacco products furnished by manufacturers of such products for use or consumption by their employees, or for experimental purposes, and tobacco products, processed tobacco, and cigarette papers and tubes transferred to the bonded premises of another manufacturer or export warehouse proprietor or released in bond from customs custody for delivery to a manufacturer of tobacco products, processed tobacco, or cigarette papers and tubes, may be exempted from subsections (a) and (b) in accordance with such regulations as the Secretary shall prescribe.

Amendments

• **2009, Children's Health Insurance Program Reauthorization Act of 2009 (P.L. 111-3)**

P.L. 111-3, §702(a)(2)(C):

Amended Code Sec. 5723 by inserting ", processed tobacco," after "tobacco products" each place it appears. **Effective** 4-1-2009.

• **1976, Tax Reform Act of 1976 (P.L. 94-455)**

P.L. 94-455, §1906(b)(13)(A):

Amended 1954 Code by substituting "Secretary" for "Secretary or his delegate" each place it appeared. **Effective** 2-1-77.

• **1958, Excise Tax Technical Changes Act of 1958 (P.L. 85-859)**

P.L. 85-859, §202:

Amended Code Sec. 5723. **Effective** 9-3-58. Prior to amendment, Code Sec. 5723 read as follows:

SEC. 5723. PACKAGES, LABELS, NOTICES, AND STAMPS.

(a) Packages, Labels, Notices, and Stamps.—All articles shall, before removal, be put up in packages having such labels, notices, and stamps as the Secretary or his delegate shall by regulation prescribe.

(b) Lottery Features.—No certificate, coupon, or other device purporting to be or to represent a ticket, chance, share, or an interest in, or dependent on, the event of a lottery shall be contained in, attached to, or stamped, marked, written or printed on any package of articles.

(c) Indecent or Immoral Material Prohibited.—No indecent or immoral picture, print, or representation shall be contained in, attached to, or stamped, marked, written, or printed on any package of articles.

(d) Exceptions.—Tobacco products furnished for employee use or consumption or for experimental purposes, and articles removed for shipment to a foreign country, Puerto Rico, the Virgin Islands, or a possession of the United States, and so shipped, may be exempted from subsections (a) and (b) in accordance with such regulations as the Secretary or his delegate shall prescribe.

Subchapter D—Occupational Tax

Sec. 5731.	Imposition and rate of tax.
Sec. 5732.	Payment of tax.
Sec. 5733.	Provisions relating to liability for occupational taxes.
Sec. 5734.	Application of State laws.

[Sec. 5731]

SEC. 5731. IMPOSITION AND RATE OF TAX.

[Sec. 5731(a)]

(a) GENERAL RULE.—Every person engaged in business as—

(1) a manufacturer of tobacco products,

(2) a manufacturer of cigarette papers and tubes, or

(3) an export warehouse proprietor,

shall pay a tax of $1,000 per year in respect of each premises at which such business is carried on.

TOBACCO TAXES—OCCUPATIONAL TAX

[Sec. 5731(b)]

(b) REDUCED RATES FOR SMALL PROPRIETORS.—

(1) IN GENERAL.—Subsection (a) shall be applied by substituting "$500" for "$1,000" with respect to any taxpayer the gross receipts of which (for the most recent taxable year ending before the 1st day of the taxable period to which the tax imposed by subsection (a) relates) are less than $500,000.

(2) CONTROLLED GROUP RULES.—All persons treated as 1 taxpayer under section 5061(e)(3) shall be treated as 1 taxpayer for purposes of paragraph (1).

(3) CERTAIN RULES TO APPLY.—For purposes of paragraph (1), rules similar to the rules of subparagraphs (B) and (C) of section 448(c)(3) shall apply.

[Sec. 5731(c)—Stricken]

(c) CERTAIN OCCUPATIONAL TAX RULES TO APPLY.—Rules similar to the rules of subpart G of part II of subchapter A of chapter 51 shall apply for purposes of this section.

Amendments

• 2005, Safe, Accountable, Flexible, Efficient Transportation Equity Act: A Legacy for Users (P.L. 109-59)

P.L. 109-59, §11125(b)(20)(E):

Amended Code Sec. 5731 by striking subsection (c) and by redesignating subsection (d) as subsection (c). **Effective** 7-1-2008, but not applicable to taxes imposed for periods before such date. Prior to being stricken, Code Sec. 5731(c) read as follows:

[Sec. 5731(c)]

(c) PENALTY FOR FAILURE TO REGISTER.—Any person engaged in a business referred to in subsection (a) who willfully fails to pay the tax imposed by subsection (a) shall be fined not more than $5,000, or imprisoned not more than 2 years, or both, for each such offense.

Amendments

• 2005, Safe, Accountable, Flexible, Efficient Transportation Equity Act: A Legacy for Users (P.L. 109-59)

P.L. 109-59, §11125(b)(20)(E):

Amended Code Sec. 5731 by redesignating subsection (d) as subsection (c). **Effective** 7-1-2008, but not applicable to taxes imposed for periods before such date.

• 1987, Revenue Act of 1987 (P.L. 100-203)

P.L. 100-203, §10512(f)(1):

Amended chapter 52 by redesignating subchapters D, E, and F as subchapters E, F, and G, respectively, and by inserting after subchapter C a new subchapter D (Code Sec. 5731). For the **effective** date, see Act Sec. 10512(h), below.

P.L. 100-203, §10512(h), provides:

(h) EFFECTIVE DATE.—

(1) IN GENERAL.—The amendments made by this section shall take effect on January 1, 1988.

(2) All Taxpayers Treated as Commencing in Business on January 1, 1988—

(A) IN GENERAL.—Any person engaged on January 1, 1988, in any trade or business which is subject to an occupational tax shall be treated for purposes of such tax as having 1st engaged in such trade or business on such date.

(B) LIMITATION ON AMOUNT OF TAX.—In the case of a taxpayer who paid an occupational tax in respect of any premises for any taxable period which began before January 1, 1988, and includes such date, the amount of the occupational tax imposed by reason of subparagraph (A) in respect of such premises shall not exceed an amount equal to $1/2$ the excess (if any) of—

(i) the rate of such tax as in effect on January 1, 1988, over

(ii) the rate of such tax as in effect on December 31, 1987.

(C) OCCUPATIONAL TAX.—For purposes of this paragraph, the term "occupational tax" means any tax imposed under part II of subchapter A of chapter 51, section 5276, section 5731, or section 5801 of the Internal Revenue Code of 1986 (as amended by this section).

(D) DUE DATE OF TAX.—The amount of any tax required to be paid by reason of this paragraph shall be due on April 1, 1988.

[Sec. 5732]

SEC. 5732. PAYMENT OF TAX.

[Sec. 5732(a)]

(a) CONDITION PRECEDENT TO CARRYING ON BUSINESS.—No person shall be engaged in or carry on any trade or business subject to tax under this subchapter until he has paid the special tax therefor.

Amendments

• 2005, Safe, Accountable, Flexible, Efficient Transportation Equity Act: A Legacy for Users (P.L. 109-59)

P.L. 109-59, §11125(b)(20)(A):

Redesignated Code Sec. 5142 as Code Sec. 5732 and amended Code Sec. 5732 [as so redesignated] by striking "this part" each place it appears and inserting "this subchapter". **Effective** 7-1-2008, but not applicable to taxes imposed for periods before such date.

P.L. 109-59, §11125(b)(20)(B):

Amended Code Sec. 5732, as redesignated by Act Sec. 11125(b)(20)(A) [and amended by Act Sec. 11125(b)(20)(A)], by striking "(except the tax imposed by section 5131)" each place it appears. **Effective** 7-1-2008, but not applicable to taxes imposed for periods before such date. Prior to amendment, Code Sec. 5732(a) read as follows:

(a) CONDITION PRECEDENT TO CARRYING ON BUSINESS.—No person shall be engaged in or carry on any trade or business subject to tax under this subchapter (except the tax imposed by section 5131) until he has paid the special tax therefor.

[Sec. 5732(b)]

(b) COMPUTATION.—All special taxes under this subchapter shall be imposed as of on the first day of July in each year, or on commencing any trade or business on which such tax is imposed. In the former case the tax shall be reckoned for 1 year, and in the latter case it shall be reckoned proportionately, from the first day of the month in which the liability to a special tax commenced, to and including the 30th day of June following.

Amendments

• 2005, Safe, Accountable, Flexible, Efficient Transportation Equity Act: A Legacy for Users (P.L. 109-59)

P.L. 109-59, §11125(b)(20)(A):

Amended Code Sec. 5732 [as redesignated] by striking "this part" each place it appears and inserting "this subchapter". **Effective** 7-1-2008, but not applicable to taxes imposed for periods before such date.

P.L. 109-59, §11125(b)(20)(B):

Amended Code Sec. 5732, as redesignated by Act Sec. 11125(b)(20)(A) [and amended by Act Sec. 11125(b)(20)(A)], by striking "(except the tax imposed by section 5131)" each place it appears. **Effective** 7-1-2008, but not applicable to taxes imposed for periods before such date. Prior to amendment, Code Sec. 5732(b) read as follows:

(b) COMPUTATION.—All special taxes under this subchapter (except the tax imposed by section 5131) shall be imposed as of on the first day of July in each year, or on commencing any trade or business on which such tax is imposed. In the former case the tax shall be reckoned for 1 year, and in the latter case it shall be reckoned proportionately, from the first day of the month in which the liability to a special tax commenced, to and including the 30th day of June following.

[Sec. 5732(c)]

(c) HOW PAID.—

(1) PAYMENT BY RETURN.—The special taxes imposed by this subchapter shall be paid on the basis of a return under such regulations as the Secretary shall prescribe.

(2) STAMP DENOTING PAYMENT OF TAX.—After receiving a properly executed return and remittance of any special tax imposed by this subchapter, the Secretary shall issue to the taxpayer an appropriate stamp as a receipt denoting payment of the tax. This paragraph shall not apply in the case of a return covering liability for a past period.

TOBACCO TAXES—OCCUPATIONAL TAX

Amendments

• **2007, Tax Technical Corrections Act of 2007 (P.L. 110-172)**

P.L. 110-172, §11(a)(32):

Amended Code Sec. 5732(c)(2), as redesignated by section 11125(b)(20)(A) of the Safe, Accountable, Flexible, Efficient Transportation Equity Act: A Legacy for Users (P.L. 109-59), by striking "this subpart" and inserting "this subchapter". **Effective** 12-29-2007.

• **2005, Safe, Accountable, Flexible, Efficient Transportation Equity Act: A Legacy for Users (P.L. 109-59)**

P.L. 109-59, §11125(b)(20)(A):

Amended Code Sec. 5732 [as redesignated] by striking "this part" each place it appears and inserting "this subchapter". **Effective** 7-1-2008, but not applicable to taxes imposed for periods before such date.

• **1976, Tax Reform Act of 1976 (P.L. 94-455)**

P.L. 94-455, §1905(a)(12):

Amended Code Sec. 5142(c). **Effective** 2-1-77. Prior to amendment, Code Sec. 5142(c) read as follows:

(c) How Paid.—

(1) Stamp.—All special taxes imposed by this part shall be paid by stamps denoting the tax.

(2) Assessment.—

For authority of the Secretary or his delegate to make assessments where the special taxes have not been duly paid by stamp at the time and in the manner provided by law, see subtitle F.

[Sec. 5733]

SEC. 5733. PROVISIONS RELATING TO LIABILITY FOR OCCUPATIONAL TAXES.

[Sec. 5733(a)]

(a) PARTNERS.—Any number of persons doing business in partnership at any one place shall be required to pay but one special tax.

[Sec. 5733(b)]

(b) DIFFERENT BUSINESSES OF SAME OWNERSHIP AND LOCATION.—Whenever more than one of the pursuits or occupations described in this suchapter are carried on in the same place by the same person at the same time, except as otherwise provided in this subchapter, the tax shall be paid for each according to the rates severally prescribed.

Amendments

• **2005, Safe, Accountable, Flexible, Efficient Transportation Equity Act: A Legacy for Users (P.L. 109-59)**

P.L. 109-59, §11125(b)(20)(A):

Amended Code Sec. 5733 [as redesignated] by striking "this part" each place it appears and inserting "this subchapter". **Effective** 7-1-2008, but not applicable to taxes imposed for periods before such date.

[Sec. 5733(c)]

(c) BUSINESSES IN MORE THAN ONE LOCATION.—

(1) LIABILITY FOR TAX.—The payment of a special tax imposed by this subchapter shall not exempt from an additional special tax the person carrying on a trade or business in any other place than that stated in the register kept in the office of the official in charge of the internal revenue district.

(2) STORAGE.—Nothing contained in paragraph (1) shall require a special tax for the storage of tobacco products and cigarette papers and tubes at a location other than the place where tobacco products and cigarette papers and tubes are sold or offered for sale.

(3) DEFINITION OF PLACE.—The term "place" as used in this section means the entire office, plant or area of the business in any one location under the same proprietorship; and passageways, streets, highways, rail crossings, waterways, or partitions dividing the premises, shall not be deemed sufficient separation to require additional special tax, if the various divisions are otherwise contiguous.

Amendments

• **2005, Safe, Accountable, Flexible, Efficient Transportation Equity Act: A Legacy for Users (P.L. 109-59)**

P.L. 109-59, §11125(b)(20)(A):

Amended Code Sec. 5733 [as redesignated] by striking "this part" each place it appears and inserting "this subchapter". **Effective** 7-1-2008, but not applicable to taxes imposed for periods before such date.

P.L. 109-59, §11125(b)(20)(C):

Amended Code Sec. 5733(c)(2), as redesignated by Act Sec. 11125(b)(20)(A), by striking "liquors" both places it appears and inserting "tobacco products and cigarette papers and tubes". **Effective** 7-1-2008, but not applicable to taxes imposed for periods before such date.

[Sec. 5733(d)]

(d) DEATH OR CHANGE OF LOCATION.—Certain persons, other than the person who has paid the special tax under this subchapter for the carrying on of any business at any place, may secure the right to carry on, without incurring additional special tax, the same business at the same place for the remainder of the taxable period for which the special tax was paid. The persons who may secure such right are:

(1) the surviving spouse or child, or executor or administrator or other legal representative, of a deceased taxpayer;

(2) a husband or wife succeeding to the business of his or her living spouse;

(3) a receiver or trustee in bankruptcy, or an assignee for benefit of creditors; and

(4) the partner or partners remaining after death or withdrawal of a member of a partnership.

When any person moves to any place other than the place for which special tax was paid for the carrying on of any business, he may secure the right to carry on, without incurring additional special tax, the same business at his new location for the remainder of the taxable period for which the special tax was paid. To secure the right to carry on the business without incurring additional special tax, the successor, or the person relocating his business, must register the succession or relocation with the Secretary in accordance with regulations prescribed by the Secretary.

Amendments

• **2005, Safe, Accountable, Flexible, Efficient Transportation Equity Act: A Legacy for Users (P.L. 109-59)**

P.L. 109-59, §11125(b)(20)(A):

Amended Code Sec. 5733 [as redesignated] by striking "this part" each place it appears and inserting "this subchapter". **Effective** 7-1-2008, but not applicable to taxes imposed for periods before such date.

• **1976, Tax Reform Act of 1976 (P.L. 94-455)**

P.L. 94-455, §1906(b)(13)(A):

Amended 1954 Code by substituting "Secretary" for "Secretary or his delegate" each place it appeared. **Effective** 2-1-77.

[Sec. 5733(e)]

(e) FEDERAL AGENCIES OR INSTRUMENTALITIES.—Any tax imposed by this subchapter shall apply to any agency or instrumentality of the United States unless such agency or instrumentality is granted by statute a specific exemption from such tax.

TOBACCO TAXES—RECORDS

Amendments

• **2005, Safe, Accountable, Flexible, Efficient Transportation Equity Act: A Legacy for Users (P.L. 109-59)**

P.L. 109-59, § 11125(b)(20)(A):

Redesignated Code Sec. 5143 as Code Sec. 5733 and amended Code Sec. 5733 [as so redesignated] by striking "this part" each place it appears and inserting "this subchapter". **Effective** 7-1-2008, but not applicable to taxes imposed for periods before such date.

[Sec. 5734]

SEC. 5734. APPLICATION OF STATE LAWS.

The payment of any tax imposed by this subchapter for carrying on any trade or business shall not be held to exempt any person from any penalty or punishment provided by the laws of any State for carrying on such trade or business within such State, or in any manner to authorize the commencement or continuance of such trade or business contrary to the laws of such State or in places prohibited by municipal law; nor shall the payment of any such tax be held to prohibit any State from placing a duty or tax on the same trade or business, for State or other purposes.

Amendments

• **2005, Safe, Accountable, Flexible, Efficient Transportation Equity Act: A Legacy for Users (P.L. 109-59)**

P.L. 109-59, § 11125(b)(20)(A):

Redesignated Code Sec. 5145 as Code Sec. 5734 and amended Code Sec. 5734 [as so redesignated] by striking "this part" each place it appears and inserting "this subchapter". **Effective** 7-1-2008, but not applicable to taxes imposed for periods before such date.

Subchapter E—Records of Manufacturers and Importers of Tobacco Products and Cigarette Papers and Tubes, and Export Warehouse Proprietors

Sec. 5741.   Records to be maintained.

[Sec. 5741]

SEC. 5741. RECORDS TO BE MAINTAINED.

Every manufacturer of tobacco products, processed tobacco, or cigarette papers and tubes, every importer, and every export warehouse proprietor shall keep such records in such manner as the Secretary shall by regulation prescribe. The records required under this section shall be available for inspection by any internal revenue officer during business hours.

Amendments

• **2009, Children's Health Insurance Program Reauthorization Act of 2009 (P.L. 111-3)**

P.L. 111-3, § 702(a)(3):

Amended Code Sec. 5741 by inserting ", processed tobacco," after "tobacco products". **Effective** 4-1-2009.

• **1976, Tax Reform Act of 1976 (P.L. 94-455)**

P.L. 94-455, § 2128(c):

Amended Code Sec. 5741. **Effective** 2-1-77. Prior to amendment, Code Sec. 5741 read as follows:

Every manufacturer of tobacco products or cigarette papers and tubes and every export warehouse proprietor shall keep such records in such manner as the Secretary or his delegate shall by regulation prescribe.

• **1965, Excise Tax Reduction Act of 1965 (P.L. 89-44)**

P.L. 89-44, § 502(b)(9):

Amended Code Sec. 5741. **Effective** for tax years beginning after 1-1-66. Prior to amendment, Code Sec. 5741 read as follows:

Every manufacturer of tobacco products or cigarette papers and tubes, every export warehouse proprietor, and every dealer in tobacco materials shall keep such records in such manner as the Secretary or his delegate shall by regulation prescribe.

• **1958, Excise Tax Technical Changes Act of 1958 (P.L. 85-859)**

P.L. 85-859, § 202:

Amended Code Sec. 5741. **Effective** 9-3-58. Prior to amendment, Code Sec. 5741 read as follows:

SEC. 5741. RECORDS TO BE MAINTAINED.

Every manufacturer of articles and dealer in tobacco materials shall keep such records in such form as the Secretary or his delegate shall by regulation prescribe.

Subchapter F—General Provisions

Sec. 5751.   Purchase, receipt, possession, or sale of tobacco products and cigarette papers and tubes, after removal.
Sec. 5752.   Restrictions relating to marks, labels, notices, and packages.
Sec. 5753.   Disposal of forfeited, condemned, and abandoned tobacco products, and cigarette papers and tubes.
Sec. 5754.   Restriction on importation of previously exported tobacco products.

[Sec. 5751]

SEC. 5751. PURCHASE, RECEIPT, POSSESSION, OR SALE OF TOBACCO PRODUCTS AND CIGARETTE PAPERS AND TUBES, AFTER REMOVAL.

[Sec. 5751(a)]

(a) RESTRICTION.—No person shall—

(1) with intent to defraud the United States, purchase, receive, possess, offer for sale, or sell or otherwise dispose of, after removal, any tobacco products or cigarette papers or tubes—

(A) upon which the tax has not been paid or determined in the manner and at the time prescribed by this chapter or regulations thereunder; or

(B) which, after removal without payment of tax pursuant to section 5704, have been diverted from the applicable purpose or use specified in that section; or

(2) with intent to defraud the United States, purchase, receive, possess, offer for sale, or sell or otherwise dispose of, after removal, any tobacco products or cigarette papers or tubes, which are not put up in packages as required under section 5723 or which are put up in packages not bearing the marks, labels, and notices, as required under such section; or

(3) otherwise than with intent to defraud the United States, purchase, receive, possess, offer for sale, or sell or otherwise dispose of, after removal, any tobacco products or cigarette papers or tubes, which are not put up in packages as required under section 5723 or which are put up in packages not bearing the marks, labels, and notices, as required under such section. This paragraph shall not prevent the sale or delivery of tobacco products or cigarette papers or tubes directly to consumers from proper packages, nor apply to such articles when so sold or delivered.

TOBACCO TAXES—GENERAL PROVISIONS

Amendments

• **1976, Tax Reform Act of 1976 (P.L. 94-455)**

P.L. 94-455, §1905(b)(7)(A):

Substituted "and notices" for "notices, and stamps" in Code Secs. 5751(a)(2) and 5751(a)(3). **Effective** 2-1-77.

[Sec. 5751(b)]

(b) LIABILITY TO TAX.—Any person who possesses tobacco products or cigarette papers or tubes in violation of subsection (a)(1) or (a)(2) shall be liable for a tax equal to the tax on such articles.

Amendments

• **1958, Excise Tax Technical Changes Act of 1958 (P.L. 85-859)**

P.L. 85-859, §202:

Amended Sec. 5751. **Effective** 9-3-58. Prior to amendment, Sec. 5751 read as follows:

SEC. 5751. PURCHASE, RECEIPT, POSSESSION, OR SALE OF ARTICLES, AFTER REMOVAL, NOT EXEMPT FROM TAX.

(a) Restriction.—No person shall purchase, receive, possess, sell, or offer for sale any articles not exempt from tax, after removal, which are not put up in packages bearing the labels, notices, or stamps, prescribed by the Secretary or his delegate: *Provided, however,* That this section is not intended to prevent the sale of articles at retail, directly from proper packages, nor to apply to such articles when so sold.

(b) Liability to Tax.—Any person who possesses articles in violation of subsection (a) of this section, shall incur liability to the tax thereon in addition to the penalties prescribed elsewhere in this title.

[Sec. 5752]

SEC. 5752. RESTRICTIONS RELATING TO MARKS, LABELS, NOTICES, AND PACKAGES.

No person shall, with intent to defraud the United States, destroy, obliterate, or detach any mark, label, or notice prescribed or authorized, by this chapter or regulations thereunder, to appear on, or be affixed to, any package of tobacco products or cigarette papers or tubes, before such package is emptied.

Amendments

• **1976, Tax Reform Act of 1976 (P.L. 94-455)**

P.L. 94-455, §1905(b)(7)(B)(i):

Amended Code Sec. 5752. **Effective** 2-1-77. Prior to amendment, Code Sec. 5752 read as follows:

SEC. 5752. RESTRICTIONS RELATING TO MARKS, LABELS, NOTICES, STAMPS, AND PACKAGES.

No person shall, with intent to defraud the United States—

(a) destroy, obliterate, or detach any mark, label, notice, or stamp prescribed or authorized, by this chapter or regulations thereunder, to appear on, or be affixed to, any package of tobacco products or cigarette papers or tubes, before such package is emptied; or

(b) empty any package of tobacco products or cigarette papers or tubes without destroying any stamp thereon to evidence the tax or indicate compliance with this chapter, prescribed by this chapter or regulations thereunder to be affixed to such package; or

(c) detach, or cause to be detached, from any package of tobacco products or cigarette papers or tubes any stamp, prescribed by this chapter or regulations thereunder, to evidence the tax or indicate compliance with this chapter, or purchase, receive, possess, sell, or dispose of, by gift or otherwise, any such stamp which has been so detached; or

(d) purchase, receive, possess, sell, or dispose of, by gift or otherwise, any package which previously contained tobacco products or cigarette papers or tubes which has been emptied, and upon which any stamp prescribed by this chapter or regulations thereunder, to evidence the tax or indicate compliance with this chapter, has not been destroyed.

• **1958, Excise Tax Technical Changes Act of 1958 (P.L. 85-859)**

P.L. 85-859, §202:

Amended Code Sec. 5752. **Effective** 9-3-58. Prior to amendment, Code Sec. 5752 read as follows:

SEC. 5752. RESTRICTIONS RELATING TO USED LABELS, STAMPS, AND PACKAGES.

If the Secretary or his delegate shall, by regulation, prescribe that a label or stamp be affixed to any package of articles, no person shall—

(1) empty any such package without destroying such label or stamp; or

(2) remove, or cause to be removed, any such label or stamp, or purchase, receive, possess, sell, or dispose of, by gift or otherwise, any such label or stamp which has been so removed; or

(3) purchase, receive, possess, sell, or dispose of, by gift or otherwise, any such package which has been emptied, upon which the label or stamp has not been destroyed.

[Sec. 5753]

SEC. 5753. DISPOSAL OF FORFEITED, CONDEMNED, AND ABANDONED TOBACCO PRODUCTS, AND CIGARETTE PAPERS AND TUBES.

If it appears that any forfeited, condemned, or abandoned tobacco products, or cigarette papers and tubes, when offered for sale, will not bring a price equal to the tax due and payable thereon, and the expenses incident to the sale thereof, such articles shall not be sold for consumption in the United States but shall be disposed of in accordance with such regulations as the Secretary shall prescribe.

Amendments

• **1976, Tax Reform Act of 1976 (P.L. 94-455)**

P.L. 94-455, §1906(b)(13)(A):

Amended 1954 Code by substituting "Secretary" for "Secretary or his delegate" each place it appeared. **Effective** 2-1-77.

• **1965, Excise Tax Reduction Act of 1965 (P.L. 89-44)**

P.L. 89-44, §502(b)(11):

Amended Code Sec. 5753. **Effective** for tax years beginning after 1-1-66. Prior to amendment, Code Sec. 5753 read as follows:

SEC. 5753. DISPOSAL OF FORFEITED, CONDEMNED, AND ABANDONED TOBACCO PRODUCTS, CIGARETTE PAPERS AND TUBES, AND TOBACCO MATERIALS.

If it appears that any forfeited, condemned, or abandoned tobacco products, cigarette papers and tubes, or tobacco materials, when offered for sale, will not bring a price equal to the tax due and payable thereon, and the expenses incident to the sale thereof, such articles and tobacco materials shall not be sold for consumption in the United States but shall be disposed of in accordance with such regulations as the Secretary or his delegate shall prescribe.

• **1958, Excise Tax Technical Changes Act of 1958 (P.L. 85-859)**

P.L. 85-859, §202:

Amended Sec. 5753 by striking out, in the heading, the word "ARTICLES" and substituting "TOBACCO PRODUCTS AND CIGARETTE PAPERS AND TUBES,", and by striking out, in the text, the phrase "articles and" and substituting "tobacco products and cigarette papers and tubes, or". **Effective** 9-3-58.

[Sec. 5754]

SEC. 5754. RESTRICTION ON IMPORTATION OF PREVIOUSLY EXPORTED TOBACCO PRODUCTS.

[Sec. 5754(a)]

(a) EXPORT-LABELED TOBACCO PRODUCTS.—

(1) IN GENERAL.—Tobacco products and cigarette papers and tubes manufactured in the United States and labeled for exportation under this chapter—

(A) may be transferred to or removed from the premises of a manufacturer or an export warehouse proprietor only if such articles are being transferred or removed without tax in accordance with section 5704;

(B) may be imported or brought into the United States, after their exportation, only if such articles either are eligible to be released from customs custody with the partial duty exemption provided in section 5704(d) or are returned to the original manufacturer of such article as provided in section 5704(c); and

(C) may not be sold or held for sale for domestic consumption in the United States unless such articles are removed from their export packaging and repackaged by the original manufacturer into new packaging that does not contain an export label.

(2) ALTERATIONS BY PERSONS OTHER THAN ORIGINAL MANUFACTURER.—This section shall apply to articles labeled for export even if the packaging or the appearance of such packaging to the consumer of such articles has been modified or altered by a person other than the

TOBACCO TAXES—PENALTIES

original manufacturer so as to remove or conceal or attempt to remove or conceal (including by the placement of a sticker over) any export label.

(3) EXPORTS INCLUDE SHIPMENTS TO PUERTO RICO.—For purposes of this section, section 5704(d), section 5761, and such other provisions as the Secretary may specify by regulations, references to exportation shall be treated as including a reference to shipment to the Commonwealth of Puerto Rico.

[Sec. 5754(b)]

(b) EXPORT LABEL.—For purposes of this section, an article is labeled for export or contains an export label if it bears the mark, label, or notice required under section 5704(b).

[Sec. 5754(c)]

(c) CROSS REFERENCES.—

(1) For exception to this section for personal use, see section 5761(d).

(2) For civil penalties related to violations of this section, see section 5761(c).

(3) For a criminal penalty applicable to any violation of this section, see section 5762(b).

(4) For forfeiture provisions related to violations of this section, see section 5761(c).

Amendments

• **2006, Tax Relief and Health Care Act of 2006 (P.L. 109-432)**

P.L. 109-432, Division C, §401(f)(2)(B):

Amended Code Sec. 5754(c)(1) by striking "section 5761(c)" and inserting "section 5761(d)". **Effective** with respect to goods entered, or withdrawn from warehouse for consumption, on or after the 15th day after 12-20-2006.

• **2000, Imported Cigarette Compliance Act of 2000 (P.L. 106-476)**

P.L. 106-476, §4002(a):

Amended Code Sec. 5754. **Effective** 2-7-2001. Prior to amendment, Code Sec. 5754 read as follows:

(a) IN GENERAL.—Tobacco products and cigarette papers and tubes previously exported from the United States may be imported or brought into the United States only as provided in section 5704(d). For purposes of this section, section 5704(d), section 5761, and such other provisions as the Secretary may specify by regulations, references to exportation shall be treated as including a reference to shipment to the Commonwealth of Puerto Rico.

(b) CROSS REFERENCE.—For penalty for the sale of tobacco products and cigarette papers and tubes in the United States which are labeled for export, see section 5761(c).

P.L. 106-476, §4002(e), provides:

(e) STUDY.—The Secretary of the Treasury shall report to Congress on the impact of requiring export warehouses to be authorized by the original manufacturer to receive relanded export-labeled cigarettes.

• **1997, Balanced Budget Act of 1997 (P.L. 105-33)**

P.L. 105-33, §9302(h)(1)(E)(i):

Amended subpart F of chapter 53 by adding at the end a new Code Sec. 5754. **Effective**, generally, for articles removed (as defined in Code Sec. 5702(k)) after 12-31-99. For a transitional rule, see Act Sec. 9302(i)(2) in the amendment notes following Code Sec. 5701(a), above.

Subchapter G—Penalties and Forfeitures

Sec. 5761.   Civil penalties.
Sec. 5762.   Criminal penalties.
Sec. 5763.   Forfeitures.

[Sec. 5761]

SEC. 5761. CIVIL PENALTIES.

[Sec. 5761(a)]

(a) OMITTING THINGS REQUIRED OR DOING THINGS FORBIDDEN.—Whoever willfully omits, neglects, or refuses to comply with any duty imposed upon him by this chapter, or to do, or cause to be done, any of the things required by this chapter, or does anything prohibited by this chapter, shall, in addition to any other penalty provided in this title, be liable to a penalty of $1,000, to be recovered, with costs of suit, in a civil action, except where a penalty under subsection (b) or (c) or under section 6651 or 6653 or part II of subchapter A of chapter 68 may be collected from such person by assessment.

Amendments

• **1997, Balanced Budget Act of 1997 (P.L. 105-33)**

P.L. 105-33, §9302(h)(1)(C):

Amended Code Sec. 5761(a) by striking "subsection (b)" and inserting "subsection (b) or (c)". **Effective**, generally, for articles removed (as defined in Code Sec. 5702(k)) after 12-31-99. For a transitional rule, see Act Sec. 9302(i)(2) in the amendment notes following Code Sec. 5701(a).

• **1989, Omnibus Budget Reconciliation Act of 1989 (P.L. 101-239)**

P.L. 101-239, §7721(c)(4):

Amended Code Sec. 5761(a) by striking "or 6653" and inserting "or 6653 or part II of subchapter A of chapter 68". **Effective** for returns the due date for which (determined without regard to extensions) is after 12-31-89.

[Sec. 5761(b)]

(b) FAILURE TO PAY TAX.—Whoever fails to pay any tax imposed by this chapter at the time prescribed by law or regulations, shall, in addition to any other penalty provided in this title, be liable to a penalty of 5 percent of the tax due but unpaid.

[Sec. 5761(c)]

(c) SALE OF TOBACCO PRODUCTS AND CIGARETTE PAPERS AND TUBES FOR EXPORT.—Except as provided in subsections (b) and (d) of section 5704—

(1) every person who sells, relands, or receives within the jurisdiction of the United States any tobacco products or cigarette papers or tubes which have been labeled or shipped for exportation under this chapter,

(2) every person who sells or receives such relanded tobacco products or cigarette papers or tubes, and

(3) every person who aids or abets in such selling, relanding, or receiving,

shall, in addition to the tax and any other penalty provided in this title, be liable for a penalty equal to the greater of $1,000 or 5 times the amount of the tax imposed by this chapter. All tobacco products and cigarette papers and tubes relanded within the jurisdiction of the United States shall be forfeited to the United States and destroyed. All vessels, vehicles, and aircraft used in such relanding or in removing such products, papers, and tubes from the place where relanded, shall be forfeited to the United States.

This subsection and section 5754 shall not apply to any person who relands or receives tobacco products in the quantity allowed entry free of tax and duty under chapter 98 of the Harmonized Tariff Schedule of the United States, and such person may voluntarily relinquish to the Secretary at the time of entry any excess of such quantity without incurring the penalty under this subsection. No quantity of tobacco products other than the quantity referred to in the preceding sentence may be relanded or received as a personal use quantity.

Amendments

• **2006, Tax Relief and Health Care Act of 2006 (P.L. 109-432)**

P.L. 109-432, Division C, §401(f)(2)(A):

Amended Code Sec. 5761(c) by striking the last two sentences. **Effective** with respect to goods entered, or withdrawn from warehouse for consumption, on or after the 15th day after 12-20-2006. Prior to being stricken, the last two sentences of Code Sec. 5761(c) read as follows:

Sec. 5754(a)(3)

TOBACCO TAXES—PENALTIES

• **2000, Community Renewal Tax Relief Act of 2000 (P.L. 106-554)**

P.L. 106-554, § 315(a)(3):

Amended Code Sec. 5761(c) by adding at the end the last two sentences. **Effective** as if included in section 9302 of P.L. 105-33 [effective, generally, for articles removed after 12-31-99.—CCH]. [Note: The last two sentences were already enacted by P.L. 106-476, § 4003(a), in substantially the same format.] As added by P.L. 106-476, the last two sentences of Code Sec. 5761(c) read as follows:

This subsection and section 5754 shall not apply to any person who relands or receives tobacco products in the quantity allowed entry free of tax and duty under subchapter IV of chapter 98 of the Harmonized Tariff Schedule of the United States. No quantity of tobacco products other than the quantity referred to in the preceding sentence may be relanded or received as a personal use quantity.

• **2000, Imported Cigarette Compliance Act of 2000 (P.L. 106-476)**

P.L. 106-476, § 4002(c):

Amended the last sentence of Code Sec. 5761(c) by striking "the jurisdiction of the United States" and all that follows through the period and adding new text. **Effective** 2-7-2001. Prior to amendment, the last sentence of Code Sec. 5761(c) read as follows:

All tobacco products and cigarette papers and tubes relanded within the jurisdiction of the United States, and all vessels, vehicles, and aircraft used in such relanding or in removing such products, papers, and tubes from the place where relanded, shall be forfeited to the United States.

P.L. 106-476, § 4003(a):

Amended Code Sec. 5761(c) by adding at the end the last two sentences. **Effective** as if included in section 9302 of P.L. 105-33 [effective, generally, for articles removed after 12-31-99.—CCH].

• **1997, Balanced Budget Act of 1997 (P.L. 105-33)**

P.L. 105-33, § 9302(h)(1)(B):

Amended Code Sec. 5761 by redesignating subsections (c) and (d) as subsections (d) and (e), respectively, and by inserting after subsection (b) as new subsection (c). **Effective**, generally, for articles removed (as defined in Code Sec. 5702(k)) after 12-31-99. For a transitional rule, see Act Sec. 9302(i)(2) in the amendment notes following Code Sec. 5701(a).

[Sec. 5761(d)]

(d) PERSONAL USE QUANTITIES.—

(1) IN GENERAL.—No quantity of tobacco products other than the quantity referred to in paragraph (2) may be relanded or received as a personal use quantity.

(2) EXCEPTION FOR PERSONAL USE QUANTITY.—Subsection (c) and section 5754 shall not apply to any person who relands or receives tobacco products in the quantity allowed entry free of tax and duty under chapter 98 of the Harmonized Tariff Schedule of the United States, and such person may voluntarily relinquish to the Secretary at the time of entry any excess of such quantity without incurring the penalty under subsection (c).

(3) SPECIAL RULE FOR DELIVERY SALES.—

(A) IN GENERAL.—Paragraph (2) shall not apply to any tobacco product sold in connection with a delivery sale.

(B) DELIVERY SALE.—For purposes of subparagraph (A), the term "delivery sale" means any sale of a tobacco product to a consumer if—

(i) the consumer submits the order for such sale by means of a telephone or other method of voice transmission, the mail, or the Internet or other online service, or the seller is otherwise not in the physical presence of the buyer when the request for purchase or order is made, or

(ii) the tobacco product is delivered by use of a common carrier, private delivery service, or the mail, or the seller is not in the physical presence of the buyer when the buyer obtains personal possession of the tobacco product.

Amendments

• **2006, Tax Relief and Health Care Act of 2006 (P.L. 109-432)**

P.L. 109-432, Division C, § 401(f)(1):

Amended Code Sec. 5761 by redesignating subsections (d) and (e) as subsections (e) and (f), respectively, and inserting after subsection (c) a new subsection (d). **Effective** with respect to goods entered, or withdrawn from warehouse for consumption, on or after the 15th day after 12-20-2006.

[Sec. 5761(e)]

(e) APPLICABILITY OF SECTION 6665.—The penalties imposed by subsections (b) and (c) shall be assessed, collected, and paid in the same manner as taxes, as provided in section 6665(a).

Amendments

• **2006, Tax Relief and Health Care Act of 2006 (P.L. 109-432)**

P.L. 109-432, Division C, § 401(f)(1):

Amended Code Sec. 5761 by redesignating subsection (d) as subsection (e). **Effective** with respect to goods entered, or withdrawn from warehouse for consumption, on or after the 15th day after 12-20-2006.

• **1997, Balanced Budget Act of 1997 (P.L. 105-33)**

P.L. 105-33, § 9302(h)(1)(B):

Amended Code Sec. 5761 by redesignating subsection (c) as subsection (d). **Effective**, generally, for articles removed (as defined in Code Sec. 5702(k)) after 12-31-99. For a transitional rule, see Act Sec. 9302(i)(2) in the amendment notes following Code Sec. 5701(a).

P.L. 105-33, § 9302(h)(1)(D):

Amended Code Sec. 5761(d), as redesignated by Act Sec. 9302(h)(1)(B), by striking "The penalty imposed by subsection (b)" and inserting "The penalties imposed by subsections (b) and (c)". **Effective**, generally, for articles removed (as defined in Code Sec. 5702(k)) after 12-31-99. For a transitional rule, see Act Sec. 9302(i)(2) in the amendment notes following Code Sec. 5701(a).

• **1989, Omnibus Budget Reconciliation Act of 1989 (P.L. 101-239)**

P.L. 101-239, § 7721(c)(5)(A)-(B):

Amended Code Sec. 5761(c) by striking "6662(a)" and inserting "6665(a)", and by striking "6662" in the subsection heading and inserting "6665". **Effective** for returns the due date for which (determined without regard to extensions) is after 12-31-89.

• **1984, Deficit Reduction Act of 1984 (P.L. 98-369)**

P.L. 98-369, § 714(h)(2):

Amended Code Sec. 5761(c) by striking out "Section 6660" in the heading and inserting in lieu thereof "Section 6662", and by striking out "section 6660(a)" in the text and inserting in lieu thereof "section 6662(a)". **Effective** as if included in the provision of P.L. 97-248 to which it relates.

• **1983, Technical Corrections Act of 1982 (P.L. 97-448)**

P.L. 97-448, § 107(b):

Amended Code Sec. 5761(c) by striking out "section 6659(a)" and inserting in lieu thereof "section 6660(a)," and by striking out "Section 6659" in the heading and inserting in lieu thereof "Section 6660." **Effective** as if included in the provision of P.L. 97-34 to which it relates.

[Sec. 5761(f)]

(f) CROSS REFERENCES.—

For penalty for failure to make deposits or for overstatement of deposits, see section 6656.

Amendments

• **2006, Tax Relief and Health Care Act of 2006 (P.L. 109-432)**

P.L. 109-432, Division C, § 401(f)(1):

Amended Code Sec. 5761 by redesignating subsection (e) as subsection (f). **Effective** with respect to goods entered, or withdrawn from warehouse for consumption, on or after the 15th day after 12-20-2006.

• **1997, Balanced Budget Act of 1997 (P.L. 105-33)**

P.L. 105-33, § 9302(h)(1)(B):

Amended Code Sec. 5761 by redesignating subsection (d) as subsection (e). **Effective**, generally, for articles removed (as defined in Code Sec. 5702(k)) after 12-31-99. For a transitional rule, see Act Sec. 9302(i)(2) in the amendment notes following Code Sec. 5701(a).

• **1981, Economic Recovery Tax Act of 1981 (P.L. 97-34)**

P.L. 97-34, § 722(a)(3):

Amended the heading and text of Code Sec. 5761(d) by striking out "6659" and inserting "6660". **Effective** for returns filed after 12-31-81.

P.L. 97-34, § 724(b)(5):

Amended Code Sec. 5761(c) and (d). **Effective** for returns filed after 8-13-81. Prior to amendment, Code Sec. 5761(c) and (d) (as previously amended by P.L. 97-34) read as follows:

(c) FAILURE TO MAKE DEPOSIT OF TAXES.—Section 6656 relating to failure to make deposit of taxes shall apply to the failure to make any deposit of taxes imposed under subchapter A on the date prescribed therefor, except that the penalty for such failure

TOBACCO TAXES—PENALTIES

shall be 5 percent of the amount of the underpayment in lieu of the penalty provided by such section.

(d) APPLICABILITY OF SECTION 6660.—The penalties imposed by subsections (b) and (c) shall be assessed, collected, and paid in the same manner as taxes, as provided in section 6660(a).

- **1958, Excise Tax Technical Changes Act of 1958 (P.L. 85-859)**

P.L. 85-859, §202:

Amended Sec. 5761. **Effective** 9-3-58. Prior to amendment, Sec. 5761 read as follows:

SEC. 5761. CIVIL PENALTIES.

(a) Omitting Things Required or Doing Things Forbidden.—Whoever willfully omits, neglects, or refuses to comply with any duty imposed upon him by this chapter, or to do, or cause to be done, any of the things required by this chapter, or does anything prohibited by this chapter, shall, in addition to any other penalty provided in this title, be liable to a penalty of $1,000, to be recovered, with costs of suit, in a civil action, except where a penalty under subsection (b) of this section or under section 6651, 6652, or 6653 may be collected from such person by assessment.

(b) Willfully Failing to Pay Tax.—Whoever willfully omits, neglects, or refuses to pay any tax imposed by this chapter, or attempts in any manner to evade or defeat any such tax or the payment thereof, shall, in addition to any other penalty provided in this title, be liable to a penalty of the amount of tax evaded, or not paid, which penalty shall be added to the tax and assessed and collected at the same time, in the same manner, and as a part of the tax.

(c) Failing to Pay Tax.—Whoever fails to pay tax at the time prescribed shall, in addition to any other penalty provided in this title, be liable to a penalty of 5 percent of the tax due but unpaid, together with interest at the rate of 6 percent per annum upon such tax from the time the tax became due; but no interest for a fraction of a month shall be demanded. The penalties provided in this subsection shall be added to the tax and assessed and collected at the same time, in the same manner, and as a part of the tax.

[Sec. 5762]

SEC. 5762. CRIMINAL PENALTIES.

[Sec. 5762(a)]

(a) FRAUDULENT OFFENSES.—Whoever, with intent to defraud the United States—

(1) ENGAGING IN BUSINESS UNLAWFULLY.—Engages in business as a manufacturer or importer of tobacco products or cigarette papers and tubes or as an export warehouse proprietor, without filing the bond and obtaining the permit where required by this chapter or regulations thereunder; or

(2) FAILING TO FURNISH INFORMATION OR FURNISHING FALSE INFORMATION.—Fails to keep or make any record, return, report, or inventory, or keeps or makes any false or fraudulent record, return, report or inventory, required by this chapter or regulations thereunder; or

(3) REFUSING TO PAY OR EVADING TAX.—Refuses to pay any tax imposed by this chapter, or attempts in any manner to evade or defeat the tax or the payment thereof; or

(4) REMOVING TOBACCO PRODUCTS OR CIGARETTE PAPERS OR TUBES UNLAWFULLY.—Removes, contrary to this chapter or regulations thereunder, any tobacco products or cigarette papers or tubes subject to tax under this chapter; or

(5) PURCHASING, RECEIVING, POSSESSING, OR SELLING TOBACCO PRODUCTS OR CIGARETTE PAPERS OR TUBES UNLAWFULLY.—Violates any provision of section 5751(a)(1) or (a)(2); or

(6) DESTROYING, OBLITERATING, OR DETACHING MARKS, LABELS, OR NOTICES BEFORE PACKAGES ARE EMPTIED.—Violates any provision of section 5752;

shall, for each such offense, be fined not more than $10,000, or imprisoned not more than 5 years, or both.

Amendments

- **1997, Balanced Budget Act of 1997 (P.L. 105-33)**

P.L. 105-33, §9302(h)(2)(A):

Amended Code Sec. 5762(a)(1) by inserting "or importer" after "manufacturer". **Effective**, generally, for articles removed (as defined in Code Sec. 5702(k)) after 12-31-99. For a transitional rule, see Act Sec. 9302(i)(2) in the amendment notes following Code Sec. 5701(a).

- **1976, Tax Reform Act of 1976 (P.L. 94-455)**

P.L. 94-455, §1905(b)(7)(B)(ii):

Substituted paragraph (6) for paragraphs (6), (7), (8), (9), (10), and (11) in Code Sec. 5762(a). **Effective** 2-1-77. Prior to amendment, Code Sec. 5762(a)(6)-(11) read as follows:

(6) AFFIXING IMPROPER STAMPS.—Affixes to any package containing tobacco products or cigarette papers or tubes any improper or counterfeit stamp, or a stamp prescribed by this chapter or regulations thereunder which has been previously used on a package of such articles; or

(7) DESTROYING, OBLITERATING, OR DETACHING MARKS, LABELS, NOTICES, OR STAMPS BEFORE PACKAGES ARE EMPTIED.—Violates any provision of section 5752(a); or

(8) EMPTYING PACKAGES WITHOUT DESTROYING STAMPS.—Violates any provision of section 5752(b); or

(9) POSSESSING EMPTIED PACKAGES BEARING STAMP.—Violates any provision of section 5752(d); or

(10) REFILLING PACKAGES BEARING STAMPS.—Puts tobacco products or cigarette papers or tubes into any package which previously contained such articles and which bears a stamp prescribed by this chapter or regulations thereunder without destroying such stamp; or

(11) DETACHING STAMPS OR POSSESSING USED STAMPS.—Violates any provision of section 5752(c);

- **1965, Excise Tax Reduction Act of 1965 (P.L. 89-44)**

P.L. 89-44, §502(b)(12):

Amended Code Sec. 5762(a)(1). **Effective** for tax years beginning after 1-1-66. Prior to amendment, Code Sec. 5762(a)(1) read as follows:

(1) Engaging in Business Unlawfully.—Engages in business as a manufacturer of tobacco products or cigarette papers and tubes, as an export warehouse proprietor, or as a dealer in tobacco materials without filing the bond and obtaining the permit where required by this chapter or regulations thereunder; or

P.L. 89-44, §502(b)(12):

Amended Code Sec. 5762(a)(2). **Effective** for tax years beginning after 1-1-66. Prior to amendment, Code Sec. 5762(a)(2) read as follows:

(2) Failing to Furnish Information or Furnishing False Information.—Fails to keep or make any record, return, report, inventory, or statement, or keeps or makes any false or fraudulent record, return, report, inventory, or statement, required by this chapter or regulations thereunder; or

[Sec. 5762(b)]

(b) OTHER OFFENSES.—Whoever, otherwise than as provided in subsection (a), violates any provision of this chapter, or of regulations prescribed thereunder, shall, for each such offense, be fined not more than $1,000, or imprisoned not more than 1 year, or both.

Amendments

- **1958, Excise Tax Technical Changes Act of 1958 (P.L. 85-859)**

P.L. 85-859, §202:

Amended Code Sec. 5762. **Effective** 9-3-58. Prior to amendment, Code Sec. 5762 read as follows:

SEC. 5762. CRIMINAL PENALTIES.

(a) Whoever, with intent to defraud the United States—

(1) Engaging in business unlawfully.—Engages in business as a manufacturer of articles or dealer in tobacco materials without filing the bond and obtaining the permit required by this chapter or regulations thereunder; or

(2) Failing to furnish information or furnishing false information.—Fails to keep or make any record, return, report, inventory, or statement, or keeps or makes any false or fraudulent record, return, report, inventory, or statement, required by this chapter or regulations thereunder; or

(3) Refusing to pay or evading tax.—Refuses to pay any tax imposed by this chapter, or attempts in any manner to evade or defeat the tax or the payment thereof; or

(4) Removing articles unlawfully.—Removes any articles subject to tax under this chapter, contrary to this chapter or regulations thereunder; or

(5) Purchasing, Receiving, possessing, or selling articles unlawfully.—Purchases, receives, possesses, or sells articles not exempt from tax under this chapter, upon which the tax has not been paid in the manner and at the time prescribed by this chapter or regulations thereunder, or which, after removal, are not put up in packages bearing proper labels, stamps, or notices, prescribed; or

(6) Affixing improper labels or stamps.—Affixes to any package containing articles subject to tax any improper or counterfeit label or stamp, or a label or stamp, prescribed by this chapter or regulations thereunder, which has been previously used on a package; or

(7) Packaging with improper notices.—Puts articles subject to tax into any package bearing an improper notice to evidence the tax; or

(8) Refilling packages bearing labels, stamps, or notices.—Puts articles subject to tax into any package which previously contained such articles, without destroying the label, stamp, or notice, prescribed by this chapter or regulations thereunder, and affixing a new one thereto; or

(9) Removing labels or stamps or possessing used labels or stamps.—Removes, or causes to be removed, from any package any label or stamp, prescribed by this chapter or regulations thereunder, or purchases, receives, or has in his possession any such label or stamp which has been so removed, with intent to reuse the same; or

(10) Possessing emptied packages bearing labels, stamps, or notices.—Purchases, receives, or has in his possession any emptied package which previously contained articles subject to tax, upon which the label, stamp, or notice, prescribed by this chapter or regulations thereunder, has not been destroyed, with intent to reuse the

TOBACCO TAXES—FORFEITURES

same, shall, for each such offense, be fined not more than $10,000 or imprisoned not more than 5 years, or both.

(b) Whoever otherwise violates any provision of this chapter, or of regulations prescribed thereunder, shall, for each such offense, be fined not more than $1,000, or imprisoned not more than 1 year, or both.

[Sec. 5763]

SEC. 5763. FORFEITURES.

[Sec. 5763(a)]

(a) TOBACCO PRODUCTS AND CIGARETTE PAPERS AND TUBES UNLAWFULLY POSSESSED.—

(1) TOBACCO PRODUCTS AND CIGARETTE PAPERS AND TUBES POSSESSED WITH INTENT TO DEFRAUD.—All tobacco products and cigarette papers and tubes which, after removal, are possessed with intent to defraud the United States shall be forfeited to the United States.

(2) TOBACCO PRODUCTS AND CIGARETTE PAPERS AND TUBES NOT PROPERLY PACKAGED.—All tobacco products and cigarette papers and tubes not in packages as required under section 5723 or which are in packages not bearing the marks, labels, and notices, as required under such section, which, after removal, are possessed otherwise than with intent to defraud the United States, shall be forfeited to the United States. This paragraph shall not apply to tobacco products or cigarette papers or tubes sold or delivered directly to consumers from proper packages.

Amendments

• **1976, Tax Reform Act of 1976 (P.L. 94-455)**

P.L. 94-455, § 1905(b)(7)(C)(i):

Substituted "and notices" for "notices, and stamps" in Code Sec. 5763(a)(2). **Effective** 2-1-77.

[Sec. 5763(b)]

(b) PERSONAL PROPERTY OF QUALIFIED MANUFACTURERS, QUALIFIED IMPORTERS, AND EXPORT WAREHOUSE PROPRIETORS, ACTING WITH INTENT TO DEFRAUD.—All tobacco products and cigarette papers and tubes, packages, machinery, fixtures, equipment, and all other materials and personal property on the premises of any qualified manufacturer or importer of tobacco products or cigarette papers and tubes, or export warehouse proprietor, who, with intent to defraud the United States, fails to keep or make any record, return, report, or inventory, or keeps or makes any false or fraudulent record, return, report, or inventory, required by this chapter; or refuses to pay any tax imposed by this chapter, or attempts in any manner to evade or defeat the tax or the payment thereof; or removes, contrary to any provision of this chapter, any article subject to tax under this chapter, shall be forfeited to the United States.

Amendments

• **1997, Balanced Budget Act of 1997 (P.L. 105-33)**

P.L. 105-33, § 9302(h)(2)(A):

Amended Code Sec. 5763(b) by inserting "or importer" after "manufacturer". **Effective**, generally, for articles removed (as defined in Code Sec. 5702(k)) after 12-31-99. For a transitional rule, see Act Sec. 9302(i)(2) in the amendment notes following Code Sec. 5701(a).

P.L. 105-33, § 9302(h)(2)(B):

Amended the heading of Code Sec. 5763(b) by inserting "QUALIFIED IMPORTERS," after "MANUFACTURERS,". **Effective**, generally, for articles removed (as defined in Code Sec. 5702(k)) after 12-31-99. For a transitional rule, see Act Sec. 9302(i)(2) in the amendment notes following Code Sec. 5701(a).

• **1976, Tax Reform Act of 1976 (P.L. 94-455)**

P.L. 94-455, § 1905(b)(7)(C)(ii):

Struck out "internal revenue stamps," following "packages," at the beginning of Code Sec. 5763(b). **Effective** 2-1-77.

• **1965, Excise Tax Reduction Act of 1965 (P.L. 89-44)**

P.L. 89-44, § 502(b)(13):

Amended Code Sec. 5763(b). **Effective** for tax years beginning after 1-1-66. Prior to amendment, Code Sec. 5763(b) read as follows:

"(b) Personal Property of Qualified Manufacturers, Export Warehouse Proprietors, and Dealers Acting with Intent to Defraud.—All tobacco products and cigarette papers and tubes, tobacco materials, packages, internal revenue stamps, machinery, fixtures, equipment, and all other materials and personal property on the premises of any qualified manufacturer of tobacco products or cigarette papers and tubes, export warehouse proprietor, or dealer in tobacco materials who, with intent to defraud the United States, fails to keep or make any record, return, report, inventory, or statement, or keeps or makes any false or fraudulent record return, report, inventory, or statement, required by this chapter; or refuses to pay any tax imposed by this chapter, or attempts in any manner to evade or defeat the tax or the payment thereof; or removes, contrary to any provision of this chapter, any article subject to tax under this chapter, shall be forfeited to the United States."

[Sec. 5763(c)]

(c) REAL AND PERSONAL PROPERTY OF ILLICIT OPERATORS.—All tobacco products, cigarette papers and tubes, machinery, fixtures, equipment, and other materials and personal property on the premises of any person engaged in business as a manufacturer or importer of tobacco products or cigarette papers and tubes, or export warehouse proprietor, without filing the bond or obtaining the permit, as required by this chapter, together with all his right, title, and interest in the building in which such business is conducted, and the lot or tract of ground on which the building is located, shall be forfeited to the United States.

Amendments

• **1997, Balanced Budget Act of 1997 (P.L. 105-33)**

P.L. 105-33, § 9302(h)(2)(A):

Amended Code Sec. 5763(c) by inserting "or importer" after "manufacturer". **Effective**, generally, for articles removed (as defined in Code Sec. 5702(k)) after 12-31-99. For a transitional rule, see Act Sec. 9302(i)(2) in the amendment notes following Code Sec. 5701(a).

• **1965, Excise Tax Reduction Act of 1965 (P.L. 89-44)**

P.L. 89-44, § 502(b)(13):

Amended Code Sec. 5763(c). **Effective** for tax years beginning after 1-1-66. Prior to amendment, Code Sec. 5763(c) read as follows:

(c) Real and Personal Property of Illicit Operators.—All tobacco products, cigarette papers and tubes, tobacco materials, machinery, fixtures, equipment, and other materials and personal property on the premises of any person engaged in business as a manufacturer of tobacco products or cigarette papers and tubes, export warehouse proprietor, or dealer in tobacco materials, without filing the bond or obtaining the permit, as required by this chapter, together with all his right, title, and interest in the building in which such business is conducted, and the lot or tract of ground on which the building is located, shall be forfeited to the United States.

[Sec. 5763(d)]

(d) GENERAL.—All property intended for use in violating the provisions of this chapter, or regulations thereunder, or which has been so used, shall be forfeited to the United States as provided in section 7302.

Amendments

• **1958, Excise Tax Technical Changes Act of 1958 (P.L. 85-859)**

P.L. 85-859, § 202:

Amended Sec. 5763. **Effective** 9-3-58. Prior to amendment, Sec. 5763 read as follows:

SEC. 5763. FORFEITURES.

(a) Articles Unlawfully Possessed.—All articles not exempt from tax which, after removal, are possessed with intent to defraud, or which, regardless of intent, are not put up in packages bearing proper labels, notices, and stamps, prescribed pursuant to section 5723, shall be forfeited to the United States: Provided, however, That this section shall not apply to articles sold at retail directly from proper packages.

(b) Personal Property of Qualified Manufacturers and Dealers With Intent to Defraud.—All articles, tobacco materials, packages, internal revenue stamps, machinery, fixtures, equipment, and all other materials and personal property on the premises of any qualified manufacturer of articles or dealer in tobacco materials who, with intent to defraud, fails to keep or make any record, return, report, inventory, or statement, or keeps or makes any false or fraudulent record, return, report, inventory, or statement, required by this chapter; or refuses to pay any tax imposed by this chapter, or attempts in any manner to evade or defeat the tax or the payment thereof; or removes any articles subject to tax under this chapter, contrary to any provision of this chapter, shall be forfeited to the United States.

(c) Real and Personal Property of Illicit Operators.—All articles, tobacco materials, machinery, fixtures, equipment, and other materials and personal property on the

FIREARMS—TAXES

premises of any person engaged in business as a manufacturer of articles or dealer in tobacco materials without filing the bond and obtaining the permit required by this chapter, together with all his right, title, and interest in the building in which such business is conducted, and the lot or tract of ground on which the building is located, shall be forfeited to the United States.

(d) GENERAL.—All property intended for use in violating the provisions of this chapter, or which has been so used, shall be forfeited to the United States as provided in section 7302.

CHAPTER 53—MACHINE GUNS, DESTRUCTIVE DEVICES, AND CERTAIN OTHER FIREARMS

SUBCHAPTER A.	Taxes.
SUBCHAPTER B.	General provisions and exemptions.
SUBCHAPTER C.	Prohibited acts.
SUBCHAPTER D.	Penalties and forfeitures.

Subchapter A—Taxes

Part I.	Special (occupational) taxes.
Part II.	Tax on transferring firearms.
Part III.	Tax on making firearms.

PART I—SPECIAL (OCCUPATIONAL) TAXES

Sec. 5801.	Imposition of tax.
Sec. 5802.	Registration of importers, manufacturers, and dealers.

[Sec. 5801]

SEC. 5801. IMPOSITION OF TAX.

[Sec. 5801(a)]

(a) GENERAL RULE.—On 1st engaging in business and thereafter on or before July 1 of each year, every importer, manufacturer, and dealer in firearms shall pay a special (occupational) tax for each place of business at the following rates:

(1) Importers and manufacturers: $1,000 a year or fraction thereof.

(2) Dealers: $500 a year or fraction thereof.

[Sec. 5801(b)]

(b) REDUCED RATES OF TAX FOR SMALL IMPORTERS AND MANUFACTURERS.—

(1) IN GENERAL.—Paragraph (1) of subsection (a) shall be applied by substituting "$500" for "$1,000" with respect to any taxpayer the gross receipts of which (for the most recent taxable year ending before the 1st day of the taxable period to which the tax imposed by subsection (a) relates) are less than $500,000.

(2) CONTROLLED GROUP RULES.—All persons treated as 1 taxpayer under section 5061(e)(3) shall be treated as 1 taxpayer for purposes of paragraph (1).

(3) CERTAIN RULES TO APPLY.—For purposes of paragraph (1), rules similar to the rules of subparagraphs (B) and (C) of section 448(c)(3) shall apply.

Amendments

- **1987, Revenue Act of 1987 (P.L. 100-203)**

P.L. 100-203, §10512(g)(1):

Amended Code Sec. 5801. For the **effective** date, see Act Sec. 10512(h), below. Prior to amendment, Code Sec. 5801 read as follows:

SEC. 5801. TAX.

On first engaging in business and thereafter on or before the first day of July of each year, every importer, manufacturer, and dealer in firearms shall pay a special (occupational) tax for each place of business at the following rates.

(1) IMPORTERS.—$500 a year or fraction thereof;

(2) MANUFACTURERS.—$500 a year or fraction thereof;

(3) DEALERS.—$200 a year or fraction thereof.

Except an importer, manufacturer, or dealer who imports, manufactures, or deals in only weapons classified as "any other weapon" under section 5845(e), shall pay a special (occupational) tax for each place of business at the following rates: Importers, $25 a year or fraction thereof; manufacturers, $25 a year or fraction thereof; dealers, $10 a year or fraction thereof.

P.L. 100-203, §10512(h), provides:

(h) EFFECTIVE DATE.—

(1) IN GENERAL.—The amendments made by this section shall take effect on January 1, 1988.

(2) ALL TAXPAYERS TREATED AS COMMENCING IN BUSINESS ON JANUARY 1, 1988.—

(A) IN GENERAL.—Any person engaged on January 1, 1988, in any trade or business which is subject to an occupational tax shall be treated for purposes of such tax as having 1st engaged in such trade or business on such date.

(B) LIMITATION ON AMOUNT OF TAX.—In the case of a taxpayer who paid an occupational tax in respect of any premises for any taxable period which began before January 1, 1988, and includes such date, the amount of the occupational tax imposed by reason of subparagraph (A) in respect of such premises shall not exceed an amount equal to $1/2$ the excess (if any) of—

(i) the rate of such tax as in effect on January 1, 1988, over

(ii) the rate of such tax as in effect on December 31, 1987.

(C) OCCUPATIONAL TAX.—For purposes of this paragraph, the term "occupational tax" means any tax imposed under part II of subchapter A of chapter 51, section 5276, section 5731, or section 5801 of the Internal Revenue Code of 1986 (as amended by this section).

(D) DUE DATE OF TAX.—The amount of any tax required to be paid by reason of this paragraph shall be due on April 1, 1988.

- **1968, Gun Control Act of 1968 (P.L. 90-618)**

P.L. 90-618, §201:

Amended Code Sec. 5801. **Effective** 11-1-68. Prior to amendment, Code Sec. 5801 read as follows:

"(a) Rate.—On first engaging in business, and thereafter on or before the first day of July of each year, every importer, manufacturer, and dealer in firearms shall pay a special tax at the following rates:

"(1) Importers or Manufacturers.—Importers or manufacturers, $500 a year or fraction thereof;

"(2) Dealers other than pawnbrokers.—Dealers, other than pawnbrokers, $200 a year or fraction thereof;

"(3) Pawnbrokers.—Pawnbrokers, $300 a year or fraction thereof:

Provided, That manufacturers and dealers in guns with combination shotgun and rifle barrels, 12 inches or more but less than 18 inches in length, from which only a single discharge can be made from either barrel without manual reloading, and manufacturers and dealers in guns classified as 'any other weapon' under section 5848(5) shall pay the following taxes: Manufacturers, $25 a year or fraction thereof; dealers, $10 a year or fraction thereof.

"(b) Cross Reference.—

"For license to transport, ship, or receive firearms or ammunition under the Federal Firearms Act, see section 3 of the Act of June 30, 1938 (52 Stat. 1251; 15 U. S. C. 903)."

- **1960 (P.L. 86-478)**

P.L. 86-478, §[1]:

Amended Code Sec. 5801(a) by adding the phrase "or fraction thereof" in paragraphs (1), (2), and (3) and by amending the material beginning with the word "*Provided*". Prior to amendment that material read as follows: "*Provided*, That manufacturers and dealers in guns with combination shotgun and rifle barrels, 12 inches or more but less than 18 inches in length, from which only a single discharge can be made from either barrel without manual reloading, guns designed to be held in one hand when fired and having a barrel 12 inches or more but less than 18 inches in length, from which only a single discharge can be made without manual reloading, or guns of both types, shall pay the following taxes: Manufacturers, $25 a year; dealers, $1 a year or any part thereof."

FIREARMS—TAXES

P.L. 86-478:

Repealed former Code Sec. 5801(b) and redesignated former Code Sec. 5801(c) as Code Sec. 5801(b). **Effective** 7-1-60. Prior to its repeal, former Code Sec. 5801(b) read as follows:

"(b) Computation of Tax.—Where the tax is payable on the first day of July in any year it shall be computed for 1 year; where the tax is payable on any other day it shall be computed proportionately from the first day of the month in which the liability to the tax accrued to the first day of July following. This subsection shall not apply to the special tax imposed at the rate of $1 a year or any part thereof."

• **1958, Excise Tax Technical Changes Act of 1958 (P.L. 85-859)**

P.L. 85-859, §203(a):

Amended Sec. 5801(a) by striking out, at the end thereof, the phrase "dealers, $1 a year" and substituting the phrase "dealers, $1 a year or any part thereof", and added the last sentence in Code Sec. 5801(b). **Effective** 9-3-58.

[Sec. 5802]

SEC. 5802. REGISTRATION OF IMPORTERS, MANUFACTURERS, AND DEALERS.

On first engaging in business and thereafter on or before the first day of July of each year, each importer, manufacturer, and dealer in firearms shall register with the Secretary in each internal revenue district in which such business is to be carried on, his name, including any trade name, and the address of each location in the district where he will conduct such business. An individual required to register under this section shall include a photograph and fingerprints of the individual with the initial application. Where there is a change during the taxable year in the location of, or the trade name used in, such business, the importer, manufacturer, or dealer shall file an application with the Secretary to amend his registration. Firearms operations of an importer, manufacturer, or dealer may not be commenced at the new location or under a new trade name prior to approval by the Secretary of the application.

Amendments

• **1994, Violent Crime Control and Law Enforcement Act of 1994 (P.L. 103-322)**

P.L. 103-322, §110301:

Amended Code Sec. 5802 by adding after the first sentence a new sentence. **Effective** 9-13-94.

• **1976, Tax Reform Act of 1976 (P.L. 94-455)**

P.L. 94-455, §1906(b)(13)(A):

Amended 1954 Code by substituting "Secretary" for "Secretary or his delegate" each place it appeared. **Effective** 2-1-77.

• **1968, Gun Control Act of 1968 (P.L. 90-618)**

P.L. 90-618, §201:

Amended Code Sec. 5802. **Effective** 11-1-68. Prior to amendment Code Sec. 5802 read as follows:

SEC. 5802. REGISTRATION.

Importers, Manufacturers, and Dealers.—On first engaging in business, and thereafter on or before the first day of July of each year, every importer, manufacturer, and dealer in firearms shall register with the Secretary or his delegate in each internal revenue district in which such business is to be carried on his name or style, principal place of business, and places of business in such district.

PART II—TAX ON TRANSFERRING FIREARMS

Sec. 5811.   Transfer tax.
Sec. 5812.   Transfers.

[Sec. 5811]

SEC. 5811. TRANSFER TAX.

[Sec. 5811(a)]

(a) RATE.—There shall be levied, collected, and paid on firearms transferred a tax at the rate of $200 for each firearm transferred, except, the transfer tax on any firearm classified as "any other weapon" under section 5845(e) shall be at the rate of $5 for each such firearm transferred.

Amendments

• **1968, Gun Control Act of 1968 (P.L. 90-618)**

P.L. 90-618, §201:

Amended Code Sec. 5811(a). **Effective** 11-1-68. Prior to amendment, Code Sec. 5811(a) read as follows:

"(a) Rate.—There shall be levied, collected, and paid on firearms transferred in the United States a tax at the rate of $200 for each firearm: *Provided,* That the transfer tax on any gun with combination shotgun and rifle barrels, 12 inches or more but less than 18 inches in length, from which only a single discharge can be made from either barrel without manual reloading, and on any gun classified as 'any other weapon' under section 5848(5), shall be at the rate of $5. The tax imposed by this section shall be in addition to any import duty imposed on such firearm."

• **1960 (P.L. 86-478)**

P.L. 86-478, §2:

Amended Code Sec. 5811(a). **Effective** 7-1-60. Prior to amendment, Code Sec. 5811(a) read as follows:

"(a) Rate.—There shall be levied, collected, and paid on firearms transferred in the United States a tax at the rate of $200 for each firearm: *Provided,* That the transfer tax on any gun with combination shotgun and rifle barrels, 12 inches or more but less than 18 inches in length, from which only a single discharge can be made from either barrel without manual reloading, or any gun designed to be held in one hand when fired and having a barrel 12 inches or more but less than 18 inches in length from which only a single discharge can be made without manual reloading, shall be at the rate of $1. The tax imposed by this section shall be in addition to any import duty imposed on such firearm."

• **1958, Excise Tax Technical Changes Act of 1958 (P.L. 85-859)**

P.L. 85-859, §203(b):

Amended Sec. 5811(a) by inserting after "12 inches" (the second place it appears) the phrase "or more". **Effective** 9-3-58.

[Sec. 5811(b)]

(b) BY WHOM PAID.—The tax imposed by subsection (a) of this section shall be paid by the transferor.

Amendments

• **1968, Gun Control Act of 1968 (P.L. 90-618)**

P.L. 90-618, §201:

Amended Code Sec. 5811(b). **Effective** 11-1-68. Prior to amendment, Code Sec. 5811(b) read as follows:

"(b) By Whom Paid.—Such tax shall be paid by the transferor: *Provided,* That if a firearm is transferred without payment of such tax the transferor and transferee shall become jointly and severally liable for such tax."

• **1960 (P.L. 86-478)**

P.L. 86-478, §2:

Amended Code Sec. 5811(b) by adding the material beginning with the word "*Provided*". **Effective** 7-1-60.

[Sec. 5811(c)]

(c) PAYMENT.—The tax imposed by subsection (a) of this section shall be payable by the appropriate stamps prescribed for payment by the Secretary.

Amendments

• **1976, Tax Reform Act of 1976 (P.L. 94-455)**

P.L. 94-455, §1906(b)(13)(A):

Amended 1954 Code by substituting "Secretary" for "Secretary or his delegate" each place it appeared. **Effective** 2-1-77.

• **1968, Gun Control Act of 1968 (P.L. 90-618)**

P.L. 90-618, §201:

Amended Code Sec. 5811(c). **Effective** 11-1-68. Prior to amendment, Code Sec. 5811(c) read as follows:

"(c) How Paid.

"(1) Stamps.—Payment of the tax herein provided shall be represented by appropriate stamps to be provided by the Secretary or his delegate."

FIREARMS—TAXES

[Sec. 5811(d)—Repealed]

Amendments

• **1968, Gun Control Act of 1968 (P.L. 90-618)**

P.L. 90-618, § 201:

Repealed Code Sec. 5811(d). **Effective** 11-1-68. Prior to repeal, Code Sec. 5811(d) read as follows:

(d) CROSS REFERENCE.—

(1) For assessment in case of omitted taxes payable by stamp, see sections 6155(a), 6201(a)(2)(A), 6601(c)(4), and 6201(a).

(2) For requirements as to registration and special tax, see sections 5801 and 5802.

(3) For excise tax on pistols, revolvers and firearms, see section 4181.

[Sec. 5812]

SEC. 5812. TRANSFERS.

[Sec. 5812(a)]

(a) APPLICATION.—A firearm shall not be transferred unless (1) the transferor of the firearm has filed with the Secretary a written application, in duplicate, for the transfer and registration of the firearm to the transferee on the application form prescribed by the Secretary; (2) any tax payable on the transfer is paid as evidenced by the proper stamp affixed to the original application form; (3) the transferee is identified in the application form in such manner as the Secretary may by regulations prescribe, except that, if such person is an individual, the identification must include his fingerprints and his photograph; (4) the transferor of the firearm is identified in the application form in such manner as the Secretary may by regulations prescribe; (5) the firearm is identified in the application form in such manner as the Secretary may by regulations prescribe; and (6) the application form shows that the Secretary has approved the transfer and the registration of the firearm to the transferee. Applications shall be denied if the transfer, receipt, or possession of the firearm would place the transferee in violation of law.

Amendments

• **1976, Tax Reform Act of 1976 (P.L. 94-455)**

P.L. 94-455, § 1906(b)(13)(A):

Amended 1954 Code by substituting "Secretary" for "Secretary or his delegate" each place it appeared. **Effective** 2-1-77.

[Sec. 5812(b)]

(b) TRANSFER OF POSSESSION.—The transferee of a firearm shall not take possession of the firearm unless the Secretary has approved the transfer and registration of the firearm to the transferee as required by subsection (a) of this section.

Amendments

• **1976, Tax Reform Act of 1976 (P.L. 94-455)**

P.L. 94-455, § 1906(b)(13)(A):

Amended 1954 Code by substituting "Secretary" for "Secretary or his delegate" each place it appeared. **Effective** 2-1-77.

• **1968, Gun Control Act of 1968 (P.L. 90-618)**

P.L. 90-618, § 201:

Amended Code Sec. 5812. **Effective** 11-1-68. Prior to amendment, Code Sec. 5812 read as follows:

SEC. 5812. EXEMPTIONS.

(a) Transfers Exempt.—This chapter shall not apply to the transfer of firearms—

(1) to the United States Government, any State, Territory, or possession of the United States, or to any political subdivision thereof, or to the District of Columbia;

(2) to any peace officer or any Federal officer designated by regulations of the Secretary or his delegate;

(3) to the transfer of any firearm which is unserviceable and which is transferred as a curiosity or ornament.

(b) Notice of Exemption.—If the transfer of a firearm is exempted as provided in subsection (a), the person transferring such firearm shall notify the Secretary or his delegate of the name and address of the applicant, the number or other mark identifying such firearm, and the date of its transfer, and shall file with the Secretary or his delegate such documents in proof thereof as the Secretary or his delegate may by regulations prescribe.

(c) Exemption from Other Taxes.—

For exemption from excise tax on pistols, revolvers, and firearms, see section 4182(a).

PART III—TAX ON MAKING FIREARMS

Sec. 5821.   Making tax.
Sec. 5822.   Making.

[Sec. 5821]

SEC. 5821. MAKING TAX.

[Sec. 5821(a)]

(a) RATE.—There shall be levied, collected, and paid upon the making of a firearm a tax at the rate of $200 for each firearm made.

[Sec. 5821(b)]

(b) BY WHOM PAID.—The tax imposed by subsection (a) of this section shall be paid by the person making the firearm.

[Sec. 5821(c)]

(c) PAYMENT.—The tax imposed by subsection (a) of this section shall be payable by the stamp prescribed for payment by the Secretary.

Amendments

• **1976, Tax Reform Act of 1976 (P.L. 94-455)**

P.L. 94-455, § 1906(b)(13)(A):

Amended 1954 Code by substituting "Secretary" for "Secretary or his delegate" each place it appeared. **Effective** 2-1-77.

• **1968, Gun Control Act of 1968 (P.L. 90-618)**

P.L. 90-618, § 201:

Amended Code Sec. 5821. **Effective** 11-1-68. Prior to amendment, Code Sec. 5821 read as follows:

"(a) Rate.—There shall be levied, collected, and paid upon the making in the United States of any firearm (whether by manufacture, putting together, alteration, any combination thereof, or otherwise) a tax at the rate of $200 for each firearm so made.

"(b) Exceptions.—The tax imposed by subsection (a) shall not apply to the making of a firearm—

"(1) by any person who is engaged within the United States in the business of manufacturing firearms;

"(2) from another firearm with respect to which a tax has been paid, prior to such making, under subsection (a) of this section; or

"(3) for the use of—

"(A) the United States Government, any State, Territory, or possession of the United States, any political subdivision thereof, or the District of Columbia, or

"(B) any peace officer or any Federal officer designated by regulations of the Secretary or his delegate.

Any person who makes a firearm in respect of which the tax imposed by subsection (a) does not apply by reason of the preceding sentence shall make such report in respect thereof as the Secretary or his delegate may by regulations prescribe.

"(c) By Whom Paid; When Paid.—The tax imposed by subsection (a) shall be paid by the person making the firearm. Such tax shall be paid in advance of the making of the firearm.

"(d) How Paid.—Payment of the tax imposed by subsection (a) shall be represented by appropriate stamps to be provided by the Secretary or his delegate.

"(e) Declaration.—It shall be unlawful for any person subject to the tax imposed by subsection (a) to make a firearm unless, prior to such making, he has declared in writing his intention to make a firearm, has affixed the stamp described in subsection (d) to the original of such declaration, and has filed such original and a copy thereof. The declaration required by the preceding sentence shall be filed at such place, and shall be in such form and contain such information, as the Secretary or his delegate may by regulations prescribe. The original of the declaration, with the stamp affixed, shall be returned to the person making the declaration. If the person making the declaration is an individual, there shall be included as part of the declaration the fingerprints and a photograph of such individual."

Sec. 5811(d)—Repealed

FIREARMS—REGISTRATION

• **1958, Excise Tax Technical Changes Act of 1958 (P.L. 85-859)**

P.L. 85-859, §203(d)(1):

Amended Code Sec. 5821(a) by striking out at the end thereof the phrase "that rate provided in section 5811(a) which would apply to any transfer of the firearm so made" and substituting "the rate of $200 for each firearm so made". **Effective** 9-3-58.

P.L. 85-859, §203(d)(1):

Amended Sec. 5821(b)(2) by striking out the phrase "under either section 5811(a) or" where it preceded the phrase "under subsection (a)". **Effective** 9-3-58.

[Sec. 5822]

SEC. 5822. MAKING.

No person shall make a firearm unless he has (a) filed with the Secretary a written application, in duplicate, to make and register the firearm on the form prescribed by the Secretary; (b) paid any tax payable on the making and such payment is evidenced by the proper stamp affixed to the original application form; (c) identified the firearm to be made in the application form in such manner as the Secretary may by regulations prescribe; (d) identified himself in the application form in such manner as the Secretary may by regulations prescribe, except that, if such person is an individual, the identification must include his fingerprints and his photograph; and (e) obtained the approval of the Secretary to make and register the firearm and the application form shows such approval. Applications shall be denied if the making or possession of the firearm would place the person making the firearm in violation of law.

Amendments

• **1976, Tax Reform Act of 1976 (P.L. 94-455)**

P.L. 94-455, §1906(b)(13)(A):

Amended 1954 Code by substituting "Secretary" for "Secretary or his delegate" each place it appeared. **Effective** 2-1-77.

• **1968, Gun Control Act of 1968 (P.L. 90-618)**

P.L. 90-618, §201:

Added Code Sec. 5822. **Effective** 11-1-68.

Subchapter B—General Provisions and Exemptions

Part I. General provisions.
Part II. Exemptions.

PART I—GENERAL PROVISIONS

Sec. 5841.   Registration of firearms.
Sec. 5842.   Identification of firearms.
Sec. 5843.   Records and returns.
Sec. 5844.   Importation.
Sec. 5845.   Definitions.
Sec. 5846.   Other laws applicable.
Sec. 5847.   Effect on other laws.
Sec. 5848.   Restrictive use of information.
Sec. 5849.   Citation of chapter.

[Sec. 5841]

SEC. 5841. REGISTRATION OF FIREARMS.

[Sec. 5841(a)]

(a) CENTRAL REGISTRY.—The Secretary shall maintain a central registry of all firearms in the United States which are not in the possession or under the control of the United States. This registry shall be known as the National Firearms Registration and Transfer Record. The registry shall include—

(1) identification of the firearm;

(2) date of registration; and

(3) identification and address of person entitled to possession of the firearm.

Amendments

• **1976, Tax Reform Act of 1976 (P.L. 94-455)**

P.L. 94-455, §1906(b)(13)(A):

Amended 1954 Code by substituting "Secretary" for "Secretary or his delegate" each place it appeared. **Effective** 2-1-77.

[Sec. 5841(b)]

(b) BY WHOM REGISTERED.—Each manufacturer, importer, and maker shall register each firearm he manufactures, imports, or makes. Each firearm transferred shall be registered to the transferee by the transferor.

[Sec. 5841(c)]

(c) HOW REGISTERED.—Each manufacturer shall notify the Secretary of the manufacture of a firearm in such manner as may by regulations be prescribed and such notification shall effect the registration of the firearm required by this section. Each importer, maker, and transferor of a firearm shall, prior to importing, making, or transferring a firearm, obtain authorization in such manner as required by this chapter or regulations issued thereunder to import, make, or transfer the firearm, and such authorization shall effect the registration of the firearm required by this section.

Amendments

• **1976, Tax Reform Act of 1976 (P.L. 94-455)**

P.L. 94-455, §1906(b)(13)(A):

Amended 1954 Code by substituting "Secretary" for "Secretary or his delegate" each place it appeared. **Effective** 2-1-77.

[Sec. 5841(d)]

(d) FIREARMS REGISTERED ON EFFECTIVE DATE OF THIS ACT.—A person shown as possessing a firearm by the records maintained by the Secretary pursuant to the National Firearms Act in force on the day immediately prior to the effective date of the National Firearms Act of 1968 shall be considered to have registered under this section the firearms in his possession which are disclosed by that record as being in his possession.

FIREARMS—IDENTIFICATION

Amendments

- **1976, Tax Reform Act of 1976 (P.L. 94-455)**

P.L. 94-455, §1906(b)(13)(A):

Amended 1954 Code by substituting "Secretary" for "Secretary or his delegate" each place it appeared. **Effective** 2-1-77.

[Sec. 5841(e)]

(e) PROOF OF REGISTRATION.—A person possessing a firearm registered as required by this section shall retain proof of registration which shall be made available to the Secretary upon request.

Amendments

- **1976, Tax Reform Act of 1976 (P.L. 94-455)**

P.L. 94-455, §1906(b)(13)(A):

Amended 1954 Code by substituting "Secretary" for "Secretary or his delegate" each place it appeared. **Effective** 2-1-77.

- **1968, Gun Control Act of 1968 (P.L. 90-618)**

P.L. 90-618, §201:

Amended Code Sec. 5841. **Effective** 11-1-68. Prior to amendment by P.L. 90-618, Code Sec. 5841 read as follows:

SEC. 5841. REGISTRATION OF PERSONS IN GENERAL.

Every person possessing a firearm shall register, with the Secretary or his delegate, the number or other mark identifying such firearm, together with his name, address, place where such firearm is usually kept, and place of business or employment, and, if such person is other than a natural person, the name and home address of an executive officer thereof. No person shall be required to register under this section with respect to a firearm which such person acquired by transfer or importation or which such person made, if provisions of this chapter applied to such transfer, importation, or making, as the case may be, and if the provisions which applied thereto were complied with.

P.L. 90-618, §207(b), provides:

(b) Notwithstanding the provisions of subsection (a) [regarding the effective date of §201 of P.L. 90-618] or any other provision of law, any person possessing a firearm as defined in section 5845(a) of the Internal Revenue Code of 1954 (as amended by this title) which is not registered to him in the National Firearms Registration and Transfer Record shall register each firearm so possessed with the Secretary of the Treasury or his delegate in such form and manner as the Secretary or his delegate may require within the thirty days immediately following the effective date of section 201 of this Act. Such registrations shall become a part of the National Firearms Registration and Transfer Record required to be maintained by section 5841 of the Internal Revenue Code of 1954 (as amended by this title). No information or evidence required to be submitted or retained by a natural person to register a firearm under this section shall be used, directly or indirectly, as evidence against such person in any criminal proceeding with respect to a prior or concurrent violation of law.

[Sec. 5842]

SEC. 5842. IDENTIFICATION OF FIREARMS.

[Sec. 5842(a)]

(a) IDENTIFICATION OF FIREARMS OTHER THAN DESTRUCTIVE DEVICES.—Each manufacturer and importer and anyone making a firearm shall identify each firearm, other than a destructive device, manufactured, imported, or made by a serial number which may not be readily removed, obliterated, or altered, the name of the manufacturer, importer, or maker, and such other identification as the Secretary may by regulations prescribe.

Amendments

- **1976, Tax Reform Act of 1976 (P.L. 94-455)**

P.L. 94-455, §1906(b)(13)(A):

Amended 1954 Code by substituting "Secretary" for "Secretary or his delegate" each place it appeared. **Effective** 2-1-77.

[Sec. 5842(b)]

(b) FIREARMS WITHOUT SERIAL NUMBER.—Any person who possesses a firearm, other than a destructive device, which does not bear the serial number and other information required by subsection (a) of this section shall identify the firearm with a serial number assigned by the Secretary and any other information the Secretary may by regulations prescribe.

Amendments

- **1976, Tax Reform Act of 1976 (P.L. 94-455)**

P.L. 94-455, §1906(b)(13)(A):

Amended 1954 Code by substituting "Secretary" for "Secretary or his delegate" each place it appeared. **Effective** 2-1-77.

[Sec. 5842(c)]

(c) IDENTIFICATION OF DESTRUCTIVE DEVICE.—Any firearm classified as a destructive device shall be identified in such manner as the Secretary may by regulations prescribe.

Amendments

- **1976, Tax Reform Act of 1976 (P.L. 94-455)**

P.L. 94-455, §1906(b)(13)(A):

Amended 1954 Code by substituting "Secretary" for "Secretary or his delegate" each place it appeared. **Effective** 2-1-77.

- **1968, Gun Control Act of 1968 (P.L. 90-618)**

P.L. 90-618, §201:

Amended Code Sec. 5842. **Effective** 11-1-68. Prior to amendment, Code Sec. 5842 read as follows:

SEC. 5842. BOOKS, RECORDS AND RETURNS.

Importers, manufacturers, and dealers shall keep such books and records and render such returns in relation to the transactions in firearms specified in this chapter as the Secretary or his delegate may by regulations require.

[Sec. 5843]

SEC. 5843. RECORDS AND RETURNS.

Importers, manufacturers, and dealers shall keep such records of, and render such returns in relation to, the importation, manufacture, making, receipt, and sale, or other disposition, of firearms as the Secretary may by regulations prescribe.

Amendments

- **1976, Tax Reform Act of 1976 (P.L. 94-455)**

P.L. 94-455, §1906(b)(13)(A):

Amended 1954 Code by substituting "Secretary" for "Secretary or his delegate" each place it appeared. **Effective** 2-1-77.

- **1968, Gun Control Act of 1968 (P.L. 90-618)**

P.L. 90-618, §201:

Amended Code Sec. 5843. **Effective** 11-1-68. Prior to amendment, Code Sec. 5843 read as follows:

SEC. 5843. IDENTIFICATION OF FIREARMS.

Each manufacturer and importer of a firearm shall identify it with a number and other identification marks approved by the Secretary or his delegate, such number and marks to be stamped or otherwise placed thereon in a manner approved by the Secretary or his delegate.

- **1958, Excise Tax Technical Changes Act of 1958 (P.L. 85-859)**

P.L. 85-859, §203(e):

Amended Code Sec. 5843 by striking out the phrase "number or other identification mark" and substituting the phrase "number and other identification marks", and by striking out the phrase "such number or mark" and substituting the phrase "such number and marks". **Effective** 9-3-58.

FIREARMS—DEFINITIONS

[Sec. 5844]

SEC. 5844. IMPORTATION.

No firearm shall be imported or brought into the United States or any territory under its control or jurisdiction unless the importer establishes, under regulations as may be prescribed by the Secretary, that the firearm to be imported or brought in is—

(1) being imported or brought in for the use of the United States or any department, independent establishment, or agency thereof or any State or possession or any political subdivision thereof; or

(2) being imported or brought in for scientific or research purposes; or

(3) being imported or brought in solely for testing or use as a model by a registered manufacturer or solely for use as a sample by a registered importer or registered dealer;

except that the Secretary may permit the conditional importation or bringing in of a firearm for examination and testing in connection with classifying the firearm.

Amendments

• **1976, Tax Reform Act of 1976 (P.L. 94-455)**

P.L. 94-455, §1906(b)(13)(A):

Amended 1954 Code by substituting "Secretary" for "Secretary or his delegate" each place it appeared. **Effective** 2-1-77.

• **1968, Gun Control Act of 1968 (P.L. 90-618)**

P.L. 90-618, §201:

Amended Code Sec. 5844. **Effective** 11-1-68. Prior to amendment, Code Sec. 5844 read as follows:

SEC. 5844. EXPORTATION.

Under such regulations as the Secretary or his delegate may prescribe, and upon proof of the exportation of any firearm to any foreign country (whether exported as part of another article or not) with respect to which the transfer tax under section 5811 has been paid by the manufacturer, the Secretary or his delegate shall refund to the manufacturer the amount of the tax so paid or, if the manufacturer waives all claim for the amount to be refunded, the refund shall be made to the exporter.

[Sec. 5845]

SEC. 5845. DEFINITIONS.

For the purpose of this chapter—

[Sec. 5845(a)]

(a) FIREARM.—The term "firearm" means (1) a shotgun having a barrel or barrels of less than 18 inches in length; (2) a weapon made from a shotgun if such weapon as modified has an overall length of less than 26 inches or a barrel or barrels of less than 18 inches in length; (3) a rifle having a barrel or barrels of less than 16 inches in length; (4) a weapon made from a rifle if such weapon as modified has an overall length of less than 26 inches or a barrel or barrels of less than 16 inches in length; (5) any other weapon, as defined in subsection (e); (6) a machine gun; (7) any silencer (as defined in section 921 of title 18, United States Code); and (8) a destructive device. The term "firearm" shall not include an antique firearm or any device (other than a machine gun or destructive device) which, although designed as a weapon, the Secretary finds by reason of the date of its manufacture, value, design, and other characteristics is primarily a collector's item and is not likely to be used as a weapon.

Amendments

• **1986, Firearms Owner's Protection Act (P.L. 99-308)**

P.L. 99-308, §109(b):

Amended Code Sec. 5845(a)(7). For the **effective** date, see Act Sec. 110(a), below. Prior to amendment, Code Sec. 5845(a)(7) read as follows:

(7) a muffler or a silencer for any firearm whether or not such firearm is included within this definition;

P.L. 99-308, §110(a), provides:

SEC. 110. EFFECTIVE DATE.

(a) IN GENERAL.—The amendments made by this Act shall become effective one hundred and eighty days after the date of the enactment of this Act. Upon their becoming effective, the Secretary shall publish and provide to all licensees a compilation of the State laws and published ordinances of which licensees are presumed to have knowledge pursuant to chapter 44 of title 18, United States Code, as amended by this Act. All amendments to such State laws and published ordinances as contained in the aforementioned compilation shall be published in the Federal Register, revised annually, and furnished to each person licensed under chapter 44 of title 18, United States Code, as amended by this Act.

• **1976, Tax Reform Act of 1976 (P.L. 94-455)**

P.L. 94-455, §1906(b)(13)(A):

Amended 1954 Code by substituting "Secretary" for "Secretary or his delegate" each place it appeared. **Effective** 2-1-77.

[Sec. 5845(b)]

(b) MACHINE GUN.—The term "machine gun" means any weapon which shoots, is designed to shoot, or can be readily restored to shoot, automatically more than one shot, without manual reloading, by a single function of the trigger. The term shall also include the frame or receiver of any such weapon, any part designed and intended solely and exclusively, or combination of parts designed and intended, for use in converting a weapon into a machine gun, and any combination of parts from which a machine gun can be assembled if such parts are in the possession or under the control of a person.

Amendments

• **1986, Firearms Owner's Protection Act (P.L. 99-308)**

P.L. 99-308, §109(a):

Amended Code Sec. 5845(b) by striking out "any combination of parts designed and intended for use in converting a weapon into a machine gun," and inserting in lieu thereof "any part designed and intended solely and exclusively, or combination of parts designed and intended, for use in converting a weapon into a machine gun,". For the **effective** date, see Act Sec. 110(a), below.

P.L. 99-308, §110(a), provides:

SEC. 110. EFFECTIVE DATE.

(a) IN GENERAL.—The amendments made by this Act shall become effective one hundred and eighty days after the date of the enactment of this Act. Upon their becoming effective, the Secretary shall publish and provide to all licensees a compilation of the State laws and published ordinances of which licensees are presumed to have knowledge pursuant to chapter 44 of title 18, United States Code, as amended by this Act. All amendments to such State laws and published ordinances as contained in the aforementioned compilation shall be published in the Federal Register, revised annually, and furnished to each person licensed under chapter 44 of title 18, United States Code, as amended by this Act.

[Sec. 5845(c)]

(c) RIFLE.—The term "rifle" means a weapon designed or redesigned, made or remade, and intended to be fired from the shoulder and designed or redesigned and made or remade to use the energy of the explosive in a fixed cartridge to fire only a single projectile through a rifled bore for each single pull of the trigger, and shall include any such weapon which may be readily restored to fire a fixed cartridge.

[Sec. 5845(d)]

(d) SHOTGUN.—The term "shotgun" means a weapon designed or redesigned, made or remade, and intended to be fired from the shoulder and designed or redesigned and made or remade to use the energy of the explosive in a fixed shotgun shell to fire through a smooth bore either a number of projectiles (ball shot) or a single projectile for each pull of the trigger, and shall include any such weapon which may be readily restored to fire a fixed shotgun shell.

[Sec. 5845(e)]

(e) ANY OTHER WEAPON.—The term "any other weapon" means any weapon or device capable of being concealed on the person from which a shot can be discharged through the energy of an explosive, a pistol or revolver having a barrel with a smooth bore designed or redesigned to fire a fixed shotgun shell, weapons with combination shotgun and rifle barrels 12 inches or more, less than 18 inches in length, from which only a single

FIREARMS—OTHER LAWS

discharge can be made from either barrel without manual reloading, and shall include any such weapon which may be readily restored to fire. Such term shall not include a pistol or a revolver having a rifled bore, or rifled bores, or weapons designed, made, or intended to be fired from the shoulder and not capable of firing fixed ammunition.

[Sec. 5845(f)]

(f) DESTRUCTIVE DEVICE.—The term "destructive device" means (1) any explosive, incendiary, or poison gas (A) bomb, (B) grenade, (C) rocket having a propellant charge of more than four ounces, (D) missile having an explosive or incendiary charge of more than one-quarter ounce, (E) mine, or (F) similar device; (2) any type of weapon by whatever name known which will, or which may be readily converted to, expel a projectile by the action of an explosive or other propellant, the barrel or barrels of which have a bore of more than one-half inch in diameter, except a shotgun or shotgun shell which the Secretary finds is generally recognized as particularly suitable for sporting purposes; and (3) any combination of parts either designed or intended for use in converting any device into a destructive device as defined in subparagraphs (1) and (2) and from which a destructive device may be readily assembled. The term "destructive device" shall not include any device which is neither designed nor redesigned for use as a weapon; any device, although originally designed for use as a weapon, which is redesigned for use as a signaling, pyrotechnic, line throwing, safety, or similar device; surplus ordnance sold, loaned, or given by the Secretary of the Army pursuant to the provisions of section 7684(2), 7685, or 7686 of title 10, United States Code; or any other device which the Secretary finds is not likely to be used as a weapon, or is an antique or is a rifle which the owner intends to use solely for sporting purposes.

Amendments

• **2018, John S. McCain National Defense Authorization Act for Fiscal Year 2019 (P.L. 115-232)**

P.L. 115-232, §809(h)(3), Div. A:

Amended Code Sec. 5845(f) by striking "section 4684(2), 4685, or 4686 of title 10 of the United States Code" and inserting "section 7684(2), 7685, or 7686 of title 10, United States Code". **Effective** 8-13-2018.

• **1976, Tax Reform Act of 1976 (P.L. 94-455)**

P.L. 94-455, §1906(b)(13)(A):

Amended 1954 Code by substituting "Secretary" for "Secretary or his delegate" each place it appeared. **Effective** 2-1-77.

P.L. 94-455, §1906(b)(13)(J):

Struck out "of the Treasury or his delegate" before "finds is not likely to be used as a weapon" in the last sentence of Code Sec. 5845(f). **Effective** 2-1-77.

[Sec. 5845(g)]

(g) ANTIQUE FIREARM.—The term "antique firearm" means any firearm not designed or redesigned for using rim fire or conventional center fire ignition with fixed ammunition and manufactured in or before 1898 (including any matchlock, flintlock, percussion cap, or similar type of ignition system or replica thereof, whether actually manufactured before or after the year 1898) and also any firearm using fixed ammunition manufactured in or before 1898, for which ammunition is no longer manufactured in the United States and is not readily available in the ordinary channels of commercial trade.

[Sec. 5845(h)]

(h) UNSERVICEABLE FIREARM.—The term "unserviceable firearm" means a firearm which is incapable of discharging a shot by means of an explosive and incapable of being readily restored to a firing condition.

[Sec. 5845(i)]

(i) MAKE.—The term "make", and the various derivatives of such word, shall include manufacturing (other than by one qualified to engage in such business under this chapter), putting together, altering, any combination of these, or otherwise producing a firearm.

[Sec. 5845(j)]

(j) TRANSFER.—The term "transfer" and the various derivatives of such word, shall include selling, assigning, pledging, leasing, loaning, giving away, or otherwise disposing of.

[Sec. 5845(k)]

(k) DEALER.—The term "dealer" means any person, not a manufacturer or importer, engaged in the business of selling, renting, leasing, or loaning firearms and shall include pawnbrokers who accept firearms as collateral for loans.

[Sec. 5845(l)]

(l) IMPORTER.—The term "importer" means any person who is engaged in the business of importing or bringing firearms into the United States.

[Sec. 5845(m)]

(m) MANUFACTURER.—The term "manufacturer" means any person who is engaged in the business of manufacturing firearms.

Amendments

• **1968, Gun Control Act of 1968 (P.L. 90-618)**

P.L. 90-618, §201:

Amended Code Sec. 5845. **Effective** 11-1-68. Prior to amendment, Code Sec. 5845 read as follows:

SEC. 5845. IMPORTATION.

No firearm shall be imported or brought into the United States or any territory under its control or jurisdiction, except that, under regulations prescribed by the Secretary or his delegate, any firearm may be so imported or brought in when—

(1) the purpose thereof is shown to be lawful and

(2) such firearm is unique or of a type which cannot be obtained within the United States or such territory.

[Sec. 5846]

SEC. 5846. OTHER LAWS APPLICABLE.

All provisions of law relating to special taxes imposed by chapter 51 and to engraving, issuance, sale, accountability, cancellation, and distribution of stamps for tax payment shall, insofar as not inconsistent with the provisions of this chapter, be applicable with respect to the taxes imposed by sections 5801, 5811, and 5821.

Amendments

• **1968, Gun Control Act of 1968 (P.L. 90-618)**

P.L. 90-618, §201:

Amended Code Sec. 5846. **Effective** 11-1-68. Prior to amendment, Code Sec. 5846 read as follows:

"All provisions of law (including those relating to special taxes, to the assessment, collection, remission, and refund of internal revenue taxes, to the engraving, issuance, sale, accountability, cancellation, and distribution of taxpaid stamps provided for in the internal revenue laws, and to penalties) applicable with respect to the taxes imposed by sections 4701 and 4721, and all other provisions of the internal revenue laws shall, insofar as not inconsistent with the provisions of this chapter, be applicable with respect to the taxes imposed by sections 5811(a), 5821(a), and 5801."

[Sec. 5847]

SEC. 5847. EFFECT ON OTHER LAWS.

Nothing in this chapter shall be construed as modifying or affecting the requirements of section 38 of the Arms Export Control Act (22 U.S.C. 2778), as amended, with respect to the manufacture, exportation, and importation of arms, ammunition, and implements of war.

Sec. 5845(f)

FIREARMS—EXEMPTIONS

Amendments
- **2018, Tax Technical Corrections Act of 2018 (P.L. 115-141)**

P.L. 115-141, §401(a)(252), Div. U:

Amended Code Sec. 5847 by striking "section 414 of the Mutual Security Act of 1954" and inserting "section 38 of the Arms Export Control Act (22 U.S.C. 2778)". **Effective** 3-23-2018.

- **1968, Gun Control Act of 1968 (P.L. 90-618)**

P.L. 90-618, §201:

Amended Code Sec. 5847. **Effective** 11-1-68. Prior to amendment, Code Sec. 5847 read as follows:

SEC. 5847. REGULATIONS.

The Secretary or his delegate shall prescribe such regulations as may be necessary for carrying the provisions of this chapter into effect.

[Sec. 5848]

SEC. 5848. RESTRICTIVE USE OF INFORMATION.

[Sec. 5848(a)]

(a) GENERAL RULE.—No information or evidence obtained from an application, registration, or records required to be submitted or retained by a natural person in order to comply with any provision of this chapter or regulations issued thereunder, shall, except as provided in subsection (b) of this section, be used, directly or indirectly, as evidence against that person in a criminal proceeding with respect to a violation of law occurring prior to or concurrently with the filing of the application or registration, or the compiling of the records containing the information or evidence.

[Sec. 5848(b)]

(b) FURNISHING FALSE INFORMATION.—Subsection (a) of this section shall not preclude the use of any such information or evidence in a prosecution or other action under any applicable provision of law with respect to the furnishing of false information.

Amendments
- **1968, Gun Control Act of 1968 (P.L. 90-618)**

P.L. 90-618, §201:

Amended Code Sec. 5848. **Effective** 11-1-68. Prior to amendment, Code Sec. 5848 read as follows:

SEC. 5848. DEFINITIONS.

For purposes of this chapter—

(1) Firearm.—The term "firearm" means a shotgun having a barrel or barrels of less than 18 inches in length, or a rifle having a barrel or barrels of less than 16 inches in length, or any weapon made from a rifle or shotgun (whether by alteration, modification, or otherwise) if such weapon as modified has an overall length of less than 26 inches, or any other weapon, except a pistol or revolver, from which a shot is discharged by an explosive if such weapon is capable of being concealed on the person, or a machine gun, and includes a muffler or silencer for any firearm whether or not such firearm is included within the foregoing definition.

(2) Machine gun.—The term "machine gun" means any weapon which shoots, or is designed to shoot, automatically or semi-automatically, more than one shot, without manual reloading, by a single function of the trigger.

(3) Rifle.—The term "rifle" means a weapon designed or redesigned, made or remade, and intended to be fired from the shoulder and designed or redesigned and made or remade to use the energy of the explosive in a fixed metallic cartridge to fire only a single projectile through a rifled bore for each single pull of the trigger.

(4) Shotgun.—The term "shotgun" means a weapon designed or redesigned, made or remade, and intended to be fired from the shoulder and designed or redesigned and made or remade to use the energy of the explosive in a fixed shotgun shell to fire through a smooth bore either a number of ball shot or a single projectile for each single pull of the trigger.

(5) Any other weapon.—The term "any other weapon" means any weapon or device capable of being concealed on the person from which a shot can be discharged through the energy of an explosive, but such term shall not include pistols or revolvers or weapons designed, made or intended to be fired from the shoulder and not capable of being fired with fixed ammunition.

(6) Importer.—The term "importer" means any person who imports or brings firearms into the United States for sale.

(7) Manufacturer.—The term "manufacturer" means any person who is engaged within the United States in the business of manufacturing firearms, or who otherwise produces therein any firearm for sale or disposition.

(8) Dealer.—The term "dealer" means any person not a manufacturer or importer, engaged within the United States in the business of selling firearms. The term "dealer" shall include wholesalers, pawnbrokers, and dealers in used firearms.

(9) Interstate commerce.—The term "interstate commerce" means transportation from any State or Territory or District, or any insular possession of the United States, to any other State or to the District of Columbia.

(10) To transfer or transferred.—The term "to transfer" or "transferred" shall include to sell, assign, pledge, lease, loan, give away, or otherwise dispose of.

(11) Person.—The term "person" includes a partnership, company, association, or corporation, as well as a natural person.

- **1960 (P.L. 86-478)**

P.L. 86-478, §3:

Amended paragraph (1) of Code Sec. 5848. **Effective** 7-1-60. Prior to amendment, paragraph (1) read as follows:

"(1) Firearm.—The term `firearm' means a shotgun or rifle having a barrel of less than 18 inches in length, or any other weapon, except a pistol or revolver, from which a shot is discharged by an explosive if such weapon is capable of being concealed on the person, or a machine gun, and includes a muffler or silencer for any firearm whether or not such firearm is included within the foregoing definition, but does not include any rifle which is within the foregoing provisions solely by reason of the length of its barrel if the caliber of such rifle is .22 or smaller and if its barrel is 16 inches or more in length."

- **1958, Excise Tax Technical Changes Act of 1958 (P.L. 85-859)**

P.L. 85-859, §203(f):

Amended paragraphs (3) and (4) of Code Sec. 5848 by striking out the phrase "designed and made" and substituting "designed or redesigned and made or remade", and amended paragraph (7) of Code Sec. 5848. **Effective** 9-3-58. Prior to amendment, paragraph (7) read as follows:

"(7) Manufacturer.—The term `manufacturer' means any person who is engaged within the United States in the manufacture of firearms, or who otherwise produces therein any firearm for sale or disposition."

[Sec. 5849]

SEC. 5849. CITATION OF CHAPTER.

This chapter may be cited as the "National Firearms Act" and any reference in any other provision of law to the "National Firearms Act" shall be held to refer to the provisions of this chapter.

Amendments
- **1958, Excise Tax Technical Changes Act of 1958 (P.L. 85-859)**

P.L. 85-859, §203(g):

Added Sec. 5849. **Effective** 9-3-58.

PART II—EXEMPTIONS

Sec. 5851.	Special (occupational) tax exemption.
Sec. 5852.	General transfer and making tax exemption.
Sec. 5853.	Transfer and making tax exemption available to certain governmental entities.
Sec. 5854.	Exportation of firearms exempt from transfer tax.

[Sec. 5851]

SEC. 5851. SPECIAL (OCCUPATIONAL) TAX EXEMPTION.

[Sec. 5851(a)]

(a) BUSINESS WITH UNITED STATES.—Any person required to pay special (occupational) tax under section 5801 shall be relieved from payment of that tax if he establishes to the satisfaction of the Secretary that his business is conducted exclusively with, or on behalf of, the United States or any department, independent establishment, or agency thereof. The Secretary may relieve any person manufacturing firearms for, or on behalf of, the United States from compliance with any provision of this chapter in the conduct of such business.

FIREARMS—EXEMPTIONS

Amendments

• **1976, Tax Reform Act of 1976 (P.L. 94-455)**

P.L. 94-455, §1906(b)(13)(A):

Amended 1954 Code by substituting "Secretary" for "Secretary or his delegate" each place it appeared. **Effective** 2-1-77.

[Sec. 5851(b)]

(b) APPLICATION.—The exemption provided for in subsection (a) of this section may be obtained by filing with the Secretary an application on such form and containing such information as may by regulations be prescribed. The exemptions must thereafter be renewed on or before July 1 of each year. Approval of the application by the Secretary shall entitle the applicant to the exemptions stated on the approved application.

Amendments

• **1976, Tax Reform Act of 1976 (P.L. 94-455)**

P.L. 94-455, §1906(b)(13)(A):

Amended 1954 Code by substituting "Secretary" for "Secretary or his delegate" each place it appeared. **Effective** 2-1-77.

• **1968, Gun Control Act of 1968 (P.L. 90-618)**

P.L. 90-618, §201:

Amended Code Sec. 5851. **Effective** 11-1-68. For former Code Sec. 5851, see the amendment note for P.L. 90-618 under Code Sec. 5861.

[Sec. 5852]

SEC. 5852. GENERAL TRANSFER AND MAKING TAX EXEMPTION.

[Sec. 5852(a)]

(a) TRANSFER.—Any firearm may be transferred to the United States or any department, independent establishment, or agency thereof, without payment of the transfer tax imposed by section 5811.

[Sec. 5852(b)]

(b) MAKING BY A PERSON OTHER THAN A QUALIFIED MANUFACTURER.—Any firearm may be made by, or on behalf of, the United States, or any department, independent establishment, or agency thereof, without payment of the making tax imposed by section 5821.

[Sec. 5852(c)]

(c) MAKING BY A QUALIFIED MANUFACTURER.—A manufacturer qualified under this chapter to engage in such business may make the type of firearm which he is qualified to manufacture without payment of the making tax imposed by section 5821.

[Sec. 5852(d)]

(d) TRANSFERS BETWEEN SPECIAL (OCCUPATIONAL) TAXPAYERS.—A firearm registered to a person qualified under this chapter to engage in business as an importer, manufacturer, or dealer may be transferred by that person without payment of the transfer tax imposed by section 5811 to any other person qualified under this chapter to manufacture, import, or deal in that type of firearm.

[Sec. 5852(e)]

(e) UNSERVICEABLE FIREARM.—An unserviceable firearm may be transferred as a curio or ornament without payment of the transfer tax imposed by section 5811, under such requirements as the Secretary may by regulations prescribe.

Amendments

• **1976, Tax Reform Act of 1976 (P.L. 94-455)**

P.L. 94-455, §1906(b)(13)(A):

Amended 1954 Code by substituting "Secretary" for "Secretary or his delegate" each place it appeared. **Effective** 2-1-77.

[Sec. 5852(f)]

(f) RIGHT TO EXEMPTION.—No firearm may be transferred or made exempt from tax under the provisions of this section unless the transfer or making is performed pursuant to an application in such form and manner as the Secretary may by regulations prescribe.

Amendments

• **1976, Tax Reform Act of 1976 (P.L. 94-455)**

P.L. 94-455, §1906(b)(13)(A):

Amended 1954 Code by substituting "Secretary" for "Secretary or his delegate" each place it appeared. **Effective** 2-1-77.

• **1968, Gun Control Act of 1968 (P.L. 90-618)**

P.L. 90-618, §201:

Amended Code Sec. 5852. **Effective** 11-1-68. For former Code Sec. 5852, see the amendment note for P.L. 90-618 under Code Sec. 5861.

[Sec. 5853]

SEC. 5853. TRANSFER AND MAKING TAX EXEMPTION AVAILABLE TO CERTAIN GOVERNMENTAL ENTITIES.

[Sec. 5853(a)]

(a) TRANSFER.—A firearm may be transferred without the payment of the transfer tax imposed by section 5811 to any State, possession of the United States, any political subdivision thereof, or any official police organization of such a government entity engaged in criminal investigations.

[Sec. 5853(b)]

(b) MAKING.—A firearm may be made without payment of the making tax imposed by section 5821 by, or on behalf of, any State, or possession of the United States, any political subdivision thereof, or any official police organization of such a government entity engaged in criminal investigations.

[Sec. 5853(c)]

(c) RIGHT TO EXEMPTION.—No firearm may be transferred or made exempt from tax under this section unless the transfer or making is performed pursuant to an application in such form and manner as the Secretary may by regulations prescribe.

Amendments

• **1976, Tax Reform Act of 1976 (P.L. 94-455)**

P.L. 94-455, §1906(b)(13)(A):

Amended 1954 Code by substituting "Secretary" for "Secretary or his delegate" each place it appeared. **Effective** 2-1-77.

• **1968, Gun Control Act of 1968 (P.L. 90-618)**

P.L. 90-618, §201:

Amended Code Sec. 5853. **Effective** 11-1-68. For former Code Sec. 5853, see the amendment note for P.L. 90-618 under Code Sec. 5861.

[Sec. 5854]

SEC. 5854. EXPORTATION OF FIREARMS EXEMPT FROM TRANSFER TAX.

A firearm may be exported without payment of the transfer tax imposed under section 5811 provided that proof of the exportation is furnished in such form and manner as the Secretary may by regulations prescribe.

FIREARMS—FORFEITURES

Amendments

• 1976, Tax Reform Act of 1976 (P.L. 94-455)

P.L. 94-455, §1906(b)(13)(A):

Amended 1954 Code by substituting "Secretary" for "Secretary or his delegate" each place it appeared. **Effective** 2-1-77.

• 1968, Gun Control Act of 1968 (P.L. 90-618)

P.L. 90-618, §201:

Amended Code Sec. 5854. **Effective** 11-1-68. For former Code Sec. 5854, see the amendment note for P.L. 90-618 under Code Sec. 5861.

Subchapter C—Prohibited Acts

Sec. 5861.   Prohibited acts.

[Sec. 5861]

SEC. 5861. PROHIBITED ACTS.

It shall be unlawful for any person—

(a) to engage in business as a manufacturer or importer of, or dealer in, firearms without having paid the special (occupational) tax required by section 5801 for his business or having registered as required by section 5802; or

(b) to receive or possess a firearm transferred to him in violation of the provisions of this chapter; or

(c) to receive or possess a firearm made in violation of the provisions of this chapter; or

(d) to receive or possess a firearm which is not registered to him in the National Firearms Registration and Transfer Record; or

(e) to transfer a firearm in violation of the provisions of this chapter; or

(f) to make a firearm in violation of the provisions of this chapter; or

(g) to obliterate, remove, change, or alter the serial number or other identification of a firearm required by this chapter; or

(h) to receive or possess a firearm having the serial number or other identification required by this chapter obliterated, removed, changed, or altered; or

(i) to receive or possess a firearm which is not identified by a serial number as required by this chapter; or

(j) to transport, deliver, or receive any firearm in interstate commerce which has not been registered as required by this chapter; or

(k) to receive or possess a firearm which has been imported or brought into the United States in violation of section 5844; or

(l) to make, or cause the making of, a false entry on any application, return, or record required by this chapter, knowing such entry to be false.

Amendments

• 1968, Gun Control Act of 1968 (P.L. 90-618)

P.L. 90-618, §201:

Amended Subchapter C. **Effective** 11-1-68. (For former Code Sec. 5861, see the amendment note for P.L. 90-618 under Code Sec. 5872.) Prior to amendment, Subchapter C read as follows:

Subchapter C—Unlawful Acts

Sec. 5851. Possessing firearms illegally.
Sec. 5852. Removing or changing identification marks.
Sec. 5853. Importing firearms illegally.
Sec. 5854. Failure to register and pay special tax.
Sec. 5855. Unlawful transportation in interstate commerce.

Sec. 5851. Possessing Firearms Illegally.

It shall be unlawful for any person to receive or possess any firearm which has at any time been transferred in violation of sections 5811, 5812(b), 5813, 5814, 5844, or 5846, or which has at any time been made in violation of section 5821, or to possess any firearm which has not been registered as required by section 5841. Whenever on trial for a violation of this section the defendant is shown to have or to have had possession of such firearm, such possession shall be deemed sufficient evidence to authorize conviction, unless the defendant explains such possession to the satisfaction of the jury.

Sec. 5852. Removing or Changing Identification Marks.

It shall be unlawful for anyone to obliterate, remove, change, or alter the number or other identification mark required by section 5843. Whenever on trial for a violation of this section the defendant is shown to have or to have had possession of any firearm upon which such number or mark shall have been obliterated, removed, changed, or altered, such possession shall be deemed sufficient evidence to authorize conviction, unless the defendant explains such possession to the satisfaction of the jury.

Sec. 5853. Importing Firearms Illegally.

It shall be unlawful—

(1) fraudulently or knowingly to import or bring any firearm into the United States or any territory under its control or jurisdiction, in violation of the provisions of this chapter; or

(2) knowingly to assist in so doing; or

(3) to receive, conceal, buy, sell, or in any manner facilitate the transportation, concealment, or sale of any such firearm after being imported or brought in, knowing the same to have been imported or brought in contrary to law.

Whenever on trial for a violation of this section the defendant is shown to have or to have had possession of such firearm, such possession shall be deemed sufficient evidence to authorize conviction, unless the defendant explains such possession to the satisfaction of the jury.

Sec. 5854. Failure to Register and Pay Special Tax.

It shall be unlawful for any person required to register under the provisions of section 5802 to import, manufacture, or deal in firearms without having registered and paid the tax imposed by section 5801.

Subchapter D—Penalties and Forfeitures

Sec. 5871.   Penalties.
Sec. 5872.   Forfeitures.

[Sec. 5871]

SEC. 5871. PENALTIES.

Any person who violates or fails to comply with any provision of this chapter shall, upon conviction, be fined not more than $10,000, or be imprisoned not more than ten years, or both.

Amendments

• 1984 (P.L. 98-473)

P.L. 98-473, §227:

Amended Code Sec. 5871 by deleting ", and shall become eligible for parole as the Board of Parole shall determine" after "both". **Effective** 11-1-86.

[Sec. 5872]

SEC. 5872. FORFEITURES.

[Sec. 5872(a)]

(a) LAWS APPLICABLE.—Any firearm involved in any violation of the provisions of this chapter shall be subject to seizure and forfeiture, and (except as provided in subsection (b)) all the provisions of internal revenue laws relating to searches, seizures, and forfeitures of unstamped articles are extended to and made to apply to the articles taxed under this chapter, and the persons to whom this chapter applies.

GREENMAIL—DEFINITIONS

[Sec. 5872(b)]

(b) DISPOSAL.—In the case of the forfeiture of any firearm by reason of a violation of this chapter, no notice of public sale shall be required; no such firearm shall be sold at public sale; if such firearm is forfeited for a violation of this chapter and there is no remission or mitigation of forfeiture thereof, it shall be delivered by the Secretary to the Administrator of General Services, General Services Administration, who may order such firearm destroyed or may sell it to any State, or possession, or political subdivision thereof, or at the request of the Secretary, may authorize its retention for official use of the Treasury Department, or may transfer it without charge to any executive department or independent establishment of the Government for use by it.

Amendments
- **1976, Tax Reform Act of 1976 (P.L. 94-455)**

P.L. 94-455, §1906(b)(13)(A):

Amended 1954 Code by substituting "Secretary" for "Secretary or his delegate" each place it appeared. **Effective** 2-1-77.

- **1968, Gun Control Act of 1968 (P.L. 90-618)**

P.L. 90-618, §201:

Amended Subchapter D. **Effective** 11-1-68. Prior to amendment, Subchapter D read as follows:

"Subchapter D—Penalties and Forfeitures.
"Sec. 5861. Penalties.
"Sec. 5862. Forfeitures.
"Sec. 5861. Penalties.

"Any person who violates or fails to comply with any of the requirements of this chapter shall, upon conviction, be fined not more than $2,000, or be imprisoned for not more than 5 years, or both, in the discretion of the court.

"Sec. 5862. Forfeitures.

"(a) Laws Applicable.—Any firearm involved in any violation of the provisions of this chapter or any regulation promulgated thereunder shall be subject to seizure and forfeiture, and (except as provided in subsection (b)) all the provisions of internal revenue laws relating to searches, seizures, and forfeiture of unstamped articles are extended to and made to apply to the articles taxed under this chapter, and the persons to whom this chapter applies.

"(b) Disposal.—In the case of the forfeiture of any firearm by reason of a violation of this chapter: No notice of public sale shall be required; no such firearm shall be sold at public sale; if such firearm is forfeited for a violation of this chapter and there is no remission or mitigation of forfeiture thereof, it shall be delivered by the Secretary or his delegate to the Administrator of General Services, General Services Administration, who may order such firearm destroyed or may sell it to any State, Territory, or possession, or political subdivision thereof, or the District of Columbia, or at the request of the Secretary or his delegate may authorize its retention for official use of the Treasury Department, or may transfer it without charge to any executive department or independent establishment of the Government for use by it."

CHAPTER 54—GREENMAIL

Sec. 5881.   Greenmail.

[Sec. 5881]

SEC. 5881. GREENMAIL.

[Sec. 5881(a)]

(a) IMPOSITION OF TAX.—There is hereby imposed on any person who receives greenmail a tax equal to 50 percent of gain or other income of such person by reason of such receipt.

Amendments
- **1988, Technical and Miscellaneous Revenue Act of 1988 (P.L. 100-647)**

P.L. 100-647, §2004(o)(1)(A):

Amended Code Sec. 5881(a) by striking out "gain realized by such person on such receipt" and inserting in lieu thereof "gain or other income of such person by reason of such receipt". **Effective** as if included in the provision of P.L. 100-203 to which it relates.

[Sec. 5881(b)]

(b) GREENMAIL.—For purposes of this section, the term "greenmail" means any consideration transferred by a corporation (or any person acting in concert with such corporation) to directly or indirectly acquire stock of such corporation from any shareholder if—

(1) such shareholder held such stock (as determined under section 1223) for less than 2 years before entering into the agreement to make the transfer,

(2) at some time during the 2-year period ending on the date of such acquisition—

(A) such shareholder,

(B) any person acting in concert with such shareholder, or

(C) any person who is related to such shareholder or person described in subparagraph (B), made or threatened to make a public tender offer for stock of such corporation, and

(3) such acquisition is pursuant to an offer which was not made on the same terms to all shareholders.

For purposes of the preceding sentence, payments made in connection with, or in transactions related to, an acquisition shall be treated as paid in such acquisition.

Amendments
- **1988, Technical and Miscellaneous Revenue Act of 1988 (P.L. 100-647)**

P.L. 100-647, §2004(o)(1)(B)(i):

Amended Code Sec. 5881(b) by striking out "a corporation to directly or indirectly acquire its stock" and inserting in lieu thereof "a corporation (or any person acting in concert with such corporation) to directly or indirectly acquire stock of such corporation". **Effective** for transactions occurring on or after 3-31-88.

[Sec. 5881(c)]

(c) OTHER DEFINITIONS.—For purposes of this section—

(1) PUBLIC TENDER OFFER.—The term "public tender offer" means any offer to purchase or otherwise acquire stock or assets in a corporation if such offer was or would be required to be filed or registered with any Federal or State agency regulating securities.

(2) RELATED PERSON.—A person is related to another person if the relationship between such persons would result in the disallowance of losses under section 267 or 707(b).

[Sec. 5881(d)]

(d) TAX APPLIES WHETHER OR NOT AMOUNT RECOGNIZED.—The tax imposed by this section shall apply whether or not the gain or other income referred to in subsection (a) is recognized.

Amendments
- **1988, Technical and Miscellaneous Revenue Act of 1988 (P.L. 100-647)**

P.L. 100-647, §2004(o)(1)(C)(i)-(ii):

Amended Code Sec. 5881(d) by striking out "the gain" and inserting in lieu thereof "the gain or other income", and by striking out "GAIN RECOGNIZED" in the subsection heading and inserting in lieu thereof "AMOUNT RECOGNIZED". **Effective** as if included in the provision of P.L. 100-203 to which it relates.

- **1987, Revenue Act of 1987 (P.L. 100-203)**

P.L. 100-203, §10228(a):

Amended subtitle E by adding new Code Sec. 5881. **Effective** for consideration received after 12-22-87 in tax years ending after such date; except that such amendments shall not apply in the case of any acquisition pursuant to a written binding contract in effect on 12-15-87, and at all times thereafter before the acquisition.

STRUCTURED SETTLEMENT FACTORING TRANSACTIONS

[Sec. 5881(e)]

(e) ADMINISTRATIVE PROVISIONS.—For purposes of the deficiency procedures of subtitle F, any tax imposed by this section shall be treated as a tax imposed by subtitle A.

Amendments

• **1988, Technical and Miscellaneous Revenue Act of 1988 (P.L. 100-647)**

P.L. 100-647, § 2004(o)(2):

Amended Code Sec. 5881 by adding at the end thereof new subsection (e).
Effective as if included in the provision of P.L. 100-203 to which it relates.

CHAPTER 55—STRUCTURED SETTLEMENT FACTORING TRANSACTIONS

Sec. 5891.   Structured settlement factoring transactions.

[Sec. 5891]

SEC. 5891. STRUCTURED SETTLEMENT FACTORING TRANSACTIONS.

[Sec. 5891(a)]

(a) IMPOSITION OF TAX.—There is hereby imposed on any person who acquires directly or indirectly structured settlement payment rights in a structured settlement factoring transaction a tax equal to 40 percent of the factoring discount as determined under subsection (c)(4) with respect to such factoring transaction.

[Sec. 5891(b)]

(b) EXCEPTION FOR CERTAIN APPROVED TRANSACTIONS.—

(1) IN GENERAL.—The tax under subsection (a) shall not apply in the case of a structured settlement factoring transaction in which the transfer of structured settlement payment rights is approved in advance in a qualified order.

(2) QUALIFIED ORDER.—For purposes of this section, the term "qualified order" means a final order, judgment, or decree which—

(A) finds that the transfer described in paragraph (1)—

(i) does not contravene any Federal or State statute or the order of any court or responsible administrative authority, and

(ii) is in the best interest of the payee, taking into account the welfare and support of the payee's dependents, and

(B) is issued—

(i) under the authority of an applicable State statute by an applicable State court, or

(ii) by the responsible administrative authority (if any) which has exclusive jurisdiction over the underlying action or proceeding which was resolved by means of the structured settlement.

(3) APPLICABLE STATE STATUTE.—For purposes of this section, the term "applicable State statute" means a statute providing for the entry of an order, judgment, or decree described in paragraph (2)(A) which is enacted by—

(A) the State in which the payee of the structured settlement is domiciled, or

(B) if there is no statute described in subparagraph (A), the State in which either the party to the structured settlement (including an assignee under a qualified assignment under section 130) or the person issuing the funding asset for the structured settlement is domiciled or has its principal place of business.

(4) APPLICABLE STATE COURT.—For purposes of this section—

(A) IN GENERAL.—The term "applicable State court" means, with respect to any applicable State statute, a court of the State which enacted such statute.

(B) SPECIAL RULE.—In the case of an applicable State statute described in paragraph (3)(B), such term also includes a court of the State in which the payee of the structured settlement is domiciled.

(5) QUALIFIED ORDER DISPOSITIVE.—A qualified order shall be treated as dispositive for purposes of the exception under this subsection.

[Sec. 5891(c)]

(c) DEFINITIONS.—For purposes of this section—

(1) STRUCTURED SETTLEMENT.—The term "structured settlement" means an arrangement—

(A) which is established by—

(i) suit or agreement for the periodic payment of damages excludable from the gross income of the recipient under section 104(a)(2), or

(ii) agreement for the periodic payment of compensation under any workers' compensation law excludable from the gross income of the recipient under section 104(a)(1), and

(B) under which the periodic payments are—

(i) of the character described in subparagraphs (A) and (B) of section 130(c)(2), and

(ii) payable by a person who is a party to the suit or agreement or to the workers' compensation claim or by a person who has assumed the liability for such periodic payments under a qualified assignment in accordance with section 130.

(2) STRUCTURED SETTLEMENT PAYMENT RIGHTS.—The term "structured settlement payment rights" means rights to receive payments under a structured settlement.

(3) STRUCTURED SETTLEMENT FACTORING TRANSACTION.—

(A) IN GENERAL.—The term "structured settlement factoring transaction" means a transfer of structured settlement payment rights (including portions of structured settlement payments) made for consideration by means of sale, assignment, pledge, or other form of encumbrance or alienation for consideration.

(B) EXCEPTION.—Such term shall not include—

(i) the creation or perfection of a security interest in structured settlement payment rights under a blanket security agreement entered into with an insured depository institution in the absence of any action to redirect the structured settlement payments to such institution (or agent or successor thereof) or otherwise to enforce such blanket security interest as against the structured settlement payment rights, or

(ii) a subsequent transfer of structured settlement payment rights acquired in a structured settlement factoring transaction.

(4) FACTORING DISCOUNT.—The term "factoring discount" means an amount equal to the excess of—

STRUCTURED SETTLEMENT FACTORING TRANSACTIONS

(A) the aggregate undiscounted amount of structured settlement payments being acquired in the structured settlement factoring transaction, over

(B) the total amount actually paid by the acquirer to the person from whom such structured settlement payments are acquired.

(5) RESPONSIBLE ADMINISTRATIVE AUTHORITY.—The term "responsible administrative authority" means the administrative authority which had jurisdiction over the underlying action or proceeding which was resolved by means of the structured settlement.

(6) STATE.—The term "State" includes the Commonwealth of Puerto Rico and any possession of the United States.

[Sec. 5891(d)]

(d) COORDINATION WITH OTHER PROVISIONS.—

(1) IN GENERAL.—If the applicable requirements of sections 72, 104(a)(1), 104(a)(2), 130, and 461(h) were satisfied at the time the structured settlement involving structured settlement payment rights was entered into, the subsequent occurrence of a structured settlement factoring transaction shall not affect the application of the provisions of such sections to the parties to the structured settlement (including an assignee under a qualified assignment under section 130) in any taxable year.

(2) NO WITHHOLDING OF TAX.—The provisions of section 3405 regarding withholding of tax shall not apply to the person making the payments in the event of a structured settlement factoring transaction.

Amendments

• 2002, Victims of Terrorism Tax Relief Act of 2001 (P.L. 107-134)

P.L. 107-134, § 115(a):

Amended subtitle E by adding at the end a new chapter 55 (Code Sec. 5891). For the **effective** date and a transition rule, see Act Sec. 115(c), below.

P.L. 107-134, § 115(c), provides:

(c) EFFECTIVE DATES.—

(1) IN GENERAL.—The amendments made by this section (other than the provisions of section 5891(d) of the Internal Revenue Code of 1986, as added by this section) shall apply to structured settlement factoring transactions (as defined in section 5891(c) of such Code (as so added)) entered into on or after the 30th day following the date of the enactment of this Act.

(2) CLARIFICATION OF EXISTING LAW.—Section 5891(d) of such Code (as so added) shall apply to structured settlement factoring transactions (as defined in section 5891(c) of such Code (as so added)) entered into before, on, or after such 30th day.

(3) TRANSITION RULE.—In the case of a structured settlement factoring transaction entered into during the period beginning on the 30th day following the date of the enactment of this Act and ending on July 1, 2002, no tax shall be imposed under section 5891(a) of such Code if—

(A) the structured settlement payee is domiciled in a State (or possession of the United States) which has not enacted a statute providing that the structured settlement factoring transaction is ineffective unless the transaction has been approved by an order, judgment, or decree of a court (or where applicable, a responsible administrative authority) which finds that such transaction—

(i) does not contravene any Federal or State statute or the order of any court (or responsible administrative authority); and

(ii) is in the best interest of the structured settlement payee or is appropriate in light of a hardship faced by the payee; and

(B) the person acquiring the structured settlement payment rights discloses to the structured settlement payee in advance of the structured settlement factoring transaction the amounts and due dates of the payments to be transferred, the aggregate amount to be transferred, the consideration to be received by the structured settlement payee for the transferred payments, the discounted present value of the transferred payments (including the present value as determined in the manner described in section 7520 of such Code), and the expenses required under the terms of the structured settlement factoring transaction to be paid by the structured settlement payee or deducted from the proceeds of such transaction.

[The next page is 4301.]

Sec. 5891(c)(4)(A)

Subtitle F—Procedure and Administration

CHAPTER 61.	Information and returns.
CHAPTER 62.	Time and place for paying tax.
CHAPTER 63.	Assessment.
CHAPTER 64.	Collection.
CHAPTER 65.	Abatements, credits, and refunds.
CHAPTER 66.	Limitations.
CHAPTER 67.	Interest.
CHAPTER 68.	Additions to the tax, additional amounts, and assessable penalties.
CHAPTER 69.	General provisions relating to stamps.
CHAPTER 70.	Jeopardy, receiverships, etc.
CHAPTER 71.	Transferees and fiduciaries.
CHAPTER 72.	Licensing and registration.
CHAPTER 73.	Bonds.
CHAPTER 74.	Closing agreements and compromises.
CHAPTER 75.	Crimes, other offenses, and forfeitures.
CHAPTER 76.	Judicial proceedings.
CHAPTER 77.	Miscellaneous provisions.
CHAPTER 78.	Discovery of liability and enforcement of title.
CHAPTER 79.	Definitions.
CHAPTER 80.	General rules.

CHAPTER 61—INFORMATION AND RETURNS

SUBCHAPTER A.	Returns and records.
SUBCHAPTER B.	Miscellaneous provisions.

Subchapter A—Returns and Records

Part I.	Records, statements, and special returns.
Part II.	Tax returns or statements.
Part III.	Information returns.
Part IV.	Signing and verifying of returns and other documents.
Part V.	Time for filing returns and other documents.
Part VI.	Extension of time for filing returns.
Part VII.	Place for filing returns or other documents.
Part VIII.	Designation of income tax payments to Presidential Election Campaign Fund.

PART I—RECORDS, STATEMENTS, AND SPECIAL RETURNS

Sec. 6001.	Notice or regulations requiring records, statements, and special returns.

[Sec. 6001]

SEC. 6001. NOTICE OR REGULATIONS REQUIRING RECORDS, STATEMENTS, AND SPECIAL RETURNS.

Every person liable for any tax imposed by this title, or for the collection thereof, shall keep such records, render such statements, make such returns, and comply with such rules and regulations as the Secretary may from time to time prescribe. Whenever in the judgment of the Secretary it is necessary, he may require any person, by notice served upon such person or by regulations, to make such returns, render such statements, or keep such records, as the Secretary deems sufficient to show whether or not such person is liable for tax under this title. The only records which an employer shall be required to keep under this section in connection with charged tips shall be charge receipts, records necessary to comply with section 6053(c), and copies of statements furnished by employees under section 6053(a).

Amendments

• **1982, Tax Equity and Fiscal Responsibility Act of 1982 (P.L. 97-248)**

P.L. 97-248, §314(d):

Amended Code Sec. 6001 by adding ", records necessary to comply with section 6053(c)," after "charge receipts". **Effective** for tax years beginning after 12-31-82. For a special rule for 1983, see the amendment note for P.L. 97-248, following Code Sec. 6053(c).

• **1978, Revenue Act of 1978 (P.L. 95-600)**

P.L. 95-600, §501(a):

Amended Code Sec. 6001 by adding the last sentence. **Effective** for payments made after 12-31-78.

• **1976, Tax Reform Act of 1976 (P.L. 94-455)**

P.L. 94-455, §1906(b)(13)(A):

Amended 1954 Code by substituting "Secretary" for "Secretary or his delegate" each place it appeared. **Effective** 2-1-77.

PART II—TAX RETURNS OR STATEMENTS

Subpart A.	General requirement.
Subpart B.	Income tax returns.
Subpart C.	Estate and gift tax returns.
Subpart D.	Miscellaneous provisions.

Subpart A—General Requirement

Sec. 6011.	General requirement of return, statement, or list.

RETURNS—GENERAL REQUIREMENT

[Sec. 6011]

SEC. 6011. GENERAL REQUIREMENT OF RETURN, STATEMENT, OR LIST.

[Sec. 6011(a)]

(a) GENERAL RULE.—When required by regulations prescribed by the Secretary any person made liable for any tax imposed by this title, or with respect to the collection thereof, shall make a return or statement according to the forms and regulations prescribed by the Secretary. Every person required to make a return or statement shall include therein the information required by such forms or regulations.

Amendments

• **1988, Technical and Miscellaneous Revenue Act of 1988 (P.L. 100-647)**

P.L. 100-647, §1015(q)(1):

Amended Code Sec. 6011(a) by striking out "for the collection thereof" and inserting in lieu thereof "with respect to the collection thereof". **Effective** 11-10-88.

• **1976, Tax Reform Act of 1976 (P.L. 94-455)**

P.L. 94-455, §1906(b)(13)(A):

Amended 1954 Code by substituting "Secretary" for "Secretary or his delegate" each place it appeared. **Effective** 2-1-77.

[Sec. 6011(b)]

(b) IDENTIFICATION OF TAXPAYER.—The Secretary is authorized to require such information with respect to persons subject to the taxes imposed by chapter 21 or chapter 24 as is necessary or helpful in securing proper identification of such person.

Amendments

• **1976, Tax Reform Act of 1976 (P.L. 94-455)**

P.L. 94-455, §1906(b)(13)(A):

Amended 1954 Code by substituting "Secretary" for "Secretary or his delegate" each place it appeared. **Effective** 2-1-77.

[Sec. 6011(c)]

(c) RETURNS, ETC., OF DISCS AND FORMER DISCS AND FORMER FSC'S.—

(1) RECORDS AND INFORMATION.—A DISC, former DISC, or former FSC (as defined in section 922 as in effect before its repeal by the FSC Repeal and Extraterritorial Income Exclusion Act of 2000) shall for the taxable year—

(A) furnish such information to persons who were shareholders at any time during such taxable year, and to the Secretary, and

(B) keep such records, as may be required by regulations prescribed by the Secretary.

(2) RETURNS.—A DISC shall file for the taxable year such returns as may be prescribed by the Secretary by forms or regulations.

Amendments

• **2007, Tax Technical Corrections Act of 2007 (P.L. 110-172)**

P.L. 110-172, §11(g)(19)(A):

Amended Code Sec. 6011(c)(1) by striking "or former DISC or a FSC or former FSC" and inserting ", former DISC, or former FSC (as defined in section 922 as in effect before its repeal by the FSC Repeal and Extraterritorial Income Exclusion Act of 2000)". **Effective** 12-29-2007.

P.L. 110-172, §11(g)(19)(B):

Amended the heading of Code Sec. 6011(c) by striking "AND FSC's" following "FORMER DISCS". **Effective** 12-29-2007.

• **1984, Deficit Reduction Act of 1984 (P.L. 98-369)**

P.L. 98-369, §801(d)(12):

Amended Code Sec. 6011(c) by inserting "or a FSC or former FSC" after "former DISC" in paragraph (1), and by inserting "and FSCs and Former FSCs" after "Former DISCs" in the heading thereof. **Effective** for transactions after 12-31-84, in tax years ending after such date.

• **1976, Tax Reform Act of 1976 (P.L. 94-455)**

P.L. 94-455, §1904(b)(10)(A)(ii):

Repealed former Code Sec. 6011(d) and redesignated Code Sec. 6011(e) as Code Sec. 6011(c). **Effective** 2-1-77, except that the repeal of paragraph (2) of Code Sec. 6011(d) shall apply with respect to loans and commitments made after 6-30-74. Prior to repeal, Code Sec. 6011(d) read as follows:

(d) INTEREST EQUALIZATION TAX RETURNS, ETC.—

(1) IN GENERAL.—

(A) Every person shall make a return for each calendar quarter during which he incurs liability for the tax imposed by section 4911, or would so incur liability but for the provisions of section 4918. The return shall, in addition to such other information as the Secretary or his delegate may by regulations require, include a list of all acquisitions made by such person during the calendar quarter for which exemption is claimed under section 4918 accompanied by a copy of any return made during such quarter under subparagraph (B). No return or accompanying evidence shall be required under this paragraph, in connection with any acquisition with respect to which—

(i) an IET clean confirmation is obtained in accordance with the provisions of section 4918(b),

(ii) a validation certificate described in section 4918(b) issued to the person from whom such acquisition was made is obtained, and such certificate was filed in accordance with the requirements prescribed by the Secretary or his delegate, or

(iii) a validation certificate was obtained by the acquiring person after such acquisition and before the date prescribed by section 6076(a) for the filing of the return,

nor shall any such acquisition be required to be listed in any return made under this paragraph.

(B) Every person who incurs liability for the tax imposed by section 4911 shall, if he disposes of the stock or debt obligation with respect to which such liability was incurred prior to the filing of the return required by subparagraph (A) (unless such disposition is made under circumstances which entitle such person to a credit under the provisions of section 4919), make a return of such tax.

(2) INFORMATION RETURNS OF COMMERCIAL BANKS.—Every United States person (as defined in section 4920(a)(4)) which is a commercial bank shall file a return with respect to loans and commitments to foreign obligors at such times, in such manner, and setting forth such information as the Secretary or his delegate shall by forms and regulations prescribe.

(3) REPORTING REQUIREMENTS FOR CERTAIN MEMBERS OF EXCHANGES AND ASSOCIATIONS.—Every member or member organization of a national securities exchange or of a national securities association registered with the Securities and Exchange Commission, which is not subject to the provisions of section 4918(c), shall keep such records and file such information as the Secretary or his delegate may by forms or regulations prescribe in connection with acquisitions and sales effected by such member or member organization, as a broker or for his own account, of stock of a foreign issuer or debt obligations of a foreign obligor—

(A) with respect to which a validation certificate described in section 4918(b)(1)(A) has been received by such member or member organization; or

(B) with respect to which an acquiring United States person is subject to the tax imposed by section 4911.

P.L. 94-455, §1906(b)(13)(A):

Amended 1954 Code by substituting "Secretary" for "Secretary or his delegate" each place it appeared. **Effective** 2-1-77.

• **1971, Revenue Act of 1971 (P.L. 92-178)**

P.L. 92-178, §504(a):

Added new Code Sec. 6011(e) and redesignated former Code Sec. 6011(e) as Code Sec. 6011(f). **Effective** date is governed by the **effective** date for Code Sec. 992.

• **1969, Interest Equalization Tax Extension Act of 1969 (P.L. 91-128)**

P.L. 91-128, §4(f):

Amended Code Sec. 6011(d)(1)(B) by inserting "(unless such disposition is made under circumstances which entitle such person to a credit under the provisions of section 4919)" after "subparagraph (A)."

P.L. 91-128, §4(g):

Amended Code Sec. 6011(d)(3). **Effective** with respect to acquisitions made after 11-26-69. Prior to amendment, Code Sec. 6011(d)(3) read as follows:

(3) Reporting requirements for members of exchanges and associations.—Every member or member organization of a national securities exchange or of a national securities association registered with the Securities and Exchange Commission shall keep such records and file such information as the Secretary or his delegate may by regulations prescribe in connection with acquisitions and sales effected by such member or member organization as a broker, and acquisitions made for the account of such member or member organization, of stock or debt obligations—

(A) as to which a certificate of American ownership or blanket certificate of American ownership is executed and filed with such member or member organization as prescribed under section 4918(e); and

(B) as to which a written confirmation is furnished to a United States person stating that the acquisition—

(i) in the case of a transaction on a national securities exchange, was made subject to a special contract, or

(ii) in the case of a transaction not on a national securities exchange, was from a person who had not filed a certificate of American ownership with respect to such stock or debt obligation or a blanket certificate of American ownership with respect to the account from which such stock or debt obligation was sold.

RETURNS—GENERAL REQUIREMENT

• **1967, Interest Equalization Tax Extension Act of 1969 (P.L. 90-59)**

P.L. 90-59, §4(b):

Amended Code Sec. 6011(d)(1). **Effective** with respect to acquisitions of stock and debt obligations made after 7-14-67. Prior to amendment, Code Sec. 6011(d)(1) read as follows:

"(1) IN GENERAL.—Every person shall make a return for each calendar quarter during which he incurs liability for the tax imposed by section 4911, or would so incur liability but for the provisions of section 4918. The return shall, in addition to such other information as the Secretary or his delegate may by regulations require, include a list of all acquisitions made by such person during the calendar quarter which are exempt under the provisions of section 4918, and shall, with respect to each such acquisition, be accompanied either (A) by a certificate of American ownership which complies with the provisions of section 4918(e), or (B) in the case of an acquisition for which other proof of exemption is permitted under section 4918(f), by a statement setting forth a summary of the evidence establishing such exemption and the reasons for the person's inability to establish prior American ownership under subsection (b), (c), or (d) of section 4918. No return or accompanying evidence shall be required under this paragraph in connection with any acquisition with respect to which a written confirmation, furnished in accordance with the requirements described in section 4918(c) or (d), is treated as conclusive proof of prior American ownership; nor shall any such acquisition be required to be listed in any return made under this paragraph."

• **1964, Interest Equalization Tax Act (P.L. 88-563)**

P.L. 88-563, §3(a):

Added Code Sec. 6011(d) and redesignated former Code Sec. 6011(d) as Code 6011(e). The first period for which returns shall be made shall be the period commencing 7-19-63, and ending at the close of the calendar quarter in which the enactment of this Act occurs, 9-2-64.

[Sec. 6011(d)]

(d) AUTHORITY TO REQUIRE INFORMATION CONCERNING SECTION 912 ALLOWANCES.—The Secretary may by regulations require any individual who receives allowances which are excluded from gross income under section 912 for any taxable year to include on his return of the taxes imposed by subtitle A for such taxable year such information with respect to the amount and type of such allowances as the Secretary determines to be appropriate.

Amendments

• **1978, Tax Treatment Extension Act of 1978 (P.L. 95-615)**

P.L. 95-615, §207(c):

Added Code Sec. 6011(d). **Effective** for tax years beginning after 12-31-77.

[Sec. 6011(e)]

(e) REGULATIONS REQUIRING RETURNS ON MAGNETIC MEDIA, ETC.—

(1) IN GENERAL.—The Secretary shall prescribe regulations providing standards for determining which returns must be filed on magnetic media or in other machine-readable form. Except as provided in paragraph (3), the Secretary may not require returns of any tax imposed by subtitle A on individuals, estates, and trusts to be other than on paper forms supplied by the Secretary.

(2) REQUIREMENTS OF REGULATIONS.—In prescribing regulations under paragraph (1), the Secretary—

(A) shall not require any person to file returns on magnetic media unless such person is required to file at least the applicable number of returns during the calendar year, and

(B) shall take into account (among other relevant factors) the ability of the taxpayer to comply at reasonable cost with the requirements of such regulations.

(3) SPECIAL RULE FOR TAX RETURN PREPARERS.—

(A) IN GENERAL.—The Secretary shall require that any individual income tax return prepared by a tax return preparer be filed on magnetic media if—

(i) such return is filed by such tax return preparer, and

(ii) such tax return preparer is a specified tax return preparer for the calendar year during which such return is filed.

(B) SPECIFIED TAX RETURN PREPARER.—For purposes of this paragraph, the term "specified tax return preparer" means, with respect to any calendar year, any tax return preparer unless such preparer reasonably expects to file 10 or fewer individual income tax returns during such calendar year.

(C) INDIVIDUAL INCOME TAX RETURN.—For purposes of this paragraph, the term "individual income tax return" means any return of the tax imposed by subtitle A on individuals, estates, or trusts.

(D) EXCEPTION FOR CERTAIN PREPARERS LOCATED IN AREAS WITHOUT INTERNET ACCESS.—The Secretary may waive the requirement of subparagraph (A) if the Secretary determines, on the basis of an application by the tax return preparer, that the preparer cannot meet such requirement by reason of being located in a geographic area which does not have access to internet service (other than dial-up or satellite service).

(4) SPECIAL RULE FOR RETURNS FILED BY FINANCIAL INSTITUTIONS WITH RESPECT TO WITHHOLDING ON FOREIGN TRANSFERS.—The numerical limitation under paragraph (2)(A) shall not apply to any return filed by a financial institution (as defined in section 1471(d)(5)) with respect to tax for which such institution is made liable under section 1461 or 1474(a).

(5) APPLICABLE NUMBER.—

(A) IN GENERAL.—For purposes of paragraph (2)(A), the applicable number shall be—

(i) except as provided in subparagraph (B), in the case of calendar years before 2021, 250,

(ii) in the case of calendar year 2021, 100, and

(iii) in the case of calendar years after 2021, 10.

(B) SPECIAL RULE FOR PARTNERSHIPS FOR 2018, 2019, 2020, AND 2021.—In the case of a partnership, for any calendar year before 2022, the applicable number shall be—

(i) in the case of calendar year 2018, 200,

(ii) in the case of calendar year 2019, 150,

(iii) in the case of calendar year 2020, 100, and

(iv) in the case of calendar year 2021, 50.

(6) PARTNERSHIPS REQUIRED TO FILE ON MAGNETIC MEDIA.—Notwithstanding paragraph (2)(A), the Secretary shall require partnerships having more than 100 partners to file returns on magnetic media.

(6)[(7)] APPLICATION OF NUMERICAL LIMITATION TO RETURNS RELATING TO DEFERRED COMPENSATION PLANS.—For purposes of applying the numerical limitation under paragraph (2)(A) to any return required under section 6058, information regarding each plan for which information is provided on such return shall be treated as a separate return.

RETURNS—GENERAL REQUIREMENT

Amendments

• **2019, Setting Every Community Up for Retirement Enhancement Act of 2019 (P.L. 116-94)**

P.L. 116-94, §202(d)(1), Div. O:

Amended Code Sec. 6011(e) by adding at the end a new paragraph (6)[(7)]. **Effective** for returns required be filed with respect to plan years beginning after 12-31-2019.

• **2019, Taxpayer First Act (P.L. 116-25)**

P.L. 116-25, §2301(a):

Amended Code Sec. 6011(e)(2)(A) by striking "250" and inserting "the applicable number of". **Effective** 7-1-2019.

P.L. 116-25, §2301(b):

Amended Code Sec. 6011(e) by striking paragraph (5) and inserting new paragraphs (5) and (6). **Effective** 7-1-2019. Prior to being stricken, Code Sec. 6011(e)(5) read as follows:

(5) SPECIAL RULES FOR PARTNERSHIPS.—

(A) PARTNERSHIPS PERMITTED TO BE REQUIRED TO FILE ON MAGNETIC MEDIA.—In the case of a partnership, paragraph (2)(A) shall be applied by substituting for "250" the following amount:

(i) In the case of returns and statements relating to calendar year 2018, "200".

(ii) In the case of returns and statements relating to calendar year 2019, "150".

(iii) In the case of returns and statements relating to calendar year 2020, "100".

(iv) In the case of returns and statements relating to calendar year 2021, "50".

(v) In the case of returns and statements relating to calendar years after 2021, "20".

(B) PARTNERSHIPS REQUIRED TO FILE ON MAGNETIC MEDIA.—Notwithstanding subparagraph (A) and paragraph (2)(A), the Secretary shall require partnerships having more than 100 partners to file returns on magnetic media.

P.L. 116-25, §2301(c):

Amended Code Sec. 6011(e)(3) by adding at the end a new subparagraph (D). **Effective** 7-1-2019.

• **2018, Tax Technical Corrections Act of 2018 (P.L. 115-141)**

P.L. 115-141, §301(a)(1), Div. U:

Amended Code Sec. 6011(e) by adding at the end a new paragraph (5). **Effective** as if included in section 1101 of the Bipartisan Budget Act of 2015 [effective generally for returns filed for partnership tax years beginning after 12-31-2017.—CCH].

P.L. 115-141, §301(a)(2), Div. U:

Amended Code Sec. 6011(e)(2) by striking the last sentence. **Effective** as if included in section 1101 of the Bipartisan Budget Act of 2015 [effective generally for returns filed for partnership tax years beginning after 12-31-2017.—CCH]. Prior to being stricken, the last sentence of Code Sec. 6011(e)(2) read as follows:

Notwithstanding the preceding sentence, the Secretary shall require partnerships having more than 100 partners to file returns on magnetic media.

• **2014, Tax Technical Corrections Act of 2014 (P.L. 113-295)**

P.L. 113-295, §220(t), Division A:

Amended Code Sec. 6011(e)(3) by striking "shall require than" and inserting "shall require that". **Effective** 12-19-2014.

• **2010, Hiring Incentives to Restore Employment Act (P.L. 111-147)**

P.L. 111-147, §522(a):

Amended Code Sec. 6011(e) by adding at the end a new paragraph (4). **Effective** for returns the due date for which (determined without regard to extensions) is after 3-18-2010.

• **2009, Worker, Homeownership, and Business Assistance Act of 2009 (P.L. 111-92)**

P.L. 111-92, §17(a):

Amended Code Sec. 6011(e) by adding at the end a new paragraph (3). **Effective** for returns filed after 12-31-2010.

P.L. 111-92, §17(b):

Amended Code Sec. 6011(e)(1) by striking "The Secretary may not" and inserting "Except as provided in paragraph (3), the Secretary may not". **Effective** for returns filed after 12-31-2010.

• **1997, Taxpayer Relief Act of 1997 (P.L. 105-34)**

P.L. 105-34, §1224:

Amended Code Sec. 6011(e)(2) by adding at the end a new sentence. **Effective** for partnership tax years beginning after 12-31-97 [effective date changed by P.L. 105-206, §6012(e)].

• **1989, Omnibus Budget Reconciliation Act of 1989 (P.L. 101-239)**

P.L. 101-239, §7713(a):

Amended Code Sec. 6011(e). **Effective** for returns the due date for which (determined without regard to extensions) is after 12-31-89. Prior to amendment, Code Sec. 6011(e) read as follows:

(e) REGULATIONS REQUIRING RETURNS ON MAGNETIC TAPE, ETC.—

(1) IN GENERAL.—The Secretary shall prescribe regulations providing standards for determining which returns must be filed on magnetic media or in other machine-readable form. The Secretary may not require returns of any tax imposed by subtitle A on individuals, estates, and trusts to be other than on paper forms supplied by the Secretary. In prescribing such regulations, the Secretary shall take into account (among other relevant factors) the ability of the taxpayer to comply at reasonable cost with such a filing requirement.

(2) CERTAIN RETURNS MUST BE FILED ON MAGNETIC MEDIA.—

(A) IN GENERAL.—In the case of any person who is required to file returns under sections 6042(a), 6044(a), and 6049(a) with respect to more than 50 payees for any calendar year, all returns under such sections shall be on magnetic media.

(B) HARDSHIP EXCEPTION.—Subparagraph (A) shall not apply to any person for any period if such person establishes to the satisfaction of the Secretary that its application to such person for such period would result in undue hardship.

• **1983, Interest and Dividend Tax Compliance Act of 1983 (P.L. 98-67)**

P.L. 98-67, §109(a):

Amended Code Sec. 6011(e). **Effective** with respect to payments made after 12-31-83. Prior to amendment, Sec. 6011(e) read as follows:

(e) REGULATIONS REQUIRING RETURNS ON MAGNETIC TAPE, ETC.—The Secretary shall prescribe regulations providing standards for determining which returns must be filed on magnetic media or in other machine-readable form. The Secretary may not require returns of any tax imposed by subtitle A on individuals, estates, and trusts to be other than on paper forms supplied by the Secretary. In prescribing such regulations, the Secretary shall take into account (among other relevant factors) the ability of the taxpayer to comply at a reasonable cost with such a filing requirement.

P.L. 98-67, §109(b), provides:

(b) STUDY OF WAGE RETURNS ON MAGNETIC TAPE.—

(1) STUDY.—The Secretary of the Treasury, in consultation with the Secretary of Health and Human Services, shall conduct a study of the feasibility of requiring persons to file, on magnetic media, returns under section 6011 of the Internal Revenue Code of 1954 containing information described in section 6051(a) of such code (relating to W-2s).

(2) REPORT TO CONGRESS.—Not later than July 1, 1984, the Secretary of the Treasury shall submit to the Committee on Ways and Means of the House of Representatives and the Committee on Finance of the Senate the results of the study conducted under paragraph (1).

• **1982, Tax Equity and Fiscal Responsibility Act of 1982 (P.L. 97-248)**

P.L. 97-248, §314(d):

Added Code Sec. 6011(e).

[Sec. 6011(f)]

(f) PROMOTION OF ELECTRONIC FILING.—

(1) IN GENERAL.—The Secretary is authorized to promote the benefits of and encourage the use of electronic tax administration programs, as they become available, through the use of mass communications and other means.

(2) INCENTIVES.—The Secretary may implement procedures to provide for the payment of appropriate incentives for electronically filed returns.

Amendments

• **1998, IRS Restructuring and Reform Act of 1998 (P.L. 105-206)**

P.L. 105-206, §2001(c):

Amended Code Sec. 6011 by redesignating subsection (f) as subsection (g) and by inserting after subsection (e) a new subsection (f). **Effective** 7-22-98.

P.L. 105-206, §2001(a)-(b) and (d), provides:

(a) IN GENERAL.—It is the policy of Congress that—

(1) paperless filing should be the preferred and most convenient means of filing Federal tax and information returns;

(2) it should be the goal of the Internal Revenue Service to have at least 80 percent of all such returns filed electronically by the year 2007; and

(3) the Internal Revenue Service should cooperate with and encourage the private sector by encouraging competition to increase electronic filing of such returns.

(b) STRATEGIC PLAN.—

(1) IN GENERAL.—Not later than 180 days after the date of the enactment of this Act, the Secretary of the Treasury or the Secretary's delegate (hereafter in this section referred to as the "Secretary") shall establish a plan to eliminate barriers, provide incentives, and use competitive market forces to increase electronic filing gradually over the next 10 years while maintaining processing times for paper returns at 40 days. To the extent practicable, such plan shall provide that all returns prepared electronically for taxable years beginning after 2001 shall be filed electronically.

(2) ELECTRONIC COMMERCE ADVISORY GROUP.—To ensure that the Secretary receives input from the private sector in the development and implementation of the plan required by paragraph (1), the Secretary shall convene an electronic commerce advisory group to include representatives from the small business community and from the tax practitioner, preparer, and computerized tax processor communities and other representatives from the electronic filing industry.

* * *

RETURNS—GENERAL REQUIREMENT

(d) ANNUAL REPORTS.—Not later than June 30 of each calendar year after 1998, the Chairperson of the Internal Revenue Service Oversight Board, the Secretary of the Treasury, and the Chairperson of the electronic commerce advisory group established under subsection (b)(2) shall report to the Committees on Ways and Means, Appropriations, Government Reform and Oversight, and Small Business of the House of Representatives and the Committees on Finance, Appropriations, Governmental Affairs, and Small Business of the Senate on—

(1) the progress of the Internal Revenue Service in meeting the goal of receiving electronically 80 percent of tax and information returns by 2007;

(2) the status of the plan required by subsection (b);

(3) the legislative changes necessary to assist the Internal Revenue Service in meeting such goal; and

(4) the effects on small businesses and the self-employed of electronically filing tax and information returns.

P.L. 105-206, § 2003(c)-(e), provides:

(c) ESTABLISHMENT OF PROCEDURES FOR OTHER INFORMATION.—In the case of taxable periods beginning after December 31, 1999, the Secretary of the Treasury or the Secretary's delegate shall, to the extent practicable, establish procedures to accept, in electronic form, any other information, statements, elections, or schedules, from taxpayers filing returns electronically, so that such taxpayers will not be required to file any paper.

(d) INTERNET AVAILABILITY.—In the case of taxable periods beginning after December 31, 1998, the Secretary of the Treasury or the Secretary's delegate shall establish procedures for all tax forms, instructions, and publications created in the most recent 5-year period to be made available electronically on the Internet in a searchable database at approximately the same time such records are available to the public in paper form. In addition, in the case of taxable periods beginning after December 31, 1998, the Secretary of the Treasury or the Secretary's delegate shall, to the extent practicable, establish procedures for other taxpayer guidance to be made available electronically on the Internet in a searchable database at approximately the same time such guidance is available to the public in paper form.

(e) PROCEDURES FOR AUTHORIZING DISCLOSURE ELECTRONICALLY.—The Secretary shall establish procedures for any taxpayer to authorize, on an electronically filed return, the Secretary to disclose information under section 6103(c) of the Internal Revenue Code of 1986 to the preparer of the return.

[Sec. 6011(g)]

(g) DISCLOSURE OF REPORTABLE TRANSACTION TO TAX-EXEMPT ENTITY.—Any taxable party to a prohibited tax shelter transaction (as defined in section 4965(e)(1)) shall by statement disclose to any tax-exempt entity (as defined in section 4965(c)) which is a party to such transaction that such transaction is such a prohibited tax shelter transaction.

Amendments

• 2006, Tax Increase Prevention and Reconciliation Act of 2005 (P.L. 109-222)

P.L. 109-222, § 516(b)(2):

Amended Code Sec. 6011 by redesignating subsection (g) as subsection (h) and by inserting after subsection (f) a new subsection (g). **Effective** for disclosures the due date for which are after 5-17-2006.

[Sec. 6011(h)]

(h) MANDATORY E-FILING OF UNRELATED BUSINESS INCOME TAX RETURN.—Any organization required to file an annual return under this section which relates to any tax imposed by section 511 shall file such return in electronic form.

Amendments

• 2019, Taxpayer First Act (P.L. 116-25)

P.L. 116-25, § 3101(b)(2):

Amended Code Sec. 6011 by redesignating subsection (h) as subsection (i) and by inserting after subsection (g) a new subsection (h). **Effective** generally for tax years beginning after 7-1-2019. For a transition rule, see Act Sec. 3101(d)(2), below.

P.L. 116-25, § 3101(d)(2), provides:

(2) TRANSITIONAL RELIEF.—

(A) SMALL ORGANIZATIONS.—

(i) IN GENERAL.—In the case of any small organizations, or any other organizations for which the Secretary of the Treasury or the Secretary's delegate (hereafter referred to in this paragraph as the "Secretary") determines the application of the amendments made by this section would cause undue burden without a delay, the Secretary may delay the application of such amendments, but such delay shall not apply to any taxable year beginning on or after the date that is 2 years after the enactment of this Act.

(ii) SMALL ORGANIZATION.—For purposes of clause (i), the term "small organization" means any organization—

(I) the gross receipts of which for the taxable year are less than $200,000; and

(II) the aggregate gross assets of which at the end of the taxable year are less than $500,000.

(B) ORGANIZATIONS FILING FORM 990-T.—In the case of any organization described in section 511(a)(2) of the Internal Revenue Code of 1986 which is subject to the tax imposed by section 511(a)(1) of such Code on its unrelated business taxable income, or any organization required to file a return under section 6033 of such Code and include information under subsection (e) thereof, the Secretary may delay the application of the amendments made by this section, but such delay shall not apply to any taxable year beginning on or after the date that is 2 years after the enactment of this Act.

[Sec. 6011(i)]

(i) INCOME, ESTATE, AND GIFT TAXES.—For requirement that returns of income, estate, and gift taxes be made whether or not there is tax liability, see subparts B and C.

Amendments

• 2019, Taxpayer First Act (P.L. 116-25)

P.L. 116-25, § 3101(b)(2):

Amended Code Sec. 6011 by redesignating subsection (h) as subsection (i). **Effective** generally for tax years beginning after 7-1-2019.

• 2006, Tax Increase Prevention and Reconciliation Act of 2005 (P.L. 109-222)

P.L. 109-222, § 516(b)(2):

Amended Code Sec. 6011 by redesignating subsection (g) as subsection (h). **Effective** for disclosures the due date for which are after 5-17-2006.

• 1998, IRS Restructuring and Reform Act of 1998 (P.L. 105-206)

P.L. 105-206, § 2001(c):

Amended Code Sec. 6011 by redesignating subsection (f) as subsection (g). **Effective** 7-22-98.

• 1986, Tax Reform Act of 1986 (P.L. 99-514)

P.L. 99-514, § 1899A(52):

Amended Code Sec. 6011(f) by striking out "sections 6012 to 6019, inclusive" and inserting in lieu thereof "subparts B and C". **Effective** 10-22-86.

• 1982, Tax Equity and Fiscal Responsibility Act of 1982 (P.L. 97-248)

P.L. 97-248, § 314(d):

Redesignated subsection (e) as subsection (f).

• 1978, Tax Treatment Extension Act of 1978 (P.L. 95-615)

P.L. 95-615, § 207(c):

Redesignated Code Sec. 6011(d) as Code Sec. 6011(e).

• 1976, Tax Reform Act of 1976 (P.L. 94-455)

P.L. 94-455, § 1904(b)(10)(A)(ii):

Redesignated Code Sec. 6011(f) as Code Sec. 6011(d).

• 1971, Revenue Act of 1971 (P.L. 92-178)

P.L. 92-178, § 504(a):

Redesignated subsection (e) of Code Sec. 6011 as subsection (f).

• 1964, Interest Equalization Tax Act (P.L. 88-563)

P.L. 88-563, § 3(a):

Redesignated subsection (d) of Code Sec. 6011 as subsection (e).

• 1958, Excise Tax Technical Changes Act of 1958 (P.L. 85-859)

P.L. 85-859, § 161:

Redesignated subsection (c) of Code Sec. 6011 as subsection (d).

Subpart B—Income Tax Returns

Sec. 6012.	Persons required to make returns of income.
Sec. 6013.	Joint returns of income tax by husband and wife.
Sec. 6014.	Income tax return—tax not computed by taxpayer.
Sec. 6015.	Relief from joint and several liability on print return.

RETURNS—INCOME TAX

Sec. 6017.   Self-employment tax returns.

[Sec. 6012]
SEC. 6012. PERSONS REQUIRED TO MAKE RETURNS OF INCOME.
[Sec. 6012(a)]

(a) GENERAL RULE.—Returns with respect to income taxes under subtitle A shall be made by the following:

(1)(A) Every individual having for the taxable year gross income which equals or exceeds the exemption amount, except that a return shall not be required of an individual—

(i) who is not married (determined by applying section 7703), is not a surviving spouse (as defined in section 2(a)), is not a head of a household (as defined in section 2(b)), and for the taxable year has gross income of less than the sum of the exemption amount plus the basic standard deduction applicable to such an individual,

(ii) who is a head of a household (as so defined) and for the taxable year has gross income of less than the sum of the exemption amount plus the basic standard deduction applicable to such an individual,

(iii) who is a surviving spouse (as so defined) and for the taxable year has gross income of less than the sum of the exemption amount plus the basic standard deduction applicable to such an individual, or

(iv) who is entitled to make a joint return and whose gross income, when combined with the gross income of his spouse, is, for the taxable year, less than the sum of twice the exemption amount plus the basic standard deduction applicable to a joint return, but only if such individual and his spouse, at the close of the taxable year, had the same household as their home.

Clause (iv) shall not apply if for the taxable year such spouse makes a separate return or any other taxpayer is entitled to an exemption for such spouse under section 151(c).

(B) The amount specified in clause (i), (ii), or (iii) of subparagraph (A) shall be increased by the amount of 1 additional standard deduction (within the meaning of section 63(c)(3)) in the case of an individual entitled to such deduction by reason of section 63(f)(1)(A) (relating to individuals age 65 or more), and the amount specified in clause (iv) of subparagraph (A) shall be increased by the amount of the additional standard deduction for each additional standard deduction to which the individual or his spouse is entitled by reason of section 63(f)(1).

(C) The exception under subparagraph (A) shall not apply to any individual—

(i) who is described in section 63(c)(5) and who has—

(I) income (other than earned income) in excess of the sum of the amount in effect under section 63(c)(5)(A) plus the additional standard deduction (if any) to which the individual is entitled, or

(II) total gross income in excess of the standard deduction, or

(ii) for whom the standard deduction is zero under section 63(c)(6).

(D) For purposes of this subsection—

(i) The terms "standard deduction", "basic standard deduction" and "additional standard deduction" have the respective meanings given such terms by section 63(c).

(ii) The term "exemption amount" has the meaning given such term by section 151(d). In the case of an individual described in section 151(d)(2), the exemption amount shall be zero.

(2) Every corporation subject to taxation under subtitle A;

(3) Every estate the gross income of which for the taxable year is $600 or more;

(4) Every trust having for the taxable year any taxable income, or having gross income of $600 or over, regardless of the amount of taxable income;

(5) Every estate or trust of which any beneficiary is a nonresident alien;

(6) Every political organization (within the meaning of section 527(e)(1)), and every fund treated under section 527(g) as if it constituted a political organization, which has political organization taxable income (within the meaning of section 527(c)(1)) for the taxable year;

(7) Every homeowners association (within the meaning of section 528(c)(1)) which has homeowners association taxable income (within the meaning of section 528(d)) for the taxable year; and

(8) Every estate of an individual under chapter 7 or 11 of title 11 of the United States Code (relating to bankruptcy) the gross income of which for the taxable year is not less than the sum of the exemption amount plus the basic standard deduction under section 63(c)(2)(C);

except that subject to such conditions, limitations, and exceptions and under such regulations as may be prescribed by the Secretary, nonresident alien individuals subject to the tax imposed by section 871 and foreign corporations subject to the tax imposed by section 881 may be exempted from the requirement of making returns under this section.

Amendments

• **2018, Tax Technical Corrections Act of 2018 (P.L. 115-141)**

P.L. 115-141, §401(a)(255), Div. U:

Amended Code Sec. 6012(a)(6) by striking "and" at the end. **Effective** 3-23-2018.

P.L. 115-141, §401(a)(256), Div. U:

Amended Code Sec. 6012(a)(7) by striking the period at the end and inserting "; and". **Effective** 3-23-2018.

P.L. 115-141, §401(a)(257), Div. U:

Amended Code Sec. 6012(a)(8) by striking "section 63(c)(2)(D)." and inserting "section 63(c)(2)(C);". **Effective** 3-23-2018.

• **2010, (P.L. 111-226)**

P.L. 111-226, §219(b)(1):

Amended Code Sec. 6012(a) by striking paragraph (8) and by redesignating paragraph (9) as paragraph (8). **Effective** for tax years beginning after 12-31-2010. Prior to being stricken, Code Sec. 6012(a)(8) read as follows:

(8) Every individual who receives payments during the calendar year in which the taxable year begins under section 3507 (relating to advance payment of earned income credit).

• **2002 (P.L. 107-276)**

P.L. 107-276, §3(a):

Amended Code Sec. 6012(a)(6) by striking "or which has" and all that follows through "section)". **Effective** as if included in the amendments made by P.L. 106-230

[**effective** for returns for tax years beginning after 6-30-2000.—CCH]. Prior to amendment, Code Sec. 6012(a)(6) read as follows:

(6) Every political organization (within the meaning of section 527(e)(1)), and every fund treated under section 527(g) as if it constituted a political organization, which has political organization taxable income (within the meaning of section 527(c)(1)) for the taxable year or which has gross receipts of $25,000 or more for the taxable year (other than an organization to which section 527 applies solely by reason of subsection (f)(1) of such section); and

• **2000 (P.L. 106-230)**

P.L. 106-230, §3(a)(1):

Amended Code Sec. 6012(a)(6) by inserting "or which has gross receipts of $25,000 or more for the taxable year (other than an organization to which section 527 applies solely by reason of subsection (f)(1) of such section)" after "taxable year". **Effective** for returns for tax years beginning after 6-30-2000.

• **1998, IRS Restructuring and Reform Act of 1998 (P.L. 105-206)**

P.L. 105-206, §2004 [repealed by P.L. 116-25, §2401], provides:

SEC. 2004. RETURN-FREE TAX SYSTEM.

(a) IN GENERAL.—The Secretary of the Treasury or the Secretary's delegate shall develop procedures for the implementation of a return-free tax system under which appropriate individuals would be permitted to comply with the Internal Revenue Code of 1986 without making the return required under section 6012 of such Code for taxable years beginning after 2007.

(b) REPORT.—Not later than June 30 of each calendar year after 1999, the Secretary shall report to the Committee on Ways and Means of the House of Representatives and the Committee on Finance of the Senate on—

(1) what additional resources the Internal Revenue Service would need to implement such a system;

(2) the changes to the Internal Revenue Code of 1986 that could enhance the use of such a system;

(3) the procedures developed pursuant to subsection (a); and

(4) the number and classes of taxpayers that would be permitted to use the procedures developed pursuant to subsection (a).

- **1988, Technical and Miscellaneous Revenue Act of 1988 (P.L. 100-647)**

P.L. 100-647, §1001(b)(2):

Amended Code Sec. 6012(a)(1)(C)(i)(I). **Effective** as if included in the provision of P.L. 99-514 to which it relates. Prior to amendment, Code Sec. 6012(a)(1)(C)(i)(I) read as follows:

(I) income (other than earned income) in excess of the amount in effect under section 63(c)(5)(A) (relating to limitation on standard deduction in the case of certain dependents), or

- **1986, Tax Reform Act of 1986 (P.L. 99-514)**

P.L. 99-514, §104(a)(1)(A):

Amended Code Sec. 6012(a)(1). **Effective** for tax years beginning after 12-31-86. Prior to amendment, Code Sec. 6012(a)(1) read as follows:

(1)(A) Every individual having for the taxable year a gross income of the exemption amount or more, except that a return shall not be required of an individual (other than an individual described in subparagraph (C))—

(i) who is not married (determined by applying section 143), is not a surviving spouse (as defined in section 2(a)), and for the taxable year has a gross income of less than the sum of the exemption amount plus the zero bracket amount applicable to such an individual,

(ii) who is a surviving spouse (as so defined) and for the taxable year has a gross income of less than the sum of the exemption amount plus the zero bracket amount applicable to such an individual, or

(iii) who is entitled to make a joint return under section 6013 and whose gross income, when combined with the gross income of his spouse, is, for the taxable year, less than the sum of twice the exemption amount plus the zero bracket amount applicable to a joint return but only if such individual and his spouse, at the close of the taxable year, had the same household as their home.

Clause (iii) shall not apply if for the taxable year such spouse makes a separate return or any other taxpayer is entitled to an exemption for such spouse under section 151(e).

(B) The amount specified in clause (i) or (ii) of subparagraph (A) shall be increased by the exemption amount in the case of an individual entitled to an additional personal exemption under section 151(c)(1), and the amount specified in clause (iii) of subparagraph (A) shall be increased by the exemption amount for each additional personal exemption to which the individual or his spouse is entitled under section 151(c).

(C) The exemption under subparagraph (A) shall not apply to—

(i) a nonresident alien individual;

(ii) a citizen of the United States entitled to the benefits of section 931;

(iii) an individual making a return under section 443(a)(1) for a period of less than 12 months on account of a change in his annual accounting period;

(iv) an individual who has income (other than earned income) of the exemption amount or more and who is described in section 63(e)(1)(D); or

(v) an estate or trust.

(D) For purposes of this paragraph—

(i) The term "zero bracket amount" has the meaning given to such term by section 63(d).

(ii) The term "exemption amount" has the meaning given to such term by section 151(f).

P.L. 99-514, §104(a)(1)(B):

Amended Code Sec. 6012(a)(9) by striking out "$2,700 or more" and inserting in lieu thereof "not less than the sum of the exemption amount plus the basic standard deduction under section 63(c)(2)(D)". **Effective** for tax years beginning after 12-31-86.

- **1983, Surface Transportation Act of 1983 (P.L. 97-424)**

P.L. 97-424, §542, provides:

SEC. 542. NO RETURN REQUIRED OF INDIVIDUAL WHOSE ONLY GROSS INCOME IS GRANT OF $1,000 FROM STATE.

(a) IN GENERAL.—Nothing in section 6012(a) of the Internal Revenue Code of 1954 shall be construed to require the filing of a return with respect to income taxes under subtitle A of such code by an individual whose only gross income for the taxable year is a grant of $1,000 received from a State which made such grants generally to residents of such State.

(b) EFFECTIVE DATE.—Subsection (a) shall apply to taxable years beginning after December 31, 1981.

- **1981, Economic Recovery Tax Act of 1981 (P.L. 97-34)**

P.L. 97-34, §104(d)(1)(A)-(E):

Amended Code Sec. 6012(a)(1)(A)(i) by striking out "$3,300" and inserting in lieu thereof "the sum of the exemption amount plus the zero bracket amount applicable to such an individual". Amended Code Sec. 6012(a)(1)(A)(ii) by striking out "$4,400" and inserting in lieu thereof "the sum of the exemption amount plus the zero bracket amount applicable to such an individual". Amended Code Sec. 6012(a)(1)(A)(iii) by striking out "$5,400" and inserting in lieu thereof "the sum of twice the exemption amount plus the zero bracket amount applicable to a joint return". Amended Code Sec. 6012(a)(1) by striking out "$1,000" each place it appeared and inserting in lieu thereof "the exemption amount". Amended Code Sec. 6012(a)(1) by adding at the end thereof new subparagraph (D). **Effective** for tax years beginning after 12-31-84.

- **1980, Bankruptcy Tax Act of 1980 (P.L. 96-589)**

P.L. 96-589, §3(b)(1):

Amended Code Sec. 6012(a) by adding a new paragraph (9). **Effective** for bankruptcy cases commencing on or after 3-25-81.

- **1978, Revenue Act of 1978 (P.L. 95-600)**

P.L. 95-600, §§101(c), 102(b)(1):

Amended Code Sec. 6012(a)(1). **Effective** for tax years beginning after 12-31-78. Prior to amendment, Code Sec. 6012(a)(1) read as follows:

"(a) GENERAL RULE.—Returns with respect to income taxes under subtitle A shall be made by the following:

"(1)(A) Every individual having for the taxable year a gross income of $750 or more, except that a return shall not be required of an individual (other than an individual described in subparagraph (C))—

"(i) who is not married (determined by applying section 143), is not a surviving spouse (as defined in section 2(a)), and for the taxable year has a gross income of less than $2,950,

"(ii) who is a surviving spouse (as so defined) and for the taxable year has a gross income of less than $3,950, or

"(iii) who is entitled to make a joint return under section 6013 and whose gross income, when combined with the gross income of his spouse, is, for the taxable year, less than $4,700, but only if such individual and his spouse, at the close of the taxable year, had the same household as their home.

Clause (iii) shall not apply if for the taxable year such spouse makes a separate return or any other taxpayer is entitled to an exemption for such spouse under section 151(e).

"(B) The amount specified in clause (i) or (ii) of subparagraph (A) shall be increased by $750 in the case of an individual entitled to an additional personal exemption under section 151(c)(1), and the amount specified in clause (iii) of subparagraph (A) shall be increased by $750 for each additional personal exemption to which the individual or his spouse is entitled under section 151(c).

"(C) The exception under subparagraph (A) shall not apply to—

"(i) a nonresident alien individual;

"(ii) a citizen of the United States entitled to the benefits of section 931;

"(iii) an individual making a return under section 443(a)(1) for a period of less than 12 months on account of a change in his annual accounting period;

"(iv) an individual who has income (other than earned income) of $750 or more and who is described in section 63(e)(1)(D); or

"(v) an estate or trust."

P.L. 95-600, §105(d):

Amended Code Sec. 6012(a) by adding new paragraph (8). **Effective** for tax years beginning after 12-31-78.

- **1977, Tax Reduction and Simplification Act of 1977 (P.L. 95-30)**

P.L. 95-30, §104:

Amended Code Sec. 6012(a)(1)(A). **Effective** for tax years beginning after 12-31-76, Prior to amendment, Sec. 6012(a)(1)(A) read as follows:

"(1)(A) Every individual having for the taxable year a gross income of $750 or more, except that a return shall not be required of an individual (other than an individual referred to in section 142(b))—

"(i) who is not married (determined by applying section 143), is not a surviving spouse (as defined in section 2(a)), and for the taxable year has a gross income of less than $2,450,

"(ii) who is a surviving spouse (as so defined) and for the taxable year has a gross income of less than $2,850, or

"(iii) who is entitled to make a joint return under section 6013 and whose gross income, when combined with the gross income of his spouse, is, for the taxable year, less than $3,600 but only if such individual and his spouse, at the close of the taxable year, had the same household as their home.

Clause (iii) shall not apply if for the taxable year such spouse makes a separate return or any other taxpayer is entitled to an exemption for such spouse under section 151(e).

"(B) The amount specified in clause (i) or (ii) of subparagraph (A) shall be increased by $750 in the case of an individual entitled to an additional personal exemption under section 151(c)(1), and the amount specified in clause (iii) of subparagraph (A) shall be increased by $750 for each additional personal exemption to which the individual or his spouse is entitled under section 151(c);

"(C) Every individual having for the taxable year a gross income of $750 or more and to whom section 141(e) (relating to limitations in case of certain dependent taxpayers) applies;"

- **1976, Tax Reform Act of 1976 (P.L. 94-455)**

P.L. 94-455, §401(b)(3):

Amended Code Sec. 6012(a)(1)(A) and (B). **Effective** for tax years ending after 12-31-75. For text of Code Sec. 6012(a)(1)(A) and (B) as it read before the amendment, see below.

P.L. 94-455, §1906(b)(13)(A):

Amended 1954 Code by substituting "Secretary" for "Secretary or his delegate" each place it appeared. **Effective** 2-1-77.

P.L. 94-455, §2101(c):

Added paragraph (7). **Effective** for tax years beginning after 12-31-73.

RETURNS—INCOME TAX

● **1975, Revenue Adjustment Act of 1975 (P.L. 94-164)**

P.L. 94-164, §2(a)(2):

Amended Code Sec. 6012(a)(1)(A) and (B) to read as follows:

(1)(A) Every individual having for the taxable year a gross income of $750 or more, except that a return shall not be required of an individual (other than an individual referred to in section 142(b))—

(i) who is not married (determined by applying section 143), is not a surviving spouse (as defined in section 2(a)), and for the taxable year has a gross income of less than $2,450,

(ii) who is a surviving spouse (as so defined) and for the taxable year has a gross income of less than $2,850, or

(iii) who is entitled to make a joint return under section 6013 and whose gross income, when combined with the gross income of his spouse, is, for the taxable year, less than $3,600 but only if such individual and his spouse, at the close of the taxable year, had the same household as their home.

Clause (iii) shall not apply if for the taxable year such spouse makes a separate return or any other taxpayer is entitled to an exemption for such spouse under section 151(e).

(B) The amount specified in clause (i) or (ii) of subparagraph (A) shall be increased by $750 in the case of an individual entitled to an additional personal exemption under section 151(c)(1), and the amount specified in clause (iii) of subparagraph (A) shall be increased by $750 for each additional personal exemption to which the individual or his spouse is entitled under section 151(c);

Effective for tax years ending after 1975 and before 1977.

● **1975, Tax Reduction Act of 1975 (P.L. 94-12)**

P.L. 94-12, §201(b):

Amended Code Sec. 6012(a)(1)(A) and (B) to read as follows:

(1)(A) Every individual having for the taxable year a gross income of $750 or more, except that a return shall not be required of an individual (other than an individual referred to in section 142(b))—

(i) who is not married (determined by applying section 143), is not a surviving spouse (as defined in section 2(a)), and for the taxable year has a gross income of less than $2,350,

(ii) who is a surviving spouse (as so defined) and for the taxable year has a gross income of less than $2,650, or

(iii) who is entitled to make a joint return under section 6013 and whose gross income, when combined with the gross income of his spouse, is, for the taxable year, less than $3,400 but only if such individual and his spouse, at the close of the taxable year, had the same household as their home.

Clause (iii) shall not apply if for the taxable year such spouse makes a separate return or any other taxpayer is entitled to an exemption for such spouse under section 151(e).

(B) The amount specified in clause (i) or (ii) of subparagraph (A) shall be increased by $750 in the case of an individual entitled to an additional personal exemption under section 151(c)(1), and the amount specified in clause (iii) of subparagraph (A) shall be increased by $750 for each additional personal exemption to which the individual or his spouse is entitled under section 151(c);

Effective for tax years ending in 1975.

Code Sec. 6012(a)(1)(A) and (B), as it existed prior to amendment by P.L. 94-12, was again scheduled to become effective for taxable years ending after 1976. Such text of Code Sec. 6012(a)(1)(A) and (B) is reproduced below:

(1)(A) Every individual having for the taxable year a gross income of $750 or more, except that a return shall not be required of an individual (other than an individual referred to in section 142(b))—

(i) who is not married (determined by applying section 143(a)) and for the taxable year has a gross income of less than $2,050, or

(ii) who is entitled to make a joint return under section 6013 and whose gross income, when combined with the gross income of his spouse, is, for the taxable year, less than $2,800 but only if such individual and his spouse, at the close of the taxable year, had the same household as their home.

Clause (ii) shall not apply if for the taxable year such spouse makes a separate return or any other taxpayer is entitled to an exemption for such spouse under section 151(e).

(B) The $2,050 amount specified in subparagraph (A)(i) shall be increased to $2,800 in the case of an individual entitled to an additional personal exemption under section 151(c)(1), and the $2,800 amount specified in subparagraph (A)(ii) shall be increased by $750 for each additional personal exemption to which the individual or his spouse is entitled under section 151(c);

● **1975 (P.L. 93-625)**

P.L. 93-625, §10(b):

Amended Code Sec. 6012(a) by deleting "and" at the end of paragraph (4), adding "and" at the end of paragraph (5), adding paragraph (6), and deleting from the end of Code Sec. 6012(a) the following: "The Secretary or his delegate shall, by regulation, exempt from the requirement of making returns under this section any political committee (as defined in section 301(d) of the Federal Election Campaign Act of 1971) having no gross income for the taxable year." **Effective** for tax years beginning after 12-31-74.

P.L. 93-625, §10(f), provides:

"(f) Exemption From Filing Requirement for Prior Years Where Income of Political Party Was $100 or Less.—In the case of a taxable year beginning after December 31, 1971, and before January 1, 1975, nothing in the Internal Revenue Code of 1954 shall be deemed to require any organization described in section 527(e)(1) of such Code to file a return for the taxable year under such Code if such organization would be exempt from so filing under section 6012(a)(6) of such Code if such section applied to such taxable year."

● **1974, Federal Election Campaign Act Amendments of 1974 (P.L. 93-443)**

P.L. 93-443, §407:

Amended Code Sec. 6012(a) by adding the last sentence. **Effective** for tax years beginning after 12-31-71.

● **1971, Revenue Act of 1971 (P.L. 92-178)**

P.L. 92-178, §204(a):

Amended Code Sec. 6012(a)(1). **Effective** for tax years beginning after 12-31-71. Prior to amendment, Code Sec. 6012(a)(1) read as follows:

"(1)(A) Every individual having for the taxable year a gross income of $600 or more, except that a return shall not be required of an individual (other than an individual referred to in section 142(b))—

"(i) who is not married (determined by applying section 143(a)) and for the taxable year has a gross income of less than $1,700, or

"(ii) who is entitled to make a joint return under section 6013 and whose gross income, when combined with the gross income of his spouse, is, for the taxable year, less than $2,300 but only if such individual and his spouse, at the close of the taxable year, had the same household as their home.

Clause (ii) shall not apply if for the taxable year such spouse makes a separate return or any other taxpayer is entitled to an exemption for such spouse under section 151(e).

"(B) The $1,700 amount specified in subparagraph (A)(i) shall be increased to $2,300 in the case of an individual entitled to an additional personal exemption under section 151(c)(1), and the $2,300 amount specified in subparagraph (A)(ii) shall be increased by $600 for each additional personal exemption to which the individual or his spouse is entitled under section 151(c);"

● **1969, Tax Reform Act of 1969 (P.L. 91-172)**

P.L. 91-172, §941(a):

Amended Code Sec. 6012(a)(1). **Effective** for tax years beginning after 12-31-69. Prior to amendment, Code Sec. 6012(a)(1) read as follows:

"(a)(1) Every individual having for the taxable year a gross income of $600 or more (except that any individual who has attained the age of 65 before the close of his taxable year shall be required to make a return only if he has for the taxable year a gross income of $1,200 or more);"

P.L. 91-172, §941(d):

Amended Code Sec. 6012(a)(1) by substituting "$750", "$1,750", and "$2,500" in lieu of "$600", "$1,700", and "$2,300". **Effective** for tax years beginning after 12-31-72.

[Sec. 6012(b)]

(b) RETURNS MADE BY FIDUCIARIES AND RECEIVERS.—

(1) RETURNS OF DECEDENTS.—If an individual is deceased, the return of such individual required under subsection (a) shall be made by his executor, administrator, or other person charged with the property of such decedent.

(2) PERSONS UNDER A DISABILITY.—If an individual is unable to make a return required under subsection (a), the return of such individual shall be made by a duly authorized agent, his committee, guardian, fiduciary or other person charged with the care of the person or property of such individual. The preceding sentence shall not apply in the case of a receiver appointed by authority of law in possession of only a part of the property of an individual.

(3) RECEIVERS, TRUSTEES AND ASSIGNEES FOR CORPORATIONS.—In a case where a receiver, trustee in a case under title 11 of the United States Code or assignee, by order of a court of competent jurisdiction, by operation of law or otherwise, has possession of or holds title to all or substantially all the property or business of a corporation, whether or not such property or business is being operated, such receiver, trustee, or assignee shall make the return of income for such corporation in the same manner and form as corporations are required to make such returns.

(4) RETURNS OF ESTATES AND TRUSTS.—Returns of an estate, a trust, or an estate of an individual under chapter 7 or 11 of title 11 of the United States Code shall be made by the fiduciary thereof.

(5) JOINT FIDUCIARIES.—Under such regulations as the Secretary may prescribe, a return made by one of two or more joint fiduciaries shall be sufficient compliance with the requirements of this section. A return made pursuant to this paragraph shall contain a statement that the fiduciary has sufficient knowledge of the affairs of the person for whom the return is made to enable him to make the return, and that the return is, to the best of his knowledge and belief, true and correct.

(6) IRA SHARE OF PARTNERSHIP INCOME.—In the case of a trust which is exempt from taxation under section 408(e), for purposes of this section, the trust's distributive share of items of gross income and gain of any partnership to which subchapter C or D of chapter 63 applies shall be treated as equal to the trust's distributive share of the taxable income of such partnership.

Amendments

• **1997, Taxpayer Relief Act of 1997 (P.L. 105-34)**

P.L. 105-34, §1225:

Amended Code Sec. 6012(b) by adding at the end a new paragraph (6). **Effective** for partnership tax years beginning after 12-31-97 [effective date changed by P.L. 105-206, §6012(e)].

• **1984, Deficit Reduction Act of 1984 (P.L. 98-369)**

P.L. 98-369, §412(b)(3):

Amended Code Sec. 6012(b)(2) by striking out "or section 6015(a)" following "subsection (a)". **Effective** with respect to tax years beginning after 12-31-84.

• **1980, Bankruptcy Tax Act of 1980 (P.L. 96-589)**

P.L. 96-589, §6(i)(5):

Amended Code Sec. 6012(b)(3) by striking out "trustee in bankruptcy" and inserting in lieu thereof "trustee in a case under title 11 of the United States Code". **Effective** 10-1-79, but inapplicable to any proceeding under the Bankruptcy Act commenced before that date.

P.L. 96-589, §3(b)(2):

Amended Code Sec. 6012(b)(4) by striking out "an estate or a trust" and inserting in lieu thereof "an estate, a trust, or an individual under chapter 7 or 11 of title 11 of the United States Code". **Effective** for bankruptcy cases commencing after 3-25-81.

• **1976, Tax Reform Act of 1976 (P.L. 94-455)**

P.L. 94-455, §1906(b)(13)(A):

Amended 1954 Code by substituting "Secretary" for "Secretary or his delegate" each place it appeared. **Effective** 2-1-77.

[Sec. 6012(c)]

(c) CERTAIN INCOME EARNED ABROAD OR FROM SALE OF RESIDENCE.—For purposes of this section, gross income shall be computed without regard to the exclusion provided for in section 121 (relating to gain from sale of principal residence) and without regard to the exclusion provided for in section 911 (relating to citizens or residents of the United States living abroad).

Amendments

• **1997, Taxpayer Relief Act of 1997 (P.L. 105-34)**

P.L. 105-34, §312(d)(11):

Amended Code Sec. 6012(c) by striking "(relating to one-time exclusion of gain from sale of principal residence by individual who has attained age 55)" and inserting "(relating to gain from sale of principal residence)". **Effective**, generally, for sales and exchanges after 5-6-97.

• **1981, Economic Recovery Tax Act of 1981 (P.L. 97-34)**

P.L. 97-34, §111(b)(3):

Amended Code Sec. 6012(c) by striking out "relating to income earned by employees in certain camps" and inserting in lieu thereof "relating to citizens or residents of the United States living abroad". **Effective** with respect to tax years beginning after 12-31-81.

• **1978, Tax Treatment Extension Act of 1978 (P.L. 95-615)**

P.L. 95-615, §202(f)(5):

Amended Code Sec. 6012(c) by striking out "relating to earned income from sources without the United States" and inserting in place thereof "relating to income earned by employees of certain camps". **Effective** for tax years beginning after 12-31-77.

• **1978, Revenue Act of 1978 (P.L. 95-600)**

P.L. 95-600, §404(c)(8):

Amended Code Sec. 6012(c) by striking out "relating to sale of residence by individual who has attained age 65" and inserting in place thereof "relating to one-time exclusion of gain from sale of principal residence by individual who has attained age 55". **Effective** for sales or exchanges after 7-26-78, in tax years ending after such date.

• **1964, Revenue Act of 1964 (P.L. 88-272)**

P.L. 88-272, §206(b)(1):

Amended subsection (c). **Effective** for dispositions after 12-31-63, in tax years ending after such date. Prior to amendment, subsection (c) read as follows:

"(c) Certain Income Earned Abroad.—For purposes of this section, gross income shall be computed without regard to the exclusion provided for in section 911 (relating to earned income from sources without the United States)."

• **1958, Technical Amendments Act of 1958 (P.L. 85-866)**

P.L. 85-866, §72(a):

Redesignated Code Sec. 6012(c) as Code Sec. 6012(d) and added new Code Sec. 6012(c). **Effective** for tax years beginning after 12-31-57.

[Sec. 6012(d)]

(d) TAX-EXEMPT INTEREST REQUIRED TO BE SHOWN ON RETURN.—Every person required to file a return under this section for the taxable year shall include on such return the amount of interest received or accrued during the taxable year which is exempt from the tax imposed by chapter 1.

Amendments

• **1986, Tax Reform Act of 1986 (P.L. 99-514)**

P.L. 99-514, §1525(a):

Amended Code Sec. 6012 by redesignating subsection (d) as subsection (e) and by inserting after subsection (c) new subsection (d). **Effective** for tax years beginning after 12-31-86.

[Sec. 6012(e)]

(e) CONSOLIDATED RETURNS.—

For provisions relating to consolidated returns by affiliated corporations, see chapter 6.

Amendments

• **1986, Tax Reform Act of 1986 (P.L. 99-514)**

P.L. 99-514, §1525(a):

Redesignated former subsection (d) as (e). **Effective** for tax years beginning after 12-31-86.

• **1958, Technical Amendments Act of 1958 (P.L. 85-866)**

P.L. 85-866, §72(a):

Redesignated Code Sec. 6012(c) as Code Sec. 6012(d). **Effective** for tax years beginning after 12-31-57.

[Sec. 6012(f)]

(f) SPECIAL RULE FOR TAXABLE YEARS 2018 THROUGH 2025.—In the case of a taxable year beginning after December 31, 2017, and before January 1, 2026, subsection (a)(1) shall not apply, and every individual who has gross income for the taxable year shall be required to make returns with respect to income taxes under subtitle A, except that a return shall not be required of—

(1) an individual who is not married (determined by applying section 7703) and who has gross income for the taxable year which does not exceed the standard deduction applicable to such individual for such taxable year under section 63, or

(2) an individual entitled to make a joint return if—

(A) the gross income of such individual, when combined with the gross income of such individual's spouse, for the taxable year does not exceed the standard deduction which would be applicable to the taxpayer for such taxable year under section 63 if such individual and such individual's spouse made a joint return,

(B) such individual and such individual's spouse have the same household as their home at the close of the taxable year,

(C) such individual's spouse does not make a separate return, and

(D) neither such individual nor such individual's spouse is an individual described in section 63(c)(5) who has income (other than earned income) in excess of the amount in effect under section 63(c)(5)(A).

RETURNS—INCOME TAX

Amendments

- 2017, Tax Cuts and Jobs Act (P.L. 115-97)

P.L. 115-97, § 11041(e).
Amended Code Sec. 6012 by adding at the end a new subsection (f). **Effective** for tax years beginning after 12-31-2017.

[Sec. 6013]

SEC. 6013. JOINT RETURNS OF INCOME TAX BY HUSBAND AND WIFE.

[Sec. 6013(a)]

(a) JOINT RETURNS.—A husband and wife may make a single return jointly of income taxes under subtitle A, even though one of the spouses has neither gross income nor deductions, except as provided below:

(1) no joint return shall be made if either the husband or wife at any time during the taxable year is a nonresident alien;

(2) no joint return shall be made if the husband and wife have different taxable years; except that if such taxable years begin on the same day and end on different days because of the death of either or both, then the joint return may be made with respect to the taxable year of each. The above exception shall not apply if the surviving spouse remarries before the close of his taxable year, nor if the taxable year of either spouse is a fractional part of a year under section 443(a)(1);

(3) in the case of death of one spouse or both spouses the joint return with respect to the decedent may be made only by his executor or administrator; except that in the case of the death of one spouse the joint return may be made by the surviving spouse with respect to both himself and the decedent if no return for the taxable year has been made by the decedent, no executor or administrator has been appointed, and no executor or administrator is appointed before the last day prescribed by law for filing the return of the surviving spouse. If an executor or administrator of the decedent is appointed after the making of the joint return by the surviving spouse, the executor or administrator may disaffirm such joint return by making, within 1 year after the last day prescribed by law for filing the return of the surviving spouse, a separate return for the taxable year of the decedent with respect to which the joint return was made, in which case the return made by the survivor shall constitute his separate return.

[Sec. 6013(b)]

(b) JOINT RETURN AFTER FILING SEPARATE RETURN.—

(1) IN GENERAL.—Except as provided in paragraph (2), if an individual has filed a separate return for a taxable year for which a joint return could have been made by him and his spouse under subsection (a) and the time prescribed by law for filing the return for such taxable year has expired, such individual and his spouse may nevertheless make a joint return for such taxable year. A joint return filed by the husband and wife under this subsection shall constitute the return of the husband and wife for such taxable year, and all payments, credits, refunds, or other repayments made or allowed with respect to the separate return of either spouse for such taxable year shall be taken into account in determining the extent to which the tax based upon the joint return has been paid. If a joint return is made under this subsection, any election (other than the election to file a separate return) made by either spouse in his separate return for such taxable year with respect to the treatment of any income, deduction, or credit of such spouse shall not be changed in the making of the joint return where such election would have been irrevocable if the joint return had not been made. If a joint return is made under this subsection after the death of either spouse, such return with respect to the decedent can be made only by his executor or administrator.

(2) LIMITATIONS FOR MAKING OF ELECTION.—The election provided for in paragraph (1) may not be made—

(A) after the expiration of 3 years from the last date prescribed by law for filing the return for such taxable year (determined without regard to any extension of time granted to either spouse); or

(B) after there has been mailed to either spouse, with respect to such taxable year, a notice of deficiency under section 6212, if the spouse, as to such notice, files a petition with the Tax Court within the time prescribed in section 6213; or

(C) after either spouse has commenced a suit in any court for the recovery of any part of the tax for such taxable year; or

(D) after either spouse has entered into a closing agreement under section 7121 with respect to such taxable year, or after any civil or criminal case arising against either spouse with respect to such taxable year has been compromised under section 7122.

(3) WHEN RETURN DEEMED FILED.—

(A) ASSESSMENT AND COLLECTION.—For purposes of section 6501 (relating to periods of limitations on assessment and collection), and for purposes of section 6651 (relating to delinquent returns), a joint return made under this subsection shall be deemed to have been filed—

(i) Where both spouses filed separate returns prior to making the joint return—on the date the last separate return was filed (but not earlier than the last date prescribed by law for filing the return of either spouse);

(ii) Where only one spouse filed a separate return prior to the making of the joint return, and the other spouse had less than the exemption amount of gross income for such taxable year—on the date of the filing of such separate return (but not earlier than the last date prescribed by law for the filing of such separate return); or

(iii) Where only one spouse filed a separate return prior to the making of the joint return, and the other spouse had gross income of the exemption amount or more for such taxable year—on the date of the filing of such joint return.

For purposes of this subparagraph, the term "exemption amount" has the meaning given to such term by section 151(d). For purposes of clauses (ii) and (iii), if the spouse whose gross income is being compared to the exemption amount is 65 or over, such clauses shall be applied by substituting "the sum of the exemption amount and the additional standard deduction under section 63(c)(2) by reason of section 63(f)(1)(A) for "the exemption amount".

(B) CREDIT OR REFUND.—For purposes of section 6511, a joint return made under this subsection shall be deemed to have been filed on the last date prescribed by law for filing the return for such taxable year (determined without regard to any extension of time granted to either spouse).

(4) ADDITIONAL TIME FOR ASSESSMENT.—If a joint return is made under this subsection, the periods of limitations provided in sections 6501 and 6502 on the making of assessments and the beginning of levy or a proceeding in court for collection shall with respect to such return include one year immediately after the date of the filing of such joint return (computed without regard to the provisions of paragraph (3)).

(5) ADDITIONS TO THE TAX AND PENALTIES.—

(A) COORDINATION WITH PART II OF SUBCHAPTER A OF CHAPTER 68.—For purposes of part II of subchapter A of chapter 68, where the sum of the amounts shown as tax on the separate returns of each spouse is less than the amount shown as tax on the joint return made under this subsection—

(i) such sum shall be treated as the amount shown on the joint return,

(ii) any negligence (or disregard of rules or regulations) on either separate return shall be treated as negligence (or such disregard) on the joint return, and

(iii) any fraud on either separate return shall be treated as fraud on the joint return.

RETURNS—INCOME TAX

(B) CRIMINAL PENALTY.—For purposes of section 7206(1) and (2) and section 7207 (relating to criminal penalties in the case of fraudulent returns) the term "return" includes a separate return filed by a spouse with respect to a taxable year for which a joint return is made under this subsection after the filing of such separate return.

Amendments

• **1996, Taxpayer Bill of Rights 2 (P.L. 104-168)**

P.L. 104-168, §402(a):

Amended Code Sec. 6013(b)(2) by striking subparagraph (A) and redesignating the following subparagraphs accordingly. **Effective** for tax years beginning after 7-30-96. Prior to amendment, Code Sec. 6013(b)(2)(A) read as follows:

(A) unless there is paid in full at or before the time of the filing of the joint return the amount shown as tax upon such joint return; or

• **1989, Omnibus Budget Reconciliation Act of 1989 (P.L. 101-239)**

P.L. 101-239, §7721(c)(6)(A)-(B):

Amended Code Sec. 6013(b)(5)(A) by striking out "section 6653" and inserting "part II of subchapter A of chapter 68", and by striking "section 6653" in the subparagraph heading and inserting "part II of subchapter A of chapter 68". **Effective** for returns the due date for which (determined without regard to extensions) is after 12-31-89.

• **1988, Technical and Miscellaneous Revenue Act of 1988 (P.L. 100-647)**

P.L. 100-647, §1015(b)(1):

Amended Code Sec. 6013(b)(5)(A). **Effective** for returns the due date for which (determined without regard to extensions) is after 12-31-88. Prior to amendment, Code Sec. 6013(b)(5)(A) read as follows:

(A) ADDITIONS TO THE TAX.—Where the amount shown as the tax by the husband and wife on a joint return made under this subsection exceeds the aggregate of the amounts shown as the tax upon the separate return of each spouse—

(i) NEGLIGENCE.—If any part of such excess is attributable to negligence or intentional disregard of rules and regulations (but without intent to defraud) at the time of the making of such separate return, then 5 percent of the total amount of such excess shall be added to the tax;

(ii) FRAUD.—If any part of such excess is attributable to fraud with intent to evade tax at the time of the making of such separate return, then 50 percent of the total amount of such excess shall be added to the tax.

• **1986, Tax Reform Act of 1986 (P.L. 99-514)**

P.L. 99-514, §104(a)(2)(A)-(C):

Amended Code Sec. 6013(b)(3)(A) by striking out "(twice the exemption amount in case such spouse was 65 or over)" each place it appears, by striking out "section 151(f)" and inserting in lieu thereof "section 151(d)", and by adding at the end thereof a new sentence. **Effective** for tax years beginning after 12-31-86.

• **1981, Economic Recovery Tax Act of 1981 (P.L. 97-34)**

P.L. 97-34, §104(d)(2):

Amended Code Sec. 6013(b)(3)(A) by striking out "$1,000" each place it appeared and inserting in lieu thereof "the exemption amount", by striking out "$2,000" each place it appeared and inserting in lieu thereof "twice the exemption amount", and by adding at the end thereof "For purposes of this subparagraph, the term `exemption amount' has the meaning given to such term by section 151(f)." **Effective** for tax years beginning after 12-31-84.

• **1978, Revenue Act of 1978 (P.L. 95-600)**

P.L. 95-600, §102(b)(2):

Amended Code Sec. 6013(b)(3)(A) by striking out "$750" and "$1,500" each place they appeared and inserting in lieu thereof "$1,000" and "$2,000", respectively. **Effective** for tax years beginning after 12-31-78.

• **1976, Tax Reform Act of 1976 (P.L. 94-455)**

P.L. 94-455, §1906(a)(1):

Struck out "of the United States" after "Tax Court" in Code Sec. 6013(b)(2)(C). **Effective** for tax years beginning after 12-31-76.

• **1971, Revenue Act of 1971 (P.L. 92-178)**

P.L. 92-178, §201(a)(2):

Substituted "$675" for "$650" and "$1,350" for "$1,300" in clauses (ii) and (iii) of Code Sec. 6013(b)(3). (Note: The $650 and $1,300 figures were scheduled to take effect in 1971 under the Tax Reform Act of 1969 (P.L. 91-172).) **Effective** for tax years beginning after 12-31-70, and before 1-1-72.

P.L. 92-178, §201(b)(2), provides:

"(2) section 6013(b)(3)(A) (relating to assessment and collection in the case of certain returns of husband and wife) is amended by striking out `$675' each place it appears and inserting in lieu thereof `$750'; and by striking out `$1,350' each place it appears and inserting in lieu thereof `$1,500'." **Effective** for tax years beginning after 12-31-71.

• **1969, Tax Reform Act of 1969 (P.L. 91-172)**

P.L. 91-172, §801:

Amended Code Sec. 6013(b)(3)(A) by substituting "$625" for "$600" wherever it appeared and by substituting "$1,250" for "$1,200" wherever it appeared. **Effective** for tax years beginning after 12-31-69 and before 1-1-71.

P.L. 91-172 also scheduled changes for 1971 and later years but such changes were repealed and replaced by the changes noted under the amendatory note for P.L. 92-178, above.

• **1958, Technical Amendments Act of 1958 (P.L. 85-866)**

P.L. 85-866, §73:

Amended Sec. 6013(b)(2)(C) by striking out the phrase "such section" and substituting the phrase "section 6213". **Effective** 1-1-54.

[Sec. 6013(c)]

(c) TREATMENT OF JOINT RETURN AFTER DEATH OF EITHER SPOUSE.—For purposes of sections 15, 443, and 7851(a)(1)(A), where the husband and wife have different taxable years because of the death of either spouse, the joint return shall be treated as if the taxable years of both spouses ended on the date of the closing of the surviving spouse's taxable year.

Amendments

• **1984, Deficit Reduction Act of 1984 (P.L. 98-369)**

P.L. 98-369, §474(b)(2):

Amended Code Sec. 6013(c) by striking out "21" and inserting in lieu thereof "15". **Effective** for tax years beginning after 12-31-83, and to carrybacks from such years.

[Sec. 6013(d)]

(d) SPECIAL RULES.—For purposes of this section—

(1) the status as husband and wife of two individuals having taxable years beginning on the same day shall be determined—

(A) if both have the same taxable year—as of the close of such year; or

(B) if one dies before the close of the taxable year of the other—as of the time of such death;

(2) an individual who is legally separated from his spouse under a decree of divorce or of separate maintenance shall not be considered as married; and

(3) if a joint return is made, the tax shall be computed on the aggregate income and the liability with respect to the tax shall be joint and several.

Amendments

• **1976, Tax Reform Act of 1976 (P.L. 94-455)**

P.L. 94-455, §1906(a)(1):

Struck out the heading "DEFINITIONS" and added a new heading, struck out "and" at the end of subparagraph (1)(A) and inserted "or" in its place, and struck out "and" at the end of subparagraph (1)(B). **Effective** for tax years beginning after 12-31-76.

[Sec. 6013(e)—Stricken]

Amendments

• **1998, IRS Restructuring and Reform Act of 1998 (P.L. 105-206)**

P.L. 105-206, §3201(e)(1):

Amended Code Sec. 6013 by striking subsection (e). **Effective** for any liability for tax arising after 7-22-98, and any liability for tax arising on or before such date but remaining unpaid as of such date. For a special rule, see Act Sec. 3201(g)(2), below. Prior to being stricken, Code Sec. 6013(e) read as follows:

(e) SPOUSE RELIEVED OF LIABILITY IN CERTAIN CASES.—

(1) IN GENERAL.—Under regulations prescribed by the Secretary, if—

(A) a joint return has been made under this section for a taxable year,

(B) on such return there is a substantial understatement of tax attributable to grossly erroneous items of one spouse,

(C) the other spouse establishes that in signing the return he or she did not know, and had no reason to know, that there was such substantial understatement, and

RETURNS—INCOME TAX

(D) taking into account all the facts and circumstances, it is inequitable to hold the other spouse liable for the deficiency in tax for such taxable year attributable to such substantial understatement,

then the other spouse shall be relieved of liability for tax (including interest, penalties, and other amounts) for such taxable year to the extent such liability is attributable to such substantial understatement.

(2) GROSSLY ERRONEOUS ITEMS.—For purposes of this subsection, the term "grossly erroneous items" means, with respect to any spouse—

(A) any item of gross income attributable to such spouse which is omitted from gross income, and

(B) any claim of a deduction, credit, or basis by such spouse in an amount for which there is no basis in fact or law.

(3) SUBSTANTIAL UNDERSTATEMENT.—For purposes of this subsection, the term "substantial understatement" means any understatement (as defined in section 6662(d)(2)(A)) which exceeds $500.

(4) UNDERSTATEMENT MUST EXCEED SPECIFIED PERCENTAGE OF SPOUSE'S INCOME.—

(A) ADJUSTED GROSS INCOME OF $20,000 OR LESS.—If the spouse's adjusted gross income for the preadjustment year is $20,000 or less, this subsection shall apply only if the liability described in paragraph (1) is greater than 10 percent of such adjusted gross income.

(B) ADJUSTED GROSS INCOME OF MORE THAN $20,000.—If the spouse's adjusted gross income for the preadjustment year is more than $20,000, subparagraph (A) shall be applied by substituting "25 percent" for "10 percent".

(C) PREADJUSTMENT YEAR.—For purposes of this paragraph, the term "preadjustment year" means the most recent taxable year of the spouse ending before the date the deficiency notice is mailed.

(D) COMPUTATION OF SPOUSE'S ADJUSTED GROSS INCOME.—If the spouse is married to another spouse at the close of the preadjustment year, the spouse's adjusted gross income shall include the income of the new spouse (whether or not they file a joint return).

(E) EXCEPTION FOR OMISSIONS FROM GROSS INCOME.—This paragraph shall not apply to any liability attributable to the omission of an item from gross income.

(5) SPECIAL RULE FOR COMMUNITY PROPERTY INCOME.—For purposes of this subsection, the determination of the spouse to whom items of gross income (other than gross income from property) are attributable shall be made without regard to community property laws.

P.L. 105-206, § 3201(g)(2), provides:

(2) 2-YEAR PERIOD.—The 2-year period under subsection (b)(1)(E) or (c)(3)(B) of section 6015 of the Internal Revenue Code of 1986 shall not expire before the date which is 2 years after the date of the first collection activity after the date of the enactment of this Act.

• **1990, Omnibus Budget Reconciliation Act of 1990 (P.L. 101-508)**

P.L. 101-508, § 11704(a)(22):

Amended Code Sec. 6013(e)(3) by striking "section 6661(b)(2)(A)" and inserting "section 6662(d)(2)(A)". **Effective** 11-5-90.

• **1984, Deficit Reduction Act of 1984 (P.L. 98-369)**

P.L. 98-369, § 424(a):

Amended Code Sec. 6013(e). **Effective** for all tax years to which the Internal Revenue Code of 1954 applies. Corresponding provisions shall be deemed to be included in the Internal Revenue Code of 1939 and shall apply to all tax years to which such Code applies. Prior to amendment, Code Sec. 6013(e) read as follows:

(e) SPOUSE RELIEVED OF LIABILITY IN CERTAIN CASES.—

(1) In General. Under regulations prescribed by the Secretary, if—

(A) a joint return has been made under this section for a taxable year and on such return there was omitted from gross income an amount properly includable therein which is attributable to one spouse and which is in excess of 25 percent of the amount of gross income stated in the return,

(B) the other spouse establishes that in signing the return he or she did not know of, and had no reason to know of, such omission, and

(C) taking into account whether or not the other spouse significantly benefited directly or indirectly from the items omitted from gross income and taking into account all other facts and circumstances, it is inequitable to hold the other spouse liable for the deficiency in tax for such taxable year attributable to such omission, then the other spouse shall be relieved of liability for tax (including interest, penalties, and other amounts) for such taxable year to the extent that such liability is attributable to such omission from gross income.

(2) Special Rules.—For purposes of paragraph (1)—

(A) the determination of the spouse to whom items of gross income (other than gross income from property) are attributable shall be made without regard to community property laws, and

(B) the amount omitted from gross income shall be determined in the manner provided by section 6501(e)(1)(A).

• **1976, Tax Reform Act of 1976 (P.L. 94-455)**

P.L. 94-455, § 1906(b)(13)(A):

Amended 1954 Code by substituting "Secretary" for "Secretary or his delegate" each place it appeared. **Effective** 2-1-77.

P.L. 94-455, § 2114(a):

Amended the **effective** date provisions of P.L. 91-679 by adding at the end thereof the following:

Upon application by a taxpayer, the Secretary of the Treasury shall redetermine the liability for tax (including interest, penalties, and other amounts) of such taxpayer for taxable years beginning after December 31, 1961, and ending before January 13, 1971. The preceding sentence shall apply solely to a taxpayer to whom the application of the provisions of section 6013(e) of the Internal Revenue Code of 1954, as added by this Act, for such taxable years is prevented by the operation of res judicata, and such redetermination shall be made without regard to such rule of law. Any overpayment of tax by such taxpayer for such taxable years resulting from the redetermination made under this Act shall be refunded to such taxpayer.

P.L. 94-455, § 2114(b), provided:

(b) EFFECTIVE DATE.—The application permitted under the amendment made by subsection (a) of this section must be filed with the Secretary of the Treasury during the first calendar year beginning after the date of the enactment of this Act.

• **1971 (P.L. 91-679)**

P.L. 91-679, § 1:

Added subsection 6013(e). **Effective** for all tax years to which the Internal Revenue Code of 1954 applies. Corresponding provisions shall be deemed to be included in the Internal Revenue Code of 1939 and shall apply to all tax years to which such Code applies.

[Sec. 6013(f)]

(f) JOINT RETURN WHERE INDIVIDUAL IS IN MISSING STATUS.—For purposes of this section and subtitle A—

(1) ELECTION BY SPOUSE.—If—

(A) an individual is in a missing status (within the meaning of paragraph (3)) as a result of service in a combat zone (as determined for purposes of section 112), and

(B) the spouse of such individual is otherwise entitled to file a joint return for any taxable year which begins on or before the day which is 2 years after the date designated under section 112 as the date of termination of combatant activities in such zone,

then such spouse may elect under subsection (a) to file a joint return for such taxable year. With respect to service in the combat zone designated for purposes of the Vietnam conflict, such election may be made for any taxable year while an individual is in missing status.

(2) EFFECT OF ELECTION.—If the spouse of an individual described in paragraph (1)(A) elects to file a joint return under subsection (a) for a taxable year, then, until such election is revoked—

(A) such election shall be valid even if such individual died before the beginning of such year, and

(B) except for purposes of section 692 (relating to income taxes of members of the Armed Forces, astronauts, and victims of certain terrorist attacks on death), the income tax liability of such individual, his spouse, and his estate shall be determined as if he were alive throughout the taxable year.

(3) MISSING STATUS.—For purposes of this subsection—

(A) UNIFORMED SERVICES.—A member of a uniformed service (within the meaning of section 101(3) of title 37 of the United States Code) is in a missing status for any period for which he is entitled to pay and allowances under section 552 of such title 37.

(B) CIVILIAN EMPLOYEES.—An employee (within the meaning of section 5561(2) of title 5 of the United States Code) is in a missing status for any period for which he is entitled to pay and allowances under section 5562 of such title 5.

(4) MAKING OF ELECTION; REVOCATION.—An election described in this subsection with respect to any taxable year may be made by filing a joint return in accordance with subsection (a) and under such regulations as may be prescribed by the Secretary. Such an election may be revoked by either spouse on or before the due date (including extensions) for such taxable year, and, in the case of an executor or administrator, may be revoked by disaffirming as provided in the last sentence of subsection (a)(3).

Amendments

• **2017, Tax Cuts and Jobs Act (P.L. 115-97)**

P.L. 115-97, § 11026, provides:

For a special rule, see Act Sec. 11026 in the amendment notes for Code Sec. 112(c).

• **2003, Military Family Tax Relief Act of 2003 (P.L. 108-121)**

P.L. 108-121, § 110(a)(2)(B):

Amended Code Sec. 6013(f)(2)(B) by inserting ", astronauts," after "Forces". **Effective** with respect to any astronaut whose death occurs after 12-31-2002.

RETURNS—INCOME TAX

- **2002, Victims of Terrorism Tax Relief Act of 2001 (P.L. 107-134)**

P.L. 107-134, §101(b)(2):

Amended Code Sec. 6013(f)(2)(B) by inserting "and victims of certain terrorist attacks" before "on death". **Effective** for tax years ending before, on, or after 9-11-2001. For a waiver of limitations, see Act Sec. 101(d)(2), below.

P.L. 107-134, §101(d)(2), provides:

(2) WAIVER OF LIMITATIONS.—If refund or credit of any overpayment of tax resulting from the amendments made by this section is prevented at any time before the close of the 1-year period beginning on the date of the enactment of this Act by the operation of any law or rule of law (including res judicata), such refund or credit may nevertheless be made or allowed if claim therefor is filed before the close of such period.

- **1999 (P.L. 106-21)**

P.L. 106-21, §1(a)(7), (b) and (d)(1), provide:

SECTION 1. AVAILABILITY OF CERTAIN TAX BENEFITS FOR SERVICES AS PART OF OPERATION ALLIED FORCE.

(a) GENERAL RULE.—For purposes of the following provisions of the Internal Revenue Code of 1986, a qualified hazardous duty area shall be treated in the same manner as if it were a combat zone (as determined under section 112 of such Code):

* * *

(7) Section 6013(f)(1) (relating to joint return where individual is in missing status).

* * *

(b) QUALIFIED HAZARDOUS DUTY AREA.—For purposes of this section, the term "qualified hazardous duty area" means any area of the Federal Republic of Yugoslavia (Serbia/Montenegro), Albania, the Adriatic Sea, and the northern Ionian Sea (above the 39th parallel) during the period (which includes the date of the enactment of this Act) that any member of the Armed Forces of the United States is entitled to special pay under section 310 of title 37, United States Code (relating to special pay: duty subject to hostile fire or imminent danger) for services performed in such area.

* * *

(d) EFFECTIVE DATES.—

(1) IN GENERAL.—Except as provided in paragraph (2), this section shall take effect on March 24, 1999.

- **1996 (P.L. 104-117)**

P.L. 104-117, §1(a)(7), (b) and (e)(1), provide:

SECTION 1. TREATMENT OF CERTAIN INDIVIDUALS PERFORMING SERVICES IN CERTAIN HAZARDOUS DUTY AREAS.

(a) GENERAL RULE.—For purposes of the following provisions of the Internal Revenue Code of 1986, a qualified hazardous duty area shall be treated in the same manner as if it were a combat zone (as determined under section 112 of such Code):

* * *

(7) Section 6013(f)(1) (relating to joint return where individual is in missing status).

* * *

(b) QUALIFIED HAZARDOUS DUTY AREA.—For purposes of this section, the term "qualified hazardous duty area" means Bosnia and Herzegovina, Croatia, or Macedonia, if as of the date of the enactment of this section any member of the Armed Forces of the United States is entitled to special pay under section 310 of title 37, United States Code (relating to special pay; duty subject to hostile fire or imminent danger) for services performed in such country. Such term includes any such country only during the period such entitlement is in effect. Solely for purposes of applying section 7508 of the Internal Revenue Code of 1986, in the case of an individual who is performing services as part of Operation Joint Endeavor outside the United States while deployed away from such individual's permanent duty station, the term "qualified hazardous duty area" includes, during the period for which such entitlement is in effect, any area in which such services are performed.

* * *

(e) EFFECTIVE DATE.—

(1) IN GENERAL.—Except as provided in paragraph (2), the provisions of and amendments made by this section shall take effect on November 21, 1995.

- **1986, Tax Reform Act of 1986 (P.L. 99-514)**

P.L. 99-514, §1708(a)(3):

Amended Code Sec. 6013(f)(1) by striking out "no such election may be made for any taxable year beginning after December 31, 1982" in the last sentence thereof and inserting in lieu thereof "such election may be made for any taxable year while an individual is in missing status". **Effective** for tax years beginning after 12-31-82.

- **1983, Technical Corrections Act of 1982 (P.L. 97-448)**

P.L. 97-448, §307(c):

Amended Code Sec. 6013(f)(1) by striking out "January 2, 1978" and inserting in lieu thereof "December 31, 1982".

- **1976 (P.L. 94-569)**

P.L. 94-569, §3(d):

Substituted "after January 2, 1978" for "more than 2 years after the date of the enactment of this sentence" in Code Sec. 6013(f)(1).

- **1976, Tax Reform Act of 1976 (P.L. 94-455)**

P.L. 94-455, §1906(b)(13)(A):

Amended 1954 Code by substituting "Secretary" for "Secretary or his delegate" each place it appeared. **Effective** 2-1-77.

- **1974 (P.L. 93-597)**

P.L. 93-597, §3(a):

Added Code Sec. 6013(f). **Effective** with respect to tax years ending on or after 2-28-61.

[Sec. 6013(g)]

(g) ELECTION TO TREAT NONRESIDENT ALIEN INDIVIDUAL AS RESIDENT OF THE UNITED STATES.—

(1) IN GENERAL.—A nonresident alien individual with respect to whom this subsection is in effect for the taxable year shall be treated as a resident of the United States—

(A) for purposes of chapter 1 for all of such taxable year, and

(B) for purposes of chapter 24 (relating to wage withholding) for payments of wages made during such taxable year.

(2) INDIVIDUALS WITH RESPECT TO WHOM THIS SUBSECTION IS IN EFFECT.—This subsection shall be in effect with respect to any individual who, at the close of the taxable year for which an election under this subsection was made, was a nonresident alien individual married to a citizen or resident of the United States, if both of them made such election to have the benefits of this subsection apply to them.

(3) DURATION OF ELECTION.—An election under this subsection shall apply to the taxable year for which made and to all subsequent taxable years until terminated under paragraph (4) or (5); except that any such election shall not apply for any taxable year if neither spouse is a citizen or resident of the United States at any time during such year.

(4) TERMINATION OF ELECTION.—An election under this subsection shall terminate at the earliest of the following times:

(A) REVOCATION BY TAXPAYERS.—If either taxpayer revokes the election, as of the first taxable year for which the last day prescribed by law for filing the return of tax under chapter 1 has not yet occurred.

(B) DEATH.—In the case of the death of either spouse, as of the beginning of the first taxable year of the spouse who survives following the taxable year in which such death occurred; except that if the spouse who survives is a citizen or resident of the United States who is a surviving spouse entitled to the benefits of section 2, the time provided by this subparagraph shall be as of the close of the last taxable year for which such individual is entitled to the benefits of section 2.

(C) LEGAL SEPARATION.—In the case of the legal separation of the couple under a decree of divorce or of separate maintenance, as of the beginning of the taxable year in which such legal separation occurs.

(D) TERMINATION BY SECRETARY.—At the time provided in paragraph (5).

(5) TERMINATION BY SECRETARY.—The Secretary may terminate any election under this subsection for any taxable year if he determines that either spouse has failed—

(A) to keep such books and records,

(B) to grant such access to such books and records, or

(C) to supply such other information,

as may be reasonably necessary to ascertain the amount of liability for taxes under chapter 1 of either spouse for such taxable year.

(6) ONLY ONE ELECTION.—If any election under this subsection for any two individuals is terminated under paragraph (4) or (5) for any taxable year, such two individuals shall be ineligible to make an election under this subsection for any subsequent taxable year.

RETURNS—INCOME TAX

Amendments

• **1998, IRS Restructuring and Reform Act of 1998 (P.L. 105-206)**

P.L. 105-206, §6011(e)(2):

Amended Code Sec. 6013 by striking "chapters 1 and 5" each place it appears in paragraphs (1)(A) and (5) of subsection (g) and inserting "chapter 1". **Effective** as if included in the provision of P.L. 105-34 to which it relates [**effective** 8-5-97.—CCH].

• **1983, Interest and Dividend Tax Compliance Act of 1983 (P.L. 98-67)**

P.L. 98-67, §102(a):

Repealed the amendment made to Code Sec. 6013(g)(1)(B) by P.L. 97-248. **Effective** as of the close of 6-30-83, as though it had not been enacted.

• **1982, Tax Equity and Fiscal Responsibility Act of 1982 (P.L. 97-248)**

P.L. 97-248, §307(a)(4):

Amended Code Sec. 6013(g)(1)(B) by striking out "(relating to wage withholding)" and inserting "(relating to withholding on wages, interest, dividends, and patronage dividends)" and by striking out "of wages". **Effective** 7-1-83.

• **1978, Revenue Act of 1978 (P.L. 95-600)**

P.L. 95-600, §701(u)(15)(A):

Amended Code Sec. 6013(g)(1). **Effective** as set forth in P.L. 95-600, §701(u)(15)(E). Prior to amendment, Code Sec. 6013(g)(1) read as follows:

"(1) IN GENERAL.—A nonresident alien individual with respect to whom this subsection is in effect for the taxable year shall be treated as a resident of the United States for purposes of chapter 1 for all of such taxable year."

P.L. 95-600, §701(u)(15)(B):

Amended Code Sec. 6013(g)(5) by striking out "chapter 1" and inserting in lieu thereof "chapters 1 and 5". **Effective** for tax years ending on or after 12-31-75.

P.L. 95-600, §701(u)(15)(E), provides:

(E) EFFECTIVE DATES.—The amendments made by this paragraph—

(i) to the extent that they relate to chapter 1 or 5 of the Internal Revenue Code of 1954, shall apply to taxable years ending on or after December 31, 1975, and

(ii) to the extent that they relate to wage withholding under chapter 24 of such Code, shall apply to remuneration paid on or after the first day of the first month which begins more than 90 days after the date of the enactment of this Act.

P.L. 95-600, §701(u)(16):

Amended Code Sec. 6013(g)(2) by striking out "who, at the time an election was made under this subsection," and inserting in lieu thereof "who, at the close of the taxable year for which an election under this subsection was made,". **Effective** for tax years beginning after 12-31-75.

• **1976, Tax Reform Act of 1976 (P.L. 94-455).**

P.L. 94-455, §1012(a):

Added Code Sec. 6013(g). **Effective** for tax years ending on or after 12-31-75.

[Sec. 6013(h)]

(h) JOINT RETURN, ETC., FOR YEAR IN WHICH NONRESIDENT ALIEN BECOMES RESIDENT OF UNITED STATES.—

(1) IN GENERAL.—If—

(A) any individual is a nonresident alien individual at the beginning of any taxable year but is a resident of the United States at the close of such taxable year,

(B) at the close of such taxable year, such individual is married to a citizen or resident of the United States, and

(C) both individuals elect the benefits of this subsection at the time and in the manner prescribed by the Secretary by regulation,

then the individual referred to in subparagraph (A) shall be treated as a resident of the United States for purposes of chapter 1 for all of such taxable year, and for purposes of chapter 24 (relating to wage withholding) for payments of wages made during such taxable year.

(2) ONLY ONE ELECTION.—If any election under this subsection applies for any 2 individuals for any taxable year, such 2 individuals shall be ineligible to make an election under this subsection for any subsequent taxable year.

Amendments

• **1998, IRS Restructuring and Reform Act of 1998 (P.L. 105-206)**

P.L. 105-206, §6011(e)(2):

Amended Code Sec. 6013 by striking "chapters 1 and 5" in subsection (h)(1) and inserting "chapter 1". **Effective** as if included in the provision of P.L. 105-34 to which it relates [**effective** 8-5-97.—CCH].

• **1983, Interest and Dividend Tax Compliance Act of 1983 (P.L. 98-67)**

P.L. 98-67, §102(a):

Repealed the amendment made to Code Sec. 6013(h)(1) by P.L. 97-248. **Effective** as of the close of 6-30-83, as though it had not been enacted.

• **1982, Tax Equity and Fiscal Responsibility Act of 1982 (P.L. 97-248)**

P.L. 97-248, §307(a)(5):

Amended Code Sec. 6013(h)(1) by striking out "(relating to wage withholding)" and by inserting "(relating to withholding on wages, interest, dividends, and patronage dividends)" and by striking out "of wages". **Effective** 7-1-83.

• **1978, Revenue Act of 1978 (P.L. 95-600)**

P.L. 95-600, §701(u)(15)(C):

Amended Code Sec. 6013(h)(1) by striking out "chapter 1" and inserting in lieu thereof "chapters 1 and 5", and by inserting before the period at the end thereof ", and for purposes of chapter 24 (relating to wage withholding) for payments of wages made during such taxable year". **Effective** as set forth in P.L. 95-600, §701(u)(15)(E). See historical comment on P.L. 95-600, §701(o)(15)(E), under Code Sec. 6013(g).

• **1976, Tax Reform Act of 1976 (P.L. 94-455)**

P.L. 94-455, §1012(a):

Added Code Sec. 6013(h). **Effective** for tax years ending on or after 12-31-75.

[Sec. 6014]

SEC. 6014. INCOME TAX RETURN—TAX NOT COMPUTED BY TAXPAYER.

[Sec. 6014(a)]

(a) ELECTION BY TAXPAYER.—An individual who does not itemize his deductions and who is not described in section 6012(a)(1)(C)(i), whose gross income is less than $10,000 and includes no income other than remuneration for services performed by him as an employee, dividends or interest, and whose gross income other than wages, as defined in section 3401(a), does not exceed $100, shall at his election not be required to show on the return the tax imposed by section 1. Such election shall be made by using the form prescribed for purposes of this section. In such case the tax shall be computed by the Secretary who shall mail to the taxpayer a notice stating the amount determined as payable.

Amendments

• **1986, Tax Reform Act of 1986 (P.L. 99-514)**

P.L. 99-514, §104(b)(16)(A):

Amended Code Sec. 6014(a) by striking out "who does not have an unused zero bracket amount (determined under section 63(e))" and inserting in lieu thereof "who is not described in section 6012(a)(1)(C)(i)". **Effective** for tax years beginning after 12-31-86.

• **1977, Tax Reduction and Simplification Act of 1977 (P.L. 95-30)**

P.L. 95-30, §101(d)(13):

Amended Code Sec. 6014(a) by striking out "entitled to take" through "section 141(e))" in the first sentence thereof and inserting in lieu thereof "who does not itemize his deductions and who does not have an unused zero bracket amount (determined under section 63(e))," and by striking out "and shall constitute an election to take the standard deduction" in the second sentence thereof. **Effective** for tax years beginning after 12-31-77.

• **1976, Tax Reform Act of 1976 (P.L. 94-455)**

P.L. 94-455, §501(b)(8):

Amended Code Sec. 6014(a) by striking out "entitled to elect to pay the tax imposed by section 3" and inserting "entitled to take the standard deduction provided by section 141 (other than an individual described in section 141(e))" in its place in the first sentence, and striking out "pay the tax imposed by section 3" and inserting "take the standard deduction" in its place in the second sentence. **Effective** for tax years beginning after 12-31-75.

P.L. 94-455, §503(b):

Amended Code Sec. 6014(a) by striking out the last sentence. **Effective** for tax years beginning after 12-31-75. Prior to repeal, the last sentence of Code Sec. 6014(a) read as follows:

In determining the amount payable, the credit against such tax provided for by section 37 shall not be allowed.

RETURNS—INCOME TAX

P.L. 94-455, §1906(b)(13)(A):

Amended 1954 Code by substituting "Secretary" for "Secretary or his delegate" each place it appeared. **Effective** 2-1-77.

• **1969, Tax Reform Act of 1969 (P.L. 91-172)**

P.L. 91-172, §803(d)(1):

Amended Code Sec. 6014(a) by inserting "$10,000" in place of "$5,000" in the first sentence and by deleting the last two sentences. **Effective** for tax years beginning after 12-31-69. Prior to amendment, Code Sec. 6014(a) read as follows:

(a) Election by Taxpayer.—An individual entitled to elect to pay the tax imposed by section 3 whose gross income is less than $5,000 and includes no income other than remuneration for services performed by him as an employee, dividends or interest, and whose gross income other than wages, as defined in section 3401(a), does not exceed $100, shall at his election not be required to show on the return the tax imposed by section 1. Such election shall be made by using the form prescribed for purposes of this section and shall constitute an election to pay the tax imposed by section 3. In such case the tax shall be computed by the Secretary or his delegate who shall mail to the taxpayer a notice stating the amount determined as payable. In determining the amount payable, the credit against such tax provided for by section 34 or 37 shall not be allowed. In the case of a head of household (as defined in section 1(b)) or a surviving spouse (as defined in section 2(b)) electing the benefits of this subsection, the tax shall be computed by the Secretary or his delegate without regard to the taxpayer's status as a head of household or as a surviving spouse. In the case of a married individual filing a separate return and electing the benefits of this subsection, neither Table V in section 3(a) nor Table V in section 3(b) shall apply.

• **1964, Revenue Act of 1964 (P.L. 88-272)**

P.L. 88-272, §201(d)(14):

Amended Code Sec. 6014(a) by deleting "34 or" [shown in boldface italic type] in the fourth sentence. **Effective** with respect to dividends received after 12-31-64, in tax years ending after such date.

P.L. 88-272, §301(b)(2):

Added the last sentence to Code Sec. 6014(a). **Effective** for tax years beginning after 12-31-63.

[Sec. 6014(b)]

(b) REGULATIONS.—The Secretary shall prescribe regulations for carrying out this section, and such regulations may provide for the application of the rules of this section—

(1) to cases where the gross income includes items other than those enumerated by subsection (a),

(2) to cases where the gross income from sources other than wages on which the tax has been withheld at the source is more than $100,

(3) to cases where the gross income is $10,000 or more, or

(4) to cases where the taxpayer itemizes his deductions or where the taxpayer claims a reduced standard deduction by reason of section 63(c)(5).

Such regulations shall provide for the application of this section in the case of husband and wife, including provisions determining when a joint return under this section may be permitted or required, whether the liability shall be joint and several, and whether one spouse may make return under this section and the other without regard to this section.

Amendments

• **1986, Tax Reform Act of 1986 (P.L. 99-514)**

P.L. 99-514, §104(b)(16)(B):

Amended Code Sec. 6014(b)(4). **Effective** for tax years beginning after 12-31-86. Prior to amendment, Code Sec. 6014(b)(4) read as follows:

(4) to cases where the taxpayer itemizes his deductions or has an unused zero bracket amount.

• **1977, Tax Reduction and Simplification Act of 1977 (P.L. 95-30)**

P.L. 95-30, §101(d)(14):

Amended Code Sec. 6014(b)(4). **Effective** for tax years beginning after 12-31-76. Prior to amendment, Code Sec. 6014(b)(4) read as follows:

"(4) to cases where the taxpayer does not elect the standard deduction or where the taxpayer elects the standard deduction but is subject to the provisions of section 141(e) (relating to limitations in case of certain dependent taxpayers)."

• **1976, Tax Reform Act of 1976 (P.L. 94-455)**

P.L. 94-455, §501(b):

Amended paragraph (5). **Effective** for tax years beginning after 12-31-75. Prior to amendment, Code Sec. 6014(b)(5) read as follows:

(5) to cases where the taxpayer does not elect the standard deduction.

P.L. 94-455, §503(b):

Struck out paragraph (4), redesignated paragraph (5) as paragraph (4), and inserted "or" at the end of paragraph (3). **Effective** for tax years beginning after 12-31-75. Prior to repeal, Code Sec. 6014(b)(4) read as follows:

(4) to cases where the taxpayer is entitled to the credit provided by section 37 (relating to retirement income credit), or

P.L. 94-455, §1906(b)(13)(A):

Amended 1954 Code by substituting "Secretary" for "Secretary or his delegate" each place it apppeared. **Effective** 2-1-77.

• **1969, Tax Reform Act of 1969 (P.L. 91-172)**

P.L. 91-172, §942(a):

Amended the first sentence of Sec. 6014(b). **Effective** for tax years beginning after 12-31-69. Prior to amendment, the first sentence read as follows:

"The Secretary or his delegate shall prescribe regulations for carrying out this section, and such regulations may provide for the application of the rules of this section to cases where the gross income includes items other than those enumerated by subsection (a), to cases where the gross income from sources other than wages on which the tax has been withheld at the source is more than $100 but not more than $200, and to cases where the gross income is $5,000 or more but not more than $5,200. Such regulations shall provide for the application of this section in the case of husband and wife, including provisions determining when a joint return under this section may be permitted or required, whether the liability shall be joint and several, and whether one spouse may make return under this section and the other without regard to this section."

[Sec. 6015]

SEC. 6015. RELIEF FROM JOINT AND SEVERAL LIABILITY ON JOINT RETURN.

[Sec. 6015(a)]

(a) IN GENERAL.—Notwithstanding section 6013(d)(3)—

(1) an individual who has made a joint return may elect to seek relief under the procedures prescribed under subsection (b); and

(2) if such individual is eligible to elect the application of subsection (c), such individual may, in addition to any election under paragraph (1), elect to limit such individual's liability for any deficiency with respect to such joint return in the manner prescribed under subsection (c).

Any determination under this section shall be made without regard to community property laws.

[Sec. 6015(b)]

(b) PROCEDURES FOR RELIEF FROM LIABILITY APPLICABLE TO ALL JOINT FILERS.—

(1) IN GENERAL.—Under procedures prescribed by the Secretary, if—

(A) a joint return has been made for a taxable year;

(B) on such return there is an understatement of tax attributable to erroneous items of 1 individual filing the joint return;

(C) the other individual filing the joint return establishes that in signing the return he or she did not know, and had no reason to know, that there was such understatement;

(D) taking into account all the facts and circumstances, it is inequitable to hold the other individual liable for the deficiency in tax for such taxable year attributable to such understatement; and

(E) the other individual elects (in such form as the Secretary may prescribe) the benefits of this subsection not later than the date which is 2 years after the date the Secretary has begun collection activities with respect to the individual making the election,

then the other individual shall be relieved of liability for tax (including interest, penalties, and other amounts) for such taxable year to the extent such liability is attributable to such understatement.

(2) APPORTIONMENT OF RELIEF.—If an individual who, but for paragraph (1)(C), would be relieved of liability under paragraph (1), establishes that in signing the return such individual did not know, and had no reason to know, the extent of such understatement, then such

RETURNS—INCOME TAX

individual shall be relieved of liability for tax (including interest, penalties, and other amounts) for such taxable year to the extent that such liability is attributable to the portion of such understatement of which such individual did not know and had no reason to know.

(3) UNDERSTATEMENT.—For purposes of this subsection, the term "understatement" has the meaning given to such term by section 6662(d)(2)(A).

[Sec. 6015(c)]

(c) PROCEDURES TO LIMIT LIABILITY FOR TAXPAYERS NO LONGER MARRIED OR TAXPAYERS LEGALLY SEPARATED OR NOT LIVING TOGETHER.—

(1) IN GENERAL.—Except as provided in this subsection, if an individual who has made a joint return for any taxable year elects the application of this subsection, the individual's liability for any deficiency which is assessed with respect to the return shall not exceed the portion of such deficiency properly allocable to the individual under subsection (d).

(2) BURDEN OF PROOF.—Except as provided in subparagraph (A)(ii) or (C) of paragraph (3), each individual who elects the application of this subsection shall have the burden of proof with respect to establishing the portion of any deficiency allocable to such individual.

(3) ELECTION.—

(A) INDIVIDUALS ELIGIBLE TO MAKE ELECTION.—

(i) IN GENERAL.—An individual shall only be eligible to elect the application of this subsection if—

(I) at the time such election is filed, such individual is no longer married to, or is legally separated from, the individual with whom such individual filed the joint return to which the election relates; or

(II) such individual was not a member of the same household as the individual with whom such joint return was filed at any time during the 12-month period ending on the date such election is filed.

(ii) CERTAIN TAXPAYERS INELIGIBLE TO ELECT.—If the Secretary demonstrates that assets were transferred between individuals filing a joint return as part of a fraudulent scheme by such individuals, an election under this subsection by either individual shall be invalid (and section 6013(d)(3) shall apply to the joint return).

(B) TIME FOR ELECTION.—An election under this subsection for any taxable year may be made at any time after a deficiency for such year is asserted but not later than 2 years after the date on which the Secretary has begun collection activities with respect to the individual making the election.

(C) ELECTION NOT VALID WITH RESPECT TO CERTAIN DEFICIENCIES.—If the Secretary demonstrates that an individual making an election under this subsection had actual knowledge, at the time such individual signed the return, of any item giving rise to a deficiency (or portion thereof) which is not allocable to such individual under subsection (d), such election shall not apply to such deficiency (or portion). This subparagraph shall not apply where the individual with actual knowledge establishes that such individual signed the return under duress.

(4) LIABILITY INCREASED BY REASON OF TRANSFERS OF PROPERTY TO AVOID TAX.—

(A) IN GENERAL.—Notwithstanding any other provision of this subsection, the portion of the deficiency for which the individual electing the application of this subsection is liable (without regard to this paragraph) shall be increased by the value of any disqualified asset transferred to the individual.

(B) DISQUALIFIED ASSET.—For purposes of this paragraph—

(i) IN GENERAL.—The term "disqualified asset" means any property or right to property transferred to an individual making the election under this subsection with respect to a joint return by the other individual filing such joint return if the principal purpose of the transfer was the avoidance of tax or payment of tax.

(ii) PRESUMPTION.—

(I) IN GENERAL.—For purposes of clause (i), except as provided in subclause (II), any transfer which is made after the date which is 1 year before the date on which the first letter of proposed deficiency which allows the taxpayer an opportunity for administrative review in the Internal Revenue Service Independent Office of Appeals is sent shall be presumed to have as its principal purpose the avoidance of tax or payment of tax.

(II) EXCEPTIONS.—Subclause (I) shall not apply to any transfer pursuant to a decree of divorce or separate maintenance or a written instrument incident to such a decree or to any transfer which an individual establishes did not have as its principal purpose the avoidance of tax or payment of tax.

Amendments

• **2019, Taxpayer First Act (P.L. 116-25)**

P.L. 116-25, §1001(b)(1)(A):

Amended Code Sec. 6015(c)(4)(B)(ii)(I) by striking "Internal Revenue Service Office of Appeals" and inserting "Internal Revenue Service Independent Office of Appeals". **Effective** 7-1-2019.

• **2000, Community Renewal Tax Relief Act of 2000 (P.L. 106-554)**

P.L. 106-554, §313(a)(1):

Amended Code Sec. 6015(c)(3)(B) by striking "shall be made" and inserting "may be made at any time after a deficiency for such year is asserted but". **Effective** on 12-21-2000.

[Sec. 6015(d)]

(d) ALLOCATION OF DEFICIENCY.—For purposes of subsection (c)—

(1) IN GENERAL.—The portion of any deficiency on a joint return allocated to an individual shall be the amount which bears the same ratio to such deficiency as the net amount of items taken into account in computing the deficiency and allocable to the individual under paragraph (3) bears to the net amount of all items taken into account in computing the deficiency.

(2) SEPARATE TREATMENT OF CERTAIN ITEMS.—If a deficiency (or portion thereof) is attributable to—

(A) the disallowance of a credit; or

(B) any tax (other than tax imposed by section 1 or 55) required to be included with the joint return;

and such item is allocated to one individual under paragraph (3), such deficiency (or portion) shall be allocated to such individual. Any such item shall not be taken into account under paragraph (1).

(3) ALLOCATION OF ITEMS GIVING RISE TO THE DEFICIENCY.—For purposes of this subsection—

(A) IN GENERAL.—Except as provided in paragraphs (4) and (5), any item giving rise to a deficiency on a joint return shall be allocated to individuals filing the return in the same manner as it would have been allocated if the individuals had filed separate returns for the taxable year.

(B) EXCEPTION WHERE OTHER SPOUSE BENEFITS.—Under rules prescribed by the Secretary, an item otherwise allocable to an individual under subparagraph (A) shall be allocated to the other individual filing the joint return to the extent the item gave rise to a tax benefit on the joint return to the other individual.

(C) EXCEPTION FOR FRAUD.—The Secretary may provide for an allocation of any item in a manner not prescribed by subparagraph (A) if the Secretary establishes that such allocation is appropriate due to fraud of one or both individuals.

(4) LIMITATIONS ON SEPARATE RETURNS DISREGARDED.—If an item of deduction or credit is disallowed in its entirety solely because a separate return is filed, such disallowance shall be disregarded and the item shall be computed as if a joint return had been filed and then allocated between the spouses appropriately. A similar rule shall apply for purposes of section 86.

(5) CHILD'S LIABILITY.—If the liability of a child of a taxpayer is included on a joint return, such liability shall be disregarded in computing the separate liability of either spouse and such liability shall be allocated appropriately between the spouses.

[Sec. 6015(e)]

(e) PETITION FOR REVIEW BY TAX COURT.—

(1) IN GENERAL.—In the case of an individual against whom a deficiency has been asserted and who elects to have subsection (b) or (c) apply, or in the case of an individual who requests equitable relief under subsection (f)—

(A) IN GENERAL.—In addition to any other remedy provided by law, the individual may petition the Tax Court (and the Tax Court shall have jurisdiction) to determine the appropriate relief available to the individual under this section if such petition is filed—

(i) at any time after the earlier of—

(I) the date the Secretary mails, by certified or registered mail to the taxpayer's last known address, notice of the Secretary's final determination of relief available to the individual, or

(II) the date which is 6 months after the date such election is filed or request is made with the Secretary, and

(ii) not later than the close of the 90th day after the date described in clause (i)(I).

(B) RESTRICTIONS APPLICABLE TO COLLECTION OF ASSESSMENT.—

(i) IN GENERAL.—Except as otherwise provided in section 6851 or 6861, no levy or proceeding in court shall be made, begun, or prosecuted against the individual making an election under subsection (b) or (c) or requesting equitable relief under subsection (f) for collection of any assessment to which such election or request relates until the close of the 90th day referred to in subparagraph (A)(ii), or, if a petition has been filed with the Tax Court under subparagraph (A), until the decision of the Tax Court has become final. Rules similar to the rules of section 7485 shall apply with respect to the collection of such assessment.

(ii) AUTHORITY TO ENJOIN COLLECTION ACTIONS.—Notwithstanding the provisions of section 7421(a), the beginning of such levy or proceeding during the time the prohibition under clause (i) is in force may be enjoined by a proceeding in the proper court, including the Tax Court. The Tax Court shall have no jurisdiction under this subparagraph to enjoin any action or proceeding unless a timely petition has been filed under subparagraph (A) and then only in respect of the amount of the assessment to which the election under subsection (b) or (c) relates or to which the request under subsection (f) relates.

(2) SUSPENSION OF RUNNING OF PERIOD OF LIMITATIONS.—The running of the period of limitations in section 6502 on the collection of the assessment to which the petition under paragraph (1)(A) relates shall be suspended—

(A) for the period during which the Secretary is prohibited by paragraph (1)(B) from collecting by levy or a proceeding in court and for 60 days thereafter, and

(B) if a waiver under paragraph (5) is made, from the date the claim for relief was filed until 60 days after the waiver is filed with the Secretary.

(3) LIMITATION ON TAX COURT JURISDICTION.—If a suit for refund is begun by either individual filing the joint return pursuant to section 6532—

(A) the Tax Court shall lose jurisdiction of the individual's action under this section to whatever extent jurisdiction is acquired by the district court or the United States Court of Federal Claims over the taxable years that are the subject of the suit for refund, and

(B) the court acquiring jurisdiction shall have jurisdiction over the petition filed under this subsection.

(4) NOTICE TO OTHER SPOUSE.—The Tax Court shall establish rules which provide the individual filing a joint return but not making the election under subsection (b) or (c) or the request for equitable relief under subsection (f) with adequate notice and an opportunity to become a party to a proceeding under either such subsection.

(5) WAIVER.—An individual who elects the application of subsection (b) or (c) or who requests equitable relief under subsection (f) (and who agrees with the Secretary's determination of relief) may waive in writing at any time the restrictions in paragraph (1)(B) with respect to collection of the outstanding assessment (whether or not a notice of the Secretary's final determination of relief has been mailed).

(6) SUSPENSION OF RUNNING OF PERIOD FOR FILING PETITION IN TITLE 11 CASES.—In the case of a person who is prohibited by reason of a case under title 11, United States Code, from filing a petition under paragraph (1)(A) with respect to a final determination of relief under this section, the running of the period prescribed by such paragraph for filing such a petition with respect to such final determination shall be suspended for the period during which the person is so prohibited from filing such a petition, and for 60 days thereafter.

(7) STANDARD AND SCOPE OF REVIEW.—Any review of a determination made under this section shall be reviewed de novo by the Tax Court and shall be based upon—

(A) the administrative record established at the time of the determination, and

(B) any additional newly discovered or previously unavailable evidence.

Amendments

• **2019, Taxpayer First Act (P.L. 116-25)**

P.L. 116-25, § 1203(a)(1):

Amended Code Sec. 6015(e) by adding at the end a new paragraph (7). **Effective** for petitions or requests filed or pending on or after 7-1-2019.

• **2015, Protecting Americans from Tax Hikes Act of 2015 (P.L. 114-113)**

P.L. 114-113, § 424(a)(1), Div. Q:

Amended Code Sec. 6015(e) by adding at the end a new paragraph (6). **Effective** for petitions filed under Code Sec. 6015(e) after 12-18-2015.

• **2006, Tax Relief and Health Care Act of 2006 (P.L. 109-432)**

P.L. 109-432, Division C, § 408(a):

Amended Code Sec. 6015(e)(1) by inserting ", or in the case of an individual who requests equitable relief under subsection (f)" after "who elects to have subsection (b) or (c) apply". **Effective** with respect to liability for taxes arising or remaining unpaid on or after 12-20-2006.

P.L. 109-432, Division C, § 408(b)(1):

Amended Code Sec. 6015(e)(1)(A)(i)(II) by inserting "or request is made" after "election is filed". **Effective** with respect to liability for taxes arising or remaining unpaid on or after 12-20-2006.

P.L. 109-432, Division C, § 408(b)(2)(A)-(B):

Amended Code Sec. 6015(e)(1)(B)(i) by inserting "or requesting equitable relief under subsection (f)" after "making an election under subsection (b) or (c)", and by inserting "or request" after "to which such election". **Effective** with respect to liability for taxes arising or remaining unpaid on or after 12-20-2006.

P.L. 109-432, Division C, § 408(b)(3):

Amended Code Sec. 6015(e)(1)(B)(ii) by inserting "or to which the request under subsection (f) relates" after "to which the election under subsection (b) or (c) relates". **Effective** with respect to liability for taxes arising or remaining unpaid on or after 12-20-2006.

P.L. 109-432, Division C, § 408(b)(4):

Amended Code Sec. 6015(e)(4) by inserting "or the request for equitable relief under subsection (f)" after "the election under subsection (b) or (c)". **Effective** with respect to liability for taxes arising or remaining unpaid on or after 12-20-2006.

P.L. 109-432, Division C, § 408(b)(5):

Amended Code Sec. 6015(e)(5) by inserting "or who requests equitable relief under subsection (f)" after "who elects the application of subsection (b) or (c)". **Effective** with respect to liability for taxes arising or remaining unpaid on or after 12-20-2006.

RETURNS—INCOME TAX

• **2000, Community Renewal Tax Relief Act of 2000 (P.L. 106-554)**

P.L. 106-554, §313(a)(2)(B):

Amended Code Sec. 6015(e)(3). **Effective** on 12-21-2000. Prior to amendment, Code Sec. 6015(e)(3) read as follows:

(3) APPLICABLE RULES.—

(A) ALLOWANCE OF CREDIT OR REFUND.—Except as provided in subparagraph (B), notwithstanding any other law or rule of law (other than section 6512(b), 7121, or 7122), credit or refund shall be allowed or made to the extent attributable to the application of subsection (b) or (f).

(B) RES JUDICATA.—In the case of any election under subsection (b) or (c), if a decision of the Tax Court in any prior proceeding for the same taxable year has become final, such decision shall be conclusive except with respect to the qualification of the individual for relief which was not an issue in such proceeding. The exception contained in the preceding sentence shall not apply if the Tax Court determines that the individual participated meaningfully in such prior proceeding.

(C) LIMITATION ON TAX COURT JURISDICTION.—If a suit for refund is begun by either individual filing the joint return pursuant to section 6532—

(i) the Tax Court shall lose jurisdiction of the individual's action under this section to whatever extent jurisdiction is acquired by the district court or the United States Court of Federal Claims over the taxable years that are the subject of the suit for refund; and

(ii) the court acquiring jurisdiction shall have jurisdiction over the petition filed under this subsection.

P.L. 106-554, §313(a)(3)(A):

Amended Code Sec. 6015(e)(1) in the matter preceding subparagraph (A) by inserting "against whom a deficiency has been asserted and" after "individual". **Effective** on 12-21-2000.

P.L. 106-554, §313(a)(3)(B):

Amended Code Sec. 6015(e)(1)(A). **Effective** on 12-21-2000. Prior to amendment, Code Sec. 6015(e)(1)(A) read as follows:

(A) IN GENERAL.—The individual may petition the Tax Court (and the Tax Court shall have jurisdiction) to determine the appropriate relief available to the individual under this section if such petition is filed during the 90-day period beginning on the date on which the Secretary mails by certified or registered mail a notice to such individual of the Secretary's determination of relief available to the individual. Notwithstanding the preceding sentence, an individual may file such petition at any time after the date which is 6 months after the date such election is filed with the Secretary and before the close of such 90-day period.

P.L. 106-554, §313(a)(3)(C)(i)-(ii):

Amended Code Sec. 6015(e)(1)(B)(i) by striking "until the expiration of the 90-day period described in subparagraph (A)" and inserting "until the close of the 90th day referred to in subparagraph (A)(ii)", and by inserting "under subparagraph (A)" after "filed with the Tax Court". **Effective** on 12-21-2000.

P.L. 106-554, §313(a)(3)(D)(i):

Amended Code Sec. 6015(e) by adding at the end a new paragraph (5). **Effective** on 12-21-2000.

P.L. 106-554, §313(a)(3)(D)(ii):

Amended Code Sec. 6015(e)(2). **Effective** on 12-21-2000. Prior to amendment, Code Sec. 6015(e)(2) read as follows:

(2) SUSPENSION OF RUNNING OF PERIOD OF LIMITATIONS.—The running of the period of limitations in section 6502 on the collection of the assessment to which the petition under paragraph (1)(A) relates shall be suspended for the period during which the Secretary is prohibited by paragraph (1)(B) from collecting by levy or a proceeding in court and for 60 days thereafter.

• **1998, Tax and Trade Relief Extension Act of 1998 (P.L. 105-277)**

P.L. 105-277, §4002(c)(2):

Amended Code Sec. 6015(e)(3)(A) by striking "of this section" and inserting "of subsection (b) or (f)". **Effective** as if included in the provision of P.L. 105-206 to which it relates [generally **effective** for any tax liability arising after 7-22-98, and any tax liability arising on or before 7-22-98, but remaining unpaid as of such date.—CCH].

[Sec. 6015(f)]

(f) EQUITABLE RELIEF.—

(1) IN GENERAL.—Under procedures prescribed by the Secretary, if—

(A) taking into account all the facts and circumstances, it is inequitable to hold the individual liable for any unpaid tax or any deficiency (or any portion of either), and

(B) relief is not available to such individual under subsection (b) or (c),

the Secretary may relieve such individual of such liability.

(2) LIMITATION.—A request for equitable relief under this subsection may be made with respect to any portion of any liability that—

(A) has not been paid, provided that such request is made before the expiration of the applicable period of limitation under section 6502, or

(B) has been paid, provided that such request is made during the period in which the individual could submit a timely claim for refund or credit of such payment.

Amendments

• **2019, Taxpayer First Act (P.L. 116-25)**

P.L. 116-25, §1203(a)(2):

Amended Code Sec. 6015(f). **Effective** for petitions or requests filed or pending on or after 7-1-2019. Prior to amendment, Code Sec. 6015(f) read as follows:

(f) EQUITABLE RELIEF.—Under procedures prescribed by the Secretary, if—

(1) taking into account all the facts and circumstances, it is inequitable to hold the individual liable for any unpaid tax or any deficiency (or any portion of either); and

(2) relief is not available to such individual under subsection (b) or (c),

the Secretary may relieve such individual of such liability.

[Sec. 6015(g)]

(g) CREDITS AND REFUNDS.—

(1) IN GENERAL.—Except as provided in paragraphs (2) and (3), notwithstanding any other law or rule of law (other than section 6511, 6512(b), 7121, or 7122), credit or refund shall be allowed or made to the extent attributable to the application of this section.

(2) RES JUDICATA.—In the case of any election under subsection (b) or (c) or of any request for equitable relief under subsection (f), if a decision of a court in any prior proceeding for the same taxable year has become final, such decision shall be conclusive except with respect to the qualification of the individual for relief which was not an issue in such proceeding. The exception contained in the preceding sentence shall not apply if the court determines that the individual participated meaningfully in such prior proceeding.

(3) CREDIT AND REFUND NOT ALLOWED UNDER SUBSECTION (c).—No credit or refund shall be allowed as a result of an election under subsection (c).

Amendments

• **2006, Tax Relief and Health Care Act of 2006 (P.L. 109-432)**

P.L. 109-432, Division C, §408(b)(6):

Amended Code Sec. 6015(g)(2) by inserting "or of any request for equitable relief under subsection (f)" after "any election under subsection (b) or (c)". **Effective** with respect to liability for taxes arising or remaining unpaid on or after 12-20-2006.

• **2000, Community Renewal Tax Relief Act of 2000 (P.L. 106-554)**

P.L. 106-554, §313(a)(2)(A):

Amended Code Sec. 6015 by redesignating subsection (g) as subsection (h) and by inserting after subsection (f) a new subsection (g). **Effective** on 12-21-2000.

[Sec. 6015(h)]

(h) REGULATIONS.—The Secretary shall prescribe such regulations as are necessary to carry out the provisions of this section, including—

(1) regulations providing methods for allocation of items other than the methods under subsection (d)(3); and

(2) regulations providing the opportunity for an individual to have notice of, and an opportunity to participate in, any administrative proceeding with respect to an election made under subsection (b) or (c) or a request for equitable relief made under subsection (f) by the other individual filing the joint return.

Amendments

• **2006, Tax Relief and Health Care Act of 2006 (P.L. 109-432)**

P.L. 109-432, Division C, §408(b)(7):

Amended Code Sec. 6015(h)(2) by inserting "or a request for equitable relief made under subsection (f)" after "with respect to an election made under subsection (b) or (c)". **Effective** with respect to liability for taxes arising or remaining unpaid on or after 12-20-2006.

• **2000, Community Renewal Tax Relief Act of 2000 (P.L. 106-554)**

P.L. 106-554, §313(a)(2)(A):

Amended Code Sec. 6015 by redesignating subsection (g) as subsection (h). **Effective** on 12-21-2000.

RETURNS—INCOME TAX

• **1998, IRS Restructuring and Reform Act of 1998 (P.L. 105-206)**

P.L. 105-206, §3201(a):

Amended subpart B of part II of subchapter A of chapter 61 by inserting after Code Sec. 6014 a new Code Sec. 6015. **Effective**, generally, for any liability for tax arising after 7-22-98, and any liability for tax arising on or before such date but remaining unpaid as of such date. For a special rule, see Act Sec. 3201(c)-(d) and (g)(2), below.

P.L. 105-206, §3201(c)-(d) and (g)(2), provides:

(c) SEPARATE FORM FOR APPLYING FOR SPOUSAL RELIEF.—Not later than 180 days after the date of the enactment of this Act, the Secretary of the Treasury shall develop a separate form with instructions for use by taxpayers in applying for relief under section 6015(a) of the Internal Revenue Code of 1986, as added by this section.

(d) SEPARATE NOTICE TO EACH FILER.—The Secretary of the Treasury shall, wherever practicable, send any notice relating to a joint return under section 6013 of the Internal Revenue Code of 1986 separately to each individual filing the joint return.

* * *

(g) EFFECTIVE DATES.—

* * *

(2) 2-YEAR PERIOD.—The 2-year period under subsection (b)(1)(E) or (c)(3)(B) of section 6015 of the Internal Revenue Code of 1986 shall not expire before the date which is 2 years after the date of the first collection activity after the date of the enactment of this Act.

[Sec. 6015—Repealed]

Amendments

• **1984, Deficit Reduction Act of 1984 (P.L. 98-369)**

P.L. 98-369, §412(a)(1):

Repealed Code Sec. 6015. **Effective** with respect to tax years beginning after 1984. Prior to repeal, Code Sec. 6015 read as follows:

SEC. 6015. DECLARATION OF ESTIMATED INCOME TAX BY INDIVIDUALS.

[Sec. 6015(a)]

(a) REQUIREMENT OF DECLARATION.—Except as otherwise provided in this section, every individual shall make a declaration of his estimated tax for the taxable year if—

(1) the gross income for the taxable year can reasonably be expected to exceed—

(A) $20,000, in the case of—

(i) a single individual, including a head of a household (as defined in section 2(b)) or a surviving spouse (as defined in section 2(a)); or

(ii) a married individual entitled under subsection (c) to file a joint declaration with his spouse, but only if his spouse has not received wages (as defined in section 3401(a)) for the taxable year; or

(B) $10,000, in the case of a married individual entitled under subsection (c) to file a joint declaration with his spouse, but only if both he and his spouse have received wages (as defined in section 3401(a)) for the taxable year; or

(C) $5,000, in the case of a married individual not entitled under subsection (c) to file a joint declaration with his spouse; or

(2) the gross income can reasonably be expected to include more than $500 from sources other than wages (as defined in section 3401(a)).

Amendments

• **1983, Technical Corrections Act of 1982 (P.L. 97-448)**

P.L. 97-448, §107(c)(2):

Amended Code Sec. 6015(a) by striking out "entitled under subsection (b)" each place it appears and inserting in lieu thereof "entitled under subsection (c)." **Effective** as if included in the provision of P.L. 97-34 to which it relates.

• **1981, Economic Recovery Tax Act of 1981 (P.L. 97-34)**

P.L. 97-34, §725(c)(2):

Amended Code Sec. 6015(a) by striking out the last sentence. **Effective** 1-1-81. Prior to amendment, the last sentence of Code Sec. 6015(a) read as follows:

Notwithstanding the provisions of this subsection, no declaration is required if the estimated tax (as defined in subsection (c)) can reasonably be expected to be less than $100.

• **1971, Revenue Act of 1971 (P.L. 92-178)**

P.L. 92-178, §209(a):

Amended Code Sec. 6015(a). **Effective** for estimated tax for tax years beginning after 12-31-71. Prior to amendment, such section read as follows:

"(a) Requirement of Declaration.—Except as otherwise provided in subsection (i), every individual shall make a declaration of his estimated tax for the taxable year if—

"(1) the gross income for the taxable year can reasonably be expected to exceed—

"(A) $5,000, in the case of—

"(i) a single individual other than a head of a household (as defined in section 2(b)) or a surviving spouse (as defined in section 2(a)); or

"(ii) a married individual not entitled under subsection (b) to file a joint declaration with his spouse; or

"(iii) a married individual entitled under subsection (b) to file a joint declaration with his spouse, but only if the aggregate gross income of such individual and his spouse for the taxable year can reasonably be expected to exceed $10,000; or

"(B) $10,000, in the case of—

"(i) a head of a household (as defined in section 2(b)); or

"(ii) a surviving spouse (as defined in section 2(a)); or

"(2) the gross income can reasonably be expected to include more than $200 from sources other than wages (as defined in section 3401(a)).

Notwithstanding the provisions of this subsection, no declaration is required if the estimated tax (as defined in subsection (c)) can reasonably be expected to be less than $40."

• **1969, Tax Reform Act of 1969 (P.L. 91-172)**

P.L. 91-172, §803(d)(7):

Amended Code Sec. 6015(a)(1) by inserting "section 2(b)" in place of "section 1(b)(2)" wherever it appeared and by inserting "section 2(a)" in place of "section 2(b)" wherever it appeared. **Effective** for tax years beginning after 12-31-70.

• **1966, Foreign Investors Tax Act of 1966 (P.L. 89-809)**

P.L. 89-809, §103 (j)(1):

Amended that portion of Code Sec. 6015(a) that precedes paragraph (1). **Effective** 1-1-67. Prior to amendment, that portion of Sec. 6015(a) that precedes paragraph (1) read as follows:

"(a) Requirement of Declaration.—Every individual (other than a nonresident alien with respect to whose wages, as defined in section 3401(a), withholding under chapter 24 is not made applicable, but including every alien individual who is a resident of Puerto Rico during the entire taxable year) shall make a declaration of his estimated tax for the taxable year if—"

• **1960 (P.L. 86-779)**

P.L. 86-779, §5(a):

Amended Code Sec. 6015(a). **Effective** for tax years beginning after 12-31-60. Prior to amendment, Code Sec. 6015(a) read as follows:

"(a) REQUIREMENT OF DECLARATION.—Every individual (other than a nonresident alien with respect to whose wages, as defined in section 3401(a), withholding under chapter 24 is not made applicable, but including every alien individual who is a resident of Puerto Rico during the entire taxable year) shall make a declaration of his estimated tax for the taxable year if—

"(1) the gross income for the taxable year can reasonably be expected to consist of wages (as defined in section 3401(a)) and of not more than $100 from sources other than such wages, and can reasonably be expected to exceed—

"(A) $5,000, in the case of a single individual other than a head of a household (as defined in section 1(b)(2)) or a surviving spouse (as defined in section 2(b)) or in the case of a married individual not entitled to file a joint declaration with his spouse;

"(B) $10,000, in the case of a head of a household (as defined in section 1(b)(2)) or a surviving spouse (as defined in section 2(b)); or

"(C) $5,000 in the case of a married individual entitled under subsection (b) to file a joint declaration with his spouse, and the aggregate gross income of such individual and his spouse for the taxable year can reasonably be expected to exceed $10,000; or

"(2) the gross income can reasonably be expected to include more than $100 from sources other than wages (as defined in section 3401(a)) and can reasonably be expected to exceed the sum of—

"(A) the amount obtained by multiplying $600 by the number of exemptions to which he is entitled under section 151 plus

"(B) $400."

[Sec. 6015(b)]

(b) DECLARATION NOT REQUIRED IN CERTAIN CASES.—No declaration shall be required under subsection (a) if the estimated tax (as defined in subsection (d)) is less than the amount determined in accordance with the following table:

In the case of taxable years beginning in:	The amount is:
1981	$100
1982	200
1983	300
1984	400
1985 and thereafter	500

Amendments

• **1981, Economic Recovery Tax Act of 1981 (P.L. 97-34)**

P.L. 97-34, §725(a):

Added Code Sec. 6015(b). **Effective** for estimated tax for tax years ending after 12-31-80.

[Sec. 6015(c)]

(c) JOINT DECLARATION BY HUSBAND AND WIFE.—In the case of a husband and wife, a single declaration under this section may be made by them jointly, in which case the liability with respect to the estimated tax shall be joint and several. No joint declaration may be made if either the husband or the wife is a nonresident alien, if they are separated under a decree of divorce or of separate maintenance, or if they have different taxable years. If a joint declaration is made but a joint return is not made for the taxable year, the estimated tax for such year may be treated as the estimated tax of either the husband or the wife, or may be divided between them.

RETURNS—INCOME TAX

Amendments

• **1981, Economic Recovery Tax Act of 1981 (P.L. 97-34)**

P.L. 97-34, §725(a):

Redesignated Code Sec. 6015(b) as Code Sec. 6015(c). **Effective** 1-1-81.

[Sec. 6015(d)]

(d) ESTIMATED TAX.—For purposes of this title, in the case of an individual, the term "estimated tax" means—

(1) the amount which the individual estimates as the amount of the income tax imposed by chapter 1 for the taxable year (other than the tax imposed by section 55), plus

(2) the amount which the individual estimates as the amount of the self-employment tax imposed by chapter 2 for the taxable year, minus

(3) the amount which the individual estimates as the sum of—

(A) any credits against tax provided by part IV of subchapter A of chapter 1, and

(B) to the extent allowed under regulations prescribed by the Secretary, any overpayment of the tax imposed by section 4986.

Amendments

• **1983, Technical Corrections Act of 1982 (P.L. 97-448)**

P.L. 97-448, §201(j)(1):

Amended Code Sec. 6015(d)(3). **Effective** as if included in the provision of P.L. 96-223 to which it relates. Prior to amendment, Code Sec. 6015(d)(3) read as follows:

"(3) the amount which the individual estimates as the sum of any credits against tax provided by part IV of subchapter A of chapter 1."

P.L. 97-448, §306(a)(1)(A):

Amended P.L. 97-248, §201, by redesignating the second subsection (c) as subsection (d).

• **1982, Tax Equity and Fiscal Responsibility Act of 1982 (P.L. 97-248)**

P.L. 97-248, §201(d)(7):

Amended Code Sec. 6015(d)(1) by striking out "or 56" which followed "section 55". **Effective** for tax years beginning after 12-31-82.

• **1981, Economic Recovery Tax Act of 1981 (P.L. 97-34)**

P.L. 97-34, §725(a):

Redesignated Code Sec. 6015(c) as Code Sec. 6015(d). **Effective** 1-1-81.

• **1978, Revenue Act of 1978 (P.L. 95-600)**

P.L. 95-600, §421(e)(7):

Amended Code Sec. 6015(c)(1) by striking out "section 56" and inserting in lieu thereof "section 55 or 56". **Effective** for tax years beginning after 12-31-78.

• **1969, Tax Reform Act of 1969 (P.L. 91-172)**

P.L. 91-172, §301(b)(12):

Amended Code Sec. 6015(c)(1) by adding the phrase "(other than the tax imposed by section 56)." **Effective** 1-1-70.

• **1966, Tax Adjustment Act of 1966 (P.L. 89-368)**

P.L. 89-368, §102(a):

Amended Code Sec. 6015(c). **Effective** 1-1-67. Prior to amendment, Sec. 6015(c) read as follows:

"(c) Estimated Tax.—For purposes of this title, in the case of an individual, the term 'estimated tax' means the amount which the individual estimates as the amount of the income tax imposed by chapter 1 for the taxable year, minus the amount which the individual estimates as the sum of any credits against tax provided by part IV of subchapter A of chapter 1."

[Sec. 6015(e)]

(e) CONTENTS OF DECLARATION.—The declaration shall contain such pertinent information as the Secretary may by forms or regulations prescribe.

Amendments

• **1981, Economic Recovery Tax Act of 1981 (P.L. 97-34)**

P.L. 97-34, §725(a):

Redesignated Code Sec. 6015(d) as Code Sec. 6015(e). **Effective** 1-1-81.

• **1976, Tax Reform Act of 1976 (P.L. 94-455)**

P.L. 94-455, §1906(b)(13)(A):

Amended 1954 Code by substituting "Secretary" for "Secretary or his delegate" each place it appeared. **Effective** 2-1-77.

[Sec. 6015(f)]

(f) AMENDMENT OF DECLARATION.—An individual may make amendments of a declaration filed during the taxable year under regulations prescribed by the Secretary.

Amendments

• **1981, Economic Recovery Tax Act of 1981 (P.L. 97-34)**

P.L. 97-34, §725(a):

Redesignated Code Sec. 6015(e) as Code Sec. 6015(f). **Effective** 1-1-81.

• **1976, Tax Reform Act of 1976 (P.L. 94-455)**

P.L. 94-455, §1906(b)(13)(A):

Amended 1954 Code by substituting "Secretary" for "Secretary or his delegate" each place it appeared. **Effective** 2-1-77.

[Sec. 6015(g)]

(g) RETURN AS DECLARATION OR AMENDMENT.—If on or before January 31 (or March 1, in the case of an individual referred to in section 6073(b), relating to income from farming or fishing) of the succeeding taxable year the taxpayer files a return, for the taxable year for which the declaration is required, and pays in full the amount computed on the return as payable, then, under regulations prescribed by the Secretary—

(1) if the declaration is not required to be filed during the taxable year, but is required to be filed on or before January 15, such return shall be considered as such declaration; and

(2) if the tax shown on the return (reduced by the sum of the credits against tax provided by part IV of subchapter A of chapter 1) is greater than the estimated tax shown in a declaration previously made, or in the last amendment thereof, such return shall be considered as the amendment of the declaration permitted by subsection (e) to be filed on or before January 15.

In the application of this subsection in the case of a taxable year beginning on any date other than January 1, there shall be substituted, for the 15th or last day of the months specified in this subsection, the 15th or last day of the months which correspond thereto.

Amendments

• **1981, Economic Recovery Tax Act of 1981 (P.L. 97-34)**

P.L. 97-34, §725(a):

Redesignated Code Sec. 6015(f) as Code Sec. 6015(g). **Effective** 1-1-81.

• **1976, Tax Reform Act of 1976 (P.L. 94-455)**

P.L. 94-455, §1906(b)(13)(A):

Amended 1954 Code by substituting "Secretary" for "Secretary or his delegate" each place it appeared. **Effective** 2-1-77.

• **1969, Tax Reform Act of 1969 (P.L. 91-172)**

P.L. 91-172, §944(a):

Amended Sec. 6015(f) in the language preceding paragraph (1) by inserting "March 1" in lieu of "February 15". **Effective** with respect to tax years beginning after 12-31-68.

• **1962 (P.L. 87-682)**

P.L. 87-682, §1:

Amended Sec. 6015(f) by inserting "or fishing" after "from farming" in line 3.

• **1958, Technical Amendments Act of 1958 (P.L. 85-866)**

P.L. 85-866, §74:

Added the last sentence to Sec. 6015(f). **Effective** 1-1-54.

[Sec. 6015(h)]

(h) SHORT TAXABLE YEARS.—An individual with a taxable year of less than 12 months shall make a declaration in accordance with regulations prescribed by the Secretary.

Amendments

• **1981, Economic Recovery Tax Act of 1981 (P.L. 97-34)**

P.L. 97-34, §725(a):

Redesignated Code Sec. 6015(g) as Code Sec. 6015(h). **Effective** 1-1-81.

• **1976, Tax Reform Act of 1976 (P.L. 94-455)**

P.L. 94-455, §1906(b)(13)(A):

Amended 1954 Code by substituting "Secretary" for "Secretary or his delegate" each place it appeared. **Effective** 2-1-77.

[Sec. 6015(i)]

(i) ESTATES AND TRUSTS.—The provisions of this section shall not apply to an estate or trust.

Amendments

• **1981, Economic Recovery Tax Act of 1981 (P.L. 97-34)**

P.L. 97-34, §725(a):

Redesignated Code Sec. 6015(h) as Code Sec. 6015(i). **Effective** 1-1-81.

[Sec. 6015(j)]

(j) NONRESIDENT ALIEN INDIVIDUALS.—No declaration shall be required to be made under this section by a nonresident alien individual unless—

(1) withholding under chapter 24 is made applicable to the wages, as defined in section 3401(a), of such individual,

(2) such individual has income (other than compensation for personal services subject to deduction and withholding under section 1441) which is effectively connected with the conduct of a trade or business within the United States, or

(3) such individual is a resident of Puerto Rico during the entire taxable year.

Amendments

• **1983, Interest and Dividend Tax Compliance Act of 1983 (P.L. 98-67)**

P.L. 98-67, §102(a):

Repealed the amendment made to Code Sec. 6015(j)(1) by P.L. 97-248. **Effective** as of the close of 6-30-83, as though it had not been enacted.

Sec. 6015—Repealed

RETURNS—INCOME TAX

- **1982, Tax Equity and Fiscal Responsibility Act of 1982 (P.L. 97-248)**

P.L. 97-248, §307(a)(6):

Amended Code Sec. 6015(j)(1) by striking out ", as defined in section 3401(a)," and inserting "(as defined in section 3401(a)), or to the interest, dividends, and patronage dividends (as defined in section 3454),". **Effective** 7-1-83.

- **1981, Economic Recovery Tax Act of 1981 (P.L. 97-34)**

P.L. 97-34, §725(a):

Redesignated Code Sec. 6015(i) as Code Sec. 6015(j). **Effective** 1-1-81.

- **1966, Foreign Investors Tax Act of 1966 (P.L. 89-809)**

P.L. 89-809, §103(j)(2)-(3):

Redesignated former Code Sec. 6015(i) as Sec. 6015(j) and added new Code Sec. 6015(i). **Effective** 1-1-67.

[Sec. 6015(j)]

Amendments

- **1976, Tax Reform Act of 1976 (P.L. 94-455)**

P.L. 94-455, §1906(a)(2):

Repealed Code Sec. 6015(j). **Effective** 2-1-77. Prior to repeal, Code Sec. 6015(j) read as follows:

(j) APPLICABILITY.—This section shall be applicable only with respect to taxable years beginning after December 31, 1954; and sections 58, 59, and 60 of the Internal Revenue Code of 1939 shall continue in force with respect to taxable years beginning before January 1, 1955.

- **1969, Tax Reform Act of 1969 (P.L. 91-172)**

P.L. 91-172, §946(b), provides:

(b) Declarations of Estimated Tax.—In the case of a taxable year beginning before the date of the enactment of this Act, if any taxpayer is required to make a declaration or amended declaration of estimated tax, or to pay any amount or additional amount of estimated tax, by reason of the amendments made by this Act, such amount or additional amount shall be paid ratably on or before each of the remaining installment dates for the taxable year beginning with the first installment date on or after the 30th day after such date of enactment. With respect to any declaration or payment of estimated tax before such first installment date, sections 6015, 6154, 6654, and 6655 of the Internal Revenue Code of 1954 shall be applied without regard to the amendments made by this Act. For purposes of this subsection, the term "installment date" means any date on which, under section 6153 or 6154 of such Code (whichever is applicable), an installment payment of estimated tax is required to be made by the taxpayer.

- **1966, Foreign Investors Tax Act of 1966 (P.L. 89-809)**

P.L. 89-809, §103(j)(2):

Redesignated former Code Sec. 6015(i) as Sec. 6015(j).

[Sec. 6015(k)]

(k) TERMINATION.—No declaration shall be required under this section for any taxable year beginning after December 31, 1982.

Amendments

- **1982, Tax Equity and Fiscal Responsibility Act of 1982 (P.L. 97-248)**

P.L. 97-248, §328(b)(1):

Added Code Sec. 6015(k). **Effective** for tax years beginning after 12-31-82.

[Sec. 6017]

SEC. 6017. SELF-EMPLOYMENT TAX RETURNS.

Every individual (other than a nonresident alien individual) having net earnings from self-employment of $400 or more for the taxable year shall make a return with respect to the self-employment tax imposed by chapter 2. In the case of a husband and wife filing a joint return under section 6013, the tax imposed by chapter 2 shall not be computed on the aggregate income but shall be the sum of the taxes computed under such chapter on the separate self-employment income of each spouse.

[Sec. 6017A—Repealed]

Amendments

- **1989, Omnibus Budget Reconciliation Act of 1989 (P.L. 101-239)**

P.L. 101-239, §7711(b)(1):

Repealed Code Sec. 6017A. **Effective** for returns and statements the due date for which (determined without regard to extensions) is after 12-31-89. Prior to repeal, Code Sec. 6017A read as follows:

SEC. 6017A. PLACE OF RESIDENCE.

In the case of an individual, the information required on any return with respect to the taxes imposed by chapter 1 for any period shall include information as to the State, county, municipality, and any other unit of local government in which the taxpayer (and any other individual with respect to whom an exemption is claimed on such return) resided on one or more dates (determined in the manner provided by regulations prescribed by the Secretary) during such period.

- **1976, Tax Reform Act of 1976 (P.L. 94-455)**

P.L. 94-455, §1906(b)(13)(A):

Amended 1954 Code by substituting "Secretary" for "Secretary or his delegate" each place it appeared. **Effective** 2-1-77.

- **1972, State and Local Fiscal Assistance Act of 1972 (P.L. 92-512)**

P.L. 92-512, §144(a):

Added Code Sec. 6017A. **Effective** 10-20-72.

Subpart C—Estate and Gift Tax Returns

Sec. 6018.	Estate tax returns.
Sec. 6019.	Gift tax returns.

[Sec. 6018]

SEC. 6018. ESTATE TAX RETURNS.

[Sec. 6018(a)]

(a) RETURNS BY EXECUTOR.—

(1) CITIZENS OR RESIDENTS.—In all cases where the gross estate at the death of a citizen or resident exceeds the basic exclusion amount in effect under section 2010(c) for the calendar year which includes the date of death, the executor shall make a return with respect to the estate tax imposed by subtitle B.

(2) NONRESIDENTS NOT CITIZENS OF THE UNITED STATES.—In the case of the estate of every nonresident not a citizen of the United States if that part of the gross estate which is situated in the United States exceeds $60,000, the executor shall make a return with respect to the estate tax imposed by subtitle B.

(3) ADJUSTMENT FOR CERTAIN GIFTS.—The amount applicable under paragraph (1) and the amount set forth in paragraph (2) shall each be reduced (but not below zero) by the sum of—

(A) the amount of the adjusted taxable gifts (within the meaning of section 2001(b)) made by the decedent after December 31, 1976, plus

(B) the aggregate amount allowed as a specific exemption under section 2521 (as in effect before its repeal by the Tax Reform Act of 1976) with respect to gifts made by the decedent after September 8, 1976.

[Sec. 6018(b)]

(b) RETURNS BY BENEFICIARIES.—If the executor is unable to make a complete return as to any part of the gross estate of the decedent, he shall include in his return a description of such part and the name of every person holding a legal or beneficial interest therein. Upon notice from the Secretary such person shall in like manner make a return as to such part of the gross estate.

RETURNS—INCOME TAX

Amendments

• **2013, American Taxpayer Relief Act of 2012 (P.L. 112-240)**

P.L. 112-240, § 101(a)(1)-(3), provides:

SEC. 101. PERMANENT EXTENSION AND MODIFICATION OF 2001 TAX RELIEF.

(a) PERMANENT EXTENSION.—

(1) IN GENERAL.—The Economic Growth and Tax Relief Reconciliation Act of 2001 is amended by striking title IX.

(2) CONFORMING AMENDMENT.—The Tax Relief, Unemployment Insurance Reauthorization, and Job Creation Act of 2010 is amended by striking section 304.

(3) EFFECTIVE DATE.—The amendments made by this subsection shall apply to taxable, plan, or limitation years beginning after December 31, 2012, and estates of decedents dying, gifts made, or generation skipping transfers after December 31, 2012.

• **2010, Tax Relief, Unemployment Insurance Reauthorization, and Job Creation Act of 2010 (P.L. 111-312)**

P.L. 111-312, § 301(a):

Amended Code Sec. 6018 to read as such provision would read if subtitle E of title V of the Economic Growth and Tax Relief Reconciliation Act of 2001 (P.L. 107-16) had never been enacted. **Effective** for estates of decedents dying, and transfers made, after 12-31-2009. For special rules, see Act Sec. 301(c) and (d)(1), below. Prior to amendment by P.L. 111-312, Code Sec. 6018 read as follows:

SEC. 6018. RETURNS RELATING TO LARGE TRANSFERS AT DEATH.

[Sec. 6018(a)]

(a) IN GENERAL.—If this section applies to property acquired from a decedent, the executor of the estate of such decedent shall make a return containing the information specified in subsection (c) with respect to such property.

[Sec. 6018(b)]

(b) PROPERTY TO WHICH SECTION APPLIES.—

(1) LARGE TRANSFERS.—This section shall apply to all property (other than cash) acquired from a decedent if the fair market value of such property acquired from the decedent exceeds the dollar amount applicable under section 1022(b)(2)(B) (without regard to section 1022(b)(2)(C)).

(2) TRANSFERS OF CERTAIN GIFTS RECEIVED BY DECEDENT WITHIN 3 YEARS OF DEATH.—This section shall apply to any appreciated property acquired from the decedent if—

(A) subsections (b) and (c) of section 1022 do not apply to such property by reason of section 1022(d)(1)(C), and

(B) such property was required to be included on a return required to be filed under section 6019.

(3) NONRESIDENTS NOT CITIZENS OF THE UNITED STATES.—In the case of a decedent who is a nonresident not a citizen of the United States, paragraphs (1) and (2) shall be applied—

(A) by taking into account only—

(i) tangible property situated in the United States, and

(ii) other property acquired from the decedent by a United States person, and

(B) by substituting the dollar amount applicable under section 1022(b)(3) for the dollar amount referred to in paragraph (1).

(4) RETURNS BY TRUSTEES OR BENEFICIARIES.—If the executor is unable to make a complete return as to any property acquired from or passing from the decedent, the executor shall include in the return a description of such property and the name of every person holding a legal or beneficial interest therein. Upon notice from the Secretary, such person shall in like manner make a return as to such property.

[Sec. 6018(c)]

(c) INFORMATION REQUIRED TO BE FURNISHED.—The information specified in this subsection with respect to any property acquired from the decedent is—

(1) the name and TIN of the recipient of such property,

(2) an accurate description of such property,

(3) the adjusted basis of such property in the hands of the decedent and its fair market value at the time of death,

(4) the decedent's holding period for such property,

(5) sufficient information to determine whether any gain on the sale of the property would be treated as ordinary income,

(6) the amount of basis increase allocated to the property under subsection (b) or (c) of section 1022, and

(7) such other information as the Secretary may by regulations prescribe.

[Sec. 6018(d)]

(d) PROPERTY ACQUIRED FROM DECEDENT.—For purposes of this section, section 1022 shall apply for purposes of determining the property acquired from a decedent.

[Sec. 6018(e)]

(e) STATEMENTS TO BE FURNISHED TO CERTAIN PERSONS.—Every person required to make a return under subsection (a) shall furnish to each person whose name is required to be set forth in such return (other than the person required to make such return) a written statement showing—

(1) the name, address, and phone number of the person required to make such return, and

(2) the information specified in subsection (c) with respect to property acquired from, or passing from, the decedent to the person required to receive such statement.

The written statement required under the preceding sentence shall be furnished not later than 30 days after the date that the return required by subsection (a) is filed.

P.L. 111-312, § 301(c) and (d)(1), provides:

(c) SPECIAL ELECTION WITH RESPECT TO ESTATES OF DECEDENTS DYING IN 2010.—Notwithstanding subsection (a), in the case of an estate of a decedent dying after December 31, 2009, and before January 1, 2011, the executor (within the meaning of section 2203 of the Internal Revenue Code of 1986) may elect to apply such Code as though the amendments made by subsection (a) do not apply with respect to chapter 11 of such Code and with respect to property acquired or passing from such decedent (within the meaning of section 1014(b) of such Code). Such election shall be made at such time and in such manner as the Secretary of the Treasury or the Secretary's delegate shall provide. Such an election once made shall be revocable only with the consent of the Secretary of the Treasury or the Secretary's delegate. For purposes of section 2652(a)(1) of such Code, the determination of whether any property is subject to the tax imposed by such chapter 11 shall be made without regard to any election made under this subsection.

(d) EXTENSION OF TIME FOR PERFORMING CERTAIN ACTS.—

(1) ESTATE TAX.—In the case of the estate of a decedent dying after December 31, 2009, and before the date of the enactment of this Act, the due date for—

(A) filing any return under section 6018 of the Internal Revenue Code of 1986 (including any election required to be made on such a return) as such section is in effect after the date of the enactment of this Act without regard to any election under subsection (c),

(B) making any payment of tax under chapter 11 of such Code, and

(C) making any disclaimer described in section 2518(b) of such Code of an interest in property passing by reason of the death of such decedent,

shall not be earlier than the date which is 9 months after the date of the enactment of this Act.

P.L. 111-312, § 303(b)(3):

Amended Code Sec. 6018(a)(1) by striking "the applicable exclusion amount" and inserting "the basic exclusion amount". **Effective** for estates of decedents dying and gifts made after 12-31-2010.

P.L. 111-312, § 304, provides [but see P.L. 112-240, § 101(a)(2)-(3), above]:

SEC. 304. APPLICATION OF EGTRRA SUNSET TO THIS TITLE.

Section 901 of the Economic Growth and Tax Relief Reconciliation Act of 2001 shall apply to the amendments made by this title.

• **2001, Economic Growth and Tax Relief Reconciliation Act of 2001 (P.L. 107-16)**

P.L. 107-16, § 542(b)(1):

Amended so much of subpart C of part II of subchapter A of chapter 61 as precedes Code Sec. 6019 (Code Sec. 6018). **Effective** for estates of decedents dying after 12-31-2009. Prior to amendment, so much of subpart C of part II of subchapter A of chapter 61 as preceded section 6019 (Code Sec. 6018) read as follows:

SEC. 6018. ESTATE TAX RETURNS.

[Sec. 6018(a)]

(a) RETURNS BY EXECUTOR.—

(1) CITIZENS OR RESIDENTS.—In all cases where the gross estate at the death of a citizen or resident exceeds the applicable exclusion amount in effect under section 2010(c) for the calendar year which includes the date of death, the executor shall make a return with respect to the estate tax imposed by subtitle B.

(2) NONRESIDENTS NOT CITIZENS OF THE UNITED STATES.—In the case of the estate of every nonresident not a citizen of the United States if that part of the gross estate which is situated in the United States exceeds $60,000, the executor shall make a return with respect to the estate tax imposed by subtitle B.

(3) ADJUSTMENT FOR CERTAIN GIFTS.—The amount applicable under paragraph (1) and the amount set forth in paragraph (2) shall each be reduced (but not below zero) by the sum of—

(A) the amount of the adjusted taxable gifts (within the meaning of section 2001(b)) made by the decedent after December 31, 1976, plus

(B) the aggregate amount allowed as a specific exemption under section 2521 (as in effect before its repeal by the Tax Reform Act of 1976) with respect to gifts made by the decedent after September 8, 1976.

Amendments

• **1997, Taxpayer Relief Act of 1997 (P.L. 105-34)**

P.L. 105-34, § 501(a)(1)(C):

Amended Code Sec. 6018(a)(1) by striking "$600,000" and inserting "the applicable exclusion amount in effect under section 2010(c) for the calendar year which includes the date of death". **Effective** for the estates of decedents dying, and gifts made, after 12-31-97.

P.L. 105-34, § 1073(b)(4):

Amended Code Sec. 6018(a) by striking paragraph (4). **Effective** for estates of decedents dying after 12-31-96. Prior to being stricken, Code Sec. 6018(a)(4) read as follows:

(4) RETURN REQUIRED IF EXCESS RETIREMENT ACCUMULATION TAX.—The executor shall make a return with respect to the estate tax imposed by subtitle B in any case where such tax is increased by reason of section 4980A(d).

• **1990, Omnibus Budget Reconciliation Act of 1990 (P.L. 101-508)**

P.L. 101-508, § 11801(a)(43):

Repealed Code Sec. 6018(a)(3). **Effective** 11-5-90. Prior to repeal, Code Sec. 6018(a)(3) read as follows:

(3) PHASE-IN OF FILING REQUIREMENT AMOUNT. —

RETURNS—INCOME TAX

In the case of decedents dying in:	Paragraph (1) shall be applied by substituting for "$600,000" the following amount
1982	$225,000
1983	275,000
1984	325,000
1985	400,000
1986	500,000

P.L. 101-508, §11801(c)(19)(C):

Amended Code Sec. 6018(a) by redesignating paragraphs (4) and (5) as paragraphs (3) and (4) respectively. **Effective** 11-5-90.

P.L. 101-508, §11821(b), provides:

(b) SAVINGS PROVISION.—If—

(1) any provision amended or repealed by this part applied to—

(A) any transaction occurring before the date of the enactment of this Act,

(B) any property acquired before such date of enactment, or

(C) any item of income, loss, deduction, or credit taken into account before such date of enactment, and

(2) the treatment of such transaction, property, or item under such provision would (without regard to the amendments made by this part) affect liability for tax for periods ending after such date of enactment,

nothing in the amendments made by this part shall be construed to affect the treatment of such transaction, property, or item for purposes of determining liability for tax for periods ending after such date of enactment.

• **1988, Technical and Miscellaneous Revenue Act of 1988 (P.L. 100-647)**

P.L. 100-647, §1011A(g)(12):

Amended Code Sec. 6018(a) by adding at the end thereof new paragraph (5). **Effective** as if included in the provision of P.L. 99-514 to which it relates.

• **1981, Economic Recovery Tax Act of 1981 (P.L. 97-34)**

P.L. 97-34, §401(a)(2)(B):

Amended Code Sec. 6018(a)(3). **Effective** for estates of decedents dying after 12-31-81. Prior to amendment, Code Sec. 6018(a)(3) read as follows:

(3) PHASE-IN OF FILING REQUIREMENT AMOUNT.—In the case of a decedent dying before 1981, paragraph (1) shall be applied—

(A) in the case of a decedent dying during 1977, by substituting "$120,000" for "$175,000",

(B) in the case of a decedent dying during 1978, by substituting "$134,000" for "$175,000",

(C) in the case of a decedent dying during 1979, by substituting "$147,000" for "$175,000", and

(D) in the case of a decedent dying during 1980, by substituting "$161,000" for "$175,000".

• **1976, Tax Reform Act of 1976 (P.L. 94-455)**

P.L. 94-455, §2001(c)(1)(J):

Amended Code Sec. 6018(a) by substituting "$175,000" for "$60,000" in paragraph (1), substituting "$60,000" for "$30,000" in paragraph (2), and adding paragraphs (3) and (4). **Effective** for estates of decedents dying after 12-31-76.

• **1966, Foreign Investors Tax Act of 1966 (P.L. 89-809)**

P.L. 89-809, §108(g):

Amended Code Sec. 6018(a)(2) by substituting "$30,000" for "$2,000". **Effective** with respect to estates of decedents dying after 11-13-66, the date of enactment.

[Sec. 6018(b)]

(b) RETURNS BY BENEFICIARIES.—If the executor is unable to make a complete return as to any part of the gross estate of the decedent, he shall include in his return a description of such part and the name of every person holding a legal or beneficial interest therein. Upon notice from the Secretary such person shall in like manner make a return as to such part of the gross estate.

P.L. 107-16, §901(a)-(b), as amended by P.L. 111-312, §101(a)(1), provides [but see P.L. 112-240, §101(a)(1) and (3), above]:

SEC. 901. SUNSET OF PROVISIONS OF ACT.

(a) IN GENERAL.—All provisions of, and amendments made by, this Act shall not apply—

(1) to taxable, plan, or limitation years beginning after December 31, 2012, or

(2) in the case of title V, to estates of decedents dying, gifts made, or generation skipping transfers, after December 31, 2012.

(b) APPLICATION OF CERTAIN LAWS.—The Internal Revenue Code of 1986 and the Employee Retirement Income Security Act of 1974 shall be applied and administered to years, estates, gifts, and transfers described in subsection (a) as if the provisions and amendments described in subsection (a) had never been enacted.

• **1976, Tax Reform Act of 1976 (P.L. 94-455)**

P.L. 94-455, §1906(b)(13)(A):

Amended 1954 Code by substituting "Secretary" for "Secretary or his delegate" each place it appeared. **Effective** 2-1-77.

[Sec. 6018(c)—Stricken]

Amendments

• **1989, Omnibus Budget Reconciliation Act of 1989 (P.L. 101-239)**

P.L. 101-239, §7304(b)(2)(B):

Amended Code Sec. 6018 by striking subsection (c). **Effective** for estates of decedents dying after 7-12-89. Prior to amendment, Code Sec. 6018(c) read as follows:

(c) ELECTION UNDER SECTION 2210.—In all cases in which subsection (a) requires the filing of a return, if an executor elects the applications of section 2210—

(1) RETURN BY EXECUTOR.—The return which the executor is required to file under the provisions of subsection (a) shall be made with respect to that portion of estate tax imposed by subtitle B which the executor is required to pay.

(2) RETURN BY PLAN ADMINISTRATOR.—The plan administrator of an employee stock ownership plan or the eligible worker-owned cooperative, as the case may be, shall make a return with respect to that portion of the tax imposed by section 2001 which such plan or cooperative is required to pay under section 2210(b).

• **1984, Deficit Reduction Act of 1984 (P.L. 98-369)**

P.L. 98-369, §544(b)(3):

Amended Code Sec. 6018 by adding subsection (c). **Effective** for those estates of decedents which are required to file returns on a date (including any extensions) after 7-18-84.

[Sec. 6019]

SEC. 6019. GIFT TAX RETURNS.

Any individual who in any calendar year makes any transfer by gift other than—

(1) a transfer which under subsection (b) or (e) of section 2503 is not to be included in the total amount of gifts for such year,

(2) a transfer of an interest with respect to which a deduction is allowed under section 2523, or

(3) a transfer with respect to which a deduction is allowed under section 2522 but only if—

(A)(i) such transfer is of the donor's entire interest in the property transferred, and

(ii) no other interest in such property is or has been transferred (for less than adequate and full consideration in money or money's worth) from the donor to a person, or for a use, not described in subsection (a) or (b) of section 2522, or

(B) such transfer is described in section 2522(d),

shall make a return for such year with respect to the gift tax imposed by subtitle B.

Amendments

• **2013, American Taxpayer Relief Act of 2012 (P.L. 112-240)**

P.L. 112-240, §101(a)(1)-(3), provides:

SEC. 101. PERMANENT EXTENSION AND MODIFICATION OF 2001 TAX RELIEF.

(a) PERMANENT EXTENSION.—

(1) IN GENERAL.—The Economic Growth and Tax Relief Reconciliation Act of 2001 is amended by striking title IX.

(2) CONFORMING AMENDMENT.—The Tax Relief, Unemployment Insurance Reauthorization, and Job Creation Act of 2010 is amended by striking section 304.

(3) EFFECTIVE DATE.—The amendments made by this subsection shall apply to taxable, plan, or limitation years beginning after December 31, 2012, and estates of decedents dying, gifts made, or generation skipping transfers after December 31, 2012.

• **2010, Tax Relief, Unemployment Insurance Reauthorization, and Job Creation Act of 2010 (P.L. 111-312)**

P.L. 111-312, §301(a):

Amended Code Sec. 6019 to read as such provision would read if subtitle E of title V of the Economic Growth and Tax Relief Reconciliation Act of 2001 (P.L. 107-16) had never been enacted. **Effective** for estates of decedents dying, and transfers made, after 12-31-2009. For a special rule, see Act Sec. 301(c), below. Prior to amendment by P.L. 111-312, Code Sec. 6019 read as follows:

SEC. 6019. GIFT TAX RETURNS.

[Sec. 6019(a)]

(a) IN GENERAL.—Any individual who in any calendar year makes any transfer by gift other than—

(1) a transfer which under subsection (b) or (e) of section 2503 is not to be included in the total amount of gifts for such year,

(2) a transfer of an interest with respect to which a deduction is allowed under section 2523, or

(3) a transfer with respect to which a deduction is allowed under section 2522 but only if—

(A)(i) such transfer is of the donor's entire interest in the property transferred, and

(ii) no other interest in such property is or has been transferred (for less than adequate and full consideration in money or money's worth) from the donor to a person, or for a use, not described in subsection (a) or (b) of section 2522, or

(B) such transfer is described in section 2522(d),

shall make a return for such year with respect to the gift tax imposed by subtitle B.

RETURNS—MISCELLANEOUS PROVISIONS

[Sec. 6019(b)]

(b) STATEMENTS TO BE FURNISHED TO CERTAIN PERSONS.—Every person required to make a return under subsection (a) shall furnish to each person whose name is required to be set forth in such return (other than the person required to make such return) a written statement showing—

(1) the name, address, and phone number of the person required to make such return, and

(2) the information specified in such return with respect to property received by the person required to receive such statement.

The written statement required under the preceding sentence shall be furnished not later than 30 days after the date that the return required by subsection (a) is filed.

P.L. 111-312, §301(c), provides:

(c) SPECIAL ELECTION WITH RESPECT TO ESTATES OF DECEDENTS DYING IN 2010.—Notwithstanding subsection (a), in the case of an estate of a decedent dying after December 31, 2009, and before January 1, 2011, the executor (within the meaning of section 2203 of the Internal Revenue Code of 1986) may elect to apply such Code as though the amendments made by subsection (a) do not apply with respect to chapter 11 of such Code and with respect to property acquired or passing from such decedent (within the meaning of section 1014(b) of such Code). Such election shall be made at such time and in such manner as the Secretary of the Treasury or the Secretary's delegate shall provide. Such an election once made shall be revocable only with the consent of the Secretary of the Treasury or the Secretary's delegate. For purposes of section 2652(a)(1) of such Code, the determination of whether any property is subject to the tax imposed by such chapter 11 shall be made without regard to any election made under this subsection.

P.L. 111-312, §304, provides [but see P.L. 112-240, §101(a)(2)-(3), above]:

SEC. 304. APPLICATION OF EGTRRA SUNSET TO THIS TITLE.

Section 901 of the Economic Growth and Tax Relief Reconciliation Act of 2001 shall apply to the amendments made by this title.

• **2001, Economic Growth and Tax Relief Reconciliation Act of 2001 (P.L. 107-16)**

P.L. 107-16, §542(b)(2)(A):

Amended Code Sec. 6019 by striking "Any individual" and inserting "(a) IN GENERAL.—Any individual". **Effective** for estates of decedents dying after 12-31-2009.

P.L. 107-16, §542(b)(2)(B):

Amended Code Sec. 6019 by adding at the end a new subsection (b). **Effective** for estates of decedents dying after 12-31-2009.

P.L. 107-16, §901(a)-(b), as amended by P.L. 111-312, §101(a)(1), provides [but see P.L. 112-240, §101(a)(1) and (3), above]:

SEC. 901. SUNSET OF PROVISIONS OF ACT.

(a) IN GENERAL.—All provisions of, and amendments made by, this Act shall not apply—

(1) to taxable, plan, or limitation years beginning after December 31, 2012, or

(2) in the case of title V, to estates of decedents dying, gifts made, or generation skipping transfers, after December 31, 2012.

(b) APPLICATION OF CERTAIN LAWS.—The Internal Revenue Code of 1986 and the Employee Retirement Income Security Act of 1974 shall be applied and administered to years, estates, gifts, and transfers described in subsection (a) as if the provisions and amendments described in subsection (a) had never been enacted.

• **1997, Taxpayer Relief Act of 1997 (P.L. 105-34)**

P.L. 105-34, §1301(a):

Amended Code Sec. 6019 by striking "or" at the end of paragraph (1), by adding "or" at the end of paragraph (2), and by inserting after paragraph (2) a new paragraph (3). **Effective** for gifts made after 8-5-97.

• **1981, Economic Recovery Tax Act of 1981 (P.L. 97-34)**

P.L. 97-34, §403(b)(3)(A):

Amended so much of Code Sec. 6019 as followed the heading and preceded subsection (b). **Effective**, generally, for gifts made after 12-31-81. Prior to amendment, that language read as follows:

"(a) IN GENERAL.—Any individual who in any calendar quarter makes any transfers by gift (other than transfers which under section 2503(b) are not to be included in the total amount of gifts for such quarter and other than qualified charitable transfers) shall make a return for such quarter with respect to the gift tax imposed by subtitle B."

There is also a special rule applicable to certain wills or trusts, executed or created, before September 12, 1981.

[Sec. 6019(b)—Repealed]

Amendments

• **1981, Economic Recovery Tax Act of 1981 (P.L. 97-34)**

P.L. 97-34, §442(d)(2):

Repealed Code Sec. 6019(b). **Effective** with respect to estates of decedents dying after 12-31-81. Prior to repeal, Code Sec. 6019(b) read as follows:

(b) QUALIFIED CHARITABLE TRANSFERS.—

(1) RETURN REQUIREMENT.—A return shall be made of any qualified charitable transfer—

(A) for the first calendar quarter, in the calendar year in which the transfer is made, for which a return is required to be filed under subsection (a), or

(B) if no return is required to be filed under subparagraph (A), for the fourth calendar quarter in the calendar year in which such transfer is made.

A return made pursuant to the provisions of this paragraph shall be deemed to be a return with respect to any transfer reported as a qualified charitable transfer for the calendar quarter in which such transfer was made.

(2) DEFINITION OF QUALIFIED CHARITABLE TRANSFER.—For purposes of this section, the term "qualified charitable transfer" means a transfer by gift with respect to which a deduction is allowable under section 2522 in an amount equal to the amount transferred.

[Sec. 6019(c)—Repealed]

Amendments

• **1981, Economic Recovery Tax Act of 1981 (P.L. 97-34)**

P.L. 97-34, §403(c)(3)(B):

Repealed Code Sec. 6019(c). **Effective**, generally, for gifts made after 12-31-81. For the special rule applicable to wills and trusts, executed or created, before 9-12-81, see the amendment note at P.L. 97-34, §403(c)(3)(A). Prior to repeal, Code Sec. 6019(c) read as follows:

(c) TENANCY BY THE ENTIRETY.—

For provisions relating to requirement of return in the case of election as to the treatment of gift by creation of tenancy by the entirety, see section 2515(c).

P.L. 97-34, §403(e)(3), provides:

(3) If—

(A) the decedent dies after December 31, 1981,

(B) by reason of the death of the decedent property passes from the decedent or is acquired from the decedent under a will executed before the date which is 30 days after the date of the enactment of this Act, or a trust created before such date, which contains a formula expressly providing that the spouse is to receive the maximum amount of property qualifying for the marital deduction allowable by Federal law,

(C) the formula referred to in subparagraph (B) was not amended to refer specifically to an unlimited marital deduction at any time after the date which is 30 days after the date of enactment of this Act, and before the death of the decedent, and

(D) the State does not enact a statute applicable to such estate which construes this type of formula as referring to the marital deduction allowable by Federal law as amended by subsection (a),

then the amendment made by subsection (a) [relating to the unlimited marital deduction (Code Sec. 2056, as amended by P.L. 97-34)] shall not apply to the estate of such decedent.

• **1970, Excise, Estate, and Gift Tax Adjustment Act of 1970 (P.L. 91-614)**

P.L. 91-614, §102(d)(3):

Amended Code Sec. 6019 by redesignating former subsection (b) as subsection (c) and by substituting subsections (a) and (b) for the following:

"(a) In General.—Any individual who in any calendar year makes any transfers by gift (except those which under section 2503(b) are not to be included in the total amount of gifts for such year) shall make a return with respect to the gift tax imposed by subtitle B."

Effective for gifts made after 12-31-70.

Subpart D—Miscellaneous Provisions

Sec. 6020.   Returns prepared for or executed by Secretary.
Sec. 6021.   Listing by Secretary of taxable objects owned by nonresidents of internal revenue districts.

[Sec. 6020]

SEC. 6020. RETURNS PREPARED FOR OR EXECUTED BY SECRETARY.

[Sec. 6020(a)]

(a) PREPARATION OF RETURN BY SECRETARY.—If any person shall fail to make a return required by this title or by regulations prescribed thereunder, but shall consent to disclose all information necessary for the preparation thereof, then, and in that case, the Secretary may prepare such return, which, being signed by such person, may be received by the Secretary as the return of such person.

Sec. 6019(b)—Repealed

RETURNS—INFORMATION

Amendments

• **1976, Tax Reform Act of 1976 (P.L. 94-455)**

P.L. 94-455, §1906(b)(13)(A):

Amended 1954 Code by substituting "Secretary" for "Secretary or his delegate" each place it appeared. **Effective** 2-1-77.

[Sec. 6020(b)]

(b) EXECUTION OF RETURN BY SECRETARY.—

(1) AUTHORITY OF SECRETARY TO EXECUTE RETURN.—If any person fails to make any return required by any internal revenue law or regulation made thereunder at the time prescribed therefor, or makes, willfully or otherwise, a false or fraudulent return, the Secretary shall make such return from his own knowledge and from such information as he can obtain through testimony or otherwise.

(2) STATUS OF RETURNS.—Any return so made and subscribed by the Secretary shall be prima facie good and sufficient for all legal purposes.

Amendments

• **1984, Deficit Reduction Act of 1984 (P.L. 98-369)**

P.L. 98-369, §412(b)(4):

Amended Code Sec. 6020(b)(1) by striking out "(other than a declaration of estimated tax required under section 6015)". **Effective** with respect to tax years beginning after 12-31-84.

• **1976, Tax Reform Act of 1976 (P.L. 94-455)**

P.L. 94-455, §1906(b)(13)(A):

Amended 1954 Code by substituting "Secretary" for "Secretary or his delegate" each place it appeared. **Effective** 2-1-77.

• **1968, Revenue and Expenditure Control Act of 1968 (P.L. 90-364)**

P.L. 90-364, §103(e)(3):

Amended Code Sec. 6020(b) by deleting "or 6016" which formerly appeared after "section 6015". **Effective** with respect to tax years beginning after 12-31-67. However, such amendment is to be taken into account only as of 5-31-68. For the **effective** date provisions of P.L. 90-364, see the amendment note following Code Sec. 6154.

[Sec. 6021]

SEC. 6021. LISTING BY SECRETARY OF TAXABLE OBJECTS OWNED BY NONRESIDENTS OF INTERNAL REVENUE DISTRICTS.

Whenever there are in any internal revenue district any articles subject to tax, which are not owned or possessed by or under the care or control of any person within such district, and of which no list has been transmitted to the Secretary, as required by law or by regulations prescribed pursuant to law, the Secretary shall enter the premises where such articles are situated, shall make such inspection of the articles as may be necessary and make lists of the same, according to the forms prescribed. Such lists, being subscribed by the Secretary, shall be sufficient lists of such articles for all purposes.

Amendments

• **1976, Tax Reform Act of 1976 (P.L. 94-455)**

P.L. 94-455, §1906(b)(13)(A):

Amended 1954 Code by substituting "Secretary" for "Secretary or his delegate" each place it appeared. **Effective** 2-1-77.

PART III—INFORMATION RETURNS

Subpart A.	Information concerning persons subject to special provisions.
Subpart B.	Information concerning transactions with other persons.
Subpart C.	Information regarding wages paid employees.
Subpart D.	Information regarding health insurance coverage.
Subpart D.	[Repealed].
Subpart E.	Registration of and information concerning pensions, etc., plans.
Subpart F.	Information concerning income tax return preparers.

Subpart A—Information Concerning Persons Subject to Special Provisions

Sec. 6031.	Return of partnership income.
Sec. 6032.	Returns of banks with respect to common trust funds.
Sec. 6033.	Returns by exempt organizations.
Sec. 6034.	Returns by certain trusts.
Sec. 6034A.	Information to beneficiaries of estates and trusts.
Sec. 6035.	Basis information to persons acquiring property from decedent.
Sec. 6036.	Notice of qualification as executor or receiver.
Sec. 6037.	Return of S corporation.
Sec. 6038.	Information reporting with respect to certain foreign corporations and partnerships.
Sec. 6038A.	Information with respect to certain foreign-owned corporations.
Sec. 6038B.	Notice of certain transfers to foreign persons.
Sec. 6038C.	Information with respect to foreign corporations engaged in U.S. business.
Sec. 6038D.	Information with respect to foreign financial assets.
Sec. 6038E.	Information with respect to assignment of lower rates or refunds by foreign producers of beer, wine, and distilled spirits.
Sec. 6039.	Returns required in connection with certain options.
Sec. 6039C.	Returns with respect to foreign persons holding direct investments in United States real property interests.
Sec. 6039D.	Returns and records with respect to certain fringe benefit plans.
Sec. 6039E.	Information concerning resident status.
Sec. 6039F.	Notice of large gifts received from foreign persons.
Sec. 6039G.	Information on individuals losing United States citizenship.
Sec. 6039H.	Information with respect to Alaska Native Settlement Trusts and sponsoring Native Corporations.

RETURNS—INFORMATION

Sec. 6039I. Returns and records with respect to employer-owned life insurance contracts.
Sec. 6039J. Information reporting with respect to commodity credit corporation transactions.
Sec. 6040. Cross references.

[Sec. 6031]

SEC. 6031. RETURN OF PARTNERSHIP INCOME.

[Sec. 6031(a)]

(a) GENERAL RULE.—Every partnership (as defined in section 761(a)) shall make a return for each taxable year, stating specifically the items of its gross income and the deductions allowable by subtitle A, and such other information for the purpose of carrying out the provisions of subtitle A as the Secretary may by forms and regulations prescribe, and shall include in the return the names and addresses of the individuals who would be entitled to share in the taxable income if distributed and the amount of the distributive share of each individual.

Amendments

• **1982, Tax Equity and Fiscal Responsibility Act of 1982 (P.L. 97-248)**

P.L. 97-248, §403(b):

Amended Code Sec. 6031 by striking out "Every partnership" and inserting "(a) GENERAL RULE.—Every partnership". **Effective** for partnership tax years beginning after the date of the enactment of this Act, and for any partnership tax year ending after the date of the enactment of this Act if the partnership, each partner, and each indirect partner requests such application and the Secretary of the Treasury or his delegate consents to such application. However, Code Sec. 6031 does not apply to certain international satellite partnerships. See Act Sec. 406 following Code Sec. 6221.

P.L. 97-248, §404, provides:

Except as hereafter provided in regulations prescribed by the Secretary of the Treasury or his delegate, nothing in section 6031 of the Internal Revenue Code of 1954 shall be treated as excluding any partnership from the filing requirements of such section for any taxable year if the income tax liability under subtitle A of such Code of any United States person is determined in whole or in part by taking into account (directly or indirectly) partnership items of such partnership for such taxable year.

• **1976, Tax Reform Act of 1976 (P.L. 94-455)**

P.L. 94-455, §1906(b)(13)(A):

Amended 1954 Code by substituting "Secretary" for "Secretary or his delegate" each place it appeared. **Effective** 2-1-77.

[Sec. 6031(b)]

(b) COPIES TO PARTNERS.—Each partnership required to file a return under subsection (a) for any partnership taxable year shall (on or before the day on which the return for such taxable year was required to be filed) furnish to each person who is a partner or who holds an interest in such partnership as a nominee for another person at any time during such taxable year a copy of such information required to be shown on such return as may be required by regulations. Information required to be furnished by the partnership under this subsection may not be amended after the due date of the return under subsection (a) to which such information relates, except—

　(1) in the case of a partnership which has elected the application of section 6221(b) for the taxable year,

　(2) as provided in the procedures under section 6225(c),

　(3) with respect to statements under section 6226, or

　(4) as otherwise provided by the Secretary.

Amendments

• **2018, Tax Technical Corrections Act of 2018 (P.L. 115-141)**

P.L. 115-141, §206(a), Div. U:

Amended Code Sec. 6031(b) by striking the last sentence and inserting a new sentence and new paragraphs (1)-(4). **Effective** as if included in section 1101 of the Bipartisan Budget Act of 2015 [effective generally for returns filed for partnership tax years beginning after 12-31-2017.—CCH]. Prior to being stricken, the last sentence of Code Sec. 6031(b) read as follows:

Except as provided in the procedures under section 6225(c), with respect to statements under section 6226, or as otherwise provided by the Secretary, information required to be furnished by the partnership under this subsection may not be amended after the due date of the return under subsection (a) to which such information relates.

• **2015, Protecting Americans from Tax Hikes Act of 2015 (P.L. 114-113)**

P.L. 114-113, §411(d), Div. Q:

Amended Code Sec. 6031(b) [as amended by P.L. 114-74] by striking the last sentence and inserting a new sentence. **Effective** as if included in section 1101 of the Bipartisan Budget Act of 2015 (P.L. 114-74) [effective generally for returns filed for partnership tax years beginning after 12-31-2017.]. Prior to being stricken, the last sentence of Code Sec. 6031(b) read as follows:

Except as provided in the procedures under section 6225(c), with respect to statements under section 6226, or as otherwise provided by the Secretary, information required to be furnished by the partnership under this subsection may not be amended after the due date of the return under subsection (a) to which such information relates.

• **2015, Bipartisan Budget Act of 2015 (P.L. 114-74)**

P.L. 114-74, §1101(e):

Amended Code Sec. 6031(b) by adding at the end a new sentence. **Effective** generally for returns filed for partnership tax years beginning after 12-31-2017. For a special rule, see Act Sec. 1101(g)(4), below.

P.L. 114-74, §1101(f)(1):

Amended Code Sec. 6031(b) [prior to amendment by Act Sec. 1101(e)] by striking the last sentence. **Effective** generally for returns filed for partnership tax years beginning after 12-31-2017. For a special rule, see Act Sec. 1101(g)(4), below. Prior to being stricken, the last sentence of Code Sec. 6031(b) read as follows:

In the case of an electing large partnership (as defined in section 775), such information shall be furnished on or before the first March 15 following the close of such taxable year.

P.L. 114-74, §1101(g)(4), provides:

(4) ELECTION.—A partnership may elect (at such time and in such form and manner as the Secretary of the Treasury may prescribe) for the amendments made by this section (other than the election under section 6221(b) of such Code (as added by this Act)) to apply to any return of the partnership filed for partnership taxable years beginning after the date of the enactment of this Act and before January 1, 2018.

• **1997, Taxpayer Relief Act of 1997 (P.L. 105-34)**

P.L. 105-34, §1223(a):

Amended Code Sec. 6031(b) by adding at the end a new sentence. **Effective** for partnership tax years ending on or after 12-31-97.

• **1986, Tax Reform Act of 1986 (P.L. 99-514)**

P.L. 99-514, §1501(c)(16)(A)-(B):

Amended Code Sec. 6031(b) by striking out "was filed" and inserting in lieu thereof "was required to be filed" and by striking out "shown on such return" and inserting in lieu thereof "required to be shown on such return." **Effective** for returns the due date for which (determined without regard to extensions) is after 12-31-86.

• **1986, Tax Reform Act of 1986 (P.L. 99-514)**

P.L. 99-514, §1811(b)(1)(A)(i):

Amended Code Sec. 6031(b) by inserting "or who holds an interest in such partnership as a nominee for another person" after "who is a partner". **Effective** for partnership tax years beginning after 10-22-86.

• **1982, Tax Equity and Fiscal Responsibility Act of 1982 (P.L. 97-248)**

P.L. 97-248, §403(a):

Added Code Sec. 6031(b). For the **effective** date, see the amendment note for P.L. 97-248, following Code 6031(a).

[Sec. 6031(c)]

(c) NOMINEE REPORTING.—Any person who holds an interest in a partnership as a nominee for another person—

　(1) shall furnish to the partnership, in the manner prescribed by the Secretary, the name and address of such other person, and any other information for such taxable year as the Secretary may by form and regulation prescribe, and

　(2) shall furnish in the manner prescribed by the Secretary such other person the information provided by such partnership under subsection (b).

Amendments

• **1986, Tax Reform Act of 1986 (P.L. 99-514)**
P.L. 99-514, §1811(b)(1)(A)(ii):
Amended Code Sec. 6031 by adding at the end thereof new subsection (c).
Effective for partnership tax years beginning after 10-22-86.

[Sec. 6031(d)]

(d) SEPARATE STATEMENT OF ITEMS OF UNRELATED BUSINESS TAXABLE INCOME.—In the case of any partnership regularly carrying on a trade or business (within the meaning of section 512(c)(1)), the information required under subsection (b) to be furnished to its partners shall include such information as is necessary to enable each partner to compute its distributive share of partnership income or loss from such trade or business in accordance with section 512(a)(1), but without regard to the modifications described in paragraphs (8) through (15) of section 512(b).

Amendments

• **1988, Technical and Miscellaneous Revenue Act of 1988 (P.L. 100-647)**
P.L. 100-647, §5074(a):
Amended Code Sec. 6031 by adding at the end thereof a new subsection (d).
Effective for tax years beginning after 12-31-88.

[Sec. 6031(e)]

(e) FOREIGN PARTNERSHIPS.—

(1) EXCEPTION FOR FOREIGN PARTNERSHIP.—Except as provided in paragraph (2), the preceding provisions of this section shall not apply to a foreign partnership.

(2) CERTAIN FOREIGN PARTNERSHIPS REQUIRED TO FILE RETURN.—Except as provided in regulations prescribed by the Secretary, this section shall apply to a foreign partnership for any taxable year if for such year, such partnership has—

(A) gross income derived from sources within the United States, or

(B) gross income which is effectively connected with the conduct of a trade or business within the United States.

The Secretary may provide simplified filing procedures for foreign partnerships to which this section applies.

Amendments

• **1997, Taxpayer Relief Act of 1997 (P.L. 105-34)**
P.L. 105-34, §1141(a):
Amended Code Sec. 6031 by adding at the end a new subsection (e). **Effective** for tax years beginning after 8-5-97.

[Sec. 6031(f)]

(f) ELECTING INVESTMENT PARTNERSHIPS.—In the case of any electing investment partnership (as defined in section 743(e)(6)), the information required under subsection (b) to be furnished to any partner to whom section 743(e)(2) applies shall include such information as is necessary to enable the partner to compute the amount of losses disallowed under section 743(e).

Amendments

• **2004, American Jobs Creation Act of 2004 (P.L. 108-357)**

P.L. 108-357, §833(b)(4)(B):
Amended Code Sec. 6031 by adding at the end a new subsection (f). **Effective** for transfers after 10-22-2004. For a transition rule, see Act Sec. 833(d)(2)(B), below.

P.L. 108-357, §833(d)(2)(B), provides:

(B) TRANSITION RULE.—In the case of an electing investment partnership which is in existence on June 4, 2004, section 743(e)(6)(H) of the Internal Revenue Code of 1986, as added by this section, shall not apply to such partnership and section 743(e)(6)(I) of such Code, as so added, shall be applied by substituting "20 years" for "15 years".

[Sec. 6032]

SEC. 6032. RETURNS OF BANKS WITH RESPECT TO COMMON TRUST FUNDS.

Every bank (as defined in section 581) maintaining a common trust fund shall make a return for each taxable year, stating specifically, with respect to such fund, the items of gross income and the deductions allowed by subtitle A, and shall include in the return the names and addresses of the participants who would be entitled to share in the taxable income if distributed and the amount of the proportionate share of each participant. The return shall be executed in the same manner as a return made by a corporation pursuant to the requirements of sections 6012 and 6062.

[Sec. 6033]

SEC. 6033. RETURNS BY EXEMPT ORGANIZATIONS.

[Sec. 6033(a)]

(a) ORGANIZATIONS REQUIRED TO FILE.—

(1) IN GENERAL.—Except as provided in paragraph (3), every organization exempt from taxation under section 501(a) shall file an annual return, stating specifically the items of gross income, receipts, and disbursements, and such other information for the purpose of carrying out the internal revenue laws as the Secretary may by forms or regulations prescribe, and shall keep such records, render under oath such statements, make such other returns, and comply with such rules and regulations as the Secretary may from time to time prescribe; except that, in the discretion of the Secretary, any organization described in section 401(a) may be relieved from stating in its return any information which is reported in returns filed by the employer which established such organization.

(2) BEING A PARTY TO CERTAIN REPORTABLE TRANSACTIONS.—Every tax-exempt entity described in section 4965(c) shall file (in such form and manner and at such time as determined by the Secretary) a disclosure of—

(A) such entity's being a party to any prohibited tax shelter transaction (as defined in section 4965(e)), and

(B) the identity of any other party to such transaction which is known by such tax-exempt entity.

(3) EXCEPTIONS FROM FILING.—

(A) MANDATORY EXCEPTIONS.—Paragraph (1) shall not apply to—

(i) churches, their integrated auxiliaries, and conventions or associations of churches,

(ii) any organization (other than a private foundation, as defined in section 509(a)) described in subparagraph (C), the gross receipts of which in each taxable year are normally not more than $5,000, or

(iii) the exclusively religious activities of any religious order.

(B) DISCRETIONARY EXCEPTIONS.—The Secretary may relieve any organization required under paragraph (1) (other than an organization described in section 509(a)(3)) to file an information return from filing such a return where he determines that such filing is not necessary to the efficient administration of the internal revenue laws.

(C) CERTAIN ORGANIZATIONS.—The organizations referred to in subparagraph (A)(ii) are—

RETURNS—INFORMATION

(i) a religious organization described in section 501(c)(3);

(ii) an educational organization described in section 170(b)(1)(A)(ii);

(iii) a charitable organization, or an organization for the prevention of cruelty to children or animals, described in section 501(c)(3), if such organization is supported, in whole or in part, by funds contributed by the United States or any State or political subdivision thereof, or is primarily supported by contributions of the general public;

(iv) an organization described in section 501(c)(3), if such organization is operated, supervised, or controlled by or in connection with a religious organization described in clause (i);

(v) an organization described in section 501(c)(8); and

(vi) an organization described in section 501(c)(1), if such organization is a corporation wholly owned by the United States or any agency or instrumentality thereof, or a wholly owned subsidiary of such a corporation.

Amendments

• **2006, Pension Protection Act of 2006 (P.L. 109-280)**

P.L. 109-280, §1245(a):

Amended Code Sec. 6033(a)(3)(B) by inserting "(other than an organization described in section 509(a)(3))" after "paragraph (1)". **Effective** for returns filed for tax years ending after 8-17-2006.

• **2006, Tax Increase Prevention and Reconciliation Act of 2005 (P.L. 109-222)**

P.L. 109-222, §516(b)(1)(A):

Amended Code Sec. 6033(a) by redesignating paragraph (2) as paragraph (3) and by inserting after paragraph (1) a new paragraph (2). **Effective** for disclosures the due date[s] for which are after 5-17-2006.

P.L. 109-222, §516(b)(1)(B):

Amended Code Sec. 6033(a)(1) by striking "paragraph (2)" and inserting "paragraph (3)". **Effective** for disclosures the due date[s] for which are after 5-17-2006.

• **1976, Tax Reform Act of 1976 (P.L. 94-455)**

P.L. 94-455, §1906(b)(13)(A):

Amended 1954 Code by substituting "Secretary" for "Secretary or his delegate" each place it appeared. **Effective** 2-1-77.

• **1969, Tax Reform Act of 1969 (P.L. 91-172)**

P.L. 91-172, §101(d)(1):

Amended Code Sec. 6033(a). **Effective** for tax years beginning after 12-31-69. Prior to amendment, Code Sec. 6033(a) read as follows:

(a) IN GENERAL.—Every organization, except as hereinafter provided, exempt from taxation under section 501(a) shall file an annual return, stating specifically the items of gross income, receipts, and disbursements, and such other information for the purpose of carrying out the provisions of subtitle A as the Secretary or his delegate may by forms or regulations prescribe, and shall keep such records, render under oath such statements, make such other returns, and comply with such rules and regulations, as the Secretary or his delegate may from time to time prescribe, except that, in the discretion of the Secretary or his delegate, an organization described in section 401(a) may be relieved from stating in its return any information which is reported in returns filed by the employer which established such organization. No such annual return need be filed under this subsection by any organization exempt from taxation under the provisions of section 501(a)—

(1) which is a religious organization described in section 501(c)(3); or

(2) which is an educational organization described in section 501(c)(3), if such organization normally maintains a regular faculty and curriculum and normally has a regularly organized body of pupils or students in attendance at the place where its educational activities are regularly carried on; or

(3) which is a charitable organization, or an organization for the prevention of cruelty to children or animals, described in section 501(c)(3), if such organization is supported, in whole or in part, by funds contributed by the United States or any State or political subdivision thereof, or is primarily supported by contributions of the general public; or

(4) which is an organization described in section 501(c)(3), if such organization is operated, supervised, or controlled by or in connection with a religious organization described in paragraph (1); or

(5) which is an organization described in section 501(c)(8); or

(6) which is an organization described in section 501(c)(1), if such organization is a corporation wholly owned by the United States or any agency or instrumentality thereof, or a wholly-owned subsidiary of such a corporation.

[Sec. 6033(b)]

(b) CERTAIN ORGANIZATIONS DESCRIBED IN SECTION 501(c)(3).—Every organization described in section 501(c)(3) which is subject to the requirements of subsection (a) shall furnish annually information, at such time and in such manner as the Secretary may by forms or regulations prescribe, setting forth—

(1) its gross income for the year,

(2) its expenses attributable to such income and incurred within the year,

(3) its disbursements within the year for the purposes for which it is exempt,

(4) a balance sheet showing its assets, liabilities, and net worth as of the beginning of such year,

(5) the total of the contributions and gifts received by it during the year, and the names and addresses of all substantial contributors,

(6) the names and addresses of its foundation managers (within the meaning of section 4946(b)(1)) and highly compensated employees,

(7) the compensation and other payments made during the year to each individual described in paragraph (6),

(8) in the case of an organization with respect to which an election under section 501(h) is effective for the taxable year, the following amounts for such organization for such taxable year:

(A) the lobbying expenditures (as defined in section 4911(c)(1)),

(B) the lobbying nontaxable amount (as defined in section 4911(c)(2)),

(C) the grass roots expenditures (as defined in section 4911(c)(3)), and

(D) the grass roots nontaxable amount (as defined in section 4911(c)(4)),

(9) such other information with respect to direct or indirect transfers to, and other direct or indirect transactions and relationships with, other organizations described in section 501(c) (other than paragraph (3) thereof) or section 527 as the Secretary may require to prevent—

(A) diversion of funds from the organization's exempt purpose, or

(B) misallocation of revenue or expense,

(10) the respective amounts (if any) of the taxes imposed on the organization, or any organization manager of the organization, during the taxable year under any of the following provisions (and the respective amounts (if any) of reimbursements paid by the organization during the taxable year with respect to taxes imposed on any such organization manager under any of such provisions):

(A) section 4911 (relating to tax on excess expenditures to influence legislation),

(B) section 4912 (relating to tax on disqualifying lobbying expenditures of certain organizations),

(C) section 4955 (relating to taxes on political expenditures of section 501(c)(3) organizations), except to the extent that, by reason of section 4962, the taxes imposed under such section are not required to be paid or are credited or refunded, and

(D) section 4959 (relating to taxes on failures by hospital organizations),

(11) the respective amounts (if any) of—

(A) the taxes imposed with respect to the organization on any organization manager, or any disqualified person, during the taxable year under section 4958 (relating to taxes on private excess benefit from certain charitable organizations), and

(B) reimbursements paid by the organization during the taxable year with respect to taxes imposed under such section,

except to the extent that, by reason of section 4962, the taxes imposed under such section are not required to be paid or are credited or refunded,

(12) such information as the Secretary may require with respect to any excess benefit transaction (as defined in section 4958),

RETURNS—INFORMATION

(13) such information with respect to disqualified persons as the Secretary may prescribe,

(14) such information as the Secretary may require with respect to disaster relief activities,

(15) in the case of an organization to which the requirements of section 501(r) apply for the taxable year—

(A) a description of how the organization is addressing the needs identified in each community health needs assessment conducted under section 501(r)(3) and a description of any such needs that are not being addressed together with the reasons why such needs are not being addressed, and

(B) the audited financial statements of such organization (or, in the case of an organization the financial statements of which are included in a consolidated financial statement with other organizations, such consolidated financial statement), and

(16) such other information for purposes of carrying out the internal revenue laws as the Secretary may require.

For purposes of paragraph (8), if section 4911(f) applies to the organization for the taxable year, such organization shall furnish the amounts with respect to the affiliated group as well as with respect to such organization.

Amendments

• **2018, Tax Technical Corrections Act of 2018 (P.L. 115-141)**

P.L. 115-141, §401(a)(258), Div. U:

Amended Code Sec. 6033(b)(15) by striking the period at the end and inserting ", and". **Effective** 3-23-2018.

P.L. 115-141, §401(d)(6)(B)(v), Div. U:

Amended Code Sec. 6033(b)(14) by striking "including the amount and use of qualified contributions to which section 1400S(a) applies," following "disaster relief activities,". **Effective** 3-23-2018. For a special rule, see Act Sec. 401(e), Div. U, below.

P.L. 115-141, §401(e), Div. U, provides:

(e) GENERAL SAVINGS PROVISION WITH RESPECT TO DEADWOOD PROVISIONS.—If—

(1) any provision amended or repealed by the amendments made by subsection (b) or (d) applied to—

(A) any transaction occurring before the date of the enactment of this Act,

(B) any property acquired before such date of enactment, or

(C) any item of income, loss, deduction, or credit taken into account before such date of enactment, and

(2) the treatment of such transaction, property, or item under such provision would (without regard to the amendments or repeals made by such subsection) affect the liability for tax for periods ending after such date of enactment,

nothing in the amendments or repeals made by this section shall be construed to affect the treatment of such transaction, property, or item for purposes of determining liability for tax for periods ending after such date of enactment.

• **2010, Patient Protection and Affordable Care Act (P.L. 111-148)**

P.L. 111-148, §9007(d)(1):

Amended Code Sec. 6033(b) by striking "and" at the end of paragraph (14), by redesignating paragraph (15) as paragraph (16), and by inserting after paragraph (14) a new paragraph (15). **Effective** for tax years beginning after 3-23-2010.

P.L. 111-148, §9007(d)(2):

Amended Code Sec. 6033(b)(10) by striking "and" at the end of subparagraph (B), by inserting "and" at the end of subparagraph (C), and by adding at the end a new subparagraph (D). **Effective** for tax years beginning after 3-23-2010.

• **2008, Heartland Disaster Tax Relief Act of 2008 (P.L. 110-343)**

P.L. 110-343, Division C, §703(a):

Amended Code Sec. 6033(b) by striking "and" at the end of paragraph (13), by redesignating paragraph (14) as paragraph (15), and by adding after paragraph (13) a new paragraph (14). **Effective** for returns the due date for which (determined without regard to any extension) occurs after 12-31-2008.

• **1997, Taxpayer Relief Act of 1997 (P.L. 105-34)**

P.L. 105-34, §1603(b)(1)(A):

Amended Code Sec. 6033(b)(10) by striking all that precedes subparagraph (A) and inserting new material. **Effective** as if included in the provision of P.L. 104-168 to which it relates [effective for tax years beginning after 7-30-96.—CCH]. Prior to amendment, the material preceding subparagraph (A) of Code Sec. 6033(b)(10) read as follows:

(10) the respective amounts (if any) of the taxes paid by the organization during the taxable year under the following provisions:

P.L. 105-34, §1603(b)(1)(B):

Amended Code Sec. 6033(b)(10)(C) by adding "except to the extent that, by reason of section 4962, the taxes imposed under such section are not required to be paid or are credited or refunded," at the end. **Effective** as if included in the provision of P.L. 104-168 to which it relates [effective for tax years beginning after 7-30-96.—CCH].

P.L. 105-34, §1603(b)(2):

Amended Code Sec. 6033(b)(11). **Effective** as if included in the provision of P.L. 104-168 to which it relates [effective for tax years beginning after 7-30-96.—CCH]. Prior to amendment, Code Sec. 6033(b)(11) read as follows:

(11) the respective amounts (if any) of the taxes paid by the organization, or any disqualified person with respect to such organization, during the taxable year under section 4958 (relating to taxes on private excess benefit from certain charitable organizations),

• **1996, Taxpayer Bill of Rights 2 (P.L. 104-168)**

P.L. 104-168, §1312(a):

Amended Code Sec. 6033(b) by striking "and" at the end of paragraph (9), by redesignating paragraph (10) as paragraph (14), and by inserting after paragraph (9) new paragraphs (10)-(13). **Effective** for returns for tax years beginning after 7-30-96.

• **1987, Revenue Act of 1987 (P.L. 100-203)**

P.L. 100-203, §10703(a):

Amended Code Sec. 6033(b) by striking out "and" at the end of paragraph (7), by striking out the period at the end of paragraph (8) and inserting in lieu thereof a comma, and by inserting after paragraph (8) new paragraphs (9) and (10). **Effective** for returns for years beginning after 12-31-87.

• **1976, Tax Reform Act of 1976 (P.L. 94-455)**

P.L. 94-455, §1307(a)(4):

Struck out "and" at the end of paragraph (6), substituted ", and" for the period at the end of paragraph (7), and added paragraph (8) and the flush sentence. **Effective** 10-4-76.

P.L. 94-455, §1906(b)(13)(A):

Amended 1954 Code by substituting "Secretary" for "Secretary or his delegate" each place it appeared. **Effective** 2-1-77.

• **1969, Tax Reform Act of 1969 (P.L. 91-172)**

P.L. 91-172, §101(d)(2), 101(j)(30):

Amended Code Sec. 6033(b). **Effective** for tax years beginning after 12-31-69. Prior to amendment, Code Sec. 6033(b) read as follows:

(b) CERTAIN ORGANIZATIONS DESCRIBED IN SECTION 501(c)(3).—Every organization described in section 501(c)(3) which is subject to the requirements of subsection (a) shall furnish annually information, at such time and in such manner as the Secretary or his delegate may by forms or regulations prescribe, setting forth—

(1) its gross income for the year,

(2) its expenses attributable to such income and incurred within the year,

(3) its disbursements out of income within the year for the purposes for which it is exempt,

(4) its accumulation of income within the year,

(5) its aggregate accumulations of income at the beginning of the year,

(6) its disbursements out of principal in the current and prior years for the purposes for which it is exempt,

(7) a balance sheet showing its assets, liabilities, and net worth as of the beginning of such year, and

(8) the total of the contributions and gifts received by it during the year.

• **1958, Technical Amendments Act of 1958 (P.L. 85-866)**

P.L. 85-866, §75(b)

Amended Sec. 6033(b) by striking out the word "and" at the end of paragraph (6), by striking out the period at the end of paragraph (7) and inserting a comma and the word "and" in its place, and by adding paragraph (8). **Effective** for tax years ending on or after 12-31-58.

[Sec. 6033(c)]

(c) ADDITIONAL PROVISIONS RELATING TO PRIVATE FOUNDATIONS.—In the case of an organization which is a private foundation (within the meaning of section 509(a))—

(1) the Secretary shall by regulations provide that the private foundation shall include in its annual return under this section such information (not required to be furnished by subsection (b) or the forms or regulations prescribed thereunder) as would have been required to be furnished under section 6056 (relating to annual reports by private foundations) as such section 6056 was in effect on January 1, 1979, and

(2) the foundation managers shall furnish copies of the annual return under this section to such State officials, at such times, and under such conditions, as the Secretary may by regulations prescribe.

Nothing in paragraph (1) shall require the inclusion of the name and address of any recipient (other than a disqualified person within the meaning of section 4946) of 1 or more charitable gifts or grants made by the foundation to such recipient as an indigent or needy person if the aggregate of such gifts or grants made by the foundation to such recipient during the year does not exceed $1,000.

RETURNS—INFORMATION

Amendments

• **1998, Tax and Trade Relief Extension Act of 1998 (P.L. 105-277)**

P.L. 105-277, § 1004(b)(2)(A):

Amended Code Sec. 6033(c) by adding "and" at the end of paragraph (1), by striking paragraph (2), and by redesignating paragraph (3) as paragraph (2). **Effective**, generally, for requests made after the later of 12-31-98, or the 60th day after the Secretary of the Treasury first issues the regulations referred to in Code Sec. 6104(d)(4), as amended by Act Sec. 1004. For an exception, see Act Sec. 1004(b)(3)(B), below. Prior to being stricken, Code Sec. 6033(c)(2) read as follows:

(2) a copy of the notice required by section 6104(d) (relating to public inspection of private foundations' annual returns), together with proof of publication thereof, shall be filed by the foundation together with the annual return under this section, and

P.L. 105-277, § 1004(b)(3)(B), provides:

(B) PUBLICATION OF ANNUAL RETURNS.—Section 6104(d) of such Code, as in effect before the amendments made by this subsection, shall not apply to any return the due date for which is after the date such amendments take effect under subparagraph (A).

• **1980 (P.L. 96-603)**

P.L. 96-603, § 1(a):

Redesignated former Code Sec. 6033(c) as Code Sec. 6033(e), and added a new Code Sec. 6033(c). **Effective** for tax years beginning after 1980.

[Sec. 6033(d)]

(d) SECTION TO APPLY TO NONEXEMPT CHARITABLE TRUSTS AND NONEXEMPT PRIVATE FOUNDATIONS.—The following organizations shall comply with the requirements of this section in the same manner as organizations described in section 501(c)(3) which are exempt from tax under section 501(a):

(1) NONEXEMPT CHARITABLE TRUSTS.—A trust described in section 4947(a)(1) (relating to nonexempt charitable trusts).

(2) NONEXEMPT PRIVATE FOUNDATIONS.—A private foundation which is not exempt from tax under section 501(a).

Amendments

• **1980 (P.L. 96-603)**

P.L. 96-603, § 1(a):

Amended Code Sec. 6033 by adding a new subsection (d). **Effective** for tax years beginning after 1980.

[Sec. 6033(e)]

(e) SPECIAL RULES RELATING TO LOBBYING ACTIVITIES.—

(1) REPORTING REQUIREMENTS.—

(A) IN GENERAL.—If this subsection applies to an organization for any taxable year, such organization—

(i) shall include on any return required to be filed under subsection (a) for such year information setting forth the total expenditures of the organization to which section 162(e)(1) applies and the total amount of the dues or other similar amounts paid to the organization to which such expenditures are allocable, and

(ii) except as provided in paragraphs (2)(A)(i) and (3), shall, at the time of assessment or payment of such dues or other similar amounts, provide notice to each person making such payment which contains a reasonable estimate of the portion of such dues or other similar amounts to which such expenditures are so allocable.

(B) ORGANIZATIONS TO WHICH SUBSECTION APPLIES.—

(i) IN GENERAL.—This subsection shall apply to any organization which is exempt from taxation under section 501 other than an organization described in section 501(c)(3).

(ii) SPECIAL RULE FOR IN-HOUSE EXPENDITURES.—This subsection shall not apply to the in-house expenditures (within the meaning of section 162(e)(4)(B)(ii)) of an organization for a taxable year if such expenditures do not exceed $2,000. In determining whether a taxpayer exceeds the $2,000 limit under this clause, there shall not be taken into account overhead costs otherwise allocable to activities described in subparagraphs (A) and (D) of section 162(e)(1).

(iii) COORDINATION WITH SECTION 527(f).—This subsection shall not apply to any amount on which tax is imposed by reason of section 527(f).

(C) ALLOCATION.—For purposes of this paragraph—

(i) IN GENERAL.—Expenditures to which section 162(e)(1) applies shall be treated as paid out of dues or other similar amounts to the extent thereof.

(ii) CARRYOVER OF LOBBYING EXPENDITURES IN EXCESS OF DUES.—If expenditures to which section 162(e)(1) applies exceed the dues or other similar amounts for any taxable year, such excess shall be treated as expenditures to which section 162(e)(1) applies which are paid or incurred by the organization during the following taxable year.

(2) TAX IMPOSED WHERE ORGANIZATION DOES NOT NOTIFY.—

(A) IN GENERAL.—If an organization—

(i) elects not to provide the notices described in paragraph (1)(A) for any taxable year, or

(ii) fails to include in such notices the amount allocable to expenditures to which section 162(e)(1) applies (determined on the basis of actual amounts rather than the reasonable estimates under paragraph (1)(A)(ii)),

then there is hereby imposed on such organization for such taxable year a tax in an amount equal to the product of the highest rate of tax imposed by section 11 for the taxable year and the aggregate amount not included in such notices by reason of such election or failure.

(B) WAIVER WHERE FUTURE ADJUSTMENTS MADE.—The Secretary may waive the tax imposed by subparagraph (A)(ii) for any taxable year if the organization agrees to adjust its estimates under paragraph (1)(A)(ii) for the following taxable year to correct any failures.

(C) TAX TREATED AS INCOME TAX.—For purposes of this title, the tax imposed by subparagraph (A) shall be treated in the same manner as a tax imposed by chapter 1 (relating to income taxes).

(3) EXCEPTION WHERE DUES GENERALLY NONDEDUCTIBLE.—Paragraph (1)(A) shall not apply to an organization which establishes to the satisfaction of the Secretary that substantially all of the dues or other similar amounts paid by persons to such organization are not deductible without regard to section 162(e).

Amendments

• **2017, Tax Cuts and Jobs Act (P.L. 115-97)**

P.L. 115-97, § 13308(b):

Amended Code Sec. 6033(e)(1)(B)(ii) by striking "section 162(e)(5)(B)(ii)" and inserting "section 162(e)(4)(B)(ii)". **Effective** for amounts paid or incurred on or after 12-22-2017.

• **1996, Small Business Job Protection Act of 1996 (P.L. 104-188)**

P.L. 104-188, § 1703(g)(1):

Amended Code Sec. 6033(e)(1)(B) by adding at the end a new clause (iii). **Effective** as if included in the provision of P.L. 103-66 to which it relates.

P.L. 104-188, § 1703(g)(2):

Amended Code Sec. 6033(e)(1)(B)(i) by striking "this subtitle" and inserting "section 501". **Effective** as if included in the provision of P.L. 103-66 to which it relates.

• **1993, Omnibus Budget Reconciliation Act of 1993 (P.L. 103-66)**

P.L. 103-66, § 13222(c):

Amended Code Sec. 6033 by redesignating subsection (e) as subsection (f) and by inserting after subsection (d) a new subsection (e). **Effective** for amounts paid or incurred after 12-31-93.

RETURNS—INFORMATION

[Sec. 6033(f)]

(f) CERTAIN ORGANIZATIONS DESCRIBED IN SECTION 501(c)(4).—Every organization described in section 501(c)(4) which is subject to the requirements of subsection (a) shall include on the return required under subsection (a)—

(1) the information referred to in paragraphs (11), (12) and (13) of subsection (b) with respect to such organization, and

(2) in the case of the first such return filed by such an organization after submitting a notice to the Secretary under section 506(a), such information as the Secretary shall by regulation require in support of the organization's treatment as an organization described in section 501(c)(4).

Amendments

• **2015, Protecting Americans from Tax Hikes Act of 2015 (P.L. 114-113)**

P.L. 114-113, §405(b)(1)-(3), Div. Q:

Amended Code Sec. 6033(f) by striking the period at the end and inserting ", and", by striking "include on the return required under subsection (a) the information" and inserting: "include on the return required under subsection (a)—"

"(1) the information",

and by adding at the end a new paragraph (2). For the **effective** date, see Act Sec. 405(f), below.

P.L. 114-113, §405(f), Div. Q, provides:

(f) EFFECTIVE DATE.—

(1) IN GENERAL.—The amendments made by this section shall apply to organizations which are described in section 501(c)(4) of the Internal Revenue Code of 1986 and organized after the date of the enactment of this Act.

(2) CERTAIN EXISTING ORGANIZATIONS.—In the case of any other organization described in section 501(c)(4) of such Code, the amendments made by this section shall apply to such organization only if, on or before the date of the enactment of this Act—

(A) such organization has not applied for a written determination of recognition as an organization described in section 501(c)(4) of such Code, and

(B) such organization has not filed at least one annual return or notice required under subsection (a)(1) or (i) (as the case may be) of section 6033 of such Code.

In the case of any organization to which the amendments made by this section apply by reason of the preceding sentence, such organization shall submit the notice required by section 506(a) of such Code, as added by this Act, not later than 180 days after the date of the enactment of this Act.

• **1996, Taxpayer Bill of Rights 2 (P.L. 104-168)**

P.L. 104-168, §1312(b):

Amended Code Sec. 6033 by redesignating subsection (f) as subsection (g) and by inserting after subsection (e) a new subsection (f). **Effective** for returns for tax years beginning after 7-30-96.

[Sec. 6033(g)]

(g) RETURNS REQUIRED BY POLITICAL ORGANIZATIONS.—

(1) IN GENERAL.—This section shall apply to a political organization (as defined by section 527(e)(1)) which has gross receipts of $25,000 or more for the taxable year. In the case of a political organization which is a qualified State or local political organization (as defined in section 527(e)(5)), the preceding sentence shall be applied by substituting "$100,000" for "$25,000".

(2) ANNUAL RETURNS.—Political organizations described in paragraph (1) shall file an annual return—

(A) containing the information required, and complying with the other requirements, under subsection (a)(1) for organizations exempt from taxation under section 501(a), with such modifications as the Secretary considers appropriate to require only information which is necessary for the purposes of carrying out section 527, and

(B) containing such other information as the Secretary deems necessary to carry out the provisions of this subsection.

(3) MANDATORY EXCEPTIONS FROM FILING.—Paragraph (2) shall not apply to an organization—

(A) which is a State or local committee of a political party, or political committee of a State or local candidate,

(B) which is a caucus or association of State or local officials,

(C) which is an authorized committee (as defined in section 301(6) of the Federal Election Campaign Act of 1971) of a candidate for Federal office,

(D) which is a national committee (as defined in section 301(14) of the Federal Election Campaign Act of 1971) of a political party,

(E) which is a United States House of Representatives or United States Senate campaign committee of a political party committee,

(F) which is required to report under the Federal Election Campaign Act of 1971 as a political committee (as defined in section 301(4) of such Act), or

(G) to which section 527 applies for the taxable year solely by reason of subsection (f)(1) of such section.

(4) DISCRETIONARY EXCEPTION.—The Secretary may relieve any organization required under paragraph (2) to file an information return from filing such a return if the Secretary determines that such filing is not necessary to the efficient administration of the internal revenue laws.

Amendments

• **2002 (P.L. 107-276)**

P.L. 107-276, §3(c):

Amended Code Sec. 6033(g). **Effective** as if included in the amendments made by P.L. 106-230 [effective for returns for tax years beginning after 6-30-2000.—CCH]. Prior to amendment, Code Sec. 6033(g) read as follows:

(g) RETURNS REQUIRED BY POLITICAL ORGANIZATIONS.—In the case of a political organization required to file a return under section 6012(a)(6)—

(1) such organization shall file a return—

(A) containing the information required, and complying with the other requirements, under subsection (a)(1) for organizations exempt from taxation under section 501(a), and

(B) containing such other information as the Secretary deems necessary to carry out the provisions of this subsection, and

(2) subsection (a)(2)(B) (relating to discretionary exceptions) shall apply with respect to such return.

• **2000 (P.L. 106-230)**

P.L. 106-230, §3(a)(2):

Amended Code Sec. 6033 by redesignating subsection (g) as subsection (h) and inserting after subsection (f) new subsection (g). **Effective** for returns for tax years beginning after 6-30-2000.

[Sec. 6033(h)]

(h) CONTROLLING ORGANIZATIONS.—Each controlling organization (within the meaning of section 512(b)(13)) which is subject to the requirements of subsection (a) shall include on the return required under subsection (a)—

(1) any interest, annuities, royalties, or rents received from each controlled entity (within the meaning of section 512(b)(13)),

(2) any loans made to each such controlled entity, and

(3) any transfers of funds between such controlling organization and each such controlled entity.

Amendments

• **2006, Pension Protection Act of 2006 (P.L. 109-280)**

P.L. 109-280, §1205(b)(1):

Amended Code Sec. 6033 by redesignating subsection (h) as subsection (i) and by inserting after subsection (g) a new subsection (h). **Effective** for returns the due date (determined without regard to extensions) of which is after 8-17-2006.

[Sec. 6033(i)]

(i) ADDITIONAL NOTIFICATION REQUIREMENTS.—Any organization the gross receipts of which in any taxable year result in such organization being referred to in subsection (a)(3)(A)(ii) or (a)(3)(B)—

RETURNS—INFORMATION

(1) shall furnish annually, in electronic form, and at such time and in such manner as the Secretary may by regulations prescribe, information setting forth—

 (A) the legal name of the organization,

 (B) any name under which such organization operates or does business,

 (C) the organization's mailing address and Internet web site address (if any),

 (D) the organization's taxpayer identification number,

 (E) the name and address of a principal officer, and

 (F) evidence of the continuing basis for the organization's exemption from the filing requirements under subsection (a)(1), and

(2) upon the termination of the existence of the organization, shall furnish notice of such termination.

Amendments

• **2006, Pension Protection Act of 2006 (P.L. 109-280)**

P.L. 109-280, §1223(a):

Amended Code Sec. 6033, as amended by this Act, by redesignating subsection (i) as subsection (j) and by inserting after subsection (h) a new subsection (i). **Effective** for notices and returns with respect to annual periods beginning after 2006.

P.L. 109-280, §1223(e)(1), provides:

(1) NOTICE REQUIREMENT.—The Secretary of the Treasury shall notify in a timely manner every organization described in section 6033(i) of the Internal Revenue Code of 1986 (as added by this section) of the requirement under such section 6033(i) and of the penalty established under section 6033(j) of such Code—

(A) by mail, in the case of any organization the identity and address of which is included in the list of exempt organizations maintained by the Secretary, and

(B) by Internet or other means of outreach, in the case of any other organization.

[Sec. 6033(j)]

(j) LOSS OF EXEMPT STATUS FOR FAILURE TO FILE RETURN OR NOTICE.—

(1) IN GENERAL.—

 (A) NOTICE.—If an organization described in subsection (a)(1) or (i) fails to file the annual return or notice required under either subsection for 2 consecutive years, the Secretary shall notify the organization—

  (i) that the Internal Revenue Service has no record of such a return or notice from such organization for 2 consecutive years, and

  (ii) about the revocation that will occur under subparagraph (B) if the organization fails to file such a return or notice by the due date for the next such return or notice required to be filed.

The notification under the preceding sentence shall include information about how to comply with the filing requirements under subsections (a)(1) and (i).

 (B) REVOCATION.—If an organization described in subsection (a)(1) or (i) fails to file an annual return or notice required under either subsection for 3 consecutive years, such organization's status as an organization exempt from tax under section 501(a) shall be considered revoked on and after the date set by the Secretary for the filing of the third annual return or notice. The Secretary shall publish and maintain a list of any organization the status of which is so revoked.

(2) APPLICATION NECESSARY FOR REINSTATEMENT.—Any organization the tax-exempt status of which is revoked under paragraph (1) must apply in order to obtain reinstatement of such status regardless of whether such organization was originally required to make such an application.

(3) RETROACTIVE REINSTATEMENT IF REASONABLE CAUSE SHOWN FOR FAILURE.—If, upon application for reinstatement of status as an organization exempt from tax under section 501(a), an organization described in paragraph (1) can show to the satisfaction of the Secretary evidence of reasonable cause for the failure described in such paragraph, the organization's exempt status may, in the discretion of the Secretary, be reinstated effective from the date of the revocation under such paragraph.

Amendments

• **2019, Taxpayer First Act (P.L. 116-25)**

P.L. 116-25, §3102(a):

Amended Code Sec. 6033(j)(1) by striking "If an organization" following "IN GENERAL.—"and inserting a new paragraph (A) and

"(B) REVOCATION.—If an organization".

Effective for failures to file returns or notices for 2 consecutive years if the return or notice for the second year is required to be filed after 12-31-2019.

• **2006, Pension Protection Act of 2006 (P.L. 109-280)**

P.L. 109-280, §1223(b):

Amended Code Sec. 6033, as amended by Act Sec. 1223(a), by redesignating subsection (j) as subsection (k) and by inserting after subsection (i) a new subsection (j). **Effective** for notices and returns with respect to annual periods beginning after 2006.

P.L. 109-280, §1223(e)(2), provides:

(2) LOSS OF STATUS PENALTY FOR FAILURE TO FILE RETURN.—The Secretary of the Treasury shall publicize, in a timely manner in appropriate forms and instructions and through other appropriate means, the penalty established under section 6033(j) of such Code for the failure to file a return under subsection (a)(1) or (i) of section 6033 of such Code.

[Sec. 6033(k)]

(k) ADDITIONAL PROVISIONS RELATING TO SPONSORING ORGANIZATIONS.—Every organization described in section 4966(d)(1) shall, on the return required under subsection (a) for the taxable year—

(1) list the total number of donor advised funds (as defined in section 4966(d)(2)) it owns at the end of such taxable year,

(2) indicate the aggregate value of assets held in such funds at the end of such taxable year, and

(3) indicate the aggregate contributions to and grants made from such funds during such taxable year.

Amendments

• **2006, Pension Protection Act of 2006 (P.L. 109-280)**

P.L. 109-280, §1235(a)(1):

Amended Code Sec. 6033, as amended by this Act, by redesignating subsection (k) as subsection (l) and by inserting after subsection (j) a new subsection (k). **Effective** for returns filed for tax years ending after 8-17-2006.

[Sec. 6033(l)]

(l) ADDITIONAL PROVISIONS RELATING TO SUPPORTING ORGANIZATIONS.—Every organization described in section 509(a)(3) shall, on the return required under subsection (a)—

(1) list the supported organizations (as defined in section 509(f)(3)) with respect to which such organization provides support,

(2) indicate whether the organization meets the requirements of clause (i), (ii), or (iii) of section 509(a)(3)(B), and

(3) certify that the organization meets the requirements of section 509(a)(3)(C).

Sec. 6033(i)(1)

RETURNS—INFORMATION

Amendments

• **2006, Pension Protection Act of 2006 (P.L. 109-280)**

P.L. 109-280, §1245(b):

Amended Code Sec. 6033, as amended by this Act, by redesignating subsection (l) as subsection (m) and by inserting after subsection (k) a new subsection (l). **Effective** for returns filed for tax years ending after 8-17-2006.

[Sec. 6033(m)]

(m) ADDITIONAL INFORMATION REQUIRED FROM CO-OP INSURERS.—An organization described in section 501(c)(29) shall include on the return required under subsection (a) the following information:

(1) The amount of the reserves required by each State in which the organization is licensed to issue qualified health plans.

(2) The amount of reserves on hand.

Amendments

• **2010, Patient Protection and Affordable Care Act (P.L. 111-148)**

P.L. 111-148, §1322(h)(2):

Amended Code Sec. 6033 by redesignating subsection (m) as subsection (n) and by inserting after subsection (l) a new subsection (m). **Effective** 3-23-2010.

[Sec. 6033(n)]

(n) MANDATORY ELECTRONIC FILING.—Any organization required to file a return under this section shall file such return in electronic form.

Amendments

• **2019, Taxpayer First Act (P.L. 116-25)**

P.L. 116-25, §3101(a):

Amended Code Sec. 6033 by redesignating subsection (n) as subsection (o) and by inserting after subsection (m) a new subsection (n). **Effective** generally for tax years beginning after 7-1-2019. For a transition rule, see Act Sec. 3101(d)(2), below.

P.L. 116-25, §3101(d)(2), provides:

(2) TRANSITIONAL RELIEF.—

(A) SMALL ORGANIZATIONS.—

(i) IN GENERAL.—In the case of any small organizations, or any other organizations for which the Secretary of the Treasury or the Secretary's delegate (hereafter referred to in this paragraph as the "Secretary") determines the application of the amendments made by this section would cause undue burden without a delay, the Secretary may delay the application of such amendments, but such delay shall not apply to any taxable year beginning on or after the date that is 2 years after the enactment of this Act.

(ii) SMALL ORGANIZATION.—For purposes of clause (i), the term "small organization" means any organization—

(I) the gross receipts of which for the taxable year are less than $200,000; and

(II) the aggregate gross assets of which at the end of the taxable year are less than $500,000.

(B) ORGANIZATIONS FILING FORM 990-T.—In the case of any organization described in section 511(a)(2) of the Internal Revenue Code of 1986 which is subject to the tax imposed by section 511(a)(1) of such Code on its unrelated business taxable income, or any organization required to file a return under section 6033 of such Code and include information under subsection (e) thereof, the Secretary may delay the application of the amendments made by this section, but such delay shall not apply to any taxable year beginning on or after the date that is 2 years after the enactment of this Act.

[Sec. 6033(o)]

(o) CROSS REFERENCE.—

For provisions relating to statements, etc., regarding exempt status of organizations, see section 6001.

For reporting requirements as to certain liquidations, dissolutions, terminations, and contractions, see section 6043(b). For provisions relating to penalties for failure to file a return required by this section, see section 6652(c).

For provisions relating to information required in connection with certain plans of deferred compensation, see section 6058.

Amendments

• **2019, Taxpayer First Act (P.L. 116-25)**

P.L. 116-25, §3101(a):

Amended Code Sec. 6033 by redesignating subsection (n) as subsection (o). **Effective** generally for tax years beginning after 7-1-2019.

• **2010, Patient Protection and Affordable Care Act (P.L. 111-148)**

P.L. 111-148, §1322(h)(2):

Amended Code Sec. 6033 by redesignating subsection (m) as subsection (n). **Effective** 3-23-2010.

• **2006, Pension Protection Act of 2006 (P.L. 109-280)**

P.L. 109-280, §1205(b)(1):

Amended Code Sec. 6033 by redesignating subsection (h) as subsection (i). **Effective** for returns the due date (determined without regard to extensions) of which is after 8-17-2006.

P.L. 109-280, §1223(a):

Amended Code Sec. 6033, as amended by this Act, by redesignating subsection (i) as subsection (j). **Effective** for notices and returns with respect to annual periods beginning after 2006.

P.L. 109-280, §1223(b):

Amended Code Sec. 6033, as amended by Act Sec. 1223(a), by redesignating subsection (j) as subsection (k). **Effective** for notices and returns with respect to annual periods beginning after 2006.

P.L. 109-280, §1235(a)(1):

Amended Code Sec. 6033, as amended by this Act, by redesignating subsection (k) as subsection (l). **Effective** for returns filed for tax years ending after 8-17-2006.

P.L. 109-280, §1245(b):

Amended Code Sec. 6033, as amended by this Act, by redesignating subsection (l) as subsection (m). **Effective** for returns filed for tax years ending after 8-17-2006.

• **2000 (P.L. 106-230)**

P.L. 106-230, §3(a)(2):

Amended Code Sec. 6033 by redesignating subsection (g) as subsection (h). **Effective** for returns for tax years beginning after 6-30-2000.

• **1996, Taxpayer Bill of Rights 2 (P.L. 104-168)**

P.L. 104-168, §1312(b):

Amended Code Sec. 6033 by redesignating subsection (f) as subsection (g). **Effective** for returns for tax years beginning after 7-30-96.

• **1993, Omnibus Budget Reconciliation Act of 1993 (P.L. 103-66)**

P.L. 103-66, §13222(c):

Amended Code Sec. 6033 by redesignating subsection (e) as subsection (f). **Effective** for amounts paid or incurred after 12-31-93.

• **1986, Tax Reform Act of 1986 (P.L. 99-514)**

P.L. 99-514, §1501(d)(1)(C):

Amended Code Sec. 6033(e) by striking out "section 6652(d)" and inserting in lieu thereof "section 6652(c)". **Effective** for returns the due date for which (determined without regard to extensions) is after 12-31-86.

• **1980 (P.L. 96-603)**

P.L. 96-603, §1(a):

Redesignated Code Sec. 6033(c) as 6033(e). **Effective** for tax years beginning after 1980.

• **1974, Employee Retirement Income Security Act of 1974 (P.L. 93-406)**

P.L. 93-406, §1031(c)(3):

Amended Code Sec. 6033(c) by adding the last sentence. **Effective** 9-2-74.

• **1969, Tax Reform Act of 1969 (P.L. 91-172)**

P.L. 91-172, §101(j)(31):

Amended Code Sec. 6033(c) by adding the second paragraph. **Effective** for tax years beginning after 12-31-69.

RETURNS—INFORMATION

[Sec. 6034]

SEC. 6034. RETURNS BY CERTAIN TRUSTS.

[Sec. 6034(a)]

(a) SPLIT-INTEREST TRUSTS.—Every trust described in section 4947(a)(2) shall furnish such information with respect to the taxable year as the Secretary may by forms or regulations require.

[Sec. 6034(b)]

(b) TRUSTS CLAIMING CERTAIN CHARITABLE DEDUCTIONS.—

(1) IN GENERAL.—Every trust not required to file a return under subsection (a) but claiming a deduction under section 642(c) for the taxable year shall furnish such information with respect to such taxable year as the Secretary may by forms or regulations prescribe, including—

(A) the amount of the deduction taken under section 642(c) within such year,

(B) the amount paid out within such year which represents amounts for which deductions under section 642(c) have been taken in prior years,

(C) the amount for which such deductions have been taken in prior years but which has not been paid out at the beginning of such year,

(D) the amount paid out of principal in the current and prior years for the purposes described in section 642(c),

(E) the total income of the trust within such year and the expenses attributable thereto, and

(F) a balance sheet showing the assets, liabilities, and net worth of the trust as of the beginning of such year.

(2) EXCEPTIONS.—Paragraph (1) shall not apply to a trust for any taxable year if—

(A) all the net income for such year, determined under the applicable principles of the law of trusts, is required to be distributed currently to the beneficiaries, or

(B) the trust is described in section 4947(a)(1).

Amendments

• **2006, Pension Protection Act of 2006 (P.L. 109-280)**

P.L. 109-280, §1201(b)(1):

Amended Code Sec. 6034. **Effective** for returns for tax years beginning after 12-31-2006. Prior to amendment, Code Sec. 6034 read as follows—

SEC. 6034. RETURNS BY TRUSTS DESCRIBED IN SECTION 4947(a)(2) OR CLAIMING CHARITABLE DEDUCTIONS UNDER SECTION 642(c).

[Sec. 6034(a)]

(a) GENERAL RULE.—Every trust described in section 4947(a)(2) or claiming a charitable, etc., deduction under section 642(c) for the taxable year shall furnish such information with respect to such taxable year as the Secretary may by forms or regulations prescribe, including—

(1) the amount of the charitable, etc., deduction taken under section 642(c) within such year,

(2) the amount paid out within such year which represents amounts for which charitable, etc., deductions under section 642(c) have been taken in prior years,

(3) the amount for which charitable, etc., deductions have been taken in prior years but which has not been paid out at the beginning of such year,

(4) the amount paid out of principal in the current and prior years for charitable, etc., purposes,

(5) the total income of the trust within such year and the expenses attributable thereto, and

(6) a balance sheet showing the assets, liabilities, and net worth of the trust as of the beginning of such year.

Amendments

• **1980 (P.L. 96-603)**

P.L. 96-603, §1(d)(1):

Amended Code Sec. 6034(a) by striking out "section 4947(a)" and inserting in lieu thereof "section 4947(a)(2)", and amended the title of Code Sec. 6034 by striking out "SECTION 4947(a)" and inserting in lieu thereof "SECTION 4947(a)(2)". **Effective** for tax years beginning after 1980.

• **1976, Tax Reform Act of 1976 (P.L. 94-455)**

P.L. 94-455, §1906(b)(13)(A):

Amended 1954 Code by substituting "Secretary" for "Secretary or his delegate" each place it appeared. **Effective** 2-1-77.

• **1969, Tax Reform Act of 1969 (P.L. 91-172)**

P.L. 91-172, §101(j)(32), (33):

Amended the matter preceding paragraph (2) in Code Sec. 6034. **Effective** for tax years beginning after 12-31-69. Prior to amendment, Code Sec. 6034 read as follows:

SEC. 6034. RETURNS BY TRUSTS CLAIMING CHARITABLE DEDUCTIONS UNDER SECTION 642(c).

(a) General Rule.—Every trust claiming a charitable, etc., deduction under section 642(c) for the taxable year shall furnish such information with respect to such taxable year as the Secretary or his delegate may by forms or regulations prescribe, setting forth—

(1) the amount of the charitable, etc., deduction taken under section 642(c) within such year (showing separately the amount of such deduction which was paid out and the amount which was permanently set aside for charitable, etc., purposes during such year),

[Sec. 6034(b)]

(b) EXCEPTIONS.—This section shall not apply in the case of a taxable year if all the net income for such year, determined under the applicable principles of the law of trusts, is required to be distributed currently to the beneficiaries. This section shall not apply in the case of a trust described in section 4947(a)(1).

Amendments

• **1980 (P.L. 96-603)**

P.L. 96-603, §1(d)(1):

Amended Code Sec. 6034(b) by striking out "EXCEPTION" in the heading and inserting in lieu thereof "EXCEPTIONS" and by adding a new last sentence. **Effective** for tax years beginning after 1980.

[Sec. 6034(c)]

(c) CROSS REFERENCE.—

For provisions relating to penalties for failure to file a return required by this section, see section 6652(c).

Amendments

• **1986, Tax Reform Act of 1986 (P.L. 99-514)**

P.L. 99-514, §1501(d)(1)(C):

Amended Code Sec. 6034(c) by striking out "section 6652(d)" and inserting in lieu thereof "section 6652(c)". **Effective** for returns the due date for which (determined without regard to extensions) is after 12-31-86.

• **1969, Tax Reform Act of 1969 (P.L. 91-172)**

P.L. 91-172, §101(j)(34):

Added Code Sec. 6034(c). **Effective** for tax years beginning after 12-31-69.

[Sec. 6034A]

SEC. 6034A. INFORMATION TO BENEFICIARIES OF ESTATES AND TRUSTS.

[Sec. 6034A(a)]

(a) GENERAL RULE.—The fiduciary of any estate or trust required to file a return under section 6012(a) for any taxable year shall, on or before the date on which such return was required to be filed, furnish to each beneficiary (or nominee thereof)—

(1) who receives a distribution from such estate or trust with respect to such taxable year, or

(2) to whom any item with respect to such taxable year is allocated,

a statement containing such information required to be shown on such return as the Secretary may prescribe.

RETURNS—INFORMATION

Amendments
• **1986, Tax Reform Act of 1986 (P.L. 99-514)**

P.L. 99-514, §1501(c)(15)(A)-(C):
Amended Code Sec. 6034A(a) by striking out "making the return required to be filed" and inserting in lieu thereof "required to file a return", by striking out "was filed" and inserting in lieu thereof "was required to be filed", and by striking out "shown on such return" and inserting in lieu thereof "required to be shown on such return". **Effective** for returns the due date for which (determined without regard to extensions) is after 12-31-86.

P.L. 99-514, §1875(d)(3)[4](A)(i)-(iii):
Amended Code Sec. 6034A by striking out "The fiduciary" and inserting in lieu thereof "(a) General Rule.—The fiduciary", by striking out "each beneficiary" and inserting in lieu thereof "each beneficiary (or nominee thereof)", and by adding at the end of Code Sec. 6034A subsection (b). **Effective** for tax years of estates and trusts beginning after 10-22-86.

[Sec. 6034A(b)]

(b) NOMINEE REPORTING.—Any person who holds an interest in an estate or trust as a nominee for another person—

(1) shall furnish to the estate or trust, in the manner prescribed by the Secretary, the name and address of such other person, and any other information for the taxable year as the Secretary may by form and regulations prescribe, and

(2) shall furnish in the manner prescribed by the Secretary to such other person the information provided by the estate or trust under subsection (a).

Amendments
• **1984, Deficit Reduction Act of 1984 (P.L. 98-369)**

P.L. 98-369, §714(q)(1):
Added Code Sec. 6034A. **Effective** for tax years beginning after 12-31-84.

[Sec. 6034A(c)]

(c) BENEFICIARY'S RETURN MUST BE CONSISTENT WITH ESTATE OR TRUST RETURN OR SECRETARY NOTIFIED OF INCONSISTENCY.—

(1) IN GENERAL.—A beneficiary of any estate or trust to which subsection (a) applies shall, on such beneficiary's return, treat any reported item in a manner which is consistent with the treatment of such item on the applicable entity's return.

(2) NOTIFICATION OF INCONSISTENT TREATMENT.—

(A) IN GENERAL.—In the case of any reported item, if—

(i)(I) the applicable entity has filed a return but the beneficiary's treatment on such beneficiary's return is (or may be) inconsistent with the treatment of the item on the applicable entity's return, or

(II) the applicable entity has not filed a return, and

(ii) the beneficiary files with the Secretary a statement identifying the inconsistency,

paragraph (1) shall not apply to such item.

(B) BENEFICIARY RECEIVING INCORRECT INFORMATION.—A beneficiary shall be treated as having complied with clause (ii) of subparagraph (A) with respect to a reported item if the beneficiary—

(i) demonstrates to the satisfaction of the Secretary that the treatment of the reported item on the beneficiary's return is consistent with the treatment of the item on the statement furnished under subsection (a) to the beneficiary by the applicable entity, and

(ii) elects to have this paragraph apply with respect to that item.

(3) EFFECT OF FAILURE TO NOTIFY.—In any case—

(A) described in subparagraph (A)(i)(I) of paragraph (2), and

(B) in which the beneficiary does not comply with subparagraph (A)(ii) of paragraph (2), any adjustment required to make the treatment of the items by such beneficiary consistent with the treatment of the items on the applicable entity's return shall be treated as arising out of mathematical or clerical errors and assessed according to section 6213(b)(1). Paragraph (2) of section 6213(b) shall not apply to any assessment referred to in the preceding sentence.

(4) DEFINITIONS.—For purposes of this subsection—

(A) REPORTED ITEM.—The term "reported item" means any item for which information is required to be furnished under subsection (a).

(B) APPLICABLE ENTITY.—The term "applicable entity" means the estate or trust of which the taxpayer is the beneficiary.

(5) ADDITION TO TAX FOR FAILURE TO COMPLY WITH SECTION.—For addition to tax in the case of a beneficiary's negligence in connection with, or disregard of, the requirements of this section, see part II of subchapter A of chapter 68.

Amendments
• **1997, Taxpayer Relief Act of 1997 (P.L. 105-34)**

P.L. 105-34, §1027(a):
Amended Code Sec. 6034A by adding at the end a new subsection (c). **Effective** for returns of beneficiaries and owners filed after 8-5-97.

[Sec. 6035]

SEC. 6035. BASIS INFORMATION TO PERSONS ACQUIRING PROPERTY FROM DECEDENT.

[Sec. 6035(a)]

(a) INFORMATION WITH RESPECT TO PROPERTY ACQUIRED FROM DECEDENTS.—

(1) IN GENERAL.—The executor of any estate required to file a return under section 6018(a) shall furnish to the Secretary and to each person acquiring any interest in property included in the decedent's gross estate for Federal estate tax purposes a statement identifying the value of each interest in such property as reported on such return and such other information with respect to such interest as the Secretary may prescribe.

(2) STATEMENTS BY BENEFICIARIES.—Each person required to file a return under section 6018(b) shall furnish to the Secretary and to each other person who holds a legal or beneficial interest in the property to which such return relates a statement identifying the information described in paragraph (1).

(3) TIME FOR FURNISHING STATEMENT.—

(A) IN GENERAL.—Each statement required to be furnished under paragraph (1) or (2) shall be furnished at such time as the Secretary may prescribe, but in no case at a time later than the earlier of—

(i) the date which is 30 days after the date on which the return under section 6018 was required to be filed (including extensions, if any), or

(ii) the date which is 30 days after the date such return is filed.

RETURNS—INFORMATION

(B) ADJUSTMENTS.—In any case in which there is an adjustment to the information required to be included on a statement filed under paragraph (1) or (2) after such statement has been filed, a supplemental statement under such paragraph shall be filed not later than the date which is 30 days after such adjustment is made.

[Sec. 6035(b)]

(b) REGULATIONS.—The Secretary shall prescribe such regulations as necessary to carry out this section, including regulations relating to—

(1) the application of this section to property with regard to which no estate tax return is required to be filed, and

(2) situations in which the surviving joint tenant or other recipient may have better information than the executor regarding the basis or fair market value of the property.

Amendments

• **2015, Surface Transportation and Veterans Health Care Choice Improvement Act of 2015 (P.L. 114-41)**

P.L. 114-41, § 2004(b)(1):

Amended subpart A of part III of subchapter A of chapter 61 by inserting after Code Sec. 6034A a new Code Sec. 6035. **Effective** for property with respect to which an estate tax return is filed after 7-31-2015.

[Sec. 6035—Repealed]

Amendments

• **2004, American Jobs Creation Act of 2004 (P.L. 108-357)**

P.L. 108-357, § 413(c)(26):

Repealed Code Sec. 6035. **Effective** for tax years of foreign corporations beginning after 12-31-2004 and for tax years of United States shareholders with or within which such tax years of foreign corporations end. Prior to repeal, Code Sec. 6035 read as follows:

SEC. 6035. RETURNS OF OFFICERS, DIRECTORS, AND SHAREHOLDERS OF FOREIGN PERSONAL HOLDING COMPANIES.

[Sec. 6035(a)]

(a) GENERAL RULE.—Each United States citizen or resident who is an officer, director, or 10-percent shareholder of a corporation which was a foreign personal holding company (as defined in section 552) for any taxable year shall file a return with respect to such taxable year setting forth—

(1) the shareholder information required by subsection (b),

(2) the income information required by subsection (c), and

(3) such other information with respect to such corporation as the Secretary shall by forms or regulations prescribe as necessary for carrying out the purposes of this title.

[Sec. 6035(b)]

(b) SHAREHOLDER INFORMATION.—The shareholder information required by this subsection with respect to any taxable year shall be—

(1) the name and address of each person who at any time during such taxable year held any share in the corporation,

(2) a description of each class of shares and the total number of shares of such class outstanding at the close of the taxable year,

(3) the number of shares of each class held by each person, and

(4) any changes in the holdings of shares during the taxable year.

For purposes of paragraphs (1), (3), and (4), the term "share" includes any security convertible into a share in the corporation and any option granted by the corporation with respect to any share in the corporation.

[Sec. 6035(c)]

(c) INCOME INFORMATION.—The income information required by this subsection for any taxable year shall be the gross income, deductions, credits, taxable income, and undistributed foreign personal holding company income of the corporation for the taxable year.

[Sec. 6035(d)]

(d) TIME AND MANNER FOR FURNISHING INFORMATION.—The information required under subsection (a) shall be furnished at such time and in such manner as the Secretary shall by forms and regulations prescribe.

[Sec. 6035(e)]

(e) DEFINITION AND SPECIAL RULES.—

(1) 10-PERCENT SHAREHOLDER.—For purposes of this section, the term "10-percent shareholder" means any individual who owns directly or indirectly (within the meaning of section 554) 10 percent or more in value of the outstanding stock of a foreign corporation.

(2) TIME FOR MAKING DETERMINATIONS.—

(A) IN GENERAL.—Except as provided in subparagraph (B), the determination of whether any person is an officer, director, or 10-percent shareholder with respect to any foreign corporation shall be made as of the date on which the return is required to be filed.

(B) SPECIAL RULE.—If after the application of subparagraph (A) no person is required to file a return under subsection (a) with respect to any foreign corporation for any taxable year, the determination of whether any person is an officer, director, or 10-percent shareholder with respect to such foreign corporation shall be made on the last day of such taxable year on which there was such a person who was a United States citizen or resident.

(3) 2 OR MORE PERSONS REQUIRED TO FURNISH INFORMATION WITH RESPECT TO SAME FOREIGN CORPORATION.—If, but for this paragraph, 2 or more persons would be required to furnish information under subsection (a) with respect to the same foreign corporation for the same taxable year, the Secretary may by regulations provide that such information shall be required only from 1 person.

Amendments

• **1982, Tax Equity and Fiscal Responsibility Act of 1982 (P.L. 97-248)**

P.L. 97-248, § 340(a):

Amended Code Sec. 6035. **Effective** for tax years beginning after the date of enactment. Prior to amendment, Code Sec. 6035 read as follows:

SEC. 6035. RETURNS OF OFFICERS, DIRECTORS, AND SHAREHOLDERS OF FOREIGN PERSONAL HOLDING COMPANIES.

(a) OFFICERS AND DIRECTORS.—

(1) MONTHLY RETURNS.—On the 15th day of each month each individual who on such day is an officer or a director of a foreign corporation which, with respect to its taxable year preceding the taxable year in which such month occurs, was a foreign personal holding company (as defined in section 552), shall make a return setting forth with respect to the preceding calendar month the name and address of each shareholder, the class and number of shares held by each, together with any changes in stockholdings during such period, the name and address of any holder of securities convertible into stock of such corporation, and such other information with respect to the stock and securities of the corporation as the Secretary shall by forms or regulations prescribe as necessary for carrying out the provisions of this title. The Secretary may by regulations prescribe, as the period with respect to which returns shall be made, a longer period than a month. In such case the return shall be due on the 15th day of the succeeding period, and shall be made by the individuals who on such day are officers or directors of the corporation.

(2) ANNUAL RETURNS.—On the 60th day after the close of the taxable year of a foreign personal holding company (as defined in section 552), each individual who on such 60th day is an officer or director of the corporation shall make a return setting forth—

(A) in complete detail the gross income, deductions and credits, taxable income, and undistributed foreign personal holding company income of such foreign personal holding company for such taxable year; and

(B) the same information with respect to such taxable year as is required in paragraph (1), except that if all the required returns with respect to such year have been filed under paragraph (1), no information under this subparagraph need be set forth in the return filed under this paragraph.

(b) SHAREHOLDERS.—

(1) MONTHLY RETURNS.—On the 15th day of each month each United States shareholder, by or for whom 50 percent or more in value of the outstanding stock of a foreign corporation is owned directly or indirectly (including, in the case of an individual, stock owned by the members of his family as defined in section 544(a)(2)), if such foreign corporation with respect to its taxable year preceding the taxable year in which such month occurs was a foreign personal holding company (as defined in section 552), shall make a return setting forth with respect to the preceding calendar month the name and address of each shareholder, the class and number of shares held by each, together with any changes in stockholdings during such period, the name and address of any holder of securities convertible into stock of such corporation, and such other information with respect to the stock and securities of the corporation as the Secretary shall by forms or regulations prescribe as necessary for carrying out the provisions of this title. The Secretary may by regulations prescribe, as the period with respect to which returns shall be made, a longer period than a month. In such case the return shall be due on the 15th day of the succeeding period, and shall be made by the persons who on such day are United States shareholders.

(2) ANNUAL RETURNS.—On the 60th day after the close of the taxable year of a foreign personal holding company (as defined in section 552) each United States shareholder by or for whom on such 60th day 50 percent or more in value of the outstanding stock of such company is owned directly or indirectly (including, in the case of an individual, stock owned by members of his family as defined in section 544(a)(2)) shall make a return setting forth the same information with respect to such taxable year as is required in paragraph (1), except that, if all the required returns with respect to such year have been made under paragraph (1), no return shall be required under this paragraph.

• **1976, Tax Reform Act of 1976 (P.L. 94-455)**

P.L. 94-455, § 1906(b)(13)(A):

Amended 1954 Code by substituting "Secretary" for "Secretary or his delegate" each place it appeared. **Effective** 2-1-77.

Sec. 6035(a)(3)(B)

RETURNS—INFORMATION

[Sec. 6036]
SEC. 6036. NOTICE OF QUALIFICATION AS EXECUTOR OR RECEIVER.

Every receiver, trustee in a case under title 11 of the United States Code, assignee for benefit of creditors, or other like fiduciary, and every executor (as defined in section 2203), shall give notice of his qualification as such to the Secretary in such manner and at such time as may be required by regulations of the Secretary. The Secretary may by regulation provide such exemptions from the requirements of this section as the Secretary deems proper.

Amendments

• **1980, Bankruptcy Tax Act of 1980 (P.L. 96-589)**

P.L. 96-589, §6(i)(6):

Amended Code Sec. 6036 by striking out "trustee in bankruptcy" and inserting in lieu thereof "trustee in a case under title 11 of the United States Code". **Effective** 10-1-79 but inapplicable to any proceeding under the Bankruptcy Act commenced before that date.

• **1976, Tax Reform Act of 1976 (P.L. 94-455)**

P.L. 94-455, §1906(b)(13)(A):

Amended 1954 Code by substituting "Secretary" for "Secretary or his delegate" each place it appeared. **Effective** 2-1-77.

[Sec. 6037]
SEC. 6037. RETURN OF S CORPORATION.

[Sec. 6037(a)]

(a) IN GENERAL.—Every S corporation shall make a return for each taxable year, stating specifically the items of its gross income and the deductions allowable by subtitle A, the names and addresses of all persons owning stock in the corporation at any time during the taxable year, the number of shares of stock owned by each shareholder at all times during the taxable year, the amount of money and other property distributed by the corporation during the taxable year to each shareholder, the date of each such distribution, each shareholder's pro rata share of each item of the corporation for the taxable year, and such other information, for the purpose of carrying out the provisions of subchapter S of chapter 1, as the Secretary may by forms and regulations prescribe. Any return filed pursuant to this section shall, for purposes of chapter 66 (relating to limitations), be treated as a return filed by the corporation under section 6012.

[Sec. 6037(b)]

(b) COPIES TO SHAREHOLDERS.—Each S corporation required to file a return under subsection (a) for any taxable year shall (on or before the day on which the return for such taxable year was filed) furnish to each person who is a shareholder at any time during such taxable year a copy of such information shown on such return as may be required by regulations.

Amendments

• **1984, Deficit Reduction Act of 1984 (P.L. 98-369)**

P.L. 98-369, §714(q)(2):

Amended Code Sec. 6037 by striking out "Every" and inserting in lieu thereof "(a) In General.—Every" and by adding subsection (b). **Effective** for tax years beginning after 12-31-84.

• **1982, Subchapter S Revision Act of 1982 (P.L. 97-354)**

P.L. 97-354, §5(a)(39)(A):

Amended Code Sec. 6037 by striking out "Every electing small business corporation (as defined in section 1371(b))" and inserting in lieu thereof "Every S corporation", by striking out "and such other information" and inserting in lieu thereof "each shareholder's pro rata share of each item of the corporation for the taxable year, and such other information", and by striking out "ELECTING SMALL BUSINESS CORPORATION" in the section heading and inserting in lieu thereof "S CORPORATION". **Effective** for tax years beginning after 12-31-82.

• **1976, Tax Reform Act of 1976 (P.L. 94-455)**

P.L. 94-455, §1906(a)(3):

Substituted "section 1371(b)" for "section 1371(a)(2)". **Effective** for tax years beginning after 12-31-76.

P.L. 94-455, §1906(b)(13)(A):

Amended 1954 Code by substituting "Secretary" for "Secretary or his delegate" each place it appeared. **Effective** 2-1-77.

• **1958, Technical Amendments Act of 1958 (P.L. 85-866)**

P.L. 85-866, §64(c):

Redesignated Code Sec. 6037 as Code Sec. 6038 and added new Code Sec. 6037. **Effective** for tax years beginning after 12-31-57.

[Sec. 6037(c)]

(c) SHAREHOLDER'S RETURN MUST BE CONSISTENT WITH CORPORATE RETURN OR SECRETARY NOTIFIED OF INCONSISTENCY.—

(1) IN GENERAL.—A shareholder of an S corporation shall, on such shareholder's return, treat a subchapter S item in a manner which is consistent with the treatment of such item on the corporate return.

(2) NOTIFICATION OF INCONSISTENT TREATMENT.—

(A) IN GENERAL.—In the case of any subchapter S item, if—

(i)(I) the corporation has filed a return but the shareholder's treatment on his return is (or may be) inconsistent with the treatment of the item on the corporate return, or

(II) the corporation has not filed a return, and

(ii) the shareholder files with the Secretary a statement identifying the inconsistency,

paragraph (1) shall not apply to such item.

(B) SHAREHOLDER RECEIVING INCORRECT INFORMATION.—A shareholder shall be treated as having complied with clause (ii) of subparagraph (A) with respect to a subchapter S item if the shareholder—

(i) demonstrates to the satisfaction of the Secretary that the treatment of the subchapter S item on the shareholder's return is consistent with the treatment of the item on the schedule furnished to the shareholder by the corporation, and

(ii) elects to have this paragraph apply with respect to that item.

(3) EFFECT OF FAILURE TO NOTIFY.—In any case—

(A) described in subparagraph (A)(i)(I) of paragraph (2), and

(B) in which the shareholder does not comply with subparagraph (A)(ii) of paragraph (2),

any adjustment required to make the treatment of the items by such shareholder consistent with the treatment of the items on the corporate return shall be treated as arising out of mathematical or clerical errors and assessed according to section 6213(b)(1). Paragraph (2) of section 6213(b) shall not apply to any assessment referred to in the preceding sentence.

(4) SUBCHAPTER S ITEM.—For purposes of this subsection, the term "subchapter S item" means any item of an S corporation to the extent that regulations prescribed by the Secretary provide that, for purposes of this subtitle, such item is more appropriately determined at the corporation level than at the shareholder level.

(5) ADDITION TO TAX FOR FAILURE TO COMPLY WITH SECTION.—For addition to tax in the case of a shareholder's negligence in connection with, or disregard of, the requirements of this section, see part II of subchapter A of chapter 68.

RETURNS—INFORMATION

Amendments

• **1996, Small Business Job Protection Act of 1996 (P.L. 104-188)**

P.L. 104-188, § 1307(c)(2):

Amended Code Sec. 6037 by adding at the end a new subsection (c). **Effective** for tax years beginning after 12-31-96.

[Sec. 6038]

SEC. 6038. INFORMATION REPORTING WITH RESPECT TO CERTAIN FOREIGN CORPORATIONS AND PARTNERSHIPS.

[Sec. 6038(a)]

(a) REQUIREMENT.—

(1) IN GENERAL.—Every United States person shall furnish, with respect to any foreign business entity which such person controls, such information as the Secretary may prescribe relating to—

(A) the name, the principal place of business, and the nature of business of such entity, and the country under whose laws such entity is incorporated (or organized in the case of a partnership);

(B) in the case of a foreign corporation, its post-1986 undistributed earnings (as defined in section 902(c));

(C) a balance sheet for such entity listing assets, liabilities, and capital;

(D) transactions between such entity and—

(i) such person,

(ii) any corporation or partnership which such person controls, and

(iii) any United States person owning, at the time the transaction takes place—

(I) in the case of a foreign corporation, 10 percent or more of the value of any class of stock outstanding of such corporation, and

(II) in the case of a foreign partnership, at least a 10-percent interest in such partnership; and

(E) (i) in the case of a foreign corporation, a description of the various classes of stock outstanding, and a list showing the name and address of, and number of shares held by, each United States person who is a shareholder of record owning at any time during the annual accounting period 5 percent or more in value of any class of stock outstanding of such foreign corporation, and

(ii) information comparable to the information described in clause (i) in the case of a foreign partnership.

The Secretary may also require the furnishing of any other information which is similar or related in nature to that specified in the preceding sentence or which the Secretary determines to be appropriate to carry out the provisions of this title.

(2) PERIOD FOR WHICH INFORMATION IS TO BE FURNISHED, ETC.—The information required under paragraph (1) shall be furnished for the annual accounting period of the foreign business entity ending with or within the United States person's taxable year. The information so required shall be furnished at such time and in such manner as the Secretary shall prescribe.

(3) LIMITATION.—No information shall be required to be furnished under this subsection with respect to any foreign business entity for any annual accounting period unless the Secretary has prescribed the furnishing of such information on or before the first day of such annual accounting period.

(4) INFORMATION REQUIRED FROM CERTAIN SHAREHOLDERS IN CERTAIN CASES.—If any foreign corporation is treated as a controlled foreign corporation for any purpose under subpart F of part III of subchapter N of chapter 1, the Secretary may require any United States person treated as a United States shareholder of such corporation for any purpose under subpart F to furnish the information required under paragraph (1).

(5) INFORMATION REQUIRED FROM 10-PERCENT PARTNER OF CONTROLLED FOREIGN PARTNERSHIP.—In the case of a foreign partnership which is controlled by United States persons holding at least 10-percent interests (but not by any one United States person), the Secretary may require each United States person who holds a 10-percent interest in such partnership to furnish information relating to such partnership, including information relating to such partner's ownership interests in the partnership and allocations to such partner of partnership items.

Amendments

• **1998, IRS Restructuring and Reform Act of 1998 (P.L. 105-206)**

P.L. 105-206, § 6011(f)(1):

Amended Code Sec. 6038(a)(2) by striking "by regulations" following "Secretary shall". **Effective** as if included in the provision of P.L. 105-34 to which it relates [**effective** for annual accounting periods beginning after 8-5-97.—CCH].

P.L. 105-206, § 6011(f)(2):

Amended Code Sec. 6038(a)(3) by striking "such information" and all that follows through the period and inserting "the Secretary has prescribed the furnishing of such information on or before the first day of such annual accounting period." **Effective** as if included in the provision of P.L. 105-34 to which it relates [**effective** for annual accounting periods beginning after 8-5-97.—CCH]. Prior to amendment, Code Sec. 6038(a)(3) read as follows:

(3) LIMITATION.—No information shall be required to be furnished under this subsection with respect to any foreign business entity for any annual accounting period unless such information was required to be furnished under regulations in effect on the first day of such annual accounting period.

• **1997, Taxpayer Relief Act of 1997 (P.L. 105-34)**

P.L. 105-34, § 1142(a):

Amended so much of Code Sec. 6038(a) as precedes paragraph (2). **Effective** for annual accounting periods beginning after 8-5-97. Prior to amendment, that portion of Code Sec. 6038(a) read as follows:

SEC. 6038. INFORMATION WITH RESPECT TO CERTAIN FOREIGN CORPORATIONS.

(a) REQUIREMENT.—

(1) IN GENERAL.—Every United States person shall furnish, with respect to any foreign corporation which such person controls (within the meaning of subsection (e)(1)), such information as the Secretary may prescribe by regulations relating to—

(A) the name, the principal place of business, and the nature of business of such foreign corporation, and the country under whose laws incorporated;

(B) the post-1986 undistributed earnings (as defined in section 902(c)) of such foreign corporation;

(C) a balance sheet for such foreign corporation listing assets, liabilities, and capital;

(D) transactions between such foreign corporation and—

(i) such person,

(ii) any other corporation which such person controls, and

(iii) any United States person owning, at the time the transaction takes place, 10 percent or more of the value of any class of stock outstanding of such foreign corporation; and

(E) a description of the various classes of stock outstanding, and a list showing the name and address of, and number of shares held by, each United States person who is a shareholder of record owning at any time during the annual accounting period 5 percent or more in value of any class of stock outstanding of such foreign corporation.

The Secretary may also require the furnishing of any other information which is similar or related in nature to that specified in the preceding sentence or which the Secretary determines to be appropriate to carry out the provisions of this title.

P.L. 105-34, § 1142(d):

Amended Code Sec. 6038(a) by adding at the end a new paragraph (5). **Effective** for annual accounting periods beginning after 8-5-97.

P.L. 105-34, § 1142(e)(1)(A):

Amended Code Sec. 6038(a)(2) and (3) by striking "foreign corporation" each place it appears and inserting "foreign business entity". **Effective** for annual accounting periods beginning after 8-5-97.

• **1996, Small Business Job Protection Act of 1996 (P.L. 104-188)**

P.L. 104-188, § 1704(f)(5)(A):

Amended Code Sec. 6038(a)(1) by striking ", and" at the end of subparagraph (E) and inserting a period, and by striking subparagraph (F). **Effective** 8-20-96. Prior to amendment, Code Sec. 6038(a)(1)(F) read as follows:

(F) such information as the Secretary may require for purposes of carrying out the provisions of section 453C.

RETURNS—INFORMATION

- **1989, Omnibus Budget Reconciliation Act of 1989 (P.L. 101-239)**

P.L. 101-239, §7712(a)(1):

Amended Code Sec. 6038(a) by adding at the end thereof a new paragraph (4). **Effective** for returns and statements the due date for which (determined without regard to extensions) is after 12-31-89.

P.L. 101-239, §7712(a)(2):

Amended Code Sec. 6038(a)(1) by inserting "or which the Secretary determines to be appropriate to carry out the provisions of this title," before the period at the end thereof. **Effective** for returns and statements the due date for which (determined without regard to extensions) is after 12-31-89.

- **1986, Tax Reform Act of 1986 (P.L. 99-514)**

P.L. 99-514, §1202(c)(1):

Amended Code Sec. 6038(a)(1)(B). **Effective** for distributions by foreign corporations out of, and to inclusions under Code Sec. 951(a) attributable to, earnings and profits for tax years beginning after 12-31-86. Prior to amendment, Code Sec. 6038(a)(1)(B) read as follows:

(B) the accumulated profits (as defined in section 902(c)) of such foreign corporation, including the items of income (whether or not included in gross income under chapter 1), deductions (whether or not allowed in computing taxable income under chapter 1), and any other items taken into account in computing such accumulated profits;

P.L. 99-514, §1245(b)(5):

Amended Code Sec. 6038(a)(1) by striking out "and" at the end of subparagraph (D), by striking out the period at end of subparagraph (E) and inserting in lieu thereof ", and", and by inserting after subparagraph (E) new subparagraph (F). **Effective** for tax years beginning after 12-31-86.

- **1982, Tax Equity and Fiscal Responsibility Act of 1982 (P.L. 97-248)**

P.L. 97-248, §338(c)(2):

Amended paragraph (1) of Code Sec. 6038(a) by striking out "within the meaning of subsection (d)(1)" and inserting "within the meaning of subsection (e)(1)". **Effective** with respect to information for annual accounting periods ending after 9-3-82.

- **1976, Tax Reform Act of 1976 (P.L. 94-455)**

P.L. 94-455, §1906(b)(13)(A):

Amended 1954 Code by substituting "Secretary" for "Secretary or his delegate" each place it appeared. **Effective** 2-1-77.

- **1962, Revenue Act of 1962 (P.L. 87-834)**

P.L. 87-834, §20:

Amended Code Sec. 6038(a). **Effective** with respect to annual accounting periods of foreign corporations beginning after 12-31-62. Prior to amendment, Sec. 6038(a) read as follows:

(a) REQUIREMENT.—

(1) IN GENERAL.—A domestic corporation shall furnish, with respect to any foreign corporation which it controls (within the meaning of subsection (c)(1)) and with respect to any foreign subsidiary of any such foreign corporation (within the meaning of subsection (c)(2)), such information as the Secretary or his delegate may prescribe by regulations relating to—

(A) the name, the principal place of business, and the nature of business of such foreign corporation or foreign subsidiary, and the country under whose laws incorporated;

(B) the accumulated profits (as defined in section 902(c)) of such foreign corporation or foreign subsidiary, including the items of income (whether or not included in gross income under chapter 1), deductions (whether or not allowed in computing taxable income under chapter 1), and any other items taken into account in computing such accumulated profits;

(C) a balance sheet for such foreign corporation or foreign subsidiary, listing assets, liabilities, and capital;

(D) transactions between such foreign corporation or foreign subsidiary and—

(i) any foreign corporation controlled by the domestic corporation,

(ii) any foreign subsidiary of a foreign corporation controlled by the domestic corporation, and

(iii) the domestic corporation or any shareholder of the domestic corporation owning at the time the transaction takes place the 10 percent or more of the value of any class of stock outstanding of the domestic corporation; and

(E) a description of the various classes of stock outstanding, and a list showing the name and address of, and number of shares held by, each citizen or resident of the United States and each domestic corporation who is a shareholder of record owning at any time during the annual accounting period 5 percent or more in value of any class of stock outstanding of such foreign corporation or foreign subsidiary.

(2) PERIOD FOR WHICH INFORMATION IS TO BE FURNISHED, ETC.—The information required under paragraph (1) shall be furnished—

(A) in the case of a foreign corporation, for its annual accounting period ending with or within the domestic corporation's taxable year, and

(B) in the case of any foreign subsidiary of such foreign corporation, for such subsidiary's annual accounting period ending with or within such foreign corporation's annual accounting period described in subparagraph (A).

The information required under this subsection shall be furnished at such time and in such manner as the Secretary or his delegate shall by regulations prescribe.

(3) LIMITATION.—No information shall be required to be furnished under this subsection with respect to any foreign corporation or foreign subsidiary for any annual accounting period unless such information was required to be furnished under regulations in effect on the first day of such annual accounting period.

[Sec. 6038(b)]

(b) DOLLAR PENALTY FOR FAILURE TO FURNISH INFORMATION.—

(1) IN GENERAL.—If any person fails to furnish, within the time prescribed under paragraph (2) of subsection (a), any information with respect to any foreign business entity required under paragraph (1) of subsection (a), such person shall pay a penalty of $10,000 for each annual accounting period with respect to which such failure exists.

(2) INCREASE IN PENALTY WHERE FAILURE CONTINUES AFTER NOTIFICATION.—If any failure described in paragraph (1) continues for more than 90 days after the day on which the Secretary mails notice of such failure to the United States person, such person shall pay a penalty (in addition to the amount required under paragraph (1)) of $10,000 for each 30-day period (or fraction thereof) during which such failure continues with respect to any annual accounting period after the expiration of such 90-day period. The increase in any penalty under this paragraph shall not exceed $50,000.

Amendments

- **1997, Taxpayer Relief Act of 1997 (P.L. 105-34)**

P.L. 105-34, §1142(c)(1)(A)-(B):

Amended Code Sec. 6038(b) by striking "$1,000" each place it appears and inserting "$10,000", and by striking "$24,000" and inserting "$50,000". **Effective** for annual accounting periods beginning after 8-5-97.

P.L. 105-34, §1142(e)(1)(B):

Amended Code Sec. 6038(b) by striking "foreign corporation" each place it appears and inserting "foreign business entity". **Effective** for annual accounting periods beginning after 8-5-97.

- **1982, Tax Equity and Fiscal Responsibility Act of 1982 (P.L. 97-248)**

P.L. 97-248, §338(a):

Added Code Sec. 6038(b). **Effective** with respect to information for annual accounting periods ending after the date of enactment.

[Sec. 6038(c)]

(c) PENALTY OF REDUCING FOREIGN TAX CREDIT.—

(1) IN GENERAL.—If a United States person fails to furnish, within the time prescribed under paragraph (2) of subsection (a), any information with respect to any foreign business entity required under paragraph (1) of subsection (a), then—

(A) in applying section 901 (relating to taxes of foreign countries and possessions of the United States) to such United States person for the taxable year, the amount of taxes (other than taxes reduced under subparagraph (B)) paid or deemed paid (other than those deemed paid under section 904(c)) to any foreign country or possession of the United States for the taxable year shall be reduced by 10 percent, and

(B) in the case of a foreign business entity which is a foreign corporation, in applying section 960 to any such United States person which is a corporation (or to any person who acquires from any other person any portion of the interest of such other person in any such foreign corporation, but only to the extent of such portion) for any taxable year, the amount of taxes paid or deemed paid by each foreign corporation with respect to which such person is required to furnish information during the annual accounting period or periods with respect to which such information is required under paragraph (2) of subsection (a) shall be reduced by 10 percent.

If such failure continues 90 days or more after notice of such failure by the Secretary to the United States person, then the amount of the reduction under this paragraph shall be 10 percent plus an additional 5 percent for each 3-month period, or fraction thereof, during which such failure to furnish information continues after the expiration of such 90-day period.

RETURNS—INFORMATION

(2) LIMITATION.—The amount of the reduction under paragraph (1) for each failure to furnish information with respect to a foreign business entity required under subsection (a)(1) shall not exceed whichever of the following amounts is the greater:

(A) $10,000, or

(B) the income of the foreign business entity for its annual accounting period with respect to which the failure occurs.

(3) COORDINATION WITH SUBSECTION (b).—The amount of the reduction which (but for this paragraph) would be made under paragraph (1) with respect to any annual accounting period shall be reduced by the amount of the penalty imposed by subsection (b) with respect to such period.

(4) SPECIAL RULES.—

(A) No taxes shall be reduced under this subsection more than once for the same failure.

(B) For purposes of this subsection and subsection (b), the time prescribed under paragraph (2) of subsection (a) to furnish information (and the beginning of the 90-day period after notice by the Secretary) shall be treated as being not earlier than the last day on which (as shown to the satisfaction of the Secretary) reasonable cause existed for failure to furnish such information.

Amendments

- **2017, Tax Cuts and Jobs Act (P.L. 115-97)**

P.L. 115-97, §14301(c)(36):

Amended Code Sec. 6038(c)(1)(B) by striking "sections 902 (relating to foreign tax credit for corporate stockholder in foreign corporation) and 960 (relating to special rules for foreign tax credit)" and inserting "section 960". **Effective** for tax years of foreign corporations beginning after 12-31-2017, and to tax years of United States shareholders in which or with which such tax years of foreign corporations end.

P.L. 115-97, §14301(c)(37):

Amended Code Sec. 6038(c)(4) by striking subparagraph (C). **Effective** for tax years of foreign corporations beginning after 12-31-2017, and to tax years of United States shareholders in which or with which such tax years of foreign corporations end. Prior to being stricken, Code Sec. 6038(c)(4)(C) read as follows:

(C) In applying subsections (a) and (b) of section 902, and in applying subsection (a) of section 960, the reduction provided by this subsection shall not apply for purposes of determining the amount of post-1986 undistributed earnings.

- **1997, Taxpayer Relief Act of 1997 (P.L. 105-34)**

P.L. 105-34, §1142(e)(1)(C):

Amended Code Sec. 6038(c) (other than paragraph (1)(B)) by striking "foreign corporation" each place it appears and inserting "foreign business entity". **Effective** for annual accounting periods beginning after 8-5-97.

P.L. 105-34, §1142(e)(2):

Amended Code Sec. 6038(c)(1)(B) by inserting "in the case of a foreign business entity which is a foreign corporation," after "(B)". **Effective** for annual accounting periods beginning after 8-5-97.

- **1986, Tax Reform Act of 1986 (P.L. 99-514)**

P.L. 99-514, §1202(c)(2):

Amended Code Sec. 6038(c)(4)(C) by striking out all that follows "the amount of" and inserting in lieu thereof "post-1986 undistributed earnings." **Effective** for distributions by foreign corporations out of, and for inclusions under Code Sec. 951(a) attributable to, earnings and profits for tax years beginning after 12-31-86.

- **1982, Tax Equity and Fiscal Responsibility Act of 1982 (P.L. 97-248)**

P.L. 97-248, §338(a):

Amended Code Sec. 6038 by redesignating subsections (b), (c), and (d), as subsections (c), (d), and (e), respectively, and by adding a new subsection (b). **Effective** with respect to information for annual accounting periods ending after the date of enactment.

P.L. 97-248, §338(b):

Amended Code Sec. 6038(c) (as redesignated by P.L. 97-248, §338(a)) by inserting "and subsection (b)" after "subsection" in paragraph (3)(B), and by redesignating paragraph (3) as paragraph (4) and adding a new paragraph (3). **Effective** with respect to information for annual accounting periods ending after the date of enactment.

P.L. 97-248, §338(c)(1):

Amended Code Sec. 6038(c) (as redesignated by P.L. 97-248, §338(a)) by striking out the subsection (b) heading "EFFECT OF FAILURE TO FURNISH INFORMATION" and inserting a new subsection heading. **Effective** with respect to information for annual accounting periods ending after the date of enactment.

P.L. 97-248, §338(c)(3):

Amended Code Sec. 6038(c) (as redesignated by P.L. 97-248, §338(a)) by striking out in paragraph (1) "notice" and inserting "notice of such failure". **Effective** with respect to information for annual accounting periods ending after the date of enactment.

- **1976, Tax Reform Act of 1976 (P.L. 94-455)**

P.L. 94-455, §1031(b)(5):

Substituted "section 904(c)" for "section 904(d)". **Effective** for tax years beginning after 12-31-75.

P.L. 94-455, §1906(b)(13)(A):

Amended 1954 Code by substituting "Secretary" for "Secretary or his delegate" each place it appeared. **Effective** 2-1-77.

- **1962, Revenue Act of 1962 (P.L. 87-834)**

P.L. 87-834, §20:

Amended Code Sec. 6038(b). **Effective** with respect to annual accounting periods of foreign corporations beginning after 12-31-62. Prior to amendment, Sec. 6038(b) read as follows:

"(b) Effect of Failure to Furnish Information.—If a domestic corporation fails to furnish, within the time prescribed under paragraph (2) of subsection (a), any information with respect to any foreign corporation or foreign subsidiary required under paragraph (1) of subsection (a), then, in applying section 902 (relating to foreign tax credit for corporate stockholder in foreign corporation) to such domestic corporation (or to any person who acquires from any person any portion of the interest of such domestic corporation in any such foreign corporation or foreign subsidiary, but only to the extent of such portion) for any taxable year, the amount of taxes paid or deemed paid by each foreign corporation and foreign subsidiary with respect to which the domestic corporation is required to furnish information during the annual accounting period or periods with respect to which such information is required under such paragraph (2) of subsection (a) shall be reduced by 10 percent. If such failure continues 90 days or more after notice by the Secretary or his delegate to the domestic corporation, then the amount of the reduction under this subsection shall be 10 percent plus an additional 5 percent for each 3 month period, or fraction thereof, during which such failure to furnish information continues after the expiration of such 90-day period. No taxes shall be reduced under this subsection more than once for the same failure. For purposes of this subsection, the time prescribed under paragraph (2) of subsection (a) to furnish information (and the beginning of the 90-day period after notice by the Secretary) shall be treated as being not earlier than the last day on which (as shown to the satisfaction of the Secretary or his delegate) reasonable cause existed for failure to furnish such information."

[Sec. 6038(d)]

(d) TWO OR MORE PERSONS REQUIRED TO FURNISH INFORMATION WITH RESPECT TO SAME FOREIGN BUSINESS ENTITY.—Where, but for this subsection, two or more United States persons would be required to furnish information under subsection (a) with respect to the same foreign business entity for the same period, the Secretary may by regulations provide that such information shall be required only from one person. To the extent practicable, the determination of which person shall furnish the information shall be made on the basis of actual ownership of stock.

Amendments

- **1997, Taxpayer Relief Act of 1997 (P.L. 105-34)**

P.L. 105-34, §1142(e)(1)(D):

Amended Code Sec. 6038(d) by striking "foreign corporation" each place it appears and inserting "foreign business entity". **Effective** for annual accounting periods beginning after 8-5-97.

- **1982, Tax Equity and Fiscal Responsibility Act of 1982 (P.L. 97-248)**

P.L. 97-248, §338(a):

Redesignated subsection (c) as subsection (d).

- **1976, Tax Reform Act of 1976 (P.L. 94-455)**

P.L. 94-455, §1906(b)(13)(A):

Amended 1954 Code by substituting "Secretary" for "Secretary or his delegate" each place it appeared. **Effective** 2-1-77.

- **1962, Revenue Act of 1962 (P.L. 87-834)**

P.L. 87-834, §20:

Amended Code Sec. 6038(c). **Effective** with respect to annual accounting periods of foreign corporations beginning after 12-31-62. Prior to amendment, Code Sec. 6038(c) read as follows:

"(c) Control, Etc.—For purposes of this section—

(1) If at any time during its taxable year a domestic corporation owns more than 50 percent of the voting stock of a foreign corporation, it shall be deemed to be in control of such foreign corporation.

(2) If at any time during its annual accounting period a foreign corporation owns more than 50 percent of the voting stock of another foreign corporation, such other corporation shall be considered a foreign subsidiary of the corporation owning such stock."

[Sec. 6038(e)]

(e) DEFINITIONS.—For purposes of this section—

(1) FOREIGN BUSINESS ENTITY.—The term "foreign business entity" means a foreign corporation and a foreign partnership.

RETURNS—INFORMATION

(2) CONTROL OF CORPORATION.—A person is in control of a corporation if such person owns stock possessing more than 50 percent of the total combined voting power of all classes of stock entitled to vote, or more than 50 percent of the total value of shares of all classes of stock, of a corporation. If a person is in control (within the meaning of the preceding sentence) of a corporation which in turn owns more than 50 percent of the total combined voting power of all classes of stock entitled to vote of another corporation, or owns more than 50 percent of the total value of the shares of all classes of stock of another corporation, then such person shall be treated as in control of such other corporation. For purposes of this paragraph, the rules prescribed by section 318(a) for determining ownership of stock shall apply; except that—

(A) subparagraphs (A), (B), and (C) of section 318(a)(3) shall not be applied so as to consider a United States person as owning stock which is owned by a person who is not a United States person, and

(B) in applying subparagraph (C) of section 318(a)(2), the phrase "10 percent" shall be substituted for the phrase "50 percent" used in subparagraph (C).

(3) PARTNERSHIP-RELATED DEFINITIONS.—

(A) CONTROL.—A person is in control of a partnership if such person owns directly or indirectly more than a 50 percent interest in such partnership.

(B) 50-PERCENT INTEREST.—For purposes of subparagraph (A), a 50-percent interest in a partnership is—

(i) an interest equal to 50 percent of the capital interest, or 50 percent of the profits interest, in such partnership, or

(ii) to the extent provided in regulations, an interest to which 50 percent of the deductions or losses of such partnership are allocated.

For purposes of the preceding sentence, rules similar to the rules of section 267(c) (other than paragraph (3)) shall apply.

(C) 10-PERCENT INTEREST.—A 10-percent interest in a partnership is an interest which would be described in subparagraph (B) if "10 percent" were substituted for "50 percent" each place it appears.

(4) ANNUAL ACCOUNTING PERIOD.—The annual accounting period of a foreign business entity is the annual period on the basis of which such foreign business entity regularly computes its income in keeping its books. In the case of a specified foreign business entity (as defined in section 898), the taxable year of such foreign business entity shall be treated as its annual accounting period.

Amendments

• **1998, IRS Restructuring and Reform Act of 1998 (P.L. 105-206)**

P.L. 105-206, § 6011(f)(3):

Amended Code Sec. 6038(e)(4) by striking "corporation" and inserting "foreign business entity" each place it appears. **Effective** as if included in the provision of P.L. 105-34 to which it relates [effective for annual accounting periods beginning after 8-5-97.—CCH].

• **1997, Taxpayer Relief Act of 1997 (P.L. 105-34)**

P.L. 105-34, § 1142(b)(1)(A)-(C):

Amended Code Sec. 6038(e) by redesignating paragraphs (1) and (2) as paragraphs (2) and (4), respectively, by inserting before paragraph (2) (as so redesignated) a new paragraph (1), and by inserting after paragraph (2) (as so redesignated) a new paragraph (3). **Effective** for annual accounting periods beginning after 8-5-97.

P.L. 105-34, § 1142(b)(2):

Amended Code Sec. 6038(e)(2) (as redesignated by Act Sec. 932(b)(1)(A)) by inserting "OF CORPORATION" after "CONTROL" in the heading. **Effective** for annual accounting periods beginning after 8-5-97.

P.L. 105-34, § 1142(e)(1)(E):

Amended Code Sec. 6038(e)(4) (as redesignated by Act Sec. 1142(b)(1)(A)) by striking "foreign corporation" each place it appears and inserting "foreign business entity". **Effective** for annual accounting periods beginning after 8-5-97.

• **1990, Omnibus Budget Reconciliation Act of 1990 (P.L. 101-508)**

P.L. 101-508, § 11701(f):

Amended Code Sec. 6038(e)(2) by adding at the end thereof a new sentence. **Effective** as if included in the provision of P.L. 101-239 to which it relates.

• **1982, Tax Equity and Fiscal Responsibility Act of 1982 (P.L. 97-248)**

P.L. 97-248, § 338(a):

Redesignated subsection (d) as subsection (e).

• **1964 (P.L. 88-554)**

P.L. 88-554, § 5(b)(6):

Amended Code Sec. 6038(d)(1) by substituting "subparagraphs (A), (B), and (C) of section 318(a)(3)" for "the second sentence of subparagraphs (A) and (B), and clause (ii) of subparagraph (C), of section 318(a)(2)" in subparagraph (A) and by deleting "clause (i) of" in subparagraph (B). **Effective** 8-31-64.

• **1962, Revenue Act of 1962 (P.L. 87-834)**

P.L. 87-834, § 20:

Amended Code Sec. 6038(d). **Effective** with respect to annual accounting periods of foreign corporations beginning after 12-31-62. Prior to amendment, Code Sec. 6038(d) read as follows:

"(d) Annual Accounting Period.—For purposes of this section, the annual accounting period of a foreign corporation or of a foreign subsidiary is the annual period on the basis of which such foreign corporation or such foreign subsidiary regularly computes its income in keeping its books."

[Sec. 6038(f)]

(f) CROSS REFERENCES.—

(1) For provisions relating to penalties for violations of this section, see section 7203.

(2) For definition of the term "United States person", see section 7701(a)(30).

Amendments

• **1996, Small Business Job Protection Act of 1996 (P.L. 104-188)**

P.L. 104-188, § 1704(t)(40):

Amended Code Sec. 6038 by redesignating the subsection relating to cross references as subsection (f). **Effective** 8-20-96.

• **1962, Revenue Act of 1962 (P.L. 87-834)**

P.L. 87-834, § 20:

Amended Code Sec. 6038(e). **Effective** with respect to annual accounting periods of foreign corporations beginning after 12-31-62. Prior to amendment, Code Sec. 6038(e) read as follows:

"(e) Cross References.—

For provisions relating to penalties for violations of this section, see section 7203."

• **1960 (P.L. 86-780)**

P.L. 86-780, § 6(a):

Added Code Sec. 6038. **Effective** for tax years of domestic corporations beginning after 12-31-60, with respect to information relating to a foreign corporation or a foreign subsidiary described in section 6038(a) for its annual accounting periods beginning after 12-31-60.

[Sec. 6038A]

SEC. 6038A. INFORMATION WITH RESPECT TO CERTAIN FOREIGN-OWNED CORPORATIONS.

[Sec. 6038A(a)]

(a) REQUIREMENT.—If, at any time during a taxable year, a corporation (hereinafter in this section referred to as the "reporting corporation")—

(1) is a domestic corporation, and

(2) is 25-percent foreign-owned,

such corporation shall furnish, at such time and in such manner as the Secretary shall by regulations prescribe, the information described in subsection (b) and such corporation shall maintain (in the location, in the manner, and to the extent prescribed in regulations) such records as may be appropriate to determine the correct treatment of transactions with related parties as the Secretary shall by regulations prescribe (or shall cause another person to so maintain such records).

Internal Revenue Code

RETURNS—INFORMATION

Amendments

• **1990, Omnibus Budget Reconciliation Act of 1990 (P.L. 101-508)**

P.L. 101-508, §11314, provides:

SEC. 11314, APPLICATION OF AMENDMENTS MADE BY SECTION 7403 OF REVENUE RECONCILIATION ACT OF 1989 TO TAXABLE YEARS BEGINNING ON OR BEFORE JULY 10, 1989.

(a) GENERAL RULE.—The amendments made by section 7403 of the Revenue Reconciliation Act of 1989 shall apply to—

(1) any requirement to furnish information under section 6038A(a) of the Internal Revenue Code of 1986 (as amended by such section 7403) if the time for furnishing such information under such section is after the date of the enactment of this Act,

(2) any requirement under such section 6038A(a) to maintain records which were in existence on or after March 20, 1990,

(3) any requirement to authorize a corporation to act as a limited agent under section 6038A(e)(1) of such Code (as so amended) if the time for authorizing such action is after the date of the enactment of this Act, and

(4) any summons issued after such date of enactment, without regard to when the taxable year (to which the information, records, authorization, or summons relates) began. Such amendments shall also apply in any case to which they would apply without regard to this section.

(b) CONTINUATION OF OLD FAILURES.—In the case of any failure with respect to a taxable year beginning on or before July 10, 1989, which first occurs on or before the date of the enactment of this Act but which continues after such date of enactment, section 6038A(d)(2) of the Internal Revenue Code of 1986 (as amended by subsection (c) of such section 7403) shall apply for purposes of determining the amount of the penalty imposed for 30-day periods referred to in such section 6038A(d)(2) which begin after the date of the enactment of this Act.

P.L. 101-508, §11315(b)(1):

Amended Code Sec. 6038A(a)(1) by striking "or is a foreign corporation engaged in trade or business within the United States" after "is a domestic corporation". For the **effective** date, see Act Sec. 11315(c), below.

P.L. 101-508, §11315(c), provides:

(c) EFFECTIVE DATE.—The amendments made by this section shall apply to—

(1) any requirement to furnish information under section 6038C(a) of the Internal Revenue Code of 1986 (as added by this section) if the time for furnishing such information under such section is after the date of the enactment of this Act,

(2) any requirement under such section 6038C(a) to maintain records which were in existence on or after March 20, 1990,

(3) any requirement to authorize a corporation to act as a limited agent under section 6038C(d)(1) of such Code (as so added) if the time for authorizing such action is after the date of the enactment of this Act, and

(4) any summons issued after such date of enactment,

without regard to when the taxable year (to which the information, records, authorization, or summons relates) began.

• **1989, Omnibus Budget Reconciliation Act of 1989 (P.L. 101-239)**

P.L. 101-239, §7403(a)(1):

Amended Code Sec. 6038A(a)(2). **Effective** for tax years beginning after 7-10-89. Prior to amendment, Code Sec. 6038A(a)(2) read as follows:

(2) is controlled by a foreign person,

P.L. 101-239, §7403(b):

Amended Code Sec. 6038A(a) by inserting "and such corporation shall maintain (in the location, in the manner, and to the extent prescribed in regulations) such records as may be appropriate to determine the correct treatment of transactions with related parties as the Secretary shall by regulations prescribe (or shall cause another person to so maintain such records)" before the period at the end thereof. **Effective** for tax years beginning after 7-10-89.

[Sec. 6038A(b)]

(b) REQUIRED INFORMATION.—

(1) IN GENERAL.—For purposes of subsection (a), the information described in this subsection is such information as the Secretary prescribes by regulations relating to—

(A) the name, principal place of business, nature of business, and country or countries in which organized or resident, of each person which—

(i) is a related party to the reporting corporation, and

(ii) had any transaction with the reporting corporation during its taxable year,

(B) the manner in which the reporting corporation is related to each person referred to in subparagraph (A), and

(C) transactions between the reporting corporation and each foreign person which is a related party to the reporting corporation.

(2) ADDITIONAL INFORMATION REGARDING BASE EROSION PAYMENTS.—For purposes of subsection (a) and section 6038C, if the reporting corporation or the foreign corporation to whom section 6038C applies is an applicable taxpayer, the information described in this subsection shall include—

(A) such information as the Secretary determines necessary to determine the base erosion minimum tax amount, base erosion payments, and base erosion tax benefits of the taxpayer for purposes of section 59A for the taxable year, and

(B) such other information as the Secretary determines necessary to carry out such section.

For purposes of this paragraph, any term used in this paragraph which is also used in section 59A shall have the same meaning as when used in such section.

Amendments

• **2017, Tax Cuts and Jobs Act (P.L. 115-97)**

P.L. 115-97, §14401(b)(1):

Amended Code Sec. 6038A(b). **Effective** for base erosion payments (as defined in Code Sec. 59A(d), as added by Act. Sec. 14401) paid or accrued in tax years beginning after 12-31-2017. Prior to amendment, Code Sec. 6038A(b) read as follows:

(b) REQUIRED INFORMATION.—For purposes of subsection (a), the information described in this subsection is such information as the Secretary may prescribe by regulations relating to—

(1) the name, principal place of business, nature of business, and country or countries in which organized or resident, of each person which—

(A) is a related party to the reporting corporation, and

(B) had any transaction with the reporting corporation during its taxable year,

(2) the manner in which the reporting corporation is related to each person referred to in paragraph (1), and

(3) transactions between the reporting corporation and each foreign person which is a related party to the reporting corporation.

• **1996, Small Business Job Protection Act of 1996 (P.L. 104-188)**

P.L. 104-188, §1704(f)(5)(B):

Amended Code Sec. 6038A(b) by adding "and" at the end of paragraph (2), by striking ", and" at the end of paragraph (3) and inserting a period, and by striking paragraph (4). **Effective** 8-20-96. Prior to amendment, Code Sec. 6038A(b)(4) read as follows:

(4) such information as the Secretary may require for purposes of carrying out the provisions of section 453C.

• **1986, Tax Reform Act of 1986 (P.L. 99-514)**

P.L. 99-514, §1245(a)(1)-(2):

Amended Code Sec. 6038A(b)(1) by striking out "each corporation" in the matter preceding subparagraph (A) and inserting in lieu thereof "each person", and by amending subparagraph (A). **Effective** for tax years beginning after 12-31-86. Prior to amendment, Code Sec. 6038A(b)(1)(A) read as follows:

(A) is a member of the same controlled group as the reporting corporation, and

P.L. 99-514, §1245(b)(1):

Amended Code Sec. 6038A(b)(2) by striking out "each corporation" and inserting in lieu thereof "each person". **Effective** for tax years beginning after 12-31-86.

P.L. 99-514, §1245(b)(2):

Amended Code Sec. 6038A(b)(3). **Effective** for tax years beginning after 12-31-86. Prior to amendment, Code Sec. 6038A(b)(3) read as follows:

(3) transactions between the reporting corporation and each foreign corporation which is a member of the same controlled group as the reporting corporation.

P.L. 99-514, §1245(b)(3):

Amended Code Sec. 6038A(b) by striking out "and" at the end of paragraph (2), by striking out the period at the end of paragraph (3) and inserting in lieu thereof ", and", and by adding at the end thereof new paragraph (4). **Effective** for tax years beginning after 12-31-86.

[Sec. 6038A(c)]

(c) DEFINITIONS.—For purposes of this section—

(1) 25-PERCENT FOREIGN-OWNED.—A corporation is 25-percent foreign-owned if at least 25 percent of—

(A) the total voting power of all classes of stock of such corporation entitled to vote, or

(B) the total value of all classes of stock of such corporation,

is owned at any time during the taxable year by 1 foreign person (hereinafter in this section referred to as a "25-percent foreign shareholder").

(2) RELATED PARTY.—The term "related party" means—

(A) any 25-percent foreign shareholder of the reporting corporation,

(B) any person who is related (within the meaning of section 267(b) or 707(b)(1)) to the reporting corporation or to a 25-percent foreign shareholder of the reporting corporation, and

(C) any other person who is related (within the meaning of section 482) to the reporting corporation.

(3) FOREIGN PERSON.—The term "foreign person" means any person who is not a United States person. For purposes of the preceding sentence, the term "United States person" has the meaning given to such term by section 7701(a)(30), except that any individual who is a citizen of any possession of the United States (but not otherwise a citizen of the United States) and who is not a resident of the United States shall not be treated as a United States person.

(4) RECORDS.—The term "records" includes any books, papers, or other data.

(5) SECTION 318 TO APPLY.—Section 318 shall apply for purposes of paragraph (1) and (2), except that—

(A) "10 percent" shall be substituted for "50 percent" in section 318(a)(2)(C), and

(B) subparagraphs (A), (B), and (C) of section 318(a)(3) shall not be applied so as to consider a United States person as owning stock which is owned by a person who is not a United States person.

Amendments

• **1990, Omnibus Budget Reconciliation Act of 1990 (P.L. 101-508)**

P.L. 101-508, §11704(a)(23):

Amended Code Sec. 6038A(c) by redesignating paragraphs (4), (5), and (6) as paragraphs (3), (4), and (5), respectively. **Effective** 11-5-90.

• **1989, Omnibus Budget Reconciliation Act of 1989 (P.L. 101-239)**

P.L. 101-239, §7403(a)(2):

Amended Code Sec. 6038A(c). **Effective** for tax years beginning after 7-10-89. Prior to amendment, Code Sec. 6038A(c) read as follows:

(c) DEFINITIONS.—For purposes of this section—

(1) CONTROL.—The term "control" has the meaning given to such term by section 6038(e)(1); except that "at least 50 percent" shall be substituted for "more than 50 percent" each place it appears in such section.

(2) RELATED PARTY.—The term "related party" means—

(A) any person who is related to the reporting corporation within the meaning of section 267(b) or 707(b)(1), and

(B) any other person who is related (within the meaning of section 482) to the reporting corporation.

(3) FOREIGN PERSON.—The term "foreign person" means any person who is not a United States person. For purposes of the preceding sentence, the term "United States person" has the meaning given to such term by section 7701(a)(30); except that any individual who is a citizen of any possession of the United States (but not otherwise a citizen of the United States) and who is not a resident of the United States shall not be treated as a United States person.

• **1986, Tax Reform Act of 1986 (P.L. 99-514)**

P.L. 99-514, §1245(b)(4):

Amended Code Sec. 6038A(c)(2). **Effective** for tax years beginning after 12-31-86. Prior to amendment, Code Sec. 6038A(c)(2) read as follows:

(2) CONTROLLED GROUP.—The term "controlled group" means any controlled group of corporations within the meaning of section 1563(a); except that—

(A) "at least 50 percent" shall be substituted—

(i) for "at least 80 percent" each place it appears in section 1563(a)(1), and

(ii) for "more than 50 percent" each place it appears in section 1563(a)(2)(B), and

(B) the determination shall be made without regard to subsections (a)(4), (b)(2)(C), and (e)(3)(C) of section 1563.

• **1984, Deficit Reduction Act of 1984 (P.L. 98-369)**

P.L. 98-369, §714(l):

Amended Code Sec. 6038A(c)(1) by striking out "section 6038(d)(1)" and inserting in lieu thereof "section 6038(e)(1)". **Effective** as if included in the provision of P.L. 97-248 to which it relates.

• **1983, Technical Corrections Act of 1982 (P.L. 97-448)**

P.L. 97-448, §306(b)(4):

Amended Code Sec. 6038A(c)(2)(B) by inserting ", (b)(2)(C)," after "(a)(4)". **Effective** as if included in the provision of P.L. 97-248 to which it relates.

[Sec. 6038A(d)]

(d) PENALTY FOR FAILURE TO FURNISH INFORMATION OR MAINTAIN RECORDS.—

(1) IN GENERAL.—If a reporting corporation—

(A) fails to furnish (within the time prescribed by regulations) any information described in subsection (b), or

(B) fails to maintain (or cause another to maintain) records as required by subsection (a),

such corporation shall pay a penalty of $25,000 for each taxable year with respect to which such failure occurs.

(2) INCREASE IN PENALTY WHERE FAILURE CONTINUES AFTER NOTIFICATION.—If any failure described in paragraph (1) continues for more than 90 days after the day on which the Secretary mails notice of such failure to the reporting corporation, such corporation shall pay a penalty (in addition to the amount required under paragraph (1)) of $25,000 for each 30-day period (or fraction thereof) during which such failure continues after the expiration of such 90-day period.

(3) REASONABLE CAUSE.—For purposes of this subsection, the time prescribed by regulations to furnish information or maintain records (and the beginning of the 90-day period after notice by the Secretary) shall be treated as not earlier than the last day on which (as shown to the satisfaction of the Secretary) reasonable cause existed for failure to furnish the information or maintain the records.

Amendments

• **2017, Tax Cuts and Jobs Act (P.L. 115-97)**

P.L. 115-97, §14401(b)(2):

Amended Code Sec. 6038A(d)(1) and (2) by striking "$10,000" and inserting "$25,000". **Effective** for base erosion payments (as defined in Code Sec. 59A(d), as added by Act. Sec. 14401) paid or accrued in tax years beginning after 12-31-2017.

• **1989, Omnibus Budget Reconciliation Act of 1989 (P.L. 101-239)**

P.L. 101-239, §7403(c):

Amended Code Sec. 6038A(d). **Effective** for tax years beginning after 7-10-89. Prior to amendment, Code Sec. 6038A(d) read as follows:

(d) PENALTY FOR FAILURE TO FURNISH INFORMATION.—

(1) IN GENERAL.—If a reporting corporation fails to furnish (within the time prescribed by regulations) any information described in subsection (b), such corporation shall pay a penalty of $1,000 for each taxable year with respect to which such failure occurs.

(2) INCREASE IN PENALTY WHERE FAILURE CONTINUES AFTER NOTIFICATION.—If any failure described in paragraph (1) continues for more than 90 days after the day on which the Secretary mails notice of such failure to the reporting corporation, such corporation shall pay a penalty (in addition to the amount required under paragraph (1)) of $1,000 for each 30-day period (or fraction thereof) during which such failure continues after the expiration of such 90-day period. The increase in any penalty under this paragraph shall not exceed $24,000.

(3) REASONABLE CAUSE.—For purposes of this subsection, the time prescribed by regulations to furnish information (and the beginning of the 90-day period after notice by the Secretary) shall be treated as not earlier than the last day on which (as shown to the satisfaction of the Secretary) reasonable cause existed for failure to furnish the information.

[Sec. 6038A(e)]

(e) ENFORCEMENT OF REQUESTS FOR CERTAIN RECORDS.—

(1) AGREEMENT TO TREAT CORPORATION AS AGENT.—The rules of paragraph (3) shall apply to any transaction between the reporting corporation and any related party who is a foreign person unless such related party agrees (in such manner and at such time as the Secretary shall prescribe) to authorize the reporting corporation to act as such related party's limited agent solely for purposes of applying sections 7602, 7603, and 7604 with respect to any request by the Secretary to examine records or produce testimony related to any such transaction or with respect to any summons by the Secretary for such records or testimony. The appearance of persons or production of records by reason of the reporting corporation being such an agent shall not subject such persons or records to legal process for any purpose other than determining the correct treatment under this title of any transaction between the reporting corporation and such related party.

(2) RULES WHERE INFORMATION NOT FURNISHED.—If—

RETURNS—INFORMATION

(A) for purposes of determining the correct treatment under this title of any transaction between the reporting corporation and a related party who is a foreign person, the Secretary issues a summons to such corporation to produce (either directly or as agent for such related party) any records or testimony,

(B) such summons is not quashed in a proceeding begun under paragraph (4) and is not determined to be invalid in a proceeding begun under section 7604(b) to enforce such summons, and

(C) the reporting corporation does not substantially comply in a timely manner with such summons and the Secretary has sent by certified or registered mail a notice to such reporting corporation that such reporting corporation has not so substantially complied,

the Secretary may apply the rules of paragraph (3) with respect to such transaction (whether or not the Secretary begins a proceeding to enforce such summons). If the reporting corporation fails to maintain (or cause another to maintain) records as required by subsection (a), and by reason of that failure, the summons is quashed in a proceeding described in subparagraph (B) or the reporting corporation is not able to provide the records requested in the summons, the Secretary may apply the rules of paragraph (3) with respect to any transaction to which the records relate.

(3) APPLICABLE RULES IN CASES OF NONCOMPLIANCE.—If the rules of this paragraph apply to any transaction—

(A) the amount of the deduction allowed under subtitle A for any amount paid or incurred by the reporting corporation to the related party in connection with such transaction, and

(B) the cost to the reporting corporation of any property acquired in such transaction from the related party (or transferred by such corporation in such transaction to the related party),

shall be the amount determined by the Secretary in the Secretary's sole discretion from the Secretary's own knowledge or from such information as the Secretary may obtain through testimony or otherwise.

(4) JUDICIAL PROCEEDINGS.—

(A) PROCEEDINGS TO QUASH.—Notwithstanding any law or rule of law, any reporting corporation to which the Secretary issues a summons referred to in paragraph (2)(A) shall have the right to begin a proceeding to quash such summons not later than the 90th day after such summons was issued. In any such proceeding, the Secretary may seek to compel compliance with such summons.

(B) REVIEW OF SECRETARIAL DETERMINATION OF NONCOMPLIANCE.—Notwithstanding any law or rule of law, any reporting corporation which has been notified by the Secretary that the Secretary has determined that such corporation has not substantially complied with a summons referred to in paragraph (2) shall have the right to begin a proceeding to review such determination not later than the 90th day after the day on which the notice referred to in paragraph (2)(C) was mailed. If such a proceeding is not begun on or before such 90th day, such determination by the Secretary shall be binding and shall not be reviewed by any court.

(C) JURISDICTION.—The United States district court for the district in which the person (to whom the summons is issued) resides or is found shall have jurisdiction to hear any proceeding brought under subparagraph (A) or (B). Any order or other determination in such a proceeding shall be treated as a final order which may be appealed.

(D) SUSPENSION OF STATUTE OF LIMITATIONS.—If the reporting corporation brings an action under subparagraph (A) or (B), the running of any period of limitations under section 6501 (relating to assessment and collection of tax) or under section 6531 (relating to criminal prosecutions) with respect to any affected taxable year shall be suspended for the period during which such proceeding, and appeals therein, are pending. In no event shall any such period expire before the 90th day after the day on which there is a final determination in such proceeding. For purposes of this subparagraph, the term "affected taxable year" means any taxable year if the determination of the amount of tax imposed for such taxable year is affected by the treatment of the transaction to which the summons relates.

Amendments

- **1996, Small Business Job Protection Act of 1996 (P.L. 104-188)**

P.L. 104-188, §1702(c)(5)(A)-(B):

Amended Code Sec. 6038A(e)(4)(D) by striking "any transaction to which the summons relates" and inserting "any affected taxable year", and by adding at the end a new sentence. **Effective** as if included in the provision of P.L. 101-508 to which it relates.

- **1989, Omnibus Budget Reconciliation Act of 1989 (P.L. 101-239)**

P.L. 101-239, §7403(d):

Amended Code Sec. 6038A by redesignating subsection (e) as subsection (f) and by inserting after subsection (d) a new subsection (e). **Effective** for tax years beginning after 7-10-89.

[Sec. 6038A(f)]

(f) CROSS REFERENCE.—

For provisions relating to criminal penalties for violation of this section, see section 7203.

Amendments

- **1989, Omnibus Budget Reconciliation Act of 1989 (P.L. 101-239)**

P.L. 101-239, §7403(d):

Amended Code Sec. 6038A by redesignating subsection (e) as subsection (f). **Effective** for tax years beginning after 7-10-89.

- **1982, Tax Equity and Fiscal Responsibility Act of 1982 (P.L. 97-248)**

P.L. 97-248, §339(a):

Added Code Sec. 6038A. **Effective** for tax years beginning after 12-31-82.

[Sec. 6038B]

SEC. 6038B. NOTICE OF CERTAIN TRANSFERS TO FOREIGN PERSONS.

[Sec. 6038B(a)]

(a) IN GENERAL.—Each United States person who—

(1) transfers property to—

(A) a foreign corporation in an exchange described in section 332, 351, 354, 355, 356, or 361, or

(B) a foreign partnership in a contribution described in section 721 or in any other contribution described in regulations prescribed by the Secretary, or

(2) makes a distribution described in section 336 to a person who is not a United States person,

shall furnish to the Secretary, at such time and in such manner as the Secretary shall by regulations prescribe, such information with respect to such exchange or distribution as the Secretary may require in such regulations.

Amendments

- **2005, Gulf Opportunity Zone Act of 2005 (P.L. 109-135)**

P.L. 109-135, §409(c):

Amended Code Sec. 6038B(a)(1)(B) by inserting "or" at the end. **Effective** as if included in the provision of the Taxpayer Relief Act of 1997 (P.L. 105-34) to which it relates [**effective**, generally, for transfers made after 8-5-97.—CCH].

- **1997, Taxpayer Relief Act of 1997 (P.L. 105-34)**

P.L. 105-34, §1144(a):

Amended Code Sec. 6038B(a)(1). **Effective**, generally, for transfers made after 8-5-97. For a special rule, see Act Sec. 1144(d)(2), below. Prior to amendment, Code Sec. 6038B(a)(1) read as follows:

Sec. 6038A(e)(2)(A)

RETURNS—INFORMATION

(1) transfers property to a foreign corporation in an exchange described in section 332, 351, 354, 355, 356, or 361, or

P.L. 105-34, §1144(d)(2), provides:

(2) ELECTION OF RETROACTIVE EFFECT.—Section 1494(c) of the Internal Revenue Code of 1986 shall not apply to any transfer after August 20, 1996, if all applicable reporting requirements under section 6038B of such Code (as amended by this section) are satisfied. The Secretary of the Treasury or his delegate may prescribe simplified reporting requirements under the preceding sentence.

[Sec. 6038B(b)]

(b) EXCEPTIONS FOR CERTAIN TRANSFERS TO FOREIGN PARTNERSHIPS; SPECIAL RULE.—

(1) EXCEPTIONS.—Subsection (a)(1)(B) shall apply to a transfer by a United States person to a foreign partnership only if—

(A) the United States person holds (immediately after the transfer) directly or indirectly at least a 10-percent interest (as defined in section 6046A(d)) in the partnership, or

(B) the value of the property transferred (when added to the value of the property transferred by such person or any related person to such partnership or a related partnership during the 12-month period ending on the date of the transfer) exceeds $100,000.

For purposes of the preceding sentence, the value of any transferred property is its fair market value at the time of its transfer.

(2) SPECIAL RULE.—If by reason of an adjustment under section 482 or otherwise, a contribution described in subsection (a)(1) is deemed to have been made, such contribution shall be treated for purposes of this section as having been made not earlier than the date specified by the Secretary.

Amendments

• **1997, Taxpayer Relief Act of 1997 (P.L. 105-34)**

P.L. 105-34, §1144(b):

Amended Code Sec. 6038B by redesignating subsection (b) as subsection (c) and by inserting after subsection (a) a new subsection (b). **Effective**, generally, for transfers made after 8-5-97. For a special rule, see Act Sec. 1144(d)(2), below.

P.L. 105-34, §1144(d)(2), provides:

(2) ELECTION OF RETROACTIVE EFFECT.—Section 1494(c) of the Internal Revenue Code of 1986 shall not apply to any transfer after August 20, 1996, if all applicable reporting requirements under section 6038B of such Code (as amended by this section) are satisfied. The Secretary of the Treasury or his delegate may prescribe simplified reporting requirements under the preceding sentence.

[Sec. 6038B(c)]

(c) PENALTY FOR FAILURE TO FURNISH INFORMATION.—

(1) IN GENERAL.—If any United States person fails to furnish the information described in subsection (a) at the time and in the manner required by regulations, such person shall pay a penalty equal to 10 percent of the fair market value of the property at the time of the exchange (and, in the case of a contribution described in subsection (a)(1)(B), such person shall recognize gain as if the contributed property had been sold for such value at the time of such contribution).

(2) REASONABLE CAUSE EXCEPTION.—Paragraph (1) shall not apply to any failure if the United States person shows such failure is due to reasonable cause and not to willful neglect.

(3) LIMIT ON PENALTY.—The penalty under paragraph (1) with respect to any exchange shall not exceed $100,000 unless the failure with respect to such exchange was due to intentional disregard.

Amendments

• **1997, Taxpayer Relief Act of 1997 (P.L. 105-34)**

P.L. 105-34, §1144(b):

Amended Code Sec. 6038B by redesignating subsection (b) as subsection (c). **Effective** for transfers made after 8-5-97. For a special rule, see Act Sec. 1144(d)(2), below.

P.L. 105-34, §1144(c)(1) (as amended by P.L. 105-206, §6011(g)):

Amended Code Sec. 6038B(c)(1), as redesignated by Act Sec. 1144(b), by striking "equal to" and all that follows and inserting "equal to 10 percent of the fair market value of the property at the time of the exchange (and, in the case of a contribution described in subsection (a)(1)(B), such person shall recognize gain as if the contributed property had been sold for such value at the time of such contribution).". **Effective** for transfers made after 8-5-97. For a special rule, see Act Sec. 1144(d)(2), below. Prior to amendment, Code Sec. 6038B(b)(1) read as follows:

(1) IN GENERAL.—If any United States person fails to furnish the information described in subsection (a) at the time and in the manner required by regulations, such person shall pay a penalty equal to 25 percent of the amount of the gain realized on the exchange.

P.L. 105-34, §1144(c)(2) (as amended by P.L. 105-206, §6011(g)):

Amended Code Sec. 6038B(c), as redesignated by Act Sec. 1144(b), by adding at the end a new paragraph (3). **Effective** for transfers made after 8-5-97. For a special rule, see Act Sec. 1144(d)(2), below.

P.L. 105-34, §1144(d)(2), provides:

(2) ELECTION OF RETROACTIVE EFFECT.—Section 1494(c) of the Internal Revenue Code of 1986 shall not apply to any transfer after August 20, 1996, if all applicable reporting requirements under section 6038B of such Code (as amended by this section) are satisfied. The Secretary of the Treasury or his delegate may prescribe simplified reporting requirements under the preceding sentence.

• **1984, Deficit Reduction Act of 1984 (P.L. 98-369)**

P.L. 98-369, §131(d)(1):

Amended Subpart A of part III of subchapter A of chapter 61 by adding a new section 6038B. **Effective** for transfers or exchanges after 12-31-84, in tax years ending after such date. See Act Sec. 131(g)(2)-(3) under the amendment notes for Code Sec. 367 for special rules.

[Sec. 6038C]

SEC. 6038C. INFORMATION WITH RESPECT TO FOREIGN CORPORATIONS ENGAGED IN U.S. BUSINESS.

[Sec. 6038C(a)]

(a) REQUIREMENT.—If a foreign corporation (hereinafter in this section referred to as the "reporting corporation") is engaged in a trade or business within the United States at any time during a taxable year—

(1) such corporation shall furnish (at such time and in such manner as the Secretary shall by regulations prescribe) the information described in subsection (b), and

(2) such corporation shall maintain (at the location, in the manner, and to the extent prescribed in regulations) such records as may be appropriate to determine the liability of such corporation for tax under this title as the Secretary shall by regulations prescribe (or shall cause another person to so maintain such records).

[Sec. 6038C(b)]

(b) REQUIRED INFORMATION.—For purposes of subsection (a), the information described in this subsection is—

(1) the information described in section 6038A(b), and

(2) such other information as the Secretary may prescribe by regulations relating to any item not directly connected with a transaction for which information is required under paragraph (1).

[Sec. 6038C(c)]

(c) PENALTY FOR FAILURE TO FURNISH INFORMATION OR MAINTAIN RECORDS.—The provisions of subsection (d) of section 6038A shall apply to—

(1) any failure to furnish (within the time prescribed by regulations) any information described in subsection (b), and

(2) any failure to maintain (or cause another to maintain) records as required by subsection (a),

in the same manner as if such failure were a failure to comply with the provisions of section 6038A.

RETURNS—INFORMATION

[Sec. 6038C(d)]

(d) ENFORCEMENT OF REQUESTS FOR CERTAIN RECORDS.—

(1) AGREEMENT TO TREAT CORPORATION AS AGENT.—The rules of paragraph (3) shall apply to any transaction between the reporting corporation and any related party who is a foreign person unless such related party agrees (in such manner and at such time as the Secretary shall prescribe) to authorize the reporting corporation to act as such related party's limited agent solely for purposes of applying sections 7602, 7603, and 7604 with respect to any request by the Secretary to examine records or produce testimony related to any such transaction or with respect to any summons by the Secretary for such records or testimony. The appearance of persons or production of records by reason of the reporting corporation being such an agent shall not subject such persons or records to legal process for any purpose other than determining the correct treatment under this title of any transaction between the reporting corporation and such related party.

(2) RULES WHERE INFORMATION NOT FURNISHED.—If—

(A) for purposes of determining the amount of the reporting corporation's liability for tax under this title, the Secretary issues a summons to such corporation to produce (either directly or as an agent for a related party who is a foreign person) any records or testimony,

(B) such summons is not quashed in a proceeding begun under paragraph (4) of section 6038A(e) (as made applicable by paragraph (4) of this subsection) and is not determined to be invalid in a proceeding begun under section 7604(b) to enforce such summons, and

(C) the reporting corporation does not substantially comply in a timely manner with such summons and the Secretary has sent by certified or registered mail a notice to such reporting corporation that such reporting corporation has not so substantially complied,

the Secretary may apply the rules of paragraph (3) with respect to any transaction or item to which such summons relates (whether or not the Secretary begins a proceeding to enforce such summons). If the reporting corporation fails to maintain (or cause another to maintain) records as required by subsection (a), and by reason of that failure, the summons is quashed in a proceeding described in subparagraph (B) or the reporting corporation is not able to provide the records requested in the summons, the Secretary may apply the rules of paragraph (3) with respect to any transaction or item to which the records relate.

(3) APPLICABLE RULES.—If the rules of this paragraph apply to any transaction or item, the treatment of such transaction (or the amount and treatment of any such item) shall be determined by the Secretary in the Secretary's sole discretion from the Secretary's own knowledge or from such information as the Secretary may obtain through testimony or otherwise.

(4) JUDICIAL PROCEEDINGS.—The provisions of section 6038A(e)(4) shall apply with respect to any summons referred to in paragraph (2)(A); except that subparagraph (D) of such section shall be applied by substituting "transaction or item" for "transaction".

[Sec. 6038C(e)]

(e) DEFINITIONS.—For purposes of this section, the terms "related party", "foreign person", and "records" have the respective meanings given to such terms by section 6038A(c).

Amendments

• **1990, Omnibus Budget Reconciliation Act of 1990 (P.L. 101-508)**

P.L. 101-508, § 11315(a):

Amended subpart A of part III of subchapter A of chapter 61 by inserting after Code Sec. 6038B a new Code Sec. 6038C. For the **effective** date, see Act Sec. 11315(c), below.

P.L. 101-508, § 11315(c), provides:

(c) EFFECTIVE DATE.—The amendments made by this section shall apply to—

(1) any requirement to furnish information under section 6038C(a) of the Internal Revenue Code of 1986 (as added by this section) if the time for furnishing such information under such section is after the date of the enactment of this Act,

(2) any requirement under such section 6038C(a) to maintain records which were in existence on or after March 20, 1990,

(3) any requirement to authorize a corporation to act as a limited agent under section 6038C(d)(1) of such Code (as so added) if the time for authorizing such action is after the date of the enactment of this Act, and

(4) any summons issued after such date of enactment,

without regard to when the taxable year (to which the information, records, authorization, or summons relates) began.

[Sec. 6038D]

SEC. 6038D. INFORMATION WITH RESPECT TO FOREIGN FINANCIAL ASSETS.

[Sec. 6038D(a)]

(a) IN GENERAL.—Any individual who, during any taxable year, holds any interest in a specified foreign financial asset shall attach to such person's return of tax imposed by subtitle A for such taxable year the information described in subsection (c) with respect to each such asset if the aggregate value of all such assets exceeds $50,000 (or such higher dollar amount as the Secretary may prescribe).

[Sec. 6038D(b)]

(b) SPECIFIED FOREIGN FINANCIAL ASSETS.—For purposes of this section, the term "specified foreign financial asset" means—

(1) any financial account (as defined in section 1471(d)(2)) maintained by a foreign financial institution (as defined in section 1471(d)(4)), and

(2) any of the following assets which are not held in an account maintained by a financial institution (as defined in section 1471(d)(5))—

(A) any stock or security issued by a person other than a United States person,

(B) any financial instrument or contract held for investment that has an issuer or counterparty which is other than a United States person, and

(C) any interest in a foreign entity (as defined in section 1473).

[Sec. 6038D(c)]

(c) REQUIRED INFORMATION.—The information described in this subsection with respect to any asset is:

(1) In the case of any account, the name and address of the financial institution in which such account is maintained and the number of such account.

(2) In the case of any stock or security, the name and address of the issuer and such information as is necessary to identify the class or issue of which such stock or security is a part.

(3) In the case of any other instrument, contract, or interest—

(A) such information as is necessary to identify such instrument, contract, or interest, and

(B) the names and addresses of all issuers and counterparties with respect to such instrument, contract, or interest.

(4) The maximum value of the asset during the taxable year.

RETURNS—INFORMATION

[Sec. 6038D(d)]

(d) PENALTY FOR FAILURE TO DISCLOSE.—

(1) IN GENERAL.—If any individual fails to furnish the information described in subsection (c) with respect to any taxable year at the time and in the manner described in subsection (a), such person shall pay a penalty of $10,000.

(2) INCREASE IN PENALTY WHERE FAILURE CONTINUES AFTER NOTIFICATION.—If any failure described in paragraph (1) continues for more than 90 days after the day on which the Secretary mails notice of such failure to the individual, such individual shall pay a penalty (in addition to the penalties under paragraph (1)) of $10,000 for each 30-day period (or fraction thereof) during which such failure continues after the expiration of such 90-day period. The penalty imposed under this paragraph with respect to any failure shall not exceed $50,000.

[Sec. 6038D(e)]

(e) PRESUMPTION THAT VALUE OF SPECIFIED FOREIGN FINANCIAL ASSETS EXCEEDS DOLLAR THRESHOLD.—If—

(1) the Secretary determines that an individual has an interest in one or more specified foreign financial assets, and

(2) such individual does not provide sufficient information to demonstrate the aggregate value of such assets,

then the aggregate value of such assets shall be treated as being in excess of $50,000 (or such higher dollar amount as the Secretary prescribes for purposes of subsection (a)) for purposes of assessing the penalties imposed under this section.

[Sec. 6038D(f)]

(f) APPLICATION TO CERTAIN ENTITIES.—To the extent provided by the Secretary in regulations or other guidance, the provisions of this section shall apply to any domestic entity which is formed or availed of for purposes of holding, directly or indirectly, specified foreign financial assets, in the same manner as if such entity were an individual.

[Sec. 6038D(g)]

(g) REASONABLE CAUSE EXCEPTION.—No penalty shall be imposed by this section on any failure which is shown to be due to reasonable cause and not due to willful neglect. The fact that a foreign jurisdiction would impose a civil or criminal penalty on the taxpayer (or any other person) for disclosing the required information is not reasonable cause.

[Sec. 6038D(h)]

(h) REGULATIONS.—The Secretary shall prescribe such regulations or other guidance as may be necessary or appropriate to carry out the purposes of this section, including regulations or other guidance which provide appropriate exceptions from the application of this section in the case of—

(1) classes of assets identified by the Secretary, including any assets with respect to which the Secretary determines that disclosure under this section would be duplicative of other disclosures,

(2) nonresident aliens, and

(3) bona fide residents of any possession of the United States.

Amendments

• **2010, Hiring Incentives to Restore Employment Act (P.L. 111-147)**

P.L. 111-147, §511(a):

Amended subpart A of part III of subchapter A of chapter 61 by inserting after Code Sec. 6038C a new Code Sec. 6038D. **Effective** for tax years beginning after 3-18-2010.

[Sec. 6038E]

SEC. 6038E. INFORMATION WITH RESPECT TO ASSIGNMENT OF LOWER RATES OR REFUNDS BY FOREIGN PRODUCERS OF BEER, WINE, AND DISTILLED SPIRITS.

Any foreign producer that elects to make an assignment described in section 5001(c), 5041(c), or 5051(a) shall provide such information, at such time and in such manner, as the Secretary may prescribe in order to make such assignment, including information about the controlled group structure of such foreign producer.

Amendments

• **2020, Taxpayer Certainty and Disaster Tax Relief Act of 2020 (P.L. 116-260)**

P.L. 116-260, §107(d)(1), Div. EE:

Amended subpart A of part III of subchapter A of chapter 61 by inserting after Code Sec. 6038D a new Code Sec. 6038E. **Effective** for elections to make an assignment under Code Sec. 5001(c), 5041(c), or 5051(a) after 12-31-2020. For a special rule, see Act Sec. 107(e)-(g), Div. EE, below.

P.L. 116-260, §107(e)-(g), Div. EE, provides:

(e) ADMINISTRATION OF REFUNDS.—The Secretary of the Treasury (or the Secretary's delegate within the Department of the Treasury) shall implement and administer sections 5001(c)(4), 5041(c)(7), and 5051(a)(6) of the Internal Revenue Code of 1986, as added by this Act, in coordination with the United States Customs and Border Protection of the Department of Homeland Security.

(f) REGULATIONS.—The Secretary of the Treasury (or the Secretary's delegate within the Department of the Treasury) shall prescribe such regulations as may be necessary or appropriate to carry out the purposes of this section, including regulations to require foreign producers to provide information necessary to enforce the volume limitations under sections 5001(c), 5041(c), and 5051(a) of such Code.

(g) REPORT.—Not later than 180 days after the date of the enactment of this Act, the Secretary of the Treasury (or the Secretary's delegate within the Department of the Treasury) shall, in coordination with the United States Customs and Border Protection of the Department of Homeland Security, prepare, submit to Congress, and make publicly available a report detailing the plans for implementing and administering sections 5001(c)(4), 5041(c)(7), and 5051(a)(6) of such Code, as added by this Act.

[Sec. 6039]

SEC. 6039. RETURNS REQUIRED IN CONNECTION WITH CERTAIN OPTIONS.

[Sec. 6039(a)]

(a) REQUIREMENT OF REPORTING.—Every corporation—

(1) which in any calendar year transfers to any person a share of stock pursuant to such person's exercise of an incentive stock option, or

(2) which in any calendar year records (or has by its agent recorded) a transfer of the legal title of a share of stock acquired by the transferor pursuant to his exercise of an option described in section 423(c) (relating to special rule where option price is between 85 percent and 100 percent of value of stock),

shall, for such calendar year, make a return at such time and in such manner, and setting forth such information, as the Secretary may by regulations prescribe.

RETURNS—INFORMATION

Amendments

• **2006, Tax Relief and Health Care Act of 2006 (P.L. 109-432)**

P.L. 109-432, Division A, §403(a):

Amended so much of Code Sec. 6039(a) as follows paragraph (2). **Effective** for calendar years beginning after 12-20-2006. Prior to amendment, so much of Code Sec. 6039(a) as followed paragraph (2) read as follows:

shall (on or before January 31 of the following calendar year) furnish to such person a written statement in such manner and setting forth such information as the Secretary may by regulations prescribe.

P.L. 109-432, Division A, §403(c)(3):

Amended the heading of Code Sec. 6039 by striking "Information" and inserting "Returns". **Effective** for calendar years beginning after 12-20-2006.

P.L. 109-432, Division A, §403(c)(4):

Amended the heading of Code Sec. 6039(a) by striking "FURNISHING OF INFORMATION" and inserting "REQUIREMENT OF REPORTING". **Effective** for calendar years beginning after 12-20-2006.

• **1998, IRS Restructuring and Reform Act of 1998 (P.L. 105-206)**

P.L. 105-206, §6023(20):

Amended Code Sec. 6039(a)(1) by inserting "to any person" after "transfers". **Effective** 7-22-98.

• **1990, Omnibus Budget Reconciliation Act of 1990 (P.L. 101-508)**

P.L. 101-508, §11801(c)(9)(J)(i):

Amended Code Sec. 6039(a) by striking paragraphs (1) and (2) and inserting new paragraphs (1) and (2). **Effective** 11-5-90. Prior to amendment, Code Sec. 6039(a)(1) and (2) read as follows:

(1) which in any calendar year transfers a share of stock to any person pursuant to such person's exercise of a qualified stock option, an incentive stock option, or a restricted stock option, or

(2) which in any calendar year records (or has by its agent recorded) a transfer of the legal title of a share of stock—

(A) acquired by the transfer or pursuant to his exercise of an option described in section 423(c) (relating to special rule where option price is between 85 percent and 100 percent of value of stock), or

(B) acquired by the transferor pursuant to his exercise of a restricted stock option described in section 424(c)(1) (relating to options under which option price is between 85 percent and 95 percent of value of stock),

P.L. 101-508, §11821(b), provides:

(b) SAVINGS PROVISION.—If—

(1) any provision amended or repealed by this part applied to—

(A) any transaction occurring before the date of the enactment of this Act,

(B) any property acquired before such date of enactment, or

(C) any item of income, loss, deduction, or credit taken into account before such date of enactment, and

(2) the treatment of such transaction, property, or item under such provision would (without regard to the amendments made by this part) affect liability for tax for periods ending after such date of enactment,

nothing in the amendments made by this part shall be construed to affect the treatment of such transaction, property, or item for purposes of determining liability for tax for periods ending after such date of enactment.

• **1981, Economic Recovery Tax Act of 1981 (P.L. 97-34)**

P.L. 97-34, §251(b)(5)(A):

Amended Code Sec. 6039(a)(1) by inserting ", an incentive stock option," after "qualified stock option". For the **effective** date and transitional rules, see the historical comment for P.L. 97-34 following Code Sec. 422A(a).

• **1979 (P.L. 96-167)**

P.L. 96-167, §7:

Amended Code Sec. 6039(a). **Effective** for calendar years beginning after 12-31-79. Prior to amendment, Code Sec. 6039(a) read as follows:

(a) REQUIREMENT OF REPORTING.—Every corporation—

(1) which in any calendar year transfers a share of stock to any person pursuant to such person's exercise of a qualified stock option or a restricted stock option, or

(2) which in any calendar year records (or has by its agent recorded) a transfer of the legal title of a share of stock—

(A) acquired by the transferor pursuant to his exercise of an option described in section 423(c) (relating to special rule where option price is between 85 percent and 100 percent of value of stock), or

(B) acquired by the transferor pursuant to his exercise of a restricted stock option described in section 424(c)(1) (relating to options under which option price is between 85 percent and 95 percent of value of stock),

shall, for such calendar year, make a return at such time and in such manner, and setting forth such information, as the Secretary may by regulations prescribe. For purposes of the preceding sentence, any option which a corporation treats as a qualified stock option, a restricted stock option, or an option granted under an employee stock purchase plan, shall be deemed to be such an option. A return is required by reason of a transfer described in paragraph (2) of a share only with respect to the first transfer of such share by the person who exercised the option.

• **1976, Tax Reform Act of 1976 (P.L. 94-455)**

P.L. 94-455, §1906(b)(13)(A):

Amended 1954 Code by substituting "Secretary" for "Secretary or his delegate" each place it appeared. **Effective** 2-1-77.

[Sec. 6039(b)]

(b) STATEMENTS TO BE FURNISHED TO PERSONS WITH RESPECT TO WHOM INFORMATION IS REPORTED.—Every corporation making a return under subsection (a) shall furnish to each person whose name is set forth in such return a written statement setting forth such information as the Secretary may by regulations prescribe. The written statement required under the preceding sentence shall be furnished to such person on or before January 31 of the year following the calendar year for which the return under subsection (a) was made.

Amendments

• **2006, Tax Relief and Health Care Act of 2006 (P.L. 109-432)**

P.L. 109-432, Division A, §403(b):

Amended Code Sec. 6039 by redesignating subsections (b) and (c) as subsections (c) and (d), respectively, and by inserting after subsection (a) a new subsection (b). **Effective** for calendar years beginning after 12-20-2006.

[Sec. 6039(c)]

(c) SPECIAL RULES.—For purposes of this section—

(1) TREATMENT BY EMPLOYER TO BE DETERMINATIVE.—Any option which the corporation treats as an incentive stock option or an option granted under an employee stock purchase plan shall be deemed to be such an option.

(2) SUBSECTION (a)(2) APPLIES ONLY TO FIRST TRANSFER DESCRIBED THEREIN.—A statement is required by reason of a transfer described in subsection (a)(2) of a share only with respect to the first transfer of such share by the person who exercised the option.

(3) IDENTIFICATION OF STOCK.—Any corporation which transfers any share of stock pursuant to the exercise of any option described in subsection (a)(2) shall identify such stock in a manner adequate to carry out the purposes of this section.

Amendments

• **2006, Tax Relief and Health Care Act of 2006 (P.L. 109-432)**

P.L. 109-432, Division A, §403(b):

Amended Code Sec. 6039 by redesignating subsection (b) as subsection (c). **Effective** for calendar years beginning after 12-20-2006.

• **1990, Omnibus Budget Reconciliation Act of 1990 (P.L. 101-508)**

P.L. 101-508, §11801(c)(9)(J)(ii):

Amended Code Sec. 6039(b)(1) by striking "a qualified stock option, incentive stock option, a restricted stock option, or an" and inserting "an incentive stock option or an". **Effective** on 11-5-90.

P.L. 101-508, §11821(b), provides:

(b) SAVINGS PROVISION.—If—

(1) any provision amended or repealed by this part applied to—

(A) any transaction occurring before the date of the enactment of this Act,

(B) any property acquired before such date of enactment, or

(C) any item of income, loss, deduction, or credit taken into account before such date of enactment, and

(2) the treatment of such transaction, property, or item under such provision would (without regard to the amendments made by this part) affect liability for tax for periods ending after such date of enactment,

nothing in the amendments made by this part shall be construed to affect the treatment of such transaction, property, or item for purposes of determining liability for tax for periods ending after such date of enactment.

• **1981, Economic Recovery Tax Act of 1981 (P.L. 97-34)**

P.L. 97-34, §251(b)(5)(B):

Amended Code Sec. 6039(b)(1) by inserting "incentive stock option," after "qualified stock option,". For the **effective** date and transitional rules, see the historical comment for P.L. 97-34 following Code Sec. 422A(a).

• **1979 (P.L. 96-167)**

P.L. 96-167, §7:

Amended Code Sec. 6039(b). **Effective** for calendar years beginning after 12-31-79. Prior to amendment, Code Sec. 6039(b) read as follows:

(b) STATEMENTS TO BE FURNISHED TO PERSONS WITH RESPECT TO WHOM INFORMATION IS FURNISHED.—Every corporation making a return under subsection (a) shall furnish to

RETURNS—INFORMATION

each person whose name is set forth in such return a written statement setting forth such information as the Secretary may by regulations prescribe. The written statement required under the preceding sentence shall be furnished to the person on or before January 31 of the year following the calendar year for which the return under subsection (a) was made.

[Sec. 6039(d)]

(d) CROSS REFERENCES.—

For definition of—

(1) the term "incentive stock option", see section 422(b), and

(2) the term "employee stock purchase plan", see section 423(b).

Amendments

• **2018, Tax Technical Corrections Act of 2018 (P.L. 115-141)**

P.L. 115-141, §401(a)(259), Div. U:

Amended Code Sec. 6039(d)(2). **Effective** 3-23-2018. Prior to amendment, Code Sec. 6039(d)(2) read as follows:

(2) the term "employee stock purchase plan" see section 423(b).

• **2006, Tax Relief and Health Care Act of 2006 (P.L. 109-432)**

P.L. 109-432, Division A, §403(b):

Amended Code Sec. 6039 by redesignating subsection (c) as subsection (d). **Effective** for calendar years beginning after 12-20-2006.

• **1990, Omnibus Budget Reconciliation Act of 1990 (P.L. 101-508)**

P.L. 101-508, §11801(c)(9)(J)(iii):

Amended Code Sec. 6039(c). **Effective** on 11-5-90. Prior to amendment, Code Sec. 6039(c) read as follows:

(c) CROSS REFERENCES.—

For definition of—

(1) The term "qualified stock option", see section 422(b).

(2) The term "employee stock purchase plan", see section 423(b).

(3) The term "restricted stock option", see section 424(b).

(4) The term "incentive stock option", see section 422A(b).

P.L. 101-508, §11821(b), provides:

(b) SAVINGS PROVISION.—If—

(1) any provision amended or repealed by this part applied to—

(A) any transaction occurring before the date of the enactment of this Act,

(B) any property acquired before such date of enactment, or

(C) any item of income, loss, deduction, or credit taken into account before such date of enactment, and

(2) the treatment of such transaction, property, or item under such provision would (without regard to the amendments made by this part) affect liability for tax for periods ending after such date of enactment,

nothing in the amendments made by this part shall be construed to affect the treatment of such transaction, property, or item for purposes of determining liability for tax for periods ending after such date of enactment.

• **1981, Economic Recovery Tax Act of 1981 (P.L. 97-34)**

P.L. 97-34, §251(b)(5)(C):

Amended Code Sec. 6039 by adding at the end of subsection (c) new paragraph (4). For the **effective** date and transitional rules, see the historical comment for P.L. 97-34 following Code Sec. 422A(a).

• **1979 (P.L. 96-167)**

P.L. 96-167, §7:

Redesignated Code Sec. 6039(c) as Code Sec. 6039(b)(3) and renumbered Code Sec. 6039(d) as Code Sec. 6039(c). **Effective** for calendar years beginning after 1979. Prior to amendment Code Sec. 6039(c) and 6039(d) read as follows:

(c) IDENTIFICATION OF STOCK.—Any corporation which transfers any share of stock pursuant to the exercise of an option described in subsection (a)(2) shall identify such stock in a manner adequate to carry out the purposes of this section.

(d) CROSS REFERENCES.—

For definition of—

(1) The term "qualified stock option", see section 422(b).

(2) The term "employee stock purchase plan", see section 423(b).

(3) The term "restricted stock option", see section 424(b).

• **1964, Revenue Act of 1964 (P.L. 88-272)**

P.L. 88-272, §221(b)(1):

Renumbered Code Sec. 6039 as Code Sec. 6040 and added new Code Sec. 6039. **Effective** for tax years ending after 12-31-63.

[Sec. 6039A—Repealed]

Amendments

• **1980, Crude Oil Windfall Profit Tax Act of 1980 (P.L. 96-223)**

P.L. 96-223, §401(a):

Repealed Code Sec. 6039A as added by P.L. 94-455, Act Sec. 2005(d)(1). **Effective** with respect to decedents dying after 12-31-76. However, see the amendment note for P.L. 96-223, §401(a), that follows Code Sec. 1014(d) that authorizes the election of the carryover basis rules in the case of a decedent dying after 12-31-76 and before 11-7-78. Prior to repeal, Code Sec. 6039A read as follows:

SEC. 6039A. INFORMATION REGARDING CARRYOVER BASIS PROPERTY ACQUIRED FROM A DECEDENT.

(a) IN GENERAL.—Every executor (as defined in section 2203) shall furnish the Secretary such information with respect to carryover basis property to which section 1023 applies as the Secretary may by regulation prescribe.

(b) STATEMENT TO BE FURNISHED TO PERSONS WHO ACQUIRE PROPERTY FROM A DECEDENT.—Every executor who is required to furnish information under subsection (a) shall furnish in writing to each person acquiring an item of such property from the decedent (or to whom the item passes from the decedent) the adjusted basis of such item.

• **1976, Tax Reform Act of 1976 (P.L. 94-455)**

P.L. 94-455, §2005(d)(f)(1):

Added Code Sec. 6039A. **Effective** in respect of decedents dying after 12-31-79 (as amended by P.L. 95-600, Act Sec. 515(6)).

[Sec. 6039B—Repealed]

Amendments

• **1986, Tax Reform Act of 1986 (P.L. 99-514)**

P.L. 99-514, §1303(b)(5):

Repealed Code Sec. 6039B. **Effective** 10-22-86. However, for special transitional rules, see the text of Act Secs. 1312 through 1318 reproduced under the amendment notes for Code Sec. 103. Prior to repeal, Code Sec. 6039B read as follows:

SEC. 6039B. RETURN OF GENERAL STOCK OWNERSHIP CORPORATION.

Every general stock ownership corporation (as defined in section 1391) which makes the election provided by section 1392 shall make a return for each taxable year, stating specifically the items of its gross income and the deductions allowable by subtitle A, the amount of investment credit or additional tax, as the case may be, the names and addresses of all persons owning stock in the corporation at any time during the taxable year, the number of shares of stock owned by each shareholder at all times during the taxable year, the amount of money and other property distributed by the corporation during the taxable year to each shareholder, the date of each such distribution, and such other information, for the purpose of carrying out the provisions of subchapter U of chapter 1, as the Secretary may by regulation prescribe. Any return filed pursuant to this section shall, for purposes of chapter 66 (relating to limitations), be treated as a return filed by the corporation under section 6012. Every electing GSOC shall file an annual report with the Secretary summarizing its operations for such year.

• **1980 (P.L. 96-595)**

P.L. 96-595, §3(b):

Amended Code Sec. 6039B by inserting "electing" after "Every" in the last sentence. **Effective** for corporations chartered after 1978 and before 1984.

• **1978, Revenue Act of 1978 (P.L. 95-600)**

P.L. 95-600, §601(b)(4):

Added Code Sec. 6039B. **Effective** with respect to corporations chartered after 12-31-78, and before 1-1-84.

• **1976, Tax Reform Act of 1976 (P.L. 94-455)**

P.L. 94-455, §1906(b)(13)(A):

Amended 1954 Code by substituting "Secretary" for "Secretary or his delegate" each place it appeared. **Effective** 2-1-77.

[Sec. 6039C]

SEC. 6039C. RETURNS WITH RESPECT TO FOREIGN PERSONS HOLDING DIRECT INVESTMENTS IN UNITED STATES REAL PROPERTY INTERESTS.

[Sec. 6039C(a)]

(a) GENERAL RULE.—To the extent provided in regulations, any foreign person holding direct investments in United States real property interests for the calendar year shall make a return setting forth—

(1) the name and address of such person,

(2) a description of all United States real property interests held by such person at any time during the calendar year, and

RETURNS—INFORMATION

(3) such other information as the Secretary may by regulations prescribe.

[Sec. 6039C(b)]

(b) DEFINITION OF FOREIGN PERSONS HOLDING DIRECT INVESTMENTS IN UNITED STATES REAL PROPERTY INTERESTS.—For purposes of this section, a foreign person shall be treated as holding direct investments in United States real property interests during any calendar year if—

(1) such person did not engage in a trade or business in the United States at any time during such calendar year, and

(2) the fair market value of the United States real property interests held directly by such person at any time during such year equals or exceeds $50,000.

[Sec. 6039C(c)]

(c) DEFINITIONS AND SPECIAL RULES.—For purposes of this section—

(1) UNITED STATES REAL PROPERTY INTEREST.—The term "United States real property interest" has the meaning given to such term by section 897(c).

(2) FOREIGN PERSON.—The term "foreign person" means any person who is not a United States person.

(3) ATTRIBUTION OF OWNERSHIP.—For purposes of subsection (b)(2)—

(A) INTERESTS HELD BY PARTNERSHIPS, ETC.—United States real property interests held by a partnership, trust, or estate shall be treated as owned proportionately by its partners or beneficiaries.

(B) INTERESTS HELD BY FAMILY MEMBERS.—United States real property interests held by the spouse or any minor child of an individual shall be treated as owned by such individual.

(4) TIME AND MANNER OF FILING RETURN.—All returns required to be made under this section shall be made at such time and in such manner as the Secretary shall by regulations prescribe.

[Sec. 6039C(d)]

(d) SPECIAL RULE FOR UNITED STATES INTEREST AND VIRGIN ISLANDS INTEREST.—A nonresident alien individual or foreign corporation subject to tax under section 897(a) (and any person required to withhold tax under section 1445) shall pay any tax and file any return required by this title—

(1) to the United States, in the case of any interest in real property located in the United States and an interest (other than an interest solely as a creditor) in a domestic corporation (with respect to the United States) described in section 897(c)(1)(A)(ii), and

(2) to the Virgin Islands, in the case of any interest in real property located in the Virgin Islands and an interest (other than an interest solely as a creditor) in a domestic corporation (with respect to the Virgin Islands) described in section 897(c)(1)(A)(ii).

Amendments

- **1986, Tax Reform Act of 1986 (P.L. 99-514)**

P.L. 99-514, § 1810(f)(7):

Amended Code Sec. 6039C(d) by striking out "subject to tax under section 897(a)" and inserting in lieu thereof "subject to tax under section 897(a) (and any person required to withhold tax under section 1445)". **Effective** as if included in the provision of P.L. 98-369 to which it relates.

- **1984, Deficit Reduction Act of 1984 (P.L. 98-369)**

P.L. 98-369, § 129(b)(1):

Amended Code Sec. 6039C. **Effective** for calendar year 1980 and subsequent calendar years. Prior to amendment, Code Sec. 6039C read as follows:

SEC. 6039C. RETURNS WITH RESPECT TO UNITED STATES REAL PROPERTY INTERESTS.

[Sec. 6039C(a)]

(a) RETURN OF CERTAIN DOMESTIC CORPORATIONS HAVING FOREIGN SHAREHOLDERS.—

(1) GENERAL RULE.—

(A) RETURN REQUIREMENT.—If this subsection applies to a domestic corporation for the calendar year, such corporation shall make a return for the calendar year setting forth—

(i) the name and address (if known by the corporation) of each person who was a shareholder at any time during the calendar year and who is known by the corporation to be a foreign person,

(ii) such information with respect to transfers of stock in such corporation to or from foreign persons during the calendar year as the Secretary may by regulations prescribe, and

(iii) such other information as the Secretary may by regulations prescribe.

(B) CORPORATIONS TO WHICH SUBSECTION APPLIES.—This subsection applies to any domestic corporation for the calendar year if—

(i) at any time during the calendar year 1 or more of the shareholders of such corporation is a foreign person, and

(ii) at any time during the calendar year or during any of the 4 immediately preceding calendar years, such corporation was a United States real property holding corporation (as defined in section 897(c)(2)).

(2) SUBSECTION DOES NOT APPLY TO PUBLICLY TRADED CORPORATIONS.—This subsection shall not apply to a corporation the stock of which is regularly traded on an established securities market at all times during the calendar year.

(3) STOCK HELD BY NOMINEES.—If—

(A) a nominee holds stock in a domestic corporation for a foreign person, and

(B) such foreign person does not furnish the information required to be furnished pursuant to paragraph (1)(A) with respect to such stock,

the nominee shall file a return under this subsection with respect to such stock.

[Sec. 6039C(b)]

(b) RETURN OF CERTAIN PERSONS HOLDING UNITED STATES REAL PROPERTY INTERESTS.—

(1) RETURN REQUIREMENT.—If any entity to which this subsection applies has at any time during the calendar year a substantial investor in United States real property, such entity shall make a return for the calendar year setting forth—

(A) the name and address of each such substantial investor,

(B) such information with respect to the assets of the entity during the calendar year as the Secretary may by regulations prescribe, and

(C) such other information as the Secretary may by regulations prescribe.

(2) EXCEPTION WHERE SECURITY FURNISHED.—This subsection shall not apply to any entity for the calendar year if such entity furnishes to the Secretary such security as the Secretary determines to be necessary to ensure that any tax imposed by chapter 1 with respect to United States real property interests held by such entity will be paid.

(3) STATEMENTS TO BE FURNISHED TO SUBSTANTIAL INVESTOR IN UNITED STATES REAL PROPERTY.—Every entity making a return under paragraph (1) shall furnish to each substantial investor in United States real property a statement showing—

(A) the name and address of the entity making such return,

(B) such substantial investor's pro rata share of the United States real property interests held by such entity, and

(C) such other information as the Secretary shall by regulations prescribe.

(4) DEFINITIONS.—For purposes of this subsection—

(A) ENTITIES TO WHICH THIS SUBSECTION APPLIES.—This subsection shall apply to any foreign corporation and to any partnership, trust, or estate (whether foreign or domestic).

(B) SUBSTANTIAL INVESTOR IN UNITED STATES REAL PROPERTY.—

(i) IN GENERAL.—The term "substantial investor in United States real property" means any foreign person who at any time during the calendar year held an interest in the entity but only if the fair market value of such person's pro rata share of the United States real property interests held by such entity exceeded $50,000.

(ii) SPECIAL RULE FOR CORPORATIONS.—In the case of any foreign corporation, clause (i) shall be applied by substituting "person (whether foreign or domestic)" for "foreign person".

(C) INDIRECT HOLDINGS.—For purposes of determining whether an entity to which this subsection applies has a substantial investor in United States real property, the assets of any person shall include the person's pro rata share of the United States real property interest held by any corporation (whether domestic or foreign) if the person's pro rata share of the United States real property interest exceeded $50,000.

Amendments

- **1981, Economic Recovery Tax Act of 1981 (P.L. 97-34)**

P.L. 97-34, § 831(e):

Amended Code Sec. 6039C(b)(4)(C). **Effective** for dispositions after 6-18-80, in tax years ending after that date. Prior to amendment, Code Sec. 6039C(b)(4)(C) read as follows:

(C) INDIRECT HOLDINGS.—The assets of any entity to which this subsection applies shall include its pro rata share of the United States real property interests held by any corporation in which the entity is a substantial investor in United States real property.

[Sec. 6039C(c)]

(c) RETURN OF CERTAIN FOREIGN PERSONS HOLDING DIRECT INVESTMENTS IN UNITED STATES REAL PROPERTY INTERESTS.—

(1) RETURN REQUIREMENT.—If this subsection applies to any foreign person for the calendar year, such person shall make a return for the calendar year setting forth—

(A) the name and address of such person,

(B) a description of all United States real property interests held by such person at any time during the calendar year, and

(C) such other information as the Secretary may by regulations prescribe.

(2) PERSONS TO WHOM THIS SUBSECTION APPLIES.—This subsection applies to any foreign person for the calendar year if—

(A) such person did not engage in a trade or business in the United States at any time during the calendar year,

RETURNS—INFORMATION

(B) the fair market value of the United States real property interests held by such person at any time during such year equals or exceeds $50,000, and

(C) such person is not required to file a return under subsection (b) for such year.

[Sec. 6039C(d)]

(d) DEFINITIONS.—For purposes of this section—

(1) UNITED STATES REAL PROPERTY INTEREST.—The term "United States real property interest" has the meaning given to such term by section 897(c).

(2) FOREIGN PERSON.—The term "foreign person" means any person who is not a United States person.

[Sec. 6039C(e)]

(e) SPECIAL RULES.—

(1) ATTRIBUTION OF OWNERSHIP.—For purposes of subsection (b)(4) and (c)(2)(B)—

(A) INTERESTS HELD BY PARTNERSHIPS, ETC.—United States real property interests held by a partnership, trust, or estate shall be treated as owned proportionately by its partners or beneficiaries.

(B) INTERESTS HELD BY FAMILY MEMBERS.—United States real property interests held by the spouse or any minor child of an individual shall be treated as owned by such individual.

(2) RETURNS, ETC.—All returns, statements, and information required to be made or furnished under this section shall be made or furnished at such time and in such manner as the Secretary shall by regulations prescribe.

Amendments

• **1980, Omnibus Reconciliation Act of 1980 (P.L. 96-499)**

P.L. 96-499, §1123(a):

Added Code Sec. 6039C. **Effective** for 1980 and subsequent calendar years. Calendar year 1980 shall be treated as beginning on 6-19-80, and ending on 12-31-80.

[Sec. 6039C(f)]

(f) SPECIAL RULE FOR UNITED STATES INTEREST AND VIRGIN ISLANDS INTEREST.—A nonresident alien individual or foreign corporation subject to tax under section 897(a) shall pay any tax and file any return required by this title—

(1) to the United States, in the case of any interest in real property located in the United States and an interest (other than an interest solely as a creditor) in a domestic corporation (with respect to the United States) described in section 897(c)(1)(A)(ii), and

(2) to the Virgin Islands, in the case of an interest in real property located in the Virgin Islands and an interest (other than an interest solely as a creditor) in a domestic corporation (with respect to the Virgin Islands) described in section 897(c)(1)(A)(ii).

Amendments

• **1981, Economic Recovery Tax Act of 1981 (P.L. 97-34)**

P.L. 97-34, §831(a)(3):

Added Code Sec. 6039C(f). **Effective** for dispositions after 6-18-80, in tax years ending after that date.

[Sec. 6039D]

SEC. 6039D. RETURNS AND RECORDS WITH RESPECT TO CERTAIN FRINGE BENEFIT PLANS.

[Sec. 6039D(a)]

(a) IN GENERAL.—Every employer maintaining a specified fringe benefit plan during any year for any portion of which the applicable exclusion applies, shall file a return (at such time and in such manner as the Secretary shall by regulations prescribe) with respect to such plan showing for such year—

(1) the number of employees of the employer,

(2) the number of employees of the employer eligible to participate under the plan,

(3) the number of employees participating under the plan,

(4) the total cost of the plan during the year, and

(5) the name, address, and taxpayer identification number of the employer and the type of business in which the employer is engaged, and

(6) the number of highly compensated employees among the employees described in paragraphs (1), (2), and (3).

Amendments

• **2014, Tax Technical Corrections Act of 2014 (P.L. 113-295)**

P.L. 113-295, §221(a)(108), Division A:

Amended Code Sec. 6039D(a) by striking "beginning after December 31, 1984," following "during any year". **Effective** generally 12-19-2014. For a special rule, see Act Sec. 221(b)(2), Division A, below.

P.L. 113-295, §221(b)(2), Division A, provides:

(2) SAVINGS PROVISION.—If—

(A) any provision amended or repealed by the amendments made by this section applied to—

(i) any transaction occurring before the date of the enactment of this Act,

(ii) any property acquired before such date of enactment, or

(iii) any item of income, loss, deduction, or credit taken into account before such date of enactment, and

(B) the treatment of such transaction, property, or item under such provision would (without regard to the amendments or repeals made by this section) affect the liability for tax for periods ending after date of enactment, nothing in the amendments or repeals made by this section shall be construed to affect the treatment of such transaction, property, or item for purposes of determining liability for tax for periods ending after such date of enactment.

• **1986, Tax Reform Act of 1986 (P.L. 99-514)**

P.L. 99-514, §1151(h)(2):

Amended Code Sec. 6039D(a) by striking out "and" at the end of paragraph (4), by striking out the period at the end of paragraph (5) and inserting in lieu thereof ", and" and by inserting after paragraph (5) new paragraph (6). For the **effective** date, see Act Sec. 1151(k)(1), reproduced under Code Sec. 6039D(d). For special rules and an exception, see the text of Act Sec. 1151(k)(2)-(4) reproduced under the amendment notes for Code Sec. 89.

[Sec. 6039D(b)]

(b) RECORDKEEPING REQUIREMENT.—Each employer maintaining a specified fringe benefit plan during any year shall keep such records as may be necessary for purposes of determining whether the requirements of the applicable exclusion are met.

[Sec. 6039D(c)]

(c) ADDITIONAL INFORMATION WHEN REQUIRED BY THE SECRETARY.—Any employer—

(1) who maintains a specified fringe benefit plan during any year for which a return is required under subsection (a), and

(2) who is required by the Secretary to file an additional return for such year,

shall file such additional return. Such additional return shall be filed at such time and in such manner as the Secretary shall prescribe and shall contain such information as the Secretary shall prescribe. The Secretary may require returns under this subsection only from a representative group of employers.

Amendments

• **1986, Tax Reform Act of 1986 (P.L. 99-514)**

P.L. 99-514, §1151(h)(3):

Amended Code Sec. 6039D(c) by adding at the end thereof a new sentence. For the **effective** date, see Act Sec. 1151(k)(1), reproduced under Code Sec. 6039D(d). For special rules and an exception, see the text of Act Sec. 1151(k)(2)-(4) reproduced under the amendment notes for Code Sec. 89.

[Sec. 6039D(d)]

(d) DEFINITIONS AND SPECIAL RULES.—For purposes of this section—

(1) SPECIFIED FRINGE BENEFIT PLAN.—The term "specified fringe benefit plan" means any plan under section 79, 105, 106, 125, 127, 129, or 137.

(2) APPLICABLE EXCLUSION.—The term "applicable exclusion" means, with respect to any specified fringe benefit plan, the section specified under paragraph (1) under which benefits under such plan are excludable from gross income.

(3) SPECIAL RULE FOR MULTIEMPLOYER PLANS.—In the case of a multiemployer plan, the plan shall be required to provide any information required by this section which the Secretary determines, on the basis of the agreement between the plan and employer, is held by the plan (and not the employer).

RETURNS—INFORMATION

Amendments

- **2014, Tax Technical Corrections Act of 2014 (P.L. 113-295)**

P.L. 113-295, §221(a)(19)(B)(vii), Division A:

Amended Code Sec. 6039D(d)(1) by striking "120," following "106,". **Effective** generally 12-19-2014. For a special rule, see Act Sec. 221(b)(2), Division A, below.

P.L. 113-295, §221(b)(2), Division A, provides:

(2) SAVINGS PROVISION.—If—

(A) any provision amended or repealed by the amendments made by this section applied to—

(i) any transaction occurring before the date of the enactment of this Act,

(ii) any property acquired before such date of enactment, or

(iii) any item of income, loss, deduction, or credit taken into account before such date of enactment, and

(B) the treatment of such transaction, property, or item under such provision would (without regard to the amendments or repeals made by this section) affect the liability for tax for periods ending after date of enactment, nothing in the amendments or repeals made by this section shall be construed to affect the treatment of such transaction, property, or item for purposes of determining liability for tax for periods ending after such date of enactment.

- **1997, Taxpayer Relief Act of 1997 (P.L. 105-34)**

P.L. 105-34, §1601(h)(2)(D)(iii):

Amended Code Sec. 6039D(d)(1) by striking "or 129" and inserting "129, or 137". **Effective** as if included in the provision of P.L. 104-188 to which it relates [**effective** for tax years beginning after 12-31-96.—CCH].

- **1990, Omnibus Budget Reconciliation Act of 1990 (P.L. 101-508)**

P.L. 101-508, §11704(a)(24):

Amended Code Sec. 6039D(d)(3) by striking all that follows "plan (and not" and inserting "the employer)." Prior to amendment, all that followed "plan (and not" in Code Sec. 6039D(d)(3) read as follows: "the employer)". **Effective** 11-5-90.

- **1989 (P.L. 101-136)**

P.L. 101-136, §528, provides:

SEC. 528. No monies appropriated by this Act may be used to implement or enforce section 1151 of the Tax Reform Act of 1986 or the amendments made by such section.

- **1988, Technical and Miscellaneous Revenue Act of 1988 (P.L. 100-647)**

P.L. 100-647, §3021(a)(15)(A)(i)-(ii):

Amended Code Sec. 6039D(d) by adding at the end thereof a new paragraph (3), and by inserting "AND SPECIAL RULES" after "DEFINITIONS" in the heading thereof. **Effective** for years beginning after 1984.

- **1986, Tax Reform Act of 1986 (P.L. 99-514)**

P.L. 99-514, §1151(h)(1):

Amended Code Sec. 6039D(d). For the **effective** date, see Act Sec. 1151(k)(1), below. For special rules and an exception, see the text of Act Sec. 1151(k)(2)-(4) reproduced under the amendment notes for Code Sec. 89. Prior to amendment Code Sec. 6039D(d) read as follows:

(d) DEFINITIONS.—For purposes of this section—

(1) SPECIAL FRINGE BENEFIT PLAN.—The term "specified fringe benefit plan" means—

(A) any qualified group legal services plan (as defined in section 120),

(B) any cafeteria plan (as defined in section 125), and

(C) any educational assistance plan (as defined in section 127).

(2) APPLICABLE EXCLUSION.—The term "applicable exclusion" means—

(A) section 120 in the case of a qualified group legal services plan,

(B) section 125 in the case of a cafeteria plan, and

(C) section 127 in the case of an educational assistance plan.

P.L. 99-514, §1151(k)(1), provides:

(k) EFFECTIVE DATES.—

(1) IN GENERAL.—The amendments made by this section shall apply to years beginning after the later of—

(A) December 31, 1987, or

(B) the earlier of—

(i) the date which is 3 months after the date on which the Secretary of the Treasury or his delegate issues such regulations as are necessary to carry out the provisions of section 89 of the Internal Revenue Code of 1986 (as added by this section), or

(ii) December 31, 1988.

Notwithstanding the preceding sentence, the amendments made by subsections (e)(1) and (i)(3)(C) shall, to the extent they relate to section 162(i)(2) and 162(k) of the Internal Revenue Code of 1986, apply to years beginning after 1986.

P.L. 99-514, §1879(d)(1):

Amended Code Sec. 6039D(d). **Effective** as if included in the provision of P.L. 98-369 to which it relates. Prior to amendment, Code Sec. 6039D(d) read as follows:

(d) DEFINITIONS.—For purposes of this section—

(1) SPECIFIED FRINGE BENEFIT PLAN.—The term "specified fringe benefit plan" means—

(A) any cafeteria plan (as defined in section 125), and

(B) any educational assistance program (as defined in section 127).

(2) APPLICABLE EXCLUSION.—The term "applicable exclusion" means—

(A) section 125, in the case of a cafeteria plan, and

(B) section 127, in the case of an educational assistance program.

P.L. 99-514, §1879(d)(2):

Repealed the Code Sec. 6039D added by section 1 of P.L. 98-612. **Effective** as if included in the provision of P.L. 98-369 to which it relates. Prior to repeal, the Code Sec. 6039D added by P.L. 98-612 read as follows:

SEC. 6039D. RETURNS AND RECORDS WITH RESPECT TO CERTAIN FRINGE BENEFIT PLANS.

(a) IN GENERAL.—Every employer maintaining a specified fringe benefit plan during any year beginning after December 31, 1984, for any portion of which the applicable exclusion applies, shall file a return (at such time and in such manner as the Secretary shall by regulations prescribe) with respect to such plan showing for such year—

(1) the number of employees of the employer,

(2) the number of employees of the employer eligible to participate under the plan,

(3) the number of employees participating under the plan,

(4) the total cost of the plan during the year, and

(5) the name, address, and taxpayer identification number of the employer and the type of business in which the employer is engaged.

(b) RECORDKEEPING REQUIREMENT.—Each employer maintaining a specified fringe benefit plan during any year shall keep such records as may be necessary for purposes of determining whether the requirements of the applicable exclusion are met.

(c) ADDITIONAL INFORMATION WHEN REQUIRED BY THE SECRETARY.—Any employer—

(1) who maintains a specified fringe benefit plan during any year for which a return is required under subsection (a), and

(2) who is required by the Secretary to file an additional return for such year,

shall file such additional return. Such additional return shall be filed at such time and in such manner as the Secretary shall prescribe and shall contain such information as the Secretary shall prescribe.

(d) DEFINITIONS.—For purposes of this section—

(1) SPECIFIED FRINGE BENEFIT PLAN.—The term "specified fringe benefit plan" means—

(A) any qualified group legal services plan (as defined in section 120), and

(B) any cafeteria plan (as defined in section 125).

(2) APPLICABLE EXCLUSION.—The term "applicable exclusion" means—

(A) section 120, in the case of a qualified group legal services plan, and

(B) section 125, in the case of a cafeteria plan.

- **1984 (P.L. 98-612)**

P.L. 98-612, §1(b)(1):

Amended Subpart A of part III of subchapter A of chapter 61 by adding Code Sec. 6039D. [Note: P.L. 98-611 added a Code Sec. 6039D earlier, the text of which was identical with the exception of subsection (d). A technical correction will, therefore, need to be made.]

- **1984 (P.L. 98-611)**

P.L. 98-611, §1(d)(1):

Amended Subpart A of part III of subchapter A of chapter 61 by adding Code Sec. 6039D. [Note: P.L. 98-612 also added a Code Sec. 6039D, the text of which is identical with the exception of subsection (d).]

[Sec. 6039E]

SEC. 6039E. INFORMATION CONCERNING RESIDENT STATUS.

[Sec. 6039E(a)]

(a) GENERAL RULE.—Notwithstanding any other provision of law, any individual who—

(1) applies for a United States passport (or a renewal thereof), or

(2) applies to be lawfully accorded the privilege of residing permanently in the United States as an immigrant in accordance with the immigration laws,

shall include with any such application a statement which includes the information described in subsection (b).

[Sec. 6039E(b)]

(b) INFORMATION TO BE PROVIDED.—Information required under subsection (a) shall include—

(1) the taxpayer's TIN (if any),

(2) in the case of a passport applicant, any foreign country in which such individual is residing,

(3) in the case of an individual seeking permanent residence, information with respect to whether such individual is required to file a return of the tax imposed by chapter 1 for such individual's most recent 3 taxable years, and

(4) such other information as the Secretary may prescribe.

[Sec. 6039E(c)]

(c) PENALTY.—Any individual failing to provide a statement required under subsection (a) shall be subject to a penalty equal to $500 for each such failure, unless it is shown that such failure is due to reasonable cause and not to willful neglect.

[Sec. 6039E(d)]

(d) INFORMATION TO BE PROVIDED TO SECRETARY.—Notwithstanding any other provision of law, any agency of the United States which collects (or is required to collect) the statement under subsection (a) shall—

(1) provide any such statement to the Secretary, and

(2) provide to the Secretary the name (and any other identifying information) of any individual refusing to comply with the provisions of subsection (a).

Nothing in the preceding sentence shall be construed to require the disclosure of information which is subject to section 245A of the Immigration and Nationality Act (as in effect on the date of the enactment of this sentence).

Amendments

• 1988, Technical and Miscellaneous Revenue Act of 1988 (P.L. 100-647)

P.L. 100-647, §1012(o):

Amended Code Sec. 6039E(d) by adding at the end thereof a new sentence. **Effective** as if included in the provision of P.L. 99-514 to which it relates.

[Sec. 6039E(e)]

(e) EXEMPTION.—The Secretary may by regulations exempt any class of individuals from the requirements of this section if he determines that applying this section to such individuals is not necessary to carry out the purposes of this section.

Amendments

• 1986, Tax Reform Act of 1986 (P.L. 99-514)

P.L. 99-514, §1234(a)(1):

Amended subpart A of part III of subchapter A of chapter 61 by inserting after Code Sec. 6039D new Code Sec. 6039E. **Effective** for applications submitted after 12-31-87 (or, if earlier, the **effective** date (which shall not be earlier than 1-1-87) of the initial regulations issued under Code Sec. 6039E).

[Sec. 6039F]

SEC. 6039F. NOTICE OF LARGE GIFTS RECEIVED FROM FOREIGN PERSONS.

[Sec. 6039F(a)]

(a) IN GENERAL.—If the value of the aggregate foreign gifts received by a United States person (other than an organization described in section 501(c) and exempt from tax under section 501(a)) during any taxable year exceeds $10,000, such United States person shall furnish (at such time and in such manner as the Secretary shall prescribe) such information as the Secretary may prescribe regarding each foreign gift received during such year.

[Sec. 6039F(b)]

(b) FOREIGN GIFT.—For purposes of this section, the term "foreign gift" means any amount received from a person other than a United States person which the recipient treats as a gift or bequest. Such term shall not include any qualified transfer (within the meaning of section 2503(e)(2)) or any distribution properly disclosed in a return under section 6048(c).

[Sec. 6039F(c)]

(c) PENALTY FOR FAILURE TO FILE INFORMATION.—

(1) IN GENERAL.—If a United States person fails to furnish the information required by subsection (a) with respect to any foreign gift within the time prescribed therefor (including extensions)—

(A) the tax consequences of the receipt of such gift shall be determined by the Secretary, and

(B) such United States person shall pay (upon notice and demand by the Secretary and in the same manner as tax) an amount equal to 5 percent of the amount of such foreign gift for each month for which the failure continues (not to exceed 25 percent of such amount in the aggregate).

(2) REASONABLE CAUSE EXCEPTION.—Paragraph (1) shall not apply to any failure to report a foreign gift if the United States person shows that the failure is due to reasonable cause and not due to willful neglect.

[Sec. 6039F(d)]

(d) COST-OF-LIVING ADJUSTMENT.—In the case of any taxable year beginning after December 31, 1996, the $10,000 amount under subsection (a) shall be increased by an amount equal to the product of such amount and the cost-of-living adjustment for such taxable year under section 1(f)(3), except that subparagraph (A)(ii) thereof shall be applied by substituting "1995" for "2016".

Amendments

• 2017, Tax Cuts and Jobs Act (P.L. 115-97)

P.L. 115-97, §11002(d)(13):

Amended Code Sec. 6039F(d) by striking "subparagraph (B) thereof shall be applied by substituting '1995' for '1992'" and inserting "subparagraph (A)(ii) thereof shall be applied by substituting '1995' for '2016'". **Effective** for tax years beginning after 12-31-2017.

[Sec. 6039F(e)]

(e) REGULATIONS.—The Secretary shall prescribe such regulations as may be necessary or appropriate to carry out the purposes of this section.

Amendments

• 1996, Small Business Job Protection Act of 1996 (P.L. 104-188)

P.L. 104-188, §1905(a):

Amended subpart A of part III of subchapter A of chapter 61 by inserting after section 6039E a new section 6039F. **Effective** for amounts received after 8-20-96, in tax years ending after such date.

RETURNS—INFORMATION

[Sec. 6039G]

SEC. 6039G. INFORMATION ON INDIVIDUALS LOSING UNITED STATES CITIZENSHIP.

[Sec. 6039G(a)]

(a) IN GENERAL.—Notwithstanding any other provision of law, any individual to whom section 877(b) or 877A applies for any taxable year shall provide a statement for such taxable year which includes the information described in subsection (b).

Amendments

• **2008, Heroes Earnings Assistance and Relief Tax Act of 2008 (P.L. 110-245)**

P.L. 110-245, §301(e)(1):

Amended Code Sec. 6039G(a) by inserting "or 877A" after "section 877(b)". **Effective** for any individual whose expatriation date (as so defined) is on or after 6-17-2008.

• **2004, American Jobs Creation Act of 2004 (P.L. 108-357)**

P.L. 108-357, §804(e)(1):

Amended Code Sec. 6039G(a). **Effective** for individuals who expatriate after 6-3-2004. Prior to amendment, Code Sec. 6039G(a) read as follows:

(a) IN GENERAL.—Notwithstanding any other provision of law, any individual who loses United States citizenship (within the meaning of section 877(a)) shall provide a statement which includes the information described in subsection (b). Such statement shall be—

(1) provided not later than the earliest date of any act referred to in subsection (c), and

(2) provided to the person or court referred to in subsection (c) with respect to such act.

[Sec. 6039G(b)]

(b) INFORMATION TO BE PROVIDED.—Information required under subsection (a) shall include—

(1) the taxpayer's TIN,

(2) the mailing address of such individual's principal foreign residence,

(3) the foreign country in which such individual is residing,

(4) the foreign country of which such individual is a citizen,

(5) information detailing the income, assets, and liabilities of such individual,

(6) the number of days during any portion of which that the individual was physically present in the United States during the taxable year, and

(7) such other information as the Secretary may prescribe.

Amendments

• **2004, American Jobs Creation Act of 2004 (P.L. 108-357)**

P.L. 108-357, §804(e)(2):

Amended Code Sec. 6039G(b). **Effective** for individuals who expatriate after 6-3-2004. Prior to amendment, Code Sec. 6039G(b) read as follows:

(b) INFORMATION TO BE PROVIDED.—Information required under subsection (a) shall include—

(1) the taxpayer's TIN,

(2) the mailing address of such individual's principal foreign residence,

(3) the foreign country in which such individual is residing,

(4) the foreign country of which such individual is a citizen,

(5) in the case of an individual having a net worth of at least the dollar amount applicable under section 877(a)(2)(B), information detailing the assets and liabilities of such individual, and

(6) such other information as the Secretary may prescribe.

[Sec. 6039G(c)—Stricken]

(1) the individual's renunciation of his United States nationality before a diplomatic or consular officer of the United States pursuant to paragraph (5) of section 349(a) of the Immigration and Nationality Act (8 U.S.C. 1481(a)(5)),

(2) the individual's furnishing to the United States Department of State a signed statement of voluntary relinquishment of United States nationality confirming the performance of an act of expatriation specified in paragraph (1), (2), (3), or (4) of section 349(a) of the Immigration and Nationality Act (8 U.S.C. 1481(a)(1)-(4)),

(3) the issuance by the United States Department of State of a certificate of loss of nationality to the individual, or

(4) the cancellation by a court of the United States of a naturalized citizen's certificate of naturalization.

Amendments

• **2004, American Jobs Creation Act of 2004 (P.L. 108-357)**

P.L. 108-357, §804(e)(4):

Amended Code Sec. 6039G by striking subsections (c), (f), and (g) and by redesignating subsections (d) and (e) as subsections (c) and (d), respectively. **Effective** for individuals who expatriate after 6-3-2004. Prior to being stricken, Code Sec. 6039G(c) read as follows:

(c) ACTS DESCRIBED.—For purposes of this section, the acts referred to in this subsection are—

[Sec. 6039G(c)]

(c) PENALTY.—If—

(1) an individual is required to file a statement under subsection (a) for any taxable year, and

(2) fails to file such a statement with the Secretary on or before the date such statement is required to be filed or fails to include all the information required to be shown on the statement or includes incorrect information,

such individual shall pay a penalty of $10,000 unless it is shown that such failure is due to reasonable cause and not to willful neglect.

Amendments

• **2004, American Jobs Creation Act of 2004 (P.L. 108-357)**

P.L. 108-357, §804(e)(3):

Amended Code Sec. 6039G(d). **Effective** for individuals who expatriate after 6-3-2004. Prior to amendment, Code Sec. 6039G(d) read as follows:

(d) PENALTY.—Any individual failing to provide a statement required under subsection (a) shall be subject to a penalty for each year (of the 10-year period beginning on the date of loss of United States citizenship) during any portion of which such failure continues in an amount equal to the greater of—

(1) 5 percent of the tax required to be paid under section 877 for the taxable year ending during such year, or

(2) $1,000,

unless it is shown that such failure is due to reasonable cause and not to willful neglect.

P.L. 108-357, §804(e)(4):

Amended Code Sec. 6039G by redesignating subsection (d) as subsection (c). **Effective** for individuals who expatriate after 6-3-2004.

[Sec. 6039G(d)]

(d) INFORMATION TO BE PROVIDED TO SECRETARY.—Notwithstanding any other provision of law—

(1) any Federal agency or court which collects (or is required to collect) the statement under subsection (a) shall provide to the Secretary—

(A) a copy of any such statement, and

(B) the name (and any other identifying information) of any individual refusing to comply with the provisions of subsection (a),

(2) the Secretary of State shall provide to the Secretary a copy of each certificate as to the loss of American nationality under section 358 of the Immigration and Nationality Act which is approved by the Secretary of State, and

(3) the Federal agency primarily responsible for administering the immigration laws shall provide to the Secretary the name of each lawful permanent resident of the United States (within the meaning of section 7701(b)(6)) whose status as such has been revoked or has been administratively or judicially determined to have been abandoned.

RETURNS—INFORMATION

Notwithstanding any other provision of law, not later than 30 days after the close of each calendar quarter, the Secretary shall publish in the Federal Register the name of each individual losing United States citizenship (within the meaning of section 877(a) or 877A) with respect to whom the Secretary receives information under the preceding sentence during such quarter.

Amendments

- **2008, Heroes Earnings Assistance and Relief Tax Act of 2008 (P.L. 110-245)**

P.L. 110-245, §301(e)(2):

Amended Code Sec. 6039G(d) by inserting "or 877A" after "section 877(a)". **Effective** for any individual whose expatriation date (as so defined) is on or after 6-17-2008.

Amendments

- **2004, American Jobs Creation Act of 2004 (P.L. 108-357)**

P.L. 108-357, §804(e)(4):

Amended Code Sec. 6039G by striking subsection (f). **Effective** for individuals who expatriate after 6-3-2004. Prior to being stricken, Code Sec. 6039G(f) read as follows:

Amendments

- **2004, American Jobs Creation Act of 2004 (P.L. 108-357)**

P.L. 108-357, §804(e)(4):

Amended Code Sec. 6039G by striking subsection (g). **Effective** for individuals who expatriate after 6-3-2004. Prior to being stricken, Code Sec. 6039G(g) read as follows:

(g) EXEMPTION.—The Secretary may by regulations exempt any class of individuals from the requirements of this section if he determines that applying this section to such individuals is not necessary to carry out the purposes of this section.

- **1997, Taxpayer Relief Act of 1997 (P.L. 105-34)**

P.L. 105-34, §1602(h)(1):

Amended subpart A of part III of subchapter A of chapter 61 by redesignating Code Sec. 6039F[G] (as added by Act Sec. 512 of P.L. 104-191) as Code Sec. 6039G, and by moving such Code Sec. 6039G to immediately after Code Sec. 6039F (as added by P.L. 104-191). **Effective** as if included in the provision of P.L. 104-191 to which it relates [effective, generally, for individuals losing U.S. citizenship on or after 2-6-95, and long-term U.S. residents who end U.S. residency or begin foreign residency on or after 2-6-95.—CCH].

Amendments

- **2004, American Jobs Creation Act of 2004 (P.L. 108-357)**

P.L. 108-357, §804(e)(4):

Amended Code Sec. 6039G by redesignating subsection (e) as subsection (d). **Effective** for individuals who expatriate after 6-3-2004.

(f) REPORTING BY LONG-TERM LAWFUL PERMANENT RESIDENTS WHO CEASE TO BE TAXED AS RESIDENTS.—In lieu of applying the last sentence of subsection (a), any individual who is required to provide a statement under this section by reason of section 877(e)(1) shall provide such statement with the return of tax imposed by chapter 1 for the taxable year during which the event described in such section occurs.

[Sec. 6039G(g)—Stricken]

- **1996, Health Insurance Portability and Accountability Act of 1996 (P.L. 104-191)**

P.L. 104-191, §512(a):

Amended subpart A of part III of subchapter A of chapter 61 by inserting after Code Sec. 6039E a new Code Sec. 6039F[G]. For the **effective** date, see Act Sec. 512(c), below.

P.L. 104-191, §512(c), provides:

(c) EFFECTIVE DATE.—The amendments made by this section shall apply to—

(1) individuals losing United States citizenship (within the meaning of section 877 of the Internal Revenue Code of 1986) on or after February 6, 1995, and

(2) long-term residents of the United States with respect to whom an event described in subparagraph (A) or (B) of section 877(e)(1) of such Code occurs on or after such date.

In no event shall any statement required by such amendments be due before the 90th day after the date of the enactment of this Act.

[Sec. 6039H]

SEC. 6039H. INFORMATION WITH RESPECT TO ALASKA NATIVE SETTLEMENT TRUSTS AND NATIVE CORPORATIONS.

[Sec. 6039H(a)]

(a) REQUIREMENT.—The fiduciary of an electing Settlement Trust (as defined in section 646(h)(1)) shall include with the return of income of the trust a statement containing the information required under subsection (c).

Amendments

- **2017, Tax Cuts and Jobs Act (P.L. 115-97)**

P.L. 115-97, §13821(c)(1)(A):

Amended Code Sec. 6039H by striking "**SPONSORING**" before "**NATIVE CORPORATIONS**" in the heading. **Effective** for tax years beginning after 12-31-2016.

[Sec. 6039H(b)]

(b) APPLICATION WITH OTHER REQUIREMENTS.—The filing of any statement under this section shall be in lieu of the reporting requirements under section 6034A to furnish any statement to a beneficiary regarding amounts distributed to such beneficiary (and such other reporting rules as the Secretary deems appropriate).

[Sec. 6039H(c)]

(c) REQUIRED INFORMATION.—The information required under this subsection shall include—

(1) the amount of distributions made during the taxable year to each beneficiary,

(2) the treatment of such distribution under the applicable provision of section 646, including the amount that is excludable from the recipient beneficiary's gross income under section 646, and

(3) the amount (if any) of any distribution during such year that is deemed to have been made by the sponsoring Native Corporation (as defined in section 646(h)(5)).

[Sec. 6039H(d)]

(d) SPONSORING NATIVE CORPORATION.—

(1) IN GENERAL.—The electing Settlement Trust shall, on or before the date on which the statement under subsection (a) is required to be filed, furnish such statement to the sponsoring Native Corporation (as so defined).

(2) DISTRIBUTEES.—The sponsoring Native Corporation shall furnish each recipient of a distribution described in section 646(e)(3) a statement containing the amount deemed to have been distributed to such recipient by such corporation for the taxable year.

- **2013, American Taxpayer Relief Act of 2012 (P.L. 112-240)**

P.L. 112-240, §101(a)(1) and (3), provides:

SEC. 101. PERMANENT EXTENSION AND MODIFICATION OF 2001 TAX RELIEF.

(a) PERMANENT EXTENSION.—

(1) IN GENERAL.—The Economic Growth and Tax Relief Reconciliation Act of 2001 is amended by striking title IX.

***

(3) EFFECTIVE DATE.—The amendments made by this subsection shall apply to taxable, plan, or limitation years beginning after December 31, 2012, and estates of decedents dying, gifts made, or generation skipping transfers after December 31, 2012.

- **2001, Economic Growth and Tax Relief Reconciliation Act of 2001 (P.L. 107-16)**

P.L. 107-16, §671(b):

Amended subpart A of part III of subchapter A of chapter 61 of subtitle F by inserting after Code Sec. 6039G a new Code Sec. 6039H. **Effective** for tax years ending after 6-7-2001, and to contributions made to electing Settlement Trusts for such year or any subsequent year.

RETURNS—INFORMATION

P.L. 107-16, §901(a)-(b), as amended by P.L. 111-312, §101(a)(1), provides [but see P.L. 112-240, §101(a)(1) and (3), above]:

SEC. 901. SUNSET OF PROVISIONS OF ACT.

(a) IN GENERAL.—All provisions of, and amendments made by, this Act shall not apply—

(1) to taxable, plan, or limitation years beginning after December 31, 2012, or

(2) in the case of title V, to estates of decedents dying, gifts made, or generation skipping transfers, after December 31, 2012.

(b) APPLICATION OF CERTAIN LAWS.—The Internal Revenue Code of 1986 and the Employee Retirement Income Security Act of 1974 shall be applied and administered to years, estates, gifts, and transfers described in subsection (a) as if the provisions and amendments described in subsection (a) had never been enacted.

[Sec. 6039H(e)]

(e) DEDUCTIBLE CONTRIBUTIONS BY NATIVE CORPORATIONS TO ALASKA NATIVE SETTLEMENT TRUSTS.—

(1) IN GENERAL.—Any Native Corporation (as defined in subsection (m) of section 3 of the Alaska Native Claims Settlement Act (43 U.S.C. 1602(m))) which has made a contribution to a Settlement Trust (as defined in subsection (t) of such section) to which an election under subsection (e) of section 247 applies shall provide such Settlement Trust with a statement regarding such election not later than January 31 of the calendar year subsequent to the calendar year in which the contribution was made.

(2) CONTENT OF STATEMENT.—The statement described in paragraph (1) shall include—

(A) the total amount of contributions to which the election under subsection (e) of section 247 applies,

(B) for each contribution, whether such contribution was in cash,

(C) for each contribution which consists of property other than cash, the date that such property was acquired by the Native Corporation and the adjusted basis and fair market value of such property on the date such property was contributed to the Settlement Trust,

(D) the date on which each contribution was made to the Settlement Trust, and

(E) such information as the Secretary determines to be necessary or appropriate for the identification of each contribution and the accurate inclusion of income relating to such contributions by the Settlement Trust.

Amendments

• **2017, Tax Cuts and Jobs Act (P.L. 115-97)**

P.L. 115-97, §13821(c)(1)(B):

Amended Code Sec. 6039H by adding at the end a new subsection (e). **Effective** for tax years beginning after 12-31-2016.

[Sec. 6039I]

SEC. 6039I. RETURNS AND RECORDS WITH RESPECT TO EMPLOYER-OWNED LIFE INSURANCE CONTRACTS.

[Sec. 6039I(a)]

(a) IN GENERAL.—Every applicable policyholder owning 1 or more employer-owned life insurance contracts issued after the date of the enactment of this section shall file a return (at such time and in such manner as the Secretary shall by regulations prescribe) showing for each year such contracts are owned—

(1) the number of employees of the applicable policyholder at the end of the year,

(2) the number of such employees insured under such contracts at the end of the year,

(3) the total amount of insurance in force at the end of the year under such contracts,

(4) the name, address, and taxpayer identification number of the applicable policyholder and the type of business in which the policyholder is engaged, and

(5) that the applicable policyholder has a valid consent for each insured employee (or, if all such consents are not obtained, the number of insured employees for whom such consent was not obtained).

[Sec. 6039I(b)]

(b) RECORDKEEPING REQUIREMENT.—Each applicable policyholder owning 1 or more employer-owned life insurance contracts during any year shall keep such records as may be necessary for purposes of determining whether the requirements of this section and section 101(j) are met.

[Sec. 6039I(c)]

(c) DEFINITIONS.—Any term used in this section which is used in section 101(j) shall have the same meaning given such term by section 101(j).

Amendments

• **2006, Pension Protection Act of 2006 (P.L. 109-280)**

P.L. 109-280, §863(b):

Amended subpart A of part III of subchapter A of chapter 61 by inserting after Code Sec. 6039H a new Code Sec. 6039I. **Effective** for life insurance contracts issued after 8-17-2006, except for a contract issued after such date pursuant to an exchange described in Code Sec. 1035 for a contract issued on or prior to that date. For purposes of the preceding sentence, any material increase in the death benefit or other material change shall cause the contract to be treated as a new contract except that, in the case of a master contract (within the meaning of Code Sec. 264(f)(4)(E)), the addition of covered lives shall be treated as a new contract only with respect to such additional covered lives.

[Sec. 6039J]

SEC. 6039J. INFORMATION REPORTING WITH RESPECT TO COMMODITY CREDIT CORPORATION TRANSACTIONS.

[Sec. 6039J(a)]

(a) REQUIREMENT OF REPORTING.—The Commodity Credit Corporation, through the Secretary of Agriculture, shall make a return, according to the forms and regulations prescribed by the Secretary of the Treasury, setting forth any market gain realized by a taxpayer during the taxable year in relation to the repayment of a loan issued by the Commodity Credit Corporation, without regard to the manner in which such loan was repaid.

[Sec. 6039J(b)]

(b) STATEMENTS TO BE FURNISHED TO PERSONS WITH RESPECT TO WHOM INFORMATION IS REQUIRED.—The Secretary of Agriculture shall furnish to each person whose name is required to be set forth in a return required under subsection (a) a written statement showing the amount of market gain reported in such return.

Amendments

• **2008, Heartland, Habitat, Harvest, and Horticulture Act of 2008 (P.L. 110-246)**

P.L. 110-246, §15353(a):

Amended subpart A of part III of subchapter A of chapter 61 by inserting after Code Sec. 6039I a new Code Sec. 6039J. **Effective** for loans repaid on or after 1-1-2007.

RETURNS—INFORMATION

[Sec. 6040]

SEC. 6040. CROSS REFERENCES.

(1) For the notice required of persons acting in a fiduciary capacity for taxpayers or for transferees, see sections 6212, 6901(g), and 6903.

(2) For application by fiduciary for determination of tax and discharge from personal liability therefor, see section 2204.

(3) For the notice required of taxpayers for redetermination of taxes claimed as credits, see sections 905(c) and 2016.

(4) For exemption certificates required to be furnished to employers by employees, see section 3402(f)(2), (3), (4), and (5).

(5) For receipts, constituting information returns, required to be furnished to employees, see section 6051.

(6) [Repealed].

(7) For information required with respect to the redemption of stamps, see section 6805.

(8) For the statement required to be filed by a corporation expecting a net operating loss carryback or unused excess profits credit carryback, see section 6164.

(9) For the application, which a taxpayer may file for a tentative carryback adjustment of income taxes, see section 6411.

Amendments

• **1970, Excise, Estate, and Gift Tax Adjustment Act of 1970 (P.L. 91-614)**

P.L. 91-614, §101(d)(2):

Amended Code Sec. 6040(2) by substituting "fiduciary" for "executor." **Effective** 1-1-71.

• **1965, Excise Tax Reduction Act of 1965 (P.L. 89-44)**

P.L. 89-44, §305(b):

Repealed subsection (6) of Sec. 6040. **Effective** noon on 12-31-65. Prior to repeal, subsection (6) of Sec. 6040 read as follows:

(6) For the requirement to print the price of an admission on a ticket, see section 4234.

• **1964, Revenue Act of 1964 (P.L. 88-272)**

P.L. 88-272, §221(b)(1):

The above section was renumbered from 6039 to 6040.

• **1960 (P.L. 86-780)**

P.L. 86-780, §6(a):

The above section was formerly Sec. 6038 prior to its redesignation by Act Sec. 6(a). **Effective** 1-1-61.

• **1958, Technical Amendments Act of 1958 (P.L. 85-866)**

P.L. 85-866, §64(c):

Redesignated Code Sec. 6037 as 6038. **Effective** for tax years ending after 12-31-57.

Subpart B—Information Concerning Transactions With Other Persons

Sec. 6041.	Information at source.
Sec. 6041A.	Returns regarding payments of remuneration for services and direct sales.
Sec. 6042.	Returns regarding payments of dividends and corporate earnings and profits.
Sec. 6043.	Liquidating, etc., transactions.
Sec. 6043A.	Returns relating to taxable mergers and acquisitions.
Sec. 6044.	Returns regarding payments of patronage dividends.
Sec. 6045.	Returns of brokers.
Sec. 6045A.	Information required in connection with transfers of covered securities to brokers.
Sec. 6045B.	Returns relating to actions affecting basis of specified securities.
Sec. 6046.	Returns as to organization or reorganization of foreign corporations and as to acquisitions of their stock.
Sec. 6046A.	Returns as to interests in foreign partnerships.
Sec. 6047.	Information relating to certain trusts and annuity plans.
Sec. 6048.	Information with respect to certain foreign trusts.
Sec. 6049.	Returns regarding payments of interest.
Sec. 6050A.	Reporting requirements of certain fishing boat operators.
Sec. 6050B.	Returns relating to unemployment compensation.
Sec. 6050D.	Returns relating to energy grants and financing.
Sec. 6050E.	State and local income tax refunds.
Sec. 6050F.	Returns relating to social security benefits.
Sec. 6050G.	Returns relating to certain railroad retirement benefits.
Sec. 6050H.	Returns relating to mortgage interest received in trade or business from individuals.
Sec. 6050I.	Returns relating to cash received in trade or business, etc.
Sec. 6050J.	Returns relating to foreclosures and abandonments of security.
Sec. 6050K.	Returns relating to exchanges of certain partnership interests.
Sec. 6050L.	Returns relating to certain donated property.
Sec. 6050M.	Returns relating to persons receiving contracts from Federal executive agencies.
Sec. 6050N.	Returns regarding payments of royalties.
Sec. 6050P.	Returns relating to the cancellation of indebtedness by certain entities.
Sec. 6050Q.	Certain long-term care benefits.
Sec. 6050R.	Returns relating to certain purchases of fish.
Sec. 6050S.	Returns relating to higher education tuition and related expenses.
Sec. 6050T.	Returns relating to credit for health insurance costs of eligible individuals.
Sec. 6050U.	Charges or payments for qualified long-term care insurance contracts under combined arrangements.
Sec. 6050V.	Returns relating to applicable insurance contracts in which certain exempt organizations hold interests.
Sec. 6050W.	Returns relating to payments made in settlement of payment card and third party network transactions.
Sec. 6050X.	Information with respect to certain fines, penalties, and other amounts.
Sec. 6050Y.	Returns relating to certain life insurance contract transactions.
Sec. 6050Z.	Reports relating to long-term care premium statements.

RETURNS—INFORMATION

[Sec. 6041]

SEC. 6041. INFORMATION AT SOURCE.

[Sec. 6041(a)]

(a) PAYMENTS OF $600 OR MORE.—All persons engaged in a trade or business and making payment in the course of such trade or business to another person, of rent, salaries, wages, premiums, annuities, compensations, remunerations, emoluments, or other fixed or determinable gains, profits, and income (other than payments to which section 6042(a)(1), 6044(a)(1), 6047(e)[d], 6049(a), or 6050N(a) applies, and other than payments with respect to which a statement is required under the authority of section 6042(a)(2), 6044(a)(2), or 6045), of $600 or more in any taxable year, or, in the case of such payments made by the United States, the officers or employees of the United States having information as to such payments and required to make returns in regard thereto by the regulations hereinafter provided for, shall render a true and accurate return to the Secretary, under such regulations and in such form and manner and to such extent as may be prescribed by the Secretary, setting forth the amount of such gains, profits, and income, and the name and address of the recipient of such payment.

Amendments

• **2011, Comprehensive 1099 Taxpayer Protection and Repayment of Exchange Subsidy Overpayments Act of 2011 (P.L. 112-9)**

P.L. 112-9, § 2(b)(1)-(2):

Amended Code Sec. 6041(a) by striking "amounts in consideration for property," following "wages,", and by striking "gross proceeds," after "emoluments, or other" and "setting forth the amount of such". **Effective** for payments made after 12-31-2011.

• **2010, Patient Protection and Affordable Care Act (P.L. 111-148)**

P.L. 111-148, § 9006(b)(1)-(3):

Amended Code Sec. 6041(a) by inserting "amounts in consideration for property," after "wages,", by inserting "gross proceeds," after "emoluments, or other" and "setting forth the amount of such". **Effective** for payments made after 12-31-2011.

• **2002, Job Creation and Worker Assistance Act of 2002 (P.L. 107-147)**

P.L. 107-147, § 401, provides:

SEC. 401. ALLOWANCE OF ELECTRONIC 1099's.

Any person required to furnish a statement under any section of subpart B of part III of subchapter A of chapter 61 of the Internal Revenue Code of 1986 for any taxable year ending after the date of the enactment of this Act, may electronically furnish such statement (without regard to any first class mailing requirement) to any recipient who has consented to the electronic provision of the statement in a manner similar to the one permitted under regulations issued under section 6051 of such Code or in such other manner as provided by the Secretary.

• **1986, Tax Reform Act of 1986 (P.L. 99-514)**

P.L. 99-514, § 1523(b)(2):

Amended Code Sec. 6041(a) by striking out "or 6049(a)" and inserting in lieu thereof "6049(a), or 6050N(a)". **Effective** with respect to payments made after 12-31-86.

• **1984, Deficit Reduction Act of 1984 (P.L. 98-369)**

P.L. 98-369, § 722(h)(4)(B):

Amended Code Sec. 6041(a) by inserting "6047(e)," after "6044(a)(1),". **Effective** for payments or distributions after 12-31-84, unless the payor elects to have such amendments apply to payments or distributions before 1-1-85.

• **1982, Tax Equity and Fiscal Responsibility Act of 1982 (P.L. 97-248)**

P.L. 97-248, § 309(b)(1):

Amended Code Sec. 6041(a) by striking out "6049(a)(1)" and inserting "6049(a)" and by striking out "6045, 6049(a)(2), or 6049(a)(3)" and inserting "or 6045". **Effective** for amounts paid (or treated as paid) after 12-31-82.

• **1976, Tax Reform Act of 1976 (P.L. 94-455)**

P.L. 94-455, § 1906(b)(13)(A):

Amended 1954 Code by substituting "Secretary" for "Secretary or his delegate" each place it appeared. **Effective** 2-1-77.

P.L. 94-455, § 2111(a), provided:

"(a) SUSPENSION OF RULINGS.—Until January 1, 1979, the law with respect to the duty of an employer under section 6041(a) of the Internal Revenue Code of 1954 to report charge account tips of employees to the Internal Revenue Service (other than charge account tips included in statements furnished to the employer under section 6053(a) of such Code) shall be administered—

"(1) without regard to Revenue Rulings 75-400 and 76-231, and

"(2) in accordance with the manner in which such law was administered before the issuance of such rulings."

Effective 1-1-76.

• **1962, Revenue Act of 1962 (P.L. 87-834)**

P.L. 87-834, § 19(f):

Amended Code Sec. 6041(a) by substituting "(other than payments to which section 6042(a)(1), 6044(a)(1), or 6049(a)(1) applies, and other than payments with respect to which a statement is required under the authority of section 6042(a)(2), 6044(a)(2), 6045, 6049(a)(2), or 6049(a)(3))" for "(other than payments described in section 6042(1) or section 6045)". **Effective** 10-17-62.

[Sec. 6041(b)]

(b) COLLECTION OF FOREIGN ITEMS.—In the case of collections of items (not payable in the United States) of interest upon the bonds of foreign countries and interest upon the bonds of and dividends from foreign corporations by any person undertaking as a matter of business or for profit the collection of foreign payments of such interest or dividends by means of coupons, checks, or bills of exchange, such person shall make a return according to the forms or regulations prescribed by the Secretary, setting forth the amount paid and the name and address of the recipient of each such payment.

Amendments

• **1976, Tax Reform Act of 1976 (P.L. 94-455)**

P.L. 94-455, § 1906(b)(13)(A):

Amended 1954 Code by substituting "Secretary" for "Secretary or his delegate" each place it appeared. **Effective** 2-1-77.

[Sec. 6041(c)]

(c) RECIPIENT TO FURNISH NAME AND ADDRESS.—When necessary to make effective the provisions of this section, the name and address of the recipient of income shall be furnished upon demand of the person paying the income.

Amendments

• **1978, Revenue Act of 1978 (P.L. 95-600)**

P.L. 95-600, § 501(b):

Redesignated the former Code Sec. 6041(d) as 6041(c) and added a new Code Sec. 6041(d). **Effective** for payments made after 12-31-78.

• **1962, Revenue Act of 1962 (P.L. 87-834)**

P.L. 87-834, § 19(f):

Repealed Code Sec. 6041(c). **Effective** 10-17-62. Prior to repeal, Code Sec. 6041(c) read as follows:

"(c) Payments of Interest by Corporations.—Every corporation making payments of interest, regardless of amounts, shall, when required by regulations of the Secretary or his delegate, make a return according to the forms or regulations prescribed by the Secretary or his delegate, setting forth the amount paid and the name and address of the recipient of each such payment."

[Sec. 6041(d)]

(d) STATEMENTS TO BE FURNISHED TO PERSONS WITH RESPECT TO WHOM INFORMATION IS REQUIRED.—Every person required to make a return under subsection (a) shall furnish to each person with respect to whom such a return is required a written statement showing—

(1) the name, address, and phone number of the information contact of the person required to make such return, and

(2) the aggregate amount of payments to the person required to be shown on the return.

The written statement required under the preceding sentence shall be furnished to the person on or before January 31 of the year following the calendar year for which the return under subsection (a) was required to be made. To the extent provided in regulations prescribed by the Secretary, this subsection shall also apply to persons required to make returns under subsection (b).

Amendments

• **1996, Taxpayer Bill of Rights 2 (P.L. 104-168)**

P.L. 104-168, §1201(a)(1):

Amended Code Sec. 6041(d)(1) by striking "name and address" and inserting "name, address, and phone number of the information contact". **Effective** for statements required to be furnished after 12-31-96 (determined without regard to any extension).

• **1986, Tax Reform Act of 1986 (P.L. 99-514)**

P.L. 99-514, §1501(c)(1):

Amended Code Sec. 6041(d). **Effective** for returns the due date for which (determined without regard to extensions) is after 12-31-86. Prior to amendment, Code Sec. 6041(d) read as follows:

(d) STATEMENT TO BE FURNISHED TO PERSONS WITH RESPECT TO WHOM INFORMATION IS FURNISHED.—Every person making a return under subsection (a) shall furnish to each person whose name is set forth in such return a written statement showing—

(1) the name, address, and identification number of the person making such return, and

(2) the aggregate amount of payments to the person shown on the return.

The written statement required under the preceding sentence shall be furnished to the person on or before January 31 of the year following the calendar year for which the return under subsection (a) was made. To the extent provided in regulations prescribed by the Secretary, this subsection shall also apply to persons making returns under subsection (b).

• **1981, Economic Recovery Tax Act of 1981 (P.L. 97-34)**

P.L. 97-34, §723(b)(1):

Added Code Sec. 6041(d). **Effective** for returns and statements required to be furnished after 12-31-81.

[Sec. 6041(e)]

(e) SECTION DOES NOT APPLY TO CERTAIN TIPS.—This section shall not apply to tips with respect to which section 6053(a) (relating to reporting of tips) applies.

Amendments

• **1981, Economic Recovery Tax Act of 1981 (P.L. 97-34)**

P.L. 97-34, §723(b)(1):

Redesignated Code Sec. 6041(d) as Code Sec. 6041(e). **Effective** for returns and statements required to be furnished after 12-31-81.

• **1978, Revenue Act of 1978 (P.L. 95-600)**

P.L. 95-600, §501(b):

Redesignated the former Code Sec. 6041(d) as 6041(c) and added a new Code Sec. 6041(d). **Effective** for payments made after 12-31-78.

[Sec. 6041(f)]

(f) SECTION DOES NOT APPLY TO CERTAIN HEALTH ARRANGEMENTS.—This section shall not apply to any payment for medical care (as defined in section 213(d)) made under—

(1) a flexible spending arrangement (as defined in section 106(c)(2)), or

(2) a health reimbursement arrangement which is treated as employer-provided coverage under an accident or health plan for purposes of section 106.

Amendments

• **2003, Medicare Prescription Drug, Improvement, and Modernization Act of 2003 (P.L. 108-173)**

P.L. 108-173, §1203(a):

Amended Code Sec. 6041 by adding at the end a new subsection (f). **Effective** for payments made after 12-31-2002.

[Sec. 6041(g)]

(g) NONQUALIFIED DEFERRED COMPENSATION.—Subsection (a) shall apply to—

(1) any deferrals for the year under a nonqualified deferred compensation plan (within the meaning of section 409A(d)), whether or not paid, except that this paragraph shall not apply to deferrals which are required to be reported under section 6051(a)(13) (without regard to any de minimis exception), and

(2) any amount includible under section 409A and which is not treated as wages under section 3401(a).

Amendments

• **2004, American Jobs Creation Act of 2004 (P.L. 108-357)**

P.L. 108-357, §885(b)(3):

Amended Code Sec. 6041 by adding at the end a new subsection (g). **Effective** generally for amounts deferred after 12-31-2004. For special rules, see Act Sec. 885(d)(2)-(3), (e), and (f), below.

P.L. 108-357, §885(d)(2)-(3), (e), and (f), provide:

(2) SPECIAL RULES.—

(A) EARNINGS.—The amendments made by this section shall apply to earnings on deferred compensation only to the extent that such amendments apply to such compensation.

(B) MATERIAL MODIFICATIONS.—For purposes of this subsection, amounts deferred in taxable years beginning before January 1, 2005, shall be treated as amounts deferred in a taxable year beginning on or after such date if the plan under which the deferral is made is materially modified after October 3, 2004, unless such modification is pursuant to the guidance issued under subsection (f).

(3) EXCEPTION FOR NONELECTIVE DEFERRED COMPENSATION.—The amendments made by this section shall not apply to any nonelective deferred compensation to which section 457 of the Internal Revenue Code of 1986 does not apply by reason of section 457(e)(12) of such Code, but only if such compensation is provided under a nonqualified deferred compensation plan—

(A) which was in existence on May 1, 2004,

(B) which was providing nonelective deferred compensation described in such section 457(e)(12) on such date, and

(C) which is established or maintained by an organization incorporated on July 2, 1974.

If, after May 1, 2004, a plan described in the preceding sentence adopts a plan amendment which provides a material change in the classes of individuals eligible to participate in the plan, this paragraph shall not apply to any nonelective deferred compensation provided under the plan on or after the date of the adoption of the amendment.

(e) GUIDANCE RELATING TO CHANGE OF OWNERSHIP OR CONTROL.—Not later than 90 days after the date of the enactment of this Act, the Secretary of the Treasury shall issue guidance on what constitutes a change in ownership or effective control for purposes of section 409A of the Internal Revenue Code of 1986, as added by this section.

(f) GUIDANCE RELATING TO TERMINATION OF CERTAIN EXISTING ARRANGEMENTS.—Not later than 60 days after the date of the enactment of this Act, the Secretary of the Treasury shall issue guidance providing a limited period during which a nonqualified deferred compensation plan adopted before December 31, 2004, may, without violating the requirements of paragraphs (2), (3), and (4) of section 409A(a) of the Internal Revenue Code of 1986 (as added by this section), be amended—

(1) to provide that a participant may terminate participation in the plan, or cancel an outstanding deferral election with regard to amounts deferred after December 31, 2004, but only if amounts subject to the termination or cancellation are includible in income of the participant as earned (or, if later, when no longer subject to substantial risk of forfeiture), and

(2) to conform to the requirements of such section 409A with regard to amounts deferred after December 31, 2004.

[Sec. 6041(h)—Stricken]

Amendments

• **2011, Comprehensive 1099 Taxpayer Protection and Repayment of Exchange Subsidy Overpayments Act of 2011 (P.L. 112-9)**

P.L. 112-9, §3(a):

Amended Code Sec. 6041 by striking subsection (h). **Effective** for payments made after 12-31-2010. Prior to being stricken, Code Sec. 6041(h) read as follows:

(h) TREATMENT OF RENTAL PROPERTY EXPENSE PAYMENTS.—

(1) IN GENERAL.—Solely for purposes of subsection (a) and except as provided in paragraph (2), a person receiving rental income from real estate shall be considered to be engaged in a trade or business of renting property.

(2) EXCEPTIONS.—Paragraph (1) shall not apply to—

(A) any individual, including any individual who is an active member of the uniformed services or an employee of the intelligence community (as defined in section 121(d)(9)(C)(iv)), if substantially all rental income is derived from renting the principal residence (within the meaning of section 121) of such individual on a temporary basis,

(B) any individual who receives rental income of not more than the minimal amount, as determined under regulations prescribed by the Secretary, and

(C) any other individual for whom the requirements of this section would cause hardship, as determined under regulations prescribed by the Secretary.

RETURNS—INFORMATION

- **2010, Creating Small Business Jobs Act of 2010 (P.L. 111-240)**

P.L. 111-240, §2101(a):

Amended Code Sec. 6041, as amended by section 9006 of the Patient Protection and Affordable Care Act [P.L. 111-148], by redesignating subsections (h) and (i) as subsections (i) and (j), respectively, and by inserting after subsection (g) a new subsection (h). **Effective** for payments made after 12-31-2010.

[Sec. 6041(i)—Stricken]

Amendments

- **2011, Comprehensive 1099 Taxpayer Protection and Repayment of Exchange Subsidy Overpayments Act of 2011 (P.L. 112-9)**

P.L. 112-9, §2(a):

Amended Code Sec. 6041 by striking subsection (i). **Effective** for payments made after 12-31-2011. Prior to being stricken, Code Sec. 6041(i) read as follows:

(i) APPLICATION TO CORPORATIONS.—Notwithstanding any regulation prescribed by the Secretary before the date of the enactment of this subsection, for purposes of this section the term "person" includes any corporation that is not an organization exempt from tax under section 501(a).

- **2010, Creating Small Business Jobs Act of 2010 (P.L. 111-240)**

P.L. 111-240, §2101(a):

Amended Code Sec. 6041, as amended by section 9006 of the Patient Protection and Affordable Care Act [P.L. 111-148], by redesignating subsection (h) as subsection (i). **Effective** for payments made after 12-31-2010.

- **2010, Patient Protection and Affordable Care Act (P.L. 111-148)**

P.L. 111-148, §9006(a):

Amended Code Sec. 6041 by adding at the end a new subsection (h). **Effective** for payments made after 12-31-2011.

[Sec. 6041(j)—Stricken]

Amendments

- **2011, Comprehensive 1099 Taxpayer Protection and Repayment of Exchange Subsidy Overpayments Act of 2011 (P.L. 112-9)**

P.L. 112-9, §2(a):

Amended Code Sec. 6041 by striking subsection (j). **Effective** for payments made after 12-31-2011. Prior to being stricken, Code Sec. 6041(j) read as follows:

(j) REGULATIONS.—The Secretary may prescribe such regulations and other guidance as may be appropriate or necessary to carry out the purposes of this section, including rules to prevent duplicative reporting of transactions.

- **2010, Creating Small Business Jobs Act of 2010 (P.L. 111-240)**

P.L. 111-240, §2101(a):

Amended Code Sec. 6041, as amended by section 9006 of the Patient Protection and Affordable Care Act [P.L. 111-148], by redesignating subsection (i) as subsection (j). **Effective** for payments made after 12-31-2010.

- **2010, Patient Protection and Affordable Care Act (P.L. 111-148)**

P.L. 111-148, §9006(a):

Amended Code Sec. 6041 by adding at the end a new subsection (i). **Effective** for payments made after 12-31-2011.

[Sec. 6041A]

SEC. 6041A. RETURNS REGARDING PAYMENTS OF REMUNERATION FOR SERVICES AND DIRECT SALES.

[Sec. 6041A(a)]

(a) RETURNS REGARDING REMUNERATION FOR SERVICES.—If—

(1) any service-recipient engaged in a trade or business pays in the course of such trade or business during any calendar year remuneration to any person for services performed by such person, and

(2) the aggregate of such remuneration paid to such person during such calendar year is $600 or more,

then the service-recipient shall make a return, according to the forms or regulations prescribed by the Secretary, setting forth the aggregate amount of such payments and the name and address of the recipient of such payments. For purposes of the preceding sentence, the term "service-recipient" means the person for whom the service is performed.

[Sec. 6041A(b)]

(b) DIRECT SALES OF $5,000 OR MORE.—

(1) IN GENERAL.—If—

(A) any person engaged in a trade or business in the course of such trade or business during any calendar year sells consumer products to any buyer on a buy-sell basis, a deposit-commission basis, or any similar basis which the Secretary prescribes by regulations, for resale (by the buyer or any other person) in the home or otherwise than in a permanent retail establishment, and

(B) the aggregate amount of the sales to such buyer during such calendar year is $5,000 or more,

then such person shall make a return, according to the forms or regulations prescribed by the Secretary, setting forth the name and address of the buyer to whom such sales are made.

(2) DEFINITIONS.—For purposes of paragraph (1)—

(A) BUY-SELL BASIS.—A transaction is on a buy-sell basis if the buyer performing the services is entitled to retain part or all of the difference between the price at which the buyer purchases the product and the price at which the buyer sells the product as part or all of the buyer's remuneration for the services, and

(B) DEPOSIT-COMMISSION BASIS.—A transaction is on a deposit-commission basis if the buyer performing the services is entitled to retain part or all of a purchase deposit paid by the consumer in connection with the transaction as part or all of the buyer's remuneration for the services.

[Sec. 6041A(c)]

(c) CERTAIN SERVICES NOT INCLUDED.—No return shall be required under subsection (a) or (b) if a statement with respect to the services is required to be furnished under section 6051, 6052, or 6053.

[Sec. 6041A(d)]

(d) APPLICATIONS TO GOVERNMENTAL UNITS.—

(1) TREATED AS PERSONS.—The term "person" includes any governmental unit (and any agency or instrumentality thereof).

(2) SPECIAL RULES.—In the case of any payment by a governmental entity or any agency or instrumentality thereof—

(A) subsection (a) shall be applied without regard to the trade or business requirement contained therein, and

(B) any return under this section shall be made by the officer or employee having control of the payment or appropriately designated for the purpose of making such return.

(3) PAYMENTS TO CORPORATIONS BY FEDERAL EXECUTIVE AGENCIES.—

(A) IN GENERAL.—Notwithstanding any regulation prescribed by the Secretary before the date of the enactment of this paragraph, subsection (a) shall apply to remuneration paid to a corporation by any Federal executive agency (as defined in section 6050M(b)).

(B) EXCEPTION.—Subparagraph (A) shall not apply to—

(i) services under contracts described in section 6050M(e)(3) with respect to which the requirements of section 6050M(e)(2) are met, and

(ii) such other services as the Secretary may specify in regulations prescribed after the date of the enactment of this paragraph.

RETURNS—INFORMATION

Amendments

• **1997, Taxpayer Relief Act of 1997 (P.L. 105-34)**

P.L. 105-34, §1022(a):

Amended Code Sec. 6041A(d) by adding at the end a new paragraph (3). **Effective** for returns the due date for which (determined without regard to any extension) is more than 90 days after 8-5-97.

[Sec. 6041A(e)]

(e) STATEMENTS TO BE FURNISHED TO PERSONS WITH RESPECT TO WHOM INFORMATION IS REQUIRED TO BE FURNISHED.—Every person required to make a return under subsection (a) or (b) shall furnish to each person whose name is required to be set forth in such return a written statement showing—

(1) the name, address, and phone number of the information contact of the person required to make such return, and

(2) in the case of subsection (a), the aggregate amount of payments to the person required to be shown on such return.

The written statement required under the preceding sentence shall be furnished to the person on or before January 31 of the year following the calendar year for which the return under subsection (a) was made.

Amendments

• **1996, Taxpayer Bill of Rights 2 (P.L. 104-168)**

P.L. 104-168, §1201(a)(2):

Amended Code Sec. 6041A(e)(1) by striking "name and address" and inserting "name, address, and phone number of the information contact". **Effective** for statements required to be furnished after 12-31-96 (determined without regard to any extension).

[Sec. 6041A(f)]

(f) RECIPIENT TO FURNISH NAME, ADDRESS, AND IDENTIFICATION NUMBER; INCLUSION ON RETURN.—

(1) FURNISHING OF INFORMATION.—Any person with respect to whom a return or statement is required under this section to be made by another person shall furnish to such other person his name, address, and identification number at such time and in such manner as the Secretary may prescribe by regulations.

(2) INCLUSION ON RETURN.—The person to whom an identification number is furnished under paragraph (1) shall include such number on any return which such person is required to file under this section and to which such identification number relates.

Amendments

• **1982, Tax Equity and Fiscal Responsibility Act of 1982 (P.L. 97-248)**

P.L. 97-248, §312(a):

Added Code Sec. 6041A. **Effective** with respect to payments and sales made after 12-31-82.

[Sec. 6042]

SEC. 6042. RETURNS REGARDING PAYMENTS OF DIVIDENDS AND CORPORATE EARNINGS AND PROFITS.

[Sec. 6042(a)]

(a) REQUIREMENT OF REPORTING.—

(1) IN GENERAL.—Every person—

(A) who makes payments of dividends aggregating $10 or more to any other person during any calendar year, or

(B) who receives payments of dividends as a nominee and who makes payments aggregating $10 or more during any calendar year to any other person with respect to the dividends so received,

shall make a return according to the forms or regulations prescribed by the Secretary, setting forth the aggregate amount of such payments and the name and address of the person to whom paid.

(2) RETURNS REQUIRED BY THE SECRETARY.—Every person who makes payments of dividends aggregating less than $10 to any other person during any calendar year shall, when required by the Secretary, make a return setting forth the aggregate amount of such payments, and the name and address of the person to whom paid.

Amendments

• **1983, Interest and Dividend Tax Compliance Act of 1983 (P.L. 98-67)**

P.L. 98-67, §102(a):

Repealed the amendments to Code Sec. 6042(a)(1), which were made by P.L. 97-248, as though they had not been made. **Effective** as of the close of 6-30-83. Code Sec. 6042(a)(1), as amended by P.L. 97-248, read as follows:

(1) IN GENERAL.—Every person—

(A) who makes payments of dividends aggregating $10 or more to any other person during any calendar year,

(B) who receives payments of dividends as a nominee and who makes payments aggregating $10 or more during any calendar year to any other person with respect to the dividend so received, *or*

(C) who is required to withhold tax under section 3451 on any payment of dividends,

shall make a return according to the forms or regulations prescribed by the Secretary, setting forth the aggregate amount of such payments and the name and address of the person to whom paid and, in the case of a payment upon which tax is withheld, the amount of tax withheld.

• **1982, Tax Equity and Fiscal Responsibility Act of 1982 (P.L. 97-248)**

P.L. 97-248, §303(a)(1):

Amended Code Sec. 6042(a)(1) to read as noted under the historical comment for P.L. 98-67. **Effective** 7-1-83.

• **1976, Tax Reform Act of 1976 (P.L. 94-455)**

P.L. 94-455, §1906(b)(13)(A):

Amended 1954 Code by substituting "Secretary" for "Secretary or his delegate" each place it appeared. **Effective** 2-1-77.

[Sec. 6042(b)]

(b) DIVIDEND DEFINED.—

(1) GENERAL RULE.—For purposes of this section, the term "dividend" means—

(A) any distribution by a corporation which is a dividend (as defined in section 316); and

(B) any payment made by a stockbroker to any person as a substitute for a dividend (as so defined).

(2) EXCEPTIONS.—For purposes of this section, the term "dividend" does not include any distribution or payment—

(A) to the extent provided in regulations prescribed by the Secretary—

(i) by a foreign corporation, or

(ii) to a foreign corporation, a nonresident alien, or a partnership not engaged in a trade or business in the United States and composed in whole or in part of nonresident aliens, or

(B) except to the extent otherwise provided in regulations prescribed by the Secretary, to any person described in section 6049(b)(4).

RETURNS—INFORMATION

(3) SPECIAL RULE.—If the person making any payment described in subsection (a)(1)(A) or (B) is unable to determine the portion of such payment which is a dividend or is paid with respect to a dividend, he shall, for purposes of subsection (a)(1), treat the entire amount of such payment as a dividend or as an amount paid with respect to a dividend.

Amendments

• **1984, Deficit Reduction Act of 1984 (P.L. 98-369)**

P.L. 98-369, § 714(d):

Amended Code Sec. 6042(b)(2). **Effective** as if included in the provision of P.L. 97-248 to which it relates. Prior to amendment, it read as follows:

(2) EXCEPTIONS.—For purposes of this section, to the extent provided in regulations prescribed by the Secretary, the term "dividend" does not include any distribution or payment—

(A) by a foreign corporation, or

(B) to a foreign corporation, a nonresident alien, or a partnership not engaged in a trade or business in the United States and composed in whole or in part of nonresident aliens.

• **1982, Subchapter S Revision Act of 1982 (P.L. 97-354)**

P.L. 97-354, § 5(a)(40):

Amended Code Sec. 6042(b)(2). **Effective** for tax years beginning after 12-31-82. Prior to amendment, it read as follows:

(2) EXCEPTIONS.—For purposes of this section, the term "dividend" does not include—

(A) to the extent provided in regulations prescribed by the Secretary, any distribution or payment—

(i) by a foreign corporation, or

(ii) to a foreign corporation, a nonresident alien, or a partnership not engaged in trade or business in the United States and composed in whole or in part of nonresident aliens; and

(B) any amount described in section 1373 (relating to undistributed taxable income of electing small business corporations).

• **1976, Tax Reform Act of 1976 (P.L. 94-455)**

P.L. 94-455, § 1906(b)(13)(A):

Amended 1954 Code by substituting "Secretary" for "Secretary or his delegate" each place it appeared. **Effective** 2-1-77.

[Sec. 6042(c)]

(c) STATEMENTS TO BE FURNISHED TO PERSONS WITH RESPECT TO WHOM INFORMATION IS REQUIRED.—Every person required to make a return under subsection (a) shall furnish to each person whose name is required to be set forth in such return a written statement showing—

(1) the name, address, and phone number of the information contact of the person required to make such return, and

(2) the aggregate amount of payments to the person required to be shown on the return.

The written statement required under the preceding sentence shall be furnished (either in person or in a statement mailing by first-class mail which includes adequate notice that the statement is enclosed) to the person on or before January 31 of the year following the calendar year for which the return under subsection (a) was required to be made and shall be in such form as the Secretary may prescribe by regulations.

Amendments

• **1996, Taxpayer Bill of Rights 2 (P.L. 104-168)**

P.L. 104-168, § 1201(a)(3):

Amended Code Sec. 6042(c)(1) by striking "name and address" and inserting "name, address, and phone number of the information contact". **Effective** for statements required to be furnished after 12-31-96 (determined without regard to any extension).

• **1986, Tax Reform Act of 1986 (P.L. 99-514)**

P.L. 99-514, § 1501(c)(2):

Amended Code Sec. 6042(c). **Effective** for returns the due date for which (determined without regard to extensions) is after 10-22-86. Prior to amendment, Code Sec. 6042(c) read as follows:

(c) STATEMENTS TO BE FURNISHED TO PERSONS WITH RESPECT TO WHOM INFORMATION IS FURNISHED.—Every person making a return under subsection (a)(1) shall furnish to each person whose name is set forth in such return a written statement showing—

(1) the name and address of the person making such return, and

(2) the aggregate amount of payments to the person as shown on such return.

The written statement required under the preceding sentence shall be furnished (either in person or in a separate mailing by first-class mail) to the person on or before January 31 of the year following the calendar year for which the return under subsection (a) was made, and shall be in such form as the Secretary may prescribe by regulations.

• **1983, Interest and Dividend Tax Compliance Act of 1983 (P.L. 98-67)**

P.L. 98-67, § 102(a):

Repealed the amendments made by P.L. 97-248 to the first text of Code Sec. 6042(c) as though such amendments had not been enacted. **Effective** as of the close of 6-30-83.

P.L. 98-67, § 108(b):

Amended Code Sec. 6042(c). **Effective** with respect to payments made after 12-31-83. Prior to amendment, Code Sec. 6042(c) read as follows:

(c) STATEMENTS TO BE FURNISHED TO PERSONS WITH RESPECT TO WHOM INFORMATION IS FURNISHED.—Every person making a return under subsection (a)(1) shall furnish to each person whose name is set forth in such return a written statement showing—

(1) the name and address of the person making such return, and

(2) the aggregate amount of payments to the person as shown on such return.

The written statement required under the preceding sentence shall be furnished to the person on or before January 31 of the year following the calendar year for which the return under subsection (a)(1) was made. No statement shall be required to be furnished to any person under this subsection if the aggregate amount of payments to such person as shown on the return made under subsection (a)(1) is less than $10.

• **1982, Tax Equity and Fiscal Responsibility Act of 1982 (P.L. 97-248)**

P.L. 97-248, § 303(a)(2):

Amended Code Sec. 6042(c) by striking out "and" at the end of paragraph (1), by striking out the period at the end of paragraph (2) and inserting ", and", by inserting paragraph (3), and by striking out "No statement" in the last sentence and inserting "Except in the case of a return required by reason of subparagraph (C) of subsection (a)(1), no statement". **Effective** 7-1-83.

[Sec. 6042(d)]

(d) STATEMENTS TO BE FURNISHED BY CORPORATIONS TO SECRETARY.—Every corporation shall, when required by the Secretary—

(1) furnish to the Secretary a statement stating the name and address of each shareholder, and the number of shares owned by each shareholder;

(2) furnish to the Secretary a statement of such facts as will enable him to determine the portion of the earnings and profits of the corporation (including gains, profits, and income not taxed) accumulated during such periods as the Secretary may specify, which have been distributed or ordered to be distributed, respectively, to its shareholders during such taxable years as the Secretary may specify; and

(3) furnish to the Secretary a statement of its accumulated earnings and profits and the names and addresses of the individuals or shareholders who would be entitled to such accumulated earnings and profits if divided or distributed, and of the amounts that would be payable to each.

Amendments

• **1976, Tax Reform Act of 1976 (P.L. 94-455)**

P.L. 94-455, § 1906(b)(13)(A):

Amended 1954 Code by substituting "Secretary" for "Secretary or his delegate" each place it appeared. **Effective** 2-1-77.

• **1962, Revenue Act of 1962 (P.L. 87-834)**

P.L. 87-834, § 19(a):

Amended Code Sec. 6042. **Effective** with respect to payments made on or after 1-1-63. Prior to amendment, Sec. 6042 read as follows:

SEC. 6042. RETURNS REGARDING CORPORATE DIVIDENDS, EARNINGS, AND PROFITS.

Every corporation shall, when required by the Secretary or his delegate—

(1) Make a return of its payments of dividends, stating the name and address of, the number of shares owned by, and the amount of dividends paid to, each shareholder;

(2) Furnish to the Secretary or his delegate a statement of such facts as will enable him to determine the portion of the earnings or profits of the corporation (including gains, profits, and income not taxed) accumulated during such periods as the Secretary or his delegate may specify, which have been distributed or ordered to be distributed, respectively, to its shareholders during such taxable years as the Secretary or his delegate may specify; and

(3) Furnish to the Secretary or his delegate a statement of its accumulated earnings and profits and the names and addresses of the individuals or shareholders who would be entitled to such accumulated earnings and profits if divided or distributed, and of the amounts that would be payable to each.

RETURNS—INFORMATION

[Sec. 6042(e)—Repealed]

Amendments

• **1983, Interest and Dividend Tax Compliance Act of 1983 (P.L. 98-67)**

P.L. 98-67, §102(a):

Repealed Code Sec. 6042(e) as though it had not been enacted. Former Code Sec. 6042(e) read:

(e) DUPLICATE OF SUBSECTION(c) STATEMENT MAY BE REQUIRED TO BE FILED WITH SECRETARY.—A duplicate of any statement made pursuant to subsection (c) which is required to set forth an amount withheld under section 3451 shall, when required by regulations prescribed by the Secretary, be filed with the Secretary.

• **1982, Tax Equity and Fiscal Responsibility Act of 1982 (P.L. 97-248)**

P.L. 97-248, §303(a)(3):

Added Code Sec. 6042(e). **Effective** 7-1-83.

[Sec. 6043]

SEC. 6043. LIQUIDATING, ETC., TRANSACTIONS.

[Sec. 6043(a)]

(a) CORPORATE LIQUIDATING, ETC., TRANSACTIONS.—Every corporation shall—

(1) Within 30 days after the adoption by the corporation of a resolution or plan for the dissolution of the corporation or for the liquidation of the whole or any part of its capital stock, make a return setting forth the terms of such resolution or plan and such other information as the Secretary shall by forms or regulations prescribe; and

(2) When required by the Secretary, make a return regarding its distributions in liquidation, stating the name and address of, the number and class of shares owned by, and the amount paid to, each shareholder, or, if the distribution is in property other than money, the fair market value (as of the date the distribution is made) of the property distributed to each shareholder.

Amendments

• **1996, Small Business Job Protection Act of 1996 (P.L. 104-188)**

P.L. 104-188, §1704(t)(17):

Amended Code Sec. 6043 by striking the semicolon in the section heading and inserting a comma. **Effective** 8-20-96.

• **1989, Omnibus Budget Reconciliation Act of 1989 (P.L. 101-239)**

P.L. 101-239, §7208(b)(3)(A):

Amended Code Sec. 6043(a) by striking "CORPORATIONS" in the heading and inserting "CORPORATE LIQUIDATING, ETC., TRANSACTIONS". **Effective** for transactions after 3-31-90.

P.L. 101-239, §7208(b)(3)(B):

Amended the heading of Code Sec. 6043. **Effective** for transactions after 3-31-90. Prior to amendment, the heading for Code Sec. 6043 read as follows:

SEC. 6043. RETURNS REGARDING LIQUIDATION, DISSOLUTION, TERMINATION, OR CONTRACTION.

• **1976, Tax Reform Act of 1976 (P.L. 94-455)**

P.L. 94-455, §1906(b)(13)(A):

Amended 1954 Code by substituting "Secretary" for "Secretary or his delegate" each place it appeared. **Effective** 2-1-77.

• **1969, Tax Reform Act of 1969 (P.L. 91-172)**

P.L. 91-172, §101(j)(35):

Amended the heading of Code Sec. 6043 and added "(a) Corporations.—" at the beginning of Code Sec. 6043. **Effective** for tax years beginning after 12-31-69. Prior to amendment, such heading read:

"RETURN REGARDING CORPORATE DISSOLUTION OR LIQUIDATION."

[Sec. 6043(b)]

(b) EXEMPT ORGANIZATIONS.—Every organization which for any of its last 5 taxable years preceding its liquidation, dissolution, termination, or substantial contraction was exempt from taxation under section 501(a) shall file such return and other information with respect to such liquidation, dissolution, termination, or substantial contraction as the Secretary shall by forms or regulations prescribe; except that—

(1) no return shall be required under this subsection from churches, their integrated auxiliaries, conventions or associations of churches, or any organization which is not a private foundation (as defined in section 509(a)) and the gross receipts of which in each taxable year are normally not more than $5,000, and

(2) the Secretary may relieve any organization from such filing where he determines that such filing is not necessary to the efficient administration of the internal revenue laws or, with respect to an organization described in section 401(a), where the employer who established such organization files such a return.

Amendments

• **1976, Tax Reform Act of 1976 (P.L. 94-455)**

P.L. 94-455, §1906(b)(13)(A):

Amended 1954 Code by substituting "Secretary" for "Secretary or his delegate" each place it appeared. **Effective** 2-1-77.

• **1969, Tax Reform Act of 1969 (P.L. 91-172)**

P.L. 91-172, §101(j)(35):

Added Code Sec. 6043(b). **Effective** for tax years beginning after 12-31-69.

[Sec. 6043(c)]

(c) CHANGES IN CONTROL AND RECAPITALIZATIONS.—If—

(1) control (as defined in section 304(c)(1)) of a corporation is acquired by any person (or group of persons) in a transaction (or series of related transactions), or

(2) there is a recapitalization of a corporation or other substantial change in the capital structure of a corporation,

when required by the Secretary, such corporation shall make a return (at such time and in such manner as the Secretary may prescribe) setting forth the identity of the parties to the transaction, the fees involved, the changes in the capital structure involved, and such other information as the Secretary may require with respect to such transaction.

Amendments

• **1989, Omnibus Budget Reconciliation Act of 1989 (P.L. 101-239)**

P.L. 101-239, §7208(b)(1):

Amended Code Sec. 6043 by striking subsection (c) and adding a new subsection (c). **Effective** for transactions after 3-31-90. Prior to amendment, Code Sec. 6043(c) read as follows:

(c) CROSS REFERENCE.—

For provisions relating to penalties for failure to file a return required by subsection (b), see section 6652(c).

• **1986, Tax Reform Act of 1986 (P.L. 99-514)**

P.L. 99-514, §1501(d)(1)(C):

Amended Code Sec. 6043(c) by striking out "section 6652(d)" and inserting in lieu thereof "section 6652(c)". **Effective** for returns the due date for which (determined without regard to extensions) is after 12-31-86.

• **1969, Tax Reform Act of 1969 (P.L. 91-172)**

P.L. 91-172, §101(j)(35):

Added Code Sec. 6043(c). **Effective** for tax years beginning after 12-31-69.

[Sec. 6043(d)]

(d) CROSS REFERENCES.—

For provisions relating to penalties for failure to file—

(1) a return under subsection (b), see section 6652(c), or

(2) a return under subsection (c), see section 6652(l).

RETURNS—INFORMATION

Amendments

• **1989, Omnibus Budget Reconciliation Act of 1989 (P.L. 101-239)**

P.L. 101-239, §7208(b)(1):

Amended Code Sec. 6043 by adding new subsections (c) and (d). **Effective** for transactions after 3-31-90.

[Sec. 6043A]

SEC. 6043A. RETURNS RELATING TO TAXABLE MERGERS AND ACQUISITIONS.

[Sec. 6043A(a)]

(a) IN GENERAL.—According to the forms or regulations prescribed by the Secretary, the acquiring corporation in any taxable acquisition shall make a return setting forth—

(1) a description of the acquisition,

(2) the name and address of each shareholder of the acquired corporation who is required to recognize gain (if any) as a result of the acquisition,

(3) the amount of money and the fair market value of other property transferred to each such shareholder as part of such acquisition, and

(4) such other information as the Secretary may prescribe.

To the extent provided by the Secretary, the requirements of this section applicable to the acquiring corporation shall be applicable to the acquired corporation and not to the acquiring corporation.

[Sec. 6043A(b)]

(b) NOMINEES.—According to the forms or regulations prescribed by the Secretary:

(1) REPORTING.—Any person who holds stock as a nominee for another person shall furnish in the manner prescribed by the Secretary to such other person the information provided by the corporation under subsection (d).

(2) REPORTING TO NOMINEES.—In the case of stock held by any person as a nominee, references in this section (other than in subsection (c)) to a shareholder shall be treated as a reference to the nominee.

[Sec. 6043A(c)]

(c) TAXABLE ACQUISITION.—For purposes of this section, the term "taxable acquisition" means any acquisition by a corporation of stock in or property of another corporation if any shareholder of the acquired corporation is required to recognize gain (if any) as a result of such acquisition.

[Sec. 6043A(d)]

(d) STATEMENTS TO BE FURNISHED TO SHAREHOLDERS.—According to the forms or regulations prescribed by the Secretary, every person required to make a return under subsection (a) shall furnish to each shareholder whose name is required to be set forth in such return a written statement showing—

(1) the name, address, and phone number of the information contact of the person required to make such return,

(2) the information required to be shown on such return with respect to such shareholder, and

(3) such other information as the Secretary may prescribe.

The written statement required under the preceding sentence shall be furnished to the shareholder on or before January 31 of the year following the calendar year during which the taxable acquisition occurred.

Amendments

• **2004, American Jobs Creation Act of 2004 (P.L. 108-357)**

P.L. 108-357, §805(a):

Amended subpart B of part III of subchapter A of chapter 61 by inserting after Code Sec. 6043 a new Code Sec. 6043A. **Effective** for acquisitions after 10-22-2004.

[Sec. 6044]

SEC. 6044. RETURNS REGARDING PAYMENTS OF PATRONAGE DIVIDENDS.

[Sec. 6044(a)]

(a) REQUIREMENT OF REPORTING.—

(1) IN GENERAL.—Except as otherwise provided in this section, every cooperative to which part I of subchapter T of chapter 1 applies, which makes payments of amounts described in subsection (b) aggregating $10 or more to any person during any calendar year, shall make a return according to the forms or regulations prescribed by the Secretary, setting forth the aggregate amount of such payments and the name and address of the person to whom paid.

(2) RETURNS REQUIRED BY THE SECRETARY.—Every such cooperative which makes payments of amounts described in subsection (b) aggregating less than $10 to any person during any calendar year shall, when required by the Secretary, make a return setting forth the aggregate amount of such payments and the name and address of the person to whom paid.

Amendments

• **1983, Interest and Dividend Tax Compliance Act of 1983 (P.L. 98-67)**

P.L. 98-67, §102(a):

Repealed Code Sec. 6044(a)(1) as though such amendments had not been enacted. **Effective** as of the close of 6-30-83, Prior to repeal, Code Sec. 6044(a)(1) read as follows:

(1) IN GENERAL.—Except as otherwise provided in this section, every cooperative to which part I of subchapter T of chapter 1 applies which—

(A) makes payments of amounts described in subsection (b) aggregating $10 or more to any person during any calendar year, or

(B) is required to withhold any tax under section 3451, shall make a return according to the forms or regulations prescribed by the Secretary, setting forth the aggregate amount of such payments, the name and address of the person to whom paid, and the amount of tax withheld.

• **1982, Tax Equity and Fiscal Responsibility Act of 1982 (P.L. 97-248)**

P.L. 97-248, §304(a):

Amended Code Sec. 6044(a)(1). **Effective** for patronage dividends paid or credited after 6-30-83.

• **1976, Tax Reform Act of 1976 (P.L. 94-455)**

P.L. 94-455, §1906(b)(13)(A):

Amended 1954 Code by substituting "Secretary" for "Secretary or his delegate" each place it appeared. **Effective** 2-1-77.

• **1962, Revenue Act of 1962 (P.L. 87-834)**

P.L. 87-834, §19(b):

Amended Code Sec. 6044(a). **Effective** with respect to payments made on or after 1-1-63, with respect to patronage occurring on or after the first day of the first tax year of the cooperative beginning on or after 1-1-63. Prior to amendment, Sec. 6044(a) read as follows:

(a) PAYMENTS OF $100 OR MORE.—Any corporation allocating amounts as patronage dividends, rebates, or refunds (whether in cash, merchandise, capital stock, revolving fund certificates, retain certificates, certificates of indebtedness, letters of advice, or in some other manner that discloses to each patron the amount of such dividend, refund, or rebate) shall make a return showing—

(1) The name and address of each patron to whom it has made such allocations amounting to $100 or more during the calendar year; and

(2) The amount of such allocations to each patron.

RETURNS—INFORMATION

[Sec. 6044(b)]

(b) AMOUNTS SUBJECT TO REPORTING.—

(1) GENERAL RULE.—Except as otherwise provided in this section, the amounts subject to reporting under subsection (a) are—

(A) the amount of any patronage dividend (as defined in section 1388(a)) which is paid in money, qualified written notices of allocation (as defined in section 1388(c)), or other property (except nonqualified written notices of allocation as defined in section 1388(d)),

(B) any amount described in section 1382(c)(2)(A) (relating to certain nonpatronage distributions) which is paid in money, qualified written notices of allocation, or other property (except nonqualified written notices of allocation) by an organization exempt from tax under section 521 (relating to exemption of farmers' cooperatives from tax),

(C) any amount described in section 1382(b)(2) (relating to redemption of nonqualified written notices of allocation) and, in the case of an organization described in section 1381(a)(1), any amount described in section 1382(c)(2)(B) (relating to redemption of nonqualified written notices of allocation paid with respect to earnings derived from sources other than patronage), and

(D) the amount of any per-unit retain allocation (as defined in section 1388(f)) which is paid in qualified per-unit retain certificates (as defined in section 1388(h)), and

(E) any amount described in section 1382(b)(4) (relating to redemption of nonqualified per-unit retain certificates).

(2) EXCEPTIONS.—The provisions of subsection (a) shall not apply, to the extent provided in regulations prescribed by the Secretary, to any payment—

(A) by a foreign corporation, or

(B) to a foreign corporation, a nonresident alien, or a partnership not engaged in trade or business in the United States and composed in whole or in part of nonresident aliens.

Amendments

• **1983, Interest and Dividend Tax Compliance Act of 1983 (P.L. 98-67)**

P.L. 98-67, §102(a):

Repealed the amendment made to Code Sec. 6044(b) by P.L. 97-248 as though such amendment had not been enacted. **Effective** as of the close of 6-30-83.

• **1982, Tax Equity and Fiscal Responsibility Act of 1982 (P.L. 97-248)**

P.L. 97-248, §304(b):

Amended Code Sec. 6044(b)(1) by striking out "under subsection (a)" and inserting "under paragraph (1)(A) or (2) of subsection (a)". **Effective** with respect to patronage dividends paid or credited after 6-30-83.

• **1976, Tax Reform Act of 1976 (P.L. 94-455)**

P.L. 94-455, §1906(b)(13)(A):

Amended 1954 Code by substituting "Secretary" for "Secretary or his delegate" each place it appeared. **Effective** 2-1-77.

• **1966, Foreign Investors Tax Act of 1966 (P.L. 89-809)**

P.L. 89-809, §211(d)(1):

Amended Code Sec. 6044(b)(1) by striking out "and" at the end of subparagraph (B), by substituting ", and" for the period at the end of subparagraph (C), and by adding new subparagraphs (D) and (E). **Effective** for calendar years after 1966.

• **1962, Revenue Act of 1962 (P.L. 87-834)**

P.L. 87-834, §19(b):

Amended Code Sec. 6044(b). **Effective** with respect to payments made on or after 1-1-63, with respect to patronage occurring on or after the first day of the first tax year of the cooperative beginning on or after 1-1-63. Prior to amendment, Sec. 6044(b) read as follows:

(b) PAYMENTS REGARDLESS OF AMOUNT.—If required by the Secretary or his delegate, any such corporation shall make a return of all patronage dividends, rebates, or refunds made during the calendar year to its patrons.

[Sec. 6044(c)]

(c) EXEMPTION FOR CERTAIN CONSUMER COOPERATIVES.—A cooperative which the Secretary determines is primarily engaged in selling at retail goods or services of a type that are generally for personal, living, or family use shall, upon application to the Secretary, be granted exemption from the reporting requirements imposed by subsection (a). Application for exemption under this subsection shall be made in accordance with regulations prescribed by the Secretary.

Amendments

• **1976, Tax Reform Act of 1976 (P.L. 94-455)**

P.L. 94-455, §1906(b)(13)(A):

Amended 1954 Code by substituting "Secretary" for "Secretary or his delegate" each place it appeared. **Effective** 2-1-77.

• **1962, Revenue Act of 1962 (P.L. 87-834)**

P.L. 87-834, §19(b):

Amended Code Sec. 6044(c). **Effective** with respect to payments made on or after 1-1-63, with respect to patronage occurring on or after the first day of the first tax year of the cooperative beginning on or after 1-1-63. Prior to amendment, Sec. 6044(c) read as follows:

(c) EXCEPTIONS.—This section shall not apply in the case of any corporation (including any cooperative or nonprofit corporation engaged in rural electrification) described in section 501(c)(12) or (15) which is exempt from tax under section 501(a), or in the case of any corporation subject to a tax imposed by subchapter L of chapter 1.

[Sec. 6044(d)]

(d) DETERMINATION OF AMOUNT PAID.—For purposes of this section, in determining the amount of any payment—

(1) property (other than a qualified written notice of allocation or a qualified per-unit retain certificate) shall be taken into account at its fair market value, and

(2) a qualified written notice of allocation or a qualified per-unit retain certificate shall be taken into account at its stated dollar amount.

Amendments

• **1966, Foreign Investors Tax Act of 1966 (P.L. 89-809)**

P.L. 89-809, §211(d)(2):

Amended Code Sec. 6044(d) by inserting "or a qualified per-unit retain certificate" immediately after "allocation" in paragraphs (1) and (2). **Effective** for calendar years after 1966.

• **1962, Revenue Act of 1962 (P.L. 87-834)**

P.L. 87-834, §19(b):

Added Code Sec. 6044(d). **Effective** with respect to payments made on or after 1-1-63, with respect to patronage occurring on or after the first day of the first tax year of the cooperative beginning on or after 1-1-63.

[Sec. 6044(e)]

(e) STATEMENTS TO BE FURNISHED TO PERSONS WITH RESPECT TO WHOM INFORMATION IS REQUIRED.—Every cooperative required to make a return under subsection (a) shall furnish to each person whose name is required to be set forth in such return a written statement showing—

(1) the name, address, and phone number of the information contact of the cooperative required to make such return, and

(2) the aggregate amount of payments to the person required to be shown on the return.

The written statement required under the preceding sentence shall be furnished (either in person or in a statement mailing by first-class mail which includes adequate notice that the statement is enclosed) to the person on or before January 31 of the year following the calendar year for which the return under subsection (a) was required to be made and shall be in such form as the Secretary may prescribe by regulations.

Amendments

• **1996, Taxpayer Bill of Rights 2 (P.L. 104-168)**

P.L. 104-168, §1201(a)(4):

Amended Code Sec. 6044(e)(1) by striking "name and address" and inserting "name, address, and phone number of the information contact". **Effective** for statements required to be furnished after 12-31-96 (determined without regard to any extension).

RETURNS—INFORMATION

- **1986, Tax Reform Act of 1986 (P.L. 99-514)**

P.L. 99-514, §1501(c)(3):

Amended Code Sec. 6044(e). **Effective** for returns the due date for which (determined without regard to extensions) is after 10-22-86. Prior to amendment, Code Sec. 6044(e) read as follows:

(e) STATEMENTS TO BE FURNISHED TO PERSONS WITH RESPECT TO WHOM INFORMATION IS FURNISHED.—Every cooperative making a return under subsection (a)(1) shall furnish to each person whose name is set forth in such return a written statement showing—

(1) the name and address of the cooperative making such return,

(2) the aggregate amount of payments to the person as shown on such return.

The written statement required under the preceding sentence shall be furnished (either in person or in a separate mailing by first-class mail) to the person on or before January 31 of the year following the calendar year for which the return under subsection (a) was made, and shall be in such form as the Secretary may prescribe by regulation.

- **1983, Interest and Dividend Tax Compliance Act of 1983 (P.L. 98-67)**

P.L. 98-67, §102(a):

Repealed the amendments made to Code Sec. 6044(e) by P.L. 97-248 and that would have become effective 7-1-83. **Effective** as of the close of 6-30-83. The amendments, therefore, did not go into effect. Under the repealed amendments, Code Sec. 6044(e) would have read as follows:

(e) STATEMENTS TO BE FURNISHED TO PERSONS WITH RESPECT TO WHOM INFORMATION IS FURNISHED.—Every cooperative making a return under subsection (a)(1) shall furnish to each person whose name is set forth in such return a written statement showing—

(1) the name and address of the cooperative making such return,

(2) the aggregate amount of payments to the person as shown on such return, and

(3) the amount of tax withheld under section 3451.

The written statement required under the preceding sentence shall be furnished to the person on or before January 31 of the year following the calendar year for which the return under subsection (a)(1) was made. Except in the case of a return required by reason of subparagraph (B) of subsection (a)(1), no statement shall be required to

Amendments

- **1983, Interest and Dividend Tax Compliance Act of 1983 (P.L. 98-67)**

P.L. 98-67, §102(a):

Repealed Code Sec. 6044(f) as though it had not been enacted by P.L. 97-248. **Effective** as of the close of 6-30-83. Prior to repeal, Code Sec. 6044(f) read as follows:

(f) DUPLICATE OF SUBSECTION (e) STATEMENT MAY BE REQUIRED TO BE FILED WITH SECRETARY.—A duplicate of any statement made pursuant to subsection (e) which is

be furnished to any person under this subsection if the aggregate amount of payments to such person as shown on the return made under subsection (a)(1) is less than $10.

P.L. 98-67, §108(c):

Amended Code Sec. 6044(e). **Effective** with respect to payments made after 12-31-83.

- **1982, Tax Equity and Fiscal Responsibility Act of 1982 (P.L. 97-248)**

P.L. 97-248, §304(c):

Amended Code Sec. 6044(e) by striking out "and" at the end of paragraph (1), by inserting ", and" in lieu of the period at the end of paragraph (2), by inserting paragraph (3), and by striking out "No statement" in the last sentence and inserting in lieu thereof "Except in the case of a return required by reason of subparagraph (B) of subsection (a)(1), no statement". **Effective** for patronage dividends paid or credited after 6-30-83. Prior to amendment, Sec. 6044(e) read as follows:

(e) STATEMENTS TO BE FURNISHED TO PERSONS WITH RESPECT TO WHOM INFORMATION IS FURNISHED.—Every cooperative making a return under subsection (a)(1) shall furnish to each person whose name is set forth in such return a written statement showing—

(1) the name and address of the cooperative making such return, and

(2) the aggregate amount of payments to the person as shown on such return.

The written statement required under the preceding sentence shall be furnished to the person on or before January 31 of the year following the calendar year for which the return under subsection (a)(1) was made. No statement shall be required to be furnished to any person under this subsection if the aggregate amount of payments to such person as shown on the return made under subsection (a)(1) is less than $10.

- **1962, Revenue Act of 1962 (P.L. 87-834)**

P.L. 87-834, §19(b):

Added Code Sec. 6044(e). **Effective** with respect to payments made on or after 1-1-63, with respect to patronage occurring on or after the first day of the first tax year of the cooperative beginning on or after 1-1-63.

[Sec. 6044(f)—Repealed]

required to set forth an amount withheld under section 3451 shall, when required by regulations prescribed by the Secretary, be filed with the Secretary.

- **1982, Tax Equity and Fiscal Responsibility Act of 1982 (P.L. 97-248)**

P.L. 97-248, §304(d):

Added Code Sec. 6044(f) to read as noted under P.L. 98-67. **Effective** with respect to patronage dividends paid or credited after 6-30-83.

[Sec. 6045]

SEC. 6045. RETURNS OF BROKERS.

[Sec. 6045(a)]

(a) GENERAL RULE.—Every person doing business as a broker shall, when required by the Secretary, make a return, in accordance with such regulations as the Secretary may prescribe, showing the name and address of each customer, with such details regarding gross proceeds and such other information as the Secretary may by forms or regulations require with respect to such business.

[Sec. 6045(b)]

(b) STATEMENTS TO BE FURNISHED TO CUSTOMERS.—Every person required to make a return under subsection (a) shall furnish to each customer whose name is required to be set forth in such return a written statement showing—

(1) the name, address and phone number of the information contact of the person required to make such return, and

(2) the information required to be shown on such return with respect to such customer.

The written statement required under the preceding sentence shall be furnished to the customer on or before February 15 of the year following the calendar year for which the return under subsection (a) was required to be made. In the case of a consolidated reporting statement (as defined in regulations) with respect to any customer, any statement which would otherwise be required to be furnished on or before January 31 of a calendar year with respect to any item reportable to the taxpayer shall instead be required to be furnished on or before February 15 of such calendar year if furnished with such consolidated reporting statement.

Amendments

- **2008, Energy Improvement and Extension Act of 2008 (P.L. 110-343)**

P.L. 110-343, Division B, §403(a)(3)(A):

Amended Code Sec. 6045(b) by striking "January 31" and inserting "February 15". **Effective** for statements required to be furnished after 12-31-2008.

P.L. 110-343, Division B, §403(a)(3)(C):

Amended Code Sec. 6045(b) by adding at the end a new sentence. **Effective** for statements required to be furnished after 12-31-2008.

- **1996, Taxpayer Bill of Rights 2 (P.L. 104-168)**

P.L. 104-168, §1201(a)(5):

Amended Code Sec. 6045(b)(1) by striking "name and address" and inserting "name, address, and phone number of the information contact". **Effective** for statements required to be furnished after 12-31-96 (determined without regard to any extension).

- **1986, Tax Reform Act of 1986 (P.L. 99-514)**

P.L. 99-514, §1501(c)(4):

Amended Code Sec. 6045(b). **Effective** for returns the due date for which (determined without regard to extensions) is after 12-31-86. Prior to amendment, Code Sec. 6045(b) read as follows:

(b) STATEMENTS TO BE FURNISHED TO CUSTOMERS.—Every person making a return under subsection (a) shall furnish to each customer whose name is set forth in such return a written statement showing—

(1) the name and address of the person making such return, and

(2) the information shown on such return with respect to such customer.

The written statement required under the preceding sentence shall be furnished to the customer on or before January 31 of the year following the calendar year for which the return under subsection (a) was made.

[Sec. 6045(c)]

(c) DEFINITIONS.—For purposes of this section—

(1) BROKER.—The term "broker" includes—

(A) a dealer,

(B) a barter exchange,

(C) any person who (for consideration) regularly acts as a middleman with respect to property or services, and

(D) any person who (for consideration) is responsible for regularly providing any service effectuating transfers of digital assets on behalf of another person.

A person shall not be treated as a broker with respect to activities consisting of managing a farm on behalf of another person.

(2) CUSTOMER.—The term "customer" means any person for whom the broker has transacted any business.

(3) BARTER EXCHANGE.—The term "barter exchange" means any organization of members providing property or services who jointly contract to trade or barter such property or services.

(4) PERSON.—The term "person" includes any governmental unit and any agency or instrumentality thereof.

Amendments

• **2021, Infrastructure Investment and Jobs Act (P.L. 117-58)**

P.L. 117-58, §80603(a)(1)-(3), Div. H,

Amended Code Sec. 6045(c)(1) by striking "and" at the end of subparagraph (B), by striking "any other person who (for a consideration)" and inserting "any person who (for consideration)", and by striking the period at the end and inserting ", and" in subparagraph (C), and by inserting after subparagraph (C) a new subparagraph (D). **Effective** for returns required to be filed, and statements required to be furnished, after 12-31-2023. For a special rule, see Act Sec. 80603(d)(1)-(2), Div. H, below.

P.L. 117-58, §80603(d)(1)-(2), Div. H, provides:

(d) RULE OF CONSTRUCTION.—Nothing in this section or the amendments made by this section shall be construed to create any inference, for any period prior to the effective date of such amendments, with respect to—

(1) whether any person is a broker under section 6045(c)(1) of the Internal Revenue Code of 1986, or

(2) whether any digital asset is property which is a specified security under section 6045(g)(3)(B) of such Code.

• **1988, Technical and Miscellaneous Revenue Act of 1988 (P.L. 100-647)**

P.L. 100-647, §1015(e)(1)(A):

Amended Code Sec. 6045(c)(1) by adding at the end thereof a new sentence. **Effective** as if included in the amendments made by section 311(a)(1) of P.L. 97-248 to which it relates.

• **1984, Deficit Reduction Act of 1984 (P.L. 98-369)**

P.L. 98-369, §714(e)(1):

Amended Code Sec. 6045(c) by adding new paragraph (4). **Effective** as if included in the provision of P.L. 97-248 to which it relates. See the special rule under Act Sec. 714(e)(2), below.

P.L. 98-369, §714(e)(2), provides:

(2) No Penalty for Payments Before January 1, 1985.—No penalty shall be imposed under the Internal Revenue Code of 1954 with respect to any person required (by reason of the amendment made by paragraph (1)) to file a return under section 6045 of such Code with respect to any payment before January 1, 1985.

[Sec. 6045(d)]

(d) STATEMENTS REQUIRED IN CASE OF CERTAIN SUBSTITUTE PAYMENTS.—If any broker—

(1) transfers securities of a customer for use in a short sale or similar transaction, and

(2) receives (on behalf of the customer) a payment in lieu of—

(A) a dividend,

(B) tax-exempt interest, or

(C) such other items as the Secretary may prescribe by regulations,

during the period such short sale or similar transaction is open, the broker shall furnish such customer a written statement (in the manner as the Secretary shall prescribe by regulations) identifying such payment as being in lieu of the dividend, tax-exempt interest, or such other item. The written statement required under the preceding sentence shall be furnished on or before February 15 of the year following the calendar year in which the payment was made. The Secretary may prescribe regulations which require the broker to make a return which includes the information contained in such written statement.

Amendments

• **2008, Energy Improvement and Extension Act of 2008 (P.L. 110-343)**

P.L. 110-343, Division B, §403(a)(3)(B)(i)-(ii):

Amended Code Sec. 6045(d) by striking "at such time and" before "in the manner", and by inserting after "other item." a new sentence. **Effective** for statements required to be furnished after 12-31-2008.

• **1984, Deficit Reduction Act of 1984 (P.L. 98-369)**

P.L. 98-369, §150(a):

Amended Code Sec. 6045 by adding at the end thereof a new subsection (d). **Effective** for payments received after 12-31-84.

[Sec. 6045(e)]

(e) RETURN REQUIRED IN THE CASE OF REAL ESTATE TRANSACTIONS.—

(1) IN GENERAL.—In the case of a real estate transaction, the real estate reporting person shall file a return under subsection (a) and a statement under subsection (b) with respect to such transaction.

(2) REAL ESTATE REPORTING PERSON.—For purposes of this subsection, the term "real estate reporting person" means any of the following persons involved in a real estate transaction in the following order:

(A) the person (including any attorney or title company) responsible for closing the transaction,

(B) the mortgage lender,

(C) the seller's broker,

(D) the buyer's broker, or

(E) such other person designated in regulations prescribed by the Secretary.

Any person treated as a real estate reporting person under the preceding sentence shall be treated as a broker for purposes of subsection (c)(1).

(3) PROHIBITION OF SEPARATE CHARGE FOR FILING RETURN.—It shall be unlawful for any real estate reporting person to separately charge any customer for complying with any requirement of paragraph (1). Nothing in this paragraph shall be construed to prohibit the real estate reporting person from taking into account its cost of complying with such requirement in establishing its charge (other than a separate charge for complying with such requirement) to any customer for performing services in the case of a real estate transaction.

(4) ADDITIONAL INFORMATION REQUIRED.—In the case of a real estate transaction involving a residence, the real estate reporting person shall include the following information on the return under subsection (a) and on the statement under subsection (b):

(A) The portion of any real property tax which is treated as a tax imposed on the purchaser by reason of section 164(d)(1)(B).

(B) Whether or not the financing (if any) of the seller was federally-subsidized indebtedness (as defined in section 143(m)(3)).

(5) EXCEPTION FOR SALES OR EXCHANGES OF CERTAIN PRINCIPAL RESIDENCES.—

(A) IN GENERAL.—Paragraph (1) shall not apply to any sale or exchange of a residence for $250,000 or less if the person referred to in paragraph (2) receives written assurance in a form acceptable to the Secretary from the seller that—

(i) such residence is the principal residence (within the meaning of section 121) of the seller,

(ii) if the Secretary requires the inclusion on the return under subsection (a) of information as to whether there is federally subsidized mortgage financing assistance with respect to the mortgage on residences, that there is no such assistance with respect to the mortgage on such residence, and

(iii) the full amount of the gain on such sale or exchange is excludable from gross income under section 121.

RETURNS—INFORMATION

If such assurance includes an assurance that the seller is married, the preceding sentence shall be applied by substituting "$500,000" for "$250,000". The Secretary may by regulation increase the dollar amounts under this subparagraph if the Secretary determines that such an increase will not materially reduce revenues to the Treasury.

(B) SELLER.—For purposes of this paragraph, the term "seller" includes the person relinquishing the residence in an exchange.

Amendments

• **2005, Gulf Opportunity Zone Act of 2005 (P.L. 109-135)**

P.L. 109-135, §412(xx):

Amended the matter following Code Sec. 6045(e)(5)(A)(iii) by striking "for '$250,000'." and all that follows through "to the Treasury." and inserting "for '$250,000'. The Secretary may by regulation increase the dollar amounts under this subparagraph if the Secretary determines that such an increase will not materially reduce revenues to the Treasury.". **Effective** 12-21-2005. Prior to amendment, the matter following Code Sec. 6045(e)(5)(A)(iii) read as follows:

If such assurance includes an assurance that the seller is married, the preceding sentence shall be applied by substituting "$500,000" for "$250,000".

The Secretary may by regulation increase the dollar amounts under this subparagraph if the Secretary determines that such an increase will not materially reduce revenues to the Treasury.

• **1997, Taxpayer Relief Act of 1997 (P.L. 105-34)**

P.L. 105-34, §312(c):

Amended Code Sec. 6045(e) by adding at the end a new paragraph (5). For the **effective** date, see Act Sec. 312(d)[(e)], below.

P.L. 105-34, §312(d)[(e)], as amended by P.L. 105-206, §6005(e)(3), provides:

(d) EFFECTIVE DATE.—

(1) IN GENERAL.—The amendments made by this section shall apply to sales and exchanges after May 6, 1997.

(2) SALES ON OR BEFORE DATE OF ENACTMENT.—At the election of the taxpayer, the amendments made by this section shall not apply to any sale or exchange on or before the date of the enactment of this Act.

(3) CERTAIN SALES WITHIN 2 YEARS AFTER DATE OF ENACTMENT.—Section 121 of the Internal Revenue Code of 1986 (as amended by this section) shall be applied without regard to subsection (c)(2)(B) thereof in the case of any sale or exchange of property during the 2-year period beginning on the date of the enactment of this Act if the taxpayer held such property on the date of the enactment of this Act and fails to meet the ownership and use requirements of subsection (a) thereof with respect to such property.

(4) BINDING CONTRACTS.—At the election of the taxpayer, the amendments made by this section shall not apply to a sale or exchange after the date of the enactment of this Act, if—

(A) such sale or exchange is pursuant to a contract which was binding on such date, or

(B) without regard to such amendments, gain would not be recognized under section 1034 of the Internal Revenue Code of 1986 (as in effect on the day before the date of the enactment of this Act) on such sale or exchange by reason of a new residence acquired on or before such date or with respect to the acquisition of which by the taxpayer a binding contract was in effect on such date.

This paragraph shall not apply to any sale or exchange by an individual if the treatment provided by section 877(a)(1) of the Internal Revenue Code of 1986 applies to such individual.

• **1996, Small Business Job Protection Act of 1996 (P.L. 104-188)**

P.L. 104-188, §1704(o)(1):

Amended Code Sec. 6045(e)(3) by adding at the end a new sentence. **Effective** as if included in section 1015(e)(2)(A) of P.L. 100-647.

• **1992, Energy Policy Act of 1992 (P.L. 102-486)**

P.L. 102-486, §1939(a):

Amended Code Sec. 6045(e)(4). **Effective** for transactions after 12-31-92. Prior to amendment, Code Sec. 6045(e)(4) read as follows:

(4) WHETHER SELLER'S FINANCING WAS FEDERALLY-SUBSIDIZED.—In the case of a real estate transaction involving a residence, the real estate reporting person shall specify on the return under subsection (a) and the statement under subsection (b) whether or not the financing (if any) of the seller was federally-subsidized indebtedness (as defined in section 143(m)(3)).

• **1990, Omnibus Budget Reconciliation Act of 1990 (P.L. 101-508)**

P.L. 101-508, §11704(a)(25):

Amended Code Sec. 6045(e)(4) by striking "broker" and inserting "reporting person." **Effective** 11-5-90.

• **1989, Omnibus Budget Reconciliation Act of 1989 (P.L. 101-239)**

P.L. 101-239, §7814(c)(1):

Amended Code Sec. 6045(e) by redesignating paragraph (3), as added by §4005 of P.L. 100-647, as paragraph (4). **Effective** as if included in the provision of P.L. 100-647 to which it relates.

• **1988, Technical and Miscellaneous Revenue Act of 1988 (P.L. 100-647)**

P.L. 100-647, §1015(e)(2)(A):

Amended Code Sec. 6045(e) by adding at the end thereof new paragraph (3). **Effective** 11-10-88.

P.L. 100-647, §1015(e)(3)(A)-(B):

Amended Code Sec. 6045(e) by striking out "real estate broker" each place it appears in the text and inserting in lieu thereof "real estate reporting person", and by striking out "Real estate broker" in the heading of paragraph (2) and inserting in lieu thereof "Real estate reporting person". **Effective** as if included in the provision of P.L. 99-514 to which it relates.

P.L. 100-647, §4005(g)(3):

Amended Code Sec. 6045(e) by adding at the end thereof a new paragraph (3)[4]. **Effective** for financing provided, and mortgage credit certificates issued, after 12-31-90. However, for an exception see Act Sec. 4005(h)(3)(B) below.

P.L. 100-647, §4005(h)(3)(B), provides:

(B) EXCEPTION.—The amendments made by subsection (g) shall not apply to financing provided pursuant to a binding contract (entered into before June 23, 1988) with a homebuilder, lender, or mortgagor if the bonds (the proceeds of which are used to provide such financing) are issued—

(i) before June 23, 1988, or

(ii) before August 1, 1988, pursuant to a written application (made before July 1, 1988) for State bond volume authority.

• **1986, Tax Reform Act of 1986 (P.L. 99-514)**

P.L. 99-514, §1521(a):

Amended Code Sec. 6045 by adding at the end thereof new subsection (e). **Effective** for real estate transactions closing after 12-31-86.

• **1982, Tax Equity and Fiscal Responsibility Act of 1982 (P.L. 97-248)**

P.L. 97-248, §311(a)(1):

Amended Code Sec. 6045. **Effective** on the date of enactment, except that regulations relating to reporting by commodities and securities brokers shall be issued under Code Sec. 6045, as amended, within six months after the date of enactment, and such regulations will not apply to transactions occurring before 1-1-83. Prior to amendment, Code Sec. 6045 read as follows:

SEC. 6045. RETURNS OF BROKERS.

Every person doing business as a broker shall, when required by the Secretary, make a return, in accordance with such regulations as the Secretary may prescribe, showing the names of customers for whom such person has transacted any business, with such details regarding the profits and losses and such other information as the Secretary may by forms or regulations require with respect to each customer as will enable the Secretary to determine the amount of such profits or losses.

• **1976, Tax Reform Act of 1976 (P.L. 94-455)**

P.L. 94-455, §1906(b)(13)(A):

Amended 1954 Code by substituting "Secretary" for "Secretary or his delegate" each place it appeared. **Effective** 2-1-77.

[Sec. 6045(f)]

(f) RETURN REQUIRED IN THE CASE OF PAYMENTS TO ATTORNEYS.—

(1) IN GENERAL.—Any person engaged in a trade or business and making a payment (in the course of such trade or business) to which this subsection applies shall file a return under subsection (a) and a statement under subsection (b) with respect to such payment.

(2) APPLICATION OF SUBSECTION.—

(A) IN GENERAL.—This subsection shall apply to any payment to an attorney in connection with legal services (whether or not such services are performed by the payor).

(B) EXCEPTION.—This subsection shall not apply to the portion of any payment which is required to be reported under section 6041(a) (or would be so required but for the dollar limitation contained therein) or section 6051.

Amendments

• **1997, Taxpayer Relief Act of 1997 (P.L. 105-34)**

P.L. 105-34, §1021(a):

Amended Code Sec. 6045 by adding at the end thereof a new subsection (f). **Effective** for payments made after 12-31-97.

[Sec. 6045(g)]

(g) ADDITIONAL INFORMATION REQUIRED IN THE CASE OF SECURITIES TRANSACTIONS, ETC.—

(1) IN GENERAL.—If a broker is otherwise required to make a return under subsection (a) with respect to the gross proceeds of the sale of a covered security, the broker shall include in such return the information described in paragraph (2).

(2) ADDITIONAL INFORMATION REQUIRED.—

(A) IN GENERAL.—The information required under paragraph (1) to be shown on a return with respect to a covered security of a customer shall include the customer's adjusted basis in such security and whether any gain or loss with respect to such security is long-term or short-term (within the meaning of section 1222).

(B) DETERMINATION OF ADJUSTED BASIS.—For purposes of subparagraph (A)—

(i) IN GENERAL.—The customer's adjusted basis shall be determined—

(I) in the case of any security (other than any stock for which an average basis method is permissible under section 1012), in accordance with the first-in first-out method unless the customer notifies the broker by means of making an adequate identification of the stock sold or transferred, and

(II) in the case of any stock for which an average basis method is permissible under section 1012, in accordance with the broker's default method unless the customer notifies the broker that he elects another acceptable method under section 1012 with respect to the account in which such stock is held.

(ii) EXCEPTION FOR WASH SALES.—Except as otherwise provided by the Secretary, the customer's adjusted basis shall be determined without regard to section 1091 (relating to loss from wash sales of stock or securities) unless the transactions occur in the same account with respect to identical securities.

(iii) TREATMENT OF UNCORRECTED DE MINIMIS ERRORS.—Except as otherwise provided by the Secretary, the customer's adjusted basis shall be determined by treating any incorrect dollar amount which is not required to be corrected by reason of section 6721(c)(3) or section 6722(c)(3) as the correct amount.

(3) COVERED SECURITY.—For purposes of this subsection—

(A) IN GENERAL.—The term "covered security" means any specified security acquired on or after the applicable date if such security—

(i) was acquired through a transaction in the account in which such security is held, or

(ii) was transferred to such account from an account in which such security was a covered security, but only if the broker received a statement under section 6045A with respect to the transfer.

(B) SPECIFIED SECURITY.—The term "specified security" means—

(i) any share of stock in a corporation,

(ii) any note, bond, debenture, or other evidence of indebtedness,

(iii) any commodity, or contract or derivative with respect to such commodity, if the Secretary determines that adjusted basis reporting is appropriate for purposes of this subsection,

(iv) any digital asset, and

(v) any other financial instrument with respect to which the Secretary determines that adjusted basis reporting is appropriate for purposes of this subsection.

(C) APPLICABLE DATE.—The term "applicable date" means—

(i) January 1, 2011, in the case of any specified security which is stock in a corporation (other than any stock described in clause (ii)),

(ii) January 1, 2012, in the case of any stock for which an average basis method is permissible under section 1012,

(iii) January 1, 2023, in the case of any specified security which is a digital asset, and

(iv) January 1, 2013, or such later date determined by the Secretary in the case of any other specified security.

(D) DIGITAL ASSET.—Except as otherwise provided by the Secretary, the term "digital asset" means any digital representation of value which is recorded on a cryptographically secured distributed ledger or any similar technology as specified by the Secretary.

(4) TREATMENT OF S CORPORATIONS.—In the case of the sale of a covered security acquired by an S corporation (other than a financial institution) after December 31, 2011, such S corporation shall be treated in the same manner as a partnership for purposes of this section.

(5) SPECIAL RULES FOR SHORT SALES.—In the case of a short sale, reporting under this section shall be made for the year in which such sale is closed.

(6) SPECIAL RULE FOR CERTAIN STOCK HELD IN CONNECTION WITH DIVIDEND REINVESTMENT PLAN.—For purposes of this subsection, stock acquired before January 1, 2012, in connection with a dividend reinvestment plan shall be treated as stock described in clause (ii) of paragraph (3)(C) (unless the broker with respect to such stock elects not to have this paragraph apply with respect to such stock).

Amendments

- **2021, Infrastructure Investment and Jobs Act (P.L. 117-58)**

P.L. 117-58, §80603(b)(1)(A), Div. H:

Amended Code Sec. 6045(g)(3)(B) by striking "and" at the end of clause (iii), by redesignating clause (iv) as clause (v), and by inserting after clause (iii) a new clause (iv). **Effective** for returns required to be filed, and statements required to be furnished, after 12-31-2023. For a special rule, see Act Sec. 80603(d)(1)-(2), Div. H, below.

P.L. 117-58, §80603(b)(1)(B), Div. H:

Amended Code Sec. 6045(g)(3) by adding at the end a new subparagraph (D). **Effective** for returns required to be filed, and statements required to be furnished, after 12-31-2023. For a special rule, see Act Sec. 80603(d)(1)-(2), Div. H, below.

P.L. 117-58, §80603(b)(1)(C)(i)-(iii), Div. H:

Amended Code Sec. 6045(g)(3)(C) by striking "and" at the end of clause (ii), by redesignating clause (iii) as clause (iv), and by inserting after clause (ii) a new clause (iii). **Effective** for returns required to be filed, and statements required to be furnished, after 12-31-2023. For a special rule, see Act Sec. 80603(d)(1)-(2), Div. H, below.

P.L. 117-58, §80603(d)(1)-(2), Div. H, provides:

(d) RULE OF CONSTRUCTION.—Nothing in this section or the amendments made by this section shall be construed to create any inference, for any period prior to the effective date of such amendments, with respect to—

(1) whether any person is a broker under section 6045(c)(1) of the Internal Revenue Code of 1986, or

(2) whether any digital asset is property which is a specified security under section 6045(g)(3)(B) of such Code.

- **2015, Protecting Americans from Tax Hikes Act of 2015 (P.L. 114-113)**

P.L. 114-113, §202(c), Div. Q:

Amended Code Sec. 6045(g)(2)(B) by adding at the end a new clause (iii). **Effective** for returns required to be filed, and payee statements required to be furnished, after 12-31-2016 [effective date changed by P.L. 115-141, §101(f)(3), Div. U.—CCH].

- **2014, Tax Technical Corrections Act of 2014 (P.L. 113-295)**

P.L. 113-295, §210(f)(4), Division A:

Amended Code Sec. 6045(g) by adding at the end a new paragraph (6). **Effective** as if included in the provision of the Energy Improvement and Extension Act of 2008 (P.L. 110-343) to which it relates [effective 1-1-2011.—CCH].

- **2008, Energy Improvement and Extension Act of 2008 (P.L. 110-343)**

P.L. 110-343, Division B, §403(a)(1):

Amended Code Sec. 6045 by adding at the end a new subsection (g). **Effective** 1-1-2011.

RETURNS—INFORMATION

[Sec. 6045(h)]

(h) APPLICATION TO OPTIONS ON SECURITIES.—

(1) EXERCISE OF OPTION.—For purposes of this section, if a covered security is acquired or disposed of pursuant to the exercise of an option that was granted or acquired in the same account as the covered security, the amount received with respect to the grant or paid with respect to the acquisition of such option shall be treated as an adjustment to gross proceeds or as an adjustment to basis, as the case may be.

(2) LAPSE OR CLOSING TRANSACTION.—In the case of the lapse (or closing transaction (as defined in section 1234(b)(2)(A))) of an option on a specified security or the exercise of a cash-settled option on a specified security, reporting under subsections (a) and (g) with respect to such option shall be made for the calendar year which includes the date of such lapse, closing transaction, or exercise.

(3) PROSPECTIVE APPLICATION.—Paragraphs (1) and (2) shall not apply to any option which is granted or acquired before January 1, 2013.

(4) DEFINITIONS.—For purposes of this subsection, the terms "covered security" and "specified security" shall have the meanings given such terms in subsection (g)(3).

Amendments

• **2008, Energy Improvement and Extension Act of 2008 (P.L. 110-343)**

P.L. 110-343, Division B, §403(a)(2):

Amended Code Sec. 6045, as amended by Act Sec. 403(a), by adding at the end a new subsection (h). **Effective** 1-1-2011.

[Sec. 6045A]

SEC. 6045A. INFORMATION REQUIRED IN CONNECTION WITH TRANSFERS OF COVERED SECURITIES TO BROKERS.

[Sec. 6045A(a)]

(a) FURNISHING OF INFORMATION.—Every applicable person which transfers to a broker (as defined in section 6045(c)(1)) a covered security (as defined in section 6045(g)(3)) in the hands of such applicable person shall furnish to such broker a written statement in such manner and setting forth such information as the Secretary may by regulations prescribe for purposes of enabling such broker to meet the requirements of section 6045(g).

Amendments

• **2021, Infrastructure Investment and Jobs Act (P.L. 117-58)**

P.L. 117-58, §80603(b)(2)(A)(i), Div. H:

Amended Code Sec. 6045A(a) by striking "a security which is" following "(as defined in section 6045(c)(1))". **Effective** for returns required to be filed, and statements required to be furnished, after 12-31-2023. For a special rule, see Act Sec. 80603(d)(1)-(2), Div. H, below.

P.L. 117-58, §80603(d)(1)-(2), Div. H, provides:

(d) RULE OF CONSTRUCTION.—Nothing in this section or the amendments made by this section shall be construed to create any inference, for any period prior to the effective date of such amendments, with respect to—

(1) whether any person is a broker under section 6045(c)(1) of the Internal Revenue Code of 1986, or

(2) whether any digital asset is property which is a specified security under section 6045(g)(3)(B) of such Code.

[Sec. 6045A(b)]

(b) APPLICABLE PERSON.—For purposes of subsection (a), the term "applicable person" means—

(1) any broker (as defined in section 6045(c)(1)), and

(2) any other person as provided by the Secretary in regulations.

[Sec. 6045A(c)]

(c) TIME FOR FURNISHING STATEMENT.—Except as otherwise provided by the Secretary, any statement required by subsection (a) shall be furnished not later than 15 days after the date of the transfer described in such subsection.

Amendments

• **2008, Energy Improvement and Extension Act of 2008 (P.L. 110-343)**

P.L. 110-343, Division B, §403(c)(1):

Amended subpart B of part III of subchapter A of chapter 61 by inserting after Code Sec. 6045 a new Code Sec. 6045A. **Effective** 1-1-2011.

[Sec. 6045A(d)]

(d) RETURN REQUIREMENT FOR CERTAIN TRANSFERS OF DIGITAL ASSETS NOT OTHERWISE SUBJECT TO REPORTING.—Any broker, with respect to any transfer (which is not part of a sale or exchange executed by such broker) during a calendar year of a covered security which is a digital asset from an account maintained by such broker to an account which is not maintained by, or an address not associated with, a person that such broker knows or has reason to know is also a broker, shall make a return for such calendar year, in such form as determined by the Secretary, showing the information otherwise required to be furnished with respect to transfers subject to subsection (a).

Amendments

• **2021, Infrastructure Investment and Jobs Act (P.L. 117-58)**

P.L. 117-58, §80603(b)(2)(A)(ii), Div. H:

Amended Code Sec. 6045A by adding at the end a new subsection (d). **Effective** for returns required to be filed, and statements required to be furnished, after 12-31-2023. For a special rule, see Act Sec. 80603(d)(1)-(2), Div. H, below.

P.L. 117-58, §80603(d)(1)-(2), Div. H, provides:

(d) RULE OF CONSTRUCTION.—Nothing in this section or the amendments made by this section shall be construed to create any inference, for any period prior to the effective date of such amendments, with respect to—

(1) whether any person is a broker under section 6045(c)(1) of the Internal Revenue Code of 1986, or

(2) whether any digital asset is property which is a specified security under section 6045(g)(3)(B) of such Code.

[Sec. 6045B]

SEC. 6045B. RETURNS RELATING TO ACTIONS AFFECTING BASIS OF SPECIFIED SECURITIES.

[Sec. 6045B(a)]

(a) IN GENERAL.—According to the forms or regulations prescribed by the Secretary, any issuer of a specified security shall make a return setting forth—

(1) a description of any organizational action which affects the basis of such specified security of such issuer,

(2) the quantitative effect on the basis of such specified security resulting from such action, and

(3) such other information as the Secretary may prescribe.

[Sec. 6045B(b)]

(b) TIME FOR FILING RETURN.—Any return required by subsection (a) shall be filed not later than the earlier of—

(1) 45 days after the date of the action described in subsection (a), or

(2) January 15 of the year following the calendar year during which such action occurred.

RETURNS—INFORMATION

[Sec. 6045B(c)]

(c) STATEMENTS TO BE FURNISHED TO HOLDERS OF SPECIFIED SECURITIES OR THEIR NOMINEES.—According to the forms or regulations prescribed by the Secretary, every person required to make a return under subsection (a) with respect to a specified security shall furnish to the nominee with respect to the specified security (or certificate holder if there is no nominee) a written statement showing—

(1) the name, address, and phone number of the information contact of the person required to make such return,

(2) the information required to be shown on such return with respect to such security, and

(3) such other information as the Secretary may prescribe.

The written statement required under the preceding sentence shall be furnished to the holder on or before January 15 of the year following the calendar year during which the action described in subsection (a) occurred.

[Sec. 6045B(d)]

(d) SPECIFIED SECURITY.—For purposes of this section, the term "specified security" has the meaning given such term by section 6045(g)(3)(B). No return shall be required under this section with respect to actions described in subsection (a) with respect to a specified security which occur before the applicable date (as defined in section 6045(g)(3)(C)) with respect to such security.

[Sec. 6045B(e)]

(e) PUBLIC REPORTING IN LIEU OF RETURN.—The Secretary may waive the requirements under subsections (a) and (c) with respect to a specified security, if the person required to make the return under subsection (a) makes publicly available, in such form and manner as the Secretary determines necessary to carry out the purposes of this section—

(1) the name, address, phone number, and email address of the information contact of such person, and

(2) the information described in paragraphs (1), (2), and (3) of subsection (a).

Amendments

• **2008, Energy Improvement and Extension Act of 2008 (P.L. 110-343)**

P.L. 110-343, Division B, §403(d)(1):

Amended subpart B of part III of subchapter A of chapter 61, as amended by Act Sec. 403(b)[(c)], by inserting after Code Sec. 6045A a new Code Sec. 6045B. **Effective** 1-1-2011.

[Sec. 6046]

SEC. 6046. RETURNS AS TO ORGANIZATION OR REORGANIZATION OF FOREIGN CORPORATIONS AND AS TO ACQUISITIONS OF THEIR STOCK.

[Sec. 6046(a)]

(a) REQUIREMENT OF RETURN.—

(1) IN GENERAL.—A return complying with the requirements of subsection (b) shall be made by—

(A) each United States citizen or resident who becomes an officer or director of a foreign corporation if a United States person (as defined in section 7701(a)(30)) meets the stock ownership requirements of paragraph (2) with respect to such corporation,

(B) each United States person—

(i) who acquires stock which, when added to any stock owned on the date of such acquisition, meets the stock ownership requirements of paragraph (2) with respect to a foreign corporation, or

(ii) who acquires stock which, without regard to stock owned on the date of such acquisition, meets the stock ownership requirements of paragraph (2) with respect to a foreign corporation,

(C) each person (not described in subparagraph (B)) who is treated as a United States shareholder under section 953(c) with respect to a foreign corporation, and

(D) each person who becomes a United States person while meeting the stock ownership requirements of paragraph (2) with respect to stock of a foreign corporation.

In the case of a foreign corporation with respect to which any person is treated as a United States shareholder under section 953(c), subparagraph (A) shall be treated as including a reference to each United States person who is an officer or director of such corporation.

(2) STOCK OWNERSHIP REQUIREMENTS.—A person meets the stock ownership requirements of this paragraph with respect to any corporation if such person owns 10 percent or more of—

(A) the total combined voting power of all classes of stock of such corporation entitled to vote, or

(B) the total value of the stock of such corporation.

Amendments

• **1997, Taxpayer Relief Act of 1997 (P.L. 105-34)**

P.L. 105-34, §1146(a):

Amended Code Sec. 6046(a). **Effective** 1-1-98. Prior to amendment, Code Sec. 6046(a) read as follows:

(a) REQUIREMENT OF RETURN.—A return complying with the requirements of subsection (b) shall be made by—

(1) each United States citizen or resident who is on January 1, 1963, an officer or director of a foreign corporation, 5 percent or more in value of the stock of which is owned by a United States person (as defined in section 7701(a)(30)), or who becomes such an officer or director at any time after such date,

(2) each United States person who on January 1, 1963, owns 5 percent or more in value of the stock of a foreign corporation, or who, at any time after such date—

(A) acquires stock which, when added to any stock owned on January 1, 1963, has a value equal to 5 percent or more of the value of the stock of a foreign corporation, or

(B) acquires an additional 5 percent or more in value of the stock of a foreign corporation,

(3) each person (not described in paragraph (2)) who, at any time after January 1, 1987, is treated as a United States shareholder under section 953(c) with respect to a foreign corporation, and

(4) each person who at any time after January 1, 1963, becomes a United States person while owning 5 percent or more in value of the stock of a foreign corporation.

In the case of a foreign corporation with respect to which any person is treated as a United States shareholder under section 953(c), paragraph (1) shall be treated as including a reference to each United States person who is an officer or director of such corporation.

• **1988, Technical and Miscellaneous Revenue Act of 1988 (P.L. 100-647)**

P.L. 100-647, §1012(i)(19)(A):

Amended Code Sec. 6046(a) by striking out "and" at the end of paragraph (2), by redesignating paragraph (3) as paragraph (4), and by inserting after paragraph (2) a new paragraph (3). **Effective** as if included in the provision of P.L. 99-514 to which it relates.

P.L. 100-647, §1012(i)(19)(C):

Amended Code Sec. 6046(a) by adding at the end thereof a new sentence. **Effective** as if included in the provision of P.L. 99-514 to which it relates.

• **1962, Revenue Act of 1962 (P.L. 87-834)**

P.L. 87-834, §20:

Amended Code Sec. 6046(a). **Effective** 2-1-63. Prior to amendment, Code Sec. 6046(a) read as follows:

SEC. 6046. RETURNS AS TO CREATION OR ORGANIZATION, OR REORGANIZATION, OF FOREIGN CORPORATIONS.

(a) General Rule.—On or before the 90th day after the creation or organization, or reorganization, of any foreign corporation—

(1) Each United States citizen or resident who was an officer or director of the corporation at any time within 60 days after the creation or organization, or reorganization thereof, and

RETURNS—INFORMATION

(2) Each United States shareholder of the corporation by or for whom, at any time within 60 days after the creation or organization or reorganization of the corporation, 5 percent or more in value of the stock of the corporation then outstanding was owned directly or indirectly (including, in the case of an individual, stock owned by members of his family).

shall make a return in compliance with the provisions of subsection (b).

[Sec. 6046(b)]

(b) FORM AND CONTENTS OF RETURNS.—The returns required by subsection (a) shall be in such form and shall set forth, in respect of the foreign corporation, such information as the Secretary prescribes by forms or regulations as necessary for carrying out the provisions of the income tax laws, except that in the case of persons described only in subsection (a)(1)(A) the information required shall be limited to the names and addresses of persons described in subparagraph (B) or (C) of subsection (a)(1).

Amendments

• **2007, Tax Technical Corrections Act of 2007 (P.L. 110-172)**

P.L. 110-172, §11(a)(33)(A)-(B):

Amended Code Sec. 6046(b) by striking "subsection (a)(1)" and inserting "subsection (a)(1)(A)", and by striking "paragraph (2) or (3) of subsection (a)" and inserting "subparagraph (B) or (C) of subsection (a)(1)". **Effective** 12-29-2007.

• **1988, Technical and Miscellaneous Revenue Act of 1988 (P.L. 100-647)**

P.L. 100-647, §1012(i)(19)(B):

Amended Code Sec. 6046(b) by striking out "subsection (a)(2)" and inserting in lieu thereof "paragraph (2) or (3) of subsection (a)". **Effective** as if included in the provision of P.L. 99-514 to which it relates.

• **1976, Tax Reform Act of 1976 (P.L. 94-455)**

P.L. 94-455, §1906(b)(13)(A):

Amended 1954 Code by substituting "Secretary" for "Secretary or his delegate" each place it appeared. **Effective** 2-1-77.

• **1960 (P.L. 86-780)**

P.L. 86-780, §7(a):

Amended Code Sec. 6046(a). **Effective** with respect to foreign corporations created or organized, or reorganized, after 9-14-60. Prior to amendment, it read as follows:

(a) Requirement.—Every attorney, accountant, fiduciary, bank, trust company, financial institution, or other person, who aids, assists, counsels, or advises in, or with respect to, the formation, organization, or reorganization of any foreign corporation, shall, within 30 days thereafter, make a return in accordance with regulations prescribed by the Secretary or his delegate.

• **1962, Revenue Act of 1962 (P.L. 87-834)**

P.L. 87-834, §20:

Amended Code Sec. 6046(b). **Effective** 1-1-63. Prior to amendment, Code Sec. 6046(b) read as follows:

(b) Form and Contents of Returns.—The returns required by subsection (a) shall be in such form and shall set forth, in respect of the foreign corporation, such information as the Secretary or his delegate prescribes by forms or regulations as necessary for carrying out the provisions of the income tax laws.

• **1960 (P.L. 86-780)**

P.L. 86-780, §7(a):

Amended Code Sec. 6046(b). **Effective** with respect to foreign corporations created or organized, or reorganized, after 9-14-60. Prior to amendment, Code Sec. 6046(b) read as follows:

(b) Form and Contents of Return.—Such return shall be in such form, and shall set forth, in respect of each such corporation, to the full extent of the information within the possession or knowledge or under the control of the person required to make the return, such information as the Secretary or his delegate prescribes by forms or regulations as necessary for carrying out the provisions of the income tax laws.

[Sec. 6046(c)]

(c) OWNERSHIP OF STOCK.—For purposes of subsection (a), stock owned directly or indirectly by a person (including, in the case of an individual, stock owned by members of his family) shall be taken into account. For purposes of the preceding sentence, the family of an individual shall be considered as including only his brothers and sisters (whether by the whole or half blood), spouse, ancestors, and lineal descendants.

Amendments

• **1962, Revenue Act of 1962 (P.L. 87-834)**

P.L. 87-834, §20:

Amended Code Sec. 6046(c). **Effective** 1-1-63. Prior to amendment, Sec. 6046(c) read as follows:

"(c) Meaning of Terms.—For the purpose of this section—

"(1) United States shareholder.—The term `United States shareholder' includes a citizen or resident of the United States, a domestic corporation, a domestic partnership or an estate or trust (other than an estate or trust the gross income of which under subtitle A includes only income from sources within the United States).

"(2) Members of family.—The family of an individual shall be considered as including only his brothers and sisters (whether by the whole or half blood), spouse, ancestors, and lineal descendants."

• **1960 (P.L. 86-780)**

P.L. 86-780, §7(a):

Amended Code Sec. 6046(c). **Effective** with respect to foreign corporations created or organized, or reorganized, after 9-14-60. Prior to amendment, Code Sec. 6046(c) read as follows:

"(c) Privileged Communications.—Nothing in this section shall be construed to require the making of a return by an attorney-at-law with respect to any advice given or information obtained through the relationship of attorney and client."

[Sec. 6046(d)]

(d) TIME FOR FILING.—Any return required by subsection (a) shall be filed on or before the 90th day after the day on which, under any provision of subsection (a), the United States citizen, resident, or person becomes liable to file such return (or on or before such later day as the Secretary may by forms or regulations prescribe).

Amendments

• **1982, Tax Equity and Fiscal Responsibility Act of 1982 (P.L. 97-248)**

P.L. 97-248, §341(a):

Amended Code Sec. 6046(d) by inserting at the end of the subsection before the period "(or in or before such later day as the Secretary may by forms or regulations prescribe)". **Effective** for returns filed after 9-3-82.

• **1962, Revenue Act of 1962 (P.L. 87-834)**

P.L. 87-834, §20:

Amended Code Sec. 6046(d). **Effective** 1-1-63. Prior to amendment, Code Sec. 6046(d) read as follows:

"(d) Cross References.—

For provisions relating to penalties for violation of this section, see section 7203."

[Sec. 6046(e)]

(e) LIMITATION.—No information shall be required to be furnished under this section with respect to any foreign corporation unless such information was required to be furnished under regulations which have been in effect for at least 90 days before the date on which the United States citizen, resident, or person becomes liable to file a return required under subsection (a).

Amendments

• **1976, Tax Reform Act of 1976 (P.L. 94-455)**

P.L. 94-455, §1906(a)(4):

Amended Code Sec. 6046(e). **Effective** for tax years beginning after 12-31-76. Prior to amendment, Code Sec. 6046(e) read as follows:

"(e) LIMITATION.—

(1) GENERAL RULE.—Except as provided in paragraph (2), no information shall be required to be furnished under this section with respect to any foreign corporation unless such information was required to be furnished under regulations which have been in effect for at least 90 days before the date on which the United States citizen, resident, or person becomes liable to file a return required under subsection (a).

(2) EXCEPTION.—In the case of liability to file a return under subsection (a) arising on or after January 1, 1963, and before June 1, 1963—

(A) no information shall be required to be furnished under this section with respect to any foreign corporation unless such information was required to be furnished under regulations in effect on or before March 1, 1963, and

(B) if the date on which such regulations become effective is later than the day on which such liability arose, any return required by subsection (a) shall (in lieu of the time prescribed by subsection (d)) be filed on or before the 90th day after such date."

• **1962, Revenue Act of 1962 (P.L. 87-834)**

P.L. 87-834, §20:

Added Code Sec. 6046(e). **Effective** 1-1-63.

RETURNS—INFORMATION

[Sec. 6046(f)]

(f) CROSS REFERENCES.—
For provisions relating to penalties for violations of this section, see sections 6679 and 7203.

Amendments

• 1962, Revenue Act of 1962 (P.L. 87-834)

P.L. 87-834, §20:
Added Code Sec. 6046(f). **Effective** 1-1-63.

[Sec. 6046A]

SEC. 6046A. RETURNS AS TO INTERESTS IN FOREIGN PARTNERSHIPS.

[Sec. 6046A(a)]

(a) REQUIREMENT OF RETURN.—Any United States person, except to the extent otherwise provided by regulations—
(1) who acquires any interest in a foreign partnership,
(2) who disposes of any portion of his interest in a foreign partnership, or
(3) whose proportional interest in a foreign partnership changes substantially,

shall file a return. Paragraphs (1) and (2) shall apply to any acquisition or disposition only if the United States person directly or indirectly holds at least a 10-percent interest in such partnership either before or after such acquisition or disposition, and paragraph (3) shall apply to any change only if the change is equivalent to at least a 10-percent interest in such partnership.

Amendments

• 1997, Taxpayer Relief Act of 1997 (P.L. 105-34)

P.L. 105-34, §1143(a)(1):
Amended Code Sec. 6046A(a) by adding at the end a new sentence. **Effective** for transfers and changes after 8-5-97.

[Sec. 6046A(b)]

(b) FORM AND CONTENTS OF RETURN.—Any return required by subsection (a) shall be in such form and set forth such information as the Secretary shall by regulations prescribe.

[Sec. 6046A(c)]

(c) TIME FOR FILING RETURN.—Any return required by subsection (a) shall be filed on or before the 90th day (or on or before such later day as the Secretary may by regulations prescribe) after the day on which the United States person becomes liable to file such return.

[Sec. 6046A(d)]

(d) 10-PERCENT INTEREST.—For purposes of subsection (a), a 10-percent interest in a partnership is an interest described in section 6038(e)(3)(C).

Amendments

• 1997, Taxpayer Relief Act of 1997 (P.L. 105-34)

P.L. 105-34, §1143(a)(2):
Amended Code Sec. 6046A by redesignating subsection (d) as subsection (e) and by inserting after subsection (c) a new subsection (d). **Effective** for transfers and changes after 8-5-97.

[Sec. 6046A(e)]

(e) CROSS REFERENCE.—
For provisions relating to penalties for violations of this section, see sections 6679 and 7203.

Amendments

• 1997, Taxpayer Relief Act of 1997 (P.L. 105-34)

P.L. 105-34, §1143(a)(2):
Amended Code Sec. 6046A by redesignating subsection (d) as subsection (e). **Effective** for transfers and changes after 8-5-97.

• 1982, Tax Equity and Fiscal Responsibility Act of 1982 (P.L. 97-248)

P.L. 97-248, §405:
Added Code Sec. 6046A. **Effective** with respect to acquisitions or dispositions of, or substantial changes in, interests in foreign partnerships occurring after 9-3-82. However, see under Code Sec. 6221, for a special rule for certain international satellite partnerships.

[Sec. 6047]

SEC. 6047. INFORMATION RELATING TO CERTAIN TRUSTS AND ANNUITY PLANS.

[Sec. 6047(a)]

(a) TRUSTEES AND INSURANCE COMPANIES.—The trustee of a trust described in section 401(a) which is exempt from tax under section 501(a) to which contributions have been paid under a plan on behalf of any owner-employee (as defined in section 401(c)(3)), and each insurance company or other person which is the issuer of a contract purchased by such a trust, or purchased under a plan described in section 403(a), contributions for which have been paid on behalf of any owner-employee, shall file such returns (in such form and at such times), keep such records, make such identification of contracts and funds (and accounts within such funds), and supply such information, as the Secretary shall by forms or regulations prescribe.

Amendments

• 1984, Deficit Reduction Act of 1984 (P.L. 98-369)

P.L. 98-369, §491(d)(57):
Amended the section heading for Code Sec. 6047 by striking out "AND BOND PURCHASE" between the words "ANNUITY" and "PLANS". **Effective** for obligations issued after 12-31-83.

• 1976, Tax Reform Act of 1976 (P.L. 94-455)

P.L. 94-455, §1906(b)(13)(A):
Amended 1954 Code by substituting "Secretary" for "Secretary or his delegate" each place it appeared. **Effective** 2-1-77.

[Sec. 6047(b)]

(b) OWNER-EMPLOYEES.—Every individual on whose behalf contributions have been paid as an owner-employee (as defined in section 401(c)(3))—
(1) to a trust described in section 401(a) which is exempt from tax under section 501(a), or
(2) to an insurance company or other person under a plan described in section 403(a),

shall furnish the trustee, insurance company, or other person, as the case may be, such information at such times and in such form and manner as the Secretary shall prescribe by forms or regulations.

RETURNS—INFORMATION

Amendments

• **1976, Tax Reform Act of 1976 (P.L. 94-455)**

P.L. 94-455, § 1906(b)(13)(A):

Amended 1954 Code by substituting "Secretary" for "Secretary or his delegate" each place it appeared. **Effective** 2-1-77.

[Sec. 6047(c)]

(c) OTHER PROGRAMS.—To the extent provided by regulations prescribed by the Secretary, the provisions of this section apply with respect to any payment described in section 219 and to transactions of any trust described in section 408(a) or under an individual retirement annuity described in section 408(b).

Amendments

• **1984, Deficit Reduction Act of 1984 (P.L. 98-369)**

P.L. 98-369, § 491(d)(47):

Amended Code Sec. 6047 by striking out subsection (c) and by redesignating subsections (d), (e) and (f) as subsections (c), (d), and (e), respectively. **Effective** for obligations issued after 12-31-83. Prior to amendment, subsection (c) read as follows:

(c) EMPLOYEES UNDER QUALIFIED BOND PURCHASE PLANS.—Every individual in whose name a bond described in section 405(b)(1) is purchased by his employer under a qualified bond purchase plan described in section 405(a), or by a trust described in section 401(a) which is exempt from tax under section 501(a), shall furnish—

(1) to his employer or to such trust, and

(2) to the Secretary (or to such person as the Secretary may by regulations prescribe),

such information as the Secretary shall by forms or regulations prescribe.

• **1983, Technical Corrections Act of 1982 (P.L. 97-448)**

P.L. 97-448, § 103(c)(12)(C):

Amended Code Sec. 6047(d) by striking out "section 219(a)" and inserting in lieu thereof "section 219". **Effective** as if included in the provision of P.L. 97-34 to which it relates.

• **1981, Economic Recovery Tax Act of 1981 (P.L. 97-34)**

P.L. 97-34, § 311(h)(8):

Amended Code Sec. 6047(d) by striking out "section 219(a) or 220(a)" and inserting "section 219(a)". **Effective** for tax years beginning after 12-31-81. The transitional rule provides, that, for purposes of the 1954 Code, any amount allowed as a deduction under section 220 of the Code (as in effect before its repeal by P.L. 97-34) shall be treated as if it were allowed by section 219 of the Code.

• **1976, Tax Reform Act of 1976 (P.L. 94-455)**

P.L. 94-455, § 1501(b)(9):

Added "or 220(a)" after "219(a)". **Effective** for tax years beginning after 12-31-76.

P.L. 94-455, § 1906(b)(13)(A):

Amended 1954 Code by substituting "Secretary" for "Secretary or his delegate" each place it appeared. **Effective** 2-1-77.

[Sec. 6047(d)]

(d) REPORTS BY EMPLOYERS, PLAN ADMINISTRATORS, ETC.—

(1) IN GENERAL.—The Secretary shall by forms or regulations require that—

(A) the employer maintaining, or the plan administrator (within the meaning of section 414(g)) of, a plan from which designated distributions (as defined in section 3405(e)(1)) may be made, and

(B) any person issuing any contract under which designated distributions (as so defined) may be made,

make returns and reports regarding such plan (or contract) to the Secretary, to the participants and beneficiaries of such plan (or contract), and to such other persons as the Secretary may by regulations prescribe. No return or report may be required under the preceding sentence with respect to distributions to any person during any year unless such distributions aggregate $10 or more.

(2) FORM, ETC., OF REPORTS.—Such reports shall be in such form, made at such time, and contain such information as the Secretary may prescribe by forms or regulations.

Amendments

• **1996, Small Business Job Protection Act of 1996 (P.L. 104-188)**

P.L. 104-188, § 1455(b)(2):

Amended Code Sec. 6047(d)(1) by adding at the end a new sentence. **Effective** for returns, reports, and other statements the due date for which (determined without regard to extensions) is after 12-31-96.

• **1992, Unemployment Compensation Amendments of 1992 (P.L. 102-318)**

P.L. 102-318, § 522(b)(2)(D):

Amended Code Sec. 6047(d)(1) by striking "section 3405(d)(1)" and inserting "section 3405(e)(1)". **Effective** for distributions after 12-31-92.

P.L. 102-318, § 522(b)(2)(E):

Amended Code Sec. 6047(d)(1)(A) by striking "section 3405(d)(1)" and inserting "section 3405(d)(3)". [This amendment conflicts with the amendment made by P.L. 102-318, § 522(b)(2)(D).—CCH.]

• **1984, Deficit Reduction Act of 1984 (P.L. 98-369)**

P.L. 98-369, § 491(d)(47):

Amended Code Sec. 6047 by striking out subsection (c) and by redesignating subsections (d), (e) and (f) as subsections (c), (d), and (e), respectively. **Effective** for obligations issued after 12-31-83.

• **1982, Tax Equity and Fiscal Responsibility Act of 1982 (P.L. 97-248)**

P.L. 97-248, § 334(b):

Added Code Sec. 6047(e). **Effective** 1-1-83, except that in the case of periodic payments beginning before 1-1-83, the first periodic payment made after 12-31-82, will be treated as the first such periodic payment.

[Sec. 6047(e)]

(e) EMPLOYEE STOCK OWNERSHIP PLANS.—The Secretary shall require—

(1) any employer maintaining, or the plan administrator (within the meaning of section 414(g)) of, an employee stock ownership plan which holds stock with respect to which section 404(k) applies to dividends paid on such stock, or

(2) both such employer or plan administrator,

to make returns and reports regarding such plan, transaction, or loan to the Secretary and to such other persons as the Secretary may prescribe. Such returns and reports shall be made in such form, shall be made at such time, and shall contain such information as the Secretary may prescribe.

Amendments

• **1996, Small Business Job Protection Act of 1996 (P.L. 104-188)**

P.L. 104-188, § 1602(b)(6):

Amended Code Sec. 6047(e) by striking paragraphs (1), (2), and (3) and inserting new paragraphs (1) and (2). For the **effective** date, see Act Sec. 1602(c), below. Prior to amendment, Code Sec. 6047(e)(1)-(3) read as follows:

(1) any employer maintaining, or the plan administrator (within the meaning of section 414(g)) of, an employee stock ownership plan—

(A) which acquired stock in a transaction to which section 133 applies, or

(B) which holds stock with respect to which section 404(k) applies to dividends paid on such stock,

(2) any person making or holding a loan to which section 133 applies, or

(3) both such employer or plan administrator and such person,

P.L. 104-188, § 1602(c), provides:

(c) EFFECTIVE DATE.—

(1) IN GENERAL.—The amendments made by this section shall apply to loans made after the date of the enactment of this Act.

(2) REFINANCINGS.—The amendments made by this section shall not apply to loans made after the date of the enactment of this Act to refinance securities acquisition loans (determined without regard to section 133(b)(1)(B) of the Internal Revenue Code of 1986, as in effect on the day before the date of the enactment of this Act) made on or before such date or to refinance loans described in this paragraph if—

(A) the refinancing loans meet the requirements of section 133 of such Code (as so in effect),

(B) immediately after the refinancing the principal amount of the loan resulting from the refinancing does not exceed the principal amount of the refinanced loan (immediately before the refinancing), and

RETURNS—INFORMATION

(C) the term of such refinancing loan does not extend beyond the last day of the term of the original securities acquisition loan.

For purposes of this paragraph, the term "securities acquisition loan" includes a loan from a corporation to an employee stock ownership plan described in section 133(b)(3) of such Code (as so in effect).

(3) EXCEPTION.—Any loan made pursuant to a binding written contract in effect before June 10, 1996, and at all times thereafter before such loan is made, shall be treated for purposes of paragraphs (1) and (2) as a loan made on or before the date of the enactment of this Act.

- **1989, Omnibus Budget Reconciliation Act of 1989 (P.L. 101-239)**

P.L. 101-239, §7301(e):

Amended Code Sec. 6047 by redesignating subsection (e) as subsection (f) and by inserting after subsection (d) a new subsection (e). **Effective**, generally, for loans made after 7-10-89. However, for exceptions, see Act Sec. 7301(f)(2), below.

P.L. 101-239, §7301(f)(2), provides:

(2) BINDING COMMITMENT EXCEPTIONS.—

(A) The amendments made by this section shall not apply to any loan—

(i) which is made pursuant to a binding written commitment in effect on June 6, 1989, and at all times thereafter before such loan is made, or

(ii) to the extent that the proceeds of such loan are used to acquire employer securities pursuant to a written binding contract (or tender offer registered with the Securities and Exchange Commission) in effect on June 6, 1989, and at all times thereafter before such securities are acquired.

(B) The amendments made by this section shall not apply to any loan to which subparagraph (A) does not apply which is made pursuant to a binding written commitment in effect on July 10, 1989, and at all times thereafter before such loan is made. The preceding sentence shall only apply to the extent that the proceeds of such loan are used to acquire employer securities pursuant to a written binding contract (or tender offer registered with the Securities and Exchange Commission) in effect on July 10, 1989, and at all times thereafter before such securities are acquired.

(C) The amendments made by this section shall not apply to any loan made on or before July 10, 1992, pursuant to a written agreement entered into on or before July 10, 1989, if such agreement evidences the intent of the borrower on a periodic basis to enter into securities acquisition loans described in section 133(b)(1)(B) of the Internal Revenue Code of 1986 (as in effect on the day before the date of the enactment of this Act). The preceding sentence shall apply only if one or more securities acquisition loans were made to the borrower on or before July 10, 1989.

[Sec. 6047(f)]

(f) DESIGNATED ROTH CONTRIBUTIONS.—The Secretary shall require the plan administrator of each applicable retirement plan (as defined in section 402A) to make such returns and reports regarding designated Roth contributions (as defined in section 402A) to the Secretary, participants and beneficiaries of the plan, and such other persons as the Secretary may prescribe.

Amendments

- **2006, Pension Protection Act of 2006 (P.L. 109-280)**

P.L. 109-280, §811, provides:

SEC. 811. PENSIONS AND INDIVIDUAL RETIREMENT ARRANGEMENT PROVISIONS OF ECONOMIC GROWTH AND TAX RELIEF RECONCILIATION ACT OF 2001 MADE PERMANENT.

Title IX of the Economic Growth and Tax Relief Reconciliation Act of 2001 [P.L. 107-16] shall not apply to the provisions of, and amendments made by, subtitles A through F of title VI [§§ 601-666]of such Act (relating to pension and individual retirement arrangement provisions).

- **2001, Economic Growth and Tax Relief Reconciliation Act of 2001 (P.L. 107-16)**

P.L. 107-16, §617(d)(2):

Amended Code Sec. 6047 by redesignating subsection (f) as subsection (g) and by inserting after subsection (e) a new subsection (f). **Effective** for tax years beginning after 12-31-2005.

P.L. 107-16, §901(a)-(b), provides [but see P.L. 109-280, §811, above]:

SEC. 901. SUNSET OF PROVISIONS OF ACT.

(a) IN GENERAL.—All provisions of, and amendments made by, this Act shall not apply—

(1) to taxable, plan, or limitation years beginning after December 31, 2010, or

(2) in the case of title V, to estates of decedents dying, gifts made, or generation skipping transfers, after December 31, 2010.

(b) APPLICATION OF CERTAIN LAWS.—The Internal Revenue Code of 1986 and the Employee Retirement Income Security Act of 1974 shall be applied and administered to years, estates, gifts, and transfers described in subsection (a) as if the provisions and amendments described in subsection (a) had never been enacted.

[Sec. 6047(g)]

(g) INFORMATION RELATING TO LIFE INSURANCE CONTRACT TRANSACTIONS.—This section shall not apply to any information which is required to be reported under section 6050Y.

Amendments

- **2017, Tax Cuts and Jobs Act (P.L. 115-97)**

P.L. 115-97, §13520(c)(2)(A)-(B):

Amended Code Sec. 6047 by redesignating subsection (g) as subsection (h) and by inserting after subsection (f) a new subsection (g). For the **effective** date, see Act Sec. 13520(d), below.

P.L. 115-97, §13520(d), provides:

(d) EFFECTIVE DATE.—The amendments made by this section shall apply to—

(1) reportable policy sales (as defined in section 6050Y(d)(2) of the Internal Revenue Code of 1986 (as added by subsection (a)) after December 31, 2017, and

(2) reportable death benefits (as defined in section 6050Y(d)(4) of such Code (as added by subsection (a)) paid after December 31, 2017.

[Sec. 6047(h)]

(h) CROSS REFERENCES.—

(1) For provisions relating to penalties for failures to file returns and reports required under this section, see sections 6652(e), 6721, and 6722.

(2) For criminal penalty for furnishing fraudulent information, see section 7207.

(3) For provisions relating to penalty for failure to comply with the provisions of subsection (d), see section 6704.

(4) For provisions requiring reporting of information relating to certain life insurance contract transactions, see section 6050Y.

Amendments

- **2017, Tax Cuts and Jobs Act (P.L. 115-97)**

P.L. 115-97, §13520(c)(2)(A), (C):

Amended Code Sec. 6047 by redesignating subsection (g) as subsection (h) and by adding at the end of subsection (h), as so redesignated, a new paragraph (4). For the **effective** date, see Act Sec. 13520(d), below.

P.L. 115-97, §13520(d), provides:

(d) EFFECTIVE DATE.—The amendments made by this section shall apply to—

(1) reportable policy sales (as defined in section 6050Y(d)(2) of the Internal Revenue Code of 1986 (as added by subsection (a)) after December 31, 2017, and

(2) reportable death benefits (as defined in section 6050Y(d)(4) of such Code (as added by subsection (a)) paid after December 31, 2017.

- **2006, Pension Protection Act of 2006 (P.L. 109-280)**

P.L. 109-280, §811, provides:

SEC. 811. PENSIONS AND INDIVIDUAL RETIREMENT ARRANGEMENT PROVISIONS OF ECONOMIC GROWTH AND TAX RELIEF RECONCILIATION ACT OF 2001 MADE PERMANENT.

Title IX of the Economic Growth and Tax Relief Reconciliation Act of 2001 [P.L. 107-16] shall not apply to the provisions of, and amendments made by, subtitles A through F of title VI [§§ 601-666]of such Act (relating to pension and individual retirement arrangement provisions).

- **2001, Economic Growth and Tax Relief Reconciliation Act of 2001 (P.L. 107-16)**

P.L. 107-16, §617(d)(2):

Amended Code Sec. 6047 by redesignating subsection (f) as subsection (g). **Effective** for tax years beginning after 12-31-2005.

P.L. 107-16, §901(a)-(b), provides [but see P.L. 109-280, §811, above]:

SEC. 901. SUNSET OF PROVISIONS OF ACT.

(a) IN GENERAL.—All provisions of, and amendments made by, this Act shall not apply—

(1) to taxable, plan, or limitation years beginning after December 31, 2010, or

(2) in the case of title V, to estates of decedents dying, gifts made, or generation skipping transfers, after December 31, 2010.

(b) APPLICATION OF CERTAIN LAWS.—The Internal Revenue Code of 1986 and the Employee Retirement Income Security Act of 1974 shall be applied and administered to years, estates, gifts, and transfers described in subsection (a) as if the provisions and amendments described in subsection (a) had never been enacted.

RETURNS—INFORMATION

- **1996, Small Business Job Protection Act of 1996 (P.L. 104-188)**

P.L. 104-188, §1455(d)(1):

Amended Code Sec. 6047(f)(1). **Effective** for returns, reports, and other statements the due date for which (determined without regard to extensions) is after 12-31-96. Prior to amendment, Code Sec. 6047(f)(1) read as follows:

(1) For provisions relating to penalties for failure to file a return required by this section, see section 6652(e).

- **1989, Omnibus Budget Reconciliation Act of 1989 (P.L. 101-239)**

P.L. 101-239, §7301(e):

Amended Code Sec. 6047 by redesignating subsection (e) as subsection (f). **Effective** for loans made after 7-10-89. However, for exceptions, see Act Sec. 7301(f)(2) in the amendment notes following Code Sec. 6047(e).

- **1986, Tax Reform Act of 1986 (P.L. 99-514)**

P.L. 99-514, §1501(d)(1)(D):

Amended Code Sec. 6047(e)(1) by striking out "section 6652(f)" and inserting in lieu thereof "section 6652(e)". **Effective** for returns the due date for which (determined without regard to extensions) is after 12-31-86.

P.L. 99-514, §1848(e)(2):

Amended Code Sec. 6047(e) by adding at the end thereof new paragraph (3). **Effective** as if included in the provision of P.L. 98-369 to which it relates.

- **1984, Deficit Reduction Act of 1984 (P.L. 98-369)**

P.L. 98-369, §491(d)(47):

Amended Code Sec. 6047 by striking out subsection (c) and by redesignating subsections (d), (e) and (f) as subsections (c), (d), and (e), respectively. **Effective** for obligations issued after 12-31-83.

- **1982, Tax Equity and Fiscal Responsibility Act of 1982 (P.L. 97-248)**

P.L. 97-248, §334(b):

Redesignated subsection (e) as subsection (f). **Effective** 1-1-83.

- **1974, Employee Retirement Income Security Act of 1974 (P.L. 93-406)**

P.L. 93-406, §1031(c)(3):

Amended Code Sec. 6047(d). **Effective** 9-2-74. Prior to amendment, Code Sec. 6047(d) read as follows:

(d) CROSS REFERENCE.—

For criminal penalty for furnishing fraudulent information, see section 7207.

P.L. 93-406, §2002(g)(8):

Amended Code Sec. 6047 further by redesignating subsection (d) as subsection (e) and by adding new subsection (d). **Effective** 1-1-75.

- **Self-Employed Individuals Tax Retirement Act of 1962 (P.L. 87-792)**

P.L. 87-792, §7:

Added Code Sec. 6047. **Effective** 1-1-63.

[Sec. 6048]

SEC. 6048. INFORMATION WITH RESPECT TO CERTAIN FOREIGN TRUSTS.

[Sec. 6048(a)]

(a) NOTICE OF CERTAIN EVENTS.—

(1) GENERAL RULE.—On or before the 90th day (or such later day as the Secretary may prescribe) after any reportable event, the responsible party shall provide written notice of such event to the Secretary in accordance with paragraph (2).

(2) CONTENTS OF NOTICE.—The notice required by paragraph (1) shall contain such information as the Secretary may prescribe, including—

(A) the amount of money or other property (if any) transferred to the trust in connection with the reportable event, and

(B) the identity of the trust and of each trustee and beneficiary (or class of beneficiaries) of the trust.

(3) REPORTABLE EVENT.—For purposes of this subsection—

(A) IN GENERAL.—The term "reportable event" means—

(i) the creation of any foreign trust by a United States person,

(ii) the transfer of any money or property (directly or indirectly) to a foreign trust by a United States person, including a transfer by reason of death, and

(iii) the death of a citizen or resident of the United States if—

(I) the decedent was treated as the owner of any portion of a foreign trust under the rules of subpart E of part I of subchapter J of chapter 1, or

(II) any portion of a foreign trust was included in the gross estate of the decedent.

(B) EXCEPTIONS.—

(i) FAIR MARKET VALUE SALES.—Subparagraph (A)(ii) shall not apply to any transfer of property to a trust in exchange for consideration of at least the fair market value of the transferred property. For purposes of the preceding sentence, consideration other than cash shall be taken into account at its fair market value and the rules of section 679(a)(3) shall apply.

(ii) DEFERRED COMPENSATION AND CHARITABLE TRUSTS.—Subparagraph (A) shall not apply with respect to a trust which is—

(I) described in section 402(b), 404(a)(4), or 404A, or

(II) determined by the Secretary to be described in section 501(c)(3).

(4) RESPONSIBLE PARTY.—For purposes of this subsection, the term "responsible party" means—

(A) the grantor in the case of the creation of an inter vivos trust,

(B) the transferor in the case of a reportable event described in paragraph (3)(A)(ii) other than a transfer by reason of death, and

(C) the executor of the decedent's estate in any other case.

[Sec. 6048(b)]

(b) UNITED STATES OWNER OF FOREIGN TRUST.—

(1) IN GENERAL.—If, at any time during any taxable year of a United States person, such person is treated as the owner of any portion of a foreign trust under the rules of subpart E of part I of subchapter J of chapter 1, such person shall submit such information as the Secretary may prescribe with respect to such trust for such year and shall be responsible to ensure that—

(A) such trust makes a return for such year which sets forth a full and complete accounting of all trust activities and operations for the year, the name of the United States agent for such trust, and such other information as the Secretary may prescribe, and

(B) such trust furnishes such information as the Secretary may prescribe to each United States person (i) who is treated as the owner of any portion of such trust or (ii) who receives (directly or indirectly) any distribution from the trust.

(2) TRUSTS NOT HAVING UNITED STATES AGENT.—

(A) IN GENERAL.—If the rules of this paragraph apply to any foreign trust, the determination of amounts required to be taken into account with respect to such trust by a United States person under the rules of subpart E of part I of subchapter J of chapter 1 shall be determined by the Secretary.

(B) UNITED STATES AGENT REQUIRED.—The rules of this paragraph shall apply to any foreign trust to which paragraph (1) applies unless such trust agrees (in such manner, subject to such conditions, and at such time as the Secretary shall prescribe) to authorize a United States person to act as such trust's limited agent solely for purposes of applying sections 7602, 7603, and 7604 with respect to—

(i) any request by the Secretary to examine records or produce testimony related to the proper treatment of amounts required to be taken into account under the rules referred to in subparagraph (A), or

(ii) any summons by the Secretary for such records or testimony.

RETURNS—INFORMATION

The appearance of persons or production of records by reason of a United States person being such an agent shall not subject such persons or records to legal process for any purpose other than determining the correct treatment under this title of the amounts required to be taken into account under the rules referred to in subparagraph (A). A foreign trust which appoints an [agent] described in this subparagraph shall not be considered to have an office or a permanent establishment in the United States, or to be engaged in a trade or business in the United States, solely because of the activities of such agent pursuant to this subsection.

(C) OTHER RULES TO APPLY.—Rules similar to the rules of paragraphs (2) and (4) of section 6038A(e) shall apply for purposes of this paragraph.

Amendments

• **2010, Hiring Incentives to Restore Employment Act (P.L. 111-147)**

P.L. 111-147, §534(a):

Amended Code Sec. 6048(b)(1) by inserting "shall submit such information as the Secretary may prescribe with respect to such trust for such year and" before "shall be responsible to ensure". **Effective** for tax years beginning after 3-18-2010.

• **1997, Taxpayer Relief Act of 1997 (P.L. 105-34)**

P.L. 105-34, §1601(i)(1):

Amended Code Sec. 6048(b) by striking "GRANTOR" in the heading and inserting "OWNER". **Effective** as if included in the provision of P.L. 104-188 to which it relates [**effective** for tax years of U.S. persons beginning after 12-31-95.—CCH].

[Sec. 6048(c)]

(c) REPORTING BY UNITED STATES BENEFICIARIES OF FOREIGN TRUSTS.—

(1) IN GENERAL.—If any United States person receives (directly or indirectly) during any taxable year of such person any distribution from a foreign trust, such person shall make a return with respect to such trust for such year which includes—

(A) the name of such trust,

(B) the aggregate amount of the distributions so received from such trust during such taxable year, and

(C) such other information as the Secretary may prescribe.

(2) INCLUSION IN INCOME IF RECORDS NOT PROVIDED.—

(A) IN GENERAL.—If adequate records are not provided to the Secretary to determine the proper treatment of any distribution from a foreign trust, such distribution shall be treated as an accumulation distribution includible in the gross income of the distributee under chapter 1. To the extent provided in regulations, the preceding sentence shall not apply if the foreign trust elects to be subject to rules similar to the rules of subsection (b)(2)(B).

(B) APPLICATION OF ACCUMULATION DISTRIBUTION RULES.—For purposes of applying section 668 in a case to which subparagraph (A) applies, the applicable number of years for purposes of section 668(a) shall be 1/2 of the number of years the trust has been in existence.

[Sec. 6048(d)]

(d) SPECIAL RULES.—

(1) DETERMINATION OF WHETHER UNITED STATES PERSON MAKES TRANSFER OR RECEIVES DISTRIBUTION.—For purposes of this section, in determining whether a United States person makes a transfer to, or receives a distribution from, a foreign trust, the fact that a portion of such trust is treated as owned by another person under the rules of subpart E of part I of subchapter J of chapter 1 shall be disregarded.

(2) DOMESTIC TRUSTS WITH FOREIGN ACTIVITIES.—To the extent provided in regulations, a trust which is a United States person shall be treated as a foreign trust for purposes of this section and section 6677 if such trust has substantial activities, or holds substantial property, outside the United States.

(3) TIME AND MANNER OF FILING INFORMATION.—Any notice or return required under this section shall be made at such time and in such manner as the Secretary shall prescribe.

(4) MODIFICATION OF RETURN REQUIREMENTS.—The Secretary is authorized to suspend or modify any requirement of this section if the Secretary determines that the United States has no significant tax interest in obtaining the required information.

(5) UNITED STATES PERSON'S RETURN MUST BE CONSISTENT WITH TRUST RETURN OR SECRETARY NOTIFIED OF INCONSISTENCY.—Rules similar to the rules of section 6034A(c) shall apply to items reported by a trust under subsection (b)(1)(B) and to United States persons referred to in such subsection.

Amendments

• **1997, Taxpayer Relief Act of 1997 (P.L. 105-34)**

P.L. 105-34, §1027(b):

Amended Code Sec. 6048(d) by adding at the end a new paragraph (5). **Effective** for returns of beneficiaries and owners filed after 8-5-97.

• **1996, Small Business Job Protection Act of 1996 (P.L. 104-188)**

P.L. 104-188, §1901(a):

Amended Code Sec. 6048. For the **effective** date, see Act Sec. 1901(d), below.

P.L. 104-188, §1901(d), provides:

(d) EFFECTIVE DATES.—

(1) REPORTABLE EVENTS.—To the extent related to subsection (a) of section 6048 of the Internal Revenue Code of 1986, as amended by this section, the amendments made by this section shall apply to reportable events (as defined in such section 6048) occurring after the date of the enactment of this Act.

(2) GRANTOR TRUST REPORTING.—To the extent related to subsection (b) of such section 6048, the amendments made by this section shall apply to taxable years of United States persons beginning after December 31, 1995.

(3) REPORTING BY UNITED STATES BENEFICIARIES.—To the extent related to subsection (c) of such section 6048, the amendments made by this section shall apply to distributions received after the date of the enactment of this Act.

Prior to amendment, Code Sec. 6048 read as follows:

SEC. 6048. RETURNS AS TO CERTAIN FOREIGN TRUSTS.

[Sec. 6048(a)]

(a) GENERAL RULE.—On or before the 90th day (or on or before such later day as the Secretary may by regulations prescribe) after—

(1) the creation of any foreign trust by a United States person, or

(2) the transfer of any money or property to a foreign trust by a United States person,

the grantor in the case of an inter vivos trust, the fiduciary of an estate in the case of a testamentary trust, or the transferor, as the case may be, shall make a return in compliance with the provisions of subsection (b).

• **1982, Tax Equity and Fiscal Responsibility Act of 1982 (P.L. 97-248)**

P.L. 97-248, §341(b):

Amended Code Sec. 6048(a) by inserting "(or on or before such later day as the Secretary may by regulations prescribe)" after "the 90th day". **Effective** for returns filed after 9-3-82.

• **1976, Tax Reform Act of 1976 (P.L. 94-455)**

P.L. 94-455, §1013(e):

Amended the heading to Code Sec. 6048. Prior to amendment, the heading read as follows:

SEC. 6048. RETURNS AS TO CREATION OF OR TRANSFER TO CERTAIN FOREIGN TRUSTS.

[Sec. 6048(b)]

(b) FORM AND CONTENTS OF RETURNS.—The returns required by subsection (a) shall be in such form and shall set forth, in respect of the foreign trust, such information as the Secretary prescribes by regulation as necessary for carrying out the provisions of the income tax laws.

Amendments

• **1976, Tax Reform Act of 1976 (P.L. 94-455)**

P.L. 94-455, §1906(b)(13)(A):

Amended 1954 Code by substituting "Secretary" for "Secretary or his delegate" each place it appeared. **Effective** 2-1-77.

[Sec. 6048(c)]

(c) ANNUAL RETURNS FOR FOREIGN TRUSTS HAVING ONE OR MORE UNITED STATES BENEFICIARIES.—Each taxpayer subject to tax under section 679 (relating to foreign trusts having one or more United States beneficiaries) for his taxable year with respect to any trust shall make a return with respect to such trust for such year at such time and in such manner, and setting forth such information, as the Secretary may by regulations prescribe.

RETURNS—INFORMATION

Amendments

• **1976, Tax Reform Act of 1976 (P.L. 94-455)**

P.L. 94-455, §1013(d):

Redesignated former Code Sec. 6048(c) as Code Sec. 6048(d) and added a new Code Sec. 6048(c). **Effective** for tax years ending after 12-31-75, but only in the case of—(A) foreign trusts created after 5-21-74, and (B) transfers of property to foreign trusts after 5-21-74.

[Sec. 6048(d)]

(d) CROSS REFERENCE.—

For provisions relating to penalties for violation of this section, see sections 6677 and 7203.

Amendments

• **1976, Tax Reform Act of 1976 (P.L. 94-455)**

P.L. 94-455, §1013(d):

Redesignated former Code Sec. 6048(c) as Code Sec. 6048(d). **Effective** for tax years ending after 12-31-75, but only in the case of—(A) foreign trusts created after 5-21-74, and (B) transfers of property to foreign trusts after 5-21-74.

P.L. 94-455, §1013(e):

Amended redesignated Code Sec. 6048(d). **Effective** for tax years ending after 12-31-75, but only in the case of—(A) foreign trusts created after 5-21-74, and (B) transfers of property to foreign trusts after 5-21-74. Prior to amendment, redesignated Code. Sec. 6048(d) read as follows:

(d) CROSS REFERENCES.—

(1) For provisions relating to penalties for violations of this section, see sections 6677 and 7203.

(2) For definition of the term "foreign trust created by a United States person", see section 643(d).

• **1962, Revenue Act of 1962 (P.L. 87-834)**

P.L. 87-834, §7:

Added Code Sec. 6048. **Effective** 10-17-62.

[Sec. 6049]

SEC. 6049. RETURNS REGARDING PAYMENTS OF INTEREST.

[Sec. 6049(a)]

(a) REQUIREMENT OF REPORTING.—Every person—

(1) who makes payments of interest (as defined in subsection (b)) aggregating $10 or more to any other person during any calendar year, or

(2) who receives payments of interest (as so defined) as a nominee and who makes payments aggregating $10 or more during any calendar year to any other person with respect to the interest so received,

shall make a return according to the forms or regulations prescribed by the Secretary, setting forth the aggregate amount of such payments and the name and address of the person to whom paid.

Amendments

• **1983, Interest and Dividend Tax Compliance Act of 1983 (P.L. 98-67)**

P.L. 98-67, §102(e)(1):

Amended Code Sec. 6049(a). **Effective** as of the close of 6-30-83. Prior to amendment, Code Sec. 6049(a) read as follows:

(a) REQUIREMENT OF REPORTING.—Every person—

(1) who makes payments of interest (as defined in subsection (b)) aggregating $10 or more to any other person during any calendar year,

(2) who receives payments of interest (as so defined) as a nominee and who makes payments aggregating $10 or more during any calendar year to any other person with respect to the interest so received, or

(3) who is required under subchapter B of chapter 24 to withhold tax on the payment of any interest,

shall make a return according to the forms or regulations prescribed by the Secretary, setting forth the aggregate amount of such payments, tax deducted and withheld, and the name and address of the person to whom paid or from whom withheld.

• **1982, Tax Equity and Fiscal Responsibility Act of 1982 (P.L. 97-248)**

P.L. 97-248, §309(a):

Amended Code Sec. 6049(a). **Effective** for amounts paid or treated as paid after 12-31-82. Prior to its amendment, Code Sec. 6049(a) read as follows:

(a) REQUIREMENT OF REPORTING.—

(1) IN GENERAL.—Every person—

(A) who makes payments of interest (as defined in subsection (b)) aggregating $10 or more to any other person during any calendar year,

(B) who receives payments of interest as a nominee and who makes payments aggregating $10 or more during any calendar year to any other person with respect to the interest so received, or

(C) which is a corporation that has outstanding any bond, debenture, note, or certificate or other evidence of indebtedness in registered form as to which there is during any calendar year an amount of original issue discount aggregating $10 or more includible in the gross income of any holder under section 1232(a)(3) without regard to subparagraph (B) thereof,

shall make a return according to the forms or regulations prescribed by the Secretary, setting forth the aggregate amount of such payments and such aggregate amount includible in the gross income of any holder and the name and address of the person to whom paid or such holder.

(2) RETURNS REQUIRED BY THE SECRETARY.—Every person who makes payments of interest (as defined in subsection (b)) aggregating less than $10 to any other person during any calendar year shall, when required by the Secretary, make a return setting forth the aggregate amount of such payments and the name and address of the person to whom paid.

(3) OTHER RETURNS REQUIRED BY SECRETARY.—Every corporation making payments, regardless of amounts, of interest other than interest as defined in subsection (b) shall, when required by regulations prescribed by the Secretary, make a return according to the forms or regulations prescribed by the Secretary, setting forth the amount paid and the name and address of the recipient of each such payment.

• **1976, Tax Reform Act of 1976 (P.L. 94-455)**

P.L. 94-455, §1906(b)(13)(A):

Amended 1954 Code by substituting "Secretary" for "Secretary or his delegate" each place it appeared. **Effective** 2-1-77.

• **1969, Tax Reform Act of 1969 (P.L. 91-172)**

P.L. 91-172, §413(c):

Amended by deleting "or" from the end of subparagraph (a)(1)(A), by adding "or" at the end of subparagraph (a)(1)(B), by adding new subparagraph (a)(1)(C), and by inserting "and such aggregate amount includible in the gross income of any holder" in the concluding language of paragraph (a)(1). **Effective** with respect to bonds and other evidences of indebtedness issued after 5-27-69 (other than evidences of indebtedness issued pursuant to a written commitment which was binding on 5-27-69, and at all times thereafter).

[Sec. 6049(b)]

(b) INTEREST DEFINED.—

(1) GENERAL RULE.—For purposes of subsection (a), the term "interest" means—

(A) interest on any obligation—

(i) issued in registered form, or

(ii) of a type offered to the public,

other than any obligation with a maturity (at issue) of not more than 1 year which is held by a corporation,

(B) interest on deposits with persons carrying on the banking business,

(C) amounts (whether or not designated as interest) paid by a mutual savings bank, savings and loan association, building and loan association, cooperative bank, homestead association, credit union, industrial loan association or bank, or similar organization, in respect of deposits, investment certificates, or withdrawable or repurchasable shares,

(D) interest on amounts held by an insurance company under an agreement to pay interest thereon,

(E) interest on deposits with brokers (as defined in section 6045(c)),

(F) interest paid on amounts held by investment companies (as defined in section 3 of the Investment Company Act of 1940 (15 U.S.C. 80a-3)) and on amounts invested in other pooled funds or trusts, and

(G) to the extent provided in regulations prescribed by the Secretary, any other interest (which is not described in paragraph (2)).

(2) EXCEPTIONS.—For purposes of subsection (a), the term "interest" does not include—

(A) interest on any obligation issued by a natural person,

(B) except to the extent otherwise provided in regulations—
　(i) any amount paid to any person described in paragraph (4), or
　(ii) any amount described in paragraph (5), and
(C) except to the extent otherwise provided in regulations, any amount not described in subparagraph (B) of this paragraph which is income from sources outside the United States or which is paid by—
　(i) a foreign government or international organization or any agency or instrumentality thereof,
　(ii) a foreign central bank of issue,
　(iii) a foreign corporation not engaged in a trade or business in the United States,
　(iv) a foreign corporation, the interest payments of which would be exempt from withholding under subchapter A of chapter 3 if paid to a person who is not a United States person, or
　(v) a partnership not engaged in a trade or business in the United States and composed in whole of nonresident alien individuals and persons described in clause (i), (ii), or (iii).

(3) PAYMENTS BY UNITED STATES NOMINEES ETC., OF UNITED STATES PERSON.—If, within the United States, a United States person—
(A) collects interest (or otherwise acts as a middleman between the payor and payee) from a foreign person described in paragraph (2)(D) or collects interest from a United States person which is income from sources outside the United States for a second person who is a United States person, or
(B) makes payments of such interest to such second United States person,
notwithstanding paragraph (2)(D), such payment shall be subject to the requirements of subsection (a) with respect to such second United States person.

(4) PERSONS DESCRIBED IN THIS PARAGRAPH.—A person is described in this paragraph if such person is—
(A) a corporation,
(B) an organization exempt from taxation under section 501(a) or an individual retirement plan,
(C) the United States or any wholly owned agency or instrumentality thereof,
(D) a State, the District of Columbia, a possession of the United States, any political subdivision of any of the foregoing, or any wholly owned agency or instrumentality of any one or more of the foregoing,
(E) a foreign government, a political subdivision of a foreign government, or any wholly owned agency or instrumentality of any one or more of the foregoing,
(F) an international organization or any wholly owned agency or instrumentality thereof,
(G) a foreign central bank of issue,
(H) a dealer in securities or commodities required to register as such under the laws of the United States or a State, the District of Columbia, or a possession of the United States,
(I) a real estate investment trust (as defined in section 856),
(J) an entity registered at all times during the taxable year under the Investment Company Act of 1940,
(K) a common trust fund (as defined in section 584(a)), or
(L) any trust which—
　(i) is exempt from tax under section 664(c), or
　(ii) is described in section 4947(a)(1).

(5) AMOUNTS DESCRIBED IN THIS PARAGRAPH.—An amount is described in this paragraph if such amount—
(A) is subject to withholding under subchapter A of chapter 3 (relating to withholding of tax on nonresident aliens and foreign corporations) by the person paying such amount, or
(B) would be subject to withholding under subchapter A of chapter 3 by the person paying such amount but for the fact that—
　(i) such amount is income from sources outside the United States,
　(ii) the payor thereof is exempt from the application of section 1441(a) by reason of section 1441(c) or a tax treaty,
　(iii) such amount is original issue discount (within the meaning of section 1273(a)), or
　(iv) such amount is described in section 871(i)(2).

Amendments

• **2006, Tax Increase Prevention and Reconciliation Act of 2005 (P.L. 109-222)**

P.L. 109-222, §502(a):

Amended Code Sec. 6049(b)(2) by striking subparagraph (B) and by redesignating subparagraphs (C) and (D) as subparagraphs (B) and (C), respectively. **Effective** for interest paid after 12-31-2005. Prior to being stricken, Code Sec. 6049(b)(2)(B) read as follows:

(B) interest on any obligation if such interest is exempt from tax under section 103(a) or if such interest is exempt from tax (without regard to the identity of the holder) under any other provision of this title,

P.L. 109-222, §502(b):

Amended Code Sec. 6049(b)(2)(C), as redesignated by Act Sec. 502(a), by striking "subparagraph (C)" and inserting "subparagraph (B)". **Effective** for interest paid after 12-31-2005.

• **1986, Tax Reform Act of 1986 (P.L. 99-514)**

P.L. 99-514, §1214(c)(4):

Amended Code Sec. 6049(b)(5)(B) by striking out "or" at the end of clause (ii), by striking out the period at the end of clause (iii) and inserting in lieu thereof ", or", and by adding at the end thereof new clause (iv). **Effective**, generally, for payments after 12-31-86. However, see Act Sec. 1214(d)(2)-(4) at Code Sec. 861 for special rules.

P.L. 99-514, §1803(a)(14)(C):

Amended Code Sec. 6049(b)(5)(B)(iii) by striking out "section 1232(b)(1)" and inserting in lieu thereof "section 1273(a)". **Effective** as if included in the provision of P.L. 98-369 to which it relates.

• **1984, Deficit Reduction Act of 1984 (P.L. 98-369)**

P.L. 98-369, §474(r)(29)(J):

Amended Code Sec. 6049(b)(2) by adding "and" at the end of subparagraph (C), by striking out ", and" at the end of subparagraph (D) and inserting in lieu thereof a period, and by striking out subparagraph (E). **Effective** for tax years beginning after 12-31-83, and to carrybacks from such years. However, it does not apply with respect to obligations issued before 1-1-84. Prior to amendment, subparagraph (E) read as follows:

(E) any amount on which the person making payment is required to deduct and withhold a tax under section 1451 (relating to tax-free covenant bonds), or would be so required but for section 1451(d) (relating to benefit of personal exemptions).

• **1983, Interest and Dividend Tax Compliance Act of 1983 (P.L. 98-67)**

P.L. 98-67, §102(e)(2):

Amended Code Sec. 6049(b)(2)(C) and added Code Sec. 6049(b)(4) and (b)(5). **Effective** as of the close of 6-30-83. Prior to amendment, Code Sec. 6049(b)(2)(C) read as follows:

(C) except to the extent otherwise provided in regulations—

　(i) any amount paid to any person referred to in paragraph (2) of section 3452(c) (other than subparagraphs (J) and (K) thereof), or

　(ii) any amount described in section 3454(a)(2)(D) or (E),

• **1982, Surface Transportation Act of 1982 (P.L. 97-424)**

P.L. 97-424, §547(b)(4):

Amended Code Sec. 6049(b)(2)(B) by striking out "law" and inserting "this title". **Effective** 1-6-83.

RETURNS—INFORMATION

- **1982, Tax Equity and Fiscal Responsibility Act of 1982 (P.L. 97-248)**

P.L. 97-248, § 309(a):

Amended Code Sec. 6049(b). **Effective** for amounts paid or treated as paid after 12-31-82. Prior to amendment, Code Sec. 6049(b) read as follows:

"(b) INTEREST DEFINED.—

(1) GENERAL RULE.—For purposes of subsections (a)(1) and (2), the term `interest' means—

(A) interest on evidences of indebtedness (including bonds, debentures, notes, and certificates) issued by a corporation in registered form, and, to the extent provided in regulations prescribed by the Secretary, interest on other evidences of indebtedness issued by a corporation of a type offered by corporations to the public;

(B) interest on deposits with persons carrying on the banking business;

(C) amounts (whether or not designated as interest) paid by a mutual savings bank, savings and loan association, building and loan association, cooperative bank, homestead association, credit union, or similar organization, in respect of deposits, investment certificates, or withdrawable or repurchasable shares;

(D) interest on amounts held by an insurance company under an agreement to pay interest thereon; and

(E) interest on deposits with stockbrokers and dealers in securities.

(2) EXCEPTIONS.—For purposes of subsections (a)(1) and (2), the term `interest' does not include—

(A) interest on obligations described in section 103(a) (relating to interest on certain governmental obligations);

(B) to the extent provided in regulations prescribed by the Secretary, any amount paid by or to a foreign corporation, a nonresident alien, or a partnership not engaged in trade or business in the United States and composed in whole or in part of nonresident aliens; and

(C) any amount on which the person making payment is required to deduct and withhold a tax under section 1451 (relating to tax-free covenant bonds), or would be so required but for section 1451(d) (relating to benefit of personal exemptions)."

- **1976, Tax Reform Act of 1976 (P.L. 94-455)**

P.L. 94-455, § 1901(b)(6):

Substituted "section 103(a)" for "section 103(a)(1) or (3)". **Effective** for tax years beginning after 12-31-76.

P.L. 94-455, § 1906(b)(13)(A):

Amended 1954 Code by substituting "Secretary" for "Secretary or his delegate" each place it appeared. **Effective** 2-1-77.

[Sec. 6049(c)]

(c) STATEMENTS TO BE FURNISHED TO PERSONS WITH RESPECT TO WHOM INFORMATION IS REQUIRED.—

(1) IN GENERAL.—Every person required to make a return under subsection (a) shall furnish to each person whose name is required to be set forth in such return a written statement showing—

(A) the name, address and phone number of the information contact of the person required to make such return, and

(B) the aggregate amount of payments to, or the aggregate amount includible in the gross income of, the person required to be shown on the return.

(2) TIME AND FORM OF STATEMENT.—The written statement under paragraph (1)—

(A) shall be furnished (either in person or in a statement mailing by first-class mail which includes adequate notice that the statement is enclosed) to the person on or before January 31 of the year following the calendar year for which the return under subsection (a) was required to be made, and

(B) shall be in such form as the Secretary may prescribe by regulations.

Amendments

- **1996, Taxpayer Bill of Rights 2 (P.L. 104-168)**

P.L. 104-168, § 1201(a)(6):

Amended Code Sec. 6049(c)(1)(A) by striking "name and address" and inserting "name, address, and phone number of the information contact". **Effective** for statements required to be furnished after 12-31-96 (determined without regard to any extension).

- **1986, Tax Reform Act of 1986 (P.L. 99-514)**

P.L. 99-514, § 1501(c)(5):

Amended Code Sec. 6049(c). **Effective** for returns the due date for which (determined without regard to extensions) is after 10-22-86. Prior to amendment, Code Sec. 6049(c) read as follows:

(c) STATEMENTS TO BE FURNISHED TO PERSONS WITH RESPECT TO WHOM INFORMATION IS FURNISHED.—

(1) IN GENERAL.—Every person making a return under subsection (a) shall furnish to each person whose name is set forth in such return a written statement showing—

(A) the name and address of the person making such return, and

(B) the aggregate amount of payments to, or the aggregate amount includible in the gross income of, the person as shown on such return, and

(C) the aggregate amount of tax deducted and withheld with respect to such person under subchapter B of chapter 24.

(2) TIME AND FORM OF STATEMENT.—The written statement under paragraph (1)—

(A) shall be furnished (either in person or in a separate mailing by first-class mail) to the person on or before January 31 of the year following the calendar year for which the return under subsection (a) was made, and

(B) shall be in such form as the Secretary may prescribe by regulations.

(3) NO STATEMENT REQUIRED WHERE INTEREST IS LESS THAN $10.—No statement with respect to payments of interest to any person shall be required to be furnished to any person under this subsection if the aggregate amount of payments to such person shown on the return made with respect to paragraph (1) or (2), as the case may be, of subsection (a) is less than $10.

- **1983, Interest and Dividend Tax Compliance Act of 1983 (P.L. 98-67)**

P.L. 98-67, § 102(e)(3):

Amended Code Sec. 6049(c)(1) by adding "and" at the end of subparagraph (A), by substituting a period for ", and" at the end of subparagraph (B). **Effective** as of the close of 6-30-83. Prior to deletion, former subparagraph (C) read as follows:

"(C) the aggregate amount of tax deducted and withheld with respect to such person under subchapter B of chapter 24.".

P.L. 98-67, § 108(a):

Amended Code Sec. 6049(c). **Effective** with respect to payments made after 12-31-83. Prior to amendment, Code Sec. 6049(c) read as follows:

(c) STATEMENTS TO BE FURNISHED TO PERSONS WITH RESPECT TO WHOM INFORMATION IS FURNISHED.—

(1) IN GENERAL.—Every person making a return under subsection (a) shall furnish to each person whose name is set forth in such return a written statement showing—

(A) the name and address of the person making such return, and

(B) the aggregate amount of payments to, or the aggregate amount includible in the gross income of, the person as shown on such return.

(2) STATEMENT MUST BE FURNISHED ON OR BEFORE JANUARY 31.—The written statement required under the preceding sentence shall be furnished to the person on or before January 31 of the year following the calendar year for which the return under subsection (a) was made.

(3) NO STATEMENT REQUIRED WHERE INTEREST IS LESS THAN $10.—No statement with respect to payments of interest to any person shall be required to be furnished to any person under this subsection if the aggregate amount of payments to such person shown on the return made with respect to paragraph (1) or (2), as the case may be, of subsection (a) is less than $10.

- **1982, Tax Equity and Fiscal Responsibility Act of 1982 (P.L. 97-248)**

P.L. 97-248, § 309(b):

Amended Code Sec. 6049(c). **Effective** for amounts paid or treated as paid after 12-31-82. Prior to amendment, Code Sec. 6049(c) read as follows:

"(c) STATEMENTS TO BE FURNISHED TO PERSONS WITH RESPECT TO WHOM INFORMATION IS FURNISHED.—Every person making a return under subsection (a)(1) shall furnish to each person whose name is set forth in such return a written statement showing—

(1) the name and address of the person making such return, and

(2) the aggregate amount of payments to, or the aggregate amount includible in the gross income of, the person as shown on such return.

The written statement required under the preceding sentence shall be furnished to the person on or before January 31 of the year following the calendar year for which the return under subsection (a)(1) was made. No statement shall be required to be furnished to any person under this subsection if the aggregate amount of payments to, or the aggregate amount includible in the gross income of, such person shown on the return made with respect to subparagraph (A), (B), or (C), as the case may be, of subsection (a)(1) is less than $10."

- **1969, Tax Reform Act of 1969 (P.L. 91-172)**

P.L. 91-172, § 413(d):

Amended subsection (c) by inserting ", or the aggregate amount includible in the gross income of," in paragraph (2), and by inserting the last sentence of subsection (c) in lieu of the following sentence: "No statement shall be required to be furnished to any person under this subsection if the aggregate amount of payments to such person as shown on the return made under subsection (a)(1) is less than $10.". **Effective** with respect to bonds and other evidences of indebtedness issued after 5-27-69 (other than evidences of indebtedness issued pursuant to a written commitment which was binding on 5-27-69, and at all times thereafter).

- **1962, Revenue Act of 1962 (P.L. 87-834)**

P.L. 87-834, § 19(c):

Added Code Sec. 6049. **Effective** with respect to payments made on or after 1-1-63.

[Sec. 6049(d)]

(d) DEFINITIONS AND SPECIAL RULES.—For purposes of this section—

(1) PERSON.—The term "person" includes any governmental unit and any agency or instrumentality thereof and any international organization and any agency or instrumentality thereof.

(2) OBLIGATION.—The term "obligation" includes bonds, debentures, notes, certificates, and other evidences of indebtedness.

Sec. 6049(c)

RETURNS—INFORMATION

(3) PAYMENTS BY GOVERNMENTAL UNITS.—In the case of payments made by any governmental unit or any agency or instrumentality thereof, the officer or employee having control of the payment of interest (or the person appropriately designated for purposes of this section) shall make the returns and statements required by this section.

(4) FINANCIAL INSTITUTIONS, BROKERS, ETC., COLLECTING INTEREST MAY BE SUBSTITUTED FOR PAYOR.—To the extent and in the manner provided by regulations, in the case of any obligation—

(A) a financial institution, broker, or other person specified in such regulations which collects interest on such obligation for the payee (or otherwise acts as a middleman between the payor and the payee) shall comply with the requirements of subsections (a) and (c), and

(B) no other person shall be required to comply with the requirements of subsections (a) and (c) with respect to any interest on such obligation for which reporting is required pursuant to subparagraph (A).

(5) INTEREST ON CERTAIN OBLIGATIONS MAY BE TREATED ON A TRANSACTIONAL BASIS.—

(A) IN GENERAL.—To the extent and in the manner provided in regulations, this section shall apply with respect to—

(i) any person described in paragraph (4)(A), and

(ii) in the case of any United States savings bonds, any Federal agency making payments thereon,

on any transactional basis rather than on an annual aggregation basis.

(B) SEPARATE RETURNS AND STATEMENTS.—If subparagraph (A) applies to interest on any obligation, the return under subsection (a) and the statement furnished under subsection (c) with respect to such transaction may be made separately, but any such statement shall be furnished to the payee at such time as the Secretary may prescribe by regulations but not later than January 31 of the next calendar year.

(C) STATEMENT TO PAYEE REQUIRED IN CASE OF TRANSACTIONS INVOLVING $10 OR MORE.—In the case of any transaction to which this paragraph applies which involves the payment of $10 or more of interest, a statement of the transaction may be provided to the payee of such interest in lieu of the statement required under subsection (c). Such statement shall be provided during January of the year following the year in which such payment is made.

(6) TREATMENT OF ORIGINAL ISSUE DISCOUNT.—

(A) IN GENERAL.—Original issue discount on any obligation shall be reported—

(i) as if paid at the time it is includible in gross income under section 1272 (except that for such purpose the amount reportable with respect to any subsequent holder shall be determined as if he were the original holder), and

(ii) if section 1272 does not apply to the obligation, at maturity (or, if earlier, on redemption).

In the case of any obligation not in registered form issued before January 1, 1983, clause (ii) and not clause (i) shall apply.

(B) ORIGINAL ISSUE DISCOUNT.—For purposes of this paragraph, the term "original issue discount" has the meaning given to such term by section 1273(a).

(7) INTERESTS IN REMIC'S AND CERTAIN OTHER DEBT INSTRUMENTS.—

(A) IN GENERAL.—For purposes of subsection (a), the term "interest" includes amounts includible in gross income with respect to regular interests in REMIC's (and such amounts shall be treated as paid when includible in gross income under section 860B(b)).

(B) REPORTING TO CORPORATIONS, ETC.—Except as otherwise provided in regulations, in the case of any interest described in subparagraph (A) of this paragraph and any other debt instrument to which section 1272(a)(6) applies, subsection (b)(4) of this section shall be applied without regard to subparagraphs (A), (H), (I), (J), (K), and (L)(i).

(C) ADDITIONAL INFORMATION.—Except as otherwise provided in regulations, any return or statement required to be filed or furnished under this section with respect to interest income described in subparagraph (A) and interest on any other debt instrument to which section 1272(a)(6) applies shall also provide information setting forth the adjusted issue price of the interest to which the return or statement relates at the beginning of each accrual period with respect to which interest income is required to be reported on such return or statement and information necessary to compute accrual of market discount.

(D) REGULATORY AUTHORITY.—The Secretary may prescribe such regulations as are necessary or appropriate to carry out the purposes of this subparagraph, including regulations which require more frequent or more detailed reporting.

(8) REPORTING OF CREDIT ON CLEAN RENEWABLE ENERGY BONDS.—

(A) IN GENERAL.—For purposes of subsection (a), the term "interest" includes amounts includible in gross income under section 54(g) and such amounts shall be treated as paid on the credit allowance date (as defined in section 54(b)(4)).

(B) REPORTING TO CORPORATIONS, ETC.—Except as otherwise provided in regulations, in the case of any interest described in subparagraph (A), subsection (b)(4) shall be applied without regard to subparagraphs (A), (H), (I), (J), (K), and (L)(i) of such subsection.

(C) REGULATORY AUTHORITY.—The Secretary may prescribe such regulations as are necessary or appropriate to carry out the purposes of this paragraph, including regulations which require more frequent or more detailed reporting.

(9) REPORTING OF CREDIT ON QUALIFIED TAX CREDIT BONDS.—

(A) IN GENERAL.—For purposes of subsection (a), the term "interest" includes amounts includible in gross income under section 54A and such amounts shall be treated as paid on the credit allowance date (as defined in section 54A(e)(1)).

(B) REPORTING TO CORPORATIONS, ETC.—Except as otherwise provided in regulations, in the case of any interest described in subparagraph (A) of this paragraph, subsection (b)(4) of this section shall be applied without regard to subparagraphs (A), (H), (I), (J), (K), and (L)(i).

(C) REGULATORY AUTHORITY.—The Secretary may prescribe such regulations as are necessary or appropriate to carry out the purposes of this paragraph, including regulations which require more frequent or more detailed reporting.

Amendments

- **2018, Tax Technical Corrections Act of 2018 (P.L. 115-141)**

P.L. 115-141, § 401(d)(6)(B)(vi)(I)-(II), Div. U:

Amended Code Sec. 6049(d)(8)(A) by striking "or 1400N(l)(6)" following "section 54(g)", and by striking "or 1400N(l)(2)(D), as the case may be" following "as defined in section 54(b)(4)". **Effective** 3-23-2018. For a special rule, see Act Sec. 401(e), Div. U, below.

P.L. 115-141, § 401(e), Div. U, provides:

(e) GENERAL SAVINGS PROVISION WITH RESPECT TO DEADWOOD PROVISIONS.—If—

(1) any provision amended or repealed by the amendments made by subsection (b) or (d) applied to—

(A) any transaction occurring before the date of the enactment of this Act,

(B) any property acquired before such date of enactment, or

(C) any item of income, loss, deduction, or credit taken into account before such date of enactment, and

(2) the treatment of such transaction, property, or item under such provision would (without regard to the amendments or repeals made by such subsection) affect the liability for tax for periods ending after such date of enactment,

nothing in the amendments or repeals made by this section shall be construed to affect the treatment of such transaction, property, or item for purposes of determining liability for tax for periods ending after such date of enactment.

RETURNS—INFORMATION

• **2008, Heartland, Habitat, Harvest, and Horticulture Act of 2008 (P.L. 110-246)**

P.L. 110-246, §15316(b):

Amended Code Sec. 6049(d) by adding at the end a new paragraph (9). **Effective** for obligations issued after 5-22-2008.

• **2005, Gulf Opportunity Zone Act of 2005 (P.L. 109-135)**

P.L. 109-135, §101(b)(2)(A)-(B):

Amended Code Sec. 6049(d)(8)(A) by inserting "or 1400N(l)(6)" after "section 54(g)", and by inserting "or 1400N(l)(2)(D), as the case may be" after "section 54(b)(4)". **Effective** for tax years ending on or after 8-28-2005.

• **2005, Energy Tax Incentives Act of 2005 (P.L. 109-58)**

P.L. 109-58, §1303(b):

Amended Code Sec. 6049(d) by adding at the end a new paragraph (8). **Effective** for bonds issued after 12-31-2005.

• **1988, Technical and Miscellaneous Revenue Act of 1988 (P.L. 100-647)**

P.L. 100-647, §1006(t)(24):

Amended Code Sec. 6049(d)(7)(C) by striking out "the issue price" and inserting in lieu thereof "the adjusted issue price". **Effective** as if included in the provision of P.L. 99-514 to which it relates.

Amendments

• **1983, Interest and Dividend Tax Compliance Act of 1983 (P.L. 98-67)**

P.L. 98-67, §102(a):

Repealed Code Sec. 6049(e) as though it had not been enacted by P.L. 97-248. **Effective** as of the close of 6-30-83. Prior to repeal, Code Sec. 6049(e) read as follows:

(e) DUPLICATE OF SUBSECTION (c) STATEMENT MAY BE REQUIRED TO BE FILED WITH SECRETARY.—A duplicate of any statement made pursuant to subsection (c) which is required to set forth an amount withheld under section 3451 shall, when required by regulations prescribed by the Secretary, be filed with the Secretary.

• **1982, Tax Equity and Fiscal Responsibility Act of 1982 (P.L. 97-248)**

P.L. 97-248, §303(b):

Added Code Sec. 6049(e). **Effective** for payments of interest paid or credited after 6-30-83.

P.L. 100-647, §1006(v):

Amended Code Sec. 6049(d)(7)(A) by inserting "(and such amounts shall be treated as paid when includible in gross income under section 860B(b))" before the period at the end thereof. **Effective** as if included in the provision of P.L. 99-514 to which it relates.

• **1986, Tax Reform Act of 1986 (P.L. 99-514)**

P.L. 99-514, §674:

Amended Code Sec. 6049(d) by adding at the end thereof new paragraph (7). **Effective** 1-1-87 [effective date changed by P.L. 100-647, §1006(w)(1)].

• **1984, Deficit Reduction Act of 1984 (P.L. 98-369)**

P.L. 98-369, §42(a)(14):

Amended Code Sec. 6049(d)(6) by striking out "section 1232A" each place it appeared in subparagraph (A) and inserting in lieu thereof "section 1272", and by striking out "section 1232(b)(1)" and inserting in lieu thereof "section 1273(a)". **Effective** for tax years ending after 7-18-84.

• **1982, Tax Equity and Fiscal Responsibility Act of 1982 (P.L. 97-248)**

P.L. 97-248, §309(a):

Added Code Sec. 6049(d). **Effective** with respect to amounts paid or treated as paid after 12-31-82.

[Sec. 6049(e)—Repealed]

[Sec. 6050—Repealed]

Secretary prescribes by regulations as necessary for carrying out the provisions of the income tax laws.

• **1976, Tax Reform Act of 1976 (P.L. 94-455)**

P.L. 94-455, §1906(b)(13)(A):

Amended 1954 Code by substituting "Secretary" for "Secretary or his delegate" each place it appeared. **Effective** 2-1-77.

• **1969, Tax Reform Act of 1969 (P.L. 91-172)**

P.L. 91-172, §121(e)(1):

Added Code Sec. 6050. **Effective** with respect to transfers of property after 12-31-69.

Amendments

• **1979 (P.L. 96-167)**

P.L. 96-167, §5:

Repealed Code Sec. 6050. **Effective** with respect to transfers made after 12-29-79. Prior to its repeal, Code Sec. 6050 read as follows:

SEC. 6050. RETURNS RELATING TO CERTAIN TRANSFERS TO EXEMPT ORGANIZATIONS.

(a) GENERAL RULE.—On or before the 90th day after the transfer of income producing property, the transferor shall make a return in compliance with the provisions of subsection (b) if the transferee is known by the transferor to be an organization referred to in section 511(a) or (b) and the property (without regard to any lien) has a fair market value in excess of $50,000.

(b) FORM AND CONTENTS OF RETURNS.—The return required by subsection (a) shall be in such form and shall set forth, in respect of the transfer, such information as the

[Sec. 6050A]

SEC. 6050A. REPORTING REQUIREMENTS OF CERTAIN FISHING BOAT OPERATORS.

[Sec. 6050A(a)]

(a) REPORTS.—The operator of a boat on which one or more individuals, during a calendar year, perform services described in section 3121(b)(20) shall submit to the Secretary (at such time, and in such manner and form, as the Secretary shall by regulations prescribe) information respecting—

(1) the identity of each individual performing such services;

(2) the percentage of each such individual's share of the catches of fish or other forms of aquatic animal life, and the percentage of the operator's share of such catches;

(3) if such individual receives his share in kind, the type and weight of such share, together with such other information as the Secretary may prescribe by regulations reasonably necessary to determine the value of such shares;

(4) if such individual receives a share of the proceeds of such catches, the amount so received; and

(5) any cash remuneration described in section 3121(b)(20)(A).

Amendments

• **1996, Small Business Job Protection Act of 1996 (P.L. 104-188)**

P.L. 104-188, §1116(a)(1)(C):

Amended Code Sec. 6050A(a) by striking "and" at the end of paragraph (3), by striking the period at the end of paragraph (4) and inserting "; and", and by adding at the end thereof a new paragraph (5). **Effective** for remuneration paid after 12-31-96.

[Sec. 6050A(b)]

(b) WRITTEN STATEMENT.—Every person required to make a return under subsection (a) shall furnish to each person whose name is required to be set forth in such return a written statement showing the information relating to such person required to be contained in such return. The written statement required under the preceding sentence shall be furnished to the person on or before January 31 of the year following the calendar year for which the return under subsection (a) was required to be made.

Amendments

• **1986, Tax Reform Act of 1986 (P.L. 99-514)**

P.L. 99-514, §1501(c)(6):

Amended Code Sec. 6050A(b). **Effective** for returns the due date for which (determined without regard to extensions) is after 12-31-86. Prior to amendment, Code Sec. 6050A(b) read as follows:

(b) WRITTEN STATEMENT.—Every person making a return under subsection (a) shall furnish to each person whose name is set forth in such return a written statement showing the information relating to such person contained in such return. The written statement required under the preceding sentence shall be furnished to the person on or before January 31 of the year following the calendar year for which the return under subsection (a) was made.

• **1976, Tax Reform Act of 1976 (P.L. 94-455)**

P.L. 94-455, §1207(e)(3):

Added Code Sec. 6050A. **Effective** for calendar years beginning after 10-4-76.

RETURNS—INFORMATION

[Sec. 6050B]
Sec. 6050B. RETURNS RELATING TO UNEMPLOYMENT COMPENSATION.

[Sec. 6050B(a)]

(a) REQUIREMENT OF REPORTING.—Every person who makes payments of unemployment compensation aggregating $10 or more to any individual during any calendar year shall make a return according to the forms or regulations prescribed by the Secretary, setting forth the aggregate amount of such payments and the name and address of the individual to whom paid.

[Sec. 6050B(b)]

(b) STATEMENTS TO BE FURNISHED TO INDIVIDUALS WITH RESPECT TO WHOM INFORMATION IS REQUIRED.—Every person required to make a return under subsection (a) shall furnish to each individual whose name is required to be set forth in such return a written statement showing—

(1) the name, address, and phone number of the information contact of the person required to make such return, and

(2) the aggregate amount of payments to the individual required to be shown on such return.

The written statement required under the preceding sentence shall be furnished to the individual on or before January 31 of the year following the calendar year for which the return under subsection (a) was required to be made.

Amendments

- **1996, Taxpayer Bill of Rights 2 (P.L. 104-168)**

P.L. 104-168, §1201(a)(7):

Amended Code Sec. 6050B(b)(1) by striking "name and address" and inserting "name, address, and phone number of the information contact". **Effective** for statements required to be furnished after 12-31-96 (determined without regard to any extension).

- **1986, Tax Reform Act of 1986 (P.L. 99-514)**

P.L. 99-514, §1501(c)(7):

Amended Code Sec. 6050B(b). **Effective** for returns the due date for which (determined without regard to extensions) is after 12-31-86. Prior to amendment, Code Sec. 6050B(b) read as follows:

(b) STATEMENTS TO BE FURNISHED TO INDIVIDUALS WITH RESPECT TO WHOM INFORMATION IS FURNISHED.—Every person making a return under subsection (a) shall furnish to each individual whose name is set forth in such return a written statement showing—

(1) the name and address of the person making such return, and

(2) the aggregate amount of payments to the individual as shown on such return.

The written statement required under the preceding sentence shall be furnished to the individual on or before January 31 of the year following the calendar year for which the return under subsection (a) was made. No statement shall be required to be furnished to any individual under this subsection if the aggregate amount of payments to such individual shown on the return made under subsection (a) is less than $10.

[Sec. 6050B(c)]

(c) DEFINITIONS.—For purposes of this section—

(1) UNEMPLOYMENT COMPENSATION.—The term "unemployment compensation" has the meaning given to such term by section 85(b).

(2) PERSON.—The term "person" means the officer or employee having control of the payment of the unemployment compensation, or the person appropriately designated for purposes of this section.

Amendments

- **1996, Small Business Job Protection Act of 1996 (P.L. 104-188)**

P.L. 104-188, §1704(t)(14):

Amended Code Sec. 6050B(c)(1) by striking "section 85(c)" and inserting "section 85(b)". **Effective** 8-20-96.

- **1978, Revenue Act of 1978 (P.L. 95-600)**

P.L. 95-600, §112(b):

Added Code Sec. 6050B. **Effective** for payments of unemployment compensation made after 12-31-78, in tax years ending after such date.

[Sec. 6050C—Repealed]

Amendments

- **1988, Omnibus Trade and Competitiveness Act of 1988 (P.L. 100-418)**

P.L. 100-418, §1941(b)(1):

Repealed Code Sec. 6050C. **Effective** for crude oil removed from the premises on or after 8-23-88. Prior to repeal, Code Sec. 6050C read as follows:

SEC. 6050C. INFORMATION REGARDING WINDFALL PROFIT TAX ON DOMESTIC CRUDE OIL.

(a) CERTIFICATION FURNISHED BY OPERATOR.—Under regulations prescribed by the Secretary, the operator of a property from which domestic crude oil was produced shall certify (at such time and in such manner as the Secretary shall by regulations prescribe) to the purchaser—

(1) the adjusted base price (within the meaning of section 4989) with respect to such crude oil,

(2) the tier and category of such crude oil for purposes of the tax imposed by section 4986,

(3) if any certification is furnished to the operator by the producer with respect to whether such oil is exempt oil or independent producer oil, a copy of such certification,

(4) the amount of such crude oil, and

(5) such other information as the Secretary by regulations may require.

(b) AGREEMENT BETWEEN OPERATOR AND PURCHASER.—The Secretary may by regulations provide that, if the operator and purchaser agree thereto, the operator shall be relieved of the duty of furnishing some or all of the information required under subsection (a).

(c) SPECIAL RULE FOR OIL NOT SUBJECT TO WITHHOLDING.—If the tax imposed by section 4986 with respect to any oil for which withholding is not required under section 4995(a)—

(1) subsections (a) and (b) shall be applied by substituting "producer" for "purchaser", and

(2) paragraph (3) of subsection (a) shall not apply.

(d) CROSS REFERENCES.—

(1) For additions to tax for failure to furnish information required under this section, see section 6722.

(2) For penalty for willful failure to supply information required under this section, see section 7241.

- **1986, Tax Reform Act of 1986 (P.L. 99-514)**

P.L. 99-514, §1501(d)(1)(E):

Amended Code Sec. 6050C(d)(1) by striking out "section 6652(b)" and inserting in lieu thereof "section 6722". **Effective** for returns the due date for which (determined without regard to extensions) is after 12-31-86.

- **1980, Crude Oil Windfall Profit Tax Act of 1980 (P.L. 96-223)**

P.L. 96-223, §101(d)(1):

Added Code Sec. 6050C. For the **effective** date and transitional rules, see P.L. 96-223, §101(i).

[Sec. 6050D]
SEC. 6050D. RETURNS RELATING TO ENERGY GRANTS AND FINANCING.

[Sec. 6050D(a)]

(a) IN GENERAL.—Every person who administers a Federal, State, or local program a principal purpose of which is to provide subsidized financing or grants for projects to conserve or produce energy shall, to the extent required under regulations prescribed by the Secretary, make a return setting forth the name and address of each taxpayer receiving financing or a grant under such program and the aggregate amount so received by such individual.

[Sec. 6050D(b)]

(b) DEFINITION OF PERSON.—For purposes of this section, the term "person" means the officer or employee having control of the program, or the person appropriately designated for purposes of this section.

RETURNS—INFORMATION

Amendments
• **1980, Crude Oil Windfall Profit Tax Act of 1980 (P.L. 96-223)**

P.L. 96-223, §203(b)(1):

Added Code Sec. 6050D. **Effective** for tax years beginning after 12-31-80, but only with respect to financing or grants made after such date.

[Sec. 6050E]

SEC. 6050E. STATE AND LOCAL INCOME TAX REFUNDS.

[Sec. 6050E(a)]

(a) REQUIREMENT OF REPORTING.—Every person who, with respect to any individual, during any calendar year makes payments of refunds of State or local income taxes (or allows credits or offsets with respect to such taxes) aggregating $10 or more shall make a return according to forms or regulations prescribed by the Secretary setting forth the aggregate amount of such payments, credits, or offsets, and the name and address of the individual with respect to whom such payment, credit, or offset was made.

[Sec. 6050E(b)]

(b) STATEMENTS TO BE FURNISHED TO INDIVIDUALS WITH RESPECT TO WHOM INFORMATION IS REQUIRED.—Every person required to make a return under subsection (a) shall furnish to each individual whose name is required to be set forth in such return a written statement showing—

(1) the name of the State or political subdivision thereof, and

(2) the information required to be shown on the return with respect to refunds, credits, and offsets to the individual.

The written statement required under the preceding sentence shall be furnished to the individual during January of the calendar year following the calendar year for which the return under subsection (a) was required to be made. No statement shall be required under this subsection with respect to any individual if it is determined (in the manner provided by regulations) that such individual did not claim itemized deductions under chapter 1 of the taxable year giving rise to the refund, credit, or offset.

Amendments
• **1986, Tax Reform Act of 1986 (P.L. 99-514)**

P.L. 99-514, §1501(c)(8):

Amended Code Sec. 6050E(b). **Effective** for returns the due date for which (determined without regard to extensions) is after 12-31-86. Prior to amendment, Code Sec. 6050E(b) read as follows:

(b) STATEMENTS TO BE FURNISHED TO INDIVIDUALS WITH RESPECT TO WHOM INFORMATION IS FURNISHED.—Every person making a return under subsection (a) shall furnish to each individual whose name is set forth in such return a written statement showing—

(1) the name of the State or political subdivision thereof, and

(2) the aggregate amount shown on the return of refunds, credits, and offsets to the individual.

The written statement required under the preceding sentence shall be furnished to the individual during January of the calendar year following the calendar year for which the return under subsection (a) was made. No statement shall be required under this subsection with respect to any individual if it is determined (in the manner provided by regulations) that such individual did not claim itemized deductions under chapter 1 for the taxable year giving rise to the refund, credit, or offset.

• **1984, Deficit Reduction Act of 1984 (P.L. 98-369)**

P.L. 98-369, §151(a):

Amended Code Sec. 6050E(b) by adding at the end thereof a new sentence. **Effective** for payments of refunds, and credits and offsets made, after 12-31-82.

[Sec. 6050E(c)]

(c) PERSON DEFINED.—For purposes of this section, the term "person" means the officer or employee having control of the payment of the refunds (or the allowance of the credits or offsets) or the person appropriately designated for purposes of this section.

Amendments
• **1982, Tax Equity and Fiscal Responsibility Act of 1982 (P.L. 97-248)**

P.L. 97-248, §313(a):

Added Code Sec. 6050E. **Effective** for payments of refunds, and credits and offsets made, after 12-31-82.

[Sec. 6050F]

SEC. 6050F. RETURNS RELATING TO SOCIAL SECURITY BENEFITS.

[Sec. 6050F(a)]

(a) REQUIREMENT OF REPORTING.—The appropriate Federal official shall make a return, according to the forms and regulations prescribed by the Secretary, setting forth—

(1) the—

(A) aggregate amount of social security benefits paid with respect to any individual during any calendar year,

(B) aggregate amount of social security benefits repaid by such individual during such calendar year, and

(C) aggregate reductions under section 224 of the Social Security Act (or under section 3(a)(1) of the Railroad Retirement Act of 1974) in benefits which would otherwise have been paid to such individual during the calendar year on account of amounts received under a workmen's compensation act, and

(2) the name and address of such individual.

Amendments
• **1989, Medicare Catastrophic Coverage Repeal Act of 1989 (P.L. 101-234)**

P.L. 101-234, §102(a), provides that:

Section 111 of the Medicare Catastrophic Coverage Act of 1988 (P.L. 100-360) is repealed and the provisions of law amended by such sections are restored or revived as if such sections had not been enacted. **Effective** for tax years beginning after 12-31-88. Therefore, Code Sec. 6050F(a) is restored as if P.L. 100-360 had not been enacted. Code Sec. 6050F(a) as amended by Act Sec. 111(b)(1) of P.L. 100-360 read as follows:

(a) REQUIREMENT OF REPORTING.—The appropriate Federal official shall make a return, according to the forms and regulations prescribed by the Secretary, setting forth—

(1) the—

(A) aggregate amount of social security benefits paid with respect to any individual during any calendar year,

(B) aggregate amount of social security benefits repaid by such individual during such calendar year, and

(C) aggregate reductions under section 224 of the Social Security Act (or under section 3(a)(1) of the Railroad Retirement Act of 1974) in benefits which would otherwise have been paid to such individual during the calendar year on account of amounts received under a workmen's compensation act,

(2) whether any individual meets the requirements of section 59B(b)(1) with respect to the calendar year (determined without regard to section 59B(f)(1)(B)(ii)), and

(3) the name and address of such individual.

• **1988, Medicare Catastrophic Coverage Act of 1988 (P.L. 100-360)**

P.L. 100-360, §111(b)(1):

Amended Code Sec. 6050F(a) by striking "and" at the end of paragraph (1), by redesignating paragraph (2) as paragraph (3), and by inserting after paragraph (1) new paragraph (2) For the **effective** date, see Act Sec. 111(e), below.

P.L. 100-360, §111(e), provides:

(e) EFFECTIVE DATE.—

(1) IN GENERAL.—The amendments made by this section shall apply to taxable years beginning after December 31, 1988.

(2) WAIVER OF ESTIMATED TAX REQUIREMENT FOR YEARS BEGINNING IN 1989.—In the case of a taxable year beginning in 1989, the premium imposed by section 59B of the Internal Revenue Code of 1986 (as added by this section) shall not be treated as a tax for purposes of applying section 6654 of such Code.

RETURNS—INFORMATION

[Sec. 6050F(b)]

(b) STATEMENTS TO BE FURNISHED WITH RESPECT TO WHOM INFORMATION IS REQUIRED.—Every person required to make a return under subsection (a) shall furnish to each individual whose name is required to set forth in such return a written statement showing—

    (1) the name of the agency making the payments, and

    (2) the aggregate amount of payments, of repayments, and of reductions, with respect to the individual required to be shown on such return.

The written statement required under the preceding sentence shall be furnished to the individual on or before January 31 of the year following the calendar year for which the return under subsection (a) was required to be made.

Amendments

• **1989, Medicare Catastrophic Coverage Repeal Act of 1989 (P.L. 101-234)**

P.L. 101-234, § 102(a), provides that:

Section 111 of the Medicare Catastrophic Coverage Act of 1988 (P.L. 100-360) is repealed and the provisions of law amended by such sections are restored or revived as if such sections had not been enacted. **Effective** for tax years beginning after 12-31-88. Therefore, Code Sec. 6050F(b) is restored as if P.L. 100-360 had not been enacted. Code Sec. 6050F(b) as amended by Act Sec. 111(b)(2(A)-(B) of P.L. 100-360 read as follows:

(a) STATEMENTS TO BE FURNISHED WITH RESPECT TO WHOM INFORMATION IS REQUIRED.—Every person required to make a return under subsection (a) shall furnish to each individual whose name is required to set forth in such return a written statement showing—

(1) the name of the agency making the payments or making the determination under subsection (a)(2), and

(2) the aggregate amount of payments, of repayments, and of reductions and the information required under subsection (a)(2), with respect to the individual required to be shown on such return.

The written statement required under the preceding sentence shall be furnished to the individual on or before January 31 of the year following the calendar year for which the return under subsection (a) was required to be made.

• **1988, Medicare Catastrophic Coverage Act of 1988 (P.L. 100-360)**

P.L. 100-360, § 111(b)(2)(A)-(B):

Amended Code Sec. 6050F(b) by inserting "or making the determination under subsection (a)(2)" after "payments" in paragraph (1), and by inserting "and the information required under subsection (a)(2)," after "reductions" in paragraph (2). For the **effective** date, see Act Sec. 111(e), below.

P.L. 100-360, § 111(e), provides:

(e) EFFECTIVE DATE.—

(1) IN GENERAL.—The amendments made by this section shall apply to taxable years beginning after December 31, 1988.

(2) WAIVER OF ESTIMATED TAX REQUIREMENT FOR YEARS BEGINNING IN 1989.—In the case of a taxable year beginning in 1989, the premium imposed by section 59B of the Internal Revenue Code of 1986 (as added by this section) shall not be treated as a tax for purposes of applying section 6654 of such Code.

• **1986, Tax Reform Act of 1986 (P.L. 99-514)**

P.L. 99-514, § 1501(c)(9):

Amended Code Sec. 6050F(b). **Effective** for returns the due date for which (determined without regard to extensions) is after 12-31-86. Prior to amendment, Code Sec. 6050F(b) read as follows:

(b) STATEMENTS TO BE FURNISHED TO INDIVIDUALS WITH RESPECT TO WHOM INFORMATION IS FURNISHED.—Every person making a return under subsection (a) shall furnish to each individual whose name is set forth in such return a written statement showing—

(1) the name of the agency making the payments, and

(2) the aggregate amount of payments, of repayments, and of reductions, with respect to the individual as shown on such return.

The written statement required under the preceding sentence shall be furnished to the individual on or before January 31 of the year following the calendar year for which the return under subsection (a) was made.

[Sec. 6050F(c)]

(c) DEFINITIONS.—For purposes of this section—

    (1) APPROPRIATE FEDERAL OFFICIAL.—The term "appropriate Federal official" means—

        (A) the Commissioner of Social Security in the case of social security benefits described in section 86(d)(1)(A), and

        (B) the Railroad Retirement Board in the case of social security benefits described in section 86(d)(1)(B).

    (2) SOCIAL SECURITY BENEFIT.—The term "social security benefit" has the meaning given to such term by section 86(d)(1).

Amendments

• **1994, Social Security Independence and Program Improvements Act of 1994 (P.L. 103-296)**

P.L. 103-296, § 108(h)(4):

Amended Code Sec. 6050F(c)(1)(A) by striking "Secretary of Health and Human Services" and inserting "Commissioner of Social Security". **Effective** 3-31-95.

• **1989, Medicare Catastrophic Coverage Repeal Act of 1989 (P.L. 101-234)**

P.L. 101-234, § 102(a), provides:

Section 111 of the Medicare Catastrophic Coverage Act of 1988 (P.L. 100-360) is repealed and the provisions of law amended by such sections are restored or revived as if such sections had not been enacted. **Effective** for tax years beginning after 12-31-88. Therefore, Code Sec. 6050F(c)(1)(A) is restored as if P.L. 100-360 had not been enacted and reads as so above. Code Sec. 6050F(c)(1)(A) as amended by Act Sec. 111(b)(3) of P.L. 100-360 read as follows:

(A) the Secretary of Health and Human Services in the case of social security benefits described in section 86(d)(1)(A) and the information required under subsection (a)(2), and

• **1988, Medicare Catastrophic Coverage Act of 1988 (P.L. 100-360)**

P.L. 100-360, § 111(b)(3):

Amended Code Sec. 6050F(c)(1)(A) by inserting "and the information required under subsection (a)(2)" after "section 86(d)(1)(A)". For the **effective** date, see Act Sec. 111(e), below.

P.L. 100-360, § 111(e), provides:

(e) EFFECTIVE DATE.—

(1) IN GENERAL.—The amendments made by this section shall apply to taxable years beginning after December 31, 1988.

(2) WAIVER OF ESTIMATED TAX REQUIREMENT FOR YEARS BEGINNING IN 1989.—In the case of a taxable year beginning in 1989, the premium imposed by section 59B of the Internal Revenue Code of 1986 (as added by this section) shall not be treated as a tax for purposes of applying section 6654 of such Code.

• **1983, Social Security Amendments of 1983 (P.L. 98-21)**

P.L. 98-21, § 121(b):

Added Code Sec. 6050F. **Effective** for benefits received after 12-31-83, in tax years ending after such date. Amendments made by Act Sec. 121 shall not apply to any portion of a lump-sum payment of social security benefits (as defined in Code Sec. 86(d)) received after 12-31-83 if the generally applicable payment date for such portion was before 1-1-84.

[Sec. 6050G]

SEC. 6050G. RETURNS RELATING TO CERTAIN RAILROAD RETIREMENT BENEFITS.

[Sec. 6050G(a)]

(a) IN GENERAL.—The Railroad Retirement Board shall make a return, according to the forms and regulations prescribed by the Secretary, setting forth—

    (1) the aggregate amount of benefits paid under the Railroad Retirement Act of 1974 (other than tier 1 railroad retirement benefits, as defined in section 86(d)(4)) to any individual during any calendar year,

    (2) the employee contributions which are treated as having been paid for purposes of section 72(r),

    (3) the name and address of such individual, and

    (4) such other information as the Secretary may require.

Amendments

• **2018, Tax Technical Corrections Act of 2018 (P.L. 115-141)**

P.L. 115-141, § 401(b)(45), Div. U:

Amended Code Sec. 6050G(a)(2) by striking "(to the extent not previously taken into account under section 72(d)(1))" following "the employee contributions". **Effective** 3-23-2018. For a special rule, see Act Sec. 401(e), Div. U, below.

P.L. 115-141, § 401(e), Div. U, provides:

(e) GENERAL SAVINGS PROVISION WITH RESPECT TO DEADWOOD PROVISIONS.—If—

(1) any provision amended or repealed by the amendments made by subsection (b) or (d) applied to—

(A) any transaction occurring before the date of the enactment of this Act,

(B) any property acquired before such date of enactment, or

RETURNS—INFORMATION

(C) any item of income, loss, deduction, or credit taken into account before such date of enactment, and

(2) the treatment of such transaction, property, or item under such provision would (without regard to the amendments or repeals made by such subsection) affect the liability for tax for periods ending after such date of enactment,

nothing in the amendments or repeals made by this section shall be construed to affect the treatment of such transaction, property, or item for purposes of determining liability for tax for periods ending after such date of enactment.

[Sec. 6050G(b)]

(b) STATEMENTS TO BE FURNISHED TO PERSONS WITH RESPECT TO WHOM INFORMATION IS REQUIRED.—The Railroad Retirement Board shall furnish to each individual whose name is required to be set forth in the return under subsection (a) a written statement showing—

(1) the aggregate amount of payments to such individual, and of employee contributions with respect thereto, required to be shown on the return, and

(2) such other information as the Secretary may require.

The written statement required under the preceding sentence shall be furnished to the individual on or before January 31 of the year following the calendar year for which the return under subsection (a) was required to be made.

Amendments

• **1986, Tax Reform Act of 1986 (P.L. 99-514)**

P.L. 99-514, §1501(c)(10):

Amended Code Sec. 6050G(b). **Effective** for returns the due date for which (determined without regard to extensions) is after 12-31-86. Prior to amendment, Code Sec. 6050G(b) read as follows:

(b) STATEMENTS TO BE FURNISHED TO INDIVIDUALS WITH RESPECT TO WHOM INFORMATION IS FURNISHED.—The Railroad Retirement Board shall furnish to each individual whose name is set forth in the return under subsection (a) a written statement showing—

(1) the aggregate amount of payments to such individual, and of employee contributions with respect thereto, as shown on such return, and

(2) such other information as the Secretary may require.

The written statement required under the preceding sentence shall be furnished to the individual on or before January 31 of the year following the calendar year for which the return under subsection (a) was made.

• **1983, Railroad Retirement Solvency Act of 1983 (P.L. 98-76)**

P.L. 98-76, §224(b)(1):

Added Code Sec. 6050G. **Effective** for benefits received after 12-31-83, in tax years ending after such date.

[Sec. 6050H]

SEC. 6050H. RETURNS RELATING TO MORTGAGE INTEREST RECEIVED IN TRADE OR BUSINESS FROM INDIVIDUALS.

[Sec. 6050H(a)]

(a) MORTGAGE INTEREST OF $600 OR MORE.—Any person—

(1) who is engaged in a trade or business, and

(2) who, in the course of such trade or business, receives from any individual interest aggregating $600 or more for any calendar year on any mortgage,

shall make the return described in subsection (b) with respect to each individual from whom such interest was received at such time as the Secretary may by regulations prescribe.

[Sec. 6050H(b)]

(b) FORM AND MANNER OF RETURNS.—A return is described in this subsection if such return—

(1) is in such form as the Secretary may prescribe, [and]

(2) contains—

(A) the name and address of the individual from whom the interest described in subsection (a)(2) was received,

(B) the amount of such interest (other than points) received for the calendar year,

(C) the amount of points on the mortgage received during the calendar year and whether such points were paid directly by the borrower,

(D) the amount of outstanding principal on the mortgage as of the beginning of such calendar year,

(E) the date of the origination of the mortgage,

(F) the address (or other description in the case of property without an address) of the property which secures the mortgage, and

(G) such other information as the Secretary may prescribe.

Amendments

• **2015, Surface Transportation and Veterans Health Care Choice Improvement Act of 2015 (P.L. 114-41)**

P.L. 114-41, §2003(a):

Amended Code Sec. 6050H(b)(2) by striking "and" at the end of subparagraph (C), by redesignating subparagraph (D) as subparagraph (G) and by inserting after subparagraph (C) new subparagraphs (D)-(F). **Effective** for returns required to be made, and statements required to be furnished, after 12-31-2016.

• **1989, Omnibus Budget Reconciliation Act of 1989 (P.L. 101-239)**

P.L. 101-239, §7646(a):

Amended Code Sec. 6050H(b)(2) by striking "and" at the end of subparagraph (B), by redesignating subparagraph (C) as subparagraph (D) and by inserting after subparagraph (B) a new subparagraph (C). **Effective** for returns and statements the due date for which (determined without regard to extensions) is after 12-31-91.

P.L. 101-239, §7646(b)(1) (as amended by P.L. 104-188, §1704(t)(23)):

Amended Code Sec. 6050H(b)(2)(B) by inserting "(other than points)" after "such interest". **Effective** for returns and statements the due date for which (determined without regard to extensions) is after 12-31-91.

[Sec. 6050H(c)]

(c) APPLICATION TO GOVERNMENTAL UNITS.—For purposes of subsection (a)—

(1) TREATED AS PERSONS.—The term "person" includes any governmental unit (and any agency or instrumentality thereof).

(2) SPECIAL RULES.—In the case of a governmental unit or any agency or instrumentality thereof—

(A) subsection (a) shall be applied without regard to the trade or business requirement contained therein, and

(B) any return required under subsection (a) shall be made by the officer or employee appropriately designated for the purpose of making such return.

[Sec. 6050H(d)]

(d) STATEMENTS TO BE FURNISHED TO INDIVIDUALS WITH RESPECT TO WHOM INFORMATION IS REQUIRED.—Every person required to make a return under subsection (a) shall furnish to each individual whose name is required to be set forth in such return a written statement showing—

(1) the name, address, and phone number of the information contact of the person required to make such return, and

(2) the aggregate amount of interest described in subsection (a)(2) (other than points) received by the person required to make such return from the individual to whom the statement is required to be furnished (and the information required under subparagraphs (C), (D), (E), and (F) of subsection (b)(2)).

The written statement required under the preceding sentence shall be furnished on or before January 31 of the year following the calendar year for which the return under subsection (a) was required to be made.

Sec. 6050G(b)

RETURNS—INFORMATION

Amendments

• **2015, Surface Transportation and Veterans Health Care Choice Improvement Act of 2015 (P.L. 114-41)**

P.L. 114-41, §2003(b):

Amended Code Sec. 6050H(d)(2) by striking "subsection (b)(2)(C)" and inserting "subparagraphs (C), (D), (E), and (F) of subsection (b)(2)". **Effective** for returns required to be made, and statements required to be furnished, after 12-31-2016.

• **1996, Taxpayer Bill of Rights 2 (P.L. 104-168)**

P.L. 104-168, §1201(a)(8):

Amended Code Sec. 6050H(d)(1) by striking "name and address" and inserting "name, address, and phone number of the information contact". **Effective** for statements required to be furnished after 12-31-96 (determined without regard to any extension).

• **1989, Omnibus Budget Reconciliation Act of 1989 (P.L. 101-239)**

P.L. 101-239, §7646(b)(2)(A)-(B):

Amended Code Sec. 6050H(d)(2) by inserting "(other than points)" after "subsection (a)(2)", and by inserting "(and the information required under subsection (b)(2)(C))" before the period at the end thereof. **Effective** for returns and statements the due date for which (determined without regard to extensions) is after 12-31-91.

• **1986, Tax Reform Act of 1986 (P.L. 99-514)**

P.L. 99-514, §1501(c)(11):

Amended Code Sec. 6050H(d). **Effective** for returns the due date for which (determined without regard to extensions) is after 12-31-86. Prior to amendment, Code Sec. 6050H(d) read as follows:

(d) STATEMENTS TO BE FURNISHED TO INDIVIDUALS WITH RESPECT TO WHOM INFORMATION IS FURNISHED.—Every person making a return under subsection (a) shall furnish to each individual whose name is set forth in such return a written statement showing—

(1) the name and address of the person making such return, and

(2) the aggregate amount of interest described in subsection (a)(2) received by the person making such return from the individual to whom the statement is furnished.

The written statement required under the preceding sentence shall be furnished on or before January 31 of the year following the calendar year for which the return under subsection (a) was made.

[Sec. 6050H(e)]

(e) MORTGAGE DEFINED.—For purposes of this section, except as provided in regulations prescribed by the Secretary, the term "mortgage" means any obligation secured by real property.

[Sec. 6050H(f)]

(f) RETURNS WHICH WOULD BE REQUIRED TO BE MADE BY 2 OR MORE PERSONS.—Except to the extent provided in regulations prescribed by the Secretary, in the case of interest received by any person on behalf of another person, only the person first receiving such interest shall be required to make the return under subsection (a).

[Sec. 6050H(g)]

(g) SPECIAL RULES FOR COOPERATIVE HOUSING CORPORATIONS.—For purposes of subsection (a), an amount received by a cooperative housing corporation from a tenant-stockholder shall be deemed to be interest received on a mortgage in the course of a trade or business engaged in by such corporation, to the extent of the tenant-stockholder's proportionate share of interest described in section 216(a)(2). Terms used in the preceding sentence shall have the same meanings as when used in section 216.

Amendments

• **1986, Tax Reform Act of 1986 (P.L. 99-514)**

P.L. 99-514, §1811(a)(1):

Amended Code Sec. 6050H by adding at the end thereof new subsection (g). **Effective** as if included in the provision of P.L. 98-369 to which it relates.

• **1984, Deficit Reduction Act of 1984 (P.L. 98-369)**

P.L. 98-369, §145(a):

Amended Subpart B of part III of subchapter A of chapter 61 by adding at the end thereof a new section 6050H. **Effective**, generally, for amounts received after 12-31-84. However, in the case of any obligation in existence on 12-31-84, no penalty shall be imposed under section 6676 of the Internal Revenue Code of 1954 by reason of the amendments made by this section on any failure to supply a taxpayer identification number with respect to amounts received before 1-1-86 [**effective** date changed by P.L. 99-514, §1811].

[Sec. 6050H(h)]

(h) RETURNS RELATING TO MORTGAGE INSURANCE PREMIUMS.—

(1) IN GENERAL.—The Secretary may prescribe, by regulations, that any person who, in the course of a trade or business, receives from any individual premiums for mortgage insurance aggregating $600 or more for any calendar year, shall make a return with respect to each such individual. Such return shall be in such form, shall be made at such time, and shall contain such information as the Secretary may prescribe.

(2) STATEMENT TO BE FURNISHED TO INDIVIDUALS WITH RESPECT TO WHOM INFORMATION IS REQUIRED.—Every person required to make a return under paragraph (1) shall furnish to each individual with respect to whom a return is made a written statement showing such information as the Secretary may prescribe. Such written statement shall be furnished on or before January 31 of the year following the calendar year for which the return under paragraph (1) was required to be made.

(3) SPECIAL RULES.—For purposes of this subsection—

(A) rules similar to the rules of subsection (c) shall apply, and

(B) the term "mortgage insurance" means—

(i) mortgage insurance provided by the Department of Veterans Affairs, the Federal Housing Administration, or the Rural Housing Service, and

(ii) private mortgage insurance (as defined by section 2 of the Homeowners Protection Act of 1998 (12 U.S.C. 4901), as in effect on the date of the enactment of this subsection).

Amendments

• **2018, Tax Technical Corrections Act of 2018 (P.L. 115-141)**

P.L. 115-141, §401(a)(2)(C), Div. U:

Amended Code Sec. 6050H(h)(3)(B)(i) by striking "Veterans Administration" and inserting "Department of Veterans Affairs". **Effective** 3-23-2018.

P.L. 115-141, §401(a)(263), Div. U:

Amended Code Sec. 6050H(h)(3)(B)(i) by striking "Rural Housing Administration" and inserting "Rural Housing Service". **Effective** 3-23-2018.

• **2006, Tax Relief and Health Care Act of 2006 (P.L. 109-432)**

P.L. 109-432, Division A, §419(c):

Amended Code Sec. 6050H by adding at the end a new subsection (h). **Effective** for amounts paid or accrued after 12-31-2006.

[Sec. 6050I]

SEC. 6050I. RETURNS RELATING TO CASH RECEIVED IN TRADE OR BUSINESS, ETC.

[Sec. 6050I(a)]

(a) CASH RECEIPTS OF MORE THAN $10,000.—Any person—

(1) who is engaged in a trade or business, and

(2) who, in the course of such trade or business, receives more than $10,000 in cash in 1 transaction (or 2 or more related transactions),

shall make the return described in subsection (b) with respect to such transaction (or related transactions) at such time as the Secretary may by regulations prescribe.

RETURNS—INFORMATION

Amendments

• **1994, Violent Crime Control and Law Enforcement Act of 1994 (P.L. 103-322)**

P.L. 103-322, §20415(b)(3):

Amended Code Sec. 6050I by striking "BUSINESS" and inserting "BUSINESS, ETC." in the heading. For the **effective** date, see Act Sec. 20415(c)-(d), below.

P.L. 103-322, §20415(c)-(d), provides:

(c) REGULATIONS.—The Secretary of the Treasury or the Secretary's delegate shall prescribe temporary regulations under the amendments made by this section within 90 days after the date of enactment of this Act.

(d) EFFECTIVE DATE.—The amendments made by this section shall take effect on the 60th day after the date on which the temporary regulations are prescribed under subsection (c).

[Sec. 6050I(b)]

(b) FORM AND MANNER OF RETURNS.—A return is described in this subsection if such return—

(1) is in such form as the Secretary may prescribe,

(2) contains—

(A) the name, address, and TIN of the person from whom the cash was received,

(B) the amount of cash received,

(C) the date and nature of the transaction, and

(D) such other information as the Secretary may prescribe.

[Sec. 6050I(c)]

(c) EXCEPTIONS.—

(1) CASH RECEIVED BY FINANCIAL INSTITUTIONS.—Subsection (a) shall not apply to—

(A) cash received in a transaction reported under title 31, United States Code, if the Secretary determines that reporting under this section would duplicate the reporting to the Treasury under title 31, United States Code, or

(B) cash received by any financial institution (as defined in subparagraphs (A), (B), (C), (D), (E), (F), (G), (J), (K), (R), and (S) of section 5312(a)(2) of title 31, United States Code).

(2) TRANSACTIONS OCCURRING OUTSIDE THE UNITED STATES.—Except to the extent provided in regulations prescribed by the Secretary, subsection (a) shall not apply to any transaction if the entire transaction occurs outside the United States.

[Sec. 6050I(d)]

(d) CASH INCLUDES FOREIGN CURRENCY AND CERTAIN MONETARY INSTRUMENTS.—For purposes of this section, the term "cash" includes—

(1) foreign currency,

(2) to the extent provided in regulations prescribed by the Secretary, any monetary instrument (whether or not in bearer form) with a face amount of not more than $10,000, and

(3) any digital asset (as defined in section 6045(g)(3)(D)).

Paragraph (2) shall not apply to any check drawn on the account of the writer in a financial institution referred to in subsection (c)(1)(B).

Amendments

• **2021, Infrastructure Investment and Jobs Act (P.L. 117-58)**

P.L. 117-58, §80603(b)(3), Div. H:

Amended Code Sec. 6050I(d) by striking "and" at the end of paragraph (1), by striking the period at the end of paragraph (2) and inserting ", and", and by inserting after paragraph (2) a new paragraph (3). **Effective** for returns required to be filed, and statements required to be furnished, after 12-31-2023. For special rule, see Act Sec. 80603(d)(1)-(2), Div. H, below.

P.L. 117-58, §80603(d)(1)-(2), Div. H, provides:

(d) RULE OF CONSTRUCTION.—Nothing in this section or the amendments made by this section shall be construed to create any inference, for any period prior to the effective date of such amendments, with respect to—

(1) whether any person is a broker under section 6045(c)(1) of the Internal Revenue Code of 1986, or

(2) whether any digital asset is property which is a specified security under section 6045(g)(3)(B) of such Code.

• **1990, Omnibus Budget Reconciliation Act of 1990 (P.L. 101-508)**

P.L. 101-508, §11318(a):

Amended Code Sec. 6050I(d). **Effective** for amounts received after 11-5-90. Prior to amendment, Code Sec. 6050I(d) read as follows:

(d) CASH INCLUDES FOREIGN CURRENCY.—For purposes of this section, the term "cash" includes foreign currency.

[Sec. 6050I(e)]

(e) STATEMENTS TO BE FURNISHED TO PERSONS WITH RESPECT TO WHOM INFORMATION IS REQUIRED.—Every person required to make a return under subsection (a) shall furnish to each person whose name is required to be set forth in such return a written statement showing—

(1) the name, address, and phone number of the information contact of the person required to make such return, and

(2) the aggregate amount of cash described in subsection (a) received by the person required to make such return.

The written statement required under the preceding sentence shall be furnished to the person on or before January 31 of the year following the calendar year for which the return under subsection (a) was required to be made.

Amendments

• **1996, Taxpayer Bill of Rights 2 (P.L. 104-168)**

P.L. 104-168, §1201(a)(9):

Amended Code Sec. 6050I(e)(1) by striking "name and address" and inserting "name, address, and phone number of the information contact". **Effective** for statements required to be furnished after 12-31-96 (determined without regard to any extension).

• **1986, Tax Reform Act of 1986 (P.L. 99-514)**

P.L. 99-514, §1501 (c)(12):

Amended Code Sec. 6050I(e). **Effective** for returns the due date for which (determined without regard to extensions) is after 12-31-86. Prior to amendment, Code Sec. 6050I(e) read as follows:

(e) STATEMENTS TO BE FURNISHED TO PERSONS WITH RESPECT TO WHOM INFORMATION IS REQUIRED.—Every person making a return under subsection (a) shall furnish to each person whose name is set forth in such return a written statement showing—

(1) the name and address of the person making such return, and

(2) the aggregate amount of cash described in subsection (a) received by the person making such return.

The written statement required under the preceding sentence shall be furnished to the person on or before January 31 of the year following the calendar year for which the return under subsection (a) was made.

• **1984, Deficit Reduction Act of 1984 (P.L. 98-369)**

P.L. 98-369, §146(a):

Amended Subpart B of part III of subchapter A of chapter 61 by adding at the end thereof new Code Sec. 6050I. **Effective** for amounts received after 12-31-84.

[Sec. 6050I(f)]

(f) STRUCTURING TRANSACTIONS TO EVADE REPORTING REQUIREMENTS PROHIBITED.—

(1) IN GENERAL.—No person shall for the purpose of evading the return requirements of this section—

(A) cause or attempt to cause a trade or business to fail to file a return required under this section,

(B) cause or attempt to cause a trade or business to file a return required under this section that contains a material omission or misstatement of fact, or

RETURNS—INFORMATION

(C) structure or assist in structuring, or attempt to structure or assist in structuring, any transaction with one or more trades or businesses.

(2) PENALTIES.—A person violating paragraph (1) of this subsection shall be subject to the same civil and criminal sanctions applicable to a person which fails to file or completes a false or incorrect return under this section.

Amendments

• **1990, Omnibus Budget Reconciliation Act of 1990 (P.L. 101-508)**

P.L. 101-508, §11318(c):

Amended the heading of Code Sec. 6050I(f). **Effective** 11-5-90. Prior to amendment, the heading of Code Sec. 6050I(f) read as follows:

(f) ACTIONS BY PAYORS.—

P.L. 101-508, §11318(d), provides:

(d) STUDY.—The Secretary of the Treasury or his delegate shall conduct a study on the operation of section 6050I of the Internal Revenue Code of 1986. Such study shall include an examination of—

(1) the extent of compliance with the provisions of such section,

(2) the effectiveness of the penalties in ensuring compliance with the provisions of such section,

(3) methods to increase compliance with the provisions of such section and ways Form 8300 could be simplified, and

(4) appropriate methods to increase the usefulness and availability of information submitted under the provisions of such section.

Not later than March 31, 1991, the Secretary shall submit to the Committee on Ways and Means of the House of Representatives and the Committee on Finance of the Senate a report on the study conducted under this subsection, together with such recommendations as he may deem advisable.

• **1988, Anti-Drug Abuse Act of 1988 (P.L. 100-690)**

P.L. 100-690, §7601(a)(1):

Amended Code Sec. 6050I by adding at the end thereof new subsection (f). **Effective** for actions after 11-18-88.

P.L. 100-690, §7601(a)(4), provides:

(4) NO INFERENCE.—No inference shall be drawn from the amendment made by paragraph (1) on the application of the Internal Revenue Code of 1986 without regard to such amendment.

[Sec. 6050I(g)]

(g) CASH RECEIVED BY CRIMINAL COURT CLERKS.—

(1) IN GENERAL.—Every clerk of a Federal or State criminal court who receives more than $10,000 in cash as bail for any individual charged with a specified criminal offense shall make a return described in paragraph (2) (at such time as the Secretary may by regulations prescribe) with respect to the receipt of such bail.

(2) RETURN.—A return is described in this paragraph if such return—

(A) is in such form as the Secretary may prescribe, and

(B) contains—

(i) the name, address, and TIN of—

(I) the individual charged with the specified criminal offense, and

(II) each person posting the bail (other than a person licensed as a bail bondsman),

(ii) the amount of cash received,

(iii) the date the cash was received, and

(iv) such other information as the Secretary may prescribe.

(3) SPECIFIED CRIMINAL OFFENSE.—For purposes of this subsection, the term "specified criminal offense" means—

(A) any Federal criminal offense involving a controlled substance,

(B) racketeering (as defined in section 1951, 1952, or 1955 of title 18, United States Code),

(C) money laundering (as defined in section 1956 or 1957 of such title), and

(D) any State criminal offense substantially similar to an offense described in subparagraph (A), (B), or (C).

(4) INFORMATION TO FEDERAL PROSECUTORS.—Each clerk required to include on a return under paragraph (1) the information described in paragraph (2)(B) with respect to an individual described in paragraph (2)(B)(i)(I) shall furnish (at such time as the Secretary may by regulations prescribe) a written statement showing such information to the United States Attorney for the jurisdiction in which such individual resides and the jurisdiction in which the specified criminal offense occurred.

(5) INFORMATION TO PAYORS OF BAIL.—Each clerk required to make a return under paragraph (1) shall furnish (at such time as the Secretary may by regulations prescribe) to each person whose name is required to be set forth in such return by reason of paragraph (2)(B)(i)(II) a written statement showing—

(A) the name and address of the clerk's office required to make the return, and

(B) the aggregate amount of cash described in paragraph (1) received by such clerk.

Amendments

• **1994, Violent Crime Control and Law Enforcement Act of 1994 (P.L. 103-322)**

P.L. 103-322, §20415(a):

Amended Code Sec. 6050I by adding at the end a new subsection (g). For the **effective** date, see Act Sec. 20415(c)-(d) below.

P.L. 103-322, §20415(c)-(d), provides:

(c) REGULATIONS.—The Secretary of the Treasury or the Secretary's delegate shall prescribe temporary regulations under the amendments made by this section within 90 days after the date of enactment of this Act.

(d) EFFECTIVE DATE.—The amendments made by this section shall take effect on the 60th day after the date on which the temporary regulations are prescribed under subsection (c).

[Sec. 6050J]

SEC. 6050J. RETURNS RELATING TO FORECLOSURES AND ABANDONMENTS OF SECURITY.

[Sec. 6050J(a)]

(a) IN GENERAL.—Any person who, in connection with a trade or business conducted by such person, lends money secured by property and who—

(1) in full or partial satisfaction of any indebtedness, acquires an interest in any property which is security for such indebtedness, or

(2) has reason to know that the property in which such person has a security interest has been abandoned,

shall make a return described in subsection (c) with respect to each of such acquisitions or abandonments, at such time as the Secretary may by regulations prescribe.

[Sec. 6050J(b)]

(b) EXCEPTION.—Subsection (a) shall not apply to any loan to an individual secured by an interest in tangible personal property which is not held for investment and which is not used in a trade or business.

RETURNS—INFORMATION

[Sec. 6050J(c)]

(c) FORM AND MANNER OF RETURN.—The return required under subsection (a) with respect to any acquisition or abandonment of property—

(1) shall be in such form as the Secretary may prescribe,

(2) shall contain—

(A) the name and address of each person who is a borrower with respect to the indebtedness which is secured,

(B) a general description of the nature of such property and such indebtedness,

(C) in the case of a return required under subsection (a)(1)—

(i) the amount of such indebtedness at the time of such acquisition, and

(ii) the amount of indebtedness satisfied in such acquisition,

(D) in the case of a return required under subsection (a)(2), the amount of such indebtedness at the time of such abandonment, and

(E) such other information as the Secretary may prescribe.

[Sec. 6050J(d)]

(d) APPLICATIONS TO GOVERNMENTAL UNITS.—For purposes of this section—

(1) TREATED AS PERSONS.—The term "person" includes any governmental unit (and any agency or instrumentality thereof).

(2) SPECIAL RULES.—In the case of a governmental unit or any agency or instrumentality thereof—

(A) subsection (a) shall be applied without regard to the trade or business requirement contained therein, and

(B) any return under this section shall be made by the officer or employee appropriately designated for the purpose of making such return.

[Sec. 6050J(e)]

(e) STATEMENTS TO BE FURNISHED TO PERSONS WITH RESPECT TO WHOM INFORMATION IS REQUIRED TO BE FURNISHED.—Every person required to make a return under subsection (a) shall furnish to each person whose name is required to be set forth in such return a written statement showing the name, address, and phone number of the information contact of the person required to make such return. The written statement required under the preceding sentence shall be furnished to the person on or before January 31 of the year following the calendar year for which the return under subsection (a) was made.

Amendments

- **1996, Taxpayer Bill of Rights 2 (P.L. 104-168)**

P.L. 104-168, §1201(a)(10):

Amended Code Sec. 6050J(e) by striking "name and address" and inserting "name, address, and phone number of the information contact". **Effective** for statements required to be furnished after 12-31-96 (determined without regard to any extension).

[Sec. 6050J(f)]

(f) TREATMENT OF OTHER DISPOSITIONS.—To the extent provided by regulations prescribed by the Secretary, any transfer of the property which secures the indebtedness to a person other than the lender shall be treated as an abandonment of such property.

Amendments

- **1984, Deficit Reduction Act of 1984 (P.L. 98-369)**

P.L. 98-369, §148(a):

Amended Subpart B of part III of subchapter A of chapter 61 by adding at the end thereof a new section 6050J. **Effective** with respect to acquisitions of property and abandonments of property after 12-31-84.

[Sec. 6050K]

SEC. 6050K. RETURNS RELATING TO EXCHANGES OF CERTAIN PARTNERSHIP INTERESTS.

[Sec. 6050K(a)]

(a) IN GENERAL.—Except as provided in regulations prescribed by the Secretary, if there is an exchange described in section 751(a) of any interest in a partnership during any calendar year, such partnership shall make a return for such calendar year stating—

(1) the name and address of the transferee and transferor in such exchange, and

(2) such other information as the Secretary may by regulations prescribe.

Such return shall be made at such time and in such manner as the Secretary may require by regulations.

[Sec. 6050K(b)]

(b) STATEMENTS TO BE FURNISHED TO TRANSFEROR AND TRANSFEREE.—Every partnership required to make a return under subsection (a) shall furnish to each person whose name is required to be set forth in such return a written statement showing—

(1) the name, address, and phone number of the information contact of the partnership required to make such return, and

(2) the information required to be shown on the return with respect to such person.

The written statement required under the preceding sentence shall be furnished to the person on or before January 31 of the year following the calendar year for which the return under subsection (a) was required to be made.

Amendments

- **1996, Taxpayer Bill of Rights 2 (P.L. 104-168)**

P.L. 104-168, §1201(a)(11):

Amended Code Sec. 6050K(b)(1) by striking "name and address" and inserting "name, address, and phone number of the information contact". **Effective** for statements required to be furnished after 12-31-96 (determined without regard to any extension).

- **1986, Tax Reform Act of 1986 (P.L. 99-514)**

P.L. 99-514, §1501(c)(13):

Amended Code Sec. 6050K(b). **Effective** for returns the due date for which (determined without regard to extensions) is after 12-31-86. Prior to amendment, Code Sec. 6050K(b) read as follows:

(b) STATEMENT TO BE FURNISHED TO TRANSFEROR AND TRANSFEREE.—Every partnership making a return under subsection (a) shall furnish to each person whose name is set forth in such return a written statement showing—

(1) the name and address of the partnership making the return, and

(2) the information shown on the return with respect to such person.

The statement required under the preceding sentence shall be furnished to the person on or before January 31 following the calendar year for which the return under subsection (a) was made.

RETURNS—INFORMATION

[Sec. 6050K(c)]

(c) REQUIREMENT THAT TRANSFEROR NOTIFY PARTNERSHIP.—

(1) IN GENERAL.—In the case of any exchange described in subsection (a), the transferor of the partnership interest shall promptly notify the partnership of such exchange.

(2) PARTNERSHIP NOT REQUIRED TO MAKE RETURN UNTIL NOTICE.—A partnership shall not be required to make a return under this subsection with respect to any exchange until the partnership is notified of such exchange.

Amendments

• 1986, Tax Reform Act of 1986 (P.L. 99-514)

P.L. 99-514, § 1811(b)(2):

Amended Code Sec. 6050K(c)(2) by striking out "this subsection" and inserting in lieu thereof "this section". **Effective** as if included in the provision of P.L. 98-369 to which it relates.

• 1984, Deficit Reduction Act of 1984 (P.L. 98-369)

P.L. 98-369, § 149(a):

Amended subpart B of part III of subchapter A of chapter 61 by adding at the end thereof new Code Sec. 6050K. **Effective** with respect to exchanges after 12-31-84.

[Sec. 6050L]

SEC. 6050L. RETURNS RELATING TO CERTAIN DONATED PROPERTY.

[Sec. 6050L(a)]

(a) DISPOSITIONS OF DONATED PROPERTY.—

(1) IN GENERAL.—If the donee of any charitable deduction property sells, exchanges, or otherwise disposes of such property within 3 years after its receipt, the donee shall make a return (in accordance with forms and regulations prescribed by the Secretary) showing—

(A) the name, address, and TIN of the donor,

(B) a description of the property,

(C) the date of the contribution,

(D) the amount received on the disposition,

(E) the date of such disposition,

(F) a description of the donee's use of the property, and

(G) a statement indicating whether the use of the property was related to the purpose or function constituting the basis for the donee's exemption under section 501.

In any case in which the donee indicates that the use of applicable property (as defined in section 170(e)(7)(C)) was related to the purpose or function constituting the basis for the exemption of the donee under section 501 under subparagraph (G), the donee shall include with the return the certification described in section 170(e)(7)(D) if such certification is made under section 170(e)(7).

(2) DEFINITIONS.—For purposes of this subsection:

(A) CHARITABLE DEDUCTION PROPERTY.—The term "charitable deduction property" means any property (other than publicly traded securities) contributed in a contribution for which a deduction was claimed under section 170 if the claimed value of such property (plus the claimed value of all similar items of property donated by the donor to 1 or more donees) exceeds $5,000.

(B) PUBLICLY TRADED SECURITIES.—The term "publicly traded securities" means securities for which (as of the date of the contribution) market quotations are readily available on an established securities market.

Amendments

• 2006, Pension Protection Act of 2006 (P.L. 109-280)

P.L. 109-280, § 1215(b)(1)-(2):

Amended Code Sec. 6050L(a)(1) by striking "2 years" and inserting "3 years", and by striking "and" at the end of subparagraph (D), by striking the period at the end of subparagraph (E) and inserting a comma, and by inserting at the end new subparagraphs (F) and (G) and a new flush sentence. **Effective** for returns filed after 9-1-2006.

[Sec. 6050L(b)]

(b) QUALIFIED INTELLECTUAL PROPERTY CONTRIBUTIONS.—

(1) IN GENERAL.—Each donee with respect to a qualified intellectual property contribution shall make a return (at such time and in such form and manner as the Secretary may by regulations prescribe) with respect to each specified taxable year of the donee showing—

(A) the name, address, and TIN of the donor,

(B) a description of the qualified intellectual property contributed,

(C) the date of the contribution, and

(D) the amount of net income of the donee for the taxable year which is properly allocable to the qualified intellectual property (determined without regard to paragraph (10)(B) of section 170(m) and with the modifications described in paragraphs (5) and (6) of such section).

(2) DEFINITIONS.—For purposes of this subsection:

(A) IN GENERAL.—Terms used in this subsection which are also used in section 170(m) have the respective meanings given such terms in such section.

(B) SPECIFIED TAXABLE YEAR.—The term "specified taxable year" means, with respect to any qualified intellectual property contribution, any taxable year of the donee any portion of which is part of the 10-year period beginning on the date of such contribution.

[Sec. 6050L(c)]

(c) STATEMENT TO BE FURNISHED TO DONORS.—Every person making a return under subsection (a) or (b) shall furnish a copy of such return to the donor at such time and in such manner as the Secretary may by regulations prescribe.

Amendments

• 2004, American Jobs Creation Act of 2004 (P.L. 108-357)

P.L. 108-357, § 882(c)(1):

Amended Code Sec. 6050L. **Effective** for contributions made after 6-3-2004. Prior to amendment, Code Sec. 6050L read as follows:

SEC. 6050L. RETURNS RELATING TO CERTAIN DISPOSITIONS OF DONATED PROPERTY.

[Sec. 6050L(a)]

(a) GENERAL RULE.—If the donee of any charitable deduction property sells, exchanges, or otherwise disposes of such property within 2 years after its receipt, the donee shall make a return (in accordance with forms and regulations prescribed by the Secretary) showing—

(1) the name, address, and TIN of the donor,

(2) a description of the property,

(3) the date of the contribution,

(4) the amount received on the disposition, and

(5) the date of such disposition.

[Sec. 6050L(b)]

(b) CHARITABLE DEDUCTION PROPERTY.—For purposes of this section, the term "charitable deduction property" means any property (other than publicly traded securities) contributed in a contribution for which a deduction was claimed under section 170 if the claimed value of such property (plus the claimed value of all similar items of property donated by the donor to 1 or more donees) exceeds $5,000.

RETURNS—INFORMATION

[Sec. 6050L(c)]

(c) STATEMENT TO BE FURNISHED TO DONORS.—Every person making a return under subsection (a) shall furnish a copy of such return to the donor at such time and in such manner as the Secretary may by regulations prescribe.

[Sec. 6050L(d)]

(d) DEFINITION OF PUBLICLY TRADED SECURITIES.—The term "publicly traded securities" means securities for which (as of the date of the contribution) market quotations are readily available on an established securities market.

Amendments

• **1984, Deficit Reduction Act of 1984 (P.L. 98-369)**

P.L. 98-369, §155(b)(1):

Amended subpart B of part III of subchapter A of chapter 61 by adding at the end thereof new Code Sec. 6050L. **Effective** for contributions made after 12-31-84, in tax years ending after such date.

[Sec. 6050M]

SEC. 6050M. RETURNS RELATING TO PERSONS RECEIVING CONTRACTS FROM FEDERAL EXECUTIVE AGENCIES.

[Sec. 6050M(a)]

(a) REQUIREMENT OF REPORTING.—The head of every Federal executive agency which enters into any contract shall make a return (at such time and in such form as the Secretary may by regulations prescribe) setting forth—

(1) the name, address, and TIN of each person with which such agency entered into a contract during the calendar year, and

(2) such other information as the Secretary may require.

[Sec. 6050M(b)]

(b) FEDERAL EXECUTIVE AGENCY.—For purposes of this section, the term "Federal executive agency" means—

(1) any Executive agency (as defined in section 105 of title 5, United States Code) other than the Government Accountability Office,

(2) any military department (as defined in section 102 of such title), and

(3) the United States Postal Service and the Postal Rate Commission.

Amendments

• **2005, Gulf Opportunity Zone Act of 2005 (P.L. 109-135)**

P.L. 109-135, §412(rr)(2):

Amended Code Sec. 6050M(b)(1) by striking "General Accounting Office" each place it appears therein and inserting "Government Accountability Office". **Effective** 12-21-2005.

[Sec. 6050M(c)]

(c) AUTHORITY TO EXTEND REPORTING TO LICENSES AND SUBCONTRACTS.—To the extent provided in regulations, this section also shall apply to—

(1) licenses granted by Federal executive agencies, and

(2) subcontracts under contracts to which subsection (a) applies.

[Sec. 6050M(d)]

(d) AUTHORITY TO PRESCRIBE MINIMUM AMOUNTS.—This section shall not apply to contracts or licenses in any class which are below a minimum amount or value which may be prescribed by the Secretary by regulations for such class.

Amendments

• **1986, Tax Reform Act of 1986 (P.L. 99-514)**

P.L. 99-514, §1522(a):

Amended subpart B of part III of subchapter A of chapter 61 by adding at the end thereof new section 6050M. **Effective** for contracts and subcontracts entered into, and licenses granted, before, on, or after 1-1-87.

[Sec. 6050M(e)]

(e) EXCEPTION FOR CERTAIN CLASSIFIED OR CONFIDENTIAL CONTRACTS.—

(1) IN GENERAL.—Except as provided in paragraph (2), this section shall not apply in the case of a contract described in paragraph (3).

(2) REPORTING REQUIREMENT.—Each Federal executive agency which has entered into a contract described in paragraph (3) shall, upon a request of the Secretary which identifies a particular person, acknowledge whether such person has entered into such a contract with such agency and, if so, provide to the Secretary—

(A) the information required under this section with respect to such person, and

(B) such other information with respect to such person which the Secretary and the head of such Federal executive agency agree is appropriate.

(3) DESCRIPTION OF CONTRACT.—For purposes of this subsection, a contract between a Federal executive agency and another person is described in this paragraph if—

(A) the fact of the existence of such contract or the subject matter of such contract has been designated and clearly marked or clearly represented, pursuant to the provisions of Federal law or an Executive order, as requiring a specific degree of protection against unauthorized disclosure for reasons of national security, or

(B) the head of such Federal executive agency (or his designee) pursuant to regulations issued by such agency determines, in writing, that filing the required return under this section would interfere with the effective conduct of a confidential law enforcement or foreign counterintelligence activity.

Amendments

• **1988, Technical and Miscellaneous Revenue Act of 1988 (P.L. 100-647)**

P.L. 100-647, §1015(f):

Amended Code Sec. 6050M by adding at the end thereof new subsection (e). **Effective** as if included in the provision of P.L. 99-514 to which it relates.

[Sec. 6050N]

SEC. 6050N. RETURNS REGARDING PAYMENTS OF ROYALTIES.

[Sec. 6050N(a)]

(a) REQUIREMENT OF REPORTING.—Every person—

(1) who makes payments of royalties (or similar amounts) aggregating $10 or more to any other person during any calendar year, or

(2) who receives payments of royalties (or similar amounts) as a nominee and who makes payments aggregating $10 or more during any calendar year to any other person with respect to the royalties (or similar amounts) so received,

shall make a return according to the forms or regulations prescribed by the Secretary, setting forth the aggregate amount of such payments and the name and address of the person to whom paid.

[Sec. 6050N(b)]

(b) STATEMENTS TO BE FURNISHED TO PERSONS WITH RESPECT TO WHOM INFORMATION IS FURNISHED.—Every person required to make a return under subsection (a) shall furnish to each person whose name is required to be set forth in such return a written statement showing—

(1) the name, address, and phone number of the information contact of the person required to make such return, and

(2) the aggregate amount of payments to the person required to be shown on such return.

The written statement required under the preceding sentence shall be furnished (either in person or in a statement mailing by first-class mail which includes adequate notice that the statement is enclosed) to the person on or before January 31 of the year following the calendar year for which the return under subsection (a) was made and shall be in such form as the Secretary may prescribe by regulations.

Amendments

• **1996, Taxpayer Bill of Rights 2 (P.L. 104-168)**

P.L. 104-168, §1201(a)(12):

Amended Code Sec. 6050N(b)(1) by striking "name and address" and inserting "name, address, and phone number of the information contact". **Effective** for statements required to be furnished after 12-31-96 (determined without regard to any extension).

[Sec. 6050N(c)]

(c) EXCEPTION FOR PAYMENTS TO CERTAIN PERSONS.—Except to the extent otherwise provided in regulations, this section shall not apply to any amount paid to a person described in subparagraph (A), (B), (C), (D), (E), or (F) of section 6049(b)(4).

Amendments

• **1986, Tax Reform Act of 1986 (P.L. 99-514)**

P.L. 99-514, §1523(a):

Amended subpart B of part III of subchapter A of chapter 61 by adding at the end thereof new section 6050N. **Effective** with respect to payments made after 12-31-86.

[Sec. 6050P]

SEC. 6050P. RETURNS RELATING TO THE CANCELLATION OF INDEBTEDNESS BY CERTAIN ENTITIES.

[Sec. 6050P(a)]

(a) IN GENERAL.—Any applicable entity which discharges (in whole or in part) the indebtedness of any person during any calendar year shall make a return (at such time and in such form as the Secretary may by regulations prescribe) setting forth—

(1) the name, address, and TIN of each person whose indebtedness was discharged during such calendar year,

(2) the date of the discharge and the amount of the indebtedness discharged, and

(3) such other information as the Secretary may prescribe.

Amendments

• **1996, Debt Collection Improvement Act of 1996 (P.L. 104-134)**

P.L. 104-134, §31001(m)(2)(A):

Amended Code Sec. 6050P(a) by striking "applicable financial entity" and inserting "applicable entity". **Effective** 4-26-96.

P.L. 104-134, §31001(m)(2)(D)(ii):

Amended the heading of Code Sec. 6050P. **Effective** 4-26-96. Prior to amendment, the heading for Code Sec. 6050P read as follows:

SEC. 6050P. RETURNS RELATING TO THE CANCELLATION OF INDEBTEDNESS BY CERTAIN FINANCIAL ENTITIES.

[Sec. 6050P(b)]

(b) EXCEPTION.—Subsection (a) shall not apply to any discharge of less than $600.

[Sec. 6050P(c)]

(c) DEFINITIONS AND SPECIAL RULES.—For purposes of this section—

(1) APPLICABLE ENTITY.—The term "applicable entity" means—

(A) an executive, judicial, or legislative agency (as defined in section 3701(a)(4) of title 31, United States Code), and

(B) an applicable financial entity.

(2) APPLICABLE FINANCIAL ENTITY.—The term "applicable financial entity" means—

(A) any financial institution described in section 581 or 591(a) and any credit union,

(B) the Federal Deposit Insurance Corporation, the Resolution Trust Corporation, the National Credit Union Administration, and any other Federal executive agency (as defined in section 6050M), and any successor or subunit of any of the foregoing,

(C) any other corporation which is a direct or indirect subsidiary of an entity referred to in subparagraph (A) but only if, by virtue of being affiliated with such entity, such other corporation is subject to supervision and examination by a Federal or State agency which regulates entities referred to in subparagraph (A), and

(D) any organization a significant trade or business of which is the lending of money.

(3) GOVERNMENTAL UNITS.—In the case of an entity described in paragraph (1)(A) or (2)(B), any return under this section shall be made by the officer or employee appropriately designated for the purpose of making such return.

Amendments

• **1999, Tax Relief Extension Act of 1999 (P.L. 106-170)**

P.L. 106-170, §533(a):

Amended Code Sec. 6050P(c)(2) by striking "and" at the end of subparagraph (B), by striking the period at the end of subparagraph (C) and inserting ", and", and by inserting after subparagraph (C) a new subparagraph (D). **Effective** for discharges of indebtedness after 12-31-99.

• **1996, Debt Collection Improvement Act of 1996 (P.L. 104-134)**

P.L. 104-134, §31001(m)(2)(B)(i)-(ii):

Amended Code Sec. 6050P(c) by redesignating paragraphs (1) and (2) as paragraphs (2) and (3), respectively, and inserting before paragraph (2) (as so redesignated) a new paragraph (1), and by striking "(1)(B)" in paragraph (3) (as so redesignated) and inserting "(1)(A) or (2)(B)". **Effective** 4-26-96.

[Sec. 6050P(d)]

(d) STATEMENTS TO BE FURNISHED TO PERSONS WITH RESPECT TO WHOM INFORMATION IS REQUIRED TO BE FURNISHED.—Every applicable entity required to make a return under subsection (a) shall furnish to each person whose name is required to be set forth in such return a written statement showing—

(1) the name and address of the entity required to make such return, and

(2) the information required to be shown on the return with respect to such person.

The written statement required under the preceding sentence shall be furnished to the person on or before January 31 of the year following the calendar year for which the return under subsection (a) was made.

RETURNS—INFORMATION

Amendments

- **1996, Debt Collection Improvement Act of 1996 (P.L. 104-134)**

P.L. 104-134, §31001(m)(2)(D)(i):

Amended Code Sec. 6050P(d) by striking "applicable financial entity" and inserting "applicable entity". Effective 4-26-96.

- **1993, Omnibus Budget Reconciliation Act of 1993 (P.L. 103-66)**

P.L. 103-66, §13252(a):

Amended subpart B of part III of subchapter A of chapter 61 by adding at the end thereof new Code Sec. 6050P. For the **effective** date, see Act Sec. 13252(d), below.

P.L. 103-66, §13252(d), provides:

(d) EFFECTIVE DATE.—

(1) IN GENERAL.—Except as provided in paragraph (2), the amendments made by this section shall apply to discharges of indebtedness after December 31, 1993.

(2) GOVERNMENTAL ENTITIES.—In the case of an entity referred to in section 6050P(c)(1)(B) of the Internal Revenue Code of 1986 (as added by this section), the amendments made by this section shall apply to discharges of indebtedness after the date of the enactment of this Act.

[Sec. 6050P(e)]

(e) ALTERNATIVE PROCEDURE.—In lieu of making a return required under subsection (a), an agency described in subsection (c)(1)(A) may submit to the Secretary (at such time and in such form as the Secretary may by regulations prescribe) information sufficient for the Secretary to complete such a return on behalf of such agency. Upon receipt of such information, the Secretary shall complete such return and provide a copy of such return to such agency.

Amendments

- **1996, Debt Collection Improvement Act of 1996 (P.L. 104-134)**

P.L. 104-134, §31001(m)(2)(C):

Amended Code Sec. 6050P by adding at the end a new subsection (e). **Effective** 4-26-96.

[Sec. 6050Q]

SEC. 6050Q. CERTAIN LONG-TERM CARE BENEFITS.

[Sec. 6050Q(a)]

(a) REQUIREMENT OF REPORTING.—Any person who pays long-term care benefits shall make a return, according to the forms or regulations prescribed by the Secretary, setting forth—

(1) the aggregate amount of such benefits paid by such person to any individual during any calendar year,

(2) whether or not such benefits are paid in whole or in part on a per diem or other periodic basis without regard to the expenses incurred during the period to which the payments relate,

(3) the name, address, and TIN of such individual, and

(4) the name, address, and TIN of the chronically ill or terminally ill individual on account of whose condition such benefits are paid.

[Sec. 6050Q(b)]

(b) STATEMENTS TO BE FURNISHED TO PERSONS WITH RESPECT TO WHOM INFORMATION IS REQUIRED.—Every person required to make a return under subsection (a) shall furnish to each individual whose name is required to be set forth in such return a written statement showing—

(1) the name, address, and phone number of the information contact of the person making the payments, and

(2) the aggregate amount of long-term care benefits paid to the individual which are required to be shown on such return.

The written statement required under the preceding sentence shall be furnished to the individual on or before January 31 of the year following the calendar year for which the return under subsection (a) was required to be made.

Amendments

- **1997, Taxpayer Relief Act of 1997 (P.L. 105-34)**

P.L. 105-34, §1602(d)(1):

Amended Code Sec. 6050Q(b)(1) by inserting ", address, and phone number of the information contact" after "name". **Effective** as if included in the provision of P.L. 104-191 to which it relates [**effective** for benefits paid after 12-31-96.—CCH].

[Sec. 6050Q(c)]

(c) LONG-TERM CARE BENEFITS.—For purposes of this section, the term "long-term care benefit" means—

(1) any payment under a product which is advertised, marketed, or offered as long-term care insurance, and

(2) any payment which is excludable from gross income by reason of section 101(g).

Amendments

- **1996, Health Insurance Portability and Accountability Act of 1996 (P.L. 104-191)**

P.L. 104-191, §323(a):

Amended subpart B of part III of subchapter A of chapter 61 by adding at the end a new Code Sec. 6050Q. **Effective** for benefits paid after 12-31-96.

[Sec. 6050R]

SEC. 6050R. RETURNS RELATING TO CERTAIN PURCHASES OF FISH.

[Sec. 6050R(a)]

(a) REQUIREMENT OF REPORTING.—Every person—

(1) who is engaged in the trade or business of purchasing fish for resale from any person engaged in the trade or business of catching fish; and

(2) who makes payments in cash in the course of such trade or business to such a person of $600 or more during any calendar year for the purchase of fish,

shall make a return (at such times as the Secretary may prescribe) described in subsection (b) with respect to each person to whom such a payment was made during such calendar year.

[Sec. 6050R(b)]

(b) RETURN.—A return is described in this subsection if such return—

(1) is in such form as the Secretary may prescribe, and

(2) contains—

(A) the name, address, and TIN of each person to whom a payment described in subsection (a)(2) was made during the calendar year,

RETURNS—INFORMATION

(B) the aggregate amount of such payments made to such person during such calendar year and the date and amount of each such payment, and

(C) such other information as the Secretary may require.

Amendments

• **1998, IRS Restructuring and Reform Act of 1998 (P.L. 105-206)**

P.L. 105-206, § 6023(21):

Amended Code Sec. 6050R(b)(2)(A) by striking the semicolon at the end thereof and inserting a comma. **Effective** 7-22-98.

[Sec. 6050R(c)]

(c) STATEMENT TO BE FURNISHED WITH RESPECT TO WHOM INFORMATION IS REQUIRED.—Every person required to make a return under subsection (a) shall furnish to each person whose name is required to be set forth in such return a written statement showing—

(1) the name, address, and phone of the information contact required to make such a return, and

(2) the aggregate amount of payments to the person required to be shown on the return.

The written statement required under the preceding sentence shall be furnished to the person on or before January 31 of the year following the calendar year for which the return under subsection (a) is required to be made.

Amendments

• **1997, Taxpayer Relief Act of 1997 (P.L. 105-34)**

P.L. 105-34, § 1601(a)(1):

Amended Code Sec. 6050R(c)(1) by striking "name and address" and inserting "name, address, and phone number of the information contact". **Effective** as if included in the provision of P.L. 104-188 to which it relates [**effective** for payments made after 12-31-97.—CCH].

[Sec. 6050R(d)]

(d) DEFINITIONS.—For purposes of this section:

(1) CASH.—The term "cash" has the meaning given such term by section 6050I(d).

(2) FISH.—The term "fish" includes other forms of aquatic life.

Amendments

• **1996, Small Business Job Protection Act of 1996 (P.L. 104-188)**

P.L. 104-188, § 1116(b)(1), as amended by P.L. 105-34, § 1601(a)(2):

Amended subpart B of part III of subchapter A of chapter 61 by inserting after Code Sec. 6050Q a new Code Sec. 6050R. **Effective** for payments made after 12-31-97.

[Sec. 6050S]

SEC. 6050S. RETURNS RELATING TO HIGHER EDUCATION TUITION AND RELATED EXPENSES.

[Sec. 6050S(a)]

(a) IN GENERAL.—Any person—

(1) which is an eligible educational institution which enrolls any individual for any academic period;

(2) which is engaged in a trade or business of making payments to any individual under an insurance arrangement as reimbursements or refunds (or similar amounts) of qualified tuition and related expenses; or

(3) except as provided in regulations, which is engaged in a trade or business and, in the course of which, receives from any individual interest aggregating $600 or more for any calendar year on one or more qualified education loans,

shall make the return described in subsection (b) with respect to the individual at such time as the Secretary may by regulations prescribe.

Amendments

• **2002 (P.L. 107-131)**

P.L. 107-131, § 1(a):

Amended Code Sec. 6050S(a)(1). **Effective** for expenses paid or assessed after 12-31-2002 (in tax years ending after such date), for education furnished in academic periods beginning after such date. Prior to amendment, Code Sec. 6050S(a)(1) read as follows:

(1) which is an eligible educational institution—

(A) which receives payments for qualified tuition and related expenses with respect to any individual for any calendar year; or

(B) which makes reimbursements or refunds (or similar amounts) to any individual of qualified tuition and related expenses;

• **1998, IRS Restructuring and Reform Act of 1998 (P.L. 105-206)**

P.L. 105-206, § 6004(a)(2):

Amended Code Sec. 6050S(a). **Effective** as if included in the provision of P.L. 105-34 to which it relates [**effective** for expenses paid after 12-31-97 (in tax years ending after such date), for education furnished in academic periods beginning after such date.—CCH]. Prior to amendment, Code Sec. 6050S(a) read as follows:

(a) IN GENERAL.—Any person—

(1) which is an eligible educational institution which receives payments for qualified tuition and related expenses with respect to any individual for any calendar year, or

(2) which is engaged in a trade or business and which, in the course of such trade or business—

(A) makes payments during any calendar year to any individual which constitutes reimbursements or refunds (or similar amounts) of qualified tuition and related expenses of such individual, or

(B) except as provided in regulations, receives from any individual interest aggregating $600 or more for any calendar year on 1 or more qualified education loans,

shall make the return described in subsection (b) with respect to the individual at such time as the Secretary may by regulations prescribe.

• **1997, Taxpayer Relief Act of 1997 (P.L. 105-34)**

P.L. 105-34, § 202(c)(1):

Amended Code Sec. 6050S(a)(2). For the **effective** date, see Act Sec. 202(e), below. Prior to amendment, Code Sec. 6050S(a)(2) read as follows:

(2) which is engaged in a trade or business and which, in the course of such trade or business, makes payments during any calendar year to any individual which constitute reimbursements or refunds (or similar amounts) of qualified tuition and related expenses of such individual,

P.L. 105-34, § 202(e), provides:

(e) EFFECTIVE DATE.—The amendments made by this section shall apply to any qualified education loan (as defined in section 221(e)(1) of the Internal Revenue Code of 1986, as added by this section) incurred on, before, or after the date of the enactment of this Act, but only with respect to—

(1) any loan interest payment due and paid after December 31, 1997, and

(2) the portion of the 60-month period referred to in section 221(d) of the Internal Revenue Code of 1986 (as added by this section) after December 31, 1997.

[Sec. 6050S(b)]

(b) FORM AND MANNER OF RETURNS.—A return is described in this subsection if such return—

(1) is in such form as the Secretary may prescribe, and

(2) contains—

(A) the name, address, and TIN of any individual—

(i) who is or has been enrolled at the institution and with respect to whom transactions described in subparagraph (B) are made during the calendar year, or

(ii) with respect to whom payments described in subsection (a)(2) or (a)(3) were made or received,

(B) the—

RETURNS—INFORMATION

(i) aggregate amount of payments received for qualified tuition and related expenses with respect to the individual described in subparagraph (A) during the calendar year,

(ii) aggregate amount of grants received by such individual for payment of costs of attendance that are administered and processed by the institution during such calendar year,

(iii) amount of any adjustments to the aggregate amounts reported by the institution pursuant to clause (i) or (ii) with respect to such individual for a prior calendar year,

(iv) aggregate amount of reimbursements or refunds (or similar amounts) paid to such individual during the calendar year by a person engaged in a trade or business described in subsection (a)(2), and

(v) aggregate amount of interest received for the calendar year from such individual,

(C) the employer identification number of the institution, and

(D) such other information as the Secretary may prescribe.

Amendments

• **2015, Protecting Americans from Tax Hikes Act of 2015 (P.L. 114-113)**

P.L. 114-113, §211(b), Div. Q:

Amended Code Sec. 6050S(b)(2) by striking "and" at the end of subparagraph (B), by redesignating subparagraph (C) as subparagraph (D), and by inserting after subparagraph (B) a new subparagraph (C). **Effective** for expenses paid after 12-31-2015, for education furnished in academic periods beginning after such date.

P.L. 114-113, §212(a), Div. Q:

Amended Code Sec. 6050S(b)(2)(B)(i) by striking "or the aggregate amount billed" after "payments received". **Effective** for expenses paid after 12-31-2015, for education furnished in academic periods beginning after such date.

• **2002 (P.L. 107-131)**

P.L. 107-131, §1(b)(1):

Amended Code Sec. 6050S(b)(1) by inserting "and" after the comma at the end. **Effective** for expenses paid or assessed after 12-31-2002 (in tax years ending after such date), for education furnished in academic periods beginning after such date.

P.L. 107-131, §1(b)(2):

Amended Code Sec. 6050S(b)(2)(A). **Effective** for expenses paid or assessed after 12-31-2002 (in tax years ending after such date), for education furnished in academic periods beginning after such date. Prior to amendment, Code Sec. 6050S(b)(2)(A) read as follows:

(A) the name, address, and TIN of the individual with respect to whom payments or interest described in subsection (a) were received from (or were paid to),

P.L. 107-131, §1(b)(3):

Amended Code Sec. 6050S(b)(2) by striking subparagraph (B) and redesignating subparagraphs (C) and (D) as subparagraphs (B) and (C), respectively. **Effective** for expenses paid or assessed after 12-31-2002 (in tax years ending after such date), for education furnished in academic periods beginning after such date. Prior to being stricken, Code Sec. 6050S(b)(2)(B) read as follows:

(B) the name, address, and TIN of any individual certified by the individual described in subparagraph (A) as the taxpayer who will claim the individual as a dependent for purposes of the deduction allowable under section 151 for any taxable year ending with or within the calendar year, and

P.L. 107-131, §1(b)(4):

Amended Code Sec. 6050S(b)(2)(B), as redesignated by Act Sec. 1(b)(3). **Effective** for expenses paid or assessed after 12-31-2002 (in tax years ending after such date), for education furnished in academic periods beginning after such date. Prior to amendment, Code Sec. 6050S(b)(2)(B) read as follows:

(B) the—

(i) aggregate amount of payments for qualified tuition and related expenses received with respect to the individual described in subparagraph (A) during the calendar year,

(ii) the amount of any grant received by such individual for payment of costs of attendance and processed by the person making such return during such calendar year,

(iii) aggregate amount of reimbursements or refunds (or similar amounts) paid to such individual during the calendar year by the person making such return, and

(iv) aggregate amount of interest received for the calendar year from such individual, and

• **1998, IRS Restructuring and Reform Act of 1998 (P.L. 105-206)**

P.L. 105-206, §3712(a)(1):

Amended Code Sec. 6050S(b)(2)(C) by redesignating clauses (ii) and (iii) as clauses (iii) and (iv), respectively, and by inserting after clause (i) a new clause (ii). **Effective** for returns required to be filed with respect to tax years beginning after 12-31-98.

P.L. 105-206, §3712(a)(2):

Amended Code Sec. 6050S(b)(2)(C)(iii), as redesignated by Act Sec. 3712(a)(1), by inserting "by the person making such return" after "year". **Effective** for returns required to be filed with respect to tax years beginning after 12-31-98.

P.L. 105-206, §3712(a)(3):

Amended Code Sec. 6050S(b)(2)(C)(iv), as redesignated by Act Sec. 3712(a)(1), by inserting "and" at the end. **Effective** for returns required to be filed with respect to tax years beginning after 12-31-98.

• **1997, Taxpayer Relief Act of 1997 (P.L. 105-34)**

P.L. 105-34, §202(c)(2)(A):

Amended Code Sec. 6050S(b)(2)(A) by inserting "or interest" after "payments". For the **effective** date, see Act Sec. 202(e) in the amendment notes following Code Sec. 6050S(a).

P.L. 105-34, §202(c)(2)(B):

Amended Code Sec. 6050S(b)(2)(C) by striking "and" at the end of clause (i), by inserting "and" at the end of clause (ii), and by inserting after clause (ii) a new clause (iii). For the **effective** date, see Act Sec. 202(e) in the amendment notes following Code Sec. 6050S(a).

[Sec. 6050S(c)]

(c) APPLICATION TO GOVERNMENTAL UNITS.—For purposes of this section—

(1) a governmental unit or any agency or instrumentality thereof shall be treated as a person, and

(2) any return required under subsection (a) by such governmental entity shall be made by the officer or employee appropriately designated for the purpose of making such return.

[Sec. 6050S(d)]

(d) STATEMENTS TO BE FURNISHED TO INDIVIDUALS WITH RESPECT TO WHOM INFORMATION IS REQUIRED.—Every person required to make a return under subsection (a) shall furnish to each individual whose name is required to be set forth in such return under subparagraph (A) of subsection (b)(2) a written statement showing—

(1) the name, address, and phone number of the information contact of the person required to make such return, and

(2) the information required by subsection (b)(2).

The written statement required under the preceding sentence shall be furnished on or before January 31 of the year following the calendar year for which the return under subsection (a) was required to be made.

Amendments

• **2015, Trade Preferences Extension Act of 2015 (P.L. 114-27)**

P.L. 114-27, §804(c):

Amended Code Sec. 6050S(d)(2). **Effective** for tax years beginning after 6-29-2015. Prior to amendment, Code Sec. 6050S(d)(2) read as follows:

(2) the amounts described in subparagraph (B) of subsection (b)(2).

• **2002 (P.L. 107-131)**

P.L. 107-131, §1(c)(1)-(2):

Amended Code Sec. 6050S(d) by striking "or (B)" following "under subparagraph (A)" in the matter preceding paragraph (1); and in paragraph (2), by striking "subparagraph (C)" and inserting "subparagraph (B)". **Effective** for expenses paid or assessed after 12-31-2002 (in tax years ending after such date), for education furnished in academic periods beginning after such date.

• **1998, IRS Restructuring and Reform Act of 1998 (P.L. 105-206)**

P.L. 105-206, §3712(b)(1):

Amended Code Sec. 6050S(d)(2) by striking "aggregate" before "amounts". **Effective** for returns required to be filed with respect to tax years beginning after 12-31-98.

RETURNS—INFORMATION

[Sec. 6050S(e)]

(e) DEFINITIONS.—For purposes of this section, the terms "eligible educational institution" and "qualified tuition and related expenses" have the meanings given such terms by section 25A (without regard to subsection (g)(2) thereof), and except as provided in regulations, the term "qualified education loan" has the meaning given such term by section 221(d)(1).

Amendments

• 2013, American Taxpayer Relief Act of 2012 (P.L. 112-240)

P.L. 112-240, §101(a)(1) and (3), provides:

SEC. 101. PERMANENT EXTENSION AND MODIFICATION OF 2001 TAX RELIEF.

(a) PERMANENT EXTENSION.—

(1) IN GENERAL.—The Economic Growth and Tax Relief Reconciliation Act of 2001 is amended by striking title IX.

***

(3) EFFECTIVE DATE.—The amendments made by this subsection shall apply to taxable, plan, or limitation years beginning after December 31, 2012, and estates of decedents dying, gifts made, or generation skipping transfers after December 31, 2012.

• 2001, Economic Growth and Tax Relief Reconciliation Act of 2001 (P.L. 107-16)

P.L. 107-16, §412(a)(2):

Amended Code Sec. 6050S(e) by striking "section 221(e)(1)" and inserting "section 221(d)(1)". **Effective** with respect to any loan interest paid after 12-31-2001, in tax years ending after such date.

P.L. 107-16, §901(a)-(b), as amended by P.L. 111-312, §101(a)(1), provides [but see P.L. 112-240, §101(a)(1) and (3), above]:

SEC. 901. SUNSET OF PROVISIONS OF ACT.

(a) IN GENERAL.—All provisions of, and amendments made by, this Act shall not apply—

(1) to taxable, plan, or limitation years beginning after December 31, 2012, or

(2) in the case of title V, to estates of decedents dying, gifts made, or generation skipping transfers, after December 31, 2012.

(b) APPLICATION OF CERTAIN LAWS.—The Internal Revenue Code of 1986 and the Employee Retirement Income Security Act of 1974 shall be applied and administered to years, estates, gifts, and transfers described in subsection (a) as if the provisions and amendments described in subsection (a) had never been enacted.

• 1998, IRS Restructuring and Reform Act of 1998 (P.L. 105-206)

P.L. 105-206, §3712(b)(2):

Amended Code Sec. 6050S(e) by inserting "(without regard to subsection (g)(2) thereof)" after "section 25A". **Effective** for returns required to be filed with respect to tax years beginning after 12-31-98.

• 1997, Taxpayer Relief Act of 1997 (P.L. 105-34)

P.L. 105-34, §202(c)(3):

Amended Code Sec. 6050S(e) by inserting ", and except as provided in regulations, the term `qualified education loan' has the meaning given such term by section 221(e)(1)" after "section 25A". For the **effective** date, see Act Sec. 202(e) in the amendment notes following Code Sec. 6050S(a).

[Sec. 6050S(f)]

(f) RETURNS WHICH WOULD BE REQUIRED TO BE MADE BY 2 OR MORE PERSONS.—Except to the extent provided in regulations prescribed by the Secretary, in the case of any amount received by any person on behalf of another person, only the person first receiving such amount shall be required to make the return under subsection (a).

[Sec. 6050S(g)]

(g) REGULATIONS.—The Secretary shall prescribe such regulations as may be necessary to carry out the provisions of this section. No penalties shall be imposed under part II of subchapter B of chapter 68 with respect to any return or statement required under this section until such time as such regulations are issued.

Amendments

• 1997, Taxpayer Relief Act of 1997 (P.L. 105-34)

P.L. 105-34, §201(c)(1):

Amended subpart B of part III of subchapter A of chapter 61 by inserting after Code Sec. 6050R a new Code Sec. 6050S. **Effective** for expenses paid after 12-31-97 (in tax years ending after such date), for education furnished in academic periods beginning after such date.

[Sec. 6050T]

SEC. 6050T. RETURNS RELATING TO CREDIT FOR HEALTH INSURANCE COSTS OF ELIGIBLE INDIVIDUALS.

[Sec. 6050T(a)]

(a) REQUIREMENT OF REPORTING.—Every person who is entitled to receive payments for any month of any calendar year under section 7527 (relating to advance payment of credit for health insurance costs of eligible individuals) with respect to any certified individual (as defined in section 7527(c)) shall, at such time as the Secretary may prescribe, make the return described in subsection (b) with respect to each such individual.

[Sec. 6050T(b)]

(b) FORM AND MANNER OF RETURNS.—A return is described in this subsection if such return—

(1) is in such form as the Secretary may prescribe, and

(2) contains—

(A) the name, address, and TIN of each individual referred to in subsection (a),

(B) the number of months for which amounts were entitled to be received with respect to such individual under section 7527 (relating to advance payment of credit for health insurance costs of eligible individuals),

(C) the amount entitled to be received for each such month, and

(D) such other information as the Secretary may prescribe.

[Sec. 6050T(c)]

(c) STATEMENTS TO BE FURNISHED TO INDIVIDUALS WITH RESPECT TO WHOM INFORMATION IS REQUIRED.—Every person required to make a return under subsection (a) shall furnish to each individual whose name is required to be set forth in such return a written statement showing—

(1) the name and address of the person required to make such return and the phone number of the information contact for such person, and

(2) the information required to be shown on the return with respect to such individual.

The written statement required under the preceding sentence shall be furnished on or before January 31 of the year following the calendar year for which the return under subsection (a) is required to be made.

Amendments

• 2002, Trade Act of 2002 (P.L. 107-210)

P.L. 107-210, §202(c)(1):

Amended subpart B of part III of subchapter A by inserting after Code Sec. 6050S a new Code Sec. 6050T. **Effective** 8-6-2002.

RETURNS—INFORMATION

[Sec. 6050U]

SEC. 6050U. CHARGES OR PAYMENTS FOR QUALIFIED LONG-TERM CARE INSURANCE CONTRACTS UNDER COMBINED ARRANGEMENTS.

[Sec. 6050U(a)]

(a) REQUIREMENT OF REPORTING.—Any person who makes a charge against the cash value of an annuity contract, or the cash surrender value of a life insurance contract, which is excludible from gross income under section 72(e)(11) shall make a return, according to the forms or regulations prescribed by the Secretary, setting forth—

(1) the amount of the aggregate of such charges against each such contract for the calendar year,

(2) the amount of the reduction in the investment in each such contract by reason of such charges, and

(3) the name, address, and TIN of the individual who is the holder of each such contract.

[Sec. 6050U(b)]

(b) STATEMENTS TO BE FURNISHED TO PERSONS WITH RESPECT TO WHOM INFORMATION IS REQUIRED.—Every person required to make a return under subsection (a) shall furnish to each individual whose name is required to be set forth in such return a written statement showing—

(1) the name, address, and phone number of the information contact of the person making the payments, and

(2) the information required to be shown on the return with respect to such individual.

The written statement required under the preceding sentence shall be furnished to the individual on or before January 31 of the year following the calendar year for which the return under subsection (a) was required to be made.

Amendments

• 2006, Pension Protection Act of 2006 (P.L. 109-280)

P.L. 109-280, § 844(d)(1):

Amended subpart B of part III of subchapter A of chapter 61 by adding at the end a new Code Sec. 6050U. **Effective** for charges made after 12-31-2009.

[Sec. 6050V]

SEC. 6050V. RETURNS RELATING TO APPLICABLE INSURANCE CONTRACTS IN WHICH CERTAIN EXEMPT ORGANIZATIONS HOLD INTERESTS.

[Sec. 6050V(a)]

(a) IN GENERAL.—Each applicable exempt organization which makes a reportable acquisition shall make the return described in subsection (c).

[Sec. 6050V(b)]

(b) TIME FOR MAKING RETURN.—Any applicable exempt organization required to make a return under subsection (a) shall file such return at such time as may be established by the Secretary.

[Sec. 6050V(c)]

(c) FORM AND MANNER OF RETURNS.—A return is described in this subsection if such return—

(1) is in such form as the Secretary prescribes,

(2) contains the name, address, and taxpayer identification number of the applicable exempt organization and the issuer of the applicable insurance contract, and

(3) contains such other information as the Secretary may prescribe.

[Sec. 6050V(d)]

(d) DEFINITIONS.—For purposes of this section—

(1) REPORTABLE ACQUISITION.—The term "reportable acquisition" means the acquisition by an applicable exempt organization of a direct or indirect interest in any applicable insurance contract in any case in which such acquisition is a part of a structured transaction involving a pool of such contracts.

(2) APPLICABLE INSURANCE CONTRACT.—

(A) IN GENERAL.—The term "applicable insurance contract" means any life insurance, annuity, or endowment contract with respect to which both an applicable exempt organization and a person other than an applicable exempt organization have directly or indirectly held an interest in the contract (whether or not at the same time).

(B) EXCEPTIONS.—Such term shall not include a life insurance, annuity, or endowment contract if—

(i) all persons directly or indirectly holding any interest in the contract (other than applicable exempt organizations) have an insurable interest in the insured under the contract independent of any interest of an applicable exempt organization in the contract,

(ii) the sole interest in the contract of an applicable exempt organization or each person other than an applicable exempt organization is as a named beneficiary, or

(iii) the sole interest in the contract of each person other than an applicable exempt organization is—

(I) as a beneficiary of a trust holding an interest in the contract, but only if the person's designation as such beneficiary was made without consideration and solely on a purely gratuitous basis, or

(II) as a trustee who holds an interest in the contract in a fiduciary capacity solely for the benefit of applicable exempt organizations or persons otherwise described in subclause (I) or clause (i) or (ii).

(3) APPLICABLE EXEMPT ORGANIZATION.—The term "applicable exempt organization" means—

(A) an organization described in section 170(c),

(B) an organization described in section 168(h)(2)(A)(iv), or

(C) an organization not described in paragraph (1) or (2) which is described in section 2055(a) or section 2522(a).

[Sec. 6050V(e)]

(e) TERMINATION.—This section shall not apply to reportable acquisitions occurring after the date which is 2 years after the date of the enactment of this section.

Amendments

• 2006, Pension Protection Act of 2006 (P.L. 109-280)

P.L. 109-280, §1211(a)(1):

Amended subpart B of part III of subchapter A of chapter 61, as amended by this Act, by adding at the end a new Code Sec. 6050V. **Effective** for acquisitions of contracts after 8-17-2006.

[Sec. 6050W]

SEC. 6050W. RETURNS RELATING TO PAYMENTS MADE IN SETTLEMENT OF PAYMENT CARD AND THIRD PARTY NETWORK TRANSACTIONS.

[Sec. 6050W(a)]

(a) IN GENERAL.—Each payment settlement entity shall make a return for each calendar year setting forth—

(1) the name, address, and TIN of each participating payee to whom one or more payments in settlement of reportable payment transactions are made, and

(2) the gross amount of the reportable payment transactions with respect to each such participating payee.

Such return shall be made at such time and in such form and manner as the Secretary may require by regulations.

[Sec. 6050W(b)]

(b) PAYMENT SETTLEMENT ENTITY.—For purposes of this section—

(1) IN GENERAL.—The term "payment settlement entity" means—

(A) in the case of a payment card transaction, the merchant acquiring entity, and

(B) in the case of a third party network transaction, the third party settlement organization.

(2) MERCHANT ACQUIRING ENTITY.—The term "merchant acquiring entity" means the bank or other organization which has the contractual obligation to make payment to participating payees in settlement of payment card transactions.

(3) THIRD PARTY SETTLEMENT ORGANIZATION.—The term "third party settlement organization" means the central organization which has the contractual obligation to make payment to participating payees of third party network transactions.

(4) SPECIAL RULES RELATED TO INTERMEDIARIES.—For purposes of this section—

(A) AGGREGATED PAYEES.—In any case where reportable payment transactions of more than one participating payee are settled through an intermediary—

(i) such intermediary shall be treated as the participating payee for purposes of determining the reporting obligations of the payment settlement entity with respect to such transactions, and

(ii) such intermediary shall be treated as the payment settlement entity with respect to the settlement of such transactions with the participating payees.

(B) ELECTRONIC PAYMENT FACILITATORS.—In any case where an electronic payment facilitator or other third party makes payments in settlement of reportable payment transactions on behalf of the payment settlement entity, the return under subsection (a) shall be made by such electronic payment facilitator or other third party in lieu of the payment settlement entity.

[Sec. 6050W(c)]

(c) REPORTABLE PAYMENT TRANSACTION.—For purposes of this section—

(1) IN GENERAL.—The term "reportable payment transaction" means any payment card transaction and any third party network transaction.

(2) PAYMENT CARD TRANSACTION.—The term "payment card transaction" means any transaction in which a payment card is accepted as payment.

(3) THIRD PARTY NETWORK TRANSACTION.—The term "third party network transaction" means any transaction described in subsection (d)(3)(A)(iii) which is settled through a third party payment network.

Amendments

• 2021, American Rescue Plan Act of 2021 (P.L. 117-2)

P.L. 117-2, §9674(b):

Amended Code Sec. 6050W(c)(3) by inserting "described in subsection (d)(3)(A)(iii)" after "any transaction". **Effective** for transactions after 3-11-2021.

[Sec. 6050W(d)]

(d) OTHER DEFINITIONS.—For purposes of this section—

(1) PARTICIPATING PAYEE.—

(A) IN GENERAL.—The term "participating payee" means—

(i) in the case of a payment card transaction, any person who accepts a payment card as payment, and

(ii) in the case of a third party network transaction, any person who accepts payment from a third party settlement organization in settlement of such transaction.

(B) EXCLUSION OF FOREIGN PERSONS.—Except as provided by the Secretary in regulations or other guidance, such term shall not include any person with a foreign address. Notwithstanding the preceding sentence, a person with only a foreign address shall not be treated as a participating payee with respect to any payment settlement entity solely because such person receives payments from such payment settlement entity in dollars.

(C) INCLUSION OF GOVERNMENTAL UNITS.—The term "person" includes any governmental unit (and any agency or instrumentality thereof).

(2) PAYMENT CARD.—The term "payment card" means any card which is issued pursuant to an agreement or arrangement which provides for—

(A) one or more issuers of such cards,

(B) a network of persons unrelated to each other, and to the issuer, who agree to accept such cards as payment, and

(C) standards and mechanisms for settling the transactions between the merchant acquiring entities and the persons who agree to accept such cards as payment.

The acceptance as payment of any account number or other indicia associated with a payment card shall be treated for purposes of this section in the same manner as accepting such payment card as payment.

RETURNS—INFORMATION

(3) THIRD PARTY PAYMENT NETWORK.—The term "third party payment network" means any agreement or arrangement—

(A) which involves the establishment of accounts with a central organization by a substantial number of persons who—

(i) are unrelated to such organization,

(ii) provide goods or services, and

(iii) have agreed to settle transactions for the provision of such goods or services pursuant to such agreement or arrangement,

(B) which provides for standards and mechanisms for settling such transactions, and

(C) which guarantees persons providing goods or services pursuant to such agreement or arrangement that such persons will be paid for providing such goods or services.

Such term shall not include any agreement or arrangement which provides for the issuance of payment cards.

Amendments

• **2018, Bipartisan Budget Act of 2018 (P.L. 115-123)**

P.L. 115-123, §41117(a), Div. D:

Amended Code Sec. 6050W(d)(1)(B) by adding at the end a new sentence. **Effective** for returns for calendar years beginning after 12-31-2017.

[Sec. 6050W(e)]

(e) DE MINIMIS EXCEPTION FOR THIRD PARTY SETTLEMENT ORGANIZATIONS.—A third party settlement organization shall not be required to report any information under subsection (a) with respect to third party network transactions of any participating payee if the amount which would otherwise be reported under subsection (a)(2) with respect to such transactions does not exceed $600.

Amendments

• **2021, American Rescue Plan Act of 2021 (P.L. 117-2)**

P.L. 117-2, §9674(a):

Amended Code Sec. 6050W(e). **Effective** for returns for calendar years beginning after 12-31-2021. Prior to amendment, Code Sec. 6050W(e) read as follows:

(e) EXCEPTION FOR DE MINIMIS PAYMENTS BY THIRD PARTY SETTLEMENT ORGANIZATIONS.—A third party settlement organization shall be required to report any information under subsection (a) with respect to third party network transactions of any participating payee only if—

(1) the amount which would otherwise be reported under subsection (a)(2) with respect to such transactions exceeds $20,000, and

(2) the aggregate number of such transactions exceeds 200.

[Sec. 6050W(f)]

(f) STATEMENTS TO BE FURNISHED TO PERSONS WITH RESPECT TO WHOM INFORMATION IS REQUIRED.—Every person required to make a return under subsection (a) shall furnish to each person with respect to whom such a return is required a written statement showing—

(1) the name, address, and phone number of the information contact of the person required to make such return, and

(2) the gross amount of the reportable payment transactions with respect to the person required to be shown on the return.

The written statement required under the preceding sentence shall be furnished to the person on or before January 31 of the year following the calendar year for which the return under subsection (a) was required to be made. Such statement may be furnished electronically, and if so, the email address of the person required to make such return may be shown in lieu of the phone number.

[Sec. 6050W(g)]

(g) REGULATIONS.—The Secretary may prescribe such regulations or other guidance as may be necessary or appropriate to carry out this section, including rules to prevent the reporting of the same transaction more than once.

Amendments

• **2008, Housing Assistance Tax Act of 2008 (P.L. 110-289)**

P.L. 110-289, §3091(a):

Amended subpart B of part III of subchapter A of chapter 61 by adding at the end a new Code Sec. 6050W. **Effective** generally for returns for calendar years beginning after 12-31-2010. For a special rule, see Act Sec. 3091(e)(2)(B), below.

P.L. 110-289, §3091(e)(2)(B), provides:

(B) ELIGIBILITY FOR TIN MATCHING PROGRAM.—Solely for purposes of carrying out any TIN matching program established by the Secretary under section 3406(i) of the Internal Revenue Code of 1986—

(i) the amendments made [by] this section shall be treated as taking effect on the date of the enactment of this Act [7-30-2008.—CCH], and

(ii) each person responsible for setting the standards and mechanisms referred to in section 6050W(d)(2)(C) of such Code, as added by this section, for settling transactions involving payment cards shall be treated in the same manner as a payment settlement entity.

[Sec. 6050X]

SEC. 6050X. INFORMATION WITH RESPECT TO CERTAIN FINES, PENALTIES, AND OTHER AMOUNTS.

[Sec. 6050X(a)]

(a) REQUIREMENT OF REPORTING.—

(1) IN GENERAL.—The appropriate official of any government or any entity described in section 162(f)(5) which is involved in a suit or agreement described in paragraph (2) shall make a return in such form as determined by the Secretary setting forth—

(A) the amount required to be paid as a result of the suit or agreement to which paragraph (1) of section 162(f) applies,

(B) any amount required to be paid as a result of the suit or agreement which constitutes restitution or remediation of property, and

(C) any amount required to be paid as a result of the suit or agreement for the purpose of coming into compliance with any law which was violated or involved in the investigation or inquiry.

(2) SUIT OR AGREEMENT DESCRIBED.—

(A) IN GENERAL.—A suit or agreement is described in this paragraph if—

(i) it is—

(I) a suit with respect to a violation of any law over which the government or entity has authority and with respect to which there has been a court order, or

(II) an agreement which is entered into with respect to a violation of any law over which the government or entity has authority, or with respect to an investigation or inquiry by the government or entity into the potential violation of any law over which such government or entity has authority, and

(ii) the aggregate amount involved in all court orders and agreements with respect to the violation, investigation, or inquiry is $600 or more.

(B) ADJUSTMENT OF REPORTING THRESHOLD.—The Secretary shall adjust the $600 amount in subparagraph (A)(ii) as necessary in order to ensure the efficient administration of the internal revenue laws.

(3) TIME OF FILING.—The return required under this subsection shall be filed at the time the agreement is entered into, as determined by the Secretary.

RETURNS—INFORMATION

[Sec. 6050X(b)]

(b) STATEMENTS TO BE FURNISHED TO INDIVIDUALS INVOLVED IN THE SETTLEMENT.—Every person required to make a return under subsection (a) shall furnish to each person who is a party to the suit or agreement a written statement showing—

(1) the name of the government or entity, and

(2) the information supplied to the Secretary under subsection (a)(1).

The written statement required under the preceding sentence shall be furnished to the person at the same time the government or entity provides the Secretary with the information required under subsection (a).

[Sec. 6050X(c)]

(c) APPROPRIATE OFFICIAL DEFINED.—For purposes of this section, the term "appropriate official" means the officer or employee having control of the suit, investigation, or inquiry or the person appropriately designated for purposes of this section.

Amendments

• **2017, Tax Cuts and Jobs Act (P.L. 115-97)**

P.L. 115-97, §13306(b)(1):

Amended subpart B of part III of subchapter A of chapter 61 by inserting after Code Sec. 6050W a new Code Sec. 6050X. For the **effective** date, see Act Sec. 13306(b)(3), below.

P.L. 115-97, §13306(b)(3), provides:

(3) EFFECTIVE DATE.—The amendments made by this subsection shall apply to amounts paid or incurred on or after the date of the enactment of this Act, except that such amendments shall not apply to amounts paid or incurred under any binding order or agreement entered into before such date. Such exception shall not apply to an order or agreement requiring court approval unless the approval was obtained before such date.

[Sec. 6050Y]

SEC. 6050Y. RETURNS RELATING TO CERTAIN LIFE INSURANCE CONTRACT TRANSACTIONS.

[Sec. 6050Y(a)]

(a) REQUIREMENT OF REPORTING OF CERTAIN PAYMENTS.—

(1) IN GENERAL.—Every person who acquires a life insurance contract or any interest in a life insurance contract in a reportable policy sale during any taxable year shall make a return for such taxable year (at such time and in such manner as the Secretary shall prescribe) setting forth—

(A) the name, address, and TIN of such person,

(B) the name, address, and TIN of each recipient of payment in the reportable policy sale,

(C) the date of such sale,

(D) the name of the issuer of the life insurance contract sold and the policy number of such contract, and

(E) the amount of each payment.

(2) STATEMENT TO BE FURNISHED TO PERSONS WITH RESPECT TO WHOM INFORMATION IS REQUIRED.—Every person required to make a return under this subsection shall furnish to each person whose name is required to be set forth in such return a written statement showing—

(A) the name, address, and phone number of the information contact of the person required to make such return, and

(B) the information required to be shown on such return with respect to such person, except that in the case of an issuer of a life insurance contract, such statement is not required to include the information specified in paragraph (1)(E).

[Sec. 6050Y(b)]

(b) REQUIREMENT OF REPORTING OF SELLER'S BASIS IN LIFE INSURANCE CONTRACTS.—

(1) IN GENERAL.—Upon receipt of the statement required under subsection (a)(2) or upon notice of a transfer of a life insurance contract to a foreign person, each issuer of a life insurance contract shall make a return (at such time and in such manner as the Secretary shall prescribe) setting forth—

(A) the name, address, and TIN of the seller who transfers any interest in such contract in such sale,

(B) the investment in the contract (as defined in section 72(e)(6)) with respect to such seller, and

(C) the policy number of such contract.

(2) STATEMENT TO BE FURNISHED TO PERSONS WITH RESPECT TO WHOM INFORMATION IS REQUIRED.—Every person required to make a return under this subsection shall furnish to each person whose name is required to be set forth in such return a written statement showing—

(A) the name, address, and phone number of the information contact of the person required to make such return, and

(B) the information required to be shown on such return with respect to each seller whose name is required to be set forth in such return.

[Sec. 6050Y(c)]

(c) REQUIREMENT OF REPORTING WITH RESPECT TO REPORTABLE DEATH BENEFITS.—

(1) IN GENERAL.—Every person who makes a payment of reportable death benefits during any taxable year shall make a return for such taxable year (at such time and in such manner as the Secretary shall prescribe) setting forth—

(A) the name, address, and TIN of the person making such payment,

(B) the name, address, and TIN of each recipient of such payment,

(C) the date of each such payment,

(D) the gross amount of each such payment, and

(E) such person's estimate of the investment in the contract (as defined in section 72(e)(6)) with respect to the buyer.

(2) STATEMENT TO BE FURNISHED TO PERSONS WITH RESPECT TO WHOM INFORMATION IS REQUIRED.—Every person required to make a return under this subsection shall furnish to each person whose name is required to be set forth in such return a written statement showing—

(A) the name, address, and phone number of the information contact of the person required to make such return, and

(B) the information required to be shown on such return with respect to each recipient of payment whose name is required to be set forth in such return.

[Sec. 6050Y(d)]

(d) DEFINITIONS.—For purposes of this section:

(1) PAYMENT.—The term "payment" means, with respect to any reportable policy sale, the amount of cash and the fair market value of any consideration transferred in the sale.

RETURNS—INFORMATION

(2) REPORTABLE POLICY SALE.—The term "reportable policy sale" has the meaning given such term in section 101(a)(3)(B).

(3) ISSUER.—The term "issuer" means any life insurance company that bears the risk with respect to a life insurance contract on the date any return or statement is required to be made under this section.

(4) REPORTABLE DEATH BENEFITS.—The term "reportable death benefits" means amounts paid by reason of the death of the insured under a life insurance contract that has been transferred in a reportable policy sale.

Amendments

• 2017, Tax Cuts and Jobs Act (P.L. 115-97)

P.L. 115-97, § 13520(a):

Amended subpart B of part III of subchapter A of chapter 61, as amended by Act Sec. 13306, by adding at the end a new Code Sec. 6050Y. For the **effective** date, see Act Sec. 13520(d), below.

P.L. 115-97, § 13520(d), provides:

(d) EFFECTIVE DATE.—The amendments made by this section shall apply to—

(1) reportable policy sales (as defined in section 6050Y(d)(2) of the Internal Revenue Code of 1986 (as added by subsection (a)) after December 31, 2017, and

(2) reportable death benefits (as defined in section 6050Y(d)(4) of such Code (as added by subsection (a)) paid after December 31, 2017.

➤➤➤ Caution: Code Sec. 6050Z, below, as added by P.L. 117-328, applies to distributions made after the date which is 3 years after December 29, 2022.

SEC. 6050Z. REPORTS RELATING TO LONG-TERM CARE PREMIUM STATEMENTS

[Sec. 6050Z(a)]

(a) REQUIREMENT OF REPORTING.—Any issuer of certified long-term care insurance (as defined in section 401(a)(39)(C)) who provides a long-term care premium statement with respect to any purchaser pursuant to section 401(a)(39)(E) for a calendar year, shall make a return not later than February 1 of the succeeding calendar year, according to forms or regulations prescribed by the Secretary, setting forth with respect to each such purchaser—

(1) the name and taxpayer identification number of such issuer,

(2) a statement that the coverage is certified long-term care insurance as defined in section 401(a)(39)(C),

(3) the name of the owner of such coverage,

(4) identification of the individual covered and such individual's relationship to the owner,

(5) the premiums paid for the coverage for the calendar year, and

(6) such other information as the Secretary may require.

[Sec. 6050Z(b)]

(b) STATEMENT TO BE FURNISHED TO PERSONS WITH RESPECT TO WHOM INFORMATION IS REQUIRED.—Every person required to make a return under subsection (a) shall furnish to each individual whose name is required to be set forth in such return a written statement showing—

(1) the name, address, and phone number of the information contact of the issuer of the contract or coverage, and

(2) the aggregate amount of premiums and charges paid under the contract or coverage covering the insured individual during the calendar year.

The written statement required under the preceding sentence shall be furnished to the individual or individuals on or before January 31 of the year following the calendar year for which the return required under subsection (a) was required to be made.

[Sec. 6050Z(c)]

(c) CONTRACTS OR COVERAGE COVERING MORE THAN ONE INSURED.—In the case of contracts or coverage covering more than one insured, the return and statement required by subsections (a) and (b) shall identify only the portion of the premium that is properly allocable to the insured in respect of whom the return or statement is made.

[Sec. 6050Z(d)]

(d) STATEMENT TO BE FURNISHED ON REQUEST.—If any individual to whom a return is required to be furnished under subsection (b) requests that such a return be furnished at any time before the close of the calendar year, the person required to make the return under subsection (b) shall comply with such request and shall furnish to the Secretary at such time a copy of the return so provided.

Amendments

• 2022, SECURE 2.0 Act of 2022 (P.L. 117-328)

P.L. 117-328, § 334(d)(1):

Amended subpart B of part III of subchapter A of chapter 61 by adding at the end new Code Sec. 6050Z. **Effective** for distributions made after the date which is 3 years after 12-29-2022.

Subpart C—Information Regarding Wages Paid Employees

Sec. 6051. Receipts for employees.
Sec. 6052. Returns regarding payment of wages in the form of group-term life insurance.
Sec. 6053. Reporting of tips.

[Sec. 6051]

SEC. 6051. RECEIPTS FOR EMPLOYEES.

[Sec. 6051(a)]

(a) REQUIREMENT.—Every person required to deduct and withhold from an employee a tax under section 3101 or 3402, or who would have been required to deduct and withhold a tax under section 3402 (determined without regard to subsection (n)) if the employee had claimed no more than one withholding exemption, or every employer engaged in a trade or business who pays remuneration for services performed by an employee, including the cash value of such remuneration paid in any medium other than cash, shall furnish to each such employee in respect of the remuneration paid by such person to such employee during the calendar year, on or before January 31 of the succeeding year, or, if his employment is terminated before the close of such calendar year, within 30 days after the date of receipt of a written request from the employee if such 30-day period ends before January 31, a written statement showing the following:

(1) the name of such person,

(2) the name of the employee (and an identifying number for the employee if wages as defined in section 3121(a) have been paid),

(3) the total amount of wages as defined in section 3401(a),

(4) the total amount deducted and withheld as tax under section 3402,

(5) the total amount of wages as defined in section 3121(a),

(6) the total amount deducted and withheld as tax under section 3101,

Sec. 6050Y(d)(2)

RETURNS—INFORMATION

(7) [Repealed.]

(8) the total amount of elective deferrals (within the meaning of section 402(g)(3)) and compensation deferred under section 457, including the amount of designated Roth contributions (as defined in section 402A),

(9) the total amount incurred for dependent care assistance with respect to such employee under a dependent care assistance program described in section 129(d),

(10) in the case of an employee who is a member of the Armed Forces of the United States, such employee's earned income as determined for purposes of section 32 (relating to earned income credit),

(11) the amount contributed to any Archer MSA (as defined in section 220(d)) of such employee or such employee's spouse,

(12) the amount contributed to any health savings account (as defined in section 223(d)) of such employee or such employee's spouse,

(13) the total amount of deferrals for the year under a nonqualified deferred compensation plan (within the meaning of section 409A(d)),

(14) the aggregate cost (determined under rules similar to the rules of section 4980B(f)(4)) of applicable employer-sponsored coverage (as defined in subsection (g)), except that this paragraph shall not apply to—

(A) coverage to which paragraphs (11) and (12) apply, or

(B) the amount of any salary reduction contributions to a flexible spending arrangement (within the meaning of section 125),

(15) the total amount of permitted benefit (as defined in section 9831(d)(3)(C)) for the year under a qualified small employer health reimbursement arrangement (as defined in section 9831(d)(2)) with respect to the employee,

(16) the amount includible in gross income under subparagraph (A) of section 83(i)(1) with respect to an event described in subparagraph (B) of such section which occurs in such calendar year, and

(17) the aggregate amount of income which is being deferred pursuant to elections under section 83(i), determined as of the close of the calendar year.

In the case of compensation paid for service as a member of a uniformed service, the statement shall show, in lieu of the amount required to be shown by paragraph (5), the total amount of wages as defined in section 3121(a), computed in accordance with such section and section 3121(i)(2). In the case of compensation paid for service as a volunteer or volunteer leader within the meaning of the Peace Corps Act, the statement shall show, in lieu of the amount required to be shown by paragraph (5), the total amount of wages as defined in section 3121(a), computed in accordance with such section and section 3121(i)(3). In the case of tips received by an employee in the course of his employment, the amounts required to be shown by paragraphs (3) and (5) shall include only such tips as are included in statements furnished to the employer pursuant to section 6053(a). The amounts required to be shown by paragraph (5) shall not include wages which are exempted pursuant to sections 3101(c) and 3111(c) from the taxes imposed by section 3101 and 3111. In the case of the amounts required to be shown by paragraph (13), the Secretary may (by regulation) establish a minimum amount of deferrals below which paragraph (13) does not apply.

Amendments

• **2019, Further Consolidated Appropriations Act, 2020 (P.L. 116-94)**

P.L. 116-94, §503(b)(1)(A), Div. N:

Amended Code Sec. 6051(a)(14) by striking "section 4980I(d)(1)" and inserting "subsection (g)". **Effective** for tax years beginning after 12-31-2019.

• **2017, Tax Cuts and Jobs Act (P.L. 115-97)**

P.L. 115-97, §13603(d):

Amended Code Sec. 6051(a) by striking "and" at the end of paragraph (14)(B), by striking the period at the end of paragraph (15) and inserting a comma, and by inserting after paragraph (15) new paragraphs (16) and (17). **Effective** generally for stock attributable to options exercised, or restricted stock units settled, after 12-31-2017. For a transition rule, see Act Sec. 13603(g), below.

P.L. 115-97, §13603(g), provides:

(g) TRANSITION RULE.—Until such time as the Secretary (or the Secretary's delegate) issues regulations or other guidance for purposes of implementing the requirements of paragraph (2)(C)(i)(II) of section 83(i) of the Internal Revenue Code of 1986 (as added by this section), or the requirements of paragraph (6) of such section, a corporation shall be treated as being in compliance with such requirements (respectively) if such corporation complies with a reasonable good faith interpretation of such requirements.

• **2016, 21st Century Cures Act (P.L. 114-255)**

P.L. 114-255, §18001(a)(6)(A):

Amended Code Sec. 6051(a) by striking "and" at the end of paragraph (13), by striking the period at the end of paragraph (14) and inserting ", and", and by inserting after paragraph (14) a new paragraph (15). **Effective** for calendar years beginning after 12-31-2016.

• **2015, Protecting Americans from Tax Hikes Act of 2015 (P.L. 114-113)**

P.L. 114-113, §409(a), Div. Q:

Amended Code Sec. 6051(a)(2) by striking "his social security account number" and inserting "an identifying number for the employee". **Effective** 12-18-2015.

• **2010, (P.L. 111-226)**

P.L. 111-226, §219(a)(3):

Repealed Code Sec. 6051(a)(7). **Effective** for tax years beginning after 12-31-2010. Prior to repeal, Code Sec. 6051(a)(7) read as follows:

(7) the total amount paid to the employee under section 3507 (relating to advance payment of earned income credit),

• **2010, Patient Protection and Affordable Care Act (P.L. 111-148)**

P.L. 111-148, §9002(a):

Amended Code Sec. 6051(a) by striking "and" at the end of paragraph (12), by striking the period at the end of paragraph (13) and inserting ", and", and by adding after paragraph (13) a new paragraph (14). **Effective** for tax years beginning after 12-31-2010.

• **2006, Pension Protection Act of 2006 (P.L. 109-280)**

P.L. 109-280, §811, provides:

SEC. 811. PENSIONS AND INDIVIDUAL RETIREMENT ARRANGEMENT PROVISIONS OF ECONOMIC GROWTH AND TAX RELIEF RECONCILIATION ACT OF 2001 MADE PERMANENT.

Title IX of the Economic Growth and Tax Relief Reconciliation Act of 2001 [P.L. 107-16] shall not apply to the provisions of, and amendments made by, subtitles A through F of title VI [§§601-666]of such Act (relating to pension and individual retirement arrangement provisions).

• **2004, American Jobs Creation Act of 2004 (P.L. 108-357)**

P.L. 108-357, §885(b)(1)(A):

Amended Code Sec. 6051(a) by striking "and" at the end of paragraph (11), by striking the period at the end of paragraph (12) and inserting ", and", and by inserting after paragraph (12) a new paragraph (13). **Effective** for amounts deferred after 12-31-2004. For special rules, see Act Sec. 885(d)(2)-(3), (e)-(f), below.

P.L. 108-357, §885(b)(1)(B):

Amended Code Sec. 6051(a) by adding at the end a new sentence. **Effective** for amounts deferred after 12-31-2004. For special rules, see Act Sec. 885(d)(2)-(3), (e)-(f), below.

P.L. 108-357, §885(d)(2)-(3), (e)-(f), provides:

(2) SPECIAL RULES.—

(A) EARNINGS.—The amendments made by this section shall apply to earnings on deferred compensation only to the extent that such amendments apply to such compensation.

(B) MATERIAL MODIFICATIONS.—For purposes of this subsection, amounts deferred in taxable years beginning before January 1, 2005, shall be treated as amounts deferred in a taxable year beginning on or after such date if the plan under which the deferral is made is materially modified after October 3, 2004, unless such modification is pursuant to the guidance issued under subsection (f).

(3) EXCEPTION FOR NONELECTIVE DEFERRED COMPENSATION.—The amendments made by this section shall not apply to any nonelective deferred compensation to which section 457 of the Internal Revenue Code of 1986 does not apply by reason of section 457(e)(12) of such Code, but only if such compensation is provided under a nonqualified deferred compensation plan—

(A) which was in existence on May 1, 2004,

(B) which was providing nonelective deferred compensation described in such section 457(e)(12) on such date, and

(C) which is established or maintained by an organization incorporated on July 2, 1974.

If, after May 1, 2004, a plan described in the preceding sentence adopts a plan amendment which provides a material change in the classes of individuals eligible to participate in the plan, this paragraph shall not apply to any nonelective deferred compensation provided under the plan on or after the date of the adoption of the amendment.

(e) GUIDANCE RELATING TO CHANGE OF OWNERSHIP OR CONTROL.—Not later than 90 days after the date of the enactment of this Act, the Secretary of the Treasury shall issue guidance on what constitutes a change in ownership or effective control for purposes of section 409A of the Internal Revenue Code of 1986, as added by this section.

(f) GUIDANCE RELATING TO TERMINATION OF CERTAIN EXISTING ARRANGEMENTS.—Not later than 60 days after the date of the enactment of this Act, the Secretary of the Treasury shall issue guidance providing a limited period during which a nonqualified deferred compensation plan adopted before December 31, 2004, may, without violating the requirements of paragraphs (2), (3), and (4) of section 409A(a) of the Internal Revenue Code of 1986 (as added by this section), be amended—

(1) to provide that a participant may terminate participation in the plan, or cancel an outstanding deferral election with regard to amounts deferred after December 31,

RETURNS—INFORMATION

2004, but only if amounts subject to the termination or cancellation are includible in income of the participant as earned (or, if later, when no longer subject to substantial risk of forfeiture), and

(2) to conform to the requirements of such section 409A with regard to amounts deferred after December 31, 2004.

• **2003, Medicare Prescription Drug, Improvement, and Modernization Act of 2003 (P.L. 108-173)**

P.L. 108-173, §1201(d)(3):

Amended Code Sec. 6051(a) by striking "and" at the end of paragraph (10), by striking the period at the end of paragraph (11) and inserting ", and", and by inserting after paragraph (11) a new paragraph (12). **Effective** for tax years beginning after 12-31-2003.

• **2001, Economic Growth and Tax Relief Reconciliation Act of 2001 (P.L. 107-16)**

P.L. 107-16, §617(d)(1):

Amended Code Sec. 6051(a)(8) by inserting ", including the amount of designated Roth contributions (as defined in section 402A)" before the comma at the end. **Effective** for tax years beginning after 12-31-2005.

P.L. 107-16, §901(a)-(b), provides [but see P.L. 109-280, §811, above]:

SEC. 901. SUNSET OF PROVISIONS OF ACT.

(a) IN GENERAL.—All provisions of, and amendments made by, this Act shall not apply—

(1) to taxable, plan, or limitation years beginning after December 31, 2010, or

(2) in the case of title V, to estates of decedents dying, gifts made, or generation skipping transfers, after December 31, 2010.

(b) APPLICATION OF CERTAIN LAWS.—The Internal Revenue Code of 1986 and the Employee Retirement Income Security Act of 1974 shall be applied and administered to years, estates, gifts, and transfers described in subsection (a) as if the provisions and amendments described in subsection (a) had never been enacted.

• **2000, Community Renewal Tax Relief Act of 2000 (P.L. 106-554)**

P.L. 106-554, §202(a)(9):

Amended Code Sec. 6051(a)(11) by striking "medical savings account" and inserting "Archer MSA". **Effective** 12-21-2000.

• **1996, Health Insurance Portability and Accountability Act of 1996 (P.L. 104-191)**

P.L. 104-191, §301(c)(3):

Amended Code Sec. 6051(a) by striking "and" at the end of paragraph (9), by striking the period at the end of paragraph (10) and inserting ", and", and by inserting after paragraph (10) a new paragraph (11). **Effective** for tax years beginning after 12-31-96.

• **1994, Uruguay Round Agreements Act (P.L. 103-465)**

P.L. 103-465, §721(b):

Amended Code Sec. 6051(a) by striking "and" at the end of paragraph (8), by striking the period at the end of paragraph (9) and by inserting ", and", and by inserting after paragraph (9) a new paragraph (10). **Effective** for remuneration paid after 12-31-94.

• **1988, Technical and Miscellaneous Revenue Act of 1988 (P.L. 100-647)**

P.L. 100-647, §1011B(c)(2)(B):

Amended Code Sec. 6051(a) by striking out the period at the end of paragraph (8) and inserting in lieu thereof ", and", and by adding at the end thereof new paragraph (9). **Effective** for tax years beginning after 12-31-87.

P.L. 100-647, §1018(u)(33):

Amended Code Sec. 6051(a)(7) by adding a comma at the end thereof. **Effective** as if included in the provision of P.L. 99-514 to which it relates.

• **1986, Tax Reform Act of 1986 (P.L. 99-514)**

P.L. 99-514, §1105(b):

Amended Code Sec. 6051(a) by striking "and" at the end of paragraph (6), by striking the period at the end of paragraph (7), and by inserting after paragraph (7) new paragraph (8). **Effective**, generally, for tax years beginning after 12-31-86. For special rules, see Act Sec. 1105(c)(2)-(5) following Code Sec. 402.

• **1982, Miscellaneous Revenue Act of 1982 (P.L. 97-362)**

P.L. 97-362, §107(a):

Amended Code Sec. 6051(a) by striking out "on the day on which the last payment of remuneration is made" and inserting in lieu thereof "within 30 days after the date of receipt of a written request from the employee if such 30-day period ends before January 31". **Effective** with respect to employees whose employment is terminated after 10-25-82.

• **1980, Technical Corrections Act of 1979 (P.L. 96-222)**

P.L. 96-222, §101(a)(2)(D):

Amended Act Sec. 105(g)(2) of P.L. 95-600 to change the **effective** date of the amendment of Code Sec. 6051(a) from 6-30-78, to 6-30-79.

• **1978, Revenue Act of 1978 (P.L. 95-600)**

P.L. 95-600, §105(c):

Amended Code Sec. 6051(a) by striking out "and" at the end of paragraph (5), by striking out the period at the end of paragraph (6) and inserting in lieu thereof ", and", and by adding a new paragraph (7). **Effective** for remuneration paid after 6-30-78.

• **1977 (P.L. 95-216)**

P.L. 95-216, §317(b)(3):

Amended Code Sec. 6051(a) by adding the last sentence. **Effective** 12-20-77.

• **1976, Tax Reform Act of 1976 (P.L. 94-455)**

P.L. 94-455, §1906(a)(5):

Struck out "and" at the end of paragraph (6). **Effective** for tax years beginning after 12-31-76.

• **1974, Employee Retirement Income Security Act of 1974 (P.L. 93-406)**

P.L. 93-406, §1022(k):

Amended Code Sec. 6051(a) by adding after "exemption," "or every employer engaged in a trade or business who pays remuneration for services performed by an employee, including the cash value of such remuneration paid in any medium other than cash,". **Effective** 9-2-74.

• **1972, Social Security Amendments of 1972 (P.L. 92-603)**

P.L. 92-603, §293(a):

Amended Code Sec. 6051(a) by deleting ", 3201," in the second line thereof, adding "and" at the end of paragraph (5), substituting a period for a comma at the end of paragraph (6), and deleting former paragraphs (7) and (8). **Effective** with respect to remuneration paid after 12-31-71. Prior to amendment, paragraphs (7) and (8) read as follows:

"(7) the total amount of compensation with respect to which the tax imposed by section 3201 was deducted, and

"(8) the total amount deducted as tax under section 3201."

• **1969, Tax Reform Act of 1969 (P.L. 91-172)**

P.L. 91-172, §805(f)(2):

Amended the first sentence of Sec. 6051 by inserting the parenthetical clause. **Effective** with respect to wages paid after 4-30-70.

• **1968, Social Security Amendments of 1967 (P.L. 90-248)**

P.L. 90-248, §502(c)(1):

Amended Sec. 6051(a) by adding ", 3201," in the second line, by deleting "and" at the end of subparagraph (5), by substituting a comma for the period at the end of subparagraph (6), and by adding new subparagraphs (7) and (8). **Effective** in respect of remuneration paid after 12-31-67.

• **1965, Social Security Amendments of 1965 (P.L. 89-97)**

P.L. 89-97, §313(e):

Added the last sentence of Sec. 6051(a). **Effective** with respect to tips received by employees after 1965.

• **1961, Peace Corps Act (P.L. 87-293)**

P.L. 87-293, §202(a)(4):

Amended Sec. 6051(a) by adding the last sentence. **Effective** with respect to services performed after 9-22-61.

• **1956, Servicemen's and Veteran's Survivor Benefits Act (P.L. 881. 84th Cong.)**

P.L. 881, 84th Cong., 2nd Sess., §412(a):

Amended Sec 6051(a) by adding the last sentence. **Effective** 1-1-57.

[Sec. 6051(b)]

(b) SPECIAL RULE AS TO COMPENSATION OF MEMBERS OF ARMED FORCES.—In the case of compensation paid for service as a member of the Armed Forces, the statement required by subsection (a) shall be furnished if any tax was withheld during the calendar year under section 3402, or if any of the compensation paid during such year is includible in gross income under chapter 1, or if during the calendar year any amount was required to be withheld as tax under section 3101. In lieu of the amount required to be shown by paragraph (3) of subsection (a), such statement shall show as wages paid during the calendar year the amount of such compensation paid during the calendar year which is not excluded from gross income under chapter 1 (whether or not such compensation constituted wages as defined in section 3401(a)).

Amendments

• **1956, Servicemen's and Veteran's Survivor Benefits Act (P.L. 881. 84th Cong.)**

P.L. 881, 84th Cong., 2nd Sess., §412(b):

Amended Sec. 6051(b). **Effective** 1-1-57. Prior to amendment, Sec. 6051(b) read as follows:

"(b) Special Rule as to Compensation of Members of Armed Forces.—In the case of compensation paid for service as a member of the Armed Forces, the statement shall show, as wages paid during the calendar year, the amount of such compensation paid during the calendar year which is not excluded from gross income under chapter 1 (whether or not such compensation constituted wages as defined in section 3401(a)); such statement to be furnished if any tax was withheld during the calendar

RETURNS—INFORMATION

year or if any of the compensation paid is includible under chapter 1 in gross income."

[Sec. 6051(c)]

(c) ADDITIONAL REQUIREMENTS.—The statements required to be furnished pursuant to this section in respect of any remuneration shall be furnished at such other times, shall contain such other information, and shall be in such form as the Secretary may by regulations prescribe. The statements required under this section shall also show the proportion of the total amount withheld as tax under section 3101 which is for financing the cost of hospital insurance benefits under part A of title XVIII of the Social Security Act.

Amendments

• **1976, Tax Reform Act of 1976 (P.L. 94-455)**

P.L. 94-455, § 1906(b)(13)(A):

Amended 1954 Code by substituting "Secretary" for "Secretary or his delegate" each place it appeared. **Effective** 2-1-77.

• **1972, Social Security Amendments of 1972 (P.L. 92-603)**

P.L. 92-603, § 293(b):

Amended Code Sec. 6051(c) by substituting "section 3101" for "sections 3101 and 3201". **Effective** with respect to remuneration paid after 12-31-71.

• **1968, Social Security Amendments of 1967 (P.L. 90-248)**

P.L. 90-248, § 502(c)(2):

Amended Sec. 6051(c) by substituting "sections 3101 and 3201" for "section 3101". **Effective** in respect of remuneration paid after 12-31-67.

• **1965, Social Security Amendments of 1965 (P.L. 89-97)**

P.L. 89-97, § 107:

Amended Sec. 6051(c) by adding the last sentence. **Effective** 7-31-65.

[Sec. 6051(d)]

(d) STATEMENTS TO CONSTITUTE INFORMATION RETURNS.—A duplicate of any statement made pursuant to this section and in accordance with regulations prescribed by the Secretary shall, when required by such regulations, be filed with the Secretary.

Amendments

• **1976, Tax Reform Act of 1976 (P.L. 94-455)**

P.L. 94-455, § 1906(b)(13)(A):

Amended 1954 Code by substituting "Secretary" for "Secretary or his delegate" each place it appeared. **Effective** 2-1-77.

[Sec. 6051(e)]

(e) RAILROAD EMPLOYEES.—

(1) ADDITIONAL REQUIREMENT.—Every person required to deduct and withhold tax under section 3201 from an employee shall include on or with the statement required to be furnished such employee under subsection (a) a notice concerning the provisions of this title with respect to the allowance of a credit or refund of the tax on wages imposed by section 3101(b) and the tax on compensation imposed by section 3201 or 3211 which is treated as a tax on wages imposed by section 3101(b).

(2) INFORMATION TO BE SUPPLIED TO EMPLOYEES.—Each person required to deduct and withhold tax under section 3201 during any year from an employee who has also received wages during such year subject to the tax imposed by section 3101(b) shall, upon request of such employee, furnish to him a written statement showing—

(A) the total amount of compensation with respect to which the tax imposed by section 3201 was deducted,

(B) the total amount deducted as tax under section 3201, and

(C) the portion of the total amount deducted as tax under section 3201 which is for financing the cost of hospital insurance under part A of title XVIII of the Social Security Act.

Amendments

• **1972, Social Security Amendments of 1972 (P.L. 92-603)**

P.L. 92-603, § 293(c):

Added Code Sec. 6051(e). **Effective** with respect to remuneration paid after 12-31-71.

[Sec. 6051(f)]

(f) STATEMENTS REQUIRED IN CASE OF SICK PAY PAID BY THIRD PARTIES.—

(1) STATEMENTS REQUIRED FROM PAYOR.—

(A) IN GENERAL.—If, during any calendar year, any person makes a payment of third-party sick pay to an employee, such person shall, on or before January 15 of the succeeding year, furnish a written statement to the employer in respect of whom such payment was made showing—

(i) the name and, if there is withholding under section 3402(o), the social security number of such employee,

(ii) the total amount of the third-party sick pay paid to such employee during the calendar year, and

(iii) the total amount (if any) deducted and withheld from such sick pay under section 3402.

For purposes of the preceding sentence, the term "third-party sick pay" means any sick pay (as defined in section 3402(o)(2)(C)) which does not constitute wages for purposes of chapter 24 (determined without regard to section 3402(o)(1)).

(B) SPECIAL RULES.—

(i) STATEMENTS ARE IN LIEU OF OTHER REPORTING REQUIREMENTS.—The reporting requirements of subparagraph (A) with respect to any payments shall, with respect to such payments, be in lieu of the requirements of subsection (a) and of section 6041.

(ii) PENALTIES MADE APPLICABLE.—For purposes of sections 6674 and 7204, the statements required to be furnished by subparagraph (A) shall be treated as statements required under this section to be furnished to employees.

(2) INFORMATION REQUIRED TO BE FURNISHED BY EMPLOYER.—Every employer who receives a statement under paragraph (1)(A) with respect to sick pay paid to any employee during any calendar year shall, on or before January 31 of the succeeding year, furnish a written statement to such employee showing—

(A) the information shown on the statement furnished under paragraph (1)(A), and

(B) if any portion of the sick pay is excludable from gross income under section 104(a)(3), the portion which is not so excludable and the portion which is so excludable.

To the extent practicable, the information required under the preceding sentence shall be furnished on or with the statement (if any) required under subsection (a).

Amendments

• **1983, Interest and Dividend Tax Compliance Act of 1983 (P.L. 98-67)**

P.L. 98-67, § 102(a):

Repealed the amendment made to Code Sec. 6051(f)(1) by P.L. 97-248 as though such amendment had not been enacted. **Effective** as of the close of 6-30-83.

• **1982, Tax Equity and Fiscal Responsibility Act of 1982 (P.L. 97-248)**

P.L. 97-248, § 307(a)(7):

Amended Code Sec. 6051(f)(1)(A) by inserting "subchapter A of" before "chapter 24". **Effective** 7-1-83.

RETURNS—INFORMATION

- **1980 (P.L. 96-601)**

P.L. 96-601, §4(e):

Amended Code Sec. 6501 by adding a new subsection (f). **Effective** for payments made on or after 5-1-81.

[Sec. 6051(g)]

(g) APPLICABLE EMPLOYER-SPONSORED COVERAGE.—For purposes of subsection (a)(14)—

(1) IN GENERAL.—The term "applicable employer-sponsored coverage" means, with respect to any employee, coverage under any group health plan made available to the employee by an employer which is excludable from the employee's gross income under section 106, or would be so excludable if it were employer-provided coverage (within the meaning of such section 106).

(2) EXCEPTIONS.—The term "applicable employer-sponsored coverage" shall not include—

(A) any coverage (whether through insurance or otherwise) described in section 9832(c)(1) (other than subparagraph (G) thereof) or for long-term care,

(B) any coverage under a separate policy, certificate, or contract of insurance which provides benefits substantially all of which are for treatment of the mouth (including any organ or structure within the mouth) or for treatment of the eye, or

(C) any coverage described in section 9832(c)(3) the payment for which is not excludable from gross income and for which a deduction under section 162(l) is not allowable.

(3) COVERAGE INCLUDES EMPLOYEE PAID PORTION.—Coverage shall be treated as applicable employer-sponsored coverage without regard to whether the employer or employee pays for the coverage.

(4) GOVERNMENTAL PLANS INCLUDED.—Applicable employer-sponsored coverage shall include coverage under any group health plan established and maintained primarily for its civilian employees by the Government of the United States, by the government of any State or political subdivision thereof, or by any agency or instrumentality of any such government.

Amendments

- **2019, Further Consolidated Appropriations Act, 2020 (P.L. 116-94)**

P.L. 116-94, §503(b)(1)(B), Div. N:

Amended Code Sec. 6051 by adding at the end a new subsection (g). **Effective** for tax years beginning after 12-31-2019.

[Sec. 6052]

SEC. 6052. RETURNS REGARDING PAYMENT OF WAGES IN THE FORM OF GROUP-TERM LIFE INSURANCE.

[Sec. 6052(a)]

(a) REQUIREMENT OF REPORTING.—Every employer who during any calendar year provides group-term life insurance on the life of an employee during part or all of such calendar year under a policy (or policies) carried directly or indirectly by such employer shall make a return according to the forms or regulations prescribed by the Secretary, setting forth the cost of such insurance and the name and address of the employee on whose life such insurance is provided, but only to the extent that the cost of such insurance is includible in the employee's gross income under section 79(a). For purposes of this section, the extent to which the cost of group-term life insurance is includible in the employee's gross income under section 79(a) shall be determined as if the employer were the only employer paying such employee remuneration in the form of such insurance.

Amendments

- **1976, Tax Reform Act of 1976 (P.L. 94-455)**

P.L. 94-455, §1906(b)(13)(A):

Amended 1954 Code by substituting "Secretary" for "Secretary or his delegate" each place it appeared. **Effective** 2-1-77.

[Sec. 6052(b)]

(b) STATEMENTS TO BE FURNISHED TO EMPLOYEES WITH RESPECT TO WHOM INFORMATION IS REQUIRED.—Every employer required to make a return under subsection (a) shall furnish to each employee whose name is required to be set forth in such return a written statement showing the cost of the group-term life insurance shown on such return. The written statement required under the preceding sentence shall be furnished to the employee on or before January 31 of the year following the calendar year for which the return under subsection (a) was required to be made.

Amendments

- **1986, Tax Reform Act of 1986 (P.L. 99-514)**

P.L. 99-514, §1501(c)(14):

Amended Code Sec. 6052(b). **Effective** for returns the due date for which (determined without regard to extensions) is after 12-31-86. Prior to amendment, Code Sec. 6052(b) read as follows:

(b) STATEMENTS TO BE FURNISHED TO EMPLOYEES WITH RESPECT TO WHOM INFORMATION IS FURNISHED.—Every employer making a return under subsection (a) shall furnish to each employee whose name is set forth in such return a written statement showing the cost of the group-term life insurance shown on such return. The written statement required under the preceding sentence shall be furnished to the employee on or before January 31 of the year following the calendar year to which the return under subsection (a) was made.

- **1964, Revenue Act of 1964 (P.L. 88-272)**

P.L. 88-272, §204(c)(1):

Added Code Sec. 6052. **Effective** with respect to group-term life insurance provided after 12-31-63, in tax years ending after such date.

[Sec. 6053]

SEC. 6053. REPORTING OF TIPS.

[Sec. 6053(a)]

(a) REPORTS BY EMPLOYEES.—Every employee who, in the course of his employment by an employer, receives in any calendar month tips which are wages (as defined in section 3121(a) or section 3401(a)) or which are compensation (as defined in section 3231(e)) shall report all such tips in one or more written statements furnished to his employer on or before the 10th day following such month. Such statements shall be furnished by the employee under such regulations, at such other times before such 10th day, and in such form and manner, as may be prescribed by the Secretary.

Amendments

- **1976, Tax Reform Act of 1976 (P.L. 94-455)**

P.L. 94-455, §1906(b)(13)(A):

Amended 1954 Code by substituting "Secretary" for "Secretary or his delegate" each place it appeared. **Effective** 2-1-77.

- **1965 (P.L. 89-212)**

P.L. 89-212, §2(d):

Inserted "or which are compensation (as defined in section 3231(e))" immediately after "or section 3401(a))". **Effective** with respect to tips received after 1965.

[Sec. 6053(b)]

(b) STATEMENTS FURNISHED BY EMPLOYERS.—If the tax imposed by section 3101 or section 3201 (as the case may be) with respect to tips reported by an employee pursuant to subsection (a) exceeds the tax which can be collected by the employer pursuant to section 3102 or section 3202 (as the case may be), the employer shall furnish to the employee a written statement showing the amount of such excess. The statement required to be

RETURNS—INFORMATION

furnished pursuant to this subsection shall be furnished at such time, shall contain such other information, and shall be in such form as the Secretary may by regulations prescribe. When required by such regulations, a duplicate of any such statement shall be filed with the Secretary.

Amendments

• **1976, Tax Reform Act of 1976 (P.L. 94-455)**

P.L. 94-455, §1906(b)(13)(A):

Amended 1954 Code by substituting "Secretary" for "Secretary or his delegate" each place it appeared. **Effective** 2-1-77.

• **1965 (P.L. 89-212)**

P.L. 89-212, §2(d):

Amended Code Sec. 6053(b) by inserting "or section 3201 (as the case may be)" immediately after "section 3101" and "or section 3202 (as the case may be)" immediately after "section 3102". **Effective** with respect to tips received after 1965.

• **1965, Social Security Amendments of 1965 (P.L. 89-97)**

P.L. 89-97, §313(e):

Added Code Sec. 6053. **Effective** with respect to tips received by employees after 1965.

[Sec. 6053(c)]

(c) REPORTING REQUIREMENTS RELATING TO CERTAIN LARGE FOOD OR BEVERAGE ESTABLISHMENTS.—

(1) REPORT TO SECRETARY.—In the case of a large food or beverage establishment, each employer shall report to the Secretary, at such time and manner as the Secretary may prescribe by regulation, the following information with respect to each calendar year:

(A) The gross receipts of such establishment from the provision of food and beverages (other than nonallocable receipts).

(B) The aggregate amount of charge receipts (other than nonallocable receipts).

(C) The aggregate amount of charged tips shown on such charge receipts.

(D) The sum of—

(i) the aggregate amount reported by employees to the employer under subsection (a), plus

(ii) the amount the employer is required to report under section 6051 with respect to service charges of less than 10 percent.

(E) With respect to each employee, the amount allocated to such employee under paragraph (3).

(2) FURNISHING OF STATEMENT TO EMPLOYEES.—Each employer described in paragraph (1) shall furnish, in such manner as the Secretary may prescribe by regulations, to each employee of the large food or beverage establishment a written statement for each calendar year showing the following information:

(A) The name and address of such employer.

(B) The name of the employee.

(C) The amount allocated to the employee under paragraph (3) for all payroll periods ending within the calendar year.

Any statement under this paragraph shall be furnished to the employee during January of the calendar year following the calendar year for which such statement is made.

(3) EMPLOYEE ALLOCATION OF 8 PERCENT OF GROSS RECEIPTS.—

(A) IN GENERAL.—For purposes of paragraphs (1)(E) and (2)(C), the employer of a large food or beverage establishment shall allocate (as tips for purposes of the requirements of this subsection) among employees performing services during any payroll period who customarily receive tip income an amount equal to the excess of—

(i) 8 percent of the gross receipts (other than nonallocable receipts) of such establishment for the payroll period, over

(ii) the aggregate amount reported by such employees to the employer under subsection (a) for such period.

(B) METHOD OF ALLOCATION.—The employer shall allocate the amount under subparagraph (A)—

(i) on the basis of a good faith agreement by the employer and the employees, or

(ii) in the absence of an agreement under clause (i), in the manner determined under regulations prescribed by the Secretary.

(C) THE SECRETARY MAY LOWER THE PERCENTAGE REQUIRED TO BE ALLOCATED.—Upon the petition of the employer or the majority of employees of such employer, the Secretary may reduce (but not below 2 percent) the percentage of gross receipts required to be allocated under subparagraph (A) where he determines that the percentage of gross receipts constituting tips is less than 8 percent.

(4) LARGE FOOD OR BEVERAGE ESTABLISHMENT.—For purposes of this subsection, the term "large food or beverage establishment" means any trade or business (or portion thereof)—

(A) which provides food or beverages,

(B) with respect to which the tipping of employees serving food or beverages by customers is customary, and

(C) which normally employed more than 10 employees on a typical business day during the preceding calendar year.

For purposes of subparagraph (C), rules similar to the rules of subsections (a) and (b) of section 52 shall apply under regulations prescribed by the Secretary, and an individual who owns 50 percent or more in value of the stock of the corporation operating the establishment shall not be treated as an employee.

(5) EMPLOYER NOT TO BE LIABLE FOR WRONG ALLOCATIONS.—The employer shall not be liable to any person if any amount is improperly allocated under paragraph (3)(B) if such allocation is done in accordance with the regulations prescribed under paragraph (3)(B).

(6) NONALLOCABLE RECEIPTS DEFINED.—For purposes of this subsection, the term "nonallocable receipts" means receipts which are allocable to—

(A) carryout sales, or

(B) services with respect to which a service charge of 10 percent or more is added.

(7) APPLICATION TO NEW BUSINESSES.—The Secretary shall prescribe regulations for the application of this subsection to new businesses.

(8) CERTIFIED PROFESSIONAL EMPLOYER ORGANIZATIONS.—For purposes of any report required by this subsection, in the case of a certified professional employer organization that is treated under section 3511 as the employer of a work site employee, the customer with respect to whom a work site employee performs services shall be the employer for purposes of reporting under this section and the certified professional employer organization shall furnish to the customer and the Secretary any information the Secretary prescribes as necessary to complete such reporting no later than such time as the Secretary shall prescribe.

Amendments

• **2014, Stephen Beck, Jr., Achieving a Better Life Experience Act of 2014 (P.L. 113-295)**

P.L. 113-295, §206(c)(3), Division B:

Amended Code Sec. 6053(c) by adding at the end a new paragraph (8). **Effective** generally for wages for services performed on or after January 1 of the first calendar year beginning more than 12 months 12-19-2014. For a special rule, see Act Sec. 206(h), below.

P.L. 113-295, §206(h), Division B, provides:

(h) NO INFERENCE.—Nothing contained in this section or the amendments made by this section shall be construed to create any inference with respect to the determination of who is an employee or employer—

(1) for Federal tax purposes (other than the purposes set forth in the amendments made by this section), or

(2) for purposes of any other provision of law.

RETURNS—INFORMATION

- **1998, IRS Restructuring and Reform Act of 1998 (P.L. 105-206)**

P.L. 105-206, § 3414, provides:

SEC. 3414. THREAT OF AUDIT PROHIBITED TO COERCE TIP REPORTING ALTERNATIVE COMMITMENT AGREEMENTS.

The Secretary of the Treasury or the Secretary's delegate shall instruct employees of the Internal Revenue Service that they may not threaten to audit any taxpayer in an attempt to coerce the taxpayer into entering into a Tip Reporting Alternative Commitment Agreement.

- **1986, Tax Reform Act of 1986 (P.L. 99-514)**

P.L. 99-514, § 1571, provides:

SEC. 1571. MODIFICATION OF TIPS ALLOCATION METHOD.

Effective for any payroll period beginning after December 31, 1986, an establishment may utilize the optional method of tips allocation described in the last sentence of section 31.6053-3(f)(1)(iv) of the Internal Revenue Regulations only if such establishment employs less than the equivalent of 25 full-time employees during such payroll period.

- **1984, Deficit Reduction Act of 1984 (P.L. 98-369)**

P.L. 98-369, § 1072(a):

Amended Code Sec. 6053(c)(3)(C) by striking out "The Secretary" and inserting in lieu thereof "Upon the petition of the employer or the majority of employees of such employer, the Secretary", and by striking out "5 percent" and inserting in lieu thereof "2 percent". **Effective** 7-18-84. However, Act Sec. 1072(b) provides that the Secretary of the Treasury shall prescribe by regulations within 1 year after 7-18-84, the applicable recordkeeping requirements for tipped employees.

P.L. 98-369, § 1072(c)(1):

Amended Code Sec. 6053(c)(4) by inserting ", and an individual who owns 50 percent or more in value of the stock of the corporation operating the establishment shall not be treated as an employee" before the period at the end of the last sentence. **Effective** for calendar years beginning after 12-31-82.

- **1982, Tax Equity and Fiscal Responsibility Act of 1982 (P.L. 97-248)**

P.L. 97-248, § 314(a):

Added Code Sec. 6053(c). **Effective** for calendar years beginning after 12-31-82. However, in case of payroll periods ending before 4-1-83, an employer must only report with respect to such periods amounts described in subparagraphs (A), (B), (C), and (D) of Code Sec. 6053(c)(1) and the name, and identification number, wages paid to, and tips reported by, each tipped employee.

P.L. 97-248, § 314(c), provides:

(c) STUDY OF TIP COMPLIANCE.—The Secretary of the Treasury or his delegate shall submit before January 1, 1987, to the Committee on Ways and Means of the House of Representatives and to the Committee on Finance of the Senate a report with respect to tip compliance in the food and beverage service industry. Such study shall include, but not be limited to, an analysis of tipping patterns, tip-sharing arrangements, and tip compliance patterns.

Subpart D—Information Regarding Health Insurance Coverage

Sec. 6055.   Reporting of health insurance coverage.
Sec. 6056.   Large employers required to report on health insurance coverage.

[Sec. 6055]

SEC. 6055. REPORTING OF HEALTH INSURANCE COVERAGE.

[Sec. 6055(a)]

(a) IN GENERAL.—Every person who provides minimum essential coverage to an individual during a calendar year shall, at such time as the Secretary may prescribe, make a return described in subsection (b).

[Sec. 6055(b)]

(b) FORM AND MANNER OF RETURN.—

(1) IN GENERAL.—A return is described in this subsection if such return—

(A) is in such form as the Secretary may prescribe, and

(B) contains—

(i) the name, address and TIN of the primary insured and the name and TIN of each other individual obtaining coverage under the policy,

(ii) the dates during which such individual was covered under minimum essential coverage during the calendar year,

(iii) in the case of minimum essential coverage which consists of health insurance coverage, information concerning—

(I) whether or not the coverage is a qualified health plan offered through an Exchange established under section 1311 of the Patient Protection and Affordable Care Act, and

(II) in the case of a qualified health plan, the amount (if any) of any advance payment under section 1412 of the Patient Protection and Affordable Care Act of any cost-sharing reduction under section 1402 of such Act or of any premium tax credit under section 36B with respect to such coverage, and

(iv) such other information as the Secretary may require.

(2) INFORMATION RELATING TO EMPLOYER-PROVIDED COVERAGE.—If minimum essential coverage provided to an individual under subsection (a) consists of health insurance coverage of a health insurance issuer provided through a group health plan of an employer, a return described in this subsection shall include—

(A) the name, address, and employer identification number of the employer maintaining the plan,

(B) the portion of the premium (if any) required to be paid by the employer, and

(C) if the health insurance coverage is a qualified health plan in the small group market offered through an Exchange, such other information as the Secretary may require for administration of the credit under section 45R (relating to credit for employee health insurance expenses of small employers).

[Sec. 6055(c)]

(c) STATEMENTS TO BE FURNISHED TO INDIVIDUALS WITH RESPECT TO WHOM INFORMATION IS REPORTED.—

(1) IN GENERAL.—Every person required to make a return under subsection (a) shall furnish to each individual whose name is required to be set forth in such return a written statement showing—

(A) the name and address of the person required to make such return and the phone number of the information contact for such person, and

(B) the information required to be shown on the return with respect to such individual.

(2) TIME FOR FURNISHING STATEMENTS.—The written statement required under paragraph (1) shall be furnished on or before January 31 of the year following the calendar year for which the return under subsection (a) was required to be made.

[Sec. 6055(d)]

(d) COVERAGE PROVIDED BY GOVERNMENTAL UNITS.—In the case of coverage provided by any governmental unit or any agency or instrumentality thereof, the officer or employee who enters into the agreement to provide such coverage (or the person appropriately designated for purposes of this section) shall make the returns and statements required by this section.

[Sec. 6055(e)]

(e) MINIMUM ESSENTIAL COVERAGE.—For purposes of this section, the term "minimum essential coverage" has the meaning given such term by section 5000A(f).

RETURNS—INFORMATION

Amendments
• **2010, Patient Protection and Affordable Care Act (P.L. 111-148)**

P.L. 111-148, § 1502(a):

Amended part III of subchapter A of chapter 61 by inserting after subpart C a new subpart D (Code Sec. 6055). **Effective** for calendar years beginning after 2013.

[Sec. 6056]

SEC. 6056. CERTAIN EMPLOYERS REQUIRED TO REPORT ON HEALTH INSURANCE COVERAGE.

[Sec. 6056(a)]

(a) IN GENERAL.—Every applicable large employer required to meet the requirements of section 4980H with respect to its full-time employees during a calendar year shall, at such time as the Secretary may prescribe, make a return described in subsection (b).

Amendments
• **2011, Department of Defense and Full-Year Continuing Appropriations Act, 2011 (P.L. 112-10)**

P.L. 112-10, § 1858(b)(5)(A):

Amended Code Sec. 6056(a) by striking "and every offering employer" before "shall". **Effective** as if included in the provision of, and the amendments made by, the provision of the Patient Protection and Affordable Care Act (P.L. 111-148) to which it relates [**effective** for periods beginning after 12-31-2013.—CCH].

• **2010, Patient Protection and Affordable Care Act (P.L. 111-148)**

P.L. 111-148, § 10108(j)(1):

Amended Code Sec. 6056(a), as added by Act Sec. 1514, by inserting "and every offering employer" before "shall". **Effective** for periods beginning after 12-31-2013.

P.L. 111-148, § 10108(j)(3)(A):

Amended the heading of Code Sec. 6056, as added by Act Sec. 1514, by striking "**LARGE**" and inserting "**CERTAIN**". **Effective** for periods beginning after 12-31-2013.

[Sec. 6056(b)]

(b) FORM AND MANNER OF RETURN.—A return is described in this subsection if such return—

(1) is in such form as the Secretary may prescribe, and

(2) contains—

(A) the name, date, and employer identification number of the employer,

(B) a certification as to whether the employer offers to its full-time employees (and their dependents) the opportunity to enroll in minimum essential coverage under an eligible employer-sponsored plan (as defined in section 5000A(f)(2)),

(C) if the employer certifies that the employer did offer to its full-time employees (and their dependents) the opportunity to so enroll—

(i) the length of any waiting period (as defined in section 2701(b)(4) of the Public Health Service Act) with respect to such coverage,

(ii) the months during the calendar year for which coverage under the plan was available,

(iii) the monthly premium for the lowest cost option in each of the enrollment categories under the plan, and

(iv) the employer's share of the total allowed costs of benefits provided under the plan,

(D) the number of full-time employees for each month during the calendar year,

(E) the name, address, and TIN of each full-time employee during the calendar year and the months (if any) during which such employee (and any dependents) were covered under any such health benefits plans, and

(F) such other information as the Secretary may require.

The Secretary shall have the authority to review the accuracy of the information provided under this subsection, including the applicable large employer's share under paragraph (2)(C)(iv).

Amendments
• **2011, Department of Defense and Full-Year Continuing Appropriations Act, 2011 (P.L. 112-10)**

P.L. 112-10, § 1858(b)(5)(B)(i)-(iv):

Amended Code Sec. 6056(b)(2)(C) by striking "in the case of an applicable large employer," before "the length" in clause (i), by inserting "and" at the end of clause (iii), by striking "and" at the end of clause (iv), and by striking clause (v). **Effective** as if included in the provision of, and the amendments made by, the provision of the Patient Protection and Affordable Care Act (P.L. 111-148) to which it relates [**effective** for periods beginning after 12-31-2013.—CCH]. Prior to being stricken, Code Sec. 6056(b)(2)(C)(v) read as follows:

(v) in the case of an offering employer, the option for which the employer pays the largest portion of the cost of the plan and the portion of the cost paid by the employer in each of the enrollment categories under such option,

• **2010, Patient Protection and Affordable Care Act (P.L. 111-148)**

P.L. 111-148, § 10106(g):

Amended Code Sec. 6056(b), as added by Act Sec. 1514(a), by adding at the end a new flush sentence. **Effective** 3-23-2010.

P.L. 111-148, § 10108(j)(3)(B)(i)-(v):

Amended Code Sec. 6056(b)(2)(C) by inserting "in the case of an applicable large employer," before "the length" in clause (i); by striking "and" at the end of clause (iii); by striking "applicable large employer" in clause (iv) and inserting "employer"; by inserting "and" at the end of clause (iv); and by inserting at the end a new clause (v). **Effective** for periods beginning after 12-31-2013.

[Sec. 6056(c)]

(c) STATEMENTS TO BE FURNISHED TO INDIVIDUALS WITH RESPECT TO WHOM INFORMATION IS REPORTED.—

(1) IN GENERAL.—Every person required to make a return under subsection (a) shall furnish to each full-time employee whose name is required to be set forth in such return under subsection (b)(2)(E) a written statement showing—

(A) the name and address of the person required to make such return and the phone number of the information contact for such person, and

(B) the information required to be shown on the return with respect to such individual.

(2) TIME FOR FURNISHING STATEMENTS.—The written statement required under paragraph (1) shall be furnished on or before January 31 of the year following the calendar year for which the return under subsection (a) was required to be made.

[Sec. 6056(d)]

(d) COORDINATION WITH OTHER REQUIREMENTS.—To the maximum extent feasible, the Secretary may provide that—

(1) any return or statement required to be provided under this section may be provided as part of any return or statement required under section 6051 or 6055, and

(2) in the case of an applicable large employer offering health insurance coverage of a health insurance issuer, the employer may enter into an agreement with the issuer to include information required under this section with the return and statement required to be provided by the issuer under section 6055.

RETURNS—INFORMATION

Amendments

• **2011, Department of Defense and Full-Year Continuing Appropriations Act, 2011 (P.L. 112-10)**

P.L. 112-10, § 1858(b)(5)(C):

Amended Code Sec. 6056(d)(2) by striking "or offering employer" after "applicable large employer". **Effective** as if included in the provision of, and the amendments made by, the provision of the Patient Protection and Affordable Care Act (P.L. 111-148) to which it relates [**effective** for periods beginning after 12-31-2013.—CCH].

• **2010, Patient Protection and Affordable Care Act (P.L. 111-148)**

P.L. 111-148, § 10108(j)(3)(C):

Amended Code Sec. 6056(d)(2) by inserting "or offering employer" after "applicable large employer". **Effective** for periods beginning after 12-31-2013.

[Sec. 6056(e)]

(e) COVERAGE PROVIDED BY GOVERNMENTAL UNITS.—In the case of any applicable large employer which is a governmental unit or any agency or instrumentality thereof, the person appropriately designated for purposes of this section shall make the returns and statements required by this section.

Amendments

• **2011, Department of Defense and Full-Year Continuing Appropriations Act, 2011 (P.L. 112-10)**

P.L. 112-10, § 1858(b)(5)(C):

Amended Code Sec. 6056(e) by striking "or offering employer" after "applicable large employer". **Effective** as if included in the provision of, and the amendments made by, the provision of the Patient Protection and Affordable Care Act (P.L. 111-148) to which it relates [**effective** for periods beginning after 12-31-2013.—CCH].

• **2010, Patient Protection and Affordable Care Act (P.L. 111-148)**

P.L. 111-148, § 10108(j)(3)(D):

Amended Code Sec. 6056(e) by inserting "or offering employer" after "applicable large employer". **Effective** for periods beginning after 12-31-2013.

[Sec. 6056(f)]

(f) DEFINITIONS.—For purposes of this section, any term used in this section which is also used in section 4980H shall have the meaning given such term by section 4980H.

Amendments

• **2011, Department of Defense and Full-Year Continuing Appropriations Act, 2011 (P.L. 112-10)**

P.L. 112-10, § 1858(b)(5)(D):

Amended Code Sec. 6056(f). **Effective** as if included in the provision of, and the amendments made by, the provision of the Patient Protection and Affordable Care Act (P.L. 111-148) to which it relates [**effective** for periods beginning after 12-31-2013.—CCH]. Prior to amendment, Code Sec. 6056(f) read as follows:

(f) DEFINITIONS.—For purposes of this section—

(1) OFFERING EMPLOYER.—

(A) IN GENERAL.—The term "offering employer" means any offering employer (as defined in section 10108(b) of the Patient Protection and Affordable Care Act) if the required contribution (within the meaning of section 5000A(e)(1)(B)(i)) of any employee exceeds 8 percent of the wages (as defined in section 3121(a)) paid to such employee by such employer.

(B) INDEXING.—In the case of any calendar year beginning after 2014, the 8 percent under subparagraph (A) shall be adjusted for the calendar year to reflect the rate of premium growth between the preceding calendar year and 2013 over the rate of income growth for such period.

(2) OTHER DEFINITIONS.—Any term used in this section which is also used in section 4980H shall have the meaning given such term by section 4980H.

• **2010, Patient Protection and Affordable Care Act (P.L. 111-148)**

P.L. 111-148, § 1514(a):

Amended subpart D of part III of subchapter A of chapter 61, as added by Act Sec. 1502, by inserting after Code Sec. 6055 a new Code Sec. 6056. **Effective** for periods beginning after 12-31-2013.

P.L. 111-148, § 10108(j)(2):

Amended Code Sec. 6056(f), as added by Act Sec. 1514. **Effective** for periods beginning after 12-31-2013. Prior to amendment, Code Sec. 6056(f) read as follows:

(f) DEFINITIONS.—For purposes of this section, any term used in this section which is also used in section 4980H shall have the meaning given such term by section 4980H.

[Sec. 6056—Repealed]

Amendments

• **1980 (P.L. 96-603)**

P.L. 96-603, § 1(d):

Repealed subpart D of part III of subchapter A of chapter 61 of the Internal Revenue Code. **Effective** for tax years beginning after 1980. Prior to its repeal, Code Sec. 6056 read as follows:

"SEC. 6056. ANNUAL REPORTS BY PRIVATE FOUNDATIONS.

(a) GENERAL.—The foundation managers (within the meaning of section 4946(b)) of every organization which is a private foundation (within the meaning of section 509(a)) having at least $5,000 of assets at any time during a taxable year shall file an annual report as of the close of the taxable year at such time and in such manner as the Secretary may by regulations prescribe.

(b) CONTENTS.—The foundation managers of the private foundation shall set forth in the annual report required under subsection (a) the following information:

(1) its gross income for the year,

(2) its expenses attributable to such income and incurred within the year,

(3) its disbursements (including administrative expenses) within the year,

(4) a balance sheet showing its assets, liabilities, and net worth as of the beginning of the year,

(5) an itemized statement of its securities and all other assets at the close of the year, showing both book and market value,

(6) the total of the contributions and gifts received by it during the year,

(7) an itemized list of all grants and contributions made or approved for future payment during the year, showing the amount of each such grant or contribution, the name and address of the recipient, any relationship between any individual recipient and the foundation's managers or substantial contributors, and a concise statement of the purpose of each such grant or contribution,

(8) the address of the principal office of the foundation and (if different) of the place where its books and records are maintained,

(9) the names and addresses of its foundation managers (within the meaning of section 4946(b)), and

(10) a list of all persons described in paragraph (9) that are substantial contributors (within the meaning of section 507(d)(2)) or that own 10 percent or more of the stock of any corporation of which the foundation owns 10 percent or more of the stock, or corresponding interests in partnerships or other entities, in which the foundation has a 10 percent or greater interest.

(c) FORM.—The annual report may be prepared in printed, typewritten, or any other legible form the foundation chooses. The Secretary shall provide forms which may be used by a private foundation for purposes of the annual report.

(d) SPECIAL RULES.—

(1) The annual report required to be filed under this section is in addition to and not in lieu of the information required to be filed under section 6033 (relating to returns by exempt organizations) and shall be filed at the same time as such information.

(2) A copy of the notice required by section 6104(d) (relating to public inspection of private foundations' annual reports), together with proof of publication thereof, shall be filed by the foundation managers together with the annual report.

(3) The foundation managers shall furnish copies of the annual report required by this section to such State officials and other persons, at such times and under such conditions, as the Secretary may by regulations prescribe."

• **1976, Tax Reform Act of 1976 (P.L. 94-455)**

P.L. 94-455, § 1906(b)(13)(A):

Amended 1954 Code by substituting "Secretary" for "Secretary or his delegate" each place it appeared. **Effective** 2-1-77.

• **1969, Tax Reform Act of 1969 (P.L. 91-172)**

P.L. 91-172, § 101(d)(3):

Added Code Sec. 6056. **Effective** for tax years beginning after 12-31-69.

Subpart E—Registration of and Information Concerning Pension, Etc., Plans

Sec. 6057.	Annual registration, etc.
Sec. 6058.	Information required in connection with certain plans of deferred compensation.
Sec. 6059.	Periodic report of actuary.

RETURNS—INFORMATION

[Sec. 6057]

SEC. 6057. ANNUAL REGISTRATION, ETC.

[Sec. 6057(a)]

(a) ANNUAL REGISTRATION.—

(1) GENERAL RULE.—Within such period after the end of a plan year as the Secretary may by regulations prescribe, the plan administrator (within the meaning of section 414(g)) of each plan to which the vesting standards of section 203 of part 2 of subtitle B of title I of the Employee Retirement Income Security Act of 1974 applies for such plan year shall file a registration statement with the Secretary.

(2) CONTENTS.—The registration statement required by paragraph (1) shall set forth—

(A) the name of the plan,

(B) the name and address of the plan administrator,

(C) the name and taxpayer identifying number of each participant in the plan—

(i) who, during such plan year, separated from the service covered by the plan,

(ii) who is entitled to a deferred vested benefit under the plan as of the end of such plan year, and

(iii) with respect to whom retirement benefits were not paid under the plan during such plan year,

(D) the nature, amount, and form of the deferred vested benefit to which such participant is entitled, and

(E) such other information as the Secretary may require.

At the time he files the registration statement under this subsection, the plan administrator shall furnish evidence satisfactory to the Secretary that he has complied with the requirement contained in subsection (e).

Amendments

• **1976, Tax Reform Act of 1976 (P.L. 94-455)**

P.L. 94-455, § 1906(b)(13)(A):

Amended 1954 Code by substituting "Secretary" for "Secretary or his delegate" each place it appeared. **Effective** 2-1-77.

[Sec. 6057(b)]

(b) NOTIFICATION OF CHANGE IN STATUS.—Any plan administrator required to register under subsection (a) shall also notify the Secretary, at such time as may be prescribed by regulations, of—

(1) any change in the name of the plan,

(2) any change in the name or address of the plan administrator,

(3) the termination of the plan, or

(4) the merger or consolidation of the plan with any other plan or its division into two or more plans.

Amendments

• **1976, Tax Reform Act of 1976 (P.L. 94-455)**

P.L. 94-455, § 1906(b)(13)(A):

Amended 1954 Code by substituting "Secretary" for "Secretary or his delegate" each place it appeared. **Effective** 2-1-77.

[Sec. 6057(c)]

(c) VOLUNTARY REPORTS.—To the extent provided in regulations prescribed by the Secretary, the Secretary may receive from—

(1) any plan to which subsection (a) applies, and

(2) any other plan (including any governmental plan or church plan (within the meaning of section 414)),

such information (including information relating to plan years beginning before January 1, 1974) as the plan administrator may wish to file with respect to the deferred vested benefit rights of any participant separated from the service covered by the plan during any plan year.

Amendments

• **1976, Tax Reform Act of 1976 (P.L. 94-455)**

P.L. 94-455, § 1906(b)(13)(A):

Amended 1954 Code by substituting "Secretary" for "Secretary or his delegate" each place it appeared. **Effective** 2-1-77.

[Sec. 6057(d)]

(d) TRANSMISSION OF INFORMATION TO COMMISSIONER OF SOCIAL SECURITY.—The Secretary shall transmit copies of any statements, notifications, reports, or other information obtained by him under this section to the Commissioner of Social Security.

Amendments

• **1994, Social Security Independence and Program Improvements Act of 1994 (P.L. 103-296)**

P.L. 103-296, § 108(h)(5):

Amended Code Sec. 6057(d) by striking "Secretary of Health and Human Services" each place it appears and inserting "Commissioner of Social Security". **Effective** 3-31-95.

• **1984, Deficit Reduction Act of 1984 (P.L. 98-369)**

P.L. 98-369, § 2663(j)(5)(D):

Amended Code Sec. 6057(d) by striking out "Health, Education, and Welfare" each place it appeared and inserting in lieu thereof "Health and Human Services". Effective 7-18-84, but does not change or affect any right, liability, status, or interpretation which existed (under the provisions of law involved) before that date.

• **1976, Tax Reform Act of 1976 (P.L. 94-455)**

P.L. 94-455, § 1906(b)(13)(A):

Amended 1954 Code by substituting "Secretary" for "Secretary or his delegate" each place it appeared. **Effective** 2-1-77.

[Sec. 6057(e)]

(e) INDIVIDUAL STATEMENT TO PARTICIPANT.—Each plan administrator required to file a registration statement under subsection (a) shall, before the expiration of the time prescribed for the filing of such registration statement, also furnish to each participant described in subsection (a)(2)(C) an individual statement setting forth the information with respect to such participant required to be contained in such registration statement. Such statement shall also include a notice to the participant of any benefits which are forfeitable if the participant dies before a certain date.

RETURNS—INFORMATION

Amendments

- **1984, Retirement Equity Act of 1984 (P.L. 98-397)**

P.L. 98-397, §206:

Amended Code Sec. 6057(e) by adding the sentence at the end thereof. **Effective** for plan years beginning after 12-31-84. Special rules appear in the notes for P.L. 98-397, following Code Sec. 401(a).

[Sec. 6057(f)]

(f) REGULATIONS.—

(1) IN GENERAL.—The Secretary, after consultation with the Commissioner of Social Security, may prescribe such regulations as may be necessary to carry out the provisions of this section.

(2) PLANS TO WHICH MORE THAN ONE EMPLOYER CONTRIBUTES.—This section shall apply to any plan to which more than one employer is required to contribute only to the extent provided in regulations prescribed under this subsection.

Amendments

- **1994, Social Security Independence and Program Improvements Act of 1994 (P.L. 103-296)**

P.L. 103-296, §108(h)(5):

Amended Code Sec. 6057(f) by striking "Secretary of Health and Human Services" each place it appears and inserting "Commissioner of Social Security". **Effective** 3-31-95.

- **1984, Deficit Reduction Act of 1984 (P.L. 98-369)**

P.L. 98-369, §2663(j)(5)(D)

Amended Code Sec. 6057(f) by striking out "Health, Education, and Welfare" and inserting in lieu thereof "Health and Human Services". **Effective** 7-18-84, but does not change or affect any right, liability, status, or interpretation which existed (under the provisions of law involved) before that date.

[Sec. 6057(g)]

(g) 403(b) MULTIPLE EMPLOYER PLANS TREATED AS ONE PLAN.—In the case of annuity contracts to which this section applies and to which section 403(b) applies by reason of the plan under which such contracts are purchased meeting the requirements of paragraph (15) thereof, such plan shall be treated as a single plan for purposes of this section.

Amendments

- **2022, SECURE 2.0 Act of 2022 (P.L. 117-328)**

P.L. 117-328, §106(b):

Amended Code Sec. 6057 by redesignating subsection (g) as subsection (h) and by inserting after subsection (f) a new subsection (g). **Effective** for plan years beginning after 12-31-2022.

[Sec. 6057(h)]

(h) CROSS REFERENCES.—

For provisions relating to penalties for failure to register or furnish statements required by this section, see section 6652(d) and section 6690.

For coordination between Department of the Treasury and the Department of Labor with regard to administration of this section, see section 3004 of the Employee Retirement Income Security Act of 1974.

Amendments

- **2022, SECURE 2.0 Act of 2022 (P.L. 117-328)**

P.L. 117-328, §106(b):

Amended Code Sec. 6057 by redesignating subsection (g) as subsection (h). **Effective** for plan years beginning after 12-31-2022.

- **1986, Tax Reform Act of 1986 (P.L. 99-514)**

P.L. 99-514, §1501(d)(1)(F):

Amended Code Sec. 6057(g) by striking out "section 6652(e)" and inserting in lieu thereof "section 6652(d)". **Effective** for returns the due date for which (determined without regard to extensions) is after 12-31-86.

- **1974, Employee Retirement Income Security Act of 1974 (P.L. 93-406)**

P.L. 93-406, §1031(a):

Added Code Sec. 6057. **Effective** for plan years beginning after 12-31-75.

[Sec. 6058]

SEC. 6058. INFORMATION REQUIRED IN CONNECTION WITH CERTAIN PLANS OF DEFERRED COMPENSATION.

[Sec. 6058(a)]

(a) IN GENERAL.—Every employer who maintains a pension, annuity, stock bonus, profit-sharing, or other funded plan of deferred compensation described in part I of subchapter D of chapter 1, or the plan administrator (within the meaning of section 414(g)) of the plan, shall file an annual return stating such information as the Secretary may by regulations prescribe with respect to the qualification, financial condition, and operations of the plan; except that, in the discretion of the Secretary, the employer may be relieved from stating in its return any information which is reported in other returns.

Amendments

- **2022, SECURE 2.0 Act of 2022 (P.L. 117-328)**

P.L. 117-328, §103(c)(2), provides:

(2) REPORTING.—The Secretary of the Treasury shall amend the forms relating to reports required under section 6058 of the Internal Revenue Code of 1986 to require—

(A) separate reporting of the aggregate amount of contributions received by the plan during the year under section 6433 of the Internal Revenue Code of 1986 (as added by this section), and

(B) similar reporting with respect to individual retirement accounts (as defined in section 408 of such Code) and individual retirement annuities (as defined in section 408(b) of such Code).

- **2019, Setting Every Community Up for Retirement Enhancement Act of 2019 (P.L. 116-94)**

P.L. 116-94, §202(a)-(c), (e), Div. O, (as amended by P.L. 117-328, §345(a)(1)-(3)), provides:

SEC. 202. COMBINED ANNUAL REPORT FOR GROUP OF PLANS.

(a) IN GENERAL.—The Secretary of the Treasury and the Secretary of Labor shall, in cooperation, modify the returns required under section 6058 of the Internal Revenue Code of 1986 and the reports required by section 104 of the Employee Retirement Income Security Act of 1974 (29 U.S.C. 1024) so that—

(1) all members of a group of plans described in subsection (c) may file a single aggregated annual return or report satisfying the requirements of both such sections; and

(2) any opinions required by section 103(a)(3) of the Employee Retirement Income Security Act of 1974 (29 U.S.C. 1023(a)(3)) shall relate only to each individual plan which would otherwise be subject to the requirements of such section 103(a)(3).

(b) ADMINISTRATIVE REQUIREMENTS.—In developing the consolidated return or report under subsection (a), the Secretary of the Treasury and the Secretary of Labor may require such return or report to include any information regarding each plan in the group as such Secretaries determine is necessary or appropriate for the enforcement and administration of the Internal Revenue Code of 1986 and the Employee Retirement Income Security Act of 1974 and shall require such information as will enable a participant in a plan to identify any aggregated return or report filed with respect to the plan.

(c) PLANS DESCRIBED.—A group of plans is described in this subsection if all plans in the group—

(1) are individual account plans or defined contribution plans (as defined in section 3(34) of the Employee Retirement Income Security Act of 1974 (29 U.S.C. 1002(34)) or in section 414(i) of the Internal Revenue Code of 1986);

(2) have—

(A) the same trustee (as described in section 403(a) of such Act (29 U.S.C. 1103(a)));

(B) the same one or more named fiduciaries (as described in section 402(a) of such Act (29 U.S.C. 1102(a)));

(C) the same administrator (as defined in section 3(16)(A) of such Act (29 U.S.C. 1002(16)(A))) and plan administrator (as defined in section 414(g) of the Internal Revenue Code of 1986); and

(D) plan years beginning on the same date; and

(3) provide the same investments or investment options to participants and beneficiaries.

A plan not subject to title I of the Employee Retirement Income Security Act of 1974 shall be treated as meeting the requirements of paragraph (2) as part of a group of plans if the same person that performs each of the functions described in such paragraph, as applicable, for all other plans in such group performs each of such functions for such plan.

* * *

(e) EFFECTIVE DATE.—The modification required by subsection (a) shall be implemented not later than January 1, 2022, and shall apply to returns and reports for plan years beginning after December 31, 2021.

• **1976, Tax Reform Act of 1976 (P.L. 94-455)**

P.L. 94-455, §1906(b)(13)(A):

Amended 1954 Code by substituting "Secretary" for "Secretary or his delegate" each place it appeared. **Effective** 2-1-77.

[Sec. 6058(b)]

(b) ACTUARIAL STATEMENT IN CASE OF MERGERS, ETC.—Not less than 30 days before a merger, consolidation, or transfer of assets or liabilities of a plan described in subsection (a) to another plan, the plan administrator (within the meaning of section 414(g)) shall file an actuarial statement of valuation evidencing compliance with the requirements of section 401(a)(12).

[Sec. 6058(c)]

(c) EMPLOYER.—For purposes of this section, the term "employer" includes a person described in section 401(c)(4) and an individual who establishes an individual retirement plan.

Amendments

• **1978, Revenue Act of 1978 (P.L. 95-600)**

P.L. 95-600, §157(k):

Amended Code Sec. 6058(c). **Effective** for returns for tax years beginning after 12-31-77. Prior to amendment, Code Sec. 6058(c) read as follows:

"(c) EMPLOYER.—For purposes of this section, the term `employer' includes a person described in section 401(c)(4) and an individual who establishes an individual retirement account or annuity described in section 408."

[Sec. 6058(d)]

(d) COORDINATION WITH INCOME TAX RETURNS, ETC.—An individual who establishes an individual retirement plan shall not be required to file a return under this section with respect to such plan for any taxable year for which there is—

(1) no special IRP tax, and

(2) no plan activity other than—

(A) the making of contributions (other than rollover contributions), and

(B) the making of distributions.

Amendments

• **1978, Revenue Act of 1978 (P.L. 95-600)**

P.L. 95-600, §157(k):

Redesignated Code Sec. 6058(d) as 6058(f) and added a new Code Sec. 6058(d). **Effective** for returns for tax years beginning after 12-31-77.

[Sec. 6058(e)]

(e) SPECIAL IRP TAX DEFINED.—For purposes of this section, the term "special IRP tax" means a tax imposed by—

(1) section 4973, or

(2) section 4974.

Amendments

• **2018, Tax Technical Corrections Act of 2018 (P.L. 115-141)**

P.L. 115-141, §401(a)(264), Div. U:

Amended Code Sec. 6058(e) by striking paragraph (1) and by redesignating paragraphs (2) and (3) as paragraphs (1) and (2), respectively. **Effective** 3-23-2018. Prior to being stricken, Code Sec. 6058(e)(1) read as follows:

(1) section 408(f),

• **1984, Deficit Reduction Act of 1984 (P.L. 98-369)**

P.L. 98-369, §491(d)(48):

Amended Code Sec. 6058(e) by striking out paragraph (2) and by redesignating paragraphs (3) and (4) as paragraphs (2) and (3), respectively. **Effective** for obligations issued after 12-31-83. Prior to amendment, paragraph (2) read as follows:

(2) section 409(c),

• **1978, Revenue Act of 1978 (P.L. 95-600)**

P.L. 95-600, §157(k):

Added a new Code Sec. 6058(e). **Effective** for returns for tax years beginning after 12-31-77.

[Sec. 6058(f)]

(f) 403(b) MULTIPLE EMPLOYER PLANS TREATED AS ONE PLAN.—In the case of annuity contracts to which this section applies and to which section 403(b) applies by reason of the plan under which such contracts are purchased meeting the requirements of paragraph (15) thereof, such plan shall be treated as a single plan for purposes of this section.

Amendments

• **2022, SECURE 2.0 Act of 2022 (P.L. 117-328)**

P.L. 117-328, §106(c):

Amended Code Sec. 6058 by redesignating subsection (f) as subsection (g) and by inserting after subsection (e) a new subsection (f). **Effective** for plan years beginning after 12-31-2022.

[Sec. 6058(g)]

(g) CROSS REFERENCES.—

For provisions relating to penalties for failure to file a return required by this section, see section 6652(e).

For coordination between the Department of the Treasury and the Department of Labor with respect to the information required under this section, see section 3004 of title III of the Employee Retirement Income Security Act of 1974.

Amendments

• **2022, SECURE 2.0 Act of 2022 (P.L. 117-328)**

P.L. 117-328, §106(c):

Amended Code Sec. 6058 by redesignating subsection (f) as subsection (g). **Effective** for plan years beginning after 12-31-2022.

• **1986, Tax Reform Act of 1986 (P.L. 99-514)**

P.L. 99-514, §1501(d)(1)(D):

Amended Code Sec. 6058(f) by striking out "section 6652(f)" and inserting in lieu thereof "section 6652(e)". **Effective** for returns the due date for which (determined without regard to extensions) is after 12-31-86.

• **1978, Revenue Act of 1978 (P.L. 95-600)**

P.L. 95-600, §157(k):

Redesignated Code Sec. 6058(d) as 6058(f). **Effective** 11-7-78.

• **1974, Employee Retirement Income Security Act of 1974 (P.L. 93-406)**

P.L. 93-406, §1031(a):

Added Code Sec. 6058. **Effective** 9-2-74.

RETURNS—TAX RETURN PREPARERS

[Sec. 6059]

SEC. 6059. PERIODIC REPORT OF ACTUARY.

[Sec. 6059(a)]

(a) GENERAL RULE.—The actuarial report described in subsection (b) shall be filed by the plan administrator (as defined in section 414(g)) of each defined benefit plan to which section 412 applies, for the first plan year for which section 412 applies to the plan and for each third plan year thereafter (or more frequently if the Secretary determines that more frequent reports are necessary).

Amendments

• **1976, Tax Reform Act of 1976 (P.L. 94-455)**

P.L. 94-455, §1906(b)(13)(A):

Amended 1954 Code by substituting "Secretary" for "Secretary or his delegate" each place it appeared. **Effective** 2-1-77.

[Sec. 6059(b)]

(b) ACTUARIAL REPORT.—The actuarial report of a plan required by subsection (a) shall be prepared and signed by an enrolled actuary (within the meaning of section 7701(a)(35)) and shall contain—

(1) a description of the funding method and actuarial assumptions used to determine costs under the plan,

(2) a certification of the contribution necessary to reduce the minimum required contribution determined under section 430, the accumulated funding deficiency under section 433, or the accumulated funding deficiency determined under section 431, to zero,

(3) a statement—

(A) that to the best of his knowledge the report is complete and accurate, and

(B) that the requirements for reasonable actuarial assumptions under section 430(h)(1), 431(c)(3), or 433(c)(3), whichever are applicable, have been complied with,

(4) such other information as may be necessary to fully and fairly disclose the actuarial position of the plan, and

(5) such other information regarding the plan as the Secretary may by regulations require.

Amendments

• **2018, Tax Technical Corrections Act of 2018 (P.L. 115-141)**

P.L. 115-141, §401(a)(265)(A)-(B), Div. U:

Amended Code Sec. 6059(b)(3)(B) by striking "the requirements" and inserting "that the requirements", and by striking the period at the end and inserting a comma. **Effective** 3-23-2018.

• **2014, Cooperative and Small Employer Charity Pension Flexibility Act (P.L. 113-97)**

P.L. 113-97, §202(c)(10)(A):

Amended Code Sec. 6059(b)(2) by striking "430," and inserting "430, the accumulated funding deficiency under section 433,". **Effective** for years beginning after 12-31-2013.

P.L. 113-97, §202(c)(10)(B):

Amended Code Sec. 6059(b)(3)(B) by striking "430(h)(1) or 431(c)(3)" and inserting "430(h)(1), 431(c)(3), or 433(c)(3)". **Effective** for years beginning after 12-31-2013.

• **2006, Pension Protection Act of 2006 (P.L. 109-280)**

P.L. 109-280, §114(f)(1)-(2):

Amended Code Sec. 6059(b) by striking "the accumulated funding deficiency (as defined in section 412(a))" in paragraph (2) and inserting "the minimum required contribution determined under section 430, or the accumulated funding deficiency determined under section 431,", and by striking paragraph (3)(B) and inserting a new paragraph (3)(B). **Effective** for plan years beginning after 2007 [**effective** date amended by P.L. 110-458, §101(d)(3).—CCH]. Prior to being stricken, Code Sec. 6059(b)(3)(B) read as follows:

(B) the requirements of section 412(c) (relating to reasonable actuarial assumptions) have been complied with,

• **1976, Tax Reform Act of 1976 (P.L. 94-455)**

P.L. 94-455, §1906(b)(13)(A):

Amended 1954 Code by substituting "Secretary" for "Secretary or his delegate" each place it appeared. **Effective** 2-1-77.

[Sec. 6059(c)]

(c) TIME AND MANNER OF FILING.—The actuarial report and statement required by this section shall be filed at the time and in the manner provided by regulations prescribed by the Secretary.

Amendments

• **1976, Tax Reform Act of 1976 (P.L. 94-455)**

P.L. 94-455, §1906(b)(13)(A):

Amended 1954 Code by substituting "Secretary" for "Secretary or his delegate" each place it appeared. **Effective** 2-1-77.

[Sec. 6059(d)]

(d) CROSS REFERENCE.—

For coordination between the Department of the Treasury and the Department of Labor with respect to the report required to be filed under this section, see section 3004 of title III of the Employee Retirement Income Security Act of 1974.

Amendments

• **1974, Employee Retirement Income Security Act of 1974 (P.L. 93-406)**

P.L. 93-406, §1033(a):

Added Code Sec. 6059. For **effective** date, see amendment note for Code Sec. 410.

Subpart F—Information Concerning Tax Return Preparers

Sec. 6060.   Information returns of tax return preparers.

[Sec. 6060]

SEC. 6060. INFORMATION RETURNS OF TAX RETURN PREPARERS.

[Sec. 6060(a)]

(a) GENERAL RULE.—Any person who employs a tax return preparer to prepare any return or claim for refund other than for such person at any time during a return period shall make a return setting forth the name, taxpayer identification number, and place of work of each tax return preparer employed by him at any time during such period. For purposes of this section, any individual who in acting as a tax return preparer is not the employee of another tax return preparer shall be treated as his own employer. The return required by this section shall be filed, in such manner as the Secretary may by regulations prescribe, on or before the first July 31 following the end of such return period.

RETURNS—SIGNING AND VERIFYING

Amendments

• 2007, Small Business and Work Opportunity Tax Act of 2007 (P.L. 110-28)

P.L. 110-28, § 8246(a)(2)(A)(i):

Amended Code Sec. 6060 by striking "INCOME TAX RETURN PREPARERS" in the heading and inserting "TAX RETURN PREPARERS". **Effective** for returns prepared after 5-25-2007.

P.L. 110-28, § 8246(a)(2)(A)(ii)(I)-(III):

Amended Code Sec. 6060(a) by striking "an income tax return preparer" each place it appears and inserting "a tax return preparer", by striking "each income tax return preparer" and inserting "each tax return preparer", and by striking "another income tax return preparer" and inserting "another tax return preparer". **Effective** for returns prepared after 5-25-2007.

[Sec. 6060(b)]

(b) ALTERNATIVE REPORTING.—In lieu of the return required by subsection (a), the Secretary may approve an alternative reporting method if he determines that the necessary information is available to him from other sources.

[Sec. 6060(c)]

(c) RETURN PERIOD DEFINED.—For purposes of subsection (a), the term "return period" means the 12-month period beginning on July 1 of each year.

Amendments

• 2014, Tax Technical Corrections Act of 2014 (P.L. 113-295)

P.L. 113-295, § 221(a)(109), Division A:

Amended Code Sec. 6060(c) by striking "'year'" and all that follows and inserting "year.". **Effective** generally 12-19-2014. For a special rule, see Act Sec. 221(b)(2), Division A, below. Prior to being stricken, "'year'" and all that follows read as follows:

year, except that the first return period shall be the 6-month period beginning on January 1, 1977, and ending on June 30, 1977.

P.L. 113-295, § 221(b)(2), Division A, provides:

(2) SAVINGS PROVISION.—If—

(A) any provision amended or repealed by the amendments made by this section applied to—

(i) any transaction occurring before the date of the enactment of this Act,

(ii) any property acquired before such date of enactment, or

(iii) any item of income, loss, deduction, or credit taken into account before such date of enactment, and

(B) the treatment of such transaction, property, or item under such provision would (without regard to the amendments or repeals made by this section) affect the liability for tax for periods ending after date of enactment, nothing in the amendments or repeals made by this section shall be construed to affect the treatment of such transaction, property, or item for purposes of determining liability for tax for periods ending after such date of enactment.

• 1976, Tax Reform Act of 1976 (P.L. 94-455)

P.L. 94-455, § 1203(e):

Added Code Sec. 6060. **Effective** for documents prepared after 12-31-76.

PART IV—SIGNING AND VERIFYING OF RETURNS AND OTHER DOCUMENTS

Sec. 6061. Signing of returns and other documents.
Sec. 6062. Signing of corporation returns.
Sec. 6063. Signing of partnership returns.
Sec. 6064. Signature presumed authentic.
Sec. 6065. Verification of returns.

[Sec. 6061]

SEC. 6061. SIGNING OF RETURNS AND OTHER DOCUMENTS.

[Sec. 6061(a)]

(a) GENERAL RULE.—Except as otherwise provided by subsection (b) and sections 6062 and 6063, any return, statement, or other document required to be made under any provision of the internal revenue laws or regulations shall be signed in accordance with forms or regulations prescribed by the Secretary.

Amendments

• 1998, IRS Restructuring and Reform Act of 1998 (P.L. 105-206)

P.L. 105-206, § 2003(a)(1):

Amended Code Sec. 6061 by striking "Except as otherwise provided by" and inserting "(a) GENERAL RULE.—Except as otherwise provided by subsection (b) and". **Effective** 7-22-98.

• 1976, Tax Reform Act of 1976 (P.L. 94-455)

P.L. 94-455, § 1906(b)(13)(A):

Amended 1954 Code by substituting "Secretary" for "Secretary or his delegate" each place it appeared. **Effective** 2-1-77.

[Sec. 6061(b)]

(b) ELECTRONIC SIGNATURES.—

(1) IN GENERAL.—The Secretary shall develop procedures for the acceptance of signatures in digital or other electronic form. Until such time as such procedures are in place, the Secretary may—

(A) waive the requirement of a signature for; or

(B) provide for alternative methods of signing or subscribing,

a particular type or class of return, declaration, statement, or other document required or permitted to be made or written under internal revenue laws and regulations.

(2) TREATMENT OF ALTERNATIVE METHODS.—Notwithstanding any other provision of law, any return, declaration, statement, or other document filed and verified, signed, or subscribed under any method adopted under paragraph (1)(B) shall be treated for all purposes (both civil and criminal, including penalties for perjury) in the same manner as though signed or subscribed.

(3) PUBLISHED GUIDANCE.—

(A) IN GENERAL.—The Secretary shall publish guidance as appropriate to define and implement any waiver of the signature requirements or any method adopted under paragraph (1).

(B) ELECTRONIC SIGNATURES FOR DISCLOSURE AUTHORIZATIONS TO, AND OTHER AUTHORIZATIONS OF, PRACTITIONERS.—Not later than 6 months after the date of the enactment of this subparagraph, the Secretary shall publish guidance to establish uniform standards and procedures for the acceptance of taxpayers' signatures appearing in electronic form with respect to any request for disclosure of a taxpayer's return or return information under section 6103(c) to a practitioner or any power of attorney granted by a taxpayer to a practitioner.

(C) PRACTITIONER.—For purposes of subparagraph (B), the term "practitioner" means any individual in good standing who is regulated under section 330 of title 31, United States Code.

Amendments

• 2019, Taxpayer First Act (P.L. 116-25)

P.L. 116-25, § 2302:

Amended Code Sec. 6061(b)(3). **Effective** 7-1-2019. Prior to amendment, Code Sec. 6061(b)(3) read as follows:

(3) PUBLISHED GUIDANCE.—The Secretary shall publish guidance as appropriate to define and implement any waiver of the signature requirements or any method adopted under paragraph (1).

RETURNS—TIME FOR FILING

• **1998, IRS Restructuring and Reform Act of 1998 (P.L. 105-206)**

P.L. 105-206, § 2003(a)(2):

Amended Code Sec. 6061 by adding at the end a new subsection (b). **Effective** 7-22-98. For a special rule, see Act Sec. 2003(c)-(e), below.

P.L. 105-206, § 2003(c)-(e), provides:

(c) ESTABLISHMENT OF PROCEDURES FOR OTHER INFORMATION.—In the case of taxable periods beginning after December 31, 1999, the Secretary of the Treasury or the Secretary's delegate shall, to the extent practicable, establish procedures to accept, in electronic form, any other information, statements, elections, or schedules, from taxpayers filing returns electronically, so that such taxpayers will not be required to file any paper.

(d) INTERNET AVAILABILITY.—In the case of taxable periods beginning after December 31, 1998, the Secretary of the Treasury or the Secretary's delegate shall establish procedures for all tax forms, instructions, and publications created in the most recent 5-year period to be made available electronically on the Internet in a searchable database at approximately the same time such records are available to the public in paper form. In addition, in the case of taxable periods beginning after December 31, 1998, the Secretary of the Treasury or the Secretary's delegate shall, to the extent practicable, establish procedures for other taxpayer guidance to be made available electronically on the Internet in a searchable database at approximately the same time such guidance is available to the public in paper form.

(e) PROCEDURES FOR AUTHORIZING DISCLOSURE ELECTRONICALLY.—The Secretary shall establish procedures for any taxpayer to authorize, on an electronically filed return, the Secretary to disclose information under section 6103(c) of the Internal Revenue Code of 1986 to the preparer of the return.

[Sec. 6062]

SEC. 6062. SIGNING OF CORPORATION RETURNS.

The return of a corporation with respect to income shall be signed by the president, vice-president, treasurer, assistant treasurer, chief accounting officer or any other officer duly authorized so to act. In the case of a return made for a corporation by a fiduciary pursuant to the provisions of section 6012(b)(3), such fiduciary shall sign the return. The fact that an individual's name is signed on the return shall be prima facie evidence that such individual is authorized to sign the return on behalf of the corporation.

[Sec. 6063]

SEC. 6063. SIGNING OF PARTNERSHIP RETURNS.

The return of a partnership made under section 6031 shall be signed by any one of the partners. The fact that a partner's name is signed on the return shall be prima facie evidence that such partner is authorized to sign the return on behalf of the partnership.

[Sec. 6064]

SEC. 6064. SIGNATURE PRESUMED AUTHENTIC.

The fact that an individual's name is signed to a return, statement, or other document shall be prima facie evidence for all purposes that the return, statement, or other document was actually signed by him.

[Sec. 6065]

SEC. 6065. VERIFICATION OF RETURNS.

Except as otherwise provided by the Secretary, any return, declaration, statement, or other document required to be made under any provision of the internal revenue laws or regulations shall contain or be verified by a written declaration that it is made under the penalties of perjury.

Amendments

• **1976, Tax Reform Act of 1976 (P.L. 94-455)**

P.L. 94-455, § 1906(a)(6):

Amended Code Sec. 6065 by striking out subsection (b) and striking out "(a) PENALTIES OF PERJURY.—" in subsection (a). **Effective** for tax years beginning after 12-31-76. Prior to repeal, Code Sec. 6065(b) read as follows:

(b) OATH.—The Secretary or his delegate may by regulations require that any return, statement, or other document required to be made under any provision of the internal revenue laws or regulations shall be verified by an oath. This subsection shall not apply to returns and declarations with respect to income taxes made by individuals.

P.L. 94-455, § 1906(b)(13)(A):

Amended the 1954 Code by substituting "Secretary" for "Secretary or his delegate" each place it appeared. **Effective** 2-1-77.

PART V—TIME FOR FILING RETURNS AND OTHER DOCUMENTS

Sec. 6071.   Time for filing returns and other documents.
Sec. 6072.   Time for filing income tax returns.
Sec. 6075.   Time for filing estate and gift tax returns.

[Sec. 6071]

SEC. 6071. TIME FOR FILING RETURNS AND OTHER DOCUMENTS.

[Sec. 6071(a)]

(a) GENERAL RULE.—When not otherwise provided for by this title, the Secretary shall by regulations prescribe the time for filing any return, statement, or other document required by this title or by regulations.

Amendments

• **1976, Tax Reform Act of 1976 (P.L. 94-455)**

P.L. 94-455, § 1906(b)(13)(A):

Amended 1954 Code by substituting "Secretary" for "Secretary or his delegate" each place it appeared. **Effective** 2-1-77.

[Sec. 6071(b)]

(b) ELECTRONICALLY FILED INFORMATION RETURNS.—Returns made under subpart B of part III of this subchapter (other than returns and statements required to be filed with respect to nonemployee compensation) which are filed electronically shall be filed on or before March 31 of the year following the calendar year to which such returns relate.

Amendments

• **2015, Protecting Americans from Tax Hikes Act of 2015 (P.L. 114-113)**

P.L. 114-113, § 201(c), Div. Q:

Amended Code Sec. 6071(b) by striking "subparts B and C of part III of this subchapter" and inserting "subpart B of part III of this subchapter (other than returns and statements required to be filed with respect to nonemployee compensation)". **Effective** for returns and statements relating to calendar years beginning after 12-18-2015.

• **1998, IRS Restructuring and Reform Act of 1998 (P.L. 105-206)**

P.L. 105-206, § 2002(b):

Amended Code Sec. 6071 by redesignating subsection (b) as subsection (c) and by inserting after subsection (a) a new subsection (b). **Effective** for returns required to be filed after 12-31-99. For a special rule, see Act Sec. 2002(b)(1)-(2), below.

P.L. 105-206, § 2002(b)(1)-(2), provides:

(1) IN GENERAL.—The Secretary of the Treasury shall conduct a study evaluating the effect of extending the deadline for providing statements to persons with respect to whom information is required to be furnished under subparts B and C of part III of subchapter A of chapter 61 of the Internal Revenue Code of 1986 (other than section 6051 of such Code) from January 31 to February 15 of the year in which the return to which the statement relates is required to be filed.

(2) REPORT.—Not later than June 30, 1999, the Secretary of the Treasury shall submit a report on the study under paragraph (1) to the Committee on Ways and Means of the House of Representatives and the Committee on Finance of the Senate.

RETURNS—TIME FOR FILING

[Sec. 6071(c)]

(c) RETURNS AND STATEMENTS RELATING TO EMPLOYEE WAGE INFORMATION AND NONEMPLOYEE COMPENSATION.—Forms W–2 and W–3 and any returns or statements required by the Secretary to report nonemployee compensation shall be filed on or before January 31 of the year following the calendar year to which such returns relate.

Amendments

• **2015, Protecting Americans from Tax Hikes Act of 2015 (P.L. 114-113)**

P.L. 114-113, §201(a), Div. Q:

Amended Code Sec. 6071 by redesignating subsection (c) as subsection (d), and by inserting after subsection (b) a new subsection (c). **Effective** for returns and statements relating to calendar years beginning after 12-18-2015.

[Sec. 6071(d)]

(d) SPECIAL TAXES.—For payment of special taxes before engaging in certain trades and businesses, see section 4901 and section 5732.

Amendments

• **2015, Protecting Americans from Tax Hikes Act of 2015 (P.L. 114-113)**

P.L. 114-113, §201(a), Div. Q:

Amended Code Sec. 6071 by redesignating subsection (c) as subsection (d). **Effective** for returns and statements relating to calendar years beginning after 12-18-2015.

• **2005, Safe, Accountable, Flexible, Efficient Transportation Equity Act: A Legacy for Users (P.L. 109-59)**

P.L. 109-59, §11125(b)(21):

Amended Code Sec. 6071(c) by striking "section 5142" and inserting "section 5732". **Effective** 7-1-2008, but not applicable to taxes imposed for periods before such date.

• **1998, IRS Restructuring and Reform Act of 1998 (P.L. 105-206)**

P.L. 105-206, §2002(a):

Amended Code Sec. 6071 by redesignating subsection (b) as subsection (c). **Effective** for returns required to be filed after 12-31-99.

• **1958, Excise Tax Technical Changes Act of 1958 (P.L. 85-859)**

P.L. 85-859, §204(l):

Added the phrase "and section 5142" at the end of Sec. 6071(b). **Effective** 9-3-58.

SEC. 6072. TIME FOR FILING INCOME TAX RETURNS.

[Sec. 6072(a)]

(a) GENERAL RULE.—In the case of returns under section 6012, 6013, or 6017 (relating to income tax under subtitle A), returns made on the basis of the calendar year shall be filed on or before the 15th day of April following the close of the calendar year and returns made on the basis of a fiscal year shall be filed on or before the 15th day of the fourth month following the close of the fiscal year, except as otherwise provided in the following subsections of this section.

Amendments

• **2015, Surface Transportation and Veterans Health Care Choice Improvement Act of 2015 (P.L. 114-41)**

P.L. 114-41, §2006(a)(1)(B):

Amended Code Sec. 6072(a) by striking "6017, or 6031" and inserting "or 6017". **Effective** generally for returns for tax years beginning after 12-31-2015. For an exception, see Act Sec. 2006(a)(3)(B), below.

P.L. 114-41, §2006(a)(3)(B), provides:

(B) SPECIAL RULE FOR C CORPORATIONS WITH FISCAL YEARS ENDING ON JUNE 30.—In the case of any C corporation with a taxable year ending on June 30, the amendments made by this subsection shall apply to returns for taxable years beginning after December 31, 2025.

[Sec. 6072(b)]

(b) RETURNS OF PARTNERSHIPS AND S CORPORATIONS.—Returns of partnerships under section 6031 and returns of S corporations under sections 6012 and 6037 made on the basis of the calendar year shall be filed on or before the 15th day of March following the close of the calendar year, and such returns made on the basis of a fiscal year shall be filed on or before the 15th day of the third month following the close of the fiscal year. Returns required for a taxable year by section 6011(c)(2) (relating to returns of a DISC) shall be filed on or before the fifteenth day of the ninth month following the close of the taxable year.

Amendments

• **2015, Surface Transportation and Veterans Health Care Choice Improvement Act of 2015 (P.L. 114-41)**

P.L. 114-41, §2006(a)(1)(A):

Amended so much of Code Sec. 6072(b) as precedes the second sentence. **Effective** generally for returns for tax years beginning after 12-31-2015. For an exception, see Act Sec. 2006(a)(3)(B), below. Prior to amendment, so much of Code Sec. 6072(b) as precedes the second sentence read as follows:

(b) RETURNS OF CORPORATIONS.—Returns of corporations under section 6012 made on the basis of the calendar year shall be filed on or before the 15th day of March following the close of the calendar year, and such returns made on the basis of a fiscal year shall be filed on or before the 15th day of the third month following the close of the fiscal year.

P.L. 114-41, §2006(a)(3)(B), provides:

(B) SPECIAL RULE FOR C CORPORATIONS WITH FISCAL YEARS ENDING ON JUNE 30.—In the case of any C corporation with a taxable year ending on June 30, the amendments made by this subsection shall apply to returns for taxable years beginning after December 31, 2025.

• **2014, Tax Technical Corrections Act of 2014 (P.L. 113-295)**

P.L. 113-295, §220(u), Division A:

Amended Code Sec. 6072(b) by striking "6011(e)(2)" and inserting "6011(c)(2)". **Effective** 12-19-2014.

• **1971, Revenue Act of 1971 (P.L. 92-178)**

P.L. 92-178, §504(b):

Added the last sentence to Code Sec. 6072(b). **Effective** date is governed by the effective date for Code Sec. 992.

[Sec. 6072(c)]

(c) RETURNS BY CERTAIN NONRESIDENT ALIEN INDIVIDUALS AND FOREIGN CORPORATIONS.—Returns made by nonresident alien individuals (other than those whose wages are subject to withholding under chapter 24) and foreign corporations (other than those having an office or place of business in the United States or a former FSC (as defined in section 922 as in effect before its repeal by the FSC Repeal and Extraterritorial Income Exclusion Act of 2000)) under section 6012 on the basis of a calendar year shall be filed on or before the 15th day of June following the close of the calendar year and such returns made on the basis of a fiscal year shall be filed on or before the 15th day of the 6th month following the close of the fiscal year.

Amendments

• **2007, Tax Technical Corrections Act of 2007 (P.L. 110-172)**

P.L. 110-172, §11(g)(20):

Amended Code Sec. 6072(c) by striking "a FSC or former FSC" and inserting "a former FSC (as defined in section 922 as in effect before its repeal by the FSC Repeal and Extraterritorial Income Exclusion Act of 2000)". **Effective** 12-29-2007.

• **1984, Deficit Reduction Act of 1984 (P.L. 98-369)**

P.L. 98-369, §801(d)(13):

Amended Code Sec. 6072(c) by inserting "or a FSC or former FSC" after "United States". **Effective** for transactions after 12-31-84, in tax years ending after such date.

[Sec. 6072(d)]

(d) RETURNS OF COOPERATIVE ASSOCIATIONS.—In the case of an income tax return of—

RETURNS—TIME FOR FILING

(1) an exempt cooperative association described in section 1381(a)(1), or

(2) an organization described in section 1381(a)(2) which is under an obligation to pay patronage dividends (as defined in section 1388(a)) in an amount equal to at least 50 percent of its net earnings from business done with or for its patrons, or which paid patronage dividends in such an amount out of the net earnings from business done with or for patrons during the most recent taxable year for which it had such net earnings,

a return made on the basis of a calendar year shall be filed on or before the 15th day of September following the close of the calendar year, and a return made on the basis of a fiscal year shall be filed on or before the 15th day of the 9th month following the close of the fiscal year.

Amendments

• **1962, Revenue Act of 1962 (P.L. 87-834)**

P.L. 87-834, §17(b)(3):

Amended Code Sec. 6072(d). **Effective** with respect to tax years beginning after 12-31-62. Prior to amendment Sec. 6072(d) read as follows:

"(d) RETURNS OF EXEMPT COOPERATIVE ASSOCIATIONS.—In the case of income tax returns of exempt cooperative associations taxable under the provisions of section 522, returns made on the basis of a calendar year shall be filed on or before the 15th day of September following the close of the calendar year and returns made on the basis of a fiscal year shall be filed on or before the 15th day of the 9th month following the close of the fiscal year."

[Sec. 6072(e)]

(e) ORGANIZATIONS EXEMPT FROM TAXATION UNDER SECTION 501(a).—In the case of an income tax return of an organization exempt from taxation under section 501(a) (other than an employees' trust described in section 401(a)), a return shall be filed on or before the 15th day of the 5th month following the close of the taxable year.

Amendments

• **1978 (P.L. 95-628)**

P.L. 95-628, §6(a), (b):

Added new Code Sec. 6072(e). **Effective** for returns for tax years beginning after 11-10-78.

• **1976, Tax Reform Act of 1976 (P.L. 94-455)**

P.L. 94-455, §1053(d)(3):

Repealed Code Sec. 6072(e). **Effective** with respect to tax years beginning after 12-31-77. Prior to repeal, Code Sec. 6072(e) read as follows:

(e) INCOME TAX DUE DATES POSTPONED IN CASE OF CHINA TRADE ACT CORPORATIONS.—In the case of any taxable year beginning after December 31, 1948, and ending before October 1, 1956, no Federal income tax return of any corporation organized under the China Trade Act, 1922 (42 Stat. 849, U.S.C., title 15, chapter 4), as amended, shall become due until December 31, 1956, but only with respect to any such corporation and any such taxable year which the Secretary or his delegate may determine reasonable under the circumstances in China pursuant to such regulations as may be prescribed. Such due date shall be subject to the power of the Secretary or his delegate to extend the time for filing such return, as in other cases.

[Sec. 6073—Repealed]

Amendments

• **1984, Deficit Reduction Act of 1984 (P.L. 98-369)**

P.L. 98-369, §412(a)(2):

Repealed Code Sec. 6073. **Effective** with respect to tax years beginning after 1984. Prior to repeal, Code Sec. 6073 read as follows:

SEC. 6073. TIME FOR FILING DECLARATIONS OF ESTIMATED INCOME TAX BY INDIVIDUALS.

[Sec. 6073(a)]

(a) INDIVIDUALS OTHER THAN FARMERS OR FISHERMEN.—Declarations of estimated tax required by section 6015 from individuals regarded as neither farmers nor fishermen for the purpose of that section shall be filed on or before April 15 of the taxable year, except that if the requirements of section 6015 are first met—

(1) After April 1 and before June 2 of the taxable year, the declaration shall be filed on or before June 15 of the taxable year, or

(2) After June 1 and before September 2 of the taxable year, the declaration shall be filed on or before September 15 of the taxable year, or

(3) After September 1 of the taxable year, the declaration shall be filed on or before January 15 of the succeeding taxable year.

In the case of a nonresident alien described in section 6072(c), the requirements of section 6015 shall be deemed to be first met no earlier than after April 1 and before June 2 of the taxable year.

Amendments

• **1976, Tax Reform Act of 1976 (P.L. 94-455)**

P.L. 94-455, §1012(c):

Added the last sentence to Code Sec. 6073(a). **Effective** for tax years beginning after 12-31-76.

P.L. 87-682 (H.R. 6413), 87th Cong., §1:

Amended Sec. 6073(a) by inserting "OR FISHERMEN" after "FARMERS" in line 1 and by substituting "individuals regarded as neither farmers nor fishermen" for "individuals not regarded as farmers."

[Sec. 6073(b)]

(b) FARMERS OR FISHERMEN.—Declarations of estimated tax required by section 6015 from any individual—

(1) whose estimated gross income from farming or fishing (including oyster farming) for the taxable year is at least two-thirds of the total estimated gross income from all sources for the taxable year, or

(2) whose gross income from farming or fishing (including oyster farming) shown on the return of the individual for the preceding taxable year is at least two-thirds of the total gross income from all sources shown on such return,

may, in lieu of the time prescribed in subsection (a), be filed at any time on or before January 15 of the taxable year succeeding the taxable year.

Amendments

• **1978 (P.L. 95-628)**

P.L. 95-628, §7(a), (b):

Amended Sec. 6073(b). **Effective** for declarations of estimated tax for tax years beginning after 11-10-78. Before amendment, subsection (b) read:

(b) FARMERS OR FISHERMEN.—Declarations of estimated tax required by section 6015 from individuals whose estimated gross income from farming or fishing (including oyster farming) for the taxable year is at least two-thirds of the total estimated gross income from all sources for the taxable year may, in lieu of the time prescribed in subsection (a), be filed at any time on or before January 15 of the succeeding taxable year.

P.L. 87-682 (H.R. 6413), 87th Cong., §1:

Amended Sec. 6073(b) by inserting "OR FISHERMEN" after "FARMERS" in and by inserting "or fishing" after "from farming".

[Sec. 6073(c)]

(c) AMENDMENT.—An amendment of a declaration may be filed in any interval between installment dates prescribed for that taxable year, but only one amendment may be filed in each such interval.

[Sec. 6073(d)]

(d) SHORT TAXABLE YEARS.—The application of this section to taxable years of less than 12 months shall be in accordance with regulations prescribed by the Secretary.

Amendments

• **1976, Tax Reform Act of 1976 (P.L. 94-455)**

P.L. 94-455, §1906(b)(13)(A):

Amended 1954 Code by substituting "Secretary" for "Secretary or his delegate" each place it appeared. **Effective** 2-1-77.

[Sec. 6073(e)]

(e) FISCAL YEARS.—In the application of this section to the case of a taxable year beginning on any date other than January 1, there shall be substituted, for the months specified in this section, the months which correspond thereto.

[Sec. 6073(f)]

(f) TERMINATION.—This section shall not apply to any taxable year beginning after December 31, 1982.

Amendments

• **1982, Tax Equity and Fiscal Responsibility Act of 1982 (P.L. 97-248)**

P.L. 97-248, §328(b)(2):

Added Code Sec. 6073(f). **Effective** for tax years beginning after 12-31-82.

[Sec. 6075]

SEC. 6075. TIME FOR FILING ESTATE AND GIFT TAX RETURNS.

[Sec. 6075(a)]

(a) ESTATE TAX RETURNS.—Returns made under section 6018(a) (relating to estate taxes) shall be filed within 9 months after the date of the decedent's death.

RETURNS—TIME FOR FILING

Amendments

• **2013, American Taxpayer Relief Act of 2012 (P.L. 112-240)**

P.L. 112-240, §101(a)(1)-(3), provides:

SEC. 101. PERMANENT EXTENSION AND MODIFICATION OF 2001 TAX RELIEF.

(a) PERMANENT EXTENSION.—

(1) IN GENERAL.—The Economic Growth and Tax Relief Reconciliation Act of 2001 is amended by striking title IX.

(2) CONFORMING AMENDMENT.—The Tax Relief, Unemployment Insurance Reauthorization, and Job Creation Act of 2010 is amended by striking section 304.

(3) EFFECTIVE DATE.—The amendments made by this subsection shall apply to taxable, plan, or limitation years beginning after December 31, 2012, and estates of decedents dying, gifts made, or generation skipping transfers after December 31, 2012.

• **2010, Tax Relief, Unemployment Insurance Reauthorization, and Job Creation Act of 2010 (P.L. 111-312)**

P.L. 111-312, §301(a):

Amended Code Sec. 6075(a) to read as such provision would read if subtitle E of title V of the Economic Growth and Tax Relief Reconciliation Act of 2001 (P.L. 107-16) had never been enacted. **Effective** for estates of decedents dying, and transfers made, after 12-31-2009. For a special rule, see Act Sec. 301(c), below. Prior to amendment by P.L. 111-312, Code Sec. 6075(a) read as follows:

(a) RETURNS RELATING TO LARGE TRANSFERS AT DEATH.—The return required by section 6018 with respect to a decedent shall be filed with the return of the tax imposed by chapter 1 for the decedent's last taxable year or such later date specified in regulations prescribed by the Secretary.

P.L. 111-312, §301(c), provides:

(c) SPECIAL ELECTION WITH RESPECT TO ESTATES OF DECEDENTS DYING IN 2010.—Notwithstanding subsection (a), in the case of an estate of a decedent dying after December 31, 2009, and before January 1, 2011, the executor (within the meaning of section 2203 of the Internal Revenue Code of 1986) may elect to apply such Code as though the amendments made by subsection (a) do not apply with respect to chapter 11 of such Code and with respect to property acquired or passing from such decedent (within the meaning of section 1014(b) of such Code). Such election shall be made at such time and in such manner as the Secretary of the Treasury or the Secretary's delegate shall provide. Such an election once made shall be revocable only with the consent of the Secretary of the Treasury or the Secretary's delegate. For purposes of section 2652(a)(1) of such Code, the determination of whether any property is subject to the tax imposed by such chapter 11 shall be made without regard to any election made under this subsection.

P.L. 111-312, §304, provides [but see P.L. 112-240, §101(a)(2)-(3), above]:

SEC. 304. APPLICATION OF EGTRRA SUNSET TO THIS TITLE.

Section 901 of the Economic Growth and Tax Relief Reconciliation Act of 2001 shall apply to the amendments made by this title.

• **2001, Economic Growth and Tax Relief Reconciliation Act of 2001 (P.L. 107-16)**

P.L. 107-16, §542(b)(3)(A):

Amended Code Sec. 6075(a). **Effective** for estates of decedents dying after 12-31-2009. Prior to amendment, Code Sec. 6075(a) read as follows:

(a) ESTATE TAX RETURNS.—Returns made under section 6018 (relating to estate taxes) shall be filed within 9 months after the date of the decedent's death.

P.L. 107-16, §901(a)-(b), as amended by P.L. 111-312, §101(a)(1), provides [but see P.L. 112-240, §101(a)(1) and (3), above]:

SEC. 901. SUNSET OF PROVISIONS OF ACT.

(a) IN GENERAL.—All provisions of, and amendments made by, this Act shall not apply—

(1) to taxable, plan, or limitation years beginning after December 31, 2012, or

(2) in the case of title V, to estates of decedents dying, gifts made, or generation skipping transfers, after December 31, 2012.

(b) APPLICATION OF CERTAIN LAWS.—The Internal Revenue Code of 1986 and the Employee Retirement Income Security Act of 1974 shall be applied and administered to years, estates, gifts, and transfers described in subsection (a) as if the provisions and amendments described in subsection (a) had never been enacted.

• **Excise, Estate, and Gift Tax Adjustment Act of 1970 (P.L. 91-614)**

P.L. 91-614, §101(b):

Amended Code Sec. 6075(a) by substituting "9 months" for "15 months." **Effective** with respect to decedents dying after 12-31-70.

[Sec. 6075(b)]

(b) GIFT TAX RETURNS.—

(1) GENERAL RULE.—Returns made under section 6019 (relating to gift taxes) shall be filed on or before the 15th day of April following the close of the calendar year.

(2) EXTENSION WHERE TAXPAYER GRANTED EXTENSION FOR FILING INCOME TAX RETURN.—Any extension of time granted the taxpayer for filing the return of income taxes imposed by subtitle A for any taxable year which is a calendar year shall be deemed to be also an extension of time granted the taxpayer for filing the return under section 6019 for such calendar year.

(3) COORDINATION WITH DUE DATE FOR ESTATE TAX RETURN.—Notwithstanding paragraphs (1) and (2), the time for filing the return made under section 6019 for the calendar year which includes the date of death of the donor shall not be later than the time (including extensions) for filing the return made under section 6018 (relating to estate tax returns) with respect to such donor.

Amendments

• **2013, American Taxpayer Relief Act of 2012 (P.L. 112-240)**

P.L. 112-240, §101(a)(1)-(3), provides:

SEC. 101. PERMANENT EXTENSION AND MODIFICATION OF 2001 TAX RELIEF.

(a) PERMANENT EXTENSION.—

(1) IN GENERAL.—The Economic Growth and Tax Relief Reconciliation Act of 2001 is amended by striking title IX.

(2) CONFORMING AMENDMENT.—The Tax Relief, Unemployment Insurance Reauthorization, and Job Creation Act of 2010 is amended by striking section 304.

(3) EFFECTIVE DATE.—The amendments made by this subsection shall apply to taxable, plan, or limitation years beginning after December 31, 2012, and estates of decedents dying, gifts made, or generation skipping transfers after December 31, 2012.

• **2010, Tax Relief, Unemployment Insurance Reauthorization, and Job Creation Act of 2010 (P.L. 111-312)**

P.L. 111-312, §301(a):

Amended Code Sec. 6075(b)(3) to read as such provision would read if subtitle E of title V of the Economic Growth and Tax Relief Reconciliation Act of 2001 (P.L. 107-16) had never been enacted. **Effective** for estates of decedents dying, and transfers made, after 12-31-2009. For a special rule, see Act Sec. 301(c), below. Prior to amendment by P.L. 111-312, Code Sec. 6075(b)(3) read as follows:

(3) COORDINATION WITH DUE DATE FOR SECTION 6018 RETURN.—Notwithstanding paragraphs (1) and (2), the time for filing the return made under section 6019 for the calendar year which includes the date of death of the donor shall not be later than the time (including extensions) for filing the return made under section 6018 (relating to returns relating to large transfers at death) with respect to such donor.

P.L. 111-312, §301(c), provides:

(c) SPECIAL ELECTION WITH RESPECT TO ESTATES OF DECEDENTS DYING IN 2010.—Notwithstanding subsection (a), in the case of an estate of a decedent dying after December 31, 2009, and before January 1, 2011, the executor (within the meaning of section 2203 of the Internal Revenue Code of 1986) may elect to apply such Code as though the amendments made by subsection (a) do not apply with respect to chapter 11 of such Code and with respect to property acquired or passing from such decedent (within the meaning of section 1014(b) of such Code). Such election shall be made at such time and in such manner as the Secretary of the Treasury or the Secretary's delegate shall provide. Such an election once made shall be revocable only with the consent of the Secretary of the Treasury or the Secretary's delegate. For purposes of section 2652(a)(1) of such Code, the determination of whether any property is subject to the tax imposed by such chapter 11 shall be made without regard to any election made under this subsection.

P.L. 111-312, §304, provides [but see P.L. 112-240, §101(a)(2)-(3), above]:

SEC. 304. APPLICATION OF EGTRRA SUNSET TO THIS TITLE.

Section 901 of the Economic Growth and Tax Relief Reconciliation Act of 2001 shall apply to the amendments made by this title.

• **2001, Economic Growth and Tax Relief Reconciliation Act of 2001 (P.L. 107-16)**

P.L. 107-16, §542(b)(3)(B)(i)-(ii):

Amended Code Sec. 6075(b)(3) by striking "ESTATE TAX RETURN" in the heading and inserting "SECTION 6018 RETURN", and by striking "(relating to estate tax returns)" and inserting "(relating to returns relating to large transfers at death)". **Effective** for estates of decedents dying after 12-31-2009.

P.L. 107-16, §901(a)-(b), as amended by P.L. 111-312, §101(a)(1), provides [but see P.L. 112-240, §101(a)(1) and (3), above]:

SEC. 901. SUNSET OF PROVISIONS OF ACT.

(a) IN GENERAL.—All provisions of, and amendments made by, this Act shall not apply—

(1) to taxable, plan, or limitation years beginning after December 31, 2012, or

(2) in the case of title V, to estates of decedents dying, gifts made, or generation skipping transfers, after December 31, 2012.

(b) APPLICATION OF CERTAIN LAWS.—The Internal Revenue Code of 1986 and the Employee Retirement Income Security Act of 1974 shall be applied and administered to years, estates, gifts, and transfers described in subsection (a) as if the provisions and amendments described in subsection (a) had never been enacted.

• **1981, Economic Recovery Tax Act of 1981 (P.L. 97-34)**

P.L. 97-34, §442(d)(3):

Amended Code Sec. 6075(b). **Effective** with respect to estates of decedents dying after 12-31-81. Prior to amendment, Code Sec. 6075(b) read as follows:

(b) GIFT TAX RETURNS.—

(1) GENERAL RULE.—Except as provided in paragraph (2), returns made under section 6019 (relating to gift taxes) shall be filed on or before—

(A) in the case of a return for the first, second, or third calendar quarter of any calendar year, the 15th day of the second month following the close of the calendar quarter, or

RETURNS—EXTENSION OF TIME FOR FILING

(B) in the case of a return for the fourth calendar quarter of any calendar year, the 15th day of the fourth month following the close of the calendar quarter.

(2) SPECIAL RULE WHERE GIFTS IN A CALENDAR QUARTER TOTAL $25,000 OR LESS.—If the total amount of taxable gifts made by a person during a calendar quarter is $25,000 or less, the return under section 6019 for such quarter shall be filed on or before the date prescribed by paragraph (1) for filing the return for—

(A) the first subsequent calendar quarter in the calendar year in which the sum of—

(i) the taxable gifts made during such subsequent quarter, plus

(ii) all other taxable gifts made during the calendar year and for which a return has not yet been required to be filed under this subsection,

exceeds $25,000, or

(B) if a return is not required to be filed under subparagraph (A), the fourth calendar quarter of the calendar year.

(3) EXTENSION WHERE TAXPAYER GRANTED EXTENSION FOR FILING INCOME TAX RETURN.—Any extension of time granted the taxpayer for filing the return of income taxes imposed by subtitle A for any taxable year which is a calendar year shall be deemed to be also an extension of time granted the taxpayer for filing the return under section 6019 for the fourth calendar quarter of such taxable year.

(4) NONRESIDENTS NOT CITIZENS OF THE UNITED STATES.—In the case of a nonresident not a citizen of the United States, paragraph (2) shall be applied by substituting "$12,500" for "$25,000" each place it appears.

• 1979 (P.L. 96-167)

P.L. 96-167, §8:

Amended Code Sec. 6075(b). **Effective** for returns for gifts made in calendar years ending after 12-29-79. Prior to amendment, Code Sec. 6075(b) read as follows:

(b) GIFT TAX RETURNS.—

(1) GENERAL RULE.—Except as provided in paragraph (2), returns made under section 6019 (relating to gift taxes) shall be filed on or before the 15th day of the second month following the close of the calendar quarter.

Amendments

• 1988, Omnibus Trade and Competitiveness Act of 1988 (P.L. 100-418)

P.L. 100-418, §1941(b)(1):

Repealed Code Sec. 6076. **Effective** for crude oil removed from the premises on or after 8-23-88. Prior to repeal, Code Sec. 6076 read as follows:

SEC. 6076. TIME FOR FILING RETURN OF WINDFALL PROFIT TAX.

(a) GENERAL RULE.—Except in the case of a return required by regulations prescribed under section 4995(a)(5), each return—

(1) of the tax imposed by section 4986 (relating to windfall profit tax) for any taxable period (within the meaning of section 4996(b)(7)), or

(2) by a person required under section 4995(a) to withhold the windfall profit tax for any taxable period,

(2) SPECIAL RULE WHERE GIFTS IN A CALENDAR QUARTER TOTAL $25,000 OR LESS.—If the total amount of taxable gifts made by a person during a calendar quarter is $25,000 or less, the return under section 6019 for such quarter shall be filed on or before the 15th day of the second month after—

(A) the close of the first subsequent calendar quarter in the calendar year in which the sum of—

(i) the taxable gifts made during such subsequent quarter, plus

(ii) all other taxable gifts made during the calendar year and for which a return has not yet been required to be filed under this subsection,

exceeds $25,000, or

(B) if a return is not required to be filed under subparagraph (A), the close of the fourth calendar quarter of the calendar year.

(3) NONRESIDENTS NOT CITIZENS OF THE UNITED STATES.—In the case of a nonresident not a citizen of the United States, paragraph (2) shall be applied by substituting "$12,500" for "$25,000" each place it appears.

• 1976, Tax Reform Act of 1976 (P.L. 94-455)

P.L. 94-455, §2008(b):

Amended Code Sec. 6075(b). **Effective** for gifts made after 12-31-76. Prior to amendment, Code Sec. 6075(b) read as follows:

(b) GIFT TAX RETURNS.—Returns made under section 6019 (relating to gift taxes) shall be filed on or before the 15th day of the second month following the close of the calendar quarter.

• Excise, Estate, and Gift Tax Adjustment Act of 1970 (P.L. 91-614)

P.L. 91-614, §102(d)(4):

Amended Code Sec. 6075(b) by substituting "the second month following the close of the calendar quarter" for "April following the close of the calendar year.". **Effective** for gifts made after 12-31-70.

[Sec. 6076—Repealed]

shall be filed not later than the last day of the second month following the close of the taxable period.

(b) CROSS REFERENCE.—

For depositary requirements applicable to the tax imposed by section 4986, see section 4995(b).

• 1980, Crude Oil Windfall Profit Tax Act of 1980 (P.L. 96-223)

P.L. 96-223, §101(c)(1)(A):

Added Code Sec. 6076. **Effective** for periods after 2-29-80.

PART VI—EXTENSION OF TIME FOR FILING RETURNS

Sec. 6081. Extension of time for filing returns.

[Sec. 6081]

SEC. 6081. EXTENSION OF TIME FOR FILING RETURNS.

[Sec. 6081(a)]

(a) GENERAL RULE.—The Secretary may grant a reasonable extension of time for filing any return, declaration, statement, or other document required by this title or by regulations. Except in the case of taxpayers who are abroad, no such extension shall be for more than 6 months.

Amendments

• 1976, Tax Reform Act of 1976 (P.L. 94-455)

P.L. 94-455, §1906(b)(13)(A):

Amended 1954 Code by substituting "Secretary" for "Secretary or his delegate" each place it appeared. **Effective** 2-1-77.

[Sec. 6081(b)]

(b) AUTOMATIC EXTENSION FOR CORPORATION INCOME TAX RETURNS.—An extension of 6 months for the filing of the return of income taxes imposed by subtitle A shall be allowed any corporation if, in such manner and at such time as the Secretary may by regulations prescribe, there is filed on behalf of such corporation the form prescribed by the Secretary, and if such corporation pays, on or before the date prescribed for payment of the tax, the amount properly estimated as its tax; but this extension may be terminated at any time by the Secretary by mailing to the taxpayer notice of such termination at least 10 days prior to the date for termination fixed in such notice. In the case of any return for a taxable year of a C corporation which ends on December 31 and begins before January 1, 2026, the first sentence of this subsection shall be applied by substituting "5 months" for "6 months". In the case of any return for a taxable year of a C corporation which ends on June 30 and begins before January 1, 2026, the first sentence of this subsection shall be applied by substituting "7 months" for "6 months".

Amendments

• 2015, Surface Transportation and Veterans Health Care Choice Improvement Act of 2015 (P.L. 114-41)

P.L. 114-41, §2006(c)(1)(A)-(B):

Amended Code Sec. 6081(b) by striking "3 months" and inserting "6 months", and by adding at the end two new sentences. **Effective** for returns for tax years beginning after 12-31-15.

• 1982, Tax Equity and Fiscal Responsibility Act of 1982 (P.L. 97-248)

P.L. 97-248, §234(b)(2)(B):

Amended Code Sec. 6081(b) by striking out "or the first installment thereof required under section 6152" after "estimated as its tax". **Effective** for tax years beginning after 12-31-82.

• 1976, Tax Reform Act of 1976 (P.L. 94-455)

P.L. 94-455, §1906(b)(13)(A):

Amended 1954 Code by substituting "Secretary" for "Secretary or his delegate" each place it appeared. **Effective** 2-1-77.

Sec. 6076—Repealed

RETURNS—PLACE FOR FILING

[Sec. 6081(c)]

(c) CROSS REFERENCES.—

For time for performing certain acts postponed by reason of war, see section 7508, and by reason of Presidentially declared disaster or terroristic or military action, see section 7508A.

Amendments

• **2002, Victims of Terrorism Tax Relief Act of 2001 (P.L. 107-134)**

P.L. 107-134, §112(d)(2):

Amended Code Sec. 6081(c). **Effective** for disasters and terroristic or military actions occurring on or after 9-11-2001, with respect to any action of the Secretary of the Treasury, the Secretary of Labor, or the Pension Benefit Guaranty Corporation occurring on or after 1-23-2002. Prior to amendment, Code Sec. 6081(c) read as follows:

(c) POSTPONEMENT BY REASON OF WAR.—

For time for performing certain acts postponed by reason of war, see section 7508.

PART VII—PLACE FOR FILING RETURNS OR OTHER DOCUMENTS

Sec. 6091.   Place for filing returns or other documents.

[Sec. 6091]

SEC. 6091. PLACE FOR FILING RETURNS OR OTHER DOCUMENTS.

[Sec. 6091(a)]

(a) GENERAL RULE.—When not otherwise provided for by this title, the Secretary shall by regulations prescribe the place for the filing of any return, declaration, statement, or other document, or copies thereof, required by this title or by regulations.

Amendments

• **1976, Tax Reform Act of 1976 (P.L. 94-455)**

P.L. 94-455, §1906(b)(13)(A):

Amended 1954 Code by substituting "Secretary" for "Secretary or his delegate" each place it appeared. **Effective** 2-1-77.

[Sec. 6091(b)]

(b) TAX RETURNS.—In the case of returns of tax required under authority of part II of this subchapter—

(1) PERSONS OTHER THAN CORPORATIONS.—

(A) GENERAL RULE.—Except as provided in subparagraph (B), a return (other than a corporation return) shall be made to the Secretary—

(i) in the internal revenue district in which is located the legal residence or principal place of business of the person making the return, or

(ii) at a service center serving the internal revenue district referred to in clause (i), as the Secretary may by regulations designate.

(B) EXCEPTION.—Returns of—

(i) persons who have no legal residence or principal place of business in any internal revenue district,

(ii) citizens of the United States whose principal place of abode for the period with respect to which the return is filed is outside the United States,

(iii) persons who claim the benefits of section 911 (relating to citizens or residents of the United States living abroad), section 931 (relating to income from sources within Guam, American Samoa, or the Northern Mariana Islands), or section 933 (relating to income from sources within Puerto Rico),

(iv) nonresident alien persons, and

(v) persons with respect to whom an assessment was made under section 6851(a) or 6852(a) (relating to termination assessments) with respect to the taxable year,

shall be made at such place as the Secretary may by regulations designate.

(2) CORPORATIONS.—

(A) GENERAL RULE.—Except as provided in subparagraph (B), a return of a corporation shall be made to the Secretary—

(i) in the internal revenue district in which is located the principal place of business or principal office or agency of the corporation, or

(ii) at a service center serving the internal revenue district referred to in clause (i), as the Secretary may by regulations designate.

(B) EXCEPTION.—Returns of—

(i) corporations which have no principal place of business or principal office or agency in any internal revenue district,

(ii) foreign corporations, and

(iii) corporations with respect to which an assessment was made under section 6851(a) (relating to termination assessments) with respect to the taxable year,

shall be made at such place as the Secretary may by regulations designate.

(3) ESTATE TAX RETURNS.—

(A) GENERAL RULE.—Except as provided in subparagraph (B), returns of estate tax required under section 6018 shall be made to the Secretary—

(i) in the internal revenue district in which was the domicile of the decedent at the time of his death, or

(ii) at a service center serving the internal revenue district referred to in clause (i), as the Secretary may by regulations designate.

(B) EXCEPTION.—If the domicile of the decedent was not in an internal revenue district, or if he had no domicile, the estate tax return required under section 6018 shall be made at such place as the Secretary may by regulations designate.

(4) HAND-CARRIED RETURNS.—Notwithstanding paragraph (1), (2), or (3), a return to which paragraph (1)(A), (2)(A), or (3)(A) would apply, but for this paragraph, which is made to the Secretary by hand carrying shall, under regulations prescribed by the Secretary, be made in the internal revenue district referred to in paragraph (1)(A)(i), (2)(A)(i), or (3)(A)(i), as the case may be.

(5) EXCEPTIONAL CASES.—Notwithstanding paragraph (1), (2), (3), or (4) of this subsection, the Secretary may permit a return to be filed in any internal revenue district, and may require the return of any officer or employee of the Treasury Department to be filed in any internal revenue district selected by the Secretary.

(6) ALCOHOL, TOBACCO, AND FIREARMS RETURNS, ETC.—In the case of any return of tax imposed by section 4181 or subtitle E (relating to taxes on alcohol, tobacco, and firearms), subsection (a) shall apply (and this subsection shall not apply).

RETURNS—CAMPAIGN FUNDS

Amendments

- **2018, Tax Technical Corrections Act of 2018 (P.L. 115-141)**

P.L. 115-141, §401(a)(266), Div. U:

Amended Code Sec. 6091(b)(2)(B)(ii) by striking "and" at the end. **Effective** 3-23-2018.

P.L. 115-141, §401(d)(1)(D)(xviii), Div. U:

Amended Code Sec. 6091(b)(2)(B) by striking clause (ii) and by redesignating clauses (iii) and (iv) as clauses (ii) and (iii), respectively. **Effective** 3-23-2018. For a special rule, see Act Sec. 401(e), Div. U, below. Prior to being stricken, Code Sec. 6091(b)(2)(B)(ii) read as follows:

(ii) corporations which claim the benefits of section 936 (relating to possession tax credit),

P.L. 115-141, §401(e), Div. U, provides:

(e) GENERAL SAVINGS PROVISION WITH RESPECT TO DEADWOOD PROVISIONS.—If—

(1) any provision amended or repealed by the amendments made by subsection (b) or (d) applied to—

(A) any transaction occurring before the date of the enactment of this Act,

(B) any property acquired before such date of enactment, or

(C) any item of income, loss, deduction, or credit taken into account before such date of enactment, and

(2) the treatment of such transaction, property, or item under such provision would (without regard to the amendments or repeals made by such subsection) affect the liability for tax for periods ending after such date of enactment,

nothing in the amendments or repeals made by this section shall be construed to affect the treatment of such transaction, property, or item for purposes of determining liability for tax for periods ending after such date of enactment.

- **1989, Omnibus Budget Reconciliation Act of 1989 (P.L. 101-239)**

P.L. 101-239, §7841(f):

Amended Code Sec. 6091(b)(6) by inserting "section 4181 or" before "subtitle E". **Effective** 12-19-89.

- **1987, Revenue Act of 1987 (P.L. 100-203)**

P.L. 100-203, §10713(b)(2)(A):

Amended Code Sec. 6091(b)(1)(B)(v) by striking out "section 6851(a)" and inserting in lieu thereof "section 6851(a) or 6852(a)". **Effective** 12-22-87.

- **1986, Tax Reform Act of 1986 (P.L. 99-514)**

P.L. 99-514, §1272(d)(10):

Amended Code Sec. 6091(b)(1)(B)(iii) by striking out "possessions of the United States" and inserting in lieu thereof "Guam, American Samoa, or the Northern Mariana Islands". **Effective**, generally, for tax years beginning after 12-31-86. For a special rule, see Act Sec. 1277(b), below.

P.L. 99-514, §1277(b), provides:

(b) SPECIAL RULE FOR GUAM, AMERICAN SAMOA, AND THE NORTHERN MARIANA ISLANDS.—The amendments made by this subtitle shall apply with respect to Guam, American Samoa, or the Northern Mariana Islands (and to residents thereof and corporations created or organized therein) only if (and so long as) an implementing agreement under section 1271 is in effect between the United States and such possession.

See also Act Sec. 1277(e) following Code Sec. 48 for a special rule regarding treatment of certain U.S. persons.

P.L. 99-514, §1879(r)(1):

Amended Code Sec. 6091(b) by adding at the end thereof new paragraph (6). **Effective** on the first day of the first calendar month which begins more than 90 days after 10-22-86.

- **1981, Economic Recovery Tax Act of 1981 (P.L. 97-34)**

P.L. 97-34, §111(b)(3):

Amended Code Sec. 6091(b)(1)(B)(iii) by striking out "relating to income earned by employees in certain camps" and inserting in lieu thereof "relating to citizens or residents of the United States living abroad". **Effective** with respect to tax years beginning after 12-31-81.

P.L. 97-34, §112(b)(6):

Amended Code Sec. 6091(b)(1)(B) by striking out "section 913 (relating to deduction for certain expenses of living abroad)". **Effective** with respect to tax years beginning after 12-31-81.

- **1978, Tax Treatment Extension Act of 1978 (P.L. 95-615)**

P.L. 95-615, §202(f)(5):

Amended Code Sec. 6091(b)(1)(B)(iii) by striking out "relating to earned income from sources without the United States" and inserting in lieu thereof "relating to income earned by employees in certain camps". **Effective** for tax years beginning after 12-31-77.

P.L. 95-615, §207(b):

Amended Code Sec. 6091(b)(1)(B)(iii) by inserting "section 913 (relating to deduction for certain expenses of living abroad)," before "section 931". **Effective** for tax years beginning after 12-31-77.

- **1976 (P.L. 94-528)**

P.L. 94-528, §2(a):

Amended the **effective** date of §1204 of the Tax Reform Act (see below) to change the date from December 31, 1976 to February 28, 1977. **Effective** 10-4-76.

- **1976, Tax Reform Act of 1976 (P.L. 94-455)**

P.L. 94-455, §§1051(h), 1052(c), 1053(d):

Amended Code Sec. 6091(b)(2)(B)(ii). **Effective** for tax years beginning after 12-31-75.

P.L. 94-455, §1204(c):

Struck out "and" at the end of paragraph (1)(B)(iii), struck out paragraph (1)(B)(iv), and inserted the material following paragraph (1)(B)(iii). **Effective** with respect to action taken under Code Sec. 6851, 6861, or 6862 of the Internal Revenue Code of 1954 where the notice and demand takes place after 12-31-76 (however, see P.L. 94-528 above). Prior to repeal, Code Sec. 6091(b)(1)(B)(iv) read as follows:

(iv) nonresident alien persons, shall be made at such place as the Secretary or his delegate may by regulations designate.

P.L. 94-455, §1204(c):

Also struck out "and" at the end of paragraph (2)(B)(ii), struck out paragraph (2)(B)(iii), and inserted the material following paragraph (2)(B)(ii). **Effective** with respect to action taken under Code Sec. 6851, 6861, or 6862 of the Internal Revenue Code of 1954 where the notice and demand takes place after 12-31-76 (however, see P.L. 94-528 above). Prior to repeal, Code Sec. 6091(b)(2)(B)(iii) read as follows:

(iii) foreign corporations, shall be made at such place as the Secretary or his delegate may by regulations designate.

P.L. 94-455, §1906(b)(13)(A):

Amended 1954 Code by substituting "Secretary" for "Secretary or his delegate" each place it appeared. **Effective** 2-1-77.

- **1970, Excise, Estate, and Gift Tax Adjustment Act of 1970 (P.L. 91-614)**

P.L. 91-614, §101(i)(2):

Amended paragraphs (3) and (4). **Effective** 1-1-71. Prior to amendment, paragraphs (3) and (4) read as follows:

(3) Estate tax returns.—Returns of estate tax required under section 6018 shall be made to the Secretary or his delegate in the internal revenue district in which was the domicile of the decedent at the time of his death or, if there was no such domicile in an internal revenue district, then at such place as the Secretary or his delegate may by regulations prescribe.

(4) Hand-carried returns.—Notwithstanding paragraph (1) or (2), a return to which paragraph (1)(A) or (2)(A) would apply, but for this paragraph, which is made to the Secretary or his delegate by handcarrying shall, under regulations prescribed by the Secretary or his delegate, be made in the internal revenue district referred to in paragraph (1)(A)(i) or (2)(A)(i), as the case may be.

- **1966 (P.L. 89-713)**

P.L. 89-713, §1(a):

Redesignated paragraph (4) as paragraph (5), substituted "(3), or (4)" for "or (3)" in newly designated paragraph (5), added a new paragraph (4), and amended paragraphs (1) and (2). **Effective** 11-2-66. Prior to amendment, paragraphs (1) and (2) read as follows:

(1) Individuals.—Returns (other than corporation returns) shall be made to the Secretary or his delegate in the internal revenue district in which is located the legal residence or principal place of business of the person making the return, or, if he has no legal residence or principal place of business in any internal revenue district, then at such place as the Secretary or his delegate may by regulations prescribe.

(2) Corporations.—Returns of corporations shall be made to the Secretary or his delegate in the internal revenue district in which is located the principal place of business or principal office or agency of the corporation, or, if it has no principal place of business or principal office or agency in any internal revenue district, then at such place as the Secretary or his delegate may be regulations prescribe.

PART VIII—DESIGNATION OF INCOME TAX PAYMENTS TO PRESIDENTIAL ELECTION CAMPAIGN FUND

Sec. 6096.   Designation by individuals.

[Sec. 6096]

SEC. 6096. DESIGNATION BY INDIVIDUALS.

[Sec. 6096(a)]

(a) IN GENERAL.—Every individual (other than a nonresident alien) whose income tax liability for the taxable year is $3 or more may designate that $3 shall be paid over to the Presidential Election Campaign Fund in accordance with the provisions of section 9006(a). In the case of a joint return of husband and wife having an income tax liability of $6 or more, each spouse may designate that $3 shall be paid to the fund.

RETURNS—CAMPAIGN FUNDS

Amendments

• **1993, Omnibus Budget Reconciliation Act of 1993 (P.L. 103-66)**

P.L. 103-66, §13441(a)(1)-(2):

Amended Code Sec. 6096(a) by striking "$1" each place it appears and inserting "$3", and by striking "$2" and inserting "$6". **Effective** with respect to tax returns required to be filed after 12-31-93.

[Sec. 6096(b)]

(b) INCOME TAX LIABILITY.—For purposes of subsection (a), the income tax liability of an individual for any taxable year is the amount of the tax imposed by chapter 1 on such individual for such taxable year (as shown on his return), reduced by the sum of the credits (as shown in his return) allowable under part IV of subchapter A of chapter 1 (other than subpart C thereof).

Amendments

• **1984, Deficit Reduction Act of 1984 (P.L. 98-369)**

P.L. 98-369, §474(r)(31):

Amended Code Sec. 6096(b) by striking out "allowable under sections 33, 37, 38, 40, 41, 42, 44, 44A, 44B, 44C, 44D, 44E, 44F, 44G, and 44H" and inserting in lieu thereof "allowable under part IV of subchapter A of Chapter 1 (other than subpart C thereof)". **Effective** for tax years beginning after 12-31-83, and to carrybacks from such years.

• **1983, Orphan Drug Act of 1982 (P.L. 97-414)**

P.L. 97-414, §4(c)(2):

Amended Code Sec. 6096(b) by striking out "and 44G" and inserting "44G, and 44H". **Effective** for amounts paid or incurred after 12-31-82, in tax years ending after such date.

• **1981, Economic Recovery Tax Act of 1981 (P.L. 97-34)**

P.L. 97-34, §221(c)(1), as amended by P.L. 99-514, §231:

Amended Code Sec. 6096(b) by striking out "and 44E" and inserting in lieu thereof "44E, and 44F". **Effective** for amounts paid or incurred after 6-30-81 [effective date changed by P.L. 99-514, §231(a)(2)].

P.L. 97-34, §221(d)(2), as amended by P.L. 99-514, §231, provides:

(2) TRANSITIONAL RULE.—

(A) IN GENERAL.—If, with respect to the first taxable year to which the amendments made by this section apply and which ends in 1981 or 1982, the taxpayer may only take into account qualified research expenses paid or incurred during a portion of such taxable year, the amount of the qualified research expenses taken into account for the base period of such taxable year shall be the amount which bears the same ratio to the total qualified research expenses for such base period as the number of months in such portion of such taxable year bears to the total number of months in such taxable year.

(B) DEFINITIONS.—For purposes of the preceding sentence, the terms "qualified research expenses" and "base period" have the meanings given to such terms by section 44F of the Internal Revenue Code of 1954 (as added by this section).

P.L. 97-34, §331(e)(1):

Amended Code Sec. 6096(b) by striking out "and 44F" and inserting in lieu thereof "44F, and 44G". **Effective** for tax years beginning after 12-31-81.

• **1980, Crude Oil Windfall Profit Tax Act of 1980 (P.L. 96-223)**

P.L. 96-223, §232(b)(3)(C):

Amended Code Sec. 6096(b), as amended by P.L. 96-223, §231(b)(2), by striking out "and 44D" and inserting "44D, and 44E". **Effective** for sales and uses after 9-30-80, in tax years ending after such date.

P.L. 96-223, §231(b)(2):

Amended Code Sec. 6096(b) by striking out "and 44C" and inserting "44C, and 44D". **Effective** for tax years ending after 12-31-79.

• **1978, Energy Tax Act of 1978 (P.L. 95-618)**

P.L. 95-618, §101(b)(4):

Amended Code Sec. 6096(b) by substituting ", 44B and 44C" for "and 44B". **Effective** for tax years ending on or after 4-20-77.

• **1977, Tax Reduction and Simplification Act of 1977 (P.L. 95-30)**

P.L. 95-30, §202(d)(6):

Amended Code Sec. 6096(b) by substituting "44A and 44B" for "and 44A". **Effective** for tax years beginning after 12-31-76, and for credit carrybacks from such years.

• **1976, Tax Reform Act of 1976 (P.L. 94-455)**

P.L. 94-455, §401(a)(2)(C):

Substituted "41, and 42" for "and 41". **Effective** for tax years ending after 12-31-75 and shall cease to apply to tax years ending after 12-31-77.

P.L. 94-455, §504(c)(2):

Substituted ", 44, and 44A" for "and 44". **Effective** for tax years beginning after 12-31-75.

P.L. 94-455, §1906(b)(13)(A):

Amended 1954 Code by substituting "Secretary" for "Secretary or his delegate" each place it appeared. **Effective** 2-1-77.

• **1975, Tax Reduction Act of 1975 (P.L. 94-12)**

P.L. 94-12, §§203(b), 208(d):

Amended Code Sec. 6096(b) by deleting "and 41" and inserting in lieu thereof, "41, 42 and 44." For **effective** date, see Code Secs. 42 and 44.

P.L. 94-12, §208(d):

Amended Code Sec. 6096(b) by deleting "and 42" and inserting in lieu thereof "42, and 44".

[Sec. 6096(c)]

(c) MANNER AND TIME OF DESIGNATION.—A designation under subsection (a) may be made with respect to any taxable year—

(1) at the time of filing the return of the tax imposed by chapter 1 for such taxable year, or

(2) at any other time (after the time of filing the return of the tax imposed by chapter 1 for such taxable year) specified in regulations prescribed by the Secretary.

Such designation shall be made in such manner as the Secretary prescribes by regulations except that, if such designation is made at the time of filing the return of the tax imposed by chapter 1 for such taxable year, such designation shall be made either on the first page of the return or on the page bearing the taxpayer's signature.

Amendments

• **1973 (P.L. 93-53)**

P.L. 93-53, §6(a):

Amended Code Sec. 6096. **Effective** for tax years beginning after 12-31-72. The **effective** date provision of P.L. 93-53 also provided that: "Any designation made under section 6096 of the Internal Revenue Code of 1954 (as in effect for taxable years beginning before January 1, 1973) for the account of the candidates of any specified political party shall, for purposes of section 9006(a) of such Code (as amended by subsection (b)), be treated solely as a designation to the Presidential Election Campaign Fund." Prior to amendment, Code Sec. 6096 read as follows:

"(a) In General.—Every individual (other than a nonresident alien) whose income tax liability for any taxable year is $1 or more may designate that $1 shall be paid over to the Presidential Election Campaign Fund for the account of the candidates of any specified political party for President and Vice President of the United States, or if no specific account is designated by such individual, for a general account for all candidates for election to the offices of President and Vice President of the United States, in accordance with the provisions of section 9006(a)(1). In the case of a joint return of husband and wife having an income tax liability of $2 or more, each spouse may designate that $1 shall be paid to any such account in the fund.

"(b) Income Tax Liability.—For purposes of subsection (a), the income tax liability of an individual for any taxable year is the amount of the tax imposed by chapter 1 on such individual for such taxable year (as shown on his return), reduced by the sum of the credits (as shown in his return) allowable under sections 32(2), 33, 35, 37, and 38.

"(c) Manner and Time of Designation.—A designation under subsection (a) may be made with respect to any taxable year, in such manner as the Secretary or his delegate may prescribe by regulations—

"(1) at the time of filing the return of the tax imposed by chapter 1 for such taxable year, or

"(2) at any other time (after the time of filing the return of the tax imposed by chapter 1 for such taxable year) specified in regulations prescribed by the Secretary or his delegate."

• **1971, Revenue Act of 1971 (P.L. 92-178)**

P.L. 92-178, §802(a):

Amended Code Sec. 6096(a). **Effective** for tax years ending on or after 12-31-72. Prior to amendment, Code Sec 6096(a) read:

"(a) IN GENERAL.—Every individual (other than a nonresident alien) whose income tax liability for any taxable year is $1 or more may designate that $1 shall be paid into the Presidential Election Campaign Fund established by section 303 of the Presidential Election Campaign Fund Act of 1966."

• **1967 (P.L. 90-26)**

P.L. 90-26, §5, provides:

(a) Funds which become available under the Presidential Election Campaign Fund Act of 1966 shall be appropriated and disbursed only after the adoption by law of guidelines governing their distribution. Section 6096 of the Internal Revenue Code of 1954 shall become applicable only after the adoption by law of such guidelines.

(b) Guidelines adopted in accordance with this section shall state expressly that they are intended to comply with this section.

RETURNS—MISCELLANEOUS PROVISIONS

• **1966, Foreign Investors Tax Act of 1966 (P.L. 89-809)**

P.L. 89-809, § 302(a):
Added Code Sec. 6096. **Effective** with respect to income tax liability for tax years beginning after 12-31-66.

Subchapter B—Miscellaneous Provisions

Sec. 6101.	Period covered by returns or other documents.
Sec. 6102.	Computations on returns or other documents.
Sec. 6103.	Confidentiality and disclosure of returns and return information.
Sec. 6104.	Publicity of information required from certain exempt organizations and certain trusts.
Sec. 6105.	Confidentiality of information arising under treaty obligations.
Sec. 6107.	Tax return preparer must furnish copy of return to taxpayer and must retain a copy or list.
Sec. 6108.	Statistical publications and studies.
Sec. 6109.	Identifying numbers.
Sec. 6110.	Public inspection of written determinations.
Sec. 6111.	Disclosure of reportable transactions.
Sec. 6112.	Material advisors of reportable transactions must keep lists of advisees, etc.
Sec. 6113.	Disclosure of nondeductibility of contributions.
Sec. 6114.	Treaty-based return positions.
Sec. 6115.	Disclosure related to quid pro quo contributions.
Sec. 6116.	Requirement for prisons located in United States to provide information for tax administration.
Sec. 6117.	Cross reference.

[Sec. 6101]

SEC. 6101. PERIOD COVERED BY RETURNS OR OTHER DOCUMENTS.

When not otherwise provided for by this title, the Secretary may by regulations prescribe the period for which, or the date as of which, any return, statement, or other document required by this title or by regulations, shall be made.

Amendments

• **1976, Tax Reform Act of 1976 (P.L. 94-455)**

P.L. 94-455, § 1906(b)(13)(A):
Amended 1954 Code by substituting "Secretary" for "Secretary or his delegate" each place it appeared. **Effective** 2-1-77.

[Sec. 6102]

SEC. 6102. COMPUTATIONS ON RETURNS OR OTHER DOCUMENTS.

[Sec. 6102(a)]

(a) AMOUNTS SHOWN ON INTERNAL REVENUE FORMS.—The Secretary is authorized to provide with respect to any amount required to be shown on a form prescribed for any internal revenue return, statement, or other document, that if such amount of such item is other than a whole-dollar amount, either—

(1) the fractional part of a dollar shall be disregarded; or

(2) the fractional part of a dollar shall be disregarded unless it amounts to one-half dollar or more, in which case the amount (determined without regard to the fractional part of a dollar) shall be increased by $1.

Amendments

• **1976, Tax Reform Act of 1976 (P.L. 94-455)**

P.L. 94-455, § 1906(b)(13)(A):
Amended 1954 Code by substituting "Secretary" for "Secretary or his delegate" each place it appeared. **Effective** 2-1-77.

[Sec. 6102(b)]

(b) ELECTION NOT TO USE WHOLE DOLLAR AMOUNTS.—Any person making a return, statement, or other document shall be allowed, under regulations prescribed by the Secretary, to make such return, statement, or other document without regard to subsection (a).

Amendments

• **1976, Tax Reform Act of 1976 (P.L. 94-455)**

P.L. 94-455, § 1906(b)(13)(A):
Amended 1954 Code by substituting "Secretary" for "Secretary or his delegate" each place it appeared. **Effective** 2-1-77.

[Sec. 6102(c)]

(c) INAPPLICABILITY TO COMPUTATION OF AMOUNT.—The provisions of subsections (a) and (b) shall not be applicable to items which must be taken into account in making the computations necessary to determine the amount required to be shown on a form, but shall be applicable only to such final amount.

[Sec. 6103]

SEC. 6103. CONFIDENTIALITY AND DISCLOSURE OF RETURNS AND RETURN INFORMATION.

[Sec. 6103(a)]

(a) GENERAL RULE.—Returns and return information shall be confidential, and except as authorized by this title—

(1) no officer or employee of the United States,

(2) no officer or employee of any State, any local law enforcement agency receiving information under subsection (i)(1)(C) or (7)(A), any local child support enforcement agency, or any local agency administering a program listed in subsection (l)(7)(D) who has or had access to returns or return information under this section or section 6104(c), and

RETURNS—MISCELLANEOUS PROVISIONS

(3) no other person (or officer or employee thereof) who has or had access to returns or return information under subsection (c), subsection (e)(1)(D)(iii), paragraph (10), (13), (14), or (15) of subsection (k), paragraph (6), (10), (12), (13) (other than subparagraphs (D)(v) and (D)(vi) thereof), (16), (19), (20), or (21) of subsection (l), paragraph (2) or (4)(B) of subsection (m), or subsection (n), shall disclose any return or return information obtained by him in any manner in connection with his service as such an officer or an employee or otherwise or under the provisions of this section. For purposes of this subsection, the term "officer or employee" includes a former officer or employee.

Amendments

- **2020, COVID-related Tax Relief Act of 2020 (P.L. 116-260)**

P.L. 116-260, §283(b)(2)(A), Div. N:

Amended Code Sec. 6103(a)(3) by striking "or (14)" and inserting "(14), or (15)". **Effective** for disclosures made on or after 12-27-2020.

P.L. 116-260, §284(a)(3)(A), Div. N:

Amended Code Sec. 6103(a)(3), as amended by section 3516(a)(1) of the CARES Act (P.L. 116-136), by striking "(13)(A), (13)(B), (13)(C), (13)(D)(i)," and inserting "(13) (other than subparagraphs (D)(v) and (D)(vi) thereof),". **Effective** for disclosures made after the date of the enactment of the FUTURE Act (P.L. 116-91) [effective for disclosures made after 12-19-2019.—CCH].

- **2020, Consolidated Appropriations Act, 2021 (P.L. 116-260)**

P.L. 116-260, §102(b)(2)(A), Div. FF:

Amended Code Sec. 6103(a)(3) by striking "or (14)" and inserting "(14), or (15)". [Note: An identical amendment was made by P.L. 116-260, Act Sec. 283(b)(2)(A), Div. N. Therefore, this amendment cannot be made.—CCH] **Effective** for disclosures made on or after 12-27-2020.

P.L. 116-260, §103(a)(3)(A), Div. FF:

Amended Code Sec. 6103(a)(3), as amended by section 3516(a)(1) of the CARES Act (P.L. 116-136), by striking "(13)(A), (13)(B), (13)(C), (13)(D)(i)," and inserting "(13) (other than subparagraphs (D)(v) and (D)(vi) thereof),". [Note: An identical amendment was made by P.L. 116-260, Act Sec. 284(a)(3)(A), Div. N. Therefore, this amendment cannot be made.—CCH] **Effective** for disclosures made after the date of the enactment of the FUTURE Act (P.L. 116-91) [effective for disclosures made after 12-19-2019.—CCH].

- **2020, Coronavirus Aid, Relief, and Economic Security (CARES) Act (P.L. 116-136)**

P.L. 116-136, §3516(a)(1):

Amended Code Sec. 6103(a)(3), as amended by the FUTURE Act (P.L. 116-91), by striking "(13), (16)" and inserting "(13)(A), (13)(B), (13)(C), (13)(D)(i), (16)". **Effective** as if included in the enactment of the FUTURE Act (P.L. 116-91) [effective for disclosures after 12-19-2019.—CCH].

- **2019, Fostering Undergraduate Talent by Unlocking Resources for Education (FUTURE) Act (P.L. 116-91)**

P.L. 116-91, §3(b):

Amended Code Sec. 6103(a)(3) by inserting ", (13)" after "(12)". **Effective** for disclosures after 12-19-2019.

- **2019, Taxpayer First Act (P.L. 116-25)**

P.L. 116-25, §1405(a)(2)(A):

Amended Code Sec. 6103(a)(3) by striking "subsection (k)(10)" and inserting "paragraph (10) or (13) of subsection (k)". **Effective** for disclosures made after 7-1-2019.

P.L. 116-25, §2003(c)(2)(A):

Amended Code Sec. 6103(a)(3), as amended by this Act, by striking "or (13)" and inserting ", (13), or (14)". **Effective** 7-1-2019.

P.L. 116-25, §2202(b):

Amended Code Sec. 6103(a)(3) by inserting "subsection (c)," after "return information under". **Effective** for disclosures made after the date which is 180 days after 7-1-2019.

- **2016, Recovering Missing Children Act (P.L. 114-184)**

P.L. 114-184, §2(b)(2)(A):

Amended Code Sec. 6103(a)(2) by striking "subsection (i)(7)(A)" and inserting "subsection (i)(1)(C) or (7)(A)". **Effective** for disclosures made after 6-30-2016.

- **2013, American Taxpayer Relief Act of 2012 (P.L. 112-240)**

P.L. 112-240, §209(b)(1):

Amended Code Sec. 6103(a)(3) by inserting "subsection (k)(10)," after "subsection (e)(1)(D)(iii),". **Effective** 1-2-2013.

- **2010, Patient Protection and Affordable Care Act (P.L. 111-148)**

P.L. 111-148, §1414(b):

Amended Code Sec. 6103(a)(3) by striking "or (20)" and inserting "(20), or (21)". **Effective** 3-23-2010.

- **2008, SSI Extension for Elderly and Disabled Refugees Act (P.L. 110-328)**

P.L. 110-328, §3(b)(1):

Amended Code Sec. 6103(a)(3) by inserting "(10)," after "(6),". **Effective** for refunds payable under Code Sec. 6402 on or after 9-30-2008.

- **2006, Pension Protection Act of 2006 (P.L. 109-280)**

P.L. 109-280, §1224(b)(1):

Amended Code Sec. 6103(a)(2) by inserting "or section 6104(c)" after "this section". **Effective** 8-17-2006 but shall not apply to requests made before such date.

- **2003, Medicare Prescription Drug, Improvement, and Modernization Act of 2003 (P.L. 108-173)**

P.L. 108-173, §105(e)(2):

Amended Code Sec. 6103(a)(3) by striking "or (16)" and inserting "(16), or (19)". **Effective** 12-8-2003.

P.L. 108-173, §811(c)(2)(A):

Amended Code Sec. 6103(a)(3), as amended by Act Sec. 105(e)(1)[(2)], by striking "or (19)" and inserting "(19), or (20)". **Effective** 12-8-2003.

- **2002, Victims of Terrorism Tax Relief Act of 2001 (P.L. 107-134)**

P.L. 107-134, §201(c)(1):

Amended Code Sec. 6103(a)(2) by inserting "any local law enforcement agency receiving information under subsection (i)(7)(A)," after "State,". **Effective** for disclosures made on or after 1-23-2002.

- **1997, Balanced Budget Act of 1997 (P.L. 105-33)**

P.L. 105-33, §11024(b)(2):

Amended Code Sec. 6103(a)(3) by striking "(6) or (12)" and inserting "(6), (12), or (16)". For the **effective** date, see Act Sec. 11721, below.

P.L. 105-33, §11721, provides:

Except as otherwise provided in this title, the provisions of this title shall take effect on the later of October 1, 1997, or the day the District of Columbia Financial Responsibility and Management Assistance Authority certifies that the financial plan and budget for the District government for fiscal year 1998 meet the requirements of section 201(c)(1) of the District of Columbia Financial Responsibility and Management Assistance Act of 1995, as amended by this title.

- **1996, Personal Responsibility and Work Opportunity Reconciliation Act of 1996 (P.L. 104-193)**

P.L. 104-193, §316(g)(4)(B)(i):

Amended Code Sec. 6103(a)(3) by striking "(l)(12)" and inserting "paragraph (6) or (12) of subsection (l)". **Effective** 8-22-96.

- **1989, Omnibus Budget Reconciliation Act of 1989 (P.L. 101-239)**

P.L. 101-239, §6202(a)(1)(B)(i):

Amended Code Sec. 6103(a)(3) by inserting "(l)(12)," after "(e)(1)(D)(iii),". **Effective** 12-19-89.

- **1984, Deficit Reduction Act of 1984 (P.L. 98-369)**

P.L. 98-369, §2651(k)(2):

Amended Code Sec. 6103(a)(2) by striking out "or of any local child support enforcement agency" and inserting in lieu thereof ", any local child support enforcement agency, or any local agency administering a program listed in subsection (l)(7)(D)". **Effective** 7-18-84.

- **1982, Debt Collection Act of 1982 (P.L. 97-365)**

P.L. 97-365, §8(c)(1):

Amended Code Sec. 6103(a)(3) by striking out "subsection (m)(4)(B)" and inserting in lieu thereof "paragraph (2) or (4)(B) of subsection (m)". **Effective** 10-25-82.

- **1978, Revenue Act of 1978 (P.L. 95-600)**

P.L. 95-600, §701(bb)(1)(B):

Amended Code Sec. 6103(a)(3) by inserting ", subsection (m)(4)(B)," after "subsection (e)(1)(D)(iii)". **Effective** 1-1-77.

- **1976, Tax Reform Act of 1976 (P.L. 94-455)**

P.L. 94-455, §1202(a):

Amended Code Sec. 6103(a). **Effective** 1-1-77. Prior to amendment, Code Sec. 6103(a) read as follows:

(a) PUBLIC RECORD AND INSPECTION.—

(1) Returns made with respect to taxes imposed by chapters 1, 2, 3, and 6 upon which the tax has been determined by the Secretary or his delegate shall constitute public records; but, except as hereinafter provided in this section, they shall be open to inspection only upon order of the President and under rules and regulations prescribed by the Secretary or his delegate and approved by the President.

(2) All returns made with respect to the taxes imposed by chapters 1, 2, 3, 5, 6, 11, 12, and 32, subchapters B and C of chapter 33, subchapter B of chapter 37, and chapter 41 shall constitute public records and shall be open to public examination and inspection to such extent as shall be authorized in rules and regulations promulgated by the President.

(3) Whenever a return is open to the inspection of any person, a certified copy thereof shall, upon request, be furnished to such person under rules and regulations prescribed by the Secretary or his delegate. The Secretary or his delegate may prescribe a reasonable fee for furnishing such copy.

RETURNS—MISCELLANEOUS PROVISIONS

- **1966 (P.L. 89-713)**

P.L. 89-713, §4(a):

Amended the heading to Code Sec. 6103 by substituting "AND DISCLOSURE OF INFORMATION AS TO PERSONS FILING INCOME TAX RETURNS" for "LISTS OF TAXPAYERS". **Effective** 11-2-66.

- **1965, Excise Tax Reduction Act of 1965 (P.L. 89-44)**

P.L. 89-44, §601(a):

Amended Sec. 6103(a) by substituting "B and C" for "B, C, and D" in paragraph (2).

- **1964, Interest Equalization Tax Act (P.L. 88-563)**

P.L. 88-563, §3(c):

Amended Code Sec. 6103(a)(2) by substituting "subchapter B of chapter 37, and chapter 41" for "and subchapter B of chapter 37".

[Sec. 6103(b)]

(b) DEFINITIONS.—For purposes of this section—

(1) RETURN.—The term "return" means any tax or information return, declaration of estimated tax, or claim for refund required by, or provided for or permitted under, the provisions of this title which is filed with the Secretary by, on behalf of, or with respect to any person, and any amendment or supplement thereto, including supporting schedules, attachments, or lists which are supplemental to, or part of, the return so filed.

(2) RETURN INFORMATION.—The term "return information" means—

(A) a taxpayer's identity, the nature, source, or amount of his income, payments, receipts, deductions, exemptions, credits, assets, liabilities, net worth, tax liability, tax withheld, deficiencies, overassessments, or tax payments, whether the taxpayer's return was, is being, or will be examined or subject to other investigation or processing, or any other data, received by, recorded by, prepared by, furnished to, or collected by the Secretary with respect to a return or with respect to the determination of the existence, or possible existence, of liability (or the amount thereof) of any person under this title for any tax, penalty, interest, fine, forfeiture, or other imposition, or offense,

(B) any part of any written determination or any background file document relating to such written determination (as such terms are defined in section 6110(b)) which is not open to public inspection under section 6110,

(C) any advance pricing agreement entered into by a taxpayer and the Secretary and any background information related to such agreement or any application for an advance pricing agreement, and

(D) any agreement under section 7121, and any similar agreement, and any background information related to such an agreement or request for such an agreement,

but such term does not include data in a form which cannot be associated with, or otherwise identify, directly or indirectly, a particular taxpayer. Nothing in the preceding sentence, or in any other provision of law, shall be construed to require the disclosure of standards used or to be used for the selection of returns for examination, or data used or to be used for determining such standards, if the Secretary determines that such disclosure will seriously impair assessment, collection, or enforcement under the internal revenue laws.

(3) TAXPAYER RETURN INFORMATION.—The term "taxpayer return information" means return information as defined in paragraph (2) which is filed with, or furnished to, the Secretary by or on behalf of the taxpayer to whom such return information relates.

(4) TAX ADMINISTRATION.—The term "tax administration"—

(A) means—

(i) the administration, management, conduct, direction, and supervision of the execution and application of the internal revenue laws or related statutes (or equivalent laws and statutes of a State) and tax conventions to which the United States is a party, and

(ii) the development and formulation of Federal tax policy relating to existing or proposed internal revenue laws, related statutes, and tax conventions, and

(B) includes assessment, collection, enforcement, litigation, publication, and statistical gathering functions under such laws, statutes, or conventions.

(5) STATE.—

(A) IN GENERAL.—The term "State" means—

(i) any of the 50 States, the District of Columbia, the Commonwealth of Puerto Rico, the Virgin Islands, Guam, American Samoa, and the Commonwealth of the Northern Mariana Islands,

(ii) for purposes of subsections (a)(2), (b)(4), (d)(1), (h)(4), and (p), any municipality—

(I) with a population in excess of 250,000 (as determined under the most recent decennial United States census data available),

(II) which imposes a tax on income or wages, and

(III) with which the Secretary (in his sole discretion) has entered into an agreement regarding disclosure, and

(iii) for purposes of subsections (a)(2), (b)(4), (d)(1), (h)(4), and (p), any governmental entity—

(I) which is formed and operated by a qualified group of municipalities, and

(II) with which the Secretary (in his sole discretion) has entered into an agreement regarding disclosure.

(B) REGIONAL INCOME TAX AGENCIES.—For purposes of subparagraph (A)(iii)—

(i) QUALIFIED GROUP OF MUNICIPALITIES.—The term "qualified group of municipalities" means, with respect to any governmental entity, 2 or more municipalities—

(I) each of which imposes a tax on income or wages,

(II) each of which, under the authority of a State statute, administers the laws relating to the imposition of such taxes through such entity, and

(III) which collectively have a population in excess of 250,000 (as determined under the most recent decennial United States census data available).

(ii) REFERENCES TO STATE LAW, ETC.—For purposes of applying subparagraph (A)(iii) to the subsections referred to in such subparagraph, any reference in such subsections to State law, proceedings, or tax returns shall be treated as references to the law, proceedings, or tax returns, as the case may be, of the municipalities which form and operate the governmental entity referred to in such subparagraph.

(iii) DISCLOSURE TO CONTRACTORS AND OTHER AGENTS.—Notwithstanding any other provision of this section, no return or return information shall be disclosed to any contractor or other agent of a governmental entity referred to in subparagraph (A)(iii) unless such entity, to the satisfaction of the Secretary—

RETURNS—MISCELLANEOUS PROVISIONS

(I) has requirements in effect which require each such contractor or other agent which would have access to returns or return information to provide safeguards (within the meaning of subsection (p)(4)) to protect the confidentiality of such returns or return information,

(II) agrees to conduct an on-site review every 3 years (or a mid-point review in the case of contracts or agreements of less than 3 years in duration) of each contractor or other agent to determine compliance with such requirements,

(III) submits the findings of the most recent review conducted under subclause (II) to the Secretary as part of the report required by subsection (p)(4)(E), and

(IV) certifies to the Secretary for the most recent annual period that such contractor or other agent is in compliance with all such requirements.

The certification required by subclause (IV) shall include the name and address of each contractor and other agent, a description of the contract or agreement with such contractor or other agent, and the duration of such contract or agreement. The requirements of this clause shall not apply to disclosures pursuant to subsection (n) for purposes of Federal tax administration and a rule similar to the rule of subsection (p)(8)(B) shall apply for purposes of this clause.

(6) TAXPAYER IDENTITY.—The term "taxpayer identity" means the name of a person with respect to whom a return is filed, his mailing address, his taxpayer identifying number (as described in section 6109), or a combination thereof.

(7) INSPECTION.—The terms "inspected" and "inspection" mean any examination of a return or return information.

(8) DISCLOSURE.—The term "disclosure" means the making known to any person in any manner whatever a return or return information.

(9) FEDERAL AGENCY.—The term "Federal agency" means an agency within the meaning of section 551(1) of title 5, United States Code.

(10) CHIEF EXECUTIVE OFFICER.—The term "chief executive officer" means, with respect to any municipality, any elected official and the chief official (even if not elected) of such municipality.

(11) TERRORIST INCIDENT, THREAT, OR ACTIVITY.—The term "terrorist incident, threat, or activity" means an incident, threat, or activity involving an act of domestic terrorism (as defined in section 2331(5) of title 18, United States Code) or international terrorism (as defined in section 2331(1) of such title).

Amendments

- **2007, Tax Technical Corrections Act of 2007 (P.L. 110-172)**

P.L. 110-172, §11(a)(34)(A):

Amended Code Sec. 6103(b)(5)(A) by striking "the Canal Zone," following "the Virgin Islands,". **Effective** 12-29-2007.

- **2006, Tax Relief and Health Care Act of 2006 (P.L. 109-432)**

P.L. 109-432, Division A, §421(a):

Amended Code Sec. 6103(b)(5). **Effective** for disclosures made after 12-31-2006. Prior to amendment, Code Sec. 6103(b)(5) read as follows:

(5) STATE.—The term "State" means—

(A) any of the 50 States, the District of Columbia, the Commonwealth of Puerto Rico, the Virgin Islands, the Canal Zone, Guam, American Samoa, and the Commonwealth of the Northern Mariana Islands, and

(B) for purposes of subsections (a)(2), (b)(4), (d)(1), (h)(4), and (p) any municipality—

(i) with a population in excess of 250,000 (as determined under the most recent decennial United States census data available),

(ii) which imposes a tax on income or wages, and

(iii) with which the Secretary (in his sole discretion) has entered into an agreement regarding disclosure.

- **2002, Victims of Terrorism Tax Relief Act of 2001 (P.L. 107-134)**

P.L. 107-134, §201(c)(2):

Amended Code Sec. 6103(b) by adding at the end a new paragraph (11). **Effective** for disclosures made on or after 1-23-2002.

- **2000, Community Renewal Tax Relief Act of 2000 (P.L. 106-554)**

P.L. 106-554, §304(a):

Amended Code Sec. 6103(b)(2) by striking "and" at the end of subparagraph (B), by inserting "and" at the end of subparagraph (C), and by inserting after subparagraph (C) a new subparagraph (D). **Effective** 12-21-2000.

- **1999, Tax Relief Extension Act of 1999 (P.L. 106-170)**

P.L. 106-170, §521(a)(1):

Amended Code Sec. 6103(b)(2) by striking "and" at the end of subparagraph (A), by inserting "and" at the end of subparagraph (B), and by inserting after subparagraph (B) a new subparagraph (C). **Effective** 12-17-99.

P.L. 106-170, §521(b)-(c), provides:

(b) ANNUAL REPORT REGARDING ADVANCE PRICING AGREEMENTS.—

(1) IN GENERAL.—Not later than 90 days after the end of each calendar year, the Secretary of the Treasury shall prepare and publish a report regarding advance pricing agreements.

(2) CONTENTS OF REPORT.—The report shall include the following for the calendar year to which such report relates:

(A) Information about the structure, composition, and operation of the advance pricing agreement program office.

(B) A copy of each model advance pricing agreement.

(C) The number of—

(i) applications filed during such calendar year for advance pricing agreements;

(ii) advance pricing agreements executed cumulatively to date and during such calendar year;

(iii) renewals of advance pricing agreements issued;

(iv) pending requests for advance pricing agreements;

(v) pending renewals of advance pricing agreements;

(vi) for each of the items in clauses (ii) through (v), the number that are unilateral, bilateral, and multilateral, respectively;

(vii) advance pricing agreements revoked or canceled, and the number of withdrawals from the advance pricing agreement program; and

(viii) advance pricing agreements finalized or renewed by industry.

(D) General descriptions of—

(i) the nature of the relationships between the related organizations, trades, or businesses covered by advance pricing agreements;

(ii) the covered transactions and the business functions performed and risks assumed by such organizations, trades, or businesses;

(iii) the related organizations, trades, or businesses whose prices or results are tested to determine compliance with transfer pricing methodologies prescribed in advance pricing agreements;

(iv) methodologies used to evaluate tested parties and transactions and the circumstances leading to the use of those methodologies;

(v) critical assumptions made and sources of comparables used;

(vi) comparable selection criteria and the rationale used in determining such criteria;

(vii) the nature of adjustments to comparables or tested parties;

(viii) the nature of any ranges agreed to, including information regarding when no range was used and why, when interquartile ranges were used, and when there was a statistical narrowing of the comparables;

(ix) adjustment mechanisms provided to rectify results that fall outside of the agreed upon advance pricing agreement range;

(x) the various term lengths for advance pricing agreements, including rollback years, and the number of advance pricing agreements with each such term length;

(xi) the nature of documentation required; and

(xii) approaches for sharing of currency or other risks.

(E) Statistics regarding the amount of time taken to complete new and renewal advance pricing agreements.

(F) A detailed description of the Secretary of the Treasury's efforts to ensure compliance with existing advance pricing agreements.

(3) CONFIDENTIALITY.—The reports required by this subsection shall be treated as authorized by the Internal Revenue Code of 1986 for purposes of section 6103 of such Code, but the reports shall not include information—

(A) which would not be permitted to be disclosed under section 6110(c) of such Code if such report were a written determination as defined in section 6110 of such Code; or

(B) which can be associated with, or otherwise identify, directly or indirectly, a particular taxpayer.

(4) FIRST REPORT.—The report for calendar year 1999 shall include prior calendar years after 1990.

(c) REGULATIONS.—The Secretary of the Treasury or the Secretary's delegate shall prescribe such regulations as may be necessary or appropriate to carry out the purposes of section 6103(b)(2)(C), and the last sentence of section 6110(b)(1), of the Internal Revenue Code of 1986, as added by this section.

- **1988, Technical and Miscellaneous Revenue Act of 1988 (P.L. 100-647)**

P.L. 100-647, §1012(bb)(3)(B):

Amended Code Sec. 6103(b)(5)(A) by striking out "the Commonwealth of the Northern Mariana Islands, the Republic of the Marshall Islands, the Federated States of Micronesia, and the Republic of Palau" and inserting in lieu thereof "and the Commonwealth of the Northern Mariana Islands". **Effective** 10-22-86.

P.L. 100-647, §6251:

Amended Code Sec. 6103(b)(5)(B)(i) by striking out "2,000,000" and inserting in lieu thereof "[ ]$250,000". **Effective** 11-10-88.

RETURNS—MISCELLANEOUS PROVISIONS

• **1986, Tax Reform Act of 1986 (P.L. 99-514)**

P.L. 99-514, § 1568(a)(1) and (a)(2):

Amended Code Sec. 6103(b) by striking out paragraph (5) and adding new paragraph (5), and by adding at the end thereof new paragraph (10). **Effective** 10-22-86. Prior to amendment, Code Sec. 6103(b)(5) read as follows:

(5) STATE.—The term "State" means any of the 50 States, the District of Columbia, the Commonwealth of Puerto Rico, the Virgin Islands, the Canal Zone, Guam, American Samoa, the Commonwealth of the Northern Mariana Islands, and the Trust Territory of the Pacific Islands.

• **1981, Economic Recovery Tax Act of 1981 (P.L. 97-34)**

P.L. 97-34, § 701:

Added the last sentence to Code Sec. 6103(b)(2). **Effective** for disclosures after 7-19-81.

• **1976, Tax Reform Act of 1976 (P.L. 94-455)**

P.L. 94-455, § 1202(a):

Amended Code Sec. 6103(b). **Effective** 1-1-77. Prior to amendment, Code Sec. 6103(b) read as follows:

(b) INSPECTION BY STATES.—

(1) STATE OFFICERS.—The proper officers of any State may, upon the request of the governor thereof, have access to the returns of any corporation, or to an abstract thereof showing the name and income of any corporation, at such times and in such manner as the Secretary or his delegate may prescribe.

(2) STATE BODIES OR COMMISSIONS.—All income returns filed with respect to the taxes imposed by chapters 1, 2, 3, and 6 (or copies thereof, if so prescribed by regulations made under this subsection), shall be open to inspection by any official, body, or commission, lawfully charged with the administration of any State tax law, if the inspection is for the purpose of such administration or for the purpose of obtaining information to be furnished to local taxing authorities as provided in this paragraph. The inspection shall be permitted only upon written request of the governor of such State, designating the representative of such official, body, or commission to make the inspection on behalf of such official, body, or commission. The inspection shall be made in such manner, and at such times and places, as shall be prescribed by regulations made by the Secretary or his delegate. Any information thus secured by any official, body, or commission of any State may be used only for the administration of the tax laws of such State, except that upon written request of the governor of such State any such information may be furnished to any official, body, or commission of any political subdivision of such State, lawfully charged with the administration of the tax laws of such political subdivision, but may be furnished only for the purpose of, and may be used only for, the administration of such tax laws.

[Sec. 6103(c)]

(c) DISCLOSURE OF RETURNS AND RETURN INFORMATION TO DESIGNEE OF TAXPAYER.—The Secretary may, subject to such requirements and conditions as he may prescribe by regulations, disclose the return of any taxpayer, or return information with respect to such taxpayer, to such person or persons as the taxpayer may designate in a request for or consent to such disclosure, or to any other person at the taxpayer's request to the extent necessary to comply with a request for information or assistance made by the taxpayer to such other person. However, return information shall not be disclosed to such person or persons if the Secretary determines that such disclosure would seriously impair Federal tax administration. Persons designated by the taxpayer under this subsection to receive return information shall not use the information for any purpose other than the express purpose for which consent was granted and shall not disclose return information to any other person without the express permission of, or request by, the taxpayer.

Amendments

• **2019, Taxpayer First Act (P.L. 116-25)**

P.L. 116-25, § 2201, provides:

SEC. 2201. DISCLOSURE OF TAXPAYER INFORMATION FOR THIRD-PARTY INCOME VERIFICATION.

(a) IN GENERAL.—Not later than 1 year after the close of the 2-year period described in subsection (d)(1), the Secretary of the Treasury or the Secretary's delegate (hereafter referred to in this section as the "Secretary") shall implement a program to ensure that any qualified disclosure—

(1) is fully automated and accomplished through the internet; and

(2) is accomplished in as close to real-time as is practicable.

(b) QUALIFIED DISCLOSURE.—For purposes of this section, the term "qualified disclosure" means a disclosure under section 6103(c) of the Internal Revenue Code of 1986 of returns or return information by the Secretary to a person seeking to verify the income or creditworthiness of a taxpayer who is a borrower in the process of a loan application.

(c) APPLICATION OF SECURITY STANDARDS.—The Secretary shall ensure that the program described in subsection (a) complies with applicable security standards and guidelines.

(d) USER FEE.—

(1) IN GENERAL.—During the 2-year period beginning on the first day of the sixth calendar month beginning after the date of the enactment of this Act, the Secretary shall assess and collect a fee for qualified disclosures (in addition to any other fee assessed and collected for such disclosures) at such rates as the Secretary determines are sufficient to cover the costs related to implementing the program described in subsection (a), including the costs of any necessary infrastructure or technology.

(2) DEPOSIT OF COLLECTIONS.—Amounts received from fees assessed and collected under paragraph (1) shall be deposited in, and credited to, an account solely for the purpose of carrying out the activities described in subsection (a). Such amounts shall be available to carry out such activities without need of further appropriation and without fiscal year limitation.

P.L. 116-25, § 2202(a):

Amended Code Sec. 6103(c) by adding at the end a new sentence. **Effective** for disclosures made after the date which is 180 days after 7-1-2019.

• **1998, IRS Restructuring and Reform Act of 1998 (P.L. 105-206)**

P.L. 105-206, § 2003(e), provides:

(e) PROCEDURES FOR AUTHORIZING DISCLOSURE ELECTRONICALLY.—The Secretary shall establish procedures for any taxpayer to authorize, on an electronically filed return, the Secretary to disclose information under section 6103(c) of the Internal Revenue Code of 1986 to the preparer of the return.

• **1996, Taxpayer Bill of Rights 2 (P.L. 104-168)**

P.L. 104-168, § 1207:

Amended Code Sec. 6103(c) by striking "written request for or consent to such disclosure" and inserting "request for or consent to such disclosure". **Effective** 7-30-96.

• **1976, Tax Reform Act of 1976 (P.L. 94-455)**

P.L. 94-455, § 1202(a):

Amended Code Sec. 6103(c). **Effective** 1-1-77. Prior to amendment, Code Sec. 6103(c) read as follows:

(c) INSPECTION BY SHAREHOLDERS.—All bona fide shareholders of record owning 1 percent or more of the outstanding stock of any corporation shall, upon making request of the Secretary or his delegate, be allowed to examine the annual income returns of such corporation and of its subsidiaries.

[Sec. 6103(d)]

(d) DISCLOSURE TO STATE TAX OFFICIALS AND STATE AND LOCAL LAW ENFORCEMENT AGENCIES.—

(1) IN GENERAL.—Returns and return information with respect to taxes imposed by chapters 1, 2, 6, 11, 12, 21, 23, 24, 31, 32, 44, 51 and 52 and subchapter D of chapter 36 shall be open to inspection by, or disclosure to, any State agency, body, or commission, or its legal representative, which is charged under the laws of such State with responsibility for the administration of State tax laws for the purpose of, and only to the extent necessary in, the administration of such laws, including any procedures with respect to locating any person who may be entitled to a refund. Such inspection shall be permitted, or such disclosure made, only upon written request by the head of such agency, body, or commission, and only to the representatives of such agency, body, or commission designated in such written request as the individuals which are to inspect or to receive the returns or return information on behalf of such agency, body, or commission. Such representatives shall not include any individual who is the chief executive officer of such State or who is neither an employee or legal representative of such agency, body, or commission nor a person described in subsection (n). However, such return information shall not be disclosed to the extent that the Secretary determines that such disclosure would identify a confidential informant or seriously impair any civil or criminal tax investigation.

(2) DISCLOSURE TO STATE AUDIT AGENCIES.—

(A) IN GENERAL.—Any returns or return information obtained under paragraph (1) by any State agency, body, or commission may be open to inspection by, or disclosure to, officers and employees of the State audit agency for the purpose of, and only to the extent necessary in, making an audit of the State agency, body, or commission referred to in paragraph (1).

(B) STATE AUDIT AGENCY.—For purposes of subparagraph (A), the term "State audit agency" means any State agency, body, or commission which is charged under the laws of the State with the responsibility of auditing State revenues and programs.

(3) EXCEPTION FOR REIMBURSEMENT UNDER SECTION 7624.—Nothing in this section shall be construed to prevent the Secretary from disclosing to any State or local law enforcement agency which may receive a payment under section 7624 the amount of the recovered taxes with respect to which such a payment may be made.

RETURNS—MISCELLANEOUS PROVISIONS

(4) AVAILABILITY AND USE OF DEATH INFORMATION.—

(A) IN GENERAL.—No returns or return information may be disclosed under paragraph (1) to any agency, body, or commission of any State (or any legal representative thereof) during any period during which a contract meeting the requirements of subparagraph (B) is not in effect between such State and the Secretary of Health and Human Services.

(B) CONTRACTUAL REQUIREMENTS.—A contract meets the requirements of this subparagraph if—

(i) such contract requires the State to furnish the Secretary of Health and Human Services information concerning individuals with respect to whom death certificates (or equivalent documents maintained by the State of any subdivision thereof) have been officially filed with it, and

(ii) such contract does not include any restriction on the use of information obtained by such Secretary pursuant to such contract, except that such contract may provide that such information is only to be used by the Secretary (or any other Federal agency) for purposes of ensuring that Federal benefits or other payments are not erroneously paid to deceased individuals.

Any information obtained by the Secretary of Health and Human Services under such a contract shall be exempt from disclosure under section 552 of title 5, United States Code, and from the requirements of section 552a of such title 5.

(C) SPECIAL EXCEPTION.—The provisions of subparagraph (A) shall not apply to any State which on July 1, 1993, was not, pursuant to a contract, furnishing the Secretary of Health and Human Services information concerning individuals with respect to whom death certificates (or equivalent documents maintained by the State or any subdivision thereof) have been officially filed with it.

(5) DISCLOSURE FOR COMBINED EMPLOYMENT TAX REPORTING.—

(A) IN GENERAL.—The Secretary may disclose taxpayer identity information and signatures to any agency, body, or commission of any State for the purpose of carrying out with such agency, body, or commission a combined Federal and State employment tax reporting program approved by the Secretary. Subsections (a)(2) and (p)(4) and sections 7213 and 7213A shall not apply with respect to disclosures or inspections made pursuant to this paragraph.

(B) TERMINATION.—The Secretary may not make any disclosure under this paragraph after December 31, 2007.

(6) LIMITATION ON DISCLOSURE REGARDING REGIONAL INCOME TAX AGENCIES TREATED AS STATES.—For purposes of paragraph (1), inspection by or disclosure to an entity described in subsection (b)(5)(A)(iii) shall be for the purpose of, and only to the extent necessary in, the administration of the laws of the member municipalities in such entity relating to the imposition of a tax on income or wages. Such entity may not redisclose any return or return information received pursuant to paragraph (1) to any such member municipality.

Amendments

• **2006, Tax Relief and Health Care Act of 2006 (P.L. 109-432)**

P.L. 109-432, Division A, §122(a)(1):

Amended Code Sec. 6103(d)(5)(B) by striking "2006" and inserting "2007". **Effective** for disclosures after 12-31-2006.

P.L. 109-432, Division A, §421(b):

Amended Code Sec. 6103(d) by adding at the end a new paragraph (6). **Effective** for disclosures made after 12-31-2006.

• **2005, Gulf Opportunity Zone Act of 2005 (P.L. 109-135)**

P.L. 109-135, §305(a)(1):

Amended Code Sec. 6103(d)(5)(B) by striking "December 31, 2005" and inserting "December 31, 2006". **Effective** for disclosures after 12-31-2005.

• **2004, Working Families Tax Relief Act of 2004 (P.L. 108-311)**

P.L. 108-311, §311(a):

Amended Code Sec. 6103(d)(5). **Effective** 10-4-2004. Prior to amendment, Code Sec. 6103(d)(5) read as follows:

(5) DISCLOSURE FOR CERTAIN COMBINED REPORTING PROJECT.—The Secretary shall disclose taxpayer identities and signatures for purposes of the demonstration project described in section 976 of the Taxpayer Relief Act of 1997. Subsections (a)(2) and (p)(4) and sections 7213 and 7213A shall not apply with respect to disclosures or inspections made pursuant to this paragraph.

• **1998, IRS Restructuring and Reform Act of 1998 (P.L. 105-206)**

P.L. 105-206, §6009(d):

Amended Code Sec. 6103(d)(5) by striking "section 967 of the Taxpayer Relief Act of 1997." and inserting "section 976 of the Taxpayer Relief Act of 1997. Subsections (a)(2) and (p)(4) and sections 7213 and 7213A shall not apply with respect to disclosures or inspections made pursuant to this paragraph." **Effective** as if included in the provision of P.L. 105-34 to which it relates [effective 8-5-97.—CCH].

• **1997, Taxpayer Relief Act of 1997 (P.L. 105-34)**

P.L. 105-34, §976(c):

Amended Code Sec. 6103(d) by adding at the end a new paragraph (5). **Effective** 8-5-97.

• **1993, Omnibus Budget Reconciliation Act of 1993 (P.L. 103-66)**

P.L. 103-66, §13444(a):

Amended Code Sec. 6103(d) by adding at the end thereof a new paragraph (4). For the **effective** date, see Act Sec. 13444(b), below.

P.L. 103-66, §13444(b), provides:

(b) EFFECTIVE DATE.—

(1) IN GENERAL.—Except as provided in paragraph (2), the amendment made by subsection (a) shall take effect on the date one year after the date of the enactment of this Act.

(2) SPECIAL RULE.—The amendment made by subsection (a) shall take effect on the date 2 years after the date of the enactment of this Act in the case of any State if it is established to the satisfaction of the Secretary of the Treasury that—

(A) under the law of such State as in effect on the date of the enactment of this Act, it is impossible for such State to enter into an agreement meeting the requirements of section 6103(d)(4)(B) of the Internal Revenue Code of 1986 (as added by subsection (a)), and

(B) it is likely that such State will enter into such an agreement during the extension period under this paragraph.

• **1989, Omnibus Budget Reconciliation Act of 1989 (P.L. 101-239)**

P.L. 101-239, §7841(d)(1):

Amended Code Sec. 6103(d)(1) by striking "45," after "44,". **Effective** 12-19-89.

• **1988, Anti-Drug Abuse Act of 1988 (P.L. 100-690)**

P.L. 100-690, §7602(c):

Amended Code Sec. 6103(d) by adding at the end thereof new paragraph (3). **Effective** for information first provided more than 90 days after the date of the enactment of this Act.

P.L. 100-690, §7602(d)(2):

Amended the heading of Code Sec. 6103(d). **Effective** for information first provided more than 90 days after the date of the enactment of this Act. Prior to amendment, the heading for Code Sec. 6103(d) read as follows:

DISCLOSURE TO STATE TAX OFFICIALS.—

P.L. 100-690, §7602(g), provides:

(g) REGULATIONS.—The Secretary of the Treasury shall, not later than 90 days after the date of enactment of this Act, prescribe such rules and regulations as shall be necessary and proper to carry out the provisions of this section, including regulations relating to the definition of information which substantially contributes to the recovery of Federal taxes and the substantiation of expenses required in order to receive a reimbursement.

• **1984, Deficit Reduction Act of 1984 (P.L. 98-369)**

P.L. 98-369, §449(a):

Amended Code Sec. 6103(d)(1) by striking out "44, 51" and inserting in lieu thereof "44, 45, 51". **Effective** 7-18-84.

• **1980 (P.L. 96-598)**

P.L. 96-598, §3(a):

Amended Code Sec. 6103(d). **Effective** 12-24-80. Prior to amendment, Code Sec. 6103(d) read:

(d) DISCLOSURE TO STATE TAX OFFICIALS.—Returns and return information with respect to taxes imposed by chapters 1, 2, 6, 11, 12, 21, 23, 24, 31, 44, 51, and 52 and subchapter D of chapter 36, shall be open to inspection by or disclosure to any State agency, body, or commission, or its legal representative, which is charged under the laws of such State with responsibility for the administration of State tax laws for the purpose of, and only to the extent necessary in, the administration of such laws, including any procedures with respect to locating any person who may be entitled to a refund. Such inspection shall be permitted, or such disclosure made, only upon written request by the head of such agency, body, or commission, and only to the representatives of such agency, body, or commission designated in such written request as the individuals who are to inspect or to receive the return or return information on behalf of such agency, body, or commission. Such representatives shall not include any individual who is the chief executive officer of such State or who is neither an employee or legal representative of such agency, body, or commission nor a person described in subsection (n). However, such return information shall not be disclosed to the extent that the Secretary determines that such disclosure would identify a confidential informant or seriously impair any civil or criminal tax investigation.

• **1978, Revenue Act of 1978 (P.L. 95-600)**

P.L. 95-600, §701(bb)(2):

Amended Code Sec. 6103(d) by inserting "31," after "24,". **Effective** 1-1-77.

RETURNS—MISCELLANEOUS PROVISIONS

• 1976, Tax Reform Act of 1976 (P.L. 94-455)
P.L. 94-455, §1202(a):
Amended Code Sec. 6103(d). **Effective** 1-1-77. Prior to amendment, Code Sec. 6103(d) read as follows:

(d) INSPECTION BY COMMITTEES OF CONGRESS.—

(1) COMMITTEES ON WAYS AND MEANS AND FINANCE.—

(A) The Secretary and any officer or employee of the Treasury Department, upon request from the Committee on Ways and Means of the House of Representatives, the Committee on Finance of the Senate, or a select committee of the Senate or House specially authorized to investigate returns by a resolution of the Senate or House, or a joint committee so authorized by concurrent resolution, shall furnish such committee sitting in executive session with any data of any character contained in or shown by any return.

(B) Any such committee shall have the right, acting directly as a committee, or by or through such examiners or agents as it may designate or appoint, to inspect any or all of the returns at such times and in such manner as it may determine.

(C) Any relevant or useful information thus obtained may be submitted by the committee obtaining it to the Senate or the House, or to both the Senate and the House, as the case may be.

(2) JOINT COMMITTEE ON INTERNAL REVENUE TAXATION.—The Joint Committee on Internal Revenue Taxation shall have the same right to obtain data and to inspect returns as the Committee on Ways and Means or the Committee on Finance, and to submit any relevant or useful information thus obtained to the Senate, the House of Representatives, the Committee on Ways and Means, or the Committee on Finance. The Committee on Ways and Means or the Committee on Finance may submit such information to the House or to the Senate, or to both the House and the Senate, as the case may be.

[Sec. 6103(e)]

(e) DISCLOSURE TO PERSONS HAVING MATERIAL INTEREST.—

(1) IN GENERAL.—The return of a person shall, upon written request, be open to inspection by or disclosure to—

(A) in the case of the return of an individual—

(i) that individual,

(ii) the spouse of that individual if the individual and such spouse have signified their consent to consider a gift reported on such return as made one-half by him and one-half by the spouse pursuant to the provisions of section 2513, or,

(iii) the child of that individual (or such child's legal representative) to the extent necessary to comply with the provisions of section (1)(g);

(B) in the case of an income tax return filed jointly, either of the individuals with respect to whom the return is filed;

(C) in the case of the return of a partnership, any person who was a member of such partnership during any part of the period covered by the return;

(D) in the case of the return of a corporation or a subsidiary thereof—

(i) any person designated by resolution of its board of directors or other similar governing body,

(ii) any officer or employee of such corporation upon written request signed by any principal officer and attested to by the secretary or other officer,

(iii) any bona fide shareholder of record owning 1 percent or more of the outstanding stock of such corporation,

(iv) if the corporation was an S corporation, any person who was a shareholder during any part of the period covered by such return during which an election under section 1362(a) was in effect, or

(v) if the corporation has been dissolved, any person authorized by applicable State law to act for the corporation or any person who the Secretary finds to have a material interest which will be affected by information contained therein;

(E) in the case of the return of an estate—

(i) the administrator, executor, or trustee of such estate, and

(ii) any heir at law, next of kin, or beneficiary under the will, of the decedent, but only if the Secretary finds that such heir at law, next of kin, or beneficiary has a material interest which will be affected by information contained therein; and

(F) in the case of the return of a trust—

(i) the trustee or trustees, jointly or separately, and

(ii) any beneficiary of such trust, but only if the Secretary finds that such beneficiary has a material interest which will be affected by information contained therein.

(2) INCOMPETENCY.—If an individual described in paragraph (1) is legally incompetent, the applicable return shall, upon written request, be open to inspection by or disclosure to the committee, trustee, or guardian of his estate.

(3) DECEASED INDIVIDUALS.—The return of a decedent shall, upon written request, be open to inspection by or disclosure to—

(A) the administrator, executor, or trustee of his estate, and

(B) any heir at law, next of kin, or beneficiary under the will, of such decedent, or a donee of property, but only if the Secretary finds that such heir at law, next of kin, beneficiary, or donee has a material interest which will be affected by information contained therein.

(4) TITLE 11 CASES AND RECEIVERSHIP PROCEEDINGS.—If—

(A) there is a trustee in a title 11 case in which the debtor is the person with respect to whom the return is filed, or

(B) substantially all of the property of the person with respect to whom the return is filed is in the hands of a receiver,

such return or returns for prior years of such person shall, upon written request, be open to inspection by or disclosure to such trustee or receiver, but only if the Secretary finds that such trustee or receiver, in his fiduciary capacity, has a material interest which will be affected by information contained therein.

(5) INDIVIDUAL'S TITLE 11 CASE.—

(A) IN GENERAL.—In any case to which section 1398 applies (determined without regard to section 1398(b)(1)), any return of the debtor for the taxable year in which the case commenced or any preceding taxable year shall, upon written request, be open to inspection by or disclosure to the trustee in such case.

(B) RETURN OF ESTATE AVAILABLE TO DEBTOR.—Any return of an estate in a case to which section 1398 applies shall, upon written request, be open to inspection by or disclosure to the debtor in such case.

(C) SPECIAL RULE FOR INVOLUNTARY CASES.—In an involuntary case, no disclosure shall be made under subparagraph (A) until the order for relief has been entered by the court having jurisdiction of such case unless such court finds that such disclosure is appropriate for purposes of determining whether an order for relief should be entered.

(6) ATTORNEY IN FACT.—Any return to which this subsection applies shall, upon written request, also be open to inspection by or disclosure to the attorney in fact duly authorized in writing by any of the persons described in paragraph (1), (2), (3), (4), (5), (8), or (9) to inspect the return or receive the information on his behalf, subject to the conditions provided in such paragraphs.

(7) RETURN INFORMATION.—Return information with respect to any taxpayer may be open to inspection by or disclosure to any person authorized by this subsection to inspect any return of such taxpayer if the Secretary determines that such disclosure would not seriously impair Federal tax administration.

(8) DISCLOSURE OF COLLECTION ACTIVITIES WITH RESPECT TO JOINT RETURN.—If any deficiency of tax with respect to a joint return is assessed and the individuals filing such return are no longer married or no longer reside in the same household, upon request in writing by either of such individuals, the Secretary shall disclose in writing to the individual making the request whether the Secretary has attempted to collect such

RETURNS—MISCELLANEOUS PROVISIONS

deficiency from such other individual, the general nature of such collection activities, and the amount collected. The preceding sentence shall not apply to any deficiency which may not be collected by reason of section 6502.

(9) DISCLOSURE OF CERTAIN INFORMATION WHERE MORE THAN 1 PERSON SUBJECT TO PENALTY UNDER SECTION 6672.—If the Secretary determines that a person is liable for a penalty under section 6672(a) with respect to any failure, upon request in writing of such person, the Secretary shall disclose in writing to such person—

(A) the name of any other person whom the Secretary has determined to be liable for such penalty with respect to such failure, and

(B) whether the Secretary has attempted to collect such penalty from such other person, the general nature of such collection activities, and the amount collected.

(10) LIMITATION ON CERTAIN DISCLOSURES UNDER THIS SUBSECTION.—In the case of an inspection or disclosure under this subsection relating to the return of a partnership, S corporation, trust, or an estate, the information inspected or disclosed shall not include any supporting schedule, attachment, or list which includes the taxpayer identity information of a person other than the entity making the return or the person conducting the inspection or to whom the disclosure is made.

(11) DISCLOSURE OF INFORMATION REGARDING STATUS OF INVESTIGATION OF VIOLATION OF THIS SECTION.—In the case of a person who provides to the Secretary information indicating a violation of section 7213, 7213A, or 7214 with respect to any return or return information of such person, the Secretary may disclose to such person (or such person's designee)—

(A) whether an investigation based on the person's provision of such information has been initiated and whether it is open or closed,

(B) whether any such investigation substantiated such a violation by any individual, and

(C) whether any action has been taken with respect to such individual (including whether a referral has been made for prosecution of such individual).

Amendments

• **2015, Protecting Americans from Tax Hikes Act of 2015 (P.L. 114-113)**

P.L. 114-113, §403(a), Div. Q:

Amended Code Sec. 6103(e) by adding at the end a new paragraph (11). **Effective** for disclosures made on or after 12-18-2015.

• **2007, Mortgage Forgiveness Debt Relief Act of 2007 (P.L. 110-142)**

P.L. 110-142, §8(c)(1):

Amended Code Sec. 6103(e) by adding at the end a new paragraph (10). **Effective** 12-20-2007.

• **2004, American Jobs Creation Act of 2004 (P.L. 108-357)**

P.L. 108-357, §413(c)(27):

Amended Code Sec. 6103(e)(1)(D) by striking clause (iv) and redesignating clauses (v) and (vi) as clauses (iv) and (v), respectively. **Effective** for disclosures of return or return information with respect to tax years beginning after 12-31-2004. Prior to being stricken, Code Sec. 6103(e)(1)(D)(iv) read as follows:

(iv) if the corporation was a foreign personal holding company, as defined by section 552, any person who was a shareholder during any part of a period covered by such return if with respect to that period, or any part thereof, such shareholder was required under section 551 to include in his gross income undistributed foreign personal holding company income of such company,

• **2000, Community Renewal Tax Relief Act of 2000 (P.L. 106-554)**

P.L. 106-554, §319(8)(B):

Amended Code Sec. 6103(e)(1)(D)(v). **Effective** 12-21-2000. Prior to amendment, Code Sec. 6103(e)(1)(D)(v) read as follows:

(v) if the corporation was an electing small business corporation under subchapter S of chapter 1, any person who was a shareholder during any part of the period covered by such return during which an election was in effect, or

• **1998, IRS Restructuring and Reform Act of 1998 (P.L. 105-206)**

P.L. 105-206, §6007(f)(4):

Amended Code Sec. 6103(e)(1)(A) by striking clause (ii) and by redesignating clauses (iii) and (iv) as clauses (ii) and (iii), respectively. **Effective** as if included in the provision of P.L. 105-34 to which it relates [effective for sales or exchanges after 8-5-97.—CCH]. Prior to being stricken, Code Sec. 6103(e)(1)(A)(ii) read as follows:

(ii) if property transferred by that individual to a trust is sold or exchanged in a transaction described in section 644, the trustee or trustees, jointly or separately, of such trust to the extent necessary to ascertain any amount of tax imposed upon the trust by section 644,

P.L. 105-206, §6019(c):

Amended Code Sec. 6103(e)(6) by striking "or (5)" and inserting "(5), (8), or (9)". **Effective** 7-22-98.

• **1997, Taxpayer Relief Act of 1997 (P.L. 105-34)**

P.L. 105-34, §1201(b)(2):

Amended Code Sec. 6103(e)(1)(A)(iv) by striking "or 59(j)" after "section (1)(g)". **Effective** for tax years beginning after 12-31-97.

• **1996, Small Business Job Protection Act of 1996 (P.L. 104-188)**

P.L. 104-188, §1704(t)(41):

Amended Code Sec. 6103(e)(1)(A)(iv) by striking all that follows "provisions of" and inserting "section (1)(g) or 59(j)". **Effective** 8-20-96. Prior to amendment, Code Sec. 6103(e)(1)(A)(iv) read as follows:

(iv) the child of that individual (or such child's legal representative) to the extent necessary to comply with the provisions of section 1(g) or 59(j);

• **1996, Taxpayer Bill of Rights 2 (P.L. 104-168)**

P.L. 104-168, §403(a):

Amended Code Sec. 6103(e) by adding at the end a new paragraph (8). **Effective** for requests made after 7-30-96.

P.L. 104-168, §902(a):

Amended Code Sec. 6103(e), as amended by Act Sec. 403, by adding at the end a new paragraph (9). **Effective** 7-30-96.

• **1990, Omnibus Budget Reconciliation Act of 1990 (P.L. 101-508)**

P.L. 101-508, §11101(d)(6):

Amended Code Sec. 6103(e)(1)(A)(iv) by striking "section 1(j)" and inserting "section 1(g)". **Effective** for tax years beginning after 12-31-90.

• **1988, Technical and Miscellaneous Revenue Act of 1988 (P.L. 100-647)**

P.L. 100-647, §1014(e)(4):

Amended Code Sec. 6103(e)(1)(A)(iv) by striking out "section 1(j)" and inserting in lieu thereof "section 1(j) or 59(j)". **Effective** as if included in the provision of P.L. 99-514 to which it relates.

• **1986, Tax Reform Act of 1986 (P.L. 99-514)**

P.L. 99-514, §1411(b):

Amended Code Sec. 6103(e)(1)(A) by striking out "or" at the end of clause (ii), by inserting "or" at the end of clause (iii), and by adding at the end thereof new clause (iv). **Effective** for tax years beginning after 12-31-86.

• **1980, Bankruptcy Tax Act of 1980 (P.L. 96-589)**

P.L. 96-589, §3(c)(1), (2):

Amended Code Sec. 6103(e) by striking out paragraph (4), redesignating paragraphs (5) and (6) as (6) and (7) and adding new paragraphs (4) and (5). **Effective** for bankruptcy cases commencing on or after 3-25-81. Prior to amendment, Code Sec. 6103(e)(4) provided:

(4) BANKRUPTCY.—If substantially all of the property of the person with respect to whom the return is filed is in the hands of a trustee in bankruptcy or receiver, such return or returns for prior years of such person shall, upon written request, be open to inspection by or disclosure to such trustee or receiver, but only if the Secretary finds that such receiver or trustee, in his fiduciary capacity, has a material interest which will be affected by information contained therein.

P.L. 96-589, §3(c)(2):

Amended Code Sec. 6103(e)(6), as redesignated, by striking out "or (4)" and inserting "(4), or (5)". **Effective** for bankruptcy cases commencing on or after 3-25-81.

• **1976, Tax Reform Act of 1976 (P.L. 94-455)**

P.L. 94-455, §1202(a):

Amended Code Sec. 6103(e). **Effective** 1-1-77. Prior to amendment, Code Sec. 6103(e) read as follows:

(e) DECLARATIONS OF ESTIMATED TAX.—For purposes of this section, a declaration of estimated tax shall be held and considered a return under this chapter.

[Sec. 6103(f)]

(f) DISCLOSURE TO COMMITTEES OF CONGRESS.—

(1) COMMITTEE ON WAYS AND MEANS, COMMITTEE ON FINANCE, AND JOINT COMMITTEE ON TAXATION.—Upon written request from the chairman of the Committee on Ways and Means of the House of Representatives, the chairman of the Committee on Finance of the Senate, or the chairman of the Joint Committee on Taxation, the Secretary shall furnish such committee with any return or return information specified in such request, except that any return or return information which can be associated with, or otherwise identify, directly or indirectly, a particular taxpayer

RETURNS—MISCELLANEOUS PROVISIONS

shall be furnished to such committee only when sitting in closed executive session unless such taxpayer otherwise consents in writing to such disclosure.

(2) CHIEF OF STAFF OF JOINT COMMITTEE ON TAXATION.—Upon written request by the Chief of Staff of the Joint Committee on Taxation, the Secretary shall furnish him with any return or return information specified in such request. Such Chief of Staff may submit such return or return information to any committee described in paragraph (1), except that any return or return information which can be associated with, or otherwise identify, directly or indirectly, a particular taxpayer shall be furnished to such committee only when sitting in closed executive session unless such taxpayer otherwise consents in writing to such disclosure.

(3) OTHER COMMITTEES.—Pursuant to an action by, and upon written request by the chairman of, a committee of the Senate or the House of Representatives (other than a committee specified in paragraph (1)) specially authorized to inspect any return or return information by a resolution of the Senate or the House of Representatives or, in the case of a joint committee (other than the joint committee specified in paragraph (1)), by concurrent resolution, the Secretary shall furnish such committee, or a duly authorized and designated subcommittee thereof, sitting in closed executive session, with any return or return information which such resolution authorizes the committee or subcommittee to inspect. Any resolution described in this paragraph shall specify the purpose for which the return or return information is to be furnished and that such information cannot reasonably be obtained from any other source.

(4) AGENTS OF COMMITTEES AND SUBMISSION OF INFORMATION TO SENATE OR HOUSE OF REPRESENTATIVES.—

(A) COMMITTEES DESCRIBED IN PARAGRAPH (1).—Any committee described in paragraph (1) or the Chief of Staff of the Joint Committee on Taxation shall have the authority, acting directly, or by or through such examiners or agents as the chairman of such committee or such chief of staff may designate or appoint, to inspect returns and return information at such time and in such manner as may be determined by such chairman or chief of staff. Any return or return information obtained by or on behalf of such committee pursuant to the provisions of this subsection may be submitted by the committee to the Senate or the House of Representatives, or to both. The Joint Committee on Taxation may also submit such return or return information to any other committee described in paragraph (1), except that any return or return information which can be associated with, or otherwise identify, directly or indirectly, a particular taxpayer shall be furnished to such committee only when sitting in closed executive session unless such taxpayer otherwise consents in writing to such disclosure.

(B) OTHER COMMITTEES.—Any committee or subcommittee described in paragraph (3) shall have the right, acting directly, or by or through no more than four examiners or agents, designated or appointed in writing in equal numbers by the chairman and ranking minority member of such committee or subcommittee, to inspect returns and return information at such time and in such manner as may be determined by such chairman and ranking minority member. Any return or return information obtained by or on behalf of such committee or subcommittee pursuant to the provisions of this subsection may be submitted by the committee to the Senate or the House of Representatives, or to both, except that any return or return information which can be associated with, or otherwise identify, directly or indirectly, a particular taxpayer, shall be furnished to the Senate or the House of Representatives only when sitting in closed executive session unless such taxpayer otherwise consents in writing to such disclosure.

(5) DISCLOSURE BY WHISTLEBLOWER.—Any person who otherwise has or had access to any return or return information under this section may disclose such return or return information to a committee referred to in paragraph (1) or any individual authorized to receive or inspect information under paragraph (4)(A) if such person believes such return or return information may relate to possible misconduct, maladministration, or taxpayer abuse.

Amendments

• **1998, IRS Restructuring and Reform Act of 1998 (P.L. 105-206)**

P.L. 105-206, § 3708(a):

Amended Code Sec. 6103(f) by adding at the end a new paragraph (5). **Effective** 7-22-98.

• **1976, Tax Reform Act of 1976 (P.L. 94-455)**

P.L. 94-455, § 1202(a):

Amended Code Sec. 6103(f). **Effective** 1-1-77. Prior to amendment, Code Sec. 6103(f) read as follows:

(f) DISCLOSURE OF INFORMATION AS TO PERSONS FILING INCOME TAX RETURNS.—The Secretary or his delegate shall, upon inquiry as to whether any person has filed an income tax return in a designated internal revenue district for a particular taxable year, furnish to the inquirer, in such manner as the Secretary or his delegate may determine, information showing that such person has, or has not, filed an income tax return in such district for such taxable year.

• **1966 (P.L. 89-713)**

P.L. 89-713, § 4(a):

Amended Code Sec. 6103(f). **Effective** 11-2-66. Prior to amendment, Sec. 6103(f) read as follows:

"(f) Inspection of List of Taxpayers.—The Secretary or his delegate shall as soon as practicable in each year cause to be prepared and made available to public inspection in such manner as he may determine, in the office of the principal internal revenue officer for the internal revenue district in which the return was filed, and in such other places as he may determine, lists containing the name and the post-office address of each person making an income tax return in such district."

[Sec. 6103(g)]

(g) DISCLOSURE TO PRESIDENT AND CERTAIN OTHER PERSONS.—

(1) IN GENERAL.—Upon written request by the President, signed by him personally, the Secretary shall furnish to the President, or to such employee or employees of the White House Office as the President may designate by name in such request, a return or return information with respect to any taxpayer named in such request. Any such request shall state—

(A) the name and address of the taxpayer whose return or return information is to be disclosed,

(B) the kind of return or return information which is to be disclosed,

(C) the taxable period or periods covered by such return or return information, and

(D) the specific reason why the inspection or disclosure is requested.

(2) DISCLOSURE OF RETURN INFORMATION AS TO PRESIDENTIAL APPOINTEES AND CERTAIN OTHER FEDERAL GOVERNMENT APPOINTEES.—The Secretary may disclose to a duly authorized representative of the Executive Office of the President or to the head of any Federal agency, upon written request by the President or head of such agency, or to the Federal Bureau of Investigation on behalf of and upon the written request by the President or such head, return information with respect to an individual who is designated as being under consideration for appointment to a position in the executive or judicial branch of the Federal Government. Such return information shall be limited to whether such an individual—

(A) has filed returns with respect to the taxes imposed under chapter 1 for not more than the immediately preceding 3 years;

(B) has failed to pay any tax within 10 days after notice and demand, or has been assessed any penalty under this title for negligence, in the current year or immediately preceding 3 years;

(C) has been or is under investigation for possible criminal offenses under the internal revenue laws and the results of any such investigation; or

(D) has been assessed any civil penalty under this title for fraud.

Within 3 days of the receipt of any request for any return information with respect to any individual under this paragraph, the Secretary shall notify such individual in writing that such information has been requested under the provisions of this paragraph.

(3) RESTRICTION ON DISCLOSURE.—The employees to whom returns and return information are disclosed under this subsection shall not disclose such returns and return information to any other person except the President or the head of such agency without the personal written direction of the President or the head of such agency.

RETURNS—MISCELLANEOUS PROVISIONS

(4) RESTRICTION ON DISCLOSURE TO CERTAIN EMPLOYEES.—Disclosure of returns and return information under this subsection shall not be made to any employee whose annual rate of basic pay is less than the annual rate of basic pay specified for positions subject to section 5316 of title 5, United States Code.

(5) REPORTING REQUIREMENTS.—Within 30 days after the close of each calendar quarter, the President and the head of any agency requesting returns and return information under this subsection shall each file a report with the Joint Committee on Taxation setting forth the taxpayers with respect to whom such requests were made during such quarter under this subsection, the returns or return information involved, and the reasons for such requests. The President shall not be required to report on any request for returns and return information pertaining to an individual who was an officer or employee of the executive branch of the Federal Government at the time such request was made. Reports filed pursuant to this paragraph shall not be disclosed unless the Joint Committee on Taxation determines that disclosure thereof (including identifying details) would be in the national interest. Such reports shall be maintained by the Joint Committee on Taxation for a period not exceeding 2 years unless, within such period, the Joint Committee on Taxation determines that a disclosure to the Congress is necessary.

Amendments

• **1976, Tax Reform Act of 1976 (P.L. 94-455)**

P.L. 94-455, §1202(a):

Amended Code Sec. 6103(g). **Effective** 1-1-77. Prior to amendment, Code Sec. 6103(g) read as follows:

(g) DISCLOSURE OF INFORMATION WITH RESPECT TO DEFERRED COMPENSATION PLANS.—The Secretary or his delegate is authorized to furnish—

(1) returns with respect to any tax imposed by this title or information with respect to such returns to the proper officers and employees of the Department of Labor and the Pension Benefit Guaranty Corporation for purposes of administration of Titles I and IV of the Employee Retirement Income Security Act of 1974, and

(2) registration statements (as described in section 6057) and information with respect to such statements to the proper officers and employees of the Department of Health, Education, and Welfare for purposes of administration of section 1131 of the Social Security Act.

• **1974, Employee Retirement Income Security Act of 1974 (P.L. 93-406)**

P.L. 93-406, §1022(h):

Added Code Sec. 6103(g). **Effective** 9-2-74.

[Sec. 6103(h)]

(h) DISCLOSURE TO CERTAIN FEDERAL OFFICERS AND EMPLOYEES FOR PURPOSES OF TAX ADMINISTRATION, ETC.—

(1) DEPARTMENT OF THE TREASURY.—Returns and return information shall, without written request, be open to inspection by or disclosure to officers and employees of the Department of the Treasury whose official duties require such inspection or disclosure for tax administration purposes.

(2) DEPARTMENT OF JUSTICE.—In a matter involving tax administration, a return or return information shall be open to inspection by or disclosure to officers and employees of the Department of Justice (including United States attorneys) personally and directly engaged in, and solely for their use in, any proceeding before a Federal grand jury or preparation for any proceeding (or investigation which may result in such a proceeding) before a Federal grand jury or any Federal or State court, but only if—

(A) the taxpayer is or may be a party to the proceeding, or the proceeding arose out of, or in connection with, determining the taxpayer's civil or criminal liability, or the collection of such civil liability in respect of any tax imposed under this title;

(B) the treatment of an item reflected on such return is or may be related to the resolution of an issue in the proceeding or investigation; or

(C) such return or return information relates or may relate to a transactional relationship between a person who is or may be a party to the proceeding and the taxpayer which affects, or may affect, the resolution of an issue in such proceeding or investigation.

(3) FORM OF REQUEST.—In any case in which the Secretary is authorized to disclose a return or return information to the Department of Justice pursuant to the provisions of this subsection—

(A) if the Secretary has referred the case to the Department of Justice, or if the proceeding is authorized by subchapter B of chapter 76, the Secretary may make such disclosure on his own motion, or

(B) if the Secretary receives a written request from the Attorney General, the Deputy Attorney General, or an Assistant Attorney General, for a return of, or return information relating to, a person named in such request and setting forth the need for the disclosure, the Secretary shall disclose return or return the information so requested.

(4) DISCLOSURE IN JUDICIAL AND ADMINISTRATIVE TAX PROCEEDINGS.—A return or return information may be disclosed in a Federal or State judicial or administrative proceeding pertaining to tax administration, but only—

(A) if the taxpayer is a party to the proceeding, or the proceeding arose out of, or in connection with, determining the taxpayer's civil or criminal liability, or the collection of such civil liability, in respect of any tax imposed under this title;

(B) if the treatment of an item reflected on such return is directly related to the resolution of an issue in the proceeding;

(C) if such return or return information directly relates to a transactional relationship between a person who is a party to the proceeding and the taxpayer which directly affects the resolution of an issue in the proceeding; or

(D) to the extent required by order of a court pursuant to section 3500 of title 18, United States Code, or rule 16 of the Federal Rules of Criminal Procedure, such court being authorized in the issuance of such order to give due consideration to congressional policy favoring the confidentiality of returns and return information as set forth in this title.

However, such return or return information shall not be disclosed as provided in subparagraph (A), (B), or (C) if the Secretary determines that such disclosure would identify a confidential informant or seriously impair a civil or criminal tax investigation.

(5) WITHHOLDING OF TAX FROM SOCIAL SECURITY BENEFITS.—Upon written request of the payor agency, the Secretary may disclose available return information from the master files of the Internal Revenue Service with respect to the address and status of an individual as a nonresident alien or as a citizen or resident of the United States to the Social Security Administration or the Railroad Retirement Board (whichever is appropriate) for purposes of carrying out its responsibilities for withholding tax under section 1441 from social security benefits (as defined in section 86(d)).

(6) INTERNAL REVENUE SERVICE OVERSIGHT BOARD.—

(A) IN GENERAL.—Notwithstanding paragraph (1), and except as provided in subparagraph (B), no return or return information may be disclosed to any member of the Oversight Board described in subparagraph (A) or (D) of section 7802(b)(1) or to any employee or detailee of such Board by reason of their service with the Board. Any request for information not permitted to be disclosed under the preceding sentence, and any contact relating to a specific taxpayer, made by any such individual to an officer or employee of the Internal Revenue Service shall be reported by such officer or employee to the Secretary, the Treasury Inspector General for Tax Administration, and the Joint Committee on Taxation.

(B) EXCEPTION FOR REPORTS TO THE BOARD.—If—

(i) the Commissioner or the Treasury Inspector General for Tax Administration prepares any report or other matter for the Oversight Board in order to assist the Board in carrying out its duties, and

(ii) the Commissioner or such Inspector General determines it is necessary to include any return or return information in such report or other matter to enable the Board to carry out such duties, such return or return information (other than information

RETURNS—MISCELLANEOUS PROVISIONS

regarding taxpayer identity) may be disclosed to members, employees, or detailees of the Board solely for the purpose of carrying out such duties.

Amendments

• **1998, Tax and Trade Relief Extension Act of 1998 (P.L. 105-277)**

P.L. 105-277, §4002(a):

Amended Code Sec. 6103(h) by redesignating paragraph (5) as paragraph (6). **Effective** as if included in the provision of P.L. 105-206 to which it relates [generally effective on 7-22-98.—CCH].

• **1998, IRS Restructuring and Reform Act of 1998 (P.L. 105-206)**

P.L. 105-206, §1101(b):

Amended Code Sec. 6103(h) by adding at the end a new paragraph (5)[(6)]. **Effective** 7-22-98. For a special rule, see Act Sec. 1101(d)(2)-(3), below.

P.L. 105-206, §1101(d)(2)-(3), provides:

(2) INITIAL NOMINATIONS TO INTERNAL REVENUE SERVICE OVERSIGHT BOARD.—The President shall submit the initial nominations under section 7802 of the Internal Revenue Code of 1986, as added by this section, to the Senate not later than 6 months after the date of the enactment of this Act.

(3) EFFECT ON ACTIONS PRIOR TO APPOINTMENT OF OVERSIGHT BOARD.—Nothing in this section shall be construed to invalidate the actions and authority of the Internal Revenue Service prior to the appointment of the members of the Internal Revenue Service Oversight Board.

P.L. 105-206, §6023(22):

Amended Code Sec. 6103(h)(4)(A) by inserting "if" before "the taxpayer is a party to". **Effective** 7-22-98.

• **1997, Taxpayer Relief Act of 1997 (P.L. 105-34)**

P.L. 105-34, §1283(a):

Amended Code Sec. 6103(h) by striking paragraph (5) and by redesignating paragraph (6) as paragraph (5). **Effective** for judicial proceedings commenced after 8-5-97. Prior to amendment, Code Sec. 6103(h)(5) read as follows:

(5) PROSPECTIVE JURORS.—In connection with any judicial proceeding described in paragraph (4) to which the United States is a party, the Secretary shall respond to a written inquiry from an attorney of the Department of Justice (including a United States attorney) involved in such proceeding or any person (or his legal representative) who is a party to such proceeding as to whether an individual who is a prospective juror in such proceeding has or has not been the subject of any audit or other tax investigation by the Internal Revenue Service. The Secretary shall limit such response to an affirmative or negative reply to such inquiry.

• **1983, Social Security Amendments of 1983 (P.L. 98-21)**

P.L. 98-21, §121(c)(3)(A):

Amended Code Sec. 6103(h) by adding paragraph (6). **Effective** for benefits received after 12-31-83 in tax years ending after such date. The amendments made by Act Sec. 121 of P.L. 98-21 shall not apply to any portion of a lump-sum payment of social security benefits (as defined in Code Sec. 86(d)) received after 12-31-83 if the generally applicable payment date for such portion was before 1-1-84.

• **1978, Revenue Act of 1978 (P.L. 95-600)**

P.L. 95-600, §503(a), (b)(1):

Amended Code Sec. 6103(h)(2). **Effective** 11-7-78. Prior to amendment, Code Sec. 6103(h)(2) read as follows:

"(2) DEPARTMENT OF JUSTICE.—A return or return information shall be open to inspection by or disclosure to attorneys of the Department of Justice (including United States attorneys) personally and directly engaged in, and solely for their use in, preparation for any proceeding (or investigation which may result in such a proceeding) before a Federal grand jury or any Federal or State court in a matter involving tax administration, but only if—

(A) the taxpayer is or may be a party to such proceeding;

(B) the treatment of an item reflected on such return is or may be related to the resolution of an issue in the proceeding or investigation; or

(C) such return or return information relates or may relate to a transactional relationship between a person who is or may be a party to the proceeding and the taxpayer which affects, or may affect, the resolution of an issue in such proceeding or investigation."

P.L. 95-600, §503(b)(2):

Amended Code Sec. 6103(h)(4)(A) by striking out "(A) if the taxpayer is a party to such proceedings," and inserting a new subparagraph (A). **Effective** 11-7-78.

• **1976, Tax Reform Act of 1976 (P.L. 94-455)**

P.L. 94-455, §1202(a):

Added Code Sec. 6103(h). **Effective** 1-1-77.

[Sec. 6103(i)]

(i) DISCLOSURE TO FEDERAL OFFICERS OR EMPLOYEES FOR ADMINISTRATION OF FEDERAL LAWS NOT RELATING TO TAX ADMINISTRATION.—

(1) DISCLOSURE OF RETURNS AND RETURN INFORMATION FOR USE IN CRIMINAL INVESTIGATIONS.—

(A) IN GENERAL.—Except as provided in paragraph (6), any return or return information with respect to any specified taxable period or periods shall, pursuant to and upon the grant of an ex parte order by a Federal district court judge or magistrate under subparagraph (B), be open (but only to the extent necessary as provided in such order) to inspection by, or disclosure to, officers and employees of any Federal agency who are personally and directly engaged in—

(i) preparation for any judicial or administrative proceeding pertaining to the enforcement of a specifically designated Federal criminal statute (not involving tax administration) to which the United States or such agency is or may be a party, or pertaining to the case of a missing or exploited child,

(ii) any investigation which may result in such a proceeding, or

(iii) any Federal grand jury proceeding pertaining to enforcement of such a criminal statute to which the United States or such agency is or may be a party, or to such a case of a missing or exploited child,

solely for the use of such officers and employees in such preparation, investigation, or grand jury proceeding.

(B) APPLICATION FOR ORDER.—The Attorney General, the Deputy Attorney General, the Associate Attorney General, any Assistant Attorney General, any United States attorney, any special prosecutor appointed under section 593 of title 28, United States Code, or any attorney in charge of a criminal division organized crime strike force established pursuant to section 510 of title 28, United States Code, may authorize an application to a Federal district court judge or magistrate for the order referred to in subparagraph (A). Upon such application, such judge or magistrate may grant such order if he determines on the basis of the facts submitted by the applicant that—

(i) there is reasonable cause to believe, based upon information believed to be reliable, that a specific criminal act has been committed,

(ii) there is reasonable cause to believe that the return or return information is or may be relevant to a matter relating to the commission of such act, and

(iii) the return or return information is sought exclusively for use in a Federal criminal investigation or proceeding concerning such act (or any criminal investigation or proceeding, in the case of a matter relating to a missing or exploited child), and the information sought to be disclosed cannot reasonably be obtained, under the circumstances, from another source.

(C) DISCLOSURE TO STATE AND LOCAL LAW ENFORCEMENT AGENCIES IN THE CASE OF MATTERS PERTAINING TO A MISSING OR EXPLOITED CHILD.—

(i) IN GENERAL.—In the case of an investigation pertaining to a missing or exploited child, the head of any Federal agency, or his designee, may disclose any return or return information obtained under subparagraph (A) to officers and employees of any State or local law enforcement agency, but only if—

(I) such State or local law enforcement agency is part of a team with the Federal agency in such investigation, and

(II) such information is disclosed only to such officers and employees who are personally and directly engaged in such investigation.

(ii) LIMITATION ON USE OF INFORMATION.—Information disclosed under this subparagraph shall be solely for the use of such officers and employees in locating the missing child, in a grand jury proceeding, or in any preparation for, or investigation which may result in, a judicial or administrative proceeding.

(iii) MISSING CHILD.—For purposes of this subparagraph, the term "missing child" shall have the meaning given such term by section 403 of the Missing Children's Assistance Act (42 U.S.C. 5772).

(iv) EXPLOITED CHILD.—For purposes of this subparagraph, the term "exploited child" means a minor with respect to whom there is reason to believe that a specified offense against a minor (as defined by section 111(7) of the Sex Offender Registration and Notification Act (42 U.S.C. 16911(7))) has or is occurring.

(2) DISCLOSURE OF RETURN INFORMATION OTHER THAN TAXPAYER RETURN INFORMATION FOR USE IN CRIMINAL INVESTIGATIONS.—

(A) IN GENERAL.—Except as provided in paragraph (6), upon receipt by the Secretary of a request which meets the requirements of subparagraph (B) from the head of any Federal agency or the Inspector General thereof, or, in the case of the Department of Justice, the Attorney General, the Deputy Attorney General, the Associate Attorney General, any Assistant Attorney General, the Director of the Federal Bureau of Investigation, the Administrator of the Drug Enforcement Administration, any United States attorney, any special prosecutor appointed under section 593 of title 28, United States Code, or any attorney in charge of a criminal division organized crime strike force established pursuant to section 510 of title 28, United States Code, the Secretary shall disclose return information (other than taxpayer return information) to officers and employees of such agency who are personally and directly engaged in—

(i) preparation for any judicial or administrative proceeding described in paragraph (1)(A)(i),

(ii) any investigation which may result in such a proceeding, or

(iii) any grand jury proceeding described in paragraph (1)(A)(iii),

solely for the use of such officers and employees in such preparation, investigation, or grand jury proceeding.

(B) REQUIREMENTS.—A request meets the requirements of this subparagraph if the request is in writing and sets forth—

(i) the name and address of the taxpayer with respect to whom the requested return information relates;

(ii) the taxable period or periods to which such return information relates;

(iii) the statutory authority under which the proceeding or investigation described in subparagraph (A) is being conducted; and

(iv) the specific reason or reasons why such disclosure is, or may be, relevant to such proceeding or investigation.

(C) TAXPAYER IDENTITY.—For purposes of this paragraph, a taxpayer's identity shall not be treated as taxpayer return information.

(3) DISCLOSURE OF RETURN INFORMATION TO APPRISE APPROPRIATE OFFICIALS OF CRIMINAL OR TERRORIST ACTIVITIES OR EMERGENCY CIRCUMSTANCES.—

(A) POSSIBLE VIOLATIONS OF FEDERAL CRIMINAL LAW.—

(i) IN GENERAL.—Except as provided in paragraph (6), the Secretary may disclose in writing return information (other than taxpayer return information) which may constitute evidence of a violation of any Federal criminal law (not involving tax administration) to the extent necessary to apprise the head of the appropriate Federal agency charged with the responsibility of enforcing such law. The head of such agency may disclose such return information to officers and employees of such agency to the extent necessary to enforce such law.

(ii) TAXPAYER IDENTITY.—If there is return information (other than taxpayer return information) which may constitute evidence of a violation by any taxpayer of any Federal criminal law (not involving tax administration), such taxpayer's identity may also be disclosed under clause (i).

(B) EMERGENCY CIRCUMSTANCES.—

(i) DANGER OF DEATH OR PHYSICAL INJURY.—Under circumstances involving an imminent danger of death or physical injury to any individual, the Secretary may disclose return information to the extent necessary to apprise appropriate officers or employees of any Federal or State law enforcement agency of such circumstances.

(ii) FLIGHT FROM FEDERAL PROSECUTION.—Under circumstances involving the imminent flight of any individual from Federal prosecution, the Secretary may disclose return information to the extent necessary to apprise appropriate officers or employees of any Federal law enforcement agency of such circumstances.

(C) TERRORIST ACTIVITIES, ETC.—

(i) IN GENERAL.—Except as provided in paragraph (6), the Secretary may disclose in writing return information (other than taxpayer return information) that may be related to a terrorist incident, threat, or activity to the extent necessary to apprise the head of the appropriate Federal law enforcement agency responsible for investigating or responding to such terrorist incident, threat, or activity. The head of the agency may disclose such return information to officers and employees of such agency to the extent necessary to investigate or respond to such terrorist incident, threat, or activity.

(ii) DISCLOSURE TO THE DEPARTMENT OF JUSTICE.—Returns and taxpayer return information may also be disclosed to the Attorney General under clause (i) to the extent necessary for, and solely for use in preparing, an application under paragraph (7)(D).

(iii) TAXPAYER IDENTITY.—For purposes of this subparagraph, a taxpayer's identity shall not be treated as taxpayer return information.

(4) USE OF CERTAIN DISCLOSED RETURNS AND RETURN INFORMATION IN JUDICIAL OR ADMINISTRATIVE PROCEEDINGS.—

(A) RETURNS AND TAXPAYER RETURN INFORMATION.—Except as provided in subparagraph (C), any return or taxpayer return information obtained under paragraph (1) or (7)(C) may be disclosed in any judicial or administrative proceeding pertaining to enforcement of a specifically designated Federal criminal statute or related civil forfeiture (not involving tax administration) to which the United States or a Federal agency is a party—

(i) if the court finds that such return or taxpayer return information is probative of a matter in issue relevant in establishing the commission of a crime or the guilt or liability of a party, or

(ii) to the extent required by order of the court pursuant to section 3500 of title 18, United States Code, or rule 16 of the Federal Rules of Criminal Procedure.

(B) RETURN INFORMATION (OTHER THAN TAXPAYER RETURN INFORMATION).—Except as provided in subparagraph (C), any return information (other than taxpayer return information) obtained under paragraph (1), (2), (3)(A) or (C), or (7) may be disclosed in any judicial or administrative proceeding pertaining to enforcement of a specifically designated Federal criminal statute or related civil forfeiture (not involving tax administration) to which the United States or a Federal agency is a party.

(C) CONFIDENTIAL INFORMANT; IMPAIRMENT OF INVESTIGATIONS.—No return or return information shall be admitted into evidence under subparagraph (A)(i) or (B) if the Secretary determines and notifies the Attorney General or his delegate or the head of the Federal agency that such admission would identify a confidential informant or seriously impair a civil or criminal tax investigation.

(D) CONSIDERATION OF CONFIDENTIALITY POLICY.—In ruling upon the admissibility of returns or return information, and in the issuance of an order under subparagraph (A)(ii), the court shall give due consideration to congressional policy favoring the confidentiality of returns and return information as set forth in this title.

(E) REVERSIBLE ERROR.—The admission into evidence of any return or return information contrary to the provisions of this paragraph shall not, as such, constitute reversible error upon appeal of a judgment in the proceeding.

RETURNS—MISCELLANEOUS PROVISIONS

(5) DISCLOSURE TO LOCATE FUGITIVES FROM JUSTICE.—

(A) IN GENERAL.—Except as provided in paragraph (6), the return of an individual or return information with respect to such individual shall, pursuant to and upon the grant of an ex parte order by a Federal district court judge or magistrate under subparagraph (B), be open (but only to the extent necessary as provided in such order) to inspection by, or disclosure to, officers and employees of any Federal agency exclusively for use in locating such individual.

(B) APPLICATION FOR ORDER.—Any person described in paragraph (1)(B) may authorize an application to a Federal district court judge or magistrate for an order referred to in subparagraph (A). Upon such application, such judge or magistrate may grant such order if he determines on the basis of the facts submitted by the applicant that—

(i) a Federal arrest warrant relating to the commission of a Federal felony offense has been issued for an individual who is a fugitive from justice,

(ii) the return of such individual or return information with respect to such individual is sought exclusively for use in locating such individual, and

(iii) there is reasonable cause to believe that such return or return information may be relevant in determining the location of such individual.

(6) CONFIDENTIAL INFORMANTS; IMPAIRMENT OF INVESTIGATIONS.—The Secretary shall not disclose any return or return information under paragraph (1), (2), (3)(A) or (C), (5), (7), or (8) if the Secretary determines (and, in the case of a request for disclosure pursuant to a court order described in paragraph (1)(B) or (5)(B), certifies to the court) that such disclosure would identify a confidential informant or seriously impair a civil or criminal tax investigation.

(7) DISCLOSURE UPON REQUEST OF INFORMATION RELATING TO TERRORIST ACTIVITIES, ETC.—

(A) DISCLOSURE TO LAW ENFORCEMENT AGENCIES.—

(i) IN GENERAL.—Except as provided in paragraph (6), upon receipt by the Secretary of a written request which meets the requirements of clause (iii), the Secretary may disclose return information (other than taxpayer return information) to officers and employees of any Federal law enforcement agency who are personally and directly engaged in the response to or investigation of any terrorist incident, threat, or activity.

(ii) DISCLOSURE TO STATE AND LOCAL LAW ENFORCEMENT AGENCIES.—The head of any Federal law enforcement agency may disclose return information obtained under clause (i) to officers and employees of any State or local law enforcement agency but only if such agency is part of a team with the Federal law enforcement agency in such response or investigation and such information is disclosed only to officers and employees who are personally and directly engaged in such response or investigation.

(iii) REQUIREMENTS.—A request meets the requirements of this clause if—

(I) the request is made by the head of any Federal law enforcement agency (or his delegate) involved in the response to or investigation of any terrorist incident, threat, or activity, and

(II) the request sets forth the specific reason or reasons why such disclosure may be relevant to a terrorist incident, threat, or activity.

(iv) LIMITATION ON USE OF INFORMATION.—Information disclosed under this subparagraph shall be solely for the use of the officers and employees to whom such information is disclosed in such response or investigation.

(v) TAXPAYER IDENTITY.—For purposes of this subparagraph, a taxpayer's identity shall not be treated as taxpayer return information.

(B) DISCLOSURE TO INTELLIGENCE AGENCIES.—

(i) IN GENERAL.—Except as provided in paragraph (6), upon receipt by the Secretary of a written request which meets the requirements of clause (ii), the Secretary may disclose return information (other than taxpayer return information) to those officers and employees of the Department of Justice, the Department of the Treasury, and other Federal intelligence agencies who are personally and directly engaged in the collection or analysis of intelligence and counterintelligence information or investigation concerning any terrorist incident, threat, or activity. For purposes of the preceding sentence, the information disclosed under the preceding sentence shall be solely for the use of such officers and employees in such investigation, collection, or analysis.

(ii) REQUIREMENTS.—A request meets the requirements of this subparagraph if the request—

(I) is made by an individual described in clause (iii), and

(II) sets forth the specific reason or reasons why such disclosure may be relevant to a terrorist incident, threat, or activity.

(iii) REQUESTING INDIVIDUALS.—An individual described in this subparagraph is an individual—

(I) who is an officer or employee of the Department of Justice or the Department of the Treasury who is appointed by the President with the advice and consent of the Senate or who is the Director of the United States Secret Service, and

(II) who is responsible for the collection and analysis of intelligence and counterintelligence information concerning any terrorist incident, threat, or activity.

(iv) TAXPAYER IDENTITY.—For purposes of this subparagraph, a taxpayer's identity shall not be treated as taxpayer return information.

(C) DISCLOSURE UNDER EX PARTE ORDERS.—

(i) IN GENERAL.—Except as provided in paragraph (6), any return or return information with respect to any specified taxable period or periods shall, pursuant to and upon the grant of an ex parte order by a Federal district court judge or magistrate under clause (ii), be open (but only to the extent necessary as provided in such order) to inspection by, or disclosure to, officers and employees of any Federal law enforcement agency or Federal intelligence agency who are personally and directly engaged in any investigation, response to, or analysis of intelligence and counterintelligence information concerning any terrorist incident, threat, or activity. Return or return information opened to inspection or disclosure pursuant to the preceding sentence shall be solely for the use of such officers and employees in the investigation, response, or analysis, and in any judicial, administrative, or grand jury proceedings, pertaining to such terrorist incident, threat, or activity.

(ii) APPLICATION FOR ORDER.—The Attorney General, the Deputy Attorney General, the Associate Attorney General, any Assistant Attorney General, or any United States attorney may authorize an application to a Federal district court judge or magistrate for the order referred to in clause (i). Upon such application, such judge or magistrate may grant such order if he determines on the basis of the facts submitted by the applicant that—

(I) there is reasonable cause to believe, based upon information believed to be reliable, that the return or return information may be relevant to a matter relating to such terrorist incident, threat, or activity, and

(II) the return or return information is sought exclusively for use in a Federal investigation, analysis, or proceeding concerning any terrorist incident, threat, or activity.

Sec. 6103(i)(5)

RETURNS—MISCELLANEOUS PROVISIONS

(D) SPECIAL RULE FOR EX PARTE DISCLOSURE BY THE IRS.—

(i) IN GENERAL.—Except as provided in paragraph (6), the Secretary may authorize an application to a Federal district court judge or magistrate for the order referred to in subparagraph (C)(i). Upon such application, such judge or magistrate may grant such order if he determines on the basis of the facts submitted by the applicant that the requirements of subparagraph (C)(ii)(I) are met.

(ii) LIMITATION ON USE OF INFORMATION.—Information disclosed under clause (i)—

(I) may be disclosed only to the extent necessary to apprise the head of the appropriate Federal law enforcement agency responsible for investigating or responding to a terrorist incident, threat, or activity, and

(II) shall be solely for use in a Federal investigation, analysis, or proceeding concerning any terrorist incident, threat, or activity.

The head of such Federal agency may disclose such information to officers and employees of such agency to the extent necessary to investigate or respond to such terrorist incident, threat, or activity.

(8) COMPTROLLER GENERAL.—

(A) RETURNS AVAILABLE FOR INSPECTION.—Except as provided in subparagraph (C), upon written request by the Comptroller General of the United States, returns and return information shall be open to inspection by, or disclosure to, officers and employees of the Government Accountability Office for the purpose of, and to the extent necessary in, making—

(i) an audit of the Internal Revenue Service, the Bureau of Alcohol, Tobacco, Firearms, and Explosives, Department of Justice, or the Tax and Trade Bureau, Department of the Treasury, which may be required by section 713 of title 31, United States Code, or

(ii) any audit authorized by subsection (p)(6),

except that no such officer or employee shall, except to the extent authorized by subsection (f) or (p)(6), disclose to any person, other than another officer or employee of such office whose official duties require such disclosure, any return or return information described in section 4424(a) in a form which can be associated with, or otherwise identify, directly or indirectly, a particular taxpayer, nor shall such officer or employee disclose any other return or return information, except as otherwise expressly provided by law, to any person other than such other officer or employee of such office in a form which can be associated with, or otherwise identify, directly or indirectly, a particular taxpayer.

(B) AUDITS OF OTHER AGENCIES.—

(i) IN GENERAL.—Nothing in this section shall prohibit any return or return information obtained under this title by any Federal agency (other than an agency referred to in subparagraph (A)) or by a Trustee as defined in the District of Columbia Retirement Protection Act of 1997, for use in any program or activity from being open to inspection by, or disclosure to, officers and employees of the Government Accountability Office if such inspection or disclosure is—

(I) for purposes of, and to the extent necessary in, making an audit authorized by law of such program or activity, and

(II) pursuant to a written request by the Comptroller General of the United States to the head of such Federal agency.

(ii) INFORMATION FROM SECRETARY.—If the Comptroller General of the United States determines that the returns or return information available under clause (i) are not sufficient for purposes of making an audit of any program or activity of a Federal agency (other than an agency referred to in subparagraph (A)), upon written request by the Comptroller General to the Secretary, returns and return information (of the type authorized by subsection (l) or (m) to be made available to the Federal agency for use in such program or activity) shall be open to inspection by, or disclosure to, officers and employees of the Government Accountability Office for the purpose of, and to the extent necessary in, making such audit.

(iii) REQUIREMENT OF NOTIFICATION UPON COMPLETION OF AUDIT.—Within 90 days after the completion of an audit with respect to which returns or return information were opened to inspection or disclosed under clause (i) or (ii), the Comptroller General of the United States shall notify in writing the Joint Committee on Taxation of such completion. Such notice shall include—

(I) a description of the use of the returns and return information by the Federal agency involved,

(II) such recommendations with respect to the use of returns and return information by such Federal agency as the Comptroller General deems appropriate, and

(III) a statement on the impact of any such recommendations on confidentiality of returns and return information and the administration of this title.

(iv) CERTAIN RESTRICTIONS MADE APPLICABLE.—The restrictions contained in subparagraph (A) on the disclosure of any returns or return information open to inspection or disclosed under such subparagraph shall also apply to returns and return information open to inspection or disclosed under this subparagraph.

(C) DISAPPROVAL BY JOINT COMMITTEE ON TAXATION.—Returns and return information shall not be open to inspection or disclosed under subparagraph (A) or (B) with respect to an audit—

(i) unless the Comptroller General of the United States notifies in writing the Joint Committee on Taxation of such audit, and

(ii) if the Joint Committee on Taxation disapproves such audit by a vote of at least two-thirds of its members within the 30-day period beginning on the day the Joint Committee on Taxation receives such notice.

Amendments

• **2016, Recovering Missing Children Act (P.L. 114-184)**

P.L. 114-184, § 2(a)(1)-(3):

Amended Code Sec. 6103(i)(1) by inserting "or pertaining to the case of a missing or exploited child," after "may be a party," in subparagraph (A)(i); by inserting "or to such a case of a missing or exploited child," after "may be a party," in subparagraph (A)(iii); and by inserting "(or any criminal investigation or proceeding, in the case of a matter relating to a missing or exploited child)" after "concerning such act" in subparagraph (B)(iii). **Effective** for disclosures made after 6-30-2016.

P.L. 114-184, § 2(b)(1):

Amended Code Sec. 6103(i)(1) by adding at the end a new subparagraph (C). **Effective** for disclosures made after 6-30-2016.

• **2008, Tax Extenders and Alternative Minimum Tax Relief Act of 2008 (P.L. 110-343)**

P.L. 110-343, Division C, § 402(a):

Amended Code Sec. 6103(i)(3)(C) by striking clause (iv). **Effective** for disclosures after 10-3-2008. Prior to being stricken, Code Sec. 6103(i)(3)(C)(iv) read as follows:

(iv) TERMINATION.—No disclosure may be made under this subparagraph after December 31, 2007.

P.L. 110-343, Division C, § 402(b):

Amended Code Sec. 6103(i)(7) by striking paragraph (E). **Effective** for disclosures after 10-3-2008. Prior to being stricken, Code Sec. 6103(i)(7)(E) read as follows:

(E) TERMINATION.—No disclosure may be made under this paragraph after December 31, 2007.

• **2006, Tax Relief and Health Care Act of 2006 (P.L. 109-432)**

P.L. 109-432, Division A, § 122(b)(1):

Amended Code Sec. 6103(i)(3)(C)(iv) and (i)(7)(E) by striking "2006" and inserting "2007". **Effective** for disclosures after 12-31-2006.

• **2005, Gulf Opportunity Zone Act of 2005 (P.L. 109-135)**

P.L. 109-135, § 305(b)(1):

Amended Code Sec. 6103(i)(3)(C)(iv) and (i)(7)(E) by striking "December 31, 2005" and inserting "December 31, 2006". **Effective** for disclosures after 12-31-2005.

P.L. 109-135, § 412(rr)(3):

Amended Code Sec. 6103(i)(8)(A), (i)(8)(B)(i), and (i)(8)(B)(ii) by striking "General Accounting Office" each place it appears therein and inserting "Government Accountability Office". **Effective** 12-21-2005.

RETURNS—MISCELLANEOUS PROVISIONS

• **2004, Working Families Tax Relief Act of 2004 (P.L. 108-311)**

P.L. 108-311, § 320(a):

Amended Code Sec. 6103(i)(3)(C)(iv) and (7)(E) by striking "December 31, 2003" and inserting "December 31, 2005". **Effective** for disclosures on or after 10-4-2004.

P.L. 108-311, § 320(b):

Amended Code Sec. 6103(i)(7)(A) by adding at the end a new clause (v). **Effective** as if included in section 201 of the Victims of Terrorism Tax Relief Act of 2001 (P.L. 107-134) [effective for disclosures made on or after 1-23-2002.—CCH].

• **2002, Homeland Security Act of 2002 (P.L. 107-296)**

P.L. 107-296, § 1112(j):

Amended Code Sec. 6103(i)(8)(A)(i) by striking "or the Bureau of Alcohol, Tobacco and Firearms" and inserting ", the Bureau of Alcohol, Tobacco, Firearms, and Explosives, Department of Justice, or the Tax and Trade Bureau, Department of the Treasury,". **Effective** 60 days after 11-25-2002.

• **2002, Victims of Terrorism Tax Relief Act of 2001 (P.L. 107-134)**

P.L. 107-134, § 201(a):

Amended Code Sec. 6103(i)(3) by adding at the end a new subparagraph (C). **Effective** for disclosures made on or after 1-23-2002.

P.L. 107-134, § 201(b):

Amended Code Sec. 6103(i) by redesignating paragraph (7) as paragraph (8) and by inserting after paragraph (6) a new paragraph (7). **Effective** for disclosures made on or after 1-23-2002.

P.L. 107-134, § 201(c)(3):

Amended the heading of Code Sec. 6103(i)(3) by inserting "OR TERRORIST" after "CRIMINAL". **Effective** for disclosures made on or after 1-23-2002.

P.L. 107-134, § 201(c)(4)(A)-(B):

Amended Code Sec. 6103(i)(4) in subparagraph (A) by inserting "or (7)(C)" after "paragraph (1)"; and in subparagraph (B) by striking "or (3)(A)" and inserting "(3)(A) or (C), or (7)". **Effective** for disclosures made on or after 1-23-2002.

P.L. 107-134, § 201(c)(5)(A)-(B):

Amended Code Sec. 6103(i)(6) by striking "(3)(A)" and inserting "(3)(A) or (C)"; and by striking "or (7)" and inserting "(7), or (8)". **Effective** for disclosures made on or after 1-23-2002.

• **1997, Balanced Budget Act of 1997 (P.L. 105-33)**

P.L. 105-33, § 11024(b)(3):

Amended Code Sec. 6103(i)(7)(B)(i) by inserting after "(other than an agency referred to in subparagraph (A))" and before the word "for" the words "or by a Trustee as defined in the District of Columbia Retirement Protection Act of 1997,". For the **effective** date, see Act Sec. 11721, below.

P.L. 105-33, § 11721, provides:

Except as otherwise provided in this title, the provisions of this title shall take effect on the later of October 1, 1997, or the day the District of Columbia Financial Responsibility and Management Assistance Authority certifies that the financial plan and budget for the District government for fiscal year 1998 meet the requirements of section 201(c)(1) of the District of Columbia Financial Responsibility and Management Assistance Act of 1995, as amended by this title.

• **1996, Taxpayer Bill of Rights 2 (P.L. 104-168)**

P.L. 104-168, § 1206(b)(1):

Amended Code Sec. 6103(i) by striking paragraph (8). **Effective** 7-30-96. Prior to being stricken, Code Sec. 6103(i)(8) read as follows:

(8) DISCLOSURE OF RETURNS FILED UNDER SECTION 6050I.—The Secretary may, upon written request, disclose returns filed under section 6050I to officers and employees of any Federal agency whose official duties require such disclosure for the administration of Federal criminal statutes not related to tax administration.

• **1988, Anti-Drug Abuse Act of 1988 (P.L. 100-690)**

P.L. 100-690, § 7601(b)(1):

Amended Code Sec. 6103(i) by adding at the end thereof new paragraph (8). **Effective** for requests made on or after 11-18-88, but disclosures may be made pursuant to such amendments only during the 2-year period beginning on such date.

• **1984, Deficit Reduction Act of 1984 (P.L. 98-369)**

P.L. 98-369, § 453(b)(5):

Amended P.L. 96-249, § 127(a)(1), by redesignating Code Sec. 6103(i)(7), as added by that Act, as Code Sec. 6103(l)(7). **Effective** on the first day of the first calendar month which begins more than 90 days after 7-18-84.

• **1982 (P.L. 97-258)**

P.L. 97-258, § 3(f)(4):

Amended Code Sec. 6103(i)(6)[7](A)(i) by striking out "section 117 of the Budget and Accounting Procedures Act of 1950 (31 U.S.C. 67)" and substituting "section 713 of title 31, United States Code". **Effective** 9-13-82.

• **1982, Tax Equity and Fiscal Responsibility Act of 1982 (P.L. 97-248)**

P.L. 97-248, § 356(a):

Amended Code Sec. 6103(i) by redesignating paragraph (6) as paragraph (7) and by striking out paragraphs (1), (2), (3), (4), and (5) and inserting new paragraphs (1)-(6). **Effective** 9-4-82. Prior to amendment, Code Sec. 6103(i)(1) through (5) read as follows:

(1) NONTAX CRIMINAL INVESTIGATION.—

(A) INFORMATION FROM TAXPAYER.—A return or taxpayer return information shall, pursuant to, and upon the grant of, an ex parte order by a Federal district court judge as provided by this paragraph, be open, but only to the extent necessary as provided in such order, to officers and employees of a Federal agency personally and directly engaged in and solely for their use in, preparation for any administrative or judicial proceeding (or investigation which may result in such a proceeding) pertaining to the enforcement of a specifically designated Federal criminal statute (not involving tax administration) to which the United States or such agency is or may be a party.

(B) APPLICATION FOR ORDER.—The head of any Federal agency described in subparagraph (A) or, in the case of the Department of Justice, the Attorney General, the Deputy Attorney General, or an Assistant Attorney General, may authorize an application to a Federal district court judge for the order referred to in subparagraph (A). Upon such application, such judge may grant such order if he determines on the basis of the facts submitted by the applicant that—

(i) there is reasonable cause to believe, based upon information believed to be reliable, that a specific criminal act has been committed;

(ii) there is reason to believe that such return or return information is probative evidence of a matter in issue related to the commission of such criminal act; and

(iii) the information sought to be disclosed cannot reasonably be obtained from any other source, unless it is determined that, notwithstanding the reasonable availability of the information from another source, the return or return information sought constitutes the most probative evidence of a matter in issue relating to the commission of such criminal act.

However, the Secretary shall not disclose any return or return information under this paragraph if he determines and certifies to the court that such disclosure would identify a confidential informant or seriously impair a civil or criminal tax investigation.

(2) RETURN INFORMATION OTHER THAN TAXPAYER RETURN INFORMATION.—Upon written request from the head of a Federal agency described in paragraph (1)(A), or in the case of the Department of Justice, the Attorney General, the Deputy Attorney General, or an Assistant Attorney General, the Secretary shall disclose return information (other than taxpayer return information) to officers and employees of such agency personally and directly engaged in, and solely for their use in preparation for any administrative or judicial proceeding (or investigation which may result in such a proceeding) described in paragraph (1)(A). Such request shall set forth—

(A) the name and address of the taxpayer with respect to whom such return information relates;

(B) the taxable period or periods to which the return information relates;

(C) the statutory authority under which the proceeding or investigation is being conducted; and

(D) the specific reason or reasons why such disclosure is or may be material to the proceeding or investigation.

However, the Secretary shall not disclose any return or return information under this paragraph if he determines that such disclosure would identify a confidential informant or seriously impair a civil or criminal tax investigation. For purposes of this paragraph, the name and address of the taxpayer shall not be treated as taxpayer return information.

(3) DISCLOSURE OF RETURN INFORMATION CONCERNING POSSIBLE CRIMINAL ACTIVITIES.—The Secretary may disclose in writing return information, other than taxpayer return information, which may constitute evidence of a violation of Federal criminal laws to the extent necessary to apprise the head of the appropriate Federal agency charged with the responsibility for enforcing such laws. For purposes of the preceding sentence, the name and address of the taxpayer shall not be treated as taxpayer return information if there is return information (other than taxpayer return information) which may constitute evidence of a violation of Federal criminal laws.

(4) USE IN JUDICIAL OR ADMINISTRATIVE PROCEEDING.—Any return or return information obtained under paragraph (1), (2), or (3) may be entered into evidence in any administrative or judicial proceeding pertaining to enforcement of a specifically designated Federal criminal statute (not involving tax administration) to which the United States or an agency described in paragraph (1)(A) is a party but, in the case of any return or return information obtained under paragraph (1), only if the court finds that such return or return information is probative of a matter in issue relevant in establishing the commission of a crime or the guilt of a party. However, any return or return information obtained under paragraph (1), (2), or (3) shall not be admitted into evidence in such proceeding if the Secretary determines and notifies the Attorney General or his delegate or the head of such agency that such admission would identify a confidential informant or seriously impair a civil or criminal tax investigation. The admission into evidence of any return or return information contrary to the provisions of this paragraph shall not, as such, constitute reversible error upon appeal of a judgment in such proceeding.

(5) RENEGOTIATION OF CONTRACTS.—A return or return information with respect to the tax imposed by chapter 1 upon a taxpayer subject to the provisions of the Renegotiation Act of 1951 shall, upon request in writing by the Chairman of the Renegotiation Board, be open to officers and employees of such board personally and directly engaged in, and solely for their use in, verifying or analyzing financial information required by such Act to be filed with, or otherwise disclosed to, the board, or to the extent necessary to implement the provisions of section 1481 or 1482. The Chairman of the Renegotiation Board may, upon referral of any matter with respect to such Act to the Department of Justice for further legal action, disclose such return and return information to any employee of such department charged with the responsibility for handling such matters.

P.L. 97-248, § 358(a):

Amended Code Sec. 6103(i)(7) (as redesignated by P.L. 97-248, § 356(a)) by redesignating subparagraph (B) as subparagraph (C) and by adding a new subparagraph (B). **Effective** 9-4-82.

P.L. 97-248, § 358(b)(1):

Amended Code Sec. 6103(i)(7)(A) (as redesignated by P.L. 97-248, § 356(a)) by striking out "subparagraph (B)" and inserting "subparagraph (C)". **Effective** 9-4-82.

P.L. 97-248, § 358(b)(2):

Amended Code Sec. 6102(i)(7)(C) (as redesignated by P.L. 97-248) by striking out "subparagraph (A)" and inserting "subparagraph (A) or (B)". **Effective** 9-4-82.

RETURNS—MISCELLANEOUS PROVISIONS

• 1980, Food Stamp Act Amendments of 1980 (P.L. 96-249)

P.L. 96-249, §127(a)(i):

Erroneously amended Code Sec. 6103(i) by adding a new subsection (7). The new subsection (7) was intended to be added to Code Sec. 6103(l) and is, therefore, reflected at that location.

• 1978, Revenue Act of 1978 (P.L. 95-600)

P.L. 95-600, §701(bb)(3):

Added a new last sentence to Code Sec. 6103(i)(2). **Effective** 1-1-77.

P.L. 95-600, §701(bb)(4):

Added a new last sentence to Code Sec. 6103(i)(3). **Effective** 1-1-77.

• 1976, Tax Reform Act of 1976 (P.L. 94-455)

P.L. 94-455, §1202(a):

Added Code Sec. 6103(i). **Effective** 1-1-77.

[Sec. 6103(j)]

(j) STATISTICAL USE.—

(1) DEPARTMENT OF COMMERCE.—Upon request in writing by the Secretary of Commerce, the Secretary shall furnish—

(A) such returns, or return information reflected thereon, to officers and employees of the Bureau of the Census, and

(B) such return information reflected on returns of corporations to officers and employees of the Bureau of Economic Analysis,

as the Secretary may prescribe by regulation for the purpose of, but only to the extent necessary in, the structuring of censuses and national economic accounts and conducting related statistical activities authorized by law.

(2) FEDERAL TRADE COMMISSION.—Upon request in writing by the Chairman of the Federal Trade Commission, the Secretary shall furnish such return information reflected on any return of a corporation with respect to the tax imposed by chapter 1 to officers and employees of the Division of Financial Statistics of the Bureau of Economics of such commission as the Secretary may prescribe by regulation for the purpose of, but only to the extent necessary in, administration by such division of legally authorized economic surveys of corporations.

(3) DEPARTMENT OF TREASURY.—Returns and return information shall be open to inspection by or disclosure to officers and employees of the Department of the Treasury whose official duties require such inspection or disclosure for the purpose of, but only to the extent necessary in, preparing economic or financial forecasts, projections, analyses, and statistical studies and conducting related activities. Such inspection or disclosure shall be permitted only upon written request which sets forth the specific reason or reasons why such inspection or disclosure is necessary and which is signed by the head of the bureau or office of the Department of the Treasury requesting the inspection or disclosure.

(4) ANONYMOUS FORM.—No person who receives a return or return information under this subsection shall disclose such return or return information to any person other than the taxpayer to whom it relates except in a form which cannot be associated with, or otherwise identify, directly or indirectly, a particular taxpayer.

(5) DEPARTMENT OF AGRICULTURE.—Upon request in writing by the Secretary of Agriculture, the Secretary shall furnish such returns, or return information reflected thereon, as the Secretary may prescribe by regulation to officers and employees of the Department of Agriculture whose official duties require access to such returns or information for the purpose of, but only to the extent necessary in, structuring, preparing, and conducting the census of agriculture pursuant to the Census of Agriculture Act of 1997 (Public Law 105-113).

(6) CONGRESSIONAL BUDGET OFFICE.—Upon written request by the Director of the Congressional Budget Office, the Secretary shall furnish to officers and employees of the Congressional Budget Office return information for the purpose of, but only to the extent necessary for, long-term models of the social security and medicare programs.

Amendments

• 2000, Community Renewal Tax Relief Act of 2000 (P.L. 106-554)

P.L. 106-554, §310(a)(1):

Amended Code Sec. 6103(j) by adding at the end a new paragraph (6). **Effective** 12-21-2000.

• 1998, Tax and Trade Relief Extension Act of 1998 (P.L. 105-277)

P.L. 105-277, §4006(a)(1):

Amended Code Sec. 6103(j) by adding at the end a new paragraph (5). **Effective** for requests made on or after 10-21-98.

• 1976, Tax Reform Act of 1976 (P.L. 94-455)

P.L. 94-455, §1202(a):

Added Code Sec. 6103(j). **Effective** 1-1-77.

[Sec. 6103(k)]

(k) DISCLOSURE OF CERTAIN RETURNS AND RETURN INFORMATION FOR TAX ADMINISTRATION PURPOSES.—

(1) DISCLOSURE OF ACCEPTED OFFERS-IN-COMPROMISE.—Return information shall be disclosed to members of the general public to the extent necessary to permit inspection of any accepted offer-in-compromise under section 7122 relating to the liability for a tax imposed by this title.

(2) DISCLOSURE OF AMOUNT OF OUTSTANDING LIEN.—If a notice of lien has been filed pursuant to section 6323(f), the amount of the outstanding obligation secured by such lien may be disclosed to any person who furnishes satisfactory written evidence that he has a right in the property subject to such lien or intends to obtain a right in such property.

(3) DISCLOSURE OF RETURN INFORMATION TO CORRECT MISSTATEMENTS OF FACT.—The Secretary may, but only following approval by the Joint Committee on Taxation, disclose such return information or any other information with respect to any specific taxpayer to the extent necessary for tax administration purposes to correct a misstatement of fact published or disclosed with respect to such taxpayer's return or any transaction of the taxpayer with the Internal Revenue Service.

(4) DISCLOSURE TO COMPETENT AUTHORITY UNDER TAX CONVENTION.—A return or return information may be disclosed to a competent authority of a foreign government which has an income tax or gift and estate tax convention or other convention or bilateral agreement relating to the exchange of tax information with the United States but only to the extent provided in, and subject to the terms and conditions of, such convention or bilateral agreement.

(5) STATE AGENCIES REGULATING TAX RETURN PREPARERS.—Taxpayer identity information with respect to any tax return preparer, and information as to whether or not any penalty has been assessed against such tax return preparer under section 6694, 6695, or 7216, may be furnished to any agency, body, or commission lawfully charged under any State or local law with the licensing, registration, or regulation of tax return preparers. Such information may be furnished only upon written request by the head of such agency, body, or commission designating the officers or employees to whom such information is to be furnished. Information may be furnished and used under this paragraph only for purposes of the licensing, registration, or regulation of tax return preparers.

(6) DISCLOSURE BY CERTAIN OFFICERS AND EMPLOYEES FOR INVESTIGATIVE PURPOSES.—An internal revenue officer or employee and an officer or employee of the Office of Treasury Inspector General for Tax Administration may, in connection with his official duties relating to any audit, collection activity, or civil or criminal tax investigation or any other offense under the internal revenue laws, disclose return information to the extent that such disclosure is necessary in obtaining information, which is not otherwise reasonably available, with respect to the correct determination of tax, liability for tax, or the amount to be collected or with respect to the enforcement of any other provision of this title. Such disclosures shall be made only in such situations and under such conditions as the Secretary may prescribe by regulation. This paragraph shall not apply to any disclosure to an individual providing information relating to any purpose described in paragraph (1) or (2) of section 7623(a) which is made under paragraph (13)(A).

(7) DISCLOSURE OF EXCISE TAX REGISTRATION INFORMATION.—To the extent the Secretary determines that disclosure is necessary to permit the effective administration of subtitle D, the Secretary may disclose—

(A) the name, address, and registration number of each person who is registered under any provision of subtitle D (and, in the case of a registered terminal operator, the address of each terminal operated by such operator), and

(B) the registration status of any person.

(8) LEVIES ON CERTAIN GOVERNMENT PAYMENTS.—

(A) DISCLOSURE OF RETURN INFORMATION IN LEVIES ON FINANCIAL MANAGEMENT SERVICE.—In serving a notice of levy, or release of such levy, with respect to any applicable government payment, the Secretary may disclose to officers and employees of the Financial Management Service—

(i) return information, including taxpayer identity information,

(ii) the amount of any unpaid liability under this title (including penalties and interest), and

(iii) the type of tax and tax period to which such unpaid liability relates.

(B) RESTRICTION ON USE OF DISCLOSED INFORMATION.—Return information disclosed under subparagraph (A) may be used by officers and employees of the Financial Management Service only for the purpose of, and to the extent necessary in, transferring levied funds in satisfaction of the levy, maintaining appropriate agency records in regard to such levy or the release thereof, notifying the taxpayer and the agency certifying such payment that the levy has been honored, or in the defense of any litigation ensuing from the honor of such levy.

(C) APPLICABLE GOVERNMENT PAYMENT.—For purposes of this paragraph, the term "applicable government payment" means—

(i) any Federal payment (other than a payment for which eligibility is based on the income or assets (or both) of a payee) certified to the Financial Management Service for disbursement, and

(ii) any other payment which is certified to the Financial Management Service for disbursement and which the Secretary designates by published notice.

(9) DISCLOSURE OF INFORMATION TO ADMINISTER SECTION 6311.—The Secretary may disclose returns or return information to financial institutions and others to the extent the Secretary deems necessary for the administration of section 6311. Disclosures of information for purposes other than to accept payments by checks or money orders shall be made only to the extent authorized by written procedures promulgated by the Secretary.

(10) DISCLOSURE OF CERTAIN RETURNS AND RETURN INFORMATION TO CERTAIN PRISON OFFICIALS.—

(A) IN GENERAL.—Under such procedures as the Secretary may prescribe, the Secretary may disclose to officers and employees of the Federal Bureau of Prisons and of any State agency charged with the responsibility for administration of prisons any returns or return information with respect to individuals incarcerated in Federal or State prison systems whom the Secretary has determined may have filed or facilitated the filing of a false or fraudulent return to the extent that the Secretary determines that such disclosure is necessary to permit effective Federal tax administration.

(B) DISCLOSURE TO CONTRACTOR-RUN PRISONS.—Under such procedures as the Secretary may prescribe, the disclosures authorized by subparagraph (A) may be made to contractors responsible for the operation of a Federal or State prison on behalf of such Bureau or agency.

(C) RESTRICTIONS ON USE OF DISCLOSED INFORMATION.—Any return or return information received under this paragraph shall be used only for the purposes of and to the extent necessary in taking administrative action to prevent the filing of false and fraudulent returns, including administrative actions to address possible violations of administrative rules and regulations of the prison facility and in administrative and judicial proceedings arising from such administrative actions.

(D) RESTRICTIONS ON REDISCLOSURE AND DISCLOSURE TO LEGAL REPRESENTATIVES.—Notwithstanding subsection (h)—

(i) RESTRICTIONS ON REDISCLOSURE.—Except as provided in clause (ii), any officer, employee, or contractor of the Federal Bureau of Prisons or of any State agency charged with the responsibility for administration of prisons shall not disclose any information obtained under this paragraph to any person other than an officer or employee or contractor of such Bureau or agency personally and directly engaged in the administration of prison facilities on behalf of such Bureau or agency.

(ii) DISCLOSURE TO LEGAL REPRESENTATIVES.—The returns and return information disclosed under this paragraph may be disclosed to the duly authorized legal representative of the Federal Bureau of Prisons, State agency, or contractor charged with the responsibility for administration of prisons, or of the incarcerated individual accused of filing the false or fraudulent return who is a party to an action or proceeding described in subparagraph (C), solely in preparation for, or for use in, such action or proceeding.

(11) DISCLOSURE OF RETURN INFORMATION TO DEPARTMENT OF STATE FOR PURPOSES OF PASSPORT REVOCATION UNDER SECTION 7345.—

(A) IN GENERAL.—The Secretary shall, upon receiving a certification described in section 7345, disclose to the Secretary of State return information with respect to a taxpayer who has a seriously delinquent tax debt described in such section. Such return information shall be limited to—

(i) the taxpayer identity information with respect to such taxpayer, and

(ii) the amount of such seriously delinquent tax debt.

(B) RESTRICTION ON DISCLOSURE.—Return information disclosed under subparagraph (A) may be used by officers and employees of the Department of State for the purposes of, and to the extent necessary in, carrying out the requirements of section 32101 of the FAST Act.

(12) QUALIFIED TAX COLLECTION CONTRACTORS.—Persons providing services pursuant to a qualified tax collection contract under section 6306 may, if speaking to a person who has identified himself or herself as having the name of the taxpayer to which a tax receivable (within the meaning of such section) relates, identify themselves as contractors of the Internal Revenue Service and disclose the business name of the contractor, and the nature, subject, and reason for the contact. Disclosures under this paragraph shall be made only in such situations and under such conditions as have been approved by the Secretary.

(13) DISCLOSURE TO WHISTLEBLOWERS.—

(A) IN GENERAL.—The Secretary may disclose, to any individual providing information relating to any purpose described in paragraph (1) or (2) of section 7623(a), return information related to the investigation of any taxpayer with respect to whom the individual has provided such information, but only to the extent that such disclosure is necessary in obtaining information, which is not otherwise reasonably available, with respect to the correct determination of tax liability for tax, or the amount to be collected with respect to the enforcement of any other provision of this title.

(B) UPDATES ON WHISTLEBLOWER INVESTIGATIONS.—The Secretary shall disclose to an individual providing information relating to any purpose described in paragraph (1) or (2) of section 7623(a) the following:

(i) Not later than 60 days after a case for which the individual has provided information has been referred for an audit or examination, a notice with respect to such referral.

(ii) Not later than 60 days after a taxpayer with respect to whom the individual has provided information has made a payment of tax with respect to tax liability to which such information relates, a notice with respect to such payment.

(iii) Subject to such requirements and conditions as are prescribed by the Secretary, upon a written request by such individual—

(I) information on the status and stage of any investigation or action related to such information, and

RETURNS—MISCELLANEOUS PROVISIONS

(II) in the case of a determination of the amount of any award under section 7623(b), the reasons for such determination.

Clause (iii) shall not apply to any information if the Secretary determines that disclosure of such information would seriously impair Federal tax administration. Information described in clauses (i), (ii), and (iii) may be disclosed to a designee of the individual providing such information in accordance with guidance provided by the Secretary.

(14) DISCLOSURE OF RETURN INFORMATION FOR PURPOSES OF CYBERSECURITY AND THE PREVENTION OF IDENTITY THEFT TAX REFUND FRAUD.—

(A) IN GENERAL.—Under such procedures and subject to such conditions as the Secretary may prescribe, the Secretary may disclose specified return information to specified ISAC participants to the extent that the Secretary determines such disclosure is in furtherance of effective Federal tax administration relating to the detection or prevention of identity theft tax refund fraud, validation of taxpayer identity, authentication of taxpayer returns, or detection or prevention of cybersecurity threats.

(B) SPECIFIED ISAC PARTICIPANTS.—For purposes of this paragraph—

(i) IN GENERAL.—The term "specified ISAC participant" means—

(I) any person designated by the Secretary as having primary responsibility for a function performed with respect to the information sharing and analysis center described in section 2003(a) of the Taxpayer First Act, and

(II) any person subject to the requirements of section 7216 and which is a participant in such information sharing and analysis center.

(ii) INFORMATION SHARING AGREEMENT.—Such term shall not include any person unless such person has entered into a written agreement with the Secretary setting forth the terms and conditions for the disclosure of information to such person under this paragraph, including requirements regarding the protection and safeguarding of such information by such person.

(C) SPECIFIED RETURN INFORMATION.—For purposes of this paragraph, the term "specified return information" means—

(i) in the case of a return which is in connection with a case of potential identity theft refund fraud—

(I) in the case of such return filed electronically, the internet protocol address, device identification, email domain name, speed of completion, method of authentication, refund method, and such other return information related to the electronic filing characteristics of such return as the Secretary may identify for purposes of this subclause, and

(II) in the case of such return prepared by a tax return preparer, identifying information with respect to such tax return preparer, including the preparer taxpayer identification number and electronic filer identification number of such preparer,

(ii) in the case of a return which is in connection with a case of a [sic] identity theft refund fraud which has been confirmed by the Secretary (pursuant to such procedures as the Secretary may provide), the information referred to in subclauses (I) and (II) of clause (i), the name and taxpayer identification number of the taxpayer as it appears on the return, and any bank account and routing information provided for making a refund in connection with such return, and

(iii) in the case of any cybersecurity threat to the Internal Revenue Service, information similar to the information described in subclauses (I) and (II) of clause (i) with respect to such threat.

(D) RESTRICTION ON USE OF DISCLOSED INFORMATION.—

(i) DESIGNATED THIRD PARTIES.—Any return information received by a person described in subparagraph (B)(i)(I) shall be used only for the purposes of and to the extent necessary in—

(I) performing the function such person is designated to perform under such subparagraph,

(II) facilitating disclosures authorized under subparagraph (A) to persons described in subparagraph (B)(i)(II), and

(III) facilitating disclosures authorized under subsection (d) to participants in such information sharing and analysis center.

(ii) RETURN PREPARERS.—Any return information received by a person described in subparagraph (B)(i)(II) shall be treated for purposes of section 7216 as information furnished to such person for, or in connection with, the preparation of a return of the tax imposed under chapter 1.

(E) DATA PROTECTION AND SAFEGUARDS.—Return information disclosed under this paragraph shall be subject to such protections and safeguards as the Secretary may require in regulations or other guidance or in the written agreement referred to in subparagraph (B)(ii). Such written agreement shall include a requirement that any unauthorized access to information disclosed under this paragraph, and any breach of any system in which such information is held, be reported to the Treasury Inspector General for Tax Administration.

(15) DISCLOSURES TO SOCIAL SECURITY ADMINISTRATION TO IDENTIFY TAX RECEIVABLES NOT ELIGIBLE FOR COLLECTION PURSUANT TO QUALIFIED TAX COLLECTION CONTRACTS.—In the case of any individual involved with a tax receivable which the Secretary has identified for possible collection pursuant to a qualified tax collection contract (as defined in section 6306(b)), the Secretary may disclose the taxpayer identity and date of birth of such individual to officers, employees, and contractors of the Social Security Administration to determine if such tax receivable is not eligible for collection pursuant to such a qualified tax collection contract by reason of section 6306(d)(3)(E).

Amendments

• **2020, COVID-related Tax Relief Act of 2020 (P.L. 116-260)**

P.L. 116-260, § 283(b)(1), Div. N:

Amended Code Sec. 6103(k) by adding at the end a new paragraph (15). **Effective** for disclosures made on or after 12-27-2020.

• **2020, Consolidated Appropriations Act, 2021 (P.L. 116-260)**

P.L. 116-260, § 102(b)(1), Div. FF:

Amended Code Sec. 6103(k) by adding at the end a new paragraph (15). [Note: An identical amendment was made by P.L. 116-260, Act Sec. 283(b)(1), Div. N. Therefore, this amendment cannot be made.—CCH] **Effective** for disclosures made on or after 12-27-2020.

• **2019, Taxpayer First Act (P.L. 116-25)**

P.L. 116-25, § 1405(a)(1):

Amended Code Sec. 6103(k) by adding at the end a new paragraph (13). **Effective** for disclosures made after 7-1-2019.

P.L. 116-25, § 1405(a)(2)(C):

Amended Code Sec. 6103(k)(6) by adding at the end a new sentence. **Effective** for disclosures made after 7-1-2019.

P.L. 116-25, § 2003(a)-(b), provides:

(a) IN GENERAL.—The Secretary of the Treasury (or the Secretary's delegate) may participate in an information sharing and analysis center to centralize, standardize, and enhance data compilation and analysis to facilitate sharing actionable data and information with respect to identity theft tax refund fraud.

(b) DEVELOPMENT OF PERFORMANCE METRICS.—The Secretary of the Treasury (or the Secretary's delegate) shall develop metrics for measuring the success of such center in detecting and preventing identity theft tax refund fraud.

P.L. 116-25, § 2003(c)(1):

Amended Code Sec. 6103(k), as amended by this Act, by adding at the end a new paragraph (14). **Effective** 7-1-2019.

• **2015, Fixing America's Surface Transportation Act (P.L. 114-94)**

P.L. 114-94, § 32101(c)(1):

Amended Code Sec. 6103(k) by adding at the end a new paragraph (11). **Effective** 12-4-2015.

P.L. 114-94, § 32102(d):

Amended Code Sec. 6103(k), as amended by Act Sec. 32101[(c)(1)], by adding at the end a new paragraph (12). **Effective** for disclosures made after 12-4-2015.

• **2013, American Taxpayer Relief Act of 2012 (P.L. 112-240)**

P.L. 112-240, § 209(a):

Amended Code Sec. 6103(k)(10). **Effective** 1-2-2013. Prior to amendment, Code Sec. 6103(k)(10) read as follows:

(10) DISCLOSURE OF CERTAIN RETURN INFORMATION TO CERTAIN PRISON OFFICIALS.—

(A) IN GENERAL.—Under such procedures as the Secretary may prescribe, the Secretary may disclose to the head of the Federal Bureau of Prisons and the head of any State agency charged with the responsibility for administration of prisons any return information with respect to individuals incarcerated in Federal or State prison whom the Secretary has determined may have filed or facilitated the filing of a false

RETURNS—MISCELLANEOUS PROVISIONS

return to the extent that the Secretary determines that such disclosure is necessary to permit effective Federal tax administration.

(B) RESTRICTION ON REDISCLOSURE.—Notwithstanding subsection (n), the head of the Federal Bureau of Prisons and the head of any State agency charged with the responsibility for administration of prisons may not disclose any information obtained under subparagraph (A) to any person other than an officer or employee of such Bureau or agency.

(C) RESTRICTION ON USE OF DISCLOSED INFORMATION.—Return information received under this paragraph shall be used only for purposes of and to the extent necessary in taking administrative action to prevent the filing of false and fraudulent returns, including administrative actions to address possible violations of administrative rules and regulations of the prison facility.

(D) TERMINATION.—No disclosure may be made under this paragraph after December 31, 2011.

• **2010, Homebuyer Assistance and Improvement Act of 2010 (P.L. 111-198)**

P.L. 111-198, §4(a)(1)-(2):

Amended Code Sec. 6103(k)(10)(A) by inserting "and the head of any State agency charged with the responsibility for administration of prisons" after "the head of the Federal Bureau of Prisons", and by striking "Federal prison" and inserting "Federal or State prison". **Effective** for disclosures made after 7-2-2010.

P.L. 111-198, §4(b)(1)-(2):

Amended Code Sec. 6103(k)(10)(B) by inserting "and the head of any State agency charged with the responsibility for administration of prisons" after "the head of the Federal Bureau of Prisons", and by inserting "or agency" after "such Bureau". **Effective** for disclosures made after 7-2-2010.

P.L. 111-198, §4(d):

Amended the heading of Code Sec. 6103(k)(10) by striking "OF PRISONERS TO FEDERAL BUREAU OF PRISONS" and inserting "TO CERTAIN PRISON OFFICIALS". **Effective** for disclosures made after 7-2-2010.

• **2008, Inmate Tax Fraud Prevention Act of 2008 (P.L. 110-428)**

P.L. 110-428, §2(a):

Amended Code Sec. 6103(k) by adding at the end a new paragraph (10). **Effective** for disclosures made after 12-31-2008.

P.L. 110-428, §2(e), provides:

(e) ANNUAL REPORTS.—The Secretary of the Treasury shall annually submit to Congress and make publicly available a report on the filing of false and fraudulent returns by individuals incarcerated in Federal and State prisons. Such report shall include statistics on the number of false and fraudulent returns associated with each Federal and State prison.

• **2007, Small Business and Work Opportunity Tax Act of 2007 (P.L. 110-28)**

P.L. 110-28, §8246(a)(2)(B)(i)-(ii):

Amended Code Sec. 6103(k)(5) by striking "income tax return preparer" each place it appears and inserting "tax return preparer", and by striking "income tax return preparers" each place it appears and inserting "tax return preparers". **Effective** for returns prepared after 5-25-2007.

• **2000, Community Renewal Tax Relief Act of 2000 (P.L. 106-554)**

P.L. 106-554, §313(c)(1)-(2):

Amended Code Sec. 6103(k)(6) by inserting "and an officer or employee of the Office of Treasury Inspector General for Tax Administration" after "internal revenue officer or employee", and by striking "INTERNAL REVENUE" in the heading and inserting "CERTAIN". **Effective** as if included in the provision of P.L. 105-206 to which it relates [effective 7-22-98.—CCH].

• **1998, IRS Restructuring and Reform Act of 1998 (P.L. 105-206)**

P.L. 105-206, §6012(b)(2):

Amended Code Sec. 6103(k) by redesignating paragraph (8) (as added by Act Sec. 1205(c)(1) of P.L. 105-34) as paragraph (9). **Effective** as if included in the provision of P.L. 105-34 to which it relates [effective 5-5-98.—CCH].

• **1997, Taxpayer Relief Act of 1997 (P.L. 105-34)**

P.L. 105-34, §1026(a):

Amended Code Sec. 6103(k) by adding at the end a new paragraph (8). **Effective** for levies issued after 8-5-97.

P.L. 105-34, §1205(c)(1):

Amended Code Sec. 6103(k) by adding at the end a new paragraph (8)[(9)]. **Effective** on the day 9 months after 8-5-97.

• **1990, Omnibus Budget Reconciliation Act of 1990 (P.L. 101-508)**

P.L. 101-508, §11212(b)(3):

Amended Code Sec. 6103(k) by adding at the end thereof a new paragraph (7). **Effective** 12-1-90.

• **1988, Technical and Miscellaneous Revenue Act of 1988 (P.L. 100-647)**

P.L. 100-647, §1012(bb)(3)(A)(i)-(ii):

Amended Code Sec. 6103(k)(4) by striking out "or other convention" and inserting in lieu thereof "or other convention or bilateral agreement", and by striking out "such convention" and inserting in lieu thereof "such convention or bilateral agreement". **Effective** 10-22-86.

• **1978, Revenue Act of 1978 (P.L. 95-600)**

P.L. 95-600, §701(bb)(5):

Amended Code Sec. 6103(k)(4). **Effective** 1-1-77. Prior to amendment, Code Sec. 6103(k)(4) read as follows:

(4) DISCLOSURE TO COMPETENT AUTHORITY UNDER INCOME TAX CONVENTION.—A return or return information may be disclosed to a competent authority of a foreign government which has an income tax convention with the United States but only to the extent provided in, and subject to the terms and conditions of, such convention.

• **1976, Tax Reform Act of 1976 (P.L. 94-455)**

P.L. 94-455, §1202(a):

Added Code Sec. 6103(k). **Effective** 1-1-77.

[Sec. 6103(l)]

(l) DISCLOSURE OF RETURNS AND RETURN INFORMATION FOR PURPOSES OTHER THAN TAX ADMINISTRATION.—

(1) DISCLOSURE OF CERTAIN RETURNS AND RETURN INFORMATION TO SOCIAL SECURITY ADMINISTRATION AND RAILROAD RETIREMENT BOARD.—The Secretary may, upon written request, disclose returns and return information with respect to—

(A) taxes imposed by chapters 2, 21, and 24, to the Social Security Administration for purposes of its administration of the Social Security Act;

(B) a plan to which part I of subchapter D of chapter 1 applies, to the Social Security Administration for purposes of carrying out its responsibility under section 1131 of the Social Security Act, limited, however to return information described in section 6057(d); and

(C) taxes imposed by chapter 22, to the Railroad Retirement Board for purposes of its administration of the Railroad Retirement Act.

(2) DISCLOSURE OF RETURNS AND RETURN INFORMATION TO THE DEPARTMENT OF LABOR AND PENSION BENEFIT GUARANTY CORPORATION.—The Secretary may, upon written request, furnish returns and return information to the proper officers and employees of the Department of Labor and the Pension Benefit Guaranty Corporation for purposes of, but only to the extent necessary in, the administration of titles I and IV of the Employee Retirement Income Security Act of 1974.

(3) DISCLOSURE THAT APPLICANT FOR FEDERAL LOAN HAS TAX DELINQUENT ACCOUNT.—

(A) IN GENERAL.—Upon written request, the Secretary may disclose to the head of the Federal agency administering any included Federal loan program whether or not an applicant for a loan under such program has a tax delinquent account.

(B) RESTRICTION ON DISCLOSURE.—Any disclosure under subparagraph (A) shall be made only for the purpose of, and to the extent necessary in, determining the creditworthiness of the applicant for the loan in question.

(C) INCLUDED FEDERAL LOAN PROGRAM DEFINED.—For purposes of this paragraph, the term "included Federal loan program" means any program under which the United States or a Federal agency makes, guarantees, or insures loans.

(4) DISCLOSURE OF RETURNS AND RETURN INFORMATION FOR USE IN PERSONNEL OR CLAIMANT REPRESENTATIVE MATTERS.—The Secretary may disclose returns and return information—

(A) upon written request—

(i) to an employee or former employee of the Department of the Treasury, or to the duly authorized legal representative of such employee or former employee, who is or may be a party to any administrative action or proceeding affecting the personnel rights of such employee or former employee; or

(ii) to any person, or to the duly authorized legal representative of such person, whose rights are or may be affected by an administrative action or proceeding under section 330 of title 31, United States Code,

solely for use in the action or proceeding, or in preparation for the action or proceeding, but only to the extent that the Secretary determines that such returns or return information is or may be relevant and material to the action or proceeding; or

(B) to officers and employees of the Department of the Treasury for use in any action or proceeding described in subparagraph (A), or in preparation for such action or proceeding, to the extent necessary to advance or protect the interests of the United States.

(5) SOCIAL SECURITY ADMINISTRATION.—Upon written request by the Commissioner of Social Security, the Secretary may disclose information returns filed pursuant to part III of subchapter A of chapter 61 of this subtitle for the purpose of—

(A) carrying out, in accordance with an agreement entered into pursuant to section 232 of the Social Security Act, an effective return processing program; or

(B) providing information regarding the mortality status of individuals for epidemiological and similar research in accordance with section 1106(d) of the Social Security Act.

(6) DISCLOSURE OF RETURN INFORMATION TO FEDERAL, STATE, AND LOCAL CHILD SUPPORT ENFORCEMENT AGENCIES.—

(A) RETURN INFORMATION FROM INTERNAL REVENUE SERVICE.—The Secretary may, upon written request, disclose to the appropriate Federal, State, or local child support enforcement agency—

(i) available return information from the master files of the Internal Revenue Service relating to the social security account number (or numbers, if the individual involved has more than one such number), address, filing status, amounts and nature of income, and the number of dependents reported on any return filed by, or with respect to, any individual with respect to whom child support obligations are sought to be established or enforced pursuant to the provisions of part D of title IV of the Social Security Act and with respect to any individual to whom such support obligations are owing, and

(ii) available return information reflected on any return filed by, or with respect to, any individual described in clause (i) relating to the amount of such individual's gross income (as defined in section 61) or consisting of the names and addresses of payors of such income and the names of any dependents reported on such return, but only if such return information is not reasonably available from any other source.

(B) DISCLOSURE TO CERTAIN AGENTS.—The following information disclosed to any child support enforcement agency under subparagraph (A) with respect to any individual with respect to whom child support obligations are sought to be established or enforced may be disclosed by such agency to any agent of such agency which is under contract with such agency to carry out the purposes described in subparagraph (C):

(i) The address and social security account number (or numbers) of such individual.

(ii) The amount of any reduction under section 6402(c) (relating to offset of past-due support against overpayments) in any overpayment otherwise payable to such individual.

(C) RESTRICTION ON DISCLOSURE.—Information may be disclosed under this paragraph only for purposes of, and to the extent necessary in, establishing and collecting child support obligations from, and locating, individuals owing such obligations.

(7) DISCLOSURE OF RETURN INFORMATION TO FEDERAL, STATE, AND LOCAL AGENCIES ADMINISTERING CERTAIN PROGRAMS UNDER THE SOCIAL SECURITY ACT, THE FOOD AND NUTRITION ACT OF 2008, OR TITLE 38, UNITED STATES CODE, OR CERTAIN HOUSING ASSISTANCE PROGRAMS.—

(A) RETURN INFORMATION FROM SOCIAL SECURITY ADMINISTRATION.—The Commissioner of Social Security shall, upon written request, disclose return information from returns with respect to net earnings from self-employment (as defined in section 1402), wages (as defined in section 3121(a) or 3401(a)), and payments of retirement income, which have been disclosed to the Social Security Administration as provided by paragraph (1) or (5) of this subsection, to any Federal, State, or local agency administering a program listed in subparagraph (D).

(B) RETURN INFORMATION FROM INTERNAL REVENUE SERVICE.—The Secretary shall, upon written request, disclose current return information from returns with respect to unearned income from the Internal Revenue Service files to any Federal, State, or local agency administering a program listed in subparagraph (D).

(C) RESTRICTION ON DISCLOSURE.—The Commissioner of Social Security and the Secretary shall disclose return information under subparagraphs (A) and (B) only for purposes of, and to the extent necessary in, determining eligibility for, or the correct amount of, benefits under a program listed in subparagraph (D).

(D) PROGRAMS TO WHICH RULE APPLIES.—The programs to which this paragraph applies are:

(i) a State program funded under part A of title IV of the Social Security Act;

(ii) medical assistance provided under a State plan approved under title XIX of the Social Security Act or subsidies provided under section 1860D-14 of such Act;

(iii) supplemental security income benefits provided under title XVI of the Social Security Act, and federally administered supplementary payments of the type described in section 1616(a) of such Act (including payments pursuant to an agreement entered into under section 212(a) of Public Law 93-66);

(iv) any benefits provided under a State plan approved under title I, X, XIV, or XVI of the Social Security Act (as those titles apply to Puerto Rico, Guam, and the Virgin Islands);

(v) unemployment compensation provided under a State law described in section 3304 of this title;

(vi) assistance provided under the Food and Nutrition Act of 2008;

(vii) State-administered supplementary payments of the type described in section 1616(a) of the Social Security Act (including payments pursuant to an agreement entered into under section 212(a) of Public Law 93-66);

(viii)(I) any needs-based pension provided under chapter 15 of title 38, United States Code, or under any other law administered by the Secretary of Veterans Affairs;

(II) parents' dependency and indemnity compensation provided under section 1315 of title 38, United States Code;

(III) health-care services furnished under sections 1710(a)(2)(G), 1710(a)(3), and 1710(b) of such title; and

(IV) compensation paid under chapter 11 of title 38, United States Code, at the 100 percent rate based solely on unemployability and without regard to the fact that the disability or disabilities are not rated as 100 percent disabling under the rating schedule; and

(ix) any housing assistance program administered by the Department of Housing and Urban Development that involves initial and periodic review of an applicant's or participant's income, except that return information may be disclosed under this clause only on written request by the Secretary of Housing and Urban Development and only for use by officers and employees of the Department of Housing and Urban Development with respect to applicants for and participants in such programs.

Only return information from returns with respect to net earnings from self-employment and wages may be disclosed under this paragraph for use with respect to any program described in clause (viii)(IV).

(8) DISCLOSURE OF CERTAIN RETURN INFORMATION BY SOCIAL SECURITY ADMINISTRATION TO FEDERAL, STATE, AND LOCAL CHILD SUPPORT ENFORCEMENT AGENCIES.—

(A) IN GENERAL.—Upon written request, the Commissioner of Social Security shall disclose directly to officers and employees of a Federal or State or local child support enforcement agency return information from returns with respect to social security account

RETURNS—MISCELLANEOUS PROVISIONS

numbers[,]net earnings from self-employment (as defined in section 1402), wages (as defined in section 3121(a) or 3401(a)), and payments of retirement income which have been disclosed to the Social Security Administration as provided by paragraph (1) or (5) of this subsection.

(B) RESTRICTION ON DISCLOSURE.—The Commissioner of Social Security shall disclose return information under subparagraph (A) only for purposes of, and to the extent necessary in, establishing and collecting child support obligations from, and locating, individuals owing such obligations. For purposes of the preceding sentence, the term "child support obligations" only includes obligations which are being enforced pursuant to a plan described in section 454 of the Social Security Act which has been approved by the Secretary of Health and Human Services under part D of title IV of such Act.

(C) STATE OR LOCAL CHILD SUPPORT ENFORCEMENT AGENCY.—For purposes of this paragraph, the term "State or local child support enforcement agency" means any agency of a State or political subdivision thereof operating pursuant to a plan described in subparagraph (B).

(9) DISCLOSURE OF ALCOHOL FUEL PRODUCERS TO ADMINISTRATORS OF STATE ALCOHOL LAWS.—Notwithstanding any other provision of this section, the Secretary may disclose—

(A) the name and address of any person who is qualified to produce alcohol for fuel use under section 5181, and

(B) the location of any premises to be used by such person in producing alcohol for fuel,

to any State agency, body, or commission, or its legal representative, which is charged under the laws of such State with responsibility for administration of State alcohol laws solely for use in the administration of such laws.

(10) DISCLOSURE OF CERTAIN INFORMATION TO AGENCIES REQUESTING A REDUCTION UNDER SUBSECTION (c), (d), (e), OR (f) OF SECTION 6402.—

(A) RETURN INFORMATION FROM INTERNAL REVENUE SERVICE.—The Secretary may, upon receiving a written request, disclose to officers and employees of any agency seeking a reduction under subsection (c), (d), (e) or (f) of section 6402, to officers and employees of the Department of Labor for purposes of facilitating the exchange of data in connection with a notice submitted under subsection (f)(5)(C) of section 6402, and to officers and employees of the Department of the Treasury in connection with such reduction—

(i) taxpayer identity information with respect to the taxpayer against whom such a reduction was made or not made and with respect to any other person filing a joint return with such taxpayer,

(ii) the fact that a reduction has been made or has not been made under such subsection with respect to such taxpayer,

(iii) the amount of such reduction,

(iv) whether such taxpayer filed a joint return, and

(v) the fact that a payment was made (and the amount of the payment) to the spouse of the taxpayer on the basis of a joint return.

(B) RESTRICTION ON USE OF DISCLOSED INFORMATION.—(i) Any officers and employees of an agency receiving return information under subparagraph (A) shall use such information only for the purposes of, and to the extent necessary in, establishing appropriate agency records, locating any person with respect to whom a reduction under subsection (c), (d), (e), or (f) of section 6402 is sought for purposes of collecting the debt with respect to which the reduction is sought, or in the defense of any litigation or administrative procedure ensuing from a reduction made under subsection (c), (d), (e), or (f) of section 6402.

(ii) Notwithstanding clause (i), return information disclosed to officers and employees of the Department of Labor may be accessed by agents who maintain and provide technological support to the Department of Labor's Interstate Connection Network (ICON) solely for the purpose of providing such maintenance and support.

(11) DISCLOSURE OF RETURN INFORMATION TO CARRY OUT FEDERAL EMPLOYEES' RETIREMENT SYSTEM.—

(A) IN GENERAL.—The Commissioner of Social Security shall, on written request, disclose to the Office of Personnel Management return information from returns with respect to net earnings from self-employment (as defined in section 1402), wages (as defined in section 3121(a) or 3401(a)), and payments of retirement income, which have been disclosed to the Social Security Administration as provided by paragraph (1) or (5).

(B) RESTRICTION ON DISCLOSURE.—The Commissioner of Social Security shall disclose return information under subparagraph (A) only for purposes of, and to the extent necessary in, the administration of chapters 83 and 84 of title 5, United States Code.

(12) DISCLOSURE OF CERTAIN TAXPAYER IDENTITY INFORMATION FOR VERIFICATION OF EMPLOYMENT STATUS OF MEDICARE BENEFICIARY AND SPOUSE OF MEDICARE BENEFICIARY.—

(A) RETURN INFORMATION FROM INTERNAL REVENUE SERVICE.—The Secretary shall, upon written request from the Commissioner of Social Security, disclose to the Commissioner available filing status and taxpayer identity information from the individual master files of the Internal Revenue Service relating to whether any medicare beneficiary identified by the Commissioner was a married individual (as defined in section 7703) for any specified year after 1986, and, if so, the name of the spouse of such individual and such spouse's TIN.

(B) RETURN INFORMATION FROM SOCIAL SECURITY ADMINISTRATION.—The Commissioner of Social Security shall, upon written request from the Administrator of the Centers for Medicare & Medicaid Services, disclose to the Administrator the following information:

(i) The name and TIN of each medicare beneficiary who is identified as having received wages (as defined in section 3401(a)), above an amount (if any) specified by the Secretary of Health and Human Services, from a qualified employer in a previous year.

(ii) For each medicare beneficiary who was identified as married under subparagraph (A) and whose spouse is identified as having received wages, above an amount (if any) specified by the Secretary of Health and Human Services, from a qualified employer in a previous year—

(I) the name and TIN of the medicare beneficiary, and

(II) the name and TIN of the spouse.

(iii) With respect to each such qualified employer, the name, address, and TIN of the employer and the number of individuals with respect to whom written statements were furnished under section 6051 by the employer with respect to such previous year.

(C) DISCLOSURE BY CENTERS FOR MEDICARE & MEDICAID SERVICES.—With respect to the information disclosed under subparagraph (B), the Administrator of the Centers for Medicare & Medicaid Services may disclose—

(i) to the qualified employer referred to in such subparagraph the name and TIN of each individual identified under such subparagraph as having received wages from the employer (hereinafter, in this subparagraph referred to as the "employee") for purposes of determining during what period such employee or the employee's spouse may be (or have been) covered under a group health plan of the employer and what benefits are or were covered under the plan (including the name, address, and identifying number of the plan),

(ii) to any group health plan which provides or provided coverage to such an employee or spouse, the name of such employee and the employee's spouse (if the spouse is a medicare beneficiary) and the name and address of the employer, and, for the purpose of presenting a claim to the plan—

(I) the TIN of such employee if benefits were paid under title XVIII of the Social Security Act with respect to the employee during a period in which the plan was a primary plan (as defined in section 1862(b)(2)(A) of the Social Security Act) and

RETURNS—MISCELLANEOUS PROVISIONS

(II) the TIN of such spouse if benefits were paid under such title with respect to the spouse during such period, and

(iii) to any agent of such Administrator the information referred to in subparagraph (B) for purposes of carrying out clauses (i) and (ii) on behalf of such Administrator.

(D) SPECIAL RULES.—

(i) RESTRICTIONS ON DISCLOSURE.—Information may be disclosed under this paragraph only for purposes of, and to the extent necessary in, determining the extent to which any medicare beneficiary is covered under any group health plan.

(ii) TIMELY RESPONSE TO REQUESTS.—Any request made under subparagaph (A) or (B) shall be complied with as soon as possible but in no event later than 120 days afer the date the request was made.

(E) DEFINITIONS.—For purposes of this paragraph—

(i) MEDICARE BENEFICIARY.—The term "medicare beneficiary" means an individual entitled to benefits under part A, or enrolled under part B, of title XVIII of the Social Security Act, but does not include such an individual enrolled in part A under section 1818.

(ii) GROUP HEALTH PLAN.—The term "group health plan" means any group health plan (as defined in section 5000(b)(1)).

(iii) QUALIFIED EMPLOYER.—The term "qualified employer" means, for a calendar year, an employer which has furnished written statements under section 6051 with respect to at least 20 individuals for wages paid in the year.

(13) DISCLOSURE OF RETURN INFORMATION TO CARRY OUT THE HIGHER EDUCATION ACT OF 1965.—

(A) APPLICATIONS AND RECERTIFICATIONS FOR INCOME-CONTINGENT OR INCOME-BASED REPAYMENT.—The Secretary shall, upon written request from the Secretary of Education, disclose to any authorized person, only for the purpose of (and to the extent necessary in) determining eligibility for, or repayment obligations under, income-contingent or income-based repayment plans under title IV of the Higher Education Act of 1965 with respect to loans under part D of such title, the following return information from returns (for any taxable year specified by the Secretary of Education as relevant to such purpose) of an individual certified by the Secretary of Education as having provided approval under section 494(a)(2) of such Act (as in effect on the date of enactment of this paragraph) for such disclosure:

(i) Taxpayer identity information.

(ii) Filing status.

(iii) Adjusted gross income.

(iv) Total number of exemptions claimed, if applicable.

(v) Number of dependents taken into account in determining the credit allowed under section 24.

(vi) If applicable, the fact that there was no return filed.

(B) DISCHARGE OF LOAN BASED ON TOTAL AND PERMANENT DISABILITY.—The Secretary shall, upon written request from the Secretary of Education, disclose to any authorized person, only for the purpose of (and to the extent necessary in) monitoring and reinstating loans under title IV of the Higher Education Act of 1965 that were discharged based on a total and permanent disability (within the meaning of section 437(a) of such Act), the following return information from returns (for any taxable year specified by the Secretary of Education as relevant to such purpose) of an individual certified by the Secretary of Education as having provided approval under section 494(a)(3) of such Act (as in effect on the date of enactment of this paragraph) for such disclosure:

(i) The return information described in clauses (i), (ii), and (vi) of subparagraph (A).

(ii) The return information described in subparagraph (C)(ii).

(C) FEDERAL STUDENT FINANCIAL AID.—The Secretary shall, upon written request from the Secretary of Education, disclose to any authorized person, only for the purpose of (and to the extent necessary in) determining eligibility for, and amount of, Federal student financial aid under a program authorized under subpart 1 of part A, part C, or part D of title IV of the Higher Education Act of 1965 the following return information from returns (for the taxable year used for purposes of section 480(a) of such Act) of an individual certified by the Secretary of Education as having provided approval under section 494(a)(1) of such Act (as in effect on the date of enactment of this paragraph) for such disclosure:

(i) Return information described in clauses (i) through (vi) of subparagraph (A).

(ii) The amount of any net earnings from self employment (as defined in section 1402(a)), wages (as defined in section 3121(a) or 3401(a)), and taxable income from a farming business (as defined in section 263A(e)(4)).

(iii) Amount of total income tax.

(iv) Amount of any credit allowed under section 25A.

(v) Amount of individual retirement account distributions not included in adjusted gross income.

(vi) Amount of individual retirement account contributions and payments to self-employed SEP, Keogh, and other qualified plans which were deducted from income.

(vii) Amount of tax-exempt interest received.

(viii) Amounts from retirement pensions and annuities not included in adjusted gross income.

(ix) If applicable, the fact that any of the following schedules (or equivalent successor schedules) were filed with the return:

(I) Schedule A.

(II) Schedule B.

(III) Schedule D.

(IV) Schedule E.

(V) Schedule F.

(VI) Schedule H.

(x) If applicable, the amount reported on Schedule C (or an equivalent successor schedule) as net profit or loss.

(D) ADDITIONAL USES OF DISCLOSED INFORMATION.—

(i) IN GENERAL.—In addition to the purposes for which information is disclosed under subparagraphs (A), (B), and (C), return information so disclosed may be used by an authorized person, with respect to income-contingent or income-based repayment plans, awards of Federal student financial aid under a program authorized under subpart 1 of part A, part C, or part D of title IV of the Higher Education Act of 1965, and discharges of loans based on a total and permanent disability (within the meaning of section 437(a) of such Act), for purposes of—

(I) reducing the net cost of improper payments under such plans, relating to such awards, or relating to such discharges,

(II) oversight activities by the Office of Inspector General of the Department of Education as authorized by the Inspector General Act of 1978, and

(III) conducting analyses and forecasts for estimating costs related to such plans, awards, or discharges.

(ii) LIMITATION.—The purposes described in clause (i) shall not include the conduct of criminal investigations or prosecutions.

RETURNS—MISCELLANEOUS PROVISIONS

(iii) REDISCLOSURE TO INSTITUTIONS OF HIGHER EDUCATION, STATE HIGHER EDUCATION AGENCIES, AND DESIGNATED SCHOLARSHIP ORGANIZATIONS.—Authorized persons may redisclose return information received under subparagraph (C), solely for the use in the application, award, and administration of financial aid awarded by the Federal government or awarded by a person described in subclause (I), (II), or (III), to the following persons:

(I) An institution of higher education participating in a program under subpart 1 of part A, part C, or part D of title IV of the Higher Education Act of 1965.

(II) A State higher education agency.

(III) A scholarship organization which is an entity designated (prior to the date of the enactment of this clause) by the Secretary of Education under section 483(a)(3)(E) of such Act.

This clause shall only apply to the extent that the taxpayer with respect to whom the return information relates provides written consent for such redisclosure to the Secretary of Education. Under such terms and conditions as may be prescribed by the Secretary, after consultation with the Department of Education, an institution of higher education described in subclause (I) or a State higher education agency described in subclause (II) may designate a contractor of such institution or state agency to receive return information on behalf of such institution or state agency to administer aspects of the institution's or state agency's activities for the application, award, and administration of such financial aid.

(iv) REDISCLOSURE TO OFFICE OF INSPECTOR GENERAL, INDEPENDENT AUDITORS, AND CONTRACTORS.—Any return information which is redisclosed under clause (iii)—

(I) may be further disclosed by persons described in subclauses (I), (II), or (III) of clause (iii) or persons designated in the last sentence of clause (iii) to the Office of Inspector General of the Department of Education and independent auditors conducting audits of such person's administration of the programs for which the return information was received, and

(II) may be further disclosed by persons described in subclauses (I), (II), or (III) of clause (iii) to contractors of such entities,

but only to the extent necessary in carrying out the purposes described in such clause (iii).

(v) REDISCLOSURE TO FAMILY MEMBERS.—In addition to the purposes for which information is disclosed and used under subparagraphs (A) and (C), or redisclosed under clause (iii), any return information so disclosed or redisclosed may be further disclosed to any individual certified by the Secretary of Education as having provided approval under paragraph (1) or (2) of section 494(a) of the Higher Education Act of 1965, as the case may be, for disclosure related to the income-contingent or income-based repayment plan under subparagraph (A) or the eligibility for, and amount of, Federal student financial aid described in subparagraph (C).

(vi) REDISCLOSURE OF FAFSA INFORMATION.—Return information received under subparagraph (C) may be redisclosed in accordance with subsection (c) of section 494 of the Higher Education Act of 1965 as in effect on the date of enactment of the Consolidated Appropriations Act, 2021 to carry out the purposes specified in such subsection.

(E) AUTHORIZED PERSON.—For purposes of this paragraph, the term 'authorized person' means, with respect to information disclosed under subparagraph (A), (B), or (C), any person who—

(i) is an officer, employee, or contractor, of the Department of Education, and

(ii) is specifically authorized and designated by the Secretary of Education for purposes of such subparagraph (applied separately with respect to each such subparagraph).

(F) JOINT RETURNS.—In the case of a joint return, any disclosure authorized under subparagraph (A), (B), or (C), and any redisclosure authorized under clause (iii), (iv)[,] (v), or (vi) of subparagraph (D), with respect to an individual shall be treated for purposes of this paragraph as applying with respect to the taxpayer.

(14) DISCLOSURE OF RETURN INFORMATION TO UNITED STATES CUSTOMS SERVICE.—The Secretary may, upon written request from the Commissioner of the United States Customs Service, disclose to officers and employees of the Department of the Treasury such return information with respect to taxes imposed by chapters 1 and 6 as the Secretary may prescribe by regulations, solely for the purpose of, and only to the extent necessary in—

(A) ascertaining the correctness of any entry in audits as provided for in section 509 of the Tariff Act of 1930 (19 U.S.C. 1509), or

(B) other actions to recover any loss of revenue, or to collect duties, taxes, and fees, determined to be due and owing pursuant to such audits.

(15) DISCLOSURE OF RETURNS FILED UNDER SECTION 6050I.—The Secretary may, upon written request, disclose to officers and employees of—

(A) any Federal agency,

(B) any agency of a State or local government, or

(C) any agency of the government of a foreign country,

information contained on returns filed under section 6050I. Any such disclosure shall be made on the same basis, and subject to the same conditions, as apply to disclosures of information on reports filed under section 5313 of title 31, United States Code; except that no disclosure under this paragraph shall be made for purposes of the administration of any tax law.

(16) DISCLOSURE OF RETURN INFORMATION FOR PURPOSES OF ADMINISTERING THE DISTRICT OF COLUMBIA RETIREMENT PROTECTION ACT OF 1997.—

(A) IN GENERAL.—Upon written request available return information (including such information disclosed to the Social Security Administration under paragraph (1) or (5) of this subsection), relating to the amount of wage income (as defined in section 3121(a) or 3401(a)), the name, address, and identifying number assigned under section 6109, of payors of wage income, taxpayer identity (as defined in section 6103(b)(6)), and the occupational status reflected on any return filed by, or with respect to, any individual with respect to whom eligibility for, or the correct amount of, benefits under the District of Columbia Retirement Protection Act of 1997, is sought to be determined, shall be disclosed by the Commissioner of Social Security, or to the extent not available from the Social Security Administration, by the Secretary, to any duly authorized officer or employee of the Department of the Treasury, or a Trustee or any designated officer or employee of a Trustee (as defined in the District of Columbia Retirement Protection Act of 1997), or any actuary engaged by a Trustee under the terms of the District of Columbia Retirement Protection Act of 1997, whose official duties require such disclosure, solely for the purpose of, and to the extent necessary in, determining an individual's eligibility for, or the correct amount of, benefits under the District of Columbia Retirement Protection Act of 1997.

(B) DISCLOSURE FOR USE IN JUDICIAL OR ADMINISTRATIVE PROCEEDINGS.—Return information disclosed to any person under this paragraph may be disclosed in a judicial or administrative proceeding relating to the determination of an individual's eligibility for, or the correct amount of, benefits under the District of Columbia Retirement Protection Act of 1997.

(17) DISCLOSURE TO NATIONAL ARCHIVES AND RECORDS ADMINISTRATION.—The Secretary shall, upon written request from the Archivist of the United States, disclose or authorize the disclosure of returns and return information to officers and employees of the National Archives and Records Administration for purposes of, and only to the extent necessary in, the appraisal of records for destruction or retention. No such officer or employee shall, except to the extent authorized by subsection (f), (i)(8), or (p), disclose any return or return information disclosed under the preceding sentence to any person other than to the Secretary, or to another officer or employee of the National Archives and Records Administration whose official duties require such disclosure for purposes of such appraisal.

RETURNS—MISCELLANEOUS PROVISIONS

(18) DISCLOSURE OF RETURN INFORMATION FOR PURPOSES OF CARRYING OUT A PROGRAM FOR ADVANCE PAYMENT OF CREDIT FOR HEALTH INSURANCE COSTS OF ELIGIBLE INDIVIDUALS.—The Secretary may disclose to providers of health insurance for any certified individual (as defined in section 7527(c)) return information with respect to such certified individual only to the extent necessary to carry out the program established by section 7527 (relating to advance payment of credit for health insurance costs of eligible individuals).

(19) DISCLOSURE OF RETURN INFORMATION FOR PURPOSES OF PROVIDING TRANSITIONAL ASSISTANCE UNDER MEDICARE DISCOUNT CARD PROGRAM.—

(A) IN GENERAL.—The Secretary, upon written request from the Secretary of Health and Human Services pursuant to carrying out section 1860D-31 of the Social Security Act, shall disclose to officers, employees, and contractors of the Department of Health and Human Services with respect to a taxpayer for the applicable year—

(i) (I) whether the adjusted gross income, as modified in accordance with specifications of the Secretary of Health and Human Services for purposes of carrying out such section, of such taxpayer and, if applicable, such taxpayer's spouse, for the applicable year, exceeds the amounts specified by the Secretary of Health and Human Services in order to apply the 100 and 135 percent of the poverty lines under such section, (II) whether the return was a joint return, and (III) the applicable year, or

(ii) if applicable, the fact that there is no return filed for such taxpayer for the applicable year.

(B) DEFINITION OF APPLICABLE YEAR.—For the purposes of this subsection, the term "applicable year" means the most recent taxable year for which information is available in the Internal Revenue Service's taxpayer data information systems, or, if there is no return filed for such taxpayer for such year, the prior taxable year.

(C) RESTRICTION ON USE OF DISCLOSED INFORMATION.—Return information disclosed under this paragraph may be used only for the purposes of determining eligibility for and administering transitional assistance under section 1860D-31 of the Social Security Act.

(20) DISCLOSURE OF RETURN INFORMATION TO CARRY OUT MEDICARE PART B PREMIUM SUBSIDY ADJUSTMENT AND PART D BASE BENEFICIARY PREMIUM INCREASE.—

(A) IN GENERAL.—The Secretary shall, upon written request from the Commissioner of Social Security, disclose to officers, employees, and contractors of the Social Security Administration return information of a taxpayer whose premium (according to the records of the Secretary) may be subject to adjustment under section 1839(i) or increase under section 1860D-13(a)(7) of the Social Security Act. Such return information shall be limited to—

(i) taxpayer identity information with respect to such taxpayer,

(ii) the filing status of such taxpayer,

(iii) the adjusted gross income of such taxpayer,

(iv) the amounts excluded from such taxpayer's gross income under sections 135 and 911 to the extent such information is available,

(v) the interest received or accrued during the taxable year which is exempt from the tax imposed by chapter 1 to the extent such information is available,

(vi) the amounts excluded from such taxpayer's gross income by sections 931 and 933 to the extent such information is available,

(vii) such other information relating to the liability of the taxpayer as is prescribed by the Secretary by regulation as might indicate in the case of a taxpayer who is an individual described in subsection (i)(4)(B)(iii) of section 1839 of the Social Security Act that the amount of the premium of the taxpayer under such section may be subject to adjustment under subsection (i) of such section or increase under section 1860D-13(a)(7) of such Act and the amount of such adjustment, and

(viii) the taxable year with respect to which the preceding information relates.

(B) RESTRICTION ON USE OF DISCLOSED INFORMATION.—

(i) IN GENERAL.—Return information disclosed under subparagraph (A) may be used by officers, employees, and contractors of the Social Security Administration only for the purposes of, and to the extent necessary in, establishing the appropriate amount of any premium adjustment under such section 1839(i) or increase under such section 1860D-13(a)(7) or for the purpose of resolving taxpayer appeals with respect to any such premium adjustment or increase.

(ii) DISCLOSURE TO OTHER AGENCIES.—Officers, employees, and contractors of the Social Security Administration may disclose—

(I) the taxpayer identity information and the amount of the premium subsidy adjustment or premium increase with respect to a taxpayer described in subparagraph (A) to officers, employees, and contractors of the Centers for Medicare and Medicaid Services, to the extent that such disclosure is necessary for the collection of the premium subsidy amount or the increased premium amount,

(II) the taxpayer identity information and the amount of the premium subsidy adjustment or the increased premium amount with respect to a taxpayer described in subparagraph (A) to officers and employees of the Office of Personnel Management and the Railroad Retirement Board, to the extent that such disclosure is necessary for the collection of the premium subsidy amount or the increased premium amount,

(III) return information with respect to a taxpayer described in subparagraph (A) to officers and employees of the Department of Health and Human Services to the extent necessary to resolve administrative appeals of such premium subsidy adjustment or increased premium, and

(IV) return information with respect to a taxpayer described in subparagraph (A) to officers and employees of the Department of Justice for use in judicial proceedings to the extent necessary to carry out the purposes described in clause (i).

(21) DISCLOSURE OF RETURN INFORMATION TO CARRY OUT ELIGIBILITY REQUIREMENTS FOR CERTAIN PROGRAMS.—

(A) IN GENERAL.—The Secretary, upon written request from the Secretary of Health and Human Services, shall disclose to officers, employees, and contractors of the Department of Health and Human Services return information of any taxpayer whose income is relevant in determining any premium tax credit under section 36B or any cost-sharing reduction under section 1402 of the Patient Protection and Affordable Care Act or eligibility for participation in a State medicaid program under title XIX of the Social Security Act, a State's children's health insurance program under title XXI of the Social Security Act, or a basic health program under section 1331 of Patient Protection and Affordable Care Act. Such return information shall be limited to—

(i) taxpayer identity information with respect to such taxpayer,

(ii) the filing status of such taxpayer,

(iii) the number of individuals for whom a deduction is allowed under section 151 with respect to the taxpayer (including the taxpayer and the taxpayer's spouse),

(iv) the modified adjusted gross income (as defined in section 36B) of such taxpayer and each of the other individuals included under clause (iii) who are required to file a return of tax imposed by chapter 1 for the taxable year,

(v) such other information as is prescribed by the Secretary by regulation as might indicate whether the taxpayer is eligible for such credit or reduction (and the amount thereof), and

RETURNS—MISCELLANEOUS PROVISIONS

(vi) the taxable year with respect to which the preceding information relates or, if applicable, the fact that such information is not available.

(B) INFORMATION TO EXCHANGE AND STATE AGENCIES.—The Secretary of Health and Human Services may disclose to an Exchange established under the Patient Protection and Affordable Care Act or its contractors, or to a State agency administering a State program described in subparagraph (A) or its contractors, any inconsistency between the information provided by the Exchange or State agency to the Secretary and the information provided to the Secretary under subparagraph (A).

(C) RESTRICTION ON USE OF DISCLOSED INFORMATION.—Return information disclosed under subparagraph (A) or (B) may be used by officers, employees, and contractors of the Department of Health and Human Services, an Exchange, or a State agency only for the purposes of, and to the extent necessary in—

(i) establishing eligibility for participation in the Exchange, and verifying the appropriate amount of, any credit or reduction described in subparagraph (A),

(ii) determining eligibility for participation in the State programs described in subparagraph (A).

(22) DISCLOSURE OF RETURN INFORMATION TO DEPARTMENT OF HEALTH AND HUMAN SERVICES FOR PURPOSES OF ENHANCING MEDICARE PROGRAM INTEGRITY.—

(A) IN GENERAL.—The Secretary shall, upon written request from the Secretary of Health and Human Services, disclose to officers and employees of the Department of Health and Human Services return information with respect to a taxpayer who has applied to enroll, or reenroll, as a provider of services or supplier under the Medicare program under title XVIII of the Social Security Act. Such return information shall be limited to—

(i) the taxpayer identity information with respect to such taxpayer;

(ii) the amount of the delinquent tax debt owed by that taxpayer; and

(iii) the taxable year to which the delinquent tax debt pertains.

(B) RESTRICTION ON DISCLOSURE.—Return information disclosed under subparagraph (A) may be used by officers and employees of the Department of Health and Human Services for the purposes of, and to the extent necessary in, establishing the taxpayer's eligibility for enrollment or reenrollment in the Medicare program, or in any administrative or judicial proceeding relating to, or arising from, a denial of such enrollment or reenrollment, or in determining the level of enhanced oversight to be applied with respect to such taxpayer pursuant to section 1866(j)(3) of the Social Security Act.

(C) DELINQUENT TAX DEBT.—For purposes of this paragraph, the term "delinquent tax debt" means an outstanding debt under this title for which a notice of lien has been filed pursuant to section 6323, but the term does not include a debt that is being paid in a timely manner pursuant to an agreement under section 6159 or 7122, or a debt with respect to which a collection due process hearing under section 6330 is requested, pending, or completed and no payment is required.

Amendments

- **2020, COVID-related Tax Relief Act of 2020 (P.L. 116-260)**

P.L. 116-260, §284(a)(1)(A)-(B), Div. N:

Amended Code Sec. 6103(l)(13)(D) by inserting at the end of clause (iii) a new sentence, and by adding at the end new clauses (iv)-(vi). **Effective** for disclosures made after the date of the enactment of the FUTURE Act (P.L. 116-91) [**effective** for disclosures made after 12-19-2019.—CCH].

P.L. 116-260, §284(a)(2), Div. N:

Amended Code Sec. 6103(l)(13)(F) by inserting ", and any redisclosure authorized under clause (iii), (iv)[,] (v), or (vi) of subparagraph (D),'" after "or (C)". **Effective** for disclosures made after the date of the enactment of the FUTURE Act (P.L. 116-91) [**effective** for disclosures made after 12-19-2019.—CCH].

- **2020, Consolidated Appropriations Act, 2021 (P.L. 116-260)**

P.L. 116-260, §103(a)(1)(A)-(B), Div. FF:

Amended Code Sec. 6103(l)(13)(D) by inserting at the end of clause (iii) a new sentence, and by adding at the end new clauses (iv)-(vi). [Note: With the exception of the text of new clause (vi), an identical amendment was made by P.L. 116-260, Act Sec. 284(a)(1)(A)-(B), Div. N. Therefore, this amendment cannot be made except for the text of new clause (vi).—CCH] **Effective** for disclosures made after the date of the enactment of the FUTURE Act (P.L. 116-91) [**effective** for disclosures made after 12-19-2019.—CCH]. Prior to amendment, Code Sec. 6103(l)(13)(d)(vi) read as follows:

(vi) REDISCLOSURE OF FAFSA INFORMATION.—Return information received under subparagraph (C) may be redisclosed in accordance with subsection (c) of section 494 of the Higher Education Act of 1965 (as in effect on the date of enactment of the COVID-related Tax Relief Act of 2020) to carry out the purposes specified in such subsection.

P.L. 116-260, §103(a)(2), Div. FF:

Amended Code Sec. 6103(l)(13)(F) by inserting ", and any redisclosure authorized under clause (iii), (iv)[,] (v), or (vi) of subparagraph (D)," after "or (C)". [Note: An identical amendment was made by P.L. 116-260, Act Sec. 284(a)(2), Div. N. Therefore, this amendment cannot be made.—CCH] **Effective** for disclosures made after the date of the enactment of the FUTURE Act (P.L. 116-91) [**effective** for disclosures made after 12-19-2019.—CCH].

- **2020, Coronavirus Aid, Relief, and Economic Security (CARES) Act (P.L. 116-136)**

P.L. 116-136, §3516(a)(5):

Amended Code Sec. 6103(l)(13)(C)(ii), as added by the FUTURE Act (P.L. 116-91), by striking "section 236A(e)(4)" and inserting "section 263A(e)(4)". **Effective** as if included in the enactment of the FUTURE Act (P.L. 116-91) [**effective** for disclosures after 12-19-2019.—CCH].

- **2019, Fostering Undergraduate Talent by Unlocking Resources for Education (FUTURE) Act (P.L. 116-91)**

P.L. 116-91, §3(a):

Amended Code Sec. 6103(l)(13). **Effective** for disclosures after 12-19-2019. Prior to amendment, Code Sec. 6103(l)(13) read as follows:

(13) DISCLOSURE OF RETURN INFORMATION TO CARRY OUT INCOME CONTINGENT REPAYMENT OF STUDENT LOANS.—

(A) IN GENERAL.—The Secretary may, upon written request from the Secretary of Education, disclose to officers and employees of the Department of Education return information with respect to a taxpayer who has received an applicable student loan and whose loan repayment amounts are based in whole or in part on the taxpayer's income. Such return information shall be limited to—

(i) taxpayer identity information with respect to such taxpayer,

(ii) the filing status of such taxpayer, and

(iii) the adjusted gross income of such taxpayer.

(B) RESTRICTION ON USE OF DISCLOSED INFORMATION.—Return information disclosed under subparagraph (A) may be used by officers and employees of the Department of Education only for the purposes of, and to the extent necessary in, establishing the appropriate income contingent repayment amount for an applicable student loan.

(C) APPLICABLE STUDENT LOAN.—For purposes of this paragraph, the term "applicable student loan" means—

(i) any loan made under the program authorized under part D of title IV of the Higher Education Act of 1965, and

(ii) any loan made under part B or E of title IV of the Higher Education Act of 1965 which is in default and has been assigned to the Department of Education.

(D) TERMINATION.—This paragraph shall not apply to any request made after December 31, 2007.

P.L. 116-91, §3(e)-(g), provides:

(e) REQUIREMENT TO DESIGNATE THE INSPECTOR GENERAL OF THE DEPARTMENT OF EDUCATION AS AN AUTHORIZED PERSON.— The Secretary of Education shall authorize and designate the Inspector General of the Department of Education as an authorized person under subparagraph (E)(ii) of section 6103(l)(13) of the Internal Revenue Code of 1986 for purposes of subparagraphs (A), (B), and (C) of such section.

(f) REPORT TO TREASURY.—The Secretary of Education shall annually submit a written report to the Secretary of the Treasury—

(1) regarding redisclosures of return information under subparagraph (D)(iii) of section 6103(l)(13) of the Internal Revenue Code of 1986, including the number of such redisclosures; and

(2) regarding any unauthorized use, access, or disclosure of return information disclosed under such section.

(g) REPORT TO CONGRESS.—The Secretary of the Treasury (or the Secretary's designee) shall annually submit a written report to Congress regarding disclosures under section 6103(l)(13) of the Internal Revenue Code of 1986, including information provided to the Secretary under subsection (f).

- **2018, Tax Technical Corrections Act of 2018 (P.L. 115-141)**

P.L. 115-141, §401(a)(267), Div. U:

Amended Code Sec. 6103(l)(7) by striking "OF 1977" following "NUTRITION ACT OF 2008" in the heading thereof. **Effective** 3-23-2018.

P.L. 115-141, §401(a)(268), Div. U:

Amended Code Sec. 6103(l)(10)(A) by striking "request made under subsection (f)(5)" and inserting "notice submitted under subsection (f)(5)(C)". **Effective** 3-23-2018.

P.L. 115-141, §401(a)(269), Div. U:

Amended Code Sec. 6103(l)(10) by striking so much of subparagraph (B) as precedes "Any" and inserting

"(B) RESTRICTION ON USE OF DISCLOSED INFORMATION.—(i)".

Effective 3-23-2018. Prior to being stricken, so much of subparagraph (B) as precedes "Any" read as follows:

(B)(i) RESTRICTION ON USE OF DISCLOSED INFORMATION.—

RETURNS—MISCELLANEOUS PROVISIONS

P.L. 115-141, §401(a)(270), Div. U:

Amended Code Sec. 6103(l)(16)(A) by striking "subsection 6103(b)(6)" and inserting "section 6103(b)(6)". **Effective** 3-23-2018.

• **2010, Preservation of Access to Care for Medicare Beneficiaries and Pension Relief Act of 2010 (P.L. 111-192)**

P.L. 111-192, §103(a)(1):

Amended Code Sec. 6103(l) by adding at the end a new paragraph (22). **Effective** 6-25-2010.

• **2010, Health Care and Education Reconciliation Act of 2010 (P.L. 111-152)**

P.L. 111-152, §1004(a)(1)(B):

Amended Code Sec. 6103(l)(21)(A)(iv), as added by section 1414 of the Patient Protection and Affordable Care Act (P.L. 111-148), by striking "modified gross" and inserting "modified adjusted gross". **Effective** 3-30-2010.

• **2010, Patient Protection and Affordable Care Act (P.L. 111-148)**

P.L. 111-148, §1414(a)(1):

Amended Code Sec. 6103(l) by adding at the end a new paragraph (21). **Effective** 3-23-2010.

P.L. 111-148, §3308(b)(2)(A)-(C):

Amended Code Sec. 6103(l)(20), in the heading, by inserting "AND PART D BASE BENEFICIARY PREMIUM INCREASE" after "PART B PREMIUM SUBSIDY ADJUSTMENT"; in subparagraph (A), in the matter preceding clause (i), by inserting "or increase under section 1860D–13(a)(7)" after "1839(i)"; and in clause (vii), by inserting "or increase under section 1860D–13(a)(7) of such Act" after "subsection (i) of such section"; and in subparagraph (B), by striking "Return information" and inserting "(i) IN GENERAL.—Return information"; by inserting "or increase under such section 1860D–13(a)(7)" before the period at the end; and, as amended by Act Sec. 3308(b)(2)(C)(i), by inserting "or for the purpose of resolving taxpayer appeals with respect to any such premium adjustment or increase" before the period at the end; and by adding at the end a new clause (ii). **Effective** 3-23-2010.

• **2008, SSI Extension for Elderly and Disabled Refugees Act (P.L. 110-328)**

P.L. 110-328, §3(b)(2)(A)-(C):

Amended Code Sec. 6103(l)(10) by striking "(c), (d), or (e)" each place it appears in the heading and text and inserting "(c), (d), (e), or (f)", in subparagraph (A) by inserting ", to officers and employees of the Department of Labor for purposes of facilitating the exchange of data in connection with a request made under subsection (f)(5) of section 6402," after "section 6402," and in subparagraph (B) by inserting "(i)" after "(B)"; and by adding at the end a new clause (ii). **Effective** for refunds payable under Code Sec. 6402 on or after 9-30-2008.

• **2008, Food, Conservation, and Energy Act of 2008 (P.L. 110-246)**

P.L. 110-246, §4002(b)(1)(B) and (H):

Amended Code Sec. 6103(l)(7) by striking "Food Stamp Act of 1977" and inserting "Food and Nutrition Act of 2008"; and by striking "FOOD STAMP ACT" [sic] in the heading and inserting "FOOD AND NUTRITION ACT OF 2008". **Effective** 10-1-2008.

• **2008, Heroes Earnings Assistance and Relief Tax Act of 2008 (P.L. 110-245)**

P.L. 110-245, §108(a):

Amended Code Sec. 6103(l)(7) by striking the last sentence. **Effective** for requests made after 9-30-2008. Prior to being stricken, the last sentence of Code Sec. 6103(l)(7) read as follows:

Clause (viii) shall not apply after September 30, 2008.

P.L. 110-245, §108(b):

Amended Code Sec. 6103(l)(7)(D)(viii)(III) by striking "sections 1710(a)(1)(I), 1710(a)(2), 1710(b), and 1712(a)(2)(B)" and inserting "sections 1710(a)(1)(G), 1710(a)(3), and 1710(b)". **Effective** 6-17-2008.

• **2006, Tax Relief and Health Care Act of 2006 (P.L. 109-432)**

P.L. 109-432, Division A, §122(c)(1):

Amended Code Sec. 6103(l)(13)(D) by striking "2006" and inserting "2007". **Effective** for requests made after 12-31-2006.

• **2005, Gulf Opportunity Zone Act of 2005 (P.L. 109-135)**

P.L. 109-135, §305(c)(1):

Amended Code Sec. 6103(l)(13)(D) by striking "December 31, 2005" and inserting "December 31, 2006". **Effective** for requests made after 12-31-2005.

P.L. 109-135, §406(a):

Amended Code Sec. 6103(l)(17) by striking "subsection (f), (i)(7), or (p)" and inserting "subsection (f), (i)(8), or (p)". **Effective** as if included in section 201 of the Victims of Terrorism Tax Relief Act of 2001 (P.L. 107-34) [effective for disclosures made on or after 1-23-2002.—CCH].

• **2004, Working Families Tax Relief Act of 2004 (P.L. 108-311)**

P.L. 108-311, §317:

Amended Code Sec. 6103(l)(13)(D) by striking "December 31, 2004" and inserting "December 31, 2005". **Effective** 10-4-2004.

• **2003, Medicare Prescription Drug, Improvement, and Modernization Act of 2003 (P.L. 108-173)**

P.L. 108-173, §101(e)(6):

Amended Code Sec. 6103(l)(7)(D)(ii) by inserting "or subsidies provided under section 1860D-14 of such Act" after "Social Security Act". **Effective** 12-8-2003.

P.L. 108-173, §105(e)(1):

Amended Code Sec. 6103(l) by adding at the end a new paragraph (19). **Effective** 12-8-2003.

P.L. 108-173, §811(c)(1):

Amended Code Sec. 6103(l), as amended by Act Sec. 105(e), by adding at the end a new paragraph (20). **Effective** 12-8-2003.

P.L. 108-173, §900(e)(3)(A)-(B):

Amended Code Sec. 6103(l)(12) in subparagraph (B) by striking "Health Care Financing Administration" in the matter preceding clause (i) and inserting "Centers for Medicare & Medicaid Services"; and in subparagraph (C) by striking "HEALTH CARE FINANCING ADMINISTRATION" in the heading and inserting "CENTERS FOR MEDICARE & MEDICAID SERVICES"; and by striking "Health Care Financing Administration" in the matter preceding clause (i) and inserting "Centers for Medicare & Medicaid Services". **Effective** 12-8-2003.

• **2003 (P.L. 108-89)**

P.L. 108-89, §201(a):

Amended Code Sec. 6103(l)(13)(D) by striking "September 30, 2003" and inserting "December 31, 2004". **Effective** for requests made after 9-30-2003.

• **2002, Veterans Benefits Act of 2002 (P.L. 107-330)**

P.L. 107-330, §306:

Amended Code Sec. 6103(l)(7)(D) by striking "September 30, 2003" in the second sentence after clause (ix) and inserting "September 30, 2008". **Effective** 12-6-2002.

• **2002, Trade Act of 2002 (P.L. 107-210)**

P.L. 107-210, §202(b)(1):

Amended Code Sec. 6103(l) by adding at the end a new paragraph (18). **Effective** 8-6-2002.

• **2002, Job Creation and Worker Assistance Act of 2002 (P.L. 107-147)**

P.L. 107-147, §416(c)(1)(A)-(B):

Amended the heading for Code Sec. 6103(l)(8) by striking "STATE AND LOCAL" and inserting "FEDERAL, STATE, AND LOCAL", and in subparagraph (A), by inserting "Federal or" before "State or local". **Effective** 3-9-2002.

• **1998, Tax and Trade Relief Extension Act of 1998 (P.L. 105-277)**

P.L. 105-277, §1006:

Amended Code Sec. 6103(l)(13)(D) by striking "September 30, 1998" and inserting "September 30, 2003". **Effective** 10-21-98.

• **1998, IRS Restructuring and Reform Act of 1998 (P.L. 105-206)**

P.L. 105-206, §3702(a):

Amended Code Sec. 6103(l) by adding at the end a new paragraph (17). **Effective** for requests made by the Archivist of the United States after 7-22-98.

P.L. 105-206, §3711(b)(1):

Amended Code Sec. 6103(l)(10) by striking "(c) or (d)" each place it appears and inserting "(c), (d), or (e)". **Effective** for refunds payable under Code Sec. 6402 after 12-31-99.

P.L. 105-206, §3711(b)(2):

Amended the paragraph heading of Code Sec. 6103(l)(10) by striking "SECTION 6402(c) OR 6402(d)" and inserting "SUBSECTION (c), (d), OR (e) OF SECTION 6402". **Effective** for refunds payable under Code Sec. 6402 after 12-31-99.

• **1997, Departments of Labor, Health and Human Services and Education, and Related Agencies Appropriations Act, 1998 (P.L. 105-65)**

P.L. 105-65, §542(b):

Amended Code Sec. 6103(l)(7)(D) by striking the last sentence. **Effective** 10-27-97. Prior to being stricken, the last sentence of Code Sec. 6103(l)(7)(D) read as follows:

Clause (ix) shall not apply after September 30, 1998.

• **1997, Taxpayer Relief Act of 1997 (P.L. 105-34)**

P.L. 105-34, §1023(a):

Amended Code Sec. 6103(l)(7)(D)(viii) by striking "1998" and inserting "2003". **Effective** 8-5-97.

• **1997, Balanced Budget Act of 1997 (P.L. 105-33)**

P.L. 105-33, §4631(c)(2):

Amended Code Sec. 6103(l)(12) by striking subparagraph (F). **Effective** 8-5-97. Prior to amendment, Code Sec. 6103(l)(12)(F) read as follows:

(F) TERMINATION.—Subparagraphs (A) and (B) shall not apply to—

(i) any request made after September 30, 1988, and

(ii) any request made before such date for information relating to—

(I) 1997 or thereafter in the case of subparagraph (A), or

(II) 1998 or thereafter in the case of subparagraph (B).

P.L. 105-33, §5514(a)(1):

Struck the amendment made by Act. Sec. 110(l)(4)(A)-(B) of P.L. 104-193, which amended Code Sec. 6103(l)(10) by striking "(c) or (d)" each place it appeared and inserting "(c), (d), or (e)" and which added at the end of subparagraph (B) a new last sentence. Thus, the provisions of law amended by such section are restored as if such section had not been enacted. **Effective** 7-1-97. Prior to the amendment's being stricken, the last sentence of Code Sec. 6103(l)(10)(B), as added by P.L. 104-193, read as follows:

Any return information disclosed with respect to section 6402(e) shall only be disclosed to officers and employees of the State agency requesting such information.

RETURNS—MISCELLANEOUS PROVISIONS

P.L. 105-33, § 11024(b)(1):

Amended Code Sec. 6103(l) by adding at the end a new paragraph (16). For the **effective** date, see Act Sec. 11721, below.

P.L. 105-33, § 11721, provides:

Except as otherwise provided in this title, the provisions of this title shall take effect on the later of October 1, 1997, or the day the District of Columbia Financial Responsibility and Management Assistance Authority certifies that the financial plan and budget for the District government for fiscal year 1998 meet the requirements of section 201(c)(1) of the District of Columbia Financial Responsibility and Management Assistance Act of 1995, as amended by this title.

- **1996, Personal Responsibility and Work Opportunity Reconciliation Act of 1996 (P.L. 104-193)**

P.L. 104-193, § 110(l)(3):

Amended Code Sec. 6103(l)(7)(D)(i) by striking "aid to families with dependent children provided under a State plan approved" and inserting "a State program funded". **Effective** 7-1-97.

P.L. 104-193, § 110(l)(4)(A)-(B):

Amended Code Sec. 6103(l)(10) by striking "(c) or (d)" each place it appears and inserting "(c), (d), or (e)"; and by adding at the end of subparagraph (B) a new sentence. **Effective** 7-1-97.

P.L. 104-193, § 316(g)(4)(A):

Amended Code Sec. 6103(l)(6) by redesignating subparagraph (B) as subparagraph (C) and by inserting after subparagraph (A) a new subparagraph (B). **Effective** 8-22-96.

P.L. 104-193, § 316(g)(4)(B)(ii):

Amended Code Sec. 6103(l)(6)(C), as redesignated by subsection (a) [subparagraph (A)]. **Effective** 8-22-96. Prior to amendment, Code Sec. 6103(l)(6)(C) read as follows:

(C) RESTRICTION ON DISCLOSURE.—The Secretary shall disclose return information under subparagraph (A) only for purposes of, and to the extent necessary in, establishing and collecting child support obligations from, and locating, individuals owing such obligations.

- **1996, Taxpayer Bill of Rights 2 (P.L. 104-168)**

P.L. 104-168, § 1206(a):

Amended Code Sec. 6103(l) by adding at the end a new paragraph (15). **Effective** 7-30-96.

- **1996, Debt Collection Improvement Act of 1996 (P.L. 104-134)**

P.L. 104-134, § 31001(g)(2):

Amended Code Sec. 6103(l)(10)(A) by inserting "and to officers and employees of the Department of the Treasury in connection with such reduction" after "6402". **Effective** 4-26-96.

P.L. 104-134, § 31001(i)(2):

Amended Code Sec. 6103(l)(3)(C). **Effective** 4-26-96. Prior to amendment, Code Sec. 6103(l)(3)(C) read as follows:

(C) INCLUDED FEDERAL LOAN PROGRAM DEFINED.—For purposes of this paragraph, the term "included Federal loan program" means any program—

(i) under which the United States or a Federal agency makes, guarantees, or insures loans, and

(ii) with respect to which there is in effect a determination by the Director of the Office of Management and Budget (which has been published in the Federal Register) that the application of this paragraph to such program will substantially prevent or reduce future delinquencies under such program.

- **1994, Social Security Independence and Program Improvements Act of 1994 (P.L. 103-296)**

P.L. 103-296, § 108(h)(6)(A)-(B):

Amended Code Sec. 6103(l)(5) by striking "DEPARTMENT OF HEALTH AND HUMAN SERVICES" in the heading and inserting "SOCIAL SECURITY ADMINISTRATION" and by striking "Secretary of Health and Human Services" and inserting "Commissioner of Social Security". **Effective** 3-31-95.

P.L. 103-296, § 311(b)(1)-(4):

Amended Code Sec. 6103(l)(5) by striking "for the purpose of" and inserting "for the purpose of—", by striking "carrying out, in accordance with an agreement" and inserting "(A) carrying out, in accordance with an agreement", by striking "program." and inserting "program; or", and by adding at the end thereof a new subparagraph (B). **Effective** with respect to requests for information made after 8-15-94.

- **1993, North American Free Trade Agreement Implementation Act (P.L. 103-182)**

P.L. 103-182, § 522(a):

Amended Code Sec. 6103(l) by adding at the end thereof new paragraph (14). **Effective** on the date the Agreement enters into force with respect to the United States.

P.L. 103-182, § 522(c)(2), provides:

(2) REGULATIONS.—Not later than 90 days after the date of the enactment of this Act, the Secretary of the Treasury or his delegate shall issue temporary regulations to carry out section 6103(l)(14) of the Internal Revenue Code of 1986, as added by this section.

- **1993, Omnibus Budget Reconciliation Act of 1993 (P.L. 103-66)**

P.L. 103-66, § 13401(a):

Amended Code Sec. 6103(l)(7)(D) by striking "September 30, 1997" in the second sentence following clause (viii) and inserting "September 30, 1998". **Effective** 8-10-93.

P.L. 103-66, § 13402(a):

Amended Code Sec. 6103(l) by adding at the end thereof new paragraph (13). **Effective** 8-10-93.

P.L. 103-66, § 13403(a)(1)-(4):

Amended Code Sec. 6103(l)(7)(D) by striking "and" at the end of clause (vii); by striking the period at the end of clause (viii) and inserting "; and"; by inserting after clause (viii) a new clause (ix), and by adding at the end of subparagraph (D) a new sentence. **Effective** 8-10-93.

P.L. 103-66, § 13403(b):

Amended Code Sec. 6103(l)(7) by inserting ", OR CERTAIN HOUSING ASSISTANCE PROGRAMS" after "CODE" in the heading. **Effective** 8-10-93.

P.L. 103-66, § 13561(a)(2)(A)-(C):

Amended Code Sec. 6103(l)(12) by inserting ", above an amount (if any) specified by the Secretary of Health and Human Services," after "section 3401 (a))" in subparagraph (B)(i); by inserting ", above an amount (if any) specified by the Secretary of Health and Human Services," after "wages" in the matter preceding subclause (I) in subparagraph (B)(ii); and in subparagraph (F) by striking "1995" and inserting "1988" in clause (i), by striking "1994" and inserting "1997" in clause (ii)(I), and by striking "1995" and inserting "1998" in clause (ii)(II). **Effective** 8-10-93.

P.L. 103-66, § 13561(e)(2)(B):

Amended Code Sec. 6103(l)(12)(E)(ii). **Effective** 8-10-93. Prior to amendment, Code Sec. 6103(l)(12)(E)(ii) read as follows:

(ii) GROUP HEALTH PLAN.—The term "group health plan" means—

(I) any group health plan (as defined in section 5000(b)(1)), and

(II) any large group health plan (as defined in section 5000(b)(2)).

- **1992, Veteran's Benefits Act of 1992 (P.L. 102-568)**

P.L. 102-568, § 602(b)(1):

Amended Code Sec. 6103(l)(7)(D) by striking out "September 30, 1992" in the last sentence and inserting in lieu thereof "September 30, 1997". **Effective** 10-29-92.

P.L. 102-568, § 602(b)(2)(A)-(B):

Amended Code Sec. 6103(l)(7)(D)(viii) by striking "section 415" in subclause (II) and inserting in lieu thereof "section 1315"; and by striking out "section 610(a)(1)(I), 610(a)(2), 610(b), and 612(a)(2)(B)" in subclause (III) and inserting in lieu thereof "sections 1710(a)(1)(I), 1710(a)(2), 1710(b), and 1712(a)(2)(B)". **Effective** 10-29-92.

- **1991, Emergency Unemployment Compensation Act of 1991 (P.L. 102-164)**

P.L. 102-164, § 401(a):

Amended section 2653(c) of P.L. 98-369 (regarding the **effective** date), as amended by P.L. 100-485, by striking "and on or before January 10, 1994". **Effective** 10-1-91.

- **1990, Omnibus Budget Reconciliation Act of 1990 (P.L. 101-508)**

P.L. 101-508, § 4203(a)(2)(A)-(C):

Amended Code Sec. 6103(l)(12)(F) by striking "September 30, 1991" in clause (i) and inserting "September 30, 1995"; by striking "1990" in clause (ii)(I) and inserting "1994"; and by striking "1991" in clause (ii)(II) and inserting "1995". **Effective** 11-5-90, and the amendment made by subsection (a)(2)(B) applies to requests made on or after such date.

P.L. 101-508, § 8051(a)(1)(A):

Amended Code Sec. 6103(l)(7)(D) by striking out "and" at the end of clause (vi). **Effective** 11-5-90.

P.L. 101-508, § 8051(a)(1)(B):

Amended Code Sec. 6103(l)(7)(D) by striking out the period at the end of clause (vii) and inserting in lieu thereof "; and". **Effective** 11-5-90.

P.L. 101-508, § 8051(a)(1)(C):

Amended Code Sec. 6103(l)(7)(D) by adding at the end thereof a new clause (viii) and concluding material at the end of subparagraph (D). **Effective** 11-5-90.

P.L. 101-508, § 8051(a)(2):

Amended Code Sec. 6103(l)(7) by striking out "OR THE FOOD STAMP ACT OF 1977" and inserting in lieu thereof ", THE FOOD STAMP ACT OF 1977, OR TITLE 38, UNITED STATES CODE". **Effective** 11-5-90.

- **1989, Omnibus Budget Reconciliation Act of 1989 (P.L. 101-239)**

P.L. 101-239, § 6202(a)(1)(A):

Amended Code Sec. 6103(l) by adding at the end thereof a new paragraph (12). **Effective** 12-19-89.

- **1988, Family Support Act of 1988 (P.L. 100-485)**

P.L. 100-485, § 701(a):

Amended section 2653(c) of P.L. 98-369 (regarding the **effective** date) by striking "before July 1, 1988" and inserting "on or before January 10, 1994". For the **effective** date, see Act Sec. 701(b)(3), below.

P.L. 100-485, § 701(b)(1):

Amended Code Sec. 6103(l)(10). **Effective**, generally, 10-13-88. However, for a special rule, see Act Sec. 701(b)(3)(B), below. Prior to amendment, Code Sec. 6103(l)(10) read as follows:

(10) DISCLOSURE OF CERTAIN INFORMATION TO AGENCIES REQUESTING A REDUCTION UNDER SECTION 6402(c) OR 6402(d)—

(A) RETURN INFORMATION FROM INTERNAL REVENUE SERVICE.—The Secretary may, upon receiving a written request, disclose to officers and employees of an agency seeking a reduction under section 6402(c) or 6402(d)—

(i) the fact that a reduction has been made or has not been made under such subsection with respect to any person,

RETURNS—MISCELLANEOUS PROVISIONS

(ii) the amount of such reduction, and

(iii) taxpayer identifying information of the person against whom a reduction was made or not made.

(B) RESTRICTION ON USE OF DISCLOSED INFORMATION.—Any officers and employees of an agency receiving return information under subparagraph (A) shall use such information only for the purposes of, and to the extent necessary in, establishing appropriate agency records or in the defense of any litigation or administrative procedure ensuing from reduction made under section 6402(c) or section 6402(d).

P.L. 100-485, §701(b)(2)(A):

Amended Code Sec. 6103(l) by striking paragraph (11) and redesignating paragraph (12) as paragraph (11). **Effective**, generally, 10-13-88. However, for a special rule, see Act. Sec. 701(b)(3)(B), below. Prior to amendment, Code Sec. 6103(l)(11) read as follows:

(11) DISCLOSURE OF CERTAIN INFORMATION TO AGENCIES REQUESTING A REDUCTION UNDER SECTION 6402(c).—

(A) RETURN INFORMATION FROM INTERNAL REVENUE SERVICE.—The Secretary shall, upon receiving a written request, disclose to officers and employees of a State agency seeking a reduction under section 6402(c)—

(i) the fact that a reduction has been made or has not been made under such subsection with respect to any taxpayer,

(ii) the amount of such reduction,

(iii) whether such taxpayer filed a joint return,

(iv) Taxpayer Identity information with respect to the taxpayer against whom a reduction was made or not made and of any other person filing a joint return with such taxpayer; and

(v) the fact that a payment was made (and the amount of the payment) on the basis of a joint return in accordance with section 464(a)(3) of the Social Security Act.

(B) RESTRICTION ON USE OF DISCLOSED INFORMATION.—Any officers and employees of an agency receiving return information under subparagraph (A) shall use such information only for the purposes of, and to the extent necessary in, establishing appropriate agency records or in the defense of any litigation or administrative procedure ensuing from a reduction made under section 6402(c).

P.L. 100-485, §701(b)(3), provides:

(3) EFFECTIVE DATES.—

(A) IN GENERAL.—The amendments made by this subsection shall take effect on the date of enactment of this Act.

(B) SPECIAL RULE.—Nothing in section 2653(c) of the Deficit Reduction Act of 1984 shall be construed to limit the application of paragraph (10) of section 6103(l) of the Internal Revenue Code of 1986 (as amended by this subsection).

• **1986, Tax Reform Act of 1986 (P.L. 99-514)**

P.L. 99-514, §1899A(53):

Amended Code Sec. 6103(l)(7)(D)(v) by striking out "this Code" and inserting in lieu thereof "this title". **Effective** 10-22-86.

• **1986 (P.L. 99-335)**

P.L. 99-335, §310(a):

Amended Code Sec. 6103(l) by adding at the end thereof new paragraph (12). **Effective** 6-6-86.

• **1984, Child Support Enforcement Amendments of 1984 (P.L. 98-378)**

P.L. 98-378, §19(b)(1):

Amended Code Sec. 6103(l)(6)(A)(i) by inserting "social security account number (or numbers, if the individual involved has more than one such number)," before "address". **Effective** 8-16-84.

P.L. 98-378, §19(b)(2):

Amended Code Sec. 6103(l)(8)(A) by inserting "social security account numbers[,]" before "net earnings". **Effective** 8-16-84.

P.L. 98-378, §21(f)(1):

Added Code Sec. 6103(l)(11). **Effective** with respect to refunds payable under Code Sec. 6402 after 12-31-85.

• **1984, Deficit Reduction Act of 1984 (P.L. 98-369)**

P.L. 98-369, §453(a):

Amended Code Sec. 6103(l) by adding at the end thereof a new paragraph (9). **Effective** on the first day of the first calendar month which begins more than 90 days after 7-18-84.

P.L. 98-369, §453(b)(5):

Amended P.L. 96-249, Act. Sec. 127(a)(1) by redesignating Code Sec. 6103(i)(7) as added by that Act as Code Sec. 6103(l)(7). **Effective** on the first day of the first calendar month which begins more than 90 days after 7-18-84.

P.L. 98-369, §453(b)(6):

Redesignated paragraph (7) of Code Sec. 6103(l) (added by Public Law 96-265) as paragraph (8). **Effective** on the first day of the first calendar month which begins more than 90 days after 7-18-84.

P.L. 98-369, §2651(k)(1):

Amended Code Sec. 6103(l)(7). **Effective** 7-18-84. Prior to amendment, Code Sec. 6103(l)(7) read as follows:

(7) Disclosure of Certain Return Information by Social Security Administration to Department of Agriculture and to State Food Stamp Agencies.—

(A) In General.—The Commissioner of Social Security may disclose return information from returns with respect to net earnings from self-employment (as defined in section 1402), wages (as defined in section 3121(a) or 3401(a)), and payments of retirement income which have been disclosed to the Social Security Administration as provided by paragraph (1) or (5) of this subsection—

(i) upon request, to officers and employees of the Department of Agriculture, and

(ii) upon written request, to officers and employees of a State food stamp agency.

(B) Restriction on Disclosure.—The Commissioner of Social Security shall disclose return information under subparagraph (A) only for purposes of, and to the extent necessary in, determining an individual's eligibility for benefits, or the amounts of benefits, under the food stamp program established under the Food Stamp Act of 1977.

(C) State Food Stamp Agency.—For purposes of this paragraph, the term, "State food stamp agency" means any agency described in section 3(n)(1) of the Food Stamp Act of 1977 which administers the food stamp program established under such Act.

P.L. 98-369, §2653(b)(3)(A):

Amended Code Sec. 6103(l) by adding at the end thereof new paragraph (10). **Effective** with respect to refunds payable under section 6402 of the Internal Revenue Code of 1954 after 12-31-85 [**effective** date changed by P.L. 102-164].

P.L. 98-369, §2663(j)(5)(E):

Amended Code Sec. 6103(l)(5) by striking out "Health, Education, and Welfare" each place it appeared and inserting in lieu thereof "Health and Human Services". **Effective** 7-18-84 but shall not be construed as changing or affecting any right, liability, status, or interpretation which existed (under the provisions of law involved) before that date.

• **1982, Debt Collection Act of 1982 (P.L. 97-365)**

P.L. 97-365, §7(a):

Amended Code Sec. 6103(l)(3). **Effective** in the case of loan applications made after 9-30-82.

• **1982 (P.L. 97-258)**

P.L. 97-258, §3(f)(5):

Amended Code Sec. 6103(l)(4)(A)(ii) by striking out "section 3 of the Act of July 7, 1884 (23 Stat. 258; 31 U.S.C. 1026)" and substituting "section 330 of title 31, United States Code". **Effective** 9-13-82.

• **1980, Social Security Disability Amendments of 1980 (P.L. 96-265)**

P.L. 96-265, §408(a)(1):

Amended Code Sec. 6103(l) by adding new subsection (7) [(8)]. **Effective** 6-9-80. An earlier subsection (7) was added to Code Sec. 6103(l) by P.L. 96-249, but due to an error in the enrollment of that law, the subsection was erroneously added to Code Sec. 6103(i). It is expected that two technical corrections will be enacted: the first clarifying that the earlier subsection (7) was intended to be Code Sec. 6103(l)(7), not Code Sec. 6103(i)(7); and the second redesignating the Code Sec. 6103(l)(7) added by P.L. 96-265 as Code Sec. 6103(l)(8).

• **1980, Food Stamp Act Amendments of 1980 (P.L. 96-249)**

P.L. 96-249, §127(a)(1):

Erroneously added the language in subparagraph (7) to Code Sec. 6103(i). **Effective** 5-26-80. It was intended to be added to Code Sec. 6103(l) and has been reflected here for that reason. A technical correction is expected that will correct the error in P.L. 96-249.

• **1976, Tax Reform Act of 1976 (P.L. 94-455)**

P.L. 94-455, §1202(a):

Added Code Sec. 6103(l). **Effective** 1-1-77.

[Sec. 6103(m)]

(m) DISCLOSURE OF TAXPAYER IDENTITY INFORMATION.—

(1) TAX REFUNDS.—The Secretary may disclose taxpayer identity information to the press and other media for purposes of notifying persons entitled to tax refunds when the Secretary, after reasonable effort and lapse of time, has been unable to locate such persons.

(2) FEDERAL CLAIMS.—

(A) IN GENERAL.—Except as provided in subparagraph (B), the Secretary may, upon written request, disclose the mailing address of a taxpayer for use by officers, employees, or agents of a Federal agency for purposes of locating such taxpayer to collect or compromise a Federal claim against the taxpayer in accordance with sections 3711, 3717, and 3718 of title 31.

(B) SPECIAL RULE FOR CONSUMER REPORTING AGENCY.—In the case of an agent of a Federal agency which is a consumer reporting agency (within the meaning of section 603(f) of the Fair Credit Reporting Act (15 U.S.C. 1681a(f))), the mailing address of a taxpayer may be disclosed to such agent under subparagraph (A) only for the purpose of allowing such agent to prepare a commercial credit report on the taxpayer for use by such Federal agency in accordance with sections 3711, 3717, and 3718 of title 31.

RETURNS—MISCELLANEOUS PROVISIONS

(3) NATIONAL INSTITUTE FOR OCCUPATIONAL SAFETY AND HEALTH.— Upon written request, the Secretary may disclose the mailing address of taxpayers to officers and employees of the National Institute for Occupational Safety and Health solely for the purpose of locating individuals who are, or may have been, exposed to occupational hazards in order to determine the status of their health or to inform them of the possible need for medical care and treatment.

(4) INDIVIDUALS WHO OWE AN OVERPAYMENT OF FEDERAL PELL GRANTS OR WHO HAVE DEFAULTED ON STUDENT LOANS ADMINISTERED BY THE DEPARTMENT OF EDUCATION.—

(A) IN GENERAL.—Upon written request by the Secretary of Education, the Secretary may disclose the mailing address of any taxpayer—

(i) who owes an overpayment of a grant awarded to such taxpayer under subpart 1 of part A of title IV of the Higher Education Act of 1965, or

(ii) who has defaulted on a loan—

(I) made under part B, D, or E of title IV of the Higher Education Act of 1965, or

(II) made pursuant to section 3(a)(1) of the Migration and Refugee Assistance Act of 1962 to a student at an institution of higher education,

for use only by officers, employees, or agents of the Department of Education for purposes of locating such taxpayer for purposes of collecting such overpayment or loan.

(B) DISCLOSURE TO EDUCATIONAL INSTITUTIONS, ETC.—Any mailing address disclosed under subparagraph (A)(i) may be disclosed by the Secretary of Education to—

(i) any lender, or any State or nonprofit guarantee agency, which is participating under part (B) or (D) of title IV of the Higher Education Act of 1965, or

(ii) any educational institution with which the Secretary of Education has an agreement under subpart 1 of part A, or part D or E, of title IV of such Act,

for use only by officers, employees or agents of such lender, guarantee agency, or institution whose duties relate to the collection of student loans for purposes of locating individuals who have defaulted on student loans made under such loan programs for purposes of collecting such loans.

(5) INDIVIDUALS WHO HAVE DEFAULTED ON STUDENT LOANS ADMINISTERED BY THE DEPARTMENT OF HEALTH AND HUMAN SERVICES.—

(A) IN GENERAL.—Upon written request by the Secretary of Health and Human Services, the Secretary may disclose the mailing address of any taxpayer who has defaulted on a loan made under part C of title VII of the Public Health Service Act or under subpart II of part B of title VIII of such Act, for use only by officers, employees, or agents of the Department of Health and Human Services for purposes of locating such taxpayer for purposes of collecting such loan.

(B) DISCLOSURE TO SCHOOLS AND ELIGIBLE LENDERS.—Any mailing address disclosed under subparagraph (A) may be disclosed by the Secretary of Health and Human Services to—

(i) any school with which the Secretary of Health and Human Services has an agreement under subpart II of part C of title VII of the Public Health Service Act or subpart II of part B of title VIII of such Act, or

(ii) any eligible lender (within the meaning of section 737(4) of such Act) participating under subpart I of part C of title VII of such Act,

for use only by officers, employees, or agents of such school or eligible lender whose duties relate to the collection of student loans for purposes of locating individuals who have defaulted on student loans made under such subparts for the purposes of collecting such loans.

(6) BLOOD DONOR LOCATOR SERVICE.—

(A) IN GENERAL.—Upon written request pursuant to section 1141 of the Social Security Act, the Secretary shall disclose the mailing address of taxpayers to officers and employees of the Blood Donor Locator Services in the Department of Health and Human Services.

(B) RESTRICTION ON DISCLOSURE.—The Secretary shall disclose return information under subparagraph (A) only for purposes of, and to the extent necessary in, assisting under the Blood Donor Locator Service authorized persons (as defined in section 1141(h)(1) of the Social Security Act) in locating blood donors who, as indicated by donated blood or products derived therefrom or by the history of the subsequent use of such blood or blood products, have or may have the virus for acquired immune deficiency syndrome, in order to inform such donors of the possible need for medical care and treatment.

(C) SAFEGUARDS.—The Secretary shall destroy all related blood donor records (as defined in section 1141(h)(2) of the Social Security Act) in the possession of the Department of the Treasury upon completion of their use in making the disclosure required under subparagraph (A), so as to make such records undisclosable.

(7) SOCIAL SECURITY ACCOUNT STATEMENT FURNISHED BY SOCIAL SECURITY ADMINISTRATION.—Upon written request by the Commissioner of Social Security, the Secretary may disclose the mailing address of any taxpayer who is entitled to receive a social security account statement pursuant to section 1143(c) of the Social Security Act, for use only by officers, employees or agents of the Social Security Administration for purposes of mailing such statement to such taxpayer.

Amendments

- **1993, Omnibus Budget Reconciliation Act of 1993 (P.L. 103-66)**

P.L. 103-66, § 13402(b)(1):

Amended so much of paragraph (4) of Code section 6103(m) as precedes subparagraph (B). **Effective** 8-10-93. Prior to amendment, Code Sec. 6103(m)(4) that preceded subparagraph (B) read as follows:

(4) INDIVIDUALS WHO HAVE DEFAULTED ON STUDENT LOANS ADMINISTERED BY THE DEPARTMENT OF EDUCATION.—

(A) IN GENERAL.—Upon written request by the Secretary of Education, the Secretary may disclose the mailing address of any taxpayer who has defaulted on a loan—

(i) made under part B or E of title IV of the Higher Education Act of 1965, or

(ii) made pursuant to section 3(a)(1) of the Migration and Refugee Assistance Act of 1962 to a student at an institution of higher education,

for use only by officers, employees, or agents of the Department of Education for purposes of locating such taxpayer for purposes of collecting such loan.

P.L. 103-66, § 13402(b)(2)(A)-(B):

Amended Code Sec. 6103(m)(4)(B) by striking "under part B" in clause (i) and inserting "under part B or D"; and by striking "under part E" in clause (ii) and inserting "under subpart 1 of part A, or part D or E,". **Effective** 8-10-93.

- **1990, Omnibus Budget Reconciliation Act of 1990 (P.L. 101-508)**

P.L. 101-508, § 5111(b)(1):

Amended Code Sec. 6103(m) by adding at the end thereof a new paragraph (7). **Effective** 11-5-90.

- **1988, Technical and Miscellaneous Revenue Act of 1988 (P.L. 100-647)**

P.L. 100-647, § 8008(c)(1):

Amended Code Sec. 6103(m) by adding at the end thereof a new paragraph (6). **Effective** 11-10-88.

- **1985 (P.L. 99-92)**

P.L. 99-92, § 8(h)(1) and (2):

Amended Code Sec. 6103(m) by inserting "ADMINISTERED BY THE DEPARTMENT OF EDUCATION" before the period in the paragraph heading of paragraph (4), and by adding at the end thereof new paragraph (5). **Effective** 10-1-85.

RETURNS—MISCELLANEOUS PROVISIONS

• **1983 (P.L. 97-452)**

P.L. 97-452, §2(c)(4):

Amended Code Sec. 6103(m)(2) by striking out "section 3 of the Federal Claims Collection Act of 1966 (31 U.S.C. 952)" wherever it appeared and inserting "sections 3711, 3717, and 3718 of title 31". **Effective** 1-12-83.

• **1982, Debt Collection Act of 1982 (P.L. 97-365)**

P.L. 97-365, §8(a):

Amended Code Sec. 6103(m)(2). **Effective** 10-25-82. Prior to amendment, Code Sec. 6103(m)(2) read as follows:

(2) FEDERAL CLAIMS.—Upon written request, the Secretary may disclose the mailing address of a taxpayer to officers and employees of an agency personally and directly engaged in, and solely for their use in, preparation for any administrative or judicial proceeding (or investigation which may result in such a proceeding) pertaining to the collection or compromise of a Federal claim against such taxpayer in accordance with the provisions of section 3 of the Federal Claims Collection Act of 1966.

P.L. 97-365, §8(e), provides:

(e) Except as otherwise provided in section 4 or 7 of the foregoing provisions of this section, nothing in this Act (or in the amendments made by this Act) shall apply to claims or indebtedness arising under, or amounts payable under, the Internal Revenue Code of 1954, the Social Security Act, or the tariff laws of the United States.

• **1982 (P.L. 97-258)**

P.L. 97-258, §3(f)(6):

Amended Code Sec. 6103(m)(2) by striking out "section 3 of the Federal Claims Collection Act of 1966" and substituting "section 3711 of Title 31, United States Code". **Effective** 9-13-82.

• **1980, Omnibus Reconciliation Act of 1980 (P.L. 96-499)**

P.L. 96-499, §302(a):

Amended Code Sec. 6103(m)(4). **Effective** 12-5-80. Prior to amendment, Code Sec 6103(m)(4) provided:

(4) INDIVIDUALS WHO HAVE DEFAULTED ON STUDENT LOANS.—

(A) IN GENERAL.—Upon written request by the Commissioner of Education, the Secretary may disclose the mailing address of any taxpayer who has defaulted on a loan made from the student loan fund established under part E of title IV of the Higher Education Act of 1965 for use only for purposes of locating such taxpayer for purposes of collecting such loan.

(B) DISCLOSURE TO INSTITUTIONS.—Any mailing address disclosed under subparagraph (A) may be disclosed by the Commissioner of Education to any educational institution with which he has an agreement under part E of Title IV of the Higher Education Act of 1965 only for use by officers, employees or agents of such institution whose duties relate to the collection of student loans for purposes of locating individuals who have defaulted on student loans made by such institution pursuant to such agreement for purposes of collecting such loans.

• **1978, Revenue Act of 1978 (P.L. 95-600)**

P.L. 95-600, §701(bb)(1)(A):

Added Code Sec. 6103(m)(4). **Effective** 1-1-77.

• **1977 (P.L. 95-210)**

P.L. 95-210, §5:

Amended subsection (m). **Effective** 12-13-77. Prior to amendment, subsection (m) read as follows:

(m) DISCLOSURE OF TAXPAYER IDENTITY INFORMATION.—The Secretary is authorized—

(1) to disclose taxpayer identity information to the press and other media for purposes of notifying persons entitled to tax refunds when the Secretary, after reasonable effort and lapse of time, has been unable to locate such persons, and

(2) upon written request, to disclose the mailing address of a taxpayer to officers and employees of an agency personally and directly engaged in; and solely for their use in, preparation for any administrative or judicial proceeding (or investigation which may result in such a proceeding) pertaining to the collection or compromise of a Federal claim against such taxpayer in accordance with the provisions of section 3 of the Federal Claims Collection Act of 1966.

• **1976, Tax Reform Act of 1976 (P.L. 94-455)**

P.L. 94-455, §1202(a):

Added Code Sec. 6103(m). **Effective** 1-1-77.

[Sec. 6103(n)]

(n) CERTAIN OTHER PERSONS.—Pursuant to regulations prescribed by the Secretary, returns and return information may be disclosed to any person, including any person described in section 7513(a), to the extent necessary in connection with the processing, storage, transmission, and reproduction of such returns and return information, the programming, maintenance, repair, testing, and procurement of equipment, and the providing of other services, for purposes of tax administration.

Amendments

• **1990, Omnibus Budget Reconciliation Act of 1990 (P.L. 101-508)**

P.L. 101-508, §11313(a)(1):

Amended Code Sec. 6103(n) by striking "and the programming" and inserting "the programming". **Effective** 11-5-90.

P.L. 101-508, §11313(a)(2):

Amended Code Sec. 6103(n) by inserting after "of equipment," the following "and the providing of other services,". **Effective** 11-5-90.

• **1976, Tax Reform Act of 1976 (P.L. 94-455)**

P.L. 94-455, §1202(a):

Added Code Sec. 6103(n). **Effective** 1-1-77.

[Sec. 6103(o)]

(o) DISCLOSURE OF RETURNS AND RETURN INFORMATION WITH RESPECT TO CERTAIN TAXES.—

(1) TAXES IMPOSED BY SUBTITLE E.—

(A) IN GENERAL.—Returns and return information with respect to taxes imposed by subtitle E (relating to taxes on alcohol, tobacco, and firearms) shall be open to inspection by or disclosure to officers and employees of a Federal agency whose official duties require such inspection or disclosure.

(B) USE IN CERTAIN PROCEEDINGS.—Returns and return information disclosed to a Federal agency under subparagraph (A) may be used in an action or proceeding (or in preparation for such action or proceeding) brought under section 625 of the American Jobs Creation Act of 2004 for the collection of any unpaid assessment or penalty arising under such Act.

(2) TAXES IMPOSED BY CHAPTER 35.—Returns and return information with respect to taxes imposed by chapter 35 (relating to taxes on wagering) shall, notwithstanding any other provision of this section, be open to inspection by or disclosure only to such person or persons and for such purpose or purposes as are prescribed by section 4424.

(3) TAXES IMPOSED BY SECTION 4481.—Returns and return information with respect to taxes imposed by section 4481 shall be open to inspection by or disclosure to officers and employees of United States Customs and Border Protection of the Department of Homeland Security whose official duties require such inspection or disclosure for purposes of administering such section.

Amendments

• **2019, Setting Every Community Up for Retirement Enhancement Act of 2019 (P.L. 116-94)**

P.L. 116-94, §404(a), Div. O:

Amended Code Sec. 6103(o) by adding at the end a new paragraph (3). **Effective** 12-20-2019.

• **2009, Children's Health Insurance Program Reauthorization Act of 2009 (P.L. 111-3)**

P.L. 111-3, §702(f)(1):

Amended Code Sec. 6103(o)(1) by designating the text as subparagraph (A), moving such text 2 ems to the right, striking "Returns" and inserting "(A) IN GENERAL.—Returns", and by inserting after subparagraph (A) (as so redesignated) a new subparagraph (B). **Effective** on or after 2-4-2009.

• **1976, Tax Reform Act of 1976 (P.L. 94-455)**

P.L. 94-455, §1202(a):

Added Code Sec. 6103(o). **Effective** 1-1-77.

[Sec. 6103(p)]

(p) PROCEDURE AND RECORDKEEPING.—

(1) MANNER, TIME, AND PLACE OF INSPECTIONS.—Requests for the inspection or disclosure of a return or return information and such inspection or disclosure shall be made in such manner and at such time and place as shall be prescribed by the Secretary.

RETURNS—MISCELLANEOUS PROVISIONS

(2) PROCEDURE.—

(A) REPRODUCTION OF RETURNS.—A reproduction or certified reproduction of a return shall, upon written request, be furnished to any person to whom disclosure or inspection of such return is authorized under this section. A reasonable fee may be prescribed for furnishing such reproduction or certified reproduction.

(B) DISCLOSURE OF RETURN INFORMATION.—Return information disclosed to any person under the provisions of this title may be provided in the form of written documents, reproductions of such documents, films or photoimpressions, or electronically produced tapes, disks, or records, or by any other mode or means which the Secretary determines necessary or appropriate. A reasonable fee may be prescribed for furnishing such return information.

(C) USE OF REPRODUCTIONS.—Any reproduction of any return, document, or other matter made in accordance with this paragraph shall have the same legal status as the original, and any such reproduction shall, if properly authenticated, be admissible in evidence in any judicial or administrative proceeding as if it were the original, whether or not the original is in existence.

(3) RECORDS OF INSPECTION AND DISCLOSURE.—

(A) SYSTEM OF RECORDKEEPING.—Except as otherwise provided by this paragraph, the Secretary shall maintain a permanent system of standardized records or accountings of all requests for inspection or disclosure of returns and return information (including the reasons for and dates of such requests) and of returns and return information inspected or disclosed under this section and section 6104(c). Notwithstanding the provisions of section 552a(c) of title 5, United States Code, the Secretary shall not be required to maintain a record or accounting of requests for inspection or disclosure of returns and return information, or of returns and return information inspected or disclosed, under the authority of subsection (c), (e), (f)(5), (h)(1), (3)(A), or (4), (i)(4), or (8)(A)(ii), (k)(1), (2), (6), (8), or (9), (l)(1), (4)(B), (5), (7), (8), (9), (10), (11), (12), (13)(D)(iv), (13)(D)(v), (13)(D)(vi)[,] (14), (15), (16), (17), or (18), (m), or (n). The records or accountings required to be maintained under this paragraph shall be available for examination by the Joint Committee on Taxation or the Chief of Staff of such joint committee. Such record or accounting shall also be available for examination by such person or persons as may be, but only to the extent, authorized to make such examination under section 552a(c)(3) of title 5, United States Code.

(B) REPORT BY THE SECRETARY.—The Secretary shall, within 90 days after the close of each calendar year, furnish to the Joint Committee on Taxation a report with respect to, or summary of, the records or accountings described in subparagraph (A) in such form and containing such information as such joint committee or the Chief of Staff of such joint committee may designate. Such report or summary shall not, however, include a record or accounting of any request by the President under subsection (g) for, or the disclosure in response to such request of, any return or return information with respect to any individual who, at the time of such request, was an officer or employee of the executive branch of the Federal Government. Such report or summary, or any part thereof, may be disclosed by such joint committee to such persons and for such purposes as the joint committee may, by record vote of a majority of the members of the joint committee, determine.

(C) PUBLIC REPORT ON DISCLOSURES.—The Secretary shall, within 90 days after the close of each calendar year, furnish to the Joint Committee on Taxation for disclosure to the public a report with respect to the records or accountings described in subparagraph (A) which—

(i) provides with respect to each Federal agency, each agency, body, or commission described in subsection (d), (i)(3)(B)(i) or (7)(A)(ii) or (l)(6), and the Government Accountability Office the number of—

(I) requests for disclosure of returns and return information,

(II) instances in which returns and return information were disclosed pursuant to such requests or otherwise,

(III) taxpayers whose returns, or return information with respect to whom, were disclosed pursuant to such requests, and

(ii) describes the general purposes for which such requests were made.

(4) SAFEGUARDS.—Any Federal agency described in subsection (h)(2), (h)(5), (i)(1), (2), (3), (5), or (7), (j)(1), (2), or (5), (k)(8), (10), (11), or (15), (l)(1), (2), (3), (5), (10), (11), (13)(A), (13)(B), (13)(C), (13)(D)(i), (14), (17), or (22), (o)(1)(A), or (o)(3), the Government Accountability Office, the Congressional Budget Office, or any agency, body, or commission described in subsection (d), (i)(1)(C), (3)(B)(i), or (7)(A)(ii), or (k)(10), (l)(6), (7), (8), (9), (12), (15), or (16), any appropriate State officer (as defined in section 6104(c)), or any other person described in subsection (k)(10) or (15), subsection (l)(10), (13)(A), (13)(B), (13)(C), (13)(D)(i), (16), (18), (19), or (20), or any entity described in subsection (l)(21), shall, as a condition for receiving returns or return information—

(A) establish and maintain, to the satisfaction of the Secretary, a permanent system of standardized records with respect to any request, the reason for such request, and the date of such request made by or of it and any disclosure of return or return information made by or to it;

(B) establish and maintain, to the satisfaction of the Secretary, a secure area or place in which such returns or return information shall be stored;

(C) restrict, to the satisfaction of the Secretary, access to the returns or return information only to persons whose duties or responsibilities require access and to whom disclosure may be made under the provisions of this title;

(D) provide such other safeguards which the Secretary determines (and which he prescribes in regulations) to be necessary or appropriate to protect the confidentiality of the returns or return information;

(E) furnish a report to the Secretary, at such time and containing such information as the Secretary may prescribe, which describes the procedures established and utilized by such agency, body, or commission, the Government Accountability Office, or the Congressional Budget Office for ensuring the confidentiality of returns and return information required by this paragraph; and

(F) upon completion of use of such returns or return information—

(i) in the case of an agency, body, or commission described in subsection (d), (i)(3)(B)(i), (k)(10), or (l)(6), (7), (8), (9), or (16), any appropriate State officer (as defined in section 6104(c)), or any other person described in subsection (k)(10) or (15) or subsection (l)(10), (13)(A), (13)(B), (13)(C), (13)(D)(i), (16), (18), (19), or (20) return to the Secretary such returns or return information (along with any copies made there-from) or make such returns or return information undisclosable in any manner and furnish a written report to the Secretary describing such manner,

(ii) in the case of an agency described in subsection (h)(2), (h)(5), (i)(1), (2), (3), (5) or (7), (j)(1), (2), or (5), (k)(8), (10), (11), or (15), (l)(1), (2), (3), (5), (10), (11), (12), (13)(A), (13)(B), (13)(C), (13)(D)(i), (14), (15), (17), or (22), (o)(1)(A), or (o)(3) or any entity described in subsection (l)(21), the Government Accountability Office, or the Congressional Budget Office, either—

(I) return to the Secretary such returns or return information (along with any copies made therefrom),

(II) otherwise make such returns or return information undisclosable, or

(III) to the extent not so returned or made undisclosable, ensure that the conditions of subparagraphs (A), (B), (C), (D), and (E) of this paragraph continue to be met with respect to such returns or return information, and

(iii) in the case of the Department of Health and Human Services for purposes of subsection (m)(6), destroy all such return information upon completion of its use in providing the notification for which the information was obtained, so as to make such information undisclosable;

except that the conditions of subparagraphs (A), (B), (C), (D), and (E) shall cease to apply with respect to any return or return information if, and to the extent that, such return or return information is disclosed in the course of any judicial or administrative proceeding and made a part of the public record thereof. If the Secretary determines that any such agency, body, or commission, including an agency, an appropriate State officer (as defined in section 6104(c)), or any other person described in subsection (k)(10) or (15) or subsection (l)(10), (13)(A), (13)(B), (13)(C), (13)(D)(i), (16), (18), (19), or (20) or any entity described in subsection (l)(21), or the Government Accountability Office or the Congressional Budget Office, has failed to, or does not, meet the requirements of this paragraph, he may, after any proceedings for review established under paragraph (7), take such actions as are necessary to ensure such requirements are met, including refusing to disclose returns or return information to such agency, body, or commission, including an agency, an appropriate State officer (as defined in section 6104(c)), or any other person described in subsection (k)(10) or (15) or subsection (l)(10), (13)(A), (13)(B), (13)(C), (13)(D)(i), (16), (18), (19), or (20) or any entity described in subsection (l)(21), or the Government Accountability Office or the Congressional Budget Office, until he determines that such requirements have been or will be met. In the case of any agency which receives any mailing address under paragraph (2), (4), (6), or (7) of subsection (m) and which discloses any such mailing address to any agent or which receives any information under paragraph (6)(A), (10), (12)(B), or (16) of subsection (l) and which discloses any such information to any agent, or any person including an agent described in subsection (l)(10), (13)(A), (13)(B), (13)(C), (13)(D)(i), or (16), this paragraph shall apply to such agency and each such agent or other person (except that, in the case of an agent, or any person including an agent described in subsection (l)(10), (13)(A), (13)(B), (13)(C), (13)(D)(i), or (16), any report to the Secretary or other action with respect to the Secretary shall be made or taken through such agency). For purposes of applying this paragraph in any case to which subsection (m)(6) applies, the term "return information" includes related blood donor records (as defined in section 1141(h)(2) of the Social Security Act).

(5) REPORT ON PROCEDURES AND SAFEGUARDS.—After the close of each calendar year, the Secretary shall furnish to each committee described in subsection (f)(1) a report which describes the procedures and safeguards established and utilized by such agencies, bodies, or commissions, the Government Accountability Office, and the Congressional Budget Office for ensuring the confidentiality of returns and return information as required by this subsection. Such report shall also describe instances of deficiencies in, and failure to establish or utilize, such procedures.

(6) AUDIT OF PROCEDURES AND SAFEGUARDS.—

(A) AUDIT BY COMPTROLLER GENERAL.—The Comptroller General may audit the procedures and safeguards established by such agencies, bodies, or commissions and the Congressional Budget Office pursuant to this subsection to determine whether such safeguards and procedures meet the requirements of this subsection and ensure the confidentiality of returns and return information. The Comptroller General shall notify the Secretary before any such audit is conducted.

(B) RECORDS OF INSPECTION AND REPORTS BY THE COMPTROLLER GENERAL.—The Comptroller General shall—

(i) maintain a permanent system of standardized records and accountings of returns and return information inspected by officers and employees of the Government Accountability Office under subsection (i)(8)(A)(ii) and shall, within 90 days after the close of each calendar year, furnish to the Secretary a report with respect to, or summary of, such records or accountings in such form and containing such information as the Secretary may prescribe, and

(ii) furnish an annual report to each committee described in subsection (f) and to the Secretary setting forth his findings with respect to any audit conducted pursuant to subparagraph A.

The Secretary may disclose to the Joint Committee any report furnished to him under clause (i).

(7) ADMINISTRATIVE REVIEW.—The Secretary shall by regulations prescribe procedures which provide for administrative review of any determination under paragraph (4) that any agency, body, or commission described in subsection (d) has failed to meet the requirements of such paragraph.

(8) STATE LAW REQUIREMENTS.—

(A) SAFEGUARDS.—Notwithstanding any other provision of this section, no return or return information shall be disclosed after December 31, 1978, to any officer or employee of any State which requires a taxpayer to attach to, or include in, any State tax return a copy of any portion of his Federal return, or information reflected on such Federal return, unless such State adopts provisions of law which protect the confidentiality of the copy of the Federal return (or portion thereof) attached to, or the Federal return information reflected on, such State tax return.

(B) DISCLOSURE OF RETURNS OR RETURN INFORMATION IN STATE RETURNS.—Nothing in subparagraph (A) or paragraph (9) shall be construed to prohibit the disclosure by an officer or employee of any State of any copy of any portion of a Federal return or any information on a Federal return which is required to be attached or included in a State return to another officer or employee of such State (or political subdivision of such State) if such disclosure is specifically authorized by State law.

(9) DISCLOSURE TO CONTRACTORS AND OTHER AGENTS.—Notwithstanding any other provision of this section, no return or return information shall be disclosed to any contractor or other agent of a Federal, State, or local agency unless such agency, to the satisfaction of the Secretary—

(A) has requirements in effect which require each such contractor or other agent which would have access to returns or return information to provide safeguards (within the meaning of paragraph (4)) to protect the confidentiality of such returns or return information,

(B) agrees to conduct an on-site review every 3 years (or a mid-point review in the case of contracts or agreements of less than 3 years in duration) of each contractor or other agent to determine compliance with such requirements,

(C) submits the findings of the most recent review conducted under subparagraph (B) to the Secretary as part of the report required by paragraph (4)(E), and

(D) certifies to the Secretary for the most recent annual period that such contractor or other agent is in compliance with all such requirements.

The certification required by subparagraph (D) shall include the name and address of each contractor or other agent, a description of the contract or agreement with such contractor or other agent, and the duration of such contract or agreement. The requirements of this paragraph shall not apply to disclosures pursuant to subsection (n) for purposes of Federal tax administration.

Amendments

• **2020, COVID-related Tax Relief Act of 2020 (P.L. 116-260)**

P.L. 116-260, § 283(b)(2)(B)(i)-(ii), Div. N:

Amended Code Sec. 6103(p)(4) by striking "(k)(8), (10)[sic] or (11)" both places it appears and inserting "(k)(8), (10), (11), or (15)", and by striking "any other person described in subsection (k)(10)" each place it appears and inserting "any other person described in subsection (k)(10) or (15)". **Effective** for disclosures made on or after 12-27-2020.

P.L. 116-260, § 284(a)(3)(B), Div. N:

Amended Code Sec. 6103(p)(3)(A), as amended by section 3516(a)(2) of the CARES Act (P.L. 116-136), by striking "(13)(A), (13)(B), (13)(C), (13)(D)(i),[sic]" and inserting "(13)(D)(iv), (13)(D)(v), (13)(D)(vi)". **Effective** for disclosures made after the date of the enactment of the FUTURE Act (P.L. 116-91) [**effective** for disclosures made after 12-19-2019.—CCH].

• **2020, Consolidated Appropriations Act, 2021 (P.L. 116-260)**

P.L. 116-260, § 102(b)(2)(B)(i)-(ii), Div. FF:

Amended Code Sec. 6103(p)(4) by striking "(k)(8), (10)[sic] or (11)" both place it appears and inserting "(k)(8), (10), (11), or (15)", and by striking "any other person described in subsection (k)(10)" each place it appears and inserting "any other person described in subsection (k)(10) or (15)". [Note: An identical amendment was made by P.L. 116-260, Act Sec. 283(b)(2)(B)(i)-(ii), Div. N. Therefore, this amendment cannot be made.—CCH] **Effective** for disclosures made on or after 12-27-2020.

P.L. 116-260, § 103(a)(3)(B), Div. FF:

Amended Code Sec. 6103(p)(3)(A), as amended by section 3516(a)(2) of the CARES Act (P.L. 116-136), by striking "(13)(A), (13)(B), (13)(C), (13)(D)(i),[sic]" and inserting "(13)(D)(iv), (13)(D)(v), (13)(D)(vi)". [Note: An identical amendment was made by P.L. 116-260, Act Sec. 284(a)(3)(B), Div. N. Therefore, this amendment cannot be

RETURNS—MISCELLANEOUS PROVISIONS

made.—CCH] **Effective** for disclosures made after the date of the enactment of the FUTURE Act (P.L. 116-91) [**effective** for disclosures made after 12-19-2019.—CCH].

• **2020, Coronavirus Aid, Relief, and Economic Security (CARES) Act (P.L. 116-136)**

P.L. 116-136, §3516(a)(2):

Amended Code Sec. 6103(p)(3)(A), as amended by the FUTURE Act (P.L. 116-91), by striking "(12)," and inserting "(12), (13)(A), (13)(B), (13)(C), (13)(D)(i)". **Effective** as if included in the enactment of the FUTURE Act (P.L. 116-91) [**effective** for disclosures after 12-19-2019.—CCH].

P.L. 116-136, §3516(a)(3):

Amended Code Sec. 6103(p)(4), as amended by the FUTURE Act (P.L. 116-91), by striking "(13) or (16)" each place it appears and inserting "(13), or (16)". **Effective** as if included in the enactment of the FUTURE Act (P.L. 116-91) [**effective** for disclosures after 12-19-2019.—CCH].

P.L. 116-136, §3516(a)(4):

Amended Code Sec. 6103(p)(4), as amended by the FUTURE Act (P.L. 116-91) and by Act Sec. 3516(a)(3), by striking "(13)" each place it appears and inserting "(13)(A), (13)(B), (13)(C), (13)(D)(i)". **Effective** as if included in the enactment of the FUTURE Act (P.L. 116-91) [**effective** for disclosures after 12-19-2019.—CCH].

• **2019, Fostering Undergraduate Talent by Unlocking Resources for Education (FUTURE) Act (P.L. 116-91)**

P.L. 116-91, §3(c)(1):

Amended Code Sec. 6103(p)(3)(A) of such Code by striking "(13)" following "(12),". **Effective** for disclosures after 12-19-2019.

P.L. 116-91, §3(c)(2):

Amended Code Sec. 6103(p)(4) of such Code by inserting ", (13)" after "(l)(10)" each place it appears. **Effective** for disclosures after 12-19-2019.

• **2019, Setting Every Community Up for Retirement Enhancement Act of 2019 (P.L. 116-94)**

P.L. 116-94, §404(b), Div. O:

Amended Code Sec. 6103(p)(4) by striking "or (o)(1)(A)" each place it appears and inserting ", (o)(1)(A), or (o)(3)". **Effective** 12-20-2019.

• **2019, Taxpayer First Act (P.L. 116-25)**

P.L. 116-25, §2004(a):

Amended Code Sec. 6103(p) by adding at the end a new paragraph (9). **Effective** for disclosures made after 12-31-2022.

P.L. 116-25, §2004(b):

Amended Code Sec. 6103(p)(8)(B) by inserting "or paragraph (9)" after "subparagraph (A)". **Effective** for disclosures made after 12-31-2022.

• **2018, Tax Technical Corrections Act of 2018 (P.L. 115-141)**

P.L. 115-141, §401(a)(271), Div. U:

Amended Code Sec. 6103(p)(3)(A) by striking "subsections" and inserting "subsection". **Effective** 3-23-2018.

P.L. 115-141, §401(a)(272), Div. U:

Amended Code Sec. 6103(p)(3)(C)(ii) by striking the comma at the end and inserting a period. **Effective** 3-23-2018.

P.L. 115-141, §401(a)(273), Div. U:

Amended Code Sec. 6103(p)(4) by striking "7(A)(ii)" in the matter preceding subparagraph (A) and inserting "(7)(A)(ii)". **Effective** 3-23-2018.

P.L. 115-141, §401(a)(274)(A)-(B), Div. U:

Amended Code Sec. 6103(p)(4)(F)(ii) by striking "subsections" and inserting "subsection", and by striking "subsection (l)(21),,,," and inserting "subsection (l)(21),". **Effective** 3-23-2018.

P.L. 115-141, §401(a)(275), Div. U:

Amended Code Sec. 6103(p)(4) by striking "subsection (l)(21),," both places it appears in the flush matter at the end and inserting "subsection (l)(21),". **Effective** 3-23-2018.

• **2016, Recovering Missing Children Act (P.L. 114-184)**

P.L. 114-184, §2(b)(2)(B):

Amended Code Sec. 6103(p)(4) by striking "(i)(3)(B)(i)" in the matter preceding subparagraph (A) and inserting "(i)(1)(C), (3)(B)(i),". **Effective** for disclosures made after 6-30-2016.

• **2015, Fixing America's Surface Transportation Act (P.L. 114-94)**

P.L. 114-94, §32101(c)(2):

Amended Code Sec. 6103(p)(4) by striking "or (10)" each place it appears in subparagraph (F)(ii) and in the matter preceding subparagraph (A) and inserting ", (10), or (11)". **Effective** 12-4-2015.

• **2013, American Taxpayer Relief Act of 2012 (P.L. 112-240)**

P.L. 112-240, §209(b)(2)(A)-(C):

Amended Code Sec. 6103(p)(4) by inserting "subsection (k)(10)," before "subsection (l)(10)," in the matter preceding subparagraph (A), in subparagraph (F)(i) by inserting "(k)(10)," before "or (l)(6),", and by inserting "subsection (k)(10) or" before "subsection (l)(10)," and by inserting "subsection (k)(10) or" before "subsection (l)(10)," both places it appears in the matter following subparagraph (F)(iii). **Effective** 1-2-2013.

Sec. 6103(p)(9)(D)

• **2010, Homebuyer Assistance and Improvement Act of 2010 (P.L. 111-198)**

P.L. 111-198, §4(c):

Amended Code Sec. 6103(p)(4) by inserting "(k)(10)," before "(l)(6)," in the matter preceding subparagraph (A). **Effective** for disclosures made after 7-2-2010.

• **2010, Preservation of Access to Care for Medicare Beneficiaries and Pension Relief Act of 2010 (P.L. 111-192)**

P.L. 111-192, §103(a)(2):

Amended Code Sec. 6103(p)(4), as amended by sections 1414 and 3308 of P.L. 111-148, in the matter preceding subparagraph (A) and in subparagraph (F)(ii), by striking "or (17)" and inserting "(17), or (22)" each place it appears. **Effective** 6-25-2010.

• **2010, Patient Protection and Affordable Care Act (P.L. 111-148)**

P.L. 111-148, §1414(c)(1)-(3):

Amended Code Sec. 6103(p)(4) by inserting ", or any entity described in subsection (l)(21)," after "or (20)" in the matter preceding subparagraph (A), by inserting "or any entity described in subsection (l)(21)," after "or (o)(1)(A)" in subparagraph (F)(ii), and by inserting "or any entity described in subsection (l)(21)," after "or (20)" both places it appears in the matter after subparagraph (F). **Effective** 3-23-2010.

• **2009, Children's Health Insurance Program Reauthorization Act of 2009 (P.L. 111-3)**

P.L. 111-3, §702(f)(2):

Amended Code Sec. 6103(p)(4) by striking "(o)(1)" both places it appears and inserting "(o)(1)(A)". **Effective** on or after 2-4-2009.

• **2008, Inmate Tax Fraud Prevention Act of 2008 (P.L. 110-428)**

P.L. 110-428, §2(b):

Amended Code Sec. 6103(p)(4) by striking "(k)(8)" both places it appears and inserting "(k)(8) or (10)". **Effective** for disclosures made after 12-31-2008.

• **2008, SSI Extension for Elderly and Disabled Refugees Act (P.L. 110-328)**

P.L. 110-328, §3(b)(3)(A)-(C):

Amended Code Sec. 6103(p)(4) in the matter preceding subparagraph (A), by striking "(l)(16)," and inserting "(l)(10), (16),"; in subparagraph (F)(i), by striking "(l)(16)," and inserting "(l)(10), (16),"; and in the matter following subparagraph (F)(iii), in each of the first two places it appears, by striking "(l)(16)," and inserting "(l)(10), (16),"; by inserting "(10)," after "paragraph (6)(A),"; and in each of the last two places it appears, by striking "(l)(16)" and inserting "(l)(10) or (16)". **Effective** for refunds payable under Code Sec. 6402 on or after 9-30-2008.

• **2006, Pension Protection Act of 2006 (P.L. 109-280)**

P.L. 109-280, §1224(b)(2):

Amended Code Sec. 6103(p)(3)(A) by inserting "and section 6104(c)" after "section" in the first sentence. **Effective** 8-17-2006 but shall not apply to requests made before such date.

P.L. 109-280, §1224(b)(3)(A)-(C):

Amended Code Sec. 6103(p)(4) by inserting ", any appropriate State officer (as defined in section 6104(c))," before "or any other person" in the matter preceding subparagraph (A), by inserting "any appropriate State officer (as defined in section 6104(c))," before "or any other person" in subparagraph (F)(i), and by inserting ", an appropriate State officer (as defined in section 6104(c))," after "including an agency" each place it appears in the matter following subparagraph (F). **Effective** 8-17-2006 but shall not apply to requests made before such date.

• **2005, Gulf Opportunity Zone Act of 2005 (P.L. 109-135)**

P.L. 109-135, §412(rr)(4):

Amended Code Sec. 6103(p)(3)(C)(i), (p)(4), (p)(5) and (p)(6)(B) by striking "General Accounting Office" each place it appears and inserting "Government Accountability Office". **Effective** 12-21-2005.

P.L. 109-135, §412(yy)(1):

Amended so much of Code Sec. 6103(p)(4) as precedes subparagraph (A). **Effective** 12-21-2005. Prior to amendment, so much of Code Sec. 6103(p)(4) as preceded subparagraph (A) read as follows:

(4) SAFEGUARDS.—Any Federal agency described in subsection (h)(2), (h)(5), (i)(1), (2), (3), (5), or (7), (j)(1), (2), or (5), (k)(8), (l)(1), (2), (3), (5), (10), (11), (13), (14), or (17), or (o)(1), the Government Accountability Office, the Congressional Budget Office, or any agency, body, or commission described in subsection (d), (i)(3)(B)(i) or (7)(A)(ii), or (l)(6), (7), (8), (9), (12), (15), or (16) or any other person described in subsection (l)(16), (18), (19), or (20) shall, as a condition for receiving returns or return information—

P.L. 109-135, §412(yy)(2):

Amended Code Sec. 6103(p)(4)(F)(i). **Effective** 12-21-2005. Prior to amendment, Code Sec. 6103(p)(4)(F)(i) read as follows:

(i) in the case of an agency, body, or commission described in subsection (d), (i)(3)(B)(i), or (l)(6), (7), (8), (9), or (16), or any other person described in subsection (l)(16), (18), (19), or (20) return to the Secretary such returns or return information (along with any copies made therefrom) or make such returns or return information undisclosable in any manner and furnish a written report to the Secretary describing such manner,

RETURNS—MISCELLANEOUS PROVISIONS

P.L. 109-135, §412(yy)(3):

Amended Code Sec. 6103(p)(4) by striking the first full sentence in the matter following subparagraph (F) and inserting a new sentence. **Effective** 12-21-2005. Prior to amendment, the first full sentence in the matter following Code Sec. 6103(p)(4)(F) read as follows:

If the Secretary determines that any such agency, body, or commission, including an agency or any other person described in subsection (l)(16), (18), (19), or (20), or the Government Accountability Office or the Congressional Budget Office has failed to, or does not, meet the requirements of this paragraph, he may, after any proceedings for review established under paragraph (7), take such actions as are necessary to ensure such requirements are met, including refusing to disclose returns or return information to such agency, body, or commission, including an agency or any other person described in subsection (l)(16), (18), (19), or (20), or the Government Accountability Office or the Congressional Budget Office, until he determines that such requirements have been or will be met.

• **2004, Miscellaneous Trade and Technical Corrections Act of 2004 (P.L. 108-429)**

P.L. 108-429, §2004(a)(22):

Amended Code Sec. 6103(p)(4), as amended by Act Sec. 202(b)(2)(B) of the Trade Act of 2002 (P.L. 107-210), by striking "or (17)" after "any other person described in subsection (l)(16)" each place it appears and inserting "or (18)". **Effective** 12-3-2004.

• **2004, Working Families Tax Relief Act of 2004 (P.L. 108-311)**

P.L. 108-311, §408(a)(24):

Amended Code Sec. 6103(p)(4) by striking "subsection (l)(16) or (17)" each place it appears and inserting "subsection (l)(16) or (18)". **Effective** 10-4-2004. [P.L. 108-173, §105(e)(3), struck "(l)(16) or (17)" and inserted "(l)(16), (17), or (19)". Therefore, this amendment cannot be made. However, see the amendment made by P.L. 108-429, §2004(a)(22), above.—CCH.]

• **2003, Medicare Prescription Drug, Improvement, and Modernization Act of 2003 (P.L. 108-173)**

P.L. 108-173, §105(e)(3):

Amended Code Sec. 6103(p)(4) by striking "(l)(16) or (17)" each place it appears and inserting "(l)(16), (17), or (19)". **Effective** 12-8-2003.

P.L. 108-173, §811(c)(2)(B):

Amended Code Sec. 6103(p)(4), as amended by Act Sec. 105(e)(3), by striking "(l)(16), (17), or (19)" each place it appears and inserting "(l)(16), (17), (19), or (20)". **Effective** 12-8-2003.

• **2002, Trade Act of 2002 (P.L. 107-210)**

P.L. 107-210, §202(b)(2)(A)-(B):

Amended Code Sec. 6103(p) by striking "or (17)" and inserting "(17), or (18)" in paragraph (3)(A), and by inserting "or (17)" after "any other person described in subsection (l)(16)" each place it appears in paragraph (4). **Effective** 8-6-2002.

• **2002, Victims of Terrorism Tax Relief Act of 2001 (P.L. 107-134)**

P.L. 107-134, §201(c)(6)(A)-(B):

Amended Code Sec. 6103(p)(3) in subparagraph (A) by striking "(7)(A)(ii)" and inserting "(8)(A)(ii)"; and in subparagraph (C) by striking "(i)(3)(B)(i)" and inserting "(i)(3)(B)(i) or (7)(A)(ii)". **Effective** for disclosures made on or after 1-23-2002.

P.L. 107-134, §201(c)(7)(A)-(B):

Amended Code Sec. 6103(p)(4) in the matter preceding subparagraph (A) by striking "or (5)," the first place it appears and inserting "(5), or (7),"; and by striking "(i)(3)(B)(i)," and inserting "(i)(3)(B)(i) or (7)(A)(ii),"; and in subparagraph (F)(ii) by striking "or (5)," the first place it appears and inserting "(5) or (7),". **Effective** for disclosures made on or after 1-23-2002.

P.L. 107-134, §201(c)(8):

Amended Code Sec. 6103(p)(6)(B)(i) by striking "(i)(7)(A)(ii)" and inserting "(i)(8)(A)(ii)". **Effective** for disclosures made on or after 1-23-2002.

• **2000, Community Renewal Tax Relief Act of 2000 (P.L. 106-554)**

P.L. 106-554, §310(a)(2)(A)(i)-(iv):

Amended Code Sec. 6103(p)(4) by inserting "the Congressional Budget Office," after "General Accounting Office," in the matter preceding subparagraph (A), by striking "commission or the General Accounting Office" and inserting "commission, the General Accounting Office, or the Congressional Budget Office" in subparagraph (E), by striking "or the General Accounting Office," and inserting "the General Accounting Office, or the Congressional Budget Office," in subparagraph (F)(ii), and by inserting "or the Congressional Budget Office" after "General Accounting Office" both places it appears in the matter following subparagraph (F). **Effective** 12-21-2000.

P.L. 106-554, §310(a)(2)(B):

Amended Code Sec. 6103(p)(5) by striking "commissions and the General Accounting Office" and inserting "commissions, the General Accounting Office, and the Congressional Budget Office". **Effective** 12-21-2000.

P.L. 106-554, §310(a)(2)(C):

Amended Code Sec. 6103(p)(6)(A) by inserting "and the Congressional Budget Office" after "commissions". **Effective** 12-21-2000.

P.L. 106-554, §319(17)(A):

Amended Code Sec. 6103(p) by striking the second comma after "(13)", and by striking "(7)" and all that follows through "shall, as a condition" and inserting "(7), (8), (9), (12), (15), or (16) or any other person described in subsection (l)(16) shall, as a condition" in the matter preceding subparagraph (4)(A). **Effective** 12-21-2000. Prior to amendment, the matter preceding subparagraph (A) of Code Sec. 6103(p)(4) read as follows:

(4) SAFEGUARDS.—Any Federal agency described in subsection (h)(2), (h)(5), (i)(1), (2), (3), or (5), (j)(1), (2), or (5), (k)(8), (l)(1), (2), (3), (5), (10), (11), (13), (14), or (17), or (o)(1), the General Accounting Office, or any agency, body, or commission described in subsection (d), (i)(3)(B)(i), or (l)(6), (7), (8), (9), (12), or [sic] (15), or (16), or any other person described in subsection (l)(16) shall, as a condition for receiving returns or return information—

P.L. 106-554, §319(17)(B):

Amended Code Sec. 6103(p)(4)(F)(ii) by striking the second comma after "(14)". **Effective** 12-21-2000.

• **1998, Tax and Trade Relief Extension Act of 1998 (P.L. 105-277)**

P.L. 105-277, §4002(h):

Amended Code Sec. 6103(p)(3)(A) by inserting "(f)(5)," after "(c), (e),". **Effective** as if included in the provision of P.L. 105-206 to which it relates [**effective** 7-22-98.—CCH].

P.L. 105-277, §4006(a)(2):

Amended Code Sec. 6103(p)(4) by striking "(j)(1) or (2)" in the material preceding subparagraph (A) and in [clause (ii) of]subparagraph (F) and inserting "(j)(1), (2), or (5)". **Effective** for requests made on or after 10-21-98.

• **1998, IRS Restructuring and Reform Act of 1998 (P.L. 105-206)**

P.L. 105-206, §3702(b)(1):

Amended Code Sec. 6103(p)(3)(A) by striking "or (16)" and inserting "(16), or (17)". **Effective** for requests made by the Archivist of the United States after 7-22-98.

P.L. 105-206, §3702(b)(2):

Amended Code Sec. 6103(p)(4) by striking "or (14)" and inserting ", (14), or (17)". **Effective** for requests made by the Archivist of the United States after 7-22-98.

P.L. 105-206, §3702(b)(3):

Amended Code Sec. 6103(p)(4)(F)(ii) by striking "or (15)" and inserting ", (15), or (17)". **Effective** for requests made by the Archivist of the United States after 7-22-98.

P.L. 105-206, §6012(b)(4), provides:

Act Sec. 1205(c)(3) of P.L. 105-34 shall be applied as if the amendment to Code Sec. 6103(p)(3)(A) struck "or (8)" and inserted "(8), or (9)". **Effective** 5-5-98.

P.L. 105-206, §2003(e), provides:

(e) PROCEDURES FOR AUTHORIZING DISCLOSURE ELECTRONICALLY.—The Secretary shall establish procedures for any taxpayer to authorize, on an electronically filed return, the Secretary to disclose information under section 6103(c) of the Internal Revenue Code of 1986 to the preparer of the return.

P.L. 105-206, §2005, provides:

SEC. 2005. ACCESS TO ACCOUNT INFORMATION.

(a) IN GENERAL.—Not later than December 31, 2006, the Secretary of the Treasury or the Secretary's delegate shall develop procedures under which a taxpayer filing returns electronically (and their designees under section 6103(c) of the Internal Revenue Code of 1986) would be able to review the taxpayer's account electronically, but only if all necessary safeguards to ensure the privacy of such account information are in place.

(b) REPORT.—Not later than December 31, 2003, the Secretary of the Treasury shall report on the progress the Secretary is making on the development of procedures under subsection (a) to the Committee on Ways and Means of the House of Representatives and the Committee on Finance of the Senate.

P.L. 105-206, §3508, provides:

SEC. 3508. DISCLOSURE TO TAXPAYERS.

The Secretary of the Treasury or the Secretary's delegate shall ensure that any instructions booklet accompanying an individual Federal income tax return form (including forms 1040, 1040A, 1040EZ, and any similar or successor forms) shall include, in clear language, in conspicuous print, and in a conspicuous place, a concise description of the conditions under which return information may be disclosed to any party outside the Internal Revenue Service, including disclosure to any State or agency, body, or commission (or legal representative) thereof.

• **1997, Taxpayer Relief Act of 1997 (P.L. 105-34)**

P.L. 105-34, §1026(b)(1)(A):

Amended Code Sec. 6103(p)(3)(A) by striking "(2), or (6)" and inserting "(2), (6), or (8)". **Effective** for levies issued after 8-5-97.

P.L. 105-34, §1026(b)(1)(B):

Amended Code Sec. 6103(p)(4) by inserting "(k)(8)," after "(j)(1) or (2)," each place it appears. **Effective** for levies issued after 8-5-97.

P.L. 105-34, §1205(c)(3):

Amended Code Sec. 6103(p)(3)(A) by striking "or (6)" [sic] and inserting "(6), or (8)". **Effective** on the day 9 months after 8-5-97.

P.L. 105-34, §1283(b):

Amended Code Sec. 6103(p)(4) by striking "(h)(6)" each place it appears and inserting "(h)(5)". **Effective** for judicial proceedings commenced after 8-5-97.

• **1997, Balanced Budget Act of 1997 (P.L. 105-33)**

P.L. 105-33, §5514(a)(1):

Struck the amendment made by Act Sec. 110(l)(5)(A)-(B) of P.L. 104-193, which amended Code Sec. 6103(p)(4) in the matter preceding subparagraph (A) by striking "(5), (10)" and inserting "(5)" and by striking "(9), or (12)" and inserting "(9), (10), or (12)". Thus, the provisions of law amended by such section are restored as if such section had not been enacted. **Effective** 7-1-97.

P.L. 105-33, §11024(b)(4):

Amended Code Sec. 6103(p)(3)(A) by striking "or (15)" and inserting "(15), or (16)". For the **effective** date, see Act Sec. 11721, below.

RETURNS—MISCELLANEOUS PROVISIONS

P.L. 105-33, §11024(b)(5):

Amended Code Sec. 6103(p)(4) in the matter preceding subparagraph (A) by striking "or (12)" and inserting "(12), or (16), or any other person described in subsection (l)(16)". For the **effective** date, see Act Sec. 11721, below.

P.L. 105-33, §11024(b)(6):

Amended Code Sec. 6103(p)(4)(F)(i) by striking "or (9)," and inserting "(9), or (16), or any other person described in subsection (l)(16)". For the **effective** date, see Act Sec. 11721, below.

P.L. 105-33, §11024(b)(7)(A)-(F):

Amended Code Sec. 6103(p)(4)(F) in the matter following clause (iii) by inserting after "any such agency, body or commission" and before the words "for [or] the General Accounting Office" the words ", including an agency or any other person described in subsection (l)(16),"; by striking "to such agency, body, or commission" and inserting "to such agency, body, or commission, including an agency or any other person described in subsection (l)(16),"; by striking "or (12)(B)" and inserting ", (12)(B), or (16)"; by inserting after the words "any agent," and before the words "this paragraph shall" the words "or any person including an agent described in subsection (l)(16),"; by inserting after the words "such agent" and before "(except that" the words "or other person"; and by inserting after the words "an agent," and before the words "any report" the words "or any person including an agent described in subsection (l)(16),". For the **effective** date, see Act Sec. 11721, below.

P.L. 105-33, §11721, provides:

Except as otherwise provided in this title, the provisions of this title shall take effect on the later of October 1, 1997, or the day the District of Columbia Financial Responsibility and Management Assistance Authority certifies that the financial plan and budget for the District government for fiscal year 1998 meet the requirements of section 201(c)(1) of the District of Columbia Financial Responsibility and Management Assistance Act of 1995, as amended by this title.

• **1996, Personal Responsibility and Work Opportunity Reconciliation Act of 1996 (P.L. 104-193)**

P.L. 104-193, §110(l)(5)(A)-(B):

Amended Code Sec. 6103(p)(4) in the matter preceding subparagraph (A) by striking "(5), (10)" and inserting "(5)"; and by striking "(9), or (12)" and inserting "(9), (10), or (12)". **Effective** 7-1-97.

P.L. 104-193, §316(g)(4)(B)(iii):

Amended Code Sec. 6103(p)(4) in the material following subparagraph (F) by striking "subsection (l)(12)(B)" and inserting "paragraph (6)(A) or (12)(B) of subsection (l)". **Effective** 8-22-96.

• **1996, Taxpayer Bill of Rights 2 (P.L. 104-168)**

P.L. 104-168, §1206(b)(2)(A)-(B):

Amended Code Sec. 6103(p)(3)(A) by striking "(7)(A)(ii), or (8)" and inserting "or (7)(A)(ii),", and by striking "or (14)" and inserting "(14), or (15)". **Effective** 7-30-96.

P.L. 104-168, §1206(b)(3)(A)-(C):

Amended the material preceding Code Sec. 6103(p)(4)(A) by striking "(5), or (8)" and inserting "or (5)", by striking "(i)(3)(B)(i), or (8)" and inserting "(i)(3)(B)(i),", and by striking "or (12)" and inserting "(12), or (15)". **Effective** 7-30-96.

P.L. 104-168, §1206(b)(4)(A)-(B):

Amended Code Sec. 6103(p)(4)(F)(ii) by striking "(5), or (8)" and inserting "or (5)", and by striking "or (14)" and inserting "(14), or (15)". **Effective** 7-30-96.

• **1993, North American Free Trade Agreement Implementation Act (P.L. 103-182)**

P.L. 103-182, §522(b):

Amended Code Sec. 6103(p)(3)(A) and (4) by striking "or (13) each place it appears and inserting "(13), or (14)". **Effective** on the date the Agreement enters into force with respect to the United States.

• **1993, Omnibus Budget Reconciliation Act of 1993 (P.L. 103-66)**

P.L. 103-66, §13402(b)(3)(A):

Amended Code Sec. 6103(p)(3)(A) by striking "(11), or (12), (m)" and inserting "(11), (12), or (13), (m)". **Effective** 8-10-93.

P.L. 103-66, §13402(b)(3)(B)(i):

Amended Code Sec. 6103(p)(4) in the matter preceding subparagraph (A), by striking out "(10), or (11)," and inserting "(10), (11), or (13),". **Effective** 8-10-93.

P.L. 103-66, §13402(b)(3)(B)(ii):

Amended Code Sec. 6103(p)(4)(F)(ii) by striking out "(11), or (12)," and inserting "(11), (12), or (13),". **Effective** 8-10-93.

• **1990, Omnibus Budget Reconciliation Act of 1990 (P.L. 101-508)**

P.L. 101-508, §5111(b)(2):

Amended Code Sec. 6103(p)(4) in the matter following subparagraph (F)(iii) by striking "subsection (m)(2), (4), or (6)" and inserting "paragraph (2), (4), (6), or (7) of subsection (m)". **Effective** 11-5-90.

• **1989, Omnibus Budget Reconciliation Act of 1989 (P.L. 101-239)**

P.L. 101-239, §6202(a)(1)(B)(ii):

Amended Code Sec. 6103(p)(3)(A) by striking "or (11)" and inserting "(11), or (12)". **Effective** 12-19-89.

P.L. 101-239, §6202(a)(1)(B)(iii):

Amended Code Sec. 6103(p)(4) by striking "or (9) shall" in the material preceding subparagraph (A) and inserting "(9), or (12) shall". **Effective** 12-19-89.

P.L. 101-239, §6202(a)(1)(B)(iv):

Amended Code Sec. 6103(p)(4)(F)(ii) by striking "or (11)" and inserting "(11), or (12)". **Effective** 12-19-89.

P.L. 101-239, §6202(a)(1)(B)(v):

Amended Code Sec. 6103(p)(4) in the next to last sentence by inserting "or which receives any information under subsection (l)(12)(B) and which discloses any such information to any agent" before ", this paragraph". **Effective** 12-19-89.

• **1988, Anti-Drug Abuse Act of 1988 (P.L. 100-690)**

P.L. 100-690, §7601(b)(2)(A):

Amended Code Sec. 6103(p)(3)(A) by striking out "or (7)(A)(ii)" and inserting in lieu thereof", (7)(A)(ii), or (8)". **Effective** for requests made on or after 11-18-88, but disclosures may be made pursuant to such amendments only during the 2-year period beginning on such date.

P.L. 100-690, §7601(b)(2)(B)(i)-(ii):

Amended Code Sec. 6103(p)(4) by striking out in the material preceding subparagraph (A) "or (5)" and inserting in lieu thereof "(5), or (8)", and by striking out "(i)(3)(B)(i)," and inserting in lieu thereof "(i)(3)(B)(i), or (8)". **Effective** for requests made on or after 11-18-88, but disclosures may be made pursuant to such amendments only during the 2-year period beginning on such date.

P.L. 100-690, §7601(b)(2)(C):

Amended Code Sec. 6103(p)(4)(F)(ii) by striking out "or (5)" and inserting in lieu thereof "(5), or (8)". **Effective** for requests made on or after 11-18-88, but disclosures may be made pursuant to such amendments only during the 2-year period beginning on such date.

• **1988, Technical and Miscellaneous Revenue Act of 1988 (P.L. 100-647)**

P.L. 100-647, §8008(c)(2)(A)(i)-(iii):

Amended Code Sec. 6103(p)(4) in subparagraph (F) by striking "manner; and" at the end of clause (i) and inserting "manner,"; by adding "and" at the end of clause (ii)(III); and by inserting after clause (ii)(III) a new clause (iii); in the last sentence, by striking "subsection (m)(2) or (4)" and inserting "subsection (m)(2), (4), or (6)"; and by adding at the end a new sentence. **Effective** 11-10-88.

P.L. 100-647, §5021, provides:

SEC. 5021. REPEAL OF RULES PERMITTING LOSS TRANSFERS BY ALASKA NATIVE CORPORATIONS.

(a) GENERAL RULE.—Nothing in section 60(b)(5) of the Tax Reform Act of 1984 (as amended by section 1804(e)(4) of the Tax Reform Act of 1986)—

(1) shall allow any loss (or credit) of any corporation which arises after April 26, 1988, to be used to offset the income (or tax) of another corporation if such use would not be allowable without regard to such section 60(b)(5) as so amended, or

(2) shall allow any loss (or credit) of any corporation which arises on or before such date to be used to offset disqualified income (or tax attributable to such income) of another corporation if such use would not be allowable without regard to such section 60(b)(5) as so amended.

(b) EXCEPTION FOR EXISTING CONTRACTS.—

(1) IN GENERAL.—Subsection (a) shall not apply to any loss (or credit) of any corporation if—

(A) such corporation was in existence on April 26, 1988, and

(B) such loss (or credit) is used to offset income assigned (or attributable to property contributed) pursuant to a binding contract entered into before July 26, 1988.

(2) $40,000,000 LIMITATION.—The aggregate amount of losses (and the deduction equivalent of credits as determined in the same manner as under section 469(j)(5) of the 1986 Code) to which paragraph (1) applies with respect to any corporation shall not exceed $40,000,000. For purposes of this paragraph, a Native Corporation and all other corporations all of the stock of which is owned directly by such corporation shall be treated as 1 corporation.

(3) SPECIAL RULE FOR CORPORATIONS UNDER TITLE 11.—In the case of a corporation which on April 26, 1988, was under the jurisdiction of a Federal district court under title 11 of the United States Code—

(A) paragraph (1)(B) shall be applied by substituting the date 1 year after the date of the enactment of this Act for "July 26, 1988",

(B) paragraph (1) shall not apply to any loss or credit which arises on or after the date 1 year after the date of the enactment of this Act, and

(C) paragraph (2) shall be applied by substituting "$99,000,000" for "$40,000,000".

(c) SPECIAL ADMINISTRATIVE RULES.—

(1) NOTICE TO NATIVE CORPORATIONS OF PROPOSED TAX ADJUSTMENTS.—Notwithstanding section 6103 of the 1986 Code, the Secretary of the Treasury or his delegate shall notify a Native Corporation or its designated representative of any proposed adjustment—

(A) of the tax liability of a taxpayer which has contracted with the Native Corporation (or other corporation all of the stock of which is owned directly by the Native Corporation) for the use of loses of such Native Corporation (or such other corporation), and

(B) which is attributable to an asserted overstatement of losses by, or misassignment of income (or income attributable to property contributed) to, an affiliated group of which the Native Corporation (or such other corporation) is a member.

Such notice shall only include information with respect to the transaction between the taxpayer and the Native Corporation.

(2) RIGHTS OF NATIVE CORPORATION.—

(A) IN GENERAL.—If a Native Corporation receives a notice under paragraph (1), the Native Corporation shall have the right to—

(i) submit to the Secretary of the Treasury or his delegate a written statement regarding the proposed adjustment, and

(ii) meet with the Secretary of the Treasury or his delegate with respect to such proposed adjustment.

The Secretary of the Treasury or his delegate may discuss such proposed adjustment with the Native Corporation or its designated representative.

Sec. 6103(p)(9)(D)

RETURNS—MISCELLANEOUS PROVISIONS

(B) EXTENSION OF STATUTE OF LIMITATIONS.—Subparagraph (A) shall not apply if the Secretary of the Treasury or his delegate determines that an extension of the statute of limitation is necessary to permit the participation described in subparagraph (A) and the taxpayer and the Secretary or his delegate have not agreed to such extension.

(3) JUDICIAL PROCEEDINGS.—In the case of any proceeding in a Federal court or the United States Tax Court involving a proposed adjustment under paragraph (1), the Native Corporation, subject to the rules of such court, may file an amicus brief concerning such adjustment.

(4) FAILURES.—For purposes of the 1986 Code, any failure by the Secretary of the Treasury or his delegate to comply with the provisions of this subsection shall not affect the validity of the determination of the Internal Revenue Service of any adjustment of tax liability of any taxpayer described in paragraph (1).

(d) DISQUALIFIED INCOME DEFINED.—For purposes of subsection (a), the term "disqualified income" means any income assigned (or attributable to property contributed) after April 26, 1988, by a person who is not a Native Corporation or a corporation all the stock of which is owned directly by a Native Corporation.

(e) BASIS DETERMINATION.—For purposes of determining basis for Federal tax purposes, no provision in any law (whether enacted before, on, or after the date of the enactment of this Act) shall affect the date on which the transfer to the Native Corporation is made. The preceding sentence shall apply to all taxable years whether beginning before, on, or after such date of enactment.

- **1988, Family Support Act of 1988 (P.L. 100-485)**

P.L. 100-485, § 701(b)(2)(B):

Amended Code Sec. 6103(p)(3)(A) and (4) by striking "(10), (11), or (12)" each place it appears and inserting "(10), or (11)". **Effective**, generally, 10-13-88. However, for a special rule, see Act Sec. 701(b)(3)(B), below.

P.L. 100-485, § 701(b)(3)(B), provides:

(B) SPECIAL RULE.—Nothing in section 2653(c) of the Deficit Reduction Act of 1984 shall be construed to limit the application of paragraph (10) of section 6103(l) of the Internal Revenue Code of 1986 (as amended by this subsection).

- **1986, Congressional Reports Elimination act of 1986 (P.L. 99-386)**

P.L. 99-386, § 206(b):

Amended Code Sec. 6103(p)(5) by striking out "quarter" and inserting in lieu thereof "year". **Effective** 8-22-86.

- **1986 (P.L. 99-335)**

P.L. 99-335, § 310(b)(1):

Amended Code Sec. 6103(p)(3)(A) by striking out "(10), or (11)" and inserting in lieu thereof "(10), (11), or (12)". **Effective** 6-6-86.

P.L. 99-335, § 310(b)(2)(A) and (B):

Amended Code Sec 6103(p)(4) by striking out "(10), or (11)" in the material preceding subparagraph (A) and inserting in lieu thereof "(10), (11), or (12)", and by striking out "(10), or (11)" in subparagraph (F)(ii) and inserting in lieu thereof "(10), (11), or (12)". **Effective** 6-6-86.

- **1984, Child Support Enforcement Amendments of 1984 (P.L. 98-378)**

P.L. 98-378, § 21(f)(2):

Amended, Code Sec. 6103(p)(3)(A) by striking out "or (10)" and inserting in lieu thereof "(10), or (11)". **Effective** with respect to refunds payable under Code Sec. 6402 after 12-31-85.

P.L. 98-378, § 21(f)(3):

Amended Code Sec. 6103(p)(4) by striking out "or (10)" and inserting in lieu thereof "(10), or (11)". **Effective** with respect to refunds payable under Code Sec. 6402 after 12-31-85.

P.L. 98-378, § 21(f)(4):

Amended Code Sec. 6103(p)(4)(F)(ii) by striking out "or (10)" and inserting in lieu thereof "(10), or (11)". **Effective** with respect to refunds payable under Code Sec. 6402 after 12-31-85.

- **1984, Deficit Reduction Act of 1984 (P.L. 98-369)**

P.L. 98-369, § 453(b)(1):

Amended Code Sec. 6103(p)(3)(A) by striking out "(5), or (7)" and inserting in lieu thereof "(5), (7), (8), or (9)". **Effective** on the first day of the first calendar month which begins more than 90 days after 7-18-84.

P.L. 98-369, § 453(b)(2):

Amended Code Sec. 6103(p)(4) by striking out, in the material preceding subparagraph (A), "or 7" and inserting in lieu thereof "(7), (8), or (9)". **Effective** on the first day of the first calendar month which begins more than 90 days after 7-18-84.

P.L. 98-369, § 453(b)(3):

Amended Code Sec. 6103(p)(4)(F)(i) by striking out "(l)(6) or (7)" and inserting in lieu thereof "(l)(6), (7), (8), or (9)". **Effective** on the first day of the first calendar month which begins more than 90 days after 7-18-84.

P.L. 98-369, § 2653(b)(3)(B)(i):

Amended Code Sec. 6103(p)(3)(A) as so amended by striking out "or (9)" and inserting in lieu thereof "(9), or (10)". **Effective** with respect to refunds payable under section 6402 of the Internal Revenue Code of 1954 after 12-31-85, and on or before 1-10-94 [**effective** date changed by P.L. 100-485].

P.L. 98-369, § 2653(b)(3)(B)(ii):

Amended Code Sec. 6103(p)(4), as so amended, by striking out "(l)(1), (2), (3), or (5)" and inserting in lieu thereof "(l)(1), (2), (3), (5), or (10)". **Effective** with respect to refunds payable under section 6402 of the Internal Revenue Code of 1954 after 12-31-85, and on or before 1-10-94 [**effective** date changed by P.L. 100-485].

P.L. 98-369, § 2653(b)(3)(B)(iii):

Amended Code Sec. 6103(p)(4)(F)(ii) by striking out "(l)(1), (2), (3), or (5)" and inserting in lieu thereof "(l)(1), (2), (3), (5), or (10)". **Effective** with respect to refunds payable under section 6402 of the Internal Revenue Code of 1954 after 12-31-85, and on or before 1-10-94 [**effective** date changed by P.L. 100-485].

- **1983, Social Security Amendments of 1983 (P.L. 98-21)**

P.L. 98-21, § 121(c)(3)(B):

Amended Code Sec. 6103(p)(4) by inserting "(h)(6)," after "(h)(2)," in the material preceding subparagraph (A) and in subparagraph (F)(ii) thereof. **Effective** for benefits received after 12-31-83, in tax years ending after such date. The amendments made by Act Sec. 121 do not apply to any portion of a lump-sum payment of social security benefits (as defined in Code Sec. 86(d)) received after 12-31-83, if the generally applicable payment date for such portion was before 1-1-84.

- **1982, Debt Collection Act of 1982 (P.L. 97-365)**

P.L. 97-365, § 7(b)(1):

Amended Code Sec. 6103(p)(3)(C)(i) by striking out "(l)(3) or (6)" and inserting in lieu thereof "(l)(6)". **Effective** in the case of loan applications made after 9-30-82.

P.L. 97-365, § 7(b)(2):

Amended Code Sec. 6103(p)(4) by striking out "(l)(1), (2)," in the matter preceding subparagraph (A) and inserting in lieu thereof "(l)(1), (2), (3),", by striking out "(l)(3), (6)," and inserting in lieu thereof "(l)(6),", and by striking out "(l)(1), (2), or (5), or (o)(1), the commission described in subsection (l)(3)" in subparagraph (F)(ii) and inserting in lieu thereof "(l)(1), (2), (3), or (5), or (o)(1),". **Effective** in the case of loan applications made after 9-30-82.

P.L. 97-365, § 8(b):

Amended Code Sec. 6103(p)(4) by adding the last sentence. **Effective** 10-25-82.

- **1982, Tax Equity and Fiscal Responsibility Act of 1982 (P.L. 97-248)**

P.L. 97-248, § 356(b)(1):

Amended Code Sec. 6103(p) by striking out "(6)(A)(ii)" in paragraph (3)(A) and inserting "(7)(A)(ii)", by striking out "(d)" in paragraph (3)(C)(i) and inserting "(d), (i)(3)(B)(i),", by striking out "such requests" in paragraph (3)(C)(i)(II) and inserting "such requests or otherwise", by striking out "(i)(1), (2), or (5)" each place it appears in paragraph (4) and inserting "(i)(1), (2), (3), or (5)", by striking out "(d)" each place it appears in paragraph (4) and inserting "(d), (i)(3)(B)(i),", and by striking out "subsection (i)(6)(A)(ii)" in paragraph (6)(B)(i) and inserting "subsection (i)(7)(A)(ii)". **Effective** 9-4-82.

- **1980, Social Security Disability Amendments of 1980 (P.L. 96-265)**

P.L. 96-265, § 408(a)(2)(A), (B) and (C):

Amended Code Sec. 6103(p)(3)(A) by striking out "(l)(1) or (4)(B) or (5)" and substituting "(l)(1), (4)(B), (5), or (7)"; amended Code Sec. 6103(p)(4) by striking out "(l)(3) or (6)" in the first sentence and substituting "(l)(3), (6), or (7)"; and amended Code Sec. 6103(p)(4)(F)(i) by striking out "(l)(6)" and substituting "(l)(6) or (7)". **Effective** 6-9-80. These amendments duplicate prior amendments made to Code Sec. 6103(p) by P.L. 96-249, which added an earlier Code Sec. 6103(l)(7). However, due to an error in the enrollment of P.L. 96-249, the new subsection (7) was added to Code Sec. 6103(i), instead of 6103(l), even though the changes made to Code Sec. 6103(p) properly referred to Code Sec. 6103(l) as the section amended by P.L. 96-249. Thus, P.L. 96-265 added a second Code Sec. 6103(l)(7) because of this error. It is expected that technical corrections will be made, redesignating the subsection (7) added by P.L. 96-265 as subsection (8), and correcting the references contained in Code Sec. 6103(p).

- **1980, Food Stamp Act Amendments of 1980 (P.L. 96-249)**

P.L. 96-249, § 127(a)(2)(A):

Amended Code Sec. 6103(p)(3)(A) by striking out "(l)(1) or (4)(B) or (5)" and inserting in lieu thereof "(l)(1), (4)(B), (5), or (7)". **Effective** 5-26-80.

P.L. 96-249, § 127(a)(2)(B):

Amended Code Sec. 6103(p)(4) by striking out "(l)(3) or (6)" in so much of such paragraph as precedes subparagraph (A), and inserting in lieu thereof "(l)(3), (6), or (7)". **Effective** 5-26-80.

P.L. 96-249, § 127(a)(2)(C):

Amended Code Sec. 6103(p)(4)(F)(i) by striking out "(l)(6)" and inserting in lieu thereof "(l)(6) or (7)". **Effective** 5-26-80.

- **1976, Tax Reform Act of 1976 (P.L. 94-455)**

P.L. 94-455, § 1202(a):

Added Code Sec. 6103(p). **Effective** 1-1-77.

[Sec. 6103(q)]

(q) REGULATIONS.—The Secretary is authorized to prescribe such other regulations as are necessary to carry out the provisions of this section.

Amendments

- **1976, Tax Reform Act of 1976 (P.L. 94-455)**

P.L. 94-455, § 1202(a):

Added Code Sec. 6103(q). **Effective** 1-1-77.

RETURNS—MISCELLANEOUS PROVISIONS

[Sec. 6104]

SEC. 6104. PUBLICITY OF INFORMATION REQUIRED FROM CERTAIN EXEMPT ORGANIZATIONS AND CERTAIN TRUSTS.

[Sec. 6104(a)]

(a) INSPECTION OF APPLICATIONS FOR TAX EXEMPTION OR NOTICE OF STATUS.—

(1) PUBLIC INSPECTION.—

(A) ORGANIZATIONS DESCRIBED IN SECTION 501 OR 527.—If an organization described in section 501(c) or (d) is exempt from taxation under section 501(a) for any taxable year or a political organization is exempt from taxation under section 527 for any taxable year, the application filed by the organization with respect to which the Secretary made his determination that such organization was entitled to exemption under section 501(a) or notice of status filed by the organization under section 527(i), together with any papers submitted in support of such application or notice, and any letter or other document issued by the Internal Revenue Service with respect to such application or notice shall be open to public inspection at the national office of the Internal Revenue Service. In the case of any application or notice filed after the date of the enactment of this subparagraph, a copy of such application or notice and such letter or document shall be open to public inspection at the appropriate field office of the Internal Revenue Service (determined under regulations prescribed by the Secretary). Any inspection under this subparagraph may be made at such times, and in such manner, as the Secretary shall by regulations prescribe. After the application of any organization for exemption from taxation under section 501(a) has been opened to public inspection under this subparagraph, the Secretary shall, on the request of any person with respect to such organization, furnish a statement indicating the subsection and paragraph of section 501 which it has been determined describes such organization.

(B) PENSION, ETC., PLANS.—The following shall be open to public inspection at such times and in such places as the Secretary may prescribe;

(i) any application filed with respect to the qualification of a pension, profit-sharing, or stock bonus plan under section 401(a) or 403(a), an individual retirement account described in section 408(a), or an individual retirement annuity described in section 408(b),

(ii) any application filed with respect to the exemption from tax under section 501(a) of an organization forming part of a plan or account referred to in clause (i),

(iii) any papers submitted in support of an application referred to in clause (i) or (ii), and

(iv) any letter or other document issued by the Internal Revenue Service and dealing with the qualification referred to in clause (i) or the exemption from tax referred to in clause (ii).

Except in the case of a plan participant, this subparagraph shall not apply to any plan referred to in clause (i) having not more than 25 participants.

(C) CERTAIN NAMES AND COMPENSATION NOT TO BE OPENED TO PUBLIC INSPECTION.—In the case of any application, document, or other papers, referred to in subparagraph (B), information from which the compensation (including deferred compensation) of any individual may be ascertained shall not be opened to public inspection under subparagraph (B).

(D) WITHHOLDING OF CERTAIN OTHER INFORMATION.—Upon request of the organization submitting any supporting papers described in subparagraph (A) or (B), the Secretary shall withhold from public inspection any information contained therein which he determines relates to any trade secret, patent, process, style of work, or apparatus, of the organization, if he determines that public disclosure of such information would adversely affect the organization. The Secretary shall withhold from public inspection any information contained in supporting papers described in subparagraph (A) or (B) the public disclosure of which he determines would adversely affect the national defense.

(2) INSPECTION BY COMMITTEE OF CONGRESS.—Section 6103(f) shall apply with respect to—

(A) the application for exemption of any organization described in section 501(c) or (d) which is exempt from taxation under section 501(a) for any taxable year or notice of status of any political organization which is exempt from taxation under section 527 for any taxable year, and any application referred to in subparagraph (B) of subsection (a)(1) of this section, and

(B) any other papers which are in the possession of the Secretary and which relate to such application,

as if such papers constituted returns.

(3) INFORMATION AVAILABLE ON INTERNET AND IN PERSON.—

(A) IN GENERAL.—The Secretary shall make publicly available, on the Internet and at the offices of the Internal Revenue Service—

(i) a list of all political organizations which file a notice with the Secretary under section 527(i), and

(ii) the name, address, electronic mailing address, custodian of records, and contact person for such organization.

(B) TIME TO MAKE INFORMATION AVAILABLE.—The Secretary shall make available the information required under subparagraph (A) not later than 5 business days after the Secretary receives a notice from a political organization under section 527(i).

Amendments

- **2000 (P.L. 106-230)**

P.L. 106-230, § 1(b)(1)(A)(i)-(vi):

Amended Code Sec. 6104(a)(1)(A) by inserting "or a political organization is exempt from taxation under section 527 for any taxable year" after "taxable year"; by inserting "or notice of status filed by the organization under section 527(i)" before ", together"; by inserting "or notice" after "such application" each place it appeared; by inserting "or notice" after "any application"; by inserting "for exemption from taxation under section 501(a)" after "any organization" in the last sentence; and by inserting "OR 527" after "SECTION 501" in the heading. **Effective** 7-1-2000. For an exception, see Act Sec. 1(d)(2), below.

P.L. 106-230, § 1(b)(1)(B):

Amended the heading for Code Sec. 6104(a) by inserting "OR NOTICE OF STATUS" before the period. **Effective** 7-1-2000. For an exception, see Act Sec. 1(d)(2), below.

P.L. 106-230, § 1(b)(2):

Amended Code Sec. 6104(a) by adding at the end new paragraph (3). **Effective** 8-15-2000.

P.L. 106-230, § 1(b)(3):

Amended Code Sec. 6104(a)(2) by inserting "or notice of status of any political organization which is exempt from taxation under section 527 for any taxable year" after "taxable year". **Effective** 7-1-2000. For an exception, see Act Sec. 1(d)(2), below.

P.L. 106-230, § 1(d)(2), provides:

(2) ORGANIZATIONS ALREADY IN EXISTENCE.—In the case of an organization established before the date of the enactment of this section, the time to file the notice under section 527(i)(2) of the Internal Revenue Code of 1986, as added by this section, shall be 30 days after the date of the enactment of this section.

- **1984, Deficit Reduction Act of 1984 (P.L. 98-369)**

P.L. 98-369, § 491(d)(49):

Amended Code Sec. 6104(a)(B)(i) by striking out ", 403(a) or 405(a)" and inserting in lieu thereof "or 403(a)". **Effective** for obligations issued after 12-31-83.

- **1978, Revenue Act of 1978 (P.L. 95-600)**

P.L. 95-600, § 703(m):

Amended Code Sec. 6104(a)(2) by striking out "Section 6103(d)" and inserting in lieu thereof "Section 6103(f)". **Effective** 10-4-76.

- **1978 (P.L. 95-488)**

P.L. 95-488, § 1(d)(1), (e):

Amended the first sentence of Code Sec. 6104(a)(1)(A) by striking out "(other than in paragraph (21) thereof)" after "section 501(c)". **Effective** for tax years beginning after 12-31-77.

- **1978, Black Lung Benefits Revenue Act of 1977 (P.L. 95-227)**

P.L. 95-227, § 4(e)(1):

Amended Code Sec. 6104(a)(1)(A) by adding "(other than in paragraph (21) thereof)" after "section 501(c)". For **effective** date, see the historical comment for P.L. 95-227 under Code Sec. 501(c).

- **1976, Tax Reform Act of 1976 (P.L. 94-455)**

P.L. 94-455, § 1201(d):

Inserted "and any letter or other document issued by the Internal Revenue Service with respect to such application" in the first sentence and "and such letter or document" in the second sentence. **Effective** for any letter or other document issued with respect to applications filed after 10-31-76.

P.L. 94-455, §1906(b)(13)(A):

Amended 1954 Code by substituting "Secretary" for "Secretary or his delegate" each place it appeared. **Effective** 2-1-77.

- **1974, Employee Retirement Income Security Act of 1974 (P.L. 93-406)**

P.L. 93-406, §1022(g)(1), (2):

Amended Code Sec. 6104(a). **Effective** with respect to applications filed (or documents issued) after 9-2-74. Prior to amendment, Code Sec. 6104(a) read as follows:

"(a) Inspection of Applications for Tax Exemption.—

"(1) Public inspection.—

"(A) In general.—If an organization described in section 501(c) or (d) is exempt from taxation under section 501(a) for any taxable year, the application filed by the organization with respect to which the Secretary or his delegate made his determination that such organization was entitled to exemption under section 501(a), together with any papers submitted in support of such application, shall be open to public inspection at the national office of the Internal Revenue Service. In the case of any application filed after the date of the enactment of this subparagraph, a copy of such application shall be open to public inspection at the appropriate field office of the Internal Revenue Service (determined under regulations prescribed by the Secretary or his delegate). Any inspection under this subparagraph may be made at such times, and in such manner, as the Secretary or his delegate shall by regulations prescribe. After the application of any organization has been opened to public inspection under this subparagraph, the Secretary or his delegate shall, on the request of any person with respect to such organization, furnish a statement indicating the subsection and paragraph of section 501 which it has been determined describes such organization.

"(B) Withholding of certain information.—Upon request of the organization submitting any supporting papers described in subparagraph (A), the Secretary or his delegate shall withhold from public inspection any information contained therein which he determines relates to any trade secret, patent, process, style of work, or apparatus, of the organization, if he determines that public disclosure of such information would adversely affect the organization. The Secretary or his delegate shall withhold from public inspection any information contained in supporting papers described in subparagraph (A) the public disclosure of which he determines would adversely affect the national defense.

"(2) Inspection by committee of congress.—Section 6103(d) shall apply with respect to—

"(A) the application for exemption of any organization described in section 501(c) or (d) which is exempt from taxation under section 501(a) for any taxable year, and

"(B) any other papers which are in the possession of the Secretary or his delegate and which relate to such application,

as if such papers constituted returns."

[Sec. 6104(b)]

(b) INSPECTION OF ANNUAL RETURNS.—The information required to be furnished by sections 6033, 6034, and 6058, together with the names and addresses of such organizations and trusts, shall be made available to the public at such times and in such places as the Secretary may prescribe. Nothing in this subsection shall authorize the Secretary to disclose the name or address of any contributor to any organization or trust (other than a private foundation, as defined in section 509(a) or a political organization exempt from taxation under section 527) which is required to furnish such information. In the case of an organization described in section 501(d), this subsection shall not apply to copies referred to in section 6031(b) with respect to such organization. In the case of a trust which is required to file a return under section 6034(a), this subsection shall not apply to information regarding beneficiaries which are not organizations described in section 170(c). Any annual return which is filed under section 6011 by an organization described in section 501(c)(3) and which relates to any tax imposed by section 511 (relating to imposition of tax on unrelated business income of charitable, etc., organizations) shall be treated for purposes of this subsection in the same manner as if furnished under section 6033. Any annual return required to be filed electronically under section 6033(n) shall be made available by the Secretary to the public as soon as practicable in a machine readable format.

Amendments

- **2019, Taxpayer First Act (P.L. 116-25)**

P.L. 116-25, §3101(c):

Amended Code Sec. 6104(b) by adding at the end a new sentence. **Effective** generally for tax year beginning after 7-1-2019. For a transition rule, see Act Sec. 3101(d)(2), below.

P.L. 116-25, §3101(d)(2), provides:

(2) TRANSITIONAL RELIEF.—

(A) SMALL ORGANIZATIONS.—

(i) IN GENERAL.—In the case of any small organizations, or any other organizations for which the Secretary of the Treasury or the Secretary's delegate (hereafter referred to in this paragraph as the "Secretary") determines the application of the amendments made by this section would cause undue burden without a delay, the Secretary may delay the application of such amendments, but such delay shall not apply to any taxable year beginning on or after the date that is 2 years after the enactment of this Act.

(ii) SMALL ORGANIZATION.—For purposes of clause (i), the term "small organization" means any organization—

(I) the gross receipts of which for the taxable year are less than $200,000; and

(II) the aggregate gross assets of which at the end of the taxable year are less than $500,000.

(B) ORGANIZATIONS FILING FORM 990-T.—In the case of any organization described in section 511(a)(2) of the Internal Revenue Code of 1986 which is subject to the tax imposed by section 511(a)(1) of such Code on its unrelated business taxable income, or any organization required to file a return under section 6033 of such Code and include information under subsection (e) thereof, the Secretary may delay the application of the amendments made by this section, but such delay shall not apply to any taxable year beginning on or after the date that is 2 years after the enactment of this Act.

- **2007, Tax Technical Corrections Act of 2007 (P.L. 110-172)**

P.L. 110-172, §3(g)(1)(A)-(B):

Amended Code Sec. 6104(b) by striking "INFORMATION" before "RETURNS" in the heading, and by adding at the end a new sentence. **Effective** as if included in the provision of the Pension Protection Act of 2006 (P.L. 109-280) to which it relates [**effective** for returns filed after 8-17-2006.—CCH].

- **2006, Pension Protection Act of 2006 (P.L. 109-280)**

P.L. 109-280, §1201(b)(3):

Amended Code Sec. 6104(b) by adding at the end a new sentence. **Effective** for returns for tax years beginning after 12-31-2006.

- **2002 (P.L. 107-276)**

P.L. 107-276, §3(b)(1):

Amended Code Sec. 6104(b) by striking "6012(a)(6)," following "to be furnished by sections". **Effective** as if included in the amendments made by P.L. 106-230 [**effective** for returns for tax years beginning after 6-30-2000.—CCH].

- **2000 (P.L. 106-230)**

P.L. 106-230, §3(b)(1)(A):

Amended Code Sec. 6104(b) by inserting "6012(a)(6)," before "6033". **Effective** for tax years beginning after 6-30-2000.

P.L. 106-230, §3(b)(1)(B):

Amended Code Sec. 6104(b) by inserting "or a political organization exempt from taxation under section 527" after "509(a)". **Effective** for tax years beginning after 6-30-2000.

- **1998, IRS Restructuring and Reform Act of 1998 (P.L. 105-206)**

P.L. 105-206, §6019(a):

Amended Code Sec. 6104(b) by adding at the end a new sentence. **Effective** 7-22-98.

- **1980 (P.L. 96-603)**

P.L. 96-603, §1(d)(3):

Amended Code Sec. 6104(b) by striking out "6056," after "6034," in the first sentence. **Effective** for tax years beginning after 1980.

- **1978 (P.L. 95-488)**

P.L. 95-488, §1(d)(2), (e):

Amended Code Sec. 6104(b) by striking out the last sentence, which read, "This subsection shall not apply to information required to be furnished by a trust described in section 501(c).". **Effective** for tax years beginning after 12-31-77.

P.L. 95-488, §1(e), provides:

"(e) The amendments made by this section shall apply to taxable years beginning after December 31, 1977. Nothing in the amendments made by subsection (d) to section 6104 of the Internal Revenue Code of 1954 shall be construed to permit the disclosure under such section 6104 of confidential business information of contributors to any trust described in section 501(c)(21) of such Code."

- **1978, Black Lung Benefits Revenue Act of 1977 (P.L. 95-227)**

P.L. 95-227, §4(e)(2):

Added the last sentence to Code Sec. 6104(b). For **effective** date, see the historical comment for P.L. 95-227 under Code Sec. 501(c)(21).

- **1976, Tax Reform Act of 1976 (P.L. 94-455)**

P.L. 94-455, §1906(b)(13)(A):

Amended 1954 Code by substituting "Secretary" for "Secretary or his delegate" each place it appeared. **Effective** 2-1-77.

- **1974, Employee Retirement Income Security Act of 1974 (P.L. 93-406)**

P.L. 93-406, §1022(g)(3):

Amended Code Sec. 6104(b) by changing "and 6056" to "6056, and 6058". **Effective** for applications filed (or documents issued) after 9-2-74.

RETURNS—MISCELLANEOUS PROVISIONS

• **1969, Tax Reform Act of 1969 (P.L. 91-172)**

P.L. 91-172, §101(e)(1), 101(j)(36):

Amended Code Sec. 6104(b) by substituting "sections 6033, 6034, and 6056," for "sections 6033(b) and 6034," in the first sentence and by adding the last sentence. **Effective** 1-1-70.

• **1958, Technical Amendments Act of 1958 (P.L. 85-866)**

P.L. 85-866, §75(a):

Amended Code Sec. 6104. **Effective** 11-1-58. Prior to amendment, Code Sec. 6104 read as follows:

Sec. 6104. Publicity of Information Required from Certain Exempt Organizations and Certain Trusts.

"The information required to be furnished by sections 6033(b) and 6034, together with the names and addresses of such organizations and trusts, shall be made available to the public at such times and in such places as the Secretary or his delegate may prescribe."

[Sec. 6104(c)]

(c) PUBLICATION TO STATE OFFICIALS.—

(1) GENERAL RULE FOR CHARITABLE ORGANIZATIONS.—In the case of any organization which is described in section 501(c)(3) and exempt from taxation under section 501(a), or has applied under section 508(a) for recognition as an organization described in section 501(c)(3), the Secretary at such times and in such manner as he may by regulations prescribe shall—

(A) notify the appropriate State officer of a refusal to recognize such organization as an organization described in section 501(c)(3), or of the operation of such organization in a manner which does not meet, or no longer meets, the requirements of its exemption,

(B) notify the appropriate State officer of the mailing of a notice of deficiency of tax imposed under section 507 or chapter 41 or 42, and

(C) at the request of such appropriate State officer, make available for inspection and copying such returns, filed statements, records, reports, and other information, relating to a determination under subparagraph (A) or (B) as are relevant to any determination under State law.

(2) DISCLOSURE OF PROPOSED ACTIONS RELATED TO CHARITABLE ORGANIZATIONS.—

(A) SPECIFIC NOTIFICATIONS.—In the case of an organization to which paragraph (1) applies, the Secretary may disclose to the appropriate State officer—

(i) a notice of proposed refusal to recognize such organization as an organization described in section 501(c)(3) or a notice of proposed revocation of such organization's recognition as an organization exempt from taxation,

(ii) the issuance of a letter of proposed deficiency of tax imposed under section 507 or chapter 41 or 42, and

(iii) the names, addresses, and taxpayer identification numbers of organizations which have applied for recognition as organizations described in section 501(c)(3).

(B) ADDITIONAL DISCLOSURES.—Returns and return information of organizations with respect to which information is disclosed under subparagraph (A) may be made available for inspection by or disclosed to an appropriate State officer.

(C) PROCEDURES FOR DISCLOSURE.—Information may be inspected or disclosed under subparagraph (A) or (B) only—

(i) upon written request by an appropriate State officer, and

(ii) for the purpose of, and only to the extent necessary in, the administration of State laws regulating such organizations.

Such information may only be inspected by or disclosed to a person other than the appropriate State officer if such person is an officer or employee of the State and is designated by the appropriate State officer to receive the returns or return information under this paragraph on behalf of the appropriate State officer.

(D) DISCLOSURES OTHER THAN BY REQUEST.—The Secretary may make available for inspection or disclose returns and return information of an organization to which paragraph (1) applies to an appropriate State officer of any State if the Secretary determines that such returns or return information may constitute evidence of noncompliance under the laws within the jurisdiction of the appropriate State officer.

(3) DISCLOSURE WITH RESPECT TO CERTAIN OTHER EXEMPT ORGANIZATIONS.—Upon written request by an appropriate State officer, the Secretary may make available for inspection or disclosure returns and return information of any organization described in section 501(c) (other than organizations described in paragraph (1) or (3) thereof) for the purpose of, and only to the extent necessary in, the administration of State laws regulating the solicitation or administration of the charitable funds or charitable assets of such organizations. Such information may only be inspected by or disclosed to a person other than the appropriate State officer if such person is an officer or employee of the State and is designated by the appropriate State officer to receive the returns or return information under this paragraph on behalf of the appropriate State officer.

(4) USE IN CIVIL JUDICIAL AND ADMINISTRATIVE PROCEEDINGS.—Returns and return information disclosed pursuant to this subsection may be disclosed in civil administrative and civil judicial proceedings pertaining to the enforcement of State laws regulating such organizations in a manner prescribed by the Secretary similar to that for tax administration proceedings under section 6103(h)(4).

(5) NO DISCLOSURE IF IMPAIRMENT.—Returns and return information shall not be disclosed under this subsection, or in any proceeding described in paragraph (4), to the extent that the Secretary determines that such disclosure would seriously impair Federal tax administration.

(6) DEFINITIONS.—For purposes of this subsection—

(A) RETURN AND RETURN INFORMATION.—The terms "return" and "return information" have the respective meanings given to such terms by section 6103(b).

(B) APPROPRIATE STATE OFFICER.—The term "appropriate State officer" means—

(i) the State attorney general,

(ii) the State tax officer,

(iii) in the case of an organization to which paragraph (1) applies, any other State official charged with overseeing organizations of the type described in section 501(c)(3), and

(iv) in the case of an organization to which paragraph (3) applies, the head of an agency designated by the State attorney general as having primary responsibility for overseeing the solicitation of funds for charitable purposes.

Amendments

• **2006, Pension Protection Act of 2006 (P.L. 109-280)**

P.L. 109-280, §1224(a):

Amended Code Sec. 6104(c) by striking paragraph (2) and inserting new paragraphs (2)-(6). **Effective** 8-17-2006 but shall not apply to requests made before such date. Prior to being stricken, Code Sec. 6104(c)(2) read as follows:

(2) APPROPRIATE STATE OFFICER.—For purposes of this subsection, the term "appropriate State officer" means the State attorney general, State tax officer, or any State official charged with overseeing organizations of the type described in section 501(c)(3).

P.L. 109-280, §1224(b)(4):

Amended the heading for Code Sec. 6104(c)(1) by inserting "FOR CHARITABLE ORGANIZATIONS" after "RULE". **Effective** 8-17-2006 but shall not apply to requests made before such date.

• **1976, Tax Reform Act of 1976 (P.L. 94-455)**

P.L. 94-455, §1307(d):

Substituted "chapter 41 or 42" for "chapter 42" in Code Sec. 6104(c)(1)(B). **Effective** for tax years beginning after 12-31-76.

P.L. 94-455, §1906(b)(13)(A):

Amended 1954 Code by substituting "Secretary" for "Secretary or his delegate" each place it appeared. **Effective** 2-1-77.

• **1969, Tax Reform Act of 1969 (P.L. 91-172)**

P.L. 91-172, §101(e)(2):

Added Code Sec. 6104(c). **Effective** 1-1-70.

[Sec. 6104(d)]

(d) PUBLIC INSPECTION OF CERTAIN ANNUAL RETURNS, REPORTS, APPLICATIONS FOR EXEMPTION, AND NOTICES OF STATUS.—

(1) IN GENERAL.—In the case of an organization described in subsection (c) or (d) of section 501 and exempt from taxation under section 501(a) or an organization exempt from taxation under section 527(a)—

(A) a copy of—

(i) the annual return filed under section 6033 (relating to returns by exempt organizations) by such organization,

(ii) any annual return which is filed under section 6011 by an organization described in section 501(c)(3) and which relates to any tax imposed by section 511 (relating to imposition of tax on unrelated business income of charitable, etc., organizations),

(iii) if the organization filed an application for recognition of exemption under section 501 or notice of status under section 527(i), the exempt status application materials or any notice materials of such organization, and

(iv) the reports filed under section 527(j) (relating to required disclosure of expenditures and contributions) by such organization,

shall be made available by such organization for inspection during regular business hours by any individual at the principal office of such organization and, if such organization regularly maintains 1 or more regional or district offices having 3 or more employees, at each such regional or district office, and

(B) upon request of an individual made at such principal office or such a regional or district office, a copy of such annual return, reports, and exempt status application materials or such notice materials shall be provided to such individual without charge other than a reasonable fee for any reproduction and mailing costs.

The request described in subparagraph (B) must be made in person or in writing. If such request is made in person, such copy shall be provided immediately and, if made in writing, shall be provided within 30 days.

(2) 3-YEAR LIMITATION ON INSPECTION OF RETURNS.—Paragraph (1) shall apply to an annual return filed under section 6011 or 6033 only during the 3-year period beginning on the last day prescribed for filing such return (determined with regard to any extension of time for filing).

(3) EXCEPTIONS FROM DISCLOSURE REQUIREMENT.—

(A) NONDISCLOSURE OF CONTRIBUTORS, ETC.—In the case of an organization which is not a private foundation (within the meaning of section 509(a)) or a political organization exempt from taxation under section 527, paragraph (1) shall not require the disclosure of the name or address of any contributor to the organization. In the case of an organization described in section 501(d), paragraph (1) shall not require the disclosure of the copies referred to in section 6031(b) with respect to such organization.

(B) NONDISCLOSURE OF CERTAIN OTHER INFORMATION.—Paragraph (1) shall not require the disclosure of any information if the Secretary withheld such information from public inspection under subsection (a)(1)(D).

(4) LIMITATION ON PROVIDING COPIES.—Paragraph (1)(B) shall not apply to any request if, in accordance with regulations promulgated by the Secretary, the organization has made the requested documents widely available, or the Secretary determines, upon application by an organization, that such request is part of a harassment campaign and that compliance with such request is not in the public interest.

(5) EXEMPT STATUS APPLICATION MATERIALS.—For purposes of paragraph (1), the term "exempt status application materials" means the application for recognition of exemption under section 501 and any papers submitted in support of such application and any letter or other document issued by the Internal Revenue Service with respect to such application.

(6) NOTICE MATERIALS.—For purposes of paragraph (1), the term "notice materials" means the notice of status filed under section 527(i) and any papers submitted in support of such notice and any letter or other document issued by the Internal Revenue Service with respect to such notice.

(7) DISCLOSURE OF REPORTS BY INTERNAL REVENUE SERVICE.—Any report filed by an organization under section 527(j) (relating to required disclosure of expenditures and contributions) shall be made available to the public at such times and in such places as the Secretary may prescribe.

(8) APPLICATION TO NONEXEMPT CHARITABLE TRUSTS AND NONEXEMPT PRIVATE FOUNDATIONS.—The organizations referred to in paragraphs (1) and (2) of section 6033(d) shall comply with the requirements of this subsection relating to annual returns filed under section 6033 in the same manner as the organizations referred to in paragraph (1).

Amendments

• **2014, Tax Technical Corrections Act of 2014 (P.L. 113-295)**

P.L. 113-295, §220(v), Division A:

Amended Code Sec. 6104(d) by redesignating the second paragraph (6) (relating to disclosure of reports by the Internal Revenue Service) and third paragraph (6) (relating to application to nonexempt charitable trusts and nonexempt private foundations) as paragraphs (7) and (8), respectively. **Effective** 12-19-2014.

• **2007, Tax Technical Corrections Act of 2007 (P.L. 110-172)**

P.L. 110-172, §3(g)(2):

Amended Code Sec. 6104(d)(1)(A)(ii). **Effective** as if included in the provision of the Pension Protection Act of 2006 (P.L. 109-280) to which it relates [effective for returns filed after 8-17-2006.—CCH]. Prior to amendment, Code Sec. 6104(d)(1)(A)(ii) read as follows:

(ii) any annual return filed under section 6011 which relates to any tax imposed by section 511 (relating to imposition of tax on unrelated business income of charitable, etc., organizations) by such organization, but only if such organization is described in section 501(c)(3),

P.L. 110-172, §3(g)(3):

Amended Code Sec. 6104(d)(2) by striking "section 6033" and inserting "section 6011 or 6033". **Effective** as if included in the provision of the Pension Protection Act of 2006 (P.L. 109-280) to which it relates [effective for returns filed after 8-17-2006.—CCH]

• **2006, Pension Protection Act of 2006 (P.L. 109-280)**

P.L. 109-280, §1225(a):

Amended Code Sec. 6104(d)(1)(A) by redesignating clauses (ii) and (iii) as clauses (iii) and (iv), respectively, and by inserting after clause (i) a new clause (ii). **Effective** for returns filed after 8-17-2006.

• **2002 (P.L. 107-276)**

P.L. 107-276, §3(b)(2)(A)-(B):

Amended Code Sec. 6104(d) in paragraph (1)(A)(i) by striking "or section 6012(a)(6) (relating to returns by political organizations)" following "by exempt organizations)", and in subparagraph [paragraph](2) by striking "or section 6012(a)(6)" following "section 6033". **Effective** as if included in the amendments made by P.L. 106-230 [effective for returns for tax years beginning after 6-30-2000.—CCH].

P.L. 107-276, §7, provides:

SEC. 7. EFFECT OF AMENDMENTS ON EXISTING DISCLOSURES.

Notices, reports, or returns that were required to be filed with the Secretary of the Treasury before the date of the enactment of the amendments made by this Act and that were disclosed by the Secretary of the Treasury consistent with the law in effect at the time of disclosure shall remain subject on and after such date to the disclosure provisions of section 6104 of the Internal Revenue Code of 1986.

• **2000, Community Renewal Tax Relief Act of 2000 (P.L. 106-554)**

P.L. 106-554, §312(a):

Amended Code Sec. 6104(d) by adding at the end a new paragraph (6)[(8)]. **Effective** as if included in the provision of P.L. 105-277 to which it relates [effective for requests made after the later of 12-31-98, or the 60th day after the Treasury first issues the regulations referred to in Code Sec. 6104(d)(4).—CCH].

• **2000 (P.L. 106-230)**

P.L. 106-230, §1(b)(4)(A)-(D):

Amended Code Sec. 6104(d) by striking "AND APPLICATIONS FOR EXEMPTION" and inserting ", APPLICATIONS FOR EXEMPTION, AND NOTICES OF STATUS" in the heading; by inserting "or notice of status under section 527(i)" after "section 501" and by inserting "or any notice materials" after "materials" in paragraph (1)(A)(ii); by inserting "or

RETURNS—MISCELLANEOUS PROVISIONS

such notice materials" after "materials" in paragraph (1)(B); and by adding at the end a new paragraph (6). **Effective** 7-1-2000. For an exception, see Act Sec. 1(d)(2), below.

P.L. 106-230, § 1(d)(2), provides:

(2) ORGANIZATIONS ALREADY IN EXISTENCE.—In the case of an organization established before the date of the enactment of this section, the time to file the notice under section 527(i)(2) of the Internal Revenue Code of 1986, as added by this section, shall be 30 days after the date of the enactment of this section.

P.L. 106-230, § 2(b)(1)(A)-(C):

Amended Code Sec. 6104(d), as amended by Act Sec. 1(b)(4), by inserting "REPORTS," after "RETURNS," in the heading; by striking "and" at the end of clause (i), by inserting "and" at the end of clause (ii), and by inserting after clause (ii) a new clause (iii) in paragraph (1)(A); and by inserting ", reports," after "return" in paragraph (1)(B). **Effective** 7-1-2000.

P.L. 106-230, § 2(b)(2):

Amended Code Sec. 6104(d)(3)(A) by inserting "or a political organization exempt from taxation under section 527" after "509(a))". **Effective** 7-1-2000.

P.L. 106-230, § 2(b)(3):

Amended Code Sec. 6104(d) by adding at the end new paragraph (6)[(7)]. **Effective** 7-1-2000.

P.L. 106-230, § 3(b)(2)(A):

Amended Code Sec. 6104(d)(1)(A)(i) by inserting "or section 6012(a)(6) (relating to returns by political organizations)" after "organizations)". **Effective** for tax years beginning after 6-30-2000.

P.L. 106-230, § 3(b)(2)(B)(i):

Amended Code Sec. 6104(d)(1) in the matter preceding subparagraph (A) by inserting "or an organization exempt from taxation under section 527(a)" after "501(a)". **Effective** for tax years beginning after 6-30-2000.

P.L. 106-230, § 3(b)(2)(B)(ii):

Amended Code Sec. 6104(d)(2) by inserting "or section 6012(a)(6)" after "section 6033". **Effective** for tax years beginning after 6-30-2000.

• **1998, Tax and Trade Relief Extension Act of 1998 (P.L. 105-277)**

P.L. 105-277, § 1004(b)(1):

Amended Code Sec. 6104 by striking subsection (d) and inserting after subsection (c) a new subsection (d). **Effective**, generally, for requests made after the later of 12-31-98, or the 60th day after the Secretary of the Treasury first issues the regulations referred to in Code Sec. 6104(d)(4), as amended by Act Sec. 1004. For an exception, see Act Sec. 1004(b)(3)(B), below. Prior to being stricken, Code Sec. 6104(d) read as follows:

(d) PUBLIC INSPECTION OF PRIVATE FOUNDATIONS' ANNUAL RETURNS.—The annual return required to be filed under section 6033 (relating to returns by exempt organizations) by any organization which is a private foundation within the meaning of section 509(a) shall be made available by the foundation managers for inspection at the principal office of the foundation during regular business hours by any citizen on request made within 180 days after the date of the publication of notice of its availability. Such notice shall be published, not later than the day prescribed for filing such annual return (determined with regard to any extension of time for filing), in a newspaper having general circulation in the county in which the principal office of the private foundation is located. The notice shall state that the annual return of the private foundation is available at its principal office for inspection during regular business hours by any citizen who requests it within 180 days after the date of such publication, and shall state the address and the telephone number of the private foundation's principal office and the name of its principal manager.

P.L. 105-277, § 1004(b)(3)(B), provides:

(B) PUBLICATION OF ANNUAL RETURNS.—Section 6104(d) of such Code, as in effect before the amendments made by this subsection, shall not apply to any return the due date for which is after the date such amendments take effect under subparagraph (A).

• **1984, Deficit Reduction Act of 1984 (P.L. 98-369)**

P.L. 98-369, § 306(b):

Amended Code Sec. 6104(d) by striking out "shall state the address of the private foundation's principal office" and inserting in lieu thereof "shall state the address and the telephone number of the private foundation's principal office". **Effective** 1-1-85.

• **1980 (P.L. 96-603)**

P.L. 96-603, § 1(b):

Amended the first sentence of Code Sec. 6104(d), substituted "ANNUAL RETURNS" for "ANNUAL REPORTS" in the title of subsection (d), and substituted "annual return" for "annual report" each place it appeared in sentences two and three of subsection (d). **Effective** for tax years beginning after 1980. Prior to amendment, the first sentence of Code Sec. 6104(d) provided:

"The annual report required to be filed under section 6056 (relating to annual reports by private foundations) shall be made available by the foundation managers for inspection at the principal office of the foundation during regular business hours by any citizen on request made within 180 days after the publication of notice of its availability."

• **1969, Tax Reform Act of 1969 (P.L. 91-172)**

P.L. 91-172, § 101(e)(3):

Added Code Sec. 6104(d). **Effective** 1-1-70.

[Sec. 6104(e)—Stricken]

Amendments

• **1998, Tax and Trade Relief Extension Act of 1998 (P.L. 105-277)**

P.L. 105-277, § 1004(b)(1):

Amended Code Sec. 6104 by striking subsection (e). **Effective**, generally, for requests made after the later of 12-31-98, or the 60th day after the Secretary of the Treasury first issues the regulations referred to in Code Sec. 6104(d)(4), as amended by Act Sec. 1004. For an exception, see Act Sec. 1004(b)(3)(B), below. Prior to being stricken, Code Sec. 6104(e) read as follows:

(e) PUBLIC INSPECTION OF CERTAIN ANNUAL RETURNS AND APPLICATIONS FOR EXEMPTION.—

(1) ANNUAL RETURNS.—

(A) IN GENERAL.—During the 3-year period beginning on the filing date—

(i) a copy of the annual return filed under section 6033 (relating to returns by exempt organizations) by any organization to which this paragraph applies shall be made available by such organization for inspection during regular business hours by any individual at the principal office of such organization and, if such organization regularly maintains 1 or more regional or district offices having 3 or more employees, at each such regional or district office, and

(ii) upon request of an individual made at such principal office or such a regional or district office, a copy of such annual return shall be provided to such individual without charge other than a reasonable fee for any reproduction and mailing costs. The request described in clause (ii) must be made in person or in writing. If the request under clause (ii) is made in person, such copy shall be provided immediately and, if made in writing, shall be provided within 30 days.

(B) ORGANIZATIONS TO WHICH PARAGRAPH APPLIES.—This paragraph shall apply to any organization which—

(i) is described in subsection (c) or (d) of section 501 and exempt from taxation under section 501(a), and

(ii) is not a private foundation (within the meaning of section 509(a).

(C) NONDISCLOSURE OF CONTRIBUTORS.—Subparagraph (A) shall not require the disclosure of the name or address of any contributor to the organization. In the case of an organization described in section 501(d), subparagraph (A) shall not require the disclosure of the copies referred to in section 6031(b) with respect to such organization.

(D) FILING DATE.—For purposes of subparagraph (A), the term "filing date" means the last day prescribed for filing the return under section 6033 (determined with regard to any extension of time for filing).

(2) APPLICATION FOR EXEMPTION.—

(A) IN GENERAL.—If—

(i) an organization described in subsection (c) or (d) of section 501 is exempt from taxation under section 501(a), and

(ii) such organization filed an application for recognition of exemption under section 501, a copy of such application (together with a copy of any papers submitted in support of such application and any letter or other document issued by the Internal Revenue Service with respect to such application) shall be made available by the organization for inspection during regular business hours by any individual at the principal office of the organization and, if the organization regularly maintains 1 or more regional or [or] district offices having 3 or more employees, at each such regional or district office (and, upon request of an individual made at such principal office or such a regional or district office, a copy of the material requested to be available for inspection under this subparagraph shall be provided (in accordance with the last sentence of paragraph (1)(A)) to such individual without charge other than reasonable fee for any reproduction and mailing costs).

(B) NONDISCLOSURE OF CERTAIN INFORMATION.—Subparagraph (A) shall not require the disclosure of any information if the Secretary withheld such information from public inspection under subsection (a)(1)(D).

(3) LIMITATION.—Paragraph (1)(A)(ii) (and the corresponding provision of paragraph (2)) shall not apply to any request if, in accordance with regulations promulgated by the Secretary, the organization has made the requested documents widely available, or, the Secretary determines, upon application by an organization, that such request is part of a harassment campaign and that compliance with such request is not in the public interest.

P.L. 105-277, § 1004(b)(3)(B), provides:

(B) PUBLICATION OF ANNUAL RETURNS.—Section 6104(d) of such Code, as in effect before the amendments made by this subsection, shall not apply to any return the due date for which is after the date such amendments take effect under subparagraph (A).

• **1998, IRS Restructuring and Reform Act of 1998 (P.L. 105-206)**

P.L. 105-206, § 6019(b):

Amended Code Sec. 6104(e)(1)(C) by adding at the end a new sentence. **Effective** 7-22-98.

• **1996, Taxpayer Bill of Rights 2 (P.L. 104-168)**

P.L. 104-168, § 1313(a)(1):

Amended Code Sec. 6104(e)(1)(A). **Effective** for requests made on or after the 60th day after the Secretary of the Treasury first issues the regulations referred to [in] Code Sec. 6104(e)(3) of the Internal Revenue Code of 1986. Prior to amendment, Code Sec. 6104(e)(1)(A) read as follows:

(A) IN GENERAL.—During the 3-year period beginning on the filing date, a copy of the annual return filed under section 6033 (relating to returns by exempt organizations) by any organization to which this paragraph applies shall be made available by such organization for inspection during regular business hours by any individual at the principal office of the organization and, if such organization regularly maintains 1 or more regional or district offices having 3 or more employees, at each such regional or district office.

RETURNS—MISCELLANEOUS PROVISIONS

P.L. 104-168, § 1313(a)(2):

Amended Code Sec. 6104(e)(2)(A)(ii) by inserting before the period at the end "(and, upon request of an individual made at such principal office or such a regional or district office, a copy of the material requested to be available for inspection under this subparagraph shall be provided (in accordance with the last sentence of paragraph (1)(A)) to such individual without charge other than reasonable fee for and reproduction and mailing costs)". **Effective** for requests made on or after the 60th day after the Secretary of the Treasury first issues the regulations referred to [in] Code Sec. 6104(e)(3) of the Internal Revenue Code of 1986.

P.L. 104-168, § 1313(a)(3):

Amended Code Sec. 6104(e) by adding at the end a new paragraph (3). **Effective** for requests made on or after the 60th day after the Secretary of the Treasury first issues the regulations referred to [in] Code Sec. 6104(e)(3) of the Internal Revenue Code of 1986.

• **1987, Revenue Act of 1987 (P.L. 100-203)**

P.L. 100-203, § 10702(a):

Amended Code Sec. 6104 by adding at the end thereof a new subsection (e). For the **effective** date, see Act Sec. 10702(b), below.

P.L. 100-203, § 10702(b), provides:

(b) EFFECTIVE DATE.—The amendment made by subsection (a) shall apply—

(1) to returns for years beginning after Deember 31, 1986, and

(2) on and after the 30th day after the date of the enactment of this Act in the case of applications submitted to the Internal Revenue Service—

(A) after July 15, 1987, or

(B) on or before July 15, 1987, if the organization has a copy of the application on July 15, 1987.

[Sec. 6105]

SEC. 6105. CONFIDENTIALITY OF INFORMATION ARISING UNDER TREATY OBLIGATIONS.

[Sec. 6105(a)]

(a) IN GENERAL.—Tax convention information shall not be disclosed.

[Sec. 6105(b)]

(b) EXCEPTIONS.—Subsection (a) shall not apply—

(1) to the disclosure of tax convention information to persons or authorities (including courts and administrative bodies) which are entitled to such disclosure pursuant to a tax convention,

(2) to any generally applicable procedural rules regarding applications for relief under a tax convention,

(3) to the disclosure of tax convention information on the same terms as return information may be disclosed under paragraph (3)(C) or (7) of section 6103(i), except that in the case of tax convention information provided by a foreign government, no disclosure may be made under this paragraph without the written consent of the foreign government, or

(4) in any case not described in paragraph (1), (2), or (3), to the disclosure of any tax convention information not relating to a particular taxpayer if the Secretary determines, after consultation with each other party to the tax convention, that such disclosure would not impair tax administration.

Amendments

• **2002, Victims of Terrorism Tax Relief Act of 2001 (P.L. 107-134)**

P.L. 107-134, § 201(c)(9)(A)-(D):

Amended Code Sec. 6105(b) by striking "or" at the end of paragraph (2); by striking "paragraphs (1) or (2)" in paragraph (3) and inserting "paragraph (1), (2), or (3)"; by redesignating paragraph (3) as paragraph (4); and by inserting after paragraph (2) a new paragraph (3). **Effective** for disclosures made on or after 1-23-2002.

[Sec. 6105(c)]

(c) DEFINITIONS.—For purposes of this section—

(1) TAX CONVENTION INFORMATION.—The term "tax convention information" means any—

(A) agreement entered into with the competent authority of one or more foreign governments pursuant to a tax convention,

(B) application for relief under a tax convention,

(C) background information related to such agreement or application,

(D) document implementing such agreement, and

(E) other information exchanged pursuant to a tax convention which is treated as con-fidential or secret under the tax convention.

(2) TAX CONVENTION.—The term "tax convention" means—

(A) any income tax or gift and estate tax convention, or

(B) any other convention or bilateral agreement (including multilateral conventions and agreements and any agreement with a possession of the United States) providing for the avoidance of double taxation, the prevention of fiscal evasion, nondiscrimination with respect to taxes, the exchange of tax relevant information with the United States, or mutual assistance in tax matters.

Amendments

• **2002, Job Creation and Worker Assistance Act of 2002 (P.L. 107-147)**

P.L. 107-147, § 417(18):

Amended Code Sec. 6105(c)(1) by striking "any" preceding "background" in subparagraph (C) and by striking "any" preceding "other information" in subparagraph (E). **Effective** 3-9-2002.

[Sec. 6105(d)]

(d) CROSS REFERENCES.—

For penalties for the unauthorized disclosure of tax convention information which is return or return information, see sections 7213, 7213A, and 7431.

Amendments

• **2000, Community Renewal Tax Relief Act of 2000 (P.L. 106-554)**

P.L. 106-554, § 304(b)(1):

Amended subchapter B of chapter 61 by inserting after Code Sec. 6104 a new Code Sec. 6105. **Effective** 12-21-2000.

[Sec. 6106—Repealed]

Amendments

• **1976, Tax Reform Act of 1976 (P.L. 94-455)**

P.L. 94-455, § 1202(h):

Repealed Code Sec. 6106. **Effective** 1-1-77. Prior to repeal, Code Sec. 6106 read as follows:

SEC. 6106. PUBLICITY OF UNEMPLOYMENT TAX RETURNS.

Returns filed with respect to the tax imposed by chapter 23 shall be open to inspection in the same manner, to the same extent, and subject to the same provisions of law, including penalties, as returns described in section 6103, except that paragraph (2) of subsections (a) and (b) of section 6103 and section 7213(a)(2) shall not apply.

RETURNS—MISCELLANEOUS PROVISIONS

[Sec. 6107]

SEC. 6107. TAX RETURN PREPARER MUST FURNISH COPY OF RETURN TO TAXPAYER AND MUST RETAIN A COPY OR LIST.

[Sec. 6107(a)]

(a) FURNISHING COPY TO TAXPAYER.—Any person who is a tax return preparer with respect to any return or claim for refund shall furnish a completed copy of such return or claim to the taxpayer not later than the time such return or claim is presented for such taxpayer's signature.

Amendments

• 2007, Small Business and Work Opportunity Tax Act of 2007 (P.L. 110-28)

P.L. 110-28, §8246(a)(2)(C)(i)(I):

Amended Code Sec. 6107 by striking "INCOME TAX RETURN PREPARER" in the heading and inserting "TAX RETURN PREPARER". **Effective** for returns prepared after 5-25-2007.

P.L. 110-28, §8246(a)(2)(C)(i)(II):

Amended Code Sec. 6107(a) by striking "an income tax return preparer" each place it appears and inserting "a tax return preparer". **Effective** for returns prepared after 5-25-2007.

[Sec. 6107(b)]

(b) COPY OR LIST TO BE RETAINED BY TAX RETURN PREPARER.—Any person who is a tax return preparer with respect to a return or claim for refund shall, for the period ending 3 years after the close of the return period—

(1) retain a completed copy of such return or claim, or retain, on a list, the name and taxpayer identification number of the taxpayer for whom such return or claim was prepared, and

(2) make such copy or list available for inspection upon request by the Secretary.

Amendments

• 2007, Small Business and Work Opportunity Tax Act of 2007 (P.L. 110-28)

P.L. 110-28, §8246(a)(2)(C)(i)(II)-(III):

Amended Code Sec. 6107(b) by striking "an income tax return preparer" each place it appears and inserting "a tax return preparer", and by striking "INCOME TAX RETURN PREPARER" in the heading and inserting "TAX RETURN PREPARER". **Effective** for returns prepared after 5-25-2007.

[Sec. 6107(c)]

(c) REGULATIONS.—The Secretary shall prescribe regulations under which, in cases where 2 or more persons are tax return preparers with respect to the same return or claim for refund, compliance with the requirements of subsection (a) or (b), as the case may be, of one such person shall be deemed to be compliance with the requirements of such subsection by the other persons.

Amendments

• 2007, Small Business and Work Opportunity Tax Act of 2007 (P.L. 110-28)

P.L. 110-28, §8246(a)(2)(C)(i)(IV):

Amended Code Sec. 6107(c) by striking "income tax return preparers" and inserting "tax return preparers". **Effective** for returns prepared after 5-25-2007.

[Sec. 6107(d)]

(d) DEFINITIONS.—For purposes of this section, the terms "return" and "claim for refund" have the respective meanings given to such terms by section 6696(e), and the term "return period" has the meaning given to such term by section 6060(c).

Amendments

• 1976, Tax Reform Act of 1976 (P.L. 94-455)

P.L. 94-455, §1203(c):

Added Code Sec. 6107. **Effective** for documents prepared after 12-31-76.

[Sec. 6108]

SEC. 6108. STATISTICAL PUBLICATIONS AND STUDIES.

[Sec. 6108(a)]

(a) PUBLICATION OR OTHER DISCLOSURE OF STATISTICS OF INCOME.—The Secretary shall prepare and publish not less than annually statistics reasonably available with respect to the operations of the internal revenue laws, including classifications of taxpayers and of income, the amounts claimed or allowed as deductions, exemptions, and credits, and any other facts deemed pertinent and valuable.

[Sec. 6108(b)]

(b) SPECIAL STATISTICAL STUDIES.—The Secretary may, upon written request by any party or parties, make special statistical studies and compilations involving return information (as defined in section 6103(b)(2)) and furnish to such party or parties transcripts of any such special statistical study or compilation. A reasonable fee may be prescribed for the cost of the work or services performed for such party or parties.

[Sec. 6108(c)]

(c) ANONYMOUS FORM.—No publication or other disclosure of statistics or other information required or authorized by subsection (a) or special statistical study authorized by subsection (b) shall in any manner permit the statistics, study, or any information so published, furnished, or otherwise disclosed to be associated with, or otherwise identify, directly or indirectly, a particular taxpayer.

Amendments

• 1976, Tax Reform Act of 1976 (P.L. 94-455)

P.L. 94-455, §1202(b):

Amended Code Sec. 6108. **Effective** 1-1-77. Prior to amendment, Code Sec. 6108 read as follows:

"SEC. 6108. PUBLICATION OF STATISTICS OF INCOME.

"The Secretary or his delegate shall prepare and publish annually statistics reasonably available with respect to the operation of the income tax laws, including classifications of taxpayers and of income, the amounts allowed as deductions, exemptions, and credits, and any other facts deemed pertinent and valuable."

[Sec. 6108(d)]

(d) STATISTICAL SUPPORT FOR NATIONAL TAXPAYER ADVOCATE.—Upon request of the National Taxpayer Advocate, the Secretary shall, to the extent practicable, provide the National Taxpayer Advocate with statistical support in connection with the preparation by the National Taxpayer Advocate of the annual report described in section 7803(c)(2)(B)(ii). Such statistical support shall include statistical studies, compilations, and the review of information provided by the National Taxpayer Advocate for statistical validity and sound statistical methodology.

RETURNS—MISCELLANEOUS PROVISIONS

Amendments

• **2019, Taxpayer First Act (P.L. 116-25)**

P.L. 116-25, §1301(b)(3)(A):

Amended Code Sec. 6108 by adding at the end a new subsection (d). **Effective** 7-1-2019.

[Sec. 6109]

SEC. 6109. IDENTIFYING NUMBERS.

[Sec. 6109(a)]

(a) SUPPLYING OF IDENTIFYING NUMBERS.—When required by regulations prescribed by the Secretary:

(1) INCLUSION IN RETURNS.—Any person required under the authority of this title to make a return, statement, or other document shall include in such return, statement, or other document such identifying number as may be prescribed for securing proper identification of such person.

(2) FURNISHING NUMBER TO OTHER PERSONS.—Any person with respect to whom a return, statement, or other document is required under the authority of this title to be made by another person or whose identifying number is required to be shown on a return of another person shall furnish to such other person such identifying number as may be prescribed for securing his proper identification.

(3) FURNISHING NUMBER OF ANOTHER PERSON.—Any person required under the authority of this title to make a return, statement, or other document with respect to another person shall request from such other person, and shall include in any such return, statement, or other document, such identifying number as may be prescribed for securing proper identification of such other person.

(4) FURNISHING IDENTIFYING NUMBER OF TAX RETURN PREPARER.—Any return or claim for refund prepared by a tax return preparer shall bear such identifying number for securing proper identification of such preparer, his employer, or both, as may be prescribed. For purposes of this paragraph, the terms "return" and "claim for refund" have the respective meanings given to such terms by section 6696(e).

For purposes of paragraphs (1), (2), and (3), the identifying number of an individual (or his estate) shall be such individual's social security account number.

Amendments

• **2007, Small Business and Work Opportunity Tax Act of 2007 (P.L. 110-28)**

P.L. 110-28, §8246(a)(2)(D)(i)-(ii):

Amended Code Sec. 6109(a)(4) by striking "an income tax return preparer" and inserting "a tax return preparer", and by striking "INCOME RETURN PREPARER" in the heading and inserting "TAX RETURN PREPARER". **Effective** for returns prepared after 5-25-2007.

• **1998, IRS Restructuring and Reform Act of 1998 (P.L. 105-206)**

P.L. 105-206, §3710(a):

Amended the last sentence of Code Sec. 6109(a) by striking "For purposes of this subsection" and inserting "For purposes of paragraphs (1), (2), and (3)". **Effective** 7-22-98.

• **1988, Family Support Act of 1988 (P.L. 100-485)**

P.L. 100-485, §703(c)(3):

Amended Code Sec. 6109(a)(2) by striking "shall furnish" and inserting "or whose identifying number is required to be shown on a return of another person shall furnish". **Effective** for tax years beginning after 12-31-88.

• **1976, Tax Reform Act of 1976 (P.L. 94-455)**

P.L. 94-455, §1203(d):

Added paragraph (4). **Effective** for documents prepared after 12-31-76.

P.L. 94-455, §1906(b)(13)(A):

Amended 1954 Code by substituting "Secretary" for "Secretary or his delegate" each place it appeared. **Effective** 2-1-77.

[Sec. 6109(b)]

(b) LIMITATION.—

(1) Except as provided in paragraph (2), a return of any person with respect to his liability for tax, or any statement or other document in support thereof, shall not be considered for purposes of paragraphs (2) and (3) of subsection (a) as a return, statement, or other document with respect to another person.

(2) For purposes of paragraphs (2) and (3) of subsection (a), a return of an estate or trust with respect to its liability for tax, and any statement or other document in support thereof, shall be considered as a return, statement, or other document with respect to each beneficiary of such estate or trust.

[Sec. 6109(c)]

(c) REQUIREMENT OF INFORMATION.—For purposes of this section, the Secretary is authorized to require such information as may be necessary to assign an identifying number to any person.

Amendments

• **1976, Tax Reform Act of 1976 (P.L. 94-455)**

P.L. 94-455, §1906(b)(13)(A):

Amended 1954 Code by substituting "Secretary" for "Secretary or his delegate" each place it appeared. **Effective** 2-1-77.

• **1961 (P.L. 87-397)**

P.L. 87-397, §[1](a):

Added Code Sec. 6109. For the **effective** date, see P.L. 87-397, §[1](d), below.

P.L. 87-397, §[1](d):

(d) EFFECTIVE DATE.—Paragraph (1) of section 6109(a) of the Internal Revenue Code of 1954, as added by subsection (a) of this section, shall apply only in respect of returns, statements, and other documents relating to periods commencing after December 31, 1961. Paragraphs (2) and (3) of such section 6109(a) shall apply only in respect of returns, statements, or other documents relating to periods commencing after December 31, 1962.

[Sec. 6109(d)]

(d) USE OF SOCIAL SECURITY ACCOUNT NUMBER.—The social security account number issued to an individual for purposes of section 205(c)(2)(A) of the Social Security Act shall, except as shall otherwise be specified under regulations of the Secretary, be used as the identifying number for such individual for purposes of this title.

Amendments

• **1976, Tax Reform Act of 1976 (P.L. 94-455)**

P.L. 94-455, §1211(c):

Added Code Sec. 6109(d). **Effective** 10-4-76.

[Sec. 6109(e)—Repealed]

Amendments

• **1996, Small Business Job Protection Act of 1996 (P.L. 104-188)**

P.L. 104-188, §1615(a)(2)(A):

Repealed Code Sec. 6109(e). **Effective**, generally, with respect to returns the due date for which (without regard to extensions) is on or after the 30th day after 8-20-96. For a special rule, see Act Sec. 1615(d)(2), below. Prior to repeal, Code Sec. 6109(e) read as follows:

(e) FURNISHING NUMBER FOR DEPENDENTS.—Any taxpayer who claims an exemption under section 151 for any dependent on a return for any taxable year shall include on such return the identifying number (for purposes of this title) of such dependent.

P.L. 104-188, §1615(d)(2), provides:

(2) SPECIAL RULE FOR 1995 AND 1996.—In the case of returns for taxable years beginning in 1995 or 1996, a taxpayer shall not be required by the amendments made by this section to provide a taxpayer identification number for a child who is born

RETURNS—MISCELLANEOUS PROVISIONS

after October 31, 1995, in the case of a taxable year beginning in 1995 or November 30, 1996, in the case of a taxable year beginning in 1996.

- **1994, Uruguay Round Agreements Act (P.L. 103-465)**

P.L. 103-465, §742(b):

Amended Code Sec. 6109(e). **Effective** for returns for tax years beginning after 12-31-94. For exceptions, see Act Sec. 742(c)(2), below. Prior to amendment, Code Sec. 6109(e) read as follows:

(e) FURNISHING NUMBER FOR CERTAIN DEPENDENTS.—If—

(1) any taxpayer claims an exemption under section 151 for any dependent on a return for any taxable year, and

(2) such dependent has attained the age of 1 year before the close of such taxable year,

such taxpayer shall include on such return the identifying number (for purposes of this title) of such dependent.

P.L. 103-465, §742(c)(2), provides:

(2) EXCEPTION.—The amendments made by this section shall not apply to—

(A) returns for taxable years beginning in 1995 with respect to individuals who are born after October 31, 1995, and

(B) returns for taxable years beginning in 1996 with respect to individuals who are born after November 30, 1996.

- **1990, Omnibus Budget Reconciliation Act of 1990 (P.L. 101-508)**

P.L. 101-508, §11112(a):

Amended Code Sec. 6109(e)(2) by striking "2 years" and inserting "1 year". **Effective** for returns for tax years beginning after 12-31-90.

- **1988, Family Support Act of 1988 (P.L. 100-485)**

P.L. 100-485, §704(a):

Amended Code Sec. 6109(e)(2) by striking "age of 5" and inserting "age of 2". **Effective** for returns the due date for which (determined without regard to extensions) is after 12-31-89.

- **1986, Tax Reform Act of 1986 (P.L. 99-514)**

P.L. 99-514, §1524(a):

Amended Code Sec. 6109 by adding at the end thereof new subsection (e). **Effective** for returns the due date for which (determined without regard to extensions) is after 12-31-87.

[Sec. 6109(f)]

(f) ACCESS TO EMPLOYER IDENTIFICATION NUMBERS BY SECRETARY OF AGRICULTURE FOR PURPOSES OF FOOD AND NUTRITION ACT OF 2008.—

(1) IN GENERAL.—In the administration of section 9 of the Food and Nutrition Act of 2008 (7 U.S.C. 2018) involving the determination of the qualifications of applicants under such Act, the Secretary of Agriculture may, subject to this subsection, require each applicant retail store or wholesale food concern to furnish to the Secretary of Agriculture the employer identification number assigned to the store or concern pursuant to this section. The Secretary of Agriculture shall not have access to any such number for any purpose other than the establishment and maintenance of a list of the names and employer identification numbers of the stores and concerns for use in determining those applicants who have been previously sanctioned or convicted under section 12 or 15 of such Act (7 U.S.C. 2021 or 2024).

(2) SHARING OF INFORMATION AND SAFEGUARDS.—

(A) SHARING OF INFORMATION.—The Secretary of Agriculture may share any information contained in any list referred to in paragraph (1) with any other agency or instrumentality of the United States which otherwise has access to employer identification numbers in accordance with this section or other applicable Federal law, except that the Secretary of Agriculture may share such information only to the extent that such Secretary determines such sharing would assist in verifying and matching such information against information maintained by such other agency or instrumentality. Any such information shared pursuant to this subparagraph may be used by such other agency or instrumentality only for the purpose of effective administration and enforcement of the Food and Nutrition Act of 2008 or for the purpose of investigation of violations of other Federal laws or enforcement of such laws.

(B) SAFEGUARDS.—The Secretary of Agriculture, and the head of any other agency or instrumentality referred to in subparagraph (A), shall restrict, to the satisfaction of the Secretary of the Treasury, access to employer identification numbers obtained pursuant to this subsection only to officers and employees of the United States whose duties or responsibilities require access for the purposes described in subparagraph (A). The Secretary of Agriculture, and the head of any agency or instrumentality with which information is shared pursuant to subparagraph (A), shall provide such other safeguards as the Secretary of the Treasury determines to be necessary or appropriate to protect the confidentiality of the employer identification numbers.

(3) CONFIDENTIALITY AND NONDISCLOSURE RULES.—Employer identification numbers that are obtained or maintained pursuant to this subsection by the Secretary of Agriculture or the head of any agency or instrumentality with which this information is shared pursuant to paragraph (2) shall be confidential, and no officer or employee of the United States who has or had access to the employer identification numbers shall disclose any such employer identification number obtained thereby in any manner. For purposes of this paragraph, the term "officer or employee" includes a former officer or employee.

(4) SANCTIONS.—Paragraphs (1), (2), and (3) of section 7213(a) shall apply with respect to the unauthorized willful disclosure to any person of employer identification numbers maintained pursuant to this subsection by the Secretary of Agriculture or any agency or instrumentality with which information is shared pursuant to paragraph (2) in the same manner and to the same extent as such paragraphs apply with respect to unauthorized disclosures of return and return information described in such paragraphs. Paragraph (4) of section 7213(a) shall apply with respect to the willful offer of any item of material value in exchange for any such employer identification number in the same manner and to the same extent as such paragraph applies with respect to offers (in exchange for any return or return information) described in such paragraph.

Amendments

- **2018, Tax Technical Corrections Act of 2018 (P.L. 115-141)**

P.L. 115-141, §401(a)(276), Div. U:

Amended Code Sec. 6109(f) by striking "OF 1977" following "NUTRITION ACT OF 2008" in the heading thereof. **Effective** 3-23-2018.

- **2008, Food, Conservation, and Energy Act of 2008 (P.L. 110-246)**

P.L. 110-246, §4002(b)(1)(B) and (G):

Amended Code Sec. 6109(f) by striking "Food Stamp Act of 1977" each place it appears and inserting "Food and Nutrition Act of 2008"; by striking "FOOD STAMP ACT" [sic] in the heading and inserting "FOOD AND NUTRITION ACT OF 2008". **Effective** 10-1-2008.

- **1994, Social Security Independence and Program Improvements Act of 1994 (P.L. 103-296)**

P.L. 103-296, §316(b):

Amended Code Sec. 6109(f) by striking out paragraph (2) and adding a new paragraph (2), by striking out "by the Secretary of Agriculture pursuant to this subsection" and inserting "pursuant to this subsection by the Secretary of Agriculture or the head of any agency or instrumentality with which information is shared pursuant to paragraph (2)", and by striking "social security account numbers" and inserting "employer identification numbers" in paragraph (3); and by striking "by the Secretary of Agriculture pursuant to this subsection" and inserting "pursuant to this subsection by the Secretary of Agriculture or any agency or instrumentality with which information is shared pursuant to paragraph (2)" in paragraph (4). **Effective** 8-15-94. Prior to amendment, Code Sec. 6109(f)(2) read as follows:

(2) SAFEGUARDS.—The Secretary of Agriculture shall restrict, to the satisfaction of the Secretary of the Treasury, access to employer identification numbers obtained pursuant to paragraph (1) only to officers and employees of the United States whose duties or responsibilities require access for the administration or enforcement of the Food Stamp Act of 1977. The Secretary of Agriculture shall provide such other safeguards as the Secretary of the Treasury determines to be necessary or appropriate to protect the confidentiality of the employer identification numbers.

- **1990, Food, Agriculture, Conservation, and Trade Act of 1990 (P.L. 101-624)**

P.L. 101-624, §1735(c):

Amended Code Sec. 6109 by adding at the end thereof new subsection (f). **Effective** and implemented the 1st day of the month beginning 120 days after the publication of implementing regulations. Such regulations shall be promulgated not later than 10-1-91.

[Sec. 6109(g)]

(g) ACCESS TO EMPLOYER IDENTIFICATION NUMBERS BY FEDERAL CROP INSURANCE CORPORATION FOR PURPOSES OF THE FEDERAL CROP INSURANCE ACT.—

(1) IN GENERAL.—In the administration of section 506 of the Federal Crop Insurance Act, the Federal Crop Insurance Corporation may require each policyholder and each reinsured company to furnish to the insurer or to the Corporation the employer identification number of such policyholder, subject to the requirements of this paragraph. No officer or employee of the Federal Crop Insurance Corporation, or

RETURNS—MISCELLANEOUS PROVISIONS

authorized person shall have access to any such number for any purpose other than the establishment of a system of records necessary to the effective administration of such Act. The Manager of the Corporation may require each policyholder to provide to the Manager or authorized person, at such times and in such manner as prescribed by the Manager, the employer identification number of each entity that holds or acquires a substantial beneficial interest in the policyholder. For purposes of this subclause, the term "substantial beneficial interest" means not less than 5 percent of all beneficial interest in the policyholder. The Secretary of Agriculture shall restrict, to the satisfaction of the Secretary of the Treasury, access to employer identification numbers obtained pursuant to this paragraph only to officers and employees of the United States or authorized persons whose duties or responsibilities require access for the administration of the Federal Crop Insurance Act.

(2) CONFIDENTIALITY AND NONDISCLOSURE RULES.—Employer identification numbers maintained by the Secretary of Agriculture or Federal Crop Insurance Corporation pursuant to this subsection shall be confidential, and except as authorized by this subsection, no officer or employee of the United States or authorized person who has or had access to such employer identification numbers shall disclose any such employer identification number obtained thereby in any manner. For purposes of this paragraph, the term "officer or employee" includes a former officer or employee. For purposes of this subsection, the term "authorized person" means an officer or employee of an insurer whom the Manager of the Corporation designates by rule, subject to appropriate safeguards including a prohibition against the release of such social security account numbers (other than to the Corporations) by such person.

(3) SANCTIONS.—Paragraphs (1), (2), and (3) of section 7213 shall apply with respect to the unauthorized willful disclosure to any person of employer identification numbers maintained by the Secretary of Agriculture or the Federal Crop Insurance Corporation pursuant to this subsection in the same manner and to the same extent as such paragraphs apply with respect to unauthorized disclosures of return and return information described in such paragraphs. Paragraph (4) of section 7213(a) shall apply with respect to the willful offer of any item of material value in exchange for any such employer identification number in the same manner and to the same extent as such paragraph applies with respect to offers (in exchange for any return or return information) described in such paragraph.

Amendments

• **1996, Small Business Job Protection Act of 1996 (P.L. 104-188)**

P.L. 104-188, §1704(t)(42):

Amended Code Sec. 6109 by redesignating subsection (f), as added by section 2201(d) of P.L. 101-624, as subsection (g). **Effective** 8-20-96.

• **1990, Food, Agriculture, Conservation, and Trade Act of 1990 (P.L. 101-624)**

P.L. 101-624, §2201(d):

Amended Code Sec. 6109 by adding at the end thereof new subsection (f)[g]. **Effective** 11-28-90.

[Sec. 6109(h)]

(h) IDENTIFYING INFORMATION REQUIRED WITH RESPECT TO CERTAIN SELLER-PROVIDED FINANCING.—

(1) PAYOR.—If any taxpayer claims a deduction under section 163 for qualified residence interest on any seller-provided financing, such taxpayer shall include on the return claiming such deduction the name, address, and TIN of the person to whom such interest is paid or accrued.

(2) RECIPIENT.—If any person receives or accrues interest referred to in paragraph (1), such person shall include on the return for the taxable year in which such interest is so received or accrued the name, address, and TIN of the person liable for such interest.

(3) FURNISHING OF INFORMATION BETWEEN PAYOR AND RECIPIENT.—If any person is required to include the TIN of another person on a return under paragraph (1) or (2), such other person shall furnish his TIN to such person.

(4) SELLER-PROVIDED FINANCING.—For purposes of this subsection, the term "seller-provided financing" means any indebtedness incurred in acquiring any residence if the person to whom such indebtedness is owed is the person from whom such residence was acquired.

Amendments

• **1992, Energy Policy Act of 1992 (P.L. 102-486)**

P.L. 102-486, §1933(a):

Amended Code Sec. 6109 by adding at the end thereof new subsection (h). **Effective** for tax years beginning after 12-31-91.

[Sec. 6109(i)]

(i) SPECIAL RULES RELATING TO THE ISSUANCE OF ITINs.—

(1) IN GENERAL.—The Secretary is authorized to issue an individual taxpayer identification number to an individual only if the applicant submits an application, using such form as the Secretary may require and including the required documentation—

(A) in the case of an applicant not described in subparagraph (B)—

(i) in person to an employee of the Internal Revenue Service or a community-based certifying acceptance agent approved by the Secretary, or

(ii) by mail, pursuant to rules prescribed by the Secretary, or

(B) in the case of an applicant who resides outside of the United States, by mail or in person to an employee of the Internal Revenue Service, a community-based certifying acceptance agent approved by the Secretary, or a designee of the Secretary at a United States diplomatic mission or consular post.

(2) REQUIRED DOCUMENTATION.—For purposes of this subsection—

(A) IN GENERAL.—The term "required documentation" includes such documentation as the Secretary may require that proves the individual's identity, foreign status, and residency.

(B) VALIDITY OF DOCUMENTS.—The Secretary may accept only original documents or certified copies meeting the requirements of the Secretary.

(3) TERM OF ITIN.—

(A) IN GENERAL.—An individual taxpayer identification number issued after December 31, 2012, shall remain in effect unless the individual to whom such number is issued does not file a return of tax (or is not included as a dependent on the return of tax of another taxpayer) for 3 consecutive taxable years ending after the issuance of such number. In the case of an individual described in the preceding sentence, such number shall expire on the day after the due date for the return of tax for such third consecutive taxable year.

(B) SPECIAL RULE FOR EXISTING ITINS.—In the case of an individual with respect to whom an individual taxpayer identification number was issued before January 1, 2013, such number shall remain in effect until the earlier of—

(i) the applicable date, or

(ii) if the individual does not file a return of tax (or is not included as a dependent on the return of tax of another taxpayer) for 3 consecutive taxable years at least one of which ends after December 18, 2015, the due date for the return of tax for such third consecutive taxable year.

(C) APPLICABLE DATE.—For purposes of subparagraph (B), the term "applicable date" means—

(i) January 1, 2017, in the case of an individual taxpayer identification number issued before January 1, 2008,

(ii) January 1, 2018, in the case of an individual taxpayer identification number issued in 2008,

(iii) January 1, 2019, in the case of an individual taxpayer identification number issued in 2009 or 2010, and

RETURNS—MISCELLANEOUS PROVISIONS

(iv) January 1, 2020, in the case of an individual taxpayer identification number issued in 2011 or 2012.

(4) DISTINGUISHING ITINS ISSUED SOLELY FOR PURPOSES OF TREATY BENEFITS.—The Secretary shall implement a system that ensures that individual taxpayer identification numbers issued solely for purposes of claiming tax treaty benefits are used only for such purposes, by distinguishing such numbers from other individual taxpayer identification numbers issued.

Amendments

• **2018, Tax Technical Corrections Act of 2018 (P.L. 115-141)**

P.L. 115-141, §101(g)(1), Div. U:

Amended Code Sec. 6109(i)(1)(A)(i) by striking "community-based certified acceptance agent" and inserting "community-based certifying acceptance agent". **Effective** as if included in the provision of the Protecting Americans from Tax Hikes Act of 2015 to which it relates [**effective**, except to the extent provided in Code Sec. 6109(i)(3), for applications for individual taxpayer identification numbers made after 12-18-2015.—CCH].

P.L. 115-141, §101(g)(2), Div. U:

Amended Code Sec. 6109(i)(1)(B) by striking "Internal Revenue Service" and inserting "Internal Revenue Service, a community-based certifying acceptance agent approved by the Secretary". **Effective** as if included in the provision of the Protecting Americans from Tax Hikes Act of 2015 to which it relates [**effective**, except to the extent provided in Code Sec. 6109(i)(3), for applications for individual taxpayer identification numbers made after 12-18-2015.—CCH].

P.L. 115-141, §101(g)(3)(A)-(B), Div. U:

Amended Code Sec. 6109(i)(3) in subparagraph (A) by inserting "ending after the issuance of such number" before the period at the end of the first sentence, and by striking "on the last day of such third consecutive taxable year" and inserting "on the day after the due date for the return of tax for such third consecutive taxable year", and by striking subparagraph (B)(ii) and inserting a new clause (ii). **Effective** as if included in the provision of the Protecting Americans from Tax Hikes Act of 2015 to which it relates [**effective**, except to the extent provided in Code Sec. 6109(i)(3), for applications for individual taxpayer identification numbers made after 12-18-2015.—CCH]. Prior to being stricken, Code Sec. 6109(i)(3)(B)(ii) read as follows:

(ii) if the individual does not file a return of tax (or is not included as a dependent on the return of tax of another taxpayer) for 3 consecutive taxable years, the earlier of—

(I) the last day of such third consecutive taxable year, or

(II) the last day of the taxable year that includes the date of the enactment of this subsection.

• **2015, Protecting Americans from Tax Hikes Act of 2015 (P.L. 114-113)**

P.L. 114-113, §203(a), Div. Q:

Amended Code Sec. 6109 by adding at the end a new subsection (i). **Effective**, except to the extent provided in Code Sec. 6109(i)(3), for applications for individual taxpayer identification numbers made after 12-18-2015 [**effective** date changed by P.L. 115-141, §101(g)(5), Div. U.—CCH].

[Sec. 6110]

SEC. 6110. PUBLIC INSPECTION OF WRITTEN DETERMINATIONS.

[Sec. 6110(a)]

(a) GENERAL RULE.—Except as otherwise provided in this section, the text of any written determination and any background file document relating to such written determination shall be open to public inspection at such place as the Secretary may by regulations prescribe.

[Sec. 6110(b)]

(b) DEFINITIONS.—For purposes of this section—

(1) WRITTEN DETERMINATION.—

(A) IN GENERAL.—The term "written determination" means a ruling, determination letter, technical advice memorandum, or Chief Counsel advice.

(B) EXCEPTIONS.—Such term shall not include any matter referred to in subparagraph (C) or (D) of section 6103(b)(2).

(2) BACKGROUND FILE DOCUMENT.—The term "background file document" with respect to a written determination includes the request for that written determination, any written material submitted in support of the request, and any communication (written or otherwise) between the Internal Revenue Service and persons outside the Internal Revenue Service in connection with such written determination (other than any communication between the Department of Justice and the Internal Revenue Service relating to a pending civil or criminal case or investigation) received before issuance of the written determination.

(3) REFERENCE AND GENERAL WRITTEN DETERMINATIONS.—

(A) REFERENCE WRITTEN DETERMINATION.—The term "reference written determination" means any written determination which has been determined by the Secretary to have significant reference value.

(B) GENERAL WRITTEN DETERMINATION.—The term "general written determination" means any written determination other than a reference written determination.

Amendments

• **2000, Community Renewal Tax Relief Act of 2000 (P.L. 106-554)**

P.L. 106-554, §304(c)(1):

Amended Code Sec. 6110(b)(1). **Effective** 12-21-2000. Prior to amendment, Code Sec. 6110(b)(1) read as follows:

(1) WRITTEN DETERMINATION.—The term "written determination" means a ruling, determination letter, technical advice memorandum, or Chief Counsel advice. Such term shall not include any advance pricing agreement entered into by a taxpayer and the Secretary and any background information related to such agreement or any application for an advance pricing agreement.

• **1999, Tax Relief Extension Act of 1999 (P.L. 106-170)**

P.L. 106-170, §521(a)(2):

Amended Code Sec. 6110(b)(1) by adding at the end a new sentence. **Effective** 12-17-99.

P.L. 106-170, §521(c), provides:

(c) REGULATIONS.—The Secretary of the Treasury or the Secretary's delegate shall prescribe such regulations as may be necessary or appropriate to carry out the purposes of section 6103(b)(2)(C), and the last sentence of section 6110(b)(1), of the Internal Revenue Code of 1986, as added by this section.

• **1998, IRS Restructuring and Reform Act of 1998 (P.L. 105-206)**

P.L. 105-206, §3509(a):

Amended Code Sec. 6110(b)(1) by striking "or technical advice memorandum" and inserting "technical advice memorandum, or Chief Counsel advice". **Effective** for any Chief Counsel advice issued more than 90 days after 7-22-98. For transition rules, see Act Sec. 3509(d)(2)-(4), below.

P.L. 105-206, §3509(d)(2)-(4), provides:

(2) TRANSITION RULES.—The amendments made by this section shall apply to any Chief Counsel advice issued after December 31, 1985, and before the 91st day after the date of the enactment of this Act by the offices of the associate chief counsel for domestic, employee benefits and exempt organizations, and international, except that any such Chief Counsel advice shall be treated as made available on a timely basis if such advice is made available for public inspection not later than the following dates:

(A) One year after the date of the enactment of this Act, in the case of all litigation guideline memoranda, service center advice, tax litigation bulletins, criminal tax bulletins, and general litigation bulletins.

(B) Eighteen months after such date of enactment, in the case of field service advice and technical assistance to the field issued on or after January 1, 1994.

(C) Three years after such date of enactment, in the case of field service advice and technical assistance to the field issued on or after January 1, 1992, and before January 1, 1994.

(D) Six years after such date of enactment, in the case of any other Chief Counsel advice issued after December 31, 1985.

(3) DOCUMENTS TREATED AS CHIEF COUNSEL ADVICE.—If the Secretary of the Treasury by regulation provides pursuant to section 6110(i)(2) of the Internal Revenue Code of 1986, as added by this section, that any additional advice or instruction issued by the Office of Chief Counsel shall be treated as Chief Counsel advice, such additional advice or instruction shall be made available for public inspection pursuant to section 6110 of such Code, as amended by this section, only in accordance with the effective date set forth in such regulation.

(4) CHIEF COUNSEL ADVICE TO BE AVAILABLE ELECTRONICALLY.—The Internal Revenue Service shall make any Chief Counsel advice issued more than 90 days after the date of the enactment of this Act and made available for public inspection pursuant to section 6110 of such Code, as amended by this section, also available by computer telecommunications within 1 year after issuance.

[Sec. 6110(c)]

(c) EXEMPTIONS FROM DISCLOSURE.—Before making any written determination or background file document open or available to public inspection under subsection (a), the Secretary shall delete—

RETURNS—MISCELLANEOUS PROVISIONS

(1) the names, addresses, and other identifying details of the person to whom the written determination pertains and of any other person, other than a person with respect to whom a notation is made under subsection (d)(1), identified in the written determination or any background file document;

(2) information specifically authorized under criteria established by an Executive order to be kept secret in the interest of national defense or foreign policy, and which is in fact properly classified pursuant to such Executive order;

(3) information specifically exempted from disclosure by any statute (other than this title) which is applicable to the Internal Revenue Service;

(4) trade secrets and commercial or financial information obtained from a person and privileged or confidential;

(5) information the disclosure of which would constitute a clearly unwarranted invasion of personal privacy;

(6) information contained in or related to examination, operating, or condition reports prepared by, or on behalf of, or for use of an agency responsible for the regulation or supervision of financial institutions; and

(7) geological and geophysical information and data, including maps, concerning wells.

The Secretary shall determine the appropriate extent of such deletions and, except in the case of intentional or willful disregard of this subsection, shall not be required to make such deletions (nor be liable for failure to make deletions) unless the Secretary has agreed to such deletions or has been ordered by a court (in a proceeding under subsection (f)(3)) to make such deletions.

[Sec. 6110(d)]

(d) PROCEDURES WITH REGARD TO THIRD PARTY CONTACTS.—

(1) NOTATIONS.—If, before the issuance of a written determination, the Internal Revenue Service receives any communication (written or otherwise) concerning such written determination, any request for such determination, or any other matter involving such written determination from a person other than an employee of the Internal Revenue Service or the person to whom such written determination pertains (or his authorized representative with regard to such written determination), the Internal Revenue Service shall indicate, on the written determination open to public inspection, the category of the person making such communication and the date of such communication.

(2) EXCEPTION.—Paragraph (1) shall not apply to any communication made by the Chief of Staff of the Joint Committee on Taxation.

(3) DISCLOSURE OF IDENTITY.—In the case of any written determination to which paragraph (1) applies, any person may file a petition in the United States Tax Court or file a complaint in the United States District Court for the District of Columbia for an order requiring that the identity of any person to whom the written determination pertains be disclosed. The court shall order disclosure of such identity if there is evidence in the record from which one could reasonably conclude that an impropriety occurred or undue influence was exercised with respect to such written determination by or on behalf of such person. The court may also direct the Secretary to disclose any portion of any other deletions made in accordance with subsection (c) where such disclosure is in the public interest. If a proceeding is commenced under this paragraph, the person whose identity is subject to being disclosed and the person about whom a notation is made under paragraph (1) shall be notified of the proceeding in accordance with the procedures described in subsection (f)(4)(B) and shall have the right to intervene in the proceeding (anonymously, if appropriate).

(4) PERIOD IN WHICH TO BRING ACTION.—No proceeding shall be commenced under paragraph (3) unless a petition is filed before the expiration of 36 months after the first day that the written determination is open to public inspection.

[Sec. 6110(e)]

(e) BACKGROUND FILE DOCUMENTS.—Whenever the Secretary makes a written determination open to public inspection under this section, he shall also make available to any person, but only upon the written request of that person, any background file document relating to the written determination.

[Sec. 6110(f)]

(f) RESOLUTION OF DISPUTES RELATING TO DISCLOSURE.—

(1) NOTICE OF INTENTION TO DISCLOSE.—Except as otherwise provided by subsection (i), the Secretary shall upon issuance of any written determination, or upon receipt of a request for a background file document, mail a notice of intention to disclose such determination or document to any person to whom the written determination pertains (or a successor in interest, executor, or other person authorized by law to act for or on behalf of such person).

(2) ADMINISTRATIVE REMEDIES.—The Secretary shall prescribe regulations establishing administrative remedies with respect to—

(A) requests for additional disclosure of any written determination or any background file document, and

(B) requests to restrain disclosure.

(3) ACTION TO RESTRAIN DISCLOSURE.—

(A) CREATION OF REMEDY.—Any person—

(i) to whom a written determination pertains (or a successor in interest, executor, or other person authorized by law to act for or on behalf of such person), or who has a direct interest in maintaining the confidentiality of any such written determination or background file document (or portion thereof),

(ii) who disagrees with any failure to make a deletion with respect to that portion of any written determination or any background file document which is to be open or available to public inspection, and

(iii) who has exhausted his administrative remedies as prescribed pursuant to paragraph (2),

may, within 60 days after the mailing by the Secretary of a notice of intention to disclose any written determination or background file document under paragraph (1), together with the proposed deletions, file a petition in the United States Tax Court (anonymously, if appropriate) for a determination with respect to that portion of such written determination or background file document which is to be open to public inspection.

(B) NOTICE TO CERTAIN PERSONS.—The Secretary shall notify any person to whom a written determination pertains (unless such person is the petitioner) of the filing of a petition under this paragraph with respect to such written determination or related background file document, and any such person may intervene (anonymously, if appropriate) in any proceeding conducted pursuant to this paragraph. The Secretary shall send such notice by registered or certified mail to the last known address of such person within 15 days after such petition is served on the Secretary. No person who has received such a notice may thereafter file any petition under this paragraph with respect to such written determination or background file document with respect to which such notice was received.

(4) ACTION TO OBTAIN ADDITIONAL DISCLOSURE.—

(A) CREATION OF REMEDY.—Any person who has exhausted the administrative remedies prescribed pursuant to paragraph (2) with respect to a request for disclosure may file a petition in the United States Tax Court or a complaint in the United States District Court for the District of Columbia for an order requiring that any written determination or background file document (or portion thereof) be made open or available to public inspection. Except where inconsistent with subparagraph (B), the provisions of subparagraphs (C), (D), (E), (F), and (G) of section 552(a)(4) of title 5, United States Code, shall apply to any proceeding under this paragraph. The Court shall examine the

RETURNS—MISCELLANEOUS PROVISIONS

matter de novo and without regard to a decision of a court under paragraph (3) with respect to such written determination or background file document, and may examine the entire text of such written determination or background file document in order to determine whether such written determination or background file document or any part thereof shall be open or available to public inspection under this section. The burden of proof with respect to the issue of disclosure of any information shall be on the Secretary and any other person seeking to restrain disclosure.

(B) INTERVENTION.—If a proceeding is commenced under this paragraph with respect to any written determination or background file document, the Secretary shall, within 15 days after notice of the petition filed under subparagraph (A) is served on him, send notice of the commencement of such proceeding to all persons who are identified by name and address in such written determination or background file document. The Secretary shall send such notice by registered or certified mail to the last known address of such person. Any person to whom such determination or background file document pertains may intervene in the proceeding (anonymously, if appropriate). If such notice is sent, the Secretary shall not be required to defend the action and shall not be liable for public disclosure of the written determination or background file document (or any portion thereof) in accordance with the final decision of the court.

(5) EXPEDITION OF DETERMINATION.—The Tax Court shall make a decision with respect to any petition described in paragraph (3) at the earliest practicable date.

(6) PUBLICITY OF TAX COURT PROCEEDINGS.—Notwithstanding sections 7458 and 7461, the Tax Court may, in order to preserve the anonymity, privacy, or confidentiality of any person under this section, provide by rules adopted under section 7453 that portions of hearings, testimony, evidence, and reports in connection with proceedings under this section may be closed to the public or to inspection by the public.

Amendments

- **1998, IRS Restructuring and Reform Act of 1998 (P.L. 105-206)**

P.L. 105-206, §3509(c)(1):

Amended Code Sec. 6110(f)(1) by striking "The Secretary" and inserting "Except as otherwise provided by subsection (i), the Secretary". **Effective** for any Chief Counsel advice issued more than 90 days after 7-22-98. For transition rules, see Act Sec. 3509(d)(2)-(4) under the amendment notes to subsection (b), above.

- **1984 (P.L. 98-620)**

P.L. 98-620, §402(28)(B):

Amended Code Sec. 6110(f)(5) by striking out "and the Court of Appeals shall expedite any review of such decision in every way possible". **Not effective** for cases pending on 11-8-84.

[Sec. 6110(g)]

(g) TIME FOR DISCLOSURE.—

(1) IN GENERAL.—Except as otherwise provided in this section, the text of any written determination or any background file document (as modified under subsection (c)) shall be open or available to public inspection—

(A) no earlier than 75 days, and no later than 90 days, after the notice provided in subsection (f)(1) is mailed, or, if later,

(B) within 30 days after the date on which a court decision under subsection (f)(3) becomes final.

(2) POSTPONEMENT BY ORDER OF COURT.—The court may extend the period referred to in paragraph (1)(B) for such time as the court finds necessary to allow the Secretary to comply with its decision.

(3) POSTPONEMENT OF DISCLOSURE FOR UP TO 90 DAYS.—At the written request of the person by whom or on whose behalf the request for the written determination was made, the period referred to in paragraph (1)(A) shall be extended (for not to exceed an additional 90 days) until the day which is 15 days after the date of the Secretary's determination that the transaction set forth in the written determination has been completed.

(4) ADDITIONAL 180 DAYS.—If—

(A) the transaction set forth in the written determination is not completed during the period set forth in paragraph (3), and

(B) the person by whom or on whose behalf the request for the written determination was made establishes to the satisfaction of the Secretary that good cause exists for additional delay in opening the written determination to public inspection,

the period referred to in paragraph (3) shall be further extended (for not to exceed an additional 180 days) until the day which is 15 days after the date of the Secretary's determination that the transaction set forth in the written determination has been completed.

(5) SPECIAL RULES FOR CERTAIN WRITTEN DETERMINATIONS, ETC.—Notwithstanding the provisions of paragraph (1), the Secretary shall not be required to make available to the public—

(A) any technical advice memorandum, any Chief Counsel advice, and any related background file document involving any matter which is the subject of a civil fraud or criminal investigation or jeopardy or termination assessment until after any action relating to such investigation or assessment is completed, or

(B) any general written determination and any related background file document that relates solely to approval of the Secretary of any adoption or change of—

(i) the funding method or plan year of a plan under section 412,

(ii) a taxpayer's annual accounting period under section 442,

(iii) a taxpayer's method of accounting under section 446(e), or

(iv) a partnership's or partner's taxable year under section 706,

but the Secretary shall make any such written determination and related background file document available upon the written request of any person after the date on which (except for this subparagraph) such determination would be open to public inspection.

Amendments

- **2000, Community Renewal Tax Relief Act of 2000 (P.L. 106-554)**

P.L. 106-554, §313(e):

Amended Code Sec. 6110(g)(5)(A) by inserting ", any Chief Counsel advice," after "technical advice memorandum". **Effective** as if included in the provision of P.L. 105-206 to which it relates [effective for Chief Counsel advice issued after 10-20-98, generally.—CCH].

[Sec. 6110(h)]

(h) DISCLOSURE OF PRIOR WRITTEN DETERMINATIONS AND RELATED BACKGROUND FILE DOCUMENTS.—

(1) IN GENERAL.—Except as otherwise provided in this subsection, a written determination issued pursuant to a request made before November 1, 1976, and any background file document relating to such written determination shall be open or available to public inspection in accordance with this section.

(2) TIME FOR DISCLOSURE.—In the case of any written determination or background file document which is to be made open or available to public inspection under paragraph (1)—

(A) subsection (g) shall not apply, but

(B) such written determination or background file document shall be made open or available to public inspection at the earliest practicable date after funds for that purpose have been appropriated and made available to the Internal Revenue Service.

(3) ORDER OF RELEASE.—Any written determination or background file document described in paragraph (1) shall be open or available to public inspection in the following order starting with the most recent written determination in each category:

RETURNS—MISCELLANEOUS PROVISIONS

(A) reference written determinations issued under this title;

(B) general written determinations issued after July 4, 1967; and

(C) reference written determinations issued under the Internal Revenue Code of 1939 or corresponding provisions of prior law.

General written determinations not described in subparagraph (B) shall be open to public inspection on written request, but not until after the written determinations referred to in subparagraphs (A), (B), and (C) are open to public inspection.

(4) NOTICE THAT PRIOR WRITTEN DETERMINATIONS ARE OPEN TO PUBLIC INSPECTION.—Notwithstanding the provisions of subsections (f)(1) and (f)(3)(A), not less than 90 days before making any portion of a written determination described in this subsection open to public inspection, the Secretary shall issue public notice in the Federal Register that such written determination is to be made open to public inspection. The person who received a written determination may, within 75 days after the date of publication of notice under this paragraph, file a petition in the United States Tax Court (anonymously, if appropriate) for a determination with respect to that portion of such written determination which is to be made open to public inspection. The provisions of subsections (f)(3)(B), (5), and (6) shall apply if such a petition is filed. If no petition is filed, the text of any written determination shall be open to public inspection no earlier than 90 days, and no later than 120 days, after notice is published in the Federal Register.

(5) EXCLUSION.—Subsection (d) shall not apply to any written determination described in paragraph (1).

Amendments

• **1976, Tax Reform Act of 1976 (P.L. 94-455)**

P.L. 94-455, § 1201(b), provides:

(b) EFFECT UPON PENDING REQUESTS.—Any written determination or background file document which is the subject of a judicial proceeding pursuant to section 552 of title 5, United States Code, commenced before January 1, 1976, shall not be treated as a written determination subject to subsection (h)(1), but shall be available to the complainant along with the background file document, if requested, as soon as practicable after July 1, 1976.

[Sec. 6110(i)]

(i) SPECIAL RULES FOR DISCLOSURE OF CHIEF COUNSEL ADVICE.—

(1) CHIEF COUNSEL ADVICE DEFINED.—

(A) IN GENERAL.—For purposes of this section, the term "Chief Counsel advice" means written advice or instruction, under whatever name or designation, prepared by any national office component of the Office of Chief Counsel which—

(i) is issued to field or service center employees of the Service or regional or district employees of the Office of Chief Counsel; and

(ii) conveys—

(I) any legal interpretation of a revenue provision;

(II) any Internal Revenue Service or Office of Chief Counsel position or policy concerning a revenue provision; or

(III) any legal interpretation of State law, foreign law, or other Federal law relating to the assessment or collection of any liability under a revenue provision.

(B) REVENUE PROVISION DEFINED.—For purposes of subparagraph (A), the term "revenue provision" means any existing or former internal revenue law, regulation, revenue ruling, revenue procedure, other published or unpublished guidance, or tax treaty, either in general or as applied to specific taxpayers or groups of specific taxpayers.

(2) ADDITIONAL DOCUMENTS TREATED AS CHIEF COUNSEL ADVICE.—The Secretary may by regulation provide that this section shall apply to any advice or instruction prepared and issued by the Office of Chief Counsel which is not described in paragraph (1).

(3) DELETIONS FOR CHIEF COUNSEL ADVICE.—In the case of Chief Counsel advice and related background file documents open to public inspection pursuant to this section—

(A) paragraphs (2) through (7) of subsection (c) shall not apply, but

(B) the Secretary may make deletions of material in accordance with subsections (b) and (c) of section 552 of title 5, United States Code, except that in applying subsection (b)(3) of such section, no statutory provision of this title shall be taken into account.

(4) NOTICE OF INTENTION TO DISCLOSE.—

(A) NONTAXPAYER-SPECIFIC CHIEF COUNSEL ADVICE.—In the case of Chief Counsel advice which is written without reference to a specific taxpayer or group of specific taxpayers—

(i) subsection (f)(1) shall not apply; and

(ii) the Secretary shall, within 60 days after the issuance of the Chief Counsel advice, complete any deletions described in subsection (c)(1) or paragraph (3) and make the Chief Counsel advice, as so edited, open for public inspection.

(B) TAXPAYER-SPECIFIC CHIEF COUNSEL ADVICE.—In the case of Chief Counsel advice which is written with respect to a specific taxpayer or group of specific taxpayers, the Secretary shall, within 60 days after the issuance of the Chief Counsel advice, mail the notice required by subsection (f)(1) to each such taxpayer. The notice shall include a copy of the Chief Counsel advice on which is indicated the information that the Secretary proposes to delete pursuant to subsection (c)(1). The Secretary may also delete from the copy of the text of the Chief Counsel advice any of the information described in paragraph (3), and shall delete the names, addresses, and other identifying details of taxpayers other than the person to whom the advice pertains, except that the Secretary shall not delete from the copy of the Chief Counsel advice that is furnished to the taxpayer any information of which that taxpayer was the source.

Amendments

• **2007, Tax Technical Corrections Act of 2007 (P.L. 110-172)**

P.L. 110-172, § 10(a):

Amended Code Sec. 6110(i)(3) by inserting "and related background file documents" after "Chief Counsel advice" in the matter preceding subparagraph (A). **Effective** as if included in the provision of the Internal Revenue Service Restructuring and Reform Act of 1998 (P.L. 105-206) to which it relates [effective generally for any Chief Counsel advice issued more than 90 days after 7-22-98. For transition rules, see P.L. 105-206, § 3509(d)(2)-(4), in the amendment notes for Code Sec. 6110(b).—CCH].

• **1998, IRS Restructuring and Reform Act of 1998 (P.L. 105-206)**

P.L. 105-206, § 3509(b):

Amended Code Sec. 6110 by redesignating subsections (i), (j), (k), and (l) as subsections (j), (k), (l), and (m), respectively, and by inserting after subsection (h) a new subsection (i). **Effective** for any Chief Counsel advice issued more than 90 days after 7-22-98. For transition rules, see Act Sec. 3509(d)(2)-(4) in the amendment notes to Code Sec. 6110(b).

[Sec. 6110(j)]

(j) CIVIL REMEDIES.—

(1) CIVIL ACTION.—Whenever the Secretary—

(A) fails to make deletions required in accordance with subsection (c), or

(B) fails to follow the procedures in subsection (g) or (i)(4)(B), the recipient of the written determination or any person identified in the written determination shall have as an exclusive civil remedy an action against the Secretary in the United States Court of Federal Claims, which shall have jurisdiction to hear any action under this paragraph.

(2) DAMAGES.—In any suit brought under the provisions of paragraph (1)(A) in which the Court determines that an employee of the Internal Revenue Service intentionally or willfully failed to delete in accordance with subsection (c), or in any suit brought under

RETURNS—MISCELLANEOUS PROVISIONS

subparagraph (1)(B) in which the Court determines that an employee intentionally or willfully failed to act in accordance with subsection (g) or (i)(4)(B), the United States shall be liable to the person in an amount equal to the sum of—

    (A) actual damages sustained by the person but in no case shall a person be entitled to receive less than the sum of $1,000, and

    (B) the costs of the action together with reasonable attorney's fees as determined by the Court.

Amendments

• **2018, Tax Technical Corrections Act of 2018 (P.L. 115-141)**

P.L. 115-141, § 401(a)(325)(A), Div. U:

Amended Code Sec. 6110(j)(1)(B) by striking "United States Claims Court" and inserting "United States Court of Federal Claims". [Note: Code Sec. 6110(j)(1)(B) does not contain the text "United States Claims Court". Therefore, this amendment cannot be made.—CCH] **Effective** 3-23-2018.

• **1998, IRS Restructuring and Reform Act of 1998 (P.L. 105-206)**

P.L. 105-206, § 3509(b):

Amended Code Sec. 6110 by redesignating subsection (i) as subsection (j). **Effective** for any Chief Counsel advice issued more than 90 days after 7-22-98. For transition rules, see Act Sec. 3509(d)(2)-(4) in the amendment notes to subsection (b).

P.L. 105-206, § 3509(c)(2):

Amended Code Sec. 6110(j)(1)(B) and (2), as redesignated, by striking " subsection (g)" each place it appears and inserting "subsection (g) or (i)(4)(B)". **Effective** for any Chief Counsel advice issued more than 90 days after 7-22-98. For transition rules, see Act Sec. 3509(d)(2)-(4) in the amendment notes to Code Sec. 6110(b).

• **1992, Court of Federal Claims Technical and Procedural Improvements Act of 1992 (P.L. 102-572)**

P.L. 102-572, § 902(b)(1):

Amended Code Sec. 6110(j)(1)(B) by striking "United States Claims Court" and inserting "United States Court of Federal Claims". **Effective** 10-29-92.

• **1982, Federal Courts Improvement Act of 1982 (P.L. 97-164)**

P.L. 97-164, § 160(a)(9):

Amended Code Sec. 6110(i)(1) by striking out "Court of Claims" and inserting in lieu thereof "United States Claims Court". **Effective** 10-1-82.

P.L. 97-164, § 403, provides:

SEC. 403. (a) Any case pending before the Court of Claims on the effective date of this Act in which a report on the merits has been filed by a commissioner, or in which there is pending a request for review, and upon which the court has not acted, shall be transferred to the United States Court of Appeals for the Federal Circuit.

(b) Any matter pending before the United States Court of Customs and Patent Appeals on the effective date of this Act shall be transferred to the United States Court of Appeals for the Federal Circuit.

(c) Any petition for rehearing, reconsideration, alteration, modification, or other change in any decision of the United States Court of Claims or the United States Court of Customs and Patent Appeals rendered prior to the effective date of this Act that has not been determined by either of those courts on that date, or that is filed after that date, shall be determined by the United States Court of Appeals for the Federal Circuit.

(d) Any matter pending before a commissioner of the United States Court of Claims on the effective date of this Act, or any pending dispositive motion that the United States Court of Claims has not determined on that date, shall be determined by the United States Claims Court.

(e) Any case in which a notice of appeal has been filed in a district court of the United States prior to the effective date of this Act shall be decided by the court of appeals to which the appeal was taken.

[Sec. 6110(k)]

(k) SPECIAL PROVISIONS.—

  (1) FEES.—The Secretary is authorized to assess actual costs—

    (A) for duplication of any written determination or background file document made open or available to the public under this section, and

    (B) incurred in searching for and making deletions required under subsection (c)(1) or (i)(3) from any written determination or background file document which is available to public inspection only upon written request.

The Secretary shall furnish any written determination or background file document without charge or at a reduced charge if he determines that waiver or reduction of the fee is in the public interest because furnishing such determination or background file document can be considered as primarily benefiting the general public.

  (2) RECORDS DISPOSAL PROCEDURES.—Nothing in this section shall prevent the Secretary from disposing of any general written determination or background file document described in subsection (b) in accordance with established records disposition procedures, but such disposal shall, except as provided in the following sentence, occur not earlier than 3 years after such written determination is first made open to public inspection. In the case of any general written determination described in subsection (h), the Secretary may dispose of such determination and any related background file document in accordance with such procedures but such disposal shall not occur earlier than 3 years after such written determination is first made open to public inspection if funds are appropriated for such purpose before January 20, 1979, or not earlier than January 20, 1979, if funds are not appropriated before such date. The Secretary shall not dispose of any reference written determinations and related background file documents.

  (3) PRECEDENTIAL STATUS.—Unless the Secretary otherwise establishes by regulations, a written determination may not be used or cited as precedent. The preceding sentence shall not apply to change the precedential status (if any) of written determinations with regard to taxes imposed by subtitle D of this title.

Amendments

• **1998, IRS Restructuring and Reform Act of 1998 (P.L. 105-206)**

P.L. 105-206, § 3509(b):

Amended Code Sec. 6110 by redesignating subsection (j) as subsection (k). **Effective** for any Chief Counsel advice issued more than 90 days after 7-22-98. For transition rules, see Act Sec. 3509(d)(2)-(4) in the amendment notes to Code Sec. 6110(b).

P.L. 105-206, § 3509(c)(3):

Amended Code Sec. 6110(k)(1)(B), as redesignated, by striking "subsection (c)" and inserting "subsection (c)(1) or (i)(3)". **Effective** for any Chief Counsel advice issued more than 90 days after 7-22-98. For transition rules, see Act Sec. 3509(d)(2)-(4) in the amendment notes to Code Sec. 6110(b).

[Sec. 6110(l)]

(l) SECTION NOT TO APPLY.—This section shall not apply to—

  (1) any matter to which section 6104 or 6105 applies, or

  (2) any—

    (A) written determination issued pursuant to a request made before November 1, 1976, with respect to the exempt status under section 501(a) of an organization described in section 501(c) or (d), the status of an organization as a private foundation under section 509(a), or the status of an organization as an operating foundation under section 4942(j)(3),

    (B) written determination described in subsection (g)(5)(B) issued pursuant to a request made before November 1, 1976,

    (C) determination letter not otherwise described in subparagraph (A), (B), or (E) issued pursuant to a request made before November 1, 1976,

    (D) background file document relating to any general written determination issued before July 5, 1967, or

    (E) letter or other document described in section 6104(a)(1)(B)(iv) issued before September 2, 1974.

Amendments

• **2000, Community Renewal Tax Relief Act of 2000 (P.L. 106-554)**

P.L. 106-554, § 304(c)(2):

Amended Code Sec. 6110(l)(1) by inserting "or 6105" after "6104". **Effective** 12-21-2000.

• **1998, IRS Restructuring and Reform Act of 1998 (P.L. 105-206)**

P.L. 105-206, § 3509(b):

Amended Code Sec. 6110 by redesignating subsection (k) as subsection (l). **Effective** for any Chief Counsel Advice issued more than 90 days after 7-22-98. For transition rules, see Act Sec. 3509(d)(2)-(4) in the amendment notes to Code Sec. 6110(b).

RETURNS—MISCELLANEOUS PROVISIONS

[Sec. 6110(m)]

(m) EXCLUSIVE REMEDY.—Except as otherwise provided in this title, or with respect to a discovery order made in connection with a judicial proceeding, the Secretary shall not be required by any Court to make any written determination or background file document open or available to public inspection, or to refrain from disclosure of any such documents.

Amendments

• 1998, IRS Restructuring and Reform Act of 1998 (P.L. 105-206)

P.L. 105-206, §3509(b):

Amended Code Sec. 6110 by redesignating subsection (l) as subsection (m). Effective for any Chief Counsel advice issued more than 90 days after 7-22-98. For transition rules, see Act Sec. 3509(d)(2)-(4) in the amendment notes to Code Sec. 6110(b).

• 1976, Tax Reform Act of 1976 (P.L. 94-455)

P.L. 94-455, §1201(a):

Added Code Sec 6110. Effective 11-1-76.

[Sec. 6111]

SEC. 6111. DISCLOSURE OF REPORTABLE TRANSACTIONS.

[Sec. 6111(a)]

(a) IN GENERAL.—Each material advisor with respect to any reportable transaction shall make a return (in such form as the Secretary may prescribe) setting forth—

(1) information identifying and describing the transaction,

(2) information describing any potential tax benefits expected to result from the transaction, and

(3) such other information as the Secretary may prescribe.

Such return shall be filed not later than the date specified by the Secretary.

[Sec. 6111(b)]

(b) DEFINITIONS.—For purposes of this section—

(1) MATERIAL ADVISOR.—

(A) IN GENERAL.—The term "material advisor" means any person—

(i) who provides any material aid, assistance, or advice with respect to organizing, managing, promoting, selling, implementing, insuring, or carrying out any reportable transaction, and

(ii) who directly or indirectly derives gross income in excess of the threshold amount (or such other amount as may be prescribed by the Secretary) for such aid, assistance, or advice.

(B) THRESHOLD AMOUNT.—For purposes of subparagraph (A), the threshold amount is—

(i) $50,000 in the case of a reportable transaction substantially all of the tax benefits from which are provided to natural persons, and

(ii) $250,000 in any other case.

(2) REPORTABLE TRANSACTION.—The term "reportable transaction" has the meaning given to such term by section 6707A(c).

Amendments

• 2005, Gulf Opportunity Zone Act of 2005 (P.L. 109-135)

P.L. 109-135, §412(zz):

Amended Code Sec. 6111(b)(1)(A)(ii) by striking "advice or assistance" and inserting "aid, assistance, or advice". Effective 12-21-2005.

[Sec. 6111(c)]

(c) REGULATIONS.—The Secretary may prescribe regulations which provide—

(1) that only 1 person shall be required to meet the requirements of subsection (a) in cases in which 2 or more persons would otherwise be required to meet such requirements,

(2) exemptions from the requirements of this section, and

(3) such rules as may be necessary or appropriate to carry out the purposes of this section.

Amendments

• 2004, American Jobs Creation Act of 2004 (P.L. 108-357)

P.L. 108-357, §815(a):

Amended Code Sec. 6111. Effective for transactions with respect to which material aid, assistance, or advice referred to in Code Sec. 6111(b)(1)(A)(i) (as added by this section) is provided after 10-22-2004. Prior to amendment, Code Sec. 6111 read as follows:

SEC. 6111. REGISTRATION OF TAX SHELTERS.

[Sec. 6111(a)]

(a) REGISTRATION.—

(1) IN GENERAL.—Any tax shelter organizer shall register the tax shelter with the Secretary (in such form and in such manner as the Secretary may prescribe) not later than the day on which the first offering for sale of interests in such tax shelter occurs.

(2) INFORMATION INCLUDED IN REGISTRATION.—Any registration under paragraph (1) shall include—

(A) information identifying and describing the tax shelter,

(B) information describing the tax benefits of the tax shelter represented (or to be represented) to investors, and

(C) such other information as the Secretary may prescribe.

[Sec. 6111(b)]

(b) FURNISHING OF TAX SHELTER IDENTIFICATION NUMBER; INCLUSION ON RETURN.—

(1) SELLERS, ETC.—Any person who sells (or otherwise transfers) an interest in a tax shelter shall (at such times and in such manner as the Secretary shall prescribe) furnish to each investor who purchases (or otherwise acquires) an interest in such tax shelter from such person the identification number assigned by the Secretary to such tax shelter.

(2) INCLUSION OF NUMBER ON RETURN.—Any person claiming any deduction, credit, or other tax benefit by reason of a tax shelter shall include (in such manner as the Secretary may prescribe) on the return of tax on which such deduction, credit, or other benefit is claimed the identification number assigned by the Secretary to such tax shelter.

[Sec. 6111(c)]

(c) TAX SHELTER.—For purposes of this section—

(1) IN GENERAL.—The term "tax shelter" means any investment—

(A) with respect to which any person could reasonably infer from the representations made, or to be made, in connection with the offering for sale of interests in the investment that the tax shelter ratio for any investor as of the close of any of the first 5 years ending after the date on which such investment is offered for sale may be greater than 2 to 1, and

(B) which is—

(i) required to be registered under a Federal or State law regulating securities,

(ii) sold pursuant to an exemption from registration requiring the filing of a notice with a Federal or State agency regulating the offering or sale of securities, or

(iii) a substantial investment.

(2) TAX SHELTER RATIO DEFINED.—For purposes of this subsection, the term "tax shelter ratio" means, with respect to any year, the ratio which—

(A) the aggregate amount of the deductions and 350 percent of the credits which are represented to be potentially allowable to any investor under subtitle A for all periods up to (and including) the close of such year, bears to

(B) the investment base as of the close of such year.

(3) INVESTMENT BASE.—

(A) IN GENERAL.—Except as provided in this paragraph, the term "investment base" means, with respect to any year, the amount of money and the adjusted basis of other property (reduced by any liability to which such other property is subject) contributed by the investor as of the close of such year.

(B) CERTAIN BORROWED AMOUNTS EXCLUDED.—For purposes of subparagraph (A), there shall not be taken into account any amount borrowed from any person—

(i) who participated in the organization, sale, or management of the investment, or

RETURNS—MISCELLANEOUS PROVISIONS

(ii) who is a related person (as defined in section 465(b)(3)(C)) to any person described in clause (i),

unless such amount is unconditionally required to be repaid by the investor before the close of the year for which the determination is being made.

(C) CERTAIN OTHER AMOUNTS INCLUDED OR EXCLUDED.—

(i) AMOUNTS HELD IN CASH EQUIVALENTS, ETC.—No amount shall be taken into account under subparagraph (A) which is to be held in cash equivalent or marketable securities.

(ii) AMOUNTS INCLUDED OR EXCLUDED BY SECRETARY.—The Secretary may by regulation—

(I) exclude from the investment base any amount described in subparagraph (A), or

(II) include in the investment base any amount not described in subparagraph (A), if the Secretary determines that such exclusion or inclusion is necessary to carry out the purposes of this section.

(4) SUBSTANTIAL INVESTMENT.—An investment is a substantial investment if—

(A) the aggregate amount which may be offered for sale exceeds $250,000, and

(B) there are expected to be 5 or more investors.

Amendments

- **1986, Tax Reform Act of 1986 (P.L. 99-514)**

P.L. 99-514, § 201(d)(13):

Amended Code Sec. 6111(c)(3)(B)(ii) by striking out "section 168(e)(4)" and inserting in lieu thereof "section 465(b)(3)(C). **Effective**, generally, for property placed in service after 12-31-86, in tax years ending after such date. For special rules see Act Secs. 203(a)(1)(B)-(e), 204 and 251(d) following Code Sec. 168(i).

P.L. 99-514, § 1531(a):

Amended Code Sec. 6111(c)(2)(A) by striking out "200 percent" and inserting in lieu thereof "350 percent". **Effective** for any tax shelter (within the meaning of section 6111 of the Internal Revenue Code of 1986) interests in which are first offered for sale after 12-31-86.

[Sec. 6111(d)]

(d) CERTAIN CONFIDENTIAL ARRANGEMENTS TREATED AS TAX SHELTERS.—

(1) IN GENERAL.—For purposes of this section, the term "tax shelter" includes any entity, plan, arrangement, or transaction—

(A) a significant purpose of the structure of which is the avoidance or evasion of Federal income tax for a direct or indirect participant which is a corporation,

(B) which is offered to any potential participant under conditions of confidentiality, and

(C) for which the tax shelter promoters may receive fees in excess of $100,000 in the aggregate.

(2) CONDITIONS OF CONFIDENTIALITY.—For purposes of paragraph (1)(B), an offer is under conditions of confidentiality if—

(A) the potential participant to whom the offer is made (or any other person acting on behalf of such participant) has an understanding or agreement with or for the benefit of any promoter of the tax shelter that such participant (or such other person) will limit disclosure of the tax shelter or any significant tax features of the tax shelter, or

(B) any promoter of the tax shelter—

(i) claims, knows, or has reason to know,

(ii) knows or has reason to know that any other person (other than the potential participant) claims, or

(iii) causes another person to claim, that the tax shelter (or any aspect thereof) is proprietary to any person other than the potential participant or is otherwise protected from disclosure to or use by others.

For purposes of this subsection, the term "promoter" means any person or any related person (within the meaning of section 267 or 707) who participates in the organization, management, or sale of the tax shelter.

(3) PERSONS OTHER THAN PROMOTER REQUIRED TO REGISTER IN CERTAIN CASES.—

(A) IN GENERAL.—If—

(i) the requirements of subsection (a) are not met with respect to any tax shelter (as defined in paragraph (1)) by any tax shelter promoter, and

(ii) no tax shelter promoter is a United States person,

then each United States person who discussed participation in such shelter shall register such shelter under subsection (a).

(B) EXCEPTION.—Subparagraph (A) shall not apply to a United States person who discussed participation in a tax shelter if—

(i) such person notified the promoter in writing (not later than the close of the 90th day after the day on which such discussions began) that such person would not participate in such shelter, and

(ii) such person does not participate in such shelter.

(4) OFFER TO PARTICIPATE TREATED AS OFFER FOR SALE.—For purposes of subsections (a) and (b), an offer to participate in a tax shelter (as defined in paragraph (1)) shall be treated as an offer for sale.

Amendments

- **1997, Taxpayer Relief Act of 1997 (P.L. 105-34)**

P.L. 105-34, § 1028(a):

Amended Code Sec. 6111 by redesignating subsections (d) and (e) as subsections (e) and (f), respectively, and by inserting after subsection (c) a new subsection (d). **Effective** for any tax shelter (as defined in Code Sec. 6111(d), as amended by Act Sec. 1028(a)) interests in which are offered to potential participants after the Secretary of the Treasury prescribes guidance with respect to meeting requirements added by such amendment.

[Sec. 6111(e)]

(e) OTHER DEFINITIONS.—For purposes of this section—

(1) TAX SHELTER ORGANIZER.—The term "tax shelter organizer" means—

(A) the person principally responsible for organizing the tax shelter,

(B) if the requirements of subsection (a) are not met by a person described in subparagraph (A) at the time prescribed therefor, any other person who participated in the organization of the tax shelter, and

(C) if the requirements of subsection (a) are not met by a person described in subparagraph (A) or (B) at the time prescribed therefor, any person participating in the sale or management of the investment at a time when the tax shelter was not registered under subsection (a).

(2) YEAR.—The term "year" means—

(A) the taxable year of the tax shelter, or

(B) if the tax shelter has no taxable year, the calendar year.

Amendments

- **1997, Taxpayer Relief Act of 1997 (P.L. 105-34)**

P.L. 105-34, § 1028(a):

Amended Code Sec. 6111 by redesignating subsection (d) as subsection (e). **Effective** for any tax shelter (as defined in Code Sec. 6111(d), as amended by Act Sec. 1028(a)) interests in which are offered to potential participants after the Secretary of the Treasury prescribes guidance with respect to meeting requirements added by such amendment.

- **1986, Tax Reform Act of 1986 (P.L. 99-514)**

P.L. 99-514, § 1899A(54):

Amended Code Sec. 6111(d)(1)(B) by striking out "subpargraph" and inserting in lieu thereof "subparagraph". **Effective** 10-22-86.

[Sec. 6111(f)]

(f) REGULATIONS.—The Secretary may prescribe regulations which provide—

(1) rules for the aggregation of similar investments offered by the same person or persons for purposes of applying subsection (c)(4),

(2) that only 1 person shall be required to meet the requirements of subsection (a) in cases in which 2 or more persons would otherwise be required to meet such requirements,

(3) exemptions from the requirements of this section, and

(4) such rules as may be necessary or appropriate to carry out the purposes of this section in the case of foreign tax shelters.

Amendments

- **1997, Taxpayer Relief Act of 1997 (P.L. 105-34)**

P.L. 105-34, § 1028(a):

Amended Code Sec. 6111 by redesignating subsection (e) as subsection (f). **Effective** for any tax shelter (as defined in Code Sec. 6111(d), as amended by Act Sec. 1028(a)) interests in which are offered to potential participants after the Secretary of the Treasury prescribes guidance with respect to meeting requirements added by such amendment.

- **1984, Deficit Reduction Act of 1984 (P.L. 98-369)**

P.L. 98-369, § 141(a):

Redesignated former Code Sec. 6111 as Code Sec. 6112 and added new Code Sec. 6111. **Effective** for any tax shelter (within the meaning of Code Sec. 6111) any interest in which is first sold to any investor after 8-31-84. However, see Act Sec. 141(d)(2)-(3), below, for special rules.

P.L. 98-369, § 141(d)(2)-(3), provides:

(2) SUBSTANTIAL INVESTMENT TEST.—For purposes of determining whether any investment is a tax shelter by reason of section 6111(c)(1)(B)(iii) of such Code (as added by this section), only offers for sale after August 31, 1984, shall be taken into account.

(3) FURNISHING OF SHELTER IDENTIFICATION NUMBER FOR INTERESTS SOLD BEFORE SEPTEMBER 1, 1984.—With respect to interests sold before September 1, 1984, any liability to act under paragraph (1) of section 6111(b) of such Code (as added by this section) which would (but for this sentence) arise before such date shall be deemed to arise on December 31, 1984.

[Sec. 6112]

SEC. 6112. MATERIAL ADVISORS OF REPORTABLE TRANSACTIONS MUST KEEP LISTS OF ADVISEES, ETC.

[Sec. 6112(a)]

(a) IN GENERAL.—Each material advisor (as defined in section 6111) with respect to any reportable transaction (as defined in section 6707A(c)) shall (whether or not required to file a return under section 6111 with respect to such transaction) maintain (in such manner as the Secretary may by regulations prescribe) a list—

(1) identifying each person with respect to whom such advisor acted as a material advisor with respect to such transaction, and

(2) containing such other information as the Secretary may by regulations require.

RETURNS—MISCELLANEOUS PROVISIONS

Amendments

• **2004, American Jobs Creation Act of 2004 (P.L. 108-357)**

P.L. 108-357, § 815(b)(2):

Amended so much of Code Sec. 6112 as precedes subsection (c). **Effective** for transactions with respect to which material aid, assistance, or advice referred to in Code Sec. 6111(b)(1)(A)(i), as added by Act Sec. 815, is provided after 10-22-2004. Prior to amendment, so much of Code Sec. 6112 as precedes subsection (c) read as follows:

SEC. 6112. ORGANIZERS AND SELLERS OF POTENTIALLY ABUSIVE TAX SHELTERS MUST KEEP LISTS OF INVESTORS.

(a) IN GENERAL.—Any person who—

(1) organizes any potentially abusive tax shelter, or

(2) sells any interest in such a shelter,

shall maintain (in such manner as the Secretary may by regulations prescribe) a list identifying each person who was sold an interest in such shelter and containing such other information as the Secretary may by regulations require.

(b) POTENTIALLY ABUSIVE TAX SHELTER.—For purposes of this section, the term "potentially abusive tax shelter" means—

(1) any tax shelter (as defined in section 6111) with respect to which registration is required under section 6111, and

(2) any entity, investment plan or arrangement, or other plan or arrangement which is of a type which the Secretary determines by regulations as having a potential for tax avoidance or evasion.

[Sec. 6112(b)]

(b) SPECIAL RULES.—

(1) AVAILABILITY FOR INSPECTION; RETENTION OF INFORMATION ON LIST.—Any person who is required to maintain a list under subsection (a) (or was required to maintain a list under subsection (a) as in effect before the enactment of the American Jobs Creation Act of 2004)—

(A) shall make such list available to the Secretary for inspection upon written request by the Secretary, and

(B) except as otherwise provided under regulations prescribed by the Secretary, shall retain any information which is required to be included on such list for 7 years.

(2) LISTS WHICH WOULD BE REQUIRED TO BE MAINTAINED BY 2 OR MORE PERSONS.—The Secretary may prescribe regulations which provide that, in cases in which 2 or more persons are required under subsection (a) to maintain the same list (or portion thereof), only 1 person shall be required to maintain such list (or portion).

Amendments

• **2005, Gulf Opportunity Zone Act of 2005 (P.L. 109-135)**

P.L. 109-135, § 403(z):

Amended Code Sec. 6112(b)(1) by inserting "(or was required to maintain a list under subsection (a) as in effect before the enactment of the American Jobs Creation Act of 2004)" after "a list under subsection (a)". **Effective** as if included in the provision of the American Jobs Creation Act of 2004 (P.L. 108-357) to which it relates [**effective** for transactions with respect to which material aid, assistance, or advice referred to in Code Sec. 6111(b)(1)(A)(i) is provided after 10-22-2004.—CCH].

• **2004, American Jobs Creation Act of 2004 (P.L. 108-357)**

P.L. 108-357, § 815(b)(3)(A)-(C):

Amended Code Sec. 6112 by redesignating subsection (c) as subsection (b), by inserting "written" before "request" in subsection (b)(1) (as so redesignated), and by striking "shall prescribe" in subsection (b)(2) (as so redesignated) and inserting "may prescribe". **Effective** for transactions with respect to which material aid, assistance, or advice referred to in Code Sec. 6111(b)(1)(A)(i), as added by Act Sec. 815, is provided after 10-22-2004.

• **1984, Deficit Reduction Act of 1984 (P.L. 98-369)**

P.L. 98-369, § 142(a):

Redesignated Code Sec. 6112, as redesignated by Act Sec. 141(a), as Code Sec. 6113 and added new Code Sec. 6112. **Effective** for any interest which is first sold to any investor after 8-31-84.

[Sec. 6113]
SEC. 6113. DISCLOSURE OF NONDEDUCTIBILITY OF CONTRIBUTIONS.

[Sec. 6113(a)]

(a) GENERAL RULE.—Each fundraising solicitation by (or on behalf of) an organization to which this section applies shall contain an express statement (in a conspicuous and easily recognizable format) that contributions or gifts to such organization are not deductible as charitable contributions for Federal income tax purposes.

[Sec. 6113(b)]

(b) ORGANIZATION TO WHICH SECTION APPLIES.—

(1) IN GENERAL.—Except as otherwise provided in this subsection, this section shall apply to any organization which is not described in section 170(c) and which—

(A) is described in subsection (c) (other than paragraph (1) thereof) or (d) of section 501 and exempt from taxation under section 501(a),

(B) is a political organization (as defined in section 527(e)), or

(C) was an organization described in subparagraph (A) or (B) at any time during the 5-year period ending on the date of the fundraising solicitation or is a successor to an organization so described at any time during such 5-year period.

(2) EXEMPTION FOR SMALL ORGANIZATIONS.—

(A) ANNUAL GROSS RECEIPTS DO NOT EXCEED $100,000.—This section shall not apply to any organization the gross receipts of which in each taxable year are normally not more than $100,000.

(B) MULTIPLE ORGANIZATION RULE.—The Secretary may treat any group of 2 or more organizations as 1 organization for purposes of subparagraph (A) where necessary or appropriate to prevent the avoidance of this section through the use of multiple organizations.

(3) SPECIAL RULE FOR CERTAIN FRATERNAL ORGANIZATIONS.—For purposes of paragraph (1), an organization described in section 170(c)(4) shall be treated as described in section 170(c) only with respect to solicitations for contributions or gifts which are to be used exclusively for purposes referred to in section 170(c)(4).

[Sec. 6113(c)]

(c) FUNDRAISING SOLICITATION.—For purposes of this section—

(1) IN GENERAL.—Except as provided in paragraph (2), the term "fundraising solicitation" means any solicitation of contributions or gifts which is made—

(A) in written or printed form,

(B) by television or radio, or

(C) by telephone.

(2) EXCEPTION FOR CERTAIN LETTERS OR CALLS.—The term "fundraising solicitation" shall not include any letter or telephone call if such letter or call is not part of a coordinated fundraising campaign soliciting more than 10 persons during the calendar year.

RETURNS—MISCELLANEOUS PROVISIONS

Amendments

• **1987, Revenue Act of 1987 (P.L. 100-203)**

P.L. 100-203, § 10701(a):

Amended subchapter B of chapter 61 by redesignating section 6113 as section 6114 and by inserting after section 6112 a new section 6113. **Effective** for solicitations after 1-31-88.

[Sec. 6114]

SEC. 6114. TREATY-BASED RETURN POSITIONS.

[Sec. 6114(a)]

(a) IN GENERAL.—Each taxpayer who, with respect to any tax imposed by this title, takes the position that a treaty of the United States overrules (or otherwise modifies) an internal revenue law of the United States shall disclose (in such manner as the Secretary may prescribe) such position—

(1) on the return of tax for such tax (or any statement attached to such return), or

(2) if no return of tax is required to be filed, in such form as the Secretary may prescribe.

[Sec. 6114(b)]

(b) WAIVER AUTHORITY.—The Secretary may waive the requirements of subsection (a) with respect to classes of cases for which the Secretary determines that the waiver will not impede the assessment and collection of tax.

Amendments

• **1990, Omnibus Budget Reconciliation Act of 1990 (P.L. 101-508)**

P.L. 101-508, § 11702(c):

Amended Code Sec. 6114(b) by striking "by regulations" after "the Secretary may". **Effective** as if included in the provision of P.L. 101-647 to which it relates.

[Sec. 6115]

SEC. 6115. DISCLOSURE RELATED TO QUID PRO QUO CONTRIBUTIONS.

[Sec. 6115(a)]

(a) DISCLOSURE REQUIREMENT.—If an organization described in section 170(c) (other than paragraph (1) thereof) receives a quid pro quo contribution in excess of $75, the organization shall, in connection with the solicitation or receipt of the contribution, provide a written statement which—

(1) informs the donor that the amount of the contribution that is deductible for Federal income tax purposes is limited to the excess of the amount of any money and the value of any property other than money contributed by the donor over the value of the goods or services provided by the organization, and

(2) provides the donor with a good faith estimate of the value of such goods or services.

[Sec. 6115(b)]

(b) QUID PRO QUO CONTRIBUTION.—For purposes of this section, the term "quid pro quo contribution" means a payment made partly as a contribution and partly in consideration for goods or services provided to the payor by the donee organization. A quid pro quo contribution does not include any payment made to an organization, organized exclusively for religious purposes, in return for which the taxpayer receives solely an intangible religious benefit that generally is not sold in a commercial transaction outside the donative context.

Amendments

• **1993, Omnibus Budget Reconciliation Act of 1993 (P.L. 103-66)**

P.L. 103-66, § 13173(a):

Amended subchapter B of chapter 61 by redesignating Code Sec. 6115 as Code Sec. 6116 and by inserting after Code Sec. 6114 a new Code Sec. 6115. **Effective** for quid pro quo contributions made on or after 1-1-94.

• **1988, Technical and Miscellaneous Revenue Act of 1988 (P.L. 100-647)**

P.L. 100-647, § 1012(aa)(5)(A):

Amended subchapter B of chapter 61 by redesignating section 6114 as section 6115 and inserting after section 6113 new section 6114. **Effective** for tax periods the due date for filing returns for which (without extension) occurs after 12-31-88.

[Sec. 6116]

SEC. 6116. REQUIREMENT FOR PRISONS LOCATED IN UNITED STATES TO PROVIDE INFORMATION FOR TAX ADMINISTRATION.

[Sec. 6116(a)]

(a) IN GENERAL.—Not later than September 15, 2012, and annually thereafter, the head of the Federal Bureau of Prisons and the head of any State agency charged with the responsibility for administration of prisons shall provide to the Secretary in electronic format a list with the information described in subsection (b) of all the inmates incarcerated within the prison system for any part of the prior 2 calendar years or the current calendar year through August 31.

[Sec. 6116(b)]

(b) INFORMATION.—The information with respect to each inmate is—

(1) first, middle, and last name,
(2) date of birth,
(3) institution of current incarceration or, for released inmates, most recent incarceration,
(4) prison assigned inmate number,
(5) the date of incarceration,
(6) the date of release or anticipated date of release,
(7) the date of work release,
(8) taxpayer identification number and whether the prison has verified such number,
(9) last known address, and
(10) any additional information as the Secretary may request.

[Sec. 6116(c)]

(c) FORMAT.—The Secretary shall determine the electronic format of the information described in subsection (b).

TAX PAYMENT—PLACE AND DUE DATE

Amendments

• **2011, United States–Korea Free Trade Agreement Implementation Act (P.L. 112-41)**

P.L. 112-41, §502(a):

Amended subchapter B of chapter 61 by redesignating Code Sec. 6116 as Code Sec. 6117 and by inserting after Code Sec. 6115 a new Code Sec. 6116. **Effective** 10-21-2011.

[Sec. 6117]

SEC. 6117. CROSS REFERENCE.

For inspection of records, returns, etc., concerning gasoline or lubricating oils, see section 4102.

Amendments

• **2011, United States–Korea Free Trade Agreement Implementation Act (P.L. 112-41)**

P.L. 112-41, §502(a):

Amended subchapter B of chapter 61 by redesignating Code Sec. 6116 as Code Sec. 6117. **Effective** 10-21-2011.

• **1993, Omnibus Budget Reconciliation Act of 1993 (P.L. 103-66)**

P.L. 103-66, §13173(a):

Redesignated Code Sec. 6115 as Code Sec. 6116. **Effective** for quid pro quo contributions made on or after 1-1-94.

• **1988, Technical and Miscellaneous Revenue Act of 1988 (P.L. 100-647)**

P.L. 100-647, §1012(aa)(5)(A):

Amended subchapter B of Chapter 61 by redesignating section 6114 as section 6115. **Effective** for tax periods the due date for filing returns for which (without extension) occurs after 12-31-88.

• **1987, Revenue Act of 1987 (P.L. 100-203)**

P.L. 100-203, §10701(a):

Amended subchapter B of Chapter 61 by redesignating section 6113 as section 6114. **Effective** for solicitations after 1-31-88.

• **1984, Deficit Reduction Act of 1984 (P.L. 98-369)**

P.L. 98-369, §141(a):

Redesignated Code Sec. 6111 as Code Sec. 6112. **Effective** 7-18-84.

P.L. 98-369, §142(a):

Redesignated Code Sec. 6112, as redesignated by Act Sec. 141(a), as Code Sec. 6113. **Effective** 7-18-84.

• **1976, Tax Reform Act of 1976 (P.L. 94-455)**

P.L. 94-455, §1906(a)(8):

Redesignated Code Sec. 6110 as Code Sec. 6111 and amended redesignated Code Sec. 6111. **Effective** for tax years beginning after 12-31-76. Prior to redesignation and amendment, Code Sec. 6111 read as follows:

SEC. 6110. CROSS REFERENCES.

(1) For reports of Secretary of Agriculture concerning cotton futures, see section 4876.

(2) For inspection of returns, order forms, and prescriptions concerning narcotics, see section 4773.

(3) For inspection of returns, order forms, and prescriptions concerning marihuana, see section 4773.

(4) For authority of Secretary or his delegate to furnish list of special taxpayers, see section 4775.

(5) For inspection of records, returns, etc., concerning gasoline or lubricating oils, see section 4102.

• **1961 (P.L. 87-397)**

P.L. 87-397, §1(a):

Redesignated Code Sec. 6109 as Code Sec. 6110.

CHAPTER 62—TIME AND PLACE FOR PAYING TAX

SUBCHAPTER A.   Place and due date for payment of tax.
SUBCHAPTER B.   Extensions of time for payment.

Subchapter A—Place and Due Date for Payment of Tax

Sec. 6151.   Time and place for paying tax shown on returns.
Sec. 6155.   Payment on notice and demand.
Sec. 6157.   Payment of Federal unemployment tax on quarterly or other time period basis.
Sec. 6159.   Agreements for payment of tax liability in installments.

[Sec. 6151]

SEC. 6151. TIME AND PLACE FOR PAYING TAX SHOWN ON RETURNS.

[Sec. 6151(a)]

(a) GENERAL RULE.—Except as otherwise provided in this subchapter, when a return of tax is required under this title or regulations, the person required to make such return shall, without assessment or notice and demand from the Secretary, pay such tax to the internal revenue officer with whom the return is filed, and shall pay such tax at the time and place fixed for filing the return (determined without regard to any extension of time for filing the return).

Amendments

• **1976, Tax Reform Act of 1976 (P.L. 94-455)**

P.L. 94-455, §1906(b)(13)(A):

Amended 1954 Code by substituting "Secretary" for "Secretary or his delegate" each place it appeared. **Effective** 2-1-77.

• **1976, Bank Holding Company Tax Act of 1976 (P.L. 94-452)**

P.L. 94-452, §3(c)(2):

Amended Code Sec. 6151(a) by substituting "subchapter" for "section". **Effective** 10-1-77, with respect to sales after 7-7-70, in tax years ending after 7-7-70, but only in the case of qualified bank holding corporations.

• **1966 (P.L. 89-713)**

P.L. 89-713, §1(b):

Amended Code Sec. 6151(a) by substituting "to the internal revenue officer with whom the return is filed" for "to the principal internal revenue officer for the internal revenue district in which the return is required to be filed". **Effective** 11-2-66.

[Sec. 6151(b)]

(b) EXCEPTIONS.—

(1) INCOME TAX NOT COMPUTED BY TAXPAYER.—If the taxpayer elects under section 6014 not to show the tax on the return, the amount determined by the Secretary as payable shall be paid within 30 days after the mailing by the Secretary to the taxpayer of a notice stating such amount and making demand therefor.

(2) USE OF GOVERNMENT DEPOSITARIES.—For authority of the Secretary to require payments to Government depositaries, see section 6302(c).

Internal Revenue Code   **Sec. 6151(b)(2)**

TAX PAYMENT—PLACE AND DUE DATE

Amendments

• **1976, Tax Reform Act of 1976 (P.L. 94-455)**

P.L. 94-455, §1906(b)(13)(A):

Amended 1954 Code by substituting "Secretary" for "Secretary or his delegate" each place it appeared. **Effective** 2-1-77.

[Sec. 6151(c)]

(c) DATE FIXED FOR PAYMENT OF TAX.—In any case in which a tax is required to be paid on or before a certain date, or within a certain period, any reference in this title to the date fixed for payment of such tax shall be deemed a reference to the last day fixed for such payment (determined without regard to any extension of time for paying the tax).

[Sec. 6152—Repealed]

Amendments

• **1986, Tax Reform Act of 1986 (P.L. 99-514)**

P.L. 99-514, §1404(c)(1):

Repealed Code Sec. 6152. **Effective** for tax years beginning after 12-31-86. Reproduced immediately below is text of Code Sec. 6152 prior to repeal.

SEC. 6152. INSTALLMENT PAYMENTS.

[Sec. 6152(a)]

(a) PRIVILEGE TO ELECT TO MAKE FOUR INSTALLMENT PAYMENTS BY DECEDENT'S ESTATE.—A decedent's estate subject to the tax imposed by chapter 1 may elect to pay such tax in four equal installments.

Amendments

• **1982, Tax Equity and Fiscal Responsibility Act of 1982 (P.L. 97-248)**

P.L. 97-248, §234(b)(1):

Amended Code Sec. 6152(a). **Effective** for tax years beginning after 12-31-82. Prior to amendment, Code Sec. 6152(a) read as follows:

(a) PRIVILEGE TO ELECT TO MAKE INSTALLMENT PAYMENTS.—

(1) CORPORATIONS.—A corporation subject to the taxes imposed by Chapter 1 may elect to pay the unpaid amount of such taxes in two equal installments.

(2) ESTATES OF DECEDENTS.—A decedent's estate subject to the tax imposed by chapter 1 may elect to pay such tax in four equal installments.

• **1976, Tax Reform Act of 1976 (P.L. 94-455)**

P.L. 94-455, §1906(a)(9):

Amended Code Sec. 6152(a)(1). **Effective** 2-1-77. Prior to amendment, Code Sec. 6152(a)(1) read as follows:

(1) CORPORATIONS.—A corporation subject to the taxes imposed by chapter 1 may elect to pay the unpaid amount of such taxes in installments as follows:

(A) with respect to taxable years ending before December 31, 1954, four installments, the first two of which shall be 45 percent, respectively, of such taxes and the last two of which shall be 5 percent, respectively, of such taxes;

(B) with respect to taxable years ending on or after December 31, 1954, two equal installments.

• **1954 (P.L. 767, 83rd Cong.)**

P.L. 767, 83rd Cong., §3:

Repealed Code Sec. 6152(a)(3). **Effective** with respect to tax years beginning after 1954. Prior to repeal, Code Sec. 6152(a)(3) read as follows:

(3) EMPLOYERS SUBJECT TO UNEMPLOYMENT TAX.—An employer subject to the tax imposed by section 3301 may elect to pay such tax in four equal installments.

[Sec. 6152(b)]

(b) DATES PRESCRIBED FOR PAYMENT OF FOUR INSTALLMENTS.—In any case (other than payment of estimated income tax) in which the tax may be paid in four installments, the first installment shall be paid on the date prescribed for the payment of the tax, the second installment shall be paid on or before 3 months, the third installment on or before 6 months, and the fourth installment on or before 9 months, after such date.

Amendments

• **1982, Tax Equity and Fiscal Responsibility Act of 1982 (P.L. 97-248)**

P.L. 97-248, §234(b)(1):

Amended Code Sec. 6152(b). **Effective** for tax years beginning after 12-31-82. Prior to amendment, Code Sec. 6152(b) read as follows:

(b) DATES PRESCRIBED FOR PAYMENT OF INSTALLMENTS.—

(1) FOUR INSTALLMENTS.—In any case (other than payment of estimated income tax) in which the tax may be paid in four installments, the first installment shall be paid on the date prescribed for the payment of the tax, the second installment shall be paid on or about 3 months, the third installment on or before 6 months, and the fourth installment on or before 9 months, after such date.

(2) TWO INSTALLMENTS.—In any case (other than payment of estimated income tax) in which the tax may be paid in two installments, the first installment shall be paid on the date prescribed for the payment of the tax, and the second installment shall be paid on or before 3 months after such date.

[Sec. 6152(c)]

(c) PRORATION OF DEFICIENCY TO INSTALLMENTS.—If an election has been made to pay the tax imposed by chapter 1 in installments and a deficiency has been assessed, the deficiency shall be prorated to such installments. Except as provided in section 6861 (relating to jeopardy assessments), that part of the deficiency so prorated to any installment the date for payment of which has not arrived shall be collected at the same time as and as part of such installment. That part of the deficiency so prorated to any installment the date for payment of which has arrived shall be paid upon notice and demand from the Secretary.

Amendments

• **1976, Tax Reform Act of 1976 (P.L. 94-455)**

P.L. 94-455, §1906(b)(13)(A):

Amended 1954 Code by substituting "Secretary" for "Secretary or his delegate" each place it appeared. **Effective** 2-1-77.

[Sec. 6152(d)]

(d) ACCELERATION OF PAYMENT.—If any installment (other than an installment of estimated income tax) is not paid on or before the date fixed for its payment, the whole of the unpaid tax shall be paid upon notice and demand from the Secretary.

Amendments

• **1976, Tax Reform Act of 1976 (P.L. 94-455)**

P.L. 94-455, §1906(b)(13)(A):

Amended 1954 Code by substituting "Secretary" for "Secretary or his delegate" each place it appeared. **Effective** 2-1-77.

[Sec. 6153—Repealed]

Amendments

• **1984, Deficit Reduction Act of 1984 (P.L. 98-369)**

P.L. 98-369, §412(a)(3):

Repealed Code Sec. 6153. **Effective** with respect to tax years beginning after 12-31-84. Prior to repeal, Code Sec. 6153 read as follows:

SEC. 6153. INSTALLMENT PAYMENTS OF ESTIMATED INCOME TAX BY INDIVIDUALS.

[Sec. 6153(a)]

(a) GENERAL RULE.—The amount of estimated tax (as defined in section 6015(d)) with respect to which a declaration is required under section 6015 shall be paid as follows:

(1) If the declaration is filed on or before April 15 of the taxable year, the estimated tax shall be paid in four equal installments. The first installment shall be paid at the time of the filing of the declaration, the second and third on June 15 and September 15, respectively, of the taxable year, and the fourth on January 15 of the succeeding taxable year.

(2) If the declaration is filed after April 15 and not after June 15 of the taxable year, and is not required by section 6073 (a) to be filed on or before April 15 of the taxable year, the estimated tax shall be paid in three equal installments. The first installment shall be paid at the time of the filing of the declaration, the second on September 15 of the taxable year, and the third on January 15 of the succeeding taxable year.

(3) If the declaration is filed after June 15 and not after September 15 of the taxable year, and is not required by section 6073 (a) to be filed on or before June 15 of the taxable year, the estimated tax shall be paid in two equal installments. The first installment shall be paid at the time of the filing of the declaration, and the second on January 15 of the succeeding taxable year.

(4) If the declaration is filed after September 15 of the taxable year, and is not required by section 6073(a) to be filed on or before September 15 of the taxable year, the estimated tax shall be paid in full at the time of the filing of the declaration.

(5) If the declaration is filed after the time prescribed in section 6073(a) (including cases in which an extension of time for filing the declaration has been granted under section 6081), paragraphs (2), (3), and (4) of this subsection shall not apply, and there shall be paid at the time of such filing all installments of estimated tax which would have been payable on or before such time if the declaration had been filed within the time prescribed in section 6073(a), and the remaining installments shall be paid at the times at which, and in the amounts in which, they would have been payable if the declaration had been so filed.

Amendments

• **1981, Economic Recovery Tax Act of 1981 (P.L. 97-34)**

P.L. 97-34, §725(c)(3):

Amended Code Sec. 6153(a) by striking out "6015(c)" and inserting "6015(d)". **Effective** 1-1-81.

[Sec. 6153(b)]

(b) FARMERS OR FISHERMEN.—If an individual referred to in section 6073(b) (relating to income from farming or fishing) makes a declaration of estimated tax after September 15 of the taxable year and on or before January 15 of the succeeding taxable year, the estimated tax shall be paid in full at the time of the filing of the declaration.

TAX PAYMENT—PLACE AND DUE DATE

Amendments

• **1962 (P.L. 87-682)**

P.L. 87-682, §1:

Amended Sec. 6153(b) by inserting "OR FISHERMEN" after "FARMERS" in line 1 and by inserting "or fishing" after "from farming" in line 2. **Effective** for tax years beginning after 1962.

[Sec. 6153(c)]

(c) AMENDMENTS OF DECLARATION.—If any amendment of a declaration is filed, the remaining installments, if any, shall be ratably increased or decreased, as the case may be, to reflect the increase or decrease, as the case may be, in the estimated tax by reason of such amendment, and if any amendment is made after September 15 of the taxable year, any increase in the estimated tax by reason thereof shall be paid at the time of making such amendment.

[Sec. 6153(d)]

(d) APPLICATION TO SHORT TAXABLE YEARS.—The application of this section to taxable years of less than 12 months shall be in accordance with regulations prescribed by the Secretary.

Amendments

• **1976, Tax Reform Act of 1976 (P.L. 94-455)**

P.L. 94-455, §1906(b)(13)(A):

Amended 1954 Code by substituting "Secretary" for "Secretary or his delegate" each place it appeared. **Effective** 2-1-77.

[Sec. 6153(e)]

(e) FISCAL YEARS.—In the application of this section to the case of a taxable year beginning on any date other than January 1, there shall be substituted, for the months specified in this section, the months which correspond thereto.

[Sec. 6153(f)]

(f) INSTALLMENTS PAID IN ADVANCE.—At the election of the individual, any installment of the estimated tax may be paid prior to the date prescribed for its payment.

[Sec. 6153(g)]

(g) SPECIAL RULES FOR TAXABLE YEARS BEGINNING AFTER 1982.—In the case of taxable years beginning after 1982—

(1) this section shall be applied as if the requirements of sections 6015 and 6073 remained in effect, and

(2) the amount of the estimated tax taken into account under this section shall be determined under rules similar to the rules of subsections (b) and (d) of section 6654.

Amendments

• **1982, Tax Equity and Fiscal Responsibility Act of 1982 (P.L. 97-248)**

P.L. 97-248, §328(b)(3):

Amended Code Sec. 6153(g). **Effective** for tax years beginning after 12-31-82. Prior to amendment, Code Sec. 6153(g) read as follows:

(g) SIX-MONTH [EIGHT-MONTH] APPLICATION OF REVENUE ADJUSTMENT ACT OF 1975 CHANGES.—In the case of a taxpayer who has as his taxable year the calendar year 1976, the amount of any installment the payment of which is required to be made after December 31, 1975, and before October 1, 1976, may be computed without regard to section 42(a)(2), 43(a)(2), 43(b)(2), 141(b)(2), or 141(c)(2).

• **1976 (P.L. 94-414)**

P.L. 94-414, §2:

Amended Code Sec. 6153(g) by substituting "October 1, 1976" for "September 15, 1976."

• **1976 (P.L. 94-396)**

P.L. 94-396, §2(a)(2):

Amended Code Sec. 6153(g) by substituting "September 15, 1976" for "September 1, 1976."

• **1976 (P.L. 94-331)**

P.L. 94-331, §3(b):

Amended Code Sec. 6153(g) by substituting "September 1, 1976" for "July 1, 1976."

• **1975, Revenue Adjustment Act of 1975 (P.L. 94-164)**

P.L. 94-164, §5(b):

Added subsection (g).

[Sec. 6154—Repealed]

Amendments

• **1987, Revenue Act of 1987 (P.L. 100-203)**

P.L. 100-203, §10301(b)(1):

Repealed Code Sec. 6154. **Effective** for tax years beginning after 12-31-87. Prior to repeal, Code Sec. 6154 read as follows:

SEC. 6154. INSTALLMENT PAYMENTS OF ESTIMATED INCOME TAX BY CORPORATIONS.

[Sec. 6154(a)]

(a) CORPORATIONS REQUIRED TO PAY ESTIMATED INCOME TAX.—Every corporation subject to taxation under section 11, 55, 59A, or 1201(a), or subchapter L of chapter 1 (relating to insurance companies), shall make payments of estimated tax (as defined in subsection (c)) during its taxable year as provided in subsection (b) of its estimated tax for such taxable year can reasonably be expected to be $40 or more.

Amendments

• **1988, Technical and Miscellaneous Revenue Act of 1988 (P.L. 100-647)**

P.L. 100-647, §1007(g)(10):

Amended Code Sec. 6154(a) by striking out "11, 59A" and inserting in lieu thereof "11, 55, 59A". **Effective** as if included in the provision of P.L. 99-514 to which it relates.

• **1986, Superfund Amendments and Reauthorization Act of 1986 (P.L. 99-499)**

P.L. 99-499, §516(b)(4)(A)(ii):

Amended Code Sec. 6154(a) by striking out "section 11" and inserting "section 11, 59A,". **Effective** for tax years beginning after 12-31-86.

[Sec. 6154(b)]

(b) PAYMENT IN INSTALLMENTS.—Any corporation required under subsection (a) to make payments of estimated tax (as defined in subsection (c)) shall make such payments in installments as follows:

	The following percentages of the estimated tax shall be paid on the 15th day of the—			
If the requirements of subsection (a) are first met—	4th month	6th month	9th month	12th month
Before the 1st day of the 4th month of the taxable year...	25	25	25	25
After the last day of the 3rd month and before the 1st day of the 6th month of the taxable year..............	—	33 1/3	33 1/3	33 1/3
After the last day of the 5th month and before the 1st day of the 9th month of the taxable year..............	—	—	50	50
After the last day of the 8th month and before the 1st day of the 12th month of the taxable year..............	—	—	—	100

[Sec. 6154(c)]

(c) ESTIMATED TAX DEFINED.—For purposes of this title, in the case of a corporation the term "estimated tax" means the excess of—

(1) the amount which the corporation estimates as the sum of—

(A) the income tax imposed by section 11 or 1201(a), or subchapter L of chapter 1, whichever applies,

(B) the minimum tax imposed by section 55, and

(C) the environmental tax imposed by section 59A, over

(2) the amount which the corporation estimates as the sum of—

(A) any credits against tax provided by part IV of subchapter A of chapter 1, and

(B) to the extent allowed under regulations prescribed by the Secretary, any overpayment of the tax imposed by section 4986.

Amendments

• **1986, Tax Reform Act of 1986 (P.L. 99-514)**

P.L. 99-514, §701(d)(1):

Amended Code Sec. 6154(c)(1). **Effective**, generally, for tax years beginning after 12-31-86. For exceptions, see Act Sec. 701(f)(2)-(7) following Code Sec. 56. Prior to amendment, Code Sec. 6154(c)(1) read as follows:

(1) the amount which the corporation estimates as the amount of the income tax imposed by section 11 or 1201(a), or subchapter L of chapter 1, whichever is applicable, over

• **1986, Superfund Amendments and Reauthorization Act of 1986 (P.L. 99-499)**

P.L. 99-499, §516(b)(4)(A)(i):

Amended Code Sec. 6154(c)(1) by striking out "and" at the end of subparagraph (A), by striking out "over" at the end of subparagraph (B) and inserting in lieu thereof "and", and by adding at the end thereof new subparagraph (C). **Effective** for tax years beginning after 12-31-86.

TAX PAYMENT—PLACE AND DUE DATE

- **1983, Technical Corrections Act of 1982 (P.L. 97-448)**

P.L. 97-448, § 201(j)(2):

Amended Code Sec. 6154(c)(2). **Effective** as if included in the provision of P.L. 96-223 to which it relates. Prior to amendment, Code Sec. 6154(c)(2) read as follows:

"(2) the amount which the corporation estimates as the sum of the credits against tax provided by part IV of subchapter A of chapter 1."

- **1978, Revenue Act of 1978 (P.L. 95-600)**

P.L. 95-600, § 301(b)(20)(A):

Amended Code Sec. 6154(c). **Effective** for tax years beginning after 12-31-78. Prior to amendment, Code Sec. 6154(c) read as follows:

(c) ESTIMATED TAX DEFINED.—

(1) IN GENERAL.—For purposes of this title, in the case of a corporation, the term 'estimated tax' means the excess of—

(A) the amount which the corporation estimates as the amount of the income tax imposed by section 11 or 1201(a), or subchapter L of chapter 1, whichever is applicable, over

(B) the sum of—

(i) the amount which the corporation estimates as the sum of the credits against tax provided by part IV of subchapter A of chapter 1, and

(ii) in the case of a taxable year beginning before January 1, 1977, the amount of the corporation's temporary estimated tax exemption for such year.

(2) TEMPORARY ESTIMATED TAX EXEMPTION.—

(A) IN GENERAL.—For purposes of clause (ii) of paragraph (1)(B), the amount of a corporation's temporary estimated tax exemption for a taxable year equals the applicable percentage (determined under subparagraph (B)) multiplied by the lesser of—

(i) an amount equal to 22 percent of the amount which the corporation estimates as its surtax exemption (as defined in section 11(d)) for such year, or

(ii) the excess determined under paragraph (1) without regard to clause (ii) of paragraph (1)(B).

(B) APPLICABLE PERCENTAGE.—For purposes of subparagraph (A) and section 6655(e)(2), the applicable percentage is—

In the case of a taxable year beginning in—	
1975	40 percent
1976	20 percent

- **1976, Tax Reform Act of 1976 (P.L. 94-455)**

P.L. 94-455, § 1906(a)(10)(A):

Added "and" at the end of Code Sec. 6154(c)(1)(B)(i) and substituted new Code Sec. 6154(c)(1)(B)(ii) for former Code Sec. 6154(c)(1)(B)(ii) and 6154(c)(1)(B)(iii). **Effective** 2-1-77. Prior to amendment, Code Sec. 6154(c)(1)(B)(ii) and 6154(c)(1)(B)(iii) read as follows:

(ii) in the case of a taxable year beginning after December 31, 1967, and before January 1, 1977, the amount of the corporation's temporary estimated tax exemption for such year, and

(iii) in the case of a taxable year beginning after December 31, 1967, and before January 1, 1972, the amount of the corporation's transitional exemption for such year.

P.L. 94-455, § 1906(a)(10)(B):

Substituted "clause (ii)" for "clauses (ii) and (iii)" in Code Sec. 6154(c)(2)(A)(ii). **Effective** 2-1-77.

P.L. 94-455, § 1906(a)(10)(C):

Struck out the following in Code Sec. 6154(c)(2)(B):

1968, 1969, 1970, 1971, and 1972	100 percent
1973	80 percent
1974	60 percent

Effective 2-1-77.

P.L. 94-455, § 1906(a)(10)(D):

Struck out Code Sec. 6154(c)(3). **Effective** 2-1-77. Prior to striking, Code Sec. 6154(c)(3) read as follows:

(3) TRANSITIONAL EXEMPTION.—

(A) IN GENERAL.—For purposes of clause (iii) of paragraph (1)(B), the amount of a corporation's transitional exemption for a taxable year equals the exclusion percentage (determined under subparagraph (B)) multiplied by the lesser of—

(i) $100,000 reduced by the amount of the corporation's temporary estimated tax exemption for such year, or

(ii) the excess determined under paragraph (1) without regard to clause (iii) of paragraph (1)(B).

(B) EXCLUSION PERCENTAGE.—For purposes of subparagraph (A) and section 6655(e)(3), the exclusion percentage is—

In the case of a taxable year beginning in—	
1968	80 percent
1969	60 percent
1970	40 percent
1971	20 percent

Sec. 6154—Repealed

[Sec. 6154(d)]

(d) RECOMPUTATION OF ESTIMATED TAX.—If, after paying any installment of estimated tax, the taxpayer makes a new estimate, the amount of each remaining installment (if any) shall be the amount which would have been payable if the new estimate had been made when the first estimate for the taxable year was made, increased or decreased (as the case may be) by the amount computed by dividing—

(1) the difference between—

(A) the amount of estimated tax required to be paid before the date on which the new estimate is made, and

(B) the amount of estimated tax which would have been required to be paid before such date if the new estimate had been made when the first estimate was made, by

(2) the number of installments remaining to be paid on or after the date on which the new estimate is made.

[Sec. 6154(e)]

(e) APPLICATION TO SHORT TAXABLE YEAR.—The application of this section to taxable years of less than 12 months shall be in accordance with regulations prescribed by the Secretary.

Amendments

- **1976, Tax Reform Act of 1976 (P.L. 94-455)**

P.L. 94-455, § 1906(b)(13)(A):

Amended 1954 Code by substituting "Secretary" for "Secretary or his delegate" each place it appeared. **Effective** 2-1-77.

[Sec. 6154(f)]

(f) INSTALLMENTS PAID IN ADVANCE.—At the election of the corporation, any installment of the estimated tax may be paid before the date prescribed for its payment.

[Sec. 6154(g)]

(g) CERTAIN FOREIGN CORPORATIONS.—For purposes of this section and section 6655, in the case of a foreign corporation subject to taxation under section 11 or 1201(a), or under subchapter L of chapter 1, the tax imposed by section 881 shall be treated as a tax imposed by section 11.

[Sec. 6154(h)]

(h) CERTAIN TAX-EXEMPT ORGANIZATIONS.—For purposes of this section and section 6655—

(1) any organization subject to the tax imposed by section 511, and any private foundation, shall be treated as a corporation subject to tax under section 11.

(2) any tax imposed by section 511, and any tax imposed by section 1 or 4940 on a private foundation, shall be treated as a tax imposed by section 11, and

(3) any reference to taxable income shall be treated as including a reference to unrelated business taxable income or net investment income (as the case may be).

In the case of an organization described in paragraph (1), subsection (c) of section 6655 shall be applied by substituting "5th month" for "third month" and subsection (d)(3)(A) of section 6655 shall be applied by substituting "2 months" for "3 months" in clause (i), by substituting "4 months" for "5 months, in clause (ii), by substituting "7 months" for "8 months" in clause (iii), and by substituting "10 months" for "11 months" in clause (iv).

Amendments

- **1988, Technical and Miscellaneous Revenue Act of 1988 (P.L. 100-647)**

P.L. 100-647, § 1015(h)(1)-(3):

Amended Code Sec. 6154(h) (as in effect before its repeal by P.L. 100-203) by striking out "subject to the tax imposed by section 4940" after "private foundation" in paragraph (1), by amending paragraph (2), and by adding at the end thereof a new sentence. **Effective** as if included in the provision of P.L. 99-514 to which it relates. Prior to amendment, Code Sec. 6154(h)(2) read as follows:

(2) any tax imposed by section 511 or 4940 shall be treated as a tax imposed by section 11, and

- **1986, Tax Reform Act of 1986 (P.L. 99-514)**

P.L. 99-514, § 1542(a):

Amended Code Sec. 6154 by inserting at the end thereof new subsection (h). **Effective** for tax years beginning after 12-31-86.

- **1976, Tax Reform Act of 1976 (P.L. 94-455)**

P.L. 94-455, § 901(c)(3):

Struck out Code Sec. 6154(h). **Effective** for tax years ending after 12-31-75. Prior to striking, Code Sec. 6154(h) read as follows:

(h) SIX-MONTH APPLICATION OF REVENUE ADJUSTMENT ACT OF 1975 CHANGES.—In the case of a corporation which has as its taxable year the calendar year 1976, the amount of any installment the payment of which is required to be made after December 31, 1975, and before October 1, 1976, may be computed without regard to sections 11(b)(2), 11(c)(2), and 11(d)(2).

- **1976 (P.L. 94-414)**

P.L. 94-414, § 2:

Amended Code Sec. 6154(h) by substituting "October 1, 1976" for "September 15, 1976."

- **1976 (P.L. 94-396)**

P.L. 94-396, § 2(a)(3):

Amended Code Sec. 6154(h) by substituting "September 15, 1976" for "September 1, 1976." **Effective** 8-31-76.

TAX PAYMENT—PLACE AND DUE DATE

- **1976 (P.L. 94-331)**

P.L. 94-331, §3(c):

Amended Code Sec. 6154(h) by substituting "September 1, 1976" for "July 1, 1976." **Effective** 6-30-76.

- **1975, Revenue Adjustment Act of 1975 (P.L. 94-164)**

P.L. 94-164, §5(c):

Amended Code Sec. 6154 by adding subsection (h).

- **1968, Revenue and Expenditure Control Act of 1968 (P.L. 90-364)**

P.L. 90-364, §103(b):

Amended Code Sec. 6154. **Effective** 5-31-68. Prior to amendment by P.L. 90-364, Code Sec. 6154 read as follows:

"(a) Amount and Time for Payment of Each Installment.—The amount of estimated tax (as defined in section 6016(b)) with respect to which a declaration is required under section 6016 shall be paid as follows:

"(1) Taxable years beginning in 1966.—With respect to taxable years beginning after December 31, 1965, and before January 1, 1967, such estimated tax shall be paid in installments in accordance with the following table:

If the declaration is timely filed on or before the 15th day of the—	The following percentages of the estimated tax shall be paid on the 15th day of the—			
	4th month	6th month	9th month	12th month
4th month of the taxable year	12	12	25	25
6th month of the taxable year (but after the 15th day of the 4th month)	—	16	29	29
9th month of the taxable year (but after the 15th day of the 6th month)	—	—	37	37
12th month of the taxable year (but after the 15th day of the 9th month)	—	—	—	74

"(2) Taxable years beginning after 1966.—With respect to taxable years beginning after December 31, 1966, such estimated tax shall be paid in installments in accordance with the following table:

If the declaration is timely filed on or before the 15th day of the—	The following percentages of the estimated tax shall be paid on the 15th day of the—			
	4th month	6th month	9th month	12th month
4th month of the taxable year	25	25	25	25
6th month of the taxable year (but after the 15th day of the 4th month)	—	$33^{1}/_{3}$	$33^{1}/_{3}$	$33^{1}/_{3}$
9th month of the taxable year (but after the 15th day of the 6th month)	—	—	50	50
12th month of the taxable year (but after the 15th day of the 9th month)	—	—	—	100

"(3) Timely filing.—A declaration is timely filed for the purposes of paragraphs (1) and (2) if it is not required by section 6074(a) to be filed on a date (determined without regard to any extension of time for filing the declaration under section 6081) before the date it is actually filed.

"(4) Late filing.—If the declaration is filed after the time prescribed in section 6074(a) (determined without regard to any extension of time for filing the declaration under section 6081), there shall be paid at the time of such filing all installments of estimated tax which would have been payable on or before such time if the declaration had been filed within the time prescribed in section 6074(a), and the remaining installments shall be paid at the times at which, and in the amounts in which, they would have been payable if the declaration had been so filed.

"(b) Amendment of Declaration.—If any amendment of a declaration is filed, the amount of each remaining installment (if any) shall be the amount which would have been payable if the new estimate had been made when the first estimate for the taxable year was made, increased or decreased (as the case may be), by the amount computed by dividing—

"(1) the difference between (A) the amount of estimated tax required to be paid before the date on which the amendment is made, and (B) the amount of estimated tax which would have been required to be paid before such date if the new estimate had been made when the first estimate was made, by

"(2) the number of installments remaining to be paid on or after the date on which the amendment is made.

"(c) Application to Short Taxable Year.—The application of this section to taxable years of less than 12 months shall be in accordance with regulations prescribed by the Secretary or his delegate.

"(d) Installments Paid in Advance.—At the election of the corporation, any installment of the estimated tax may be paid before the date prescribed for its payment."

P.L. 90-364, §104(a), provides:

"Payment of Estimated Tax for Taxable Years Beginning Before Date of Enactment.—In determining whether any taxpayer is required to make a declaration or amended declaration of estimated tax, or to pay any amount or additional amount of estimated tax, by reason of the amendments made by sections 102 and 103—

"(1) such amendments shall apply (A) in the case of an individual, only if the taxable year ends on or after September 30, 1968, and (B) in the case of a corporation, only if the taxable year ends on or after June 30, 1968,

"(2) in applying sections 6015, 6073, and 6654 of the Internal Revenue Code of 1954, such amendments shall first be taken into account as of September 1, 1968, and

"(3) in applying sections 6016, 6074, 6154, and 6655 of such Code, such amendments shall first be taken into account as of May 31, 1968.

In the case of any amount or additional amount of estimated tax payable, by reason of such amendments, by a corporation on or after June 15, 1968, and before the 15th day of the date of the enactment of this Act, the time prescribed for payment of such amount or additional amount shall not expire before such date (not earlier than the 15th day after the date of the enactment of this Act) as the Secretary of the Treasury or his delegate shall prescribe."

- **1966, Tax Adjustment Act of 1966 (P.L. 89-368)**

P.L. 89-368, §104(a):

Amended Code Sec. 6154(a). **Effective** 1-1-66. Prior to amendment, Sec. 6154(a) read as follows:

"(a) Amount and Time for Payment of Each Installment.—The amount of estimated tax (as defined in section 6016(b)) with respect to which a declaration is required under section 6016 shall be paid as follows:

"(1) Payment in 4 installments.—If the declaration is filed on or before the 15th day of the 4th month of the taxable year, the estimated tax shall be paid in 4 installments. The amount and time for payment of each installment shall be determined in accordance with the following table:

If the taxable year begins in—	The following percentages of the estimated tax shall be paid on the 15th day of the—			
	4th month	6th month	9th month	12th month
1964	1	1	25	25
1965	4	4	25	25
1966	9	9	25	25
1967	14	14	25	25
1968	19	19	25	25
1969	22	22	25	25
1970 or any subsequent year	25	25	25	25

"(2) Payment in 3 installments.—If the declaration is filed after the 15th day of the 4th month and not after the 15th day of the 6th month of the taxable year, and is not required by section 6074(a) to be filed on or before the 15th day of such 4th month, the estimated tax shall be paid in 3 installments. The amount and time for payment of each installment shall be determined in accordance with the following table:

If the taxable year begins in—	The following percentages of the estimated tax shall be paid on the 15th day of the—		
	6th month	9th month	12th month
1964	$1^{1}/_{3}$	$25^{1}/_{3}$	$25^{1}/_{3}$
1965	$5^{1}/_{3}$	$26^{1}/_{3}$	$26^{1}/_{3}$
1966	12	28	28
1967	$18^{2}/_{3}$	$29^{2}/_{3}$	$29^{2}/_{3}$
1968	$25^{1}/_{3}$	$31^{1}/_{3}$	$31^{1}/_{3}$
1969	$29^{1}/_{3}$	$32^{1}/_{3}$	$32^{1}/_{3}$
1970 or any subsequent year	$33^{1}/_{3}$	$33^{1}/_{3}$	$33^{1}/_{3}$

"(3) Payment in 2 installments.—If the declaration of estimated tax is filed after the 15th day of the 6th month and not after the 15th day of the 9th month of the taxable year, and is not required by section 6074(a) to be filed on or before the 15th day of such 6th month, the estimated tax shall be paid in 2 installments. The amount and time for payment of each installment shall be determined in accordance with the following table:

If the taxable year begins in—	The following percentages of the estimated tax shall be paid on the 15th day of the—	
	9th month	12th month
1964	26	26
1965	29	29
1966	34	34
1967	39	39
1968	44	44

TAX PAYMENT—PLACE AND DUE DATE

If the taxable year begins in—	The following percentages of the estimated tax shall be paid on the 15th day of the—	
1969	47	47
1970 or any subsequent year	50	50

"(4) Payment in 1 installment.—If the declaration of estimated tax is filed after the 15th day of the 9th month of the taxable year, and is not required by section 6074(a) to be filed on or before the 15th day of such 9th month, the estimated tax shall be paid in 1 installment. The amount and time for payment of the installment shall be determined in accordance with the following table:

If the taxable year begins in—	The following percentages of the estimated tax shall be paid on the 15th day of the 12th month
1964	52
1965	58
1966	68
1967	78
1968	88
1969	94
1970 or any subsequent year	100

"(5) Late filing.—If the declaration is filed after the time prescribed in section 6074(a) (determined without regard to any extension of time for filing the declaration under section 6081), paragraphs (2), (3), and (4) of this subsection shall not apply, and there shall be paid at the time of such filing all installments of estimated tax which would have been payable on or before such time if the declaration had been filed within the time prescribed in section 6074(a), and the remaining installments shall be paid at the times at which, and in the amounts in which, they would have been payable if the declaration had been so filed."

• 1964, Revenue Act of 1964 (P.L. 88-272)

P.L. 88-272, § 122(a):

Amended Sec. 6154. **Effective** for tax years beginning after 12-31-63. Prior to amendment, Code Sec. 6154 read as follows:

"(a) Amount of Estimated Income Tax Required to Be Paid.—The amount of estimated tax (as defined in section 6016(b)) with respect to which a declaration is required under section 6016 shall be paid as follows:

If the taxable year ends—	The amount required to be paid shall be the following percentage of the estimated tax:
On or after December 31, 1955 and before December 31, 1956	10
On or after December 31, 1956 and before December 31, 1957	20
On or after December 31, 1957 and before December 31, 1958	30
On or after December 31, 1958 and before December 31, 1959	40
On or after December 31, 1959	50

"(b) Time for Payment of Installment.—If the declaration is filed on or before the 15th day of the 9th month of the taxable year, the amount determined under subsection (a) shall be paid in two equal installments. The first installment shall be paid on or before the 15th day of the 9th month of the taxable year, and the second installment shall be paid on or before the 15th day of the 12th month of the taxable year. If the declaration is filed after the 15th day of the 9th month of the taxable year, the amount determined under subsection (a) shall be paid in full on or before the 15th day of the 12th month of the taxable year.

"(c) Amendment of Declaration.—If any amendment of a declaration is filed, installments payable on the 15th day of the 12th month, if any, shall be ratably increased or decreased, as the case may be, to reflect the increase or decrease, as the case may be, in the estimated tax by reason of such amendment.

"(d) Application to Short Taxable Year.—The application of this section to taxable years of less than 12 months shall be in accordance with regulations prescribed by the Secretary or his delegate.

"(e) Installments Paid in Advance.—At the election of the corporation, any installment of the estimated tax may be paid prior to the date prescribed for its payment."

[Sec. 6155]

SEC. 6155. PAYMENT ON NOTICE AND DEMAND.

[Sec. 6155(a)]

(a) GENERAL RULE.—Upon receipt of notice and demand from the Secretary, there shall be paid at the place and time stated in such notice the amount of any tax (including any interest, additional amounts, additions to tax, and assessable penalties) stated in such notice and demand.

Amendments
• 1976, Tax Reform Act of 1976 (P.L. 94-455)

P.L. 94-455, § 1906(b)(13)(A):

Amended 1954 Code by substituting "Secretary" for "Secretary or his delegate" each place it appeared. **Effective** 2-1-77.

[Sec. 6155(b)]

(b) CROSS REFERENCES.—

(1) For restrictions on assessment and collection of deficiency assessments of taxes subject to the jurisdiction of the Tax Court, see sections 6212 and 6213.

(2) For provisions relating to assessment of claims allowed in a receivership proceeding, see section 6873.

(3) For provisions relating to jeopardy assessments, see subchapter A of chapter 70.

Amendments
• 1980, Bankruptcy Tax Act of 1980 (P.L. 96-589)

P.L. 96-589, § 6(i)(7):

Amended Code Sec. 6155(b)(2) by striking out "bankruptcy or". **Effective** 10-1-79 but inapplicable to any proceeding under the Bankruptcy Act commenced before that date. Prior to amendment, Code Sec. 6155(b)(2) provided:

"(2) For provisions relating to assessment of claims allowed in a bankruptcy or receivership proceeding, see section 6873.".

[Sec. 6156—Repealed]

Amendments
• 2004, American Jobs Creation Act of 2004 (P.L. 108-357)

P.L. 108-357, § 867(b)(1):

Repealed Code Sec. 6156. **Effective** for tax periods beginning after 10-22-2004. Prior to repeal, Code Sec. 6156 read as follows:

SEC. 6156. INSTALLMENT PAYMENTS OF TAX ON USE OF HIGHWAY MOTOR VEHICLES.

[Sec. 6156(a)]

(a) PRIVILEGE TO PAY TAX IN INSTALLMENTS.—If the taxpayer files a return of the tax imposed by section 4481 on or before the date prescribed for the filing of such return, he may elect to pay the tax shown on such return in equal installments in accordance with the following table:

If liability is incurred in—	The number of installments shall be—
July, August, or September	4
October, November, or December	3
January, February, or March	2

Amendments
• 1982, Tax Equity and Fiscal Responsibility Act of 1982 (P.L. 97-248)

P.L. 97-248, § 280(c)(2)(C):

Amended Code Sec. 6156(a) by striking out " or 4491" after "section 4481". **Effective** 9-1-82.

TAX PAYMENT—PLACE AND DUE DATE

P.L. 97-248, §280(c)(2)(E):

Amended the section heading. **Effective** 9-1-82. Prior to amendment, the section heading read as follows:

"INSTALLMENT PAYMENTS OF TAX ON USE OF HIGHWAY MOTOR VEHICLES AND CIVIL AIRCRAFT."

[Sec. 6156(b)]

(b) DATES FOR PAYING INSTALLMENTS.—In the case of any tax payable in installments by reason of an election under subsection (a)—

(1) the first installment shall be paid on the date prescribed for payment of the tax,

(2) the second installment shall be paid on or before the last day of the third month following the calendar quarter in which the liability was incurred,

(3) the third installment (if any) shall be paid on or before the last day of the sixth month following the calendar quarter in which the liability was incurred, and

(4) the fourth installment (if any) shall be paid on or before the last day of the ninth month following the calendar quarter in which the liability was incurred.

[Sec. 6156(c)]

(c) PRORATION OF ADDITIONAL TAX TO INSTALLMENTS.—If an election has been made under subsection (a) in respect of tax reported on a return filed by the taxpayer and tax required to be shown but not shown on such return is assessed before the date prescribed for payment of the last installment, the additional tax shall be prorated equally to the installments for which the election was made. That part of the additional tax so prorated to any installment the date for payment of which has not arrived shall be collected at the same time as and as part of such installment. That part of the additional tax so prorated to any installment the date for payment of which has arrived shall be paid upon notice and demand from the Secretary.

Amendments

• **1976, Tax Reform Act of 1976 (P.L. 94-455)**

P.L. 94-455, §1906(b)(13)(A):

Amended 1954 Code by substituting "Secretary" for "Secretary or his delegate" each place it appeared. **Effective** 2-1-77.

[Sec. 6156(d)]

(d) ACCELERATION OF PAYMENTS.—If the taxpayer does not pay any installment under this section on or before the date prescribed for its payment, the whole of the unpaid tax shall be paid upon notice and demand from the Secretary.

Amendments

• **1976, Tax Reform Act of 1976 (P.L. 94-455)**

P.L. 94-455, §1906(b)(13)(A):

Amended 1954 Code by substituting "Secretary" for "Secretary or his delegate" each place it appeared. **Effective** 2-1-77.

[Sec. 6156(e)]

(e) SECTION INAPPLICABLE TO CERTAIN LIABILITIES.—This section shall not apply to any liability for tax incurred in—

(1) April, May, or June of any year, or

(2) July, August, or September of 2005.

Amendments

• **1998, Transportation Equity Act for the 21st Century (P.L. 105-178)**

P.L. 105-178, §9002(a)(2)(B):

Amended Code Sec. 6156(e)(2) by striking "1999" and inserting "2005". **Effective** 6-9-98.

• **1991, Intermodal Surface Transportation Efficiency Act of 1991 (P.L. 102-240)**

P.L. 102-240, §8002(c)(2):

Amended Code Sec. 6156(e)(2) by striking "1995" and inserting "1999". **Effective** 12-18-91.

• **1990, Omnibus Budget Reconciliation Act of 1990 (P.L. 101-508)**

P.L. 101-508, §11211(f)(2):

Amended Code Sec. 6156(e)(2) by striking "1993" and inserting "1995". **Effective** 11-5-90.

• **1987, Surface Transportation and Uniform Relocation Assistance Act of 1987 (P.L. 100-17)**

P.L. 100-17, §502(d)(2):

Amended Code Sec. 6156(e)(2) by striking out "1988" and inserting in lieu thereof "1993". **Effective** 4-2-87.

• **1983, Surface Transportation Act of 1982 (P.L. 97-424)**

P.L. 97-424, §516(a)(6):

Amended Code Sec. 6156(e)(2) by striking out "1984" and inserting "1988". **Effective** 1-6-83.

• **1982, Tax Equity and Fiscal Responsibility Act of 1982 (P.L. 97-248)**

P.L. 97-248, §280(c)(2)(D):

Amended Code Sec. 6156(e)(2) by striking out at the end "in the case of the tax imposed by section 4481". **Effective** 9-1-82.

• **1978, Surface Transportation Assistance Act of 1978 (P.L. 95-599)**

P.L. 95-599, §502(a)(9):

Substituted "1984" for "1979" in Code Sec. 6156(e)(2). **Effective** 11-7-78.

• **1976 (P.L. 94-280)**

P.L. 94-280, §303(a)(10):

Amended Code Sec. 6156(e)(2) by substituting "1979" for "1977."

• **1970, Federal-Aid Highway Act of 1970 (P.L. 91-605)**

P.L. 91-605, §303(a)(10):

Amended Code Sec. 6156(e)(2) by substituting "1977" for "1972."

• **1970 (P.L. 91-258)**

P.L. 91-258, §206(b):

Amended Code Sec. 6156 by adding "AND CIVIL AIRCRAFT" in the heading, by adding "or 4491" in subsection (a), and by adding "in the case of the tax imposed by section 4481" at the end of subsection (e). **Effective** 7-1-70.

• **1961, Federal-Aid Highway Act of 1961 (P.L. 87-61)**

P.L. 87-61, §203(c):

Amended subchapter A of chapter 62 by renumbering Sec. 6156 as 6157 and adding new Sec. 6156. **Effective** 7-1-61.

[Sec. 6157]

SEC. 6157. PAYMENT OF FEDERAL UNEMPLOYMENT TAX ON QUARTERLY OR OTHER TIME PERIOD BASIS.

[Sec. 6157(a)]

(a) GENERAL RULE.—Every person who for the calendar year is an employer (as defined in section 3306(a)) shall—

(1) if the person is such an employer for the preceding calendar year (determined by only taking into account wages paid and employment during such preceding calendar year), compute the tax imposed by section 3301 for each of the first 3 calendar quarters in the calendar year on wages paid for services with respect to which the person is such an employer for such preceding calendar year (as so determined), and

(2) if the person is not such an employer for the preceding calendar year with respect to any services (as so determined), compute the tax imposed by section 3301 on wages paid for services with respect to which the person is not such an employer for the preceding calendar year (as so determined)—

(A) for the period beginning with the first day of the calendar year and ending with the last day of the calendar quarter (excluding the last calendar quarter) in which such person becomes such an employer with respect to such services, and

(B) for the third calendar quarter of such year, if the period specified in subparagraph (A) includes only the first two calendar quarters of the calendar year.

The tax for any calendar quarter or other period shall be computed as provided in subsection (b) and the tax as so computed shall, except as otherwise provided in subsection (c), be paid in such manner and at such time as may be provided in regulations prescribed by the Secretary.

Amendments

• **1989, Omnibus Budget Reconciliation Act of 1989 (P.L. 101-239)**

P.L. 101-239, §7841(d)(12):

Amended Code Sec. 6157(a) by striking "subsections (c) and (d)" and inserting "subsection (c)" in the last sentence. **Effective** 12-19-89. [Note: This amendment was superfluous as Code Sec. 6157(a) already read as noted in the preceding sentence.—CCH].

• **1976, Unemployment Compensation Amendments of 1976 (P.L. 94-566)**

P.L. 94-566, §114(b):

Amended Code Sec. 6157(a). **Effective** with respect to remuneration paid after 12-31-77, for services performed after that date. Prior to amendment, Code Sec. 6157(a) read as follows:

Internal Revenue Code   **Sec. 6157(a)(2)(B)**

TAX PAYMENT—PLACE AND DUE DATE

(a) GENERAL RULE.—Every person who for the calendar year is an employer (as defined in section 3306(a)) shall—

(1) if the person

(A) during any calendar quarter in the preceding calendar year paid wages of $1,500 or more, or

(B) on each of some 20 days during the preceding calendar year, each day being in a different calendar week, employed at least one individual in employment,

compute the tax imposed by section 3301 for each of the first three calendar quarters in the calendar year, and

(2) if paragraph (1) does not apply, compute the tax imposed by section 3301—

(A) for the period beginning with the first day of the calendar year and ending with the last day of the calendar quarter (excluding the last calendar quarter) in which such person becomes such an employer, and

(B) for the third calendar quarter of such year, if the period specified in subparagraph (A) includes only the first two calendar quarters of the calendar year.

The tax for any calendar quarter or other period shall be computed as provided in subsection (b) and the tax as so computed shall, except as otherwise provided in subsection (c), be paid in such manner and at such time as may be provided in regulations prescribed by the Secretary.

[Sec. 6157(b)]

(b) COMPUTATION OF TAX.—The tax for any calendar quarter or other period referred to in paragraph (1) or (2) of subsection (a) shall be computed by multiplying the amount of wages (as defined in section 3306(b)) paid in such calendar quarter or other period by 0.6 percent. In the case of wages paid in any calendar quarter or other period during a calendar year to which paragraph (1) of section 3301 applies, the amount of such wages shall be multiplied by 0.8 percent in lieu of 0.6 percent.

Amendments

• **1982, Tax Equity and Fiscal Responsibility Act of 1982 (P.L. 97-248)**

P.L. 97-248, §271(b)(2)(C):

Amended Code Sec. 6157(b) by striking out "0.7 percent" and inserting "0.8 percent". **Effective** for remuneration paid after 12-31-82.

P.L. 97-248, §271(c)(3)(C):

Amended Code Sec. 6157(b) by striking out each place it appears "0.5 percent" and inserting "0.6 percent". **Effective** for remuneration paid after 12-31-84.

• **1976, Unemployment Compensation Amendments of 1976 (P.L. 94-566)**

P.L. 94-566, §211(c)(3):

Amended the last sentence of Sec. 6157(b). **Effective** 10-20-76. Prior to amendment it read as follows:

"In the case of wages paid in any calendar quarter or other period during 1973, the amount of such wages shall be multiplied by 0.58 percent in lieu of 0.5 percent."

[Sec. 6157(c)]

(c) SPECIAL RULE WHERE ACCUMULATED AMOUNT DOES NOT EXCEED $100.—Nothing in this section shall require the payment of tax with respect to any calendar quarter or other period if the tax under section 3301 for such period, plus any unpaid amounts for prior periods in the calendar year, does not exceed $100.

Amendments

• **1976, Tax Reform Act of 1976 (P.L. 94-455)**

P.L. 94-455, §1906(a)(11)(A):

Struck out former Code Sec. 6157(c) and redesignated former Code Sec. 6157(d) as Code Sec. 6157(c). **Effective** 2-1-77. Prior to striking, Code Sec. 6157(c) read as follows:

(c) SPECIAL RULE FOR CALENDAR YEARS 1970 AND 1971.—For purposes of subsection (a), the tax computed as provided in subsection (b) for any calendar quarter or other period shall be reduced (1) by 66$^{2}/_{3}$ percent if such quarter or period is in 1970, and (2) by 33$^{1}/_{3}$ percent if such quarter or period is in 1971.

• **1969 (P.L. 91-53)**

P.L. 91-53, §2(a):

Amended Code Sec. 6157. **Effective** for calendar years beginning after 12-31-69. Prior to amendment, Code Sec. 6157 read as follows:

[Sec. 6157(d)—Repealed]

Amendments

• **1988, Technical and Miscellaneous Revenue Act of 1988 (P.L. 100-647)**

P.L. 100-647, §7106(c)(1):

Repealed Code Sec. 6157(d). **Effective** for remuneration paid after 12-31-88. Prior to repeal, Code Sec. 6157(d) read as follows:

(d) QUARTERLY PAYMENT OF RAILROAD UNEMPLOYMENT REPAYMENT TAX.—

(1) IN GENERAL.—Every rail employer shall compute the tax imposed by section 3321 for each calendar quarter in any taxable period in the manner provided in paragraph (2). The tax so computed shall, except as otherwise provided in paragraph (3), be paid in such manner and at such time as may be provided in regulations prescribed by the Secretary.

(2) COMPUTATION OF TAX.—The tax for any calendar quarter shall be computed by multiplying the aggregate amount of rail wages paid in such calendar quarter by the applicable percentage determined under section 3321(c).

[Sec. 6158—Repealed]

Amendments

• **1990, Omnibus Budget Reconciliation Act of 1990 (P.L. 101-508)**

P.L. 101-508, §11801(a)(44):

Repealed Code Sec. 6158. **Effective** on 11-5-90.

• **1976, Tax Reform Act of 1976 (P.L. 94-455)**

P.L. 94-455, §1906(a)(11)(B):

Substituted "subsection (c)" for "subsections (c) and (d)" in Code Sec. 6157(a). **Effective** 2-1-77.

P.L. 94-455, §1906(b)(13)(A):

Amended 1954 Code by substituting "Secretary" for "Secretary or his delegate" each place it appeared. **Effective** 2-1-77.

• **1970, Employment Security Amendments of 1970 (P.L. 91-373)**

P.L. 91-373, §101(b):

Amended Code Sec. 6157(a)(1) to read as prior to amendment by P.L. 94-455 and P.L. 94-566. Prior to amendment, Code Sec. 6157(a)(1) read as follows:

(1) if the person in the preceding calendar year employed 4 or more employees in employment (within the meaning of section 3306(c) and (d)) on each of some 20 days during such preceding calendar year, each such day being in a different calendar week, compute the tax imposed by section 3301 for each of the first three calendar quarters in the calendar year, and

• **1972 (P.L. 92-329)**

P.L. 92-329, §2(b):

Added the last sentence of Code Sec. 6157(b).

• **1970, Employment Security Amendments of 1970 (P.L. 91-373)**

P.L. 91-373, §101(b):

Substituted "0.5 percent" for "the number of percentage points (including fractional points) by which the rate of tax specified in section 3301 exceeds 2.7 percent" in Code Sec. 6157(b). **Effective** for calendar years beginning after 12-31-69.

P.L. 91-373, §301(b), provides:

"(b) For purposes of section 6157 of the Internal Revenue Code of 1954 (relating to payment of Federal unemployment tax on quarterly or other time period basis), in computing tax as required by subsections (a)(1) and (2) of such section, the percentage contained in subsection (b) of such section applicable with respect to wages paid in any calendar quarter in 1970 ending before the date of the enactment of this Act [August 10, 1970] shall be treated as being 0.4 percent."

SEC. 6157. PAYMENT OF TAXES UNDER PROVISIONS OF THE TARIFF ACT.

For collection under the provisions of the Tariff Act of 1930 of the taxes imposed by section 4501(b), and subchapters A, B, C, D, and E of chapter 38, see sections 4504 and 4601, respectively.

• **1961, Federal-Aid Highway Act of 1961 (P.L. 87-61)**

P.L. 87-61, §203(c):

Amended subchapter A of chapter 62 by renumbering Sec. 6156 as 6157 and adding new Sec. 6156. **Effective** 7-1-61.

(3) EXCEPTIONS.—No payment shall be required under this subsection—

(A) for the last calendar quarter in any taxable period, and

(B) for any calendar quarter if the tax under section 3321 for such quarter, plus any unpaid amounts for prior calendar quarters in the taxable period, does not exceed $100.

(4) DEFINITIONS.—For purposes of this subsection, the terms "taxable period", "rail employer", and "rail wages" have the same respective meanings as when used in chapter 23A.

• **1983, Railroad Retirement Solvency Act of 1983 (P.L. 98-76)**

P.L. 98-76, §231(b)(1):

Added Code Sec. 6157(d). **Effective** for remuneration paid after 6-30-86.

P.L. 101-508, §11821(b)(1)-(2), provides:

(b) SAVINGS PROVISION.—If—

(1) any provision amended or repealed by this part applied to—

(A) any transaction occurring before the date of the enactment of this Act,

Sec. 6157(b)

(B) any property acquired before such date of enactment, or

(C) any item of income, loss, deduction, or credit taken into account before such date of enactment,

(2) the treatment of such transaction, property, or item under such provision would (without regard to the amendments made by this part) affect liability for tax for periods ending after such date of enactment,

nothing in the amendments made by this part shall be construed to affect the treatment of such transaction, property, or item for purposes of determining liability for tax for periods ending after such date of enactment.

Prior to repeal, Code Sec. 6158 read as follows:

SEC. 6158. INSTALLMENT PAYMENT OF TAX ATTRIBUTABLE TO DIVESTITURES PURSUANT TO BANK HOLDING COMPANY ACT AMENDMENTS OF 1970.

(a) ELECTION OF EXTENSION.—If, after July 7, 1970, a qualified bank holding corporation sells bank property or prohibited property, the divestiture of either of which the Board certifies, before such sale, is necessary or appropriate to effectuate section 4 or the policies of the Bank Holding Company Act, the tax under chapter 1 attributable to such sale shall, at the election of the taxpayer, be payable in equal annual installments beginning with the due date (determined without extension) for the taxpayer's return of tax under chapter 1 for the taxable year in which the sale occurred and ending with the corresponding date in 1985. If the number of installments determined under the preceding sentence is less than 10, such number shall be increased to 10 equal annual installments which begin as provided in the preceding sentence and which end on the corresponding date 10 years later. An election under this subsection shall be made at such time and in such manner as the Secretary may by regulations prescribe.

(b) LIMITATIONS.—

(1) TREATMENT NOT AVAILABLE TO TAXPAYER FOR BOTH BANK PROPERTY AND PROHIBITED PROPERTY.—This section shall not apply to any sale of prohibited property if the taxpayer (or a corporation having control of the taxpayer or a subsidiary of the taxpayer) has made an election under subsection (a) with respect to bank property or has made any distribution pursuant to section 1101(b). This section shall not apply to bank property if the taxpayer (or a corporation having control of the taxpayer or a subsidiary of the taxpayer) has made an election under subsection (a) with respect to prohibited property or has made any distribution pursuant to section 1101(a).

(2) TREATMENT NOT AVAILABLE FOR CERTAIN INSTALLMENT SALES.—No election may be made under subsection (a) with respect to a sale if the income from such sale is being returned at the time and in the manner provided in section 453 (relating to installment method).

(c) ACCELERATION OF PAYMENTS.—If an election is made under subsection (a) and before the tax attributable to such sale is paid in full—

(1) any installment under this section is not paid on or before the date fixed by this section for its payment, or

(2) the Board fails to make a certification similar to the applicable certification provided in section 1101(e) within the time prescribed therein (for this purpose treating the last such sale as constituting the last distribution),

then the extension of time for payment of tax provided in this section shall cease to apply, and any portion of the tax payable in installments shall be paid on notice and demand from the Secretary.

(d) PRORATION OF DEFICIENCY TO INSTALLMENTS.—If an election is made under subsection (a) and a deficiency attributable to the sale has been assessed, the deficiency shall be prorated to such installments. The part of the deficiency so prorated to any installment the date for payment of which has not arrived shall be collected at the same time as, and as part of, such installment. The part of the deficiency so prorated to any installment the date for payment of which has arrived shall be paid on notice and demand from the Secretary. This subsection shall not apply if the deficiency is due to negligence, to intentional disregard of rules and regulations, or to fraud with intent to evade tax.

(e) BOND MAY BE REQUIRED.—If an election is made under this section, section 6165 shall apply as though the Secretary were extending the time for payment of the tax.

(f) DEFINITIONS.—For purposes of this section—

(1) TERMS HAVE MEANINGS GIVEN TO THEM BY SECTION 1103.—The terms "qualified bank holding corporation", "Bank Holding Company Act", "Board", "control", and "subsidiary" have the respective meanings given to such terms by section 1103.

(2) PROHIBITED PROPERTY.—The term "prohibited property" means property held by a qualified bank holding corporation which could be distributed without recognition of gain under section 1101(a)(1).

(3) BANK PROPERTY.—The term "bank property" means property held by a qualified bank holding corporation which could be distributed without recognition of gain under section 1101(b)(1).

(g) CROSS REFERENCES.—

(1) SECURITY.—For authority of the Secretary to require security in the case of an extension under this section, see section 6165.

(2) PERIOD OF LIMITATION.—For extension of the period of limitation in the case of an extension under this section, see section 6503(i).

• **1976, Tax Reform Act of 1976 (P.L. 94-455)**

P.L. 94-455, §1906(b)(13)(A):

Amended 1954 Code by substituting "Secretary" for "Secretary or his delegate" each place it appeared. **Effective** 2-1-77.

• **1976, Bank Holding Company Tax Act of 1976 (P.L. 94-452)**

P.L. 94-452, §3(a):

Added Code Sec. 6158. **Effective**, generally, 10-1-77, with respect to sales after 7-7-70, in tax years ending after 7-7-70, but only in the case of qualified bank holding corporations with the following exceptions: (1) For purposes of Code Sec. 6158(a), in the case of any sale which takes place on or before 12-31-76, a certification by the Federal Reserve Board shall be treated as made before the sale if application for such certification is made before the close of 12-31-76; (2) If any tax attributable to a sale which occurred before 10-1-77, is payable in annual installments by reason of an election under Code Sec. 6158(a), any portion of such tax for which the due date of the installment does not occur before 10-1-77, shall on application of the taxpayer, be treated as an overpayment of tax; (3) For purposes of Code Sec. 6611(b), in the case of any overpayment attributable to (2), above, the date of the overpayment shall be the day which is 6 months after the latest of (a) the date on which application for refund or credit of overpayment is filed; (b) the due date prescribed by law (determined without extensions) for filing the return of tax under chapter 1 of the 1954 Internal Revenue Code for the taxable year the tax of which is being refunded or credited, or (c) 10-2-76. Further, if any refund or credit of tax attributable to the application of (2), above, is prevented any time before 10-1-78, refund or credit of such overpayment may be made or allowed if claim therefor is filed before 10-1-78.

[Sec. 6159]

SEC. 6159. AGREEMENTS FOR PAYMENT OF TAX LIABILITY IN INSTALLMENTS.

[Sec. 6159(a)]

(a) AUTHORIZATION OF AGREEMENTS.—The Secretary is authorized to enter into written agreements with any taxpayer under which such taxpayer is allowed to make payment on any tax in installment payments if the Secretary determines that such agreement will facilitate full or partial collection of such liability.

Amendments

• **2004, American Jobs Creation Act of 2004 (P.L. 108-357)**

P.L. 108-357, §843(a)(1)(A)-(B):

Amended Code Sec. 6159(a) by striking "satisfy liability for payment of" and inserting "make payment on", and by inserting "full or partial" after "facilitate". **Effective** for agreements entered into on or after 10-22-2004.

[Sec. 6159(b)]

(b) EXTENT TO WHICH AGREEMENTS REMAIN IN EFFECT.—

(1) IN GENERAL.—Except as otherwise provided in this subsection, any agreement entered into by the Secretary under subsection (a) shall remain in effect for the term of the agreement.

(2) INADEQUATE INFORMATION OR JEOPARDY.—The Secretary may terminate any agreement entered into by the Secretary under subsection (a) if—

(A) information which the taxpayer provided to the Secretary prior to the date such agreement was entered into was inaccurate or incomplete, or

(B) the Secretary believes that collection of any tax to which an agreement under this section relates is in jeopardy.

(3) SUBSEQUENT CHANGE IN FINANCIAL CONDITIONS.—If the Secretary makes a determination that the financial condition of a taxpayer with whom the Secretary has entered into an agreement under subsection (a) has significantly changed, the Secretary may alter, modify, or terminate such agreement.

(4) FAILURE TO PAY AN INSTALLMENT OR ANY OTHER TAX LIABILITY WHEN DUE OR TO PROVIDE REQUESTED FINANCIAL INFORMATION.—The Secretary may alter, modify, or terminate an agreement entered into by the Secretary under subsection (a) in the case of the failure of the taxpayer—

(A) to pay any installment at the time such installment payment is due under such agreement,

(B) to pay any other tax liability at the time such liability is due, or

(C) to provide a financial condition update as requested by the Secretary.

TAX PAYMENT—PLACE AND DUE DATE

(5) NOTICE REQUIREMENTS.—The Secretary may not take any action under paragraph (2), (3), or (4) unless—

(A) a notice of such action is provided to the taxpayer not later than the day 30 days before the date of such action, and

(B) such notice includes an explanation why the Secretary intends to take such action.

The preceding sentence shall not apply in any case in which the Secretary believes that collection of any tax to which an agreement under this section relates is in jeopardy.

Amendments

• **1996, Taxpayer Bill of Rights 2 (P.L. 104-168)**

P.L. 104-168, § 201(a):

Amended Code Sec. 6159(b) by adding at the end a new paragraph (5). **Effective** on the date 6 months after 7-30-96.

P.L. 104-168, § 201(b):

Amended Code Sec. 6159(b)(3). **Effective** on the date 6 months after 7-30-96. Prior to amendment, Code Sec. 6159(b)(3) read as follows:

(3) SUBSEQUENT CHANGE IN FINANCIAL CONDITIONS.—

(A) IN GENERAL.—If the Secretary makes a determination that the financial condition of a taxpayer with whom the Secretary has entered into an agreement under subsection (a) has significantly changed, the Secretary may alter, modify, or terminate such agreement.

(B) NOTICE.—Action may be taken by the Secretary under subparagraph (A) only if—

(i) notice of such determination is provided to the taxpayer no later than 30 days prior to the date of such action, and

(ii) such notice includes the reasons why the Secretary believes a significant change in the financial condition of the taxpayer has occurred.

• **1988, Technical and Miscellaneous Revenue Act of 1988 (P.L. 100-647)**

P.L. 100-647, § 6234(a):

Amended subchapter A of chapter 62 by adding at the end thereof a new Section 6159. **Effective** for agreements entered into after 11-10-88.

[Sec. 6159(c)]

(c) SECRETARY REQUIRED TO ENTER INTO INSTALLMENT AGREEMENTS IN CERTAIN CASES.—In the case of a liability for tax of an individual under subtitle A, the Secretary shall enter into an agreement to accept the full payment of such tax in installments if, as of the date the individual offers to enter into the agreement—

(1) the aggregate amount of such liability (determined without regard to interest, penalties, additions to the tax, and additional amounts) does not exceed $10,000;

(2) the taxpayer (and, if such liability relates to a joint return, the taxpayer's spouse) has not, during any of the preceding 5 taxable years—

(A) failed to file any return of tax imposed by subtitle A;

(B) failed to pay any tax required to be shown on any such return; or

(C) entered into an installment agreement under this section for payment of any tax imposed by subtitle A,

(3) the Secretary determines that the taxpayer is financially unable to pay such liability in full when due (and the taxpayer submits such information as the Secretary may require to make such determination);

(4) the agreement requires full payment of such liability within 3 years; and

(5) the taxpayer agrees to comply with the provisions of this title for the period such agreement is in effect.

Amendments

• **2004, American Jobs Creation Act of 2004 (P.L. 108-357)**

P.L. 108-357, § 843(a)(2):

Amended the matter preceding paragraph (1) of Code Sec. 6159(c) by inserting "full" before "payment". **Effective** for agreements entered into on or after 10-22-2004.

• **1998, IRS Restructuring and Reform Act of 1998 (P.L. 105-206)**

P.L. 105-206, § 3467(a):

Amended Code Sec. 6159 by redesignating subsection (c) as subsection (d) and by inserting after subsection (b) a new subsection (c). **Effective** 7-22-98.

P.L. 105-206, § 3506 (as amended by P.L. 106-554, § 302(a)), provides:

SEC. 3506. STATEMENTS REGARDING INSTALLMENT AGREEMENTS.

The Secretary of the Treasury or the Secretary's delegate shall, beginning not later than July 1, 2000, provide each taxpayer who has an installment agreement in effect under section 6159 of the Internal Revenue Code of 1986 an annual statement setting forth the initial balance at the beginning of the year, the payments made during the year, and the remaining balance as of the end of the year.

[Sec. 6159(d)]

(d) SECRETARY REQUIRED TO REVIEW INSTALLMENT AGREEMENTS FOR PARTIAL COLLECTION EVERY TWO YEARS.—In the case of an agreement entered into by the Secretary under subsection (a) for partial collection of a tax liability, the Secretary shall review the agreement at least once every 2 years.

Amendments

• **2004, American Jobs Creation Act of 2004 (P.L. 108-357)**

P.L. 108-357, § 843(b):

Amended Code Sec. 6159 by redesignating subsections (d) and (e) as subsections (e) and (f), respectively, and inserting after subsection (c) a new subsection (d). **Effective** for agreements entered into on or after 10-22-2004.

[Sec. 6159(e)]

(e) ADMINISTRATIVE REVIEW.—The Secretary shall establish procedures for an independent administrative review of terminations of installment agreements under this section for taxpayers who request such a review.

Amendments

• **2004, American Jobs Creation Act of 2004 (P.L. 108-357)**

P.L. 108-357, § 843(b):

Amended Code Sec. 6159 by redesignating subsection (d) as subsection (e). **Effective** for agreements entered into on or after 10-22-2004.

• **1998, IRS Restructuring and Reform Act of 1998 (P.L. 105-206)**

P.L. 105-206, § 3467(a):

Amended Code Sec. 6159 by redesignating subsection (c) as subsection (d). **Effective** 7-22-98.

• **1996, Taxpayer Bill of Rights 2 (P.L. 104-168)**

P.L. 104-168, § 202(a):

Amended Code Sec. 6159 by adding at the end a new subsection (c). **Effective** 1-1-97.

[Sec. 6159(f)]

(f) INSTALLMENT AGREEMENT FEES.—

(1) LIMITATION ON FEE AMOUNT.—The amount of any fee imposed on an installment agreement under this section may not exceed the amount of such fee as in effect on the date of the enactment of this subsection.

(2) WAIVER OR REIMBURSEMENT.—In the case of any taxpayer with an adjusted gross income, as determined for the most recent year for which such information is available, which does not exceed 250 percent of the applicable poverty level (as determined by the Secretary)—

(A) if the taxpayer has agreed to make payments under the installment agreement by electronic payment through a debit instrument, no fee shall be imposed on an installment agreement under this section, and

TAX PAYMENT—EXTENSIONS OF TIME

(B) if the taxpayer is unable to make payments under the installment agreement by electronic payment through a debit instrument, the Secretary shall, upon completion of the installment agreement, pay the taxpayer an amount equal to any such fees imposed.

Amendments

• **2018, Bipartisan Budget Act of 2018 (P.L. 115-123)**

P.L. 115-123, §41105(a), Div. D:

Amended Code Sec. 6159 by redesignating subsection (f) as subsection (g) and by inserting after subsection (e) a new subsection (f). **Effective** for agreements entered into on or after the date which is 60 days after 2-9-2018.

[Sec. 6159(g)]

(g) CROSS REFERENCE.—

For rights to administrative review and appeal, see section 7122(e).

Amendments

• **2018, Bipartisan Budget Act of 2018 (P.L. 115-123)**

P.L. 115-123, §41105(a), Div. D:

Amended Code Sec. 6159 by redesignating subsection (f) as subsection (g). **Effective** for agreements entered into on or after the date which is 60 days after 2-9-2018.

• **2006, Tax Increase Prevention and Reconciliation Act of 2005 (P.L. 109-222)**

P.L. 109-222, §509(c):

Amended Code Sec. 6159(f) by striking "section 7122(d)" and inserting "section 7122(e)". **Effective** for offers-in-compromise submitted on and after the date which is 60 days after 5-17-2006.

• **2004, American Jobs Creation Act of 2004 (P.L. 108-357)**

P.L. 108-357, §843(b):

Amended Code Sec. 6159 by redesignating subsection (e) as subsection (f). **Effective** for agreements entered into on or after 10-22-2004.

• **1998, Tax and Trade Relief Extension Act of 1998 (P.L. 105-277)**

P.L. 105-277, §4002(g):

Amended Code Sec. 6159 by redesignating the subsection (d) relating to cross reference as subsection (e). **Effective** as if included in the provision of P.L. 105-206 to which it relates [**effective** 7-22-98.—CCH].

• **1998, IRS Restructuring and Reform Act of 1998 (P.L. 105-206)**

P.L. 105-206, §3462(c)(2):

Amended Code Sec. 6159 by adding at the end a new subsection (d) [(e)]. **Effective** for proposed offers-in-compromise and installment agreements submitted after 7-22-98.

Subchapter B—Extensions of Time for Payment

Sec. 6161.	Extension of time for paying tax.
Sec. 6163.	Extension of time for payment of estate tax on value of reversionary or remainder interest in property.
Sec. 6164.	Extension of time for payment of taxes by corporations expecting carrybacks.
Sec. 6165.	Bonds where time to pay tax or deficiency has been extended.
Sec. 6166.	Extension of time for payment of estate tax where estate consists largely of interest in closely held business.
Sec. 6167.	Extension of time for payment of tax attributable to recovery of foreign expropriation losses.

[Sec. 6161]

SEC. 6161. EXTENSION OF TIME FOR PAYING TAX.

[Sec. 6161(a)]

(a) AMOUNT DETERMINED BY TAXPAYER ON RETURN.—

(1) GENERAL RULE.—The Secretary, except as otherwise provided in this title, may extend the time for payment of the amount of the tax shown, or required to be shown, on any return or declaration required under authority of this title (or any installment thereof), for a reasonable period not to exceed 6 months (12 months in the case of estate tax) from the date fixed for payment thereof. Such extension may exceed 6 months in the case of a taxpayer who is abroad.

(2) ESTATE TAX.—The Secretary may, for reasonable cause, extend the time for payment of—

(A) any part of the amount determined by the executor as the tax imposed by chapter 11, or

(B) any part of any installment under section 6166 (including any part of a deficiency prorated to any installment under such section),

for a reasonable period not in excess of 10 years from the date prescribed by section 6151(a) for payment of the tax (or, in the case of an amount referred to in subparagraph (B), if later, not beyond the date which is 12 months after the due date for the last installment).

Amendments

• **1981, Economic Recovery Tax Act of 1981 (P.L. 97-34)**

P.L. 97-34, §422(e)(1):

Amended Code Sec. 6161(a) by striking out "or 6166A". **Effective** for estates of decedents dying after 12-31-81.

• **1976, Tax Reform Act of 1976 (P.L. 94-455)**

P.L. 94-455, §1906(b)(13)(A):

Amended 1954 Code by substituting "Secretary" for "Secretary or his delegate" each place it appeared. **Effective** 2-1-77.

P.L. 94-455, §2004(c)(1):

Amended Code Sec. 6161(a)(2). **Effective** for the estates of decedents dying after 12-31-76. Prior to amendment, Code Sec. 6161(a)(2) read as follows:

(2) ESTATE TAX.—If the Secretary or his delegate finds—

(A) that the payment, on the due date, of any part of the amount determined by the executor as the tax imposed by chapter 11,

(B) that the payment, on the date fixed for the payment of any installment under section 6166, of any part of such installment (including any part of a deficiency prorated to an installment the date for payment of which had not arrived), or

(C) that the payment upon notice and demand of any part of a deficiency prorated under the provisions of section 6166 to installments the date for payment of which had arrived,

would result in undue hardship to the estate, he may extend the time for payment for a reasonable period not in excess of 10 years from the date prescribed by section 6151(a) for payment of the tax.

• **1970, Excise, Estate, and Gift Tax Adjustment Act of 1970 (P.L. 91-614)**

P.L. 91-614, §101(h):

Amended Code Sec. 6161(a) by adding "(12 months in the case of estate tax)" in the first sentence of paragraph (1). **Effective** 1-1-71.

• **1958, Technical Amendments Act of 1958 (P.L. 85-866)**

P.L. 85-866, §206(c):

Amended paragraph (2) of Sec. 6161(a). For **effective** date, see Act Sec. 206(f), below. Prior to amendment, paragraph (2) read as follows:

"(2) Estate Tax.—If the Secretary or his delegate finds that the payment on the due date of any part of the amount determined by the executor as the tax imposed by chapter 11 would result in undue hardship to the estate, he may extend the time for payment for a reasonable period not in excess of 10 years from the date fixed for payment of the tax."

P.L. 85-866, §206(f), provides:

"The amendments made by this section shall apply to estates of decedents with respect to which the date for the filing of the estate tax return (including extensions thereof) prescribed by section 6075(a) of the Internal Revenue Code of 1954 is after the date of the enactment of this Act; except that (1) section 6166(i) of such Code as added by this section shall apply to estates of decedents dying after August 16, 1954, but only if the date for the filing of the estate tax return (including extensions thereof) expired on or before the date of the enactment of this Act, and (2) notwithstanding section 6166(a) of such Code, if an election under such section is required to be made before the sixtieth day after the date of the enactment of this Act such an election shall be considered timely if made on or before such sixtieth day."

TAX PAYMENT—EXTENSIONS OF TIME

[Sec. 6161(b)]

(b) AMOUNT DETERMINED AS DEFICIENCY.—

(1) INCOME, GIFT, AND CERTAIN OTHER TAXES.—Under regulations prescribed by the Secretary, the Secretary may extend the time for the payment of the amount determined as a deficiency of a tax imposed by chapter 1, 12, 41, 42, 43, or 44 for a period not to exceed 18 months from the date fixed for the payment of the deficiency, and in exceptional cases, for a further period not to exceed 12 months. An extension under this paragraph may be granted only where it is shown to the satisfaction of the Secretary that payment of a deficiency upon the date fixed for the payment thereof will result in undue hardship to the taxpayer in the case of a tax imposed by chapter 1, 41, 42, 43, or 44, or to the donor in the case of a tax imposed by chapter 12.

(2) ESTATE TAX.—Under regulations prescribed by the Secretary, the Secretary may, for reasonable cause, extend the time for the payment of any deficiency of a tax imposed by chapter 11 for a reasonable period not to exceed 4 years from the date otherwise fixed for the payment of the deficiency.

(3) NO EXTENSION FOR CERTAIN DEFICIENCIES.—No extension shall be granted under this subsection for any deficiency if the deficiency is due to negligence, to intentional disregard of rules and regulations, or to fraud with intent to evade tax.

Amendments

• **1988, Omnibus Trade and Competitiveness Act of 1988 (P.L. 100-418)**

P.L. 100-418, § 1941(b)(2)(B)(viii):

Amended Code Sec. 6161(b)(1) by striking "44, or 45" each place it appears and inserting "or 44". **Effective** for crude oil removed from the premises on or after 8-23-88.

• **1980, Crude Oil Windfall Profit Tax Act of 1980 (P.L. 96-223)**

P.L. 96-223, § 101(f)(1)(H):

Amended Code Sec. 6161(b)(1) by striking out "or 44" and inserting "44, or 45". For the **effective** date and transitional rules, see P.L. 96-223, § 101(i), following Code Sec. 4986.

• **1976, Tax Reform Act of 1976 (P.L. 94-455)**

P.L. 94-455, § 2004(c)(2):

Amended Code Sec. 6161(b). **Effective** for the estates of decedents dying after 12-31-76. Prior to amendment, Code Sec. 6161(b) read as follows:

(b) AMOUNT DETERMINED AS DEFICIENCY.—Under regulations prescribed by the Secretary or his delegate, the Secretary or his delegate may extend, to the extent provided below, the time for payment of the amount determined as a deficiency:

(1) In the case of a tax imposed by chapter 1, 12, 42 or 43, for a period not to exceed 18 months from the date fixed for payment of the deficiency, and, in exceptional cases, for a further period not to exceed 12 months;

(2) In the case of a tax imposed by chapter 11, for a period not to exceed 4 years from the date otherwise fixed for payment of the deficiency.

An extension under this subsection may be granted only where it is shown to the satisfaction of the Secretary or his delegate that the payment of a deficiency upon the date fixed for the payment thereof will result in undue hardship to the taxpayer in the case of a tax imposed by chapter 1, 42, or chapter 43, to the estate in the case of a tax imposed by chapter 11, or to the donor in the case of a tax imposed by chapter 12. No extension shall be granted if the deficiency is due to negligence, to intentional disregard of rules and regulations, or to fraud with intent to evade tax.

P.L. 94-455, § 1307(d):

Amended former Code Sec. 6161(b) by substituting "12, 41" for "12" in paragraph (1) and by substituting "41, 42," for "42" in the second sentence of paragraph (1). The amendments are incorporated in the amendment made by P.L. 94-455, § 2004(c)(2). **Effective** 10-4-76.

P.L. 94-455, § 1605(b)(3):

Amended Code Sec. 6161(b)(1) (as amended by P.L. 94-455, § 1307(d)) by substituting "42, 43, or 44" for "42 or 43" and by substituting "43, or 44" for "or chapter 43". The amendments are incorporated in the amendment made by P.L. 94-455, § 2004(c)(2). **Effective** for tax years of real estate investment trusts beginning after 10-4-76.

• **1974, Employee Retirement Income Security Act of 1974 (P.L. 93-406)**

P.L. 93-406, § 1016(a)(7):

Amended Code Sec. 6161(b) by changing "or 42" to "42 or 43" in paragraph (1) and by changing "or 42" to "42, or chapter 43" in the second sentence of subsection (b). For **effective** date, see amendment note for P.L. 93-406 under Code Sec. 410.

• **1969, Tax Reform Act of 1969 (P.L. 91-172)**

P.L. 91-172, § 101(j)(37):

Amended Code Sec. 6161(b) by substituting "chapter 1, 12, or 42," for "chapter 1 or 12," in paragraph (1) and by substituting "chapter 1 or 42," in the first sentence following paragraph (2). **Effective** 1-1-70.

[Sec. 6161(c)]

(c) CLAIMS IN CASES UNDER TITLE 11 OF THE UNITED STATES CODE OR IN RECEIVERSHIP PROCEEDINGS.—Extensions of time for payment of any portion of a claim for tax under chapter 1 or chapter 12, allowed in cases under title 11 of the United States Code or in receivership proceedings, which is unpaid, may be had in the same manner and subject to the same provisions and limitations as provided in subsection (b) in respect of a deficiency in such tax.

Amendments

• **1980, Bankruptcy Tax Act of 1980 (P.L. 96-589)**

P.L. 96-589, § 6(i)(8):

Amended Code Sec. 6161(c). **Effective** 10-1-79 but inapplicable to any proceeding under the Bankruptcy Act commenced before that date. Prior to amendment, Code Sec. 6161(c) provided:

"(c) CLAIMS IN BANKRUPTCY OR RECEIVERSHIP PROCEEDINGS.—Extensions of time for payment of any portion of a claim for tax under chapter 1 or chapter 12, allowed in bankruptcy or receivership proceedings, which is unpaid, may be had in the same manner and subject to the same provisions and limitations as provided in subsection (b) in respect of a deficiency in such tax."

[Sec. 6161(d)]

(d) CROSS REFERENCES.—

(1) PERIOD OF LIMITATION.—

For extension of the period of limitation in case of an extension under subsection (a)(2) or subsection (b)(2), see section 6503(d).

(2) SECURITY.—

For authority of the Secretary to require security in case of an extension under subsection (a)(2) or subsection (b), see section 6165.

(3) POSTPONEMENT OF CERTAIN ACTS.—

For time for performing certain acts postponed by reason of war, see section 7508, and by reason of Presidentially declared disaster or terroristic or military action, see section 7508A.

Amendments

• **2002, Victims of Terrorism Tax Relief Act of 2001 (P.L. 107-134)**

P.L. 107-134, § 112(d)(3):

Amended Code Sec. 6161(d) by adding at the end a new paragraph (3). **Effective** for disasters and terroristic or military actions occurring on or after 9-11-01, with respect to any action of the Secretary of the Treasury, the Secretary of Labor, or the Pension Benefit Guaranty Corporation occurring on or after 1-23-02.

• **1976, Tax Reform Act of 1976 (P.L. 94-455)**

P.L. 94-455, § 1906(b)(13)(A):

Amended 1954 Code by substituting "Secretary" for "Secretary or his delegate" each place it appeared. **Effective** 2-1-77.

[Sec. 6163]

SEC. 6163. EXTENSION OF TIME FOR PAYMENT OF ESTATE TAX ON VALUE OF REVERSIONARY OR REMAINDER INTEREST IN PROPERTY.

[Sec. 6163(a)]

(a) EXTENSION PERMITTED.—If the value of a reversionary or remainder interest in property is included under chapter 11 in the value of the gross estate, the payment of the part of the tax under chapter 11 attributable to such interest may, at the election of the executor, be postponed until 6 months after the termination of the precedent interest or interests in the property, under such regulations as the Secretary may prescribe.

TAX PAYMENT—EXTENSIONS OF TIME

Amendments

• **1976, Tax Reform Act of 1976 (P.L. 94-455)**

P.L. 94-455, § 1906(b)(13)(A):

Amended 1954 Code by substituting "Secretary" for "Secretary or his delegate" each place it appeared. **Effective** 2-1-77.

[Sec. 6163(b)]

(b) EXTENSION FOR REASONABLE CAUSE.—At the expiration of the period of postponement provided for in subsection (a), the Secretary may, for reasonable cause, extend the time for payment for a reasonable period or periods not in excess of 3 years from the expiration of the period of postponement provided in subsection (a).

Amendments

• **1976, Tax Reform Act of 1976 (P.L. 94-455)**

P.L. 94-455, § 2004(c)(3):

Amended Code Sec. 6163(b). **Effective** for the estates of decedents dying after 12-31-76. Prior to amendment, Code Sec. 6163(b) read as follows:

(b) EXTENSION TO PREVENT UNDUE HARDSHIP.—If the Secretary or his delegate finds that the payment of the tax at the expiration of the period of postponement provided for in subsection (a) would result in undue hardship to the estate, he may extend the time for payment for a reasonable period or periods not in excess of 3 years from the expiration of such period of postponement.

• **1964, Revenue Act of 1964 (P.L. 88-272)**

P.L. 88-272, § 240(a):

Amended subsection (b) to insert "or periods not in excess of 3 years" in lieu of "not in excess of 2 years". **Effective** in the case of any reversionary or remainder interest only if the time for payment of the tax under chapter 11 attributable to such interest, including any extensions thereof, has not expired on 2-26-64.

• **1958, Technical Amendments Act of 1958 (P.L. 85-866)**

P.L. 85-866, § 66(b)(1):

Redesignated subsection (b) of Sec. 6163 as subsection (c) and added a new subsection (b). **Effective** in the case of any reversionary or remainder interest only if the precedent interest or interests in the property did not terminate before the beginning of the 6-month period which ends on 9-2-58.

[Sec. 6163(c)]

(c) CROSS REFERENCE.—

For authority of the Secretary to require security in the case of an extension under this section, see section 6165.

Amendments

• **1976, Tax Reform Act of 1976 (P.L. 94-455)**

P.L. 94-455, § 1906(b)(13)(A):

Amended 1954 Code by substituting "Secretary" for "Secretary or his delegate" each place it appeared. **Effective** 2-1-77.

• **1975 (P.L. 93-625)**

P.L. 93-625, § 7(d)(1):

Amended Code Sec. 6163(c). **Effective** 7-1-75. Prior to amendment, this section read as follows:

"(c) Cross References.—

"(1) Interest.—

"For provisions requiring the payment of interest for the period of such extension, see section 6601(b).

"(2) Security.—

"For authority of the Secretary or his delegate to require security in the case of such extension, see section 6165."

• **1958, Technical Amendments Act of 1958 (P.L. 85-866)**

P.L. 85-866, § 66(b)(1):

Redesignated old subsection (b) as subsection (c). **Effective** 9-2-58.

[Sec. 6164]

SEC. 6164. EXTENSION OF TIME FOR PAYMENT OF TAXES BY CORPORATIONS EXPECTING CARRYBACKS.

[Sec. 6164(a)]

(a) IN GENERAL.—If a corporation, in any taxable year, files with the Secretary a statement, as provided in subsection (b), with respect to an expected net operating loss carryback from such taxable year, the time for payment of all or part of any tax imposed by subtitle A for the taxable year immediately preceding such taxable year shall be extended, to the extent and subject to the conditions and limitations hereinafter provided in this section.

Amendments

• **1976, Tax Reform Act of 1976 (P.L. 94-455)**

P.L. 94-455, § 1906(b)(13)(A):

Amended 1954 Code by substituting "Secretary" for "Secretary or his delegate" each place it appeared. **Effective** 2-1-77.

[Sec. 6164(b)]

(b) CONTENTS OF STATEMENT.—The statement shall be filed at such time and in such manner and form as the Secretary may by regulations prescribe. Such statement shall set forth that the corporation expects to have a net operating loss carryback, as provided in section 172(b), from the taxable year in which such statement is made, and shall set forth, in such detail and with such supporting data and explanation as such regulations shall require—

(1) the estimated amount of the expected net operating loss;

(2) the reasons, facts, and circumstances which cause the corporation to expect such net operating loss;

(3) the amount of the reduction of the tax previously determined attributable to the expected carryback, such tax previously determined being ascertained in accordance with the method prescribed in section 1314(a); and such reduction being determined by applying the expected carryback in the manner provided by law to the items on the basis of which such tax was determined;

(4) the tax and the part thereof the time for payment of which is to be extended; and

(5) such other information for purposes of carrying out the provisions of this section as may be required by such regulations.

The Secretary shall, upon request, furnish a receipt for any statement filed, which shall set forth the date of such filing.

Amendments

• **1976, Tax Reform Act of 1976 (P.L. 94-455)**

P.L. 94-455, § 1906(b)(13)(A):

Amended 1954 Code by substituting "Secretary" for "Secretary or his delegate" each place it appeared. **Effective** 2-1-77.

[Sec. 6164(c)]

(c) AMOUNT TO WHICH EXTENSION RELATES AND INSTALLMENT PAYMENTS.—The amount the time for payment of which may be extended under subsection (a) with respect to any tax shall not exceed the amount of such tax shown on the return, increased by any amount assessed as a deficiency (or as interest or addition to the tax) prior to the date of filing the statement and decreased by any amount paid or required to be paid prior to the date of such filing, and the total amount of the tax the time for payment of which may be extended shall not exceed the amount stated under subsection (b)(3). For purposes of this subsection, an amount shall not be considered as required to be paid unless shown on the return or assessed as a deficiency (or as interest or addition to the tax), and an amount assessed as a deficiency (or as interest or addition to the tax) shall be

TAX PAYMENT—EXTENSIONS OF TIME

considered to be required to be paid prior to the date of filing of the statement if the 10th day after notice and demand for its payment occurs prior to such date. If an extension of time under this section relates to only a part of the tax, the time for payment of the remainder shall be the date on which payment would have been required if such remainder had been the tax.

Amendments

• **1982, Tax Equity and Fiscal Responsibility Act of 1982 (P.L. 97-248)**

P.L. 97-248, §234(b)(2)(C)(i):

Amended Code Sec. 6164(c) by striking out the last sentence and inserting a new last sentence. **Effective** for tax years beginning after 12-31-82. Prior to amendment, the last sentence of Code Sec. 6164(c) read as follows:

"If an extension of time under this section relates to only a part of the tax, the time for payment of the remainder shall be considered to be the dates on which payments would have been required if such remainder had been the tax and the taxpayer had elected to pay the tax in installments as provided in section 6152."

[Sec. 6164(d)]

(d) PERIOD OF EXTENSION.—The extension of time for payment provided in this section shall expire—

(1) on the last day of the month in which falls the last date prescribed by law (including any extension of time granted the taxpayer) for the filing of the return for the taxable year of the expected net operating loss, or

(2) if an application for tentative carryback adjustment provided in section 6411 with respect to such loss is filed before the expiration of the period prescribed in paragraph (1), on the date on which notice is mailed by certified mail or registered mail by the Secretary to the taxpayer that such application is allowed or disallowed in whole or in part.

Amendments

• **1976, Tax Reform Act of 1976 (P.L. 94-455)**

P.L. 94-455, §1906(b)(13)(A):

Amended 1954 Code by substituting "Secretary" for "Secretary or his delegate" each place it appeared. **Effective** 2-1-77.

• **1958, Technical Amendments Act of 1958 (P.L. 85-866)**

P.L. 85-866, §89(b):

Amended Sec. 6164(d)(2) by striking out "registered mail" and substituting "certified mail or registered mail". **Effective** 9-3-58, but only if mailing occurs after 9-2-58.

[Sec. 6164(e)]

(e) REVISED STATEMENTS.—Each statement filed under subsection (a) with respect to any taxable year shall be in lieu of the last statement previously filed with respect to such year. If the amount the time for payment of which is extended under a statement filed is less than the amount under the last statement previously filed, the extension of time shall be terminated as to the difference between the two amounts.

[Sec. 6164(f)]

(f) TERMINATION.—The Secretary is not required to make any examination of the statement, but he may make such examination thereof as he deems necessary and practicable. The Secretary shall terminate the extension as to any part of the amount to which it relates which he deems should be terminated because, upon such examination, he believes that, as of the time such examination is made, all or any part of the statement clearly is in a material respect erroneous or unreasonable.

Amendments

• **1976, Tax Reform Act of 1976 (P.L. 94-455)**

P.L. 94-455, §1906(b)(13)(A):

Amended 1954 Code by substituting "Secretary" for "Secretary or his delegate" each place it appeared. **Effective** 2-1-77.

[Sec. 6164(g)]

(g) PAYMENTS ON TERMINATION.—If an extension of time is terminated under subsection (e) or (f) with respect to any amount, then—

(1) no further extension of time shall be made under this section with respect to such amount, and

(2) the time for payment of such amount shall be considered to be the date on which payment would have been required if there had been no extension with respect to such amount.

Amendments

• **1982, Tax Equity and Fiscal Responsibility Act of 1982 (P.L. 97-248)**

P.L. 97-248, §234(b)(2)(C)(ii):

Amended Code Sec. 6164(g)(2). **Effective** for tax years beginning after 12-31-82. Prior to amendment, Code Sec. 6164(g)(2) read as follows:

"(2) the time for payment of such amount shall be considered to be the dates on which payments would have been required if there had been no extension with respect to such amount and the taxpayer had elected to pay the tax in installments as provided in section 6152."

[Sec. 6164(h)]

(h) JEOPARDY.—If the Secretary believes that collection of the amount to which an extension under this section relates is in jeopardy, he shall immediately terminate such extension, and notice and demand shall be made by him for payment of such amount.

Amendments

• **1976, Tax Reform Act of 1976 (P.L. 94-455)**

P.L. 94-455, §1906(b)(13)(A):

Amended 1954 Code by substituting "Secretary" for "Secretary or his delegate" each place it appeared. **Effective** 2-1-77.

[Sec. 6164(i)]

(i) CONSOLIDATED RETURNS.—If the corporation seeking an extension of time under this section made or was required to make a consolidated return, either for the taxable year within which the net operating loss arises or for the preceding taxable year affected by such loss, the provisions of such section shall apply only to such extent and subject to such conditions, limitations, and exceptions as the Secretary may by regulations prescribe.

Amendments

• **1976, Tax Reform Act of 1976 (P.L. 94-455)**

P.L. 94-455, §1906(b)(13)(A):

Amended 1954 Code by substituting "Secretary" for "Secretary or his delegate" each place it appeared. **Effective** 2-1-77.

[Sec. 6165]

SEC. 6165. BONDS WHERE TIME TO PAY TAX OR DEFICIENCY HAS BEEN EXTENDED.

In the event the Secretary grants any extension of time within which to pay any tax or any deficiency therein, the Secretary may require the taxpayer to furnish a bond in such amount (not exceeding double the amount with respect to which the extension is granted) conditioned upon the payment of the amount extended in accordance with the terms of such extension.

TAX PAYMENT—EXTENSIONS OF TIME

Amendments

• **1976, Tax Reform Act of 1976 (P.L. 94-455)**

P.L. 94-455, §1906(b)(13)(A):

Amended 1954 Code by substituting "Secretary" for "Secretary or his delegate" each place it appeared. **Effective** 2-1-77.

[Sec. 6166]

SEC. 6166. EXTENSION OF TIME FOR PAYMENT OF ESTATE TAX WHERE ESTATE CONSISTS LARGELY OF INTEREST IN CLOSELY HELD BUSINESS.

[Sec. 6166(a)]

(a) 5-YEAR DEFERRAL; 10-YEAR INSTALLMENT PAYMENT.—

(1) IN GENERAL.—If the value of an interest in a closely held business, which is included in determining the gross estate of a decedent who was (at the date of his death) a citizen or resident of the United States exceeds 35 percent of the adjusted gross estate, the executor may elect to pay part or all of the tax imposed by section 2001 in 2 or more (but not exceeding 10) equal installments.

(2) LIMITATION.—The maximum amount of tax which may be paid in installments under this subsection shall be an amount which bears the same ratio to the tax imposed by section 2001 (reduced by the credits against such tax) as—

(A) the closely held business amount, bears to

(B) the amount of the adjusted gross estate.

(3) DATE FOR PAYMENT OF INSTALLMENTS.—If an election is made under paragraph (1), the first installment shall be paid on or before the date selected by the executor which is not more than 5 years after the date prescribed by section 6151(a) for payment of the tax, and each succeeding installment shall be paid on or before the date which is 1 year after the date prescribed by this paragraph for payment of the preceding installment.

Amendments

• **1981, Economic Recovery Tax Act of 1981 (P.L. 97-34)**

P.L. 97-34, §422(a)(1):

Amended Code Sec. 6166(a)(1) by striking out "65 percent" and inserting "35 percent". **Effective** for estates of decedents dying after 12-31-81.

P.L. 97-34, §422(e)(5)(A):

Repealed Code Sec. 6166(a)(4). **Effective** for estates of decedents dying after 12-31-81. Prior to its repeal, Code Sec. 6166(a)(4) read as follows:

(4) ELIGIBILITY FOR ELECTION.—No election may be made under this section by the executor of the estate of any decedent if an election under section 6166A applies with respect to the estate of such decedent.

P.L. 97-34, §422(e)(5)(B):

Amended Code Sec. 6166 by striking out "ALTERNATE" in the heading. **Effective** for estates of decedents dying after 12-31-81.

[Sec. 6166(b)]

(b) DEFINITIONS AND SPECIAL RULES.—

(1) INTEREST IN CLOSELY HELD BUSINESS.—For purposes of this section, the term "interest in a closely held business" means—

(A) an interest as a proprietor in a trade or business carried on as a proprietorship;

(B) an interest as a partner in a partnership carrying on a trade or business, if—

(i) 20 percent or more of the total capital interest in such partnership is included in determining the gross estate of the decedent, or

(ii) such partnership had 45 or fewer partners; or

(C) stock in a corporation carrying on a trade or business if—

(i) 20 percent or more in value of the voting stock of such corporation is included in determining the gross estate of the decedent, or

(ii) such corporation had 45 or fewer shareholders.

(2) RULES FOR APPLYING PARAGRAPH (1).—For purposes of paragraph (1)—

(A) TIME FOR TESTING.—Determinations shall be made as of the time immediately before the decedent's death.

(B) CERTAIN INTERESTS HELD BY HUSBAND AND WIFE.—Stock or a partnership interest which—

(i) is community property of a husband and wife (or the income from which is community income) under the applicable community property law of a State, or

(ii) is held by a husband and wife as joint tenants, tenants by the entirety, or tenants in common,

shall be treated as owned by one shareholder or one partner, as the case may be.

(C) INDIRECT OWNERSHIP.—Property owned, directly or indirectly, by or for a corporation, partnership, estate, or trust shall be considered as being owned proportionately by or for its shareholders, partners, or beneficiaries. For purposes of the preceding sentence, a person shall be treated as a beneficiary of any trust only if such person has a present interest in the trust.

(D) CERTAIN INTERESTS HELD BY MEMBERS OF DECEDENT'S FAMILY.—All stock and all partnership interests held by the decedent or by any member of his family (within the meaning of section 267(c)(4)) shall be treated as owned by the decedent.

(3) FARMHOUSES AND CERTAIN OTHER STRUCTURES TAKEN INTO ACCOUNT.—For purposes of the 35-percent requirement of subsection (a)(1), an interest in a closely held business which is the business of farming includes an interest in residential buildings and related improvements on the farm which are occupied on a regular basis by the owner or lessee of the farm or by persons employed by such owner or lessee for purposes of operating or maintaining the farm.

(4) VALUE.—For purposes of this section, value shall be value determined for purposes of chapter 11 (relating to estate tax).

(5) CLOSELY HELD BUSINESS AMOUNT.—For purposes of this section, the term "closely held business amount" means the value of the interest in a closely held business which qualifies under subsection (a)(1).

(6) ADJUSTED GROSS ESTATE.—For purposes of this section, the term "adjusted gross estate" means the value of the gross estate reduced by the sum of the amounts allowable as a deduction under section 2053 or 2054. Such sum shall be determined on the basis of the facts and circumstances in existence on the date (including extensions) for filing the return of tax imposed by section 2001 (or, if earlier, the date on which such return is filed).

(7) PARTNERSHIP INTERESTS AND STOCK WHICH IS NOT READILY TRADABLE.—

(A) IN GENERAL.—If the executor elects the benefits of this paragraph (at such time and in such manner as the Secretary shall by regulations prescribe), then—

(i) for purposes of paragraph (1)(B)(i) or (1)(C)(i) (whichever is appropriate) and for purposes of subsection (c), any capital interest in a partnership and any non-readily-tradable stock which (after the application of paragraph (2)) is treated as owned by the decedent shall be treated as included in determining the value of the decedent's gross estate,

(ii) the executor shall be treated as having selected under subsection (a)(3) the date prescribed by section 6151(a), and

(iii) for purposes of applying section 6601(j), the 2-percent portion (as defined in such section) shall be treated as being zero.

(B) NON-READILY-TRADABLE STOCK DEFINED.—For purposes of this paragraph, the term "non-readily-tradable stock" means stock for which, at the time of the decedent's death, there was no market on a stock exchange or in an over-the-counter market.

(8) STOCK IN HOLDING COMPANY TREATED AS BUSINESS COMPANY STOCK IN CERTAIN CASES.—

(A) IN GENERAL.—If the executor elects the benefits of this paragraph, then—

(i) HOLDING COMPANY STOCK TREATED AS BUSINESS COMPANY STOCK.—For purposes of this section, the portion of the stock of any holding company which represents direct ownership (or indirect ownership through 1 or more other holding companies) by such company in a business company shall be deemed to be stock in such business company.

(ii) 5-YEAR DEFERRAL FOR PRINCIPAL NOT TO APPLY.—The executor shall be treated as having selected under subsection (a)(3) the date prescribed by section 6151(a).

(iii) 2-PERCENT INTEREST RATE NOT TO APPLY.—For purposes of applying section 6601(j), the 2-percent portion (as defined in such section) shall be treated as being zero.

(B) ALL STOCK MUST BE NON-READILY-TRADABLE STOCK.—

(i) IN GENERAL.—No stock shall be taken into account for purposes of applying this paragraph unless it is non-readily-tradable stock (within the meaning of paragraph (7)(B)).

(ii) SPECIAL APPLICATION WHERE ONLY HOLDING COMPANY STOCK IS NON-READILY-TRADABLE STOCK.—If the requirements of clause (i) are not met, but all of the stock of each holding company taken into account is non-readily-tradable, then this paragraph shall apply, but subsection (a)(1) shall be applied by substituting "5" for "10".

(C) APPLICATION OF VOTING STOCK REQUIREMENT OF PARAGRAPH (1)(c)(i).—For purposes of clause (i) of paragraph (1)(C), the deemed stock resulting from the application of subparagraph (A) shall be treated as voting stock to the extent that voting stock in the holding company owns directly (or through the voting stock of 1 of more other holding companies) voting stock in the business company.

(D) DEFINITIONS.—For purposes of this paragraph—

(i) HOLDING COMPANY.—The term "holding company" means any corporation holding stock in another corporation.

(ii) BUSINESS COMPANY.—The term "business company" means any corporation carrying on a trade or business.

(9) DEFERRAL NOT AVAILABLE FOR PASSIVE ASSETS.—

(A) IN GENERAL.—For purposes of subsection (a)(1) and determining the closely held business amount (but not for purposes of subsection (g)), the value of any interest in a closely held business shall not include the value of that portion of such interest which is attributable to passive assets held by the business.

(B) PASSIVE ASSET DEFINED.—For purposes of this paragraph—

(i) IN GENERAL.—The term "passive asset" means any asset other than an asset used in carrying on a trade or business.

(ii) STOCK TREATED AS PASSIVE ASSET.—The term "passive asset" includes any stock in another corporation unless—

(I) such stock is treated as held by the decedent by reason of an election under paragraph (8), and

(II) such stock qualified under subsection (a)(1).

(iii) EXCEPTION FOR ACTIVE CORPORATIONS.—If—

(I) a corporation owns 20 percent or more in value of the voting stock of another corporation, or such other corporation has 45 or fewer shareholders, and

(II) 80 percent or more of the value of the assets of each such corporation is attributable to assets used in carrying on a trade or business,

then such corporations shall be treated as 1 corporation for purposes of clause (ii). For purposes of applying subclause (II) to the corporation holding the stock of the other corporation, such stock shall not be taken into account.

(10) STOCK IN QUALIFYING LENDING AND FINANCE BUSINESS TREATED AS STOCK IN AN ACTIVE TRADE OR BUSINESS COMPANY.—

(A) IN GENERAL.—If the executor elects the benefits of this paragraph, then—

(i) STOCK IN QUALIFYING LENDING AND FINANCE BUSINESS TREATED AS STOCK IN AN ACTIVE TRADE OR BUSINESS COMPANY.—For purposes of this section, any asset used in a qualifying lending and finance business shall be treated as an asset which is used in carrying on a trade or business.

(ii) 5-YEAR DEFERRAL FOR PRINCIPAL NOT TO APPLY.—The executor shall be treated as having selected under subsection (a)(3) the date prescribed by section 6151(a).

(iii) 5 EQUAL INSTALLMENTS ALLOWED.—For purposes of applying subsection (a)(1), "5" shall be substituted for "10".

(B) DEFINITIONS.—For purposes of this paragraph—

(i) QUALIFYING LENDING AND FINANCE BUSINESS.—The term "qualifying lending and finance business" means a lending and finance business, if—

(I) based on all the facts and circumstances immediately before the date of the decedent's death, there was substantial activity with respect to the lending and finance business, or

(II) during at least 3 of the 5 taxable years ending before the date of the decedent's death, such business had at least 1 full-time employee substantially all of whose services were the active management of such business, 10 full-time, nonowner employees substantially all of whose services were directly related to such business, and $5,000,000 in gross receipts from activities described in clause (ii).

(ii) LENDING AND FINANCE BUSINESS.—The term "lending and finance business" means a trade or business of—

(I) making loans,

(II) purchasing or discounting accounts receivable, notes, or installment obligations,

(III) engaging in rental and leasing of real and tangible personal property, including entering into leases and purchasing, servicing, and disposing of leases and leased assets,

(IV) rendering services or making facilities available in the ordinary course of a lending or finance business, and

(V) rendering services or making facilities available in connection with activities described in subclauses (I) through (IV) carried on by the corporation rendering services or making facilities available, or another corporation which is a member of the same affiliated group (as defined in section 1504 without regard to section 1504(b)(3)).

(iii) LIMITATION.—The term "qualifying lending and finance business" shall not include any interest in an entity, if the stock or debt of such entity or a controlled group (as defined in section 267(f)(1)) of which such entity was a member was readily tradable on

TAX PAYMENT—EXTENSIONS OF TIME

an established securities market or secondary market (as defined by the Secretary) at any time within 3 years before the date of the decedent's death.

Amendments

• **2013, American Taxpayer Relief Act of 2012 (P.L. 112-240)**

P.L. 112-240, §101(a)(1) and (3), provides:

SEC. 101. PERMANENT EXTENSION AND MODIFICATION OF 2001 TAX RELIEF.

(a) PERMANENT EXTENSION.—

(1) IN GENERAL.—The Economic Growth and Tax Relief Reconciliation Act of 2001 is amended by striking title IX.

* * *

(3) EFFECTIVE DATE.—The amendments made by this subsection shall apply to taxable, plan, or limitation years beginning after December 31, 2012, and estates of decedents dying, gifts made, or generation skipping transfers after December 31, 2012.

• **2001, Economic Growth and Tax Relief Reconciliation Act of 2001 (P.L. 107-16)**

P.L. 107-16, §571(a):

Amended Code Sec. 6166(b)(1)(B)(ii), (b)(1)(C)(ii), and (b)(9)(B)(iii)(I) by striking "15" and inserting "45". **Effective** for estates of decedents dying after 12-31-2001.

P.L. 107-16, §572(a):

Amended Code Sec. 6166(b) by adding at the end a new paragraph (10). **Effective** for estates of decedents dying after 12-31-2001.

P.L. 107-16, §573(a):

Amended Code Sec. 6166(b)(8)(B). **Effective** for estates of decedents dying after 12-31-2001. Prior to amendment, Code Sec. 6166(b)(8)(B) read as follows:

(B) ALL STOCK MUST BE NON-READILY-TRADABLE STOCK.—No stock shall be taken into account for purposes of applying this paragraph unless it is non-readily-tradable stock (within the meaning of paragraph (7)(B)).

P.L. 107-16, §901(a)-(b), as amended by P.L. 111-312, §101(a)(1), provides [but see P.L. 112-240, §101(a)(1) and (3), above]:

SEC. 901. SUNSET OF PROVISIONS OF ACT.

(a) IN GENERAL.—All provisions of, and amendments made by, this Act shall not apply—

(1) to taxable, plan, or limitation years beginning after December 31, 2012, or

(2) in the case of title V, to estates of decedents dying, gifts made, or generation skipping transfers, after December 31, 2012.

(b) APPLICATION OF CERTAIN LAWS.—The Internal Revenue Code of 1986 and the Employee Retirement Income Security Act of 1974 shall be applied and administered to years, estates, gifts, and transfers described in subsection (a) as if the provisions and amendments described in subsection (a) had never been enacted.

• **1998, IRS Restructuring and Reform Act of 1998 (P.L. 105-206)**

P.L. 105-206, §6007(c)(1):

Amended Code Sec. 6166(b)(7)(A)(iii). **Effective** as if included in the provision of P.L. 105-34 to which it relates [**effective** for estates of decedents dying after 12-31-97.—CCH]. Prior to amendment, Code Sec. 6166(b)(7)(A)(iii) read as follows:

(iii) section 6601(j) (relating to 2-percent rate of interest) shall not apply.

P.L. 105-206, §6007(c)(2):

Amended Code Sec. 6166(b)(8)(A)(iii). **Effective** for estates of decedents dying after 12-31-97. Prior to amendment, Code Sec. 6166(b)(8)(A)(iii) read as follows:

(iii) 2-PERCENT INTEREST RATE NOT TO APPLY.—Section 6601(j) (relating to 2-percent rate of interest) shall not apply.

• **1997, Taxpayer Relief Act of 1997 (P.L. 105-34)**

P.L. 105-34, §503(c)(1):

Amended Code Sec. 6166(b)(7)(A)(iii) and (8)(A)(iii) by striking "4-percent" each place it appears (including the heading) and inserting "2-percent". **Effective** for estates of decedents dying after 12-31-97.

• **1984, Deficit Reduction Act of 1984 (P.L. 98-369)**

P.L. 98-369, §1021(a):

Amended Code Sec. 6166(b) by adding new paragraph (8). **Effective** with respect to estates of decedents dying after 7-18-84. However, see Act Sec. 1021(d)[(e)](2) following Code Sec. 6166(g) for special rules.

P.L. 98-369, §1021(b):

Amended Code Sec. 6166(b) by adding at the end thereof new paragraph (9). **Effective** with respect to estates of decedents dying after 7-18-84. However, see Act Sec. 1021(d)[(e)](2) following Code Sec. 6166(g) for special rules.

• **1983, Technical Corrections Act of 1982 (P.L. 97-448)**

P.L. 97-448, §104(c)(1):

Amended Code Sec. 6166(b)(3) by striking out "65-percent requirement" and inserting in lieu thereof "35-percent requirement". **Effective** as if included in the provision of P.L. 97-34 to which it relates.

• **1978, Revenue Act of 1978 (P.L. 95-600)**

P.L. 95-600, §512(a), (b):

Added Code Secs. 6166(b)(2)(D) and (b)(7). **Effective** with respect to estates of decedents dying after 11-6-78.

[Sec. 6166(c)]

(c) SPECIAL RULE FOR INTEREST IN 2 OR MORE CLOSELY HELD BUSINESSES.—For purposes of this section, interests in 2 or more closely held businesses, with respect to each of which there is included in determining the value of the decedent's gross estate 20 percent or more of the total value of each such business, shall be treated as an interest in a single closely held business. For purposes of the 20-percent requirement of the preceding sentence, an interest in a closely held business which represents the surviving spouse's interest in property held by the decedent and the surviving spouse as community property or as joint tenants, tenants by the entirety, or tenants in common shall be treated as having been included in determining the value of the decedent's gross estate.

Amendments

• **1981, Economic Recovery Tax Act of 1981 (P.L. 97-34)**

P.L. 97-34, §422(a)(2):

Amended Code Sec. 6166(c) by striking out "more than 20 percent" and inserting "20 percent or more". **Effective** for estates of decedents dying after 12-31-81.

[Sec. 6166(d)]

(d) ELECTION.—Any election under subsection (a) shall be made not later than the time prescribed by section 6075(a) for filing the return of tax imposed by section 2001 (including extensions thereof), and shall be made in such manner as the Secretary shall by regulations prescribe. If an election under subsection (a) is made, the provisions of this subtitle shall apply as though the Secretary were extending the time for payment of the tax.

[Sec. 6166(e)]

(e) PRORATION OF DEFICIENCY TO INSTALLMENTS.—If an election is made under subsection (a) to pay any part of the tax imposed by section 2001 in installments and a deficiency has been assessed, the deficiency shall (subject to the limitation provided by subsection (a)(2)) be prorated to the installments payable under subsection (a). The part of the deficiency so prorated to any installment the date for payment of which has not arrived shall be collected at the same time as, and as a part of, such installment. The part of the deficiency so prorated to any installment the date for payment of which has arrived shall be paid upon notice and demand from the Secretary. This subsection shall not apply if the deficiency is due to negligence, to intentional disregard of rules and regulations, or to fraud with intent to evade tax.

[Sec. 6166(f)]

(f) TIME FOR PAYMENT OF INTEREST.—If the time for payment of any amount of tax has been extended under this section—

(1) INTEREST FOR FIRST 5 YEARS.—Interest payable under section 6601 of any unpaid portion of such amount attributable to the first 5 years after the date prescribed by section 6151(a) for payment of the tax shall be paid annually.

(2) INTEREST FOR PERIODS AFTER FIRST 5 YEARS.—Interest payable under section 6601 on any unpaid portion of such amount attributable to any period after the 5-year period referred to in paragraph (1) shall be paid annually at the same time as, and as a part of, each installment payment of the tax.

(3) INTEREST IN THE CASE OF CERTAIN DEFICIENCIES.—In the case of a deficiency to which subsection (e) applies which is assessed after the close of the 5-year period referred to in paragraph (1), interest attributable to such 5-year period, and interest assigned under paragraph (2) to any

TAX PAYMENT—EXTENSIONS OF TIME

installment the date for payment of which has arrived on or before the date of the assessment of the deficiency, shall be paid upon notice and demand from the Secretary.

(4) SELECTION OF SHORTER PERIOD.—If the executor has selected a period shorter than 5 years under subsection (a)(3), such shorter period shall be substituted for 5 years in paragraphs (1), (2), and (3) of this subsection.

[Sec. 6166(g)]

(g) ACCELERATION OF PAYMENT.—

(1) DISPOSITION OF INTEREST; WITHDRAWAL OF FUNDS FROM BUSINESS.—

(A) If—

(i)(I) any portion of an interest in a closely held business which qualifies under subsection (a)(1) is distributed, sold, exchanged, or otherwise disposed of, or

(II) money and other property attributable to such an interest is withdrawn from such trade or business, and

(ii) the aggregate of such distributions, sales, exchanges, or other dispositions and withdrawals equals or exceeds 50 percent of the value of such interest,

then the extension of time for payment of tax provided in subsection (a) shall cease to apply, and the unpaid portion of the tax payable in installments shall be paid upon notice and demand from the Secretary.

(B) In the case of a distribution in redemption of stock to which section 303 (or so much of section 304 as relates to section 303) applies—

(i) the redemption of such stock, and the withdrawal of money and other property distributed in such redemption, shall not be treated as a distribution or withdrawal for purposes of subparagraph (A), and

(ii) for purposes of subparagraph (A), the value of the interest in the closely held business shall be considered to be such value reduced by the value of the stock redeemed.

This subparagraph shall apply only if, on or before the date prescribed by subsection (a)(3) for the payment of the first installment which becomes due after the date of the distribution (or, if earlier, on or before the day which is 1 year after the date of the distribution), there is paid an amount of the tax imposed by section 2001 not less than the amount of money and other property distributed.

(C) Subparagraph (A)(i) does not apply to an exchange of stock pursuant to a plan of reorganization described in subparagraph (D), (E), or (F) of section 368(a)(1) nor to an exchange to which section 355 (or so much of section 356 as relates to section 355) applies; but any stock received in such an exchange shall be treated for purposes of subparagraph (A)(i) as an interest qualifying under subsection (a)(1).

(D) Subparagraph (A)(i) does not apply to a transfer of property of the decedent to a person entitled by reason of the decedent's death to receive such property under the decedent's will, the applicable law of descent and distribution, or a trust created by the decedent. A similar rule shall apply in the case of a series of subsequent transfers of the property by reason of death so long as each transfer is to a member of the family (within the meaning of section 267(c)(4)) of the transferor in such transfer.

(E) CHANGES IN INTEREST IN HOLDING COMPANY.—If any stock in a holding company is treated as stock in a business company by reason of subsection (b)(8)(A)—

(i) any disposition of any interest in such stock in such holding company which was included in determining the gross estate of the decedent, or

(ii) any withdrawal of any money or other property from such holding company attributable to any interest included in determining the gross estate of the decedent,

shall be treated for purposes of subparagraph (A) as a disposition of (or a withdrawal with respect to) the stock qualifying under subsection (a)(1).

(F) CHANGES IN INTEREST IN BUSINESS COMPANY.—If any stock in a holding company is treated as stock in a business company by reason of subsection (b)(8)(A)—

(i) any disposition of any interest in such stock in the business company by such holding company, or

(ii) any withdrawal of any money or other property from such business company attributable to such stock by such holding company owning such stock,

shall be treated for purposes of subparagraph (A) as a disposition of (or a withdrawal with respect to) the stock qualifying under subsection (a)(1).

(2) UNDISTRIBUTED INCOME OF ESTATE.—

(A) If an election is made under this section and the estate has undistributed net income for any taxable year ending on or after the due date for the first installment, the executor shall, on or before the date prescribed by law for filing the income tax return for such taxable year (including extensions thereof), pay an amount equal to such undistributed net income in liquidation of the unpaid portion of the tax payable in installments.

(B) For purposes of subparagraph (A), the undistributed net income of the estate for any taxable year is the amount by which the distributable net income of the estate for such taxable year (as defined in section 643) exceeds the sum of—

(i) the amounts for such taxable year specified in paragraphs (1) and (2) of section 661(a) (relating to deduction for distributions, etc.);

(ii) the amount of tax imposed for the taxable year on the estate under chapter 1; and

(iii) the amount of the tax imposed by section 2001 (including interest) paid by the executor during the taxable year (other than any amount paid pursuant to this paragraph).

(C) For purposes of this paragraph, if any stock in a corporation is treated as stock in another corporation by reason of subsection (b)(8)(A), any dividends paid by such other corporation to the corporation shall be treated as paid to the estate of the decedent to the extent attributable to the stock qualifying under subsection (a)(1).

(3) FAILURE TO MAKE PAYMENT OF PRINCIPAL OR INTEREST.—

(A) IN GENERAL.—Except as provided in subparagraph (B), if any payment of principal or interest under this section is not paid on or before the date fixed for its payment by this section (including any extension of time), the unpaid portion of the tax payable in installments shall be paid upon notice and demand from the Secretary.

(B) PAYMENT WITHIN 6 MONTHS.—If any payment of principal or interest under this section is not paid on or before the date determined under subparagraph (A) but is paid within 6 months of such date—

(i) the provisions of subparagraph (A) shall not apply with respect to such payment,

(ii) the provisions of section 6601(j) shall not apply with respect to the determination of interest on such payment, and

(iii) there is imposed a penalty in an amount equal to the product of—

(I) 5 percent of the amount of such payment, multiplied by

TAX PAYMENT—EXTENSIONS OF TIME

(II) the number of months (or fractions thereof) after such date and before payment is made.

The penalty imposed under clause (iii) shall be treated in the same manner as a penalty imposed under subchapter B of chapter 68.

Amendments

• **1984, Deficit Reduction Act of 1984 (P.L. 98-369)**

P.L. 98-369, §1021(c):

Amended Code Sec. 6166(g)(1) by adding at the end thereof new subparagraphs (E) and (F). **Effective** with respect to estates of decedents dying after 7-18-84. However, see Act Sec. 1021(d)[(e)](2), below, for special rules.

P.L. 98-369, §1021(d):

Amended Code Sec. 6166(g)(2) by adding at the end thereof a new subparagraph (C). **Effective** with respect to estates of decedents dying after 7-18-84. However, see Act Sec. 1021(d)[(e)](2), below, for special rules.

P.L. 98-369, §1021(e)(2), provides:

(2) Special Rule.—

(A) In General.—At the election of the executor, if—

(i) a corporation has 15 or fewer shareholders on June 22, 1984, and at all times thereafter before the date of the decedent's death, and

(ii) stock of such corporation is included in the gross estate of the decedent,

then all other corporations all of the stock of which is owned directly or indirectly by the corporation described in clauses (i) and (ii) shall be treated as one corporation for purposes of section 6166 of the Internal Revenue Code of 1954.

(B) Effect of Election.—Any executor who elects the application of this paragraph shall be treated as having made the election under paragraph (8) of section 6166(b) of such Code.

• **1983, Technical Corrections Act of 1982 (P.L. 97-448)**

P.L. 97-448, §104(c)(2):

Amended clauses (i) and (ii) of the first sentence of Code Sec. 6166(g)(1)(B). **Effective** as if included in the provision of P.L. 97-34 to which it relates. Prior to amendment, clauses (i) and (ii) of the first sentence of Code Sec. 6166(g)(1)(B) read as follows:

"(i) subparagraph (A)(i) does not apply with respect to the stock redeemed; and for purposes of such subparagraph the interest in the closely held business shall be considered to be such interest reduced by the value of the stock redeemed, and

(ii) subparagraph (A)(ii) does not apply with respect to withdrawals of money and other property distributed; and for purposes of such subparagraph the value of the trade or business shall be considered to be such value reduced by the amount of money and other property distributed."

• **1981, Economic Recovery Tax Act of 1981 (P.L. 97-34)**

P.L. 97-34, §422(c)(1):

Amended Code Sec. 6166(g)(1)(A). **Effective** for estates of decedents dying after 12-31-81. Prior to amendment, Code Sec. 6166(g)(1)(A) read as follows:

(A) If—

(i) one-third or more in value of an interest in a closely held business which qualifies under subsection (a)(1) is distributed, sold, exchanged, or otherwise disposed of, or

(ii) aggregate withdrawals of money and other property from the trade or business, an interest in which qualifies under subsection (a)(1), made with respect to such interest, equal or exceed one-third of the value of such trade or business,

then the extension of time for payment of tax provided in subsection (a) shall cease to apply, and any unpaid portion of the tax payable in installments shall be paid upon notice and demand from the Secretary.

P.L. 97-34, §422(c)(2):

Amended Code Sec. 6166(g)(3). **Effective** for estates of decedents dying after 12-31-81. Prior to amendment, Code Sec. 6166(g)(3) read as follows:

(3) FAILURE TO PAY INSTALLMENT.—If any installment under this section is not paid on or before the date fixed for its payment by this section (including any extension of time for the payment of such installment), the unpaid portion of the tax payable in installments shall be paid upon notice and demand from the Secretary.

P.L. 97-34, §422(c)(3):

Amended Code Sec. 6166(g)(1)(D) by adding the last sentence. **Effective** for transfers after 12-31-81.

[Sec. 6166(h)]

(h) ELECTION IN CASE OF CERTAIN DEFICIENCIES.—

(1) IN GENERAL.—If—

(A) a deficiency in the tax imposed by section 2001 is assessed,

(B) the estate qualifies under subsection (a)(1), and

(C) the executor has not made an election under subsection (a),

the executor may elect to pay the deficiency in installments. This subsection shall not apply if the deficiency is due to negligence, to intentional disregard of rules and regulations, or to fraud with intent to evade tax.

(2) TIME OF ELECTION.—An election under this subsection shall be made not later than 60 days after issuance of notice and demand by the Secretary for the payment of the deficiency, and shall be made in such manner as the Secretary shall by regulations prescribe.

(3) EFFECT OF ELECTION ON PAYMENT.—If an election is made under this subsection, the deficiency shall (subject to the limitation provided by subsection (a)(2)) be prorated to the installments which would have been due if an election had been timely made under subsection (a) at the time the estate tax return was filed. The part of the deficiency so prorated to any installment the date for payment of which would have arrived shall be paid at the time of the making of the election under this subsection. The portion of the deficiency so prorated to installments the date for payment of which would not have so arrived shall be paid at the time such installments would have been due if such an election had been made.

[Sec. 6166(i)]

(i) SPECIAL RULE FOR CERTAIN DIRECT SKIPS.—To the extent that an interest in a closely held business is the subject of a direct skip (within the meaning of section 2612(c)) occurring at the same time as and as a result of the decedent's death, then for purposes of this section any tax imposed by section 2601 on the transfer of such interest shall be treated as if it were additional tax imposed by section 2001.

Amendments

• **1986, Tax Reform Act of 1986 (P.L. 99-514)**

P.L. 99-514, §1432(e):

Amended Code Sec. 6166 by redesignating subsection (i) and (j) as subsections (j) and (k), respectively, and by inserting after subsection (h), new subsection (i).

Effective, generally, for any generation-skipping transfer (within the meaning of section 2611 of the Internal Revenue Code of 1986) made after the date of the enactment of this Act. For special rules, see Act Sec. 1433(b)-(d) following Code Sec. 2601.

[Sec. 6166(j)]

(j) REGULATIONS.—The Secretary shall prescribe such regulations as may be necessary to the application of this section.

Amendments

• **1986, Tax Reform Act of 1986 (P.L. 99-514)**

P.L. 99-514, §1432(e):

Amended Code Sec. 6166 by redesignating subsection (i) and (j) as subsections (j) and (k), respectively, and by inserting after subsection (h), new subsection (i).

Effective, generally, for any generation-skipping transfer (within the meaning of section 2611 of the Internal Revenue Code of 1986) made after 10-22-86. For special rules, see Act Sec. 1433(b)-(d) following Code Sec. 2601.

[Sec. 6166(k)]

(k) CROSS REFERENCES.—

(1) SECURITY.—For authority of the Secretary to require security in the case of an extension under this section, see section 6165.

(2) LIEN.—For special lien (in lieu of bond) in the case of an extension under this section, see section 6324A.

(3) PERIOD OF LIMITATION.—For extension of the period of limitation in the case of an extension under this section, see section 6503(d).

(4) INTEREST.—For provisions relating to interest on tax payable in installments under this section, see subsection (j) of section 6601.

(5) TRANSFERS WITHIN 3 YEARS OF DEATH.—For special rule for qualifying an estate under this section where property has been transferred within 3 years of decedent's death, see section 2035(c)(2).

TAX PAYMENT—EXTENSIONS OF TIME

Amendments

• **2000, Community Renewal Tax Relief Act of 2000 (P.L. 106-554)**

P.L. 106-554, §319(18):

Amended Code Sec. 6166(k)(5) by striking "2035(d)(4)" and inserting "2035(c)(2)". **Effective** on 12-21-00.

• **1996, Small Business Job Protection Act of 1996 (P.L. 104-188)**

P.L. 104-188, §1704(t)(15):

Amended Code Sec. 6166(k) by striking paragraph (6). **Effective** 8-20-96. Prior to being stricken, Code Sec. 6166(k)(6) read as follows:

(6) PAYMENT OF ESTATE TAX BY EMPLOYEE STOCK OWNERSHIP PLAN OR ELIGIBLE WORKER-OWNED COOPERATIVE.—For provision allowing plan administrator or eligible worker-owned cooperative to elect to pay a certain portion of the estate tax in installments under the provisions of this section, see section 2210(c).

• **1986, Tax Reform Act of 1986 (P.L. 99-514)**

P.L. 99-514, §1432(e):

Amended Code Sec. 6166 by redesignating subsection (i) and (j) as subsections (j) and (k), respectively, and by inserting after subsection (h), new subsection (i).

Amendments

• **1981, Economic Recovery Tax Act of 1981 (P.L. 97-34)**

P.L. 97-34, §422(d):

Repealed Code Sec. 6166A. **Effective** for estates of decedents dying after 12-31-81. Prior to its repeal, Code Sec. 6166A read as follows:

SEC. 6166A. EXTENSION OF TIME FOR PAYMENT OF ESTATE TAX WHERE ESTATE CONSISTS LARGELY OF INTEREST IN CLOSELY HELD BUSINESS.

[Sec. 6166A(a)]

(a) EXTENSION PERMITTED.—If the value of an interest in a closely held business which is included in determining the gross estate of a decedent who was (at the date of his death) a citizen or resident of the United States exceeds either—

(1) 35 percent of the value of the gross estate of such decedent, or

(2) 50 percent of the taxable estate of such decedent,

the executor may elect to pay part or all of the tax imposed by section 2001 in two or more (but not exceeding 10) equal installments. Any such election shall be made not later than the time prescribed by section 6075(a) for filing the return of such tax (including extensions thereof), and shall be made in such manner as the Secretary shall by regulations prescribe. If an election under this section is made, the provisions of this subtitle shall apply as though the Secretary were extending the time for payment of the tax. For purposes of this section, value shall be value determined for Federal estate tax purposes.

Amendments

• **1976, Tax Reform Act of 1976 (P.L. 94-455)**

P.L. 94-455, §1906(b)(13)(A):

Amended 1954 Code by substituting "Secretary" for "Secretary or his delegate" each place it appeared. **Effective** 2-1-77.

[Sec. 6166A(b)]

(b) LIMITATION.—The maximum amount of tax which may be paid in installments as provided in this section shall be an amount which bears the same ratio to the tax imposed by section 2001 (reduced by the credits against such tax) as the value of the interest in a closely held business which qualifies under subsection (a) bears to the value of the gross estate.

[Sec. 6166A(c)]

(c) CLOSELY HELD BUSINESS.—For purposes of this section, the term "interest in a closely held business" means—

(1) an interest as a proprietor in a trade or business carried on as a proprietorship.

(2) an interest as a partner in a partnership carrying on a trade or business, if—

(A) 20 percent or more of the total capital interest in such partnership is included in determining the gross estate of the decedent, or

(B) such partnership had 10 or less partners,

(3) stock in a corporation carrying on a trade or business, if—

(A) 20 percent or more in value of the voting stock of such corporation is included in determining the gross estate of the decedent, or

(B) such corporation had 10 or less shareholders.

For purposes of this subsection, determinations shall be made as of the time immediately before the decedent's death.

[Sec. 6166A(d)]

(d) SPECIAL RULE FOR INTERESTS IN TWO OR MORE CLOSELY HELD BUSINESSES.—For purposes of subsections (a), (b), and (h)(1), interests in two or more closely held businesses, with respect to each of which there is included in determining the value of the decedent's gross estate more than 50 percent of the total value of each such business, shall be treated as an interest in a single closely held business. For purposes of the 50 percent requirement of the preceding sentence, an interest in a closely held business which represents the surviving spouse's interest in property held by the decedent and the surviving spouse as community property shall be treated as having been included in determining the value of the decedent's gross estate.

[Sec. 6166A(e)]

(e) DATE FOR PAYMENT OF INSTALLMENTS.—If an election is made under subsection (a), the first installment shall be paid on or before the date prescribed by section 6151(a) for payment of the tax, and each succeeding installment shall be paid on or before the date which is one year after the date prescribed by this subsection for payment of the preceeding installment.

Effective, generally, for any generation-skipping transfer (within the meaning of section 2611 of the Internal Revenue Code of 1986) made after 10-22-86. For special rules, see Act Sec. 1433(b)-(d) following Code Sec. 2601.

• **1984, Deficit Reduction Act of 1984 (P.L. 98-369)**

P.L. 98-369 §544(b)(4):

Amended Code Sec. 6166(j) by adding new paragraph (6). **Effective** for those estates of decedents required to file returns on a date (including any extensions) after 7-18-84.

• **1983, Technical Corrections Act of 1982 (P.L. 97-448)**

P.L. 97-448, §104(d)(1)(B):

Amended Code Sec. 6166(j) by adding at the end thereof new paragraph (5). **Effective** as if included in the provision of P.L. 97-34 to which it relates.

• **1976, Tax Reform Act of 1976 (P.L. 94-455)**

P.L. 94-455, §2004(a):

Redesignated former Code Sec. 6166 as Code Sec. 6166A and added a new Code Sec. 6166, including Code Sec. 6166(j). **Effective** for estates of decedents dying after 12-31-76.

[Sec. 6166A—Repealed]

[Sec. 6166A(f)]

(f) PRORATION OF DEFICIENCY TO INSTALLMENTS.—If an election is made under subsection (a) to pay any part of the tax imposed by section 2001 in installments and a deficiency has been assessed, the deficiency shall (subject to the limitation provided by subsection (b)) be prorated to such installments. The part of the deficiency so prorated to any installment the date for payment of which has not arrived shall be collected at the same time as, and as a part of, such installment. The part of the deficiency so prorated to any installment the date for payment of which has arrived shall be paid upon notice and demand from the Secretary. This subsection shall not apply if the deficiency is due to negligence, to intentional disregard of rules and regulations, or to fraud with intent to evade tax.

Amendments

• **1976, Tax Reform Act of 1976 (P.L. 94-455)**

P.L. 94-455, §1906(b)(13)(A):

Amended 1954 Code by substituting "Secretary" for "Secretary or his delegate" each place it appeared. **Effective** 2-1-77.

[Sec. 6166A(g)]

(g) TIME FOR PAYMENT OF INTEREST.—If the time for payment of any amount of tax has been extended under this section, interest payable under section 6601 on any unpaid portion of such amount shall be paid annually at the same time as, and as a part of, each installment payment of the tax. Interest, on that part of a deficiency prorated under this section to any installment the date for payment of which has not arrived, for the period before the date fixed for the last installment preceding the assessment of the deficiency, shall be paid upon notice and demand from the Secretary.

Amendments

• **1976, Tax Reform Act of 1976 (P.L. 94-455)**

P.L. 94-455, §1906(b)(13)(A):

Amended 1954 Code by substituting "Secretary" for "Secretary or his delegate" each place it appeared. **Effective** 2-1-77.

• **1975 (P.L. 93-625)**

P.L. 93-625, §7(d)(2):

Amended Code Sec. 6166(g) by deleting the following from the end thereof: "In applying section 6601(b) (relating to the application of the 4-percent rate of interest in the case of certain extensions of time to pay estate tax) in the case of a deficiency, the entire amount which is prorated to installments under this section shall be treated as an amount of tax the payment of which is extended under this section." **Effective** 7-1-75.

[Sec. 6166A(h)]

(h) ACCELERATION OF PAYMENT.—

(1) WITHDRAWAL OF FUNDS FROM BUSINESS; DISPOSITION OF INTEREST.—

(A) If—

(i) aggregate withdrawals of money and other property from the trade or business, an interest in which qualifies under subsection (a), made with respect to such interest, equal or exceed 50 percent of the value of such trade or business, or

(ii) 50 percent or more in value of an interest in a closely held business which qualifies under subsection (a) is distributed, sold, exchanged, or otherwise disposed of,

then the extension of time for payment of tax provided in this section shall cease to apply, and any unpaid portion of the tax payable in installments shall be paid upon notice and demand from the Secretary.

(B) In the case of a distribution in redemption of stock to which section 303 (or so much of section 304 as relates to section 303) applies—

(i) subparagraph (A)(i) does not apply with respect to withdrawals of money and other property distributed; and for purposes of such subparagraph the value of the trade or business shall be considered to be such value reduced by the amount of money and other property distributed, and

(ii) subparagraph (A)(ii) does not apply with respect to the stock redeemed; and for purposes of such subparagraph the interest in the closely held business shall be considered to be such interest reduced by the value of the stock redeemed.

TAX PAYMENT—EXTENSIONS OF TIME

This subparagraph shall apply only if, on or before the date prescribed by subsection (e) for payment on the first installment which becomes due after the date of the distribution, there is paid an amount of the tax imposed by section 2001 not less than the amount of money and other property distributed.

(C) Subparagraph (A)(ii) does not apply to an exchange of stock pursuant to a plan of reorganization described in subparagraph (D), (E), or (F) of section 368(a)(1) nor to an exchange to which section 355 (or so much of section 356 as relates to section 355) applies; but any stock received in such an exchange shall be treated for purposes of such subparagraph as an interest qualifying under subsection (a).

(D) Subparagraph (A)(ii) does not apply to a transfer of property of the decedent by the executor to a person entitled to receive such property under the decedent's will or under the applicable law of descent and distribution.

(2) UNDISTRIBUTED INCOME OF ESTATE.—

(A) If an election is made under this section and the estate has undistributed net income for any taxable year after its fourth taxable year, the executor shall, on or before the date prescribed by law for filing the income tax return for such taxable year (including extensions thereof), pay an amount equal to such undistributed net income in liquidation of the unpaid portion of the tax payable in installments.

(B) For purposes of subparagraph (A), the undistributed net income of the estate for any taxable year is the amount by which the distributable net income of the estate for such taxable year (as defined in section 643) exceeds the sum of—

(i) the amounts for such taxable year specified in paragraphs (1) and (2) of section 661(a) (relating to deduction for distributions, etc.);

(ii) the amount of tax imposed for the taxable year on the estate under chapter 1; and,

(iii) the amount of the Federal estate tax (including interest) paid by the executor during the taxable year (other than any amount paid pursuant to this paragraph).

(3) FAILURE TO PAY INSTALLMENT.—If any installment under this section is not paid on or before the date fixed for its payment by this section (including any extension of time for the payment of such installment), the unpaid portion of the tax payable in installments shall be paid upon notice and demand from the Secretary.

Amendments

• **1976, Tax Reform Act of 1976 (P.L. 94-455)**

P.L. 94-455, §1906(b)(13)(A):

Amended 1954 Code by substituting "Secretary" for "Secretary or his delegate" each place it appeared. **Effective** 2-1-77.

[Sec. 6166A(i)]

(i) TRANSITIONAL RULES.—

(1) IN GENERAL.—If—

(A) a deficiency in the tax imposed by section 2001 is assessed after the date of the enactment of this section, and

(B) the estate qualifies under paragraph (1) or (2) of subsection (a),

the executor may elect to pay the deficiency in installments. This subsection shall not apply if the deficiency is due to negligence, to intentional disregard of rules and regulations, or to fraud with intent to evade tax.

(2) TIME OF ELECTION.—An election under this subsection shall be made not later than 60 days after issuance of notice and demand by the Secretary for the payment of the deficiency, and shall be made in such manner as the Secretary shall by regulations prescribe.

(3) EFFECT OF ELECTION ON PAYMENT.—If an election is made under this subsection, the deficiency shall (subject to the limitation provided by subsection (b)) be prorated to the installments which would have been due if an election had been timely made under this section at the time the estate tax return was filed. The part of the deficiency so prorated to any installment the date for payment of which would have arrived shall be paid at the time of the making of the election under this subsection. The portion of the deficiency so prorated to installments the date for payment of which would not have so arrived shall be paid at the time such installments would have been due if such an election had been made.

(4) APPLICATION OF SUBSECTION (h)(2).—In the case of an election under this subsection, subsection (h)(2) shall not apply with respect to undistributed net income for any taxable year ending before January 1, 1960.

Amendments

• **1976, Tax Reform Act of 1976 (P.L. 94-455)**

P.L. 94-455, §1906(b)(13)(A):

Amended 1954 Code by substituting "Secretary" for "Secretary or his delegate" each place it appeared. **Effective** 2-1-77.

[Sec. 6166A(j)]

(j) REGULATIONS.—The Secretary shall prescribe such regulations as may be necessary to the application of this section.

Amendments

P.L. 94-455, §1906(b)(13)(A):

Amended 1954 Code by substituting "Secretary" for "Secretary or his delegate" each place it appeared. **Effective** 2-1-77.

[Sec. 6166A(k)]

(k) CROSS REFERENCES.—

(1) SECURITY.—

For authority of the Secretary to require security in the case of an extension under this section, see section 6165.

(2) PERIOD OF LIMITATION.—

For extension of the period of limitation in the case of an extension under this section, see section 6503(d).

Amendments

• **1976, Tax Reform Act of 1976 (P.L. 94-455)**

P.L. 94-455, §1906(b)(13)(A):

Amended 1954 Code by substituting "Secretary" for "Secretary or his delegate" each place it appeared. **Effective** 2-1-77.

• **1975 (P.L. 93-625)**

P.L. 93-625, §7(d)(3):

Amended Code Sec. 6166(k) by deleting former paragraph (1) and renumbering former paragraphs (2) and (3) to be paragraphs (1) and (2), respectively. **Effective** 7-1-75. Prior to amendment, paragraph (1) read as follows:

"(1) Interest.—

"For provisions requiring the payment of interest at the rate of 4 percent per annum for the period of an extension, see section 6601(b)."

• **1958, Technical Amendments Act of 1958 (P.L. 85-866)**

P.L. 85-866, §206(a):

Added Sec. 6166. For **effective** date, see Act Sec. 206(f), below.

P.L. 85-866, §206(f), provides:

"The amendments made by this section shall apply to estates of decedents with respect to which the date for the filing of the estate tax return (including extensions thereof) prescribed by section 6075(a) of the Internal Revenue Code of 1954 is after the date of the enactment of this Act; except that (1) section 6166(i) of such Code as added by this section shall apply to estates of decedents dying after August 16, 1954, but only if the date for the filing of the estate tax return (including extensions thereof) expired on or before the date of the enactment of this Act, and (2) notwithstanding section 6166(a) of such Code, if an election under such section is required to be made before the sixtieth day after the date of the enactment of this Act such an election shall be considered timely if made on or before such sixtieth day."

[Sec. 6167]

SEC. 6167. EXTENSION OF TIME FOR PAYMENT OF TAX ATTRIBUTABLE TO RECOVERY OF FOREIGN EXPROPRIATION LOSSES.

[Sec. 6167(a)]

(a) EXTENSION ALLOWED BY ELECTION.—If—

(1) a corporation has a recovery of a foreign expropriation loss to which section 1351 applies, and

(2) the portion of the recovery received in money is less than 25 percent of the amount of such recovery (as defined in section 1351(c)) and is not greater than the tax attributable to such recovery,

the tax attributable to such recovery shall, at the election of the taxpayer, be payable in 10 equal installments on the 15th day of the fourth month of each of the taxable years following the taxable year of the recovery. Such election shall be made at such time and in such manner as the Secretary may prescribe by regulations. If an election is made under this subsection, the provisions of this subtitle shall apply as though the Secretary were extending the time for payment of such tax.

Amendments

• **2015, Surface Transportation and Veterans Health Care Choice Improvement Act of 2015 (P.L. 114-41)**

P.L. 114-41, §2006(a)(2)(D):

Amended Code Sec. 6167(a) by striking "third month" and inserting "fourth month". **Effective** generally for returns for tax years beginning after 12-31-2015. For an exception, see Act Sec. 2006(a)(3)(B), below.

P.L. 114-41, §2006(a)(3)(B), provides:

(B) SPECIAL RULE FOR C CORPORATIONS WITH FISCAL YEARS ENDING ON JUNE 30.—In the case of any C corporation with a taxable year ending on June 30, the amendments made by this subsection shall apply to returns for taxable years beginning after December 31, 2025.

• **1976, Tax Reform Act of 1976 (P.L. 94-455)**

P.L. 94-455, §1906(b)(13)(A):

Amended 1954 Code by substituting "Secretary" for "Secretary or his delegate" each place it appeared. **Effective** 2-1-77.

TAX PAYMENT—EXTENSIONS OF TIME

[Sec. 6167(b)]

(b) EXTENSION PERMITTED BY SECRETARY.—If a corporation has a recovery of a foreign expropriation loss to which section 1351 applies and if an election is not made under subsection (a), the Secretary may, upon finding that the payment of the tax attributable to such recovery at the time otherwise provided in this subtitle would result in undue hardship, extend the time for payment of such tax for a reasonable period or periods not in excess of 9 years from the date on which such tax is otherwise payable.

Amendments
- **1976, Tax Reform Act of 1976 (P.L. 94-455)**

P.L. 94-455, §1906(b)(13)(A):

Amended 1954 Code by substituting "Secretary" for "Secretary or his delegate" each place it appeared. **Effective** 2-1-77.

[Sec. 6167(c)]

(c) ACCELERATION OF PAYMENTS.—If—

   (1) an election is made under subsection (a),

   (2) during any taxable year before the tax attributable to such recovery is paid in full—

      (A) any property (other than money) received on such recovery is sold or exchanged, or

      (B) any property (other than money) received on any sale or exchange described in subparagraph (A) is sold or exchanged, and

   (3) the amount of money received on such sale or exchange (reduced by the amount of the tax imposed under chapter 1 with respect to such sale or exchange), when added to the amount of money—

      (A) received on such recovery, and

      (B) received on previous sales or exchanges described in subparagraphs (A) and (B) of paragraph (2) (as so reduced),

exceeds the amount of money which may be received under subsection (a)(2), an amount of the tax attributable to such recovery equal to such excess shall be payable on the 15th day of the fourth month of the taxable year following the taxable year in which such sale or exchange occurs. The amount of such tax so paid shall be treated, for purposes of this section, as a payment of the first unpaid installment or installments (or portion thereof) which become payable under subsection (a) following such taxable year.

Amendments
- **2015, Surface Transportation and Veterans Health Care Choice Improvement Act of 2015 (P.L. 114-41)**

P.L. 114-41, §2006(a)(2)(D):

Amended Code Sec. 6167(c) by striking "third month" and inserting "fourth month". **Effective** generally for returns for tax years beginning after 12-31-2015. For an exception, see Act Sec. 2006(a)(3)(B), below.

P.L. 114-41, §2006(a)(3)(B), provides:

(B) SPECIAL RULE FOR C CORPORATIONS WITH FISCAL YEARS ENDING ON JUNE 30.—In the case of any C corporation with a taxable year ending on June 30, the amendments made by this subsection shall apply to returns for taxable years beginning after December 31, 2025.

[Sec. 6167(d)]

(d) PRORATION OF DEFICIENCY TO INSTALLMENTS.—If an election is made under subsection (a), and a deficiency attributable to the recovery of a foreign expropriation loss has been assessed, the deficiency shall be prorated to such installments. The part of the deficiency so prorated to any installment the date for payment of which has not arrived shall be collected at the same time as, and as part of, such installment. The part of the deficiency so prorated to any installment the date for payment of which has arrived shall be paid upon notice and demand from the Secretary. This subsection shall not apply if the deficiency is due to negligence, to intentional disregard of rules and regulations, or to fraud with intent to evade tax.

Amendments
- **1976, Tax Reform Act of 1976 (P.L. 94-455)**

P.L. 94-455, §1906(b)(13)(A):

Amended 1954 Code by substituting "Secretary" for "Secretary or his delegate" each place it appeared. **Effective** 2-1-77.

[Sec. 6167(e)]

(e) TIME FOR PAYMENT OF INTEREST.—If the time for payment for any amount of tax has been extended under this section, interest payable under section 6601 on any unpaid portion of such amount shall be paid annually at the same time as, and as part of, each installment payment of the tax. Interest, on that part of a deficiency prorated under this section to any installment the date for payment of which has not arrived, for the period before the date fixed for the last installment preceding the assessment of the deficiency, shall be paid upon notice and demand from the Secretary.

Amendments
- **1976, Tax Reform Act of 1976 (P.L. 94-455)**

P.L. 94-455, §1906(b)(13)(A):

Amended 1954 Code by substituting "Secretary" for "Secretary or his delegate" each place it appeared. **Effective** 2-1-77.

[Sec. 6167(f)]

(f) TAX ATTRIBUTABLE TO RECOVERY OF FOREIGN EXPROPRIATION LOSS.—For purposes of this section, the tax attributable to a recovery of a foreign expropriation loss is the sum of—

   (1) the additional tax imposed by section 1351(d)(1) on such recovery, and

   (2) the amount by which the tax imposed under subtitle A is increased by reason of the gain on such recovery which under section 1351(e) is considered as gain on the involuntary conversion of property.

[Sec. 6167(g)]

(g) FAILURE TO PAY INSTALLMENT.—If any installment under this section is not paid on or before the date fixed for its payment by this section (including any extension of time for the payment of such installment), the unpaid portion of the tax payable in installments shall be paid upon notice and demand from the Secretary.

Amendments
- **1976, Tax Reform Act of 1976 (P.L. 94-455)**

P.L. 94-455, §1906(b)(13)(A):

Amended 1954 Code by substituting "Secretary" for "Secretary or his delegate" each place it appeared. **Effective** 2-1-77.

ASSESSMENT—IN GENERAL

[Sec. 6167(h)]

(h) CROSS REFERENCES.—

(1) SECURITY.—For authority of the Secretary to require security in the case of an extension under this section, see section 6165.

(2) PERIOD OF LIMITATION.—For extension of the period of limitation in the case of an extension under this section, see section 6503(e).

Amendments

• **1976, Tax Reform Act of 1976 (P.L. 94-455)**

P.L. 94-455, §1902(b)(2)(B):

Substituted "section 6503(e)" for "section 6503(f)" in Code Sec. 6167(h)(2). **Effective** for estates of decedents dying after 10-4-76.

P.L. 94-455, §1906(b)(13)(A):

Amended 1954 Code by substituting "Secretary" for "Secretary or his delegate" each place it appeared. **Effective** 2-1-77.

• **1975 (P.L. 93-625)**

P.L. 93-625, §7(d)(2):

Amended Code Sec. 6167(e) by deleting the following from the end thereof: "In applying section 6601(j) (relating to the application of the 4-percent rate of interest in the case of recoveries of foreign expropriation losses to which this section applies) in the case of a deficiency, the entire amount which is prorated to installments under this section shall be treated as an amount of tax the payment of which is extended under this section." Effective 7-1-75.

P.L. 93-625, §7(d)(3):

Amended Code Sec. 6167(h) by deleting former paragraph (1) and renumbering former paragraphs (2) and (3) to be paragraphs (1) and (2), respectively. **Effective** 7-1-75. Prior to deletion, paragraph (1) read as follows:

"(1) Interest.—For provisions requiring the payment of interest at the rate of 4 percent per annum for the period of an extension, see section 6601(j)."

• **1966 (P.L. 89-384)**

P.L. 89-384, §1(d):

Added new Code Sec. 6167. **Effective** with respect to amounts received after 12-31-64, in respect of foreign expropriation losses sustained after 12-31-58.

CHAPTER 63—ASSESSMENT

SUBCHAPTER A.	In general.
SUBCHAPTER B.	Deficiency procedures in the case of income, estate, gift, and certain excise taxes.
SUBCHAPTER C.	Tax treatment of partnership items.
SUBCHAPTER D.	Treatment of electing large partnerships.

Subchapter A—In General

Sec. 6201.	Assessment authority.
Sec. 6202.	Establishment by regulations of mode or time of assessment.
Sec. 6203.	Method of assessment.
Sec. 6204.	Supplemental assessments.
Sec. 6205.	Special rules applicable to certain employment taxes.
Sec. 6206.	Special rules applicable to excessive claims under certain sections.
Sec. 6207.	Cross references.

[Sec. 6201]

SEC. 6201. ASSESSMENT AUTHORITY.

[Sec. 6201(a)]

(a) AUTHORITY OF SECRETARY.—The Secretary is authorized and required to make the inquiries, determinations, and assessments of all taxes (including interest, additional amounts, additions to the tax, and assessable penalties) imposed by this title, or accruing under any former internal revenue law, which have not been duly paid by stamp at the time and in the manner provided by law. Such authority shall extend to and include the following:

(1) TAXES SHOWN ON RETURN.—The Secretary shall assess all taxes determined by the taxpayer or by the Secretary as to which returns or lists (or payments under section 6225(c)(2)(B)(i)) are made under this title.

(2) UNPAID TAXES PAYABLE BY STAMP.—

(A) OMITTED STAMPS.—Whenever any article upon which a tax is required to be paid by means of a stamp is sold or removed for sale or use by the manufacturer thereof or whenever any transaction or act upon which a tax is required to be paid by means of a stamp occurs without the use of the proper stamp, it shall be the duty of the Secretary, upon such information as he can obtain, to estimate the amount of tax which has been omitted to be paid and to make assessment therefor upon the person or persons the Secretary determines to be liable for such tax.

(B) CHECK OR MONEY ORDER NOT DULY PAID.—In any case in which a check or money order received under authority of section 6311 as payment for stamps is not duly paid, the unpaid amount may be immediately assessed as if it were a tax imposed by this title, due at the time of such receipt, from the person who tendered such check or money order.

(3) ERRONEOUS INCOME TAX PREPAYMENT CREDITS.—If on any return or claim for refund of income taxes under subtitle A there is an overstatement of the credit for income tax withheld at the source, or of the amount paid as estimated income tax, the amount so overstated which is allowed against the tax shown on the return or which is allowed as a credit or refund may be assessed by the Secretary in the same manner as in the case of a mathematical or clerical error appearing upon the return, except that the provisions of section 6213(b)(2) (relating to abatement of mathematical or clerical error assessments) shall not apply with regard to any assessment under this paragraph.

(4) CERTAIN ORDERS OF CRIMINAL RESTITUTION.—

(A) IN GENERAL.—The Secretary shall assess and collect the amount of restitution under an order pursuant to section 3556 of title 18, United States Code, for failure to pay any tax imposed under this title in the same manner as if such amount were such tax.

(B) TIME OF ASSESSMENT.—An assessment of an amount of restitution under an order described in subparagraph (A) shall not be made before all appeals of such order are concluded and the right to make all such appeals has expired.

(C) RESTRICTION ON CHALLENGE OF ASSESSMENT.—The amount of such restitution may not be challenged by the person against whom assessed on the basis of the existence or amount of the underlying tax liability in any proceeding authorized under this title (including in any suit or proceeding in court permitted under section 7422).

Amendments

• **2018, Tax Technical Corrections Act of 2018 (P.L. 115-141)**

P.L. 115-141, §203(b), Div. U:

Amended Code Sec. 6201(a)(1) by inserting "(or payments under section 6225(c)(2)(B)(i))" after "returns or lists". **Effective** as if included in section 1101 of the Bipartisan Budget Act of 2015 [**effective** generally for returns filed for partnership tax years beginning after 12-31-2017.—CCH].

ASSESSMENT—IN GENERAL

- **2010, Firearms Excise Tax Improvement Act of 2010 (P.L. 111-237)**

P.L. 111-237, §3(a):

Amended Code Sec. 6201(a) by adding at the end a new paragraph (4). **Effective** for restitution ordered after 8-16-2010.

- **1988, Technical and Miscellaneous Revenue Act of 1988 (P.L. 100-647)**

P.L. 100-647, §1015(r)(1):

Amended Code Sec. 6201(a) by striking out paragraph (4). **Effective** for notices of deficiencies mailed after 11-10-88. Prior to amendment, Code Sec. 6201(a)(4) read as follows:

(4) ERRONEOUS CREDIT UNDER SECTION 32 OR 34.—If on any return or claim for refund of income taxes under subtitle A there is an overstatement of the credit allowable by section 34 (relating to certain uses of gasoline and special fuels) or section 32 (relating to earned income), the amount so overstated which is allowed against the tax shown on the return or which is allowed as a credit or refund may be assessed by the Secretary in the same manner as in the case of a mathematical or clerical error appearing upon the return, except that the provisions of section 6213(b)(2) (relating to abatement of mathematical or clerical error assessments) shall not apply with regard to any assessment under this paragraph.

- **1984, Deficit Reduction Act of 1984 (P.L. 98-369)**

P.L. 98-369, §474(r)(32):

Amended Code Sec. 6201(a)(4) by striking out "section 39" and inserting in lieu thereof "section 34", by striking out "section 43" and inserting in lieu thereof "section 32", and by striking out "Section 39 or 43" in the paragraph heading and inserting in lieu thereof "Section 32 or 34". **Effective** for tax years beginning after 12-31-83, and to carrybacks from such years.

- **1983, Surface Transportation Act of 1983 (P.L. 97-424)**

P.L. 97-424, §515(b)(6)(E):

Amended Code Sec. 6201(a)(4) by striking out ", special fuels, and lubricating oil" and inserting "and special fuels". **Effective** with respect to articles sold after 1-6-83.

- **1976, Tax Reform Act of 1976 (P.L. 94-455)**

P.L. 94-455, §1206(c)(2)(A):

Substituted "mathematical or clerical error" for "mathematical error" in Code Sec. 6201(a)(3) and 6201(a)(4). **Effective** with respect to returns filed after 12-31-76.

P.L. 94-455, §1206(c)(2)(B):

Added ", except that the provisions of section 6213(b)(2) (relating to abatement of mathematical or clerical error assessments) shall not apply with regard to any assessment under this paragraph" immediately before the period at the end of Code Sec. 6201(a)(3) and 6201(a)(4). **Effective** with respect to returns filed after 12-31-76.

P.L. 94-455, §1906(b)(13)(A):

Amended 1954 Code by substituting "Secretary" for "Secretary or his delegate" each place it appeared. **Effective** 2-1-77.

- **1975, Tax Reduction Act of 1975 (P.L. 94-12)**

P.L. 94-12, §204(b)(2):

Amended Code Sec. 6201(a)(4) by inserting "or 43" after "section 39" in the caption of the section and by deleting "oil)," and inserting in lieu thereof "oil) or section 43 (relating to earned income),". **Effective** only for tax years beginning after 1974 (as amended by P.L. 95-600, §103(a), and P.L. 94-164, §2(f)).

- **1970 (P.L. 91-258)**

P.L. 91-258, §207(d)(1), (2:

Amended Code Sec. 6201(a)(4) by substituting "UNDER SECTION 39" for "FOR USE OF GASOLINE" in the heading and by adding ", special fuels," in the parenthetical matter in the body. **Effective** 7-1-70.

- **1965, Excise Tax Reduction Act of 1965 (P.L. 89-44)**

P.L. 89-44, §809(d)(4):

Amended Sec. 6201(a) by adding paragraph (4). **Effective** 7-1-65.

[Sec. 6201(b)]

(b) AMOUNT NOT TO BE ASSESSED.—

(1) ESTIMATED INCOME TAX.—No unpaid amount of estimated income tax required to be paid under section 6654 or 6655 shall be assessed.

(2) FEDERAL UNEMPLOYMENT TAX.—No unpaid amount of Federal unemployment tax for any calendar quarter or other period of a calendar year, computed as provided in section 6157, shall be assessed.

Amendments

- **1988, Technical and Miscellaneous Revenue Act of 1988 (P.L. 100-647)**

P.L. 100-647, §7106(c)(2):

Amended Code Sec. 6201(b)(2) by striking out "or tax imposed by section 3321" after the words "Federal unemployment tax". **Effective** for remuneration paid after 12-31-88.

- **1987, Revenue Act of 1987 (P.L. 100-203)**

P.L. 100-203, §10301(b)(3):

Amended Code Sec. 6201(b)(1) by striking out "section 6154 or 6654" and inserting in lieu thereof "section 6654 or 6655". **Effective** for tax years beginning after 12-31-87.

- **1984, Deficit Reduction Act of 1984 (P.L. 98-369)**

P.L. 98-369, §412(b)(5):

Amended Code Sec. 6201(b)(1). **Effective** with respect to tax years beginning after 12-31-84. Prior to amendment, paragraph (1) read as follows:

(1) Estimated Income Tax.—No unpaid amount of estimated tax under section 6153 or 6154 shall be assessed.

- **1983, Railroad Retirement Solvency Act of 1983 (P.L. 98-76)**

P.L. 98-76, §231(b)(2)(A):

Amended Code Sec. 6201(b). **Effective** for remuneration paid after 6-30-86.

- **1969 (P.L. 91-53)**

P.L. 91-53, §2(b):

Amended Code Sec. 6201(b). **Effective** for calendar years beginning after 12-31-69. Prior to amendment, Code Sec. 6201(b) read as follows:

"(b) Estimated Income Tax.—No unpaid amount of estimated tax under section 6153 or 6154 shall be assessed."

[Sec. 6201(c)]

(c) COMPENSATION OF CHILD.—Any income tax under chapter 1 assessed against a child, to the extent attributable to amounts includible in the gross income of the child, and not of the parent, solely by reason of section 73(a), shall, if not paid by the child, for all purposes be considered as having also been properly assessed against the parent.

[Sec. 6201(d)]

(d) REQUIRED REASONABLE VERIFICATION OF INFORMATION RETURNS.—In any court proceeding, if a taxpayer asserts a reasonable dispute with respect to any item of income reported on an information return filed with the Secretary under subpart B or C of part III of subchapter A of chapter 61 by a third party and the taxpayer has fully cooperated with the Secretary (including providing, within a reasonable period of time, access to and inspection of all witnesses, information, and documents within the control of the taxpayer as reasonably requested by the Secretary), the Secretary shall have the burden of producing reasonable and probative information concerning such deficiency in addition to such information return.

Amendments

- **1996, Taxpayer Bill of Rights 2 (P.L. 104-168)**

P.L. 104-168, §602(a):

Amended Code Sec. 6201 by redesignating subsection (d) as subsection (e) and by inserting after subsection (c) a new subsection (d). **Effective** 7-30-96.

[Sec. 6201(e)]

(e) DEFICIENCY PROCEEDINGS.—

For special rules applicable to deficiencies of income, estate, gift, and certain excise taxes, see subchapter B.

Amendments

- **1996, Taxpayer Bill of Rights 2 (P.L. 104-168)**

P.L. 104-168, §602(a):

Amended Code Sec. 6201 by redesignating subsection (d) as subsection (e). **Effective** 7-30-96.

- **1976, Tax Reform Act of 1976 (P.L. 94-455)**

P.L. 94-455, §1307(d)(2)(D):

Substituted "and certain excise taxes" for "chapter 42, and chapter 43 taxes" in Code Sec. 6201(d). **Effective** 10-4-76.

Sec. 6201(b)

ASSESSMENT—IN GENERAL

• **1974, Employee Retirement Income Security Act of 1974 (P.L. 93-406)**

P.L. 93-406, § 1016(a)(8):

Amended Code Sec. 6201(d) by changing "and chapter 42" to "chapter 42, and chapter 43". For **effective** date, see amendment note for Code Sec. 410.

• **1969, Tax Reform Act of 1969 (P.L. 91-172)**

P.L. 91-172, § 101(j)(38):

Amended Code Sec. 6201(d) by substituting "gift, and chapter 42 taxes," for "and gift taxes,". **Effective** 1-1-70.

[Sec. 6202]

SEC. 6202. ESTABLISHMENT BY REGULATIONS OF MODE OR TIME OF ASSESSMENT.

If the mode or time for the assessment of any internal revenue tax (including interest, additional amounts, additions to the tax, and assessable penalties) is not otherwise provided for, the Secretary may establish the same by regulations.

Amendments

• **1976, Tax Reform Act of 1976 (P.L. 94-455)**

P.L. 94-455, § 1906(b)(13)(A):

Amended 1954 Code by substituting "Secretary" for "Secretary or his delegate" each place it appeared. **Effective** 2-1-77.

[Sec. 6203]

SEC. 6203. METHOD OF ASSESSMENT.

The assessment shall be made by recording the liability of the taxpayer in the office of the Secretary in accordance with rules or regulations prescribed by the Secretary. Upon request of the taxpayer, the Secretary shall furnish the taxpayer a copy of the record of the assessment.

Amendments

• **1976, Tax Reform Act of 1976 (P.L. 94-455)**

P.L. 94-455, § 1906(b)(13)(A):

Amended 1954 Code by substituting "Secretary" for "Secretary or his delegate" each place it appeared. **Effective** 2-1-77.

[Sec. 6204]

SEC. 6204. SUPPLEMENTAL ASSESSMENTS.

[Sec. 6204(a)]

(a) GENERAL RULE.—The Secretary may, at any time within the period prescribed for assessment, make a supplemental assessment whenever it is ascertained that any assessment is imperfect or incomplete in any material respect.

Amendments

• **1976, Tax Reform Act of 1976 (P.L. 94-455)**

P.L. 94-455, § 1906(b)(13)(A):

Amended 1954 Code by substituting "Secretary" for "Secretary or his delegate" each place it appeared. **Effective** 2-1-77.

[Sec. 6204(b)]

(b) RESTRICTIONS ON ASSESSMENT.—

For restrictions on assessment of deficiencies in income, estate, gift, and certain excise taxes, see section 6213.

Amendments

• **1974, Employee Retirement Income Security Act of 1974 (P.L. 93-406)**

P.L. 93-406, § 1016(a)(27):

Amended Code Sec. 6204(b) by changing "and gift taxes," to "gift, and certain excise taxes". For **effective** date, see amendment note for Code Sec. 410.

[Sec. 6205]

SEC. 6205. SPECIAL RULES APPLICABLE TO CERTAIN EMPLOYMENT TAXES.

[Sec. 6205(a)]

(a) ADJUSTMENT OF TAX.—

(1) GENERAL RULE.—If less than the correct amount of tax imposed by section 3101, 3111, 3201, 3221, or 3402 is paid with respect to any payment of wages or compensation, proper adjustments, with respect to both the tax and the amount to be deducted, shall be made, without interest, in such manner and at such times as the Secretary may by regulations prescribe.

(2) UNITED STATES AS EMPLOYER.—For purposes of this subsection, in the case of remuneration received from the United States or a wholly-owned instrumentality thereof during any calendar year, each head of a Federal agency or instrumentality who makes a return pursuant to section 3122 and each agent, designated by the head of a Federal agency or instrumentality, who makes a return pursuant to such section shall be deemed a separate employer.

(3) GUAM OR AMERICAN SAMOA AS EMPLOYER.—For purposes of this subsection, in the case of remuneration received during any calendar year from the Government of Guam, the Government of American Samoa, a political subdivision of either, or any instrumentality of any one or more of the foregoing which is wholly owned thereby, the Governor of Guam, the Governor of American Samoa, and each agent designated by either who makes a return pursuant to section 3125 shall be deemed a separate employer.

(4) DISTRICT OF COLUMBIA AS EMPLOYER.—For purposes of this subsection, in the case of remuneration received during any calendar year from the District of Columbia or any instrumentality which is wholly owned thereby, the Mayor of the District of Columbia and each agent designated by him who makes a return pursuant to section 3125 shall be deemed a separate employer.

(5) STATES AND POLITICAL SUBDIVISIONS AS EMPLOYER.—For purposes of this subsection, in the case of remuneration received from a State or any political subdivision thereof (or any instrumentality of any one or more of the foregoing which is wholly owned thereby) during any calendar year, each head of an agency or instrumentality, and each agent designated by either, who makes a return pursuant to section 3125 shall be deemed a separate employer.

Amendments

• **1986, Consolidated Omnibus Budget Reconciliation Act of 1985, (P.L. 99-272)**

P.L. 99-272, § 13205(a)(2)(D):

Amended Code Sec. 6205(a) by adding at the end thereof new paragraph (5). **Effective** for services performed after 3-31-86.

• **1976, Tax Reform Act of 1976 (P.L. 94-455)**

P.L. 94-455, § 1906(a)(13):

Substituted "Mayor of the District of Columbia and each agent designated by him" for "Commissioners of the District of Columbia and each agent designated by them" in Code Sec. 6205(a)(4). **Effective** 2-1-77.

ASSESSMENT—IN GENERAL

P.L. 94-455, § 1906(b)(13)(A):

Amended 1954 Code by substituting "Secretary" for "Secretary or his delegate" each place it appeared. **Effective** 2-1-77.

- **1965, Social Security Amendments of 1965 (P.L. 89-97)**

P.L. 89-97, § 317(d):

Added Sec. 6205(a)(4) to read as prior to amendment by P.L. 94-455. **Effective** with respect to service performed after the calendar quarter in which this section is enacted (7-30-65) and after the calendar quarter in which the Secretary of the Treasury receives a certification from the Commissioners of the District of Columbia expressing their desire to have the insurance system established by title II (and part A of title XVIII) of the Social Security Act extended to the officers and employees coming under these provisions.

- **1960, Social Security Amendments of 1960 (P.L. 86-778)**

P.L. 86-778, § 103(r):

Added a new paragraph (3) to Code Sec. 6205(a). **Effective** only with respect to (1) service in the employ of the Government of Guam or any political subdivision thereof, or any instrumentality of any one or more of the foregoing wholly owned thereby, which is performed after 1960 and after the calendar quarter in which the Secretary of the Treasury receives a certification by the Governor of Guam that legislation has been enacted by the Government of Guam expressing its desire to have the insurance system established by title II of the Social Security Act extended to the officers and employees of such Government and such political subdivisions and instrumentalities, and (2) service in the employ of the Government of American Samoa or any political subdivision thereof, or any instrumentality of any one or more of the foregoing wholly owned thereby, which is performed after 1960 and after the calendar quarter in which the Secretary of the Treasury receives a certification by the Governor of American Samoa that the Government of American Samoa desires to have the insurance system established by such title II extended to the officers and employees of such Government and such political subdivisions and instrumentalities.

[Sec. 6205(b)]

(b) UNDERPAYMENTS.—If less than the correct amount of tax imposed by section 3101, 3111, 3201, 3221, or 3402 is paid or deducted with respect to any payment of wages or compensation and the underpayment cannot be adjusted under subsection (a) of this section, the amount of the underpayment shall be assessed and collected in such manner and at such times (subject to the statute of limitations properly applicable thereto) as the Secretary may by regulations prescribe.

Amendments

- **1976, Tax Reform Act of 1976 (P.L. 94-455)**

P.L. 94-455, § 1906(b)(13)(A):

Amended 1954 Code by substituting "Secretary" for "Secretary or his delegate" each place it appeared. **Effective** 2-1-77.

[Sec. 6206]

SEC. 6206. SPECIAL RULES APPLICABLE TO EXCESSIVE CLAIMS UNDER CERTAIN SECTIONS.

Any portion of a refund made under section 6416(a)(4) and any portion of a payment made under section 6420, 6421, or 6427 which constitutes an excessive amount (as defined in section 6675(b)), and any civil penalty provided by section 6675, may be assessed and collected as if it were a tax imposed by section 4081 (with respect to refunds under section 6416(a)(4) and payments under sections 6420 and 6421), or 4041 or 4081 (with respect to payments under section 6427) and as if the person who made the claim were liable for such tax. The period for assessing any such portion, and for assessing any such penalty, shall be 3 years from the last day prescribed for the filing of the claim under section 6416(a)(4), 6420, 6421, or 6427 as the case may be.

Amendments

- **2005, Safe, Accountable, Flexible, Efficient Transportation Equity Act: A Legacy for Users (P.L. 109-59)**

P.L. 109-59, § 11163(d)(1)(A)-(D):

Amended Code Sec. 6206 by striking "Any portion" in the first sentence and inserting "Any portion of a refund made under section 6416(a)(4) and any portion", by striking "payments under sections 6420" in the first sentence and inserting "refunds under section 6416(a)(4) and payments under sections 6420", by striking "section 6420" in the second sentence and inserting "section 6416(a)(4), 6420", and by striking "SECTIONS 6420, 6421, AND 6427" in the heading thereof and inserting "CERTAIN SECTIONS". **Effective** for sales after 12-31-2005.

- **2004, American Jobs Creation Act of 2004 (P.L. 108-357)**

P.L. 108-357, § 853(d)(2)(F):

Amended Code Sec. 6206 by striking ", 4081, or 4091" and inserting "or 4081". **Effective** for aviation-grade kerosene removed, entered, or sold after 12-31-2004.

- **1993, Omnibus Budget Reconciliation Act of 1993 (P.L. 103-66)**

P.L. 103-66, § 13242(d)(14):

Amended Code Sec. 6206 by striking "4041 or 4091" and inserting "4041, 4081, or 4091". **Effective** 1-1-94.

- **1987, Revenue Act of 1987 (P.L. 100-203)**

P.L. 100-203, § 10502(d)(5):

Amended Code Sec. 6206 by striking out "or 4041" and inserting in lieu thereof "or 4041 or 4091". **Effective** for sales after 3-31-88.

- **1983, Surface Transportation Act of 1983 (P.L. 97-424)**

P.L. 97-424, § 515(b)(3)(A):

Amended Code Sec. 6206 by striking out "4091 (with respect to payments under section 6424)," and by striking out "6424," each place it appears in the heading and in the text. **Effective** with respect to articles sold after 1-6-83.

- **1970 (P.L. 91-258)**

P.L. 91-258, § 207(d)(3):

Amended Code Sec. 6206. **Effective** 7-1-70. Prior to amendment, this section read as follows:

"SEC. 6206. SPECIAL RULES APPLICABLE TO EXCESSIVE CLAIMS UNDER SECTIONS 6420, 6421, AND 6424.

"Any portion of a payment made under section 6420, 6421, or 6424 which constitutes an excessive amount (as defined in section 6675(b)), and any civil penalty provided by section 6675, may be assessed and collected as if it were a tax imposed by section 4081 (or, in the case of lubricating oil, by section 4091) and as if the person who made the claim were liable for such tax. The period for assessing any such portion, and for assessing any such penalty, shall be 3 years from the last day prescribed for the filing of the claim under section 6420, 6421, or 6424, as the case may be."

- **1965, Excise Tax Reduction Act of 1965 (P.L. 89-44)**

P.L. 89-44, § 202(c)(2)(A):

Amended Sec. 6206 by inserting "6420, 6421, and 6424" in lieu of "6420 and 6421" in the heading; by inserting "6420, 6421, or 6424" in lieu of "6420 or 6421" wherever it appeared in the section; and by inserting the parenthetical comment after "4081." **Effective** 1-1-66.

- **1956 (P.L. 627, 84th Cong.)**

P.L. 627, 84th Cong., 2nd Sess., § 208(d)(1):

Amended Sec. 6206 by (1) striking out "Section 6420" in the heading and substituting "Sections 6420 and 6421"; (2) inserting after "6420" in the first sentence "or 6421"; and (3) inserting after "6420" in the second sentence "or 6421, as the case may be". **Effective** 7-1-56.

- **1956 (P.L. 466, 84th Cong.)**

P.L. 466, 84th Cong., 2nd Sess., § 4(b):

Added Code Sec. 6206, and amended table of sections for subchapter A to reflect new section 6206. See also amendment note following Code Sec. 6207.

[Sec. 6207]

SEC. 6207. CROSS REFERENCES.

(1) For prohibition of suits to restrain assessment of any tax, see section 7421.

(2) For prohibition of assessment of taxes against insolvent banks, see section 7507.

(3) For assessment where property subject to tax has been sold in a distraint proceeding without the tax having been assessed prior to such sale, see section 6342.

(4) For assessment with respect to taxes required to be paid by chapter 52, see section 5703.

(5) For assessment in case of distilled spirits removed from place where distilled and not deposited in bonded warehouse, see section 5006(c).

(6) For period of limitation upon assessment, see chapter 66.

Amendments

• **1976, Tax Reform Act of 1976 (P.L. 94-455)**

P.L. 94-455, §1906(a)(14):

Struck out Code Sec. 6207(7). **Effective** 2-1-77. Prior to striking, Code Sec. 6207(7) read as follows:

(7) For assessment under the provisions of the Tariff Act of 1930 of the taxes imposed by section 4501(b), and subchapters A, B, C, D, and E of chapter 38, see sections 4504 and 4601, respectively.

• **1958, Excise Tax Technical Changes Act of 1958 (P.L. 85-859)**

P.L. 85-859, §204(2):

Amended paragraph (4) of Sec. 6207. **Effective** 9-3-58. Prior to amendment, paragraph (4) read as follows:

"(4) For assessment in case of sale or removal of tobacco, snuff, cigars, and cigarettes without the use of proper stamps, see section 5703(d)."

P.L. 85-859, §204(3):

Struck out paragraphs (6) and (7) of Sec. 6207, and renumbered paragraphs (8) and (9) as (6) and (7), respectively. **Effective** 9-3-58.

• **1956 (P.L. 466, 84th Cong.)**

P.L. 466, 84th Cong., 2nd Sess., §4(b):

Renumbered Section 6206 as 6207.

Subchapter B—Deficiency Procedures in the Case of Income, Estate, Gift, and Certain Excise Taxes

Sec. 6211. Definition of a deficiency.
Sec. 6212. Notice of deficiency.
Sec. 6213. Restrictions applicable to deficiencies; petition to Tax Court.
Sec. 6214. Determinations by Tax Court.
Sec. 6215. Assessment of deficiency found by Tax Court.
Sec. 6216. Cross references.

[Sec. 6211]

SEC. 6211. DEFINITION OF A DEFICIENCY.

[Sec. 6211(a)]

(a) IN GENERAL.—For purposes of this title in the case of income, estate, and gift taxes imposed by subtitles A and B and excise taxes imposed by chapters 41, 42, 43, and 44 the term "deficiency" means the amount by which the tax imposed by subtitle A or B, or chapter 41, 42, 43, or 44 exceeds the excess of—

(1) the sum of

(A) the amount shown as the tax by the taxpayer upon his return, if a return was made by the taxpayer and an amount was shown as the tax by the taxpayer thereon, plus

(B) the amounts previously assessed (or collected without assessment) as a deficiency, over—

(2) the amount of rebates, as defined in subsection (b)(2), made.

Amendments

• **1988, Omnibus Trade and Competitiveness Act of 1988 (P.L. 100-418)**

P.L. 100-418, §1941(b)(2)(B)(i):

Amended Code Sec. 6211(a) by striking "44, or 45" each place it appears and inserting "or 44". **Effective** for crude oil removed from the premises on or after 8-23-88.

P.L. 100-418, §1941(b)(2)(C):

Amended Code Sec. 6211(a) by striking "44, and 45" and inserting "and 44". **Effective** for crude oil removed from the premises on or after 8-23-88.

• **1980, Crude Oil Windfall Profit Tax Act of 1980 (P.L. 96-223)**

P.L. 96-223, §101(f)(1)(A), (f)(2):

Amended Code Sec. 6211(a) by striking out "or 44" and inserting "44, or 45" and by striking out "and 44" and inserting "44, and 45". For the **effective** date and the transitional rules see P.L. 96-223, §101(i), following Code Sec. 4986.

• **1976, Tax Reform Act of 1976 (P.L. 94-455)**

P.L. 94-455, §1307(d)(2)(E):

Substituted "chapters 41, 42," for "chapters 42" in Code Sec. 6211(a). **Effective** 10-4-76.

P.L. 94-455, §1307(d)(2)(F)(i):

Substituted "chapter 41, 42," for "chapter 42" in Code Sec. 6211(a).

P.L. 94-455, §1605(b)(4)(A):

Substituted "43, and 44" for "and 43" in Code Sec. 6211(a).

P.L. 94-455, §1608(d), provides:

(d) OTHER AMENDMENTS.—

(1) Except as provided in paragraphs (2) and (3), the amendments made by sections 1603, 1604, and 1605 shall apply to taxable years of real estate investment trusts beginning after the date of the enactment of this Act.

(2) If, as a result of a determination (as defined in section 859(c) of the Internal Revenue Code of 1954) occurring after the date of enactment of this Act, with respect to the real estate investment trust, such trust does not meet the requirement of section 856(a)(4) of the Internal Revenue Code of 1954 (as in effect before the amendment of such section by this Act) for any taxable year beginning on or before the date of the enactment of this Act, such trust may elect, within 60 days after such determination in the manner provided in regulations prescribed by the Secretary of the Treasury or his delegate, to have the provisions of section 1603 (other than paragraphs (1), (2), (3), and (4) of section 1603(c)) apply with respect to such taxable year. Where the provisions of section 1603 apply to a real estate investment trust with respect to any taxable year beginning on or before the date of the enactment of this Act—

(A) credit or refund of any overpayment of tax which results from the application of section 1603 to such taxable year shall be made as if on the date of the determination (as defined in section 859(c) of the Internal Revenue Code of 1954) 2 years remained before the expiration of the period of limitation prescribed by section 6511 of such Code on the filing of claim for refund for the taxable year to which the overpayment relates,

(B) the running of the statute of limitations provided in section 6501 of such Code on the making of assessments, and the bringing of distraint or a proceeding in court for collection, in respect of any deficiency (as defined in section 6211 of such Code) established by such a determination, and all interest, additions to tax, additional amounts, or assessable penalties in respect thereof, shall be suspended for a period of 2 years after the date of such determination, and

(C) the collection of any deficiency (as defined in section 6211 of such Code) established by such determination and all interest, additions to tax, additional amounts, and assessable penalties in respect thereof shall, except in cases of jeopardy, be stayed until the expiration of 60 days after the date of such determination.

No distraint or proceeding in court shall be begun for the collection of an amount the collection of which is stayed under subparagraph (C) during the period for which the collection of such amount is stayed.

(3) Section 856 (g)(3) of the Internal Revenue Code of 1954, as added by section 1604 of this Act, shall not apply with respect to a termination of an election, filed by a taxpayer under section 856(c)(1) of such Code on or before the date of the enactment of this Act, unless the provisions of part II of subchapter M of chapter 1 of subtitle A of such Code apply to such taxpayer for a taxable year ending after the date of the enactment of this Act for which such election is in effect.

P.L. 94-455, §1605(b)(4)(B):

Substituted "43, or 44" for "or 43" in Code Sec. 6211(a). For **effective** date information, see amendatory note for P.L. 94-455, §1605(b)(4)(A).

• **1974, Employee Retirement Income Security Act of 1974 (P.L. 93-406)**

P.L. 93-406, §1016(a)(9):

Amended Code Sec. 6211(a) by changing so much of subsection (a) as precedes paragraph (1) to read as prior to amendment by P.L. 94-455. For **effective** date, see amendment note for Code Sec. 410. Prior to amendment it read as follows:

"(a) In General.—For purposes of this title in the case of income, estate, gift, and excise taxes, imposed by subtitles A and B, and chapter 42, the term 'deficiency' means the amount by which the tax imposed by subtitle A or B or chapter 42 exceeds the excess of—"

• **1969, Tax Reform Act of 1969 (P.L. 91-172)**

P.L. 91-172, §101(f)(1):

Amended Code Sec. 6211(a). **Effective** 1-1-70. Prior to amendment, the matter preceding paragraph (1) in Code Sec. 6211(a) read as follows:

"(a) In General.—For purposes of this title in the case of income, estate, and gift taxes, imposed by subtitles A and B, the term 'deficiency' means the amount by which the tax imposed by subtitles A or B exceeds the excess of—"

ASSESSMENT—DEFICIENCY PROCEDURES

[Sec. 6211(b)]

(b) RULES FOR APPLICATION OF SUBSECTION (a).—For purposes of this section—

(1) The tax imposed by subtitle A and the tax shown on the return shall both be determined without regard to payment on account of estimated tax, without regard to the credit under section 31, without regard to the credit under section 33, and without regard to any credits resulting from the collection of amounts assessed under section 6851 or 6852 (relating to termination assessments).

(2) The term "rebate" means so much of an abatement, credit, refund, or other repayment, as was made on the ground that the tax imposed by subtitle A or B or chapter 41, 42, 43, or 44 was less than the excess of the amount specified in subsection (a)(1) over the rebates previously made.

(3) The computation by the Secretary, pursuant to section 6014, of the tax imposed by chapter 1 shall be considered as having been made by the taxpayer and the tax so computed considered as shown by the taxpayer upon his return.

⟫→ *Caution: Code Sec. 6211(b)(4), below, prior to amendment by P.L. 117-328, applies to tax years on or before after December 31, 2026.*

(4) For purposes of subsection (a)—

(A) any excess of the sum of the credits allowable under sections 21 by reason of subsection (g) thereof, 24 by reason of subsections (d) and (i)(1) thereof, 25A by reason of subsection (i) thereof, 32, 34, 35, 36, 36B, 6428, 6428A, 6428B, and 7527A over the tax imposed by subtitle A (determined without regard to such credits), and

(B) any excess of the sum of such credits as shown by the taxpayer on his return over the amount shown as the tax by the taxpayer on such return (determined without regard to such credits),

shall be taken into account as negative amounts of tax.

⟫→ *Caution: Code Sec. 6211(b)(4), below, as amended by P.L. 117-328, applies to tax years beginning after December 31, 2026.*

(4) For purposes of subsection (a)—

(A) any excess of the sum of the credits allowable under sections 21 by reason of subsection (g) thereof, 24 by reason of subsections (d) and (i)(1) thereof, 25A by reason of subsection (i) thereof, 32, 34, 35, 36, 36B, 6428, 6428A, 6428B, 7527A, and 6433 over the tax imposed by subtitle A (determined without regard to such credits), and

(B) any excess of the sum of such credits as shown by the taxpayer on his return over the amount shown as the tax by the taxpayer on such return (determined without regard to such credits),

shall be taken into account as negative amounts of tax.

Amendments

- **2022, SECURE 2.0 Act of 2022 (P.L. 117-328)**

P.L. 117-328, §103(c)(1):

Amended Code Sec. 6211(b)(4) by striking "and 7527A" and inserting "7527A, and 6433". **Effective** for tax years beginning after 12-31-2026.

- **2021, American Rescue Plan Act of 2021 (P.L. 117-2)**

P.L. 117-2, §9601(c)(1):

Amended Code Sec. 6211(b)(4)(A) by striking "6428, and 6428A" and inserting "6428, 6428A, and 6428B". **Effective** 3-11-2021.

P.L. 117-2, §9611(b)(4)(B)(i)-(ii):

Amended Code Sec. 6211(b)(4)(A), as amended by the preceding provisions of this subtitle, by striking "24(d)" and inserting "24 by reason of subsections (d) and (i)(1) thereof", and by striking "and 6428B" and inserting "6428B, and 7527A". **Effective** for tax years beginning after 12-31-2020.

P.L. 117-2, §9631(c)(1):

Amended Code Sec. 6211(b)(4)(A), as amended by the preceding provisions of this Act, by inserting "21 by reason of subsection (g) thereof," before "24". **Effective** for tax years beginning after 12-31-2020.

- **2020, COVID-related Tax Relief Act of 2020 (P.L. 116-260)**

P.L. 116-260, §272(b)(1), Div. N:

Amended Code Sec. 6211(b)(4)(A) by striking "and 6428" and inserting "6428, and 6428A". **Effective** 12-27-2020.

- **2020, Coronavirus Aid, Relief, and Economic Security (CARES) Act (P.L. 116-136)**

P.L. 116-136, §2201(b)(1):

Amended Code Sec. 6211(b)(4)(A) by striking "and 36B, 168(k)(4)" and inserting "36B, and 6428". **Effective** 3-27-2020.

- **2018, Tax Technical Corrections Act of 2018 (P.L. 115-141)**

P.L. 115-141, §101(l)(17), Div. U:

Amended Code Sec. 6211(b)(4)(A), as amended by this Act, by striking "subsection (i)(5)" and inserting "subsection (i)". **Effective** as if included in the provision of the Protecting Americans from Tax Hikes Act of 2015 to which it relates [effective for tax years beginning after 12-18-2015.—CCH].

P.L. 115-141, §106(a), Div. U:

Amended Code Sec. 6211(b)(4)(A) by striking "subsection (i)(6)" and inserting "subsection (i)(5)". **Effective** as if included in section 104 of the American Taxpayer Relief Act of 2012 [effective for tax years beginning after 12-31-2011.—CCH].

- **2017, Tax Cuts and Jobs Act (P.L. 115-97)**

P.L. 115-97, §13404(c)(3):

Amended Code Sec. 6211(b)(4)(A) by striking ", and 6431" following ", 168(k)(4)" and inserting "and" before "36B". **Effective** for bonds issued after 12-31-2017.

- **2014, Tax Technical Corrections Act of 2014 (P.L. 113-295)**

P.L. 113-295, §221(a)(5)(B), Division A:

Amended Code Sec. 6211(b)(4)(A) by striking ", 36A" following "36". **Effective** generally 12-19-2014. For a special rule, see Act Sec. 221(b)(2), Division A, below.

P.L. 113-295, §221(a)(8)(B), Division A:

Amended Code Sec. 6211(b)(4) by striking ", 53(e)" following "36B". **Effective** generally 12-19-2014. For a special rule, see Act Sec. 221(b)(2), Division A, below.

P.L. 113-295, §221(a)(112)(B), Division A:

Amended Code Sec. 6211(b)(4)(A) by striking "6428," following "168(k)(4),". **Effective** generally 12-19-2014. For a special rule, see Act Sec. 221(b)(2), Division A, below.

P.L. 113-295, §221(b)(2), Division A, provides:

(2) SAVINGS PROVISION.—If—

(A) any provision amended or repealed by the amendments made by this section applied to—

(i) any transaction occurring before the date of the enactment of this Act,

(ii) any property acquired before such date of enactment, or

(iii) any item of income, loss, deduction, or credit taken into account before such date of enactment, and

(B) the treatment of such transaction, property, or item under such provision would (without regard to the amendments or repeals made by this section) affect the liability for tax for periods ending after date of enactment, nothing in the amendments or repeals made by this section shall be construed to affect the treatment of such transaction, property, or item for purposes of determining liability for tax for periods ending after such date of enactment.

- **2013, American Taxpayer Relief Act of 2012 (P.L. 112-240)**

P.L. 112-240, §101(a)(1) and (3), provides:

SEC. 101. PERMANENT EXTENSION AND MODIFICATION OF 2001 TAX RELIEF.

(a) PERMANENT EXTENSION.—

(1) IN GENERAL.—The Economic Growth and Tax Relief Reconciliation Act of 2001 is amended by striking title IX.

* * *

(3) EFFECTIVE DATE.—The amendments made by this subsection shall apply to taxable, plan, or limitation years beginning after December 31, 2012, and estates of decedents dying, gifts made, or generation skipping transfers after December 31, 2012.

- **2010, Tax Relief, Unemployment Insurance Reauthorization, and Job Creation Act of 2010 (P.L. 111-312)**

P.L. 111-312, §101(b)(1):

Amended Code Sec. 6211(b)(4)(A) to read as such provision would read if section 10909 of the Patient Protection and Affordable Care Act (P.L. 111-148) had never been enacted. **Effective** for tax years beginning after 12-31-2011.

- **2010, Patient Protection and Affordable Care Act (P.L. 111-148)**

P.L. 111-148, §10105(d):

Amended Act Sec. 1401(d) by adding at the end a new Act Sec. 1401(d)(3), which amends Code Sec. 6211(b)(4)(A) by inserting "36B," after "36A,". **Effective** 3-23-2010.

P.L. 111-148, §10909(b)(2)(N):

Amended Code Sec. 6211(b)(4)(A) by inserting "36C," before "53(e)". **Effective** for tax years beginning after 12-31-2009.

P.L. 111-148, §10909(c), as amended by P.L. 111-312, §101(b)(1), provides:

(c) SUNSET PROVISION.—Each provision of law amended by this section is amended to read as such provision would read if this section had never been enacted. The amendments made by the preceding sentence shall apply to taxable years beginning after December 31, 2011.

ASSESSMENT—DEFICIENCY PROCEDURES

- **2009, American Recovery and Reinvestment Tax Act of 2009 (P.L. 111-5)**

P.L. 111-5, §1001(e)(1):

Amended Code Sec. 6211(b)(4)(A) by inserting "36A," after "36,". **Effective** for tax years beginning after 12-31-2008.

P.L. 111-5, §1004(b)(7):

Amended Code Sec. 6211(b)(4)(A) by inserting "25A by reason of subsection (i)(6) thereof," after "24(d),". **Effective** for tax years beginning after 12-31-2008.

P.L. 111-5, §1201(a)(3)(B):

Amended Code Sec. 6211(b)(4)(A) by inserting "168(k)(4)," after "53(e),". **Effective** for tax years ending after 3-31-2008.

P.L. 111-5, §1201(b)(2):

Amended Code Sec. 6211(b)(4)(A) by inserting "168(k)(4)," after "53(e),". **Effective** for tax years ending after 3-31-2008. [This amendment cannot be made because the same amendment was made by P.L. 111-5, §1201(a)(3)(B).—CCH].

P.L. 111-5, §1531(c)(4):

Amended Code Sec. 6211(b)(4)(A) by striking "and 6428" and inserting "6428, and 6431". **Effective** for obligations issued after 2-17-2009.

- **2008, Housing Assistance Tax Act of 2008 (P.L. 110-289)**

P.L. 110-289, §3011(b)(2):

Amended Code Sec. 6211(b)(4)(A) by striking "34," and all that follows through "6428" and inserting "34, 35, 36, 53(e), and 6428". **Effective** for residences purchased on or after 4-9-2008, in tax years ending on or after such date. Prior to being stricken, "34," and all that follows through "6428" read as follows:

"34, and 35, 53(e), and 6428"

- **2008, Economic Stimulus Act of 2008 (P.L. 110-185)**

P.L. 110-185, §101(b)(1):

Amended Code Sec. 6211(b)(4)(A) by striking "and 53(e)" and inserting "53(e), and 6428". **Effective** 2-13-2008.

- **2007, Tax Technical Corrections Act of 2007 (P.L. 110-172)**

P.L. 110-172, §11(a)(35):

Amended Code Sec. 6211(b)(4)(A) by striking "and 34" [sic]and inserting "34, and 35". **Effective** 12-29-2007.

- **2006, Tax Relief and Health Care Act of 2006 (P.L. 109-432)**

P.L. 109-432, Division A, §402(b)(1):

Amended Code Sec. 6211(b)(4)(A) by striking "and 34" and inserting "34, and 53(e)". **Effective** for tax years beginning after 12-20-2006.

- **2000, Community Renewal Tax Relief Act of 2000 (P.L. 106-554)**

P.L. 106-554, §314(a):

Amended Code Sec. 6211(b)(4) by striking "sections 32 and 34" and inserting "sections 24(d), 32, and 34". **Effective** as if included in the provision of the Taxpayer Relief Act of 1997 (P.L. 105-34) to which it relates [effective for tax years beginning after 12-31-97.—CCH].

- **1988, Technical and Miscellaneous Revenue Act of 1988 (P.L. 100-647)**

P.L. 100-647, §1015(r)(2):

Amended Code Sec. 6211(b)(4). **Effective** for notices of deficiencies mailed after 11-10-88. Prior to amendment, Code Sec. 6211(b)(4) read as follows:

(4) The tax imposed by subtitle A and the tax shown on the return shall both be determined without regard to the credit under section 34, unless, without regard to such credit, the tax imposed by subtitle A exceeds the excess of the amount specified in subsection (a)(1) over the amount specified in subsection (a)(2).

- **1988, Omnibus Trade and Competitiveness Act of 1988 (P.L. 100-418)**

P.L. 100-418, §1941(b)(2)(B)(ii):

Amended Code Sec. 6211(b)(2) by striking "44, or 45" each place it appears and inserting "or 44". **Effective** for crude oil removed from the premises on or after 8-23-88.

P.L. 100-418, §1941(b)(2)(D):

Amended Code Sec. 6211(b) by striking paragraphs (5) and (6). **Effective** for crude oil removed from the premises on or after 8-23-88. Prior to amendment, Code Sec. 6211(b)(5) and (6) read as follows:

(5) The amount withheld under section 4995(a) from amounts payable to any producer for crude oil removed during any taxable period (as defined in section 4996(b)(7)) which is not otherwise shown on a return by such producer shall be treated as tax shown by the producer on a return for the taxable period.

(6) Any liability to pay amounts required to be withheld under section 4995(a) shall not be treated as a tax imposed by chapter 45.

- **1987, Revenue Act of 1987 (P.L. 100-203)**

P.L. 100-203, §0713(b)(2)(B):

Amended Code Sec. 6211(b)(1) by striking out "section 6851" and inserting in lieu thereof "section 6851 or 6852". **Effective** 12-22-87.

- **1984, Deficit Reduction Act of 1984 (P.L. 98-369)**

P.L. 98-369, §474(r)(33)(A):

Amended Code Sec. 6211(b)(1) by striking out "without regard to so much of the credit under section 32 as exceeds 2 percent of the interest on obligations described in section 1451" and inserting in lieu thereof "without regard to the credit under section 33". **Effective** for tax years beginning after 12-31-83, and to carrybacks from such years.

P.L. 98-369, §474(r)(33)(B):

Amended Code Sec. 6211(b)(4) by striking out "section 39" and inserting in lieu thereof "section 34". **Effective** for tax years beginning after 12-31-83, and to carrybacks from such years.

- **1980, Crude Oil Windfall Profit Tax Act of 1980 (P.L. 96-223)**

P.L. 96-223, §101(f)(1)(B); (f)(3):

Amended Code Sec. 6211(b) by striking out in paragraph (2) "or 44" and inserting "44, or 45" and by adding paragraphs (5) and (6). For the **effective** date and transitional rules, see P.L. 96-223, §101(i), following Code Sec. 4986.

- **1976, Tax Reform Act of 1976 (P.L. 94-455)**

P.L. 94-455, §1204(a)(4):

Struck out "and" following "31," in Code Sec. 6211(b)(1) and added ",and without regard to any credits resulting from the collection of amounts assessed under section 6851 (relating to termination assessments)" before the period at the end of Code Sec. 6211(b)(1). **Effective** with respect to action taken under Code Secs. 6851, 6861, or 6862 where the notice and demand takes place after 2-28-77. [effective date changed by P.L. 94-528, §2(a).

P.L. 94-455, §1307(d)(2)(F)(i):

Substituted "chapter 41, 42," for "chapter 42" in Code Sec. 6211(b)(2). **Effective** 10-4-76.

P.L. 94-455, §1605(b)(4)(C):

Substituted "43, or 44" for "or 43" in Code Sec. 6211(b)(2). For **effective** date, see amendatory note for P.L. 94-455, §1605(b)(4)(A), following Code Sec. 6211(a).

P.L. 94-455, §1906(b)(13)(A):

Amended 1954 Code by substituting "Secretary" for "Secretary or his delegate" each place it appeared. **Effective** 2-1-77.

- **1974, Employee Retirement Income Security Act of 1974 (P.L. 93-406)**

P.L. 93-406, §1016(a)(9):

Amended Code Sec. 6211(b)(2) by changing "chapter 42" to "chapter 42 or 43". For **effective** date, see amendment note for Code Sec. 410.

- **1969, Tax Reform Act of 1969 (P.L. 91-172)**

P.L. 91-172, §101(j)(39):

Amended Code Sec. 6211(b) by substituting "subtitle A or B or chapter 42" for "subtitles A or B" in paragraph (2). **Effective** 1-1-70.

- **1966, Tax Adjustment Act of 1966 (P.L. 89-368)**

P.L. 89-368, §102(b)(4):

Amended Code Sec. 6211(b)(1) by substituting "subtitle A" for "chapter 1". **Effective** 1-1-67.

- **1965, Excise Tax Reduction Act of 1965 (P.L. 89-44)**

P.L. 89-44, §809(d)(5):

Amended Code Sec. 6211(b) by adding paragraph (4). **Effective** 7-1-65.

[Sec. 6211(c)]

(c) COORDINATION WITH SUBCHAPTER C.—In determining the amount of any deficiency for purposes of this subchapter, adjustments to partnership-related items shall be made only as provided in subchapter C.

Amendments

- **2018, Tax Technical Corrections Act of 2018 (P.L. 115-141)**

P.L. 115-141, §201(c)(1), Div. U:

Amended Code Sec. 6211(c). **Effective** as if included in section 1101 of the Bipartisan Budget Act of 2015 [effective generally for returns filed for partnership tax years beginning after 12-31-2017.—CCH]. Prior to amendment, Code Sec. 6211(c) read as follows:

(c) COORDINATION WITH SUBCHAPTERS C AND D.—In determining the amount of any deficiency for purposes of this subchapter, adjustments to partnership items shall be made only as provided in subchapters C and D.

- **1998, IRS Restructuring and Reform Act of 1998 (P.L. 105-206)**

P.L. 105-206, §6012(f)(1)-(2):

Amended Code Sec. 6211(c) by striking "SUBCHAPTER C" in the heading and inserting "SUBCHAPTERS C AND D", and by striking "subchapter C" in the text and inserting "subchapters C and D". **Effective** as if included in the provision of P.L. 105-34 to which it relates [effective for partnership tax years ending after 8-5-97.—CCH].

- **1997, Taxpayer Relief Act of 1997 (P.L. 105-34)**

P.L. 105-34, §1231(b):

Amended Code Sec. 6211 by adding at the end a new subsection (c). **Effective** for partnership tax years ending after 8-5-97.

ASSESSMENT—DEFICIENCY PROCEDURES

[Sec. 6212]

SEC. 6212. NOTICE OF DEFICIENCY.

[Sec. 6212(a)]

(a) IN GENERAL.—If the Secretary determines that there is a deficiency in respect of any tax imposed by subtitle A or B or chapter 41, 42, 43, or 44, he is authorized to send notice of such deficiency to the taxpayer by certified mail or registered mail. Such notice shall include a notice to the taxpayer of the taxpayer's right to contact a local office of the taxpayer advocate and the location and phone number of the appropriate office.

Amendments

• **1998, IRS Restructuring and Reform Act of 1998 (P.L. 105-206)**

P.L. 105-206, §1102(b):

Amended Code Sec. 6212(a) by adding at the end a new sentence. **Effective** 7-22-98. For a special rule, see Act Sec. 1102(f)(3)-(4), below.

P.L. 105-206, §1102(f)(3)-(4), provides:

(3) NATIONAL TAXPAYER ADVOCATE.—Notwithstanding section 7803(c)(1)(B)(iv) of such Code, as added by this section, in appointing the first National Taxpayer Advocate after the date of the enactment of this Act, the Secretary of the Treasury—

(A) shall not appoint any individual who was an officer or employee of the Internal Revenue Service at any time during the 2-year period ending on the date of appointment, and

(B) need not consult with the Internal Revenue Service Oversight Board if the Oversight Board has not been appointed.

(4) CURRENT OFFICERS.—

(A) In the case of an individual serving as Commissioner of Internal Revenue on the date of the enactment of this Act who was appointed to such position before such date, the 5-year term required by section 7803(a)(1) of such Code, as added by this section, shall begin as of the date of such appointment.

(B) Clauses (ii), (iii), and (iv) of section 7803(c)(1)(B) of such Code, as added by this section, shall not apply to the individual serving as Taxpayer Advocate on the date of the enactment of this Act.

P.L. 105-206, §3463(a), provides:

SEC. 3463. NOTICE OF DEFICIENCY TO SPECIFY DEADLINES FOR FILING TAX COURT PETITION.

(a) IN GENERAL.—The Secretary of the Treasury or the Secretary's delegate shall include on each notice of deficiency under section 6212 of the Internal Revenue Code of 1986 the date determined by such Secretary (or delegate) as the last day on which the taxpayer may file a petition with the Tax Court.

P.L. 105-206, §3504, provides:

SEC. 3504. EXPLANATIONS OF APPEALS AND COLLECTION PROCESS.

The Secretary of the Treasury or the Secretary's delegate shall, as soon as practicable, but not later than 180 days after the date of the enactment of this Act, include with any first letter of proposed deficiency which allows the taxpayer an opportunity for administrative review in the Internal Revenue Service Office of Appeals an explanation of the entire process from examination through collection with respect to such proposed deficiency, including the assistance available to the taxpayer from the National Taxpayer Advocate at various points in the process.

• **1988, Omnibus Trade and Competitiveness Act of 1988 (P.L. 100-418)**

P.L. 100-418, §1941(b)(2)(B)(iii):

Amended Code Sec. 6212(a) by striking "44, or 45" each place it appears and inserting "or 44". **Effective** for crude oil removed from the premises on or after 8-23-88.

• **1980, Crude Oil Windfall Profit Tax Act of 1980 (P.L. 96-223)**

P.L. 96-223, §101(f)(1)(C):

Amended Code Sec. 6212(a) by striking out "or 44" and inserting "44, or 45". For the **effective** date and transitional rules, see P.L. 96-223, §101(i), following Code Sec. 4986.

• **1976, Tax Reform Act of 1976 (P.L. 94-455)**

P.L. 94-455, §1307(d)(2)(F)(ii):

Substituted "chapter 41, 42," for "chapter 42" in Code Sec. 6212(a). **Effective** 10-4-76.

P.L. 94-455, §1605(b)(5)(A):

Substituted "43, or 44" for "or 43" in Code Sec. 6212(a). For **effective** date, see amendatory note for P.L. 94-455, §1605(b)(4)(A), following Code Sec. 6211(a).

P.L. 94-455, §1906(b)(13)(A):

Amended 1954 Code by substituting "Secretary" for "Secretary or his delegate" each place it appeared. **Effective** 2-1-77.

• **1974, Employee Retirement Income Security Act of 1974 (P.L. 93-406)**

P.L. 93-406, §1016(a)(10):

Amended Code Sec. 6212(a) by changing "chapter 42" to "chapter 42 or 43". For **effective** date, see amendment note for Code Sec. 410.

• **1969, Tax Reform Act of 1969 (P.L. 91-172)**

P.L. 91-172, §101(j)(40):

Amended Sec. 6212(a) by substituting "subtitle A or B or chapter 42," for "subtitles A or B,". **Effective** 1-1-70.

• **1958, Technical Amendments Act of 1958 (P.L. 85-866)**

P.L. 85-866, §89(b):

Amended Sec. 6212(a) by striking out "registered mail" and substituting "certified mail or registered mail". **Effective** only for mailing after 9-2-58.

[Sec. 6212(b)]

(b) ADDRESS FOR NOTICE OF DEFICIENCY.—

(1) INCOME AND GIFT TAXES AND CERTAIN EXCISE TAXES.—In the absence of notice to the Secretary under section 6903 of the existence of a fiduciary relationship, notice of a deficiency in respect of a tax imposed by subtitle A, chapter 12, chapter 42, chapter 43, or chapter 44 if mailed to the taxpayer at his last known address, shall be sufficient for purposes of subtitle A, chapter 12, chapter 42, chapter 43, chapter 44, and this chapter even if such taxpayer is deceased, or is under a legal disability, or, in the case of a corporation, has terminated its existence.

(2) JOINT INCOME TAX RETURN.—In the case of a joint income tax return filed by husband and wife, such notice of deficiency may be a single joint notice, except that if the Secretary has been notified by either spouse that separate residences have been established, then, in lieu of the single joint notice, a duplicate original of the joint notice shall be sent by certified mail or registered mail to each spouse at his last known address.

(3) ESTATE TAX.—In the absence of notice to the Secretary under section 6903 of the existence of a fiduciary relationship, notice of a deficiency in respect of a tax imposed by chapter 11, if addressed in the name of the decedent or other person subject to liability and mailed to his last known address, shall be sufficient for purposes of chapter 11 and of this chapter.

Amendments

• **1988, Omnibus Trade and Competitiveness Act of 1988 (P.L. 100-418)**

P.L. 100-418, §1941(b)(2)(E)(i)-(ii):

Amended Code Sec. 6212(b)(1) by striking "chapter 44, or 45" and inserting "or chapter 44", and by striking "chapter 44, chapter 45, and this chapter" and inserting "chapter 44, and this chapter". **Effective** for crude oil removed from the premises on or after 8-23-88.

• **1980, Crude Oil Windfall Profit Tax Act of 1980 (P.L. 96-223)**

P.L. 96-223, §101(f)(4):

Amended Code Sec. 6212(b) by striking out in paragraph (1) "or chapter 44" and "chapter 44, and this chapter" and inserting "chapter 44, or chapter 45" and "chapter 44, chapter 45, and this chapter", respectively, and by striking out "TAXES IMPOSED BY CHAPTER 42" in the paragraph heading and inserting "CERTAIN EXCISE TAXES". For the **effective** date and transitional rules, see P.L. 96-223, §101(i), following Code Sec. 4986.

• **1976, Tax Reform Act of 1976 (P.L. 94-455)**

P.L. 94-455, §1605(b)(5)(B):

Substituted "chapter 43, or chapter 44" for "or chapter 43" in Code Sec. 6212(b)(1). For **effective** date, see amendatory note for P.L. 94-455, §1605(b)(4)(A), following Code Sec. 6211(a).

P.L. 94-455, §1605(b)(5)(C):

Substituted "chapter 43, chapter 44, and this chapter" for "chapter 43, and this chapter" in Code Sec. 6212(b)(1). For **effective** date, see amendatory note for P.L. 94-455, §1605(b)(4)(A), following Code Sec. 6211(a).

P.L. 94-455, §1906(b)(13)(A):

Amended 1954 Code by substituting "Secretary" for "Secretary or his delegate" each place it appeared. **Effective** 2-1-77.

• **1974, Employee Retirement Income Security Act of 1974 (P.L. 93-406)**

P.L. 93-406, §1016(a)(10):

Amended Code Sec. 6212(b)(1) by changing "or chapter 42" to "chapter 42, or chapter 43" and by changing "chapter 42, and this chapter" to "chapter 42, chapter 43, and this chapter". For **effective** date, see amendment note for Code Sec. 410.

• **1969, Tax Reform Act of 1969 (P.L. 91-172)**

P.L. 91-172, §101(j)(41):

Amended paragraph (1) of Code Sec. 6212(b) by adding "and taxes imposed by chapter 42" in the heading thereof, by substituting "chapter 12, or chapter 42," for "or chapter 12,", and by adding "chapter 42," after "chapter 12," the last place it appears. **Effective** 1-1-70.

ASSESSMENT—DEFICIENCY PROCEDURES

- **1958, Technical Amendments Act of 1958 (P.L. 85-866)**

P.L. 85-866, §76:

Amended Sec. 6212(b) by striking out "chapter 1 or 12" where that phrase followed "a tax imposed by" and substituting "subtitle A or chapter 12", and by striking out "such chapter and" where that phrase followed "for purposes of" and substituting "subtitle A, chapter 12, and". **Effective** 1-1-54.

P.L. 85-866, §89(b):

Amended Sec. 6212(b)(2) by striking out "registered mail" and substituting "certified mail or registered mail". **Effective** only if the mailing occurs after 9-2-58.

[Sec. 6212(c)]

(c) FURTHER DEFICIENCY LETTERS RESTRICTED.—

(1) GENERAL RULE.—If the Secretary has mailed to the taxpayer a notice of deficiency as provided in subsection (a), and the taxpayer files a petition with the Tax Court within the time prescribed in section 6213(a), the Secretary shall have no right to determine any additional deficiency of income tax for the same taxable year, of gift tax for the same calendar year, of estate tax in respect of the taxable estate of the same decedent, of chapter 41 tax for the same taxable year, of chapter 43 tax for the same taxable year, of chapter 44 tax for the same taxable year, of section 4940 tax for the same taxable year, or of chapter 42 tax (other than under section 4940) with respect to any act (or failure to act) to which such petition relates, except in the case of fraud, and except as provided in section 6214(a) (relating to assertion of greater deficiencies before the Tax Court), in section 6213(b)(1) (relating to mathematical or clerical errors), in section 6851 or 6852 (relating to termination assessments), or in section 6861(c) (relating to the making of jeopardy assessments).

(2) CROSS REFERENCES.—

For assessment as a deficiency notwithstanding the prohibition of further deficiency letters, in the case of—

(A) Deficiency attributable to change of treatment with respect to itemized deductions, see section 63(e)(3).

(B) Deficiency attributable to gain on involuntary conversion, see section 1033(a)(2)(C) and (D).

(C) Deficiency attributable to activities not engaged in for profit, see section 183(e)(4).

For provisions allowing determination of tax in title 11 cases, see section 505(a) of title 11 of the United States Code.

Amendments

- **1997, Taxpayer Relief Act of 1997 (P.L. 105-34)**

P.L. 105-34, §312(d)(12):

Amended Code Sec. 6212(c)(2) by striking subparagraph (C) and by redesignating the succeeding subparagraphs accordingly. **Effective** for sales and exchanges after 5-6-97. Prior to being stricken, Code Sec. 6212(c)(2)(C) read as follows:

(C) Deficiency attributable to gain on sale or exchange of principal residence, see section 1034(j).

- **1988, Omnibus Trade and Competitiveness Act of 1988 (P.L. 100-418)**

P.L. 100-418, §1941(b)(2)(F)(i)-(ii):

Amended Code Sec. 6212(c)(1) by striking out "of chapter 42 tax" and inserting "or of chapter 42 tax", and by striking ", or of chapter 45 tax for the same taxable period" before ", except in the case of fraud". **Effective** for crude oil removed from the premises on or after 8-23-88.

- **1987, Revenue Act of 1987 (P.L. 100-203)**

P.L. 100-203, §10713(b)(2)(C):

Amended Code Sec. 6212(c)(1) by striking out "section 6851" and inserting in lieu thereof "section 6851 or 6852". **Effective** 12-22-87.

- **1986, Tax Reform Act of 1986 (P.L. 99-514)**

P.L. 99-514, §104(b)(17):

Amended Code Sec. 6212(c)(2)(A). **Effective** for tax years beginning after 12-31-86. Prior to amendment, Code Sec. 6212(c)(2)(A) read as follows:

(A) Deficiency attributable to change of treatment with respect to itemized deductions and zero bracket amount, see section 63(g)(5).

- **1984, Economic Recovery Tax Act of 1981 (P.L. 97-34)**

P.L. 97-34, §442(d)(4):

Amended Code Sec. 6212(c) by striking out "calendar quarter" and inserting "calendar year". **Effective** with respect to estates of decedents dying after 12-31-81.

- **1980, Bankruptcy Tax Act of 1980 (P.L. 96-589)**

P.L. 96-589, §6(d)(2):

Amended Code Sec. 6212(c)(2) by adding a new last sentence. **Effective** 10-1-79, but inapplicable to any proceeding under the Bankruptcy Act commenced before that date.

- **1980, Crude Oil Windfall Profit Tax Act of 1980 (P.L. 96-223)**

P.L. 96-223, §101(f)(5):

Amended Code Sec. 6212(c) by striking out "or of chapter 42 tax" and inserting "of chapter 42 tax" and by inserting ", or of chapter 45 tax for the same taxable period" after "to which such petition relates". For the **effective** date and transitional rules, see P.L. 96-223, §101(i), following Code Sec. 4986.

- **1978, Revenue Act of 1978 (P.L. 95-600)**

P.L. 95-600, §405(c)(5):

Amended Code Sec. 6212(c)(2)(C) by striking out "personal residence" and inserting in lieu thereof "principal residence". **Effective** for sales and exchanges of residences after 7-26-78, in tax years ending after such date.

- **1977, Tax Reduction and Simplification Act of 1977 (P.L. 95-30)**

P.L. 95-30, §101(d)(15):

Amended Code Sec. 6212(c)(2)(A). **Effective** for tax years beginning after 12-31-76. Prior to amendment, Code Sec. 6212(c)(2)(A) read as follows:

"(A) Deficiency attributable to change of election with respect to the standard deduction where taxpayer and his spouse made separate returns, see section 144(b)."

- **1976, Tax Reform Act of 1976 (P.L. 94-455)**

P.L. 94-455, §214(b):

Added Code Sec. 6212(c)(2)(E). **Effective** for tax years beginning after 12-31-69; except that Code Sec. 6212(c)(2)(E) shall not apply to any tax year ending before 10-4-76, with respect to which the period for assessing a deficiency has expired before such date.

P.L. 94-455, §1204(c)(5):

Added "in section 6851 (relating to termination assessments)," after "errors)," in Code Sec. 6212(c)(1). P.L. 94-455, §1204(d) provides that the amendment shall be **effective** for action taken under Code Secs. 6851, 6861, or 6862 where the notice or demand takes place after 12-31-76; but P.L. 94-528, §2(a), **effective** 10-4-76, substitutes "February 28, 1977" for "December 31, 1976" in P.L. 94-455, §1204(d).

P.L. 94-455, §1206(c)(3):

Substituted "(relating to mathematical or clerical errors)" for "(relating to mathematical errors)" in Code Sec. 6212(c)(1). **Effective** with respect to returns filed after 12-31-76.

P.L. 94-455, §1605(b)(5)(D):

Added "of chapter 43 tax for the same taxable year, of chapter 44 tax for the same taxable year," in place of "of chapter 43 tax for the same taxable years," (as amended by P.L. 95-600, Sec. 701(t)(3)(B)) in Code Sec. 6212(c)(1). For **effective** date, see amendatory note for P.L. 94-455, §1605(b)(4)(A), following Code Sec. 6211(a).

P.L. 94-455, §1901(b)(31)(C):

Substituted "1033(a)(2)(C) and (D)" for "1033(a)(3)(C) and (D)" in Code Sec. 6212(c)(2)(B). **Effective** for tax years beginning after 12-31-76.

P.L. 94-455, §1901(b)(37)(C):

Struck out Code Sec. 6212(c)(2)(D) (but did not renumber (E)). **Effective** for tax years beginning after 12-31-76. Prior to striking, Code Sec. 6212(c)(2)(D) read as follows:

"(D) Deficiency attributable to war loss recoveries where prior benefit rule is elected, see section 1335."

P.L. 94-455, §1906(b)(13)(A):

Amended 1954 Code by substituting "Secretary" for "Secretary or his delegate" each place it appeared. **Effective** 2-1-77.

- **1974, Employee Retirement Income Security Act of 1974 (P.L. 93-406)**

P.L. 93-406, §1016(a)(10):

Amended Code Sec. 6212(c)(1) by changing "of the same decedent," to "of the same decedent, of chapter 43 for the same taxable years,". For **effective** date, see amendment note for Code Sec. 410.

- **1970, Excise, Estate, and Gift Tax Adjustment Act of 1970 (P.L. 91-614)**

P.L. 91-614, §102(d)(5):

Amended Code Sec. 6212(c)(1) by substituting "calendar quarter" for "calendar year" in the sixth line. **Effective** for gifts made after 12-31-70.

- **1969, Tax Reform Act of 1969 (P.L. 91-172)**

P.L. 91-172, §101(f)(2):

Amended Code Sec. 6212(c)(1). **Effective** 1-1-70. Prior to amendment, paragraph (1) of Code Sec. 6212(c) read as follows:

"(1) General rule.—If the Secretary or his delegate has mailed to the taxpayer a notice of deficiency as provided in subsection (a), and the taxpayer files a petition with the Tax Court within the time prescribed in section 6213(a), the Secretary or his delegate shall have no right to determine any additional deficiency of income tax for the same taxable year, of gift tax for the same calendar year, or of estate tax in respect of the taxable estate of the same decedent, except in the case of fraud, and except as provided in section 6214(a) (relating to assertion of greater deficiencies before the Tax

ASSESSMENT—DEFICIENCY PROCEDURES

Court), in section 6213(b)(1) (relating to mathematical errors), or in section 6861(c) (relating to the making of jeopardy assessments)."

• **1964, Revenue Act of 1964 (P.L. 88-272)**

P.L. 88-272, §112(d)(1):

Amended subparagraph (A) by striking out "to take" and inserting in lieu thereof "with respect to the". **Effective** 1-1-64.

[Sec. 6212(d)]

(d) AUTHORITY TO RESCIND NOTICE OF DEFICIENCY WITH TAXPAYER'S CONSENT.—The Secretary may, with the consent of the taxpayer, rescind any notice of deficiency mailed to the taxpayer. Any notice so rescinded shall not be treated as a notice of deficiency for purposes of subsection (c)(1) (relating to further deficiency letters restricted), section 6213(a) (relating to restrictions applicable to deficiencies; petition to Tax Court), and section 6512(a) (relating to limitations in case of petition to Tax Court), and the taxpayer shall have no right to file a petition with the Tax Court based on such notice. Nothing in this subsection shall affect any suspension of the running of any period of limitations during any period during which the rescinded notice was outstanding.

Amendments

• **1988, Technical and Miscellaneous Revenue Act of 1988 (P.L. 100-647)**

P.L. 100-647, §1015(m):

Amended Code Sec. 6212(d) by adding at the end thereof a new sentence. **Effective** as if included in the provision of P.L. 99-514 to which it relates.

• **1986, Tax Reform Act of 1986 (P.L. 99-514)**

P.L. 99-514, §1562(a):

Amended Code Sec. 6212 by adding at the end thereof new paragraph (d). **Effective** for notices of deficiency issued on or after 1-1-86.

[Sec. 6213]

SEC. 6213. RESTRICTIONS APPLICABLE TO DEFICIENCIES; PETITION TO TAX COURT.

[Sec. 6213(a)]

(a) TIME FOR FILING PETITION AND RESTRICTION ON ASSESSMENT.—Within 90 days, or 150 days if the notice is addressed to a person outside the United States, after the notice of deficiency authorized in section 6212 is mailed (not counting Saturday, Sunday, or a legal holiday in the District of Columbia as the last day), the taxpayer may file a petition with the Tax Court for a redetermination of the deficiency. Except as otherwise provided in section 6851, 6852, or 6861 no assessment of a deficiency in respect of any tax imposed by subtitle A or B, chapter 41, 42, 43, or 44 and no levy or proceeding in court for its collection shall be made, begun, or prosecuted until such notice has been mailed to the taxpayer, nor until the expiration of such 90-day or 150-day period, as the case may be, nor, if a petition has been filed with the Tax Court, until the decision of the Tax Court has become final. Notwithstanding the provisions of section 7421(a), the making of such assessment or the beginning of such proceeding or levy during the time such prohibition is in force may be enjoined by a proceeding in the proper court, including the Tax Court, and a refund may be ordered by such court of any amount collected within the period during which the Secretary is prohibited from collecting by levy or through a proceeding in court under the provisions of this subsection. The Tax Court shall have no jurisdiction to enjoin any action or proceeding or order any refund under this subsection unless a timely petition for a redetermination of the deficiency has been filed and then only in respect of the deficiency that is the subject of such petition. Any petition filed with the Tax Court on or before the last date specified for filing such petition by the Secretary in the notice of deficiency shall be treated as timely filed.

Amendments

• **1998, IRS Restructuring and Reform Act of 1998 (P.L. 105-206)**

P.L. 105-206, §3463(b):

Amended Code Sec. 6213(a) by adding at the end a new sentence. **Effective** for notices mailed after 12-31-98.

P.L. 105-206, §3464(a)(1)-(2):

Amended Code Sec. 6213(a) by striking ", including the Tax Court." and inserting ", including the Tax Court, and a refund may be ordered by such court of any amount collected within the period during which the Secretary is prohibited from collecting by levy or through a proceeding in court under the provisions of this subsection.", and by striking "to enjoin any action or proceeding" and inserting "to enjoin any action or proceeding or order any refund". **Effective** 7-22-98.

• **1988, Technical and Miscellaneous Revenue Act of 1988 (P.L. 100-647)**

P.L. 100-647, §6243(a):

Amended Code Sec. 6213(a) by striking out the period at the end of the last sentence and inserting in lieu thereof ", including the Tax Court. The Tax Court shall have no jurisdiction to enjoin any action or proceeding under this subsection unless a timely petition for a redetermination of the deficiency has been filed and then only in respect of the deficiency that is the subject of such petition." **Effective** for orders entered after 11-10-88.

• **1988, Omnibus Trade and Competitiveness Act of 1988 (P.L. 100-418)**

P.L. 100-418, §1941(b)(2)(B)(iv):

Amended Code Sec. 6213(a) by striking "44, or 45" each place it appears and inserting "or 44". **Effective** for crude oil removed from the premises on or after 8-23-88.

• **1987, Revenue Act of 1987 (P.L. 100-203)**

P.L. 100-203, §10713(b)(2)(D):

Amended Code Sec. 6213(a) by striking out "section 6851 or section 6861" and inserting in lieu thereof "section 6851, 6852, or 6861". **Effective** 12-22-87.

• **1980, Crude Oil Windfall Profit Tax Act of 1980 (P.L. 96-223)**

P.L. 96-223, §101(f)(1)(D):

Amended Code Sec. 6213(a) by striking out "or 44" and inserting "44, or 45". For the **effective** date and transitional rules, see P.L. 96-223, §101(i), following Code Sec. 4986.

• **1976, Tax Reform Act of 1976 (P.L. 94-455)**

P.L. 94-455, §1204(c)(6):

Added "section 6851 or" before "section 6861" in Code Sec. 6213(a). **Effective** for action taken under Code Sec. 6851, 6861, or 6862 where the notice and demand takes place after 2-28-77. [P.L. 94-528, §2(a) amended the **effective** date.]

P.L. 94-455, §1307(d)(2)(F)(iii):

Substituted "chapter 41, 42," for "chapter 42" in Code Sec. 6213(a). **Effective** 10-4-76.

P.L. 94-455, §1605(b)(6):

Substituted "43, or 44" for "or 43" in Code Sec. 6213(a). For **effective** date, see amendment note for P.L. 94-455, §1605(b)(4)(A), following Code Sec. 6211(a).

P.L. 94-455, §1906(a)(15):

Substituted "United States" for "States of the Union and the District of Columbia" in Code Sec. 6213(a). **Effective** 2-1-77.

• **1974, Employee Retirement Income Security Act of 1974 (P.L. 93-406)**

P.L. 93-406, §1016(a)(11):

Amended Code Sec. 6213(a) by changing "chapter 42" to "chapter 42 or 43". For **effective** date, see amendment note for Code Sec. 410.

• **1969, Tax Reform Act of 1969 (P.L. 91-172)**

P.L. 91-172, §101(j)(42):

Amended Code Sec. 6213(a) by adding "or chapter 42" after "subtitle A or B". **Effective** 1-1-70.

[Sec. 6213(b)]

(b) EXCEPTIONS TO RESTRICTIONS ON ASSESSMENT.—

(1) ASSESSMENTS ARISING OUT OF MATHEMATICAL OR CLERICAL ERRORS.—If the taxpayer is notified that, on account of a mathematical or clerical error appearing on the return, an amount of tax in excess of that shown on the return is due, and that an assessment of the tax has been or will be made on the basis of what would have been the correct amount of tax but for the mathematical or clerical error, such notice shall not be considered as a notice of deficiency for the purposes of subsection (a) (prohibiting assessment and collection until notice of the deficiency has been mailed), or of section 6212(c)(1) (restricting further deficiency letters), or of section 6512(a) (prohibiting credits or refunds after petition to the Tax Court), and the taxpayer shall have no right to file a petition with the Tax Court based on such notice, nor shall such assessment or collection be prohibited by the provisions of subsection (a) of this section. Each notice under this paragraph shall set forth the error alleged and an explanation thereof.

Sec. 6212(d)

ASSESSMENT—DEFICIENCY PROCEDURES

(2) ABATEMENT OF ASSESSMENT OF MATHEMATICAL OR CLERICAL ERRORS.—

(A) REQUEST FOR ABATEMENT.—Notwithstanding section 6404(b), a taxpayer may file with the Secretary within 60 days after notice is sent under paragraph (1) a request for an abatement of any assessment specified in such notice, and upon receipt of such request, the Secretary shall abate the assessment. Any reassessment of the tax with respect to which an abatement is made under this subparagraph shall be subject to the deficiency procedures prescribed by this subchapter.

(B) STAY OF COLLECTION.—In the case of any assessment referred to in paragraph (1), notwithstanding paragraph (1), no levy or proceeding in court for the collection of such assessment shall be made, begun, or prosecuted during the period in which such assessment may be abated under this paragraph.

(3) ASSESSMENTS ARISING OUT OF TENTATIVE CARRYBACK OR REFUND ADJUSTMENTS.—If the Secretary determines that the amount applied, credited, or refunded under section 6411 is in excess of the overassessment attributable to the carryback or the amount described in section 1341(b)(1) with respect to which such amount was applied, credited, or refunded, he may assess without regard to the provisions of paragraph (2) the amount of the excess as a deficiency as if it were due to a mathematical or clerical error appearing on the return.

(4) ASSESSMENT OF AMOUNT PAID.—Any amount paid as a tax or in respect of a tax may be assessed upon the receipt of such payment notwithstanding the provisions of subsection (a). In any case where such amount is paid after the mailing of a notice of deficiency under section 6212, such payment shall not deprive the Tax Court of jurisdiction over such deficiency determined under section 6211 without regard to such assessment.

(5) CERTAIN ORDERS OF CRIMINAL RESTITUTION.—If the taxpayer is notified that an assessment has been or will be made pursuant to section 6201(a)(4)—

(A) such notice shall not be considered as a notice of deficiency for the purposes of subsection (a) (prohibiting assessment and collection until notice of the deficiency has been mailed), section 6212(c)(1) (restricting further deficiency letters), or section 6512(a) (prohibiting credits or refunds after petition to the Tax Court), and

(B) subsection (a) shall not apply with respect to the amount of such assessment.

Amendments

• **2019, Taxpayer Certainty and Disaster Tax Relief Act of 2019 (P.L. 116-94)**

P.l. 116-94, § 204(c), Div. Q, provides:

For a special rule, see Act Sec. 204(c), Div. Q, in the amendment notes for Code Sec. 1400S.

• **2018, Bipartisan Budget Act of 2018 (P.L. 115-123)**

P.L. 115-123, § 20104(c), Div. B, provides:

For a special rule, see Act Sec. 20104(c), Div. B, in the amendment notes for Code Sec. 1400S(d).

• **2017, Disaster Tax Relief and Airport and Airway Extension Act of 2017 (P.L. 115-63)**

P.L. 115-63, § 504(c), provides:

For a special rule, see Act Sec. 504(c) in the amendment notes for Code Sec. 1400S(d).

• **2010, Firearms Excise Tax Improvement Act of 2010 (P.L. 111-237)**

P.L. 111-237, § 3(b)(1):

Amended Code Sec. 6213(b) by adding at the end a new paragraph (5). **Effective** for restitution ordered after 8-16-2010.

• **2005, Katrina Emergency Tax Relief Act of 2005 (P.L. 109-73)**

P.L. 109-73, § 406 [repealed by P.L. 109-135, § 201(b)(4)(B)], provides:

SEC. 406. SPECIAL RULE FOR DETERMINING EARNED INCOME.

(a) IN GENERAL.—In the case of a qualified individual, if the earned income of the taxpayer for the taxable year which includes August 25, 2005, is less than the earned income of the taxpayer for the preceding taxable year, the credits allowed under sections 24(d) and 32 of the Internal Revenue Code of 1986 may, at the election of the taxpayer, be determined by substituting—

(1) such earned income for the preceding taxable year, for

(2) such earned income for the taxable year which includes August 25, 2005.

(b) QUALIFIED INDIVIDUAL.—For purposes of this section, the term "qualified individual" means any individual whose principal place of abode on August 25, 2005, was located—

(1) in the core disaster area, or

(2) in the Hurricane Katrina disaster area (but outside the core disaster area) and such individual was displaced from such principal place of abode by reason of Hurricane Katrina.

(c) EARNED INCOME.—For purposes of this section, the term "earned income" has the meaning given such term under section 32(c) of such Code.

(d) SPECIAL RULES.

(1) APPLICATION TO JOINT RETURNS.—For purpose of subsection (a), in the case of a joint return for a taxable year which includes August 25, 2005—

(A) such subsection shall apply if either spouse is a qualified individual, and

(B) the earned income of the taxpayer for the preceding taxable year shall be the sum of the earned income of each spouse for such preceding taxable year.

(2) UNIFORM APPLICATION OF ELECTION.—Any election made under subsection (a) shall apply with respect to both section 24(d) and section 32 of such Code.

(3) ERRORS TREATED AS MATHEMATICAL ERROR.—For purposes of section 6213 of such Code, an incorrect use on a return of earned income pursuant to subsection (a) shall be treated as a mathematical or clerical error.

(4) NO EFFECT ON DETERMINATION OF GROSS INCOME, ETC.—Except as otherwise provided in this section, the Internal Revenue Code of 1986 shall be applied without regard to any substitution under subsection (a).

• **1978, Revenue Act of 1978 (P.L. 95-600)**

P.L. 95-600, § 504(b)(2)(A), (B), (c):

Amended Code Sec. 6213(b)(3). **Effective** for tentative refund claims filed on and after 11-6-78. Prior to amendment, paragraph (3) read:

"(3) ASSESSMENTS ARISING OUT OF TENTATIVE CARRYBACK ADJUSTMENTS.—If the Secretary determines that the amount applied, credited, or refunded under section 6411 is in excess of the overassessment attributable to the carryback with respect to which such amount was applied, credited, or refunded, he may assess without regard to the provisions of paragraph (2) the amount of the excess as a deficiency as if it were due to a mathematical or clerical error appearing on the return."

• **1976, Tax Reform Act of 1976 (P.L. 94-455)**

P.L. 94-455, § 1206(a):

Amended Code Sec. 6213(b) by redesignating paragraph (2) as paragraph (3), redesignating paragraph (3) as paragraph (4), and by substituting paragraphs (1) and (2) above for paragraph (1). **Effective** with respect to returns filed after 12-31-76. Prior to amendment, Code Sec. 6213(b)(1) read as follows:

"(1) MATHEMATICAL ERRORS.—If the taxpayer is notified that, on account of a mathematical error appearing upon the return, an amount of tax in excess of that shown upon the return is due, and that an assessment of the tax has been or will be made on the basis of what would have been the correct amount of tax but for the mathematical error, such notice shall not be considered as a notice of deficiency for the purposes of subsection (a) (prohibiting assessment and collection until notice of the deficiency has been mailed), or of section 6212(c)(1) (restricting further deficiency letters), or section 6512(a) (prohibiting credits or refunds after petition to the Tax Court), and the taxpayer shall have no right to file a petition with the Tax Court based on such notice, nor shall such assessment or collection be prohibited by the provisions of subsection (a) of this section."

P.L. 94-455, § 1206(c)(1):

Substituted "he may assess without regard to the provisions of paragraph (2)" for "he may assess" in Code Sec. 6213(b)(3) (as redesignated), and substituted "mathematical or clerical error" for "mathematical error" in Code Sec. 6213(b)(3). **Effective** with respect to returns filed after 12-31-76.

P.L. 94-455, § 1906(b)(13)(A):

Amended 1954 Code by substituting "Secretary" for "Secretary or his delegate" each place it appeared. **Effective** 2-1-77.

[Sec. 6213(c)]

(c) FAILURE TO FILE PETITION.—If the taxpayer does not file a petition with the Tax Court within the time prescribed in subsection (a), the deficiency, notice of which has been mailed to the taxpayer, shall be assessed, and shall be paid upon notice and demand from the Secretary.

Amendments

• **1976, Tax Reform Act of 1976 (P.L. 94-455)**

P.L. 94-455, § 1906(b)(13)(A):

Amended 1954 Code by substituting "Secretary" for "Secretary or his delegate" each place it appeared. **Effective** 2-1-77.

ASSESSMENT—DEFICIENCY PROCEDURES

[Sec. 6213(d)]

(d) WAIVER OF RESTRICTIONS.—The taxpayer shall at any time (whether or not a notice of deficiency has been issued) have the right, by a signed notice in writing filed with the Secretary, to waive the restrictions provided in subsection (a) on the assessment and collection of the whole or any part of the deficiency.

Amendments

• **1976, Tax Reform Act of 1976 (P.L. 94-455)**

P.L. 94-455, §1906(b)(13)(A):

Amended 1954 Code by substituting "Secretary" for "Secretary or his delegate" each place it appeared. **Effective** 2-1-77.

[Sec. 6213(e)]

(e) SUSPENSION OF FILING PERIOD FOR CERTAIN EXCISE TAXES.—The running of the time prescribed by subsection (a) for filing a petition in the Tax Court with respect to the taxes imposed by section 4941 (relating to taxes on self-dealing), 4942 (relating to taxes on failure to distribute income), 4943 (relating to taxes on excess business holdings), 4944 (relating to investments which jeopardize charitable purpose), 4945 (relating to taxes on taxable expenditures), 4951 (relating to taxes on self-dealing) or 4952 (relating to taxes on taxable expenditures), 4955 (relating to taxes on political expenditures), 4958 (relating to private excess benefit), 4971 (relating to excise taxes on failure to meet minimum funding standard), [or] 4975 (relating to excise taxes on prohibited transactions) shall be suspended for any period during which the Secretary has extended the time allowed for making correction under section 4963(e).

Amendments

• **1996, Taxpayer Bill of Rights 2 (P.L. 104-168)**

P.L. 104-168, §1311(c)(3):

Amended Code Sec. 6213(e) by inserting "4958 (relating to private excess benefit)," before "4971". For the **effective** date, see Act Sec. 1311(d)(1)-(2), below.

P.L. 104-168, §1311(d)(1)-(2), provides:

(d) EFFECTIVE DATES.—

(1) IN GENERAL.—The amendments made by this section (other than subsection (b)) shall apply to excess benefit transactions occurring on or after September 14, 1995.

(2) BINDING CONTRACTS.—The amendments referred to in paragraph (1) shall not apply to any benefit arising from a transaction pursuant to any written contract which was binding on September 13, 1995, and at all times thereafter before such transaction occurred.

• **1987, Revenue Act of 1987 (P.L. 100-203)**

P.L. 100-203, §10712(c)(1):

Amended Code Sec. 6213(e) by striking out "4971" and inserting in lieu thereof "4955 (relating to taxes on political expenditures), 4971". **Effective** for tax years beginning after 12-22-87.

• **1984, Deficit Reduction Act of 1984 (P.L. 98-369)**

P.L. 98-369, §305(b)(4):

Amended Code Sec. 6213(e) by striking out "section 4962(e)" and inserting in lieu thereof "section 4963(e)". **Effective** for taxable events occurring after 12-31-84.

• **1980 (P.L. 96-596)**

P.L. 96-596, §2(a)(3):

Amended Code Sec. 6213(e) by striking out "section 4941(e)(4), 4942(j)(2), 4943(d)(3), 4944(e)(3), 4945(i)(2), 4951(e)(4), 4952(e)(2), 4971(c)(3), or 4975(f)(6)." and inserting in lieu thereof "section 4962(e).". **Effective** 12-24-80.

• **1978, Black Lung Benefits Revenue Act of 1977 (P.L. 95-227)**

P.L. 95-227, §4(d)(1):

Amended Code Sec. 6213(e) by adding "4951 (relating to taxes on selfdealing), or 4952 (relating to taxes on taxable expenditures)," before "4975 (relating to excise taxes on prohibited transactions", by adding "4951(e)(4), 4952(e)(2)" after "4945(i)(2)", and by substituting "4975(f)(6)" for "4975(f)(4)". For **effective** date, see the historical comment for P.L. 95-227 under Code Sec. 4951.

• **1976, Tax Reform Act of 1976 (P.L. 94-455)**

P.L. 94-455, §1906(b)(13)(A):

Amended 1954 Code by substituting "Secretary" for "Secretary or his delegate" each place it appeared. **Effective** 2-1-77.

• **1974, Employee Retirement Income Security Act of 1974 (P.L. 93-406)**

P.L. 93-406, §1016(a)(11):

Amended Code Sec. 6213(e) by changing "or 4945 (relating to taxes on taxable expenditures)" to "4945 (relating to taxes on taxable expenditures), 4971 (relating to excise taxes on failure to meet minimum funding standard), 4975 (relating to excise taxes on prohibited transactions)". For **effective** date, see amendment note for Code Sec. 410.

• **1969, Tax Reform Act of 1969 (P.L. 91-172)**

P.L. 91-172, §101(f)(3):

Added Code Sec. 6213(e). **Effective** 1-1-70.

[Sec. 6213(f)]

(f) COORDINATION WITH TITLE 11.—

(1) SUSPENSION OF RUNNING OF PERIOD FOR FILING PETITION IN TITLE 11 CASES.—In any case under title 11 of the United States Code, the running of the time prescribed by subsection (a) for filing a petition in the Tax Court with respect to any deficiency shall be suspended for the period during which the debtor is prohibited by reason of such case from filing a petition in the Tax Court with respect to such deficiency, and for 60 days thereafter.

(2) CERTAIN ACTION NOT TAKEN INTO ACCOUNT.—For purposes of the second and third sentences of subsection (a), the filing of a proof of claim or request for payment (or the taking of any other action) in a case under title 11 of the United States Code shall not be treated as action prohibited by such second sentence.

Amendments

• **1980, Bankruptcy Tax Act of 1980 (P.L. 96-589)**

P.L. 96-589, §6(b)(1):

Redesignated former Code Sec. 6213(f) as Code Sec. 6213(g) and added a new Code Sec. 6213(f). **Effective** 10-1-79, but inapplicable to any proceeding under the Bankruptcy Act commenced before that date.

[Sec. 6213(g)]

(g) DEFINITIONS.—For purposes of this section—

(1) RETURN.—The term "return" includes any return, statement, schedule, or list, and any amendment or supplement thereto, filed with respect to any tax imposed by subtitle A or B, or chapter 41, 42, 43, or 44.

(2) MATHEMATICAL OR CLERICAL ERROR.—The term "mathematical or clerical error" means—

(A) an error in addition, subtraction, multiplication or division shown on any return,

(B) an incorrect use of any table provided by the Internal Revenue Service with respect to any return if such incorrect use is apparent from the existence of other information on the return,

(C) an entry on a return of an item which is inconsistent with another entry of the same or another item on such return,

(D) an omission of information which is required to be supplied on the return to substantiate an entry on the return,

(E) an entry on a return of a deduction or credit in an amount which exceeds a statutory limit imposed by subtitle A or B, or chapter 41, 42, 43, or 44, if such limit is expressed—

(i) as a specified monetary amount, or

(ii) as a percentage, ratio, or fraction,

ASSESSMENT—DEFICIENCY PROCEDURES

and if the items entering into the application of such limit appear on such return,

(F) an omission of a correct taxpayer identification number required under section 32 (relating to the earned income credit) to be included on a return,

(G) an entry on a return claiming the credit under section 32 with respect to net earnings from self-employment described in section 32(c)(2)(A) to the extent the tax imposed by section 1401 (relating to self-employment tax) on such net earnings has not been paid,

(H) an omission of a correct TIN required under section 21 (relating to expenses for household and dependent care services necessary for gainful employment) or section 151 (relating to allowance of deductions for personal exemptions),

(I) an omission of a correct TIN required under section 24(e) (relating to child tax credit) to be included on a return,

(J) an omission of a correct TIN required under section 25A(g)(1) (relating to higher education tuition and related expenses) to be included on a return,

(K) an omission of information required by section 32(k)(2) (relating to taxpayers making improper prior claims of earned income credit) or an entry on the return claiming the credit under section 32 for a taxable year for which the credit is disallowed under subsection (k)(1) thereof,

(L) the inclusion on a return of a TIN required to be included on the return under section 21, 24, 32, 6428, or 6428A if—

(i) such TIN is of an individual whose age affects the amount of the credit under such section, and

(ii) the computation of the credit on the return reflects the treatment of such individual as being of an age different from the individual's age based on such TIN,

(M) the entry on the return claiming the credit under section 32 with respect to a child if, according to the Federal Case Registry of Child Support Orders established under section 453(h) of the Social Security Act, the taxpayer is a non-custodial parent of such child,

(N) an omission of any increase required under section 36(f) with respect to the recapture of a credit allowed under section 36,

(O) the inclusion on a return of an individual taxpayer identification number issued under section 6109(i) which has expired, been revoked by the Secretary, or is otherwise invalid,

(P) an omission of information required by section 24(g)(2) or an entry on the return claiming the credit under section 24 for a taxable year for which the credit is disallowed under subsection (g)(1) thereof,

(Q) an omission of information required by section 25A(b)(4)(B) or an entry on the return claiming the American Opportunity Tax Credit for a taxable year for which such credit is disallowed under section 25A(b)(4)(A),

(R) an omission of information or documentation required under section 25C(b)(6)(B) (relating to home energy audits) to be included on a return,

»»→ Caution: Code Sec. 6213(g)(2)(S), below, as added by P.L. 117-169, applies to property placed in service after December 31, 2024.

(S) an omission of a correct product identification number required under section 25C(h) (relating to credit for nonbusiness energy property) to be included on a return,

(T) an omission of a correct vehicle identification number required under section 30D(f)(9) (relating to credit for new clean vehicles) to be included on a return,

(U) an omission of a correct vehicle identification number required under section 25E(d) (relating to credit for previously-owned clean vehicles) to be included on a return, and

(V) an omission of a correct vehicle identification number required under section 45W(e) (relating to commercial clean vehicle credit) to be included on a return.

A taxpayer shall be treated as having omitted a correct TIN for purposes of the preceding sentence if information provided by the taxpayer on the return with respect to the individual whose TIN was provided differs from the information the Secretary obtains from the person issuing the TIN.

Amendments

• **2022, Inflation Reduction Act of 2022 (P.L. 117-169)**

P.L. 117-169, § 13301(f)(4)(A)-(C):

Amended Code Sec. 6213(g)(2) by striking "and" at the end of subparagraph (P), by striking the period at the end of subparagraph (Q) and inserting ", and", and by inserting after subparagraph (Q) a new subparagraph (R). **Effective** for property placed in service after 12-31-2022.

P.L. 117-169, § 13301(g)(2)(A)-(C):

Amended Code Sec. 6213(g)(2), as amended by the preceding provisions of this Act, by striking "and" at the end of subparagraph (Q), by striking the period at the end of subparagraph (R) and inserting ", and", and by inserting after subparagraph (R) a new subparagraph (S). **Effective** for property placed in service after 12-31-2024.

P.L. 117-169, § 13401(i)(4)(A)-(C):

Amended Code Sec. 6213(g)(2), as amended by the preceding provisions of this Act, by striking "and" at the end of subparagraph (R), by striking the period at the end of subparagraph (S) and inserting ", and", and by inserting after subparagraph (S) a new subparagraph (T). **Effective** for vehicles placed in service after 12-31-2022.

P.L. 117-169, § 13402(c)(1)-(3):

Amended Code Sec. 6213(g)(2), as amended by the preceding provisions of this Act, by striking "and" at the end of subparagraph (S), by striking the period at the end of subparagraph (T) and inserting ", and", and by inserting after subparagraph (T) a new subparagraph (U). **Effective** for vehicles acquired after 12-31-2022.

P.L. 117-169, § 13403(b)(2)(A)-(C):

Amended Code Sec. 6213(g)(2), as amended by the preceding provisions of this Act, by striking "and" at the end of subparagraph (T), by striking the period at the end of subparagraph (U) and inserting ", and", and by inserting after subparagraph (U) a new subparagraph (V). **Effective** for vehicles acquired after 12-31-2022.

• **2020, COVID-related Tax Relief Act of 2020 (P.L. 116-260)**

P.L. 116-260, § 272(b)(2), Div. N:

Amended Code Sec. 6213(g)(2)(L) by striking "or 6428" and inserting "6428, or 6428A". **Effective** 12-27-2020.

• **2020, Coronavirus Aid, Relief, and Economic Security (CARES) Act (P.L. 116-136)**

P.L. 116-136, § 2201(b)(2):

Amended Code Sec. 6213(g)(2)(L) by striking "or 32" and inserting "32, or 6428". **Effective** 3-27-2020.

• **2018, Tax Technical Corrections Act of 2018 (P.L. 115-141)**

P.L. 115-141, § 101(l)(18), Div. U:

Amended Code Sec. 6213(g)(2)(Q). **Effective** as if included in the provision of the Protecting Americans from Tax Hikes Act of 2015 to which it relates [effective for tax years beginning after 12-18-2015.—CCH]. Prior to amendment, Code Sec. 6213(g)(2)(Q) read as follows:

(Q) an omission of information required by section 25A(i)(8)(B) [25A(i)(7)(B)] or an entry on the return claiming the credit determined under section 25A(i) for a taxable year for which the credit is disallowed under paragraph (8)(A) [(7)(A)] thereof.

P.L. 115-141, § 401(a)(277), Div. U:

Amended Code Sec. 6213(g)(2)(O) by adding a comma at the end. **Effective** 3-23-2018.

P.L. 115-141, § 401(a)(278)(A)-(B), Div. U:

Amended Code Sec. 6213(g)(2)(P) by striking "section 24(h)(2)" and inserting "section 24(g)(2)", and by striking "subsection (h)(1)" and inserting "subsection (g)(1)". **Effective** 3-23-2018.

• **2015, Protecting Americans from Tax Hikes Act of 2015 (P.L. 114-113)**

P.L. 114-113, § 203(e), Div. Q:

Amended Code Sec. 6213(g)(2) by striking "and" at the end subparagraph (M), by striking the period at the end of subparagraph (N) and inserting ", and", and by inserting after subparagraph (N) a new subparagraph (O). **Effective**, except to the extent provided in Code Sec. 6109(i)(3), for applications for individual taxpayer identification numbers made after 12-18-2015 [effective date changed by P.L. 115-141, § 101(g)(5), Div. U.—CCH].

ASSESSMENT—DEFICIENCY PROCEDURES

P.L. 114-113, §208(b)(1), Div. Q:

Amended Code Sec. 6213(g)(2)(K) by inserting before the comma at the end "or an entry on the return claiming the credit under section 32 for a taxable year for which the credit is disallowed under subsection (k)(1) thereof". **Effective** for tax years beginning after 12-31-2015.

P.L. 114-113, §208(b)(2), Div. Q:

Amended Code Sec. 6213(g)(2), as amended by this Act, by striking "and" at the end of subparagraph (N), by striking the period at the end of subparagraph (O), and by inserting after subparagraph (O) new subparagraphs (P)-(Q). **Effective** for tax years beginning after 12-31-2015.

• **2014, Tax Technical Corrections Act of 2014 (P.L. 113-295)**

P.L. 113-295, §214(a)(1)-(2), Division A:

Amended Code Sec. 6213(g)(2) by striking "32, or 6428" in subparagraph (L) and inserting "or 32", and by striking "and" at the end of subparagraph (O), by striking the period at the end of subparagraph (P) and inserting ", and", and by inserting after subparagraph (P) a new subparagraph (Q). **Effective** as if included in the provision of the Economic Stimulus Act of 2008 (P.L. 110-185) to which it relates [effective 2-13-2008.—CCH].

P.L. 113-295, §221(a)(4), Division A:

Amended Code Sec. 6213(g)(2), as amended by Act Sec. 214(a)(2), by striking subparagraph (P). **Effective** generally 12-19-2014. For a special rule, see Act Sec. 221(b)(2), Division A, below. Prior to being stricken, Code Sec. 6213(g)(2)(P) read as follows:

(P) an entry on a return claiming the credit under section 36 if—

(i) the Secretary obtains information from the person issuing the TIN of the taxpayer that indicates that the taxpayer does not meet the age requirement of section 36(b)(4),

(ii) information provided to the Secretary by the taxpayer on an income tax return for at least one of the 2 preceding taxable years is inconsistent with eligibility for such credit, or

(iii) the taxpayer fails to attach to the return the form described in section 36(d)(4), and

P.L. 113-295, §221(a)(5)(C), Division A:

Amended Code Sec. 6213(g)(2) by striking subparagraph (N). **Effective** generally 12-19-2014. For a special rule, see Act Sec. 221(b)(2), Division A, below. Prior to being stricken, Code Sec. 6213(g)(2)(N) read as follows:

(N) an omission of the reduction required under section 36A(c) with respect to the credit allowed under section 36A or an omission of the correct social security account number required under section 36A(d)(1)(B),

P.L. 113-295, §221(a)(112)(C), Division A:

Amended Code Sec. 6213(g)(2), as amended by Act Sec. 214(a)(2) and Act Sec. 221(a)(4) and (5)(C), by striking subparagraph (Q), by redesignating subparagraph (O) as subparagraph (N), by inserting "and" at the end of subparagraph (M), and by striking the comma at the end of subparagraph (N) (as so redesignated) and inserting a period. **Effective** generally 12-19-2014. For a special rule, see Act Sec. 221(b)(2), Division A, below. Prior to being stricken, Code Sec. 6213(g)(2)(Q) read as follows:

(Q) an omission of a correct valid identification number required under section 6428(h) (relating to 2008 recovery rebates for individuals) to be included on a return.

P.L. 113-295, §221(b)(2), Division A, provides:

(2) SAVINGS PROVISION.—If—

(A) any provision amended or repealed by the amendments made by this section applied to—

(i) any transaction occurring before the date of the enactment of this Act,

(ii) any property acquired before such date of enactment, or

(iii) any item of income, loss, deduction, or credit taken into account before such date of enactment, and

(B) the treatment of such transaction, property, or item under such provision would (without regard to the amendments or repeals made by this section) affect the liability for tax for periods ending after date of enactment, nothing in the amendments or repeals made by this section shall be construed to affect the treatment of such transaction, property, or item for purposes of determining liability for tax for periods ending after such date of enactment.

• **2013, American Taxpayer Relief Act of 2012 (P.L. 112-240)**

P.L. 112-240, §101(a)(1) and (3), provides:

SEC. 101. PERMANENT EXTENSION AND MODIFICATION OF 2001 TAX RELIEF.

(a) PERMANENT EXTENSION.—

(1) IN GENERAL.—The Economic Growth and Tax Relief Reconciliation Act of 2001 is amended by striking title IX.

* * *

(3) EFFECTIVE DATE.—The amendments made by this subsection shall apply to taxable, plan, or limitation years beginning after December 31, 2012, and estates of decedents dying, gifts made, or generation skipping transfers after December 31, 2012.

• **2009, Worker, Homeownership, and Business Assistance Act of 2009 (P.L. 111-92)**

P.L. 111-92, §11(h)(1)-(3):

Amended Code Sec. 6213(g)(2) by striking "and" at the end of subparagraph (M), by striking the period at the end of subparagraph (N) and inserting ", and", and by inserting after subparagraph (N) a new subparagraph (O). **Effective** for tax years ending on or after 4-9-2008.

P.L. 111-92, §12(d):

Amended Code Sec. 6213(g)(2), as amended by this Act, by striking "and" at the end of subparagraph (N), by striking the period at the end of subparagraph (O) and inserting ", and", and by inserting after subparagraph (O) a new subparagraph (P). **Effective** for returns for tax years ending on or after 4-9-2008.

• **2009, American Recovery and Reinvestment Tax Act of 2009 (P.L. 111-5)**

P.L. 111-5, §1001(d):

Amended Code Sec. 6213(g)(2) by striking "and" at the end of subparagraph (L)(ii), by striking the period at the end of subparagraph (M) and inserting ", and", and by adding at the end a new subparagraph (N). **Effective** for tax years beginning after 12-31-2008.

• **2008, Economic Stimulus Act of 2008 (P.L. 110-185)**

P.L. 110-185, §101(b)(2):

Amended Code Sec. 6213(g)(2)(L) by striking "or 32" and inserting "32, or 6428". **Effective** 2-13-2008.

• **2001, Economic Growth and Tax Relief Reconciliation Act of 2001 (P.L. 107-16)**

P.L. 107-16, §303(g):

Amended Code Sec. 6213(g)(2) by striking "and" at the end of subparagraph (K), by striking the period at the end of subparagraph (L) and inserting ", and", and by inserting after subparagraph (L) a new subparagraph (M). **Effective** 1-1-2004.

P.L. 107-16, §901(a)-(b), as amended by P.L. 111-312, §101(a)(1), provides [but see P.L. 112-240, §101(a)(1) and (3), above]:

SEC. 901. SUNSET OF PROVISIONS OF ACT.

(a) IN GENERAL.—All provisions of, and amendments made by, this Act shall not apply—

(1) to taxable, plan, or limitation years beginning after December 31, 2012, or

(2) in the case of title V, to estates of decedents dying, gifts made, or generation skipping transfers, after December 31, 2012.

(b) APPLICATION OF CERTAIN LAWS.—The Internal Revenue Code of 1986 and the Employee Retirement Income Security Act of 1974 shall be applied and administered to years, estates, gifts, and transfers described in subsection (a) as if the provisions and amendments described in subsection (a) had never been enacted.

• **1998, Tax and Trade Relief Extension Act of 1998 (P.L. 105-277)**

P.L. 105-277, §3003(a):

Amended Code Sec. 6213(g)(2) by adding at the end a new flush sentence. **Effective** for tax years ending after 10-21-98.

P.L. 105-277, §3003(b):

Amended Code Sec. 6213(g)(2) by striking "and" at the end of subparagraph (J), by striking the period at the end of subparagraph (K) and inserting ", and", and by inserting after subparagraph (K) a new subparagraph (L). **Effective** for tax years ending after 10-21-98.

• **1997, Taxpayer Relief Act of 1997 (P.L. 105-34)**

P.L. 105-34, §101(d)(2):

Amended Code Sec. 6213(g)(2) by striking "and" at the end of subparagraph (G), by striking the period at the end of subparagraph (H) and inserting ", and", and by inserting after subparagraph (H) a new subparagraph (I). **Effective** for tax years beginning after 12-31-97.

P.L. 105-34, §201(b):

Amended Code Sec. 6213(g)(2), as amended by Act Sec. 101(d)(2), by striking "and" at the end of subparagraph (H), by striking the period at the end of subparagraph (I) and inserting ", and", and by inserting after subparagraph (I) a new subparagraph (J). **Effective** for expenses paid after 12-31-97 (in tax years ending after such date), for education furnished in academic periods beginning after such date.

P.L. 105-34, §1085(a)(3) (as amended by P.L. 105-206, §6010 (p)(3)):

Amended Code Sec. 6213(g)(2) by striking "and" at the end of subparagraph (I), by striking the period at the end of subparagraph (J) and inserting ", and", and by inserting after subparagraph (J) a new subparagraph (K). **Effective** for tax years beginning after 12-31-96.

• **1996, Personal Responsibility and Work Opportunity Reconciliation Act of 1996 (P.L. 104-193)**

P.L. 104-193, §451(c):

Amended Code Sec. 6213(g)(2) by striking "and" at the end of subparagraph (D), by striking the period at the end of subparagraph (E) and inserting a comma, and by inserting after subparagraph (E) new subparagraphs (F) and (G). **Effective** with respect to returns the due date for which (without regard to extensions) is more than 30 days after 8-22-96.

• **1996, Small Business Job Protection Act of 1996 (P.L. 104-188)**

P.L. 104-188, §1615(c):

Amended Code Sec. 6213(g)(2), as amended by P.L. 104-193, by striking "and" at the end of subparagraph (F), by striking the period at the end of subparagraph (G) and inserting ", and", and by inserting at the end a new subparagraph (H). **Effective**, generally, with respect to returns the due date for which (without regard to extensions) is on or after the 30th day after 8-20-96. For a special rule, see Act Sec. 1615(d)(2), below.

P.L. 104-188, §1615(d)(2), provides:

(2) SPECIAL RULE FOR 1995 AND 1996.—In the case of returns for taxable years beginning in 1995 or 1996, a taxpayer shall not be required by the amendments made by this section to provide a taxpayer identification number for a child who is born after October 31, 1995, in the case of a taxable year beginning in 1995 or November 30, 1996, in the case of a taxable year beginning in 1996.

ASSESSMENT—DEFICIENCY PROCEDURES

• **1988, Omnibus Trade and Competitiveness Act of 1988 (P.L. 100-418)**

P.L. 100-418, §1941(b)(2)(B)(v):

Amended Code Sec. 6213(g) by striking "44, or 45" each place it appears and inserting "or 44". **Effective** for crude oil removed from the premises on or after 8-23-88.

• **1980, Bankruptcy Tax Act of 1980 (P.L. 96-589)**

P.L. 96-589, §6(b)(1):

Redesignated Code Sec. 6213(f) as 6213(g). **Effective** 10-1-79, but inapplicable to any proceeding under the Bankruptcy Act commenced before 10-1-79.

• **1980, Crude Oil Windfall Profit Tax Act of 1980 (P.L. 96-223)**

P.L. 96-223, §101(f)(1)(E):

Amended Code Sec. 6213(f)(2)(E) by striking out "or 44" and inserting "44, or 45". For the **effective** date and transitional rules, see P.L. 96-223, §101(i), following Code Sec. 4986.

• **1978, Black Lung Benefits Revenue Act of 1977 (P.L. 95-227)**

P.L. 95-227, §4(d)(2):

Amended Code Sec. 6213(f) by substituting "chapter 41, 42, 43, or 44" for "chapter 42 or 43" in paragraphs (1) and (2)(E). For **effective** date, see the historical comment from P.L. 95-227 under Code Sec. 4951.

• **1976, Tax Reform Act of 1976 (P.L. 94-455)**

P.L. 94-455, §1206(b):

Redesignated former Code Sec. 6213(f) as Code Sec. 6213(g) and added a new Code Sec. 6213(f). **Effective** with respect to returns filed after 12-31-76.

[Sec. 6213(h)]

(h) CROSS REFERENCES.—

(1) For assessment as if a mathematical error on the return, in the case of erroneous claims for income tax prepayment credits, see section 6201(a)(3).

(2) For assessments without regard to restrictions imposed by this section in the case of—

(A) Recovery of foreign income taxes, see section 905(c).

(B) Recovery of foreign estate tax, see section 2016.

(3) For provisions relating to application of this subchapter in the case of certain partnership items, etc., see section 6230(a).

Amendments

• **1988, Technical and Miscellaneous Revenue Act of 1988 (P.L. 100-647)**

P.L. 100-647, §1015(r)(3):

Amended Code Sec. 6213(h) by striking out paragraph (3) and by redesignating paragraph (4) as paragraph (3). **Effective** for notices of deficiencies mailed after 11-10-88. Prior to amendment, Code Sec. 6213(h)(3) read as follows:

(3) For assessment as if a mathematical error on the return, in the case of erroneous claims for credits under section 32 or 34, see section 6201(a)(4).

• **1986, Tax Reform Act of 1986 (P.L. 99-514)**

P.L. 99-514, §1875(d)(2)(B)(i):

Amended Code Sec. 6213(h)(4). **Effective** as if it were included in P.L. 97-248. Prior to amendment, paragraph (4) read as follows:

(4) For provision that this subchapter shall not apply in the case of computational adjustments attributable to partnership items, see section 6230(a).

• **1984, Deficit Reduction Act of 1984 (P.L. 98-369)**

P.L. 98-369, §474(r)(34):

Amended Code Sec. 6213(h)(3) by striking out "section 39" and inserting in lieu thereof "section 32 or 34". **Effective** for tax years beginning after 12-31-83, and to carrybacks from such years.

• **1982, Tax Equity and Fiscal Responsibility Act of 1982 (P.L. 97-248)**

P.L. 97-248, §402(c)(2):

Amended Code Sec. 6213(h) by adding paragraph (4). **Effective** for partnership tax years beginning after 9-3-82.

• **1980, Bankruptcy Tax Act of 1980 (P.L. 96-589)**

P.L. 96-589, §6(b)(1):

Redesignated Code Sec. 6213(g) as 6213(h). **Effective** 10-1-79, but inapplicable to any proceeding under the Bankruptcy Act commenced before 10-1-79.

• **1976, Tax Reform Act of 1976 (P.L. 94-455)**

P.L. 94-455, §1206(b):

Redesignated former Code Sec. 6213(f) to be Code Sec. 6213(g). **Effective** with respect to returns filed after 12-31-76.

• **1969, Tax Reform Act of 1969 (P.L. 91-172)**

P.L. 91-172, §101(f)(3):

Redesignated Code Sec. 6213(e) as 6213(f). **Effective** 1-1-70.

• **1965, Excise Tax Reduction Act of 1965 (P.L. 89-44)**

P.L. 89-44, §809(d)(4):

Added paragraph (3). **Effective** 7-1-65.

[Sec. 6214]

SEC. 6214. DETERMINATIONS BY TAX COURT.

[Sec. 6214(a)]

(a) JURISDICTION AS TO INCREASE OF DEFICIENCY, ADDITIONAL AMOUNTS, OR ADDITIONS TO THE TAX.—Except as provided by section 7463, the Tax Court shall have jurisdiction to redetermine the correct amount of the deficiency even if the amount so redetermined is greater than the amount of the deficiency, notice of which has been mailed to the taxpayer, and to determine whether any additional amount, or any addition to the tax should be assessed, if claim therefor is asserted by the Secretary at or before the hearing or a rehearing.

Amendments

• **1986, Tax Reform Act of 1986 (P.L. 99-514)**

P.L. 99-514, §1554(a):

Amended Code Sec. 6214(a) by striking out "addition to the tax" and inserting in lieu thereof "any addition to the tax". **Effective** for any action or proceeding in the Tax Court with respect to which a decision has not become final (as determined under section 7481 of the Internal Revenue Code of 1954) before 10-22-86.

• **1976, Tax Reform Act of 1976 (P.L. 94-455)**

P.L. 94-455, §1906(b)(13)(A):

Amended 1954 Code by substituting "Secretary" for "Secretary or his delegate" each place it appeared. **Effective** 2-1-77.

• **1969, Tax Reform Act of 1969 (P.L. 91-172)**

P.L. 91-172, §960(a):

Amended Code Sec. 6214(a) by adding the introductory phrase "Except as provided by section 7463,". **Effective** 12-30-70.

[Sec. 6214(b)]

(b) JURISDICTION OVER OTHER YEARS AND QUARTERS.—The Tax Court in redetermining a deficiency of income tax for any taxable year or of gift tax for any calendar year or calendar quarter shall consider such facts with relation to the taxes for other years or calendar quarters as may be necessary correctly to redetermine the amount of such deficiency, but in so doing shall have no jurisdiction to determine whether or not the tax for any other year or calendar quarter has been overpaid or underpaid. Notwithstanding the preceding sentence, the Tax Court may apply the doctrine of equitable recoupment to the same extent that it is available in civil tax cases before the district courts of the United States and the United States Court of Federal Claims.

Amendments

• **2006, Pension Protection Act of 2006 (P.L. 109-280)**

P.L. 109-280, §858(a):

Amended Code Sec. 6214(b) by adding at the end a new sentence. **Effective** for any action or proceeding in the United States Tax Court with respect to which a decision has not become final (as determined under Code Sec. 7481) as of 8-17-2006.

• **1970, Excise, Estate, and Gift Tax Adjustment Act of 1970 (P.L. 91-614)**

P.L. 91-614, §102(d)(6):

Amended Code Sec. 6214(b). **Effective** 1-1-71 for gifts made after 12-31-70. Prior to amendment, the section read as follows:

(b) JURISDICTION OVER OTHER YEARS.—The Tax Court in redetermining a deficiency of income tax for any taxable year or of gift tax for any calendar year shall consider such

ASSESSMENT—DEFICIENCY PROCEDURES

facts with relation to the taxes for other years as may be necessary correctly to redetermine the amount of such deficiency, but in so doing shall have no jurisdiction to determine whether or not the tax for any other year has been overpaid or underpaid.

[Sec. 6214(c)]

(c) TAXES IMPOSED BY SECTION 507 OR CHAPTER 41, 42, 43, OR 44.—The Tax Court, in redetermining a deficiency of any tax imposed by section 507 or chapter 41, 42, 43, or 44 for any period, act, or failure to act, shall consider such facts with relation to the taxes under chapter 41, 42, 43, or 44 for other periods, acts, or failures to act as may be necessary correctly to redetermine the amount of such deficiency, but in so doing shall have no jurisdiction to determine whether or not the taxes under chapter 41, 42, 43, or 44 for any other period, act, or failure to act have been overpaid or underpaid. The Tax Court, in redetermining a deficiency of any second tier tax (as defined in section 4963(b)), shall make a determination with respect to whether the taxable event has been corrected.

Amendments

- **1988, Omnibus Trade and Competitiveness Act of 1988 (P.L. 100-418)**

P.L. 100-418, § 1941(b)(2)(B)(vi):

Amended Code Sec. 6214(c) by striking "44, or 45" each place it appears and inserting "or 44". **Effective** for crude oil removed from the premises on or after 8-23-88.

- **1986, Tax Reform Act of 1986 (P.L. 99-514)**

P.L. 99-514, § 1833:

Amended Code Sec. 6214(c) by striking out "section 4962(b)" and inserting in lieu thereof "section 4963(b)". **Effective** as if included in the provision of P.L. 98-369 to which it relates.

- **1980 (P.L. 96-596)**

P.L. 96-596, § 2(b):

Amended Code Sec. 6214(c) by adding the last sentence. **Effective** with respect to second tier taxes assessed after 12-24-80 (except in cases where there is a court decision with regard to which res judicata applies on that date).

- **1980, Crude Oil Windfall Profit Tax Act of 1980 (P.L. 96-223)**

P.L. 96-223, § 101(f)(1)(F):

Amended Code Sec. 6214(c) by striking out each place it appears "or 44" and inserting ", 44, or 45". For the **effective** date and transitional rules, see P.L. 96-223, § 101(i), following Code Sec. 4986.

- **1976, Tax Reform Act of 1976 (P.L. 94-455)**

P.L. 94-455, § 1307(d)(2)(F)(iv):

Substituted "chapter 41, 42," for "chapter 42" each place it appeared in Code Sec. 6214(c). **Effective** 10-4-76.

P.L. 94-455, § 1605(b)(7)(A), (B):

Substituted "43, or 44" for "or 43" each place it appeared in Code Sec. 6214(c). For **effective** date, see amendment note for P.L. 94-455, § 1605(b)(4)(A), following Code Sec. 6211(a).

- **1974, Employee Retirement Income Security Act of 1974 (P.L. 93-406)**

P.L. 93-406, § 1016(a)(12):

Amended Code Sec. 6214(c) by changing "chapter 42" to "chapter 42 or 43" each place it appears. For **effective** date, see amendment note for Code Sec. 410.

- **1969, Tax Reform Act of 1969 (P.L. 91-172)**

P.L. 91-172, § 101(j)(43):

Added Code Sec. 6214(c). **Effective** 1-1-70.

[Sec. 6214(d)]

(d) FINAL DECISIONS OF TAX COURT.—For purposes of this chapter, chapter 41, 42, 43, or 44 and subtitles A or B the date on which a decision of the Tax Court becomes final shall be determined according to the provisions of section 7481.

Amendments

- **1988, Omnibus Trade and Competitiveness Act of 1988 (P.L. 100-418)**

P.L. 100-418, § 1941(b)(2)(B)(vii):

Amended Code Sec. 6214(d) by striking "44, or 45" each place it appears and inserting "or 44". **Effective** for crude oil removed from the premises on or after 8-23-88.

- **1980, Crude Oil Windfall Profit Tax Act of 1980 (P.L. 96-223)**

P.L. 96-223, § 101(f)(1)(G):

Amended Code Sec. 6214(d) by striking out "or 44" and inserting "44, or 45". For the **effective** date and transitional rules, see P.L. 96-223, § 101(i), following Code Sec. 4986.

- **1976, Tax Reform Act of 1976 (P.L. 94-455)**

P.L. 94-455, § 1307(d)(2)(F)(iv):

Substituted "chapter 41, 42," for "chapter 42" in Code Sec. 6214(d). **Effective** 10-4-76.

P.L. 94-455, § 1605(b)(7)(C):

Substituted "43, or 44" for "or 43" in Code Sec. 6214(d). For **effective** date, see amendatory note for P.L. 94-455, § 1605(b)(4)(A), following Code Sec. 6211(a).

- **1974, Employee Retirement Income Security Act of 1974 (P.L. 93-406)**

P.L. 93-406, § 1016(a)(12):

Amended Code Sec. 6214(d) by changing "chapter 42" to "chapter 42 or 43". For **effective** date, see amendment note for Code Sec. 410.

- **1969, Tax Reform Act of 1969 (P.L. 91-172)**

P.L. 91-172, § 101(j)(43), (44):

Redesignated former Code Sec. 6214(c) as Code Sec. 6214(d) and added ", chapter 42," after "chapter". **Effective** 1-1-70.

[Sec. 6214(e)]

(e) CROSS REFERENCE.—

For provision giving Tax Court jurisdiction to order a refund of an overpayment and to award sanctions, see section 6512(b)(2).

Amendments

- **1996, Small Business Job Protection Act of 1996 (P.L. 104-188)**

P.L. 104-188, § 1704(t)(16):

Amended Code Sec. 6214(e). **Effective** 8-20-96. Prior to amendment, Code Sec. 6214(e) read as follows:

(e) CROSS REFERENCES.—

(1) For provision giving Tax Court jurisdiction to determine whether any portion of deficiency is a substantial underpayment attributable to tax motivated transactions, see section 6621(c)(4).

(2) For provision giving Tax Court jurisdiction to order a refund of an overpayment and to award sanctions, see section 6512(b)(2).

- **1988, Technical and Miscellaneous Revenue Act of 1988 (P.L. 100-647)**

P.L. 100-647, § 6244(b)(1):

Amended Code Sec. 6214(e) by striking out "REFERENCE.—" and inserting in lieu thereof "REFERENCES.—" in the heading, by designating the undesignated paragraph as paragraph (1), and by adding at the end thereof new paragraph (2). **Effective** for overpayments determined by the Tax Court that have not yet been refunded by the 90th day after 11-10-88.

- **1986, Tax Reform Act of 1986 (P.L. 99-514)**

P.L. 99-514, § 1511(c)(8):

Amended Code Sec. 6214(e) by striking out "section 6621(d)(4)" and inserting in lieu thereof "section 6621(c)(4)". **Effective** for purposes of determining interest for periods after 12-31-86.

- **1984, Deficit Reduction Act of 1984 (P.L. 98-369)**

P.L. 98-369, § 144(b):

Amended Code Sec. 6214 by adding new subsection (e). **Effective** with respect to interest accruing after 12-31-84.

[Sec. 6215]

SEC. 6215. ASSESSMENT OF DEFICIENCY FOUND BY TAX COURT.

[Sec. 6215(a)]

(a) GENERAL RULE.—If the taxpayer files a petition with the Tax Court, the entire amount redetermined as the deficiency by the decision of the Tax Court which has become final shall be assessed and shall be paid upon notice and demand from the Secretary. No part of the amount determined as a deficiency by the Secretary but disallowed as such by the decision of the Tax Court which has become final shall be assessed or be collected by levy or by proceeding in court with or without assessment.

Sec. 6214(c)

ASSESSMENT—TREATMENT OF PARTNERSHIPS

Amendments

• **1976, Tax Reform Act of 1976 (P.L. 94-455)**

P.L. 94-455, §1906(b)(13)(A):

Amended 1954 Code by substituting "Secretary" for "Secretary or his delegate" each place it appeared. **Effective** 2-1-77.

[Sec. 6215(b)]

(b) CROSS REFERENCES.—

(1) For assessment or collection of the amount of the deficiency determined by the Tax Court pending appellate court review, see section 7485.

(2) For dismissal of petition by Tax Court as affirmation of deficiency as determined by the Secretary, see section 7459(d).

(3) For decision of Tax Court that tax is barred by limitation as its decision that there is no deficiency, see section 7459(e).

(4) For assessment of damages awarded by Tax Court for instituting proceedings merely for delay, see section 6673.

(5) For rules applicable to Tax Court proceedings, see generally subchapter C of chapter 76.

(6) For extension of time for paying amount determined as deficiency, see section 6161(b).

Amendments

• **2018, Tax Technical Corrections Act of 2018 (P.L. 115-141)**

P.L. 115-141, §401(b)(46), Div. U:

Amended Code Sec. 6215(b) by striking paragraph (5) and by redesignating paragraphs (6) and (7) as paragraphs (5) and (6), respectively. **Effective** 3-23-2018. For a special rule, see Act Sec. 401(e), Div. U, below. Prior to being stricken, Code Sec. 6215(b)(5) read as follows:

(5) For treatment of certain deficiencies as having been paid, in connection with sale of surplus war-built vessels, see section 9(b)(8) of the Merchant Ship Sales Act of 1946 (50 U.S.C. App. 1742).

P.L. 115-141, §401(e), Div. U, provides:

(e) GENERAL SAVINGS PROVISION WITH RESPECT TO DEADWOOD PROVISIONS.—If—

(1) any provision amended or repealed by the amendments made by subsection (b) or (d) applied to—

(A) any transaction occurring before the date of the enactment of this Act,

(B) any property acquired before such date of enactment, or

(C) any item of income, loss, deduction, or credit taken into account before such date of enactment, and

(2) the treatment of such transaction, property, or item under such provision would (without regard to the amendments or repeals made by such subsection) affect the liability for tax for periods ending after such date of enactment,

nothing in the amendments or repeals made by this section shall be construed to affect the treatment of such transaction, property, or item for purposes of determining liability for tax for periods ending after such date of enactment.

• **1986, Tax Reform Act of 1986 (P.L. 99-514)**

P.L. 99-514, §1404(c)(2):

Amended Code Sec. 6215(b) by striking out paragraph (7) and redesignating paragraph (8) as paragraph (7). **Effective** for tax years beginning after 12-31-86. Prior to amendment, Code Sec. 6215(b)(7) read as follows:

(7) For proration of deficiency to installments, see section 6152(c).

• **1976, Tax Reform Act of 1976 (P.L. 94-455)**

P.L. 94-455, §1906(a)(16):

Struck out "60 Stat. 48;" before "50 U.S.C. App. 1742" in Code Sec. 6215(b)(5). **Effective** 2-1-77.

[Sec. 6216]

SEC. 6216. CROSS REFERENCES.

(1) For procedures relating to receivership proceedings, see subchapter B of chapter 70.

(2) For procedures relating to jeopardy assessments, see subchapter A of chapter 70.

(3) For procedures relating to claims against transferees and fiduciaries, see chapter 71.

(4) For procedures relating to partnership items, see subchapter C.

Amendments

• **1982, Tax Equity and Fiscal Responsibility Act of 1982 (P.L. 97-248)**

P.L. 97-248, §402(c)(3):

Added paragraph (4). **Effective** for partnership tax years beginning after 9-3-82.

• **1980, Bankruptcy Tax Act of 1980 (P.L. 96-589)**

P.L. 96-589, §6(i)(9):

Amended paragraph (1) of Code Sec. 6216. **Effective** 10-1-79 but inapplicable to any proceeding under the Bankruptcy Act commenced before that date. Prior to amendment, paragraph (1) provided:

(1) For procedures relating to bankruptcy and receivership, see subchapter B of chapter 70.

Subchapter C—Treatment of Partnerships

Part I.	In General.
Part II.	Partnership Adjustments
Part III.	Procedure.
Part IV.	Definitions and Special Rules.

PART I—IN GENERAL

Sec. 6221.	Determination at partnership level.
Sec. 6222.	Partner's return must be consistent with partnership return.
Sec. 6223.	Designation of partnership representative. [sic]

SEC. 6221. DETERMINATION AT PARTNERSHIP LEVEL.

[Sec. 6221(a)]

(a) IN GENERAL.—Any adjustment to a partnership-related item shall be determined, and any tax attributable thereto shall be assessed and collected, and the applicability of any penalty, addition to tax, or additional amount which relates to an adjustment to any such item shall be determined, at the partnership level, except to the extent otherwise provided in this subchapter.

Amendments

• **2018, Tax Technical Corrections Act of 2018 (P.L. 115-141)**

P.L. 115-141, §201(c)(2), Div. U:

Amended Code Sec. 6221(a). **Effective** as if included in section 1101 of the Bipartisan Budget Act of 2015 [effective generally for returns filed for partnership tax years beginning after 12-31-2017.—CCH]. Prior to amendment, Code Sec. 6221(a) read as follows:

(a) IN GENERAL.—Any adjustment to items of income, gain, loss, deduction, or credit of a partnership for a partnership taxable year (and any partner's distributive share thereof) shall be determined, any tax attributable thereto shall be assessed and collected, and the applicability of any penalty, addition to tax, or additional amount which relates to an adjustment to any such item or share shall be determined, at the partnership level pursuant to this subchapter.

[Sec. 6221(b)]

(b) ELECTION OUT FOR CERTAIN PARTNERSHIPS WITH 100 OR FEWER PARTNERS, ETC.—

(1) IN GENERAL.—This subchapter shall not apply with respect to any partnership for any taxable year if—

ASSESSMENT—TREATMENT OF PARTNERSHIPS

(A) the partnership elects the application of this subsection for such taxable year,

(B) for such taxable year the partnership is required to furnish 100 or fewer statements under section 6031(b) with respect to its partners,

(C) each of the partners of such partnership is an individual, a C corporation, any foreign entity that would be treated as a C corporation were it domestic, an S corporation, or an estate of a deceased partner,

(D) the election—

(i) is made with a timely filed return for such taxable year, and

(ii) includes (in the manner prescribed by the Secretary) a disclosure of the name and taxpayer identification number of each partner of such partnership, and

(E) the partnership notifies each such partner of such election in the manner prescribed by the Secretary.

(2) SPECIAL RULES RELATING TO CERTAIN PARTNERS.—

(A) S CORPORATION PARTNERS.—In the case of a partner that is an S corporation—

(i) the partnership shall only be treated as meeting the requirements of paragraph (1)(C) with respect to such partner if such partnership includes (in the manner prescribed by the Secretary) a disclosure of the name and taxpayer identification number of each person with respect to whom such S corporation is required to furnish a statement under section 6037(b) for the taxable year of the S corporation ending with or within the partnership taxable year for which the application of this subsection is elected, and

(ii) the statements such S corporation is required to so furnish shall be treated as statements furnished by the partnership for purposes of paragraph (1)(B).

(B) FOREIGN PARTNERS.—For purposes of paragraph (1)(D)(ii), the Secretary may provide for alternative identification of any foreign partners.

(C) OTHER PARTNERS.—The Secretary may by regulation or other guidance prescribe rules similar to the rules of subparagraph (A) with respect to any partners not described in such subparagraph or paragraph (1)(C).

Amendments

• **2015, Bipartisan Budget Act of 2015 (P.L. 114-74)**

P.L. 114-74, §1101(c)(1):

Amended chapter 63, as amended by this Act, by inserting after subchapter B a new subchapter C (Code Secs. 6221-6241). **Effective** generally for returns filed for partnership tax years beginning after 12-31-2017. For a special rule, see Act Sec. 1101(g)(4), below.

P.L. 114-74, §1101(g)(4), provides:

(4) ELECTION.—A partnership may elect (at such time and in such form and manner as the Secretary of the Treasury may prescribe) for the amendments made by this section (other than the election under section 6221(b) of such Code (as added by this Act)) to apply to any return of the partnership filed for partnership taxable years beginning after the date of the enactment of this Act and before January 1, 2018.

SEC. 6222. PARTNER'S RETURN MUST BE CONSISTENT WITH PARTNERSHIP RETURN.

[Sec. 6222(a)]

(a) IN GENERAL.—A partner shall, on the partner's return, treat any partnership-related item in a manner which is consistent with the treatment of such item on the partnership return.

Amendments

• **2018, Tax Technical Corrections Act of 2018 (P.L. 115-141)**

P.L. 115-141, §201(c)(3), Div. U:

Amended Code Sec. 6222(a). **Effective** as if included in section 1101 of the Bipartisan Budget Act of 2015 [**effective** generally for returns filed for partnership tax years beginning after 12-31-2017.—CCH]. Prior to amendment, Code Sec. 6222(a) read as follows:

(a) IN GENERAL.—A partner shall, on the partner's return, treat each item of income, gain, loss, deduction, or credit attributable to a partnership in a manner which is consistent with the treatment of such income, gain, loss, deduction, or credit on the partnership return.

[Sec. 6222(b)]

(b) UNDERPAYMENT DUE TO INCONSISTENT TREATMENT ASSESSED AS MATH ERROR.—Any underpayment of tax by a partner by reason of failing to comply with the requirements of subsection (a) shall be assessed and collected in the same manner as if such underpayment were on account of a mathematical or clerical error appearing on the partner's return. Paragraph (2) of section 6213(b) shall not apply to any assessment of an underpayment referred to in the preceding sentence.

[Sec. 6222(c)]

(c) EXCEPTION FOR NOTIFICATION OF INCONSISTENT TREATMENT.—

(1) IN GENERAL.—In the case of any item referred to in subsection (a), if—

(A)(i) the partnership has filed a return but the partner's treatment on the partner's return is (or may be) inconsistent with the treatment of the item on the partnership return, or

(ii) the partnership has not filed a return, and

(B) the partner files with the Secretary a statement identifying the inconsistency,

subsections (a) and (b) shall not apply to such item.

(2) PARTNER RECEIVING INCORRECT INFORMATION.—A partner shall be treated as having complied with subparagraph (B) of paragraph (1) with respect to an item if the partner—

(A) demonstrates to the satisfaction of the Secretary that the treatment of the item on the partner's return is consistent with the treatment of the item on the statement furnished to the partner by the partnership, and

(B) elects to have this paragraph apply with respect to that item.

[Sec. 6222(d)]

(d) FINAL DECISION ON CERTAIN POSITIONS NOT BINDING ON PARTNERSHIP.—Any final decision with respect to an inconsistent position identified under subsection (c) in a proceeding to which the partnership is not a party shall not be binding on the partnership.

[Sec. 6222(e)]

(e) ADDITION TO TAX FOR FAILURE TO COMPLY WITH SECTION.—For addition to tax in the case of a partner's disregard of the requirements of this section, see part II of subchapter A of chapter 68.

Amendments

• **2015, Bipartisan Budget Act of 2015 (P.L. 114-74)**

P.L. 114-74, §1101(c)(1):

Amended chapter 63, as amended by this Act, by inserting after subchapter B a new subchapter C (Code Secs. 6221-6241). **Effective** generally for returns filed for partnership tax years beginning after 12-31-2017. For a special rule, see Act Sec. 1101(g)(4), below.

P.L. 114-74, §1101(g)(4), provides:

(4) ELECTION.—A partnership may elect (at such time and in such form and manner as the Secretary of the Treasury may prescribe) for the amendments made by this

ASSESSMENT—TREATMENT OF PARTNERSHIPS

section (other than the election under section 6221(b) of such Code (as added by this Act)) to apply to any return of the partnership filed for partnership taxable years beginning after the date of the enactment of this Act and before January 1, 2018.

SEC. 6223. PARTNERS BOUND BY ACTIONS OF PARTNERSHIP.

[Sec. 6223(a)]

(a) DESIGNATION OF PARTNERSHIP REPRESENTATIVE.—Each partnership shall designate (in the manner prescribed by the Secretary) a partner (or other person) with a substantial presence in the United States as the partnership representative who shall have the sole authority to act on behalf of the partnership under this subchapter. In any case in which such a designation is not in effect, the Secretary may select any person as the partnership representative.

[Sec. 6223(b)]

(b) BINDING EFFECT.—A partnership and all partners of such partnership shall be bound—
  (1) by actions taken under this subchapter by the partnership, and
  (2) by any final decision in a proceeding brought under this subchapter with respect to the partnership.

Amendments

• 2015, Bipartisan Budget Act of 2015 (P.L. 114-74)

P.L. 114-74, §1101(c)(1):

Amended chapter 63, as amended by this Act, by inserting after subchapter B a new subchapter C (Code Secs. 6221-6241). **Effective** generally for returns filed for partnership tax years beginning after 12-31-2017. For a special rule, see Act Sec. 1101(g)(4), below.

P.L. 114-74, §1101(g)(4), provides:

(4) ELECTION.—A partnership may elect (at such time and in such form and manner as the Secretary of the Treasury may prescribe) for the amendments made by this section (other than the election under section 6221(b) of such Code (as added by this Act)) to apply to any return of the partnership filed for partnership taxable years beginning after the date of the enactment of this Act and before January 1, 2018.

PART II—PARTNERSHIP ADJUSTMENTS

Sec. 6225. Partnership adjustment by Secretary.
Sec. 6226. Alternative to payment of imputed underpayment by partnership.
Sec. 6227. Administrative adjustment request by partnership.

SEC. 6225. PARTNERSHIP ADJUSTMENT BY SECRETARY.

[Sec. 6225(a)]

(a) IN GENERAL.—In the case of any adjustments by the Secretary to any partnership-related items with respect to any reviewed year of a partnership—
  (1) if such adjustments result in an imputed underpayment, the partnership shall pay an amount equal to such imputed underpayment in the adjustment year as provided in section 6232, and
  (2) if such adjustments do not result in an imputed underpayment, such adjustments shall be taken into account by the partnership in the adjustment year.

Amendments

• 2018, Tax Technical Corrections Act of 2018 (P.L. 115-141)

P.L. 115-141, §202(c)(1), Div. U:

Amended Code Sec. 6225(a). **Effective** as if included in section 1101 of the Bipartisan Budget Act of 2015 [effective generally for returns filed for partnership tax years beginning after 12-31-2017.—CCH]. Prior to amendment, Code Sec. 6225(a) read as follows:

(a) IN GENERAL.—In the case of any adjustment by the Secretary in the amount of any item of income, gain, loss, deduction, or credit of a partnership, or any partner's distributive share thereof—

(1) the partnership shall pay any imputed underpayment with respect to such adjustment in the adjustment year as provided in section 6232, and

(2) any adjustment that does not result in an imputed underpayment shall be taken into account by the partnership in the adjustment year—

(A) except as provided in subparagraph (B), as a reduction in non-separately stated income or an increase in non-separately stated loss (whichever is appropriate) under section 702(a)(8), or

(B) in the case of an item of credit, as a separately stated item.

[Sec. 6225(b)]

(b) DETERMINATION OF IMPUTED UNDERPAYMENTS.—For purposes of this subchapter—
  (1) IN GENERAL.—Except as otherwise provided in this section, any imputed underpayment with respect to any reviewed year shall be determined by the Secretary by—
    (A) appropriately netting all partnership adjustments with respect to such reviewed year, and
    (B) applying the highest rate of tax in effect for the reviewed year under section 1 or 11.
  (2) ADJUSTMENTS TO DISTRIBUTIVE SHARES OF PARTNERS NOT NETTED.—In the case of any adjustment which reallocates the distributive share of any item from one partner to another, such adjustment shall be taken into account by disregarding so much of such adjustment as results in a decrease in the amount of the imputed underpayment.
  (3) ADJUSTMENTS SEPARATELY NETTED BY CATEGORY.—For purposes of paragraph (1)(A), partnership adjustments for any reviewed year shall first be separately determined (and netted as appropriate) within each category of items that are required to be taken into account separately under section 702(a) or other provision of this title.
  (4) LIMITATION ON ADJUSTMENTS THAT MAY BE TAKEN INTO ACCOUNT.—If any adjustment would (but for this paragraph)—
    (A) result in a decrease in the amount of the imputed underpayment, and
    (B) could be subject to any additional limitation under the provisions of this title (or not allowed, in whole or in part, against ordinary income) if such adjustment were taken into account by any person,
such adjustment shall not be taken into account under paragraph (1)(A) except to the extent otherwise provided by the Secretary.

Amendments

• 2018, Tax Technical Corrections Act of 2018 (P.L. 115-141)

P.L. 115-141, §202(a), Div. U:

Amended Code Sec. 6225(b). **Effective** as if included in section 1101 of the Bipartisan Budget Act of 2015 [effective generally for returns filed for partnership tax years beginning after 12-31-2017.—CCH]. Prior to amendment, Code Sec. 6225(b) read as follows:

(b) DETERMINATION OF IMPUTED UNDERPAYMENTS.—For purposes of this subchapter—

(1) IN GENERAL.—Except as provided in subsection (c), any imputed underpayment with respect to any partnership adjustment for any reviewed year shall be determined—

(A) by netting all adjustments of items of income, gain, loss, or deduction and multiplying such net amount by the highest rate of tax in effect for the reviewed year under section 1 or 11,

(B) by treating any net increase or decrease in loss under subparagraph (A) as a decrease or increase, respectively, in income, and

(C) by taking into account any adjustments to items of credit as an increase or decrease, as the case may be, in the amount determined under subparagraph (A).

(2) ADJUSTMENTS TO DISTRIBUTIVE SHARES OF PARTNERS NOT NETTED.—In the case of any adjustment which reallocates the distributive share of any item from one partner to another, such adjustment shall be taken into account under paragraph (1) by disregarding—

ASSESSMENT—TREATMENT OF PARTNERSHIPS

(A) any decrease in any item of income or gain, and

(B) any increase in any item of deduction, loss, or credit.

[Sec. 6225(c)]

(c) MODIFICATION OF IMPUTED UNDERPAYMENTS.—

(1) IN GENERAL.—The Secretary shall establish procedures under which the imputed underpayment amount may be modified consistent with the requirements of this subsection.

(2) PROCEDURES FOR PARTNERS TO TAKE ADJUSTMENTS INTO ACCOUNT.—

(A) AMENDED RETURNS OF PARTNERS.—Such procedures shall provide that if—

(i) one or more partners file returns for the taxable year of the partners which includes the end of the reviewed year of the partnership (and for any taxable year with respect to which any tax attribute is affected by reason of any adjustment referred to in clause (ii)),

(ii) such returns take into account all adjustments under subsection (a) properly allocable to such partners (and the effect of such adjustments on any tax attributes), and

(iii) payment of any tax due is included with such returns,

then the imputed underpayment amount shall be determined without regard to the portion of the adjustments so taken into account.

(B) ALTERNATIVE PROCEDURE TO FILING AMENDED RETURNS.—Such procedures shall provide that, with respect to any partner referred to in subparagraph (A), the requirements of subparagraph (A) shall be treated as satisfied with respect to adjustments properly allocable to such partner if, in lieu of filing the returns described in such subparagraph—

(i) the amounts described in subparagraph (A)(iii) are paid by the partner,

(ii) the partner agrees to take into account, in the form and manner prescribed by the Secretary, the adjustments to the tax attributes of such partner referred to in subparagraph (A)(ii), and

(iii) such partner provides, in the form and manner specified by the Secretary (including, if the Secretary so specifies, in the same form as on an amended return), such information as the Secretary may require to carry out this subparagraph.

(C) REALLOCATION OF DISTRIBUTIVE SHARE.—In the case of any adjustment which reallocates the distributive share of any item from one partner to another, this paragraph shall apply with respect to any such partner only if the requirements of subparagraph (A) or (B) are satisfied with respect to all partners affected by such adjustment.

(D) APPLICATION OF STATUTE OF LIMITATIONS.—In the case of adjustments referred to in subparagraph (A)(ii), sections 6501 and 6511 shall not apply with respect to any return filed for purposes of subparagraph (A)(i) or any amount paid under subparagraph (A)(iii) or (B)(i).

(E) ADJUSTMENTS TO TAX ATTRIBUTES BINDING FOR AFFECTED TAXABLE YEARS OF PARTNER.—The adjustments to the tax attributes of any partner provided for in subparagraph (A)(ii) or (B)(ii) shall be binding with respect to the taxable year of the partner which includes the end of the reviewed year of the partnership and any taxable years for which any tax attribute is affected by such adjustment. Any failure to so treat any such tax attribute shall be treated for purposes of this title in the same manner as a failure to treat a partnership-related item in a manner which is consistent with the treatment of such item on the partnership return within the meaning of section 6222.

(F) APPLICATION TO PARTNERSHIPS AND S CORPORATIONS IN TIERED STRUCTURES.—

(i) IN GENERAL.—In the case of any partnership any partner of which is a partnership, subparagraph (A) or (B) may apply with respect to any partner (hereafter in this subparagraph referred to as the "relevant partner") in the chain of ownership of such partnerships if—

(I) such information as the Secretary may require is furnished to the Secretary for purposes of carrying out this paragraph with respect to such partnerships (including any information the Secretary may require with respect to any chain of ownership of the relevant partner), and

(II) to such extent as the Secretary may require, each partnership in the chain of ownership between the relevant partner and the audited partnership satisfies the requirements of subparagraph (A) or (B).

(ii) TREATMENT OF S CORPORATIONS.—For purposes of clause (i), an S corporation and its shareholders shall be treated in the same manner as a partnership and its partners.

(F)[(G)] ADJUSTMENTS NOT TREATED AS AMENDED RETURN.—An administrative adjustment request under section 6227 and a partnership adjustment tracking report under section 6226(b)(4)(A) shall not be treated as a return for purposes of this paragraph.

(3) TAX-EXEMPT PARTNERS.—Such procedures shall provide for determining the imputed underpayment without regard to the portion of the adjustment that the partnership demonstrates is allocable to a partner that would not owe tax by reason of its status as a tax-exempt entity (as defined in section 168(h)(2)).

(4) MODIFICATION OF APPLICABLE HIGHEST TAX RATES.—

(A) IN GENERAL.—Such procedures shall provide for taking into account a rate of tax lower than the rate of tax described in subsection (b)(1)(A) with respect to any portion of the adjustment that the partnership demonstrates is allocable to a partner which—

(i) is a C corporation, or

(ii) in the case of a capital gain or qualified dividend, is an individual.

In no event shall the lower rate determined under the preceding sentence be less than the highest rate in effect with respect to the income and taxpayer described in clause (i) or clause (ii), as the case may be. For purposes of clause (ii), an S corporation shall be treated as an individual.

(B) PORTION OF IMPUTED UNDERPAYMENT TO WHICH LOWER RATE APPLIES.—

(i) IN GENERAL.—Except as provided in clause (ii), the portion of the imputed underpayment to which the lower rate applies with respect to a partner under subparagraph (A) shall be determined by reference to the partners' distributive share of items to which the imputed underpayment relates.

(ii) RULE IN CASE OF VARIED TREATMENT OF ITEMS AMONG PARTNERS.—If the imputed underpayment is attributable to the adjustment of more than 1 item, and any partner's distributive share of such items is not the same with respect to all such items, then the portion of the imputed underpayment to which the lower rate applies with respect to a partner under subparagraph (A) shall be determined by reference to the amount which would have been the partner's distributive share of net gain or loss if the partnership had sold all of its assets at their fair market value as of the close of the reviewed year of the partnership.

(5) CERTAIN PASSIVE LOSSES OF PUBLICLY TRADED PARTNERSHIPS.—

(A) IN GENERAL.—In the case of a publicly traded partnership (as defined in section 469(k)(2)), such procedures shall provide—

(i) for determining the imputed underpayment without regard to the portion of the adjustment that the partnership demonstrates is attributable to a net decrease in a specified passive activity loss which is allocable to a specified partner, and

(ii) for the partnership to take such net decrease into account as an adjustment in the adjustment year with respect to the specified partners to which such net decrease relates.

ASSESSMENT—TREATMENT OF PARTNERSHIPS

(B) SPECIFIED PASSIVE ACTIVITY LOSS.—For purposes of this paragraph, the term "specified passive activity loss" means, with respect to any specified partner of such publicly traded partnership, the lesser of—

(i) the passive activity loss of such partner which is separately determined with respect to such partnership under section 469(k) with respect to such partner's taxable year in which or with which the reviewed year of such partnership ends, or

(ii) such passive activity loss so determined with respect to such partner's taxable year in which or with which the adjustment year of such partnership ends.

(C) SPECIFIED PARTNER.—For purposes of this paragraph, the term "specified partner" means any person if such person—

(i) is a partner of the publicly traded partnership referred to in subparagraph (A),

(ii) is described in section 469(a)(2), and

(iii) has a specified passive activity loss with respect to such publicly traded partnership,

with respect to each taxable year of such person which is during the period beginning with the taxable year of such person in which or with which the reviewed year of such publicly traded partnership ends and ending with the taxable year of such person in which or with which the adjustment year of such publicly traded partnership ends.

(6) OTHER PROCEDURES FOR MODIFICATION OF IMPUTED UNDERPAYMENT.—The Secretary may by regulations or guidance provide for additional procedures to modify imputed underpayment amounts on the basis of such other factors as the Secretary determines are necessary or appropriate to carry out the purposes of this subsection.

(7) YEAR AND DAY FOR SUBMISSION TO SECRETARY.—Anything required to be filed or submitted under this subsection shall be submitted to the Secretary not later than the close of the 270-day period beginning on the date on which the notice of a proposed partnership adjustment is mailed under section 6231 unless such period is extended with the consent of the Secretary.

(8) DECISION OF SECRETARY.—Any modification of the imputed underpayment amount under this subsection shall be made only upon approval of such modification by the Secretary.

(9) MODIFICATION OF ADJUSTMENTS NOT RESULTING IN AN IMPUTED UNDERPAYMENT.—The Secretary shall establish procedures under which the adjustments described in subsection (a)(2) may be modified in such manner as the Secretary determines appropriate.

Amendments

• **2018, Tax Technical Corrections Act of 2018 (P.L. 115-141)**

P.L. 115-141, §202(b)(1), Div. U:

Amended Code Sec. 6225(c)(3) by striking "without regard to the portion thereof" and inserting "without regard to the portion of the adjustment". **Effective** as if included in section 1101 of the Bipartisan Budget Act of 2015 [**effective** generally for returns filed for partnership tax years beginning after 12-31-2017.—CCH].

P.L. 115-141, §202(b)(2), Div. U:

Amended Code Sec. 6225(c)(4)(A) by striking "with respect to any portion of the imputed underpayment" and inserting "with respect to any portion of the adjustment". **Effective** as if included in section 1101 of the Bipartisan Budget Act of 2015 [**effective** generally for returns filed for partnership tax years beginning after 12-31-2017.—CCH].

P.L. 115-141, §202(b)(3), Div. U:

Amended Code Sec. 6225(c)(5)(A)(i) by striking "without regard to the portion thereof" and inserting "without regard to the portion of the adjustment". **Effective** as if included in section 1101 of the Bipartisan Budget Act of 2015 [**effective** generally for returns filed for partnership tax years beginning after 12-31-2017.—CCH].

P.L. 115-141, §202(c)(2), Div. U:

Amended Code Sec. 6225(c) by adding at the end a new paragraph (9). **Effective** as if included in section 1101 of the Bipartisan Budget Act of 2015 [**effective** generally for returns filed for partnership tax years beginning after 12-31-2017.—CCH].

P.L. 115-141, §203(a), Div. U:

Amended Code Sec. 6225(c)(2). **Effective** as if included in section 1101 of the Bipartisan Budget Act of 2015 [**effective** generally for returns filed for partnership tax years beginning after 12-31-2017.—CCH]. Prior to amendment, Code Sec. 6225(c)(2) read as follows:

(2) AMENDED RETURNS OF PARTNERS.—

(A) IN GENERAL.—Such procedures shall provide that if—

(i) one or more partners file returns (notwithstanding section 6511) for the taxable year of the partners which includes the end of the reviewed year of the partnership,

(ii) such returns take into account all adjustments under subsection (a) properly allocable to such partners (and for any other taxable year with respect to which any tax attribute is affected by reason of such adjustments), and

(iii) payment of any tax due is included with such return,

then the imputed underpayment amount shall be determined without regard to the portion of the adjustments so taken into account.

(B) REALLOCATION OF DISTRIBUTIVE SHARE.—In the case of any adjustment which reallocates the distributive share of any item from one partner to another, paragraph (2) shall apply only if returns are filed by all partners affected by such adjustment.

P.L. 115-141, §206(b), Div. U:

Amended Code Sec. 6225(c)(2), as amended by the preceding provisions of this Act, by adding a new subparagraph (F)[(G)]. **Effective** as if included in section 1101 of the Bipartisan Budget Act of 2015 [**effective** generally for returns filed for partnership tax years beginning after 12-31-2017.—CCH].

P.L. 115-141, §206(p)(1), Div. U:

Amended Code Sec. 6225(c)(7) by striking "submitted pursuant to paragraph (1)" and inserting "filed or submitted under this subsection". **Effective** as if included in section 1101 of the Bipartisan Budget Act of 2015 [**effective** generally for returns filed for partnership tax years beginning after 12-31-2017.—CCH].

• **2015, Protecting Americans from Tax Hikes Act of 2015 (P.L. 114-113)**

P.L. 114-113, §411(a)(1), Div. Q:

Amended Code Sec. 6225(c)(4)(A)(i) by striking "in the case of ordinary income," before "is a C corporation". **Effective** as if included in section 1101 of the Bipartisan Budget Act of 2015 (P.L. 114-74) [**effective** generally for returns filed for partnership tax years beginning after 12-31-2017].

P.L. 114-113, §411(a)(2), Div. Q:

Amended Code Sec. 6225(c) by redesignating paragraphs (5)-(7) as paragraphs (6)-(8), respectively, and by inserting after paragraph (4) a new paragraph (5). **Effective** as if included in section 1101 of the Bipartisan Budget Act of 2015 (P.L. 114-74) [**effective** generally for returns filed for partnership tax years beginning after 12-31-2017].

[Sec. 6225(d)]

(d) DEFINITIONS.—For purposes of this subchapter—

(1) REVIEWED YEAR.—The term "reviewed year" means the partnership taxable year to which the item being adjusted relates.

(2) ADJUSTMENT YEAR.—The term "adjustment year" means the partnership taxable year in which—

(A) in the case of an adjustment pursuant to the decision of a court in a proceeding brought under section 6234, such decision becomes final,

(B) in the case of an administrative adjustment request under section 6227, such administrative adjustment request is made, or

(C) in any other case, notice of the final partnership adjustment is mailed under section 6231.

Amendments

• **2015, Bipartisan Budget Act of 2015 (P.L. 114-74)**

P.L. 114-74, §1101(c)(1):

Amended chapter 63, as amended by this Act, by inserting after subchapter B a new subchapter C (Code Secs. 6221-6241). **Effective** generally for returns filed for partnership tax years beginning after 12-31-2017. For a special rule, see Act Sec. 1101(g)(4), below.

P.L. 114-74, §1101(g)(4), provides:

(4) ELECTION.—A partnership may elect (at such time and in such form and manner as the Secretary of the Treasury may prescribe) for the amendments made by this section (other than the election under section 6221(b) of such Code (as added by this Act)) to apply to any return of the partnership filed for partnership taxable years beginning after the date of the enactment of this Act and before January 1, 2018.

SEC. 6226. ALTERNATIVE TO PAYMENT OF IMPUTED UNDERPAYMENT BY PARTNERSHIP.

[Sec. 6226(a)]

(a) IN GENERAL.—If the partnership—

(1) not later than 45 days after the date of the notice of final partnership adjustment, elects the application of this section with respect to an imputed underpayment, and

ASSESSMENT—TREATMENT OF PARTNERSHIPS

(2) at such time and in such manner as the Secretary may provide, furnishes to each partner of the partnership for the reviewed year and to the Secretary a statement of the partner's share of any adjustment to a partnership-related item (as determined in the notice of final partnership adjustment),

section 6225 shall not apply with respect to such underpayment (and no assessment of tax, levy, or proceeding in any court for the collection of such underpayment shall be made against such partnership) and each such partner shall take such adjustment into account as provided in subsection (b). The election under paragraph (1) shall be made in such manner as the Secretary may provide and, once made, shall be revocable only with the consent of the Secretary.

Amendments

• **2018, Tax Technical Corrections Act of 2018 (P.L. 115-141)**

P.L. 115-141, §201(c)(4), Div. U:

Amended Code Sec. 6226(a)(2) by striking "any adjustment to income, gain, loss, deduction, or credit" and inserting "any adjustment to a partnership-related item". **Effective** as if included in section 1101 of the Bipartisan Budget Act of 2015 [**effective** generally for returns filed for partnership tax years beginning after 12-31-2017.—CCH].

P.L. 115-141, §206(d), Div. U:

Amended Code Sec. 6226(a) by inserting "(and no assessment of tax, levy, or proceeding in any court for the collection of such underpayment shall be made against such partnership)" after "section 6225 shall not apply with respect to such underpayment". **Effective** as if included in section 1101 of the Bipartisan Budget Act of 2015 [**effective** generally for returns filed for partnership tax years beginning after 12-31-2017.—CCH].

[Sec. 6226(b)]

(b) ADJUSTMENTS TAKEN INTO ACCOUNT BY PARTNER.—

(1) TAX IMPOSED IN YEAR OF STATEMENT.—Except as provided in paragraph (4), each partner's tax imposed by chapter 1 for the taxable year which includes the date the statement was furnished under subsection (a) shall be adjusted by the aggregate of the correction amounts determined under paragraph (2) for the taxable years referred to therein.

(2) CORRECTION AMOUNTS.—The correction amounts determined under this paragraph are—

(A) in the case of the taxable year of the partner which includes the end of the reviewed year, the amount by which the tax imposed under chapter 1 would increase or decrease if the partner's share of the adjustments described in subsection (a) were taken into account for such taxable year, and

(B) in the case of any taxable year after the taxable year referred to in subparagraph (A) and before the taxable year referred to in paragraph (1), the amount by which the tax imposed under chapter 1 would increase or decrease by reason of the adjustment to tax attributes under paragraph (3).

(3) ADJUSTMENT OF TAX ATTRIBUTES.—Any tax attribute which would have been affected if the adjustments described in subsection (a) were taken into account for the taxable year referred to in paragraph (2)(A) shall—

(A) in the case of any taxable year referred to in paragraph (2)(B), be appropriately adjusted for purposes of applying such paragraph, and

(B) in the case of any subsequent taxable year, be appropriately adjusted.

(4) TREATMENT OF PARTNERSHIPS AND S CORPORATIONS IN TIERED STRUCTURES.—

(A) IN GENERAL.—If a partner which receives a statement under subsection (a)(2) is a partnership or an S corporation, such partner shall, with respect to the partner's share of the adjustment—

(i) file with the Secretary a partnership adjustment tracking report which includes such information as the Secretary may require, and

(ii)(I) furnish statements under rules similar to the rules of subsection (a)(2), or

(II) if no such statements are furnished, compute and pay an imputed underpayment under rules similar to the rules of section 6225 (other than paragraphs (2), (7), and (9) of subsection (c) thereof).

(B) DUE DATE.—For purposes of subparagraph (A), with respect to a partner's share of the adjustment, the partnership adjustment tracking report shall be filed, and the imputed underpayment shall be paid or statements shall be furnished, not later than the due date for the return for the adjustment year of the audited partnership.

(C) PARTNERSHIP PAYMENT OF TAX IF ELECTED OUT OF SUBCHAPTER.—In the case of a partnership which has elected the application of section 6221(b) with respect to the taxable year of the partnership which includes the end of the reviewed year of the audited partnership, this paragraph shall apply notwithstanding such election.

(D) AUDITED PARTNERSHIP.—For purposes of this paragraph, the term "audited partnership" means, with respect to any partner described in subparagraph (A), the partnership in the chain of ownership originally electing the application of this section.

(E) TREATMENT OF TRUSTS.—The Secretary shall prescribe such rules as may be necessary with respect to trusts which receive a statement under subsection (a)(2).

Amendments

• **2018, Tax Technical Corrections Act of 2018 (P.L. 115-141)**

P.L. 115-141, §204(a), Div. U:

Amended Code Sec. 6226(b) by adding at the end a new paragraph (4). **Effective** as if included in section 1101 of the Bipartisan Budget Act of 2015 [**effective** generally for returns filed for partnership tax years beginning after 12-31-2017.—CCH].

P.L. 115-141, §204(b)(1), Div. U:

Amended Code Sec. 6226(b)(1) by striking "Each partner's" and inserting "Except as provided in paragraph (4), each partner's". **Effective** as if included in section 1101 of the Bipartisan Budget Act of 2015 [**effective** generally for returns filed for partnership tax years beginning after 12-31-2017.—CCH].

P.L. 115-141, §206(e)(1)-(5), Div. U:

Amended Code Sec. 6226(b) by striking "increased" in paragraph (1) and inserting "adjusted", by striking "adjustment amounts" each place it appears in paragraphs (1) and (2) and inserting "correction amounts", by striking "increase" each place it appears in subparagraphs (A) and (B) of paragraph (2) and inserting "increase or decrease", by striking "plus" at the end of paragraph (2)(A) and inserting "and", and by striking "ADJUSTMENT AMOUNTS" in the heading of paragraph (2) and inserting "CORRECTION AMOUNTS". **Effective** as if included in section 1101 of the Bipartisan Budget Act of 2015 [**effective** generally for returns filed for partnership tax years beginning after 12-31-2017.—CCH].

[Sec. 6226(c)]

(c) PENALTIES AND INTEREST.—

(1) PENALTIES.—Notwithstanding subsections (a) and (b), any penalties, additions to tax, or additional amount shall be determined as provided under section 6221 and the partners of the partnership for the reviewed year shall be liable for any such penalty, addition to tax, or additional amount.

(2) INTEREST.—In the case of an imputed underpayment with respect to which the application of this section is elected, or which is described in subsection (b)(4)(A)(ii)(I), interest shall be determined—

(A) at the partner level,

(B) from the due date of the return for the taxable year to which the increase is attributable (determined by taking into account any increases attributable to a change in tax attributes for a taxable year under subsection (b)(2)), and

(C) at the underpayment rate under section 6621(a)(2), determined by substituting "5 percentage points" for "3 percentage points" in subparagraph (B) thereof.

ASSESSMENT—TREATMENT OF PARTNERSHIPS

Amendments

- **2018, Tax Technical Corrections Act of 2018 (P.L. 115-141)**

P.L. 115-141, §204(b)(2), Div. U:

Amended Code Sec. 6226(c)(2) by inserting "or which is described in subsection (b)(4)(A)(ii)(I)," after "is elected,". **Effective** as if included in section 1101 of the Bipartisan Budget Act of 2015 [**effective** generally for returns filed for partnership tax years beginning after 12-31-2017.—CCH].

- **2015, Bipartisan Budget Act of 2015 (P.L. 114-74)**

P.L. 114-74, §1101(c)(1):

Amended chapter 63, as amended by this Act, by inserting after subchapter B a new subchapter C (Code Secs. 6221-6241). **Effective** generally for elections with respect to returns filed for partnership tax years beginning after 12-31-2017. For a special rule, see Act Sec. 1101(g)(4), below.

P.L. 114-74, §1101(g)(4), provides:

(4) ELECTION.—A partnership may elect (at such time and in such form and manner as the Secretary of the Treasury may prescribe) for the amendments made by this section (other than the election under section 6221(b) of such Code (as added by this Act)) to apply to any return of the partnership filed for partnership taxable years beginning after the date of the enactment of this Act and before January 1, 2018.

[Sec. 6226(d)]

(d) JUDICIAL REVIEW.—For the time period within which a partnership may file a petition for a readjustment, see section 6234(a).

Amendments

- **2015, Protecting Americans from Tax Hikes Act of 2015 (P.L. 114-113)**

P.L. 114-113, §411(b)(1), Div. Q:

Amended Code Sec. 6226 by adding at the end a new subsection (d). **Effective** as if included in section 1101 of the Bipartisan Budget Act of 2015 (P.L. 114-74) [**effective** generally for elections with respect to returns filed for partnership tax years beginning after 12-31-2017].

SEC. 6227. ADMINISTRATIVE ADJUSTMENT REQUEST BY PARTNERSHIP.

[Sec. 6227(a)]

(a) IN GENERAL.—A partnership may file a request for an administrative adjustment in the amount of one or more partnership-related items for any partnership taxable year.

Amendments

- **2018, Tax Technical Corrections Act of 2018 (P.L. 115-141)**

P.L. 115-141, §201(c)(5), Div. U:

Amended Code Sec. 6227(a) by striking "items of income, gain, loss, deduction, or credit of the partnership" and inserting "partnership-related items". **Effective** as if included in section 1101 of the Bipartisan Budget Act of 2015 [**effective** generally for returns filed for partnership tax years beginning after 12-31-2017.—CCH].

[Sec. 6227(b)]

(b) ADJUSTMENT.—Any such adjustment under subsection (a) shall be determined and taken into account for the partnership taxable year in which the administrative adjustment request is filed—

(1) by the partnership under rules similar to the rules of section 6225 (other than paragraphs (2), (7), and (9) of subsection (c) thereof) for the partnership taxable year in which the administrative adjustment request is filed, or

(2) by the partnership and partners under rules similar to the rules of section 6226 (determined without regard to the substitution described in subsection (c)(2)(C) thereof).

In the case of an adjustment that would not result in an imputed underpayment, paragraph (1) shall not apply and paragraph (2) shall apply with appropriate adjustments.

Amendments

- **2018, Tax Technical Corrections Act of 2018 (P.L. 115-141)**

P.L. 115-141, §206(p)(2), Div. U:

Amended Code Sec. 6227(b) by striking "is made" both places it appears and inserting "is filed". **Effective** as if included in section 1101 of the Bipartisan Budget Act of 2015 [**effective** generally for returns filed for partnership tax years beginning after 12-31-2017.—CCH].

P.L. 115-141, §206(p)(3), Div. U:

Amended Code Sec. 6227(b)(1) by striking "paragraphs (2), (6), and (7)" and inserting "paragraphs (2), (7), and (9)". **Effective** as if included in section 1101 of the Bipartisan Budget Act of 2015 [**effective** generally for returns filed for partnership tax years beginning after 12-31-2017.—CCH].

[Sec. 6227(c)]

(c) PERIOD OF LIMITATIONS.—A partnership may not file such a request more than 3 years after the later of—

(1) the date on which the partnership return for such year is filed, or

(2) the last day for filing the partnership return for such year (determined without regard to extensions).

In no event may a partnership file such a request after a notice of an administrative proceeding with respect to the taxable year is mailed under section 6231.

Amendments

- **2015, Bipartisan Budget Act of 2015 (P.L. 114-74)**

P.L. 114-74, §1101(c)(1):

Amended chapter 63, as amended by this Act, by inserting after subchapter B a new subchapter C (Code Secs. 6221-6241). **Effective** generally for requests with respect to returns filed for partnership tax years beginning after 12-31-2017. For a special rule, see Act Sec. 1101(g)(4), below.

P.L. 114-74, §1101(g)(4), provides:

(4) ELECTION.—A partnership may elect (at such time and in such form and manner as the Secretary of the Treasury may prescribe) for the amendments made by this section (other than the election under section 6221(b) of such Code (as added by this Act)) to apply to any return of the partnership filed for partnership taxable years beginning after the date of the enactment of this Act and before January 1, 2018.

[Sec. 6227(d)]

(d) COORDINATION WITH ADJUSTMENTS RELATED TO FOREIGN TAX CREDITS.—The Secretary shall issue regulations or other guidance which provide for the proper coordination of this section and section 905(c).

Amendments

- **2018, Tax Technical Corrections Act of 2018 (P.L. 115-141)**

P.L. 115-141, §206(f), Div. U:

Amended Code Sec. 6227 by adding at the end a new subsection (d). **Effective** as if included in section 1101 of the Bipartisan Budget Act of 2015 [**effective** generally for returns filed for partnership tax years beginning after 12-31-2017.—CCH].

PART III—PROCEDURE

Sec. 6231.	Notice of proceedings and adjustment.
Sec. 6232.	Assessment, collection, and payment.
Sec. 6233.	Interest and penalties.
Sec. 6234.	Judicial review of partnership adjustment.
Sec. 6235.	Period of limitations on making adjustments.

ASSESSMENT—TREATMENT OF PARTNERSHIPS

SEC. 6231. NOTICE OF PROCEEDINGS AND ADJUSTMENT.

[Sec. 6231(a)]

(a) IN GENERAL.—The Secretary shall mail to the partnership and the partnership representative—

(1) notice of any administrative proceeding initiated at the partnership level with respect to an adjustment of any partnership-related item for any partnership taxable year, or any partner's distributive share thereof,

(2) notice of any proposed partnership adjustment resulting from such proceeding, and

(3) notice of any final partnership adjustment resulting from such proceeding.

Any notice of a final partnership adjustment shall be sufficient if mailed to the last known address of the partnership representative or the partnership (even if the partnership has terminated its existence). The first sentence shall apply to any proceeding with respect to an administrative adjustment request filed by a partnership under section 6227.

Amendments

• **2018, Tax Technical Corrections Act of 2018 (P.L. 115-141)**

P.L. 115-141, §201(c)(6), Div. U:

Amended Code Sec. 6231(a)(1) by striking "any item of income, gain, loss, deduction, or credit of a partnership for a partnership taxable year" and inserting "any partnership-related item for any partnership taxable year". **Effective** as if included in section 1101 of the Bipartisan Budget Act of 2015 [**effective** generally for returns filed for partnership tax years beginning after 12-31-2017.—CCH].

P.L. 115-141, §206(h)(2), Div. U:

Amended Code Sec. 6231(a) by striking "Any notice of a final partnership adjustment" and all that follows through "Such notices" [in the flush text] and inserting "Any notice of a final partnership adjustment". **Effective** as if included in section 1101 of the Bipartisan Budget Act of 2015 [**effective** generally for returns filed for partnership tax years beginning after 12-31-2017.—CCH]. Prior to amendment, the flush text of Code Sec. 6231(a) read as follows:

Any notice of a final partnership adjustment shall not be mailed earlier than 270 days after the date on which the notice of the proposed partnership adjustment is mailed. Such notices shall be sufficient if mailed to the last known address of the partnership representative or the partnership (even if the partnership has terminated its existence). The first sentence shall apply to any proceeding with respect to an administrative adjustment request filed by a partnership under section 6227.

[Sec. 6231(b)]

(b) TIMING OF NOTICES.—

(1) NOTICE OF PROPOSED PARTNERSHIP ADJUSTMENT.—Any notice of a proposed partnership adjustment shall not be mailed later than the date determined under section 6235 (determined without regard to paragraphs (2) and (3) of subsection (a) thereof).

(2) NOTICE OF FINAL PARTNERSHIP ADJUSTMENT.—

(A) IN GENERAL.—Except to the extent that the partnership elects to waive the application of this subparagraph, any notice of a final partnership adjustment shall not be mailed earlier than 270 days after the date on which the notice of the proposed partnership adjustment is mailed.

(B) STATUTE OF LIMITATIONS ON ADJUSTMENT.—For the period of limitations on making adjustments, see section 6235.

Amendments

• **2018, Tax Technical Corrections Act of 2018 (P.L. 115-141)**

P.L. 115-141, §206(h)(1), Div. U:

Amended Code Sec. 6231 by redesignating subsections (b) and (c) as subsections (c) and (d), respectively, and by inserting after subsection (a) a new subsection (b). **Effective** as if included in section 1101 of the Bipartisan Budget Act of 2015 [**effective** generally for returns filed for partnership tax years beginning after 12-31-2017.—CCH].

[Sec. 6231(c)]

(c) FURTHER NOTICES RESTRICTED.—If the Secretary mails a notice of a final partnership adjustment to any partnership for any partnership taxable year and the partnership files a petition under section 6234 with respect to such notice, in the absence of a showing of fraud, malfeasance, or misrepresentation of a material fact, the Secretary shall not mail another such notice to such partnership with respect to such taxable year.

Amendments

• **2018, Tax Technical Corrections Act of 2018 (P.L. 115-141)**

P.L. 115-141, §206(h)(1), Div. U:

Amended Code Sec. 6231 by redesignating subsection (b) as subsection (c). **Effective** as if included in section 1101 of the Bipartisan Budget Act of 2015 [**effective** generally for returns filed for partnership tax years beginning after 12-31-2017.—CCH].

[Sec. 6231(d)]

(d) AUTHORITY TO RESCIND NOTICE WITH PARTNERSHIP CONSENT.—The Secretary may, with the consent of the partnership, rescind any notice of a partnership adjustment mailed to such partnership. Any notice so rescinded shall not be treated as a notice of a partnership adjustment for purposes of this subchapter, and the taxpayer shall have no right to bring a proceeding under section 6234 with respect to such notice.

Amendments

• **2018, Tax Technical Corrections Act of 2018 (P.L. 115-141)**

P.L. 115-141, §206(h)(1), Div. U:

Amended Code Sec. 6231 by redesignating subsection (c) as subsection (d). **Effective** as if included in section 1101 of the Bipartisan Budget Act of 2015 [**effective** generally for returns filed for partnership tax years beginning after 12-31-2017.—CCH].

• **2015, Bipartisan Budget Act of 2015 (P.L. 114-74)**

P.L. 114-74, §1101(c)(1):

Amended chapter 63, as amended by this Act, by inserting after subchapter B a new subchapter C (Code Secs. 6221-6241). **Effective** generally for returns filed for partnership tax years beginning after 12-31-2017. For a special rule, see Act Sec. 1101(g)(4), below.

P.L. 114-74, §1101(g)(4), provides:

(4) ELECTION.—A partnership may elect (at such time and in such form and manner as the Secretary of the Treasury may prescribe) for the amendments made by this section (other than the election under section 6221(b) of such Code (as added by this Act)) to apply to any return of the partnership filed for partnership taxable years beginning after the date of the enactment of this Act and before January 1, 2018.

SEC. 6232. ASSESSMENT, COLLECTION, AND PAYMENT.

[Sec. 6232(a)]

(a) IN GENERAL.—Any imputed underpayment shall be assessed and collected in the same manner as if it were a tax imposed for the adjustment year by subtitle A, except that—

(1) subchapter B of chapter 63 shall not apply, and

(2) in the case of an administrative adjustment request to which section 6227(b)(1) applies, the underpayment shall be paid and may be assessed when the request is filed.

ASSESSMENT—TREATMENT OF PARTNERSHIPS

Amendments

• **2018, Tax Technical Corrections Act of 2018 (P.L. 115-141)**

P.L. 115-141, §206(g)(1), Div. U:

Amended Code Sec. 6232(a) by striking "except that in the case of" and all that follows and inserting "except that—"

and new subparagraphs (1) and (2). **Effective** as if included in section 1101 of the Bipartisan Budget Act of 2015 [**effective** generally for returns filed for partnership tax years beginning after 12-31-2017.—CCH]. Prior to being stricken, "except that in the case of" and all that follows in Code Sec. 6232(a) read as follows:

except that in the case of an administrative adjustment request to which section 6227(b)(1) applies, the underpayment shall be paid when the request is filed.

[Sec. 6232(b)]

(b) LIMITATION ON ASSESSMENT.—Except as otherwise provided in this subtitle (other than subchapter B of this chapter), no assessment of an imputed underpayment may be made (and no levy or proceeding in any court for the collection of any amount resulting from such adjustment may be made, begun or prosecuted) before—

(1) the close of the 90th day after the day on which a notice of a final partnership adjustment was mailed, and

(2) if a petition is filed under section 6234 with respect to such notice, the decision of the court has become final.

The preceding sentence shall not apply in the case of a specified similar amount (as defined in subsection (f)(2)).

Amendments

• **2018, Tax Technical Corrections Act of 2018 (P.L. 115-141)**

P.L. 115-141, §206(g)(2)(A)-(B), Div. U:

Amended Code Sec. 6232(b) by striking "assessment of a deficiency" and inserting "assessment of an imputed underpayment", and by adding at the end new flush matter. **Effective** as if included in section 1101 of the Bipartisan Budget Act of 2015 [**effective** generally for returns filed for partnership tax years beginning after 12-31-2017.—CCH].

P.L. 115-141, §206(p)(4), Div. U:

Amended Code Sec. 6232(b) by striking "this chapter" and inserting "this subtitle (other than subchapter B of this chapter)". **Effective** as if included in section 1101 of the Bipartisan Budget Act of 2015 [**effective** generally for returns filed for partnership tax years beginning after 12-31-2017.—CCH].

[Sec. 6232(c)]

(c) PREMATURE ACTION MAY BE ENJOINED.—Notwithstanding section 7421(a), any action which violates subsection (b) may be enjoined in the proper court, including the Tax Court. The Tax Court shall have no jurisdiction to enjoin any action under this subsection unless a timely petition has been filed under section 6234 and then only in respect of the adjustments that are the subject of such petition.

[Sec. 6232(d)]

(d) EXCEPTIONS TO RESTRICTIONS ON ADJUSTMENTS.—

(1) ADJUSTMENTS ARISING OUT OF MATH OR CLERICAL ERRORS.—

(A) IN GENERAL.—If the partnership is notified that, on account of a mathematical or clerical error appearing on the partnership return, an adjustment to an item is required, rules similar to the rules of paragraphs (1) and (2) of section 6213(b) shall apply to such adjustment.

(B) SPECIAL RULE.—If a partnership is a partner in another partnership, any adjustment on account of such partnership's failure to comply with the requirements of section 6222(a) with respect to its interest in such other partnership shall be treated as an adjustment referred to in subparagraph (A), except that paragraph (2) of section 6213(b) shall not apply to such adjustment.

(2) PARTNERSHIP MAY WAIVE RESTRICTIONS.—The partnership may at any time (whether or not any notice of partnership adjustment has been issued), by a signed notice in writing filed with the Secretary, waive the restrictions provided in subsection (b) on the making of any partnership adjustment.

Amendments

• **2018, Tax Technical Corrections Act of 2018 (P.L. 115-141)**

P.L. 115-141, §206(p)(5), Div. U:

Amended Code Sec. 6232(d)(1)(A) by striking "a item" and inserting "an item". **Effective** as if included in section 1101 of the Bipartisan Budget Act of 2015 [**effective** generally for returns filed for partnership tax years beginning after 12-31-2017.—CCH].

[Sec. 6232(e)]

(e) LIMIT WHERE NO PROCEEDING BEGUN.—If no proceeding under section 6234 is begun with respect to any notice of a final partnership adjustment during the 90-day period described in subsection (b), the amount for which the partnership is liable under section 6225 shall not exceed the amount determined in accordance with such notice.

Amendments

• **2018, Tax Technical Corrections Act of 2018 (P.L. 115-141)**

P.L. 115-141, §206(p)(6), Div. U:

Amended Code Sec. 6232(e) by striking "thereof" following "subsection (b)". **Effective** as if included in section 1101 of the Bipartisan Budget Act of 2015 [**effective** generally for returns filed for partnership tax years beginning after 12-31-2017.—CCH].

• **2015, Bipartisan Budget Act of 2015 (P.L. 114-74)**

P.L. 114-74, §1101(c)(1):

Amended chapter 63, as amended by this Act, by inserting after subchapter B a new subchapter C (Code Secs. 6221-6241). **Effective** generally for returns filed for partnership tax years beginning after 12-31-2017. For a special rule, see Act Sec. 1101(g)(4), below.

P.L. 114-74, §1101(g)(4), provides:

(4) ELECTION.—A partnership may elect (at such time and in such form and manner as the Secretary of the Treasury may prescribe) for the amendments made by this section (other than the election under section 6221(b) of such Code (as added by this Act)) to apply to any return of the partnership filed for partnership taxable years beginning after the date of the enactment of this Act and before January 1, 2018.

[Sec. 6232(f)]

(f) FAILURE TO PAY IMPUTED UNDERPAYMENT.—

(1) IN GENERAL.—If any amount of any imputed underpayment to which section 6225 applies or any specified similar amount (or any interest or penalties with respect to any such amount) has not been paid by the date which is 10 days after the date on which the Secretary provides notice and demand for such payment—

(A) section 6621(a)(2)(B) shall be applied by substituting "5 percentage points" for "3 percentage points" with respect to such amount, and

(B) the Secretary may assess upon each partner of the partnership (determined as of the close of the adjustment year or, if the partnership has ceased to exist as of such time, the former partners of the partnership as determined for purposes of section 6241(7)) a tax equal to such partner's proportionate share of such amount (including any such interest or penalties, determined after application of subparagraph (A)).

(2) SPECIFIED SIMILAR AMOUNT.—For purposes of this subsection, the term "specified similar amount" means—

(A) the amount described in subclause (II) of section 6226(b)(4)(A)(ii) (including any failure to satisfy the requirement of subclause (I) of such section which is treated as a failure to pay such amount under section 6651(i)), and

(B) any amount assessed under paragraph (1)(B) upon a partner which is a partnership.

ASSESSMENT—TREATMENT OF PARTNERSHIPS

(3) PROPORTIONATE SHARE.—For purposes of paragraph (1), a partner's proportionate share is such percentage as the Secretary may determine on the basis of such partner's distributive share. The Secretary shall make determinations under the preceding sentence such that the aggregate proportionate shares so determined total 100 percent.

(4) COORDINATION WITH PARTNERSHIP LIABILITY.—The liability of the partnership for any amount with respect to which a partner is made liable under paragraph (1) shall be reduced upon payment by the partner of such amount. Paragraph (1)(B) shall not apply with respect to any amount after the date on which such amount is paid by the partnership.

(5) S CORPORATIONS.—For purposes of this subsection, an S corporation and its shareholders shall be treated in the same manner as a partnership and its partners.

(6) RULES RELATED TO ASSESSMENT AND COLLECTION.—

   (A) DEFICIENCY PROCEDURES NOT APPLICABLE.—Subchapter B shall not apply to any assessment or collection under this paragraph.

   (B) LIMITATION ON ASSESSMENT.—Except as otherwise provided in this subtitle, no assessment may be made (or proceeding in court begun without assessment) with respect to any partner with respect to an amount under paragraph (1) after the date which is 2 years after the date on which the Secretary provides the notice and demand referred to in paragraph (1) with respect to such amount.

Amendments

- **2018, Tax Technical Corrections Act of 2018 (P.L. 115-141)**

P.L. 115-141, § 205(a), Div. U:

Amended Code Sec. 6232 by adding at the end a new subsection (f). **Effective** as if included in section 1101 of the Bipartisan Budget Act of 2015 [**effective** generally for returns filed for partnership tax years beginning after 12-31-2017.—CCH].

SEC. 6233. INTEREST AND PENALTIES.

[Sec. 6233(a)]

(a) INTEREST AND PENALTIES DETERMINED FROM REVIEWED YEAR.—

   (1) IN GENERAL.—Except to the extent provided in section 6226(c), in the case of a partnership adjustment for a reviewed year—

      (A) interest shall be computed under paragraph (2), and

      (B) the partnership shall be liable for any penalty, addition to tax, or additional amount as provided in paragraph (3).

   (2) DETERMINATION OF AMOUNT OF INTEREST.—The interest computed under this paragraph with respect to any partnership adjustment is the interest which would be determined under chapter 67 for the period beginning on the day after the return due date for the reviewed year and ending on the return due date for the adjustment year (or, if earlier, the date payment of the imputed underpayment is made). Proper adjustments in the amount determined under the preceding sentence shall be made for adjustments required for partnership taxable years after the reviewed year and before the adjustment year by reason of such partnership adjustment.

   (3) PENALTIES.—Any penalty, addition to tax, or additional amount shall be determined at the partnership level as if such partnership had been an individual subject to tax under chapter 1 for the reviewed year and the imputed underpayment were an actual underpayment (or understatement) for such year.

[Sec. 6233(b)]

(b) INTEREST AND PENALTIES WITH RESPECT TO ADJUSTMENT YEAR RETURN.—

   (1) IN GENERAL.—In the case of any failure to pay an imputed underpayment on the date prescribed therefor, the partnership shall be liable—

      (A) for interest as determined under paragraph (2), and

      (B) for any penalty, addition to tax, or additional amount as determined under paragraph (3).

   (2) INTEREST.—Interest determined under this paragraph is the interest that would be determined by treating the imputed underpayment as an underpayment of tax imposed in the adjustment year.

   (3) PENALTIES.—Penalties, additions to tax, or additional amounts determined under this paragraph are the penalties, additions to tax, or additional amounts that would be determined—

      (A) by applying section 6651(a)(2) to such failure to pay, and

      (B) by treating the imputed underpayment as an underpayment of tax for purposes of part II of subchapter A of chapter 68.

Amendments

- **2015, Bipartisan Budget Act of 2015 (P.L. 114-74)**

P.L. 114-74, § 1101(c)(1):

Amended chapter 63, as amended by this Act, by inserting after subchapter B a new subchapter C (Code Secs. 6221-6241). **Effective** generally for returns filed for partnership tax years beginning after 12-31-2017. For a special rule, see Act Sec. 1101(g)(4), below.

P.L. 114-74, § 1101(g)(4), provides:

(4) ELECTION.—A partnership may elect (at such time and in such form and manner as the Secretary of the Treasury may prescribe) for the amendments made by this section (other than the election under section 6221(b) of such Code (as added by this Act)) to apply to any return of the partnership filed for partnership taxable years beginning after the date of the enactment of this Act and before January 1, 2018.

[Sec. 6233(c)]

(c) DEPOSIT TO SUSPEND INTEREST.—For rules allowing deposits to suspend running of interest on potential underpayments, see section 6603.

Amendments

- **2018, Tax Technical Corrections Act of 2018 (P.L. 115-141)**

P.L. 115-141, § 206(i), Div. U:

Amended Code Sec. 6233 by adding at the end a new subsection (c). **Effective** as if included in section 1101 of the Bipartisan Budget Act of 2015 [**effective** generally for returns filed for partnership tax years beginning after 12-31-2017.—CCH].

SEC. 6234. JUDICIAL REVIEW OF PARTNERSHIP ADJUSTMENT.

[Sec. 6234(a)]

(a) IN GENERAL.—Within 90 days after the date on which a notice of a final partnership adjustment is mailed under section 6231 with respect to any partnership taxable year, the partnership may file a petition for a readjustment for such taxable year with—

   (1) the Tax Court,

   (2) the district court of the United States for the district in which the partnership's principal place of business is located, or

   (3) the Court of Federal Claims.

ASSESSMENT—TREATMENT OF PARTNERSHIPS

Amendments

• **2015, Protecting Americans from Tax Hikes Act of 2015 (P.L. 114-113)**

P.L. 114-113, §411(b)(2), Div. Q:

Amended Code Sec. 6234(a)(3) by striking "the Claims Court" and inserting "the Court of Federal Claims". **Effective** as if included in section 1101 of the Bipartisan Budget Act of 2015 (P.L. 114-74) [**effective** generally for returns filed for partnership tax years beginning after 12-31-2017].

[Sec. 6234(b)]

(b) JURISDICTIONAL REQUIREMENT FOR BRINGING ACTION IN DISTRICT COURT OR COURT OF FEDERAL CLAIMS.—

(1) IN GENERAL.—A readjustment petition under this section may be filed in a district court of the United States or the Court of Federal Claims only if the partnership filing the petition deposits with the Secretary, on or before the date the petition is filed, the amount of (as of the date of the filing of the petition) the imputed underpayment, penalties, additions to tax, and additional amounts with respect to such imputed underpayment if the partnership adjustment was made as provided by the notice of final partnership adjustment. The court may by order provide that the jurisdictional requirements of this paragraph are satisfied where there has been a good faith attempt to satisfy such requirement and any shortfall of the amount required to be deposited is timely corrected.

(2) INTEREST PAYABLE.—Any amount deposited under paragraph (1), while deposited, shall not be treated as a payment of tax for purposes of this title (other than chapter 67).

Amendments

• **2018, Tax Technical Corrections Act of 2018 (P.L. 115-141)**

P.L. 115-141, §206(j), Div. U:

Amended the first sentence of Code Sec. 6234(b) by striking "the amount of the imputed underpayment (as of the date of the filing of the petition)" and inserting "the amount of (as of the date of the filing of the petition) the imputed underpayment, penalties, additions to tax, and additional amounts with respect to such imputed underpayment". **Effective** as if included in section 1101 of the Bipartisan Budget Act of 2015 [**effective** generally for returns filed for partnership tax years beginning after 12-31-2017.—CCH].

• **2015, Protecting Americans from Tax Hikes Act of 2015 (P.L. 114-113)**

P.L. 114-113, §411(b)(2), Div. Q:

Amended Code Sec. 6234(b)(1) striking "the Claims Court" and inserting "the Court of Federal Claims". **Effective** as if included in section 1101 of the Bipartisan Budget Act of 2015 (P.L. 114-74) [**effective** generally for returns filed for partnership tax years beginning after 12-31-2017].

P.L. 114-113, §411(b)(3), Div. Q:

Amended the heading for Code Sec. 6234(b) by striking "CLAIMS COURT" and inserting "COURT OF FEDERAL CLAIMS". **Effective** as if included in section 1101 of the Bipartisan Budget Act of 2015 (P.L. 114-74) [**effective** generally for returns filed for partnership tax years beginning after 12-31-2017].

[Sec. 6234(c)]

(c) SCOPE OF JUDICIAL REVIEW.—A court with which a petition is filed in accordance with this section shall have jurisdiction to determine all partnership-related items for the partnership taxable year to which the notice of final partnership adjustment relates, the proper allocation of such items among the partners, and the applicability of any penalty, addition to tax, or additional amount for which the partnership may be liable under this subchapter.

Amendments

• **2018, Tax Technical Corrections Act of 2018 (P.L. 115-141)**

P.L. 115-141, §201(c)(7), Div. U:

Amended Code Sec. 6234(c) by striking "all items of income, gain, loss, deduction, or credit of the partnership" and inserting "all partnership-related items". **Effective** as if included in section 1101 of the Bipartisan Budget Act of 2015 [**effective** generally for returns filed for partnership tax years beginning after 12-31-2017.—CCH].

[Sec. 6234(d)]

(d) DETERMINATION OF COURT REVIEWABLE.—Any determination by a court under this section shall have the force and effect of a decision of the Tax Court or a final judgment or decree of the district court or the Court of Federal Claims, as the case may be, and shall be reviewable as such. The date of any such determination shall be treated as being the date of the court's order entering the decision.

Amendments

• **2015, Protecting Americans from Tax Hikes Act of 2015 (P.L. 114-113)**

P.L. 114-113, §411(b)(2), Div. Q:

Amended Code Sec. 6234(d) by striking "the Claims Court" and inserting "the Court of Federal Claims". **Effective** as if included in section 1101 of the Bipartisan Budget Act of 2015 (P.L. 114-74) [**effective** generally for returns filed for partnership tax years beginning after 12-31-2017].

[Sec. 6234(e)]

(e) EFFECT OF DECISION DISMISSING ACTION.—If an action brought under this section is dismissed other than by reason of a rescission under section 6231(c), the decision of the court dismissing the action shall be considered as its decision that the notice of final partnership adjustment is correct, and an appropriate order shall be entered in the records of the court.

Amendments

• **2015, Bipartisan Budget Act of 2015 (P.L. 114-74)**

P.L. 114-74, §1101(c)(1):

Amended chapter 63, as amended by this Act, by inserting after subchapter B a new subchapter C (Code Secs. 6221-6241). **Effective** generally for returns filed for partnership tax years beginning after 12-31-2017. For a special rule, see Act Sec. 1101(g)(4), below.

P.L. 114-74, §1101(g)(4), provides:

(4) ELECTION.—A partnership may elect (at such time and in such form and manner as the Secretary of the Treasury may prescribe) for the amendments made by this section (other than the election under section 6221(b) of such Code (as added by this Act)) to apply to any return of the partnership filed for partnership taxable years beginning after the date of the enactment of this Act and before January 1, 2018.

SEC. 6235. PERIOD OF LIMITATIONS ON MAKING ADJUSTMENTS.

[Sec. 6235(a)]

(a) IN GENERAL.—Except as otherwise provided in this section or section 905(c), no adjustment under this subchapter for any partnership taxable year may be made after the later of—

(1) the date which is 3 years after the latest of—

(A) the date on which the partnership return for such taxable year was filed,

(B) the return due date for the taxable year, or

(C) the date on which the partnership filed an administrative adjustment request with respect to such year under section 6227, or

(2) in the case of any modification of an imputed underpayment under section 6225(c), the date that is 270 days (plus the number of days of any extension consented to by the Secretary under paragraph (7) thereof) after the date on which everything required to be submitted to the Secretary pursuant to such section is so submitted, or

(3) in the case of any notice of a proposed partnership adjustment under section 6231(a)(2), the date that is 330 days (plus the number of days of any extension consented to by the Secretary under section 6225(c)(7)) after the date of such notice.

ASSESSMENT—TREATMENT OF PARTNERSHIPS

Amendments

• **2018, Tax Technical Corrections Act of 2018 (P.L. 115-141)**

P.L. 115-141, §206(k)(1)(A)-(B), Div. U:

Amended Code Sec. 6235(a) by inserting "or section 905(c)" after "Except as otherwise provided in this section", and by striking "subpart" and inserting "subchapter". **Effective** as if included in section 1101 of the Bipartisan Budget Act of 2015 [**effective** generally for returns filed for partnership tax years beginning after 12-31-2017.—CCH].

P.L. 115-141, §206(k)(2), Div. U:

Amended Code Sec. 6235(a)(3) by striking "section 6225(c)(7)" and inserting "section 6225(c)(7))". **Effective** as if included in section 1101 of the Bipartisan Budget Act of 2015 [**effective** generally for returns filed for partnership tax years beginning after 12-31-2017.—CCH].

• **2015, Protecting Americans from Tax Hikes Act of 2015 (P.L. 114-113)**

P.L. 114-113, §411(c)(1), Div. Q:

Amended Code Sec. 6235(a)(2) by striking "paragraph (4)" and inserting "paragraph (7)". **Effective** as if included in section 1101 of the Bipartisan Budget Act of 2015 (P.L. 114-74) [**effective** generally for returns filed for partnership tax years beginning after 12-31-2017].

P.L. 114-113, §411(c)(2), Div. Q:

Amended Code Sec. 6235(a)(3) by striking "270 days" and inserting "330 days (plus the number of days of any extension consented to by the Secretary under section 6225(c)(7))". **Effective** as if included in section 1101 of the Bipartisan Budget Act of 2015 (P.L. 114-74) [**effective** generally for returns filed for partnership tax years beginning after 12-31-2017].

[Sec. 6235(b)]

(b) EXTENSION BY AGREEMENT.—The period described in subsection (a) (including an extension period under this subsection) may be extended by an agreement entered into by the Secretary and the partnership before the expiration of such period.

[Sec. 6235(c)]

(c) SPECIAL RULE IN CASE OF FRAUD, ETC.—

(1) FALSE RETURN.—In the case of a false or fraudulent partnership return with intent to evade tax, the adjustment may be made at any time.

(2) SUBSTANTIAL OMISSION OF INCOME.—If any partnership omits from gross income an amount properly includible therein and such amount is described in subparagraph (A) or (C) of section 6501(e)(1), subsection (a) shall be applied by substituting "6 years" for "3 years".

(3) NO RETURN.—In the case of a failure by a partnership to file a return for any taxable year, the adjustment may be made at any time.

(4) RETURN FILED BY SECRETARY.—For purposes of this section, a return executed by the Secretary under subsection (b) of section 6020 on behalf of the partnership shall not be treated as a return of the partnership.

(5) INFORMATION REQUIRED TO BE REPORTED.—In the case of a partnership that is required to report any information described in section 6501(c)(8), the time for making any adjustment under this subchapter with respect to any tax return, event, or period to which such information relates shall not expire before the date that is determined under section 6501(c)(8).

(6) LISTED TRANSACTIONS.—If a partnership fails to include on any return or statement any information with respect to a listed transaction as described in section 6501(c)(10), the time for making any adjustment under this subchapter with respect to such transaction shall not expire before the date that is determined under section 6501(c)(10).

Amendments

• **2018, Tax Technical Corrections Act of 2018 (P.L. 115-141)**

P.L. 115-141, §206(k)(3), Div. U:

Amended Code Sec. 6235(c)(2) by striking "section 6501(e)(1)(A)" and inserting "subparagraph (A) or (C) of section 6501(e)(1)". **Effective** as if included in section 1101 of the Bipartisan Budget Act of 2015 [**effective** generally for returns filed for partnership tax years beginning after 12-31-2017.—CCH].

P.L. 115-141, §206(k)(4), Div. U:

Amended Code Sec. 6235(c) by adding at the end new subparagraphs (5) and (6). **Effective** as if included in section 1101 of the Bipartisan Budget Act of 2015 [**effective** generally for returns filed for partnership tax years beginning after 12-31-2017.—CCH].

[Sec. 6235(d)—Stricken]

(2) for 1 year thereafter.

Amendments

• **2018, Tax Technical Corrections Act of 2018 (P.L. 115-141)**

P.L. 115-141, §206(k)(5), Div. U:

Amended Code Sec. 6235 by striking subsection (d). **Effective** as if included in section 1101 of the Bipartisan Budget Act of 2015 [**effective** generally for returns filed for partnership tax years beginning after 12-31-2017.—CCH]. Prior to being stricken, subsection (d) read as follows:

(d) SUSPENSION WHEN SECRETARY MAILS NOTICE OF ADJUSTMENT.—If notice of a final partnership adjustment with respect to any taxable year is mailed under section 6231, the running of the period specified in subsection (a) (as modified by the other provisions of this section) shall be suspended—

(1) for the period during which an action may be brought under section 6234 (and, if a petition is filed under such section with respect to such notice, until the decision of the court becomes final), and

• **2015, Bipartisan Budget Act of 2015 (P.L. 114-74)**

P.L. 114-74, §1101(c)(1):

Amended chapter 63, as amended by this Act, by inserting after subchapter B a new subchapter C (Code Secs. 6221-6241). **Effective** generally for returns filed for partnership tax years beginning after 12-31-2017. For a special rule, see Act Sec. 1101(g)(4), below.

P.L. 114-74, §1101(g)(4), provides:

(4) ELECTION.—A partnership may elect (at such time and in such form and manner as the Secretary of the Treasury may prescribe) for the amendments made by this section (other than the election under section 6221(b) of such Code (as added by this Act)) to apply to any return of the partnership filed for partnership taxable years beginning after the date of the enactment of this Act and before January 1, 2018.

PART IV—DEFINITIONS AND SPECIAL RULES

Sec. 6241. Definitions and special rules.

SEC. 6241. DEFINITIONS AND SPECIAL RULES.

For purposes of this subchapter—

(1) PARTNERSHIP.—The term "partnership" means any partnership required to file a return under section 6031(a).

(2) PARTNERSHIP ADJUSTMENT.—

(A) IN GENERAL.—The term "partnership adjustment" means any adjustment to a partnership-related item.

(B) PARTNERSHIP-RELATED ITEM.—The term "partnership-related item" means—

(i) any item or amount with respect to the partnership (without regard to whether or not such item or amount appears on the partnership's return and including an imputed underpayment and any item or amount relating to any transaction with, basis in, or liability of, the partnership) which is relevant (determined without regard to this subchapter) in determining the tax liability of any person under chapter 1, and

(ii) any partner's distributive share of any item or amount described in clause (i).

(3) RETURN DUE DATE.—The term "return due date" means, with respect to the taxable year, the date prescribed for filing the partnership return for such taxable year (determined without regard to extensions).

(4) PAYMENTS NONDEDUCTIBLE.—No deduction shall be allowed under subtitle A for any payment required to be made by a partnership under this subchapter.

ASSESSMENT—TREATMENT OF PARTNERSHIPS

(5) PARTNERSHIPS HAVING PRINCIPAL PLACE OF BUSINESS OUTSIDE UNITED STATES.—For purposes of section 6234, a principal place of business located outside the United States shall be treated as located in the District of Columbia.

(6) PARTNERSHIPS IN CASES UNDER TITLE 11 OF UNITED STATES CODE.—

(A) SUSPENSION OF PERIOD OF LIMITATIONS ON MAKING ADJUSTMENT, ASSESSMENT, OR COLLECTION.—The running of any period of limitations provided in this subchapter on making a partnership adjustment (or provided by section 6501 or 6502 on the assessment or collection of any imputed underpayment determined under this subchapter) shall, in a case under title 11 of the United States Code, be suspended during the period during which the Secretary is prohibited by reason of such case from making the adjustment (or assessment or collection) and—

(i) for adjustment or assessment, 60 days thereafter, and

(ii) for collection, 6 months thereafter.

A rule similar to the rule of section 6213(f)(2) shall apply for purposes of section 6232(b).

(B) SUSPENSION OF PERIOD OF LIMITATION FOR FILING FOR JUDICIAL REVIEW.—The running of the period specified in section 6234 shall, in a case under title 11 of the United States Code, be suspended during the period during which the partnership is prohibited by reason of such case from filing a petition under section 6234 and for 60 days thereafter.

(7) TREATMENT WHERE PARTNERSHIP CEASES TO EXIST.—If a partnership ceases to exist before a partnership adjustment under this subchapter takes effect, such adjustment shall be taken into account by the former partners of such partnership under regulations prescribed by the Secretary.

(8) EXTENSION TO ENTITIES FILING PARTNERSHIP RETURN.—If a partnership return is filed by an entity for a taxable year but it is determined that the entity is not a partnership (or that there is no entity) for such year, then, to the extent provided in regulations, the provisions of this subchapter are hereby extended in respect of such year to such entity and its items and to persons holding an interest in such entity.

(9) COORDINATION WITH OTHER CHAPTERS.—

(A) IN GENERAL.—This subchapter shall not apply with respect to any tax imposed (including any amount required to be deducted or withheld) under chapter 2, 2A, 3, or 4, except that any partnership adjustment determined under this subchapter for purposes of chapter 1 shall be taken into account for purposes of determining any such tax to the extent that such adjustment is relevant to such determination.

(B) TIMING OF WITHHOLDING.—In the case of any tax imposed (including any amount required to be deducted or withheld) under chapter 3 or 4, which is determined with respect to an adjustment described in subparagraph (A), such tax—

(i) shall be so determined with respect to the reviewed year, and

(ii) shall be so imposed (or so required to be deducted or withheld) with respect to the adjustment year.

(C) STATUTE OF LIMITATION ON ASSESSMENT.—For special rule with respect to limitation on assessment of taxes under chapter 2 or 2A which are attributable to any partnership adjustment, see section 6501(c)(12).

(10) AUTHORITY TO REQUIRE ELECTRONIC FILING.—Notwithstanding section 6011(e), the Secretary may require that anything required to be filed or submitted under section 6225(c), or to be furnished to or filed with the Secretary under section 6226, be so filed, submitted, or furnished by magnetic media or in other machine-readable form.

(11) TREATMENT OF SPECIAL ENFORCEMENT MATTERS.—

(A) IN GENERAL.—In the case of partnership-related items which involve special enforcement matters, the Secretary may prescribe regulations pursuant to which—

(i) this subchapter (or any portion thereof) does not apply to such items, and

(ii) such items are subject to such special rules (including rules related to assessment and collection) as the Secretary determines to be necessary for the effective and efficient enforcement of this title.

(B) SPECIAL ENFORCEMENT MATTERS.—For purposes of subparagraph (A), the term "special enforcement matters" means—

(i) failure to comply with the requirements of section 6226(b)(4)(A)(ii),

(ii) assessments under section 6851 (relating to termination assessments of income tax) or section 6861 (relating to jeopardy assessments of income, estate, gift, and certain excise taxes),

(iii) criminal investigations,

(iv) indirect methods of proof of income,

(v) foreign partners or partnerships, and

(vi) other matters that the Secretary determines by regulation present special enforcement considerations.

(12) UNITED STATES SHAREHOLDERS AND CERTAIN OTHER PERSONS TREATED AS PARTNERS.—

(A) IN GENERAL.—Except as otherwise provided by the Secretary, in the case of any controlled foreign corporation (as defined in section 957 or 953(c)(1)) which is a partner of a partnership, each United States shareholder (as defined in section 951(b) or 953(c)(1)) with respect to such controlled foreign corporation shall be treated for purposes of this subchapter as a partner of such partnership. For purposes of the preceding sentence, any distributive share of any such United States shareholder with respect to such partnership shall, except as otherwise provided by the Secretary, be equal to such United States shareholder's pro rata share with respect to such controlled foreign corporation (determined under rules similar to the rules of section 951(a)(2)).

(B) PASSIVE FOREIGN INVESTMENT COMPANIES.—For purposes of subparagraph (A), in the case of a passive foreign investment company (as defined in section 1297), each taxpayer that makes an election under section 1295 with respect to such company shall be treated in the same manner as United States shareholders under subparagraph (A), except that such taxpayer's pro rata share with respect to the passive foreign investment company shall be determined under rules similar to the rules of section 1293(b).

(C) REGULATIONS OR OTHER GUIDANCE.—The Secretary shall issue such regulations or other guidance as is necessary or appropriate to carry out the purposes of this paragraph, including regulations which apply the rules of subparagraph (A) in similar circumstances or with respect to similarly situated persons.

Amendments

• **2018, Tax Technical Corrections Act of 2018 (P.L. 115-141)**

P.L. 115-141, § 201(a), Div. U:

Amended Code Sec. 6241(2). **Effective** as if included in section 1101 of the Bipartisan Budget Act of 2015 [**effective** generally for returns filed for partnership tax years beginning after 12-31-2017.—CCH]. Prior to amendment, Code Sec. 6241(2) read as follows:

(2) PARTNERSHIP ADJUSTMENT.—The term "partnership adjustment" means any adjustment in the amount of any item of income, gain, loss, deduction, or credit of a partnership, or any partner's distributive share thereof.

P.L. 115-141, § 201(b)(1), Div. U:

Amended Code Sec. 6241 by adding at the end a new paragraph (9). **Effective** as if included in section 1101 of the Bipartisan Budget Act of 2015 [**effective** generally for returns filed for partnership tax years beginning after 12-31-2017.—CCH].

P.L. 115-141, § 206(c), Div. U:

Amended Code Sec. 6241, as amended by this Act, by adding at the end a new paragraph (10). **Effective** as if included in section 1101 of the Bipartisan Budget Act of 2015 [**effective** generally for returns filed for partnership tax years beginning after 12-31-2017.—CCH].

ASSESSMENT—PARTNERSHIP ITEMS

P.L. 115-141, § 206(l), Div. U:

Amended Code Sec. 6241, as amended by this Act, by adding at the end a new paragraph (11). **Effective** as if included in section 1101 of the Bipartisan Budget Act of 2015 [**effective** generally for returns filed for partnership tax years beginning after 12-31-2017.—CCH].

P.L. 115-141, § 206(m), Div. U:

Amended Code Sec. 6241, as amended by this Act, by adding at the end a new paragraph (12). **Effective** as if included in section 1101 of the Bipartisan Budget Act of 2015 [**effective** generally for returns filed for partnership tax years beginning after 12-31-2017.—CCH].

P.L. 115-141, § 206(p)(7), Div. U:

Amended Code Sec. 6241(5) by striking "sections 6234" and inserting "section 6234". **Effective** as if included in section 1101 of the Bipartisan Budget Act of 2015 [**effective** generally for returns filed for partnership tax years beginning after 12-31-2017.—CCH].

• **2015, Bipartisan Budget Act of 2015 (P.L. 114-74)**

P.L. 114-74, § 1101(c)(1):

Amended chapter 63, as amended by this Act, by inserting after subchapter B a new subchapter C (Code Secs. 6221-6241). **Effective** generally for returns filed for partnership tax years beginning after 12-31-2017. For a special rule, see Act Sec. 1101(g)(4), below.

P.L. 114-74, § 1101(g)(4), provides:

(4) ELECTION.—A partnership may elect (at such time and in such form and manner as the Secretary of the Treasury may prescribe) for the amendments made by this section (other than the election under section 6221(b) of such Code (as added by this Act)) to apply to any return of the partnership filed for partnership taxable years beginning after the date of the enactment of this Act and before January 1, 2018.

Subchapter C—Tax Treatment of Partnership Items—[Stricken]

[Sec. 6221—Stricken]

Amendments

• **2015, Bipartisan Budget Act of 2015 (P.L. 114-74)**

P.L. 114-74, § 1101(a):

Amended chapter 63 by striking subchapter C (Code Secs. 6221-6234). **Effective** generally for returns filed for partnership tax years beginning after 12-31-2017. For a special rule, see Act Sec. 1101(g)(4), below.

P.L. 114-74, § 1101(g)(4), provides:

(4) ELECTION.—A partnership may elect (at such time and in such form and manner as the Secretary of the Treasury may prescribe) for the amendments made by this section (other than the election under section 6221(b) of such Code (as added by this Act)) to apply to any return of the partnership filed for partnership taxable years beginning after the date of the enactment of this Act and before January 1, 2018.

Prior to being stricken, Code Sec. 6221 read as follows:

SEC. 6221. TAX TREATMENT DETERMINED AT PARTNERSHIP LEVEL.

Except as otherwise provided in this subchapter, the tax treatment of any partnership item (and the applicability of any penalty, addition to tax, or additional amount which relates to an adjustment to a partnership item) shall be determined at the partnership level.

Amendments

• **1997, Taxpayer Relief Act of 1997 (P.L. 105-34)**

P.L. 105-34, § 1238(a):

Amended Code Sec. 6221 by striking "item" and inserting "item (and the applicability of any penalty, addition to tax, or additional amount which relates to an adjustment to a partnership item)". **Effective** for partnership tax years ending after 8-5-97.

• **1982, Tax Equity and Fiscal Responsibility Act of 1982 (P.L. 97-248)**

P.L. 97-248, § 402(a):

Added Code Sec. 6221. **Effective** for partnership tax years beginning after 9-3-82 and **effective** for any partnership taxable year ending after 9-3-82 if the partnership, each partner, and each indirect partner requests such application and the Secretary or his delegate consents to such application.

P.L. 97-248, § 406, provides:

Subchapter C of chapter 63 of the Internal Revenue Code of 1954 (relating to tax treatment of partnership items), section 6031 of such Code (relating to returns of partnership income), and section 6046A of such Code (relating to returns as to interest in foreign partnerships) shall not apply to the International Telecommunications Satellite Organization, the International Maritime Satellite Organization, and any organization which is a successor of either of such organizations.

• **1997, Taxpayer Relief Act of 1997 (P.L. 105-34)**

P.L. 105-34, § 1238(a):

Amended Code Sec. 6221 by striking "item" and inserting "item (and the applicability of any penalty, addition to tax, or additional amount which relates to an adjustment to a partnership item)". **Effective** for partnership tax years ending after 8-5-97.

• **1982, Tax Equity and Fiscal Responsibility Act of 1982 (P.L. 97-248)**

P.L. 97-248, § 402(a):

Added Code Sec. 6221. **Effective** for partnership tax years beginning after 9-3-82 and **effective** for any partnership taxable year ending after 9-3-82 if the partnership, each partner, and each indirect partner requests such application and the Secretary or his delegate consents to such application.

P.L. 97-248, § 406, provides:

Subchapter C of chapter 63 of the Internal Revenue Code of 1954 (relating to tax treatment of partnership items), section 6031 of such Code (relating to returns of partnership income), and section 6046A of such Code (relating to returns as to interest in foreign partnerships) shall not apply to the International Telecommunications Satellite Organization, the International Maritime Satellite Organization, and any organization which is a successor of either of such organizations.

[Sec. 6222—Stricken]

Amendments

• **2015, Bipartisan Budget Act of 2015 (P.L. 114-74)**

P.L. 114-74, § 1101(a):

Amended chapter 63 by striking subchapter C (Code Secs. 6221-6234). **Effective** generally for returns filed for partnership tax years beginning after 12-31-2017. For a special rule, see Act Sec. 1101(g)(4), below.

P.L. 114-74, § 1101(g)(4), provides:

(4) ELECTION.—A partnership may elect (at such time and in such form and manner as the Secretary of the Treasury may prescribe) for the amendments made by this section (other than the election under section 6221(b) of such Code (as added by this Act)) to apply to any return of the partnership filed for partnership taxable years beginning after the date of the enactment of this Act and before January 1, 2018.

Prior to being stricken, Code Sec. 6222 read as follows:

SEC. 6222. PARTNER'S RETURN MUST BE CONSISTENT WITH PARTNERSHIP RETURN OR SECRETARY NOTIFIED OF INCONSISTENCY.

[Sec. 6222(a)]

(a) IN GENERAL.—A partner shall, on the partner's return, treat a partnership item in a manner which is consistent with the treatment of such partnership item on the partnership return.

[Sec. 6222(b)]

(b) NOTIFICATION OF INCONSISTENT TREATMENT.—

(1) IN GENERAL.—In the case of any partnership item, if—

(A)(i) the partnership has filed a return but the partner's treatment on his return is (or may be) inconsistent with the treatment of the item on the partnership return, or

(ii) the partnership has not filed a return, and

(B) the partner files with the Secretary a statement identifying the inconsistency, subsection (a) shall not apply to such item.

(2) PARTNER RECEIVING INCORRECT INFORMATION.—A partner shall be treated as having complied with subparagraph (B) of paragraph (1) with respect to a partnership item if the partner—

(A) demonstrates to the satisfaction of the Secretary that the treatment of the partnership item on the partner's return is consistent with the treatment of the item on the schedule furnished to the partner by the partnership, and

(B) elects to have this paragraph apply with respect to that item.

[Sec. 6222(c)]

(c) EFFECT OF FAILURE TO NOTIFY.—In any case—

(1) described in paragraph (1)(A)(i) of subsection (b), and

(2) in which the partner does not comply with paragraph (1)(B) of subsection (b),

section 6225 shall not apply to any part of a deficiency attributable to any computational adjustment required to make the treatment of the items by such partner consistent with the treatment of the items on the partnership return.

[Sec. 6222(d)]

(d) ADDITION TO TAX FOR FAILURE TO COMPLY WITH SECTION.—

For addition to tax in the case of a partner's disregard of requirements of this section, see part II of subchapter A of chapter 68.

Amendments

• **1989, Omnibus Budget Reconciliation Act of 1989 (P.L. 101-239)**

P.L. 101-239, § 7721(c)(7):

Amended Code Sec. 6222(d) by striking "section 6653(a)" and inserting "part II of subchapter A of chapter 68". **Effective** for returns the due date for which (determined without regard to extensions) is after 12-31-89.

• **1986, Tax Reform Act of 1986 (P.L. 99-514)**

P.L. 99-514, § 1503(c)(1):

Amended Code Sec. 6222(d) by striking out "intentional or negligent" following "of a partner's". **Effective** for returns the due date for which (determined without regard to extensions) is after 12-31-86.

Sec. 6221

ASSESSMENT—PARTNERSHIP ITEMS

- **1982, Tax Equity and Fiscal Responsibility Act of 1982 (P.L. 97-248)**

P.L. 97-248, § 402(a):

Added Code Sec. 6222. **Effective** for partnership tax years beginning after 9-3-82, and **effective** for any partnership tax year ending after 9-3-82, if the partnership, each partner, and each indirect partner requests such application and the Secretary or his delegate consents to such application. For a special rule for certain international satellite partnerships, see the amendment note for P.L. 97-248, under Code Sec. 6221.

Amendments

[Sec. 6223—Stricken]

- **2015, Bipartisan Budget Act of 2015 (P.L. 114-74)**

P.L. 114-74, § 1101(a):

Amended chapter 63 by striking subchapter C (Code Secs. 6221-6234). **Effective** generally for returns filed for partnership tax years beginning after 12-31-2017. For a special rule, see Act Sec. 1101(g)(4), below.

P.L. 114-74, § 1101(g)(4), provides:

(4) ELECTION.—A partnership may elect (at such time and in such form and manner as the Secretary of the Treasury may prescribe) for the amendments made by this section (other than the election under section 6221(b) of such Code (as added by this Act)) to apply to any return of the partnership filed for partnership taxable years beginning after the date of the enactment of this Act and before January 1, 2018.

Prior to being stricken, Code Sec. 6223 read as follows:

SEC. 6223. NOTICE TO PARTNERS OF PROCEEDINGS.

[Sec. 6223(a)]

(a) SECRETARY MUST GIVE PARTNERS NOTICE OF BEGINNING AND COMPLETION OF ADMINISTRATIVE PROCEEDINGS.—The Secretary shall mail to each partner whose name and address is furnished to the Secretary notice of—

(1) the beginning of an administrative proceeding at the partnership level with respect to a partnership item, and

(2) the final partnership administrative adjustment resulting from any such proceeding.

A partner shall not be entitled to any notice under this subsection unless the Secretary has received (at least 30 days before it is mailed to the tax matters partner) sufficient information to enable the Secretary to determine that such partner is entitled to such notice and to provide such notice to such partner.

[Sec. 6223(b)]

(b) SPECIAL RULES FOR PARTNERSHIP WITH MORE THAN 100 PARTNERS.—

(1) PARTNER WITH LESS THAN 1 PERCENT INTEREST.—Except as provided in paragraph (2), subsection (a) shall not apply to a partner if—

(A) the partnership has more than 100 partners, and

(B) the partner has a less than 1 percent interest in the profits of the partnership.

(2) SECRETARY MUST GIVE NOTICE TO NOTICE GROUP.—If a group of partners in the aggregate having a 5 percent or more interest in the profits of a partnership so request and designate one of their members to receive the notice, the member so designated shall be treated as a partner to whom subsection (a) applies.

[Sec. 6223(c)]

(c) INFORMATION BASE FOR SECRETARY'S NOTICES, ETC.—For purposes of this subchapter—

(1) INFORMATION ON PARTNERSHIP RETURN.—Except as provided in paragraphs (2) and (3), the Secretary shall use the names, addresses, and profits interests shown on the partnership return.

(2) USE OF ADDITIONAL INFORMATION.—The Secretary shall use additional information furnished to him by the tax matters partner or any other person in accordance with regulations prescribed by the Secretary.

(3) SPECIAL RULE WITH RESPECT TO INDIRECT PARTNERS.—If any information furnished to the Secretary under paragraph (1) or (2)—

(A) shows that a person has a profits interest in the partnership by reason of ownership of an interest through 1 or more pass-thru partners, and

(B) contains the name, address, and profits interest of such person,

then the Secretary shall use the name, address, and profits interest of such person with respect to such partnership interest (in lieu of the names, addresses, and profits interests of the pass-thru partners).

[Sec. 6223(d)]

(d) PERIOD FOR MAILING NOTICE.—

(1) NOTICE OF BEGINNING OF PROCEEDINGS.—The Secretary shall mail the notice specified in paragraph (1) of subsection (a) to each partner entitled to such notice not later than the 120th day before the day on which the notice specified in paragraph (2) of subsection (a) is mailed to the tax matters partner.

(2) NOTICE OF FINAL PARTNERSHIP ADMINISTRATIVE ADJUSTMENT.—The Secretary shall mail the notice specified in paragraph (2) of subsection (a) to each partner entitled to such notice not later than the 60th day after the day on which the notice specified in such paragraph (2) was mailed to the tax matters partner.

[Sec. 6223(e)]

(e) EFFECT OF SECRETARY'S FAILURE TO PROVIDE NOTICE.—

(1) APPLICATION OF SUBSECTION.—

(A) IN GENERAL.—This subsection applies where the Secretary has failed to mail any notice specified in subsection (a) to a partner entitled to such notice within the period specified in subsection (d).

(B) SPECIAL RULES FOR PARTNERSHIPS WITH MORE THAN 100 PARTNERS.—For purposes of subparagraph (A), any partner described in paragraph (1) of subsection (b) shall be treated as entitled to notice specified in subsection (a). The Secretary may provide such notice—

(i) except as provided in clause (ii), by mailing notice to the tax matters partner, or

(ii) in the case of a member of a notice group which qualifies under paragraph (2) of subsection (b), by mailing notice to the partner designated for such purpose by the group.

(2) PROCEEDINGS FINISHED.—In any case to which this subsection applies, if at the time the Secretary mails the partner notice of the proceeding—

(A) the period within which a petition for review of a final partnership administrative adjustment under section 6226 may be filed has expired and no such petition has been filed, or

(B) the decision of a court in an action begun by such a petition has become final,

the partner may elect to have such adjustment, such decision, or a settlement agreement described in paragraph (2) of section 6224(c) with respect to the partnership taxable year to which the adjustment relates apply to such partner. If the partner does not make an election under the preceding sentence, the partnership items of the partner for the partnership taxable year to which the proceeding relates shall be treated as nonpartnership items.

(3) PROCEEDINGS STILL GOING ON.—In any case to which this subsection applies, if paragraph (2) does not apply, the partner shall be a party to the proceeding unless such partner elects—

(A) to have a settlement agreement described in paragraph (2) of section 6224(c) with respect to the partnership taxable year to which the proceeding relates apply to the partner, or

(B) to have the partnership items of the partner for the partnership taxable year to which the proceeding relates treated as nonpartnership items.

[Sec. 6223(f)]

(f) ONLY ONE NOTICE OF FINAL PARTNERSHIP ADMINISTRATIVE ADJUSTMENT.—If the Secretary mails a notice of final partnership administrative adjustment for a partnership taxable year with respect to a partner, the Secretary may not mail another such notice to such partner with respect to the same taxable year of the same partnership in the absence of a showing of fraud, malfeasance, or misrepresentation of a material fact.

[Sec. 6223(g)]

(g) TAX MATTERS PARTNER MUST KEEP PARTNERS INFORMED OF PROCEEDINGS.—To the extent and in the manner provided by regulations, the tax matters partner of a partnership shall keep each partner informed of all administrative and judicial proceedings for the adjustment at the partnership level of partnership items.

[Sec. 6223(h)]

(h) PASS-THRU PARTNER REQUIRED TO FORWARD NOTICE.—

(1) IN GENERAL.—If a pass-thru partner receives a notice with respect to a partnership proceeding from the Secretary, the tax matters partner, or another pass-thru partner, the pass-thru partner shall, within 30 days of receiving that notice, forward a copy of that notice to the person or persons holding an interest (through the pass-thru partner) in the profits or losses of the partnership for the partnership taxable year to which the notice relates.

(2) PARTNERSHIP AS PASS-THRU PARTNER.—In the case of a pass-thru partner which is a partnership, the tax matters partner of such partnership shall be responsible for forwarding copies of the notice to the partners of such partnership.

Amendments

- **1982, Tax Equity and Fiscal Responsibility Act of 1982 (P.L. 97-248)**

P.L. 97-248, § 402(a):

Added Code Sec. 6223. **Effective** for partnership tax years beginning after 9-3-82, and **effective** for any partnership tax year ending after 9-3-82, if the partnership, each partner, and each indirect partner requests such application and the Secretary or his delegate consents to such application. For a special rule for certain international satellite partnerships, see the amendment note for P.L. 97-248, following Code Sec. 6221.

[Sec. 6224—Stricken]

Amendments

- **2015, Bipartisan Budget Act of 2015 (P.L. 114-74)**

P.L. 114-74, § 1101(a):

Amended chapter 63 by striking subchapter C (Code Secs. 6221-6234). **Effective** generally for returns filed for partnership tax years beginning after 12-31-2017. For a special rule, see Act Sec. 1101(g)(4), below.

P.L. 114-74, § 1101(g)(4), provides:

(4) ELECTION.—A partnership may elect (at such time and in such form and manner as the Secretary of the Treasury may prescribe) for the amendments made by this section (other than the election under section 6221(b) of such Code (as added by this Act)) to apply to any return of the partnership filed for partnership taxable years beginning after the date of the enactment of this Act and before January 1, 2018.

Prior to being stricken, Code Sec. 6224 read as follows:

SEC. 6224. PARTICIPATION IN ADMINISTRATIVE PROCEEDINGS; WAIVERS; AGREEMENTS.

[Sec. 6224(a)]

(a) PARTICIPATION IN ADMINISTRATIVE PROCEEDINGS.—Any partner has the right to participate in any administrative proceeding relating to the determination of partnership items at the partnership level.

ASSESSMENT—PARTNERSHIP ITEMS

[Sec. 6224(b)]

(b) PARTNER MAY WAIVE RIGHTS.—

(1) IN GENERAL.—A partner may at any time waive—

(A) any right such partner has under this subchapter, and

(B) any restriction under this subchapter on action by the Secretary.

(2) FORM.—Any waiver under paragraph (1) shall be made by a signed notice in writing filed with the Secretary.

[Sec. 6224(c)]

(c) SETTLEMENT AGREEMENT.—In the absence of a showing of fraud, malfeasance, or misrepresentation of fact—

(1) BINDS ALL PARTIES.—A settlement agreement between the Secretary or the Attorney General (or his delegate) and 1 or more partners in a partnership with respect to the determination of partnership items for any partnership taxable year shall (except as otherwise provided in such agreement) be binding on all parties to such agreement with respect to the determination of partnership items for such partnership taxable year. An indirect partner is bound by any such agreement entered into by the pass-thru partner unless the indirect partner has been identified as provided in section 6223(c)(3).

(2) OTHER PARTNERS HAVE RIGHT TO ENTER INTO CONSISTENT AGREEMENTS.—If the Secretary or the Attorney General (or his delegate) enters into a settlement agreement with any partner with respect to partnership items for any partnership taxable year, the Secretary or the Attorney General (or his delegate) shall offer to any other partner who so requests settlement terms for the partnership taxable year which are consistent with those contained in such settlement agreement. Except in the case of an election under paragraph (2) or (3) of section 6223(e) to have a settlement agreement described in this paragraph apply, this paragraph shall apply with respect to a settlement agreement entered into with a partner before notice of a final partnership administrative adjustment is mailed to the tax matters partner only if such other partner makes the request before the expiration of 150 days after the day on which such notice is mailed to the tax matters partner.

Amendments

• **2015, Bipartisan Budget Act of 2015 (P.L. 114-74)**

P.L. 114-74, § 1101(a):

Amended chapter 63 by striking subchapter C (Code Secs. 6221-6234). **Effective** generally for returns filed for partnership tax years beginning after 12-31-2017. For a special rule, see Act Sec. 1101(g)(4), below.

P.L. 114-74, § 1101(g)(4), provides:

(4) ELECTION.—A partnership may elect (at such time and in such form and manner as the Secretary of the Treasury may prescribe) for the amendments made by this section (other than the election under section 6221(b) of such Code (as added by this Act)) to apply to any return of the partnership filed for partnership taxable years beginning after the date of the enactment of this Act and before January 1, 2018.

Prior to being stricken, Code Sec. 6225 read as follows:

SEC. 6225. ASSESSMENTS MADE ONLY AFTER PARTNERSHIP LEVEL PROCEEDINGS ARE COMPLETED.

[Sec. 6225(a)]

(a) RESTRICTION ON ASSESSMENT AND COLLECTION.—Except as otherwise provided in this subchapter, no assessment of a deficiency attributable to any partnership item may be made (and no levy or proceeding in any court for the collection of any such deficiency may be made, begun, or prosecuted) before—

(1) the close of the 150th day after the day on which a notice of a final partnership administrative adjustment was mailed to the tax matters partner, and

(2) if a proceeding is begun in the Tax Court under section 6226 during such 150-day period, the decision of the court in such proceeding has become final.

[Sec. 6225(b)]

(b) PREMATURE ACTION MAY BE ENJOINED.—Notwithstanding section 7421(a), any action which violates subsection (a) may be enjoined in the proper court, including the Tax Court. The Tax Court shall have no jurisdiction to enjoin any action or

(3) TAX MATTERS PARTNER MAY BIND CERTAIN OTHER PARTNERS.—

(A) IN GENERAL.—A partner who is not a notice partner (and not a member of a notice group described in subsection (b)(2) of section 6223) shall be bound by any settlement agreement—

(i) which is entered into by the tax matters partner, and

(ii) in which the tax matters partner expressly states that such agreement shall bind the other partners.

(B) EXCEPTION.—Subparagraph (A) shall not apply to any partner who (within the time prescribed by the Secretary) files a statement with the Secretary providing that the tax matters partner shall not have the authority to enter into a settlement agreement on behalf of such partner.

Amendments

• **2002, Job Creation and Worker Assistance Act of 2002 (P.L. 107-147)**

P.L. 107-147, § 416(d)(1)(A):

Amended Code Sec. 6224(c)(1)-(2) by inserting "or the Attorney General (or his delegate)" after "Secretary" each place it appears. **Effective** with respect to settlement agreements entered into after 3-9-2002.

• **1982, Tax Equity and Fiscal Responsibility Act of 1982 (P.L. 97-248)**

P.L. 97-248, § 402(a):

Added Code Sec. 6224. **Effective** for partnership tax years beginning after 9-3-82, and **effective** for any partnership tax year ending after 9-3-82, if the partnership, each partner, and each indirect partner requests such application and the Secretary or his delegate consents to such application. For a special rule for certain international satellite partnerships, see the amendment note for P.L. 97-248, following Code Sec. 6221.

[Sec. 6225—Stricken]

proceeding under this subsection unless a timely petition for a readjustment of the partnership items for the taxable year has been filed and then only in respect of the adjustments that are the subject of such petition.

Amendments

• **1997, Taxpayer Relief Act of 1997 (P.L. 105-34)**

P.L. 105-34, § 1239(a):

Amended Code Sec. 6225(b) by striking "the proper court." and inserting "the proper court, including the Tax Court. The Tax Court shall have no jurisdiction to enjoin any action or proceeding under this subsection unless a timely petition for a readjustment of the partnership items for the taxable year has been filed and then only in respect of the adjustments that are the subject of such petition.". **Effective** for partnership tax years ending after 8-5-97.

[Sec. 6225(c)]

(c) LIMIT WHERE NO PROCEEDING BEGUN.—If no proceeding under section 6226 is begun with respect to any final partnership administrative adjustment during the 150-day period described in subsection (a), the deficiency assessed against any partner with respect to the partnership items to which such adjustment relates shall not exceed the amount determined in accordance with such adjustment.

Amendments

• **1982, Tax Equity and Fiscal Responsibility Act of 1982 (P.L. 97-248)**

P.L. 97-248, § 402(a):

Added Code Sec. 6225. **Effective** for partnership tax years beginning after 9-3-82, and **effective** for partnership tax years ending after 9-3-82, if the partnership, each partner, and each indirect partner requests such application and if the Secretary or his delegate consents to such application. For a special rule for certain international satellite partnerships, see the amendment note for P.L. 97-248, following Code Sec. 6221.

[Sec. 6226—Stricken]

Amendments

• **2015, Bipartisan Budget Act of 2015 (P.L. 114-74)**

P.L. 114-74, § 1101(a):

Amended chapter 63 by striking subchapter C (Code Secs. 6221-6234). **Effective** generally for returns filed for partnership tax years beginning after 12-31-2017. For a special rule, see Act Sec. 1101(g)(4), below.

P.L. 114-74, § 1101(g)(4), provides:

(4) ELECTION.—A partnership may elect (at such time and in such form and manner as the Secretary of the Treasury may prescribe) for the amendments made by this section (other than the election under section 6221(b) of such Code (as added by this Act)) to apply to any return of the partnership filed for partnership taxable years beginning after the date of the enactment of this Act and before January 1, 2018.

Prior to being stricken, Code Sec. 6226 read as follows:

SEC. 6226. JUDICIAL REVIEW OF FINAL PARTNERSHIP ADMINISTRATIVE ADJUSTMENTS.

[Sec. 6226(a)]

(a) PETITION BY TAX MATTERS PARTNER.—Within 90 days after the day on which a notice of a final partnership administrative adjustment is mailed to the tax matters partner, the tax matters partner may file a petition for a readjustment of the partnership items for such taxable year with—

(1) the Tax Court,

(2) the district court of the United States for the district in which the partnership's principal place of business is located, or

(3) the Court of Federal Claims.

Amendments

• **1992, Court of Federal Claims Technical and Procedural Improvements Act of 1992 (P.L. 102-572)**

P.L. 102-572, § 902(b)(2):

Amended Code Sec. 6226(a)(3) by striking "Claims Court" and inserting "Court of Federal Claims". **Effective** 10-29-92.

[Sec. 6226(b)]

(b) PETITION BY PARTNER OTHER THAN TAX MATTERS PARTNER.—

(1) IN GENERAL.—If the tax matters partner does not file a readjustment petition under subsection (a) with respect to any final partnership administrative adjustment, any notice partner (and any 5-percent group) may, within 60 days after the close of the 90-day period set forth in subsection (a), file a petition for a readjustment of the partnership items for the taxable year involved with any of the courts described in subsection (a).

(2) PRIORITY OF THE TAX COURT ACTION.—If more than 1 action is brought under paragraph (1) with respect to any partnership for any partnership taxable year, the first such action brought in the Tax Court shall go forward.

Sec. 6225—Stricken

ASSESSMENT—PARTNERSHIP ITEMS

(3) PRIORITY OUTSIDE THE TAX COURT.—If more than 1 action is brought under paragraph (1) with respect to any partnership for any taxable year but no such action is brought in the Tax Court, the first such action brought shall go forward.

(4) DISMISSAL OF OTHER ACTIONS.—If an action is brought under paragraph (1) in addition to the action which goes forward under paragraph (2) or (3), such action shall be dismissed.

(5) TREATMENT OF PREMATURE PETITIONS.—If—

(A) a petition for a readjustment of partnership items for the taxable year involved is filed by a notice partner (or a 5-percent group) during the 90-day period described in subsection (a), and

(B) no action is brought under paragraph (1) during the 60-day period described therein with respect to such taxable year which is not dismissed,

such petition shall be treated for purposes of paragraph (1) as filed on the last day of such 60-day period.

(6) TAX MATTERS PARTNER MAY INTERVENE.—The tax matters partner may intervene in any action brought under this subsection.

Amendments

• **1997, Taxpayer Relief Act of 1997 (P.L. 105-34)**

P.L. 105-34, §1240(a):

Amended Code Sec. 6226(b) by redesignating paragraph (5) as paragraph (6) and by inserting after paragraph (4) a new paragraph (5). **Effective** for petitions filed after 8-5-97.

[Sec. 6226(c)]

(c) PARTNERS TREATED AS PARTIES.—If an action is brought under subsection (a) or (b) with respect to a partnership for any partnership taxable year—

(1) each person who was a partner in such partnership at any time during such year shall be treated as a party to such action, and

(2) the court having jurisdiction of such action shall allow each such person to participate in the action.

[Sec. 6226(d)]

(d) PARTNER MUST HAVE INTEREST IN OUTCOME.—

(1) IN ORDER TO BE PARTY TO ACTION.—Subsection (c) shall not apply to a partner after the day on which—

(A) the partnership items of such partner for the partnership taxable year became nonpartnership items by reason of 1 or more of the events described in subsection (b) of section 6231, or

(B) the period within which any tax attributable to such partnership items may be assessed against that partner expired.

Notwithstanding subparagraph (B), any person treated under subsection (c) as a party to an action shall be permitted to participate in such action (or file a readjustment petition under subsection (b) or paragraph (2) of this subsection) solely for the purpose of asserting that the period of limitations for assessing any tax attributable to partnership items has expired with respect to such person, and the court having jurisdiction of such action shall have jurisdiction to consider such assertion.

(2) TO FILE PETITION.—No partner may file a readjustment petition under subsection (b) unless such partner would (after the application of paragraph (1) of this subsection) be treated as a party to the proceeding.

Amendments

• **1997, Taxpayer Relief Act of 1997 (P.L. 105-34)**

P.L. 105-34, §1239(b):

Amended Code Sec. 6226(d)(1) by adding at the end a new sentence. **Effective** for partnership tax years ending after 8-5-97.

[Sec. 6226(e)]

(e) JURISDICTIONAL REQUIREMENT FOR BRINGING ACTION IN DISTRICT COURT OR COURT OF FEDERAL CLAIMS.—

(1) IN GENERAL.—A readjustment petition under this section may be filed in a district court of the United States or the Court of Federal Claims only if the partner filing the petition deposits with the Secretary, on or before the day the petition is filed, the amount by which the tax liability of the partner would be increased if the treatment of partnership items on the partner's return were made consistent with the treatment of partnership items on the partnership return, as adjusted by the final partnership administrative adjustment. In the case of a petition filed by a 5-percent group, the requirement of the preceding sentence shall apply to each member of the group. The court may by order provide that the jurisdictional requirements of this paragraph are satisfied where there has been a good faith attempt to satisify such requirements and any shortfall in the amount required to be deposited is timely corrected.

(2) REFUND ON REQUEST.—If an action brought in a district court of the United States or in the Court of Federal Claims is dismissed by reason of the priority of a Tax Court action under paragraph (2) of subsection (b), the Secretary shall, at the request of the partner who made the deposit, refund the amount deposited under paragraph (1).

(3) INTEREST PAYABLE.—Any amount deposited under paragraph (1), while deposited, shall not be treated as a payment of tax for purposes of this title (other than chapter 67).

Amendments

• **1992, Court of Federal Claims Technical and Procedural Improvements Act of 1992 (P.L. 102-572)**

P.L. 102-572, §902(b)(2):

Amended Code Sec. 6226(e) by striking "Claims Court" and inserting "Court of Federal Claims" each place it appears in the heading and text thereof. **Effective** 10-29-92.

[Sec. 6226(f)]

(f) SCOPE OF JUDICIAL REVIEW.—A court with which a petition is filed in accordance with this section shall have jurisdiction to determine all partnership items of the partnership for the partnership taxable year to which the notice of final partnership administrative adjustment relates, the proper allocation of such items among the partners, and the applicability of any penalty, addition to tax, or additional amount which relates to an adjustment to a partnership item.

Amendments

• **1997, Taxpayer Relief Act of 1997 (P.L. 105-34)**

P.L. 105-34, §1238(b)(1)(A)-(B):

Amended Code Sec. 6226(f) by striking "relates and" and inserting "relates,", and by inserting before the period ", and the applicability of any penalty, addition to tax, or additional amount which relates to an adjustment to a partnership item". **Effective** for partnership tax years ending after 8-5-97.

[Sec. 6226(g)]

(g) DETERMINATION OF COURT REVIEWABLE.—Any determination by a court under this section shall have the force and effect of a decision of the Tax Court or a final judgment or decree of the district court or the Court of Federal Claims, as the case may be, and shall be reviewable as such. With respect to the partnership, only the tax matters partner, a notice partner, or a 5-percent group may seek review of a determination by a court under this section.

Amendments

• **1992, Court of Federal Claims Technical and Procedural Improvements Act of 1992 (P.L. 102-572)**

P.L. 102-572, §902(b)(2):

Amended Code Sec. 6226(g) by striking "Claims Court" and inserting "Court of Federal Claims". **Effective** 10-29-92.

[Sec. 6226(h)]

(h) EFFECT OF DECISION DISMISSING ACTION.—If an action brought under this section is dismissed (other than under paragraph (4) of subsection (b)), the decision of the court dismissing the action shall be considered as its decision that the notice of final partnership administrative adjustment is correct, and an appropriate order shall be entered in the records of the court.

Amendments

• **1983, Technical Corrections Act of 1982 (P.L. 97-448)**

P.L. 97-448, §306(c)(1)(A):

Amended the second sentence of Code Sec. 6226(g) by striking out "Only" and inserting in lieu thereof "With respect to the partnership, only". **Effective** as if included in the provision of P.L. 97-248 to which it relates.

• **1982, Tax Equity and Fiscal Responsibility Act of 1982 (P.L. 97-248)**

P.L. 97-248, §402(a):

Added Code Sec. 6226. **Effective** for partnership tax years beginning after 9-3-82, and for partnership tax years ending after 9-3-82, if the partnership, each partner, and each indirect partner requests such application and the Secretary or his delegate consents to such application. For a special rule for certain international satellite partnerships, see the amendment note for P.L. 97-248, following Code Sec. 6221.

• **1992, Court of Federal Claims Technical and Procedural Improvements Act of 1992 (P.L. 102-572)**

P.L. 102-572, §902(b)(2):

Amended Code Sec. 6226(a)(3) by striking "Claims Court" and inserting "Court of Federal Claims". **Effective** 10-29-92.

[Sec. 6227—Stricken]

Amendments

• **2015, Bipartisan Budget Act of 2015 (P.L. 114-74)**

P.L. 114-74, §1101(a):

Amended chapter 63 by striking subchapter C (Code Secs. 6221-6234). **Effective** generally for requests with respect to returns filed for partnership tax years beginning after 12-31-2017. For a special rule, see Act Sec. 1101(g)(4), below.

P.L. 114-74, §1101(g)(4), provides:

(4) ELECTION.—A partnership may elect (at such time and in such form and manner as the Secretary of the Treasury may prescribe) for the amendments made by this section (other than the election under section 6221(b) of such Code (as added by this Act)) to apply to any return of the partnership filed for partnership taxable years beginning after the date of the enactment of this Act and before January 1, 2018.

Prior to being stricken, Code Sec. 6227 read as follows:

SEC. 6227. ADMINISTRATIVE ADJUSTMENT REQUESTS.

[Sec. 6227(a)]

(a) GENERAL RULE.—A partner may file a request for an administrative adjustment of partnership items for any partnership taxable year at any time which is—

(1) within 3 years after the later of—

(A) the date on which the partnership return for such year is filed, or

(B) the last day for filing the partnership return for such year (determined without regard to extensions), and

(2) before the mailing to the tax matters partner of a notice of final partnership administrative adjustment with respect to such taxable year.

ASSESSMENT—PARTNERSHIP ITEMS

[Sec. 6227(b)]

(b) SPECIAL RULE IN CASE OF EXTENSION OF PERIOD OF LIMITATIONS UNDER SECTION 6229.—The period prescribed by subsection (a)(1) for filing of a request for an administrative adjustment shall be extended—

(1) for the period within which an assessment may be made pursuant to an agreement (or any extension thereof) under section 6229(b), and

(2) for 6 months thereafter.

Amendments

• **1997, Taxpayer Relief Act of 1997 (P.L. 105-34)**

P.L. 105-34, §1236(a):

Amended Code Sec. 6227 by redesignating subsections (b) and (c) as subsections (c) and (d), respectively, and by inserting after subsection (a) a new subsection (b). **Effective** as if included in the amendments made by section 403 of P.L. 97-248 [generally **effective** for partnership tax years beginning after 9-3-82.—CCH].

[Sec. 6227(c)]

(c) REQUESTS BY TAX MATTERS PARTNER ON BEHALF OF PARTNERSHIP.—

(1) SUBSTITUTED RETURN.—If the tax matters partner—

(A) files a request for an administrative adjustment, and

(B) asks that the treatment shown on the request be substituted for the treatment of partnership items on the partnership return to which the request relates,

the Secretary may treat the changes shown on such request as corrections of mathematical or clerical errors appearing on the partnership return.

(2) REQUESTS NOT TREATED AS SUBSTITUTED RETURNS.—

(A) IN GENERAL.—If the tax matters partner files an administrative adjustment request on behalf of the partnership which is not treated as a substituted return under paragraph (1), the Secretary may, with respect to all or any part of the requested adjustments—

(i) without conducting any proceeding, allow or make to all partners the credits or refunds arising from the requested adjustments,

(ii) conduct a partnership proceeding under this subchapter, or

(iii) take no action on the request.

(B) EXCEPTIONS.—Clause (i) of subparagraph (A) shall not apply with respect to a partner after the day on which the partnership items become nonpartnership items by reason of 1 or more of the events described in subsection (b) of section 6231.

(3) REQUEST MUST SHOW EFFECT ON DISTRIBUTIVE SHARES.—The tax matters partner shall furnish with any administrative adjustment request on behalf of the partnership revised schedules showing the effect of such request on the distributive shares of the partners and such other information as may be required under regulations.

Amendments

• **1997, Taxpayer Relief Act of 1997 (P.L. 105-34)**

P.L. 105-34, §1236(a):

Amended Code Sec. 6227 by redesignating subsection (b) as subsection (c). **Effective** as if included in the amendments made by section 402 of P.L. 97-248 [generally **effective** for partnership tax years beginning after 9-3-82.—CCH].

[Sec. 6227(d)]

(d) OTHER REQUESTS.—If any partner files a request for an administrative adjustment (other than a request described in subsection (c)), the Secretary may—

(1) process the request in the same manner as a claim for credit or refund with respect to items which are not partnership items,

(2) assess any additional tax that would result from the requested adjustments,

(3) mail to the partner, under subparagraph (A) of section 6231(b)(1) (relating to items becoming nonpartnership items), a notice that all partnership items of the partner for the partnership taxable year to which such request relates shall be treated as nonpartnership items, or

(4) conduct a partnership proceeding.

Amendments

• **2002, Job Creation and Worker Assistance Act of 2002 (P.L. 107-147)**

P.L. 107-147, §417(19)(A):

Amended Code Sec. 6227(d) by striking "subsection (b)" and inserting "subsection (c)". Effective 3-9-2002.

• **1997, Taxpayer Relief Act of 1997 (P.L. 105-34)**

P.L. 105-34, §1236(a):

Amended Code Sec. 6227 by redesignating subsection (c) as subsection (d). **Effective** as if included in the amendments made by section 402 of P.L. 97-248 [generally **effective** for partnership tax years beginning after 9-3-82.—CCH].

• **1982, Tax Equity and Fiscal Responsibility Act of 1982 (P.L. 97-248)**

P.L. 97-248, §402(a):

Added Code Sec. 6227. **Effective** for partnership tax years beginning after 9-3-82, and also for partnership tax years ending after 9-3-82, if the partnership, each partner, and each indirect partner requests such application and the Secretary or his delegate consents to such application. For a special rule for certain international satellite partnerships, see the amendment note for P.L. 97-248, following Code Sec. 6221.

[Sec. 6227(e)]

(e) REQUESTS WITH RESPECT TO BAD DEBTS OR WORTHLESS SECURITIES.—In the case of that portion of any request for an administrative adjustment which relates to the deductibility by the partnership under section 166 of a debt as a debt which became worthless, or under section 165(g) of a loss from worthlessness of a security, the period prescribed in subsection (a)(1) shall be 7 years from the last day for filing the partnership return for the year with respect to which such request is made (determined without regard to extensions).

Amendments

• **1997, Taxpayer Relief Act of 1997 (P.L. 105-34)**

P.L. 105-34, §1243(a):

Amended Code Sec. 6227 by adding at the end a new subsection (e). **Effective** as if included in the amendments made by section 402 of P.L. 97-248 [generally **effective** for partnership tax years beginning after 9-3-82.—CCH]. For a special rule, see Act Sec. 1243(b)(2)(A)-(C), below.

P.L. 105-34, §1243(b)(2)(A)-(C), provides:

(2) TREATMENT OF REQUESTS FILED BEFORE DATE OF ENACTMENT.—In the case of that portion of any request (filed before the date of the enactment of this Act) for an administrative adjustment which relates to the deductibility of a debt as a debt which became worthless or the deductibility of a loss from the worthlessness of a security—

(A) paragraph (2) of section 6227(a) of the Internal Revenue Code of 1986 shall not apply,

(B) the period for filing a petition under section 6228 of the Internal Revenue Code of 1986 with respect to such request shall not expire before the date 6 months after the date of the enactment of this Act, and

(C) such a petition may be filed without regard to whether there was a notice of the beginning of an administrative proceeding or a final partnership administrative adjustment.

[Sec. 6228—Stricken]

Amendments

• **2015, Bipartisan Budget Act of 2015 (P.L. 114-74)**

P.L. 114-74, §1101(a):

Amended chapter 63 by striking subchapter C (Code Secs. 6221-6234). **Effective** generally for returns filed for partnership tax years beginning after 12-31-2017. For a special rule, see Act Sec. 1101(g)(4), below.

P.L. 114-74, §1101(g)(4), provides:

(4) ELECTION.—A partnership may elect (at such time and in such form and manner as the Secretary of the Treasury may prescribe) for the amendments made by this section (other than the election under section 6221(b) of such Code (as added by this Act)) to apply to any return of the partnership filed for partnership taxable years beginning after the date of the enactment of this Act and before January 1, 2018.

Prior to being stricken, Code Sec. 6228 read as follows:

SEC. 6228. JUDICIAL REVIEW WHERE ADMINISTRATIVE ADJUSTMENT REQUEST IS NOT ALLOWED IN FULL.

[Sec. 6228(a)]

(a) REQUEST ON BEHALF OF PARTNERSHIP.—

(1) IN GENERAL.—If any part of an administrative adjustment request filed by the tax matters partner under subsection (c) of section 6227 is not allowed by the Secretary, the tax matters partner may file a petition for an adjustment with respect to the partnership items to which such part of the request relates with—

(A) the Tax Court,

(B) the district court of the United States for the district in which the principal place of business of the partnership is located, or

(C) the Court of Federal Claims.

(2) PERIOD FOR FILING PETITION.—

(A) IN GENERAL.—A petition may be filed under paragraph (1) with respect to partnership items for a partnership taxable year only—

(i) after the expiration of 6 months from the date of filing of the request under section 6227, and

(ii) before the date which is 2 years after the date of such request.

(B) NO PETITION AFTER NOTICE OF BEGINNING OF ADMINISTRATIVE PROCEEDING.—No petition may be filed under paragraph (1) after the day the Secretary mails to the partnership a notice of the beginning of an administrative proceeding with respect to the partnership taxable year to which such request relates.

(C) FAILURE BY SECRETARY TO ISSUE TIMELY NOTICE OF ADJUSTMENT.—If the Secretary—

(i) mails the notice referred to in subparagraph (B) before the expiration of the 2-year period referred to in clause (ii) of subparagraph (A), and

(ii) fails to mail a notice of final partnership administrative adjustment with respect to the partnership taxable year to which the request relates before the expiration of the period described in section 6229(a) (including any extension by agreement),

subparagraph (B) shall cease to apply with respect to such request, and the 2-year period referred to in clause (ii) of subparagraph (A) shall not expire before the date 6 months after the expiration of the period described in section 6229(a) (including any extension by agreement).

(D) EXTENSION OF TIME.—The 2-year period described in subparagraph (A)(ii) shall be extended for such period as may be agreed upon in writing between the tax matters partner and the Secretary.

(3) COORDINATION WITH ADMINISTRATIVE ADJUSTMENT.—

(A) ADMINISTRATIVE ADJUSTMENT BEFORE FILING OF PETITION.—No petition may be filed under this subsection after the Secretary mails to the tax matters partner a notice of final partnership administrative adjustment for the partnership taxable year to which the request under section 6227 relates.

(B) ADMINISTRATIVE ADJUSTMENT AFTER FILING BUT BEFORE HEARING OF PETITION.—If the Secretary mails to the tax matters partner a notice of final partnership administrative adjustment for the partnership taxable year to which the request under section 6227 relates after the filing of a petition under this subsection but before the hearing of

ASSESSMENT—PARTNERSHIP ITEMS

such petition, such petition shall be treated as an action brought under section 6226 with respect to that administrative adjustment, except that subsection (e) of section 6226 shall not apply.

(C) NOTICE MUST BE BEFORE EXPIRATION OF STATUTE OF LIMITATIONS.—A notice of final partnership administrative adjustment for the partnership taxable year shall be taken into account under subparagraphs (A) and (B) only if such notice is mailed before the expiration of the period prescribed by section 6229 for making assessments of tax attributable to partnership items for such taxable year.

(4) PARTNERS TREATED AS PARTY TO ACTION.—

(A) IN GENERAL.—If an action is brought by the tax matters partner under paragraph (1) with respect to any request for an adjustment of a partnership item for any taxable year—

(i) each person who was a partner in such partnership at any time during the partnership taxable year involved shall be treated as a party to such action, and

(ii) the court having jurisdiction of such action shall allow each such person to participate in the action.

(B) PARTNERS MUST HAVE INTEREST IN OUTCOME.—For purposes of subparagraph (A), rules similar to the rules of paragraph (1) of section 6226(d) shall apply.

(5) SCOPE OF JUDICIAL REVIEW.—Except in the case described in subparagraph (B) of paragraph (3), a court with which a petition is filed in accordance with this subsection shall have jurisdiction to determine only those partnership items to which the part of the request under section 6227 not allowed by the Secretary relates and those items with respect to which the Secretary asserts adjustments as offsets to the adjustments requested by the tax matters partner.

(6) DETERMINATION OF COURT REVIEWABLE.—Any determination by a court under this subsection shall have the force and effect of a decision of the Tax Court or a final judgment or decree of the district court or the Court of Federal Claims, as the case may be, and shall be reviewable as such. With respect to the partnership, only the tax matters partner, a notice partner, or a 5-percent group may seek review of a determination by a court under this subsection.

Amendments

• **2002, Job Creation and Worker Assistance Act of 2002 (P.L. 107-147)**

P.L. 107-147, §417(19)(B)(i):

Amended Code Sec. 6228(a)(1) by striking "subsection (b) of section 6227" and inserting "subsection (c) of section 6227". **Effective** 3-9-2002.

P.L. 107-147, §417(19)(B)(ii):

Amended Code Sec. 6228(a)(3)(A) by striking "subsection (b) of" preceding "section 6227". **Effective** 3-9-2002.

• **1992, Court of Federal Claims Technical and Procedural Improvements Act of 1992 (P.L. 102-572)**

P.L. 102-572, §902(b)(2):

Amended Code Sec. 6228(a) by striking "Claims Court" and inserting "Court of Federal Claims" each place it appears. **Effective** 10-29-92.

• **1983, Technical Corrections Act of 1982 (P.L. 97-448)**

P.L. 97-448, §306(c)(1)(B):

Amended the second sentence of Code Sec. 6228(a)(6) by striking out "Only" and inserting in lieu thereof "With respect to the partnership, only". **Effective** as if included in the provision of P.L. 97-248 to which it relates.

[Sec. 6228(b)]

(b) OTHER REQUESTS.—

(1) NOTICE PROVIDING THAT ITEMS BECOME NONPARTNERSHIP ITEMS.—If the Secretary mails to a partner, under subparagraph (A) of section 6231(b)(1) (relating to items ceasing to be partnership items), a notice that all partnership items of the partner for the partnership taxable year to which a timely request for administrative adjustment under subsection (d) of section 6227 relates shall be treated as nonpartnership items—

(A) such request shall be treated as a claim for credit or refund of an overpayment attributable to nonpartnership items, and

(B) the partner may bring an action under section 7422 with respect to such claim at any time within 2 years of the mailing of such notice.

(2) OTHER CASES.—

(A) IN GENERAL.—If the Secretary fails to allow any part of an administrative adjustment request filed under subsection (d) of section 6227 by a partner and paragraph (1) does not apply—

(i) such partner may, pursuant to section 7422, begin a civil action for refund of any amount due by reason of the adjustments described in such part of the request, and

(ii) on the beginning of such civil action, the partnership items of such partner for the partnership taxable year to which such part of such request relates shall be treated as nonpartnership items for purposes of this subchapter.

(B) PERIOD FOR FILING PETITION.—

(i) IN GENERAL.—An action may be begun under subparagraph (A) with respect to an administrative adjustment request for a partnership taxable year only—

(I) after the expiration of 6 months from the date of filing of the request under section 6227, and

(II) before the date which is 2 years after the date of filing of such request.

(ii) EXTENSION OF TIME.—The 2-year period described in subclause (II) of clause (i) shall be extended for such period as may be agreed upon in writing between the partner and the Secretary.

(C) ACTION BARRED AFTER PARTNERSHIP PROCEEDING HAS BEGUN.—No petition may be filed under subparagraph (A) with respect to an administrative adjustment request for a partnership taxable year after the Secretary mails to the partnership a notice of the beginning of a partnership proceeding with respect to such year.

(D) FAILURE BY SECRETARY TO ISSUE TIMELY NOTICE OF ADJUSTMENT.—If the Secretary—

(i) mails the notice referred to in subparagraph (C) before the expiration of the 2-year period referred to in clause (i)(II) of subparagraph (B), and

(ii) fails to mail a notice of final partnership administrative adjustment with respect to the partnership taxable year to which the request relates before the expiration of the period described in section 6229(a) (including any extension by agreement),

subparagraph (C) shall cease to apply with respect to such request, and the 2-year period referred to in clause (i)(II) of subparagraph (B) shall not expire before the date 6 months after the expiration of the period described in section 6229(a) (including any extension by agreement).

Amendments

• **2002, Job Creation and Worker Assistance Act of 2002 (P.L. 107-147)**

P.L. 107-147, §417(19)(B)(iii):

Amended Code Sec. 6228(b)(1) and Code Sec. 6228(b)(2)(A) by striking "subsection (c) of section 6227" and inserting "subsection (d) of section 6227". **Effective** 3-9-2002.

• **1982, Tax Equity and Fiscal Responsibility Act of 1982 (P.L. 97-248)**

P.L. 97-248, §402(a):

Added Code Sec. 6228. **Effective** for partnership tax years beginning after 9-3-82, and also for partnership tax years ending after 9-3-1982, if the partnership, each partner, and each indirect partner requests such application and if the Secretary or his delegate consents to such application. For a special rule for certain international satellite partnerships, see the amendment note for P.L. 97-248, following Code Sec. 6221.

• **2002, Job Creation and Worker Assistance Act of 2002 (P.L. 107-147)**

P.L. 107-147, §417(19)(B)(i):

Amended Code Sec. 6228(a)(1) by striking "subsection (b) of section 6227" and inserting "subsection (c) of section 6227". **Effective** 3-9-2002.

P.L. 107-147, §417(19)(B)(ii):

Amended Code Sec. 6228(a)(3)(A) by striking "subsection (b) of" preceding "section 6227". **Effective** 3-9-2002.

• **1992, Court of Federal Claims Technical and Procedural Improvements Act of 1992 (P.L. 102-572)**

P.L. 102-572, §902(b)(2):

Amended Code Sec. 6228(a) by striking "Claims Court" and inserting "Court of Federal Claims" each place it appears. **Effective** 10-29-92.

• **1983, Technical Corrections Act of 1982 (P.L. 97-448)**

P.L. 97-448, §306(c)(1)(B):

Amended the second sentence of Code Sec. 6228(a)(6) by striking out "Only" and inserting in lieu thereof "With respect to the partnership, only". **Effective** as if included in the provision of P.L. 97-248 to which it relates.

[Sec. 6229—Stricken]

Amendments

• **2015, Bipartisan Budget Act of 2015 (P.L. 114-74)**

P.L. 114-74, §1101(a):

Amended chapter 63 by striking subchapter C (Code Secs. 6221-6234). **Effective** generally for returns filed for partnership tax years beginning after 12-31-2017. For a special rule, see Act Sec. 1101(g)(4), below.

P.L. 114-74, §1101(g)(4), provides:

(4) ELECTION.—A partnership may elect (at such time and in such form and manner as the Secretary of the Treasury may prescribe) for the amendments made by this section (other than the election under section 6221(b) of such Code (as added by this Act)) to apply to any return of the partnership filed for partnership taxable years beginning after the date of the enactment of this Act and before January 1, 2018.

Prior to being stricken, Code Sec. 6229 read as follows:

SEC. 6229. PERIOD OF LIMITATIONS FOR MAKING ASSESSMENTS.

[Sec. 6229(a)]

(a) GENERAL RULE.—Except as otherwise provided in this section, the period for assessing any tax imposed by subtitle A with respect to any person which is attributable to any partnership item (or affected item) for a partnership taxable year shall not expire before the date which is 3 years after the later of—

(1) the date on which the partnership return for such taxable year was filed, or

(2) the last day for filing such return for such year (determined without regard to extensions).

[Sec. 6229(b)]

(b) EXTENSION BY AGREEMENT.—

(1) IN GENERAL.—The period described in subsection (a) (including an extension period under this subsection) may be extended—

(A) with respect to any partner, by an agreement entered into by the Secretary and such partner, and

(B) with respect to all partners, by an agreement entered into by the Secretary and the tax matters partner (or any other person authorized by the partnership in writing to enter into such an agreement),

before the expiration of such period.

(2) SPECIAL RULE WITH RESPECT TO DEBTORS IN TITLE 11 CASES.—Notwithstanding any other law or rule of law, if an agreement is entered into under paragraph (1)(B) and

ASSESSMENT—PARTNERSHIP ITEMS

the agreement is signed by a person who would be the tax matters partner but for the fact that, at the time that the agreement is executed, the person is a debtor in a bankruptcy proceeding under title 11 of the United States Code, such agreement shall be binding on all partners in the partnership unless the Secretary has been notified of the bankruptcy proceeding in accordance with regulations prescribed by the Secretary.

(3) COORDINATION WITH SECTION 6501(c)(4).—Any agreement under section 6501(c)(4) shall apply with respect to the period described in subsection (a) only if the agreement expressly provides that such agreement applies to tax attributable to partnership items.

Amendments

• **1997, Taxpayer Relief Act of 1997 (P.L. 105-34)**

P.L. 105-34, §1233(c):

Amended Code Sec. 6229(b) by redesignating paragraph (2) as paragraph (3) and by inserting after paragraph (1) a new paragraph (2). **Effective** for agreements entered into after 8-5-97.

[Sec. 6229(c)]

(c) SPECIAL RULE IN CASE OF FRAUD, ETC.—

(1) FALSE RETURN.—If any partner has, with the intent to evade tax, signed or participated directly or indirectly in the preparation of a partnership return which includes a false or fraudulent item—

(A) in the case of partners so signing or participating in the preparation of the return, any tax imposed by subtitle A which is attributable to any partnership item (or affected item) for the partnership taxable year to which the return relates may be assessed at any time, and

(B) in the case of all other partners, subsection (a) shall be applied with respect to such return by substituting "6 years" for "3 years."

(2) SUBSTANTIAL OMISSION OF INCOME.—If any partnership omits from gross income an amount properly includible therein and such amount is described in clause (i) or (ii) of section 6501(e)(1)(A), subsection (a) shall be applied by substituting "6 years" for "3 years".

(3) NO RETURN.—In the case of a failure by a partnership to file a return for any taxable year, any tax attributable to a partnership item (or affected item) arising in such year may be assessed at any time.

(4) RETURN FILED BY SECRETARY.—For purposes of this section, a return executed by the Secretary under subsection (b) of section 6020 on behalf of the partnership shall not be treated as a return of the partnership.

Amendments

• **2010, Hiring Incentives to Restore Employment Act (P.L. 111-147)**

P.L. 111-147, §513(a)(2)(B):

Amended Code Sec. 6229(c)(2) by striking "which is in excess of 25 percent of the amount of gross income stated in its return" and inserting "and such amount is described in clause (i) or (ii) of section 6501(e)(1)(A)". For the **effective** date, see Act Sec. 513(d), below.

P.L. 111-147, §513(d), provides:

(d) EFFECTIVE DATE.—The amendments made by this section shall apply to—

(1) returns filed after the date of the enactment of this Act; and

(2) returns filed on or before such date if the period specified in section 6501 of the Internal Revenue Code of 1986 (determined without regard to such amendments) for assessment of such taxes has not expired as of such date.

[Sec. 6229(d)]

(d) SUSPENSION WHEN SECRETARY MAKES ADMINISTRATIVE ADJUSTMENT.—If notice of a final partnership administrative adjustment with respect to any taxable year is mailed to the tax matters partner, the running of the period specified in subsection (a) (as modified by other provisions of this section) shall be suspended—

(1) for the period during which an action may be brought under section 6226 (and, if a petition is filed under section 6226 with respect to such administrative adjustment, until the decision of the court becomes final), and

(2) for 1 year thereafter.

Amendments

• **1997, Taxpayer Relief Act of 1997 (P.L. 105-34)**

P.L. 105-34, §1233(a):

Amended Code Sec. 6229(d)(1) by striking all that follows "section 6226" and inserting "(and, if a petition is filed under section 6226 with respect to such administrative adjustment, until the decision of the court becomes final), and". **Effective** for partnership tax years with respect to which the period under Code Sec. 6229 for assessing tax has not expired on or before 8-5-97. Prior to amendment, Code Sec. 6229(d)(1) read as follows:

(1) for the period during which an action may be brought under section 6226 (and, if an action with respect to such administrative adjustment is brought during such period, until the decision of the court in such action becomes final), and

[Sec. 6229(e)]

(e) UNIDENTIFIED PARTNER.—If—

(1) the name, address, and taxpayer identification number of a partner are not furnished on the partnership return for a partnership taxable year, and

(2)(A) the Secretary, before the expiration of the period otherwise provided under this section with respect to such partner, mails to the tax matters partner the notice specified in paragraph (2) of section 6223(a) with respect to such taxable year, or

(B) the partner has failed to comply with subsection (b) of section 6222 (relating to notification of inconsistent treatment) with respect to any partnership item for such taxable year,

the period for assessing any tax imposed by subtitle A which is attributable to any partnership item (or affected item) for such taxable year shall not expire with respect to such partner before the date which is 1 year after the date on which the name, address, and taxpayer identification number of such partner are furnished to the Secretary.

[Sec. 6229(f)]

(f) SPECIAL RULES.—

(1) ITEMS BECOMING NONPARTNERSHIP ITEMS.—If, before the expiration of the period otherwise provided in this section for assessing any tax imposed by subtitle A with respect to the partnership items of a partner for the partnership taxable year, such items become nonpartnership items by reason of 1 or more of the events described in subsection (b) of section 6231, the period for assessing any tax imposed by subtitle A which is attributable to such items (or any item affected by such items) shall not expire before the date which is 1 year after the date on which the items become nonpartnership items. The period described in the preceding sentence (including any extension period under this sentence) may be extended with respect to any partner by agreement entered into by the Secretary and such partner.

(2) SPECIAL RULE FOR PARTIAL SETTLEMENT AGREEMENTS.—If a partner enters into a settlement agreement with the Secretary or the Attorney General (or his delegate) with respect to the treatment of some of the partnership items in dispute for a partnership taxable year but other partnership items for such year remain in dispute, the period of limitations for assessing any tax attributable to the settled items shall be determined as if such agreement had not been entered into.

Amendments

• **2002, Job Creation and Worker Assistance Act of 2002 (P.L. 107-147)**

P.L. 107-147, §416(d)(1)(B):

Amended Code Sec. 6229(f)(2) by inserting "or the Attorney General (or his delegate)" after "Secretary". **Effective** with respect to settlement agreements entered into after 3-9-2002.

• **1997, Taxpayer Relief Act of 1997 (P.L. 105-34)**

P.L. 105-34, §1235(a)(1)-(3):

Amended Code Sec. 6229(f) by striking "(f) ITEMS BECOMING NONPARTNERSHIP ITEMS.—If" and inserting "(f) SPECIAL RULES.—(1) ITEMS BECOMING NONPARTNERSHIP ITEMS.—If", by moving the text of such subsection 2 ems to the right, and by adding at the end a new paragraph (2). **Effective** for settlements entered into after 8-5-97.

• **1988, Technical and Miscellaneous Revenue Act of 1988 (P.L. 100-647)**

P.L. 100-647, §1018(o)(3):

Amended Code Sec. 6229(f) by adding at the end thereof a new sentence. **Effective** as if included in the provision of P.L. 99-514 to which it relates.

• **1982, Tax Equity and Fiscal Responsibility Act of 1982 (P.L. 97-248)**

P.L. 97-248, §402(a):

Added Code Sec. 6229. **Effective** for partnership tax years beginning after 9-3-82, and also for partnership tax years ending after 9-3-82, if the partnership, each partner, and each indirect partner requests such application and the Secretary or his delegate consents to such application. For a special rule for certain international satellite partnerships, see the amendment note for P.L. 97-248, following Code Sec. 6221.

[Sec. 6229(g)]

(g) PERIOD OF LIMITATIONS FOR PENALTIES.—The provisions of this section shall apply also in the case of any addition to tax or an additional amount imposed under subchapter A of chapter 68 which arises with respect to any tax imposed under subtitle A in the same manner as if such addition or additional amount were a tax imposed by subtitle A.

Amendments

• **1986, Tax Reform Act of 1986 (P.L. 99-514)**

P.L. 99-514, §1875(d)(1):

Amended Code Sec. 6229 by adding at the end thereof new subsection (g). **Effective** as if included in the provision of P.L. 98-369 to which it relates.

[Sec. 6229(h)]

(h) SUSPENSION DURING PENDENCY OF BANKRUPTCY PROCEEDING.—If a petition is filed naming a partner as a debtor in a bankruptcy proceeding under title 11 of the United States Code, the running of the period of limitations provided in this section with respect to such partner shall be suspended—

(1) for the period during which the Secretary is prohibited by reason of such bankruptcy proceeding from making an assessment, and

(2) for 60 days thereafter.

Amendments

• **1997, Taxpayer Relief Act of 1997 (P.L. 105-34)**

P.L. 105-34, §1233(b):

Amended Code Sec. 6229 by adding at the end a new subsection (h). **Effective** for partnership tax years with respect to which the period under Code Sec. 6229 for assessing tax has not expired on or before 8-5-97.

Sec. 6229—Stricken

ASSESSMENT—PARTNERSHIP ITEMS

[Sec. 6230—Stricken]

Amendments

• **2015, Bipartisan Budget Act of 2015 (P.L. 114-74)**

P.L. 114-74, §1101(a):

Amended chapter 63 by striking subchapter C (Code Secs. 6221-6234). **Effective** generally for returns filed for partnership tax years beginning after 12-31-2017. For a special rule, see Act Sec. 1101(g)(4), below.

P.L. 114-74, §1101(g)(4), provides:

(4) ELECTION.—A partnership may elect (at such time and in such form and manner as the Secretary of the Treasury may prescribe) for the amendments made by this section (other than the election under section 6221(b) of such Code (as added by this Act)) to apply to any return of the partnership filed for partnership taxable years beginning after the date of the enactment of this Act and before January 1, 2018.

Prior to being stricken, Code Sec. 6230 read as follows:

SEC. 6230. ADDITIONAL ADMINISTRATIVE PROVISIONS.

[Sec. 6230(a)]

(a) COORDINATION WITH DEFICIENCY PROCEEDINGS.—

(1) IN GENERAL.—Except as provided in paragraph (2) or (3), subchapter B of this chapter shall not apply to the assessment or collection of any computational adjustment.

(2) DEFICIENCY PROCEEDINGS TO APPLY IN CERTAIN CASES.—

(A) Subchapter B shall apply to any deficiency attributable to—

(i) affected items which require partner level determinations (other than penalties, additions to tax, and additional amounts that relate to adjustments to partnership items), or

(ii) items which have become nonpartnership items (other than by reason of section 6231(b)(1)(C) and are described in section 6231(e)(1)(B).

(B) Subchapter B shall be applied separately with respect to each deficiency described in subparagraph (A) attributable to each partnership.

(C) Notwithstanding any other law or rule of law, any notice or proceeding under subchapter B with respect to a deficiency described in this paragraph shall not preclude or be precluded by any other notice, proceeding, or determination with respect to a partner's tax liability for a taxable year.

(3) SPECIAL RULE IN CASE OF ASSERTION BY PARTNER'S SPOUSE OF INNOCENT SPOUSE RELIEF.—

(A) Notwithstanding section 6404(b), if the spouse of a partner asserts that section 6015 applies with respect to a liability that is attributable to any adjustment to a partnership item (including any liability for any penalties, additions to tax, or additional amounts relating to such adjustment), then such spouse may file with the Secretary within 60 days after the notice of computational adjustment is mailed to the spouse a request for abatement of the assessment specified in such notice. Upon receipt of such request, the Secretary shall abate the assessment. Any reassessment of the tax with respect to which an abatement is made under this subparagraph shall be subject to the deficiency procedures prescribed by subchapter B. The period for making any such reassessment shall not expire before the expiration of 60 days after the date of such abatement.

(B) If the spouse files a petition with the Tax Court pursuant to section 6213 with respect to the request for abatement described in subparagraph (A), the Tax Court shall only have jurisdiction pursuant to this section to determine whether the requirements of section 6015 have been satisfied. For purposes of such determination, the treatment of partnership items (and the applicability of any penalties, additions to tax, or additional amounts) under the settlement, the final partnership administrative adjustment, or the decision of the court (whichever is appropriate) that gave rise to the liability in question shall be conclusive.

(C) Rules similar to the rules contained in subparagraphs (B) and (C) of paragraph (2) shall apply for purposes of this paragraph.

Amendments

• **2007, Tax Technical Corrections Act of 2007 (P.L. 110-172)**

P.L. 110-172, §11(a)(36):

Amended Code Sec. 6230(a)(3)(A) and (B) by striking "section 6013(e)" and inserting "section 6015". **Effective** 12-29-2007.

• **1997, Taxpayer Relief Act of 1997 (P.L. 105-34)**

P.L. 105-34, §1237(a):

Amended Code Sec. 6230(a) by adding at the end a new paragraph (3). **Effective** as if included in the amendments made by section 402 of P.L. 97-248 [generally **effective** for partnership tax years beginning after 9-3-82.—CCH].

P.L. 105-34, §1237(c)(1):

Amended Code Sec. 6230(a)(1) by striking "paragraph (2)" and inserting "paragraph (2) or (3)". **Effective** as if included in the amendments made by section 402 of P.L. 97-248 [generally **effective** for partnership tax years beginning after 9-3-82.—CCH].

P.L. 105-34, §1238(b)(2):

Amended Code Sec. 6230(a)(2)(A)(i). **Effective** for partnership tax years ending after 8-5-97. Prior to amendment, Code Sec. 6230(a)(2)(A)(i) read as follows:

(i) affected items which require partner level determinations, or

P.L. 105-34, §1238(b)(3)(A):

Amended Code Sec. 6230(a)(3)(A), as added by Act Sec. 1237(a), by inserting "(including any liability for any penalties, additions to tax, or additional amounts relating to such adjustment)" after "partnership item". **Effective** for partnership tax years ending after 8-5-97.

P.L. 105-34, §1238(b)(3)(B):

Amended Code Sec. 6230(a)(3)(B), as added by Act Sec. 1237(a), by inserting "(and the applicability of any penalties, additions to tax, or additional amounts)" after "partnership items". **Effective** for partnership tax years ending after 8-5-97.

• **1988, Technical and Miscellaneous Revenue Act of 1988 (P.L. 100-647)**

P.L. 100-647, §1018(o)(1):

Amended Code Sec. 6230(a)(2)(A)(ii) by striking out "nonpartnership items" and inserting in lieu thereof "nonpartnership items (other than by reason of section 6231(b)(1)(C))". **Effective** as if included in the provision of P.L. 99-514 to which it relates.

• **1986, Tax Reform Act of 1986 (P.L. 99-514)**

P.L. 99-514, §1875(d)(2)(A):

Amended Code Sec. 6230(a). **Effective** as if it were included in P.L. 97-248. Prior to amendment, Code Sec. 6230(a) read as follows:

(a) NORMAL DEFICIENCY PROCEEDINGS DO NOT APPLY TO COMPUTATIONAL ADJUSTMENTS.—Subchapter B of this chapter shall not apply to the assessment or collection of any computational adjustment.

[Sec. 6230(b)]

(b) MATHEMATICAL AND CLERICAL ERRORS APPEARING ON PARTNERSHIP RETURN.—

(1) IN GENERAL.—Section 6225 shall not apply to any adjustment necessary to correct a mathematical or clerical error (as defined in section 6213(g)(2)) appearing on the partnership return.

(2) EXCEPTION.—Paragraph (1) shall not apply to a partner if, within 60 days after the day on which notice of the correction of the error is mailed to the partner, such partner files with the Secretary a request that the correction not be made.

[Sec. 6230(c)]

(c) CLAIMS ARISING OUT OF ERRONEOUS COMPUTATIONS, ETC.—

(1) IN GENERAL.—A partner may file a claim for refund on the grounds that—

(A) the Secretary erroneously computed any computational adjustment necessary—

(i) to make the partnership items on the partner's return consistent with the treatment of the partnership items on the partnership return, or

(ii) to apply to the partner a settlement, a final partnership administrative adjustment, or the decision of a court in an action brought under section 6226 or section 6228(a),

(B) the Secretary failed to allow a credit or to make a refund to the partner in the amount of the overpayment attributable to the application to the partner of a settlement, a final partnership administrative adjustment, or the decision of a court in an action brought under section 6226 or section 6228(a), or

(C) the Secretary erroneously imposed any penalty, addition to tax, or additional amount which relates to an adjustment to a partnership item.

(2) TIME FOR FILING CLAIM.—

(A) UNDER PARAGRAPH (1)(A) OR (C).—Any claim under subparagraph (A) or (C) of paragraph (1) shall be filed within 6 months after the day on which the Secretary mails the notice of computational adjustment to the partner.

(B) UNDER PARAGRAPH (1)(B).—Any claim under paragraph (1)(B) shall be filed within 2 years after whichever of the following days is appropriate:

(i) the day on which the settlement is entered into,

(ii) the day on which the period during which an action may be brought under section 6226 with respect to the final partnership administrative adjustment expires, or

(iii) the day on which the decision of the court becomes final.

(3) SUIT IF CLAIM NOT ALLOWED.—If any portion of a claim under paragraph (1) is not allowed, the partner may bring suit with respect to such portion within the period specified in subsection (a) of section 6532 (relating to periods of limitations on refund suits).

(4) NO REVIEW OF SUBSTANTIVE ISSUES.—For purposes of any claim or suit under this subsection, the treatment of partnership items on the partnership return, under the settlement, under the final partnership administrative adjustment, or under the decision of the court (whichever is appropriate) shall be conclusive. In addition, the determination under the final partnership administrative adjustment or under the decision of the court (whichever is appropriate) concerning the applicability of any penalty, addition to tax, or additional amount which relates to an adjustment to a partnership item shall also be conclusive. Notwithstanding the preceding sentence, the partner shall be allowed to assert any partner level defenses that may apply or to challenge the amount of the computational adjustment.

(5) RULES FOR SEEKING INNOCENT SPOUSE RELIEF.—

(A) IN GENERAL.—The spouse of a partner may file a claim for refund on the ground that the Secretary failed to relieve the spouse under section 6015 from a liability that is attributable to an adjustment to a partnership item (including any liability for any penalties, additions to tax, or additional amounts relating to such adjustment).

(B) TIME FOR FILING CLAIM.—Any claim under subparagraph (A) shall be filed within 6 months after the day on which the Secretary mails to the spouse the notice of computational adjustment referred to in subsection (a)(3)(A).

(C) SUIT IF CLAIM NOT ALLOWED.—If the claim under subparagraph (B) is not allowed, the spouse may bring suit with respect to the claim within the period specified in paragraph (3).

(D) PRIOR DETERMINATIONS ARE BINDING.—For purposes of any claim or suit under this paragraph, the treatment of partnership items (and the applicability of any penalties, additions to tax, or additional amounts) under the settlement, the final partnership administrative adjustment, or the decision of the court (whichever is appropriate) that gave rise to the liability in question shall be conclusive.

ASSESSMENT—PARTNERSHIP ITEMS

Amendments

• **1998, IRS Restructuring and Reform Act of 1998 (P.L. 105-206)**

P.L. 105-206, §3201(e)(2):

Amended Code Sec. 6230(c)(5)(A) by striking "section 6013(e)" and inserting "section 6015". **Effective** for any liability for tax arising after 7-22-98 and any liability for tax arising on or before such date but remaining unpaid as of such date.

• **1997, Taxpayer Relief Act of 1997 (P.L. 105-34)**

P.L. 105-34, §1237(b):

Amended Code Sec. 6230(c) by adding at the end a new paragraph (5). **Effective** as if included in the amendments made by section 402 of P.L. 97-248 [generally **effective** for partnership tax years beginning after 9-3-82.—CCH]

P.L. 105-34, §1238(b)(3)(C):

Amended Code Sec. 6230(c)(5)(A), as added by Act Sec. 1237(b), by inserting before the period "(including any liability for any penalties, additions to tax, or additional amounts relating to such adjustment)". **Effective** for partnership tax years ending after 8-5-97.

P.L. 105-34, §1238(b)(3)(D):

Amended Code Sec. 6230(c)(5)(D), as added by Act Sec. 1237(b), by inserting "(and the applicability of any penalties, additions to tax, or additional amounts)" after "partnership items". **Effective** for partnership tax years ending after 8-5-97.

P.L. 105-34, §1238(b)(4):

Amended Code Sec. 6230(c)(1) by striking "or" at the end of subparagraph (A), by striking the period at the end of subparagraph (B) and inserting ", or", and by adding at the end a new subparagraph (C). **Effective** for partnership tax years ending after 8-5-97.

P.L. 105-34, §1238(b)(5):

Amended so much of Code Sec. 6230(c)(2)(A) as precedes "shall be filed". **Effective** for partnership tax years ending after 8-5-97. Prior to amendment, Code Sec. 6230(c)(2)(A) read as follows:

(A) UNDER PARAGRAPH (1)(A).—Any claim under paragraph (1)(A) shall be filed within 6 months after the day on which the Secretary mails the notice of computational adjustment to the partner.

P.L. 105-34, §1238(b)(6):

Amended Code Sec. 6230(c)(4) by adding at the end two new sentences. **Effective** for partnership tax years ending after 8-5-97.

• **1984, Deficit Reduction Act of 1984 (P.L. 98-369)**

P.L. 98-369, §714(p)(2)(A):

Amended Code Sec. 6230(c)(1)(B) by striking out "(or erroneously computed the amount of any such credit or refund)". **Effective** as if included in the provision of P.L. 97-248 to which it relates.

[Sec. 6230(d)]

(d) SPECIAL RULES WITH RESPECT TO CREDITS OR REFUNDS ATTRIBUTABLE TO PARTNERSHIP ITEMS.—

(1) IN GENERAL.—Except as otherwise provided in this subsection, no credit or refund of an overpayment attributable to a partnership item (or an affected item) for a partnership taxable year shall be allowed or made to any partner after the expiration of the period of limitation prescribed in section 6229 with respect to such partner for assessment of any tax attributable to such item.

(2) ADMINISTRATIVE ADJUSTMENT REQUEST.—If a request for an administrative adjustment under section 6227 with respect to a partnership item is timely filed, credit or refund of any overpayment attributable to such partnership item (or an affected item) may be allowed or made at any time before the expiration of the period prescribed in section 6228 for bringing suit with respect to such request.

(3) CLAIM UNDER SUBSECTION (c).—If a timely claim is filed under subsection (c) for a credit or refund of an overpayment attributable to a partnership item (or affected item), credit or refund of such overpayment may be allowed or made at any time before the expiration of the period specified in section 6532 (relating to periods of limitations on suits) for bringing suit with respect to such claim.

(4) TIMELY SUIT.—Paragraph (1) shall not apply to any credit or refund of any overpayment attributable to a partnership item (or an item affected by such partnership item) if a partner brings a timely suit with respect to a timely administrative adjustment request under section 6228 or a timely claim under subsection (c) relating to such overpayment.

(5) OVERPAYMENTS REFUNDED WITHOUT REQUIREMENT THAT PARTNER FILE CLAIM.—In the case of any overpayment by a partner which is attributable to a partnership item (or an affected item) and which may be refunded under this subchapter, to the extent practicable credit or refund of such overpayment shall be allowed or made without any requirement that the partner file a claim therefor.

(6) SUBCHAPTER B OF CHAPTER 66 NOT APPLICABLE.—Subchapter B of chapter 66 (relating to limitations on credit or refund) shall not apply to any credit or refund of an overpayment attributable to a partnership item.

Amendments

• **1997, Taxpayer Relief Act of 1997 (P.L. 105-34)**

P.L. 105-34, §1239(c)(1):

Amended Code Sec. 6230(d)(6) by striking "(or an affected item)" before the period at the end of the sentence. **Effective** for partnership tax years ending after 8-5-97.

[Sec. 6230(e)]

(e) TAX MATTERS PARTNER REQUIRED TO FURNISH NAMES OF PARTNERS TO SECRETARY.—If the Secretary mails to any partnership the notice specified in paragraph (1) of section 6223(a) with respect to any partnership taxable year, the tax matters partner shall furnish to the Secretary the name, address, profits interest, and taxpayer identification number of each person who was a partner in such partnership at any time during such taxable year. If the tax matters partner later discovers that the information furnished to the Secretary was incorrect or incomplete, the tax matters partner shall furnish such revised or additional information as may be necessary.

[Sec. 6230(f)]

(f) FAILURE OF TAX MATTERS PARTNER, ETC., TO FULFILL RESPONSIBILITY DOES NOT AFFECT APPLICABILITY OF PROCEEDING.—The failure of the tax matters partner, a pass-thru partner, the representative of a notice group, or any other representative of a partner to provide any notice or perform any act required under this subchapter or under regulations prescribed under this subchapter on behalf of such partner does not affect the applicability of any proceeding or adjustment under this subchapter to such partner.

[Sec. 6230(g)]

(g) DATE DECISION OF COURT BECOMES FINAL.—For purposes of section 6229(d)(1) and section 6230(c)(2)(B), the principles of section 7481(a) shall be applied in determining the date on which a decision of a district court or the Court of Federal Claims becomes final.

Amendments

• **1992, Court of Federal Claims Technical and Procedural Improvements Act of 1992 (P.L. 102-572)**

P.L. 102-572, §902(b)(2):

Amended Code Sec. 6230(g) by striking "Claims Court" and inserting "Court of Federal Claims". **Effective** 10-29-92.

[Sec. 6230(h)]

(h) EXAMINATION AUTHORITY NOT LIMITED.—Nothing in this subchapter shall be construed as limiting the authority granted to the Secretary under section 7602.

[Sec. 6230(i)]

(i) TIME AND MANNER OF FILING STATEMENTS, MAKING ELECTIONS, ETC.—Except as otherwise provided in this subchapter, each—

(1) statement,

(2) election,

(3) request, and

(4) furnishing of information,

shall be filed or made at such time, in such manner, and at such place as may be prescribed in regulations.

[Sec. 6230(j)]

(j) PARTNERSHIPS HAVING PRINCIPAL PLACE OF BUSINESS OUTSIDE THE UNITED STATES.—For purposes of sections 6226 and 6228, a principal place of business located outside the United States shall be treated as located in the District of Columbia.

[Sec. 6230(k)]

(k) REGULATIONS.—The Secretary shall prescribe such regulations as may be necessary to carry out the purposes of this subchapter. Any reference in this subchapter to regulations is a reference to regulations prescribed by the Secretary.

[Sec. 6230(l)]

(l) COURT RULES.—Any action brought under any provision of this subchapter shall be conducted in accordance with such rules of practice and procedure as may be prescribed by the Court in which the action is brought.

Amendments

• **1982, Tax Equity and Fiscal Responsibility Act of 1982 (P.L. 97-248)**

P.L. 97-248, §402(a):

Added Code Sec. 6230. **Effective** for partnership tax years beginning after 9-3-82, and also for partnership tax years ending after 9-3-82, if the partnership, each partner, and each indirect partner, requests such application and if the Secretary consents to such application. For a special rule for certain international satellite partnerships, see the amendment note for P.L. 97-248, following Code Sec. 6221.

• **2007, Tax Technical Corrections Act of 2007 (P.L. 110-172)**

P.L. 110-172, §11(a)(36):

Amended Code Sec. 6230(a)(3)(A) and (B) by striking "section 6013(e)" and inserting "section 6015". **Effective** 12-29-2007.

• **1997, Taxpayer Relief Act of 1997 (P.L. 105-34)**

P.L. 105-34, §1237(a):

Amended Code Sec. 6230(a) by adding at the end a new paragraph (3). **Effective** as if included in the amendments made by section 402 of P.L. 97-248 [generally **effective** for partnership tax years beginning after 9-3-82.—CCH].

P.L. 105-34, §1237(c)(1):

Amended Code Sec. 6230(a)(1) by striking "paragraph (2)" and inserting "paragraph (2) or (3)". **Effective** as if included in the amendments made by section 402 of P.L. 97-248 [generally **effective** for partnership tax years beginning after 9-3-82.—CCH].

P.L. 105-34, §1238(b)(2):

Amended Code Sec. 6230(a)(2)(A)(i). **Effective** for partnership tax years ending after 8-5-97. Prior to amendment, Code Sec. 6230(a)(2)(A)(i) read as follows:

(i) affected items which require partner level determinations, or

P.L. 105-34, §1238(b)(3)(A):

Amended Code Sec. 6230(a)(3)(A), as added by Act Sec. 1237(a), by inserting "(including any liability for any penalties, additions to tax, or additional amounts relating to such adjustment)" after "partnership item". **Effective** for partnership tax years ending after 8-5-97.

Sec. 6230—Stricken

P.L. 105-34, §1238(b)(3)(B):

Amended Code Sec. 6230(a)(3)(B), as added by Act Sec. 1237(a), by inserting "(and the applicability of any penalties, additions to tax, or additional amounts)" after "partnership items". **Effective** for partnership tax years ending after 8-5-97.

- **1988, Technical and Miscellaneous Revenue Act of 1988 (P.L. 100-647)**

P.L. 100-647, §1018(o)(1):

Amended Code Sec. 6230(a)(2)(A)(ii) by striking out "nonpartnership items" and inserting in lieu thereof "nonpartnership items (other than by reason of section 6231(b)(1)(C))". **Effective** as if included in the provision of P.L. 99-514 to which it relates.

[Sec. 6231—Stricken]

Amendments

- **2015, Bipartisan Budget Act of 2015 (P.L. 114-74)**

P.L. 114-74, §1101(a):

Amended chapter 63 by striking subchapter C (Code Secs. 6221-6234). **Effective** generally for returns filed for partnership tax years beginning after 12-31-2017. For a special rule, see Act Sec. 1101(g)(4), below.

P.L. 114-74, §1101(g)(4), provides:

(4) ELECTION.—A partnership may elect (at such time and in such form and manner as the Secretary of the Treasury may prescribe) for the amendments made by this section (other than the election under section 6221(b) of such Code (as added by this Act)) to apply to any return of the partnership filed for partnership taxable years beginning after the date of the enactment of this Act and before January 1, 2018.

Prior to being stricken, Code Sec. 6231 read as follows:

SEC. 6231. DEFINITIONS AND SPECIAL RULES.

[Sec. 6231(a)]

(a) DEFINITIONS.—For purposes of this subchapter—

(1) PARTNERSHIP.—

(A) IN GENERAL.—Except as provided in subparagraph (B), the term "partnership" means any partnership required to file a return under section 6031(a).

(B) EXCEPTION FOR SMALL PARTNERSHIPS.—

(i) IN GENERAL.—The term "partnership" shall not include any partnership having 10 or fewer partners each of whom is an individual (other than a nonresident alien), a C corporation, or an estate of a deceased partner. For purposes of the preceding sentence, a husband and wife (and their estates) shall be treated as 1 partner.

(ii) ELECTION TO HAVE SUBCHAPTER APPLY.—A partnership (within the meaning of subparagraph (A)) may for any taxable year elect to have clause (i) not apply. Such election shall apply for such taxable year and all subsequent taxable years unless revoked with the consent of the Secretary.

(2) PARTNER.—The term "partner" means—

(A) a partner in the partnership, and

(B) any other person whose income tax liability under subtitle A is determined in whole or in part by taking into account directly or indirectly partnership items of the partnership.

(3) PARTNERSHIP ITEM.—The term "partnership item" means, with respect to a partnership, any item required to be taken into account for the partnership's taxable year under any provision of subtitle A to the extent regulations prescribed by the Secretary provide that, for purposes of this subtitle, such item is more appropriately determined at the partnership level than at the partner level.

(4) NONPARTNERSHIP ITEM.—The term "nonpartnership item" means an item which is (or is treated as) not a partnership item.

(5) AFFECTED ITEM.—The term "affected item" means any item to the extent such item is affected by a partnership item.

(6) COMPUTATIONAL ADJUSTMENT.—The term "computational adjustment" means the change in the tax liability of a partner which properly reflects the treatment under this subchapter of a partnership item. All adjustments required to apply the results of a proceeding with respect to a partnership under this subchapter to an indirect partner shall be treated as computational adjustments.

(7) TAX MATTERS PARTNER.—The tax matters partner of any partnership is—

(A) the general partner designated as the tax matters partner as provided in regulations, or

(B) if there is no general partner who has been so designated, the general partner having the largest profits interest in the partnership at the close of the taxable year involved (or, where there is more than 1 such partner, the 1 of such partners whose name would appear first in an alphabetical listing).

If there is no general partner designated under subparagraph (A) and the Secretary determines that it is impracticable to apply subparagraph (B), the partner selected by the Secretary shall be treated as the tax matters partner. The Secretary shall, within 30 days of selecting a tax matters partner under the preceding sentence, notify all partners required to receive notice under section 6223(a) of the name and address of the person selected.

(8) NOTICE PARTNER.—The term "notice partner" means a partner who, at the time in question, would be entitled to notice under subsection (a) of section 6223 (determined without regard to subsections (b)(2) and (e)(1)(B) thereof).

(9) PASS-THRU PARTNER.—The term "pass-thru partner" means a partnership, estate, trust, S corporation, nominee, or other similar person through whom other persons hold an interest in the partnership with respect to which proceedings under this subchapter are conducted.

(10) INDIRECT PARTNER.—The term "indirect partner" means a person holding an interest in a partnership through 1 or more pass-thru partners.

(11) 5-PERCENT GROUP.—A 5-percent group is a group of partners who for the partnership taxable year involved had profits interests which aggregated 5 percent or more.

- **1986, Tax Reform Act of 1986 (P.L. 99-514)**

P.L. 99-514, §1875(d)(2)(A):

Amended Code Sec. 6230(a). **Effective** as if it were included in P.L. 97-248. Prior to amendment, Code Sec. 6230(a) read as follows:

(a) NORMAL DEFICIENCY PROCEEDINGS DO NOT APPLY TO COMPUTATIONAL ADJUSTMENTS.—Subchapter B of this chapter shall not apply to the assessment or collection of any computational adjustment.

(12) HUSBAND AND WIFE.—Except to the extent otherwise provided in regulations, a husband and wife who have a joint interest in a partnership shall be treated as 1 person.

Amendments

- **1998, IRS Restructuring and Reform Act of 1998 (P.L. 105-206)**

P.L. 105-206, §3507(a):

Amended Code Sec. 6231(a)(7) by adding at the end a new sentence. **Effective** for selections of tax matters partners made by the Secretary of the Treasury after 7-22-98.

- **1997, Taxpayer Relief Act of 1997 (P.L. 105-34)**

P.L. 105-34, §1234(a):

Amended Code Sec. 6231(a)(1)(B)(i). **Effective** for partnership tax years ending after 8-5-97. Prior to amendment, Code Sec. 6231(a)(1)(B)(i) read as follows:

(i) IN GENERAL.—The term "partnership" shall not include any partnership if—

(I) such partnership has 10 or fewer partners each of whom is a natural person (other than a nonresident alien) or an estate, and

(II) each partner's share of each partnership item is the same as his share of every other item.

For purposes of the preceding sentence, a husband and wife (and their estates) shall be treated as 1 partner.

- **1984, Deficit Reduction Act of 1984 (P.L. 98-369)**

P.L. 98-369, §714(p)(2)(B):

Amended Code Sec. 6231(a)(9) by striking out "electing small business corporation" and inserting in lieu thereof "S corporation". **Effective** as if included in the provision of P.L. 97-248 to which it relates.

[Sec. 6231(b)]

(b) ITEMS CEASE TO BE PARTNERSHIP ITEMS IN CERTAIN CASES.—

(1) IN GENERAL.—For purposes of this subchapter, the partnership items of a partner for a partnership taxable year shall become nonpartnership items as of the date—

(A) the Secretary mails to such partner a notice that such items shall be treated as nonpartnership items,

(B) the partner files suit under section 6228(b) after the Secretary fails to allow an administrative adjustment request with respect to any of such items,

(C) the Secretary or the Attorney General (or his delegate) enters into a settlement agreement with the partner with respect to such items, or

(D) such change occurs under subsection (e) of section 6223 (relating to effect of Secretary's failure to provide notice) or under subsection (c) of this section.

(2) CIRCUMSTANCES IN WHICH NOTICE IS PERMITTED.—The Secretary may mail the notice referred to in subparagraph (A) of paragraph (1) to a partner with respect to partnership items for a partnership taxable year only if—

(A) such partner—

(i) has complied with subparagraph (B) of section 6222(b)(1) (relating to notification of inconsistent treatment) with respect to one or more of such items, and

(ii) has not, as of the date on which the Secretary mails the notice, filed a request for administrative adjustments which would make the partner's treatment of the item or items with respect to which the partner complied with subparagraph (B) of section 6222(b)(1) consistent with the treatment of such item or items on the partnership return, or

(B)(i) such partner has filed a request under section 6227(d) for administrative adjustment of one or more of such items, and

(ii) the adjustments requested would not make such partner's treatment of such items consistent with the treatment of such items on the partnership return.

(3) NOTICE MUST BE MAILED BEFORE BEGINNING OF PARTNERSHIP PROCEEDING.—Any notice to a partner under subparagraph (A) of paragraph (1) with respect to partnership items for a partnership taxable year shall be mailed before the day on which the Secretary mails to the tax matters partner a notice of the beginning of an administrative proceeding at the partnership level with respect to such items.

Amendments

- **2002, Job Creation and Worker Assistance Act of 2002 (P.L. 107-147)**

P.L. 107-147, §416(d)(1)(C):

Amended Code Sec. 6231(b)(1)(C) by inserting "or the Attorney General (or his delegate)" after "Secretary". **Effective** with respect to settlement agreements entered into after 3-9-2002.

P.L. 107-147, §417(19)(C):

Amended Code Sec. 6231(b)(2)(B)(i) by striking "section 6227(c)" and inserting "section 6227(d)". **Effective** 3-9-2002.

ASSESSMENT—PARTNERSHIP ITEMS

• **1984, Deficit Reduction Act of 1984 (P.L. 98-369)**

P.L. 98-369, §714(p)(2)(I):

Amended Code Sec. 6231(b)(2)(B) by striking out "section 6227(b)" and inserting in lieu thereof "section 6227(c)". **Effective** as if included in the provision of P.L. 97-248 to which it relates.

[Sec. 6231(c)]

(c) REGULATIONS WITH RESPECT TO CERTAIN SPECIAL ENFORCEMENT AREAS.—

(1) APPLICABILITY OF SUBSECTION.—This subsection applies in the case of—

(A) assessments under section 6851 (relating to termination assessments of income tax) or section 6861 (relating to jeopardy assessments of income, estate, gift, and certain excise taxes),

(B) criminal investigations,

(C) indirect methods of proof of income,

(D) foreign partnerships, and

(E) other areas that the Secretary determines by regulation to present special enforcement considerations.

(2) ITEMS MAY BE TREATED AS NONPARTNERSHIP ITEMS.—To the extent that the Secretary determines and provides by regulations that to treat items as partnership items will interfere with the effective and efficient enforcement of this title in any case described in paragraph (1), such items shall be treated as non-partnership items for purposes of this subchapter.

(3) SPECIAL RULES.—The Secretary may prescribe by regulation such special rules as the Secretary determines to be necessary to achieve the purposes of this subchapter in any case described in paragraph (1).

[Sec. 6231(d)]

(d) TIME FOR DETERMINING PARTNER'S PROFITS INTEREST IN PARTNERSHIP.—

(1) IN GENERAL.—For purposes of section 6223(b) (relating to special rules for partnerships with more than 100 partners) and paragraph (11) of subsection (a) (relating to 5-percent group), the interest of a partner in the profits of a partnership for a partnership taxable year shall be determined—

(A) in the case of a partner whose entire interest in the partnership is disposed of during such partnership taxable year, as of the moment immediately before such disposition, or

(B) in the case of any other partner, as of the close of the partnership taxable year.

(2) INDIRECT PARTNERS.—The Secretary shall prescribe regulations consistent with the principles of paragraph (1) to be applied in the case of indirect partners.

Amendments

• **1984, Deficit Reduction Act of 1984 (P.L. 98-369)**

P.L. 98-369, §714(p)(2)(C):

Amended Code Sec. 6231(d)(1)(A). **Effective** as if included in the provision of P.L. 97-248 to which it relates. Prior to amendment, Code Sec. 6231(d)(1)(A) read as follows:

(A) in the case of a partner whose entire interest in the partnership is liquidated, sold, or exchanged during such partnership taxable year, as of the moment immediately before such liquidation, sale, or exchange, or

[Sec. 6231(e)]

(e) EFFECT OF JUDICIAL DECISIONS IN CERTAIN PROCEEDINGS.—

(1) DETERMINATIONS AT PARTNER LEVEL.—No judicial determination with respect to the income tax liability of any partner not conducted under this subchapter shall be a bar to any adjustment in such partner's income tax liability resulting from—

(A) a proceeding with respect to partnership items under this subchapter, or

(B) a proceeding with respect to items which become nonpartnership items—

(i) by reason of 1 or more of the events described in subsection (b), and

(ii) after the appropriate time for including such items in any other proceeding with respect to nonpartnership items.

(2) PROCEEDINGS UNDER SECTION 6228(a).—No judicial determination in any proceeding under subsection (a) of section 6228 with respect to any partnership item shall be a bar to any adjustment in any other partnership item.

[Sec. 6231(f)]

(f) SPECIAL RULE FOR DEDUCTIONS, LOSSES, AND CREDITS OF FOREIGN PARTNERSHIPS.—Except to the extent otherwise provided in regulations, in the case of any partnership the tax matters partner of which resides outside the United States or the books of which are maintained outside the United States, no deduction, loss, or credit shall be allowable to any partner unless section 6031 is complied with for the partnership's taxable year in which such deduction, loss, or credit arose at such time as the Secretary prescribes by regulations.

Amendments

• **1997, Taxpayer Relief Act of 1997 (P.L. 105-34)**

P.L. 105-34, §1141(b)(1)-(2):

Amended Code Sec. 6231(f) by striking "LOSSES AND" in the heading and inserting "DEDUCTIONS, LOSSES, AND", and by striking "loss or" each place it apppears and inserting "deduction, loss, or". **Effective** for tax years beginning after 8-5-97.

• **1984, Deficit Reduction Act of 1984 (P.L. 98-369)**

P.L. 98-369, §714(p)(2)(D):

Amended Code Sec. 6231(f) by striking out "such deduction or credit" and inserting in lieu thereof "such loss or credit". **Effective** as if included in the provision of P.L. 97-248 to which it relates.

• **1982, Tax Equity and Fiscal Responsibility Act of 1982 (P.L. 97-248)**

P.L. 97-248, §402(a):

Added Code Sec. 6231. **Effective** for partnership tax years beginning after 9-3-82, and also for partnership tax years ending after 9-3-82, if the partnership, each partner, and each indirect partner requests such application and the Secretary or his delegate consents to such application. For a special rule for certain international satellite partnerships, see the amendment note for P.L. 97-248, following Code Sec. 6221.

[Sec. 6231(g)]

(g) PARTNERSHIP RETURN TO BE DETERMINATIVE OF WHETHER SUBCHAPTER APPLIES.—

(1) DETERMINATION THAT SUBCHAPTER APPLIES.—If, on the basis of a partnership return for a taxable year, the Secretary reasonably determines that this subchapter applies to such partnership for such year but such determination is erroneous, then the provisions of this subchapter are hereby extended to such partnership (and its items) for such taxable year and to partners of such partnership.

(2) DETERMINATION THAT SUBCHAPTER DOES NOT APPLY.—If, on the basis of a partnership return for a taxable year, the Secretary reasonably determines that this subchapter does not apply to such partnership for such year but such determination is erroneous, then the provisions of this subchapter shall not apply to such partnership (and its items) for such taxable year or to partners of such partnership.

Amendments

• **1997, Taxpayer Relief Act of 1997 (P.L. 105-34)**

P.L. 105-34, §1232(a):

Amended Code Sec. 6231 by adding at the end a new subsection (g). **Effective** for partnership tax years ending after 8-5-97.

• **1998, IRS Restructuring and Reform Act of 1998 (P.L. 105-206)**

P.L. 105-206, §3507(a):

Amended Code Sec. 6231(a)(7) by adding at the end a new sentence. **Effective** for selections of tax matters partners made by the Secretary of the Treasury after 7-22-98.

• **1997, Taxpayer Relief Act of 1997 (P.L. 105-34)**

P.L. 105-34, §1234(a):

Amended Code Sec. 6231(a)(1)(B)(i). **Effective** for partnership tax years ending after 8-5-97. Prior to amendment, Code Sec. 6231(a)(1)(B)(i) read as follows:

(i) IN GENERAL.—The term "partnership" shall not include any partnership if—

(I) such partnership has 10 or fewer partners each of whom is a natural person (other than a nonresident alien) or an estate, and

(II) each partner's share of each partnership item is the same as his share of every other item.

For purposes of the preceding sentence, a husband and wife (and their estates) shall be treated as 1 partner.

• **1984, Deficit Reduction Act of 1984 (P.L. 98-369)**

P.L. 98-369, §714(p)(2)(B):

Amended Code Sec. 6231(a)(9) by striking out "electing small business corporation" and inserting in lieu thereof "S corporation". **Effective** as if included in the provision of P.L. 97-248 to which it relates.

[Sec. 6232—Repealed]

Amendments

• **1988, Omnibus Trade and Competitiveness Act of 1988 (P.L. 100-418)**

P.L. 100-418, §1941(b)(1):

Repealed Code Sec. 6232. **Effective** for crude oil removed from the premises on or after 8-23-88. Prior to repeal, Code Sec. 6232 read as follows:

SEC. 6232. EXTENSION OF SUBCHAPTER TO WINDFALL PROFIT TAX.

(a) INCLUSION AS PARTNERSHIP ITEM.—For purposes of applying this subchapter to the tax imposed by chapter 45 (relating to the windfall profit tax), the term "partnership item" means any item relating to the determination of the tax imposed by chapter 45 to the extent regulations prescribed by the Secretary provide that, for purposes of this subtitle, such item is more appropriately determined at the partnership level than at the partner level.

(b) SEPARATE APPLICATION.—This subchapter shall be applied separately with respect to—

(1) partnership items described in subsection (a), and

(2) partnership items described in section 6231(a)(3).

(c) PARTNERSHIP AUTHORIZED TO ACT FOR PARTNERS.—

(1) IN GENERAL.—For purposes of chapter 45 and so much of this subtitle as relates to chapter 45, to the extent and in the manner provided in regulations, a partnership shall be treated as authorized to act for each partner with respect to the determination, assessment, or collection of the tax imposed by chapter 45.

(2) PARTNERS ENTITLED TO 5 PERCENT OR MORE OF INCOME MAY ELECT OUT OF SUBSECTION.—Paragraph (1) shall not apply to any partnership if partners entitled to 5 percent or more of the income of the partnership elect (at the time and in the manner provided in regulations) not to have paragraph (1) apply to the partnership.

(3) PARTNER'S RIGHTS PRESERVED.—Nothing in paragraph (1) shall be construed to take away from any person any right granted to such person by the foregoing sections of this subchapter.

• **1982, Tax Equity and Fiscal Responsibility Act of 1982 (P.L. 97-248)**

P.L. 97-248, §402(a):

Added Code Sec. 6232. **Effective** for partnership tax years beginning after 9-3-82, and also for partnership tax years ending after 9-3-82, if the partnership, each partner, and each indirect partner requests such application and the Secretary or his delegate consents to such application. For a special rule for certain international

ASSESSMENT—PARTNERSHIP ITEMS

satellite partnerships, see the amendment note for P.L. 97-248, following Code Sec. 6221.

[Sec. 6233—Stricken]

Amendments

• **2015, Bipartisan Budget Act of 2015 (P.L. 114-74)**

P.L. 114-74, §1101(a):

Amended chapter 63 by striking subchapter C (Code Secs. 6221-6234). **Effective** generally for returns filed for partnership tax years beginning after 12-31-2017. For a special rule, see Act Sec. 1101(g)(4), below.

P.L. 114-74, §1101(g)(4), provides:

(4) ELECTION.—A partnership may elect (at such time and in such form and manner as the Secretary of the Treasury may prescribe) for the amendments made by this section (other than the election under section 6221(b) of such Code (as added by this Act)) to apply to any return of the partnership filed for partnership taxable years beginning after the date of the enactment of this Act and before January 1, 2018.

Prior to being stricken, Code Sec. 6233 read as follows:

SEC. 6233. EXTENSION TO ENTITIES FILING PARTNERSHIP RETURNS, ETC.

[Sec. 6233(a)]

(a) GENERAL RULE.—If a partnership return is filed by an entity for a taxable year but it is determined that the entity is not a partnership for such year, then, to the extent provided in regulations, the provisions of this subchapter are hereby extended in respect of such year to such entity and its items and to persons holding an interest in such entity.

[Sec. 6233(b)]

(b) SIMILAR RULES IN CERTAIN CASES.—If a partnership return is filed for any taxable year but it is determined that there is no entity for such taxable year, to the extent provided in regulations, rules similar to the rules of subsection (a) shall apply.

Amendments

• **1996, Small Business Job Protection Act of 1996 (P.L. 104-188)**

P.L. 104-188, §1307(c)(3)(B):

Amended Code Sec. 6233(b). **Effective** for tax years beginning after 12-31-96. Prior to amendment, Code Sec. 6233(b) read as follows:

(b) SIMILAR RULES IN CERTAIN CASES.—If for any taxable year—

(1) an entity files a return as an S corporation but it is determined that the entity was not an S corporation for such year, or

(2) a partnership return or S corporation return is filed but it is determined that there is no entity for such taxable year,

then, to the extent provided in regulations, rules similar to the rules of subsection (a) shall apply.

• **1984, Deficit Reduction Act of 1984 (P.L. 98-369)**

P.L. 98-369, §714(p)(1):

Amended subchapter C of chapter 63 by adding at the end thereof a new section 6233. **Effective** as if included in the provision of P.L. 97-248 to which it relates.

[Sec. 6234—Stricken]

Amendments

• **2015, Bipartisan Budget Act of 2015 (P.L. 114-74)**

P.L. 114-74, §1101(a):

Amended chapter 63 by striking subchapter C (Code Secs. 6221-6234). **Effective** generally for returns filed for partnership tax years beginning after 12-31-2017. For a special rule, see Act Sec. 1101(g)(4), below.

P.L. 114-74, §1101(g)(4), provides:

(4) ELECTION.—A partnership may elect (at such time and in such form and manner as the Secretary of the Treasury may prescribe) for the amendments made by this section (other than the election under section 6221(b) of such Code (as added by this Act)) to apply to any return of the partnership filed for partnership taxable years beginning after the date of the enactment of this Act and before January 1, 2018.

Prior to being stricken, Code Sec. 6234 read as follows:

SEC. 6234. DECLARATORY JUDGMENT RELATING TO TREATMENT OF ITEMS OTHER THAN PARTNERSHIP ITEMS WITH RESPECT TO AN OVERSHELTERED RETURN.

[Sec. 6234(a)]

(a) GENERAL RULE.—If—

(1) a taxpayer files an oversheltered return for a taxable year,

(2) the Secretary makes a determination with respect to the treatment of items (other than partnership items) of such taxpayer for such taxable year, and

(3) the adjustments resulting from such determination do not give rise to a deficiency (as defined in section 6211) but would give rise to a deficiency if there were no net loss from partnership items, the Secretary is authorized to send a notice of adjustment reflecting such determination to the taxpayer by certified or registered mail.

[Sec. 6234(b)]

(b) OVERSHELTERED RETURN.—For purposes of this section, the term "oversheltered return" means an income tax return which—

(1) shows no taxable income for the taxable year, and

(2) shows a net loss from partnership items.

[Sec. 6234(c)]

(c) JUDICIAL REVIEW IN THE TAX COURT.—Within 90 days, or 150 days if the notice is addressed to a person outside the United States, after the day on which the notice of adjustment authorized in subsection (a) is mailed to the taxpayer, the taxpayer may file a petition with the Tax Court for redetermination of the adjustments. Upon the filing of such a petition, the Tax Court shall have jurisdiction to make a declaration with respect to all items (other than partnership items and affected items which require partner level determinations as described in section 6230(a)(2)(A)(i)) for the taxable year to which the notice of adjustment relates, in accordance with the principles of section 6214(a). Any such declaration shall have the force and effect of a decision of the Tax Court and shall be reviewable as such.

[Sec. 6234(d)]

(d) FAILURE TO FILE PETITION.—

(1) IN GENERAL.—Except as provided in paragraph (2), if the taxpayer does not file a petition with the Tax Court within the time prescribed in subsection (c), the determination of the Secretary set forth in the notice of adjustment that was mailed to the taxpayer shall be deemed to be correct.

(2) EXCEPTION.—Paragraph (1) shall not apply after the date that the taxpayer—

(A) files a petition with the Tax Court within the time prescribed in subsection (c) with respect to a subsequent notice of adjustment relating to the same taxable year, or

(B) files a claim for refund of an overpayment of tax under section 6511 for the taxable year involved.

If a claim for refund is filed by the taxpayer, then solely for purposes of determining (for the taxable year involved) the amount of any computational adjustment in connection with a partnership proceeding under this subchapter (other than under this section) or the amount of any deficiency attributable to affected items in a proceeding under section 6230(a)(2), the items that are the subject of the notice of adjustment shall be presumed to have been correctly reported on the taxpayer's return during the pendency of the refund claim (and, if within the time prescribed by section 6532 the taxpayer commences a civil action for refund under section 7422, until the decision in the refund action becomes final).

[Sec. 6234(e)]

(e) LIMITATIONS PERIOD.—

(1) IN GENERAL.—Any notice to a taxpayer under subsection (a) shall be mailed before the expiration of the period prescribed by section 6501 (relating to the period of limitations on assessment).

(2) SUSPENSION WHEN SECRETARY MAILS NOTICE OF ADJUSTMENT.—If the Secretary mails a notice of adjustment to the taxpayer for a taxable year, the period of limitations on the making of assessments shall be suspended for the period during which the Secretary is prohibited from making the assessment (and, in any event, if a proceeding in respect of the notice of adjustment is placed on the docket of the Tax Court, until the decision of the Tax Court becomes final), and for 60 days thereafter.

(3) RESTRICTIONS ON ASSESSMENT.—Except as otherwise provided in section 6851, 6852, or 6861, no assessment of a deficiency with respect to any tax imposed by subtitle A attributable to any item (other than a partnership item or any item affected by a partnership item) shall be made—

(A) until the expiration of the applicable 90-day or 150-day period set forth in subsection (c) for filing a petition with the Tax Court, or

(B) if a petition has been filed with the Tax Court, until the decision of the Tax Court has become final.

[Sec. 6234(f)]

(f) FURTHER NOTICES OF ADJUSTMENT RESTRICTED.—If the Secretary mails a notice of adjustment to the taxpayer for a taxable year and the taxpayer files a petition with the Tax Court within the time prescribed in subsection (c), the Secretary may not mail another such notice to the taxpayer with respect to the same taxable year in the absence of a showing of fraud, malfeasance, or misrepresentation of a material fact.

[Sec. 6234(g)]

(g) COORDINATION WITH OTHER PROCEEDINGS UNDER THIS SUBCHAPTER.—

(1) IN GENERAL.—The treatment of any item that has been determined pursuant to subsection (c) or (d) shall be taken into account in determining the amount of any computational adjustment that is made in connection with a partnership proceeding under this subchapter (other than under this section), or the amount of any deficiency attributable to affected items in a proceeding under section 6230(a)(2), for the taxable year involved. Notwithstanding any other law or rule of law pertaining to the period of limitations on the making of assessments, for purposes of the preceding sentence, any adjustment made in accordance with this section shall be taken into account regardless of whether any assessment has been made with respect to such adjustment.

(2) SPECIAL RULE IN CASE OF COMPUTATIONAL ADJUSTMENT.—In the case of a computational adjustment that is made in connection with a partnership proceeding under this subchapter (other than under this section), the provisions of paragraph (1) shall apply only if the computational adjustment is made within the period prescribed by section 6229 for assessing any tax under subtitle A which is attributable to any partnership item or affected item for the taxable year involved.

(3) CONVERSION TO DEFICIENCY PROCEEDING.—If—

(A) after the notice referred to in subsection (a) is mailed to a taxpayer for a taxable year but before the expiration of the period for filing a petition with the Tax Court under subsection (c) (or, if a petition is filed with the Tax Court, before the Tax Court makes a declaration for that taxable year), the treatment of any partnership item for the taxable year is finally determined, or any such item ceases to be a partnership item pursuant to section 6231(b), and

(B) as a result of that final determination or cessation, a deficiency can be determined with respect to the items that are the subject of the notice of adjustment,

ASSESSMENT—ELECTING LARGE PARTNERSHIPS

the notice of adjustment shall be treated as a notice of deficiency under section 6212 and any petition filed in respect of the notice shall be treated as an action brought under section 6213.

(4) FINALLY DETERMINED.—For purposes of this subsection, the treatment of partnership items shall be treated as finally determined if—

(A) the Secretary or the Attorney General (or his delegate) enters into a settlement agreement (within the meaning of section 6224) with the taxpayer regarding such items,

(B) a notice of final partnership administrative adjustment has been issued and—

(i) no petition has been filed under section 6226 and the time for doing so has expired, or

(ii) a petition has been filed under section 6226 and the decision of the court has become final, or

(C) the period within which any tax attributable to such items may be assessed against the taxpayer has expired.

Amendments

• 2002, Job Creation and Worker Assistance Act of 2002 (P.L. 107-147)

P.L. 107-147, §416(d)(1)(D):

Amended Code Sec. 6234(g)(4)(A) by inserting "or the Attorney General (or his delegate)" after "Secretary". **Effective** with respect to settlement agreements entered into after 3-9-2002.

[Sec. 6234(h)]

(h) SPECIAL RULES IF SECRETARY INCORRECTLY DETERMINES APPLICABLE PROCEDURE.—

(1) SPECIAL RULE IF SECRETARY ERRONEOUSLY MAILS NOTICE OF ADJUSTMENT.—If the Secretary erroneously determines that subchapter B does not apply to a taxable year of a taxpayer and consistent with that determination timely mails a notice of adjustment to the taxpayer pursuant to subsection (a) of this section, the notice of adjustment shall be treated as a notice of deficiency under section 6212 and any petition that is filed in respect of the notice shall be treated as an action brought under section 6213.

(2) SPECIAL RULE IF SECRETARY ERRONEOUSLY MAILS NOTICE OF DEFICIENCY.—If the Secretary erroneously determines that subchapter B applies to a taxable year of a taxpayer and consistent with that determination timely mails a notice of deficiency to the taxpayer pursuant to section 6212, the notice of deficiency shall be treated as a notice of adjustment under subsection (a) and any petition that is filed in respect of the notice shall be treated as an action brought under subsection (c).

Amendments

• 1997, Taxpayer Relief Act of 1997 (P.L. 105-34)

P.L. 105-34, §1231(a):

Amended subchapter C of chapter 63 by adding at the end a new Code Sec. 6234. **Effective** for partnership tax years ending after 8-5-97.

Subchapter D—Treatment of Electing Large Partnerships—[Stricken]

Part I.   Treatment of partnership items and adjustments.
Part II.   Partnership level adjustments.
Part III.   Definitions and special rules.

PART I—TREATMENT OF PARTNERSHIP ITEMS AND ADJUSTMENTS—[Stricken]

[Sec. 6240—Stricken]

Amendments

• 2015, Bipartisan Budget Act of 2015 (P.L. 114-74)

P.L. 114-74, §1101(b)(2):

Amended chapter 63 by striking subchapter D (Code Secs. 6240-6255). **Effective** generally for returns filed for partnership tax years beginning after 12-31-2017. For a special rule, see Act Sec. 1101(g)(4), below.

P.L. 114-74, §1101(g)(4), provides:

(4) ELECTION.—A partnership may elect (at such time and in such form and manner as the Secretary of the Treasury may prescribe) for the amendments made by this section (other than the election under section 6221(b) of such Code (as added by this Act)) to apply to any return of the partnership filed for partnership taxable years beginning after the date of the enactment of this Act and before January 1, 2018.

Prior to being stricken, Code Sec. 6240 read as follows:

SEC. 6240. APPLICATION OF SUBCHAPTER.

[Sec. 6240(a)]

(a) GENERAL RULE.—This subchapter shall only apply to electing large partnerships and partners in such partnerships.

Amendments

• 2015, Bipartisan Budget Act of 2015 (P.L. 114-74)

P.L. 114-74, §1101(b)(2):

Amended chapter 63 by striking subchapter D (Code Secs. 6240-6255). **Effective** generally for returns filed for partnership tax years beginning after 12-31-2017. For a special rule, see Act Sec. 1101(g)(4), below.

P.L. 114-74, §1101(g)(4), provides:

(4) ELECTION.—A partnership may elect (at such time and in such form and manner as the Secretary of the Treasury may prescribe) for the amendments made by this section (other than the election under section 6221(b) of such Code (as added by this Act)) to apply to any return of the partnership filed for partnership taxable years beginning after the date of the enactment of this Act and before January 1, 2018.

Prior to being stricken, Code Sec. 6241 read as follows:

SEC. 6241. PARTNER'S RETURN MUST BE CONSISTENT WITH PARTNERSHIP RETURN.

[Sec. 6241(a)]

(a) GENERAL RULE.—A partner of any electing large partnership shall, on the partner's return, treat each partnership item attributable to such partnership in a manner which is consistent with the treatment of such partnership item on the partnership return.

[Sec. 6241(b)]

(b) UNDERPAYMENT DUE TO INCONSISTENT TREATMENT ASSESSED AS MATH ERROR.—Any underpayment of tax by a partner by reason of failing to comply with the requirements of subsection (a) shall be assessed and collected in the same manner as if such underpayment were on account of a mathematical or clerical error appearing on the partner's return. Paragraph (2) of section 6213(b) shall not apply to any assessment of an underpayment referred to in the preceding sentence.

[Sec. 6241(c)]

(c) ADJUSTMENTS NOT TO AFFECT PRIOR YEAR OF PARTNERS.—

(1) IN GENERAL.—Except as provided in paragraph (2), subsections (a) and (b) shall apply without regard to any adjustment to the partnership item under part II.

[Sec. 6240(b)]

(b) COORDINATION WITH OTHER PARTNERSHIP AUDIT PROCEDURES.—

(1) IN GENERAL.—Subchapter C of this chapter shall not apply to any electing large partnership other than in its capacity as a partner in another partnership which is not an electing large partnership.

(2) TREATMENT WHERE PARTNER IN OTHER PARTNERSHIP.—If an electing large partnership is a partner in another partnership which is not an electing large partnership—

(A) subchapter C of this chapter shall apply to items of such electing large partnership which are partnership items with respect to such other partnership, but

(B) any adjustment under such subchapter C shall be taken into account in the manner provided by section 6242.

Amendments

• 1997, Taxpayer Relief Act of 1997 (P.L. 105-34)

P.L. 105-34, §1222(a):

Amended chapter 63 by adding at the end a new subchapter D, part I (Code Secs. 6240-6242). **Effective** for partnership tax years beginning after 12-31-97 [effective date changed by P.L. 105-206, §6012(e)].

[Sec. 6241—Stricken]

(2) CERTAIN CHANGES IN DISTRIBUTIVE SHARE TAKEN INTO ACCOUNT BY PARTNER.—

(A) IN GENERAL.—To the extent that any adjustment under part II involves a change under section 704 in a partner's distributive share of the amount of any partnership item shown on the partnership return, such adjustment shall be taken into account in applying this title to such partner for the partner's taxable year for which such item was required to be taken into account.

(B) COORDINATION WITH DEFICIENCY PROCEDURES.—

(i) IN GENERAL.—Subchapter B shall not apply to the assessment or collection of any underpayment of tax attributable to an adjustment referred to in subparagraph (A).

(ii) ADJUSTMENT NOT PRECLUDED.—Notwithstanding any other law or rule of law, nothing in subchapter B (or in any proceeding under subchapter B) shall preclude the assessment or collection of any underpayment of tax (or the allowance of any credit or refund of any overpayment of tax) attributable to an adjustment referred to in subparagraph (A) and such assessment or collection or allowance (or any notice thereof) shall not preclude any notice, proceeding, or determination under subchapter B.

(C) PERIOD OF LIMITATIONS.—The period for—

(i) assessing any underpayment of tax, or

(ii) filing a claim for credit or refund of any overpayment of tax,

attributable to an adjustment referred to in subparagraph (A) shall not expire before the close of the period prescribed by section 6248 for making adjustments with respect to the partnership taxable year involved.

(D) TIERED STRUCTURES.—If the partner referred to in subparagraph (A) is another partnership or an S corporation, the rules of this paragraph shall also apply to persons holding interests in such partnership or S corporation (as the case may be); except that, if such partner is an electing large partnership, the adjustment referred to in subparagraph (A) shall be taken into account in the manner provided by section 6242.

[Sec. 6241(d)]

(d) ADDITION TO TAX FOR FAILURE TO COMPLY WITH SECTION.—

For addition to tax in case of partner's disregard of requirements of this section, see part II of subchapter A of chapter 68.

ASSESSMENT—ELECTING LARGE PARTNERSHIPS

Amendments

• **1997, Taxpayer Relief Act of 1997 (P.L. 105-34)**

P.L. 105-34, §1222(a):

Added Code Sec. 6241. **Effective** for partnership tax years beginning after 12-31-97 [**effective** date changed by P.L. 105-206, §6012(e)].

Amendments

• **1996, Small Business Job Protection Act of 1996 (P.L. 104-188)**

P.L. 104-188, §1307(c)(1):

Repealed subchapter D of chapter 63 (Code Secs. 6241-6245). **Effective** for tax years beginning after 12-31-96. Prior to repeal, Code Sec. 6241 read as follows:

SEC. 6241. TAX TREATMENT DETERMINED AT CORPORATE LEVEL.

Amendments

• **2015, Bipartisan Budget Act of 2015 (P.L. 114-74)**

P.L. 114-74, §1101(b)(2):

Amended chapter 63 by striking subchapter D (Code Secs. 6240-6255). **Effective** generally for returns filed for partnership tax years beginning after 12-31-2017. For a special rule, see Act Sec. 1101(g)(4), below.

P.L. 114-74, §1101(g)(4), provides:

(4) ELECTION.—A partnership may elect (at such time and in such form and manner as the Secretary of the Treasury may prescribe) for the amendments made by this section (other than the election under section 6221(b) of such Code (as added by this Act)) to apply to any return of the partnership filed for partnership taxable years beginning after the date of the enactment of this Act and before January 1, 2018.

Prior to being stricken, Code Sec. 6242 read as follows:

SEC. 6242. PROCEDURES FOR TAKING PARTNERSHIP ADJUSTMENTS INTO ACCOUNT.

[Sec. 6242(a)]

(a) ADJUSTMENTS FLOW THROUGH TO PARTNERS FOR YEAR IN WHICH ADJUSTMENT TAKES EFFECT.—

(1) IN GENERAL.—If any partnership adjustment with respect to any partnership item takes effect (within the meaning of subsection (d)(2)) during any partnership taxable year and if an election under paragraph (2) does not apply to such adjustment, such adjustment shall be taken into account in determining the amount of such item for the partnership taxable year in which such adjustment takes effect. In applying this title to any person who is (directly or indirectly) a partner in such partnership during such partnership taxable year, such adjustment shall be treated as an item actually arising during such taxable year.

(2) PARTNERSHIP LIABLE IN CERTAIN CASES.—If—

(A) a partnership elects under this paragraph to not take an adjustment into account under paragraph (1),

(B) a partnership does not make such an election but in filing its return for any partnership taxable year fails to take fully into account any partnership adjustment as required under paragraph (1), or

(C) any partnership adjustment involves a reduction in a credit which exceeds the amount of such credit determined for the partnership taxable year in which the adjustment takes effect,

the partnership shall pay to the Secretary an amount determined by applying the rules of subsection (b)(4) to the adjustments not so taken into account and any excess referred to in subparagraph (C).

(3) OFFSETTING ADJUSTMENTS TAKEN INTO ACCOUNT.—If a partnership adjustment requires another adjustment in a taxable year after the adjusted year and before the partnership taxable year in which such partnership adjustment takes effect, such other adjustment shall be taken into account under this subsection for the partnership taxable year in which such partnership adjustment takes effect.

(4) COORDINATION WITH PART II.—Amounts taken into account under this subsection for any partnership taxable year shall continue to be treated as adjustments for the adjusted year for purposes of determining whether such amounts may be readjusted under part II.

[Sec. 6242(b)]

(b) PARTNERSHIP LIABLE FOR INTEREST AND PENALTIES.—

(1) IN GENERAL.—If a partnership adjustment takes effect during any partnership taxable year and such adjustment results in an imputed underpayment for the adjusted year, the partnership—

(A) shall pay to the Secretary interest computed under paragraph (2), and

(B) shall be liable for any penalty, addition to tax, or additional amount as provided in paragraph (3).

(2) DETERMINATION OF AMOUNT OF INTEREST.—The interest computed under this paragraph with respect to any partnership adjustment is the interest which would be determined under chapter 67—

(A) on the imputed underpayment determined under paragraph (4) with respect to such adjustment,

(B) for the period beginning on the day after the return due date for the adjusted year and ending on the return due date for the partnership taxable year in which such adjustment takes effect (or, if earlier, in the case of any adjustment to which subsection (a)(2) applies, the date on which the payment under subsection (a)(2) is made).

Proper adjustments in the amount determined under the preceding sentence shall be made for adjustments required for partnership taxable years after the adjusted year and before the year in which the partnership adjustment takes effect by reason of such partnership adjustment.

(3) PENALTIES.—A partnership shall be liable for any penalty, addition to tax, or additional amount for which it would have been liable if such partnership had been an individual subject to tax under chapter 1 for the adjusted year and the imputed underpayment determined under paragraph (4) were an actual underpayment (or understatement) for such year.

(4) IMPUTED UNDERPAYMENT.—For purposes of this subsection, the imputed underpayment determined under this paragraph with respect to any partnership adjustment is the underpayment (if any) which would result—

(A) by netting all adjustments to items of income, gain, loss, or deduction and by treating any net increase in income as an underpayment equal to the amount of such net increase multiplied by the highest rate of tax in effect under section 1 or 11 for the adjusted year, and

(B) by taking adjustments to credits into account as increases or decreases (whichever is appropriate) in the amount of tax.

For purposes of the preceding sentence, any net decrease in a loss shall be treated as an increase in income and a similar rule shall apply to a net increase in a loss.

[Sec. 6242(c)]

(c) ADMINISTRATIVE PROVISIONS.—

(1) IN GENERAL.—Any payment required by subsection (a)(2) or (b)(1)(A)—

(A) shall be assessed and collected in the same manner as if it were a tax imposed by subtitle C, and

(B) shall be paid on or before the return due date for the partnership taxable year in which the partnership adjustment takes effect.

(2) INTEREST.—For purposes of determining interest, any payment required by subsection (a)(2) or (b)(1)(A) shall be treated as an underpayment of tax.

(3) PENALTIES.—

(A) IN GENERAL.—In the case of any failure by any partnership to pay on the date prescribed therefor any amount required by subsection (a)(2) or (b)(1)(A), there is hereby imposed on such partnership a penalty of 10 percent of the underpayment. For purposes of the preceding sentence, the term "underpayment" means the excess of any payment required under this section over the amount (if any) paid on or before the date prescribed therefor.

(B) ACCURACY-RELATED AND FRAUD PENALTIES MADE APPLICABLE.—For purposes of part II of subchapter A of chapter 68, any payment required by subsection (a)(2) shall be treated as an underpayment of tax.

[Sec. 6242(d)]

(d) DEFINITIONS AND SPECIAL RULES.—For purposes of this section—

(1) PARTNERSHIP ADJUSTMENT.—The term "partnership adjustment" means any adjustment in the amount of any partnership item of an electing large partnership.

(2) WHEN ADJUSTMENT TAKES EFFECT.—A partnership adjustment takes effect—

(A) in the case of an adjustment pursuant to the decision of a court in a proceeding brought under part II, when such decision becomes final,

(B) in the case of an adjustment pursuant to any administrative adjustment request under section 6251, when such adjustment is allowed by the Secretary, or

(C) in any other case, when such adjustment is made.

(3) ADJUSTED YEAR.—The term "adjusted year" means the partnership taxable year to which the item being adjusted relates.

(4) RETURN DUE DATE.—The term "return due date" means, with respect to any taxable year, the date prescribed for filing the partnership return for such taxable year (determined without regard to extensions).

(5) ADJUSTMENTS INVOLVING CHANGES IN CHARACTER.—Under regulations, appropriate adjustments in the application of this section shall be made for purposes of taking into account partnership adjustments which involve a change in the character of any item of income, gain, loss, or deduction.

[Sec. 6242(e)]

(e) PAYMENTS NONDEDUCTIBLE.—No deduction shall be allowed under subtitle A for any payment required to be made by an electing large partnership under this section.

Amendments

• **1997, Taxpayer Relief Act of 1997 (P.L. 105-34)**

P.L. 105-34, §1222(a):

Added Code Sec. 6242. **Effective** for partnership tax years beginning after 12-31-97 [**effective** date changed by P.L. 105-206, §6012(e)].

ASSESSMENT—ELECTING LARGE PARTNERSHIPS

[Sec. 6242—Repealed]

Amendments

• **1996, Small Business Job Protection Act of 1996 (P.L. 104-188)**

P.L. 104-188, §1307(c)(1):

Repealed subchapter D of chapter 63 (Code Secs. 6241-6245). **Effective** for tax years beginning after 12-31-96. Prior to repeal, Code Sec. 6242 read as follows:

SEC. 6242. SHAREHOLDER'S RETURN MUST BE CONSISTENT WITH CORPORATE RETURN OR SECRETARY NOTIFIED OF INCONSISTENCY.

A shareholder of an S corporation shall, on such shareholder's return, treat a subchapter S item in a manner which is consistent with the treatment of such item on the corporate return unless the shareholder notifies the Secretary (at the time and in the manner prescribed by regulations) of the inconsistency.

• **1982, Subchapter S Revision Act of 1982 (P.L. 97-354)**

P.L. 97-354, §4(a):

Added Code Sec. 6242. **Effective** for tax years beginning after 12-31-82.

[Sec. 6243—Repealed]

Amendments

• **1996, Small Business Job Protection Act of 1996 (P.L. 104-188)**

P.L. 104-188, §1307(c)(1):

Repealed subchapter D of chapter 63 (Code Secs. 6241-6245). **Effective** for tax years beginning after 12-31-96. Prior to repeal, Code Sec. 6243 read as follows:

SEC. 6243. ALL SHAREHOLDERS TO BE NOTIFIED OF PROCEEDINGS AND GIVEN OPPORTUNITY TO PARTICIPATE.

In the manner and at the time prescribed in regulations, each shareholder in a corporation shall be given notice of, and the right to participate in, any administrative or judicial proceeding for the determination at the corporate level of any subchapter S item.

• **1982, Subchapter S Revision Act of 1982 (P.L. 97-354)**

P.L. 97-354, §4(a):

Added Code Sec. 6243. **Effective** for tax years beginning after 12-31-82.

[Sec. 6244—Repealed]

Amendments

• **1996, Small Business Job Protection Act of 1996 (P.L. 104-188)**

P.L. 104-188, §1307(c)(1):

Repealed subchapter D of chapter 63 (Code Secs. 6241-6245), applicable to tax years beginning after 12-31-96. Prior to repeal, Code Sec. 6244 read as follows:

SEC. 6244. CERTAIN PARTNERSHIP PROVISIONS MADE APPLICABLE.

The provisions of—

(1) subchapter C which relate to—

(A) assessing deficiencies, and filing claims for credit or refund, with respect to partnership items, and

(B) judicial determination of partnership items, and

(2) so much of the other provisions of this subtitle as relate to partnership items,

are (except to the extent modified or made inapplicable in regulations) hereby extended to and made applicable to subchapter S items.

• **1982, Subchapter S Revision Act of 1982 (P.L. 97-354)**

P.L. 97-354, §4(a):

Added Code Sec. 6244. **Effective** for tax years beginning after 12-31-82.

PART II—PARTNERSHIP LEVEL ADJUSTMENTS—[Stricken]

Subpart A.   Adjustments by Secretary.
Subpart B.   Claims for adjustments by partnership.

Subpart A—Adjustments by Secretary—[Stricken]

[Sec. 6245—Stricken]

Amendments

• **2015, Bipartisan Budget Act of 2015 (P.L. 114-74)**

P.L. 114-74, §1101(b)(2):

Amended chapter 63 by striking subchapter D (Code Secs. 6240-6255). **Effective** generally for returns filed for partnership tax years beginning after 12-31-2017. For a special rule, see Act Sec. 1101(g)(4), below.

P.L. 114-74, §1101(g)(4), provides:

(4) ELECTION.—A partnership may elect (at such time and in such form and manner as the Secretary of the Treasury may prescribe) for the amendments made by this section (other than the election under section 6221(b) of such Code (as added by this Act)) to apply to any return of the partnership filed for partnership taxable years beginning after the date of the enactment of this Act and before January 1, 2018.

Prior to being stricken, Code Sec. 6245 read as follows:

SEC. 6245. SECRETARIAL AUTHORITY.

[Sec. 6245(a)]

(a) GENERAL RULE.—The Secretary is authorized and directed to make adjustments at the partnership level in any partnership item to the extent necessary to have such item be treated in the manner required.

[Sec. 6245(b)]

(b) NOTICE OF PARTNERSHIP ADJUSTMENT.—

(1) IN GENERAL.—If the Secretary determines that a partnership adjustment is required, the Secretary is authorized to send notice of such adjustment to the partnership by certified mail or registered mail. Such notice shall be sufficient if mailed to the partnership at its last known address even if the partnership has terminated its existence.

(2) FURTHER NOTICES RESTRICTED.—If the Secretary mails a notice of a partnership adjustment to any partnership for any partnership taxable year and the partnership files a petition under section 6247 with respect to such notice, in the absence of a showing of fraud, malfeasance, or misrepresentation of a material fact, the Secretary shall not mail another such notice to such partnership with respect to such taxable year.

(3) AUTHORITY TO RESCIND NOTICE WITH PARTNERSHIP CONSENT.—The Secretary may, with the consent of the partnership, rescind any notice of a partnership adjustment mailed to such partnership. Any notice so rescinded shall not be treated as a notice of a partnership adjustment, for purposes of this section, section 6246, and section 6247, and the taxpayer shall have no right to bring a proceeding under section 6247 with respect to such notice. Nothing in this subsection shall affect any suspension of the running of any period of limitations during any period during which the rescinded notice was outstanding.

Amendments

• **1997, Taxpayer Relief Act of 1997 (P.L. 105-34)**

P.L. 105-34, §1222(a):

Amended chapter 63 by adding at the end a new subchapter D, part II, subpart A (Code Secs. 6245-6248). **Effective** for partnership tax years beginning after 12-31-97 [effective date changed by P.L. 105-206, §6012(e)].

[Sec. 6245—Repealed]

Amendments

• **1996, Small Business Job Protection Act of 1996 (P.L. 104-188)**

P.L. 104-188, §1307(c)(1):

Repealed subchapter D of chapter 63 (Code Secs. 6241-6245). **Effective** for tax years beginning after 12-31-96. Prior to repeal, Code Sec. 6245 read as follows:

SEC. 6245. SUBCHAPTER S ITEM DEFINED.

For purposes of this subchapter, the term "subchapter S item" means any item of an S corporation to the extent regulations prescribed by the Secretary provide that, for purposes of this subtitle, such item is more appropriately determined at the corporate level than at the shareholder level.

• **1982, Subchapter S Revision Act of 1982 (P.L. 97-354)**

P.L. 97-354, §4(a):

Added Code Sec. 6245. **Effective** for tax years beginning after 12-31-82.

ASSESSMENT—ELECTING LARGE PARTNERSHIPS

[Sec. 6246—Stricken]

Amendments

• **2015, Bipartisan Budget Act of 2015 (P.L. 114-74)**

P.L. 114-74, §1101(b)(2):

Amended chapter 63 by striking subchapter D (Code Secs. 6240-6255). **Effective** generally for returns filed for partnership tax years beginning after 12-31-2017. For a special rule, see Act Sec. 1101(g)(4), below.

P.L. 114-74, §1101(g)(4), provides:

(4) ELECTION.—A partnership may elect (at such time and in such form and manner as the Secretary of the Treasury may prescribe) for the amendments made by this section (other than the election under section 6221(b) of such Code (as added by this Act)) to apply to any return of the partnership filed for partnership taxable years beginning after the date of the enactment of this Act and before January 1, 2018.

Prior to being stricken, Code Sec. 6246 read as follows:

SEC. 6246. RESTRICTIONS ON PARTNERSHIP ADJUSTMENTS.

[Sec. 6246(a)]

(a) GENERAL RULE.—Except as otherwise provided in this chapter, no adjustment to any partnership item may be made (and no levy or proceeding in any court for the collection of any amount resulting from such adjustment may be made, begun or prosecuted) before—

(1) the close of the 90th day after the day on which a notice of a partnership adjustment was mailed to the partnership, and

(2) if a petition is filed under section 6247 with respect to such notice, the decision of the court has become final.

[Sec. 6246(b)]

(b) PREMATURE ACTION MAY BE ENJOINED.—Notwithstanding section 7421(a), any action which violates subsection (a) may be enjoined in the proper court, including the Tax Court. The Tax Court shall have no jurisdiction to enjoin any action under this subsection unless a timely petition has been filed under section 6247 and then only in respect of the adjustments that are the subject of such petition.

[Sec. 6246(c)]

(c) EXCEPTIONS TO RESTRICTIONS ON ADJUSTMENTS.—

(1) ADJUSTMENTS ARISING OUT OF MATH OR CLERICAL ERRORS.—

(A) IN GENERAL.—If the partnership is notified that, on account of a mathematical or clerical error appearing on the partnership return, an adjustment to a partnership item is required, rules similar to the rules of paragraphs (1) and (2) of section 6213(b) shall apply to such adjustment.

(B) SPECIAL RULE.—If an electing large partnership is a partner in another electing large partnership, any adjustment on account of such partnership's failure to comply with the requirements of section 6241(a) with respect to its interest in such other partnership shall be treated as an adjustment referred to in subparagraph (A), except that paragraph (2) of section 6213(b) shall not apply to such adjustment.

(2) PARTNERSHIP MAY WAIVE RESTRICTIONS.—The partnership shall at any time (whether or not a notice of partnership adjustment has been issued) have the right, by a signed notice in writing filed with the Secretary, to waive the restrictions provided in subsection (a) on the making of any partnership adjustment.

[Sec. 6246(d)]

(d) LIMIT WHERE NO PROCEEDING BEGUN.—If no proceeding under section 6247 is begun with respect to any notice of a partnership adjustment during the 90-day period described in subsection (a), the amount for which the partnership is liable under section 6242 (and any increase in any partner's liability for tax under chapter 1 by reason of any adjustment under section 6242(a)) shall not exceed the amount determined in accordance with such notice.

Amendments

• **1997, Taxpayer Relief Act of 1997 (P.L. 105-34)**

P.L. 105-34, §1222(a):

Added Code Sec. 6246. **Effective** for partnership tax years beginning after 12-31-97 [**effective** date changed by P.L. 105-206, §6012(e)].

[Sec. 6247—Stricken]

Amendments

• **2015, Bipartisan Budget Act of 2015 (P.L. 114-74)**

P.L. 114-74, §1101(b)(2):

Amended chapter 63 by striking subchapter D (Code Secs. 6240-6255). **Effective** generally for returns filed for partnership tax years beginning after 12-31-2017. For a special rule, see Act Sec. 1101(g)(4), below.

P.L. 114-74, §1101(g)(4), provides:

(4) ELECTION.—A partnership may elect (at such time and in such form and manner as the Secretary of the Treasury may prescribe) for the amendments made by this section (other than the election under section 6221(b) of such Code (as added by this Act)) to apply to any return of the partnership filed for partnership taxable years beginning after the date of the enactment of this Act and before January 1, 2018.

Prior to being stricken, Code Sec. 6247 read as follows:

SEC. 6247. JUDICIAL REVIEW OF PARTNERSHIP ADJUSTMENT.

[Sec. 6247(a)]

(a) GENERAL RULE.—Within 90 days after the date on which a notice of a partnership adjustment is mailed to the partnership with respect to any partnership taxable year, the partnership may file a petition for a readjustment of the partnership items for such taxable year with—

(1) the Tax Court,

(2) the district court of the United States for the district in which the partnership's principal place of business is located, or

(3) the Claims Court.

[Sec. 6247(b)]

(b) JURISDICTIONAL REQUIREMENT FOR BRINGING ACTION IN DISTRICT COURT OR CLAIMS COURT.—

(1) IN GENERAL.—A readjustment petition under this section may be filed in a district court of the United States or the Claims Court only if the partnership filing the petition deposits with the Secretary, on or before the date the petition is filed, the amount for which the partnership would be liable under section 6242(b) (as of the date of the filing of the petition) if the partnership items were adjusted as provided by the notice of partnership adjustment. The court may by order provide that the jurisdictional requirements of this paragraph are satisfied where there has been a good faith attempt to satisfy such requirement and any shortfall of the amount required to be deposited is timely corrected.

(2) INTEREST PAYABLE.—Any amount deposited under paragraph (1), while deposited, shall not be treated as a payment of tax for purposes of this title (other than chapter 67).

[Sec. 6247(c)]

(c) SCOPE OF JUDICIAL REVIEW.—A court with which a petition is filed in accordance with this section shall have jurisdiction to determine all partnership items of the partnership for the partnership taxable year to which the notice of partnership adjustment relates and the proper allocation of such items among the partners (and the applicability of any penalty, addition to tax, or additional amount for which the partnership may be liable under section 6242(b)).

[Sec. 6247(d)]

(d) DETERMINATION OF COURT REVIEWABLE.—Any determination by a court under this section shall have the force and effect of a decision of the Tax Court or a final judgment or decree of the district court or the Claims Court, as the case may be, and shall be reviewable as such. The date of any such determination shall be treated as being the date of the court's order entering the decision.

[Sec. 6247(e)]

(e) EFFECT OF DECISION DISMISSING ACTION.—If an action brought under this section is dismissed other than by reason of a rescission under section 6245(b)(3), the decision of the court dismissing the action shall be considered as its decision that the notice of partnership adjustment is correct, and an appropriate order shall be entered in the records of the court.

Amendments

• **1997, Taxpayer Relief Act of 1997 (P.L. 105-34)**

P.L. 105-34, §1222(a):

Added Code Sec. 6247. **Effective** for partnership tax years beginning after 12-31-97 [**effective** date changed by P.L. 105-206, §6012(e)].

[Sec. 6248—Stricken]

Amendments

• **2015, Bipartisan Budget Act of 2015 (P.L. 114-74)**

P.L. 114-74, §1101(b)(2):

Amended chapter 63 by striking subchapter D (Code Secs. 6240-6255). **Effective** generally for returns filed for partnership tax years beginning after 12-31-2017. For a special rule, see Act Sec. 1101(g)(4), below.

P.L. 114-74, §1101(g)(4), provides:

(4) ELECTION.—A partnership may elect (at such time and in such form and manner as the Secretary of the Treasury may prescribe) for the amendments made by this section (other than the election under section 6221(b) of such Code (as added by this Act)) to apply to any return of the partnership filed for partnership taxable years beginning after the date of the enactment of this Act and before January 1, 2018.

Prior to being stricken, Code Sec. 6248 read as follows:

SEC. 6248. PERIOD OF LIMITATIONS FOR MAKING ADJUSTMENTS.

[Sec. 6248(a)]

(a) GENERAL RULE.—Except as otherwise provided in this section, no adjustment under this subpart to any partnership item for any partnership taxable year may be made after the date which is 3 years after the later of—

(1) the date on which the partnership return for such taxable year was filed, or

(2) the last day for filing such return for such year (determined without regard to extensions).

[Sec. 6248(b)]

(b) EXTENSION BY AGREEMENT.—The period described in subsection (a) (including an extension period under this subsection) may be extended by an agreement entered into by the Secretary and the partnership before the expiration of such period.

ASSESSMENT—ELECTING LARGE PARTNERSHIPS

[Sec. 6248(c)]

(c) SPECIAL RULE IN CASE OF FRAUD, ETC.—

(1) FALSE RETURN.—In the case of a false or fraudulent partnership return with intent to evade tax, the adjustment may be made at any time.

(2) SUBSTANTIAL OMISSION OF INCOME.—If any partnership omits from gross income an amount properly includible therein which is in excess of 25 percent of the amount of gross income stated in its return, subsection (a) shall be applied by substituting "6 years" for "3 years".

(3) NO RETURN.—In the case of a failure by a partnership to file a return for any taxable year, the adjustment may be made at any time.

(4) RETURN FILED BY SECRETARY.—For purposes of this section, a return executed by the Secretary under subsection (b) of section 6020 on behalf of the partnership shall not be treated as a return of the partnership.

[Sec. 6248(d)]

(d) SUSPENSION WHEN SECRETARY MAILS NOTICE OF ADJUSTMENT.—If notice of a partnership adjustment with respect to any taxable year is mailed to the partnership, the running of the period specified in subsection (a) (as modified by the other provisions of this section) shall be suspended—

(1) for the period during which an action may be brought under section 6247 (and, if a petition is filed under section 6247 with respect to such notice, until the decision of the court becomes final), and

(2) for 1 year thereafter.

Amendments

• **1997, Taxpayer Relief Act of 1997 (P.L. 105-34)**

P.L. 105-34, § 1222(a):

Added Code Sec. 6248. **Effective** for partnership tax years beginning after 12-31-97 [**effective** date changed by P.L. 105-206, § 6012(e)].

Subpart B—Claims for Adjustments by Partnership—[Stricken]

[Sec. 6251—Stricken]

Amendments

• **2015, Bipartisan Budget Act of 2015 (P.L. 114-74)**

P.L. 114-74, § 1101(b)(2):

Amended chapter 63 by striking subchapter D (Code Secs. 6240-6255). **Effective** generally for returns filed for partnership tax years beginning after 12-31-2017. For a special rule, see Act Sec. 1101(g)(4), below.

P.L. 114-74, § 1101(g)(4), provides:

(4) ELECTION.—A partnership may elect (at such time and in such form and manner as the Secretary of the Treasury may prescribe) for the amendments made by this section (other than the election under section 6221(b) of such Code (as added by this Act)) to apply to any return of the partnership filed for partnership taxable years beginning after the date of the enactment of this Act and before January 1, 2018.

Prior to being stricken, Code Sec. 6251 read as follows:

SEC. 6251. ADMINISTRATIVE ADJUSTMENT REQUESTS.

[Sec. 6251(a)]

(a) GENERAL RULE.—A partnership may file a request for an administrative adjustment of partnership items for any partnership taxable year at any time which is—

(1) within 3 years after the later of—

(A) the date on which the partnership return for such year is filed, or

(B) the last day for filing the partnership return for such year (determined without regard to extensions), and

(2) before the mailing to the partnership of a notice of a partnership adjustment with respect to such taxable year.

[Sec. 6251(b)]

(b) SECRETARIAL ACTION.—If a partnership files an administrative adjustment request under subsection (a), the Secretary may allow any part of the requested adjustments.

[Sec. 6251(c)]

(c) SPECIAL RULE IN CASE OF EXTENSION UNDER SECTION 6248.—If the period described in section 6248(a) is extended pursuant to an agreement under section 6248(b), the period prescribed by subsection (a)(1) shall not expire before the date 6 months after the expiration of the extension under section 6248(b).

Amendments

• **1997, Taxpayer Relief Act of 1997 (P.L. 105-34)**

P.L. 105-34, § 1222(a):

Amended chapter 63 by adding at the end a new subchapter D, part II, subpart B (Code Secs. 6251-6252). **Effective** for partnership tax years beginning after 12-31-97 [**effective** date changed by P.L. 105-206, § 6012(e)].

[Sec. 6252—Stricken]

Amendments

• **2015, Bipartisan Budget Act of 2015 (P.L. 114-74)**

P.L. 114-74, § 1101(b)(2):

Amended chapter 63 by striking subchapter D (Code Secs. 6240-6255). **Effective** generally for returns filed for partnership tax years beginning after 12-31-2017. For a special rule, see Act Sec. 1101(g)(4), below.

P.L. 114-74, § 1101(g)(4), provides:

(4) ELECTION.—A partnership may elect (at such time and in such form and manner as the Secretary of the Treasury may prescribe) for the amendments made by this section (other than the election under section 6221(b) of such Code (as added by this Act)) to apply to any return of the partnership filed for partnership taxable years beginning after the date of the enactment of this Act and before January 1, 2018.

Prior to being stricken, Code Sec. 6252 read as follows:

SEC. 6252. JUDICIAL REVIEW WHERE ADMINISTRATIVE ADJUSTMENT REQUEST IS NOT ALLOWED IN FULL.

[Sec. 6252(a)]

(a) IN GENERAL.—If any part of an administrative adjustment request filed under section 6251 is not allowed by the Secretary, the partnership may file a petition for an adjustment with respect to the partnership items to which such part of the request relates with—

(1) the Tax Court,

(2) the district court of the United States for the district in which the principal place of business of the partnership is located, or

(3) the Claims Court.

[Sec. 6252(b)]

(b) PERIOD FOR FILING PETITION.—A petition may be filed under subsection (a) with respect to partnership items for a partnership taxable year only—

(1) after the expiration of 6 months from the date of filing of the request under section 6251, and

(2) before the date which is 2 years after the date of such request.

The 2-year period set forth in paragraph (2) shall be extended for such period as may be agreed upon in writing by the partnership and the Secretary.

[Sec. 6252(c)]

(c) COORDINATION WITH SUBPART A.—

(1) NOTICE OF PARTNERSHIP ADJUSTMENT BEFORE FILING OF PETITION.—No petition may be filed under this section after the Secretary mails to the partnership a notice of a partnership adjustment for the partnership taxable year to which the request under section 6251 relates.

(2) NOTICE OF PARTNERSHIP ADJUSTMENT AFTER FILING BUT BEFORE HEARING OF PETITION.—If the Secretary mails to the partnership a notice of a partnership adjustment for the partnership taxable year to which the request under section 6251 relates after the filing of a petition under this subsection but before the hearing of such petition, such petition shall be treated as an action brought under section 6247 with respect to such notice, except that subsection (b) of section 6247 shall not apply.

(3) NOTICE MUST BE BEFORE EXPIRATION OF STATUTE OF LIMITATIONS.—A notice of a partnership adjustment for the partnership taxable year shall be taken into account under paragraphs (1) and (2) only if such notice is mailed before the expiration of the period prescribed by section 6248 for making adjustments to partnership items for such taxable year.

[Sec. 6252(d)]

(d) SCOPE OF JUDICIAL REVIEW.—Except in the case described in paragraph (2) of subsection (c), a court with which a petition is filed in accordance with this section shall have jurisdiction to determine only those partnership items to which the part of the request under section 6251 not allowed by the Secretary relates and those items with respect to which the Secretary asserts adjustments as offsets to the adjustments requested by the partnership.

[Sec. 6252(e)]

(e) DETERMINATION OF COURT REVIEWABLE.—Any determination by a court under this section shall have the force and effect of a decision of the Tax Court or a final judgment or decree of the district court or the Claims Court, as the case may be, and shall be reviewable as such. The date of any such determination shall be treated as being the date of the court's order entering the decision.

Amendments

• **1997, Taxpayer Relief Act of 1997 (P.L. 105-34)**

P.L. 105-34, § 1222(a):

Added Code Sec. 6252. **Effective** for partnership tax years beginning after 12-31-97 [**effective** date changed by P.L. 105-206, § 6012(e)].

COLLECTION—GENERAL PROVISIONS

PART III—DEFINITIONS AND SPECIAL RULES—[Stricken]

[Sec. 6255—Stricken]

Amendments

• 2015, Bipartisan Budget Act of 2015 (P.L. 114-74)

P.L. 114-74, §1101(b)(2):

Amended chapter 63 by striking subchapter D (Code Secs. 6240-6255). **Effective** generally for returns filed for partnership tax years beginning after 12-31-2017. For a special rule, see Act Sec. 1101(g)(4), below.

P.L. 114-74, §1101(g)(4), provides:

(4) ELECTION.—A partnership may elect (at such time and in such form and manner as the Secretary of the Treasury may prescribe) for the amendments made by this section (other than the election under section 6221(b) of such Code (as added by this Act)) to apply to any return of the partnership filed for partnership taxable years beginning after the date of the enactment of this Act and before January 1, 2018.

Prior to being stricken, Code Sec. 6255 read as follows:

SEC. 6255. DEFINITIONS AND SPECIAL RULES.

[Sec. 6255(a)]

(a) DEFINITIONS.—For purposes of this subchapter—

(1) ELECTING LARGE PARTNERSHIP.—The term "electing large partnership" has the meaning given to such term by section 775.

(2) PARTNERSHIP ITEM.—The term "partnership item" has the meaning given to such term by section 6231(a)(3).

[Sec. 6255(b)]

(b) PARTNERS BOUND BY ACTIONS OF PARTNERSHIP, ETC.—

(1) DESIGNATION OF PARTNER.—Each electing large partnership shall designate (in the manner prescribed by the Secretary) a partner (or other person) who shall have the sole authority to act on behalf of such partnership under this subchapter. In any case in which such a designation is not in effect, the Secretary may select any partner as the partner with such authority.

(2) BINDING EFFECT.—An electing large partnership and all partners of such partnership shall be bound—

(A) by actions taken under this subchapter by the partnership, and

(B) by any decision in a proceeding brought under this subchapter.

[Sec. 6255(c)]

(c) PARTNERSHIPS HAVING PRINCIPAL PLACE OF BUSINESS OUTSIDE THE UNITED STATES.—For purposes of sections 6247 and 6252, a principal place of business located outside the United States shall be treated as located in the District of Columbia.

[Sec. 6255(d)]

(d) TREATMENT WHERE PARTNERSHIP CEASES TO EXIST.—If a partnership ceases to exist before a partnership adjustment under this subchapter takes effect, such adjustment shall be taken into account by the former partners of such partnership under regulations prescribed by the Secretary.

[Sec. 6255(e)]

(e) DATE DECISION BECOMES FINAL.—For purposes of this subchapter, the principles of section 7481(a) shall be applied in determining the date on which a decision of a district court or the Claims Court becomes final.

[Sec. 6255(f)]

(f) PARTNERSHIPS IN CASES UNDER TITLE 11 OF THE UNITED STATES CODE.—

(1) SUSPENSION OF PERIOD OF LIMITATIONS ON MAKING ADJUSTMENT, ASSESSMENT, OR COLLECTION.—The running of any period of limitations provided in this subchapter on making a partnership adjustment (or provided by section 6501 or 6502 on the assessment or collection of any amount required to be paid under section 6242) shall, in a case under title 11 of the United States Code, be suspended during the period during which the Secretary is prohibited by reason of such case from making the adjustment (or assessment or collection) and—

(A) for adjustment or assessment, 60 days thereafter, and

(B) for collection, 6 months thereafter.

A rule similar to the rule of section 6213(f)(2) shall apply for purposes of section 6246.

(2) SUSPENSION OF PERIOD OF LIMITATION FOR FILING FOR JUDICIAL REVIEW.—The running of the period specified in section 6247(a) or 6252(b) shall, in a case under title 11 of the United States Code, be suspended during the period during which the partnership is prohibited by reason of such case from filing a petition under section 6247 or 6252 and for 60 days thereafter.

[Sec. 6255(g)]

(g) REGULATIONS.—The Secretary shall prescribe such regulations as may be necessary to carry out the provisions of this subchapter, including regulations—

(1) to prevent abuse through manipulation of the provisions of this subchapter, and

(2) providing that this subchapter shall not apply to any case described in section 6231(c)(1) (or the regulations prescribed thereunder) where the application of this subchapter to such a case would interfere with the effective and efficient enforcement of this title.

In any case to which this subchapter does not apply by reason of paragraph (2), rules similar to the rules of sections 6229(f) and 6255(f) shall apply.

Amendments

• 1997, Taxpayer Relief Act of 1997 (P.L. 105-34)

P.L. 105-34, §1222(a):

Amended chapter 63 by adding at the end a new subchapter D, part III (Code Sec. 6255). **Effective** for partnership tax years beginning after 12-31-97 [effective date changed by P.L. 105-206, §6012(e)].

CHAPTER 64—COLLECTION

SUBCHAPTER A.	General provisions.
SUBCHAPTER B.	Receipt of payment.
SUBCHAPTER C.	Lien for taxes.
SUBCHAPTER D.	Seizure of property for collection of taxes.

Subchapter A—General Provisions

Sec. 6301.	Collection authority.
Sec. 6302.	Mode or time of collection.
Sec. 6303.	Notice and demand for tax.
Sec. 6304.	Fair tax collection practices.
Sec. 6305.	Collection of certain liability.
Sec. 6306.	Qualified tax collection contracts.
Sec. 6307.	Special compliance personnel program account.

[Sec. 6301]

SEC. 6301. COLLECTION AUTHORITY.

The Secretary shall collect the taxes imposed by the internal revenue laws.

Amendments

• 1976, Tax Reform Act of 1976 (P.L. 94-455)

P.L. 94-455, §1906(b)(13)(A):

Amended 1954 Code by substituting "Secretary" for "Secretary or his delegate" each place it appeared. **Effective** 2-1-77.

[Sec. 6302]

SEC. 6302. MODE OR TIME OF COLLECTION.

[Sec. 6302(a)]

(a) ESTABLISHMENT BY REGULATIONS.—If the mode or time for collecting any tax is not provided for by this title, the Secretary may establish the same by regulations.

COLLECTION—GENERAL PROVISIONS

Amendments

• **1983, Railroad Retirement Solvency Act of 1983 (P.L. 98-76)**

P.L. 98-76, §226, provides:

SEC. 226. DEPOSITARY SCHEDULES.

Effective on and after January 1, 1984, the times for making payments prescribed under section 6302 of the Internal Revenue Code of 1954 with respect to the taxes imposed by chapter 22 of such Code shall be the same as the times prescribed under such section which apply to the taxes imposed by chapters 21 and 24 of such Code.

• **1976, Tax Reform Act of 1976 (P.L. 94-455)**

P.L. 94-455, §1906(b)(13)(A):

Amended 1954 Code by substituting "Secretary" for "Secretary or his delegate" each place it appeared. **Effective** 2-1-77.

[Sec. 6302(b)]

(b) DISCRETIONARY METHOD.—Whether or not the method of collecting any tax imposed by chapter 21, 31, 32, or 33, or by section 4481, is specifically provided for by this title, any such tax may, under regulations prescribed by the Secretary, be collected by means of returns, stamps, coupons, tickets, books, or such other reasonable devices or methods as may be necessary or helpful in securing a complete and proper collection of the tax.

Amendments

• **1990, Omnibus Budget Reconciliation Act of 1990 (P.L. 101-508)**

P.L. 101-508, §11801(c)(22)(A) (as amended by P.L. 104-188, §1704(t)(52)):

Amended Code Sec. 6302(b) by striking "chapters 21" and all that follows down through "chapter 37," and inserting "chapter 21, 31, 32, or 33, or by section 4481". **Effective** 11-5-90. Prior to amendment, Code Sec. 6302(b) read as follows:

(b) DISCRETIONARY METHOD.—Whether or not the method of collecting any tax imposed by chapters 21, 31, 32, 33, section 4481 of chapter 36, [or] section 4501(a) of chapter 37, is specifically provided for by this title, any such tax may, under regulations prescribed by the Secretary, be collected by means of returns, stamps, coupons, tickets, books, or such other reasonable devices or methods as may be necessary or helpful in securing a complete and proper collection of the tax.

P.L. 101-508, §11821(b), provides:

(b) SAVINGS PROVISION.—If—

(1) any provision amended or repealed by this part applied to—

(A) any transaction occurring before the date of the enactment of this Act,

(B) any property acquired before such date of enactment, or

(C) any item of income, loss, deduction, or credit taken into account before such date of enactment, and

(2) the treatment of such transaction, property, or item under such provision would (without regard to the amendments made by this part) affect liability for tax periods ending after such date of enactment,

nothing in the amendments made by this part shall be construed to affect the treatment of such transaction, property, or item for purposes of determining liability for tax for periods ending after such date of enactment.

• **1976, Tax Reform Act of 1976 (P.L. 94-455)**

P.L. 94-455, §1906(a)(17):

Substituted "section 4501(a) of chapter 37" for "sections 4501(a) or 4511 of chapter 37, or section 4701 or 4721 of chapter 39" in Code Sec. 6302(b). **Effective** 2-1-77.

P.L. 94-455, §1906(b)(13)(A):

Amended 1954 Code by substituting "Secretary" for "Secretary or his delegate" each place it appeared. **Effective** 2-1-77.

• **1956 (P.L. 627, 84th Cong.)**

P.L. 627, 84th Cong., §206(b):

Amended subsection (b) by inserting "section 4481 of Chapter 36," after "33,". **Effective** 7-1-56.

[Sec. 6302(c)]

(c) USE OF GOVERNMENT DEPOSITARIES.—The Secretary may authorize Federal Reserve banks, and incorporated banks, trust companies, domestic building and loan associations, or credit unions which are depositaries or financial agents of the United States, to receive any tax imposed under the internal revenue laws, in such manner, at such times, and under such conditions as he may prescribe; and he shall prescribe the manner, times, and conditions under which the receipt of such tax by such banks, trust companies, domestic building and loan associations, and credit unions is to be treated as payment of such tax to the Secretary.

Amendments

• **1977 (P.L. 95-147)**

P.L. 95-147, §3(a):

Amended Code Sec. 6302(c) by substituting "trust companies, domestic building and loan associations, or credit unions" for "or trust companies" and by substituting "trust companies, domestic building and loan associations, and credit unions" for "and trust companies". **Effective** for amounts deposited after 10-28-77.

• **1976, Tax Reform Act of 1976 (P.L. 94-455)**

P.L. 94-455, §1906(b)(13)(A):

Amended 1954 Code by substituting "Secretary" for "Secretary or his delegate" each place it appeared. **Effective** 2-1-77.

[Sec. 6302(d)]

(d) TIME FOR PAYMENT OF MANUFACTURERS' EXCISE TAX ON RECREATIONAL EQUIPMENT.—The taxes imposed by subchapter D of chapter 32 of this title (relating to taxes on recreational equipment) shall be due and payable on the date for filing the return for such taxes.

Amendments

• **2010, Firearms Excise Tax Improvement Act of 2010 (P.L. 111-237)**

P.L. 111-237, §2(a):

Amended Code Sec. 6302(d). **Effective** for articles sold by the manufacturer, producer, or importer after 8-16-2010. Prior to amendment, Code Sec. 6302(d) read as follows:

(d) TIME FOR PAYMENT OF MANUFACTURERS' EXCISE TAX ON SPORTING GOODS.—The taxes imposed by subsections (a) and (b) of section 4161 (relating to taxes on sporting goods) shall be due and payable on the date for filing the return for such taxes.

• **1988, Technical and Miscellaneous Revenue Act of 1988 (P.L. 100-647)**

P.L. 100-647, §6107(a):

Amended Code Sec. 6302(d). **Effective** with respect to articles sold by the manufacturer, producer, or importer after 12-31-88. Prior to amendment, Code Sec. 6302(d) read as follows:

(d) TIME FOR PAYMENT OF MANUFACTURERS EXCISE TAX ON SPORT FISHING EQUIPMENT.—The tax imposed by section 4161(a) (relating to manufacturers excise tax on sport fishing equipment) shall be due and payable on the date for filing the return for such tax.

• **1984, Deficit Reduction Act of 1984 (P.L. 98-369)**

P.L. 98-369, §1015(c):

Amended Code Sec. 6302 by redesignating subsection (d) as subsection (e) and by inserting after subsection (c) new subsection (d). **Effective** with respect to articles sold by the manufacturer, producer, or importer after 9-30-84.

[Sec. 6302(e)]

(e) TIME FOR DEPOSIT OF TAXES ON COMMUNICATIONS SERVICES AND AIRLINE TICKETS.—

(1) IN GENERAL.—Except as provided in paragraph (2), if, under regulations prescribed by the Secretary, a person is required to make deposits of any tax imposed by section 4251 or subsection (a) or (b) of section 4261 with respect to amounts considered collected by such person during any semi-monthly period, such deposit shall be made not later than the 3rd day (not including Saturdays, Sundays, or legal holidays) after the close of the 1st week of the 2nd semimonthly period following the period to which such amounts relate.

(2) SPECIAL RULE FOR TAX DUE IN SEPTEMBER.—

(A) AMOUNTS CONSIDERED COLLECTED.—In the case of a person required to make deposits of the tax imposed by section 4251, 4261, or 4271 with respect to amounts considered collected by such person during any semimonthly period, the amount of such tax included in bills rendered or tickets sold during the period beginning on September 1 and ending on September 11 shall be deposited not later than September 29.

(B) SPECIAL RULE WHERE SEPTEMBER 29 IS ON SATURDAY OR SUNDAY.—If September 29 falls on a Saturday or Sunday, the due date under subparagraph (A) shall be—

(i) in the case of Saturday, the preceding day, and

(ii) in the case of Sunday, the following day.

COLLECTION—GENERAL PROVISIONS

(C) TAXPAYERS NOT REQUIRED TO USE ELECTRONIC FUNDS TRANSFER.—In the case of deposits not required to be made by electronic funds transfer, subparagraphs (A) and (B) shall be applied by substituting "September 10" for "September 11" and "September 28" for "September 29".

Amendments

• **2018, Tax Technical Corrections Act of 2018 (P.L. 115-141)**

P.L. 115-141, §401(a)(279), Div. U:

Amended Code Sec. 6302(e)(2)(A) by striking "sections" and inserting "section". **Effective** 3-23-2018.

• **2014, Tax Technical Corrections Act of 2014 (P.L. 113-295)**

P.L. 113-295, §221(a)(110)(A), Division A:

Amended Code Sec. 6302(e)(2)[(A)] by striking "imposed by" and all that follows through "with respect to" and inserting "imposed by sections 4251, 4261, or 4271 with respect to". **Effective** generally 12-19-2014. For a special rule, see Act Sec. 221(b)(2), Division A, below. Prior to amendment, Code Sec. 6302(e)(2)(A) read as follows:

(A) AMOUNTS CONSIDERED COLLECTED.—In the case of a person required to make deposits of the tax imposed by—

(i) section 4251, or

(ii) effective on January 1, 1997, section 4261 or 4271,

with respect to amounts considered collected by such person during any semimonthly period, the amount of such tax included in bills rendered or tickets sold during the period beginning on September 1 and ending on September 11 shall be deposited not later than September 29.

P.L. 113-295, §221(b)(2), Division A, provides:

(2) SAVINGS PROVISION.—If—

(A) any provision amended or repealed by the amendments made by this section applied to—

(i) any transaction occurring before the date of the enactment of this Act,

(ii) any property acquired before such date of enactment, or

(iii) any item of income, loss, deduction, or credit taken into account before such date of enactment, and

(B) the treatment of such transaction, property, or item under such provision would (without regard to the amendments or repeals made by this section) affect the liability for tax for periods ending after date of enactment, nothing in the amendments or repeals made by this section shall be construed to affect the treatment of such transaction, property, or item for purposes of determining liability for tax for periods ending after such date of enactment.

• **2001, Tax-Related Provisions in the Air Transportation Safety and System Stabilization Act (P.L. 107-42)**

P.L. 107-42, §301 (as amended by P.L. 107-134, §114), provides:

SEC. 301. EXTENSION OF DUE DATE FOR EXCISE TAX DEPOSITS; TREATMENT OF LOSS COMPENSATION.

(a) EXTENSION OF DUE DATE FOR EXCISE TAX DEPOSITS.—

(1) IN GENERAL.—In the case of an eligible air carrier, any airline-related deposit required under section 6302 of the Internal Revenue Code of 1986 to be made after September 10, 2001, and before November 15, 2001, shall be treated for purposes of such Code as timely made if such deposit is made on or before November 15, 2001. If the Secretary of the Treasury so prescribes, the preceding sentence shall be applied by substituting for "November 15, 2001" each place it appears—

(A) "January 15, 2002"; or

(B) such earlier date after November 15, 2001, as such Secretary may prescribe.

(2) ELIGIBLE AIR CARRIER.—For purposes of this subsection, the term "eligible air carrier" means any domestic corporation engaged in the trade or business of transporting (for hire) persons by air if such transportation is available to the general public.

(3) AIRLINE-RELATED DEPOSIT.—For purposes of this subsection, the term "airline-related deposit" means any deposit of taxes imposed by subchapter C of chapter 33 of such Code (relating to transportation by air).

(b) TREATMENT OF LOSS COMPENSATION.—Nothing in any provision of law shall be construed to exclude from gross income under the Internal Revenue Code of 1986 any compensation received under section 101(a)(2) of this Act.

• **1994, Uruguay Round Agreements Act (P.L. 103-465)**

P.L. 103-465, §712(d):

Amended Code Sec. 6302(e). **Effective** 1-1-95. Prior to amendment, Code Sec. 6302(e) read as follows:

(e) TIME FOR DEPOSIT OF TAXES ON COMMUNICATION SERVICES AND AIRLINE TICKETS.—If, under regulations prescribed by the Secretary, a person is required to make deposits of any tax imposed by section 4251 or subsection (a) or (b) of section 4261 with respect to amounts considered collected by such person during any semimonthly period, such deposit shall be made not later than the 3rd day (not including Saturdays, Sundays, or legal holidays) after the close of the 1st week of the 2nd semimonthly period following the period to which such amounts relate.

• **1990, Omnibus Budget Reconciliation Act of 1990 (P.L. 101-508)**

P.L. 101-508, §11217(b)(1)(A)-(B):

Amended Code Sec. 6302(e) by inserting "COMMUNICATIONS SERVICES AND" before "AIRLINE", and by inserting "section 4251 or" before "subsection (a) or (b)". **Effective** for payments of taxes considered collected during semimonthly periods beginning after 12-31-90.

• **1989, Omnibus Budget Reconciliation Act of 1989 (P.L. 101-239)**

P.L. 101-239, §7502(a):

Amended Code Sec. 6302 by redesignating subsection (e) as subsection (f) and by inserting after subsection (d) a new subsection (e). **Effective** for payments of taxes considered collected for semimonthly periods beginning after 6-30-90.

[Sec. 6302(f)]

(f) TIME FOR DEPOSIT OF CERTAIN EXCISE TAXES.—

(1) GENERAL RULE.—Except as otherwise provided in this subsection and subsection (e), if any person is required under regulations to make deposits of taxes under subtitle D with respect to semi-monthly periods, such person shall make deposits of such taxes for the period beginning on September 16 and ending on September 26 not later than September 29.

(2) TAXES ON OZONE DEPLETING CHEMICALS.—If any person is required under regulations to make deposits of taxes under subchapter D of chapter 38 with respect to semimonthly periods, in lieu of paragraph (1), such person shall make deposits of such taxes for—

(A) the second semimonthly period in August, and

(B) the period beginning on September 1 and ending on September 11,

not later than September 29.

(3) TAXPAYERS NOT REQUIRED TO USE ELECTRONIC FUNDS TRANSFER.—In the case of deposits not required to be made by electronic funds transfer, paragraphs (1) and (2) shall be applied by substituting "September 25" for "September 26", "September 10" for "September 11", and "September 28" for "September 29".

(4) SPECIAL RULE WHERE DUE DATE ON SATURDAY OR SUNDAY.—If, but for this paragraph, the due date under paragraph (1), (2), or (3) would fall on a Saturday or Sunday, such due date shall be deemed to be—

(A) in the case of Saturday, the preceding day, and

(B) in the case of Sunday, the following day.

Amendments

• **2014, Tax Technical Corrections Act of 2014 (P.L. 113-295)**

P.L. 113-295, §221(a)(110)(B), Division A:

Amended Code Sec. 6302(f)(1) by striking the last sentence. **Effective** generally 12-19-2014. For a special rule, see Act Sec. 221(b)(2), Division A, below. Prior to being stricken, the last sentence of Code Sec. 6302(f)(1) read as follows:

In the case of taxes imposed by sections 4261 and 4271, this paragraph shall not apply to periods before January 1, 1997.

P.L. 113-295, §221(b)(2), Division A, provides:

(2) SAVINGS PROVISION.—If—

(A) any provision amended or repealed by the amendments made by this section applied to—

(i) any transaction occurring before the date of the enactment of this Act,

(ii) any property acquired before such date of enactment, or

(iii) any item of income, loss, deduction, or credit taken into account before such date of enactment, and

(B) the treatment of such transaction, property, or item under such provision would (without regard to the amendments or repeals made by this section) affect the liability for tax for periods ending after date of enactment, nothing in the amendments or repeals made by this section shall be construed to affect the treatment of such transaction, property, or item for purposes of determining liability for tax for periods ending after such date of enactment.

• **1994, Uruguay Round Agreements Act (P.L. 103-465)**

P.L. 103-465, §712(a):

Amended Code Sec. 6302(f). **Effective** 1-1-95. Prior to amendment, Code Sec. 6302(f) read as follows:

(f) TIME FOR DEPOSIT OF TAXES ON GASOLINE AND DIESEL FUEL.—

(1) GENERAL RULE.—Notwithstanding section 518 of the Highway Revenue Act of 1982, any person whose liability for tax under section 4081 is payable with respect to semimonthly periods shall, not later than September 27, make deposits of such tax for the period beginning on September 16 and ending on September 22.

(2) SPECIAL RULE WHERE DUE DATE FALLS ON SATURDAY, SUNDAY, OR HOLIDAY.—If, but for this paragraph, the due date under paragraph (1) would fall on a Saturday, Sunday, or holiday in the District of Columbia, such due date shall be deemed to be the immediately preceding day which is not a Saturday, Sunday, or such a holiday.

COLLECTION—GENERAL PROVISIONS

- **1993, Omnibus Budget Reconciliation Act of 1993 (P.L. 103-66)**

P.L. 103-66, § 13242(d)(15):

Amended Code Sec. 6302(f) by inserting "AND DIESEL FUEL" after "GASOLINE" in the heading. **Effective** 1-1-94.

- **1989, Omnibus Budget Reconciliation Act of 1989 (P.L. 101-239)**

P.L. 101-239, § 7502(a):

Amended Code Sec. 6302 by redesignating subsection (e) as subsection (f). **Effective** for payments of taxes considered collected for semimonthly periods beginning after 6-30-90.

P.L. 101-239, § 7507(a):

Amended Code Sec. 6302 by redesignating subsection (f) as subsection (g) and by inserting after subsection (e) a new subsection (f). **Effective** for payments of taxes for tax periods beginning after 12-31-89.

[Sec. 6302(g)]

(g) DEPOSITS OF SOCIAL SECURITY TAXES AND WITHHELD INCOME TAXES.—If, under regulations prescribed by the Secretary, a person is required to make deposits of taxes imposed by chapters 21, 22, and 24 on the basis of eighth-month periods, such person shall make deposits of such taxes on the 1st banking day after any day on which such person has $100,000 or more of such taxes for deposit.

Amendments

- **1996, Small Business Job Protection Act of 1996 (P.L. 104-188)**

P.L. 104-188, § 1702(c)(3):

Amended Code Sec. 6302(g) by inserting ", 22," after "chapters 21". **Effective** as if included in the provision of P.L. 101-508 to which it relates.

P.L. 104-188, § 1809, provides:

Notwithstanding any other provision of law, the increase in the applicable required percentages for fiscal year 1997 in clauses (i)(IV) and (ii)(IV) of section 6302(h)(2)(C) of the Internal Revenue Code of 1986 shall not take effect before July 1, 1997.

- **1990, Omnibus Budget Reconciliation Act of 1990 (P.L. 101-508)**

P.L. 101-508, § 11334(a):

Amended Code Sec. 6302(g). **Effective** for amounts required to be deposited after 12-31-90. Prior to amendment, Code Sec. 6302(g) read as follows:

(g) DEPOSITS OF SOCIAL SECURITY TAXES AND WITHHELD INCOME TAXES.—

(1) IN GENERAL.—If, under regulations prescribed by the Secretary, a person is required to make deposits of taxes imposed by chapters 21 and 24 on the basis of eighth-month periods, such person shall, for the years specified in paragraph (2), make deposits of such taxes on the applicable banking day after any day on which such person has $100,000 or more of such taxes for deposit.

(2) SPECIFIED YEARS.—For purposes of paragraph (1)—

In the case of:	The applicable banking day is:
1990	1st
1991	2d
1992	3rd
1993	1st
1994	1st.

- **1989, Omnibus Budget Reconciliation Act of 1989 (P.L. 101-239)**

P.L. 101-239, § 7507(a):

Amended Code Sec. 6302 by redesignating subsection (f) as subsection (g). **Effective** for payments of taxes for tax periods beginning after 12-31-89.

P.L. 101-239, § 7632(a):

Amended Code Sec. 6302 by redesignating subsection (g) as subsection (h) and by inserting after subsection (f) a new subsection (g). **Effective** for amounts required to be deposited after 7-31-90.

[Sec. 6302(h)]

(h) USE OF ELECTRONIC FUND TRANSFER SYSTEM FOR COLLECTION OF CERTAIN TAXES.—

(1) ESTABLISHMENT OF SYSTEM.—

(A) IN GENERAL.—The Secretary shall prescribe such regulations as may be necessary for the development and implementation of an electronic fund transfer system which is required to be used for the collection of depository taxes. Such system shall be designed in such manner as may be necessary to ensure that such taxes are credited to the general account of the Treasury on the date on which such taxes would otherwise have been required to be deposited under the Federal tax deposit system.

(B) EXEMPTIONS.—The regulations prescribed under subparagraph (A) may contain such exemptions as the Secretary may deem appropriate.

(2) DEFINITIONS.—For purposes of this subsection—

(A) DEPOSITORY TAX.—The term "depository tax" means any tax if the Secretary is authorized to require deposits of such tax.

(B) ELECTRONIC FUND TRANSFER.—The term "electronic fund transfer" means any transfer of funds, other than a transaction originated by check, draft, or similar paper instrument, which is initiated through an electronic terminal, telephonic instrument, or computer or magnetic tape so as to order, instruct, or authorize a financial institution or other financial intermediary to debit or credit an account.

(3) COORDINATION WITH OTHER ELECTRONIC FUND TRANSFER REQUIREMENTS.—Under regulations, any tax required to be paid by electronic fund transfer under section 5061(e) or 5703(b) shall be paid in such a manner as to ensure that the requirements of the second sentence of paragraph (1)(A) of this subsection are satisfied.

Amendments

- **2014, Tax Technical Corrections Act of 2014 (P.L. 113-295)**

P.L. 113-295, § 221(a)(110)(C)(i)-(ii), Division A:

Amended Code Sec. 6302(h) by striking paragraph (2) and redesignating paragraphs (3) and (4) as paragraphs (2) and (3), respectively, and by amending paragraph (3) (as so redesignated). **Effective** generally 12-19-2014. For a special rule, see Act Sec. 221(b)(2), Division A, below. Prior to being stricken and amended, respectively, Code Sec. 6302(h)(2) and (3) (as redesignated) read as follows:

(2) PHASE-IN REQUIREMENTS.—

(A) IN GENERAL.—Except as provided in subparagraph (B), the regulations referred to in paragraph (1)—

(i) shall contain appropriate procedures to assure that an orderly conversion from the Federal tax deposit system to the electronic fund transfer system is accomplished, and

(ii) may provide for a phase-in of such electronic fund transfer system by classes of taxpayers based on the aggregate undeposited taxes of such taxpayers at the close of specified periods and any other factors the Secretary may deem appropriate.

(B) PHASE-IN REQUIREMENTS.—The phase-in of the electronic fund transfer system shall be designed in such manner as may be necessary to ensure that—

(i) during each fiscal year beginning after September 30, 1993, at least the applicable required percentage of the total depository taxes imposed by chapters 21, 22, and 24 shall be collected by means of electronic fund transfer, and

(ii) during each fiscal year beginning after September 30, 1993, at least the applicable required percentage of the total other depository taxes shall be collected by means of electronic fund transfer.

(C) APPLICABLE REQUIRED PERCENTAGE.—

(i) In the case of the depository taxes imposed by chapters 21, 22, and 24, the applicable required percentage is—

(I) 3 percent for fiscal year 1994,

(II) 16.9 percent for fiscal year 1995,

(III) 20.1 percent for fiscal year 1996,

(IV) 58.3 percent for fiscal years 1997 and 1998, and

(V) 94 percent for fiscal year 1999 and all fiscal years thereafter.

(ii) In the case of other depository taxes, the applicable required percentage is—

(I) 3 percent for fiscal year 1994,

(II) 20 percent for fiscal year 1995,

(III) 30 percent for fiscal year 1996,

(IV) 60 percent for fiscal years 1997 and 1998, and

(V) 94 percent for fiscal year 1999 and all fiscal years thereafter.

(3) COORDINATION WITH OTHER ELECTRONIC FUND TRANSFER REQUIREMENTS.—

(A) COORDINATION WITH CERTAIN EXCISE TAXES.—In determining whether the requirements of subparagraph (B) of paragraph (2) are met, taxes required to be paid by electronic fund transfer under sections 5061(e) and 5703(b) shall be disregarded.

(B) ADDITIONAL REQUIREMENT.—Under regulations, any tax required to be paid by electronic fund transfer under section 5061(e) or 5703(b) shall be paid in such a manner as to ensure that the requirements of the second sentence of paragraph (1)(A) of this subsection are satisfied.

Sec. 6302(g)

COLLECTION—GENERAL PROVISIONS

P.L. 113-295, §221(b)(2), Division A, provides:

(2) SAVINGS PROVISION.—If—

(A) any provision amended or repealed by the amendments made by this section applied to—

(i) any transaction occurring before the date of the enactment of this Act,

(ii) any property acquired before such date of enactment, or

(iii) any item of income, loss, deduction, or credit taken into account before such date of enactment, and

(B) the treatment of such transaction, property, or item under such provision would (without regard to the amendments or repeals made by this section) affect the liability for tax for periods ending after date of enactment, nothing in the amendments or repeals made by this section shall be construed to affect the treatment of such transaction, property, or item for purposes of determining liability for tax for periods ending after such date of enactment.

• **1997, Taxpayer Relief Act of 1997 (P.L. 105-34)**

P.L. 105-34, §931, provides:

ACT SEC. 931. WAIVER OF PENALTY THROUGH JUNE 30, 1998, ON SMALL BUSINESSES FAILING TO MAKE ELECTRONIC FUND TRANSFERS OF TAXES.

No penalty shall be imposed under the Internal Revenue Code of 1986 solely by reason of a failure by a person to use the electronic fund transfer system established under section 6302(h) of such Code if—

Amendments

• **2010, (P.L. 111-226)**

P.L. 111-226, §219(b)(2):

Amended Code Sec. 6302 by striking subsection (i). **Effective** for tax years beginning after 12-31-2010. Prior to being stricken, Code Sec. 6302(i) read as follows:

(i) CROSS REFERENCES.—

For treatment of earned income advance amounts as payment of withholding and FICA taxes, see section 3507(d).

• **1993, North American Free Trade Agreement Implementation Act (P.L. 103-182)**

P.L. 103-182, §523(a):

Amended Code Sec. 6302 by redesignating subsection (h) as subsection (i). **Effective** on the date the Agreement enters into force with respect to the United States.

• **1989, Omnibus Budget Reconciliation Act of 1989 (P.L. 101-239)**

P.L. 101-239, §7632(a):

Amended Code Sec. 6302 by redesignating subsection (g) as subsection (h). **Effective** for amounts required to be deposited after 7-31-90.

• **1988, Omnibus Trade and Competitiveness Act of 1988 (P.L. 100-418)**

P.L. 100-418, §1941(b)(2)(G)(i)-(ii):

Amended Code Sec. 6302(e) by striking "(1) For" and inserting "For", and by striking out paragraph (2). **Effective** for crude oil removed from the premises on or after 8-23-88. Prior to amendment, Code Sec. 6320(e)(2) read as follows:

(1) such person is a member of a class of taxpayers first required to use such system on or after July 1, 1997, and

(2) such failure occurs before July 1, 1998.

• **1993, North American Free Trade Agreement Implementation Act (P.L. 103-182)**

P.L. 103-182, §523(a):

Amended Code Sec. 6302 by redesignating subsection (h) as subsection (i) and by inserting after subsection (g) new subsection (h). **Effective** on the date the Agreement enters into force with respect to the United States.

P.L. 103-182, §523(b)(2), provides:

(2) REGULATIONS.—Not later than 210 days after the date of the enactment of this Act, the Secretary of the Treasury or his delegate shall prescribe temporary regulations under section 6302(h) of the Internal Revenue Code of 1986 (as added by this section).

[Sec. 6302(i)—Stricken]

(2) For depositary requirements applicable to the windfall profit tax imposed by section 4986, see section 4995(b).

• **1984, Deficit Reduction Act of 1984 (P.L. 98-369)**

P.L. 98-369, §1015(c):

Amended Code Sec. 6302 by redesignating subsection (d) as subsection (e). **Effective** with respect to articles sold by the manufacturer, producer, or importer after 9-30-84.

• **1980, Technical Corrections Act of 1979 (P.L. 96-222)**

P.L. 96-222, §101(a)(2)(D):

Amended Act Sec. 105(g)(2) of P.L. 95-600 to change the **effective** date of the addition of Code Sec. 6302(d) from 6-30-78, to 6-30-79.

• **1980, Crude Oil Windfall Profit Tax Act of 1980 (P.L. 96-223)**

P.L. 96-223, §101(c)(2):

Amended Code Sec. 6302(d). **Effective** for periods after 2-29-80. Prior to amendment, Code Sec. 6302(d) read:

(d) CROSS REFERENCE.—

For treatment of payment of earned income advance amounts as payment of withholding and FICA taxes, see section 3507(d).

• **1978, Revenue Act of 1978 (P.L. 95-600)**

P.L. 95-600, §105(e), (g)(2):

Added Code Sec. 6302(d). **Effective** for remuneration paid after 6-30-78.

[Sec. 6303]

SEC. 6303. NOTICE AND DEMAND FOR TAX.

[Sec. 6303(a)]

(a) GENERAL RULE.—Where it is not otherwise provided by this title, the Secretary shall, as soon as practicable, and within 60 days, after the making of an assessment of a tax pursuant to section 6203, give notice to each person liable for the unpaid tax, stating the amount and demanding payment thereof. Such notice shall be left at the dwelling or usual place of business of such person, or shall be sent by mail to such person's last known address.

Amendments

• **1976, Tax Reform Act of 1976 (P.L. 94-455)**

P.L. 94-455, §1906(b)(13)(A):

Amended 1954 Code by substituting "Secretary" for "Secretary or his delegate" each place it appeared. **Effective** 2-1-77.

[Sec. 6303(b)]

(b) ASSESSMENT PRIOR TO LAST DATE FOR PAYMENT.—Except where the Secretary believes collection would be jeopardized by delay, if any tax is assessed prior to the last date prescribed for payment of such tax, payment of such tax shall not be demanded under subsection (a) until after such date.

Amendments

• **1976, Tax Reform Act of 1976 (P.L. 94-455)**

P.L. 94-455, §1906(b)(13)(A):

Amended 1954 Code by substituting "Secretary" for "Secretary or his delegate" each place it appeared. **Effective** 2-1-77.

[Sec. 6304]

SEC. 6304. FAIR TAX COLLECTION PRACTICES.

[Sec. 6304(a)]

(a) COMMUNICATION WITH THE TAXPAYER.—Without the prior consent of the taxpayer given directly to the Secretary or the express permission of a court of competent jurisdiction, the Secretary may not communicate with a taxpayer in connection with the collection of any unpaid tax—

(1) at any unusual time or place or a time or place known or which should be known to be inconvenient to the taxpayer;

Internal Revenue Code

COLLECTION—GENERAL PROVISIONS

(2) if the Secretary knows the taxpayer is represented by any person authorized to practice before the Internal Revenue Service with respect to such unpaid tax and has knowledge of, or can readily ascertain, such person's name and address, unless such person fails to respond within a reasonable period of time to a communication from the Secretary or unless such person consents to direct communication with the taxpayer; or

(3) at the taxpayer's place of employment if the Secretary knows or has reason to know that the taxpayer's employer prohibits the taxpayer from receiving such communication.

In the absence of knowledge of circumstances to the contrary, the Secretary shall assume that the convenient time for communicating with a taxpayer is after 8 a.m. and before 9 p.m., local time at the taxpayer's location.

[Sec. 6304(b)]

(b) PROHIBITION OF HARASSMENT AND ABUSE.—The Secretary may not engage in any conduct the natural consequence of which is to harass, oppress, or abuse any person in connection with the collection of any unpaid tax. Without limiting the general application of the foregoing, the following conduct is a violation of this subsection:

(1) The use or threat of use of violence or other criminal means to harm the physical person, reputation, or property of any person.

(2) The use of obscene or profane language or language the natural consequence of which is to abuse the hearer or reader.

(3) Causing a telephone to ring or engaging any person in telephone conversation repeatedly or continuously with intent to annoy, abuse, or harass any person at the called number.

(4) Except as provided under rules similar to the rules in section 804 of the Fair Debt Collection Practices Act (15 U.S.C. 1692b), the placement of telephone calls without meaningful disclosure of the caller's identity.

[Sec. 6304(c)]

(c) CIVIL ACTION FOR VIOLATIONS OF SECTION.—

For civil action for violations of this section, see section 7433.

Amendments

• **1998, IRS Restructuring and Reform Act of 1998 (P.L. 105-206)**

P.L. 105-206, §3466(a):

Amended subchapter A of chapter 64 by inserting after Code Sec. 6303 a new Code Sec. 6304. **Effective** 7-22-98.

[Sec. 6304—Repealed]

Amendments

• **1976, Tax Reform Act of 1976 (P.L. 94-455)**

P.L. 94-455, §1906(a)(20):

Repealed Code Sec. 6304. **Effective** 2-1-77. Prior to repeal, Code Sec. 6304 read as follows:

SEC. 6304. COLLECTION UNDER THE TARIFF ACT.

For collection under the provisions of the Tariff Act of 1930 of the taxes imposed by section 4501(b), and subchapters A, B, C, D, and E of chapter 38, see sections 4504 and 4601, respectively.

[Sec. 6305]

SEC. 6305. COLLECTION OF CERTAIN LIABILITY.

[Sec. 6305(a)]

(a) IN GENERAL.—Upon receiving a certification from the Secretary of Health and Human Services, under section 452(b) of the Social Security Act with respect to any individual, the Secretary shall assess and collect the amount certified by the Secretary of Health and Human Services, in the same manner, with the same powers, and (except as provided in this section) subject to the same limitations as if such amount were a tax imposed by subtitle C the collection of which would be jeopardized by delay, except that—

(1) no interest or penalties shall be assessed or collected,

(2) for such purposes, paragraphs (4), (6), and (8) of section 6334(a) (relating to property exempt from levy) shall not apply,

(3) there shall be exempt from levy so much of the salary, wages, or other income of an individual as is being withheld therefrom in garnishment pursuant to a judgment entered by a court of competent jurisdiction for the support of his minor children,

(4) in the case of the first assessment against an individual for delinquency under a court or administrative order against such individual for a particular person or persons, the collection shall be stayed for a period of 60 days immediately following notice and demand as described in section 6303, and

(5) no additional fee may be assessed for adjustments to an amount previously certified pursuant to such section 452(b) with respect to the same obligor.

Amendments

• **1996, Personal Responsibility and Work Opportunity Reconciliation Act of 1996 (P.L. 104-193)**

P.L. 104-193, §361(a)(1)-(4):

Amended Code Sec. 6305(a) by striking "and" at the end of paragraph (3); by striking the period at the end of paragraph (4) and inserting ", and"; by adding at the end a new paragraph (5); and by striking "Secretary of Health, Education and Welfare" each place it appears and inserting "Secretary of Health and Human Services". **Effective** 10-1-97.

• **1981, Omnibus Budget Reconciliation act of 1981 (P.L. 97-35)**

P.L. 97-35, §2332(g):

Amended Code Sec. 6305(a)(4) by striking out "court order" and inserting in lieu thereof "court or administrative order". **Effective** 10-1-81.

• **1976, Tax Reform Act of 1976 (P.L. 94-455)**

P.L. 94-455, §1906(b)(13)(A):

Amended 1954 Code by substituting "Secretary" for "Secretary or his delegate" each place it appeared. **Effective** 2-1-77.

[Sec. 6305(b)]

(b) REVIEW OF ASSESSMENTS AND COLLECTIONS.—No court of the United States, whether established under article I or article III of the Constitution, shall have jurisdiction of any action, whether legal or equitable, brought to restrain or review the assessment and collection of amounts by the Secretary under subsection (a), nor shall any such assessment and collection be subject to review by the Secretary in any proceeding. This subsection does not preclude any legal, equitable, or administrative action against the State by an individual in any State court or before any State agency to determine his liability for any amount assessed against him and collected, or to recover any such amount collected from him, under this section.

Amendments

• **1976, Tax Reform Act of 1976 (P.L. 94-455)**

P.L. 94-455, §1906(b)(13)(A):

Amended 1954 Code by substituting "Secretary" for "Secretary or his delegate" each place it appeared. **Effective** 2-1-77.

• **1975, Social Security Act of 1975 (P.L. 93-647)**

P.L. 93-647, §101(b)(1):

Added Code Sec. 6305. **Effective** 7-1-75.

COLLECTION—GENERAL PROVISIONS

[Sec. 6306]
SEC. 6306. QUALIFIED TAX COLLECTION CONTRACTS.

[Sec. 6306(a)]

(a) IN GENERAL.—Nothing in any provision of law shall be construed to prevent the Secretary from entering into a qualified tax collection contract.

[Sec. 6306(b)]

(b) QUALIFIED TAX COLLECTION CONTRACT.—For purposes of this section, the term "qualified tax collection contract" means any contract which—

(1) is for the services of any person (other than an officer or employee of the Treasury Department)—

(A) to locate and contact any taxpayer specified by the Secretary,

(B) to request full payment from such taxpayer of an amount of Federal tax specified by the Secretary and, if such request cannot be met by the taxpayer, to offer the taxpayer an installment agreement providing for full payment of such amount during a period not to exceed 7 years, and

(C) to obtain financial information specified by the Secretary with respect to such taxpayer,

(2) prohibits each person providing such services under such contract from committing any act or omission which employees of the Internal Revenue Service are prohibited from committing in the performance of similar services,

(3) prohibits subcontractors from—

(A) having contacts with taxpayers,

(B) providing quality assurance services, and

(C) composing debt collection notices, and

(4) permits subcontractors to perform other services only with the approval of the Secretary.

Amendments

• **2019, Taxpayer First Act (P.L. 116-25)**

P.L. 116-25, §1205(c):

Amended Code Sec. 6306(b)(1)(B) by striking "5 years" and inserting "7 years". **Effective** for contracts entered into after 7-1-2019.

[Sec. 6306(c)]

(c) COLLECTION OF INACTIVE TAX RECEIVABLES.—

(1) IN GENERAL.—Notwithstanding any other provision of law, the Secretary shall enter into one or more qualified tax collection contracts for the collection of all outstanding inactive tax receivables.

(2) INACTIVE TAX RECEIVABLES.—For purposes of this section—

(A) IN GENERAL.—The term "inactive tax receivable" means any tax receivable if—

(i) at any time after assessment, the Internal Revenue Service removes such receivable from the active inventory for lack of resources or inability to locate the taxpayer,

(ii) more than 2 years has passed since assessment and such receivable has not been assigned for collection to any employee of the Internal Revenue Service, or

(iii) in the case of a receivable which has been assigned for collection, more than 365 days have passed without interaction with the taxpayer or a third party for purposes of furthering the collection of such receivable.

(B) TAX RECEIVABLE.—The term "tax receivable" means any outstanding assessment which the Internal Revenue Service includes in potentially collectible inventory.

Amendments

• **2019, Taxpayer First Act (P.L. 116-25)**

P.L. 116-25, §1205(b):

Amended Code Sec. 6306(c)(2)(A)(ii) by striking "more than 1/3 of the period of the applicable statute of limitation has lapsed" and inserting "more than 2 years has passed since assessment". **Effective** for tax receivables identified by the Secretary (or the Secretary's delegate) after 12-31-2020.

• **2015, Fixing America's Surface Transportation Act (P.L. 114-94)**

P.L. 114-94, §32102(a):

Amended Code Sec. 6306 by redesignating subsections (c)-(f) as subsections (d)-(g), respectively, and by inserting after subsection (b) a new subsection (c). **Effective** for tax receivables identified by the Secretary after 12-4-2015.

[Sec. 6306(d)]

(d) CERTAIN TAX RECEIVABLES NOT ELIGIBLE FOR COLLECTION UNDER QUALIFIED TAX COLLECTIONS CONTRACTS.—A tax receivable shall not be eligible for collection pursuant to a qualified tax collection contract if such receivable—

(1) is subject to a pending or active offer-in-compromise or installment agreement,

(2) is classified as an innocent spouse case,

(3) involves a taxpayer identified by the Secretary as being—

(A) deceased,

(B) under the age of 18,

(C) in a designated combat zone,

(D) a victim of tax-related identity theft,

(E) a taxpayer substantially all of whose income consists of disability insurance benefits under section 223 of the Social Security Act or supplemental security income benefits under title XVI of the Social Security Act (including supplemental security income benefits of the type described in section 1616 of such Act or section 212 of Public Law 93-66), or

(F) a taxpayer who is an individual with adjusted gross income, as determined for the most recent taxable year for which such information is available, which does not exceed 200 percent of the applicable poverty level (as determined by the Secretary),

(4) is currently under examination, litigation, criminal investigation, or levy, or

(5) is currently subject to a proper exercise of a right of appeal under this title.

COLLECTION—GENERAL PROVISIONS

Amendments

• **2019, Taxpayer First Act (P.L. 116-25)**

P.L. 116-25, §1205(a):

Amended Code Sec. 6306(d)(3) by striking "or" at the end of subparagraph (C) and by inserting after subparagraph (D) new subparagraphs (E)-(F). **Effective** for tax receivables identified by the Secretary (or the Secretary's delegate) after 12-31-2020.

• **2015, Fixing America's Surface Transportation Act (P.L. 114-94)**

P.L. 114-94, §32102(b):

Amended Code Sec. 6306, as amended by Act Sec. 32102(a), by redesignating subsections (d)-(g) as subsections (e)-(h), respectively, and by inserting after subsection (c) a new subsection (d). **Effective** for tax receivables identified by the Secretary after 12-4-2015.

[Sec. 6306(e)]

(e) FEES.—The Secretary may retain and use—

(1) an amount not in excess of 25 percent of the amount collected under any qualified tax collection contract for the costs of services performed under such contract, and

(2) an amount not in excess of 25 percent of such amount collected to fund the special compliance personnel program account under section 6307.

The Secretary shall keep adequate records regarding amounts so retained and used. The amount credited as paid by any taxpayer shall be determined without regard to this subsection.

Amendments

• **2015, Fixing America's Surface Transportation Act (P.L. 114-94)**

P.L. 114-94, §32102(a):

Amended Code Sec. 6306 by redesignating subsection (c) as subsection (d). **Effective** for tax receivables identified by the Secretary after 12-4-2015.

P.L. 114-94, §32102(b):

Amended Code Sec. 6306, as amended by Act Sec. 32102(a), by redesignating subsection (d) as subsection (e). **Effective** for tax receivables identified by the Secretary after 12-4-2015.

P.L. 114-94, §32103(a):

Amended Code Sec. 6306(e), as redesignated by Act Sec. 32102, by striking "for collection enforcement activities of the Internal Revenue Service" in paragraph (2) and inserting "to fund the special compliance personnel program account under section 6307". **Effective** for amounts collected and retained by the Secretary after 12-4-2015.

[Sec. 6306(f)]

(f) NO FEDERAL LIABILITY.—The United States shall not be liable for any act or omission of any person performing services under a qualified tax collection contract.

Amendments

• **2015, Fixing America's Surface Transportation Act (P.L. 114-94)**

P.L. 114-94, §32102(a):

Amended Code Sec. 6306 by redesignating subsection (d) as subsection (e). **Effective** for tax receivables identified by the Secretary after 12-4-2015.

P.L. 114-94, §32102(b):

Amended Code Sec. 6306, as amended by Act Sec. 32102(a), by redesignating subsection (e) as subsection (f). **Effective** for tax receivables identified by the Secretary after 12-4-2015.

[Sec. 6306(g)]

(g) APPLICATION OF FAIR DEBT COLLECTION PRACTICES ACT.—The provisions of the Fair Debt Collection Practices Act (15 U.S.C. 1692 et seq.) shall apply to any qualified tax collection contract, except to the extent superseded by section 6304, section 7602(c), or by any other provision of this title.

Amendments

• **2015, Fixing America's Surface Transportation Act (P.L. 114-94)**

P.L. 114-94, §32102(a):

Amended Code Sec. 6306 by redesignating subsection (e) as subsection (f). **Effective** for tax receivables identified by the Secretary after 12-4-2015.

P.L. 114-94, §32102(b):

Amended Code Sec. 6306, as amended by Act Sec. 32102(a), by redesignating subsection (f) as subsection (g). **Effective** for tax receivables identified by the Secretary after 12-4-2015.

[Sec. 6306(h)]

(h) CONTRACTING PRIORITY.—In contracting for the services of any person under this section, the Secretary shall utilize private collection contractors and debt collection centers on the schedule required under section 3711(g) of title 31, United States Code, including the technology and communications infrastructure established therein, to the extent such private collection contractors and debt collection centers are appropriate to carry out the purposes of this section.

Amendments

• **2015, Fixing America's Surface Transportation Act (P.L. 114-94)**

P.L. 114-94, §32102(c):

Amended Code Sec. 6306, as amended by Act Sec. 32102(a)-(b), by redesignating subsection (h) as subsection (i) and by inserting after subsection (g) a new subsection (h). For the **effective** date, see Act Sec. 32102(g)(2), below.

P.L. 114-94, §32102(g)(2), provides:

(2) CONTRACTING PRIORITY.—The Secretary shall begin entering into contracts and agreements as described in the amendment made by subsection (c) within 3 months after the date of the enactment of this Act.

[Sec. 6306(i)]

(i) TAXPAYERS IN PRESIDENTIALLY DECLARED DISASTER AREAS.—The Secretary may prescribe procedures under which a taxpayer determined to be affected by a Federally declared disaster (as defined by section 165(i)(5)) may request—

(1) relief from immediate collection measures by contractors under this section, and

(2) a return of the inactive tax receivable to the inventory of the Internal Revenue Service to be collected by an employee thereof.

Amendments

• **2015, Fixing America's Surface Transportation Act (P.L. 114-94)**

P.L. 114-94, §32102(e):

Amended Code Sec. 6306, as amended by Act Sec. 32102(a)-(c), by redesignating subsection (i) as subsection (j) and by inserting after subsection (h) a new subsection (i). **Effective** 12-4-2015.

[Sec. 6306(j)]

(j) REPORT TO CONGRESS.—Not later than 90 days after the last day of each fiscal year (beginning with the first such fiscal year ending after the date of the enactment of this subsection), the Secretary shall submit to the Committee on Ways and Means of the House of Representatives and the Committee on Finance of the Senate a report with respect to qualified tax collection contracts under this section which shall include—

(1) annually, with respect to such fiscal year—

(A) the total number and amount of tax receivables provided to each contractor for collection under this section,

(B) the total amounts collected (and amounts of installment agreements entered into under subsection (b)(1)(B)) with respect to each contractor and the collection costs incurred (directly and indirectly) by the Internal Revenue Service with respect to such amounts,

(C) the impact of such contracts on the total number and amount of unpaid assessments, and on the number and amount of assessments collected by Internal Revenue Service personnel after initial contact by a contractor,

COLLECTION—GENERAL PROVISIONS

(D) the amount of fees retained by the Secretary under subsection (e) and a description of the use of such funds, and

(E) a disclosure safeguard report in a form similar to that required under section 6103(p)(5), and

(2) biannually (beginning with the second report submitted under this subsection)—

(A) an independent evaluation of contractor performance, and

(B) a measurement plan that includes a comparison of the best practices used by the private collectors to the collection techniques used by the Internal Revenue Service and mechanisms to identify and capture information on successful collection techniques used by the contractors that could be adopted by the Internal Revenue Service.

• 2015, Fixing America's Surface Transportation Act (P.L. 114-94)

P.L. 114-94, §32102(f)(1):

Amended Code Sec. 6306, as amended by Act Sec. 32102(a)-(c) and (e), by redesignating subsection (j) as subsection (k) and by inserting after subsection (i) a new subsection (j). **Effective** 12-4-2015.

[Sec. 6306(k)]

(k) CROSS REFERENCES.—

(1) For damages for certain unauthorized collection actions by persons performing services under a qualified tax collection contract, see section 7433A.

(2) For application of Taxpayer Assistance Orders to persons performing services under a qualified tax collection contract, see section 7811(g).

Amendments

• 2015, Fixing America's Surface Transportation Act (P.L. 114-94)

P.L. 114-94, §32102(a):

Amended Code Sec. 6306 by redesignating subsection (f) as subsection (g). **Effective** for tax receivables identified by the Secretary after 12-4-2015.

P.L. 114-94, §32102(b):

Amended Code Sec. 6306, as amended by Act Sec. 32102(a), by redesignating subsection (g) as subsection (h). **Effective** for tax receivables identified by the Secretary after 12-4-2015.

P.L. 114-94, §32102(c):

Amended Code Sec. 6306, as amended by Act Sec. 32102(a)-(b), by redesignating subsection (h) as subsection (i). For the **effective** date, see Act Sec. 32102(g)(2), below.

P.L. 114-94, §32102(e):

Amended Code Sec. 6306, as amended by Act Sec. 32102(a)-(c), by redesignating subsection (i) as subsection (j). **Effective** 12-4-2015.

P.L. 114-94, §32102(f)(1):

Amended Code Sec. 6306, as amended by Act Sec. 32102(a)-(c) and (e), by redesignating subsection (j) as subsection (k). **Effective** 12-4-2015.

P.L. 114-94, §32102(g)(2), provides:

(2) CONTRACTING PRIORITY.—The Secretary shall begin entering into contracts and agreements as described in the amendment made by subsection (c) within 3 months after the date of the enactment of this Act.

• 2004, American Jobs Creation Act of 2004 (P.L. 108-357)

P.L. 108-357, §881(a)(1):

Amended subchapter A of chapter 64 by adding at the end a new Code Sec. 6306. **Effective** 10-22-2004.

[Sec. 6307]

SEC. 6307. SPECIAL COMPLIANCE PERSONNEL PROGRAM ACCOUNT.

[Sec. 6307(a)]

(a) ESTABLISHMENT OF A SPECIAL COMPLIANCE PERSONNEL PROGRAM ACCOUNT.—The Secretary shall establish an account within the Department for carrying out a program consisting of the hiring, training, and employment of special compliance personnel, and shall transfer to such account from time to time amounts retained by the Secretary under section 6306(e)(2).

[Sec. 6307(b)]

(b) RESTRICTIONS.—The program described in subsection (a) shall be subject to the following restrictions:

(1) No funds shall be transferred to such account except as described in subsection (a).

(2) No other funds from any other source shall be expended for special compliance personnel employed under such program.

(3) Notwithstanding any other authority, the Secretary is prohibited from spending funds out of such account for other than program costs.

Amendments

• 2019, Taxpayer First Act (P.L. 116-25)

P.L. 116-25, §1205(d)(1)(A)-(B):

Amended Code Sec. 6307(b) in paragraph (2), by striking all that follows "under such program" and inserting a period, and in paragraph (3), by striking all that follows "out of such account" and inserting "for other than program costs.". **Effective** for amounts expended from the special compliance personnel program account after 7-1-2019. Prior to amendment, Code Sec. 6307(b)(2)-(3) read as follows:

(2) No other funds from any other source shall be expended for special compliance personnel employed under such program, and no funds from such account shall be expended for the hiring of any personnel other than special compliance personnel.

(3) Notwithstanding any other authority, the Secretary is prohibited from spending funds out of such account for any purpose other than for costs under such program associated with the employment of special compliance personnel and the retraining and reassignment of current noncollections personnel as special compliance personnel, and to reimburse the Internal Revenue Service or other government agencies for the cost of administering qualified tax collection contracts under section 6306.

[Sec. 6307(c)]

(c) REPORTING.—Not later than March of each year, the Commissioner of Internal Revenue shall submit a report to the Committees on Finance and Appropriations of the Senate and the Committees on Ways and Means and Appropriations of the House of Representatives consisting of the following:

(1) For the preceding fiscal year, all funds received in the account established under subsection (a), administrative and program costs for the program described in such subsection, the number of special compliance personnel hired and employed under the program, and the amount of revenue actually collected by such personnel.

(2) For the current fiscal year, all actual and estimated funds received or to be received in the account, all actual and estimated administrative and program costs, the number of all actual and estimated special compliance personnel hired and employed under the program, and the actual and estimated revenue actually collected or to be collected by such personnel.

(3) For the following fiscal year, an estimate of all funds to be received in the account, all estimated administrative and program costs, the estimated number of special compliance personnel hired and employed under the program, and the estimated revenue to be collected by such personnel.

[Sec. 6307(d)]

(d) DEFINITIONS.—For purposes of this section—

(1) SPECIAL COMPLIANCE PERSONNEL.—The term "special compliance personnel" means individuals employed by the Internal Revenue Service as field function collection officers or in a similar position, or employed to collect taxes using the automated collection system or an equivalent replacement system.

(2) PROGRAM COSTS.—The term "program costs" means—

COLLECTION—RECEIPT OF PAYMENT

        (A) total salaries (including locality pay and bonuses), benefits, and employment taxes for special compliance personnel employed or trained under the program described in subsection (a),

        (B) direct overhead costs, salaries, benefits, and employment taxes relating to support staff, rental payments, office equipment and furniture, travel, data processing services, vehicle costs, utilities, communications, software, technology, postage, printing and reproduction, supplies and materials, lands and structures, insurance claims, and indemnities for special compliance personnel hired and employed under this section, and

        (C) reimbursement of the Internal Revenue Service or other government agencies for the cost of administering the qualified tax collection program under section 6306.

For purposes of subparagraph (B), the cost of management and supervision of special compliance personnel shall be taken into account as direct overhead costs to the extent such costs, when included in total program costs under this paragraph, do not represent more than 10 percent of such total costs.

Amendments

- **2019, Taxpayer First Act (P.L. 116-25)**

P.L. 116-25, §1205(d)(2):
Amended Code Sec. 6307(d)(2)(B) by striking "telecommunications" and inserting "communications, software, technology". **Effective** for amounts expended from the special compliance personnel program account after 7-1-2019.

P.L. 116-25, §1205(d)(3):
Amended Code Sec. 6307(d)(2) by striking "and" at the end of subparagraph (A), by striking the period at the end of subparagraph (B) and inserting ", and", and by inserting after subparagraph (B) a new subparagraph (C). **Effective** for amounts expended from the special compliance personnel program account after 7-1-2019.

- **2015, Fixing America's Surface Transportation Act (P.L. 114-94)**

P.L. 114-94, §32103(b):
Amended subchapter A of chapter 64 by adding at the end a new Code Sec. 6307. **Effective** for amounts collected and retained by the Secretary after 12-4-2015.

Subchapter B—Receipt of Payment

Sec. 6311.	Payment of tax by commercially acceptable means.
Sec. 6312.	[Repealed].
Sec. 6313.	Fractional parts of a cent.
Sec. 6314.	Receipt for taxes.
Sec. 6315.	Payments of estimated income tax.
Sec. 6316.	Payment by foreign currency.
Sec. 6317.	Payments of Federal unemployment tax for calendar quarter.

[Sec. 6311]

SEC. 6311. PAYMENT OF TAX BY COMMERCIALLY ACCEPTABLE MEANS.

[Sec. 6311(a)]

    (a) AUTHORITY TO RECEIVE.—It shall be lawful for the Secretary to receive for internal revenue taxes (or in payment for internal revenue stamps) any commercially acceptable means that the Secretary deems appropriate to the extent and under the conditions provided in regulations prescribed by the Secretary.

[Sec. 6311(b)]

    (b) ULTIMATE LIABILITY.—If a check, money order, or other method of payment, including payment by credit card, debit card, or charge card so received is not duly paid, or is paid and subsequently charged back to the Secretary, the person by whom such check, or money order, or other method of payment has been tendered shall remain liable for the payment of the tax or for the stamps, and for all legal penalties and additions, to the same extent as if such check, money order, or other method of payment had not been tendered.

[Sec. 6311(c)]

    (c) LIABILITY OF BANKS AND OTHERS.—If any certified, treasurer's, or cashier's check (or other guaranteed draft), or any money order, or any other means of payment that has been guaranteed by a financial institution (such as a credit card, debit card, or charge card transaction which has been guaranteed expressly by a financial institution) so received is not duly paid, the United States shall, in addition to its right to exact payment from the party originally indebted therefor, have a lien for—

        (1) the amount of such check (or draft) upon all assets of the financial institution on which drawn,

        (2) the amount of such money order upon all the assets of the issuer thereof, or

        (3) the guaranteed amount of any other transaction upon all the assets of the institution making such guarantee,

and such amount shall be paid out of such assets in preference to any other claims whatsoever against such financial institution, issuer, or guaranteeing institution, except the necessary costs and expenses of administration and the reimbursement of the United States for the amount expended in the redemption of the circulating notes of such financial institution.

[Sec. 6311(d)]

    (d) PAYMENT BY OTHER MEANS.—

        (1) AUTHORITY TO PRESCRIBE REGULATIONS.—The Secretary shall prescribe such regulations as the Secretary deems necessary to receive payment by commercially acceptable means, including regulations that—

            (A) specify which methods of payment by commercially acceptable means will be acceptable,

            (B) specify when payment by such means will be considered received,

            (C) identify types of nontax matters related to payment by such means that are to be resolved by persons ultimately liable for payment and financial intermediaries, without the involvement of the Secretary, and

            (D) ensure that tax matters will be resolved by the Secretary, without the involvement of financial intermediaries.

        (2) AUTHORITY TO ENTER INTO CONTRACTS.—Notwithstanding section 3718(f) of title 31, United States Code, the Secretary is authorized to enter into contracts to obtain services related to receiving payment by other means where cost beneficial to the Government. The Secretary may not pay any fee or provide any other consideration under any such contract for the use of credit, debit, or charge cards for the payment of taxes imposed by subtitle A. The preceding sentence shall not apply to the extent that the Secretary ensures that any such fee or other consideration

COLLECTION—RECEIPT OF PAYMENT

is fully recouped by the Secretary in the form of fees paid to the Secretary by persons paying taxes imposed under subtitle A with credit, debit, or charge cards pursuant to such contract. Notwithstanding the preceding sentence, the Secretary shall seek to minimize the amount of any fee or other consideration that the Secretary pays under any such contract.

(3) SPECIAL PROVISIONS FOR USE OF CREDIT CARDS.—If use of credit cards is accepted as a method of payment of taxes pursuant to subsection (a)—

(A) a payment of internal revenue taxes (or a payment for internal revenue stamps) by a person by use of a credit card shall not be subject to section 161 of the Truth in Lending Act (15 U.S.C. 1666), or to any similar provisions of State law, if the error alleged by the person is an error relating to the underlying tax liability, rather than an error relating to the credit card account such as a computational error or numerical transposition in the credit card transaction or an issue as to whether the person authorized payment by use of the credit card,

(B) a payment of internal revenue taxes (or a payment for internal revenue stamps) shall not be subject to section 170 of the Truth in Lending Act (15 U.S.C. 1666i), or to any similar provisions of State law,

(C) a payment of internal revenue taxes (or a payment for internal revenue stamps) by a person by use of a debit card shall not be subject to section 908 of the Electronic Fund Transfer Act (15 U.S.C. 1693f), or to any similar provisions of State law, if the error alleged by the person is an error relating to the underlying tax liability, rather than an error relating to the debit card account such as a computational error or numerical transposition in the debit card transaction or an issue as to whether the person authorized payment by use of the debit card,

(D) the term "creditor" under section 103(g) of the Truth in Lending Act (15 U.S.C. 1602(g)) shall not include the Secretary with respect to credit card transactions in payment of internal revenue taxes (or payment for internal revenue stamps), and

(E) notwithstanding any other provision of law to the contrary, in the case of payment made by credit card or debit card transaction of an amount owed to a person as the result of the correction of an error under section 161 of the Truth in Lending Act (15 U.S.C. 1666) or section 908 of the Electronic Fund Transfer Act (15 U.S.C. 1693f), the Secretary is authorized to provide such amount to such person as a credit to that person's credit card or debit card account through the applicable credit card or debit card system.

Amendments

• **2019, Taxpayer First Act (P.L. 116-25)**

P.L. 116-25, §2303:

Amended Code Sec. 6311(d)(2) by adding at the end two new sentences. **Effective** 7-1-2019.

• **2018, Tax Technical Corrections Act of 2018 (P.L. 115-141)**

P.L. 115-141, §401(a)(280)(A)-(B), Div. U:

Amended Code Sec. 6311(d)(3)(D) by striking "section 103(f)" and inserting "section 103(g)", and by striking "1602(f)" and inserting "1602(g)". **Effective** 3-23-2018.

• **1998, Tax and Trade Relief Extension Act of 1998 (P.L. 105-277)**

P.L. 105-277, §4003(k):

Amended Code Sec. 6311(d)(2) by striking "under such contracts" in the last sentence and inserting "under any such contract for the use of credit, debit, or charge cards for the payment of taxes imposed by subtitle A". **Effective** as if included in the provision of P.L. 105-34 to which it relates [**effective** 5-5-98.—CCH].

[Sec. 6311(e)]

(e) CONFIDENTIALITY OF INFORMATION.—

(1) IN GENERAL.—Except as otherwise authorized by this subsection, no person may use or disclose any information relating to credit or debit card transactions obtained pursuant to section 6103(k)(9) other than for purposes directly related to the processing of such transactions, or the billing or collection of amounts charged or debited pursuant thereto.

(2) EXCEPTIONS.—

(A) Debit or credit card issuers or others acting on behalf of such issuers may also use and disclose such information for purposes directly related to servicing an issuer's accounts.

(B) Debit or credit card issuers or others directly involved in the processing of credit or debit card transactions or the billing or collection of amounts charged or debited thereto may also use and disclose such information for purposes directly related to—

(i) statistical risk and profitability assessment;

(ii) transferring receivables, accounts, or interest therein;

(iii) auditing the account information;

(iv) complying with Federal, State, or local law; and

(v) properly authorized civil, criminal, or regulatory investigation by Federal, State, or local authorities.

(3) PROCEDURES.—Use and disclosure of information under this paragraph shall be made only to the extent authorized by written procedures promulgated by the Secretary.

(4) CROSS REFERENCE.—

For provision providing for civil damages for violation of paragraph (1), see section 7431.

Amendments

• **1998, IRS Restructuring and Reform Act of 1998 (P.L. 105-206)**

P.L. 105-206, §6012(b)(1):

Amended Code Sec. 6311(e)(1) by striking "section 6103(k)(8)" and inserting "section 6103(k)(9)". **Effective** as if included in the provision of P.L. 105-34 to which it relates [**effective** 5-5-98.—CCH].

P.L. 105-206, §3703, provides:

SEC. 3703. PAYMENT OF TAXES.

The Secretary of the Treasury or the Secretary's delegate shall establish such rules, regulations, and procedures as are necessary to allow payment of taxes by check or money order made payable to the United States Treasury.

• **1997, Taxpayer Relief Act of 1997 (P.L. 105-34)**

P.L. 105-34, §1205(a):

Amended Code Sec. 6311. **Effective** on the day 9 months after 8-5-97. Prior to amendment, Code Sec. 6311 read as follows:

SEC. 6311. PAYMENT BY CHECK OR MONEY ORDER.

[Sec. 6311(a)]

(a) AUTHORITY TO RECEIVE.—It shall be lawful for the Secretary to receive for internal revenue taxes, or in payment for internal revenue stamps, checks or money orders, to the extent and under the conditions provided in regulations prescribed by the Secretary.

Amendments

• **1976, Tax Reform Act of 1976 (P.L. 94-455)**

P.L. 94-455, §1906(b)(13)(A):

Amended 1954 Code by substituting "Secretary" for "Secretary or his delegate" each place it appeared. **Effective** 2-1-77.

[Sec. 6311(b)]

(b) CHECK OR MONEY ORDER UNPAID.—

(1) ULTIMATE LIABILITY.—If a check or money order so received is not duly paid, the person by whom such check or money order has been tendered shall remain liable for the payment of the tax or for the stamps, and for all legal penalties and additions, to the same extent as if such check or money order had not been tendered.

(2) LIABILITY OF BANKS AND OTHERS.—If any certified, treasurer's, or cashier's check (or other guaranteed draft) or any money order so received is not duly paid, the United States shall, in addition to its right to exact payment from the party originally indebted therefor, have a lien for the amount of such check (or draft) upon all the assets of the financial institution on which drawn or for the amount of such money order upon all the assets of the issuer thereof; and such amount shall be paid out of such assets in preference to any other claims whatsoever against such financial institution or issuer except the necessary costs and expenses of administration and the reimbursement of the United States for the amount expended in the redemption of the circulating notes of such financial institution.

COLLECTION—RECEIPT OF PAYMENT

Amendments

• **1984, Deficit Reduction Act of 1984 (P.L. 98-369)**

P.L. 98-369, § 448(a):

Amended Code Sec. 6311(b)(2) by striking out "or cashier's check" and inserting in lieu thereof "or cashier's check (or other guaranteed draft)", by striking out "the amount of such check" and inserting in lieu thereof "the amount of such check (or draft)", by striking out "the bank or trust company" and inserting in lieu thereof "the financial institution", and by striking out "such bank" each place it appeared and inserting in lieu thereof "such financial institution". **Effective** 7-18-84.

[Sec. 6312—Repealed]

Amendments

• **1971 (P.L. 92-5)**

P.L. 92-5, § 4(a)(2):

Repealed Code Sec. 6312. **Effective** with respect to obligations issued after 3-3-71. Prior to repeal, Code Sec. 6312 read as follows:

SEC. 6312. PAYMENT BY UNITED STATES NOTES AND CERTIFICATES OF INDEBTEDNESS.

(a) GENERAL RULE.—It shall be lawful for the Secretary or his delegate to receive, at par with an adjustment for accrued interest, Treasury bills, notes and certificates of indebtedness issued by the United States in payment of any internal revenue taxes, or in payment for internal revenue stamps, to the extent and under the conditions provided in regulations prescribed by the Secretary or his delegate.

(b) CROSS REFERENCES.—

(1) For authority to receive silver certificates, see section 5 of the act of June 19, 1934 (48 Stat. 1178; 31 U.S.C. 405a).

(2) For full legal tender status of all coins and currencies of the United States, see section 43(b)(1) of the Agricultural Adjustment Act, as amended (48 Stat. 52, 113; 31 U.S.C. 462).

(3) For authority to receive obligations under the Second Liberty Bond Act, see section 20(b) of that act, as amended (56 Stat. 189; 31 U.S.C. 754b).

[Sec. 6313]

SEC. 6313. FRACTIONAL PARTS OF A CENT.

In the payment of any tax imposed by this title, a fractional part of a cent shall be disregarded unless it amounts to one-half cent or more, in which case it shall be increased to 1 cent.

Amendments

• **1976, Tax Reform Act of 1976 (P.L. 94-455)**

P.L. 94-455, § 1906(a)(19):

Struck out "not payable by stamp" following "any tax imposed by this title" in Code Sec. 6313. **Effective** 2-1-77.

[Sec. 6314]

SEC. 6314. RECEIPT FOR TAXES.

[Sec. 6314(a)]

(a) GENERAL RULE.—The Secretary shall, upon request, give receipts for all sums collected by him, excepting only when the same are in payment for stamps sold and delivered; but no receipt shall be issued in lieu of a stamp representing a tax.

Amendments

• **1976, Tax Reform Act of 1976 (P.L. 94-455)**

P.L. 94-455, § 1906(b)(13)(A):

Amended 1954 Code by substituting "Secretary" for "Secretary or his delegate" each place it appeared. **Effective** 2-1-77.

[Sec. 6314(b)]

(b) DUPLICATE RECEIPTS FOR PAYMENT OF ESTATE TAXES.—The Secretary shall, upon request, give to the person paying the tax under chapter 11 (relating to the estate tax) duplicate receipts, either of which shall be sufficient evidence of such payment, and shall entitle the executor to be credited and allowed the amount thereof by any court having jurisdiction to audit or settle his accounts.

Amendments

• **1976, Tax Reform Act of 1976 (P.L. 94-455)**

P.L. 94-455, § 1906(b)(13)(A):

Amended 1954 Code by substituting "Secretary" for "Secretary or his delegate" each place it appeared. **Effective** 2-1-77.

[Sec. 6314(c)]

(c) CROSS REFERENCES.—

(1) For receipt required to be furnished by employer to employee with respect to employment taxes, see section 6051.

(2) For receipt of discharge of fiduciary from personal liability, see section 2204.

Amendments

• **1970, Excise, Estate, and Gift Tax Adjustment Act of 1970 (P.L. 91-614)**

P.L. 91-614, § 101(d)(2):

Amended Code Sec. 6314(c)(2) by substituting "fiduciary" for "executor." **Effective** 1-1-71.

[Sec. 6315]

SEC. 6315. PAYMENTS OF ESTIMATED INCOME TAX.

Payment of the estimated income tax, or any installment thereof, shall be considered payment on account of the income taxes imposed by subtitle A for the taxable year.

[Sec. 6316]

SEC. 6316. PAYMENT BY FOREIGN CURRENCY.

The Secretary is authorized in his discretion to allow payment of taxes in the currency of a foreign country under such circumstances and subject to such conditions as the Secretary may by regulations prescribe.

Amendments

• **1976, Tax Reform Act of 1976 (P.L. 94-455)**

P.L. 94-455, § 1906(b)(13)(A):

Amended 1954 Code by substituting "Secretary" for "Secretary or his delegate" each place it appeared. **Effective** 2-1-77.

COLLECTION—LIEN FOR TAXES

[Sec. 6317]
SEC. 6317. PAYMENTS OF FEDERAL UNEMPLOYMENT TAX FOR CALENDAR QUARTER.

Payment of Federal unemployment tax for a calendar quarter or other period within a calendar year pursuant to section 6157 shall be considered payment on account of the tax imposed by chapter 23 of such calendar year.

Amendments

• **1988, Technical and Miscellaneous Revenue Act of 1988 (P.L. 100-647)**

P.L. 100-647, §7106(c)(3)(A)-(B):

Amended Code Sec. 6317 by striking out "or tax imposed by section 3321" following the phrase "Payment of Federal unemployment tax", and by striking out "and [or] 23A, as the case may be," following the phrase "by chapter 23". **Effective** for remuneration paid after 12-31-88.

• **1983, Railroad Retirement Solvency Act of 1983 (P.L. 98-76)**

P.L. 98-76, §231(b)(2)(B):

Amended Code Sec. 6317. **Effective** for remuneration paid after 6-30-86. Prior to amendment, Code Sec. 6317 read as follows:

Payment of Federal unemployment tax for a calendar quarter or other period within a calendar year pursuant to section 6157 shall be considered payment on account of the tax imposed by chapter 23 of such calendar year.

• **1969 (P.L. 91-53)**

P.L. 91-53, §2(c):

Added Code Sec. 6317. **Effective** for calendar years beginning after 12-31-69.

Subchapter C—Lien for Taxes

Part I.   Due process for liens.
Part II.   Liens.

PART I—DUE PROCESS FOR LIENS

Sec. 6320.   Notice and opportunity for hearing upon filing of notice of lien.

[Sec. 6320]
SEC. 6320. NOTICE AND OPPORTUNITY FOR HEARING UPON FILING OF NOTICE OF LIEN.

[Sec. 6320(a)]

(a) REQUIREMENT OF NOTICE.—

(1) IN GENERAL.—The Secretary shall notify in writing the person described in section 6321 of the filing of a notice of lien under section 6323.

(2) TIME AND METHOD FOR NOTICE.—The notice required under paragraph (1) shall be—

(A) given in person;

(B) left at the dwelling or usual place of business of such person; or

(C) sent by certified or registered mail to such person's last known address,

not more than 5 business days after the day of the filing of the notice of lien.

(3) INFORMATION INCLUDED WITH NOTICE.—The notice required under paragraph (1) shall include in simple and nontechnical terms—

(A) the amount of unpaid tax;

(B) the right of the person to request a hearing during the 30-day period beginning on the day after the 5-day period described in paragraph (2);

(C) the administrative appeals available to the taxpayer with respect to such lien and the procedures relating to such appeals;

(D) the provisions of this title and procedures relating to the release of liens on property; and

(E) the provisions of section 7345 relating to the certification of seriously delinquent tax debts and the denial, revocation, or limitation of passports of individuals with such debts pursuant to section 32101 of the FAST Act.

Amendments

• **2015, Fixing America's Surface Transportation Act (P.L. 114-94)**

P.L. 114-94, §32101(b)(1):

Amended Code Sec. 6320(a)(3) by striking "and" at the end of subparagraph (C), by striking the period at the end of subparagraph (D) and inserting "; and", and by adding at the end a new subparagraph (E). **Effective** 12-4-2015.

[Sec. 6320(b)]

(b) RIGHT TO FAIR HEARING.—

(1) IN GENERAL.—If the person requests a hearing in writing under subsection (a)(3)(B) and states the grounds for the requested hearing, such hearing shall be held by the Internal Revenue Service Independent Office of Appeals.

(2) ONE HEARING PER PERIOD.—A person shall be entitled to only one hearing under this section with respect to the taxable period to which the unpaid tax specified in subsection (a)(3)(A) relates.

(3) IMPARTIAL OFFICER.—The hearing under this subsection shall be conducted by an officer or employee who has had no prior involvement with respect to the unpaid tax specified in subsection (a)(3)(A) before the first hearing under this section or section 6330. A taxpayer may waive the requirement of this paragraph.

(4) COORDINATION WITH SECTION 6330.—To the extent practicable, a hearing under this section shall be held in conjunction with a hearing under section 6330.

Amendments

• **2019, Taxpayer First Act (P.L. 116-25)**

P.L. 116-25, §1001(b)(1)(B):

Amended Code Sec. 6320(b)(1) by striking "Internal Revenue Service Office of Appeals" and inserting "Internal Revenue Service Independent Office of Appeals". **Effective** 7-1-2019.

• **2006, Tax Relief and Health Care Act of 2006 (P.L. 109-432)**

P.L. 109-432, Division A, §407(c)(1):

Amended Code Sec. 6320(b)(1) by striking "under subsection (a)(3)(B)" and inserting "in writing under subsection (a)(3)(B) and states the grounds for the requested hearing". **Effective** for submissions made and issues raised after the date on which the Secretary first prescribes a list under Code Sec. 6702(c), as amended by Act Sec. 407(a).

[Sec. 6320(c)]

(c) CONDUCT OF HEARING; REVIEW; SUSPENSIONS.—For purposes of this section, subsections (c), (d) (other than paragraph (3)(B) thereof), (e), and (g) of section 6330 shall apply.

COLLECTION—LIEN FOR TAXES

Amendments

• **2015, Protecting Americans from Tax Hikes Act of 2015 (P.L. 114-113)**

P.L. 114-113, §424(c), Div. Q:

Amended Code Sec. 6320(c) by striking "(2)(B)" and inserting "(3)(B)". **Effective** 12-18-2015.

• **2006, Tax Relief and Health Care Act of 2006 (P.L. 109-432)**

P.L. 109-432, Division A, §407(c)(2):

Amended Code Sec. 6320(c) by striking "and (e)" and inserting "(e), and (g)". **Effective** for submissions made and issues raised after the date on which the Secretary first prescribes a list under Code Sec. 6702(c), as amended by Act Sec. 407(a).

• **1998, IRS Restructuring and Reform Act of 1998 (P.L. 105-206)**

P.L. 105-206, §3401(a):

Amended subchapter C of chapter 64 by inserting a new Code Sec. 6320. **Effective** for collection actions initiated after the date which is 180 days after 7-22-98.

PART II—LIENS

Sec. 6321.   Lien for taxes.
Sec. 6322.   Period of lien.
Sec. 6323.   Validity and priority against certain persons.
Sec. 6324.   Special liens for estate and gift taxes.
Sec. 6324A. Special lien for estate tax deferred under section 6166.
Sec. 6324B. Special lien for additional estate tax attributable to farm, etc., valuation
Sec. 6325.   Release of lien or discharge of property.
Sec. 6326.   Administrative appeal of liens.
Sec. 6327.   Cross references.

[Sec. 6321]

SEC. 6321. LIEN FOR TAXES.

If any person liable to pay any tax neglects or refuses to pay the same after demand, the amount (including any interest, additional amount, addition to tax, or assessable penalty, together with any costs that may accrue in addition thereto) shall be a lien in favor of the United States upon all property and rights to property, whether real or personal, belonging to such person.

Amendments

• **1998, IRS Restructuring and Reform Act of 1998 (P.L. 105-206)**

P.L. 105-206, §3421, provides:

ACT SEC. 3421. APPROVAL PROCESS FOR LIENS, LEVIES, AND SEIZURES.

(a) IN GENERAL.—The Commissioner of Internal Revenue shall develop and implement procedures under which—

(1) a determination by an employee to file a notice of lien or levy with respect to, or to levy or seize, any property or right to property would, where appropriate, be required to be reviewed by a supervisor of the employee before the action was taken; and

(2) appropriate disciplinary action would be taken against the employee or supervisor where the procedures under paragraph (1) were not followed.

(b) REVIEW PROCESS.—The review process under subsection (a)(1) may include a certification that the employee has—

(1) reviewed the taxpayer's information;

(2) verified that a balance is due; and

(3) affirmed that the action proposed to be taken is appropriate given the taxpayer's circumstances, considering the amount due and the value of the property or right to property.

(c) EFFECTIVE DATES.—

(1) IN GENERAL.—Except as provided in paragraph (2), this section shall take effect on the date of the enactment of this Act.

(2) AUTOMATED COLLECTION SYSTEM ACTIONS.—In the case of any action under an automated collection system, this section shall apply to actions initiated after December 31, 2000.

[Sec. 6322]

SEC. 6322. PERIOD OF LIEN.

Unless another date is specifically fixed by law, the lien imposed by section 6321 shall arise at the time the assessment is made and shall continue until the liability for the amount so assessed (or a judgment against the taxpayer arising out of such liability) is satisfied or becomes unenforceable by reason of lapse of time.

Amendments

• **1966, Federal Tax Lien Act of 1966 (P.L. 89-719)**

P.L. 89-719, §113(a):

Amended Code Sec. 6322 by inserting "(or a judgment against the taxpayer arising out of such liability)" immediately after "liability for the amount so assessed".

Effective, generally, after 11-2-66. However, see the amendment note for Code Sec. 6323 for exceptions to this **effective** date.

[Sec. 6323]

SEC. 6323. VALIDITY AND PRIORITY AGAINST CERTAIN PERSONS.

[Sec. 6323(a)]

(a) PURCHASERS, HOLDERS OF SECURITY INTERESTS, MECHANIC'S LIENORS, AND JUDGMENT LIEN CREDITORS.—The lien imposed by section 6321 shall not be valid as against any purchaser, holder of a security interest, mechanic's lienor, or judgment lien creditor until notice thereof which meets the requirements of subsection (f) has been filed by the Secretary.

Amendments

• **1990, Omnibus Budget Reconciliation Act of 1990 (P.L. 101-508)**

P.L. 101-508, §11704(a)(26):

Amended Code Sec. 6323(a) by striking "Purchases" in the heading and inserting "Purchasers". **Effective** on the date of enactment of this Act.

• **1976, Tax Reform Act of 1976 (P.L. 94-455)**

P.L. 94-455, §1906(b)(13)(A):

Amended 1954 Code by substituting "Secretary" for "Secretary or his delegate" each place it appeared. **Effective** 2-1-77.

[Sec. 6323(b)]

(b) PROTECTION FOR CERTAIN INTERESTS EVEN THOUGH NOTICE FILED.—Even though notice of a lien imposed by section 6321 has been filed, such lien shall not be valid—

(1) SECURITIES.—With respect to a security (as defined in subsection (h)(4))—

(A) as against a purchaser of such security who at the time of purchase did not have actual notice or knowledge of the existence of such lien; and

(B) as against a holder of a security interest in such security who, at the time such interest came into existence, did not have actual notice or knowledge of the existence of such lien.

(2) MOTOR VEHICLES.—With respect to a motor vehicle (as defined in subsection (h)(3)), as against a purchaser of such motor vehicle, if—

(A) at the time of the purchase such purchaser did not have actual notice or knowledge of the existence of such lien, and

(B) before the purchaser obtains such notice or knowledge, he has acquired possession of such motor vehicle and has not thereafter relinquished possession of such motor vehicle to the seller or his agent.

(3) PERSONAL PROPERTY PURCHASED AT RETAIL.—With respect to tangible personal property purchased at retail, as against a purchaser in the ordinary course of the seller's trade or business, unless at the time of such purchase such purchaser intends such purchase to (or knows such purchase will) hinder, evade, or defeat the collection of any tax under this title.

(4) PERSONAL PROPERTY PURCHASED IN CASUAL SALE.—With respect to household goods, personal effects, or other tangible personal property described in section 6334(a) purchased (not for resale) in a casual sale for less than $1,000, as against the purchaser, but only if such purchaser does not have actual notice or knowledge (A) of the existence of such lien, or (B) that this sale is one of a series of sales.

(5) PERSONAL PROPERTY SUBJECT TO POSSESSORY LIEN.—With respect to tangible personal property subject to a lien under local law securing the reasonable price of the repair or improvement of such property, as against a holder of such a lien, if such holder is, and has been, continuously in possession of such property from the time such lien arose.

(6) REAL PROPERTY TAX AND SPECIAL ASSESSMENT LIENS.—With respect to real property, as against a holder of a lien upon such property, if such lien is entitled under local law to priority over security interests in such property which are prior in time, and such lien secures payment of—

(A) a tax of general application levied by any taxing authority based upon the value of such property;

(B) a special assessment imposed directly upon such property by any taxing authority, if such assessment is imposed for the purpose of defraying the cost of any public improvement; or

(C) charges for utilities or public services furnished to such property by the United States, a State or political subdivision thereof, or an instrumentality of any one or more of the foregoing.

(7) RESIDENTIAL PROPERTY SUBJECT TO A MECHANIC'S LIEN FOR CERTAIN REPAIRS AND IMPROVEMENTS.—With respect to real property subject to a lien for repair or improvement of a personal residence (containing not more than four dwelling units) occupied by the owner of such residence, as against a mechanic's lienor, but only if the contract price on the contract with the owner is not more than $5,000.

(8) ATTORNEYS' LIENS.—With respect to a judgment or other amount in settlement of a claim or of a cause of action, as against an attorney who, under local law, holds a lien upon or a contract enforcible against such judgment or amount, to the extent of his reasonable compensation for obtaining such judgment or procuring such settlement, except that this paragraph shall not apply to any judgment or amount in settlement of a claim or of a cause of action against the United States to the extent that the United States offsets such judgment or amount against any liability of the taxpayer to the United States.

(9) CERTAIN INSURANCE CONTRACTS.—With respect to a life insurance, endowment, or annuity contract, as against the organization which is the insurer under such contract, at any time—

(A) before such organization had actual notice or knowledge of the existence of such lien;

(B) after such organization had such notice or knowledge, with respect to advances required to be made automatically to maintain such contract in force under an agreement entered into before such organization had such notice or knowledge; or

(C) after satisfaction of a levy pursuant to section 6332(b), unless and until the Secretary delivers to such organization a notice, executed after the date of such satisfaction, of the existence of such lien.

(10) DEPOSIT-SECURED LOANS.—With respect to a savings deposit, share, or other account, with an institution described in section 581 or 591, to the extent of any loan made by such institution without actual notice or knowledge of the existence of such lien, as against such institution, if such loan is secured by such account.

Amendments

• **1998, IRS Restructuring and Reform Act of 1998 (P.L. 105-206)**

P.L. 105-206, §3435(a)(1)(A)-(B):

Amended Code Sec. 6323(b) by striking "$250" and inserting "$1,000" in paragraph (4), and by striking "$1,000" and inserting "$5,000" in paragraph (7). **Effective 7-22-98.**

P.L. 105-206, §3435(b)(1)-(3):

Amended Code Sec. 6323(b)(10) by striking "PASSBOOK LOANS" in the heading and inserting "DEPOSIT-SECURED LOANS", by striking ", evidenced by a passbook,", and by striking all that follows "secured by such account" and inserting a period. **Effective 7-22-98.** Prior to amendment, Code Sec. 6323(b)(10) read as follows:

(10) PASSBOOK LOANS.—With respect to a savings deposit, share, or other account, evidenced by a passbook, with an institution described in section 581 or 591, to the extent of any loan made by such institution without actual notice or knowledge of the existence of such lien, as against such institution, if such loan is secured by such account and if such institution has been continuously in possession of such passbook from the time the loan is made.

• **1976, Tax Reform Act of 1976 (P.L. 94-455)**

P.L. 94-455, §1906(b)(13)(A):

Amended 1954 Code by substituting "Secretary" for "Secretary or his delegate" each place it appeared. **Effective 2-1-77.**

[Sec. 6323(c)]

(c) PROTECTION FOR CERTAIN COMMERCIAL TRANSACTIONS FINANCING AGREEMENTS, ETC.—

(1) IN GENERAL.—To the extent provided in this subsection, even though notice of a lien imposed by section 6321 has been filed, such lien shall not be valid with respect to a security interest which came into existence after tax lien filing but which—

(A) is in qualified property covered by the terms of a written agreement entered into before tax lien filing and constituting—

(i) a commercial transactions financing agreement,

(ii) a real property construction or improvement financing agreement, or

(iii) an obligatory disbursement agreement, and

(B) is protected under local law against a judgment lien arising, as of the time of tax lien filing, out of an unsecured obligation.

(2) COMMERCIAL TRANSACTIONS FINANCING AGREEMENT.—For purposes of this subsection—

(A) DEFINITION.—The term "commercial transactions financing agreement" means an agreement (entered into by a person in the course of his trade or business)—

(i) to make loans to the taxpayer to be secured by commercial financing security acquired by the taxpayer in the ordinary course of his trade or business, or

(ii) to purchase commercial financing security (other than inventory) acquired by the taxpayer in the ordinary course of his trade or business;

but such an agreement shall be treated as coming within the term only to the extent that such loan or purchase is made before the 46th day after the date of tax lien filing or (if earlier) before the lender or purchaser had actual notice or knowledge of such tax lien filing.

(B) LIMITATION ON QUALIFIED PROPERTY.—The term "qualified property", when used with respect to a commercial transactions financing agreement, includes only commercial financing security acquired by the taxpayer before the 46th day after the date of tax lien filing.

(C) COMMERCIAL FINANCING SECURITY DEFINED.—The term "commercial financing security" means (i) paper of a kind ordinarily arising in commercial transactions, (ii) accounts receivable, (iii) mortgages on real property, and (iv) inventory.

(D) PURCHASER TREATED AS ACQUIRING SECURITY INTEREST.—A person who satisfies subparagraph (A) by reason of clause (ii) thereof shall be treated as having acquired a security interest in commercial financing security.

COLLECTION—LIEN FOR TAXES

(3) REAL PROPERTY CONSTRUCTION OR IMPROVEMENT FINANCING AGREEMENT.—For purposes of this subsection—

(A) DEFINITION.—The term "real property construction or improvement financing agreement" means an agreement to make cash disbursements to finance—

(i) the construction or improvement of real property,

(ii) a contract to construct or improve real property, or

(iii) the raising or harvesting of a farm crop or the raising of livestock or other animals.

For purposes of clause (iii), the furnishing of goods and services shall be treated as the disbursement of cash.

(B) LIMITATION ON QUALIFIED PROPERTY.—The term "qualified property", when used with respect to a real property construction or improvement financing agreement, includes only—

(i) in the case of subparagraph (A)(i), the real property with respect to which the construction or improvement has been or is to be made,

(ii) in the case of subparagraph (A)(ii), the proceeds of the contract described therein, and

(iii) in the case of subparagraph (A)(iii), property subject to the lien imposed by section 6321 at the time of tax lien filing and the crop or the livestock or other animals referred to in subparagraph (A)(iii).

(4) OBLIGATORY DISBURSEMENT AGREEMENT.—For purposes of this subsection—

(A) DEFINITION.—The term "obligatory disbursement agreement" means an agreement (entered into by a person in the course of his trade or business) to make disbursements, but such an agreement shall be treated as coming within the term only to the extent of disbursements which are required to be made by reason of the intervention of the rights of a person other than the taxpayer.

(B) LIMITATION ON QUALIFIED PROPERTY.—The term "qualified property", when used with respect to an obligatory disbursement agreement, means property subject to the lien imposed by section 6321 at the time of tax lien filing and (to the extent that the acquisition is directly traceable to the disbursements referred to in subparagraph (A)) property acquired by the taxpayer after tax lien filing.

(C) SPECIAL RULES FOR SURETY AGREEMENTS.—Where the obligatory disbursement agreement is an agreement ensuring the performance of a contract between the taxpayer and another person—

(i) the term "qualified property" shall be treated as also including the proceeds of the contract the performance of which was ensured, and

(ii) if the contract the performance of which was ensured was a contract to construct or improve real property, to produce goods, or to furnish services, the term "qualified property" shall be treated as also including any tangible personal property used by the taxpayer in the performance of such ensured contract.

[Sec. 6323(d)]

(d) 45-DAY PERIOD FOR MAKING DISBURSEMENTS.—Even though notice of a lien imposed by section 6321 has been filed, such lien shall not be valid with respect to a security interest which came into existence after tax lien filing by reason of disbursements made before the 46th day after the date of tax lien filing, or (if earlier) before the person making such disbursements had actual notice or knowledge of tax lien filing, but only if such security interest—

(1) is in property (A) subject, at the time of tax lien filing, to the lien imposed by section 6321, and (B) covered by the terms of a written agreement entered into before tax lien filing, and

(2) is protected under local law against a judgment lien arising, as of the time of tax lien filing, out of an unsecured obligation.

[Sec. 6323(e)]

(e) PRIORITY OF INTEREST AND EXPENSES.—If the lien imposed by section 6321 is not valid as against a lien or security interest, the priority of such lien or security interest shall extend to—

(1) any interest or carrying charges upon the obligation secured,

(2) the reasonable charges and expenses of an indenture trustee or agent holding the security interest for the benefit of the holder of the security interest,

(3) the reasonable expenses, including reasonable compensation for attorneys, actually incurred in collecting or enforcing the obligation secured,

(4) the reasonable costs of insuring, preserving, or repairing the property to which the lien or security interest relates,

(5) the reasonable costs of insuring payment of the obligation secured, and

(6) amounts paid to satisfy any lien on the property to which the lien or security interest relates, but only if the lien so satisfied is entitled to priority over the lien imposed by section 6321,

to the extent that, under local law, any such item has the same priority as the lien or security interest to which it relates.

[Sec. 6323(f)]

(f) PLACE FOR FILING NOTICE; FORM.—

(1) PLACE FOR FILING.—The notice referred to in subsection (a) shall be filed—

(A) UNDER STATE LAWS.—

(i) REAL PROPERTY.—In the case of real property, in one office within the State (or the county, or other governmental subdivision), as designated by the laws of such State, in which the property subject to the lien is situated; and

(ii) PERSONAL PROPERTY.—In the case of personal property, whether tangible or intangible, in one office within the State (or the county, or other governmental subdivision), as designated by the laws of such State, in which the property subject to the lien is situated, except that State law merely conforming to or reenacting Federal law establishing a national filing system does not constitute a second office for filing as designated by the laws of such State;

(B) WITH CLERK OF DISTRICT COURT.—In the office of the clerk of the United States district court for the judicial district in which the property subject to the lien is situated, whenever the State has not by law designated one office which meets the requirements of subparagraph (A); or

(C) WITH RECORDER OF DEEDS OF THE DISTRICT OF COLUMBIA.—In the office of the Recorder of Deeds of the District of Columbia, if the property subject to the lien is situated in the District of Columbia.

(2) SITUS OF PROPERTY SUBJECT TO LIEN.—For purposes of paragraphs (1) and (4), property shall be deemed to be situated—

(A) REAL PROPERTY.—In the case of real property, at its physical location; or

(B) PERSONAL PROPERTY.—In the case of personal property, whether tangible or intangible, at the residence of the taxpayer at the time the notice of lien is filed.

COLLECTION—LIEN FOR TAXES

For purposes of paragraph (2)(B), the residence of a corporation or partnership shall be deemed to be the place at which the principal executive office of the business is located, and the residence of a taxpayer whose residence is without the United States shall be deemed to be in the District of Columbia.

(3) FORM.—The form and content of the notice referred to in subsection (a) shall be prescribed by the Secretary. Such notice shall be valid notwithstanding any other provision of law regarding the form or content of a notice of lien.

(4) INDEXING REQUIRED WITH RESPECT TO CERTAIN REAL PROPERTY.—In the case of real property, if—

(A) under the laws of the State in which the real property is located, a deed is not valid as against a purchaser of the property who (at the time of purchase) does not have actual notice or knowledge of the existence of such deed unless the fact of filing of such deed has been entered and recorded in a public index at the place of filing in such a manner that a reasonable inspection of the index will reveal the existence of the deed, and

(B) there is maintained (at the applicable office under paragraph (1)) an adequate system for the public indexing of Federal tax liens,

then the notice of lien referred to in subsection (a) shall not be treated as meeting the filing requirements under paragraph (1) unless the fact of filing is entered and recorded in the index referred to in subparagraph (B) in such a manner that a reasonable inspection of the index will reveal the existence of the lien.

(5) NATIONAL FILING SYSTEMS.—The filing of a notice of lien shall be governed solely by this title and shall not be subject to any other Federal law establishing a place or places for the filing of liens or encumbrances under a national filing system.

Amendments

• **1988, Technical and Miscellaneous Revenue Act of 1988 (P.L. 100-647)**

P.L. 100-647, §1015(s)(1)(A)-(B):

Amended Code Sec. 6323(f) by inserting ", except that State law merely conforming to or reenacting Federal law establishing a national filing system does not constitute a second office for filing as designated by the laws of such State" after "situated" in paragraph (1)(A)(ii) and by adding at the end thereof new paragraph (5). **Effective** 11-10-88.

• **1978, Revenue Act of 1978 (P.L. 95-600)**

P.L. 95-600, §702(q)(1), (q)(3):

Amended Code Sec. 6323(f)(4). **Effective** as indicated in Act Sec. 702(q)(3), below. Prior to amendment, paragraph (4) read:

"(4) INDEX.—The notice of lien referred to in subsection (a) shall not be treated as meeting the filing requirements under paragraph (1) unless the fact of filing is entered and recorded in a public index at the district office of the Internal Revenue Service for the district in which the property subject to the lien is situated."

P.L. 95-600, §702(q)(3), provides:

"(3) EFFECTIVE DATE.—

(A) The amendments made by this subsection shall apply with respect to liens, other security interests, and other interests in real property acquired after November 6, 1978.

(B) If, after November 6, 1978, there is a change in the application (or nonapplication) of section 6323(f)(4) of the Internal Revenue Code of 1954 (as amended by paragraph (1)) with respect to any filing jurisdiction, such change shall apply only with respect to liens, other security interests, and other interests in real property acquired after the date of such change."

• **1976, Tax Reform Act of 1976 (P.L. 94-455)**

P.L. 94-455, §1906(b)(13)(A):

Amended 1954 Code by substituting "Secretary" for "Secretary or his delegate" each place it appeared. **Effective** 2-1-77.

P.L. 94-455, §2008(c)(1)(A):

Added Code Sec. 6323(f)(4). **Effective**, in the case of liens filed before 10-4-76, on 7-1-77. **Effective**, in the case of liens filed on or after 10-4-76, on 2-1-77.

P.L. 94-455, §2008(c)(1)(B):

Substituted "paragraphs (1) and (4)" for "paragraph (1)" in Code Sec. 6323(f)(2). **Effective**, in the case of liens filed before 10-4-76, on 7-1-77. **Effective**, in the case of liens filed on or after 10-4-76, on 2-1-77.

[Sec. 6323(g)]

(g) REFILING OF NOTICE.—For purposes of this section—

(1) GENERAL RULE.—Unless notice of lien is refiled in the manner prescribed in paragraph (2) during the required refiling period, such notice of lien shall be treated as filed on the date on which it is filed (in accordance with subsection (f)) after the expiration of such refiling period.

(2) PLACE FOR FILING.—A notice of lien refiled during the required refiling period shall be effective only—

(A) if—

(i) such notice of lien is refiled in the office in which the prior notice of lien was filed, and

(ii) in the case of real property, the fact of refiling is entered and recorded in an index to the extent required by subsection (f)(4); and

(B) in any case in which, 90 days or more prior to the date of a refiling of notice of lien under subparagraph (A), the Secretary received written information (in the manner prescribed in regulations issued by the Secretary) concerning a change in the taxpayer's residence, if a notice of such lien is also filed in accordance with subsection (f) in the State in which such residence is located.

(3) REQUIRED REFILING PERIOD.—In the case of any notice of lien, the term "required refiling period" means—

(A) the one-year period ending 30 days after the expiration of 10 years after the date of the assessment of the tax, and

(B) the one-year period ending with the expiration of 10 years after the close of the preceding required refiling period for such notice of lien.

(4) TRANSITIONAL RULE.—Notwithstanding paragraph (3), if the assessment of the tax was made before January 1, 1962, the first required refiling period shall be the calendar year 1967.

Amendments

• **1990, Omnibus Budget Reconciliation Act of 1990 (P.L. 101-508)**

P.L. 101-508, §11317(b):

Amended Code Sec. 6323(g)(3) by striking "6 years" each place it appears and inserting "10 years". For the **effective** date, see Act Sec. 11317(c), below.

P.L. 101-508, §11317(c), provides:

(c) EFFECTIVE DATE.—The amendments made by this section shall apply to—

(1) taxes assessed after the date of the enactment of this Act, and

(2) taxes assessed on or before such date if the period specified in section 6502 of the Internal Revenue Code of 1986 (determined without regard to the amendments made by subsection (a)) for collection of such taxes has not expired as of such date.

• **1978, Revenue Act of 1978 (P.L. 95-600)**

P.L. 95-600, §702(q)(2), (3):

Amended Code Sec. 6323(g)(2)(A). **Effective**, generally, for liens, other security interests, and other interests in real property acquired after 11-6-78 [see Act Sec. 702(q)(3) in the amendment notes following Code Sec. 6323(f)]. Prior to amendment, subparagraph (A) read:

"(A) if such notice of lien is refiled in the office in which the prior notice of lien was filed and the fact of refiling is entered and recorded in an index in accordance with subsection (f)(4); and"

• **1976, Tax Reform Act of 1976 (P.L. 94-455)**

P.L. 94-455, §1906(b)(13)(A):

Amended 1954 Code by substituting "Secretary" for "Secretary or his delegate" each place it appeared. **Effective** 2-1-77.

P.L. 94-455, §2008(c)(2):

Amended Code Sec. 6323(g)(2)(A). **Effective**, in the case of liens filed before 10-4-76, on 7-1-77. **Effective**, in the case of liens filed on or after 10-4-76, on 2-1-77. Prior to amendment, Code Sec. 6323(g)(2)(A) read as follows:

(A) if such notice of lien is refiled in the office in which the prior notice of lien was filed; and

[Sec. 6323(h)]

(h) DEFINITIONS.—For purposes of this section and section 6324—

(1) SECURITY INTEREST.—The term "security interest" means any interest in property acquired by contract for the purpose of securing payment or performance of an obligation or indemnifying against loss or liability. A security interest exists at any time (A) if, at such time the

COLLECTION—LIEN FOR TAXES

property is in existence and the interest has become protected under local law against a subsequent judgment lien arising out of an unsecured obligation, and (B) to the extent that, at such time, the holder has parted with money or money's worth.

(2) MECHANIC'S LIENOR.—The term "mechanic's lienor" means any person who under local law has a lien on real property (or on the proceeds of a contract relating to real property) for services, labor, or materials furnished in connection with the construction or improvement of such property. For purposes of the preceding sentence, a person has a lien on the earliest date such lien becomes valid under local law against subsequent purchasers without actual notice, but not before he begins to furnish the services, labor, or materials.

(3) MOTOR VEHICLE.—The term "motor vehicle" means a self-propelled vehicle which is registered for highway use under the laws of any State or foreign country.

(4) SECURITY.—The term "security" means any bond, debenture, note, or certificate or other evidence of indebtedness, issued by a corporation or a government or political subdivision thereof, with interest coupons or in registered form, share of stock, voting trust certificate, or any certificate of interest or participation in, certificate of deposit or receipt for, temporary or interim certificate for, or warrant or right to subscribe to or purchase, any of the foregoing; negotiable instrument; or money.

(5) TAX LIEN FILING.—The term "tax lien filing" means the filing of notice (referred to in subsection (a)) of the lien imposed by section 6321.

(6) PURCHASER.—The term "purchaser" means a person who, for adequate and full consideration in money or money's worth, acquires an interest (other than a lien or security interest) in property which is valid under local law against subsequent purchasers without actual notice. In applying the preceding sentence for purposes of subsection (a) of this section, and for purposes of section 6324—

(A) a lease of property,

(B) a written executory contract to purchase or lease property,

(C) an option to purchase or lease property or any interest therein, or

(D) an option to renew or extend a lease of property,

which is not a lien or security interest shall be treated as an interest in property.

[Sec. 6323(i)]

(i) SPECIAL RULES.—

(1) ACTUAL NOTICE OR KNOWLEDGE.—For purposes of this subchapter, an organization shall be deemed for purposes of a particular transaction to have actual notice or knowledge of any fact from the time such fact is brought to the attention of the individual conducting such transaction, and in any event from the time such fact would have been brought to such individual's attention if the organization had exercised due diligence. An organization exercises due diligence if it maintains reasonable routines for communicating significant information to the person conducting the transaction and there is reasonable compliance with the routines. Due diligence does not require an individual acting for the organization to communicate information unless such communication is part of his regular duties or unless he has reason to know of the transaction and that the transaction would be materially affected by the information.

(2) SUBROGATION.—Where, under local law, one person is subrogated to the rights of another with respect to a lien or interest, such person shall be subrogated to such rights for purposes of any lien imposed by section 6321 or 6324.

(3) FORFEITURES.—For purposes of this subchapter, a forfeiture under local law of property seized by a law enforcement agency of a State, county, or other local governmental subdivision shall relate back to the time of seizure, except that this paragraph shall not apply to the extent that under local law the holder of an intervening claim or interest would have priority over the interest of the State, county, or other local governmental subdivision in the property.

(4) COST-OF-LIVING ADJUSTMENT.—In the case of notices of liens imposed by section 6321 which are filed in any calendar year after 1998, each of the dollar amounts under paragraph (4) or (7) of subsection (b) shall be increased by an amount equal to—

(A) such dollar amount, multiplied by

(B) the cost-of-living adjustment determined under section 1(f)(3) for the calendar year, determined by substituting "calendar year 1996" for "calendar year 2016" in subparagraph (A)(ii) thereof.

If any amount as adjusted under the preceding sentence is not a multiple of $10, such amount shall be rounded to the nearest multiple of $10.

Amendments

- **2017, Tax Cuts and Jobs Act (P.L. 115-97)**

P.L. 115-97, § 11002(d)(1)(HH):

Amended Code Sec. 6323(i)(4)(B) by striking "for 'calendar year 1992' in subparagraph (B)" and inserting "for 'calendar year 2016' in subparagraph (A)(ii)". **Effective** for tax years beginning after 12-31-2017.

- **1998, IRS Restructuring and Reform Act of 1998 (P.L. 105-206)**

P.L. 105-206, § 3435(a)(2):

Amended Code Sec. 6323(i) by adding at the end a new paragraph (4). **Effective** 7-22-98.

- **1986, Tax Reform Act of 1986 (P.L. 99-514)**

P.L. 99-514, § 1569(a):

Amended Code Sec. 6323(i) by adding at the end thereof new paragraph (3). **Effective** 10-22-86.

- **1976, Tax Reform Act of 1976 (P.L. 94-455)**

P.L. 94-455, § 1202(h)(2):

Struck out Code Sec. 6323(i)(3). **Effective** 1-1-77. Prior to striking, Code Sec. 6323(i)(3) read as follows:

(3) DISCLOSURE OF AMOUNT OF OUTSTANDING LIEN.—If a notice of lien has been filed pursuant to subsection (f), the Secretary or his delegate is authorized to provide by regulations the extent to which, and the conditions under which, information as to the amount of outstanding obligation secured by the lien may be disclosed.

- **1966, Federal Tax Lien Act of 1966 (P.L. 89-719)**

P.L. 89-719, § 101(a):

Amended Code Sec. 6323. Prior to amendment, Sec. 6323 read as follows:

SEC. 6323. VALIDITY AGAINST MORTGAGEES, PLEDGEES, PURCHASERS, AND JUDGMENT CREDITORS.

(a) Invalidity of Lien Without Notice.—Except as otherwise provided in subsections (c) and (d), the lien imposed by section 6321 shall not be valid as against any mortgagee, pledgee, purchaser, or judgment creditor until notice thereof has been filed by the Secretary of his delegate—

(1) Under state or territorial laws.—In the office designated by the law of the State or Territory in which the property subject to the lien is situated, whenever the State or Territory has by law designated an office within the State or Territory for the filing of such notice; or

(2) With clerk of district court.—In the office of the clerk of the United States district court for the judicial district in which the property subject to the lien is situated, whenever the State or Territory has not by law designated an office within the State or Territory for the filing of such notice; or

(3) With Recorder of Deeds of the District of Columbia.—In the office of the Recorder of Deeds of the District of Columbia, if the property subject to the lien is situated in the District of Columbia.

(b) Form of Notice.—If the notice filed pursuant to subsection (a)(1) is in such form as would be valid if filed with the clerk of the United States district court pursuant to subsection (a)(2), such notice shall be valid notwithstanding any law of the State or Territory regarding the form or content of a notice of lien.

(c) Exception in Case of Securities.—

(1) Exception.—Even though notice of a lien provided in section 6321 has been filed in the manner prescribed in subsection (a) of this section, the lien shall not be valid with respect to a security, as defined in paragraph (2) of this subsection, as against any mortgagee, pledgee, or purchaser of such security, for an adequate and full consideration in money or money's worth, if at the time of such mortgage, pledge, or purchase such mortgagee, pledgee, or purchaser is without notice or knowledge of the existence of such lien.

(2) Definition of security.—As used in this subsection, the term 'security' means any bond, debenture, note, or certificate or other evidence of indebtedness, issued by any corporation (incuding one issued by a government or political subdivision thereof), with interest coupons or in registered form, share of stock, voting trust certificate, or any certificate of interest or participation in, certificate of deposit or receipt for, temporary or interim certificate for, or warrant or right to subscribe to or purchase, any of the foregoing; negotiable instrument; or money.

(d) Exception in Case of Motor Vehicles.—

(1) EXCEPTION.—Even though notice of a lien provided in section 6321 has been filed in the manner prescribed in subsection (a) of this section, the lien shall not be valid with respect to a motor vehicle, as defined in paragraph (2) of this subsection, as against any purchaser of such motor vehicle for an adequate and full consideration in money or money's worth if—

(A) at the time of the purchase the purchaser is without notice or knowledge of the existence of such lien, and

(B) before the purchaser obtains such notice or knowledge, he has acquired possession of such motor vehicle and has not thereafter relinquished possession of such motor vehicle to the seller or his agent.

(2) DEFINITION OF MOTOR VEHICLE.—As used in this subsection, the term "motor vehicle" means a self-propelled vehicle which is registered for highway use under the laws of any State or foreign country.

(e) DISCLOSURE OF AMOUNT OF OUTSTANDING LIEN.—If a notice of lien has been filed under subsection (a), the Secretary or his delegate is authorized to provide by rules or regulations the extent to which, and the conditions under which, information as to the amount of the outstanding obligation secured by the lien may be disclosed.

Effective generally after 11-2-66, regardless of when a lien or title of the U. S. arose or when a lien or interest of any other person was acquired. However, the Act provides certain exceptions to the effective date as follows:

(1) The amendments made by the Act are not to apply in any case where the Government has, in effect, completed enforcement of its interest arising under a lien. Thus, the amendments are not to apply where the enforcement proceeding has reached the stage of a civil action or suit which has become final by judgment, sale, or agreement, before the date of enactment.

(2) The amendments are not to apply to any case where they would impair a priority of any person holding a lien or interest prior to the date of enactment;

increase the liability of any person; or, shorten the time for bringing suit with respect to any transaction occurring before the date of enactment.

(3) The amendments imposing a liability on third persons who pay wages of employees of another or supply funds for the specific purpose of paying wages of the employees of another are to apply only with respect to wages paid on or after January 1, 1967.

(4) The amendments requiring performance bonds on public works contracts to provide for the payment of withholding are to apply only to contracts entered into pursuant to invitations for bids made by the Government after June 30, 1967.

(5) Where a person has commenced a civil action to clear title to property under the present law (sec. 7424 which, in effect, is repealed by this Act), the action is to be determined in accordance with that section without regard to this Act.

• **1966 (P.L. 89-493)**

P.L. 89-493, §17(a):

Amended Code Sec. 6323(a)(3) by substituting "Recorder of Deeds of the District of Columbia" for "Clerk of the United States District Court of the District of Columbia". **Effective** on the first day of the first month which is at least 90 days after 7-5-66.

• **1964, Revenue Act of 1964 (P.L. 88-272)**

P.L. 88-272, §236(c)(1):

Amended the first sentence to subsection (a) by inserting "subsections (c) and (d)" in lieu of "subsection (c)". **Effective** with respect to purchases made after 2-26-64.

P.L. 88-272, §236(a):

Added new subsection (d), and redesignated former subsection (d) as subsection (e). **Effective** with respect to purchases made after 2-26-64.

[Sec. 6323(j)]

(j) WITHDRAWAL OF NOTICE IN CERTAIN CIRCUMSTANCES.—

(1) IN GENERAL.—The Secretary may withdraw a notice of a lien filed under this section and this chapter shall be applied as if the withdrawn notice had not been filed, if the Secretary determines that—

(A) the filing of such notice was premature or otherwise not in accordance with administrative procedures of the Secretary,

(B) the taxpayer has entered into an agreement under section 6159 to satisfy the tax liability for which the lien was imposed by means of installment payments, unless such agreement provides otherwise,

(C) the withdrawal of such notice will facilitate the collection of the tax liability, or

(D) with the consent of the taxpayer or the National Taxpayer Advocate, the withdrawal of such notice would be in the best interests of the taxpayer (as determined by the National Taxpayer Advocate) and the United States.

Any such withdrawal shall be made by filing notice at the same office as the withdrawn notice. A copy of such notice of withdrawal shall be provided to the taxpayer.

(2) NOTICE TO CREDIT AGENCIES, ETC.—Upon written request by the taxpayer with respect to whom a notice of a lien was withdrawn under paragraph (1), the Secretary shall promptly make reasonable efforts to notify credit reporting agencies, and any financial institution or creditor whose name and address is specified in such request, of the withdrawal of such notice. Any such request shall be in such form as the Secretary may prescribe.

Amendments

• **1998, IRS Restructuring and Reform Act of 1998 (P.L. 105-206)**

P.L. 105-206, §1102(d)(1)(A):

Amended Code Sec. 6323(j)(1)(D) by striking "Taxpayer Advocate" each place it appears and inserting "National Taxpayer Advocate". **Effective** 7-22-98. For special rules, see Act Sec. 1102(f)(3)-(4) in the amendment notes following Code Sec. 7803.

• **1996, Taxpayer Bill of Rights 2 (P.L. 104-168)**

P.L. 104-168, §501(a):

Amended Code Sec. 6323 by adding at the end a new subsection (j). **Effective** 7-30-96.

[Sec. 6324]

SEC. 6324. SPECIAL LIENS FOR ESTATE AND GIFT TAXES.

[Sec. 6324(a)]

(a) LIENS FOR ESTATE TAX.—Except as otherwise provided in subsection (c)—

(1) UPON GROSS ESTATE.—Unless the estate tax imposed by chapter 11 is sooner paid in full, or becomes unenforceable by reason of lapse of time, it shall be a lien upon the gross estate of the decedent for 10 years from the date of death, except that such part of the gross estate as is used for the payment of charges against the estate and expenses of its administration, allowed by any court having jurisdiction thereof, shall be divested of such lien.

(2) LIABILITY OF TRANSFEREES AND OTHERS.—If the estate tax imposed by chapter 11 is not paid when due, then the spouse, transferee, trustee (except the trustee of an employees' trust which meets the requirements of section 401(a)), surviving tenant, person in possession of the property by reason of the exercise, nonexercise, or release of a power of appointment, or beneficiary, who receives, or has on the date of the decedent's death, property included in the gross estate under sections 2034 to 2042, inclusive, to the extent of the value, at the time of the decedent's death, of such property, shall be personally liable for such tax. Any part of such property transferred by (or transferred by a transferee of) such spouse, transferee, trustee, surviving tenant, person in possession, or beneficiary, to a purchaser or holder of a security interest shall be divested of the lien provided in paragraph (1) and a like lien shall then attach to all the property of such spouse, transferee, trustee, surviving tenant, person in possession, or beneficiary, or transferee of any such person, except any part transferred to a purchaser or a holder of a security interest.

(3) CONTINUANCE AFTER DISCHARGE OF FIDUCIARY.—The provisions of section 2204 (relating to discharge of fiduciary from personal liability) shall not operate as a release of any part of the gross estate from the lien for any deficiency that may thereafter be determined to be due, unless such part of the gross estate (or any interest therein) has been transferred to a purchaser or a holder of a security interest, in which case such part (or such interest) shall not be subject to a lien or to any claim or demand for any such deficiency, but the lien shall attach to the consideration received from such purchaser or holder of a security interest, by the heirs, legatees, devisees, or distributees.

Amendments

• **1970, Excise, Estate, and Gift Tax Adjustment Act of 1970 (P.L. 91-614)**

P.L. 91-614, §101(d)(2):

Amended Code Sec. 6324(a)(3) by substituting "fiduciary" for "executor" in the heading and in the text. **Effective** for gifts made after 12-31-70.

COLLECTION—LIEN FOR TAXES

[Sec. 6324(b)]

(b) LIEN FOR GIFT TAX.—Except as otherwise provided in subsection (c), unless the gift tax imposed by chapter 12 is sooner paid in full or becomes unenforceable by reason of lapse of time, such tax shall be a lien upon all gifts made during the period for which the return was filed, for 10 years from the date the gifts are made. If the tax is not paid when due, the donee of any gift shall be personally liable for such tax to the extent of the value of such gift. Any part of the property comprised in the gift transferred by the donee (or by a transferee of the donee) to a purchaser or holder of a security interest shall be divested of the lien imposed by this subsection and such lien, to the extent of the value of such gift, shall attach to all the property (including after-acquired property) of the donee (or the transferee) except any part transferred to a purchaser or holder of a security interest.

Amendments

• 1970, Excise, Estate, and Gift Tax Adjustment Act of 1970 (P.L. 91-614)

P.L. 91-614, §102(d)(7):

Amended Code Sec. 6324(b) by substituting "period for which the return was filed" for "calendar year" in the first sentence. **Effective** for gifts made after 12-31-70.

[Sec. 6324(c)]

(c) EXCEPTIONS.—

(1) The lien imposed by subsection (a) or (b) shall not be valid as against a mechanic's lienor and, subject to the conditions provided by section 6323(b) (relating to protection for certain interests even though notice filed), shall not be valid with respect to any lien or interest described in section 6323(b).

(2) If a lien imposed by subsection (a) or (b) is not valid as against a lien or security interest, the priority of such lien or security interest shall extend to any item described in section 6323(e) (relating to priority of interest and expenses) to the extent that, under local law, such item has the same priority as the lien or security interest to which it relates.

[Sec. 6324(d)—Repealed]

Amendments

• 1966, Federal Tax Lien Act of 1966 (P.L. 89-719)

P.L. 89-719, §102:

Amended Code Sec. 6324. **Effective**, generally, after 11-2-66, regardless of when a lien or title of the U. S. arose or when a lien or interest of any other person was acquired. However, see the amendment note for Code Sec. 6323 for exceptions to this **effective** date. Prior to amendment, Sec. 6324 read as follows:

Sec. 6324. Special Liens for Estate and Gift Taxes.

(a) Liens for Estate Tax.—Except as otherwise provided in subsection (c) (relating to transfers of securities) and subsection (d) (relating to purchases of motor vehicles)—

(1) Upon gross estate.—Unless the estate tax imposed by chapter 11 is sooner paid in full, it shall be a lien for 10 years upon the gross estate of the decedent, except that such part of the gross estate as is used for the payment of charges against the estate and expenses of its administration, allowed by any court having jurisdiction thereof, shall be divested of such lien.

(2) Liability of transferees and others.—If the estate tax imposed by chapter 11 is not paid when due, then the spouse, transferee, trustee (except the trustee of an employee's [sic]trust which meets the requirements of section 401(a)), surviving tenant, person in possession of the property by reason of the exercise, nonexercise, or release of a power of appointment, or beneficiary, who receives, or has on the date of the decedent's death, property included in the gross estate under sections 2034 to 2042, inclusive, to the extent of the value, at the time of the decedent's death, of such property, shall be personally liable for such tax. Any part of such property transferred by (or transferred by a transferee of) such spouse, transferee, trustee, surviving tenant, person in possession of property by reason of the exercise, nonexercise, or release of a power of appointment, or beneficiary, to a bona fide purchaser, mortgagee, or pledgee, for an adequate and full consideration in money or money's worth shall be divested of the lien provided in paragraph (1) and a like lien shall then attach to all the property of such spouse, transferee, trustee, surviving tenant, person in possession, beneficiary, or transferee of any such person, except any part transferred to a bona fide purchaser, mortgagee, or pledgee for an adequate and full consideration in money or money's worth.

(3) Continuance after discharge of executor.—The provisions of section 2204 (relating to discharge of executor from personal liability) shall not operate as a release of any part of the gross estate from the lien for any deficiency that may thereafter be determined to be due, unless such part of the gross estate (or any interest therein) has been transferred to a bona fide purchaser, mortgagee, or pledgee for an adequate and full consideration in money, or money's worth, in which case such part (or such interest) shall not be subject to a lien or to any claim or demand for any such deficiency, but the lien shall attach to the consideration received from such purchaser, mortgagee, or pledgee by the heirs, legatees, devisees, or distributees.

(b) Lien for Gift Tax.—Except as otherwise provided in subsection (c) (relating to transfers of securities) and subsection (d) (relating to purchases of motor vehicles), the gift tax imposed by chapter 12 shall be a lien upon all gifts made during the calendar year, for 10 years from the time the gifts are made. If the tax is not paid when due, the donee of any gift shall be personally liable for such tax to the extent of the value of such gift. Any part of the property comprised in the gift transferred by the donee (or by a transferee of the donee) to a bona fide purchaser, mortgagee, or pledgee for an adequate and full consideration in money or money's worth shall be divested of the lien herein imposed and the lien, to the extent of the value of such gift, shall attach to all the property (including after-acquired property) of the donee (or the transferee) except any part transferred to a bona fide purchaser, mortgagee, or pledgee for an adequate and full consideration in money or money's worth.

(c) Exception in Case of Securities.—The lien imposed by subsection (a) or (b) shall not be valid with respect to a security, as defined in section 6323(c)(2), as against any mortgagee, pledgee, or purchaser of any such security, for an adequate and full consideration in money or money's worth, if at the time of such mortgage, pledge, or purchase such mortgagee, pledgee, or purchaser is without notice or knowledge of the existence of such lien.

(d) Exception in Case of Motor Vehicles.—The lien imposed by subsection (a) or (b) shall not be valid with respect to a motor vehicle, as defined in section 6323(d)(2), as against any purchaser of such motor vehicle for an adequate and full consideration in money or money's worth—

(1) at the time of the purchase the purchaser is without notice or knowledge of the existence of such lien, and

(2) before the purchaser obtains such notice or knowledge, he has acquired possession of such motor vehicle and has not thereafter relinquished possession of such motor vehicle to the seller or his agent."

• 1964, Revenue Act of 1964 (P.L. 88-272)

P.L. 88-272, §236(c)(2):

Amended subsections (a) and (b) by adding in the first sentence of each "and subsection (d) (relating to purchases of motor vehicles)". **Effective** with respect to purchases made after 2-26-64.

P.L. 88-272, §236(b):

Added subsection (d). **Effective** for purchases made after 2-26-64.

[Sec. 6324A]

SEC. 6324A. SPECIAL LIEN FOR ESTATE TAX DEFERRED UNDER SECTION 6166.

[Sec. 6324A(a)]

(a) GENERAL RULE.—In the case of any estate with respect to which an election has been made under section 6166, if the executor makes an election under this section (at such time and in such manner as the Secretary shall by regulations prescribe) and files the agreement referred to in subsection (c), the deferred amount (plus any interest, additional amount, addition to tax, assessable penalty, and costs attributable to the deferred amount) shall be a lien in favor of the United States on the section 6166 lien property.

Amendments

• 1981, Economic Recovery Tax Act of 1981 (P.L. 97-34)

P.L. 97-34, §422(e)(6)(A):

Amended Code Sec. 6324A(a) by striking out "6166 or 6166A" and inserting "6166". **Effective** for estates of decedents dying after 12-31-81.

P.L. 97-34, §422(e)(6)(C):

Amended Code Sec. 6324A by striking out in the section heading "OR 6166A". **Effective** for estates of decedents dying after 12-31-81.

[Sec. 6324A(b)]

(b) SECTION 6166 LIEN PROPERTY.—

(1) IN GENERAL.—For purposes of this section, the term "section 6166 lien property" means interests in real and other property to the extent such interests—

(A) can be expected to survive the deferral period, and

COLLECTION—LIEN FOR TAXES

(B) are designated in the agreement referred to in subsection (c).

(2) MAXIMUM VALUE OF REQUIRED PROPERTY.—The maximum value of the property which the Secretary may require as section 6166 lien property with respect to any estate shall be a value which is not greater than the sum of—

(A) the deferred amount, and

(B) the required interest amount.

For purposes of the preceding sentence, the value of any property shall be determined as of the date prescribed by section 6151(a) for payment of the tax imposed by chapter 11 and shall be determined by taking into account any encumbrance such as a lien under section 6324B.

(3) PARTIAL SUBSTITUTION OF BOND FOR LIEN.—If the value required as section 6166 lien property pursuant to paragraph (2) exceeds the value of the interests in property covered by the agreement referred to in subsection (c), the Secretary may accept bond in an amount equal to such excess conditioned on the payment of the amount extended in accordance with the terms of such extension.

Amendments
• **1978, Revenue Act of 1978 (P.L. 95-600)**

P.L. 95-600, §702(e)(1)(B), (e)(2):

Amended Code Sec. 6324A(b)(2)(B) by striking out "aggregate interest amount" and inserting in place thereof "required interest amount". **Effective** for estates of decedents dying after 12-31-76.

[Sec. 6324A(c)]

(c) AGREEMENT.—The agreement referred to in this subsection is a written agreement signed by each person in being who has an interest (whether or not in possession) in any property designated in such agreement—

(1) consenting to the creation of the lien under this section with respect to such property, and

(2) designating a responsible person who shall be the agent for the beneficiaries of the estate and for the persons who have consented to the creation of the lien in dealings with the Secretary on matters arising under section 6166 or this section.

Amendments
• **1981, Economic Recovery Tax Act of 1981 (P.L. 97-34)**

P.L. 97-34, §422(e)(6)(A):

Amended Code Sec. 6324A(c)(2) by striking out "or 6166A" after "section 6166". **Effective** for estates of decedents dying after 12-31-81.

[Sec. 6324A(d)]

(d) SPECIAL RULES.—

(1) REQUIREMENT THAT LIEN BE FILED.—The lien imposed by this section shall not be valid as against any purchaser, holder of a security interest, mechanic's lien, or judgment lien creditor until notice thereof which meets the requirements of section 6323(f) has been filed by the Secretary. Such notice shall not be required to be refiled.

(2) PERIOD OF LIEN.—The lien imposed by this section shall arise at the time the executor is discharged from liability under section 2204 (or, if earlier, at the time notice is filed pursuant to paragraph (1)) and shall continue until the liability for the deferred amount is satisfied or becomes unenforceable by reason of lapse of time.

(3) PRIORITIES.—Even though notice of a lien imposed by this section has been filed as provided in paragraph (1), such lien shall not be valid—

(A) REAL PROPERTY TAX AND SPECIAL ASSESSMENT LIENS.—To the extent provided in section 6323(b)(6).

(B) REAL PROPERTY SUBJECT TO A MECHANIC'S LIEN FOR REPAIRS AND IMPROVEMENTS.—In the case of any real property subject to a lien for repair or improvement, as against a mechanic's lienor.

(C) REAL PROPERTY CONSTRUCTION OR IMPROVEMENT FINANCING AGREEMENT.—As against any security interest set forth in paragraph (3) of section 6323(c) (whether such security interest came into existence before or after tax lien filing).

Subparagraphs (B) and (C) shall not apply to any security interest which came into existence after the date on which the Secretary filed notice (in a manner similar to notice filed under section 6323(f)) that payment of the deferred amount has been accelerated under section 6166(g).

(4) LIEN TO BE IN LIEU OF SECTION 6324 LIEN.—If there is a lien under this section on any property with respect to any estate, there shall not be any lien under section 6324 on such property with respect to the same estate.

(5) ADDITIONAL LIEN PROPERTY REQUIRED IN CERTAIN CASES.—If at any time the value of the property covered by the agreement is less than the unpaid portion of the deferred amount and the required interest amount, the Secretary may require the addition of property to the agreement (but he may not require under this paragraph that the value of the property covered by the agreement exceed such unpaid portion). If property having the required value is not added to the property covered by the agreement (or if other security equal to the required value is not furnished) within 90 days after notice and demand therefor by the Secretary, the failure to comply with the preceding sentence shall be treated as an act accelerating payment of the installments under section 6166(g).

(6) LIEN TO BE IN LIEU OF BOND.—The Secretary may not require under section 6165 the furnishing of any bond for the payment of any tax to which an agreement which meets the requirements of subsection (c) applies.

Amendments

• **1981, Economic Recovery Tax Act of 1981 (P.L. 97-34)**

P.L. 97-34, §422(e)(6)(B):

Amended Code Sec. 6324A(d)(3) and (5) by striking out "section 6166(g) or 6166A(h)" and inserting "section 6166(g)". **Effective** for estates of decedents dying after 12-31-81.

• **1978, Revenue Act of 1978 (P.L. 95-600)**

P.L. 95-600, §702(e)(1)(C), (e)(2):

Amended Code Sec. 6324A(d)(5). **Effective** for estates of decedents dying after 12-31-76, by striking out "aggregate interest amount" and inserting in place thereof "required interest amount".

[Sec. 6324A(e)]

(e) DEFINITIONS.—For purposes of this section—

(1) DEFERRED AMOUNT.—The term "deferred amount" means the aggregate amount deferred under section 6166 (determined as of the date prescribed by section 6151(a) for payment of the tax imposed by chapter 11).

(2) REQUIRED INTEREST AMOUNT.—The term "required interest amount" means the aggregate amount of interest which will be payable over the first 4 years of the deferral period with respect to the deferred amount (determined as of the date prescribed by section 6151(a) for the payment of the tax imposed by chapter 11).

(3) DEFERRAL PERIOD.—The term "deferral period" means the period for which the payment of tax is deferred pursuant to the election under section 6166.

COLLECTION—LIEN FOR TAXES

(4) APPLICATION OF DEFINITIONS IN CASE OF DEFICIENCIES.—In the case of a deficiency, a separate deferred amount, required interest amount, and deferral period shall be determined as of the due date of the first installment after the deficiency is prorated to installments under section 6166.

Amendments

• 1981, Economic Recovery Tax Act of 1981 (P.L. 97-34)

P.L. 97-34, §422(e)(6)(A):

Amended Code Sec. 6324A(e) by striking out "section 6166 or 6166A" and inserting "section 6166" each place it appears. **Effective** for estates of decedents dying after 12-31-81.

• 1978, Revenue Act of 1978 (P.L. 95-600)

P.L. 95-600, §702(e)(1)(A), 702(e)(2):

Amended Code Sec. 6324A(e)(2). **Effective** for estates of decedents dying after 12-31-76. Prior to amendment, paragraph (2) read:

"(2) AGGREGATE INTEREST AMOUNT.—The term 'aggregate interest amount' means the aggregate amount of interest which will be payable over the deferral period with respect to the deferred amount (determined as of the date prescribed by section 6151(a) for payment of the tax imposed by chapter 11)."

P.L. 95-600, §702(e)(1)(D), 702(e)(2):

Amended Code Sec. 6324A(e)(4) by striking out "aggregate interest amount" and inserting in place thereof "required interest amount". **Effective** for estates of decedents dying after 12-31-76.

• 1976, Tax Reform Act of 1976 (P.L. 94-455)

P.L. 94-455, §2004(d)(1):

Added new Code Sec. 6324A. **Effective** for estates of decedents dying after 12-31-76.

[Sec. 6324B]

SEC. 6324B. SPECIAL LIEN FOR ADDITIONAL ESTATE TAX ATTRIBUTABLE TO FARM, ETC., VALUATION.

[Sec. 6324B(a)]

(a) GENERAL RULE.—In the case of any interest in qualified real property (within the meaning of section 2032A(b)), an amount equal to the adjusted tax difference attributable to such interest (within the meaning of section 2032A(c)(2)(B)) shall be a lien in favor of the United States on the property in which such interest exists.

[Sec. 6324B(b)]

(b) PERIOD OF LIEN.—The lien imposed by this section shall arise at the time an election is filed under section 2032A and shall continue with respect to any interest in the qualified real property—

(1) until the liability for tax under subsection (c) of section 2032A with respect to such interest has been satisfied or has become unenforceable by reason of lapse of time, or

(2) until it is established to the satisfaction of the Secretary that no further tax liability may arise under section 2032A(c) with respect to such interest.

Amendments

• 1978, Revenue Act of 1978 (P.L. 95-600)

P.L. 95-600, §702(r)(4), (5):

Amended Code Sec. 6324B(b). **Effective** for estates of decedents dying after 12-31-76, by striking out "qualified farm real property" and inserting in place thereof "qualified real property".

[Sec. 6324B(c)]

(c) CERTAIN RULES AND DEFINITIONS MADE APPLICABLE.—

(1) IN GENERAL.—The rule set forth in paragraphs (1), (3), and (4) of section 6324A(d) shall apply with respect to the lien imposed by this section as if it were a lien imposed by section 6324A.

(2) QUALIFIED REAL PROPERTY.—For purposes of this section, the term "qualified real property" includes qualified replacement property (within the meaning of section 2032A(h)(3)(B)) and qualified exchange property (within the meaning of section 2032A(i)(3)).

Amendments

• 1981, Economic Recovery Tax Act of 1981 (P.L. 97-34)

P.L. 97-34, §421(d)(2)(B):

Amended Code Sec. 6324B(c)(2) by adding before the period "and qualified exchange property (within the meaning of section 2032A(i)(3))". **Effective** with respect to exchanges after 12-31-81.

• 1980, Technical Corrections Act of 1979 (P.L. 96-222)

P.L. 96-222, §108(d):

Amended Code Sec. 6342B(c). Prior to amendment, Code Sec. 6342B(c) read as follows:

(c) CERTAIN RULES MADE APPLICABLE.—The rules set forth in paragraphs (1), (3), and (4) of section 6324A(d) shall apply with respect to the lien imposed by this section as if it were a lien imposed by section 6324A.

[Sec. 6324B(d)]

(d) SUBSTITUTION OF SECURITY FOR LIEN.—To the extent provided in regulations prescribed by the Secretary the furnishing of security may be substituted for the lien imposed by this section.

Amendments

• 1976, Tax Reform Act of 1976 (P.L. 94-455)

P.L. 94-455, §2003(b):

Added new Code Sec. 6324B. **Effective** for estates of decedents dying after 12-31-76.

[Sec. 6325]

SEC. 6325. RELEASE OF LIEN OR DISCHARGE OF PROPERTY.

[Sec. 6325(a)]

(a) RELEASE OF LIEN.—Subject to such regulations as the Secretary may prescribe, the Secretary shall issue a certificate of release of any lien imposed with respect to any internal revenue tax not later than 30 days after the day on which—

(1) LIABILITY SATISFIED OR UNENFORCEABLE.—The Secretary finds that the liability for the amount assessed, together with all interest in respect thereof, has been fully satisfied or has become legally unenforceable; or

(2) BOND ACCEPTED.—There is furnished to the Secretary and accepted by him a bond that is conditioned upon the payment of the amount assessed, together with all interest in respect thereof, within the time prescribed by law (including any extension of such time), and that is in accordance with such requirements relating to terms, conditions, and form of the bond and sureties thereon, as may be specified by such regulations.

Sec. 6324A(e)(4)

COLLECTION—LIEN FOR TAXES

Amendments

• **1982, Tax Equity and Fiscal Responsibility Act of 1982 (P.L. 97-248)**

P.L. 97-248, §348(a):

Amended so much of subsection (a) as precedes paragraph (1). **Effective** with respect to liens which are filed after 12-31-82 which are satisfied after 12-31-82, or with respect to which the taxpayer after 12-31-82, requests the Secretary of the Treasury or his delegate to issue a certificate of release on the grounds that the liability was satisfied or legally unenforceable. Prior to amendment, so much of subsection (a) as precedes paragraph (1) read as follows:

"(a) RELEASE OF LIEN.—Subject to such regulations as the Secretary may prescribe, the Secretary may issue a certificate of release of any lien imposed with respect to any internal revenue tax if—"

• **1976, Tax Reform Act of 1976 (P.L. 94-455)**

P.L. 94-455, §1906(b)(13)(A):

Amended 1954 Code by substituting "Secretary" for "Secretary or his delegate" each place it appeared. **Effective** 2-1-77.

[Sec. 6325(b)]

(b) DISCHARGE OF PROPERTY.—

(1) PROPERTY DOUBLE THE AMOUNT OF THE LIABILITY.—Subject to such regulations as the Secretary may prescribe, the Secretary may issue a certificate of discharge of any part of the property subject to any lien imposed under this chapter if the Secretary finds that the fair market value of that part of such property remaining subject to the lien is at least double the amount of the unsatisfied liability secured by such lien and the amount of all other liens upon such property which have priority over such lien.

(2) PART PAYMENT; INTEREST OF UNITED STATES VALUELESS.—Subject to such regulations as the Secretary may prescribe, the Secretary may issue a certificate of discharge of any part of the property subject to the lien if—

(A) there is paid over to the Secretary in partial satisfaction of the liability secured by the lien an amount determined by the Secretary, which shall not be less than the value, as determined by the Secretary, of the interest of the United States in the part to be so discharged, or

(B) the Secretary determines at any time that the interest of the United States in the part to be so discharged has no value.

In determining the value of the interest of the United States in the part to be so discharged, the Secretary shall give consideration to the value of such part and to such liens thereon as have priority over the lien of the United States.

(3) SUBSTITUTION OF PROCEEDS OF SALE.—Subject to such regulations as the Secretary may prescribe, the Secretary may issue a certificate of discharge of any part of the property subject to the lien if such part of the property is sold and, pursuant to an agreement with the Secretary, the proceeds of such sale are to be held, as a fund subject to the liens and claims of the United States, in the same manner and with the same priority as such liens and claims had with respect to the discharged property.

(4) RIGHT OF SUBSTITUTION OF VALUE.—

(A) IN GENERAL.—At the request of the owner of any property subject to any lien imposed by this chapter, the Secretary shall issue a certificate of discharge of such property if such owner—

(i) deposits with the Secretary an amount of money equal to the value of the interest of the United States (as determined by the Secretary) in the property; or

(ii) furnishes a bond acceptable to the Secretary in a like amount.

(B) REFUND OF DEPOSIT WITH INTEREST AND RELEASE OF BOND.—The Secretary shall refund the amount so deposited (and shall pay interest at the overpayment rate under section 6621), and shall release such bond, to the extent that the Secretary determines that—

(i) the unsatisfied liability giving rise to the lien can be satisfied from a source other than such property; or

(ii) the value of the interest of the United States in the property is less than the Secretary's prior determination of such value.

(C) USE OF DEPOSIT, ETC., IF ACTION TO CONTEST LIEN NOT FILED.—If no action is filed under section 7426(a)(4) within the period prescribed therefor, the Secretary shall, within 60 days after the expiration of such period—

(i) apply the amount deposited, or collect on such bond, to the extent necessary to satisfy the unsatisfied liability secured by the lien; and

(ii) refund (with interest as described in subparagraph (B)) any portion of the amount deposited which is not used to satisfy such liability.

(D) EXCEPTION.—Subparagraph (A) shall not apply if the owner of the property is the person whose unsatisfied liability gave rise to the lien.

Amendments

• **1998, IRS Restructuring and Reform Act of 1998 (P.L. 105-206)**

P.L. 105-206, §3106(a):

Amended Code Sec. 6325(b) by adding at the end a new paragraph (4). **Effective** 7-22-98.

• **1976, Tax Reform Act of 1976 (P.L. 94-455)**

P.L. 94-455, §1906(b)(13)(A):

Amended 1954 Code by substituting "Secretary" for "Secretary or his delegate" each place it appeared. **Effective** 2-1-77.

[Sec. 6325(c)]

(c) ESTATE OR GIFT TAX.—Subject to such regulations as the Secretary may prescribe, the Secretary may issue a certificate of discharge of any or all of the property subject to any lien imposed by section 6324 if the Secretary finds that the liability secured by such lien has been fully satisfied or provided for.

Amendments

• **1976, Tax Reform Act of 1976 (P.L. 94-455)**

P.L. 94-455, §1906(b)(13)(A):

Amended 1954 Code by substituting "Secretary" for "Secretary or his delegate" each place it appeared. **Effective** 2-1-77.

[Sec. 6325(d)]

(d) SUBORDINATION OF LIEN.—Subject to such regulations as the Secretary may prescribe, the Secretary may issue a certificate of subordination of any lien imposed by this chapter upon any part of the property subject to such lien if—

(1) there is paid over to the Secretary an amount equal to the amount of the lien or interest to which the certificate subordinates the lien of the United States,

(2) the Secretary believes that the amount realizable by the United States from the property to which the certificate relates, or from any other property subject to the lien, will ultimately be increased by reason of the issuance of such certificate and that the ultimate collection of the tax liability will be facilitated by such subordination, or

(3) in the case of any lien imposed by section 6324B, if the Secretary determines that the United States will be adequately secured after such subordination.

Amendments

• **1978, Revenue Act of 1978 (P.L. 95-600)**

P.L. 95-600, §513(a), (b):

Added Code Sec. 6325(d)(3). **Effective** for estates of decedents dying after 12-31-76.

• **1976, Tax Reform Act of 1976 (P.L. 94-455)**

P.L. 94-455, §1906(b)(13)(A):

Amended 1954 Code by substituting "Secretary" for "Secretary or his delegate" each place it appeared. **Effective** 2-1-77.

COLLECTION—LIEN FOR TAXES

[Sec. 6325(e)]

(e) NONATTACHMENT OF LIEN.—If the Secretary determines that, because of confusion of names or otherwise, any person (other than the person against whom the tax was assessed) is or may be injured by the appearance that a notice of lien filed under section 6323 refers to such person, the Secretary may issue a certificate that the lien does not attach to the property of such person.

Amendments

• **1976, Tax Reform Act of 1976 (P.L. 94-455)**

P.L. 94-455, § 1906(b)(13)(A):

Amended 1954 Code by substituting "Secretary" for "Secretary or his delegate" each place it appeared. **Effective** 2-1-77.

[Sec. 6325(f)]

(f) EFFECT OF CERTIFICATE.—

(1) CONCLUSIVENESS.—Except as provided in paragraphs (2) and (3), if a certificate is issued pursuant to this section by the Secretary and is filed in the same office as the notice of lien to which it relates (if such notice of lien has been filed) such certificate shall have the following effect:

(A) in the case of a certificate of release, such certificate shall be conclusive that the lien referred to in such certificate is extinguished;

(B) in the case of a certificate of discharge, such certificate shall be conclusive that the property covered by such certificate is discharged from the lien;

(C) in the case of a certificate of subordination, such certificate shall be conclusive that the lien or interest to which the lien of the United States is subordinated is superior to the lien of the United States; and

(D) in the case of a certificate of nonattachment, such certificate shall be conclusive that the lien of the United States does not attach to the property of the person referred to in such certificate.

(2) REVOCATION OF CERTIFICATE OF RELEASE OR NONATTACHMENT.—If the Secretary determines that a certificate of release or nonattachment of a lien imposed by section 6321 was issued erroneously or improvidently, or if a certificate of release of such lien was issued pursuant to a collateral agreement entered into in connection with a compromise under section 7122 which has been breached, and if the period of limitation on collection after assessment has not expired, the Secretary may revoke such certificate and reinstate the lien—

(A) by mailing notice of such revocation to the person against whom the tax was assessed at his last known address, and

(B) by filing notice of such revocation in the same office in which the notice of lien to which it relates was filed (if such notice of lien had been filed).

Such reinstated lien (i) shall be effective on the date notice of revocation is mailed to the taxpayer in accordance with the provisions of subparagraph (A), but not earlier than the date on which any required filing of notice of revocation is filed in accordance with the provisions of subparagraph (B), and (ii) shall have the same force and effect (as of such date), until the expiration of the period of limitation on collection after assessment, as a lien imposed by section 6321 (relating to lien for taxes).

(3) CERTIFICATES VOID UNDER CERTAIN CONDITIONS.—Notwithstanding any other provision of this subtitle, any lien imposed by this chapter shall attach to any property with respect to which a certificate of discharge has been issued if the person liable for the tax reacquires such property after such certificate has been issued.

Amendments

• **1976, Tax Reform Act of 1976 (P.L. 94-455)**

P.L. 94-455, § 1906(b)(13)(A):

Amended 1954 Code by substituting "Secretary" for "Secretary or his delegate" each place it appeared. **Effective** 2-1-77.

[Sec. 6325(g)]

(g) FILING OF CERTIFICATES AND NOTICES.—If a certificate or notice issued pursuant to this section may not be filed in the office designated by State law in which the notice of lien imposed by section 6321 is filed, such certificate or notice shall be effective if filed in the office of the clerk of the United States district court for the judicial district in which such office is situated.

[Sec. 6325(h)]

(h) CROSS REFERENCE.—

For provisions relating to bonds, see chapter 73 (sec. 7101 and following).

Amendments

• **1966, Federal Tax Lien Act of 1966 (P.L. 89-719)**

P.L. 89-719, § 103(a):

Amended Code Sec. 6325 to read as prior to amendment by P.L. 94-455. **Effective**, generally, after 11-2-66, regardless of when a lien or title of the U.S. arose or when a lien or interest of any other person was acquired. However, see the amendment note for Code Sec. 6323 for exceptions to this **effective** date. Prior to amendment, Code Sec. 6325 read as follows:

"Sec. 6325. Release of Lien or Partial Discharge of Property.

"(a) Release of Lien.—Subject to such rules or regulations as the Secretary or his delegate may prescribe, the Secretary or his delegate may issue a certificate of release of any lien imposed with respect to any internal revenue tax if—

"(1) Liability satisfied or unenforceable.—The Secretary or his delegate finds that the liability for the amount assessed, together with all interest in respect thereof, has been fully satisfied or has become legally unenforceable; or

"(2) Bond accepted.—There is furnished to the Secretary or his delegate and accepted by him a bond that is conditioned upon the payment of the amount assessed, together with all interest in respect thereof, within the time prescribed by law (including any extension of such time), and that is in accordance with such requirements relating to terms, conditions, and form of the bond and sureties thereon, as may be specified by such rules or regulations.

"(b) Partial Discharge of Property.—

"(1) Property double the amount of the liability.—Subject to such rules or regulations as the Secretary or his delegate may prescribe, the Secretary or his delegate may issue a certificate of discharge of any part of the property subject to any lien imposed under this chapter if the Secretary or his delegate finds that the fair market value of that part of such property remaining subject to the lien is at least double the amount of the unsatisfied liability secured by such lien and the amount of all other liens upon such property which have priority to such lien.

"(2) Part payment or interest of United States valueless.—Subject to such rules or regulations as the Secretary or his delegate may prescribe, the Secretary or his delegate may issue a certificate of discharge of any part of the property subject to the lien if—

"(A) there is paid over to the Secretary or his delegate in part satisfaction of the liability secured by the lien an amount determined by the Secretary or his delegate, which shall not be less than the value, as determined by the Secretary or his delegate, of the interest of the United States in the part to be so discharged, or

"(B) the Secretary or his delegate determines at any time that the interest of the United States in the part to be so discharged has no value.

In determining the value of the interest of the United States in the part to be so discharged, the Secretary or his delegate shall give consideration to the fair market value of such part and to such liens thereon as have priority to the lien of the United States.

"(c) Estate or Gift Tax.—Subject to such rules or regulations as the Secretary or his delegate may prescribe, the Secretary or his delegate may issue a certificate of discharge of any or all of the property subject to any lien imposed by section 6324 if the Secretary or his delegate finds that the liability secured by such lien has been fully satisfied or provided for.

"(d) Effect of Certificate of Release or Discharge.—A certificate of release or of discharge issued under this section shall be held conclusive that the lien upon the property covered by the certificate is extinguished.

"(e) Cross References.—

"(1) For single bond complying with the requirements of both subsection (a)(2) and section 6165, see section 7102.

"(2) For other provisions relating to bonds, see generally chapter 73.

"(3) For provisions relating to suits to enforce lien, see section 7403.

"(4) For provisions relating to suits to clear title to realty, see section 7424."

COLLECTION—SEIZURE OF PROPERTY

- **1958, Technical Amendments Act of 1958 (P.L. 85-866)**

P.L. 85-866, §77(1):

Amended Code Sec. 6325(a)(1). **Effective** 1-1-54. Prior to amendment, Code Sec. 6325 (a)(1) read as follows:

"(1) Liability Satisfied or Unenforceable.—The Secretary or his delegate finds that the liability for the amount assessed, together with all interest in respect thereof, has been fully satisfied, has become legally unenforceable, or, in the case of the estate tax imposed by chapter 11 or the gift tax imposed by chapter 12, has been fully satisifed or provided for; or"

P.L. 85-866, §77(2), (3):

Amended Code Sec. 6325 by redesignating subsections (c) and (d) as (d) and (e), respectively, added a new subsection (c), and struck out the word "Partial" where it appeared in the heading and text preceding "Discharge". **Effective** 1-1-54.

[Sec. 6326]

SEC. 6326. ADMINISTRATIVE APPEAL OF LIENS.

[Sec. 6326(a)]

(a) IN GENERAL.—In such form and at such time as the Secretary shall prescribe by regulations, any person shall be allowed to appeal to the Secretary after the filing of a notice of a lien under this subchapter on the property or the rights to property of such person for a release of such lien alleging an error in the filing of the notice of such lien.

[Sec. 6326(b)]

(b) CERTIFICATE OF RELEASE.—If the Secretary determines that the filing of the notice of any lien was erroneous, the Secretary shall expeditiously (and, to the extent practicable, within 14 days after such determination) issue a certificate of release of such lien and shall include in such certificate a statement that such filing was erroneous.

Amendments

- **1988, Technical and Miscellaneous Revenue Act of 1988 (P.L. 100-647)**

P.L. 100-647, §6238(a):

Redesignated Code Sec. 6326 as Code Sec. 6327 and inserted new Code Sec. 6326. **Effective** on the date which is 60 days after the date regulations are issued under Act Sec. 6238(b).

P.L. 100-647, §6238(b), provides:

(b) REGULATIONS.—The Secretary of the Treasury or the Secretary's delegate shall prescribe the regulations necessary to implement the administrative appeal provided for in the amendment made by subsection (a) within 180 days after the date of the enactment of this Act.

[Sec. 6327]

SEC. 6327. CROSS REFERENCES.

(1) For lien in case of tax on distilled spirits, see section 5004.

(2) For exclusion of tax liability from discharge in cases under title 11 of the United States Code, see section 523 of such title 11.

(3) For recognition of tax liens in cases under title 11 of the United States Code, see sections 545 and 724 of such title 11.

(4) For collection of taxes in connection with plans for individuals with regular income in cases under title 11 of the United States Code, see section 1328 of such title 11.

(5) For provisions permitting the United States to be made party defendant in a proceeding in a State court for the foreclosure of a lien upon real estate where the United States may have a claim upon the premises involved, see section 2410 of title 28 of the United States Code.

(6) For priority of lien of the United States in case of insolvency, see section 3713(a) of title 31, United States Code.

Amendments

- **1988, Technical and Miscellaneous Revenue Act of 1988 (P.L. 100-647)**

P.L. 100-647, §6238(a):

Redesignated Code Sec. 6326 as Code Sec. 6327. **Effective** on the date which is 60 days after the date regulations are issued under Act Sec. 6238(b).

P.L. 100-647, §6238(b), provides:

(b) REGULATIONS.—The Secretary of the Treasury or the Secretary's delegate shall prescribe the regulations necessary to implement the administrative appeal provided for in the amendment made by subsection (a) within 180 days after the date of the enactment of this Act.

- **1982 (P.L. 97-258)**

P.L. 97-258, §3(f)(7):

Amended Code Sec. 6326(6) by striking out "R.S. 3466 (31 U.S.C. 191)" and substituting "section 3713(a) of title 31, United States Code". **Effective** 9-13-82.

- **1980, Bankruptcy Tax Act of 1980 (P.L. 96-589)**

P.L. 96-589, §6(i)(10):

Amended Code Sec. 6326 by striking out paragraphs (2) through (5) and inserting new paragraphs (2) through (4). Redesignated former paragraphs (6) and (7) as (5) and (6), respectively. **Effective** 10-1-79, but are inapplicable to any proceeding under the Bankruptcy Act commenced before that date. Prior to amendment, paragraphs (2) through (5) provided:

"(2) For exclusion of tax liability from discharge in bankruptcy, see section 17 of the Bankruptcy Act, as amended (11 U.S.C. 35).

(3) For limit on amount allowed in bankruptcy proceedings on debts owing to the United States, see section 57(j) of the Bankruptcy Act, as amended (11 U.S.C. 93).

(4) For recognition of tax liens in proceedings under the Bankruptcy Act, see section 67(b) and (c) of that act, as amended (11 U.S.C. 107).

(5) For collection of taxes in connection with wage earners' plans in bankruptcy courts, see section 680 of the Bankruptcy Act, as added by the act of June 22, 1938 (11 U.S.C. 1080).".

- **1976, Tax Reform Act of 1976 (P.L. 94-455)**

P.L. 94-455, §1906(a)(20)(A):

Struck out "52 Stat. 851;" before "11 U.S.C. 35" in Code Sec. 6326(2). **Effective** 2-1-77.

P.L. 94-455, §1906(a)(20)(B):

Struck out "52 Stat. 867;" before "11 U.S.C. 93" in Code Sec. 6326(3). **Effective** 2-1-77.

P.L. 94-455, §1906(a)(20)(C):

Struck out "52 Stat. 876-877;" before "11 U.S.C. 107" in Code Sec. 6326(4). **Effective** 2-1-77.

P.L. 94-455, §1906(a)(20)(D):

Struck out "52 Stat. 938;" before "11 U.S.C. 1080" in Code Sec. 6326(5). **Effective** 2-1-77.

Subchapter D—Seizure of Property for Collection of Taxes

Part I.   Due process for collections.
Part II.   Levy.

PART I—DUE PROCESS FOR COLLECTIONS

Sec. 6330.   Notice and opportunity for hearing before levy.

[Sec. 6330]

SEC. 6330. NOTICE AND OPPORTUNITY FOR HEARING BEFORE LEVY.

[Sec. 6330(a)]

(a) REQUIREMENT OF NOTICE BEFORE LEVY.—

(1) IN GENERAL.—No levy may be made on any property or right to property of any person unless the Secretary has notified such person in writing of their right to a hearing under this section before such levy is made. Such notice shall be required only once for the taxable period to which the unpaid tax specified in paragraph (3)(A) relates.

COLLECTION—SEIZURE OF PROPERTY

(2) TIME AND METHOD FOR NOTICE.—The notice required under paragraph (1) shall be—

(A) given in person;

(B) left at the dwelling or usual place of business of such person; or

(C) sent by certified or registered mail, return receipt requested, to such person's last known address,

not less than 30 days before the day of the first levy with respect to the amount of the unpaid tax for the taxable period.

(3) INFORMATION INCLUDED WITH NOTICE.—The notice required under paragraph (1) shall include in simple and nontechnical terms—

(A) the amount of unpaid tax;

(B) the right of the person to request a hearing during the 30-day period under paragraph (2); and

(C) the proposed action by the Secretary and the rights of the person with respect to such action, including a brief statement which sets forth—

(i) the provisions of this title relating to levy and sale of property;

(ii) the procedures applicable to the levy and sale of property under this title;

(iii) the administrative appeals available to the taxpayer with respect to such levy and sale and the procedures relating to such appeals;

(iv) the alternatives available to taxpayers which could prevent levy on property (including installment agreements under section 6159); and

(v) the provisions of this title and procedures relating to redemption of property and release of liens on property.

[Sec. 6330(b)]

(b) RIGHT TO FAIR HEARING.—

(1) IN GENERAL.—If the person requests a hearing in writing under subsection (a)(3)(B) and states the grounds for the requested hearing, such hearing shall be held by the Internal Revenue Service Independent Office of Appeals.

(2) ONE HEARING PER PERIOD.—A person shall be entitled to only one hearing under this section with respect to the taxable period to which the unpaid tax specified in subsection (a)(3)(A) relates.

(3) IMPARTIAL OFFICER.—The hearing under this subsection shall be conducted by an officer or employee who has had no prior involvement with respect to the unpaid tax specified in subsection (a)(3)(A) before the first hearing under this section or section 6320. A taxpayer may waive the requirement of this paragraph.

Amendments

• **2019, Taxpayer First Act (P.L. 116-25)**

P.L. 116-25, §1001(b)(1)(C):

Amended Code Sec. 6330(b)(1) by striking "Internal Revenue Service Office of Appeals" and inserting "Internal Revenue Service Independent Office of Appeals". **Effective** 7-1-2019.

• **2006, Tax Relief and Health Care Act of 2006 (P.L. 109-432)**

P.L. 109-432, Division A, §407(b)(3):

Amended Code Sec. 6330(b)(1) by striking "under subsection (a)(3)(B)" and inserting "in writing under subsection (a)(3)(B) and states the grounds for the requested hearing". **Effective** for submissions made and issues raised after the date on which the Secretary first prescribes a list under Code Sec. 6702(c), as amended by Act Sec. 407(a).

[Sec. 6330(c)]

(c) MATTERS CONSIDERED AT HEARING.—In the case of any hearing conducted under this section—

(1) REQUIREMENT OF INVESTIGATION.—The appeals officer shall at the hearing obtain verification from the Secretary that the requirements of any applicable law or administrative procedure have been met.

(2) ISSUES AT HEARING.—

(A) IN GENERAL.—The person may raise at the hearing any relevant issue relating to the unpaid tax or the proposed levy, including—

(i) appropriate spousal defenses;

(ii) challenges to the appropriateness of collection actions; and

(iii) offers of collection alternatives, which may include the posting of a bond, the substitution of other assets, an installment agreement, or an offer-in-compromise.

(B) UNDERLYING LIABILITY.—The person may also raise at the hearing challenges to the existence or amount of the underlying tax liability for any tax period if the person did not receive any statutory notice of deficiency for such tax liability or did not otherwise have an opportunity to dispute such tax liability.

(3) BASIS FOR THE DETERMINATION.—The determination by an appeals officer under this subsection shall take into consideration—

(A) the verification presented under paragraph (1);

(B) the issues raised under paragraph (2); and

(C) whether any proposed collection action balances the need for the efficient collection of taxes with the legitimate concern of the person that any collection action be no more intrusive than necessary.

(4) CERTAIN ISSUES PRECLUDED.—An issue may not be raised at the hearing if—

(A)(i) the issue was raised and considered at a previous hearing under section 6320 or in any other previous administrative or judicial proceeding; and

(ii) the person seeking to raise the issue participated meaningfully in such hearing or proceeding;

(B) the issue meets the requirement of clause (i) or (ii) of section 6702(b)(2)(A); or

(C) a final determination has been made with respect to such issue in a proceeding brought under subchapter C of chapter 63.

This paragraph shall not apply to any issue with respect to which subsection (d)(3)(B) applies.

Amendments

• **2018, Tax Technical Corrections Act of 2018 (P.L. 115-141)**

P.L. 115-141, §401(a)(281), Div. U:

Amended Code Sec. 6330(c) by striking "subsection (d)(2)(B)" in the last sentence and inserting "subsection (d)(3)(B)". **Effective** 3-23-2018.

• **2015, Bipartisan Budget Act of 2015 (P.L. 114-74)**

P.L. 114-74, §1101(d):

Amended Code Sec. 6330(c)(4) by striking "or" at the end of subparagraph (A), by striking the period at the end of subparagraph (B) and inserting "; or", and by inserting after subparagraph (B) a new subparagraph (C). **Effective** generally for returns filed for partnership tax years beginning after 12-31-2017. For a special rule, see Act Sec. 1101(g)(4), below.

P.L. 114-74, §1101(g)(4), provides:

(4) ELECTION.—A partnership may elect (at such time and in such form and manner as the Secretary of the Treasury may prescribe) for the amendments made by this section (other than the election under section 6221(b) of such Code (as added by this Act)) to apply to any return of the partnership filed for partnership taxable years beginning after the date of the enactment of this Act and before January 1, 2018.

• **2006, Tax Relief and Health Care Act of 2006 (P.L. 109-432)**

P.L. 109-432, Division A, §407(b)(2)(A)-(D):

Amended Code Sec. 6330(c)(4) by striking "(A)" and inserting "(A)(i)"; by striking "(B)" and inserting "(ii)"; by striking the period at the end of the first sentence [of subparagraph (A)(ii), as so redesignated] and inserting "; or"; and by inserting after subparagraph (A)(ii) (as so redesignated) a new subparagraph (B). **Effective** for submissions made and issues raised after the date on which the Secretary first prescribes a list under Code Sec. 6702(c), as amended by Act Sec. 407(a).

COLLECTION—SEIZURE OF PROPERTY

[Sec. 6330(d)]

(d) PROCEEDING AFTER HEARING.—

(1) PETITION FOR REVIEW BY TAX COURT.—The person may, within 30 days of a determination under this section, petition the Tax Court for review of such determination (and the Tax Court shall have jurisdiction with respect to such matter).

(2) SUSPENSION OF RUNNING OF PERIOD FOR FILING PETITION IN TITLE 11 CASES.—In the case of a person who is prohibited by reason of a case under title 11, United States Code, from filing a petition under paragraph (1) with respect to a determination under this section, the running of the period prescribed by such subsection for filing such a petition with respect to such determination shall be suspended for the period during which the person is so prohibited from filing such a petition, and for 30 days thereafter.

(3) JURISDICTION RETAINED AT IRS INDEPENDENT OFFICE OF APPEALS.—The Internal Revenue Service Independent Office of Appeals shall retain jurisdiction with respect to any determination made under this section, including subsequent hearings requested by the person who requested the original hearing on issues regarding—

(A) collection actions taken or proposed with respect to such determination; and

(B) after the person has exhausted all administrative remedies, a change in circumstances with respect to such person which affects such determination.

Amendments

• **2019, Taxpayer First Act (P.L. 116-25)**

P.L. 116-25, §1001(b)(1)(C):

Amended Code Sec. 6330(d)(3) by striking "Internal Revenue Service Office of Appeals" and inserting "Internal Revenue Service Independent Office of Appeals". **Effective** 7-1-2019.

P.L. 116-25, §1001(b)(3):

Amended the heading of Code Sec. 6330(d)(3) by inserting "INDEPENDENT" after "IRS". **Effective** 7-1-2019.

• **2018, Tax Technical Corrections Act of 2018 (P.L. 115-141)**

P.L. 115-141, §401(a)(282), Div. U:

Amended Code Sec. 6330(d)(2) by striking ", and" at the end and inserting a period. **Effective** 3-23-2018.

• **2015, Protecting Americans from Tax Hikes Act of 2015 (P.L. 114-113)**

P.L. 114-113, §424(b)(1)(A)-(D), Div. Q:

Amended Code Sec. 6330(d) by striking "appeal such determination to the Tax Court" in paragraph (1) and inserting "petition the Tax Court for review of such determination", by striking "JUDICIAL REVIEW OF DETERMINATION" in the heading of paragraph (1) and inserting "PETITION FOR REVIEW BY TAX COURT", by redesignating paragraph (2) as paragraph (3), and by inserting after paragraph (1) a new paragraph (2). **Effective** for petitions filed under Code Sec. 6330 after 12-18-2015.

• **2006, Pension Protection Act of 2006 (P.L. 109-280)**

P.L. 109-280, §855(a):

Amended Code Sec. 6330(d)(1). **Effective** for determinations made after the date which is 60 days after 8-17-2006. Prior to amendment, Code Sec. 6330(d)(1) read as follows:

(1) JUDICIAL REVIEW OF DETERMINATION.—The person may, within 30 days of a determination under this section, appeal such determination—

(A) to the Tax Court (and the Tax Court shall have jurisdiction with respect to such matter); or

(B) if the Tax Court does not have jurisdiction of the underlying tax liability, to a district court of the United States.

If a court determines that the appeal was to an incorrect court, a person shall have 30 days after the court determination to file such appeal with the correct court.

• **2000, Community Renewal Tax Relief Act of 2000 (P.L. 106-554)**

P.L. 106-554, §313(d):

Amended Code Sec. 6330(d)(1)(A) by striking "to hear" and inserting "with respect to". **Effective** as if included in the provision of P.L. 105-206 to which it relates [**effective** for collection actions initiated after 1-18-99.—CCH].

[Sec. 6330(e)]

(e) SUSPENSION OF COLLECTIONS AND STATUTE OF LIMITATIONS.—

(1) IN GENERAL.—Except as provided in paragraph (2), if a hearing is requested under subsection (a)(3)(B), the levy actions which are the subject of the requested hearing and the running of any period of limitations under section 6502 (relating to collection after assessment), section 6531 (relating to criminal prosecutions), or section 6532 (relating to other suits) shall be suspended for the period during which such hearing, and appeals therein, are pending. In no event shall any such period expire before the 90th day after the day on which there is a final determination in such hearing. Notwithstanding the provisions of section 7421(a), the beginning of a levy or proceeding during the time the suspension under this paragraph is in force may be enjoined by a proceeding in the proper court, including the Tax Court. The Tax Court shall have no jurisdiction under this paragraph to enjoin any action or proceeding unless a timely appeal has been filed under subsection (d)(1) and then only in respect of the unpaid tax or proposed levy to which the determination being appealed relates.

(2) LEVY UPON APPEAL.—Paragraph (1) shall not apply to a levy action while an appeal is pending if the underlying tax liability is not at issue in the appeal and the court determines that the Secretary has shown good cause not to suspend the levy.

Amendments

• **2000, Community Renewal Tax Relief Act of 2000 (P.L. 106-554)**

P.L. 106-554, §313(b)(2)(A):

Amended Code Sec. 6330(e)(1) by adding at the end the last two sentences. **Effective** 12-21-2000.

[Sec. 6330(f)]

(f) EXCEPTIONS.—If—

(1) the Secretary has made a finding under the last sentence of section 6331(a) that the collection of tax is in jeopardy,

(2) the Secretary has served a levy on a State to collect a Federal tax liability from a State tax refund,

(3) the Secretary has served a disqualified employment tax levy, or

(4) the Secretary has served a Federal contractor levy,

this section shall not apply, except that the taxpayer shall be given the opportunity for the hearing described in this section within a reasonable period of time after the levy.

Amendments

• **2010, Creating Small Business Jobs Act of 2010 (P.L. 111-240)**

P.L. 111-240, §2104(a):

Amended Code Sec. 6330(f) by striking "or" at the end of paragraph (2), by inserting "or" at the end of paragraph (3), and by inserting after paragraph (3) a new paragraph (4). **Effective** for levies issued after 9-27-2010.

P.L. 111-240, §2104(c):

Amended the heading of Code Sec. 6330(f) by striking "JEOPARDY AND STATE REFUND COLLECTION" and inserting "EXCEPTIONS". **Effective** for levies issued after 9-27-2010.

• **2007, Small Business and Work Opportunity Tax Act of 2007 (P.L. 110-28)**

P.L. 110-28, §8243(a)(1)-(3):

Amended Code Sec. 6330(f) by striking "; or" at the end of paragraph (1) and inserting a comma, by adding "or" at the end of paragraph (2), and by inserting after paragraph (2) a new paragraph (3). **Effective** for levies served on or after the date that is 120 days after 5-25-2007.

• **1998, IRS Restructuring and Reform Act of 1998 (P.L. 105-206)**

P.L. 105-206, §3401(b):

Amended subchapter D of chapter 64 by inserting a new Code Sec. 6330. **Effective** for collection actions initiated after the date which is 180 days after 7-22-98.

COLLECTION—SEIZURE OF PROPERTY

[Sec. 6330(g)]

(g) FRIVOLOUS REQUESTS FOR HEARING, ETC.—Notwithstanding any other provision of this section, if the Secretary determines that any portion of a request for a hearing under this section or section 6320 meets the requirement of clause (i) or (ii) of section 6702(b)(2)(A), then the Secretary may treat such portion as if it were never submitted and such portion shall not be subject to any further administrative or judicial review.

Amendments

• **2006, Tax Relief and Health Care Act of 2006 (P.L. 109-432)**

P.L. 109-432, Division A, § 407(b)(1):

Amended Code Sec. 6330 by adding at the end a new subsection (g). **Effective** for submissions made and issues raised after the date on which the Secretary first prescribes a list under Code Sec. 6702(c), as amended by Act Sec. 407(a).

[Sec. 6330(h)]

(h) DEFINITIONS RELATED TO EXCEPTIONS.—For purposes of subsection (f)—

(1) DISQUALIFIED EMPLOYMENT TAX LEVY.—A disqualified employment tax levy is any levy in connection with the collection of employment taxes for any taxable period if the person subject to the levy (or any predecessor thereof) requested a hearing under this section with respect to unpaid employment taxes arising in the most recent 2-year period before the beginning of the taxable period with respect to which the levy is served. For purposes of the preceding sentence, the term "employment taxes" means any taxes under chapter 21, 22, 23, or 24.

(2) FEDERAL CONTRACTOR LEVY.—A Federal contractor levy is any levy if the person whose property is subject to the levy (or any predecessor thereof) is a Federal contractor.

Amendments

• **2010, Creating Small Business Jobs Act of 2010 (P.L. 111-240)**

P.L. 111-240, § 2104(b)(1)-(2):

Amended Code Sec. 6330(h) by striking all that precedes "any levy in connection with the collection" and by inserting

"(h) DEFINITIONS RELATED TO EXCEPTIONS.—For purposes of subsection (f)—"

"(1) DISQUALIFIED EMPLOYMENT TAX LEVY.—A disqualified employment tax levy is";

and by adding at the end a new paragraph (2). **Effective** for levies issued after 9-27-2010. Prior to being stricken, all that preceded "any levy in connection with the collection" read as follows:

(h) DISQUALIFIED EMPLOYMENT TAX LEVY.—For purposes of subsection (f), a disqualified employment tax levy is

• **2007, Small Business and Work Opportunity Tax Act of 2007 (P.L. 110-28)**

P.L. 110-28, § 8243(b):

Amended Code Sec. 6330 by adding at the end a new subsection (h). **Effective** for levies served on or after the date that is 120 days after 5-25-2007.

PART II—LEVY

Sec. 6331.	Levy and distraint.
Sec. 6332.	Surrender of property subject to levy.
Sec. 6333.	Production of books.
Sec. 6334.	Property exempt from levy.
Sec. 6335.	Sale of seized property.
Sec. 6336.	Sale of perishable goods.
Sec. 6337.	Redemption of property.
Sec. 6338.	Certificate of sale; deed of real property.
Sec. 6339.	Legal effect of certificate of sale of personal property and deed of real property.
Sec. 6340.	Records of sale.
Sec. 6341.	Expense of levy and sale.
Sec. 6342.	Application of proceeds of levy.
Sec. 6343.	Authority to release levy and return property.
Sec. 6344.	Cross references.

[Sec. 6331]

SEC. 6331. LEVY AND DISTRAINT.

[Sec. 6331(a)]

(a) AUTHORITY OF SECRETARY.—If any person liable to pay any tax neglects or refuses to pay the same within 10 days after notice and demand, it shall be lawful for the Secretary to collect such tax (and such further sum as shall be sufficient to cover the expenses of the levy) by levy upon all property and rights to property (except such property as is exempt under section 6334) belonging to such person or on which there is a lien provided in this chapter for the payment of such tax. Levy may be made upon the accrued salary or wages of any officer, employee, or elected official, of the United States, the District of Columbia, or any agency or instrumentality of the United States or the District of Columbia, by serving a notice of levy on the employer (as defined in section 3401(d)) of such officer, employee, or elected official. If the Secretary makes a finding that the collection of such tax is in jeopardy, notice and demand for immediate payment of such tax may be made by the Secretary and, upon failure or refusal to pay such tax, collection thereof by levy shall be lawful without regard to the 10-day period provided in this section.

Amendments

• **1998, IRS Restructuring and Reform Act of 1998 (P.L. 105-206)**

P.L. 105-206, § 3421, provides:

SEC. 3421. APPROVAL PROCESS FOR LIENS, LEVIES, AND SEIZURES.

(a) IN GENERAL.—The Commissioner of Internal Revenue shall develop and implement procedures under which—

(1) a determination by an employee to file a notice of lien or levy with respect to, or to levy or seize, any property or right to property would, where appropriate, be required to be reviewed by a supervisor of the employee before the action was taken; and

(2) appropriate disciplinary action would be taken against the employee or supervisor where the procedures under paragraph (1) were not followed.

(b) REVIEW PROCESS.—The review process under subsection (a)(1) may include a certification that the employee has—

(1) reviewed the taxpayer's information;

(2) verified that a balance is due; and

(3) affirmed that the action proposed to be taken is appropriate given the taxpayer's circumstances, considering the amount due and the value of the property or right to property.

(c) EFFECTIVE DATES.—

(1) IN GENERAL.—Except as provided in paragraph (2), this section shall take effect on the date of the enactment of this Act.

(2) AUTOMATED COLLECTION SYSTEM ACTIONS.—In the case of any action under an automated collection system, this section shall apply to actions initiated after December 31, 2000.

• **1976, Tax Reform Act of 1976 (P.L. 94-455)**

P.L. 94-455, § 1906(b)(13)(A):

Amended 1954 Code by substituting "Secretary" for "Secretary or his delegate" each place it appeared. **Effective** 2-1-77.

COLLECTION—SEIZURE OF PROPERTY

[Sec. 6331(b)]

(b) SEIZURE AND SALE OF PROPERTY.—The term "levy" as used in this title includes the power of distraint and seizure by any means. Except as otherwise provided in subsection (e), a levy shall extend only to property possessed and obligations existing at the time thereof. In any case in which the Secretary may levy upon property or rights to property, he may seize and sell such property or rights to property (whether real or personal, tangible or intangible).

Amendments

• **1984, Deficit Reduction Act of 1984 (P.L. 98-369)**

P.L. 98-369, §714(o):

Amended Code Sec. 6331(b) by striking out "subsection (d)(3)" and inserting in lieu thereof "subsection (e)". **Effective** as if included in the provision of P.L. 97-248 to which it relates.

• **1976, Tax Reform Act of 1976 (P.L. 94-455)**

P.L. 94-455, §1209(d)(2):

Substituted "Except as otherwise provided in subsection (d)(3), a levy" for "A levy" in the second sentence of Code Sec. 6331(b). **Effective** for levies made after 12-31-76; but P.L. 94-528, §2(c), **effective** 10-4-76, substituted "February 28, 1977" for "December 31, 1976" in P.L. 94-455, §1209(e).

P.L. 94-455, §1906(b)(13)(A):

Amended 1954 Code by substituting "Secretary" for "Secretary or his delegate" each place it appeared. **Effective** 2-1-77.

• **1966, Federal Tax Lien Act of 1966 (P.L. 89-719)**

P.L. 89-719, §104(a):

Amended Code Sec. 6331(b) by adding the second sentence. **Effective**, generally, after 11-2-66, the date of enactment. However, see the amendment note for Code Sec. 6323 for exceptions to this **effective** date.

[Sec. 6331(c)]

(c) SUCCESSIVE SEIZURES.—Whenever any property or right to property upon which levy has been made by virtue of subsection (a) is not sufficient to satisfy the claim of the United States for which levy is made, the Secretary may, thereafter, and as often as may be necessary, proceed to levy in like manner upon any other property liable to levy of the person against whom such claim exists, until the amount due from him, together with all expenses, is fully paid.

Amendments

• **1976, Tax Reform Act of 1976 (P.L. 94-455)**

P.L. 94-455, §1906(b)(13)(A):

Amended 1954 Code by substituting "Secretary" for "Secretary or his delegate" each place it appeared. **Effective** 2-1-77.

[Sec. 6331(d)]

(d) REQUIREMENT OF NOTICE BEFORE LEVY.—

(1) IN GENERAL.—Levy may be made under subsection (a) upon the salary or wages or other property of any person with respect to any unpaid tax only after the Secretary has notified such person in writing of his intention to make such levy.

(2) 30-DAY REQUIREMENT.—The notice required under paragraph (1) shall be—

(A) given in person,

(B) left at the dwelling or usual place of business of such person, or

(C) sent by certified or registered mail to such person's last known address,

no less than 30 days before the day of the levy.

(3) JEOPARDY.—Paragraph (1) shall not apply to a levy if the Secretary has made a finding under the last sentence of subsection (a) that the collection of tax is in jeopardy.

(4) INFORMATION INCLUDED WITH NOTICE.—The notice required under paragraph (1) shall include a brief statement which sets forth in simple and nontechnical terms—

(A) the provisions of this title relating to levy and sale of property,

(B) the procedures applicable to the levy and sale of property under this title,

(C) the administrative appeals available to the taxpayer with respect to such levy and sale and the procedures relating to such appeals,

(D) the alternatives available to taxpayers which could prevent levy on the property (including installment agreements under section 6159),

(E) the provisions of this title relating to redemption of property and release of liens on property,

(F) the procedures applicable to the redemption of property and the release of a lien on property under this title, and

(G) the provisions of section 7345 relating to the certification of seriously delinquent tax debts and the denial, revocation, or limitation of passports of individuals with such debts pursuant to section 32101 of the FAST Act.

Amendments

• **2015, Fixing America's Surface Transportation Act (P.L. 114-94)**

P.L. 114-94, §32101(b)(2):

Amended Code Sec. 6331(d)(4) by striking "and" at the end of subparagraph (E), by striking the period at the end of subparagraph (F) and inserting ", and", and by adding at the end a new subparagraph (G). **Effective** 12-4-2015.

• **1988, Technical and Miscellaneous Revenue Act of 1988 (P.L. 100-647)**

P.L. 100-647, §6236(a)(1)-(3):

Amended Code Sec. 6331(d) by striking out "10 days" in paragraph (2) and inserting in lieu thereof "30 days"; by striking out "10-DAY REQUIREMENT" in the heading of paragraph (2) and inserting in lieu thereof "30-DAY REQUIREMENT", and by adding at the end thereof new paragraph (4). **Effective** for levies issued on or after 7-1-89.

• **1982, Tax Equity and Fiscal Responsibility Act of 1982 (P.L. 97-248)**

P.L. 97-248, §349(a):

Amended Code Sec. 6331(d). **Effective** for levies made after 12-31-82. Prior to amendment, Code Sec. 6331(d) read as follows:

"(d) SALARY AND WAGES.—

(1) IN GENERAL.—Levy may be made under subsection (a) upon the salary or wages of an individual with respect to any unpaid tax only after the Secretary has notified such individual in writing of his intention to make such levy. Such notice shall be given in person, left at the dwelling or usual place of business of such individual, or shall be sent by mail to such individual's last known address, no less than 10 days before the day of levy.

(2) JEOPARDY.—Paragraph (1) shall not apply to a levy if the Secretary has made a finding under the last sentence of subsection (a) that the collection of tax is in jeopardy.

(3) CONTINUING LEVY ON SALARY AND WAGES.—

(A) EFFECT OF LEVY.—The effect of a levy on salary or wages payable to or received by a taxpayer shall be continuous from the date such levy is first made until the liability out of which such levy arose is satisfied or becomes unenforceable by reason of lapse of time.

(B) RELEASE AND NOTICE OF RELEASE.—With respect to a levy described in subparagraph (A), the Secretary shall promptly release the levy when the liability out of which such levy arose is satisfied or becomes unenforceable by reason of lapse of time, and shall promptly notify the person upon whom such levy was made that such levy has been released."

• **1976, Tax Reform Act of 1976 (P.L. 94-455)**

P.L. 94-455, §1209(d)(1):

Added Code Sec. 6331(d)(3). **Effective** for levies made after 2-28-77. [**effective** date amended by P.L. 94-528, §2(c)].

P.L. 94-455, §1209(d)(4):

Struck out the last sentence of Code Sec. 6331(d)(1). For **effective** date, see amendment note for P.L. 94-455, §1209(d)(1). Prior to striking, the last sentence of Code Sec. 6331(d)(1) read as follows:

No additional notice shall be required in the case of successive levies with respect to such tax.

COLLECTION—SEIZURE OF PROPERTY

P.L. 94-455, §1906(b)(13)(A):

Amended 1954 Code by substituting "Secretary" for "Secretary or his delegate" each place it appeared. **Effective** 2-1-77.

• **1971, Revenue Act of 1971 (P.L. 92-178)**

P.L. 92-178, §211(a):

Added Code Sec. 6331(d) and redesignated former Code Sec. 6331(d) as Code Sec. 6331(e). **Effective** for levies made after 3-31-72.

[Sec. 6331(e)]

(e) CONTINUING LEVY ON SALARY AND WAGES.—The effect of a levy on salary or wages payable to or received by a taxpayer shall be continuous from the date such levy is first made until such levy is released under section 6343.

Amendments

• **1988, Technical and Miscellaneous Revenue Act of 1988 (P.L. 100-647)**

P.L. 100-647, §6236(b)(1):

Amended Code Sec. 6331(e). **Effective** for levies issued on or after 7-1-89. Prior to amendment, Code Sec. 6331(e) read as follows:

(e) CONTINUING LEVY ON SALARY AND WAGES.—

(1) EFFECT OF LEVY.—The effect of a levy on salary or wages payable to or received by a taxpayer shall be continuous from the date such levy is first made until the liability out of which such levy arose is satisfied or becomes unenforceable by reason of lapse of time.

(2) RELEASE AND NOTICE OF RELEASE.—With respect to a levy described in paragraph (1), the Secretary shall promptly release the levy when the liability out of which such levy arose is satisfied or becomes unenforceable by reason of lapse of time, and shall promptly notify the person upon whom such levy was made that such levy has been released.

• **1982, Tax Equity and Fiscal Responsibility Act of 1982 (P.L. 97-248)**

P.L. 97-248, §349(a):

Added Code Sec. 6331(e). **Effective** for levies made after 12-31-82.

[Sec. 6331(f)]

(f) UNECONOMICAL LEVY.—No levy may be made on any property if the amount of the expenses which the Secretary estimates (at the time of levy) would be incurred by the Secretary with respect to the levy and sale of such property exceeds the fair market value of such property at the time of levy.

Amendments

• **1988, Technical and Miscellaneous Revenue Act of 1988 (P.L. 100-647)**

P.L. 100-647, §6236(d):

Amended Code Sec. 6331 by redesignating subsection (f) as subsection (h), and adding new subsection (f). **Effective** for levies issued on or after 7-1-89.

[Sec. 6331(g)]

(g) LEVY ON APPEARANCE DATE OF SUMMONS.—

(1) IN GENERAL.—No levy may be made on the property of any person on any day on which such person (or officer or employee of such person) is required to appear in response to a summons issued by the Secretary for the purpose of collecting any underpayment of tax.

(2) NO APPLICATION IN CASE OF JEOPARDY.—This subsection shall not apply if the Secretary finds that the collection of tax is in jeopardy.

Amendments

• **1988, Technical and Miscellaneous Revenue Act of 1988 (P.L. 100-647)**

P.L. 100-647, §6236(d):

Amended Code Sec. 6331 by adding new subsection (g). **Effective** for levies issued on or after 7-1-89.

[Sec. 6331(h)]

(h) CONTINUING LEVY ON CERTAIN PAYMENTS.—

(1) IN GENERAL.—If the Secretary approves a levy under this subsection, the effect of such levy on specified payments to or received by a taxpayer shall be continuous from the date such levy is first made until such levy is released. Notwithstanding section 6334, such continuous levy shall attach to up to 15 percent of any specified payment due to the taxpayer.

(2) SPECIFIED PAYMENT.—For the purposes of paragraph (1), the term "specified payment" means—

(A) any Federal payment other than a payment for which eligibility is based on the income or assets (or both) of a payee,

(B) any payment described in paragraph (4), (7), (9), or (11) of section 6334(a), and

(C) any annuity or pension payment under the Railroad Retirement Act or benefit under the Railroad Unemployment Insurance Act.

(3) INCREASE IN LEVY FOR CERTAIN PAYMENTS.—Paragraph (1) shall be applied by substituting "100 percent" for "15 percent" in the case of any specified payment due to a vendor of property, goods, or services sold or leased to the Federal Government and by substituting "100 percent" for "15 percent" in the case of any specified payment due to a Medicare provider or supplier under title XVIII of the Social Security Act.

Amendments

• **2015, Medicare Access and CHIP Reauthorization Act of 2015 (P.L. 114-10)**

P.L. 114-10, §413(a):

Amended Code Sec. 6331(h)(3) by striking "30 percent" and inserting "100 percent". **Effective** for payments made after 180 days after 4-16-2015.

• **2014, Stephen Beck, Jr., Achieving a Better Life Experience Act of 2014 (P.L. 113-295)**

P.L. 113-295, §209(a), Division B:

Amended Code Sec. 6331(h)(3) by striking the period at the end and inserting "and by substituting '30 percent' for '15 percent' in the case of any specified payment due to a Medicare provider or supplier under title XVIII of the Social Security Act.". **Effective** for payments made after 180 days after 12-19-2014.

• **2011, VOW to Hire Heroes Act of 2011 (P.L. 112-56)**

P.L. 112-56, §301(a):

Amended Code Sec. 6331(h)(3) by striking "goods or services" and inserting "property, goods, or services". **Effective** for levies issued after 11-21-2011.

• **2004, American Jobs Creation Act of 2004 (P.L. 108-357)**

P.L. 108-357, §887(a):

Amended Code Sec. 6331(h) by adding at the end a new paragraph (3). **Effective** 10-22-2004.

• **1998, IRS Restructuring and Reform Act of 1998 (P.L. 105-206)**

P.L. 105-206, §6010(f):

Amended Code Sec. 6331(h)(1) by striking "The effect of a levy" and inserting "If the Secretary approves a levy under this subsection, the effect of such levy". **Effective** as if included in the provision of P.L. 105-34 to which it relates [**effective** for levies issued after 8-5-97.—CCH].

P.L. 105-206, §3421, provides:

SEC. 3421. APPROVAL PROCESS FOR LIENS, LEVIES, AND SEIZURES.

(a) IN GENERAL.—The Commissioner of Internal Revenue shall develop and implement procedures under which—

(1) a determination by an employee to file a notice of lien or levy with respect to, or to levy or seize, any property or right to property would, where appropriate, be required to be reviewed by a supervisor of the employee before the action was taken; and

(2) appropriate disciplinary action would be taken against the employee or supervisor where the procedures under paragraph (1) were not followed.

(b) REVIEW PROCESS.—The review process under subsection (a)(1) may include a certification that the employee has—

(1) reviewed the taxpayer's information;

(2) verified that a balance is due; and

(3) affirmed that the action proposed to be taken is appropriate given the taxpayer's circumstances, considering the amount due and the value of the property or right to property.

Sec. 6331(e)

COLLECTION—SEIZURE OF PROPERTY

(c) EFFECTIVE DATES.—

(1) IN GENERAL.—Except as provided in paragraph (2), this section shall take effect on the date of the enactment of this Act.

(2) AUTOMATED COLLECTION SYSTEM ACTIONS.—In the case of any action under an automated collection system, this section shall apply to actions initiated after December 31, 2000.

• **1997, Taxpayer Relief Act of 1997 (P.L. 105-34)**

P.L. 105-34, §1024(a)(1)-(2):

Amended Code Sec. 6331 by redesignating subsection (h) as subsection (i), and by inserting after subsection (g) a new subsection (h). **Effective** for levies issued after 8-5-97.

[Sec. 6331(i)]

(i) NO LEVY DURING PENDENCY OF PROCEEDINGS FOR REFUND OF DIVISIBLE TAX.—

(1) IN GENERAL.—No levy may be made under subsection (a) on the property or rights to property of any person with respect to any unpaid divisible tax during the pendency of any proceeding brought by such person in a proper Federal trial court for the recovery of any portion of such divisible tax which was paid by such person if—

(A) the decision in such proceeding would be res judicata with respect to such unpaid tax; or

(B) such person would be collaterally estopped from contesting such unpaid tax by reason of such proceeding.

(2) DIVISIBLE TAX.—For purposes of paragraph (1), the term "divisible tax" means—

(A) any tax imposed by subtitle C; and

(B) the penalty imposed by section 6672 with respect to any such tax.

(3) EXCEPTIONS.—

(A) CERTAIN UNPAID TAXES.—This subsection shall not apply with respect to any unpaid tax if—

(i) the taxpayer files a written notice with the Secretary which waives the restriction imposed by this subsection on levy with respect to such tax; or

(ii) the Secretary finds that the collection of such tax is in jeopardy.

(B) CERTAIN LEVIES.—This subsection shall not apply to—

(i) any levy to carry out an offset under section 6402; and

(ii) any levy which was first made before the date that the applicable proceeding under this subsection commenced.

(4) LIMITATION ON COLLECTION ACTIVITY; AUTHORITY TO ENJOIN COLLECTION.—

(A) LIMITATION ON COLLECTION.—No proceeding in court for the collection of any unpaid tax to which paragraph (1) applies shall be begun by the Secretary during the pendency of a proceeding under such paragraph. This subparagraph shall not apply to—

(i) any counterclaim in a proceeding under such paragraph; or

(ii) any proceeding relating to a proceeding under such paragraph.

(B) AUTHORITY TO ENJOIN.—Notwithstanding section 7421(a), a levy or collection proceeding prohibited by this subsection may be enjoined (during the period such prohibition is in force) by the court in which the proceeding under paragraph (1) is brought.

(5) SUSPENSION OF STATUTE OF LIMITATIONS ON COLLECTION.—The period of limitations under section 6502 shall be suspended for the period during which the Secretary is prohibited under this subsection from making a levy.

(6) PENDENCY OF PROCEEDING.—For purposes of this subsection, a proceeding is pending beginning on the date such proceeding commences and ending on the date that a final order or judgment from which an appeal may be taken is entered in such proceeding.

Amendments

• **1998, IRS Restructuring and Reform Act of 1998 (P.L. 105-206)**

P.L. 105-206, §3433(a):

Amended Code Sec. 6331 by redesignating subsection (i) as subsection (j) and by inserting after subsection (h) a new subsection (i). **Effective** for unpaid tax attributable to tax periods beginning after 12-31-98.

• **1997, Taxpayer Relief Act of 1997 (P.L. 105-34)**

P.L. 105-34, §1024(a)(1):

Amended Code Sec. 6331 by redesignating subsection (h) as subsection (i). **Effective** for levies issued after 8-5-97.

• **1988, Technical and Miscellaneous Revenue Act of 1988 (P.L. 100-647)**

P.L. 100-647, §6236(d):

Amended Code Sec. 6331 by redesignating subsection (f) as subsection (h). **Effective** for levies issued on or after 7-1-89.

P.L. 100-647, §6236(b)(2):

Amended Code Sec. 6331(f), prior to amendment by Act Sec. 6236(d), by adding at the end thereof new paragraph (3). **Effective** for levies issued on or after 7-1-89.

• **1982, Tax Equity and Fiscal Responsibility Act of 1982 (P.L. 97-248)**

P.L. 97-248, §349(a):

Redesignated Code Sec. 6331(e) as Code Sec. 6331(f).

• **1971, Revenue Act of 1971 (P.L. 92-178)**

P.L. 92-178, §211(a):

Redesignated Code Sec. 6331(d) as Code Sec. 6331(e).

[Sec. 6331(j)]

(j) NO LEVY BEFORE INVESTIGATION OF STATUS OF PROPERTY.—

(1) IN GENERAL.—For purposes of applying the provisions of this subchapter, no levy may be made on any property or right to property which is to be sold under section 6335 until a thorough investigation of the status of such property has been completed.

(2) ELEMENTS IN INVESTIGATION.—For purposes of paragraph (1), an investigation of the status of any property shall include—

(A) a verification of the taxpayer's liability;

(B) the completion of an analysis under subsection (f);

(C) the determination that the equity in such property is sufficient to yield net proceeds from the sale of such property to apply to such liability; and

(D) a thorough consideration of alternative collection methods.

Amendments

• **1998, IRS Restructuring and Reform Act of 1998 (P.L. 105-206)**

P.L. 105-206, §3444(a):

Amended Code Sec. 6331, as amended by Act Sec. 3433, by redesignating subsection (j) as subsection (k) and by inserting after subsection (i) a new subsection (j). **Effective** 7-22-98.

[Sec. 6331(k)]

(k) NO LEVY WHILE CERTAIN OFFERS PENDING OR INSTALLMENT AGREEMENT PENDING OR IN EFFECT.—

(1) OFFER-IN-COMPROMISE PENDING.—No levy may be made under subsection (a) on the property or rights to property of any person with respect to any unpaid tax—

COLLECTION—SEIZURE OF PROPERTY

(A) during the period that an offer-in-compromise by such person under section 7122 of such unpaid tax is pending with the Secretary; and

(B) if such offer is rejected by the Secretary, during the 30 days thereafter (and, if an appeal of such rejection is filed within such 30 days, during the period that such appeal is pending).

For purposes of subparagraph (A), an offer is pending beginning on the date the Secretary accepts such offer for processing.

(2) INSTALLMENT AGREEMENTS.—No levy may be made under subsection (a) on the property or rights to property of any person with respect to any unpaid tax—

(A) during the period that an offer by such person for an installment agreement under section 6159 for payment of such unpaid tax is pending with the Secretary;

(B) if such offer is rejected by the Secretary, during the 30 days thereafter (and, if an appeal of such rejection is filed within such 30 days, during the period that such appeal is pending);

(C) during the period that such an installment agreement for payment of such unpaid tax is in effect; and

(D) if such agreement is terminated by the Secretary, during the 30 days thereafter (and, if an appeal of such termination is filed within such 30 days, during the period that such appeal is pending).

(3) CERTAIN RULES TO APPLY.—Rules similar to the rules of—

(A) paragraphs (3) and (4) of subsection (i), and

(B) except in the case of paragraph (2)(C), paragraph (5) of subsection (i),

shall apply for purposes of this subsection.

Amendments

• **2002, Job Creation and Worker Assistance Act of 2002 (P.L. 107-147)**

P.L. 107-147, §416(e)(1):

Amended Code Sec. 6331(k)(3). **Effective** 3-9-2002. Prior to amendment, Code Sec. 6331(k)(3) read as follows:

(3) CERTAIN RULES TO APPLY.—Rules similar to the rules of paragraphs (3) and (4) of subsection (i) shall apply for purposes of this subsection.

• **2000, Community Renewal Tax Relief Act of 2000 (P.L. 106-554)**

P.L. 106-554, §313(b)(3):

Amended Code Sec. 6331(k)(3) by striking "(3), (4), and (5)" and inserting "(3) and (4)". **Effective** 12-21-2000.

• **1998, IRS Restructuring and Reform Act of 1998 (P.L. 105-206)**

P.L. 105-206, §3462(b):

Amended Code Sec. 6331, as amended by Act Secs. 3433 and 3444, by redesignating subsection (k) as subsection (l) and by inserting after subsection (j) a new subsection (k). **Effective** for offers-in-compromise pending on or made after 12-31-99.

[Sec. 6331(l)]

(l) CROSS REFERENCES.—

(1) For provisions relating to jeopardy, see subchapter A of chapter 70.

(2) For proceedings applicable to sale of seized property, see section 6335.

(3) For release and notice of release of levy, see section 6343.

Amendments

• **1998, IRS Restructuring and Reform Act of 1998 (P.L. 105-206)**

P.L. 105-206, §3433(a):

Amended Code Sec. 6331 by redesignating subsection (i) as subsection (j). **Effective** for unpaid tax attributable to tax periods beginning after 12-31-98.

P.L. 105-206, §3444(a):

Amended Code Sec. 6331, as amended by Act Sec. 3433, by redesignating subsection (j) as subsection (k). **Effective** 7-22-98.

P.L. 105-206, §3462(b):

Amended Code Sec. 6331, as amended by Act Secs. 3433 and 3444, by redesignating subsection (k) as subsection (l). **Effective** for offers-in-compromise pending on or made after 12-31-99.

[Sec. 6332]

SEC. 6332. SURRENDER OF PROPERTY SUBJECT TO LEVY.

[Sec. 6332(a)]

(a) REQUIREMENT.—Except as otherwise provided in this section, any person in possession of (or obligated with respect to) property or rights to property subject to levy upon which a levy has been made shall, upon demand of the Secretary, surrender such property or rights (or discharge such obligation) to the Secretary, except such part of the property or rights as is, at the time of such demand, subject to an attachment or execution under any judicial process.

Amendments

• **1990, Omnibus Budget Reconciliation Act of 1990 (P.L. 101-508)**

P.L. 101-508, §11704(a)(27):

Amended Code Sec. 6332(a) by striking "subsections (b) and (c)" and inserting "this section". **Effective** 11-5-90.

• **1988, Technical and Miscellaneous Revenue Act of 1988 (P.L. 100-647)**

P.L. 100-647, §6236(e)(2)(A):

Amended Code Sec. 6332(a) by striking out "subsection (b)" and inserting in lieu thereof "subsections (b) and (c)". **Effective** for levies issued on or after 7-1-89.

• **1976, Tax Reform Act of 1976 (P.L. 94-455)**

P.L. 94-455, §1906(b)(13)(A):

Amended 1954 Code by substituting "Secretary" for "Secretary or his delegate" each place it appeared. **Effective** 2-1-77.

• **1966, Federal Tax Lien Act of 1966 (P.L. 89-719)**

P.L. 89-719, §104(b):

Amended Code Sec. 6332(a) by substituting "Except as otherwise provided in subsection (b), any person" for "Any person". **Effective**, generally, after 11-2-66. However, see the amendment note for Code Sec. 6323 for exceptions to this **effective** date.

[Sec. 6332(b)]

(b) SPECIAL RULE FOR LIFE INSURANCE AND ENDOWMENT CONTRACTS.—

(1) IN GENERAL.—A levy on an organization with respect to a life insurance or endowment contract issued by such organization shall, without necessity for the surrender of the contract document, constitute a demand by the Secretary for payment of the amount described in paragraph (2) and the exercise of the right of the person against whom the tax is assessed to the advance of such amount. Such organization shall pay over such amount 90 days after service of notice of levy. Such notice shall include a certification by the Secretary that a copy of such notice has been mailed to the person against whom the tax is assessed at his last known address.

(2) SATISFACTION OF LEVY.—Such levy shall be deemed to be satisfied if such organization pays over to the Secretary the amount which the person against whom the tax is assessed could have had advanced to him by such organization on the date prescribed in paragraph (1) for the satisfaction of such levy, increased by the amount of any advance (including contractual interest thereon) made to such person on or after the date such organization had actual notice or knowledge (within the meaning of section 6323(i)(1)) of the existence of the lien with respect to

COLLECTION—SEIZURE OF PROPERTY

which such levy is made, other than an advance (including contractual interest thereon) made automatically to maintain such contract in force under an agreement entered into before such organization had such notice or knowledge.

(3) ENFORCEMENT PROCEEDINGS.—The satisfaction of a levy under paragraph (2) shall be without prejudice to any civil action for the enforcement of any lien imposed by this title with respect to such contract.

Amendments

• **1976, Tax Reform Act of 1976 (P.L. 94-455)**

P.L. 94-455, §1906(b)(13)(A):

Amended 1954 Code by substituting "Secretary" for "Secretary or his delegate" each place it appeared. **Effective** 2-1-77.

• **1966, Federal Tax Lien Act of 1966 (P.L. 89-719)**

P.L. 89-719, §104(b):

Amended Code Sec. 6332(b). **Effective**, generally, after 11-2-66. However, see the amendment note for Code Sec. 6323 for exceptions to this **effective** date. Prior to amendment, Code Sec. 6332(b) read as follows:

"(b) Penalty for Violation.—Any person who fails or refuses to surrender as required by subsection (a) any property or rights to property, subject to levy, upon demand by the Secretary or his delegate, shall be liable in his own person and estate to the United States in a sum equal to the value of the property or rights not so surrendered, but not exceeding the amount of the taxes for the collection of which such levy has been made, together with costs and interest on such sum at the rate of 6 percent per annum from the date of such levy."

[Sec. 6332(c)]

(c) SPECIAL RULE FOR BANKS.—Any bank (as defined in section 408(n)) shall surrender (subject to an attachment or execution under judicial process) any deposits (including interest thereon) in such bank only after 21 days after service of levy.

Amendments

• **1988, Technical and Miscellaneous Revenue Act of 1988 (P.L. 100-647)**

P.L. 100-647, §6236(e)(1):

Amended Code Sec. 6332, as amended by title I of this Act, by redesignating subsections (c), (d), and (e) as subsections (d), (e), and (f), respectively, and by inserting after subsection (b) new subsection (c). **Effective** for levies issued on or after 7-1-89.

[Sec. 6332(d)]

(d) ENFORCEMENT OF LEVY.—

(1) EXTENT OF PERSONAL LIABILITY.—Any person who fails or refuses to surrender any property or rights to property, subject to levy, upon demand by the Secretary, shall be liable in his own person and estate to the United States in a sum equal to the value of the property or rights not so surrendered, but not exceeding the amount of taxes for the collection of which such levy has been made, together with costs and interest on such sum at the underpayment rate established under section 6621 from the date of such levy (or, in the case of a levy described in section 6331(d)(3), from the date such person would otherwise have been obligated to pay over such amounts to the taxpayer). Any amount (other than costs) recovered under this paragraph shall be credited against the tax liability for the collection of which levy was made.

(2) PENALTY FOR VIOLATION.—In addition to the personal liability imposed by paragraph (1), if any person required to surrender property or rights to property fails or refuses to surrender such property or rights to property without reasonable cause, such person shall be liable for a penalty equal to 50 percent of the amount recoverable under paragraph (1). No part of such penalty shall be credited against the tax liability for the collection of which such levy was made.

Amendments

• **1988, Technical and Miscellaneous Revenue Act of 1988 (P.L. 100-647)**

P.L. 100-647, §6236(e)(1):

Amended Code Sec. 6332, as amended by title I of this Act, by redesignating subsection (c) as subsection (d). **Effective** for levies issued on or after 7-1-89.

• **1986, Tax Reform Act of 1986 (P.L. 99-514)**

P.L. 99-514, §1511(c)(9):

Amended Code Sec. 6332(c)(1) by striking out "an annual rate established under section 6621" and inserting in lieu thereof "the underpayment rate established under section 6621". **Effective** for purposes of determining interest for periods after 12-31-86.

• **1976, Tax Reform Act of 1976 (P.L. 94-455)**

P.L. 94-455, §1209(d)(3):

Added "(or, in the case of a levy described in section 6331(d)(3), from the date such person would otherwise have been obligated to pay over such amounts to the taxpayer)" immediately before the period at the end of the first sentence of Code Sec. 6332(c)(1). **Effective** for levies made after 2-28-77. [**effective** date changed by P.L. 94-528, §2(c)].

P.L. 94-455, §1906(b)(13)(A):

Amended 1954 Code by substituting "Secretary" for "Secretary or his delegate" each place it appeared. **Effective** 2-1-77.

• **1975 (P.L. 93-625)**

P.L. 93-625, §7(a)(2):

Amended Code Sec. 6332(c)(1) by substituting "an annual rate established under section 6621" for "the rate of 6 percent per annum". For **effective** date, see the historical comment for P.L. 93-625 following the text of Code Sec. 6621.

[Sec. 6332(e)]

(e) EFFECT OF HONORING LEVY.—Any person in possession of (or obligated with respect to) property or rights to property subject to levy upon which a levy has been made who, upon demand by the Secretary, surrenders such property or rights to property (or discharges such obligation) to the Secretary (or who pays a liability under subsection (d)(1)) shall be discharged from any obligation or liability to the delinquent taxpayer and any other person with respect to such property or rights to property arising from such surrender or payment.

Amendments

• **1988, Technical and Miscellaneous Revenue Act of 1988 (P.L. 100-647)**

P.L. 100-647, §1015(t)(1)(A)-(B):

Amended Code Sec. 6332(d), prior to its redesignation by Act Sec. 6236(e)(1), by inserting "and any other person" after "delinquent taxpayer", and by striking out the last sentence thereof. **Effective** for levies issued after 11-10-88. Prior to being struck out, the last sentence of Code Sec. 6332(d) read as follows:

In the case of a levy which is satisfied pursuant to subsection (b), such organization shall also be discharged from any obligation or liability to any beneficiary arising from such surrender or payment.

P.L. 100-647, §6236(e)(1):

Amended Code Sec. 6332, as amended by title I of this Act, by redesignating subsection (d) as subsection (e). **Effective** for levies issued on or after 7-1-89.

P.L. 100-647, §6236(e)(2)(B):

Amended Code Sec. 6332(e), as redesignated, by striking out "subsection (c)(1)" and inserting in lieu thereof "subsection (d)(1)". **Effective** for levies issued on or after 7-1-89.

• **1976, Tax Reform Act of 1976 (P.L. 94-455)**

P.L. 94-455, §1906(b)(13)(A):

Amended 1954 Code by substituting "Secretary" for "Secretary or his delegate" each place it appeared. **Effective** 2-1-77.

• **1966, Federal Tax Lien Act of 1966 (P.L. 89-719)**

P.L. 89-719, §104(b):

Added Code Secs. 6332(c) and (d), and redesignated former Code Sec. 6332(c) as Code Sec. 6332(e). **Effective**, generally, after 11-2-66. However, see amendment note for Code Sec. 6323 for exceptions to this **effective** date.

COLLECTION—SEIZURE OF PROPERTY

[Sec. 6332(f)]

(f) PERSON DEFINED.—The term "person," as used in subsection (a), includes an officer or employee of a corporation or a member or employee of a partnership, who as such officer, employee, or member is under a duty to surrender the property or rights to property, or to discharge the obligation.

Amendments

• **1988, Technical and Miscellaneous Revenue Act of 1988 (P.L. 100-647)**

P.L. 100-647, § 6326(e)(1):

Amended Code Sec. 6332, as amended by title I of this Act, by redesignating subsection (e) as subsection (f). **Effective** for levies issued on or after 7-1-89.

• **1966, Federal Tax Lien Act of 1966 (P.L. 89-719)**

P.L. 89-719, § 104(b):

Redesignated former Code Sec. 6332(c) as Code Sec. 6332(e). **Effective**, generally, after 11-2-66. However, see the amendment note for Code Sec. 6323 for exceptions to this **effective** date.

[Sec. 6333]

SEC. 6333. PRODUCTION OF BOOKS.

If a levy has been made or is about to be made on any property, or right to property, any person having custody or control of any books or records, containing evidence or statements relating to the property or right to property subject to levy, shall, upon demand of the Secretary, exhibit such books or records to the Secretary.

Amendments

• **1976, Tax Reform Act of 1976 (P.L. 94-455)**

P.L. 94-455, § 1906(b)(13)(A):

Amended 1954 Code by substituting "Secretary" for "Secretary or his delegate" each place it appeared. **Effective** 2-1-77.

[Sec. 6334]

SEC. 6334. PROPERTY EXEMPT FROM LEVY.

[Sec. 6334(a)]

(a) ENUMERATION.—There shall be exempt from levy—

(1) WEARING APPAREL AND SCHOOL BOOKS.—Such items of wearing apparel and such school books as are necessary for the taxpayer or for members of his family;

(2) FUEL, PROVISIONS, FURNITURE, AND PERSONAL EFFECTS.—So much of the fuel, provisions, furniture, and personal effects in the taxpayer's household, and of the arms for personal use, livestock, and poultry of the taxpayer, as does not exceed $6,250 in value;

(3) BOOKS AND TOOLS OF A TRADE, BUSINESS, OR PROFESSION.—So many of the books and tools necessary for the trade, business, or profession of the taxpayer as do not exceed in the aggregate $3,125 in value.

(4) UNEMPLOYMENT BENEFITS.—Any amount payable to an individual with respect to his unemployment (including any portion thereof payable with respect to dependents) under an unemployment compensation law of the United States, of any State, or of the District of Columbia or of the Commonwealth of Puerto Rico.

(5) UNDELIVERED MAIL.—Mail, addressed to any person, which has not been delivered to the addressee.

(6) CERTAIN ANNUITY AND PENSION PAYMENTS.—Annuity or pension payments under the Railroad Retirement Act, benefits under the Railroad Unemployment Insurance Act, special pension payments received by a person whose name has been entered on the Army, Navy, Air Force, and Coast Guard Medal of Honor roll (38 U. S. C. 562), and annuities based on retired or retainer pay under chapter 73 of title 10 of the United States Code.

(7) WORKMEN'S COMPENSATION.—Any amount payable to an individual as workmen's compensation (including any portion thereof payable with respect to dependents) under a workmen's compensation law of the United States, any State, the District of Columbia, or the Commonwealth of Puerto Rico.

(8) JUDGMENTS FOR SUPPORT OF MINOR CHILDREN.—If the taxpayer is required by judgment of a court of competent jurisdiction, entered prior to the date of levy, to contribute to the support of his minor children, so much of his salary, wages, or other income as is necessary to comply with such judgment.

(9) MINIMUM EXEMPTION FOR WAGES, SALARY, AND OTHER INCOME.—Any amount payable to or received by an individual as wages or salary for personal services, or as income derived from other sources, during any period, to the extent that the total of such amounts payable to or received by him during such period does not exceed the applicable exempt amount determined under subsection (d).

(10) CERTAIN SERVICE-CONNECTED DISABILITY PAYMENTS.—Any amount payable to an individual as a service-connected (within the meaning of section 101(16) of title 38, United States Code) disability benefit under—

(A) subchapter II, III, IV, V, or VI of chapter 11 of such title 38, or

(B) chapter 13, 21, 23, 31, 32, 34, 35, 37, or 39 of such title 38.

(11) CERTAIN PUBLIC ASSISTANCE PAYMENTS.—Any amount payable to an individual as a recipient of public assistance under—

(A) title IV or title XVI (relating to supplemental security income for the aged, blind, and disabled) of the Social Security Act, or

(B) State or local government public assistance or public welfare programs for which eligibility is determined by a needs or income test.

(12) ASSISTANCE UNDER JOB TRAINING PARTNERSHIP ACT.—Any amount payable to a participant under the Job Training Partnership Act (29 U.S.C. 1501 et seq.) from funds appropriated pursuant to such Act.

(13) RESIDENCES EXEMPT IN SMALL DEFICIENCY CASES AND PRINCIPAL RESIDENCES AND CERTAIN BUSINESS ASSETS EXEMPT IN ABSENCE OF CERTAIN APPROVAL OR JEOPARDY.—

(A) RESIDENCES IN SMALL DEFICIENCY CASES.—If the amount of the levy does not exceed $5,000—

(i) any real property used as a residence by the taxpayer; or

(ii) any real property of the taxpayer (other than real property which is rented) used by any other individual as a residence.

(B) PRINCIPAL RESIDENCES AND CERTAIN BUSINESS ASSETS.—Except to the extent provided in subsection (e)—

(i) the principal residence of the taxpayer (within the meaning of section 121); and

(ii) tangible personal property or real property (other than real property which is rented) used in the trade or business of an individual taxpayer.

Amendments

• **2018, Tax Technical Corrections Act of 2018 (P.L. 115-141)**

P.L. 115-141, § 401(a)(283), Div. U:

Amended Code Sec. 6334(a)(10)(A) by striking "V,," and inserting "V,". **Effective** 3-23-2018.

• **1998, IRS Restructuring and Reform Act of 1998 (P.L. 105-206)**

P.L. 105-206, § 3431(a):

Amended Code Sec. 6334(a)(2) by striking "$2,500" and inserting "$6,250". **Effective** with respect to levies issued after 7-22-98.

COLLECTION—SEIZURE OF PROPERTY

P.L. 105-206, § 3431(b):

Amended Code Sec. 6334(a)(3) by striking "$1,250" and inserting "$3,125". **Effective** with respect to levies issued after 7-22-98.

P.L. 105-206, § 3445(a):

Amended Code Sec. 6334(a)(13). **Effective** 7-22-98. Prior to amendment, Code Sec. 6334(a)(13) read as follows:

(13) PRINCIPAL RESIDENCE EXEMPT IN ABSENCE OF CERTAIN APPROVAL OR JEOPARDY.—Except to the extent provided in subsection (e), the principal residence of the taxpayer (within the meaning of section 121).

• **1997, Taxpayer Relief Act of 1997 (P.L. 105-34)**

P.L. 105-34, § 312(d)(1):

Amended Code Sec. 6334(a)(13) by striking "section 1034" and inserting "section 121". **Effective** for sales and exchanges after 5-6-97.

• **1996, Personal Responsibility and Work Opportunity Reconciliation Act of 1996 (P.L. 104-193)**

P.L. 104-193, § 110(l)(6):

Amended Code Sec. 6334(a)(11)(A) by striking "(relating to aid to families with dependent children)" after "title IV". **Effective** 7-1-97.

• **1996, Taxpayer Bill of Rights 2 (P.L. 104-168)**

P.L. 104-168, § 502(a)(1)-(3):

Amended Code Sec. 6334(a)(2) by striking "If the taxpayer is the head of a family, so" and inserting "So", by striking "his household" and inserting "the taxpayer's household", and by striking "$1,650 ($1,550 in the case of levies issued during 1989)" and inserting "$2,500". **Effective** with respect to levies issued after 12-31-96.

P.L. 104-168, § 502(b):

Amended Code Sec. 6334(a)(3) by striking "$1,100 ($1,050 in the case of levies issued during 1989)" and inserting "$1,250". **Effective** with respect to levies issued after 12-31-96.

• **1988, Technical and Miscellaneous Revenue Act of 1988 (P.L. 100-647)**

P.L. 100-647, § 1015(o)(1)-(3):

Amended Code Sec. 6334(a)(10) in subparagraph (A) by striking out "IV" and inserting in lieu thereof "III, IV, V," and by adding "or" at the end thereof, in subparagraph (C) by striking out "21," and inserting in lieu thereof "13, 21, 23," and by striking out subparagraph (B) and redesignating subparagraph (C) as subparagraph (B). **Effective** as if included in the provision of P.L. 99-514 to which it relates. Prior to amendment, Code Sec. 6334(a)(10)(B) read as follows:

(B) subchapter I, II, or III of chapter 19 of such title 38, or

P.L. 100-647, § 6236(c)(1):

Amended Code Sec. 6334(a)(2) by striking out "$1,500" and inserting in lieu thereof "$1,650 ($1,550 in the case of levies issued during 1989)". **Effective** for levies issued on or after 7-1-89.

P.L. 100-647, § 6236(c)(2):

Amended Code Sec. 6334(a)(3) by striking out "$1,000" and inserting in lieu thereof "$1,100 ($1,050 in the case of levies issued during 1989)". **Effective** for levies issued on or after 7-1-89.

P.L. 100-647, § 6236(c)(4)(A):

Amended Code Sec. 6334(a) by adding at the end thereof new paragraphs (11)-(13). **Effective** for levies issued on or after 7-1-89.

• **1986, Tax Reform Act of 1986 (P.L. 99-514)**

P.L. 99-514, § 1565(a):

Amended Code Sec. 6334(a) by adding at the end thereof new paragraph (10). **Effective** for amounts payable after 12-31-86.

• **1982, Tax Equity and Fiscal Responsibility Act of 1982 (P.L. 97-248)**

P.L. 97-248, § 347(a)(1):

Amended Code Sec. 6334(a)(2) by striking out "$500" and inserting "$1,500". **Effective** for levies made after 12-31-82.

P.L. 97-248, § 347(a)(2):

Amended Code Sec. 6334(a)(3) by striking out "$250" and inserting "$1,000". **Effective** for levies made after 12-31-82.

• **1976, Tax Reform Act of 1976 (P.L. 94-455)**

P.L. 94-455, § 1209(a):

Added Code Sec. 6334(a)(9). **Effective** for levies made after 2-28-77. [effective date changed by P.L. 94-528, § 2(c)].

P.L. 94-455, § 1209(c):

Amended the heading of Code Sec. 6334(a)(8). For **effective** date, see amendatory note for P.L. 94-455, § 1209(a). Prior to amendment, the heading of Code Sec. 6334(a)(8) read as follows:

"(8) SALARY, WAGES, OR OTHER INCOME.—"

• **1969, Tax Reform Act of 1969 (P.L. 91-172)**

P.L. 91-172, § 945(a):

Added paragraph (a)(8). **Effective** with respect to levies made 30 days or more after 12-30-69.

• **1966, Federal Tax Lien Act of 1966 (P.L. 89-719)**

P.L. 89-719, § 104(c):

Amended Code Sec. 6334(a) by deleting "or Territory" in paragraph (4) and by adding new paragraphs (6) and (7). **Effective**, generally, after 11-2-66. However, see the amendment note for Code Sec. 6323 for exceptions to this **effective** date.

• **1965, Excise Tax Reduction Act of 1965 (P.L. 89-44)**

P.L. 89-44, § 812(a):

Added paragraph (5) to Code Sec. 6334(a). **Effective** 6-21-65.

• **1958, Social Security Amendments of 1958 (P.L. 85-840)**

P.L. 85-840, § 406:

Added paragraph (4) to Code Sec. 6334(a). **Effective** 8-28-58.

[Sec. 6334(b)]

(b) APPRAISAL.—The officer seizing property of the type described in subsection (a) shall appraise and set aside to the owner the amount of such property declared to be exempt. If the taxpayer objects at the time of the seizure to the valuation fixed by the officer making the seizure, the Secretary shall summon three disinterested individuals who shall make the valuation.

Amendments

• **1976, Tax Reform Act of 1976 (P.L. 94-455)**

P.L. 94-455, § 1906(b)(13)(A):

Amended 1954 Code by substituting "Secretary" for "Secretary or his delegate" each place it appeared. **Effective** 2-1-77.

[Sec. 6334(c)]

(c) NO OTHER PROPERTY EXEMPT.—Notwithstanding any other law of the United States (including section 207 of the Social Security Act), no property or rights to property shall be exempt from levy other than the property specifically made exempt by subsection (a).

Amendments

• **1984, Deficit Reduction Act of 1984 (P.L. 98-369)**

P.L. 98-369, § 2661(o)(5):

Amended Code Sec. 6334(c) by adding "(including section 207 of the Social Security Act)" after "United States". **Effective** as if included in P.L. 98-21.

[Sec. 6334(d)]

(d) EXEMPT AMOUNT OF WAGES, SALARY, OR OTHER INCOME.—

(1) INDIVIDUALS ON WEEKLY BASIS.—In the case of an individual who is paid or receives all of his wages, salary, and other income on a weekly basis, the amount of the wages, salary, and other income payable to or received by him during any week which is exempt from levy under subsection (a)(9) shall be the exempt amount.

(2) EXEMPT AMOUNT.—For purposes of paragraph (1), the term "exempt amount" means an amount equal to—

(A) the sum of—

(i) the standard deduction, and

(ii) the aggregate amount of the deductions for personal exemptions allowed the taxpayer under section 151 in the taxable year in which such levy occurs, divided by

(B) 52.

COLLECTION—SEIZURE OF PROPERTY

Unless the taxpayer submits to the Secretary a written and properly verified statement specifying the facts necessary to determine the proper amount under subparagraph (A), subparagraph (A) shall be applied as if the taxpayer were a married individual filing a separate return with only 1 personal exemption.

(3) INDIVIDUALS ON BASIS OTHER THAN WEEKLY.—In the case of any individual not described in paragraph (1), the amount of the wages, salary, and other income payable to or received by him during any applicable pay period or other fiscal period (as determined under regulations prescribed by the Secretary) which is exempt from levy under subsection (a)(9) shall be an amount (determined under such regulations) which as nearly as possible will result in the same total exemption from levy for such individual over a period of time as he would have under paragraph (1) if (during such period of time) he were paid or received such wages, salary, and other income on a regular weekly basis.

(4) YEARS WHEN PERSONAL EXEMPTION AMOUNT IS ZERO.—

(A) IN GENERAL.—In the case of any taxable year in which the exemption amount under section 151(d) is zero, paragraph (2) shall not apply and for purposes of paragraph (1) the term "exempt amount" means an amount equal to—

(i) the sum of the amount determined under subparagraph (B) and the standard deduction, divided by

(ii) 52.

(B) AMOUNT DETERMINED.—For purposes of subparagraph (A), the amount determined under this subparagraph is $4,150 multiplied by the number of the taxpayer's dependents for the taxable year in which the levy occurs.

(C) INFLATION ADJUSTMENT.—In the case of any taxable year beginning in a calendar year after 2018, the $4,150 amount in subparagraph (B) shall be increased by an amount equal to—

(i) such dollar amount, multiplied by

(ii) the cost-of-living adjustment determined under section 1(f)(3) for the calendar year in which the taxable year begins, determined by substituting "2017" for "2016" in subparagraph (A)(ii) thereof.

If any increase determined under the preceding sentence is not a multiple of $100, such increase shall be rounded to the next lowest multiple of $100.

(D) VERIFIED STATEMENT.—Unless the taxpayer submits to the Secretary a written and properly verified statement specifying the facts necessary to determine the proper amount under subparagraph (A), subparagraph (A) shall be applied as if the taxpayer were a married individual filing a separate return with no dependents.

Amendments

• **2017, Tax Cuts and Jobs Act (P.L. 115-97)**

P.L. 115-97, §11041(d):

Amended Code Sec. 6334(d) by adding at the end a new paragraph (4). **Effective** for tax years beginning after 12-31-2017.

• **1988, Technical and Miscellaneous Revenue Act of 1988 (P.L. 100-647)**

P.L. 100-647, §6236(c)(3)(A):

Amended Code Sec. 6334(d)(1). **Effective** for levies issued on or after 7-1-89. Prior to amendment, Code Sec. 6334(d)(1) read as follows:

(1) INDIVIDUALS ON WEEKLY BASIS.—In the case of an individual who is paid or receives all of his wages, salary, and other income on a weekly basis, the amount of the wages, salary, and other income payable to or received by him during any week which is exempt from levy under subsection (a)(9) shall be—

(A) $75, plus

(B) $25 for each individual who is specified in a written statement which is submitted to the person on whom notice of levy is served and which is verified in such manner as the Secretary shall prescribe by regulations and—

(i) over half of whose support for the payroll period was received from the taxpayer,

(ii) who is the spouse of the taxpayer, or who bears a relationship to the taxpayer specified in paragraphs (1) through (9) of section 152(a) (relating to definition of dependents), and

(iii) who is not a minor child of the taxpayer with respect to whom amounts are exempt from levy under subsection (a)(8) for the payroll period.

For purposes of subparagraph (B)(ii) of the preceding sentence, "payroll period" shall be substituted for "taxable year" each place it appears in paragraph (9) of section 152(a).

P.L. 100-647, §6236(c)(3)(B):

Amended Code Sec. 6334(d) by redesignating paragraph (2) as paragraph (3) and by inserting after paragraph (1) new paragraph (2). **Effective** for levies issued on or after 7-1-89.

• **1982, Tax Equity and Fiscal Responsibility Act of 1982 (P.L. 97-248)**

P.L. 97-248, §347(a)(3):

Amended Code Sec. 6334(d)(1)(A) by striking out "$50" and inserting "$75" and by striking out "$15" and inserting "$25". **Effective** for levies made after 12-31-82.

• **1976, Tax Reform Act of 1976 (P.L. 94-455)**

P.L. 94-455, §1209(b):

Added Code Sec. 6334(d). For **effective** date, see amendatory note for P.L. 94-455, §1209(a), following Code Sec. 6334(a).

[Sec. 6334(e)]

(e) LEVY ALLOWED ON PRINCIPAL RESIDENCES AND CERTAIN BUSINESS ASSETS IN CERTAIN CIRCUMSTANCES.—

(1) PRINCIPAL RESIDENCES.—

(A) APPROVAL REQUIRED.—A principal residence shall not be exempt from levy if a judge or magistrate of a district court of the United States approves (in writing) the levy of such residence.

(B) JURISDICTION.—The district courts of the United States shall have exclusive jurisdiction to approve a levy under subparagraph (A).

(2) CERTAIN BUSINESS ASSETS.—Property (other than a principal residence) described in subsection (a)(13)(B) shall not be exempt from levy if—

(A) a district director or assistant district director of the Internal Revenue Service personally approves (in writing) the levy of such property; or

(B) the Secretary finds that the collection of tax is in jeopardy.

An official may not approve a levy under subparagraph (A) unless the official determines that the taxpayer's other assets subject to collection are insufficient to pay the amount due, together with expenses of the proceedings.

Amendments

• **1998, IRS Restructuring and Reform Act of 1998 (P.L. 105-206)**

P.L. 105-206, §3445(b):

Amended Code Sec. 6334(e). **Effective** 7-22-98. Prior to amendment, Code Sec. 6334(e) read as follows:

(e) LEVY ALLOWED ON PRINCIPAL RESIDENCE IN CASE OF JEOPARDY OR CERTAIN APPROVAL.—Property described in subsection (a)(13) shall not be exempt from levy if—

(1) a district director or assistant district director of the Internal Revenue Service personally approves (in writing) the levy of such property, or

(2) the Secretary finds that the collection of tax is in jeopardy.

P.L. 105-206, §3445(c)(1)-(2), provides:

(1) IN GENERAL.—With respect to permits issued by a State and required under State law for the harvest of fish or wildlife in the trade or business of an individual taxpayer, the term "other assets" as used in section 6334(e)(2) of the Internal Revenue Code of 1986 shall include future income which may be derived by such taxpayer from the commercial sale of fish or wildlife under such permit.

(2) CONSTRUCTION.—Paragraph (1) shall not be construed to invalidate or in any way prejudice any assertion that the privilege embodied in permits described in paragraph (1) is not property or a right to property under the Internal Revenue Code of 1986.

• **1988, Technical and Miscellaneous Revenue Act of 1988 (P.L. 100-647)**

P.L. 100-647, §6236(c)(4)(B):

Amended Code Sec. 6334 by adding at the end thereof new subsection (e). **Effective** for levies issued on or after 7-1-89.

COLLECTION—SEIZURE OF PROPERTY

[Sec. 6334(f)]

(f) LEVY ALLOWED ON CERTAIN SPECIFIED PAYMENTS.—Any payment described in subparagraph (B) or (C) of section 6331(h)(2) shall not be exempt from levy if the Secretary approves the levy thereon under section 6331(h).

Amendments

• **1997, Taxpayer Relief Act of 1997 (P.L. 105-34)**

P.L. 105-34, §1025(a):

Amended Code Sec. 6334 by redesignating subsection (f) as subsection (g) and by inserting after subsection (e) a new subsection (f). **Effective** for levies issued after 8-5-97.

[Sec. 6334(g)]

(g) INFLATION ADJUSTMENT.—

(1) IN GENERAL.—In the case of any calendar year beginning after 1999, each dollar amount referred to in paragraphs (2) and (3) of subsection (a) shall be increased by an amount equal to—

(A) such dollar amount, multiplied by

(B) the cost-of-living adjustment determined under section 1(f)(3) for such calendar year, by substituting "calendar year 1998" for "calendar year 2016" in subparagraph (A)(ii) thereof.

(2) ROUNDING.—If any dollar amount after being increased under paragraph (1) is not a multiple of $10, such dollar amount shall be rounded to the nearest multiple of $10.

Amendments

• **2017, Tax Cuts and Jobs Act (P.L. 115-97)**

P.L. 115-97, §11002(d)(1)(II):

Amended Code Sec. 6334(g)(1)(B) by striking "for 'calendar year 1992'" in subparagraph (B)" and inserting "for 'calendar year 2016' in subparagraph (A)(ii)". **Effective** for tax years beginning after 12-31-2017.

• **1998, IRS Restructuring and Reform Act of 1998 (P.L. 105-206)**

P.L. 105-206, §3431(c)(1):

Amended Code Sec. 6334(g)(1) by striking "1997" and inserting "1999". **Effective** with respect to levies issued after 7-22-98.

P.L. 105-206, §3431(c)(2):

Amended Code Sec. 6334(g)(1)(B) by striking "1996" and inserting "1998". **Effective** with respect to levies issued after 7-22-98.

• **1997, Taxpayer Relief Act of 1997 (P.L. 105-34)**

P.L. 105-34, §1025(a):

Amended Code Sec. 6334 by redesignating subsection (f) as subsection (g). **Effective** for levies issued after 8-5-97.

• **1996, Taxpayer Bill of Rights 2 (P.L. 104-168)**

P.L. 104-168, §502(c):

Amended Code Sec. 6334 by adding at the end a new subsection (f). **Effective** with respect to levies issued after 12-31-96.

[Sec. 6335]

SEC. 6335. SALE OF SEIZED PROPERTY.

[Sec. 6335(a)]

(a) NOTICE OF SEIZURE.—As soon as practicable after seizure of property, notice in writing shall be given by the Secretary to the owner of the property (or, in the case of personal property, the possessor thereof), or shall be left at his usual place of abode or business if he has such within the internal revenue district where the seizure is made. If the owner cannot be readily located, or has no dwelling or place of business within such district, the notice may be mailed to his last known address. Such notice shall specify the sum demanded and shall contain, in the case of personal property, an account of the property seized and, in the case of real property, a description with reasonable certainty of the property seized.

Amendments

• **1976, Tax Reform Act of 1976 (P.L. 94-455)**

P.L. 94-455, §1906(b)(13)(A):

Amended 1954 Code by substituting "Secretary" for "Secretary or his delegate" each place it appeared. **Effective** 2-1-77.

[Sec. 6335(b)]

(b) NOTICE OF SALE.—The Secretary shall as soon as practicable after the seizure of the property give notice to the owner, in the manner prescribed in subsection (a), and shall cause a notification to be published in some newspaper published or generally circulated within the county wherein such seizure is made, or, if there be no newspaper published or generally circulated in such county, shall post such notice at the post office nearest the place where the seizure is made, and in not less than two other public places. Such notice shall specify the property to be sold, and the time, place, manner, and conditions of the sale thereof. Whenever levy is made without regard to the 10-day period provided in section 6331(a), public notice of sale of the property seized shall not be made within such 10-day period unless section 6336 (relating to sale of perishable goods) is applicable.

Amendments

• **1976, Tax Reform Act of 1976 (P.L. 94-455)**

P.L. 94-455, §1906(b)(13)(A):

Amended 1954 Code by substituting "Secretary" for "Secretary or his delegate" each place it appeared. **Effective** 2-1-77.

• **1966, Federal Tax Lien Act of 1966 (P.L. 89-719)**

P.L. 89-719, §104(d):

Amended the first sentence of Code Sec. 6335(b). **Effective**, generally, after 11-2-66. However, see the amendment note for Code Sec. 6323 for exceptions to this **effective** date. Prior to amendment, the first sentence read as follows:

"The Secretary or his delegate shall as soon as practicable after the seizure of the property give notice to the owner, in the same manner as that prescribed in subsection (a), and shall cause a notification to be published in some newspaper within the county wherein such seizure is made, or, if there be no newspaper published in such county, shall post such notice at the post office nearest the place where the seizure is made, and in not less than two other public places."

[Sec. 6335(c)]

(c) SALE OF INDIVISIBLE PROPERTY.—If any property liable to levy is not divisible, so as to enable the Secretary by sale of a part thereof to raise the whole amount of the tax and expenses, the whole of such property shall be sold.

Amendments

• **1976, Tax Reform Act of 1976 (P.L. 94-455)**

P.L. 94-455, §1906(b)(13)(A):

Amended 1954 Code by substituting "Secretary" for "Secretary or his delegate" each place it appeared. **Effective** 2-1-77.

COLLECTION—SEIZURE OF PROPERTY

[Sec. 6335(d)]

(d) TIME AND PLACE OF SALE.—The time of sale shall not be less than 10 days nor more than 40 days from the time of giving public notice under subsection (b). The place of sale shall be within the county in which the property is seized, except by special order of the Secretary.

Amendments

• **1976, Tax Reform Act of 1976 (P.L. 94-455)**

P.L. 94-455, §1906(b)(13)(A):

Amended 1954 Code by substituting "Secretary" for "Secretary or his delegate" each place it appeared. **Effective** 2-1-77.

[Sec. 6335(e)]

(e) MANNER AND CONDITIONS OF SALE.—

(1) IN GENERAL.—

(A) DETERMINATIONS RELATING TO MINIMUM PRICE.—Before the sale of property seized by levy, the Secretary shall determine—

(i) a minimum price below which such property shall not be sold (taking into account the expense of making the levy and conducting the sale), and

(ii) whether, on the basis of criteria prescribed by the Secretary, the purchase of such property by the United States at such minimum price would be in the best interest of the United States.

(B) SALE TO HIGHEST BIDDER AT OR ABOVE MINIMUM PRICE.—If, at the sale, one or more persons offer to purchase such property for not less than the amount of the minimum price, the property shall be declared sold to the highest bidder.

(C) PROPERTY DEEMED SOLD TO UNITED STATES AT MINIMUM PRICE IN CERTAIN CASES.—If no person offers the amount of the minimum price for such property at the sale and the Secretary has determined that the purchase of such property by the United States would be in the best interest of the United States, the property shall be declared to be sold to the United States at such minimum price.

(D) RELEASE TO OWNER IN OTHER CASES.—If, at the sale, the property is not declared sold under subparagraph (B) or (C), the property shall be released to the owner thereof and the expense of the levy and sale shall be added to the amount of tax for the collection of which the levy was made. Any property released under this subparagraph shall remain subject to any lien imposed by subchapter C.

(2) ADDITIONAL RULES APPLICABLE TO SALE.—The Secretary shall by regulations prescribe the manner and other conditions of the sale of property seized by levy. If one or more alternative methods or conditions are permitted by regulations, the Secretary shall select the alternatives applicable to the sale. Such regulations shall provide:

(A) That the sale shall not be conducted in any manner other than—

(i) by public auction, or

(ii) by public sale under sealed bids.

(B) In the case of the seizure of several items of property, whether such items shall be offered separately, in groups, or in the aggregate; and whether such property shall be offered both separately (or in groups) and in the aggregate, and sold under whichever method produces the highest aggregate amount.

(C) Whether the announcement of the minimum price determined by the Secretary may be delayed until the receipt of the highest bid.

(D) Whether payment in full shall be required at the time of acceptance of a bid, or whether a part of such payment may be deferred for such period (not to exceed 1 month) as may be determined by the Secretary to be appropriate.

(E) The extent to which methods (including advertising) in addition to those prescribed in subsection (b) may be used in giving notice of the sale.

(F) Under what circumstances the Secretary may adjourn the sale from time to time (but such adjournments shall not be for a period to exceed in all 1 month).

(3) PAYMENT OF AMOUNT BID.—If payment in full is required at the time of acceptance of a bid and is not then and there paid, the Secretary shall forthwith proceed to again sell the property in the manner provided in this subsection. If the conditions of the sale permit part of the payment to be deferred, and if such part is not paid within the prescribed period, suit may be instituted against the purchaser for the purchase price or such part thereof as has not been paid, together with interest at the rate of 6 percent per annum from the date of the sale; or, in the discretion of the Secretary, the sale may be declared by the Secretary to be null and void for failure to make full payment of the purchase price and the property may again be advertised and sold as provided in subsections (b) and (c) and this subsection. In the event of such readvertisement and sale any new purchaser shall receive such property or rights to property, free and clear of any claim or right of the former defaulting purchaser, of any nature whatsoever, and the amount paid upon the bid price by such defaulting purchaser shall be forfeited.

(4) CROSS REFERENCE.—

For provision providing for civil damages for violation of paragraph (1)(A)(i), see section 7433.

Amendments

• **1998, IRS Restructuring and Reform Act of 1998 (P.L. 105-206)**

P.L. 105-206, §3441(a):

Amended Code Sec. 6335(e)(1)(A)(i) by striking "a minimum price for which such property shall be sold" and inserting "a minimum price below which such property shall not be sold". **Effective** for sales made after 7-22-98.

P.L. 105-206, §3441(b):

Amended Code Sec. 6335(e) by adding a new paragraph (4). **Effective** for sales made after 7-22-98.

P.L. 105-206, §3443, provides:

SEC. 3443. UNIFORM ASSET DISPOSAL MECHANISM.

Not later than the date which is 2 years after the date of the enactment of this Act, the Secretary of the Treasury or the Secretary's delegate shall implement a uniform asset disposal mechanism for sales under section 6335 of the Internal Revenue Code of 1986. The mechanism should be designed to remove any participation in such sales by revenue officers of the Internal Revenue Service and should consider the use of outsourcing.

• **1986, Tax Reform Act of 1986 (P.L. 99-514)**

P.L. 99-514, §1570(a):

Amended Code Sec. 6335(e)(1). **Effective** for property seized after 10-22-86, and property seized on or before such date which is held by the United States on such date. Prior to amendment, paragraph (1) read as follows:

(1) MINIMUM PRICE.—Before the sale the Secretary shall determine a minimum price for which the property shall be sold, and if no person offers for such property at the sale the amount of the minimum price, the property shall be declared to be purchased at such price for the United States; otherwise the property shall be declared to be sold to the highest bidder. In determining the minimum price, the Secretary shall take into account the expense of making the levy and sale.

• **1976, Tax Reform Act of 1976 (P.L. 94-455)**

P.L. 94-455, §1906(b)(13)(A):

Amended 1954 Code by substituting "Secretary" for "Secretary or his delegate" each place it appeared. **Effective** 2-1-77.

[Sec. 6335(f)]

(f) RIGHT TO REQUEST SALE OF SEIZED PROPERTY WITHIN 60 DAYS.—The owner of any property seized by levy may request that the Secretary sell such property within 60 days after such request (or within such longer period as may be specified by the owner). The Secretary shall comply with such request unless the Secretary determines (and notifies the owner within such period) that such compliance would not be in the best interests of the United States.

COLLECTION—SEIZURE OF PROPERTY

Amendments

• **1988, Technical and Miscellaneous Revenue Act of 1988 (P.L. 100-647)**

P.L. 100-647, §6236(g):

Amended Code Sec. 6335 by redesignating subsection (f) as subsection (g) and by inserting after subsection (e) new subsection (f). **Effective** for requests made on or after 1-1-89.

[Sec. 6335(g)]

(g) STAY OF SALE OF SEIZED PROPERTY PENDING TAX COURT DECISION.—

For restrictions on sale of seized property pending Tax Court decision, see section 6863(b)(3).

Amendments

• **1988, Technical and Miscellaneous Revenue Act of 1988 (P.L. 100-647)**

P.L. 100-647, §6236(g):

Amended Code Sec. 6335 by redesignating subsection (f) as subsection (g). **Effective** for requests made on or after 1-1-89.

[Sec. 6336]

SEC. 6336. SALE OF PERISHABLE GOODS.

If the Secretary determines that any property seized is liable to perish, he shall appraise the value of such property and—

(1) RETURN TO OWNER.—If the owner of the property can be readily found, the Secretary shall give him notice of such determination of the appraised value of the property. The property shall be returned to the owner if, within such time as may be specified in the notice, the owner—

(A) Pays to the Secretary an amount equal to the appraised value, or

(B) Gives bond in such form, with such sureties, and in such amount as the Secretary shall prescribe to pay the appraised amount at such time as the Secretary determines to be appropriate in the circumstances.

(2) IMMEDIATE SALE.—If the owner does not pay such amount or furnish such bond in accordance with this section, the Secretary shall as soon as practicable make public sale of the property in accordance with such regulations as may be prescribed by the Secretary.

Amendments

• **2019, Taxpayer First Act (P.L. 116-25)**

P.L. 116-25, §1404(a):

Amended Code Sec. 6336 by striking "or become greatly reduced in price or value by keeping, or that such property cannot be kept without great expense" following "is liable to perish". **Effective** for property seized after 7-1-2019.

• **1976, Tax Reform Act of 1976 (P.L. 94-455)**

P.L. 94-455, §1906(b)(13)(A):

Amended 1954 Code by substituting "Secretary" for "Secretary or his delegate" each place it appeared. **Effective** 2-1-77.

[Sec. 6337]

SEC. 6337. REDEMPTION OF PROPERTY.

[Sec. 6337(a)]

(a) BEFORE SALE.—Any person whose property has been levied upon shall have the right to pay the amount due, together with the expenses of the proceeding, if any, to the Secretary at any time prior to the sale thereof, and upon such payment the Secretary shall restore such property to him, and all further proceedings in connection with the levy on such property shall cease from the time of such payment.

Amendments

• **1976, Tax Reform Act of 1976 (P.L. 94-455)**

P.L. 94-455, §1906(b)(13)(A):

Amended 1954 Code by substituting "Secretary" for "Secretary or his delegate" each place it appeared. **Effective** 2-1-77.

[Sec. 6337(b)]

(b) REDEMPTION OF REAL ESTATE AFTER SALE.—

(1) PERIOD.—The owners of any real property sold as provided in section 6335, their heirs, executors, or administrators, or any person having any interest therein, or a lien thereon, or any person in their behalf, shall be permitted to redeem the property sold, or any particular tract of such property, at any time within 180 days after the sale thereof.

(2) PRICE.—Such property or tract of property shall be permitted to be redeemed upon payment to the purchaser, or in case he cannot be found in the county in which the property to be redeemed is situated, then to the Secretary, for the use of the purchaser, his heirs, or assigns, the amount paid by such purchaser and interest thereon at the rate of 20 percent per annum.

Amendments

• **1982, Tax Equity and Fiscal Responsibility Act of 1982 (P.L. 97-248)**

P.L. 97-248, §349A(a):

Amended Code Sec. 6337(b)(1) by striking out "120 days" and inserting "180 days". **Effective** with respect to property sold after 9-3-82.

• **1976, Tax Reform Act of 1976 (P.L. 94-455)**

P.L. 94-455, §1906(b)(13)(A):

Amended 1954 Code by substituting "Secretary" for "Secretary or his delegate" each place it appeared. **Effective** 2-1-77.

• **1966, Federal Tax Lien Act of 1966 (P.L. 89-719)**

P.L. 89-719, §104(e):

Amended Code Sec. 6337(b)(1) by substituting "120 days" for "1 year". **Effective**, generally, after 11-2-66. However, see the amendment note for Code Sec. 6323 for exceptions to this **effective** date.

[Sec. 6337(c)]

(c) RECORD.—When any lands sold are redeemed as provided in this section, the Secretary shall cause entry of the fact to be made upon the record mentioned in section 6340, and such entry shall be evidence of such redemption.

Amendments

• **1976, Tax Reform Act of 1976 (P.L. 94-455)**

P.L. 94-455, §1906(b)(13)(A):

Amended 1954 Code by substituting "Secretary" for "Secretary or his delegate" each place it appeared. **Effective** 2-1-77.

COLLECTION—SEIZURE OF PROPERTY

[Sec. 6338]

SEC. 6338. CERTIFICATE OF SALE; DEED OF REAL PROPERTY.

[Sec. 6338(a)]

(a) CERTIFICATE OF SALE.—In the case of property sold as provided in section 6335, the Secretary shall give to the purchaser a certificate of sale upon payment in full of the purchase price. In the case of real property, such certificate shall set forth the real property purchased, for whose taxes the same was sold, the name of the purchaser, and the price paid therefor.

Amendments

• 1976, Tax Reform Act of 1976 (P.L. 94-455)

P.L. 94-455, §1906(b)(13)(A):

Amended 1954 Code by substituting "Secretary" for "Secretary or his delegate" each place it appeared. **Effective** 2-1-77.

[Sec. 6338(b)]

(b) DEED TO REAL PROPERTY.—In the case of any real property sold as provided in section 6335 and not redeemed in the manner and within the time provided in section 6337, the Secretary shall execute (in accordance with the laws of the State in which such real property is situated pertaining to sales of real property under execution) to the purchaser of such real property at such sale, upon his surrender of the certificate of sale, a deed of the real property so purchased by him, reciting the facts set forth in the certificate.

Amendments

• 1976, Tax Reform Act of 1976 (P.L. 94-455)

P.L. 94-455, §1906(b)(13)(A):

Amended 1954 Code by substituting "Secretary" for "Secretary or his delegate" each place it appeared. **Effective** 2-1-77.

[Sec. 6338(c)]

(c) REAL PROPERTY PURCHASED BY UNITED STATES.—If real property is declared purchased by the United States at a sale pursuant to section 6335, the Secretary shall at the proper time execute a deed therefor, and without delay cause such deed to be duly recorded in the proper registry of deeds.

Amendments

• 1976, Tax Reform Act of 1976 (P.L. 94-455)

P.L. 94-455, §1906(b)(13)(A):

Amended 1954 Code by substituting "Secretary" for "Secretary or his delegate" each place it appeared. **Effective** 2-1-77.

• 1966, Federal Tax Lien Act of 1966 (P.L. 89-719)

P.L. 89-719, §104(f):

Amended Code Sec. 6338(c). **Effective** generally after 11-2-66. However, see the amendment note for Code Sec. 6323 for exceptions to this **effective** date. Prior to amendment, Code Sec. 6338(c) read as follows:

"(c) Real Property Purchased by United States.—If real property is declared purchased by the United States at a sale pursuant to section 6335, the Secretary or his delegate shall at the proper time execute a deed therefor after its preparation and the endorsement of approval as to its form by the United States attorney for the district in which the property is situated, and the Secretary or his delegate shall, without delay, cause the deed to be duly recorded in the proper registry of deeds."

• 1958, Technical Amendments Act of 1958 (P.L. 85-866)

P.L. 85-866, §78:

Amended Code Sec. 6338(c) by striking out the word "district" where it appeared in the phrase "United States district attorney". **Effective** 1-1-54.

[Sec. 6339]

SEC. 6339. LEGAL EFFECT OF CERTIFICATE OF SALE OF PERSONAL PROPERTY AND DEED OF REAL PROPERTY.

[Sec. 6339(a)]

(a) CERTIFICATE OF SALE OF PROPERTY OTHER THAN REAL PROPERTY.—In all cases of sale pursuant to section 6335 of property (other than real property), the certificate of such sale—

(1) AS EVIDENCE.—Shall be prima facie evidence of the right of the officer to make such sale, and conclusive evidence of the regularity of his proceedings in making the sale; and

(2) AS CONVEYANCES.—Shall transfer to the purchaser all right, title, and interest of the party delinquent in and to the property sold; and

(3) AS AUTHORITY FOR TRANSFER OF CORPORATE STOCK.—If such property consists of stocks, shall be notice, when received, to any corporation, company, or association of such transfer, and shall be authority to such corporation, company, or association to record the transfer on its books and records in the same manner as if the stocks were transferred or assigned by the party holding the same, in lieu of any original or prior certificate, which shall be void, whether canceled or not; and

(4) AS RECEIPTS.—If the subject of sale is securities or other evidences of debt, shall be a good and valid receipt to the person holding the same, as against any person holding or claiming to hold possession of such securities or other evidences of debt; and

(5) AS AUTHORITY FOR TRANSFER OF TITLE TO MOTOR VEHICLE.—If such property consists of a motor vehicle, shall be notice, when received, to any public official charged with the registration of title to motor vehicles, of such transfer and shall be authority to such official to record the transfer on his books and records in the same manner as if the certificate of title to such motor vehicle were transferred or assigned by the party holding the same, in lieu of any original or prior certificate, which shall be void, whether canceled or not.

[Sec. 6339(b)]

(b) DEED OF REAL PROPERTY.—In the case of the sale of real property pursuant to section 6335—

(1) DEED AS EVIDENCE.—The deed of sale given pursuant to section 6338 shall be prima facie evidence of the facts therein stated; and

(2) DEED AS CONVEYANCE OF TITLE.—If the proceedings of the Secretary as set forth have been substantially in accordance with the provisions of law, such deed shall be considered and operate as a conveyance of all the right, title, and interest the party delinquent had in and to the real property thus sold at the time the lien of the United States attached thereto.

Amendments

• 1976, Tax Reform Act of 1976 (P.L. 94-455)

P.L. 94-455, §1906(b)(13)(A):

Amended 1954 Code by substituting "Secretary" for "Secretary or his delegate" each place it appeared. **Effective** 2-1-77.

• 1958, Technical Amendments Act of 1958 (P.L. 85-866)

P.L. 85-866, §79:

The heading for Code Sec. 6339(b)(2) which formerly read "Deed of Conveyance of Title.—" was amended. **Effective** 1-1-54.

[Sec. 6339(c)]

(c) EFFECT OF JUNIOR ENCUMBRANCES.—A certificate of sale of personal property given or a deed to real property executed pursuant to section 6338 shall discharge such property from all liens, encumbrances, and titles over which the lien of the United States with respect to which the levy was made had priority.

Sec. 6338

COLLECTION—SEIZURE OF PROPERTY

[Sec. 6339(d)]

(d) CROSS REFERENCES.—

(1) For distribution of surplus proceeds, see section 6342(b).

(2) For judicial procedure with respect to surplus proceeds, see section 7426(a)(2).

Amendments

• **1966, Federal Tax Lien Act of 1966 (P.L. 89-719)**

P.L. 89-719, §104(g):

Added Code Sec. 6339(c) and (d). **Effective**, generally, after 11-2-66. However, see the amendment note for Code Sec. 6323 for exceptions to this **effective** date.

[Sec. 6340]

SEC. 6340. RECORDS OF SALE.

[Sec. 6340(a)]

(a) REQUIREMENT.—The Secretary shall, for each internal revenue district, keep a record of all sales of property under section 6335 and of redemptions of such property. The record shall set forth the tax for which any such sale was made, the dates of seizure and sale, the name of the party assessed and all proceedings in making such sale, the amount of expenses, the names of the purchasers, and the date of the deed or certificate of sale of personal property.

Amendments

• **1998, IRS Restructuring and Reform Act of 1998 (P.L. 105-206)**

P.L. 105-206, §3442(a)(1)(A)-(B):

Amended Code Sec. 6340(a) by striking "real" after "sales of", and by inserting "or certificate of sale of personal property" after "deed". **Effective** for seizures occurring after 7-22-98.

• **1976, Tax Reform Act of 1976 (P.L. 94-455)**

P.L. 94-455, §1906(b)(13)(A):

Amended 1954 Code by substituting "Secretary" for "Secretary or his delegate" each place it appeared. **Effective** 2-1-77.

[Sec. 6340(b)]

(b) COPY AS EVIDENCE.—A copy of such record, or any part thereof, certified by the Secretary shall be evidence in any court of the truth of the facts therein stated.

Amendments

• **1976, Tax Reform Act of 1976 (P.L. 94-455)**

P.L. 94-455, §1906(b)(13)(A):

Amended 1954 Code by substituting "Secretary" for "Secretary or his delegate" each place it appeared. **Effective** 2-1-77.

[Sec. 6340(c)]

(c) ACCOUNTING TO TAXPAYER.—The taxpayer with respect to whose liability the sale was conducted or who redeemed the property shall be furnished—

(1) the record under subsection (a) (other than the names of the purchasers);

(2) the amount from such sale applied to the taxpayer's liability; and

(3) the remaining balance of such liability.

Amendments

• **1998, IRS Restructuring and Reform Act of 1998 (P.L. 105-206)**

P.L. 105-206, §3442(a)(2):

Amended Code Sec. 6340 by adding at the end a new subsection (c). **Effective** for seizures occurring after the date of the enactment of this Act.

[Sec. 6341]

SEC. 6341. EXPENSE OF LEVY AND SALE.

The Secretary shall determine the expenses to be allowed in all cases of levy and sale.

Amendments

• **1976, Tax Reform Act of 1976 (P.L. 94-455)**

P.L. 94-455, §1906(b)(13)(A):

Amended 1954 Code by substituting "Secretary" for "Secretary or his delegate" each place it appeared. **Effective** 2-1-77.

[Sec. 6342]

SEC. 6342. APPLICATION OF PROCEEDS OF LEVY.

[Sec. 6342(a)]

(a) COLLECTION OF LIABILITY.—Any money realized by proceedings under this subchapter (whether by seizure, by surrender under section 6332 (except pursuant to subsection (d)(2) thereof), or by sale of seized property) or by sale of property redeemed by the United States (if the interest of the United States in such property was a lien arising under the provisions of this title) shall be applied as follows:

(1) EXPENSE OF LEVY AND SALE.—First, against the expenses of the proceedings;

(2) SPECIFIC TAX LIABILITY ON SEIZED PROPERTY.—If the property seized and sold is subject to a tax imposed by any internal revenue law which has not been paid, the amount remaining after applying paragraph (1) shall then be applied against such tax liability (and, if such tax was not previously assessed, it shall then be assessed);

(3) LIABILITY OF DELINQUENT TAXPAYER.—The amount, if any, remaining after applying paragraphs (1) and (2) shall then be applied against the liability in respect of which the levy was made or the sale was conducted.

Amendments

• **2018, Tax Technical Corrections Act of 2018 (P.L. 115-141)**

P.L. 115-141, §401(a)(284), Div. U:

Amended Code Sec. 6342(a) by striking "subsection (c)(2)" and inserting "subsection (d)(2)". **Effective** 3-23-2018.

• **1966, Federal Tax Lien Act of 1966 (P.L. 89-719),**

P.L. 89-719, §104(h):

Amended Code Sec. 6342(a) (preceding paragraph (1)). **Effective**, generally, after 11-2-66. See, however, the amendment note for Code Sec. 6323 for exceptions to this

COLLECTION—SEIZURE OF PROPERTY

effective date. Prior to amendment, such portion of Code Sec. 6342 (a) read as follows:

"(a) Collection of Liability.—Any money realized by proceedings under this subchapter (whether by seizure, by surrender under section 6332, or by sale of seized property) shall be applied as follows:". Amended Code Sec. 6342(a)(1) by striking out "under this subchapter" and amended Code Sec. 6342(a)(3) by adding "or the sale was conducted" after "levy was made".

[Sec. 6342(b)]

(b) SURPLUS PROCEEDS.—Any surplus proceeds remaining after the application of subsection (a) shall, upon application and satisfactory proof in support thereof, be credited or refunded by the Secretary to the person or persons legally entitled thereto.

Amendments

• **1976, Tax Reform Act of 1976 (P.L. 94-455)**

P.L. 94-455, § 1906(b)(13)(A):

Amended 1954 Code by substituting "Secretary" for "Secretary or his delegate" each place it appeared. **Effective** 2-1-77.

[Sec. 6343]

SEC. 6343. AUTHORITY TO RELEASE LEVY AND RETURN PROPERTY.

[Sec. 6343(a)]

(a) RELEASE OF LEVY AND NOTICE OF RELEASE.—

(1) IN GENERAL.—Under regulations prescribed by the Secretary, the Secretary shall release the levy upon all, or part of, the property or rights to property levied upon and shall promptly notify the person upon whom such levy was made (if any) that such levy has been released if—

(A) the liability for which such levy was made is satisfied or becomes unenforceable by reason of lapse of time,

(B) release of such levy will facilitate the collection of such liability,

(C) the taxpayer has entered into an agreement under section 6159 to satisfy such liability by means of installment payments, unless such agreement provides otherwise,

(D) the Secretary has determined that such levy is creating an economic hardship due to the financial condition of the taxpayer, or

(E) the fair market value of the property exceeds such liability and release of the levy on a part of such property could be made without hindering the collection of such liability.

For purposes of subparagraph (C), the Secretary is not required to release such levy if such release would jeopardize the secured creditor status of the Secretary.

(2) EXPEDITED DETERMINATION ON CERTAIN BUSINESS PROPERTY.—In the case of any tangible personal property essential in carrying on the trade or business of the taxpayer, the Secretary shall provide for an expedited determination under paragraph (1) if levy on such tangible personal property would prevent the taxpayer from carrying on such trade or business.

(3) SUBSEQUENT LEVY.—The release of levy on any property under paragraph (1) shall not prevent any subsequent levy on such property.

Amendments

• **1988, Technical and Miscellaneous Revenue Act of 1988 (P.L. 100-647)**

P.L. 100-647, § 6236(f):

Amended Code Sec. 6343(a). **Effective** for levies issued on or after 7-1-89. Prior to amendment, Code Sec. 6343(a) read as follows:

(a) RELEASE OF LEVY.—It shall be lawful for the Secretary, under regulations prescribed by the Secretary, to release the levy upon all or part of the property or rights to property levied upon where the Secretary determines that such action will facilitate the collection of the liability, but such release shall not operate to prevent any subsequent levy.

• **1976, Tax Reform Act of 1976 (P.L. 94-455)**

P.L. 94-455, § 1906(b)(13)(A):

Amended 1954 Code by substituting "Secretary" for "Secretary or his delegate" each place it appeared. **Effective** 2-1-77.

[Sec. 6343(b)]

(b) RETURN OF PROPERTY.—If the Secretary determines that property has been wrongfully levied upon, it shall be lawful for the Secretary to return—

(1) the specific property levied upon,

(2) an amount of money equal to the amount of money levied upon, or

(3) an amount of money equal to the amount of money received by the United States from a sale of such property.

Property may be returned at any time. An amount equal to the amount of money levied upon or received from such sale may be returned at any time before the expiration of 2 years from the date of such levy. For purposes of paragraph (3), if property is declared purchased by the United States at a sale pursuant to section 6335(e) (relating to manner and conditions of sale), the United States shall be treated as having received an amount of money equal to the minimum price determined pursuant to such section or (if larger) the amount received by the United States from the resale of such property.

Amendments

• **2017, Tax Cuts and Jobs Act (P.L. 115-97)**

P.L. 115-97, § 11071(a):

Amended Code Sec. 6343(b) by striking "9 months" and inserting "2 years". For the **effective** date, see Act Sec. 11071(c), below.

P.L. 115-97, § 11071(c), provides:

(c) EFFECTIVE DATE.—The amendments made by this section shall apply to—

(1) levies made after the date of the enactment of this Act, and

(2) levies made on or before such date if the 9-month period has not expired under section 6343(b) of the Internal Revenue Code of 1986 (without regard to this section) as of such date.

• **1976, Tax Reform Act of 1976 (P.L. 94-455)**

P.L. 94-455, § 1906(b)(13)(A):

Amended 1954 Code by substituting "Secretary" for "Secretary or his delegate" each place it appeared. **Effective** 2-1-77.

• **1966, Federal Tax Lien Act of 1966 (P.L. 89-719)**

P.L. 89-719, § 104(i):

Amended Code Sec. 6343 by adding "AND RETURN PROPERTY" in the title, by adding "(a) Release of Levy.—" immediately before "It shall be lawful", and by adding new subsection (b). **Effective**, generally, after 11-2-66. However, see the amendment note for Code Sec. 6323 for exceptions to this **effective** date.

[Sec. 6343(c)]

(c) INTEREST.—Interest shall be allowed and paid at the overpayment rate established under section 6621—

(1) in a case described in subsection (b)(2), from the date the Secretary receives the money to a date (to be determined by the Secretary) preceding the date of return by not more than 30 days, or

(2) in a case described in subsection (b)(3), from the date of the sale of the property to a date (to be determined by the Secretary) preceding the date of return by not more than 30 days.

Sec. 6342(b)

COLLECTION—SEIZURE OF PROPERTY

Amendments

• **1986, Tax Reform Act of 1986 (P.L. 99-514)**

P.L. 99-514, §1511(c)(10):

Amended Code Sec. 6343(c) by striking out "an annual rate established under section 6621" and inserting in lieu thereof "the overpayment rate established under section 6621". **Effective** for purposes of determining interest for periods after 12-31-86.

• **1979 (P.L. 96-167)**

P.L. 96-167, §4:

Added new Code Sec. 6343(c). **Effective** for levies made after 12-29-79.

[Sec. 6343(d)]

(d) RETURN OF PROPERTY IN CERTAIN CASES.—If—

(1) any property has been levied upon, and

(2) the Secretary determines that—

(A) the levy on such property was premature or otherwise not in accordance with administrative procedures of the Secretary,

(B) the taxpayer has entered into an agreement under section 6159 to satisfy the tax liability for which the levy was imposed by means of installment payments, unless such agreement provides otherwise,

(C) the return of such property will facilitate the collection of the tax liability, or

(D) with the consent of the taxpayer or the National Taxpayer Advocate, the return of such property would be in the best interests of the taxpayer (as determined by the National Taxpayer Advocate) and the United States,

the provisions of subsection (b) shall apply in the same manner as if such property had been wrongly levied upon, except that no interest shall be allowed under subsection (c).

Amendments

• **1998, IRS Restructuring and Reform Act of 1998 (P.L. 105-206)**

P.L. 105-206, §1102(d)(1)(B):

Amended Code Sec. 6343(d)(2)(D) by striking "Taxpayer Advocate" each place it appears and inserting "National Taxpayer Advocate". **Effective** 7-22-98. For a special rule, see Act Sec. 1102 (f)(3)-(4), below.

P.L. 105-206, §1102(f)(3)-(4), provides:

(3) NATIONAL TAXPAYER ADVOCATE.—Notwithstanding section 7803(c)(1)(B)(iv) of such Code, as added by this section, in appointing the first National Taxpayer Advocate after the date of the enactment of this Act, the Secretary of the Treasury—

(A) shall not appoint any individual who was an officer or employee of the Internal Revenue Service at any time during the 2-year period ending on the date of appointment, and

(B) need not consult with the Internal Revenue Service Oversight Board if the Oversight Board has not been appointed.

(4) CURRENT OFFICERS.—

(A) In the case of an individual serving as Commissioner of Internal Revenue on the date of the enactment of this Act who was appointed to such position before such date, the 5-year term required by section 7803(a)(1) of such Code, as added by this section, shall begin as of the date of such appointment.

(B) Clauses (ii), (iii), and (iv) of section 7803(c)(1)(B) of such Code, as added by this section, shall not apply to the individual serving as Taxpayer Advocate on the date of the enactment of this Act.

• **1996, Taxpayer Bill of Rights 2 (P.L. 104-168)**

P.L. 104-168, §501(b):

Amended Code Sec. 6343 by adding at the end a new subsection (d). **Effective** 7-30-96.

[Sec. 6343(e)]

(e) RELEASE OF LEVY UPON AGREEMENT THAT AMOUNT IS NOT COLLECTIBLE.—In the case of a levy on the salary or wages payable to or received by the taxpayer, upon agreement with the taxpayer that the tax is not collectible, the Secretary shall release such levy as soon as practicable.

• **1998, IRS Restructuring and Reform Act of 1998 (P.L. 105-206)**

P.L. 105-206, §3432(a):

Amended Code Sec. 6343 by adding at the end a new subsection (e). **Effective** for levies imposed after 12-31-99.

[Sec. 6343(f)]

(f) INDIVIDUALS HELD HARMLESS ON WRONGFUL LEVY, ETC. ON RETIREMENT PLAN.—

(1) IN GENERAL.—If the Secretary determines that an individual's account or benefit under an eligible retirement plan (as defined in section 402(c)(8)(B)) has been levied upon in a case to which subsection (b) or (d)(2)(A) applies and property or an amount of money is returned to the individual—

(A) the individual may contribute such property or an amount equal to the sum of—

(i) the amount of money so returned by the Secretary, and

(ii) interest paid under subsection (c) on such amount of money,

into such eligible retirement plan if such contribution is permitted by the plan, or into an individual retirement plan (other than an endowment contract) to which a rollover contribution of a distribution from such eligible retirement plan is permitted, but only if such contribution is made not later than the due date (not including extensions) for filing the return of tax for the taxable year in which such property or amount of money is returned, and

(B) the Secretary shall, at the time such property or amount of money is returned, notify such individual that a contribution described in subparagraph (A) may be made.

(2) TREATMENT AS ROLLOVER.—The distribution on account of the levy and any contribution under paragraph (1) with respect to the return of such distribution shall be treated for purposes of this title as if such distribution and contribution were described in section 402(c), 402A(c)(3), 403(a)(4), 403(b)(8), 408(d)(3), 408A(d)(3), or 457(e)(16), whichever is applicable; except that—

(A) the contribution shall be treated as having been made for the taxable year in which the distribution on account of the levy occurred, and the interest paid under subsection (c) shall be treated as earnings within the plan after the contribution and shall not be included in gross income, and

(B) such contribution shall not be taken into account under section 408(d)(3)(B).

(3) REFUND, ETC., OF INCOME TAX ON LEVY.—

(A) IN GENERAL.—If any amount is includible in gross income for a taxable year by reason of a distribution on account of a levy referred to in paragraph (1) and any portion of such amount is treated as a rollover contribution under paragraph (2), any tax imposed by chapter 1 on such portion shall not be assessed, and if assessed shall be abated, and if collected shall be credited or refunded as an overpayment made on the due date for filing the return of tax for such taxable year.

(B) EXCEPTION.—Subparagraph (A) shall not apply to a rollover contribution under this subsection which is made from an eligible retirement plan which is not a Roth IRA or a designated Roth account (within the meaning of section 402A) to a Roth IRA or a designated Roth account under an eligible retirement plan.

(4) INTEREST.—Notwithstanding subsection (d), interest shall be allowed under subsection (c) in a case in which the Secretary makes a determination described in subsection (d)(2)(A) with respect to a levy upon an individual retirement plan.

COLLECTION—STATE INCOME TAXES

(5) TREATMENT OF INHERITED ACCOUNTS.—For purposes of paragraph (1)(A), section 408(d)(3)(C) shall be disregarded in determining whether an individual retirement plan is a plan to which a rollover contribution of a distribution from the plan levied upon is permitted.

Amendments

• **2018, Bipartisan Budget Act of 2018 (P.L. 115-123)**

P.L. 115-123, §41104(a), Div. D:

Amended Code Sec. 6343 by adding at the end a new subsection (f). **Effective** for amounts paid under Code Sec. 6343(b), (c), and (d)(2)(A) in tax years beginning after 12-31-2017.

[Sec. 6344]

SEC. 6344. CROSS REFERENCES.

[Sec. 6344(a)]

(a) LENGTH OF PERIOD.—For period within which levy may be begun in case of—

(1) Income, estate, and gift taxes, and taxes imposed by chapter 41, 42, 43, or 44, see sections 6502(a) and 6503(a)(1).

(2) Employment and miscellaneous excise taxes, see section 6502(a).

Amendments

• **1988, Omnibus Trade and Competitiveness Act of 1988 (P.L. 100-418)**

P.L. 100-418, §1941(b)(2)(B)(ix):

Amended Code Sec. 6344(a)(1) by striking "44, or 45" each place it appears and inserting "or 44". **Effective** for crude oil removed from the premises on or after 8-23-88.

• **1980, Crude Oil Windfall Profit Tax Act of 1980 (P.L. 96-223)**

P.L. 96-223, §101(f)(1)(I):

Amended Code Sec. 6433(a)(1) by striking out "or 44" and inserting "44, or 45". For the **effective** date and transitional rules, see P.L. 96-223, §101(i), following Code Sec. 4986.

• **1976, Tax Reform Act of 1976 (P.L. 94-455)**

P.L. 94-455, §1307(d)(2)(F)(v):

Substituted "chapter 41, 42," for "chapter 42" in Code Sec. 6344(a)(1). **Effective** 10-4-76.

P.L. 94-455, §1605(b)(8):

Substituted "43, or 44" for "or 43" in Code Sec. 6344(a)(1).

P.L. 94-455, §1608(d), provides:

(d) OTHER AMENDMENTS.—

(1) Except as provided in paragraphs (2) and (3), the amendments made by sections 1603, 1604, and 1605 shall apply to taxable years of real estate investment trusts beginning after the date of the enactment of this Act.

(2) If, as a result of a determination (as defined in section 859(c) of the Internal Revenue Code of 1954), occurring after the date of enactment of this Act, with respect to the real estate investment trust, such trust does not meet the requirement of section 856(a)(4) of the Internal Revenue Code of 1954 (as in effect before the amendment of such section by this Act) for any taxable year beginning on or before the date of the enactment of this Act, such trust may elect, within 60 days after such determination in the manner provided in regulations prescribed by the Secretary of the Treasury or his delegate, to have the provisions of section 1603 (other than paragraphs (1), (2), (3), and (4) of section 1603(c)) apply with respect to such taxable year. Where the provisions of section 1603 apply to a real estate investment trust with respect to any taxable year beginning on or before the date of the enactment of this Act—

(A) credit or refund of any overpayment of tax which results from the application of section 1603 to such taxable year shall be made as if on the date of the determination (as defined in section 859(c) of the Internal Revenue Code of 1954) 2 years remained before the expiration of the period of limitation prescribed by section 6511 of such Code on the filing of claim for refund for the taxable year to which the overpayment relates,

(B) the running of the statute of limitations provided in section 6501 of such Code on the making of assessments, and the bringing of distraint or a proceeding in court for collection, in respect of any deficiency (as defined in section 6211 of such Code) established by such a determination, and all interest, additions to tax, additional amounts, or assessable penalties in respect thereof, shall be suspended for a period of 2 years after the date of such determination, and

(C) the collection of any deficiency (as defined in section 6211 of such Code) established by such determination and all interest, additions to tax, additional amounts, and assessable penalties in respect thereof shall, except in cases of jeopardy, be stayed until the expiration of 60 days after the date of such determination.

No distraint or proceeding in court shall be begun for the collection of an amount the collection of which is stayed under subparagraph (C) during the period for which the collection of such amount is stayed.

(3) Section 856(g)(3) of the Internal Revenue Code of 1954, as added by section 1604 of this Act, shall not apply with respect to a termination of an election, filed by a taxpayer under section 856(c)(1) of such Code on or before the date of the enactment of this Act, unless the provisions of part II of subchapter M of chapter 1 of subtitle A of such Code apply to such taxpayer for a taxable year ending after the date of the enactment of this Act for which such election is in effect.

• **1974, Employee Retirement Income Security Act of 1974 (P.L. 93-406)**

P.L. 93-406, §1016(a)(13):

Amended Code Sec. 6344(a)(1) by changing "chapter 42" to "chapter 42 or 43". For **effective** date, see amendment note for Code Sec. 410.

• **1969, Tax Reform Act of 1969 (P.L. 91-172)**

P.L. 91-172, §101(j)(45):

Amended Code Sec. 6344(a)(1) by adding "and taxes imposed by chapter 42," after "gift taxes". **Effective** 1-1-70.

[Sec. 6344(b)]

(b) DELINQUENT COLLECTION OFFICERS.—For distraint proceedings against delinquent internal revenue officers, see section 7804(c).

Amendments

• **1998, IRS Restructuring and Reform Act of 1998 (P.L. 105-206)**

P.L. 105-206, §1104(b)(1):

Amended Code Sec. 6344(b) by striking "section 7803(d)" and inserting "section 7804(c)". **Effective** 7-22-98.

[Sec. 6344(c)]

(c) OTHER REFERENCES.—For provisions relating to—

(1) Stamps, marks and brands, see section 6807.

(2) Administration of real estate acquired by the United States, see section 7506.

Subchapter E—Collection of State Individual Income Taxes—[Repealed]

[Sec. 6361—Repealed]

Amendments

• **1990, Omnibus Budget Reconciliation Act of 1990 (P.L. 101-508)**

P.L. 101-508, §11801(a)(45):

Repealed Subchapter E of chapter 64. **Effective** 11-5-90.

P.L. 101-508, §11821(b), provides:

(b) SAVINGS PROVISION.—If—

(1) any provision amended or repealed by this part applied to—

(A) any transaction occurring before the date of the enactment of this Act,

(B) any property acquired before such date of enactment, or

(C) any item of income, loss, deduction, or credit taken into account before such date of enactment, and

(2) the treatment of such transaction, property, or item under such provision would (without regard to the amendments made by this part) affect liability for tax for periods ending after such date of enactment,

nothing in the amendments made by this part shall be construed to affect the treatment of such transaction, property, or item for purposes of determining liability for tax for periods ending after such date of enactment.

Prior to repeal, Code Sec. 6361 read as follows:

Sec. 6361. GENERAL RULES.

[Sec. 6361(a)]

(a) COLLECTION AND ADMINISTRATION.—In the case of any State which has in effect an agreement with the Secretary entered into under section 6363, the Secretary shall collect and administer the qualified State individual income taxes of such State. No

COLLECTION—STATE INCOME TAXES

fee or other charge shall be imposed upon any State for the collection or administration of the qualified State individual income taxes of such State or any other State. All provisions of this subtitle, subtitle G, and chapter 24 relating to the collection and administration of the taxes imposed by chapter 1 on the incomes of individuals (and all civil and criminal sanctions provided by this subtitle or by title 18 of the United States Code with respect to such collection and administration) shall apply to the collection and administration of qualified State individual income taxes as if such taxes were imposed by chapter 1, except to the extent that their application is modified by the Secretary by regulations necessary or appropriate to reflect the provisions of this subchapter, or to reflect differences in the taxes or differences in the situations in which liability for such taxes arises.

Amendments

• **1976, Tax Reform Act of 1976 (P.L. 94-455)**

P.L. 94-455, §1906(b)(13)(A):

Amended 1954 Code by substituting "Secretary" for "Secretary or his delegate" each place it appeared. **Effective** 2-1-77.

P.L. 94-455, §2116(c):

Added the second sentence of Code Sec. 6361(a). **Effective** 10-4-76.

[Sec. 6361(b)]

(b) CIVIL PROCEEDINGS.—Any person shall have, with respect to a qualified State individual income tax (including the current collection thereof), the same right to bring or contest a civil action and obtain review thereof, in the same court or courts and subject to the same requirements and procedures, as he would have under chapter 76, and under title 28 of the United States Code, if the tax were imposed by section 1 (or were for the current collection of the tax imposed by section 1). To the extent that the preceding sentence provides judicial procedures (including review procedures) with respect to any matter, such procedures shall replace judicial procedures under State law, except that nothing in this subchapter shall be construed in any way to affect the right or power of a State court to pass on matters involving the constitution of that State.

[Sec. 6361(c)]

(c) TRANSFERS TO STATES.—

(1) PROMPT TRANSFERS.—Any amount collected under this subchapter which is apportioned to a qualified State individual income tax shall be promptly transferred to the State on the basis of estimates by the Secretary. In the case of amounts collected under chapter 24, the estimated amount due the State shall be transferred to the State not later than the close of the third business day after the amount is deposited in a Federal Reserve bank. In the case of amounts collected pursuant to a return, a declaration of estimated tax, an amendment of such a declaration, or otherwise, the estimated amount due the State shall be transferred to the State not later than the close of the 30th day after the amount is received by the Secretary.

(2) ADJUSTMENTS.—Not less often than once each fiscal year the difference between collections (adjusted for credits and refunds) made under this subchapter during the preceding fiscal year and the transfers to the States made on account of estimates of such collections shall be determined, and such difference shall be a charge against, or an addition to, the amounts otherwise payable.

Amendments

• **1976, Tax Reform Act of 1976 (P.L. 94-455)**

P.L. 94-455, §1906(b)(13)(A):

Amended 1954 Code by substituting "Secretary" for "Secretary or his delegate" each place it appeared. **Effective** 2-1-77.

[Sec. 6361(d)]

(d) SPECIAL RULES.—

(1) UNITED STATES TO REPRESENT STATE INTEREST.—

(A) GENERAL RULE.—In all administrative proceedings, and in all judicial proceedings (whether civil or criminal), relating to the administration and collection of a State qualified individual income tax the interests of the State imposing such tax shall be represented by the United States in the same manner in which the interests of the United States are represented in corresponding proceedings involving the taxes imposed by chapter 1.

(B) EXCEPTIONS.—Subparagraph (A) shall not apply to—

(i) proceedings in a State court involving the constitution of that State, and

(ii) proceedings involving the relationship between the United States and the State.

(2) ALLOCATION OF OVERPAYMENTS AND UNDERPAYMENTS.—If the combined amount collected in respect of a qualified State individual income tax for any period and the taxes imposed by chapter 1 for such period with respect to the income of any individual is greater or less than the combined amount required to be paid for such period, the collected amount shall be divided between the accounts for such taxes on the basis of the respective amounts required to be paid.

(3) FINALITY OF ADMINISTRATIVE DETERMINATIONS.—Administrative determinations of the Secretary as to tax liabilities of, or refunds owing to, individuals with respect to qualified State individual income taxes shall not be reviewed by or enforced by any officer or employee of any State or political subdivision of a State.

Amendments

• **1976, Tax Reform Act of 1976 (P.L. 94-455)**

P.L. 94-455, §1906(b)(13)(A):

Amended 1954 Code by substituting "Secretary" for "Secretary or his delegate" each place it appeared. **Effective** 2-1-77.

• **1972, State and Local Fiscal Assistance Act of 1972 (P.L. 92-512)**

P.L. 92-512, §202(a):

Added Code Sec. 6361. **Effective** on whichever of the following is later: (1) 1-1-74, or (2) the first January 1 which is more than one year after the first date on which at least two States having residents who in the aggregate filed 5% or more of the federal individual income tax returns filed during 1972 have notified the Treasury of an election to enter into an agreement under Code Sec. 6363.

[Sec. 6362—Repealed]

Amendments

• **1990, Omnibus Budget Reconciliation Act of 1990 (P.L. 101-508)**

P.L. 101-508, §11801(a)(45):

Repealed Code Sec. 6362. **Effective** 11-5-90.

P.L. 101-508, §11821(b), provides:

(b) SAVINGS PROVISION.—If—

(1) any provision amended or repealed by this part applied to—

(A) any transaction occurring before the date of the enactment of this Act,

(B) any property acquired before such date of enactment, or

(C) any item of income, loss, deduction, or credit taken into account before such date of enactment, and

(2) the treatment of such transaction, property, or item under such provision would (without regard to the amendments made by this part) affect liability for tax for periods ending after such date of enactment,

nothing in the amendments made by this part shall be construed to affect the treatment of such transaction, property, or item for purposes of determining liability for tax for periods ending after such date of enactment.

Prior to repeal, Code Sec. 6362 read as follows:

SEC. 6362. QUALIFIED STATE INDIVIDUAL INCOME TAXES.

[Sec. 6362(a)]

(a) QUALIFIED STATE INDIVIDUAL INCOME TAXES DEFINED.—For purposes of this subchapter—

(1) IN GENERAL.—The term "qualified State individual income tax" means—

(A) a qualified resident tax, and

(B) a qualified nonresident tax.

(2) QUALIFIED RESIDENT TAX.—The term "qualified resident tax" means a tax imposed by a State on the income of individuals who are residents of such State which is either—

(A) a tax based on taxable income which meets the requirements of subsection (b), or

(B) a tax which is a percentage of the Federal tax which meets the requirements of subsection (c),

and which, in addition, meets the requirements of subsections (e) and (f).

(3) QUALIFIED NONRESIDENT TAX.—The term "qualified nonresident tax" means a tax which is imposed by a State on the wage and other business income of individuals who are not residents of such State and which meets the requirements of subsections (d), (e), and (f).

[Sec. 6362(b)]

(b) QUALIFIED RESIDENT TAX BASED ON TAXABLE INCOME.—

(1) IN GENERAL.—A tax meets the requirements of this subsection only if it is imposed on an amount equal to the individual's taxable income (as defined in section 63) for the taxable year, adjusted—

(A) by subtracting an amount equal to the amount of his interest on obligations of the United States which was included in his gross income for the year,

(B) by adding an amount equal to his net State income tax deduction for the year,

(C) by adding an amount equal to his net tax-exempt income for the year, and

(D) if a credit is allowed against such tax for State or local sales tax in accordance with paragraph (2)(C), by adding an amount equal to the amount of his deduction under section 164(a)(4) for such sales tax.

(2) PERMITTED ADJUSTMENTS.—A tax which otherwise meets the requirements of paragraph (1) shall not be deemed to fail to meet such requirements solely because it provides for one or more of the following adjustments:

(A) There is imposed a tax on the amount taxed under section 55 (relating to the minimum tax for tax preferences).

(B) A credit determined under rules prescribed by the Secretary is allowed against such tax for income tax paid to another State or a political subdivision thereof.

(C) A credit is allowed against such tax for all or a portion of any general sales tax imposed by the same State or a political subdivision thereof with respect to sales to the taxpayer or his dependents.

(3) NET STATE INCOME TAX DEDUCTION.—For purposes of this subsection and subsection (c), the term "net State income tax deduction" means the excess (if any) of (A) the amount deducted from income under section 164(a)(3) as taxes paid to a State or a political subdivision thereof, over (B) amounts included in income as recoveries of prior income taxes paid to a State or a political subdivision thereof which had been deducted under section 164(a)(3).

(4) NET TAX-EXEMPT INCOME.—For purposes of this subsection and subsection (c), the term "net tax-exempt income" means the excess (if any) of—

(A) the interest on obligations described in section 103(a) other than obligations of the State and its political subdivisions, and

(B) the interest on obligations described in such section of the State and its political subdivision which under the law of the State is subject to the individual income tax imposed by the State, over

the sum of the amount of deductions allocable to such interest which is disallowed by application of section 265, and the amount of the proper adjustment to basis allocable to such obligations which is required to be made for the taxable year under section 1016(a)(5) or (6).

COLLECTION—STATE INCOME TAXES

Amendments

- **1983, Technical Corrections Act of 1982 (P.L. 97-448)**

P.L. 97-448, §306(a)(1)(A):

Amended section 201 of P.L. 97-248 by redesignating the second subsection (c) as subsection (d).

- **1983, Surface Transportation Act of 1982 (P.L. 97-424)**

P.L. 97-424, §547(b)(5):

Amended Code Sec. 6362(b)(4)(A) by striking out "103(a)(1)" and inserting "103(a)". **Effective** 1-6-83.

- **1982, Tax Equity and Fiscal Responsibility Act of 1982 (P.L. 97-248)**

P.L. 97-248, §207(d)(7):

Amended Code Sec. 6362(b)(2)(A) by striking out "or 56". **Effective** for tax years beginning after 12-31-82.

- **1978, Revenue Act of 1978 (P.L. 95-600)**

P.L. 95-600, §421(e)(8):

Amended Code Sec. 6362(b)(2)(A). **Effective** for tax years beginning after 12-31-78, by striking out "section 56" and inserting in place thereof "section 55 or 56".

- **1976, Tax Reform Act of 1976 (P.L. 94-455)**

P.L. 94-455, §1906(b)(13)(A):

Amended 1954 Code by substituting "Secretary" for "Secretary or his delegate" each place it appeared. **Effective** 2-1-77.

P.L. 94-455, §2116(b)(1)(A):

Struck out "and" at the end of Code Sec. 6362(b)(1)(B), substituted ", and" for the period at the end of Code Sec. 6362(b)(1)(C), and added Code Sec. 6362(b)(1)(D). **Effective** 10-4-76.

P.L. 94-455, §2116(b)(1)(B):

Added Code Sec. 6362(b)(2)(C). **Effective** 10-4-76.

[Sec. 6362(c)]

(c) QUALIFIED RESIDENT TAX WHICH IS A PERCENTAGE OF THE FEDERAL TAX.—

(1) IN GENERAL.—A tax meets the requirements of this subsection only if it is imposed as a specified percentage of the excess of the taxes imposed by chapter 1 over the sum of the credits allowable under part IV of subchapter A of chapter 1 (other than the credits allowable by sections 31 and 34).

(2) REQUIRED ADJUSTMENTS.—A tax meets the requirements of this subsection only if the liability for tax is decreased by the decrease in such liability which would result from excluding from gross income an amount equal to the interest on obligations of the United States which was included in gross income for such year.

(3) PERMITTED ADJUSTMENTS.—A tax which otherwise meets the requirements of paragraphs (1) and (2) shall not be deemed to fail to meet such requirements solely because it provides for all of the following adjustments:

(A) the liability for tax is increased by the increase in such liability which would result from including as an item of gross income an amount equal to the net tax-exempt income for the year,

(B) the liability for tax is increased by the increase in such liability which would result from including as an item of gross income an amount equal to the net State income tax deduction for the year, and

(C) if a credit is allowed against such tax for State or local sales tax in accordance with paragraph (4)(B), the liability for tax is increased by the increase in such liability which would result from including as an item of income an amount equal to the amount of his deduction under section 164(a)(4) for such sales tax.

(4) FURTHER PERMITTED ADJUSTMENTS.—A tax which otherwise meets the requirements of paragraphs (1) and (2) shall not be deemed to fail to meet such requirements solely because it provides for one or both of the following adjustments:

(A) A credit determined under rules prescribed by the Secretary is allowed against such tax for income tax paid to another State or a political subdivision thereof.

(B) A credit is allowed against such tax for all or a portion of any general sales tax imposed by the same State or a political subdivision thereof with respect to sales to the taxpayer or his dependents.

Amendments

- **1984, Deficit Reduction Act of 1984 (P.L. 98-369)**

P.L. 98-369, §474(r)(35):

Amended Code Sec. 6362(c)(1) by striking out "sections 31 and 39" and inserting in lieu thereof "sections 31 and 34". **Effective** for tax years beginning after 12-31-83, and to carrybacks from such years.

- **1976, Tax Reform Act of 1976 (P.L. 94-455)**

P.L. 94-455, §2116(b)(2)(A):

Substituted "All" for "both" in Code Sec. 6362(c)(3), struck out "and" at the end of Code Sec. 6362(c)(3)(A), substituted ", and" for the period at the end of Code Sec. 6362(c)(3)(B), and added Code Sec. 6362(c)(3)(C). **Effective** 10-4-76.

P.L. 94-455, §2116(b)(2)(B):

Amended Code Sec. 6362(c)(4). **Effective** 10-4-76. Prior to amendment, Code Sec. 6362(c)(4) read as follows:

(4) FURTHER PERMITTED ADJUSTMENT.—A tax which otherwise meets the requirements of paragraphs (1) and (2) shall not be deemed to fail to meet such requirements solely because a credit determined under rules prescribed by the Secretary or his delegate is allowed against such tax for income tax paid to another State or a political subdivision thereof.

[Sec. 6362(d)]

(d) QUALIFIED NONRESIDENT TAX.—

(1) IN GENERAL.—A tax imposed by a State meets the requirements of this subsection only if it has the following characteristics—

(A) such tax is imposed by the State on the wage and other business income of individuals who are not residents of such State,

(B) such tax applies only with respect to wage and other business income derived from sources within such State,

(C) such tax applies only if 25 percent or more of the individual's wage and other business income for the taxable year is derived from sources within such State,

(D) the amount of such tax imposed with respect to any individual who is not a resident does not exceed the amount of tax for which he would be liable under such State's qualified resident tax if he were a resident of such State and if his taxable income were an amount equal to the excess of—

(i) the amount of his wage and other business income derived from sources within such State, over

(ii) that portion of the nonbusiness deductions taken into account for purposes of the State's qualified resident tax which bears the same ratio to the amount of such deductions as the income referred to in clause (i) bears to his adjusted gross income, and

(E) the State has in effect for the same period a qualified resident tax.

(2) WAGE AND OTHER BUSINESS INCOME.—The term "wage and other business income" means—

(A) wages, as defined in section 3401(a),

(B) net earnings from self-employment (within the meaning of section 1402(a)), and

(C) the distributive share of income of any trade or business carried on by a trust, estate, or an S corporation to the extent such share (i) is includible in the gross income of the individual for the taxable year, and (ii) would constitute net earnings from self-employment (within the meaning of section 1402(a)) if such trade or business were carried on by a partnership.

Amendments

- **1984, Deficit Reduction Act of 1984 (P.L. 98-369)**

P.L. 98-369, §721(x)(5):

Amended Code Sec. 6362(d)(2)(C) by striking out "electing small business corporation (within the meaning of section 1371(a))" and inserting in lieu thereof "an S corporation". **Effective** as if included in P.L. 97-354.

[Sec. 6362(e)]

(e) REQUIREMENTS RELATING TO RESIDENCE.—A tax imposed by a State meets the requirements of this subsection only if for purposes of such tax—

(1) RESIDENT INDIVIDUAL.—An individual (other than a trust or estate) is treated as a resident of such State with respect to a taxable year only if—

(A) his principal place of residence has been within such State for a period of at least 135 consecutive days and at least 30 days of such period are in such taxable year, or

(B) in the case of a citizen or resident of the United States who is not a resident (determined in the manner provided in subparagraph (A)) of any State with respect to such taxable year, such individual is domiciled in such State for at least 30 days during such taxable year.

Nothing in this subchapter shall be construed to require or authorize the treatment of a Senator, Representative, Delegate, or Resident Commissioner as a resident of a State other than the State which he represents in Congress.

(2) ESTATE.—An estate of an individual is treated as a resident of the last State of which such individual was a resident (within the meaning of paragraph (1)) before his death.

(3) TRUSTS.—

(A) TESTAMENTARY TRUST.—A trust with respect to which a deceased individual is the principal contributor by reason of property passing on his death is treated as a resident of the last State of which such individual was a resident (within the meaning of paragraph (1)) before his death.

(B) NONTESTAMENTARY TRUST.—A trust (other than a trust described in subparagraph (A)) is treated as a resident of such State with respect to a taxable year only if the principal contributor to the trust, during the 3-year period ending on the date of the creation of the trust, resided in the State for an aggregate number of days longer than the aggregate number of days he resided in any other State.

(C) SPECIAL RULES.—For purposes of this paragraph—

(i) If on any day before the close of the taxable year an existing trust received assets having a value greater than the aggregate value of all assets theretofore contributed to the trust, such trust shall be treated as created on such day. For purposes of this subparagraph, the value of any asset taken into account shall be its fair market value on the day it is contributed to the trust.

(ii) The principal contributor to the trust is the individual who contributed more (in value) of the assets contributed on the date of the creation of the trust (determined after applying clause (i)) than any other individual.

(iii) If the foregoing rules would create more than one State of residence (or no State of residence) for a trust, such trust shall be treated as a resident of the State determined under similar principles prescribed by the Secretary by regulations.

(4) LIABILITY FOR TAX ON CHANGE OF RESIDENCE.—With respect to a taxable year, in the case of an individual (other than an individual who comes into being or ceases to exist) who becomes a resident, or ceases to be a resident, of the State, his liability to such State for the resident tax is determined by multiplying the amount which would be his liability for tax (after the nonrefundable credits allowed against such tax) if he had been a resident of such State for the entire taxable year by a fraction the numerator of which is the number of days he was a resident of such State and the denominator of which is the total number of days in the taxable year. In the case of an individual who is treated as a resident of a State with respect to a taxable year by reason of paragraph (1)(B), the preceding sentence shall be applied by substituting days of domicile for days of residence.

Sec. 6362—Repealed

(5) CURRENT COLLECTION OF TAX.—In applying chapter 24 (relating to withholding) and provisions relating to estimated income tax (and amendments thereto)—

(A) in the case of a resident tax, an individual is treated as subject to the tax if he reasonably expects to reside in the State for 30 days or more or if such individual is a resident of the State (within the meaning of paragraph (1), (2), or (3)), and

(B) in the case of a nonresident tax, an individual is treated as subject to the tax if he reasonably expects to receive wage and other business income (within the meaning of subsection (d)(2)) for 30 days or more during the taxable year.

Amendments

- **1984, Deficit Reduction Act of 1984 (P.L. 98-369)**

P.L. 98-369, § 412(b)(6):

Amended Code Sec. 6362(e)(5) by striking out "and section 6015 and other provisions relating to declarations of estimated income" and inserting in lieu thereof "and provisions relating to estimated income tax". **Effective** with respect to tax years beginning after 12-31-84.

- **1976, Tax Reform Act of 1976 (P.L. 94-455)**

P.L. 94-455, § 1906(b)(13)(A):

Amended 1954 Code by substituting "Secretary" for "Secretary or his delegate" each place it appeared. **Effective** 2-1-77.

[Sec. 6362(f)]

(f) ADDITIONAL REQUIREMENTS.—A tax imposed by a State shall meet the requirements of this subsection only if—

(1) STATE AGREEMENT MUST BE IN EFFECT FOR PERIOD CONCERNED.—A State agreement entered into under section 6363 is in effect with respect to such tax for the taxable period in question.

(2) STATE LAWS MUST CONTAIN CERTAIN PROVISIONS.—Under the laws of such State—

(A) the provisions of this subchapter (and of the regulations prescribed thereunder) as in effect from time to time are made applicable for the period for which the State agreement is in effect, and

(B) any change made by the State in the tax imposed by the State will not apply to taxable years beginning in any calendar year for which the State agreement is in effect unless such change is enacted before November 1 of such calendar year.

(3) STATE LAWS TAXING INCOMES OF INDIVIDUALS CAN ONLY BE OF CERTAIN KINDS.—The State does not impose any tax on the income of individuals other than—

(A) a qualified resident tax,

(B) a qualified nonresident tax, and

(C) a separate tax on income which is not wage and other business income and which is received or accrued by individuals who are domiciled in the State but who are not residents of the State within the meaning of subsection (e)(1).

(4) TAXABLE YEARS MUST COINCIDE.—The taxable years of individuals under such tax coincide with taxable years for purposes of the taxes imposed by chapter 1.

(5) MARRIED INDIVIDUALS.—A married individual (within the meaning of section 7703)—

(A) who files a joint return for purposes of the taxes imposed by chapter 1 shall not file a separate return for purposes of such State tax, and

(B) who files a separate return for purposes of the taxes imposed by chapter 1, shall not file a joint return for purposes of such State tax.

(6) NO DOUBLE JEOPARDY UNDER STATE LAW.—The laws of such State do not provide criminal or civil sanctions for an act (or omission to act) with respect to a qualified resident tax or qualified nonresident tax other than the criminal or civil sanctions to which an individual is subjected by reason of section 6361.

(7) PARTNERSHIPS, TRUSTS, AND OTHER CONDUIT ENTITIES.—Under the State law the tax treatment of—

(A) partnerships and partners,

(B) trusts and their beneficiaries,

(C) estates and their beneficiaries,

(D) S corporations and their shareholders, and

(E) any other entity and the individuals having beneficial interests therein, to the extent that such entity is treated as a conduit for purposes of the taxes imposed by chapter 1, shall correspond to the tax treatment provided therefor in the case of the taxes imposed by chapter 1.

(8) MEMBERS OF ARMED FORCES.—The relief provided to any member of the Armed Forces of the United States by section 514 of the Soldiers' and Sailors' Civil Relief Act (50 U. S. C. App. sec. 574) is in no way diminished.

(9) WITHHOLDING ON COMPENSATION OF EMPLOYEES OF RAILROADS, MOTOR CARRIERS, AIRLINES, AND WATER CARRIERS.—There is no contravention of the provisions of section 11504 of title 49 or of section 1112 of the Federal Aviation Act of 1958 with respect to the withholding of compensation to which such sections apply for purposes of the nonresident tax.

Amendments

- **1986, Tax Reform Act of 1986 (P.L. 99-514)**

P.L. 99-514, § 1301(j)(8):

Amended Code Sec. 6362(f)(5) by striking out "section 143" and inserting in lieu thereof "section 7703". **Effective** for bonds issued after 8-15-86.

- **1982, Subchapter S Revision Act of 1982 (P.L. 97-354)**

P.L. 97-354, § 5(a)(41):

Amended Code Sec. 6362(f)(7) by striking out "electing small business corporations (within the meaning of section 1371(a))" in subparagraph (D) and inserting in lieu thereof "S corporations", and by striking out "SUBCHAPTER S CORPORATIONS," in the paragraph heading. **Effective** for tax years beginning after 12-31-82.

- **1978 (P.L. 95-473)**

P.L. 95-473, § 2(a)(2)(H):

Amended Code Sec. 6362(f)(9) by striking out "26, 226A, or 324 of the Interstate Commerce Act" and substituting "section 11504 of title 49". **Effective** 10-17-78.

- **1972, State and Local Fiscal Assistance Act of 1972 (P.L. 92-512)**

P.L. 92-512, § 202(a):

Added Code Sec. 6362. For **effective** date, see the **effective** date for Code Sec. 6361.

[Sec. 6363—Repealed]

Amendments

- **1990, Omnibus Budget Reconciliation Act of 1990 (P.L. 101-508)**

P.L. 101-508, § 11801(a)(45):

Repealed Code Sec. 6363. **Effective** on the date of enactment.

P.L. 101-508, § 11821(b), provides:

(b) SAVINGS PROVISION.—If—

(1) any provision amended or repealed by this part applied to—

(A) any transaction occurring before the date of the enactment of this Act,

(B) any property acquired before such date of enactment, or

(C) any item of income, loss, deduction, or credit taken into account before such date of enactment, and

(2) the treatment of such transaction, property, or item under such provision would (without regard to the amendments made by this part) affect liability for tax for periods ending after such date of enactment,

nothing in the amendments made by this part shall be construed to affect the treatment of such transaction, property, or item for purposes of determining liability for tax for periods ending after such date of enactment.

Prior to repeal, Code Sec. 6363 read as follows:

SEC. 6363. STATE AGREEMENTS; OTHER PROCEDURES.

[Sec. 6363(a)]

(a) STATE AGREEMENT.—If a State elects to enter into an agreement with the United States to have its individual income taxes collected and administered as provided in this subchapter, it shall file notice of such election in such manner and with such supporting information as the Secretary may prescribe by regulations. The Secretary shall enter into an agreement with such State unless the Secretary notifies the Governor of the State within 90 days after the date of the filing of the notice of the election that the State does not have a qualified State individual income tax (determined without regard to section 6362(f)(1)). The provisions of this subchapter shall apply on and after the date (not earlier than the first January 1 which is more than 6 months after the date of the notice) specified for this purpose in the agreement.

Amendments

- **1976, Tax Reform Act of 1976 (P.L. 94-455)**

P.L. 94-455, § 1906(b)(13)(A):

Amended 1954 Code by substituting "Secretary" for "Secretary or his delegate" each place it appeared. **Effective** 2-1-77.

[Sec. 6363(b)]

(b) WITHDRAWAL.—

(1) BY NOTIFICATION.—If a State wishes to withdraw from the agreement, it shall notify the Secretary of its intention to withdraw in such manner as the Secretary may prescribe by regulations. The provisions of this subchapter (other than this section) shall not apply on or after the date specified for this purpose in the notification. Except as provided in regulations, the date so specified shall not be earlier than the first January 1 which is more than 6 months after the date on which the Secretary is so notified.

(2) BY CHANGE IN STATE LAW.—Any change in State law which would (but for this subchapter) have the effect of causing a tax to cease to be a qualified State individual income tax shall be treated as an intention to withdraw from the agreement. Notification by the Secretary to the Governor of such State that the change in State law will be treated as an intention to withdraw shall be made by the Secretary in such manner as the Secretary shall by regulations prescribe. Such notification shall have the same effect as a notice under paragraph (1) of an intention to withdraw from the agreement received on the effective date of the change in State law.

Amendments

- **1976, Tax Reform Act of 1976 (P.L. 94-455)**

P.L. 94-455, § 1906(b)(13)(A):

Amended 1954 Code by substituting "Secretary" for "Secretary or his delegate" each place it appeared. **Effective** 2-1-77.

[Sec. 6363(c)]

(c) TRANSITION YEARS.—

(1) SUBCHAPTER CEASES TO APPLY DURING TAXPAYER'S YEAR.—If the provisions of this subchapter cease to apply on a day other than the last day of the taxpayer's taxable year, then amounts previously paid to the United States on account of the State's qualified individual income tax for that taxable year (whether paid by withholding, estimated tax, credit in lieu of refund, or otherwise) shall be treated as having been paid on account of the State's individual income tax law for that taxable year. Such amounts shall be transferred to the State as though the State had not withdrawn from the agreement. Returns, applications, elections, and other forms previously filed with the Secretary for that taxable year, which are thereafter required to be filed with the appropriate State official shall be treated as having been filed with the appropriate State official.

(2) PREVENTION OF UNINTENDED HARDSHIPS OR BENEFITS.—The State may by law provide for the transition to a qualified State individual income tax or from such a tax to the

COLLECTION—STATE INCOME TAXES

extent necessary to prevent double taxation or other unintended hardships, or to prevent unintended benefits, under State law.

(3) ADMINISTRATION OF SUBSECTION.—The provisions of this subsection shall be administered by the Secretary, by the State, or jointly, to the extent provided in regulations prescribed by the Secretary.

Amendments

• **1976, Tax Reform Act of 1976 (P.L. 94-455)**

P.L. 94-455, § 1906(b)(13)(A):

Amended 1954 Code by substituting "Secretary" for "Secretary or his delegate" each place it appeared. **Effective** 2-1-77.

[Sec. 6363(d)]

(d) JUDICIAL REVIEW.—

(1) IN GENERAL.—Whenever under this section the Secretary determines that a State does not have a qualified State individual income tax, such State may, within 60 days after the Governor of the State has been notified of such action, file with the United States court of appeals for the circuit in which such State is located, or with the United States Court of Appeals for the District of Columbia, a petition for review of such action. A copy of the petition shall be forthwith transmitted by the clerk of the court to the Secretary. The Secretary thereupon shall file in the court the record of the proceedings on which he based his action as provided in section 2112 of title 28, United States Code.

(2) JURISDICTION OF COURT; REVIEW.—The court shall have jurisdiction to affirm the action of the Secretary or to set it aside in whole or in part and to issue such other orders as may be appropriate with regard to taxable years which include any part of the period of litigation. The judgment of the court shall be subject to review by the Supreme Court of the United States upon certiorari or certification as provided in section 1254 of title 28, United States Code.

(3) STAY OF DECISION.—

• **1990, Omnibus Budget Reconciliation Act of 1990 (P.L. 101-508)**

P.L. 101-508, § 11801(a)(45):

Repealed Code Sec. 6364. **Effective** 11-5-90.

P.L. 101-508, § 11821(b), provides:

(b) SAVINGS PROVISION.—If—

(1) any provision amended or repealed by this part applied to—

(A) any transaction occurring before the date of the enactment of this Act,

(B) any property acquired before such date of enactment, or

(C) any item of income, loss, deduction, or credit taken into account before such date of enactment, and

(2) the treatment of such transaction, property, or item under such provision would (without regard to the amendments made by this part) affect liability for tax for periods ending after such date of enactment,

nothing in the amendments made by this part shall be construed to affect the treatment of such transaction, property, or item for purposes of determining liability for tax for periods ending after such date of enactment.

Amendments

• **1990, Omnibus Budget Reconciliation Act of 1990 (P.L. 101-508)**

P.L. 101-508, § 11801(a)(45):

Repealed Code Sec. 6365. **Effective** 11-5-90.

P.L. 101-508, § 11821(b), provides:

(b) SAVINGS PROVISION.—If—

(1) any provision amended or repealed by this part applied to—

(A) any transaction occurring before the date of the enactment of this Act,

(B) any property acquired before such date of enactment, or

(C) any item of income, loss, deduction, or credit taken into account before such date of enactment, and

(2) the treatment of such transaction, property, or item under such provision would (without regard to the amendments made by this part) affect liability for tax for periods ending after such date of enactment,

nothing in the amendments made by this part shall be construed to affect the treatment of such transaction, property, or item for purposes of determining liability for tax for periods ending after such date of enactment.

Prior to repeal, Code Sec. 6365 read as follows:
SEC. 6365. DEFINITIONS AND SPECIAL RULES.

[Sec. 6365(a)]

(a) STATE.—For purposes of this subchapter, the term "State" includes the District of Columbia.

[Sec. 6365(b)]

(b) GOVERNOR.—For purposes of this subchapter, the term "Governor" includes the Mayor of the District of Columbia.

Amendments

• **1976, Tax Reform Act of 1976 (P.L. 94-455)**

P.L. 94-455, § 1906(a)(21):

Substituted "Mayor" for "Commissioner" in Code Sec. 6365(b). **Effective** 2-1-77.

(A) If judgment on a petition to review a determination under subsection (a) includes a determination that the State has a qualified State individual income tax, then the provisions of this subchapter shall apply on and after the first January 1 which is more than 6 months after the date of the judgment.

(B) If judgment on a petition to review a determination by the Secretary under subsection (b)(2) includes a determination that the State does not have a qualified State individual income tax, then the provisions of this subchapter (other than this section) shall not apply on and after the first January 1 which is more than 6 months after the date of the judgment.

Amendments

• **1984 (P.L. 98-620)**

P.L. 98-620, § 402(28)(C):

Repealed Code Sec. 6363(d)(4). Not **effective** for cases pending on 11-8-84. Prior to repeal, Code Sec. 6363(d)(4) read as follows:

(4) PREFERENCE.—Any judicial proceedings under this section shall be entitled to and, upon request of the Secretary or the State, shall receive a preference and shall be heard and determined as expeditiously as possible.

• **1976, Tax Reform Act of 1976 (P.L. 94-455)**

P.L. 94-455, § 1906(b)(13)(A):

Amended 1954 Code by substituting "Secretary" for "Secretary or his delegate" each place it appeared. **Effective** 2-1-77.

• **1972, State and Local Fiscal Assistance Act of 1972 (P.L. 92-512)**

P.L. 92-512, § 202(a):

Added Code Sec. 6363. For the **effective** date, see the **effective** date for Code Sec. 6361.

[Sec. 6364—Repealed]

Prior to repeal, Code Sec. 6364 read as follows:

SEC. 6364. REGULATIONS.

The Secretary shall prescribe such regulations as may be necessary or appropriate to carry out the purposes of this subchapter.

• **1976, Tax Reform Act of 1976 (P.L. 94-455)**

P.L. 94-455, § 1906(b)(13)(A):

Amended 1954 Code by substituting "Secretary" for "Secretary or his delegate" each place it appeared. **Effective** 2-1-77.

• **1972, State and Local Fiscal Assistance Act of 1972 (P.L. 92-512)**

P.L. 92-512, § 202(a):

Added Code Sec. 6364. For the **effective** date, see the **effective** date for Code Sec. 6361.

[Sec. 6365—Repealed]

[Sec. 6365(c)]

(c) APPLICATION OF SUBCHAPTER.—Whenever this subchapter begins to apply, or ceases to apply, to any State tax on any January 1—

(1) except as provided in paragraph (2), such change shall apply to taxable years beginning on or after such date, and

(2) for purposes of chapter 24, such change shall apply to wages paid on or after such date.

Amendments

• **1983, Interest and Dividend Tax Compliance Act of 1983 (P.L. 98-67)**

P.L. 98-67, § 102(a):

Repealed the amendment made to Code Sec. 6365(c)(2) by P.L. 97-248 (see below). **Effective** as of the close of 6-30-83, as though such amendment had not been enacted.

• **1982, Tax Equity and Fiscal Responsibility Act of 1982 (P.L. 97-248)**

P.L. 97-248, § 307(a)(8):

Amended Code Sec. 6365(c)(2) by inserting ", interest, dividends, and patronage dividends" before "paid on or after such date". **Effective** for payments of interest, dividends, and patronage dividends made after 6-30-83.

• **1972, State and Local Fiscal Assistance Act of 1972 (P.L. 92-512)**

P.L. 92-512, § 202(a):

Added Code Sec. 6365. For the **effective** date, see the **effective** date for Code Sec. 6361.

CREDITS AND REFUNDS—GENERAL PROCEDURE

CHAPTER 65—ABATEMENTS, CREDITS, AND REFUNDS

SUBCHAPTER A.   Procedure in general.
SUBCHAPTER B.   Rules of special application.

Subchapter A—Procedure in General

Sec. 6401.   Amounts treated as overpayments.
Sec. 6402.   Authority to make credits or refunds.
Sec. 6403.   Overpayment of installment.
Sec. 6404.   Abatements.
Sec. 6405.   Reports of refunds and credits.
Sec. 6406.   Prohibition of administrative review of decisions.
Sec. 6407.   Date of allowance of refund or credit.
Sec. 6408.   State escheat laws not to apply.
Sec. 6409.   Refunds disregarded in the administration of federal programs and federally assisted programs.

[Sec. 6401]

SEC. 6401. AMOUNTS TREATED AS OVERPAYMENTS.

[Sec. 6401(a)]

(a) ASSESSMENT AND COLLECTION AFTER LIMITATION PERIOD.—The term "overpayment" includes that part of the amount of the payment of any internal revenue tax which is assessed or collected after the expiration of the period of limitation properly applicable thereto.

[Sec. 6401(b)]

(b) EXCESSIVE CREDITS.—

(1) IN GENERAL.—If the amount allowable as credits under subpart C of part IV of subchapter A of chapter 1 (relating to refundable credits) exceeds the tax imposed by subtitle A (reduced by the credits allowable under subparts A, B, D, and G of such part IV), the amount of such excess shall be considered an overpayment.

(2) SPECIAL RULE FOR CREDIT UNDER SECTION 33.—For purposes of paragraph (1), any credit allowed under section 33 (relating to withholding of tax on nonresident aliens and on foreign corporations) for any taxable year shall be treated as a credit allowable under subpart C of part IV of subchapter A of chapter 1 only if an election under subsection (g) or (h) of section 6013 is in effect for such taxable year. The preceding sentence shall not apply to any credit so allowed by reason of section 1446.

Amendments

• **2017, Tax Cuts and Jobs Act (P.L. 115-97)**

P.L. 115-97, §13404(c)(4):

Amended Code Sec. 6401(b)(1) by striking "G, H, I, and J" and inserting "and G". **Effective** for bonds issued after 12-31-2017.

• **2009, American Recovery and Reinvestment Tax Act of 2009 (P.L. 111-5)**

P.L. 111-5, §1531(c)(5):

Amended Code Sec. 6401(b)(1) by striking "and I" and inserting "I, and J". **Effective** for obligations issued after 2-17-2009.

• **2008, Heartland, Habitat, Harvest, and Horticulture Act of 2008 (P.L. 110-246)**

P.L. 110-246, §15316(c)(3):

Amended Code Sec. 6401(b)(1) by striking "and H" and inserting "H, and I". **Effective** for obligations issued after 5-22-2008.

• **2005, Energy Tax Incentives Act of 2005 (P.L. 109-58)**

P.L. 109-58, §1303(c)(4):

Amended Code Sec. 6401(b)(1) by striking "and G" and inserting "G, and H". **Effective** for tax years beginning after 12-31-2005 [effective date amended by P.L. 109-135, §402(c)(2)].

• **1998, IRS Restructuring and Reform Act of 1998 (P.L. 105-206)**

P.L. 105-206, §6022(a):

Amended Code Sec. 6401(b)(1) by striking "and D" and inserting "D, and G". **Effective** as if included in the amendments made by section 701(b) of P.L. 99-514 [effective, generally, for tax years beginning after 12-31-86.—CCH].

• **1988, Technical and Miscellaneous Revenue Act of 1988 (P.L. 100-647)**

P.L. 100-647, §1012(s)(1)(B):

Amended Code Sec. 6401(b)(2) by striking out the last sentence and inserting in lieu thereof a new sentence. For the **effective** date, see Act Sec. 1012(s)(1)(D), below. Prior to amendment, the last sentence of Code Sec. 6401(b)(2) read as follows:

The preceding sentence shall not apply to any amount deducted and withheld under section 1446.

P.L. 100-647, §1012(s)(1)(D), provides:

The above amendment applies to tax years beginning after December 31, 1987. No amount shall be required to be deducted and withheld under section 1446 of the 1986 Code (as in effect before the amendment made by subparagraph (A)).

• **1986, Tax Reform Act of 1986 (P.L. 99-514)**

P.L. 99-514, §1246(b):

Amended Code Sec. 6401(b)(2) by adding at the end thereof the last sentence. **Effective** for distributions after 12-31-87 (or, if earlier, the **effective** date (which shall not be earlier than 1-1-87) of the initial regulations issued under section 1446 of the Internal Revenue Code of 1986 as added by this section).

• **1984, Deficit Reduction Act of 1984 (P.L. 98-369)**

P.L. 98-369, §474(r)(36):

Amended Code Sec. 6401(b). **Effective** for tax years beginning after 12-31-83, and to carrybacks from such years. Prior to amendment by Act Sec. 474(r)(36), Code Sec. 6401(b) read as follows:

(b) EXCESSIVE CREDITS.—If the amount allowable as credits under sections 31 (relating to tax withheld on wages), and 39 (relating to certain uses of gasoline and special fuels), and 43 (relating to earned income credit), exceeds the tax imposed by subtitle A (reduced by the credits allowable under subpart A of part IV of subchapter A of chapter 1, other than the credits allowable under sections 31, 39 and 43), the amount of such excess shall be considered an overpayment. For purposes of the preceding sentence, any credit allowed under paragraph (1) of section 32 (relating to withholding of tax on nonresident aliens and on foreign corporations) to a nonresident alien individual for a taxable year with respect to which an election under section 6013(g) or (h) is in effect shall be treated as an amount allowable as a credit under section 31.

P.L. 98-369, §735(c)(16):

Amended Code Sec. 6401(b) by striking out ", special fuels, and lubricating oil" and inserting in lieu thereof "and special fuels". **Effective** as if included in the provision of P.L. 97-424 to which it relates.

• **1983, Interest and Dividend Tax Compliance Act of 1983 (P.L. 98-67)**

P.L. 98-67, §102(a):

Repealed the amendment made to Code Sec. 6401(b) by P.L. 97-248 (see below) as though it had not been enacted.

• **1982, Tax Equity and Fiscal Responsibility Act of 1982 (P.L. 97-248)**

P.L. 97-248, §307(a)(9):

Amended Code Sec. 6401(b) by inserting ", interest, dividends, and patronage dividends" after "tax withheld on wages". **Effective** for interest, dividends, or patronage dividends paid or credited after 6-30-83.

• **1978, Revenue Act of 1978 (P.L. 95-600)**

P.L. 95-600, §701(u)(15)(D):

Amended Code Sec. 6401(b) by adding at the end thereof a new last sentence. **Effective** for tax years ending on or after 12-31-75.

• **1976, Tax Reform Act of 1976 (P.L. 94-455)**

P.L. 94-455, §701(f)(2):

Amended Code Sec. 6401(b), as in effect before the date of enactment of the Tax Reduction Act of 1975, by substituting "wages) and" for "wages)," and, following the words "and lubricating oil" by striking the phraseology "and 667(b) (relating to taxes paid by certain trusts". **Effective** for distributions made in tax years beginning after 12-31-75.

P.L. 94-455, §701(f)(3):

Amended Code Sec. 6401(b), as amended by the Tax Reduction Act of 1975, by substituting "lubricating oil), and" for "lubricating oil)," and following the words "earned income credit)" by striking the phraseology "and 667(b) (relating to taxes

CREDITS AND REFUNDS—GENERAL PROCEDURE

paid by certain trusts)". **Effective** for distributions made in tax years beginning after 12-31-75. After amendment, Code Sec. 6401(b) read as follows:

(b) EXCESSIVE CREDITS.—If the amount allowable as credits under section 31 (relating to tax withheld on wages), 39 (relating to certain uses of gasoline, special fuels, and lubricating oil), and 43 (relating to earned income credit) exceeds the tax imposed by subtitle A (reduced by the credits allowable under subpart A of part IV of subchapter A of chapter 1, other than credits allowable under sections 31, 39 and 43), the amount of such excess shall be considered as overpayment.

• **1975, Tax Reduction Act of 1975 (P.L. 94-12)**

P.L. 94-12, §204(b), as amended by P.L. 95-600, §103(a):

Amended Code Sec. 6401(b) by inserting "43 (relating to earned income credit)," before "and 667(b)"; and by deleting "and 39" and inserting in lieu thereof a comma and ", 39 and 43". **Effective** for tax years beginning after 1974.

• **1970 (P.L. 91-258)**

P.L. 91-258, §207(d)(1):

Amended Code Sec. 6401(b) by adding, "special fuels," after "gasoline" in the second line. **Effective** 7-1-70.

• **1969, Tax Reform Act of 1969 (P.L. 91-172)**

P.L. 91-172, §331(c):

Amended Code Sec. 6401(b) by: (1) striking out "Under Sections 31 and 39" in the heading, (2) by striking out "and 39 (relating" in the text and inserting in lieu thereof ", 39 (relating", and (3) inserting after "lubricating oil)" in the text "and 667(b) (relating to taxes paid by certain trusts)". **Effective** for tax years beginning after 12-31-68.

• **1965, Excise Tax Reduction Act of 1965 (P.L. 89-44)**

P.L. 89-44, §809(d)(6):

Amended Code Sec. 6401(b). **Effective** 7-1-65. Prior to amendment, Code Sec. 6401(b) read as follows:

"(b) Excessive Withholding.—If the amount allowable as a credit under section 31 (relating to credit for tax withheld at the source under chapter 24) exceeds the taxes imposed by chapter 1 against which such credit is allowable, the amount of such excess shall be considered an overpayment."

[Sec. 6401(c)]

(c) RULE WHERE NO TAX LIABILITY.—An amount paid as tax shall not be considered not to constitute an overpayment solely by reason of the fact that there was no tax liability in respect of which such amount was paid.

[Sec. 6401(d)—Stricken]

Amendments

• **1980, Crude Oil Windfall Profit Tax Act of 1980 (P.L. 96-223)**

P.L. 96-223, §223(2):

Amended Code Sec. 6401 by striking out subsection (d). **Effective** for qualified investment for tax years beginning after 12-31-79. Prior to amendment, Code Sec. 6401(d) read:

(d) CROSS REFERENCE.—

For rule allowing refund for excess investment credit attributable to solar or wind energy property, see section 46(a)(9)(C).

• **1980, Technical Corrections Act of 1979 (P.L. 96-222)**

P.L. 96-222, §103(a)(2)(B)(iv):

Amended Code Sec. 6401(d) by striking out "46(a)(10)(C)" and inserting "46(a)(9)(C)". **Effective** for tax years beginning after 12-31-78.

• **1978, Energy Tax Act of 1978 (P.L. 95-618)**

P.L. 95-618, §301(c)(2):

Added Code Sec. 6401(d). **Effective** 11-10-78.

[Sec. 6402]

SEC. 6402. AUTHORITY TO MAKE CREDITS OR REFUNDS.

[Sec. 6402(a)]

(a) GENERAL RULE.—In the case of any overpayment, the Secretary, within the applicable period of limitations, may credit the amount of such overpayment, including any interest allowed thereon, against any liability in respect of an internal revenue tax on the part of the person who made the overpayment and shall, subject to subsections (c), (d), (e), and (f), refund any balance to such person.

Amendments

• **2018, Tax Technical Corrections Act of 2018 (P.L. 115-141)**

P.L. 115-141, §401(a)(285), Div. U:

Amended Code Sec. 6402(a) by striking "(f) refund" and inserting "(f), refund". **Effective** 3-23-2018.

• **2008, SSI Extension for Elderly and Disabled Refugees Act (P.L. 110-328)**

P.L. 110-328, §3(d)(1):

Amended Code Sec. 6402(a) by striking "(c), (d), and (e)," and inserting "(c), (d), (e), and (f)". **Effective** for refunds payable under Code Sec. 6402 on or after 9-30-2008.

• **1998, IRS Restructuring and Reform Act of 1998 (P.L. 105-206)**

P.L. 105-206, §3711(c)(1):

Amended Code Sec. 6402(a) by striking "(c) and [or] (d)" and inserting "(c), (d), and (e)". **Effective** for refunds payable under Code Sec. 6402 after 12-31-99.

• **1997, Balanced Budget Act of 1997 (P.L. 105-33)**

P.L. 105-33, §5514(a)(1):

Struck the changes made by Act Sec. 110(l)(7)(A) of P.L. 104-193, which amended Code Sec. 6402(a) by striking "(c) or (d)" each place it appeared and inserting "(c), (d), or (e)". Thus, the provisions of law amended by such section are restored as if it had not been enacted. **Effective** 7-1-97.

• **1996, Personal Responsibility and Work Opportunity Reconciliation Act of 1996 (P.L. 104-193)**

P.L. 104-193, §110(l)(7)(A):

Amended Code Sec. 6402(a) by striking "(c) and (d)" and inserting "(c), (d), and (e)". **Effective** 7-1-97.

• **1984, Deficit Reduction Act of 1984 (P.L. 98-369)**

P.L. 98-369, §2653(b)(2):

Amended Code Sec. 6402(a) by striking out "subsection (c)" and inserting in lieu thereof "subsections (c) and (d)". **Effective** with respect to refunds payable under section 6402 of the Internal Revenue Code of 1954 after 12-31-85 [effective date changed by P.L. 100-485 and P.L. 102-164].

• **1981, Omnibus Budget Reconciliation Act of 1981 (P.L. 97-35)**

P.L. 97-35, §2331(c)(1):

Amended Code Sec. 6402(a) by striking out "shall refund" and inserting in lieu thereof "shall, subject to subsection (c), refund". For the **effective** date, see the historical comment for P.L. 97-35 following Code Sec. 6402(c).

• **1976, Tax Reform Act of 1976 (P.L. 94-455)**

P.L. 94-455, §1906(b)(13)(A):

Amended 1954 Code by substituting "Secretary" for "Secretary or his delegate" each place it appeared. **Effective** 2-1-77.

[Sec. 6402(b)]

(b) CREDITS AGAINST ESTIMATED TAX.—The Secretary is authorized to prescribe regulations providing for the crediting against the estimated income tax for any taxable year of the amount determined by the taxpayer or the Secretary to be an overpayment of the income tax for a preceding taxable year.

Amendments

• **1976, Tax Reform Act of 1976 (P.L. 94-455)**

P.L. 94-455, §1906(b)(13)(A):

Amended the 1954 Code by substituting "Secretary" for "Secretary or his delegate" each place it appeared. **Effective** 2-1-77.

P.L. 94-455, §1906(b)(13)(K):

Struck out "(or his delegate)" following "or the Secretary" in Code Sec. 6402(b). **Effective** 2-1-77.

[Sec. 6402(c)]

(c) OFFSET OF PAST-DUE SUPPORT AGAINST OVERPAYMENTS.—The amount of any overpayment to be refunded to the person making the overpayment shall be reduced by the amount of any past-due support (as defined in section 464(c) of the Social Security Act) owed by that person of which the Secretary has been notified by a State in accordance with section 464 of such Act. The Secretary shall remit the amount by which the overpayment is so reduced to the State collecting such support and notify the person making the overpayment that so much of the overpayment as was necessary to satisfy his obligation for past-due support has been paid to the State. The Secretary shall apply a reduction under this subsection first to an amount certified by the State as past due support under section 464 of the Social Security Act before any other reductions allowed by law. This subsection shall be applied to an overpayment prior to its being credited to a person's future liability for an internal revenue tax.

CREDITS AND REFUNDS—GENERAL PROCEDURE

Amendments

• **2018, Tax Technical Corrections Act of 2018 (P.L. 115-141)**

P.L. 115-141, § 401(a)(286), Div. U:

Amended Code Sec. 6402(c) by striking "of of" and inserting "of". **Effective** 3-23-2018.

• **2006, Deficit Reduction Act of 2005 (P.L. 109-171)**

P.L. 109-171, § 7301(d)(1)-(2):

Amended Code Sec. 6402(c) by striking in the first sentence "the Social Security Act." and inserting "of such Act."; and by striking the third sentence and inserting the following: "The Secretary shall apply a reduction under this subsection first to an amount certified by the State as past due support under section 464 of the Social Security Act before any other reductions allowed by law.". **Effective**, generally, 10-1-2009. For a special rule, see Act Sec. 7301(e), below. Prior to being stricken the third sentence of Code Sec. 6402(c) read as follows:

A reduction under this subsection shall be applied first to satisfy any past-due support which has been assigned to the State under section 402(a)(26) or 471(a)(17) of the Social Security Act, and shall be applied to satisfy any other past-due support after any other reductions allowed by law (but before a credit against future liability for an internal revenue tax) have been made.

P.L. 109-171, § 7301(e), provides:

(e) EFFECTIVE DATE.—

(1) IN GENERAL.—Except as otherwise provided in this section, the amendments made by the preceding provisions of this section shall take effect on October 1, 2009, and shall apply to payments under parts A and D of title IV of the Social Security Act for calendar quarters beginning on or after such date, and without regard to whether regulations to implement the amendments (in the case of State programs operated under such part D) are promulgated by such date.

(2) STATE OPTION TO ACCELERATE EFFECTIVE DATE.—Notwithstanding paragraph (1), a State may elect to have the amendments made by the preceding provisions of this section apply to the State and to amounts collected by the State (and the payments under parts A and D), on and after such date as the State may select that is not earlier than October 1, 2008, and not later than September 30, 2009.

• **1984, Child Support Enforcement Amendments of 1984 (P.L. 98-378)**

P.L. 98-378, § 21(e)(1):

Amended Code Sec. 6402(c) by striking out "to which such support has been assigned" and inserting in lieu thereof "collecting such support"; and by inserting before the last sentence thereof "A reduction under this subsection shall be applied first to satisfy any past-due support which has been assigned to the State under section 402(a)(26) or 471(a)(17) of the Social Security Act, and shall be applied to satisfy any other past-due support after any other reductions allowed by law (but before a credit against future liability for an internal revenue tax) have been made." **Effective** with respect to refunds payable under Code Sec. 6402 after 12-31-85.

• **1981, Omnibus Budget Reconciliation Act of 1981 (P.L. 97-35)**

P.L. 97-35, § 2331(c)(2):

Added Code Sec. 6402(c). **Effective** as noted in Act Sec. 2336, below.

P.L. 97-35, § 2336, provides:

SEC. 2336. (a) Except as otherwise specifically provided in the preceding sections of this chapter or in subsection (b), the provisions of this chapter and the amendments and repeals made by this chapter shall become effective on October 1, 1981.

(b) If a State agency administering a plan approved under part D of title IV of the Social Security Act demonstrates, to the satisfaction of the Secretary of Health and Human Services, that it cannot, by reason of State law, comply with the requirements of an amendment made by this chapter to which the effective date specified in subsection (a) applies, the Secretary may prescribe that, in the case of such State, the amendment will become effective beginning with the first month beginning after the close of the first session of such State's legislature ending on or after October 1, 1981. For purposes of the preceding sentence, the term "session of a State's legislature" includes any regular, special, budget, or other session of a State legislature.

[Sec. 6402(d)]

(d) COLLECTION OF DEBTS OWED TO FEDERAL AGENCIES.—

(1) IN GENERAL.—Upon receiving notice from any Federal agency that a named person owes a past-due legally enforceable debt (other than past-due support subject to the provisions of subsection (c)) to such agency, the Secretary shall—

(A) reduce the amount of any overpayment payable to such person by the amount of such debt;

(B) pay the amount by which such overpayment is reduced under subparagraph (A) to such agency; and

(C) notify the person making such overpayment that such overpayment has been reduced by an amount necessary to satisfy such debt.

(2) PRIORITIES FOR OFFSET.—Any overpayment by a person shall be reduced pursuant to this subsection after such overpayment is reduced pursuant to subsection (c) with respect to past-due support collected pursuant to an assignment under section 408(a)(3) of the Social Security Act (42 U.S.C. 608(a)(3)) and before such overpayment is reduced pursuant to subsections (e) and (f) and before such overpayment is credited to the future liability for tax of such person pursuant to subsection (b). If the Secretary receives notice from a Federal agency or agencies of more than one debt subject to paragraph (1) that is owed by a person to such agency or agencies, any overpayment by such person shall be applied against such debts in the order in which such debts accrued.

(3) TREATMENT OF OASDI OVERPAYMENTS.—

(A) REQUIREMENTS.—Paragraph (1) shall apply with respect to an OASDI overpayment only if the requirements of paragraphs (1) and (2) of section 3720A(f) of title 31, United States Code, are met with respect to such overpayment.

(B) NOTICE; PROTECTION OF OTHER PERSONS FILING JOINT RETURN.—

(i) NOTICE.—In the case of a debt consisting of an OASDI overpayment, if the Secretary determines upon receipt of the notice referred to in paragraph (1) that the refund from which the reduction described in paragraph (1)(A) would be made is based upon a joint return, the Secretary shall—

(I) notify each taxpayer filing such joint return that the reduction is being made from a refund based upon such return, and

(II) include in such notification a description of the procedures to be followed, in the case of a joint return, to protect the share of the refund which may be payable to another person.

(ii) ADJUSTMENTS BASED ON PROTECTIONS GIVEN TO OTHER TAXPAYERS ON JOINT RETURN.—If the other person filing a joint return with the person owing the OASDI overpayment takes appropriate action to secure his or her proper share of the refund subject to reduction under this subsection, the Secretary shall pay such share to such other person. The Secretary shall deduct the amount of such payment from amounts which are derived from subsequent reductions in refunds under this subsection and are payable to a trust fund referred to in subparagraph (C).

(C) DEPOSIT OF AMOUNT OF REDUCTION INTO APPROPRIATE TRUST FUND.—In lieu of payment, pursuant to paragraph (1)(B), of the amount of any reduction under this subsection to the Commissioner of Social Security, the Secretary shall deposit such amount in the Federal Old-Age and Survivors Insurance Trust Fund or the Federal Disability Insurance Trust Fund, whichever is certified to the Secretary as appropriate by the Commissioner of Social Security.

(D) OASDI OVERPAYMENT.—For purposes of this paragraph, the term "OASDI overpayment" means any overpayment of benefits made to an individual under title II of the Social Security Act.

Amendments

• **2018, Tax Technical Corrections Act of 2018 (P.L. 115-141)**

P.L. 115-141, § 401(a)(287), Div. U:

Amended Code Sec. 6402(d)(2) by striking "section 402(a)(26) of the Social Security Act" and inserting "section 408(a)(3) of the Social Security Act (42 U.S.C. 608(a)(3))". **Effective** 3-23-2018.

• **2008, SSI Extension for Elderly and Disabled Refugees Act (P.L. 110-328)**

P.L. 110-328, § 3(d)(2):

Amended Code Sec. 6402(d)(2) by striking "and before such overpayment is reduced pursuant to subsection (e)" and inserting "and before such overpayment is reduced pursuant to subsections (e) and (f)". **Effective** for refunds payable under Code Sec. 6402 on or after 9-30-2008.

• **1998, IRS Restructuring and Reform Act of 1998 (P.L. 105-206)**

P.L. 105-206, § 3711(c)(2):

Amended Code Sec. 6402(d)(2) by striking "and before such overpayment" and inserting "and before such overpayment is reduced pursuant to subsection (e) and before such overpayment". **Effective** for refunds payable under Code Sec. 6402 after 12-31-99.

• **1994, Social Security Independence and Program Improvements Act of 1994 (P.L. 103-296)**

P.L. 103-296, § 108(h)(7):

Amended Code Sec. 6402(d)(3)(C) by striking "Secretary of Health and Human Services" each place it appears and inserting "Commissioner of Social Security". **Effective** 3-31-95.

CREDITS AND REFUNDS—GENERAL PROCEDURE

• **1990, Omnibus Budget Reconciliation Act of 1990 (P.L. 101-508)**

P.L. 101-508, §5129(c)(1)(A):

Amended Code Sec. 6402(d)(1) by striking "any OASDI overpayment and" after "other than". **Effective** 1-1-91, and shall not apply to refunds to which the amendments made by section 2653 of the Deficit Reduction Act of 1984 (98 Stat. 1153) do not apply.

P.L. 101-508, §5129(c)(1)(B):

Amended Code Sec. 6402(d) by striking paragraph (3) and inserting new paragraph (3). **Effective** 1-1-91, and shall not apply to refunds to which the amendments made by section 2653 of P.L. 98-369 (98 Stat. 1153) do not apply. Prior to amendment, paragraph (3) read as follows:

(3) DEFINITIONS.—For purposes of this subsection the term "OASDI overpayment" means any overpayment of benefits made to an individual under title II of the Social Security Act.

• **1984, Deficit Reduction Act of 1984 (P.L. 98-369)**

P.L. 98-369, §2653(b)(1):

Amended Code Sec. 6402 by adding subsection (d). **Effective** with respect to refunds payable under section 6402 of the Internal Revenue Code of 1954 after 12-31-85 [**effective** date changed by P.L. 100-485 and P.L. 102-164].

[Sec. 6402(e)]

(e) COLLECTION OF PAST-DUE, LEGALLY ENFORCEABLE STATE INCOME TAX OBLIGATIONS.—

(1) IN GENERAL.—Upon receiving notice from any State that a named person owes a past-due, legally enforceable State income tax obligation to such State, the Secretary shall, under such conditions as may be prescribed by the Secretary—

(A) reduce the amount of any overpayment payable to such person by the amount of such State income tax obligation;

(B) pay the amount by which such overpayment is reduced under subparagraph (A) to such State and notify such State of such person's name, taxpayer identification number, address, and the amount collected; and

(C) notify the person making such overpayment that the overpayment has been reduced by an amount necessary to satisfy a pastdue, legally enforceable State income tax obligation.

If an offset is made pursuant to a joint return, the notice under subparagraph (B) shall include the names, taxpayer identification numbers, and addresses of each person filing such return.

(2) OFFSET PERMITTED ONLY AGAINST RESIDENTS OF STATE SEEKING OFFSET.—Paragraph (1) shall apply to an overpayment by any person for a taxable year only if the address shown on the Federal return for such taxable year of the overpayment is an address within the State seeking the offset.

(3) PRIORITIES FOR OFFSET.—Any overpayment by a person shall be reduced pursuant to this subsection—

(A) after such overpayment is reduced pursuant to—

(i) subsection (a) with respect to any liability for any internal revenue tax on the part of the person who made the overpayment;

(ii) subsection (c) with respect to past-due support; and

(iii) subsection (d) with respect to any past-due, legally enforceable debt owed to a Federal agency; and

(B) before such overpayment is credited to the future liability for any Federal internal revenue tax of such person pursuant to subsection (b).

If the Secretary receives notice from one or more agencies of the State of more than one debt subject to paragraph (1) or subsection (f) that is owed by such person to such an agency, any overpayment by such person shall be applied against such debts in the order in which such debts accrued.

(4) NOTICE; CONSIDERATION OF EVIDENCE.— No State may take action under this subsection until such State—

(A) notifies by certified mail with return receipt the person owing the past-due State income tax liability that the State proposes to take action pursuant to this section;

(B) gives such person at least 60 days to present evidence that all or part of such liability is not past-due or not legally enforceable;

(C) considers any evidence presented by such person and determines that an amount of such debt is past-due and legally enforceable; and

(D) satisfies such other conditions as the Secretary may prescribe to ensure that the determination made under subparagraph (C) is valid and that the State has made reasonable efforts to obtain payment of such State income tax obligation.

(5) PAST-DUE, LEGALLY ENFORCEABLE STATE INCOME TAX OBLIGATION.—For purposes of this subsection, the term "past-due, legally enforceable State income tax obligation" means a debt—

(A)(i) which resulted from—

(I) a judgment rendered by a court of competent jurisdiction which has determined an amount of State income tax to be due; or

(II) a determination after an administrative hearing which has determined an amount of State income tax to be due; and

(ii) which is no longer subject to judicial review; or

(B) which resulted from a State income tax which has been assessed but not collected, the time for redetermination of which has expired, and which has not been delinquent for more than 10 years.

For purposes of this paragraph, the term "State income tax" includes any local income tax administered by the chief tax administration agency of the State.

(6) REGULATIONS.—The Secretary shall issue regulations prescribing the time and manner in which States must submit notices of past-due, legally enforceable State income tax obligations and the necessary information that must be contained in or accompany such notices. The regulations shall specify the types of State income taxes and the minimum amount of debt to which the reduction procedure established by paragraph (1) may be applied. The regulations may require States to pay a fee to reimburse the Secretary for the cost of applying such procedure. Any fee paid to the Secretary pursuant to the preceding sentence shall be used to reimburse appropriations which bore all or part of the cost of applying such procedure.

(7) ERRONEOUS PAYMENT TO STATE.—Any State receiving notice from the Secretary that an erroneous payment has been made to such State under paragraph (1) shall pay promptly to the Secretary, in accordance with such regulations as the Secretary may prescribe, an amount equal to the amount of such erroneous payment (without regard to whether any other amounts payable to such State under such paragraph have been paid to such State).

Amendments

• **2008, SSI Extension for Elderly and Disabled Refugees Act (P.L. 110-328)**

P.L. 110-328, §3(d)(3):

Amended the last sentence of Code Sec. 6402(e)(3) by inserting "or subsection (f)" after "paragraph (1)". **Effective** for refunds payable under Code Sec. 6402 on or after 9-30-2008.

• **1998, IRS Restructuring and Reform Act of 1998 (P.L. 105-206)**

P.L. 105-206, §3711(a):

Amended Code Sec. 6402, as amended by Act Sec. 3505(a), by redesignating subsections (e) through (j) as subsections (f) through (k), respectively, and by inserting after subsection (d) a new subsection (e). **Effective** for refunds payable under Code Sec. 6402 after 12-31-99.

CREDITS AND REFUNDS—GENERAL PROCEDURE

• **1997, Balanced Budget Act of 1997 (P.L. 105-33)**

P.L. 105-33, § 5514(a)(1):

Struck the change made by Act Sec. 110(l)(7)(C) of P.L. 104-193, which added a new Code Sec. 6402(e). Thus, subsection (e) of Code Sec. 6402 never took effect, and Code Sec. 6402 is restored as if Act Sec. 110(l)(7)(C) was never enacted. **Effective** 7-1-97. Prior to being stricken, Code Sec. 6402(e) read as follows:

(e) COLLECTION OF OVERPAYMENTS UNDER TITLE IV-A OF THE SOCIAL SECURITY ACT.—The amount of any overpayment to be refunded to the person making the overpayment shall be reduced (after reductions pursuant to subsections (c) and (d), but before a credit against future liability for an internal revenue tax) in accordance with section 405(e) of the Social Security Act (concerning recovery of overpayments to individuals under State plans approved under part A of title IV of such Act).

• **1996, Personal Responsibility and Work Opportunity Reconciliation Act of 1996 (P.L. 104-193)**

P.L. 104-193, § 110(l)(7)(B)-(C):

Amended Code Sec. 6402 by redesignating subsections (e) through (i) as subsections (f) through (j) respectively; and by inserting after subsection (d) a new subsection (e). **Effective** 7-1-97.

[Sec. 6402(f)]

(f) COLLECTION OF UNEMPLOYMENT COMPENSATION DEBTS.—

(1) IN GENERAL.—Upon receiving notice from any State that a named person owes a covered unemployment compensation debt to such State, the Secretary shall, under such conditions as may be prescribed by the Secretary—

(A) reduce the amount of any overpayment payable to such person by the amount of such covered unemployment compensation debt;

(B) pay the amount by which such overpayment is reduced under subparagraph (A) to such State and notify such State of such person's name, taxpayer identification number, address, and the amount collected; and

(C) notify the person making such overpayment that the overpayment has been reduced by an amount necessary to satisfy a covered unemployment compensation debt.

If an offset is made pursuant to a joint return, the notice under subparagraph (C) shall include information related to the rights of a spouse of a person subject to such an offset.

(2) PRIORITIES FOR OFFSET.—Any overpayment by a person shall be reduced pursuant to this subsection—

(A) after such overpayment is reduced pursuant to—

(i) subsection (a) with respect to any liability for any internal revenue tax on the part of the person who made the overpayment;

(ii) subsection (c) with respect to past-due support; and

(iii) subsection (d) with respect to any past-due, legally enforceable debt owed to a Federal agency; and

(B) before such overpayment is credited to the future liability for any Federal internal revenue tax of such person pursuant to subsection (b).

If the Secretary receives notice from a State or States of more than one debt subject to paragraph (1) or subsection (e) that is owed by a person to such State or States, any overpayment by such person shall be applied against such debts in the order in which such debts accrued.

(3) NOTICE; CONSIDERATION OF EVIDENCE.—No State may take action under this subsection until such State—

(A) notifies the person owing the covered unemployment compensation debt that the State proposes to take action pursuant to this section;

(B) provides such person at least 60 days to present evidence that all or part of such liability is not legally enforceable or is not a covered unemployment compensation debt;

(C) considers any evidence presented by such person and determines that an amount of such debt is legally enforceable and is a covered unemployment compensation debt; and

(D) satisfies such other conditions as the Secretary may prescribe to ensure that the determination made under subparagraph (C) is valid and that the State has made reasonable efforts to obtain payment of such covered unemployment compensation debt.

(4) COVERED UNEMPLOYMENT COMPENSATION DEBT.—For purposes of this subsection, the term "covered unemployment compensation debt" means—

(A) a past-due debt for erroneous payment of unemployment compensation due to fraud or the person's failure to report earnings which has become final under the law of a State certified by the Secretary of Labor pursuant to section 3304 and which remains uncollected;

(B) contributions due to the unemployment fund of a State for which the State has determined the person to be liable and which remain uncollected; and

(C) any penalties and interest assessed on such debt.

(5) REGULATIONS.—

(A) IN GENERAL.—The Secretary may issue regulations prescribing the time and manner in which States must submit notices of covered unemployment compensation debt and the necessary information that must be contained in or accompany such notices. The regulations may specify the minimum amount of debt to which the reduction procedure established by paragraph (1) may be applied.

(B) FEE PAYABLE TO SECRETARY.—The regulations may require States to pay a fee to the Secretary, which may be deducted from amounts collected, to reimburse the Secretary for the cost of applying such procedure. Any fee paid to the Secretary pursuant to the preceding sentence shall be used to reimburse appropriations which bore all or part of the cost of applying such procedure.

(C) SUBMISSION OF NOTICES THROUGH SECRETARY OF LABOR.—The regulations may include a requirement that States submit notices of covered unemployment compensation debt to the Secretary via the Secretary of Labor in accordance with procedures established by the Secretary of Labor. Such procedures may require States to pay a fee to the Secretary of Labor to reimburse the Secretary of Labor for the costs of applying this subsection. Any such fee shall be established in consultation with the Secretary of the Treasury. Any fee paid to the Secretary of Labor may be deducted from amounts collected and shall be used to reimburse the appropriation account which bore all or part of the cost of applying this subsection.

(6) ERRONEOUS PAYMENT TO STATE.—Any State receiving notice from the Secretary that an erroneous payment has been made to such State under paragraph (1) shall pay promptly to the Secretary, in accordance with such regulations as the Secretary may prescribe, an amount equal to the amount of such erroneous payment (without regard to whether any other amounts payable to such State under such paragraph have been paid to such State).

Amendments

• **2010, Tax Relief, Unemployment Insurance Reauthorization, and Job Creation Act of 2010 (P.L. 111-312)**

P.L. 111-312, § 503(a):

Amended Code Sec. 6402(f)(3)(C), as amended by section 801 of the Claims Resolution Act of 2010 (P.L. 111-291), by striking "is not a covered unemployment compensation debt" and inserting "is a covered unemployment compensation debt". **Effective** as if included in section 801 of the Claims Resolution Act of 2010 (P.L. 111-291) [effective for refunds payable under Code Sec. 6402 on or after 12-8-2010.—CCH].

• **2010, Claims Resolution Act of 2010 (P.L. 111-291)**

P.L. 111-291, § 801(a)(1)-(4):

Amended Code Sec. 6402(f) by striking "RESULTING FROM FRAUD" following "COMPENSATION DEBTS" in the heading; by striking paragraphs (3) and (8) and redesignating paragraphs (4) through (7) as paragraphs (3) through (6), respectively; in paragraph

CREDITS AND REFUNDS—GENERAL PROCEDURE

(3), as so redesignated, by striking "by certified mail with return receipt" following "notifies" in subparagraph (A); by striking "due to fraud" and inserting "is not a covered unemployment compensation debt" in subparagraph (B); by striking " due to fraud" and inserting "is not [sic] a covered unemployment compensation debt" in subparagraph (C); and in paragraph (4), as so redesignated, in subparagraph (A), by inserting "or the person's failure to report earnings" after "due to fraud"; and by striking "for not more than 10 years" following "which remains uncollected"; and in subparagraph (B), by striking "due to fraud" following "the person to be liable"; and by striking "for not more than 10 years" following "which remain uncollected". **Effective** for refunds payable under Code Sec. 6402 on or after 12-8-2010. Prior to being stricken, Code Sec. 6402(f)(3) and (8) read as follows:

(3) OFFSET PERMITTED ONLY AGAINST RESIDENTS OF STATE SEEKING OFFSET.—Paragraph (1) shall apply to an overpayment by any person for a taxable year only if the address shown on the Federal return for such taxable year of the overpayment is an address within the State seeking the offset.

(8) TERMINATION.—This section shall not apply to refunds payable after the date which is 10 years after the date of the enactment of this subsection.

***

- **2008, SSI Extension for Elderly and Disabled Refugees Act (P.L. 110-328)**

P.L. 110-328, §3(a):

Amended Code Sec. 6402 by redesignating subsections (f) through (k) as subsections (g) through (l), respectively, and by inserting after subsection (e) a new subsection (f). **Effective** for refunds payable under Code Sec. 6402 on or after 9-30-2008.

[Sec. 6402(g)]

(g) REVIEW OF REDUCTIONS.—No court of the United States shall have jurisdiction to hear any action, whether legal or equitable, brought to restrain or review a reduction authorized by subsection (c), (d), (e), or (f). No such reduction shall be subject to review by the Secretary in an administrative proceeding. No action brought against the United States to recover the amount of any such reduction shall be considered to be a suit for refund of tax. This subsection does not preclude any legal, equitable, or administrative action against the Federal agency or State to which the amount of such reduction was paid or any such action against the Commissioner of Social Security which is otherwise available with respect to recoveries of overpayments of benefits under section 204 of the Social Security Act.

Amendments

- **2008, SSI Extension for Elderly and Disabled Refugees Act (P.L. 110-328)**

P.L. 110-328, §3(a):

Amended Code Sec. 6402 by redesignating subsection (f) as subsection (g). **Effective** for refunds payable under Code Sec. 6402 on or after 9-30-2008.

P.L. 110-328, §3(d)(4):

Amended Code Sec. 6402(g), as redesignated by Act Sec. 3(a), by striking "(c), (d), or (e)" and inserting "(c), (d), (e), or (f)". **Effective** for refunds payable under Code Sec. 6402 on or after 9-30-2008.

- **1998, IRS Restructuring and Reform Act of 1998 (P.L. 105-206)**

P.L. 105-206, §3711(a):

Amended Code Sec. 6402 by redesignating subsection (e) as subsection (f). **Effective** for refunds payable under Code Sec. 6402 after 12-31-99.

P.L. 105-206, §3711(c)(3)(A)-(B):

Amended Code Sec. 6402(f), as redesignated by Act Sec. 3711(a), by striking "(c) or (d)" and inserting "(c), (d), or (e)", and by striking "Federal agency" and inserting "Federal agency or State". **Effective** for refunds payable under Code Sec. 6402 after 12-31-99.

- **1997, Balanced Budget Act of 1997 (P.L. 105-33)**

P.L. 105-33, §5514(a)(1):

Struck the change made by Act Sec. 110(l)(7)(B) of P.L. 104-193, which redesignated Code Sec. 6402(e) as Code Sec. 6402(f). The provision of law added by P.L. 104-193 is restored as if Act Sec. 110(l)(7)(B) had not been enacted. Thus, subsection (f) of Code Sec. 6402 is now designated as subsection (e) of Code Sec. 6402. **Effective** 7-1-97.

- **1996, Personal Responsibility and Work Opportunity Reconciliation Act of 1996 (P.L. 104-193)**

P.L. 104-193, §110(l)(7)(B):

Amended Code Sec. 6402 by redesignating subsection (e) as subsection (f). **Effective** 7-1-97.

- **1994, Social Security Independence and Program Improvements Act of 1994 (P.L. 103-296)**

P.L. 103-296, §108(h)(7):

Amended Code Sec. 6402(e) by striking "Secretary of Health and Human Services" each place it appears and inserting "Commissioner of Social Security". **Effective** 3-31-95.

- **1990, Omnibus Budget Reconciliation Act of 1990 (P.L. 101-508)**

P.L. 101-508, §5129(c)(2):

Amended Code Sec. 6402(e) by inserting before the period in the last sentence the following: "or any such action against the Secretary of Health and Human Services which is otherwise available with respect to recoveries of overpayments of benefits under section 204 of the Social Security Act". **Effective** 1-1-91, and shall not apply to refunds to which the Deficit Reduction Act of 1984 (98 Stat. 1153) does not apply.

- **1984, Deficit Reduction Act of 1984 (P.L. 98-369)**

P.L. 98-369, §2653(b)(1):

Amended Code Sec. 6402 by adding subsection (e). **Effective** with respect to refunds payable under section 6402 of the Internal Revenue Code of 1954 after 12-31-85 [effective date changed by P.L. 100-485 and P.L. 102-164].

[Sec. 6402(h)]

(h) FEDERAL AGENCY.—For purposes of this section, the term "Federal agency" means a department, agency, or instrumentality of the United States, and includes a Government corporation (as such term is defined in section 103 of title 5, United States Code).

Amendments

- **2008, SSI Extension for Elderly and Disabled Refugees Act (P.L. 110-328)**

P.L. 110-328, §3(a):

Amended Code Sec. 6402 by redesignating subsection (g) as subsection (h). **Effective** for refunds payable under Code Sec. 6402 on or after 9-30-2008.

- **1998, IRS Restructuring and Reform Act of 1998 (P.L. 105-206)**

P.L. 105-206, §3711(a):

Amended Code Sec. 6402 by redesignating subsection (f) as subsection (g). **Effective** for refunds payable under Code Sec. 6402 after 12-31-99.

- **1997, Balanced Budget Act of 1997 (P.L. 105-33)**

P.L. 105-33, §5514(a)(1):

Struck the change made by Act Sec. 110(l)(7)(B) of P.L. 104-193, which redesignated Code Sec. 6402(f) as Code Sec. 6402(g). The provision of law added by P.L. 104-193 is restored as if Act Sec. 110(l)(7)(B) had not been enacted. Thus, subsection (g) of Code Sec. 6402 is now designated as subsection (f) of Code Sec. 6402. **Effective** 7-1-97.

- **1996, Personal Responsibility and Work Opportunity Reconciliation Act of 1996 (P.L. 104-193)**

P.L. 104-193, §110(l)(7)(B):

Amended Code Sec. 6402 by redesignating subsection (f) as subsection (g). **Effective** 7-1-97.

- **1996, Debt Collection Improvement Act of 1996 (P.L. 104-134)**

P.L. 104-134, §31001(u)(2):

Amended Code Sec. 6402(f). **Effective** 4-26-96. Prior to amendment Code Sec. 6402(f) read as follows:

(f) FEDERAL AGENCY.—For purposes of this section, the term "Federal agency" means a department, agency, or instrumentality of the United States (other than an agency subject to section 9 of the Act of May 18, 1933 (48 Stat. 63, chapter 32; 16 U.S.C. 831h)), and includes a Government corporation (as such term is defined in section 103 of title 5, United States Code).

- **1984, Deficit Reduction Act of 1984 (P.L. 98-369)**

P.L. 98-369, §2653(b)(1):

Amended Code Sec. 6402 by adding subsection (f). **Effective** with respect to refunds payable under section 6402 of the Internal Revenue Code of 1954 after 12-31-85 [effective date changed by P.L. 100-485 and P.L. 102-164].

[Sec. 6402(i)]

(i) TREATMENT OF PAYMENTS TO STATES.—The Secretary may provide that, for purposes of determining interest, the payment of any amount withheld under subsection (c), (e), or (f) to a State shall be treated as a payment to the person or persons making the overpayment.

Amendments

- **2008, SSI Extension for Elderly and Disabled Refugees Act (P.L. 110-328)**

P.L. 110-328, §3(a):

Amended Code Sec. 6402 by redesignating subsection (h) as subsection (i). **Effective** for refunds payable under Code Sec. 6402 on or after 9-30-2008.

P.L. 110-328, §3(d)(5):

Amended Code Sec. 6402(i), as redesignated by Act Sec. 3(a), by striking "subsection (c) or (e)" and inserting "subsection (c), (e), or (f)". **Effective** for refunds payable under Code Sec. 6402 on or after 9-30-2008.

CREDITS AND REFUNDS—GENERAL PROCEDURE

• **1998, IRS Restructuring and Reform Act of 1998 (P.L. 105-206)**

P.L. 105-206, § 3711(a):

Amended Code Sec. 6402 by redesignating subsection (g) as subsection (h). **Effective** for refunds payable under Code Sec. 6402 after 12-31-99.

P.L. 105-206, § 3711(c)(4):

Amended Code Sec. 6402(h), as redesignated by Act Sec. 3711(a), by striking "subsection (c)" and inserting "subsection (c) or (e)". **Effective** for refunds payable under Code Sec. 6402 after 12-31-99.

• **1997, Balanced Budget Act of 1997 (P.L. 105-33)**

P.L. 105-33, § 5514(a)(1):

Struck the change made by Act Sec. 110(l)(7)(B) of P.L. 104-193, which redesignated Code Sec. 6402(g) as Code Sec. 6402(h). The provision of law added by P.L. 104-193 is restored as if Act Sec. 110(l)(7)(B) had not been enacted. Thus, subsection (h) of Code Sec. 6402 is now designated as subsection (g) of Code Sec. 6402. **Effective** 7-1-97.

• **1996, Personal Responsibility and Work Opportunity Reconciliation Act of 1996 (P.L. 104-193)**

P.L. 104-193, § 110(l)(7)(B):

Amended Code Sec. 6402 by redesignating subsection (g) as subsection (h). **Effective** 7-1-97.

• **1984, Child Support Enforcement Amendments of 1984 (P.L. 98-378)**

P.L. 98-378, § 21(e)(2):

Amended Code Sec. 6402 by adding at the end thereof new subsection (g). **Effective** with respect to refunds payable under Code Sec. 6402 after 12-31-85.

[Sec. 6402(j)]

(j) CROSS REFERENCE.—

For procedures relating to agency notification of the Secretary, see section 3721 of title 31, United States Code.

Amendments

• **2008, SSI Extension for Elderly and Disabled Refugees Act (P.L. 110-328)**

P.L. 110-328, § 3(a):

Amended Code Sec. 6402 by redesignating subsection (i) as subsection (j). **Effective** for refunds payable under Code Sec. 6402 on or after 9-30-2008.

• **1998, IRS Restructuring and Reform Act of 1998 (P.L. 105-206)**

P.L. 105-206, § 3711(a):

Amended Code Sec. 6402 by redesignating subsection (h) as subsection (i). **Effective** for refunds payable under Code Sec. 6402 after 12-31-99.

• **1997, Balanced Budget Act of 1997 (P.L. 105-33)**

P.L. 105-33, § 5514(a)(1):

Struck the change made by Act Sec. 110(l)(7)(B) of P.L. 104-193, which redesignated Code Sec. 6402(h) as Code Sec. 6402(i). The provision of law added by P.L. 104-193 is restored as if Act Sec. 110(l)(7)(B) had not been enacted. Thus, subsection (i) of Code Sec. 6402 is now designated as subsection (h) of Code Sec. 6402. **Effective** 7-1-97.

• **1996, Personal Responsibility and Work Opportunity Reconciliation Act of 1996 (P.L. 104-193)**

P.L. 104-193, § 110(l)(7)(B):

Amended Code Sec. 6402 by redesignating subsection (h) as subsection (i). **Effective** 7-1-97.

• **1984, Child Support Enforcement Amendments of 1984 (P.L. 98-378)**

P.L. 98-378, § 21(e)(2):

Redesignated Code Sec. 6402(g) as (h). **Effective** with respect to refunds payable under Code Sec. 6402 after 12-31-85.

• **1984, Deficit Reduction Act of 1984 (P.L. 98-369)**

P.L. 98-369, § 2653(b)(1):

Amended Code Sec. 6402 by adding subsection (g). **Effective** with respect to refunds payable under section 6402 of the Internal Revenue Code of 1954 after 12-31-85 [effective date changed by P.L. 100-485 and P.L. 102-164].

[Sec. 6402(k)]

(k) REFUNDS TO CERTAIN FIDUCIARIES OF INSOLVENT MEMBERS OF AFFILIATED GROUPS.—Notwithstanding any other provision of law, in the case of an insolvent corporation which is a member of an affiliated group of corporations filing a consolidated return for any taxable year and which is subject to a statutory or court-appointed fiduciary, the Secretary may by regulation provide that any refund for such taxable year may be paid on behalf of such insolvent corporation to such fiduciary to the extent that the Secretary determines that the refund is attributable to losses or credits of such insolvent corporation.

Amendments

• **2008, SSI Extension for Elderly and Disabled Refugees Act (P.L. 110-328)**

P.L. 110-328, § 3(a):

Amended Code Sec. 6402 by redesignating subsection (j) as subsection (k). **Effective** for refunds payable under Code Sec. 6402 on or after 9-30-2008.

• **1998, IRS Restructuring and Reform Act of 1998 (P.L. 105-206)**

P.L. 105-206, § 3711(a):

Amended Code Sec. 6402 by redesignating subsection (i) as subsection (j). **Effective** for refunds payable under Code Sec. 6402 after 12-31-99.

• **1997, Balanced Budget Act of 1997 (P.L. 105-33)**

P.L. 105-33, § 5514(a)(1):

Struck the change made by Act Sec. 110(l)(7)(B) of P.L. 104-193, which redesignated Code Sec. 6402(i) as Code Sec. 6402(j). The provision of law added by P.L. 104-193 is restored as if Act Sec. 110(l)(7)(B) had not been enacted. Thus, subsection (j) of Code Sec. 6402 is now designated as subsection (i) of Code Sec. 6402. **Effective** 7-1-97.

• **1996, Personal Responsibility and Work Opportunity Reconciliation Act of 1996 (P.L. 104-193)**

P.L. 104-193, § 110(l)(7)(B):

Amended Code Sec. 6402 by redesignating subsection (i) as subsection (j). **Effective** 7-1-97.

• **1988, Technical and Miscellaneous Revenue Act of 1988 (P.L. 100-647)**

P.L. 100-647, § 6276:

Amended Code Sec. 6402 by adding at the end thereof new subsection (i). **Effective** 11-10-88.

[Sec. 6402(l)]

(l) EXPLANATION OF REASON FOR REFUND DISALLOWANCE.—In the case of a disallowance of a claim for refund, the Secretary shall provide the taxpayer with an explanation for such disallowance.

Amendments

• **2008, SSI Extension for Elderly and Disabled Refugees Act (P.L. 110-328)**

P.L. 110-328, § 3(a):

Amended Code Sec. 6402 by redesignating subsection (k) as subsection (l). **Effective** for refunds payable under Code Sec. 6402 on or after 9-30-2008.

• **1998, IRS Restructuring and Reform Act of 1998 (P.L. 105-206)**

P.L. 105-206, § 3505(a):

Amended Code Sec. 6402 by adding at the end a new subsection (j). **Effective** for disallowances after the 180th day after 7-22-98.

P.L. 105-206, § 3711(a):

Amended Code Sec. 6402(j), as added by Act Sec. 3505(a), by redesignating subsection (j) as subsection (k). **Effective** for refunds payable under Code Sec. 6402 after 12-31-99.

[Sec. 6402(m)]

(m) EARLIEST DATE FOR CERTAIN REFUNDS.—No credit or refund of an overpayment for a taxable year shall be made to a taxpayer before the 15th day of the second month following the close of such taxable year if a credit is allowed to such taxpayer under section 24 (by reason of subsection (d) thereof) or 32 for such taxable year.

Amendments

• **2015, Protecting Americans from Tax Hikes Act of 2015 (P.L. 114-113)**

P.L. 114-113, § 201(b), Div. Q:

Amended Code Sec. 6402 by adding at the end a new subsection (m). **Effective** for credits or refunds made after 12-31-2016.

CREDITS AND REFUNDS—GENERAL PROCEDURE

[Sec. 6402(n)]

(n) MISDIRECTED DIRECT DEPOSIT REFUND.—Not later than the date which is 6 months after the date of the enactment of the Taxpayer First Act, the Secretary shall prescribe regulations to establish procedures to allow for—

(1) taxpayers to report instances in which a refund made by the Secretary by electronic funds transfer was not transferred to the account of the taxpayer;

(2) coordination with financial institutions for the purpose of—

(A) identifying the accounts to which transfers described in paragraph (1) were made; and

(B) recovery of the amounts so transferred; and

(3) the refund to be delivered to the correct account of the taxpayer.

Amendments

• **2019, Taxpayer First Act (P.L. 116-25)**

P.L. 116-25, §1407:

Amended Code Sec. 6402 by adding at the end a new subsection (n). **Effective** 7-1-2019.

[Sec. 6403]

SEC. 6403. OVERPAYMENT OF INSTALLMENT.

In the case of a tax payable in installments, if the taxpayer has paid as an installment of the tax more than the amount determined to be the correct amount of such installment, the overpayment shall be credited against the unpaid installments, if any. If the amount already paid, whether or not on the basis of installments, exceeds the amount determined to be the correct amount of the tax, the overpayment shall be credited or refunded as provided in section 6402.

[Sec. 6404]

SEC. 6404. ABATEMENTS.

[Sec. 6404(a)]

(a) GENERAL RULE.—The Secretary is authorized to abate the unpaid portion of the assessment of any tax or any liability in respect thereof, which—

(1) is excessive in amount, or

(2) is assessed after the expiration of the period of limitations properly applicable thereto, or

(3) is erroneously or illegally assessed.

Amendments

• **1976, Tax Reform Act of 1976 (P.L. 94-455)**

P.L. 94-455, §1906(b)(13)(A):

Amended 1954 Code by substituting "Secretary" for "Secretary or his delegate" each place it appeared. **Effective** 2-1-77.

[Sec. 6404(b)]

(b) NO CLAIM FOR ABATEMENT OF INCOME, ESTATE, AND GIFT TAXES.—No claim for abatement shall be filed by a taxpayer in respect of an assessment of any tax imposed under subtitle A or B.

[Sec. 6404(c)]

(c) SMALL TAX BALANCES.—The Secretary is authorized to abate the unpaid portion of the assessment of any tax, or any liability in respect thereof, if the Secretary determines under uniform rules prescribed by the Secretary that the administration and collection costs involved would not warrant collection of the amount due.

Amendments

• **1976, Tax Reform Act of 1976 (P.L. 94-455)**

P.L. 94-455, §1906(b)(13)(A):

Amended 1954 Code by substituting "Secretary" for "Secretary or his delegate" each place it appeared. **Effective** 2-1-77.

[Sec. 6404(d)]

(d) ASSESSMENTS ATTRIBUTABLE TO CERTAIN MATHEMATICAL ERRORS BY INTERNAL REVENUE SERVICE.—In the case of an assessment of any tax imposed by chapter 1 attributable in whole or in part to a mathematical error described in section 6213(g)(2)(A), if the return was prepared by an officer or employee of the Internal Revenue Service acting in his official capacity to provide assistance to taxpayers in the preparation of income tax returns, the Secretary is authorized to abate the assessment of all or any part of any interest on such deficiency for any period ending on or before the 30th day following the date of notice and demand by the Secretary for payment of the deficiency.

Amendments

• **1980, Bankruptcy Tax Act of 1980 (P.L. 96-589)**

P.L. 96-589, §6(b)(2):

Amended Code Sec. 6404(d) by striking out "section 6213(f)(2)(A)" and inserting in lieu thereof "section 6213(g)(2)(A)". **Effective** 10-1-79, but inapplicable to any proceeding under the Bankruptcy Act commenced before that date.

• **1976, Tax Reform Act of 1976 (P.L. 94-455)**

P.L. 94-455, §1212(a):

Added Code Sec. 6404(d). **Effective** with respect to returns filed for tax years ending after 10-4-76.

[Sec. 6404(e)]

(e) ABATEMENT OF INTEREST ATTRIBUTABLE TO UNREASONABLE ERRORS AND DELAYS BY INTERNAL REVENUE SERVICE.—

(1) IN GENERAL.—In the case of any assessment of interest on—

(A) any deficiency attributable in whole or in part to any unreasonable error or delay by an officer or employee of the Internal Revenue Service (acting in his official capacity) in performing a ministerial or managerial act, or

(B) any payment of any tax described in section 6212(a) to the extent that any unreasonable error or delay in such payment is attributable to such officer or employee being erroneous or dilatory in performing a ministerial or managerial act,

the Secretary may abate the assessment of all or any part of such interest for any period. For purposes of the preceding sentence, an error or delay shall be taken into account only if no significant aspect of such error or delay can be attributed to the taxpayer involved, and after the Internal Revenue Service has contacted the taxpayer in writing with respect to such deficiency or payment.

(2) INTEREST ABATED WITH RESPECT TO ERRONEOUS REFUND CHECK.—The Secretary shall abate the assessment of all interest on any erroneous refund under section 6602 until the date demand for repayment is made, unless—

(A) the taxpayer (or a related party) has in any way caused such erroneous refund, or

(B) such erroneous refund exceeds $50,000.

Amendments

• **1996, Taxpayer Bill of Rights 2 (P.L. 104-168)**

P.L. 104-168, §301(a)(1)-(2):

Amended Code Sec. 6404(e)(1) by inserting "unreasonable" before "error" each place it appears in subparagraphs (A) and (B), and by striking "in performing a ministerial act" each place it appears and inserting "in performing a ministerial or managerial act". **Effective** for interest accruing with respect to deficiencies or payments for tax years beginning after 7-30-96.

P.L. 104-168, §301(b)(1)-(2):

Amended Code Sec. 6404(e) by striking "ASSESSMENTS" and inserting "ABATEMENT", and by inserting "UNREASONABLE" before "ERRORS" in the heading. **Effective** for interest accruing with respect to deficiencies or payments for tax years beginning after 7-30-96.

• **1988, Technical and Miscellaneous Revenue Act of 1988 (P.L. 100-647)**

P.L. 100-647, §1015(n)(1)-(2):

Amended Code Sec. 6404(e)(1)(B) by inserting "error or" before "delay", and by inserting "erroneous or" before "dilatory". **Effective** as if included in the provision of P.L. 99-514 to which it relates.

• **1986, Tax Reform Act of 1986 (P.L. 99-514)**

P.L. 99-514, §1563(a):

Amended Code Sec. 6404 by adding at the end thereof new subsection (e). **Effective** for interest accruing with respect to deficiencies or payments for tax years beginning after 12-31-78. However, see Act Sec. 1563(b)(2), below.

P.L. 99-514, §1563(b)(2), provides:

(2) STATUTE OF LIMITATIONS.—If refund or credit of any amount resulting from the application of the amendment made by subsection (a) is prevented at any time before the close of the date which is 1 year after the date of the enactment of this Act by the operation of any law or rule of law (including res judicata), refund or credit of such amount (to the extent attributable to the application of the amendment made by subsection (a)) may, nevertheless, be made or allowed if claim therefore is filed before the close of such 1-year period.

[Sec. 6404(f)]

(f) ABATEMENT OF ANY PENALTY OR ADDITION TO TAX ATTRIBUTABLE TO ERRONEOUS WRITTEN ADVICE BY THE INTERNAL REVENUE SERVICE.—

(1) IN GENERAL.—The Secretary shall abate any portion of any penalty or addition to tax attributable to erroneous advice furnished to the taxpayer in writing by an officer or employee of the Internal Revenue Service, acting in such officer's or employee's official capacity.

(2) LIMITATIONS.—Paragraph (1) shall apply only if—

(A) the written advice was reasonably relied upon by the taxpayer and was in response to a specific written request of the taxpayer, and

(B) the portion of the penalty or addition to tax did not result from a failure by the taxpayer to provide adequate or accurate information.

Amendments

• **2014, Tax Technical Corrections Act of 2014 (P.L. 113-295)**

P.L. 113-295, §221(a)(111), Division A:

Amended Code Sec. 6404(f) by striking paragraph (3). **Effective** 12-19-2014. For a special rule, see Act Sec. 221(b)(2), Division A, below. Prior to being stricken, Code Sec. 6404(f)(3) read as follows:

(3) INITIAL REGULATIONS.—Within 180 days after the date of the enactment of this subsection, the Secretary shall prescribe such initial regulations as may be necessary to carry out this subsection.

P.L. 113-295, §221(b)(2), Division A, provides:

(2) SAVINGS PROVISION.—If—

(A) any provision amended or repealed by the amendments made by this section applied to—

(i) any transaction occurring before the date of the enactment of this Act,

(ii) any property acquired before such date of enactment, or

(iii) any item of income, loss, deduction, or credit taken into account before such date of enactment, and

(B) the treatment of such transaction, property, or item under such provision would (without regard to the amendments or repeals made by this section) affect the liability for tax for periods ending after date of enactment, nothing in the amendments or repeals made by this section shall be construed to affect the treatment of such transaction, property, or item for purposes of determining liability for tax for periods ending after such date of enactment.

• **1988, Technical and Miscellaneous Revenue Act of 1988 (P.L. 100-647)**

P.L. 100-647, §6229(a):

Amended Code Sec. 6404 by adding at the end thereof new subsection (f). **Effective** with respect to advice requested on or after 1-1-89.

[Sec. 6404(g)]

(g) SUSPENSION OF INTEREST AND CERTAIN PENALTIES WHERE SECRETARY FAILS TO CONTACT TAXPAYER.—

(1) SUSPENSION.—

(A) IN GENERAL.—In the case of an individual who files a return of tax imposed by subtitle A for a taxable year on or before the due date for the return (including extensions), if the Secretary does not provide a notice to the taxpayer specifically stating the taxpayer's liability and the basis for the liability before the close of the 36-month period beginning on the later of—

(i) the date on which the return is filed; or

(ii) the due date of the return without regard to extensions,

the Secretary shall suspend the imposition of any interest, penalty, addition to tax, or additional amount with respect to any failure relating to the return which is computed by reference to the period of time the failure continues to exist and which is properly allocable to the suspension period.

(B) SEPARATE APPLICATION.—This paragraph shall be applied separately with respect to each item or adjustment.

If, after the return for a taxable year is filed, the taxpayer provides to the Secretary 1 or more signed written documents showing that the taxpayer owes an additional amount of tax for the taxable year, clause (i) shall be applied by substituting the date the last of the documents was provided for the date on which the return is filed.

(2) EXCEPTIONS.—Paragraph (1) shall not apply to—

(A) any penalty imposed by section 6651;

(B) any interest, penalty, addition to tax, or additional amount in a case involving fraud;

(C) any interest, penalty, addition to tax, or additional amount with respect to any tax liability shown on the return;

(D) any interest, penalty, addition to tax, or additional amount with respect to any gross misstatement;

(E) any interest, penalty, addition to tax, or additional amount with respect to any reportable transaction with respect to which the requirement of section 6664(d)(3)(A) is not met and any listed transaction (as defined in 6707A(c)); or

(F) any criminal penalty.

(3) SUSPENSION PERIOD.—For purposes of this subsection, the term "suspension period" means the period—

(A) beginning on the day after the close of the 36-month period under paragraph (1); and

(B) ending on the date which is 21 days after the date on which notice described in paragraph (1)(A) is provided by the Secretary.

CREDITS AND REFUNDS—GENERAL PROCEDURE

Amendments

• **2018, Tax Technical Corrections Act of 2018 (P.L. 115-141)**

P.L. 115-141, §401(a)(288), Div. U:

Amended Code Sec. 6404(g)(2)(E) by striking "section 6664(d)(2)(A)" and inserting "section 6664(d)(3)(A)". **Effective** 3-23-2018.

• **2007, Small Business and Work Opportunity Tax Act of 2007 (P.L. 110-28)**

P.L. 110-28, §8242(a):

Amended Code Sec. 6404(g)(1)(A) and (3)(A) by striking "18-month period" and inserting "36-month period". **Effective** for notices provided by the Secretary of the Treasury, or his delegate, after the date which is 6 months after 5-25-2007.

• **2005, Gulf Opportunity Zone Act of 2005 (P.L. 109-135)**

P.L. 109-135, §303(b)(1):

Amended Code Sec. 6404(g)(1) by adding at the end a new sentence. **Effective** for documents provided on or after 12-21-2005.

• **2004, American Jobs Creation Act of 2004 (P.L. 108-357)**

P.L. 108-357, §903(a):

Amended Code Sec. 6404(g) by striking "1-year period (18-month period in the case of taxable years beginning before January 1, 2004)" both places it appears and inserting "18-month period". **Effective** for tax years beginning after 12-31-2003.

P.L. 108-357, §903(b):

Amended Code Sec. 6404(g)(2) by striking "or" at the end of subparagraph (C), by redesignating subparagraph (D) as subparagraph (E), and by inserting after subparagraph (C) a new subparagraph (D). **Effective** for tax years beginning after 12-31-2003.

P.L. 108-357, §903(c):

Amended Code Sec. 6404(g)(2), as amended by Act Sec. 903(b), by striking "or" at the end of subparagraph (D), by redesignating subparagraph (E) as subparagraph (F), and by inserting after subparagraph (D) a new subparagraph (E). **Effective**, generally, with respect to interest accruing after 10-3-2004. For a special rule, see Act Sec. 903(d)(2)(B), below.

P.L. 108-357, §903(d)(2)(B), as added by P.L. 109-135, §303(a)(1), and amended by P.L. 109-432, §426(b)(1), provides:

(B) SPECIAL RULE FOR CERTAIN LISTED AND REPORTABLE TRANSACTIONS.—

(i) IN GENERAL.—Except as provided in clauses (ii), (iii), and (iv), the amendments made by subsection (c) shall also apply with respect to interest accruing on or before October 3, 2004.

(ii) PARTICIPANTS IN SETTLEMENT INITIATIVES.—Clause (i) shall not apply to any transaction if, as of January 23, 2006—

(I) the taxpayer is participating in a settlement initiative described in Internal Revenue Service Announcement 2005-80 with respect to such transaction, or

(II) the taxpayer has entered into a settlement agreement pursuant to such an initiative.

Subclause (I) shall not apply to any taxpayer if, after January 23, 2006, the taxpayer withdraws from, or terminates, participation in the initiative or the Secretary of the Treasury or the Secretary's delegate determines that a settlement agreement will not be reached pursuant to the initiative within a reasonable period of time.

(iii) TAXPAYERS ACTING IN GOOD FAITH.—The Secretary of the Treasury or the Secretary's delegate may except from the application of clause (i) any transaction in which the taxpayer has acted reasonably and in good faith.

(iv) CLOSED TRANSACTIONS.—Clause (i) shall not apply to a transaction if, as of December 14, 2005—

(I) the assessment of all Federal income taxes for the taxable year in which the tax liability to which the interest relates arose is prevented by the operation of any law or rule of law, or

(II) a closing agreement under section 7121 has been entered into with respect to the tax liability arising in connection with the transaction.

• **1998, IRS Restructuring and Reform Act of 1998 (P.L. 105-206)**

P.L. 105-206, §3305(a):

Amended Code Sec. 6404 by redesignating subsection (g) as subsection (h) and by inserting after subsection (f) a new subsection (g). **Effective** for tax years ending after 7-22-98.

[Sec. 6404(h)]

(h) JUDICIAL REVIEW OF REQUEST FOR ABATEMENT OF INTEREST.—

(1) IN GENERAL.—The Tax Court shall have jurisdiction over any action brought by a taxpayer who meets the requirements referred to in section 7430(c)(4)(A)(ii) to determine whether the Secretary's failure to abate interest under this section was an abuse of discretion, and may order an abatement, if such action is brought—

(A) at any time after the earlier of—

(i) the date of the mailing of the Secretary's final determination not to abate such interest, or

(ii) the date which is 180 days after the date of the filing with the Secretary (in such form as the Secretary may prescribe) of a claim for abatement under this section, and

(B) not later than the date which is 180 days after the date described in subparagraph (A)(i).

(2) SPECIAL RULES.—

(A) DATE OF MAILING.—Rules similar to the rules of section 6213 shall apply for purposes of determining the date of the mailing referred to in paragraph (1).

(B) RELIEF.—Rules similar to the rules of section 6512(b) shall apply for purposes of this subsection.

(C) REVIEW.—An order of the Tax Court under this subsection shall be reviewable in the same manner as a decision of the Tax Court, but only with respect to the matters determined in such order.

Amendments

• **2015, Protecting Americans from Tax Hikes Act of 2015 (P.L. 114-113)**

P.L. 114-113, §421(a)(1)-(2), Div. Q:

Amended Code Sec. 6404(h) by striking "REVIEW OF DENIAL" in the heading and inserting "JUDICIAL REVIEW", and by striking "if such action is brought" and all that follows in paragraph (1) and inserting "if such action is brought—"and new subparagraphs (A)-(B). **Effective** for claims for abatement of interest filed with the Secretary of the Treasury after 12-18-2015. Prior to being stricken, "if such action is brought" and all that follows in Code Sec. 6404(h)(1) read as follows:

if such action is brought within 180 days after the date of the mailing of the Secretary's final determination not to abate such interest.

• **2002, Victims of Terrorism Tax Relief Act of 2001 (P.L. 107-134)**

P.L. 107-134, §112(d)(1)(B):

Amended Code Sec. 6404 by redesignating subsection (i) as subsection (h). **Effective** for disasters and terroristic or military actions occurring on or after 9-11-2001, with respect to any action of the Secretary of the Treasury, the Secretary of Labor, or the Pension Benefit Guaranty Corporation occurring on or after 1-23-2002.

• **1998, IRS Restructuring and Reform Act of 1998 (P.L. 105-206)**

P.L. 105-206, §3305(a):

Amended Code Sec. 6404 by redesignating subsection (g) as subsection (h). **Effective** for tax years ending after 7-22-98.

P.L. 105-206, §3309(a):

Amended Code Sec. 6404, as amended by Act Sec. 3305(a), by redesignating subsection (h) as subsection (i). **Effective** for disasters declared after 12-31-97, with respect to tax years beginning after 12-31-97. For a special rule, see Act Sec. 3309(c)(1)-(2), below.

P.L. 105-206, §3309(c)(1)-(2), provides:

(c) EMERGENCY DESIGNATION.—

(1) For the purposes of section 252(e) of the Balanced Budget and Emergency Deficit Control Act, Congress designates the provisions of this section as an emergency requirement.

(2) The amendments made by subsections (a) and (b) of this section shall only take effect upon the transmittal by the President to the Congress of a message designating the provisions of subsections (a) and (b) as an emergency requirement pursuant to section 252(e) of the Balanced Budget and Emergency Deficit Control Act.

• **1996, Taxpayer Bill of Rights 2 (P.L. 104-168)**

P.L. 104-168, §302(a):

Amended Code Sec. 6404 by adding at the end a new subsection (g). **Effective** for requests for abatement after 7-30-96.

P.L. 104-168, §701(c)(3):

Amended Code Sec. 6404(g) (as amended by Act Sec. 302(a)) by striking "section 7430(c)(4)(A)(iii)" and inserting "section 7430(c)(4)(A)(ii)". **Effective** in the case of proceedings commenced after 7-30-96.

Sec. 6404(h)

CREDITS AND REFUNDS—GENERAL PROCEDURE

[Sec. 6404(h)—Stricken]

Amendments

• **2002, Victims of Terrorism Tax Relief Act of 2001 (P.L. 107-134)**

P.L. 107-134, §112(d)(1)(A):

Amended Code Sec. 6404 by striking subsection (h). **Effective** for disasters and terroristic or military actions occurring on or after 9-11-2001, with respect to any action of the Secretary of the Treasury, the Secretary of Labor, or the Pension Benefit Guaranty Corporation occurring on or after 1-23-2002. Prior to being stricken, Code Sec. 6404(h) read as follows:

(h) ABATEMENT OF INTEREST ON UNDERPAYMENTS BY TAXPAYERS IN PRESIDENTIALLY DECLARED DISASTER AREAS.—

(1) IN GENERAL.—If the Secretary extends for any period the time for filing income tax returns under section 6081 and the time for paying income tax with respect to such returns under section 6161 for any taxpayer located in a Presidentially declared disaster area, the Secretary shall abate for such period the assessment of any interest prescribed under section 6601 on such income tax.

(2) PRESIDENTIALLY DECLARED DISASTER AREA.—For purposes of paragraph (1), the term "Presidentially declared disaster area" means, with respect to any taxpayer, any area which the President has determined warrants assistance by the Federal Government under the Robert T. Stafford Disaster Relief and Emergency Assistance Act.

• **1998, Tax and Trade Relief Extension Act of 1998 (P.L. 105-277)**

P.L. 105-277, §4003(e)(2):

Amended Code Sec. 6404(h)(2) by inserting "Robert T. Stafford" before "Disaster". **Effective** as if included in the provision of P.L. 105-34 to which it relates [**effective** for disasters declared after 12-31-96.—CCH].

• **1998, IRS Restructuring and Reform Act of 1998 (P.L. 105-206)**

P.L. 105-206, §3305(a):

Amended Code Sec. 6404 by redesignating subsection (g) as subsection (h). **Effective** for tax years ending after 7-22-98.

P.L. 105-206, §3309(a):

Amended Code Sec. 6404, as amended by Act Sec. 3305(a), by redesignating subsection (h) as subsection (i) and by inserting after subsection (g) a new subsection (h). **Effective** for disasters declared after 12-31-97, with respect to tax years beginning after 12-31-97. For a special rule, see Act Sec. 3309(c)(1)-(2), below.

P.L. 105-206, §3309(c)(1)-(2), provides:

(c) EMERGENCY DESIGNATION.—

(1) For the purposes of section 252(e) of the Balanced Budget and Emergency Deficit Control Act, Congress designates the provisions of this section as an emergency requirement.

(2) The amendments made by subsections (a) and (b) of this section shall only take effect upon the transmittal by the President to the Congress of a message designating the provisions of subsections (a) and (b) as an emergency requirement pursuant to section 252(e) of the Balanced Budget and Emergency Deficit Control Act.

[Sec. 6404(i)]

(i) CROSS REFERENCE.—

For authority to suspend running of interest, etc. by reason of Presidentially declared disaster or terroristic or military action, see section 7508A.

Amendments

• **2002, Victims of Terrorism Tax Relief Act of 2001 (P.L. 107-134)**

P.L. 107-134, §112(d)(1)(C):

Amended Code Sec. 6404 by adding at the end a new subsection (i). **Effective** for disasters and terroristic or military actions occurring on or after 9-11-2001, with respect to any action of the Secretary of the Treasury, the Secretary of Labor, or the Pension Benefit Guaranty Corporation occurring on or after 1-23-2002.

[Sec. 6405]

SEC. 6405. REPORTS OF REFUNDS AND CREDITS.

[Sec. 6405(a)]

(a) BY TREASURY TO JOINT COMMITTEE.—No refund or credit of any income, war profits, excess profits, estate, or gift tax, or any tax imposed with respect to public charities, private foundations, operators' trust funds, pension plans, or real estate investment trusts under chapter 41, 42, 43, or 44, in excess of $2,000,000 ($5,000,000 in the case of a C corporation) shall be made until after the expiration of 30 days from the date upon which a report giving the name of the person to whom the refund or credit is to be made, the amount of such refund or credit, and a summary of the facts and the decision of the Secretary, is submitted to the Joint Committee on Taxation.

Amendments

• **2014, Tax Increase Prevention Act of 2014 (P.L. 113-295)**

P.L. 113-295, §301(a), Division A:

Amended Code Sec. 6405(a) by inserting "($5,000,000 in the case of a C corporation)" after "$2,000,000". **Effective** 12-19-2014, except that such amendment shall not apply with respect to any refund or credit with respect to a report that has been made before such date under Code Sec. 6405.

• **2000, Community Renewal Tax Relief Act of 2000 (P.L. 106-554)**

P.L. 106-554, §305(a):

Amended Code Sec. 6405(a) by striking "$1,000,000" and inserting "$2,000,000". **Effective** 12-21-2000, except that such amendment shall not apply with respect to any refund or credit with respect to a report that has been made before such date under Code Sec. 6405.

• **1990, Omnibus Budget Reconciliation Act of 1990 (P.L. 101-508)**

P.L. 101-508, §11834(a):

Amended Code Sec. 6405(a) by striking "$200,000" and inserting "$1,000,000." **Effective** 11-5-90, except that such amendment shall not apply with respect to any refund or credit with respect to a report [that] has been made before such date of enactment under section 6405 of the Internal Revenue Code of 1986.

• **1978, Black Lung Benefits Revenue Act of 1977 (P.L. 95-227)**

P.L. 95-227, §4(d)(3):

Amended Code Sec. 6405(a) by substituting "public charities, private foundations, operators' trust funds, pension plans, or real estate investment trusts under chapter 41, 42, 43, or 44" for "private foundations and pension plans under chapters 42 and 43". For **effective** date, see the historical comment for P.L. 95-227 under Code Sec. 4951.

• **1976, Tax Reform Act of 1976 (P.L. 94-455)**

P.L. 94-455, §1210(a):

Amended Code Sec. 6405(a). **Effective** as indicated in Act Sec. 1210(d)(1), below. Prior to amendment Code Sec. 6405(a) read as follows:

(a) BY TREASURY TO JOINT COMMITTEE.—No refund or credit of any income, war profits, excess profits, estate, or gift tax in excess of $100,000 shall be made until after the expiration of 30 days from the date upon which a report giving the name of the person to whom the refund or credit is to be made, the amount of such refund or credit, and a summary of the facts and the decision of the Secretary or his delegate, is submitted to the Joint Committee on Internal Revenue Taxation.

P.L. 94-455, §1210(d)(1), provides:

(1) The amendments made by subsections (a) and (b) shall take effect on the date of the enactment of this Act [October 4, 1976], except that such amendments shall not apply with respect to any refund or credit with respect to which a report has been made before the date of the enactment of this Act under subsection (a) or (c) of section 6405 of the Internal Revenue Code of 1954.

[Sec. 6405(b)]

(b) TENTATIVE ADJUSTMENTS.—Any credit or refund allowed or made under section 6411 shall be made without regard to the provisions of subsection (a) of this section. In any such case, if the credit or refund, reduced by any deficiency in such tax thereafter assessed and by deficiencies in any other tax resulting from adjustments reflected in the determination of the credit or refund, is in excess of $2,000,000 ($5,000,000 in the case of a C corporation), there shall be submitted to such committee a report containing the matter specified in subsection (a) at such time after the making of the credit or refund as the Secretary shall determine the correct amount of the tax.

Amendments

• **2014, Tax Increase Prevention Act of 2014 (P.L. 113-295)**

P.L. 113-295, §301(a), Division A:

Amended Code Sec. 6405(b) by inserting "($5,000,000 in the case of a C corporation)" after "$2,000,000". **Effective** 12-19-2014, except that such amendment shall not apply with respect to any refund or credit with respect to a report that has been made before such date under Code Sec. 6405.

• **2000, Community Renewal Tax Relief Act of 2000 (P.L. 106-554)**

P.L. 106-554, §305(a):

Amended Code Sec. 6405(b) by striking "$1,000,000" and inserting "$2,000,000". **Effective** 12-21-2000, except that such amendment shall not apply with respect to any refund or credit with respect to a report that has been made before such date under Code Sec. 6405.

CREDITS AND REFUNDS—GENERAL PROCEDURE

• **1990, Omnibus Budget Reconciliation Act of 1990 (P.L. 101-508)**

P.L. 101-508, §11834(a):

Amended Code Sec. 6405(b) by striking "$200,000" and inserting "$1,000,000". **Effective** 11-5-90, except that it shall not apply to any refund or credit with respect to a report [that] has been made before such date of enactment under section 6405 of the Internal Revenue Code of 1986.

• **1986, Tax Reform Act of 1986 (P.L. 99-514)**

P.L. 99-514, §1879(e):

Amended Code Sec. 6405 by striking out subsection (b) and redesignating subsections (c), (d), and (e) as subsections (b), (c), and (d), respectively. **Effective** as if included in the provision of P.L. 98-369 to which it relates. Prior to amendment, Code Sec. 6045(b) read as follows:

(b) BY JOINT COMMITTEE TO CONGRESS.—A report to Congress shall be made annually by such committee of such refunds and credits, including the names of all persons and corporations to whom amounts are credited or payments are made, together with the amounts credited or paid to each.

• **1976, Tax Reform Act of 1976 (P.L. 94-455)**

P.L. 94-455, §1210(b):

Substituted "$200,000" for "$100,000" in Code Sec. 6405(c). **Effective** as indicated in §1210(d)(1) in the historical note to Code Sec. 6405(a).

P.L. 94-455, §1906(b)(13)(A):

Amended the 1954 Code by substituting "Secretary" for "Secretary or his delegate" each place it appeared. **Effective** 2-1-77.

[Sec. 6405(c)]

(c) REFUNDS ATTRIBUTABLE TO CERTAIN DISASTER LOSSES.—If any refund or credit of income taxes is attributable to the taxpayer's election under section 165(i) to deduct a disaster loss for the taxable year immediately preceding the taxable year in which the disaster occurred, the Secretary is authorized in his discretion to make the refund or credit, to the extent attributable to such election, without regard to the provisions of subsection (a) of this section. If such refund or credit is made without regard to subsection (a), there shall thereafter be submitted to such Joint Committee a report containing the matter specified in subsection (a) as soon as the Secretary shall determine the correct amount of the tax for the taxable year for which the refund or credit is made.

Amendments

• **1986, Tax Reform Act of 1986 (P.L. 99-514)**

P.L. 99-514, §1879(e):

Amended Code Sec. 6405 by striking out subsection (b) and redesignating subsections (c), (d), and (e) as subsections (b), (c), and (d), respectively. **Effective** as if included in the provision of P.L. 98-369 to which it relates.

• **1984, Deficit Reduction Act of 1984 (P.L. 98-369)**

P.L. 98-369, §711(c)(3):

Amended Code Sec. 6405(d) by striking out "section 165(h)" and inserting in lieu thereof "section 165(i)". **Effective** as if included in the provision of P.L. 97-248 to which it relates.

• **1976, Tax Reform Act of 1976 (P.L. 94-455)**

P.L. 94-455, §1906(b)(13)(A):

Amended 1954 Code by substituting "Secretary" for "Secretary or his delegate" each place it appeared. **Effective** 2-1-77.

[Sec. 6405(d)—Repealed]

Amendments

• **1990, Omnibus Budget Reconciliation Act of 1990 (P.L. 101-508)**

P.L. 101-508, §11801(c)(21)(A):

Repealed Code Sec. 6405(d). **Effective** 11-5-90. Prior to being stricken, Code Sec. 6405(d) read as follows:

(d) QUALIFIED STATE INDIVIDUAL INCOME TAXES.—For purposes of this section, a refund or credit made under subchapter E of chapter 64 (relating to Federal collection of qualified State individual income taxes) for a taxable year shall be treated as a portion of a refund or credit of the income tax for that taxable year.

P.L. 101-508, §11821(b), provides:

(b) SAVINGS PROVISION.—If—

(1) any provision amended or repealed by this part applied to—

(A) any transaction occurring before the date of the enactment of this Act,

(B) any property acquired before such date of enactment, or

(C) any item of income, loss, deduction, or credit taken into account before such date of enactment, and

(2) the treatment of such transaction, property, or item under such provision would (without regard to the amendments made by this part) affect liability for tax for periods ending after such date of enactment,

nothing in the amendments made by this part shall be construed to affect the treatment of such transaction, property, or item for purposes of determining liability for tax for periods ending after such date of enactment.

• **1986, Tax Reform Act of 1986 (P.L. 99-514)**

P.L. 99-514, §1879(e):

Amended Code Sec. 6405 by striking out subsection (b) and redesignating subsections (c), (d), and (e) as subsections (b), (c), and (d), respectively. **Effective** as if included in the provision of P.L. 98-369 to which it relates.

• **1972, State and Local Fiscal Assistance Act of 1972 (P.L. 92-512)**

P.L. 92-512, §203(a):

Added Code Sec. 6405(e). For **effective** date, see the amendment notes for P.L. 92-512 under Code Sec. 6361.

• **1972 (P.L. 92-418)**

P.L. 92-418, §2(b):

Added Code Sec. 6405(d). **Effective** with respect to refunds or credits made after 7-1-72.

[Sec. 6406]

SEC. 6406. PROHIBITION OF ADMINISTRATIVE REVIEW OF DECISIONS.

In the absence of fraud or mistake in mathematical calculation, the findings of fact in and the decision of the Secretary upon the merits of any claim presented under or authorized by the internal revenue laws and the allowance or nonallowance by the Secretary of interest on any credit or refund under the internal revenue laws shall not, except as provided in subchapters C and D of chapter 76 (relating to the Tax Court), be subject to review by any other administrative or accounting officer, employee, or agent of the United States.

Amendments

• **1976, Tax Reform Act of 1976 (P.L. 94-455)**

P.L. 94-455, §1906(b)(13)(A):

Amended 1954 Code by substituting "Secretary" for "Secretary or his delegate" each place it appeared. **Effective** 2-1-77.

[Sec. 6407]

SEC. 6407. DATE OF ALLOWANCE OF REFUND OR CREDIT.

The date on which the Secretary first authorizes the scheduling of an overassessment in respect of any internal revenue tax shall be considered as the date of allowance of refund or credit in respect of such tax.

Amendments

• **1976, Tax Reform Act of 1976 (P.L. 94-455)**

P.L. 94-455, §1906(b)(13)(A):

Amended 1954 Code by substituting "Secretary" for "Secretary or his delegate" each place it appeared. **Effective** 2-1-77.

[Sec. 6408]

SEC. 6408. STATE ESCHEAT LAWS NOT TO APPLY.

No overpayment of any tax imposed by this title shall be refunded (and no interest with respect to any such overpayment shall be paid) if the amount of such refund (or interest) would escheat to a State or would otherwise become the property of a State under any law relating to the disposition of unclaimed or abandoned property. No refund (or payment of interest) shall be made to the estate of any decedent unless it is affirmatively shown that such amount will not escheat to a State or otherwise become the property of a State under such a law.

CREDITS AND REFUNDS—SPECIAL RULES

Amendments

• **1987, Revenue Act of 1987 (P.L. 100-203)**

P.L. 100-203, §10621(a):

Amended subchapter A of chapter 65 by adding at the end thereof new Code Sec. 6408. **Effective** 12-22-87.

[Sec. 6409]

SEC. 6409. REFUNDS DISREGARDED IN THE ADMINISTRATION OF FEDERAL PROGRAMS AND FEDERALLY ASSISTED PROGRAMS.

Notwithstanding any other provision of law, any refund (or advance payment with respect to a refundable credit) made to any individual under this title shall not be taken into account as income, and shall not be taken into account as resources for a period of 12 months from receipt, for purposes of determining the eligibility of such individual (or any other individual) for benefits or assistance (or the amount or extent of benefits or assistance) under any Federal program or under any State or local program financed in whole or in part with Federal funds.

Amendments

• **2013, American Taxpayer Relief Act of 2012 (P.L. 112-240)**

P.L. 112-240, §103(d):

Amended Code Sec. 6409. **Effective** for amounts received after 12-31-2012. Prior to amendment, Code Sec. 6409 read as follows:

SEC. 6409. REFUNDS DISREGARDED IN THE ADMINISTRATION OF FEDERAL PROGRAMS AND FEDERALLY ASSISTED PROGRAMS.

[Sec. 6409(a)]

(a) IN GENERAL.—Notwithstanding any other provision of law, any refund (or advance payment with respect to a refundable credit) made to any individual under this title shall not be taken into account as income, and shall not be taken into account as resources for a period of 12 months from receipt, for purposes of determining the eligibility of such individual (or any other individual) for benefits or assistance (or the amount or extent of benefits or assistance) under any Federal program or under any State or local program financed in whole or in part with Federal funds.

[Sec. 6409(b)]

(b) TERMINATION.—Subsection (a) shall not apply to any amount received after December 31, 2012.

• **2010, Tax Relief, Unemployment Insurance Reauthorization, and Job Creation Act of 2010 (P.L. 111-312)**

P.L. 111-312, §728(a):

Amended subchapter A of chapter 65 by adding at the end a new Code Sec. 6409. **Effective** for amounts received after 12-31-2009.

Subchapter B—Rules of Special Application

Sec.	
Sec. 6411.	Tentative carryback and refund adjustments.
Sec. 6412.	Floor stocks refunds.
Sec. 6413.	Special rules applicable to certain employment taxes.
Sec. 6414.	Income tax withheld.
Sec. 6415.	Credits or refunds to persons who collected certain taxes.
Sec. 6416.	Certain taxes on sales and services.
Sec. 6417.	Elective payment of applicable credits.
Sec. 6418.	Transfer of certain credits.
Sec. 6419.	Excise tax on wagering.
Sec. 6420.	Gasoline used on farms.
Sec. 6421.	Gasoline used for certain nonhighway purposes, used by local transit systems, or sold for certain exempt purposes.
Sec. 6422.	Cross references.
Sec. 6423.	Conditions to allowance in the case of alcohol and tobacco taxes.
Sec. 6425.	Adjustment of overpayment of estimated income tax by corporation.
Sec. 6426.	Credit for alcohol fuel, biodiesel, and alternative fuel mixtures.
Sec. 6427.	Fuels not used for taxable purposes.
Sec. 6428.	2020 recovery rebates for individuals.
Sec. 6428A.	Additional 2020 recovery rebates for individuals.
Sec. 6428B.	2021 recovery rebates to individuals.
Sec. 6430.	Treatment of tax imposed at Leaking Underground Storage Tank Trust Fund financing rate.
Sec. 6432.	Continuation coverage premium assistance.
Sec. 6433.	Saver's match.

[Sec. 6411]

SEC. 6411. TENTATIVE CARRYBACK AND REFUND ADJUSTMENTS.

[Sec. 6411(a)]

(a) APPLICATION FOR ADJUSTMENT.—A taxpayer may file an application for a tentative carryback adjustment of the tax for the prior taxable year affected by a net operating loss carryback provided in section 172(b), by a business credit carryback provided in section 39, or by a capital loss carryback provided in subsection (a)(1) or (c) of section 1212, from any taxable year. The application shall be verified in the manner prescribed by section 6065 in the case of a return of such taxpayer and shall be filed, on or after the date of filing for the return for the taxable year of the net operating loss, net capital loss, or unused business credit from which the carryback results and within a period of 12 months after such taxable year or, with respect to any portion of a business credit carryback attributable to a net operating loss carryback or a net capital loss carryback from a subsequent taxable year, within a period of 12 months from the end of such subsequent taxable year, in the manner and form required by regulations prescribed by the Secretary. The applications shall set forth in such detail and with such supporting data and explanation as such regulations shall require—

(1) The amount of the net operating loss, net capital loss, or unused business credit;

(2) The amount of the tax previously determined for the prior taxable year affected by such carryback, the tax previously determined being ascertained in accordance with the method prescribed in section 1314(a);

(3) The amount of decrease in such tax, attributable to such carryback, such decrease being determined by applying the carryback in the manner provided by law to the items on the basis of which such tax was determined;

(4) The unpaid amount of such tax, not including any amount required to be shown under paragraph (5);

(5) The amount, with respect to the tax for the taxable year immediately preceding the taxable year from which the carryback is made, as to which an extension of time for payment under section 6164 is in effect; and

CREDITS AND REFUNDS—SPECIAL RULES

(6) Such other information for purposes of carrying out the provisions of this section as may be required by such regulations.

Except for purposes of applying section 6611(f)(4)(B), an application under this subsection shall not constitute a claim for credit or refund.

Amendments

• **2020, Coronavirus Aid, Relief, and Economic Security (CARES) Act (P.L. 116-136)**

P.L. 116-136, §2303(d)(4), provides:

(4) SPECIAL RULE.—In the case of a net operating loss arising in a taxable year beginning before January 1, 2018, and ending after December 31, 2017—

(A) an application under section 6411(a) of the Internal Revenue Code of 1986 with respect to the carryback of such net operating loss shall not fail to be treated as timely filed if filed not later than the date which is 120 days after the date of the enactment of this Act, and

(B) an election to—

(i) forgo any carryback of such net operating loss,

(ii) reduce any period to which such net operating loss may be carried back, or

(iii) revoke any election made under section 172(b) to forgo any carryback of such net operating loss,

shall not fail to be treated as timely made if made not later than the date which is 120 days after the date of the enactment of this Act.

• **2009, American Recovery and Reinvestment Tax Act of 2009 (P.L. 111-5)**

P.L. 111-5, §1211(d)(2), provides:

(2) TRANSITIONAL RULE.—In the case of a net operating loss for a taxable year ending before the date of the enactment of this Act—

(A) any election made under section 172(b)(3) of the Internal Revenue Code of 1986 with respect to such loss may (notwithstanding such section) be revoked before the applicable date,

(B) any election made under section 172(b)(1)(H) of such Code with respect to such loss shall (notwithstanding such section) be treated as timely made if made before the applicable date, and

(C) any application under section 6411(a) of such Code with respect to such loss shall be treated as timely filed if filed before the applicable date.

For purposes of this paragraph, the term "applicable date" means the date which is 60 days after the date of the enactment of this Act.

• **2005, Gulf Opportunity Zone Act of 2005 (P.L. 109-135)**

P.L. 109-135, §409(a)(1):

Amended the last sentence of Code Sec. 6411(a) by striking "6611(f)(3)(B)" and inserting "6611(f)(4)(B)". **Effective** as if included in the provision of the Taxpayer Relief Act of 1997 (P.L. 105-34) to which it relates [effective for foreign tax credit carrybacks arising in tax years beginning after 8-5-97.—CCH].

• **2004, Working Families Tax Relief Act of 2004 (P.L. 108-311)**

P.L. 108-311, §403(b)(2), provides:

(2) In the case of a net operating loss for a taxable year ending during 2001 or 2002—

(A) an application under section 6411(a) of the Internal Revenue Code of 1986 with respect to such loss shall not fail to be treated as timely filed if filed before November 1, 2002,

(B) any election made under section 172(b)(3) of such Code may (notwithstanding such section) be revoked before November 1, 2002, and

(C) any election made under section 172(j) of such Code shall (notwithstanding such section) be treated as timely made if made before November 1, 2002.

• **2000, Community Renewal Tax Relief Act of 2000 (P.L. 106-554)**

P.L. 106-554, §318(d)(1):

Amended Code Sec. 6411(a) by striking "section 1212(a)(1)" and inserting "subsection (a)(1) or (c) of section 1212". **Effective** as if included in the amendments made by section 504 of P.L. 97-34 [effective for property acquired and positions established after 6-23-81.—CCH].

• **1986, Tax Reform Act of 1986 (P.L. 99-514)**

P.L. 99-514, §231(d)(3)(H)(i)-(iv):

Amended Code Sec. 6411 by striking out "by a research credit carryback provided in section 30(g)(2)", by striking out "a research credit or carryback or", and by striking out "(or, with respect to any portion of a business credit carryback attributable to a research credit carryback from a subsequent taxable year within a period of 12 months from the end of such subsequent taxable year)" in subsection (a), and by striking out "unused research credit," each place it appeared in subsections (a) and (b). **Effective** for tax years beginning after 12-31-85. Prior to amendment (but after amendment by Act Sec. 1847(b)(10)), Code Sec. 6411(a)(1) read as follows:

(a) APPLICATION FOR ADJUSTMENT.—A taxpayer may file an application for a tentative carryback adjustment of the tax for the prior taxable year affected by a net operating loss carryback provided in section 172(b), by a business credit carryback provided in section 39, by a research credit carryback provided in section 30(g)(2) or by a capital loss carryback provided in section 1212(a)(1), from any taxable year. The application shall be verified in the manner prescribed by section 6065 in the case of a return of such taxpayer and shall be filed, on or after the date of filing for the return for the taxable year of the net operating loss, net capital loss, unused research credit, or unused business credit from which the carryback results and within a period of 12 months after such taxable year or, with respect to any portion of a research credit carryback or a business credit carryback attributable to a net operating loss carryback or a net capital loss carryback from a subsequent taxable year, within a period of 12 months from the end of such subsequent taxable year (or, with respect to any portion of a business credit carryback attributable to a research credit carryback from a subsequent taxable year within a period of 12 months from the end of such subsequent taxable year), in the manner and form required by regulations prescribed by the Secretary. The applications shall set forth in such detail and with such supporting data and explanation as such regulations shall require—

(1) The amount of the net operating loss, net capital loss, unused research credit, or unused business credit;

P.L. 99-514, §1847(b)(10):

Amended Code Sec. 6411(a) by striking out "or unused business credit" in the second sentence thereof and inserting in lieu thereof "unused research credit, or unused business credit". **Effective** as if included in the provision of P.L. 98-369 to which it relates.

• **1984, Deficit Reduction Act of 1984 (P.L. 98-369)**

P.L. 98-369, §474(r)(37)(A):

Amended so much of Code Sec. 6411(a) as preceded paragraph (2). **Effective** for tax years after 12-31-83, and to carrybacks from such years. Prior to amendment, that language read as follows:

(a) Application for Adjustment.—A taxpayer may file an application for a tentative carryback adjustment of the tax for the prior taxable year affected by a net operating loss carryback provided in section 172(b), by an investment credit carryback provided in section 46(b), by a work incentive program carryback provided in section 50A(b), by a new employee credit carryback provided in section 53(b), by a research credit carryback provided in section 44F(g)(2), by an employee stock ownership credit carryback provided by section 44G(b)(2) or by a capital loss carryback provided in section 1212(a)(1), from any taxable year. The application shall be verified in the manner prescribed by section 6065 in the case of a return of such taxpayer, and shall be filed, on or after the date of filing of the return for the taxable year of the net operating loss, net capital loss, unused investment credit, unused work incentive program credit, unused new employee credit, unused research credit, or unused employee stock ownership credit from which the carryback results and within a period of 12 months from the end of such taxable year (or, with respect to any portion of an investment credit carryback, a work incentive program carryback, a new employee credit carryback, a research credit carryback, or employee stock ownership credit carryback from a taxable year attributable to a net operating loss carryback or a capital loss carryback (or, in the case of a work incentive program carryback, to an investment credit carryback, or, in the case of a new employee credit carryback, to an investment credit carryback or a work incentive program carryback, or, in the case of a research credit carryback, to an investment credit carryback, a work incentive program carryback, or a new employee credit carryback, or, in the case of an employee stock ownership credit carryback, to an investment credit carryback, a new employee credit carryback or a research and experimental credit carryback) from a subsequent taxable year within a period of 12 months from the end of such subsequent taxable year), in the manner and form required by regulations prescribed by the Secretary. The application shall set forth in such detail and with such supporting data and explanation as such regulations shall require—

(1) The amount of the net operating loss, net capital loss, unused investment credit, unused work incentive program credit, unused new employee credit, unused research credit, or unused employee stock ownership credit;

P.L. 98-369, §714(n)(2)(B):

Amended the last sentence of Code Sec. 6411(a) by striking out "An" and inserting in lieu thereof "Except for purposes of applying section 6611(f)(3)(B), an". **Effective** only for applications filed after 7-18-84 [effective date changed by P.L. 99-514, §1875(d)(3)].

• **1981, Economic Recovery Tax Act of 1981 (P.L. 97-34)**

P.L. 97-34, §221(b)(2)(B):

Amended Code Sec. 6411(a) by striking out "or unused new employee credit" each place it appeared and inserting in lieu thereof "unused new employee credit, or unused research credit"; by inserting "by a research credit carryback provided in section 44F(g)(2)," after "53(b)," in the first sentence; by striking out "or a new employee credit carryback from" and inserting in lieu thereof "a new employee credit carryback, or a research credit carryback from"; and by striking out "work incentive program carryback" and inserting "work incentive program carryback, or, in the case of a research credit carryback, to an investment credit carryback, a work incentive program carryback, or a new employee credit carryback)". **Effective** for amounts paid or incurred after 6-30-81 [effective date changed by P.L. 99-514, §231(a)(2)].

P.L. 97-34, §221(d)(2), as amended by P.L. 99-514, §231(a)(2), provides:

(2) TRANSITIONAL RULE.—

(A) IN GENERAL.—If, with respect to the first taxable year to which the amendments made by this section apply and which ends in 1981 or 1982, the taxpayer may only take into account qualified research expenses paid or incurred during a portion of such taxable year, the amount of the qualified research expenses taken into account for the base period of such taxable year shall be the amount which bears the same ratio to the total qualified research expenses for such base period as the number of months in such portion of such taxable year bears to the total number of months in such taxable year.

(B) DEFINITIONS.—For purposes of the preceding sentence, the terms "qualified research expenses" and "base period" have the meanings given to such terms by section 44F of the Internal Revenue Code of 1954 (as added by this section).

P.L. 97-34, §331(d)(2)(B):

Amended Code Sec. 6411(a) by striking out "or unused research credit" each place it appeared and inserting "unused research credit, or unused employee stock ownership credit"; by inserting "by an employee stock ownership credit carryback provided by section 44G(b)(2)" after "by a research credit carryback provided in section 44F(g)(2)," in the first sentence; by striking out "or a research credit carryback from" and inserting "a research credit carryback, or employee stock ownership credit carryback from"; and by striking out "new employee credit carryback)" in the second sentence and inserting "new employee credit carryback, or, in the case of an employee stock ownership credit carryback, to an investment credit carryback, a new employee credit carryback or a research and experimental credit carryback)". **Effective** for tax years beginning after 12-31-81.

- **1980, Technical Corrections Act of 1979 (P.L. 96-222)**

P.L. 96-222, §103(a)(6)(G)(xiii):

Amended Code Sec. 6411(a) by striking out "53(c)" and inserting "53(b)".

- **1978, Revenue Act of 1978 (P.L. 95-600)**

P.L. 95-600, §504(b)(1)(A), (c):

Amended the heading for Code Sec. 6411 by inserting "AND REFUND" after "CARRYBACK". **Effective** for tentative refund claims filed on and after 11-6-78.

- **1977, Tax Reduction and Simplification Act of 1977 (P.L. 95-30)**

P.L. 95-30, §202(d)(5)(A):

Amended the material in Code Sec. 6411(a) preceding paragraph (2). **Effective** for tax years beginning after 12-31-76, and for credit carrybacks from such years. Prior to amendment, this material read as follows:

(a) APPLICATION FOR ADJUSTMENT.—A taxpayer may file an application for a tentative carryback adjustment of the tax for the prior taxable year affected by a net operating loss carryback provided in section 172(b), by an investment credit carryback provided in section 46(b), by a work incentive program carryback provided in section 50A(b), or by a capital loss carryback provided in section 1212(a)(1), from any taxable year. The application shall be verified in the manner prescribed by section 6065 in the case of a return of such taxpayer, and shall be filed, on or after the date of filing of the return for the taxable year of the net operating loss, net capital loss, unused investment credit, or unused work incentive program credit from which the carryback results and within a period of 12 months from the end of such taxable year (or, with respect to any portion of an investment credit carryback or a work incentive program carryback from a taxable year attributable to a net operating loss carryback or a capital loss carryback (or, in the case of a work incentive program carryback, to an investment credit carryback) from a subsequent taxable year, within a period of 12 months from the end of such subsequent taxable year), in the manner and form required by regulations prescribed by the Secretary. The application shall set forth in such detail and with such supporting data and explanation as such regulations shall require—

(1) The amount of the net operating loss, net capital loss, unused investment credit, or unused work incentive program credit;

- **1976, Tax Reform Act of 1976 (P.L. 94-455)**

P.L. 94-455, §2107(g):

Substituted "capital loss carryback (or, in the case of a work incentive program carryback, to an investment credit carryback)" for "capital loss carryback" in the second sentence of Code Sec. 6411(a). **Effective** 10-4-76.

P.L. 94-455, §1906(b)(13)(A):

Amended the 1954 Code by substituting "Secretary" for "Secretary or his delegate" each place it appeared. **Effective** 2-1-77.

- **1971, Revenue Act of 1971 (P.L. 92-178)**

P.L. 92-178, §601(e)(1):

Amended Code Sec. 6411(a). **Effective** for tax years beginning after 12-31-71. Prior to amendment, the material preceding paragraph (2) read as follows:

"(a) Application for Adjustment.—A taxpayer may file an application for a tentative carryback adjustment of the tax for the prior taxable year affected by a net operating loss carryback provided in section 172(b), by an investment credit carryback provided in section 46(b), or by a capital loss carryback provided in section 1212(a)(1), from any taxable year. The application shall be verified in the manner prescribed by section 6065 in the case of a return of such taxpayer, and shall be filed, on or after the date of filing of the return for the taxable year of the net operating loss, net capital loss, or unused investment credit from which the carryback results and within a period of 12 months from the end of such taxable year (or, with respect to any portion of an investment credit carryback from a taxable year attributable to a net operating loss carryback or a capital loss carryback from a subsequent taxable year, within a period of 12 months from the end of such subsequent taxable year), in the manner and form required by regulations prescribed by the Secretary or his delegate. The application shall set forth in such detail and with such supporting data and explanation as such regulations shall require—

"(1) The amount of the net operating loss, net capital loss, or unused investment credit;"

- **1969, Tax Reform Act of 1969 (P.L. 91-172)**

P.L. 91-172, §512(d)(1):

Amended first two sentences of Code Sec. 6411(a). **Effective** with respect to net capital loss sustained in tax years beginning after 12-31-69. Prior to amendment, the first two sentences of Code Sec. 6411(a) read as follows:

"A taxpayer may file an application for a tentative carryback adjustment of the tax for the prior taxable year affected by a net operating loss carryback provided in section 172(b), or by an investment credit carryback provided in section 46(b), from any taxable year. The application shall be verified in the manner prescribed by section 6065 in the case of a return of such taxpayer, and shall be filed, on or after the date of filing of the return for the taxable year of the net operating loss or unused investment credit from which the carryback results and within a period of 12 months from the end of such subsequent taxable year (or, with respect to any portion of an investment credit carryback from a taxable year attributable to a net operating loss carryback from a subsequent taxable year, within a period of 12 months from the end of such subsequent taxable year), in the manner and form required by regulations prescribed by the Secretary or his delegate."

P.L. 91-172, §512(d)(2):

Amended Code Sec. 6411(a)(1). **Effective** with respect to net capital loss sustained in tax years beginning after 12-31-69. Prior to amendment, Code Sec. 6411(a)(1) read "The amount of the net operating loss or unused investment credit."

- **1967 (P.L. 90-225)**

P.L. 90-225, §2(b):

Amended the second sentence of Code Sec. 6411(a) by inserting "(or, with respect to any portion of an investment credit carryback from a taxable year attributable to a net operating loss carryback from a subsequent taxable year, within a period of 12 months from the end of such subsequent taxable year)". **Effective** with respect to investment credit carrybacks attributable to net operating loss carrybacks from tax years ending after 7-31-67.

- **1966 (P.L. 89-721)**

P.L. 89-721, §2(a), (b), (c):

Amended the first sentence of Code Sec. 6411(a) by striking out the comma after "net operating loss carryback" and by inserting "or by an investment credit carryback provided in section 46(b)" immediately after "provided in section 172(b),"; amended the second sentence of Code Sec. 6411(a) by inserting "or unused investment credit" immediately after "net operating loss"; amended Code Sec. 6411(a)(1) by inserting "or unused investment credit" immediately after "net operating loss"; and amended Code Sec. 6411(a)(5) by substituting "from which the carryback is made" for "of such loss". **Effective** with respect to tax years ending after 12-31-61, but only in the case of applications filed after 11-2-66. The period of 12 months referred to in the second sentence of section 6411(a) for filing an application for a tentative carryback adjustment of tax attributable to the carryback of any unused investment credit shall not expire before the close of 12-31-66.

[Sec. 6411(b)]

(b) ALLOWANCE OF ADJUSTMENTS.—Within a period of 90 days from the date on which an application for a tentative carryback adjustment is filed under subsection (a), or from the last day of the month in which falls the last date prescribed by law (including any extension of time granted the taxpayer) for filing the return for the taxable year of the net operating loss, net capital loss, or unused business credit from which such carryback results, whichever is the later, the Secretary shall make, to the extent he deems practicable in such period, a limited examination of the application, to discover omissions and errors of computation therein, and shall determine the amount of the decrease in the tax attributable to such carryback upon the basis of the application and the examination, except that the Secretary may disallow, without further action, any application which he finds contains errors of computation which he deems cannot be corrected by him within such 90-day period or material omissions. Such decrease shall be applied against any unpaid amount of the tax decreased (including any amount of such tax as to which an extension of time under section 6164 is in effect) and any remainder shall be credited against any unsatisfied amount of any tax for the taxable year immediately preceding the taxable year of the net operating loss, net capital loss, or unused business credit the time for payment of which tax is extended under section 6164. Any remainder shall, within such 90-day period, be either credited against any tax or installment thereof then due from the taxpayer, or refunded to the taxpayer.

Amendments

- **1986, Tax Reform Act of 1986 (P.L. 99-514)**

P.L. 99-514, §231(d)(3)(H)(i)-(iv):

Amended Code Sec. 6411 by striking out "by a research credit carryback provided in section 30(g)(2)", by striking out "a research credit or carryback or", and by striking out "(or, with respect to any portion of a business credit carryback attributable to a research credit carryback from a subsequent taxable year within a period of 12 months from the end of such subsequent taxable year)" in subsection (a), and by striking out "unused research credit," each place it appeared in subsections (a) and (b). **Effective** for tax years beginning after 12-31-85. Prior to amendment Code Sec. 6411(b) read as follows:

(b) ALLOWANCE OF ADJUSTMENTS.—Within a period of 90 days from the date on which an application for a tentative carryback adjustment is filed under subsection (a), or from the last day of the month in which falls the last date prescribed by law (including any extension of time granted the taxpayer) for filing the return for the taxable year of the net operating loss, net capital loss, unused research credit, or unused business credit from which such carryback results, whichever is the later, the Secretary shall make, to the extent he deems practicable in such period, a limited examination of the application, to discover omissions and errors of computation therein, and shall determine the amount of the decrease in the tax attributable to such carryback upon the basis of the application and the examination, except that the Secretary may disallow, without further action, any application which he finds contains errors of computation which he deems cannot be corrected by him within such 90-day period or material omissions. Such decrease shall be applied against any unpaid amount of the tax decreased (including any amount of such tax as to which an extension of time under section 6164 is in effect) and any remainder shall be credited against any unsatisfied amount of any tax for the taxable year immediately preceding the taxable year of the net operating loss, net capital loss, unused research credit, or unused business credit the time for payment of which tax is extended under section 6164. Any remainder shall, within such 90-day period, be either credited against any tax or installment thereof then due from the taxpayer, or refunded to the taxpayer.

CREDITS AND REFUNDS—SPECIAL RULES

- **1984, Deficit Reduction Act of 1984 (P.L. 98-369)**

P.L. 98-369, §474(r)(37)(B):

Amended Code Sec. 6411(b) by striking out "unused investment credit, unused work incentive program credit, unused new employee credit, unused research credit, or unused employee stock ownership credit" each place it appeared and inserting in lieu thereof "unused research credit, or unused business credit". **Effective** for tax years beginning after 12-31-83, and to carrybacks from such years.

- **1981, Economic Recovery Tax Act of 1981 (P.L. 97-34)**

P.L. 97-34, §221(b)(2)(B)(i):

Amended Code Sec. 6411(b) by striking out "or unused new employee credit" each place it appeared and inserting in lieu thereof "unused new employee credit, or unused research credit". **Effective** for amounts paid or incurred after 6-30-81 [effective date changed by P.L. 99-514, §231(a)(2)].

P.L. 97-34, §221(d)(2), as amended by P.L. 99-514, §231(a)(2), provides the following transitional rule:

(2) TRANSITIONAL RULE.—

(A) IN GENERAL.—If, with respect to the first taxable year to which the amendments made by this section apply and which ends in 1981 or 1982, the taxpayer may only take into account qualified research expenses paid or incurred during a portion of such taxable year, the amount of the qualified research expenses taken into account for the base period of such taxable year shall be the amount which bears the same ratio to the total qualified research expenses for such base period as the number of months in such portion of such taxable year bears to the total number of months in such taxable year.

(B) DEFINITIONS.—For purposes of the preceding sentence, the terms "qualified research expenses" and "base period" have the meanings given to such terms by section 44F of the Internal Revenue Code of 1954 (as added by this section).

P.L. 97-34, §331(d)(2)(B)(i):

Amended Code Sec. 6411(b) by striking out "or unused research credit" each place it appeared and inserting in lieu thereof "unused research credit, or unused employee stock ownership credit". **Effective** for tax years beginning after 12-31-81.

- **1977, Tax Reduction and Simplification Act of 1977 (P.L. 95-30)**

P.L. 95-30, §202(d)(5)(A):

Amended Code Sec. 6411(b) by substituting "unused work incentive program credit, or unused new employee credit" for "or unused work incentive program credit" in the first and second sentences thereof. **Effective** for tax years beginning after 12-31-76, and for credit carrybacks from such years.

- **1976, Tax Reform Act of 1976 (P.L. 94-455)**

P.L. 94-455, §1906(b)(13)(A):

Amended 1954 Code by substituting "Secretary" for "Secretary or his delegate" each place it appeared. **Effective** 2-1-77.

- **1971, Revenue Act of 1971 (P.L. 92-178)**

P.L. 92-178, §601(e)(1):

Amended Code Sec. 6411(b). **Effective** for tax years beginning after 12-31-71, by substituting "unused investment credit, or unused work incentive program credit" for "or unused investment credit" in the first and second sentences of Code Sec. 6411(b).

- **1969, Tax Reform Act of 1969 (P.L. 91-172)**

P.L. 91-172, §512(d):

Amended Code Sec. 6411(b) by inserting ", net capital loss," between "net operating loss" and "unused investment credit." **Effective** with respect to net capital losses sustained in tax years beginning after 12-31-69.

- **1966 (P.L. 89-721)**

P.L. 89-721, §2(d):

Amended Code Sec. 6411(b) by inserting "or unused investment credit" immediately after "net operating loss" each place it appears. **Effective** with respect to tax years ending after 12-31-61, but only in the case of applications filed after 11-2-66.

[Sec. 6411(c)]

(c) CONSOLIDATED RETURNS.—If the corporation seeking a tentative carryback adjustment under this section, made or was required to make a consolidated return, either for the taxable year within which the net operating loss, net capital loss, or unused business credit arises, or for the preceding taxable year affected by such loss or credit, the provisions of this section shall apply only to such extent and subject to such conditions, limitations, and exceptions as the Secretary may by regulations prescribe.

Amendments

- **1988, Technical and Miscellaneous Revenue Act of 1988 (P.L. 100-647)**

P.L. 100-647, §1002(h)(2):

Amended Code Sec. 6411(c) by striking out "unused research credit," after "net capital loss,". **Effective** as if included in the provision of P.L. 99-514 to which it relates.

- **1984, Deficit Reduction Act of 1984 (P.L. 98-369)**

P.L. 98-369, §474(r)(37)(B):

Amended Code Sec. 6411(c) by striking out "unused investment credit, unused work incentive program credit, unused new employee credit, unused research credit, or unused employee stock ownership credit" and inserting in lieu thereof "unused research credit, or unused business credit". **Effective** for tax years after 12-31-83, and to carrybacks from such years.

- **1981, Economic Recovery Tax Act of 1981 (P.L. 97-34)**

P.L. 97-34, §221(b)(2)(B)(i):

Amended Code Sec. 6411(c), by striking out "or unused new employee credit" and inserting in lieu thereof "unused new employee credit, or unused research credit". **Effective** for amounts paid or incurred after 6-30-81 [effective date changed by P.L. 99-514, §231(a)(2)].

P.L. 97-34, §221(d)(2), as amended by P.L. 99-514, §231(a)(2), provides the following transitional rule:

(2) TRANSITIONAL RULE.—

(A) IN GENERAL.—If, with respect to the first taxable year to which the amendments made by this section apply and which ends in 1981 or 1982, the taxpayer may only take into account qualified research expenses paid or incurred during a portion of such taxable year, the amount of the qualified research expenses taken into account for the base period of such taxable year shall be the amount which bears the same ratio to the total qualified research expenses for such base period as the number of months in such portion of such taxable year bears to the total number of months in such taxable year.

(B) DEFINITIONS.—For purposes of the preceding sentence, the terms "qualified research expenses" and "base period" have the meanings given to such terms by section 44F of the Internal Revenue Code of 1954 (as added by this section).

P.L. 97-34, §331(d)(2)(B)(i):

Amended Code Sec. 6411(c) by striking out "or unused research credit" and inserting in lieu thereof "unused research credit, or unused employee stock ownership credit". **Effective** for tax years beginning after 12-31-81.

- **1977, Tax Reduction and Simplification Act of 1977 (P.L. 95-30)**

P.L. 95-30, §202(d)(5)(A):

Amended Code Sec. 6411(c) by substituting "unused work incentive program credit or unused new employee credit" for "or unused new employee program credit". **Effective** for tax years beginning after 12-31-76, and for credit carrybacks from such years.

- **1976, Tax Reform Act of 1976 (P.L. 94-455)**

P.L. 94-455, §1906(b)(13)(A):

Amended 1954 Code by substituting "Secretary" for "Secretary or his delegate" each place it appeared. **Effective** 2-1-77.

- **1971, Revenue Act of 1971 (P.L. 92-178)**

P.L. 92-178, §601(e)(1):

Amended Code Sec. 6411(c). **Effective** for tax years beginning after 12-31-71, by substituting "unused investment credit, or unused work incentive program credit" for "or unused investment credit".

- **1969, Tax Reform Act of 1969 (P.L. 91-172)**

P.L. 91-172, §512(d):

Amended Code Sec. 6411(c) by inserting ", net capital loss," between "net operating loss" and "unused investment credit." **Effective** with respect to net capital losses sustained in tax years beginning after 12-31-69.

- **1966 (P.L. 89-721)**

P.L. 89-721, §2(d), (e):

Amended Code Sec. 6411(c) by inserting "or unused investment credit" immediately after "net operating loss" and by inserting "or credit" after "such loss". **Effective** with respect to tax years ending after 12-31-61, but only in the case of applications filed after 11-2-66.

[Sec. 6411(d)]

(d) TENTATIVE REFUND OF TAX UNDER CLAIM OF RIGHT ADJUSTMENT.—

(1) APPLICATION.—A taxpayer may file an application for a tentative refund of any amount treated as an overpayment of tax for the taxable year under section 1341(b)(1). Such application shall be in such manner and form as the Secretary may prescribe by regulation and shall—

(A) be verified in the same manner as an application under subsection (a),

(B) be filed during the period beginning on the date of filing the return for such taxable year and ending on the date 12 months from the last day of such taxable year, and

(C) set forth in such detail and with such supporting data as such regulations prescribe—

(i) the amount of the tax for such taxable year computed without regard to the deduction described in section 1341(a)(2),

(ii) the amount of the tax for all prior taxable years for which the decrease in tax provided in section 1341(a)(5)(B) was computed,

(iii) the amount determined under section 1341(a)(5)(B),

(iv) the amount of the overpayment determined under section 1341(b)(1); and

(v) such other information as the Secretary may require.

(2) ALLOWANCE OF ADJUSTMENTS.—Within a period of 90 days from the date on which an application is filed under paragraph (1) or from the date of the overpayment (determined under section 1341(b)(1)), whichever is later, the Secretary shall—

(A) review the application,

(B) determine the amount of the overpayment, and

(C) apply, credit, or refund such overpayment,

in a manner similar to the manner provided in subsection (b).

(3) CONSOLIDATED RETURNS.—The provisions of subsection (c) shall apply to an adjustment under this subsection to the same extent and manner as the Secretary may by regulations provide.

Amendments

• **1980, Technical Corrections Act of 1979 (P.L. 96-222)**

P.L. 96-222, §105(a)(2):

Amended Code Sec. 6411(d)(2). **Effective** for tentative refund claims filed on and after 11-6-78. Prior to amendment, Code Sec. 6411(d)(2) read as follows:

(2) ALLOWANCE OF ADJUSTMENTS.—Within a period of 90 days from the date on which an application is filed under paragraph (1), or from the last day of the month in which falls the last date prescribed by law (including any extension of time granted the taxpayer) for filing the return for [the] taxable year in which the overpayment occurs, whichever is later, the Secretary shall—

(A) review the application,

(B) determine the amount of the overpayment, and

(C) apply, credit, or refund such overpayment in a manner similar to the manner provided in subsection (b).

• **1978, Revenue Act of 1978 (P.L. 95-600)**

P.L. 95-600, §504(a), (c):

Added Code Sec. 6411(d). **Effective** for tentative refund claims filed on and after 11-6-78.

[Sec. 6412]

SEC. 6412. FLOOR STOCKS REFUNDS.

[Sec. 6412(a)]

(a) IN GENERAL.—

(1) TIRES AND TAXABLE FUEL.—Where before October 1, 2028, any article subject to the tax imposed by section 4071 or 4081 has been sold by the manufacturer, producer, or importer and on such date is held by a dealer and has not been used and is intended for sale, there shall be credited or refunded (without interest) to the manufacturer, producer, or importer an amount equal to the difference between the tax paid by such manufacturer, producer, or importer on his sale of the article and the amount of tax made applicable to such article on and after October 1, 2028, if claim for such credit or refund is filed with the Secretary on or before March 31, 2029, based upon a request submitted to the manufacturer, producer, or importer before January 1, 2029, by the dealer who held the article in respect of which the credit or refund is claimed, and, on or before March 31, 2029, reimbursement has been made to such dealer by such manufacturer, producer, or importer for the tax reduction on such article or written consent has been obtained from such dealer to allowance of such credit or refund. No credit or refund shall be allowable under this paragraph with respect to taxable fuel in retail stocks held at the place where intended to be sold at retail, nor with respect to taxable fuel held for sale by a producer or importer of taxable fuel.

(2) DEFINITIONS.—For purposes of this section—

(A) The term "dealer" includes a wholesaler, jobber, distributor, or retailer.

(B) An article shall be considered as "held by a dealer" if title thereto has passed to such dealer (whether or not delivery to him has been made), and if for purposes of consumption title to such article or possession thereof has not at any time been transferred to any person other than a dealer.

Amendments

• **2021, Infrastructure Investment and Jobs Act (P.L. 117-58)**

P.L. 117-58, §80102(c)(1)-(3), Div. H:

Amended Code Sec. 6412(a)(1) by striking "October 1, 2022" each place it appears and inserting "October 1, 2028"; by striking "March 31, 2023" each place it appears and inserting "March 31, 2029"; and by striking "January 1, 2023" and inserting "January 1, 2029". **Effective** 10-1-2021.

• **2015, Fixing America's Surface Transportation Act (P.L. 114-94)**

P.L. 114-94, §31102(c)(1)-(3):

Amended Code Sec. 6412(a)(1) by striking "October 1, 2016" each place it appears and inserting "October 1, 2022"; by striking "March 31, 2017" each place it appears and inserting "March 31, 2023"; and by striking "January 1, 2017" and inserting "January 1, 2023". **Effective** 10-1-2016.

• **2012, Highway Investment, Job Creation, and Economic Growth Act of 2012 (P.L. 112-141)**

P.L. 112-141, §40102(c)(1)-(3):

Amended Code Sec. 6412(a)(1) by striking "July 1, 2012" each place it appears and inserting "October 1, 2016", by striking "December 31, 2012" each place it appears and inserting "March 31, 2017", and by striking "October 1, 2012" and inserting "January 1, 2017". **Effective** 7-1-2012.

• **2012, Temporary Surface Transportation Extension Act of 2012 (P.L. 112-140)**

P.L. 112-140, §1(c), provides:

(c) SPECIAL RULE FOR EXECUTION OF AMENDMENTS IN MAP-21.—On the date of enactment of the MAP-21 [P.L. 112-141]—

(1) this Act and the amendments made by this Act shall cease to be effective;

(2) the text of the laws amended by this Act shall revert back so as to read as the text read on the day before the date of enactment of this Act; and

(3) the amendments made by the MAP-21 shall be executed as if this Act had not been enacted.

P.L. 112-140, §402(b)(1)-(3):

Amended Code Sec. 6412(a)(1) by striking "July 1, 2012" each place it appears and inserting "July 7, 2012"; by striking "December 31, 2012" each place it appears and inserting "January 6, 2013"; and by striking "October 1, 2012" and inserting "October 7, 2012". **Effective** 7-1-2012. For a special rule, see Act Sec. 1(c), above.

• **2012, Surface Transportation Extension Act of 2012 (P.L. 112-102)**

P.L. 112-102, §402(c)(1)-(3):

Amended Code Sec. 6412(a)(1) by striking "April 1, 2012" each place it appears and inserting "July 1, 2012"; by striking "September 30, 2012" each place it appears and inserting "December 31, 2012"; and by striking "July 1, 2012" and inserting "October 1, 2012". **Effective** 4-1-2012.

• **2011, Surface Transportation Extension Act of 2011, Part II (P.L. 112-30)**

P.L. 112-30, §142(c)(1)-(3):

Amended Code Sec. 6412(a)(1) by striking "October 1, 2011" each place it appears and inserting "April 1, 2012"; by striking "March 31, 2012" each place it appears and inserting "September 30, 2012"; and by striking "January 1, 2012" and inserting "July 1, 2012". **Effective** 10-1-2011.

• **2005, Safe, Accountable, Flexible, Efficient Transportation Equity Act: A Legacy for Users (P.L. 109-59)**

P.L. 109-59, §11101(a)(3)(A)-(B):

Amended Code Sec. 6412(a)(1) by striking "2005" each place it appears and inserting "2011", and by striking "2006" each place it appears and inserting "2012". **Effective** 8-10-2005.

• **1998, Transportation Equity Act for the 21st Century (P.L. 105-178)**

P.L. 105-178, §9002(a)(2)(A)(i)-(ii):

Amended Code Sec. 6412(a)(1) by striking "1999" each place it appears and inserting "2005", and by striking "2000" each place it appears and inserting "2006". **Effective** 6-9-98.

• **1993, Omnibus Budget Reconciliation Act of 1993 (P.L. 103-66)**

P.L. 103-66, §13242(d)(16):

Amended Code Sec. 6412(a)(1) by striking "gasoline" each place it appears (including the heading) and inserting "taxable fuel". **Effective** 1-1-94.

CREDITS AND REFUNDS—SPECIAL RULES

- **1991, Intermodal Surface Transportation Efficiency Act of 1991 (P.L. 102-240)**

P.L. 102-240, §8002(c)(1)(A)-(B):

Amended Code Sec. 6412(a)(1) by striking "1995" each place it appears and inserting "1999", and by striking "1996" each place it appears and inserting "2000". **Effective** 12-18-91.

- **1990, Omnibus Budget Reconciliation Act of 1990 (P.L. 101-508)**

P.L. 101-508, §11211(f)(1)(A)-(B):

Amended Code Sec. 6412(a)(1) by striking "1993" each place it appears and inserting "1995", and by striking "1994" each place it appears and inserting "1996". **Effective** 11-5-90.

- **1987, Surface Transportation and Uniform Relocation Assistance Act of 1987 (P.L. 100-17)**

P.L. 100-17, §502(d)(1)(A)-(B):

Amended Code Sec. 6412(a)(1) by striking out "1988" each place it appears and inserting in lieu thereof "1993", and by striking out "1989" each place it appears and inserting in lieu thereof "1994". **Effective** 4-2-87.

- **1984, Deficit Reduction Act of 1984 (P.L. 98-369)**

P.L. 98-369, §735(c)(12)(A):

Amended so much of Code Sec. 6412(a)(1) as preceded "there shall be credited or refunded". **Effective** as if included in the provision of the Highway Revenue Act of 1982 to which it relates. Prior to amendment, that language read as follows:

(1) Trucks, Tires, Tubes, Tread Rubber, and Gasoline.—Where before October 1, 1988, any article subject to the tax imposed by section 4061(a)(1), 4071(a)(1), (3), or (4), or 4081 has been sold by the manufacturer, producer, or importer and on such date is held by a dealer and has not been used and is intended for sale (or, in the case of tread rubber, is intended for sale or is held for use),

P.L. 98-369, §735(c)(12)(B):

Amended Code Sec. 6412(a)(1) by striking out the last sentence. **Effective** as if included in the provision of the Highway Revenue Act of 1982 to which it relates. Prior to amendment, the last sentence read as follows:

No credit or refund shall be allowable under this paragraph with respect to inner tubes for bicycle tires (as defined in section 4221(e)(4)(B)).

P.L. 98-369, §735(c)(12)(C):

Amended Code Sec. 6412(a)(2)(A). **Effective** as if included in the provision of the Highway Revenue Act of 1982 to which it relates. Prior to amendment, Code Sec. 6412(a)(2)(A) read as follows:

(A) The term "dealer" includes a wholesaler, jobber, distributor, or retailer, or, in the case of tread rubber subject to tax under section 4071(a)(4), includes any person (other than the manufacturer, producer, or importer thereof) who holds such tread rubber for sale or use.

- **1983, Surface Transportation Act of 1982 (P.L. 97-424)**

P.L. 97-424, §516(a)(5):

Amended Code Sec. 6412(a)(1) by striking out "1984" each place it appeared and inserting "1988", and by striking out "1985" each place it appeared and inserting "1989". **Effective** 1-6-83. In addition, special floor stock provisions apply to the 1983 tax on gasoline (Code Sec. 4081) and to the 1984 tax on tires (Code Sec. 4071). For the special floor stock taxes, see the amendment notes for Act Sec. 521 following Code Sec. 4071 (tire tax) or 4081 (gasoline tax). Floor stock provisions, relating to the transfer of such taxes to the Highway Trust Fund, to refunds, and to definitions and special rules appear below.

P.L. 97-424, §§521–523, provide:

SEC. 521. FLOOR STOCK TAXES.

***

(e) TRANSFER OF FLOOR STOCKS TAXES TO HIGHWAY TRUST FUND.—For purposes of determining the amount transferred to the Highway Trust Fund for any period, the taxes imposed by this section shall be treated as if they were imposed by section 4081 or 4071 of the Internal Revenue Code of 1954, whichever is appropriate.

SEC. 522. FLOOR STOCKS REFUNDS.

(a) GENERAL RULE.—

(1) IN GENERAL.—Where, before the day after the date of the enactment of this Act, any tax-repealed article has been sold by the manufacturer, producer, or importer and on such day is held by a dealer and has not been used and is intended for sale, there shall be credited or refunded (without interest) to the manufacturer, producer, or importer an amount equal to the tax paid by such manufacturer, producer, or importer on his sale of the article if—

(A) claim for such credit or refund is filed with the Secretary of the Treasury or his delegate before October 1, 1983, based on a request submitted to the manufacturer, producer, or importer before July 1, 1983, by the dealer who held the article in respect of which the credit or refund is claimed, and

(B) on or before October 1, 1983, reimbursement has been made to the dealer by the manufacturer, producer, or importer in an amount equal to the tax paid on the article or written consent has been obtained from the dealer to allowance of the credit or refund.

(2) LIMITATION ON ELIGIBILITY FOR CREDIT OR REFUND.—No manufacturer, producer, or importer shall be entitled to credit or refund under paragraph (1) unless he has in his possession such evidence of the inventories with respect to which the credit or refund is claimed as may be required by regulations prescribed by the Secretary of the Treasury or his delegate under this subsection.

(3) OTHER LAWS APPLICABLE.—All provisions of law, including penalties, applicable with respect to the taxes imposed by section 4061, 4071, or 4091 (whichever is appropriate) shall, insofar as applicable and not inconsistent with paragraphs (1) and (2) of this subsection, apply in respect of the credits and refunds provided for in paragraph (1) to the same extent as if the credits or refunds constituted overpayments of the tax.

(b) REFUNDS WITH RESPECT TO CERTAIN CONSUMER PURCHASES OF TRUCKS AND TRAILERS.—

(1) IN GENERAL.—Except as otherwise provided in paragraph (2), where after December 2, 1982, and before the day after the date of the enactment of this Act, a tax-repealed article on which tax was imposed by section 4061(a) has been sold to an ultimate purchaser, there shall be credited or refunded (without interest) to the manufacturer, producer, or importer of such article an amount equal to the tax paid by such manufacturer, producer, or importer on his sale of the article.

(2) LIMITATION OF ELIGIBILITY FOR CREDIT OR REFUND.—No manufacturer, producer, or importer shall be entitled to a credit or refund under paragraph (1) with respect to an article unless—

(A) he has in his possession such evidence of the sale of the article to an ultimate purchaser, and of the reimbursement of the tax to such purchaser, as may be required by regulations prescribed by the Secretary of the Treasury or his delegate under this subsection.

(B) claim for such credit or refund is filed with the Secretary of the Treasury or his delegate before October 1, 1983, based on information submitted to the manufacturer, producer, or importer before July 1, 1983, by the person who sold the article (in respect of which the credit or refund is claimed) to the ultimate purchaser, or

(C) on or before October 1, 1983, reimbursement has been made to the ultimate purchaser in an amount equal to the tax paid on the article.

(3) OTHER LAWS APPLICABLE.—All provisions of law, including penalties, applicable with respect to the taxes imposed by section 4061(a) shall, insofar as applicable and not inconsistent with paragraph (1) or (2) of this subsection, apply in respect of the credits and refunds provided for in paragraph (1) to the same extent as if the credits or refunds constituted overpayments of the tax.

(c) CERTAIN USES BY MANUFACTURER, ETC.—In the case of any article which was subject to the tax imposed by section 4061(a) (as in effect on the day before the date of the enactment of this Act), any tax paid by reason of section 4218(a) (relating to use by manufacturer or importer considered sale) with respect to a tax-repealed article shall be deemed to be an overpayment of such tax if tax was imposed on such article after December 2, 1982, by reason of section 4218(a).

(d) TRANSFER OF FLOOR STOCKS REFUNDS FROM HIGHWAY TRUST FUND.—The Secretary of the Treasury shall pay from time to time from the Highway Trust Fund into the general fund of the Treasury amounts equivalent to the floor stocks refunds made under this section.

SEC. 523. DEFINITIONS AND SPECIAL RULE. [Includes amendments made by P.L. 98-369, §734.]

(a) IN GENERAL.—For purposes of this subtitle—

(1) The term "dealer" includes a wholesaler, jobber, distributor, or retailer.

(2) An article shall be considered as "held by a dealer" if title thereto has passed to such dealer (whether or not delivery to him has been made) and if for purposes of consumption title to such article or possession thereof has not at any time been transferred to any person other than a dealer.

(3) The term "tax-repealed article" means any article on which a tax was imposed by section 4061(a), 4061(b), or section 4091 as in effect on the day before the date of the enactment of this Act, and which will not be subject to tax under section 4061(a), 4061(b), or 4091 as in effect on the day after the date of the enactment of this Act.

(4) Except as otherwise expressly provided herein, any reference in this subtitle to a section or other provision shall be treated as a reference to a section or other provision of the Internal Revenue Code of 1954.

(b) 1984 EXTENSION OF FLOOR STOCKS REFUND TO TIRES.—

(1) IN GENERAL.—In the case of an article on which a tax was imposed by section 4071(a) as in effect on December 31, 1983, and which will not be subject to tax under such section (or will be subject to a lower rate of tax under such section) as in effect on January 1, 1984, such article shall be treated as a tax-repealed article for purposes of subsection (a) of section 522. Any tread rubber which was subject to tax under section 4071(a)(4) as in effect on December 31, 1983, and which on January 1, 1984, is part of a retread tire which is held by a dealer and has not been used and is intended for sale shall be treated as a tax-repealed article for purposes of subsection (a) of section 522.

(2) ALLOWANCE OF REFUND.—Except as provided in paragraph (3), in the case of a tax-repealed article to which paragraph (1) applies, subsection (a) of section 522 shall be applied—

(A) by treating January 1, 1984, as the day after the date of the enactment of this Act, and

(B) by substituting "1984" for "1983" each place it appears in paragraph (1) of such subsection (a).

(3) SPECIAL RULES FOR TIRES TAXED AT LOWER RATE AFTER JANUARY 1, 1984.—In the case of any tire which is a tax-repealed article solely by reason of the amendment made by subsection (a)(1) or (d) of section 734 of the Tax Reform Act of 1984—

(A) the amount of the credit or refund under subsection (a) shall not exceed the excess of—

(i) the tax imposed with respect to such tire by section 4071(a) as in effect on December 31, 1983, over

(ii) the tax which would have been imposed with respect to such tire by section 4071(a) on January 1, 1984, and

(B) paragraph (1) of section 522(a) shall be applied—

(i) by substituting "January 1, 1985" for "July 1, 1983", and

(ii) by substituting "April 1, 1985" for "October 1, 1983" each place it appears.

- **1978, Energy Tax Act of 1978 (P.L. 95-618)**

P.L. 95-618, §231(f)(1), (g)(1):

Amended the heading for Code Sec. 6412(a)(1) by deleting "AND BUSES" after "TRUCKS". **Effective** for articles sold after 11-9-78.

CREDITS AND REFUNDS—SPECIAL RULES

• **1978, Surface Transportation Assistance Act of 1978 (P.L. 95-599)**

P.L. 95-599, §502(c):

Substituted "1984" for "1979" each place it appeared, and substituted "1985" for "1980" each place it appeared. **Effective** 11-7-78.

• **1976, Tax Reform Act of 1976 (P.L. 94-455)**

P.L. 94-455, §1906(a)(22):

Redesignated paragraphs (2) and (4) as paragraphs (1) and (2) of Code Sec. 6412(a). **Effective** 2-1-77.

P.L. 94-455, §1906(b)(13)(A):

Amended the 1954 Code by substituting "Secretary" for "Secretary or his delegate" each place it appeared. **Effective** 2-1-77.

• **1976 (P.L. 94-280)**

P.L. 94-280, §303(b):

Amended Code Sec. 6412(a)(2) by substituting "October 1, 1979" for "October 1, 1977" (two places), "March 31, 1980" for "March 31, 1978" (two places), and "January 1, 1980" for "January 1, 1978" (one place).

• **1971, Revenue Act of 1971 (P.L. 92-178)**

P.L. 92-178, §401(g)(5):

Repealed Code Sec. 6412(a)(1). For **effective** date, see the amendment note for P.L. 92-178, §401(h), under Code Sec. 4061. Prior to repeal, Code Sec. 6412(a)(1) read as follows:

(1) Passenger automobiles, etc.—Where before the day after the date of the enactment of the Excise Tax Reduction Act of 1965, or before January 1, 1966, January 1 of 1973, 1974, 1978, 1979, 1980, 1981, or 1982, any article subject to the tax imposed by section 4061(a)(2) has been sold by the manufacturer, producer, or importer and on such day or such date is held by a dealer and has not been used and is intended for sale, there shall be credited or refunded (without interest) to the manufacturer, producer, or importer an amount equal to the difference between the tax paid by the manufacturer, producer, or importer on his sale of the article and the amount of tax made applicable to the article on such day or such date, if—

(A) claim for such credit or refund is filed with the Secretary or his delegate on or before the 10th day of the 8th calendar month beginning after such day or such date based upon a request submitted to the manufacturer, producer, or importer before the first day of the 7th calendar month beginning after such day or such date by the dealer who held the article in respect of which the credit or refund is claimed; and

(B) on or before such 10th day reimbursement has been made to the dealer by the manufacturer, producer, or importer for the tax reduction on the article or written consent has been obtained from the dealer to allowance of the credit or refund.

• **1971 (P.L. 91-678)**

P.L. 91-678 provides:

(a) where before January 1, 1970, and after June 30, 1968, any cement mixer subject to the tax imposed by section 4061 of the Internal Revenue Code of 1954 during such period, had been sold by the manufacturer, producer, or importer, and on January 1, 1970, was held by a dealer and had not been used and was intended for sale, there shall be credited or refunded (without interest) to the manufacturer, producer, or importer an amount equal to the tax paid by the manufacturer, producer, or importer on his sale of the cement mixer, if—

(1) claim for such credit or refund is filed with the Secretary of the Treasury or his delegate on or before the last day of the ninth calendar month beginning after the date of enactment of this Act, based upon a request submitted to the manufacturer, producer, or importer on or before the last day of the sixth calendar month beginning after the date of enactment of this Act, by the dealer who held the cement mixer in respect of which the credit or refund is claimed; and

(2) on or before the last day of the ninth calendar month beginning after the date of enactment of this Act, reimbursement has been made to the dealer by the manufacturer, producer, or importer for the tax on the cement mixer or written consent has been obtained from the dealer to allowance of the credit or refund.

(b) For the purposes of this section—

(1) The term "cement mixer" means—

(A) any article designed (i) to be placed or mounted on an automobile truck chassis or truck trailer or semitrailer chassis and (ii) to be used to process or prepare concrete, and

(B) parts or accessories designed primarily for use on or in connection with an article described in subparagraph (A).

(2) The term "dealer" includes a wholesaler, jobber, distributor, or retailer.

(3) A cement mixer shall be considered as "held by a dealer" if title thereto has passed to the dealer (whether or not delivery to him has been made), and if for purposes of consumption title to the cement mixer or possession thereof had not at any time prior to January 1, 1970, been transferred to any person other than a dealer. For purposes of subsection (a) and notwithstanding the preceding sentence, a cement mixer shall be considered as "held by a dealer" and not to have been used, although possession of such cement mixer has been transferred to another person, if such cement mixer is returned to the dealer in a transaction under which any amount paid or deposited by the transferee for such cement mixer is refunded to him (other than amounts retained by the dealer to cover damage to the cement mixer). Moreover, such a cement mixer shall be considered as held by a dealer on January 1, 1970, even though it was in the possession of the transferee on such day, if it was returned to the dealer (in a transaction described in the preceding sentence) before January 31, 1970.

• **1970, Excise, Estate, and Gift Tax Adjustment Act of 1970 (P.L. 91-614)**

P.L. 91-614, §201(a)(2):

Amended Code Sec. 6412(a)(1) by substituting "January 1 of 1973, 1974, 1978, 1979, 1980, 1981, or 1982" for "January 1, 1971, January 1, 1972, January 1, 1973, or January 1, 1974".

• **1970, Federal-Aid Highway Act of 1970 (P.L. 91-605)**

P.L. 91-605, §303(b):

Amended Code Sec. 6412(a)(2) by substituting "October 1, 1977" for "October 1, 1972" (two places), "March 31, 1978" for "February 10, 1973" (two places), and "January 1, 1978" for "January 1, 1973" (one place).

• **1969, Tax Reform Act of 1969 (P.L. 91-172)**

P.L. 91-172, §702(a)(2):

Amended Code Sec. 6412(a)(1) by substituting "January 1, 1971, January 1, 1972, January 1, 1973, or January 1, 1974" for "January 1, 1970, January 1, 1971, January 1, 1972, or January 1, 1973".

• **1968, Revenue and Expenditure Control Act of 1968 (P.L. 90-364)**

P.L. 90-364 §105(a)(2):

Amended Code Sec. 6412(a)(1) by substituting "January 1, 1970, January 1, 1971, January 1, 1972, or January 1, 1973," for "May 1, 1968, or January 1, 1969," in the first sentence. **Effective** 4-30-68.

• **1968 (P.L. 90-285)**

P.L. 90-285:

Amended Code Sec. 6412(a)(1) by substituting "May 1, 1968" for "April 1, 1968" in the third line. **Effective** 3-31-68.

• **1966, Tax Adjustment Act of 1966 (P.L. 89-368)**

P.L. 89-368, §201(b):

Amended Code Sec. 6412(a)(1) by substituting "January 1, 1966, April 1, 1968, or January 1, 1969" for "January 1, 1966, 1967, 1968, or 1969". **Effective** with respect to articles sold after 3-15-66.

• **1965, Excise Tax Reduction Act of 1965 (P.L. 89-44)**

P.L. 89-44, §209(a):

Amended subsection (a)(1) of Section 6412. **Effective** 6-22-65. Prior to amendment, subsection (a)(1) read as follows:

"(1) Passenger Automobiles, Etc.—Where before July 1, 1965, any article subject to the tax imposed by section 4061(a)(2) has been sold by the manufacturer, producer, or importer and on such date is held by a dealer and has not been used and is intended for sale, there shall be credited or refunded (without interest) to the manufacturer, producer, or importer an amount equal to the difference between the tax paid by such manufacturer, producer, or importer on his sale of the article and the amount of tax made applicable to such article on and after July 1, 1965, if claim for such credit or refund is filed with the Secretary or his delegate on or before November 10, 1965, based upon a request submitted to the manufacturer, producer or importer before October 1, 1965, by the dealer who held the article in respect of which the credit or refund is claimed, and, on or before November 10, 1965, reimbursement has been made to such dealer by such manufacturer, producer, or importer for the tax reduction on such article or written consent has been obtained from such dealer to allowance of such credit or refund."

• **1964, Excise Tax Rate Extension Act of 1964 (P.L. 88-348)**

P.L. 88-348, §2(b)(1):

Substituted "1965" for "1964" wherever it appeared in Sec. 6412(a)(1).

• **1963, Tax Rate Extension Act of 1963 (P.L. 88-52)**

P.L. 88-52, §3(b)(1):

Substituted "1964" for "1963" wherever it appeared in Sec. 6412(a)(1).

• **1962, Tax Rate Extension Act of 1962 (P.L. 87-508)**

P.L. 87-508, §3(b)(3):

Substituted "1963" for "1962" wherever it appeared in Sec. 6412(a)(1).

• **1961, Tax Rate Extension Act of 1961 (P.L. 87-72)**

P.L. 87-72, §3(b)(3):

Substituted "1962" for "1961" wherever it appeared in Sec. 6412(a)(1).

• **1961, Federal-Aid Highway Act of 1961 (P.L. 87-61)**

P.L. 87-61, §206(c):

Amended Sec. 6412(a)(2) by inserting "TUBES" in the heading; substituting "4071(a)(1), (3), or (4)" in place of "4071(a)(1) or (4)"; by substituting "October 1" for "July 1" wherever it appeared; by substituting "February 10, 1973" for "November 10, 1972" wherever it appeared; by substituting "January 1, 1973" for "October 1, 1972" wherever it appeared; and by adding the last sentence. **Effective** 6-29-61.

P.L. 87-61, §206(d):

Repealed Code Sec. 6412(a)(3). **Effective** 6-29-61. Prior to repeal, Code Sec. 6412(a)(3) read as follows:

(3) Gasoline held on July 1, 1961.—Where before July 1, 1961, any gasoline subject to the tax imposed by section 4081 has been sold by the producer or importer and on such date is held by a dealer and is intended for sale, there shall be credited or refunded (without interest) to the producer or importer an amount equal to the difference between the tax paid by such producer or importer on his sale of the gasoline and the amount of tax made applicable to such gasoline on and after July 1, 1961, if claim for such credit or refund is filed with the Secretary or his delegate on or before November 10, 1961, based upon a request submitted to the producer or importer before October 1, 1961, by the dealer who held the gasoline in respect of which the credit or refund is claimed, and, on or before November 10, 1961, reimbursement has been made to such dealer by such producer or importer for the tax reduction on such gasoline or written consent has been obtained from such dealer to allowance of such credit or refund. No credit or refund shall be allowable under this

CREDITS AND REFUNDS—SPECIAL RULES

paragraph with respect to gasoline in retail stocks held at the place where intended to be sold at retail, nor with respect to gasoline held for sale by a producer or importer of gasoline.

- **1960, Public Debt and Tax Rate Extension Act of 1960 (P.L. 86-564)**

P.L. 86-564, §202(b):

Amended 1954 Code Sec. 6412(a)(1) by striking out "1960" wherever it appeared and by substituting "1961".

- **1959, Federal-Aid Highway Act of 1959 (P.L. 86-342)**

P.L. 86-342, §201(c)(4):

Renumbered paragraph (3) of Sec. 6412(a) as paragraph (4) and added a new paragraph (3).

- **1959, Tax Rate Extension Act of 1959 (P.L. 86-75)**

P.L. 86-75, §3(b):

Amended 1954 Code Sec. 6412(a)(1) by striking out "1959" wherever it appeared, and by substituting "1960".

- **1958, Tax Rate Extension Act of 1958 (P.L. 85-475)**

P.L. 85-475, §3(b):

Substituted "July 1, 1959" for "July 1, 1958", "October 1, 1959" for "October 1, 1958", and "November 10, 1959" for "November 10, 1958" wherever these dates appeared in Sec. 6412(a)(1).

- **1957, Tax Rate Extension Act of 1957 (P.L. 85-12)**

P.L. 85-12, §3(b):

Substituted "July 1, 1958" for "April 1, 1957", "October 1, 1958" for "July 1, 1957", and "November 10, 1958" for "August 10, 1957", in Sec. 6412(a)(1).

- **1956 (P.L. 627, 84th Cong.)**

P.L. 627, 84th Cong., §208(a):

Amended subsection (a). **Effective** 7-1-56. Prior to amendment it read as follows:

(a) MOTOR VEHICLES.—

(1) IN GENERAL.—Where before April 1, 1957, any article subject to the tax imposed by section 4061(a) or (b) has been sold by the manufacturer, producer, or importer, and on such date is held by a dealer and has not been used and is intended for sale, there shall be credited or refunded (without interest) to the manufacturer, producer, or importer an amount equal to the difference between the tax paid by such manufacturer, producer, or importer on his sale of the article and the amount of tax made applicable to such article on and after April 1, 1957.

(2) DEFINITIONS.—For purposes of this subsection—

(A) The term `dealer' includes a wholesaler, jobber, distributor, or retailer.

(B) An article shall be considered as `held by a dealer' if title thereto has passed to such dealer (whether or not delivery to him has been made), and if for purposes of consumption title to such article or possession thereof has not at any time been transferred to any person other than a dealer.

(3) REFUNDS TO DEALERS.—Under regulations prescribed by the Secretary or his delegate, the refund provided by this subsection may be made to the dealer instead of the manufacturer, producer, or importer, if the manufacturer, producer, or importer waives any claim for the amount so to be refunded.

(4) REIMBURSEMENT OF DEALERS.—When the credit or refund provided for in this subsection has been allowed to the manufacturer, producer, or importer, he shall remit to the dealer to whom was sold the article in respect of which the credit or refund was allowed so much of that amount of the tax corresponding to the credit or refund as was included in or added to the price paid or agreed to be paid by the dealer.

(5) LIMITATION ON ELIGIBILITY FOR CREDIT OR REFUND.—No person shall be entitled to credit or refund under this subsection unless (A) he has in his possession such evidence of the inventories with respect to which the credit or refund is claimed as may be required by regulations prescribed under this subsection, and (B) claim for such credit or refund is filed with the Secretary or his delegate before July 1, 1957.

- **1956, Tax Rate Extension Act of 1956 (P.L. 458, 84th Cong.)**

P.L. 458, 84th Cong., §3(b)(4):

Substituted "1957" for "1956" wherever it appeared in Sec. 6412(a).

- **1955, Tax Rate Extension Act of 1955 (P.L. 18, 84th Cong.)**

P.L. 18, 84th Cong., §3(b)(4):

Substituted "1956" for "1955" wherever it appeared in Secs. 6412(a)(1) and (5). **Effective** 3-30-55.

[Sec. 6412(b)]

(b) LIMITATION ON ELIGIBILITY FOR CREDIT OR REFUND.—No manufacturer, producer, or importer shall be entitled to credit or refund under subsection (a) unless he has in his possession such evidence of the inventories with respect to which the credit or refund is claimed as may be required by regulations prescribed under this section.

Amendments

- **1956 (P.L. 627, 84th Cong.)**

P.L. 627, 84th Cong., §208(a):

Amended subsection (b). **Effective** 7-1-56. Prior to amendment subsection (b) read as follows:

(b) GASOLINE.—

(1) IN GENERAL.—With respect to any gasoline taxable under section 4081, upon which tax (including floor stocks tax) at the applicable rate has been paid, and which, on April 1, 1957, is held and intended for sale by any person, there shall be credited or refunded (without interest) to the producer or importer who paid the tax, subject to such regulations as may be prescribed by the Secretary or his delegate, an amount equal to so much of the difference between the tax so paid and the amount of tax made applicable to such gasoline on and after April 1, 1957, as has been paid by such producer or importer to such person as reimbursement for the tax reduction on such gasoline, if claim for such credit or refund is filed with the Secretary or his delegate prior to July 1, 1957. No credit or refund shall be allowable under this subsection with respect to gasoline in retail stocks held at the place where intended to be sold at retail, nor with respect to gasoline held for sale by a producer or importer of gasoline.

(2) LIMITATION ON ELIGIBILITY FOR CREDIT OR REFUND.—No producer or importer shall be entitled to a credit or refund under paragraph (1) unless he has in his possession satisfactory evidence of the inventories with respect to which he has made the reimbursements described in such paragraph, and establishes to the satisfaction of the Secretary or his delegate with respect to the quantity of gasoline as to which credit or refund is claimed under such paragraph, that on or after April 1, 1957, such quantity of gasoline was sold to the ultimate consumer at a price which reflected the amount of the tax reduction.

- **1956, Tax Rate Extension Act of 1956 (P.L. 458, 84th Cong.)**

P.L. 458, 84th Cong., 2d Sess., §3(b)(4):

Substituted "1957" for "1956" wherever it appeared in Sec. 6412(b).

- **1955, Tax Rate Extension Act of 1955 (P.L. 18, 84th Cong.)**

P.L. 18, 84th Cong., §3(b)(4):

Substituted "1956" for "1955" wherever it appeared in Sec. 6412(b). **Effective** 3-30-55.

[Sec. 6412(c)]

(c) OTHER LAWS APPLICABLE.—All provisions of law, including penalties, applicable in respect of the taxes imposed by sections 4071 and 4081 shall, insofar as applicable and not inconsistent with subsections (a) and (b) of this section, apply in respect of the credits and refunds provided for in subsection (a) to the same extent as if such credits or refunds constituted overpayments of such taxes.

Amendments

- **1984, Deficit Reduction Act of 1984 (P.L. 98-369)**

P.L. 98-369, §735(c)(12)(D):

Amended Code Sec. 6412(c) by striking out "4061, 4071," and inserting in lieu thereof "4071". **Effective** as if included in the provision of the Highway Revenue Act of 1982 to which it relates.

- **1956 (P.L. 627, 84th Cong.)**

P.L. 627, 84th Cong., §208(a):

Amended subsection (c) by (1) striking "to Certain Floor Stocks Refunds" following "Other Laws Applicable", (2) adding ", 4071," following "4061", (3) substituting "subsection (a)" for "such subsections", and (4) substituted the word "apply" for the words "be applicable". **Effective** 7-1-56.

[Sec. 6412(d)—Repealed]

Amendments

- **1962, Tariff Classification Act of 1961 (P.L. 87-456)**

P.L. 87-456, §302(d):

Repealed Sec. 6412(d). **Effective** 8-31-63. Prior to repeal, Sec. 6412 read as follows:

(d) Sugar.—With respect to any sugar or articles composed in chief value of sugar upon which tax imposed under section 4501(b) has been paid and which, on June 30, 1967, are held by the importer and intended for sale or other disposition, there shall be refunded (without interest) to such importer, subject to such regulations as may be prescribed by the Secretary or his delegate, an amount equal to the tax paid with respect to such sugar or articles composed in chief value of sugar, if claim for such refund is filed with the Secretary or his delegate on or before September 30, 1967.

- **1962, Sugar Act Amendments of 1962 (P.L. 87-535)**

P.L. 87-535, §18(b):

Amended Code Sec. 6412(d) by striking out "December 31, 1962" and inserting in lieu thereof "June 30, 1967" and by striking out "March 31, 1963" and inserting in lieu thereof "September 30, 1967".

- **1961 (P.L. 87-15)**

P.L. 87-15, §2(b):

Amended Code Sec. 6412(d) by striking out "September 30, 1961" where it first appeared therein and by substituting "December 31, 1962", and by striking out

CREDITS AND REFUNDS—SPECIAL RULES

"September 30, 1961" where it appeared therein the second time and by substituting "March 31, 1963."

• **1960 (P.L. 86-592)**

P.L. 86-592, §2:

Amended Code Sec. 6412(d) by striking out "June 30, 1961" and by inserting "September 30, 1961" in lieu thereof.

• **1958, Excise Tax Technical Changes Act of 1958 (P.L. 85-859)**

P.L. 85-859, §162(a):

Inserted a comma preceding the period at the end of Sec. 6412(d) and added the following: "if claim for such refund is filed with the Secretary or his delegate on or before September 30, 1961".

Amendments

• **1965, Excise Tax Reduction Act of 1965 (P.L. 89-44)**

P.L. 89-44, §209(d):

Repealed Code Sec. 6412(e). **Effective** 6-21-65. Prior to repeal, Code Sec. 6412(e) read as follows:

• **1956 (P.L. 545, 84th Cong.)**

P.L. 545, 84th Cong., §19:

Deleted "1957" wherever it appeared in Sec. 6412(d) and substituted "1961". **Effective** 1-1-56.

[Sec. 6412(e)—Repealed]

(e) Cross Reference.—

For floor stocks refunds in case of certain alcohol and tobacco taxes, see sections 5063 and 5707.

[Sec. 6413]

SEC. 6413. SPECIAL RULES APPLICABLE TO CERTAIN EMPLOYMENT TAXES.

[Sec. 6413(a)]

(a) ADJUSTMENT OF TAX.—

(1) GENERAL RULE.—If more than the correct amount of tax imposed by section 3101, 3111, 3201, 3221, or 3402 is paid with respect to any payment of remuneration, proper adjustments, with respect to both the tax and the amount to be deducted, shall be made, without interest, in such manner and at such times as the Secretary may by regulations prescribe.

(2) UNITED STATES AS EMPLOYER.—For purposes of this subsection, in the case of remuneration received from the United States or a wholly-owned instrumentality thereof during any calendar year, each head of a Federal agency or instrumentality who makes a return pursuant to section 3122 and each agent, designated by the head of a Federal agency or instrumentality, who makes a return pursuant to such section shall be deemed a separate employer.

(3) GUAM OR AMERICAN SAMOA AS EMPLOYER.—For purposes of this subsection, in the case of remuneration received during any calendar year from the Government of Guam, the Government of American Samoa, a political subdivision of either, or any instrumentality of any one or more of the foregoing which is wholly owned thereby, the Governor of Guam, the Governor of American Samoa, and each agent designated by either who makes a return pursuant to section 3125 shall be deemed a separate employer.

(4) DISTRICT OF COLUMBIA AS EMPLOYER.—For purposes of this subsection, in the case of remuneration received during any calendar year from the District of Columbia or any instrumentality which is wholly owned thereby, the Mayor of the District of Columbia and each agent designated by him who makes a return pursuant to section 3125 shall be deemed a separate employer.

(5) STATES AND POLITICAL SUBDIVISIONS AS EMPLOYER.—For purposes of this subsection, in the case of remuneration received from a State or any political subdivision therof (or any instrumentality of any one or more of the foregoing which is wholly owned thereby) during any calendar year, each head of an agency or instrumentality, and each agent designated by either, who makes a return pursuant to section 3125 shall be deemed a separate employer.

Amendments

• **1986, Consolidated Omnibus Budget Reconciliation Act of 1985 (P.L. 99-272)**

P.L. 99-272, §13205(a)(2)(E)(i):

Amended Code Sec. 6413(a) by adding at the end thereof new paragraph (5). **Effective** for services performed after 3-31-86.

• **1983, Interest and Dividend Tax Compliance Act of 1983 (P.L. 98-67)**

P.L. 98-67, §102(a):

Repealed the amendment made to Code Sec. 6413(a)(1) by P.L. 97-248, §307(a)(10). **Effective** as of the close of 6-30-83, as though it had not been enacted. Also repealed the amendment made in the heading of Code Sec. 6413 by P.L. 97-248, §307(a)(12), as though it had not been enacted.

• **1982, Tax Equity and Fiscal Responsibility Act of 1982 (P.L. 97-248)**

P.L. 97-248, §307(a)(10):

Amended Code Sec. 6413(a)(1) by striking out "or 3402 is paid with respect to any payment of remuneration," and inserting "3402 or 3451 is paid with respect to any payment of remuneration, interest, dividends, or other amounts,". **Effective** for payments of interest, dividends, and patronage dividends paid or credited after 6-30-83.

P.L. 97-248, §307(a)(12):

Amended the heading of Code Sec. 6413. **Effective** 7-1-83. Prior to amendment, the heading read as follows: "SPECIAL RULES APPLICABLE TO CERTAIN EMPLOYMENT TAXES"

• **1976, Tax Reform Act of 1976 (P.L. 94-455)**

P.L. 94-455, §1906(a)(23)(A):

Substituted "Mayor of the District of Columbia and each agent designated by him" for "Commissioners of the District of Columbia and each agent designated by them" in Code Sec. 6413(a)(4). **Effective** 2-1-77.

P.L. 94-455, §1906(b)(13)(A):

Amended the 1954 Code by substituting "Secretary" for "Secretary or his delegate" each place it appeared. **Effective** 2-1-77.

• **1965, Social Security Amendments of 1965 (P.L. 89-97)**

P.L. 89-97, §317(e):

Added Code Sec. 6413(a)(4). **Effective** with respect to service performed after the calendar quarter in which this section is enacted (7-30-65) and after the calendar quarter in which the Secretary of the Treasury receives a certification from the Commissioners of the District of Columbia expressing their desire to have the insurance system established by title II (and part A of title XVIII) of the Social Security Act extended to the officers and employees coming under this provision.

• **1960, Social Security Amendments of 1960 (P.L. 86-778)**

P.L. 86-778, §103(r):

Added a new paragraph (3) to Code Sec. 6413(a). **Effective** 1-1-61, but only with respect to (1) service in the employ of the Government of Guam or any political subdivision thereof, or any instrumentality of any one or more of the foregoing wholly owned thereby, which is performed after 1960 and after the calendar quarter in which the Secretary of the Treasury receives a certification by the Governor of Guam that legislation has been enacted by the Government of Guam expressing its desire to have the insurance system established by title II of the Social Security Act extended to the officers and employees of such Government and such political subdivisions and instrumentalities, and (2) service in the employ of the Government of American Samoa or any political subdivision thereof, or any instrumentality of any one or more of the foregoing wholly owned thereby, which is performed after 1960 and after the calendar quarter in which the Secretary of the Treasury receives a certification by the Governor of American Samoa that the Government of American Samoa desires to have the insurance system established by such title II extended to the officers and employees of such Government and such political subdivisions and instrumentalities.

[Sec. 6413(b)]

(b) OVERPAYMENTS OF CERTAIN EMPLOYMENT TAXES.—If more than the correct amount of tax imposed by section 3101, 3111, 3201, 3221, or 3402 is paid or deducted with respect to any payment of remuneration and the overpayment cannot be adjusted under subsection (a) of this section, the amount of the overpayment shall be refunded in such manner and at such times (subject to the statute of limitations properly applicable thereto) as the Secretary may by regulations prescribe.

CREDITS AND REFUNDS—SPECIAL RULES

Amendments

• **1983, Interest and Dividend Tax Compliance Act of 1983 (P.L. 98-67)**

P.L. 98-67, §102(a):

Repealed the amendments made to Code Sec. 6413(b) by P.L. 97-248 as though they had not been enacted. **Effective** as of the close of 6-30-83.

• **1982, Tax Equity and Fiscal Responsibility Act of 1982 (P.L. 97-248)**

P.L. 97-248, §307(a)(11)(A):

Amended Code Sec. 6413(b) by striking out from the subsection heading "of Certain Employment Taxes". **Effective** for payments of interest, dividends and patronage dividends, paid or credited after 6-30-83.

P.L. 97-248, §307(a)(11)(B):

Amended Code Sec. 6413(b) by striking out "or 3402 is paid or deducted with respect to any payment of remuneration" and inserting "3402 or 3451 is paid or deducted with respect to any payment of remuneration, interest, dividends, or other amount". **Effective** for payments of interest, dividends, and patronage dividends paid or credited after 6-30-83.

• **1976, Tax Reform Act of 1976 (P.L. 94-455)**

P.L. 94-455, §1906(b)(13)(A):

Amended 1954 Code by substituting "Secretary" for "Secretary or his delegate" each place it appeared. **Effective** 2-1-77.

[Sec. 6413(c)]

(c) SPECIAL REFUNDS.—

(1) IN GENERAL.—If by reason of an employee receiving wages from more than one employer during a calendar year the wages received by him during such year exceed the contribution and benefit base (as determined under section 230 of the Social Security Act) which is effective with respect to such year, the employee shall be entitled (subject to the provisions of section 31(b)) to a credit or refund of any amount of tax, with respect to such wages, imposed by section 3101(a) or section 3201(a) (to the extent of so much of the rate applicable under section 3201(a) as does not exceed the rate of tax in effect under section 3101(a)), or by both such sections, and deducted from the employee's wages (whether or not paid to the Secretary), which exceeds the tax with respect to the amount of such wages received in such year which is equal to such contribution and benefit base. The term "wages" as used in this paragraph shall, for purposes of this paragraph, include "compensation" as defined in section 3231(e).

(2) APPLICABILITY IN CASE OF FEDERAL AND STATE EMPLOYEES, EMPLOYEES OF CERTAIN FOREIGN AFFILIATES, AND GOVERNMENTAL EMPLOYEES IN GUAM, AMERICAN SAMOA, AND THE DISTRICT OF COLUMBIA.—

(A) FEDERAL EMPLOYEES.—In the case of remuneration received from the United States or a wholly owned instrumentality thereof during any calendar year, each head of a Federal agency or instrumentality who makes a return pursuant to section 3122 and each agent, designated by the head of a Federal agency or instrumentality, who makes a return pursuant to such section shall, for purposes of this subsection, be deemed a separate employer, and the term "wages" includes, for purposes of this subsection, the amount, not to exceed an amount equal to the contribution and benefit base (as determined under section 230 of the Social Security Act) for any calendar year with respect to which such contribution and benefit base is effective, determined by each such head or agent as constituting wages paid to an employee.

(B) STATE EMPLOYEES.—For purposes of this subsection, in the case of remuneration received during any calendar year, the term "wages" includes such remuneration for services covered by an agreement made pursuant to section 218 of the Social Security Act as would be wages if such services constituted employment; the term "employer" includes a State or any political subdivision thereof, or any instrumentality of any one or more of the foregoing; the term "tax" or "tax imposed by section 3101(a)" includes, in the case of services covered by an agreement made pursuant to section 218 of the Social Security Act, an amount equivalent to the tax which would be imposed by section 3101(a), if such services constituted employment as defined in section 3121; and the provisions of this subsection shall apply whether or not any amount deducted from the employee's remuneration as a result of an agreement made pursuant to section 218 of the Social Security Act has been paid to the Secretary.

(C) EMPLOYEES OF CERTAIN FOREIGN AFFILIATES.—For purposes of paragraph (1) of this subsection, the term "wages" includes such remuneration for services covered by an agreement made pursuant to section 3121(l) as would be wages if such services constituted employment; the term "employer" includes any American employer which has entered into an agreement pursuant to section 3121(l); the term "tax" or "tax imposed by section 3101(a)" includes, in the case of services covered by an agreement entered into pursuant to section 3121(l), an amount equivalent to the tax which would be imposed by section 3101(a), if such services constituted employment as defined in section 3121; and the provisions of paragraph (1) of this subsection shall apply whether or not any amount deducted from the employee's remuneration as a result of the agreement entered into pursuant to section 3121(l) has been paid to the Secretary.

(D) GOVERNMENTAL EMPLOYEES IN GUAM.—In the case of remuneration received from the Government of Guam or any political subdivision thereof or from any instrumentality of any one or more of the foregoing which is wholly owned thereby, during any calendar year, the Governor of Guam and each agent designated by him who makes a return pursuant to section 3125(b) shall, for purposes of this subsection, be deemed a separate employer.

(E) GOVERNMENTAL EMPLOYEES IN AMERICAN SAMOA.—In the case of remuneration received from the Government of American Samoa or any political subdivision thereof or from any instrumentality of any one or more of the foregoing which is wholly owned thereby, during any calendar year, the Governor of American Samoa and each agent designated by him who makes a return pursuant to section 3125(c) shall, for purposes of this subsection, be deemed a separate employer.

(F) GOVERNMENTAL EMPLOYEES IN THE DISTRICT OF COLUMBIA.—In the case of remuneration received from the District of Columbia or any instrumentality wholly owned thereby, during any calendar year, the Mayor of the District of Columbia and each agent designated by him who makes a return pursuant to section 3125(d), shall, for purposes of this subsection, be deemed a separate employer.

(G) EMPLOYEES OF STATES AND POLITICAL SUBDIVISIONS.—In the case of remuneration received from a State or any political subdivision thereof (or any instrumentality of any one or more of the foregoing which is wholly owned thereby) during any calendar year, each head of an agency or instrumentality, and each agent designated by either, who makes a return pursuant to section 3125(a) shall, for purposes of this subsection, be deemed a separate employer.

Amendments

• **1993, Omnibus Budget Reconciliation Act of 1993 (P.L. 103-66)**

P.L. 103-66, §13207(d)(1):

Amended Code Sec. 6413(c)(1) by striking "section 3101 or section 3201" and inserting "section 3101(a) or section 3201(a) (to the extent of so much of the rate applicable under section 3201(a) as does not exceed the rate of tax in effect under section 3101(a))". **Effective** for 1994 and later calendar years.

P.L. 103-66, §13207(d)(2):

Amended Code Sec. 6413(c)(2)(B)-(C) by striking "section 3101" each place it appears and inserting "section 3101(a)". **Effective** for 1994 and later calendar years.

P.L. 103-66, §13207(d)(3):

Amended Code Sec. 6413(c) by striking paragraph (3). **Effective** for 1994 and later calendar years. Prior to being stricken, Code Sec. 6413(c)(3) read as follows:

(3) SEPARATE APPLICATION FOR HOSPITAL INSURANCE TAXES.—In applying this subsection with respect to—

(A) the tax imposed by section 3101(b) (or any amount equivalent to such tax), and

(B) so much of the tax imposed by section 3201 as is determined at a rate not greater than the rate in effect under section 3101(b),

the applicable contribution base determined under section 3121(x)(2) for any calendar year shall be substituted for "contribution and benefit base (as determined under section 230 of the Social Security Act)" each place it appears.

• **1990, Omnibus Budget Reconciliation Act of 1990 (P.L. 101-508)**

P.L. 101-508, §11331(d)(1):

Amended Code Sec. 6413(c)(3). **Effective** for 1991 and later calendar years. Prior to amendment, Code Sec. 6413(c)(3) read as follows:

(3) APPLICABILITY WITH RESPECT TO COMPENSATION OF EMPLOYEES SUBJECT TO THE RAILROAD RETIREMENT TAX ACT.—In the case of any individual who, during any calendar year, receives wages from one or more employers and also receives compensation which is subject to the tax imposed by section 3201 or 3211, such compensation shall, solely for purposes of applying paragraph (1) with respect to the tax imposed by section 3101(b), be treated as wages received from an employer with respect to which the tax imposed by section 3101(b) was deducted.

CREDITS AND REFUNDS—SPECIAL RULES

• 1986, Consolidated Omnibus Budget Reconciliation Act of 1985, (P.L. 99-272)

P.L. 99-272, §13205(a)(2)(E)(ii)(I) and (II):

Amended Code Sec. 6413(c)(2) by striking out "3125(a)", "3125(b)", and "3125(c)" in subparagraphs (D), (E), and (F), respectively, and inserting in lieu thereof "3125(b)", "3125(c)", and "3125(d)", respectively, and by adding at the end thereof new subparagraph (G). **Effective** for services performed after 3-31-86.

• 1983, Interest and Dividend Tax Compliance Act of 1983 (P.L. 98-67)

P.L. 98-67, §102(a):

Repealed the amendment made to Code Sec. 6413(c)(1) by P.L. 97-248 as though it had not been made. **Effective** as of the close of 6-30-83.

• 1983, Social Security Amendments of 1983 (P.L. 98-21)

P.L. 98-21 §321(e)(4):

Amended Code Sec. 6413(c)(2)(C) by striking out "FOREIGN CORPORATIONS" in the heading and inserting in lieu thereof "FOREIGN AFFILIATES"; and by striking out "domestic corporation" in the text and inserting in lieu thereof "American employer.", and amended the heading of Code Sec. 6413(c)(2) by striking out "FOREIGN CORPORATIONS" and inserting in lieu thereof "FOREIGN AFFILIATES". **Effective** with respect to agreements entered into after 4-20-83, but at the election of any American employer, the amendments shall also apply to any agreement entered into on or before the date of enactment made at the time and manner to be prescribed by regulations.

• 1982, Tax Equity and Fiscal Responsibility Act of 1982 (P.L. 97-248)

P.L. 97-248, §302(c):

Amended Code Sec. 6413(c)(1) by striking out "section 31(b)" and inserting "section 31(c)". **Effective** 7-1-83.

• 1976, Tax Reform Act of 1976 (P.L. 94-455)

P.L. 94-455, §1906(a)(23)(B)(i):

Amended Code Sec. 6413(c)(1). **Effective** with respect to remuneration paid after 12-31-76. Prior to amendment Code Sec. 6413(c)(1) read as follows:

(1) IN GENERAL.—If by reason of an employee receiving wages from more than one employer during a calendar year after the calendar year 1950 and prior to the calendar year 1955, the wages received by him during such year exceed $3,600, the employee shall be entitled (subject to the provisions of section 31(b)) to a credit or refund of any amount of tax, with respect to such wages, imposed by section 1400 of the Internal Revenue Code of 1939 and deducted from the employee's wages (whether or not paid to the Secretary or his delegate), which exceeds the tax with respect to the first $3,600 of such wages received; or if by reason of an employee receiving wages from more than one employer (A) during any calendar year after the calendar year 1954 and prior to the calendar year 1959, the wages received by him during such year exceed $4,200, or (B) during any calendar year after the calendar year 1958 and prior to the calendar year 1966, the wages received by him during such year exceed $4,800, or (C) during any calendar year after the calendar year 1965 and prior to the calendar year 1968, the wages received by him during such year exceed $6,600, or (D) during any calendar year after the calendar year 1967 and prior to the calendar year 1972, the wages received by him during such year exceed $7,800, or (E) during any calendar year after the calendar year 1971 and prior to the calendar year 1973, the wages received by him during such year exceed $9,000, or (F) during any calendar year after the calendar year 1972 and prior to the calendar year 1974, the wages received by him during such year exceed $10,800, or (i)[G] during any calendar year after the calendar year 1973 and prior to the calendar year 1975, the wages received by him during such year exceed $13,200, or (H) during any during any calendar year after 1974, the wages received by him during such year exceed the contribution and benefit base (as determined under section 230 of the Social Security Act) which is effective with respect to such year; and the employee shall be entitled (subject to the provisions of section 31(b)) to a credit or refund of any amount of tax with respect to such wages, imposed by section 3101 or section 3201, or by both such sections, and deducted from the employee's wages (whether or not paid to the Secretary or his delegate), which exceeds the tax with respect to the first $4,200 of such wages received in such calendar year after 1954 and before 1959, or which exceeds the tax with respect to the first $4,800 of such wages received in such calendar year after 1958 and before 1966, or which exceeds the tax with respect to the first $6,600 of such wages received in such calendar year after 1965 and before 1968, or which exceeds the tax with respect to the first $7,800 of such wages received in such calendar year after 1967 and before 1972, or which exceeds the tax with respect to the first $9,000 of such wages received in such calendar year after 1971 and before 1973, or which exceeds the tax with respect to the first $10,800 of such wages received in such calendar year after 1972 and before 1974, or which exceeds the tax with respect to the first $13,200 of such wages received in such calendar year after 1973 and before 1975, or which exceeds the tax with respect to an amount of such wages received in such calendar year after 1974 equal to the contribution and benefit base (as determined under section 230 of the Social Security Act) which is effective with respect to such year. The term "wages" as used in this paragraph shall, for purposes of this paragraph, include "compensation" as defined in section 3231(e).

P.L. 94-455, §1906(a)(23)(B)(ii):

Amended Code Sec. 6413(c)(2)(A). **Effective** with respect to remuneration paid after 12-31-76. Prior to amendment Code Sec. 6413(c)(2)(A) read as follows:

(A) FEDERAL EMPLOYEES.—In the case of remuneration received from the United States or a wholly owned instrumentality thereof during any calendar year, each head of a Federal agency or instrumentality who makes a return pursuant to section 3122 and each agent, designated by the head of a Federal agency or instrumentality, who makes a return pursuant to such section shall, for purposes of this subsection, be deemed a separate employer, and the term "wages" includes for purposes of this subsection the amount, not to exceed $3,600 for the calendar year 1951, 1952, 1953, or 1954, $4,200 for the calendar year 1955, 1956, 1957, or 1958, $4,800 for the calendar year 1959, 1960, 1961, 1962, 1963, 1964, or 1965, $6,600 for the calendar year 1966 or 1967, $7,800 for the calendar year 1968, 1969, 1970 or 1971, or $9,000 for the calendar year 1972, $10,800 for the calendar year 1973, $13,200 for the calendar year 1974, or an amount equal to the contribution and benefit base (as determined under section 230 of the Social Security Act) for any calendar year after 1974 with respect to which such contribution and benefit base is effective, determined by each such head or agent as constituting wages paid to an employee.

P.L. 94-455, §1906(a)(23)(C):

Substituted "Mayor of the District of Columbia and each agent designated by him" for "Commissioners of the District of Columbia and each agent designated by them" in Code Sec. 6413(c)(2)(F). **Effective** 2-1-77.

P.L. 94-455, §1906(a)(23)(D):

Substituted "during any calendar year," for "during any calendar year after 1967," in Code Sec. 6413(c)(3). **Effective** with respect to remuneration paid after 12-31-76.

P.L. 94-455, §1906(b)(13)(A):

Amended the 1954 Code by substituting "Secretary" for "Secretary or his delegate" each place it appeared. **Effective** 2-1-77.

• 1974 (P.L. 93-445)

P.L. 93-445, §502:

Amended Code Sec. 6413(c) by inserting "or section 3201, or by both such sections," after "section 3101" in paragraph (1) and by adding the last sentence of paragraph (1). **Effective** 1-1-75, but only with respect to compensation paid for services rendered on or after that date.

• 1973 (P.L. 93-233)

P.L. 93-233, §5(b)(5)-(6):

Amended Code Sec. 6413(c)(1) and (c)(2)(A) by substituting "$13,200" for "$10,800." **Effective** with respect to remuneration paid after 1973.

• 1973 (P.L. 93-66)

P.L. 93-66, §203(b)(5), (6):

Amended Code Sec. 6413(c)(1) and (c)(2)(A) by substituting "$12,600" for "$12,000." (But see P.L. 93-233, above.)

• 1972 (P.L. 92-336)

P.L. 92-336, §203(b)(5) and (6):

Amended Code Secs. 6413(c)(1) and 6413(c)(2)(A). **Effective** for tax years beginning after 1972. Prior to amendment these Code Secs. read as follows:

(c) Special Refunds.—

(1) In general.—If by reason of an employee receiving wages from more than one employer during a calendar year after the calendar year 1950 and prior to the calendar year 1955, the wages received by him during such year exceed $3,600, the employee shall be entitled (subject to the provisions of section 31(b)) to a credit or refund of any amount of tax, with respect to such wages, imposed by section 1400 of the Internal Revenue Code of 1939 and deducted from the employee's wages (whether or not paid to the Secretary or his delegate), which exceeds the tax with respect to the first $3,600 of such wages received; or if by reason of an employee receiving wages from more than one employer (A) during any calendar year after the calendar year 1954 and prior to the calendar year 1959, the wages received by him during such year exceed $4,200, or (B) during any calendar year after the calendar year 1958 and prior to the calendar year 1966, the wages received by him during such year exceed $4,800, or (C) during any calendar year after the calendar year 1965 and prior to the calendar year 1968, the wages received by him during such year exceed $6,600, or (D) during any calendar year after the calendar year 1967 and prior to the calendar year 1972, the wages received by him during such year exceed $7,800, or (E) during any calendar year after the calendar year 1971, the wages received by him during such year exceed $9,000, the employee shall be entitled (subject to the provisions of section 31(b)) to a credit or refund of any amount of tax, with respect to such wages, imposed by section 3101 and deducted from the employee's wages (whether or not paid to the Secretary or his delegate), which exceeds the tax with respect to the first $4,200 of such wages received in such calendar year after 1954 and before 1959, or which exceeds the tax with respect to the first $4,800 of such wages received in such calendar year after 1958 and before 1966, or which exceeds the tax with respect to the first $6,600 of such wages received in such calendar year after 1965 and before 1968, or which exceeds the tax with respect to the first $7,800 of such wages received in such calendar year after 1967 and before 1972, or which exceeds the tax with respect to the first $9,000 of such wages received in such calendar year after 1971.

(A) Federal employees.—In the case of remuneration received from the United States or a wholly owned instrumentality thereof during any calendar year, each head of a Federal agency or instrumentality who makes a return pursuant to section 3122 and each agent, designated by the head of a Federal agency or instrumentality, who makes a return pursuant to such section shall, for purposes of this subsection, be deemed a separate employer, and the term "wages" includes for purposes of this subsection the amount, not to exceed $3,600 for the calendar year 1951, 1952, 1953, or 1954, $4,200 for the calendar year 1955, 1956, 1957, or 1958, $4,800 for the calendar year 1959, 1960, 1961, 1962, 1963, 1964, or 1965, $6,600 for the calendar year 1966 or 1967, $7,800 for the calendar year 1968, 1969, 1970 or 1971, or $9,000 for any calendar year after 1971, determined by each such head or agent as constituting wages paid to an employee.

• 1971 (P.L. 92-5)

P.L. 92-5, §203(b)(5):

Amended Sec. 6413(c)(1) by inserting "and prior to the calendar year 1972" after "after the calendar year 1967", by inserting after "exceed $7,800," the following: "or (E) during any calendar year after the calendar year 1971, the wages received by him during such year exceed $9,000," and by inserting before the period at the end the following: "and before 1972, or which exceeds the tax with respect to the first $9,000 of such wages received in such calendar year after 1971". **Effective** 1-1-72.

CREDITS AND REFUNDS—SPECIAL RULES

P.L. 92-5, § 203(b)(6):

Amended Sec. 6413(c)(2)(A) by striking out "or $7,800 for any calendar year after 1967" and inserting in lieu thereof "$7,800 for the calendar year 1968, 1969, 1970 or 1971, or $9,000 for any calendar year after 1971". **Effective** 1-1-72.

- **1968, Social Security Amendments of 1967 (P.L. 90-248)**

P.L. 90-248, § 108(b)(5):

Amended Sec. 6413(c)(1) by inserting "and prior to the calendar year 1968" after "the calendar year 1965", by inserting after "exceed $6,600" the following: "or (D) during any calendar year after the calendar year 1967, the wages received by him during such year exceed $7,800", and by inserting at the end of Sec. 6413(c)(1) the material beginning with "and before 1968,". **Effective** only with respect to remuneration paid after 12-31-67.

P.L. 90-248, § 108(b)(6):

Amended Sec. 6413(c)(2)(A) by substituting "6,600 for the calendar year 1966 or 1967, or $7,800 for any calendar year after the calendar year 1967" for "or $6,600 for any calendar year after 1965". **Effective** only with respect to remuneration paid after 12-31-67.

P.L. 90-248, § 502(a):

Amended Sec. 6413(c) by adding paragraph (3). **Effective** 1-2-68.

- **1965, Social Security Amendments of 1965 (P.L. 89-97)**

P.L. 89-97, § 317(f):

Amended Sec. 6413(c)(2) by adding subparagraph (F). **Effective** with respect to service performed after the calendar quarter in which this section is enacted (7-30-65) and after the calendar quarter in which the Secretary of the Treasury receives a certification from the Commissioners of the District of Columbia expressing their desire to have the insurance system established by title II (and part A of title XVIII) of the Social Security Act extended to officers and employees coming under this provision.

P.L. 89-97, § 320(b):

Amended Sec. 6413(c)(1) by inserting "and prior to the calendar year 1966" after "the calendar year 1958" and by inserting after "exceed $4,800," the following: "or (C) during any calendar year after the calendar year 1965, the wages received by him during such year exceed $6,600". Amended Sec. 6413(c)(2)(A) by substituting "$4,800 for the calendar year 1959, 1960, 1961, 1962, 1963, 1964, or 1965, or $6,600 for any calendar year after 1965" for "or $4,800 for any calendar year after 1958". **Effective** with respect to remuneration paid after 12-31-65.

- **1960, Social Security Amendments of 1960 (P.L. 86-778)**

P.L. 86-778, § 103(r):

Amended Code Sec. 6413(c)(2) by adding new subparagraphs (D) and (E), and amended the heading by striking out "AND EMPLOYEES OF CERTAIN FOREIGN CORPORATIONS" and by substituting ", EMPLOYEES OF CERTAIN FOREIGN CORPORATIONS, AND GOVERNMENTAL EMPLOYEES IN GUAM AND AMERICAN SAMOA." **Effective** 1-1-61, and only with respect to (1) service in the employ of the Government of Guam or any political subdivision thereof, or any instrumentality of any one or more of the foregoing wholly owned thereby, which is performed after 1960 and after the calendar quarter in which the Secretary of the Treasury receives a certification by the Governor of Guam that legislation has been enacted by the Government of Guam expressing its desire to have the insurance system established by title II of the Social Security Act extended to the officers and employees of such Government and such political subdivisions and instrumentalities, and (2) service in the employ of the Government of American Samoa or any political subdivision thereof, or any instrumentality of any one or more of the foregoing wholly owned thereby, which is performed after 1960 and after the calendar quarter in which the Secretary of the Treasury receives a certification by the Governor of American Samoa that the Government of American Samoa desires to have the insurance system established by such title II extended to the officers and employees of such Government and such political subdivisions and instrumentalities.

- **1958, Social Security Amendments of 1958 (P.L. 85-840)**

P.L. 85-840, § 402(d)(1):

Amended Sec. 6413(c)(1). **Effective** only for remuneration paid after 1958. Prior to amendment, Sec. 6413(c)(1) read as follows:

(1) In General.—If by reason of an employee receiving wages from more than one employer during a calendar year after the calendar year 1950 and prior to the calendar year 1955, the wages received by him during such year exceed $3,600, the employee shall be entitled (subject to the provisions of section 31(b)) to a credit or refund of any amount of tax, with respect to such wages, imposed by section 1400 of the Internal Revenue Code of 1939 and deducted from the employee's wages (whether or not paid to the Secretary or his delegate), which exceeds the tax with respect to the first $3,600 of such wages received; or if by reason of an employee receiving wages from more than one employer during any calendar year after the calendar year 1954, the wages received by him during such year exceed $4,200, the employee shall be entitled (subject to the provisions of section 31(b)) to a credit or refund of any amount of tax, with respect to such wages, imposed by section 3101 and deducted from the employee's wages (whether or not paid to the Secretary or his delegate), which exceeds the tax with respect to the first $4,200 of such wages received.

P.L. 85-840, § 402(d)(2):

Amended subparagraph (A) of Sec. 6413(c)(2) as follows: by deleting the semicolon after the phrase "separate employer" and inserting a comma; by deleting the comma after the phrase "the term `wages' includes"; by deleting the comma after the word "subsection" the second time it is used; by striking out "or" where it appeared preceding "$4,200"; and by inserting after the phrase "any calendar year after 1954," and substituting the phrase "the calendar year 1955, 1956, 1957, or 1958, or $4,800 for any calendar year after 1958,". **Effective** only for remuneration paid after 1958.

- **1954, Social Security Amendments of 1954 (P.L. 761, 83rd Cong.)**

P.L. 761, 83rd Cong., § 202(a):

Amended paragraph (1). **Effective** 1-1-55. Prior to amendment, paragraph (1) read as follows:

(1) In general.—If by reason of an employee receiving wages from more than one employer during any calendar year, the wages received by him during such year exceed $3,600, the employee shall be entitled (subject to the provisions of section 31(b)) to a credit or refund of any amount of tax, with respect to wages, imposed by section 3101 and deducted from the employee's wages (whether or not paid to the Secretary or his delegate), which exceeds the tax with respect to the first $3,600 of such wages received.

P.L. 761, 83rd Cong., § 202(b):

Amended the heading of paragraph (2) by adding "and employees of certain foreign corporations." Amended subparagraph (2)(A) by substituting "$3,600 for the calendar year 1951, 1952, 1953, or 1954, or $4,200 for any calendar year after 1954," for "$3,600,". Added subparagraph (2)(C). **Effective** only with respect to remuneration paid after 1954.

[Sec. 6413(d)]

(d) REFUND OR CREDIT OF FEDERAL UNEMPLOYMENT TAX.—Any credit allowable under section 3302, to the extent not previously allowed, shall be considered an overpayment, but no interest shall be allowed or paid with respect to such overpayment.

[Sec. 6414]

SEC. 6414. INCOME TAX WITHHELD.

In the case of an overpayment of tax imposed by chapter 24, or by chapter 3 or 4, refund or credit shall be made to the employer or to the withholding agent, as the case may be, only to the extent that the amount of such overpayment was not deducted and withheld by the employer or withholding agent.

Amendments

- **2010, Hiring Incentives to Restore Employment Act (P.L. 111-147)**

P.L. 111-147, § 501(c)(1):

Amended Code Sec. 6414 by inserting "or 4" after "chapter 3". **Effective** generally for payments made after 12-31-2012. For a special rule, see Act Sec. 501(d)(2), below.

P.L. 111-147, § 501(d)(2), provides:

(2) GRANDFATHERED TREATMENT OF OUTSTANDING OBLIGATIONS.—The amendments made by this section shall not require any amount to be deducted or withheld from any payment under any obligation outstanding on the date which is 2 years after the date of the enactment of this Act or from the gross proceeds from any disposition of such an obligation.

[Sec. 6415]

SEC. 6415. CREDITS OR REFUNDS TO PERSONS WHO COLLECTED CERTAIN TAXES.

[Sec. 6415(a)]

(a) ALLOWANCE OF CREDITS OR REFUNDS.—Credit or refund of any overpayment of tax imposed by section 4251, 4261, or 4271 may be allowed to the person who collected the tax and paid it to the Secretary if such person establishes, under such regulations as the Secretary may prescribe, that he has repaid the amount of such tax to the person from whom he collected it, or obtains the consent of such person to the allowance of such credit or refund.

Amendments

- **1976, Tax Reform Act of 1976 (P.L. 94-455)**

P.L. 94-455, § 1906(b)(13)(A):

Amended 1954 Code by substituting "Secretary" for "Secretary or his delegate" each place it appeared. **Effective** 2-1-77.

- **1970 (P.L. 91-258)**

P.L. 91-258, § 205(b)(2):

Amended Code Sec. 6415(a) by substituting "section 4251, 4261, or 4271" for "section 4251 or 4261." **Effective** 7-1-70.

CREDITS AND REFUNDS—SPECIAL RULES

• **1965, Excise Tax Reduction Act of 1965 (P.L. 89-44)**

P.L. 89-44, §601(b):

Amended Sec. 6415(a) by substituting "4251 or 4261" for "4231(1), 4231(2), 4231(3), 4241, 4251, 4261, or 4286" in the first sentence, and by striking out the last sentence which read as follows: "For purposes of this subsection, in the case of any payment outside the United States in respect of which tax is imposed under paragraph (1), (2), or (3) of section 4231, the person who paid for the admission or for the use of the box or seat shall be considered the person from whom the tax was collected."

• **1958, Excise Tax Technical Changes Act of 1958 (P.L. 85-859)**

P.L. 85-859, §163(d):

Amended Sec. 6415(a) by adding the last sentence. **Effective** 1-1-59.

• **1958, Tax Rate Extension Act of 1958 (P.L. 85-475)**

P.L. 85-475, §4(b):

Amended Sec. 6415(a) by deleting "4271," following "4261,". **Effective** as to amounts paid after 7-31-58.

[Sec. 6415(b)]

(b) CREDIT ON RETURNS.—Any person entitled to a refund of tax imposed by section 4251, 4261, or 4271 paid, or collected and paid, to the Secretary by him may, instead of filing a claim for refund, take credit therefor against taxes imposed by such section due upon any subsequent return.

Amendments

• **1976, Tax Reform Act of 1976 (P.L. 94-455)**

P.L. 94-455, §1906(b)(13)(A):

Amended 1954 Code by substituting "Secretary" for "Secretary or his delegate" each place it appeared. **Effective** 2-1-77.

• **1970 (P.L. 91-258)**

P.L. 91-258, §205(b)(2):

Amended Code Sec. 6415(b) by substituting "section 4251, 4261, or 4271" for "section 4251 or 4261." **Effective** 7-1-70.

• **1965, Excise Tax Reduction Act of 1965 (P.L. 89-44)**

P.L. 89-44, §601(b):

Amended Sec. 6415(b) by substituting "4251 or 4261" for "4231(1), 4231(2), 4231(3), 4241, 4251, 4261, or 4286".

• **1958, Tax Rate Extension Act of 1958 (P.L. 85-475)**

P.L. 85-475, §4(b):

Amended Sec. 6415(b) by deleting "4271," following "4261,". **Effective** as to amounts paid after 7-31-58.

[Sec. 6415(c)]

(c) REFUND OF OVERCOLLECTIONS.—In case any person required under section 4251, 4261, or 4271 to collect any tax shall make an overcollection of such tax, such person shall, upon proper application, refund such overcollection to the person entitled thereto.

Amendments

• **1970 (P.L. 91-258)**

P.L. 91-258, §205(b)(2):

Amended Code Sec. 6415(c) by substituting "section 4251, 4261, or 4271" for "section 4251 or 4261." **Effective** 7-1-70.

• **1965, Excise Tax Reduction Act of 1965 (P.L. 89-44)**

P.L. 89-44, §601(b):

Amended Sec. 6415(c) by substituting "4251 or 4261" for "4231(1), 4231(2), 4231(3), 4241, 4251, 4261, or 4286".

• **1958, Tax Rate Extension Act of 1958 (P.L. 85-475)**

P.L. 85-475, §4(b):

Amended Sec. 6415(c) by deleting "4271," following "4261,". **Effective** as to amounts paid after 7-31-58.

[Sec. 6415(d)]

(d) REFUND OF TAXABLE PAYMENT.—Any person making a refund of any payment on which tax imposed by section 4251, 4261, or 4271 has been collected may repay therewith the amount of tax collected on such payment.

Amendments

• **1970 (P.L. 91-258)**

P.L. 91-258, §205(b)(2):

Amended Code Sec. 6415(d) by substituting "section 4251, 4261, or 4271" for "section 4251 or 4261." **Effective** 7-1-70.

• **1965, Excise Tax Reduction Act of 1965 (P.L. 89-44)**

P.L. 89-44, §601(b):

Amended Sec. 6415(d) by substituting "4251 or 4261" for "4231(1), 4231(2), 4231(3), 4241, 4251, 4261, or 4286".

• **1958, Tax Rate Extension Act of 1958 (P.L. 85-475)**

P.L. 85-475, §4(b):

Amended Sec. 6415(d) by deleting "4271," following "4261,". **Effective** as to amounts paid after 7-31-58.

[Sec. 6416]

SEC. 6416. CERTAIN TAXES ON SALES AND SERVICES.

[Sec. 6416(a)]

(a) CONDITION TO ALLOWANCE.—

(1) GENERAL RULE.—No credit or refund of any overpayment of tax imposed by chapter 31 (relating to retail excise taxes), or chapter 32 (manufacturers taxes) shall be allowed or made unless the person who paid the tax establishes, under regulations prescribed by the Secretary, that he—

(A) has not included the tax in the price of the article with respect to which it was imposed and has not collected the amount of the tax from the person who purchased such article;

(B) has repaid the amount of the tax to the ultimate purchaser of the article;

(C) in the case of an overpayment under subsection (b)(2) of this section—

(i) has repaid or agreed to repay the amount of the tax to the ultimate vendor of the article, or

(ii) has obtained the written consent of such ultimate vendor to the allowance of the credit or the making of the refund; or

(D) has filed with the Secretary the written consent of the person referred to in subparagraph (B) to the allowance of the credit or the making of the refund.

(2) EXCEPTIONS.—This subsection shall not apply to—

(A) the tax imposed by section 4041 (relating to tax on special fuels) on the use of any liquid, and

(B) an overpayment of tax under paragraph (1), (3)(A), (4), (5), or (6) of subsection (b) of this section.

(3) SPECIAL RULE.—For purposes of this subsection, in any case in which the Secretary determines that an article is not taxable, the term "ultimate purchaser" (when used in paragraph (1)(B) of this subsection) includes a wholesaler, jobber, distributor, or retailer who, on the 15th day after the date of such determination, holds such article for sale; but only if claim for credit or refund by reason of this paragraph is filed on or before the date for filing the return with respect to the taxes imposed under chapter 32 for the first period which begins more than 60 days after the date of such determination.

CREDITS AND REFUNDS—SPECIAL RULES

(4) REGISTERED ULTIMATE VENDOR OR CREDIT CARD ISSUER TO ADMINISTER CREDITS AND REFUNDS OF GASOLINE TAX.—

(A) IN GENERAL.—For purposes of this subsection, except as provided in subparagraph (B), if an ultimate vendor purchases any gasoline on which tax imposed by section 4081 has been paid and sells such gasoline to an ultimate purchaser described in subparagraph (C) or (D) of subsection (b)(2) (and such gasoline is for a use described in such subparagraph), such ultimate vendor shall be treated as the person (and the only person) who paid such tax, but only if such ultimate vendor is registered under section 4101.

(B) CREDIT CARD ISSUER.—For purposes of this subsection, if the purchase of gasoline described in subparagraph (A) (determined without regard to the registration status of the ultimate vendor) is made by means of a credit card issued to the ultimate purchaser, paragraph (1) shall not apply and the person extending the credit to the ultimate purchaser shall be treated as the person (and the only person) who paid the tax, but only if such person—

(i) is registered under section 4101,

(ii) has established, under regulations prescribed by the Secretary, that such person—

(I) has not collected the amount of the tax from the person who purchased such article, or

(II) has obtained the written consent from the ultimate purchaser to the allowance of the credit or refund, and

(iii) has so established that such person—

(I) has repaid or agreed to repay the amount of the tax to the ultimate vendor,

(II) has obtained the written consent of the ultimate vendor to the allowance of the credit or refund, or

(III) has otherwise made arrangements which directly or indirectly provides the ultimate vendor with reimbursement of such tax.

If clause (i), (ii), or (iii) is not met by such person extending the credit to the ultimate purchaser, then such person shall collect an amount equal to the tax from the ultimate purchaser and only such ultimate purchaser may claim such credit or payment.

(C) TIMING OF CLAIMS.—The procedure and timing of any claim under subparagraph (A) or (B) shall be the same as for claims under section 6427(i)(4), except that the rules of section 6427(i)(3)(B) regarding electronic claims shall not apply unless the ultimate vendor or credit card issuer has certified to the Secretary for the most recent quarter of the taxable year that all ultimate purchasers of the vendor or credit card issuer are certified and entitled to a refund under subparagraph (C) or (D) of subsection (b)(2).

Amendments

- **2007, Tax Technical Corrections Act of 2007 (P.L. 110-172)**

P.L. 110-172, §11(d)(1)(A)-(B):

Amended Code Sec. 6416(a)(4)(C) by striking "ultimate vendor" and all that follows through "has certified" and inserting "ultimate vendor or credit card issuer has certified", and by striking "all ultimate purchasers of the vendor" and all that follows through "are certified" and inserting "all ultimate purchasers of the vendor or credit card issuer are certified". **Effective** as if included in the provision of the Safe, Accountable, Flexible, Efficient Transportation Equity Act: A Legacy for Users (P.L. 109-59) to which it relates [**effective** for sales after 12-31-2005.—CCH]. Prior to amendment, Code Sec. 6416(a)(4)(C) read as follows:

(C) TIMING OF CLAIMS.—The procedure and timing of any claim under subparagraph (A) or (B) shall be the same as for claims under section 6427(i)(4), except that the rules of section 6427(i)(3)(B) regarding electronic claims shall not apply unless the ultimate vendor or credit card issuer has certified to the Secretary for the most recent quarter of the taxable year that all ultimate purchasers of the vendor or credit card issuer are certified and entitled to a refund under subparagraph (C) or (D) of subsection (b)(2).

- **2005, Safe, Accountable, Flexible, Efficient Transportation Equity Act: A Legacy for Users (P.L. 109-59)**

P.L. 109-59, §11163(b)(1)(A)-(E):

Amended Code Sec. 6416(a)(4) by inserting "except as provided in subparagraph (B)," after "For purposes of this subsection," in subparagraph (A), by redesignating subparagraph (B) as subparagraph (C) and by inserting after subparagraph (A) a new subparagraph (B), by striking "subparagraph (A)" in subparagraph (C), as redesignated by Act Sec. 11163(b)(2) [Act Sec. 11163(b)(1)(B)], and inserting "subparagraph (A) or (B)", by inserting "or credit card issuer" after "vendor" in subparagraph (C), as so redesignated, and by inserting "OR CREDIT CARD ISSUER" after "VENDOR" in the heading thereof. **Effective** for sales after 12-31-2005.

- **2004, American Jobs Creation Act of 2004 (P.L. 108-357)**

P.L. 108-357, §865(a):

Amended Code Sec. 6416(a)(4). **Effective** 1-1-2005. Prior to amendment, Code Sec. 6416(a)(4) read as follows:

(4) WHOLESALE DISTRIBUTORS TO ADMINISTER CREDITS AND REFUNDS OF GASOLINE TAX.—

(A) IN GENERAL.—For purposes of this subsection, a wholesale distributor who purchases any gasoline on which tax imposed by section 4081 has been paid and who sells the gasoline to its ultimate purchaser shall be treated as the person (and the only person) who paid such tax.

(B) WHOLESALE DISTRIBUTOR.—For purposes of subparagraph (A), the term "wholesale distributor" has the meaning given such term by section 4093(b)(2) (determined by substituting "any gasoline taxable under section 4081" for "aviation fuel" therein). Such term includes any person who makes retail sales of gasoline at 10 or more retail motor fuel outlets.

- **1997, Taxpayer Relief Act of 1997 (P.L. 105-34)**

P.L. 105-34, §905(a):

Amended Code Sec. 6416(a)(4)(B) by adding at the end a new sentence. **Effective** for sales after 8-5-97.

- **1993, Omnibus Budget Reconciliation Act of 1993 (P.L. 103-66)**

P.L. 103-66, §13242(d)(17)(A):

Amended Code Sec. 6416(a)(4)(A) by striking "product" each place it appears and inserting "gasoline". **Effective** 1-1-94.

P.L. 103-66, §13242(d)(17)(B)(i)-(ii):

Amended Code Sec. 6416(a)(4)(B) by striking "section 4092(b)(2)" and inserting section 4093(b)(2)", and by striking all that follows "substituting" and inserting "`any gasoline taxable under section 4081' for `aviation fuel' therein)." **Effective** 1-1-94. Prior to amendment, Code Sec. 6416(a)(4)(B) read as follows:

(B) WHOLESALE DISTRIBUTOR.—For purposes of subparagraph (A), the term "wholesale distributor" has the meaning given such term by section 4092(b)(2) (determined by substituting "any product taxable under section 4081" for "a taxable fuel" therein).

- **1988, Technical and Miscellaneous Revenue Act of 1988 (P.L. 100-647)**

P.L. 100-647, §6102(a):

Amended Code Sec. 6416(a) by adding at the end thereof new paragraph (4). **Effective** for fuel sold by wholesale distributors (as defined in section 6416(a)(4)(B) of the 1986 Code, as added by this section) after 9-30-88.

- **1984, Deficit Reduction Act of 1984 (P.L. 98-369)**

P.L. 98-369, §734(b)(1)(B):

Amended Code Sec. 6416(a)(2)(B) by striking out "or (5)" and inserting in lieu thereof "(5), or (6)". **Effective** as if included in the provision of the Highway Revenue Act of 1982 to which it relates.

P.L. 98-369, §734(b)(2)(B)(iii):

Amended Code Sec. 6416(a)(1)(C) by striking out ", (b)(3)(C) or (D), or (b)(4)". **Effective** as if included in the provision of the Highway Revenue Act of 1982 to which it relates.

P.L. 98-369, §734(b)(2)(B)(iv):

Amended Code Sec. 6416(a)(2)(B), as amended by Act Sec. 734(b)(1)(B), by inserting "(4)," before "(5)". **Effective** as if included in the provision of the Highway Revenue Act of 1982 to which it relates.

P.L. 98-369, §734(b)(2)(B)(v):

Amended Code Sec. 6416(a)(3). **Effective** as if included in the provision of the Highway Revenue Act of 1982 to which it relates. Prior to amendment, Code Sec. 6416(a)(3) read as follows:

(3) SPECIAL RULES.—For purposes of this subsection—

(A) in any case in which the Secretary determines that an article is not taxable, the term "ultimate purchaser" (when used in paragraph (1)(B) of this subsection) includes a wholesaler, jobber, distributor, or retailer who, on the 15th day after the date of such determination, holds such article for sale; but only if claim for credit or refund by reason of this subparagraph is filed on or before the day for filing the return with respect to the taxes imposed under chapter 32 for the first period which begins more than 60 days after the date of such determination; and

(B) in applying paragraph (1)(C) to any overpayment under paragraph (2)(F), (3)(C), or (4) of subsection (b), the term "ultimate vendor" means the ultimate vendor of the other article.

P.L. 98-369, §735(c)(13)(D):

Amended Code Sec. 6416(a)(2)(B) by striking out "or (B)". **Effective** as if included in the provision of the Highway Revenue Act of 1982 to which it relates.

- **1983, Surface Transportation Act of 1983 (P.L. 97-424)**

P.L. 97-424, §512(b)(2)(D):

Amended Code Sec. 6416(a)(1) by striking out "chapter 31 (special fuels)" and inserting "chapter 31 (relating to retail excise taxes)". **Effective** 4-1-83.

- **1976, Tax Reform Act of 1976 (P.L. 94-455)**

P.L. 94-455, §1904(b)(1)(A):

Substituted "(special fuels)" for "(retailers taxes)" in Code Sec. 6416(a)(1). **Effective** 2-1-77.

P.L. 94-455, §1906(a)(24)(A):

Redesignated subparagraphs (C) and (D) as subparagraphs (A) and (B) of Code Sec. 6416(a)(3). **Effective** 2-1-77.

CREDITS AND REFUNDS—SPECIAL RULES

P.L. 94-455, § 1906(b)(13)(A):

Amended the 1954 Code by substituting "Secretary" for "Secretary or his delegate" each place it appeared. **Effective** 2-1-77.

- **1970 (P.L. 91-258)**

P.L. 91-258, § 205(b)(3):

Amended Code Sec. 6416(a)(2)(A) by substituting "section 4041 (relating to tax on special fuels) on the use of any liquid" for "section 4041(a)(2) or (b)(2) (use of diesel and special motor fuels)". **Effective** 7-1-70.

- **1965, Excise Tax Reduction Act of 1965 (P.L. 89-44)**

P.L. 89-44, § 601(b), (c):

Amended Sec. 6416(a). Prior to amendment, Sec. 6416 (a) read as follows:

(a) Condition to Allowance.—

(1) General rule.—No credit or refund of any overpayment of tax imposed by section 4231(4), (5), or (6) (cabarets, etc.), chapter 31 (retailers taxes), or chapter 32 (manufacturers taxes) shall be allowed or made unless the person who paid the tax establishes, under regulations prescribed by the Secretary or his delegate, that he—

(A) has not included the tax in the price of the article, admission, or service with respect to which it was imposed and has not collected the amount of the tax from the person who purchased such article, admission, or service;

(B) has repaid the amount of the tax—

(i) in the case of any tax imposed by chapter 31 (other than the tax imposed by section 4041(a)(1) or (b)(1)), to the purchaser of the article,

(ii) in the case of any tax imposed by chapter 32 and the tax imposed by section 4041(a)(1) or (b)(1) (diesel and special motor fuels), to the ultimate purchaser of the article, or

(iii) in the case of any tax imposed by section 4231(4), (5), or (6) (cabarets, etc.) to the person who paid for the admission, refreshment, service, or merchandise;

(C) in the case of an overpayment under subsection (b)(2), (b)(3)(C) or (D), or (b)(4) of this section—

(i) has repaid or agreed to repay the amount of the tax to the ultimate vendor of the article, or

(ii) has obtained the written consent of such ultimate vendor to the allowance of the credit or the making of the refund; or

(D) has filed with the Secretary or his delegate the written consent of the person referred to in subparagraph (B)(i), (ii), or (iii), as the case may be, to the allowance of the credit or the making of the refund.

(2) Exceptions.—This subsection shall not apply to—

(A) the tax imposed by section 4041(a)(2) or (b)(2) (use of diesel and special motor fuels), and

(B) an overpayment of tax under paragraph (1), (3)(A) or (B), or (5) of subsection (b) of this section.

(3) Special rules.—For purposes of this subsection—

(A) any tax collected under section 4231(6) from a concessionaire and paid to the Secretary or his delegate shall be treated as paid by the concessionaire;

(B) if tax under chapter 31 was paid by a supplier pursuant to an agreement under section 6011(c), either the person who (without regard to section 6011(c)) was required to return and pay the tax or the supplier may be treated as the person who paid the tax;

(C) in any case in which the Secretary or his delegate determines that an article is not taxable, the term `ultimate purchaser' (when used in paragraph (1)(B)(ii) of this subsection) includes a wholesaler, jobber, distributor, or retailer who, on the 15th day after the date of such determination, holds such article for sale; but only if claim for credit or refund by reason of this subparagraph is filed on or before the day for filing the return with respect to the taxes imposed under chapter 32 for the first period which begins more than 60 days after the date of such determination; and

(D) in applying paragraph (1)(C) to any overpayment under paragraph (2)(F), (3)(C) or (D), or (4) of subsection (b), the term `ultimate vendor' means the ultimate vendor of the other article.

- **1958, Excise Tax Technical Changes Act of 1958 (P.L. 85-859)**

P.L. 85-859, § 163(a):

Amended Sec. 6416(a). **Effective** 1-1-59. Prior to amendment, Sec. 6416(a) read as follows:

(a) Condition to Allowance.—No credit or refund of any overpayment of tax imposed by section 4231(6) or by chapter 31 (other than section 4041(a)(2) or (b)(2)) or chapter 32 (except an overpayment of tax under paragraph (1) or (3) of subsection (b) of this section) shall be allowed unless the person who paid the tax establishes under regulations prescribed by the Secretary or his delegate—

(1) That he has not included the tax in the price of the article or service with respect to which it was imposed or has not collected the amount of the tax from the vendee; or

(2) Has repaid the amount of the tax to the purchaser (in case of retailers' taxes) or to the ultimate purchaser (in the case of manufacturers' taxes and the tax under section 4041(a)(1) or (b)(1)) of the article or service or, in any case within subsection (b)(2), has repaid or has agreed to repay the amount of the tax to the ultimate vendor of the article; or

(3) Has filed with the Secretary or his delegate the written consent of such purchaser, ultimate purchaser, or ultimate vendor, as the case may be, to the allowance of the credit or refund or has obtained the written consent of such ultimate vendor thereto.

- **1958, Tax Rate Extension Act of 1958 (P.L. 85-475)**

P.L. 85-475, § 4(b), (c):

Amended Sec. 6416(a), as reproduced in the amendment note for P.L. 85-859 above, by deleting the phrase "or 4281" following "4231(6)". **Effective** only as to *amounts* paid after 7-31-58, except that in the case of transportation to which the second sentence of Sec. 4281 applies, the repeal applies only to *transportation* beginning after 7-31-58.

[Sec. 6416(b)]

(b) SPECIAL CASES IN WHICH TAX PAYMENTS CONSIDERED OVERPAYMENTS.—Under regulations prescribed by the Secretary, credit or refund (without interest) shall be allowed or made in respect of the overpayments determined under the following paragraphs:

(1) PRICE READJUSTMENTS.—

(A) IN GENERAL.—Except as provided in subparagraph (B) or (C), if the price of any article in respect of which a tax, based on such price, is imposed by chapter 31 or 32, is readjusted by reason of the return or repossession of the article or a covering or container, or by a bona fide discount, rebate, or allowance, including a readjustment for local advertising (but only to the extent provided in section 4216(e)(2) and (3)), the part of the tax proportionate to the part of the price repaid or credited to the purchaser shall be deemed to be an overpayment.

(B) FURTHER MANUFACTURE.—Subparagraph (A) shall not apply in the case of an article in respect of which tax was computed under section 4223(b)(2); but if the price for which such article was sold is readjusted by reason of the return or repossession of the article, the part of the tax proportionate to the part of such price repaid or credited to the purchaser shall be deemed to be an overpayment.

(C) ADJUSTMENT OF TIRE PRICE.—No credit or refund of any tax imposed by subsection (a) or (b) of section 4071 shall be allowed or made by reason of an adjustment of a tire pursuant to a warranty or guarantee.

(2) SPECIFIED USES AND RESALES.—The tax paid under chapter 32 (or under subsection (a) or (d) of section 4041 in respect of sales or under section 4051) in respect of any article shall be deemed to be an overpayment if such article was, by any person—

(A) exported;

(B) used or sold for use as supplies for vessels or aircraft;

(C) sold to a State or local government for the exclusive use of a State or local government;

(D) sold to a nonprofit educational organization for its exclusive use;

(E) sold to a qualified blood collector organization (as defined in section 7701(a)(49)) for such organization's exclusive use in the collection, storage, or transportation of blood;

(F) in the case of any tire taxable under section 4071(a), sold to any person for use as described in section 4221(e)(3); or

(G) in the case of gasoline, used or sold for use in the production of special fuels referred to in section 4041.

Subparagraphs (C), (D), and (E) shall not apply in the case of any tax paid under section 4064. This paragraph shall not apply in the case of any tax imposed under section 4041(a)(1) or 4081 on diesel fuel or kerosene and any tax paid under section 4121. In the case of the tax imposed by section 4131, subparagraphs (B), (C), (D), and (E) shall not apply and subparagraph (A) shall apply only if the use of the exported vaccine meets such requirements as the Secretary may by regulations prescribe. Subparagraphs (C) and (D) shall not apply in the case of any tax imposed on gasoline under section 4081 if the requirements of subsection (a)(4) are not met. In the case of taxes imposed by subchapter C or D of chapter 32, subparagraphs (E) shall not apply.

(3) TAX-PAID ARTICLES USED FOR FURTHER MANUFACTURE, ETC.—If the tax imposed by chapter 32 has been paid with respect to the sale of any article (other than coal taxable under section 4121) by the manufacturer, producer, or importer thereof and such article is sold to a subsequent manufacturer or producer before being used, such tax shall be deemed to be an overpayment by such subsequent manufacturer or producer if—

CREDITS AND REFUNDS—SPECIAL RULES

(A) in the case of any article other than any fuel taxable under section 4081, such article is used by the subsequent manufacturer or producer as material in the manufacture or production of, or as a component part of—

(i) another article taxable under chapter 32, or

(ii) an automobile bus chassis or an automobile bus body, manufactured or produced by him; or

(B) in the case of any fuel taxable under section 4081, such fuel is used by the subsequent manufacturer or producer, for nonfuel purposes, as a material in the manufacture or production of any other article manufactured or produced by him.

(4) TIRES.—If—

(A) the tax imposed by section 4071 has been paid with respect to the sale of any tire by the manufacturer, producer, or importer thereof, and

(B) such tire is sold by any person on or in connection with, or with the sale of, any other article, such tax shall be deemed to be an overpayment by such person if such other article is—

(i) an automobile bus chassis or an automobile bus body,

(ii) by such person exported, sold to a State or local government for the exclusive use of a State or local government, sold to a nonprofit educational organization for its exclusive use, or used or sold for use as supplies for vessels or aircraft, or

(iii) sold to a qualified blood collector organization for its exclusive use in connection with a vehicle the organization certifies will be primarily used in the collection, storage, or transportation of blood.

(5) RETURN OF CERTAIN INSTALLMENT ACCOUNTS.—If—

(A) tax was paid under section 4216(d)(1) in respect of any installment account,

(B) such account is, under the agreement under which the account was sold, returned to the person who sold such account, and

(C) the consideration is readjusted as provided in such agreement,

the part of the tax paid under section 4216(d)(1) allocable to the part of the consideration repaid or credited to the purchaser of such account shall be deemed to be an overpayment.

(6) TRUCK CHASSIS, BODIES, AND SEMITRAILERS USED FOR FURTHER MANUFACTURE.—If—

(A) the tax imposed by section 4051 has been paid with respect to the sale of any article, and

(B) before any other use, such article is by any person used as a component part of another article taxable under section 4051 manufactured or produced by him,

such tax shall be deemed to be an overpayment by such person. For purposes of the preceding sentence, an article shall be treated as having been used as a component part of another article if, had it not been broken or rendered useless in the manufacture or production of such other article, it would have been so used.

This subsection shall apply in respect of an article only if the exportation or use referred to in the applicable provision of this subsection occurs before any other use, or, in the case of a sale or resale, the use referred to in the applicable provision of this subsection is to occur before any other use.

Amendments

• **2019, Further Consolidated Appropriations Act, 2020 (P.L. 116-94)**

P.L. 116-94, §501(b)(2), Div. N:

Amended Code Sec. 6416(b)(2) by striking the last sentence. **Effective** for sales after 12-31-2019. Prior to being stricken, the last sentence of Code Sec. 6416(b)(2) read as follows:

In the case of the tax imposed by section 4191, subparagraphs (B), (C), (D), and (E) shall not apply.

• **2010, Health Care and Education Reconciliation Act of 2010 (P.L. 111-152)**

P.L. 111-152, §1405(b)(2):

Amended Code Sec. 6416(b)(2), by adding at the end a new sentence. **Effective** for sales after 12-31-2012.

• **2008, Energy Improvement and Extension Act of 2008 (P.L. 110-343)**

P.L. 110-343, Division B, §114, provides:

SEC. 114. SPECIAL RULES FOR REFUND OF THE COAL EXCISE TAX TO CERTAIN COAL PRODUCERS AND EXPORTERS.

(a) REFUND.—

(1) COAL PRODUCERS.—

(A) IN GENERAL.—Notwithstanding subsections (a)(1) and (c) of section 6416 and section 6511 of the Internal Revenue Code of 1986, if—

(i) a coal producer establishes that such coal producer, or a party related to such coal producer, exported coal produced by such coal producer to a foreign country or shipped coal produced by such coal producer to a possession of the United States, or caused such coal to be so exported or shipped, the export or shipment of which was other than through an exporter who meets the requirements of paragraph (2),

(ii) such coal producer filed an excise tax return on or after October 1, 1990, and on or before the date of the enactment of this Act [10-3-2008.—CCH], and

(iii) such coal producer files a claim for refund with the Secretary not later than the close of the 30-day period beginning on the date of the enactment of this Act,

then the Secretary shall pay to such coal producer an amount equal to the tax paid under section 4121 of such Code on such coal exported or shipped by the coal producer or a party related to such coal producer, or caused by the coal producer or a party related to such coal producer to be exported or shipped.

(B) SPECIAL RULES FOR CERTAIN TAXPAYERS.—For purposes of this section—

(i) IN GENERAL.—If a coal producer or a party related to a coal producer has received a judgment described in clause (iii), such coal producer shall be deemed to have established the export of coal to a foreign country or shipment of coal to a possession of the United States under subparagraph (A)(i).

(ii) AMOUNT OF PAYMENT.—If a taxpayer described in clause (i) is entitled to a payment under subparagraph (A), the amount of such payment shall be reduced by any amount paid pursuant to the judgment described in clause (iii).

(iii) JUDGMENT DESCRIBED.—A judgment is described in this subparagraph if such judgment—

(I) is made by a court of competent jurisdiction within the United States,

(II) relates to the constitutionality of any tax paid on exported coal under section 4121 of the Internal Revenue Code of 1986, and

(III) is in favor of the coal producer or the party related to the coal producer.

(2) EXPORTERS.—Notwithstanding subsections (a)(1) and (c) of section 6416 and section 6511 of the Internal Revenue Code of 1986, and a judgment described in paragraph (1)(B)(iii) of this subsection, if—

(A) an exporter establishes that such exporter exported coal to a foreign country or shipped coal to a possession of the United States, or caused such coal to be so exported or shipped,

(B) such exporter filed a tax return on or after October 1, 1990, and on or before the date of the enactment of this Act, and

(C) such exporter files a claim for refund with the Secretary not later than the close of the 30-day period beginning on the date of the enactment of this Act,

then the Secretary shall pay to such exporter an amount equal to $0.825 per ton of such coal exported by the exporter or caused to be exported or shipped, or caused to be exported or shipped, by the exporter.

(b) LIMITATIONS.—Subsection (a) shall not apply with respect to exported coal if a settlement with the Federal Government has been made with and accepted by, the coal producer, a party related to such coal producer, or the exporter, of such coal, as of the date that the claim is filed under this section with respect to such exported coal. For purposes of this subsection, the term "settlement with the Federal Government" shall not include any settlement or stipulation entered into as of the date of the enactment of this Act, the terms of which contemplate a judgment concerning which any party has reserved the right to file an appeal, or has filed an appeal.

(c) SUBSEQUENT REFUND PROHIBITED.—No refund shall be made under this section to the extent that a credit or refund of such tax on such exported or shipped coal has been paid to any person.

(d) DEFINITIONS.—For purposes of this section—

(1) COAL PRODUCER.—The term "coal producer" means the person in whom is vested ownership of the coal immediately after the coal is severed from the ground, without regard to the existence of any contractual arrangement for the sale or other disposition of the coal or the payment of any royalties between the producer and third parties. The term includes any person who extracts coal from coal waste refuse piles or from the silt waste product which results from the wet washing (or similar processing) of coal.

(2) EXPORTER.—The term "exporter" means a person, other than a coal producer, who does not have a contract, fee arrangement, or any other agreement with a producer or seller of such coal to export or ship such coal to a third party on behalf of the producer or seller of such coal and—

(A) is indicated in the shipper's export declaration or other documentation as the exporter of record, or

(B) actually exported such coal to a foreign country or shipped such coal to a possession of the United States, or caused such coal to be so exported or shipped.

(3) RELATED PARTY.—The term "a party related to such coal producer" means a person who—

(A) is related to such coal producer through any degree of common management, stock ownership, or voting control,

CREDITS AND REFUNDS—SPECIAL RULES

(B) is related (within the meaning of section 144(a)(3) of the Internal Revenue Code of 1986) to such coal producer, or

(C) has a contract, fee arrangement, or any other agreement with such coal producer to sell such coal to a third party on behalf of such coal producer.

(4) SECRETARY.—The term "Secretary" means the Secretary of Treasury or the Secretary's designee.

(e) TIMING OF REFUND.—With respect to any claim for refund filed pursuant to this section, the Secretary shall determine whether the requirements of this section are met not later than 180 days after such claim is filed. If the Secretary determines that the requirements of this section are met, the claim for refund shall be paid not later than 180 days after the Secretary makes such determination.

(f) INTEREST.—Any refund paid pursuant to this section shall be paid by the Secretary with interest from the date of overpayment determined by using the overpayment rate and method under section 6621 of the Internal Revenue Code of 1986.

(g) DENIAL OF DOUBLE BENEFIT.—The payment under subsection (a) with respect to any coal shall not exceed—

(1) in the case of a payment to a coal producer, the amount of tax paid under section 4121 of the Internal Revenue Code of 1986 with respect to such coal by such coal producer or a party related to such coal producer, and

(2) in the case of a payment to an exporter, an amount equal to $0.825 per ton with respect to such coal exported by the exporter or caused to be exported by the exporter.

(h) APPLICATION OF SECTION.—This section applies only to claims on coal exported or shipped on or after October 1, 1990, through the date of the enactment of this Act [10-3-2008.—CCH].

(i) STANDING NOT CONFERRED.—

(1) EXPORTERS.—With respect to exporters, this section shall not confer standing upon an exporter to commence, or intervene in, any judicial or administrative proceeding concerning a claim for refund by a coal producer of any Federal or State tax, fee, or royalty paid by the coal producer.

(2) COAL PRODUCERS.—With respect to coal producers, this section shall not confer standing upon a coal producer to commence, or intervene in, any judicial or administrative proceeding concerning a claim for refund by an exporter of any Federal or State tax, fee, or royalty paid by the producer and alleged to have been passed on to an exporter.

• **2006, Pension Protection Act of 2006 (P.L. 109-280)**

P.L. 109-280, §1207(e)(1)(A):

Amended Code Sec. 6416(b)(2) by redesignating subparagraphs (E) and (F) as subparagraphs (F) and (G), respectively, and by inserting after subparagraph (D) a new subparagraph (E). **Effective** 1-1-2007.

P.L. 109-280, §1207(e)(1)(B):

Amended Code Sec. 6416(b)(2) by adding at the end a new sentence. **Effective** 1-1-2007.

P.L. 109-280, §1207(e)(1)(C)(i)-(ii):

Amended Code Sec. 6416(b)(2) by striking "Subparagraphs (C) and (D)" in the second sentence and inserting "Subparagraphs (C), (D), and (E)", and by striking "(B), (C), and (D)" and inserting "(B), (C), (D), and (E)". **Effective** 1-1-2007.

P.L. 109-280, §1207(e)(2):

Amended Code Sec. 6416(b)(4)(B) by striking "or" at the end of clause (i), by striking the period at the end of clause (ii) and inserting ", or", and by adding after clause (ii) a new clause (iii). **Effective** 1-1-2007.

• **2005, Safe, Accountable, Flexible, Efficient Transportation Equity Act: A Legacy for Users (P.L. 109-59)**

P.L. 109-59, §11163(b)(2):

Amended Code Sec. 6416(b)(2) by adding at the end a new sentence. **Effective** for sales after 12-31-2005.

• **2004, American Jobs Creation Act of 2004 (P.L. 108-357)**

P.L. 108-357, §853(d)(2)(G):

Amended Code Sec. 6416(b)(2) by striking "4091 or" immediately preceding "4121". **Effective** for aviation-grade kerosene removed, entered, or sold after 12-31-2004.

P.L. 108-357, §853(d)(2)(H):

Amended Code Sec. 6416(b)(3) by striking "or 4091" after "section 4081" each place it appears. **Effective** for aviation-grade kerosene removed, entered, or sold after 12-31-2004.

• **1998, IRS Restructuring and Reform Act of 1998 (P.L. 105-206)**

P.L. 105-206, §6023(23):

Amended Code Sec. 6416(b)(5) by striking "section 4216(e)(1)" each place it appears and inserting "section 4216(d)(1)". **Effective** 7-22-98.

• **1997, Taxpayer Relief Act of 1997 (P.L. 105-34)**

P.L. 105-34, §1032(e)(6):

Amended the flush paragraph of Code Sec. 6416(b)(2) by inserting "or kerosene" after "diesel fuel". **Effective** 7-1-98.

• **1996, Small Business Job Protection Act of 1996 (P.L. 104-188)**

P.L. 104-188, §1702(b)(3):

Amended Code Sec. 6416(b)(1)[(A)] by striking "chapter 32 or section 4051" and inserting "chapter 31 or 32". **Effective** as if included in the provision of P.L. 101-508 to which it relates.

• **1993, Omnibus Budget Reconciliation Act of 1993 (P.L. 103-66)**

P.L. 103-66, §13242(d)(18):

Amended Code Sec. 6416(b)(2) by inserting "any tax imposed under section 4041(a)(1) or 4081 on diesel fuel and" after "This paragraph shall not apply in the case of" in the material following the first sentence. **Effective** 1-1-94.

P.L. 103-66, §13242(d)(19)(A):

Amended Code Sec. 6416(b)(3)(A) by striking "gasoline taxable under section 4081 and other than any fuel taxable under section 4091" and inserting "any fuel taxable under section 4081 or 4091". **Effective** 1-1-94.

P.L. 103-66, §13242(d)(19)(B):

Amended Code Sec. 6416(b)(3)(B) by striking "gasoline taxable under section 4081 or any fuel taxable under section 4091, such gasoline or fuel" and inserting "any fuel taxable under section 4081 or 4091, such fuel". **Effective** 1-1-94.

• **1988, Technical and Miscellaneous Revenue Act of 1988 (P.L. 100-647)**

P.L. 100-647, §2001(d)(1)(B):

Amended Code Sec. 6416(b)(2) by striking out "(or under paragraph (1)(A) or (2)(A) of section 4041(a) or under paragraph (1)(A) or (2)(A) of section 4041(d) or under section 4051)" and inserting in lieu thereof "(or under subsection (a) or (d) of section 4041 in respect of sales or under section 4051)". **Effective** as if included in the provision of P.L. 99-499 to which it relates.

• **1987, Revenue Act of 1987 (P.L. 100-203)**

P.L. 100-203, §9201(b)(2):

Amended Code Sec. 6416(b)(2) by adding at the end thereof a new sentence. **Effective** 1-1-88.

P.L. 100-203, §10502(d)(6)(A)-(B):

Amended Code Sec. 6416(b)(2) by striking out "(other than coal taxable under section 4121)", and by adding at the end thereof a new sentence. **Effective** for sales after 3-31-88.

P.L. 100-203, §10502(d)(7):

Amended Code Sec. 6416(b)(3)(A) by inserting "and other than any fuel taxable under section 4091" after "section 4081". **Effective** for sales after 3-31-88.

P.L. 100-203, §10502(d)(8):

Amended Code Sec. 6416(b)(3)(B) by striking out ", such gasoline" and inserting in lieu thereof "or any fuel taxable under section 4091, such gasoline or fuel". **Effective** for sales after 3-31-88.

• **1986, Superfund Amendments and Reauthorization Act of 1986 (P.L. 99-499)**

P.L. 99-499, §521(d)(5):

Amended Code Sec. 6416(b)(2) by inserting "or under paragraph (1)(A) or (2)(A) of section 4041(d)" after "section 4041(a)". **Effective** 1-1-87.

• **1984, Deficit Reduction Act of 1984 (P.L. 98-369)**

P.L. 98-369, §734(b)(1)(A):

Amended Code Sec. 6416(b) by adding after paragraph (5) new paragraph (6). **Effective** as if included in the provision of the Highway Revenue Act of 1982 to which it relates.

P.L. 98-369, §734(b)(2)(A):

Amended Code Sec. 6416(b)(4). **Effective** as if included in the provision of the Highway Revenue Act of 1982 to which it relates. Prior to amendment, Code Sec. 6416(b)(4) read as follows:

(4) Tires, Inner Tubes.—If—

(A) a tire or inner tube taxable under section 4071, or a recapped or retreaded tire in respect of which tax under section 4071(a)(4) was paid on the tread rubber used in the recapping or retreading, is sold by the manufacturer, producer, or importer thereof on or in connection with, or with the sale of, any other article manufactured or produced by him, and

(B) such other article is—

(i) an automobile bus chassis or an automobile bus body, or

(ii) by any person exported, sold to a State or local government for the exclusive use of a State or local government, sold to a nonprofit educational organization for its exclusive use, or used or sold for use as supplies for vessels or aircraft, any tax imposed by chapter 32 in respect of such tire or inner tube which has been paid by the manufacturer, producer, or importer thereof shall be deemed to be an overpayment by him.

P.L. 98-369, §734(b)(2)(B)(i):

Amended Code Sec. 6416(b)(2) by striking out subparagraph (E). **Effective** as if included in the provision of the Highway Revenue Act of 1982 to which it relates. Prior to amendment, Code Sec. 6416(b)(2)(E) read as follows:

(E) in the case of a tire or inner tube, resold for use as provided in subparagraph (C) of paragraph (3) (or in the case of the tread rubber on a recapped or retreaded tire, resold for use as provided in subparagraph (D) of paragraph (3)), and the other article referred to in such subparagraph is by any person exported or sold as provided in such subparagraph;

P.L. 98-369, §734(b)(2)(B)(ii):

Amended Code Sec. 6416(b)(3) by striking out subparagraph (C). **Effective** as if included in the provision of the Highway Revenue Act of 1982 to which it relates. Prior to amendment, Code Sec. 6416(b)(3)(C) read as follows:

(C) in the case of a tire or inner tube taxable under section 4071, such article is sold by the subsequent manufacturer or producer on or in connection with, or with the sale of, any other article manufactured or produced by him and such other article is—

CREDITS AND REFUNDS—SPECIAL RULES

(i) an automobile bus chassis or an automobile bus body, or

(ii) by any person exported, sold to a State or local government for the exclusive use of a State or local government, sold to a nonprofit educational organization for its exclusive use, or used or sold for use as supplies for vessels or aircraft;

P.L. 98-369, §734(j):

Amended Code Sec. 6416(b)(1)(A) by inserting "or by section 4051" after "by chapter 32". **Effective** as if included in the provision of the Highway Revenue Act of 1982 to which it relates.

P.L. 98-369, §735(c)(13)(A):

Amended Code Sec. 6416(b)(1)(C) by striking out "section 4071(a)(1) or (2) or section 4071(b)" and inserting in lieu thereof "subsection (a) or (b) of section 4071". **Effective** as if included in the provision of the Highway Revenue Act of 1982 to which it relates.

P.L. 98-369, §735(c)(13)(B):

Amended Code Sec. 6416(b)(2) by striking out subparagraph (F) and all that follows to the end thereof and inserting new subparagraphs (E) and (F). **Effective** as if included in the provision of the Highway Revenue Act of 1982 to which it relates. Prior to amendment, Code Sec. 6416(b)(2)(F)-(M) and the sentence at the end thereof read as follows:

(F) in the case of any article taxable under section 4061(b) (other than spark plugs and storage batteries), used or sold for use as repair or replacement parts or accessories for farm equipment (other than equipment taxable under section 4061(a));

(G) in the case of tread rubber in respect of which tax was paid under section 4071(a)(4)—

(i) used or sold for use otherwise than in the recapping or retreading of tires of the type used on highway vehicles (as defined in section 4072(c)),

(ii) destroyed, scrapped, wasted, or rendered useless in the recapping or retreading process,

(iii) used in the recapping or retreading of a tire the sale of which is later adjusted pursuant to a warranty or guarantee, in which case the overpayment shall be in proportion to the adjustment in the sales price of such tire, or

(iv) used in the recapping or retreading of a tire, if such tire is by any person exported, used or sold for use as supplies for vessels or aircraft, sold to a State or local government for the exclusive use of a State or local government, or sold to a nonprofit educational organization for its exclusive use,

unless credit or refund of such tax is allowable under paragraph (3);

(H) in the case of gasoline, used or sold for use in production of special fuels referred to in section 4041;

(I) in the case of any article taxable under section 4061(b), sold for use by the purchaser on or in connection with an automobile bus;

(J) in the case of a box, container, receptacle, bin, or other similiar article taxable under section 4061(b), sold to any person for use as described in section 4221(a)(7); or

(K) in the case of any article taxable under section 4061(b), sold on or in connection with the first retail sale of a light-duty truck, as described in section 4061(a)(2), if credit or refund of such tax is not available under any other provisions of law;

(L) in the case of any tire or inner tube taxable under paragraph (1) or (3) of section 4071(a), sold to any person for use as described in section 4221(e)(5)(A); or

(M) in the case of tread rubber taxable under paragraph (4) of section 4071(a), used in the recapping or retreading of a tire sold to any person for use on or in connection with a qualified bus (as defined in section 4221(d)(7)).

Subparagraphs (C) and (D) shall not apply in the case of any tax paid under section 4064.

P.L. 98-369, §735(c)(13)(C):

Amended Code Sec. 6416(b)(3) by striking out all subparagraphs and the last sentence thereof and inserting in lieu thereof new subparagraphs (A) and (B). **Effective** as if included in the provision of the Highway Revenue Act of 1982 to which it relates. Prior to amendment, Code Sec. 6416(b)(3)(A), (B), and (D)-(F) and the last sentence read as follows:

(A) in the case of any article other than an article to which subparagraph (B), (C), (D), or (E) applies, such article is used by the subsequent manufacturer or producer as material in the manufacture or production of, or as a component part of—

(i) another article taxable under chapter 32, or

(ii) an automobile bus chassis or an automobile bus body,

manufactured or produced by him;

(B) in the case of a part or accessory taxable under section 4061(b), such article is used by the subsequent manufacturer or producer as material in the manufacture or production of, or as a component part of, any other article manufactured or produced by him;

* * *

(D) in the case of tread rubber in respect of which tax was paid under section 4071(a)(4) used in the recapping or retreading of a tire, such tire is sold by the subsequent manufacturer or producer on or in connection with, or with the sale of, any other article manufactured or produced by him and such other article is by any person exported, sold to a State or local government for the exclusive use of a State or local government, sold to a nonprofit educational organization for its exclusive use, or used or sold for use as supplies for vessels or aircraft, unless credit or refund of such tax is allowable under subparagraph (C);

(E) in the case of—

(i) a bicycle tire (as defined in section 4221(e)(4)(B)), or

(ii) an inner tube for such a tire,

such article is used by the subsequent manufacturer or producer as material in the manufacture or production of, or as a component part of, a bicycle (other than a rebuilt or reconditioned bicycle); or

(F) in the case of gasoline taxable under section 4081, such gasoline is used by the subsequent manufacturer or producer, for nonfuel purposes, as a material in the manufacture or production of any other article manufactured or produced by him.

For purposes of subparagraphs (A) and (B), an article shall be treated as having been used as a component part of another article if, had it not been broken or rendered useless in the manufacture or production of such other article, it would have been so used.

P.L. 98-369, §735(c)(13)(F):

Amended Code Sec. 6416(b)(2)(A) by striking out "(except in any case to which subsection (g) applies)". **Effective** as if included in the provision of the Highway Revenue Act of 1982 to which it relates.

• **1983, Surface Transportation Act of 1983 (P.L. 97-424)**

P.L. 97-424, §511(g)(2)(A):

Amended Code Sec. 6416(b)(2) by striking out "section 4041(a)(1) or (b)(1)" and inserting "paragraph (1)(A) or (2)(A) of section 4041(a)". **Effective** 4-1-83.

P.L. 97-424, §512(b)(2)(C):

Amended Code Sec. 6416(b)(2) (as amended by Act Sec. 511(g)(2)(A)) by inserting "or under section 4051" after "section 4041(a)". **Effective** 4-1-83.

P.L. 97-424, §515(b)(4):

Amended Code Sec. 6416(b)(2) by striking out subparagraph (N), by striking out the next to the last sentence, by inserting "or" at the end of subparagraph (L), and by striking out "; or" at the end of subparagraph (M) and inserting a period. **Effective** with respect to articles sold after 1-6-83. Prior to amendment, subparagraph (N) and the next to the last sentence read as follows:

(N) in the case of lubricating oil taxable under section 4091 which is contained in a mixture which is rerefined oil (as defined in section 4093(b)(3)), used or sold.

The amount of the credit or refund under subparagraph (N) with respect to any lubricating oil shall be the amount which would be exempt from tax under section 4093."

P.L. 97-424, §521(c), provides:

(c) OVERPAYMENT OF FLOOR STOCKS TAXES.—Section 6416 shall apply in respect of the floor stocks taxes imposed by this section, so as to entitle, subject to all provisions of section 6416, any person paying such floor stocks taxes to a credit or refund thereof for any of the reasons specified in section 6416. All other provisions of law, including penalties, applicable with respect to the taxes imposed by section 4081 or 4071(a) (whichever is appropriate) shall apply to the floor stocks taxes imposed by this section.

For the texts of additional floor stock provisions, see the amendment note for Act Sec. 521(b) and (d)(2) following Code Sec. 4071 (tax on tires), the amendment for Act Sec. 521(a) and (d)(1) following Code Sec. 4081 (gasoline tax), and the amendment notes for Act Sec. 521(e), 522 and 523 following Code Sec. 6412 (transfer of taxes to Highway Trust Fund, floor stock refunds, definitions, and special rules).

• **1980 (P.L. 96-598)**

P.L. 96-598, §1(a):

Amended Code Sec. 6416(b)(2)(G). **Effective** 2-1-81. Prior to amendment, Code Sec. 6416(b)(2)(G) read as follows:

"(G) in the case of tread rubber in respect of which tax was paid under section 4071(a)(4), used or sold for use otherwise than in the recapping or retreading of tires of the type used on highway vehicles (as defined in section 4072(c)), unless credit or refund of such tax is allowable under subsection (b)(3);"

P.L. 96-598, §1(b)(1):

Amended Code Sec. 6416(b)(3) by inserting after subparagraph (C) new subparagraph (D). **Effective** 2-1-81.

P.L. 96-598, §1(b)(2):

Amended Code Sec. 6416(a)(1)(C) by striking out "(b)(3)(C)" and inserting in lieu thereof "(b)(3)(C) or (D)", and amended: (1) Code Sec. 6416(b)(2)(E) by inserting after "paragraph (3)" the words "(or in the case of the tread rubber on a recapped or retreaded tire, resold for use as provided in subparagraph (D) of paragraph (3)),"; (2) Code Sec. 6416(b)(3)(A) by inserting "(D)," after "(C),"; and (3) Code Sec. 6416(b)(4)(A) by striking out "section 4071" and inserting in lieu thereof "section 4071, or a recapped or retreaded tire in respect of which tax under section 4071(a)(4) was paid on the tread rubber used in the recapping or retreading,". **Effective** 2-1-81.

P.L. 96-598, §4(c):

Amended Code Sec. 6416(b)(1). **Effective** with respect to adjustments of any tire after 12-31-82. Prior to amendment, Code Sec. 6416(b)(1) read:

(1) PRICE READJUSTMENTS.—If the price of any article in respect of which a tax, based on such price, is imposed by chapter 32, is readjusted by reason of the return or repossession of the article or a covering or container, or by a bona fide discount, rebate, or allowance, including a readjustment for local advertising (but only to the extent provided in section 4216(e)(2) and (3)), the part of the tax proportionate to the part of the price repaid or credited to the purchaser shall be deemed to be an overpayment. The preceding sentence shall not apply in the case of an article in respect of which tax was computed under section 4223(b)(2); but if the price for which such article was sold is readjusted by reason of the return or repossession of the article, the part of the tax proportionate to the part of such price repaid or credited to the purchaser shall be deemed to be an overpayment.

• **1980, Technical Corrections Act of 1979 (P.L. 96-222)**

P.L. 96-222, §108(c)(2)(A):

Amended Code Sec. 6416(b)(3)(C). **Effective** for sales on or after 12-1-78. Prior to amendment, Code Sec. 6416(c)(3)(C) read as follows:

(C) in the case of a tire or inner tube taxable under section 4071, such article is sold by the subsequent manufacturer or producer on or in connection with, or with the sale of, any other article manufactured or produced by him and such other article is by any person exported, sold to a State or local government for the exclusive use of a State or local government, sold to a nonprofit educational organization for its exclusive use, or used or sold for use as supplies for vessels or aircraft;

P.L. 96-222, § 108(c)(2)(B):

Amended Code Sec. 6416(b)(4)(B). **Effective** for sales after 12-31-78, and before 10-1-84. Prior to amendment, Code Sec. 6416(b)(4)(B) read as follows:

(B) such other article is by any person exported, sold to a State or local government for the exclusive use of a State or local government, sold to a nonprofit educational organization for its exclusive use, or used or sold for use as supplies for vessels or aircraft,

any tax imposed by chapter 32 in respect of such tire or inner tube which has been paid by the manufacturer, producer, or importer thereof shall be deemed to be an overpayment by him.

P.L. 96-222, § 108(c)(3):

Amended Code Sec. 6416(b)(2) by adding subparagraph (N) and the sentence that follows. **Effective** for sales on or after 12-1-78.

P.L. 96-222, § 108(c)(4):

Amended Code Sec. 6416(b)(3)(A). **Effective** for sales on or after 12-1-78. Prior to amendment, Code Sec. 6416(b)(3)(A) read as follows:

(A) in the case of any article other than an article to which subparagraph (B), (C), or (E) applies, such article is used by the subsequent manufacturer or producer as material in the manufacture or production of, or as a component part of, another article taxable under chapter 32 manufactured or produced by him;

- **1978, Energy Tax Act of 1978 (P.L. 95-618)**

P.L. 95-618, § 201(c)(3):

Added the last sentence of Code Sec. 6416(b)(2). For **effective** date, see historical comment for P.L. 95-618, § 201(a), under Code Sec. 4064.

P.L. 95-618, § 232(b):

Amended Code Sec. 6416(b)(2)(I). **Effective** for sales on or after 12-1-78. Prior to amendment, Code Sec. 6416(b)(2)(I) read as follows:

(I) in the case of a bus chassis or body taxable under section 4061(a), sold to any person for use as described in section 4063(a)(6) or 4221(e)(5);

P.L. 95-618, § 233(c)(3):

Amended Code Sec. 6416(b)(2) by striking out the period at the end of subparagraph (K), inserting in lieu thereof a semicolon, and adding the new subparagraphs (L) and (M). **Effective** 12-1-78.

- **1978, Black Lung Benefits Revenue Act of 1977 (P.L. 95-227)**

P.L. 95-227, § 2(b)(4):

Added "(other than coal taxable under section 4121)" in the second line of Code Sec. 6416(b)(2) and (3). For **effective** date, see the historical comment for P.L. 95-227 under Code Sec. 4121.

- **1976, Tax Reform Act of 1976 (P.L. 94-455)**

P.L. 94-455, § 2108(a):

Added Code Sec. 6416(b)(2)(T) [later renumbered (K)]. **Effective** for parts and accessories sold after 10-4-76.

P.L. 94-455, § 1904(b)(2):

Substituted "section 4216(e)(2) and (3)" for "section 4216(f)(2) and (3)" in Code Sec. 6416(b)(1). **Effective** 2-1-77.

P.L. 94-455, § 1906(a)(24)(B)(i):

Repealed Code Sec. 6416(b)(2)(G), (H), (I), and (J), and redesignated subparagraphs (F), (K), (L), (M), (R), (S), and (T) as subparagraphs (E), (F), (G), (H), (I), (J), and (K), respectively. **Effective** with respect to the use or resale for use of liquids after 12-31-76. Prior to repeal, Code Sec. 6416(b)(2)(G), (H), (I), and (J), read as follows:

(G) in the case of a liquid taxable under section 4041, sold for use as fuel in a diesel-powered highway vehicle or as fuel for the propulsion of a motor vehicle, motorboat, or airplane, if before July 1, 1970(i) the vendee used such liquid otherwise than as fuel in such a vehicle, motorboat, or airplane or resold such liquid, or (ii) such liquid was (within the meaning of paragraphs (1), (2), and (3) of section 6420(c)) used on a farm for farming purposes;

(H) in the case of a liquid in respect of which tax was paid under section 4041 at the rate of 3 cents or 4 cents a gallon, used during any calendar quarter beginning before July 1, 1970, in vehicles while engaged in furnishing scheduled common carrier public passenger land transportation service along regular routes; except that (i) this subparagraph shall apply only if the 60 percent passenger fare revenue test set forth in section 6421(b)(2) is met with respect to such quarter, and (ii) the amount of such overpayment for such quarter shall be an amount determined by multiplying 1 cent (where tax was paid at the 3-cent rate) or 2 cents (where tax was paid at the 4-cent rate) for each gallon of liquid so used by the percentage which such person's commuter fare revenue (as defined in section 6421(d)(2)) derived from such scheduled service during such quarter was of his total passenger fare revenue derived from such scheduled service during such quarter;

(I) in the case of a liquid in respect of which tax was paid under section 4041(a)(1) at the rate of 3 cents or 4 cents a gallon, used or resold for use as a fuel in a diesel-powered highway vehicle (i) which (at the time of such use or resale) is not registered, and is not required to be registered, for highway use under the laws of any State or foreign country, or (ii) which, in the case of a diesel-powered highway vehicle owned by the United States, is not used on the highway; except that the amount of any overpayment by reason of this subparagraph shall not exceed an amount computed at the rate of 1 cent a gallon where tax was paid at the 3-cent rate or at the rate of 2 cents a gallon where tax was paid at the 4-cent rate;

(J) in the case of a liquid in respect of which tax was paid under section 4041(b)(1) at the rate of 3 cents or 4 cents a gallon, used or resold for use before July 1, 1970, otherwise than as a fuel for the propulsion of a highway vehicle (i) which (at the time of such use or resale) is registered, or is required to be registered, for highway use under the laws of any State or foreign country, or (ii) which, in the case of a highway vehicle owned by the United States, is used on the highway; except that the amount of any overpayment by reason of this subparagraph shall not exceed an amount

computed at the rate of 1 cent a gallon where tax was paid at the 3-cent rate or at the rate of 2 cents a gallon where tax was paid at the 4-cent rate;

P.L. 94-455, § 1906(b)(13)(A):

Amended the 1954 Code by substituting "Secretary" for "Secretary or his delegate" each place it appeared. **Effective** 2-1-77.

- **1971, Revenue Act of 1971 (P.L. 92-178)**

P.L. 92-178, § 401(a)(3)(C):

Amended Code Sec. 6416(b)(2) by adding subparagraph (S) and by substituting "section 4063(a)(6) or 4221(e)(5); or" for "section 4221(e)(5)" in subparagraph (R). For **effective** date, see the amendatory note for P.L. 92-178, § 401(h) under Code Sec. 4061.

- **1970, Excise, Estate, and Gift Tax Adjustment Act of 1970 (P.L. 91-614)**

P.L. 91-614, § 302(a)(1)(A):

Amended Code Sec. 6416(b)(3) by substituting "and such article is sold to a subsequent manufacturer or producer before being used, such tax shall be deemed to be an overpayment by such subsequent manufacturer or producer if" for "to a second manufacturer or producer, such tax shall be deemed to be an overpayment by such second manufacturer or producer if". **Effective** only with respect to claims for credit or refund filed after 12-31-70, and only if the filing of the claim is not barred on the date after 12-31-70 by any law or rule of law.

P.L. 91-614, § 302(a)(1)(B):

Amended subparagraphs (A), (B), (C), (E) and (F) of Code Sec. 6416(b)(3) by substituting "the subsequent manufacturer" for "the second manufacturer." **Effective** only with respect to claims for credit or refund filed after 12-31-70, and only if the filing of the claim is not barred on the date after 12-31-70 by any law or rule of law.

P.L. 91-614, § 302(a)(2):

Amended Code Sec. 6416(b)(2) by deleting the last sentence. **Effective** only with respect to claims for credit or refund filed after 12-31-70, and only if the filing of the claim is not barred on the day after the date of enactment by any law or rule of law. The former last sentence read as follows: "The credit provided by this subsection shall be allowable only in respect to the first sale on or in connection with, or with the sale of, another article on the sale of which tax is imposed under chapter 32."

P.L. 91-614, § 302(b):

Amended Code Sec. 6416(b)(2) by striking out subparagraph (E). **Effective** only for claims for credit or refund filed after 12-31-70, and only if the filing of the claim is not barred on the date after 12-31-70 by any law or rule of law. Prior to repeal, subparagraph (E) read as follows:

(E) resold to a manufacturer or producer for use by him as provided in subparagraph (A), (B), (E), or (F) of paragraph (3);

- **1970 (P.L. 91-258)**

P.L. 91-258, §§ 205(b)(4), 207(d)(4)-(7):

Amended Code Sec. 6416(b)(2) by (1) adding "before July 1, 1970" in subparagraphs (G), (I) and (J), (2) adding "beginning before July 1, 1970" in subparagraph (H), and substituting subparagraph (M) for the following: "(M) in the case of gasoline, used or sold for use in production of special motor fuels referred to in section 4041(b);". **Effective** 7-1-70.

- **1965, Excise Tax Reduction Act of 1965 (P.L. 89-44)**

P.L. 89-44, § 601(c)(7):

Amended Sec. 6416(b)(1). **Effective** 6-22-65. Prior to amendment, the first sentence read:

If the price of any article in respect of which a tax, based on such price, is imposed by chapter 31 or 32, is readjusted by reason of the return or repossession of the article or a covering or container, or by a bona fide discount, rebate, or allowance, including (in the case of a tax imposed by chapter 32) a readjustment for local advertising (but only to the extent provided in section 4216(f)(2) and (3)), the part of the tax proportionate to the part of the price repaid or credited to the purchaser shall be deemed to be an overpayment.

P.L. 89-44, § 601(c)(8):

Amended Sec. 6416(b)(2)(F). **Effective** 6-22-65. Prior to amendment, this subsection read as follows:

(F) in the case of a tire, inner tube, or receiving set, resold for use as provided in subparagraph (C) or (D) of paragraph (3) and the other article referred to in such subparagraph is by any person exported or sold as provided in such subparagraph;

P.L. 89-44, § 601(c)(9):

Deleted subparagraphs (N), (O), (P), and (Q) of Sec. 6416(b)(2). **Effective** 6-22-65. Prior to deletion, these subparagraphs read as follows:

(N) in the case of lubricating oil, used or sold for nonlubricating purposes;

(O) in the case of lubricating oil in respect of which tax was paid at the rate of 6 cents a gallon, used or sold for use as cutting oils (within the meaning of section 4092(b)); except that the amount of such overpayment shall not exceed an amount computed at the rate of 3 cents a gallon;

(P) in the case of any musical instrument taxable under section 4151, sold to a religious institution for exclusively religious purposes;

(Q) in the case of unexposed motion picture film, used or sold for use in the making of newsreel motion picture film.

P.L. 89-44, § 601(c)(10):

Amended Sec. 6416(b)(3) by substituting "(B), (C), or (E)" for "(B), (C), (D), or (E)" in subparagraph (A), by striking out subparagraph (D) of such subsection, and by amending subparagraphs (B) and (C). **Effective** 6-22-65. Prior to amendment, subparagraphs (B), (C), and (D) read as follows:

(B) in the case of—

(i) a part or accessory taxable under section 4061(b),

CREDITS AND REFUNDS—SPECIAL RULES

(ii) a radio or television component taxable under section 4141, or

(iii) a camera lens taxable under section 4171,

such article is used by the second manufacturer or producer as material in the manufacture or production of, or as a component part of, any other article manufactured or produced by him;

(C) in the case of—

(i) a tire or inner tube taxable under section 4071, or

(ii) an automobile radio or television receiving set taxable under section 4141,

such article is sold by the second manufacturer or producer on or in connection with, or with the sale of, any other article manufactured or produced by him and such other article is by any person exported, sold to a State or local government for the exclusive use of a State or local government, sold to a nonprofit educational organization for its exclusive use, or used or sold for use as supplies for vessels or aircraft;

(D) in the case of a radio receiving set or an automobile radio receiving set—

(i) such set is used by the second manufacturer or producer as a component part of any other article manufactured or produced by him, and

(ii) such other article is by any person exported, sold to a State or local government for the exclusive use of a State or local government, sold to a nonprofit educational organization for its exclusive use, or used or sold for use as supplies for vessels or aircraft;

P.L. 89-44, § 601(c)(11) and (12):

Amended Sec. 6416(4) and (5). **Effective** 6-22-65. Prior to amendment, subparagraphs (4) and (5) read as follows:

(4) Tires, inner tubes, and automobile radio and television receiving sets.—If—

(A)(i) a tire or inner tube taxable under section 4071, or automobile radio or television receiving set taxable under section 4141, is sold by the manufacturer, producer, or importer thereof on or in connection with, or with the sale of, any other article manufactured or produced by him, or

(ii) a radio receiving set or an automobile radio receiving set is used by the manufacturer thereof as a component part of any other article manufactured or produced by him; and

(B) such other article is by any person exported, sold to a State or local government for the exclusive use of a State or local government, sold to a nonprofit educational organization for its exclusive use, or used or sold for use as supplies for vessels or aircraft,

any tax imposed by chapter 32 in respect of such tire, inner tube, or receiving set which has been paid by the manufacturer, producer, or importer thereof shall be deemed to be an overpayment by him.

(5) Return of certain installment accounts.—If—

(A) tax was paid under section 4053(b)(1) or 4216(e)(1) in respect of any installment account,

(B) such account is, under the agreement under which the account was sold, returned to the person who sold such account, and

(C) the consideration is readjusted a provided in such agreement, the part of the tax paid under section 4053(b)(1) or 4216(e)(1) proportionate to the part of the consideration repaid or credited to the purchaser of such account shall be deemed to be an overpayment.

This subsection shall apply in respect of an article only if the exportation or use referred to in the applicable provision of this subsection occurs before any other use, or, in the case of a sale or resale, the use referred to in the applicable provision of this subsection is to occur before any other use.

P.L. 89-44 § 801(d)(2):

Amended Sec. 6416(b)(2) by adding subparagraph (R). **Effective** 6-22-65.

P.L. 89-44, § 207(c):

Amended Sec. 6416(b)(5) by inserting "allocable" in lieu of "proportionate." **Effective** 6-22-65.

• **1962, Tax Rate Extension Act of 1962 (P.L. 87-508)**

P.L. 87-508, § 5(c)(3):

Amended Code Sec. 6416(b)(2)(H). **Effective** 9-16-62. Prior to amendment, Sec. 6416(b)(2)(H) read as follows:

(H) in the case of a liquid in respect of which tax was paid under section 4041 at the rate of 3 cents or 4 cents a gallon, used during any calendar quarter in vehicles while engaged in furnishing scheduled common carrier public passenger land transportation service along regular routes; except that (i) this subparagraph shall apply only if the 60 percent passenger fare revenue test set forth in section 6421(b)(2) is met with respect to such quarter, and (ii) the amount of such overpayment for such quarter shall be an amount determined by multiplying 1 cent (where tax was paid at the 3-cent rate) or 2 cents (where tax was paid at the 4-cent rate) for each gallon of liquid so used by the percentage which such person's tax-exempt passenger fare revenue (as defined in section 6421(d)(2)) derived from such scheduled service during such quarter was of his total passenger fare revenue (not including the tax imposed by section 4261, relating to the tax on transportation of persons) derived from such scheduled service during such quarter;

• **1961, Federal-Aid Highway Act of 1961 (P.L. 87-61)**

P.L. 87-61, § 205(c) and (d):

Amended Sec. 6416(b)(2)(E) by substituting "(E), or (F)" for "or (E)", and amended Sec. 6416(b)(3) by striking "or" at the end of subparagraph (D); by substituting "; or" for a period at the end of subparagraph (E); and by adding subparagraph (F). **Effective** 10-1-61.

• **1960 (P.L. 86-781)**

P.L. 86-781, § 2:

Amended Code Sec. 6416(b)(1) by adding the following after "or allowance," in the first sentence: "including (in the case of a tax imposed by chapter 32) a readjustment for local advertising (but only to the extent provided in section 4216(f)(2) and (3)),". **Effective** for articles sold on or after 1-1-61.

• **1960 (P.L. 86-418)**

P.L. 86-418, § 3:

Amended Code Sec. 6416(b) by (1) striking out, in subparagraph (2)(E), the phrase "subparagraph (A) or (B)" and substituting the phrase "subparagraph (A), (B), or (E)"; (2) striking out, in subparagraph (3)(A) the phrase "subparagraph (B), (C), or (D)" and substituting the phrase "subparagraph (B), (C), (D), or (E)"; (3) striking out "or" at the end of subparagraph (3)(C); (4) striking out the period at the end of subparagraph (3)(D) and substituting "; or"; and (5) adding subparagraph (3)(E). **Effective** 5-1-60.

• **1959, Federal-Aid Highway Act of 1959 (P.L. 86-342)**

P.L. 86-342, § 201(d)(1):

Amended Code Sec. 6416(b)(2) by: (1) striking out "at the rate of 3 cents a gallon" each place it appeared in subparagraphs (H), (I), and (J) and substituting "at the rate of 3 cents or 4 cents a gallon"; (2) striking out "1 cent for each gallon" in subparagraph (H) and substituting "1 cent (where tax was paid at the 3-cent rate) or 2 cents (where tax was paid at the 4-cent rate) for each gallon"; and (3) striking out "at the rate of 1 cent a gallon;" at the end of subparagraphs (I) and (J) and substituting "at the rate of 1 cent a gallon where tax was paid at the 3-cent rate or at the rate of 2 cents a gallon where tax was paid at the 4-cent rate;".

• **1958, Excise Tax Technical Changes Act of 1958 (P.L. 85-859)**

P.L. 85-859, § 163(a):

Amended Sec. 6416(b), disregarding the later amendments by P.L. 86-342 and 86-418. **Effective** only with respect to articles exported, sold, or resold, on or after 1-1-59. Prior to amendment, Sec. 6416(b) read as follows:

(b) Special Cases in Which Tax Payments Considered Overpayments.—Under regulations prescribed by the Secretary or his delegate credit or refund, without interest, shall be made of the overpayments determined under the following paragraphs:

(1) Price readjustments.—If the price of any article in respect of which a tax, based on such price, is imposed by chapter 31 or 32, is readjusted by reason of the return or repossession of the article or a covering or container, or by a bona fide discount, rebate or allowance, the part of the tax proportionate to the part of the price repaid or credited to the purchaser shall be deemed to be an overpayment.

(2) Specified uses and resales.—The tax paid under subchapter E of chapter 31 or chapter 32 in respect of any article shall be deemed to be an overpayment if such article was, by any person—

(A) Resold for the exclusive use of any State, Territory of the United States, or any political subdivision of the foregoing, or the District of Columbia, or, in the case of musical instruments embraced in section 4151, resold for the use of any religious or nonprofit educational institution for exclusively religious or educational purposes;

(B) Used or resold for use for any of the purposes, but subject to the conditions, provided in section 4222;

(C) In the case of a liquid taxable under section 4041, sold for use as fuel in a diesel-powered highway vehicle or as fuel for the propulsion of a motor vehicle, motorboat, or airplane, if (i) the vendee used such liquid otherwise than as fuel in such a vehicle, motorboat, or airplane or resold such liquid, or (ii) such liquid was (within the meaning of paragraphs (1), (2), and (3) of section 6420(c)) used on a farm for farming purposes;

(D) In the case of lubricating oils, used or resold for nonlubricating purposes;

(E) In the case of unexposed motion picture films, used or resold for use in the making of newsreel motion picture films;

(F) In the case of articles taxable under section 4061(b) (other than spark plugs, storage batteries, leaf springs, coils, timers, and tire chains), used or resold for use as repair or replacement parts or accessories for farm equipment (other than equipment taxable under section 4061(a));

[(G) Repealed]

(H) In the case of gasoline, used in production of special motor fuels referred to in section 4041(b);

(I) In the case of lubricating oils in respect to which tax was paid at the rate of 6 cents a gallon, used or resold for use on or after the effective date of this subparagraph as cutting oils (within the meaning of section 4092(b)); except that the amount of such overpayment shall not exceed an amount computed at the rate of 3 cents a gallon;

(J) In the case of a liquid in respect of which tax was paid under section 4041(a)(1) at the rate of 3 cents a gallon, used or resold for use as a fuel in a diesel-powered highway vehicle (i) which (at the time of such use or resale) is not registered, and is not required to be registered, for highway use under the laws of any State or foreign country, or (ii) which, in the case of a diesel-powered highway vehicle owned by the United States, is not used on the highway; except that the amount of any overpayment by reason of this subparagraph shall not exceed an amount computed at the rate of 1 cent a gallon;

(K) In the case of a liquid in respect of which tax was paid under section 4041(b)(1) at the rate of 3 cents a gallon, used or resold for use otherwise than as a fuel for the propulsion of a highway vehicle (i) which (at the time of such use or resale) is registered, or is required to be registered, for highway use under the laws of any State or foreign country, or (ii) which, in the case of a highway vehicle owned by the United States, is used on the highway; except that the amount of any overpayment by reason of this subparagraph shall not exceed an amount computed at the rate of 1 cent a gallon;

(L) In the case of a liquid in respect of which tax was paid under section 4041 at the rate of 3 cents a gallon, used during any calendar quarter in vehicles while engaged in furnishing scheduled common carrier public passenger land transportation service along regular routes; except that (i) this subparagraph shall apply only if the 60 percent passenger fare revenue test set forth in section 6421(b)(2) is met with respect to such quarter, and (ii) the amount of such overpayment for such quarter shall be an amount determined by multiplying 1 cent for each gallon of liquid so used by the percentage which such person's tax-exempt passenger fare revenue (as defined in section 6421(d)(2)) derived from such scheduled service during such quarter was of

CREDITS AND REFUNDS—SPECIAL RULES

his total passenger fare revenue (not including the tax imposed by section 4261, relating to the tax on transportation of persons) derived from such scheduled service during such quarter;

(M) In the case of tread rubber in respect of which tax was paid under section 4071(a)(4), used or resold for use otherwise than in the recapping or retreading of tires of the type used on highway vehicles (as defined in section 4072(c)), unless credit or refund of such tax is allowable under subsection (b)(3).

(3) Tax-paid articles used for further manufacture.—If the tax imposed by chapter 32 has been paid with respect to the sale of—

(A) Any article (other than a tire, inner tube, or automobile radio or television receiving set taxable under section 4141 and other than an automobile part or accessory taxable under section 4061(b), a refrigerator component taxable under section 4111, a radio or television component taxable under section 4141, or a camera lens taxable under section 4171) purchased by a manufacturer or producer and used by him as material in the manufacture or production of, or as a component part of, an article with respect to which tax under chapter 32 has been paid, or which has been sold free of tax by virtue of section 4220 or 4224, relating to tax-free sales;

(B) An automobile part or accessory taxable under section 4061(b), a refrigerator component taxable under section 4111, a radio or television component taxable under section 4141, or a camera lens taxable under section 4171, purchased by a manufacturer or producer and used by him as material in the manufacture of, production of, or as a component part of, any article;

such tax shall be deemed an overpayment by such manufacturer or producer.

- **1956 (P.L. 627, 84th Cong.)**

P.L. 627, 84th Cong., §208(b):

Amended Sec. 6416(b)(2) by striking out the period at the end of subparagraph (I), inserting a semicolon, and adding new subparagraphs (J) through (M). **Effective** 7-1-56.

- **1956 (P.L. 466, 84th Cong.)**

P.L. 466, 84th Cong., §2(b):

Amended Code Sec. 6416(b)(2)(C). **Effective** for liquid sold after 12-31-55. Prior to amendment such section read as follows:

(C) In the case of a liquid taxable under section 4041, sold for use as fuel in a diesel-powered highway vehicle or as fuel for the propulsion of a motor vehicle, motorboat, or airplane, if the vendee used such liquid otherwise than as fuel in such a vehicle, motorboat, or airplane or resold such liquid;

- **1955 (P.L. 367, 84th Cong.)**

P.L. 367, 84th Cong., §[1](h):

Added the material in the parenthetical expression after "section 4141" in subparagraph (3)(A), as reproduced in the amendment note for P.L. 85-859.

P.L. 367, 84th Cong., §[1](i):

Amended subparagraph 3(B) to read as reproduced in the amendment note for P.L. 85-859. **Effective** for articles used after 8-31-55 by the manufacturer or producer as material in the manufacture of, production of, or as a component part of, another article. Prior to amendment, it read as follows:

(B) Any article described in sections 4142 and 4143(b) purchased by a manufacturer or producer and used by him as material in the manufacture or production of, or as a component part of, communication, detection, or navigation receivers of the type used in commercial, military, or marine installations if such receivers have been sold by him to the United States for its exclusive use;

P.L. 367, 84th Cong., §2(b):

Repealed paragraph (G). **Effective** only for articles sold by manufacturer, producer, or importer after 8-31-55. Prior to repeal, §2(b) read as follows:

(G) In the case of a communication, detection, or navigation receiver of the type used in commercial, military, or marine installations, resold to the United States for its exclusive use;

- **1955 (P.L. 355, 84th Cong.)**

P.L. 355, 84th Cong., §2:

Added new subparagraph (I) to read as reproduced in the amendment note for P.L. 85-859. **Effective** 10-1-55.

[Sec. 6416(c)]

(c) REFUND TO EXPORTER OR SHIPPER.—Under regulations prescribed by the Secretary the amount of any tax imposed by chapter 31, or chapter 32 erroneously or illegally collected in respect of any article exported to a foreign country or shipped to a possession of the United States may be refunded to the exporter or shipper thereof, if the person who paid such tax waives his claim to such amount.

Amendments

- **1984, Deficit Reduction Act of 1984 (P.L. 98-369)**

P.L. 98-369, §735(c)(13)(E):

Amended Code Sec. 6416 by striking out subsection (c) and by redesignating subsection (e) as subsection (c). **Effective** as if included in the provision of the Highway Revenue Act of 1982 to which it relates. Prior to amendment, Code Sec. 6416(c) read as follows:

(c) Credit for Tax Paid on Tires or Inner Tubes.—If tires or inner tubes on which tax has been paid under chapter 32 are sold on or in connection with, or with the sale of, another article taxable under chapter 32, there shall (under regulations prescribed by the Secretary) be credited (without interest) against the tax imposed on the sale of such other article, an amount determined by multiplying the applicable percentage rate of tax for such other article by—

(1) the purchase price (less, in the case of tires, the part of such price attributable to the metal rim or rim base) if such tires or inner tubes were taxable under section 4071 (relating to tax on tires and inner tubes); or

(2) if such tires or inner tubes were taxable under section 4218 (relating to use by manufacturer, producer, or importer), the price (less, in the case of tires, the part of such price attributable to the metal rim or rim base) at which such or similar tires or inner tubes are sold, in the ordinary course of trade, by manufacturers, producers, or importers thereof, as determined by the Secretary.

- **1976, Tax Reform Act of 1976 (P.L. 94-455)**

P.L. 94-455, §1904(b)(1)(B):

Struck out the phrase "subchapter E of" in "tax imposed by subchapter E of chapter 31" in Code Sec. 6416(e). **Effective** 2-1-77.

P.L. 94-455, §1906(b)(13)(A):

Amended 1954 Code by substituting "Secretary" for "Secretary or his delegate" each place it appeared. **Effective** 2-1-77.

- **1965, Excise Tax Reduction Act of 1965 (P.L. 89-44)**

P.L. 89-44, §601(c)(13):

Amended Sec. 6416(c). **Effective** 6-22-65. Prior to amendment, Sec. 6416(c) read as follows:

(c) Credit for Tax Paid on Tires, Inner Tubes, or Radio or Television Receiving Sets.—If tires, inner tubes, or automobile radio or television receiving sets on which tax has been paid under chapter 32 are sold on or in connection with, or with the sale of, another article taxable under chapter 32, there shall (under regulations prescribed

by the Secretary or his delegate) be credited (without interest) against the tax imposed on the sale of such other article, an amount determined by multiplying the applicable percentage rate of tax for such other article by—

(1) the purchase price (less, in the case of tires, the part of such price attributable to the metal rim or rim base) if such tires or inner tubes were taxable under section 4071 (relating to tax on tires and inner tubes) or, in the case of automobile radio or television receiving sets, if such sets were taxable under section 4141; or

(2) if such tires, inner tubes, or automobile radio or television receiving sets were taxable under section 4218 (relating to use by manufacturer, producer, or importer), the price (less, in the case of tires, the part of such price attributable to the metal rim or rim base) at which such or similar tires, inner tubes, or sets are sold, in the ordinary course of trade, by manufacturers, producers, or importers thereof, as determined by the Secretary or his delegate.

The credit provided by this subsection shall be allowable only in respect of the first sale on or in connection with or with the sale of, another article on the sale of which tax is imposed under chapter 32.

- **1958, Excise Tax Technical Changes Act of 1958 (P.L. 85-859)**

P.L. 85-859, §163(a):

Amended Sec. 6416(c). **Effective** 1-1-59. Prior to amendment, Sec. 6416(c) read as follows:

(c) Credit for Tax Paid on Tires, Inner Tubes, Radios or Television Receiving Sets.—If tires, inner tubes, or automobile radio or television receiving sets on which tax has been imposed under chapter 32 are sold on or in connection with, or with the sale of, an article taxable under section 4061(a) (relating to automobiles, trucks, etc.), there shall (under regulations prescribed by the Secretary or his delegate) be credited, without interest, against the tax under section 4061 an amount equal to, in the case of an article taxable under paragraphs (1) or (2) of subsection (a) of section 4061, the applicable percentage rate of tax provided in such subsections—

(1) Of the purchase price (less, in the case of tires, the part of such price attributable to the metal rim or rim base) if such tires or inner tubes were taxable under section 4071 (relating to tax on tires and inner tubes) or, in the case of automobile radio or television receiving sets, if such sets were taxable under section 4141; or

(2) If such tires, inner tubes, or automobile radio or television receiving sets were taxable under section 4218 (relating to use by manufacturer, producer, or importer), then of the price (less, in the case of tires, the part of such price attributable to the metal rim or rim base) at which such or similar tires, inner tubes, or sets are sold, in the ordinary course of trade, by manufacturers, producers, or importers thereof, as determined by the Secretary or his delegate.

[Sec. 6416(d)]

(d) CREDIT ON RETURNS.—Any person entitled to a refund of tax imposed by chapter 31 or 32, paid to the Secretary may, instead of filing a claim for refund, take credit therefor against taxes imposed by such chapter due on any subsequent return. The preceding sentence shall not apply to the tax imposed by section 4081 in the case of refunds described in section 4081(e).

Amendments

- **2004, American Jobs Creation Act of 2004 (P.L. 108-357)**

P.L. 108-357, §853(d)(2)(I):

Amended Code Sec. 6416(d) by striking "or to the tax imposed by section 4091 in the case of refunds described in section 4091(d)" immediately preceding the period at the end of the last sentence. **Effective** for aviation-grade kerosene removed, entered, or sold after 12-31-2004.

CREDITS AND REFUNDS—SPECIAL RULES

• **1997, Taxpayer Relief Act of 1997 (P.L. 105-34)**

P.L. 105-34, §1436(b):

Amended Code Sec. 6416(d) by inserting before the period "or to the tax imposed by section 4091 in the case of refunds described in section 4091(d)" in the last sentence. **Effective** for fuel acquired by the producer after 9-30-97.

• **1990, Omnibus Budget Reconciliation Act of 1990 (P.L. 101-508)**

P.L. 101-508, §11212(d)(2):

Amended Code Sec. 6416(d) by adding at the end thereof a new sentence. **Effective** 7-1-91.

• **1984, Deficit Reduction Act of 1984 (P.L. 98-369)**

P.L. 98-369, §735(c)(13)(E):

Amended Code Sec. 6416 by redesignating subsection (f) as subsection (d). **Effective** as if included in P.L. 97-424.

• **1976, Tax Reform Act of 1976 (P.L. 94-455)**

P.L. 94-455, §1906(b)(13)(A):

Amended 1954 Code by substituting "Secretary" for "Secretary or his delegate" each place it appeared. **Effective** 2-1-77.

• **1965, Excise Tax Reduction Act of 1965 (P.L. 89-44)**

P.L. 89-44, §601(c)(14):

Repealed Sec. 6416(d). **Effective** 6-22-65. Prior to repeal, Sec. 6416(d) read as follows:

(d) Mechanical Pencils Taxable as Jewelry.—If any article, on the sale of which tax has been paid under section 4201, is further manufactured or processed resulting in an article taxable under section 4001, the person who sells such article at retail shall, in the computation of the retailers' excise tax due on such sale, be entitled to a credit or refund, without interest, in an amount equal to the tax paid under section 4201.

• **1958, Tax Rate Extension Act of 1958 (P.L. 85-475)**

P.L. 85-475, §4(b), (c):

Amended Sec. 6416(f) by deleting the phrase "or section 4281" following the phrase "31 or 32", and by deleting the words "or section" following the word "chapter". **Effective** only as to *amounts* paid after 7-31-58, except that in the case of transportation to which the second sentence of Sec. 4281 applies, the repeal applies only to *transportation* beginning after 7-31-58.

[Sec. 6416(e)]

(e) ACCOUNTING PROCEDURES FOR LIKE ARTICLES.—Under regulations prescribed by the Secretary, if any person uses or resells like articles, then for purposes of this section the manufacturer, producer, or importer of any such article may be identified, and the amount of tax paid under chapter 32 in respect of such article may be determined—

(1) on a first-in-first-out basis,

(2) on a last-in-first-out basis, or

(3) in accordance with any other consistent method approved by the Secretary.

Amendments

• **1984, Deficit Reduction Act of 1984 (P.L. 98-369)**

P.L. 98-369, §735(C)(13)(E):

Struck out Code Sec. 6416(g) and redesignated subsection (h) as subsection (e). **Effective** as if included in P.L. 97-424. Prior to being stricken, Code Sec. 6416(g) read as follows:

(g) Trucks, Buses, Tractors, etc.—Under regulations prescribed by the Secretary, subsection (b)(2)(A) shall apply, in the case of any article subject to the tax imposed by section 4061(a) only if the article with respect to which the tax was paid was sold by the manufacturer, producer, or importer for export after receipt by him of notice of intent to export or to resell for export.

• **1976, Tax Reform Act of 1976 (P.L. 94-455)**

P.L. 94-455, §1906(b)(13)(A):

Amended 1954 Code by substituting "Secretary" for "Secretary or his delegate" each place it appeared. **Effective** 2-1-77.

• **1971, Revenue Act of 1971 (P.L. 92-178)**

P.L. 92-178, §401(g)(6):

Amended the heading of Code Sec. 6416(g). Prior to amendment, such heading read as follows: "Automobiles, etc.—".

• **1965, Excise Tax Reduction Act of 1965 (P.L. 89-44)**

P.L. 89-44, §601(c)(15):

Amended Sec. 6416(g) by substituting: "section 4061(a)" for "sections 4061(a), 4111, 4121, and 4141,". **Effective** 7-22-65.

• **1958, Excise Tax Technical Changes Act of 1958 (P.L. 85-859)**

P.L. 85-859, §163(c):

Added subsection (g) and (h). **Effective** 1-1-59.

[Sec. 6416(f)]

(f) MEANING OF TERMS.—For purposes of this section, any term used in this section has the same meaning as when used in chapter 31, 32, or 33, as the case may be.

Amendments

• **1984, Deficit Reduction Act of 1984 (P.L. 98-369)**

P.L. 98-369, §735(c)(13)(E):

Redesignated Code Sec. 6416(i) as subsection (f). **Effective** as if included in P.L. 97-424.

• **1958, Excise Tax Technical Changes Act of 1958 (P.L. 85-859)**

P.L. 85-859, §163(c):

Added subsection (i). **Effective** 1-1-59.

[Sec. 6417]

SEC. 6417. ELECTIVE PAYMENT OF APPLICABLE CREDITS.

[Sec. 6417(a)]

(a) IN GENERAL.—In the case of an applicable entity making an election (at such time and in such manner as the Secretary may provide) under this section with respect to any applicable credit determined with respect to such entity, such entity shall be treated as making a payment against the tax imposed by subtitle A (for the taxable year with respect to which such credit was determined) equal to the amount of such credit.

[Sec. 6417(b)]

(b) APPLICABLE CREDIT.—The term "applicable credit" means each of the following:

(1) So much of the credit for alternative fuel vehicle refueling property allowed under section 30C which, pursuant to subsection (d)(1) of such section, is treated as a credit listed in section 38(b).

(2) So much of the renewable electricity production credit determined under section 45(a) as is attributable to qualified facilities which are originally placed in service after December 31, 2022.

(3) So much of the credit for carbon oxide sequestration determined under section 45Q(a) as is attributable to carbon capture equipment which is originally placed in service after December 31, 2022.

(4) The zero-emission nuclear power production credit determined under section 45U(a).

(5) So much of the credit for production of clean hydrogen determined under section 45V(a) as is attributable to qualified clean hydrogen production facilities which are originally placed in service after December 31, 2012.

(6) In the case of a tax-exempt entity described in clause (i), (ii), or (iv) of section 168(h)(2)(A), the credit for qualified commercial vehicles determined under section 45W by reason of subsection (d)(3) thereof.

(7) The credit for advanced manufacturing production under section 45X(a).

(8) The clean electricity production credit determined under section 45Y(a).

(9) The clean fuel production credit determined under section 45Z(a).

(10) The energy credit determined under section 48.

(11) The qualifying advanced energy project credit determined under section 48C.

(12) The clean electricity investment credit determined under section 48E.

[Sec. 6417(c)]

(c) APPLICATION TO PARTNERSHIPS AND S CORPORATIONS.—

(1) IN GENERAL.—In the case of any applicable credit determined with respect to any facility or property held directly by a partnership or S corporation, any election under subsection (a) shall be made by such partnership or S corporation. If such partnership or S corporation makes an election under such subsection (in such manner as the Secretary may provide) with respect to such credit—

(A) the Secretary shall make a payment to such partnership or S corporation equal to the amount of such credit,

(B) subsection (e) shall be applied with respect to such credit before determining any partner's distributive share, or shareholder's pro rata share, of such credit,

(C) any amount with respect to which the election in subsection (a) is made shall be treated as tax exempt income for purposes of sections 705 and 1366, and

(D) a partner's distributive share of such tax exempt income shall be based on such partner's distributive share of the otherwise applicable credit for each taxable year.

(2) COORDINATION WITH APPLICATION AT PARTNER OR SHAREHOLDER LEVEL.—In the case of any facility or property held directly by a partnership or S corporation, no election by any partner or shareholder shall be allowed under subsection (a) with respect to any applicable credit determined with respect to such facility or property.

(3) TREATMENT OF PAYMENTS TO PARTNERSHIPS AND S CORPORATIONS.—For purposes of section 1324 of title 31, United States Code, the payments under paragraph (1)(A) shall be treated in the same manner as a refund due from a credit provision referred to in subsection (b)(2) of such section.

[Sec. 6417(d)]

(d) SPECIAL RULES.—For purposes of this section—

(1) APPLICABLE ENTITY.—

(A) IN GENERAL.—The term "applicable entity" means—

(i) any organization exempt from the tax imposed by subtitle A,

(ii) any State or political subdivision thereof,

(iii) the Tennessee Valley Authority,

(iv) an Indian tribal government (as defined in section 30D(g)(9)),

(v) any Alaska Native Corporation (as defined in section 3 of the Alaska Native Claims Settlement Act (43 U.S.C. 1602(m)), or

(vi) any corporation operating on a cooperative basis which is engaged in furnishing electric energy to persons in rural areas.

(B) ELECTION WITH RESPECT TO CREDIT FOR PRODUCTION OF CLEAN HYDROGEN.—If a taxpayer other than an entity described in subparagraph (A) makes an election under this subparagraph with respect to any taxable year in which such taxpayer has placed in service a qualified clean hydrogen production facility (as defined in section 45V(c)(3)), such taxpayer shall be treated as an applicable entity for purposes of this section for such taxable year, but only with respect to the credit described in subsection (b)(5).

(C) ELECTION WITH RESPECT TO CREDIT FOR CARBON OXIDE SEQUESTRATION.—If a taxpayer other than an entity described in subparagraph (A) makes an election under this subparagraph with respect to any taxable year in which such taxpayer has, after December 31, 2022, placed in service carbon capture equipment at a qualified facility (as defined in section 45Q(d)), such taxpayer shall be treated as an applicable entity for purposes of this section for such taxable year, but only with respect to the credit described in subsection (b)(3).

(D) ELECTION WITH RESPECT TO ADVANCED MANUFACTURING PRODUCTION CREDIT.—

(i) IN GENERAL.—If a taxpayer other than an entity described in subparagraph (A) makes an election under this subparagraph with respect to any taxable year in which such taxpayer has, after December 31, 2022, produced eligible components (as defined in section 45X(c)(1)), such taxpayer shall be treated as an applicable entity for purposes of this section for such taxable year, but only with respect to the credit described in subsection (b)(7).

(ii) LIMITATION.—

(I) IN GENERAL.—Except as provided in subclause (II), if a taxpayer makes an election under this subparagraph with respect to any taxable year, such taxpayer shall be treated as having made such election for each of the 4 succeeding taxable years ending before January 1, 2033.

(II) EXCEPTION.—A taxpayer may elect to revoke the application of the election made under this subparagraph to any taxable year described in subclause (I). Any such election, if made, shall apply to the applicable year specified in such election and each subsequent taxable year within the period described in subclause (I). Any election under this subclause may not be subsequently revoked.

(iii) PROHIBITION ON TRANSFER.—For any taxable year described in clause (ii)(I), no election may be made by the taxpayer under section 6418(a) for such taxable year with respect to eligible components for purposes of the credit described in subsection (b)(7).

(E) OTHER RULES.—

(i) IN GENERAL.—An election made under subparagraph (B), (C), or (D) shall be made at such time and in such manner as the Secretary may provide.

(ii) LIMITATION.—No election may be made under subparagraph (B), (C), or (D) with respect to any taxable year beginning after December 31, 2032.

(2) APPLICATION.—In the case of any applicable entity which makes the election described in subsection (a), any applicable credit shall be determined—

(A) without regard to paragraphs (3) and (4)(A)(i) of section 50(b), and

(B) by treating any property with respect to which such credit is determined as used in a trade or business of the applicable entity.

(3) ELECTIONS.—

(A) IN GENERAL.—

(i) DUE DATE.—Any election under subsection (a) shall be made not later than—

(I) in the case of any government, or political subdivision, described in paragraph (1) and for which no return is required under section 6011 or 6033(a), such date as is determined appropriate by the Secretary, or

(II) in any other case, the due date (including extensions of time) for the return of tax for the taxable year for which the election is made, but in no event earlier than 180 days after the date of the enactment of this section.

CREDITS AND REFUNDS—SPECIAL RULES

(ii) ADDITIONAL RULES.—Any election under subsection (a), once made, shall be irrevocable and shall apply (except as otherwise provided in this paragraph) with respect to any credit for the taxable year for which the election is made.

(B) RENEWABLE ELECTRICITY PRODUCTION CREDIT.—In the case of the credit described in subsection (b)(2), any election under subsection (a) shall—

(i) apply separately with respect to each qualified facility,

(ii) be made for the taxable year in which such qualified facility is originally placed in service, and

(iii) shall apply to such taxable year and to any subsequent taxable year which is within the period described in subsection (a)(2)(A)(ii) of section 45 with respect to such qualified facility.

(C) CREDIT FOR CARBON OXIDE SEQUESTRATION.—

(i) IN GENERAL.—In the case of the credit described in subsection (b)(3), any election under subsection (a) shall—

(I) apply separately with respect to the carbon capture equipment originally placed in service by the applicable entity during a taxable year, and

(II)(aa) in the case of a taxpayer who makes an election described in paragraph (1)(C), apply to the taxable year in which such equipment is placed in service and the 4 subsequent taxable years with respect to such equipment which end before January 1, 2033, and

(bb) in any other case, apply to such taxable year and to any subsequent taxable year which is within the period described in paragraph (3)(A) or (4)(A) of section 45Q(a) with respect to such equipment.

(ii) PROHIBITION ON TRANSFER.—For any taxable year described in clause (i)(II)(aa) with respect to carbon capture equipment, no election may be made by the taxpayer under section 6418(a) for such taxable year with respect to such equipment for purposes of the credit described in subsection (b)(3).

(iii) REVOCATION OF ELECTION.—In the case of a taxpayer who makes an election described in paragraph (1)(C) with respect to carbon capture equipment, such taxpayer may, at any time during the period described in clause (i)(II)(aa), revoke the application of such election with respect to such equipment for any subsequent taxable years during such period. Any such election, if made, shall apply to the applicable year specified in such election and each subsequent taxable year within the period described in clause (i)(II)(aa). Any election under this subclause may not be subsequently revoked.

(D) CREDIT FOR PRODUCTION OF CLEAN HYDROGEN.—

(i) IN GENERAL.—In the case of the credit described in subsection (b)(5), any election under subsection (a) shall—

(I) apply separately with respect to each qualified clean hydrogen production facility,

(II) be made for the taxable year in which such facility is placed in service (or within the 1-year period subsequent to the date of enactment of this section in the case of facilities placed in service before December 31, 2022), and

(III)(aa) in the case of a taxpayer who makes an election described in paragraph (1)(B), apply to such taxable year and the 4 subsequent taxable years with respect to such facility which end before January 1, 2033, and

(bb) in any other case, apply to such taxable year and all subsequent taxable years with respect to such facility.

(ii) PROHIBITION ON TRANSFER.—For any taxable year described in clause (i)(III)(aa) with respect to a qualified clean hydrogen production facility, no election may be made by the taxpayer under section 6418(a) for such taxable year with respect to such facility for purposes of the credit described in subsection (b)(5).

(iii) REVOCATION OF ELECTION.—In the case of a taxpayer who makes an election described in paragraph (1)(B) with respect to a qualified clean hydrogen production facility, such taxpayer may, at any time during the period described in clause (i)(III)(aa), revoke the application of such election with respect to such facility for any subsequent taxable years during such period. Any such election, if made, shall apply to the applicable year specified in such election and each subsequent taxable year within the period described in clause (i)(II)(aa). Any election under this subclause may not be subsequently revoked.

(E) CLEAN ELECTRICITY PRODUCTION CREDIT.—In the case of the credit described in subsection (b)(8), any election under subsection (a) shall—

(i) apply separately with respect to each qualified facility,

(ii) be made for the taxable year in which such facility is placed in service, and

(iii) shall apply to such taxable year and to any subsequent taxable year which is within the period described in subsection (b)(1)(B) of section 45Y with respect to such facility.

(4) TIMING.—The payment described in subsection (a) shall be treated as made on—

(A) in the case of any government, or political subdivision, described in paragraph (1) and for which no return is required under section 6011 or 6033(a), the later of the date that a return would be due under section 6033(a) if such government or subdivision were described in that section or the date on which such government or subdivision submits a claim for credit or refund (at such time and in such manner as the Secretary shall provide), and

(B) in any other case, the later of the due date (determined without regard to extensions) of the return of tax for the taxable year or the date on which such return is filed.

(5) ADDITIONAL INFORMATION.—As a condition of, and prior to, any amount being treated as a payment which is made by an applicable entity under subsection (a), the Secretary may require such information or registration as the Secretary deems necessary for purposes of preventing duplication, fraud, improper payments, or excessive payments under this section.

(6) EXCESSIVE PAYMENT.—

(A) IN GENERAL.—In the case of any amount treated as a payment which is made by the applicable entity under subsection (a), or the amount of the payment made pursuant to subsection (c), which the Secretary determines constitutes an excessive payment, the tax imposed on such entity by chapter 1 (regardless of whether such entity would otherwise be subject to tax under such chapter) for the taxable year in which such determination is made shall be increased by an amount equal to the sum of—

(i) the amount of such excessive payment, plus

(ii) an amount equal to 20 percent of such excessive payment.

(B) REASONABLE CAUSE.—Subparagraph (A)(ii) shall not apply if the applicable entity demonstrates to the satisfaction of the Secretary that the excessive payment resulted from reasonable cause.

(C) EXCESSIVE PAYMENT DEFINED.—For purposes of this paragraph, the term "excessive payment" means, with respect to a facility or property for which an election is made under this section for any taxable year, an amount equal to the excess of—

(i) the amount treated as a payment which is made by the applicable entity under subsection (a), or the amount of the payment made pursuant to subsection (c), with respect to such facility or property for such taxable year, over

(ii) the amount of the credit which, without application of this section, would be otherwise allowable (as determined pursuant to paragraph (2) and without regard to section 38(c)) under this title with respect to such facility or property for such taxable year.

[Sec. 6417(e)]

(e) DENIAL OF DOUBLE BENEFIT.—In the case of an applicable entity making an election under this section with respect to an applicable credit, such credit shall be reduced to zero and shall, for any other purposes under this title, be deemed to have been allowed to such entity for such taxable year.

[Sec. 6417(f)]

(f) MIRROR CODE POSSESSIONS.—In the case of any possession of the United States with a mirror code tax system (as defined in section 24(k)), this section shall not be treated as part of the income tax laws of the United States for purposes of determining the income tax law of such possession unless such possession elects to have this section be so treated.

[Sec. 6417(g)]

(g) BASIS REDUCTION AND RECAPTURE.—Except as otherwise provided in subsection (c)(2)(A)[(d)(2)(A)], rules similar to the rules of section 50 shall apply for purposes of this section.

[Sec. 6417(h)]

(h) REGULATIONS.—The Secretary shall issue such regulations or other guidance as may be necessary to carry out the purposes of this section, including guidance to ensure that the amount of the payment or deemed payment made under this section is commensurate with the amount of the credit that would be otherwise allowable (determined without regard to section 38(c)).

Amendments

- 2022, Inflation Reduction Act of 2022 (P.L. 117-169)

P.L. 117-169, § 13801(a):

Amended subchapter B of chapter 65 by inserting after Code Sec. 6416 a new Code Sec. 6417. **Effective** for tax years beginning after 12-31-2022.

[Sec. 6418]

SEC. 6418. TRANSFER OF CERTAIN CREDITS.

[Sec. 6418(a)]

(a) IN GENERAL.—In the case of an eligible taxpayer which elects to transfer all (or any portion specified in the election) of an eligible credit determined with respect to such taxpayer for any taxable year to a taxpayer (referred to in this section as the "transferee taxpayer") which is not related (within the meaning of section 267(b) or 707(b)(1)) to the eligible taxpayer, the transferee taxpayer specified in such election (and not the eligible taxpayer) shall be treated as the taxpayer for purposes of this title with respect to such credit (or such portion thereof).

[Sec. 6418(b)]

(b) TREATMENT OF PAYMENTS MADE IN CONNECTION WITH TRANSFER.—With respect to any amount paid by a transferee taxpayer to an eligible taxpayer as consideration for a transfer described in subsection (a), such consideration—

(1) shall be required to be paid in cash,

(2) shall not be includible in gross income of the eligible taxpayer, and

(3) with respect to the transferee taxpayer, shall not be deductible under this title.

[Sec. 6418(c)]

(c) APPLICATION TO PARTNERSHIPS AND S CORPORATIONS.—

(1) IN GENERAL.—In the case of any eligible credit determined with respect to any facility or property held directly by a partnership or S corporation, if such partnership or S corporation makes an election under subsection (a) (in such manner as the Secretary may provide) with respect to such credit—

(A) any amount received as consideration for a transfer described in such subsection shall be treated as tax exempt income for purposes of sections 705 and 1366, and

(B) a partner's distributive share of such tax exempt income shall be based on such partner's distributive share of the otherwise eligible credit for each taxable year.

(2) COORDINATION WITH APPLICATION AT PARTNER OR SHAREHOLDER LEVEL.—In the case of any facility or property held directly by a partnership or S corporation, no election by any partner or shareholder shall be allowed under subsection (a) with respect to any eligible credit determined with respect to such facility or property.

[Sec. 6418(d)]

(d) TAXABLE YEAR IN WHICH CREDIT TAKEN INTO ACCOUNT.—In the case of any credit (or portion thereof) with respect to which an election is made under subsection (a), such credit shall be taken into account in the first taxable year of the transferee taxpayer ending with, or after, the taxable year of the eligible taxpayer with respect to which the credit was determined.

[Sec. 6418(e)]

(e) LIMITATIONS ON ELECTION.—

(1) TIME FOR ELECTION.—An election under subsection (a) to transfer any portion of an eligible credit shall be made not later than the due date (including extensions of time) for the return of tax for the taxable year for which the credit is determined, but in no event earlier than 180 days after the date of the enactment of this section. Any such election, once made, shall be irrevocable.

(2) NO ADDITIONAL TRANSFERS.—No election may be made under subsection (a) by a transferee taxpayer with respect to any portion of an eligible credit which has been previously transferred to such taxpayer pursuant to this section.

[Sec. 6418(f)]

(f) DEFINITIONS.—For purposes of this section—

(1) ELIGIBLE CREDIT.—

(A) IN GENERAL.—The term "eligible credit" means each of the following:

(i) So much of the credit for alternative fuel vehicle refueling property allowed under section 30C which, pursuant to subsection (d)(1) of such section, is treated as a credit listed in section 38(b).

(ii) The renewable electricity production credit determined under section 45(a).

CREDITS AND REFUNDS—SPECIAL RULES

(iii) The credit for carbon oxide sequestration determined under section 45Q(a).

(iv) The zero-emission nuclear power production credit determined under section 45U(a).

(v) The clean hydrogen production credit determined under section 45V(a).

(vi) The advanced manufacturing production credit determined under section 45X(a).

(vii) The clean electricity production credit determined under section 45Y(a).

(viii) The clean fuel production credit determined under section 45Z(a).

(ix) The energy credit determined under section 48.

(x) The qualifying advanced energy project credit determined under section 48C.

(xi) The clean electricity investment credit determined under section 48E.

(B) ELECTION FOR CERTAIN CREDITS.—In the case of any eligible credit described in clause (ii), (iii), (v), or (vii) of subparagraph (A), an election under subsection (a) shall be made—

(i) separately with respect to each facility for which such credit is determined, and

(ii) for each taxable year during the 10-year period beginning on the date such facility was originally placed in service (or, in the case of the credit described in clause (iii), for each year during the 12-year period beginning on the date the carbon capture equipment was originally placed in service at such facility).

(C) EXCEPTION FOR BUSINESS CREDIT CARRYFORWARDS OR CARRYBACKS.—The term "eligible credit" shall not include any business credit carryforward or business credit carryback determined under section 39.

(2) ELIGIBLE TAXPAYER.—The term "eligible taxpayer" means any taxpayer which is not described in section 6417(d)(1)(A).

[Sec. 6418(g)]

(g) SPECIAL RULES.—For purposes of this section—

(1) ADDITIONAL INFORMATION.—As a condition of, and prior to, any transfer of any portion of an eligible credit pursuant to subsection (a), the Secretary may require such information (including, in such form or manner as is determined appropriate by the Secretary, such information returns) or registration as the Secretary deems necessary for purposes of preventing duplication, fraud, improper payments, or excessive payments under this section.

(2) EXCESSIVE CREDIT TRANSFER.—

(A) IN GENERAL.—In the case of any portion of an eligible credit which is transferred to a transferee taxpayer pursuant to subsection (a) which the Secretary determines constitutes an excessive credit transfer, the tax imposed on the transferee taxpayer by chapter 1 (regardless of whether such entity would otherwise be subject to tax under such chapter) for the taxable year in which such determination is made shall be increased by an amount equal to the sum of—

(i) the amount of such excessive credit transfer, plus

(ii) an amount equal to 20 percent of such excessive credit transfer.

(B) REASONABLE CAUSE.—Subparagraph (A)(ii) shall not apply if the transferee taxpayer demonstrates to the satisfaction of the Secretary that the excessive credit transfer resulted from reasonable cause.

(C) EXCESSIVE CREDIT TRANSFER DEFINED.—For purposes of this paragraph, the term "excessive credit transfer" means, with respect to a facility or property for which an election is made under subsection (a) for any taxable year, an amount equal to the excess of—

(i) the amount of the eligible credit claimed by the transferee taxpayer with respect to such facility or property for such taxable year, over

(ii) the amount of such credit which, without application of this section, would be otherwise allowable under this title with respect to such facility or property for such taxable year.

(3) BASIS REDUCTION; NOTIFICATION OF RECAPTURE.—In the case of any election under subsection (a) with respect to any portion of an eligible credit described in clauses (ix) through (xi) of subsection (f)(1)(A)—

(A) subsection (c) of section 50 shall apply to the applicable investment credit property (as defined in subsection (a)(5) of such section) as if such eligible credit was allowed to the eligible taxpayer, and

(B) if, during any taxable year, the applicable investment credit property (as defined in subsection (a)(5) of section 50) is disposed of, or otherwise ceases to be investment credit property with respect to the eligible taxpayer, before the close of the recapture period (as described in subsection (a)(1) of such section)—

(i) such eligible taxpayer shall provide notice of such occurrence to the transferee taxpayer (in such form and manner as the Secretary shall prescribe), and

(ii) the transferee taxpayer shall provide notice of the recapture amount (as defined in subsection (c)(2) of such section), if any, to the eligible taxpayer (in such form and manner as the Secretary shall prescribe).

(4) PROHIBITION ON ELECTION OR TRANSFER WITH RESPECT TO PROGRESS EXPENDITURES.—This section shall not apply with respect to any amount of an eligible credit which is allowed pursuant to rules similar to the rules of subsections (c)(4) and (d) of section 46 (as in effect on the day before the date of the enactment of the Revenue Reconciliation Act of 1990).

[Sec. 6418(h)]

(h) REGULATIONS.—The Secretary shall issue such regulations or other guidance as may be necessary to carry out the purposes of this section, including regulations or other guidance providing rules for determining a partner's distributive share of the tax exempt income described in subsection (c)(1).

Amendments

• **2022, Inflation Reduction Act of 2022 (P.L. 117-169)**

P.L. 117-169, §13801(b):

Amended subchapter B of chapter 65, as amended by Act Sec. 13801(a), by inserting after Code Sec. 6417 a new Code Sec. 6418. **Effective** for tax years beginning after 12-31-2022.

[Sec. 6418—Repealed]

Amendments

• **1990, Omnibus Budget Reconciliation Act of 1990 (P.L. 101-508)**

P.L. 101-508, §11801(c)(22)(B)(i):

Repealed Code Sec. 6418. **Effective** 11-5-90.

P.L. 101-508, §11821(b), provides:

(b) SAVINGS PROVISION.—If—

(1) any provision amended or repealed by this part applied to—

(A) any transaction occurring before the date of the enactment of this Act,

(B) any property acquired before such date of enactment, or

(C) any item of income, loss, deduction, or credit taken into account before such date of enactment, and

CREDITS AND REFUNDS—SPECIAL RULES

(2) the treatment of such transaction, property, or item under such provision would (without regard to the amendments made by this part) affect liability for tax for periods ending after such date of enactment,

nothing in the amendments made by this part shall be construed to affect the treatment of such transaction, property, or item for purposes of determining liability for tax for periods ending after such date of enactment.

Prior to repeal, Code Sec. 6418 read as follows:

SEC. 6418. SUGAR.

[Sec. 6418(a)]

(a) USE AS LIVESTOCK FEED OR FOR DISTILLATION OR PRODUCTION OF ALCOHOL.—Upon the use of any manufactured sugar, or any article manufactured therefrom, as livestock feed, or in the production of livestock feed, or for the distillation of alcohol, or for the production of alcohol (other than alcohol produced for human food consumption), there shall be paid by the Secretary to the person so using such manufactured sugar, or article manufactured therefrom, the amount of any tax paid under section 4501 with respect thereto.

Amendments

• **1976, Tax Reform Act of 1976 (P.L. 94-455)**

P.L. 94-455, §1906(b)(13)(A):

Amended 1954 Code by substituting "Secretary" for "Secretary or his delegate" each place it appeared. **Effective** 2-1-77.

• **1965, Sugar Act Amendments of 1965 (P.L. 89-331)**

P.L. 89-331, §9(b):

Amended Code Sec. 6418(a) by inserting "Or Production" after "Distillation" in the heading and by inserting "or for the production of alcohol (other than alcohol produced for human food consumption)," after "the distillation of alcohol," in the text. **Effective** 11-8-65.

• **1956 (P.L. 545, 84th Cong.)**

P.L. 545, 84th Cong., §21(b), 22:

Amended Sec. 6418(a) by striking out the "(a)" immediately following "section 4501". **Effective** 1-1-56.

[Sec. 6418(b)]

(b) EXPORTATION.—Upon the exportation from the United States to a foreign country, or the shipment from the United States to any possession of the United States except Puerto Rico, of any manufactured sugar, or any article manufactured wholly or partly from manufactured sugar, with respect to which tax under the provisions of section 4501(a) has been paid, the amount of such tax shall be paid by the Secretary to the consignor named in the bill of lading under which the article was exported or shipped to a possession, or to the shipper, or to the manufacturer of the manufactured sugar or of the articles exported, if the consignor waives any claim thereto in favor of such shipper or manufacturer.

Amendments

• **1976, Tax Reform Act of 1976 (P.L. 94-455)**

P.L. 94-455, §1906(b)(13)(A):

Amended 1954 Code by substituting "Secretary" for "Secretary or his delegate" each place it appeared. **Effective** 2-1-77.

• **1962, Tariff Classification Act of 1962 (P.L. 87-456)**

P.L. 87-456, §302(c):

Amended Code Sec. 6418(b) by deleting the following: "; except that no such payment shall be allowed with respect to any manufactured sugar, or article, upon which, through substitution or otherwise, a drawback of any tax paid under section 4501(b) has been or is to be claimed under any provisions of law made applicable by section 4504." **Effective** 8-31-63.

[Sec. 6419]

SEC. 6419. EXCISE TAX ON WAGERING.

[Sec. 6419(a)]

(a) CREDIT OR REFUND GENERALLY.—No overpayment of tax imposed by chapter 35 shall be credited or refunded (otherwise than under subsection (b)), in pursuance of a court decision or otherwise, unless the person who paid the tax establishes, in accordance with regulations prescribed by the Secretary, (1) that he has not collected (whether as a separate charge or otherwise) the amount of the tax from the person who placed the wager on which the tax was imposed, or (2) that he has repaid the amount of the tax to the person who placed such wager, or unless he files with the Secretary written consent of the person who placed such wager to the allowance of the credit or the making of the refund. In the case of any laid-off wager, no overpayment of tax imposed by chapter 35 shall be so credited or refunded to the person with whom such laid-off wager was placed unless he establishes, in accordance with regulations prescribed by the Secretary, that the provisions of the preceding sentence have been complied with both with respect to the person who placed the laidoff wager with him and with respect to the person who placed the original wager.

Amendments

• **1976, Tax Reform Act of 1976 (P.L. 94-455)**

P.L. 94-455, §1906(b)(13)(A):

Amended 1954 Code by substituting "Secretary" for "Secretary or his delegate" each place it appeared. **Effective** 2-1-77.

[Sec. 6419(b)]

(b) CREDIT OR REFUND ON WAGERS LAID-OFF BY TAXPAYER.—Where any taxpayer lays off part or all of a wager with another person who is liable for tax imposed by chapter 35 on the amount so laid off, a credit against such tax shall be allowed, or a refund shall be made to, the taxpayer laying off such amount. Such credit or refund shall be in an amount which bears the same ratio to the amount of tax which such taxpayer paid on the original wager as the amount so laid off bears to the amount of the original wager. Credit or refund under this subsection shall be allowed or made only in accordance with regulations prescribed by the Secretary; and no interest shall be allowed with respect to any amount so credited or refunded.

Amendments

• **1976, Tax Reform Act of 1976 (P.L. 94-455)**

P.L. 94-455, §1906(b)(13)(A):

Amended 1954 Code by substituting "Secretary" for "Secretary or his delegate" each place it appeared. **Effective** 2-1-77.

[Sec. 6420]

SEC. 6420. GASOLINE USED ON FARMS.

[Sec. 6420(a)]

(a) GASOLINE.—Except as provided in subsection (g), if gasoline is used on a farm for farming purposes, the Secretary shall pay (without interest) to the ultimate purchaser of such gasoline the amount determined by multiplying—

(1) the number of gallons so used, by

(2) the rate of tax on gasoline under section 4081 which applied on the date he purchased such gasoline.

Amendments

• **1976, Tax Reform Act of 1976 (P.L. 94-455)**

P.L. 94-455, §1906(a)(26)(C)(ii):

Substituted "subsection (g)" for "subsection (h)" in Code Sec. 6420(a). **Effective** 2-1-77.

P.L. 94-455, §1906(b)(13)(A):

Amended the 1954 Code by substituting "Secretary" for "Secretary or his delegate" each place it appeared. **Effective** 2-1-77.

• **1965, Excise Tax Reduction Act of 1965 (P.L. 89-44)**

P.L. 89-44, §809(a)(1):

Substituted "Except as provided in subsection (h), if" for "If" in Sec. 6420(a). **Effective** 7-1-65.

[Sec. 6420(b)]

(b) TIME FOR FILING CLAIMS; PERIOD COVERED.—Not more than one claim may be filed under this section by any person with respect to gasoline used during his taxable year, and no claim shall be allowed under this section with respect to gasoline used during any taxable year unless filed by

CREDITS AND REFUNDS—SPECIAL RULES

such person not later than the time prescribed by law for filing a claim for credit or refund of overpayment of income tax for such taxable year. For purposes of this subsection, a person's taxable year shall be his taxable year for purposes of subtitle A.

Amendments

• **1976, Tax Reform Act of 1976 (P.L. 94-455)**

P.L. 94-455, §1906(a)(26)(A):

Amended Code Sec. 6420(b). **Effective** 2-1-77. Prior to amendment, Code Sec. 6420(b) read as follows:

(b) TIME FOR FILING CLAIM; PERIOD COVERED.—

(1) GASOLINE USED BEFORE JULY 1, 1965.—Except as provided in paragraph (2), not more than one claim may be filed under this section by any person with respect to gasoline used during the one-year period ending on June 30 of any year. No claim shall be allowed under this paragraph with respect to any one-year period unless filed on or before September 30 of the year in which such one-year period ends.

(2) GASOLINE USED AFTER JUNE 30, 1965.—In the case of gasoline used after June 30, 1965—

(A) not more than one claim may be filed under this section by any person with respect to gasoline used during his taxable year; and

(B) no claim shall be allowed under this section with respect to gasoline used during any taxable year unless filed by such person not later than the time prescribed by law for filing a claim for credit or refund of overpayment of income tax for such taxable year.

For purposes of this paragraph, a person's taxable year shall be his taxable year for purposes of subtitle A, except that a person's first taxable year beginning after June 30, 1965, shall include the period after June 30, 1965, and before the beginning of such first taxable year.

• **1970 (P.L. 91-258)**

P.L. 91-258, §207(b):

Amended Code Sec. 6420(b)(2)(B) by substituting "a claim for credit or refund of overpayment of income tax" for "an income tax return". **Effective** 7-1-70.

• **1965, Excise Tax Reduction Act of 1965 (P.L. 89-44)**

P.L. 89-44, §809(a)(2):

Amended Sec. 6420(b). **Effective** 7-1-65. Prior to amendment, Sec. 6420(b) read as follows:

(b) Time for Filing Claim; Period Covered.—Not more than one claim may be filed under this section by any person with respect to gasoline used during the one-year period ending on June 30 of any year. No claim shall be allowed under this section with respect to any one-year period unless filed on or before September 30 of the year in which such one-year period ends.

[Sec. 6420(c)]

(c) MEANING OF TERMS.—For purposes of this section—

(1) USE ON A FARM FOR FARMING PURPOSES.—Gasoline shall be treated as used on a farm for farming purposes only if used (A) in carrying on a trade or business, (B) on a farm situated in the United States, and (C) for farming purposes.

(2) FARM.—The term "farm" includes stock, dairy, poultry, fruit, fur-bearing animal, and truck farms, plantations, ranches, nurseries, ranges, greenhouses or other similar structures used primarily for the raising of agricultural or horticultural commodities, and orchards.

(3) FARMING PURPOSES.—Gasoline shall be treated as used for farming purposes only if used—

(A) by the owner, tenant, or operator of a farm, in connection with cultivating the soil, or in connection with raising or harvesting any agricultural or horticultural commodity, including the raising, shearing, feeding, caring for, training, and management of livestock, bees, poultry, and fur-bearing animals and wildlife, on a farm of which he is the owner, tenant, or operator;

(B) by the owner, tenant, or operator of a farm, in handling, drying, packing, grading, or storing any agricultural or horticultural commodity in its unmanufactured state; but only if such owner, tenant, or operator produced more than one-half of the commodity which he so treated during the period with respect to which claim is filed;

(C) by the owner, tenant, or operator of a farm, in connection with—

(i) the planting, cultivating, caring for, or cutting of trees, or

(ii) the preparation (other than milling) of trees for market, incidental to farming operations; or

(D) by the owner, tenant, or operator of a farm, in connection with the operation, management, conservation, improvement, or maintenance of such farm and its tools and equipment.

(4) CERTAIN FARMING USE OTHER THAN BY OWNER, ETC.—In applying paragraph (3)(A) to a use on a farm for any purpose described in paragraph (3)(A) by any person other than the owner, tenant, or operator of such farm—

(A) the owner, tenant, or operator of such farm shall be treated as the user and ultimate purchaser of the gasoline, except that

(B) if the person so using the gasoline is an aerial or other applicator of fertilizers or other substances and is the ultimate purchaser of the gasoline, then subparagraph (A) of this paragraph shall not apply and the aerial or other applicator shall be treated as having used such gasoline on a farm for farming purposes.

In the case of an aerial applicator, gasoline shall be treated as used on a farm for farming purposes if the gasoline is used for the direct flight between the airfield and one or more farms.

(5) GASOLINE.—The term "gasoline" has the meaning given to such term by section 4083(a).

Amendments

• **2005, Safe, Accountable, Flexible, Efficient Transportation Equity Act: A Legacy for Users (P.L. 109-59)**

P.L. 109-59, §11121(a):

Amended Code Sec. 6420(c)(4)(B). **Effective** for fuel use or air transportation after 9-30-2005. Prior to amendment, Code Sec. 6420(c)(4)(B) read as follows:

(B) if—

(i) the person so using the gasoline is an aerial or other applicator of fertilizers or other substances and is the ultimate purchaser of the gasoline, and

(ii) the person described in subparagraph (A) waives (at such time and in such form and manner as the Secretary shall prescribe) his right to be treated as the user and ultimate purchaser of the gasoline,

then subparagraph (A) of this paragraph shall not apply and the aerial or other applicator shall be treated as having used such gasoline on a farm for farming purposes.

P.L. 109-59, §11121(b):

Amended Code Sec. 6420(c)(4), as amended by Act Sec. 11121(a), by adding at the end a new flush sentence. **Effective** for fuel use or air transportation after 9-30-2005.

• **1993, Omnibus Budget Reconciliation Act of 1993 (P.L. 103-66)**

P.L. 103-66, §13242(d)(20):

Amended Code Sec. 6420(c)(5) by striking "section 4082(b)" and inserting "section 4083(a)". **Effective** 1-1-94.

• **1983, Surface Transportation Act of 1983 (P.L. 97-424)**

P.L. 97-424, §511(f):

Amended Code Sec. 6420(c)(4). **Effective** 4-1-83. Prior to amendment, Code Sec. 6420(c)(4) read as follows:

(4) CERTAIN FARMING USE OTHER THAN BY OWNER, ETC.—In applying paragraph (3)(A) to a use on a farm for any purpose described in paragraph (3)(A) by any person other than the owner, tenant, or operator of such farm—

(A) the owner, tenant, or operator of such farm shall be treated as the user and ultimate purchaser of the gasoline, except that

(B) if the person so using the gasoline is an aerial applicator who is the ultimate purchaser of the gasoline and the person described in subparagraph (A) waives (at such time and in such form and manner as the Secretary shall prescribe) his right to be treated as the user and ultimate purchaser of the gasoline, then subparagraph (A) of this paragraph shall not apply and the aerial applicator shall be treated as having used such gasoline on a farm for farming purposes.

• **1978 (P.L. 95-458)**

P.L. 95-458, §3(a), (d):

Redesignated former subsection (c)(4) as subsection (c)(5) and added a new subsection (c)(4). **Effective** 4-1-79.

P.L. 95-458, §3(c), (d):

Amended subparagraph (c)(3)(A) by striking out "except that if such use is by any person other than the owner, tenant, or operator of such farm, then for purposes of this subparagraph, in applying subsection (a) to this subparagraph, the owner, tenant, or operator of the farm on which gasoline or a liquid taxable under section 4041 issued shall be treated as the user and the ultimate purchaser of such gasoline or liquid;" at the end thereof. **Effective** 4-1-79.

• **1976, Tax Reform Act of 1976 (P.L. 94-455)**

P.L. 94-455, §1906(b)(6)(A):

Amended Code Sec. 6420(c)(3)(A). **Effective** with respect to the use of liquids after 12-31-70. Prior to amendment, Code Sec. 6420(c)(3)(A) read as follows:

(A) by the owner, tenant, or operator of a farm, in connection with cultivating the soil, or in connection with raising or harvesting any agricultural or horticultural commodity, including the raising, shearing, feeding, caring for, training, and management of livestock, bees, poultry, and fur-bearing animals and wildlife, on a farm of which he is the owner, tenant, or operator; except that if such use is by any person other than the owner, tenant, or operator of such farm, then (i) for purposes of this subparagraph, in applying subsection (a) to this subparagraph, and for purposes of section 6416(b)(2)(G)(ii) (but not for purposes of section 4041), the owner, tenant, or operator of the farm on which gasoline or a liquid taxable under section 4041 is used shall be treated as the user and ultimate purchaser of such gasoline or liquid, and (ii) for purposes of applying section 6416(b)(2)(G)(ii), any tax paid under section 4041 in respect of a liquid used on a farm for farming purposes (within the meaning of this subparagraph) shall be treated as having been paid by the owner, tenant, or operator of the farm on which such liquid is used;

- **1958, Excise Tax Technical Changes Act of 1958 (P.L. 85-859)**

P.L. 85-859, §163(d)(2):

Amended Sec. 6420(c)(3)(A) by striking out "6416(b)(2)(C)(ii)" each place where it appeared and substituting "6416(b)(2)(G)(ii)". **Effective** 1-1-59.

[Sec. 6420(d)]

(d) EXEMPT SALES; OTHER PAYMENTS OR REFUNDS AVAILABLE.—No amount shall be payable under this section with respect to any gasoline which the Secretary determines was exempt from the tax imposed by section 4081. The amount which (but for this sentence) would be payable under this section with respect to any gasoline shall be reduced by any other amount which the Secretary determines is payable under this section, or is refundable under any provision of this title, to any person with respect to such gasoline.

Amendments

- **1976, Tax Reform Act of 1976 (P.L. 94-455)**

P.L. 94-455, §1906(b)(13)(A):

Amended 1954 Code by substituting "Secretary" for "Secretary or his delegate" each place it appeared. **Effective** 2-1-77.

- **1965, Excise Tax Reduction Act of 1965 (P.L. 89-44)**

P.L. 89-44, §809(a)(3):

Amended Sec. 6420(d) by substituting "payable" for "paid" in the first sentence. **Effective** 7-1-65.

[Sec. 6420(e)]

(e) APPLICABLE LAWS.—

(1) IN GENERAL.—All provisions of law, including penalties, applicable in respect of the tax imposed by section 4081 shall, insofar as applicable and not inconsistent with this section, apply in respect of the payments provided for in this section to the same extent as if such payments constituted refunds of overpayments of the tax so imposed.

(2) EXAMINATION OF BOOKS AND WITNESSES.—For the purpose of ascertaining the correctness of any claim made under this section, or the correctness of any payment made in respect of any such claim, the Secretary shall have the authority granted by paragraphs (1), (2), and (3) of section 7602(a) (relating to examination of books and witnesses) as if the claimant were the person liable for tax.

(3) FRACTIONAL PARTS OF A DOLLAR.—Section 7504 (granting the Secretary discretion with respect to fractional parts of a dollar) shall not apply.

Amendments

- **1989, Omnibus Budget Reconciliation Act of 1989 (P.L. 101-239)**

P.L. 101-239, §7841(d)(20):

Amended Code Sec. 6420(e)(2) by striking "section 7602" and inserting "section 7602(a)". **Effective** 12-31-89.

- **1976, Tax Reform Act of 1976 (P.L. 94-455)**

P.L. 94-455, §1906(a)(26)(B):

Substituted "apply in respect" for "apply in in respect" in Code Sec. 6420(e)(1). **Effective** 2-1-77.

P.L. 94-455, §1906(b)(13)(A):

Amended the 1954 Code by substituting "Secretary" for "Secretary or his delegate" each place it appeared. **Effective** 2-1-77.

[Sec. 6420(f)]

(f) REGULATIONS.—The Secretary may by regulations prescribe the conditions, not inconsistent with the provisions of this section, under which payments may be made under this section.

Amendments

- **1976, Tax Reform Act of 1976 (P.L. 94-455)**

P.L. 94-455, §1906(b)(13)(A):

Amended 1954 Code by substituting "Secretary" for "Secretary or his delegate" each place it appeared. **Effective** 2-1-77.

[Sec. 6420(g)]

(g) INCOME TAX CREDIT IN LIEU OF PAYMENT.—

(1) PERSONS NOT SUBJECT TO INCOME TAX.—Payment shall be made under subsection (a) only to—

(A) the United States or an agency or instrumentality thereof, a State, a political subdivision of a State, or an agency or instrumentality of one or more States or political subdivisions, or

(B) an organization exempt from tax under section 501(a) (other than an organization required to make a return of the tax imposed under subtitle A for its taxable year).

(2) ALLOWANCE OF CREDIT AGAINST INCOME TAX.—For allowance of credit against the tax imposed by subtitle A, see section 34.

Amendments

- **1984, Deficit Reduction Act of 1984 (P.L. 98-369)**

P.L. 98-369, §474(r)(38):

Amended Code Sec. 6420(g)(2) by striking out "section 39" and inserting in lieu thereof "section 34". **Effective** for tax years beginning after 12-31-83, and to carrybacks from such years.

- **1976, Tax Reform Act of 1976 (P.L. 94-455)**

P.L. 94-455, §1906(a)(26)(C)(ii):

Repealed Code Sec. 6420(g) and redesignated subsection (h) as Code Sec. 6420(g). **Effective** 2-1-77. Prior to repeal, Code Sec. 6420(g) read as follows:

(g) EFFECTIVE DATE.—This section shall apply only with respect to gasoline purchased after December 31, 1955.

P.L. 94-455, §1906(a)(26)(D):

Amended redesignated Code Sec. 6420(g) [formerly (h)]. **Effective** 2-1-77. Prior to amendment, redesignated Code Sec. 6420(g) read as follows:

(g) INCOME TAX CREDIT IN LIEU OF PAYMENT.—

(1) PERSONS NOT SUBJECT TO INCOME TAX.—Payment shall be made under subsection (a) with respect to gasoline used after June 30, 1965, only to—

(A) the United States or an agency or instrumentality thereof, a State, a political subdivision of a State, or an agency or instrumentality of one or more States or political subdivisions, or

(B) an organization exempt from tax under section 501(a) (other than an organization required to make a return of the tax imposed under subtitle A for its taxable year).

(2) ALLOWANCE OF CREDIT AGAINST INCOME TAX.—For allowance of credit against the tax imposed by subtitle A for gasoline used after June 30, 1965, see section 39.

- **1965, Excise Tax Reduction Act of 1965 (P.L. 89-44)**

P.L. 89-44, §809(a):

Redesignated Sec. 6420(h) as 6420(i) and added new Sec. 6420(h). **Effective** 7-1-65.

[Sec. 6420(h)—Stricken]

(h) TERMINATION.—Except with respect to taxes imposed by section 4081 at the Leaking Underground Storage Tank Trust Fund financing rate, this section shall apply only with respect to gasoline purchased before October 1, 1999.

Amendments

- **1993, Omnibus Budget Reconciliation Act of 1993 (P.L. 103-66)**

P.L. 103-66, §13241(f)(5):

Amended Code Sec. 6420 by striking subsection (h). **Effective** 10-1-93. Prior to amendment, Code Sec. 6420(h) read as follows:

CREDITS AND REFUNDS—SPECIAL RULES

• **1991, Intermodal Surface Transportation Efficiency Act of 1991 (P.L. 102-240)**

P.L. 102-240, §8002(b)(5):

Amended Code Sec. 6420(h) by striking "1995" each place it appears and inserting "1999". **Effective** 12-18-91.

• **1990, Omnibus Budget Reconciliation Act of 1990 (P.L. 101-508)**

P.L. 101-508, §11211(d)(5):

Amended Code Sec. 6420(h) by striking "1993" and inserting "1995". **Effective** 11-5-90.

• **1987, Surface Transportation and Uniform Relocation Assistance Act of 1987 (P.L. 100-17)**

P.L. 100-17, §502(b)(6):

Amended Code Sec. 6420(h) by striking out "1988" and inserting in lieu thereof "1993". **Effective** 4-2-87.

• **1986, Superfund Amendments and Reauthorization Act of 1986 (P.L. 99-499)**

P.L. 99-499, §521(c)(1):

Amended Code Sec. 6420(h) by striking out "This section" and inserting in lieu thereof "Except with respect to taxes imposed by section 4081 at the Leaking Underground Storage Tank Trust Fund financing rate, this section". **Effective** 1-1-87.

• **1983, Surface Transportation Act of 1983 (P.L. 97-424)**

P.L. 97-424, §516(b)(4):

Amended Code Sec. 6420 by redesignating subsection (h) as subsection (i) and by adding a new subsection (h). **Effective** 1-6-83.

[Sec. 6420(i)]

(i) CROSS REFERENCES.—

(1) For exemption from tax in case of special fuels used on a farm for farming purposes, see section 4041(f).

(2) For civil penalty for excessive claim under this section, see section 6675.

(3) For fraud penalties, etc., see chapter 75 (section 7201 and following, relating to crimes, other offenses, and forfeitures).

(4) For treatment of an Indian tribal government as a State (and a subdivision of an Indian tribal government as a political subdivision of a State), see section 7871.

Amendments

• **2018, Tax Technical Corrections Act of 2018 (P.L. 115-141)**

P.L. 115-141, §401(a)(289), Div. U:

Amended Code Sec. 6420(i)(4) by striking "State and" and inserting "State (and". **Effective** 3-23-2018.

• **1983 (P.L. 97-473)**

P.L. 97-473, §202(b)(12):

Added Code Sec. 6420(h)[i](4). For the **effective** date, see the amendment note for Act Sec. 204, following Code Sec. 7871.

• **1983, Surface Transportation Act of 1983 (P.L. 97-424)**

P.L. 97-424, §516(b)(4):

Redesignated subsection (h) as subsection (i). **Effective** 1-6-83.

• **1976, Tax Reform Act of 1976 (P.L. 94-455)**

P.L. 94-455, §1906(a)(26)(C)(i):

Redesignated former subsection (i) as Code Sec. 6420(h). **Effective** 2-1-77.

• **1970 (P.L. 91-258)**

P.L. 91-258, §205(c)(7):

Amended Code Sec. 6420(i)(1). **Effective** 7-1-70. Prior to amendment this section read as follows:

(1) For exemption from tax in case of diesel fuel and special motor fuels used on a farm for farming purposes, see section 4041(d).

• **1965, Excise Tax Reduction Act of 1965 (P.L. 89-44)**

P.L. 89-44, §809(a):

Redesignated Sec. 6420(h) as Sec. 6420(i). **Effective** 7-1-65.

• **1956 (P.L. 466, 84th Cong.)**

P.L. 466, 84th Cong., §1:

Added Code Sec. 6420. See also amendment note following Code Sec. 6421. **Effective** for gasoline purchased after 12-31-55.

[Sec. 6421]

SEC. 6421. GASOLINE USED FOR CERTAIN NONHIGHWAY PURPOSES, USED BY LOCAL TRANSIT SYSTEMS, OR SOLD FOR CERTAIN EXEMPT PURPOSES.

[Sec. 6421(a)]

(a) NONHIGHWAY USES.—Except as provided in subsection (i), if gasoline is used in an off-highway business use, the Secretary shall pay (without interest) to the ultimate purchaser of such gasoline an amount equal to the amount determined by multiplying the number of gallons so used by the rate at which tax was imposed on such gasoline under section 4081. Except as provided in paragraph (2) of subsection (f) of this section, in the case of gasoline used as a fuel in an aircraft, the Secretary shall pay (without interest) to the ultimate purchaser of such gasoline an amount equal to the amount determined by multiplying the number of gallons of gasoline so used by the rate at which tax was imposed on such gasoline under section 4081.

Amendments

• **1998, IRS Restructuring and Reform Act of 1998 (P.L. 105-206)**

P.L. 105-206, §6023(24)(C):

Amended Code Sec. 6421(a) by striking "subsection (j)" and inserting "subsection (i)". **Effective** 7-22-98.

• **1988, Technical and Miscellaneous Revenue Act of 1988 (P.L. 100-647)**

P.L. 100-647, §1017(c)(7):

Amended Code Sec. 6421(a) by striking out "subsection (i)" and inserting in lieu thereof "subsection (j)". **Effective** as if included in the provision of P.L. 99-514 to which it relates.

P.L. 100-647, §2001(d)(3)(F):

Amended Code Sec. 6421(a) by striking out "paragraph (3) of subsection (e)" in the second sentence and inserting in lieu thereof "paragraph (2) of subsection (f)". **Effective** as if included in the provision of P.L. 99-499 to which it relates.

• **1986, Tax Reform Act of 1986 (P.L. 99-514)**

P.L. 99-514, §1703(c)(2)(D):

Amended the heading for Code Sec. 6421. **Effective** for gasoline removed (as defined in section 4082 of the Internal Revenue Code of 1986) after 12-31-87. Prior to amendment, the heading read as follows:

SEC. 6421. GASOLINE USED FOR CERTAIN NONHIGHWAY PURPOSES OR BY LOCAL TRANSIT SYSTEMS.

• **1983, Surface Transportation Act of 1983 (P.L. 97-424)**

P.L. 97-424, §511(c)(1):

Amended Code Sec. 6421(a) by striking out the first sentence and inserting a new first sentence. **Effective** 4-1-83. Prior to amendment, the first sentence of Code Sec. 6421(a) read as follows:

Except as provided in subsection (i), if gasoline is used in a qualified business use, the Secretary shall pay (without interest) to the ultimate purchaser of such gasoline an amount equal to 1 cent for each gallon of gasoline so used on which tax was paid at the rate of 3 cents a gallon and 2 cents for each gallon of gasoline so used on which tax was paid at the rate of 4 cents a gallon.

• **1978, Energy Tax Act of 1978 (P.L. 95-618)**

P.L. 95-618, §222(a)(1)(A), (b):

Amended the first sentence of Code Sec. 6421(a). **Effective** for uses after 12-31-78. Prior to amendment, such sentence read:

Except as provided in subsection (i), if gasoline is used otherwise than as a fuel in a highway vehicle (1) which (at the time of such use) is registered, or is required to be registered, for highway use under the laws of any State or foreign country, or (2) which, in the case of a highway vehicle owned by the United States, is used on the highway, the Secretary shall pay (without interest) to the ultimate purchaser of such gasoline an amount equal to 1 cent for each gallon of gasoline so used on which tax was paid at the rate of 3 cents a gallon and 2 cents for each gallon of gasoline so used on which tax was paid at the rate of 4 cents a gallon.

• **1976, Tax Reform Act of 1976 (P.L. 94-455)**

P.L. 94-455, §1906(a)(27)(i):

Deleted "after June 30, 1970," as it appeared before "as a fuel in an aircraft," in Code Sec. 6421(a). **Effective** with respect to gasoline used as a fuel after 6-30-70.

P.L. 94-455, §1906(b)(13)(A):

Amended the 1954 Code by substituting "Secretary" for "Secretary or his delegate" each place it appeared. **Effective** 2-1-77.

• **1970 (P.L. 91-258)**

P.L. 91-258, §205(b)(1)(A):

Amended Code Sec. 6421(a) by adding the last sentence. **Effective** 7-1-70.

CREDITS AND REFUNDS—SPECIAL RULES

• **1965, Excise Tax Reduction Act of 1965 (P.L. 89-44)**

P.L. 89-44, § 809(b)(1)(A):

Amended Sec. 6421(a) by substituting "Except as provided in subsection (i), if" for "If" at the beginning of Sec. 6421(a). **Effective** 7-1-65.

• **1959, Federal-Aid Highway Act of 1959 (P.L. 86-342)**

P.L. 86-342, § 201(d)(2):

Amended Code Sec. 6421(a) by striking out "1 cent for each gallon of gasoline so used" and substituting "1 cent for each gallon of gasoline so used on which tax was paid at the rate of 3 cents a gallon and 2 cents for each gallon of gasoline so used on which tax was paid at the rate of 4 cents a gallon".

[Sec. 6421(b)]

(b) INTERCITY, LOCAL, OR SCHOOL BUSES.—

(1) ALLOWANCE.—Except as provided in paragraph (2) and subsection (i), if gasoline is used in an automobile bus while engaged in—

(A) furnishing (for compensation) passenger land transportation available to the general public, or

(B) the transportation of students and employees of schools (as defined in the last sentence of section 4221(d)(7)(C)),

the Secretary shall pay (without interest) to the ultimate purchaser of such gasoline an amount equal to the product of the number of gallons of gasoline so used multiplied by the rate at which tax was imposed on such gasoline by section 4081.

(2) LIMITATION IN CASE OF NONSCHEDULED INTERCITY OR LOCAL BUSES.—Paragraph (1)(A) shall not apply in respect of gasoline used in any automobile bus while engaged in furnishing transportation which is not scheduled and not along regular routes unless the seating capacity of such bus is at least 20 adults (not including the driver).

Amendments

• **1998, IRS Restructuring and Reform Act of 1998 (P.L. 105-206)**

P.L. 105-206, § 6023(24)(C):

Amended Code Sec. 6421(b) by striking "subsection (j)" and inserting "subsection (i)". **Effective** 7-22-98.

• **1988, Technical and Miscellaneous Revenue Act of 1988 (P.L. 100-647)**

P.L. 100-647, § 1017(c)(7):

Amended Code Sec. 6421(b)(1) by striking out "subsection (i)" and inserting in lieu thereof "subsection (j)". **Effective** as if included in the provision of P.L. 99-514 to which it relates.

• **1978, Energy Tax Act of 1978 (P.L. 95-618)**

P.L. 95-618, § 233(a)(1), (d):

Amended Code Sec. 6421(b). **Effective** 12-1-78. Prior to amendment, such section read:

"(b) LOCAL TRANSIT SYSTEMS.—

(1) ALLOWANCE.—Except as provided in subsection (i), if gasoline is used during any calendar quarter in vehicles while engaged in furnishing scheduled common carrier public passenger land transportation service along regular routes, the Secretary shall, subject to the provisions of paragraph (2), pay (without interest) to the ultimate purchaser of such gasoline the amount determined by multiplying—

(A) 1 cent for each gallon of gasoline so used on which tax was paid at the rate of 3 cents a gallon and 2 cents for each gallon of gasoline so used on which tax was paid at the rate of 4 cents a gallon, by

(B) the percentage which the ultimate purchaser's commuter fare revenue derived from such scheduled service during such quarter was of his total passenger fare revenue derived from such scheduled service during such quarter.

(2) LIMITATION.—Paragraph (1) shall apply in respect of gasoline used during any calendar quarter only if at least 60 percent of the total passenger fare revenue derived during such quarter from scheduled service described in paragraph (1) by the person filing the claim was attributable to commuter fare revenue derived during such quarter by such person from such scheduled service."

• **1976, Tax Reform Act of 1976 (P.L. 94-455)**

P.L. 94-455, § 1906(b)(13)(A):

Amended 1954 Code by substituting "Secretary" for "Secretary or his delegate" each place it appeared. **Effective** 2-1-77.

• **1965, Excise Tax Reduction Act of 1965 (P.L. 89-44)**

P.L. 89-44, § 809(b)(1)(A):

Amended Sec. 6421(b)(1) by substituting "Except as provided in subsection (i), if" for "If" at the beginning of Sec. 6421(b)(1). **Effective** 7-1-65.

• **1962, Tax Rate Extension Act of 1962 (P.L. 87-508)**

P.L. 87-508, § 5(c)(2):

Amended Code Sec. 6421(b). **Effective** 9-16-62. Prior to amendment, Sec. 6421(b) read as follows:

"(b) Local Transit Systems.—

"(1) Allowance.—If gasoline is used during any calendar quarter in vehicles while engaged in furnishing scheduled common carrier public passenger land transportation service along regular routes, the Secretary or his delegate shall, subject to the provisions of paragraph (2), pay (without interest) to the ultimate purchaser of such gasoline the amount determined by multiplying—

"(A) 1 cent for each gallon of gasoline so used on which tax was paid at the rate of 3 cents a gallon and 2 cents for each gallon of gasoline so used on which tax was paid at the rate of 4 cents a gallon, by

"(B) the percentage which the ultimate purchaser's tax-exempt passenger fare revenue derived from such scheduled service during such quarter was of his total passenger fare revenue (not including the tax imposed by section 4261, relating to the tax on transportation of persons) derived from such scheduled service during such quarter.

"(2) Limitation.—Paragraph (1) shall apply in respect of gasoline used during any calendar quarter only if at least 60 percent of the total passenger fare revenue (not including the tax imposed by section 4261, relating to the tax on transportation of persons) derived during such quarter from scheduled service described in paragraph (1) by the person filing the claim was attributable to tax-exempt passenger fare revenue derived during such quarter by such person from such scheduled service."

• **1959, Federal-Aid Highway Act of 1959 (P.L. 86-342)**

P.L. 86-342, § 201(d)(2):

Amended Code Sec. 6421(b)(1)(A) by striking out "1 cent for each gallon of gasoline so used" and substituting "1 cent for each gallon of gasoline so used on which tax was paid at the rate of 3 cents a gallon and 2 cents for each gallon of gasoline so used on which tax was paid at the rate of 4 cents a gallon".

[Sec. 6421(c)]

(c) EXEMPT PURPOSES.—If gasoline is sold to any person for any purpose described in paragraph (2), (3), (4), (5), or (6) of section 4221(a), the Secretary shall pay (without interest) to such person an amount equal to the product of the number of gallons of gasoline so sold multiplied by the rate at which tax was imposed on such gasoline by section 4081. The preceding sentence shall apply notwithstanding paragraphs (2) and (3) of subsection (f). Subsection (a) shall not apply to gasoline to which this subsection applies.

Amendments

• **2018, Tax Technical Corrections Act of 2018 (P.L. 115-141)**

P.L. 115-141, § 401(a)(290), Div. U:

Amended Code Sec. 6421(c) by striking "(4) (5)" and inserting "(4), (5)". **Effective** 3-23-2018.

• **2006, Pension Protection Act of 2006 (P.L. 109-280)**

P.L. 109-280, § 1207(b)(3)(B):

Amended Code Sec. 6421(c) by striking "or (5)" and inserting "(5), or (6)". **Effective** 1-1-2007.

• **1998, IRS Restructuring and Reform Act of 1998 (P.L. 105-206)**

P.L. 105-206, § 6010(g)(3)(A)-(B):

Amended Code Sec. 6421(c) by striking "(2)(A)" and inserting "(2)", and by adding at the end a new sentence. **Effective** as if included in the provision of P.L. 105-34 to which it relates [**effective** 10-1-97.—CCH].

• **1993, Omnibus Budget Reconciliation Act of 1993 (P.L. 103-66)**

P.L. 103-66, § 13242(d)(22):

Amended Code Sec. 6421(c) by adding at the end thereof a new sentence. **Effective** 1-1-94.

• **1986, Tax Reform Act of 1986 (P.L. 99-514)**

P.L. 99-514, § 1703(c)(1)(A), (B):

Amended Code Sec. 6421 by redesignating subsections (c), (d), (e), (f), (g), and (h) as subsections (d), (e), (f), (g), (h), and (i), respectively, and by inserting after subsection (b) new subsection (c). **Effective** for gasoline removed (as defined in section 4082 of the Internal Revenue Code of 1986) after 12-31-87.

[Sec. 6421(d)]

(d) TIME FOR FILING CLAIMS; PERIOD COVERED.—

(1) IN GENERAL.—Except as provided in paragraph (2), not more than one claim may be filed under subsection (a), not more than one claim may be filed under subsection (b), and not more than one claim may be filed under subsection (c) by any person with respect to gasoline used during his taxable year; and no claim shall be allowed under this paragraph with respect to gasoline used during any taxable year unless filed

CREDITS AND REFUNDS—SPECIAL RULES

by such person not later than the time prescribed by law for filing a claim for credit or refund of overpayment of income tax for such taxable year. For purposes of this subsection, a person's taxable year shall be his taxable year for purposes of subtitle A.

(2) EXCEPTION.—For payments per quarter based on aggregate amounts payable under this section and section 6427, see section 6427(i)(2).

(3) APPLICATION TO SALES UNDER SUBSECTION (c).—For purposes of this subsection, gasoline shall be treated as used for a purpose referred to in subsection (c) when it is sold for such a purpose.

Amendments

- **1998, Transportation Equity Act for the 21st Century (P.L. 105-178)**

P.L. 105-178, §9009(b)(3):

Amended Code Sec. 6421(d)(2). **Effective** 10-1-98. Prior to amendment, Code Sec. 6421(d)(2) read as follows:

(2) EXCEPTION.—If $1,000 or more is payable under this section to any person with respect to gasoline used during any of the first three quarters of his taxable year, a claim may be filed under this section by such person with respect to gasoline used during such quarter. No claim filed under this paragraph shall be allowed unless filed on or before the last day of the first quarter following the quarter for which the claim is filed.

- **1988, Technical and Miscellaneous Revenue Act of 1988 (P.L. 100-647)**

P.L. 100-647, §1017(c)(15):

Amended Code Sec. 6421(d) by adding at the end thereof a new paragraph (3). **Effective** as if included in the provision of P.L. 99-514 to which it relates.

- **1986, Tax Reform Act of 1986 (P.L. 99-514)**

P.L. 99-514, §1703(c)(1)(A), (B):

Amended Code Sec. 6421 by redesignating subsections (c), (d), (e), (f), (g), and (h) as subsections (d), (e), (f), (g), (h), and (i), respectively, and by inserting after subsection (b) new subsection (c). **Effective** for gasoline removed (as defined in section 4082 of the Internal Revenue Code of 1986) after 12-31-87.

P.L. 99-514, §1703(c)(2)(A):

Amended Code Sec. 6421(d)(1) as redesignated by paragraph (1) of this subsection, by striking out "and not more than one claim may be filed under subsection (b)" and inserting in lieu thereof "not more than one claim may be filed under subsection (b), and not more than one claim may be filed under subsection (c)". **Effective** for gasoline removed (as defined in section 4082 of the Internal Revenue Code of 1986) after 12-31-87.

- **1976, Tax Reform Act of 1976 (P.L. 94-455)**

P.L. 94-455, §1906(a)(27)(B):

Amended Code Sec. 6421(c). **Effective** 2-1-77. Prior to amendment, Code Sec. 6421(c) read as follows:

(c) TIME FOR FILING CLAIMS; PERIOD COVERED.—

(1) GASOLINE USED BEFORE JULY 1, 1965.—Except as provided in paragraphs (2) and (3), not more than one claim may be filed under subsection (a), and not more than one claim may be filed under subsection (b), by any person with respect to gasoline used during the oneyear period ending on June 30 of any year. No claim shall be allowed under this paragraph with respect to any oneyear period unless filed on or before September 30 of the year in which such oneyear period ends.

(2) EXCEPTION.—Except as provided in paragraph (3), if $1,000 or more is payable under this section to any person with respect to gasoline used during a calendar quarter, a claim may be filed under this section by such person with respect to gasoline used during such quarter. No claim filed under this paragraph shall be allowed unless filed on or before the last day of the first calendar quarter following the calendar quarter for which the claim is filed.

(3) GASOLINE USED AFTER JUNE 30, 1965.—

(A) IN GENERAL.—In the case of gasoline used after June 30, 1965—

(i) except as provided in subparagraph (B), not more than one claim may be filed under subsection (a), and not more than one claim may be filed under subsection (b), by any person with respect to gasoline used during his taxable year; and

(ii) no claim shall be allowed under this subparagraph with respect to gasoline used during any taxable year unless filed by such person not later than the time prescribed by law for filing a claim for credit or refund of overpayment of income tax for such taxable year.

For purposes of this paragraph, a person's taxable year shall be his taxable year for purposes of subtitle A, except that a person's first taxable year beginning after June 30, 1965, shall include the period after June 30, 1965, and before the beginning of such first taxable year.

(B) EXCEPTION.—If $1,000 or more is payable under this section to any person with respect to gasoline used during any of the first three quarters of his taxable year, a claim may be filed under this section by such person with respect to gasoline used during such quarter. No claim filed under this subparagraph shall be allowed unless filed on or before the last day of the first quarter following the quarter for which the claim is filed.

- **1970 (P.L. 91-258)**

P.L. 91-258, §207(b):

Amended Code Sec. 6421(c)(3)(A)(ii). **Effective** for tax years ending after 6-30-70, by substituting "a claim for credit or refund of overpayment of income tax" for "an income tax return".

- **1965, Excise Tax Reduction Act of 1965 (P.L. 89-44)**

P.L. 89-44, §809(b)(2):

Amended Sec. 6421(c) by substituting: "Gasoline Used Before July 1, 1965.—Except as provided in paragraphs (2) and (3)" for: "General Rule.—Except as provided in paragraph (2)" at the beginning of subsection (c)(1); by substituting: "Except as provided in paragraph (3), if" for: "If" in the first sentence of subsection (c)(2), and by adding a new paragraph (3). **Effective** 7-1-65.

- **1958, Excise Tax Technical Changes Act of 1958 (P.L. 85-859)**

P.L. 85-859, §164(a):

Amended Sec. 6421(c). **Effective** only with respect to claims the last day for the filing of which occurs after 1-1-59. Prior to amendment, Sec. 6421(c) read as follows:

(c) Time for Filing Claim; Period Covered.—Not more than one claim may be filed under subsection (a), and not more than one claim may be filed under subsection (b), by any person with respect to gasoline used during the one-year period ending on June 30 of any year. No claim shall be allowed under this section with respect to any one-year period unless filed on or before September 30 of the year in which such one-year period ends.

[Sec. 6421(e)]

(e) DEFINITIONS.—For purposes of this section—

(1) GASOLINE.—The term "gasoline" has the meaning given to such term by section 4083(a).

(2) OFF-HIGHWAY BUSINESS USE.—

(A) IN GENERAL.—The term "off-highway business use" means any use by a person in a trade or business of such person or in an activity of such person described in section 212 (relating to production of income) otherwise than as a fuel in a highway vehicle—

(i) which (at the time of such use) is registered, or is required to be registered, for highway use under the laws of any State or foreign country, or

(ii) which, in the case of a highway vehicle owned by the United States, is used on the highway.

(B) USES IN BOATS.—

(i) IN GENERAL.—Except as otherwise provided in this subparagraph, the term "off-highway business use" does not include any use in a motorboat.

(ii) FISHERIES AND WHALING.—The term "off-highway business use" shall include any use in a vessel employed in the fisheries or in the whaling business.

(C) USES IN MOBILE MACHINERY.—

(i) IN GENERAL.—The term "off-highway business use" shall include any use in a vehicle which meets the requirements described in clause (ii).

(ii) REQUIREMENTS FOR MOBILE MACHINERY.—The requirements described in this clause are—

(I) the design-based test, and

(II) the use-based test.

(iii) DESIGN-BASED TEST.—For purposes of clause (ii)(I), the design-based test is met if the vehicle consists of a chassis—

(I) to which there has been permanently mounted (by welding, bolting, riveting, or other means) machinery or equipment to perform a construction, manufacturing, processing, farming, mining, drilling, timbering, or similar operation if the operation of the machinery or equipment is unrelated to transportation on or off the public highways,

(II) which has been specially designed to serve only as a mobile carriage and mount (and a power source, where applicable) for the particular machinery or equipment involved, whether or not such machinery or equipment is in operation, and

CREDITS AND REFUNDS—SPECIAL RULES

(III) which, by reason of such special design, could not, without substantial structural modification, be used as a component of a vehicle designed to perform a function of transporting any load other than that particular machinery or equipment or similar machinery or equipment requiring such a specially designed chassis.

(iv) USE-BASED TEST.—For purposes of clause (ii)(II), the use-based test is met if the use of the vehicle on public highways was less than 7,500 miles during the taxpayer's taxable year. This clause shall be applied without regard to use of the vehicle by any organization which is described in section 501(c) and exempt from tax under section 501(a).

Amendments

• **2004, American Jobs Creation Act of 2004 (P.L. 108-357)**

P.L. 108-357, §851(d)(1):

Amended Code Sec. 6421(e)(2) by adding at the end a new subparagraph (C). **Effective** for tax years beginning after 10-22-2004.

• **1997, Taxpayer Relief Act of 1997 (P.L. 105-34)**

P.L. 105-34, §902(a):

Amended Code Sec. 6421(e)(2)(B) by striking clauses (iii) and (iv). **Effective** 1-1-98. Prior to being stricken, Code Sec. 6421(e)(2)(B)(iii)-(iv) read as follows:

(iii) EXCEPTION FOR DIESEL FUEL.—The term "off-highway business use" shall include the use of diesel fuel in a boat in the active conduct of—

(I) a trade or business of commercial fishing or transporting persons or property for compensation or hire, and

(II) except as provided in clause (iv), any other trade or business.

(iv) NONCOMMERCIAL BOATS.—In the case of a boat used predominantly in any activity which is of a type generally considered to constitute entertainment, amusement, or recreation, clause (iii)(II) shall not apply to—

(I) the taxes under sections 4041(a)(1) and 4081 for the period after December 31, 1993, and before January 1, 2000, and

(II) so much of the tax under sections 4041(a)(1) and 4081 as does not exceed 4.3 cents per gallon for the period after December 31, 1999.

• **1993, Omnibus Budget Reconciliation Act of 1993 (P.L. 103-66)**

P.L. 103-66, §13163(b):

Amended Code Sec. 6421(e)(2)(B). **Effective** 1-1-94. Prior to amendment, Code Sec. 6421(e)(2)(B) read as follows:

(B) EXCEPTION FOR USE IN MOTORBOATS.—The term "off-highway business use" does not include any use in a motorboat. The preceding sentence shall not apply to use in a vessel employed in the fisheries or in the whaling business.

P.L. 103-66, §13242(d)(20):

Amended Code Sec. 6421(e)(1) by striking "section 4082(b)" and inserting "section 4083(a)". **Effective** 1-1-94.

• **1987, Revenue Act of 1987 (P.L. 100-203)**

P.L. 100-203, §10502(d)(9):

Repealed Code Sec. 6421(e)(2)(C). **Effective** for sales after 3-31-88. Prior to repeal, Code Sec. 6421(e)(2)(C) read as follows:

(C) COMMERCIAL FISHING VESSELS.—For provisions exempting from tax gasoline and special motor fuels used for commercial fishing vessels, see—

(i) subsections (a)(3) and (d)(3) of section 4221 (relating to certain tax-free sales),

(ii) section 6416(b)(2)(B) (relating to refund or credit in case of certain uses), and

(iii) section 4041(g)(1) (relating to exemptions from tax on special fuels).

• **1986, Tax Reform Act of 1986 (P.L. 99-514)**

P.L. 99-514, §1703(c)(1)(A), (B):

Amended Code Sec. 6421 by redesignating subsections (c), (d), (e), (f), (g), and (h) as subsections (d), (e), (f), (g), (h), and (i), respectively, and by inserting after subsection (b) new subsection (c). **Effective** for gasoline removed (as defined in section 4082 of the Internal Revenue Code of 1986) after 12-31-87.

• **1983, Surface Transportation Act of 1983 (P.L. 97-424)**

P.L. 97-424, §511(c)(3)(A):

Amended Code Sec. 6421(d)(2)(A) and (B) by striking out "qualified business use" and inserting "off-highway business use". **Effective** 4-1-83.

P.L. 97-424, §511(c)(3)(B):

Amended the heading of Code Sec. 6421(d)(2) by striking out "Qualified" and inserting "Off-Highway". **Effective** 4-1-83.

P.L. 97-424, §515(b)(7):

Amended Code Sec. 6421(d)(2)(C) by striking out ", special motor fuels, and lubricating oil" and inserting "and special motor fuels". **Effective** with respect to articles sold after 1-6-83.

• **1980, Technical Corrections Act of 1979 (P.L. 96-222)**

P.L. 96-222, §108(c)(1):

Amended Code Sec. 6421(d)(2)(B) by adding the last sentence. **Effective** for uses after 12-31-78.

• **1978, Energy Tax Act of 1978 (P.L. 95-618)**

P.L. 95-618, §233(a)(3)(A), (d):

Repealed Code Sec. 6421(d)(2), and redesignated subsection (d)(3), which was added by Act Sec. 222(a)(1)(B) as subsection (d)(2). **Effective** 12-1-78. Prior to amendment, Code Sec. 6421(d)(2) read as follows:

(2) COMMUTER FARE REVENUE.—The term "commuter fare revenue" means revenue attributable to fares derived from the transportation of persons and attributable to—

(A) amounts paid for transportation which do not exceed 60 cents,

(B) amounts paid for commutation or season tickets for single trips of less than 30 miles, or

(C) amounts paid for commutation tickets for one month or less.

P.L. 95-618, §222(a)(1)(B), (b):

Added Code Sec. 6421(d)(3). **Effective** for uses after 12-31-78. [Note: subsection (d)(3) was redesignated as (d)(2) by Act Sec. 233(a)(3)(A), above, **effective** 12-1-78.]

• **1962, Tax Rate Extension Act of 1962 (P.L. 87-508)**

P.L. 87-508, §5(c)(2):

Amended Code Sec. 6421(d)(2). **Effective** 9-16-62. Prior to amendment, Sec. 6421(d)(2) read as follows:

(2) Tax-exempt Passenger Fare Revenue.—The term 'tax-exempt passenger fare revenue' means revenue attributable to fares which were exempt from the tax imposed by section 4261 by reason of section 4263(a) (relating to the exemption for commutation travel, etc.).

• **1956 (P.L. 796, 84th Cong.)**

P.L. 796, 84th Cong., §2:

Amended Sec. 6421(d)(2) by striking out "4262(b)" and substituting "4263(a)". **Effective** with respect to transportation commencing on or after 10-1-56.

[Sec. 6421(f)]

(f) EXEMPT SALES; OTHER PAYMENTS OR REFUNDS AVAILABLE.—

(1) GASOLINE USED ON FARMS.—This section shall not apply in respect of gasoline which was (within the meaning of paragraphs (1), (2), and (3) of section 6420(c)) used on a farm for farming purposes.

(2) GASOLINE USED IN AVIATION.—This section shall not apply in respect of gasoline which is used as a fuel in an aircraft—

(A) in aviation which is not commercial aviation (as defined in section 4083(b)), or

(B) in commercial aviation (as so defined) with respect to the tax imposed by section 4081 at the Leaking Underground Storage Tank Trust Fund financing rate and, in the case of fuel purchased after September 30, 1995, at so much of the rate specified in section 4081(a)(2)(A) as does not exceed 4.3 cents per gallon.

(3) GASOLINE USED IN TRAINS.—In the case of gasoline used as a fuel in a train, this section shall not apply with respect to—

(A) the Leaking Underground Storage Tank Trust Fund financing rate under section 4081, and

(B) so much of the rate specified in section 4081(a)(2)(A) as does not exceed the rate applicable under section 4041(a)(1)(C)(ii).

Amendments

• **2005, Safe, Accountable, Flexible, Efficient Transportation Equity Act: A Legacy for Users (P.L. 109-59)**

P.L. 109-59, §11151(b)(3)(A)-(B):

Amended Code Sec. 6421(f)(2) by striking "noncommercial aviation (as defined in section 4041(c)(2))" in subparagraph (A) and inserting "aviation which is not commercial aviation (as defined in section 4083(b))", and by striking "aviation which is not noncommercial aviation" in subparagraph (B) and inserting "commercial aviation". **Effective** as if included in the provision of P.L. 108-357 to which it relates [effective for aviation-grade kerosene removed, entered, or sold after 12-31-2004.—CCH].

• **2004, American Jobs Creation Act of 2004 (P.L. 108-357)**

P.L. 108-357, §241(a)(2)(C):

Amended Code Sec. 6421(f)(3)(B). **Effective** on 1-1-2005. Prior to amendment, Code Sec. 6421(f)(3)(B) read as follows:

(B) so much of the rate specified in section 4081(a)(2)(A) as does not exceed—

(i) 6.8 cents per gallon after September 30, 1993, and before October 1, 1995,

(ii) 5.55 cents per gallon after September 30, 1995, and before November 1, 1998, and

(iii) 4.3 cents per gallon after October 31, 1998.

CREDITS AND REFUNDS—SPECIAL RULES

• **1998, Transportation Equity Act for the 21st Century (P.L. 105-178)**

P.L. 105-178, § 9006(b)(1)(A)-(B):

Amended Code Sec. 6421(f)(3)(B) by striking "October 1, 1999" in clause (ii) and inserting "November 1, 1998", and by striking "September 30, 1999" in clause (iii) and inserting "October 31, 1998". **Effective** 6-9-98.

• **1996, Small Business Job Protection Act of 1996 (P.L. 104-188)**

P.L. 104-188, § 1609(g)(4)(C):

Amended Code Sec. 6421(f)(2)(A) by striking "section 4041(c)(4)" and inserting "section 4041(c)(2)". **Effective** on the 7th calendar day after 8-20-96.

• **1993, Omnibus Budget Reconciliation Act of 1993 (P.L. 103-66)**

P.L. 103-66, § 13241(f)(6):

Amended Code Sec. 6421(f)(3) by inserting "and at the deficit reduction rate" after "financing rate", and by inserting "AND DEFICIT REDUCTION TAX" after "TAX" in the heading. **Effective** 10-1-93.

P.L. 103-66, § 13242(d)(23):

Amended Code Sec. 6421(f)(2)(B) by inserting before the period "and, in the case of fuel purchased after September 30, 1995, at so much of the rate specified in section 4081(a)(2)(A) as does not exceed 4.3 cents per gallon". **Effective** 1-1-94.

P.L. 103-66, § 13242(d)(24):

Amended Code Sec. 6421(f)(3), as amended by subpart A. **Effective** 1-1-94. Prior to amendment, Code Sec. 6421(f)(3) read as follows:

(3) LEAKING UNDERGROUND STORAGE TANK TRUST FUND TAX AND DEFICIT REDUCTION TAX ON GASOLINE USED IN TRAINS.—This section shall not apply with respect to the tax imposed by section 4081 at the Leaking Underground Storage Tank Trust Fund financing rate and at the deficit reduction rate on gasoline used as a fuel in a train.

• **1988, Technical and Miscellaneous Revenue Act of 1988 (P.L. 100-647)**

P.L. 100-647, § 2001(d)(3)(E):

Amended Code Sec. 6421(f) by striking out all that follows paragraph (1) and inserting in lieu thereof new paragraphs (2)-(3). **Effective** as if included in the provision of P.L. 99-499 to which it relates. Prior to amendment, the material that followed paragraph (1) read as follows:

(2) GASOLINE USED IN NONCOMMERCIAL AVIATION.—This section shall not apply in respect of gasoline which is used as a fuel in an aircraft in noncommercial aviation (as defined in section 4041(c)(4)).

(4)[3] SECTION NOT TO APPLY TO CERTAIN OFF-HIGHWAY BUSINESS USES WITH RESPECT TO THE TAX IMPOSED BY SECTION 4081 AT THE LEAKING UNDERGROUND STORAGE TANK TRUST FUND FINANCING RATE.—This section shall not apply with respect to the tax imposed by section 4081 at the Leaking Underground Storage Tank Trust Fund financing rate on gasoline used in any off-highway business use other than use in a vessel employed in the fisheries or in the whaling business.

[Sec. 6421(g)]

(g) APPLICABLE LAWS.—

(1) IN GENERAL.—All provisions of law, including penalties, applicable in respect of the tax imposed by section 4081 shall, insofar as applicable and not inconsistent with this section, apply in respect of the payments provided for in this section to the same extent as if such payments constituted refunds of overpayments of the tax so imposed.

(2) EXAMINATION OF BOOKS AND WITNESSES.—For the purpose of ascertaining the correctness of any claim made under this section, or the correctness of any payment made in respect of any such claim, the Secretary shall have the authority granted by paragraphs (1), (2), and (3) of section 7602(a) (relating to examination of books and witnesses) as if the claimant were the person liable for tax.

Amendments

• **1989, Omnibus Budget Reconciliation Act of 1989 (P.L. 101-239)**

P.L. 101-239, § 7841(d)(20):

Amended Code Sec. 6421(g)(2) by striking "section 7602" and inserting "section 7602(a)". **Effective** 12-19-89.

• **1986, Tax Reform Act of 1986 (P.L. 99-514)**

P.L. 99-514, § 1703(c)(1)(A), (B):

Amended Code Sec. 6421 by redesignating subsections (c), (d), (e), (f), (g), and (h) as subsections (d), (e), (f), (g), (h) and (i), respectively, and by inserting after subsection (b) new subsection (c). **Effective** for gasoline removed (as defined in section 4082 of the Internal Revenue Code of 1986) after 12-31-87.

• **1986, Tax Reform Act of 1986 (P.L. 99-514)**

P.L. 99-514, § 1703(c)(1)(A), (B):

Amended Code Sec. 6421 by redesignating subsections (c), (d), (e), (f), (g), and (h) as subsections (d), (e), (f), (g), (h), and (i), respectively, and by inserting after subsection (b) new subsection (c). **Effective** for gasoline removed (as defined in section 4082 of the Internal Revenue Code of 1986) after 12-31-87.

P.L. 99-514, § 1703(c)(2)(B):

Amended Code Sec. 6421(f), as redesignated by paragraph (1) of this subsection, by striking out paragraph (1) and redesignating paragraphs (2) and (3) as paragraphs (1) and (2), respectively. **Effective** for gasoline removed (as defined in section 4082 of the Internal Revenue Code of 1986) after 12-31-87. Prior to amendment, Sec. 6421(f)(1) read as follows:

(1) EXEMPT SALES.—No amount shall be payable under this section with respect to any gasoline which the Secretary determines was exempt from the tax imposed by section 4081. The amount which (but for this sentence) would be payable under this section with respect to any gasoline shall be reduced by any other amount which the Secretary determines is payable under this section or is refundable under any provision of this title, to any person with respect to such gasoline.

• **1986, Superfund Amendments and Reauthorization Act of 1986 (P.L. 99-499)**

P.L. 99-499, § 521(c)(2)(B):

Amended Code Sec. 6421(e), as in effect on the day before the date of enactment of the Tax Reform Act of 1986, by adding at the end thereof new paragraph (4). **Effective** 1-1-87.

• **1976, Tax Reform Act of 1976 (P.L. 94-455)**

P.L. 94-455, § 1906(a)(27)(A)(i):

Struck out "after June 30, 1970," following the words "gasoline which is used" in Code Sec. 6421(e)(3). **Effective** with respect to gasoline used as a fuel after 6-30-70.

P.L. 94-455, § 1906(b)(13)(A):

Amended the 1954 Code by substituting "Secretary" for "Secretary or his delegate" each place it appeared. **Effective** 2-1-77.

• **1970 (P.L. 91-258)**

P.L. 91-258, § 205(b)(1)(B):

Amended Code Sec. 6421(e). **Effective** for transportation beginning after 6-30-70, by adding paragraph (3).

• **1965, Excise Tax Reduction Act of 1965 (P.L. 89-44)**

P.L. 89-44, § 809(b)(3):

Substituted "payable" for "paid" in the first sentence of Code Sec. 6421(e)(1). **Effective** 7-1-65.

[Sec. 6421(h)]

(h) REGULATIONS.—The Secretary may by regulations prescribe the conditions, not inconsistent with the provisions of this section, under which payments may be made under this section.

Amendments

• **1986, Tax Reform Act of 1986 (P.L. 99-514)**

P.L. 99-514, § 1703(c)(1)(A), (B):

Amended Code Sec. 6421 by redesignating subsections (c), (d), (e), (f), (g), and (h) as subsections (d), (e), (f), (g), (h), and (i), respectively, and by inserting after subsection (b) new subsection (c). **Effective** for gasoline removed (as defined in section 4082 of the Internal Revenue Code of 1986) after 12-31-87.

• **1976, Tax Reform Act of 1976 (P.L. 94-455)**

P.L. 94-455, § 1906(b)(13)(A):

Amended 1954 Code by substituting "Secretary" for "Secretary or his delegate" each place it appeared. **Effective** 2-1-77.

[Sec. 6421(i)—Stricken]

Amendments

• **1993, Omnibus Budget Reconciliation Act of 1993 (P.L. 103-66)**

P.L. 103-66, § 13241(f)(7):

Amended Code Sec. 6421 by striking subsection (i). **Effective** 10-1-93. Prior to amendment, Code Sec. 6421(i) read as follows:

(i) EFFECTIVE DATE.—Except with respect to taxes imposed by section 4081 at the Leaking Underground Storage Tank Trust Fund financing rate, this section shall apply only with respect to gasoline purchased before October 1, 1999.

• **1991, Intermodal Surface Transportation Efficiency Act of 1991 (P.L. 102-240)**

P.L. 102-240, § 8002(b)(6):

Amended Code Sec. 6421(i) by striking "1995" each place it appears and inserting "1999". **Effective** 12-18-91.

CREDITS AND REFUNDS—SPECIAL RULES

• **1990, Omnibus Budget Reconciliation Act of 1990 (P.L. 101-508)**

P.L. 101-508, §11211(d)(6):

Amended Code Sec. 6421(i) by striking "1993" and inserting "1995". **Effective** 11-5-90.

• **1987, Surface Transportation and Uniform Relocation Assistance Act of 1987 (P.L. 100-17)**

P.L. 100-17, §502(b)(7):

Amended Code Sec. 6421(h) (as in effect before its redesignation by P.L. 99-514, §1703(c)) by striking out "1988" and inserting in lieu thereof "1993". **Effective** 4-2-87.

• **1986, Tax Reform Act of 1986 (P.L. 99-514)**

P.L. 99-514, §1703(c)(1)(A), (B):

Amended Code Sec. 6421 by redesignating subsections (c), (d), (e), (f), (g), and (h) as subsections (d), (e), (f), (g), (h), and (i), respectively, and by inserting after subsection (b) new subsection (c). **Effective** for gasoline removed (as defined in section 4082 of the Internal Revenue Code of 1986) after 12-31-87.

• **1986, Superfund Amendments and Reauthorization Act of 1986 (P.L. 99-499)**

P.L. 99-499, §521(c)(2)(A):

Amended Code Sec. 6421(h), as in effect on the day before the date of the enactment of the Tax Reform Act of 1986, by striking out "This section" and inserting in lieu thereof "Except with respect to taxes imposed by section 4081 at the Leaking Underground Storage Tank Trust Fund financing rate, this section". **Effective** 1-1-87.

• **1983, Surface Transportation Act of 1983 (P.L. 97-424)**

P.L. 97-424, §516(a)(6):

Amended Code Sec. 6421(h) by striking out "1984" and inserting "1988". **Effective** 1-6-83.

• **1978, Surface Transportation Assistance Act of 1978 (P.L. 95-599)**

P.L. 95-599, §502(a)(10):

Substituted "1984" for "1979" in Code Sec. 6421(h). **Effective** 11-7-78.

• **1976, Tax Reform Act of 1976 (P.L. 94-455)**

P.L. 94-455, §1906(a)(27)(C):

Deleted "after June 30, 1956, and" before "before October 1, 1979" in Code Sec. 6421(h). **Effective** 2-1-77.

• **1976 (P.L. 94-280)**

P.L. 94-280, §303(a)(11):

Amended Code Sec. 6421(h) by substituting "1979" for "1977".

• **1970, Federal-Aid Highway Act of 1970 (P.L. 91-605)**

P.L. 91-605, §303(a)(11):

Amended Code Sec. 6421(h) by substituting "1977" for "1972."

• **1961, Federal-Aid Highway Act of 1961 (P.L. 87-61)**

P.L. 87-61, §201(e):

Amended Sec. 6421(h) by substituting "October" for "July". **Effective** 7-1-61.

[Sec. 6421(i)]

(i) INCOME TAX CREDIT IN LIEU OF PAYMENT.—

(1) PERSONS NOT SUBJECT TO INCOME TAX.—Payment shall be made under subsections (a) and (b) only to—

(A) the United States or an agency or instrumentality thereof, a State, a political subdivision of a State, or an agency or instrumentality of one or more States or political subdivisions, or

(B) an organization exempt from tax under section 501(a) (other than an organization required to make a return of the tax imposed under subtitle A for its taxable year).

(2) EXCEPTION.—Paragraph (1) shall not apply to a payment of a claim filed under subsection (d)(2).

(3) ALLOWANCE OF CREDIT AGAINST INCOME TAX.—For allowance of credit against the tax imposed by subtitle A, see section 34.

Amendments

• **1998, IRS Restructuring and Reform Act of 1998 (P.L. 105-206)**

P.L. 105-206, §6023(24)(A):

Amended Code Sec. 6421 by redesignating subsections (j) and (k) as subsections (i) and (j), respectively. **Effective** 7-22-98.

• **1988, Technical and Miscellaneous Revenue Act of 1988 (P.L. 100-647)**

P.L. 100-647, §1017(c)(6):

Amended Code Sec. 6421 by redesignating subsection (i) as subsection (j). **Effective** as if included in the provision of P.L. 99-514 to which it relates.

P.L. 100-647, §1017(c)(8):

Amended Code Sec. 6421(j)(2) (as redesignated) by striking out "subsection (c)(2)" and inserting in lieu thereof "subsection (d)(2)". **Effective** as if included in the provision of P.L. 99-514 to which it relates.

• **1984, Deficit Reduction Act of 1984 (P.L. 98-369)**

P.L. 98-369, §474(r)(38):

Amended Code Sec. 6421(i)(3) by striking out "section 39" and inserting in lieu thereof "section 34". **Effective** for tax years beginning after 12-31-83, and to carrybacks from such years.

• **1976, Tax Reform Act of 1976 (P.L. 94-455)**

P.L. 94-455, §1906(a)(27)(D)(i):

Deleted "with respect to gasoline used after June 30, 1965," before "only to" in Code Sec. 6421(i)(1). **Effective** 2-1-77.

P.L. 94-455, §1906(a)(27)(D)(ii):

Substituted "subsection (c)(2)" for "subsection (c)(3)(B)" in Code Sec. 6421(i)(2). **Effective** 2-1-77.

P.L. 94-455, §1906(a)(27)(D)(iii):

Deleted "for gasoline used after June 30, 1965" before "see section 39" in Code Sec. 6421(i)(3). **Effective** 2-1-77.

[Sec. 6421(j)]

(j) CROSS REFERENCES.—

(1) For civil penalty for excessive claims under this section, see section 6675.

(2) For fraud penalties, etc., see chapter 75 (section 7201 and following, relating to crimes, other offenses, and forfeitures).

(3) For treatment of an Indian tribal government as a State (and a subdivision of an Indian tribal government as a political subdivision of a State), see section 7871.

Amendments

• **2018, Tax Technical Corrections Act of 2018 (P.L. 115-141)**

P.L. 115-141, §401(a)(291), Div. U:

Amended Code Sec. 6421(j)(3) by striking "State and" and inserting "State (and". **Effective** 3-23-2018.

• **1998, IRS Restructuring and Reform Act of 1998 (P.L. 105-206)**

P.L. 105-206, §6023(24)(A):

Amended Code Sec. 6421 by redesignating subsection (k) as subsection (j). **Effective** 7-22-98.

• **1988, Technical and Miscellaneous Revenue Act of 1988 (P.L. 100-647)**

P.L. 100-647, §1017(c)(6):

Amended Code Sec. 6421 by redesignating subsection (j) as subsection (k). **Effective** as if included in the provision of P.L. 99-514 to which it relates.

• **1987, Revenue Act of 1987 (P.L. 100-203)**

P.L. 100-203, §10502(d)(10):

Amended Code Sec. 6421(j) by striking out paragraph (1) and by redesignating paragraphs (2), (3), and (4), as paragraphs (1), (2), and (3), respectively. **Effective** for sales after 3-31-88. Prior to amendment, paragraph (1) read as follows:

(1) For rate of tax in case of special fuels used in noncommercial aviation or for nonhighway purposes, see section 4041.

• **1983 (P.L. 97-473)**

P.L. 97-473, §202(b)(12):

Added Code Sec. 6421(j)(4). For the **effective** date, see the amendment note for P.L. 97-473, Act Sec. 204, following Code Sec. 7871.

• **1970 (P.L. 91-258)**

P.L. 91-258, §205(c)(8):

Amended Code Sec. 6421(j). **Effective** 7-1-70. Prior to amendment, this section read as follows:

(j) Cross References.—

(1) For reduced rate of tax in case of diesel fuel and special motor fuels used for certain nonhighway purposes, see subsections (a) and (b) of section 4041.

(2) For partial refund of tax in case of diesel fuel and special motor fuels used for certain nonhighway purposes, see section 6416(b)(2)(I) and (J).

(3) For partial refund of tax in case of diesel fuel and special motor fuels used by local transit systems, see section 6416(b)(2)(H).

(4) For civil penalty for excessive claims under this section, see section 6675.

(5) For fraud penalties, etc., see chapter 75 (section 7201 and following, relating to crimes, other offenses, and forfeitures).

CREDITS AND REFUNDS—SPECIAL RULES

- **1965, Excise Tax Reduction Act of 1965 (P.L. 89-44)**

P.L. 89-44, § 809(b)(1):

Redesignated subsection (i) as (j). **Effective** 7-1-65.

- **1958, Excise Tax Technical Changes Act of 1958 (P.L. 85-859)**

P.L. 85-859, § 163(d)(3):

Amended Sec. 6421(i) by striking out in paragraph (2) "section 6416(b)(2)(J) and (K)" and substituting "section 6416(b)(2)(I) and (J)"; by striking out, in paragraph (3), "section 6416(b)(2)(L)" and substituting "section 6416(b)(2)(H)".

- **1956 (P.L. 627, 84th Cong.)**

P.L. 627, 84th Cong., 2nd Sess., § 208(c):

Added Code Sec. 6421. **Effective** 7-1-56.

[Sec. 6422]

SEC. 6422. CROSS REFERENCES.

(1) For limitations on credits and refunds, see subchapter B of chapter 66.

(2) For overpayment in case of adjustments to accrued foreign taxes, see section 905(c).

(3) For credit or refund in case of deficiency dividends paid by a personal holding company, see section 547.

(4) For refund, credit, or abatement of amounts disallowed by courts upon review of Tax Court decision, see section 7486.

(5) For refund or redemption of stamps, see chapter 69.

(6) For abatement, credit, or refund in case of jeopardy assessments, see chapter 70.

(7) For restrictions on transfers and assignments of claims against the United States, see section 3727 of title 31, United States Code.

(8) For set-off of claims against amounts due the United States, see section 3728 of title 31, United States Code.

(9) For special provisions relating to alcohol and tobacco taxes, see subtitle E.

(10) For credit or refund in case of deficiency dividends paid by a regulated investment company or real estate investment trust, see section 860.

Amendments

- **2018, Tax Technical Corrections Act of 2018 (P.L. 115-141)**

P.L. 115-141, § 401(a)(292)(A)-(C), Div. U:

Amended Code Sec. 6422 by striking paragraph (7), by redesignating paragraphs (8) through (12) as paragraphs (7) through (11), respectively, and by striking "for credit" in paragraph (10) as so redesignated and inserting "For credit". [Note: Code Sec. 6422(12) was stricken by P.L. 114-74, § 1101(f)(2). Therefore, it cannot be redesignated as Code Sec. 6422(11).—CCH] **Effective** 3-23-2018. Prior to being stricken, Code Sec 6422(7) read as follows:

(7) For treatment of certain overpayments as having been refunded, in connection with sale of surplus war-built vessels, see section 9(b)(8) of the Merchant Ship Sales Act of 1946 (50 U.S.C. App. 1742).

- **2015, Bipartisan Budget Act of 2015 (P.L. 114-74)**

P.L. 114-74, § 1101(f)(2):

Amended Code Sec. 6422 by striking paragraph (12). **Effective** generally for returns filed for partnership tax years beginning after 12-31-2017. For a special rule, see Act Sec. 1101(g)(4), below. Prior to being stricken, Code Sec. 6422(12) read as follows:

(12) For special rules in the case of a credit or refund attributable to partnership items, see section 6227 and subsections (c) and (d) of section 6230.

P.L. 114-74, § 1101(g)(4), provides:

(4) ELECTION.—A partnership may elect (at such time and in such form and manner as the Secretary of the Treasury may prescribe) for the amendments made by this section (other than the election under section 6221(b) of such Code (as added by this Act)) to apply to any return of the partnership filed for partnership taxable years beginning after the date of the enactment of this Act and before January 1, 2018.

- **1997, Taxpayer Relief Act of 1997 (P.L. 105-34)**

P.L. 105-34, § 1131(c)[(d)](3):

Amended Code Sec. 6422 by striking paragraph (5) and by redesignating paragraphs (6) through (13) as paragraphs (5) through (12), respectively. **Effective** 8-5-97. Prior to being stricken, Code Sec. 6422(5) read as follows:

(5) For abatement or refund of tax on transfers to avoid income tax, see section 1494(b).

- **1990, Omnibus Budget Reconciliation Act of 1990 (P.L. 101-508)**

P.L. 101-508, § 11801(c)(17)(A):

Amended Code Sec. 6422 by striking paragraph (6) and by redesignating paragraphs (7) through (15)[(14)] as paragraphs (6) through (13). **Effective** 11-5-90. Prior to repeal, Code Sec. 6422(6) read as follows:

(6) For overpayment in certain renegotiation of war contracts, see section 1481.

P.L. 101-508, § 11821(b), provides:

(b) SAVINGS PROVISION.—If—

(1) any provision amended or repealed by this part applied to—

(A) any transaction occurring before the date of the enactment of this Act,

(B) any property acquired before such date of enactment, or

(C) any item of income, loss, deduction, or credit taken into account before such date of enactment, and

(2) the treatment of such transaction, property, or item under such provision would (without regard to the amendments made by this part) affect liability for tax for periods ending after such date of enactment,

nothing in the amendments made by this part shall be construed to affect the treatment of such transaction, property, or item for purposes of determining liability for tax for periods ending after such date of enactment.

- **1982 (P.L. 97-258)**

P.L. 97-258, § 3(f)(8):

Amended Code Sec. 6422(10) by striking out "R.S. 3477 (31 U.S.C. 203)" and substituting "section 3727 of title 31, United States Code". **Effective** 9-13-82.

P.L. 97-258, § 3(f)(9):

Amended Code Sec. 6422(11) by striking out "the Act of March 3, 1875, as amended by section 13 of the Act of March 3, 1933 (31 U.S.C. 227)" and substituting "section 3728 of title 31, United States Code". **Effective** 9-13-82.

- **1982, Tax Equity and Fiscal Responsibility Act of 1982 (P.L. 97-248)**

P.L. 97-248, § 402(c)(4):

Added Code Sec. 6422(15)[(14)]. **Effective** 9-4-82.

- **1978, Revenue Act of 1978 (P.L. 95-600)**

P.L. 95-600, § 362(d)(4)(A), (B), (e):

Amended Code Sec. 6422(14) by inserting "regulated investment company or" before "real estate investment trust", and by striking out "859" and inserting in place thereof "860". **Effective** for determinations (as defined in Code Sec. 860(d)) after 11-6-78.

- **1976, Tax Reform Act of 1976 (P.L. 94-455)**

P.L. 94-455, § 1601(f)(1):

Added Code Sec. 6422(14). **Effective** as indicated in Act Sec. 1608(a), quoted below.

P.L. 94-455, § 1608(a), provides:

(a) DEFICIENCY DIVIDEND PROCEDURES.—The amendments made by section 1601 shall apply with respect to determinations (as defined in section 859(c) of the Internal Revenue Code of 1954) occurring after the date of the enactment of this Act [October 4, 1976]. If the amendments made by section 1601 apply to a taxable year ending on or before the date of enactment of this Act:

(1) the reference to section 857(b)(3)(A)(ii) in sections 857(b)(3)(C) and 859(b)(1)(B) of such Code, as amended, shall be considered to be a reference to section 857(b)(3)(A) of such Code, as in effect immediately before the enactment of this Act [October 4, 1976], and

(2) the reference to section 857(b)(2)(B) in section 859(a) of such Code, as amended, shall be considered to be a reference to section 857(b)(2)(C) of such Code, as in effect immediately before the enactment of this Act [October 4, 1976].

P.L. 94-455, § 1901(b)(36)(B):

Deleted paragraph (2) and redesignated paragraphs (3) through (13) as paragraphs (2) through (12) in Code Sec. 6422. **Effective** with respect to tax years beginning after 12-31-76. Prior to its deletion, Code Sec. 6422(2) read as follows:

(2) For overpayment arising out of adjustments incident to involuntary liquidation of inventory, see section 1321.

P.L. 94-455, § 1906(a)(28):

Deleted "60 Stat. 48;" as appearing before "50 U.S.C. App. 1742" in redesignated Code Sec. 6422(9), and deleted "47 Stat. 1516;" as appearing before "31 U.S.C. 227" in redesignated Code Sec. 6422(11). **Effective** 2-1-77.

- **1963 (P.L. 88-36)**

P.L. 88-36, § 201(c):

Amended Code Sec. 6422 by striking out paragraph (7) and by renumbering paragraphs (8), (9), (10), (11), (12), (13), and (14), as paragraphs (7), (8), (9), (10), (11), (12), and (13). **Effective** with respect to transfers after 6-4-63. Prior to amendment, old paragraph (7) read as follows:

(7) For abatement or refund in case of tax on silver bullion, see section 4894.

- **1958, Excise Tax Technical Changes Act of 1958 (P.L. 85-859)**

P.L. 85-859, § 204(4):

Amended paragraph (14) of Sec. 6422. **Effective** 9-3-58. Prior to amendment, paragraph (14) read as follows:

"For special provisions relating to alcohol and tobacco taxes, see sections 5011, 5044, 5057, 5063, 5705, and 5707."

CREDITS AND REFUNDS—SPECIAL RULES

• **1956 (P.L. 627, 84th Cong.)**

P.L. 627, 84th Cong., 2d. Sess., § 208(c):

Amended subchapter B of chapter 65 of the 1954 Code by renumbering section 6421 as 6422. **Effective** 7-1-56.

• **1956 (P.L. 466, 84th Cong.)**

P.L. 466, 84th Cong., 2d. Sess., §§ 1 and 4(c):

Renumbered Section 6420 as Section 6421. Also, amended table of contents for subchapter B to reflect new section 6420.

[Sec. 6423]

SEC. 6423. CONDITIONS TO ALLOWANCE IN THE CASE OF ALCOHOL AND TOBACCO TAXES.

[Sec. 6423(a)]

(a) CONDITIONS.—No credit or refund shall be allowed or made, in pursuance of a court decision or otherwise, of any amount paid or collected as an alcohol or tobacco tax unless the claimant establishes (under regulations prescribed by the Secretary)—

(1) that he bore the ultimate burden of the amount claimed; or

(2) that he has unconditionally repaid the amount claimed to the person who bore the ultimate burden of such amount; or

(3) that (A) the owner of the commodity furnished him the amount claimed for payment of the tax, (B) he has filed with the Secretary the written consent of such owner to the allowance to the claimant of the credit or refund, and (C) such owner satisfies the requirements of paragraph (1) or (2).

Amendments

• **1976, Tax Reform Act of 1976 (P.L. 94-455)**

P.L. 94-455, § 1906(b)(13)(A):

Amended 1954 Code by substituting "Secretary" for "Secretary or his delegate" each place it appeared. **Effective** 2-1-77.

[Sec. 6423(b)]

(b) FILING OF CLAIMS.—No credit or refund of any amount to which subsection (a) applies shall be allowed or made unless a claim therefor has been filed by the person who paid the amount claimed, and unless such claim is filed within the time prescribed by law and in accordance with regulations prescribed by the Secretary. All evidence relied upon in support of such claim shall be clearly set forth and submitted with the claim.

Amendments

• **1976, Tax Reform Act of 1976 (P.L. 94-455)**

P.L. 94-455, § 1906(a)(29)(A):

Amended Code Sec. 6423(b). **Effective** 2-1-77. Prior to amendment Code Sec. 6423(b) read as follows:

(b) FILING OF CLAIMS.—No credit or refund of any amount to which subsection (a) applies shall be allowed or made unless a claim therefor has been filed by the person who paid the amount claimed, and except as hereinafter provided in this subsection, unless such claim is filed after April 30, 1958, and within the time prescribed by law, and in accordance with regulations prescribed by the Secretary or his delegate. All evidence relied upon in support of such claim shall be clearly set forth and submitted with the claim. Any claimant who has on or before April 30, 1958, filed a claim for any amount to which subsection (a) applies may, if such claim was not barred from allowance on April 30, 1958, file a superseding claim after April 30, 1958, and on or before April 30, 1959, conforming to the requirements of this section and covering the amount (or any part thereof) claimed in such prior claim. No claim filed before May 1, 1958, for the credit or refund of any amount to which subsection (a) applies shall be held to constitute a claim for refund or credit within the meaning of, or for purposes of, section 7422(a); except that any claimant who instituted a suit before June 15, 1957, for recovery of any amount to which subsection (a) applies shall not be barred by this subsection from the maintenance of such suit as to any amount claimed in such suit on such date if in such suit he establishes the conditions to allowance required under subsection (a) with respect to such amount.

[Sec. 6423(c)]

(c) APPLICATION OF SECTION.—This section shall apply only if the credit or refund is claimed on the grounds that an amount of alcohol or tobacco tax was assessed or collected erroneously, illegally, without authority, or in any manner wrongfully, or on the grounds that such amount was excessive. This section shall not apply to—

(1) any claim for drawback, and

(2) any claim made in accordance with any law expressly providing for credit or refund where a commodity is withdrawn from the market, returned to bond, or lost or destroyed.

Amendments

• **1976, Tax Reform Act of 1976 (P.L. 94-455)**

P.L. 94-455, § 1906(a)(29)(B):

Deleted subsection (c) and redesignated former subsection (d) as Code Sec. 6423(c). **Effective** 2-1-77. Prior to its deletion, Code Sec. 6423(c) read as follows:

(c) PERIOD NOT EXTENDED.—Any suit or proceeding, with respect to any amount to which subsection (a) applies, which is barred on April 30, 1958, shall remain barred.

No claim for credit or refund of any such amount which is barred from allowance on April 30, 1958, shall be allowed after such date in any amount.

P.L. 94-455, § 1906(a)(29)(C):

Deleted paragraph (3) of redesignated Code Sec. 6423(c). **Effective** 2-1-77. Prior to its deletion, redesignated Code Sec. 6423(c)(3) read as follows:

(3) any amount claimed with respect to a commodity which has been lost, where a suit or proceeding was instituted before June 5, 1957.

[Sec. 6423(d)]

(d) MEANING OF TERMS.—For purposes of this section—

(1) ALCOHOL OR TOBACCO TAX.—The term "alcohol or tobacco tax" means—

(A) any tax imposed by chapter 51 (other than part II of subchapter A, relating to occupational taxes) or by chapter 52 or by any corresponding provision of prior internal revenue laws, and

(B) in the case of any commodity of a kind subject to a tax described in subparagraph (A), any tax equal to any such tax, any additional tax, or any floor stocks tax.

(2) TAX.—The term "tax" includes a tax and an exaction denominated a "tax", and any penalty, addition to tax, additional amount, or interest applicable to any such tax.

(3) ULTIMATE BURDEN.—The claimant shall be treated as having borne the ultimate burden of an amount of an alcohol or tobacco tax for purposes of subsection (a)(1), and the owner referred to in subsection (a)(3) shall be treated as having borne such burden for purposes of such subsection, only if—

(A) he has not, directly or indirectly, been relieved of such burden or shifted such burden to any other person,

(B) no understanding or agreement exists for any such relief or shifting, and

(C) if he has neither sold nor contracted to sell the commodities involved in such claim, he agrees that there will be no such relief or shifting, and furnishes such bond as the Secretary may require to insure faithful compliance with his agreement.

Amendments

• **1976, Tax Reform Act of 1976 (P.L. 94-455)**

P.L. 94-455, § 1906(a)(29)(B):

Redesignated former subsection (e) as Code Sec. 6423(d). **Effective** 2-1-77.

P.L. 94-455, § 1906(b)(13)(A):

Amended the 1954 Code by substituting "Secretary" for "Secretary or his delegate" each place it appeared. **Effective** 2-1-77.

• **1958 (P.L. 85-323)**

P.L. 85-323, § 1:

Added Code Sec. 6423. **Effective** for credits or refunds allowed or made on or after 5-1-58.

CREDITS AND REFUNDS—SPECIAL RULES

[Sec. 6424—Repealed]

Amendments

• **1983, Surface Transportation Act of 1983 (P.L. 97-424)**

P.L. 97-424, § 515(b)(5):

Repealed Code Sec. 6424. **Effective** with respect to articles sold after 1-6-83. Prior to its repeal, Code Sec. 6424 read as follows:

SEC. 6424. LUBRICATING OIL USED FOR CERTAIN NONTAXABLE PURPOSES.

[Sec. 6424(a)]

(a) PAYMENTS.—Except as provided in subsection (f), if lubricating oil (other than cutting oils, as defined in section 4092(b), and other than oil which has previously been used) is used—

(1) in a qualified business use (as defined in section 6421(d)(2)), or

(2) in a qualified bus (as defined in section 4221(d)(7)),

the Secretary shall pay (without interest) to the ultimate purchaser of such lubricating oil an amount equal to 6 cents for each gallon of lubricating oil so used.

Amendments

• **1978, Energy Tax Act of 1978 (P.L. 95-618)**

P.L. 95-618, § 233(b)(1):

Amended Code Sec. 6424(a). **Effective** 12-1-78. Prior to amendment, Code Sec. 6424(a) read as follows:

(a) PAYMENTS.—Except as provided in subsection (g), if lubricating oil (other than cutting oils, as defined in section 4092(b), and other than oil which has previously been used) is used otherwise than in a highway motor vehicle, the Secretary shall pay (without interest) to the ultimate purchaser of such lubricating oil an amount equal to 6 cents for each gallon of lubricating oil so used.

P.L. 95-618, § 233(b)(2):

Amended the heading for Code Sec. 6424. **Effective** 12-1-78. Prior to amendment, the section heading read as follows:

Sec. 6424. LUBRICATING OIL NOT USED IN HIGHWAY MOTOR VEHICLES.

• **1976, Tax Reform Act of 1976 (P.L. 94-455)**

P.L. 94-455, § 1906(b)(13)(A):

Amended 1954 Code by substituting "Secretary" for "Secretary or his delegate" each place it appeared. **Effective** 2-1-77.

[Sec. 6424(b)]

(b) TIME FOR FILING CLAIMS; PERIODS COVERED.—

(1) GENERAL RULE.—Except as provided in paragraph (2), not more than one claim may be filed under subsection (a) by any person with respect to lubricating oil used during his taxable year. No claim shall be allowed under this paragraph with respect to lubricating oil used during any taxable year unless filed by such person not later than the time prescribed by law for filing a claim for credit or refund of overpayment of income tax for such taxable year. For purposes of this subsection, a person's taxable year shall be his taxable year for purposes of subtitle A.

(2) EXCEPTION.—If $1,000 or more is payable under this section to any person with respect to lubricating oil used during any of the first three quarters of his taxable year, a claim may be filed under this section by such person with respect to lubricating oil used during such quarter. No claim filed under this paragraph shall be allowed unless filed on or before the last day of the first quarter following the quarter for which the claim is filed.

Amendments

• **1976, Tax Reform Act of 1976 (P.L. 94-455)**

P.L. 94-455, § 1906(a)(30)(A):

Deleted ", except that a person's first taxable year beginning after December 31, 1965, shall include the period after December 31, 1965, and before the beginning of such first taxable year" from the end of the last sentence of Code Sec. 6424(b)(1). **Effective** 2-1-77.

• **1970 (P.L. 91-258)**

P.L. 91-258, § 207(b):

Substituted "a claim for credit or refund of overpayment of income tax" for "an income tax return" in Code Sec. 6424(b)(1). **Effective** 7-1-70.

[Sec. 6424(c)]

(c) EXEMPT SALES.—No amount shall be payable under this section with respect to any lubricating oil which the Secretary determines was exempt from the tax imposed by section 4091. The amount which (but for this sentence) would be payable under this section with respect to any lubricating oil shall be reduced by any other amount which the Secretary determines is payable under this section, or is refundable under any provision of this title, to any person with respect to such lubricating oil.

Amendments

• **1976, Tax Reform Act of 1976 (P.L. 94-455)**

P.L. 94-455, § 1906(b)(13)(A):

Amended 1954 Code by substituting "Secretary" for "Secretary or his delegate" each place it appeared. **Effective** 2-1-77.

[Sec. 6424(d)]

(d) APPLICABLE LAWS.—

(1) IN GENERAL.—All provisions of law, including penalties, applicable in respect of the tax imposed by section 4091 shall, insofar as applicable and not inconsistent with this section, apply in respect of the payments provided for in this section to the same extent as if such payments constituted refunds of overpayments of the tax so imposed.

(2) EXAMINATION OF BOOKS AND WITNESSES.—For the purpose of ascertaining the correctness of any claim made under this section, or the correctness of any payment made in respect of any claim, the Secretary shall have the authority granted by paragraphs (1), (2), and (3) of section 7602 (relating to examination of books and witnesses) as if the claimant were the person liable for tax.

Amendments

• **1976, Tax Reform Act of 1976 (P.L. 94-455)**

P.L. 94-455, § 1906(b)(13)(A):

Amended 1954 Code by substituting "Secretary" for "Secretary or his delegate" each place it appeared. **Effective** 2-1-77.

[Sec. 6424(e)]

(e) REGULATIONS.—The Secretary may by regulations prescribe the conditions, not inconsistent with the provisions of this section, under which payments may be made under this section.

Amendments

• **1976, Tax Reform Act of 1976 (P.L. 94-455)**

P.L. 94-455, § 1906(b)(13)(A):

Amended 1954 Code by substituting "Secretary" for "Secretary or his delegate" each place it appeared. **Effective** 2-1-77.

[Sec. 6424(f)]

(f) INCOME TAX CREDIT IN LIEU OF PAYMENT.—

(1) PERSONS NOT SUBJECT TO INCOME TAX.—Payment shall be made under subsection (a) only to—

(A) the United States or an agency or instrumentality thereof, a State, a political subdivision of a State, or an agency or instrumentality of one or more States or political subdivisions, or

(B) an organization exempt from tax under section 501(a) (other than an organization required to make a return of the tax imposed under subtitle A for its taxable year).

(2) EXCEPTION.—Paragraph (1) shall not apply to a payment of a claim filed under subsection (b)(2).

(3) ALLOWANCE OF CREDIT AGAINST INCOME TAX.—

For allowance of credit against the tax imposed by subtitle A for lubricating oil used, see section 39.

Amendments

• **1976, Tax Reform Act of 1976 (P.L. 94-455)**

P.L. 94-455, § 1906(a)(30)(B):

Deleted former subsection (f) and redesignated subsection (g) as Code Sec. 6424(f). **Effective** 2-1-77. Prior to deletion, Code Sec. 6424(f) read as follows:

(f) EFFECTIVE DATE.—This section shall apply only with respect to lubricating oil placed in use after December 31, 1965.

[Sec. 6424(g)]

(g) CROSS REFERENCES.—

(1) For civil penalty for excessive claims under this section, see section 6675.

(2) For fraud penalties, etc., see chapter 75 (section 7201 and following, relating to crimes, other offenses, and forfeitures).

(3) For treatment of an Indian tribal government as a State (and a subdivision of an Indian tribal government as a political subdivision of a State), see section 7871.

Amendments

• **1983 (P.L. 97-473)**

P.L. 97-473, § 202(b)(13):

Added Code Sec. 6424(g)(3). For the **effective** date, see the amendment note for Act Sec. 204 following Code Sec. 7871.

• **1976, Tax Reform Act of 1976 (P.L. 94-455)**

P.L. 94-455, § 1906(a)(30)(B):

Redesignated former subsection (h) as Code Sec. 6424(g). **Effective** 2-1-77.

• **1965, Excise Tax Reduction Act of 1965 (P.L. 89-44)**

P.L. 89-44, § 202(b):

Added Code Sec. 6424. **Effective** 1-1-66.

CREDITS AND REFUNDS—SPECIAL RULES

[Sec. 6425]
SEC. 6425. ADJUSTMENT OF OVERPAYMENT OF ESTIMATED INCOME TAX BY CORPORATION.

[Sec. 6425(a)]

(a) APPLICATION FOR ADJUSTMENT.—

(1) TIME FOR FILING.—A corporation may, after the close of the taxable year and on or before the 15th day of the fourth month thereafter, and before the day on which it files a return for such taxable year, file an application for an adjustment of an overpayment by it of estimated income tax for such taxable year. An application under this subsection shall not constitute a claim for credit or refund.

(2) FORM OF APPLICATION, ETC.—An application under this subsection shall be verified in the manner prescribed by section 6065 in the case of a return of the taxpayer, and shall be filed in the manner and form required by regulations prescribed by the Secretary. The application shall set forth—

(A) the estimated income tax paid by the corporation during the taxable year,

(B) the amount which, at the time of filing the application, the corporation estimates as its income tax liability for the taxable year,

(C) the amount of the adjustment, and

(D) such other information for purposes of carrying out the provisions of this section as may be required by such regulations.

Amendments

• **2015, Surface Transportation and Veterans Health Care Choice Improvement Act of 2015 (P.L. 114-41)**

P.L. 114-41, §2006(a)(2)(E):

Amended Code Sec. 6425(a)(1) by striking "third month" and inserting "fourth month". **Effective** generally for returns for tax years beginning after 12-31-2015. For an exception, see Act Sec. 2006(a)(3)(B), below.

P.L. 114-41, §2006(a)(3)(B), provides:

(B) SPECIAL RULE FOR C CORPORATIONS WITH FISCAL YEARS ENDING ON JUNE 30.—In the case of any C corporation with a taxable year ending on June 30, the amendments made by this subsection shall apply to returns for taxable years beginning after December 31, 2025.

• **1976, Tax Reform Act of 1976 (P.L. 94-455)**

P.L. 94-455, §1906(b)(13)(A):

Amended 1954 Code by substituting "Secretary" for "Secretary or his delegate" each place it appeared. **Effective** 2-1-77.

[Sec. 6425(b)]

(b) ALLOWANCE OF ADJUSTMENT.—

(1) LIMITED EXAMINATION OF APPLICATION.—Within a period of 45 days from the date on which an application for an adjustment is filed under subsection (a), the Secretary shall make, to the extent he deems practicable in such period, a limited examination of the application to discover omissions and errors therein, and shall determine the amount of the adjustment upon the basis of the application and the examination; except that the Secretary may disallow, without further action, any application which he finds contains material omissions or errors which he deems cannot be corrected within such 45 days.

(2) ADJUSTMENT CREDITED OR REFUNDED.—The Secretary, within the 45-day period referred to in paragraph (1), may credit the amount of the adjustment against any liability in respect of an internal revenue tax on the part of the corporation and shall refund the remainder to the corporation.

(3) LIMITATION.—No application under this section shall be allowed unless the amount of the adjustment equals or exceeds (A) 10 percent of the amount estimated by the corporation on its application as its income tax liability for the taxable year, and (B) $500.

(4) EFFECT OF ADJUSTMENT.—For purposes of this title (other than section 6655), any adjustment under this section shall be treated as a reduction, in the estimated income tax paid, made on the day the credit is allowed or the refund is paid.

Amendments

• **1976, Tax Reform Act of 1976 (P.L. 94-455)**

P.L. 94-455, §1906(b)(13)(A):

Amended 1954 Code by substituting "Secretary" for "Secretary or his delegate" each place it appeared. **Effective** 2-1-77.

[Sec. 6425(c)]

(c) DEFINITIONS.—For purposes of this section and section 6655[h] (relating to excessive adjustment)—

(1) The term "income tax liability" means the excess of—

(A) the sum of—

(i) the tax imposed by section 11 or subchapter L of chapter 1, whichever is applicable, plus

(ii) the tax imposed by section 55, plus

(iii) the tax imposed by section 59A, over

(B) the credits against tax provided by part IV of subchapter A of chapter 1.

(2) The amount of an adjustment under this section is equal to the excess of—

(A) the estimated income tax paid by the corporation during the taxable year, over

(B) the amount which, at the time of filing the application, the corporation estimates as its income tax liability for the taxable year.

Amendments

• **2022, Inflation Reduction Act of 2022 (P.L. 117-169)**

P.L. 117-169, §10101(a)(4)(F):

Amended Code Sec. 6425(c)(1)(A). **Effective** for tax years beginning after 12-31-2022. Prior to amendment, Code Sec. 6425(c)(1)(A) read as follows:

(A) the sum of—

(i) the tax imposed by section 11, or subchapter L of chapter 1, whichever is applicable, plus

(ii) the tax imposed by section 59A, over

• **2018, Tax Technical Corrections Act of 2018 (P.L. 115-141)**

P.L. 115-141, §401(a)(293), Div. U:

Amended Code Sec. 6425(c)(1)(A) by striking "The sum" and inserting "the sum". **Effective** 3-23-2018.

• **2017, Tax Cuts and Jobs Act (P.L. 115-97)**

P.L. 115-97, §12001(b)(17):

Amended Code Sec. 6425(c)(1)(A). **Effective** for tax years beginning after 12-31-2017. Prior to amendment, Code Sec. 6425(c)(1)(A) read as follows:

(A) The sum of—

(i) the tax imposed by section 11 or 1201(a), or subchapter L of chapter 1, whichever is applicable, plus

(ii) the tax imposed by section 55, over

P.L. 115-97, §13001(b)(2)(P):

Amended Code Sec. 6425(c)(1)(A), as amended by Act Sec. 12001, by striking "or 1201(a)," following "section 11". **Effective** for tax years beginning after 12-31-2017.

P.L. 115-97, §14401(d)(3):

Amended Code Sec. 6425(c)(1)(A), as amended by Act. Sec. 13001. **Effective** for base erosion payments paid or accrued in tax years beginning after 12-31-2017. Prior to amendment, Code Sec. 6425(c)(1)(A) read as follows:

(A) the tax imposed by section 11 or subchapter L of chapter 1, whichever is applicable, over

• **2014, Tax Technical Corrections Act of 2014 (P.L. 113-295)**

P.L. 113-295, §221(a)(12)(J), Division A:

Amended Code Sec. 6425(c)(1)(A) by inserting "plus" at end of clause (i), by striking "plus" and inserting "over" at the end of clause (ii), and by striking clause

CREDITS AND REFUNDS—SPECIAL RULES

(iii). **Effective** generally 12-19-2014. For a special rule, see Act Sec. 221(b)(2), Division A, below. Prior to being stricken, Code Sec. 6425(c)(1)(A)(iii) read as follows:

(iii) the tax imposed by section 59A, over

P.L. 113-295, §221(b)(2), Division A, provides:

(2) SAVINGS PROVISION.—If—

(A) any provision amended or repealed by the amendments made by this section applied to—

(i) any transaction occurring before the date of the enactment of this Act,

(ii) any property acquired before such date of enactment, or

(iii) any item of income, loss, deduction, or credit taken into account before such date of enactment, and

(B) the treatment of such transaction, property, or item under such provision would (without regard to the amendments or repeals made by this section) affect the liability for tax for periods ending after date of enactment, nothing in the amendments or repeals made by this section shall be construed to affect the treatment of such transaction, property, or item for purposes of determining liability for tax for periods ending after such date of enactment.

• **1987, Revenue Act of 1987 (P.L. 100-203)**

P.L. 100-203, §10301(b)(4):

Amended Code Sec. 6425(c) by striking out "section 6655(g)" and inserting in lieu thereof "section 6655(h)". **Effective** for tax years beginning after 12-31-87.

• **1986, Tax Reform Act of 1986 (P.L. 99-514)**

P.L. 99-514, §701(d)(2):

Amended Code Sec. 6425(c)(1)(A). **Effective**, generally, for tax years beginning after 12-31-86. However, see Act Sec. 701(f)(2)-(7) for exceptions following Code Sec. 56. Prior to amendment, Code Sec. 6425(c)(1)(A) read as follows:

(A) the tax imposed by section 11 or 1201(a), or subchapter L of chapter 1, whichever is applicable, over

• **1986, Superfund Amendments and Reauthorization Act of 1986 (P.L. 99-499)**

P.L. 99-499, §516(b)(4)(C)[B]:

Amended Code Sec. 6425(c)(1)(A), as amended by P.L. 99-514, by striking out "plus" at the end of clause (i), by striking out "over" at the end of clause (ii) and inserting in lieu thereof "plus", and by adding at the end thereof new clause (iii). **Effective** for tax years beginning after 12-31-86.

[Sec. 6425(d)]

(d) CONSOLIDATED RETURNS.—If the corporation seeking an adjustment under this section paid its estimated income tax on a consolidated basis or expects to make a consolidated return for the taxable year, this section shall apply only to such extent and subject to such conditions, limitations, and exceptions as the Secretary may by regulations prescribe.

Amendments

• **1976, Tax Reform Act of 1976 (P.L. 94-455)**

P.L. 94-455, §1906(b)(13)(A):

Amended 1954 Code by substituting "Secretary" for "Secretary or his delegate" each place it appeared. **Effective** 2-1-77.

• **1968, Revenue and Expenditure Control Act of 1968 (P.L. 90-364)**

P.L. 90-364, §103(d)(1):

Added Code Sec. 6425. **Effective** with respect to tax years beginning after 12-31-67.

SEC. 6426. CREDIT FOR ALCOHOL FUEL, BIODIESEL, AND ALTERNATIVE FUEL MIXTURES.

[Sec. 6426(a)]

(a) ALLOWANCE OF CREDITS.—There shall be allowed as a credit—

(1) against the tax imposed by section 4081 an amount equal to the sum of the credits described in subsections (b), (c), (e), and (k), and

(2) against the tax imposed by section 4041 an amount equal to the sum of the credits described in subsection (d).

No credit shall be allowed in the case of the credits described in subsections (d) and (e) unless the taxpayer is registered under section 4101.

Amendments

• **2022, Inflation Reduction Act of 2022 (P.L. 117-169)**

P.L. 117-169, §13203(d)(2)(A)(i):

Amended Code Sec. 6426(a)(1) by striking "and (e)" and inserting "(e), and (k)". **Effective** for fuel sold or used after 12-31-2022.

• **2005, Safe, Accountable, Flexible, Efficient Transportation Equity Act: A Legacy for Users (P.L. 109-59)**

P.L. 109-59, §11113(b)(1):

Amended Code Sec. 6426(a). **Effective** for any sale or use for any period after 9-30-2006. Prior to amendment, Code Sec. 6426(a) read as follows:

(a) ALLOWANCE OF CREDITS.—There shall be allowed as a credit against the tax imposed by section 4081 an amount equal to the sum of—

(1) the alcohol fuel mixture credit, plus

(2) the biodiesel mixture credit.

P.L. 109-59, §11113(b)(3)(A):

Amended the heading for Code Sec. 6426 by striking "ALCOHOL FUEL AND BIODIESEL" and inserting "ALCOHOL FUEL, BIODIESEL, AND ALTERNATIVE FUEL". **Effective** for any sale or use for any period after 9-30-2006.

[Sec. 6426(b)]

(b) ALCOHOL FUEL MIXTURE CREDIT.—

(1) IN GENERAL.—For purposes of this section, the alcohol fuel mixture credit is the product of the applicable amount and the number of gallons of alcohol used by the taxpayer in producing any alcohol fuel mixture for sale or use in a trade or business of the taxpayer.

(2) APPLICABLE AMOUNT.—For purposes of this subsection—

(A) IN GENERAL.—Except as provided in subparagraphs (B) and (C), the applicable amount is—

(i) in the case of calendar years beginning before 2009, 51 cents, and

(ii) in the case of calendar years beginning after 2008, 45 cents.

(B) MIXTURES NOT CONTAINING ETHANOL.—In the case of an alcohol fuel mixture in which none of the alcohol consists of ethanol, the applicable amount is 60 cents.

(C) REDUCTION DELAYED UNTIL ANNUAL PRODUCTION OR IMPORTATION OF 7,500,000,000 GALLONS.—In the case of any calendar year beginning after 2008, if the Secretary makes a determination described in section 40(h)(3)(B) with respect to all preceding calendar years beginning after 2007, subparagraph (A)(ii) shall be applied by substituting "51 cents" for "45 cents".

(3) ALCOHOL FUEL MIXTURE.—For purposes of this subsection, the term "alcohol fuel mixture" means a mixture of alcohol and a taxable fuel which—

(A) is sold by the taxpayer producing such mixture to any person for use as a fuel, or

(B) is used as a fuel by the taxpayer producing such mixture.

For purposes of subparagraph (A), a mixture produced by any person at a refinery prior to a taxable event which includes ethyl tertiary butyl ether or other ethers produced from alcohol shall be treated as sold at the time of its removal from the refinery (and only at such time) to another person for use as a fuel.

(4) OTHER DEFINITIONS.—For purposes of this subsection—

(A) ALCOHOL.—The term "alcohol" includes methanol and ethanol but does not include—

(i) alcohol produced from petroleum, natural gas, or coal (including peat), or

(ii) alcohol with a proof of less than 190 (determined without regard to any added denaturants).

Such term also includes an alcohol gallon equivalent of ethyl tertiary butyl ether or other ethers produced from such alcohol.

(B) TAXABLE FUEL.—The term "taxable fuel" has the meaning given such term by section 4083(a)(1).

CREDITS AND REFUNDS—SPECIAL RULES

(5) VOLUME OF ALCOHOL.—For purposes of determining under subsection (a) the number of gallons of alcohol with respect to which a credit is allowable under subsection (a), the volume of alcohol shall include the volume of any denaturant (including gasoline) which is added under any formulas approved by the Secretary to the extent that such denaturants do not exceed 2 percent of the volume of such alcohol (including denaturants).

(6) TERMINATION.—This subsection shall not apply to any sale, use, or removal for any period after December 31, 2011.

Amendments

• **2018, Tax Technical Corrections Act of 2018 (P.L. 115-141)**

P.L. 115-141, §401(a)(294), Div. U:

Amended Code Sec. 6426(b)(2)(A)(ii) by striking "cents.." and inserting "cents.". **Effective** 3-23-2018.

• **2010, Tax Relief, Unemployment Insurance Reauthorization, and Job Creation Act of 2010 (P.L. 111-312)**

P.L. 111-312, §708(b)(1):

Amended Code Sec. 6426(b)(6) by striking "December 31, 2010" and inserting "December 31, 2011". **Effective** for periods after 12-31-2010.

• **2008, Heartland, Habitat, Harvest, and Horticulture Act of 2008 (P.L. 110-246)**

P.L. 110-246, §15331(b)(1):

Amended Code Sec. 6426(b)(2)(A) by striking "the applicable amount is 51 cents" and inserting "the applicable amount is—" and new clauses (i)-(ii). **Effective** 5-22-2008.

P.L. 110-246, §15331(b)(2):

Amended Code Sec. 6426(b)(2) by adding at the end a new subparagraph (C). **Effective** 5-22-2008.

P.L. 110-246, §15331(b)(3):

Amended Code Sec. 6426(b)(2)(A) by striking "subparagraph (B)" and inserting "subparagraphs (B) and (C)". **Effective** 5-22-2008.

P.L. 110-246, §15332(b):

Amended Code Sec. 6426(b) by redesignating paragraph (5) as paragraph (6) and by inserting after paragraph (4) a new paragraph (5). **Effective** for fuel sold or used after 12-31-2008.

[Sec. 6426(c)]

(c) BIODIESEL MIXTURE CREDIT.—

(1) IN GENERAL.—For purposes of this section, the biodiesel mixture credit is the product of the applicable amount and the number of gallons of biodiesel used by the taxpayer in producing any biodiesel mixture for sale or use in a trade or business of the taxpayer.

(2) APPLICABLE AMOUNT.—For purposes of this subsection, the applicable amount is $1.00.

(3) BIODIESEL MIXTURE.—For purposes of this section, the term "biodiesel mixture" means a mixture of biodiesel and diesel fuel (as defined in section 4083(a)(3)), determined without regard to any use of kerosene, which—

(A) is sold by the taxpayer producing such mixture to any person for use as a fuel, or

(B) is used as a fuel by the taxpayer producing such mixture.

(4) CERTIFICATION FOR BIODIESEL.—No credit shall be allowed under this subsection unless the taxpayer obtains a certification (in such form and manner as prescribed by the Secretary) from the producer of the biodiesel which identifies the product produced and the percentage of biodiesel and agri-biodiesel in the product.

(5) OTHER DEFINITIONS.—Any term used in this subsection which is also used in section 40A shall have the meaning given such term by section 40A.

(6) TERMINATION.—This subsection shall not apply to any sale, use, or removal for any period after December 31, 2024.

Amendments

• **2022, Inflation Reduction Act of 2022 (P.L. 117-169)**

P.L. 117-169, §13201(b)(1):

Amended Code Sec. 6426(c)(6) by striking "December 31, 2022" and inserting "December 31, 2024". **Effective** for fuel sold or used after 12-31-2021.

• **2019, Taxpayer Certainty and Disaster Tax Relief Act of 2019 (P.L. 116-94)**

P.L. 116-94, §121(b)(1)(A), Div. Q:

Amended Code Sec. 6426(c)(6) by striking "December 31, 2017" and inserting "December 31, 2022". **Effective** for fuel sold or used after 12-31-2017. For a special rule, see Act Sec. 121(b)(3), Div. Q, below.

P.L. 116-94, §121(b)(3), Div. Q, provides:

(3) SPECIAL RULE.—Notwithstanding any other provision of law, in the case of any biodiesel mixture credit properly determined under section 6426(c) of the Internal Revenue Code of 1986 for the period beginning on January 1, 2018, and ending with the close of the last calendar quarter beginning before the date of the enactment of this Act, such credit shall be allowed, and any refund or payment attributable to such credit (including any payment under section 6427(e) of such Code) shall be made, only in such manner as the Secretary of the Treasury (or the Secretary's delegate) shall provide. Such Secretary shall issue guidance within 30 days after the date of the enactment of this Act providing for a one-time submission of claims covering periods described in the preceding sentence. Such guidance shall provide for a 180-day period for the submission of such claims (in such manner as prescribed by such Secretary) to begin not later than 30 days after such guidance is issued. Such claims shall be paid by such Secretary not later than 60 days after receipt. If such Secretary has not paid pursuant to a claim filed under this subsection within 60 days after the date of the filing of such claim, the claim shall be paid with interest from such date determined by using the overpayment rate and method under section 6621 of such Code.

• **2018, Bipartisan Budget Act of 2018 (P.L. 115-123)**

P.L. 115-123, §40407(b)(1), Div. D:

Amended Code Sec. 6426(c)(6) by striking "December 31, 2016" and inserting "December 31, 2017". **Effective** for fuel sold or used after 12-31-2016. For a special rule, see Act Sec. 40407(b)(4), below.

P.L. 115-123, §40407(b)(4), Div. D, provides:

(4) SPECIAL RULE FOR 2017.—Notwithstanding any other provision of law, in the case of any biodiesel mixture credit properly determined under section 6426(c) of the Internal Revenue Code of 1986 for the period beginning on January 1, 2017, and ending on December 31, 2017, such credit shall be allowed, and any refund or payment attributable to such credit (including any payment under section 6427(e) of such Code) shall be made, only in such manner as the Secretary of the Treasury (or the Secretary's delegate) shall provide. Such Secretary shall issue guidance within 30 days after the date of the enactment of this Act providing for a one-time submission of claims covering periods described in the preceding sentence. Such guidance shall provide for a 180-day period for the submission of such claims (in such manner as prescribed by such Secretary) to begin not later than 30 days after such guidance is issued. Such claims shall be paid by such Secretary not later than 60 days after receipt. If such Secretary has not paid pursuant to a claim filed under this subsection within 60 days after the date of the filing of such claim, the claim shall be paid with interest from such date determined by using the overpayment rate and method under section 6621 of such Code.

• **2015, Protecting Americans from Tax Hikes Act of 2015 (P.L. 114-113)**

P.L. 114-113, §185(b)(1), Div. Q:

Amended Code Sec. 6426(c)(6) by striking "December 31, 2014" and inserting "December 31, 2016". **Effective** for fuel sold or used after 12-31-2014. For a special rule, see Act Sec. 185(b)(4), below.

P.L. 114-113, §185(b)(4), Div. Q, provides:

(4) SPECIAL RULE FOR 2015.—Notwithstanding any other provision of law, in the case of any biodiesel mixture credit properly determined under section 6426(c) of the Internal Revenue Code of 1986 for the period beginning on January 1, 2015, and ending on December 31, 2015, such credit shall be allowed, and any refund or payment attributable to such credit (including any payment under section 6427(e) of such Code) shall be made, only in such manner as the Secretary of the Treasury (or the Secretary's delegate) shall provide. Such Secretary shall issue guidance within 30 days after the date of the enactment of this Act providing for a one-time submission of claims covering periods described in the preceding sentence. Such guidance shall provide for a 180-day period for the submission of such claims (in such manner as prescribed by such Secretary) to begin not later than 30 days after such guidance is issued. Such claims shall be paid by such Secretary not later than 60 days after receipt. If such Secretary has not paid pursuant to a claim filed under this subsection within 60 days after the date of the filing of such claim, the claim shall be paid with interest from such date determined by using the overpayment rate and method under section 6621 of such Code.

• **2014, Tax Increase Prevention Act of 2014 (P.L. 113-295)**

P.L. 113-295, §160(a)(1), Div. A:

Amended Code Sec. 6426(c)(6) by striking "December 31, 2013" and inserting "December 31, 2014". **Effective** for fuel sold or used after 12-31-2013. For a special rule, see Act Sec. 160(e), Div. A, below.

P.L. 113-295, §160(e), Div. A, provides:

(e) SPECIAL RULE FOR CERTAIN PERIODS DURING 2014.—Notwithstanding any other provision of law, in the case of—

(1) any biodiesel mixture credit properly determined under section 6426(c) of the Internal Revenue Code of 1986 for periods after December 31, 2013, and before the date of the enactment of this Act, and

(2) any alternative fuel credit properly determined under section 6426(d) of such Code for such periods,

CREDITS AND REFUNDS—SPECIAL RULES

such credit shall be allowed, and any refund or payment attributable to such credit (including any payment under section 6427(e) of such Code) shall be made, only in such manner as the Secretary of the Treasury (or the Secretary's delegate) shall provide. Such Secretary shall issue guidance within 30 days after the date of the enactment of this Act providing for a one-time submission of claims covering periods described in the preceding sentence. Such guidance shall provide for a 180-day period for the submission of such claims (in such manner as prescribed by such Secretary) to begin not later than 30 days after such guidance is issued. Such claims shall be paid by such Secretary not later than 60 days after receipt. If such Secretary has not paid pursuant to a claim filed under this subsection within 60 days after the date of the filing of such claim, the claim shall be paid with interest from such date determined by using the overpayment rate and method under section 6621 of such Code.

• **2013, American Taxpayer Relief Act of 2012 (P.L. 112-240)**

P.L. 112-240, §405(b)(1):

Amended Code Sec. 6426(c)(6) by striking "December 31, 2011" and inserting "December 31, 2013". **Effective** for fuel sold or used after 12-31-2011.

• **2010, Tax Relief, Unemployment Insurance Reauthorization, and Job Creation Act of 2010 (P.L. 111-312)**

P.L. 111-312, §701(b)(1):

Amended Code Sec. 6426(c)(6) by striking "December 31, 2009" and inserting "December 31, 2011". **Effective** for fuel sold or used after 12-31-2009.

P.L. 111-312, §701(c), provides:

(c) SPECIAL RULE FOR 2010.—Notwithstanding any other provision of law, in the case of any biodiesel mixture credit properly determined under section 6426(c) of the Internal Revenue Code of 1986 for periods during 2010, such credit shall be allowed, and any refund or payment attributable to such credit (including any payment under section 6427(e) of such Code) shall be made, only in such manner as the Secretary of the Treasury (or the Secretary's delegate) shall provide. Such Secretary shall issue guidance within 30 days after the date of the enactment of this Act providing for a one-time submission of claims covering periods during 2010. Such guidance shall provide for a 180-day period for the submission of such claims (in such manner as prescribed by such Secretary) to begin not later than 30 days after such guidance is issued. Such claims shall be paid by such Secretary not later than 60 days after receipt. If such Secretary has not paid pursuant to a claim filed under this subsection within 60 days after the date of the filing of such claim, the claim shall be paid with interest from such date determined by using the overpayment rate and method under section 6621 of such Code.

• **2008, Energy Improvement and Extension Act of 2008 (P.L. 110-343)**

P.L. 110-343, Div. B, §202(a):

Amended Code Sec. 6426(c)(6) by striking "December 31, 2008" and inserting "December 31, 2009". **Effective** for fuel produced, and sold or used, after 12-31-2008.

P.L. 110-343, Div. B, §202(b)(2):

Amended Code Sec. 6426(c)(2). **Effective** for fuel produced, and sold or used, after 12-31-2008. Prior to amendment, Code Sec. 6426(c)(2) read as follows:

(2) APPLICABLE AMOUNT.—For purposes of this subsection—

(A) IN GENERAL.—Except as provided in subparagraph (B), the applicable amount is 50 cents.

(B) AMOUNT FOR AGRI-BIODIESEL.—In the case of any biodiesel which is agri-biodiesel, the applicable amount is $1.00.

• **2005, Energy Tax Incentives Act of 2005 (P.L. 109-58)**

P.L. 109-58, §1344(a):

Amended Code Sec. 6426(c)(6) by striking "2006" and inserting "2008". **Effective** 8-8-2005.

[Sec. 6426(d)]

(d) ALTERNATIVE FUEL CREDIT.—

(1) IN GENERAL.—For purposes of this section, the alternative fuel credit is the product of 50 cents and the number of gallons of an alternative fuel or gasoline gallon equivalents of a nonliquid alternative fuel sold by the taxpayer for use as a fuel in a motor vehicle or motorboat, sold by the taxpayer for use as a fuel in aviation, or so used by the taxpayer.

(2) ALTERNATIVE FUEL.—For purposes of this section, the term "alternative fuel" means—

(A) liquefied petroleum gas,

(B) P Series Fuels (as defined by the Secretary of Energy under section 13211(2) of title 42, United States Code),

(C) compressed or liquefied natural gas,

(D) any liquid fuel which meets the requirements of paragraph (4) and which is derived from coal (including peat) through the Fischer-Tropsch process,

(E) compressed or liquefied gas derived from biomass (as defined in section 45K(c)(3)), and

(F) liquid fuel derived from biomass (as defined in section 45K(c)(3)).

Such term does not include ethanol, methanol, biodiesel, or any fuel (including lignin, wood residues, or spent pulping liquors) derived from the production of paper or pulp.

(3) GASOLINE GALLON EQUIVALENT.—For purposes of this subsection, the term "gasoline gallon equivalent" means, with respect to any nonliquid alternative fuel, the amount of such fuel having a Btu content of 124,800 (higher heating value).

(4) CARBON CAPTURE REQUIREMENT.—

(A) IN GENERAL.—The requirements of this paragraph are met if the fuel is certified, under such procedures as required by the Secretary, as having been derived from coal produced at a gasification facility which separates and sequesters not less than the applicable percentage of such facility's total carbon dioxide emissions.

(B) APPLICABLE PERCENTAGE.—For purposes of subparagraph (A), the applicable percentage is—

(i) 50 percent in the case of fuel produced after September 30, 2009, and on or before December 30, 2009, and

(ii) 75 percent in the case of fuel produced after December 30, 2009.

(5) TERMINATION.—This subsection shall not apply to any sale or use for any period after December 31, 2024.

Amendments

• **2022, Inflation Reduction Act of 2022 (P.L. 117-169)**

P.L. 117-169, §13201(c):

Amended Code Sec. 6426(d)(5) by striking "December 31, 2021" and inserting "December 31, 2024". **Effective** for fuel sold or used after 12-31-2021. For a special rule, see Act Sec. 13201(g), below.

P.L. 117-169, §13201(g), provides:

(g) SPECIAL RULE.—In the case of any alternative fuel credit properly determined under section 6426(d) of the Internal Revenue Code of 1986 for the period beginning on January 1, 2022, and ending with the close of the last calendar quarter beginning before the date of the enactment of this Act, such credit shall be allowed, and any refund or payment attributable to such credit (including any payment under section 6427(e) of such Code) shall be made, only in such manner as the Secretary of the Treasury (or the Secretary's delegate) shall provide. Such Secretary shall issue guidance within 30 days after the date of the enactment of this Act providing for a one-time submission of claims covering periods described in the preceding sentence. Such guidance shall provide for a 180-day period for the submission of such claims (in such manner as prescribed by such Secretary) to begin not later than 30 days after such guidance is issued. Such claims shall be paid by such Secretary not later than 60 days after receipt. If such Secretary has not paid pursuant to a claim filed under this subsection within 60 days after the date of the filing of such claim, the claim shall be paid with interest from such date determined by using the overpayment rate and method under section 6621 of such Code.

P.L. 117-169, §13204(d)(1):

Amended Code Sec. 6426(d)(2) by striking subparagraph (D) and by redesignating subparagraphs (E), (F), and (G) as subparagraphs (D), (E), and (F), respectively. **Effective** for fuel sold or used after 12-31-2022. Prior to being stricken, Code Sec. 6426(d)(2)(D) read as follows:

(D) liquefied hydrogen,

• **2020, Taxpayer Certainty and Disaster Tax Relief Act of 2020 (P.L. 116-260)**

P.L. 116-260, §147(a), Div. EE:

Amended Code Sec. 6426(d)(5) by striking "December 31, 2020" and inserting "December 31, 2021". **Effective** for fuel sold or used after 12-31-2020.

• **2019, Taxpayer Certainty and Disaster Tax Relief Act of 2019 (P.L. 116-94)**

P.L. 116-94, §133(a)(1), Div. Q:

Amended Code Sec. 6426(d)(5) by striking "December 31, 2017" and inserting "December 31, 2020". **Effective** for fuel sold or used after 12-31-2017. For a special rule, see Act Sec. 133(a)(3), Div. Q, below.

P.L. 116-94, §133(a)(3), Div. Q, provides:

(3) SPECIAL RULE.—Notwithstanding any other provision of law, in the case of any alternative fuel credit properly determined under section 6426(d) of the Internal Revenue Code of 1986 for the period beginning on January 1, 2018, and ending with the close of the last calendar quarter beginning before the date of the enactment of this Act, such credit shall be allowed, and any refund or payment attributable to such credit (including any payment under section 6427(e) of such Code) shall be made, only in such manner as the Secretary of the Treasury (or the Secretary's delegate) shall provide. Such Secretary shall issue guidance within 30 days after the date of the enactment of this Act providing for a one-time submission of claims covering periods

CREDITS AND REFUNDS—SPECIAL RULES

described in the preceding sentence. Such guidance shall provide for a 180-day period for the submission of such claims (in such manner as prescribed by such Secretary) to begin not later than 30 days after such guidance is issued. Such claims shall be paid by such Secretary not later than 60 days after receipt. If such Secretary has not paid pursuant to a claim filed under this subsection within 60 days after the date of the filing of such claim, the claim shall be paid with interest from such date determined by using the overpayment rate and method under section 6621 of such Code.

• **2018, Bipartisan Budget Act of 2018 (P.L. 115-123)**

P.L. 115-123, §40415(a)(1), Div. D:

Amended Code Sec. 6426(d)(5) by striking "December 31, 2016" and inserting "December 31, 2017". **Effective** for fuel sold or used after 12-31-2016. For a special rule, see Act Sec. 40415(b), Div. D, below.

P.L. 115-123, §40415(b), Div. D, provides:

(b) SPECIAL RULE FOR 2017.—Notwithstanding any other provision of law, in the case of any alternative fuel credit properly determined under section 6426(d) of the Internal Revenue Code of 1986 for the period beginning on January 1, 2017, and ending on December 31, 2017, such credit shall be allowed, and any refund or payment attributable to such credit (including any payment under section 6427(e) of such Code) shall be made, only in such manner as the Secretary of the Treasury (or the Secretary's delegate) shall provide. Such Secretary shall issue guidance within 30 days after the date of the enactment of this Act providing for a one-time submission of claims covering periods described in the preceding sentence. Such guidance shall provide for a 180-day period for the submission of such claims (in such manner as prescribed by such Secretary) to begin not later than 30 days after such guidance is issued. Such claims shall be paid by such Secretary not later than 60 days after receipt. If such Secretary has not paid pursuant to a claim filed under this subsection within 60 days after the date of the filing of such claim, the claim shall be paid with interest from such date determined by using the overpayment rate and method under section 6621 of such Code.

• **2015, Protecting Americans from Tax Hikes Act of 2015 (P.L. 114-113)**

P.L. 114-113, §192(a)(1), Div. Q:

Amended Code Sec. 6426(d)(5) by striking "December 31, 2014" and inserting "December 31, 2016". **Effective** for fuel sold or used after 12-31-2014. For a special rule, see Act Sec. 192(c), below.

P.L. 114-113, §192(c), Div. Q, provides:

(c) SPECIAL RULE FOR 2015.—Notwithstanding any other provision of law, in the case of any alternative fuel credit properly determined under section 6426(d) of the Internal Revenue Code of 1986 for the period beginning on January 1, 2015, and ending on December 31, 2015, such credit shall be allowed, and any refund or payment attributable to such credit (including any payment under section 6427(e) of such Code) shall be made, only in such manner as the Secretary of the Treasury (or the Secretary's delegate) shall provide. Such Secretary shall issue guidance within 30 days after the date of the enactment of this Act providing for a one-time submission of claims covering periods described in the preceding sentence. Such guidance shall provide for a 180-day period for the submission of such claims (in such manner as prescribed by such Secretary) to begin not later than 30 days after such guidance is issued. Such claims shall be paid by such Secretary not later than 60 days after receipt. If such Secretary has not paid pursuant to a claim filed under this subsection within 60 days after the date of the filing of such claim, the claim shall be paid with interest from such date determined by using the overpayment rate and method under section 6621 of such Code.

• **2014, Tax Increase Prevention Act of 2014 (P.L. 113-295)**

P.L. 113-295, §160(b)(1), Div. A:

Amended Code Sec. 6426(d)(5) by striking "December 31, 2013" and inserting "December 31, 2014". **Effective** for fuel sold or used after 12-31-2013. For a special rule, see Act Sec. 160(e), Div. A, below.

P.L. 113-295, §160(c)(1), Div. A:

Amended Code Sec. 6426(d)(5), as amended by Act Sec. 160(b), Div. A, by striking "(September 30, 2014 in the case of any sale or use involving liquefied hydrogen)" after "December 31, 2014". **Effective** for fuel sold or used after 9-30-2014. For a special rule, see Act Sec. 160(e), Div. A, below.

P.L. 113-295, §160(e), Div. A, provides:

(e) SPECIAL RULE FOR CERTAIN PERIODS DURING 2014.—Notwithstanding any other provision of law, in the case of—

(1) any biodiesel mixture credit properly determined under section 6426(c) of the Internal Revenue Code of 1986 for periods after December 31, 2013, and before the date of the enactment of this Act, and

(2) any alternative fuel credit properly determined under section 6426(d) of such Code for such periods,

such credit shall be allowed, and any refund or payment attributable to such credit (including any payment under section 6427(e) of such Code) shall be made, only in such manner as the Secretary of the Treasury (or the Secretary's delegate) shall provide. Such Secretary shall issue guidance within 30 days after the date of the enactment of this Act providing for a one-time submission of claims covering periods described in the preceding sentence. Such guidance shall provide for a 180-day period for the submission of such claims (in such manner as prescribed by such Secretary) to begin not later than 30 days after such guidance is issued. Such claims shall be paid by such Secretary not later than 60 days after receipt. If such Secretary

has not paid pursuant to a claim filed under this subsection within 60 days after the date of the filing of such claim, the claim shall be paid with interest from such date determined by using the overpayment rate and method under section 6621 of such Code.

• **2013, American Taxpayer Relief Act of 2012 (P.L. 112-240)**

P.L. 112-240, §412(a):

Amended Code Sec. 6426(d)(5) by striking "December 31, 2011" and inserting "December 31, 2013". **Effective** for fuel sold or used after 12-31-2011.

• **2010, Tax Relief, Unemployment Insurance Reauthorization, and Job Creation Act of 2010 (P.L. 111-312)**

P.L. 111-312, §704(a):

Amended Code Sec. 6426(d)(5) by striking "December 31, 2009" and inserting "December 31, 2011". **Effective** for fuel sold or used after 12-31-2009. For a special rule, see Act Sec. 704(c), below.

P.L. 111-312, §704(b):

Amended the last sentence of Code Sec. 6426(d)(2) by striking "or biodiesel" and inserting "biodiesel, or any fuel (including lignin, wood residues, or spent pulping liquors) derived from the production of paper or pulp". **Effective** for fuel sold or used after 12-31-2009. For a special rule, see Act Sec. 704(c), below:

P.L. 111-312, §704(c), provides:

(c) SPECIAL RULE FOR 2010.—Notwithstanding any other provision of law, in the case of any alternative fuel credit or any alternative fuel mixture credit properly determined under subsection (d) or (e) of section 6426 of the Internal Revenue Code of 1986 for periods during 2010, such credit shall be allowed, and any refund or payment attributable to such credit (including any payment under section 6427(e) of such Code) shall be made, only in such manner as the Secretary of the Treasury (or the Secretary's delegate) shall provide. Such Secretary shall issue guidance within 30 days after the date of the enactment of this Act providing for a one-time submission of claims covering periods during 2010. Such guidance shall provide for a 180-day period for the submission of such claims (in such manner as prescribed by such Secretary) to begin not later than 30 days after such guidance is issued. Such claims shall be paid by such Secretary not later than 60 days after receipt. If such Secretary has not paid pursuant to a claim filed under this subsection within 60 days after the date of the filing of such claim, the claim shall be paid with interest from such date determined by using the overpayment rate and method under section 6621 of such Code.

• **2008, Energy Improvement and Extension Act of 2008 (P.L. 110-343)**

P.L. 110-343, Div. B, §204(a)(1):

Amended Code Sec. 6426(d)(4) by striking "September 30, 2009" and inserting "December 31, 2009". **Effective** for fuel sold or used after 10-3-2008.

P.L. 110-343, Div. B, §204(b)(1):

Amended Code Sec. 6426(d)(2) by striking "and" at the end of subparagraph (E), by redesignating subparagraph (F) as subparagraph (G), and by inserting after subparagraph (E) a new subparagraph (F). **Effective** for fuel sold or used after 10-3-2008.

P.L. 110-343, Div. B, §204(b)(2):

Amended Code Sec. 6426(d)(1) by inserting "sold by the taxpayer for use as a fuel in aviation," after "motorboat,". **Effective** for fuel sold or used after 10-3-2008.

P.L. 110-343, Div. B, §204(c)(1):

Amended Code Sec. 6426(d), as amended by Act Sec. 204(a), by redesignating paragraph (4) as paragraph (5) and by inserting after paragraph (3) a new paragraph (4). **Effective** for fuel sold or used after 10-3-2008.

P.L. 110-343, Div. B, §204(c)(2):

Amended Code Sec. 6426(d)(2)(E) by inserting "which meets the requirements of paragraph (4) and which is" after "any liquid fuel". **Effective** for fuel sold or used after 10-3-2008.

• **2007, Tax Technical Corrections Act of 2007 (P.L. 110-172)**

P.L. 110-172, §5(a)(2):

Amended Code Sec. 6426(d)(2)(F) by striking "hydrocarbons" and inserting "fuel". **Effective** as if included in the provision of the Safe, Accountable, Flexible, Efficient Transportation Equity Act: A Legacy for Users (P.L. 109-59) to which it relates [**effective** for any sale or use for any period after 9-30-2006.—CCH]

• **2005, Safe, Accountable, Flexible, Efficient Transportation Equity Act: A Legacy for Users (P.L. 109-59)**

P.L. 109-59, §11113(b)(2):

Amended Code Sec. 6426 by redesignating subsections (d) and (e) as subsections (f) and (g) and by inserting after subsection (c) new subsections (d) and (e). **Effective** for any sale or use for any period after 9-30-2006.

P.L. 109-59, §11151(e)(2):

Amended Code Sec. 6426(d)(2)(F) [as added by Act Sec. 11113(b)(2)], by striking "section 29(c)(3)" and inserting "section 45K(c)(3)". **Effective** as if included in the provision of the Energy Tax Incentives Act of 2005 to which it relates [**effective** for credits determined under the Internal Revenue Code of 1986 for tax years ending after 12-31-2005.—CCH].

[Sec. 6426(e)]

(e) ALTERNATIVE FUEL MIXTURE CREDIT.—

(1) IN GENERAL.—For purposes of this section, the alternative fuel mixture credit is the product of 50 cents and the number of gallons of alternative fuel used by the taxpayer in producing any alternative fuel mixture for sale or use in a trade or business of the taxpayer.

CREDITS AND REFUNDS—SPECIAL RULES

(2) ALTERNATIVE FUEL MIXTURE.—For purposes of this section, the term "alternative fuel mixture" means a mixture of alternative fuel (other than a fuel described in subparagraph (A), (C), or (E) of subsection (d)(2)) and taxable fuel (as defined in subparagraph (A), (B), or (C) of section 4083(a)(1)) which—

(A) is sold by the taxpayer producing such mixture to any person for use as fuel, or

(B) is used as a fuel by the taxpayer producing such mixture.

(3) TERMINATION.—This subsection shall not apply to any sale or use for any period after December 31, 2024.

Amendments

• **2022, Inflation Reduction Act of 2022 (P.L. 117-169)**

P.L. 117-169, § 13201(d):

Amended Code Sec. 6426(e)(3) by striking "December 31, 2021" and inserting "December 31, 2024". **Effective** for fuel sold or used after 12-31-2021.

P.L. 117-169, § 13204(d)(2):

Amended Code Sec. 6426(e)(2) by striking "(F)" and inserting "(E)". **Effective** for fuel sold or used after 12-31-2022.

• **2020, Taxpayer Certainty and Disaster Tax Relief Act of 2020 (P.L. 116-260)**

P.L. 116-260, § 147(a), Div. EE:

Amended Code Sec. 6426(e)(3) by striking "December 31, 2020" and inserting "December 31, 2021". **Effective** for fuel sold or used after 12-31-2020.

• **2019, Taxpayer Certainty and Disaster Tax Relief Act of 2019 (P.L. 116-94)**

P.L. 116-94, § 133(a)(1), Div. Q:

Amended Code Sec. 6426(e)(3) by striking "December 31, 2017" and inserting "December 31, 2020". **Effective** for fuel sold or used after 12-31-2017. For a special rule, see Act Sec. 133(a)(3), Div. Q, below.

P.L. 116-94, § 133(a)(3), Div. Q, provides:

(3) SPECIAL RULE.—Notwithstanding any other provision of law, in the case of any alternative fuel credit properly determined under section 6426(d) of the Internal Revenue Code of 1986 for the period beginning on January 1, 2018, and ending on the close of the last calendar quarter beginning before the date of the enactment of this Act, such credit shall be allowed, and any refund or payment attributable to such credit (including any payment under section 6427(e) of such Code) shall be made, only in such manner as the Secretary of the Treasury (or the Secretary's delegate) shall provide. Such Secretary shall issue guidance within 30 days after the date of the enactment of this Act providing for a one-time submission of claims covering periods described in the preceding sentence. Such guidance shall provide for a 180-day period for the submission of such claims (in such manner as prescribed by such Secretary) to begin not later than 30 days after such guidance is issued. Such claims shall be paid by such Secretary not later than 60 days after receipt. If such Secretary has not paid pursuant to a claim filed under this subsection within 60 days after the date of the filing of such claim, the claim shall be paid with interest from such date determined by using the overpayment rate and method under section 6621 of such Code.

P.L. 116-94, § 133(b)(1), Div. Q:

Amended Code Sec. 6426(e)(2) by striking "mixture of alternative fuel" and inserting "mixture of alternative fuel (other than a fuel described in subparagraph (A), (C), or (F) of subsection (d)(2))". For the **effective** date, see Act Sec. 133(b)(2)(A)-(B), Div. Q, below. For a special rule, see Act Sec. 133(b)(3), Div. Q, below.

P.L. 116-94, § 133(b)(2), Div. Q, provides:

(2) EFFECTIVE DATE.—The amendment made by this subsection shall apply to—

(A) fuel sold or used on or after the date of the enactment of this Act, and

(B) fuel sold or used before such date of enactment, but only to the extent that claims for the credit under section 6426(e) of the Internal Revenue Code of 1986 with respect to such sale or use—

(i) have not been paid or allowed as of such date, and

(ii) were made on or after January 8, 2018.

P.L. 116-94, § 133(b)(3), Div. Q, provides:

(3) NO INFERENCE.—Nothing contained in this subsection or the amendments made by this subsection shall be construed to create any inference as to a change in law or guidance in effect prior to enactment of this subsection.

• **2018, Bipartisan Budget Act of 2018 (P.L. 115-123)**

P.L. 115-123, § 40415(a)(1), Div. D:

Amended Code Sec. 6426(e)(3) by striking "December 31, 2016" and inserting "December 31, 2017". **Effective** for fuel sold or used after 12-31-2016. For a special rule, see Act Sec. 40415(b), Div. D, below.

P.L. 115-123, § 40415(b), Div. D, provides:

(b) SPECIAL RULE FOR 2017.—Notwithstanding any other provision of law, in the case of any alternative fuel credit properly determined under section 6426(d) of the Internal Revenue Code of 1986 for the period beginning on January 1, 2017, and ending on December 31, 2017, such credit shall be allowed, and any refund or payment attributable to such credit (including any payment under section 6427(e) of such Code) shall be made, only in such manner as the Secretary of the Treasury (or the Secretary's delegate) shall provide. Such Secretary shall issue guidance within 30 days after the date of the enactment of this Act providing for a one-time submission of claims covering periods described in the preceding sentence. Such guidance shall provide for a 180-day period for the submission of such claims (in such manner as prescribed by such Secretary) to begin not later than 30 days after such guidance is issued. Such claims shall be paid by such Secretary not later than 60 days after receipt. If such Secretary has not paid pursuant to a claim filed under this subsection within 60 days after the date of the filing of such claim, the claim shall be paid with interest from such date determined by using the overpayment rate and method under section 6621 of such Code.

• **2015, Protecting Americans from Tax Hikes Act of 2015 (P.L. 114-113)**

P.L. 114-113, § 192(a)(1), Div. Q:

Amended Code Sec. 6426(e)(3) by striking "December 31, 2014" and inserting "December 31, 2016". **Effective** for fuel sold or used after 12-31-2014. For a special rule, see Act Sec. 192(c), below.

P.L. 114-113, § 192(c), Div. Q, provides:

(c) SPECIAL RULE FOR 2015.—Notwithstanding any other provision of law, in the case of any alternative fuel credit properly determined under section 6426(d) of the Internal Revenue Code of 1986 for the period beginning on January 1, 2015, and ending on December 31, 2015, such credit shall be allowed, and any refund or payment attributable to such credit (including any payment under section 6427(e) of such Code) shall be made, only in such manner as the Secretary of the Treasury (or the Secretary's delegate) shall provide. Such Secretary shall issue guidance within 30 days after the date of the enactment of this Act providing for a one-time submission of claims covering periods described in the preceding sentence. Such guidance shall provide for a 180-day period for the submission of such claims (in such manner as prescribed by such Secretary) to begin not later than 30 days after such guidance is issued. Such claims shall be paid by such Secretary not later than 60 days after receipt. If such Secretary has not paid pursuant to a claim filed under this subsection within 60 days after the date of the filing of such claim, the claim shall be paid with interest from such date determined by using the overpayment rate and method under section 6621 of such Code.

• **2014, Tax Increase Prevention Act of 2014 (P.L. 113-295)**

P.L. 113-295, § 160(b)(1), Div. A:

Amended Code Sec. 6426(e)(3) by striking "December 31, 2013" and inserting "December 31, 2014". **Effective** for fuel sold or used after 12-31-2013.

P.L. 113-295, § 160(c)(1), Div. A:

Amended Code Sec. 6426(e)(3), as amended by Act Sec. 160(b), Div. A, by striking "(September 30, 2014 in the case of any sale or use involving liquefied hydrogen)". **Effective** for fuel sold or used after 9-30-2014.

• **2013, American Taxpayer Relief Act of 2012 (P.L. 112-240)**

P.L. 112-240, § 412(a):

Amended Code Sec. 6426(e)(3) by striking "December 31, 2011" and inserting "December 31, 2013". **Effective** for fuel sold or used after 12-31-2011.

• **2010, Tax Relief, Unemployment Insurance Reauthorization, and Job Creation Act of 2010 (P.L. 111-312)**

P.L. 111-312, § 704(a):

Amended Code Sec. 6426(e)(3) by striking "December 31, 2009" and inserting "December 31, 2011". **Effective** for fuel sold or used after 12-31-2009. For a special rule, see Act Sec. 704(c), below.

P.L. 111-312, § 704(c), provides:

(c) SPECIAL RULE FOR 2010.—Notwithstanding any other provision of law, in the case of any alternative fuel credit or any alternative fuel mixture credit properly determined under subsection (d) or (e) of section 6426 of the Internal Revenue Code of 1986 for periods during 2010, such credit shall be allowed, and any refund or payment attributable to such credit (including any payment under section 6427(e) of such Code) shall be made, only in such manner as the Secretary of the Treasury (or the Secretary's delegate) shall provide. Such Secretary shall issue guidance within 30 days after the date of the enactment of this Act providing for a one-time submission of claims covering periods during 2010. Such guidance shall provide for a 180-day period for the submission of such claims (in such manner as prescribed by such Secretary) to begin not later than 30 days after such guidance is issued. Such claims shall be paid by such Secretary not later than 60 days after receipt. If such Secretary has not paid pursuant to a claim filed under this subsection within 60 days after the date of the filing of such claim, the claim shall be paid with interest from such date determined by using the overpayment rate and method under section 6621 of such Code.

• **2008, Energy Improvement and Extension Act of 2008 (P.L. 110-343)**

P.L. 110-343, Div. B, § 204(a)(2):

Amended Code Sec. 6426(e)(3) by striking "September 30, 2009" and inserting "December 31, 2009". **Effective** for fuel sold or used after 10-3-2008.

• **2005, Safe, Accountable, Flexible, Efficient Transportation Equity Act: A Legacy for Users (P.L. 109-59)**

P.L. 109-59, § 11113(b)(2):

Amended Code Sec. 6426 by redesignating subsections (d) and (e) as subsections (f) and (g) and by inserting after subsection (c) new subsections (d) and (e). **Effective** for any sale or use for any period after 9-30-2006.

CREDITS AND REFUNDS—SPECIAL RULES

[Sec. 6426(f)]

(f) MIXTURE NOT USED AS A FUEL, ETC.—

(1) IMPOSITION OF TAX.—If—

(A) any credit was determined under this section with respect to alcohol or biodiesel used in the production of any alcohol fuel mixture or biodiesel mixture, respectively, and

(B) any person—

(i) separates the alcohol or biodiesel from the mixture, or

(ii) without separation, uses the mixture other than as a fuel,

then there is hereby imposed on such person a tax equal to the product of the applicable amount and the number of gallons of such alcohol or biodiesel.

(2) APPLICABLE LAWS.—All provisions of law, including penalties, shall, insofar as applicable and not inconsistent with this section, apply in respect of any tax imposed under paragraph (1) as if such tax were imposed by section 4081 and not by this section.

Amendments

• **2005, Safe, Accountable, Flexible, Efficient Transportation Equity Act: A Legacy for Users (P.L. 109-59)**

P.L. 109-59, §11113(b)(2):

Amended Code Sec. 6426 by redesignating subsection (d) as subsection (f). **Effective** for any sale or use for any period after 9-30-2006.

[Sec. 6426(g)]

(g) COORDINATION WITH EXEMPTION FROM EXCISE TAX.—Rules similar to the rules under section 40(c) shall apply for purposes of this section.

Amendments

• **2005, Safe, Accountable, Flexible, Efficient Transportation Equity Act: A Legacy for Users (P.L. 109-59)**

P.L. 109-59, §11113(b)(2):

Amended Code Sec. 6426 by redesignating subsection (e) as subsection (g). **Effective** for any sale or use for any period after 9-30-2006.

• **2004, American Jobs Creation Act of 2004 (P.L. 108-357)**

P.L. 108-357, §301(a):

Amended subchapter B of chapter 65 by inserting after Code Sec. 6425 a new Code Sec. 6426. **Effective** for fuel sold or used after 12-31-2004.

[Sec. 6426(h)]

(h) DENIAL OF DOUBLE BENEFIT.—No credit shall be determined under subsection (d) or (e) with respect to any fuel with respect to which credit may be determined under subsection (b) or (c) or under section 40, 40A, or 40B.

Amendments

• **2022, Inflation Reduction Act of 2022 (P.L. 117-169)**

P.L. 117-169, §13203(d)(2)(A)(ii):

Amended Code Sec. 6426(h) by striking "under section 40 or 40A" and inserting "under section 40, 40A, or 40B". **Effective** for fuel sold or used after 12-31-2022.

• **2007, Tax Technical Corrections Act of 2007 (P.L. 110-172)**

P.L. 110-172, §5(a)(3):

Amended Code Sec. 6426 by adding at the end a new subsection (h). **Effective** as if included in the provision of the Safe, Accountable, Flexible, Efficient Transportation Equity Act: A Legacy for Users (P.L. 109-59) to which it relates [**effective** for any sale or use for any period after 9-30-2006.—CCH].

[Sec. 6426(i)]

(i) LIMITATION TO FUELS WITH CONNECTION TO THE UNITED STATES.—

(1) ALCOHOL.—No credit shall be determined under this section with respect to any alcohol which is produced outside the United States for use as a fuel outside the United States.

(2) BIODIESEL AND ALTERNATIVE FUELS.—No credit shall be determined under this section with respect to any biodiesel or alternative fuel which is produced outside the United States for use as a fuel outside the United States.

For purposes of this subsection, the term "United States" includes any possession of the United States.

Amendments

• **2008, Energy Improvement and Extension Act of 2008 (P.L. 110-343)**

P.L. 110-343, Div. B, §203(c)(1):

Amended Code Sec. 6426 by adding at the end a new subsection (i). **Effective** for claims for credit or payment made on or after 5-15-2008.

[Sec. 6426(j)]

(j) ENERGY EQUIVALENCY DETERMINATIONS FOR LIQUEFIED PETROLEUM GAS AND LIQUEFIED NATURAL GAS.—For purposes of determining any credit under this section, any reference to the number of gallons of an alternative fuel or the gasoline gallon equivalent of such a fuel shall be treated as a reference to—

(1) in the case of liquefied petroleum gas, the energy equivalent of a gallon of gasoline, as defined in section 4041(a)(2)(C), and

(2) in the case of liquefied natural gas, the energy equivalent of a gallon of diesel, as defined in section 4041(a)(2)(D).

Amendments

• **2015, Protecting Americans from Tax Hikes Act of 2015 (P.L. 114-113)**

P.L. 114-113, §342(a), Div. Q:

Amended Code Sec. 6426 by adding at the end a new subsection (j). **Effective** for fuel sold or used after 12-31-2015.

[Sec. 6426(k)]

(k) SUSTAINABLE AVIATION FUEL CREDIT.—

(1) IN GENERAL.—For purposes of this section, the sustainable aviation fuel credit for the taxable year is, with respect to any sale or use of a qualified mixture, an amount equal to the product of—

(A) the number of gallons of sustainable aviation fuel in such mixture, multiplied by

(B) the sum of—

(i) $1.25, plus

(ii) the applicable supplementary amount with respect to such sustainable aviation fuel.

(2) DEFINITIONS.—Any term used in this subsection which is also used in section 40B shall have the meaning given such term by section 40B.

(3) REGISTRATION REQUIREMENT.—For purposes of this subsection, rules similar to the rules of section 40B(f) shall apply.

CREDITS AND REFUNDS—SPECIAL RULES

Amendments

• **2022, Inflation Reduction Act of 2022 (P.L. 117-169)**

P.L. 117-169, §13203(d)(1):

Amended Code Sec. 6426 by adding at the end a new subsection (k). **Effective** for fuel sold or used after 12-31-2022.

[Sec. 6426—Repealed]

Amendments

• **1982, Tax Equity and Fiscal Responsibility Act of 1982 (P.L. 97-248)**

P.L. 97-248, §280(c)(2)(G):

Repealed Code Sec. 6426. **Effective** with respect to transportation occurring after 8-31-82, except that such amendment will not apply to any amount paid on or before that date. Prior to repeal, Code Sec. 6426 read as follows:

SEC. 6426. REFUND OF AIRCRAFT USE TAX WHERE PLANE TRANSPORTS FOR HIRE IN FOREIGN AIR COMMERCE.

[Sec. 6426(a)]

(a) GENERAL RULE.—In the case of any aircraft used in the business of transporting persons or property for compensation or hire by air, if any of such transportation during any period is transportation in foreign air commerce, the Secretary shall pay (without interest) to the person who paid the tax under section 4491 for such period the amount determined by multiplying that portion of the amount so paid for such period which is determined under section 4491(a)(2) with respect to such aircraft by a fraction—

(1) the numerator of which is the number of airport-to-airport miles such aircraft traveled in foreign air commerce during such period while engaged in such business, and

(2) the denominator of which is the total number of airport-to-airport miles such aircraft traveled during such period.

Amendments

• **1976, Tax Reform Act of 1976 (P.L. 94-455)**

P.L. 94-455, §1906(b)(13)(A):

Amended 1954 Code by substituting "Secretary" for "Secretary or his delegate" each place it appeared. **Effective** 2-1-77.

[Sec. 6426(b)]

(b) DEFINITIONS.—For purposes of this section—

(1) FOREIGN AIR COMMERCE.—The term "foreign air commerce" means any movement by air of the aircraft which does not begin and end in the United States; except that any segment of such movement in which the aircraft traveled between two ports or stations in the United States shall be treated as travel which is not foreign air commerce.

(2) AIRPORT-TO-AIRPORT MILES.—The term "airport-to-airport miles" means the official mileage distance between airports as determined under regulations prescribed by the Secretary.

Amendments

• **1976, Tax Reform Act of 1976 (P.L. 94-455)**

P.L. 94-455, §1906(b)(13)(A):

Amended 1954 Code by substituting "Secretary" for "Secretary or his delegate" each place it appeared. **Effective** 2-1-77.

[Sec. 6426(c)]

(c) PAYMENTS TO PERSONS PAYING TENTATIVE TAX.—In the case of any person who paid a tentative tax determined under section 4493(b) with respect to any aircraft for any period, the amount payable under subsection (a) with respect to such aircraft for such period—

(1) shall be computed with reference to that portion of the tax imposed under section 4491 for such period which is determined under section 4491(a)(2), and

(2) as so computed, shall be reduced by an amount equal to—

(A) the amount by which that portion of the tax imposed under section 4491 for such period which is determined under section 4491(a)(2), exceeds

(B) the amount of the tentative tax determined under section 4493(b) paid for such period.

[Sec. 6426(d)]

(d) TIME FOR FILING CLAIM.—Not more than one claim may be filed under this section by any person with respect to any year. No claim shall be allowed under this subsection with respect to any year unless filed on or before the first September 30 after the end of such year.

[Sec. 6426(e)]

(e) REGULATIONS.—The Secretary may by regulations prescribe the conditions, not inconsistent with the provisions of this section, under which payments may be made under this section or the amount to which any person is entitled under this section with respect to any period may be treated by such person as an overpayment which may be credited against the tax imposed by section 4491 with respect to such period.

Amendments

• **1976, Tax Reform Act of 1976 (P.L. 94-455)**

P.L. 94-455, §1906(b)(13)(A):

Amended 1954 Code by substituting "Secretary" for "Secretary or his delegate" each place it appeared. **Effective** 2-1-77.

• **1970 (P.L. 91-258)**

P.L. 91-258, §206(c):

Added Code Sec. 6426. **Effective** 7-1-70.

[Sec. 6427]

SEC. 6427. FUELS NOT USED FOR TAXABLE PURPOSES.

[Sec. 6427(a)]

(a) NONTAXABLE USES.—Except as provided in subsection (k), if tax has been imposed under paragraph (2) or (3) of section 4041(a) or section 4041(c) on the sale of any fuel and the purchaser uses such fuel other than for the use for which sold, or resells such fuel, the Secretary shall pay (without interest) to him an amount equal to—

(1) the amount of tax imposed on the sale of the fuel to him, reduced by

(2) if he uses the fuel, the amount of tax which would have been imposed under section 4041 on such use if no tax under section 4041 had been imposed on the sale of the fuel.

Amendments

• **1993, Omnibus Budget Reconciliation Act of 1993 (P.L. 103-66)**

P.L. 103-66, §13242(d)(21):

Amended Code Sec. 6427(a) by striking "section 4041(a) or (c)" and inserting "paragraph (2) or (3) of section 4041(a) or section 4041(c)". **Effective** 1-1-94.

• **1986, Tax Reform Act of 1986 (P.L. 99-514)**

P.L. 99-514, §1703(e)(2)(A):

Amended Code Sec. 6427(a), (b)(1), (c), (d), (e)(1), and (g)(1) by striking out "subsection (j)" and inserting in lieu thereof "subsection (k)". **Effective** for gasoline removed (as defined in section 4082 of the Internal Revenue Code of 1986) after 12-31-87.

• **1984, Deficit Reduction Act of 1984 (P.L. 98-369)**

P.L. 98-369, §911(d)[c](2)(B):

Amended Code Sec. 6427(a) by striking out "(i)" and inserting in lieu thereof "(j)". **Effective** 8-1-84.

• **1983, Surface Transportation Act of 1983 (P.L. 97-424)**

P.L. 97-424, §511(g)(2)(B):

Amended Code Sec. 6427(a) by striking out "section 4041(a), (b), or (c)" and inserting "section 4041(a) or (c)". **Effective** 4-1-83.

• **1980, Crude Oil Windfall Profit Tax Act of 1980 (P.L. 96-223)**

P.L. 96-223, §232(d)(4)(B):

Substituted "subsection (i)" for "subsection (h)" in Code Sec. 6427(a). **Effective** 1-1-79.

• **1978, Surface Transportation Assistance Act of 1978 (P.L. 95-599)**

P.L. 95-599, §505(c)(1), (d):

Substituted "(h)" for "(g)" in Code Sec. 6427(a). **Effective** 1-1-79.

• **1976 (P.L. 94-530)**

P.L. 94-530, §[1](c)(2):

Substituted "(g)" for "(f)" in Code Sec. 6427(a). **Effective** 10-1-76.

• **1976, Tax Reform Act of 1976 (P.L. 94-455)**

P.L. 94-455, §1906(a)(31)(A):

Deleted ", after June 30, 1970," following "any fuel and" in Code Sec. 6427(a). **Effective** only with respect to fuel used or resold after 6-30-70.

P.L. 94-455, §1906(b)(13)(A):

Amended the 1954 Code by substituting "Secretary" for "Secretary or his delegate" each place it appeared. **Effective** 2-1-77.

[Sec. 6427(b)]

(b) INTERCITY, LOCAL OR SCHOOL BUSES.—

(1) ALLOWANCE.—Except as otherwise provided in this subsection and subsection (k), if any fuel other than gasoline (as defined in section 4083(a)) on the sale of which tax was imposed by section 4041(a) or 4081 is used in an automobile bus while engaged in—

CREDITS AND REFUNDS—SPECIAL RULES

(A) furnishing (for compensation) passenger land transportation available to the general public, or

(B) the transportation of students and employees of schools (as defined in the last sentence of section 4221(d)(7)(C)),

the Secretary shall pay (without interest) to the ultimate purchaser of such fuel an amount equal to the product of the number of gallons of such fuel so used multiplied by the rate at which tax was imposed on such fuel by section 4041(a) or 4081, as the case may be.

(2) REDUCTION IN REFUND IN CERTAIN CASES.—

(A) IN GENERAL.—Except as provided in subparagraphs (B) and (C), the rate of tax taken into account under paragraph (1) shall be 7.4 cents per gallon less than the aggregate rate at which tax was imposed on such fuel by section 4041(a) or 4081, as the case may be.

(B) EXCEPTION FOR SCHOOL BUS TRANSPORTATION.—Subparagraph (A) shall not apply to fuel used in an automobile bus while engaged in the transportation described in paragraph (1)(B).

(C) EXCEPTION FOR CERTAIN INTRACITY TRANSPORTATION.—Subparagraph (A) shall not apply to fuel used in any automobile bus while engaged in furnishing (for compensation) intracity passenger land transportation—

(i) which is available to the general public, and

(ii) which is scheduled and along regular routes, but only if such bus is a qualified local bus.

(D) QUALIFIED LOCAL BUS.—For purposes of this paragraph, the term "qualified local bus" means any local bus—

(i) which has a seating capacity of at least 20 adults (not including the driver), and

(ii) which is under contract (or is receiving more than a nominal subsidy) from any State or local government (as defined in section 4221(d)) to furnish such transportation.

(3) LIMITATION IN CASE OF NONSCHEDULED INTERCITY OR LOCAL BUSES.—Paragraph (1)(A) shall not apply in respect of fuel used in any automobile bus while engaged in furnishing transportation which is not scheduled and not along regular routes unless the seating capacity of such bus is at least 20 adults (not including the driver).

(4) REFUNDS FOR USE OF DIESEL FUEL IN CERTAIN INTERCITY BUSES.—With respect to any fuel to which paragraph (2)(A) applies, if the ultimate purchaser of such fuel waives (at such time and in such form and manner as the Secretary shall prescribe) the right to payment under paragraph (1) and assigns such right to the ultimate vendor, then the Secretary shall pay the amount which would be paid under paragraph (1) to such ultimate vendor, but only if such ultimate vendor—

(A) is registered under section 4101, and

(B) meets the requirements of subparagraph (A), (B), or (D) of section 6416(a)(1).

Amendments

• **2004, American Jobs Creation Act of 2004 (P.L. 108-357)**

P.L. 108-357, § 857(b):

Amended Code Sec. 6427(b) by adding at the end a new paragraph (4). **Effective** for fuel sold after 12-31-2004.

• **1993, Omnibus Budget Reconciliation Act of 1993 (P.L. 103-66)**

P.L. 103-66, § 13241(f)(8)(A)-(B):

Amended Code Sec. 6427(b)(2) by striking "3.1 cents" in subparagraph (A) and inserting "7.4 cents", and by striking "3-CENT REDUCTION" in the paragraph heading and inserting "REDUCTION". **Effective** 10-1-93.

P.L. 103-66, § 13242(d)(25)(A)-(B):

Amended Code Sec. 6427(b) by striking "if any fuel" in paragraph (1) and inserting "if any fuel other than gasoline (as defined in section 4083(a))", and by striking "4091" each place it appears and inserting "4081". **Effective** 1-1-94.

• **1990, Omnibus Budget Reconciliation Act of 1990 (P.L. 101-508)**

P.L. 101-508, § 11211(b)(5):

Amended Code Sec. 6427(b)(2)(A) by striking "shall not exceed 12 cents" and inserting "shall be 3.1 cents per gallon less than the aggregate rate at which tax was imposed on such fuel by section 4041(a) or 4091, as the case may be". **Effective** 12-1-90.

• **1987, Revenue Act of 1987 (P.L. 100-203)**

P.L. 100-203, § 10502(c)(2)(A)-(B):

Amended Code Sec. 6427(b)(1) by striking out "subsection (a) of section 4041" the first place it appears and inserting in lieu thereof "section 4041(a) or 4091", and by striking out "subsection (a) of section 4041" the second place it appears and inserting in lieu thereof "section 4041(a) or 4091, as the case may be". **Effective** for sales after 3-31-88. See also Act Sec. 10502(f) in the amendment notes following Code Sec. 6427(q).

• **1986, Tax Reform Act of 1986 (P.L. 99-514)**

P.L. 99-514, § 1703(e)(2)(A):

Amended Code Sec. 6427(a), (b)(1), (c), (d), (e)(1), (f)(1), and (g)(1) by striking out "subsection (j)" and inserting in lieu thereof "subsection (k)". **Effective** for gasoline removed (as defined in section 4082 of the Internal Revenue Code of 1986) after 12-31-87.

P.L. 99-514, § 1877(b)(1):

Amended Code Sec. 6427(b)(2) by redesignating subparagraphs (B) and (C) as subparagraphs (C) and (D), respectively, and by inserting after subparagraph (A) new subparagraph (B). **Effective** as if included in the provision of P.L. 98-369 to which it relates.

P.L. 99-514, § 1877(b)(2):

Amended Code Sec. 6427(b)(2)(A) by striking out "subparagraph (B)" and inserting in lieu thereof "subparagraphs (B) and (C)". **Effective** as if included in the provision of P.L. 98-369 to which it relates.

P.L. 99-514, § 1877(b)(3):

Amended Code Sec. 6427(b)(2), as redesignated by Act Sec. 1877(b)(1), by striking out "Exception" in the heading of subparagraph (C) and inserting in lieu thereof "Exception for certain intracity transportation". **Effective** as if included in the provision of P.L. 98-369 to which it relates.

P.L. 99-514, § 1899A(55):

Amended Code Sec. 6427(b)(1) by striking out "provided in paragraph (2)" and inserting in lieu thereof "otherwise provided in this subsection". **Effective** on 10-22-86.

• **1984, Deficit Reduction Act of 1984 (P.L. 98-369)**

P.L. 98-369, § 911(d)[c](2)(B):

Amended Code Sec. 6427(b)(1) by striking out "(i)" and inserting in lieu thereof"(j)". **Effective** 8-1-84.

P.L. 98-369, § 915(a):

Amended Code Sec. 6427(b) by redesignating paragraph (2) as paragraph (3) and inserting after paragraph (1) new paragraph (2). **Effective** 8-1-84.

• **1983, Surface Transportation Act of 1983 (P.L. 97-424)**

P.L. 97-424, § 511(g)(2)(C):

Amended Code Sec. 6427(b)(1) by striking out "subsection (a) or (b) of section 4041" and inserting "subsection (a) of section 4041". **Effective** 4-1-83.

• **1980, Crude Oil Windfall Profit Tax Act of 1980 (P.L. 96-223)**

P.L. 96-223, § 232(d)(4)(B):

Substituted "subsection (i)" for "subsection (h)" in Code Sec. 6427(b)(1). **Effective** 1-1-79.

• **1978, Energy Tax Act of 1978 (P.L. 95-618)**

P.L. 95-618, § 233(a)(2), (d):

Amended Code Sec. 6427(b). **Effective** 12-1-78. Prior to amendment, Code Sec. 6427(b) read:

"(b) LOCAL TRANSIT SYSTEMS.—

"(1) ALLOWANCE.—Except as provided in subsection (g), if any fuel on the sale of which tax was imposed under section 4041(a) or (b) is used by the purchaser during any calendar quarter in vehicles while engaged in furnishing scheduled common carrier public passenger land transportation service along regular routes, the Secretary shall, subject to the provisions of paragraph (2), pay (without interest) to the purchaser the amount determined by multiplying—

"(A) 2 cents for each gallon of fuel so used on which tax was imposed at the rate of 4 cents a gallon, by

"(B) the percentage which the purchaser's commuter fare revenue (as defined in section 6421(d)(2)) derived from such scheduled service during the quarter was of his total passenger fare revenue derived from such scheduled service during the quarter.

"(2) LIMITATION.—Paragraph (1) shall apply in respect of fuel used during any calendar quarter only if at least 60 percent of the total passenger fare revenue derived during the quarter from scheduled service described in paragraph (1) by the purchaser was attributable to commuter fare revenue derived during the quarter by the purchaser from such scheduled service."

• **1978, Surface Transportation Assistance Act of 1978 (P.L. 95-599)**

P.L. 95-599, § 505(c)(2), (d):

Substituted "(h)" for "(g)" in Code Sec. 6427(b)(1). **Effective** 1-1-79.

• **1976 (P.L. 94-530)**

P.L. 94-530, § [1](c)(2):

Substituted "(g)" for "(f)" in Code Sec. 6427(b)(1). **Effective** 10-1-76.

CREDITS AND REFUNDS—SPECIAL RULES

- **1976, Tax Reform Act of 1976 (P.L. 94-455)**

P.L. 94-455, §1906(a)(31)(A):

Deleted ", after June 30, 1970," following "section 4041(a) or (b) is" in Code Sec. 6427(b)(1). **Effective** only with respect to fuel used or resold after 6-30-70.

P.L. 94-455, §1906(b)(13)(A):

Amended the 1954 Code by substituting "Secretary" for "Secretary or his delegate" each place it appeared. **Effective** 2-1-77.

[Sec. 6427(c)]

(c) USE FOR FARMING PURPOSES.—Except as provided in subsection (k), if any fuel on the sale of which tax was imposed under section paragraph (2) or (3) of section 4041(a) or section 4041(c) is used on a farm for farming purposes (within the meaning of section 6420(c)), the Secretary shall pay (without interest) to the purchaser an amount equal to the amount of the tax imposed on the sale of the fuel. For purposes of this subsection, if fuel is used on a farm by any person other than the owner, tenant, or operator of such farm, the rules of paragraph (4) of section 6420(c) shall be applied (except that "liquid taxable under section 4041" shall be substituted for "gasoline" each place it appears in such paragraph (4)).

Amendments

- **1993, Omnibus Budget Reconciliation Act of 1993 (P.L. 103-66)**

P.L. 103-66, §13242(d)(21):

Amended Code Sec. 6427(c) by striking "section 4041(a) or (c)" and inserting "paragraph (2) or (3) of section 4041(a) or section 4041(c)". **Effective** 1-1-94.

- **1986, Tax Reform Act of 1986 (P.L. 99-514)**

P.L. 99-514, §1703(e)(2)(A):

Amended Code Sec. 6427(a), (b)(1), (c), (d), (e)(1), (f)(1), and (g)(1) by striking out "subsection (j)" and inserting in lieu thereof "subsection (k)". **Effective** for gasoline removed (as defined in section 4082 of the Internal Revenue Code of 1986) after 12-31-87.

- **1984, Deficit Reduction Act of 1984 (P.L. 98-369)**

P.L. 98-369, §911(d)[c](2)(B):

Amended Code Sec. 6427(c) by striking out "(i)" and inserting in lieu thereof "(j)". **Effective** 8-1-84.

- **1983, Surface Transportation Act of 1983 (P.L. 97-424)**

P.L. 97-424, §511(g)(2)(D):

Amended Code Sec. 6427(c) by striking out "section 4041(a), (b) or (c)" and inserting "section 4041(a) or (c)".

- **1980, Crude Oil Windfall Profit Tax Act of 1980 (P.L. 96-223)**

P.L. 96-223, §232(d)(4)(B):

Substituted "subsection (i)" for "subsection (h)" in Code Sec. 6427(c). **Effective** 1-1-79.

- **1978, Surface Transportation Assistance Act of 1978 (P.L. 95-599)**

P.L. 95-599, §505(c)(2), (d):

Substituted "(h)" for "(g)" in Code Sec. 6427(c). **Effective** 1-1-79.

- **1978 (P.L. 95-458)**

P.L. 95-458, §3(b), (d):

Amended the second sentence of subsection (c). **Effective** 4-1-79. Prior to amendment, the second sentence of subsection (c) read as follows:

"For purposes of this subsection, if fuel is used on a farm by any person other than the owner, tenant, or operator of such farm, such owner, tenant, or operator shall be treated as the user and purchaser of such fuel."

- **1976 (P.L. 94-530)**

P.L. 94-530, §[1](c)(2):

Substituted "(g)" for "(f)" in Code Sec. 6427(c). **Effective** 10-1-76.

- **1976, Tax Reform Act of 1976 (P.L. 94-455)**

P.L. 94-455, §1906(a)(31)(A):

Deleted ", after June 30, 1970," following "section 4041(a), (b) or (c) is" in Code Sec. 6427(c). **Effective** only with respect to fuel used or resold after 6-30-70.

P.L. 94-455, §1906(b)(13)(A):

Amended the 1954 Code by substituting "Secretary" for "Secretary or his delegate" each place it appeared. **Effective** 2-1-77.

[Sec. 6427(d)]

(d) USE BY CERTAIN AIRCRAFT MUSEUMS OR IN CERTAIN OTHER AIRCRAFT USES.—Except as provided in subsection (k), if—

    (1) any gasoline on which tax is imposed by section 4081, or

    (2) any fuel on the sale of which tax was imposed under section 4041,

is used by an aircraft museum (as defined in section 4041(h)(2)) in an aircraft or vehicle owned by such museum and used exclusively for purposes set forth in section 4041(h)(2)(C), or is used in a helicopter or a fixed-wing aircraft for a purpose described in section 4041(1), the Secretary shall pay (without interest) to the ultimate purchaser of such gasoline or fuel an amount equal to the aggregate amount of the tax imposed on such gasoline or fuel.

Amendments

- **1998, IRS Restructuring and Reform Act of 1998 (P.L. 105-206)**

P.L. 105-206, §6016(b)(1)-(2):

Amended Code Sec. 6427(d) by striking "HELICOPTERS" in the heading and inserting "OTHER AIRCRAFT USES", and by inserting "or a fixed-wing aircraft" after "helicopter". **Effective** as if included in the provision of P.L. 105-34 to which it relates [generally effective 8-27-96.—CCH].

- **1986, Tax Reform Act of 1986 (P.L. 99-514)**

P.L. 99-514, §1703(e)(2)(A):

Amended Code Sec. 6427(a), (b)(1), (c), (d), (e)(1), (f)(1), and (g)(1) by striking out "subsection (j)" and inserting in lieu thereof "subsection (k)". **Effective** for gasoline removed (as defined in section 4082 of the Internal Revenue Code of 1986) after 12-31-87.

- **1984, Deficit Reduction Act of 1984 (P.L. 98-369)**

P.L. 98-369, §911(d)[c](2)(B):

Amended Code Sec. 6427(d) by striking out "(i)" and inserting in lieu thereof "(j)". **Effective** 8-1-84.

- **1982, Tax Equity and Fiscal Responsibility Act of 1982 (P.L. 97-248)**

P.L. 97-248, §279(b)(2)(A):

Amended Code Sec. 6427(d) by inserting "or is used in a helicopter for a purpose described in section 4041(1)," after "section 4041(h)(2)(C),". **Effective** 9-1-82.

P.L. 97-248, §279(b)(2)(B):

Amended the subsection heading by inserting "OR IN CERTAIN HELICOPTERS" after "MUSEUMS". **Effective** 9-1-82.

- **1980, Crude Oil Windfall Profit Tax Act of 1980 (P.L. 96-223)**

P.L. 96-223, §232(d)(4)(B):

Substituted "subsection (i)" for "subsection (h)" in Code Sec. 6427(d). **Effective** 1-1-79.

- **1978, Revenue Act of 1978 (P.L. 95-600)**

P.L. 95-600, §703(l)(3), (r):

Amended Code Sec. 6427(d) by striking out "Secretary or his delegate" and inserting "Secretary" in lieu thereof. **Effective** 10-4-76.

- **1978, Surface Transportation Assistance Act of 1978 (P.L. 95-599)**

P.L. 95-599, §505(c)(2), (d):

Substituted "(h)" for "(g)" in Code Sec. 6427(d). **Effective** 1-1-79.

- **1976 (P.L. 94-530)**

P.L. 94-530, §[1](b):

Added Code Sec. 6427(d). **Effective** 10-1-76.

(e) ALCOHOL, BIODIESEL, ALTERNATIVE FUEL, OR SUSTAINABLE AVIATION FUEL.—Except as provided in subsection (k)—

    (1) USED TO PRODUCE A MIXTURE.—If any person produces a mixture described in section 6426 in such person's trade or business, the Secretary shall pay (without interest) to such person an amount equal to the alcohol fuel mixture credit or the biodiesel mixture credit or the alternative fuel mixture credit or the sustainable aviation fuel mixture credit with respect to such mixture.

    (2) ALTERNATIVE FUEL.—If any person sells or uses an alternative fuel (as defined in section 6426(d)(2)) for a purpose described in section 6426(d)(1) in such person's trade or business, the Secretary shall pay (without interest) to such person an amount equal to the alternative fuel credit with respect to such fuel.

    (3) COORDINATION WITH OTHER REPAYMENT PROVISIONS.—No amount shall be payable under paragraph (1) or (2) with respect to any mixture or alternative fuel with respect to which an amount is allowed as a credit under section 6426.

CREDITS AND REFUNDS—SPECIAL RULES

(4) REGISTRATION REQUIREMENT FOR ALTERNATIVE FUELS.—The Secretary shall not make any payment under this subsection to any person with respect to any alternative fuel credit or alternative fuel mixture credit unless the person is registered under section 4101.

(5) LIMITATION TO FUELS WITH CONNECTION TO THE UNITED STATES.—No amount shall be payable under paragraph (1) or (2) with respect to any mixture or alternative fuel if credit is not allowed with respect to such mixture or alternative fuel by reason of section 6426(i).

(6) TERMINATION.—This subsection shall not apply with respect to—

(A) any alcohol fuel mixture (as defined in section 6426(b)(3)) sold or used after December 31, 2011,

(B) any biodiesel mixture (as defined in section 6426(c)(3)) sold or used after December 31, 2024,

(C) any alternative fuel (as defined in section 6426(d)(2)) sold or used after December 31, 2024,

(D) any alternative fuel mixture (as defined in section 6426(e)(2)) sold or used after December 31, 2011, and

(E) any qualified mixture of sustainable aviation fuel (as defined in section 6426(k)(3)) sold or used after December 31, 2024.

Amendments

• **2022, Inflation Reduction Act of 2022 (P.L. 117-169)**

P.L. 117-169, § 13201(b)(2):

Amended Code Sec. 6427(e)(6)(B) by striking "December 31, 2022" and inserting "December 31, 2024". **Effective** for fuel sold or used after 12-31-2021. For a special rule, see Act Sec. 13201(g), below.

P.L. 117-169, § 13201(e):

Amended Code Sec. 6427(e)(6)(C) by striking "December 31, 2021" and inserting "December 31, 2024". **Effective** for fuel sold or used after 12-31-2021. For a special rule, see Act Sec. 13201(g), below.

P.L. 117-169, § 13201(g), provides:

(g) SPECIAL RULE.—In the case of any alternative fuel credit properly determined under section 6426(d) of the Internal Revenue Code of 1986 for the period beginning on January 1, 2022, and ending with the close of the last calendar quarter beginning before the date of the enactment of this Act, such credit shall be allowed, and any refund or payment attributable to such credit (including any payment under section 6427(e) of such Code) shall be made, only in such manner as the Secretary of the Treasury (or the Secretary's delegate) shall provide. Such Secretary shall issue guidance within 30 days after the date of the enactment of this Act providing for a one-time submission of claims covering periods described in the preceding sentence. Such guidance shall provide for a 180-day period for the submission of such claims (in such manner as prescribed by such Secretary) to begin not later than 30 days after such guidance is issued. Such claims shall be paid by such Secretary not later than 60 days after receipt. If such Secretary has not paid pursuant to a claim filed under this subsection within 60 days after the date of the filing of such claim, the claim shall be paid with interest from such date determined by using the overpayment rate and method under section 6621 of such Code.

P.L. 117-169, § 13203(d)(2)(B)(i)-(iii):

Amended Code Sec. 6427(e) by striking "OR ALTERNATIVE FUEL" and inserting, "ALTERNATIVE FUEL, OR SUSTAINABLE AVIATION FUEL" in the heading, and in paragraph (1), by inserting "or the sustainable aviation fuel mixture credit" after "alternative fuel mixture credit", and in paragraph (6), by striking "and" at the end of subparagraph (C), by striking the period at the end of subparagraph (D) and inserting ", and", and by adding at the end new subparagraph (E). **Effective** for fuel sold or used after 12-31-2022.

• **2020, Taxpayer Certainty and Disaster Tax Relief Act of 2020 (P.L. 116-260)**

P.L. 116-260, § 147(b), Div. EE:

Amended Code Sec. 6427(e)(6)(C) by striking "December 31, 2020" and inserting "December 31, 2021". **Effective** for fuel sold or used after 12-31-2020.

• **2019, Taxpayer Certainty and Disaster Tax Relief Act of 2019 (P.L. 116-94)**

P.L. 116-94, § 121(b)(1)(B), Div. Q:

Amended Code Sec. 6427(e)(6)(B) by striking "December 31, 2017" and inserting "December 31, 2022". **Effective** for fuel sold or used after 12-31-2017. For a special rule, see Act 121(b)(3), Div. Q, below.

P.L. 116-94, § 121(b)(3), Div. Q, provides:

(3) SPECIAL RULE.—Notwithstanding any other provision of law, in the case of any biodiesel mixture credit properly determined under section 6426(c) of the Internal Revenue Code of 1986 for the period beginning on January 1, 2018, and ending with the close of the last calendar quarter beginning before the date of the enactment of this Act, such credit shall be allowed, and any refund or payment attributable to such credit (including any payment under section 6427(e) of such Code) shall be made, only in such manner as the Secretary of the Treasury (or the Secretary's delegate) shall provide. Such Secretary shall issue guidance within 30 days after the date of the enactment of this Act providing for a one-time submission of claims covering periods described in the preceding sentence. Such guidance shall provide for a 180-day period for the submission of such claims (in such manner as prescribed by such Secretary) to begin not later than 30 days after such guidance is issued. Such claims shall be paid by such Secretary not later than 60 days after receipt. If such Secretary has not paid pursuant to a claim filed under this subsection within 60 days after the date of the filing of such claim, the claim shall be paid with interest from such date determined by using the overpayment rate and method under section 6621 of such Code.

P.L. 116-94, § 133(a)(2), Div. Q:

Amended Code Sec. 6427(e)(6)(C) by striking "December 31, 2017" and inserting "December 31, 2020". **Effective** for fuel sold or used after 12-31-2017. For special rule, see Act Sec. 133(a)(3), Div. Q, below.

P.L. 116-94, § 133(a)(3), Div. Q, provides:

(3) SPECIAL RULE.—Notwithstanding any other provision of law, in the case of any alternative fuel credit properly determined under section 6426(d) of the Internal Revenue Code of 1986 for the period beginning on January 1, 2018, and ending with the close of the last calendar quarter beginning before the date of the enactment of this Act, such credit shall be allowed, and any refund or payment attributable to such credit (including any payment under section 6427(e) of such Code) shall be made, only in such manner as the Secretary of the Treasury (or the Secretary's delegate) shall provide. Such Secretary shall issue guidance within 30 days after the date of the enactment of this Act providing for a one-time submission of claims covering periods described in the preceding sentence. Such guidance shall provide for a 180-day period for the submission of such claims (in such manner as prescribed by such Secretary) to begin not later than 30 days after such guidance is issued. Such claims shall be paid by such Secretary not later than 60 days after receipt. If such Secretary has not paid pursuant to a claim filed under this subsection within 60 days after the date of the filing of such claim, the claim shall be paid with interest from such date determined by using the overpayment rate and method under section 6621 of such Code.

• **2018, Bipartisan Budget Act of 2018 (P.L. 115-123)**

P.L. 115-123, § 40407(b)(2), Div. D:

Amended Code Sec. 6427(e)(6)(B) by striking "December 31, 2016" and inserting "December 31, 2017". **Effective** for fuel sold or used after 12-31-2016. For a special rule, see Act Sec. 40407(b)(4), below.

P.L. 115-123, § 40407(b)(4), Div. D, provides:

(4) SPECIAL RULE FOR 2017.—Notwithstanding any other provision of law, in the case of any biodiesel mixture credit properly determined under section 6426(c) of the Internal Revenue Code of 1986 for the period beginning on January 1, 2017, and ending on December 31, 2017, such credit shall be allowed, and any refund or payment attributable to such credit (including any payment under section 6427(e) of such Code) shall be made, only in such manner as the Secretary of the Treasury (or the Secretary's delegate) shall provide. Such Secretary shall issue guidance within 30 days after the date of the enactment of this Act providing for a one-time submission of claims covering periods described in the preceding sentence. Such guidance shall provide for a 180-day period for the submission of such claims (in such manner as prescribed by such Secretary) to begin not later than 30 days after such guidance is issued. Such claims shall be paid by such Secretary not later than 60 days after receipt. If such Secretary has not paid pursuant to a claim filed under this subsection within 60 days after the date of the filing of such claim, the claim shall be paid with interest from such date determined by using the overpayment rate and method under section 6621 of such Code.

P.L. 115-123, § 40415(a)(2), Div. D:

Amended Code Sec. 6427(e)(6)(C) by striking "December 31, 2016" and inserting "December 31, 2017". **Effective** for fuel sold or used after 12-31-2016. For a special rule, see Act Sec. 40415(b), Div. D, below.

P.L. 115-123, § 40415(a), Div. D, provides:

(b) SPECIAL RULE FOR 2017.—Notwithstanding any other provision of law, in the case of any alternative fuel credit properly determined under section 6426(d) of the Internal Revenue Code of 1986 for the period beginning on January 1, 2017, and ending on December 31, 2017, such credit shall be allowed, and any refund or payment attributable to such credit (including any payment under section 6427(e) of such Code) shall be made, only in such manner as the Secretary of the Treasury (or the Secretary's delegate) shall provide. Such Secretary shall issue guidance within 30 days after the date of the enactment of this Act providing for a one-time submission of claims covering periods described in the preceding sentence. Such guidance shall provide for a 180-day period for the submission of such claims (in such manner as prescribed by such Secretary) to begin not later than 30 days after such guidance is issued. Such claims shall be paid by such Secretary not later than 60 days after receipt. If such Secretary has not paid pursuant to a claim filed under this subsection within 60 days after the date of the filing of such claim, the claim shall be paid with interest from such date determined by using the overpayment rate and method under section 6621 of such Code.

• **2015, Protecting Americans from Tax Hikes Act of 2015 (P.L. 114-113)**

P.L. 114-113, § 185(b)(2), Div. Q:

Amended Code Sec. 6427(e)(6)(B) by striking "December 31, 2014" and inserting "December 31, 2016". **Effective** for fuel sold or used after 12-31-2014. For a special rule, see Act Sec. 185(b)(4), below.

P.L. 114-113, § 185(b)(4), Div. Q, provides:

(4) SPECIAL RULE FOR 2015.—Notwithstanding any other provision of law, in the case of any biodiesel mixture credit properly determined under section 6426(c) of the Internal Revenue Code of 1986 for the period beginning on January 1, 2015, and ending on December 31, 2015, such credit shall be allowed, and any refund or payment attributable to such credit (including any payment under section 6427(e) of such Code) shall be made, only in such manner as the Secretary of the Treasury (or the Secretary's delegate) shall provide. Such Secretary shall issue guidance within 30 days after the date of the enactment of this Act providing for a one-time submission of claims covering periods described in the preceding sentence. Such guidance shall provide for a 180-day period for the submission of such claims (in such manner as prescribed by such Secretary) to begin not later than 30 days after such guidance is issued. Such claims shall be paid by such Secretary not later than 60 days after receipt. If such Secretary has not paid pursuant to a claim filed under this subsection

CREDITS AND REFUNDS—SPECIAL RULES

within 60 days after the date of the filing of such claim, the claim shall be paid with interest from such date determined by using the overpayment rate and method under section 6621 of such Code.

P.L. 114-113, §192(a)(2), Div. Q:

Amended Code Sec. 6427(e)(6)(C) by striking "December 31, 2014" and inserting "December 31, 2016". **Effective** for fuel sold or used after 12-31-2014. For a special rule, see Act Sec. 192(c), below.

P.L. 114-113, §192(c), Div. Q, provides:

(c) SPECIAL RULE FOR 2015.—Notwithstanding any other provision of law, in the case of any alternative fuel credit properly determined under section 6426(d) of the Internal Revenue Code of 1986 for the period beginning on January 1, 2015, and ending on December 31, 2015, such credit shall be allowed, and any refund or payment attributable to such credit (including any payment under section 6427(e) of such Code) shall be made, only in such manner as the Secretary of the Treasury (or the Secretary's delegate) shall provide. Such Secretary shall issue guidance within 30 days after the date of the enactment of this Act providing for a one-time submission of claims covering periods described in the preceding sentence. Such guidance shall provide for a 180-day period for the submission of such claims (in such manner as prescribed by such Secretary) to begin not later than 30 days after such guidance is issued. Such claims shall be paid by such Secretary not later than 60 days after receipt. If such Secretary has not paid pursuant to a claim filed under this subsection within 60 days after the date of the filing of such claim, the claim shall be paid with interest from such date determined by using the overpayment rate and method under section 6621 of such Code.

- **2014, Tax Increase Prevention Act of 2014 (P.L. 113-295)**

P.L. 113-295, §160(a)(2), Div. A:

Amended Code Sec. 6427(e)(6)(B) by striking "December 31, 2013" and inserting "December 31, 2014". **Effective** for fuel sold or used after 12-31-2013. For a special rule, see Act Sec. 160(e), Div. A, below.

P.L. 113-295, §160(b)(2), Div. A:

Amended Code Sec. 6427(e)(6)(C) by striking "December 31, 2013" and inserting "December 31, 2014". **Effective** for fuel sold or used after 12-31-2013. For a special rule, see Act Sec. 160(e), Div. A, below.

P.L. 113-295, §160(c)(2)(A)-(C), Div. A:

Amended Code Sec. 6427(e)(6) by striking "except as provided in subparagraph (D), any" in subparagraph (C), as amended by this Act, and inserting "any", by striking the comma at the end of subparagraph (C) and inserting ", and", and by striking subparagraph (D) and redesignating subparagraph (E) as subparagraph (D). **Effective** for fuel sold or used after 9-30-2014. For a special rule, see Act Sec. 160(e), Div. A, below. Prior to being stricken, Code Sec. 6427(e)(6)(D) read as follows:

(D) any alternative fuel (as so defined) involving liquefied hydrogen sold or used after September 30, 2014, and

P.L. 113-295, §160(e), Div. A, provides:

(e) SPECIAL RULE FOR CERTAIN PERIODS DURING 2014.—Notwithstanding any other provision of law, in the case of—

(1) any biodiesel mixture credit properly determined under section 6426(c) of the Internal Revenue Code of 1986 for periods after December 31, 2013, and before the date of the enactment of this Act, and

(2) any alternative fuel credit properly determined under section 6426(d) of such Code for such periods,

such credit shall be allowed, and any refund or payment attributable to such credit (including any payment under section 6427(e) of such Code) shall be made, only in such manner as the Secretary of the Treasury (or the Secretary's delegate) shall provide. Such Secretary shall issue guidance within 30 days after the date of the enactment of this Act providing for a one-time submission of claims covering periods described in the preceding sentence. Such guidance shall provide for a 180-day period for the submission of such claims (in such manner as prescribed by such Secretary) to begin not later than 30 days after such guidance is issued. Such claims shall be paid by such Secretary not later than 60 days after receipt. If such Secretary has not paid pursuant to a claim filed under this subsection within 60 days after the date of the filing of such claim, the claim shall be paid with interest from such date determined by using the overpayment rate and method under section 6621 of such Code.

- **2013, American Taxpayer Relief Act of 2012 (P.L. 112-240)**

P.L. 112-240, §405(b)(2):

Amended Code Sec. 6427(e)(6)(B) by striking "December 31, 2011" and inserting "December 31, 2013". **Effective** for fuel sold or used after 12-31-2011.

P.L. 112-240, §412(b)(1)-(3):

Amended Code Sec. 6427(e)(6) by striking "or alternative fuel mixture (as defined in subsection (d)(2) or (e)(3) of section 6426)" and inserting "(as defined in section 6426(d)(2))", and by striking "December 31, 2011, and" and inserting "December 31, 2013," in subparagraph (C), and by striking "or alternative fuel mixture" after "any alternative fuel", and by striking the period at the end and inserting ", and" in subparagraph (D), and by adding at the end a new subparagraph (E). **Effective** for fuel sold or used after 12-31-2011.

- **2010, Tax Relief, Unemployment Insurance Reauthorization, and Job Creation Act of 2010 (P.L. 111-312)**

P.L. 111-312, §701(b)(2):

Amended Code Sec. 6427(e)(6)(B) by striking "December 31, 2009" and inserting "December 31, 2011". **Effective** for fuel sold or used after 12-31-2009.

P.L. 111-312, §704(a):

Amended Code Sec. 6427(e)(6)(C) by striking "December 31, 2009" and inserting "December 31, 2011". **Effective** for fuel sold or used after 12-31-2009. For a special rule, see Act Sec. 704(c), below.

P.L. 111-312, §704(c), provides:

(c) SPECIAL RULE FOR 2010.—Notwithstanding any other provision of law, in the case of any alternative fuel credit or any alternative fuel mixture credit properly determined under subsection (d) or (e) of section 6426 of the Internal Revenue Code of 1986 for periods during 2010, such credit shall be allowed, and any refund or payment attributable to such credit (including any payment under section 6427(e) of such Code) shall be made, only in such manner as the Secretary of the Treasury (or the Secretary's delegate) shall provide. Such Secretary shall issue guidance within 30 days after the date of the enactment of this Act providing for a one-time submission of claims covering periods during 2010. Such guidance shall provide for a 180-day period for the submission of such claims (in such manner as prescribed by such Secretary) to begin not later than 30 days after such guidance is issued. Such claims shall be paid by such Secretary not later than 60 days after receipt. If such Secretary has not paid pursuant to a claim filed under this subsection within 60 days after the date of the filing of such claim, the claim shall be paid with interest from such date determined by using the overpayment rate and method under section 6621 of such Code.

P.L. 111-312, §708(c)(1):

Amended Code Sec. 6427(e)(6)(A) by striking "December 31, 2010" and inserting "December 31, 2011". **Effective** for sales and uses after 12-31-2010.

- **2008, Energy Improvement and Extension Act of 2008 (P.L. 110-343)**

P.L. 110-343, Div. B, §202(a):

Amended Code Sec. 6427(e)(5)(B) by striking "December 31, 2008" and inserting "December 31, 2009". **Effective** for fuel produced, and sold or used, after 12-31-2008.

P.L. 110-343, Div. B, §203(c)(2):

Amended Code Sec. 6427(e) by redesignating paragraph (5) as paragraph (6) and inserting after paragraph (4) a new paragraph (5). **Effective** for claims for credit or payment made on or after 5-15-2008.

P.L. 110-343, Div. B, §204(a)(3):

Amended Code Sec. 6427(e)(5)(C) [prior to redesignation as Code Sec. 6427(e)(6)(C) by Act Sec. 203(c)(2)] by striking "September 30, 2009" and inserting "December 31, 2009". **Effective** for fuel sold or used after 10-3-2008.

- **2007, Tax Technical Corrections Act of 2007 (P.L. 110-172)**

P.L. 110-172, §11(a)(37):

Amended Code Sec. 6427(e) by redesignating paragraph (3), as added [sic] by section 11113 of the Safe, Accountable, Flexible, Efficient Transportation Equity Act: A Legacy for Users (P.L. 109-59), as paragraph (5) and moving it after paragraph (4). **Effective** 12-29-2007.

P.L. 110-172, §11(e)(1):

Amended Code Sec. 6427(e)(5)(B), as redesignated by Act Sec. 11(a)(37), by striking "2006" and inserting "2008". [Note: Code Sec. 6427(e)(5)(B) does not contain the text "2006". Therefore, this amendment cannot be made.—CCH] **Effective** as if included in the provision of the Energy Tax Incentives Act of 2005 (P.L. 109-58) to which it relates [effective 8-8-2005.—CCH].

- **2005, Safe, Accountable, Flexible, Efficient Transportation Equity Act: A Legacy for Users (P.L. 109-59)**

P.L. 109-59, §11113(b)(3)(C)(i)-(ix):

Amended Code Sec. 6427(e) by inserting "or the alternative fuel mixture credit" after "biodiesel mixture credit" in paragraph (1), by redesignating paragraph (2) as paragraph (3) and paragraph (4)[(3)] as paragraph (5), by inserting after paragraph (1) a new paragraph (2), by striking "under paragraph (1) with respect to any mixture" in paragraph (3) (as redesignated by Act Sec. 11113(b)(3)(C)(ii)) and inserting "under paragraph (1) or (2) with respect to any mixure or alternative fuel", by inserting after paragraph (3) (as so redesignated) a new paragraph (4), by striking "and" at the end of paragraph (5)(A) (as redesignated by Act Sec. 11113(b)(3)(C)(ii)), by striking the period at the end of paragraph (5)(B) (as so redesignated) and inserting a comma, by adding at the end of paragraph (5) (as so redesignated) new subparagraphs (C) and (D), and by striking "OR BIODIESEL USED TO PRODUCE ALCOHOL FUEL AND BIODIESEL MIXTURES" in the heading and inserting ", BIODIESEL, OR ALTERNATIVE FUEL". **Effective** for any sale or use for any period after 9-30-2006.

- **2005, Energy Tax Incentives Act of 2005 (P.L. 109-58)**

P.L. 109-58, §1344(a):

Amended Code Sec. 6427(e)(4)[(3)](B) by striking "2006" and inserting "2008". **Effective** 8-8-2005.

- **2004, American Jobs Creation Act of 2004 (P.L. 108-357)**

P.L. 108-357, §301(c)(9):

Amended Code Sec. 6427 by inserting after subsection (d) a new subsection (e). **Effective** for fuel sold or used after 12-31-2004.

CREDITS AND REFUNDS—SPECIAL RULES

[Sec. 6427(e)—Repealed]

Amendments

• **1990, Omnibus Budget Reconciliation Act of 1990 (P.L. 101-508)**

P.L. 101-508, § 11801(a)(46):

Repealed Code Sec. 6427(e). **Effective** 11-5-90.

P.L. 101-508, § 11821(b), provides:

(b) SAVINGS PROVISION.—If—

(1) any provision amended or repealed by this part applied to—

(A) any transaction occurring before the date of the enactment of this Act,

(B) any property acquired before such date of enactment, or

(C) any item of income, loss, deduction, or credit taken into account before such date of enactment, and

(2) the treatment of such transaction, property, or item under such provision would (without regard to the amendments made by this part) affect liability for tax for periods ending after such date of enactment,

nothing in the amendments made by this part shall be construed to affect the treatment of such transaction, property, or item for purposes of determining liability for tax for periods ending after such date of enactment.

Prior to repeal, Code Sec. 6427(e) read as follows:

(e) USE IN CERTAIN TAXICABS.—

(1) IN GENERAL.—Except as provided in subsection (k), if—

(A) any gasoline on which tax is imposed by section 4081, or

(B) any fuel on the sale of which tax is imposed by section 4041 or 4091,

is used in a qualified taxicab while engaged exclusively in furnishing qualified taxicab services, the Secretary shall pay (without interest) to the ultimate purchaser of such gasoline or fuel an amount determined at the rate of 4 cents a gallon.

(2) DEFINITIONS.—For purposes of this subsection—

(A) QUALIFIED TAXICAB SERVICES.—The term "qualified taxicab services" means the furnishing of nonscheduled passenger land transportation for a fixed fare by a taxicab which is operated by a person who—

(i) is licensed to engage in the trade or business of furnishing such transportation by a Federal, State, or local authority having jurisdiction over a substantial portion of such transportation furnished by such person, and

(ii) is not prohibited under the laws, regulations, or procedures of such Federal, State, or local authority, and is not prohibited by company policy, from furnishing (with consent of the passengers) shared transportation.

(B) QUALIFIED TAXICAB.—Except as provided by subparagraph (C), the term "qualified taxicab" means any land vehicle the passenger capacity of which is less than 10 adults, including the driver.

(C) CERTAIN GAS-GUZZLING TAXICABS EXCLUDED.—The term "qualified taxicab" does not include any vehicle if—

(i) such vehicle was acquired by the person operating such vehicle after 1978,

(ii) the model year of such vehicle is 1978 or later, and

(iii) the fuel economy of the model type of such vehicle is less than or equal to the average fuel economy standard applicable under section 502(a) of the Motor Vehicle Information and Cost Savings Act to the model year of such vehicle.

The preceding sentence shall not apply to any vehicle manufactured by a manufacturer to which an exemption under section 502(c) of the Motor Vehicle Information and Cost Savings Act was granted (or on application could have been granted) for the model year of such vehicle. Terms used in this subparagraph shall have the same meaning as when used in title V of the Motor Vehicle Information and Cost Savings Act.

(3) TERMINATION.—This subsection shall not apply after September 30, 1988.

• **1987, Revenue Act of 1987 (P.L. 100-203)**

P.L. 100-203, § 10502(c)(3):

Amended Code Sec. 6427(e)(1)(B) by inserting "or 4091" after "section 4041". **Effective** for sales after 3-31-88. See also Act Sec. 10502(f) in the amendment notes following Code Sec. 6427(q)

• **1986, Tax Reform Act of 1986 (P.L. 99-514)**

P.L. 99-514, § 422(b):

Amended Code Sec. 6427(e)(3) by striking out "September 30, 1985" and inserting in lieu thereof "September 30, 1988". **Effective** 10-22-86.

P.L. 99-514, § 1703(e)(2)(A):

Amended Code Sec. 6427(a), (b)(1), (c), (d), (e)(1), and (f)(1), and (g)(1) by striking out "subsection (j)" and inserting in lieu thereof "subsection (k)". **Effective** for gasoline removed (as defined in section 4082 of the Internal Revenue Code of 1986) after 12-31-87.

• **1984, Deficit Reduction Act of 1984 (P.L. 98-369)**

P.L. 98-369, § 911(d)[c](2)(B):

Amended Code Sec. 6427(e)(1) by striking out "(i)" and inserting in lieu thereof "(j)". **Effective** 8-1-84.

P.L. 98-369, § 914:

Amended Code Sec. 6427(e)(3) by striking out "September 30, 1984" and inserting in lieu thereof "September 30, 1985". **Effective** 7-18-84.

• **1983, Surface Transportation Act of 1983 (P.L. 97-424)**

P.L. 97-424, § 511(e)(1):

Amended Code Sec. 6427(e)(1) by striking out "an amount equal to the aggregate amount of the tax imposed on such gasoline or fuel" and inserting "an amount determined at the rate of 4 cents a gallon". **Effective** 4-1-83.

P.L. 97-424, § 511(e)(2):

Amended Code Sec. 6427(e)(3) by stiking out "December 31, 1982" and inserting "September 30, 1984". **Effective** 1-1-83.

P.L. 97-424, § 511(e)(3):

Amended Code Sec. 6427(e)(2)(A)(ii). **Effective** with respect to fuel purchased after 12-31-82, and before 1-1-84. Prior to amendment, Code Sec. 6427(e)(2)(A)(ii) read as follows:

"(ii) is not prohibited by company policy from furnishing (with consent of the passengers) shared transportation", applicable with respect to fuel purchased after December 31, 1982, and before January 1, 1984.

P.L. 97-424, § 511(e)(4), provides:

(4) **Study.**—The Secretary of the Treasury or his delegate shall conduct a study of the reduced rate of fuels taxes provided for taxicabs by section 6427(e) of the Internal Revenue Code of 1954. Not later than January 1, 1984, the Secretary shall transmit a report on the study conducted under the preceding sentence to the Congress, together with such recommendations as he may deem advisable.

• **1980 (P.L. 96-541)**

P.L. 96-541, § 4:

Amended Code Sec. 6427(e)(3) by striking out "1980" and inserting in lieu thereof "1982". **Effective** 12-17-80.

• **1980, Crude Oil Windfall Profit Tax Act of 1980 (P.L. 96-223)**

P.L. 96-223, § 232(d)(4)(B):

Substituted "subsection (i)" for subsection (h)" in Code Sec. 6427(e)(1). **Effective** 1-1-79.

• **1978, Surface Transportation Assistance Act of 1978 (P.L. 95-599)**

P.L. 95-599, § 505(a)(2), (d):

Added Code Sec. 6427(e). **Effective** 1-1-79.

[Sec. 6427(f)—Stricken]

Amendments

• **2005, Safe, Accountable, Flexible, Efficient Transportation Equity Act: A Legacy for Users (P.L. 109-59)**

P.L. 109-59, § 11151(a)(1):

Amended Code Sec. 6427 by striking subsection (f). **Effective** as if included in the provision of P.L. 108-357 to which it relates [**effective** for fuel sold or used after 12-31-2004.—CCH]. Prior to being stricken, Code Sec. 6427(f) read as follows:

(f) GASOLINE, DIESEL FUEL, KEROSENE, AND AVIATION FUEL USED TO PRODUCE CERTAIN ALCOHOL FUELS.—

(1) IN GENERAL.—Except as provided in subsection (k), if any gasoline, diesel fuel, kerosene, or aviation fuel on which tax was imposed by section 4081 or 4091 at the regular tax rate is used by any person in producing a mixture described in section 4081(c) or 4091(c)(1)(A) (as the case may be) which is sold or used in such person's trade or business the Secretary shall pay (without interest) to such person an amount equal to the excess of the regular tax rate over the incentive tax rate with respect to such fuel.

(2) DEFINITIONS.—For purposes of paragraph (1)—

(A) REGULAR TAX RATE.—The term "regular tax rate" means—

(i) in the case of gasoline, diesel fuel, or kerosene the aggregate rate of tax imposed by section 4081 determined without regard to subsection (c) thereof, and

(ii) in the case of aviation fuel, the aggregate rate of tax imposed by section 4091 determined without regard to subsection (c) thereof.

(B) INCENTIVE TAX RATE.—The term "incentive tax rate" means—

(i) in the case of gasoline, diesel fuel, or kerosene the aggregate rate of tax imposed by section 4081 with respect to fuel described in subsection (c)(2) thereof, and

(ii) in the case of aviation fuel, the aggregate rate of tax imposed by section 4091 with respect to fuel described in subsection (c)(2) thereof.

(3) COORDINATION WITH OTHER REPAYMENT PROVISIONS.—No amount shall be payable under paragraph (1) with respect to any gasoline, diesel fuel, kerosene, or aviation fuel with respect to which an amount is payable under subsection (d) or (1) of this section or under section 6420 or 6421.

(4) TERMINATION.—This subsection shall not apply with respect to any mixture sold or used after September 30, 2007.

• **1998, IRS Restructuring and Reform Act of 1998 (P.L. 105-206)**

P.L. 105-206, § 6023(25):

Amended Code Sec. 6427(f)(3) by striking ", (e)," after "(d)". **Effective** 7-22-98.

• **1998, Transportation Equity Act for the 21st Century (P.L. 105-178)**

P.L. 105-178, § 9003(a)(2):

Amended Code Sec. 6427(f)(4) by striking "1999" and inserting "2007". **Effective** 6-9-98.

CREDITS AND REFUNDS—SPECIAL RULES

- **1997, Taxpayer Relief Act of 1997 (P.L. 105-34)**

P.L. 105-34, §1032(e)(7):

Amended Code Sec. 6427(f)(1) and (3) and the heading to (f) by inserting "kerosene," after "diesel fuel,". **Effective** 7-1-98.

P.L. 105-34, §1032(e)(8):

Amended Code Sec. 6427(f)(2) by striking "or diesel fuel" each place it appears and inserting ", diesel fuel, or kerosene". **Effective** 7-1-98.

P.L. 105-34, §1601(g)(1), provides:

(1) EXTENSION OF PERIOD FOR CLAIMING REFUNDS FOR ALCOHOL FUELS.—Notwithstanding section 6427(i)(3)(C) of the Internal Revenue Code of 1986, a claim filed under section 6427(f) of such Code for any period after September 30, 1995, and before October 1, 1996, shall be treated as timely filed if filed before the 60th day after the date of the enactment of this Act.

- **1996, Small Business Job Protection Act of 1996 (P.L. 104-188)**

P.L. 104-188, §1703(k):

Amended Code Sec. 6427(f)(4) by striking "1995" and inserting "1999". **Effective** as if included in the provision of P.L. 103-66 to which it relates.

- **1993, Omnibus Budget Reconciliation Act of 1993 (P.L. 103-66)**

P.L. 103-66, §13242(d)(26)(A):

Amended Code Sec. 6427(f)(1) by striking ", 4091(c)(1)(A), or 4091(d)(1)(A)" and inserting "or 4091(c)(1)(A)". **Effective** 1-1-94.

P.L. 103-66, §13242(d)(26)(B):

Amended Code Sec. 6427(f)(2). **Effective** 1-1-94. Prior to amendment, Code Sec. 6427(f)(2) read as follows:

(2) DEFINITIONS.—For purposes of paragraph (1)—

(A) REGULAR TAX RATE.—The term "regular tax rate" means—

(i) in the case of gasoline, the aggregate rate of tax imposed by section 4081 determined without regard to subsection (c) thereof,

(ii) in the case of diesel fuel, the aggregate rate of tax imposed by section 4091 on such fuel determined without regard to subsection (c) thereof, and

(iii) in the case of aviation fuel, the aggregate rate of tax imposed by section 4091 on such fuel determined without regard to subsection (d) thereof.

(B) INCENTIVE TAX RATE.—The term "incentive tax rate" means—

(i) in the case of gasoline, the aggregate rate of tax imposed by section 4081 with respect to fuel described in subsection (c)(1) thereof,

(ii) in the case of diesel fuel, the aggregate rate of tax imposed by section 4091 with respect to fuel described in subsection (c)(1)(B) thereof, and

(iii) in the case of aviation fuel, the aggregate rate of tax imposed by section 4091 with respect to fuel described in subsection (d)(1)(B) thereof.

(3) COORDINATION WITH OTHER REPAYMENT PROVISIONS.—No amount shall be payable under paragraph (1) with respect to any gasoline, diesel fuel, or aviation fuel with respect to which an amount is payable under subsection (d), (e), or (l) of this section or under section 6420 or 6421.

(4) TERMINATION.—This subsection shall not apply with respect to any mixture sold or used after September 30, 1995.

- **1990, Omnibus Budget Reconciliation Act of 1990 (P.L. 101-508)**

P.L. 101-508, §11213(b)(3):

Amended Code Sec. 6427(f). **Effective** 12-1-90. Prior to amendment, Code Sec. 6427(f) read as follows:

(f) GASOLINE, DIESEL FUEL, AND AVIATION FUEL USED TO PRODUCE CERTAIN ALCOHOL FUELS.—Except as provided in subsection (k)—

(1) GASOLINE AND DIESEL FUELS.—

(A) IN GENERAL.—If any gasoline or diesel fuel on which tax was imposed by section 4081 or 4091 at the regular tax rate is used by any person in producing a mixture described in section 4081(c) or in section 4091(c)(1)(A) (as the case may be) which is sold or used in such person's trade or business, the Secretary shall pay (without interest) to such person an amount equal to the excess of the regular tax rate over the incentive tax rate with respect to such fuel.

(B) DEFINITIONS.—For purposes of subparagraph (A)—

(i) REGULAR TAX RATE.—The term "regular tax rate" means—

(I) in the case of gasoline, the aggregate rate of tax imposed by section 4081 determined without regard to subsection (c) thereof, and

(II) in the case of diesel fuel, the aggregate rate of tax imposed by section 4091 on such fuel determined without regard to subsection (c) thereof.

(ii) INCENTIVE TAX RATE.—The term "incentive tax rate" means—

(I) in the case of gasoline, the aggregate rate of tax imposed by section 4081 with respect to fuel described in subsection (c)(1) thereof, and

(II) in the case of diesel fuel, the aggregate rate of tax imposed by section 4091 with respect to fuel described in subsection (c)(1)(B) thereof,

(C) COORDINATION WITH OTHER REPAYMENT PROVISIONS.—No amount shall be payable under subparagraph (A) with respect to any gasoline diesel fuel with respect to which an amount is payable under subsection (d), (e), or (l) of this section or under section 6420 or 6421.

(2) AVIATION FUEL.—If any aviation fuel on which tax was imposed by section 4091 is used by any person in producing a mixture at least 10 percent of which is alcohol (as defined in section 4081(c)(3)) which is sold or used in such person's trade or business, the Secretary shall pay (without interest) to such person an amount equal to the aggregate amount of tax (attributable to the Airport and Airway Trust Fund financing rate) imposed on such fuel under section 4091.

(3) TERMINATION.—Paragraphs (1) and (2) shall not apply with respect to any mixture sold or used after September 30, 1993.

Sec. 6427(f)—Stricken

- **1988, Technical and Miscellaneous Revenue Act of 1988 (P.L. 100-647)**

P.L. 100-647, §2001(d)(7)(B)(i)-(ii):

Amended Code Sec. 6427(f)(1)(A) by striking out "regular Highway Trust Fund financing rate" each place it appears and inserting in lieu thereof "regular tax rate", and by striking out "incentive Highway Trust Fund financing rate" and inserting in lieu thereof "incentive tax rate". **Effective** as if included in the amendments made by §10502 of P.L. 100-203.

P.L. 100-647, §2001(d)(7)(C), amended by P.L. 101-239, §7812(a):

Amended Code Sec. 6427(f)(1)(B). **Effective** as if included in the amendments made by §10502 of P.L. 100-203. Prior to amendment, Code Sec. 6427(f)(1)(B) read as follows:

(B) DEFINITIONS.—For purposes of subparagraph (A)—

(i) REGULAR HIGHWAY TRUST FUND FINANCING RATE.—The term "regular Highway Trust Fund financing rate" means—

(I) 9 cents per gallon in the case of gasoline, and

(II) 15 cents per gallon in the case of diesel fuel.

(ii) INCENTIVE HIGHWAY TRUST FUND FINANCING RATE.—The term "incentive Highway Trust Fund financing rate" means—

(I) $3^{1}/_{3}$ cents per gallon in the case of gasoline, and

(II) 10 cents per gallon in the case of diesel fuel.

- **1987, Revenue Act of 1987 (P.L. 100-203)**

P.L. 100-203, §10502(c)(4):

Amended Code Sec. 6427(f). **Effective** for sales after 3-31-88. See also Act Sec. 10502(f) in the amendment notes following Code Sec. 6427(q). Prior to amendment, Code Sec. 6427(f) read as follows:

(f) GASOLINE USED TO PRODUCE CERTAIN ALCOHOL FUELS.—

(1) IN GENERAL.—Except as provided in subsection (k), if any gasoline on which a tax is imposed by section 4081 at the Highway Trust Fund financing rate of 9 cents a gallon is used by any person in producing a mixture described in section 4081(c) which is sold or used in such person's trade or business, the Secretary shall pay (without interest) to such person an amount equal to the amount determined at the rate of $5^{2}/_{3}$ cents a gallon. The preceding sentence shall not apply with respect to any mixture sold or used after December 31, 1992.

(2) COORDINATION WITH OTHER REPAYMENT PROVISIONS.—No amount shall be payable under paragraph (1) with respect to any gasoline with respect to which an amount is payable under subsection (d) or (e) of this section or under section 6420 or 6421.

- **1986, Tax Reform Act of 1986 (P.L. 99-514)**

P.L. 99-514, §1703(e)(2)(A):

Amended Code Sec. 6427(a), (b)(1), (c), (d), (e)(1), (f)(1), and (g)(1) by striking out "subsection (j)" and inserting in lieu thereof "subsection (k)". **Effective** for gasoline removed (as defined in section 4082 of the Internal Revenue Code of 1986) after 12-31-87.

- **1986, Superfund Amendments and Reauthorization Act of 1986 (P.L. 99-499)**

P.L. 99-499, §521(c)(3)(C):

Amended Code Sec. 6427(f)(1) by striking out "at the rate" and inserting in lieu thereof "at the Highway Trust Fund financing rate". **Effective** 1-1-87.

- **1984, Deficit Reduction Act of 1984 (P.L. 98-369)**

P.L. 98-369, §732(a)(3):

Amended Code Sec. 6427(f)(1) by striking out "5 cents" and inserting in lieu thereof "$4^{5}/_{9}$ cents". **Effective** as if included in the provision of the Highway Revenue Act of 1982 to which it relates.

P.L. 98-369, §911(d)[c](2)(B):

Amended Code Sec. 6427(f)(1) by striking out "(i)" and inserting in lieu thereof "(j)". **Effective** 8-1-84.

P.L. 98-369, §912(d):

Amended Code Sec. 6427(f)(1) by striking out "$4^{5}/_{9}$ cents" and inserting in lieu thereof "$5^{2}/_{3}$ cents". **Effective** 1-1-85.

- **1983, Surface Transportation Act of 1983 (P.L. 97-424)**

P.L. 97-424, §511(d)(4):

Amended Code Sec. 6427(f). **Effective** 4-1-83. Prior to amendment, Code Sec. 6427(f) read as follows:

"(f) GASOLINE USED TO PRODUCE CERTAIN ALCOHOL FUELS.—

(1) IN GENERAL.—Except as provided in subsection (i), if any gasoline on which tax is imposed by section 4081 is used by any person in producing a mixture described in section 4081(c) which is sold or used in such person's trade or business, the Secretary shall pay (without interest) to such person an amount equal to the aggregate amount of the tax imposed on such gasoline. The preceding sentence shall not apply with respect to any mixture sold or used after December 31, 1992.

(2) COORDINATION WITH OTHER REPAYMENT PROVISIONS.—No amount shall be payable under subsection (d) or (e) of this section or under section 6420 or 6421 with respect to any gasoline with respect to which an amount is payable under paragraph (1).".

- **1980, Crude Oil Windfall Profit Tax Act of 1980 (P.L. 96-223)**

P.L. 96-223, §232(d)(1)(B):

Added Code Sec. 6427(f). **Effective**, generally, 1-1-79, but see transitional rule below.

CREDITS AND REFUNDS—SPECIAL RULES

P.L. 96-223, §232(h)(2)(B), provides:

(B) TRANSITIONAL RULE.—Any mixture sold or used on or after January 1, 1979, and before the date of the enactment of this Act which is described in section 6427(f)(1) of the Internal Revenue Code of 1954 (as amended by subsection (d)) shall, for purposes of section 6427 of such Code, be treated as sold or used on the date of the enactment of this Act [April 2, 1980].

[Sec. 6427(g)—Stricken]

Amendments

• **1996, Small Business Job Protection Act of 1996 (P.L. 104-188)**

P.L. 104-188, §1606(a):

Amended Code Sec. 6427 by striking subsection (g). **Effective** for vehicles purchased after 8-20-96. Prior to being stricken, Code Sec. 6427(g) read as follows:

(g) ADVANCE REPAYMENT OF INCREASED DIESEL FUEL TAX TO ORIGINAL PURCHASERS OF DIESEL-POWERED AUTOMOBILES AND LIGHT TRUCKS.—

(1) IN GENERAL.—Except as provided in subsection (k), the Secretary shall pay (without interest) to the original purchaser of any qualified diesel-powered highway vehicle an amount equal to the diesel fuel differential amount.

(2) QUALIFIED DIESEL-POWERED HIGHWAY VEHICLE.—For purposes of this subsection, the term "qualified diesel-powered highway vehicle" means any diesel-powered highway vehicle which—

(A) has at least 4 wheels,

(B) has a gross vehicle weight rating of 10,000 pounds or less, and

(C) is registered for highway use in the United States under the laws of any State.

(3) DIESEL FUEL DIFFERENTIAL AMOUNT.—For purposes of this subsection, the term "diesel fuel differential amount" means—

(A) except as provided in subparagraph (B), $102, or

(B) in the case of a truck or van, $198.

(4) ORIGINAL PURCHASER.—For purposes of this subsection—

(A) IN GENERAL.—Except as provided in subparagraph (B), the term "original purchaser" means the first person to purchase the qualified diesel-powered vehicle for use other than resale.

(B) EXCEPTION FOR CERTAIN PERSONS NOT SUBJECT TO FUELS TAX.—The term "original purchaser" shall not include any State or local government (as defined in section 4221(d)(4)) or any nonprofit educational organization (as defined in section 4221(d)(5)).

(C) TREATMENT OF DEMONSTRATION USE BY DEALER.—For purposes of subparagraph (A), use as a demonstrator by a dealer shall not be taken into account.

(5) VEHICLES TO WHICH SUBSECTION APPLIES.—Except as provided in paragraph (6), this subsection shall only apply to qualified diesel-powered highway vehicles originally purchased after January 1, 1985, and before January 1, 1999.

(6) SPECIAL RULE FOR CERTAIN VEHICLES HELD ON JANUARY 1, 1985.—

(A) IN GENERAL.—In the case of any person holding a qualified diesel-powered highway vehicle on January 1, 1985—

(i) such person shall be treated as if he originally purchased such vehicle on December 31, 1984, but

(ii) the amount payable under paragraph (1) to such person for such vehicle shall be the applicable fraction of the diesel fuel differential amount.

(B) APPLICABLE FRACTION.—for purposes of subparagraph (A), the applicable fraction is the fraction determined in accordance with the following table:

If the model year of the vehicle is:	The applicable fraction is:
1984 or 1985	1
1983	5/6
1982	4/6
1981	3/6
1980	2/6
1979	1/6

In the case of a 1978 or earlier model year vehicle, the applicable fraction shall be zero.

(7) BASIS REDUCTION.—For the purposes of subtitle A, the basis of any qualified diesel-powered highway vehicle shall be reduced by the amount payable under this subsection with respect to such vehicle.

• **1991, Intermodal Surface Transportation Efficiency Act of 1991 (P.L. 102-240)**

P.L. 102-240, §8002(b)(7):

Amended Code Sec. 6427(g)(5) by striking "1995" each place it appears and inserting "1999". **Effective** 12-18-91.

• **1990, Omnibus Budget Reconciliation Act of 1990 (P.L. 101-508)**

P.L. 101-508, §11211(d)(7):

Amended Code Sec. 6427(g)(5) by striking out "1993" each place it appears and inserting "1995". **Effective** 11-5-90.

• **1987, Surface Transportation and Uniform Relocation Assistance Act of 1987 (P.L. 100-17)**

P.L. 100-17, §502(b)(8):

Amended Code Sec. 6427(g)(5) by striking out "1988" each place it appears and inserting in lieu thereof "1993". **Effective** 4-2-87.

• **1986, Tax Reform Act of 1986 (P.L. 99-514)**

P.L. 99-514, §1703(e)(2)(A):

Amended Code Sec. 6427(a), (b)(1), (c), (d), (e)(1), (f)(1), and (g)(1) by striking out "subsection (j)" and inserting in lieu thereof "subsection (k)". **Effective** for gasoline removed (as defined in section 4082 of the Internal Revenue Code of 1986) after 12-31-87.

P.L. 99-514, §1899A(56):

Amended Code Sec. 6427(g)(1) by striking out "anount" and inserting in lieu thereof "amount". **Effective** 10-22-86.

• **1984, Deficit Reduction Act of 1984 (P.L. 98-369)**

P.L. 98-369, §911(b):

Added Code Sec. 6427(g). **Effective**, generally, for qualified diesel-powered highway vehicles originally purchased after 1-1-85, and before 1-1-88.

[Sec. 6427(h)]

(h) BLEND STOCKS NOT USED FOR PRODUCING TAXABLE FUEL.—

(1) GASOLINE BLEND STOCKS OR ADDITIVES NOT USED FOR PRODUCING GASOLINE.—Except as provided in subsection (k), if any gasoline blend stock or additive (within the meaning of section 4083(a)(2)) is not used by any person to produce gasoline and such person establishes that the ultimate use of such gasoline blend stock or additive is not to produce gasoline, the Secretary shall pay (without interest) to such person an amount equal to the aggregate amount of the tax imposed on such person with respect to such gasoline blend stock or additive.

(2) DIESEL FUEL BLEND STOCKS OR ADDITIVES NOT USED FOR PRODUCING DIESEL.—Except as provided in subsection (k), if any diesel fuel blend stock is not used by any person to produce diesel fuel and such person establishes that the ultimate use of such diesel fuel blend stock is not to produce diesel fuel, the Secretary shall pay (without interest) to such person an amount equal to the aggregate amount of the tax imposed on such person with respect to such diesel fuel blend stock.

Amendments

• **2004, American Jobs Creation Act of 2004 (P.L. 108-357)**

P.L. 108-357, §870(b):

Amended Code Sec. 6427(h). **Effective** for fuel removed, sold, or used after 12-31-2004. Prior to amendment, Code Sec. 6427(h) read as follows:

(h) GASOLINE BLEND STOCKS OR ADDITIVES NOT USED FOR PRODUCING GASOLINE.—Except as provided in subsection (k), if any gasoline blend stock or additive (within the meaning of section 4083(a)(2)) is not used by any person to produce gasoline and such person establishes that the ultimate use of such gasoline blend stock or additive is not to produce gasoline, the Secretary shall pay (without interest) to such person an amount equal to the aggregate amount of the tax imposed on such person with respect to such gasoline blend stock or additive.

• **1993, Omnibus Budget Reconciliation Act of 1993 (P.L. 103-66)**

P.L. 103-66, §13242(d)(27):

Amended Code Sec. 6427(h) by striking "section 4082(b)" and inserting "section 4083(a)(2)". **Effective** 1-1-94.

• **1986, Tax Reform Act of 1986 (P.L. 99-514)**

P.L. 99-514, §1703(e)(1)(A), (B):

Amended Code Sec. 6427 (as amended by P.L. 99-499) by redesignating subsections (h), (i), (j), (k), (l), (m), (n), and (o) as subsections (i), (j), (k), (l), (m), (n), (o), and (p), respectively, and by inserting after subsection (g) new subsection (h). **Effective** for gasoline removed (as defined in section 4082 of the Internal Revenue Code of 1986) after 12-31-87.

[Sec. 6427(i)]

(i) TIME FOR FILING CLAIMS; PERIOD COVERED.—

(1) GENERAL RULE.—Except as otherwise provided in this subsection, not more than one claim may be filed under subsection (a), (b), (d), (h), (l), (m), or (o) by any person with respect to fuel used during his taxable year; and no claim shall be allowed under this paragraph with respect to fuel used during any taxable year unless filed by the purchaser not later than the time prescribed by law for filing a claim for credit

CREDITS AND REFUNDS—SPECIAL RULES

or refund of overpayment of income tax for such taxable year. For purposes of this paragraph, a person's taxable year shall be his taxable year for purposes of subtitle A.

(2) EXCEPTIONS.—

(A) IN GENERAL.—If, at the close of any quarter of the taxable year of any person, at least $750 is payable in the aggregate under subsections (a), (b), (d), (h), (l), (m), and (o) of this section and section 6421 to such person with respect to fuel used during—

(i) such quarter, or

(ii) any prior quarter (for which no other claim has been filed) during such taxable year,

a claim may be filed under this section with respect to such fuel.

(B) TIME FOR FILING CLAIM.—No claim filed under this paragraph shall be allowed unless filed during the first quarter following the last quarter included in the claim.

(C) NONAPPLICATION OF PARAGRAPH.—This paragraph shall not apply to any fuel used solely in any off-highway business use described in section 6421(e)(2)(C).

(3) SPECIAL RULE FOR MIXTURE CREDITS AND THE ALTERNATIVE FUEL CREDIT.—

(A) IN GENERAL.—A claim may be filed under subsection (e)(1) by any person with respect to a mixture described in section 6426 or under subsection (e)(2) by any person with respect to an alternative fuel (as defined in section 6426(d)(2)) for any period—

(i) for which $200 or more is payable under such subsection (e)(1) or (e)(2), and

(ii) which is not less than 1 week.

In the case of an electronic claim, this subparagraph shall be applied without regard to clause (i).

(B) PAYMENT OF CLAIM.—Notwithstanding subsection (e)(1) or (e)(2), if the Secretary has not paid pursuant to a claim filed under this section within 45 days of the date of the filing of such claim (20 days in the case of an electronic claim), the claim shall be paid with interest from such date determined by using the overpayment rate and method under section 6621.

(C) TIME FOR FILING CLAIM.—No claim filed under this paragraph shall be allowed unless filed on or before the last day of the first quarter following the earliest quarter included in the claim.

(4) SPECIAL RULE FOR VENDOR REFUNDS.—

(A) IN GENERAL.—A claim may be filed under subsections (b)(4) and paragraph (4)(C) or (5) of subsection (l) by any person with respect to fuel sold by such person for any period—

(i) for which $200 or more ($100 or more in the case of kerosene) is payable under paragraph (4)(C) or (5) of subsection (l), and

(ii) which is not less than 1 week.

Notwithstanding subsection (l)(1), paragraph (3)(B) shall apply to claims filed under subsections (b)(4), (l)(4)(C)(ii), and (l)(5).

(B) TIME FOR FILING CLAIM.—No claim filed under this paragraph shall be allowed unless filed on or before the last day of the first quarter following the earliest quarter included in the claim.

Amendments

- **2007, Tax Technical Corrections Act of 2007 (P.L. 110-172)**

P.L. 110-172, § 5(a)(1)(A)-(C):

Amended Code Sec. 6427(i)(3) by inserting "or under subsection (e)(2) by any person with respect to an alternative fuel (as defined in section 6426(d)(2))" after "section 6426" in subparagraph (A), by inserting "or (e)(2)" after "subsection (e)(1)" in subparagraphs (A)(i) and (B), and by striking "ALCOHOL FUEL AND BIODIESEL MIXTURE CREDIT" and inserting "MIXTURE CREDITS AND THE ALTERNATIVE FUEL CREDIT" in the heading thereof. **Effective** as if included in the provision of the Safe, Accountable, Flexible, Efficient Transportation Equity Act: A Legacy for Users (P.L. 109-59) to which it relates [**effective** for any sale or use for any period after 9-30-2006.—CCH].

- **2006, Tax Relief and Health Care Act of 2006 (P.L. 109-432)**

P.L. 109-432, Div. A, § 420(b)(3)(A)-(B):

Amended Code Sec. 6427(i)(4)(A) by striking "paragraph (4)(B), (5), or (6)" each place it appears and inserting "paragraph (4)(C) or (5)", and by striking "(l)(5), and (l)(6)" and inserting "(l)(4)(C)(ii), and (l)(5)". **Effective** generally for kerosene sold after 9-30-2005. For special rules, see Act Sec. 420(c)(2) and (d) in the amendment notes following Code Sec. 6427(l).

- **2005, Safe, Accountable, Flexible, Efficient Transportation Equity Act: A Legacy for Users (P.L. 109-59)**

P.L. 109-59, § 11161(b)(3)(D)(i)-(ii):

Amended Code Sec. 6427(i)(4)(A) by striking "paragraph (4)(B) or (5)" both places it appears and inserting "paragraph (4)(B), (5), or (6)", and by striking "subsection (b)(4) and subsection (l)(5)" in the last sentence and inserting "subsections (b)(4), (l)(5), and (l)(6)". **Effective** for fuels or liquids removed, entered, or sold after 9-30-2005.

- **2005, Energy Tax Incentives Act of 2005 (P.L. 109-58)**

P.L. 109-58, § 1343(b)(3):

Amended Code Sec. 6427(i)(1) and (2) by inserting "(m)," after "(l),". **Effective** 1-1-2006.

- **2004, American Jobs Creation Act of 2004 (P.L. 108-357)**

P.L. 108-357, § 301(c)(10)(A)-(F):

Amended Code Sec. 6427(i)(3) by striking "subsection (f)" both places it appears in subparagraph (A) and inserting "subsection (e)(1)", by striking "gasoline, diesel fuel, or kerosene used to produce a qualified alcohol mixture (as defined in section 4081(c)(3))" in subparagraph (A) and inserting "a mixture described in section 6426", by adding at the end of subparagraph (A) a new flush sentence, by striking "subsection (f)(1)" in subparagraph (B) and inserting "subsection (e)(1)", by striking "20 days of the date of the filing of such claim" in subparagraph (B) and inserting "45 days of the date of the filing of such claim (20 days in the case of an electronic claim)", and by striking "ALCOHOL MIXTURE" in the heading and inserting "ALCOHOL FUEL AND BIODIESEL MIXTURE". **Effective** for fuel sold or used after 12-31-2004. For a special rule, see Act Sec. 301(e), below. Prior to amendment, Code Sec. 6427(i)(3) read as follows:

(3) SPECIAL RULE FOR ALCOHOL MIXTURE CREDIT.—

(A) IN GENERAL.—A claim may be filed under subsection (f) by any person with respect to gasoline, diesel fuel, or kerosene used to produce a qualified alcohol mixture (as defined in section 4081(c)(3)) for any period—

(i) for which $200 or more is payable under such subsection (f), and

(ii) which is not less than 1 week.

(B) PAYMENT OF CLAIM.—Notwithstanding subsection (f)(1), if the Secretary has not paid pursuant to a claim filed under this section within 20 days of the date of the filing of such claim, the claim shall be paid with interest from such date determined by using the overpayment rate and method under section 6621.

(C) TIME FOR FILING CLAIM.—No claim filed under this paragraph shall be allowed unless filed on or before the last day of the first quarter following the earliest quarter included in the claim.

P.L. 108-357, § 301(e), provides:

(e) FORMAT FOR FILING.—The Secretary of the Treasury shall describe the electronic format for filing claims described in section 6427(i)(3)(B) of the Internal Revenue Code of 1986 (as amended by subsection (c)(10)(C)) not later than December 31, 2004.

P.L. 108-357, § 851(d)(3):

Amended Code Sec. 6427(i)(2) by adding at the end a new subparagraph (C). **Effective** for tax years beginning after 10-22-2004.

P.L. 108-357, § 853(c)(2)(A)-(B):

Amended Code Sec. 6427(i)(4)(A) by striking "subsection (l)(5)" both places it appears and inserting "paragraph (4)(B) or (5) of subsection (l)", and by striking "the preceding sentence" and inserting "subsection (l)(5)". **Effective** for aviation-grade kerosene removed, entered, or sold after 12-31-2004. For special rules, see Act Sec. 853(f), below.

P.L. 108-357, § 853(f), provides:

(f) FLOOR STOCKS TAX.—

(1) IN GENERAL.—There is hereby imposed on aviation-grade kerosene held on January 1, 2005, by any person a tax equal to—

(A) the tax which would have been imposed before such date on such kerosene had the amendments made by this section been in effect at all times before such date, reduced by

(B) the sum of—

(i) the tax imposed before such date on such kerosene under section 4091 of the Internal Revenue Code of 1986, as in effect on such date, and

(ii) in the case of kerosene held exclusively for such person's own use, the amount which such person would (but for this clause) reasonably expect (as of such date) to be paid as a refund under section 6427(l) of such Code with respect to such kerosene.

(2) EXCEPTION FOR FUEL HELD IN AIRCRAFT FUEL TANK.—Paragraph (1) shall not apply to kerosene held in the fuel tank of an aircraft on January 1, 2005.

(3) LIABILITY FOR TAX AND METHOD OF PAYMENT.—

(A) LIABILITY FOR TAX.—The person holding the kerosene on January 1, 2005, to which the tax imposed by paragraph (1) applies shall be liable for such tax.

CREDITS AND REFUNDS—SPECIAL RULES

(B) METHOD AND TIME FOR PAYMENT.—The tax imposed by paragraph (1) shall be paid at such time and in such manner as the Secretary of the Treasury (or the Secretary's delegate) shall prescribe, including the nonapplication of such tax on de minimis amounts of kerosene.

(4) TRANSFER OF FLOOR STOCK TAX REVENUES TO TRUST FUNDS.—For purposes of determining the amount transferred to any trust fund, the tax imposed by this subsection shall be treated as imposed by section 4081 of the Internal Revenue Code of 1986—

(A) in any case in which tax was not imposed by section 4091 of such Code, at the Leaking Underground Storage Tank Trust Fund financing rate under such section to the extent of 0.1 cents per gallon, and

(B) at the rate under section 4081(a)(2)(A)(iv) of such Code to the extent of the remainder.

(5) HELD BY A PERSON.—For purposes of this subsection, kerosene shall be considered as held by a person if title thereto has passed to such person (whether or not delivery to the person has been made).

(6) OTHER LAWS APPLICABLE.—All provisions of law, including penalties, applicable with respect to the tax imposed by section 4081 of such Code shall, insofar as applicable and not inconsistent with the provisions of this subsection, apply with respect to the floor stock tax imposed by paragraph (1) to the same extent as if such tax were imposed by such section.

P.L. 108-357, §857(c):

Amended Code Sec. 6427(i)(4)(A), as amended by this Act, by inserting "subsections (b)(4) and" after "filed under". **Effective** for fuel sold after 12-31-2004.

- **1998, IRS Restructuring and Reform Act of 1998 (P.L. 105-206)**

P.L. 105-206, §6017(a):

Amended Code Sec. 6427(i)(2)(B). **Effective** as if included in the amendments made by P.L. 105-178, §9009 [effective 10-1-98.—CCH]. Prior to amendment, Code Sec. 6427(i)(2)(B) read as follows:

(B) TIME FOR FILING CLAIM.—No claim filed under this paragraph shall be allowed unless filed on or before the last day of the first quarter following the quarter for which the claim is filed.

P.L. 105-206, §6023(26)(B):

Amended Code Sec. 6427(i)(1) and (2)(A) by striking "(q)" and inserting "(o)". **Effective** 7-22-98.

- **1998, Transportation Equity Act for the 21st Century (P.L. 105-178)**

P.L. 105-178, §9009(a):

Amended Code Sec. 6427(i)(2)(A). **Effective** 10-1-98. Prior to amendment, Code Sec. 6427(i)(2)(A) read as follows:

(A) IN GENERAL.—If $1,000 or more is payable under subsections (a), (b), (d), (h), and (q) to any person with respect to fuel used, during any of the first 3 quarters of his taxable year, a claim may be filed under this section with respect to fuel used, during such quarter.

P.L. 105-178, §9009(b)(1):

Amended Code Sec. 6427(i) by striking paragraph (4) and by redesignating paragraph (5) as paragraph (4). **Effective** 10-1-98. Prior to being stricken, Code Sec. 6427(i)(4) read as follows:

(4) SPECIAL RULE FOR REFUNDS UNDER SUBSECTION (l).—

(A) IN GENERAL.—If at the close of any of the 1st 3 quarters of the taxable year of any person, at least $750 is payable under subsection (l) to such person with respect to fuel used during such quarter or any prior quarter during the taxable year (and for which no other claim has been filed), a claim may be filed under subsection (l) with respect to such fuel.

(B) TIME FOR FILING CLAIM.—No claim filed under this paragraph shall be allowed unless filed during the 1st quarter following the last quarter included in the claim.

- **1997, Taxpayer Relief Act of 1997 (P.L. 105-34)**

P.L. 105-34, §1032(c)(3)(E):

Amended Code Sec. 6427(i)(5)(A)(i) by inserting "($100 or more in the case of kerosene)" after "$200 or more". **Effective** 7-1-98.

P.L. 105-34, §1032(e)(9):

Amended Code Sec. 6427(i)(3)(A) by striking "or diesel fuel" and inserting ", diesel fuel, or kerosene". **Effective** 7-1-98.

P.L. 105-34, §1032(e)(10):

Amended the heading of Code Sec. 6427(i)(4). **Effective** 7-1-98. Prior to amendment, the heading of Code Sec. 6427(i)(4) read as follows:

(4) SPECIAL RULE FOR NONTAXABLE USES OF DIESEL FUEL AND AVIATION FUEL TAXED UNDER SECTION 4081 OR 4091.—

- **1996, Small Business Job Protection Act of 1996 (P.L. 104-188)**

P.L. 104-188, §1606(b)(2)(A)-(B):

Amended Code Sec. 6427(i)(1) and (2)(A) by striking "(g)," after "(d),", and by striking "(or a qualified diesel powered highway vehicle purchased)" after "fuel used" each place it appears. **Effective** for vehicles purchased after 8-20-96.

- **1993, Omnibus Budget Reconciliation Act of 1993 (P.L. 103-66)**

P.L. 103-66, §13242(c)(2)(A):

Amended Code Sec. 6427(i) by adding at the end thereof a new paragraph (5). **Effective** 1-1-94.

P.L. 103-66, §13242(c)(2)(B):

Amended Code Sec. 6427(i)(1) by striking "provided in paragraphs (2), (3), and (4)" and inserting "otherwise provided in this subsection". **Effective** 1-1-94.

P.L. 103-66, §13242(c)(2)(D):

Amended Code Sec. 6427(i)(3) by adding at the end thereof a new subparagraph (C). **Effective** 1-1-94.

P.L. 103-66, §13242(d)(28)(A)-(B):

Amended Code Sec. 6427(i)(3) by striking "GASOHOL" in the heading and inserting "ALCOHOL MIXTURE", and by striking "gasoline used to produce gasohol (as defined in section 4081(c)(1))" in subparagraph (A) and inserting "gasoline or diesel fuel used to produce a qualified alcohol mixture (as defined in section 4081(c)(3))". **Effective** 1-1-94.

P.L. 103-66, §13242(d)(30):

Amended Code Sec. 6427(i)(4) by inserting "4081 OR" before "4091" in the heading. **Effective** 1-1-94.

- **1990, Omnibus Budget Reconciliation Act of 1990 (P.L. 101-508)**

P.L. 101-508, §11801(c)(23):

Amended Code Sec. 6427(i) in paragraph (1) by striking "(e)" after "(d)"; in paragraph (2) by amending subparagraph (A), by striking subparagraph (B), and by redesignating subparagraph (C) as subparagraph (B). **Effective** 11-5-90. Prior to amendment, Code Sec. 6427(i)(2)(A)-(B) read as follows:

(A) IN GENERAL.—If—

(i) $1,000 or more is payable under subsections (a), (b), (d), (e), (g), (h), and (q), or[,]

(ii) $50 or more is payable under subsection (e),

to any person with respect to fuel used (or a qualified diesel powered highway vehicle purchased) during any of the first three quarters of his taxable year, a claim may be filed under this section by the purchaser with respect to fuel used (or a qualified diesel powered highway vehicle purchased) during such quarter.

(B) SPECIAL RULE.—If the requirements of subparagraph (A)(ii) are met by any person for any quarter but the requirements of subparagraph (A)(i) are not met by such person for such quarter, such person may file a claim under subparagraph (A) for such quarter only with respect to amounts referred to in subparagraph (A)(ii).

P.L. 101-508, §11821(b), provides:

(b) SAVINGS PROVISION.—If—

(1) any provision amended or repealed by this part applied to—

(A) any transaction occurring before the date of the enactment of this Act,

(B) any property acquired before such date of enactment, or

(C) any item of income, loss, deduction, or credit taken into account before such date of enactment, and

(2) the treatment of such transaction, property, or item under such provision would (without regard to the amendments made by this part) affect liability for tax periods ending after such date of enactment,

nothing in the amendments made by this part shall be construed to affect the treatment of such transaction, property, or item for purposes of determining liability for tax for periods ending after such date of enactment.

- **1989, Omnibus Budget Reconciliation Act of 1989 (P.L. 101-239)**

P.L. 101-239, §7822(b)(1):

Amended Code Sec. 6427(i)(1) by striking "subsection (a)" and all that follows through "by any person" and inserting "subsection (a), (b), (d), (e), (g), (h), (l), or (q) by any person". **Effective** as if included in the provision of P.L. 100-203 to which it relates. Prior to amendment, Code Sec. 6427(i)(1) read as follows:

(1) GENERAL RULE.—Except as provided in paragraphs (2), (3), and (4), not more than one claim may be filed under subsection (a), (b), (d), (e), (g), (h), (l), or (p), by any person with respect to fuel used (or a qualified diesel powered highway vehicle purchased) during his taxable year; and no claim shall be allowed under this paragraph with respect to fuel used (or a qualified diesel powered highway vehicle purchased) during any taxable year unless filed by the purchaser not later than the time prescribed by law for filing a claim for credit or refund of overpayment of income tax for such taxable year. For purposes of this paragraph, a person's taxable year shall be his taxable year for purposes of subtitle A.

P.L. 101-239, §7822(b)(2):

Amended Code Sec. 6427(i)(2)(A)(i). **Effective** as if included in the provision of P.L. 100-203 to which it relates. Prior to amendment, Code Sec. 6427(i)(2)(A)(i) read as follows:

(i) $1,000 or more is payable under subsections (a), (b), (d), (e), (g), (h), and (p) or

P.L. 101-239, §7822(b)(3):

Amended Code Sec. 6427(i)(2)(B). **Effective** as if included in the provision of P.L. 100-203 to which it relates. Prior to amendment, Code Sec. 6427(i)(2)(B) read as follows:

(B) SPECIAL RULE.—If the requirements of clause (ii) of subparagraph (A) are met by any person for any quarter but the requirements of subparagraph (a)(i) are not met by such person for such quarter, such person may file a claim under subparagraph (A) for such quarter only with respect to amounts referred to in the clause (or clauses) of subparagraph (A) the requirements of which are met by such person for such quarter.

- **1988, Technical and Miscellaneous Revenue Act of 1988 (P.L. 100-647)**

P.L. 100-647, §3002(a):

Amended Code Sec. 6427(i) by adding at the end thereof a new paragraph (4). **Effective** for fuel used after 12-31-88.

P.L. 100-647, §3002(c)(1):

Amended Code Sec. 6427(i)(1) by striking out "paragraph (2)" and inserting in lieu thereof "paragraphs (2), (3), and (4)". **Effective** for fuel used after 12-31-88.

P.L. 100-647, §3002(c)(2):

Amended Code Sec. 6427(i)(2)(A) by striking out "(l)," after "(h)," in clause (i). **Effective** for fuel used after 12-31-88.

CREDITS AND REFUNDS—SPECIAL RULES

- **1987, Airport and Airway Revenue Act of 1987 (P.L. 100-223)**

P.L. 100-223, §405(b)(2)(A):

Amended Code Sec. 6427(i)(1) by striking out "or (h)" and inserting in lieu thereof "(h), or (p)". **Effective** 12-30-87.

P.L. 100-223, §405(b)(2)(B):

Amended Code Sec. 6427(i)(2)(A)(i) by striking out "and (h)" and inserting in lieu thereof "(h), and (p)". **Effective** 12-30-87.

- **1987, Revenue Act of 1987 (P.L. 100-203)**

P.L. 100-203, §10502(c)(5)(A):

Amended Code Sec. 6427(i)(1) by striking out "or (h)" and inserting in lieu thereof "(h), or (l)". **Effective** for sales after 3-31-88. See also Act Sec. 10502(f) in the amendment notes following Code Sec. 6427(q).

P.L. 100-203, §10502(c)(5)(B):

Amended Code Sec. 6427(i)(2)(A)(i) by striking out "and (h)" and inserting in lieu thereof "(h), and (l)". **Effective** for sales after 3-31-88. See also Act Sec. 10502(f) in the amendment notes following Code Sec. 6427(q).

- **1986, Tax Reform Act of 1986 (P.L. 99-514)**

P.L. 99-514, §1703(d)(1)[A]:

Amended Code Sec. 6427(h) by adding at the end thereof new paragraph (3). **Effective** for gasoline removed (as defined in section 4082 of the Internal Revenue Code of 1986) after 12-31-87.

P.L. 99-514, §1703(d)(1)(B)(i):

Amended Code Sec. 6427(h)(1) by striking out "(f)". **Effective** for gasoline removed (as defined in section 4082 of the Internal Revenue Code of 1986) after 12-31-87. Prior to amendment, Code Sec. 6427(h)(1) read as follows:

(1) GENERAL RULE.—Except as provided in paragraph (2), not more than one claim may be filed under subsection (a), (b), (c), (d), (e), (f), or (g), by any person with respect to fuel used (or a qualified diesel powered highway vehicle purchased) during his taxable year; and no claim shall be allowed under this paragraph with respect to fuel used (or a qualified diesel powered highway vehicle purchased) during any taxable year unless filed by the purchaser not later than the time prescribed by law for filing a claim for credit or refund of overpayment of income tax for such taxable year. For purposes of this paragraph, a person's taxable year shall be his taxable year for purposes of subtitle A.

P.L. 99-514, §1703(d)(1)(B)(ii):

Amended Code Sec. 6427(h)(2)(A) by inserting "or" at the end of subclause (i), by striking out "or" at the end of subclause (ii), and by striking out clause (iii) and "(or clauses)". [However, "(or clauses)" does not appear. This typographical error will have to be corrected.] **Effective** for gasoline removed (as defined in section 4082 of the Internal Revenue Code of 1986) after 12-31-87.

P.L. 99-514, §1703(d)(1)(B)(iii):

Amended Code Sec. 6427(f)[h](2)(B) by striking out "or clause (iii)". **Effective** for gasoline removed (as defined in section 4082 of the Internal Revenue Code of 1986) after 12-31-87. Prior to amendment, Code Sec. 6427 (f)[h](2)(B) read as follows:

(B) SPECIAL RULE.—If the requirements of clause (ii) or clause (iii) of subparagraph (A) are met by any person for any quarter but the requirements of subparagraph (A)(i) are not met by such person for such quarter, such person may file a claim under subparagraph (A) for such quarter only with respect to amounts referred to in the clause (or clauses) of subparagraph (A) the requirements of which are met by such person for such quarter.

P.L. 99-514, §1703(e)(1)(A), (B):

Amended Code Sec. 6427 (as amended by P.L. 99-499) by redesignating subsections (h), (i), (j), (k), (l), (m), (n), and (o) as subsections (i), (j), (k), (l), (m), (n), (o), and (p), respectively, and by inserting after subsection (g) new subsection (h). **Effective** for gasoline removed (as defined in section 4082 of the Internal Revenue Code of 1986) after 12-31-87.

P.L. 99-514, §1703(e)(2)(B):

Amended Code Sec. 6427(i)(1) (as redesignated by Act Sec. 1703(e)(1)(A)) by striking out "or (g)" and inserting in lieu thereof "(g), or (h)". **Effective** for gasoline removed (as defined in section 4082 of the Internal Revenue Code of 1986) after 12-31-87.

P.L. 99-514, §1703(e)(2)(C):

Amended Code Sec. 6427(i)(2)(A)(i) (as so redesignated) by striking out "and (g)" and inserting in lieu thereof "(g), and (h)". **Effective** for gasoline removed (as defined in section 4082 of the Internal Revenue Code of 1986) after 12-31-87.

- **1984, Deficit Reduction Act of 1984 (P.L. 98-369)**

P.L. 98-369, §911(b):

Amended Code Sec. 6427 (as amended by Act Sec. 734(c)(2)) by redesignating subsection (g) as subsection (h). **Effective** date noted under Code Sec. 6427(g).

P.L. 98-369, §911(d)[c](2)(C):

Amended Code Sec. 6427(h)(1) (as redesignated by Act Sec. 911(b)) by striking out "or (f)" and inserting in lieu thereof "(f), or (g)", and by striking out "fuel used" each place it appeared and inserting in lieu thereof "fuel used (or a qualified diesel powered highway vehicle purchased)". **Effective** 8-1-84.

P.L. 98-369, §911(d)[c](2)(D):

Amended Code Sec. 6427(h)(2)(A) (as redesignated by Act Sec. 1202(c)) by striking out "and (e)" in clause (i) and inserting in lieu thereof "(e), and (g)", and by striking out "fuel used" each place it appeared and inserting in lieu thereof "fuel used (or a qualified diesel powered highway vehicle purchased)". **Effective** 8-1-84.

- **1980, Crude Oil Windfall Profit Tax Act of 1980 (P.L. 96-223)**

P.L. 96-223, §232(d)(1)(A):

Redesignated subsection (f) as Code Sec. 6427(g). **Effective** 1-1-79.

P.L. 96-223, §232(d)(2)(A):

Amended Code Sec. 6427(g)(2)(A), as redesignated, by striking out "or" at the end of clause (i), by inserting "or" at the end of clause (ii), and by inserting clause (iii). **Effective** 1-1-79.

P.L. 96-223, §232(d)(2)(B):

Amended Code Sec. 6427(g)(2)(B) as redesignated. **Effective** 1-1-79. Prior to amendment, Code Sec. 6427(g)(2)(B) read:

(B) SPECIAL RULE.—If a claim may be filed by any person under subparagraph (A)(ii) but not under subparagraph (A)(i) for any quarter, such person may file a claim under subparagraph (A) for such quarter only with respect to amounts payable under subsection (e).

P.L. 96-223, §232(d)(4)(C):

Amended Code Sec. 6427(g)(1), as redesignated, by striking out "(a), (b), (c), (d), or (e)" and inserting "(a), (b), (c), (d), (e), or (f)". **Effective** 1-1-79.

- **1978, Surface Transportation Assistance Act of 1978 (P.L. 95-599)**

P.L. 95-599, §505(a)(1), (d):

Redesignated subsection (e) as Code Sec. 6427(f). **Effective** 1-1-79.

P.L. 95-599, §505(b), (d):

Amended Code Sec. 6427(f)(2). **Effective** 1-1-79. Prior to amendment, subsection (f)(2) read:

"(2) EXCEPTION.—If $1,000 or more is payable under subsections (a), (b), and (d) to any person with respect to fuel used during any of the first three quarters of his taxable year, a claim may be filed under this section by the purchaser with respect to fuel used during such quarter. No claim filed under this paragraph shall be allowed unless filed on or before the last day of the first quarter following the quarter for which the claim is filed."

P.L. 95-599, §505(c)(3), (d):

Amended Code Sec. 6427(f)(1) by inserting "(a), (b), (c), (d), or (e)" in place of "(a), (b), (c), or (d)". **Effective** 1-1-79.

- **1976 (P.L. 94-530)**

P.L. 94-530, §[1](b):

Redesignated subsection (d) as Code Sec. 6427(e). **Effective** 10-1-76.

P.L. 94-530, §[1](c)(3):

Substituted "(a), (b), (c), or (d)" for "(a), (b), or (c)" in Code Sec. 6427(e)(1). **Effective** 10-1-76.

P.L. 94-530, §[1](c)(4):

Substituted "(a), (b), and (d)" for "(a) and (b)" in Code Sec. 6427(e)(2). **Effective** 10-1-76.

- **1976, Tax Reform Act of 1976 (P.L. 94-455)**

P.L. 94-455, §1906(b)(13)(A):

Amended 1954 Code by substituting "Secretary" for "Secretary or his delegate" each place it appeared. **Effective** 2-1-77.

[Sec. 6427(j)]

(j) APPLICABLE LAWS.—

(1) IN GENERAL.—All provisions of law, including penalties, applicable in respect of the taxes imposed by sections 4041 and 4081 shall, insofar as applicable and not inconsistent with this section, apply in respect of the payments provided for in this section to the same extent as if such payments constituted refunds of overpayments of the tax so imposed.

(2) EXAMINATION OF BOOKS AND WITNESSES.—For the purpose of ascertaining the correctness of any claim made under this section, or the correctness of any payment made in respect of any such claim, the Secretary shall have the authority granted by paragraphs (1), (2), and (3) of section 7602(a) (relating to examination of books and witnesses) as if the claimant were the person liable for tax.

Amendments

- **2004, American Jobs Creation Act of 2004 (P.L. 108-357)**

P.L. 108-357, §853(d)(2)(J):

Amended Code Sec. 6427(j)(1) by striking ", 4081, and 4091" and inserting "and 4081". **Effective** for aviation-grade kerosene removed, entered, or sold after 12-31-2004. For special rules, see Act Sec. 853(f) in the amendments for Code Sec. 6427(i).

- **1993, Omnibus Budget Reconciliation Act of 1993 (P.L. 103-66)**

P.L. 103-66, §13242(d)(29):

Amended Code Sec. 6427(j)(1) by striking "section 4041" and inserting "sections 4041, 4081, and 4091". **Effective** 1-1-94.

CREDITS AND REFUNDS—SPECIAL RULES

- **1989, Omnibus Budget Reconciliation Act of 1989 (P.L. 101-239)**

P.L. 101-239, §7841(d)(20):

Amended Code Sec. 6427(j)(2) by striking "section 7602" and inserting "section 7602(a)". **Effective** 12-19-89.

- **1986, Tax Reform Act of 1986 (P.L. 99-514)**

P.L. 99-514, §1703(e)(1)(A), (B):

Amended Code Sec. 6427 (as amended by P.L. 99-499 by redesignating subsections (h), (i), (j), (k), (l), (m), (n), and (o) as subsections (i), (j), (k), (l), (m), (n), (o), and (p), respectively, and by inserting after subsection (g) new subsection (h). **Effective** for gasoline removed (as defined in section 4082 of the Internal Revenue Code of 1986) after 12-31-87.

- **1984, Deficit Reduction Act of 1984 (P.L. 98-369)**

P.L. 98-369, §911(b):

Amended Code Sec. 6427 (as amended by Act Sec. 734(c)(2)) by redesignating subsection (h) as (i). For the **effective** date see the notes following Code Sec. 6427(g).

- **1980, Crude Oil Windfall Profit Tax Act of 1980 (P.L. 96-223)**

P.L. 96-223, §232(d)(1)(A):

Redesignated subsection (g) as Code Sec. 6427(h). **Effective** 1-1-79.

- **1978, Surface Transportation Assistance Act of 1978 (P.L. 95-599)**

P.L. 95-599, §505(a)(1), (d):

Redesignated subsection (f) as Code Sec. 6427(g). **Effective** 1-1-79.

- **1976 (P.L. 94-530)**

P.L. 94-530, §[1](b):

Redesignated subsection (e) as Code Sec. 6427(f). **Effective** 10-1-76.

[Sec. 6427(k)]

(k) INCOME TAX CREDIT IN LIEU OF PAYMENT.—

(1) PERSONS NOT SUBJECT TO INCOME TAX.—Payment shall be made under this section only to—

(A) the United States or an agency or instrumentality thereof, a State, a political subdivision of a State, or any agency or instrumentality of one or more States or political subdivisions, or

(B) an organization exempt from tax under section 501(a) (other than an organization required to make a return of the tax imposed under subtitle A for its taxable year).

(2) EXCEPTION.—Paragraph (1) shall not apply to a payment of a claim filed under paragraph (2), (3), or (4) of subsection (i).

(3) ALLOWANCE OF CREDIT AGAINST INCOME TAX.—

For allowances of credit against the income tax imposed by subtitle A for fuel used or resold by the purchaser, see section 34.

Amendments

- **1998, Transportation Equity Act for the 21st Century (P.L. 105-178)**

P.L. 105-178, §9009(b)(2):

Amended Code Sec. 6427(k)(2). **Effective** 10-1-98. Prior to amendment, Code Sec. 6427(k)(2) read as follows:

(2) EXCEPTION.—Paragraph (1) shall not apply to a payment of a claim filed under paragraph (2), (3) [,](4), or (5) of subsection (i).

- **1993, Omnibus Budget Reconciliation Act of 1993 (P.L. 103-66)**

P.L. 103-66, §13242(c)(2)(C):

Amended Code Sec. 6427(k)(2) by striking out "or (4)" and inserting "[,] (4), or (5)". **Effective** 1-1-94.

- **1988, Technical and Miscellaneous Revenue Act of 1988 (P.L. 100-647)**

P.L. 100-647, §1017(c)(10):

Amended Code Sec. 6427(k)(2) by striking out "subsection" and all that follows and inserting in lieu thereof "paragraph (2) or (3) of subsection (i)". **Effective** as if included in the provision of P.L. 99-514 to which it relates. Prior to amendment, Code Sec. 6427(k)(2) read as follows:

(2) EXCEPTION.—Paragraph (1) shall not apply to a payment of a claim filed under subsection (i)(2) or (h)[i](3).

P.L. 100-647, §3002(b):

Amended Code Sec. 6427(k)(2), as amended by title I, by striking out "paragraph (2) or (3)" and inserting in lieu thereof "paragraph (2), (3), or (4)". **Effective** for fuel used after 12-31-88.

- **1986, Tax Reform Act of 1986 (P.L. 99-514)**

P.L. 99-514, §1703(d)(1)(B)(iv):

Amended Code Sec. 6427(j)(2) by striking out "subsection (h)(2)" and inserting in lieu thereof "subsection (h)(2) or (h)(3)". **Effective** for gasoline removed (as defined in section 4082 of the Internal Revenue Code of 1986) after 12-31-87.

P.L. 99-514, §1703(e)(1)(A), (B):

Amended Code Sec. 6427 (as amended by P.L. 99-499) by redesignating subsections (h), (i), (j), (k), (l), (m), (n), and (o) as subsections (i), (j), (k), (l), (m), (n), (o), and (p), respectively, and by inserting after subsection (g) new subsection (h). **Effective** for gasoline removed (as defined in section 4082 of the Internal Revenue Code of 1986) after 12-31-87.

P.L. 99-514, §1703(e)(2)(E):

Amended Code Sec. 6427(i)[k](2) (as so redesignated) by striking out "subsection (h)(2)" and inserting in lieu thereof "(i)(2)" [note, "subsection (h)(2)" does not appear in Code Sec. 6427(i)(2), as so redesignated]. **Effective** for gasoline removed (as defined in section 4082 of the Internal Revenue Code of 1986) after 12-31-87.

- **1984, Deficit Reduction Act of 1984 (P.L. 98-369)**

P.L. 98-369, §474(r)(38):

Amended Code Sec. 6427(i)(3) [redesignated (j) by Act Sec. 911(b)]by striking out "section 39" and inserting in lieu thereof "section 34". **Effective** for tax years beginning after 12-31-83, and to carryback from such years.

P.L. 98-369, §911(b):

Amended Code Sec. 6427 (as amended by Act Sec. 734(c)(2)) by redesignating subsection (i) as (j). For the **effective** date, see the notes following Code Sec. 6427(g).

P.L. 98-369, §911(d)[c](2)(E):

Amended Code Sec. 6427(k)[j](2) (as redesignated by Act Sec. 911(b)) by striking out "(g)(2)" and inserting in lieu thereof "(h)(2)". **Effective** 8-1-84.

- **1980, Crude Oil Windfall Profit Tax Act of 1980 (P.L. 96-223)**

P.L. 96-223, §232(d)(1)(A):

Redesignated subsection (h) as Code Sec. 6427(i). **Effective** 1-1-79.

P.L. 96-223, §232(d)(4)(D):

Amended Code Sec. 6427(i)(2), as redesignated by §233(d)(1)(A), by striking out "(f)(2)" and inserting "(g)(2)". **Effective** 1-1-79.

- **1978, Surface Transportation Assistance Act of 1978 (P.L. 95-599)**

P.L. 95-599, §505(a)(1), (d):

Redesignated subsection (g) as Code Sec. 6427(h). **Effective** 1-1-79.

P.L. 95-599, §505(c)(4), (d):

Substituted "(f)(2)" for "(e)(2)" in Code Sec. 6427(h)(2). **Effective** 1-1-79.

- **1976 (P.L. 94-530)**

P.L. 94-530, §[1](b):

Redesignated subsection (f) as Code Sec. 6427(g). **Effective** 10-1-76.

P.L. 94-530, §[1](c)(5):

Substituted "(e)(2)" for "(d)(2)" in Code Sec. 6427(g)(2). **Effective** 10-1-76.

- **1976, Tax Reform Act of 1976 (P.L. 94-455)**

P.L. 94-455, §1906(b)(13)(A):

Amended 1954 Code by substituting "Secretary" for "Secretary or his delegate" each place it appeared. **Effective** 2-1-77.

[Sec. 6427(l)]

(l) NONTAXABLE USES OF DIESEL FUEL AND KEROSENE.—

(1) IN GENERAL.—Except as otherwise provided in this subsection and in subsection (k), if any diesel fuel or kerosene on which tax has been imposed by section 4041 or 4081 is used by any person in a nontaxable use, the Secretary shall pay (without interest) to the ultimate purchaser of such fuel an amount equal to the aggregate amount of tax imposed on such fuel under section 4041 or 4081, as the case may be, reduced by any payment made to the ultimate vendor under paragraph (4)(C)(i).

(2) NONTAXABLE USE.—For purposes of this subsection, the term "nontaxable use" means any use which is exempt from the tax imposed by section 4041(a)(1) other than by reason of a prior imposition of tax.

(3) REFUND OF CERTAIN TAXES ON FUEL USED IN DIESEL-POWERED TRAINS.—For purposes of this subsection, the term "nontaxable use" includes fuel used in a diesel-powered train. The preceding sentence shall not apply with respect to—

(A) the Leaking Underground Storage Tank Trust Fund financing rate under sections 4041 and 4081, and

(B) so much of the rate specified in section 4081(a)(2)(A) as does not exceed the rate applicable under section 4041(a)(1)(C)(ii).

CREDITS AND REFUNDS—SPECIAL RULES

The preceding sentence shall not apply in the case of fuel sold for exclusive use by a State or any political subdivision thereof.

(4) REFUNDS FOR KEROSENE USED IN AVIATION.—

(A) KEROSENE USED IN COMMERCIAL AVIATION.—In the case of kerosene used in commercial aviation (as defined in section 4083(b)) (other than supplies for vessels or aircraft within the meaning of section 4221(d)(3)), paragraph (1) shall not apply to so much of the tax imposed by section 4041 or 4081, as the case may be, as is attributable to—

(i) the Leaking Underground Storage Tank Trust Fund financing rate imposed by such section, and

(ii) so much of the rate of tax specified in section 4041(c) or 4081(a)(2)(A)(iii), as the case may be, as does not exceed 4.3 cents per gallon.

(B) KEROSENE USED IN NONCOMMERCIAL AVIATION.—In the case of kerosene used in aviation that is not commercial aviation (as so defined) (other than any use which is exempt from the tax imposed by section 4041(c) other than by reason of a prior imposition of tax), paragraph (1) shall not apply to—

(i) any tax imposed by subsection (c) or (d)(2) of section 4041, and

(ii) so much of the tax imposed by section 4081 as is attributable to—

(I) the Leaking Underground Storage Tank Trust Fund financing rate imposed by such section, and

(II) so much of the rate of tax specified in section 4081(a)(2)(A)(iii) as does not exceed the rate specified in section 4081(a)(2)(C)(ii).

(C) PAYMENTS TO ULTIMATE, REGISTERED VENDOR.—

(i) IN GENERAL.—With respect to any kerosene used in aviation (other than kerosene described in clause (ii) or kerosene to which paragraph (5) applies), if the ultimate purchaser of such kerosene waives (at such time and in such form and manner as the Secretary shall prescribe) the right to payment under paragraph (1) and assigns such right to the ultimate vendor, then the Secretary shall pay the amount which would be paid under paragraph (1) to such ultimate vendor, but only if such ultimate vendor—

(I) is registered under section 4101, and

(II) meets the requirements of subparagraph (A), (B), or (D) of section 6416(a)(1).

(ii) PAYMENTS FOR KEROSENE USED IN NONCOMMERCIAL AVIATION.—The amount which would be paid under paragraph (1) with respect to any kerosene to which subparagraph (B) applies shall be paid only to the ultimate vendor of such kerosene. A payment shall be made to such vendor if such vendor—

(I) is registered under section 4101, and

(II) meets the requirements of subparagraph (A), (B), or (D) of section 6416(a)(1).

(5) REGISTERED VENDORS TO ADMINISTER CLAIMS FOR REFUND OF DIESEL FUEL OR KEROSENE SOLD TO STATE AND LOCAL GOVERNMENTS.—

(A) IN GENERAL.—Paragraph (1) shall not apply to diesel fuel or kerosene used by a State or local government.

(B) SALES OF KEROSENE NOT FOR USE IN MOTOR FUEL.—Paragraph (1) shall not apply to kerosene (other than kerosene used in aviation) sold by a vendor—

(i) for any use if such sale is from a pump which (as determined under regulations prescribed by the Secretary) is not suitable for use in fueling any diesel-powered highway vehicle or train, or

(ii) to the extent provided by the Secretary, for blending with heating oil to be used during periods of extreme or unseasonable cold.

(C) PAYMENT TO ULTIMATE, REGISTERED VENDOR.—Except as provided in subparagraph (D), the amount which would (but for subparagraph (A) or (B)) have been paid under paragraph (1) with respect to any fuel shall be paid to the ultimate vendor of such fuel, if such vendor—

(i) is registered under section 4101, and

(ii) meets the requirements of subparagraph (A), (B), or (D) of section 6416(a)(1).

(D) CREDIT CARD ISSUER.—For purposes of this paragraph, if the purchase of any fuel described in subparagraph (A) (determined without regard to the registration status of the ultimate vendor) is made by means of a credit card issued to the ultimate purchaser, the Secretary shall pay to the person extending the credit to the ultimate purchaser the amount which would have been paid under paragraph (1) (but for subparagraph (A)), but only if such person meets the requirements of clauses (i), (ii), and (iii) of section 6416(a)(4)(B). If such clause (i), (ii), or (iii) is not met by such person extending the credit to the ultimate purchaser, then such person shall collect an amount equal to the tax from the ultimate purchaser and only such ultimate purchaser may claim such amount.

Amendments

- **2020, Coronavirus Aid, Relief, and Economic Security (CARES) Act (P.L. 116-136)**

P.L. 116-136, § 4007(b)-(c), provides:

(b) USE OF KEROSENE IN COMMERCIAL AVIATION.—In the case of kerosene used in commercial aviation (as defined in section 4083 of the Internal Revenue Code of 1986) during the excise tax holiday period—

(1) no tax shall be imposed on such kerosene under—

(A) section 4041(c) of the Internal Revenue Code of 1986, or

(B) section 4081 of such Code (other than at the rate provided in subsection (a)(2)(B) thereof), and

(2) section 6427(l) of such Code shall be applied—

(A) by treating such use as a nontaxable use, and

(B) without regard to paragraph (4)(A)(ii) thereof.

(c) EXCISE TAX HOLIDAY PERIOD.—For purposes of this section, the term "excise tax holiday period" means the period beginning after the date of the enactment of this section and ending before January 1, 2021.

- **2007, Tax Technical Corrections Act of 2007 (P.L. 110-172)**

P.L. 110-172, § 11(a)(38):

Amended Code Sec. 6427(l)(4)(A)(ii) by striking "section 4081(a)(2)(iii)" and inserting "section 4081(a)(2)(A)(iii)". [Note: Code Sec. 6427(l)(4)(A)(ii) does not contain the text "section 4081(a)(2)(iii)"; therefore, this amendment cannot be made.—CCH]. **Effective** 12-29-2007.

- **2006, Tax Relief and Health Care Act of 2006 (P.L. 109-432)**

P.L. 109-432, Div. A, § 420(a):

Amended Code Sec. 6427(l)(4). **Effective** generally for kerosene sold after 9-30-2005. For special rules, see Act Sec. 420(c)(2) and (d), below. Prior to amendment, Code Sec. 6427(l)(4) read as follows:

(4) REFUNDS FOR KEROSENE USED IN COMMERCIAL AVIATION.—

(A) NO REFUND OF CERTAIN TAXES ON FUEL USED IN COMMERCIAL AVIATION.—In the case of kerosene used in commercial aviation (as defined in section 4083(b)) (other than supplies for vessels or aircraft within the meaning of section 4221(d)(3)), paragraph (1) shall not apply to so much of the tax imposed by section 4081 as is attributable to—

(i) the Leaking Underground Storage Tank Trust Fund financing rate imposed by such section, and

(ii) so much of the rate of tax specified in section 4081(a)(2)[A](iii) as does not exceed 4.3 cents per gallon.

(B) PAYMENT TO ULTIMATE, REGISTERED VENDOR.—With respect to kerosene used in commercial aviation as described in subparagraph (A), if the ultimate purchaser of such kerosene waives (at such time and in such form and manner as the Secretary shall prescribe) the right to payment under paragraph (1) and assigns such right to the ultimate vendor, then the Secretary shall pay the amount which would be paid under paragraph (1) to such ultimate vendor, but only if such ultimate vendor—

(i) is registered under section 4101, and

(ii) meets the requirements of subparagraph (A), (B), or (D) of section 6416(a)(1).

CREDITS AND REFUNDS—SPECIAL RULES

P.L. 109-432, Div. A, § 420(b)(1):

Amended Code Sec. 6427(l) by striking paragraph (5) and by redesignating paragraph (6) as paragraph (5). **Effective** generally for kerosene sold after 9-30-2005. For special rules, see Act Sec. 420(c)(2) and (d), below. Prior to being stricken, Code Sec. 6427(l)(5) read as follows:

(5) REFUNDS FOR KEROSENE USED IN NONCOMMERCIAL AVIATION.—

(A) IN GENERAL.—In the case of kerosene used in aviation not described in paragraph (4)(A) (other than any use which is exempt from the tax imposed by section 4041(c) other than by reason of a prior imposition of tax), paragraph (1) shall not apply to so much of the tax imposed by section 4081 as is attributable to—

(i) the Leaking Underground Storage Tank Trust Fund financing rate imposed by such section, and

(ii) so much of the rate of tax specified in section 4081(a)(2)(A)(iii) as does not exceed the rate specified in section 4081(a)(2)(C)(ii).

(B) PAYMENT TO ULTIMATE, REGISTERED VENDOR.—The amount which would be paid under paragraph (1) with respect to any kerosene shall be paid only to the ultimate vendor of such kerosene. A payment shall be made to such vendor if such vendor—

(i) is registered under section 4101, and

(ii) meets the requirements of subparagraph (A), (B), or (D) of section 6416(a)(1).

P.L. 109-432, Div. A, § 420(b)(4):

Amended Code Sec. 6427(l)(1) by striking "paragraph (4)(B)" and inserting "paragraph (4)(C)(i)". **Effective** generally for kerosene sold after 9-30-2005. For special rules, see Act Sec. 420(c)(2) and (d), below.

P.L. 109-432, Div. A, § 420(c)(2) and (d), provide:

(c) EFFECTIVE DATE.—

* * *

(2) SPECIAL RULE FOR PENDING CLAIMS.—In the case of kerosene sold for use in aviation (other than kerosene to which section 6427(l)(4)(C)(ii) of the Internal Revenue Code of 1986 (as added by subsection (a)) applies or kerosene to which section 6427(l)(5) of such Code (as redesignated by subsection (b)) applies) after September 30, 2005, and before the date of the enactment of this Act, the ultimate purchaser shall be treated as having waived the right to payment under section 6427(l)(1) of such Code and as having assigned such right to the ultimate vendor if such ultimate vendor has met the requirements of subparagraph (A), (B), or (D) of section 6416(a)(1) of such Code.

(d) SPECIAL RULE FOR KEROSENE USED IN AVIATION ON A FARM FOR FARMING PURPOSES.—

(1) REFUNDS FOR PURCHASES AFTER DECEMBER 31, 2004, AND BEFORE OCTOBER 1, 2005.—The Secretary of the Treasury shall pay to the ultimate purchaser of any kerosene which is used in aviation on a farm for farming purposes and which was purchased after December 31, 2004, and before October 1, 2005, an amount equal to the aggregate amount of tax imposed on such fuel under section 4041 or 4081 of the Internal Revenue Code of 1986, as the case may be, reduced by any payment to the ultimate vendor under section 6427(l)(5)(C) of such Code (as in effect on the day before the date of the enactment of the Safe, Accountable, Flexible, Efficient Transportation Equity Act: a Legacy for Users).

(2) USE ON A FARM FOR FARMING PURPOSES.—For purposes of paragraph (1), kerosene shall be treated as used on a farm for farming purposes if such kerosene is used for farming purposes (within the meaning of section 6420(c)(3) of the Internal Revenue Code of 1986) in carrying on a trade or business on a farm situated in the United States. For purposes of the preceding sentence, rules similar to the rules of section 6420(c)(4) of such Code shall apply.

(3) TIME FOR FILING CLAIMS.—No claim shall be allowed under paragraph (1) unless the ultimate purchaser files such claim before the date that is 3 months after the date of the enactment of this Act.

(4) NO DOUBLE BENEFIT.—No amount shall be paid under paragraph (1) or section 6427(l) of the Internal Revenue Code of 1986 with respect to any kerosene described in paragraph (1) to the extent that such amount is in excess of the tax imposed on such kerosene under section 4041 or 4081 of such Code, as the case may be.

(5) APPLICABLE LAWS.—For purposes of this subsection, rules similar to the rules of section 6427(j) of the Internal Revenue Code of 1986 shall apply.

• **2005, Safe, Accountable, Flexible, Efficient Transportation Equity Act: A Legacy for Users (P.L. 109-59)**

P.L. 109-59, § 11161(b)(2)(A):

Amended Code Sec. 6427(l)(2). **Effective** for fuels or liquids removed, entered, or sold after 9-30-2005. Prior to amendment, Code Sec. 6427(l)(2) read as follows:

(2) NONTAXABLE USE.—For purposes of this subsection, the term "nontaxable use" means—

(A) in the case of diesel fuel or kerosene, any use which is exempt from the tax imposed by section 4041(a)(1) other than by reason of a prior imposition of tax, and

(B) in the case of aviation-grade kerosene—

(i) any use which is exempt from the tax imposed by section 4041(c) other than by reason of a prior imposition of tax, or

(ii) any use in commercial aviation (within the meaning of section 4083(b)).

P.L. 109-59, § 11161(b)(2)(B):

Amended Code Sec. 6427(l) by redesignating paragraph (5) as paragraph (6) and by inserting after paragraph (4) a new paragraph (5). **Effective** for fuels or liquids removed, entered, or sold after 9-30-2005.

P.L. 109-59, § 11161(b)(3)(B):

Amended the heading for Code Sec. 6427(l) by striking ", KEROSENE AND AVIATION FUEL" and inserting "AND KEROSENE". **Effective** for fuels or liquids removed, entered, or sold after 9-30-2005.

P.L. 109-59, § 11161(b)(3)(E)(i)-(iv):

Amended Code Sec. 6427(l)(4) by striking "aviation-grade" before "kerosene" in subparagraph (A), by striking "section 4081(a)(2)(A)(iv)" and inserting "section 4081(a)(2)[A](iii)", by striking "aviation-grade kerosene" in subparagraph (B) and inserting "kerosene used in commercial aviation as described in subparagraph (A)", and by striking "AVIATION-GRADE KEROSENE" in the heading thereof and inserting "KEROSENE USED IN COMMERCIAL AVIATION". **Effective** for fuels or liquids removed, entered, or sold after 9-30-2005.

P.L. 109-59, § 11161(b)(3)(F):

Amended Code Sec. 6427(l)(6)(B), as redesignated by Act Sec. 11161(b)(2)(B), by striking "aviation-grade kerosene" and inserting "kerosene used in aviation". **Effective** for fuels or liquids removed, entered, or sold after 9-30-2005.

P.L. 109-59, § 11162(a):

Amended Code Sec. 6427(l)(6)(A), as redesignated by Act Sec. 11161. **Effective** for sales after 9-30-2005. Prior to amendment, Code Sec. 6427(l)(6)(A) read as follows:

(A) IN GENERAL.—Paragraph (1) shall not apply to diesel fuel or kerosene used—

(i) on a farm for farming purposes (within the meaning of section 6420(c)), or

(ii) by a State or local government.

P.L. 109-59, § 11162(b):

Amended the heading of Code Sec. 6427(l)(6), as redesignated by Act Sec. 11161, by striking "FARMERS AND" before "STATE AND LOCAL". **Effective** for sales after 9-30-2005.

P.L. 109-59, § 11163(c)(1)-(2):

Amended Code Sec. 6427(l)(6), as redesignated by Act Sec. 11161, by striking "The amount" in subparagraph (C) and inserting "Except as provided in subparagraph (D), the amount", and by adding at the end a new subparagraph (D). **Effective** for sales after 12-31-2005.

• **2004, American Jobs Creation Act of 2004 (P.L. 108-357)**

P.L. 108-357, § 241(a)(2)(D):

Amended Code Sec. 6427(l)(3)(B). **Effective** on 1-1-2005. Prior to amendment, Code Sec. 6427(l)(3)(B) read as follows:

(B) so much of the rate specified in section 4081(a)(2)(A) as does not exceed—

(i) 6.8 cents per gallon after September 30, 1993, and before October 1, 1995,

(ii) 5.55 cents per gallon after September 30, 1995, and before November 1, 1998, and

(iii) 4.3 cents per gallon after October 31, 1998.

P.L. 108-357, § 853(c)(1):

Amended Code Sec. 6427(l)(4). **Effective** for aviation-grade kerosene removed, entered, or sold after 12-31-2004. For special rules, see Act Sec. 853(f) in the amendments for Code Sec. 6427(i). Prior to amendment, Code Sec. 6427(l)(4) read as follows:

(4) NO REFUND OF CERTAIN TAXES ON FUEL USED IN COMMERCIAL AVIATION.—In the case of fuel used in commercial aviation (as defined in section 4092(b)) (other than supplies for vessels or aircraft within the meaning of section 4221(d)(3)), paragraph (1) shall not apply to so much of the tax imposed by section 4091 as is attributable to—

(A) the Leaking Underground Storage Tank Trust Fund financing rate imposed by such section, and

(B) in the case of fuel purchased after September 30, 1995, so much of the rate of tax specified in section 4091(b)(1) as does not exceed 4.3 cents per gallon.

P.L. 108-357, § 853(c)(3):

Amended Code Sec. 6427(l)(2)(B). **Effective** for aviation-grade kerosene removed, entered, or sold after 12-31-2004. For special rules, see Act Sec. 853(f) in the amendments for Code Sec. 6427(i). Prior to amendment, Code Sec. 6427(l)(2)(B) read as follows:

(B) in the case of aviation fuel, any use which is exempt from the tax imposed by section 4041(c)(1) other than by reason of a prior imposition of tax.

P.L. 108-357, § 853(d)(2)(K)(i):

Amended Code Sec. 6427(l)(1). **Effective** for aviation-grade kerosene removed, entered, or sold after 12-31-2004. For special rules, see Act Sec. 853(f) in the amendments for Code Sec. 6427(i). Prior to amendment, Code Sec. 6427(l)(1) read as follows:

(1) IN GENERAL.—Except as otherwise provided in this subsection and in subsection (k), if—

(A) any diesel fuel or kerosene on which tax has been imposed by section 4041 or 4081, or

(B) any aviation fuel on which tax has been imposed by section 4091,

is used by any person in a nontaxable use, the Secretary shall pay (without interest) to the ultimate purchaser of such fuel an amount equal to the aggregate amount of tax imposed on such fuel under section 4041, 4081, or 4091, as the case may be.

P.L. 108-357, § 853(d)(2)(K)(ii):

Amended Code Sec. 6427(l)(5)(B) by striking "Paragraph (1)(A) shall not apply to kerosene" and inserting "Paragraph (1) shall not apply to kerosene (other than aviation-grade kerosene)". **Effective** for aviation-grade kerosene removed, entered, or sold after 12-31-2004. For special rules, see Act Sec. 853(f) in the amendments for Code Sec. 6427(i).

• **1998, Transportation Equity Act for the 21st Century (P.L. 105-178)**

P.L. 105-178, § 9006(b)(2)(A)-(B):

Amended Code Sec. 6427(l)(3)(B) by striking "October 1, 1999" in clause (ii) and inserting "November 1, 1998", and by striking "September 30, 1999" in clause (iii) and inserting "October 31, 1998". **Effective** 6-9-98.

• **1997, Taxpayer Relief Act of 1997 (P.L. 105-34)**

P.L. 105-34, § 1032(c)(3)(A):

Amended Code Sec. 6427(l) by inserting "or kerosene" after "diesel fuel" each place it appears in paragraphs (1), (2), and (5) (including the heading for paragraph (5)). **Effective** 7-1-98.

P.L. 105-34, § 1032(c)(3)(B):

Amended Code Sec. 6427(l)(5) by redesignating subparagraph (B) as subparagraph (C) and by inserting after subparagraph (A) a new subparagraph (B). **Effective** 7-1-98.

CREDITS AND REFUNDS—SPECIAL RULES

P.L. 105-34, § 1032(c)(3)(C):

Amended Code Sec. 6427(l)(5)(C), as redesignated by subparagraph (B) of Act Sec. 1032(c)(3), by striking "subparagraph (A)" and inserting "subparagraph (A) or (B)". **Effective** 7-1-98.

P.L. 105-34, § 1032(c)(3)(D):

Amended Code Sec. 6427(l) by inserting ", KEROSENE" after "DIESEL FUEL" in the heading. **Effective** 7-1-98.

• **1996, Small Business Job Protection Act of 1996 (P.L. 104-188)**

P.L. 104-188, § 1702(b)(2)(B):

Amended Code Sec. 6427(l)(4), as in effect prior to amendment by P.L. 103-66, by inserting before the period "unless such fuel was used by a State or any political subdivision thereof". **Effective** as if included in the provision of P.L. 101-508 to which it relates.

• **1993, Omnibus Budget Reconciliation Act of 1993 (P.L. 103-66)**

P.L. 103-66, § 13241(f)(9):

Amended Code Sec. 6427(l) by striking paragraphs (3) and (4) and inserting new paragraphs (3) and (4). **Effective** 10-1-93. Prior to amendment, Code Sec. 6427(l)(3)-(4) read as follows:

(3) NO REFUND OF LEAKING UNDERGROUND STORAGE TANK TRUST FUND FINANCING TAX.—Paragraph (1) shall not apply to so much of the tax imposed by section 4091 as is attributable in the Leaking Underground Storage Tank Trust Fund financing rate imposed by such section in the case of—

(A) fuel used in a diesel-powered train, and

(B) fuel used in any aircraft (except as supplies for vessels or aircraft within the meaning of section 4221(d)(3)).

(4) NO REFUND OF DEFICIT REDUCTION TAX ON FUEL USED IN TRAINS.—In the case of fuel used in a diesel-powered train, paragraph (1) also shall not apply to so much of the tax imposed by section 4091 as is attributable to the diesel fuel deficit reduction rate imposed by such section unless such fuel was used by a State or any political subdivision thereof.

P.L. 103-66, § 13242(c)(1):

Amended Code Sec. 6427(l) by adding at the end a new paragraph (5). **Effective** 1-1-94.

P.L. 103-66, § 13242(d)(31):

Amended Code Sec. 6427(l), as previously amended by this part. **Effective** 1-1-94. Prior to amendment, Code Sec. 6427(l) read as follows:

(l) NONTAXABLE USES OF DIESEL FUEL AND AVIATION FUEL TAXED UNDER SECTION 4091.—

(1) IN GENERAL.—Except as provided in subsection (k) and in paragraphs (3) and (4) of this subsection, if any fuel on which tax has been imposed by section 4091 is used by any person in a nontaxable use, the Secretary shall pay (without interest) to the ultimate purchaser of such fuel an amount equal to the aggregate amount of tax imposed on such fuel under section 4091.

(2) NONTAXABLE USE.—For purposes of this subsection, the term "nontaxable use" means, with respect to any fuel, any use of such fuel if such use is exempt under section 4041 from the taxes imposed by subsections (a)(1) and (c)(1) of section 4041 (other than by reason of the imposition of tax on any sale thereof).

Amendments

• **1993, Omnibus Budget Reconciliation Act of 1993 (P.L. 103-66)**

P.L. 103-66, § 13241(f)(10):

Amended Code Sec. 6427 by striking subsection (m). **Effective** 10-1-93. Prior to amendment, Code Sec. 6427(m) read as follows:

(m) SPECIAL RULES WITH RESPECT TO NONCOMMERCIAL AVIATION.—

For purposes of subsection (a), in the case of gasoline.—

(1) on which tax was imposed under section 4041(c)(2),

(2) on which tax was not imposed under section 4081, and

(3) which was not used as an off-highway business use (within the meaning of section 6421(e)(2)),

the amount of the payment under subsection (a) shall be an amount equal to the amount of gasoline used as described in subsection (a) or resold multiplied by the rate equal to the excess of the rate of tax imposed by section 4041(c)(2) over the rate of tax imposed by section 4081.

• **1988, Technical and Miscellaneous Revenue Act of 1988 (P.L. 100-647)**

P.L. 100-647, § 1017(c)(3):

Amended Code Sec. 6427(m)(3) by striking out "6421(d)(2)" and inserting in lieu thereof "section 6421(e)(2)". **Effective** as if included in the provision of P.L. 99-514 to which it relates.

• **1987, Revenue Act of 1987 (P.L. 100-203)**

P.L. 100-203, § 10502(c)(1):

Amended Code Sec. 6427 by redesignating subsection (l) as subsection (m). **Effective** for sales after 3-31-88.

(3) NO REFUND OF CERTAIN TAXES ON FUEL USED IN DIESEL-POWERED TRAINS.—In the case of fuel used in a diesel-powered train, paragraph (1) shall not apply to so much of the tax imposed by section 4091 as is attributable to the Leaking Underground Storage Tank Trust Fund financing rate and the diesel fuel deficit reduction rate imposed by such section. The preceding sentence shall not apply in the case of fuel sold for exclusive use by a State or any political subdivision thereof.

(4) NO REFUND OF LEAKING UNDERGROUND STORAGE TANK TRUST FUND TAXES ON FUEL USED IN COMMERCIAL AVIATION.—In the case of fuel used in commercial aviation (as defined in section 4093(c)(2)(B)) (other than supplies for vessels or aircraft within the meaning of section 4221(d)(3)), paragraph (1) shall not apply to so much of the tax imposed by section 4091 as is attributable to the Leaking Underground Storage Tank Trust Fund financing rate imposed by such section.

• **1990, Omnibus Budget Reconciliation Act of 1990 (P.L. 101-508)**

P.L. 101-508, § 11211(b)(4)(B)(i):

Amended Code Sec. 6427(l) by adding at the end thereof a new paragraph (4). **Effective** 12-1-90.

P.L. 101-508, § 11211(b)(4)(B)(ii):

Amended Code Sec. 6427(l)(1) by striking "paragraph (3)" and inserting "paragraphs (3) and (4)". **Effective** 12-1-90.

• **1988, Technical and Miscellaneous Revenue Act of 1988 (P.L. 100-647)**

P.L. 100-647, § 2001(d)(7)(D):

Amended Code Sec. 6427(l)(2) by inserting "under section 4041" after "exempt". **Effective** as if included in the amendments made by section 10502 of P.L. 100-203.

P.L. 100-647, § 2004(e)(2):

Amended Code Sec. 6427(l)(3)(B) by inserting "(except as supplies for vessels or aircraft within the meaning of section 4221(d)(3))" after "aircraft". **Effective** as if included in the provision of P.L. 100-203 to which it relates.

• **1987, Revenue Act of 1987 (P.L. 100-203)**

P.L. 100-203, § 10502(c)(1):

Amended Code Sec. 6427 by redesignating subsections (l) through (p) as subsections (m) through (q), respectively, and by inserting after subsection (k) new subsection (l). **Effective** for sales after 3-31-88.

• **1986, Tax Reform Act of 1986 (P.L. 99-514)**

P.L. 99-514, § 1703(e)(1)(A), (B):

Amended Code Sec. 6427 (as amended by P.L. 99-499) by redesignating subsections (h), (i), (j), (k),(l), (m), (n), and (o) as subsections (i), (j), (k), (l), (m), (n), (o), and (p), respectively, and by inserting after subsection (g) new subsection (h). **Effective** for gasoline removed (as defined in section 4082 of the Internal Revenue Code of 1986) after 12-31-87.

• **1984, Deficit Reduction Act of 1984 (P.L. 98-369)**

P.L. 98-369, § 734(c)(2):

Amended Code Sec. 6427 by redesignating subsections (j), (k), and (l) as subsections (k), (l), and (m) respectively, and by inserting new subsection (j). **Effective** on the first day of the first calendar quarter beginning after 7-18-84.

[Sec. 6427(m)—Stricken]

• **1986, Tax Reform Act of 1986 (P.L. 99-514)**

P.L. 99-514, § 1703(e)(1)(A), (B):

Amended Code Sec. 6427 (as amended by P.L. 99-499) by redesignating subsections (h), (i), (j), (k), (l), (m), (n), and (o) as subsections (i), (j), (k), (l), (m), (n), (o), and (p), respectively, and by inserting after subsection (g) new subsection (h). **Effective** for gasoline removed (as defined in section 4082 of the Internal Revenue Code of 1986) after 12-31-87.

• **1984, Deficit Reduction Act of 1984 (P.L. 98-369)**

P.L. 98-369, § 734(c)(2):

Redesignated Code Sec. 6427(j) as (k). For the **effective** date, see the notes following Code Sec. 6427(k).

P.L. 98-369, § 911(b):

Amended Code Sec. 6427 (as amended by Act Sec. 734(c)(2)) by redesignating subsection (k) as (l). For the **effective** date, see the notes following Code Sec. 6427(g).

• **1980, Crude Oil Windfall Profit Tax Act of 1980 (P.L. 96-223)**

P.L. 96-223, § 232(d)(1)(A):

Redesignated subsection (i) as Code Sec. 6427(j). **Effective** 1-1-79.

• **1978, Surface Transportation Assistance Act of 1978 (P.L. 95-599)**

P.L. 95-599, § 505(a)(1), (d):

Redesignated subsection (h) as Code Sec. 6427(i). **Effective** 1-1-79.

• **1976 (P.L. 94-530)**

P.L. 94-530, § [1](b):

Redesignated subsection (g) as Code Sec. 6427(h). **Effective** 10-1-76.

[Sec. 6427(m)]

(m) DIESEL FUEL USED TO PRODUCE EMULSION.—

(1) IN GENERAL.—Except as provided in subsection (k), if any diesel fuel on which tax was imposed by section 4081 at the regular tax rate is used by any person in producing an emulsion described in section 4081(a)(2)(D) which is sold or used in such person's trade or business, the Secretary shall pay (without interest) to such person an amount equal to the excess of the regular tax rate over the incentive tax rate with respect to such fuel.

(2) DEFINITIONS.—For purposes of paragraph (1)—

Sec. 6427(m)—Stricken

(A) REGULAR TAX RATE.—The term "regular tax rate" means the aggregate rate of tax imposed by section 4081 determined without regard to section 4081(a)(2)(D).

(B) INCENTIVE TAX RATE.—The term "incentive tax rate" means the aggregate rate of tax imposed by section 4081 determined with regard to section 4081(a)(2)(D).

Amendments

• **2005, Energy Tax Incentives Act of 2005 (P.L. 109-58)**

P.L. 109-58, §1343(b)(1):

Amended Code Sec. 6427 by redesignating subsections (m) through (p) as subsections (n) through (q), respectively, and by inserting after subsection (l) a new subsection (m). **Effective** 1-1-2006.

[Sec. 6427(n)]

(n) REGULATIONS.—The Secretary may by regulations prescribe the conditions, not inconsistent with the provisions of this section, under which payments may be made under this section.

Amendments

• **2005, Energy Tax Incentives Act of 2005 (P.L. 109-58)**

P.L. 109-58, §1343(b)(1):

Amended Code Sec. 6427 by redesignating subsection (m) as subsection (n). **Effective** 1-1-2006.

• **1998, IRS Restructuring and Reform Act of 1998 (P.L. 105-206)**

P.L. 105-206, §6023(26)(A):

Amended Code Sec. 6427, as amended by Act Sec. 6023(16), by redesignating subsections (n), (p), (q), and (r) as subsections (m), (n), (o), and (p), respectively. **Effective** 7-22-98.

• **1987, Revenue Act of 1987 (P.L. 100-203)**

P.L. 100-203, §10502(c)(1):

Amended Code Sec. 6427 by redesignating subsection (m) as subsection (n). **Effective** for sales after 3-31-88. See also Act Sec. 10502(f) in the amendment notes following Code Sec. 6427(q).

• **1987, Surface Transportation and Uniform Relocation Assistance Act of 1987 (P.L. 100-17)**

P.L. 100-17, §502(b)(9):

Amended Code Sec. 6427(m) (as in effect prior to redesignation by P.L. 99-514, §1703(e)(1)) by striking out "1988" and inserting in lieu thereof "1993". **Effective** 4-2-87

• **1986, Tax Reform Act of 1986 (P.L. 99-514)**

P.L. 99-514, §1703(e)(1)(A), (B):

Amended Code Sec. 6427 (as amended by P.L. 99-499) by redesignating subsections (h), (i), (j), (k), (l), (m), (n), and (o) as subsections (i), (j), (k), (l), (m), (n), (o), and (p), respectively, and by inserting after subsection (g) new subsection (h). **Effective** for gasoline removed (as defined in section 4082 of the Internal Revenue Code of 1986) after 12-31-87.

P.L. 99-514, §1703(e)(2)(C):

Amended Code Sec. 6427(n) (as so redesignated) by striking out "and (g)" and inserting in lieu thereof "(g), and (h)". **Effective** for gasoline removed (as defined in section 4082 of the Internal Revenue Code of 1986) after 12-31-87.

P.L. 99-514, §1703(e)(2)(D):

Amended Code Sec. 6427(n) (as so redesignated) by striking out "AND (g)" and inserting in lieu thereof "(g), AND (h)". **Effective** for gasoline removed (as defined in section 4082 of the Internal Revenue Code of 1986) after 12-31-87.

• **1986, Superfund Amendments and Reauthorization Act of 1986 (P.L. 99-499)**

P.L. 99-499, §521(c)(3)(A):

Amended Code Sec. 6427(m), as in effect on the day before the date of the enactment of P.L. 99-514, by striking out "Subsections" and inserting in lieu thereof "Except with respect to taxes imposed by section 4041(d) and section 4081 at the Leaking Underground Storage Tank Trust Fund financing rate, subsections". **Effective** 1-1-87.

• **1984, Deficit Reduction Act of 1984 (P.L. 98-369)**

P.L. 98-369, §734(c)(2):

Redesignated Code Sec. 6427(k) as (l). For the **effective** date, see the notes following Code Sec. 6427(k).

P.L. 98-369, §911(b):

Amended Code Sec. 6427 (as amended by Act Sec. 734(c)(2)) by redesignating subsection (l) as (m). For the **effective** date, see the notes following Code Sec. 6427(g).

P.L. 98-369, §911(d)[c](2)(F):

Amended Code Sec. 6427(m) (as redesignated by Act Sec. 911(b)) by striking out "and (d)" each place it appeared and inserting in lieu thereof "(d), and (g)". **Effective** 8-1-84.

• **1983, Surface Transportation Act of 1983 (P.L. 97-424)**

P.L. 97-424, §516(b)(5):

Amended Code Sec. 6427 by redesignating subsection (k) as subsection (l) and by adding a new subsection (k). **Effective** 1-6-83.

[Sec. 6427(o)]

(o) PAYMENTS FOR TAXES IMPOSED BY SECTION 4041(d).—For purposes of subsections (a), (b), and (c), the taxes imposed by section 4041(d) shall be treated as imposed by section 4041(a).

Amendments

• **2005, Energy Tax Incentives Act of 2005 (P.L. 109-58)**

P.L. 109-58, §1343(b)(1):

Amended Code Sec. 6427 by redesignating subsection (n) as subsection (o). **Effective** 1-1-2006.

• **1998, IRS Restructuring and Reform Act of 1998 (P.L. 105-206)**

P.L. 105-206, §6023(26)(A):

Amended Code Sec. 6427 by redesignating subsection (p) as subsection (n). **Effective** 7-22-98.

• **1989, Omnibus Budget Reconciliation Act of 1989 (P.L. 101-239)**

P.L. 101-239, §7822(b)(4):

Amended Code Sec. 6427 by redesignating the subsection relating to payments for taxes imposed by section 4041(d) as subsection (p). [This subsection was already redesignated (p) by Act Sec. 10502(c)(1) of P.L. 100-203.—CCH.] **Effective** as if included in the provision of P.L. 100-203 to which it relates.

• **1987, Revenue Act of 1987 (P.L. 100-203)**

P.L. 100-203, §10502(c)(1):

Amended Code Sec. 6427 by redesignating subsection (o) as subsection (p). **Effective** for sales after 3-31-88. See also Act Sec. 10502(f) in the amendment notes following Code Sec. 6427(q).

[Sec. 6427(o)—Stricken]

Amendments

• **1993, Omnibus Budget Reconciliation Act of 1993 (P.L. 103-66)**

P.L. 103-66, §13241(f)(10):

Amended Code Sec. 6427 by striking subsection (o). **Effective** 10-1-93. Prior to amendment, Code Sec. 6427(o) read as follows:

(o) TERMINATION OF CERTAIN PROVISIONS.—Except with respect to taxes imposed by section 4041(d) and sections 4081 and 4091 at the Leaking Underground Storage Tank Trust Fund financing rate, subsections (a), (b), (c), (d), (g), (h), and (l) shall only apply with respect to fuels purchased before October 1, 1999.

• **1991, Intermodal Surface Transportation Efficiency Act of 1991 (P.L. 102-240)**

P.L. 102-240, §8002(b)(8):

Amended Code Sec. 6427(o) by striking "1995" each place it appears and inserting "1999". **Effective** 12-18-91.

CREDITS AND REFUNDS—SPECIAL RULES

• **1990, Omnibus Budget Reconciliation Act of 1990 (P.L. 101-508)**

P.L. 101-508, §11211(d)(8):

Amended Code Sec. 6427(o) by striking "1993" and inserting "1995". **Effective** on 11-5-90.

• **1987, Revenue Act of 1987 (P.L. 100-203)**

P.L. 100-203, §10502(c)(1):

Amended Code Sec. 6427 by redesignating subsection (n) as subsection (o). **Effective** for sales after 3-31-88. See also Act Sec. 10502(f) in the amendment notes following Code Sec. 6427(q).

P.L. 100-203, §10502(c)(6):

Amended Code Sec. 6427(o) (as redesignated by paragraph (1)). **Effective** for sales after 3-31-88. Prior to amendment Code Sec. 6427(o) read as follows:

(o) TERMINATION OF SUBSECTIONS (a), (b), (c), (d), (g), AND (h).—Except with respect to taxes imposed by section 4041(d) and section 4081 at the Leaking Underground Storage Tank Trust Fund financing rate, subsections (a), (b), (c), (d), (g), and (h) shall only apply with respect to fuels purchased before October 1, 1993.

• **1986, Tax Reform Act of 1986 (P.L. 99-514)**

P.L. 99-514, §1703(e)(1)(A), (B):

Amended Code Sec. 6427 (as amended by P.L. 99-499) by redesignating subsections (h), (i), (j), (k), (l), (m), (n), and (o) as subsections (i), (j), (k), (l), (m), (n), (o), and (p), respectively, and by inserting after subsection (g) new subsection (h). **Effective** for gasoline removed (as defined in section 4082 of the Internal Revenue Code of 1986) after 12-31-87.

• **1986, Superfund Amendments and Reauthorization Act of 1986 (P.L. 99-499)**

P.L. 99-499, §521(c)(3)(B)(i):

Amended Code Sec. 6427 by redesignating subsection (n) as subsection (o) and by inserting after subsection (m) new subsection (n). **Effective** 1-1-87.

[Sec. 6427(p)—Stricken]

Amendments

• **2007, Tax Technical Corrections Act of 2007 (P.L. 110-172)**

P.L. 110-172, §11(a)(39)(A):

Amended Code Sec. 6427, as amended by section 1343(b)(1) of the Energy Policy Act of 2005 (P.L. 109-58), by striking subsection (p) and redesignating subsection (q) as subsection (p). **Effective** 12-29-2007. Prior to being stricken, Code Sec. 6427(p) read as follows:

(p) GASOHOL USED IN NONCOMMERCIAL AVIATION.—Except as provided in subsection (k), if—

(1) any tax is imposed by section 4081 at a rate determined under subsection (c) thereof on gasohol (as defined in such subsection), and

(2) such gasohol is used as a fuel in any aircraft in noncommercial aviation (as defined in section 4041(c)(2)),

the Secretary shall pay (without interest) to the ultimate purchaser of such gasohol an amount equal to 1.4 cents (2 cents in the case of a mixture none of the alcohol in which consists of ethanol) multiplied by the number of gallons of gasohol so used.

P.L. 110-172, §11(a)(39)(B), provides:

(B) The Internal Revenue Code of 1986 shall be applied and administered as if the amendments made by paragraph (2) of section 11151(a) of the SAFETEA-LU [P.L. 109-59] had never been enacted.

• **2005, Safe, Accountable, Flexible, Efficient Transportation Equity Act: A Legacy for Users (P.L. 109-59)**

P.L. 109-59, §11151(a)(2) [but see P.L. 110-172, §11(a)(39)(B), above]:

Amended Code Sec. 6427 by striking subsection (o). **Effective** as if included in the provision of P.L. 108-357 to which it relates [**effective** for fuel sold or used after 12-31-2004.—CCH]. Prior to being stricken, Code Sec. 6427(o) read as follows:

(o) GASOHOL USED IN NONCOMMERCIAL AVIATION.—Except as provided in subsection (k), if—

(1) any tax is imposed by section 4081 at a rate determined under subsection (c) thereof on gasohol (as defined in such subsection), and

(2) such gasohol is used as a fuel in any aircraft in noncommercial aviation (as defined in section 4041(c)(2)),

the Secretary shall pay (without interest) to the ultimate purchaser of such gasohol an amount equal to 1.4 cents (2 cents in the case of a mixture none of the alcohol in which consists of ethanol) multiplied by the number of gallons of gasohol so used.

• **2005, Energy Tax Incentives Act of 2005 (P.L. 109-58)**

P.L. 109-58, §1343(b)(1):

Amended Code Sec. 6427 by redesignating subsection (o) as subsection (p). [This amendment did not need to be made in light of the striking of Code Sec. 6427(o) by P.L. 109-59.—CCH] **Effective** 1-1-2006.

• **1998, IRS Restructuring and Reform Act of 1998 (P.L. 105-206)**

P.L. 105-206, §6023(16):

Amended Code Sec. 6427(q)(2) by striking "section 4041(c)(4)" and inserting "section 4041(c)(2)". **Effective** 7-22-98.

P.L. 105-206, §6023(26)(A):

Amended Code Sec. 6427, as amended by Act Sec. 6023(16), by redesignating subsection (q) as subsection (o). **Effective** 7-22-98.

• **1990, Omnibus Budget Reconciliation Act of 1990 (P.L. 101-508)**

P.L. 101-508, §11211(b)(6)(E)(ii):

Amended Code Sec. 6427(q). **Effective** 12-1-90. Prior to amendment, Code Sec. 6427(q) read as follows:

(q) GASOLINE USED IN NONCOMMERCIAL AVIATION DURING PERIOD RATE REDUCTION IN EFFECT.—Except as provided in subsection (k), if—

(1) any tax is imposed by section 4081 on any gasoline,

(2) such gasoline is used during 1991 as a fuel in any aircraft in noncommercial aviation (as defined in section 4041(c)(4)), and

(3) no tax is imposed by section 4041(c)(2) on taxable events occurring during 1991 by reason of section 4283,

the Secretary shall pay (without interest) to the ultimate purchaser of such gasoline an amount equal to the excess of the aggregate amount of tax paid under section 4081 on the gasoline so used over an amount equal to 6 cents multiplied by the number of gallons of gasoline so used.

• **1989, Omnibus Budget Reconciliation Act of 1989 (P.L. 101-239)**

P.L. 101-239, §7501(b)(3):

Amended Code Sec. 6427(q) by striking "1990" each place it appears and inserting "1991". **Effective** 12-19-89.

• **1988, Technical and Miscellaneous Revenue Act of 1988 (P.L. 100-647)**

P.L. 100-647, §2004(s)(3):

Amended Code Sec. 6427 by redesignating subsection (p) (relating to gasoline used in noncommercial aviation during period rate reduction in effect) as subsection (q). **Effective** as if included in the provision of P.L. 100-203 to which it relates.

• **1987, Airport and Airway Revenue Act of 1987 (P.L. 100-223)**

P.L. 100-223, §405(b)(1):

Amended Code Sec. 6427 by redesignating subsection (p)[q] as subsection (q)[r] and by inserting after subsection (p) a new subsection (p)[q]. **Effective** on 12-30-87.

[Sec. 6427(p)]

(p) CROSS REFERENCES.—

(1) For civil penalty for excessive claims under this section, see section 6675.

(2) For fraud penalties, etc., see chapter 75 (section 7201 and following, relating to crimes, other offenses, and forfeitures).

(3) For treatment of an Indian tribal government as a State (and a subdivision of an Indian tribal government as a political subdivision of a State), see section 7871.

Amendments

• **2007, Tax Technical Corrections Act of 2007 (P.L. 110-172)**

P.L. 110-172, §11(a)(39)(A):

Amended Code Sec. 6427, as amended by section 1343(b)(1) of the Energy Policy Act of 2005 (P.L. 109-58), by redesignating subsection (q) as subsection (p). **Effective** 12-29-2007.

P.L. 110-172, §11(a)(39)(B), provides:

(B) The Internal Revenue Code of 1986 shall be applied and administered as if the amendments made by paragraph (2) of section 11151(a) of the SAFETEA-LU [P.L. 109-59] had never been enacted.

• **2005, Safe, Accountable, Flexible, Efficient Transportation Equity Act: A Legacy for Users (P.L. 109-59)**

P.L. 109-59, §11151(a)(2) [but see P.L. 110-172, §11(a)(39)(B), above]:

Amended Code Sec. 6427 by striking subsection (o) and redesignating subsection (p) as subsection (o). [Note, however, subsection (p) was redesignated as subsection (q) by P.L. 109-58, effective 1-1-2006.—CCH.] **Effective** as if included in the provision of P.L. 108-357 to which it relates [**effective** for fuel sold or used after 12-31-2004.—CCH].

• **2005, Energy Tax Incentives Act of 2005 (P.L. 109-58)**

P.L. 109-58, §1343(b)(1):

Amended Code Sec. 6427 by redesignating subsection (p) as subsection (q). [This amendment did not account for the striking of Code Sec. 6427(o) by P.L. 109-59. As a result, the redesignation by P.L. 109-58 in the manner provided for by Congress is alphabetically incorrect.—CCH.] **Effective** 1-1-2006.

• **1998, IRS Restructuring and Reform Act of 1998 (P.L. 105-206)**

P.L. 105-206, §6023(26)(A):

Amended Code Sec. 6427 by redesignating subsection (r) as subsection (p). **Effective** 7-22-98.

CREDITS AND REFUNDS—SPECIAL RULES

- **1988, Technical and Miscellaneous Revenue Act of 1988 (P.L. 100-647)**

P.L. 100-647, §2004(s)(3):

Amended Code Sec. 6427 by redesignating subsection (q) (relating to cross references) as subsection (r). **Effective** as if included in the provision of P.L. 100-203 to which it relates.

- **1987, Airport and Airway Revenue Act of 1987 (P.L. 100-223)**

P.L. 100-223, §405(b)(1):

Redesignated subsection (p)[q] as subsection (q)[r]. **Effective** on the date of the enactment of this Act.

- **1987, Revenue Act of 1987 (P.L. 100-203)**

P.L. 100-203, §10502(c)(1):

Amended Code Sec. 6427 by redesignating subsections (l) through (p) as subsections (m) through (q), respectively, and by inserting after subsection (k) new subsection (l). **Effective** for sales after 3-31-88.

P.L. 100-203, §10502(f), provides:

(f) FLOOR STOCKS TAX.—

(1) IMPOSITION OF TAX.—On any taxable fuel which on April 1, 1988, is held by a taxable person, there is hereby imposed a floor stocks tax at the rate of tax which would be imposed if such fuel were sold on such date in a sale subject to tax under section 4091 of the Internal Revenue Code of 1986 (as added by this section).

(2) OVERPAYMENT OF FLOOR STOCKS TAXES, ETC.—Sections 6416 and 6427 of such Code shall apply in respect of the floor stocks taxes imposed by this subsection so as to entitle, subject to all provisions of such sections, any person paying such floor stocks taxes to a credit or refund thereof for any reason specified in such sections. All provisions of law, including penalties, applicable with respect to the taxes imposed by section 4091 of such Code (as so added) shall apply to the floor stocks taxes imposed by this subsection.

(3) DUE DATE OF TAX.—The taxes imposed by this subsection shall be paid before June 16, 1988.

(4) DEFINITIONS.—For purposes of this subsection—

(A) TAXABLE FUEL.—

(i) IN GENERAL.—The term "taxable fuel" means any taxable fuel (as defined in section 4092 of such Code, as added by this section) on which no tax has been imposed under section 4041 of such Code.

(ii) EXCEPTION FOR FUEL HELD FOR NONTAXABLE USES.—The term "taxable fuel" shall not include fuel held exclusively for any use which is a nontaxable use (as defined in section 6427(l) of such Code, as added by this section).

(B) TAXABLE PERSON.—The term "taxable person" means any person other than a producer (as defined in section 4092 of such Code, as so added) or importer of taxable fuel.

(C) HELD BY A TAXABLE PERSON.—An article shall be treated as held by a person if title thereto has passed to such person (whether or not delivery to such person has been made).

(5) SPECIAL RULE FOR FUEL HELD FOR USE IN TRAINS AND COMMERCIAL AIRCRAFT.—Only the Leaking Underground Storage Tank Trust Fund financing rate under section 4091 of such Code shall apply for purposes of this subsection with respect to—

(A) diesel fuel held exclusively for use as a fuel in a diesel-powered train, and

(B) aviation fuel held exclusively for use as a fuel in an aircraft not in noncommercial aviation (as defined in section 4041(c)(4) of such code).

(6) TRANSFER OF FLOOR STOCK REVENUES TO TRUST FUNDS.—For purposes of determining the amount transferred to any trust fund, the tax imposed by this subsection shall be treated as imposed by section 4091 of such Code (as so added).

- **1986, Tax Reform Act of 1986 (P.L. 99-514)**

P.L. 99-514, §1703(e)(1)(A), (B):

Amended Code Sec. 6427 (as amended by P.L. 99-499) by redesignating subsections (h), (i), (j), (k), (l), (m), (n), and (o) as subsections (i), (j), (k), (l), (m), (n), (o), and (p), respectively, and by inserting after subsection (g) new subsection (h). **Effective** for gasoline removed (as defined in section 4082 of the Internal Revenue Code of 1986) after 12-31-87.

- **1986, Superfund Amendments and Reauthorization Act of 1986 (P.L. 99-499)**

P.L. 99-499, §521(c)(3)(B)(i):

Amended Code Sec. 6427 by redesignating subsection (n) as subsection (o) and by inserting after subsection (m) new subsection (n). **Effective** 1-1-87.

- **1984, Deficit Reduction Act of 1984 (P.L. 98-369)**

P.L. 98-369, §734(c)(2):

Redesignated Code Sec. 6427 (l) as (m). For the **effective** date, see the notes following Code Sec. 6427(k).

P.L. 98-369, §911(b):

Amended Code Sec. 6427 (as amended by Act Sec. 734(c)(2)) by redesignating subsection (m) as (n). For the **effective** date, see the notes following Code Sec. 6427(g).

- **1983 (P.L. 97-473)**

P.L. 97-473, §202(b)(13):

Added Code Sec. 6427(k)[l]. For the **effective** date, see the amendment note for Act Sec. 204 following Code Sec. 7871.

- **1983, Surface Transportation Act of 1983 (P.L. 97-424)**

P.L. 97-424, §516(b)(5):

Redesignated Code Sec. 6427(k) as Code Sec. 6427(l).

- **1980, Crude Oil Windfall Profit Tax Act of 1980 (P.L. 96-223)**

P.L. 96-223, §232(d)(1)(A):

Redesignated subsection (j) as Code Sec. 6427(k). **Effective** 1-1-79.

- **1978, Surface Transportation Assistance Act of 1978 (P.L. 95-599)**

P.L. 95-599, §505(a)(1), (d):

Redesignated subsection (i) as Code Sec. 6427(j). **Effective** 1-1-79.

- **1976 (P.L. 94-530)**

P.L. 94-530, §[1](b):

Redesignated subsection (h) as Code Sec. 6427(i). **Effective** 10-1-76.

- **1970 (P.L. 91-258)**

P.L. 91-258, §207(a):

Added Code Sec. 6427. **Effective** 7-1-70.

[Sec. 6428]

SEC. 6428. 2020 RECOVERY REBATES FOR INDIVIDUALS.

[Sec. 6428(a)]

(a) IN GENERAL.—In the case of an eligible individual, there shall be allowed as a credit against the tax imposed by subtitle A for the first taxable year beginning in 2020 an amount equal to the sum of—

(1) $1,200 ($2,400 in the case of eligible individuals filing a joint return), plus

(2) an amount equal to the product of $500 multiplied by the number of qualifying children (within the meaning of section 24(c) of the taxpayer.

[Sec. 6428(b)]

(b) TREATMENT OF CREDIT.—The credit allowed by subsection (a) shall be treated as allowed by subpart C of part IV of subchapter A of chapter 1.

[Sec. 6428(c)]

(c) LIMITATION BASED ON ADJUSTED GROSS INCOME.—The amount of the credit allowed by subsection (a) (determined without regard to this subsection and subsection (e)) shall be reduced (but not below zero) by 5 percent of so much of the taxpayer's adjusted gross income as exceeds—

(1) $150,000 in the case of a joint return or a surviving spouse (as defined in section 2(a)),

(2) $112,500 in the case of a head of household, and

(3) $75,000 in the case of a taxpayer not described in paragraph (1) or (2).

Amendments

- **2020, COVID-related Tax Relief Act of 2020 (P.L. 116-260)**

P.L. 116-260, §273(a)(1), Div. N:

Amended Code Sec. 6428(c)(1) by inserting "or a surviving spouse (as defined in section 2(a))" after "joint return". **Effective** as if included in Act Sec. 2201 of the CARES Act (P.L. 116-136) [effective 3-27-2020.—CCH].

[Sec. 6428(d)]

(d) ELIGIBLE INDIVIDUAL.—For purposes of this section, the term "eligible individual" means any individual other than—

(1) any nonresident alien individual,

CREDITS AND REFUNDS—SPECIAL RULES

(2) any individual with respect to whom a deduction under section 151 is allowable to another taxpayer for a taxable year beginning in the calendar year in which the individual's taxable year begins, and

(3) an estate or trust.

[Sec. 6428(e)]

(e) COORDINATION WITH ADVANCE REFUNDS OF CREDIT.—

(1) IN GENERAL.—The amount of credit which would (but for this paragraph) be allowable under this section shall be reduced (but not below zero) by the aggregate refunds and credits made or allowed to the taxpayer under subsection (f). Any failure to so reduce the credit shall be treated as arising out of a mathematical or clerical error and assessed according to section 6213(b)(1).

(2) JOINT RETURNS.—In the case of a refund or credit made or allowed under subsection (f) with respect to a joint return, half of such refund or credit shall be treated as having been made or allowed to each individual filing such return.

[Sec. 6428(f)]

(f) ADVANCE REFUNDS AND CREDITS.—

(1) IN GENERAL.—Subject to paragraph (5), each individual who was an eligible individual for such individual's first taxable year beginning in 2019 shall be treated as having made a payment against the tax imposed by chapter 1 for such taxable year in an amount equal to the advance refund amount for such taxable year.

(2) ADVANCE REFUND AMOUNT.—For purposes of paragraph (1), the advance refund amount is the amount that would have been allowed as a credit under this section for such taxable year if this section (other than subsection (e) and this subsection) had applied to such taxable year.

(3) TIMING AND MANNER OF PAYMENTS.—

(A) TIMING.—The Secretary shall, subject to the provisions of this title, refund or credit any overpayment attributable to this subsection as rapidly as possible. No refund or credit shall be made or allowed under this subsection after December 31, 2020.

(B) DELIVERY OF PAYMENTS.—Notwithstanding any other provision of law, the Secretary may certify and disburse refunds payable under this subsection electronically to any account to which the payee authorized, on or after January 1, 2018, the delivery of a refund of taxes under this title or of a Federal payment (as defined in section 3332 of title 31, United States Code).

(C) WAIVER OF CERTAIN RULES.—Notwithstanding section 3325 of title 31, United States Code, or any other provision of law, with respect to any payment of a refund under this subsection, a disbursing official in the executive branch of the United States Government may modify payment information received from an officer or employee described in section 3325(a)(1)(B) of such title for the purpose of facilitating the accurate and efficient delivery of such payment. Except in cases of fraud or reckless neglect, no liability under sections 3325, 3527, 3528, or 3529 of title 31, United States Code, shall be imposed with respect to payments made under this subparagraph.

(4) NO INTEREST.—No interest shall be allowed on any overpayment attributable to this subsection.

(5) ALTERNATE TAXABLE YEAR.—In the case of an individual who, at the time of any determination made pursuant to paragraph (3), has not filed a tax return for the year described in paragraph (1), the Secretary may—

(A) apply such paragraph by substituting "2018" for "2019", and

(B) if the individual has not filed a tax return for such individual's first taxable year beginning in 2018, use information with respect to such individual for calendar year 2019 provided in—

(i) Form SSA-1099, Social Security Benefit Statement, or

(ii) Form RRB-1099, Social Security Equivalent Benefit Statement.

(6) PAYMENT TO REPRESENTATIVE PAYEES AND FIDUCIARIES.—

(A) IN GENERAL.—In the case of any individual for which payment information is provided to the Secretary by the Commissioner of Social Security, the Railroad Retirement Board, or the Secretary of Veterans Affairs, the payment by the Secretary under paragraph (3) with respect to such individual may be made to such individual's representative payee or fiduciary and the entire payment shall be—

(i) provided to the individual who is entitled to the payment, or

(ii) used only for the benefit of the individual who is entitled to the payment.

(B) APPLICATION OF ENFORCEMENT PROVISIONS.—

(i) In the case of a payment described in subparagraph (A) which is made with respect to a social security beneficiary or a supplemental security income recipient, section 1129(a)(3) of the Social Security Act (42 U.S.C. 1320a-8(a)(3)) shall apply to such payment in the same manner as such section applies to a payment under title II or XVI of such Act.

(ii) In the case of a payment described in subparagraph (A) which is made with respect to a railroad retirement beneficiary, section 13 of the Railroad Retirement Act (45 U.S.C. 231l) shall apply to such payment in the same manner as such section applies to a payment under such Act.

(iii) In the case of a payment described in subparagraph (A) which is made with respect to a veterans beneficiary, sections 5502, 6106, and 6108 of title 38, United States Code, shall apply to such payment in the same manner as such sections apply to a payment under such title.

(7) NOTICE TO TAXPAYER.—Not later than 15 days after the date on which the Secretary distributed any payment to an eligible taxpayer pursuant to this subsection, notice shall be sent by mail to such taxpayer's last known address. Such notice shall indicate the method by which such payment was made, the amount of such payment, and a phone number for the appropriate point of contact at the Internal Revenue Service to report any failure to receive such payment.

Amendments

• **2020, COVID-related Tax Relief Act of 2020 (P.L. 116-260)**

P.L. 116-260, §273(a)(2)(A)-(C), Div. N:

Amended Code Sec. 6428(f), in paragraph 3(A), by striking "section" and inserting "subsection", in paragraph (4), by striking "section" and inserting "subsection", and by redesignating paragraph (6) as paragraph (7) and by inserting after paragraph (5) a new paragraph (6). **Effective** as if included in Act Sec. 2201 of the CARES Act (P.L. 116-136) [effective 3-27-2020.—CCH].

[Sec. 6428(g)]

(g) IDENTIFICATION NUMBER REQUIREMENT.—

(1) REQUIREMENTS FOR CREDIT.—Subject to paragraph (2), with respect to the credit allowed under subsection (a), the following provisions shall apply:

(A) IN GENERAL.—In the case of a return other than a joint return, the $1,200 amount in subsection (a)(1) shall be treated as being zero unless the taxpayer includes the valid identification number of the taxpayer on the return of tax for the taxable year.

(B) JOINT RETURNS.—In the case of a joint return, the $2,400 amount in subsection (a)(1) shall be treated as being—

(i) $1,200 if the valid identification number of only 1 spouse is included on the return of tax for the taxable year, and

(ii) zero if the valid identification number of neither spouse is so included.

CREDITS AND REFUNDS—SPECIAL RULES

(C) QUALIFYING CHILD.—A qualifying child of a taxpayer shall not be taken into account under subsection (a)(2) unless—

(i) the taxpayer includes the valid identification number of such taxpayer (or, in the case of a joint return, the valid identification number of at least 1 spouse) on the return of tax for the taxable year, and

(ii) the valid identification number of such qualifying child is included on the return of tax for the taxable year.

(2) REQUIREMENTS FOR ADVANCE REFUNDS.—No refund shall be payable under subsection (f) to an eligible individual who does not include on the return of tax for the taxable year—

(A) such individual's valid identification number,

(B) in the case of a joint return, the valid identification number of such individual's spouse, and

(C) in the case of any qualifying child taken into account under subsection (a)(2), the valid identification number of such qualifying child.

(3) VALID IDENTIFICATION NUMBER.—

(A) IN GENERAL.—For purposes of this subsection, the term "valid identification number" means a social security number (as such term is defined in section 24(h)(7)).

(B) ADOPTION TAXPAYER IDENTIFICATION NUMBER.—For purposes of paragraphs (1)(C) and (2)(C), in the case of a qualifying child who is adopted or placed for adoption, the term "valid identification number" shall include the adoption taxpayer identification number of such child.

(4) SPECIAL RULE FOR MEMBERS OF THE ARMED FORCES.—Paragraphs (1)(B) and (2)(B) shall not apply in the case where at least 1 spouse was a member of the Armed Forces of the United States at any time during the taxable year and the valid identification number of at least 1 spouse is included on the return of tax for the taxable year.

(5) MATHEMATICAL OR CLERICAL ERROR AUTHORITY.—Any omission of a correct valid identification number required under this subsection shall be treated as a mathematical or clerical error for purposes of applying section 6213(g)(2) to such omission.

Amendments

• **2020, COVID-related Tax Relief Act of 2020 (P.L. 116-260)**

P.L. 116-260, §273(a)(3), Div. N:

Amended Code Sec. 6428 by striking subsection (g) and inserting a new subsection (g). **Effective** as if included in Act Sec. 2201 of the CARES Act (P.L. 116-136) [**effective** 3-27-2020.—CCH]. Prior to being stricken, Code Sec. 6428(g) read as follows:

(g) IDENTIFICATION NUMBER REQUIREMENT.—

(1) IN GENERAL.—No credit shall be allowed under subsection (a) to an eligible individual who does not include on the return of tax for the taxable year—

(A) such individual's valid identification number,

(B) in the case of a joint return, the valid identification number of such individual's spouse, and

(C) in the case of any qualifying child taken into account under subsection (a)(2), the valid identification number of such qualifying child.

(2) VALID IDENTIFICATION NUMBER.—

(A) IN GENERAL.—For purposes of paragraph (1), the term "valid identification number" means a social security number (as such term is defined in section 24(h)(7)).

(B) ADOPTION TAXPAYER IDENTIFICATION NUMBER.—For purposes of paragraph (1)(C), in the case of a qualifying child who is adopted or placed for adoption, the term "valid identification number" shall include the adoption taxpayer identification number of such child.

(3) SPECIAL RULE FOR MEMBERS OF THE ARMED FORCES.—Paragraph (1)(B) shall not apply in the case where at least 1 spouse was a member of the Armed Forces of the United States at any time during the taxable year and at least 1 spouse satisfies paragraph (1)(A).

(4) MATHEMATICAL OR CLERICAL ERROR AUTHORITY.—Any omission of a correct valid identification number required under this subsection shall be treated as a mathematical or clerical error for purposes of applying section 6213(g)(2) to such omission.

[Sec. 6428(g)—Stricken]

Amendments

• **2020, COVID-related Tax Relief Act of 2020 (P.L. 116-260)**

P.L. 116-260, §273(a)(3), Div. N:

Amended Code Sec. 6428 by striking subsection (g) and inserting a new subsection (g). **Effective** as if included in Act Sec. 2201 of the CARES Act (P.L. 116-136) [**effective** 3-27-2020.—CCH]. Prior to being stricken, Code Sec. 6428(g) read as follows:

(g) IDENTIFICATION NUMBER REQUIREMENT.—

(1) IN GENERAL.—No credit shall be allowed under subsection (a) to an eligible individual who does not include on the return of tax for the taxable year—

(A) such individual's valid identification number,

(B) in the case of a joint return, the valid identification number of such individual's spouse, and

(C) in the case of any qualifying child taken into account under subsection (a)(2), the valid identification number of such qualifying child.

(2) VALID IDENTIFICATION NUMBER.—

(A) IN GENERAL.—For purposes of paragraph (1), the term "valid identification number" means a social security number (as such term is defined in section 24(h)(7)).

(B) ADOPTION TAXPAYER IDENTIFICATION NUMBER.—For purposes of paragraph (1)(C), in the case of a qualifying child who is adopted or placed for adoption, the term "valid identification number" shall include the adoption taxpayer identification number of such child.

(3) SPECIAL RULE FOR MEMBERS OF THE ARMED FORCES.—Paragraph (1)(B) shall not apply in the case where at least 1 spouse was a member of the Armed Forces of the United States at any time during the taxable year and at least 1 spouse satisfies paragraph (1)(A).

(4) MATHEMATICAL OR CLERICAL ERROR AUTHORITY.—Any omission of a correct valid identification number required under this subsection shall be treated as a mathematical or clerical error for purposes of applying section 6213(g)(2) to such omission.

[Sec. 6428(h)]

(h) REGULATIONS.—The Secretary shall prescribe such regulations or other guidance as may be necessary to carry out the purposes of this section, including any such measures as are deemed appropriate to avoid allowing multiple credits or rebates to a taxpayer.

Amendments

• **2020, Coronavirus Aid, Relief, and Economic Security (CARES) Act (P.L. 116-136)**

P.L. 116-136, §2201(a):

Amended subchapter B of chapter 65 of subtitle F by inserting after Code Sec. 6427 a new Code Sec. 6428. **Effective** 3-27-2020. For special rules, see Act Sec. 2201(c)-(e), below.

P.L. 116-136, §2201(c)-(e) (as amended by P.L. 116-260, §273(b)(1), Div. N), provides:

(c) TREATMENT OF POSSESSIONS.—

(1) PAYMENTS TO POSSESSIONS.—

(A) MIRROR CODE POSSESSION.—The Secretary of the Treasury shall pay to each possession of the United States which has a mirror code tax system amounts equal to the loss (if any) to that possession by reason of the amendments made by this section. Such amounts shall be determined by the Secretary of the Treasury based on information provided by the government of the respective possession.

(B) OTHER POSSESSIONS.—The Secretary of the Treasury shall pay to each possession of the United States which does not have a mirror code tax system amounts estimated by the Secretary of the Treasury as being equal to the aggregate benefits (if any) that would have been provided to residents of such possession by reason of the amendments made by this section if a mirror code tax system had been in effect in such possession. The preceding sentence shall not apply unless the respective possession has a plan, which has been approved by the Secretary of the Treasury, under which such possession will promptly distribute such payments to its residents.

(2) COORDINATION WITH CREDIT ALLOWED AGAINST UNITED STATES INCOME TAXES.—No credit shall be allowed against United States income taxes under section 6428 of the Internal Revenue Code of 1986 (as added by this section) to any person—

(A) to whom a credit is allowed against taxes imposed by the possession by reason of the amendments made by this section, or

(B) who is eligible for a payment under a plan described in paragraph (1)(B).

(3) DEFINITIONS AND SPECIAL RULES.—

(A) POSSESSION OF THE UNITED STATES.— For purposes of this subsection, the term "possession of the United States" includes the Commonwealth of Puerto Rico and the Commonwealth of the Northern Mariana Islands.

(B) MIRROR CODE TAX SYSTEM.—For purposes of this subsection, the term "mirror code tax system" means, with respect to any possession of the United States, the income tax system of such possession if the income tax liability of the residents of such possession under such system is determined by reference to the income tax laws of the United States as if such possession were the United States.

(C) TREATMENT OF PAYMENTS.—For purposes of section 1324 of title 31, United States Code, the payments under this subsection shall be treated in the same manner as a refund due from a credit provision referred to in subsection (b)(2) of such section.

CREDITS AND REFUNDS—SPECIAL RULES

(d) EXCEPTION FROM REDUCTION OR OFFSET.—Any refund payable by reason of section 6428(f) of the Internal Revenue Code of 1986 (as added by this section), or any such refund payable by reason of subsection (c) of this section, shall not be—

(1) subject to reduction or offset pursuant to section 3716 or 3720A of title 31, United States Code,

(2) subject to reduction or offset pursuant to subsection (d), (e), or (f) of section 6402 of the Internal Revenue Code of 1986, or

(3) reduced or offset by other assessed Federal taxes that would otherwise be subject to levy or collection.

Amendments

• **2014, Tax Technical Corrections Act of 2014 (P.L. 113-295)**

P.L. 113-295, § 221(a)(112)(A), Division A:

Amended subchapter B of chapter 65 by striking Code Sec. 6428. **Effective** generally 12-19-2014. For a special rule, see Act Sec. 221(b)(2), Division A, below.

P.L. 113-295, § 221(b)(2), Division A, provides:

(2) SAVINGS PROVISION.—If—

(A) any provision amended or repealed by the amendments made by this section applied to—

(i) any transaction occurring before the date of the enactment of this Act,

(ii) any property acquired before such date of enactment, or

(iii) any item of income, loss, deduction, or credit taken into account before such date of enactment, and

(B) the treatment of such transaction, property, or item under such provision would (without regard to the amendments or repeals made by this section) affect the liability for tax for periods ending after date of enactment, nothing in the amendments or repeals made by this section shall be construed to affect the treatment of such transaction, property, or item for purposes of determining liability for tax for periods ending after such date of enactment.

Prior to being stricken, Code Sec. 6428 read as follows:

SEC. 6428. 2008 RECOVERY REBATES FOR INDIVIDUALS.

[Sec. 6428(a)]

(a) IN GENERAL.—In the case of an eligible individual, there shall be allowed as a credit against the tax imposed by subtitle A for the first taxable year beginning in 2008 an amount equal to the lesser of—

(1) net income tax liability, or

(2) $600 ($1,200 in the case of a joint return).

[Sec. 6428(b)]

(b) SPECIAL RULES.—

(1) IN GENERAL.—In the case of a taxpayer described in paragraph (2)—

(A) the amount determined under subsection (a) shall not be less than $300 ($600 in the case of a joint return), and

(B) the amount determined under subsection (a) (after the application of subparagraph (A)) shall be increased by the product of $300 multiplied by the number of qualifying children (within the meaning of section 24(c)) of the taxpayer.

(2) TAXPAYER DESCRIBED.—A taxpayer is described in this paragraph if the taxpayer—

(A) has qualifying income of at least $3,000, or

(B) has—

(i) net income tax liability which is greater than zero, and

(ii) gross income which is greater than the sum of the basic standard deduction plus the exemption amount (twice the exemption amount in the case of a joint return).

[Sec. 6428(c)]

(c) TREATMENT OF CREDIT.—The credit allowed by subsection (a) shall be treated as allowed by subpart C of part IV of subchapter A of chapter 1.

[Sec. 6428(d)]

(d) LIMITATION BASED ON ADJUSTED GROSS INCOME.—The amount of the credit allowed by subsection (a) (determined without regard to this subsection and subsection (f)) shall be reduced (but not below zero) by 5 percent of so much of the taxpayer's adjusted gross income as exceeds $75,000 ($150,000 in the case of a joint return).

[Sec. 6428(e)]

(e) DEFINITIONS.—For purposes of this section—

(1) QUALIFYING INCOME.—The term "qualifying income" means—

(A) earned income,

(B) social security benefits (within the meaning of section 86(d)), and

(C) any compensation or pension received under chapter 11, chapter 13, or chapter 15 of title 38, United States Code.

(2) NET INCOME TAX LIABILITY.—The term "net income tax liability" means the excess of—

(A) the sum of the taxpayer's regular tax liability (within the meaning of section 26(b)) and the tax imposed by section 55 for the taxable year, over

(B) the credits allowed by part IV (other than section 24 and subpart C thereof) of sub-chapter A of chapter 1.

(3) ELIGIBLE INDIVIDUAL.—The term "eligible individual" means any individual other than—

(A) any nonresident alien individual,

(B) any individual with respect to whom a deduction under section 151 is allowable to another taxpayer for a taxable year beginning in the calendar year in which the individual's taxable year begins, and

(e) PUBLIC AWARENESS CAMPAIGN.—The Secretary of the Treasury (or the Secretary's delegate) shall conduct a public awareness campaign, in coordination with the Commissioner of Social Security and the heads of other relevant Federal agencies, to provide information regarding the availability of the credit and rebate allowed under section 6428 of the Internal Revenue Code of 1986 (as added by this section), including information with respect to individuals who may not have filed a tax return for taxable year 2018 or 2019.

[Sec. 6428—Stricken]

(C) an estate or trust.

(4) EARNED INCOME.—The term "earned income" has the meaning set forth in section 32(c)(2) except that such term shall not include net earnings from self-employment which are not taken into account in computing taxable income.

(5) BASIC STANDARD DEDUCTION; EXEMPTION AMOUNT.—The terms "basic standard deduction" and "exemption amount" shall have the same respective meanings as when used in section 6012(a).

Amendments

• **2008, Heroes Earnings Assistance and Relief Tax Act of 2008 (P.L. 110-245)**

P.L. 110-245, § 102(b):

Amended Code Sec. 6428(e)(4) by striking "except that—"and all that follows through "(B) such term shall" and inserting "except that such term shall". **Effective** for tax years ending after 12-31-2007. Prior to amendment, Code Sec. 6428(e)(4) read as follows:

(4) EARNED INCOME.—The term "earned income" has the meaning set forth in section 32(c)(2) except that—

(A) subclause (II) of subparagraph (B)(vi) thereof shall be applied by substituting "January 1, 2009" for "January 1, 2008", and

(B) such term shall not include net earnings from self-employment which are not taken into account in computing taxable income.

[Sec. 6428(f)]

(f) COORDINATION WITH ADVANCE REFUNDS OF CREDIT.—

(1) IN GENERAL.—The amount of credit which would (but for this paragraph) be allowable under this section shall be reduced (but not below zero) by the aggregate refunds and credits made or allowed to the taxpayer under subsection (g). Any failure to so reduce the credit shall be treated as arising out of a mathematical or clerical error and assessed according to section 6213(b)(1).

(2) JOINT RETURNS.—In the case of a refund or credit made or allowed under subsection (g) with respect to a joint return, half of such refund or credit shall be treated as having been made or allowed to each individual filing such return.

[Sec. 6428(g)]

(g) ADVANCE REFUNDS AND CREDITS.—

(1) IN GENERAL.—Each individual who was an eligible individual for such individual's first taxable year beginning in 2007 shall be treated as having made a payment against the tax imposed by chapter 1 for such first taxable year in an amount equal to the advance refund amount for such taxable year.

(2) ADVANCE REFUND AMOUNT.—For purposes of paragraph (1), the advance refund amount is the amount that would have been allowed as a credit under this section for such first taxable year if this section (other than subsection (f) and this subsection) had applied to such taxable year.

(3) TIMING OF PAYMENTS.—The Secretary shall, subject to the provisions of this title, refund or credit any overpayment attributable to this section as rapidly as possible. No refund or credit shall be made or allowed under this subsection after December 31, 2008.

(4) NO INTEREST.—No interest shall be allowed on any overpayment attributable to this section.

[Sec. 6428(h)]

(h) IDENTIFICATION NUMBER REQUIREMENT.—

(1) IN GENERAL.—No credit shall be allowed under subsection (a) to an eligible individual who does not include on the return of tax for the taxable year—

(A) such individual's valid identification number,

(B) in the case of a joint return, the valid identification number of such individual's spouse, and

(C) in the case of any qualifying child taken into account under subsection (b)(1)(B), the valid identification number of such qualifying child.

(2) VALID IDENTIFICATION NUMBER.—For purposes of paragraph (1), the term "valid identification number" means a social security number issued to an individual by the Social Security Administration. Such term shall not include a TIN issued by the Internal Revenue Service.

(3) SPECIAL RULE FOR MEMBERS OF THE ARMED FORCES.—Paragraph (1) shall not apply to a joint return where at least 1 spouse was a member of the Armed Forces of the United States at any time during the taxable year.

Amendments

• **2008, Heroes Earnings Assistance and Relief Tax Act of 2008 (P.L. 110-245)**

P.L. 110-245, § 101(a):

Amended Code Sec. 6428(h) by adding at the end a new paragraph (3). **Effective** as if included in the amendments made by section 101 of the Economic Stimulus Act of 2008 (P.L. 110-185) [**effective** 2-13-2008.—CCH].

CREDITS AND REFUNDS—SPECIAL RULES

• **2008, Economic Stimulus Act of 2008 (P.L. 110-185)**

P.L. 110-185, §101(a):

Amended Code Sec. 6428. **Effective** 2-13-2008. Prior to amendment, Code Sec. 6428 read as follows:

SEC. 6428. ACCELERATION OF 10 PERCENT INCOME TAX RATE BRACKET BENEFIT FOR 2001.

[Sec. 6428(a)]

(a) IN GENERAL.—In the case of an eligible individual, there shall be allowed as a credit against the tax imposed by chapter 1 for the taxpayer's first taxable year beginning in 2001 an amount equal to 5 percent of so much of the taxpayer's taxable income as does not exceed the initial bracket amount (as defined in section 1(i)(1)(B)).

[Sec. 6428(b)]

(b) CREDIT TREATED AS NONREFUNDABLE PERSONAL CREDIT.—For purposes of this title, the credit allowed under this section shall be treated as a credit allowable under subpart A of part IV of subchapter A of chapter 1.

Amendments

• **2002, Job Creation and Worker Assistance Act of 2002 (P.L. 107-147)**

P.L. 107-147, §411(a)(1):

Amended Code Sec. 6428(b). **Effective** as if included in the provision of P.L. 107-16 to which it relates [**effective** for tax years beginning after 12-31-2000.—CCH]. Prior to amendment, Code Sec. 6428(b) read as follows:

(b) LIMITATION BASED ON AMOUNT OF TAX.—The credit allowed by subsection (a) shall not exceed the excess (if any) of—

(1) the sum of the regular tax liability (as defined in section 26(b)) plus the tax imposed by section 55, over

(2) the sum of the credits allowable under part IV of subchapter A of chapter 1 (other than the credits allowable under subpart C thereof, relating to refundable credits).

• **2001, Economic Growth and Tax Relief Reconciliation Act of 2001 (P.L. 107-16)**

P.L. 107-16, §901(a)-(b), as amended by P.L. 111-312, §101(a)(1), provides:

SEC. 901. SUNSET OF PROVISIONS OF ACT.

(a) IN GENERAL.—All provisions of, and amendments made by, this Act shall not apply—

(1) to taxable, plan, or limitation years beginning after December 31, 2012, or

(2) in the case of title V, to estates of decedents dying, gifts made, or generation skipping transfers, after December 31, 2012.

(b) APPLICATION OF CERTAIN LAWS.—The Internal Revenue Code of 1986 and the Employee Retirement Income Security Act of 1974 shall be applied and administered to years, estates, gifts, and transfers described in subsection (a) as if the provisions and amendments described in subsection (a) had never been enacted.

[Sec. 6428(c)]

(c) ELIGIBLE INDIVIDUAL.—For purposes of this section, the term "eligible individual" means any individual other than—

(1) any estate or trust,

(2) any nonresident alien individual, and

(3) any individual with respect to whom a deduction under section 151 is allowable to another taxpayer for a taxable year beginning in the calendar year in which the individual's taxable year begins.

[Sec. 6428(d)]

(d) COORDINATION WITH ADVANCE REFUNDS OF CREDIT.—

(1) IN GENERAL.—The amount of credit which would (but for this paragraph) be allowable under this section shall be reduced (but not below zero) by the aggregate refunds and credits made or allowed to the taxpayer under subsection (e). Any failure to so reduce the credit shall be treated as arising out of a mathematical or clerical error and assessed according to section 6213(b)(1).

(2) JOINT RETURNS.—In the case of a refund or credit made or allowed under subsection (e) with respect to a joint return, half of such refund or credit shall be treated as having been made or allowed to each individual filing such return.

Amendments

• **2002, Job Creation and Worker Assistance Act of 2002 (P.L. 107-147)**

P.L. 107-147, §411(a)(2)(A):

Amended Code Sec. 6428(d). **Effective** as if included in the provision of P.L. 107-16 to which it relates [**effective** for tax years beginning after 12-31-2000.—CCH]. Prior to amendment, Code Sec. 6428(d) read as follows:

(d) SPECIAL RULES.—

(1) COORDINATION WITH ADVANCE REFUNDS OF CREDIT.—

(A) IN GENERAL.—The amount of credit which would (but for this paragraph) be allowable under this section shall be reduced (but not below zero) by the aggregate refunds and credits made or allowed to the taxpayer under subsection (e). Any failure to so reduce the credit shall be treated as arising out of a mathematical or clerical error and assessed according to section 6213(b)(1).

(B) JOINT RETURNS.—In the case of a refund or credit made or allowed under subsection (e) with respect to a joint return, half of such refund or credit shall be treated as having been made or allowed to each individual filing such return.

(2) COORDINATION WITH ESTIMATED TAX.—The credit under this section shall be treated for purposes of section 6654(f) in the same manner as a credit under subpart A of part IV of subchapter A of chapter 1.

• **2001, Economic Growth and Tax Relief Reconciliation Act of 2001 (P.L. 107-16)**

P.L. 107-16, §901(a)-(b), as amended by P.L. 111-312, §101(a)(1), provides:

SEC. 901. SUNSET OF PROVISIONS OF ACT.

(a) IN GENERAL.—All provisions of, and amendments made by, this Act shall not apply—

(1) to taxable, plan, or limitation years beginning after December 31, 2012, or

(2) in the case of title V, to estates of decedents dying, gifts made, or generation skipping transfers, after December 31, 2012.

(b) APPLICATION OF CERTAIN LAWS.—The Internal Revenue Code of 1986 and the Employee Retirement Income Security Act of 1974 shall be applied and administered to years, estates, gifts, and transfers described in subsection (a) as if the provisions and amendments described in subsection (a) had never been enacted.

[Sec. 6428(e)]

(e) ADVANCE REFUNDS OF CREDIT BASED ON PRIOR YEAR DATA.—

(1) IN GENERAL.—Each individual who was an eligible individual for such individual's first taxable year beginning in 2000 shall be treated as having made a payment against the tax imposed by chapter 1 for such first taxable year in an amount equal to the advance refund amount for such taxable year.

(2) ADVANCE REFUND AMOUNT.—For purposes of paragraph (1), the advance refund amount is the amount that would have been allowed as a credit under this section for such first taxable year if—

(A) this section (other than subsections (b) and (d) and this subsection) had applied to such taxable year, and

(B) the credit for such taxable year were not allowed to exceed the excess (if any) of—

(i) the sum of the regular tax liability (as defined in section 26(b)) plus the tax imposed by section 55, over

(ii) the sum of the credits allowable under part IV of subchapter A of chapter 1 (other than the credits allowable under subpart C thereof, relating to refundable credits).

(3) TIMING OF PAYMENTS.—In the case of any overpayment attributable to this subsection, the Secretary shall, subject to the provisions of this title, refund or credit such overpayment as rapidly as possible and, to the extent practicable, before October 1, 2001. No refund or credit shall be made or allowed under this subsection after December 31, 2001.

(4) NO INTEREST.—No interest shall be allowed on any overpayment attributable to this subsection.

Amendments

• **2002, Job Creation and Worker Assistance Act of 2002 (P.L. 107-147)**

P.L. 107-147, §411(a)(2)(B):

Amended Code Sec. 6428(e)(2). **Effective** as if included in the provision of P.L. 107-16 to which it relates [**effective** for tax years beginning after 12-31-2000.—CCH]. Prior to amendment, Code Sec. 6428(e)(2) read as follows:

(2) ADVANCE REFUND AMOUNT.—For purposes of paragraph (1), the advance refund amount is the amount that would have been allowed as a credit under this section for such first taxable year if this section (other than subsection (d) and this subsection) had applied to such taxable year.

• **2001, Economic Growth and Tax Relief Reconciliation Act of 2001 (P.L. 107-16)**

P.L. 107-16, §101(b)(1):

Amended subchapter B of chapter 65 by adding at the end a new Code Sec. 6428. **Effective** for tax years beginning after 12-31-2000.

P.L. 107-16, §901(a)-(b), as amended by P.L. 111-312, §101(a)(1), provides:

SEC. 901. SUNSET OF PROVISIONS OF ACT.

(a) IN GENERAL.—All provisions of, and amendments made by, this Act shall not apply—

(1) to taxable, plan, or limitation years beginning after December 31, 2012, or

(2) in the case of title V, to estates of decedents dying, gifts made, or generation skipping transfers, after December 31, 2012.

(b) APPLICATION OF CERTAIN LAWS.—The Internal Revenue Code of 1986 and the Employee Retirement Income Security Act of 1974 shall be applied and administered to years, estates, gifts, and transfers described in subsection (a) as if the provisions and amendments described in subsection (a) had never been enacted.

P.L. 110-185, §101(c)-(d), provides:

(c) TREATMENT OF POSSESSIONS.—

(1) PAYMENTS TO POSSESSIONS.—

(A) MIRROR CODE POSSESSION.—The Secretary of the Treasury shall make a payment to each possession of the United States with a mirror code tax system in an amount equal to the loss to that possession by reason of the amendments made by this section. Such amount shall be determined by the Secretary of the Treasury based on information provided by the government of the respective possession.

(B) OTHER POSSESSIONS.—The Secretary of the Treasury shall make a payment to each possession of the United States which does not have a mirror code tax system in an amount estimated by the Secretary of the Treasury as being equal to the aggregate benefits that would have been provided to residents of such possession by reason of the amendments made by this section if a mirror code tax system had been in effect in such possession. The preceding sentence shall not apply with respect to any possession of the United States unless such possession has a plan, which has been

CREDITS AND REFUNDS—SPECIAL RULES

approved by the Secretary of the Treasury, under which such possession will promptly distribute such payment to the residents of such possession.

(2) COORDINATION WITH CREDIT ALLOWED AGAINST UNITED STATES INCOME TAXES.—No credit shall be allowed against United States income taxes under section 6428 of the Internal Revenue Code of 1986 (as amended by this section) to any person—

(A) to whom a credit is allowed against taxes imposed by the possession by reason of the amendments made by this section, or

(B) who is eligible for a payment under a plan described in paragraph (1)(B).

(3) DEFINITIONS AND SPECIAL RULES.—

(A) POSSESSION OF THE UNITED STATES.—For purposes of this subsection, the term "possession of the United States" includes the Commonwealth of Puerto Rico and the Commonwealth of the Northern Mariana Islands.

(B) MIRROR CODE TAX SYSTEM.—For purposes of this subsection, the term "mirror code tax system" means, with respect to any possession of the United States, the income tax system of such possession if the income tax liability of the residents of such possession under such system is determined by reference to the income tax laws of the United States as if such possession were the United States.

(C) TREATMENT OF PAYMENTS.—For purposes of section 1324(b)(2) of title 31, United States Code, the payments under this subsection shall be treated in the same manner as a refund due from the credit allowed under section 6428 of the Internal Revenue Code of 1986 (as amended by this section).

(d) REFUNDS DISREGARDED IN THE ADMINISTRATION OF FEDERAL PROGRAMS AND FEDERALLY ASSISTED PROGRAMS.—Any credit or refund allowed or made to any individual by reason of section 6428 of the Internal Revenue Code of 1986 (as amended by this section) or by reason of subsection (c) of this section shall not be taken into account as income and shall not be taken into account as resources for the month of receipt and the following 2 months, for purposes of determining the eligibility of such individual or any other individual for benefits or assistance, or the amount or extent of benefits or assistance, under any Federal program or under any State or local program financed in whole or in part with Federal funds.

[Sec. 6428—Repealed]

Amendments

• **1990, Omnibus Budget Reconciliation Act of 1990 (P.L. 101-508)**

P.L. 101-508, §11801(a)(47):

Repealed Code Sec. 6428. **Effective** 11-5-90.

P.L. 101-508, §11821(b), provides:

(b) SAVINGS PROVISION.—If—

(1) any provision amended or repealed by this part applied to—

(A) any transaction occurring before the date of the enactment of this Act,

(B) any property acquired before such date of enactment, or

(C) any item of income, loss, deduction, or credit taken into account before such date of enactment, and

(2) the treatment of such transaction, property, or item under such provision would (without regard to the amendments made by this part) affect liability for tax for periods ending after such date of enactment,

nothing in the amendments made by this part shall be construed to affect the treatment of such transaction, property, or item for purposes of determining liability for tax for periods ending after such date of enactment.

Prior to repeal, Code Sec. 6428 read as follows:

SEC. 6428. 1981 RATE REDUCTION TAX CREDIT.

(a) ALLOWANCE OF CREDIT.—There shall be allowed as a credit against the tax imposed by section 1, or against a tax imposed in lieu of the tax imposed by section 1, for any taxable year beginning in 1981, an amount equal to the product of—

(1) 1.25 percent, multiplied by

(2) the amount of tax imposed by section 1 (or in lieu thereof) for such taxable year.

(b) SPECIAL RULES FOR APPLICATION OF THIS SECTION.—

(1) APPLICATION WITH OTHER CREDITS.—In determining any credit allowed under subpart A of part IV of subchapter A of chapter 1 (other than under sections 31, 39, and 43), the tax imposed by chapter 1 shall (before any other reductions) be reduced by the credit allowed under subsection (a).

(2) CREDIT TREATED AS SUBPART A CREDIT.—For purposes of this title, the credit allowed under subsection (a) shall be treated as a credit allowed under subpart A of part IV of subchapter A of chapter 1.

(c) TABLES TO REFLECT CREDIT.—

(1) SECTION 3 TABLES.—The tables prescribed by the Secretary under section 3 shall reflect the credit allowed under subsection (a).

(2) OTHER TABLES.—In order to reflect the amount of the credit under subsection (a) for different levels of tax or taxable income, the Secretary may—

(A) modify the tables under section 1, or

(B) prescribe such other tables as he determines necessary.

(d) SPECIAL RULES.—For purposes of this section—

(1) INDIVIDUALS TO WHOM 50 PERCENT MAXIMUM RATE OR 20 PERCENT CAPITAL GAIN RATE APPLIES.—

(A) IN GENERAL.—In the case of any individual to whom this paragraph applies, in determining the amount of the credit allowable under subsection (a)—

(i) the portion of the tax imposed by section 1 determined under section 1348(a)(2) (as in effect before its repeal by the Economic Recovery Tax Act of 1981), and

(ii) the portion of the tax imposed by section 1 determined under subsection (a)(2)(B) of section 102 of the Economic Recovery Tax Act of 1981,

shall not be taken into account.

(B) INDIVIDUALS TO WHOM PARAGRAPH APPLIES.—This paragraph applies to any individual if the tax imposed by section 1 for the taxable year is determined under—

(i) section 1348 (as in effect before its repeal by the Economic Recovery Tax Act of 1981), or

(ii) section 102(a)(2) of the Economic Recovery Tax Act of 1981.

(2) SPECIAL RULE FOR TAX IMPOSED BY SECTION 402(e).—The tax imposed by subsection (e) of section 402 shall be treated as a tax imposed by section 1.

• **1983, Technical Corrections Act of 1982 (P.L. 97-448)**

P.L. 97-448, §101(a)(2):

Added Code Sec. 6428(d). **Effective** as if included in the provision of P.L. 97-34 to which it relates.

• **1981, Economic Recovery Tax Act of 1981 (P.L. 97-34)**

P.L. 97-34, §101(b):

Amended Code Sec. 6428. Prior to amendment, Code Sec. 6428 read as follows:

SEC. 6428. REFUND OF 1974 INDIVIDUAL INCOME TAXES.

(a) GENERAL RULE.—Except as otherwise provided in this section, each individual shall be treated as having made a payment against the tax imposed by chapter 1 for his first taxable year beginning in 1974 in an amount equal to 10 percent of the amount of his liability for tax for such taxable year.

(b) MINIMUM PAYMENT.—The amount treated as paid by reason of this section shall not be less than the lesser of—

(1) the amount of the taxpayer's liability for tax for his first taxable year beginning in 1974, or

(2) $100 ($50 in the case of a married individual filing a separate return).

(c) MAXIMUM PAYMENT.—

(1) IN GENERAL.—The amount treated as paid by reason of this section shall not exceed $200 ($100 in the case of a married individual filing a separate return).

(2) LIMITATION BASED ON ADJUSTED GROSS INCOME.—The excess (if any) of—

(A) the amount which would (but for this paragraph) be treated as paid by reason of this section, over

(B) the applicable minimum payment provided by subsection (b),

shall be reduced (but not below zero) by an amount which bears the same ratio to such excess as the adjusted gross income for the taxable year in excess of $20,000 bears to $10,000. In the case of a married individual filing a separate return, the preceding sentence shall be applied by substituting "$10,000" for "$20,000" and by substituting "$5,000" for "$10,000".

(d) LIABILITY FOR TAX.—For purposes of this section, the liability for tax for the taxable year shall be the sum of—

(1) the tax imposed by chapter 1 for such year, reduced by the sum of the credits allowable under—

(A) section 33 (relating to foreign tax credit),

(B) section 37 (relating to retirement income),

(C) section 38 (relating to investment in certain depreciable property),

(D) section 40 (relating to expenses of work incentive programs), and

(E) section 41 (relating to contributions to candidates for public office), plus

(2) the tax on amounts described in section 3102(c) or 3202(c) which are required to be shown on the taxpayer's return of the chapter 1 tax for the taxable year.

(e) DATE PAYMENT DEEMED MADE.—The payment provided by this section shall be deemed made on whichever of the following dates is the later:

(1) the date prescribed by law (determined without extensions) for filing the return of tax under chapter 1 for the taxable year, or

(2) the date on which the taxpayer files his return of tax under chapter 1 for the taxable year.

(f) JOINT RETURN.—For purposes of this section, in the case of a joint return under section 6013 both spouses shall be treated as one individual.

(g) MARITAL STATUS.—The determination of marital status for purposes of this section shall be made under section 143.

(h) CERTAIN PERSONS NOT ELIGIBLE.—This section shall not apply to any estate or trust, nor shall it apply to any nonresident alien individual.

• **1975, Tax Reduction Act of 1975 (P.L. 94-12)**

P.L. 94-12, §101(a):

Added Code Sec. 6428. **Effective** 3-29-75.

P.L. 94-12, §102, provides:

SEC. 102. REFUNDS DISREGARDED IN THE ADMINISTRATION OF FEDERAL PROGRAMS AND FEDERALLY ASSISTED PROGRAMS.

Any payment considered to have been made by any individual by reason of section 6428 of the Internal Revenue Code of 1954 shall not be taken into account as income or receipts for purposes of determining the eligibility of such individual or any other individual for benefits or assistance, or the amount or extent of benefits or assistance, under any Federal program or under any State or local program financed in whole or in part with Federal funds.

CREDITS AND REFUNDS—SPECIAL RULES

[Sec. 6428A]

SEC. 6428A. ADDITIONAL 2020 RECOVERY REBATES FOR INDIVIDUALS.

[Sec. 6428A(a)]

(a) IN GENERAL.—In addition to the credit allowed under section 6428, in the case of an eligible individual, there shall be allowed as a credit against the tax imposed by subtitle A for the first taxable year beginning in 2020 an amount equal to the sum of—

(1) $600 ($1,200 in the case of eligible individuals filing a joint return), plus

(2) an amount equal to the product of $600 multiplied by the number of qualifying children (within the meaning of section 24(c)) of the taxpayer.

[Sec. 6428A(b)]

(b) TREATMENT OF CREDIT.—The credit allowed by subsection (a) shall be treated as allowed by subpart C of part IV of subchapter A of chapter 1.

[Sec. 6428A(c)]

(c) LIMITATION BASED ON ADJUSTED GROSS INCOME.—The amount of the credit allowed by subsection (a) (determined without regard to this subsection and subsection (e)) shall be reduced (but not below zero) by 5 percent of so much of the taxpayer's adjusted gross income as exceeds—

(1) $150,000 in the case of a joint return or a surviving spouse (as defined in section 2(a)),

(2) $112,500 in the case of a head of household (as defined in section 2(b)), and

(3) $75,000 in the case of a taxpayer not described in paragraph (1) or (2).

[Sec. 6428A(d)]

(d) ELIGIBLE INDIVIDUAL.—For purposes of this section, the term "eligible individual" means any individual other than—

(1) any nonresident alien individual,

(2) any individual with respect to whom a deduction under section 151 is allowable to another taxpayer for a taxable year beginning in the calendar year in which the individual's taxable year begins, and

(3) an estate or trust.

[Sec. 6428A(e)]

(e) COORDINATION WITH ADVANCE REFUNDS OF CREDIT.—

(1) IN GENERAL.—The amount of the credit which would (but for this paragraph) be allowable under this section shall be reduced (but not below zero) by the aggregate refunds and credits made or allowed to the taxpayer under subsection (f). Any failure to so reduce the credit shall be treated as arising out of a mathematical or clerical error and assessed according to section 6213(b)(1).

(2) JOINT RETURNS.—Except as otherwise provided by the Secretary, in the case of a refund or credit made or allowed under subsection (f) with respect to a joint return, half of such refund or credit shall be treated as having been made or allowed to each individual filing such return.

[Sec. 6428A(f)]

(f) ADVANCE REFUNDS AND CREDITS.—

(1) IN GENERAL.—Each individual who was an eligible individual for such individual's first taxable year beginning in 2019 shall be treated as having made a payment against the tax imposed by chapter 1 for such taxable year in an amount equal to the advance refund amount for such taxable year.

(2) ADVANCE REFUND AMOUNT.—For purposes of paragraph (1), the advance refund amount is the amount that would have been allowed as a credit under this section for such taxable year if this section (other than subsection (e) and this subsection) had applied to such taxable year. For purposes of determining the advance refund amount with respect to such taxable year—

(A) any individual who was deceased before January 1, 2020, shall be treated for purposes of applying subsection (g) in the same manner as if the valid identification number of such person was not included on the return of tax for such taxable year, and

(B) no amount shall be determined under this subsection with respect to any qualifying child of the taxpayer if—

(i) the taxpayer was deceased before January 1, 2020, or

(ii) in the case of a joint return, both taxpayers were deceased before January 1, 2020.

(3) TIMING AND MANNER OF PAYMENTS.—

(A) TIMING.—

(i) IN GENERAL.—The Secretary shall, subject to the provisions of this title, refund or credit any overpayment attributable to this subsection as rapidly as possible.

(ii) DEADLINE.—

(I) IN GENERAL.—Except as provided in subclause (II), no refund or credit shall be made or allowed under this subsection after January 15, 2021.

(II) EXCEPTION FOR MIRROR CODE POSSESSIONS.—In the case of a possession of the United States which has a mirror code tax system (as such terms are defined in section 272(c) of the COVID-related Tax Relief Act of 2020), no refund or credit shall be made or allowed under this subsection after the earlier of—

(aa) such date as is determined appropriate by the Secretary, or

(bb) September 30, 2021.

(B) DELIVERY OF PAYMENTS.—Notwithstanding any other provision of law, the Secretary may certify and disburse refunds payable under this subsection electronically to—

(i) any account to which the payee authorized, on or after January 1, 2019, the delivery of a refund of taxes under this title or of a Federal payment (as defined in section 3332 of title 31, United States Code),

(ii) any account belonging to a payee from which that individual, on or after January 1, 2019, made a payment of taxes under this title, or

(iii) any Treasury-sponsored account (as defined in section 208.2 of title 31, Code of Federal Regulations).

(C) WAIVER OF CERTAIN RULES.—Notwithstanding section 3325 of title 31, United States Code, or any other provision of law, with respect to any payment of a refund under this subsection, a disbursing official in the executive branch of the United States Government may modify payment information received from an officer or employee described in section 3325(a)(1)(B) of such title for the purpose of

CREDITS AND REFUNDS—SPECIAL RULES

facilitating the accurate and efficient delivery of such payment. Except in cases of fraud or reckless neglect, no liability under sections 3325, 3527, 3528, or 3529 of title 31, United States Code, shall be imposed with respect to payments made under this subparagraph.

(4) NO INTEREST.—No interest shall be allowed on any overpayment attributable to this subsection.

(5) APPLICATION TO CERTAIN INDIVIDUALS WHO DO NOT FILE A RETURN OF TAX FOR 2019.—

(A) IN GENERAL.—In the case of a specified individual who, at the time of any determination made pursuant to paragraph (3), has not filed a tax return for the year described in paragraph (1), the Secretary may use information with respect to such individual which is provided by—

(i) in the case of a specified social security beneficiary or a specified supplemental security income recipient, the Commissioner of Social Security,

(ii) in the case of a specified railroad retirement beneficiary, the Railroad Retirement Board, and

(iii) in the case of a specified veterans beneficiary, the Secretary of Veterans Affairs (in coordination with, and with the assistance of, the Commissioner of Social Security if appropriate).

(B) SPECIFIED INDIVIDUAL.—For purposes of this paragraph, the term "specified individual" means any individual who is—

(i) a specified social security beneficiary,

(ii) a specified supplemental security income recipient,

(iii) a specified railroad retirement beneficiary, or

(iv) a specified veterans beneficiary.

(C) SPECIFIED SOCIAL SECURITY BENEFICIARY.—

(i) IN GENERAL.—For purposes of this paragraph, the term "specified social security beneficiary" means any individual who, for the last month for which the Secretary has available information as of the date of enactment of this section, is entitled to any monthly insurance benefit payable under title II of the Social Security Act (42 U.S.C. 401 et seq.), including payments made pursuant to sections 202(d), 223(g), and 223(i)(7) of such Act.

(ii) EXCEPTION.—For purposes of this paragraph, the term "specified social security beneficiary" shall not include any individual if such benefit is not payable for such month by reason of section 202(x)(1)(A) of the Social Security Act (42 U.S.C. 402(x)(1)(A)) or section 1129A of such Act (42 U.S.C. 1320a–8a).

(D) SPECIFIED SUPPLEMENTAL SECURITY INCOME RECIPIENT.—

(i) IN GENERAL.—For purposes of this paragraph, the term "specified supplemental security income recipient" means any individual who, for the last month for which the Secretary has available information as of the date of enactment of this section, is eligible for a monthly benefit payable under title XVI of the Social Security Act (42 U.S.C. 1381 et seq.), including—

(I) payments made pursuant to section 1614(a)(3)(C) of such Act (42 U.S.C. 1382c(a)(3)(C)),

(II) payments made pursuant to section 1619(a) (42 U.S.C. 1382h(a)) or subsections (a)(4), (a)(7), or (p)(7) of section 1631 (42 U.S.C. 1383) of such Act, and

(III) State supplementary payments of the type referred to in section 1616(a) of such Act (42 U.S.C. 1382e(a)) (or payments of the type described in section 212(a) of Public Law 93–66) which are paid by the Commissioner under an agreement referred to in such section 1616(a) (or section 212(a) of Public Law 93–66).

(ii) EXCEPTION.—For purposes of this paragraph, the term "specified supplemental security income recipient" shall not include any individual if such monthly benefit is not payable for such month by reason of section 1611(e)(1)(A) of the Social Security Act (42 U.S.C. 1382(e)(1)(A)) or section 1129A of such Act (42 U.S.C. 1320a–8a).

(E) SPECIFIED RAILROAD RETIREMENT BENEFICIARY.—For purposes of this paragraph, the term "specified railroad retirement beneficiary" means any individual who, for the last month for which the Secretary has available information as of the date of enactment of this section, is entitled to a monthly annuity or pension payment payable (without regard to section 5(a)(ii) of the Railroad Retirement Act of 1974 (45 U.S.C. 231d(a)(ii))) under—

(i) section 2(a)(1) of such Act (45 U.S.C. 231a(a)(1)),

(ii) section 2(c) of such Act (45 U.S.C. 231a(c)),

(iii) section 2(d)(1) of such Act (45 U.S.C. 231a(d)(1)), or

(iv) section 7(b)(2) of such Act (45 U.S.C. 231f(b)(2)) with respect to any of the benefit payments described in subparagraph (C)(i).

(F) SPECIFIED VETERANS BENEFICIARY.—

(i) IN GENERAL.—For purposes of this paragraph, the term "specified veterans beneficiary" means any individual who, for the last month for which the Secretary has available information as of the date of enactment of this section, is entitled to a compensation or pension payment payable under—

(I) section 1110, 1117, 1121, 1131, 1141, or 1151 of title 38, United States Code,

(II) section 1310, 1312, 1313, 1315, 1316, or 1318 of title 38, United States Code,

(III) section 1513, 1521, 1533, 1536, 1537, 1541, 1542, or 1562 of title 38, United States Code, or

(IV) section 1805, 1815, or 1821 of title 38, United States Code,

to a veteran, surviving spouse, child, or parent as described in paragraph (2), (3), (4)(A)(ii), or (5) of section 101, title 38, United States Code.

(ii) EXCEPTION.—For purposes of this paragraph, the term "specified veterans beneficiary" shall not include any individual if such compensation or pension payment is not payable, or was reduced, for such month by reason of section 1505 or 5313 of title 38, United States Code.

(G) SUBSEQUENT DETERMINATIONS AND REDETERMINATIONS NOT TAKEN INTO ACCOUNT.—For purposes of this section, any individual's status as a specified social security beneficiary, a specified supplemental security income recipient, a specified railroad retirement beneficiary, or a specified veterans beneficiary shall be unaffected by any determination or redetermination of any entitlement to, or eligibility for, any benefit, payment, or compensation, if such determination or redetermination occurs after the last month for which the Secretary has available information as of the date of enactment of this section.

(H) PAYMENT TO REPRESENTATIVE PAYEES AND FIDUCIARIES.—

(i) IN GENERAL.—If the benefit, payment, or compensation referred to in subparagraph (C)(i), (D)(i), (E), or (F)(i) with respect to any specified individual is paid to a representative payee or fiduciary, payment by the Secretary under paragraph (3) with respect to such specified individual shall be made to such individual's representative payee or fiduciary and the entire payment shall be used only for the benefit of the individual who is entitled to the payment.

CREDITS AND REFUNDS—SPECIAL RULES

(ii) APPLICATION OF ENFORCEMENT PROVISIONS.—

(I) In the case of a payment described in clause (i) which is made with respect to a specified social security beneficiary or a specified supplemental security income recipient, section 1129(a)(3) of the Social Security Act (42 U.S.C. 1320a–8(a)(3)) shall apply to such payment in the same manner as such section applies to a payment under title II or XVI of such Act.

(II) In the case of a payment described in clause (i) which is made with respect to a specified railroad retirement beneficiary, section 13 of the Railroad Retirement Act (45 U.S.C. 231l) shall apply to such payment in the same manner as such section applies to a payment under such Act.

(III) In the case of a payment described in clause (i) which is made with respect to a specified veterans beneficiary, sections 5502, 6106, and 6108 of title 38, United States Code, shall apply to such payment in the same manner as such sections apply to a payment under such title.

(I) INELIGIBILITY FOR SPECIAL RULE NOT TO BE INTERPRETED AS GENERAL INELIGIBILITY.—An individual shall not fail to be treated as an eligible individual for purposes of this subsection or subsection (a) merely because such individual is not a specified individual (including by reason of subparagraph (C)(ii), (D)(ii), or (F)(ii)).

(6) NOTICE TO TAXPAYER.—As soon as practicable after the date on which the Secretary distributed any payment to an eligible taxpayer pursuant to this subsection, the Secretary shall send notice by mail to such taxpayer's last known address. Such notice shall indicate the method by which such payment was made, the amount of such payment, and a phone number for the appropriate point of contact at the Internal Revenue Service to report any failure to receive such payment.

Amendments

• 2020, COVID-related Tax Relief Act of 2020 (P.L. 116-260)

P.L. 116-260, § 272(d)(1)-(2), Div. N, provides:

(d) ADMINISTRATIVE PROVISIONS.—

(1) EXCEPTION FROM REDUCTION OR OFFSET.—Any refund payable by reason of section 6428A(f) of the Internal Revenue Code of 1986 (as added by this section), or any such refund payable by reason of subsection (c) of this section, shall not be—

(A) subject to reduction or offset pursuant to section 3716 or 3720A of title 31, United States Code,

(B) subject to reduction or offset pursuant to subsection (c), (d), (e), or (f) of section 6402 of the Internal Revenue Code of 1986, or

(C) reduced or offset by other assessed Federal taxes that would otherwise be subject to levy or collection.

(2) ASSIGNMENT OF BENEFITS.—

(A) IN GENERAL.—The right of any person to any applicable payment shall not be transferable or assignable, at law or in equity, and no applicable payment shall be subject to, execution, levy, attachment, garnishment, or other legal process, or the operation of any bankruptcy or insolvency law.

(B) ENCODING OF PAYMENTS.—In the case of an applicable payment described in subparagraph (E)(iii)(I) that is paid electronically by direct deposit through the Automated Clearing House (ACH) network, the Secretary of the Treasury (or the Secretary's delegate) shall—

(i) issue the payment using a unique identifier that is reasonably sufficient to allow a financial institution to identify the payment as an applicable payment, and

(ii) further encode the payment pursuant to the same specifications as required for a benefit payment defined in section 212.3 of title 31, Code of Federal Regulations.

(C) GARNISHMENT.—

(i) ENCODED PAYMENTS.—In the case of a garnishment order that applies to an account that has received an applicable payment that is encoded as provided in subparagraph (B), a financial institution shall follow the requirements and procedures set forth in part 212 of title 31, Code of Federal Regulations, except—

(I) notwithstanding section 212.4 of title 31, Code of Federal Regulations (and except as provided in subclause (II)), a financial institution shall not fail to follow the procedures of sections 212.5 and 212.6 of such title with respect to a garnishment order merely because such order has attached, or includes, a notice of right to garnish federal benefits issued by a State child support enforcement agency, and

(II) a financial institution shall not, with regard to any applicable payment, be required to provide the notice referenced in sections 212.6 and 212.7 of title 31, Code of Federal Regulations.

(ii) OTHER PAYMENTS.—In the case of a garnishment order (other than an order that has been served by the United States) that has been received by a financial institution and that applies to an account into which an applicable payment that has not been encoded as provided in subparagraph (B) has been deposited electronically on any date during the lookback period or into which an applicable payment that has been deposited by check on any date in the lookback period, the financial institution, upon the request of the account holder, shall treat the amount of the funds in the account at the time of the request, up to the amount of the applicable payment (in addition to any amounts otherwise protected under part 212 of title 31, Code of Federal Regulations), as exempt from a garnishment order without requiring the consent of the party serving the garnishment order or the judgment creditor.

(iii) LIABILITY.—A financial institution that acts in good faith in reliance on clauses (i) or (ii) shall not be subject to liability or regulatory action under any Federal or State law, regulation, court or other order, or regulatory interpretation for actions concerning any applicable payments.

(D) NO RECLAMATION RIGHTS.—This paragraph shall not alter the status of applicable payments as tax refunds or other nonbenefit payments for purpose of any reclamation rights of the Department of the Treasury or the Internal Revenue Service as per part 210 of title 31, Code of Federal Regulations.

(E) DEFINITIONS.—For purposes of this paragraph—

(i) ACCOUNT HOLDER.—The term "account holder" means a natural person whose name appears in a financial institution's records as the direct or beneficial owner of an account.

(ii) ACCOUNT REVIEW.—The term "account review" means the process of examining deposits in an account to determine if an applicable payment has been deposited into the account during the lookback period. The financial institution shall perform the account review following the procedures outlined in section 212.5 of title 31, Code of Federal Regulations and in accordance with the requirements of section 212.6 of title 31, Code of Federal Regulations.

(iii) APPLICABLE PAYMENT.—The term "applicable payment" means—

(I) any advance refund amount paid pursuant to section 6428A(f) of Internal Revenue Code of 1986 (as added by this section),

(II) any payment made by a possession of the United States with a mirror code tax system (as defined in subsection (c) of this section) pursuant to such subsection which corresponds to a payment described in subclause (I), and

(III) any payment made by a possession of the United States without a mirror code tax system (as so defined) pursuant to subsection (c) of this section.

(iv) GARNISHMENT.—The term "garnishment" means execution, levy, attachment, garnishment, or other legal process.

(v) GARNISHMENT ORDER.—The term "garnishment order" means a writ, order, notice, summons, judgment, levy, or similar written instruction issued by a court, a State or State agency, a municipality or municipal corporation, or a State child support enforcement agency, including a lien arising by operation of law for overdue child support or an order to freeze the assets in an account, to effect a garnishment against a debtor.

(vi) LOOKBACK PERIOD.—The term "lookback period" means the two month period that begins on the date preceding the date of account review and ends on the corresponding date of the month two months earlier, or on the last date of the month two months earlier if the corresponding date does not exist.

[Sec. 6428A(g)]

(g) IDENTIFICATION NUMBER REQUIREMENT.—

(1) IN GENERAL.—In the case of a return other than a joint return, the $600 amount in subsection (a)(1) shall be treated as being zero unless the taxpayer includes the valid identification number of the taxpayer on the return of tax for the taxable year.

(2) JOINT RETURNS.—In the case of a joint return, the $1,200 amount in subsection (a)(1) shall be treated as being—

(A) $600 if the valid identification number of only 1 spouse is included on the return of tax for the taxable year, and

(B) zero if the valid identification number of neither spouse is so included.

(3) QUALIFYING CHILD.—A qualifying child of a taxpayer shall not be taken into account under subsection (a)(2) unless—

(A) the taxpayer includes the valid identification number of such taxpayer (or, in the case of a joint return, the valid identification number of at least 1 spouse) on the return of tax for the taxable year, and

(B) the valid identification number of such qualifying child is included on the return of tax for the taxable year.

(4) VALID IDENTIFICATION NUMBER.—

(A) IN GENERAL.—For purposes of this subsection, the term "valid identification number" means a social security number (as such term is defined in section 24(h)(7)).

(B) ADOPTION TAXPAYER IDENTIFICATION NUMBER.—For purposes of paragraph (3)(B), in the case of a qualifying child who is adopted or placed for adoption, the term "valid identification number" shall include the adoption taxpayer identification number of such child.

CREDITS AND REFUNDS—SPECIAL RULES

(5) SPECIAL RULE FOR MEMBERS OF THE ARMED FORCES.—Paragraph (2) shall not apply in the case where at least 1 spouse was a member of the Armed Forces of the United States at any time during the taxable year and the valid identification number of at least 1 spouse is included on the return of tax for the taxable year.

(6) COORDINATION WITH CERTAIN ADVANCE PAYMENTS.—In the case of any payment under subsection (f) which is based on information provided under paragraph (5) of such subsection, a valid identification number shall be treated for purposes of this subsection as included on the taxpayer's return of tax if such valid identification number is provided pursuant to subsection (f)(5).

(7) MATHEMATICAL OR CLERICAL ERROR AUTHORITY.—Any omission of a correct valid identification number required under this subsection shall be treated as a mathematical or clerical error for purposes of applying section 6213(g)(2) to such omission.

[Sec. 6428A(h)]

(h) REGULATIONS.—The Secretary shall prescribe such regulations or other guidance as may be necessary to carry out the purposes of this section, including any such measures as are deemed appropriate to avoid allowing multiple credits or rebates to a taxpayer.

Amendments

- 2020, COVID-related Tax Relief Act of 2020 (P.L. 116-260)

P.L. 116-260, §272(a), Div. N:

Amended subchapter B of chapter 65 of subtitle F by inserting after Code Sec. 6428 a new Code Sec. 6428A. **Effective** 12-27-2020.

[Sec. 6428B]

SEC. 6428B. 2021 RECOVERY REBATES TO INDIVIDUALS.

[Sec. 6428B(a)]

(a) IN GENERAL.—In the case of an eligible individual, there shall be allowed as a credit against the tax imposed by subtitle A for the first taxable year beginning in 2021 an amount equal to the 2021 rebate amount determined for such taxable year.

[Sec. 6428B(b)]

(b) 2021 REBATE AMOUNT.—For purposes of this section, the term "2021 rebate amount" means, with respect to any taxpayer for any taxable year, the sum of—

(1) $1,400 ($2,800 in the case of a joint return), plus

(2) $1,400 multiplied by the number of dependents of the taxpayer for such taxable year.

[Sec. 6428B(c)]

(c) ELIGIBLE INDIVIDUAL.—For purposes of this section, the term "eligible individual" means any individual other than—

(1) any nonresident alien individual,

(2) any individual who is a dependent of another taxpayer for a taxable year beginning in the calendar year in which the individual's taxable year begins, and

(3) an estate or trust.

[Sec. 6428B(d)]

(d) LIMITATION BASED ON ADJUSTED GROSS INCOME.—

(1) IN GENERAL.—The amount of the credit allowed by subsection (a) (determined without regard to this subsection and subsection (f)) shall be reduced (but not below zero) by the amount which bears the same ratio to such credit (as so determined) as—

(A) the excess of—

(i) the taxpayer's adjusted gross income for such taxable year, over

(ii) $75,000, bears to

(B) $5,000.

(2) SPECIAL RULES.—

(A) JOINT RETURN OR SURVIVING SPOUSE.—In the case of a joint return or a surviving spouse (as defined in section 2(a)), paragraph (1) shall be applied by substituting "$150,000" for "$75,000" and "$10,000" for "$5,000".

(B) HEAD OF HOUSEHOLD.—In the case of a head of household (as defined in section 2(b)), paragraph (1) shall be applied by substituting "$112,500" for "$75,000" and "$7,500" for "$5,000".

[Sec. 6428B(e)]

(e) DEFINITIONS AND SPECIAL RULES.—

(1) DEPENDENT DEFINED.—For purposes of this section, the term "dependent" has the meaning given such term by section 152.

(2) IDENTIFICATION NUMBER REQUIREMENT.—

(A) IN GENERAL.—In the case of a return other than a joint return, the $1,400 amount in subsection (b)(1) shall be treated as being zero unless the taxpayer includes the valid identification number of the taxpayer on the return of tax for the taxable year.

(B) JOINT RETURNS.—In the case of a joint return, the $2,800 amount in subsection (b)(1) shall be treated as being—

(i) $1,400 if the valid identification number of only 1 spouse is included on the return of tax for the taxable year, and

(ii) zero if the valid identification number of neither spouse is so included.

(C) DEPENDENTS.—A dependent shall not be taken into account under subsection (b)(2) unless the valid identification number of such dependent is included on the return of tax for the taxable year.

(D) VALID IDENTIFICATION NUMBER.—

(i) IN GENERAL.—For purposes of this paragraph, the term "valid identification number" means a social security number issued to an individual by the Social Security Administration on or before the due date for filing the return for the taxable year.

(ii) ADOPTION TAXPAYER IDENTIFICATION NUMBER.—For purposes of subparagraph (C), in the case of a dependent who is adopted or placed for adoption, the term "valid identification number" shall include the adoption taxpayer identification number of such dependent.

(E) SPECIAL RULE FOR MEMBERS OF THE ARMED FORCES.—Subparagraph (B) shall not apply in the case where at least 1 spouse was a member of the Armed Forces of the United States at any time during the taxable year and the valid identification number of at least 1 spouse is included on the return of tax for the taxable year.

Sec. 6428A(g)(5)

CREDITS AND REFUNDS—SPECIAL RULES

(F) COORDINATION WITH CERTAIN ADVANCE PAYMENTS.—In the case of any payment determined pursuant to subsection (g)(6), a valid identification number shall be treated for purposes of this paragraph as included on the taxpayer's return of tax if such valid identification number is available to the Secretary as described in such subsection.

(G) MATHEMATICAL OR CLERICAL ERROR AUTHORITY.—Any omission of a correct valid identification number required under this paragraph shall be treated as a mathematical or clerical error for purposes of applying section 6213(g)(2) to such omission.

(3) CREDIT TREATED AS REFUNDABLE.—The credit allowed by subsection (a) shall be treated as allowed by subpart C of part IV of subchapter A of chapter 1.

[Sec. 6428B(f)]

(f) COORDINATION WITH ADVANCE REFUNDS OF CREDIT.—

(1) REDUCTION OF REFUNDABLE CREDIT.—The amount of the credit which would (but for this paragraph) be allowable under subsection (a) shall be reduced (but not below zero) by the aggregate refunds and credits made or allowed to the taxpayer (or, except as otherwise provided by the Secretary, any dependent of the taxpayer) under subsection (g). Any failure to so reduce the credit shall be treated as arising out of a mathematical or clerical error and assessed according to section 6213(b)(1).

(2) JOINT RETURNS.—Except as otherwise provided by the Secretary, in the case of a refund or credit made or allowed under subsection (g) with respect to a joint return, half of such refund or credit shall be treated as having been made or allowed to each individual filing such return.

[Sec. 6428B(g)]

(g) ADVANCE REFUNDS AND CREDITS.—

(1) IN GENERAL.—Subject to paragraphs (5) and (6), each individual who was an eligible individual for such individual's first taxable year beginning in 2019 shall be treated as having made a payment against the tax imposed by chapter 1 for such taxable year in an amount equal to the advance refund amount for such taxable year.

(2) ADVANCE REFUND AMOUNT.—

(A) IN GENERAL.—For purposes of paragraph (1), the advance refund amount is the amount that would have been allowed as a credit under this section for such taxable year if this section (other than subsection (f) and this subsection) had applied to such taxable year.

(B) TREATMENT OF DECEASED INDIVIDUALS.—For purposes of determining the advance refund amount with respect to such taxable year—

(i) any individual who was deceased before January 1, 2021, shall be treated for purposes of applying subsection (e)(2) in the same manner as if the valid identification number of such person was not included on the return of tax for such taxable year (except that subparagraph (E) thereof shall not apply),

(ii) notwithstanding clause (i), in the case of a joint return with respect to which only 1 spouse is deceased before January 1, 2021, such deceased spouse was a member of the Armed Forces of the United States at any time during the taxable year, and the valid identification number of such deceased spouse is included on the return of tax for the taxable year, the valid identification number of 1 (and only 1) spouse shall be treated as included on the return of tax for the taxable year for purposes of applying subsection (e)(2)(B) with respect to such joint return, and

(iii) no amount shall be determined under subsection (e)(2) with respect to any dependent of the taxpayer if the taxpayer (both spouses in the case of a joint return) was deceased before January 1, 2021.

(3) TIMING AND MANNER OF PAYMENTS.—The Secretary shall, subject to the provisions of this title and consistent with rules similar to the rules of subparagraphs (B) and (C) of section 6428A(f)(3), refund or credit any overpayment attributable to this subsection as rapidly as possible, consistent with a rapid effort to make payments attributable to such overpayments electronically if appropriate. No refund or credit shall be made or allowed under this subsection after December 31, 2021.

(4) NO INTEREST.—No interest shall be allowed on any overpayment attributable to this subsection.

(5) APPLICATION TO INDIVIDUALS WHO HAVE FILED A RETURN OF TAX FOR 2020.—

(A) APPLICATION TO 2020 RETURNS FILED AT TIME OF INITIAL DETERMINATION.—If, at the time of any determination made pursuant to paragraph (3), the individual referred to in paragraph (1) has filed a return of tax for the individual's first taxable year beginning in 2020, paragraph (1) shall be applied with respect to such individual by substituting "2020" for "2019".

(B) ADDITIONAL PAYMENT.—

(i) IN GENERAL.—In the case of any individual who files, before the additional payment determination date, a return of tax for such individual's first taxable year beginning in 2020, the Secretary shall make a payment (in addition to any payment made under paragraph (1)) to such individual equal to the excess (if any) of—

(I) the amount which would be determined under paragraph (1) (after the application of subparagraph (A)) by applying paragraph (1) as of the additional payment determination date, over

(II) the amount of any payment made with respect to such individual under paragraph (1).

(ii) ADDITIONAL PAYMENT DETERMINATION DATE.—The term "additional payment determination date" means the earlier of—

(I) the date which is 90 days after the 2020 calendar year filing deadline, or

(II) September 1, 2021.

(iii) 2020 CALENDAR YEAR FILING DEADLINE.—The term "2020 calendar year filing deadline" means the date specified in section 6072(a) with respect to returns for calendar year 2020. Such date shall be determined after taking into account any period disregarded under section 7508A if such disregard applies to substantially all returns for calendar year 2020 to which section 6072(a) applies.

(6) APPLICATION TO CERTAIN INDIVIDUALS WHO HAVE NOT FILED A RETURN OF TAX FOR 2019 OR 2020 AT TIME OF DETERMINATION.—In the case of any individual who, at the time of any determination made pursuant to paragraph (3), has filed a tax return for neither the year described in paragraph (1) nor for the year described in paragraph (5)(A), the Secretary shall, consistent with rules similar to the rules of section 6428A(f)(5)(H)(i), apply paragraph (1) on the basis of information available to the Secretary and shall, on the basis of such information, determine the advance refund amount with respect to such individual without regard to subsection (d) unless the Secretary has reason to know that such amount would otherwise be reduced by reason of such subsection.

(7) SPECIAL RULE RELATED TO TIME OF FILING RETURN.—Solely for purposes of this subsection, a return of tax shall not be treated as filed until such return has been processed by the Internal Revenue Service.

(8) RESTRICTION ON USE OF CERTAIN PREVIOUSLY ISSUED PREPAID DEBIT CARDS.—Payments made by the Secretary to individuals under this section shall not be in the form of an increase in the balance of any previously issued prepaid debit card if, as of the time of the issuance of such card, such card was issued solely for purposes of making payments under section 6428 or 6428A.

CREDITS AND REFUNDS—SPECIAL RULES

[Sec. 6428B(h)]

(h) REGULATIONS.—The Secretary shall prescribe such regulations or other guidance as may be necessary or appropriate to carry out the purposes of this section, including—

(1) regulations or other guidance providing taxpayers the opportunity to provide the Secretary information sufficient to allow the Secretary to make payments to such taxpayers under subsection (g) (including the determination of the amount of such payment) if such information is not otherwise available to the Secretary, and

(2) regulations or other guidance to ensure to the maximum extent administratively practicable that, in determining the amount of any credit under subsection (a) and any credit or refund under subsection (g), an individual is not taken into account more than once, including by different taxpayers and including by reason of a change in joint return status or dependent status between the taxable year for which an advance refund amount is determined and the taxable year for which a credit under subsection (a) is determined.

[Sec. 6428B(i)]

(i) OUTREACH.—The Secretary shall carry out a robust and comprehensive outreach program to ensure that all taxpayers described in subsection (h)(1) learn of their eligibility for the advance refunds and credits under subsection (g); are advised of the opportunity to receive such advance refunds and credits as provided under subsection (h)(1); and are provided assistance in applying for such advance refunds and credits.

Amendments

• 2021, American Rescue Plan Act of 2021 (P.L. 117-2)

P.L. 117-2, § 9601(a):

Amended subchapter B of chapter 65 by inserting after Code Sec. 6428A a new Code Sec. 6428B. **Effective** 3-11-2021. For a special rule, see Act Sec. 9601(c)(2), below.

Amendments

• 2014, Tax Technical Corrections Act of 2014 (P.L. 113-295)

P.L. 113-295, § 221(a)(113), Division A:

Amended subchapter B of chapter 65 by striking Code Sec. 6429. **Effective** generally 12-19-2014. For a special rule, see Act Sec. 221(b)(2), Division A, below.

P.L. 113-295, § 221(b)(2), Division A, provides:

(2) SAVINGS PROVISION.—If—

(A) any provision amended or repealed by the amendments made by this section applied to—

(i) any transaction occurring before the date of the enactment of this Act,

(ii) any property acquired before such date of enactment, or

(iii) any item of income, loss, deduction, or credit taken into account before such date of enactment, and

(B) the treatment of such transaction, property, or item under such provision would (without regard to the amendments or repeals made by this section) affect the liability for tax for periods ending after date of enactment, nothing in the amendments or repeals made by this section shall be construed to affect the treatment of such transaction, property, or item for purposes of determining liability for tax for periods ending after such date of enactment.

Prior to being stricken, Code Sec. 6429 read as follows:

SEC. 6429. ADVANCE PAYMENT OF PORTION OF INCREASED CHILD CREDIT FOR 2003.

[Sec. 6429(a)]

(a) IN GENERAL.—Each taxpayer who was allowed a credit under section 24 on the return for the taxpayer's first taxable year beginning in 2002 shall be treated as having made a payment against the tax imposed by chapter 1 for such taxable year in an amount equal to the child tax credit refund amount (if any) for such taxable year.

[Sec. 6429(b)]

(b) CHILD TAX CREDIT REFUND AMOUNT.—For purposes of this section, the child tax credit refund amount is the amount by which the aggregate credits allowed under part IV of subchapter A of chapter 1 for such first taxable year would have been increased if—

(1) the per child amount under section 24(a)(2) for such year were $1,000,

(2) only qualifying children (as defined in section 24(c)) of the taxpayer for such year who had not attained age 17 as of December 31, 2003, were taken into account, and

(3) section 24(d)(1)(B)(ii) did not apply.

[Sec. 6429(c)]

(c) TIMING OF PAYMENTS.—In the case of any overpayment attributable to this section, the Secretary shall, subject to the provisions of this title, refund or credit such overpayment as rapidly as possible and, to the extent practicable, before October 1, 2003. No refund or credit shall be made or allowed under this section after December 31, 2003.

[Sec. 6429(d)]

(d) COORDINATION WITH CHILD TAX CREDIT.—

(1) IN GENERAL.—The amount of credit which would (but for this subsection and section 26) be allowed under section 24 for the taxpayer's first taxable year beginning in 2003 shall be reduced (but not below zero) by the payments made to the taxpayer under this section. Any failure to so reduce the credit shall be treated as arising out of a mathematical or clerical error and assessed according to section 6213(b)(1).

(2) JOINT RETURNS.—In the case of a payment under this section with respect to a joint return, half of such payment shall be treated as having been made to each individual filing such return.

[Sec. 6429(e)]

(e) NO INTEREST.—No interest shall be allowed on any overpayment attributable to this section.

Amendments

• 2013, American Taxpayer Relief Act of 2012 (P.L. 112-240)

P.L. 112-240, § 101(a)(1) and (3), provides:

SEC. 101. PERMANENT EXTENSION AND MODIFICATION OF 2001 TAX RELIEF.

(a) PERMANENT EXTENSION.—

(1) IN GENERAL.—The Economic Growth and Tax Relief Reconciliation Act of 2001 is amended by striking title IX.

* * *

(3) EFFECTIVE DATE.—The amendments made by this subsection shall apply to taxable, plan, or limitation years beginning after December 31, 2012, and estates of decedents dying, gifts made, or generation skipping transfers after December 31, 2012.

• 2003, Jobs and Growth Tax Relief Reconciliation Act of 2003 (P.L. 108-27)

P.L. 108-27, § 101(b)(1):

Amended subchapter B of chapter 65 by inserting after Code Sec. 6428 a new Code Sec. 6429. **Effective** on 5-28-2003.

P.L. 108-27, § 107, provides:

SEC. 107. APPLICATION OF EGTRRA SUNSET TO THIS TITLE.

Each amendment made by this title shall be subject to title IX of the Economic Growth and Tax Relief Reconciliation Act of 2001 to the same extent and in the same manner as the provision of such Act to which such amendment relates.

• 2001, Economic Growth and Tax Relief Reconciliation Act of 2001 (P.L. 107-16)

P.L. 107-16, § 901(a)-(b), as amended by P.L. 111-312, § 101(a)(1), provides [but see P.L. 112-240, § 101(a)(1) and (3), above]:

SEC. 901. SUNSET OF PROVISIONS OF ACT.

(a) IN GENERAL.—All provisions of, and amendments made by, this Act shall not apply—

(1) to taxable, plan, or limitation years beginning after December 31, 2012, or

(2) in the case of title V, to estates of decedents dying, gifts made, or generation skipping transfers, after December 31, 2012.

(b) APPLICATION OF CERTAIN LAWS.—The Internal Revenue Code of 1986 and the Employee Retirement Income Security Act of 1974 shall be applied and administered to years, estates, gifts, and transfers described in subsection (a) as if the provisions and amendments described in subsection (a) had never been enacted.

[Sec. 6429—Repealed]

SEC. 6429. CREDIT AND REFUND OF CHAPTER 45 TAXES PAID BY ROYALTY OWNERS.

[Sec. 6429(a)]

(a) TREATMENT AS OVERPAYMENT.—In the case of a qualified royalty owner, that portion of the tax imposed by section 4986 which is paid in connection with qualified

Amendments

• 1988, Omnibus Trade and Competitiveness Act of 1988 (P.L. 100-418)

P.L. 100-418, § 1941(b)(1):

Repealed Code Sec. 6429. **Effective** for crude oil removed from the premises on or after 8-23-88. Prior to repeal, Code Sec. 6429 read as follows:

CREDITS AND REFUNDS—SPECIAL RULES

royalty production removed from the premises during calendar year 1981 shall be treated as an overpayment of the tax imposed by section 4986.

Amendments

• **1981, Economic Recovery Tax Act of 1981 (P.L. 97-34)**

P.L. 97-34, § 601(a)(1):

Amended Code Sec. 6429(a). **Effective** 1-1-81. Prior to amendment, Code Sec. 6429(a) read as follows:

(a) TREATMENT AS OVERPAYMENT.—In the case of a qualified royalty owner, that portion of the tax imposed by section 4986 which is paid in connection with qualified royalty production shall be treated as an overpayment of the tax imposed by section 4986.

[Sec. 6429(b)]

(b) CREDITS AND REFUNDS.—

(1) IN GENERAL.—Under regulations prescribed by the Secretary, any amount treated as an overpayment of tax under subsection (a) shall be credited against the tax imposed by section 4986 or refunded to the qualified royalty owner.

(2) CLAIM FOR CREDIT OR REFUND.—Any claim for credit or refund under this section shall be filed in such form and manner, and at such time, as the Secretary may prescribe by regulations.

[Sec. 6429(c)]

(c) $2,500 LIMITATION ON CREDIT OR REFUND.—

(1) IN GENERAL.—The aggregate amount which may be treated as an overpayment under subsection (a) with respect to any qualified royalty owner for production removed from the premises during calendar year 1981 shall not exceed $2,500.

(2) ALLOCATION WITHIN A FAMILY.—In the case of individuals who are members of the same family (within the meaning of section 4992(e)(3)(C)) at any time during the calendar year, the $2,500 amount in paragraph (1) shall be reduced for each such individual by allocating such amount among all such individuals in proportion to their respective qualified royalty production.

(3) ALLOCATION BETWEEN CORPORATIONS AND INDIVIDUALS.—

(A) IN GENERAL.—In the case of an individual who owns at any time during the calendar year stock in a qualified family farm corporation, the $2,500 amount in paragraph (1) applicable to such individual shall be reduced by the amount which bears the same ratio to the credit or refund allowable to the corporation under this section (determined after the application of paragraph (4)) as the fair market value of the shares owned by such individual during such period bears to the fair market value of all shares of the corporation.

(B) SPECIAL RULE FOR FAMILY MEMBERS.—In the case of individuals who are members of the same family (within the meaning of section 4992(e)(3)(C)) at any time during the calendar year—

(i) for purposes of subparagraph (A), all such individuals shall be treated as 1 individual, and

(ii) the amount allocated among such individuals under paragraph (2) shall be $2,500, reduced by the amount determined under subparagraph (A).

(4) ALLOCATION BETWEEN CORPORATIONS.—If at any time after June 24, 1980, any individual owns stock in two or more qualified family farm corporations, the $2,500 amount in paragraph (1) shall be reduced for each such corporation by allocating such amount among all such corporations in proportion to their respective qualified royalty production.

Amendments

• **1981, Economic Recovery Tax Act of 1981 (P.L. 97-34)**

P.L. 97-34, § 601(a)(2):

Amended Code Sec. 6429(c)(1). **Effective** 1-1-81. Prior to amendment, Code Sec. 6429(c)(1) read as follows:

(1) In General.—The aggregate amount which may be treated as an overpayment under subsection (a) with respect to any qualified royalty owner shall not exceed $1,000.

P.L. 97-34, § 601(a)(3):

Amended Code Sec. 6429(c) by striking out "$1,000" each place it appears and inserting "$2,500" and by striking out "qualified period" each place it appears and inserting "calendar year". **Effective** 1-1-81.

[Sec. 6429(d)]

(d) DEFINITIONS AND SPECIAL RULES.—For purposes of this section—

(1) QUALIFIED ROYALTY OWNER.—The term "qualified royalty owner" means a producer (within the meaning of section 4996(a)(1)), but only if such producer is an individual, an estate, or a qualified family farm corporation.

(2) QUALIFIED ROYALTY PRODUCTION.—The term "qualified royalty production" means, with respect to any qualified royalty owner, taxable crude oil which is attributable to an economic interest of such royalty owner other than an operating mineral interest (within the meaning of section 614(d)). Such term does not include taxable crude oil attributable to any overriding royalty interest, production payment, net profits interest, or similar interest of the qualified royalty owner which—

(A) is created after June 9, 1981, out of an operating mineral interest in property which is proven oil or gas property (within the meaning of section 613A(c)(9)(A)) on the date such interest is created, and

(B) is not created pursuant to a binding contract entered into prior to June 10, 1981.

(3) PRODUCTION FROM TRANSFERRED PROPERTY.—

(A) IN GENERAL.—In the case of a transfer of an interest in any property, the qualified royalty production of the transferee shall not include any production attributable to an interest that has been transferred after June 9, 1981, in a transfer which—

(i) is described in section 613A(c)(9)(A), and

(ii) is not described in section 613A(c)(9)(B).

(B) EXCEPTIONS.—Subparagraph (A) shall not apply in the case of any transfer so long as the transferor and the transferee are required by paragraph (3) or (4) of subsection (c) to share the $2,500 amount in subsection (c)(1). The preceding sentence shall apply to the case of any property only if the production from the property was qualified royalty production of the transferor.

(C) TRANSFERS INCLUDE SUBLEASES.—For purposes of this paragraph, a sublease shall be treated as a transfer.

(4) QUALIFIED FAMILY FARM CORPORATION.—The term "qualified family farm corporation" means a corporation—

(A) all the outstanding shares of stock of which at all times during the calendar year are held by members of the same family (within the meaning of section 2032A(e)(2)), and

(B) 80 percent in value of the assets of which (other than royalty interests from which there is qualified royalty production determined by treating such corporation as a qualified royalty owner) are held by the corporation at all times during such calendar year for use for farming purposes (within the meaning of section 2032A(e)(5)).

Amendments

• **1983, Technical Corrections Act of 1982 (P.L. 97-448)**

P.L. 97-448, § 106(a)(1):

Amended Code Sec. 6429(d)(3) by striking out subparagraph (D). **Effective** as if included in the provision of P.L. 97-34 to which it relates. Prior to being stricken, subparagraph (D) read as follows:

"(D) Estates.—For purposes of this paragraph, property held by any estate shall be treated as owned both by such estate and proportionately by the beneficiaries of such estate."

P.L. 97-448, § 106(a)(3):

Amended Code Sec. 6429(d)(4)(B) by striking out "other than royalty interests described in paragraph (2)(A)" and inserting in lieu thereof "other than royalty interests from which there is qualified royalty production determined by treating such corporation as a qualified royalty owner". **Effective** as if included in the provision of P.L. 97-34 to which it relates.

• **1981, Economic Recovery Tax Act of 1981 (P.L. 97-34)**

P.L. 97-34, § 601(a)(4):

Amended Code Sec. 6429(d)(2) and (3). **Effective** 1-1-81. Prior to amendment, Code Sec. 6429(d)(2) and (3) read as follows:

(2) QUALIFIED ROYALTY PRODUCTION.—The term "qualified royalty production" means, with respect to any qualified royalty owner, taxable crude oil which—

(A) is attributable to an economic interest of such royalty owner other than an operating mineral interest (within the meaning of section 614(d)), and

(B) is removed from the premises during the qualified period.

(3) QUALIFIED PERIOD.—The term "qualified period" means the period beginning March 1, 1980, and ending December 31, 1980.

P.L. 97-34, § 601(a)(5):

Amended Code Sec. 6429(d)(4). **Effective** 1-1-81. Prior to amendment, Code Sec. 6429(d)(4) read as follows:

(4) QUALIFIED FAMILY FARM CORPORATION.—The term "qualified family farm corporation" means a corporation—

(A) which was in existence on June 25, 1980,

(B) all of the outstanding shares of stock of which at all times after June 24, 1980, and before January 1, 1981, were held by members of the same family (within the meaning of section 2032A(e)(2)), and

(C) 80 percent in value of the assets of which (other than royalty interests described in paragraph (2)(A)) were held by the corporation on such date for use for farming purposes (within the meaning of section 2032A(e)(5)).

[Sec. 6429(e)]

(e) CROSS REFERENCE.—

For the holder of the economic interest in the case of a production payment, see section 636.

Amendments

• **1980, Omnibus Reconciliation Act of 1980 (P.L. 96-499)**

P.L. 96-499, § 1131(a)(1):

Added Code Sec. 6429. **Effective** for tax years ending after 2-29-80.

[Sec. 6430]

SEC. 6430. TREATMENT OF TAX IMPOSED AT LEAKING UNDERGROUND STORAGE TANK TRUST FUND FINANCING RATE.

No refunds, credits, or payments shall be made under this subchapter for any tax imposed at the Leaking Underground Storage Tank Trust Fund financing rate, except in the case of fuels—

(1) which are exempt from tax under section 4081(a) by reason of section 4082(f)(2),

(2) which are exempt from tax under section 4041(d) by reason of the last sentence of paragraph (5) thereof, or

(3) with respect to which the rate increase under section 4081(a)(2)(B) is zero by reason of section 4082(e)(2).

CREDITS AND REFUNDS—SPECIAL RULES

Amendments

• **2007, Tax Technical Corrections Act of 2007 (P.L. 110-172)**

P.L. 110-172, § 6(d)(2)(D):

Amended Code Sec. 6430. **Effective** as if included in the provision of the Energy Tax Incentives Act of 2005 (P.L. 109-58) to which it relates [**effective** for fuel entered, removed, or sold after 9-30-2005.—CCH]. Prior to amendment, Code Sec. 6430 read as follows:

SEC. 6430. TREATMENT OF TAX IMPOSED AT LEAKING UNDERGROUND STORAGE TANK TRUST FUND FINANCING RATE.

No refunds, credits, or payments shall be made under this subchapter for any tax imposed at the Leaking Underground Storage Tank Trust Fund financing rate, except in the case of fuels destined for export.

• **2005, Energy Tax Incentives Act of 2005 (P.L. 109-58)**

P.L. 109-58, § 1362(b)(3)(A):

Amended subchapter B of chapter 65 by adding at the end a new Code Sec. 6430. **Effective** for fuel entered, removed, or sold after 9-30-2005.

[Sec. 6430—Repealed]

Amendments

• **1988, Omnibus Trade and Competitiveness Act of 1988 (P.L. 100-418)**

P.L. 100-418, § 1941(b)(1):

Repealed Code Sec. 6430. **Effective** for crude oil removed from the premises on or after 8-23-88. Prior to repeal, Code Sec. 6430 read as follows:

SEC. 6430. CREDIT OR REFUND OF WINDFALL PROFIT TAXES TO CERTAIN TRUST BENEFICIARIES.

(a) GENERAL RULE.—That portion of the tax imposed by section 4986 (relating to crude oil windfall profit tax) which is paid by any trust with respect to any qualified beneficiary's allocable trust production shall be treated as an overpayment of such tax by such qualified beneficiary. Any such overpayment shall be credited against the tax imposed by section 4986 or refunded to such qualified beneficiary.

(b) COORDINATION WITH ROYALTY EXEMPTION.—

(1) IN GENERAL.—If the aggregate amount of the allocable trust production of any qualified beneficiary for any calendar year exceeds such beneficiary's unused exempt royalty limit for such calendar year, then the amount treated as an overpayment under subsection (a) with respect to such qualified beneficiary shall be reduced by an amount which bears the same ratio to the amount which (but for this paragraph) would be so treated as—

(A) the amount of such excess, bears to

(B) the aggregate amount of such allocable trust production.

(2) UNUSED EXEMPT ROYALTY LIMIT.—The unused exempt royalty limit of any qualified beneficiary for any calendar year is the excess of—

(A) the number of days in such calendar year, multiplied by the limitation in barrels determined under the table contained in section 4994(f)(2)(A)(ii), over

(B) the amount of exempt royalty oil (within the meaning of section 4994(f))—

(i) with respect to which such qualified beneficiary is the producer, and

(ii) which is removed from the premises during such calendar year.

(3) ALLOCATION.—Rules similar to the rules of paragraphs (2), (3), and (4) of section 6429(c) shall apply to the amount determined under paragraph (2)(A).

(c) ALLOCABLE TRUST PRODUCTION.—For purposes of this section—

(1) IN GENERAL.—The term "allocable trust production" means, with respect to any qualified beneficiary, the qualified royalty production of any trust which—

(A) is removed from the premises during the calendar year, and

(B) is allocated to such qualified beneficiary under paragraph (2).

(2) ALLOCATION OF PRODUCTION.—

(A) IN GENERAL.—The qualified royalty production of a trust for any calendar year shall be allocated between the trust and its income beneficiaries as follows:

(i) there shall be allocated to the trust an amount of production based on the amount of any reserve for depletion for the calendar year with respect to qualified royalty production, and

(ii) production not allocated under clause (i) shall be allocated between the trust and the income beneficiaries in accordance with their respective shares of the adjusted distributable net income for the calendar year.

(B) DEFINITION AND SPECIAL RULE.—For purposes of this paragraph—

(i) ADJUSTED DISTRIBUTABLE NET INCOME.—The term "adjusted distributable net income" means distributable net income (as defined in section 643) for the calendar year reduced by the excess (if any) of—

(I) any reserve for depletion for such year with respect to qualified royalty production, over

(II) the amount allowable as a deduction for depletion to the trust for such year with respect to qualified royalty production.

(ii) ALLOCATION PRO RATA FROM EACH UNIT OF PRODUCTION.—Allocations under subparagraph (A) shall be treated as made pro rata from each unit of the qualified royalty production.

(3) PRODUCTION FROM TRANSFERRED PROPERTY.—

(A) IN GENERAL.—The allocable trust production of any qualified beneficiary shall not include any production attributable to an interest in property which has been transferred after June 9, 1981, in a transfer which—

(i) is described in section 613A(c)(9)(A), and

(ii) is not described in section 613A(c)(9)(B).

(B) EXCEPTIONS.—Subparagraph (A) shall not apply in the case of any transfer so long as the transferor and the qualified beneficiary are required by subsection (b)(3) to share the amount determined under subsection (b)(2)(A). The preceding sentence shall apply to the transfer of any property only if the production attributable to the property was allocable trust production or qualified royalty production of the transferor.

(d) DEFINITIONS.—For purposes of this section—

(1) QUALIFIED BENEFICIARY.—The term "qualified beneficiary" means any individual or estate which is a beneficiary of any trust which is a producer.

(2) QUALIFIED ROYALTY PRODUCTION.—The term "qualified royalty production" means, with respect to any person, taxable crude oil (within the meaning of section 4991(a)) which is attributable to an economic interest of such person other than an operating mineral interest (within the meaning of section 614(d)). Such term does not include taxable crude oil attributable to any overriding royalty interest, production payment, net profits interest, or similar interest of the person which—

(A) is created after June 9, 1981, out of an operating mineral interest in property which is proven oil or gas property (within the meaning of section 613A(c)(9)(A)) on the date such interest is created, and

(B) is not created pursuant to a binding contract entered into before June 10, 1981.

(3) PRODUCER.—The term "producer" has the meaning given to such term by section 4996(a)(1).

(e) REGULATIONS.—The Secretary shall prescribe such regulations as may be necessary or appropriate to carry out the purposes of this section.

• **1983, Technical Corrections Act of 1982 (P.L. 97-448)**

P.L. 97-448, § 106(a)(4)(A):

Added Code Sec. 6430. **Effective** with respect to calendar years beginning after 12-31-81.

[Sec. 6431—Stricken]

Amendments

• **2017, Tax Cuts and Jobs Act (P.L. 115-97)**

P.L. 115-97, § 13404(b):

Amended subchapter B of chapter 65 by striking Code Sec. 6431. **Effective** for bonds issued after 12-31-2017. Prior to being stricken, Code Sec. 6431 read as follows:

SEC. 6431. CREDIT FOR QUALIFIED BONDS ALLOWED TO ISSUER.

[Sec. 6431(a)]

(a) IN GENERAL.—In the case of a qualified bond issued before January 1, 2011, the issuer of such bond shall be allowed a credit with respect to each interest payment under such bond which shall be payable by the Secretary as provided in subsection (b).

[Sec. 6431(b)]

(b) PAYMENT OF CREDIT.—The Secretary shall pay (contemporaneously with each interest payment date under such bond) to the issuer of such bond (or to any person who makes such interest payments on behalf of the issuer) 35 percent of the interest payable under such bond on such date.

[Sec. 6431(c)]

(c) APPLICATION OF ARBITRAGE RULES.—For purposes of section 148, the yield on a qualified bond shall be reduced by the credit allowed under this section.

[Sec. 6431(d)]

(d) INTEREST PAYMENT DATE.—For purposes of this subsection, the term "interest payment date" means each date on which interest is payable by the issuer under the terms of the bond.

[Sec. 6431(e)]

(e) QUALIFIED BOND.—For purposes of this subsection, the term "qualified bond" has the meaning given such term in section 54AA(g).

[Sec. 6431(f)]

(f) APPLICATION OF SECTION TO CERTAIN QUALIFIED TAX CREDIT BONDS.—

(1) IN GENERAL.—In the case of any specified tax credit bond—

(A) such bond shall be treated as a qualified bond for purposes of this section,

(B) subsection (a) shall be applied without regard to the requirement that the qualified bond be issued before January 1, 2011,

(C) the amount of the payment determined under subsection (b) with respect to any interest payment due under such bond shall be equal to the lesser of—

(i) the amount of interest payable under such bond on such date, or

(ii) the amount of interest which would have been payable under such bond on such date if such interest were determined at the applicable credit rate determined under section 54A(b)(3),

(D) interest on any such bond shall be includible in gross income for purposes of this title,

(E) no credit shall be allowed under section 54A with respect to such bond,

(F) any payment made under subsection (b) shall not be includible as income for purposes of this title, and

(G) the deduction otherwise allowed under this title to the issuer of such bond with respect to interest paid under such bond shall be reduced by the amount of the payment made under this section with respect to such interest.

Sec. 6430—Repealed

(2) SPECIAL RULE FOR NEW CLEAN RENEWABLE ENERGY BONDS AND QUALIFIED ENERGY CONSERVATION BONDS.—In the case of any specified tax credit bond described in clause (i) or (ii) of paragraph (3)(A), the amount determined under paragraph (1)(C)(ii) shall be 70 percent of the amount so determined without regard to this paragraph and sections 54C(b) and 54D(b).

(3) SPECIFIED TAX CREDIT BOND.—For purposes of this subsection, the term "specified tax credit bond" means any qualified tax credit bond (as defined in section 54A(d)) if—

(A) such bond is—

(i) a new clean renewable energy bond (as defined in section 54C),

(ii) a qualified energy conservation bond (as defined in section 54D),

(iii) a qualified zone academy bond (as defined in section 54E) determined without regard to any allocation relating to the national zone academy bond limitation for years after 2010 or any carryforward of any such allocation, or

(iv) a qualified school construction bond (as defined in section 54F), and

(B) the issuer of such bond makes an irrevocable election to have this subsection apply.

Amendments

• **2014, Tax Technical Corrections Act of 2014 (P.L. 113-295)**

P.L. 113-295, §202(d)(1)-(2), Division A:

Amended Code Sec. 6431(f)(3)(A)(iii) by striking "2011" and inserting "years after 2010", and by striking "of such allocation" and inserting "of any such allocation". **Effective** as if included in the provision of the American Taxpayer Relief Act of 2012 (P.L. 112-240) to which it relates [**effective** for obligations issued after 12-31-2010.—CCH].

• **2010, Tax Relief, Unemployment Insurance Reauthorization, and Job Creation Act of 2010 (P.L. 111-312)**

P.L. 111-312, §758(b):

Amended Code Sec. 6431(f)(3)(A)(iii) by inserting "determined without regard to any allocation relating to the national zone academy bond limitation for 2011 or any carryforward of such allocation" after "54E)". **Effective** for obligations issued after 12-31-2010.

• **2010, Hiring Incentives to Restore Employment Act (P.L. 111-147)**

P.L. 111-147, §301(a):

Amended Code Sec. 6431 by adding at the end a new subsection (f). **Effective** for bonds issued after 3-18-2010.

• **2009, American Recovery and Reinvestment Tax Act of 2009 (P.L. 111-5)**

P.L. 111-5, §1531(b):

Amended subchapter B of chapter 65 by adding at the end a new Code Sec. 6431. **Effective** for obligations issued after 2-17-2009.

P.L. 111-5, §1531(d), provides:

(d) TRANSITIONAL COORDINATION WITH STATE LAW.—Except as otherwise provided by a State after the date of the enactment of this Act, the interest on any build America bond (as defined in section 54AA of the Internal Revenue Code of 1986, as added by this section) and the amount of any credit determined under such section with respect to such bond shall be treated for purposes of the income tax laws of such State as being exempt from Federal income tax.

[Sec. 6432]

SEC. 6432. CONTINUATION COVERAGE PREMIUM ASSISTANCE.

[Sec. 6432(a)]

(a) IN GENERAL.—The person to whom premiums are payable for continuation coverage under section 9501(a)(1) of the American Rescue Plan Act of 2021 shall be allowed as a credit against the tax imposed by section 3111(b), or so much of the taxes imposed under section 3221(a) as are attributable to the rate in effect under section 3111(b), for each calendar quarter an amount equal to the premiums not paid by assistance eligible individuals for such coverage by reason of such section 9501(a)(1) with respect to such calendar quarter.

[Sec. 6432(b)]

(b) PERSON TO WHOM PREMIUMS ARE PAYABLE.—For purposes of subsection (a), except as otherwise provided by the Secretary, the person to whom premiums are payable under such continuation coverage shall be treated as being—

(1) in the case of any group health plan which is a multiemployer plan (as defined in section 3(37) of the Employee Retirement Income Security Act of 1974), the plan,

(2) in the case of any group health plan not described in paragraph (1)—

(A) which is subject to the COBRA continuation provisions contained in—

(i) the Internal Revenue Code of 1986,

(ii) the Employee Retirement Income Security Act of 1974, or

(iii) the Public Health Service Act, or

(B) under which some or all of the coverage is not provided by insurance,

the employer maintaining the plan, and

(3) in the case of any group health plan not described in paragraph (1) or (2), the insurer providing the coverage under the group health plan.

[Sec. 6432(c)]

(c) LIMITATIONS AND REFUNDABILITY.—

(1) CREDIT LIMITED TO CERTAIN EMPLOYMENT TAXES.—The credit allowed by subsection (a) with respect to any calendar quarter shall not exceed the tax imposed by section 3111(b), or so much of the taxes imposed under section 3221(a) as are attributable to the rate in effect under section 3111(b), for such calendar quarter (reduced by any credits allowed against such taxes under sections 3131, 3132, and 3134) on the wages paid with respect to the employment of all employees of the employer.

(2) REFUNDABILITY OF EXCESS CREDIT.—

(A) CREDIT IS REFUNDABLE.—If the amount of the credit under subsection (a) exceeds the limitation of paragraph (1) for any calendar quarter, such excess shall be treated as an overpayment that shall be refunded under sections 6402(a) and 6413(b).

(B) CREDIT MAY BE ADVANCED.—In anticipation of the credit, including the refundable portion under subparagraph (A), the credit may be advanced, according to forms and instructions provided by the Secretary, up to an amount calculated under subsection (a) through the end of the most recent payroll period in the quarter.

(C) TREATMENT OF DEPOSITS.—The Secretary shall waive any penalty under section 6656 for any failure to make a deposit of the tax imposed by section 3111(b), or so much of the taxes imposed under section 3221(a) as are attributable to the rate in effect under section 3111(b), if the Secretary determines that such failure was due to the anticipation of the credit allowed under this section.

(D) TREATMENT OF PAYMENTS.—For purposes of section 1324 of title 31, United States Code, any amounts due to an employer under this paragraph shall be treated in the same manner as a refund due from a credit provision referred to in subsection (b)(2) of such section.

(3) OVERSTATEMENTS.—Any overstatement of the credit to which a person is entitled under this section (and any amount paid by the Secretary as a result of such overstatement) shall be treated as an underpayment by such person of the taxes described in paragraph (1) and may be assessed and collected by the Secretary in the same manner as such taxes.

[Sec. 6432(d)]

(d) GOVERNMENTAL ENTITIES.—For purposes of this section, the term "person" includes the government of any State or political subdivision thereof, any Indian tribal government (as defined in section 139E(c)(1)), any agency or instrumentality of any of the foregoing, and any agency or instrumentality of the Government of the United States that is described in section 501(c)(1) and exempt from taxation under section 501(a).

CREDITS AND REFUNDS—SPECIAL RULES

[Sec. 6432(e)]

(e) DENIAL OF DOUBLE BENEFIT.—For purposes of chapter 1, the gross income of any person allowed a credit under this section shall be increased for the taxable year which includes the last day of any calendar quarter with respect to which such credit is allowed by the amount of such credit. No credit shall be allowed under this section with respect to any amount which is taken into account as qualified wages under section 2301 of the CARES Act or section 3134 of this title or as qualified health plan expenses under section 7001(d) or 7003(d) of the Families First Coronavirus Response Act or section 3131 or 3132 of this title.

[Sec. 6432(f)]

(f) EXTENSION OF LIMITATION ON ASSESSMENT.—Notwithstanding section 6501, the limitation on the time period for the assessment of any amount attributable to a credit claimed under this section shall not expire before the date that is 5 years after the later of—

(1) the date on which the original return which includes the calendar quarter with respect to which such credit is determined is filed, or

(2) the date on which such return is treated as filed under section 6501(b)(2).

[Sec. 6432(g)]

(g) REGULATIONS.—The Secretary shall issue such regulations, or other guidance, forms, instructions, and publications, as may be necessary or appropriate to carry out this section, including—

(1) the requirement to report information or the establishment of other methods for verifying the correct amounts of reimbursements under this section,

(2) the application of this section to group health plans that are multiemployer plans (as defined in section 3(37) of the Employee Retirement Income Security Act of 1974),

(3) to allow the advance payment of the credit determined under subsection (a), subject to the limitations provided in this section, based on such information as the Secretary shall require,

(4) to provide for the reconciliation of such advance payment with the amount of the credit at the time of filing the return of tax for the applicable quarter or taxable year, and

(5) allowing the credit to third party payors (including professional employer organizations, certified professional employer organizations, or agents under section 3504).

Amendments

• **2021, American Rescue Plan Act of 2021 (P.L. 117-2)**

P.L. 117-2, §9501(a)(1)(A), provides:

(a) PREMIUM ASSISTANCE FOR COBRA CONTINUATION COVERAGE FOR INDIVIDUALS AND THEIR FAMILIES.—

(1) PROVISION OF PREMIUM ASSISTANCE.—

(A) REDUCTION OF PREMIUMS PAYABLE.—In the case of any premium for a period of coverage during the period beginning on the first day of the first month beginning after the date of the enactment of this Act, and ending on September 30, 2021, for COBRA continuation coverage with respect to any assistance eligible individual described in paragraph (3), such individual shall be treated for purposes of any COBRA continuation provision as having paid in full the amount of such premium.

P.L. 117-2, §9501(b)(1)(A):

Amended subchapter B of chapter 65 by adding at the end a new Code Sec. 6432. For the **effective date** and a special rule, see Act Sec. 9501(b)(1)(C)-(D), below.

P.L. 117-2, §9501(b)(1)(C)-(D), provides:

(C) EFFECTIVE DATE.—The amendments made by this paragraph shall apply to premiums to which subsection (a)(1)(A) applies and wages paid on or after April 1, 2021.

(D) SPECIAL RULE IN CASE OF EMPLOYEE PAYMENT THAT IS NOT REQUIRED UNDER THIS SECTION.—

(i) IN GENERAL.—In the case of an assistance eligible individual who pays, with respect any period of coverage to which subsection (a)(1)(A) applies, any amount of the premium for such coverage that the individual would have (but for this Act) been required to pay, the person to whom such payment is payable shall reimburse such individual for the amount of such premium paid.

(ii) CREDIT OF REIMBURSEMENT.—A person to which clause (i) applies shall be allowed a credit in the manner provided under section 6432 of the Internal Revenue Code of 1986 for any payment made to the employee under such clause.

(iii) PAYMENT OF CREDITS.—Any person to which clause (i) applies shall make the payment required under such clause to the individual not later than 60 days after the date on which such individual made the premium payment.

[Sec. 6432—Stricken]

Amendments

• **2018, Tax Technical Corrections Act of 2018 (P.L. 115-141)**

P.L. 115-141, §401(d)(7)(A), Div. U:

Amended subchapter B of chapter 65 by striking Code Sec. 6432. **Effective** 3-23-2018. For a special rule, see Act Sec. 401(e), Div. U, below. Prior to being stricken, Code Sec. 6432 read as follows:

SEC. 6432. COBRA PREMIUM ASSISTANCE.

[Sec. 6432(a)]

(a) IN GENERAL.—The person to whom premiums are payable under COBRA continuation coverage shall be reimbursed as provided in subsection (c) for the amount of premiums not paid by assistance eligible individuals by reason of section 3001(a) of title III of division B of the American Recovery and Reinvestment Act of 2009.

Amendments

• **2010, Temporary Extension Act of 2010 (P.L. 111-144)**

P.L. 111-144, §3(b)(5)(C)(i):

Amended Code Sec. 6432(a) by striking "section 3002(a) of the Health Insurance Assistance for the Unemployed Act of 2009" and inserting "section 3001(a) of title III of division B of the American Recovery and Reinvestment Act of 2009". **Effective** as if included in the provision of section 3001 of division B of the American Recovery and Reinvestment Act of 2009 to which it relates [**effective** generally for premiums for a period of coverage beginning on or after 2-17-2009.—CCH].

[Sec. 6432(b)]

(b) PERSON ENTITLED TO REIMBURSEMENT.—For purposes of subsection (a), except as otherwise provided by the Secretary, the person to whom premiums are payable under COBRA continuation coverage shall be treated as being—

(1) in the case of any group health plan which is a multiemployer plan (as defined in section 3(37) of the Employee Retirement Income Security Act of 1974), the plan,

(2) in the case of any group health plan not described in paragraph (1)—

(A) which is subject to the COBRA continuation provisions contained in—

(i) the Internal Revenue Code of 1986,

(ii) the Employee Retirement Income Security Act of 1974,

(iii) the Public Health Service Act, or

(iv) title 5, United States Code, or

(B) under which some or all of the coverage is not provided by insurance,

the employer maintaining the plan, and

(3) in the case of any group health plan not described in paragraph (1) or (2), the insurer providing the coverage under the group health plan.

[Sec. 6432(c)]

(c) METHOD OF REIMBURSEMENT.—Except as otherwise provided by the Secretary—

(1) TREATMENT AS PAYMENT OF PAYROLL TAXES.—Each person entitled to reimbursement under subsection (a) (and filing a claim for such reimbursement at such time and in such manner as the Secretary may require) shall be treated for purposes of this title and section 1324(b)(2) of title 31, United States Code, as having paid to the Secretary, on the date that the assistance eligible individual's premium payment is received, payroll taxes in an amount equal to the portion of such reimbursement which relates to such premium. To the extent that the amount treated as paid under the preceding sentence exceeds the amount of such person's liability for such taxes, the Secretary shall credit or refund such excess in the same manner as if it were an overpayment of such taxes.

(2) OVERSTATEMENTS.—Any overstatement of the reimbursement to which a person is entitled under this section (and any amount paid by the Secretary as a result of such overstatement) shall be treated as an underpayment of payroll taxes by such person and may be assessed and collected by the Secretary in the same manner as payroll taxes.

(3) REIMBURSEMENT CONTINGENT ON PAYMENT OF REMAINING PREMIUM.—No reimbursement may be made under this section to a person with respect to any assistance eligible individual until after the reduced premium required under section 3001(a)(1)(A) of title III of division B of the American Recovery and Reinvestment Act of 2009 with respect to such individual has been received.

Amendments

• **2010, Temporary Extension Act of 2010 (P.L. 111-144)**

P.L. 111-144, §3(b)(5)(C)(ii):

Amended Code Sec. 6432(c)(3) by striking "section 3002(a)(1)(A) of such Act" and inserting "section 3001(a)(1)(A) of title III of division B of the American Recovery and Reinvestment Act of 2009". **Effective** as if included in the provision of section 3001 of division B of the American Recovery and Reinvestment Act of 2009 to which it **relates** [**effective** generally for premiums for a period of coverage beginning on or after 2-17-2009.—CCH].

[Sec. 6432(d)]

(d) DEFINITIONS.—For purposes of this section—

CREDITS AND REFUNDS—SPECIAL RULES

(1) PAYROLL TAXES.—The term "payroll taxes" means—

(A) amounts required to be deducted and withheld for the payroll period under section 3402 (relating to wage withholding),

(B) amounts required to be deducted for the payroll period under section 3102 (relating to FICA employee taxes), and

(C) amounts of the taxes imposed for the payroll period under section 3111 (relating to FICA employer taxes).

(2) PERSON.—The term "person" includes any governmental entity.

[Sec. 6432(e)]

(e) EMPLOYER DETERMINATION OF QUALIFYING EVENT AS INVOLUNTARY TERMINATION.—For purposes of this section, in any case in which—

(1) based on a reasonable interpretation of section 3001(a)(3)(C) of division B of the American Recovery and Reinvestment Act of 2009 and administrative guidance thereunder, an employer determines that the qualifying event with respect to COBRA continuation coverage for an individual was involuntary termination of a covered employee's employment, and

(2) the employer maintains supporting documentation of the determination, including an attestation by the employer of involuntary termination with respect to the covered employee,

the qualifying event for the individual shall be deemed to be involuntary termination of the covered employee's employment.

Amendments

• **2010, Temporary Extension Act of 2010 (P.L. 111-144)**

P.L. 111-144, §3(b)(5)(C)(iii):

Amended Code Sec. 6432 by redesignating subsections (e) and (f) as subsections (f) and (g), respectively, and inserting after subsection (d) a new subsection (e). **Effective** as if included in the provision of section 3001 of division B of the American Recovery and Reinvestment Act of 2009 to which it relates [**effective** generally for premiums for a period of coverage beginning on or after 2-17-2009.—CCH].

[Sec. 6432(f)]

(f) REPORTING.—Each person entitled to reimbursement under subsection (a) for any period shall submit such reports (at such time and in such manner) as the Secretary may require, including—

(1) an attestation of involuntary termination of employment for each covered employee on the basis of whose termination entitlement to reimbursement is claimed under subsection (a),

(2) a report of the amount of payroll taxes offset under subsection (a) for the reporting period and the estimated offsets of such taxes for the subsequent reporting period in connection with reimbursements under subsection (a), and

(3) a report containing the TINs of all covered employees, the amount of subsidy reimbursed with respect to each covered employee and qualified beneficiaries, and a designation with respect to each covered employee as to whether the subsidy reimbursement is for coverage of 1 individual or 2 or more individuals.

Amendments

• **2010, Temporary Extension Act of 2010 (P.L. 111-144)**

P.L. 111-144, §3(b)(5)(C)(iii):

Amended Code Sec. 6432 by redesignating subsection (e) as subsection (f). **Effective** as if included in the provision of section 3001 of division B of the American Recovery and Reinvestment Act of 2009 to which it relates [**effective** generally for premiums for a period of coverage beginning on or after 2-17-2009.—CCH].

[Sec. 6432(g)]

(g) REGULATIONS.—The Secretary shall issue such regulations or other guidance as may be necessary or appropriate to carry out this section, including—

(1) the requirement to report information or the establishment of other methods for verifying the correct amounts of reimbursements under this section, and

(2) the application of this section to group health plans that are multiemployer plans (as defined in section 3(37) of the Employee Retirement Income Security Act of 1974).

Amendments

• **2010, Temporary Extension Act of 2010 (P.L. 111-144)**

P.L. 111-144, §3(b)(5)(C)(iii):

Amended Code Sec. 6432 by redesignating subsection (f) as subsection (g). **Effective** as if included in the provision of section 3001 of division B of the American Recovery and Reinvestment Act of 2009 to which it relates [**effective** generally for premiums for a period of coverage beginning on or after 2-17-2009.—CCH].

• **2009, American Recovery and Reinvestment Tax Act of 2009 (P.L. 111-5)**

P.L. 111-5, §3001(a)(12)(A):

Amended subchapter B of chapter 65, as amended by this Act, by adding at the end a new Code Sec. 6432. **Effective** generally for premiums for a period of coverage beginning on or after 2-17-2009.

P.L. 115-141, §401(e), Div. U, provides:

(e) GENERAL SAVINGS PROVISION WITH RESPECT TO DEADWOOD PROVISIONS.—If—

(1) any provision amended or repealed by the amendments made by subsection (b) or (d) applied to—

(A) any transaction occurring before the date of the enactment of this Act,

(B) any property acquired before such date of enactment, or

(C) any item of income, loss, deduction, or credit taken into account before such date of enactment, and

(2) the treatment of such transaction, property, or item under such provision would (without regard to the amendments or repeals made by such subsection) affect the liability for tax for periods ending after such date of enactment,

nothing in the amendments or repeals made by this section shall be construed to affect the treatment of such transaction, property, or item for purposes of determining liability for tax for periods ending after such date of enactment.

⟫⟫→ *Caution: Code Sec. 6433, below, as added by P.L. 117-328, applies to tax years beginning after December 31, 2026.*

SEC. 6433. SAVER'S MATCH.

[Sec. 6433(a)]

(a) IN GENERAL.—

(1) ALLOWANCE OF MATCH.—Any eligible individual who makes qualified retirement savings contributions for the taxable year shall be allowed a matching contribution for such taxable year in an amount equal to the applicable percentage of so much of the qualified retirement savings contributions made by such eligible individual for the taxable year as does not exceed $2,000.

(2) PAYMENT OF MATCH.—

(A) IN GENERAL.—Except as provided in subparagraph (B), the matching contribution under this section shall be allowed as a credit which shall be payable by the Secretary as a contribution (as soon as practicable after the eligible individual has filed a tax return making a claim for such matching contribution for the taxable year) to the applicable retirement savings vehicle of the eligible individual.

(B) EXCEPTION.—In the case of an eligible individual who elects the application of this subparagraph and with respect to whom the matching contribution determined under paragraph (1) is greater than zero but less than $100 for the taxable year, subparagraph (A) shall not apply and such matching contribution shall be treated as a credit allowed by subpart C of part IV of subchapter A of chapter 1.

[Sec. 6433(b)]

(b) APPLICABLE PERCENTAGE.—For purposes of this section—

(1) IN GENERAL.—Except as provided in paragraph (2), the applicable percentage is 50 percent.

(2) PHASEOUT.—The percentage under paragraph (1) shall be reduced (but not below zero) by the number of percentage points which bears the same ratio to 50 percentage points as—

(A) the excess of—

(i) the taxpayer's modified adjusted gross income for such taxable year, over

(ii) the applicable dollar amount, bears to

(B) the phaseout range.

If any reduction determined under this paragraph is not a whole percentage point, such reduction shall be rounded to the next lowest whole percentage point.

(3) APPLICABLE DOLLAR AMOUNT; PHASEOUT RANGE.—

(A) JOINT RETURNS AND SURVIVING SPOUSES.—Except as provided in subparagraph (B)—

(i) the applicable dollar amount is $41,000, and

(ii) the phaseout range is $30,000.

(B) OTHER RETURNS.—In the case of—

CREDITS AND REFUNDS—SPECIAL RULES

(i) a head of a household (as defined in section 2(b)), the applicable dollar amount and the phaseout range shall be $3/4$ of the amounts applicable under subparagraph (A) (as adjusted under subsection (h)), and

(ii) any taxpayer who is not filing a joint return, who is not a head of a household (as so defined), and who is not a surviving spouse (as defined in section 2(a)), the applicable dollar amount and the phaseout range shall be $1/2$ of the amounts applicable under subparagraph (A) (as so adjusted).

[Sec. 6433(c)]

(c) ELIGIBLE INDIVIDUAL.—For purposes of this section—

(1) IN GENERAL.—The term "eligible individual" means any individual if such individual has attained the age of 18 as of the close of the taxable year.

(2) DEPENDENTS AND FULL-TIME STUDENTS NOT ELIGIBLE.—The term "eligible individual" shall not include—

(A) any individual with respect to whom a deduction under section 151 is allowed to another taxpayer for a taxable year beginning in the calendar year in which such individual's taxable year begins, and

(B) any individual who is a student (as defined in section 152(f)(2)).

(3) NONRESIDENT ALIENS NOT ELIGIBLE.—The term "eligible individual" shall not include any individual who is a nonresident alien individual for any portion of the taxable year unless such individual is treated for such taxable year as a resident of the United States for purposes of chapter 1 by reason of an election under subsection (g) or (h) of section 6013.

[Sec. 6433(d)]

(d) QUALIFIED RETIREMENT SAVINGS CONTRIBUTIONS.—For purposes of this section—

(1) IN GENERAL.—The term "qualified retirement savings contributions" means, with respect to any taxable year, the sum of—

(A) the amount of the qualified retirement contributions (as defined in section 219(e)) made by the eligible individual,

(B) the amount of—

(i) any elective deferrals (as defined in section 402(g)(3)) of such individual, and

(ii) any elective deferral of compensation by such individual under an eligible deferred compensation plan (as defined in section 457(b)) of an eligible employer described in section 457(e)(1)(A), and

(C) the amount of voluntary employee contributions by such individual to any qualified retirement plan (as defined in section 4974(c)).

Such term shall not include any amount attributable to a payment under subsection (a)(2).

(2) REDUCTION FOR CERTAIN DISTRIBUTIONS.—

(A) IN GENERAL.—The qualified retirement savings contributions determined under paragraph (1) for a taxable year shall be reduced (but not below zero) by the aggregate distributions received by the individual during the testing period from any entity of a type to which contributions under paragraph (1) may be made.

(B) TESTING PERIOD.—For purposes of subparagraph (A), the testing period, with respect to a taxable year, is the period which includes—

(i) such taxable year,

(ii) the 2 preceding taxable years, and

(iii) the period after such taxable year and before the due date (including extensions) for filing the return of tax for such taxable year.

(C) EXCEPTED DISTRIBUTIONS.—There shall not be taken into account under subparagraph (A)—

(i) any distribution referred to in section 72(p), 401(k)(8), 401(m)(6), 402(g)(2), 404(k), or 408(d)(4),

(ii) any distribution to which section 408(d)(3) or 408A(d)(3) applies, and

(iii) any portion of a distribution if such portion is transferred or paid in a rollover contribution (as defined in section 402(c), 403(a)(4), 403(b)(8), 408A(e), or 457(e)(16)) to an account or plan to which qualified retirement savings contributions can be made.

(D) TREATMENT OF DISTRIBUTIONS RECEIVED BY SPOUSE OF INDIVIDUAL.—For purposes of determining distributions received by an individual under subparagraph (A) for any taxable year, any distribution received by the spouse of such individual shall be treated as received by such individual if such individual and spouse file a joint return for such taxable year and for the taxable year during which the spouse receives the distribution.

[Sec. 6433(e)]

(e) APPLICABLE RETIREMENT SAVINGS VEHICLE.—

(1) IN GENERAL.—The term "applicable retirement savings vehicle" means an account or plan elected by the eligible individual under paragraph (2).

(2) ELECTION.—Any such election to have contributed the amount determined under subsection (a) shall be to an account or plan which—

(A) is—

(i) the portion of a plan which—

(I) is described in clause (v) of section 402(c)(8)(B), is a qualified cash or deferred arrangement (within the meaning of section 401(k)), or is an annuity contract described in section 403(b) which is purchased under a salary reduction agreement, and

(II) does not consist of a qualified Roth contribution program (as defined in section 402A(b)), or

(ii) an individual retirement plan which is not a Roth IRA,

(B) is for the benefit of the eligible individual,

(C) accepts contributions made under this section, and

(D) is designated by such individual (in such form and manner as the Secretary may provide).

[Sec. 6433(f)]

(f) OTHER DEFINITIONS AND SPECIAL RULES.—

(1) MODIFIED ADJUSTED GROSS INCOME.—For purposes of this section, the term "modified adjusted gross income" means adjusted gross income—

(A) determined without regard to sections 911, 931, and 933, and

(B) determined without regard to any exclusion or deduction allowed for any qualified retirement savings contribution made during the taxable year.

(2) TREATMENT OF CONTRIBUTIONS.—In the case of any contribution under subsection (a)(2)—

(A) except as otherwise provided in this section or by the Secretary under regulations, such contribution shall be treated as—

(i) an elective deferral made by the individual, if contributed to an applicable retirement savings vehicle described in subsection (e)(2)(A)(i), or

(ii) as an individual retirement plan contribution made by such individual, if contributed to such a plan,

(B) such contribution shall not be taken into account with respect to any applicable limitation under sections 402(g)(1), 403(b), 408(a)(1), 408(b)(2)(B), 408A(c)(2), 414(v)(2), 415(c), or 457(b)(2), and shall be disregarded for purposes of sections 401(a)(4), 401(k)(3), 401(k)(11)(B)(i)(III), and 416, and

(C) such contribution shall not be treated as an amount that may be paid, made available, or distributable to the participant under section 401(k)(2)(B)(i)(IV), 403(b)(7)(A)(i)(V), or 457(d)(1)(A)(iii).

(3) TREATMENT OF QUALIFIED PLANS, ETC.—A plan or arrangement to which a contribution is made under this section shall not be treated as violating any requirement under section 401, 403, 408, or 457 solely by reason of accepting such contribution.

(4) ERRONEOUS MATCHING CONTRIBUTIONS.—

(A) IN GENERAL.—If any contribution is erroneously paid under subsection (a)(2), including a payment that is not made to an applicable retirement savings vehicle, the amount of such erroneous payment shall be treated as an underpayment of tax (other than for purposes of part II of subchapter A of chapter 68) for the taxable year in which the Secretary determines the payment is erroneous.

(B) DISTRIBUTION OF ERRONEOUS MATCHING CONTRIBUTIONS.—In the case of a contribution to which subparagraph (A) applies—

(i) section 402(a), 403(a)(1), 403(b)(1), 408(d)(1), or 457(a)(1), whichever is applicable, shall not apply to any distribution of such contribution, and section 72(t) shall not apply to the distribution of such contribution or any income attributable thereto, if such distribution is received not later than the day prescribed by law (including extensions of time) for filing the individual's return for such taxable year, and

(ii) any plan or arrangement from which such a distribution is made under this subparagraph shall not be treated as violating any requirement under section 401, 403, or 457 solely by reason of making such distribution.

(5) EXCEPTION FROM REDUCTION OR OFFSET.—Any payment made to any individual under this section shall not be—

(A) subject to reduction or offset pursuant to subsection (c), (d), (e), or (f) of section 6402 or any similar authority permitting offset, or

(B) reduced or offset by other assessed Federal taxes that would otherwise be subject to levy or collection.

(6) SAVER'S MATCH RECOVERY PAYMENTS.—

(A) IN GENERAL.—In the case of an applicable retirement savings vehicle to which contributions have been made under subsection (a)(2), and from which a specified early distribution has been made during the taxable year, if the aggregate amount of such contributions exceeds the account balance of such savings vehicle at the end of the such taxable year, the tax imposed by chapter 1 shall be increased by an amount equal to such excess (reduced by the amount by which the tax under such chapter was increased under section 72(t)(1) with respect to such distribution).

(B) SPECIFIED EARLY DISTRIBUTION.—For purposes of this paragraph, the term "specified early distribution" means any portion of a distribution—

(i) which is from such applicable retirement savings vehicle to which a contribution has been made under subsection (a)(2),

(ii) which is includible in gross income, and

(iii) to which 72(t)(1) applies.

(C) EXCESS MAY BE REPAID.—

(i) IN GENERAL.—The increase in tax for any taxable year under subparagraph (A) shall be reduced (but not below zero) by so much of such specified early distribution as the individual elects to contribute to an applicable retirement savings vehicle not later than the day prescribed by law (including extensions of time) for filing such individual's return for such taxable year.

(ii) CONTRIBUTION OF EXCESS.—Any individual who elects to contribute an amount under clause (i) may make one or more contributions in an aggregate amount not to exceed the amount of the specified early distribution to which the election relates to an applicable retirement savings vehicle and to which a rollover contribution of such distribution could be made under section 402(c), 403(b)(8), 408(d)(3), or 457(e)(16), as the case may be.

(iii) LIMITATION ON CONTRIBUTIONS TO APPLICABLE RETIREMENT SAVINGS VEHICLE OTHER THAN IRAS.—The aggregate amount of contributions made by an individual under clause (ii) to any applicable savings retirement vehicle which is not an individual retirement plan shall not exceed the aggregate amount of specified early retirement distributions which are made from such savings retirement vehicle to such individual. Clause (ii) shall not apply to contributions to any applicable retirement savings vehicle which is not an individual retirement plan unless the individual is eligible to make contributions (other than those described in clause (ii)) to such retirement savings vehicle.

(iv) TREATMENT OF REPAYMENTS OF DISTRIBUTIONS FROM APPLICABLE ELIGIBLE RETIREMENT PLANS OTHER THAN IRAS.—If a contribution is made under clause (ii) with respect to a specified early distribution from an applicable savings retirement vehicle other than an individual retirement plan, then the taxpayer shall, to the extent of the amount of the contribution, be treated as having received such distribution in an eligible rollover distribution (as defined in section 402(c)(4)) and as having transferred the amount to the savings retirement vehicle in a direct trustee to trustee transfer within 60 days of the distribution.

(v) TREATMENT OF REPAYMENTS FOR DISTRIBUTIONS FROM IRAS.—If a contribution is made under clause (ii) with respect to a specified early distribution from an individual retirement plan, then, to the extent of the amount of the contribution, such distribution shall be treated as a distribution described in section 408(d)(3) and as having been transferred to the applicable retirement savings vehicle in a direct trustee to trustee transfer within 60 days of the distribution.

(D) RULES TO ACCOUNT FOR INVESTMENT LOSS.—The Secretary shall prescribe such rules as may be appropriate to reduce any increase in tax otherwise made under subparagraph (A) to properly account for the extent to which any portion of the excess described in such subparagraph is allocable to investment loss in the retirement savings vehicle.

[Sec. 6433(g)]

(g) PROVISION BY SECRETARY OF INFORMATION RELATING TO CONTRIBUTIONS.—In the case of an amount elected by an eligible individual to be contributed to an account or plan under subsection (e)(2), the Secretary shall provide general guidance applicable to the custodian of the account or the plan sponsor, as the case may be, detailing the treatment of such contribution under subsection (f)(2) and the reporting requirements with respect to such contribution under section 6058, particularly as such requirements are modified pursuant to section 102(c)(2) of the SECURE 2.0 Act of 2022.

LIMITATIONS—ASSESSMENT AND COLLECTION

[Sec. 6433(h)]

(h) INFLATION ADJUSTMENTS.—

(1) IN GENERAL.—In the case of any taxable year beginning in a calendar year after 2027, the $41,000 amount in subsection (b)(3)(A)(i) shall be increased by an amount equal to—

(A) such dollar amount, multiplied by

(B) the cost-of-living adjustment determined under section 1(f)(3) for the calendar year in which the taxable year begins, determined by substituting "calendar year 2026" for "calendar year 2016" in subparagraph (A)(ii) thereof.

(2) ROUNDING.—Any increase determined under paragraph (1) shall be rounded to the nearest multiple of $1,000.

Amendments

• 2022, SECURE 2.0 Act of 2022 (P.L. 117-328)

P.L. 117-328, § 103(a):

Amended subchapter B of chapter 65 by adding at the end a new Code Sec. 6433. **Effective** for tax years beginning after 12-31-2026.

CHAPTER 66—LIMITATIONS

SUBCHAPTER A.	Limitations on assessment and collection.
SUBCHAPTER B.	Limitations on credit or refund.
SUBCHAPTER C.	Mitigation of effect of period of limitations.
SUBCHAPTER D.	Periods of limitation in judicial proceedings.

Subchapter A—Limitations on Assessment and Collection

Sec. 6501.	Limitations on assessment and collection.
Sec. 6502.	Collection after assessment.
Sec. 6503.	Suspension of running of period of limitation.
Sec. 6504.	Cross references.

[Sec. 6501]

SEC. 6501. LIMITATIONS ON ASSESSMENT AND COLLECTION.

[Sec. 6501(a)]

(a) GENERAL RULE.—Except as otherwise provided in this section, the amount of any tax imposed by this title shall be assessed within 3 years after the return was filed (whether or not such return was filed on or after the date prescribed) or, if the tax is payable by stamp, at any time after such tax became due and before the expiration of 3 years after the date on which any part of such tax was paid, and no proceeding in court without assessment for the collection of such tax shall be begun after the expiration of such period. For purposes of this chapter, the term "return" means the return required to be filed by the taxpayer (and does not include a return of any person from whom the taxpayer has received an item of income, gain, loss, deduction, or credit).

Amendments

• 1997, Taxpayer Relief Act of 1997 (P.L. 105-34)

P.L. 105-34, § 1284(a):

Amended Code Sec. 6501(a) by adding at the end a new sentence. **Effective** for tax years beginning after 8-5-97.

• 1958, Excise Tax Technical Changes Act of 1958 (P.L. 85-859)

P.L. 85-859, § 165(a):

Amended Code Sec. 6501(a) by striking out "within 3 years after such tax became due," and substituting "at any time after such tax became due and before the expiration of 3 years after the date on which any part of such tax was paid,".

[Sec. 6501(b)]

(b) TIME RETURN DEEMED FILED.—

(1) EARLY RETURN.—For purposes of this section, a return of tax imposed by this title, except tax imposed by chapter 3, 4, 21, or 24, filed before the last day prescribed by law or by regulations promulgated pursuant to law for the filing thereof, shall be considered as filed on such last day.

(2) RETURN OF CERTAIN EMPLOYMENT AND WITHHOLDING TAXES.—For purposes of this section, if a return of tax imposed by chapter 3, 4, 21 or 24 for any period ending with or within a calendar year is filed before April 15 of the succeeding calendar year, such return shall be considered filed on April 15 of such calendar year.

(3) RETURN EXECUTED BY SECRETARY.—Notwithstanding the provisions of paragraph (2) of section 6020(b), the execution of a return by the Secretary pursuant to the authority conferred by such section shall not start the running of the period of limitations on assessment and collection.

(4) RETURN OF EXCISE TAXES.—For purposes of this section, the filing of a return for a specified period on which an entry has been made with respect to a tax imposed under a provision of subtitle D (including a return on which an entry has been made showing no liability for such tax for such period) shall constitute the filing of a return of all amounts of such tax which, if properly paid, would be required to be reported on such return for such period.

Amendments

• 2010, Hiring Incentives to Restore Employment Act (P.L. 111-147)

P.L. 111-147, § 501(c)(2):

Amended Code Sec. 6501(b)(1) by inserting "4," after "chapter 3,". **Effective** generally for payments made after 12-31-2012. For a special rule, see Act Sec. 501(d)(2), below.

P.L. 111-147, § 501(c)(3)(A)-(B):

Amended Code Sec. 6501(b)(2) by inserting "4," after "chapter 3," in the text thereof, and by striking "TAXES AND TAX IMPOSED BY CHAPTER 3" in the heading thereof and inserting "AND WITHHOLDING TAXES". **Effective** generally for payments made after 12-31-2012. For a special rule, see Act Sec. 501(d)(2), below.

P.L. 111-147, § 501(d)(2), provides:

(2) GRANDFATHERED TREATMENT OF OUTSTANDING OBLIGATIONS.—The amendments made by this section shall not require any amount to be deducted or withheld from any payment under any obligation outstanding on the date which is 2 years after the date of the enactment of this Act or from the gross proceeds from any disposition of such an obligation.

• 1976, Tax Reform Act of 1976 (P.L. 94-455)

P.L. 94-455, § 1906(b)(13)(A):

Amended 1954 Code by substituting "Secretary" for "Secretary or his delegate" each place it appeared. **Effective** 2-1-77.

• 1966, Foreign Investors Tax Act of 1966 (P.L. 89-809)

P.L. 89-809, § 105(f)(3):

Amended Code Sec. 6501(b)(1) and (2) by substituting "chapter 3, 21, or 24" for "chapter 21 or 24" and amended Code Sec. 6501(b)(2) by inserting "and Tax Imposed by Chapter 3" after "Taxes" in the heading. **Effective** 11-13-66.

• 1965, Excise Tax Reduction Act of 1965 (P.L. 89-44)

P.L. 89-44, § 810(a):

Amended Sec. 6501(b) by adding paragraph (4). **Effective** 7-1-65.

LIMITATIONS—ASSESSMENT AND COLLECTION

[Sec. 6501(c)]

(c) EXCEPTIONS.—

(1) FALSE RETURN.—In the case of a false or fraudulent return with the intent to evade tax, the tax may be assessed, or a proceeding in court for collection of such tax may be begun without assessment, at any time.

(2) WILLFUL ATTEMPT TO EVADE TAX.—In case of a willful attempt in any manner to defeat or evade tax imposed by this title (other than tax imposed by subtitle A or B), the tax may be assessed, or a proceeding in court for the collection of such tax may be begun without assessment, at any time.

(3) NO RETURN.—In the case of failure to file a return, the tax may be assessed, or a proceeding in court for the collection of such tax may be begun without assessment, at any time.

(4) EXTENSION BY AGREEMENT.—

(A) IN GENERAL.—Where before the expiration of the time prescribed for the assessment of any tax imposed by this title, except the estate tax provided in chapter 11, both the Secretary and the taxpayer have consented in writing to its assessment after such time, the tax may be assessed at any time prior to the expiration of the period agreed upon. The period so agreed upon may be extended by subsequent agreements in writing made before the expiration of the period previously agreed upon.

(B) NOTICE TO TAXPAYER OF RIGHT TO REFUSE OR LIMIT EXTENSION.—The Secretary shall notify the taxpayer of the taxpayer's right to refuse to extend the period of limitations, or to limit such extension to particular issues or to a particular period of time, on each occasion when the taxpayer is requested to provide such consent.

(5) TAX RESULTING FROM CHANGES IN CERTAIN INCOME TAX OR ESTATE TAX CREDITS.—For special rules applicable in cases where the adjustment of certain taxes allowed as a credit against income taxes or estate taxes results in additional tax, see section 905(c) (relating to the foreign tax credit for income tax purposes) and section 2016 (relating to taxes of foreign countries, States, etc., claimed as credit against estate taxes).

(6) TERMINATION OF PRIVATE FOUNDATION STATUS.—In the case of a tax on termination of private foundation status under section 507, such tax may be assessed, or a proceeding in court for the collection of such tax may be begun without assessment, at any time.

(7) SPECIAL RULE FOR CERTAIN AMENDED RETURNS.—Where, within the 60-day period ending on the day on which the time prescribed in this section for the assessment of any tax imposed by subtitle A for any taxable year would otherwise expire, the Secretary receives a written document signed by the taxpayer showing that the taxpayer owes an additional amount of such tax for such taxable year, the period for the assessment of such additional amount shall not expire before the day 60 days after the day on which the Secretary receives such document.

(8) FAILURE TO NOTIFY SECRETARY OF CERTAIN FOREIGN TRANSFERS.—

(A) IN GENERAL.—In the case of any information which is required to be reported to the Secretary pursuant to an election under section 1295(b) or under section 1298(f), 6038, 6038A, 6038B, 6038D, 6046, 6046A, or 6048, the time for assessment of any tax imposed by this title with respect to any tax return, event, or period to which such information relates shall not expire before the date which is 3 years after the date on which the Secretary is furnished the information required to be reported under such section.

(B) APPLICATION TO FAILURES DUE TO REASONABLE CAUSE.—If the failure to furnish the information referred to in subparagraph (A) is due to reasonable cause and not willful neglect, subparagraph (A) shall apply only to the item or items related to such failure.

(9) GIFT TAX ON CERTAIN GIFTS NOT SHOWN ON RETURN.—If any gift of property the value of which (or any increase in taxable gifts required under section 2701(d) which) is required to be shown on a return of tax imposed by chapter 12 (without regard to section 2503(b)), and is not shown on such return, any tax imposed by chapter 12 on such gift may be assessed, or a proceeding in court for the collection of such tax may be begun without assessment, at any time. The preceding sentence shall not apply to any item which is disclosed in such return, or in a statement attached to the return, in a manner adequate to apprise the Secretary of the nature of such item.

(10) LISTED TRANSACTIONS.—If a taxpayer fails to include on any return or statement for any taxable year any information with respect to a listed transaction (as defined in section 6707A(c)(2)) which is required under section 6011 to be included with such return or statement, the time for assessment of any tax imposed by this title with respect to such transaction shall not expire before the date which is 1 year after the earlier of—

(A) the date on which the Secretary is furnished the information so required, or

(B) the date that a material advisor meets the requirements of section 6112 with respect to a request by the Secretary under section 6112(b) relating to such transaction with respect to such taxpayer.

(11) CERTAIN ORDERS OF CRIMINAL RESTITUTION.—In the case of any amount described in section 6201(a)(4), such amount may be assessed, or a proceeding in court for the collection of such amount may be begun without assessment, at any time.

(12) CERTAIN TAXES ATTRIBUTABLE TO PARTNERSHIP ADJUSTMENTS.—In the case of any partnership adjustment determined under subchapter C of chapter 63, the period for assessment of any tax imposed under chapter 2 or 2A which is attributable to such adjustment shall not expire before the date that is 1 year after—

(A) in the case of an adjustment pursuant to the decision of a court in a proceeding brought under section 6234, such decision becomes final, or

(B) in any other case, 90 days after the date on which the notice of the final partnership adjustment is mailed under section 6231.

Amendments

• **2018, Tax Technical Corrections Act of 2018 (P.L. 115-141)**

P.L. 115-141, § 201(b)(2), Div. U:

Amended Code Sec. 6501(c) by adding at the end a new paragraph (12). **Effective** as if included in section 1101 of the Bipartisan Budget Act of 2015 [**effective** generally for returns filed for partnership tax years beginning after 12-31-2017.—CCH].

P.L. 115-141, § 205(b), Div. U:

Amended Code Sec. 6501(c)(4)(A) by striking "in this section" before "for the assessment". **Effective** as if included in section 1101 of the Bipartisan Budget Act of 2015 [**effective** generally for returns filed for partnership tax years beginning after 12-31-2017.—CCH].

• **2010, Firearms Excise Tax Improvement Act of 2010 (P.L. 111-237)**

P.L. 111-237, § 3(b)(2):

Amended Code Sec. 6501(c) by adding at the end a new paragraph (11). **Effective** for restitution ordered after 8-16-2010.

• **2010, (P.L. 111-226)**

P.L. 111-226, § 218(a)(1)-(2):

Amended Code Sec. 6501(c)(8) by striking "In the case of any information" and inserting

"(A) IN GENERAL.—In the case of any information"; and

by adding at the end a new subparagraph (B). **Effective** as if included in section 513 of the Hiring Incentives to Restore Employment Act (P.L. 111-147) [**effective** for returns filed after the date of the enactment of P.L. 111-147 [3-18-2010]; and returns filed on or before such date if the period specified in Code Sec. 6501 (determined without regard to the amendment made by section 513) for assessment of such taxes has not expired as of such date.—CCH].

• **2010, Hiring Incentives to Restore Employment Act (P.L. 111-147)**

P.L. 111-147, § 513(b)(1)-(3):

Amended Code Sec. 6501(c)(8) by inserting "pursuant to an election under section 1295(b) or" before "under section 6038", by inserting "1298(f)," before "6038", and by inserting "6038D," after "6038B,". For the **effective** date, see Act Sec. 513(d), below.

P.L. 111-147, § 513(c):

Amended Code Sec. 6501(c)(8) by striking "event" and inserting "tax return, event,". For the **effective** date, see Act Sec. 513(d), below.

P.L. 111-147, § 513(d), provides:

(d) EFFECTIVE DATE.—The amendments made by this section shall apply to—

(1) returns filed after the date of the enactment of this Act; and

(2) returns filed on or before such date if the period specified in section 6501 of the Internal Revenue Code of 1986 (determined without regard to such amendments) for assessment of such taxes has not expired as of such date.

LIMITATIONS—ASSESSMENT AND COLLECTION

• **2005, Gulf Opportunity Zone Act of 2005 (P.L. 109-135)**

P.L. 109-135, § 403(y):

Amended Code Sec. 6501(c)(10)(B) by striking "(as defined in section 6111)" after "material advisor". **Effective** as if included in the provision of the American Jobs Creation Act of 2004 (P.L. 108-357) to which it relates [**effective** for tax years with respect to which the period for assessing a deficiency did not expire before 10-22-2004.—CCH.]

• **2004, American Jobs Creation Act of 2004 (P.L. 108-357)**

P.L. 108-357, § 814(a):

Amended Code Sec. 6501(c) by adding at the end a new paragraph (10). **Effective** for tax years with respect to which the period for assessing a deficiency did not expire before 10-22-2004.

• **1998, IRS Restructuring and Reform Act of 1998 (P.L. 105-206)**

P.L. 105-206, § 3461(b)(1)-(2):

Amended Code Sec. 6501(c)(4) by striking "Where" and inserting "(A) IN GENERAL.—Where", and by adding at the end a new subparagraph (B). **Effective** for requests to extend the period of limitations made after 12-31-99. For a special rule, see Act Sec. 3461(c)(2), below.

P.L. 105-206, § 3461(c)(2), provides:

(2) PRIOR REQUEST.—If, in any request to extend the period of limitations made on or before December 31, 1999, a taxpayer agreed to extend such period beyond the 10-year period referred to in section 6502(a) of the Internal Revenue Code of 1986, such extension shall expire on the latest of—

(A) the last day of such 10-year period;

(B) December 31, 2002; or

(C) in the case of an extension in connection with an installment agreement, the 90th day after the end of the period of such extension.

P.L. 105-206, § 6007(e)(2)(A):

Amended Code Sec. 6501(c)(9) by striking the last sentence. **Effective** as if included in the provision of P.L. 105-34 to which it relates [**effective** for gifts made in calendar years ending after 8-5-97.—CCH]. Prior to being stricken, the last sentence of Code Sec. 6501(c)(9) read as follows:

The value of any item which is so disclosed may not be redetermined by the Secretary after the expiration of the period under subsection (a).

• **1997, Taxpayer Relief Act of 1997 (P.L. 105-34)**

P.L. 105-34, § 506(b):

Amended Code Sec. 6501(c)(9). **Effective** for gifts made in calendar years ending after 8-5-97. Prior to amendment, Code Sec. 6501(c)(9) read as follows:

(9) GIFT TAX ON CERTAIN GIFTS NOT SHOWN ON RETURN.—If any gift of property the value of which is determined under section 2701 or 2702 (or any increase in taxable gifts required under section 2701(d)) is required to be shown on a return of tax imposed by chapter 12 (without regard to section 2503(b)), and is not shown on such return, any tax imposed by chapter 12 on such gift may be assessed, or a proceeding in court for the collection of such tax may be begun without assessment, at any time. The preceding sentence shall not apply to any item not shown as a gift on such return if such item is disclosed in such return, or in a statement attached to the return, in a manner adequate to apprise the Secretary of the nature of such item.

P.L. 105-34, § 1145(a):

Amended Code Sec. 6501(c)(8). **Effective** for information the due date for the reporting of which is after 8-5-97. Prior to amendment, Code Sec. 6501(c)(8) read as follows:

(8) FAILURE TO NOTIFY SECRETARY UNDER SECTION 6038B.—In the case of any tax imposed on any exchange or distribution by reason of subsection (a), (d), or (e) of section 367, the time for assessment of such tax shall not expire before the date which is 3 years after the date on which the Secretary is notified of such exchange or distribution under section 6038B(a).

• **1990, Omnibus Budget Reconciliation Act of 1990 (P.L. 101-508)**

P.L. 101-508, § 11602(b):

Amended Code Sec. 6501(c) by adding at the end thereof a new paragraph (9). **Effective** for gifts after 10-8-90.

• **1986, Tax Reform Act of 1986 (P.L. 99-514)**

P.L. 99-514, § 1810(g)(3)(A), (B):

Amended Code Sec. 6501(c)(8) by striking out "subsection (a) or (d)" and inserting in lieu thereof "subsection (a), (d), or (e)", and by striking out "exchange" each place it appears and inserting in lieu thereof "exchange or distribution". **Effective** as if included in the provision of P.L. 98-369 to which it relates.

• **1984, Deficit Reduction Act of 1984 (P.L. 98-369)**

P.L. 98-369, § 131(d)(2):

Amended Code Sec. 6501(c) by adding new paragraph (8). **Effective** for transfers or exchanges after 12-31-84, in tax years ending after such date. Special rules appear in Act Sec. 131(g)(2) and (3) following Code Sec. 367.

P.L. 98-369, § 211(b)(24)(A):

Amended Code Sec. 6501(c) by striking out paragraph (6) and by redesignating paragraph (7) as paragraph (6). **Effective** for tax years beginning after 12-31-83. Prior to amendment, paragraph (6) read as follows:

(6) Tax Resulting from Certain Distributions or from Termination as Life Insurance Company.—In the case of any tax imposed under section 802(a) by reason of section 802(b)(3) on account of a termination of the taxpayer as an insurance company or as a life insurance company to which section 815(d)(2)(A) applies, or on account of a distribution by the taxpayer to which section 815(d)(2)(B) applies, such tax may be assessed within 3 years after the return was filed (whether or not such return was filed on or after the date prescribed) for the taxable year for which the taxpayer ceases to be an insurance company, the second taxable year for which the taxpayer is not a life insurance company, or the taxable year in which the distribution is actually made, as the case may be.

P.L. 98-369, § 447(a):

Amended Code Sec. 6501(c) by adding new paragraph (7). **Effective** with respect to documents received by the Secretary of the Treasury (or his delegate) after 7-18-84.

• **1976, Tax Reform Act of 1976 (P.L. 94-455)**

P.L. 94-455, § 1906(b)(13)(A):

Amended 1954 Code by substituting "Secretary" for "Secretary or his delegate" each place it appeared. **Effective** 2-1-77.

• **1969, Tax Reform Act of 1969 (P.L. 91-172)**

P.L. 91-172, § 101(g)(2):

Added paragraph (7) to Code Sec. 6501(c). **Effective** 1-1-70.

• **1962 (P.L. 87-858)**

P.L. 87-858, § 3(b)(4):

Amended Code Sec. 6501(c)(6) by substituting "802(a)" for "802(a)(1)". **Effective** 1-1-62.

• **1959, Life Insurance Company Income Tax Act of 1959 (P.L. 86-69)**

P.L. 86-69, § 3(g):

Amended Code Sec. 6501(c) by adding a new paragraph (6). **Effective** for tax years beginning after 12-31-57.

[Sec. 6501(d)]

(d) REQUEST FOR PROMPT ASSESSMENT.—Except as otherwise provided in subsection (c), (e), or (f), in the case of any tax (other than the tax imposed by chapter 11 of subtitle B, relating to estate taxes) for which return is required in the case of a decedent, or by his estate during the period of administration, or by a corporation, the tax shall be assessed, and any proceeding in court without assessment for the collection of such tax shall be begun, within 18 months after written request therefor (filed after the return is made and filed in such manner and such form as may be prescribed by regulations of the Secretary) by the executor, administrator, or other fiduciary representing the estate of such decedent, or by the corporation, but not after the expiration of 3 years after the return was filed. This subsection shall not apply in the case of a corporation unless—

(1)(A) such written request notifies the Secretary that the corporation contemplates dissolution at or before the expiration of such 18-month period, (B) the dissolution is in good faith begun before the expiration of such 18-month period, and (C) the dissolution is completed;

(2)(A) such written request notifies the Secretary that a dissolution has in good faith been begun, and (B) the dissolution is completed; or

(3) a dissolution has been completed at the time such written request is made.

Amendments

• **1976, Tax Reform Act of 1976 (P.L. 94-455)**

P.L. 94-455, § 1906(b)(13)(A):

Amended 1954 Code by substituting "Secretary" for "Secretary or his delegate" each place it appeared. **Effective** 2-1-77.

• **1958, Technical Amendments Act of 1958 (P.L. 85-866)**

P.L. 85-866, § 80(a):

Amended the first sentence of Sec. 6501(d) by striking out "subsection (c)" and substituting "subsection (c), (e), or (f)". **Effective** 1-1-54.

P.L. 85-866, § 80(b):

Amended paragraphs (1), (2) and (3) of Sec. 6501(d). **Effective** 1-1-54. Prior to amendment, those paragraphs read as follows:

"(1) Such written request notifies the Secretary or his delegate that the corporation contemplates dissolution at or before the expiration of such 18-month period; and

"(2) The dissolution is in good faith begun before the expiration of such 18-month period; and

"(3) The dissolution is completed."

[Sec. 6501(e)]

(e) SUBSTANTIAL OMISSION OF ITEMS.—Except as otherwise provided in subsection (c)—

(1) INCOME TAXES.—In the case of any tax imposed by subtitle A—

(A) GENERAL RULE.—If the taxpayer omits from gross income an amount properly includible therein and—

(i) such amount is in excess of 25 percent of the amount of gross income stated in the return, or

(ii) such amount—

(I) is attributable to one or more assets with respect to which information is required to be reported under section 6038D (or would be so required if such section were applied without regard to the dollar threshold specified in subsection (a) thereof and without regard to any exceptions provided pursuant to subsection (h)(1) thereof), and

(II) is in excess of $5,000,

the tax may be assessed, or a proceeding in court for collection of such tax may be begun without assessment, at any time within 6 years after the return was filed.

(B) DETERMINATION OF GROSS INCOME.—For purposes of subparagraph (A)—

(i) In the case of a trade or business, the term "gross income" means the total of the amounts received or accrued from the sale of goods or services (if such amounts are required to be shown on the return) prior to diminution by the cost of such sales or services;

(ii) An understatement of gross income by reason of an overstatement of unrecovered cost or other basis is an omission from gross income; and

(iii) In determining the amount omitted from gross income (other than in the case of an overstatement of unrecovered cost or other basis), there shall not be taken into account any amount which is omitted from gross income stated in the return if such amount is disclosed in the return, or in a statement attached to the return, in a manner adequate to apprise the Secretary of the nature and amount of such item.

(C) CONSTRUCTIVE DIVIDENDS.—If the taxpayer omits from gross income an amount properly includible therein under section 951(a), the tax may be assessed, or a proceeding in court for the collection of such tax may be done without assessing, at any time within 6 years after the return was filed.

(2) ESTATE AND GIFT TAXES.—In the case of a return of estate tax under chapter 11 or a return of gift tax under chapter 12, if the taxpayer omits from the gross estate or from the total amount of the gifts made during the period for which the return was filed items includible in such gross estate or such total gifts, as the case may be, as exceed in amount 25 percent of the gross estate stated in the return or the total amount of gifts stated in the return, the tax may be assessed, or a proceeding in court for the collection of such tax may be begun without assessment, at any time within 6 years after the return was filed. In determining the items omitted from the gross estate or the total gifts, there shall not be taken into account any item which is omitted from the gross estate or from the total gifts stated in the return if such item is disclosed in the return, or in a statement attached to the return, in a manner adequate to apprise the Secretary of the nature and amount of such item.

(3) EXCISE TAXES.—In the case of a return of a tax imposed under a provision of subtitle D, if the return omits an amount of such tax properly includible thereon which exceeds 25 percent of the amount of such tax reported thereon, the tax may be assessed, or a proceeding in court for the collection of such tax may be begun without assessment, at any time within 6 years after the return is filed. In determining the amount of tax omitted on a return, there shall not be taken into account any amount of tax imposed by chapter 41, 42, 43, or 44 which is omitted from the return if the transaction giving rise to such tax is disclosed in the return, or in a statement attached to the return, in a manner adequate to apprise the Secretary of the existence and nature of such item.

Amendments

- **2015, Surface Transportation and Veterans Health Care Choice Improvement Act of 2015 (P.L. 114-41)**

P.L. 114-41, §2005(a)(1)-(2)

Amended Code Sec. 6501(e)(1)(B) by striking "and" at the end of clause (i), by redesignating clause (ii) as clause (iii), and by inserting after clause (i) a new clause (ii), and by inserting "(other than in the case of an overstatement of unrecovered cost or other basis)" in clause (iii) (as so redesignated) after "In determining the amount omitted from gross income". For the **effective** date, see Act Sec. 2005(b)(1)-(2), below.

P.L. 114-41, §2005(b)(1)-(2), provides:

(b) EFFECTIVE DATE.—The amendments made by this section shall apply to—

(1) returns filed after the date of the enactment of this Act, and

(2) returns filed on or before such date if the period specified in section 6501 of the Internal Revenue Code of 1986 (determined without regard to such amendments) for assessment of the taxes with respect to which such return relates has not expired as of such date.

- **2010, Hiring Incentives to Restore Employment Act (P.L. 111-147)**

P.L. 111-147, §513(a)(1):

Amended Code Sec. 6501(e)(1) by redesignating subparagraphs (A) and (B) as subparagraphs (B) and (C), respectively, and by inserting before subparagraph (B) (as so redesignated) a new subparagraph (A). For the **effective** date, see Act Sec. 513(d), below.

P.L. 111-147, §513(a)(2)(A):

Amended Code Sec. 6501(e)(1)(B), as redesignated by Act Sec. 513(a)(1), by striking all that precedes clause (i) and inserting "(B) DETERMINATION OF GROSS INCOME.—For purposes of subparagraph (A)—". For the **effective** date, see Act Sec. 513(d), below. Prior to being stricken, all that precedes clause (i) of Code Sec. 6501(e)(1)(B) read as follows:

(B) GENERAL RULE.—If the taxpayer omits from gross income an amount properly includible therein which is in excess of 25 percent of the amount of gross income stated in the return, the tax may be assessed, or a proceeding in court for the collection of such tax may be begun without assessment, at any time within 6 years after the return was filed. For purposes of this subparagraph—

P.L. 111-147, §513(d), provides:

(d) EFFECTIVE DATE.—The amendments made by this section shall apply to—

(1) returns filed after the date of the enactment of this Act; and

(2) returns filed on or before such date if the period specified in section 6501 of the Internal Revenue Code of 1986 (determined without regard to such amendments) for assessment of such taxes has not expired as of such date.

- **2004, American Jobs Creation Act of 2004 (P.L. 108-357)**

P.L. 108-357, §413(c)(28):

Amended Code Sec. 6501(e)(1)(B). **Effective** for tax years of foreign corporations beginning after 12-31-2004, and for tax years of United States shareholders with or within which such tax years of foreign corporations end. Prior to amendment, Code Sec. 6501(e)(1)(B) read as follows:

(B) CONSTRUCTIVE DIVIDENDS.—If the taxpayer omits from gross income an amount properly includible therein under section 551(b) (relating to the inclusion in the gross income of United States shareholders of their distributive shares of the undistributed foreign personal holding company income), the tax may be assessed, or a proceeding in court for the collection of such tax may be begun without assessment, at any time within 6 years after the return was filed.

- **1978, Revenue Act of 1978 (P.L. 95-600)**

P.L. 95-600, §701(t)(3)(A):

Amended Code Sec. 6501(e)(3) by changing ", or 43" to "43, or 44". **Effective** 10-4-76.

- **1978, Black Lung Benefits Revenue Act of 1977 (P.L. 95-227)**

P.L. 95-227, §4(d)(4):

Amended Code Sec. 6501(e)(3) by substituting "43, or 44" for "or 43" in the second sentence thereof. For **effective** date, see the historical comment for P.L. 95-227 under Code Sec. 4951.

- **1976, Tax Reform Act of 1976 (P.L. 94-455)**

P.L. 94-455, §1307(d)(2)(F)(vi):

Substituted "chapter 41, 42," for "chapter 42" in Code Sec. 6501(e)(3). **Effective** 10-4-76.

P.L. 94-455, §1906(b)(13)(A):

Amended the 1954 Code by substituting "Secretary" for "Secretary or his delegate" each place it appeared. **Effective** 2-1-77.

- **1974, Employee Retirement Income Security Act of 1974 (P.L. 93-406)**

P.L. 93-406, §1016(a)(14):

Amended Code Sec. 6501(e)(3) by changing "chapter 42" to "chapter 42 or 43". For **effective** date, see amendment note for Code Sec. 410.

- **1970, Excise, Estate, and Gift Tax Adjustment Act of 1970 (P.L. 91-614)**

P.L. 91-614, §102(d)(8):

Amended Code Sec. 6501(e) by substituting "period for which the return was filed" for "year" in the first sentence of paragraph (2). **Effective** for gifts made after 12-31-70.

- **1969, Tax Reform Act of 1969 (P.L. 91-172)**

P.L. 91-172, §101(g)(3):

Added the last sentence in Code Sec. 6501(e)(3). **Effective** 1-1-70.

- **1965, Excise Tax Reduction Act of 1965 (P.L. 89-44)**

P.L. 89-44, §810(b):

Amended Code Sec. 6501(e) by adding paragraph (3). **Effective** 7-1-65.

LIMITATIONS—ASSESSMENT AND COLLECTION

[Sec. 6501(f)]

(f) PERSONAL HOLDING COMPANY TAX.—If a corporation which is a personal holding company for any taxable year fails to file with its return under chapter 1 for such year a schedule setting forth—

(1) the items of gross income and adjusted ordinary gross income, described in section 543, received by the corporation during such year, and

(2) the names and addresses of the individuals who owned, within the meaning of section 544 (relating to rules for determining stock ownership), at any time during the last half of such year more than 50 percent in value of the outstanding capital stock of the corporation,

the personal holding company tax for such year may be assessed, or a proceeding in court for the collection of such tax may be begun without assessment, at any time within 6 years after the return for such year was filed.

Amendments

• **1964, Revenue Act of 1964 (P.L. 88-272)**

P.L. 88-272, §225(k)(6):

Amended Code Sec. 6501(f) by striking out "gross income, described in section 543(a)," and inserting in lieu thereof "gross income and adjusted ordinary gross income, described in section 543,". **Effective** 1-1-64.

[Sec. 6501(g)]

(g) CERTAIN INCOME TAX RETURNS OF CORPORATIONS.—

(1) TRUSTS OR PARTNERSHIPS.—If a taxpayer determines in good faith that it is a trust or partnership and files a return as such under subtitle A, and if such taxpayer is thereafter held to be a corporation for the taxable year for which the return is filed, such return shall be deemed the return of the corporation for purposes of this section.

(2) EXEMPT ORGANIZATIONS.—If a taxpayer determines in good faith that it is an exempt organization and files a return as such under section 6033, and if such taxpayer is thereafter held to be a taxable organization for the taxable year for which the return is filed, such return shall be deemed the return of the organization for purposes of this section.

(3) DISC.—If a corporation determines in good faith that it is a DISC (as defined in section 992(a)) and files a return as such under section 6011(c)(2) and if such corporation is thereafter held to be a corporation which is not a DISC for the taxable year for which the return is filed, such return shall be deemed the return of a corporation which is not a DISC for purposes of this section.

Amendments

• **1984, Deficit Reduction Act of 1984 (P.L. 98-369)**

P.L. 98-369, §801(d)(14):

Amended Code Sec. 6501(g)(3) by striking out "section 6011(e)(2)" and inserting in lieu thereof "section 6011(c)(2)." **Effective** for transactions after 12-31-84, in tax years ending after such date.

• **1971, Revenue Act of 1971 (P.L. 92-178)**

P.L. 92-178, §504(c):

Amended Code Sec. 6501(g) by adding paragraph (3). **Effective** date is governed by the **effective** date for Code Sec. 992.

• **1958, Technical Amendments Act of 1958 (P.L. 85-866)**

P.L. 85-866, §81(a):

Amended Code Sec. 6501(g)(2) by striking out "corporation" each place it appeared and substituting "organization". The word "corporation" previously appeared in the 3rd and last lines. **Effective** 1-1-54.

[Sec. 6501(h)]

(h) NET OPERATING LOSS OR CAPITAL LOSS CARRYBACKS.—In the case of a deficiency attributable to the application to the taxpayer of a net operating loss carryback or a capital loss carryback (including deficiencies which may be assessed pursuant to the provisions of section 6213(b)(3)), such deficiency may be assessed at any time before the expiration of the period within which a deficiency for the taxable year of the net operating loss or net capital loss which results in such carryback may be assessed.

Amendments

• **1978, Revenue Act of 1978 (P.L. 95-600)**

P.L. 95-600, §§703(n), 703(p)(2):

Amended Code Sec. 6501(h) by changing "section 6213(b)(2)" to "section 6213(b)(3)" and by striking the last sentence. **Effective** 10-4-76. Prior to being stricken, the last sentence read as follows:

"In the case of a deficiency attributable to the application of a net operating loss carryback, such deficiency may be assessed within 18 months after the date on which the taxpayer files in accordance with section 172(b)(3) a copy of the certification (with respect to the taxable year of the net operating loss) issued under section 317 of the Trade Expansion Act of 1962, if later than the date prescribed by the preceding sentence."

• **1969, Tax Reform Act of 1969 (P.L. 91-172)**

P.L. 91-172, §512(e)(1):

Amended Code Sec. 6501(h) by adding "or Capital Loss" between "Loss" and "Carryback" in heading; by adding "or a capital loss carryback" after "loss carryback"; by adding "or net capital loss" between "net operating loss" and "which"; and by striking out all after "assessed, or within 18 months" and inserting above. **Effective** with respect to net capital losses sustained in tax years beginning after 12-31-69. Prior to amendment, Code Sec. 6501(h) read as follows:

"(h) Net Operating Loss Carrybacks.—In the case of a deficiency attributable to the application to the taxpayer of a net operating loss carryback (including deficiencies which may be assessed pursuant to the provisions of section 6213(b)(2)), such deficiency may be assessed at any time before the expiration of the period within which a deficiency for the taxable year of the net operating loss which results in such carryback may be assessed, or within 18 months after the date on which the taxpayer files in accordance with section 172(b)(3) a copy of the certification (with respect to such taxable year) issued under section 317 of the Trade Expansion Act of 1962, whichever is later."

• **1962, Trade Expansion Act of 1962 (P.L. 87-794)**

P.L. 87-794, §317(c):

Amended Code Sec. 6501(h). **Effective** with respect to net operating losses for tax years ending after 12-31-55. Prior to amendment, Code Sec. 6501(h) read as follows:

"(h) Net Operating Loss Carrybacks.—In the case of a deficiency attributable to the application to the taxpayer of a net operating loss carryback (including deficiencies which may be assessed pursuant to the provisions of section 6213(b)(2)), such deficiency may be assessed at any time before the expiration of the period within which a deficiency for the taxable year of the net operating loss which results in such carryback may be assessed."

• **1958, Technical Amendments Act of 1958 (P.L. 85-866)**

P.L. 85-866, §81(b):

Redesignated Sec. 6501(h) as Code Sec. 6501(i) (now (j)) and added new Sec. 6501(h). **Effective** 1-1-54.

[Sec. 6501(i)]

(i) FOREIGN TAX CARRYBACKS.—In the case of a deficiency attributable to the application to the taxpayer of a carryback under section 904(c) (relating to carryback and carryover of excess foreign taxes), or under section 907(f) (relating to carryback and carryover of disallowed foreign oil and gas taxes), such deficiency may be assessed at any time before the expiration of one year after the expiration of the period within which a deficiency may be assessed for the taxable year of the excess taxes described in section 904(c) or 907(f) which result in such carryback.

Amendments

• **2008, Energy Improvement and Extension Act of 2008 (P.L. 110-343)**

P.L. 110-343, Division B, §402(d):

Amended Code Sec. 6501(i) by striking "oil and gas extraction taxes" and inserting "foreign oil and gas taxes". **Effective** for tax years beginning after 12-31-2008.

• **1976, Tax Reform Act of 1976 (P.L. 94-455)**

P.L. 94-455, §1031(b)(5):

Substituted "section 904(c)" for "section 904(d)" each place it appeared in Code Sec. 6501(i). **Effective** for tax years beginning after 12-31-75.

LIMITATIONS—ASSESSMENT AND COLLECTION

P.L. 94-455, §1035(d)(3)(A):

Substituted "excess foreign taxes) or under section 907(f) (relating to carryback and carryover of disallowed oil and gas extraction taxes)" for "excess foreign taxes)" in Code Sec. 6501(i). **Effective** for taxes paid or accrued during tax years ending after 10-4-76.

P.L. 94-455, §1035(d)(3)(B):

Substituted "section 904(c) or 907(f)" for "section 904(c)" in the second place it appeared in Code Sec. 6501(i). **Effective** for taxes paid or accrued during tax years ending after 10-4-76.

- **1960 (P.L. 86-780)**

P.L. 86-780, §3(c):

Redesignated Sec. 6501(i) as Sec. 6501(j) and added a new Code Sec. 6501(i). **Effective** for tax years beginning after 12-31-57.

[Sec. 6501(j)]

(j) CERTAIN CREDIT CARRYBACKS.—

(1) IN GENERAL.—In the case of a deficiency attributable to the application to the taxpayer of a credit carryback (including deficiencies which may be assessed pursuant to the provisions of section 6213(b)(3)), such deficiency may be assessed at any time before the expiration of the period within which a deficiency for the taxable year of the unused credit which results in such carryback may be assessed, or with respect to any portion of a credit carryback from a taxable year attributable to a net operating loss carryback, capital loss carryback, or other credit carryback from a subsequent taxable year, at any time before the expiration of the period within which a deficiency for such subsequent taxable year may be assessed.

(2) CREDIT CARRYBACK DEFINED.—For purposes of this subsection, the term "credit carryback" has the meaning given such term by section 6511(d)(4)(C).

Amendments

- **1978 (P.L. 95-628)**

P.L. 95-628, §8(c)(1):

Amended Code Sec. 6501(j). **Effective** for carrybacks arising in tax years beginning after 11-10-78. Prior to amendment, Code Sec. 6501(j) read as follows:

"(j) INVESTMENT CREDIT CARRYBACKS.—In the case of a deficiency attributable to the application to the taxpayer of an investment credit carryback (including deficiencies which may be assessed pursuant to the provisions of section 6213(b)(3)), such deficiency may be assessed at any time before the expiration of the period within which a deficiency for the taxable year of the unused investment credit which results in such carryback may be assessed, or, with respect to any portion of an investment credit carryback from a taxable year attributable to a net operating loss carryback or a capital loss carryback from a subsequent taxable year, at any time before the expiration of the period within which a deficiency for such subsequent taxable year may be assessed."

- **1978, Revenue Act of 1978 (P.L. 95-600)**

P.L. 95-600, §703(n):

Amended Code Sec. 6501(j) by changing "section 6213(b)(2)" to "section 6213(b)(3)". **Effective** 10-4-76.

- **1969, Tax Reform Act of 1969 (P.L. 91-172)**

P.L. 91-172, §512(e)(1):

Amended Code Sec. 6501(j) by adding "or a capital loss carryback" after "loss carryback". **Effective** with respect to net capital losses sustained in tax years beginning after 12-31-69.

- **1967 (P.L. 90-225)**

P.L. 90-225, §2(c):

Amended Code Sec. 6501(j) by inserting at the end thereof the following: ", or, with respect to any portion of an investment credit carryback from a taxable year attributable to a net operating loss carryback from a subsequent taxable year, at any time before the expiration of the period within which a deficiency for such subsequent taxable year may be assessed". **Effective** with respect to investment credit carrybacks attributable to net operating loss carrybacks from tax years ending after 7-31-67.

- **1966 (P.L. 89-721)**

P.L. 89-721, §2(f):

Amended Code Sec. 6501(j) by inserting "(including deficiencies which may be assessed pursuant to the provisions of section 6213(b)(2))" immediately after "investment credit carryback". **Effective** for tax years ending after 12-31-61, but only in the case of applications filed after 11-2-66, the date of enactment.

- **1962, Revenue Act of 1962 (P.L. 87-834)**

P.L. 87-834, §2:

Redesignated Code Sec. 6501(j) as Code Sec. 6501(k) and added a new Code Sec. 6501(j). **Effective** for tax years ending after 12-31-61.

[Sec. 6501(k)]

(k) TENTATIVE CARRYBACK ADJUSTMENT ASSESSMENT PERIOD.—In a case where an amount has been applied, credited, or refunded under section 6411 (relating to tentative carryback and refund adjustments) by reason of a net operating loss carryback, a capital loss carryback, or a credit carryback, (as defined in section 6511(d)(4)(C)) to a prior taxable year, the period described in subsection (a) of this section for assessing a deficiency for such prior taxable year shall be extended to include the period described in subsection (h) or (j), whichever is applicable; except that the amount which may be assessed solely by reason of this subsection shall not exceed the amount so applied, credited, or refunded under section 6411, reduced by any amount which may be assessed solely by reason of subsection (h) or (j), as the case may be.

Amendments

- **1986, Tax Reform Act of 1986 (P.L. 99-514)**

P.L. 99-514, §1847(b)(14):

Amended Code Sec. 6501(k) by striking out "an investment credit carryback, or a work incentive program carryback, or a new employee credit carryback" and inserting in lieu thereof "or a credit carryback (as defined in section 6511(d)(4)(C))". **Effective** as if included in the provision of P.L. 98-369 to which it relates.

- **1984, Deficit Reduction Act of 1984 (P.L. 98-369)**

P.L. 98-369, §163(b)(1):

Redesignated Code Sec. 6501(m) as (k). **Effective** for expenditures with respect to which the second tax year described in Code Sec. 118(b)(2)(B) ends after 12-31-84.

P.L. 98-369, §211(b)(24)(B):

Repealed Code Sec. 6501(k). **Effective** for tax years beginning after 12-31-83. Prior to repeal, it read as follows:

(k) Reductions of Policyholders Surplus Account of Life Insurance Companies.—In the case of a deficiency attributable to the application to the taxpayer of section 815(d)(5) (relating to reductions of policyholders surplus account of life insurance companies for certain unused deductions), such deficiency may be assessed at any time before the expiration of the period within which a deficiency for the last taxable year to which the loss described in section 815(d)(5)(A) is carried under section 812(b)(2) may be assessed.

- **1978 (P.L. 95-628)**

P.L. 95-628, §8(b):

Amended Code Sec. 6501(m) by striking out "subsection (h), (j), (o), or (p)" each place it appeared and inserting in lieu thereof "subsection (h) or (j)". **Effective** for carrybacks arising in tax years beginning after 11-10-78.

- **1978, Revenue Act of 1978 (P.L. 95-600)**

P.L. 95-600, §504(b)(3):

Amended Code Sec. 6501(m) by inserting "and refund" after "carryback" the first place it appears. **Effective** for tentative refund claims filed on and after 11-6-78.

- **1977, Tax Reduction and Simplification Act of 1977 (P.L. 95-30)**

P.L. 95-30, §202(d)(5)(B):

Amended Code Sec. 6501(m) by substituting "a work incentive program carryback, or a new employee credit carryback" for "or a work incentive program carryback" and also substituting "(j), (o), or (p)" for "(j) or (o)". **Effective** for tax years beginning after 12-31-76, or for credit carrybacks from such years.

- **1971, Revenue Act of 1971 (P.L. 92-178)**

P.L. 92-178, §601(e)(2):

Amended Code Sec. 6501(m) by substituting "an investment credit carryback, or a work incentive program carryback" for "or an investment credit carryback" and by substituting "(h), (j), or (o)" for "(h) or (j)" in each of the two places such words appear. **Effective** for tax years beginning after 12-31-71.

- **1969, Tax Reform Act of 1969 (P.L. 91-172)**

P.L. 91-172, §512(e)(1):

Amended Code Sec. 6501(m) by adding ", a capital loss carryback," after "loss carryback". **Effective** with respect to net capital losses sustained in tax years beginning after 12-31-69.

LIMITATIONS—ASSESSMENT AND COLLECTION

• 1966 (P.L. 89-721)

P.L. 89-721, §3(a):

Added new Code Sec. 6501(m). **Effective** in any case where the application under Code Sec. 6411 is filed after 11-2-66.

• 1964 (P.L. 88-571)

P.L. 88-571, §3(b):

Amended Code Sec. 6501 by adding subsection (k), and by redesignating Subsection (k) as (l). **Effective** with respect to amounts added to policyholders surplus accounts for taxable years beginning after 12-31-58.

[Sec. 6501(l)]

(l) SPECIAL RULE FOR CHAPTER 42 AND SIMILAR TAXES.—

(1) IN GENERAL.—For purposes of any tax imposed by section 4912, by chapter 42 (other than section 4940) or by section 4975, the return referred to in this section shall be the return filed by the private foundation, plan, trust, or other organization (as the case may be) for the year in which the act (or failure to act) giving rise to liability for such tax occurred. For purposes of section 4940, such return is the return filed by the private foundation for the taxable year for which the tax is imposed.

(2) CERTAIN CONTRIBUTIONS TO SECTION 501(c)(3) ORGANIZATIONS.—In the case of a deficiency of tax of a private foundation making a contribution in the manner provided in section 4942(g)(3) (relating to certain contributions to section 501(c)(3) organizations) attributable to the failure of a section 501(c)(3) organization to make the distribution prescribed by section 4942(g)(3), such deficiency may be assessed at any time before the expiration of one year after the expiration of the period within which a deficiency may be assessed for the taxable year with respect to which the contribution was made.

(3) CERTAIN SET-ASIDES DESCRIBED IN SECTION 4942(g)(2).—In the case of a deficiency attributable to the failure of an amount set aside by a private foundation for a specific project to be treated as a qualifying distribution under the provisions of section 4942(g)(2)(B)(ii), such deficiency may be assessed at any time before the expiration of 2 years after the expiration of the period within which a deficiency may be assessed for the taxable year to which the amount set aside relates.

(4) INDIVIDUAL RETIREMENT PLANS.—

(A) IN GENERAL.—For purposes of any tax imposed by section 4973 or 4974 in connection with an individual retirement plan, the return referred to in this section shall include the income tax return filed by the person on whom the tax under such section is imposed for the year in which the act (or failure to act) giving rise to the liability for such tax occurred.

(B) RULE IN CASE OF INDIVIDUALS NOT REQUIRED TO FILE RETURN.—In the case of a person who is not required to file an income tax return for such year—

(i) the return referred to in this section shall be the income tax return that such person would have been required to file but for the fact that such person was not required to file such return, and

(ii) the 3-year period referred to in subsection (a) with respect to the return shall be deemed to begin on the date by which the return would have been required to be filed (excluding any extension thereof).

(C) PERIOD FOR ASSESSMENT IN CASE OF INCOME TAX RETURN.—In any case in which the return with respect to a tax imposed by section 4973 is the individual's income tax return for purposes of this section, subsection (a) shall be applied by substituting a 6-year period in lieu of the 3-year period otherwise referred to in such subsection.

(D) EXCEPTION FOR CERTAIN ACQUISITIONS OF PROPERTY.—In the case of any tax imposed by section 4973 that is attributable to acquiring property for less than fair market value, subparagraph (A) shall not apply.

Amendments

• 2022, SECURE 2.0 Act of 2022 (P.L. 117-328)

P.L. 117-328, §313(a):

Amended Code Sec. 6501(l) by adding at the end a new paragraph (4). **Effective** 12-29-2022.

• 1987, Revenue Act of 1987 (P.L. 100-203)

P.L. 100-203, §10712(c)(2):

Amended Code Sec. 6501(l)(1) by striking out "plan, or trust" and inserting in lieu thereof "plan, trust, or other organization." **Effective** for tax years beginning after 12-22-87.

P.L. 100-203, §10714(c):

Amended Code Sec. 6501(l)(1) by striking out "by chapter 42 (other than section 4940)" and inserting in lieu thereof "by section 4912, by chapter 42 (other than section 4940),". **Effective** for tax years beginning after 12-22-87.

• 1984, Deficit Reduction Act of 1984 (P.L. 98-369)

P.L. 98-369, §163(b)(1):

Amended Code Sec. 6501 by striking subsection (l) and redesignating subsection (n) as (l). **Effective** for expenditures with respect to which the second tax year described in Code Sec. 118(b)(2)(B) ends after 12-31-84. Prior to being stricken, subsection (l) read as follows:

(l) Joint Income Return After Separate Return.—For period of limitations for assessment and collection in the case of a joint income return filed after separate returns have been filed, see section 6013(b)(3) and (4).

P.L. 98-369, §314(a)(3):

Amended Code Sec. 6501(n)(3) [prior to its redesignation as (l)] by striking out "section 4942(g)(2)(B)(i)(II)" and inserting in lieu thereof "section 4942(g)(2)(B)(ii)".

• 1978, Black Lung Benefits Revenue Act of 1977 (P.L. 95-227)

P.L. 95-227, §4(d)(5):

Amended Code Sec. 6501(n) by adding "AND SIMILAR" in the heading and by substituting the first sentence for the following: "For purposes of any tax imposed by chapter 42 (other than section 4940), the return referred to in this section shall be the return filed by the private foundation for the year in which the act (or failure to act) giving rise to liability for such tax occurred." For **effective** date, see the historical comment for P.L. 95-227 under Code Sec. 4951.

• 1976, Tax Reform Act of 1976 (P.L. 94-455)

P.L. 94-455, §1302(b):

Added Code Sec. 6501(n)(3). **Effective** for tax years beginning after 12-31-74.

• 1969, Tax Reform Act of 1969 (P.L. 91-172)

P.L. 91-172, §101(g)(1):

Added Code Sec. 6501(n). **Effective** 1-1-70.

• 1964 (P.L. 88-571)

P.L. 88-571, §3(b):

Redesignated former Code Sec. 6501(k) as Sec. 6501(l).

• 1962, Revenue Act of 1962 (P.L. 87-834)

P.L. 87-834, §2:

Redesignated Code Sec. 6501(j) as 6501(k). **Effective** for tax years ending after 12-31-61.

• 1960 (P.L. 86-780)

P.L. 86-780, §3(c):

Redesignated Sec. 6501(i) as 6501(j). **Effective** for tax years beginning after 12-31-57.

• 1958, Technical Amendments Act of 1958 (P.L. 85-866)

P.L. 85-866, §81(b):

Redesignated Sec. 6501(h) as 6501(i). **Effective** 1-1-54.

[Sec. 6501(m)]

(m) DEFICIENCIES ATTRIBUTABLE TO ELECTION OF CERTAIN CREDITS.—The period for assessing a deficiency attributable to any election under section 30B(h)(9), 30C(e)(4), 30D(f)(6), 35(g)(11), 40(f), 43, 45B, 45C(d)(4), 45H(g), or 51(j) (or any revocation thereof) shall not expire before the date 1 year after the date on which the Secretary is notified of such election (or revocation).

Amendments

• 2022, Inflation Reduction Act of 2022 (P.L. 117-169)

P.L. 117-169, §13401(i)(5):

Amended Code Sec. 6501(m) by striking "30D(e)(4)" and inserting "30D(f)(6)". **Effective** for vehicles placed in service after 12-31-2022.

• 2018, Tax Technical Corrections Act of 2018 (P.L. 115-141)

P.L. 115-141, §401(a)(295), Div. U:

Amended Code Sec. 6501(m) by striking "any election" and all that follows through "(or any" and inserting "any election under section 30B(h)(9), 30C(e)(4), 30D(e)(4), 35(g)(11), 40(f), 43, 45B, 45C(d)(4), 45H(g), or 51(j) (or any". **Effective**

LIMITATIONS—ASSESSMENT AND COLLECTION

3-23-2018. Prior to being stricken, "any election" and all that follows through "(or any" read as follows:

any election under [section] 30B(h)(9), 30C(e)(5) [30C(e)(4)], 30D(e)(4), 35(g)(11), 40(f), 43, 45B, 45C(d)(4), 45H(g), 45S(h), or 51(j) (or any

- **2017, Tax Cuts and Jobs Act (P.L. 115-97)**

P.L. 115-97, §13403(d)(2):

Amended Code Sec. 6501(m) by inserting "45S(h)," after "45H(g),". **Effective** for wages paid in tax years beginning after 12-31-2017.

- **2015, Trade Adjustment Assistance Reauthorization Act of 2015 (P.L. 114-27)**

P.L. 114-27, §407(e):

Amended Code Sec. 6501(m) by inserting ", 35(g)(11)" after "30D(e)(4)". **Effective** generally for coverage months in tax years beginning after 12-31-2013. For a transition rule, see Act Sec. 407(f)(3), below.

P.L. 114-27, §407(f)(3), provides:

(3) TRANSITION RULE.—Notwithstanding section 35(g)(11)(B)(i) of the Internal Revenue Code of 1986 (as added by this title), an election to apply section 35 of such Code to an eligible coverage month (as defined in section 35(b) of such Code) (and not to claim the credit under section 36B of such Code with respect to such month) in a taxable year beginning after December 31, 2013, and before the date of the enactment of this Act—

(A) may be made at any time on or after such date of enactment and before the expiration of the 3-year period of limitation prescribed in section 6511(a) with respect to such taxable year; and

(B) may be made on an amended return.

- **2014, Tax Technical Corrections Act of 2014 (P.L. 113-295)**

P.L. 113-295, §221(a)(2)(E), Division A:

Amended Code Sec. 6501(m) by striking "section 30(e)(6)," before "30B(h)(9),". **Effective** generally 12-19-2014. For a special rule, see Act Sec. 221(b)(2), Division A, below.

P.L. 113-295, §221(b)(2), Division A, provides:

(2) SAVINGS PROVISION.—If—

(A) any provision amended or repealed by the amendments made by this section applied to—

(i) any transaction occurring before the date of the enactment of this Act,

(ii) any property acquired before such date of enactment, or

(iii) any item of income, loss, deduction, or credit taken into account before such date of enactment, and

(B) the treatment of such transaction, property, or item under such provision would (without regard to the amendments or repeals made by this section) affect the liability for tax for periods ending after date of enactment, nothing in the amendments or repeals made by this section shall be construed to affect the treatment of such transaction, property, or item for purposes of determining liability for tax for periods ending after such date of enactment.

- **2009, American Recovery and Reinvestment Tax Act of 2009 (P.L. 111-5)**

P.L. 111-5, §1141(b)(4):

Amended Code Sec. 6501(m) by striking "section [sic] 30D(e)(9)" and inserting "section [sic] 30D(e)(4)". **Effective** for vehicles acquired after 12-31-2009.

P.L. 111-5, §1142(b)(7):

Amended Code Sec. 6501(m) by striking "section 30(d)(4)" and inserting "section 30(e)(6)". **Effective** for vehicles acquired after 2-17-2009. For a transitional rule, see Act Sec. 1142(d) in the amendment notes for Code Sec. 30.

- **2008, Energy Improvement and Extension Act of 2008 (P.L. 110-343)**

P.L. 110-343, Division B, §205(d)(3):

Amended Code Sec. 6501(m) by inserting "30D(e)(9)," after "30C(e)(5),". **Effective** for tax years beginning after 12-31-2008.

[Sec. 6501(m)—Stricken]

Amendments

- **1996, Small Business Job Protection Act of 1996 (P.L. 104-188)**

P.L. 104-188, §1702(e)(3)(A):

Amended Code Sec. 6501 by striking subsection (m) and by redesignating subsections (n) and (o) as subsections (m) and (n), respectively. [Note: Code Sec. 6501(m) was already stricken by P.L. 100-418, applicable to crude oil removed from the premises on or after August 23, 1988.—CCH.] **Effective** as if included in the provision of P.L. 101-508 to which it relates.

- **1988, Omnibus Trade and Competitiveness Act of 1988 (P.L. 100-418)**

P.L. 100-418, §1941(b)(2)(H):

Amended Code Sec. 6501 by striking subsection (m). **Effective** for crude oil removed from the premises on or after 8-23-88. Prior to amendment, Code Sec. 6501(m) read as follows:

(m) SPECIAL RULES FOR WINDFALL PROFIT TAX—

(1) OIL SUBJECT TO WITHHOLDING.—

(A) IN GENERAL.—In the case of any oil to which section 4995(a) applies and with respect to which no return is required, the return referred to in this section shall be the return (of the person liable for the tax imposed by section 4986) of the taxes imposed by subtitle A for the taxable year in which the removal year ends.

(B) REMOVAL YEAR.—For purposes of subparagraph (A), the term "removal year" means the calendar year in which the oil is removed from the premises.

(2) EXTENSION OF LIABILITY ATTRIBUTABLE TO DOE RECLASSIFICATION.—

- **2007, Tax Technical Corrections Act of 2007 (P.L. 110-172)**

P.L. 110-172, §7(a)(2)(B):

Amended Code Sec. 6501(m) by inserting "45H(g)," after "45C(d)(4),". **Effective** as if included in the provision of the American Jobs Creation Act of 2004 (P.L. 108-357) to which it relates [effective for expenses paid or incurred after 12-31-2002, in tax years ending after such date.—CCH].

- **2005, Energy Tax Incentives Act of 2005 (P.L. 109-58)**

P.L. 109-58, §1341(b)(4):

Amended Code Sec. 6501(m) by inserting "30B(h)(9)," after "30(d)(4),". **Effective** for property placed in service after 12-31-2005, in tax years ending after such date.

P.L. 109-58, §1342(b)(4):

Amended Code Sec. 6501(m) by inserting "30C(e)(5)," after "30B(h)(9),". **Effective** for property placed in service after 12-31-2005, in tax years ending after such date.

- **1998, IRS Restructuring and Reform Act of 1998 (P.L. 105-206)**

P.L. 105-206, §6023(27):

Amended Code Sec. 6501(m) by striking "election under" and all that follows through "(or any" and inserting "election under section 30(d)(4), 40(f), 43, 45B, 45C(d)(4), or 51(j) (or any". **Effective** 7-22-98. Prior to amendment, Code Sec. 6501(m) read as follows:

(m) DEFICIENCIES ATTRIBUTABLE TO ELECTION OF CERTAIN CREDITS.—The period for assessing a deficiency attributable to any election under section 30(d)(4), 40(f), 43, 45B, or 51(j) (or any revocation thereof) shall not expire before the date 1 year after the date on which the Secretary is notified of such election (or revocation).

- **1996, Small Business Job Protection Act of 1996 (P.L. 104-188)**

P.L. 104-188, §1702(e)(3)(A):

Amended Code Sec. 6501 by striking subsection (m) and by redesignating subsections (n) and (o) as subsections (m) and (n), respectively. **Effective** as if included in the provision of P.L. 101-508 to which it relates.

P.L. 104-188, §1702(e)(3)(B):

Amended Code Sec. 6501(m), as redesignated by Act Sec. 1702(e)(3)(A), by striking "section 40(f) or 51(j)" and inserting "section 40(f), 43, or 51(j)". **Effective** as if included in the provision of P.L. 101-508 to which it relates.

P.L. 104-188, §1703(n)(8):

Amended Code Sec. 6501(m), as redesignated by Act Sec. 1702(e)(3)(A), by striking "or 51(j)" and inserting "45B, or 51(j)". **Effective** as if included in the provision of P.L. 103-66 to which it relates.

P.L. 104-188, §1704(j)(4)(B):

Amended Code Sec. 6501(m), as redesignated by Act Sec. 1703(e)(3)(A), by striking "section 40(f)" and inserting "section 30(d)(4), 40(f)". **Effective** 8-20-96.

- **1989, Omnibus Budget Reconciliation Act of 1989 (P.L. 101-239)**

P.L. 101-239, §7814(e)(2)(E):

Amended Code Sec. 6501(n) by striking ", 41(h)," after "40(f)". **Effective** as if included in the provision of P.L. 100-647 to which it relates.

- **1988, Technical and Miscellaneous Revenue Act of 1988 (P.L. 100-647)**

P.L. 100-647, §4008(c)(2):

Amended Code Sec. 6501(n) by striking out "or 51(j)" and inserting in lieu thereof ", 41(h), or 51(j)". **Effective** for tax years beginning after 12-31-88.

- **1986, Tax Reform Act of 1986 (P.L. 99-514)**

P.L. 99-514, §1847(b)(13):

Amended Code Sec. 6501 by redesignating subsection (n) as subsection (o) and by inserting after subsection (m) new subsection (n). **Effective** as if included in the provision of P.L. 98-369 to which it relates.

(A) IN GENERAL.—In the case of the tax imposed by chapter 45, if a Department of Energy change becomes final, the period for assessing any deficiency attributable to such change shall not expire before the date which is 1 year after the date on which such change becomes final.

(B) DEPARTMENT OF ENERGY CHANGE.—For purposes of subparagraph (A) and section 6511(h)(2), the term "Department of Energy change" means any change by the Department of Energy in the classification under the June 1979 energy regulations (as defined in section 4996(b)(8)(C)) of a property or of domestic crude oil from a property.

(3) CROSS REFERENCE.—

For extension of period for windfall profit tax items of partnerships, see section 6229 as made applicable by section 6232.

- **1984, Deficit Reduction Act of 1984 (P.L. 98-369)**

P.L. 98-369, §163(b)(1):

Redesignated Code Sec. 6501(p) as (m). **Effective** for expenditures with respect to which the second tax year described in Code Sec. 118(b)(2)(B) ends after 12-31-84.

P.L. 98-369, §474(r)(39):

Amended Code Sec. 6501 by striking out subsection (p) and by redesignating subsection (q) as subsection (p). **Effective** for tax years beginning after 12-31-83, and to carrybacks from such years. Prior to amendment, subsection (p) read as follows:

(p) DEFICIENCY ATTRIBUTABLE TO ELECTION UNDER SECTION 43 OR 44B.—The period for assessing a deficiency attributable to any election under section 43 or 44B (or any

LIMITATIONS—ASSESSMENT AND COLLECTION

revocation thereof) shall not expire before the date 1 year after the date on which the Secretary is notified of such election (or revocation).

P.L. 98-369, §714(p)(2)(F):

Amended Code Sec. 6501(q)(3) (prior to redesignation by Act Secs. 163(b)(1) and 474(r)(39)). **Effective** as if included in the provision of P.L. 97-248 to which it relates. Prior to amendment, Code Sec. 6501(q)(3) read as follows:

(3) PARTNERSHIP ITEMS OF FEDERALLY REGISTERED PARTNERSHIPS.—Under regulations prescribed by the Secretary, rules similar to the rules of subsection (o) shall apply to the tax imposed by section 4986.

- **1990, Omnibus Budget Reconciliation Act of 1990 (P.L. 101-508)**

P.L. 101-508, §11511(c)(2):

Amended Code Sec. 6501(m)[p] by striking "44B" each place it appears and inserting "43 or 44B". **Effective** for costs paid or incurred in tax years beginning after 12-31-90.

- **1980, Crude Oil Windfall Profit Tax Act of 1980 (P.L. 96-223)**

P.L. 96-223, §101(g)(1):

Added Code Sec. 6501(q). For the **effective** date and transitional rules, see P.L. 96-223, §101(i), following Code Sec. 4986.

- **1980, Technical Corrections Act of 1979 (P.L. 96-222)**

P.L. 96-222, §103(a)(6)(G)(x):

Redesignated Act Sec. 6501(q) as (p). **Effective** for amounts paid or incurred after 12-31-78, in tax years ending after such date.

[Sec. 6501(n)]

(n) CROSS REFERENCES.—For period of limitations for assessment and collection in the case of a joint income return filed after separate returns have been filed, see section 6013(b)(3) and (4).

Amendments

- **2015, Bipartisan Budget Act of 2015 (P.L. 114-74)**

P.L. 114-74, §1101(f)(3):

Amended Code Sec. 6501(n) by striking paragraphs (2)-(3) and by striking "CROSS REFERENCES" and all that follows through "For period of limitations" and inserting "CROSS REFERENCE.—For period of limitations". **Effective** generally for returns filed for partnership tax years beginning after 12-31-2017. For a special rule, see Act Sec. 1101(g)(4), below. Prior to amendment, Code Sec. 6501(n) read as follows:

(n) CROSS REFERENCES.—

(1) For period of limitations for assessment and collection in the case of a joint income return filed after separate returns have been filed, see section 6013(b)(3) and (4).

(2) For extension of period in the case of partnership items (as defined in section 6231(a)(3)), see section 6229.

(3) For declaratory judgment relating to treatment of items other than partnership items with respect to an oversheltered return, see section 6234.

P.L. 114-74, §1101(g)(4), provides:

(4) ELECTION.—A partnership may elect (at such time and in such form and manner as the Secretary of the Treasury may prescribe) for the amendments made by this section (other than the election under section 6221(b) of such Code (as added by this Act)) to apply to any return of the partnership filed for partnership taxable years beginning after the date of the enactment of this Act and before January 1, 2018.

- **1997, Taxpayer Relief Act of 1997 (P.L. 105-34)**

P.L. 105-34, §1239(e)(2):

Amended Code Sec. 6501(o)[(n)] by adding at the end a new paragraph (3). **Effective** for partnership tax years ending after 8-5-97.

- **1996, Small Business Job Protection Act of 1996 (P.L. 104-188)**

P.L. 104-188, §1702(e)(3)(A):

Amended Code Sec. 6501 by redesignating subsection (o) as subsection (n). **Effective** as if included in the provision of P.L. 101-508 to which it relates.

- **1988, Technical and Miscellaneous Revenue Act of 1988 (P.L. 100-647)**

P.L. 100-647, §1008(j)(1):

Amended Code Sec. 6501(o) by striking out paragraph (3). **Effective** as if included in the provision of P.L. 99-514 to which it relates. Prior to amendment, Code Sec. 6501(o)(3) read as follows:

(3) For extension of period in the case of certain contributions in aid of construction, see section 118(c).

- **1986, Tax Reform Act of 1986 (P.L. 99-514)**

P.L. 99-514, §1847(b)(13):

Amended Code Sec. 6501 by redesignating subsection (n) as subsection (o). **Effective** as if included in the provision of P.L. 98-369 to which it relates.

- **1984, Deficit Reduction Act of 1984 (P.L. 98-369)**

P.L. 98-369, §163(b)(1):

Amended Code Sec. 6501 by striking out subsection (o), and by inserting after subsection (m) a new subsection (n). **Effective** for expenditures with respect to which the second tax year described in Code Sec. 118(b)(2)(B) ends after 12-31-84. Prior to being stricken, Code Sec. 6501(o) read as follows:

(o) SPECIAL RULES FOR PARTNERSHIP ITEMS.—For extension of period in the case of partnership items (as defined in section 6231(a)(3)), see section 6229.

- **1978, Revenue Act of 1978 (P.L. 95-600)**

P.L. 95-600, §321(b)(2):

Added Code Sec. 6501(q) [6501(r)]. **Effective** for amounts paid or incurred after 12-31-78, in tax years ending after such date.

- **1978 (P.L. 95-628)**

P.L. 95-628, §8(b):

Repealed Code Sec. 6501(p). **Effective** for carrybacks arising in tax years beginning after 11-10-78. Prior to repeal, Code Sec. 6501(p) read as follows:

"(p) NEW EMPLOYEE CREDIT CARRYBACKS.—In the case of a deficiency attributable to the application to the taxpayer of a new employee credit carryback (including deficiencies which may be assessed pursuant to the provisions of section 6213(b)(3)), such deficiency may be assessed at any time before the expiration of the period within which a deficiency for the taxable year of the unused new employee credit which results in such carryback may be assessed, or, with respect to any portion of a new employee credit carryback from a taxable year attributable to a net operating loss carryback, an investment credit carryback, a work incentive program credit carryback, or a capital loss carryback from a subsequent taxable year, at any time before the expiration of the period within which a deficiency for such subsequent taxable year may be assessed."

- **1977, Tax Reduction and Simplification Act of 1977 (P.L. 95-30)**

P.L. 95-30, §202(d)(4)(A):

Added Code Sec. 6501(p). **Effective** for tax years beginning after 12-31-76, and for credit carrybacks from such years.

- **1982, Tax Equity and Fiscal Responsibility Act of 1982 (P.L. 97-248)**

P.L. 97-248, §402(c)(5):

Amended Code Sec. 6501(o). **Effective** for partnership tax years beginning after 9-3-82, and also to partnership tax years ending after 9-3-82, if the partnership, each partner, and each indirect partner requests such application and the Secretary or his delegate consents to such application. Prior to amendment, Code Sec. 6501(o) read as follows:

"(o) SPECIAL RULES FOR PARTNERSHIP ITEMS OF FEDERALLY REGISTERED PARTNERSHIPS.—

(1) IN GENERAL.—In the case of any tax imposed by subtitle A with respect to any person, the period for assessing a deficiency attributable to any partnership item of a federally registered partnership shall not expire before the later of—

(A) the date which is 4 years after the date on which the partnership return of the federally registered partnership for the partnership taxable year in which the item arose was filed (or, later, if the date prescribed for filing the return), or

(B) if the name or address of such person does not appear on the partnership return, the date which is 1 year after the date on which such information is furnished to the Secretary in such manner and at such place as he may prescribe by regulations.

(2) PARTNERSHIP ITEM DEFINED.—For purposes of this subsection, the term `partnership item' means—

(A) any item required to be taken into account for the partnership taxable year under any provision of subchapter K of chapter 1 to the extent that regulations prescribed by the Secretary provide that for purposes of this subtitle such item is more appropriately determined at the partnership level than at the partner level, and

(B) any other item to the extent affected by an item described in subparagraph (A).

(3) EXTENSION BY AGREEMENT.—The extensions referred to in subsection (c)(4), insofar as they relate to partnership items, may, with respect to any person, be consented to—

(A) except to the extent the Secretary is otherwise notified by the partnership, by a general partner of the partnership, or

(B) by any person authorized to do so by the partnership in writing.

(4) FEDERALLY REGISTERED PARTNERSHIP.—For purposes of this subsection, the term `federally registered partnership' means, with respect to any partnership taxable year, any partnership—

(A) interests in which have been offered for sale at any time during such taxable year or a prior taxable year in any offering required to be registered with the Securities and Exchange Commission, or

(B) which, at any time during such taxable year or a prior taxable year, was subject to the annual reporting requirements of the Securities and Exchange Commission which relate to the protection of investors in the partnership."

- **1980, Technical Corrections Act of 1979 (P.L. 96-222)**

P.L. 96-222, §102(a)(2)(A):

Redesignated Code Sec. 6501(q) as (o). **Effective** for partnership items arising in partnership tax years beginning after 12-31-78.

- **1978 (P.L. 95-628)**

P.L. 95-628, §8(b):

Repealed Code Sec. 6501(o). **Effective** for carrybacks arising in tax years beginning after 11-10-78. Prior to repeal, Code Sec. 6501(o) read as follows:

(o) WORK INCENTIVE PROGRAM CREDIT CARRYBACKS.—In the case of a deficiency attributable to the application to the taxpayer of a work incentive program credit carryback (including deficiencies which may be assessed pursuant to the provisions of section 6213(b)(3)), such deficiency may be assessed at any time before the expiration of the period within which a deficiency for the taxable year of the unused work incentive program credit which results in such carryback may be assessed, or, with respect to any portion of a work incentive program credit carryback from a taxable year attributable to a net operating loss carryback, an investment credit carryback, or a capital loss carryback from a subsequent taxable year, at any time before the expiration of the period within which a deficiency for such subsequent taxable year may be assessed.

• **1978, Revenue Act of 1978 (P.L. 95-600)**

P.L. 95-600, §212(a):

Added Code Sec. 6501(q). **Effective** for partnership items arising in partnership tax years beginning after 12-31-78.

P.L. 95-600, §703(n):

Amended Code Sec. 6501(o) by changing "section 6213(b)(2)" to "section 6213(b)(3)". **Effective** 10-4-76.

• **1976, Tax Reform Act of 1976 (P.L. 94-455)**

P.L. 94-455, §2107(g)(2):

Inserted ", an investment credit carryback," after "net operating loss carryback" in Code Sec. 6501(o). **Effective** 10-4-76.

• **1971, Revenue Act of 1971 (P.L. 92-178)**

P.L. 92-178, §601(d)(1):

Added Code Sec. 6501(o). **Effective** for tax years beginning after 12-31-71.

[Sec. 6502]

SEC. 6502. COLLECTION AFTER ASSESSMENT.

[Sec. 6502(a)]

(a) LENGTH OF PERIOD.—Where the assessment of any tax imposed by this title has been made within the period of limitation properly applicable thereto, such tax may be collected by levy or by a proceeding in court, but only if the levy is made or the proceeding begun—

(1) within 10 years after the assessment of the tax, or

(2) if—

(A) there is an installment agreement between the taxpayer and the Secretary, prior to the date which is 90 days after the expiration of any period for collection agreed upon in writing by the Secretary and the taxpayer at the time the installment agreement was entered into; or

(B) there is a release of levy under section 6343 after such 10-year period, prior to the expiration of any period for collection agreed upon in writing by the Secretary and the taxpayer before such release.

If a timely proceeding in court for the collection of a tax is commenced, the period during which such tax may be collected by levy shall be extended and shall not expire until the liability for the tax (or a judgment against the taxpayer arising from such liability) is satisfied or becomes unenforceable.

Amendments

• **1998, IRS Restructuring and Reform Act of 1998 (P.L. 105-206)**

P.L. 105-206, §3461(a)(1)-(2):

Amended Code Sec. 6502(a) by striking paragraph (2) and inserting a new paragraph (2), and by striking the first sentence in the matter following paragraph (2). **Effective** for requests to extend the period of limitations made after 12-31-99. For a special rule, see Act Sec. 3461(c)(2), below. Prior to amendment, Code Sec. 6502(a)(2) and the first sentence in the matter following paragraph (2) read as follows:

(2) prior to the expiration of any period for collection agreed upon in writing by the Secretary and the taxpayer before the expiration of such 10-year period (or, if there is a release of levy under section 6343 after such 10-year period, then before such release).

The period so agreed upon may be extended by subsequent agreements in writing made before the expiration of the period previously agreed upon.

P.L. 105-206, §3461(c)(2), provides:

(2) PRIOR REQUEST.—If, in any request to extend the period of limitations made on or before December 31, 1999, a taxpayer agreed to extend such period beyond the 10-year period referred to in section 6502(a) of the Internal Revenue Code of 1986, such extension shall expire on the latest of—

(A) the last day of such 10-year period;

(B) December 31, 2002; or

(C) in the case of an extension in connection with an installment agreement, the 90th day after the end of the period of such extension.

• **1990, Omnibus Budget Reconciliation Act of 1990 (P.L. 101-508)**

P.L. 101-508, §11317(a)(1):

Amended Code Sec. 6502(a) by striking "6 years" in paragraph (1) and inserting "10 years" and by striking "6-year period" each place it appears in paragraph (2) and inserting "10-year period". For the **effective** date, see Act Sec. 11317(c), below.

P.L. 101-508, §11317(c), provides:

(c) EFFECTIVE DATE.—The amendments made by this section shall apply to—

(1) taxes assessed after the date of the enactment of this Act, and

(2) taxes assessed on or before such date if the period specified in section 6502 of the Internal Revenue Code of 1986 (determined without regard to the amendments made by subsection (a)) for collection of such taxes has not expired as of such date.

• **1989, Omnibus Budget Reconciliation Act of 1989 (P.L. 101-239)**

P.L. 101-239, §7811(k)(2):

Amended Code Sec. 6502(a) by striking "enforceable" and inserting "unenforceable" in the last sentence. **Effective** as if included in the provision of P.L. 100-647 to which it relates.

• **1988, Technical and Miscellaneous Revenue Act of 1988 (P.L. 100-647)**

P.L. 100-647, §1015(u)(1):

Amended the last sentence of Code Sec. 6502(a). **Effective** for levies issued after 11-10-88. Prior to amendment, the last sentence read as follows:

The period provided by this subsection during which a tax may be collected by levy shall not be extended or curtailed by reason of a judgment against the taxpayer.

• **1976, Tax Reform Act of 1976 (P.L. 94-455)**

P.L. 94-455, §1906(b)(13)(A):

Amended 1954 Code by substituting "Secretary" for "Secretary or his delegate" each place it appeared. **Effective** 2-1-77.

• **1966, Federal Tax Lien Act of 1966 (P.L. 89-719)**

P.L. 89-719, §113(b):

Amended Code Sec. 6502(a) by adding the last sentence. **Effective**, generally, after 11-2-66. However, see the amendment note for Code Sec. 6323 for exceptions to this **effective** date.

[Sec. 6502(b)]

(b) DATE WHEN LEVY IS CONSIDERED MADE.—The date on which a levy on property or rights to property is made shall be the date on which the notice of seizure provided in section 6335(a) is given.

[Sec. 6503]

SEC. 6503. SUSPENSION OF RUNNING OF PERIOD OF LIMITATION.

[Sec. 6503(a)]

(a) ISSUANCE OF STATUTORY NOTICE OF DEFICIENCY.—

(1) GENERAL RULE.—The running of the period of limitations provided in section 6501 or 6502 on the making of assessments or the collection by levy or a proceeding in court, in respect of any deficiency as defined in section 6211 (relating to income, estate, gift and certain excise taxes), shall (after the mailing of a notice under section 6212(a)) be suspended for the period during which the Secretary is prohibited from making the assessment or from collecting by levy or a proceeding in court (and in any event, if a proceeding in respect of the deficiency is placed on the docket of the Tax Court, until the decision of the Tax Court becomes final), and for 60 days thereafter.

(2) CORPORATION JOINING IN CONSOLIDATED INCOME TAX RETURN.—If a notice under section 6212(a) in respect of a deficiency in tax imposed by subtitle A for any taxable year is mailed to a corporation, the suspension of the running of the period of limitations provided in paragraph (1) of this subsection shall apply in the case of corporations with which such corporation made a consolidated income tax return for such taxable year.

LIMITATIONS—ASSESSMENT AND COLLECTION

Amendments

• **2018, Tax Technical Corrections Act of 2018 (P.L. 115-141)**

P.L. 115-141, §401(a)(296), Div. U:

Amended Code Sec. 6503(a)(1) by striking "section 6230(a)." and inserting "section 6230(a))". **Effective** 3-23-2018. [Note: This amendment cannot be made to the version of Code Sec. 6503(a)(1) in effect 3-23-2018.—CCH.]

• **2015, Bipartisan Budget Act of 2015 (P.L. 114-74)**

P.L. 114-74, §1101(f)(4):

Amended Code Sec. 6503(a)(1) by striking "(or section 6229" and all that follows through "of section 6230(a))" following "or 6502". **Effective** generally for returns filed for partnership tax years beginning after 12-31-2017. For a special rule, see Act Sec. 1101(g)(4), below. Prior to being stricken, "(or section 6229" and all that follows through "of section 6230(a))" read as follows:

(or section 6229, but only with respect to a deficiency described in paragraph (2)(A) or (3) of section 6230(a))

P.L. 114-74, §1101(g)(4), provides:

(4) ELECTION.—A partnership may elect (at such time and in such form and manner as the Secretary of the Treasury may prescribe) for the amendments made by this section (other than the election under section 6221(b) of such Code (as added by this Act)) to apply to any return of the partnership filed for partnership taxable years beginning after the date of the enactment of this Act and before January 1, 2018.

• **1997, Taxpayer Relief Act of 1997 (P.L. 105-34)**

P.L. 105-34, §1237(c)(2):

Amended Code Sec. 6503(a)(1) by striking "section 6230(a)(2)(A)" and inserting "paragraph (2)(A) or (3) of section 6230(a)". **Effective** as if included in the amendments made by section 402 of P.L. 97-248 [generally effective for partnership tax years beginning after 9-3-82.—CCH].

• **1986, Tax Reform Act of 1986 (P.L. 99-514)**

P.L. 99-514, §1875(d)(2)(B)(ii):

Amended Code Sec. 6503(a)(1) by striking out "section 6501 or 6502" and inserting in lieu thereof "section 6501 or 6502 (or section 6229, but only with respect to a deficiency described in section 6230(a)(2)(A))." **Effective** as if included in P.L. 97-248.

• **1976, Tax Reform Act of 1976 (P.L. 94-455)**

P.L. 94-455, §1906(b)(13)(A):

Amended 1954 Code by substituting "Secretary" for "Secretary or his delegate" each place it appeared. **Effective** 2-1-77.

• **1974, Employee Retirement Income Security Act of 1974 (P.L. 93-406)**

P.L. 93-406, §1016(a)(15):

Amended Code Sec. 6503(a)(1) by changing "chapter 42 taxes" to "certain excise taxes". For **effective** date, see amendment note for Code Sec. 410.

• **1969, Tax Reform Act of 1969 (P.L. 91-172)**

P.L. 91-172, §101(j)(46):

Amended Code Sec. 6503(a)(1) by substituting "gift and chapter 42 taxes" for "and gift taxes". **Effective** 1-1-70.

[Sec. 6503(b)]

(b) ASSETS OF TAXPAYER IN CONTROL OR CUSTODY OF COURT.—The period of limitations on collection after assessment prescribed in section 6502 shall be suspended for the period the assets of the taxpayer are in the control or custody of the court in any proceeding before any court of the United States or of any State or of the District of Columbia, and for 6 months thereafter.

Amendments

• **1966, Federal Tax Lien Act of 1966 (P.L. 89-719)**

P.L. 89-719, §106(a):

Amended Code Sec. 6503(b) by striking out "(other than the estate of a decedent or of an incompetent)" and "or Territory". **Effective**, generally, after 11-2-66. However, see the amendment note for Code Sec. 6323 for exceptions to this **effective** date.

[Sec. 6503(c)]

(c) TAXPAYER OUTSIDE UNITED STATES.—The running of the period of limitations on collection after assessment prescribed in section 6502 shall be suspended for the period during which the taxpayer is outside the United States if such period of absence is for a continuous period of at least 6 months. If the preceding sentence applies and at the time of the taxpayer's return to the United States the period of limitations on collection after assessment prescribed in section 6502 would expire before the expiration of 6 months from the date of his return, such period shall not expire before the expiration of such 6 months.

Amendments

• **1966, Federal Tax Lien Act of 1966 (P.L. 89-719)**

P.L. 89-719, §106(b):

Amended Code Sec. 6503(c). **Effective**, generally, after 11-2-66. However, see the amendment note for Code Sec. 6323 for exceptions to this **effective** date. Prior to amendment, Code Sec. 6503(c) read as follows:

"(c) Location of Property Outside the United States or Removal of Property From the United States.—In case collection is hindered or delayed because property of the taxpayer is situated or held outside the United States or is removed from the United States, the period of limitations on collection after assessment prescribed in section 6502 shall be suspended for the period collection is so hindered or delayed. The total suspension of time under this subsection shall not in the aggregate exceed 6 years."

[Sec. 6503(d)]

(d) EXTENSIONS OF TIME FOR PAYMENT OF ESTATE TAX.—The running of the period of limitations for collection of any tax imposed by chapter 11 shall be suspended for the period of any extension of time for payment granted under the provisions of section 6161(a)(2) or (b)(2) or under provisions of section 6163, or 6166.

Amendments

• **1981, Economic Recovery Tax Act of 1981 (P.L. 97-34)**

P.L. 97-34, §422(e)(7):

Amended Code Sec. 6503(d) by striking out "6163, 6166, or 6166A" and inserting "6163, or 6166". **Effective** for estates of decedents dying after 12-31-81.

• **1976, Tax Reform Act of 1976 (P.L. 94-455)**

P.L. 94-455, §2004(c)(4):

Substituted "section 6163, 6166, or 6166A" for "section 6166" in Code Sec. 6503(d). **Effective** for estates of decedents dying after 12-31-76.

• **1958, Technical Amendments Act of 1958 (P.L. 85-866)**

P.L. 85-866, §206(d):

Amended Sec. 6503(d) by striking out "assessment or" where it preceded the word "collection", and by adding, before the period at the end thereof, the following: "or under the provisions of section 6166". For the **effective** date, see Act Sec. 206(f), below.

P.L. 85-866, §206(f), provides:

"The amendments made by this section shall apply to estates of decedents with respect to which the date for the filing of the estate tax return (including extensions thereof) prescribed by section 6075(a) of the Internal Revenue Code of 1954 is after the date of the enactment of this Act; except that (1) section 6166(i) of such Code as added by this section shall apply to estates of decedents dying after August 16, 1954, but only if the date for the filing of the estate tax return (including extensions thereof) expired on or before the date of the enactment of this Act, and (2) notwithstanding section 6166(a) of such Code, if an election under such section is required to be made before the sixtieth day after the date of the enactment of this Act such an election shall be considered timely if made on or before such sixtieth day."

[Sec. 6503(e)]

(e) EXTENSIONS OF TIME FOR PAYMENT OF TAX ATTRIBUTABLE TO RECOVERIES OF FOREIGN EXPROPRIATION LOSSES.—The running of the period of limitations for collection of the tax attributable to a recovery of a foreign expropriation loss (within the meaning of section 6167(f)) shall be suspended for the period of any extension of time for payment under subsection (a) or (b) of section 6167.

Amendments

• **1976, Tax Reform Act of 1976 (P.L. 94-455)**

P.L. 94-455, §1902(b)(2)(A):

Deleted subsection (e) and renumbered subsection (f) as Code Sec. 6503(e). **Effective** in the case of estates of decedents dying after 10-4-76. Prior to deletion Code Sec. 6503(e) read as follows:

"(e) CERTAIN POWERS OF APPOINTMENT.—The running of the period of limitations for assessment or collection of any tax imposed by chapter 11 shall be suspended in respect of the estate of a decedent claiming a deduction under section 2055(b)(2) until 30 days after the expiration of the period for assessment or collection of the tax imposed by chapter 11 on the estate of the surviving spouse.

LIMITATIONS—ASSESSMENT AND COLLECTION

• 1966 (P.L. 89-384)

P.L. 89-384, §1(e):

Added Code Sec. 6503(f) and redesignated former Sec. 6503(f) as Sec. 6503(g). **Effective** with respect to amounts received after 12-31-64, in respect of foreign expropriation losses sustained after 12-31-58.

• 1956 (P.L. 1011, 84th Cong.)

P.L. 1011, 84th Cong., §2:

Added Code Sec. 6503(e). **Effective** for decedents dying after 8-16-54.

[Sec. 6503(f)]

(f) WRONGFUL SEIZURE OF OR LIEN ON PROPERTY OF THIRD PARTY.—

(1) WRONGFUL SEIZURE.—The running of the period under section 6502 shall be suspended for a period equal to the period from the date property (including money) of a third party is wrongfully seized or received by the Secretary to the date the Secretary returns property pursuant to section 6343(b) or the date on which a judgment secured pursuant to section 7426 with respect to such property becomes final, and for 30 days thereafter. The running of such period shall be suspended under this paragraph only with respect to the amount of such assessment equal to the amount of money or the value of specific property returned.

(2) WRONGFUL LIEN.—In the case of any assessment for which a lien was made on any property, the running of the period under section 6502 shall be suspended for a period equal to the period beginning on the date any person becomes entitled to a certificate under section 6325(b)(4) with respect to such property and ending on the date which is 30 days after the earlier of—

(A) the earliest date on which the Secretary no longer holds any amount as a deposit or bond provided under section 6325(b)(4) by reason of such deposit or bond being used to satisfy the unpaid tax or being refunded or released; or

(B) the date that the judgment secured under section 7426(b)(5) becomes final.

The running of such period shall be suspended under this paragraph only with respect to the amount of such assessment equal to the value of the interest of the United States in the property plus interest, penalties, additions to the tax, and additional amounts attributable thereto.

Amendments

• 1998, IRS Restructuring and Reform Act of 1998 (P.L. 105-206)

P.L. 105-206, §3106(b)(3):

Amended Code Sec. 6503(f). **Effective** 7-22-98. Prior to amendment, Code Sec. 6503(f) read as follows:

(f) WRONGFUL SEIZURE OF PROPERTY OF THIRD PARTY.—The running of the period of limitations on collection after assessment prescribed in section 6502 shall be suspended for a period equal to the period from the date property (including money) of a third party is wrongfully seized or received by the Secretary to the date the Secretary returns property pursuant to section 6343(b) or the date on which a judgment secured pursuant to section 7426 with respect to such property becomes final, and for 30 days thereafter. The running of the period of limitations on collection after assessment shall be suspended under this subsection only with respect to the amount of such assessment equal to the amount of money or the value of specific property returned.

• 1976, Tax Reform Act of 1976 (P.L. 94-455)

P.L. 94-455, §1902(b)(2)(A):

Redesignated subsection (g) as Code Sec. 6503(f). **Effective** in the case of estates of decedents dying after 10-4-76.

P.L. 94-455, §1906(b)(13)(A):

Amended the 1954 Code by substituting "Secretary" for "Secretary or his delegate" each place it appeared. **Effective** 2-1-77.

• 1966, Federal Tax Lien Act of 1966 (P.L. 89-719)

P.L. 89-719, §106(c):

Redesignated former Code Sec. 6503(g) as Sec. 6503(h) and added new Code Sec. 6503(g). **Effective**, generally, after 11-2-66. However, see the amendment note for Code Sec. 6323 for exceptions to this **effective** date.

[Sec. 6503(g)]

(g) SUSPENSION PENDING CORRECTION.—The running of the periods of limitations provided in sections 6501 and 6502 on the making of assessments or the collection by levy or a proceeding in court in respect of any tax imposed by chapter 42 or section 507, 4971, or 4975 shall be suspended for any period described in section 507(g)(2) or during which the Secretary has extended the time for making correction under section 4963(e).

Amendments

• 1987, Revenue Act of 1987 (P.L. 100-203)

P.L. 100-203, §10712(c)(3):

Amended Code Sec. 6503(g) by striking out "4951, 4952," after "507,". **Effective** for tax years beginning after 12-22-87.

• 1984, Deficit Reduction Act of 1984 (P.L. 98-369)

P.L. 98-369, §305(b)(4):

Amended Code Sec. 6503(g) by striking out "section 4962(e)" and inserting in lieu thereof "section 4963(e)". **Effective** for tax events occurring after 12-31-84.

• 1980 (P.L. 96-596)

P.L. 96-596, §2(a)(3):

Amended Code Sec. 6503(g) by striking out "section 4941(e)(4), 4942(j)(2), 4943(d)(3), 4944(e)(3), 4951(i)(2), 4951(e)(4), 4952(e)(2), 4971(c)(3); or 4975(f)(6)." and inserting in lieu thereof "section 4962(e)." **Effective** 12-24-80.

• 1980, Technical Corrections Act of 1979 (P.L. 96-222)

P.L. 96-222, §108(b)(1)(A):

Amended Code Sec. 6503(g) by striking out "4971, 4975, 4985, or 4986" and inserting "4951, 4952, 4971, or 4975" and by striking out "4971(c)(3), 4975(f)(6), 4985(e)(4), or 4986(e)(2)" and inserting "4951(e)(4), 4952(e)(2), 4971(c)(3), or 4975(f)(6)". For the **effective** date, see the historical comment for P.L. 95-227 under Code Sec. 4951.

• 1978, Black Lung Benefits Revenue Act of 1977 (P.L. 95-227)

P.L. 95-227, §4(d)(6):

Amended Code Sec. 6503(g) by substituting "507, 4971, 4975, 4951, or 4952" for "507 or section 4971 or section 4975" and by substituting "4975(f)(6), 4951(e)(4), or 4952(e)(2)" for "or 4975(f)(4)". For **effective** date, see the historical comment for P.L. 95-227 under Code Sec. 4951.

• 1976, Tax Reform Act of 1976 (P.L. 94-455)

P.L. 94-455, §1902(b)(2)(A):

Renumbered subsection (h) as Code Sec. 6503(g). **Effective** in the case of estates of decedents dying after 10-4-76.

P.L. 94-455, §1906(b)(13)(A):

Amended the 1954 Code by substituting "Secretary" for "Secretary or his delegate" each place it appeared. **Effective** 2-1-77.

• 1974, Employee Retirement Income Security Act of 1974 (P.L. 93-406)

P.L. 93-406, §1016(a)(15):

Amended Code Sec. 6503(h) by inserting "or section 4971 or section 4975" after "section 507" and by changing "or 4945(h)(2)" to "4945(i)(2), 4971(c)(3), or 4975(f)(4)". For **effective** date, see amendment note for Code Sec. 410.

[Sec. 6503(h)—Repealed]

Amendments

• 1990, Omnibus Budget Reconciliation Act of 1990 (P.L. 101-508)

P.L. 101-508, §11801(c)(20)(A):

Repealed Code Sec. 6503(h) and redesignated subsection (i) as subsection (h). **Effective** 11-5-90. Prior to repeal, Code Sec. 6503(h) read as follows:

(h) EXTENSION OF TIME FOR COLLECTING TAX ATTRIBUTABLE TO DIVESTITURES PURSUANT TO BANK HOLDING COMPANY ACT AMENDMENTS OF 1970.—The running of the period of limitations for collection of the tax attributable to a sale with respect to which the taxpayer makes an election under section 6158(a) shall be suspended for the period during which there are any unpaid installments of such tax.

P.L. 101-508, §11821(b)(1)-(2), provides:

(b) SAVINGS PROVISION.—If—

(1) any provision amended or repealed by this part applied to—

(A) any transaction occurring before the date of the enactment of this Act,

(B) any property acquired before such date of enactment, or

(C) any item of income, loss, deduction, or credit taken into account before such date of enactment, and

(2) the treatment of such transaction, property, or item under such provision would (without regard to the amendments made by this part) affect liability for tax for periods ending after such date of enactment,

nothing in the amendments made by this part shall be construed to affect the treatment of such transaction, property, or item for purposes of determining liability for tax for periods ending after such date of enactment.

• 1976, Bank Holding Company Tax Act of 1976 (P.L. 94-452)

P.L. 94-452, §3(b):

Added Code Sec. 6503(h). **Effective** 10-1-77 with respect to sales after 7-7-70, in tax years ending after 7-7-70, but only in the case of qualified bank holding corporations.

LIMITATIONS—ASSESSMENT AND COLLECTION

- **1969, Tax Reform Act of 1969 (P.L. 91-172)**

P.L. 91-172, §101(g)(4):

Added Code Sec. 6503(h). **Effective** 1-1-70.

[Sec. 6503(h)]

(h) Cases Under Title 11 of the United States Code.—The running of the period of limitations provided in section 6501 or 6502 on the making of assessments or collection shall, in a case under title 11 of the United States Code, be suspended for the period during which the Secretary is prohibited by reason of such case from making the assessment or from collecting and—

(1) for assessment, 60 days thereafter, and

(2) for collection, 6 months thereafter.

Amendments

- **1990, Omnibus Budget Reconciliation Act of 1990 (P.L. 101-508)**

P.L. 101-508, §11801(c)(20)(A):

Amended Code Sec. 6503 by redesignating subsection (i) as subsection (h). **Effective** 11-5-90.

- **1980, Bankruptcy Tax Act of 1980 (P.L. 96-589)**

P.L. 96-589, §6(a):

Redesignated Code Sec. 6503(i) as 6503(j), and inserted a new Code Sec. 6503(i). **Effective** 10-1-79, but inapplicable to any proceeding under the Bankruptcy Act commenced before that date.

[Sec. 6503(i)]

(i) Extension of Time For Payment of Undistributed PFIC Earnings Tax Liability.—The running of any period of limitations for collection of any amount of undistributed PFIC earnings tax liability (as defined in section 1294(b)) shall be suspended for the period of any extension of time under section 1294 for payment of such amount.

Amendments

- **1990, Omnibus Budget Reconciliation Act of 1990 (P.L. 101-508)**

P.L. 101-508, §11801(c)(20)(A):

Amended Code Sec. 6503 by redesignating subsection (j) is subsection (i). **Effective** 11-5-90.

P.L. 101-508, §11821(b)(1)-(2), provides:

(b) Savings provision.—If—

(1) any provision amended or repealed by this part applied to—

(A) any transaction occurring before the date of the enactment of this Act,

(B) any property acquired before such date of enactment, or

(C) any item of income, loss, deduction, or credit taken into account before such date of enactment, and

(2) the treatment of such transaction, property, or item under such provision would (without regard to the amendments made by this part) affect liability for tax for periods ending after such date of enactment,

nothing in the amendments made by this part shall be construed to affect the treatment of such transaction, property, or item for purposes of determining liability for tax for periods ending after such date of enactment.

- **1986, Tax Reform Act of 1986 (P.L. 99-514)**

P.L. 99-514, §1235(d):

Amended Code Sec. 6503 by redesignating subsection (j) as subsection (k) and by inserting after subsection (i) new subsection (j). **Effective** for tax years of foreign corporations beginning after 12-31-86.

[Sec. 6503(j)]

(j) Extension in Case of Certain Summonses.—

(1) In general.—If any designated summons is issued by the Secretary to a corporation (or to any other person to whom the corporation has transferred records) with respect to any return of tax by such corporation for a taxable year (or other period) for which such corporation is being examined under the coordinated industry case program (or any successor program) of the Internal Revenue Service, the running of any period of limitations provided in section 6501 on the assessment of such tax shall be suspended—

(A) during any judicial enforcement period—

(i) with respect to such summons, or

(ii) with respect to any other summons

which is issued during the 30-day period which begins on the date on which such designated summons is issued and which relates to the same return as such designated summons, and

(B) if the court in any proceeding referred to in paragraph (3) requires any compliance with a summons referred to in subparagraph (A), during the 120-day period beginning with the 1st day after the close of the suspension under subparagraph (A).

If subparagraph (B) does not apply, such period shall in no event expire before the 60th day after the close of the suspension under subparagraph (A).

(2) Designated summons.—For purposes of this subsection—

(A) In general.—The term "designated summons" means any summons issued for purposes of determining the amount of any tax imposed by this title if—

(i) the issuance of such summons is preceded by a review and written approval of such issuance by the Commissioner of the relevant operating division of the Internal Revenue Service and the Chief Counsel which—

(I) states facts clearly establishing that the Secretary has made reasonable requests for the information that is the subject of the summons, and

(II) is attached to such summons,

(ii) such summons is issued at least 60 days before the day on which the period prescribed in section 6501 for the assessment of such tax expires (determined with regard to extensions), and

(iii) such summons clearly states that it is a designated summons for purposes of this subsection.

(B) Limitation.—A summons which relates to any return shall not be treated as a designated summons if a prior summons which relates to such return was treated as a designated summons for purposes of this subsection.

(3) Judicial enforcement period.—For purposes of this subsection, the term "judicial enforcement period" means, with respect to any summons, the period—

(A) which begins on the day on which a court proceeding with respect to such summons is brought, and

(B) which ends on the day on which there is a final resolution as to the summoned person's response to such summons.

(4) Establishment that reasonable requests for information were made.—In any court proceeding described in paragraph (3), the Secretary shall establish that reasonable requests were made for the information that is the subject of the summons.

Amendments

- **2019, Taxpayer First Act (P.L. 116-25)**

P.L. 116-25, §1207(a):

Amended Code Sec. 6503(j)(1) by striking "coordinated examination program" and inserting "coordinated industry case program". **Effective** for summonses issued after the date which is 45 days after 7-1-2019.

P.L. 116-25, §1207(b):

Amended Code Sec. 6503(j)(2)(A)(i). **Effective** for summonses issued after the date which is 45 days after 7-1-2019. Prior to amendment, Code Sec. 6503(j)(2)(A)(i) read as follows:

LIMITATIONS—ASSESSMENT AND COLLECTION

(i) the issuance of such summons is preceded by a review of such issuance by the regional counsel of the Office of Chief Counsel for the region in which the examination of the corporation is being conducted,

P.L. 116-25, §1207(c):

Amended Code Sec. 6503(j) by adding at the end a new paragraph (4). **Effective** for summonses issued after the date which is 45 days after 7-1-2019.

• **1996, Small Business Job Protection Act of 1996 (P.L. 104-188)**

P.L. 104-188, §1702(h)(17)(A):

Amended Code Sec. 6503 by redesignating the subsection relating to extension in case of certain summonses as subsection (j). [Note: Code Sec. 6503(j) was previously redesignated by Act Sec. 1002(c) of P.L. 104-168.—CCH.] **Effective** as if included in the provision of P.L. 101-508 to which it relates.

• **1996, Taxpayer Bill of Rights 2 (P.L. 104-168)**

P.L. 104-168, §1002(a):

Amended Code Sec. 6503(k)(2)(A) [prior to redesignation by Act Sec. 1002(c)] by redesignating clauses (i) and (ii) as clauses (ii) and (iii), respectively, and by inserting before clause (ii) (as so redesignated) a new clause (i). **Effective** for summonses issued after 7-30-96.

P.L. 104-168, §1002(b):

Amended Code Sec. 6503(k)(1) [prior to redesignation by Act Sec. 1002(c)] by striking "with respect to any return of tax by a corporation" and inserting "to a corporation (or to any other person to whom the corporation has transferred records) with respect to any return of tax by such corporation for a taxable year (or other period) for which such corporation is being examined under the coordinated examination program (or any successor program) of the Internal Revenue Service". **Effective** for summonses issued after 7-30-96.

P.L. 104-168, §1002(c):

Amended Code Sec. 6503 by redesignating subsection (k) as subsection (j). **Effective** for summonses issued after 7-30-96.

• **1990, Omnibus Budget Reconciliation Act of 1990 (P.L. 101-508)**

P.L. 101-508, §11311(a):

Amended Code Sec. 6503 by inserting after subsection (j)[i]a new subsection (k)[(j)]. **Effective** for any tax (whether imposed before, on, or after 11-5-90) if the period prescribed by section 6501 of the Internal Revenue Code of 1986 for the assessment of such tax (determined with regard to extensions) has not expired on such date of the enactment.

[Sec. 6503(k)]

(k) CROSS REFERENCES.—

For suspension in case of—

(1) Deficiency dividends of a personal holding company, see section 547(f).

(2) Receiverships, see subchapter B of chapter 70.

(3) Claims against transferees and fiduciaries, see chapter 71.

(4) Tax return preparers, see section 6694(c)(3).

(5) Deficiency dividends in the case of a regulated investment company or a real estate investment trust, see section 860(h).

Amendments

• **2007, Small Business and Work Opportunity Tax Act of 2007 (P.L. 110-28)**

P.L. 110-28, §8246(a)(2)(E):

Amended Code Sec. 6503(k)(4) by striking "Income tax return preparers" and inserting "Tax return preparers". **Effective** for returns prepared after 5-25-2007.

• **1996, Small Business Job Protection Act of 1996 (P.L. 104-188)**

P.L. 104-188, §1702(h)(17)(B):

Amended Code Sec. 6503 by redesignating the subsection relating to cross references as subsection (k). [Note: Code Sec. 6502(k) was prviously redesignated by P.L. 104-168.—CCH.] **Effective** as if included in the provision of P.L. 101-508 to which such it relates.

• **1996, Taxpayer Bill of Rights 2 (P.L. 104-168)**

P.L. 104-168, §1002(c):

Amended Code Sec. 6503 by redesignating subsection (l) as subsection (k). **Effective** for summonses issued after 7-30-96.

• **1990, Omnibus Budget Reconciliation Act of 1990 (P.L. 101-508)**

P.L. 101-508, §11311(a):

Amended Code Sec. 6503 by redesignating subsection (k)[j] as subsection (l)[k]. **Effective** for any tax (whether imposed before, on, or after 11-5-90) if the period prescribed by section 6501 of the Internal Revenue Code of 1986 for the assessment of such tax (determined with regard to extensions) has not expired on such date of the enactment.

P.L. 101-508, §11801(c)(20)(A):

Amended Code Sec. 6503 by redesignating subsection (k) as subsection (j). **Effective** 11-5-90.

P.L. 101-508, §11821(b)(1)-(2), provides:

(b) SAVINGS PROVISION.—If—

(1) any provision amended or repealed by this part applied to—

(A) any transaction occurring before the date of the enactment of this Act,

(B) any property acquired before such date of enactment, or

(C) any item of income, loss, deduction, or credit taken into account before such date of enactment, and

(2) the treatment of such transaction, property, or item under such provision would (without regard to the amendments made by this part) affect liability for tax for periods ending after such date of enactment,

nothing in the amendments made by this part shall be construed to affect the treatment of such transaction, property, or item for purposes of determining liability for tax for periods ending after such date of enactment.

• **1986, Tax Reform Act of 1986 (P.L. 99-514)**

P.L. 99-514, §1235(d):

Amended Code Sec. 6503 by redesignating subsection (j) as subsection (k) and by inserting after subsection (i) new subsection (j). **Effective** for tax years of foreign corporations beginning after 12-31-86.

• **1980 (P.L. 96-596)**

P.L. 96-596, §2(a)(4), provides:

"The amendments made by sections 1203(h)(1) and 1601(f)(2) of the Tax Reform Act of 1976, and the amendment made by section 362(d)(5) of the Revenue Act of 1978 shall be deemed to be amendments to section 6503(i) of the Internal Revenue Code of 1954 (as redesignated)". **Effective** 1-1-70.

• **1980, Bankruptcy Tax Act of 1980 (P.L. 96-589)**

P.L. 96-589, §6(a):

Redesignated Code Sec. 6503(i) as 6503(j). **Effective** 10-1-79, but inapplicable to any proceeding under the Bankruptcy Act commenced before that date.

P.L. 96-589, §6(i)(11):

Amended paragraph (2) of Code Sec. 6503(j). **Effective** 10-1-79, but inapplicable to any proceeding under the Bankruptcy Act commenced before that date. Prior to amendment, paragraph (2) provided:

"(2) Bankruptcy and receiverships, see subchapter B of chapter 70."

• **1978, Revenue Act of 1978 (P.L. 95-600)**

P.L. 95-600, §362(d)(5):

Amended Code Sec. 6503(i)(5). **Effective** with respect to determinations after 11-7-78. Prior to amendment, Code Sec. 6503(i)(5) read as follows:

"(5) Deficiency dividends in the case of a regulated investment company, see section 860(h).

• **1976, Tax Reform Act of 1976 (P.L. 94-455)**

P.L. 94-455, §1203(h)(1):

Added Code Sec. 6503(h)(4). **Effective** for documents prepared after 12-31-76.

P.L. 94-455, §1601(f)(2):

Added Code Sec. 6503(i)(5) [6503(h)(5)]. **Effective** with respect to determinations (as defined in Sec. 859(c)) occurring after 10-4-76.

P.L. 94-455, §1902(b)(2)(A):

Redesignated subsection (i) as Code Sec. 6503(h). **Effective** in the case of estates of decedents dying after 10-4-76.

The above redesignations made by P.L. 94-455 did not take into consideration the addition of Code Sec. (h), above, as added by P.L. 94-452.

• **1969, Tax Reform Act of 1969 (P.L. 91-172)**

P.L. 91-172, §101(g)(4):

Redesignated former Code Sec. 6503(h) as Code Sec. 6503(i).

• **1966, Federal Tax Lien Act of 1966 (P.L. 89-719)**

P.L. 89-719, §106(c):

Redesignated Code Sec. 6503(g) as Sec. 6503(h). **Effective**, generally, after 11-2-66. However, see the amendment note for Code Sec. 6323 for exceptions to this **effective** date.

• **1966 (P.L. 89-384)**

P.L. 89-384, §1(e):

Redesignated Code Sec. 6503(f) as Code Sec. 6503(g). **Effective** with respect to amounts received after 12-31-64, in respect of foreign expropriation losses sustained after 12-31-58.

• **1956 (P.L. 1011, 84th Cong.)**

P.L. 1011, 84th Cong., §2:

Redesignated former Code Sec. 6503(e) as Code Sec. 6503(f). **Effective** under Code Sec. 3 for decedents dying after 8-16-54.

LIMITATIONS—ASSESSMENT AND COLLECTION

[Sec. 6504]

SEC. 6504. CROSS REFERENCES.

For limitation period in case of—

(1) Adjustments to accrued foreign taxes, see section 905(c).

(2) Change of treatment with respect to itemized deductions where taxpayer and his spouse make separate returns, see section 63(e)(3).

(3) involuntary conversion of property, see section 1033(a)(2)(C) and (D).

(4) Application by fiduciary for discharge from personal liability for estate tax, see section 2204.

(5) Insolvent banks and trust companies, see section 7507.

(6) Service in a combat zone, etc., see section 7508.

(7) Claims against transferees and fiduciaries, see chapter 71.

(8) Assessments to recover excessive amounts paid under section 6420 (relating to gasoline used on farms), 6421 (relating to gasoline used for certain nonhighway purposes or by local transit systems), or 6427 (relating to fuels not used for taxable purposes) and assessments of civil penalties under section 6675 for excessive claims under section 6420, 6421, or 6427, see section 6206.

(9) Assessment and collection of interest, see section 6601(g).

(10) Assessment of civil penalties under section 6694 or 6695, see section 6696(d)(1).

Amendments

• **2015, Bipartisan Budget Act of 2015 (P.L. 114-74)**

P.L. 114-74, §1101(f)(5):

Amended Code Sec. 6504 by striking paragraph (11). **Effective** generally for returns filed for partnership tax years beginning after 12-31-2017. For a special rule, see Act Sec. 1101(g)(4), below. Prior to being stricken, Code Sec. 6504(11) read as follows:

(11) Assessments of tax attributable to partnership items, see section 6229.

P.L. 114-74, §1101(g)(4), provides:

(4) ELECTION.—A partnership may elect (at such time and in such form and manner as the Secretary of the Treasury may prescribe) for the amendments made by this section (other than the election under section 6221(b) of such Code (as added by this Act)) to apply to any return of the partnership filed for partnership taxable years beginning after the date of the enactment of this Act and before January 1, 2018.

• **1997, Taxpayer Relief Act of 1997 (P.L. 105-34)**

P.L. 105-34, §312(d)(13):

Amended Code Sec. 6504 by striking paragraph (4) and by redesignating the succeeding paragraphs accordingly. **Effective** for sales and exchanges after 5-6-97. Prior to being stricken, Code Sec. 6504(4) read as follows:

(4) Gain upon sale or exchange of principal residence, see section 1034(j).

• **1986, Tax Reform Act of 1986 (P.L. 99-514)**

P.L. 99-514, §104(b)(18):

Amended Code Sec. 6504(2). **Effective** for tax years beginning after 12-31-86. Prior to amendment, Code Sec. 6504(2) read as follows:

(2) Change of treatment with respect to itemized deductions and zero bracket amount where taxpayer and his spouse make separate returns, see section 63(g)(5).

• **1983, Surface Transportation Act of 1983 (P.L. 97-424)**

P.L. 97-424, §515(b)(10):

Amended Code Sec. 6504(9) by striking out "6424 (relating to lubricating oil used for certain nontaxable purposes)," after "local transit systems)," and by striking out "6424," after "6421,". **Effective** with respect to articles sold after 1-6-83.

• **1982, Tax Equity and Fiscal Responsibility Act of 1982 (P.L. 97-248)**

P.L. 97-248, §402(c)(6):

Added Code Sec. 6504(12). **Effective** for partnership tax years beginning after 9-3-82 and also to partnership tax years ending after that date if the partnership, each partner, and each indirect partner, requests such application and if the Secretary or his delegate consents to such application.

• **1978, Revenue Act of 1978 (P.L. 95-600)**

P.L. 95-600, §405(c)(6):

Amended Code Sec. 6504(4) by changing "residence" to "principal residence". **Effective** for sales and exchanges of residences after 7-26-78, in tax years ending after such date.

• **1978, Energy Tax Act of 1978 (P.L. 95-618)**

P.L. 95-618, §233(b)(2)(D):

Amended Code Sec. 6504(9) by changing "not used in highway motor vehicles" to "used for certain nontaxable purposes". **Effective** on the first day of the first calendar month which begins more than 10 days after 11-6-78 [12-1-78.—CCH].

• **1977, Tax Reduction and Simplification Act of 1977 (P.L. 95-30)**

P.L. 95-30, §101(d)(16):

Amended Code Sec. 6504(2). **Effective** for tax years beginning after 12-31-76. Prior to amendment, Code Sec. 6504(2) read as follows:

"(2) Change of election with respect to the standard deduction where taxpayer and his spouse make separate returns, see section 144(b)."

• **1976, Tax Reform Act of 1976 (P.L. 94-455)**

P.L. 94-455, §1203(h)(2):

Added Code Sec. 6504(11). **Effective** for documents prepared after 12-31-76.

P.L. 94-455, §901(b)(31)(D):

Substituted "1033(a)(2)(C) and (D)" for "1033(a)(3)(C) and (D)" in Code Sec. 6504(4) [6504(3)]. **Effective** with respect to tax years beginning after 12-31-76.

P.L. 94-455, §1901(b)(36)(C):

Deleted Code Sec. 6504(1). **Effective** for tax years beginning after 12-31-76. Prior to deletion, Code Sec. 6504(1) read as follows:

(1) Adjustments incident to involuntary liquidation of inventory, see section 1321.

P.L. 94-455, §1901(b)(37)(D):

Deleted Code Sec. 6504(6). **Effective** with respect to tax years beginning after 12-31-76. Prior to deletion, Code Sec. 6504(6) read as follows:

(6) War loss recoveries where prior benefit rule is elected, see section 1335.

P.L. 94-455, §1901(b)(39)(B):

Deleted Code Sec. 6504(7). **Effective** with respect to tax years beginning after 12-31-76. Prior to deletion Code Sec. 6504(7) read as follows:

(7) Recovery of unconstitutional Federal taxes, see section 1346.

P.L. 94-455, §1906(a)(32)(A):

Substituted Code Sec. 6504(13) [6504(9)] for former paragraphs (13) and (14). **Effective** 2-1-77. Prior to deletion, Code Sec. 6504(13) and (14) read as follows:

(13) Assessments to recover excessive amounts paid under section 6420 (relating to gasoline used on farms) and assessments of civil penalties under section 6675 for excessive claims under section 6420, see section 6206.

(14) Assessments to recover excessive amounts paid under section 6421 (relating to gasoline used for certain nonhighway purposes or by local transit systems) and assessments of civil penalties under section 6675 for excessive claims under section 6421, see section 6206.

P.L. 94-455, §1906(a)(32)(B):

Redesignated paragraphs (2), (3), (4), (5), (9), (10), (11), (12), (13), and (15) as Code Sec. 6504(1) through (10), respectively. **Effective** 2-1-77.

• **1975 (P.L. 93-625)**

P.L. 93-625, §7(d)(4):

Amended Code Sec. 6504(15) by substituting "section 6601(g)" for "section 6601(h)". **Effective** 7-1-75.

• **1970, Excise, Estate, and Gift Tax Adjustment Act of 1970 (P.L. 91-614)**

P.L. 91-614, §101(d)(2):

Amended Code Sec. 6504(9) by substituting "fiduciary" for "executor." **Effective** 1-1-71.

• **1969, Tax Reform Act of 1969 (P.L. 91-172)**

P.L. 91-172, §213(c)(3):

Amended Code Sec Sec. 6504 by striking out the item referring to section 270. **Effective** for tax years beginning before 12-31-69. Prior to repeal, Code Sec. 6504(8) read as follows:

"(8) Limitations on deductions allowable to individuals in certain cases, see section 270(d)."

• **1964, Revenue Act of 1964 (P.L. 88-272)**

P.L. 88-272, §112(d)(2):

Amended paragraph (3) by striking out "to take" and inserting in lieu thereof "with respect to the". **Effective** 1-1-64.

• **1958, Technical Amendments Act of 1958 (P.L. 85-866)**

P.L. 85-866, §84(b):

Added paragraph (15). **Effective** 1-1-54.

• **1956 (P.L. 627, 84th Cong.)**

P.L. 627, 84th Cong., 2d Sess., §208(e)(5):

Amended Sec. 6504 by adding paragraph (14). **Effective** 7-1-56.

• **1956 (P.L. 466, 84th Cong.)**

P.L. 466, 84th Cong., §4(d):

Added paragraph (13).

Subchapter B—Limitations on Credit or Refund

Sec. 6511. Limitations on credit or refund.
Sec. 6512. Limitations in case of petition to Tax Court.
Sec. 6513. Time return deemed filed and tax considered paid.
Sec. 6514. Credits or refunds after period of limitation.
Sec. 6515. Cross references.

[Sec. 6511]

SEC. 6511. LIMITATIONS ON CREDIT OR REFUND.

[Sec. 6511(a)]

(a) PERIOD OF LIMITATION ON FILING CLAIM.—Claim for credit or refund of an overpayment of any tax imposed by this title in respect of which tax the taxpayer is required to file a return shall be filed by the taxpayer within 3 years from the time the return was filed or 2 years from the time the tax was paid, whichever of such periods expires the later, or if no return was filed by the taxpayer, within 2 years from the time the tax was paid. Claim for credit or refund of an overpayment of any tax imposed by this title which is required to be paid by means of a stamp shall be filed by the taxpayer within 3 years from the time the tax was paid.

Amendments

• **2016, Combat-Injured Veterans Tax Fairness Act of 2016 (P.L. 114-292)**

P.L. 114-292, §3, provides:

SEC. 3. RESTORATION OF AMOUNTS IMPROPERLY WITHHELD FOR TAX PURPOSES FROM SEVERANCE PAYMENTS TO VETERANS WITH COMBAT-RELATED INJURIES.

(a) IN GENERAL.—Not later than 1 year after the date of the enactment of this Act, the Secretary of Defense shall—

(1) identify—

(A) the severance payments—

(i) that the Secretary paid after January 17, 1991;

(ii) that the Secretary computed under section 1212 of title 10, United States Code;

(iii) that were not considered gross income pursuant to section 104(a)(4) of the Internal Revenue Code of 1986; and

(iv) from which the Secretary withheld amounts for tax purposes; and

(B) the individuals to whom such severance payments were made; and

(2) with respect to each person identified under paragraph (1)(B), provide—

(A) notice of—

(i) the amount of severance payments in paragraph (1)(A) which were improperly withheld for tax purposes; and

(ii) such other information determined to be necessary by the Secretary of the Treasury to carry out the purposes of this section; and

(B) instructions for filing amended tax returns to recover the amounts improperly withheld for tax purposes.

(b) EXTENSION OF LIMITATION ON TIME FOR CREDIT OR REFUND.—

(1) PERIOD FOR FILING CLAIM.—If a claim for credit or refund under section 6511(a) of the Internal Revenue Code of 1986 relates to a specified overpayment, the 3-year period of limitation prescribed by such subsection shall not expire before the date which is 1 year after the date the information return described in subsection (a)(2) is provided. The allowable amount of credit or refund of a specified overpayment shall be determined without regard to the amount of tax paid within the period provided in section 6511(b)(2).

(2) SPECIFIED OVERPAYMENT.—For purposes of paragraph (1), the term "specified overpayment" means an overpayment attributable to a severance payment described in subsection (a)(1).

• **1958, Technical Amendments Act of 1958 (P.L. 85-866)**

P.L. 85-866, §82(a):

Amended the first sentence of Code Sec. 6511(a). **Effective** 8-17-54. Prior to amendment, that sentence read as follows:

"Claim for credit or refund of an overpayment of any tax imposed by this title in respect of which tax the taxpayer is required to file a return shall be filed by the taxpayer within 3 years from the time the return was required to be filed (determined without regard to any extension of time) or 2 years from the time the tax was paid, whichever of such periods expires the later, or if no return was filed by the taxpayer, within 2 years from the time the tax was paid."

[Sec. 6511(b)]

(b) LIMITATION ON ALLOWANCE OF CREDITS AND REFUNDS.—

(1) FILING OF CLAIM WITHIN PRESCRIBED PERIOD.—No credit or refund shall be allowed or made after the expiration of the period of limitation prescribed in subsection (a) for the filing of a claim for credit or refund, unless a claim for credit or refund is filed by the taxpayer within such period.

(2) LIMIT ON AMOUNT OF CREDIT OR REFUND.—

(A) LIMIT WHERE CLAIM FILED WITHIN 3-YEAR PERIOD.—If the claim was filed by the taxpayer during the 3-year period prescribed in subsection (a), the amount of the credit or refund shall not exceed the portion of the tax paid within the period, immediately preceding the filing of the claim, equal to 3 years plus the period of any extension of time for filing the return. If the tax was required to be paid by means of a stamp, the amount of the credit or refund shall not exceed the portion of the tax paid within the 3 years immediately preceding the filing of the claim.

(B) LIMIT WHERE CLAIM NOT FILED WITHIN 3-YEAR PERIOD.—If the claim was not filed within such 3-year period, the amount of the credit or refund shall not exceed the portion of the tax paid during the 2 years immediately preceding the filing of the claim.

(C) LIMIT IF NO CLAIM FILED.—If no claim was filed, the credit or refund shall not exceed the amount which would be allowable under subparagraph (A) or (B), as the case may be, if claim was filed on the date the credit or refund is allowed.

Amendments

• **1958, Technical Amendments Act of 1958 (P.L. 85-866)**

P.L. 85-866, §82(b):

Amended the heading and first sentence of Code Sec. 6511(b)(2)(A). **Effective** 1-1-54. Prior to amendment, they read as follows:

"(A) Limit to amount paid within 3 years.—If the claim was filed by the taxpayer during the 3-year period prescribed in subsection (a), the amount of the credit or refund shall not exceed the portion of the tax paid within the 3 years immediately preceding the filing of the claim."

P.L. 85-866, §82(c):

Amended the heading for Code Sec. 6511(b)(2)(B). **Effective** 1-1-54. Prior to amendment, it read as follows:

"(B) Limit to amount paid within 2 years.—".

[Sec. 6511(c)]

(c) SPECIAL RULES APPLICABLE IN CASE OF EXTENSION OF TIME BY AGREEMENT.—If an agreement under the provisions of section 6501(c)(4) extending the period for assessment of a tax imposed by this title is made within the period prescribed in subsection (a) for the filing of a claim for credit or refund—

(1) TIME FOR FILING CLAIM.—The period for filing claim for credit or refund or for making credit or refund if no claim is filed, provided in subsections (a) and (b)(1), shall not expire prior to 6 months after the expiration of the period within which an assessment may be made pursuant to the agreement or any extension thereof under section 6501(c)(4).

(2) LIMIT ON AMOUNT.—If a claim is filed, or a credit or refund is allowed when no claim was filed, after the execution of the agreement and within 6 months after the expiration of the period within which an assessment may be made pursuant to the agreement or any extension thereof, the amount of the credit or refund shall not exceed the portion of the tax paid after the execution of the agreement and before the filing of the claim or the making of the credit or refund, as the case may be, plus the portion of the tax paid within the period which would be applicable under subsection (b)(2) if a claim had been filed on the date the agreement was executed.

LIMITATIONS—CREDIT OR REFUND

(3) CLAIMS NOT SUBJECT TO SPECIAL RULE.—This subsection shall not apply in the case of a claim filed, or credit or refund allowed if no claim is filed, either—

(A) prior to the execution of the agreement or

(B) more than 6 months after the expiration of the period within which an assessment may be made pursuant to the agreement or any extension thereof.

[Sec. 6511(d)]

(d) SPECIAL RULES APPLICABLE TO INCOME TAXES.—

(1) SEVEN-YEAR PERIOD OF LIMITATION WITH RESPECT TO BAD DEBTS AND WORTHLESS SECURITIES.—If the claim for credit or refund relates to an overpayment of tax imposed by subtitle A on account of—

(A) The deductibility by the taxpayer, under section 166 or section 832(c), of a debt as a debt which became worthless, or, under section 165(g), of a loss from worthlessness of a security, or

(B) The effect that the deductibility of a debt or loss described in subparagraph (A) has on the application to the taxpayer of a carryover,

in lieu of the 3-year period of limitation prescribed in subsection (a), the period shall be 7 years from the date prescribed by law for filing the return for the year with respect to which the claim is made. If the claim for credit or refund relates to an overpayment on account of the effect that the deductibility of such a debt or loss has on the application to the taxpayer of a carryback, the period shall be either 7 years from the date prescribed by law for filing the return for the year of the net operating loss which results in such carryback or the period prescribed in paragaph (2) of this subsection, whichever expires the later. In the case of a claim described in this paragraph the amount of the credit or refund may exceed the portion of the tax paid within the period prescribed in subsection (b)(2) or (c), whichever is applicable, to the extent of the amount of the overpayment attributable to the deductibility of items described in this paragraph.

(2) SPECIAL PERIOD OF LIMITATION WITH RESPECT TO NET OPERATING LOSS OR CAPITAL LOSS CARRYBACKS.—

(A) PERIOD OF LIMITATION.—If the claim for credit or refund relates to an overpayment attributable to a net operating loss carryback or a capital loss carryback, in lieu of the 3-year period of limitation prescribed in subsection (a), the period shall be that period which ends 3 years after the time prescribed by law for filing the return (including extensions thereof) for the taxable year of the net operating loss or net capital loss which results in such carryback, or the period prescribed in subsection (c) in respect of such taxable year, whichever expires later.

In the case of such a claim, the amount of the credit or refund may exceed the portion of the tax paid within the period provided in subsection (b)(2) or (c), whichever is applicable, to the extent of the amount of the overpayment attributable to such carryback.

(B) APPLICABLE RULES.—

(i) IN GENERAL.—If the allowance of a credit or refund of an overpayment of tax attributable to a net operating loss carryback or a capital loss carryback is otherwise prevented by the operation of any law or rule of law other than section 7122 (relating to compromises), such credit or refund may be allowed or made, if claim therefor is filed within the period provided in subparagraph (A) of this paragraph.

(ii) TENTATIVE CARRYBACK ADJUSTMENTS.—If the allowance of an application, credit, or refund of a decrease in tax determined under section 6411(b) is otherwise prevented by the operation of any law or rule of law other than section 7122, such application, credit, or refund may be allowed or made if application for a tentative carryback adjustment is made within the period provided in section 6411(a).

(iii) DETERMINATIONS BY COURTS TO BE CONCLUSIVE.—In the case of any such claim for credit or refund or any such application for a tentative carryback adjustment, the determination by any court, including the Tax Court, in any proceeding in which the decision of the court has become final, shall be conclusive except with respect to—

(I) the net operating loss deduction and the effect of such deduction, and

(II) the determination of a short-term capital loss and the effect of such short-term capital loss, to the extent that such deduction or short-term capital loss is affected by a carryback which was not an issue in such proceeding.

(3) SPECIAL RULES RELATING TO FOREIGN TAX CREDIT.—

(A) SPECIAL PERIOD OF LIMITATION WITH RESPECT TO FOREIGN TAXES PAID OR ACCRUED.—If the claim for credit or refund relates to an overpayment attributable to any taxes paid or accrued to any foreign country or to any possession of the United States for which credit is allowed against the tax imposed by subtitle A in accordance with the provisions of section 901 or the provisions of any treaty to which the United States is a party, in lieu of the 3-year period of limitation prescribed in subsection (a), the period shall be 10 years from the date prescribed by law for filing the return for the year in which such taxes were actually paid or accrued.

(B) EXCEPTION IN THE CASE OF FOREIGN TAXES PAID OR ACCRUED.—In the case of a claim described in subparagraph (A), the amount of the credit or refund may exceed the portion of the tax paid within the period provided in subsection (b) or (c), whichever is applicable, to the extent of the amount of the overpayment attributable to the allowance of a credit for the taxes described in subparagraph (A).

(4) SPECIAL PERIOD OF LIMITATION WITH RESPECT TO CERTAIN CREDIT CARRYBACKS.—

(A) PERIOD OF LIMITATION.—If the claim for credit or refund relates to an overpayment attributable to a credit carryback, in lieu of the 3-year period of limitation prescribed in subsection (a), the period shall be that period which ends 3 years after the time prescribed by law for filing the return (including extensions thereof) for the taxable year of the unused credit which results in such carryback (or, with respect to any portion of a credit carryback from a taxable year attributable to a net operating loss carryback, capital loss carryback, or other credit carryback from a subsequent taxable year, the period shall be that period which ends 3 years after the time prescribed by law for filing the return, including extensions thereof, for such subsequent taxable year) or the period prescribed in subsection (c) in respect of such taxable year, whichever expires later. In the case of such a claim, the amount of the credit or refund may exceed the portion of the tax paid within the period provided in subsection (b)(2) or (c), whichever is applicable, to the extent of the amount of the overpayment attributable to such carryback.

(B) APPLICABLE RULES.—If the allowance of a credit or refund of an overpayment of tax attributable to a credit carryback is otherwise prevented by the operation of any law or rule of law other than section 7122, relating to compromises, such credit or refund may be allowed or made, if claim therefor is filed within the period provided in subparagraph (A) of this paragraph. In the case of any such claim for credit or refund, the determination by any court, including the Tax Court, in any proceeding in which the decision of the court has become final, shall not be conclusive with respect to any credit, and the effect of such credit, to the extent that such credit is affected by a credit carryback which was not in issue in such proceeding.

(C) CREDIT CARRYBACK DEFINED.—For purposes of this paragraph, the term "credit carryback" means any business carryback under section 39.

(5) SPECIAL PERIOD OF LIMITATION WITH RESPECT TO SELF-EMPLOYMENT TAX IN CERTAIN CASES.—If the claim for credit or refund relates to an overpayment of the tax imposed by chapter 2 (relating to the tax on self-employment income) attributable to an agreement, or modification of an agreement, made pursuant to section 218 of the Social Security Act (relating to coverage of State and local employees), and if the allowance

of a credit or refund of such overpayment is otherwise prevented by the operation of any law or rule of law other than section 7122 (relating to compromises), such credit or refund may be allowed or made if claim therefor is filed on or before the last day of the second year after the calendar year in which such agreement (or modification) is agreed to by the State and the Commissioner of Social Security.

(6) SPECIAL PERIOD OF LIMITATION WITH RESPECT TO AMOUNTS INCLUDED IN INCOME SUBSEQUENTLY RECAPTURED UNDER QUALIFIED PLAN TERMINATION.—If the claim for credit or refund relates to an overpayment of tax imposed by subtitle A on account of the recapture, under section 4045 of the Employee Retirement Income Security Act of 1974, of amounts included in income for a prior taxable year, the 3-year period of limitation prescribed in subsection (a) shall be extended, for purposes of permitting a credit or refund of the amount of the recapture, until the date which occurs one year after the date on which such recaptured amount is paid by the taxpayer.

(7) SPECIAL PERIOD OF LIMITATION WITH RESPECT TO SELF-EMPLOYMENT TAX IN CERTAIN CASES.—If—

(A) the claim for credit or refund relates to an overpayment of the tax imposed by chapter 2 (relating to the tax on self-employment income) attributable to Tax Court determination in a proceeding under section 7436, and

(B) the allowance of a credit or refund of such overpayment is otherwise prevented by the operation of any law or rule of law other than section 7122 (relating to compromises),

such credit or refund may be allowed or made if claim therefor is filed on or before the last day of the second year after the calendar year in which such determination becomes final.

(8) SPECIAL RULES WHEN UNIFORMED SERVICES RETIRED PAY IS REDUCED AS A RESULT OF AWARD OF DISABILITY COMPENSATION.—

(A) PERIOD OF LIMITATION ON FILING CLAIM.—If the claim for credit or refund relates to an overpayment of tax imposed by subtitle A on account of—

(i) the reduction of uniformed services retired pay computed under section 1406 or 1407 of title 10, United States Code, or

(ii) the waiver of such pay under section 5305 of title 38 of such Code,

as a result of an award of compensation under title 38 of such Code pursuant to a determination by the Secretary of Veterans Affairs, the 3-year period of limitation prescribed in subsection (a) shall be extended, for purposes of permitting a credit or refund based upon the amount of such reduction or waiver, until the end of the 1-year period beginning on the date of such determination.

(B) LIMITATION TO 5 TAXABLE YEARS.—Subparagraph (A) shall not apply with respect to any taxable year which began more than 5 years before the date of such determination.

Amendments

• **2008, Heroes Earnings Assistance and Relief Tax Act of 2008 (P.L. 110-245)**

P.L. 110-245, §106(a):

Amended Code Sec. 6511(d) by adding at the end a new paragraph (8). **Effective** for claims for credit or refund filed after 6-17-2008. For a transitional rule, see Act Sec. 106(c)(1)-(2), below.

P.L. 110-245, §106(c)(1)-(2) (as amended by P.L. 113-295, §213(a), Division A), provides:

(c) TRANSITION RULES.—In the case of a determination described in paragraph (8) of section 6511(d) of the Internal Revenue Code of 1986 (as added by this section) which is made by the Secretary of Veterans Affairs after December 31, 2000, and before the date of the enactment of this Act [6-17-2008.—CCH], such paragraph—

(1) shall not apply with respect to any taxable year which began before January 1, 2001, and

(2) shall be applied by substituting "June 17, 2008" for "the date of such determination" in subparagraph (A) thereof.

• **1997, Taxpayer Relief Act of 1997 (P.L. 105-34)**

P.L. 105-34, §1056(a):

Amended Code Sec. 6511(d)(3)(A) by striking "for the year with respect to which the claim is made" and inserting "for the year in which such taxes were actually paid or accrued". **Effective** for taxes paid or accrued in tax years beginning after 8-5-97.

P.L. 105-34, §1454(b)(1):

Amended Code Sec. 6511(d) by adding at the end a new paragraph (7). **Effective** 8-5-97.

• **1994, Social Security Independence and Program Improvements Act of 1994 (P.L. 103-296)**

P.L. 103-296, §108(h)(8):

Amended Code Sec. 6511(d)(5) by striking "Secretary of Health and Human Services" and inserting "Commissioner of Social Security". **Effective** 3-31-95.

• **1990, Omnibus Budget Reconciliation Act of 1990 (P.L. 101-508)**

P.L. 101-508, §11801(c)(17)(B):

Amended Code Sec. 6511(d)(2)(A) by striking "; except that" and all that follows down through the period at the end of the first sentence and inserting a period. **Effective** 11-5-90. Prior to amendment, Code Sec. 6511(d)(2)(A) read as follows:

(2) SPECIAL PERIOD OF LIMITATION WITH RESPECT TO NET OPERATING LOSS OR CAPITAL LOSS CARRYBACKS.—

(A) PERIOD OF LIMITATION.—If the claim for credit or refund relates to an overpayment attributable to a net operating loss carryback or a capital loss carryback, in lieu of the 3-year period of limitation prescribed in subsection (a), the period shall be that period which ends 3 years after the time prescribed by law for filing the return (including extensions thereof) for the taxable year of the net operating loss or net capital loss which results in such carryback, or the period prescribed in subsection (c) in respect of such taxable year, whichever expires later; except that with respect to an overpayment attributable to the creation of, or an increase in a net operating loss carryback as a result of the elimination of excessive profits by a renegotiation (as defined in section 1481(a)(1)(A)), the period shall not expire before the expiration of the 12th month following the month in which the agreement or order for the elimination of such excessive profits becomes final.

In the case of such a claim, the amount of the credit or refund may exceed the portion of the tax paid within the period provided in subsection (b)(2) or (c), whichever is applicable, to the extent of the amount of the overpayment attributable to such carryback.

P.L. 101-508, §11821(b)(1)-(2), provides:

(b) SAVINGS PROVISION.—If—

(1) any provision amended or repealed by this part applied to—

(A) any transaction occurring before the date of the enactment of this Act,

(B) any property acquired before such date of enactment, or

(C) any item of income, loss, deduction, or credit taken into account before such date of enactment, and

(2) the treatment of such transaction, property, or item under such provision would (without regard to the amendments made by this part) affect liability for tax for periods ending after such date of enactment,

nothing in the amendments made by this part shall be construed to affect the treatment of such transaction, property, or item for purposes of determining liability for tax for periods ending after such date of enactment.

• **1986, Tax Reform Act of 1986 (P.L. 99-514)**

P.L. 99-514, §141(b)(3):

Amended Code Sec. 6511(d)(2)(B). **Effective** for tax years beginning after 12-31-86. Prior to amendment, Code Sec. 6511(d)(2)(B) read as follows:

(B) APPLICABLE RULES.—

(i) If the allowance of a credit or refund of an overpayment of tax attributable to a net operating loss carryback or a capital loss carryback is otherwise prevented by the operation of any law or rule of law other than section 7122, relating to compromises, such credit or refund may be allowed or made, if claim therefor is filed within the period provided in subparagraph (A) of this paragraph. If the allowance of an application, credit, or refund of a decrease in tax determined under section 6411(b) is otherwise prevented by the operation of any law or rule of law other than section 7122, such application, credit, or refund may be allowed or made if application for a tentative carryback adjustment is made within the period provided in section 6411(a). In the case of any such claim for credit or refund or any such application for a tentative carryback adjustment, the determination by any court, including the Tax Court, in any proceeding in which the decision of the court has become final, shall be conclusive except with respect to the net operating loss deduction, and the effect of such deduction, or with respect to the determination of a short-term capital loss, and the effect of such short-term capital loss, to the extent that such deduction or short-term capital loss is affected by a carryback which was not an issue in such proceeding.

(ii) A claim for credit or refund for a computation year (as defined in section 1302(c)(1)) shall be determined to relate to an overpayment attributable to a net operating loss carryback or a capital loss carryback, as the case may be, when such carryback relates to any base period year (as defined in section 1302(c)(3)).

P.L. 99-514, §231(d)(3)(I):

Amended Code Sec. 6511(d)(4)(C) by striking out "and any research credit carryback under section 30(g)(2)". **Effective** for tax years beginning after 12-31-85.

• **1984, Deficit Reduction Act of 1984 (P.L. 98-369)**

P.L. 98-369, §211(b)(25):

Amended Code Sec. 6511(d) by striking out paragraph (6) and by redesignating paragraph (7) as paragraph (6). **Effective** for tax years beginning after 12-31-83. Prior to amendment, paragraph (6) read as follows:

(6) Special Period of Limitation with Respect to Reduction of Policyholders Surplus Account of Life Insurance Companies.—

(A) Period of Limitations.—If the claim for credit or refund relates to an overpayment arising by operation of section 815(d)(5) (relating to reduction of policyholders surplus account of life insurance companies for certain unused deductions), in lieu of the 3-year period of limitation prescribed in subsection (a), the period shall be that period which ends with the expiration of the 15th day of the 39th month following

LIMITATIONS—CREDIT OR REFUND

the end of the last taxable year to which the loss described in section 815(d)(5)(A) is carried under section 812(b)(2), or the period prescribed in subsection (c), in respect of such taxable year, whichever expires later. In the case of such a claim, the amount of the credit or refund may exceed the portion of the tax paid within the period provided in subsection (b)(2) or (c), whichever is applicable, to the extent of the amount of overpayment arising by operation of section 815(d)(5).

(B) Applicable Rules.—If the allowance of a credit or refund of an overpayment arising by operation of section 815(d)(5) is otherwise prevented by operation of any law or rule of law, other than section 7122 (relating to compromises), such credit or refund may be allowed or made, if claim therefor is filed within the period provided in subparagraph (A) of this paragraph. In the case of any such claim for credit or refund, the determination by any court, including the Tax Court, in any proceeding in which the decision of the court has become final, shall be conclusive except with respect to the effect of the operation of section 815(d)(5), to the extent such effect of the operation of section 815(d)(5) was not in issue in such proceeding.

P.L. 98-369, §474(r)(40):

Amended Code Sec. 6511(d)(4)(C). **Effective** for tax years beginning after 12-31-83, and to carrybacks from such years. Prior to amendment, it read as follows:

(C) Credit Carryback Defined.—For purposes of this paragraph, the term "credit carryback" means any investment credit carryback, work incentive program credit carryback, new employee credit carryback, research credit carryback, and employee stock ownership credit carryback.

P.L. 98-369, §2663(j)(5)(F):

Amended Code Sec. 6511(d)(5) by striking out "Health, Education, and Welfare" each place it appears and inserting in lieu thereof "Health and Human Services". **Effective** 7-18-84. However, it does not change or affect any right, liability, status, or interpretation which existed (under the provisions of law involved) before that date.

• **1981, Economic Recovery Tax Act of 1981 (P.L. 97-34)**

P.L. 97-34, §221(b)(2)(A):

Amended Code Sec. 6511(d)(4)(C) by striking out "and new employee credit carryback" and inserting in lieu thereof "new employee credit carryback, and research credit carryback". **Effective** for amounts paid or incurred after 6-30-81 [**effective** date changed by P.L. 99-514, §231(a)].

P.L. 97-34, §221(d)(2), as amended by P.L. 99-514, §231(a), provides the following transitional rule:

(2) TRANSITIONAL RULE.—

(A) IN GENERAL.—If, with respect to the first taxable year to which the amendments made by this section apply and which ends in 1981 or 1982, the taxpayer may only take into account qualified research expenses paid or incurred during a portion of such taxable year, the amount of the qualified research expenses taken into account for the base period of such taxable year shall be the amount which bears the same ratio to the total qualified research expenses for such base period as the number of months in such portion of such taxable year bears to the total number of months in such taxable year.

(B) DEFINITIONS.—For purposes of the preceding sentence, the terms "qualified research expenses" and "base period" have the meanings given to such terms by section 44F of the Internal Revenue Code of 1954 (as added by this section).

P.L. 97-34, §331(d)(2)(A):

Amended Code Sec. 6511(d)(4)(C) by striking out "and research credit carryback" and inserting in lieu thereof "research credit carryback, and employee stock ownership credit carryback". **Effective** for tax years beginning after 12-31-81.

• **1978 (P.L. 95-628)**

P.L. 95-628, §8(a):

Amended Code Sec. 6511(d)(2)(A) by striking out "with the expiration of the 15th day of the 40th month (or the 39th month, in the case of a corporation) following the end of" and inserting in lieu thereof "3 years after the time prescribed by law for filing the return (including extensions thereof) for". **Effective** for carrybacks arising in tax years beginning after 11-10-78.

P.L. 95-628, §8(b):

Amended Code Sec. 6511(d) by changing paragraph (d)(4), by deleting paragraphs (d)(7) and (d)(9) and by redesignating paragraph (d)(8) as paragraph (d)(7). **Effective** for carrybacks arising in tax years beginning after 11-10-78. Prior to amendment and deletion, paragraphs (d)(4), (d)(7) and (d)(9) read as follows:

"(4) SPECIAL PERIOD OF LIMITATION WITH RESPECT TO INVESTMENT CREDIT CARRYBACKS.—

(A) PERIOD OF LIMITATION.—If the claim for credit or refund relates to an overpayment attributable to an investment credit carryback, in lieu of the 3-year period of limitation prescribed in subsection (a), the period shall be that period which ends with the expiration of the 15th day of the 40th month (or 39th month, in the case of a corporation) following the end of the taxable year of the unused investment credit which results in such carryback (or, with respect to any portion of an investment credit carryback from a taxable year attributable to a net operating loss carryback or a capital loss carryback from a subsequent taxable year, the period shall be that period which ends with the expiration of the 15th day of the 40th month, or 39th month, in the case of a corporation, following the end of such subsequent taxable year) or the period prescribed in subsection (c) in respect of such taxable year, whichever expires later. In the case of such a claim, the amount of the credit or refund may exceed the portion of the tax paid within the period provided in subsection (b)(2) or (c), whichever is applicable, to the extent of the amount of the overpayment attributable to such carryback.

(B) APPLICABLE RULES.—If the allowance of a credit or refund of an overpayment of tax attributable to an investment credit carryback is otherwise prevented by the operation of any law or rule of law other than section 7122, relating to compromises, such credit or refund may be allowed or made, if claim therefor is filed within the period provided in subparagraph (A) of this paragraph. In the case of any such claim for credit or refund, the determination by any court, including the Tax Court, in any proceeding in which the decision of the court has become final, shall not be conclusive with respect to the investment credit, and the effect of such credit, to the extent that such credit is affected by a carryback which was not in issue in such proceeding."

"(7) SPECIAL PERIOD OF LIMITATION WITH RESPECT TO WORK INCENTIVE PROGRAM CREDIT CARRYBACKS.—

(A) PERIOD OF LIMITATION.—If the claim for credit or refund relates to an overpayment attributable to a work incentive program credit carryback, in lieu of the 3-year period of limitation prescribed in subsection (a), the period shall be that period which ends with the expiration of the 15th day of the 40th month (or 39th month, in the case of a corporation) following the end of the taxable year of the unused work incentive program credit which results in such carryback (or, with respect to any portion of a work incentive program credit carryback from a taxable year attributable to a net operating loss carryback, an investment credit carryback, or a capital loss carryback from a subsequent taxable year, the period shall be that period which ends with the expiration of the 15th day of the 40th month, or 39th month, in the case of a corporation, following the year of such taxable year) or the period prescribed in subsection (c) in respect of such taxable year, whichever expires later. In the case of such a claim, the amount of the credit or refund may exceed the portion of the tax paid within the period provided in subsection (b)(2) or (c), whichever is applicable, to the extent of the amount of the overpayment attributable to such carryback.

(B) APPLICABLE RULES.—If the allowance of a credit or refund of an overpayment of tax attributable to a work incentive program credit carryback is otherwise prevented by the operation of any law or rule of law other than section 7122, relating to compromises, such credit or refund may be allowed or made, if claim therefor is filed within the period provided in subparagraph (A) of this paragraph. In the case of any such claim for credit or refund, the determination by any court, including the Tax Court, in any proceeding in which the decision of the court has become final, shall not be conclusive with respect to the work incentive program credit, and the effect of such credit, to the extent that such credit is affected by a carryback which was not in issue in such proceeding."

"(9) SPECIAL PERIOD OF LIMITATION WITH RESPECT TO NEW EMPLOYEE CREDIT CARRYBACKS.—

(A) PERIOD OF LIMITATIONS.—Of the claim for credit or refund related to an overpayment attributable to a new employee credit carryback, in lieu of the 3-year period of limitation prescribed in subsection (a), the period shall be that period which ends with the expiration of the 15th day of the 40th month (or 39th month, in the case of a corporation) following the end of the taxable year of the unused new employee credit which results in such carryback (or, with respect to any portion of a new employee credit carryback from a taxable year attributable to a net operating loss carryback, an investment credit carryback, a work incentive program credit carryback, or a capital loss carryback from a subsequent taxable year, the period shall be that period which ends with the expiration of the 15th day of the 40th month, or 39th month, in the case of a corporation following the end of such taxable year) or the period prescribed in subsection (c) in respect of such taxable year, whichever expires later. In the case of such a claim, the amount of the credit or refund may exceed the portion of the tax paid within the period provided in subsection (b)(2) or (c), whichever is applicable, to the extent of the amount of the overpayment attributable to such carryback.

(B) APPLICABLE RULES.—If the allowance of a credit or refund of an overpayment of tax attributable to a new employee credit carryback is otherwise prevented by the operation or any law or rule of law other than section 7122, relating to compromises, such credit or refund may be allowed or made, if claim therefor is filed within the period provided in subparagraph (A) of this paragraph. In the case of any such claim for credit or refund, the determination by any court, including the Tax Court, in any proceeding in which the decision of the court has become final shall not be conclusive with respect to the new employee credit, and the effect of such credit, to the extent that such credit is affected by a carryback which was not in issue in such proceeding."

• **1978, Revenue Act of 1978 (P.L. 95-600)**

P.L. 95-600, §703(p)(3):

Amended Code Sec. 6511(d)(2)(A). **Effective** with respect to losses sustained in tax years ending after 11-7-78. Prior to amendment, Code Sec. 6511(d)(2)(A) read:

"(A) PERIOD OF LIMITATION.—If the claim for credit or refund relates to an overpayment attributable to a net operating loss carryback or a capital loss carryback, in lieu of the 3-year period of limitation prescribed in subsection (a), the period shall be that period which ends with the expiration of the 15th day of the 40th month (or the 39th month, in the case of a corporation) following the end of the taxable year of the net operating loss or net capital loss which results in such carryback, or the period prescribed in subsection (c) in respect of such taxable year, whichever expires later; except that—

"(i) with respect to an overpayment attributable to a net operating loss carryback to any year on account of a certification issued to the taxpayer under section 317 of the Trade Expansion Act of 1962, the period shall not expire before the expiration of the sixth month following the month in which such certification is issued to the taxpayer, and

"(ii) with respect to an overpayment attributable to the creation of, or an increase in, a net operating loss carryback as a result of the elimination of excessive profits by a renegotiation (as defined in section 1481(a)(1)(A)), the period shall not expire before the expiration of the twelfth month following the month in which the agreement or order for the elimination of such excessive profits becomes final."

• **1977, Tax Reduction and Simplification Act of 1977 (P.L. 95-30)**

P.L. 95-30, §202(d)(4)(B):

Amended Code Sec. 6511(d) by adding paragraph (9). **Effective** for tax years beginning after 12-31-76, and for credit carrybacks from such years.

• **1976, Tax Reform Act of 1976 (P.L. 94-455)**

P.L. 94-455, §1906(a)(33)(A):

Deleted "September 1, 1959, or" and, "whichever is the later" in Code Sec. 6511(d)(2)(A)(ii). **Effective** 2-1-77.

Sec. 6511(d)(8)(B)

LIMITATIONS—CREDIT OR REFUND

P.L. 94-455, §1906(a)(33)(B):
Deleted "the later of the following dates: (A)" and ", or (B) December 31, 1965" in Code Sec. 6511(d)(5). **Effective** 2-1-77.

P.L. 94-455, §2107(g)(2)(B):
Inserted ", an investment credit carryback," after "net operating loss carryback" in Code Sec. 6511(d)(7). **Effective** 10-4-76.

• **1974, Employee Retirement Income Security Act of 1974 (P.L. 93-406)**

P.L. 93-406, §4081(b):
Amended Code Sec. 6511(d) by adding new paragraph (8). **Effective** 9-2-74.

• **1971, Revenue Act of 1971 (P.L. 92-178)**

P.L. 92-178, §601(d)(2):
Amended Code Sec. 6511(d) by adding paragraph (7). **Effective** for tax years ending after 12-31-71.

• **1969, Tax Reform Act of 1969 (P.L. 91-172)**

P.L. 91-172, §311(d)(3):
Amended Sec. 6511(d)(2)(B)(ii) by substituting references to Code Sec. 1302(c) for references to Code Sec. 1302(e). **Effective** 1-1-70.

P.L. 91-172, §512(e)(2):
Amended Code Sec. 6511(d)(2)(A). **Effective** with respect to net capital losses sustained in tax years beginning after 12-31-69. Prior to amendment, Code Sec. 6511(d)(2)(A) read as follows:

(2) SPECIAL PERIOD OF LIMITATION WITH RESPECT TO NET OPERATING LOSS CARRYBACKS.—

(A) PERIOD OF LIMITATION.—If the claim for credit or refund relates to an overpayment attributable to a net operating loss carryback, in lieu of the 3-year period of limitation prescribed in subsection (a), the period shall be that period which ends with the expiration of the 15th day of the 40th month (or the 39th month, in the case of a corporation) following the end of the taxable year of the net operating loss which results in such carryback, or the period prescribed in subsection (c) in respect of such taxable year, whichever expires later; except that—.

P.L. 91-172, §512(e)(2):
Amended Code Sec. 6511(d)(2)(B)(i) by adding "or a capital loss carryback" after "loss carryback"; and by amending last sentence. **Effective** with respect to net capital losses sustained in tax years beginning after 12-31-69. Prior to amendment, last sentence of Code Sec. 6511(d)(2)(B)(i) read as follows:

"In the case of any such claim for credit or refund or any such application for a tentative carryback adjustment, the determination by any court, including the Tax Court, in any proceeding in which the decision of the court has become final, shall be conclusive except with respect to the net operating loss deduction, and the effect of such deduction, to the extent that such deduction is affected by a carryback which was not in issue in such proceeding."

P.L. 91-172, §512(e)(2):
Amended Code Sec. 6511(d)(2)(B)(ii) by adding "or a capital loss carryback, as the case may be," after "loss carryback". **Effective** with respect to net capital losses sustained in tax years beginning after 12-31-69.

P.L. 91-172, §512(e)(2):
Amended Code Sec. 6511(d)(4)(A) by adding "or a capital loss carryback" after "loss carryback". **Effective** with respect to net capital losses sustained in tax years beginning after 12-31-69.

• **1967 (P.L. 90-225)**

P.L. 90-225, §2(d):
Amended Code Sec. 6511(d)(4)(A) by inserting after "which results in such carryback" in the first sentence the following: "(or, with respect to any portion of a investment credit carryback from a taxable year attributable to a net operating loss carryback from a subsequent taxable year, the period shall be that period which ends with the expiration of the 15th day of the 40th month, or 39th month, in the case of a corporation, following the end of such subsequent taxable year)". **Effective** with respect to investment credit carrybacks attributable to net operating loss carrybacks from tax years ending after 7-31-67.

• **1964 (P.L. 88-571)**

P.L. 88-571, §3(c):
Amended Code Sec. 6511(d) by adding paragraph (6). **Effective** with respect to amounts added to policyholders surplus accounts for tax years beginning after 12-31-58.

• **1964, Revenue Act of 1964 (P.L. 88-272)**

P.L. 88-272, §232(d):
Amended Code Sec. 6511(d)(2)(B) by designating the first paragraph as (i) and by adding new paragraph (ii). **Effective** with respect to tax years beginning after 12-31-63.

P.L. 88-272, §239:
Added to Code Sec. 6511(d) a new paragraph (5).

• **1962, Revenue Act of 1962 (P.L. 87-834)**

P.L. 87-834, §2:
Added to Code Sec. 6511(d) a new paragraph (4). **Effective** for tax years ending after 12-31-61.

• **1962, Trade Expansion Act of 1962 (P.L. 87-794)**

P.L. 87-794, §317(d):
Amended Code Sec. 6511(d)(2)(A). **Effective** with respect to net operating losses for tax years ending after 12-31-55. Prior to amendment, Sec. 6511(d)(2)(A) read as follows:

"(A) Period of limitation.—If the claim for credit or refund relates to an overpayment attributable to a net operating loss carryback, in lieu of the 3-year period of limitation prescribed in subsection (a), the period shall be that period which ends with the expiration of the 15th day of the 40th month (or 39th month, in the case of a corporation) following the end of the taxable year of the net operating loss which results in such carryback, or the period prescribed in subsection (c) in respect of such taxable year, whichever expires later; except that, with respect to an overpayment attributable to the creation of or an increase in a net operating loss carryback as a result of the elimination of excessive profits by a renegotiation (as defined in section 1481(a)(1)(A)), the period shall not expire before September 1, 1959, or the expiration of the twelfth month following the month in which the agreement of order for the elimination of such excessive profits becomes final, whichever is the later. In the case of such a claim, the amount of the credit or refund may exceed the portion of the tax paid within the period provided in subsection (b)(2) or (c), whichever is applicable, to the extent of the amount of the overpayment attributable to such carryback."

• **1959 (P.L. 86-280)**

P.L. 86-280, §1(a):
Added the matter following the semicolon in the first sentence of Code Sec. 6511(d)(2)(A).

P.L. 86-280, §1(c), provides:
"The amendment made by subsection (a) shall apply with respect to claims for credit or refund resulting from the elimination of excessive profits by renegotiation to which section 6511(d)(2) of the Internal Revenue Code of 1954 applies."

• **1958, Technical Amendments Act of 1958 (P.L. 85-866)**

P.L. 85-866, §82(d):
Amended Sec. 6511(d)(2)(A) by striking out the phrase "15th day of the 39th month" and substituting the following: "15th day of the 40th month (or 39th month, in the case of a corporation)". **Effective** 1-1-54.

[Sec. 6511(e)—Repealed]

Amendments

• **1990, Omnibus Budget Reconciliation Act of 1990 (P.L. 101-508)**

P.L. 101-508, §11801(c)(22)(C):
Repealed Code Sec. 6511(e). **Effective** on the date of enactment of this Act. Prior to repeal, Code Sec. 6511(e) read as follows:

(e) SPECIAL RULES IN CASE OF MANUFACTURED SUGAR.—

(1) USE AS LIVESTOCK FEED OR FOR DISTILLATION OR PRODUCTION OF ALCOHOL.—No payment shall be allowed under section 6418(a) unless within 2 years after the right to such payment has accrued a claim therefor is filed by the person entitled thereto.

(2) EXPORTATION.—No payment shall be allowed under section 6418(b) unless within 2 years after the right to such payment has accrued a claim therefor is filed by the person entitled thereto.

P.L. 101-508, §11821(b)(1)-(2), provides:

(b) SAVINGS PROVISION.—If—

(1) any provision amended or repealed by this part applied to—

(A) any transaction occurring before the date of the enactment of this Act,

(B) any property acquired before such date of enactment, or

(C) any item of income, loss, deduction, or credit taken into account before such date of enactment, and

(2) the treatment of such transaction, property, or item under such provision would (without regard to the amendments made by this part) affect liability for tax for periods ending after such date of enactment,

nothing in the amendments made by this part shall be construed to affect the treatment of such transaction, property, or item for purposes of determining liability for tax for periods ending after such date of enactment.

• **1965, Sugar Act Amendments of 1965 (P.L. 89-331)**

P.L. 89-331, §9(c):
Amended Code Sec. 6511(e)(1) by inserting "Or Production" after "Distillation" in the heading. **Effective** 11-8-65.

[Sec. 6511(f)]

(f) SPECIAL RULE FOR CHAPTER 42 AND SIMILAR TAXES.—For purposes of any tax imposed by section 4912, chapter 42, or section 4975, the return referred to in subsection (a) shall be the return specified in section 6501(l)(1).

Amendments

• **1988, Technical and Miscellaneous Revenue Act of 1988 (P.L. 100-647)**

P.L. 100-647, §1018(u)(51)(A)-(B):
Amended Code Sec. 6511(f) by striking out "chapter 42" in the text and inserting in lieu thereof "section 4912, chapter 42,", and by striking out "Certain Chapter 43 Taxes" in the subsection heading and inserting in lieu thereof "Similar Taxes". **Effective** as if included in the provision of P.L. 99-514 to which it relates.

LIMITATIONS—CREDIT OR REFUND

- **1984, Deficit Reduction Act of 1984 (P.L. 98-369)**

P.L. 98-369, §163(b)(2):

Amended Code Sec. 6511(f) by striking out "section 6501(n)(1)" and inserting in lieu thereof "section 6501(l)(1)". **Effective** for expenditures with respect to which the second tax year described in Code Sec. 118(b)(2)(B) ends after 12-31-84.

Amendments

- **2015, Bipartisan Budget Act of 2015 (P.L. 114-74)**

P.L. 114-74, §1101(f)(6):

Amended Code Sec. 6511 by striking subsection (g). **Effective** generally for returns filed for partnership tax years beginning after 12-31-2017. For a special rule, see Act Sec. 1101(g)(4), below. Prior to being stricken, Code Sec. 6511(g) read as follows:

(g) SPECIAL RULE FOR CLAIMS WITH RESPECT TO PARTNERSHIP ITEMS.—In the case of any tax imposed by subtitle A with respect to any person which is attributable to any partnership item (as defined in section 6231(a)(3)), the provisions of section 6227 and subsections (c) and (d) of section 6230 shall apply in lieu of the provisions of this subchapter.

P.L. 114-74, §1101(g)(4), provides:

(4) ELECTION.—A partnership may elect (at such time and in such form and manner as the Secretary of the Treasury may prescribe) for the amendments made by this section (other than the election under section 6221(b) of such Code (as added by this Act)) to apply to any return of the partnership filed for partnership taxable years beginning after the date of the enactment of this Act and before January 1, 2018.

- **1982, Tax Equity and Fiscal Responsibility Act of 1982 (P.L. 97-248)**

P.L. 97-248, §402(c)(7):

Amended Code Sec. 6511(g). **Effective** for partnership tax years beginning after 9-3-82 and also to partnership tax years ending after that date if the partnership, each partner, and each indirect partner, requests such application and the Secretary or his delegate consents to such application. Prior to amendment, Code Sec. 6511(g) read as follows:

"(g) SPECIAL RULE FOR PARTNERSHIP ITEMS OF FEDERALLY REGISTERED PARTNERSHIPS.—

(1) IN GENERAL.—In the case of any tax imposed by subtitle A with respect to any person, the period for filing a claim for credit or refund of any overpayment attributable to any partnership item of a federally registered partnership shall not expire before the later of—

(A) the date which is 4 years after the date prescribed by law (including extensions thereof) for filing the partnership return for the partnership taxable year in which the item arose, or

(B) if an agreement under the provisions of section 6501(c)(4) extending the period for the assessment of any deficiency attributable to such partnership item is made before the date specified in subparagraph (A), the date 6 months after the expiration of such extension.

In any case to which the preceding sentence applies, the amount of the credit or refund may exceed the portion of the tax paid within the period provided in subsection (b)(2) or (c), whichever is applicable.

(2) DEFINITIONS.—For purposes of this subsection, the terms 'partnership item' and 'federally registered partnership' have the same meanings as such terms have when used in section 6501(o)."

- **1980, Technical Corrections Act of 1979 (P.L. 96-222)**

P.L. 96-222, §102(a)(2)(B):

Amended Code Sec. 6511(g)(2) by striking out "6501(q)" and inserting "6501(o)". **Effective** for partnership items arising in partnership tax years beginning after 12-31-78.

- **1978, Revenue Act of 1978 (P.L. 95-600)**

P.L. 95-600, §212(b)(1):

Added Code Sec. 6511(g). **Effective** for partnership items arising in partnership tax years beginning after 12-31-78.

- **1980, Technical Corrections Act of 1979 (P.L. 96-222)**

P.L. 96-222, §108(b)(1)(B):

Amended Code Sec. 6511(f) by adding "or section 4975" and by adding "and Certain Chapter 43" to the heading. **Effective** with respect to contributions, acts and expenditures made after 12-31-77.

- **1969, Tax Reform Act of 1969 (P.L. 91-172)**

P.L. 91-172, §101(h):

Added Code Sec. 6511(f). **Effective** 1-1-70.

[Sec. 6511(g)—Stricken]

[Sec. 6511(h)]

(h) RUNNING OF PERIODS OF LIMITATION SUSPENDED WHILE TAXPAYER IS UNABLE TO MANAGE FINANCIAL AFFAIRS DUE TO DISABILITY.—

(1) IN GENERAL.—In the case of an individual, the running of the periods specified in subsections (a), (b), and (c) shall be suspended during any period of such individual's life that such individual is financially disabled.

(2) FINANCIALLY DISABLED.—

(A) IN GENERAL.—For purposes of paragraph (1), an individual is financially disabled if such individual is unable to manage his financial affairs by reason of a medically determinable physical or mental impairment of the individual which can be expected to result in death or which has lasted or can be expected to last for a continuous period of not less than 12 months. An individual shall not be considered to have such an impairment unless proof of the existence thereof is furnished in such form and manner as the Secretary may require.

(B) EXCEPTION WHERE INDIVIDUAL HAS GUARDIAN, ETC.—An individual shall not be treated as financially disabled during any period that such individual's spouse or any other person is authorized to act on behalf of such individual in financial matters.

Amendments

- **1998, IRS Restructuring and Reform Act of 1998 (P.L. 105-206)**

P.L. 105-206, §3202(a):

Amended Code Sec. 6511 by redesignating subsection (h) as subsection (i) and by inserting after subsection (g) a new subsection (h). **Effective** for periods of disability before, on, or after 7-22-98 but does not apply to any claim for credit or refund which (without regard to such amendment) is barred by the operation of any law or rule of law (including res judicata) as of 7-22-98.

[Sec. 6511(i)]

(i) CROSS REFERENCES.—

(1) For time return deemed filed and tax considered paid, see section 6513.

(2) For limitations with respect to certain credits against estate tax, see sections 2014(b) and 2015.

(3) For limitations in case of floor stocks refunds, see section 6412.

(4) For a period of limitations for credit or refund in the case of joint income returns after separate returns have been filed, see section 6013(b)(3).

(5) For limitations in case of payments under section 6420 (relating to gasoline used on farms), see section 6420(b).

(6) For limitations in case of payments under section 6421 (relating to gasoline used for certain nonhighway purposes or by local transit systems), see section 6421(d).

(7) For a period of limitations for refund of an overpayment of penalties imposed under section 6694 or 6695, see section 6696(d)(2).

Amendments

- **2013, American Taxpayer Relief Act of 2012 (P.L. 112-240)**

P.L. 112-240, §101(a)(1) and (3), provides:

SEC. 101. PERMANENT EXTENSION AND MODIFICATION OF 2001 TAX RELIEF.

(a) PERMANENT EXTENSION.—

(1) IN GENERAL.—The Economic Growth and Tax Relief Reconciliation Act of 2001 is amended by striking title IX.

* * *

(3) EFFECTIVE DATE.—The amendments made by this subsection shall apply to taxable, plan, or limitation years beginning after December 31, 2012, and estates of decedents dying, gifts made, or generation skipping transfers after December 31, 2012.

- **2001, Economic Growth and Tax Relief Reconciliation Act of 2001 (P.L. 107-16)**

P.L. 107-16, §532(c)(11):

Amended Code Sec. 6511(i)(2) by striking "2011(c), 2014(b)," and inserting "2014(b)". **Effective** for estates of decedents dying, and generation-skipping transfers, after 12-31-2004.

Sec. 6511(g)—Stricken

LIMITATIONS—CREDIT OR REFUND

P.L. 107-16, §901(a)-(b), as amended by P.L. 111-312, §101(a)(1), provides [but see P.L. 112-240, §101(a)(1) and (3), above]:

SEC. 901. SUNSET OF PROVISIONS OF ACT.

(a) IN GENERAL.—All provisions of, and amendments made by, this Act shall not apply—

(1) to taxable, plan, or limitation years beginning after December 31, 2012, or

(2) in the case of title V, to estates of decedents dying, gifts made, or generation skipping transfers, after December 31, 2012.

(b) APPLICATION OF CERTAIN LAWS.—The Internal Revenue Code of 1986 and the Employee Retirement Income Security Act of 1974 shall be applied and administered to years, estates, gifts, and transfers described in subsection (a) as if the provisions and amendments described in subsection (a) had never been enacted.

• 1998, IRS Restructuring and Reform Act of 1998 (P.L. 105-206)

P.L. 105-206, §3202(a):

Amended Code Sec. 6511 by redesignating subsection (h) as subsection (i). Effective for periods of disability before, on, or after 7-22-98 but does not apply to any claim for credit or refund which (without regard to such amendment) is barred by the operation of any law or rule of law (including res judicata) as of 7-22-98.

• 1988, Technical and Miscellaneous Revenue Act of 1988 (P.L. 100-647)

P.L. 100-647, §1017(c)(11):

Amended Code Sec. 6511(i)[(h)](6) by striking out "section 6421(c)" and inserting in lieu thereof "section 6421(d)". Effective as if included in the provision of P.L. 99-514 to which it relates.

• 1988, Omnibus Trade and Competitiveness Act of 1988 (P.L. 100-418)

P.L. 100-418, §1941(b)(2)(I):

Amended Code Sec. 6511 by striking subsection (h) and redesignating subsection (i) as subsection (h). Effective for crude oil removed from the premises on or after 8-23-88. Prior to amendment, Code Sec. 6511(h) read as follows:

(h) SPECIAL RULES FOR WINDFALL PROFIT TAXES.—

(1) OIL SUBJECT TO WITHHOLDING.—In the case of any oil to which section 4995(a) applies and with respect to which no return is required, the return referred to in subsection (a) shall be the return (of the person liable for the tax imposed by section 4986) or the taxes imposed by subtitle A for the taxable year in which the removal year (as defined in section 6501(m)(1)(B)) ends.

(2) SPECIAL RULE FOR DOE RECLASSIFICATION.—In the case of any tax imposed by chapter 45, if a Department of Energy change (as defined in section 6501(m)(2)(B)) becomes final, the period for filing a claim for credit or refund for any overpayment attributable to such change shall not expire before the date which is 1 year after the date on which such change becomes final.

(3) CROSS REFERENCE.—

For period of limitation for windfall profit tax items of partnerships, see section 6227(a) and subsections (c) and (d) of section 6230 as made applicable by section 6232.

• 1986, Tax Reform Act of 1986 (P.L. 99-514)

P.L. 99-514, §1847(b)(15)(A) and (B):

Amended Code Sec. 6511(h) by striking out "section 6501(q)(1)(B)" in paragraph (1) and inserting in lieu thereof "section 6501(m)(1)(B)", and by striking out "section 6501(q)(2)(B)" in paragraph (2) and inserting in lieu thereof "section 6501(m)(2)(B)". Effective as if included in the provision of P.L. 98-369 to which it relates.

• 1984, Deficit Reduction Act of 1984 (P.L. 98-369)

P.L. 98-369, §714(p)(2)(G):

Amended Code Sec. 6511(h)(3). Effective as if included in P.L. 97-248. Prior to amendment, 6511(h)(3) read as follows:

(3) Partnership Items of Federally Registered Partnerships.—Under regulations prescribed by the Secretary, rules similar to the rules of subsection (g) shall apply to the tax imposed by section 4986.

P.L. 98-369, §735(c)(14):

Amended Code Sec. 6511 by striking out subsection (i) and by redesignating subsection (j) as subsection (i). Effective as if included in the provision of P.L. 97-424 to which it relates. Prior to amendment, subsection (i) read as follows:

(i) Special Rule for Certain Tread Rubber Tax Credits or Refunds.—The period for allowing a credit or making a refund of any overpayment of tax arising by reason of subparagraph (G)(iii) of section 6416(b)(2) with respect to any adjustment of sales price of a tire pursuant to a warranty or guarantee shall not expire if claim therefore is filed before the date which is one year after the day on which such adjustment is made.

• 1980 (P.L. 96-598)

P.L. 96-598, §1(c):

Redesignated Code Sec. 6511(i) as (j) and inserted a new (i). Effective 2-1-81.

• 1980, Crude Oil Windfall Profit Tax Act of 1980 (P.L. 96-223)

P.L. 96-223, §101(g)(2):

Added Code Sec. 6511(h). For the effective date and transitional rules, see P.L. 96-223, §101(i), following Code Sec. 4986.

P.L. 96-223, §101(g)(2):

Redesignated Code Sec. 6511(h) as (i). Effective for periods beginning after 2-29-80.

• 1978, Revenue Act of 1978 (P.L. 95-600)

P.L. 95-600, §212(b)(1):

Redesignated former Code Sec. 6511(g) as Code Sec. 6511(h).

• 1976, Tax Reform Act of 1976 (P.L. 94-455)

P.L. 94-455, §1203(h)(3):

Added a new paragraph (7) to Code Sec. 6511(g). Effective for documents prepared after 12-31-76.

• 1969, Tax Reform Act of 1969 (P.L. 91-172)

P.L. 91-172, §101(h):

Redesignated former Code Sec. 6511(f) as Code Sec. 6511(g). Effective 1-1-70.

• 1956 (P.L. 627, 84th Cong.)

P.L. 627, 84th Cong., §208(e)(6):

Amended subsection (f) by adding subparagraph (6). Effective 7-1-56.

• 1956 (P.L. 466, 84th Cong.)

P.L. 466, 84th Cong., §4(e):

Added subparagraph (5) to Code Sec. 6511(f).

[Sec. 6512]

SEC. 6512. LIMITATIONS IN CASE OF PETITION TO TAX COURT.

[Sec. 6512(a)]

(a) EFFECT OF PETITION TO TAX COURT.—If the Secretary has mailed to the taxpayer a notice of deficiency under section 6212(a) (relating to deficiencies of income, estate, gift, and certain excise taxes) and if the taxpayer files a petition with the Tax Court within the time prescribed in section 6213(a) (or 7481(c) with respect to a determination of statutory interest or section 7481(d) solely with respect to a determination of estate tax by the Tax Court), no credit or refund of income tax for the same taxable year, of gift tax for the same calendar year or calendar quarter, of estate tax in respect of the taxable estate of the same decedent, or of tax imposed by chapter 41, 42, 43, or 44 with respect to any act (or failure to act) to which such petition relates, in respect of which the Secretary has determined the deficiency shall be allowed or made and no suit by the taxpayer for the recovery of any part of the tax shall be instituted in any court except—

(1) As to overpayments determined by a decision of the Tax Court which has become final, and

(2) As to any amount collected in excess of an amount computed in accordance with the decision of the Tax Court which has become final, and

(3) As to any amount collected after the period of limitation upon the making of levy or beginning a proceeding in court for collection has expired; but in any such claim for credit or refund or in any such suit for refund the decision of the Tax Court which has become final, as to whether such period has expired before the notice of deficiency was mailed, shall be conclusive, and

(4) As to overpayments attributable to partnership items, in accordance with subchapter C of chapter 63, and

(5) As to any amount collected within the period during which the Secretary is prohibited from making the assessment or from collecting by levy or through a proceeding in court under the provisions of section 6213(a), and

(6) As to overpayments the Secretary is authorized to refund or credit pending appeal as provided in subsection (b).

Amendments

• 2000, Community Renewal Tax Relief Act of 2000 (P.L. 106-554)

P.L. 106-554, §319(19):

Amended Code Sec. 6512(a) by striking "; and" at the end of paragraphs (1), (2), and (5) and inserting ", and". Effective 12-21-2000.

• 1998, IRS Restructuring and Reform Act of 1998 (P.L. 105-206)

P.L. 105-206, §3464(b):

Amended Code Sec. 6512(a) by striking the period at the end of paragraph (4) and inserting ", and", and by inserting after paragraph (4) new paragraphs (5) and (6). Effective 7-22-98.

LIMITATIONS—CREDIT OR REFUND

• **1988, Technical and Miscellaneous Revenue Act of 1988 (P.L. 100-647)**

P.L. 100-647, § 6246(b)(1):

Amended Code Sec. 6512(a) by inserting after "section 6213(a)" the following: "(or 7481(c) with respect to a determination of statutory interest)". **Effective** for assessments of deficiencies redetermined by the Tax Court made after 11-10-88.

P.L. 100-647, § 6247(b)(1):

Amended Code Sec. 6512(a), as amended, by striking out "interest)" and inserting in lieu thereof "interest or section 7481(d) solely with respect to a determination of estate tax by the Tax Court)". **Effective** with respect to Tax Court cases for which the decision is not final on 11-10-88.

• **1988, Omnibus Trade and Competitiveness Act of 1988 (P.L. 100-418)**

P.L. 100-418, § 1941(b)(2)(J)(i)-(ii):

Amended Code Sec. 6512(a) by striking "of tax imposed by chapter 41" and inserting "or of tax imposed by chapter 41", and by striking, "or of tax imposed by chapter 45 for the same taxable period" after "petition relates". **Effective** for crude oil removed from the premises on or after 8-23-88.

• **1982, Tax Equity and Fiscal Responsibility Act of 1982 (P.L. 97-248)**

P.L. 97-248, § 402(c)(8):

Amended Code Sec. 6512(a) by striking out the period at the end of paragraph (3) and inserting ", and", and by inserting a new paragraph (4). **Effective** for partnership tax years beginning after 9-3-82, and also to partnership tax years ending after that date if the partnership, each partner, and each indirect partner requests such application and if the Secretary or his delegate consents to such application.

• **1980, Crude Oil Windfall Profit Tax Act of 1980 (P.L. 96-223)**

P.L. 96-223, § 101(f)(6)(A):

Amended Code Sec. 6512(a) by striking out "chapter 41, 42, 43, or 44 taxes" and inserting "certain excise taxes", by striking out "or of tax imposed by chapter 41" and inserting "of tax imposed by chapter 41", and by inserting ", or of tax imposed by chapter 45 for the same taxable period" after "to which such petition relates". For the **effective** date and transitional rules, see P.L. 96-223, § 101(i), following Code Sec. 4986.

• **1976, Tax Reform Act of 1976 (P.L. 94-455)**

P.L. 94-455, § 1307(d)(2)(F)(vii):

Substituted "chapter 41, 42," for "chapter 42" each place it appeared in Code Sec. 6512(a). **Effective** on and after 10-4-76.

P.L. 94-455, § 1605(b)(9):

Substituted "43, or 44" for "or 43" each place it appeared in Code Sec. 6512(a). **Effective** for tax years of real estate investment trusts beginning after 10-4-76.

P.L. 94-455, § 1906(b)(13)(A):

Amended 1954 Code by substituting "Secretary" for "Secretary or his delegate" each place it appeared. **Effective** 2-1-77.

• **1970, Excise, Estate, and Gift Tax Adjustment Act of 1970 (P.L. 91-614)**

P.L. 91-614, § 102(d)(9):

Amended Code Sec. 6512(a) by adding "or calendar quarter" in the sixth line thereof. **Effective** for gifts made after 12-31-70.

• **1969, Tax Reform Act of 1969 (P.L. 91-172)**

P.L. 91-172, § 101(j)(47):

Amended the first sentence of Code Sec. 6512(a) by substituting "gift, and chapter 42 taxes" for "and gift taxes" and by substituting "of estate tax in respect of the taxable estate of the same decedent, or of tax imposed by chapter 42 with respect to any act (or failure to act) to which such petition relates," for "or of estate tax in respect of the taxable estate of the same decedent,". **Effective** 1-1-70.

[Sec. 6512(b)]

(b) OVERPAYMENT DETERMINED BY TAX COURT.—

(1) JURISDICTION TO DETERMINE.—Except as provided by paragraph (3) and by section 7463, if the Tax Court finds that there is no deficiency and further finds that the taxpayer has made an overpayment of income tax for the same taxable year, of gift tax for the same calendar year or calendar quarter, of estate tax in respect of the taxable estate of the same decedent, or of tax imposed by chapter 41, 42, 43, or 44 with respect to any act (or failure to act) to which such petition relates for the same taxable period, in respect of which the Secretary determined the deficiency, or finds that there is a deficiency but that the taxpayer has made an overpayment of such tax, the Tax Court shall have jurisdiction to determine the amount of such overpayment, and such amount shall, when the decision of the Tax Court has become final, be credited or refunded to the taxpayer. If a notice of appeal in respect of the decision of the Tax Court is filed under section 7483, the Secretary is authorized to refund or credit the overpayment determined by the Tax Court to the extent the overpayment is not contested on appeal.

(2) JURISDICTION TO ENFORCE.—If, after 120 days after a decision of the Tax Court has become final, the Secretary has failed to refund the overpayment determined by the Tax Court, together with the interest thereon as provided in subchapter B of chapter 67, then the Tax Court, upon motion by the taxpayer, shall have jurisdiction to order the refund of such overpayment and interest. An order of the Tax Court disposing of a motion under this paragraph shall be reviewable in the same manner as a decision of the Tax Court, but only with respect to the matters determined in such order.

(3) LIMIT ON AMOUNT OF CREDIT OR REFUND.—No such credit or refund shall be allowed or made of any portion of the tax unless the Tax Court determines as part of its decision that such portion was paid—

(A) after the mailing of the notice of deficiency,

(B) within the period which would be applicable under section 6511(b)(2), (c), or (d), if on the date of the mailing of the notice of deficiency a claim had been filed (whether or not filed) stating the grounds upon which the Tax Court finds that there is an overpayment, or

(C) within the period which would be applicable under section 6511(b)(2), (c), or (d), in respect of any claim for refund filed within the applicable period specified in section 6511 and before the date of the mailing of the notice of deficiency—

(i) which had not been disallowed before that date,

(ii) which had been disallowed before that date and in respect of which a timely suit for refund could have been commenced as of that date, or

(iii) in respect of which a suit for refund had been commenced before that date and within the period specified in section 6532.

In a case described in subparagraph (B) where the date of the mailing of the notice of deficiency is during the third year after the due date (with extensions) for filing the return of tax and no return was filed before such date, the applicable period under subsections (a) and (b)(2) of section 6511 shall be 3 years.

(4) DENIAL OF JURISDICTION REGARDING CERTAIN CREDITS AND REDUCTIONS.—The Tax Court shall have no jurisdiction under this subsection to restrain or review any credit or reduction made by the Secretary under section 6402.

Amendments

• **2015, Bipartisan Budget Act of 2015 (P.L. 114-74)**

P.L. 114-74, § 1101(f)(7):

Amended Code Sec. 6512(b)(3) by striking the second sentence. **Effective** generally for returns filed for partnership tax years beginning after 12-31-2017. For a special rule, see Act Sec. 1101(g)(4), below. Prior to being stricken, the second sentence of Code Sec. 6512(b)(3) read as follows:

In the case of a credit or refund relating to an affected item (within the meaning of section 6231(a)(5)), the preceding sentence shall be applied by substituting the periods under sections 6229 and 6230(d) for the periods under section 6511(b)(2), (c), and (d).

P.L. 114-74, § 1101(g)(4), provides:

(4) ELECTION.—A partnership may elect (at such time and in such form and manner as the Secretary of the Treasury may prescribe) for the amendments made by this section (other than the election under section 6221(b) of such Code (as added by this Act)) to apply to any return of the partnership filed for partnership taxable years beginning after the date of the enactment of this Act and before January 1, 2018.

• **1998, IRS Restructuring and Reform Act of 1998 (P.L. 105-206)**

P.L. 105-206, § 3464(c):

Amended Code Sec. 6512(b)(1) by adding at the end a new sentence. **Effective** 7-22-98.

• **1997, Taxpayer Relief Act of 1997 (P.L. 105-34)**

P.L. 105-34, § 1239(c)(2):

Amended Code Sec. 6512(b)(3) by adding at the end a new sentence. **Effective** for partnership tax years ending after 8-5-97.

P.L. 105-34, § 1282(a):

Amended Code Sec. 6512(b)(3) by adding at the end a new flush sentence. **Effective** for claims for credit or refund for tax years ending after 8-5-97.

P.L. 105-34, § 1451(a):

Amended Code Sec. 6512(b)(2) by adding at the end a new sentence. **Effective** 8-5-97.

LIMITATIONS—CREDIT OR REFUND

P.L. 105-34, § 1451(b):

Amended Code Sec. 6512(b) by adding at the end a new paragraph (4). **Effective** 8-5-97.

• **1988, Technical and Miscellaneous Revenue Act of 1988 (P.L. 100-647)**

P.L. 100-647, § 6244(a):

Amended Code Sec. 6512(b) by striking out "paragraph (2)" and inserting in lieu thereof "paragraph (3)" in paragraph (1), by redesignating paragraph (2) as paragraph (3) and by inserting new paragraph (2). **Effective** for overpayments determined by the Tax Court which have not yet been refunded by the 90th day after 11-10-88.

• **1988, Omnibus Trade and Competitiveness Act of 1988 (P.L. 100-418)**

P.L. 100-418, § 1941(b)(2)(K)(i)-(ii):

Amended Code Sec. 6512(b)(1) by striking "of tax imposed by chapter 41" and inserting "or of tax imposed by chapter 41", and by striking ", or of tax imposed by chapter 45 for the same taxable period" after "petition relates". **Effective** for crude oil removed from the premises on or after 8-23-88.

• **1982, Tax Equity and Fiscal Responsibility Act of 1982 (P.L. 97-248)**

P.L. 97-248, § 402(c)(9):

Amended Code Sec. 6512(b)(2) by striking out "(c), (d), or (g)" each place it appeared and inserting "(c), or (d)". For the **effective** date, see the amendment note for P.L. 97-248, following Code Sec. 6512(a).

• **1980, Crude Oil Windfall Profit Tax Act of 1980 (P.L. 96-223)**

P.L. 96-223, § 101(f)(6)(B):

Amended Code Sec. 6512(b) by striking out "or of tax imposed by chapter 41" and inserting "of tax imposed by chapter 41" and by inserting ",or of chapter 45 for the same taxable period" after "to which such petition relates". For the **effective** date and transitional rules, see P.L. 96-223, § 101(i), following Code Sec. 4986.

• **1978, Revenue Act of 1978 (P.L. 95-600)**

P.L. 95-600, § 212(b)(2):

Amended Code Sec. 6512(b)(2) by changing "(c), or (d)" each place it appeared to "(c), (d), or (g)". **Effective** for partnership items arising in partnership tax years beginning after 12-31-78.

• **1976, Tax Reform Act of 1976 (P.L. 94-455)**

P.L. 94-455, § 1307(d)(2)(F)(vii):

Substituted "chapter 41, 42," for "chapter 42" each place it appeared in Code Sec. 6512(b)(1). **Effective** on and after 10-4-76.

P.L. 94-455, § 1605(b)(9):

Substituted "43, or 44" for "or 43" each place it appeared in Code Sec. 6512(b). **Effective** for tax years of real estate investment trusts beginning after 10-4-76.

P.L. 94-455, § 1906(b)(13)(A):

Amended 1954 Code by substituting "Secretary" for "Secretary or his delegate" each place it appeared. **Effective** 2-1-77.

• **1974, Employee Retirement Income Security Act of 1974 (P.L. 93-406)**

P.L. 93-406, § 1016(a)(16):

Amended Code Sec. 6512 by changing "chapter 42" to "chapter 42 or 43" each place it appears. For **effective** date, see amendment note for Code Sec. 410.

• **1970, Excise, Estate, and Gift Tax Adjustment Act of 1970 (P.L. 91-614)**

P.L. 91-614, § 102(d)(9):

Amended Code Sec. 6512(b) by adding "or calendar quarter" in paragraph (1). **Effective** for gifts made after 12-31-70.

• **1969, Tax Reform Act of 1969 (P.L. 91-172)**

P.L. 91-172, § 101(j)(48):

Amended paragraph (1) of Code Sec. 6512(b) by substituting "of estate tax in respect of the taxable estate of the same decedent, or of tax imposed by chapter 42 with respect to any act (or failure to act) to which such petition relates," for "or of estate tax in respect of the taxable estate of the same decedent,". **Effective** 1-1-70.

P.L. 91-172, § 960(b):

Amended Code Sec. 6512(b)(1) by adding the initial phrase "Except as provided by paragraph (2) and section 7463,". **Effective** 12-30-70.

• **1962 (P.L. 87-870)**

P.L. 87-870, § 4:

Amended Code Sec. 6512(b)(2) by deleting "or" at the end of subparagraph (A), by deleting the period at the end of subparagraph (B) and inserting in lieu thereof ", or", and by adding after subparagraph (B) a new subparagraph (C). **Effective** 10-24-62.

[Sec. 6512(c)]

(c) CROSS REFERENCES.—

(1) For provisions allowing determination of tax in title 11 cases, see section 505(a) of title 11 of the United States Code.

(2) For provision giving the Tax Court jurisdiction to award reasonable litigation costs in proceedings to enforce an overpayment determined by such court, see section 7430.

Amendments

• **1988, Technical and Miscellaneous Revenue Act of 1988 (P.L. 100-647)**

P.L. 100-647, § 6244(b)(2):

Amended Code Sec. 6512(c) by striking out "REFERENCE.—"and inserting in lieu thereof "REFERENCES.—" in the heading, by designating the undesignated paragraph as paragraph (1), and by adding at the end thereof new paragraph (2). **Effective** for overpayments determined by the Tax Court which have not yet been refunded by the 90th day after 11-10-88.

• **1980, Bankruptcy Tax Act of 1980 (P.L. 96-589)**

P.L. 96-589, § 6(d)(3):

Added Code Sec. 6512(c). **Effective** 10-1-79, but inapplicable to proceedings under the Bankruptcy Act commenced before that date.

[Sec. 6513]
SEC. 6513. TIME RETURN DEEMED FILED AND TAX CONSIDERED PAID.

[Sec. 6513(a)]

(a) EARLY RETURN OR ADVANCE PAYMENT OF TAX.—For purposes of section 6511, any return filed before the last day prescribed for the filing thereof shall be considered as filed on such last day. For purposes of section 6511(b)(2) and (c) and section 6512, payment of any portion of the tax made before the last day prescribed for the payment of the tax shall be considered made on such last day. For purposes of this subsection, the last day prescribed for filing the return or paying the tax shall be determined without regard to any extension of time granted the taxpayer and without regard to any election to pay the tax in installments.

[Sec. 6513(b)]

(b) PREPAID INCOME TAX.—For purposes of section 6511 or 6512—

(1) Any tax actually deducted and withheld at the source during any calendar year under chapter 24 shall, in respect of the recipient of the income, be deemed to have been paid by him on the 15th day of the fourth month following the close of his taxable year with respect to which such tax is allowable as a credit under section 31.

(2) Any amount paid as estimated income tax for any taxable year shall be deemed to have been paid on the last day prescribed for filing the return under section 6012 for such taxable year (determined without regard to any extension of time for filing such return).

(3) Any tax withheld at the source under chapter 3 or 4 shall, in respect of the recipient of the income, be deemed to have been paid by such recipient on the last day prescribed for filing the return under section 6012 for the taxable year (determined without regard to any extension of time for filing) with respect to which such tax is allowable as a credit under section 1462 or 1474(b). For this purpose, any exemption granted under section 6012 from the requirement of filing a return shall be disregarded.

LIMITATIONS—CREDIT OR REFUND

Amendments

• **2010, Hiring Incentives to Restore Employment Act (P.L. 111-147)**

P.L. 111-147, § 501(c)(4)(A)-(B):

Amended Code Sec. 6513(b)(3) by inserting "or 4" after "chapter 3", and by inserting "or 1474(b)" after "section 1462". **Effective** generally for payments made after 12-31-2012. For a special rule, see Act Sec. 501(d)(2), below.

P.L. 111-147, § 501(d)(2), provides:

(2) GRANDFATHERED TREATMENT OF OUTSTANDING OBLIGATIONS.—The amendments made by this section shall not require any amount to be deducted or withheld from any payment under any obligation outstanding on the date which is 2 years after the date of the enactment of this Act or from the gross proceeds from any disposition of such an obligation.

• **1966, Foreign Investors Tax Act of 1966 (P.L. 89-809)**

P.L. 89-809, § 105(f)(1):

Amended Code Sec. 6513(b). **Effective** 11-13-66. Prior to amendment, Code Sec. 6513(b) read as follows:

(b) PREPAID INCOME TAX.—For purposes of section 6511 or 6512, any tax actually deducted and withheld at the source during any calendar year under chapter 24 shall, in respect of the recipient of the income, be deemed to have been paid by him on the 15th day of the fourth month following the close of his taxable year with respect to which such tax is allowable as a credit under section 31. For purposes of section 6511 or 6512, any amount paid as estimated income tax for any taxable year shall be deemed to have been paid on the last day prescribed for filing the return under section 6012 for such taxable year (determined without regard to any extension of time for filing such return).

[Sec. 6513(c)]

(c) RETURN AND PAYMENT OF SOCIAL SECURITY TAXES AND INCOME TAX WITHHOLDING.—Notwithstanding subsection (a), for purposes of section 6511 with respect to any tax imposed by chapter 3, 4, 21, or 24—

(1) If a return for any period ending with or within a calendar year is filed before April 15 of the succeeding calendar year, such return shall be considered filed on April 15 of such succeeding calendar year; and

(2) If a tax with respect to remuneration or other amount paid during any period ending with or within a calendar year is paid before April 15 of the succeeding calendar year, such tax shall be considered paid on April 15 of such succeeding calendar year.

Amendments

• **2010, Hiring Incentives to Restore Employment Act (P.L. 111-147)**

P.L. 111-147, § 501(c)(5):

Amended Code Sec. 6513(c) by inserting "4," after "chapter 3,". **Effective** generally for payments made after 12-31-2012. For a special rule, see Act Sec. 501(d)(2), below.

P.L. 111-147, § 501(d)(2), provides:

(2) GRANDFATHERED TREATMENT OF OUTSTANDING OBLIGATIONS.—The amendments made by this section shall not require any amount to be deducted or withheld from any payment under any obligation outstanding on the date which is 2 years after the date of the enactment of this Act or from the gross proceeds from any disposition of such an obligation.

• **1966, Foreign Investors Tax Act of 1966 (P.L. 89-809)**

P.L. 89-809, § 105(f)(2):

Amended Code Sec. 6513(c) by substituting "chapter 3, 21, or 24" for "chapter 21 or 24" and by substituting in paragraph (2) "remuneration or other amount" for "remuneration". **Effective** 11-13-66.

[Sec. 6513(d)]

(d) OVERPAYMENT OF INCOME TAX CREDITED TO ESTIMATED TAX.—If any overpayment of income tax is, in accordance with section 6402(b), claimed as a credit against estimated tax for the succeeding taxable year, such amount shall be considered as a payment of the income tax for the succeeding taxable year (whether or not claimed as a credit in the return of estimated tax for such succeeding taxable year), and no claim for credit or refund of such overpayment shall be allowed for the taxable year in which the overpayment arises.

[Sec. 6513(e)]

(e) PAYMENTS OF FEDERAL UNEMPLOYMENT TAX.—Notwithstanding subsection (a), for purposes of section 6511 any payment of tax imposed by chapter 23 which, pursuant to section 6157, is made for a calendar quarter or other period within a calendar year shall, if made before the last day prescribed for filing the return for the calendar year (determined without regard to any extension of time for filing), be considered made on such last day.

Amendments

• **1988, Technical and Miscellaneous Revenue Act of 1988 (P.L. 100-647)**

P.L. 100-647, § 7106(c)(4):

Amended Code Sec. 6513(e) by striking out the last sentence. **Effective** for remuneration paid after 12-31-88. Prior to amendment, the last sentence of Code Sec. 6513(e) read as follows:

Notwithstanding subsection (a), for purposes of section 6511, any payment of tax imposed by chapter 23A which, pursuant to section 6157, is made for a calendar quarter within a taxable period shall, if made before the last day prescribed for filing the return for the taxable period (determined without regard to any extension of time for filing), be considered made on such last day.

• **1983, Railroad Retirement Solvency Act of 1983 (P.L. 98-76)**

P.L. 98-76, § 231(b)(2)(C):

Added the last sentence in Code Sec. 6513(e). **Effective** for remuneration paid after 6-30-86.

• **1969 (P.L. 91-53)**

P.L. 91-53, § 2(d):

Added Code Sec. 6513(e). **Effective** for calendar years beginning after 12-31-69.

[Sec. 6514]

SEC. 6514. CREDITS OR REFUNDS AFTER PERIOD OF LIMITATION.

[Sec. 6514(a)]

(a) CREDITS OR REFUNDS AFTER PERIOD OF LIMITATION.—A refund of any portion of an internal revenue tax shall be considered erroneous and a credit of any such portion shall be considered void—

(1) EXPIRATION OF PERIOD FOR FILING CLAIM.—If made after the expiration of the period of limitation for filing claim therefor, unless within such period claim was filed; or

(2) DISALLOWANCE OF CLAIM AND EXPIRATION OF PERIOD FOR FILING SUIT.—In the case of a claim filed within the proper time and disallowed by the Secretary, if the credit or refund was made after the expiration of the period of limitation for filing suit, unless within such period suit was begun by the taxpayer.

(3) RECOVERY OF ERRONEOUS REFUNDS.—

For procedure by the United States to recover erroneous refunds, see sections 6532(b) and 7405.

Amendments

• **1976, Tax Reform Act of 1976 (P.L. 94-455)**

P.L. 94-455, § 1906(b)(13)(A):

Amended 1954 Code by substituting "Secretary" for "Secretary of his delegate" each place it appeared. **Effective** 2-1-77.

[Sec. 6514(b)]

(b) CREDIT AFTER PERIOD OF LIMITATION.—Any credit against a liability in respect of any taxable year shall be void if any payment in respect of such liability would be considered an overpayment under section 6401(a).

[Sec. 6515]

SEC. 6515. CROSS REFERENCES.

For limitations in case of—

(1) Deficiency dividends of a personal holding company, see section 547.

(2) Tentative carry-back adjustments, see section 6411.
(3) Service in a combat zone, etc., see section 7508.
(4) Suits for refund by taxpayers, see section 6532(a).
(5) Deficiency dividends of a regulated investment company or real estate investment trust, see section 860.

Amendments

• **2015, Bipartisan Budget Act of 2015 (P.L. 114-74)**

P.L. 114-74, §1101(f)(8):

Amended Code Sec. 6515 by striking paragraph (6). **Effective** generally for returns filed for partnership tax years beginning after 12-31-2017. For a special rule, see Act Sec. 1101(g)(4), below. Prior to being stricken, Code Sec. 6515(6) read as follows:

(6) Refunds or credits attributable to partnership items, see section 6227 and subsections (c) and (d) of section 6230.

P.L. 114-74, §1101(g)(4), provides:

(4) ELECTION.—A partnership may elect (at such time and in such form and manner as the Secretary of the Treasury may prescribe) for the amendments made by this section (other than the election under section 6221(b) of such Code (as added by this Act)) to apply to any return of the partnership filed for partnership taxable years beginning after the date of the enactment of this Act and before January 1, 2018.

• **1990, Omnibus Budget Reconciliation Act of 1990 (P.L. 101-508)**

P.L. 101-508, §11801(c)(17)(C):

Amended Code Sec. 6515 by striking paragraph (2) and by redesignating paragraphs (3) through (7) as paragraphs (2) through (6). **Effective** 11-5-90. Prior to repeal, Code Sec. 6515(2) read as follows:

(2) Overpayment in certain renegotiations of war contracts, see section 1481.

P.L. 101-508, §11821(b)(1)-(2), provides:

(b) SAVINGS PROVISION.—If—

(1) any provision amended or repealed by this part applied to—

(A) any transaction occurring before the date of the enactment of this Act,

(B) any property acquired before such date of enactment, or

(C) any item of income, loss, deduction, or credit taken into account before such date of enactment, and

(2) the treatment of such transaction, property, or item under such provision would (without regard to the amendments made by this part) affect liability for tax for periods ending after such date of enactment,

nothing in the amendments made by this part shall be construed to affect the treatment of such transaction, property, or item for purposes of determining liability for tax for periods ending after such date of enactment.

• **1982, Tax Equity and Fiscal Responsibility Act of 1982 (P.L. 97-248)**

P.L. 97-248, §402(c)(10):

Added Code Sec. 6515(7). **Effective** for partnership tax years beginning after 9-3-82, and also to partnership tax years ending after 9-3-82, if the partnership, each partner, and each indirect partner requests such application and the Secretary or his delegate consents to such application.

• **1978, Revenue Act of 1978 (P.L. 95-600)**

P.L. 95-600, §362(d)(4):

Amended Code Sec. 6515(5). **Effective** with respect to determinations after 11-6-78. Prior to amendment, Code Sec. 6515(5) read as follows:

"(5) Deficiency dividends of a real estate investment trust, see section 860."

• **1976, Tax Reform Act of 1976 (P.L. 94-455)**

P.L. 94-455, §1601(f)(3):

Added a new paragraph (8) at the end of Code Sec. 6515.

P.L. 94-455, §1608, provides:

(a) DEFICIENCY DIVIDEND PROCEDURES.—The amendments made by section 1601 shall apply with respect to determinations (as defined in section 859(c) of the Internal Revenue Code of 1954) occurring after the date of the enactment of this Act. If the amendments made by section 1601 apply to a taxable year ending on or before the date of enactment of this Act:

(1) the reference to section 857(b)(3)(A)(ii) in sections 857(b)(3)(C) and 859(b)(1)(B) of such Code, as amended, shall be considered to be a reference to section 857(b)(3)(A) of such Code, as in effect immediately before the enactment of this Act, and

(2) the reference to section 857(b)(2)(B) in section 859(a) of such Code, as amended, shall be considered to be a reference to section 857(b)(2)(C) of such Code, as in effect immediately before the enactment of this Act.

P.L. 94-455, §1901(b)(36)(D):

Deleted paragraph (1) of Code Sec. 6515. **Effective** with respect to tax years beginning after 12-31-76. Prior to amendment, paragraph (1) read as follows:

(1) Adjustments incident to involuntary liquidation of involuntary liquidation of inventory, see section 1321.

P.L. 94-455, §1901(b)(37)(E):

Amended Code Sec. 6515, as amended by P.L. 94-455, by striking out paragraph (2); and by redesignating paragraphs (3), (4), (5), (6), (7), and (8) as paragraphs (1), (2), (3), (4), (5) and (6), respectively. **Effective** with respect to tax years beginning after 12-31-76. Prior to amendment, paragraph (2) read as follows:

(2) War loss recoveries where prior benefit rule is elected, see section 1335.

Subchapter C—Mitigation of Effect of Period of Limitations

Sec. 6521.   Mitigation of effect of limitation in case of related taxes under different chapters.

[Sec. 6521]

SEC. 6521. MITIGATION OF EFFECT OF LIMITATION IN CASE OF RELATED TAXES UNDER DIFFERENT CHAPTERS.

[Sec. 6521(a)]

(a) SELF-EMPLOYMENT TAX AND TAX ON WAGES.—In the case of the tax imposed by chapter 2 (relating to tax on self-employment income) and the tax imposed by section 3101 (relating to tax on employees under the Federal Insurance Contributions Act)—

(1) If an amount is erroneously treated as self-employment income, or if an amount is erroneously treated as wages, and

(2) If the correction of the error would require an assessment of one such tax and the refund or credit of the other tax, and

(3) If at any time the correction of the error is authorized as to one such tax but is prevented as to the other tax by any law or rule of law (other than section 7122, relating to compromises),

then, if the correction authorized is made, the amount of the assessment, or the amount of the credit or refund, as the case may be, authorized as to the one tax shall be reduced by the amount of the credit or refund, or the amount of the assessment, as the case may be, which would be required with respect to such other tax for the correction of the error if such credit or refund, or such assessment, of such other tax were not prevented by any law or rule of law (other than section 7122, relating to compromises).

[Sec. 6521(b)]

(b) DEFINITIONS.—For purposes of subsection (a), the terms "self-employment income" and "wages" shall have the same meaning as when used in section 1402(b).

Subchapter D—Periods of Limitation in Judicial Proceedings

Sec. 6531.   Periods of limitation on criminal prosecutions.
Sec. 6532.   Periods of limitation on suits.
Sec. 6533.   Cross references.

[Sec. 6531]

SEC. 6531. PERIODS OF LIMITATION ON CRIMINAL PROSECUTIONS.

No person shall be prosecuted, tried, or punished for any of the various offenses arising under the internal revenue laws unless the indictment is found or the information instituted within 3 years next after the commission of the offense, except that the period of limitation shall be 6 years—

(1) for offenses involving the defrauding or attempting to defraud the United States or any agency thereof, whether by conspiracy or not, and in any manner;

LIMITATIONS—JUDICIAL PROCEEDINGS

(2) for the offense of willfully attempting in any manner to evade or defeat any tax or the payment thereof;

(3) for the offense of willfully aiding or assisting in, or procuring, counseling, or advising, the preparation or presentation under, or in connection with any matter arising under, the internal revenue laws, of a false or fraudulent return, affidavit, claim, or document (whether or not such falsity or fraud is with the knowledge or consent of the person authorized or required to present such return, affidavit, claim, or document);

(4) for the offense of willfully failing to pay any tax, or make any return (other than a return required under authority of part III of subchapter A of chapter 61) at the time or times required by law or regulations;

(5) for offenses described in sections 7206(1) and 7207 (relating to false statements and fraudulent documents);

(6) for the offense described in section 7212(a) (relating to intimidation of officers and employees of the United States);

(7) for offenses described in section 7214(a) committed by officers and employees of the United States; and

(8) for offenses arising under section 371 of Title 18 of the United States Code, where the object of the conspiracy is to attempt in any manner to evade or defeat any tax or the payment thereof.

The time during which the person committing any of the various offenses arising under the internal revenue laws is outside the United States or is a fugitive from justice within the meaning of section 3290 of Title 18 of the United States Code, shall not be taken as any part of the time limited by law for the commencement of such proceedings. (The preceding sentence shall also be deemed an amendment to section 3748(a) of the Internal Revenue Code of 1939, and shall apply in lieu of the sentence in section 3748(a) which relates to the time during which a person committing an offense is absent from the district wherein the same is committed, except that such amendment shall apply only if the period of limitations under section 3748 would, without the application of such amendment, expire more than 3 years after the date of enactment of this title, and except that such period shall not, with the application of this amendment, expire prior to the date which is 3 years after the date of enactment of this title.) Where a complaint is instituted before a commissioner of the United States within the period above limited, the time shall be extended until the date which is 9 months after the date of the making of the complaint before the commissioner of the United States. For the purpose of determining the periods of limitation on criminal prosecutions, the rules of section 6513 shall be applicable.

[Sec. 6532]

SEC. 6532. PERIODS OF LIMITATION ON SUITS.

[Sec. 6532(a)]

(a) SUITS BY TAXPAYERS FOR REFUND.—

(1) GENERAL RULE.—No suit or proceeding under section 7422(a) for the recovery of any internal revenue tax, penalty, or other sum, shall be begun before the expiration of 6 months from the date of filing the claim required under such section unless the Secretary renders a decision thereon within that time, nor after the expiration of 2 years from the date of mailing by certified mail or registered mail by the Secretary to the taxpayer of a notice of the disallowance of the part of the claim to which the suit or proceeding relates.

(2) EXTENSION OF TIME.—The 2-year period prescribed in paragraph (1) shall be extended for such period as may be agreed upon in writing between the taxpayer and the Secretary.

(3) WAIVER OF NOTICE OF DISALLOWANCE.—If any person files a written waiver of the requirement that he be mailed a notice of disallowance, the 2-year period prescribed in paragraph (1) shall begin on the date such waiver is filed.

(4) RECONSIDERATION AFTER MAILING OF NOTICE.—Any consideration, reconsideration, or action by the Secretary with respect to such claim following the mailing of a notice by certified mail or registered mail of disallowance shall not operate to extend the period within which suit may be begun.

(5) CROSS REFERENCE.—

For substitution of 120-day period for the 6-month period contained in paragraph (1) in a title 11 case, see section 505(a)(2) of title 11 of the United States Code.

Amendments

• **1980, Bankruptcy Tax Act of 1980 (P.L. 96-589)**

P.L. 96-589, § 6(d)(4):

Amended Code Sec. 6532(a) by adding a new paragraph (5). **Effective** 10-1-79, but inapplicable to any proceeding under the Bankruptcy Act commenced before that date.

• **1976, Tax Reform Act of 1976 (P.L. 94-455)**

P.L. 94-455, § 1906(b)(13)(A):

Amended 1954 Code by substituting "Secretary" for "Secretary or his delegate" each place it appeared. **Effective** 2-1-77.

• **1958, Technical Amendments Act of 1958 (P.L. 85-866)**

P.L. 85-866, § 89(b):

Amended Sec. 6532(a)(4) by striking out "registered mail" and substituting "certified mail or registered mail". **Effective** 9-3-58.

[Sec. 6532(b)]

(b) SUITS BY UNITED STATES FOR RECOVERY OF ERRONEOUS REFUNDS.—Recovery of an erroneous refund by suit under section 7405 shall be allowed only if such suit is begun within 2 years after the making of such refund, except that such suit may be brought at any time within 5 years from the making of the refund if it appears that any part of the refund was induced by fraud or misrepresentation of a material fact.

Amendments

• **1976, Tax Reform Act of 1976 (P.L. 94-455)**

P.L. 94-455, § 1906(b)(13)(A):

Amended 1954 Code by substituting "Secretary" for "Secretary or his delegate" each place it appeared. **Effective** 2-1-77.

[Sec. 6532(c)]

(c) SUITS BY PERSONS OTHER THAN TAXPAYERS.—

(1) GENERAL RULE.—Except as provided by paragraph (2), no suit or proceeding under section 7426 shall be begun after the expiration of 2 years from the date of the levy or agreement giving rise to such action.

(2) PERIOD WHEN CLAIM IS FILED.—If a request is made for the return of property described in section 6343(b), the 2-year period prescribed in paragraph (1) shall be extended for a period of 12 months from the date of filing of such request or for a period of 6 months from the date of mailing by registered or certified mail by the Secretary to the person making such request of a notice of disallowance of the part of the request to which the action relates, whichever is shorter.

INTEREST—UNDERPAYMENTS

Amendments

• **2017, Tax Cuts and Jobs Act (P.L. 115-97)**

P.L. 115-97, §11071(b)(1)-(2):

Amended Code Sec. 6532(c) by striking "9 months" in paragraph (1) and inserting "2 years", and by striking "9-month" in paragraph (2) and inserting "2-year". For the **effective** date, see Act Sec. 11071(c), below.

P.L. 115-97, §11071(c), provides:

(c) EFFECTIVE DATE.—The amendments made by this section shall apply to—

(1) levies made after the date of the enactment of this Act, and

(2) levies made on or before such date if the 9-month period has not expired under section 6343(b) of the Internal Revenue Code of 1986 (without regard to this section) as of such date.

• **1966, Federal Tax Lien Act of 1966 (P.L. 89-719)**

P.L. 89-719, §110(b):

Added new Code Sec. 6532(c). **Effective**, generally, after 11-2-66. but see the amendment note for Code Sec. 6323 for exceptions.

[Sec. 6533]

SEC. 6533. CROSS REFERENCES.

(1) For period of limitation in respect of civil actions for fines, penalties, and forfeitures, see section 2462 of Title 28 of the United States Code.

(2) For extensions of time by reason of armed service in a combat zone, see section 7508.

(3) For suspension of running of statute until 3 years after termination of hostilities, see section 3287 of Title 18.

CHAPTER 67—INTEREST

SUBCHAPTER A.	Interest on underpayments.
SUBCHAPTER B.	Interest on overpayments.
SUBCHAPTER C.	Determination of interest rate; compounding of interest.
SUBCHAPTER D.	Notice requirements.

Subchapter A—Interest on Underpayments

Sec. 6601.	Interest on underpayment, nonpayment, or extensions of time for payment, of tax.
Sec. 6602.	Interest on erroneous refund recoverable by suit.
Sec. 6603.	Deposits made to suspend running of interest on potential underpayments, etc.

[Sec. 6601]

SEC. 6601. INTEREST ON UNDERPAYMENT, NONPAYMENT, OR EXTENSIONS OF TIME FOR PAYMENT, OF TAX.

[Sec. 6601(a)]

(a) GENERAL RULE.—If any amount of tax imposed by this title (whether required to be shown on a return, or to be paid by stamp or by some other method) is not paid on or before the last date prescribed for payment, interest on such amount at the underpayment rate established under section 6621 shall be paid for the period from such last date to the date paid.

Amendments

• **1986, Tax Reform Act of 1986 (P.L. 99-514)**

P.L. 99-514, §1511(c)(11):

Amended Code Sec. 6601(a) by striking out "an annual rate established under section 6621" and inserting in lieu thereof "the underpayment rate established under section 6621". **Effective** for purposes of determining interest for periods after 12-31-86.

• **1975 (P.L. 93-625)**

P.L. 93-625, §7(a)(2):

Amended Code Sec. 6601(a) by substituting "an annual rate established under section 6621" for "the rate of 6 percent per annum". For **effective** date, see the historical comment for P.L. 93-625 following the text of Code Sec. 6621.

[Sec. 6601(b)—Repealed]

Amendments

• **1975 (P.L. 93-625)**

P.L. 93-625, §7(b)(1):

Repealed Code Sec. 6601(b) and redesignated the remaining subsections of Code Sec. 6601. **Effective** on 7-1-75, and applicable to amounts outstanding on such date or arising thereafter. Prior to repeal, Code Sec. 6601(b) read as follows:

(b) EXTENSIONS OF TIME FOR PAYMENT OF ESTATE TAX.—If the time for payment of an amount of tax imposed by chapter 11 is extended as provided in section 6161(a)(2) or 6166, or if the time for payment of an amount of such tax is postponed or extended as provided by section 6163, interest shall be paid at the rate of 4 percent, in lieu of 6 percent as provided in subsection (a). Effective 7-1-75.

• **1958, Technical Amendments Act of 1958 (P.L. 85-866)**

P.L. 85-866, §66(c):

Amended Sec. 6601(b) by striking out the phrase "if postponement of the payment of an amount of such tax is permitted by section 6163(a)," and substituting the phrase

"if the time for payment of an amount of such tax is postponed or extended as provided by section 6163,". For the **effective** date, see Act Sec. 206(f), below.

P.L. 85-866, §206(e):

Amended Sec. 6601(b) by striking out "section 6161(a)(2)" and substituting "section 6161(a)(2) or 6166,". For the **effective** date, see Act Sec. 206(f), below.

P.L. 85-866, §206(f), provides:

"The amendments made by this section shall apply to estates of decedents with respect to which the date for the filing of the estate tax return (including extensions thereof) prescribed by section 6075(a) of the Internal Revenue Code of 1954 is after the date of the enactment of this Act; except that (1) section 6166(i) of such Code as added by this section shall apply to estates of decedents dying after August 16, 1954, but only if the date for the filing of the estate tax return (including extensions thereof) expired on or before the date of the enactment of this Act, and (2) notwithstanding section 6166(a) of such Code, if an election under such section is required to be made before the sixtieth day after the date of the enactment of this Act such an election shall be considered timely if made on or before such sixtieth day." **Effective** 1-1-54.

[Sec. 6601(b)]

(b) LAST DATE PRESCRIBED FOR PAYMENT.—For purposes of this section, the last date prescribed for payment of the tax shall be determined under chapter 62 with the application of the following rules:

(1) EXTENSIONS OF TIME DISREGARDED.—The last date prescribed for payment shall be determined without regard to any extension of time for payment or any installment agreement entered into under section 6159.

(2) JEOPARDY.—The last date prescribed for payment shall be determined without regard to any notice and demand for payment issued, by reason of jeopardy (as provided in chapter 70), prior to the last date otherwise prescribed for such payment.

(3) ACCUMULATED EARNINGS TAX.—In the case of the tax imposed by section 531 for any taxable year, the last date prescribed for payment shall be deemed to be the due date (without regard to extensions) for the return of tax imposed by subtitle A for such taxable year.

(4) LAST DATE FOR PAYMENT NOT OTHERWISE PRESCRIBED.—In the case of taxes payable by stamp and in all other cases in which the last date for payment is not otherwise prescribed, the last date for payment shall be deemed to be the date the liability for tax arises (and in no event shall be later than the date notice and demand for the tax is made by the Secretary).

Amendments

• **2018, Tax Technical Corrections Act of 2018 (P.L. 115-141)**

P.L. 115-141, §401(b)(47), Div. U:

Amended Code Sec. 6601(b) by striking paragraph (2) and by redesignating paragraphs (3) through (5) as paragraphs (2) through (4), respectively. **Effective**

3-23-2018. For a special rule, see Act Sec. 401(e), Div. U, below. Prior to being stricken, Code Sec. 6601(b)(2) read as follows:

(2) INSTALLMENT PAYMENTS.—In the case of an election under section 6156(a) to pay the tax in installments—

Internal Revenue Code   **Sec. 6601(b)(4)**

INTEREST—UNDERPAYMENTS

(A) The date prescribed for payment of each installment of the tax shown on the return shall be determined under section 6156(b), and

(B) The last date prescribed for payment of the first installment shall be deemed the last date prescribed for payment of any portion of the tax not shown on the return.

P.L. 115-141, § 401(e), Div. U, provides:

(e) GENERAL SAVINGS PROVISION WITH RESPECT TO DEADWOOD PROVISIONS.—If—

(1) any provision amended or repealed by the amendments made by subsection (b) or (d) applied to—

(A) any transaction occurring before the date of the enactment of this Act,

(B) any property acquired before such date of enactment, or

(C) any item of income, loss, deduction, or credit taken into account before such date of enactment, and

(2) the treatment of such transaction, property, or item under such provision would (without regard to the amendments or repeals made by such subsection) affect the liability for tax for periods ending after such date of enactment,

nothing in the amendments or repeals made by this section shall be construed to affect the treatment of such transaction, property, or item for purposes of determining liability for tax for periods ending after such date of enactment.

- **1990, Omnibus Budget Reconciliation Act of 1990 (P.L. 101-508)**

P.L. 101-508, § 11801(c)(20)(B)(i)-(iii):

Amended Code Sec. 6601(b)(2) by striking "or 6158(a)" in the material preceding subparagraph (A), by striking "or 6158(a), as the case may be" in subparagraph (A), and by striking the last sentence. **Effective** 11-5-90. Prior to amendment, Code Sec. 6601(b)(2) read as follows:

(2) INSTALLMENT PAYMENTS.—In the case of an election under section 6156(a) or 6158(a) to pay the tax in installments—

(A) The date prescribed for payment of each installment of the tax shown on the return shall be determined under section 6156(b) or 6158(a), as the case may be, and

(B) The last date prescribed for payment of the first installment shall be deemed the last date prescribed for payment of any portion of the tax not shown on the return.

For purposes of subparagraph (A), section 6158(a) shall be treated as providing that the date prescribed for payment of each installment shall not be later than the date prescribed for payment of the 1985 installment.

P.L. 101-508, § 11821(b)(1)-(2), provides:

(b) SAVINGS PROVISION.—If—

(1) any provision amended or repealed by this part applied to—

(A) any transaction occurring before the date of the enactment of this Act,

(B) any property acquired before such date of enactment, or

(C) any item of income, loss, deduction, or credit taken into account before such date of enactment, and

(2) the treatment of such transaction, property, or item under such provision would (without regard to the amendments made by this part) affect liability for tax for periods ending after such date of enactment,

nothing in the amendments made by this part shall be construed to affect the treatment of such transaction, property, or item for purposes of determining liability for tax for periods ending after such date of enactment.

- **1988, Technical and Miscellaneous Revenue Act of 1988 (P.L. 100-647)**

P.L. 100-647, § 6234(b)(1):

Amended Code Sec. 6601(b)(1) by inserting "or any installment agreement entered into under section 6159" after "time for payment". **Effective** for agreements entered into after 11-10-88.

- **1986, Tax Reform Act of 1986 (P.L. 99-514)**

P.L. 99-514, § 1404(c)(3)(A)-(B):

Amended Code Sec. 6601(b)(2) by striking out "6152(a), 6156(a), 6158(a)" and inserting in lieu thereof "6156(a) or 6158(a)", and by striking out "6152(b), 6156(b), or 6158(a)" in subparagraph (A) and inserting in lieu thereof "6156(b) or 6158(a)". **Effective** for tax years beginning after 12-31-86.

P.L. 99-514, § 1512(a):

Amended Code Sec. 6601(b) by redesignating paragraph (4) as paragraph (5) and by inserting after paragraph (3) new paragraph (4). **Effective** for returns the due date for which (determined without regard to extensions) is after 12-31-85.

- **1976, Tax Reform Act of 1976 (P.L. 94-455)**

P.L. 94-455, § 1906(b)(13)(A):

Amended 1954 Code by substituting "Secretary" for "Secretary or his delegate" each place it appeared. **Effective** 2-1-77.

- **1976, Bank Holding Company Tax Act of 1976 (P.L. 94-452)**

P.L. 94-452, § 3(c)(3):

Amended Code Sec. 6601(b) by striking out "or 6156(a)" and inserting in lieu thereof ", 6156(a), or 6158(a)", and by striking out "or 6156(b)" and inserting in lieu thereof ", 6156(b), or 6158(a)"; and by adding the new sentence at the end thereof. **Effective** 10-1-77, with respect to sales after 7-7-70, in tax years ending after 7-7-70, but only in the case of qualified bank holding corporations.

- **1975 (P.L. 93-625)**

P.L. 93-625, § 7(b)(1):

Redesignated Code Sec. 6601(c) as Code Sec. 6601(b). **Effective** 7-1-75.

- **1961, Federal-Aid Highway Act of 1961 (P.L. 87-61)**

P.L. 87-61, § 203(c)(2):

Amended Sec. 6601(c)(2) by adding "or 6156(a)" and "or 6156(b), as the case may be." **Effective** 7-1-61.

[Sec. 6601(c)]

(c) SUSPENSION OF INTEREST IN CERTAIN INCOME, ESTATE, GIFT, AND CERTAIN EXCISE TAX CASES.—In the case of a deficiency as defined in section 6211 (relating to income, estate, gift, and certain excise taxes), if a waiver of restrictions under section 6213(d) on the assessment of such deficiency has been filed, and if notice and demand by the Secretary for payment of such deficiency is not made within 30 days after the filing of such waiver, interest shall not be imposed on such deficiency for the period beginning immediately after such 30th day and ending with the date of notice and demand and interest shall not be imposed during such period on any interest with respect to such deficiency for any prior period.

Amendments

- **2015, Bipartisan Budget Act of 2015 (P.L. 114-74)**

P.L. 114-74, § 1101(f)(9):

Amended Code Sec. 6601(c) by striking the last sentence. **Effective** generally for returns filed for partnership tax years beginning after 12-31-2017. For a special rule, see Act Sec. 1101(g)(4), below. Prior to being stricken, the last sentence of Code Sec. 6601(c) read as follows:

In the case of a settlement under section 6224(c) which results in the conversion of partnership items to nonpartnership items pursuant to section 6231(b)(1)(C), the preceding sentence shall apply to a computational adjustment resulting from such settlement in the same manner as if such adjustment were a deficiency and such settlement were a waiver referred to in the preceding sentence.

P.L. 114-74, § 1101(g)(4), provides:

(4) ELECTION.—A partnership may elect (at such time and in such form and manner as the Secretary of the Treasury may prescribe) for the amendments made by this section (other than the election under section 6221(b) of such Code (as added by this Act)) to apply to any return of the partnership filed for partnership taxable years beginning after the date of the enactment of this Act and before January 1, 2018.

- **1997, Taxpayer Relief Act of 1997 (P.L. 105-34)**

P.L. 105-34, § 1242(a):

Amended Code Sec. 6601(c) by adding at the end a new sentence. **Effective** for adjustments with respect to partnership tax years beginning after 8-5-97.

- **1986, Tax Reform Act of 1986 (P.L. 99-514)**

P.L. 99-514, § 1564(a):

Amended Code Sec. 6601(c) by inserting before the period at the end thereof "and interest shall not be imposed during such period on any interest with respect to such deficiency for any prior period." **Effective** for interest accruing after 12-31-82. However, see Act Sec. 1564(c)(2).

P.L. 99-514, § 1564(b)(2), provides:

(2) STATUTE OF LIMITATIONS.—If refund or credit of any amount resulting from the application of the amendment made by subsection (a) is prevented at any time before the close of the date which is 1 year after the date of the enactment of this Act by the operation of any law or rule of law (including res judicata), refund or credit of such amount (to the extent attributable to the application of the amendment made by subsection (a)) may, nevertheless, be made or allowed if claim therefore is filed before the close of such 1-year period.

- **1980, Crude Oil Windfall Profit Tax Act of 1980 (P.L. 96-223)**

P.L. 96-223, § 101(f)(7):

Amended Code Sec. 6601(c) by striking out in the subsection heading "CHAPTER 41, 42, 43, OR 44 TAX" and inserting "CERTAIN EXCISE TAX". For the **effective** date and the transitional rules, see P.L. 96-223, § 101(i), following Code Sec. 4986.

- **1976, Tax Reform Act of 1976 (P.L. 94-455)**

P.L. 94-455, § 1307(d)(2)(H):

Substituted "Chapter 41, 42," for "Chapter 42" in the heading of Code Sec. 6601(c). **Effective** on and after 10-4-76.

P.L. 94-455, § 1605(b)(10):

Substituted ", 43, or 44" for "or 43" in the heading of Code Sec. 6601(c). **Effective** for tax years of real estate investment trusts beginning after 10-4-76.

P.L. 94-455, § 1906(b)(13)(A):

Amended 1954 Code by substituting "Secretary" for "Secretary or his delegate" each place it appeared. **Effective** 2-1-77.

- **1975 (P.L. 93-625)**

P.L. 93-625, § 7(b)(1):

Redesignated Code Sec. 6601(d) as Code Sec. 6601(c). **Effective** 7-1-75.

- **1974, Employee Retirement Income Security Act of 1974 (P.L. 93-406)**

P.L. 93-406, § 1016(a)(17):

Amended Code Sec. 6601(d) by adding "or 43" to the heading and by changing "chapter 42" to "certain excise". For **effective** date, see amendment note for Code Sec. 410.

INTEREST—UNDERPAYMENTS

- **1969, Tax Reform Act of 1969 (P.L. 91-172)**

P.L. 91-172, §101(j)(49):

Amended Code Sec. 6601(d) by substituting in the heading thereof "Gift, and Chapter 42 Tax Cases" for "and Gift Tax Cases" and by substituting in the body thereof "gift, and chapter 42 taxes" for "and gift taxes". **Effective** 1-1-70.

[Sec. 6601(d)]

(d) INCOME TAX REDUCED BY CARRYBACK OR ADJUSTMENT FOR CERTAIN UNUSED DEDUCTIONS.—

(1) NET OPERATING LOSS OR CAPITAL LOSS CARRYBACK.—If the amount of any tax imposed by subtitle A is reduced by reason of a carryback of a net operating loss or net capital loss, such reduction in tax shall not affect the computation of interest under this section for the period ending with the filing date for the taxable year in which the net operating loss or net capital loss arises.

(2) FOREIGN TAX CREDIT CARRYBACKS.—If any credit allowed for any taxable year is increased by reason of a carryback of tax paid or accrued to foreign countries or possessions of the United States, such increase shall not affect the computation of interest under this section for the period ending with the filing date for the taxable year in which such taxes were in fact paid or accrued, or, with respect to any portion of such credit carryback from a taxable year attributable to a net operating loss carryback or a capital loss carryback from a subsequent taxable year, such increase shall not affect the computation of interest under this section for the period ending with the filing date for such subsequent taxable year.

(3) CERTAIN CREDIT CARRYBACKS.—

(A) IN GENERAL.—If any credit allowed for any taxable year is increased by reason of a credit carryback, such increase shall not affect the computation of interest under this section for the period ending with the filing date for the taxable year in which the credit carryback arises, or, with respect to any portion of a credit carryback from a taxable year attributable to a net operating loss carryback, capital loss carryback, or other credit carryback from a subsequent taxable year, such increase shall not affect the computation of interest under this section for the period ending with the filing date for such subsequent taxable year.

(B) CREDIT CARRYBACK DEFINED.—For purposes of this paragraph, the term "credit carryback" has the meaning given such term by section 6511(d)(4)(C).

(4) FILING DATE.—For purposes of this subsection, the term "filing date" has the meaning given to such term by section 6611(f)(4)(A).

Amendments

- **2005, Gulf Opportunity Zone Act of 2005 (P.L. 109-135)**

P.L. 109-135, §409(a)(2):

Amended Code Sec. 6601(d)(4) by striking "6611(f)(3)(A)" and inserting "6611(f)(4)(A)". **Effective** as if included in the provision of the Taxpayer Relief Act of 1997 (P.L. 105-34) to which it relates [**effective** for foreign tax credit carrybacks arising in tax years beginning after 8-5-97.—CCH.]

- **1997, Taxpayer Relief Act of 1997 (P.L. 105-34)**

P.L. 105-34, §1055(a):

Amended Code Sec. 6601(d) by redesignating paragraphs (2) and (3) as paragraphs (3) and (4), respectively, and by inserting after paragraph (1) a new paragraph (2). **Effective** for foreign tax credit carrybacks arising in tax years beginning after 8-5-97.

- **1984, Deficit Reduction Act of 1984 (P.L. 98-369)**

P.L. 98-369, §211(b)(26):

Amended Code Sec. 6601(d) by striking out paragraph (3) and by redesignating paragraph (4) as paragraph (3). **Effective** for tax years beginning after 12-31-83. Prior to amendment paragraph (3) read as follows:

(3) Adjustment for Certain Unused Deductions of Life Insurance Companies.—If the amount of any tax imposed by subtitle A is reduced by operation of section 815(d)(5) (relating to reduction of policyholders surplus account of life insurance companies for certain unused deductions), such reduction in tax shall not affect the computation of interest under this section for the period ending with the last day of the last taxable year to which the loss described in section 815(d)(5)(A) is carried under section 812(b)(2).

P.L. 98-369, §714(n)(1):

Corrected an error in P.L. 97-248, Act Sec. 346(c)(2)(B). That section amended Code Sec. 6601(d)(2)(A) by striking out "the last day of the" (instead of "the last day of") and inserted in lieu thereof "the filing date for". **Effective** as if included in P.L. 97-248.

- **1982, Tax Equity and Fiscal Responsibility Act of 1982 (P.L. 97-248)**

P.L. 97-248, §346(c)(2)(A):

Amended Code Sec. 6601(d)(1) by striking out "the last day of the taxable year" and inserting "the filing date for the taxable year". **Effective** for interest accruing after 10-3-82.

P.L. 97-248, §346(c)(2)(B):

Amended Code Sec. 6601(d)(2)(A) by striking out "the last day of" each place it appeared and inserting "the filing date for". **Effective** for interest accruing after 10-3-82.

P.L. 97-248, §346(c)(2)(C):

Added Code Sec. 6601(d)(4). **Effective** for interest accruing after 10-3-82.

- **1978 (P.L. 95-628)**

P.L. 95-628, §8(c)(2)(A), (d):

Amended Code Sec. 6601(d)(2). **Effective** for carrybacks arising in tax years beginning after 11-10-78. Prior to amendment, paragraph (2) read:

"(2) INVESTMENT CREDIT CARRYBACK.—If the credit allowed by section 38 for any taxable year is increased by reason of an investment credit carryback, such increase shall not affect the computation of interest under this section for the period ending with the last day of the taxable year in which the investment credit carryback arises, or, with respect to any portion of an investment credit carryback from a taxable year attributable to a net operating loss carryback or a capital loss carryback from a subsequent taxable year, such increase shall not affect the computation of interest under this section for the period ending with the last day of such subsequent taxable year."

P.L. 95-628, §8(c)(2)(B), (d):

Repealed Code Secs. 6601(d)(4) and (5). **Effective** for carrybacks arising in tax years beginning after 11-10-78. Prior to repeal, such paragraphs read:

"(4) WORK INCENTIVE PROGRAM CREDIT CARRYBACK.—If the credit allowed by section 40 for any taxable year is increased by reason of a work incentive program credit carryback, such increase shall not affect the computation of interest under this section for the period ending with the last day of the taxable year in which the work incentive program credit carryback arises, or, with respect to any portion of a work incentive program carryback from a taxable year attributable to a net operating loss carryback, an investment credit carryback, or a capital loss carryback from a subsequent taxable year, such increase shall not affect the computation of interest under this section for the period ending with the last day of such subsequent taxable year.

"(5) NEW EMPLOYEE CREDIT CARRYBACK.—If the credit allowed by section 44B for any taxable year is increased by reason of a new employee credit carryback, such increase shall not affect the computation of interest under this section for the period ending with the last day of the taxable year in which the new employee credit carryback arises, or, with respect to any portion of a new employee credit carryback from a taxable year attributable to a net operating loss carryback, an investment credit carryback, a work incentive program credit carryback, or a capital loss carryback from a subsequent taxable year, such increase shall not affect the computation of interest under this section for the period ending with the last day of such subsequent taxable year."

- **1977, Tax Reduction and Simplification Act of 1977 (P.L. 95-30)**

P.L. 95-30, §202(d)(4)(C):

Amended Code Sec. 6601(d) by adding paragraph (5). **Effective** for tax years beginning after 12-31-76, and for credit carrybacks from such years.

- **1976, Tax Reform Act of 1976 (P.L. 94-455)**

P.L. 94-455, §2107(g)(2)(C):

Amended Code Sec. 6601(d)(4) by inserting ", an investment credit carryback," after "net operating loss carryback." **Effective** 10-4-76.

- **1975 (P.L. 93-625)**

P.L. 93-625, §7(b)(1):

Redesignated Code Sec. 6601(e) as Code Sec. 6601(d). **Effective** 7-1-75.

- **1971, Revenue Act of 1971 (P.L. 92-178)**

P.L. 92-178, §601(d)(3):

Amended Code Sec. 6601(e) by adding paragraph (4). **Effective** for tax years ending after 12-31-71.

- **1969, Tax Reform Act of 1969 (P.L. 91-172)**

P.L. 91-172, §512(e)(3):

Amended Code Sec. 6601(e)(1) by adding "or Capital Loss" after "Net Operating Loss" in heading; and by adding "or net capital loss" wherever it appears after "operating loss". Amended Code Sec. 6601(e)(2) by adding "or a capital loss carryback" after "loss carryback". **Effective** with respect to net capital losses sustained in tax years beginning after 12-31-69.

- **1967 (P.L. 90-225)**

P.L. 90-225, §2(e):

Amended Code Sec. 6601(e)(2) by inserting at the end thereof the following: ", or, with respect to any portion of an investment credit carryback from a taxable year attributable to a net operating loss carryback from a subsequent taxable year, such increase shall not affect the computation of interest under this section for the period ending with the last day of such subsequent taxable year". **Effective** with respect to

INTEREST—UNDERPAYMENTS

investment credit carrybacks attributable to net operating loss carrybacks from tax years ending after 7-31-67.

• **1964 (P.L. 88-571)**

P.L. 88-571, § 3(d):

Amended Code Sec. 6601(e) by changing the heading and by adding paragraph (3). **Effective** with respect to amounts added to policyholders surplus accounts for tax years beginning after 12-31-58.

• **1962, Revenue Act of 1962 (P.L. 87-834)**

P.L. 87-834, § 2:

Amended Code Sec. 6601(e). **Effective** for tax years ending after 12-31-61. Prior to amendment, Sec. 6601(e) read as follows:

"(e) Income Tax Reduced by Carryback.—If the amount of any tax imposed by subtitle A is reduced by reason of a carryback of a net operating loss, such reduction in tax shall not affect the computation of interest under this section for the period ending with the last day of the taxable year in which the net operating loss arises."

[Sec. 6601(e)]

(e) APPLICABLE RULES.—Except as otherwise provided in this title—

(1) INTEREST TREATED AS TAX.—Interest prescribed under this section on any tax shall be paid upon notice and demand, and shall be assessed, collected, and paid in the same manner as taxes. Any reference in this title (except subchapter B of chapter 63, relating to deficiency procedures) to any tax imposed by this title shall be deemed also to refer to interest imposed by this section on such tax.

(2) INTEREST ON PENALTIES, ADDITIONAL AMOUNTS, OR ADDITIONS TO THE TAX.—

(A) IN GENERAL.—Interest shall be imposed under subsection (a) in respect of any assessable penalty, additional amount, or addition to the tax (other than an addition to tax imposed under section 6651(a)(1) or 6653 or under part II of subchapter A of chapter 68) only if such assessable penalty, additional amount, or addition to the tax is not paid within 21 calendar days from the date of notice and demand therefor (10 business days if the amount for which such notice and demand is made equals or exceeds $100,000), and in such case interest shall be imposed only for the period from the date of the notice and demand to the date of payment.

(B) INTEREST ON CERTAIN ADDITIONS TO TAX.—Interest shall be imposed under this section with respect to any addition to tax imposed by section 6651(a)(1) or 6653 or under part II of subchapter A of chapter 68 for the period which—

(i) begins on the date on which the return of the tax with respect to which such addition to tax is imposed is required to be filed (including any extensions), and

(ii) ends on the date of payment of such addition to tax.

(3) PAYMENTS MADE WITHIN SPECIFIED PERIOD AFTER NOTICE AND DEMAND.—If notice and demand is made for payment of any amount and if such amount is paid within 21 calendar days (10 business days if the amount for which such notice and demand is made equals or exceeds $100,000) after the date of such notice and demand, interest under this section on the amount so paid shall not be imposed for the period after the date of such notice and demand.

Amendments

• **1996, Taxpayer Bill of Rights 2 (P.L. 104-168)**

P.L. 104-168, § 303(a):

Amended Code Sec. 6601(e)(3). **Effective** for any notice and demand given after 12-31-96. Prior to amendment, Code Sec. 6601(e)(3) read as follows:

(3) PAYMENTS MADE WITHIN 10 DAYS AFTER NOTICE AND DEMAND.—If notice and demand is made for payment of any amount, and if such amount is paid within 10 days after the date of such notice and demand, interest under this section on the amount so paid shall not be imposed for the period after the date of such notice and demand.

P.L. 104-168, § 303(b)(1):

Amended Code Sec. 6601(e)(2)(A) by striking "10 days from the date of notice and demand therefor" and inserting "21 calendar days from the date of notice and demand therefor (10 business days if the amount for which such notice and demand is made equals or exceeds $100,000)". **Effective** for any notice and demand given after 12-31-96.

• **1989, Omnibus Budget Reconciliation Act of 1989 (P.L. 101-239)**

P.L. 101-239, § 7721(c)(8):

Amended Code Sec. 6601(e)(2) by striking "section 6651(a)(1), 6653, 6659, 6660, or 6661" each place it appears and inserting "section 6651(a)(1) or 6653 or under part II of subchapter A of chapter 68". **Effective** for returns the due date for which (determined without regard to extensions) is after 12-31-89.

• **1988, Technical and Miscellaneous Revenue Act of 1988 (P.L. 100-647)**

P.L. 100-647, § 1015(b)(2)(C):

Amended Code Sec. 6601(e)(2) by striking out "6659" before "6660" each place it appears and inserting in lieu thereof "6653, 6659". **Effective** for returns the due date for which (determined without regard to extensions) is after 12-31-88.

• **1984, Deficit Reduction Act of 1984 (P.L. 98-369)**

P.L. 98-369, § 158(a):

Amended Code Sec. 6601(e)(2). **Effective** for interest accrued after 7-18-84, except with respect to additions to tax for which notice and demand is made before such date. Prior to amendment, Code Sec. 6601(e)(2) read as follows:

(2) Interest on Penalties, Additional Amounts, or Additions to the Tax.—Interest shall be imposed under subsection (a) in respect of any assessable penalty, additional amount, or addition to the tax only if such assessable penalty, additional amount, or addition to the tax is not paid within 10 days from the date of notice and demand therefor, and in such case interest shall be imposed only for the period from the date of the notice and demand to the date of payment.

• **1982, Tax Equity and Fiscal Responsibility Act of 1982 (P.L. 97-248)**

P.L. 97-248, § 344(b)(1):

Amended Code Sec. 6601(e) by striking out paragraph (2) and redesignating paragraphs (3) and (4) as paragraphs (2) and (3), respectively. **Effective** for interest accruing after 12-31-82. Prior to being stricken, such paragraph read:

"(2) No interest on interest.—No interest under this section shall be imposed on the interest provided by this section."

• **1975 (P.L. 93-625)**

P.L. 93-625, § 7(b)(1):

Redesignated Code Sec. 6601(f) as 6601(e). **Effective** 7-1-75.

[Sec. 6601(f)]

(f) SATISFACTION BY CREDITS.—If any portion of a tax is satisfied by credit of an overpayment, then no interest shall be imposed under this section on the portion of the tax so satisfied for any period during which, if the credit had not been made, interest would have been allowable with respect to such overpayment. The preceding sentence shall not apply to the extent that section 6621(d) applies.

Amendments

• **1998, IRS Restructuring and Reform Act of 1998 (P.L. 105-206)**

P.L. 105-206, § 3301(b):

Amended Code Sec. 6601(f) by adding at the end a new sentence. **Effective**, generally, for interest for periods beginning after 7-22-98. For a special rule, see Act Sec. 3301(c)(2), below.

P.L. 105-206, § 3301(c)(2), as amended by P.L. 105-277, § 4002(d), provides:

(2) SPECIAL RULE.—Subject to any applicable statute of limitation not having expired with regard to either a tax underpayment or a tax overpayment, the amendments made by this section shall apply to interest for periods beginning before the date of the enactment of this Act if the taxpayer—

(A) reasonably identifies and establishes periods of such tax overpayments and under-payments for which the zero rate applies; and

(B) not later than December 31, 1999, requests the Secretary of the Treasury to apply section 6621(d) of the Internal Revenue Code of 1986, as added by subsection (a), to such periods.

• **1975 (P.L. 93-625)**

P.L. 93-625, § 7(b)(1):

Redesignated Code Sec. 6601(g) as Code Sec. 6601(f). **Effective** 7-1-75.

• **1958, Technical Amendments Act of 1958 (P.L. 85-866)**

P.L. 85-866, § 83(a)(1):

Redesignated subsections (g) and (h) of Sec. 6601 as subsections (i) and (j) and added a new subsection (g). **Effective** for overpayments credited after 12-31-57.

[Sec. 6601(g)]

(g) LIMITATION ON ASSESSMENT AND COLLECTION.—Interest prescribed under this section on any tax may be assessed and collected at any time during the period within which the tax to which such interest relates may be collected.

INTEREST—UNDERPAYMENTS

Amendments

• 1975 (P.L. 93-625)

P.L. 93-625, §7(b)(1):

Redesignated Code Sec. 6601(h) as Code Sec. 6601(g). **Effective** 7-1-75.

• 1958, Technical Amendments Act of 1958 (P.L. 85-866)

P.L. 85-866, §84(a):

Added subsection (h). **Effective** 1-1-54.

[Sec. 6601(h)]

(h) EXCEPTION AS TO ESTIMATED TAX.—This section shall not apply to any failure to pay any estimated tax required to be paid by section 6654 or 6655.

Amendments

• 1987, Revenue Act of 1987 (P.L. 100-203)

P.L. 100-203, §10301(b)(5):

Amended Code Sec. 6601(h) by striking out "section 6154 or 6654" and inserting in lieu thereof "section 6654 or 6655". **Effective** for tax years beginning after 12-31-87.

• 1984, Deficit Reduction Act of 1984 (P.L. 98-369)

P.L. 98-369, §412(b)(7):

Amended Code Sec. 6601(h). **Effective** with respect to tax years beginning after 12-31-84. Prior to amendment, it read as follows:

(h) Exception as to Estimated Tax.—This section shall not apply to any failure to pay estimated tax required by section 6153 or section 6154.

• 1976, Tax Reform Act of 1976 (P.L. 94-455)

P.L. 94-455, §1906(a)(34):

Deleted "(or section 59 of the Internal Revenue Code of 1939)" in Code Sec. 6601(h). **Effective** 2-1-77.

• 1975 (P.L. 93-625)

P.L. 93-625, §7(b)(1):

Redesignated Code Sec. 6601(i) as Code Sec. 6601(h). **Effective** 7-1-75.

• 1958, Technical Amendments Act of 1958 (P.L. 85-866)

P.L. 85-866, §83(a)(1):

Redesignated Code Sec. 6601(g) as Code Sec. 6601(i). **Effective** 1-1-58.

[Sec. 6601(i)]

(i) EXCEPTION AS TO FEDERAL UNEMPLOYMENT TAX.—This section shall not apply to any failure to make a payment of tax imposed by section 3301 for a calendar quarter or other period within a taxable year required under authority of section 6157.

Amendments

• 1988, Technical and Miscellaneous Revenue Act of 1988 (P.L. 100-647)

P.L. 100-647, §7106(c)(5):

Amended Code Sec. 6601(i) by striking out "or 3321" after "3301". **Effective** for remuneration paid after 12-31-88.

• 1983, Railroad Retirement Solvency Act of 1983 (P.L. 98-76)

P.L. 98-76, §231(b)(2)(D):

Amended Code Sec. 6601(i) by adding "or 3321". **Effective** for remuneration paid after 6-30-86.

• 1975 (P.L. 93-625)

P.L. 93-625, §7(b)(1):

Redesignated Code Sec. 6601(k) as Code Sec. 6601(i). **Effective** 7-1-75.

• 1969 (P.L. 91-53)

P.L. 91-53, §2(e):

Added Code Sec. 6601(k), and redesignated former Code Sec. 6601(k) as Code Sec. 6601(l). **Effective** for calendar years beginning after 12-31-69.

[Sec. 6601(j)]

(j) 2-PERCENT RATE ON CERTAIN PORTION OF ESTATE TAX EXTENDED UNDER SECTION 6166.—

(1) IN GENERAL.—If the time for payment of an amount of tax imposed by chapter 11 is extended as provided in section 6166, then in lieu of the annual rate provided by subsection (a)—

(A) interest on the 2-percent portion of such amount shall be paid at the rate of 2 percent, and

(B) interest on so much of such amount as exceeds the 2-percent portion shall be paid at a rate equal to 45 percent of the annual rate provided by subsection (a).

For purposes of this subsection, the amount of any deficiency which is prorated to installments payable under section 6166 shall be treated as an amount of tax payable in installments under such section.

(2) 2-PERCENT PORTION.—For purposes of this subsection, the term "2-percent portion" means the lesser of—

(A)(i) the amount of the tentative tax which would be determined under the rate schedule set forth in section 2001(c) if the amount with respect to which such tentative tax is to be computed were the sum of $1,000,000 and the applicable exclusion amount in effect under section 2010(c), reduced by

(ii) the applicable credit amount in effect under section 2010(c), or

(B) the amount of the tax imposed by chapter 11 which is extended as provided in section 6166.

(3) INFLATION ADJUSTMENT.—In the case of estates of decedents dying in a calendar year after 1998, the $1,000,000 amount contained in paragraph (2)(A) shall be increased by an amount equal to—

(A) $1,000,000, multiplied by

(B) the cost-of-living adjustment determined under section 1(f)(3) for such calendar year by substituting "calendar year 1997" for "calendar year 2016" in subparagraph (A)(ii) thereof.

If any amount as adjusted under the preceding sentence is not a multiple of $10,000, such amount shall be rounded to the next lowest multiple of $10,000.

(4) TREATMENT OF PAYMENTS.—If the amount of tax imposed by chapter 11 which is extended as provided in section 6166 exceeds the 2-percent portion, any payment of a portion of such amount shall, for purposes of computing interest for periods after such payment, be treated as reducing the 2-percent portion by an amount which bears the same ratio to the amount of such payment as the amount of the 2-percent portion (determined without regard to this paragraph) bears to the amount of the tax which is extended as provided in section 6166.

Amendments

• 2017, Tax Cuts and Jobs Act (P.L. 115-97)

P.L. 115-97, §11002(d)(1)(JJ):

Amended Code Sec. 6601(j)(3)(B) by striking "for 'calendar year 1992' in subparagraph (B)" and inserting "for 'calendar year 2016' in subparagraph (A)(ii)". **Effective** for tax years beginning after 12-31-2017.

• 1997, Taxpayer Relief Act of 1997 (P.L. 105-34)

P.L. 105-34, §501(e):

Amended Code Sec. 6601(j) by redesignating paragraph (3) as paragraph (4) and by inserting after paragraph (2) a new paragraph (3). **Effective** for the estates of decedents dying, and gifts made, after 12-31-97.

P.L. 105-34, §503(a):

Amended Code Sec. 6601(j)(1)-(2). **Effective**, generally, for estates of decedents dying after 12-31-97. For a special rule, see Act Sec. 503(d)(2), below. Prior to amendment, Code Sec. 6601(j)(1)-(2) read as follows:

(1) IN GENERAL.—If the time for payment of an amount of tax imposed by chapter 11 is extended as provided in section 6166, interest on the 4-percent portion of such amount shall (in lieu of the annual rate provided by subsection (a)) be paid at the rate of 4 percent. For purposes of this subsection, the amount of any deficiency which is prorated to installments payable under section 6166 shall be treated as an amount of tax payable in installments under such section.

(2) 4-PERCENT PORTION.—For purposes of this subsection, the term "4-percent portion" means the lesser of—

(A) $345,800 reduced by the amount of the credit allowable under section 2010(a); or

(B) the amount of the tax imposed by chapter 11 which is extended as provided in section 6166.

P.L. 105-34, §503(c)(2):

Amended Code Sec. 6601(j)(4), as redesignated by Act Sec. 501(e), by striking "4-percent" each place it appears and inserting "2-percent". **Effective**, generally, for

Internal Revenue Code

Sec. 6601(j)(4)

INTEREST—UNDERPAYMENTS

estates of decedents dying after 12-31-97. For a special rule, see Act Sec. 503(d)(2), below.

P.L. 105-34, §503(c)(3):

Amended Code Sec. 6601(j) by striking "4-Percent" in the subsection heading and inserting "2-Percent". **E ffective**, generally, for estates of decedents dying after 12-31-97. For a special rule, see Act Sec. 503(d)(2), below.

P.L. 105-34, §503(d)(2), provides:

(2) Election.—In the case of the estate of any decedent dying before January 1, 1998, with respect to which there is an election under section 6166 of the Internal Revenue Code of 1986, the executor of the estate may elect to have the amendments made by this section apply with respect to installments due after the effective date of the election; except that the 2-percent portion of such installments shall be equal to the amount which would be the 4-percent portion of such installments without regard to such election. Such an election shall be made before January 1, 1999 in the manner prescribed by the Secretary of the Treasury and, once made, is irrevocable.

- **1976, Tax Reform Act of 1976 (P.L. 94-455)**

P.L. 94-455, §2004(b):

Redesignated Code Sec. 6601(j) as Code Sec. 6601(k); and inserted after subsection (i) a new subsection (j). **Effective** for estates of decedents dying after 12-31-76.

- **1975 (P.L. 93-625)**

P.L. 93-625, §7(b)(1):

Amended Code Sec. 6601 by striking out subsection (j) and redesignating subsection (l) as subsection (j). **Effective** 7-1-75, and applicable to amounts outstanding on such date or arising thereafter. Prior to being stricken, Code Sec. 6601(j) read as follows:

(j) Extension of Time for Payment of Tax Attributable to Recoveries of Foreign Expropriation Losses.—If the time for payment of an amount of the tax attributable to a recovery of a foreign expropriation loss (within the meaning of section 6167(f)) is extended as provided in subsection (a) or (b) of section 6167, interest shall be paid at the rate of 4 percent, in lieu of 6 percent as provided in subsection (a).

- **1966 (P.L. 89-384)**

P.L. 89-384, §1(f):

Added Code Sec. 6601(j), and redesignated former Code Sec. 6601(j) as Code Sec. 6601(k). **Effective** with respect to amounts received after 12-31-64, in respect of foreign expropriation losses sustained in tax years beginning after 12-31-58.

[Sec. 6601(k)]

(k) No Interest on Certain Adjustments.—

For provisions prohibiting interest on certain adjustments in tax, see section 6205(a).

Amendments

- **1976, Tax Reform Act of 1976 (P.L. 94-455)**

P.L. 94-455, §2004(b):

Redesignated Code Sec. 6601(j) as Code Sec. 6601(k). **Effective** for estates of decedents dying after 12-31-76.

- **1975 (P.L. 93-625)**

P.L. 93-625, §7(b)(1):

Redesignated Code Sec. 6601(l) as Code Sec. 6601(j). **Effective** 7-1-75.

- **1969, Tax Reform Act of 1969 (P.L. 91-172)**

P.L. 91-172, §946(a), provides:

Interest on Underpayment.—Notwithstanding section 6601 of the Internal Revenue Code of 1954, in the case of any taxable year ending before the date of the enactment of this Act, no interest on any underpayment of tax, to the extent such underpayment is attributable to the amendments made by this Act, shall be assessed or collected for any period before the 90th day after such date.

- **1969 (P.L. 91-53)**

P.L. 91-53, §2(e):

Redesignated Code Sec. 6601(k) as Code Sec. 6601(l). **Effective** 1-1-70.

- **1966 (P.L. 89-384)**

P.L. 89-384, §1(f):

Redesignated Code Sec. 6601(j) as Code Sec. 6601(k).

- **1958, Technical Amendments Act of 1958 (P.L. 85-866)**

P.L. 85-866, §83(a)(1):

Redesignated Code Sec. 6601(h) as Code Sec. 6601(i). **Effective** 1-1-58.

[Sec. 6602]

SEC. 6602. INTEREST ON ERRONEOUS REFUND RECOVERABLE BY SUIT.

Any portion of an internal revenue tax (or any interest, assessable penalty, additional amount, or addition to tax) which has been erroneously refunded, and which is recoverable by suit pursuant to section 7405, shall bear interest at the underpayment rate established under section 6621 from the date of the payment of the refund.

Amendments

- **1986, Tax Reform Act of 1986 (P.L. 99-514)**

P.L. 99-514, §1511(c)(12):

Amended Code Sec. 6602 by striking out "an annual rate established under section 6621" and inserting in lieu thereof "the underpayment rate established under section 6621". **Effective** for purposes of determining interest for periods after 12-31-86.

- **1975 (P.L. 93-625)**

P.L. 93-625, §7(a)(2):

Amended Code Sec. 6602 by substituting "an annual rate established under section 6621" for "the rate of 6 percent per annum". For **effective** date, see the historical comment for P.L. 93-625, following the text of Code Sec. 6621.

[Sec. 6603]

SEC. 6603. DEPOSITS MADE TO SUSPEND RUNNING OF INTEREST ON POTENTIAL UNDERPAYMENTS, ETC.

[Sec. 6603(a)]

(a) Authority To Make Deposits Other Than As Payment of Tax.—A taxpayer may make a cash deposit with the Secretary which may be used by the Secretary to pay any tax imposed under subtitle A or B or chapter 41, 42, 43, or 44 which has not been assessed at the time of the deposit. Such a deposit shall be made in such manner as the Secretary shall prescribe.

[Sec. 6603(b)]

(b) No Interest Imposed.—To the extent that such deposit is used by the Secretary to pay tax, for purposes of section 6601 (relating to interest on underpayments), the tax shall be treated as paid when the deposit is made.

[Sec. 6603(c)]

(c) Return of Deposit.—Except in a case where the Secretary determines that collection of tax is in jeopardy, the Secretary shall return to the taxpayer any amount of the deposit (to the extent not used for a payment of tax) which the taxpayer requests in writing.

[Sec. 6603(d)]

(d) Payment of Interest.—

(1) In general.—For purposes of section 6611 (relating to interest on overpayments), except as provided in paragraph (4), a deposit which is returned to a taxpayer shall be treated as a payment of tax for any period to the extent (and only to the extent) attributable to a disputable tax for such period. Under regulations prescribed by the Secretary, rules similar to the rules of section 6611(b)(2) shall apply.

(2) Disputable tax.—

(A) In general.—For purposes of this section, the term "disputable tax" means the amount of tax specified at the time of the deposit as the taxpayer's reasonable estimate of the maximum amount of any tax attributable to disputable items.

(B) Safe harbor based on 30-day letter.—In the case of a taxpayer who has been issued a 30-day letter, the maximum amount of tax under subparagraph (A) shall not be less than the amount of the proposed deficiency specified in such letter.

(3) Other definitions.—For purposes of paragraph (2)—

(A) Disputable item.—The term "disputable item" means any item of income, gain, loss, deduction, or credit if the taxpayer—

INTEREST—OVERPAYMENTS

(i) has a reasonable basis for its treatment of such item, and

(ii) reasonably believes that the Secretary also has a reasonable basis for disallowing the taxpayer's treatment of such item.

(B) 30-DAY LETTER.—The term "30-day letter" means the first letter of proposed deficiency which allows the taxpayer an opportunity for administrative review in the Internal Revenue Service Independent Office of Appeals.

(4) RATE OF INTEREST.—The rate of interest under this subsection shall be the Federal short-term rate determined under section 6621(b), compounded daily.

Amendments

• **2019, Taxpayer First Act (P.L. 116-25)**

P.L. 116-25, § 1001(b)(1)(D):

Amended Code Sec. 6603(d)(3)(B) by striking "Internal Revenue Service Office of Appeals" and inserting "Internal Revenue Service Independent Office of Appeals". **Effective** 7-1-2019.

[Sec. 6603(e)]

(e) USE OF DEPOSITS.—

(1) PAYMENT OF TAX.—Except as otherwise provided by the taxpayer, deposits shall be treated as used for the payment of tax in the order deposited.

(2) RETURNS OF DEPOSITS.—Deposits shall be treated as returned to the taxpayer on a last-in, first-out basis.

Amendments

• **2004, American Jobs Creation Act of 2004 (P.L. 108-357)**

P.L. 108-357, § 842(a):

Amended subchapter A of chapter 67 by adding at the end a new Code Sec. 6603. **Effective** generally for deposits made after 10-22-2004. For a special rule, see Act Sec. 842(c)(2), below.

P.L. 108-357, § 842(c)(2), provides:

(2) COORDINATION WITH DEPOSITS MADE UNDER REVENUE PROCEDURE 84-58.—In the case of an amount held by the Secretary of the Treasury or his delegate on the date of the enactment of this Act [10-22-2004.—CCH] as a deposit in the nature of a cash bond deposit pursuant to Revenue Procedure 84-58, the date that the taxpayer identifies such amount as a deposit made pursuant to section 6603 of the Internal Revenue Code (as added by this Act) shall be treated as the date such amount is deposited for purposes of such section 6603.

Subchapter B—Interest on Overpayments

Sec. 6611. Interest on overpayments.
Sec. 6612. Cross references.

[Sec. 6611]

SEC. 6611. INTEREST ON OVERPAYMENTS.

[Sec. 6611(a)]

(a) RATE.—Interest shall be allowed and paid upon any overpayment in respect of any internal revenue tax at the overpayment rate established under section 6621.

Amendments

• **1986, Tax Reform Act of 1986 (P.L. 99-514)**

P.L. 99-514, § 1511(c)(13):

Amended Code Sec. 6611(a) by striking out "an annual rate established under section 6621" and inserting in lieu thereof "the overpayment rate established under section 6621". **Effective** for purposes of determining interest for periods after 12-31-86.

• **1975 (P.L. 93-625)**

P.L. 93-625, § 7(a)(2):

Amended Code Sec. 6611(a) by substituting "an annual rate established under section 6621" for "the rate of 6 percent per annum". For **effective** date, see the historical comment for P.L. 93-625 following the text of Code Sec. 6621.

[Sec. 6611(b)]

(b) PERIOD.—Such interest shall be allowed and paid as follows:

(1) CREDITS.—In the case of a credit, from the date of the overpayment to the due date of the amount against which the credit is taken.

(2) REFUNDS.—In the case of a refund, from the date of the overpayment to a date (to be determined by the Secretary) preceding the date of the refund check by not more than 30 days, whether or not such refund check is accepted by the taxpayer after tender of such check to the taxpayer. The acceptance of such check shall be without prejudice to any right of the taxpayer to claim any additional overpayment and interest thereon.

(3) LATE RETURNS.—Notwithstanding paragraph (1) or (2) in the case of a return of tax which is filed after the last date prescribed for filing such return (determined with regard to extentions), no interest shall be allowed or paid for any day before the date on which the return is filed.

Amendments

• **1982, Tax Equity and Fiscal Responsibility Act of 1982 (P.L. 97-248)**

P.L. 97-248, § 346(a):

Added Code Sec. 6611(b)(3). **Effective** for returns filed after 10-3-82.

• **1976, Tax Reform Act of 1976 (P.L. 94-455)**

P.L. 94-455, § 1906(b)(13)(A):

Amended 1954 Code by substituting "Secretary" for "Secretary or his delegate" each place it appeared. **Effective** 2-1-77.

• **1958, Technical Amendments Act of 1958 (P.L. 85-866)**

P.L. 85-866, § 83(b):

Amended Sec. 6611(b)(1). **Effective** for overpayments credited after 12-31-57. Prior to amendment, Sec. 6611(b)(1) read as follows:

"(1) Credits.—In the case of a credit, from the date of the overpayment to the due date of the amount against which the credit is taken, but if the amount against which the credit is taken is an additional assessment, then to the date of the assessment of that amount."

[Sec. 6611(c)—Repealed]

Amendments

• **1958, Technical Amendments Act of 1958 (P.L. 85-866)**

P.L. 85-866, § 83(c):

Repealed Code Sec. 6611(c). **Effective** 1-1-58. Prior to repeal, Sec. 6611(c) read as follows:

"(c) Additional Assessment Defined.—As used in this section, the term 'additional assessment' means a further assessment for a tax of the same character previously paid in part, and includes the assessment of a deficiency (as defined in section 6211)."

[Sec. 6611(d)]

(d) ADVANCE PAYMENT OF TAX, PAYMENT OF ESTIMATED TAX, AND CREDIT FOR INCOME TAX WITHHOLDING.—The provisions of section 6513 (except the provisions of subsection (c) thereof), applicable in determining the date of payment of tax for purposes of determining the period of limitation on credit or refund, shall be applicable in determining the date of payment for purposes of subsection (a).

INTEREST—OVERPAYMENTS

[Sec. 6611(e)]

(e) DISALLOWANCE OF INTEREST ON CERTAIN OVERPAYMENTS.—

(1) REFUNDS WITHIN 45 DAYS AFTER RETURN IS FILED.—If any overpayment of tax imposed by this title is refunded within 45 days after the last day prescribed for filing the return of such tax (determined without regard to any extention of time for filing the return) or, in the case of a return filed after such last date, is refunded within 45 days after the date the return is filed, no interest shall be allowed under subsection (a) on such overpayment.

(2) REFUNDS AFTER CLAIM FOR CREDIT OR REFUND.—If—

(A) the taxpayer files a claim for a credit or refund for any overpayment of tax imposed by this title, and

(B) such overpayment is refunded within 45 days after such claim is filed,

no interest shall be allowed on such overpayment from the date the claim is filed until the day the refund is made.

(3) IRS INITIATED ADJUSTMENTS.—If an adjustment initiated by the Secretary, results in a refund or credit of an overpayment, interest on such overpayment shall be computed by subtracting 45 days from the number of days interest would otherwise be allowed with respect to such overpayment.

(4) CERTAIN WITHHOLDING TAXES.—In the case of any overpayment resulting from tax deducted and withheld under chapter 3 or 4, paragraphs (1), (2), and (3) shall be applied by substituting "180 days" for "45 days" each place it appears.

Amendments

• **2010, Hiring Incentives to Restore Employment Act (P.L. 111-147)**

P.L. 111-147, § 501(b):

Amended Code Sec. 6611(e) by adding at the end a new paragraph (4). For the **effective** date, see Act Sec. 501(d)(3), below.

P.L. 111-147, § 501(d)(3), provides:

(3) INTEREST ON OVERPAYMENTS.—The amendment made by subsection (b) shall apply—

(A) in the case of such amendment's application to paragraph (1) of section 6611(e) of the Internal Revenue Code of 1986, to returns the due date for which (determined without regard to extensions) is after the date of the enactment of this Act,

(B) in the case of such amendment's application to paragraph (2) of such section, to claims for credit or refund of any overpayment filed after the date of the enactment of this Act (regardless of the taxable period to which such refund relates), and

(C) in the case of such amendment's application to paragraph (3) of such section, to refunds paid after the date of the enactment of this Act (regardless of the taxable period to which such refund relates).

• **1993, Omnibus Budget Reconciliation Act of 1993 (P.L. 103-66)**

P.L. 103-66, § 13271(a):

Amended Code Sec. 6611(e). For the **effective** date, see Act Sec. 13271(b). Prior to amendment, Code Sec. 6611(e) read as follows:

(e) INCOME TAX REFUND WITHIN 45 DAYS AFTER RETURN IS FILED.—If any overpayment of tax imposed by subtitle A is refunded within 45 days after the last date prescribed for filing the return of such tax (determined without regard to any extension of time for filing the return) or, in case the return is filed after such last date, is refunded within 45 days after the date the return is filed, no interest shall be allowed under subsection (a) on such overpayment.

P.L. 103-66, § 13271(b), provides:

(b) EFFECTIVE DATES.—

(1) Paragraph (1) of section 6611(e) of the Internal Revenue Code of 1986 (as amended by subsection (a)) shall apply in the case of returns the due date for which (determined without regard to extensions) is on or after January 1, 1994.

(2) Paragraph (2) of section 6611(e) of such Code (as so amended) shall apply in the case of claims for credit or refund of any overpayment filed on or after January 1, 1995, regardless of the taxable period to which such refund relates.

(3) Paragraph (3) of section 6611(e) of such Code (as so amended) shall apply in the case of any refund paid on or after January 1, 1995, regardless of the taxable period to which such refund relates.

• **1975, Tax Reduction Act of 1975 (P.L. 94-12)**

P.L. 94-12, § 101(b), provides:

"(b) No Interest on Individual Income Tax Refunds for 1974 Refunded Within 60 Days After Return Is Filed.—In applying section 6611(e) of the Internal Revenue Code of 1954 (relating to income tax refund within 45 days after return is filed) in the case of any overpayment of tax imposed by subtitle A of such Code by an individual (other than an estate or trust and other than a nonresident alien individual) for a taxable year beginning in 1974, '60 days' shall be substituted for '45 days' each place it appears in such section 6611(e)."

• **1966 (P.L. 89-721)**

P.L. 89-721, § [1(a)]:

Amended Code Sec. 6611(e). **Effective** with respect to refunds made more than 45 days after 11-2-66. Prior to amendment, Code Sec. 6611(e) read as follows:

"(e) Income Tax Refund Within 45 Days of Due Date of Tax.—If any overpayment of tax imposed by subtitle A is refunded within 45 days after the last date prescribed for filing the return of such tax (determined without regard to any extension of time for filing the return), no interest shall be allowed under subsection (a) on such overpayment."

[Sec. 6611(f)]

(f) REFUND OF INCOME TAX CAUSED BY CARRYBACK OR ADJUSTMENT FOR CERTAIN UNUSED DEDUCTIONS.—

(1) NET OPERATING LOSS OR CAPITAL LOSS CARRYBACK.—For purposes of subsection (a), if any overpayment of tax imposed by subtitle A results from a carryback of a net operating loss or net capital loss, such overpayment shall be deemed not to have been made prior to the filing date for the taxable year in which such net operating loss or net capital loss arises.

(2) FOREIGN TAX CREDIT CARRYBACKS.—For purposes of subsection (a), if any overpayment of tax imposed by subtitle A results from a carryback of tax paid or accrued to foreign countries or possessions of the United States, such overpayment shall be deemed not to have been made before the filing date for the taxable year in which such taxes were in fact paid or accrued, or, with respect to any portion of such credit carryback from a taxable year attributable to a net operating loss carryback or a capital loss carryback from a subsequent taxable year, such overpayment shall be deemed not to have been made before the filing date for such subsequent taxable year.

(3) CERTAIN CREDIT CARRYBACKS.—

(A) IN GENERAL.—For purposes of subsection (a), if any overpayment of tax imposed by subtitle A results from a credit carryback, such overpayment shall be deemed not to have been made before the filing date for the taxable year in which such credit carryback arises, or, with respect to any portion of a credit carryback from a taxable year attributable to a net operating loss carryback, capital loss carryback, or other credit carryback from a subsequent taxable year, such overpayment shall be deemed not to have been made before the filing date for such subsequent taxable year.

(B) CREDIT CARRYBACK DEFINED.—For purposes of this paragraph, the term "credit carryback" has the meaning given such term by section 6511(d)(4)(C).

(4) SPECIAL RULES FOR PARAGRAPHS (1), (2), AND (3).—

(A) FILING DATE.—For purposes of this subsection, the term "filing date" means the last date prescribed for filing the return of tax imposed by subtitle A for the taxable year (determined without regard to extensions).

(B) COORDINATION WITH SUBSECTION (e).—

(i) IN GENERAL.—For purposes of subsection (e)—

(I) any overpayment described in paragraph (1), (2), or (3) shall be treated as an overpayment for the loss year, and

(II) such subsection shall be applied with respect to such overpayment by treating the return for the loss year as not filed before claim for such overpayment is filed.

(ii) LOSS YEAR.—For purposes of this subparagraph, the term "loss year" means—

(I) in the case of a carryback of a net operating loss or net capital loss, the taxable year in which such loss arises,

(II) in the case of a carryback of taxes paid or accrued to foreign countries or possessions of the United States, the taxable year in which such taxes were in fact paid or accrued (or, with respect to any portion of such carryback from a taxable year

INTEREST—OVERPAYMENTS

attributable to a net operating loss carryback or a capital loss carryback from a subsequent taxable year, such subsequent taxable year), and

(III) in the case of a credit carryback (as defined in paragraph (3)(B)), the taxable year in which such credit carryback arises (or, with respect to any portion of a credit carryback from a taxable year attributable to a net operating loss carryback, a capital loss carryback, or other credit carryback from a subsequent taxable year, such subsequent taxable year).

(C) APPLICATION OF SUBPARAGRAPH (B) WHERE SECTION 6411(a) CLAIM FILED.—For purposes of subparagraph (B)(i)(II), if a taxpayer—

(i) files a claim for refund of any overpayment described in paragraph (1), (2), or (3) with respect to the taxable year to which a loss or credit is carried back, and

(ii) subsequently files an application under section 6411(a) with respect to such overpayment,

then the claim for overpayment shall be treated as having been filed on the date the application under section 6411(a) was filed.

Amendments

• **1997, Taxpayer Relief Act of 1997 (P.L. 105-34)**

P.L. 105-34, §1055(b)(1):

Amended Code Sec. 6611(f) by redesignating paragraphs (2) and (3) as paragraphs (3) and (4), respectively, and by inserting after paragraph (1) a new paragraph (2). **Effective** for foreign tax credit carrybacks arising in tax years beginning after 8-5-97.

P.L. 105-34, §1055(b)(2)(A)(i)-(ii):

Amended Code Sec. 6611(f)(4), as so redesignated, by striking "PARAGRAPHS (1) AND (2)" [in the heading] and inserting "PARAGRAPHS (1), (2), AND (3)", and by striking "paragraph (1) or (2)" each place it appears and inserting "paragraph (1), (2), or (3)". **Effective** for foreign tax credit carrybacks arising in tax years beginning after 8-5-97.

P.L. 105-34, §1055(b)(2)(B):

Amended Code Sec. 6611(f)(4)(B)(ii), as so redesignated, by striking "and" at the end of subclause (I), by redesignating subclause (II) as subclause (III), and by inserting after subclause (I) a new subclause (II). **Effective** for foreign tax credit carrybacks arising in tax years beginning after 8-5-97.

P.L. 105-34, §1055(b)(2)(C):

Amended Code Sec. 6611(f)(4)(B)(ii)(III), as so redesignated, by inserting "(as defined in paragraph (3)(B))" after "credit carryback" the first place it appears. **Effective** for foreign tax credit carrybacks arising in tax years beginning after 8-5-97.

• **1984, Deficit Reduction Act of 1984 (P.L. 98-369)**

P.L. 98-369, §211(b)(27):

Amended Code Sec. 6611(f) by striking out paragraph (4). **Effective** for tax years beginning after 12-31-83. Prior to amendment, it read as follows:

"(4) Adjustment for Certain Unused Deductions of Life Insurance Companies.—For purposes of subsection (a), if any overpayment of tax imposed by subtitle A arises by operation of section 815(d)(5) (relating to reduction of policyholders surplus account of life insurance companies for certain unused deductions), such overpayment shall be deemed not to have been made prior to the close of the last taxable year to which the loss described in section 815(d)(5)(A) is carried under section 812(b)(2).

P.L. 98-369, §714(n)(2)(A):

Amended Code Sec. 6611(f)(3) by adding subparagraph (C). **Effective** only for applications filed after 7-18-84 [effective date changed by P.L. 99-514, §1875(d)].

• **1982, Tax Equity and Fiscal Responsibility Act of 1982 (P.L. 97-248)**

P.L. 97-248, §346(c)(1)(A):

Amended Code Sec. 6611(f)(1) by striking out "the close of the taxable year" and inserting "the filing date for the taxable year". **Effective** for interest accruing after 10-3-82.

P.L. 97-248, §346(c)(1)(B):

Amended Code Sec. 611(f)(2)(A) by striking out "the close of" each place it appeared and inserting "the filing date for". **Effective** for interest accruing after 10-3-82.

P.L. 97-248, §346(c)(1)(C):

Amended Code Sec. 611(f) by redesignating paragraph (3) as paragraph (4) and by adding a new paragraph (3). **Effective** for interest accruing after 10-3-82.

• **1978 (P.L. 95-628)**

P.L. 95-628, §8(c)(3)(A), (d):

Amended Code Sec. 6611(f)(2). **Effective** for carrybacks arising in tax years beginning after 11-10-78. Prior to amendment, paragraph (2) read:

"(2) INVESTMENT CREDIT CARRYBACK.—For purposes of subsection (a), if any overpayment of tax imposed by subtitle A results from an investment credit carryback, such overpayment shall be deemed not to have been made prior to the close of the taxable year in which such investment credit carryback arises, or, with respect to any portion of an investment credit carryback from a taxable year attributable to a net operating loss carryback or a capital loss carryback from a subsequent taxable year, such overpayment shall be deemed not to have been made prior to the close of such subsequent taxable year."

P.L. 95-628, §8(c)(3)(B), (d):

Repealed Code Secs. 6611(f)(4) and (5). **Effective** for carrybacks arising in tax years beginning after 11-10-78. Prior to amendment, paragraphs (4) and (5) read:

"(4) WORK INCENTIVE PROGRAM CREDIT CARRYBACK.—For purposes of subsection (a), if any overpayment of tax imposed by subtitle A results from a work incentive program credit carryback, such overpayment shall be deemed not to have been made prior to the close of the taxable year in which such work incentive program credit carryback arises, or, with respect to any portion of a work incentive program credit carryback from a taxable year attributable to a net operating loss carryback, an investment credit carryback, or a capital loss carryback from a subsequent taxable year, such overpayment shall be deemed not to have been made prior to the close of such subsequent taxable year.

"(5) NEW EMPLOYEE CREDIT CARRYBACK.—For purposes of subsection (a), if any overpayment of tax imposed by subtitle A results from a new employee credit carryback, such overpayment shall be deemed not to have been made before the close of the taxable year in which such new employee credit carryback arises, or, with respect to any portion of a new employee credit carryback from a taxable year attributable to a net operating loss carryback, an investment credit carryback, a work incentive program credit carryback, or a capital loss carryback from a subsequent taxable year, such overpayment shall be deemed not to have been made before the close of such subsequent taxable year."

• **1977, Tax Reduction and Simplification Act of 1977 (P.L. 95-30)**

P.L. 95-30, §202(d)(4)(D):

Amended Code Sec. 6611(f) by adding paragraph (5). **Effective** for tax years beginning after 12-31-76, and for credit carrybacks from such years.

• **1976, Tax Reform Act of 1976 (P.L. 94-455)**

P.L. 94-455, §2107(g)(2)(D):

Added ", an investment credit carryback," after "net operating loss carryback" in Code Sec. 6611(f)(4). **Effective** 10-4-76.

• **1971, Revenue Act of 1971 (P.L. 92-178)**

P.L. 92-178, §601(d)(4):

Amended Code Sec. 6611(f) by adding paragraph (4). **Effective** for tax years ending after 12-31-71.

• **1969, Tax Reform Act of 1969 (P.L. 91-172)**

P.L. 91-172, §512(e)(4):

Amended Code Sec. 6611(f)(1) by adding "or Capital Loss" after "Operating Loss" in heading; by adding "or net capital loss" after "operating loss" wherever it appeared. Amended Code Sec. 6611(f)(2) by adding "or a capital loss carryback" after "loss carryback". **Effective** with respect to net capital losses sustained in tax years beginning after 12-31-69.

• **1967 (P.L. 90-225)**

P.L. 90-225, §2(f):

Amended Code Sec. 6611(f)(2) by inserting at the end thereof the following: ", or, with respect to any portion of an investment credit carryback from a taxable year attributable to a net operating loss carryback from a subsequent taxable year, such overpayment shall be deemed not to have been made prior to the close of such subsequent taxable year". **Effective** with respect to investment credit carrybacks attributable to net operating loss carrybacks from tax years ending after 7-31-67.

• **1964 (P.L. 88-571)**

P.L. 88-571, §3(e):

Amended Code Sec. 6611(f) by changing the heading and by adding paragraph (3). **Effective** with respect to amounts added to policyholders surplus accounts in tax years beginning after 12-31-58.

• **1962, Revenue Act of 1962 (P.L. 87-834)**

P.L. 87-834, §2:

Amended Code Sec. 6611(f). **Effective** for tax years ending after 12-31-61. Prior to amendment, Sec. 6611(f) read as follows:

"(f) Refund of Income Tax Caused by Carryback.—For purposes of subsection (a), if any overpayment of tax imposed by subtitle A results from a carryback of a net operating loss, such overpayment shall be deemed not to have been made prior to the close of the taxable year in which such net operating loss arises."

[Sec. 6611(g)]

(g) NO INTEREST UNTIL RETURN IN PROCESSIBLE FORM.—

(1) For purposes of subsections (b)(3) and (e), a return shall not be treated as filed until it is filed in processible form.

(2) For purposes of paragraph (1), a return is in a processible form if—

(A) such return is filed on a permitted form, and

(B) such return contains—

(i) the taxpayer's name, address, and identifying number and the required signature, and

INTEREST—OVERPAYMENTS

(ii) sufficient required information (whether on the return or on required attachments) to permit the mathematical verification of tax liability shown on the return.

Amendments

• **2000, Community Renewal Tax Relief Act of 2000 (P.L. 106-554)**

P.L. 106-554, § 319(20):

Amended Code Sec. 6611(g)(1) by striking the comma after "(b)(3)". **Effective** 12-21-2000.

• **1998, IRS Restructuring and Reform Act of 1998 (P.L. 105-206)**

P.L. 105-206, § 6010(l):

Amended Code Sec. 6611(g)(1) by striking "(e), and (h)" and inserting "and (e)". **Effective** as if included in the provision of P.L. 105-34 to which it relates [effective for foreign tax credit carrybacks arising in tax years beginning after 8-5-97.—CCH].

• **1997, Taxpayer Relief Act of 1997 (P.L. 105-34)**

P.L. 105-34, § 1055(b)(2)(D):

Amended Code Sec. 6611 by striking subsection (g) and by redesignating subsections (h) and (i) as subsections (g) and (h), respectively. **Effective** for foreign tax credit carrybacks arising in tax years beginning after 8-5-97. Prior to being stricken, Code Sec. 6611(g) read as follows:

(g) REFUND OF INCOME TAX CAUSED BY CARRYBACK OF FOREIGN TAXES.—For purposes of subsection (a), if any overpayment of tax results from a carryback of tax paid or accrued to foreign countries or possessions of the United States, such overpayment shall be deemed not to have been paid or accrued prior to the filing date (as defined in subsection (f)(3)) for the taxable year under this subtitle in which such taxes were in fact paid or accrued.

• **1982, Tax Equity and Fiscal Responsibility Act of 1982 (P.L. 97-248)**

P.L. 97-248, § 346(c)(1)(D):

Amended Code Sec. 6611(g) by striking out "the close of the taxable year" and inserting "the filing date (as defined in subsection (f)(3)) for the taxable year". **Effective** for interest accruing after 10-3-82.

• **1958, Technical Amendments Act of 1958 (P.L. 85-866)**

P.L. 85-866, § 42(b):

Added new subsection (g) to Sec. 6611. **Effective** for tax years beginning after 12-31-57.

[Sec. 6611(h)—Stricken]

(2) SPECIAL RULE WHERE NO RETURN IS REQUIRED.—In the case of any oil for which no return of the tax imposed by section 4986 is required, the return referred to in paragraph (1) shall be the return of the tax imposed by subtitle A for the taxable year of the producer in which the removal year (with respect to which the overpayment was made) ends. For purposes of the preceding sentence, the term "removal year" means the calendar year in which the oil is removed from the premises.

• **1982, Tax Equity and Fiscal Responsibility Act of 1982 (P.L. 97-248)**

P.L. 97-248, § 346(b):

Added Code Sec. 6611(i). **Effective** for returns filed after 10-3-82.

• **1980, Crude Oil Windfall Profit Tax Act of 1980 (P.L. 96-223)**

P.L. 96-223, § 101(h):

Added Code Sec. 6611(h). For the **effective** date and transitional rules, see P.L. 96-223, § 101(i), following Code Sec. 4986.

Amendments

• **1988, Omnibus Trade and Competitiveness Act of 1988 (P.L. 100-418)**

P.L. 100-418, § 1941(b)(2)(L):

Amended Code Sec. 6611 by striking subsection (h) and redesignating subsections (i) and (j) as subsections (h) and (i), respectively. **Effective** for crude oil removed from the premises on or after 8-23-88. Prior to amendment, Code Sec. 6611(h) read as follows:

(h) SPECIAL RULE FOR WINDFALL PROFIT TAX.—

(1) IN GENERAL.—If any overpayment of tax imposed by section 4986 is refunded within 45 days after—

(A) the last date (determined without regard to any extension of time for filing the return) prescribed for filing the return of the tax imposed by section 4986 for the taxable period with respect to which the overpayment was made, or

(B) if such return is filed after such last date, the date on which the return is filed, no interest shall be allowed under subsection (a) on such overpayment.

[Sec. 6611(h)—Repealed]

Amendments

• **1976, Tax Reform Act of 1976 (P.L. 94-455)**

P.L. 94-455, § 1904(b)(10)(A)(iv):

Repealed Code Sec. 6611(h) and redesignated Code Sec. 6611(i) as Code Sec. 6611(h). **Effective** with respect to acquisitions of stock or debt obligations made after 6-30-74. Prior to repeal, Code Sec. 6611(h) read as follows:

(h) REFUND WITHIN 45 DAYS AFTER FILING CLAIM FOR REFUND OF INTEREST EQUALIZATION TAX PAID ON SECURITIES SOLD TO FOREIGNERS.—No interest shall be allowed under subsection (a) on any overpayment of the tax imposed by section 4911, arising by reason of section 4919(a), if the overpayment is refunded within 45 days after the filing of a claim for refund for that overpayment of tax with respect to a prior quarter.

• **1973, Interest Equalization Tax Extension Act of 1973 (P.L. 93-17)**

P.L. 93-17, § 3(i)(2):

Added Code Sec. 6611(h) and redesignated former Code Sec. 6611(h) as Code Sec. 6611(i). **Effective** 4-10-73.

[Sec. 6611(h)]

(h) PROHIBITION OF ADMINISTRATIVE REVIEW.—

For prohibition of administrative review, see section 6406.

Amendments

• **1997, Taxpayer Relief Act of 1997 (P.L. 105-34)**

P.L. 105-34, § 1055(b)(2)(D):

Amended Code Sec. 6611 by redesignating subsection (i) as subsection (h). **Effective** for foreign tax credit carrybacks arising in tax years beginning after 8-5-97.

• **1988, Omnibus Trade and Competitiveness Act of 1988 (P.L. 100-418)**

P.L. 100-418, § 1941(b)(2)(L):

Amended Code Sec. 6611 by redesignating subsection (j) as subsection (i). **Effective** for crude oil removed from the premises on or after 8-23-88.

• **1982, Tax Equity and Fiscal Responsibility Act of 1982 (P.L. 97-248)**

P.L. 97-248, § 346(b):

Redesignated subsection (i) as subsection (j).

• **1980, Crude Oil Windfall Profit Tax Act of 1980 (P.L. 96-223)**

P.L. 96-223, § 101(h):

Redesignated Code Sec. 6611(h) as Code Sec. 6611(i). **Effective** for periods beginning after 2-29-80.

• **1976, Tax Reform Act of 1976 (P.L. 94-455)**

P.L. 94-455, § 1904(b)(10)(A)(iv):

Redesignated Code Sec. 6611(i) as Code Sec. 6611(h). **Effective** with respect to acquisitions of stock or debt obligations made after 6-30-74.

• **1973, Interest Equalization Tax Extension Act of 1973 (P.L. 93-17)**

P.L. 93-17, § 3(i)(2):

See historical comment under the repealed Code Sec. 6611(h). **Effective** 4-10-73.

• **1958, Technical Amendments Act of 1958 (P.L. 85-866)**

P.L. 85-866, § 42(b):

Redesignated subsection (g) of Sec. 6611 as subsection (h). **Effective** for tax years beginning after 12-31-57.

[Sec. 6612]

SEC. 6612. CROSS REFERENCES.

[Sec. 6612(a)]

(a) INTEREST ON JUDGMENTS FOR OVERPAYMENTS.—For interest on judgments for overpayments, see 28 U.S.C. 2411(a).

[Sec. 6612(b)]

(b) ADJUSTMENTS.—For provisions prohibiting interest on certain adjustments in tax, see section 6413(a).

[Sec. 6612(c)]

(c) OTHER RESTRICTIONS ON INTEREST.—For other restrictions on interest, see sections 2014(e) (relating to refunds attributable to foreign tax credits), 6412 (relating to floor stock refunds), 6413(d) (relating to taxes under the Federal Unemployment Tax Act), 6416 (relating to certain taxes on sales and services), 6419 (relating to the excise tax on wagering), 6420 (relating to payments in the case of gasoline used on the farm for farming purposes) and 6421 (relating to payments in the case of gasoline used for certain nonhighway purposes or by local transit systems).

Amendments

• **2018, Tax Technical Corrections Act of 2018 (P.L. 115-141)**

P.L. 115-141, §401(a)(297)(A)-(B), Div. U:

Amended Code Sec. 6612(c) by inserting "sections" before "2014(e)", and by striking "and 6420" and inserting "6420". **Effective** 3-23-2018.

• **2013, American Taxpayer Relief Act of 2012 (P.L. 112-240)**

P.L. 112-240, §101(a)(1) and (3), provides:

SEC. 101. PERMANENT EXTENSION AND MODIFICATION OF 2001 TAX RELIEF.

(a) PERMANENT EXTENSION.—

(1) IN GENERAL.—The Economic Growth and Tax Relief Reconciliation Act of 2001 is amended by striking title IX.

* * *

(3) EFFECTIVE DATE.—The amendments made by this subsection shall apply to taxable, plan, or limitation years beginning after December 31, 2012, and estates of decedents dying, gifts made, or generation skipping transfers after December 31, 2012.

• **2001, Economic Growth and Tax Relief Reconciliation Act of 2001 (P.L. 107-16)**

P.L. 107-16, §532(c)(12):

Amended Code Sec. 6612(c) by striking "section 2011(c) (relating to refunds due to credit for State taxes)," following "For other restrictions on interest, see". **Effective** for estates of decedents dying, and generation-skipping transfers, after 12-31-2004.

P.L. 107-16, §901(a)-(b), as amended by P.L. 111-312, §101(a)(1), provides [but see P.L. 112-240, §101(a)(1) and (3), above]:

SEC. 901. SUNSET OF PROVISIONS OF ACT.

(a) IN GENERAL.—All provisions of, and amendments made by, this Act shall not apply—

(1) to taxable, plan, or limitation years beginning after December 31, 2012, or

(2) in the case of title V, to estates of decedents dying, gifts made, or generation skipping transfers, after December 31, 2012.

(b) APPLICATION OF CERTAIN LAWS.—The Internal Revenue Code of 1986 and the Employee Retirement Income Security Act of 1974 shall be applied and administered to years, estates, gifts, and transfers described in subsection (a) as if the provisions and amendments described in subsection (a) had never been enacted.

• **1956 (P.L. 627, 84th Cong.)**

P.L. 627, 84th Cong., 2nd Sess., §208(e)(7):

Amended subsection (c) by striking out "and" before "6420" and by inserting before the period at the end of subsection (c) the following: "and 6421 (relating to payments in the case of gasoline used for certain nonhighway purposes or by local transit systems)". **Effective** 7-1-56.

• **1956 (P.L. 466, 84th Cong.)**

P.L. 466, 84th Cong., 2nd Sess., §4(f):

Amended Code Sec. 6612(c) by striking out the word "and" which had appeared before the number "6419" and adding the words ", and 6420 (relating to payments in the case of gasoline used on the farm for farming purposes)" at the end of the section.

Subchapter C—Determination of Interest Rate; Compounding of Interest

Sec. 6621. Determination of rate of interest.
Sec. 6622. Interest compounded daily.

[Sec. 6621]

SEC. 6621. DETERMINATION OF RATE OF INTEREST.

[Sec. 6621(a)]

(a) GENERAL RULE.—

(1) OVERPAYMENT RATE.—The overpayment rate established under this section shall be the sum of—

(A) the Federal short-term rate determined under subsection (b), plus

(B) 3 percentage points (2 percentage points in the case of a corporation).

To the extent that an overpayment of tax by a corporation for any taxable period (as defined in subsection (c)(3), applied by substituting "overpayment" for "underpayment") exceeds $10,000, subparagraph (B) shall be applied by substituting "0.5 percentage point" for "2 percentage points".

(2) UNDERPAYMENT RATE.—The underpayment rate established under this section shall be the sum of—

(A) the Federal short-term rate determined under subsection (b), plus

(B) 3 percentage points.

Amendments

• **1998, IRS Restructuring and Reform Act of 1998 (P.L. 105-206)**

P.L. 105-206, §3302(a):

Amended Code Sec. 6621(a)(1)(B). **Effective** for interest for the second and succeeding calendar quarters beginning after 7-22-98. Prior to amendment, Code Sec. 6621(a)(1)(B) read as follows:

(B) 2 percentage points.

• **1997, Taxpayer Relief Act of 1997 (P.L. 105-34)**

P.L. 105-34, §1604(b)(1):

Amended Code Sec. 6621(a)(1) by striking "subsection (c)(3))" in the last sentence and inserting "subsection (c)(3), applied by substituting 'overpayment' for 'underpayment')". **Effective** as if included in the provision of P.L. 103-465 to which it relates [**effective** for determining interest for periods after 12-31-94.—CCH].

• **1994, Uruguay Round Agreements Act (P.L. 103-465)**

P.L. 103-465, §713(a):

Amended Code Sec. 6621(a)(1) by adding at the end a new flush sentence. **Effective** for purposes of determining interest for periods after 12-31-94.

• **1988, Technical and Miscellaneous Revenue Act of 1988 (P.L. 100-647)**

P.L. 100-647, §1015(d)(1)-(2):

Amended Code Sec. 6621 by striking out "short-term Federal rate" each place it appears in subsections (a) and (b)(1) and inserting in lieu thereof "Federal short-term rate". **Effective** as if included in the provision of P.L. 99-514 to which it relates.

• **1986, Tax Reform Act of 1986 (P.L. 99-514)**

P.L. 99-514, §1511(a):

Amended Code Sec. 6621 by striking out subsection (a) and inserting in lieu thereof new subsection (a). **Effective** for purposes of determining interest to periods after 12-31-86. Prior to amendment, Code Sec. 6621(a) read as follows:

(a) IN GENERAL.—The annual rate established under this section shall be such adjusted rate as is established by the Secretary under subsection (b).

• **1979 (P.L. 96-167)**

P.L. 96-167, §4:

Amended Code Sec. 6621(a). **Effective** 12-29-79. Prior to amendment, Sec. 6621(a) read as follows:

"(a) IN GENERAL.—The rate of interest under sections 6601(a), 6602, 6611(a), 6332(c)(1), and 7426(g) of this title, and under section 2411(a) of title 28 is 9 percent per annum, or such adjusted rate as is established by the Secretary under subsection (b)."

• **1976, Tax Reform Act of 1976 (P.L. 94-455)**

P.L. 94-455, §1906(b)(13)(A):

Amended 1954 Code by substituting "Secretary" for "Secretary or his delegate" each place it appeared. **Effective** 2-1-77.

• **1975 (P.L. 93-625)**

P.L. 93-625, §7(a)(1):

Added Code Sec. 6621(a). **Effective** for amounts outstanding on 7-1-75 or arising thereafter.

[Sec. 6621(b)]

(b) FEDERAL SHORT-TERM RATE.—For purposes of this section—

(1) GENERAL RULE.—The Secretary shall determine the Federal short-term rate for the first month in each calendar quarter.

(2) PERIOD DURING WHICH RATE APPLIES.—

(A) IN GENERAL.—Except as provided in subparagraph (B), the Federal short-term rate determined under paragraph (1) for any month shall apply during the first calendar quarter beginning after such month.

RATE OF INTEREST—COMPOUNDING OF INTEREST

(B) Special rule for individual estimated tax.—In determining the addition to tax under section 6654 for failure to pay estimated tax for any taxable year, the Federal short-term rate which applies during the 3rd month following such taxable year shall also apply during the first 15 days of the 4th month following such taxable year.

(3) Federal short-term rate.—The Federal short-term rate for any month shall be the Federal short-term rate determined during such month by the Secretary in accordance with section 1274(d). Any such rate shall be rounded to the nearest full percent (or, if a multiple of $^1/_2$ of 1 percent, such rate shall be increased to the next highest full percent).

Amendments

• **1988, Technical and Miscellaneous Revenue Act of 1988 (P.L. 100-647)**

P.L. 100-647, §1015(d)(1)-(2):

Amended Code Sec. 6621 by striking out "short-term Federal rate" each place it appears in subsections (a) and (b)(1) and inserting in lieu thereof "Federal short-term rate", and by striking out "Short-Term Federal Rate" in the heading of subsection (b) and inserting in lieu thereof "Federal Short-Term Rate". **Effective** as if included in the provision of P.L. 99-514 to which it relates.

• **1986, Tax Reform Act of 1986 (P.L. 99-514)**

P.L. 99-514, §1511(a):

Amended Code Sec. 6621 by striking out subsection (b) and inserting in lieu thereof new subsections (a) and (b). **Effective** for purposes of determining interest to periods after 12-31-86. Prior to amendment, Code Sec. 6621(b) read as follows:

(b) Adjustment of Interest Rate.—

(1) Establishment of adjusted rate.—If the adjusted prime rate charged by banks (rounded to the nearest full percent)—

(A) during the 6-month period ending on September 30 of any calendar year, or

(B) during the 6-month period ending on March 31 of any calendar year,

differs from the interest rate in effect under this section on either such date, respectively, then the Secretary shall establish, within 15 days after the close of the applicable 6-month period, an adjusted rate of interest equal to such adjusted prime rate.

(2) Effective date of adjustment.—Any adjusted rate of interest established under paragraph (1) shall become effective—

(A) on January 1, of the succeeding year in the case of an adjustment attributable to paragraph (1)(A), and

(B) on July 1 of the same year in the case of an adjustment attributable to paragraph (1)(B).

• **1982, Tax Equity and Fiscal Responsibility Act of 1982 (P.L. 97-248)**

P.L. 97-248, §345(a):

Amended Code Sec. 6621(b). **Effective** for adjustments taking effect on or after 1-1-83. [effective date changed by P.L. 98-369, §714(m).] Prior to amendment, Code Sec. 6621(b) read as follows:

"(b) Adjustment of Interest Rate.—The Secretary shall establish an adjusted rate of interest for the purpose of subsection (a) not later than October 15 of any year if the adjusted prime rate charged by banks during September of that year, rounded to the nearest full percent, is at least a full percentage point more or less than the interest rate which is then in effect. Any such adjusted rate of interest shall be equal to the adjusted prime rate charged by banks, rounded to the nearest full percent, and shall become effective on January 1 [February 1, effective until 1982] of the immediately succeeding year."

• **1981, Economic Recovery Tax Act of 1981 (P.L. 97-34)**

P.L. 97-34, §711(a):

Amended Code Sec. 6621(b) by striking out the last sentence thereof. **Effective** for adjustments made after 8-13-81. Prior to amendment, the last sentence of Code Sec. 6621(b) read as follows:

An adjustment provided for under this subsection may not be made prior to the expiration of 23 months following the date of any preceding adjustment under this subsection which changes the rate of interest.

P.L. 97-34, §711(c):

Amended Code Sec. 6621(b) by striking out "February 1" and inserting "January 1". **Effective** for adjustments made for periods after 1982.

• **1976, Tax Reform Act of 1976 (P.L. 94-455)**

P.L. 94-455, §1906(b)(13)(A):

Amended 1954 Code by substituting "Secretary" for "Secretary or his delegate" each place it appeared. **Effective** 2-1-77.

• **1975 (P.L. 93-625)**

P.L. 93-625, §7(a)(1):

Added Code Sec. 6621(b). **Effective** for amounts outstanding on 7-1-75 or arising thereafter.

[Sec. 6621(c)]

(c) Increase in Underpayment Rate for Large Corporate Underpayments.—

(1) In general.—For purposes of determining the amount of interest payable under section 6601 on any large corporate underpayment for periods after the applicable date, paragraph (2) of subsection (a) shall be applied by substituting "5 percentage points" for "3 percentage points".

(2) Applicable date.—For purposes of this subsection—

(A) In general.—The applicable date is the 30th day after the earlier of—

(i) the date on which the 1st letter of proposed deficiency which allows the taxpayer an opportunity for administrative review in the Internal Revenue Service Independent Office of Appeals is sent, or

(ii) the date on which the deficiency notice under section 6212 is sent.

The preceding sentence shall be applied without regard to any such letter or notice which is withdrawn by the Secretary.

(B) Special rules.—

(i) Nondeficiency procedures.—In the case of any underpayment of any tax imposed by this title to which the deficiency procedures do not apply, subparagraph (A) shall be applied by taking into account any letter or notice provided by the Secretary which notifies the taxpayer of the assessment or proposed assessment of the tax.

(ii) Exception where amounts paid in full.—For purposes of subparagraph (A), a letter or notice shall be disregarded if, during the 30-day period beginning on the day on which it was sent, the taxpayer makes a payment equal to the amount shown as due in such letter or notice, as the case may be.

(iii) Exception for letters or notices involving small amounts.—For purposes of this paragraph, any letter or notice shall be disregarded if the amount of the deficiency or proposed deficiency (or the assessment or proposed assessment) set forth in such letter or notice is not greater than $100,000 (determined by not taking into account any interest, penalties, or additions to tax).

(3) Large corporate underpayment.—For purposes of this subsection—

(A) In general.—The term "large corporate underpayment" means any underpayment of a tax by a C corporation for any taxable period if the amount of such underpayment for such period exceeds $100,000.

(B) Taxable period.—For purposes of subparagraph (A), the term "taxable period" means—

(i) in the case of any tax imposed by subtitle A, the taxable year, or

(ii) in the case of any other tax, the period to which the underpayment relates.

Amendments

• **2019, Taxpayer First Act (P.L. 116-25)**

P.L. 116-25, §1001(b)(1)(E):

Amended Code Sec. 6621(c)(2)(A)(i) by striking "Internal Revenue Service Office of Appeals" and inserting "Internal Revenue Service Independent Office of Appeals". **Effective** 7-1-2019.

• **1997, Taxpayer Relief Act of 1997 (P.L. 105-34)**

P.L. 105-34, §1463(a):

Amended Code Sec. 6621(c)(2)(B) by adding at the end a new clause (iii). **Effective** for purposes of determining interest for periods after 12-31-97.

Sec. 6621(b)(2)(B)

RATE OF INTEREST—COMPOUNDING OF INTEREST

• **1996, Small Business Job Protection Act of 1996 (P.L. 104-188)**

P.L. 104-188, §1702(c)(6):

Amended Code Sec. 6621(c)(2)(A) by adding at the end a new flush sentence. **Effective** as if included in the provision of P.L. 101-508 to which it relates.

P.L. 104-188, §1702(c)(7):

Amended Code Sec. 6621(c)(2)(B)(i) by striking "this subtitle" and inserting "this title". **Effective** as if included in the provision of P.L. 101-508 to which it relates.

Amendments

• **1989, Omnibus Budget Reconciliation Act of 1989 (P.L. 101-239)**

P.L. 101-239, §7721(b):

Repealed Code Sec. 6621(c). **Effective** for returns the due date for which (determined without regard to extensions) is after 12-31-89. Prior to repeal, Code Sec. 6621(c) read as follows:

(c) INTEREST ON SUBSTANTIAL UNDERPAYMENTS ATTRIBUTABLE TO TAX MOTIVATED TRANSACTIONS.—

(1) IN GENERAL.—In the case of interest payable under section 6601 with respect to any substantial underpayment attributable to tax motivated transactions, the rate of interest established under this section shall be 120 percent of the underpayment rate established under this subsection.

(2) SUBSTANTIAL UNDERPAYMENT ATTRIBUTABLE TO TAX MOTIVATED TRANSACTIONS.—For purposes of this subsection, the term "substantial underpayment attributable to tax motivated transactions" means any underpayment of taxes imposed by subtitle A for any taxable year which is attributable to 1 or more tax motivated transactions if the amount of the underpayment for such year so attributable exceeds $1,000.

(3) TAX MOTIVATED TRANSACTIONS.—

(A) IN GENERAL.—For purposes of this subsection, the term "tax motivated transaction" means—

(i) any valuation overstatement (within the meaning of section 6659(c)),

(ii) any loss disallowed by reason of section 465(a) and any credit disallowed under section 46(c)(8),

(iii) any straddle (as defined in section 1092(c) without regard to subsections (d) and (e) of section 1092),

(iv) any use of an accounting method specified in regulations prescribed by the Secretary as a use which may result in a substantial distortion of income for any period, and

(v) any sham or fraudulent transaction.

(B) REGULATORY AUTHORITY.—The Secretary may by regulations specify other types of transactions which will be treated as tax motivated for purposes of this subsection and may by regulations provide that specified transactions being treated as tax motivated will no longer be so treated. In prescribing regulations under the preceding sentence, the Secretary shall take into account—

(i) the ratio of tax benefits to cash invested,

(ii) the methods of promoting the use of this type of transaction, and

(iii) other relevant considerations.

(C) EFFECTIVE DATE FOR REGULATIONS.—Any regulations prescribed under subparagraph (A)(iv) or (B) shall apply only to interest accruing after a date (specified in such regulations) which is after the date on which such regulations are prescribed.

(4) JURISDICTION OF TAX COURT.—In the case of any proceeding in the Tax Court for a redetermination of a deficiency, the Tax Court shall also have jurisdiction to determine the portion (if any) of such deficiency which is a substantial underpayment attributable to tax motivated transactions.

• **1990, Omnibus Budget Reconciliation Act of 1990 (P.L. 101-508)**

P.L. 101-508, §11341(a):

Amended Code Sec. 6621 by adding at the end thereof a new subsection (c). **Effective** for purposes of determining interest for periods after 12-31-90.

[Sec. 6621(c)—Repealed]

• **1986, Tax Reform Act of 1986 (P.L. 99-514)**

P.L. 99-514, §1511(a):

Amended Code Sec. 6621 by striking out subsection (c). **Effective** for purposes of determining interest for periods after 12-31-86. Prior to amendment, Code Sec. 6621(c) read as follows:

(c) DEFINITION OF PRIME RATE.—For purposes of subsection (b), the term "adjusted prime rate charged by banks" means the average predominant prime rate quoted by commercial banks to large businesses, as determined by the Board of Governors of the Federal Reserve System.

P.L. 99-514, §1511(c)(1)(A)-(C):

Amended Code Sec. 6621 by redesignating subsection (d) as subsection (c), by striking out "the adjusted rate established under subsection (b)" in subsection (c)(1) (as so redesignated) and inserting in lieu thereof "the underpayment rate established under this section", and by striking out "annual" in subsection (c)(1) (as so redesignated). **Effective** for purposes of determining interest for periods after 12-31-86.

P.L. 99-514, §1535(a):

Amended Code Sec. 6621(c)(3)(A) (as so redesignated) by striking out "and" at the end of clause (iii), by striking out the period at the end of clause (iv) and inserting in lieu thereof ", and", and by adding at the end thereof new clause (v). **Effective** for interest accruing after 12-31-84, except that it shall not apply in the case of any underpayment with respect to which there was a final court decision before 10-22-86.

P.L. 99-514, §1511(b), provides:

(b) COORDINATION BY REGULATION.—The Secretary of the Treasury or his delegate may issue regulations to coordinate section 6621 of the Internal Revenue Code of 1954 (as amended by this section) with section 6601(f) of such Code. Such regulations shall not apply to any period after the date 3 years after the date of the enactment of this Act.

• **1984, Deficit Reduction Act of 1984 (P.L. 98-369)**

P.L. 98-369, §144(a):

Amended Code Sec. 6621 by adding subsection (d). **Effective** with respect to interest accruing after 12-31-84.

• **1981, Economic Recovery Tax Act of 1981 (P.L. 97-34)**

P.L. 97-34, §711(b):

Amended Code Sec. 6621(c) by striking out "90 percent of" after "`adjusted prime rate charged by banks' means". **Effective** for adjustments made after 8-13-81.

• **1976, Tax Reform Act of 1976 (P.L. 94-455)**

P.L. 94-455, §1906(b)(13)(A):

Amended 1954 Code by substituting "Secretary" for "Secretary or his delegate" each place it appeared. **Effective** 2-1-77.

• **1975 (P.L. 93-625)**

P.L. 93-625, §7(a)(1):

Added Code Sec. 6621(c). **Effective** 7-1-75, for amounts outstanding on such date or arising thereafter.

[Sec. 6621(d)]

(d) ELIMINATION OF INTEREST ON OVERLAPPING PERIODS OF TAX OVERPAYMENTS AND UNDERPAYMENTS.—To the extent that, for any period, interest is payable under subchapter A and allowable under subchapter B on equivalent underpayments and overpayments by the same taxpayer of tax imposed by this title, the net rate of interest under this section on such amounts shall be zero for such period.

Amendments

• **1998, IRS Restructuring and Reform Act of 1998 (P.L. 105-206)**

P.L. 105-206, §3301(a):

Amended Code Sec. 6621 by adding at the end a new subsection (d). **Effective**, generally, for interest for periods beginning after 7-22-98. For a special rule, see Act Sec. 3301(c)(2), below.

P.L. 105-206, §3301(c)(2), as amended by P.L. 105-277, §4002(d), provides:

(2) SPECIAL RULE.—Subject to any applicable statute of limitation not having expired with regard to either a tax underpayment or a tax overpayment, the amendments made by this section shall apply to interest for periods beginning before the date of the enactment of this Act if the taxpayer—

(A) reasonably identifies and establishes periods of such tax overpayments and under-payments for which the zero rate applies; and

(B) not later than December 31, 1999, requests the Secretary of the Treasury to apply section 6621(d) of the Internal Revenue Code of 1986, as added by subsection (a), to such periods.

[Sec. 6622]

SEC. 6622. INTEREST COMPOUNDED DAILY.

[Sec. 6622(a)]

(a) GENERAL RULE.—In computing the amount of any interest required to be paid under this title or sections 1961(c)(1) or 2411 of title 28, United States Code, by the Secretary or by the taxpayer, or any other amount determined by reference to such amount of interest, such interest and such amount shall be compounded daily.

[Sec. 6622(b)]

(b) EXCEPTION FOR PENALTY FOR FAILURE TO FILE ESTIMATED TAX.—Subsection (a) shall not apply for purposes of computing the amount of any addition to tax under section 6654 or 6655.

Internal Revenue Code   **Sec. 6622(b)**

ADDITIONS TO TAX

Amendments

• **1982, Tax Equity and Fiscal Responsibility Act of 1982 (P.L. 97-248)**

P.L. 97-248, § 344(a):

Added Code Sec. 6622. **Effective** for interest accruing after 12-31-82.

Subchapter D—Notice Requirements

Sec. 6631.   Notice requirements.

[Sec. 6631]

SEC. 6631. NOTICE REQUIREMENTS.

The Secretary shall include with each notice to an individual taxpayer which includes an amount of interest required to be paid by such taxpayer under this title information with respect to the section of this title under which the interest is imposed and a computation of the interest.

Amendments

• **1998, IRS Restructuring and Reform Act of 1998 (P.L. 105-206)**

P.L. 105-206, § 3308(a):

Amended chapter 67 by adding at the end a new subchapter D (Code Sec. 6631). **Effective** for notices issued after 12-31-2001. In the case of any notice issued after 6-3-2001, and before 7-1-2003, to which Code Sec. 6631 applies, the requirements of Code Sec. 6631 shall be treated as met if such notice contains a telephone number at which the taxpayer can request a copy of the taxpayer's payment history relating to interest amounts included in such notice [**effective** date changed by P.L. 106-554, § 302(c)].

CHAPTER 68—ADDITIONS TO THE TAX, ADDITIONAL AMOUNTS, AND ASSESSABLE PENALTIES

SUBCHAPTER A.   Additions to the tax and additional amounts.
SUBCHAPTER B.   Assessable penalties.
SUBCHAPTER C.   Procedural requirements.

Subchapter A—Additions to the Tax and Additional Amounts

Part I.   General provisions.
Part II.   Accuracy-related and fraud penalties.
Part III.   Applicable rules.

PART I—GENERAL PROVISIONS

Sec. 6651.   Failure to file tax return or to pay tax.
Sec. 6652.   Failure to file certain information returns, registration statements, etc.
Sec. 6653.   Failure to pay stamp tax.
Sec. 6654.   Failure by individual to pay estimated income tax.
Sec. 6655.   Failure by corporation to pay estimated income tax.
Sec. 6656.   Failure to make deposit of taxes.
Sec. 6657.   Bad checks.
Sec. 6658.   Coordination with title 11.

[Sec. 6651]

SEC. 6651. FAILURE TO FILE TAX RETURN OR TO PAY TAX.

[Sec. 6651(a)]

(a) ADDITION TO THE TAX.—In case of failure—

(1) to file any return required under authority of subchapter A of chapter 61 (other than part III thereof), subchapter A of chapter 51 (relating to distilled spirits, wines, and beer), or of subchapter A of chapter 52 (relating to tobacco, cigars, cigarettes, and cigarette papers and tubes) or of subchapter A of chapter 53 (relating to machine guns and certain other firearms), on the date prescribed therefor (determined with regard to any extension of time for filing), unless it is shown that such failure is due to reasonable cause and not due to willful neglect, there shall be added to the amount required to be shown as tax on such return 5 percent of the amount of such tax if the failure is for not more than 1 month, with an additional 5 percent for each additional month or fraction thereof during which such failure continues, not exceeding 25 percent in the aggregate;

(2) to pay the amount shown as tax on any return specified in paragraph (1) on or before the date prescribed for payment of such tax (determined with regard to any extension of time for payment), unless it is shown that such failure is due to reasonable cause and not due to willful neglect, there shall be added to the amount shown as tax on such return 0.5 percent of the amount of such tax if the failure is for not more than 1 month, with an additional 0.5 percent for each additional month or fraction thereof during which such failure continues, not exceeding 25 percent in the aggregate; or

(3) to pay any amount in respect of any tax required to be shown on a return specified in paragraph (1) which is not so shown (including an assessment made pursuant to section 6213(b)) within 21 calendar days from the date of notice and demand therefor (10 business days if the amount for which such notice and demand is made equals or exceeds $100,000), unless it is shown that such failure is due to reasonable cause and not due to willful neglect, there shall be added to the amount of tax stated in such notice and demand 0.5 percent of the amount of such tax if the failure is for not more than 1 month, with an additional 0.5 percent for each additional month or fraction thereof during which such failure continues, not exceeding 25 percent in the aggregate.

In the case of a failure to file a return of tax imposed by chapter 1 within 60 days of the date prescribed for filing of such return (determined with regard to any extensions of time for filing), unless it is shown that such failure is due to reasonable cause and not due to willful neglect, the addition to tax under paragraph (1) shall not be less than the lesser of $435 or 100 percent of the amount required to be shown as tax on such return.

ADDITIONS TO TAX

Amendments

• **2019, Setting Every Community Up for Retirement Enhancement Act of 2019 (P.L. 116-94)**

P.L. 116-94, §402(a), Div. O:

Amended the second sentence of Code Sec. 6651(a) by striking "$330" and inserting "$435". **Effective** for returns the due date for which (including extensions) is after 12-31-2019.

• **2019, Taxpayer First Act (P.L. 116-25)**

P.L. 116-25, §3201(a):

Amended the second sentence of Code Sec. 6651(a) by striking "$205" and inserting "$330". **Effective** for returns required to be filed after 12-31-2019.

• **2016, Trade Facilitation and Trade Enforcement Act of 2015 (P.L. 114-125)**

P.L. 114-125, §921(a):

Amended Code Sec. 6651(a) by striking "$135" in the last sentence and inserting "$205". **Effective** for returns required to be filed in calendar years after 2015.

• **2008, Heroes Earnings Assistance and Relief Tax Act of 2008 (P.L. 110-245)**

P.L. 110-245, §303(a):

Amended Code Sec. 6651(a) by striking "$100" in the last sentence and inserting "$135". **Effective** for returns required to be filed after 12-31-2008.

• **1998, IRS Restructuring and Reform Act of 1998 (P.L. 105-206)**

P.L. 105-206, §3707, provides:

SEC. 3707. ILLEGAL TAX PROTESTER DESIGNATION.

(a) PROHIBITION.—The officers and employees of the Internal Revenue Service—

(1) shall not designate taxpayers as illegal tax protesters (or any similar designation); and

(2) in the case of any such designation made on or before the date of the enactment of this Act—

(A) shall remove such designation from the individual master file; and

(B) shall disregard any such designation not located in the individual master file.

(b) DESIGNATION OF NONFILERS ALLOWED.—An officer or employee of the Internal Revenue Service may designate any appropriate taxpayer as a nonfiler, but shall remove such designation once the taxpayer has filed income tax returns for 2 consecutive taxable years and paid all taxes shown on such returns.

(c) EFFECTIVE DATE.—The provisions of this section shall take effect on July 22, 1998, except that the removal of any designation under subsection (a)(2)(A) shall not be required to begin before January 1, 1999.

• **1996, Taxpayer Bill of Rights 2 (P.L. 104-168)**

P.L. 104-168, §303(b)(2):

Amended Code Sec. 6651(a)(3) by striking "10 days of the date of the notice and demand therefor" and inserting "21 calendar days from the date of notice and demand therefor (10 business days if the amount for which such notice and demand is made equals or exceeds $100,000)". **Effective** in the case of any notice and demand given after 12-31-96.

• **1982, Tax Equity and Fiscal Responsibility Act of 1982 (P.L. 97-248)**

P.L. 97-248, §318(a):

Amended Code Sec. 6651(a) by adding at the end a new sentence. **Effective** for returns the due date for the filing of which (including extensions) is after 12-31-82.

[Sec. 6651(b)]

(b) PENALTY IMPOSED ON NET AMOUNT DUE.—For purposes of—

(1) subsection (a)(1), the amount of tax required to be shown on the return shall be reduced by the amount of any part of the tax which is paid on or before the date prescribed for payment of the tax and by the amount of any credit against the tax which may be claimed on the return,

(2) subsection (a)(2), the amount of tax shown on the return shall, for purposes of computing the addition for any month, be reduced by the amount of any part of the tax which is paid on or before the beginning of such month and by the amount of any credit against the tax which may be claimed on the return, and

(3) subsection (a)(3), the amount of tax stated in the notice and demand shall, for the purpose of computing the addition for any month, be reduced by the amount of any part of the tax which is paid before the beginning of such month.

[Sec. 6651(c)]

(c) LIMITATIONS AND SPECIAL RULE.—

(1) ADDITIONS UNDER MORE THAN ONE PARAGRAPH.—With respect to any return, the amount of the addition under paragraph (1) of subsection (a) shall be reduced by the amount of the addition under paragraph (2) of subsection (a) for any month (or fraction thereof) to which an addition to tax applies under both paragraphs (1) and (2). In any case described in the last sentence of subsection (a), the amount of the addition under paragraph (1) of subsection (a) shall not be reduced under the preceding sentence below the amount provided in such last sentence.

(2) AMOUNT OF TAX SHOWN MORE THAN AMOUNT REQUIRED TO BE SHOWN.—If the amount required to be shown as tax on a return is less than the amount shown as tax on such return, subsections (a)(2) and (b)(2) shall be applied by substituting such lower amount.

Amendments

• **1986, Tax Reform Act of 1986 (P.L. 99-514)**

P.L. 99-514, §1502(b):

Amended Code Sec. 6651(c)(1). **Effective** for amounts assessed after 12-31-86, with respect to failures to pay which begin before, on, or after such date. Prior to amendment, Code Sec. 6651(c)(1) read as follows:

(1) ADDITIONS UNDER MORE THAN ONE PARAGRAPH.—

(A) With respect to any return, the amount of the addition under paragraph (1) of subsection (a) shall be reduced by the amount of the addition under paragraph (2) of subsection (a) for any month to which an addition to tax applies under both paragraphs (1) and (2). In any case described in the last sentence of subsection (a), the amount of the addition under paragraph (1) of subsection (a) shall not be reduced under the preceding sentence below the amount provided in such last sentence.

(B) With respect to any return, the maximum amount of the addition permitted under paragraph (3) of subsection (a) shall be reduced by the amount of the addition under paragraph (1) of subsection (a) (determined without regard to the last sentence of such subsection) which is attributable to the tax for which the notice and demand is made and which is not paid within 10 days of notice and demand.

• **1982, Tax Equity and Fiscal Responsibility Act of 1982 (P.L. 97-248)**

P.L. 97-248, §318(b)(1):

Amended Code Sec. 6651(c)(1)(A) by adding at the end a new sentence. **Effective** for returns the due date for the filing of which (including extensions) is after 12-31-82.

P.L. 97-248, §318(b)(2):

Amended Code Sec. 6651(c)(1)(B) by inserting "(determined without regard to the last sentence of such subsection)" after "paragraph (1) of subsection (a)". **Effective** for returns the due date for the filing of which (including extensions) is after 12-31-82.

• **1968, Revenue and Expenditure Control Act of 1968 (P.L. 90-364)**

P.L. 90-364, §103(e)(4):

Amended Code Sec. 6651(c) by deleting "or section 6016" which formerly appeared after "section 6015". **Effective** with respect to tax years beginning after 12-31-67.

[Sec. 6651(d)]

(d) INCREASE IN PENALTY FOR FAILURE TO PAY TAX IN CERTAIN CASES.—

(1) IN GENERAL.—In the case of each month (or fraction thereof) beginning after the day described in paragraph (2) of this subsection, paragraphs (2) and (3) of subsection (a) shall be applied by substituting "1 percent" for "0.5 percent" each place it appears.

(2) DESCRIPTION.—For purposes of paragraph (1), the day described in this paragraph is the earlier of—

(A) the day 10 days after the date of which notice is given under section 6331(d), or

(B) the day on which notice and demand for immediate payment is given under the last sentence of section 6331(a).

Amendments

• **1986, Tax Reform Act of 1986 (P.L. 99-514)**

P.L. 99-514, §1502(a):

Amended Code Sec. 6651 by redesignating subsection (d) as subsection (e) and by inserting after subsection (c) new subsection (d). For the **effective** date, see Act Sec. 1502(c)(1), below.

P.L. 99-514, §1502(c)(1), provides:

(c) EFFECTIVE DATES.—

(1) SUBSECTION (a).—The amendments made by subsection (a) shall apply—

(A) to failures to pay which began after December 31, 1986, and

(B) to failures to pay which begin on or before December 31, 1986, if after December 31, 1986—

ADDITIONS TO TAX

(i) notice (or renotice) under section 6331(d) of the Internal Revenue Code of 1954 is given with respect to such failure, or

(ii) notice and demand for immediate payment of the underpayment is made under the last sentence of section 6331(a) of such Code.

In the case of a failure to pay described in subparagraph (B), paragraph (2) of section 6651(d) of such Code (as added by subsection (a)) shall be applied by taking into account the first notice (or renotice) after December 31, 1986.

[Sec. 6651(e)]

(e) EXCEPTION FOR ESTIMATED TAX.—This section shall not apply to any failure to pay any estimated tax required to be paid by section 6654 or 6655.

Amendments

• **1987, Revenue Act of 1987 (P.L. 100-203)**

P.L. 100-203, §10301(b)(6):

Amended Code Sec. 6651(e) by striking out "section 6154 or 6654" and inserting in lieu thereof "section 6654 or 6655". **Effective** for tax years beginning after 12-31-87.

• **1986, Tax Reform Act of 1986 (P.L. 99-514)**

P.L. 99-514, §1502(a):

Amended Code Sec. 6651 by redesignating subsection (d) as subsection (e). For the **effective** date, see Act Sec. 1502(c)(1), below.

P.L. 99-514, §1502(c)(1), provides:

(c) EFFECTIVE DATES.—

(1) SUBSECTION (a).—The amendments made by subsection (a) shall apply—

(A) to failures to pay which began after December 31, 1986, and

(B) to failures to pay which begin on or before December 31, 1986, if after December 31, 1986—

(i) notice (or renotice) under section 6331(d) of the Internal Revenue Code of 1954 is given with respect to such failure, or

(ii) notice and demand for immediate payment of the underpayment is made under the last sentence of section 6331(a) of such Code.

In the case of a failure to pay described in subparagraph (B), paragraph (2) of section 6651(d) of such Code (as added by subsection (a)) shall be applied by taking into account the first notice (or renotice) after December 31, 1986.

Amendments

• **1976, Tax Reform Act of 1976 (P.L. 94-455)**

P.L. 94-455, §1904(b)(10)(A)(v):

Repealed Code Sec. 6651(e). **Effective** with respect to acquisitions of stock or debt obligations made after 6-30-74. Prior to repeal, Code Sec. 6651(e) read as follows:

(e) CERTAIN INTEREST EQUALIZATION TAX RETURNS.—The provisions of this section shall apply with respect to returns of amounts withheld under section 4918(e)(7) (relating to withholding of interest equalization tax by participating firms) in the same manner and to the same extent as they apply with respect to returns specified in subsection (a)(1).

• **1971, Interest Equalization Tax Extension Act of 1971 (P.L. 92-9)**

P.L. 92-9, §3(j)(1):

Added Code Sec. 6651(e). **Effective** with respect to returns required to be filed on or after 4-1-71.

• **1984, Deficit Reduction Act of 1984 (P.L. 98-369)**

P.L. 98-369, §412(b)(8):

Amended Code Sec. 6651(d). **Effective** with respect to tax years beginning after 12-31-84. Prior to amendment, it read as follows:

(d) EXCEPTION FOR DECLARATION OF ESTIMATED TAX.—This section shall not apply to any failure to file a declaration of estimated tax required by section 6015 or to pay any estimated tax required to be paid by section 6153 or 6154.

• **1969, Tax Reform Act of 1969 (P.L. 91-172)**

P.L. 91-172, §943(a):

Amended Code Sec. 6651. **Effective** with respect to returns the date prescribed by law (without regard to any extension of time) for filing of which is after 12-31-69, and with respect to notices and demands for payment of tax made after 12-31-69. Prior to amendment, Sec. 6651 read as follows:

SEC. 6651. FAILURE TO FILE TAX RETURN.

(a) ADDITION TO THE TAX.—In case of failure to file any return required under authority of subchapter A of chapter 61 (other than part III thereof), of subchapter A of chapter 51 (relating to distilled spirits, wines, and beer), or of subchapter A of chapter 52 (relating to tobacco, cigars, cigarettes, and cigarette papers and tubes), or of subchapter A of chapter 53 (relating to machine guns and certain other firearms), on the date prescribed therefor (determined with regard to any extension of time for filing), unless it is shown that such failure is due to reasonable cause and not due to willful neglect, there shall be added to the amount required to be shown as tax on such return 5 percent of the amount of such tax if the failure is for not more than 1 month, with an additional 5 percent for each additional month or fraction thereof during which such failure continues, not exceeding 25 percent in the aggregate.

(b) PENALTY IMPOSED ON NET AMOUNT DUE.—For purposes of subsection (a), the amount of tax required to be shown on the return shall be reduced by the amount of any part of the tax which is paid on or before the date prescribed for payment of the tax and by the amount of any credit against the tax which may be claimed upon the return.

(c) EXCEPTION FOR DECLARATIONS OF ESTIMATED TAX.—This section shall not apply to any failure to file a declaration of estimated tax required by section 6015.

[Sec. 6651(e)—Repealed]

[Sec. 6651(f)]

(f) INCREASE IN PENALTY FOR FRAUDULENT FAILURE TO FILE.—If any failure to file any return is fraudulent, paragraph (1) of subsection (a) shall be applied—

(1) by substituting "15 percent" for "5 percent" each place it appears, and

(2) by substituting "75 percent" for "25 percent".

Amendments

• **1989, Omnibus Budget Reconciliation Act of 1989 (P.L. 101-239)**

P.L. 101-239, §7741(a):

Amended Code Sec. 6651 by adding at the end thereof a new subsection (f). **Effective** in the case of failures to file returns the due date for which (determined without regard to extensions) is after 12-31-89.

[Sec. 6651(g)]

(g) TREATMENT OF RETURNS PREPARED BY SECRETARY UNDER SECTION 6020(b).—In the case of any return made by the Secretary under section 6020(b)—

(1) such return shall be disregarded for purposes of determining the amount of the addition under paragraph (1) of subsection (a), but

(2) such return shall be treated as the return filed by the taxpayer for purposes of determining the amount of the addition under paragraphs (2) and (3) of subsection (a).

Amendments

• **1996, Taxpayer Bill of Rights 2 (P.L. 104-168)**

P.L. 104-168, §1301(a):

Amended Code Sec. 6651 by adding at the end a new subsection (g). **Effective** in the case of any return the due date for which (determined without regard to extensions) is after 7-30-96.

[Sec. 6651(h)]

(h) LIMITATION ON PENALTY ON INDIVIDUAL'S FAILURE TO PAY FOR MONTHS DURING PERIOD OF INSTALLMENT AGREEMENT.—In the case of an individual who files a return of tax on or before the due date for the return (including extensions), paragraphs (2) and (3) of subsection (a) shall each be applied by substituting "0.25" for "0.5" each place it appears for purposes of determining the addition to tax for any month during which an installment agreement under section 6159 is in effect for the payment of such tax.

Amendments

• **1998, IRS Restructuring and Reform Act of 1998 (P.L. 105-206)**

P.L. 105-206, §3303(a):

Amended Code Sec. 6651 by adding at the end a new subsection (h). **Effective** for purposes of determining additions to the tax for months beginning after 12-31-99.

Sec. 6651(e)

ADDITIONS TO TAX

[Sec. 6651(i)]

(i) APPLICATION TO IMPUTED UNDERPAYMENT.—For purposes of this section, any failure to comply with section 6226(b)(4)(A)(ii) shall be treated as a failure to pay the amount described in subclause (II) thereof and such amount shall be treated for purposes of this section as an amount shown as tax on a return specified in subsection (a)(1).

Amendments

- **2018, Tax Technical Corrections Act of 2018 (P.L. 115-141)**

P.L. 115-141, §206(n)(1), Div. U:

Amended Code Sec. 6651 by redesignating subsection (i) as subsection (j) and by inserting after subsection (h) a new subsection (i). **Effective** as if included in section 1101 of the Bipartisan Budget Act of 2015 [**effective** generally for returns filed for partnership tax years beginning after 12-31-2017.—CCH].

[Sec. 6651(j)]

(j) ADJUSTMENT FOR INFLATION.—

(1) IN GENERAL.—In the case of any return required to be filed in a calendar year beginning after 2020, the $435 dollar amount under subsection (a) shall be increased by an amount equal to such dollar amount multiplied by the cost-of-living adjustment determined under section 1(f)(3) for the calendar year determined by substituting "calendar year 2019" for "calendar year 2016" in subparagraph (A)(ii) thereof.

(2) ROUNDING.—If any amount adjusted under paragraph (1) is not a multiple of $5, such amount shall be rounded to the next lowest multiple of $5.

Amendments

- **2019, Setting Every Community Up for Retirement Enhancement Act of 2019 (P.L. 116-94)**

P.L. 116-94, §402(b), Div. O:

Amended Code Sec. 6651(j)(1) by striking "$330" and inserting "$435". **Effective** for returns the due date for which (including extensions) is after 12-31-2019.

- **2019, Taxpayer First Act (P.L. 116-25)**

P.L. 116-25, §3201(b)(1)-(3):

Amended Code Sec. 6651(j)(1) by striking "2014" and inserting "2020", by striking "$205" and inserting "$330", and by striking "2013" and inserting "2019". **Effective** for returns required to be filed after 12-31-2019.

- **2018, Tax Technical Corrections Act of 2018 (P.L. 115-141)**

P.L. 115-141, §206(n)(1), Div. U:

Amended Code Sec. 6651 by redesignating subsection (i) as subsection (j). **Effective** as if included in section 1101 of the Bipartisan Budget Act of 2015 [**effective** generally for returns filed for partnership tax years beginning after 12-31-2017.—CCH].

P.L. 115-141, §401(a)(299)(A), Div. U:

Amended Code Sec. 6651(i) by inserting "an amount equal to" after "increased by" and by inserting "for the calendar year" after "section 1(f)(3)". **Effective** 3-23-2018.

- **2017, Tax Cuts and Jobs Act (P.L. 115-97)**

P.L. 115-97, §11002(d)(1)(KK):

Amended Code Sec. 6651(i)(1) by striking "for 'calendar year 1992' in subparagraph (B)" and inserting "for 'calendar year 2016' in subparagraph (A)(ii)". **Effective** for tax years beginning after 12-31-2017.

- **2016, Trade Facilitation and Trade Enforcement Act of 2015 (P.L. 114-125)**

P.L. 114-125, §921(b):

Amended Code Sec. 6651(i)[(1)] by striking "$135" and inserting "$205". **Effective** for returns required to be filed in calendar years after 2015.

- **2014, Stephen Beck, Jr., Achieving a Better Life Experience Act of 2014 (P.L. 113-295)**

P.L. 113-295, §208(a), Division B:

Amended Code Sec. 6651 by adding at the end a new subsection (i). **Effective** for returns required to be filed, and statements required to be furnished, after 12-31-2014 [**effective** date changed by P.L. 115-141, §105(a)(1)-(2), Div. U.—CCH]

[Sec. 6652]

SEC. 6652. FAILURE TO FILE CERTAIN INFORMATION RETURNS, REGISTRATION STATEMENTS, ETC.

[Sec. 6652(a)]

(a) RETURNS WITH RESPECT TO CERTAIN PAYMENTS AGGREGATING LESS THAN $10.—In the case of each failure to file a statement of a payment to another person required under the authority of—

(1) section 6042(a)(2) (relating to payments of dividends aggregating less than $10), or

(2) section 6044(a)(2) (relating to payments of patronage dividends aggregating less than $10),

on the date prescribed therefor (determined with regard to any extension of time for filing), unless it is shown that such failure is due to reasonable cause and not to willful neglect, there shall be paid (upon notice and demand by the Secretary and in the same manner as tax) by the person failing to so file the statement, $1 for each such statement not so filed, but the total amount imposed on the delinquent person for all such failures during the calendar year shall not exceed $1,000.

Amendments

- **1986, Tax Reform Act of 1986 (P.L. 99-514)**

P.L. 99-514, §1501(d)(1)(A)(i)-(ii):

Amended Code Sec. 6652 by striking out subsection (a) and by redesignating subsections (b) through (k) as subsections (a) through (j), respectively, and by striking out "OTHER RETURNS" in the heading of subsection (a) (as so redesignated) and inserting in lieu thereof "RETURNS WITH RESPECT TO CERTAIN PAYMENTS AGGREGATING LESS THAN $10". **Effective** for returns the due date for which (determined without regard to extensions) is after 12-31-86. Prior to amendment (but after amendment by Act Sec. 1811(c)(2)), Code Sec. 6652(a) read as follows:

(a) RETURNS RELATING TO INFORMATION AT SOURCE, PAYMENTS OF DIVIDENDS, ETC., AND CERTAIN TRANSFERS OF STOCK.—

(1) IN GENERAL.—In the case of each failure—

(A) to file a statement of the amount of payments to another person required by—

(i) section 6041(a) or (b) (relating to certain information at source),

(ii) section 6050A(a) (relating to reporting requirements of certain fishing boat operators), or

(iii) section 6051(d) (relating to information returns with respect to income tax withheld), or

(B) to make a return required by—

(i) subsection (a) or (b) of section 6041A (relating to returns of direct sellers),

(ii) section 6045 (relating to returns of brokers),

(iii) section 6052(a) (relating to reporting payment of wages in the form of group term life insurance),

(iv) section 6053(c)(1) (relating to reporting with respect to certain tips),

(v) section 6050H(a) (relating to mortgage interest received in trade or business from individuals),

(vi) section 6050I(a) (relating to cash received in trade or business),

(vii) section 6050J(a) (relating to foreclosures and abandonments of security),

(viii) section 6050K (relating to exchanges of certain partnership interests), or

(ix) section 6050L (relating to returns relating to certain dispositions of donated property),

on the date prescribed therefor (determined with regard to any extension of time for filing), unless it is shown that such failure is due to reasonable cause and not to willful neglect, there shall be paid (upon notice and demand by the Secretary and in the same manner as tax), by the person failing to file a statement referred to in subparagraph (A) or failing to make a return referred to in subparagraph (B), $50 for each such failure, but the total amount imposed on the delinquent person for all such failures during any calendar year shall not exceed $50,000.

(2) FAILURE TO FILE RETURNS ON INTERESTS, DIVIDENDS, AND PATRONAGE DIVIDENDS.—

(A) IN GENERAL.—In the case of each failure to file a statement of the amount of payments to another person required by—

(i) section 6042(a)(1) (relating to payments of dividends),

(ii) section 6044(a)(1) (relating to payments of patronage dividends), or

(iii) section 6049(a) (relating to payments of interest),

on the date prescribed therefor (determined with regard to any extension of time for filing), there shall be paid by the person failing to file such statement a penalty of $50 for each such failure unless it is shown that such person exercised due diligence in attempting to satisfy the requirement with respect to such statement.

(B) SELF-ASSESSMENT.—Any penalty imposed under subparagraph (A) on any person—

(i) for purposes of this subtitle, shall be treated as an excise tax imposed by subtitle D, and

(ii) shall be due and payable on April 1 of the calendar year following the calendar year for which such statement is required.

(C) DEFICIENCY PROCEDURES NOT TO APPLY.—Subchapter B of chapter 63 (relating to deficiency procedures for income, estate, gift, and certain excise taxes) shall not apply in respect of the assessment or collection of any penalty imposed by subparagraph (A).

ADDITIONS TO TAX

(3) PENALTY IN CASE OF INTENTIONAL DISREGARD.—If 1 or more failures to which paragraph (1) or (2) applies are due to intentional disregard of the filing requirement, then with respect to such failures—

(A) the penalty imposed under paragraph (1) or (2) shall not be less than an amount equal to—

(i) in the case of a return not described in clauses (ii) and (iii), 10 percent of the aggregate amount of the items required to be reported,

(ii) in the case of a return required to be filed by section 6045 (other than by subsection (d) of such section), 5 percent of the gross proceeds required to be reported, and

(iii) in the case of a return required to be filed by section 6041(A)(b), 6050H, 6050I, or 6050J, $100 for each such failure, and

(B) the $50,000 limitation under paragraph (1) shall not apply.

• **1984, Deficit Reduction Act of 1984 (P.L. 98-369)**

P.L. 98-369, § 145(b)(1):

Amended Code Sec. 6652(a)(1)(B) by striking out "or" at the end of clause (iii), by inserting "or" at the end of clause (iv), and by inserting new clause (v). **Effective**, generally, for amounts received after 12-31-84. However, in the case of any obligation in existence on 12-31-84, no penalty shall be imposed under section 6676 of the Internal Revenue Code of 1954 by reason of the amendments on any failure to supply a taxpayer identification number with respect to amounts received before 1-1-86 [effective date changed by P.L. 99-514, § 1811].

P.L. 98-369, § 145(b)(2):

Amended Code Sec. 6652(a)(3)(A)(iii) by inserting "or section 6050H" after "section 6041A(b)". **Effective**, generally, for amounts received after 12-31-84. However, in the case of any obligation in existence on 12-31-84, no penalty shall be imposed under section 6676 of the Internal Revenue Code of 1954 by reason of the amendments on any failure to supply a taxpayer identification number with respect to amounts received before 1-1-86 [effective date changed by P.L. 99-514, § 1811].

P.L. 98-369, § 146(b)(1):

Amended Code Sec. 6652(a)(1)(B) by striking out "or" at the end of clause (iv), by adding "or" at the end of clause (v), and by inserting new clause (vi). **Effective** for amounts received after 12-31-84.

P.L. 98-369, § 146(b)(2):

Amended Code Sec. 6652(a)(3)(A)(iii) by striking out "or section 6050H" and inserting in lieu thereof ", section 6050H or section 6050I". **Effective** for amounts received after 12-31-84.

P.L. 98-369, § 148(b)(1):

Amended Code Sec. 6652(a)(1)(B) by striking out "or" at the end of clause (v), by adding "or" at the end of clause (vi), and by inserting new clause (vii). **Effective** with respect to acquisitions of property and abandonments of property after 12-31-84.

P.L. 98-369, § 148(b)(2):

Amended Code Sec. 6652(a)(3)(A)(iii) by striking out "or 6050I" and inserting in lieu thereof ", 6050I, or 6050J". **Effective** with respect to acquisitions of property and abandonments of property after 12-31-84.

P.L. 98-369, § 149(b)(1):

Amended Code Sec. 6652(a)(1)(B) by striking out "or" at the end of clause (vi), by adding "or" at the end of clause (vii), and by inserting after clause (vii) new clause (viii). **Effective** with respect to exchanges after 12-31-84.

P.L. 98-369, § 155(b)(2)(A):

Amended Code Sec. 6652(a)(1)(B) by striking out "or" at the end of clause (vii), by adding "or" at the end of clause (viii), and by inserting after clause (viii) new clause (ix). **Effective** for contributions made after 12-31-84, in tax years ending after such date.

• **1983, Interest and Dividend Tax Compliance Act of 1983 (P.L. 98-67)**

P.L. 98-67, § 105(b)(1)(A)-(C):

Amended Code Sec. 6652(a). **Effective** with respect to payments made after 12-31-83. For Code Sec. 6652(a) prior to amendment, see the first text of Code Sec. 6652(a).

• **1983, Technical Corrections Act of 1982 (P.L. 97-448)**

P.L. 97-448, § 201(i)(2)(A):

Amended Code Sec. 6652(a) [as in effect prior to the enactment of P.L. 97-248] by striking out "or" at the end of subparagraph (F) of paragraph (1), by adding "or" at the end of paragraph (2), and by inserting after paragraph (2) new paragraph (3). **Effective** with respect to returns and statements the due dates for which (without regard to extensions) are after 1-12-83.

P.L. 97-448, § 201(i)(2)(B):

Amended Code Sec. 6652(a) [as in effect prior to the enactment of P.L. 97-248] by striking out "paragraph (2)" and inserting in lieu thereof "paragraph (2) or (3)". **Effective** with respect to returns and statements the due dates for which (without regard to extensions) are after 1-12-83.

• **1982, Tax Equity and Fiscal Responsibility Act of 1982 (P.L. 97-248)**

P.L. 97-248, § 309(b)(2):

Amended Code Sec. 6652(b) by adding "or" at the end of paragraph (1) and by striking out paragraphs (3) and (4). **Effective** with respect to amounts paid (or treated as paid) after 12-31-82. Prior to amendment, Code Sec. 6652(b)(3) and (4) read as follows:

(3) section 6049(a)(2) (relating to payments of interest aggregating less than $10), or

(4) section 6049(a)(3) (relating to other payments of interest by corporations),

P.L. 97-248, § 315(a):

Amended Code Sec. 6652(a). **Effective** with respect to returns or statements the due date for the filing of which (without regard to extensions) is after 12-31-82. Prior to amendment, Code Sec. 6652(a) read as follows:

(a) RETURNS RELATING TO INFORMATION AT SOURCE PAYMENTS OF DIVIDENDS, ETC., AND CERTAIN TRANSFERS OF STOCK.—In the case of each failure—

(1) to file a statement of the aggregate amount of payments to another person required by—

(A) section 6041(a) or (b) (relating to certain information at source),

(B) section 6042(a)(1) (relating to payments of dividends aggregating $10 or more),

(C) section 6044(a)(1) (relating to payments of patronage dividends aggregating $10 or more),

(D) section 6049(a)(1) (relating to payments of interest aggregating $10 or more),

(E) section 6050A(a) (relating to reporting requirements of certain fishing boat operators), or

(F) section 6051(d) (relating to information returns with respect to income tax withheld),

(2) to make a return required by section 6052(a) (relating to reporting payment of wages in the form of group-term life insurance) with respect to group-term life insurance on the life of an employee, or

(3) to make a return required by section 4997(a) (relating to information with respect to windfall profit tax on crude oil),

on the date prescribed therefor (determined with regard to any extension of time for filing), unless it is shown that such failure is due to reasonable cause and not to willful neglect, there shall be paid (upon notice and demand by the Secretary and in the same manner as tax), by the person failing to file a statement referred to in paragraph (1) or failing to make a return referred to in paragraph (2) or (3), $10 for each such failure, but the total amount imposed on the delinquent person for all such failures during any calendar year shall not exceed $25,000.

• **1981, Economic Recovery Tax Act of 1981 (P.L. 97-34)**

P.L. 97-34, § 723(a)(1):

Amended Code Sec. 6652(a)(1). **Effective** for returns and statements required to be furnished after 12-31-81. Prior to amendment, Code Sec. 6652(a)(1) read as follows:

(1) to file a statement of the aggregate amount of payments to another person required by section 6042(a)(1) (relating to payments of dividends aggregating $10 or more), section 6044(a)(1) (relating to payments of patronage dividends aggregating $10 or more), or section 6049(a)(1) (relating to payments of interest aggregating $10 or more), or

P.L. 97-34, § 723(a)(3):

Amended Code Sec. 6652(b). **Effective** for returns and statements required to be furnished after 12-31-81. Prior to amendment, Code Sec. 6652(b) read as follows:

(b) OTHER RETURNS.—In the case of each failure to file a statement of a payment to another person required under authority of section 6041 (relating to ceratin information at source), section 6042(a)(2) (relating to payments of dividends aggregating less than $10), section 6044(a)(2) (relating to payments of patronage dividends aggregating less than $10), section 6049(a)(2) (relating to payments of interest aggregating less than $10), section 6049(a)(3) (relating to other payments of interest by corporations), or section 6051(d) (relating to information returns with respect to income tax withheld), in the case of each failure to make a return required by section 6050A(a) (relating to reporting requirements of certain fishing boat operators), and in the case of each failure to furnish a statement required by section 6053(b) (relating to statements furnished by employers with respect to tips), section 6050A(b) (relating to statements furnished by certain fishing boat operators), or section 6050C (relating to information regarding windfall profit tax on crude oil), on the date prescribed therefor (determined with regard to any extension of time for filing), unless it is shown that such failure is due to reasonable cause and not to willful neglect, there shall be paid (upon notice and demand by the Secretary and in the same manner as tax) by the person failing to so file the statement, $1 for each such statement not so filed, but the total amount imposed on the delinquent person for all such failures during the calendar year shall not exceed $1,000.

P.L. 97-34, § 723(a)(4):

Amended the heading of Code Sec. 6652(a) by inserting "Information at Source" before "Payments of Dividends". **Effective** for returns and statements required to be furnished after 12-31-81.

• **1980, Crude Oil Windfall Profit Tax Act of 1980 (P.L. 96-223)**

P.L. 96-223, § 101(d)(2)(A):

Amended Code Sec. 6652(b) by striking out "or section 6050A" and inserting ", section 6050A" and by inserting ", or section 6050C (relating to information regarding windfall profit tax on crude oil)" after "fishing boat operators)". **Effective** for periods after 2-29-80.

• **1979 (P.L. 96-167)**

P.L. 96-167, § 7:

Amended Code Sec. 6652(a). **Effective** for calendar years beginning after 1979. Prior to amendment, Code Sec. 6652(a) read as follows:

"(a) RETURNS RELATING TO PAYMENTS OF DIVIDENDS, ETC., AND CERTAIN TRANSFERS OF STOCK.—In the case of each failure—

"(1) to file a statement of the aggregate amount of payments to another person required by section 6042(a)(1) (relating to payments of dividends aggregating $10 or more), section 6044(a)(1) (relating to payments of patronage dividends aggregating $10 or more), or section 6049(a)(1) (relating to payments of interest aggregating $10 or more),

"(2) to make a return required by section 6039(a) (relating to reporting information in connection with certain options) with respect to a transfer of stock or a transfer of legal title to stock, or

"(3) to make a return required by section 6052(a) (relating to reporting payment of wages in the form of group-term life insurance) with respect to group-term life insurance on the life of an employee,

on the date prescribed therefor (determined with regard to any extension of time for filing), unless it is shown that such failure is due to reasonable cause and not to willful neglect, there shall be paid (upon notice and demand by the Secretary and in

ADDITIONS TO TAX

the same manner as tax), by the person failing to file a statement referred to in paragraph (1) or failing to make a return referred to in paragraph (2) or (3), $10 for each such failure, but the total amount imposed on the delinquent person for all such failures during any calendar year shall not exceed $25,000."

- **1976, Tax Reform Act of 1976 (P.L. 94-455)**

P.L. 94-455, §1207(e)(3)(B):

Amended Code Sec. 6652(b) by inserting after "withheld),", the following: "in the case of each failure to make a return required by section 6050A(a) (relating to reporting requirements of certain fishing boat operators),". **Effective** for calendar years beginning after 10-4-76.

P.L. 94-455, §1207(e)(3)(C):

Amended Code Sec. 6652(b) by inserting after "tips),", the following: "or section 6050A(b) (relating to statements furnished by certain fishing boat operators),". **Effective** for calendar years beginning after 10-4-76.

P.L. 94-455, §1906(b)(13)(A):

Amended 1954 Code by substituting "Secretary" for "Secretary or his delegate" each place it appeared. **Effective** 2-1-77.

- **1974, Employee Retirement Income Security Act of 1974 (P.L. 93-406)**

P.L. 93-406, §1031(b)(1):

Amended Code Sec. 6652 by adding "registration statement, etc." to the heading. **Effective** 9-2-74.

- **1965, Social Security Amendments of 1965 (P.L. 89-97)**

P.L. 89-97, §313(e):

Amended Code Sec. 6652(b) by inserting after "income tax withheld)," "and in the case of each failure to furnish a statement required by section 6053(b) (relating to statements furnished by employers with respect to tips),". **Effective** with respect to tips received by employees after 1965.

- **1964, Revenue Act of 1964 (P.L. 88-272)**

P.L. 88-272, §221(b)(2):

Amended Code Sec. 6652(a). **Effective** for tax years ending after 12-31-63. Prior to amendment, Code Sec. 6652(a) read as follows:

"(a) RETURNS RELATING TO PAYMENTS OF DIVIDENDS, INTEREST, AND PATRONAGE DIVIDENDS.—In the case of each failure to file a statement of the aggregate amount of payments to another person required by section 6042(a)(1) (relating to payments of dividends aggregating $10 or more), section 6044(a)(1) (relating to payments of patronage dividends aggregating $10 or more), or section 6049(a)(1) (relating to payments of interest aggregating $10 or more), on the date prescribed therefor (determined with regard to any extension of time for filing), unless it is shown that such failure is due to reasonable cause and not to willful neglect, there shall be paid (upon notice and demand by the Secretary or his delegate and in the same manner as tax), by the person failing to so file the statement, $10 for each such statement not so filed, but the total amount imposed on the delinquent person for all such failures during any calendar year shall not exceed $25,000."

- **1962, Revenue Act of 1962 (P.L. 87-834)**

P.L. 87-834, §19(d):

Amended Code Sec. 6652(a). **Effective** for payments of dividends and interest made on or after 1-1-63. **Effective** with respect to payments of patronage dividends made on or after 1-1-63, with respect to patronage occurring on or after the first day of the first tax year of the cooperative beginning on or after 1-1-63. Prior to amendment, Code Sec. 6652(a) read as follows:

"(a) ADDITIONAL AMOUNT.—In case of each failure to file a statement of a payment to another person, required under authority to section 6041 (relating to information at source), section 6042(1) (relating to payments of corporate dividends), section 6044 (relating to patronage dividends), or section 6051(d) (relating to information returns with respect to income tax withheld), on the date prescribed therefor (determined with regard to any extension of time for filing), unless it is shown that such failure is due to reasonable cause and not to willful neglect, there shall be paid (upon notice and demand by the Secretary or his delegate and in the same manner as tax), by the person failing to so file the statement, $1 for each such statement not so filed, but the total amount imposed on the delinquent person for all such failures during any calendar year shall not exceed $1,000."

- **1958, Technical Amendments Act of 1958 (P.L. 85-866)**

P.L. 85-866, §85:

Amended Code Sec. 6652(a). **Effective** 1-1-54. Prior to amendment, Code Sec. 6652(a) read as follows:

"(a) ADDITIONAL AMOUNT.—In case of each failure to file a statement of a payment to another person, required under authority of section 6041 (relating to information at source), section 6042 (relating to payments of corporate dividends), section 6044 (relating to patronage dividends), section 6045 (relating to returns of brokers), or section 6051(d) (relating to information returns with respect to income tax withheld), unless it is shown that such failure is due to reasonable cause and not to willful neglect, there shall be paid by the person failing to file the statement, upon notice and demand by the Secretary or his delegate and in the same manner as tax, $1 for each such statement not filed, but the total amount imposed on the delinquent person for all such failures during any calendar year shall not exceed $1,000."

[Sec. 6652(b)]

(b) FAILURE TO REPORT TIPS.—In the case of failure by an employee to report to his employer on the date and in the manner prescribed therefor any amount of tips required to be so reported by section 6053(a) which are wages (as defined in section 3121(a)) or which are compensation (as defined in section 3231(e)), unless it is shown that such failure is due to reasonable cause and not due to willful neglect, there shall be paid by the employee, in addition to the tax imposed by section 3101 or section 3201 (as the case may be) with respect to the amount of tips which he so failed to report, an amount equal to 50 percent of such tax.

Amendments

- **1986, Tax Reform Act of 1986 (P.L. 99-514)**

P.L. 99-514, §1501(d)(1)(A)(i) and (ii):

Amended Code Sec. 6652 by striking out subsection (a) and by redesignating subsections (b) through (k) as subsections (a) through (j), respectively. **Effective** for returns for which the due date (determined without regard to extensions) is after 12-31-86.

- **1965 (P.L. 89-212)**

P.L. 89-212, §2(e):

Amended Code Sec. 6652(c) by inserting "or which are compensation (as defined in section 3231(e))" after "which are wages (as defined in section 3121(a))" and by inserting "or section 3201 (as the case may be)" after "section 3101". **Effective** with respect to tips received after 1965.

- **1965, Social Security Amendments of 1965 (P.L. 89-97)**

P.L. 89-97, §313(e):

Redesignated former Sec. 6652(c) as (d) and added new Sec. 6652(c). **Effective** for tips received by employees after 1965.

- **1962, Revenue Act of 1962 (P.L. 87-834)**

P.L. 87-834, §19(d):

Amended Code Sec. 6652(b). **Effective** for payments of dividends and interest made on or after 1-1-63. **Effective** with respect to payments of patronage dividends made on or after 1-1-63, with respect to patronage occurring on or after the first day of the first tax year of the cooperative beginning on or after 1-1-63. Prior to amendment, Sec. 6652(b) read as follows:

(b) Alcohol and Tobacco Taxes.—

For penalties for failure to file certain information returns with respect to alcohol and tobacco taxes, see, generally, subtitle E.

[Sec. 6652(c)]

(c) RETURNS BY EXEMPT ORGANIZATIONS AND BY CERTAIN TRUSTS.—

(1) ANNUAL RETURNS UNDER SECTION 6033(a)(1) OR 6012(a)(6).—

(A) PENALTY ON ORGANIZATION.—In the case of—

(i) a failure to file a return required under section 6033(a)(1) (relating to returns by exempt organizations) or section 6012(a)(6) (relating to returns by political organizations) on the date and in the manner prescribed therefor (determined with regard to any extension of time for filing), or

(ii) a failure to include any of the information required to be shown on a return filed under section 6033(a)(1) or section 6012(a)(6) or to show the correct information,

there shall be paid by the exempt organization $20 for each day during which such failure continues. The maximum penalty under this subparagraph on failures with respect to any 1 return shall not exceed the lesser of $10,000 or 5 percent of the gross receipts of the organization for the year. In the case of an organization having gross receipts exceeding $1,000,000 for any year, with respect to the return required under section 6033(a)(1) or section 6012(a)(6) for such year, in applying the first sentence of this subparagraph, the amount of the penalty for each day during which a failure continues shall be $100 in lieu of the amount otherwise specified, and, in lieu of applying the second sentence of this subparagraph, the maximum penalty under this subparagraph shall not exceed $50,000.

(B) MANAGERS.—

(i) IN GENERAL.—The Secretary may make a written demand on any organization subject to penalty under subparagraph (A) specifying therein a reasonable future date by which the return shall be filed (or the information furnished) for purposes of this subparagraph.

ADDITIONS TO TAX

(ii) FAILURE TO COMPLY WITH DEMAND.—If any person fails to comply with any demand under clause (i) on or before the date specified in such demand, there shall be paid by the person failing to so comply $10 for each day after the expiration of the time specified in such demand during which such failure continues. The maximum penalty imposed under this subparagraph on all persons for failures with respect to any 1 return shall not exceed $5,000.

(C) PUBLIC INSPECTION OF ANNUAL RETURNS AND REPORTS.—In the case of a failure to comply with the requirements of section 6104(d) with respect to any annual return on the date and in the manner prescribed therefor (determined with regard to any extension of time for filing) or report required under section 527(j), there shall be paid by the person failing to meet such requirements $20 for each day during which such failure continues. The maximum penalty imposed under this subparagraph on all persons for failures with respect to any 1 return or report shall not exceed $10,000.

(D) PUBLIC INSPECTION OF APPLICATIONS FOR EXEMPTION AND NOTICE OF STATUS.—In the case of a failure to comply with the requirements of section 6104(d) with respect to any exempt status application materials (as defined in such section) or notice materials (as defined in such section) on the date and in the manner prescribed therefor, there shall be paid by the person failing to meet such requirements $20 for each day during which such failure continues.

(E) NO PENALTY FOR CERTAIN ANNUAL NOTICES.—This paragraph shall not apply with respect to any notice required under section 6033(i).

(2) RETURNS UNDER SECTION 6034 OR 6043.—

(A) PENALTY ON ORGANIZATION OR TRUST.—In the case of a failure to file a return required under section 6034 (relating to returns by certain trusts) or section 6043(b) (relating to terminations, etc., of exempt organizations), on the date and in the manner prescribed therefor (determined with regard to any extension of time for filing), there shall be paid by the exempt organization or trust failing so to file $10 for each day during which such failure continues, but the total amount imposed under this subparagraph on any organization or trust for failure to file any 1 return shall not exceed $5,000.

(B) MANAGERS.—The Secretary may make written demand on an organization or trust failing to file under subparagraph (A) specifying therein a reasonable future date by which such filing shall be made for purposes of this subparagraph. If such filing is not made on or before such date, there shall be paid by the person failing so to file $10 for each day after the expiration of the time specified in the written demand during which such failure continues, but the total amount imposed under this subparagraph on all persons for failure to file any 1 return shall not exceed $5,000.

(C) SPLIT-INTEREST TRUSTS.—In the case of a trust which is required to file a return under section 6034(a), subparagraphs (A) and (B) of this paragraph shall not apply and paragraph (1) shall apply in the same manner as if such return were required under section 6033, except that—

(i) the 5 percent limitation in the second sentence of paragraph (1)(A) shall not apply,

(ii) in the case of any trust with gross income in excess of $250,000, in applying the first sentence of paragraph (1)(A), the amount of the penalty for each day during which a failure continues shall be $100 in lieu of the amount otherwise specified, and in lieu of applying the second sentence of paragraph (1)(A), the maximum penalty under paragraph (1)(A) shall not exceed $50,000, and

(iii) the third sentence of paragraph (1)(A) shall be disregarded.

In addition to any penalty imposed on the trust pursuant to this subparagraph, if the person required to file such return knowingly fails to file the return, such penalty shall also be imposed on such person who shall be personally liable for such penalty.

(3) DISCLOSURE UNDER SECTION 6033(a)(2).—

(A) PENALTY ON ENTITIES.—In the case of a failure to file a disclosure required under section 6033(a)(2), there shall be paid by the tax-exempt entity (the entity manager in the case of a tax-exempt entity described in paragraph (4), (5), (6), or (7) of section 4965(c)) $100 for each day during which such failure continues. The maximum penalty under this subparagraph on failures with respect to any 1 disclosure shall not exceed $50,000.

(B) WRITTEN DEMAND.—

(i) IN GENERAL.—The Secretary may make a written demand on any entity or manager subject to penalty under subparagraph (A) specifying therein a reasonable future date by which the disclosure shall be filed for purposes of this subparagraph.

(ii) FAILURE TO COMPLY WITH DEMAND.—If any entity or manager fails to comply with any demand under clause (i) on or before the date specified in such demand, there shall be paid by such entity or manager failing to so comply $100 for each day after the expiration of the time specified in such demand during which such failure continues. The maximum penalty imposed under this subparagraph on all entities and managers for failures with respect to any 1 disclosure shall not exceed $10,000.

(C) DEFINITIONS.—Any term used in this section which is also used in section 4965 shall have the meaning given such term under section 4965.

(4) NOTICES UNDER SECTION 506.—

(A) PENALTY ON ORGANIZATION.—In the case of a failure to submit a notice required under section 506(a) (relating to organizations required to notify Secretary of intent to operate as 501(c)(4)) on the date and in the manner prescribed therefor, there shall be paid by the organization failing to so submit $20 for each day during which such failure continues, but the total amount imposed under this subparagraph on any organization for failure to submit any one notice shall not exceed $5,000.

(B) MANAGERS.—The Secretary may make written demand on an organization subject to penalty under subparagraph (A) specifying in such demand a reasonable future date by which the notice shall be submitted for purposes of this subparagraph. If such notice is not submitted on or before such date, there shall be paid by the person failing to so submit $20 for each day after the expiration of the time specified in the written demand during which such failure continues, but the total amount imposed under this subparagraph on all persons for failure to submit any one notice shall not exceed $5,000.

(5) REASONABLE CAUSE EXCEPTION.—No penalty shall be imposed under this subsection with respect to any failure if it is shown that such failure is due to reasonable cause.

(6) OTHER SPECIAL RULES.—

(A) TREATMENT AS TAX.—Any penalty imposed under this subsection shall be paid on notice and demand of the Secretary and in the same manner as tax.

(B) JOINT AND SEVERAL LIABILITY.—If more than 1 person is liable under this subsection for any penalty with respect to any failure, all such persons shall be jointly and severally liable with respect to such failure.

(C) PERSON.—For purposes of this subsection, the term "person" means any officer, director, trustee, employee, or other individual who is under a duty to perform the act in respect of which the violation occurs.

(7) ADJUSTMENT FOR INFLATION.—

(A) IN GENERAL.—In the case of any failure relating to a return required to be filed in a calendar year beginning after 2014, each of the dollar amounts under paragraphs (1), (2), and (3) shall be increased by an amount equal to such dollar amount multiplied by the cost-of-

ADDITIONS TO TAX

living adjustment determined under section 1(f)(3) for the calendar year determined by substituting "calendar year 2013" for "calendar year 2016" in subparagraph (A)(ii) thereof.

(B) ROUNDING.—If any amount adjusted under subparagraph (A)—

(i) is not less than $5,000 and is not a multiple of $500, such amount shall be rounded to the next lowest multiple of $500, and

(ii) is not described in clause (i) and is not a multiple of $5, such amount shall be rounded to the next lowest multiple of $5.

Amendments

• **2018, Tax Technical Corrections Act of 2018 (P.L. 115-141)**

P.L. 115-141, § 401(a)(299)(B), Div. U:

Amended Code Sec. 6652(c)(7)(A) by inserting "an amount equal to" after "increased by" and by inserting "for the calendar year" after "section 1(f)(3)". **Effective** 3-23-2018.

• **2017, Tax Cuts and Jobs Act (P.L. 115-97)**

P.L. 115-97, § 11002(d)(1)(LL):

Amended Code Sec. 6652(c)(7)(A) by striking "for 'calendar year 1992' in subparagraph (B)" and inserting "for 'calendar year 2016' in subparagraph (A)(ii)". **Effective** for tax years beginning after 12-31-2017.

• **2015, Protecting Americans from Tax Hikes Act of 2015 (P.L. 114-113)**

P.L. 114-113, § 405(c), Div. Q:

Amended Code Sec. 6652(c) by redesignating paragraphs (4)-(6) as paragraphs (5)-(7), respectively, and by inserting after paragraph (3) a new paragraph (4). For the **effective** date, see Act Sec. 405(f), below.

P.L. 114-113, § 405(f), Div. Q, provides:

(f) EFFECTIVE DATE.—

(1) IN GENERAL.—The amendments made by this section shall apply to organizations which are described in section 501(c)(4) of the Internal Revenue Code of 1986 and organized after the date of the enactment of this Act.

(2) CERTAIN EXISTING ORGANIZATIONS.—In the case of any other organization described in section 501(c)(4) of such Code, the amendments made by this section shall apply to such organization only if, on or before the date of the enactment of this Act—

(A) such organization has not applied for a written determination of recognition as an organization described in section 501(c)(4) of such Code, and

(B) such organization has not filed at least one annual return or notice required under subsection (a)(1) or (i) (as the case may be) of section 6033 of such Code.

In the case of any organization to which the amendments made by this section apply by reason of the preceding sentence, such organization shall submit the notice required by section 506(a) of such Code, as added by this Act, not later than 180 days after the date of the enactment of this Act.

• **2014, Stephen Beck, Jr., Achieving a Better Life Experience Act of 2014 (P.L. 113-295)**

P.L. 113-295, § 208(b)(1), Division B:

Amended Code Sec. 6652(c) by adding at the end a new paragraph (6). **Effective** for returns required to be filed, and statements required to be furnished, after 12-31-2014 [effective date changed by P.L. 115-141, § 105(a)(1)-(2), Div. U.—CCH].

P.L. 113-295, § 208(b)(2)(A), Division B:

Amended the last sentence of Code Sec. 6652(c)(1)(A) by striking "the first sentence of this subparagraph shall be applied by substituting '$100' for '$20' and" and inserting "in applying the first sentence of this subparagraph, the amount of the penalty for each day during which a failure continues shall be $100 in lieu of the amount otherwise specified, and". **Effective** for returns required to be filed, and statements required to be furnished, after 12-31-2014 [effective date changed by P.L. 115-141, § 105(a)(1)-(2), Div. U.—CCH].

P.L. 113-295, § 208(b)(2)(B), Division B:

Amended Code Sec. 6652(c)(2)(C)(ii) by striking "the first sentence of paragraph (1)(A)" and all that follows and inserting "in applying the first sentence of paragraph (1)(A), the amount of the penalty for each day during which a failure continues shall be $100 in lieu of the amount otherwise specified, and in lieu of applying the second sentence of paragraph (1)(A), the maximum penalty under paragraph (1)(A) shall not exceed $50,000, and". **Effective** for returns required to be filed, and statements required to be furnished, after 12-31-2014 [effective date changed by P.L. 115-141, § 105(a)(1)-(2), Div. U.—CCH]. Prior to being stricken, "the first sentence of paragraph (1)(A)" and all that follows read as follows:

the first sentence of paragraph (1)(A) shall be applied by substituting "$100" for "$20", and the second sentence thereof shall be applied by substituting "$50,000" for "$10,000", and

• **2006, Pension Protection Act of 2006 (P.L. 109-280)**

P.L. 109-280, § 1201(b)(2):

Amended Code Sec. 6652(c)(2) by adding at the end a new subparagraph (C). **Effective** for returns for tax years beginning after 12-31-2006.

P.L. 109-280, § 1223(d):

Amended Code Sec. 6652(c)(1) by adding at the end a new subparagraph (E). **Effective** for notices and returns with respect to annual periods beginning after 2006.

• **2006, Tax Increase Prevention and Reconciliation Act of 2005 (P.L. 109-222)**

P.L. 109-222, § 516(c)(1):

Amended Code Sec. 6652(c) by redesignating paragraphs (3) and (4) as paragraphs (4) and (5), respectively, and by inserting after paragraph (2) a new paragraph (3). **Effective** for disclosures the due date for which are after 5-17-2006.

P.L. 109-222, § 516(c)(2):

Amended Code Sec. 6652(c)(1) by striking "6033" each place it appears in the text and heading thereof and inserting "6033(a)(1)". **Effective** for disclosures the due date for which are after 5-17-2006.

• **2000 (P.L. 106-230)**

P.L. 106-230, § 1(c)(1)-(2):

Amended Code Sec. 6652(c)(1)(D) by inserting "or notice materials (as defined in such section)" after "section)" and by inserting "AND NOTICE OF STATUS" after "EXEMPTION" in the heading. **Effective** 7-1-2000. For an exception, see Act Sec. 1(d)(2), below.

P.L. 106-230, § 1(d)(2), provides:

(2) ORGANIZATIONS ALREADY IN EXISTENCE.—In the case of an organization established before the date of the enactment of this section, the time to file the notice under section 527(i)(2) of the Internal Revenue Code of 1986, as added by this section, shall be 30 days after the date of the enactment of this section.

P.L. 106-230, § 2(c)(1)-(3):

Amended Code Sec. 6652(c)(1)(C) by inserting "or report required under section 527(j)" after "filing)"; by inserting "or report" after "1 return"; and by inserting "AND REPORTS" after "RETURNS" in the heading. **Effective** 7-1-2000.

P.L. 106-230, § 3(c)(1):

Amended Code Sec. 6652(c)(1)(A)(i) by inserting "or section 6012(a)(6) (relating to returns by political organizations)" after "organizations)". **Effective** for returns for tax years beginning after 6-30-2000.

P.L. 106-230, § 3(c)(2):

Amended Code Sec. 6652(c)(1)(A)(ii) by inserting "or section 6012(a)(6)" after "section 6033". **Effective** for returns for tax years beginning after 6-30-2000.

P.L. 106-230, § 3(c)(3):

Amended Code Sec. 6652(c)(1)(A) by inserting "or section 6012(a)(6)" after "section 6033" in the third sentence. **Effective** for returns for tax years beginning after 6-30-2000.

P.L. 106-230, § 3(c)(4):

Amended Code Sec. 6652(c)(1) by inserting "OR 6012(a)(6)" after "SECTION 6033" in the heading. **Effective** for returns for tax years beginning after 6-30-2000.

• **1998, Tax and Trade Relief Extension Act of 1998 (P.L. 105-277)**

P.L. 105-277, § 1004(b)(2)(B):

Amended Code Sec. 6652(c)(1)(C) by striking "subsection (d) or (e)(1) of section 6104 (relating to public inspection of annual returns)" and inserting "section 6104(d) with respect to any annual return". **Effective**, generally, for requests made after the later of 12-31-98, or the 60th day after the Secretary of the Treasury first issues the regulations referred to in Code Sec. 6104(d)(4), as amended by Act Sec. 1004. For an exception, see Act Sec. 1004(b)(3)(B), below.

P.L. 105-277, § 1004(b)(2)(C):

Amended Code Sec. 6652(c)(1)(D) by striking "section 6104(e)(2) (relating to public inspection of applications for exemption)" and inserting "section 6104(d) with respect to any exempt status application materials (as defined in such section)". **Effective**, generally, for requests made after the later of 12-31-98, or the 60th day after the Secretary of the Treasury first issues the regulations referred to in Code Sec. 6104(d)(4), as amended by Act Sec. 1004. For an exception, see Act Sec. 1004(b)(3)(B), below.

P.L. 105-277, § 1004(b)(3)(B), provides:

(B) PUBLICATION OF ANNUAL RETURNS.—Section 6104(d) of such Code, as in effect before the amendments made by this subsection, shall not apply to any return the due date for which is after the date such amendments take effect under subparagraph (A).

• **1996, Small Business Job Protection Act of 1996 (P.L. 104-188)**

P.L. 104-188, § 1704(s)(1):

Amended Code Sec. 6652(c)(1)(C) by striking "$10" and inserting "$20", and by striking "$5,000" and inserting "$10,000". **Effective** 8-20-96.

P.L. 104-188, § 1704(s)(2):

Amended Code Sec. 6652(c)(1)(D) by striking "$10" and inserting "$20". **Effective** 8-20-96.

• **1996, Taxpayer Bill of Rights 2 (P.L. 104-168)**

P.L. 104-168, § 1314(a):

Amended Code Sec. 6652(c)(1)(A) by striking "$10" and inserting "$20" and by striking "$5,000" and inserting "$10,000". **Effective** for returns for tax years ending on or after 7-30-96.

P.L. 104-168, § 1314(b):

Amended Code Sec. 6652(c)(1)(A) by adding at the end a new sentence. **Effective** for returns for tax years ending on or after 7-30-96.

ADDITIONS TO TAX

- **1987, Revenue Act of 1987 (P.L. 100-203)**

P.L. 100-203, §10704(a):

Amended Code Sec. 6652(c). For the **effective** date, see Act Sec. 10704(d) below. Prior to amendment, Code Sec. 6652(c) read as follows:

(c) RETURNS BY EXEMPT ORGANIZATIONS AND BY CERTAIN TRUSTS.—

(1) PENALTY ON ORGANIZATION OR TRUST.—In the case of a failure to file a return required under section 6033 (relating to returns by exempt organizations), section 6034 (relating to returns by certain trusts), or section 6043(b) (relating to exempt organizations), on the date and in the manner prescribed therefor (determined with regard to any extension of time for filing), unless it is shown that such failure is due to reasonable cause there shall be paid (on notice and demand by the Secretary and in the same manner as tax) by the exempt organization or trust failing so to file, $10 for each day during which such failure continues, but the total amount imposed hereunder on any organization for failure to file any return shall not exceed $5,000.

(2) MANAGERS.—The Secretary may make written demand upon an organization failing to file under paragraph (1) specifying therein a reasonable future date by which such filing shall be made, and if such filing is not made on or before such date, and unless it is shown that failure so to file is due to reasonable cause, there shall be paid (on notice and demand by the Secretary and in the same manner as tax) by the person failing so to file, $10 for each day after the expiration of the time specified in the written demand during which such failure continues, but the total amount imposed hereunder on all persons for such failure to file shall not exceed $5,000. If more than one person is liable under this paragraph for a failure to file, all such persons shall be jointly and severally liable with respect to such failure. The term "person" as used herein means any officer, director, trustee, employee, member, or other individual who is under duty to perform the act in respect of which the violation occurs.

(3) ANNUAL RETURNS.—In the case of a failure to comply with the requirements of section 6104(d) (relating to public inspection of private foundations' annual returns) on the date and in the manner prescribed therefor (determined with regard to any extension of time for filing), unless it is shown that such failure is due to reasonable cause, there shall be paid (on notice and demand by the Secretary and in the same manner as tax) by the person failing to meet such requirement, $10 for each day during which such failure continues, but the total amount imposed hereunder on all such persons for such failure with respect to any one annual return shall not exceed $5,000. If more than one person is liable under this paragraph for a failure to file or comply with the requirements of section 6104(d), all such persons shall be jointly and severally liable with respect to such failure. The term "person" as used herein means any officer, director, trustee, employee, member, or other individual who is under a duty to perform the act in respect of which the violation occurs.

P.L. 100-203, §10704(d), provides:

(d) EFFECTIVE DATE.—The amendments made by this section shall apply—

(1) to returns for years beginning after December 31, 1986, and

(2) on and after the date of the enactment of this Act in the case of applications submitted to the Internal Revenue Service—

(A) after July 15, 1987, or

(B) on or before July 15, 1987, if the organization has a copy of the application on July 15, 1987.

- **1986, Tax Reform Act of 1986 (P.L. 99-514)**

P.L. 99-514, §1501(d)(1)(A)(i) and (ii):

Amended Code Sec. 6652 by striking out subsection (a) and by redesignating subsections (b) through (k) as subsections (a) through (j), respectively. **Effective** for returns for which the due date (determined without regard to extensions) is after 12-31-86.

- **1980 (P.L. 96-603)**

P.L. 96-603, §1(d)(2):

Amended the heading of Code Sec. 6652(d)(3) by striking out "REPORTS" and inserting in lieu thereof "RETURNS" and by amending the first sentence of such paragraph (3). **Effective** for tax years beginning after 1980. Prior to amendment, the first sentence of Code Sec. 6652(d)(3) provided:

"In the case of a failure to file a report required under section 6056 (relating to annual reports by private foundations) or to comply with the requirements of section 6104(d) (relating to public inspection of private foundations' annual reports), on the date and in the manner prescribed therefor (determined with regard to any extension of time for filing), unless it is shown that such failure is due to reasonable cause, there shall be paid (on notice and demand by the Secretary and in the same manner as tax) by the person failing so to file or meet the publicity requirement, $10 for each day during which such failure continues, but the total amount imposed hereunder on all such persons for such failure to file or comply with the requirements of section 6104(d) with regard to any one annual report shall not exceed $5,000."

- **1976, Tax Reform Act of 1976 (P.L. 94-455)**

P.L. 94-455, §1906(b)(13)(A):

Amended 1954 Code by substituting "Secretary" for "Secretary or his delegate" each place it appeared. **Effective** 2-1-77.

- **1969, Tax Reform Act of 1969 (P.L. 91-172)**

P.L. 91-172, §101(d)(4):

Added Code Sec. 6652(d). **Effective** for tax years beginning after 12-31-69.

[Sec. 6652(d)]

(d) ANNUAL REGISTRATION AND OTHER NOTIFICATION BY PENSION PLAN.—

(1) REGISTRATION.—In the case of any failure to file a registration statement required under section 6057(a) (relating to annual registration of certain plans) which includes all participants required to be included in such statement, on the date prescribed therefor (determined without regard to any extension of time for filing), unless it is shown that such failure is due to reasonable cause, there shall be paid (on notice and demand by the Secretary and in the same manner as tax) by the person failing so to file, an amount equal to $10 for each participant with respect to whom there is a failure to file, multiplied by the number of days during which such failure continues, but the total amount imposed under this paragraph on any person for any failure to file with respect to any plan year shall not exceed $50,000.

(2) NOTIFICATION OF CHANGE OF STATUS.—In the case of failure to file a notification required under section 6057(b) (relating to notification of change of status) on the date prescribed therefor (determined without regard to any extension of time for filing), unless it is shown that such failure is due to reasonable cause, there shall be paid (on notice and demand by the Secretary and in the same manner as tax) by the person failing so to file, $10 for each day during which such failure continues, but the total amounts imposed under this paragraph on any person for failure to file any notification shall not exceed $10,000.

Amendments

- **2019, Setting Every Community Up for Retirement Enhancement Act of 2019 (P.L. 116-94)**

P.L. 116-94, §403(b)(1)-(3), Div. O:

Amended Code Sec. 6652(d) by striking "$1" both places it appears in paragraphs (1) and (2) and inserting "$10"; by striking "$5,000" in paragraph (1) and inserting "$50,000"; and by striking "$1,000" in paragraph (2) and inserting "$10,000". **Effective** for returns, statements, and notifications required to be filed, and notices required to be provided, after 12-31-2019.

- **1986, Tax Reform Act of 1986 (P.L. 99-514)**

P.L. 99-514, §1501(d)(1)(A)(i) and (ii):

Amended Code Sec. 6652 by striking out subsection (a) and by redesignating subsections (b) through (k) as subsections (a) through (j), respectively. **Effective** for returns for which the due date (determined without regard to extensions) is after 12-31-86.

- **1976, Tax Reform Act of 1976 (P.L. 94-455)**

P.L. 94-455, §1906(b)(13)(A):

Amended 1954 Code by substituting "Secretary" for "Secretary or his delegate" each place it appeared. **Effective** 2-1-77.

- **1974, Employee Retirement Income Security Act of 1974 (P.L. 93-406)**

P.L. 93-406, §1031(b)(1):

Amended Code Sec. 6652 by adding subsection (e). **Effective** 9-2-74.

[Sec. 6652(e)]

(e) INFORMATION REQUIRED IN CONNECTION WITH CERTAIN PLANS OF DEFERRED COMPENSATION; ETC.—In the case of failure to file a return or statement required under section 6058 (relating to information required in connection with certain plans of deferred compensation), 6047 (relating to information relating to certain trusts and annuity and bond purchase plans), or 6039D (relating to returns and records with respect to certain fringe benefit plans) on the date and in the manner prescribed therefor (determined with regard to any extension of time for filing), unless it is shown that such failure is due to reasonable cause, there shall be paid (on notice and demand by the Secretary and in the same manner as tax) by the person failing so to file, $250 for each day during which such failure continues, but the total amount imposed under this subsection on any person for failure to file any return shall not exceed $150,000. This subsection shall not apply to any return or statement which is an information return described in section 6724(d)(1)(C)(ii) or a payee statement described in section 6724(d)(2)(AA).

ADDITIONS TO TAX

Amendments

- **2019, Setting Every Community Up for Retirement Enhancement Act of 2019 (P.L. 116-94)**

P.L. 116-94, §403(a)(1)-(2), Div. O:

Amended Code Sec. 6652(e) by striking "$25" and inserting "$250"; and by striking "$15,000" and inserting "$150,000". **Effective** for returns, statements, and notifications required to be filed, and notices required to be provided, after 12-31-2019.

- **2018, Tax Technical Corrections Act of 2018 (P.L. 115-141)**

P.L. 115-141, §401(a)(300), Div. U:

Amended Code Sec. 6652(e) by striking "section 6724(d)(2)(Y)" in the last sentence and inserting "section 6724(d)(2)(AA)". **Effective** 3-23-2018.

- **1997, Taxpayer Relief Act of 1997 (P.L. 105-34)**

P.L. 105-34, §1602(d)(2)(B):

Amended Code Sec. 6652(e) by striking "section 6724(d)(2)(X)" in the last sentence and inserting "section 6724(d)(2)(Y)". **Effective** as if included in the provision of P.L. 104-191 to which it relates [effective for benefits paid after 12-31-96.—CCH].

- **1996, Small Business Job Protection Act of 1996 (P.L. 104-188)**

P.L. 104-188, §1455(d)(2):

Amended Code Sec. 6652(e) by adding at the end a new sentence. **Effective** for returns, reports, and other statements the due date for which (determined without regard to extensions) is after 12-31-96.

- **1986, Tax Reform Act of 1986 (P.L. 99-514)**

P.L. 99-514, §1501(d)(1)(A)(i) and (ii):

Amended Code Sec. 6652 by striking out subsection (a) and by redesignating subsections (b) through (k) as subsections (a) through (j), respectively. **Effective** for returns for which the due date (determined without regard to extensions) is after 12-31-86.

- **1984 (P.L. 98-612)**

P.L. 98-612, §1(b)(2):

Erroneously amended Code Sec. 6652(f) by striking out "125(h) (relating to information with respect to cafeteria plans)" and inserting in lieu thereof "6039D (relating to returns and records with respect to certain fringe benefit plans)". P.L. 98-611 had already made this change. **Effective** 1-1-85.

- **1984 (P.L. 98-611)**

P.L. 98-611, §1(d)(2):

Amended Code Sec. 6652(f) by striking out "125(h) (relating to information with respect to cafeteria plans)" and inserting in lieu thereof "6039D (relating to returns and records with respect to certain fringe benefit plans)". **Effective** 1-1-85.

- **1984, Deficit Reduction Act of 1984 (P.L. 98-369)**

P.L. 98-369, §491(d)(50):

Amended Code Sec. 6652(f) by striking out "and bond purchase". **Effective** for obligations issued after 12-31-83.

P.L. 98-369, §531(b)(4)(B):

Amended Code Sec. 6652(f) by striking out "or 6047 (relating to information relating to certain trusts and annuity and bond purchase plans)" and inserting in lieu thereof ", 6047 (relating to information relating to certain trusts and annuity and bond purchase plans), or 125(h) (relating to information with respect to cafeteria plans)", and by striking out "Deferred Compensation.—" in the subsection heading and inserting in lieu thereof "Deferred Compensation; Etc.—". **Effective** 1-1-85.

- **1982, Tax Equity and Fiscal Responsibility Act of 1982 (P.L. 97-248)**

P.L. 97-248, §315(b):

Amended Code Sec. 6652(f) by striking out "$10" and inserting "$25" and by striking out "$5,000" and inserting "$15,000". **Effective** with respect to returns or statements the due date for the filing of which (without regard to extensions) is after 12-31-82.

- **1976, Tax Reform Act of 1976 (P.L. 94-455)**

P.L. 94-455, §1906(b)(13)(A):

Amended 1954 Code by substituting "Secretary" for "Secretary or his delegate" each place it appeared. **Effective** 2-1-77.

- **1974, Employee Retirement Income Security Act of 1974 (P.L. 93-406)**

P.L. 93-406, §1031(b)(1):

Amended Code Sec. 6652 by adding subsection (f). **Effective** 9-2-74.

[Sec. 6652(f)]

(f) RETURNS REQUIRED UNDER SECTION 6039C.—

(1) IN GENERAL.—In the case of each failure to make a return by section 6039C which contains the information required by such section on the date prescribed therefor (determined with regard to any extension of time for filing), unless it is shown that such failure is due to reasonable cause and not to willful neglect, the amount determined under paragraph (2) shall be paid (upon notice and demand by the Secretary and in the same manner as tax) by the person failing to make such return.

(2) AMOUNT OF PENALTY.—For purposes of paragraph (1), the amount determined under this paragraph with respect to any failure shall be $25 for each day during which such failure continues.

(3) LIMITATION.—The amount determined under paragraph (2) with respect to any person for failing to meet the requirements of section 6039C for any calendar year shall not exceed the lesser of—

(A) $25,000, or

(B) 5 percent of the aggregate of the fair market value of the United States real property interests owned by such person at any time during such year.

For purposes of the preceding sentence, fair market value shall be determined as of the end of the calendar year (or, in the case of any property disposed of during the calendar year, as of the date of such disposition).

Amendments

- **1986, Tax Reform Act of 1986 (P.L. 99-514)**

P.L. 99-514, §1501(d)(1)(A)(i) and (ii):

Amended Code Sec. 6652 by striking out subsection (a) and by redesignating subsections (b) through (k) as subsections (a) through (j), respectively. **Effective** for returns for which the due date (determined without regard to extensions) is after 12-31-86.

P.L. 99-514, §1810(f)(9)(A):

Amended Code Sec. 6652(g)(1). **Effective** as if included in the provision of P.L. 98-369 to which it relates. Prior to amendment, Code Sec. 6652(g)(1) read as follows:

(1) IN GENERAL.—In the case of failure

(A) to make a return required by section 6039C which contains the information required by such section, or

(B) to furnish a statement required by section 6039C(b)(3),

on the date prescribed therefor (determined with regard to any extension of time for filing), unless it is shown that such failure is due to reasonable cause and not to willful neglect, the amount determined under paragraph (2) shall be paid (upon notice and demand by the Secretary and in the same manner as tax) by the person failing to make such return or furnish such statement.

P.L. 99-514, §1810(f)(9)(B):

Amended Code Sec. 6652(g)(3). **Effective** as if included in the provision of P.L. 98-369 to which it relates. Prior to amendment, Code Sec. 6652(g)(3) read as follows:

(3) LIMITATIONS.—

(A) FOR FAILURE TO MEET REQUIREMENTS OF SUBSECTION (a) OR (b) OF SECTION 6039C.—The amount determined under paragraph (2) with respect to any person for failing to meet the requirements of subsection (a) or (b) of section 6039C for any calendar year shall not exceed $25,000 with respect to each such subsection.

(B) FOR FAILURE TO MEET REQUIREMENTS OF SECTION 6039C(c).—The amount determined under paragraph (2) with respect to any person for failing to meet the requirements of subsection (c) of section 6039C for any calendar year shall not exceed the lesser of $25,000 or 5 percent of the aggregate of the fair market value of the United States real property interests owned by such person at any time during such year. For purposes of the preceding sentence, fair market value shall be determined as of the end of the calendar year (or, in the case of any property disposed of during the calendar year, as of the date of such disposition).

P.L. 99-514, §1810(f)(9)(C):

Amended Code Sec. 6652(g) by striking out ", Etc.," in the subsection heading. **Effective** as if included in the provision of P.L. 98-369 to which it relates. Prior to amendment, the subsection heading for Code Sec. 6652(g) read as follows:

(g) RETURNS, ETC., REQUIRED UNDER SECTION 6039C.—

P.L. 99-514, §1811(c)(2):

Amended Code Sec. 6652(a)(3)(A)(ii) by inserting "(other than by subsection (d) of such section)" after "section 6045". **Effective** as if included in the provision of P.L. 98-369 to which it relates.

- **1980, Omnibus Reconciliation Act of 1980 (P.L. 96-499)**

P.L. 96-499, §1123(b):

Amended Code Sec. 6652 by redesignating subsection (g) as subsection (h), and inserting a new subsection (g). **Effective** for 1980 and subsequent calendar years. Calendar year 1980 shall be treated as beginning on 6-19-80, and ending on 12-31-80.

ADDITIONS TO TAX

[Sec. 6652(g)—Stricken]

Amendments

• **2014, Tax Technical Corrections Act of 2014 (P.L. 113-295)**

P.L. 113-295, §221(a)(39)(B), Division A:

Amended Code Sec. 6652 by striking subsection (g). **Effective** generally 12-19-2014. For a special rule, see Act Sec. 221(b)(2), below. Prior to being stricken, Code Sec. 6652(g) read as follows:

(g) INFORMATION REQUIRED IN CONNECTION WITH DEDUCTIBLE EMPLOYEE CONTRIBUTIONS.—In the case of failure to make a report required by section 219(f)(4) which contains the information required by such section on the date prescribed therefor (determined with regard to any extension of time for filing), there shall be paid (on notice and demand by the Secretary and in the same manner as tax) by the person failing so to file, an amount equal to $25 for each participant with respect to whom there was a failure to file such information, multiplied by the number of years during which such failure continues, but the total amount imposed under this subsection on any person for failure to file shall not exceed $10,000. No penalty shall be imposed under this subsection on any failure which is shown to be due to reasonable cause and not willful neglect.

P.L. 113-295, §221(b)(2), Division A, provides:

(2) SAVINGS PROVISION.—If—

(A) any provision amended or repealed by the amendments made by this section applied to—

(i) any transaction occurring before the date of the enactment of this Act,

(ii) any property acquired before such date of enactment, or

(iii) any item of income, loss, deduction, or credit taken into account before such date of enactment, and

(B) the treatment of such transaction, property, or item under such provision would (without regard to the amendments or repeals made by this section) affect the liability for tax for periods ending after date of enactment, nothing in the amendments or repeals made by this section shall be construed to affect the treatment of such transaction, property, or item for purposes of determining liability for tax for periods ending after such date of enactment.

• **1997, Taxpayer Relief Act of 1997 (P.L. 105-34)**

P.L. 105-34, §1281(a):

Amended Code Sec. 6652(g) by adding at the end a new sentence. **Effective** for tax years beginning after 8-5-97.

• **1986, Tax Reform Act of 1986 (P.L. 99-514)**

P.L. 99-514, §1501(d)(1)(A)(i) and (ii):

Amended Code Sec. 6652 by striking out subsection (a) and by redesignating subsections (b) through (k) as subsections (a) through (j), respectively. **Effective** for returns for which the due date (determined without regard to extensions) is after 12-31-86.

• **1981, Economic Recovery Tax Act of 1981 (P.L. 97-34)**

P.L. 97-34, §311(f):

Added Code Sec. 6652(h). **Effective** for tax years beginning after 12-31-81. The transitional rule provides that, for purposes of the 1954 Code, any amount allowed as a deduction under section 220 of the Code (as in effect before its repeal by P.L. 97-34) shall be treated as if it were allowed by Code Sec. 219.

[Sec. 6652(h)]

(h) FAILURE TO GIVE NOTICE TO RECIPIENTS OF CERTAIN PENSION, ETC., DISTRIBUTIONS.—In the case of each failure to provide notice as required by section 3405(e)(10)(B), at the time prescribed therefor, unless it is shown that such failure is due to reasonable cause and not to willful neglect, there shall be paid, on notice and demand of the Secretary and in the same manner as tax, by the person failing to provide such notice, an amount equal to $100 for each such failure, but the total amount imposed on such person for all such failures during any calendar year shall not exceed $50,000.

Amendments

• **2019, Setting Every Community Up for Retirement Enhancement Act of 2019 (P.L. 116-94)**

P.L. 116-94, §403(c)(1)-(2), Div. O:

Amended Code Sec. 6652(h) by striking "$10" and inserting "$100"; and by striking "$5,000" and inserting "$50,000". **Effective** for returns, statements, and notifications required to be filed, and notices required to be provided, after 12-31-2019.

• **1992, Unemployment Compensation Amendments of 1992 (P.L. 102-318)**

P.L. 102-318, §522(b)(2)(F):

Amended Code Sec. 6652(h) by striking "section 3405(d)(10)(B)" and inserting "section 3405(e)(10)(B)". **Effective** for distributions after 12-31-92.

• **1986, Tax Reform Act of 1986 (P.L. 99-514)**

P.L. 99-514, §1501(d)(1)(A)(i) and (ii):

Amended Code Sec. 6652 by striking out subsection (a) and by redesignating subsections (b) through (k) as subsections (a) through (j), respectively. **Effective** for returns for which the due date (determined without regard to extensions) is after 12-31-86.

• **1984, Deficit Reduction Act of 1984 (P.L. 98-369)**

P.L. 98-369, §714(j)(3):

Amended Code Sec. 6652 by redesignating subsection (i) as subsection (j) and by inserting a new subsection (i). **Effective** as if included in the provision of P.L. 97-248 to which it relates.

[Sec. 6652(i)]

(i) FAILURE TO GIVE WRITTEN EXPLANATION TO RECIPIENTS OF CERTAIN QUALIFYING ROLLOVER DISTRIBUTIONS.—In the case of each failure to provide a written explanation as required by section 402(f), at the time prescribed therefor, unless it is shown that such failure is due to reasonable cause and not to willful neglect, there shall be paid, on notice and demand of the Secretary and in the same manner as tax, by the person failing to provide such written explanation, an amount equal to $100 for each such failure, but the total amount imposed on such person for all such failures during any calendar year shall not exceed $50,000.

Amendments

• **1996, Small Business Job Protection Act of 1996 (P.L. 104-188)**

P.L. 104-188, §1455(c)(1)-(2):

Amended Code Sec. 6652(i) by striking "the $10" and inserting "$100", and by striking "$5,000" and inserting "$50,000". **Effective** for returns, reports, and other statements the due date for which (determined without regard to extensions) is after 12-31-96.

• **1986, Tax Reform Act of 1986 (P.L. 99-514)**

P.L. 99-514, §1501(d)(1)(A)(i) and (ii):

Amended Code Sec. 6652 by striking out subsection (a) and by redesignating subsections (b) through (k) as subsections (a) through (j), respectively. **Effective** for returns for which the due date (determined without regard to extensions) is after 12-31-86.

• **1984, Retirement Equity Act of 1984 (P.L. 98-397)**

P.L. 98-397, §207(b):

Amended Code Sec. 6652 by redesignating subsection (j) as (k) and by inserting after subsection (i) new subsection (j). **Effective** for distributions after 12-31-84. Special rules appear in the notes for P.L. 98-397, following Code Sec. 401(a).

[Sec. 6652(j)]

(j) FAILURE TO FILE CERTIFICATION WITH RESPECT TO CERTAIN RESIDENTIAL RENTAL PROJECTS.—In the case of each failure to provide a certification as required by section 142(d)(7) at the time prescribed therefor, unless it is shown that such failure is due to reasonable cause and not to willful neglect, there shall be paid, on notice and demand of the Secretary and in the same manner as tax, by the person failing to provide such certification, an amount equal to $100 for each such failure.

Amendments

• **1986, Tax Reform Act of 1986 (P.L. 99-514)**

P.L. 99-514, §1301(g):

Amended Code Sec. 6652, as amended by Act Sec. 1501, by redesignating subsection (j) as subsection (k) and by inserting after subsection (i) new subsection (j). **Effective**, generally, for bonds issued after 8-15-86. However, see the transitional rules provided by Act Secs. 1312-1318 following Code Sec. 103.

P.L. 99-514, §1702(b):

Amended Code Sec. 6652, as amended by Act Secs. 1301(g) and 1501(d), by redesignating subsection (j)[(k)] as subsection (k)[(l)]and by inserting after subsection (i)[(j)] new subsection (j)[(k)]. **Effective** for sales after the first calendar quarter beginning more than 60 days after 10-22-86.

[Sec. 6652(k)]

(k) FAILURE TO MAKE REPORTS REQUIRED UNDER SECTION 1202.—In the case of a failure to make a report required under section 1202(d)(1)(C) which contains the information required by such section on the date prescribed therefor (determined with regard to any extension of time for filing), there shall be paid (on notice and demand by the Secretary and in the same manner as tax) by the person failing to make such report, an amount equal to $50 for each report with respect to which there was such a failure. In the case of any failure due to negligence or intentional

ADDITIONS TO TAX

disregard, the preceding sentence shall be applied by substituting "$100" for "$50". In the case of a report covering periods in 2 or more years, the penalty determined under preceding provisions of this subsection shall be multiplied by the number of such years. No penalty shall be imposed under this subsection on any failure which is shown to be due to reasonable cause and not willful neglect.

Amendments

• **1997, Taxpayer Relief Act of 1997 (P.L. 105-34)**

P.L. 105-34, §1281(b):

Amended Code Sec. 6652(k) by adding at the end a new sentence. **Effective** for tax years beginning after 8-5-97.

• **1993, Omnibus Budget Reconciliation Act of 1993 (P.L. 103-66)**

P.L. 103-66, §13113(c):

Amended Code Sec. 6652 by inserting before the last subsection thereof a new subsection (k). **Effective** for stock issued after 8-10-93.

[Sec. 6652(l)]

(l) FAILURE TO FILE RETURN WITH RESPECT TO CERTAIN CORPORATE TRANSACTIONS.—In the case of any failure to make a return required under section 6043(c) containing the information required by such section on the date prescribed therefor (determined with regard to any extension of time for filing), unless it is shown that such failure is due to reasonable cause, there shall be paid (on notice and demand by the Secretary and in the same manner as tax) by the person failing to file such return, an amount equal to $500 for each day during which such failure continues, but the total amount imposed under this subsection with respect to any return shall not exceed $100,000.

Amendments

• **1989, Omnibus Budget Reconciliation Act of 1989 (P.L. 101-239)**

P.L. 101-239, §7208(b)(2):

Amended Code Sec. 6652 by redesignating subsection (l) as subsection (m) and by inserting after subsection (k) a new subsection (l). **Effective** for transactions after 3-31-90.

P.L. 101-239, §7841(d)(5)(A):

Amended Code Sec. 6652 by redesignating the subsection relating to information with respect to includible employee benefits as subsection (k). See the amendment note for P.L. 101-140, §203(a)(1) in the amendment notes following Code Sec. 6652(m)[l]. **Effective** 12-19-89.

[Sec. 6652(m)]

(m) ALCOHOL AND TOBACCO TAXES.—For penalties for failure to file certain information returns with respect to alcohol and tobacco taxes, see, generally, subtitle E.

Amendments

• **1989, Omnibus Budget Reconciliation Act of 1989 (P.L. 101-239)**

P.L. 101-239, §7208(b)(2):

Amended Code Sec. 6652 by redesignating subsection (l) as subsection (m). **Effective** for transactions after 3-31-90.

P.L. 101-239, §7841(d)(5)(B):

Amended Code Sec. 6652 by redesignating the subsection relating to alcohol and tobacco taxes as subsection (l). **Effective** 12-19-89.

• **1989 (P.L. 101-140)**

P.L. 101-140, §203(a)(1):

Provides that Code Sec. 6652(l)-(m), as amended by Section 1151(b) of P.L. 99-514, shall be applied as if the amendment had not been enacted. **Effective** as if included in section 1151 of P.L. 99-514. Code Sec. 6652(l)[k], prior to amendment by Act Sec. 1151(b) of P.L. 99-514, read as follows:

(k) INFORMATION WITH RESPECT TO INCLUDIBLE EMPLOYEE BENEFITS.—

(1) IN GENERAL.—In the case of each failure to include any amount on any statement under section 6051(a) or 6051(d) which is required to be so included under section 89(l), there shall be paid, on notice and demand of the Secretary and in the same manner as tax, the amount determined under paragraph (2).

(2) AMOUNT OF ADDITIONAL TAX.—The amount determined under this paragraph shall be equal to the product of—

(A) the highest rate of tax imposed by section 1 for taxable years beginning in the calendar year to which the return or statement relates, multiplied by

(B) the amount which bears the same ratio to the employer-provided benefit (within the meaning of section 89 without regard to subsection (g)(3)(C)(i) thereof) with respect to the employee to whom such failure relates as the amount of such benefit required to be but not shown on timely statements under sections 6051(a) and 6051(d) bears to the amount required to be shown.

(3) REASONABLE CAUSE EXCEPTION.—Paragraph (1) shall not apply to any failure if it is shown that such failure is due to reasonable cause.

(4) COORDINATION WITH OTHER PENALTIES.—Any penalty under this subsection shall be in addition to any other penalty under this section or part II of subchapter B of this chapter with respect to any failure.

(5) ONLY 1 ADDITION PER EMPLOYEE PER YEAR.—Paragraph (1) shall be applied only once if there is more than 1 failure with respect to any amount.

P.L. 101-136, §528, provides:

SEC. 528. No monies appropriated by this Act may be used to implement or enforce section 1151 of the Tax Reform Act of 1986 or the amendments made by such section.

• **1988, Technical and Miscellaneous Revenue Act of 1988 (P.L. 100-647)**

P.L. 100-647, §1011B(a)(10):

Amended Code Sec. 6652(l)[k](2)(B) by striking out "subsection (g)(3)" and inserting in lieu thereof "subsection (g)(3)(C)(i)". **Effective** as if included in the provision of P.L. 99-514 to which it relates.

P.L. 100-647, §1018(u)(36):

Amended Code Sec. 6652(k)(4) by striking out "or section 6678" and inserting in lieu thereof "or part II of subchapter B of this chapter". **Effective** as if included in the provision of P.L. 99-514 to which it relates.

P.L. 100-647, §3021(a)(10):

Amended Code Sec. 6652(k)(2)(B). **Effective** as if included in section 1151 of P.L. 99-514. Prior to amendment, Code Sec. 6652(k)(2)(B) read as follows:

(B) the employer-provided benefit (within the meaning of section 89 without regard to subsection (g)(3)(C)(i) thereof) with respect to the employee to whom such failure relates.

P.L. 100-647, §1017(b):

Amended Code Sec. 6652(j), as added by P.L. 99-514 and in effect before its repeal by P.L. 100-203, by inserting "(and the corresponding provision of section 4041(d)(1))" after "section 4041(a)(1)". **Effective** as if included in the provision of P.L. 99-514 to which it relates.

• **1987, Revenue Act of 1987 (P.L. 100-203)**

P.L. 100-203, §10502(d)(11):

Amended Code Sec. 6652 by striking out the subsection (j) added by section 1702(b) of the Tax Reform Act of 1986 and by redesignating subsections (l) and (m) as subsections (k) and (l), respectively. **Effective** for sales after 3-31-88. Prior to amendment, subsection (j) read as follows:

(j)[(k)] FAILURE TO GIVE WRITTEN NOTICE TO CERTAIN SELLERS OF DIESEL FUEL.—

(1) IN GENERAL.—If any qualified retailer fails to provide the notice described in section 4041(n)(3)(A)(ii) to any seller of diesel fuel to such retailer, unless it is shown that such failure is due to reasonable cause and not to willful neglect, there shall be paid, on notice and demand of the Secretary and in the same manner as tax, by such retailer with respect to each sale of diesel fuel to such retailer by such seller to which section 4041(n)(4) applies an amount equal to 5 percent of the tax imposed by section 4041(a)(1) (and the corresponding provision of section 4041(d)(1)) on such sale by reason of paragraphs (3) and (4)(A) of section 4041(n).

(2) DEFINITIONS.—For purposes of paragraph (1), the terms "qualified retailer" and "diesel fuel" have the respective meanings given such terms by section 4041(n).

• **1986, Tax Reform Act of 1986 (P.L. 99-514)**

P.L. 99-514, §1151(b):

Amended Code Sec. 6652 by redesignating subsection (l) as subsection (m) and by inserting after subsection (k) new subsection (l). **Effective**, generally, for years beginning after the later of—

(A) 12-31-87, or

(B) the earlier of—

(i) the date which is 3 months after the date on which the Secretary of the Treasury or his delegate issues such regulations as are necessary to carry out the provisions of section 89 of the Internal Revenue Code of 1986 (as added by this section), or

(ii) 12-31-88. However, see the special rule under the amendment notes to Code Sec. 89.

• **1984, Retirement Equity Act of 1984 (P.L. 98-397)**

P.L. 98-397, §207(b):

Amended Code Sec. 6652 by redesignating subsection (j) as (k). **Effective** for distributions after 12-31-84.

• **1984, Deficit Reduction Act of 1984 (P.L. 98-369)**

P.L. 98-369, §714(j)(3):

Redesignated Code Sec. 6652(i) as (j). **Effective** as if included in P.L. 97-248.

• **1981, Economic Recovery Tax Act of 1981 (P.L. 97-34)**

P.L. 97-34, §311(f):

Redesignated Code Sec. 6652(h) as Code Sec. 6652(i). **Effective** for tax years beginning after 12-31-81.

• **1980, Omnibus Reconciliation Act of 1980 (P.L. 96-499)**

P.L. 96-499, §1123(b):

Redesignating Code Sec. 6652(g) as 6652(h). **Effective** for 1980 and subsequent tax years. Calendar year 1980 shall be treated as beginning on 6-19-80 and ending on 12-31-80.

• **1974, Employee Retirement Income Security Act of 1974 (P.L. 93-406)**

P.L. 93-406, §1031(b)(1):

Amended Code Sec. 6652 by redesignating subsection (e) as subsection (g). **Effective** 9-2-74.

ADDITIONS TO TAX

- **1969, Tax Reform Act of 1969 (P.L. 91-172)**

P.L. 91-172, § 101(d)(4):

Redesignated Code Sec. 6652(d) as (e).

- **1965, Social Security Amendments of 1965 (P.L. 89-97)**

P.L. 89-97, § 313(e):

Redesignated Code Sec. 6652(c) as (d).

- **1962, Revenue Act of 1962 (P.L. 87-834)**

P.L. 87-834, § 19(d):

Added Code Sec. 6652(c). **Effective** 10-17-62.

[Sec. 6652(n)]

(n) FAILURE TO MAKE REPORTS REQUIRED UNDER SECTIONS 3511, 6053 (c)(8), AND 7705.—In the case of a failure to make a report required under section 3511, 6053(c)(8), or 7705 which contains the information required by such section on the date prescribed therefor (determined with regard to any extension of time for filing), there shall be paid (on notice and demand by the Secretary and in the same manner as tax) by the person failing to make such report, an amount equal to $50 for each report with respect to which there was such a failure. In the case of any failure due to negligence or intentional disregard the preceding sentence shall be applied by substituting "$100" for "$50".

Amendments

- **2014, Stephen Beck, Jr., Achieving a Better Life Experience Act of 2014 (P.L. 113-295)**

P.L. 113-295, § 206(c)(4), Division B:

Amended Code Sec. 6652 by adding at the end a new subsection (n). **Effective** generally for wages for services performed on or after January 1 of the first calendar year beginning more than 12 months after 12-19-2014. For a special rule, see Act Sec. 206(h), below.

P.L. 113-295, § 206(h), Division B, provides:

(h) NO INFERENCE.—Nothing contained in this section or the amendments made by this section shall be construed to create any inference with respect to the determination of who is an employee or employer—

(1) for Federal tax purposes (other than the purposes set forth in the amendments made by this section), or

(2) for purposes of any other provision of law.

[Sec. 6652(o)]

(o) FAILURE TO PROVIDE NOTICES WITH RESPECT TO QUALIFIED SMALL EMPLOYER HEALTH REIMBURSEMENT ARRANGEMENTS.—In the case of each failure to provide a written notice as required by section 9831(d)(4), unless it is shown that such failure is due to reasonable cause and not willful neglect, there shall be paid, on notice and demand of the Secretary and in the same manner as tax, by the person failing to provide such written notice, an amount equal to $50 per employee per incident of failure to provide such notice, but the total amount imposed on such person for all such failures during any calendar year shall not exceed $2,500.

Amendments

- **2016, 21st Century Cures Act (P.L. 114-255)**

P.L. 114-255, § 18001(a)(5):

Amended Code Sec. 6652 by adding at the end a new subsection (o). **Effective** for notices with respect to years beginning after 12-31-2016. For a special rule, see Act Sec. 18001(a)(7)(D)(ii), below.

P.L. 114-255, § 18001(a)(7)(D)(ii), provides:

(ii) TRANSITION RELIEF.—For purposes of section 6652(o) of the Internal Revenue Code of 1986 (as added by this Act), a person shall not be treated as failing to provide a written notice as required by section 9831(d)(4) of such Code if such notice is so provided not later than 90 days after the date of the enactment of this Act.

[Sec. 6652(p)]

(p) FAILURE TO PROVIDE NOTICE UNDER SECTION 83(I).—In the case of each failure to provide a notice as required by section 83(i)(6), at the time prescribed therefor, unless it is shown that such failure is due to reasonable cause and not to willful neglect, there shall be paid, on notice and demand of the Secretary and in the same manner as tax, by the person failing to provide such notice, an amount equal to $100 for each such failure, but the total amount imposed on such person for all such failures during any calendar year shall not exceed $50,000.

Amendments

- **2017, Tax Cuts and Jobs Act (P.L. 115-97)**

P.L. 115-97, § 13603(e):

Amended Code Sec. 6652 by adding at the end a new subsection (p). **Effective** generally for failures after 12-31-2017. For a transition rule, see Act Sec. 13603(g), below.

P.L. 115-97, § 13603(g), provides:

(g) TRANSITION RULE.—Until such time as the Secretary (or the Secretary's delegate) issues regulations or other guidance for purposes of implementing the requirements of paragraph (2)(C)(i)(II) of section 83(i) of the Internal Revenue Code of 1986 (as added by this section), or the requirements of paragraph (6) of such section, a corporation shall be treated as being in compliance with such requirements (respectively) if such corporation complies with a reasonable good faith interpretation of such requirements.

[Sec. 6653]

SEC. 6653. FAILURE TO PAY STAMP TAX.

Any person (as defined in section 6671(b)) who—

(1) willfully fails to pay any tax imposed by this title which is payable by stamp, coupons, tickets, books, or other devices or methods prescribed by this title or by regulations under the authority of this title, or

(2) willfully attempts in any manner to evade or defeat any such tax or the payment thereof,

shall, in addition to other penalties provided by law, be liable for a penalty of 50 percent of the total amount of the underpayment of the tax.

Amendments

- **1989, Omnibus Budget Reconciliation Act of 1989 (P.L. 101-239)**

P.L. 101-239, § 7721(c)(1):

Amended Code Sec. 6653. **Effective** for returns the due date for which (determined without regard to extensions) is after 12-31-89. Prior to amendment, Code Sec. 6653 read as follows:

SEC. 6653. ADDITIONS TO TAX FOR NEGLIGENCE AND FRAUD.

[Sec. 6653(a)]

(a) NEGLIGENCE.—

(1) IN GENERAL.—If any part of any underpayment (as defined in subsection (c)) of tax required to be shown on a return is due to negligence (or disregard of rules or regulations), there shall be added to the tax an amount equal to 5 percent of the underpayment.

(2) UNDERPAYMENT TAKEN INTO ACCOUNT REDUCED BY PORTION ATTRIBUTABLE TO FRAUD.—There shall not be taken into account under this subsection any portion of an underpayment attributable to fraud with respect to which a penalty is imposed under subsection (b).

(3) NEGLIGENCE.—For purposes of this subsection, the term "negligence" includes any failure to make a reasonable attempt to comply with the provisions of this title, and the term "disregard" includes any careless, reckless, or intentional disregard.

Amendments

- **1988, Technical and Miscellaneous Revenue Act of 1988 (P.L. 100-647)**

P.L. 100-647, § 1015(b)(2)(A):

Amended Code Sec. 6653(a)(1). **Effective** for returns the due date for which (determined without regard to extensions) is after 12-31-88. Prior to amendment, Code Sec. 6653(a)(1) read as follows:

(1) IN GENERAL.—If any part of any underpayment (as defined in subsection (c)) is due to negligence or disregard of rules or regulations, there shall be added to the tax an amount equal to the sum of—

(A) 5 percent of the underpayment, and

(B) an amount equal to 50 percent of the interest payable under section 6601 with respect to the portion of such underpayment which is attributable to negligence for the period beginning on the last date prescribed by law for payment of such underpayment (determined without regard to any extension) and ending on the date of the assessment of the tax (or, if earlier, the date of the payment of the tax).

- **1986, Tax Reform Act of 1986 (P.L. 99-514)**

P.L. 99-514, § 1503(a):

Amended Code Sec. 6653 by striking out subsection (a) and inserting a new subsection (a). **Effective** for returns, the due date for which (determined without

ADDITIONS TO TAX

regard to extensions) is after 12-31-86. Prior to amendment, Code Sec. 6653(a) read as follows:

(a) NEGLIGENCE OR INTENTIONAL DISREGARD OF RULES AND REGULATIONS WITH RESPECT TO INCOME, GIFT, OR WINDFALL PROFIT TAXES.—

(1) IN GENERAL.—If any part of any underpayment (as defined in subsection (c)(1)) of any tax imposed by subtitle A, by chapter 12 of subtitle B or by chapter 45 (relating to windfall profit tax) is due to negligence or intentional disregard of rules or regulations (but without intent to defraud), there shall be added to the tax an amount equal to 5 percent of the underpayment.

(2) ADDITIONAL AMOUNT FOR PORTION ATTRIBUTABLE TO NEGLIGENCE, ETC.—There shall be added to the tax (in addition to the amount determined under paragraph (1)) an amount equal to 50 percent of the interest payable under section 6601—

(A) with respect to the portion of the underpayment described in paragraph (1) which is attributable to the negligence or intentional disregard referred to in paragraph (1), and

(B) for the period beginning on the last date prescribed by law for payment of such underpayment (determined without regard to any extension) and ending on the date of the assessment of the tax (or, if earlier, the date of the payment of the tax).

P.L. 99-514, §1503(d)(1):

Amended the heading for Code Sec. 6653. **Effective** for returns, the due date for which (determined without regard to extensions) is after 12-31-86. Prior to amendment, the heading for Code Sec. 6653 read as follows:

SEC. 6653. FAILURE TO PAY TAX.

• **1983, Technical Corrections Act of 1982 (P.L. 97-448)**

P.L. 97-448, §107(a)(3):

Amended Code Sec. 6653(a)(2)(B) by inserting "(or, if earlier, the date of the payment of the tax)" after "assessment of the tax". **Effective** as if included in the provision of P.L. 97-34 to which it relates.

• **1981, Economic Recovery Tax Act of 1981 (P.L. 97-34)**

P.L. 97-34, §722(b)(1):

Amended Code Sec 6653(a). **Effective** for taxes the last date prescribed for payment of which is after 12-31-81. Prior to amendment, Code Sec. 6653(a) read as follows:

(a) NEGLIGENCE OR INTENTIONAL DISREGARD OF RULES AND REGULATIONS WITH RESPECT TO INCOME, GIFT, OR WINDFALL PROFIT TAXES.—If any part of any underpayment (as defined in subsection (c)(1)) of any tax imposed by subtitle A, by chapter 12 of subtitle B (relating to income taxes and gift taxes), or by chapter 45 (relating to windfall profit tax) is due to negligence or intentional disregard of rules and regulations (but without intent to defraud), there shall be added to the tax an amount equal to 5 percent of the underpayment.

• **1980, Crude Oil Windfall Profit Tax Act of 1980 (P.L. 96-223)**

P.L. 96-223, §101(f)(8):

Amended Code Sec. 6653(a) by striking out "or by chapter 12" and inserting ", by chapter 12", by striking out "is due" and inserting ", or by chapter 45 (relating to windfall profit tax) is due", and by striking out "OR GIFT" in the subsection heading and inserting ", GIFT, OR WINDFALL PROFIT". For the **effective** date and transitional rules, see P.L. 96-223, Act Sec. 101(i), following Code Sec. 4986.

[Sec. 6653(b)]

(b) FRAUD.—

(1) IN GENERAL.—If any part of any underpayment (as defined in subsection (c)) of tax required to be shown on a return is due to fraud, there shall be added to the tax an amount equal to 75 percent of the portion of the underpayment which is attributable to fraud.

(2) DETERMINATION OF PORTION ATTRIBUTABLE TO FRAUD.—If the Secretary establishes that any portion of an underpayment is attributable to fraud, the entire underpayment shall be treated as attributable to fraud, except with respect to any portion of the underpayment which the taxpayer establishes is not attributable to fraud.

(3) SPECIAL RULE FOR JOINT RETURNS.—In the case of a joint return, this subsection shall not apply with respect to a spouse unless some part of the underpayment is due to the fraud of such spouse.

Amendments

• **1988, Technical and Miscellaneous Revenue Act of 1988 (P.L. 100-647)**

P.L. 100-647, §1015(b)(2)(B):

Amended Code Sec. 6653(b)(1). **Effective** for returns the due date for which (determined without regard to extensions) is after 12-31-88. Prior to amendment, Code Sec. 6653(b)(1) read as follows:

(1) IN GENERAL.—If any part of any underpayment (as defined in subsection (c)) of tax required to be shown on a return is due to fraud, there shall be added to the tax an amount equal to the sum of—

(A) 75 percent of the portion of the underpayment which is attributable to fraud, and

(B) an amount equal to 50 percent of the interest payable under section 6601 with respect to such portion for the period beginning on the last day prescribed by law for payment of such underpayment (determined without regard to any extension) and ending on the date of the assessment of the tax or, if earlier, the date of the payment of the tax.

• **1986, Tax Reform Act of 1986 (P.L. 99-514)**

P.L. 99-514, §1503(a):

Amended by Code Sec. 6653 by striking out subsection (b) and inserting new subsection (b). **Effective** for returns the due date for which (determined without regard to extensions) is after 12-31-86. Prior to amendment, Code Sec. 6653(b) read as follows:

(b) FRAUD.—

(1) IN GENERAL.—If any part of any underpayment (as defined in subsection (c)) of tax required to be shown on a return is due to fraud, there shall be added to the tax an amount equal to 50 percent of the underpayment.

(2) ADDITIONAL AMOUNT FOR PORTION ATTRIBUTABLE TO FRAUD.—There shall be added to the tax (in addition to the amount determined under paragraph (1)) an amount equal to 50 percent of the interest payable under section 6601—

(A) with respect to the portion of the underpayment described in paragraph (1) which is attributable to fraud, and

(B) for the period beginning on the last day prescribed by law for payment of such underpayment (determining without regard to any extension) and ending on the date of the assessment of the tax (or, if earlier, the date of the payment of the tax).

(3) NO NEGLIGENCE ADDITION WHEN THERE IS ADDITION FOR FRAUD.—The addition to tax under this subsection shall be in lieu of any amount determined under subsection (a).

(4) SPECIAL RULE FOR JOINT RETURNS.—In the case of a joint return under section 6013, this subsection shall not apply with respect to the tax of the spouse unless some part of the underpayment is due to the fraud of such spouse.

• **1982, Tax Equity and Fiscal Responsibility Act of 1982 (P.L. 97-248)**

P.L. 97-248, §325(a):

Amended Code Sec. 6653(b). **Effective** with respect to taxes the last day prescribed by law for payment of which (determined without regard to any extension) is after 9-3-82. Prior to amendment, Code Sec. 6653(b) read as follows:

(b) FRAUD.—If any part of any underpayment (as defined in subsection (c)) of tax required to be shown on a return is due to fraud, there shall be added to the tax an amount equal to 50 percent of the underpayment. In the case of income taxes and gift taxes, this amount shall be in lieu of any amount determined under subsection (a). In the case of a joint return under section 6013, this subsection shall not apply with respect to the tax of a spouse unless some part of the underpayment is due to the fraud of such spouse.

• **1971 (P.L. 91-679)**

P.L. 91-679, §2:

Amended subsection 6653(b) by adding new sentence at the end thereof. **Effective** for all tax years in which the Internal Revenue Code of 1954 applies. Corresponding provisions shall be deemed to be included in the Internal Revenue Code of 1939 and shall apply to all tax years to which such Code applies.

[Sec. 6653(c)]

(c) DEFINITION OF UNDERPAYMENT.—For purposes of this section, the term "underpayment" means—

(1) INCOME, ESTATE, GIFT, AND CERTAIN EXCISE TAXES.—In the case of a tax to which section 6211 (relating to income, estate, gift, and certain excise taxes) is applicable, a deficiency as defined in that section (except that, for this purpose, the tax shown on a return referred to in section 6211(a)(1)(A) shall be taken into account only if such return was filed on or before the last day prescribed for the filing of such return, determined with regard to any extension of time for such filing), and

(2) OTHER TAXES.—In the case of any other tax, the amount by which such tax imposed by this title exceeds the excess of—

(A) The sum of—

(i) The amount shown as the tax by the taxpayer upon his return (determined without regard to any credit for an overpayment for any prior period, and without regard to any adjustment under authority of sections 6205(a) and 6413(a)), if a return was made by the taxpayer within the time prescribed for filing such return (determined with regard to any extension of time for such filing) and an amount was shown as the tax by the taxpayer thereon, plus

(ii) Any amount, not shown on the return, paid in respect of such tax, over—

(B) The amount of rebates made.

For purposes of subparagraph (B), the term "rebate" means so much of an abatement, credit, refund, or other repayment, as was made on the ground that the tax imposed was less than the excess of the amount specified in subparagraph (A) over the rebates previously made.

Amendments

• **1974, Employee Retirement Income Security Act of 1974 (P.L. 93-406)**

P.L. 93-406, §1016(a)(18):

Amended Code Sec. 6653(c)(1) by changing "chapter 42" to "certain excise". For **effective** date, see amendment note for Code Sec. 410.

• **1969, Tax Reform Act of 1969 (P.L. 91-172)**

P.L. 91-172, §101(j)(50):

Amended Code Sec. 6653(c)(1) by substituting in the heading thereof "GIFT, AND CHAPTER 42 TAXES" for "AND GIFT TAXES" and by substituting in the body thereof "gift, and chapter 42 taxes" for "and gift taxes". **Effective** 1-1-70.

• **1958, Technical Amendments Act of 1958 (P.L. 85-866)**

P.L. 85-866, §86:

Amended paragraph (1) of Sec. 6653(c) by inserting "on or" after the phrase "such return was filed". **Effective** 1-1-54.

[Sec. 6653(d)]

(d) NO DELINQUENCY PENALTY IF FRAUD ASSESSED.—If any penalty is assessed under subsection (b) (relating to fraud) for an underpayment of tax which is required to be shown on a return, no penalty under section 6651 (relating to failure to file such return or pay tax) shall be assessed with respect to the portion of the underpayment which is attributable to fraud.

ADDITIONS TO TAX

Amendments

• **1986, Tax Reform Act of 1986 (P.L. 99-514)**

P.L. 99-514, §1503(c)(2):

Amended Code Sec. 6653(d) by striking out "same underpayment" and inserting in lieu thereof "portion of the underpayment which is attributable to fraud". **Effective** for returns the due date for which (determined without regard to extensions) is after 12-31-86.

• **1969, Tax Reform Act of 1969 (P.L. 91-172)**

P.L. 91-172, §943(c)(6):

Amended Sec. 6653(d) by inserting "or pay tax" immediately following "such return". **Effective** with respect to returns the date prescribed by law (without regard to any extension of time) for filing of which is after 12-31-69, and with respect to notices and demands for payment of tax made after 12-31-69.

[Sec. 6653(e)]

(e) FAILURE TO PAY STAMP TAX.—Any person (as defined in section 6671 (b)) who willfully fails to pay any tax imposed by this title which is payable by stamp, coupons, tickets, books, or other devices or methods prescribed by this title or by regulations under authority of this title, or willfully attempts in any manner to evade or defeat any such tax or the payment thereof, shall, in addition to other penalties provided by law, be liable to a penalty of 50 percent of the total amount of the underpayment of the tax.

[Sec. 6653(f)]

(f) SPECIAL RULE IN CASES OF FAILURE TO REPORT UNRECOGNIZED GAIN ON POSITION IN PERSONAL PROPERTY.—If—

(1) a taxpayer fails to make the report required under section 1092(a)(3)(B) in the manner prescribed by such section and such failure is not due to reasonable cause, and

(2) such taxpayer has an underpayment of any tax attributable (in whole or in part) to the denial of a deduction of a loss with respect to any position (within the meaning of section 1092(d)(2)),

then such underpayment shall, for purposes of subsection (a), be treated as an underpayment due to negligence.

Amendments

• **1986, Tax Reform Act of 1986 (P.L. 99-514)**

P.L. 99-514, §1503(c)(3):

Amended Code Sec. 6653(f) by striking out "or intentional disregard of rules and regulations (but without intent to defraud)" following "negligence". **Effective** for returns the due date for which (determined without regard to extensions) is after 12-31-86.

• **1983, Technical Corrections Act of 1982 (P.L. 97-448)**

P.L. 97-448, §105(a)(1)(D)(i):

Amended Code Sec. 6653 by redesignating subsection (g) as subsection (f). **Effective** as if included in the provision of P.L. 97-34 to which it relates.

P.L. 97-448, §105(a)(1)(D)(ii):

Amended the subsection heading of Code Sec. 6653(f) by striking out "Unrealized" and inserting in lieu thereof "Unrecognized". **Effective** as if included in the provision of P.L. 97-34 to which it relates.

• **1981, Economic Recovery Tax Act of 1981 (P.L. 97-34)**

P.L. 97-34, §501(b):

Added Code Sec. 6653(g)[f]. **Effective** for property acquired or positions established after 6-23-81, in tax years ending after that date.

[Sec. 6653(g)]

(g) SPECIAL RULE FOR AMOUNTS SHOWN ON INFORMATION RETURNS.—If—

(1) any amount is shown on—

(A) an information return (as defined is section 6724(d)(1)), or

(B) a return filed under section 6031, section 6037, section 6012(a) by an estate or trust, section 6050B, or section 6050E, and

(2) the payee (or other person with respect to whom the return is made) fails to properly show such amount on his return,

any portion of an underpayment attributable to such failure shall be treated, for purposes of subsection (a), as due to negligence in the absence of clear and convincing evidence to the contrary. If any penalty is imposed under subsection (a) by reason of the preceding sentence, only the portion of the underpayment which is attributable to the failure described in the preceding sentence shall be taken into account in determining the amount of the penalty under subsection (a).

Amendments

• **1988, Technical and Miscellaneous Revenue Act of 1988 (P.L. 100-647)**

P.L. 100-647, §1015(b)(3):

Amended Code Sec. 6653(g) by adding at the end thereof a new sentence. **Effective** as if included in the provision of P.L. 99-514 to which it relates.

• **1986, Tax Reform Act of 1986 (P.L. 99-514)**

P.L. 99-514, §1503(b):

Amended Code Sec. 6653(g). **Effective** for returns the due date for which (determined without regard to extensions) is after 12-31-86. Prior to amendment, Code Sec. 6653(g) read as follows:

(g) SPECIAL RULE IN THE CASE OF INTEREST OR DIVIDEND PAYMENTS.—

(1) IN GENERAL.—If—

(A) any payment is shown on a return made by the payor under section 6042(a), 6044(a), or 6049(a) and

(B) the payee fails to include any portion of such payment in gross income,

any portion of an underpayment attributable to such failure shall be treated, for purposes of subsection (a), as due to negligence in the absence of clear and convincing evidence to the contrary.

(2) PENALTY TO APPLY ONLY TO PORTION OF UNDERPAYMENT DUE TO FAILURE TO INCLUDE INTEREST OR DIVIDEND PAYMENT.—If any penalty is imposed under subsection (a) by reason of paragraph (1), the amount of the penalty imposed by paragraph (1) of subsection (a), shall be 5 percent of the portion of the underpayment which is attributable to the failure described in paragraph (1).

• **1983, Interest and Dividend Tax Compliance Act of 1983 (P.L. 98-67)**

P.L. 98-67, §106:

Added Code Sec. 6653(g). **Effective** with respect to payments made after 12-31-83.

[Sec. 6653(h)—Repealed]

Amendments

• **1985 (P.L. 99-44)**

P.L. 99-44, §1(b):

Repealed P.L. 98-369, §179(b)(3), which amended Code Sec. 6653 by adding at the end thereof subsection (h). **Effective** as if included in the amendments made by P.L. 98-369, §179(b)(3), and the Internal Revenue Code of 1954 shall be applied and administered as if such paragraph (and the amendment made by such paragraph) had not been enacted. Prior to repeal, Code Sec. 6653(h) read as follows:

(h) SPECIAL RULE IN THE CASE OF UNDERPAYMENT ATTRIBUTABLE TO FAILURE TO MEET CERTAIN SUBSTANTIATION REQUIREMENTS.—

(1) IN GENERAL.—Any portion of an underpayment attributable to a failure to comply with the requirements of section 274(d) shall be treated, for purposes of subsection (a), as due to negligence in the absence of clear and convincing evidence to the contrary.

(2) PENALTY TO APPLY ONLY TO PORTION OF UNDERPAYMENT DUE TO FAILURE TO MEET SUBSTANTIATION REQUIREMENTS.—If any penalty is imposed under subsection (a) by reason of paragraph (1), the amount of the penalty imposed by paragraph (1) of subsection (a) shall be 5 percent of the portion of the underpayment which is attributable to the failure described in paragraph (1).

P.L. 99-44, §1(c), provides:

(c) REPEAL OF REGULATIONS.—Regulations issued before the date of the enactment of this Act to carry out the amendments made by paragraphs (1)(C), (2), and (3) of section 179(b) of the Tax Reform Act of 1984 shall have no force and effect.

P.L. 99-44, §5, provides:

Not later than October 1, 1985, the Secretary of the Treasury or his delegate shall prescribe regulations to carry out the provisions of this Act which shall fully reflect such provisions.

• **1984, Deficit Reduction Act of 1984 (P.L. 98-369)**

P.L. 98-369, §179(b)(3):

Amended Code Sec. 6653 by adding new subsection (h). **Effective** for tax years beginning after 12-31-84.

[Sec. 6654]

SEC. 6654. FAILURE BY INDIVIDUAL TO PAY ESTIMATED INCOME TAX.

[Sec. 6654(a)]

(a) ADDITION TO THE TAX.—Except as otherwise provided in this section, in the case of any underpayment of estimated tax by an individual, there shall be added to the tax under chapter 1, the tax under chapter 2, and the tax under chapter 2A for the taxable year an amount determined by applying—

(1) the underpayment rate established under section 6621,

(2) to the amount of the underpayment,

(3) for the period of the underpayment.

Amendments

• **2018, Tax Technical Corrections Act of 2018 (P.L. 115-141)**

P.L. 115-141, §401(a)(301), Div. U:

Amended Code Sec. 6654(a) by striking "chapter 1 the tax" and inserting "chapter 1, the tax". **Effective** 3-23-2018.

ADDITIONS TO TAX

• **2010, Health Care and Education Reconciliation Act of 2010 (P.L. 111-152)**

P.L. 111-152, §1402(a)(2)(A):

Amended Code Sec. 6654(a) by striking "and the tax under chapter 2" and inserting "the tax under chapter 2, and the tax under chapter 2A". **Effective** for tax years beginning after 12-31-2012.

• **1986, Tax Reform Act of 1986 (P.L. 99-514)**

P.L. 99-514, §1511(c)(14):

Amended Code Sec. 6654(a)(1) by striking out "the applicable annual rate established under section 6621" and inserting in lieu thereof "the underpayment rate established under section 6621". **Effective** for purposes of determining interest for periods after 12-31-86. For a special rule, see Act Sec. 1543 under Code Sec. 6654(j).

[Sec. 6654(b)]

(b) AMOUNT OF UNDERPAYMENT; PERIOD OF UNDERPAYMENT.—For purposes of subsection (a)—

(1) AMOUNT.—The amount of the underpayment shall be the excess of—

(A) the required installment, over

(B) the amount (if any) of the installment paid on or before the due date for the installment.

(2) PERIOD OF UNDERPAYMENT.—The period of the underpayment shall run from the due date for the installment to whichever of the following dates is the earlier—

(A) the 15th day of the 4th month following the close of the taxable year, or

(B) with respect to any portion of the underpayment, the date on which such portion is paid.

(3) ORDER OF CREDITING PAYMENTS.—For purposes of paragraph (2)(B), a payment of estimated tax shall be credited against unpaid required installments in the order in which such installments are required to be paid.

[Sec. 6654(c)]

(c) NUMBER OF REQUIRED INSTALLMENTS; DUE DATES.—For purposes of this section—

(1) PAYABLE IN 4 INSTALLMENTS.—There shall be 4 required installments for each taxable year.

(2) TIME FOR PAYMENT OF INSTALLMENTS.—

In the case of the following required installments:	The due date is:
1st	April 15
2nd	June 15
3rd	September 15
4th	January 15 of the following taxable year.

[Sec. 6654(d)]

(d) AMOUNT OF REQUIRED INSTALLMENTS.—For purposes of this section—

(1) AMOUNT.—

(A) IN GENERAL.—Except as provided in paragraph (2), the amount of any required installment shall be 25 percent of the required annual payment.

(B) REQUIRED ANNUAL PAYMENT.—For purposes of subparagraph (A), the term "required annual payment" means the lesser of—

(i) 90 percent of the tax shown on the return for the taxable year (or, if no return is filed, 90 percent of the tax for such year), or

(ii) 100 percent of the tax shown on the return of the individual for the preceding taxable year.

Clause (ii) shall not apply if the preceding taxable year was not a taxable year of 12 months or if the individual did not file a return for such preceding taxable year.

(C) LIMITATION ON USE OF PRECEDING YEAR'S TAX.—

(i) IN GENERAL.—If the adjusted gross income shown on the return of the individual for the preceding taxable year beginning in any calendar year exceeds $150,000, clause (ii) of subparagraph (B) shall be applied by substituting "110 percent" for "100 percent". For purposes of the preceding sentence, the applicable percentage shall be determined in accordance with the following table:

If the preceding taxable year begins in:	The applicable percentage is:
1998	105
1999	108.6
2000	110
2001	112
2002 or thereafter	110

This clause shall not apply in the case of a preceding taxable year beginning in calendar year 1997.

(ii) SEPARATE RETURNS.—In the case of a married individual (within the meaning of section 7703) who files a separate return for the taxable year for which the amount of the installment is being determined, clause (i) shall be applied by substituting "$75,000" for "$150,000".

(iii) SPECIAL RULE.—In the case of an estate or trust, adjusted gross income shall be determined as provided in section 67(e).

(2) LOWER REQUIRED INSTALLMENT WHERE ANNUALIZED INCOME INSTALLMENT IS LESS THAN AMOUNT DETERMINED UNDER PARAGRAPH (1).—

(A) IN GENERAL.—In the case of any required installment, if the individual establishes that the annualized income installment is less than the amount determined under paragraph (1)—

(i) the amount of such required installment shall be the annualized income installment, and

(ii) any reduction in a required installment resulting from the application of this subparagraph shall be recaptured by increasing the amount of the next required installment determined under paragraph (1) by the amount of such reduction (and by increasing subsequent required installments to the extent that the reduction has not previously been recaptured under this clause).

(B) DETERMINATION OF ANNUALIZED INCOME INSTALLMENT.—In the case of any required installment, the annualized income installment is the excess (if any) of—

(i) an amount equal to the applicable percentage of the tax for the taxable year computed by placing on an annualized basis the taxable income, alternative minimum taxable income, and adjusted self-employment income for months in the taxable year ending before the due date for the installment, over

(ii) the aggregate amount of any prior required installments for the taxable year.

ADDITIONS TO TAX

(C) SPECIAL RULES.—For purposes of this paragraph—

(i) ANNUALIZATION.—The taxable income, alternative minimum taxable income, and adjusted self-employment income shall be placed on an annualized basis under regulations prescribed by the Secretary.

(ii) APPLICABLE PERCENTAGE.—

In the case of the following required installments:	The applicable percentage is:
1st	22.5
2nd	45
3rd	67.5
4th	90

(iii) ADJUSTED SELF-EMPLOYMENT INCOME.—The term "adjusted self-employment income" means self-employment income (as defined in section 1402(b)); except that section 1402(b) shall be applied by placing wages (within the meaning of section 1402(b)) for months in the taxable year ending before the due date for the installment on an annualized basis consistent with clause (i).

(D) TREATMENT OF SUBPART F INCOME.—

(i) IN GENERAL.—Any amounts required to be included in gross income under section 951(a) (and credits properly allocable thereto) shall be taken into account in computing any annualized income installment under subparagraph (B) in a manner similar to the manner under which partnership income inclusions (and credits properly allocable thereto) are taken into account.

(ii) PRIOR YEAR SAFE HARBOR.—If a taxpayer elects to have this clause apply to any taxable year—

(I) clause (i) shall not apply, and

(II) for purposes of computing any annualized income installment for such taxable year, the taxpayer shall be treated as having received ratably during such taxable year items of income and credit described in clause (i) in an amount equal to the amount of such items shown on the return of the taxpayer for the preceding taxable year (the second preceding taxable year in the case of the first and second required installments for such taxable year).

Amendments

• **2018, Tax Technical Corrections Act of 2018 (P.L. 115-141)**

P.L. 115-141, §401(b)(48), Div. U:

Amended Code Sec. 6654(d)(1)(C)(i) by striking "by substituting" and all that follows in that sentence and inserting "by substituting '110 percent' for '100 percent'.". **Effective** 3-23-2018. For a special rule, see Act Sec. 401(e), Div. U, below. Prior to being stricken, "by substituting" and all that follows in Code Sec. 6654(d)(1)(C)(i) read as follows:

by substituting the applicable percentage for "100 percent".

P.L. 115-141, §401(b)(49), Div. U:

Amended Code Sec. 6654(d)(1) by striking subparagraph (D). **Effective** 3-23-2018. For a special rule, see Act Sec. 401(e), Div. U, below. Prior to being stricken, Code Sec. 6654(d)(1)(D) read as follows:

(D) SPECIAL RULE FOR 2009.—

(i) IN GENERAL.—Notwithstanding subparagraph (C), in the case of any taxable year beginning in 2009, clause (ii) of subparagraph (B) shall be applied in any qualified individual by substituting "90 percent" for "100 percent".

(ii) QUALIFIED INDIVIDUAL.—For purposes of this subparagraph, the term "qualified individual" means any individual if—

(I) the adjusted gross income shown on the return of such individual for the preceding taxable year is less than $500,000, and

(II) such individual certifies that more than 50 percent of the gross income shown on the return of such individual for the preceding taxable year was income from a small business.

A certification under subclause (II) shall be in such form and manner and filed at such time as the Secretary may by regulations prescribe.

(iii) INCOME FROM A SMALL BUSINESS.—For purposes of clause (ii), income from a small business means, with respect to any individual, income from a trade or business the average number of employees of which was less than 500 employees for the calendar year ending with or within the preceding taxable year of the individual.

(iv) SEPARATE RETURNS.—In the case of a married individual (within the meaning of section 7703) who files a separate return for the taxable year for which the amount of the installment is being determined, clause (ii)(I) shall be applied by substituting "$250,000" for "$500,000".

(v) ESTATES AND TRUSTS.—In the case of an estate or trust, adjusted gross income shall be determined as provided in section 67(e).

P.L. 115-141, §401(d)(1)(D)(xix)(I)-(II), Div. U:

Amended Code Sec. 6654(d)(2)(D) by striking "936(h) or" in clause (i) following "gross income under section", and by striking "AND SECTION 936" following "TREATMENT OF SUBPART F" in the heading. **Effective** 3-23-2018. For a special rule, see Act Sec. 401(e), Div. U, below.

P.L. 115-141, §401(e), Div. U, provides:

(e) GENERAL SAVINGS PROVISION WITH RESPECT TO DEADWOOD PROVISIONS.—If—

(1) any provision amended or repealed by the amendments made by subsection (b) or (d) applied to—

(A) any transaction occurring before the date of the enactment of this Act,

(B) any property acquired before such date of enactment, or

(C) any item of income, loss, deduction, or credit taken into account before such date of enactment, and

(2) the treatment of such transaction, property, or item under such provision would (without regard to the amendments or repeals made by such subsection) affect the liability for tax for periods ending after such date of enactment,

nothing in the amendments or repeals made by this section shall be construed to affect the treatment of such transaction, property, or item for purposes of determining liability for tax for periods ending after such date of enactment.

• **2009, American Recovery and Reinvestment Tax Act of 2009 (P.L. 111-5)**

P.L. 111-5, §1212:

Amended Code Sec. 6654(d)(1) by adding at the end a new subparagraph (D). **Effective** 2-17-2009.

• **1999, Tax Relief Extension Act of 1999 (P.L. 106-170)**

P.L. 106-170, §531(a):

Amended Code Sec. 6654(d)(1)(C)(i) by striking the items in the table relating to 1999 and 2000 and inserting new items. **Effective** with respect to any installment payment for tax years beginning after 12-31-99. Prior to amendment, the items in the table relating to 1999 and 2000 read as follows:

1999 or 2000	106

• **1998, Tax and Trade Relief Extension Act of 1998 (P.L. 105-277)**

P.L. 105-277, §2003(a):

Amended the table contained in Code Sec. 6654(d)(1)(C)(i) by striking the item relating to 1998, 1999, or 2000 and inserting new items. **Effective** with respect to any installment payment for tax years beginning after 12-31-99. Prior to amendment, the table contained in Code Sec. 6654(d)(1)(C)(i) read as follows:

If the preceding taxable year begins in:	The applicable percentage is:
1998, 1999, or 2000	105
2001	112
2002 or thereafter	110

• **1998, IRS Restructuring and Reform Act of 1998 (P.L. 105-206)**

P.L. 105-206, §1(c), provides:

(c) WAIVER OF ESTIMATED TAX PENALTIES.—No addition to tax shall be made under section 6654 or 6655 of the Internal Revenue Code with respect to any underpayment of an installment required to be paid on or before the 30th day after the date of the enactment of this Act to the extent such underpayment was created or increased by any provision of this Act.

• **1997, Taxpayer Relief Act of 1997 (P.L. 105-34)**

P.L. 105-34, §1091(a):

Amended Code Sec. 6654(d)(1)(C)(i). **Effective** with respect to any installment payment for tax years beginning after 12-31-97. Prior to amendment, Code Sec. 6654(d)(1)(C)(i) read as follows:

(i) IN GENERAL.—If the adjusted gross income shown on the return of the individual for the preceding taxable year exceeds $150,000, clause (ii) of subparagraph (B) shall be applied by substituting "110 percent" for "100 percent".

• **1994, Uruguay Round Agreements Act (P.L. 103-465)**

P.L. 103-465, §711(b):

Amended Code Sec. 6654(d)(2) by adding at the end a new subparagraph (D). **Effective** for purposes of determining underpayments of estimated tax for tax years beginning after 12-31-94.

• **1993, Omnibus Budget Reconciliation Act of 1993 (P.L. 103-66)**

P.L. 103-66, §13214(a):

Amended Code Sec. 6654(d)(1) by striking subparagraphs (C), (D), (E), and (F) and by inserting a new subparagraph (C). **Effective** for tax years beginning after 12-31-93. Prior to amendment, Code Sec. 6654(d)(1)(C)-(F) read as follows:

ADDITIONS TO TAX

(C) LIMITATION ON USE OF PRECEDING YEAR'S TAX.—

(i) IN GENERAL.—In any case to which this subparagraph applies, clause (ii) of subparagraph (B) shall be applied as if it read as follows:

"(ii) the greater of—

"(I) 100 percent of the tax shown on the return of the individual for the preceding taxable year, or

"(II) 90 percent of the tax shown on the return for the current year, determined by taking into account the adjustments set forth in subparagraph (D)."

(ii) CASES TO WHICH SUBPARAGRAPH APPLIES.—This subparagraph shall apply if—

(I) the modified adjusted gross income for the current year exceeds the amount of the adjusted gross income shown on the return of the individual for the preceding taxable year by more than $40,000 ($20,000 in the case of a separate return for the current year by a married individual),

(II) the adjusted gross income shown on the return for the current year exceeds $75,000 ($37,500 in the case of a married individual filing a separate return), and

(III) the taxpayer has made a payment of estimated tax (determined without regard to subsection (g) and section 6402(b)) with respect to any of the preceding 3 taxable years (or a penalty has been previously assessed under this section for a failure to pay estimated tax with respect to any of such 3 preceding taxable years).

This subparagraph shall not apply to any taxable year beginning after December 31, 1996.

(iii) MAY USE PRECEDING YEAR'S TAX FOR FIRST INSTALLMENT.—This subparagraph shall not apply for purposes of determining the amount of the 1st required installment for any taxable year. Any reduction in an installment by reason of the preceding sentence shall be recaptured by increasing the amount of the 1st succeeding required installment (with respect to which the requirements of clause (iv) are not met) by the amount of such reduction.

(iv) ANNUALIZATION EXCEPTION.—This subparagraph shall not apply to any required installment if the individual establishes that the requirements of subclauses (I) and (II) of clause (ii) would not have been satisfied if such subclauses were applied on the basis of—

(I) the annualized amount of the modified adjusted gross income for months in the current year ending before the due date for the installment determined by assuming that all items referred to in clause (i) of subparagraph (D) accrued ratably during the current year, and

(II) the annualized amount of the adjusted gross income for months in the current year ending before the due date for the installment.

Any reduction in an installment under the preceding sentence shall be recaptured by increasing the amount of the 1st succeeding required installment (with respect to which the requirements of the preceding sentence are not met) by the amount of such reduction.

(D) MODIFIED ADJUSTED GROSS INCOME FOR CURRENT YEAR.—For purposes of this paragraph, the term "modified adjusted gross income" means the amount of the adjusted gross income shown on the return for the current year determined with the following modifications:

(i) The qualified pass-thru items shown on the return for the preceding taxable year shall be treated as also shown on the return for the current year (and the actual qualified pass-thru items (if any) for the current year shall be disregarded).

(ii) The amount of any gain from any involuntary conversion (within the meaning of section 1033) which is shown on the return for the current year shall be disregarded.

(iii) The amount of any gain from the sale or exchange of a principal residence (within the meaning of section 1034) which is shown on the return for the current year shall be disregarded.

(E) QUALIFIED PASS-THRU ITEM.—For purposes of this paragraph—

(i) IN GENERAL.—Except as otherwise provided in this subparagraph, the term "qualified pass-thru item" means any item of income, gain, loss, deduction, or credit attributable to an interest in a partnership or S corporation. Such term shall not include any gain or loss from the disposition of an interest in any entity referred to in the preceding sentence.

(ii) 10-PERCENT OWNERS AND GENERAL PARTNERS EXCLUDED.—The term "qualified pass-thru item" shall not include, with respect to any year, any item attributable to—

(I) an interest in an S corporation, if at any time during such year the individual was a 10-percent owner in such corporation, or

(II) an interest in a partnership, if at any time during such year the individual was a 10-percent owner or general partner in such partnership.

(iii) 10-PERCENT OWNER.—The term "10-percent owner" means—

(I) in the case of an S corporation, an individual who owns 10 percent or more (by vote or value) of the stock in such corporation, and

(II) in the case of a partnership, an individual who owns 10 percent or more of the capital interest (or the profits interest) in such partnership.

(F) OTHER DEFINITIONS AND SPECIAL RULES.—For purposes of this paragraph—

(i) CURRENT YEAR.—The term "current year" means the taxable year for which the amount of the installment is being determined.

(ii) SPECIAL RULE.—If no return is filed for the current year, any reference in subparagraph (C) or (D) to an item shown on the return for the current year shall be treated as a reference to the actual amount of such item for such year.

(iii) MARITAL STATUS.—Marital status shall be determined under section 7703.

• **1991, Emergency Unemployment Compensation Act of 1991 (P.L. 102-164)**

P.L. 102-164, § 403(a):

Amended Code Sec. 6654(d)(1) by adding at the end thereof new subparagraphs (C)-(F). **Effective** for tax years beginning after 12-31-91.

• **1986, Tax Reform Act of 1986 (P.L. 99-514)**

P.L. 99-514, § 1541(a):

Amended Code Sec. 6654(d)(1)(B)(i) by striking out "80 percent" each place it appears and inserting in lieu thereof "90 percent". **Effective** for tax years beginning after 12-31-86. For a special rule, see Act Sec. 1543 under Code Sec. 6654(j).

P.L. 99-514, § 1541(b)(1)(A)-(D):

Amended Code Sec. 6654(d)(2)(C)(ii) by striking out "20" and inserting in lieu thereof "22.5", by striking out "40" and inserting in lieu thereof "45", by striking out "60" and inserting in lieu thereof "67.5", and by striking out "80" and inserting in lieu thereof "90" in the table contained therein. **Effective** for tax years beginning after 12-31-86. For a special rule, see Act Sec. 1543 under Code Sec. 6654(j).

[Sec. 6654(e)]

(e) EXCEPTIONS.—

(1) WHERE TAX IS SMALL AMOUNT.—No addition to tax shall be imposed under subsection (a) for any taxable year if the tax shown on the return for such taxable year (or, if no return is filed, the tax), reduced by the credit allowable under section 31, is less than $1,000.

(2) WHERE NO TAX LIABILITY FOR PRECEDING TAXABLE YEAR.—No addition to tax shall be imposed under subsection (a) for any taxable year if—

(A) the preceding taxable year was a taxable year of 12 months,

(B) the individual did not have any liability for tax for the preceding taxable year, and

(C) the individual was a citizen or resident of the United States throughout the preceding taxable year.

(3) WAIVER IN CERTAIN CASES.—

(A) IN GENERAL.—No addition to tax shall be imposed under subsection (a) with respect to any underpayment to the extent the Secretary determines that by reason of casualty, disaster, or other unusual circumstances the imposition of such addition to tax would be against equity and good conscience.

(B) NEWLY RETIRED OR DISABLED INDIVIDUALS.—No addition to tax shall be imposed under subsection (a) with respect to any underpayment if the Secretary determines that—

(i) the taxpayer—

(I) retired after having attained age 62, or

(II) became disabled,

in the taxable year for which estimated payments were required to be made or in the taxable year preceding such taxable year, and

(ii) such underpayment was due to reasonable cause and not to willful neglect.

Amendments

• **1997, Taxpayer Relief Act of 1997 (P.L. 105-34)**

P.L. 105-34, § 1202(a):

Amended Code Sec. 6654(e)(1) by striking "$500" and inserting "$1,000". **Effective** for tax years beginning after 12-31-97.

[Sec. 6654(f)]

(f) TAX COMPUTED AFTER APPLICATION OF CREDITS AGAINST TAX.—For purposes of this section, the term "tax" means—

(1) the tax imposed by chapter 1 (other than any increase in such tax by reason of section 143(m)), plus

(2) the tax imposed by chapter 2, plus

(3) the tax imposed by chapter 2A, minus

ADDITIONS TO TAX

(4) the credits against tax provided by part IV of subchapter A of chapter 1, other than the credit against tax provided by section 31 (relating to tax withheld on wages).

Amendments

• **2018, Tax Technical Corrections Act of 2018 (P.L. 115-141)**

P.L. 115-141, §401(a)(302), Div. U:

Amended Code Sec. 6654(f)(3) by striking "taxes" and inserting "tax". **Effective** 3-23-2018.

• **2010, Health Care and Education Reconciliation Act of 2010 (P.L. 111-152)**

P.L. 111-152, §1402(a)(2)(B)(i)-(ii):

Amended Code Sec. 6654(f) by striking "minus" at the end of paragraph (2) and inserting "plus"; and by redesignating paragraph (3) as paragraph (4) and inserting after paragraph (2) a new paragraph (3). **Effective** for tax years beginning after 12-31-2012.

• **1988, Technical and Miscellaneous Revenue Act of 1988 (P.L. 100-647)**

P.L. 100-647, §4005(g)(5):

Amended Code Sec. 6654(f)(1) by inserting "(other than any increase in such tax by reason of section 143(m))" after "chapter 1". **Effective** for financing provided, and mortgage credit certificates issued, after 12-31-90. However, for an exception, see Act Sec. 4005(h)(3)(B), below.

P.L. 100-647, §4005(h)(3)(B), provides:

(B) EXCEPTION.—The amendments made by subsection (g) shall not apply to financing provided pursuant to a binding contract (entered into before June 23, 1988) with a homebuilder, lender, or mortgagor if the bonds (the proceeds of which are used to provide such financing) are issued—

(i) before June 23, 1988, or

(ii) before August 1, 1988, pursuant to a written application (made before July 1, 1988) for State bond volume authority.

• **1988, Omnibus Trade and Competitiveness Act of 1988 (P.L. 100-418)**

P.L. 100-418, §1941(b)(6)(A):

Amended Code Sec. 6654(f)(3). **Effective** for crude oil removed from the premises on or after 8-23-88. Prior to amendment, Code Sec. 6654(f)(3) read as follows:

(3) the sum of—

(A) the credits against tax allowed by part IV of subchapter A of chapter 1, other than the credit against tax provided by section 31 (relating to tax withheld on wages), plus

(B) to the extent allowed under regulations prescribed by the Secretary, any overpayment of the tax imposed by section 4986 (determined without regard to section 4995(a)(4)(B))

[Sec. 6654(g)]

(g) APPLICATION OF SECTION IN CASE OF TAX WITHHELD ON WAGES.—

(1) IN GENERAL.—For purposes of applying this section, the amount of the credit allowed under section 31 for the taxable year shall be deemed a payment of estimated tax, and an equal part of such amount shall be deemed paid on each due date for such taxable year, unless the taxpayer establishes the dates on which all amounts were actually withheld, in which case the amounts so withheld shall be deemed payments of estimated tax on the dates on which such amounts were actually withheld.

(2) SEPARATE APPLICATION.—The taxpayer may apply paragraph (1) separately with respect to—

(A) wage withholding, and

(B) all other amounts withheld for which credit is allowed under section 31.

[Sec. 6654(h)]

(h) SPECIAL RULE WHERE RETURN FILED ON OR BEFORE JANUARY 31.—If, on or before January 31 of the following taxable year, the taxpayer files a return for the taxable year and pays in full the amount computed on the return as payable, then no addition to tax shall be imposed under subsection (a) with respect to any underpayment of the 4th required installment for the taxable year.

[Sec. 6654(i)]

(i) SPECIAL RULES FOR FARMERS AND FISHERMEN.—For purposes of this section—

(1) IN GENERAL.—If an individual is a farmer or fisherman for any taxable year—

(A) there shall be only 1 required installment for the taxable year,

(B) the due date for such installment shall be January 15 of the following taxable year,

(C) the amount of such installment shall be equal to the required annual payment determined under subsection (d)(1)(B) by substituting "66^{2}/$_{3}$ percent" for "90 percent" and without regard to subparagraph (C) of subsection (d)(1), and

(D) subsection (h) shall be applied—

(i) by substituting "March 1" for "January 31", and

(ii) by treating the required installment described in subparagraph (A) of this paragraph as the 4th required installment.

(2) FARMER OR FISHERMAN DEFINED.—An individual is a farmer or fisherman for any taxable year if—

(A) the individual's gross income from farming or fishing (including oyster farming) for the taxable year is at least 66^{2}/$_{3}$ percent of the total gross income from all sources for the taxable year, or

(B) such individual's gross income from farming or fishing (including oyster farming) shown on the return of the individual for the preceding taxable year is at least 66^{2}/$_{3}$ percent of the total gross income from all sources shown on such return.

Amendments

• **1991, Emergency Unemployment Compensation Act of 1991 (P.L. 102-164)**

P.L. 102-164, §403(b)(1):

Amended Code Sec. 6654(i)(1)(C). **Effective** for tax years beginning after 12-31-91. Prior to amendment, Code Sec. 6654(i)(1)(C) read as follows:

(C) the amount of such installment shall be equal to the required annual payment (determined under subsection (d)(1)(B) by substituting "66^{2}/$_{3}$ percent" for "90 percent", and

• **1986, Tax Reform Act of 1986 (P.L. 99-514)**

P.L. 99-514, §1541(b)(2):

Amended Code Sec. 6654(i)(1)(C) by striking out "80 percent" and inserting in lieu thereof "90 percent". **Effective** for tax years beginning after 12-31-86. For a special rule, see Act Sec. 1543 under Code Sec. 6654(j).

[Sec. 6654(j)]

(j) SPECIAL RULES FOR NONRESIDENT ALIENS.—In the case of a nonresident alien described in section 6072(c):

(1) PAYABLE IN 3 INSTALLMENTS.—There shall be 3 required installments for the taxable year.

(2) TIME FOR PAYMENT OF INSTALLMENTS.—The due dates for required installments under this subsection shall be determined under the following table:

In the case of the following required installments:	The due date is:
1st	June 15
2nd	September 15
3rd	January 15 of the following taxable year

ADDITIONS TO TAX

(3) AMOUNT OF REQUIRED INSTALLMENTS.—

(A) FIRST REQUIRED INSTALLMENT.—In the case of the first required installment, subsection (d) shall be applied by substituting "50 percent" for "25 percent" in subsection (d)(1)(A).

(B) DETERMINATION OF APPLICABLE PERCENTAGE.—The applicable percentage for purposes of subsection (d)(2) shall be determined under the following table:

In the case of the following required installments:	The applicable percentage is:
1st	45
2nd	67.5
3rd	90

Amendments

• **1993, Omnibus Budget Reconciliation Act of 1993 (P.L. 103-66)**

P.L. 103-66, §13214(b)(1):

Amended Code Sec. 6654(j)(3)(A) by striking "and subsection (d)(1)(C)(iii) shall not apply" after "(d)(1)(A)". **Effective** for tax years beginning after 12-31-93.

• **1991, Emergency Unemployment Compensation Act of 1991 (P.L. 102-164)**

P.L. 102-164, §403(b)(2):

Amended Code Sec. 6654(j)(3)(A) by inserting "and subsection (d)(1)(C)(iii) shall not apply" before the period at the end thereof. **Effective** for tax years beginning after 12-31-91.

• **1986, Tax Reform Act of 1986 (P.L. 99-514)**

P.L. 99-514, §1841:

Amended Code Sec. 6654 by redesignating subsections (j), (k), and (l) as subsections (k), (l), and (m), respectively, and by inserting after subsection (i) new subsection (j). **Effective** as if included in the provision of P.L. 98-369 to which it relates.

P.L. 99-514, §1879(a), provides:

(a) WAIVER OF ESTIMATED TAX PENALTIES.—No addition to tax shall be made under section 6654 or 6655 of the Internal Revenue Code of 1954 (relating to failure to pay estimated income tax) for any period before April 16, 1985 (March 16, 1985 in the case of a taxpayer subject to section 6655 of such Code), with respect to any underpayment, to the extent that such underpayment was created or increased by any provision of the Tax Reform Act of 1984.

P.L. 99-514, §1541(b)(3)(A)-(C):

Amended Code Sec. 6654(j)(3) by striking out "40" and inserting in lieu thereof "45", by striking out "60" and inserting in lieu thereof "67.5", and by striking out "80" and inserting in lieu thereof "90" in the table contained in subparagraph (B). [This change was reflected in amendment made by Act Sec. 1841.—CCH.] **Effective** for tax years beginning after 12-31-86.

P.L. 99-514, §1543 provides:

SEC. 1543. WAIVER OF ESTIMATED PENALTIES FOR 1986 UNDERPAYMENTS ATTRIBUTABLE TO THIS ACT.

No addition to tax shall be made under section 6654 or 6655 of the Internal Revenue Code of 1986 (relating to failure to pay estimated tax) for any period before April 16, 1987 (March 16, 1987, in the case of a taxpayer subject to section 6655 of such Code), with respect to any underpayment, to the extent such underpayment was created or increased by any provision of this Act.

[Sec. 6654(k)]

(k) FISCAL YEARS AND SHORT YEARS.—

(1) FISCAL YEARS.—In applying this section to a taxable year beginning on any date other than January 1, there shall be substituted, for the months specified in this section, the months which correspond thereto.

(2) SHORT TAXABLE YEAR.—This section shall be applied to taxable years of less than 12 months in accordance with regulations prescribed by the Secretary.

[Sec. 6654(l)]

(l) ESTATES AND TRUSTS.—

(1) IN GENERAL.—Except as otherwise provided in this subsection, this section shall apply to any estate or trust.

(2) EXCEPTION FOR ESTATES AND CERTAIN TRUSTS.—With respect to any taxable year ending before the date 2 years after the date of the decedent's death, this section shall not apply to—

(A) the estate of such decedent, or

(B) any trust—

(i) all of which was treated (under subpart E of part I of subchapter J of chapter 1) as owned by the decedent, and

(ii) to which the residue of the decedent's estate will pass under his will (or, if no will is admitted to probate, which is the trust primarily responsible for paying debts, taxes, and expenses of administration).

(3) EXCEPTION FOR CHARITABLE TRUSTS AND PRIVATE FOUNDATIONS.—This section shall not apply to any trust which is subject to the tax imposed by section 511 or which is a private foundation.

(4) SPECIAL RULE FOR ANNUALIZATIONS.—In the case of any estate or trust to which this section applies, subsection (d)(2)(B)(i) shall be applied by substituting "ending before the date 1 month before the due date for the installment" for "ending before the due date for the installment".

Amendments

• **1993, Omnibus Budget Reconciliation Act of 1993 (P.L. 103-66)**

P.L. 103-66, §13214(b)(2):

Amended Code Sec. 6654(l)(4) by striking "paragraphs (1)(C)(iv) and (2)(B)(i) of subsection (d)" and inserting "subsection (d)(2)(B)(i)". **Effective** for tax years beginning after 12-31-93.

• **1991, Emergency Unemployment Compensation Act of 1991 (P.L. 102-164)**

P.L. 102-164, §403(b)(3):

Amended Code Sec. 6654(l)(4) by striking "subsection (d)(2)(B)(i)" and inserting "paragraphs (1)(C)(iv) and (2)(B)(i) of subsection (d)". **Effective** for tax years beginning after 12-31-91.

• **1989, Omnibus Budget Reconciliation Act of 1989 (P.L. 101-239)**

P.L. 101-239, §7811(j)(5):

Amended Code Sec. 6654(l)(1) by striking "this subsection shall" and inserting "this section shall". **Effective** as if included in the provision of P.L. 100-647 to which it relates.

P.L. 101-239, §7811(j)(6):

Amended Code Sec. 6654(l)(2)(B)(ii) by inserting "(or, if no will is admitted to probate, which is the trust primarily responsible for paying debts, taxes, and expenses of administration)" before the period at the end thereof. **Effective** as if included in the provision of P.L. 100-647 to which it relates.

• **1988, Technical and Miscellaneous Revenue Act of 1988 (P.L. 100-647)**

P.L. 100-647, §1014(d)(2):

Amended Code Sec. 6654(l). **Effective** as if included in the provision of P.L. 99-514 to which it relates. Prior to amendment, Code Sec. 6654(l) read as follows:

(l) ESTATES AND TRUSTS.—This section shall apply to—

(1) any trust, and

(2) any estate with respect to any taxable year ending 2 or more years after the date of the death of the decedent's death.

• **1986, Tax Reform Act of 1986 (P.L. 99-514)**

P.L. 99-514, §1404(a):

Amended Code Sec. 6654(k)[l]. **Effective** for tax years beginning after 12-31-86. For a special rule, see Act Sec. 1543 under Code Sec. 6654(j). Prior to amendment, subsection (k) read as follows:

(k) ESTATES AND TRUSTS.—This section shall not apply to any estate or trust.

[Sec. 6654(m)]

(m) SPECIAL RULE FOR MEDICARE TAX.—For purposes of this section, the tax imposed under section 3101(b)(2) (to the extent not withheld) shall be treated as a tax imposed under chapter 2.

Internal Revenue Code

ADDITIONS TO TAX

Amendments

- **2010, Health Care and Education Reconciliation Act of 2010 (P.L. 111-152)**

P.L. 111-152, §1402(b)(2):

Amended Code Sec. 6654 by redesignating subsection (m) as subsection (n) and by inserting after subsection (l) a new subsection (m). **Effective** with respect to remuneration received, and tax years beginning after, 12-31-2012.

[Sec. 6654(n)]

(n) REGULATIONS.—The Secretary shall prescribe such regulations as may be necessary to carry out the purposes of this section.

Amendments

- **2010, Health Care and Education Reconciliation Act of 2010 (P.L. 111-152)**

P.L. 111-152, §1402(b)(2):

Amended Code Sec. 6654 by redesignating subsection (m) as subsection (n). **Effective** with respect to remuneration received, and tax years beginning after, 12-31-2012.

- **1986, Tax Reform Act of 1986 (P.L. 99-514)**

P.L. 99-514, §1841:

Amended Code Sec. 6654 by redesignating subsections (j), (k), and (l) as subsections (k), (l), and (m), respectively, and by inserting after subsection (i) new subsection (j). **Effective** as if included in the provision of P.L. 98-369 to which it relates.

- **1984, Deficit Reduction Act of 1984 (P.L. 98-369)**

P.L. 98-369, §413, provides:

SEC. 413. CREDITING OF INCOME TAX OVERPAYMENT AGAINST ESTIMATED TAX LIABILITY.

The application of the Internal Revenue Code of 1954 with respect to the crediting of a prior year overpayment of income tax against the estimated tax shall be determined—

(1) without regard to Revenue Ruling 83-111 (and without regard to any other regulation, ruling, or decision reaching the same result as, or a result similar to, the result set forth in such Revenue Ruling); and

(2) with full regard to the rules (including Revenue Ruling 77-475) before Revenue Ruling 83-111.

P.L. 98-369, §411:

Amended Code Sec. 6654. **Effective** for tax years beginning after 12-31-84. Prior to amendment, Code Sec. 6654 read as follows:

SEC. 6654. FAILURE BY INDIVIDUAL TO PAY ESTIMATED TAX.

[Sec. 6654(a)]

(a) ADDITION TO THE TAX.—In the case of any underpayment of estimated tax by an individual, except as provided in subsection (d), there shall be added to the tax under chapter 1 and the tax under chapter 2 for the taxable year an amount determined at an annual rate established under section 6621 upon the amount of the underpayment (determined under subsection (b) for the period of the underpayment (determined under subsection (c)).

Amendments

- **1977, Tax Reduction and Simplification Act of 1977 (P.L. 95-30)**

P.L. 95-30, §303, provides:

SEC. 303. UNDERPAYMENTS OF ESTIMATED TAX.

No addition to the tax shall be made under section 6654 or 6655 of the Internal Revenue Code of 1954 (relating to failure to pay estimated income tax) for any period before April 16, 1977 (March 16, 1977, in the case of a taxpayer subject to section 6655), with respect to any underpayment, to the extent that such underpayment was created or increased by any provision of the Tax Reform Act of 1976.

P.L. 95-30, §305, provides:

SEC. 305. INTEREST ON UNDERPAYMENTS OF TAX.

No interest shall be payable for any period before April 16, 1977 (March 16, 1977, in the case of a corporation), on any underpayment of a tax imposed by the Internal Revenue Code of 1954, to the extent that such underpayment was credited or increased by any provision of the Tax Reform Act of 1976.

- **1975 (P.L. 93-625)**

P.L. 93-625, §7(c):

Amended Code Sec. 6654(a) by substituting "an annual rate established under section 6621" for "the rate of 6 percent per annum". **Effective** 7-1-75, for amounts outstanding on such date or arising thereafter.

- **1971, Revenue Act of 1971 (P.L. 92-178)**

P.L. 92-178, §207, provides:

"(a) Waiver of Penalty.—Notwithstanding any other provision of law, section 6654(a) of the Internal Revenue Code of 1954 (relating to addition to tax for failure by individual to pay estimated income tax) shall not apply to any taxable year beginning after December 31, 1970, and ending before January 1, 1972—

"(1) if gross income for the taxable year does not exceed $10,000 in the case of—

"(A) a single individual other than a head of a household (as defined in section 9(b) of such Code) or a surviving spouse (as defined in section 2(a) of such Code); or

"(B) a married individual not entitled under section 6013 of such Code to file a joint return for the taxable year; or

"(2) if gross income for the taxable year does not exceed $20,000 in the case of—

"(A) a head of a household (as defined in section 2(b) of such Code); or

"(B) a surviving spouse (as defined in section 2(a) of such Code); or

"(3) in the case of a married individual entitled under section 6013 of such Code to file a joint return for the taxable year, if the aggregate gross income of such individual and his spouse for the taxable year does not exceed $20,000.

"(b) Limitation.—Subsection (a) shall not apply if the taxpayer has income from sources other than wages (as defined in section 3401(a) of such Code) in excess of $200 for the taxable year ($400 in the case of a husband and wife entitled to file a joint return under section 6013 of such Code for the taxable year)."

- **1966, Tax Adjustment Act of 1966 (P.L. 89-368)**

P.L. 89-368, §102(b)(1):

Amended Code Sec. 6654(a) by inserting "and the tax under chapter 2" immediately after "chapter 1". **Effective** 1-1-67.

[Sec. 6654(b)]

(b) AMOUNT OF UNDERPAYMENT.—For purposes of subsection (a), the amount of the underpayment shall be the excess of—

(1) The amount of the installment which would be required to be paid if the estimated tax were equal to 80 percent ($66^2/_3$ percent in the case of individuals referred to in section 6073(b), relating to income from farming or fishing) of the tax shown on the return for the taxable year or, if no return was filed, 80 percent ($66^2/_3$ percent in the case of individuals referred to in section 6073(b), relating to income from farming or fishing) of the tax for such year, over

(2) The amount, if any, of the installment paid on or before the last date prescribed for such payment.

Amendments

- **1966, Tax Adjustment Act of 1966 (P.L. 89-368)**

P.L. 89-368, §103(a):

Amended Code Sec. 6654(b) by substituting "80 percent" for "70 percent" each place it appears. **Effective** 1-1-67.

- **1962 (P.L. 87-682)**

P.L. 87-682, §1:

Amended Sec. 6654(b)(1) by inserting "or fishing" after "from farming". **Effective** with respect to tax years beginning after 1962.

[Sec. 6654(c)]

(c) PERIOD OF UNDERPAYMENT.—The period of the underpayment shall run from the date the installment was required to be paid to whichever of the following dates is the earlier—

(1) The 15th day of the fourth month following the close of the taxable year.

(2) With respect to any portion of the underpayment, the date on which such portion is paid.

For purposes of this paragraph, a payment of estimated tax on any installment date shall be considered a payment of any previous underpayment only to the extent such payment exceeds the amount of the installment determined under subsection (b)(1) for such installment date.

[Sec. 6654(d)]

(d) EXCEPTION.—Notwithstanding the provisions of the preceding subsections, the addition to the tax with respect to any underpayment of any installment shall not be imposed if the total amount of all payments of estimated tax made on or before the last date prescribed for the payment of such installment equals or exceeds the amount which would have been required to be paid on or before such date if the estimated tax were whichever of the following is the least—

(1) The tax shown on the return of the individual for the preceding taxable year, if a return showing a liability for tax was filed by the individual for the preceding taxable year and such preceding year was a taxable year of 12 months.

(2) An amount equal to 80 percent ($66^2/_3$ percent in the case of individuals referred to in section 6073(b), relating to income from farming or fishing) of the tax for the taxable year computed by placing on an annualized basis the taxable income for the months in the taxable year ending before the month in which the installment is required to be paid and by taking into account the adjusted self-employment income (if the net earnings from self-employment (as defined in section 1402(a)) for the taxable year equal or exceed $400). For purposes of this paragraph—

(A) The taxable income shall be placed in an annualized basis under regulations prescribed by the Secretary.

(B) The term "adjusted self-employment income" means—

(i) the net earnings from self-employment (as defined in section 1402(a)) for the months in the taxable year ending before the month in which the installment is required to be paid, but not more than

(ii) the excess of (I) an amount equal to the contribution and benefit base (as determined under section 230 of the Social Security Act) which is effective for the calendar year in which the taxable year begins, over (II) the amount determined by placing the wages (within the meaning of section 1402(b)) for the months in the taxable year ending before the month in which the installment is required to be paid on an annualized basis in a manner consistent with clauses (i) and (ii) of subparagraph (A).

ADDITIONS TO TAX

(3) An amount equal to 90 percent of the tax computed, at the rates applicable to the taxable year, on the basis of the actual taxable income and the actual self-employment income for the months in the taxable year ending before the month in which the installment is required to be paid as if such months constituted the taxable year.

(4) An amount equal to the tax computed, at the rates applicable to the taxable year, on the basis of the taxpayer's status with respect to personal exemptions under section 151 for the taxable year, but otherwise on the basis of the facts shown on his return for, and the law applicable to, the preceding taxable year.

Amendments

• **1977, Tax Reduction and Simplification Act of 1977 (P.L. 95-30)**

P.L. 95-30, §102(b)(16):

Amended subparagraph (A) of Code Sec. 6654(d)(2). **Effective** for tax years beginning after 12-31-76. Prior to amendment, subparagraph (A) of Code Sec. 6654(d)(2) read as follows:

"(A) The taxable income shall be placed on an annualized basis by—

"(i) multiplying by 12 (or, in the case of a taxable year of less than 12 months, the number of months in the taxable year) the taxable income (computed without deduction of personal exemptions) for the months in the taxable year ending before the month in which the installment is required to be paid,

"(ii) dividing the resulting amount by the number of months in the taxable year ending before the month in which such installment date falls, and

"(iii) deducting from such amount the deductions for personal exemptions allowable for the taxable year (such personal exemptions being determined as of the last date prescribed for payment of the installment)."

• **1973 (P.L. 93-233)**

P.L. 93-233, §5(b)(7):

Amended Code Sec. 6654(d)(2)(B)(ii) by substituting "$13,200" for "$10,800." **Effective** with respect to tax years beginning after 1973.

• **1973 (P.L. 93-66)**

P.L. 93-66, §203(b)(7):

Amended Code Sec. 6654(d)(2)(B)(ii) by substituting "$12,600" for "$12,000." (But see P.L. 92-336, below.)

• **1972 (P.L. 92-336)**

P.L. 92-336, §203(b)(7):

Amended Code Sec. 6654(d)(2)(B)(ii) by striking out "$9,000" and inserting in lieu thereof "$10,800". **Effective** for tax years beginning after 1972. **Effective** for tax years beginning after 1973, the $10,800 figure is changed to $13,200; and **effective** for tax years beginning after 1974, the $13,200 figure is to be stricken and replaced by "the excess of (I) an amount equal to the contribution and benefit base (as determined under section 230 of the Social Security Act) which is effective for the calendar year in which the taxable year begins, over (II) the amount".

• **1971 (P.L. 92-5)**

P.L. 92-5, §203(b)(7):

Amended Sec.6654(d)(2)(B)(ii) by changing "$6,600" to "$9,000". **Effective** for tax years beginning after 1971.

• **1966, Tax Adjustment Act of 1966 (P.L. 89-368)**

P.L. 89-368, §102(b)(2):

Amended Code Sec. 6654(d). Prior to amendment, Sec. 6654(d) read as follows:

"(d) Exception.—Notwithstanding the provisions of the preceding subsections, the addition to the tax with respect to any underpayment of any installment shall not be imposed if the total amount of all payments of estimated tax made on or before the last date prescribed for the payment of such installment equals or exceeds whichever of the following is the lesser—

"(1) The amount which would have been required to be paid on or before such date if the estimated tax were whichever of the following is the least—

"(A) The tax shown on the return of the individual for the preceding taxable year, if a return showing a liability for tax was filed by the individual for the preceding taxable year and such preceding year was a taxable year of 12 months, or

"(B) An amount equal to the tax computed, at the rates applicable to the taxable year, on the basis of the taxpayer's status with respect to personal exemptions under section 151 for the taxable year, but otherwise on the basis of the facts shown on his return for, and the law applicable to, the preceding taxable year, or

"(C) An amount to 70 percent (66⅔ percent in the case of individuals referred to in section 6073(b), relating to income from farming or fishing) of the tax for the taxable year computed by placing on an annualized basis the taxable income for the months in the taxable year ending before the month in which the installment is required to be paid. For purposes of this subparagraph, the taxable income shall be placed on an annualized basis by—

"(1) multiplying by 12 (or, in the case of a taxable year of less than 12 months, the number of months in the taxable year) the taxable income (computed without deduction of personal exemptions) for the months in the taxable year ending before the month in which the installment is required to be paid,

"(ii) dividing the resulting amount by the number of months in the taxable year ending before the month in which such installment date falls, and

"(iii) deducting from such amount the deductions for personal exemptions allowable for the taxable year (such personal exemptions being determined as of the last date prescribed for payment of the installment); or

"(2) An amount equal to 90 percent of the tax computed, at the rates applicable to the taxable year, on the basis of the actual taxable income for the months in the taxable year ending before the month in which the installment is required to be paid."

• **1966, Tax Adjustment Act of 1966 (P.L. 89-368)**

P.L. 89-368, §103(a):

Amended Code Sec. 6654(d) by substituting "80 percent" for "70 percent". **Effective** 1-1-67.

• **1962 (P.L. 87-682)**

P.L. 87-682, §1:

Amended Sec. 6654(d)(1)(C) by inserting "or fishing" after "from farming." **Effective** with respect to tax years beginning after 1962.

[Sec. 6654(e)]

Amendments

• **1984, Deficit Reduction Act of 1984 (P.L. 98-369)**

P.L. 98-369, §411:

Amended Code Sec. 6654. **Effective** with respect to tax years beginning after 1984. Code Sec. 6654(e)(3) applies with respect to underpayments for tax years beginning in 1984. Prior to amendment, Code Sec. 6654(e) read as follows:

(e) APPLICATION OF SECTION IN CASE OF TAX WITHHELD ON WAGES.—For purposes of applying this section—

(1) The estimated tax shall be computed without any reduction for the amount which the individual estimates as his credit under section 31 (relating to tax withheld at source on wages), and

(2) The amount of the credit allowed under section 31 for the taxable year shall be deemed a payment of estimated tax, and an equal part of such amount shall be deemed paid on each installment date (determined under section 6153) for such taxable year, unless the taxpayer establishes the dates on which all amounts were actually withheld, in which case the amounts so withheld shall be deemed payments of estimated tax on the dates on which such amounts were actually withheld.

• **1983, Interest and Dividend Tax Compliance Act of 1983 (P.L. 98-67)**

P.L. 98-67, §102(a):

Repealed the amendment made to Code Sec. 6654(e)(1) by P.L. 97-248 (see below). **Effective** as of the close of 6-30-83, as though such amendment had not been enacted.

P.L. 98-67, §102(d), provides:

(d) ESTIMATED TAX PAYMENTS.—For purposes of determining the amount of any addition to tax under section 6654 of the Internal Revenue Code of 1954 with respect to any installment required to be paid before July 1, 1983, the amount of the credit allowed by section 31 of such Code for any taxable year which includes any portion of the period beginning July 1, 1983, and ending December 31, 1983, shall be increased by an amount equal to 10 percent of the aggregate amount of payments—

(1) which are received during the portion of such taxable year after June 30, 1983, and before January 1, 1984, and

(2) which (but for the repeal made by subsection (a)) would have been subject to withholding under subchapter B of chapter 24 of such Code (determined without regard to any exemption described in section 3452 of such subchapter B).

• **1982, Tax Equity and Fiscal Responsibility Act of 1982 (P.L. 97-248)**

P.L. 97-248, §307(a)(14):

Amended Code Sec. 6654(e) by inserting ", interest, dividends, and patronage dividends" after "tax withheld at source on wages". **Effective** for payments of interest, dividends, and patronage dividends paid or credited after 6-30-83.

[Sec. 6654(f)]

(f) EXCEPTION WHERE TAX IS SMALL AMOUNT.—

(1) IN GENERAL.—No addition to tax shall be imposed under subsection (a) for any taxable year if the tax shown on the return for such taxable year (or, if no return is filed, the tax), reduced by the credit allowable under section 31, is less than the amount determined under the following table:

In the case of taxable years beginning in:	The amount is:
1981	$100
1982	200
1983	300
1984	400
1985 and thereafter	500

(2) SPECIAL RULE.—For purposes of subsection (b), the amount of any installment required to be paid shall be determined without regard to subsection (b) of section 6015.

Amendments

• **1983, Technical Corrections Act of 1982 (P.L. 97-448)**

P.L. 97-448, §107(c)(1):

Amended Code Sec. 6654(f)(1) by striking out "is less than" and inserting in lieu thereof ", reduced by the credit allowable under section 31, is less than". **Effective** as if included in the provision of P.L. 97-34 to which it relates.

• **1981, Economic Recovery Tax Act of 1981 (P.L. 97-34)**

P.L. 97-34, §725(b):

Added Code Sec. 6654(f). **Effective** for estimated tax for tax years beginning after 12-31-80.

Internal Revenue Code   Sec. 6654(n)

ADDITIONS TO TAX

[Sec. 6654(g)]

(g) TAX COMPUTED AFTER APPLICATION OF CREDITS AGAINST TAX.—For purposes of subsections (b), (d), (f), and (h) the term "tax" means—

(1) the tax imposed by this chapter 1 (other than by section 55), plus

(2) the tax imposed by chapter 2, minus

(3) the sum of—

(A) the credits against tax allowed by part IV of subchapter A of chapter 1, other than the credit against tax provided by section 31 (relating to tax withheld on wages), plus

(B) to the extent allowed under regulations prescribed by the Secretary, any amount which is treated under section 6429 or 6430 as an overpayment of the tax imposed by section 4986.

Amendments

• **1983, Interest and Dividend Tax Compliance Act of 1983 (P.L. 98-67)**

P.L. 98-67, § 102(a):

Repealed the amendment made to Code Sec. 6654(g)(3)(A) by P.L. 97-248, § 307(a)(14) (see below). **Effective** as of the close of 6-30-83, as though such amendment had not been enacted.

• **1983, Technical Corrections Act of 1982 (P.L. 97-448)**

P.L. 97-448, § 106(a)(4)(C):

Amended Code Sec. 6654(g)(3)(B) by inserting "or 6430" after "section 6429". **Effective** 1-1-82. See, however, the amendment note for Act Sec. 201(j)(3) below.

P.L. 97-448, § 201(j)(3):

Amended Code Sec. 6654(g)(3)(B). **Effective** as if included in the provision of P.L. 96-223 to which it relates. (See Code Sec. 4986.) Prior to amendment, Code Sec. 6654(g)(3)(B) read as follows:

"(B) to the extent allowed under regulations prescribed by theSecretary, any amount which is treated under section 6429 as an overpayment of the tax imposed by section 4986."

See, however, the amendment note for Act Sec. 106(a)(4)(C), above.

P.L. 97-448, § 306(a)(1)(A):

Amended P.L. 97-248, § 201 by redesignating the second subsection (c) as subsection (d).

• **1982, Tax Equity and Fiscal Responsibility Act of 1982 (P.L. 97-248)**

P.L. 97-248, § 201(d)(7):

Amended Code Sec. 6654(g)(1) by striking out "or 56" after "section 55". **Effective** 1-1-83.

P.L. 97-248, § 307(a)(14):

Amended Code Sec. 6654(g)(3)(A) by inserting ", interest, dividends, and patronage dividends" after "tax withheld at source on wages". **Effective** for payments of interest, dividends and patronage, dividends paid or credited after 6-30-83.

P.L. 97-248, § 328(a)(2):

Amended Code Sec. 6654(g) by striking out "and (f)" and inserting "(f), and (h)". **Effective** 1-1-83.

• **1981, Economic Recovery Tax Act of 1981 (P.L. 97-34)**

P.L. 97-34, § 601(a)(6)(A):

Amended Code Sec. 6654(f)(3). **Effective** 1-1-80. Prior to amendments, Code Sec. 6654(f)(3) read as follows:

(3) the credits against tax allowed by part IV of subchapter A of chapter 1, other than the credit against tax provided by section 31 (relating to tax withheld on wages).

P.L. 97-34, § 725(b):

Redesignated Code Sec. 6654(f) as Code Sec. 6654(g). **Effective** 1-1-81.

P.L. 97-34, § 725(c)(5):

Amended Code Sec. 6654(g), as redesignated by P.L. 97-34, by striking out "subsections (b) and (d)" and inserting "subsections (b), (d), and (f)". **Effective** 1-1-81.

• **1978, Revenue Act of 1978 (P.L. 95-600)**

P.L. 95-600, § 421(e)(9):

Amended Code Sec. 6654(f)(1) by changing "section 56" to "section 55 or 56". **Effective** for tax years beginning after 12-31-78.

• **1969, Tax Reform Act of 1969 (P.L. 91-172)**

P.L. 91-172, § 301(b)(13):

Amended Code Sec. 6654(f)(1) by adding the phrase "(other than by section 56)". **Effective** 1-1-70.

• **1966, Tax Adjustment Act of 1966 (P.L. 89-368)**

P.L. 89-368, § 102(c)(3):

Amended Code Sec. 6654(f). **Effective** 1-1-67. Prior to amendment, Code Sec. 6654(f) read as follows:

"(f) Tax Computed After Application of Credits Against Tax.—For purposes of subsections (b) and (d), the term 'tax' means the tax imposed by chapter 1 reduced by the credits against tax allowed by part IV of subchapter A of chapter 1, other than the credit against tax provided by section 31 (relating to tax withheld on wages)."

[Sec. 6654(h)]

(h) EXCEPTION WHERE NO TAX LIABILITY FOR PRECEDING TAXABLE YEAR.—No addition to tax shall be imposed under subsection (a) for any taxable year if—

(1) the individual did not have any liability for tax for the preceding taxable year,

(2) the preceding taxable year was a taxable year of 12 months, and

(3) the individual was a citizen or resident of the United States throughout the preceding taxable year.

Amendments

• **1982, Tax Equity and Fiscal Responsibility Act of 1982 (P.L. 97-248)**

P.L. 97-248, § 328(a)(1):

Added Code Sec. 6654(h). **Effective** for tax years beginning after 12-31-82.

[Sec. 6654(i)]

(i) SHORT TAXABLE YEAR.—The application of this section to taxable years of less than 12 months shall be in accordance with regulations prescribed by the Secretary.

Amendments

• **1982, Tax Equity and Fiscal Responsibility Act of 1982 (P.L. 97-248)**

P.L. 97-248, § 328(a)(1):

Redesignated subsection (h) as subsection (i). **Effective** for tax years beginning after 12-31-82.

• **1981, Economic Recovery Tax Act of 1981 (P.L. 97-34)**

P.L. 97-34, § 725(b):

Redesignated Code Sec. 6654(g) as Code Sec. 6654(h). **Effective** 1-1-81.

• **1976, Tax Reform Act of 1976 (P.L. 94-455)**

P.L. 94-455, § 1906(a)(35):

Repealed Code Sec. 6654(h). **Effective** 2-2-77. Prior to repeal, Code Sec. 6654(h) read as follows:

(h) APPLICABILITY.—This section shall apply only with respect to taxable years beginning after December 31, 1954; and section 294(d) of the Internal Revenue Code of 1939 shall continue in force with respect to taxable years beginning before January 1, 1955.

P.L. 94-455, § 1906(b)(13)(A):

Amended 1954 Code by substituting "Secretary" for "Secretary or his delegate" each place it appeared. **Effective** 2-1-77.

[Sec. 6655]

SEC. 6655. FAILURE BY CORPORATION TO PAY ESTIMATED INCOME TAX.

[Sec. 6655(a)]

(a) ADDITION TO TAX.—Except as otherwise provided in this section, in the case of any underpayment of estimated tax by a corporation, there shall be added to the tax under chapter 1 for the taxable year an amount determined by applying—

(1) the underpayment rate established under section 6621,

(2) to the amount of the underpayment,

(3) for the period of the underpayment.

[Sec. 6655(b)]

(b) AMOUNT OF UNDERPAYMENT; PERIOD OF UNDERPAYMENT.—For purposes of subsection (a)—

(1) AMOUNT.—The amount of the underpayment shall be the excess of

(A) the required installment, over

(B) the amount (if any) of the installment paid on or before the due date for the installment.

(2) PERIOD OF UNDERPAYMENT.—The period of the underpayment shall run from the due date for the installment to whichever of the following dates is the earlier—

(A) the 15th day of the 4th month following the close of the taxable year, or

(B) with respect to any portion of the underpayment, the date on which such portion is paid.

(3) ORDER OF CREDITING PAYMENTS.—For purposes of paragraph (2)(B), a payment of estimated tax shall be credited against unpaid required installments in the order in which such installments are required to be paid.

ADDITIONS TO TAX

Amendments

• **2015, Surface Transportation and Veterans Health Care Choice Improvement Act of 2015 (P.L. 114-41)**

P.L. 114-41, §2006(a)(2)(F):

Amended Code Sec. 6655(b)(2)(A) by striking "3rd month" and inserting "4th month". **Effective** generally for returns for tax years beginning after 12-31-2015. For an exception, see Act Sec. 2006(a)(3)(B), below.

P.L. 114-41, §2006(a)(3)(B), provides:

(B) SPECIAL RULE FOR C CORPORATIONS WITH FISCAL YEARS ENDING ON JUNE 30.—In the case of any C corporation with a taxable year ending on June 30, the amendments made by this subsection shall apply to returns for taxable years beginning after December 31, 2025.

[Sec. 6655(c)]

(c) NUMBER OF REQUIRED INSTALLMENTS; DUE DATES.—For purposes of this section—

(1) PAYABLE IN 4 INSTALLMENTS.—There shall be 4 required installments for each taxable year.

(2) TIME FOR PAYMENT OF INSTALLMENTS.—

In the case of the following required installments:	The due date is:
1st	April 15
2nd	June 15
3rd	September 15
4th	December 15.

[Sec. 6655(d)]

(d) AMOUNT OF REQUIRED INSTALLMENTS.—For purposes of this section—

(1) AMOUNT.—

(A) IN GENERAL.—Except as otherwise provided in this section, the amount of any required installment shall be 25 percent of the required annual payment.

(B) REQUIRED ANNUAL PAYMENT.—Except as otherwise provided in this subsection, the term "required annual payment" means the lesser of—

(i) 100 percent of the tax shown on the return for the taxable year (or, if no return is filed, 100 percent of the tax for such year), or

(ii) 100 percent of the tax shown on the return of the corporation for the preceding taxable year.

Clause (ii) shall not apply if the preceding taxable year was not a taxable year of 12 months, or the corporation did not file a return for such preceding taxable year showing a liability for tax.

(2) LARGE CORPORATIONS REQUIRED TO PAY 100 PERCENT OF CURRENT YEAR TAX.—

(A) IN GENERAL.—Except as provided in subparagraph (B), clause (ii) of paragraph (1)(B) shall not apply in the case of a large corporation.

(B) MAY USE LAST YEAR'S TAX FOR 1ST INSTALLMENT.—Subparagraph (A) shall not apply for purposes of determining the amount of the 1st required installment for any taxable year. Any reduction in such 1st installment by reason of the preceding sentence shall be recaptured by increasing the amount of the next required installment determined under paragraph (1) by the amount of such reduction.

Amendments

• **2015, Trade Preferences Extension Act of 2015 (P.L. 114-27)**

P.L. 114-27, §803 [stricken by P.L. 115-123, §41118, Div. D], provides:

SEC. 803. TIME FOR PAYMENT OF CORPORATE ESTIMATED TAXES.

Notwithstanding section 6655 of the Internal Revenue Code of 1986, in the case of a corporation with assets of not less than $1,000,000,000 (determined as of the end of the preceding taxable year)—

(1) the amount of any required installment of corporate estimated tax which is otherwise due in July, August, or September of 2020 shall be increased by 8 percent of such amount (determined without regard to any increase in such amount not contained in such Code); and

(2) the amount of the next required installment after an installment referred to in paragraph (1) shall be appropriately reduced to reflect the amount of the increase by reason of such paragraph.

• **2012, (P.L. 112-163)**

P.L. 112-163, §4, provides:

SEC. 4. TIME FOR PAYMENT OF CORPORATE ESTIMATED TAXES.

Notwithstanding section 6655 of the Internal Revenue Code of 1986—

(1) in the case of a corporation with assets of not less than $1,000,000,000 (determined as of the end of the preceding taxable year), the amount of any required installment of corporate estimated tax which is otherwise due in July, August, or September of 2017 shall be 100.25 percent of such amount; and

(2) the amount of the next required installment after an installment referred to in paragraph (1) shall be appropriately reduced to reflect the amount of the increase by reason of such paragraph.

• **2012, Middle Class Tax Relief and Job Creation Act of 2012 (P.L. 112-96)**

P.L. 112-96, §7001 (as amended by P.L. 113-295, §203(a), Division A), provides:

SEC. 7001. REPEAL OF CERTAIN SHIFTS IN THE TIMING OF CORPORATE ESTIMATED TAX PAYMENTS.

The following provisions of law (and any modification of any such provision which is contained in any other provision of law) shall not apply with respect to any installment of corporate estimated tax:

(1) Section 202(b) of the Corporate Estimated Tax Shift Act of 2009.

(2) Section 561 of the Hiring Incentives to Restore Employment Act.

(3) Section 505 of the United States-Korea Free Trade Agreement Implementation Act.

(4) Section 603 of the United States-Colombia Trade Promotion Agreement Implementation Act.

(5) Section 502 of the United States-Panama Trade Promotion Agreement Implementation Act.

• **2011, United States–Panama Trade Promotion Agreement Implementation Act (P.L. 112-43)**

P.L. 112-43, §502 [but see P.L. 112-96, §7001, above], provides:

SEC. 502. TIME FOR PAYMENT OF CORPORATE ESTIMATED TAXES.

Notwithstanding section 6655 of the Internal Revenue Code of 1986, in the case of a corporation with assets of not less than $1,000,000,000 (determined as of the end of the preceding taxable year)—

(1) the amount of any required installment of corporate estimated tax which is otherwise due in July, August, or September of 2012 shall be increased by 0.25 percent of such amount (determined without regard to any increase in such amount not contained in such Code);

(2) the amount of any required installment of corporate estimated tax which is otherwise due in July, August, or September of 2016 shall be increased by 0.25 percent of such amount (determined without regard to any increase in such amount not contained in such Code); and

(3) the amount of the next required installment after an installment referred to in paragraph (1) or (2) shall be appropriately reduced to reflect the amount of the increase by reason of such paragraph.

• **2011, United States–Colombia Trade Promotion Agreement Implementation Act (P.L. 112-42)**

P.L. 112-42, §603 [but see P.L. 112-96, §7001, above], provides:

SEC. 603. TIME FOR PAYMENT OF CORPORATE ESTIMATED TAXES.

Notwithstanding section 6655 of the Internal Revenue Code of 1986, in the case of a corporation with assets of not less than $1,000,000,000 (determined as of the end of the preceding taxable year)—

(1) the amount of any required installment of corporate estimated tax which is otherwise due in July, August, or September of 2016 shall be increased by 0.50 percent of such amount (determined without regard to any increase in such amount not contained in such Code); and

(2) the amount of the next required installment after an installment referred to in paragraph (1) shall be appropriately reduced to reflect the amount of the increase by reason of such paragraph.

• **2011, United States–Korea Free Trade Agreement Implementation Act (P.L. 112-41)**

P.L. 112-41, §505 [but see P.L. 112-96, §7001, above], provides:

SEC. 505. TIME FOR PAYMENT OF CORPORATE ESTIMATED TAXES.

ADDITIONS TO TAX

Notwithstanding section 6655 of the Internal Revenue Code of 1986, in the case of a corporation with assets of not less than $1,000,000,000 (determined as of the end of the preceding taxable year)—

(1) the amount of any required installment of corporate estimated tax which is otherwise due in July, August, or September of 2012 shall be increased by 0.25 percent of such amount (determined without regard to any increase in such amount not contained in such Code);

(2) the amount of any required installment of corporate estimated tax which is otherwise due in July, August, or September of 2016 shall be increased by 2.75 percent of such amount (determined without regard to any increase in such amount not contained in such Code); and

(3) the amount of the next required installment after an installment referred to in paragraph (1) or (2) shall be appropriately reduced to reflect the amount of the increase by reason of such paragraph.

- **2010, Hiring Incentives to Restore Employment Act (P.L. 111-147)**

P.L. 111-147, §561 (as amended by P.L. 111-171, §12(b), P.L. 111-210, §3, P.L. 111-227, §4002, P.L. 111-237, §4(a), P.L. 111-240, §2131, and P.L. 111-344, §302) [but see P.L. 112-96, §7001, above], provides:

SEC. 561. TIME FOR PAYMENT OF CORPORATE ESTIMATED TAXES.

Notwithstanding section 6655 of the Internal Revenue Code of 1986, in the case of a corporation with assets of not less than $1,000,000,000 (determined as of the end of the preceding taxable year)—

(1) the percentage under paragraph (1) of section 202(b) of the Corporate Estimated Tax Shift Act of 2009 in effect on the date of the enactment of this Act is increased by 23 percentage points,

(2) the amount of any required installment of corporate estimated tax which is otherwise due in July, August, or September of 2015 shall be 163.75 percent of such amount,

(3) the amount of any required installment of corporate estimated tax which is otherwise due in July, August, or September of 2019 shall be 106.5 percent of such amount, and

(4) the amount of the next required installment after an installment referred to in paragraph (2) or (3) shall be appropriately reduced to reflect the amount of the increase by reason of such paragraph.

- **2009, Corporate Estimated Tax Shift Act of 2009 (P.L. 111-42)**

P.L. 111-42, §202 (as amended by P.L. 111-92, §18, P.L. 111-124, §4, P.L. 111-152, §1410, and P.L. 111-171, §12(a)) [but see P.L. 111-147, §561, and P.L. 112-96, §7001, above], provides:

SEC. 202. TIME FOR PAYMENT OF CORPORATE ESTIMATED TAXES.

(a) REPEAL OF ADJUSTMENTS FOR 2010, 2011, AND 2013.—Section 401 of the Tax Increase Prevention and Reconciliation Act of 2005 (and any modification of such section contained in any other provision of law) shall not apply with respect to any installment of corporate estimated tax which (without regard to such section) would otherwise be due after December 31, 2009.

(b) ADJUSTMENT FOR 2014.—Notwithstanding section 6655 of the Internal Revenue Code of 1986—

(1) in the case of a corporation with assets of not less than $1,000,000,000 (determined as of the end of the preceding taxable year), the amount of any required installment of corporate estimated tax which is otherwise due in July, August, or September of 2014 shall be 151.25 percent of such amount; and

(2) the amount of the next required installment after an installment referred to in paragraph (1) shall be appropriately reduced to reflect the amount of the increase by reason of such paragraph.

- **2006, Tax Increase Prevention and Reconciliation Act of 2005 (P.L. 109-222)**

P.L. 109-222, §401 (as amended by P.L. 110-28, §8248, P.L. 110-42, §4, P.L. 110-52, §3, P.L. 110-89, §2(a), P.L. 110-138, §602, P.L. 110-142, §10, P.L. 110-191, §4, P.L. 110-246, §15202, P.L. 110-289, §3094, P.L. 110-436, §6, and P.L. 111-3, §704), provides [but see P.L. 111-42, §202, above]:

SEC. 401. TIME FOR PAYMENT OF CORPORATE ESTIMATED TAXES.

Notwithstanding section 6655 of the Internal Revenue Code of 1986—

(1) in the case of a corporation with assets of not less than $1,000,000,000 (determined as of the end of the preceding taxable year)—

(A) the amount of any required installment of corporate estimated tax which is otherwise due in July, August, or September of 2006 shall be 105 percent of such amount,

(B) the amount of any required installment of corporate estimated tax which is otherwise due in July, August, or September of 2012 shall be 100 percent of such amount,

(C) the amount of any required installment of corporate estimated tax which is otherwise due in July, August, or September of 2013 shall be 120.25 percent of such amount, and

(D) the amount of the next required installment after an installment referred to in subparagraph (A), (B), or (C) shall be appropriately reduced to reflect the amount of the increase by reason of such subparagraph,

(2) 20.5 percent of the amount of any required installment of corporate estimated tax which is otherwise due in September 2010 shall not be due until October 1, 2010, and

(3) 27.5 percent of the amount of any required installment of corporate estimated tax which is otherwise due in September 2011 shall not be due until October 1, 2011.

- **2003, Jobs and Growth Tax Relief Reconciliation Act of 2003 (P.L. 108-27)**

P.L. 108-27, §501, provides:

SEC. 501. TIME FOR PAYMENT OF CORPORATE ESTIMATED TAXES.

Notwithstanding section 6655 of the Internal Revenue Code of 1986, 25 percent of the amount of any required installment of corporate estimated tax which is otherwise due in September 2003 shall not be due until October 1, 2003.

- **2001, Economic Growth and Tax Relief Reconciliation Act of 2001 (P.L. 107-16)**

P.L. 107-16, §801, provides:

SEC. 801. TIME FOR PAYMENT OF CORPORATE ESTIMATED TAXES.

Notwithstanding section 6655 of the Internal Revenue Code of 1986—

(1) 100 percent of the amount of any required installment of corporate estimated tax which is otherwise due in September 2001 shall not be due until October 1, 2001; and

(2) 20 percent of the amount of any required installment of corporate estimated tax which is otherwise due in September 2004 shall not be due until October 1, 2004.

- **1993, Omnibus Budget Reconciliation Act of 1993 (P.L. 103-66)**

P.L. 103-66, §13225(a)(1):

Amended Code Sec. 6655(d)(1)(B)(i) by striking "91 percent" each place it appears and inserting "100 percent". **Effective** for tax years beginning after 12-31-93.

P.L. 103-66, §13225(a)(2)(A)(i)-(ii):

Amended Code Sec. 6655(d) by striking paragraph (3), and by striking "91 PERCENT" in the paragraph heading of paragraph (2) and inserting "100 PERCENT". **Effective** for tax years beginning after 12-31-93. Prior to amendment, Code Sec. 6655(d)(3) read as follows:

(3) TEMPORARY INCREASE IN AMOUNT OF INSTALLMENT BASED ON CURRENT YEAR TAX.—In the case of any taxable year beginning after June 30, 1992, and before 1997—

(A) paragraph (1)(B)(i) and subsection (e)(3)(A)(i) shall be applied by substituting "97 percent" for "91 percent" each place it appears, and

(B) the table contained in subsection (e)(2)(B)(ii) shall be applied by substituting "24.25", "48.50", "72.75", and "97" for "22.75", 45.50", "68.25", and "91.00", respectively.

- **1992, Unemployment Compensation Amendments of 1991 (P.L. 102-318)**

P.L. 102-318, §512(a)(1)-(3):

Amended Code Sec. 6655(d) by striking "90 percent" each place it appears in paragraph (1)(B)(i) and inserting "91 percent", by striking "90 percent" in the heading of paragraph (2) and inserting "91 percent", and by striking paragraph (3) and inserting new paragraph (3). **Effective** for tax years beginning after 6-30-92. Prior to amendment, Code Sec. 6655(d)(3) read as follows:

(3) TEMPORARY INCREASE IN AMOUNT OF INSTALLMENT BASED ON CURRENT YEAR TAX.—In the case of any taxable year beginning after 1991 and before 1997—

(A) Paragraph (1)(B)(i) and subsection (e)(3)(A)(i) shall be applied by substituting for "90 percent" each place it appears the current year percentage determined under the following table:

In the case of a taxable year beginning in:	The current year percentage is:
1992	93
1993 through 1996	95

(B) Appropriate adjustments to the table contained in subsection (e)(2)(B)(ii) shall be made to reflect the provisions of subparagraph (A).

- **1992 (P.L. 102-244)**

P.L. 102-244, §3(a):

Amended Code Sec. 6655(d)(3)(A) by striking the table contained therein and inserting a new table. **Effective** for tax years beginning after 12-31-92. Prior to being stricken, the table in Code Sec. 6655(d)(3)(A) read as follows:

In the case of a taxable year beginning in:	The current year percentage is:
1992	93
1993 or 1994	94
1995 or 1996	95

P.L. 102-244, §4, provides:

SEC. 4. EXTENSION OF TIME FOR PAYMENT OF ADDITIONAL FUTA TAXES.

(a) IN GENERAL.—Notwithstanding any other provision of law, if a qualified taxpayer is required to pay additional taxes for taxable years beginning in 1991 with respect to any employment in any State by reason of such State being declared a credit reduction State, such taxpayer may elect to defer the filing and payment of such additional taxes to a date no later than June 30, 1992.

(b) INTEREST.—Notwithstanding subsection (a), for purposes of section 6601(a) of the Internal Revenue Code of 1986, the last date prescribed for payment of any additional taxes for which an election is made under subsection (a) shall be January 31, 1992.

(c) DEFINITIONS.—For purposes of this section—

(1) QUALIFIED TAXPAYER.—The term "qualified taxpayer" means a taxpayer—

(A) in a State which has been declared a credit reduction State for taxable years beginning in 1991, and

(B) who did not receive notice of such credit reduction before December 1, 1991 from either the State unemployment compensation agency or the Internal Revenue Service.

Sec. 6655(d)(2)(B)

(2) CREDIT REDUCTION STATE.—The term "credit reduction State" means a State with respect to which the Internal Revenue Service has determined that a reduction in credits is applicable for taxable years beginning in 1991 pursuant to the provisions of section 3302 of the Internal Revenue Code of 1986.

(d) TIME AND MANNER FOR MAKING ELECTION.—An election under this section shall be made at such time and in such manner as the Secretary of the Treasury shall prescribe.

• 1991, Tax Extension Act of 1991 (P.L. 102-227)

P.L. 102-227, §201(a):

Amended Code Sec. 6655(d) by adding at the end thereof a new paragraph (3). **Effective** for tax years beginning after 12-31-91.

[Sec. 6655(e)]

(e) LOWER REQUIRED INSTALLMENT WHERE ANNUALIZED INCOME INSTALLMENT OR ADJUSTED SEASONAL INSTALLMENT IS LESS THAN AMOUNT DETERMINED UNDER SUBSECTION (d).—

(1) IN GENERAL.—In the case of any required installment, if the corporation establishes that the annualized income installment or the adjusted seasonal installment is less than the amount determined under subsection (d)(1) (as modified by paragraphs (2) and (3) of subsection (d))—

(A) the amount of such required installment shall be the annualized income installment (or, if lesser, the adjusted seasonal installment), and

(B) any reduction in a required installment resulting from the application of this paragraph shall be recaptured by increasing the amount of the next required installment determined under subsection (d)(1) (as so modified) by the amount of such reduction (and by increasing subsequent required installments to the extent that the reduction has not previously been recaptured under this subparagraph).

(2) DETERMINATION OF ANNUALIZED INCOME INSTALLMENT.—

(A) IN GENERAL.—In the case of any required installment, the annualized income installment is the excess (if any) of—

(i) an amount equal to the applicable percentage of the tax for the taxable year computed by placing on an annualized basis the taxable income, adjusted financial statement income (as defined in section 56A), and modified taxable income—

(I) for the first 3 months of the taxable year, in the case of the 1st required installment,

(II) for the first 3 months of the taxable year, in the case of the 2nd required installment,

(III) for the first 6 months of the taxable year in the case of the 3rd required installment, and

(IV) for the first 9 months of the taxable year, in the case of the 4th required installment, over

(ii) the aggregate amount of any prior required installments for the taxable year.

(B) SPECIAL RULES.—For purposes of this paragraph—

(i) ANNUALIZATION.—The taxable income, adjusted financial statement income (as defined in section 56A), and modified taxable income shall be placed on an annualized basis under regulations prescribed by the Secretary.

(ii) APPLICABLE PERCENTAGE.—

In the case of the following required installments:	*The applicable percentage is:*
1st	25
2nd	50
3rd	75
4th	100

(iii) MODIFIED TAXABLE INCOME.—The term "modified taxable income" has the meaning given such term by section 59A(c)(1).

(C) ELECTION FOR DIFFERENT ANNUALIZATION PERIODS.—

(i) If the taxpayer makes an election under this clause—

(I) subclause (I) of subparagraph (A)(i) shall be applied by substituting "2 months" for "3 months",

(II) subclause (II) of subparagraph (A)(i) shall be applied by substituting "4 months" for "3 months",

(III) subclause (III) of subparagraph (A)(i) shall be applied by substituting "7 months" for "6 months", and

(IV) subclause (IV) of subparagraph (A)(i) shall be applied by substituting "10 months" for "9 months".

(ii) If the taxpayer makes an election under this clause—

(I) subclause (II) of subparagraph (A)(i) shall be applied by substituting "5 months" for "3 months",

(II) subclause (III) of subparagraph (A)(i) shall be applied by substituting "8 months" for "6 months",

(III) subclause (IV) of subparagraph (A)(i) shall be applied by substituting "11 months" for "9 months".

(iii) An election under clause (i) or (ii) shall apply to the taxable year for which made and such an election shall be effective only if made on or before the date required for the payment of the first required installment for such taxable year.

(3) DETERMINATION OF ADJUSTED SEASONAL INSTALLMENT.—

(A) IN GENERAL.—In the case of any required installment, the amount of the adjusted seasonal installment is the excess (if any) of—

(i) 100 percent of the amount determined under subparagraph (C), over

(ii) the aggregate amount of all prior required installments for the taxable year.

(B) LIMITATION ON APPLICATION OF PARAGRAPH.—This paragraph shall apply only if the base period percentage for any 6 consecutive months of the taxable year equals or exceeds 70 percent.

(C) DETERMINATION OF AMOUNT.—The amount determined under this subparagraph for any installment shall be determined in the following manner—

(i) take the taxable income for all months during the taxable year preceding the filing month,

(ii) divide such amount by the base period percentage for all months during the taxable year preceding the filing month,

(iii) determine the tax on the amount determined under clause (ii), and

(iv) multiply the tax computed under clause (iii) by the base period percentage for the filing month and all months during the taxable year preceding the filing month.

(D) DEFINITIONS AND SPECIAL RULES.—For purposes of this paragraph—

(i) BASE PERIOD PERCENTAGE.—The base period percentage for any period of months shall be the average percent which the taxable income for the corresponding months in each of the 3 preceding taxable years bears to the taxable income for the 3 preceding taxable years.

(ii) FILING MONTH.—The term "filing month" means the month in which the installment is required to be paid.

ADDITIONS TO TAX

(iii) REORGANIZATION, ETC.—The Secretary may by regulations provide for the determination of the base period percentage in the case of reorganizations, new corporations, and other similar circumstances.

(4) TREATMENT OF SUBPART F INCOME.—

(A) IN GENERAL.—Any amounts required to be included in gross income under 951(a) (and credits properly allocable thereto) shall be taken into account in computing any annualized income installment under paragraph (2) in a manner similar to the manner under which partnership income inclusions (and credits properly allocable thereto) are taken into account.

(B) PRIOR YEAR SAFE HARBOR.—

(i) IN GENERAL.—If a taxpayer elects to have this subparagraph apply for any taxable year—

(I) subparagraph (A) shall not apply, and

(II) for purposes of computing any annualized income installment for such taxable year, the taxpayer shall be treated as having received ratably during such taxable year items of income and credit described in subparagraph (A) in an amount equal to 115 percent of the amount of such items shown on the return of the taxpayer for the preceding taxable year (the second preceding taxable year in the case of the first and second required installments for such taxable year).

(ii) SPECIAL RULE FOR NONCONTROLLING SHAREHOLDER.—

(I) IN GENERAL.—If a taxpayer making the election under clause (i) is a noncontrolling shareholder of a corporation, clause (i)(II) shall be applied with respect to items of such corporation by substituting "100 percent" for "115 percent".

(II) NONCONTROLLING SHAREHOLDER.—For purposes of subclause (I), the term "noncontrolling shareholder" means, with respect to any corporation, a shareholder which (as of the beginning of the taxable year for which the installment is being made) does not own (within the meaning of section 958(a)), and is not treated as owning (within the meaning of section 958(b)), more than 50 percent (by vote or value) of the stock in the corporation.

(5) TREATMENT OF CERTAIN REIT DIVIDENDS.—

(A) IN GENERAL.—Any dividend received from a closely held real estate investment trust by any person which owns (after application of subsection (d)(5) of section 856) 10 percent or more (by vote or value) of the stock or beneficial interests in the trust shall be taken into account in computing annualized income installments under paragraph (2) in a manner similar to the manner under which partnership income inclusions are taken into account.

(B) CLOSELY HELD REIT.—For purposes of subparagraph (A), the term "closely held real estate investment trust" means a real estate investment trust with respect to which 5 or fewer persons own (after application of subsection (d)(5) of section 856) 50 percent or more (by vote or value) of the stock or beneficial interests in the trust.

Amendments

- **2022, Inflation Reduction Act of 2022 (P.L. 117-169)**

P.L. 117-169, §10101(a)(4)(G):

Amended Code Sec. 6655(e)(2) by inserting ", adjusted financial statement income (as defined in section 56A)," before "and modified taxable income" each place it appears in subparagraphs (A)(i) and (B)(i). **Effective** for tax years beginning after 12-31-2022.

- **2018, Tax Technical Corrections Act of 2018 (P.L. 115-141)**

P.L. 115-141, §401(d)(1)(D)(xx)(I)-(II), Div. U:

Amended Code Sec. 6655(e)(4) by striking "936(h) or" following "gross income under section" in subparagraph (A), and by striking "AND SECTION 936" following "TREATMENT OF SUBPART F" in the heading. **Effective** 3-23-2018. For a special rule, see Act Sec. 401(e), Div. U, below.

P.L. 115-141, §401(e), Div. U, provides:

(e) GENERAL SAVINGS PROVISION WITH RESPECT TO DEADWOOD PROVISIONS.—If—

(1) any provision amended or repealed by the amendments made by subsection (b) or (d) applied to—

(A) any transaction occurring before the date of the enactment of this Act,

(B) any property acquired before such date of enactment, or

(C) any item of income, loss, deduction, or credit taken into account before such date of enactment, and

(2) the treatment of such transaction, property, or item under such provision would (without regard to the amendments or repeals made by such subsection) affect the liability for tax for periods ending after such date of enactment,

nothing in the amendments or repeals made by this section shall be construed to affect the treatment of such transaction, property, or item for purposes of determining liability for tax for periods ending after such date of enactment.

- **2017, Tax Cuts and Jobs Act (P.L. 115-97)**

P.L. 115-97, §12001(b)(18):

Amended Code Sec. 6655(e)(2) by striking "and alternative minimum taxable income" each place it appears in subparagraphs (A) and (B)(i). **Effective** for tax years beginning after 12-31-2017. Prior to amendment, Code Sec. 6655(e)(2)(A) and (B)(i) read as follows:

(A) IN GENERAL.—In the case of any required installment, the annualized income installment is the excess (if any) of—

(i) an amount equal to the applicable percentage of the tax for the taxable year computed by placing on an annualized basis the taxable income and alternative minimum taxable income—

(I) for the first 3 months of the taxable year, in the case of the 1st required installment,

(II) for the first 3 months of the taxable year, in the case of the 2nd required installment,

(III) for the first 6 months of the taxable year in the case of the 3rd required installment, and

(IV) for the first 9 months of the taxable year, in the case of the 4th required installment, over

(ii) the aggregate amount of any prior required installments for the taxable year.

(B) SPECIAL RULES.—For purposes of this paragraph—

(i) ANNUALIZATION.—The taxable income and alternative minimum taxable income shall be placed on an annualized basis under regulations prescribed by the Secretary.

P.L. 115-97, §14401(d)(4)(B):

Amended Code Sec. 6655(e)(2)(A)(i) and (B)(i), as amended by Act. Secs. 12001 and 13001, by inserting "and modified taxable income" after "taxable income". **Effective** for base erosion payments (as defined in Code Sec. 59A(d), as added by Act. Sec. 14401) paid or accrued in tax years beginning after 12-31-2017.

P.L. 115-97, §14401(d)(4)(C):

Amended Code Sec. 6655(e)(2)(B) by adding at the end a new clause (iii). **Effective** for base erosion payments (as defined in Code Sec. 59A(d), as added by Act. Sec. 14401) paid or accrued in tax years beginning after 12-31-2017.

- **2014, Tax Technical Corrections Act of 2014 (P.L. 113-295)**

P.L. 113-295, §221(a)(12)(K)(i)-(ii), Division A:

Amended Code Sec. 6655(e)(2) by striking "taxable income, alternative minimum taxable income, and modified alternative minimum taxable income" in subparagraphs (A)(i) and (B)(i) and inserting "taxable income and alternative minimum taxable income", and by striking clause (iii) in subparagraph (B). **Effective** generally 12-19-2014. For a special rule, see Act Sec. 221(b)(2), Division A, below. Prior to being stricken, Code Sec. 6655(e)(2)(B)(iii) read as follows:

(iii) MODIFIED ALTERNATIVE MINIMUM TAXABLE INCOME.—The term "modified alternative minimum taxable income" has the meaning given to such term by section 59A(b).

P.L. 113-295, §221(b)(2), Division A, provides:

(2) SAVINGS PROVISION.—If—

(A) any provision amended or repealed by the amendments made by this section applied to—

(i) any transaction occurring before the date of the enactment of this Act,

(ii) any property acquired before such date of enactment, or

(iii) any item of income, loss, deduction, or credit taken into account before such date of enactment, and

(B) the treatment of such transaction, property, or item under such provision would (without regard to the amendments or repeals made by this section) affect the liability for tax for periods ending after date of enactment, nothing in the amendments or repeals made by this section shall be construed to affect the treatment of such transaction, property, or item for purposes of determining liability for tax for periods ending after such date of enactment.

- **2000, Community Renewal Tax Relief Act of 2000 (P.L. 106-554)**

P.L. 106-554, §319(21):

Amended Code Sec. 6655(e)(5)(A) and (B) by striking "subsections (d)(5) and (I)(3)(B)" and inserting "subsection (d)(5)". **Effective** 12-21-2000.

- **1999, Tax Relief Extension Act of 1999 (P.L. 106-170)**

P.L. 106-170, §571(a):

Amended Code Sec. 6655(e) by adding at the end a new paragraph (5). **Effective** for estimated tax payments due on or after 12-15-99.

- **1994, Uruguay Round Agreements Act (P.L. 103-465)**

P.L. 103-465, §711(a):

Amended Code Sec. 6655(e) by adding at the end a new paragraph (4). **Effective** for purposes of determining underpayments of estimated tax for tax years beginning after 12-31-94.

ADDITIONS TO TAX

- 1993, Omnibus Budget Reconciliation Act of 1993 (P.L. 103-66)

P.L. 103-66, §13225(a)(2)(B):

Amended Code Sec. 6655(e)(2)(B)(ii) by striking the table contained therein and inserting a new table. **Effective** for tax years beginning after 12-31-93. Prior to amendment, the table contained in Code Sec. 6655(e)(2)(B)(ii) read as follows:

In the case of the following required installments:	The applicable percentage is:
1st	22.75
2nd	45.50
3rd	68.25
4th	91.00

P.L. 103-66, §13225(a)(2)(C):

Amended Code Sec. 6655(e)(3)(A)(i) by striking "91 percent" and inserting "100 percent". **Effective** for tax years beginning after 12-31-93.

P.L. 103-66, §13225(b)(1)(A)-(C):

Amended Code Sec. 6655(e)(2)(A)(i) by striking "or for the first 5 months" in subclause (II) after "3 months", by striking "or for the first 8 months" in subclause (III) after "6 months" and by striking "or for the first 11 months" in subclause (IV) after "9 months". **Effective** for tax years beginning after 12-31-93.

P.L. 103-66, §13225(b)(2):

Amended Code Sec. 6655(e)(2) by adding at the end thereof new subparagraph (C). **Effective** for tax years beginning after 12-31-93.

- 1992, Unemployment Compensation Amendments of 1992 (P.L. 102-318)

P.L. 102-318, §512(b)(1):

Amended Code Sec. 6655(e)(2)(B)(ii) by striking the table contained therein and inserting a new table. **Effective** for tax years beginning after 6-30-92. Prior to amendment Code Sec. 6655(e)(2)(B)(ii) read as follows:

In the case of the following required installments:	The applicable percentage is:
1st	22.5
2nd	45
3rd	67.5
4th	90

P.L. 102-318, §512(b)(2):

Amended Code Sec. 6655(e)(3)(A)(i) by striking "90 percent" and inserting "91 percent". **Effective** for tax years beginning after 6-30-92.

- 1991, Tax Extension Act of 1991 (P.L. 102-227)

P.L. 102-227, §201(b):

Amended Code Sec. 6655(e)(1) by striking "modified by subsection (d)(2)" and inserting "modified by paragraphs (2) and (3) of subsection (d)". **Effective** for tax years beginning after 12-31-91.

- 1989, Omnibus Budget Reconciliation Act of 1989 (P.L. 101-239)

P.L. 101-239, §7822(a):

Amended Code Sec. 6655(e)(1) by striking "section (d)(1)" and inserting "subsection (d)(1)". **Effective** as if included in the provision of P.L. 100-203 to which it relates.

- 1988, Technical and Miscellaneous Revenue Act of 1988 (P.L. 100-647)

P.L. 100-647, §5001(a):

Amended Code Sec. 6655(e)(1) by striking out the last sentence. **Effective** for installments required to be made after 12-31-88. Prior to amendment, the last sentence of Code Sec. 6655(e)(1) read as follows:

A reduction shall be treated as recaptured for purposes of subparagraph (a) if 90 percent of the reduction is recaptured.

[Sec. 6655(f)]

(f) EXCEPTION WHERE TAX IS SMALL AMOUNT.—No addition to tax shall be imposed under subsection (a) for any taxable year if the tax shown on the return for such taxable year (or, if no return is filed, the tax) is less than $500.

[Sec. 6655(g)]

(g) DEFINITIONS AND SPECIAL RULES.—

(1) TAX.—For purposes of this section, the term "tax" means the excess of—

(A) the sum of—

(i) the tax imposed by section 11 or subchapter L of chapter 1, whichever applies,

(ii) the tax imposed by section 55,

(iii) the tax imposed by section 59A, plus

(iv) the tax imposed by section 887, over

(B) the credits against tax provided by part IV of subchapter A of chapter 1.

For purposes of the preceding sentence, in the case of a foreign corporation subject to taxation under section 11 or 1201(a), or under subchapter L of chapter 1, the tax imposed by section 881 shall be treated as a tax imposed by section 11.

(2) LARGE CORPORATION.—

(A) IN GENERAL.—For purposes of this section, the term "large corporation" means any corporation if such corporation (or any predecessor corporation) had taxable income of $1,000,000 or more for any taxable year during the testing period.

(B) RULES FOR APPLYING SUBPARAGRAPH (A).—

(i) TESTING PERIOD.—For purposes of subparagraph (A), the term "testing period" means the 3 taxable years immediately preceding the taxable year involved.

(ii) MEMBERS OF CONTROLLED GROUP.—For purposes of applying subparagraph (A) to any taxable year in the testing period with respect to corporations which are component members of a controlled group of corporations for such taxable year, the $1,000,000 amount specified in subparagraph (A) shall be divided among such members under rules similar to the rules of section 1561.

(iii) CERTAIN CARRYBACKS AND CARRYOVERS NOT TAKEN INTO ACCOUNT.—For purposes of subparagraph (A), taxable income shall be determined without regard to any amount carried to the taxable year under section 172 or 1212(a).

(3) CERTAIN TAX-EXEMPT ORGANIZATIONS.—For purposes of this section—

(A) Any organization subject to the tax imposed by section 511, and any private foundation, shall be treated as a corporation subject to tax under section 11.

(B) Any tax imposed by section 511, and any tax imposed by section 1 or 4940 on a private foundation, shall be treated as a tax imposed by section 11.

(C) Any reference to taxable income shall be treated as including a reference to unrelated business taxable income or net investment income (as the case may be).

In the case of any organization described in subparagraph (A), subsection (b)(2)(A) shall be applied by substituting "5th month" for "4th month", subsection (e)(2)(A) shall be applied by substituting "2 months" for "3 months" in clause (i)(I), the election under clause (i) of subsection (e)(2)(C) may be made separately for each installment, and clause (ii) of subsection (e)(2)(C) shall not apply. In the case of a private foundation, subsection (c)(2) shall be applied by substituting "May 15" for "April 15".

(4) APPLICATION OF SECTION TO CERTAIN TAXES IMPOSED ON S CORPORATIONS.—In the case of an S corporation, for purposes of this section—

(A) The following taxes shall be treated as imposed by section 11:

(i) The tax imposed by section 1374(a).

(ii) The tax imposed by section 1375(a).

(iii) Any tax for which the S corporation is liable by reason of section 1371(d)(2).

(B) Paragraph (2) of subsection (d) shall not apply.

ADDITIONS TO TAX

(C) Clause (ii) of subsection (d)(1)(B) shall be applied as if it read as follows:

"(ii) the sum of—

"(I) the amount determined under clause (i) by only taking into account the taxes referred to in clauses (i) and (iii) of subsection (g)(4)(A), and

"(II) 100 percent of the tax imposed by section 1375(a) which was shown on the return of the corporation for the preceding taxable year."

(D) The requirement in the last sentence of subsection (d)(1)(B) that the return for the preceding taxable year show a liability for tax shall not apply.

(E) Subsection (b)(2)(A) shall be applied by substituting "3rd month" for "4th month".

(F) Any reference in subsection (e) to taxable income shall be treated as including a reference to the net recognized built-in gain or the excess passive income (as the case may be).

Amendments

• **2022, Inflation Reduction Act of 2022 (P.L. 117-169)**

P.L. 117-169, §10101(a)(4)(H):

Amended Code Sec. 6655(g)(1)(A) by redesignating clauses (ii) and (iii) as clauses (iii) and (iv), respectively, and by inserting after clause (i) new clause (ii). **Effective** for tax years beginning after 12-31-2022.

• **2017, Tax Cuts and Jobs Act (P.L. 115-97)**

P.L. 115-97, §12001(b)(19):

Amended Code Sec. 6655(g)(1)(A) by inserting "plus" at the end of clause (i), by striking clause (ii), and by redesignating clause (iii) as clause (ii). **Effective** for tax years beginning after 12-31-2017. Prior to being stricken, Code Sec. 6655(g)(1)(A)(ii) read as follows:

(ii) the tax imposed by section 55, plus

P.L. 115-97, §13001(b)(2)(P):

Amended Code Sec. 6655(g)(1)(A)(i) by striking "or 1201(a)," following "section 11". **Effective** for tax years beginning after 12-31-2017.

P.L. 115-97, §14401(d)(4)(A):

Amended Code Sec. 6655(g)(1)(A), as amended by Act. Secs. 12001 and 13001, by striking "plus" at the end of clause (i), by redesignating clause (ii) as clause (iii), and by inserting after clause (i) new clause (ii). **Effective** for base erosion payments (as defined in Code Sec. 59A(d), as added by Act. Sec. 14401) paid or accrued in tax years beginning after 12-31-2017.

• **2015, Surface Transportation and Veterans Health Care Choice Improvement Act of 2015 (P.L. 114-41)**

P.L. 114-41, §2006(a)(2)(F):

Amended Code Sec. 6655(g)(3) by striking "3rd month" and inserting "4th month". **Effective** generally for returns for tax years beginning after 12-31-2015. For an exception, see Act Sec. 2006(a)(3)(B), below.

P.L. 114-41, §2006(a)(2)(G):

Amended Code Sec. 6655(g)(4) by redesignating subparagraph (E) as subparagraph (F) and by inserting after subparagraph (D) a new subparagraph (E). **Effective** generally for returns for tax years beginning after 12-31-2015. For an exception, see Act Sec. 2006(a)(3)(B), below.

P.L. 114-41, §2006(a)(3)(B), provides:

(B) SPECIAL RULE FOR C CORPORATIONS WITH FISCAL YEARS ENDING ON JUNE 30.—In the case of any C corporation with a taxable year ending on June 30, the amendments made by this subsection shall apply to returns for taxable years beginning after December 31, 2025.

• **2014, Tax Technical Corrections Act of 2014 (P.L. 113-295)**

P.L. 113-295, §221(a)(12)(K)(iii), Division A:

Amended Code Sec. 6655(g)(1)(A) by inserting "plus" at the end of clause (ii), by striking clause (iii), and by redesignating clause (iv) as clause (iii). **Effective** generally 12-19-2014. For a special rule, see Act Sec. 221(b)(2), Division A, below. Prior to being stricken, Code Sec. 6655(g)(1)(A)(iii) read as follows:

(iii) the tax imposed by section 59A, plus

P.L. 113-295, §221(a)(114), Division A:

Amended Code Sec. 6655(g)(4)(A)(i) by striking "(or the corresponding provisions of prior law)" following "section 1374(a)". **Effective** generally 12-19-2014. For a special rule, see Act Sec. 221(b)(2), Division A, below.

P.L. 113-295, §221(b)(2), Division A, provides:

(2) SAVINGS PROVISION.—If—

(A) any provision amended or repealed by the amendments made by this section applied to—

(i) any transaction occurring before the date of the enactment of this Act,

(ii) any property acquired before such date of enactment, or

(iii) any item of income, loss, deduction, or credit taken into account before such date of enactment, and

(B) the treatment of such transaction, property, or item under such provision would (without regard to the amendments or repeals made by this section) affect the liability for tax for periods ending after date of enactment, nothing in the amendments or repeals made by this section shall be construed to affect the treatment of such transaction, property, or item for purposes of determining liability for tax for periods ending after such date of enactment.

• **1997, Taxpayer Relief Act of 1997 (P.L. 105-34)**

P.L. 105-34, §1461(a):

Amended Code Sec. 6655(g)(3) by adding at the end a new sentence. **Effective** for purposes of determining underpayments of estimated tax for tax years beginning after 8-5-97.

• **1996, Small Business Job Protection Act of 1996 (P.L. 104-188)**

P.L. 104-188, §1703(h):

Amended Code Sec. 6655(g)(3) by striking all that follows "'3rd month'" in the sentence following subparagraph (C) and inserting ", subsection (e)(2)(A) shall be applied by substituting '2 months' for '3 months' in clause (i)(I), the election under clause (i) of subsection (e)(2)(C) may be made separately for each installment, and clause (ii) of subsection (e)(2)(C) shall not apply.". **Effective** as if included in the provision of P.L. 103-66 to which it relates. Prior to amendment, the sentence following subparagraph (C) of Code Sec. 6655(g)(3) read as follows:

In the case of any organization described in subparagraph (A), subsection (b)(2)(A) shall be applied by substituting "5th month" for "3rd month", and, except in the case of an election under subsection (e)(2)(C), subsection (e)(2)(A) shall be applied by substituting "2 months" for "3 months" and in clause (i)(I), by substituting "4 months" for "5 months" in clause (i)(II), by substituting "7 months" for "8 months" in clause (i)(III), and by substituting "10 months" for "11 months" in clause (i)(IV).

• **1993, Omnibus Budget Reconciliation Act of 1993 (P.L. 103-66)**

P.L. 103-66, §13225(b)(3):

Amended Code Sec. 6655(g)(3) by striking "and subsection (e)(2)(A)" and inserting "and, except in the case of an election under subsection (e)(2)(C), subsection (e)(2)(A)". **Effective** for tax years beginning after 12-31-93.

• **1990, Omnibus Budget Reconciliation Act of 1990 (P.L. 101-508)**

P.L. 101-508, §11704(a)(28):

Amended Code Sec. 6655(g)(3) by striking all that follows "11 months" in the last sentence and inserting "in clause (i)(IV)." **Effective** 11-5-90.

• **1989, Omnibus Budget Reconciliation Act of 1989 (P.L. 101-239)**

P.L. 101-239, §7209(a):

Amended Code Sec. 6655(g) by adding at the end thereof a new paragraph (4). **Effective** for tax years beginning after 12-31-89.

• **1988, Technical and Miscellaneous Revenue Act of 1988 (P.L. 100-647)**

P.L. 100-647, §2004(r):

Amended Code Sec. 6655(g)(3) by striking out the sentence following subparagraph (C) and inserting in lieu thereof a new sentence. **Effective** as if included in the provision of P.L. 100-203 to which it relates. Prior to amendment, the sentence following subparagraph (C) read as follows:

In the case of any organization described in subparagraph (A), subsection (b)(2)(A) shall be applied by substituting "5th month" for "3rd month".

• **1988, Omnibus Trade and Competitiveness Act of 1988 (P.L. 100-418)**

P.L. 100-418, §1941(b)(6)(B):

Amended Code Sec. 6655(g)(1)(B). **Effective** for crude oil removed from the premises on or after 8-23-88. Prior to amendment, Code Sec. 6655(g)(1)(B) read as follows:

(B) the sum of—

(i) the credits against tax provided by part IV of subchapter A of chapter 1, plus

(ii) to the extent allowed under regulations prescribed by the Secretary, any overpayment of the tax imposed by section 4986 (determined without regard to section 4995(a)(4)(B)).

[Sec. 6655(h)]

(h) EXCESSIVE ADJUSTMENT UNDER SECTION 6425.—

(1) ADDITION TO TAX.—If the amount of an adjustment under section 6425 made before the 15th day of the 4th month following the close of the taxable year is excessive, there shall be added to the tax under chapter 1 for the taxable year an amount determined at the underpayment rate established under section 6621 upon the excessive amount from the date on which the credit is allowed or the refund is paid to such 15th day.

(2) EXCESSIVE AMOUNT.—For purposes of paragraph (1), the excessive amount is equal to the amount of the adjustment or (if smaller) the amount by which—

(A) the income tax liability (as defined in section 6425(c)) for the taxable year as shown on the return for the taxable year, exceeds

ADDITIONS TO TAX

(B) the estimated income tax paid during the taxable year, reduced by the amount of the adjustment.

Amendments

• **2015, Surface Transportation and Veterans Health Care Choice Improvement Act of 2015 (P.L. 114-41)**

P.L. 114-41, §2006(a)(2)(F):

Amended Code Sec. 6655(h)(1) by striking "3rd month" and inserting "4th month". **Effective** generally for returns for tax years beginning after 12-31-2015. For an exception, see Act Sec. 2006(a)(3)(B), below.

P.L. 114-41, §2006(a)(3)(B), provides:

(B) SPECIAL RULE FOR C CORPORATIONS WITH FISCAL YEARS ENDING ON JUNE 30.—In the case of any C corporation with a taxable year ending on June 30, the amendments made by this subsection shall apply to returns for taxable years beginning after December 31, 2025.

[Sec. 6655(i)]

(i) FISCAL YEARS AND SHORT YEARS.—

(1) FISCAL YEARS.—In applying this section to a taxable year beginning on any date other than January 1, there shall be substituted, for the months specified in this section, the months which correspond thereto.

(2) SHORT TAXABLE YEAR.—This section shall be applied to taxable years of less than 12 months in accordance with regulations prescribed by the Secretary.

[Sec. 6655(j)]

(j) REGULATIONS.—The Secretary shall prescribe such regulations as may be necessary to carry out the purposes of this section.

Amendments

• **1987, Revenue Act of 1987 (P.L. 100-203)**

P.L. 100-203, §10301(a):

Amended Code Sec. 6655. **Effective** for tax years beginning 12-31-87. Prior to amendment, Code Sec. 6655 read as follows:

SEC. 6655. FAILURE BY CORPORATION TO PAY ESTIMATED INCOME TAX.

[Sec. 6655(a)]

(a) ADDITION TO TAX.—Except as provided in subsections (d) and (e), in the case of any underpayment of tax by a corporation—

(1) IN GENERAL.—There shall be added to the tax under chapter 1 for the taxable year an amount determined at the underpayment rate established under section 6621 on the amount of the underpayment for the period of the underpayment.

(2) SPECIAL RULE WHERE CORPORATION PAID 80 PERCENT OR MORE OF TAX.—In any case in which there would be no underpayment if subsection (b) were applied by substituting "80 percent" for "90 percent" each place it appears, the addition to tax under paragraph (1) shall be equal to 75 percent of the amount otherwise determined under paragraph (1).

Amendments

• **1986, Tax Reform Act of 1986 (P.L. 99-514)**

P.L. 99-514, §1511(c)(15):

Amended Code Sec. 6655(a)(1) by striking out "the rate established under section 6621" and inserting in lieu thereof "the underpayment rate established under section 6621". **Effective** for purposes of determining interest for periods after 12-31-86.

• **1984, Deficit Reduction Act of 1984 (P.L. 98-369)**

P.L. 98-369, §218, provides:

SEC. 218. UNDERPAYMENTS OF ESTIMATED TAX FOR 1984.

No addition to the tax shall be made under section 6655 of the Internal Revenue Code of 1954 (relating to failure by corporation to pay estimated tax) with respect to any underpayment of an installment required to be paid before the date of the enactment of this Act [July 18, 1984] to the extent—

(1) such underpayment was created or increased by any provision of this subtitle, and

(2) such underpayment is paid in full on or before the last date prescribed for payment of the first installment of estimated tax required to be paid after the date of the enactment of this Act.

• **1982, Tax Equity and Fiscal Responsibility Act of 1982 (P.L. 97-248)**

P.L. 97-248, §234(c):

Amended Code Sec. 6655(a). **Effective** for tax years beginning after 12-31-82. Prior to amendment, Code Sec. 6655(a) read as follows:

"(a) ADDITION TO THE TAX.—In case of any underpayment of estimated tax by a corporation, except as provided in subsection (d), there shall be added to the tax under chapter 1 for the taxable year an amount determined at an annual rate established under section 6621 upon the amount of the underpayment (determined under subsection (b)) for the period of the underpayment (determined under subsection (c))."

• **1977, Tax Reduction and Simplification Act of 1977 (P.L. 95-30)**

P.L. 95-30, §303, provides:

SEC. 303. UNDERPAYMENTS OF ESTIMATED TAX.

No addition to the tax shall be made under section 6654 or 6655 of the Internal Revenue Code of 1954 (relating to failure to pay estimated income tax) for any period before April 16, 1977 (March 16, 1977, in the case of a taxpayer subject to section 6655), with respect to any underpayment, to the extent that such underpayment was created or increased by any provision of the Tax Reform Act of 1976.

P.L. 95-30, §305, provides:

SEC. 305. INTEREST ON UNDERPAYMENTS OF TAX.

No interest shall be payable for any period before April 16, 1977 (March 16, 1977, in the case of a corporation), on any underpayment of a tax imposed by the Internal Revenue Code of 1954, to the extent that such underpayment was created or increased by any provision of the Tax Reform Act of 1976.

• **1976, Tax Reform Act of 1976 (P.L. 94-455)**

P.L. 94-455, §803(g), provides:

(g) WAIVER OF PENALTY FOR UNDERPAYMENT OF ESTIMATED TAX.—If—

(1) a corporation made underpayments of estimated tax for a taxable year of the corporation which includes August 1, 1975, because the corporation intended to elect to have the provisions of subparagraph (B) of section 46(a)(1) of the Internal Revenue Code of 1954 (as it existed before the date of enactment of this Act) apply for such taxable year, and

(2) the corporation does not elect to have the provisions of such subparagraph apply for such taxable year because this Act does not contain the amendments made by section 804(a)(2) (relating to flowthrough of investment credit), or the provisions of subsection (f) of such section (relating to grace period for certain plan transfers), of the bill P.L. 108-1730612 (94th Congress, 2d Session), as amended by the Senate,

then the provisions of section 6655 of such Code (relating to failure by corporation to pay estimated income tax) shall not apply to so much of any such underpayment as the corporation can establish, to the satisfaction of the Secretary of the Treasury, is properly attributable to the inapplicability of such subparagraph (B) for such taxable year.

Effective for tax years beginning after 12-31-74.

• **1975 (P.L. 93-625)**

P.L. 93-625, §7(c):

Amended Code Sec. 6655(a) by substituting "an annual rate established under section 6621" for "the rate of 6 percent per annum". **Effective** 7-1-75, and applicable to amounts outstanding on such date or arising thereafter.

[Sec. 6655(b)]

(b) AMOUNT OF UNDERPAYMENTS.—For purposes of subsection (a), the amount of the underpayment shall be the excess of—

(1) The amount of the installment which would be required to be paid if the estimated tax were equal to 90 percent of the tax shown on the return for the taxable year or, if no return was filed, 90 percent of the tax for such year, over

(2) The amount, if any, of the installment paid on or before the last date prescribed for payment.

Amendments

• **1982, Tax Equity and Fiscal Responsibility Act of 1982 (P.L. 97-248)**

P.L. 97-248, §234(a)(1):

Amended Code Sec. 6655(a)(1) by striking out "80" each place it appeared and inserting "90". **Effective** for tax years beginning after 12-31-82.

• **1968, Revenue and Expenditure Control Act of 1968 (P.L. 90-364)**

P.L. 90-364, §103(c)(1):

Amended Code Sec. 6655(b) by substituting "80 percent" for "70 percent" in paragraph (1). **Effective** with respect to tax years beginning after 12-31-67. However, such amendment is to be taken into account only as of 5-31-68. For the **effective** date of provisions of P.L. 90-364, see the amendment note following Code Sec. 6154.

[Sec. 6655(c)]

(c) PERIOD OF UNDERPAYMENT.—The period of the underpayment shall run from the date the installment was required to be paid to whichever of the following dates is the earlier—

(1) The 15th day of the third month following the close of the taxable year.

(2) With respect to any portion of the underpayment, the date on which such portion is paid. For purposes of this paragraph, a payment of estimated tax on any installment date shall be considered a payment of any previous underpayment only to the extent such payment exceeds the amount of the installment determined under subsection (b)(1) for such installment date.

Amendments

• **1964, Revenue Act of 1964 (P.L. 88-272)**

P.L. 88-272, §122(c)(1):

Amended last sentence of paragraph (c)(2). **Effective** with respect to tax years beginning after 12-31-63. Prior to amendment, the last sentence of paragraph (c)(2) read as follows:

ADDITIONS TO TAX

For purposes of this paragraph, a payment of estimated tax on the 15th day of the 12th month shall be considered a payment of any previous underpayment only to the extent such payment exceeds the amount of the installment determined under subsection (b)(1) for the 15th day of the 12th month.

[Sec. 6655(d)]

(d) EXCEPTION.—Notwithstanding the provisions of the preceding subsections, the addition to the tax with respect to any underpayment of any installment shall not be imposed if the total amount of all payments of estimated tax made on or before the last date prescribed for the payment of such installment equals or exceeds the amount which would have been required to be paid on or before such date if the estimated tax were whichever of the following is the lesser—

(1) The tax shown on the return of the corporation for the preceding taxable year, if a return showing a liability for tax was filed by the corporation for the preceding taxable year and such preceding year was a taxable year of 12 months.

(2) An amount equal to the tax computed at the rates applicable to the taxable year but otherwise on the basis of the facts shown on the return of the corporation for, and the law applicable to, the preceding taxable year.

(3)(A) An amount equal to 90 percent of the tax for the taxable year computed by placing on an annualized basis the taxable income:

(i) for the first 3 months of the taxable year, in the case of the installment required to be paid in the 4th month,

(ii) for the first 3 months or for the first 5 months of the taxable year, in the case of the installment required to be paid in the 6th month,

(iii) for the first 6 months or for the first 8 months of the taxable year in the case of the installment required to be paid in the 9th month, and

(iv) for the first 9 months or for the first 11 months of the taxable year, in the case of the installment required to be paid in the 12th month of the taxable year.

(B) For purposes of this paragraph, the taxable income shall be placed on an annualized basis by—

(i) multiplying by 12 the taxable income referred to in subparagraph (A), and

(ii) dividing the resulting amount by the number of months in the taxable year (3, 5, 6, 8, 9, or 11, as the case may be) referred to in subparagraph (A).

Amendments

• **1982, Tax Equity and Fiscal Responsibility Act of 1982 (P.L. 97-248)**

P.L. 97-248, § 234(a)(2):

Amended Code Sec. 6655(d)(3) by striking out "80" and inserting "90". **Effective** for tax years beginning after 12-31-82.

• **1968, Revenue and Expenditure Control Act of 1968 (P.L. 90-364)**

P.L. 90-364, § 103(c)(1):

Amended Code Sec. 6655(d)(3) by substituting "80 percent" for "70 percent" in the first line thereof. **Effective** with respect to tax years beginning after 12-31-67. However, such amendment is to be taken into account only as of 5-31-68. For the **effective** date provisions of P.L. 90-364, see the amendment note following Sec. 6154.

P.L. 90-364, § 103(e)(1):

Amended Code Sec. 6655(d)(1) by deleting "reduced by $100,000" which formerly followed "taxable year" in the second line of such subsection. **Effective** with respect to tax years beginning after 12-31-67. However, such amendment is to be taken into account only as of 5-31-68. For the **effective** date provisions of P.L. 90-364, see the amendment note following Code Sec. 6154.

• **1964, Revenue Act of 1964 (P.L. 88-272)**

P.L. 88-272, § 122(c)(2):

Amended paragraph (d)(3). **Effective** with respect to tax years beginning after 12-31-63. Prior to amendment, paragraph (3) read as follows:

(3)(A) An amount equal to 70 percent of the tax for the taxable year computed by placing on an annualized basis the taxable income:

(i) for the first 6 months or for the first 8 months of the taxable year, in the case of the installment required to be paid in the ninth month, and

(ii) for the first 9 months or for the first 11 months of the taxable year, in the case of the installment required to be paid in the twelfth month.

(B) For purposes of this paragraph, the taxable income shall be placed on an annualized basis by—

(i) multiplying by 12 the taxable income referred to in subparagraph (A), and

(ii) dividing the resulting amount by the number of months in the taxable year (6 or 8, or 9 or 11, as the case may be) referred to in subparagraph (A).

[Sec. 6655(e)]

(e) ADDITIONAL EXCEPTION FOR RECURRING SEASONAL INCOME.—

(1) IN GENERAL.—Notwithstanding the preceding subsections, the addition to the tax with respect to any underpayment of any installment shall not be imposed if the total amount of all payments of estimated tax made on or before the last date prescribed for the payment of such installment equals or exceeds 90 percent of the amount determined under paragraph (2).

(2) DETERMINATION OF AMOUNT.—The amount determined under this paragraph for any installment shall be determined in the following manner—

(A) take the taxable income for all months during the taxable year preceding the filing month,

(B) divide such amount by the base period percentage for all months during the taxable year preceding the filing month,

(C) determine the tax on the amount determined under subparagraph (B), and

(D) multiply the tax computed under subparagraph (C) by the base period percentage for the filing month and all months during the taxable year preceding the filing month.

(3) DEFINITIONS AND SPECIAL RULES.—For purposes of this subsection—

(A) BASE PERIOD PERCENTAGE.—The base period percentage for any period of months shall be the average percent which the taxable income for the corresponding months in each of the 3 preceding taxable years bears to the taxable income for the 3 preceding taxable years.

(B) FILING MONTH.—The term "filing month" means the month in which the installment is required to be paid.

(C) LIMITATION ON APPLICATION OF SUBSECTION.—This subsection shall only apply if the base period percentage for any 6 consecutive months of the taxable year equals or exceeds 70 percent.

(D) REORGANIZATIONS, ETC.—The Secretary may by regulations provide for the determination of the base period percentage in the case of reorganizations, new corporations, and other similar circumstances.

Amendments

• **1982, Tax Equity and Fiscal Responsibility Act of 1982 (P.L. 97-248)**

P.L. 97-248, § 234(d)(1):

Added Code Sec. 6655(e). **Effective** for tax years beginning after 12-31-82.

[Sec. 6655(f)]

(f) DEFINITION OF TAX.—For purposes of subsections (b), (d), (e), and (i), the term "tax" means the excess of—

(1) the sum of—

(A) the tax imposed by section 11 or 1201(a), or subchapter L of chapter 1, whichever is applicable,

(B) the tax imposed by section 55, plus

(C) the tax imposed by section 59A, over

(2) the sum of—

(A) the credits against tax provided by part IV of subchapter A of chapter 1, plus

(B) to the extent allowed under regulations prescribed by the Secretary, any overpayment of the tax imposed by section 4986 (determined without regard to section 4995(a)(4)(B)).

Amendments

• **1986, Tax Reform Act of 1986 (P.L. 99-514)**

P.L. 99-514, § 701(d)(3):

Amended Code Sec. 6655(f)(1). **Effective**, generally, for tax years beginning after 12-31-86. For exceptions, see Act Sec. 701(f)(2)-(7) following Code Sec. 56. Prior to amendment, Code Sec. 6655(f)(1) read as follows:

(1) the tax imposed by section 11 or 1201(a), or subchapter L of chapter 1, whichever is applicable, over

P.L. 99-514, § 1543, provides:

SEC. 1543. WAIVER OF ESTIMATED PENALTIES FOR 1986 UNDERPAYMENTS ATTRIBUTABLE TO THIS ACT.

No addition to tax shall be made under section 6654 or 6655 of the Internal Revenue Code of 1986 (relating to failure to pay estimated tax) for any period before April 16, 1987 (March 16, 1987, in the case of a taxpayer subject to section 6655 of such Code), with respect to any underpayment, to the extent such underpayment was created or increased by any provision of this Act.

P.L. 99-514, § 1879(a), provides:

(a) WAIVER OF ESTIMATED TAX PENALTIES.—No addition to tax shall be made under section 6654 or 6655 of the Internal Revenue Code of 1954 (relating to failure to pay estimated income tax) for any period before April 16, 1985 (March 16, 1985 in the case of a taxpayer subject to section 6655 of such Code), with respect to any underpayment, to the extent that such underpayment was created or increased by any provision of the Tax Reform Act of 1984.

• **1986, Superfund Amendments and Reauthorization Act of 1986 (P.L. 99-499)**

P.L. 99-499, § 516(b)(4)(D)[C]:

Amended Code Sec. 6655(f)(1), as amended by the Tax Reform Act of 1986, by striking out "plus" at the end of subparagraph (A), by striking out "over" at the end of subparagraph (B) and inserting in lieu thereof "plus", and by adding at the end thereof new subparagraph (C). **Effective** for tax years beginning after 12-31-86.

• **1983, Technical Corrections Act of 1982 (P.L. 97-448)**

P.L. 97-448, § 201(j)(4):

Amended Code Sec. 6655(e)[f](2)(B). **Effective** as if included in the provision of P.L. 96-223 to which it relates. Prior to amendment, Code Sec. 6655(f)(2)(B) read as follows:

(B) to the extent allowed under regulations prescribed by the Secretary, any amount which is treated under section 6429 as an overpayment of the tax imposed by section 4986.

• **1982, Tax Equity and Fiscal Responsibility Act of 1982 (P.L. 97-248)**

P.L. 97-248, § 234(d)(1):

Redesignated subsection (e) as subsection (f). **Effective** 1-1-83.

P.L. 97-248, § 234(d)(2):

Amended Code Sec. 6655(f) (as redesignated by P.L. 97-248, § 234(d)(1)) by striking out "(d), and (h)" and inserting "(d), (e), and (i)". **Effective** 1-1-83.

• **1981, Economic Recovery Tax Act of 1981 (P.L. 97-34)**

P.L. 97-34, § 601(a)(6)(B):

Amended Code Sec. 6655(e)(2). **Effective** 1-1-80. Prior to amendment, Code Sec. 6655(e)(2) read as follows:

(2) the credits against tax provided by part IV of subchapter A of chapter 1.

ADDITIONS TO TAX

• **1980, Omnibus Reconciliation Act of 1980 (P.L. 96-499)**

P.L. 96-499, §1111(b):

Amended Code Sec. 6655(e) by striking out "subsections (b) and (d)" and inserting in lieu thereof "subsections (b), (d), and (h)". **Effective** for tax years beginning after 1980.

• **1978, Revenue Act of 1978 (P.L. 95-600)**

P.L. 95-600, §301(b)(20)(B):

Amended Code Sec. 6655(e). **Effective** for tax years beginning after 12-31-78. Prior to amendment, Code Sec. 6655(e) read as follows:

"(e) DEFINITION OF TAX.—

"(1) IN GENERAL.—For purposes of subsections (b) and (d), the term 'tax' means the excess of—

"(A) the tax imposed by section 11 or 1201(a), or subchapter L of chapter 1, whichever is applicable, over

"(B) the sum of—

"(i) the credits against tax provided by part IV of subchapter A of chapter 1, and

"(ii) in the case of a taxable year beginning before January 1, 1977, the amount of the corporation's estimated tax exemption for such year.

"(2) TEMPORARY ESTIMATED TAX EXEMPTION.—For purposes of clause (ii) of paragraph (1)(B), the amount of a corporation's temporary estimated tax exemption for a taxable year equals the applicable percentage (determined under section 6154(c)(2)(B)) multiplied by the lesser of—

"(A) an amount equal to 22 percent of the corporation's surtax exemption (as defined in section 11(d)) for such year, or

"(B) the excess determined under paragraph (1) without regard to clause (ii) of paragraph (1)(B).

"(3) SPECIAL RULE FOR SUBSECTION (d)(1) AND (2).—In applying this subsection for purposes of subsection (d)(1) and (2), the applicable percentage and the exclusion percentage shall be the percentage for the taxable year for which the underpayment is being determined."

• **1976, Tax Reform Act of 1976 (P.L. 94-455)**

P.L. 94-455, §1906(b)(3)(A):

Amended Code Sec. 6655(e)(1)(B) by adding "and" at the end of clause (i), and by striking out clauses (ii) and (iii) and inserting in lieu thereof a new clause (ii). **Effective** 2-1-77. Prior to amendment, clauses (ii) and (iii) read as follows:

(ii) in the case of a taxable year beginning after December 31, 1967, and before January 1, 1977, the amount of the corporation's temporary estimated tax exemption for such year, and

(iii) in the case of a taxable year beginning after December 31, 1967, and before January 1, 1972, the amount of the corporation's transitional exemption for such year.

P.L. 94-455, §1906(b)(3)(B):

Substituted "clause (ii)" for "clauses (ii) and (iii)" in Code Sec. 6655(e)(2)(B). **Effective** 2-1-77.

P.L. 94-455, §1906(b)(3)(C)(i):

Deleted paragraph (3) of Code Sec. 6655(e); and redesignated paragraph (4) as paragraph (3). **Effective** 2-1-77. Prior to amendment, paragraph (3) read as follows:

(3) TRANSITIONAL EXEMPTION.—For purposes of clause (iii) of paragraph (1)(B), the amount of a corporation's transitional exemption for a taxable year equals the exclusion percentage (determined under section 6154(c)(3)(B)) multiplied by the lesser of—

(A) $100,000, reduced by the amount of the corporation's temporary estimated tax exemption for such year, or

(B) the excess determined under paragraph (1) without regard to clause (iii) of paragraph (1)(B).

• **1968, Revenue and Expenditure Control Act of 1968 (P.L. 90-364)**

P.L. 90-364, §103(c)(2):

Amended Code Sec. 6655(e). **Effective** with respect to tax years beginning after 12-31-67. However, the amendment is to be taken into account only as of 5-31-68. For the **effective** date provisions of P.L. 90-364, see the amendment note following Code Sec. 6154. Prior to amendment, Code Sec. 6655(e) read as follows:

"(e) Definition of Tax.—For purposes of subsections (b), (d)(2), and (d)(3), the term tax means the excess of—

"(1) the tax imposed by section 11 or 1201(a), or subchapter L of chapter 1, whichever is applicable, over

"(2) the sum of—

"(A) $100,000, and

"(B) the credits against tax provided in part IV of subchapter A of chapter 1."

[Sec. 6655(g)]

(g) SHORT TAXABLE YEAR.—The application of this section to taxable years of less than 12 months shall be in accordance with regulations prescribed by the Secretary.

Amendments

• **1982, Tax Equity and Fiscal Responsibility Act of 1982 (P.L. 97-248)**

P.L. 97-248, §234(d)(1):

Redesignated subsection (f) as subsection (g). **Effective** 1-1-83.

• **1976, Tax Reform Act of 1976 (P.L. 94-455)**

P.L. 94-455, §1906(b)(13)(A):

Amended 1954 Code by substituting "Secretary" for "Secretary or his delegate" each place it appeared. **Effective** 2-1-77.

[Sec. 6655(h)]

(h) EXCESSIVE ADJUSTMENT UNDER SECTION 6425.—

(1) ADDITION TO TAX.—If the amount of an adjustment under section 6425 made before the 15th day of the third month following the close of the taxable year is excessive, there shall be added to the tax under chapter 1 for the taxable year an amount determined at an annual rate established under section 6621 upon the excessive amount from the date on which the credit is allowed or the refund is paid to such 15th day.

(2) EXCESSIVE AMOUNT.—For purposes of paragraph (1), the excessive amount is equal to the amount of the adjustment or (if smaller) the amount by which—

(A) the income tax liability (as defined in section 6425(c)) for the taxable year as shown on the return for the taxable year, exceeds

(B) the estimated income tax paid during the taxable year, reduced by the amount of the adjustment.

Amendments

• **1982, Tax Equity and Fiscal Responsibility Act of 1982 (P.L. 97-248)**

P.L. 97-248, §234(d)(1):

Redesignated subsection (g) as subsection (h). **Effective** 1-1-83.

• **1975 (P.L. 93-625)**

P.L. 93-625, §7(c):

Amended Code Sec. 6655(g)(1) by substituting "an annual rate established under section 6621" for "the rate of 6 percent per annum". **Effective** for amounts outstanding on 7-1-75 or arising thereafter.

• **1968, Revenue and Expenditure Control Act of 1968 (P.L. 90-364)**

P.L. 90-364, §103(d)(2):

Added Code Sec. 6655(g). **Effective** with respect to tax years beginning after 12-31-67.

[Sec. 6655(i)]

(i) LARGE CORPORATIONS REQUIRED TO PAY MINIMUM PERCENTAGE OF CURRENT YEAR TAX.—

(1) MINIMUM PERCENTAGE.—

(A) IN GENERAL.—Except as provided in subparagraph (B), in the case of a large corporation, paragraphs (1) and (2) of subsection (d) shall not apply.

(B) TRANSITION RULE.—For taxable years beginning before 1984, in the case of a large corporation, the amount treated as the estimated tax for the taxable year under paragraphs (1) and (2) of subsection (d) shall in no event be less than the applicable percentage of—

(i) the tax shown on the return for the taxable year, or

(ii) if no return was filed, the tax for such year.

(C) APPLICABLE PERCENTAGE.—For purposes of subparagraph (B), the applicable percentage shall be determined in accordance with the following table:

If the taxable year begins in:	The applicable percentage is:
1982	65
1983	75

(2) LARGE CORPORATION.—For purposes of this subsection, the term "large corporation" means any corporation if such corporation (or any predecessor corporation) had taxable income of $1,000,000 or more for any taxable year during the testing period.

(3) RULES FOR APPLYING PARAGRAPH (2).—

(A) TESTING PERIOD.—For purposes of this subsection, the term "testing period" means the 3 taxable years immediately preceding the taxable year involved.

(B) MEMBERS OF CONTROLLED GROUPS.—For purposes of applying paragraph (2) to any taxable year in the testing period with respect to corporations which are component members of a controlled group of corporations for such taxable year, the $1,000,000 amount specified in paragraph (2) shall be divided among such members under rules similar to the rules of section 1561.

Amendments

• **1982, Tax Equity and Fiscal Responsibility Act of 1982 (P.L. 97-248)**

P.L. 97-248, §234(d)(1):

Redesignated subsection (h) as subsection (i). **Effective** 1-1-83.

• **1981, Econcomic Recovery Tax Act of 1981 (P.L. 97-34)**

P.L. 97-34, §731(a):

Amended Code Sec. 6655(h)(1). **Effective** for tax years beginning after 12-31-81. Prior to amendment, Code Sec. 6655(h)(1) read:

(1) IN GENERAL.—In the case of a large corporation, the amount treated as the estimated tax for the taxable year under paragraphs (1) and (2) of subsection (d) shall in no event be less than 60 percent of—

(A) the tax shown on the return for the taxable year, or

(B) if no return was filed, the tax for such year.

P.L. 97-34, §731(b):

Amended the heading of Code Sec. 6655(h) by striking out "AT LEAST 60 PERCENT" and inserting "MINIMUM PERCENTAGE". E ffective for tax years beginning after 12-31-81.

• **1980, Omnibus Reconciliation Act of 1980 (P.L. 96-499)**

P.L. 96-499, §1111(a):

Added Code Sec. 6655(h). **Effective** for tax years beginning after 1980.

ADDITIONS TO TAX

P.L. 100-203, §10303(b)(2), provides:

(b) CORPORATE PROVISIONS.—

* * *

(2) CORPORATIONS ALSO MAY USE 1986 TAX TO DETERMINE AMOUNT OF CERTAIN ESTIMATED TAX INSTALLMENTS DUE ON OR BEFORE JUNE 15, 1987.—

(A) IN GENERAL.—In the case of a large corporation, no addition to tax shall be imposed by section 6655 of the Internal Revenue Code of 1986 with respect to any underpayment of an estimated tax installment to which this subsection applies if no addition would be imposed with respect to such underpayment by reason of section 6655(d)(1) of such Code if such corporation were not a large corporation. The preceding sentence shall apply only to the extent the underpayment is paid on or before the last date prescribed for payment of the most recent installment of estimated tax due on or before September 15, 1987.

(B) INSTALLMENT TO WHICH SUBSECTION APPLIES.—This subsection applies to any installment of estimated tax for a taxable year beginning after December 31, 1986, which is due on or before June 15, 1987.

(C) LARGE CORPORATION.—For purposes of this subsection, the term "large corporation" has the meaning given such term by section 6655(i)(2) of such Code (as in effect on the day before the date of the enactment of this Act).

[Sec. 6656]

SEC. 6656. FAILURE TO MAKE DEPOSIT OF TAXES.

[Sec. 6656(a)]

(a) UNDERPAYMENT OF DEPOSITS.—In the case of any failure by any person to deposit (as required by this title or by regulations of the Secretary under this title) on the date prescribed therefor any amount of tax imposed by this title in such government depository as is authorized under section 6302(c) to receive such deposit, unless it is shown that such failure is due to reasonable cause and not due to willful neglect, there shall be imposed upon such person a penalty equal to the applicable percentage of the amount of the underpayment.

Amendments

• **2020, Taxpayer Certainty and Disaster Tax Relief Act of 2020 (P.L. 116-260)**

P.L. 116-260, §303(d)(6), Div. EE, provides:

(6) TREATMENT OF DEPOSITS.—The Secretary shall waive any penalty under section 6656 of such Code for any failure to make a deposit of applicable employment taxes if the Secretary determines that such failure was due to the anticipation of the credit allowed under this subsection.

• **2020, Coronavirus Aid, Relief, and Economic Security (CARES) Act (P.L. 116-136)**

P.L. 116-136, §2301(k), provides:

(k) TREATMENT OF DEPOSITS.—The Secretary shall waive any penalty under section 6656 of the Internal Revenue Code of 1986 for any failure to make a deposit of any applicable employment taxes if the Secretary determines that such failure was due to the reasonable anticipation of the credit allowed under this section.

[Sec. 6656(b)]

(b) DEFINITIONS.—For purposes of subsection (a)—

(1) APPLICABLE PERCENTAGE.—

(A) IN GENERAL.—Except as provided in subparagraph (B), the term "applicable percentage" means—

(i) 2 percent if the failure is for not more than 5 days,

(ii) 5 percent if the failure is for more than 5 days but not more than 15 days, and

(iii) 10 percent if the failure is for more than 15 days.

(B) SPECIAL RULE.—In any case where the tax is not deposited on or before the earlier of—

(i) the day 10 days after the date of the first delinquency notice to the taxpayer under section 6303, or

(ii) the day on which notice and demand for immediate payment is given under section 6861 or 6862 or the last sentence of section 6331(a),

the applicable percentage shall be 15 percent.

(2) UNDERPAYMENT.—The term "underpayment" means the excess of the amount of the tax required to be deposited over the amount, if any, thereof deposited on or before the date prescribed therefor.

Amendments

• **1989, Omnibus Budget Reconciliation Act of 1989 (P.L. 101-239)**

P.L. 101-239, §7742(a):

Amended Code Sec. 6656. **Effective** for deposits required to be made after 12-31-89. Prior to amendment, Code Sec. 6656 read as follows:

SEC. 6656. FAILURE TO MAKE DEPOSIT OF TAXES OR OVERSTATEMENT OF DEPOSITS.

[Sec. 6656(a)]

(a) UNDERPAYMENT OF DEPOSITS.—In case of failure by any person required by this title or by regulation of the Secretary under this title to deposit on the date prescribed therefor any amount of tax imposed by this title in such government depositary as is authorized under section 6302(c) to receive such deposit, unless it is shown that such failure is due to reasonable cause and not due to willful neglect, there shall be imposed upon such person a penalty of 10 percent of the amount of the underpayment. For purposes of this subsection, the term "underpayment" means the excess of the amount of the tax required to be so deposited over the amount, if any, thereof deposited on or before the date prescribed therefor.

Amendments

• **1986, Omnibus Budget Reconciliation Act of 1986 (P.L. 99-509)**

P.L. 99-509, §8001(a):

Amended Code Sec. 6656(a) by striking out "5 percent" and inserting in lieu thereof "10 percent". **Effective** for penalties assessed after 10-21-86.

• **1981, Economic Recovery Tax Act of 1981 (P.L. 97-34)**

P.L. 97-34, §724(b)(1):

Amended the heading of Code Sec. 6656 by inserting **"OR OVERSTATEMENT OF DEPOSITS"** after **"TAXES"**. **Effective** for returns filed after 8-13-81.

P.L. 97-34, §724(b)(3):

Amended the heading of Code Sec. 6656(a) by striking out "PENALTY" and inserting "UNDERPAYMENT OF DEPOSITS". **Effective** for returns filed after 8-13-81.

• **1976, Tax Reform Act of 1976 (P.L. 94-455)**

P.L. 94-455, §1906(b)(13)(A):

Amended 1954 Code by substituting "Secretary" for "Secretary or his delegate" each place it appeared. **Effective** 2-1-77.

• **1969, Tax Reform Act of 1969 (P.L. 91-172)**

P.L. 91-172, §943(b):

Amended Sec. 6656(a) by inserting "a penalty of 5 percent of the amount of the underpayment" in lieu of "a penalty of 1 percent of the amount of the underpayment if the failure is for not more than 1 month, with an additional 1 percent for each additional month or fraction thereof during which such failure continues, not exceeding 6 percent in the aggregate" at the end of the first sentence. **Effective** with respect to deposits the time for making of which is after 12-31-69.

[Sec. 6656(b)]

(b) OVERSTATED DEPOSIT CLAIMS.—

(1) IMPOSITION OF PENALTY.—Any person who makes an overstated deposit claim shall be subject to a penalty equal to 25 percent of such claim.

(2) OVERSTATED DEPOSIT CLAIM DEFINED.—For purposes of this subsection, the term "overstated deposit claim" means the excess of—

(A) the amount of tax under this title which any person claims, in a return filed with the Secretary, that such person has deposited in a government depositary under section 6302(c) for any period, over

(B) the aggregate amount such person has deposited in a government depositary under section 6302(c), for such period, on or before the date such return is filed.

(3) PENALTY NOT IMPOSED IN CERTAIN CASES.—The penalty under paragraph (1) shall not apply if it is shown that the excess described in paragraph (2) is due to reasonable cause and not due to willful neglect.

(4) PENALTY IN ADDITION TO OTHER PENALTIES.—The penalty under paragraph (1) shall be in addition to any other penalty provided by law.

Amendments

• **1981, Economic Recovery Tax Act of 1981 (P.L. 97-34)**

P.L. 97-34, §724(a):

Amended Code Sec. 6656(b). **Effective** for returns filed after 8-13-81. Prior to amendment, Code Sec. 6656(b) read as follows:

(b) PENALTY NOT IMPOSED AFTER DUE DATE FOR RETURN.—For purposes of subsection (a), the failure shall be deemed not to continue beyond the last date (determined without regard to any extension of time) prescribed for payment of the tax required to be deposited or beyond the date the tax is paid whichever is earlier.

ADDITIONS TO TAX

[Sec. 6656(c)]

(c) EXCEPTION FOR FIRST-TIME DEPOSITORS OF EMPLOYMENT TAXES.—The Secretary may waive the penalty imposed by subsection (a) on a person's inadvertent failure to deposit any employment tax if—

(1) such person meets the requirements referred to in section 7430(c)(4)(A)(ii),

(2) such failure—

(A) occurs during the first quarter that such person was required to deposit any employment tax; or

(B) if such person is required to change the frequency of deposits of any employment tax, relates to the first deposit to which such change applies, and

(3) the return of such tax was filed on or before the due date.

For purposes of this subsection, the term "employment taxes" means the taxes imposed by subtitle C.

Amendments

• **1998, IRS Restructuring and Reform Act of 1998 (P.L. 105-206)**

P.L. 105-206, § 3304(b)(1):

Amended Code Sec. 6656(c)(2). **Effective** for deposits required to be made after the 180th day after 7-22-98. Prior to amendment, Code Sec. 6656(c)(2) read as follows:

(2) such failure occurs during the 1st quarter that such person was required to deposit any employment tax, and

• **1996, Taxpayer Bill of Rights 2 (P.L. 104-168)**

P.L. 104-168, § 304(a):

Amended Code Sec. 6656 by adding at the end a new subsection (c). **Effective** for deposits required to be made after 7-30-96.

P.L. 104-168, § 701(c)(3):

Amended Code Sec. 6656(c)(1) (as added by Act Sec. 304(a)) by striking "section 7430(c)(4)(A)(iii)" and inserting "section 7430(c)(4)(A)(ii)". **Effective** in the case of proceedings commenced after 7-30-96.

[Sec. 6656(d)]

(d) AUTHORITY TO ABATE PENALTY WHERE DEPOSIT SENT TO SECRETARY.—The Secretary may abate the penalty imposed by subsection (a) with respect to the first time a depositor is required to make a deposit if the amount required to be deposited is inadvertently sent to the Secretary instead of to the appropriate government depository.

Amendments

• **1996, Taxpayer Bill of Rights 2 (P.L. 104-168)**

P.L. 104-168, § 304(a):

Amended Code Sec. 6656 by adding at the end a new subsection (d). **Effective** for deposits required to be made after 7-30-96.

[Sec. 6656(e)]

(e) DESIGNATION OF PERIODS TO WHICH DEPOSITS APPLY.—

(1) IN GENERAL.—A deposit made under this section shall be applied to the most recent period or periods within the specified tax period to which the deposit relates, unless the person making such deposit designates a different period or periods to which such deposit is to be applied.

(2) TIME FOR MAKING DESIGNATION.—A person may make a designation under paragraph (1) only during the 90-day period beginning on the date of a notice that a penalty under subsection (a) has been imposed for the specified tax period to which the deposit relates.

Amendments

• **1998, IRS Restructuring and Reform Act of 1998 (P.L. 105-206)**

P.L. 105-206, § 3304(a):

Amended Code Sec. 6656 by adding at the end a new subsection (e). **Effective** for deposits required to be made after the 180th day after 7-22-98.

P.L. 105-206, § 3304(c):

Amended Code Sec. 6656(e)(1), as added by Act Sec. 3304(a). **Effective** for deposits required to be made after 12-31-2001. Prior to amendment, Code Sec. 6656(e)(1) read as follows:

(1) IN GENERAL.—A person may, with respect to any deposit of tax to be reported on such person's return for a specified tax period, designate the period or periods within such specified tax period to which the deposit is to be applied for purposes of this section.

[Sec. 6657]

SEC. 6657. BAD CHECKS.

If any instrument in payment, by any commercially acceptable means, of any amount receivable under this title is not duly paid, in addition to any other penalties provided by law, there shall be paid as a penalty by the person who tendered such instrument, upon notice and demand by the Secretary, in the same manner as tax, an amount equal to 2 percent of the amount of such instrument, except that if the amount of such instrument is less than $1,250, the penalty under this section shall be $25 or the amount of such instrument, whichever is the lesser. This section shall not apply if the person tendered such instrument in good faith and with reasonable cause to believe that it would be duly paid.

Amendments

• **2010, Homebuyer Assistance and Improvement Act of 2010 (P.L. 111-198)**

P.L. 111-198, § 3(a)(1)-(2):

Amended Code Sec. 6657 by striking "If any check or money order in payment of any amount" and inserting "If any instrument in payment, by any commercially acceptable means, of any amount", and by striking "such check" each place it appears and inserting "such instrument". **Effective** for instruments tendered after 7-2-2010.

• **2007, Small Business and Work Opportunity Tax Act of 2007 (P.L. 110-28)**

P.L. 110-28, § 8245(a)(1)-(2):

Amended Code Sec. 6657 by striking "$750" and inserting "$1,250", and by striking "$15" and inserting "$25". **Effective** for checks or money orders received after 5-25-2007.

• **1988, Technical and Miscellaneous Revenue Act of 1988 (P.L. 100-647)**

P.L. 100-647, § 5071(a)(1)-(3):

Amended Code Sec. 6657 by striking out "1 percent" and inserting in lieu thereof "2 percent", by striking out "$500" and inserting in lieu thereof "$750", and by striking out "$5" and inserting in lieu thereof "$15". **Effective** for checks or money orders received after 11-10-88.

• **1976, Tax Reform Act of 1976 (P.L. 94-455)**

P.L. 94-455, § 1906(b)(13)(A):

Amended 1954 Code by substituting "Secretary" for "Secretary or his delegate" each place it appeared. **Effective** 2-1-77.

[Sec. 6658]

SEC. 6658. COORDINATION WITH TITLE 11.

[Sec. 6658(a)]

(a) CERTAIN FAILURES TO PAY TAX.—No addition to the tax shall be made under section 6651, 6654, or 6655 for failure to make timely payment of tax with respect to a period during which a case is pending under title 11 of the United States Code—

(1) if such tax was incurred by the estate and the failure occurred pursuant to an order of the court finding probable insufficiency of funds of the estate to pay administrative expenses, or

(2) if—

ADDITIONS TO TAX

(A) such tax was incurred by the debtor before the earlier of the order for relief or (in the involuntary case) the appointment of a trustee, and

(B)(i) the petition was filed before the due date prescribed by law (including extensions) for filing a return of such tax, or

(ii) the date for making the addition to the tax occurs on or after the day on which the petition was filed.

Amendments

• **1980, Bankruptcy Tax Act of 1980 (P.L. 96-589)**

P.L. 96-589, §6(e)(1):

Added Code Sec. 6658(a). **Effective** 10-1-79, but inapplicable to any proceeding under the Bankruptcy Act commenced before that date.

[Sec. 6658(b)]

(b) EXCEPTION FOR COLLECTED TAXES.—Subsection (a) shall not apply to any liability for an addition to the tax which arises from the failure to pay or deposit a tax withheld or collected from others and required to be paid to the United States.

Amendments

• **1980, Bankruptcy Tax Act of 1980 (P.L. 96-589)**

P.L. 96-589, §6(e)(1):

Added Code Sec. 6658(b). **Effective** 10-1-79, but inapplicable to any proceeding under the Bankruptcy Act commenced before that date.

Amendments

• **1989, Omnibus Budget Reconciliation Act of 1989 (P.L. 101-239)**

P.L. 101-239, §7721(c)(2):

Repealed Code Sec. 6659. **Effective** for returns the due date for which (determined without regard to extensions) is after 12-31-89. Prior to repeal, Code Sec. 6659 read as follows:

SEC. 6659. ADDITION TO TAX IN THE CASE OF VALUATION OVERSTATEMENTS FOR PURPOSES OF THE INCOME TAX.

[Sec. 6659(a)]

(a) ADDITION TO THE TAX.—If—

(1) an individual, or

(2) a closely held corporation or a personal service corporation,

has an underpayment of the tax imposed by chapter 1 for the taxable year which is attributable to a valuation overstatement, then there shall be added to the tax an amount equal to the applicable percentage of the underpayment so attributable.

[Sec. 6659(b)]

(b) APPLICABLE PERCENTAGE DEFINED.—For purposes of subsection (a), the applicable percentage shall be determined under the following table:

If the valuation claimed is the following percent of the correct valuation—	The applicable percentage is:
150 percent or more but not more than 200 percent	10
More than 200 percent but not more than 250 percent	20
More than 250 percent	30

[Sec. 6659(c)]

(c) VALUATION OVERSTATEMENT DEFINED.—For purposes of this section, there is a valuation overstatement if the value of any property, or the adjusted basis of any property, claimed on any return is 150 percent or more of the amount determined to be the correct amount of such valuation or adjusted basis (as the case may be).

Amendments

• **1984, Deficit Reduction Act of 1984 (P.L. 98-369)**

P.L. 98-369, §155(c)(1)(A):

Amended Code Sec. 6659(c). Prior to amendment, Code Sec. 6659(c) read as follows:

(c) Valuation Overstatement Defined.—

(1) In General.—For purposes of this section, there is a valuation overstatement if the value of any property, or the adjusted basis of any property, claimed on any return is 150 percent or more of the amount determined to be the correct amount of such valuation or adjusted basis (as the case may be).

(2) Property Must Have Been Acquired Within Last 5 Years.—This section shall not apply to any property which, as of the close of the taxable year for which there is a valuation overstatement, has been held by the taxpayer for more than 5 years.

[Sec. 6659(d)]

(d) UNDERPAYMENT MUST BE AT LEAST $1,000.—This section shall not apply if the underpayment for the taxable year attributable to valuation overstatements is less than $1,000.

[Sec. 6659(e)]

(e) AUTHORITY TO WAIVE.—The Secretary may waive all or any part of the addition to the tax provided by this section on a showing by the taxpayer that there was a reasonable basis for the valuation or adjusted basis claimed on the return and that such claim was made in good faith.

[Sec. 6659(f)]

(f) SPECIAL RULES FOR OVERSTATEMENT OF CHARITABLE DEDUCTION.—

(1) AMOUNT OF APPLICABLE PERCENTAGE.—In the case of any underpayment attributable to a valuation overstatement with respect to charitable deduction property, the applicable percentage for purposes of subsection (a) shall be 30 percent.

• **1979 (P.L. 96-167)**

P.L. 96-167, §6:

Repealed Code Section 6658. **Effective** for violations or attempted violations occurring after 12-12-79. Prior to repeal, former Code Sec. 6658 provided:

"If a taxpayer violates or attempts to violate section 6851 (relating to termination of taxable year) there shall, in addition to all other penalties, be added as part of the tax 25 percent of the total amount of the tax or deficiency in the tax."

[Sec. 6659—Repealed]

(2) LIMITATION ON AUTHORITY TO WAIVE.—In the case of any underpayment attributable to a valuation overstatement with respect to charitable deduction property, the Secretary may not waive any portion of the addition to tax provided by this section unless the Secretary determines that—

(A) the claimed value of the property was based on a qualified appraisal made by a qualified appraiser, and

(B) in addition to obtaining such appraisal, the taxpayer made a good faith investigation of the value of the contributed property.

(3) DEFINITIONS.—For purposes of this subsection—

(A) CHARITABLE DEDUCTION PROPERTY.—The term "charitable deduction property" means any property contributed by the taxpayer in a contribution for which a deduction was claimed under section 170. For purposes of paragraph (2), such term shall not include any securities for which (as of the date of the contribution) market quotations are readily available on an established securities market.

(B) QUALIFIED APPRAISER.—The term "qualified appraiser" means any appraiser meeting the requirements of the regulations prescribed under section 170(a)(1).

(C) QUALIFIED APPRAISAL.—The term "qualified appraisal" means any appraisal meeting the requirements of the regulations prescribed under section 170(a)(1).

Amendments

• **1984, Deficit Reduction Act of 1984 (P.L. 98-369)**

P.L. 98-369, §155(c)(1)(B):

Amended Code Sec. 6659 by redesignating subsection (f) as subsection (g) and adding new subsection (f). **Effective** for returns filed after 12-31-84.

[Sec. 6659(g)]

(g) OTHER DEFINITIONS.—For purposes of this section—

(1) UNDERPAYMENT.—The term "underpayment" has the meaning given to such term by section 6653(c)(1).

(2) CLOSELY HELD CORPORATION.—The term "closely held corporation" means any corporation described in section 465(a)(1)(B).

(3) PERSONAL SERVICE CORPORATION.—The term "personal service corporation" means any corporation which is a service organization (within the meaning of section 414(m)(3)).

Amendments

• **1984, Deficit Reduction Act of 1984 (P.L. 98-369)**

P.L. 98-369, §155(c)(1)(B):

Amended Code Sec. 6659 by redesignating subsection (f) as subsection (g). **Effective** for returns filed after 12-31-84.

P.L. 98-369, §721(x)(4):

Amended Code Sec. 6659(f), prior to redesignation by Act Sec. 155(c)(1)(B), by striking out "section 465(a)(1)(C)" and inserting in lieu thereof "section 465(a)(1)(B)". **Effective** as if included in P.L. 97-354.

• **1983, Technical Corrections Act of 1982 (P.L. 97-448)**

P.L. 97-448, §107(a)(1):

Amended Code Sec. 6659(d) by striking out "the valuation overstatement" and inserting in lieu thereof "valuation overstatements". **Effective** as if included in the provision of P.L. 97-34 to which it relates.

P.L. 97-448, §107(a)(2):

Amended Code Sec. 6659(c)(1) by striking out "exceeds 150 percent of" and inserting in lieu thereof "is 150 percent or more of". **Effective** as if included in the provision of P.L. 97-34 to which it relates.

• **1981, Economic Recovery Tax Act of 1981 (P.L. 97-34)**

P.L. 97-34, §722(a)(1):

Added Code Sec. 6659. **Effective** for returns filed after 12-31-81.

ADDITIONS TO TAX

[Sec. 6659A—Repealed]

Amendments

• **1989, Omnibus Budget Reconciliation Act of 1989 (P.L. 101-239)**

P.L. 101-239, §7721(c)(2):

Repealed Code Sec. 6659A. **Effective** for returns the due date for which (determined without regard to extensions) is after 12-31-89. Prior to repeal, Code Sec. 6659A read as follows:

SEC. 6659A. ADDITION TO TAX IN CASE OF OVERSTATEMENTS OF PENSION LIABILITIES.

(a) ADDITION TO TAX.—In the case of an underpayment of the tax imposed by chapter 1 on any taxpayer for the taxable year which is attributable to an overstatement of pension liabilities, there shall be added to such tax an amount equal to the applicable percentage of the underpayment so attributable.

(b) APPLICABLE PERCENTAGE DEFINED.—For purposes of subsection (a), the applicable percentage shall be determined under the following table:

If the valuation claimed is the following percent of the correct valuation—	The applicable percentage is:
150 percent or more but not more than 200 percent	10
More than 200 percent but not more than 250 percent	20
More than 250 percent	30

(c) OVERSTATEMENT OF PENSION LIABILITIES.—For purposes of this section, there is an overstatement of pension liabilities if the actuarial determination of the liabilities taken into account for purposes of computing the deduction under paragraph (1) or (2) of section 404(a) exceeds the amount determined to be the correct amount of such liability.

(d) UNDERPAYMENT MUST BE AT LEAST $1,000.—This section shall not apply if the underpayment for the taxable year attributable to valuation overstatements is less than $1,000.

(e) AUTHORITY TO WAIVE.—The Secretary may waive all or any part of the addition to the tax provided by this section on a showing by the taxpayer that there was a reasonable basis for the valuation claimed on the return and that such claim was made in good faith.

• **1986, Tax Reform Act of 1986 (P.L. 99-514)**

P.L. 99-514, §1138(a):

Amended subchapter A of chapter 68 by inserting after section 6659 new section 6659A. **Effective** for overstatements made after 10-22-86.

[Sec. 6660—Repealed]

Amendments

• **1989, Omnibus Budget Reconciliation Act of 1989 (P.L. 101-239)**

P.L. 101-239, §7721(c)(2):

Repealed Code Sec. 6660. **Effective** for returns the due date for which (determined without regard to extensions) is after 12-31-89. Prior to repeal, Code Sec. 6660 read as follows:

SEC. 6660. ADDITION TO TAX IN THE CASE OF VALUATION UNDERSTATEMENT FOR PURPOSES OF ESTATE OR GIFT TAXES.

(a) ADDITION TO THE TAX.—In the case of any underpayment of a tax imposed by subtitle B (relating to estate and gift taxes) which is attributable to a valuation understatement, there shall be added to the tax an amount equal to the applicable percentage of the underpayment so attributed.

(b) APPLICABLE PERCENTAGE.—For purposes of subsection (a), the applicable percentage shall be determined under the following table:

If the valuation claimed is the following percent of the correct valuation—	The applicable percentage is:
50 percent or more but not more than $66^{2}/_{3}$ percent	10
40 percent or more but less than 50 percent	20
Less than 40 percent	30

(c) VALUATION UNDERSTATEMENT DEFINED.—For purposes of this section, there is a valuation understatement if the value of any property claimed on any return is $66^{2}/_{3}$ percent or less of the amount determined to be the correct amount of such valuation.

(d) UNDERPAYMENT MUST BE AT LEAST $1,000.—This section shall not apply if the underpayment is less than $1,000 for any taxable period (or, in the case of the tax imposed by chapter 11, with respect to the estate of the decedent).

(e) AUTHORITY TO WAIVE.—The Secretary may waive all or any part of the addition to the tax provided by this section on a showing by the taxpayer that there was a reasonable basis for the valuation claimed on the return and that such claim was made in good faith.

(f) UNDERPAYMENT DEFINED.—For purposes of this section, the term "underpayment" has the meaning given to such term by section 6653(c)(1).

• **1986, Tax Reform Act of 1986 (P.L. 99-514)**

P.L. 99-514, §1811(d):

Amended Code Sec. 6660 by adding at the end thereof new subsection (f). **Effective** as if included in the provision of P.L. 98-369 to which it relates.

P.L. 99-514, §1899A(57):

Amended Code Sec. 6660 by striking out "THE ESTATE" and inserting in lieu thereof "ESTATE" in the heading. **Effective** 10-22-86.

• **1984, Deficit Reduction Act of 1984 (P.L. 98-369)**

P.L. 98-369, §155(c)(2)(A):

Added Code Sec. 6660. **Effective** for returns filed after 12-31-84.

[Sec. 6661—Repealed]

Amendments

• **1989, Omnibus Budget Reconciliation Act of 1989 (P.L. 101-239)**

P.L. 101-239, §7721:

Repealed Code Sec. 6661. **Effective** for returns the due date for which (determined without regard to extensions) is after 12-31-89. Prior to repeal, Code Sec. 6661 read as follows:

SEC. 6661. SUBSTANTIAL UNDERSTATEMENT OF LIABILITY.

[Sec. 6661(a)]

(a) ADDITION TO TAX.—If there is a substantial understatement of income tax for any taxable year, there shall be added to the tax an amount equal to 25 percent of the amount of any underpayment attributable to such understatement.

Amendments

• **1986, Tax Reform Act of 1986 (P.L. 99-514)**

P.L. 99-514, §1504(a) (repealed by P.L. 99-509, §8002(c)):

Amended Code Sec. 6661(a) by striking out "10 percent" and inserting in lieu thereof "20 percent" [see amendment note below.—CCH.] **Effective** for returns the due date for which (determined without regard to extensions) is after 12-31-86.

• **1986, Omnibus Budget Reconciliation Act of 1986 (P.L. 99-509)**

P.L. 99-509, §8002(a):

Amended Code Sec. 6661(a). **Effective** for penalties assessed after 10-21-86. Prior to the repeal of P.L. 99-514, §1504(a), Code Sec. 6661(a) read as follows:

(a) ADDITION TO TAX.—If there is a substantial understatement of income tax for any taxable year, there shall be added to the tax an amount equal to 20 percent of the amount of any underpayment attributable to such understatement.

[Sec. 6661(b)]

(b) DEFINITION AND SPECIAL RULE.—

(1) SUBSTANTIAL UNDERSTATEMENT.—

(A) IN GENERAL.—For purposes of this section, there is a substantial understatement of income tax for any taxable year if the amount of the understatement for the taxable year exceeds the greater of—

(i) 10 percent of the tax required to be shown on the return for the taxable year, or

(ii) $5,000.

(B) SPECIAL RULE FOR CORPORATIONS.—In the case of a corporation other than an S corporation or a personal holding company (as defined in section 542), paragraph (1) shall be applied by substituting "$10,000" for "$5,000".

(2) UNDERSTATEMENT.—

(A) IN GENERAL.—For purposes of paragraph (1), the term "Understatement" means the excess of—

(i) the amount of the tax required to be shown on the return for the taxable year, over

(ii) the amount of the tax imposed which is shown on the return, reduced by any rebate (within the meaning of section 6211(b)(2)).

(B) REDUCTION FOR UNDERSTATEMENT DUE TO POSITION OF TAXPAYER OR DISCLOSED ITEM.—The amount of the understatement under subparagraph (A) shall be reduced by that portion of the understatement which is attributable to—

(i) the tax treatment of any item by the taxpayer if there is or was substantial authority for such treatment, or

(ii) any item with respect to which the relevant facts affecting the item's tax treatment are adequately disclosed in the return or in a statement attached to the return.

(C) SPECIAL RULES IN CASES INVOLVING TAX SHELTERS.—

(i) IN GENERAL.—In the case of any item attributable to a tax shelter—

(I) subparagraph (B)(ii) shall not apply, and

(II) subparagraph (B)(i) shall not apply unless (in addition to meeting the requirements of such subparagraph) the taxpayer reasonably believed that the tax treatment of such item by the taxpayer was more likely than not the proper treatment.

(ii) TAX SHELTER.—For purposes of clause (i), the term "tax shelter" means—

(I) a partnership or other entity,

(II) any investment plan or arrangement, or

(III) any other plan or arrangement,

if the principal purpose of such partnership, entity, plan, or arrangement is the avoidance or evasion of Federal income tax.

ACCURACY-RELATED AND FRAUD PENALTIES

(3) COORDINATION WITH PENALTY IMPOSED BY SECTION 6659.—For purposes of determining the amount of the addition to tax assessed under subsection (a), there shall not be taken into account that portion of the substantial understatement on which a penalty is imposed under section 6659 (relating to addition to tax in the case of valuation overstatements).

[Sec. 6661(c)]

(c) AUTHORITY TO WAIVE.—The Secretary may waive all or any part of the addition to tax provided by this section on a showing by the taxpayer that there was reasonable cause for the understatement (or part thereof) and that the taxpayer acted in good faith.

Amendments

• **1984, Deficit Reduction Act of 1984 (P.L. 98-369)**

P.L. 98-369, §714(h)(3):

Amended Code Sec. 6661(b)(2)(A)(ii) by inserting ", reduced by any rebate (within the meaning of section 6211(b)(2))" after "return". **Effective** as if included in the provision of P.L. 97-248 to which it relates.

• **1982, Subchapter S Revision Act of 1982 (P.L. 97-354)**

P.L. 97-354, §5(a)(42):

Amended Code Sec. 6661(b)(1)(B) by striking out "an electing small business corporation (as defined in section 1371(b))" and inserting in lieu thereof "an S corporation". **Effective** for tax years beginning after 12-31-82.

• **1982, Tax Equity and Fiscal Responsibility Act of 1982 (P.L. 97-248)**

P.L. 97-248, §323(a):

Added Code Sec. 6661. **Effective** for returns the due date (determined without regard to extension) for filing of which is after 12-31-82.

PART II—ACCURACY-RELATED AND FRAUD PENALTIES

Sec. 6662. Imposition of accuracy-related penalty on underpayments.
Sec. 6662A. Imposition of accuracy-related penalty on understatements with respect to reportable transactions.
Sec. 6663. Imposition of fraud penalty.
Sec. 6664. Definitions and special rules.

[Sec. 6662]

SEC. 6662. IMPOSITION OF ACCURACY-RELATED PENALTY ON UNDERPAYMENTS.

[Sec. 6662(a)]

(a) IMPOSITION OF PENALTY.—If this section applies to any portion of an underpayment of tax required to be shown on a return, there shall be added to the tax an amount equal to 20 percent of the portion of the underpayment to which this section applies.

Amendments

• **2004, American Jobs Creation Act of 2004 (P.L. 108-357)**

P.L. 108-357, §812(e)(1):

Amended the heading for Code Sec. 6662. **Effective** for tax years ending after 10-22-2004. Prior to amendment, the heading for Code Sec. 6662 read as follows:

SEC. 6662. IMPOSITION OF ACCURACY-RELATED PENALTY.

[Sec. 6662(b)]

(b) PORTION OF UNDERPAYMENT TO WHICH SECTION APPLIES.—This section shall apply to the portion of any underpayment which is attributable to 1 or more of the following:

(1) Negligence or disregard of rules or regulations.

(2) Any substantial understatement of income tax.

(3) Any substantial valuation misstatement under chapter 1.

(4) Any substantial overstatement of pension liabilities.

(5) Any substantial estate or gift tax valuation understatement.

(6) Any disallowance of claimed tax benefits by reason of a transaction lacking economic substance (within the meaning of section 7701(o)) or failing to meet the requirements of any similar rule of law.

(7) Any undisclosed foreign financial asset understatement.

(8) Any inconsistent estate basis.

(9) Any overstatement of the deduction provided in section 170(p).

(10) Any disallowance of a deduction by reason of section 170(h)(7).

This section shall not apply to any portion of an underpayment on which a penalty is imposed under section 6663. Except as provided in paragraph (1) or (2)(B) of section 6662A(e), this section shall not apply to the portion of any underpayment which is attributable to a reportable transaction understatement on which a penalty is imposed under section 6662A.

Amendments

• **2022, SECURE 2.0 Act of 2022 (P.L. 117-328)**

P.L. 117-328, §605(a)(2)(A):

Amended Code Sec. 6662(b) by inserting after paragraph (9) a new paragraph (10). **Effective** for contributions made after 12-29-2022. For a special rule, see Act Sec. 605(c)(2), below.

P.L. 117-328, §605(c)(2), provides:

(2) NO INFERENCE.—No inference is intended as to the appropriate treatment of contributions made in taxable years ending on or before the date specified in paragraph (1), or as to any contribution for which a deduction is not disallowed by reason of section 170(h)(7) of the Internal Revenue Code of 1986, as added by this section.

• **2020, Taxpayer Certainty and Disaster Tax Relief Act of 2020 (P.L. 116-260)**

P.L. 116-260, §212(b)(1), Div. EE:

Amended Code Sec. 6662(b) by inserting after paragraph (8) a new paragraph (9). **Effective** for tax years beginning after 12-31-2020.

• **2015, Surface Transportation and Veterans Health Care Choice Improvement Act of 2015 (P.L. 114-41)**

P.L. 114-41, §2004(c)(1):

Amended Code Sec. 6662(b) by inserting after paragraph (7) a new paragraph (8). **Effective** for property with respect to which an estate tax return is filed after 7-31-2015.

• **2010, Health Care and Education Reconciliation Act of 2010 (P.L. 111-152)**

P.L. 111-152, §1409(b)(1):

Amended Code Sec. 6662(b) by inserting after paragraph (5) a new paragraph (6). **Effective** for underpayments attributable to transactions entered into after 3-30-2010.

• **2010, Hiring Incentives to Restore Employment Act (P.L. 111-147)**

P.L. 111-147, §512(a)(1) (as amended by P.L. 113-295, §208(a), Division A):

Amended Code Sec. 6662, as amended by this Act, in subsection (b) by inserting after paragraph (5) a new paragraph (7). **Effective** for tax years beginning after 3-18-2010.

• **2005, Gulf Opportunity Zone Act of 2005 (P.L. 109-135)**

P.L. 109-135, §403(x)(1):

Amended Code Sec. 6662(b) by adding at the end a new sentence. **Effective** as if included in the provision of the American Jobs Creation Act of 2004 (P.L. 108-357) to which it relates [effective for tax years ending after 10-22-2004.—CCH].

• **1990, Omnibus Budget Reconciliation Act of 1990 (P.L. 101-508)**

P.L. 101-508, §11312(b)(1):

Amended Code Sec. 6662(b)(3). **Effective** for tax years ending after 11-5-90. Prior to amendment, Code Sec. 6662(b)(3) read as follows:

(3) Any substantial valuation overstatement under chapter 1.

ACCURACY-RELATED AND FRAUD PENALTIES

[Sec. 6662(c)]

(c) NEGLIGENCE.—For purposes of this section, the term "negligence" includes any failure to make a reasonable attempt to comply with the provisions of this title, and the term "disregard" includes any careless, reckless, or intentional disregard.

[Sec. 6662(d)]

(d) SUBSTANTIAL UNDERSTATEMENT OF INCOME TAX.—

(1) SUBSTANTIAL UNDERSTATEMENT.—

(A) IN GENERAL.—For purposes of this section, there is a substantial understatement of income tax for any taxable year if the amount of the understatement for the taxable year exceeds the greater of—

(i) 10 percent of the tax required to be shown on the return for the taxable year, or

(ii) $5,000.

(B) SPECIAL RULE FOR CORPORATIONS.—In the case of a corporation other than an S corporation or a personal holding company (as defined in section 542), there is a substantial understatement of income tax for any taxable year if the amount of the understatement for the taxable year exceeds the lesser of—

(i) 10 percent of the tax required to be shown on the return for the taxable year (or, if greater, $10,000), or

(ii) $10,000,000.

(C) SPECIAL RULE FOR TAXPAYERS CLAIMING SECTION 199A DEDUCTION.—In the case of any taxpayer who claims any deduction allowed under section 199A for the taxable year, subparagraph (A) shall be applied by substituting "5 percent" for "10 percent".

(2) UNDERSTATEMENT.—

(A) IN GENERAL.—For purposes of paragraph (1), the term "understatement" means the excess of—

(i) the amount of the tax required to be shown on the return for the taxable year, over

(ii) the amount of the tax imposed which is shown on the return, reduced by any rebate (within the meaning of section 6211(b)(2)).

The excess under the preceding sentence shall be determined without regard to items to which section 6662A applies.

(B) REDUCTION FOR UNDERSTATEMENT DUE TO POSITION OF TAXPAYER OR DISCLOSED ITEM.—The amount of the understatement under subparagraph (A) shall be reduced by that portion of the understatement which is attributable to—

(i) the tax treatment of any item by the taxpayer if there is or was substantial authority for such treatment, or

(ii) any item if—

(I) the relevant facts affecting the item's tax treatment are adequately disclosed in the return or in a statement attached to the return, and

(II) there is a reasonable basis for the tax treatment of such item by the taxpayer.

For purposes of clause (ii)(II), in no event shall a corporation be treated as having a reasonable basis for its tax treatment of an item attributable to a multiple-party financing transaction if such treatment does not clearly reflect the income of the corporation.

(C) REDUCTION NOT TO APPLY TO TAX SHELTERS.—

(i) IN GENERAL.—Subparagraph (B) shall not apply to any item attributable to a tax shelter.

(ii) TAX SHELTER.—For purposes of clause (i), the term "tax shelter" means—

(I) a partnership or other entity,

(II) any investment plan or arrangement, or

(III) any other plan or arrangement,

if a significant purpose of such partnership, entity, plan, or arrangement is the avoidance or evasion of Federal income tax.

(3) SECRETARIAL LIST.—The Secretary may prescribe a list of positions which the Secretary believes do not meet 1 or more of the standards specified in paragraph (2)(B)(i), section 6664(d)(3), and section 6694(a)(1). Such list (and any revisions thereof) shall be published in the Federal Register or the Internal Revenue Bulletin.

Amendments

• **2018, Consolidated Appropriations Act, 2018 (P.L. 115-141)**

P.L. 115-141, §101(a)(2)(A), Div. T:

Amended Code Sec. 6662(d)(1)(C) by striking "the deduction" and inserting "any deduction". **Effective** as if included in section 11011 of Public Law 115–97 [effective for tax years beginning after 12-31-2017.—CCH].

• **2018, Tax Technical Corrections Act of 2018 (P.L. 115-141)**

P.L. 115-141, §401(a)(303), Div. U:

Amended Code Sec. 6662(d)(3) by striking "section 6664(d)(2)" and inserting "section 6664(d)(3)". **Effective** 3-23-2018.

• **2017, Tax Cuts and Jobs Act (P.L. 115-97)**

P.L. 115-97, §11011(c):

Amended Code Sec. 6662(d)(1) by inserting at the end a new subparagraph (C). **Effective** for tax years beginning after 12-31-2017.

• **2005, Gulf Opportunity Zone Act of 2005 (P.L. 109-135)**

P.L. 109-135, §412(aaa):

Amended Code Sec. 6662(d)(3) by striking "the" before "1 or more". **Effective** 12-21-2005.

• **2004, American Jobs Creation Act of 2004 (P.L. 108-357)**

P.L. 108-357, §812(b):

Amended Code Sec. 6662(d)(2)(A) by adding at the end a flush sentence. **Effective** for tax years ending after 10-22-2004.

P.L. 108-357, §812(d):

Amended Code Sec. 6662(d)(2)(C). **Effective** for tax years ending after 10-22-2004. Prior to amendment, Code Sec. 6662(d)(2)(C) read as follows:

(C) SPECIAL RULES IN CASES INVOLVING TAX SHELTERS.—

(i) IN GENERAL.—In the case of any item of a taxpayer other than a corporation which is attributable to a tax shelter—

(I) subparagraph (B)(ii) shall not apply, and

(II) subparagraph (B)(i) shall not apply unless (in addition to meeting the requirements of such subparagraph) the taxpayer reasonably believed that the tax treatment of such item by the taxpayer was more likely than not the proper treatment.

(ii) SUBPARAGRAPH (B) NOT TO APPLY TO CORPORATIONS.—Subparagraph (B) shall not apply to any item of a corporation which is attributable to a tax shelter.

(iii) TAX SHELTER.—For purposes of this subparagraph, the term "tax shelter" means—

(I) a partnership or other entity,

(II) any investment plan or arrangement, or

(III) any other plan or arrangement,

if a significant purpose of such partnership, entity, plan, or arrangement is the avoidance or evasion of Federal income tax.

P.L. 108-357, §819(a):

Amended Code Sec. 6662(d)(1)(B). **Effective** for tax years beginning after 10-22-2004. Prior to amendment, Code Sec. 6662(d)(1)(B) read as follows:

(B) SPECIAL RULE FOR CORPORATIONS.—In the case of a corporation other than an S corporation or a personal holding company (as defined in section 542), paragraph (1) shall be applied by substituting "$10,000" for "$5,000".

P.L. 108-357, §819(b)(1):

Amended Code Sec. 6662(d) by adding at the end a new paragraph (3). **Effective** for tax years beginning after 10-22-2004.

P.L. 108-357, §819(b)(2):

Amended Code Sec. 6662(d)(2) by striking subparagraph (D). **Effective** for tax years beginning after 10-22-2004. Prior to being stricken, Code Sec. 6662(d)(2)(D) read as follows:

(D) SECRETARIAL LIST.—The Secretary shall prescribe (and revise not less frequently than annually) a list of positions—

(i) for which the Secretary believes there is not substantial authority, and

(ii) which affect a significant number of taxpayers.

Such list (and any revision thereof) shall be published in the Federal Register.

ACCURACY-RELATED AND FRAUD PENALTIES

• **1997, Taxpayer Relief Act of 1997 (P.L. 105-34)**

P.L. 105-34, §1028(c)(1):

Amended Code Sec. 6662(d)(2)(B) by adding at the end a new flush sentence. **Effective** for items with respect to transactions entered into after 8-5-97.

P.L. 105-34, §1028(c)(2):

Amended Code Sec. 6662(d)(2)(C)(iii) by striking "the principal purpose" and inserting "a significant purpose". **Effective** for items with respect to transactions entered into after 8-5-97.

• **1994, Uruguay Round Agreements Act (P.L. 103-465)**

P.L. 103-465, §744(a):

Amended Code Sec. 6662(d)(2)(C) by redesignating clause (ii) as clause (iii) and by inserting after clause (i) a new clause (ii). **Effective** for items related to transactions occurring after 12-8-94.

P.L. 103-465, §744(b)(1):

Amended Code Sec. 6662(d)(2)(C)(i) by striking "In the case of any item" and inserting "In the case of any item of a taxpayer other than a corporation which is". **Effective** for items related to transactions occurring after 12-8-94.

P.L. 103-465, §744(b)(2):

Amended Code Sec. 6662(d)(2)(C)(iii), as redesignated by Act Sec. 744(a), by striking "clause (i)" and inserting "this subparagraph". **Effective** for items related to transactions occurring after 12-8-94.

• **1993, Omnibus Budget Reconciliation Act of 1993 (P.L. 103-66)**

P.L. 103-66, §13251(a):

Amended Code Sec. 6662(d)(2)(B)(ii). **Effective** for returns the due dates for which (determined without regard to extensions) are after 12-31-93. Prior to amendment, Code Sec. 6662(d)(2)(B)(ii) read as follows:

(ii) any item with respect to which the relevant facts affecting the item's tax treatment are adequately disclosed in the return or in a statement attached to the return.

[Sec. 6662(e)]

(e) SUBSTANTIAL VALUATION MISSTATEMENT UNDER CHAPTER 1.—

(1) IN GENERAL.—For purposes of this section, there is a substantial valuation misstatement under chapter 1 if—

(A) the value of any property (or the adjusted basis of any property) claimed on any return of tax imposed by chapter 1 is 150 percent or more of the amount determined to be the correct amount of such valuation or adjusted basis (as the case may be), or

(B)(i) the price for any property or services (or for the use of property) claimed on any such return in connection with any transaction between persons described in section 482 is 200 percent or more (or 50 percent or less) of the amount determined under section 482 to be the correct amount of such price, or

(ii) the net section 482 transfer price adjustment for the taxable year exceeds the lesser of $5,000,000 or 10 percent of the taxpayer's gross receipts.

(2) LIMITATION.—No penalty shall be imposed by reason of subsection (b)(3) unless the portion of the underpayment for the taxable year attributable to substantial valuation misstatements under chapter 1 exceeds $5,000 ($10,000 in the case of a corporation other than an S corporation or a personal holding company (as defined in section 542)).

(3) NET SECTION 482 TRANSFER PRICE ADJUSTMENT.—For purposes of this subsection—

(A) IN GENERAL.—The term "net section 482 transfer price adjustment" means, with respect to any taxable year, the net increase in taxable income for the taxable year (determined without regard to any amount carried to such taxable year from another taxable year) resulting from adjustments under section 482 in the price for any property or services (or for the use of property).

(B) CERTAIN ADJUSTMENTS EXCLUDED IN DETERMINING THRESHOLD.—For purposes of determining whether the threshold requirements of paragraph (1)(B)(ii) are met, the following shall be excluded:

(i) Any portion of the net increase in taxable income referred to in subparagraph (A) which is attributable to any redetermination of a price if—

(I) it is established that the taxpayer determined such price in accordance with a specific pricing method set forth in the regulations prescribed under section 482 and that the taxpayer's use of such method was reasonable,

(II) the taxpayer has documentation (which was in existence as of the time of filing the return) which sets forth the determination of such price in accordance with such a method and which establishes that the use of such method was reasonable, and

(III) the taxpayer provides such documentation to the Secretary within 30 days of a request for such documentation.

(ii) Any portion of the net increase in taxable income referred to in subparagraph (A) which is attributable to a redetermination of price where such price was not determined in accordance with such a specific pricing method if—

(I) the taxpayer establishes that none of such pricing methods was likely to result in a price that would clearly reflect income, the taxpayer used another pricing method to determine such price, and such other pricing method was likely to result in a price that would clearly reflect income,

(II) the taxpayer has documentation (which was in existence as of the time of filing the return) which sets forth the determination of such price in accordance with such other method and which establishes that the requirements of subclause (I) were satisfied, and

(III) the taxpayer provides such documentation to the Secretary within 30 days of a request for such documentation.

(iii) Any portion of such net increase which is attributable to any transaction solely between foreign corporations unless, in the case of any such corporations, the treatment of such transaction affects the determination of income from sources within the United States or taxable income effectively connected with the conduct of a trade or business within the United States.

(C) SPECIAL RULE.—If the regular tax (as defined in section 55(c)) imposed by chapter 1 on the taxpayer is determined by reference to an amount other than taxable income, such amount shall be treated as the taxable income of such taxpayer for purposes of this paragraph.

(D) COORDINATION WITH REASONABLE CAUSE EXCEPTION.—For purposes of section 6664(c) the taxpayer shall not be treated as having reasonable cause for any portion of an underpayment attributable to a net section 482 transfer price adjustment unless such taxpayer meets the requirements of clause (i), (ii), or (iii) of subparagraph (B) with respect to such portion.

Amendments

• **2006, Pension Protection Act of 2006 (P.L. 109-280)**

P.L. 109-280, §1219(a)(1)(A):

Amended Code Sec. 6662(e)(1)(A) by striking "200 percent" and inserting "150 percent". **Effective** generally for returns filed after 8-17-2006. For a special rule, see Act Sec. 1219(e)(3), below.

P.L. 109-280, §1219(e)(3), provides:

(3) SPECIAL RULE FOR CERTAIN EASEMENTS.—In the case of a contribution of a qualified real property interest which is a restriction with respect to the exterior of a building described in section 170(h)(4)(C)(ii) of the Internal Revenue Code of 1986, and an appraisal with respect to the contribution, the amendments made by subsections (a) and (b) shall apply to returns filed after July 25, 2006.

• **1993, Omnibus Budget Reconciliation Act of 1993 (P.L. 103-66)**

P.L. 103-66, §13236(a):

Amended Code Sec. 6662(e)(1)(B)(ii). **Effective** for tax years beginning after 12-31-93. Prior to amendment, Code Sec. 6662(e)(1)(B)(ii) read as follows:

(ii) the net section 482 transfer price adjustment for the taxable year exceeds $10,000,000.

P.L. 103-66, §13236(b):

Amended Code Sec. 6662(e)(3)(B). **Effective** for tax years beginning after 12-31-93. Prior to amendment, Code Sec. 6662(e)(3)(B) read as follows:

Sec. 6662(e)

ACCURACY-RELATED AND FRAUD PENALTIES

(B) CERTAIN ADJUSTMENTS EXCLUDED IN DETERMINING THRESHOLD.—For purposes of determining whether the $10,000,000 threshold requirement of paragraph (1)(B)(ii) is met, there shall be excluded—

(i) any portion of the net increase in taxable income referred to in subparagraph (A) which is attributable to any redetermination of a price if it is shown that there was a reasonable cause for the taxpayer's determination of such price and that the taxpayer acted in good faith with respect to such price, and

(ii) any portion of such net increase which is attributable to any transaction solely between foreign corporations unless, in the case of any of such corporations, the treatment of such transaction affects the determination of income from sources within the United States or taxable income effectively connected with the conduct of a trade or business within the United States.

P.L. 103-66, §13236(c):

Amended Code Sec. 6662(e)(3) by adding at the end thereof a new subparagraph (D). **Effective** for tax years beginning after 12-31-93.

• 1990, Omnibus Budget Reconciliation Act of 1990 (P.L. 101-508)

P.L. 101-508, §11312(a):

Amended Code Sec. 6662(e). **Effective** for tax years ending after 11-5-90. Prior to amendment, Code Sec. 6662(e) read as follows:

(e) SUBSTANTIAL VALUATION OVERSTATEMENT UNDER CHAPTER 1.—

(1) IN GENERAL.—For purposes of this section, there is a substantial valuation overstatement under chapter 1 if the value of any property (or the adjusted basis of any property) claimed on any return of tax imposed by chapter 1 is 200 percent or more of the amount determined to be the correct amount of such valuation or adjusted basis (as the case may be).

(2) LIMITATION.—No penalty shall be imposed by reason of subsection (b)(3) unless the portion of the underpayment for the taxable year attributable to substantial valuation overstatements under chapter 1 exceeds $5,000 ($10,000 in the case of a corporation other than an S corporation or a personal holding company (as defined in section 542)).

[Sec. 6662(f)]

(f) SUBSTANTIAL OVERSTATEMENT OF PENSION LIABILITIES.—

(1) IN GENERAL.—For purposes of this section, there is a substantial overstatement of pension liabilities if the actuarial determination of the liabilities taken into account for purposes of computing the deduction under paragraph (1) or (2) of section 404(a) is 200 percent or more of the amount determined to be the correct amount of such liabilities.

(2) LIMITATION.—No penalty shall be imposed by reason of subsection (b)(4) unless the portion of the underpayment for the taxable year attributable to substantial overstatements of pension liabilities exceeds $1,000.

[Sec. 6662(g)]

(g) SUBSTANTIAL ESTATE OR GIFT TAX VALUATION UNDERSTATEMENT.—

(1) IN GENERAL.—For purposes of this section, there is a substantial estate or gift tax valuation understatement if the value of any property claimed on any return of tax imposed by subtitle B is 65 percent or less of the amount determined to be the correct amount of such valuation.

(2) LIMITATION.—No penalty shall be imposed by reason of subsection (b)(5) unless the portion of the underpayment attributable to substantial estate or gift tax valuation understatements for the taxable period (or, in the case of the tax imposed by chapter 11, with respect to the estate of the decedent) exceeds $5,000.

Amendments

• 2006, Pension Protection Act of 2006 (P.L. 109-280)

P.L. 109-280, §1219(a)(1)(B):

Amended Code Sec. 6662(g)(1) by striking "50 percent" and inserting "65 percent". **Effective** for returns filed after 8-17-2006. For a special rule, see Act Sec. 1219(e)(3), below.

P.L. 109-280, §1219(e)(3), provides:

(3) SPECIAL RULE FOR CERTAIN EASEMENTS.—In the case of a contribution of a qualified real property interest which is a restriction with respect to the exterior of a building described in section 170(h)(4)(C)(ii) of the Internal Revenue Code of 1986, and an appraisal with respect to the contribution, the amendments made by subsections (a) and (b) shall apply to returns filed after July 25, 2006.

[Sec. 6662(h)]

(h) INCREASE IN PENALTY IN CASE OF GROSS VALUATION MISSTATEMENTS.—

(1) IN GENERAL.—To the extent that a portion of the underpayment to which this section applies is attributable to one or more gross valuation misstatements, subsection (a) shall be applied with respect to such portion by substituting "40 percent" for "20 percent".

(2) GROSS VALUATION MISSTATEMENTS.—The term "gross valuation misstatements" means—

(A) any substantial valuation misstatement under chapter 1 as determined under subsection (e) by substituting—

(i) in paragraph (1)(A), "200 percent" for "150 percent",

(ii) in paragraph (1)(B)(i)—

(I) "400 percent" for "200 percent", and

(II) "25 percent" for "50 percent", and

(iii) in paragraph (1)(B)(ii)—

(I) "$20,000,000" for "$5,000,000", and

(II) "20 percent" for "10 percent",

(B) any substantial overstatement of pension liabilities as determined under subsection (f) by substituting "400 percent" for "200 percent",

(C) any substantial estate or gift tax valuation understatement as determined under subsection (g) by substituting "40 percent" for "65 percent", and

(D) any disallowance of a deduction described in subsection (b)(10).

Amendments

• 2022, SECURE 2.0 Act of 2022 (P.L. 117-328)

P.L. 117-328, §605(a)(2)(B):

Amended Code Sec. 6662(h)(2) by striking "and" at the end of subparagraph (B), by striking the period at the end of subparagraph (C) and inserting ", and", and by adding at the end a new subparagraph (D). **Effective** for contributions made after 12-29-2022. For a special rule, see Act Sec. 605(c)(2), below.

P.L. 117-328, §605(c)(2), provides:

(2) NO INFERENCE.—No inference is intended as to the appropriate treatment of contributions made in taxable years ending on or before the date specified in paragraph (1), or as to any contribution for which a deduction is not disallowed by reason of section 170(h)(7) of the Internal Revenue Code of 1986, as added by this section.

• 2006, Pension Protection Act of 2006 (P.L. 109-280)

P.L. 109-280, §1219(a)(2)(A):

Amended Code Sec. 6662(h)(2)(A)(i)-(ii). **Effective** generally for returns filed after 8-17-2006. For a special rule, see Act Sec. 1219(e)(3), below. Prior to amendment, Code Sec. 6662(h)(2)(A)(i)-(ii) read as follows:

(i) "400 percent" for "200 percent" each place it appears,

(ii) "25 percent" for "50 percent", and

P.L. 109-280, §1219(a)(2)(B):

Amended Code Sec. 6662(h)(2)(C) by striking "'25 percent' for '50 percent'" and inserting "'40 percent' for '65 percent'". **Effective** generally for returns filed after 8-17-2006. For a special rule, see Act Sec. 1219(e)(3), below.

P.L. 109-280, §1219(e)(3), provides:

(3) SPECIAL RULE FOR CERTAIN EASEMENTS.—In the case of a contribution of a qualified real property interest which is a restriction with respect to the exterior of a building described in section 170(h)(4)(C)(ii) of the Internal Revenue Code of 1986, and an appraisal with respect to the contribution, the amendments made by subsections (a) and (b) shall apply to returns filed after July 25, 2006.

• 1993, Omnibus Budget Reconciliation Act of 1993 (P.L. 103-66)

P.L. 103-66, §13236(d):

Amended Code Sec. 6662(h)(2)(A)(iii). **Effective** for tax years beginning after 12-31-93. Prior to amendment, Code Sec. 6662(h)(2)(A)(iii) read as follows:

(iii) "$20,000,000" for "$10,000,000".

• 1990, Omnibus Budget Reconciliation Act of 1990 (P.L. 101-508)

P.L. 101-508, §11312(b)(2):

Amended Code Sec. 6662(h)(2)(A). **Effective** for tax years ending after 11-5-90. Prior to amendment, Code Sec. 6662(h)(2)(A) read as follows:

ACCURACY-RELATED AND FRAUD PENALTIES

(A) any substantial valuation overstatement under chapter 1 as determined under subsection (e) by substituting "400 percent" for "200 percent",

- **1989, Omnibus Budget Reconciliation Act of 1989 (P.L. 101-239)**

P.L. 101-239, §7721(a):

Amended subchapter A of chapter 68 by striking section 6662 and inserting new Parts II and III. **Effective** for returns the due date for which (determined without regard to extensions) is after 12-31-89. Prior to amendment, Code Sec. 6662 read as follows:

SEC. 6662. APPLICABLE RULES.

(a) ADDITIONS TREATED AS TAX.—Except as otherwise provided in this title—

(1) The additions to the tax, additional amounts, and penalties provided by this chapter shall be paid upon notice and demand and shall be assessed, collected, and paid in the same manner as taxes;

(2) Any reference in this title to "tax" imposed by this title shall be deemed also to refer to the additions to the tax, additional amounts, and penalties provided by this chapter.

(b) PROCEDURE FOR ASSESSING CERTAIN ADDITIONS TO TAX.—For purposes of subchapter B of chapter 63 (relating to deficiency procedures for income, estate, gift, and certain excise taxes), subsection (a) shall not apply to any addition to tax under section 6651, 6654, or 6655; except that it shall apply—

(1) in the case of an addition described in section 6651, to that portion of such addition which is attributable to a deficiency in tax described in section 6211; or

(2) to an addition described in section 6654 or 6655, if no return is filed for the taxable year.

- **1982, Tax Equity and Fiscal Responsibility Act of 1982 (P.L. 97-248)**

P.L. 97-248, §323(a):

Redesignated Code Sec. 6660 as Code Sec. 6662. For **effective** date, see the amendment note for P.L. 97-248 following Code Sec. 6661.

- **1981, Economic Recovery Tax Act of 1981 (P.L. 97-34)**

P.L. 97-34, §722(a)(1):

Redesignated Code Sec. 6659 as Code Sec. 6660. **Effective** for returns filed after 12-31-81.

- **1974, Employee Retirement Income Security Act of 1974 (P.L. 93-406)**

P.L. 93-406, §1016(a)(19):

Amended Code Sec. 6659(b) by changing "chapter 42" to "certain excise". For **effective** date, see amendment note for Code Sec. 410.

- **1969, Tax Reform Act of 1969 (P.L. 91-172)**

P.L. 91-172, §101(j)(51):

Amended Code Sec. 6659(b) by substituting "gift, and chapter 42 taxes" for "and gift taxes". **Effective** 1-1-70.

- **1960 (P.L. 86-470)**

P.L. 86-470, §§1, 2:

Amended Code Sec. 6659(b). For **effective** date, see §2, below. Prior to amendment, Code Sec. 6659(b) read as follows:

"(b) Additions to Tax for Failure to File Return or Pay Tax.—Any addition under section 6651 or section 6653 to a tax imposed by another subtitle of this title shall be considered a part of such tax for the purpose of applying the provisions of this title relating to the assessment and collection of such tax (including the provisions of subchapter B of chapter 63, relating to deficiency procedures for income, estate, and gift taxes)."

P.L. 86-470, §2, provides:

"The amendment made by the first section of this Act shall apply with respect to assessments made after the date of the enactment of this Act. Any addition to tax under section 6651, 6654, or 6655 of the Internal Revenue Code of 1954, assessed and collected on or before the date of the enactment of this Act, shall not be considered an overpayment solely on the ground that such assessment was invalid, if such assessment would not have been invalid had the amendment made by the first section of this Act applied with respect to such assessment."

[Sec. 6662(i)]

(i) INCREASE IN PENALTY IN CASE OF NONDISCLOSED NONECONOMIC SUBSTANCE TRANSACTIONS.—

(1) IN GENERAL.—In the case of any portion of an underpayment which is attributable to one or more nondisclosed noneconomic substance transactions, subsection (a) shall be applied with respect to such portion by substituting "40 percent" for "20 percent".

(2) NONDISCLOSED NONECONOMIC SUBSTANCE TRANSACTIONS.—For purposes of this subsection, the term "nondisclosed noneconomic substance transaction" means any portion of a transaction described in subsection (b)(6) with respect to which the relevant facts affecting the tax treatment are not adequately disclosed in the return nor in a statement attached to the return.

(3) SPECIAL RULE FOR AMENDED RETURNS.—In no event shall any amendment or supplement to a return of tax be taken into account for purposes of this subsection if the amendment or supplement is filed after the earlier of the date the taxpayer is first contacted by the Secretary regarding the examination of the return or such other date as is specified by the Secretary.

Amendments

- **2018, Tax Technical Corrections Act of 2018 (P.L. 115-141)**

P.L. 115-141, §401(a)(304), Div. U:

Amended Code Sec. 6662 by moving subsection (i) before subsection (j). **Effective** 3-23-2018.

- **2010, Health Care and Education Reconciliation Act of 2010 (P.L. 111-152)**

P.L. 111-152, §1409(b)(2):

Amended Code Sec. 6662 by adding at the end a new subsection (i). **Effective** for underpayments attributable to transactions entered into after 3-30-2010.

[Sec. 6662(j)]

(j) UNDISCLOSED FOREIGN FINANCIAL ASSET UNDERSTATEMENT.—

(1) IN GENERAL.—For purposes of this section, the term "undisclosed foreign financial asset understatement" means, for any taxable year, the portion of the understatement for such taxable year which is attributable to any transaction involving an undisclosed foreign financial asset.

(2) UNDISCLOSED FOREIGN FINANCIAL ASSET.—For purposes of this subsection, the term "undisclosed foreign financial asset" means, with respect to any taxable year, any asset with respect to which information was required to be provided under section 6038, 6038B, 6038D, 6046A, or 6048 for such taxable year but was not provided by the taxpayer as required under the provisions of those sections.

(3) INCREASE IN PENALTY FOR UNDISCLOSED FOREIGN FINANCIAL ASSET UNDERSTATEMENTS.—In the case of any portion of an underpayment which is attributable to any undisclosed foreign financial asset understatement, subsection (a) shall be applied with respect to such portion by substituting "40 percent" for "20 percent".

Amendments

- **2010, Hiring Incentives to Restore Employment Act (P.L. 111-147)**

P.L. 111-147, §512(a)(2):

Amended Code Sec. 6662, as amended by this Act, by adding at the end a new subsection (j). **Effective** for tax years beginning after 3-18-2010.

[Sec. 6662(k)]

(k) INCONSISTENT ESTATE BASIS REPORTING.—For purposes of this section, the term "inconsistent estate basis" means any portion of an underpayment attributable to the failure to comply with section 1014(f).

Amendments

- **2018, Tax Technical Corrections Act of 2018 (P.L. 115-141)**

P.L. 115-141, §104(a), Div. U:

Amended Code Sec. 6662(k). **Effective** as if included in the provision of the Surface Transportation and Veterans Health Care Choice Improvement Act of 2015 to which it relates [**effective** for property with respect to which an estate tax return is filed after 7-31-2015.—CCH]. Prior to amendment, Code Sec. 6662(k) read as follows:

(k) INCONSISTENT ESTATE BASIS REPORTING.—For purposes of this section, there is an "inconsistent estate basis" if the basis of property claimed on a return exceeds the basis as determined under section 1014(f).

- **2015, Surface Transportation and Veterans Health Care Choice Improvement Act of 2015 (P.L. 114-41)**

P.L. 114-41, §2004(c)(2):

Amended Code Sec. 6662 by adding at the end a new subsection (k). **Effective** for property with respect to which an estate tax return is filed after 7-31-2015.

Sec. 6662(i)

ACCURACY-RELATED AND FRAUD PENALTIES

[Sec. 6662(l)]

(l) INCREASE IN PENALTY IN CASE OF OVERSTATEMENT OF QUALIFIED CHARITABLE CONTRIBUTIONS.—In the case of any portion of an underpayment which is attributable to one or more overstatements of the deduction provided in section 170(p), subsection (a) shall be applied with respect to such portion by substituting "50 percent" for "20 percent".

Amendments

• **2020, Taxpayer Certainty and Disaster Tax Relief Act of 2020 (P.L. 116-260)**

P.L. 116-260, §212(b)(2), Div. EE:

Amended Code Sec. 6662 by adding at the end a new subsection (l). **Effective** for tax years beginning after 12-31-2020.

[Sec. 6662A]

SEC. 6662A. IMPOSITION OF ACCURACY-RELATED PENALTY ON UNDERSTATEMENTS WITH RESPECT TO REPORTABLE TRANSACTIONS.

[Sec. 6662A(a)]

(a) IMPOSITION OF PENALTY.—If a taxpayer has a reportable transaction understatement for any taxable year, there shall be added to the tax an amount equal to 20 percent of the amount of such understatement.

[Sec. 6662A(b)]

(b) REPORTABLE TRANSACTION UNDERSTATEMENT.—For purposes of this section—

(1) IN GENERAL.—The term "reportable transaction understatement" means the sum of—

(A) the product of—

(i) the amount of the increase (if any) in taxable income which results from a difference between the proper tax treatment of an item to which this section applies and the taxpayer's treatment of such item (as shown on the taxpayer's return of tax), and

(ii) the highest rate of tax imposed by section 1 (section 11 in the case of a taxpayer which is a corporation), and

(B) the amount of the decrease (if any) in the aggregate amount of credits determined under subtitle A which results from a difference between the taxpayer's treatment of an item to which this section applies (as shown on the taxpayer's return of tax) and the proper tax treatment of such item.

For purposes of subparagraph (A), any reduction of the excess of deductions allowed for the taxable year over gross income for such year, and any reduction in the amount of capital losses which would (without regard to section 1211) be allowed for such year, shall be treated as an increase in taxable income.

(2) ITEMS TO WHICH SECTION APPLIES.—This section shall apply to any item which is attributable to—

(A) any listed transaction, and

(B) any reportable transaction (other than a listed transaction) if a significant purpose of such transaction is the avoidance or evasion of Federal income tax.

[Sec. 6662A(c)]

(c) HIGHER PENALTY FOR NONDISCLOSED LISTED AND OTHER AVOIDANCE TRANSACTIONS.—Subsection (a) shall be applied by substituting "30 percent" for "20 percent" with respect to the portion of any reportable transaction understatement with respect to which the requirement of section 6664(d)(3)(A) is not met.

Amendments

• **2014, Tax Technical Corrections Act of 2014 (P.L. 113-295)**

P.L. 113-295, §220(w), Division A:

Amended Code Sec. 6662A(c) by striking "section 6664(d)(2)(A)" and inserting "section 6664(d)(3)(A)". **Effective** 12-19-2014.

[Sec. 6662A(d)]

(d) DEFINITIONS OF REPORTABLE AND LISTED TRANSACTIONS.—For purposes of this section, the terms "reportable transaction" and "listed transaction" have the respective meanings given to such terms by section 6707A(c).

[Sec. 6662A(e)]

(e) SPECIAL RULES.—

(1) COORDINATION WITH PENALTIES, ETC., ON OTHER UNDERSTATEMENTS.—In the case of an understatement (as defined in section 6662(d)(2))—

(A) the amount of such understatement (determined without regard to this paragraph) shall be increased by the aggregate amount of reportable transaction understatements for purposes of determining whether such understatement is a substantial understatement under section 6662(d)(1), and

(B) the addition to tax under section 6662(a) shall apply only to the excess of the amount of the substantial understatement (if any) after the application of subparagraph (A) over the aggregate amount of reportable transaction understatements.

(2) COORDINATION WITH OTHER PENALTIES.—

(A) COORDINATION WITH FRAUD PENALTY.—This section shall not apply to any portion of an understatement on which a penalty is imposed under section 6663.

(B) COORDINATION WITH CERTAIN INCREASED UNDERPAYMENT PENALTIES.—This section shall not apply to any portion of an understatement on which a penalty is imposed under section 6662 if the rate of the penalty is determined under subsections [sic] (h) or (i) of section 6662.

(3) SPECIAL RULE FOR AMENDED RETURNS.—Except as provided in regulations, in no event shall any tax treatment included with an amendment or supplement to a return of tax be taken into account in determining the amount of any reportable transaction understatement if the amendment or supplement is filed after the earlier of the date the taxpayer is first contacted by the Secretary regarding the examination of the return or such other date as is specified by the Secretary.

Amendments

• **2010, Health Care and Education Reconciliation Act of 2010 (P.L. 111-152)**

P.L. 111-152, §1409(b)(3)(A)-(B):

Amended Code Sec. 6662A(e)(2)(B) by striking "section 6662(h)" and inserting "subsections [sic] (h) or (i) of section 6662"; and by striking "GROSS VALUATION MISSTATEMENT PENALTY" in the heading and inserting "CERTAIN INCREASED UNDERPAYMENT PENALTIES". **Effective** for underpayments attributable to transactions entered into after 3-30-2010.

• **2005, Gulf Opportunity Zone Act of 2005 (P.L. 109-135)**

P.L. 109-135, §403(x)(2):

Amended Code Sec. 6662A(e)(2). **Effective** as if included in the provision of the American Jobs Creation Act of 2004 (P.L. 108-357) to which it relates [effective for tax

ACCURACY-RELATED AND FRAUD PENALTIES

years ending after 10-22-2004.—CCH]. Prior to amendment, Code Sec. 6662A(e)(2) read as follows:

(2) COORDINATION WITH OTHER PENALTIES.—

(A) APPLICATION OF FRAUD PENALTY.—References to an underpayment in section 6663 shall be treated as including references to a reportable transaction understatement.

(B) NO DOUBLE PENALTY.—This section shall not apply to any portion of an understatement on which a penalty is imposed under section 6663.

(C) COORDINATION WITH VALUATION PENALTIES.—

(i) SECTION 6662(e).—Section 6662(e) shall not apply to any portion of an understatement on which a penalty is imposed under this section.

(ii) SECTION 6662(h).—This section shall not apply to any portion of an understatement on which a penalty is imposed under section 6662(h).

• 2004, American Jobs Creation Act of 2004 (P.L. 108-357)

P.L. 108-357, §812(a):

Amended [part II of]subchapter A of chapter 68 by inserting after Code Sec. 6662 a new Code Sec. 6662A. **Effective** for tax years ending after 10-22-2004.

[Sec. 6663]

SEC. 6663. IMPOSITION OF FRAUD PENALTY.

[Sec. 6663(a)]

(a) IMPOSITION OF PENALTY.—If any part of any underpayment of tax required to be shown on a return is due to fraud, there shall be added to the tax an amount equal to 75 percent of the portion of the underpayment which is attributable to fraud.

[Sec. 6663(b)]

(b) DETERMINATION OF PORTION ATTRIBUTABLE TO FRAUD.—If the Secretary establishes that any portion of an underpayment is attributable to fraud, the entire underpayment shall be treated as attributable to fraud, except with respect to any portion of the underpayment which the taxpayer establishes (by a preponderance of the evidence) is not attributable to fraud.

[Sec. 6663(c)]

(c) SPECIAL RULE FOR JOINT RETURNS.—In the case of a joint return, this section shall not apply with respect to a spouse unless some part of the underpayment is due to the fraud of such spouse.

Amendments

• **1989, Omnibus Budget Reconciliation Act of 1989 (P.L. 101-239)**

P.L. 101-239, §7721(a):

Amended subchapter A of chapter 68 by adding a new section 6663. **Effective** for returns the due date for which (determined without regard to extensions) is after 12-31-89.

[Sec. 6664]

SEC. 6664. DEFINITIONS AND SPECIAL RULES.

[Sec. 6664(a)]

(a) UNDERPAYMENT.—For purposes of this part, the term "underpayment" means the amount by which any tax imposed by this title exceeds the excess of—

(1) the sum of—

(A) the amount shown as the tax by the taxpayer on his return, plus

(B) amounts not so shown previously assessed (or collected without assessment), over

(2) the amount of rebates made.

For purposes of paragraph (2), the term "rebate" means so much of an abatement, credit, refund, or other repayment, as was made on the ground that tax imposed was less than the excess of the amount specified in paragraph (1) over the rebates previously made. A rule similar to the rule of section 6211(b)(4) shall apply for purposes of this subsection.

Amendments

• **2015, Protecting Americans from Tax Hikes Act of 2015 (P.L. 114-113)**

P.L. 114-113, §209(a), Div. Q:

Amended Code Sec. 6664(a) by adding at the end a new sentence. For the **effective** date, see Act Sec. 209(d)(1), below.

P.L. 114-113, §209(d)(1), Div. Q, provides:

(1) UNDERPAYMENT PENALTIES.—The amendment made by subsection (a) shall apply to—

(A) returns filed after the date of the enactment of this Act, and

(B) returns filed on or before such date if the period specified in section 6501 of the Internal Revenue Code of 1986 for assessment of the taxes with respect to which such return relates has not expired as of such date.

[Sec. 6664(b)]

(b) PENALTIES APPLICABLE ONLY WHERE RETURN FILED.—The penalties provided in this part shall apply only in cases where a return of tax is filed (other than a return prepared by the Secretary under the authority of section 6020(b)).

[Sec. 6664(c)]

(c) REASONABLE CAUSE EXCEPTION FOR UNDERPAYMENTS.—

(1) IN GENERAL.—No penalty shall be imposed under section 6662 or 6663 with respect to any portion of an underpayment if it is shown that there was a reasonable cause for such portion and that the taxpayer acted in good faith with respect to such portion.

(2) EXCEPTION.—Paragraph (1) shall not apply to any portion of an underpayment which is attributable to one or more transactions described in section 6662(b)(6) or to any disallowance of a deduction described in section 6662(b)(10).

(3) SPECIAL RULE FOR CERTAIN VALUATION OVERSTATEMENTS.—In the case of any underpayment attributable to a substantial or gross valuation over statement under chapter 1 with respect to charitable deduction property, paragraph (1) shall not apply. The preceding sentence shall not apply to a substantial valuation overstatement under chapter 1 if—

(A) the claimed value of the property was based on a qualified appraisal made by a qualified appraiser, and

(B) in addition to obtaining such appraisal, the taxpayer made a good faith investigation of the value of the contributed property.

(4) DEFINITIONS.—For purposes of this subsection—

(A) CHARITABLE DEDUCTION PROPERTY.—The term "charitable deduction property" means any property contributed by the taxpayer in a contribution for which a deduction was claimed under section 170. For purposes of paragraph (3), such term shall not include any securities for which (as of the date of the contribution) market quotations are readily available on an established securities market.

(B) QUALIFIED APPRAISAL.—The term "qualified appraisal" has the meaning given such term by section 170(f)(11)(E)(i).

(C) QUALIFIED APPRAISER.—The term "qualified appraiser" has the meaning given such term by section 170(f)(11)(E)(ii).

ACCURACY-RELATED AND FRAUD PENALTIES

Amendments

• **2022, SECURE 2.0 Act of 2022 (P.L. 117-328)**

P.L. 117-328, §605(a)(2)(C):

Amended Code Sec. 6664(c)(2) by inserting "or to any disallowance of a deduction described in section 6662(b)(10)" before the period at the end. **Effective** for contributions made after 12-29-2022. For a special rule, see Act Sec. 605(c)(2), below.

P.L. 117-328, §605(c)(2), provides:

(2) NO INFERENCE.—No inference is intended as to the appropriate treatment of contributions made in taxable years ending on or before the date specified in paragraph (1), or as to any contribution for which a deduction is not disallowed by reason of section 170(h)(7) of the Internal Revenue Code of 1986, as added by this section.

• **2010, Health Care and Education Reconciliation Act of 2010 (P.L. 111-152)**

P.L. 111-152, §1409(c)(1)(A)-(C):

Amended Code Sec. 6664(c) by redesignating paragraphs (2) and (3) as paragraphs (3) and (4), respectively; by striking "paragraph (2)" in paragraph (4)(A), as so redesignated, and inserting "paragraph (3)"; and by inserting after paragraph (1) a new paragraph (2). **Effective** for underpayments attributable to transactions entered into after 3-30-2010.

• **2006, Pension Protection Act of 2006 (P.L. 109-280)**

P.L. 109-280, §1219(a)(3):

Amended Code Sec. 6664(c)(2) by striking "paragraph (1) shall not apply unless" and inserting "paragraph (1) shall not apply. The preceding sentence shall not apply to a substantial valuation overstatement under chapter 1 if". **Effective** generally for returns filed after 8-17-2006. For a special rule, see Act Sec. 1219(e)(3), below.

P.L. 109-280, §1219(c)(2):

Amended Code Sec. 6664(c)(3)(B)-(C). **Effective** generally for appraisals prepared with respect to returns or submissions filed after 8-17-2006. Prior to amendment, Code Sec. 6664(c)(3)(B)-(C) read as follows:

(B) QUALIFIED APPRAISER.—The term "qualified appraiser" means any appraiser meeting the requirements of the regulations prescribed under section 170(a)(1).

(C) QUALIFIED APPRAISAL.—The term "qualified appraisal" means any appraisal meeting the requirements of the regulations prescribed under section 170(a)(1).

P.L. 109-280, §1219(e)(3), provides:

(3) SPECIAL RULE FOR CERTAIN EASEMENTS.—In the case of a contribution of a qualified real property interest which is a restriction with respect to the exterior of a building described in section 170(h)(4)(C)(ii) of the Internal Revenue Code of 1986, and an appraisal with respect to the contribution, the amendments made by subsections (a) and (b) shall apply to returns filed after July 25, 2006.

• **2004, American Jobs Creation Act of 2004 (P.L. 108-357)**

P.L. 108-357, §812(c)(2)(A):

Amended Code Sec. 6664(c)(1) by striking "this part" and inserting "section 6662 or 6663". **Effective** for tax years ending after 10-22-2004.

P.L. 108-357, §812(c)(2)(B):

Amended the heading of Code Sec. 6664(c) by inserting "FOR UNDERPAYMENTS" after "EXCEPTION". **Effective** for tax years ending after 10-22-2004.

• **1989, Omnibus Budget Reconciliation Act of 1989 (P.L. 101-239)**

P.L. 101-239, §7721(a):

Amended subchapter A of chapter 68 by adding a new section 6664. **Effective** for returns the due date for which (determined without regard to extensions) is after 12-31-89.

[Sec. 6664(d)]

(d) REASONABLE CAUSE EXCEPTION FOR REPORTABLE TRANSACTION UNDERSTATEMENTS.—

(1) IN GENERAL.—No penalty shall be imposed under section 6662A with respect to any portion of a reportable transaction understatement if it is shown that there was a reasonable cause for such portion and that the taxpayer acted in good faith with respect to such portion.

(2) EXCEPTION.—Paragraph (1) shall not apply to any portion of a reportable transaction understatement which is attributable to one or more transactions described in section 6662(b)(6).

(3) SPECIAL RULES.—Paragraph (1) shall not apply to any reportable transaction understatement unless—

(A) the relevant facts affecting the tax treatment of the item are adequately disclosed in accordance with the regulations prescribed under section 6011,

(B) there is or was substantial authority for such treatment, and

(C) the taxpayer reasonably believed that such treatment was more likely than not the proper treatment.

A taxpayer failing to adequately disclose in accordance with section 6011 shall be treated as meeting the requirements of subparagraph (A) if the penalty for such failure was rescinded under section 6707A(d).

(4) RULES RELATING TO REASONABLE BELIEF.—For purposes of paragraph (3)(C)—

(A) IN GENERAL.—A taxpayer shall be treated as having a reasonable belief with respect to the tax treatment of an item only if such belief—

(i) is based on the facts and law that exist at the time the return of tax which includes such tax treatment is filed, and

(ii) relates solely to the taxpayer's chances of success on the merits of such treatment and does not take into account the possibility that a return will not be audited, such treatment will not be raised on audit, or such treatment will be resolved through settlement if it is raised.

(B) CERTAIN OPINIONS MAY NOT BE RELIED UPON.—

(i) IN GENERAL.—An opinion of a tax advisor may not be relied upon to establish the reasonable belief of a taxpayer if—

(I) the tax advisor is described in clause (ii), or

(II) the opinion is described in clause (iii).

(ii) DISQUALIFIED TAX ADVISORS.—A tax advisor is described in this clause if the tax advisor—

(I) is a material advisor (within the meaning of section 6111(b)(1)) and participates in the organization, management, promotion, or sale of the transaction or is related (within the meaning of section 267(b) or 707(b)(1)) to any person who so participates,

(II) is compensated directly or indirectly by a material advisor with respect to the transaction,

(III) has a fee arrangement with respect to the transaction which is contingent on all or part of the intended tax benefits from the transaction being sustained, or

(IV) as determined under regulations prescribed by the Secretary, has a disqualifying financial interest with respect to the transaction.

(iii) DISQUALIFIED OPINIONS.—For purposes of clause (i), an opinion is disqualified if the opinion—

(I) is based on unreasonable factual or legal assumptions (including assumptions as to future events),

(II) unreasonably relies on representations, statements, findings, or agreements of the taxpayer or any other person,

(III) does not identify and consider all relevant facts, or

(IV) fails to meet any other requirement as the Secretary may prescribe.

Amendments

• **2010, Health Care and Education Reconciliation Act of 2010 (P.L. 111-152)**

P.L. 111-152, §1409(c)(2)(A)-(C):

Amended Code Sec. 6664(d) by redesignating paragraphs (2) and (3) as paragraphs (3) and (4), respectively; by striking "paragraph (2)(C)" in paragraph (4), as so redesignated, and inserting "paragraph (3)(C)"; and by inserting after paragraph (1) a new paragraph (2). **Effective** for understatements attributable to transactions entered into after 3-30-2010.

• **2004, American Jobs Creation Act of 2004 (P.L. 108-357)**

P.L. 108-357, §812(c)(1):

Amended Code Sec. 6664 by adding at the end a new subsection (d). **Effective** for tax years ending after 10-22-2004. For a special rule, see Act Sec. 812(f)(2), below.

P.L. 108-357, §812(f)(2), as added by P.L. 109-135, §403(x)(3), provides:

(2) DISQUALIFIED OPINIONS.—Section 6664(d)(3)(B) of the Internal Revenue Code of 1986 (as added by subsection (c)) shall not apply to the opinion of a tax advisor if—

ASSESSABLE PENALTIES

(A) the opinion was provided to the taxpayer before the date of the enactment of this Act,

(B) the opinion relates to one or more transactions all of which were entered into before such date, and

(C) the tax treatment of items relating to each such transaction was included on a return or statement filed by the taxpayer before such date.

PART III—APPLICABLE RULES

Sec. 6665.   Applicable rules.

[Sec. 6665]

SEC. 6665. APPLICABLE RULES.

[Sec. 6665(a)]

(a) ADDITIONS TREATED AS TAX.—Except as otherwise provided in this title—

(1) the additions to the tax, additional amounts, and penalties provided by this chapter shall be paid upon notice and demand and shall be assessed, collected, and paid in the same manner as taxes; and

(2) any reference in this title to "tax" imposed by this title shall be deemed also to refer to the additions to the tax, additional amounts, and penalties provided by this chapter.

[Sec. 6665(b)]

(b) PROCEDURE FOR ASSESSING CERTAIN ADDITIONS TO TAX.—For purposes of subchapter B of chapter 63 (relating to deficiency procedures for income, estate, gift, and certain excise taxes), subsection (a) shall not apply to any addition to tax under section 6651, 6654, or 6655; except that it shall apply—

(1) in the case of an addition described in section 6651, to that portion of such addition which is attributable to a deficiency in tax described in section 6211; or

(2) to an addition described in section 6654 or 6655, if no return is filed for the taxable year.

Amendments

• 1989, Omnibus Budget Reconciliation Act of 1989 (P.L. 101-239)

P.L. 101-239, §7721(a):

Amended subchapter A of chapter 68 by adding a new part III. Effective for returns the due date for which (determined without regard to extensions) is after 12-31-89.

Subchapter B—Assessable Penalties

Part I.   General provisions.
Part II. Failure to comply with certain information reporting requirements.

PART I—GENERAL PROVISIONS

Sec. 6671.   Rules for application of assessable penalties.
Sec. 6672.   Failure to collect and pay over tax, or attempt to evade or defeat tax.
Sec. 6673.   Sanctions and costs awarded by courts.
Sec. 6674.   Fraudulent statement or failure to furnish statement to employee.
Sec. 6675.   Excessive claims with respect to the use of certain fuels.
Sec. 6676.   Erroneous claim for refund or credit.
Sec. 6677.   Failure to file information returns with respect to certain foreign trusts.
Sec. 6679.   Failure to file returns, etc., with respect to foreign corporations or foreign partnerships.
Sec. 6682.   False information with respect to withholding.
Sec. 6684.   Assessable penalties with respect to liability for tax under chapter 42.
Sec. 6685.   Assessable penalty with respect to public inspection requirements for certain tax-exempt organizations.
Sec. 6686.   Failure to file returns or supply information by DISC or former FSC.
Sec. 6688.   Assessable penalties with respect to information required to be furnished under section 7654.
Sec. 6689.   Failure to file notice of redetermination of foreign tax.
Sec. 6690.   Fraudulent statement or failure to furnish statement to plan participant.
Sec. 6692.   Failure to file actuarial report.
Sec. 6693.   Failure to provide reports on certain tax-favored accounts or annuities; penalties relating to designated nondeductible contributions.
Sec. 6694.   Understatement of taxpayer's liability by tax return preparer.
Sec. 6695.   Other assessable penalties with respect to the preparation of tax returns for other persons.
Sec. 6695A.   Substantial and gross valuation misstatements attributable to incorrect appraisals.
Sec. 6696.   Rules applicable with respect to sections 6694, 6695, and 6695A.
Sec. 6698.   Failure to file partnership return.
Sec. 6699.   Failure to file S corporation return.
Sec. 6700.   Promoting abusive tax shelters, etc.
Sec. 6701.   Penalties for aiding and abetting understatement of tax liability.
Sec. 6702.   Frivolous tax submissions.
Sec. 6703.   Rules applicable to penalties under sections 6700, 6701, and 6702.
Sec. 6704.   Failure to keep records necessary to meet reporting requirements under section 6047(d).
Sec. 6705.   Failure by broker to provide notice to payors.
Sec. 6706.   Original issue discount information requirements.

ASSESSABLE PENALTIES

Sec. 6707.	Failure to furnish information regarding reportable transactions.
Sec. 6707A.	Penalty for failure to include reportable transaction information with return.
Sec. 6708.	Failure to maintain lists of advisees with respect to reportable transactions.
Sec. 6709.	Penalties with respect to mortgage credit certificates.
Sec. 6710.	Failure to disclose that contributions are nondeductible.
Sec. 6711.	Failure by tax-exempt organization to disclose that certain information or service available from Federal Government.
Sec. 6712.	Failure to disclose treaty-based return positions.
Sec. 6713.	Disclosure or use of information by preparers of returns.
Sec. 6714.	Failure to meet disclosure requirements applicable to quid pro quo contributions.
Sec. 6715.	Dyed fuel sold for use or used in taxable use, etc.
Sec. 6715A.	Tampering with or failing to maintain security requirements for mechanical dye injection systems.
Sec. 6716.	Failure to file information with respect to certain transfers at death and gifts.
Sec. 6717.	Refusal of entry.
Sec. 6718.	Failure to display tax registration on vessels.
Sec. 6719.	Failure to register or reregister.
Sec. 6720.	Fraudulent acknowledgments with respect to donations of motor vehicles, boats, and airplanes.
Sec. 6720A.	Penalty with respect to certain adulterated fuels.
Sec. 6720B.	Fraudulent identification of exempt use property.
Sec. 6720C.	Penalty for failure to notify health plan of cessation of eligibility for continuation coverage premium assistance.

[Sec. 6671]

SEC. 6671. RULES FOR APPLICATION OF ASSESSABLE PENALTIES.

[Sec. 6671(a)]

(a) PENALTY ASSESSED AS TAX.—The penalties and liabilities provided by this subchapter shall be paid upon notice and demand by the Secretary, and shall be assessed and collected in the same manner as taxes. Except as otherwise provided, any reference in this title to "tax" imposed by this title shall be deemed also to refer to the penalties and liabilities provided by this subchapter.

Amendments

• **1976, Tax Reform Act of 1976 (P.L. 94-455)**

P.L. 94-455, §1906(b)(13)(A):

Amended 1954 Code by substituting "Secretary" for "Secretary or his delegate" each place it appeared. **Effective** 2-1-77.

[Sec. 6671(b)]

(b) PERSON DEFINED.—The term "person", as used in this subchapter, includes an officer or employee of a corporation, or a member or employee of a partnership who as such officer, employee, or member is under a duty to perform the act in respect of which the violation occurs.

[Sec. 6672]

SEC. 6672. FAILURE TO COLLECT AND PAY OVER TAX, OR ATTEMPT TO EVADE OR DEFEAT TAX.

[Sec. 6672(a)]

(a) GENERAL RULE.—Any person required to collect, truthfully account for, and pay over any tax imposed by this title who willfully fails to collect such tax, or truthfully account for and pay over such tax, or willfully attempts in any manner to evade or defeat any such tax or the payment thereof, shall, in addition to other penalties provided by law, be liable to a penalty equal to the total amount of the tax evaded, or not collected, or not accounted for and paid over. No penalty shall be imposed under section 6653 or part II of subchapter A of chapter 68 for any offense to which this section is applicable.

Amendments

• **1989, Omnibus Budget Reconciliation Act of 1989 (P.L. 101-239)**

P.L. 101-239, §7721(c)(9):

Amended Code Sec. 6672(a) by striking "under section 6653" and inserting "under section 6653 or part II of subchapter A of chapter 68". **Effective** for returns the due date for which (determined without regard to extensions) is after 12-31-89.

[Sec. 6672(b)]

(b) PRELIMINARY NOTICE REQUIREMENT.—

(1) IN GENERAL.—No penalty shall be imposed under subsection (a) unless the Secretary notifies the taxpayer in writing by mail to an address as determined under section 6212(b) or in person that the taxpayer shall be subject to an assessment of such penalty.

(2) TIMING OF NOTICE.—The mailing of the notice described in paragraph (1) (or, in the case of such a notice delivered in person, such delivery) shall precede any notice and demand of any penalty under subsection (a) by at least 60 days.

(3) STATUTE OF LIMITATIONS.—If a notice described in paragraph (1) with respect to any penalty is mailed or delivered in person before the expiration of the period provided by section 6501 for the assessment of such penalty (determined without regard to this paragraph), the period provided by such section for the assessment of such penalty shall not expire before the later of—

(A) the date 90 days after the date on which such notice was mailed or delivered in person, or

(B) if there is a timely protest of the proposed assessment, the date 30 days after the Secretary makes a final administrative determination with respect to such protest.

(4) EXCEPTION FOR JEOPARDY.—This subsection shall not apply if the Secretary finds that the collection of the penalty is in jeopardy.

Amendments

• **1998, IRS Restructuring and Reform Act of 1998 (P.L. 105-206)**

P.L. 105-206, §3307(a):

Amended Code Sec. 6672(b)(1) by inserting "or in person" after "section 6212(b)". **Effective** 7-22-98.

P.L. 105-206, §3307(b)(1):

Amended Code Sec. 6672(b)(2) by inserting "(or, in the case of such a notice delivered in person, such delivery)" after "paragraph (1)". **Effective** 7-22-98.

ASSESSABLE PENALTIES

P.L. 105-206, § 3307(b)(2):

Amended Code Sec. 6672(b)(3) by inserting "or delivered in person" after "mailed" each place it appears. **Effective** 7-22-98.

• **1996, Taxpayer Bill of Rights 2 (P.L. 104-168)**

P.L. 104-168, § 901(a):

Amended Code Sec. 6672 by redesignating subsection (b) as subsection (c), and by inserting after subsection (a) a new subsection (b). **Effective** for proposed assessments made after 6-30-96.

P.L. 104-168, § 904(b), provides:

(b) PUBLIC INFORMATION REQUIREMENTS.—

(1) IN GENERAL.—The Secretary of the Treasury or the Secretary's delegate (hereafter in this subsection referred to as the "Secretary") shall take such actions as may be appropriate to ensure that employees are aware of their responsibilities under the Federal tax depository system, the circumstances under which employees may be liable for the penalty imposed by section 6672 of the Internal Revenue Code of 1986, and the responsibility to promptly report to the Internal Revenue Service any failure referred to in subsection (a) of such section 6672. Such actions shall include—

(A) printing of a warning on deposit coupon booklets and the appropriate tax returns that certain employees may be liable for the penalty imposed by such section 6672, and

(B) the development of a special information packet.

(2) DEVELOPMENT OF EXPLANATORY MATERIALS.—The Secretary shall develop materials explaining the circumstances under which board members of tax-exempt organizations (including voluntary and honorary members) may be subject to penalty under section 6672 of such Code. Such materials shall be made available to tax-exempt organizations.

(3) IRS INSTRUCTIONS.—The Secretary shall clarify the instructions to Internal Revenue Service employees on the application of the penalty under section 6672 of such Code with regard to voluntary members of boards of trustees or directors of tax-exempt organizations.

[Sec. 6672(c)]

(c) EXTENSION OF PERIOD OF COLLECTION WHERE BOND IS FILED.—

(1) IN GENERAL.—If, within 30 days after the day on which notice and demand of any penalty under subsection (a) is made against any person, such person—

(A) pays an amount which is not less than the miminum amount required to commence a proceeding in court with respect to his liability for such penalty,

(B) files a claim for refund of the amount so paid, and

(C) furnishes a bond which meets the requirements of paragraph (3),

no levy or proceeding in court for the collection of the remainder of such penalty shall be made, begun, or prosecuted until a final resolution of a proceeding begun as provided in paragraph (2). Notwithstanding the provisions of section 7421(a), the beginning of such proceeding or levy during the time such prohibition is in force may be enjoined by a proceeding in the proper court. Nothing in this paragraph shall be construed to prohibit any counterclaim for the remainder of such penalty in a proceeding begun as provided in paragraph (2).

(2) SUIT MUST BE BROUGHT TO DETERMINE LIABILITY FOR PENALTY.—If, within 30 days after the day on which his claim for refund with respect to any penalty under subsection (a) is denied, the person described in paragraph (1) fails to begin a proceeding in the appropriate United States district court (or in the Court of Federal Claims) for the determination of his liability for such penalty, paragraph (1) shall cease to apply with respect to such penalty, effective on the day following the close of the 30-day period referred to in this paragraph.

(3) BOND.—The bond referred to in paragraph (1) shall be in such form and with such sureties as the Secretary may by regulations prescribe and shall be in an amount equal to $1^{1}/_{2}$ times the amount of excess of the penalty assessed over the payment described in paragraph (1).

(4) SUSPENSION OF RUNNING OF PERIOD OF LIMITATIONS ON COLLECTION.—The running of the period of limitations provided in section 6502 on the collection by levy or by a proceeding in court in respect of any penalty described in paragraph (1) shall be suspended for the period during which the Secretary is prohibited from collecting by levy or a proceeding in court.

(5) JEOPARDY COLLECTION.—If the Secretary makes a finding that the collection of the penalty is in jeopardy, nothing in this subsection shall prevent the immediate collection of such penalty.

Amendments

• **2018, Tax Technical Corrections Act of 2018 (P.L. 115-141)**

P.L. 115-141, § 401(a)(325)(D), Div. U:

Amended Code Sec. 6672(c)(2) by striking "Court of Claims" and inserting "Court of Federal Claims". **Effective** 3-23-2018.

• **1996, Taxpayer Bill of Rights 2 (P.L. 104-168)**

P.L. 104-168, § 901(a):

Amended Code Sec. 6672 by redesignating subsection (b) as subsection (c). **Effective** for proposed assessments made after 6-30-96.

• **1989, Omnibus Budget Reconciliation Act of 1989 (P.L. 101-239)**

P.L. 101-239, § 7737(a):

Amended Code Sec. 6672(b)(1) by adding at the end thereof a new sentence. **Effective** 12-19-89.

• **1978 (P.L. 95-628)**

P.L. 95-628, § 9(a):

Amended Code Sec. 6672 by striking out "Any person" and inserting in lieu thereof "(a) GENERAL RULE.—Any person" and by adding a new Code Sec. 6672(b). **Effective** for penalties assessed after 1-9-79.

[Sec. 6672(d)]

(d) RIGHT OF CONTRIBUTION WHERE MORE THAN 1 PERSON LIABLE FOR PENALTY.—If more than 1 person is liable for the penalty under subsection (a) with respect to any tax, each person who paid such penalty shall be entitled to recover from other persons who are liable for such penalty an amount equal to the excess of the amount paid by such person over such person's proportionate share of the penalty. Any claim for such a recovery may be made only in a proceeding which is separate from, and is not joined or consolidated with—

(1) an action for collection of such penalty brought by the United States, or

(2) a proceeding in which the United States files a counterclaim or third-party complaint for the collection of such penalty.

Amendments

• **1996, Taxpayer Bill of Rights 2 (P.L. 104-168)**

P.L. 104-168, § 903(a):

Amended Code Sec. 6672 by adding at the end a new subsection (d). **Effective** for penalties assessed after 7-30-96.

[Sec. 6672(e)]

(e) EXCEPTION FOR VOLUNTARY BOARD MEMBERS OF TAX-EXEMPT ORGANIZATIONS.—No penalty shall be imposed by subsection (a) on any unpaid, volunteer member of any board of trustees or directors of an organization exempt from tax under subtitle A if such member—

(1) is solely serving in an honorary capacity,

(2) does not participate in the day-to-day or financial operations of the organization, and

(3) does not have actual knowledge of the failure on which such penalty is imposed.

The preceding sentence shall not apply if it results in no person being liable for the penalty imposed by subsection (a).

Amendments

• **1996, Taxpayer Bill of Rights 2 (P.L. 104-168)**

P.L. 104-168, § 904(a):

Amended Code Sec. 6672 by adding at the end a new subsection (e). **Effective** 7-30-96.

Sec. 6672(c)

ASSESSABLE PENALTIES

[Sec. 6673]
SEC. 6673. SANCTIONS AND COSTS AWARDED BY COURTS.

[Sec. 6673(a)]

(a) TAX COURT PROCEEDINGS.—

(1) PROCEDURES INSTITUTED PRIMARILY FOR DELAY, ETC.—Whenever it appears to the Tax Court that—

(A) proceedings before it have been instituted or maintained by the taxpayer primarily for delay,

(B) the taxpayer's position in such proceeding is frivolous or groundless, or

(C) the taxpayer unreasonably failed to pursue available administrative remedies,

the Tax Court, in its decision, may require the taxpayer to pay to the United States a penalty not in excess of $25,000.

(2) COUNSEL'S LIABILITY FOR EXCESSIVE COSTS.—Whenever it appears to the Tax Court that any attorney or other person admitted to practice before the Tax Court has multiplied the proceedings in any case unreasonably and vexatiously, the Tax Court may require—

(A) that such attorney or other person pay personally the excess costs, expenses, and attorneys' fees reasonably incurred because of such conduct, or

(B) if such attorney is appearing on behalf of the Commissioner of Internal Revenue, that the United States pay such excess costs, expenses, and attorneys' fees in the same manner as such an award by a district court.

[Sec. 6673(b)]

(b) PROCEEDINGS IN OTHER COURTS.—

(1) CLAIMS UNDER SECTION 7433.—Whenever it appears to the court that the taxpayer's position in the proceedings before the court instituted or maintained by such taxpayer under section 7433 is frivolous or groundless, the court may require the taxpayer to pay to the United States a penalty not in excess of $10,000.

(2) COLLECTION OF SANCTIONS AND COSTS.—In any civil proceeding before any court (other than the Tax Court) which is brought by or against the United States in connection with the determination, collection, or refund of any tax, interest, or penalty under this title, any monetary sanctions, penalties, or costs awarded by the court to the United States may be assessed by the Secretary and, upon notice and demand, may be collected in the same manner as a tax.

(3) SANCTIONS AND COSTS AWARDED BY A COURT OF APPEALS.—In connection with any appeal from a proceeding in the Tax Court or a civil proceeding described in paragraph (2), an order of a United States Court of Appeals or the Supreme Court awarding monetary sanctions, penalties or court costs to the United States may be registered in a district court upon filing a certified copy of such order and shall be enforceable as other district court judgments. Any such sanctions, penalties, or costs may be assessed by the Secretary and, upon notice and demand, may be collected in the same manner as a tax.

Amendments

• **1989, Omnibus Budget Reconciliation Act of 1989 (P.L. 101-239)**

P.L. 101-239, §7731(a):

Amended Code Sec. 6673. **Effective** for positions taken after 12-31-89, in proceedings which are pending on, or commenced after such date. Prior to amendment, Code Sec. 6673 read as follows:

SEC. 6673. DAMAGES ASSESSABLE FOR INSTITUTING PROCEEDINGS BEFORE THE TAX COURT PRIMARILY FOR DELAY, ETC.

(a) IN GENERAL.—Whenever it appears to the Tax Court that proceedings before it have been instituted or maintained by the taxpayer primarily for delay, that the taxpayer's position in such proceeding is frivolous or groundless, or that the taxpayer unreasonably failed to pursue available administrative remedies, damages in an amount not in excess of $5,000 shall be awarded to the United States by the Tax Court in its decision. Damages so awarded shall be assessed at the same time as the deficiency and shall be paid upon notice and demand from the Secretary and shall be collected as a part of the tax.

(b) CLAIMS UNDER SECTION 7433.—Whenever it appears to the court that the taxpayer's position in proceedings before the court instituted or maintained by such taxpayer under section 7433 is frivolous or groundless, damages in an amount not in excess of $10,000 shall be awarded to the United States by the court in the court's decision. Damages so awarded shall be assessed at the same time as the decision and shall be paid upon notice and demand from the Secretary.

• **1988, Technical and Miscellaneous Revenue Act of 1988 (P.L. 100-647)**

P.L. 100-647, §6241(b)(1):

Amended Code Sec. 6673 by inserting "(a) IN GENERAL.—" before "Whenever" and by adding at the end thereof new subsection (b). **Effective** for actions by officers or employees of the Internal Revenue Service after 11-10-88.

P.L. 100-647, §6241(b)(2):

Amended Code Sec. 6673 by striking out "TAX" before "Court" in the heading. **Effective** for actions by officers or employees of the Internal Revenue Service after 11-10-88.

• **1986, Tax Reform Act of 1986 (P.L. 99-514)**

P.L. 99-514, §1552(a):

Amended Code Sec. 6673 by striking out "or that the taxpayer's position in such proceedings is frivolous or groundless" and inserting in lieu thereof ", that the taxpayer's position in such proceeding is frivolous or groundless, or that the taxpayer unreasonably failed to pursue available administrative remedies". **Effective** for proceedings commenced after 10-22-86.

• **1982, Tax Equity and Fiscal Responsibility Act of 1982 (P.L. 97-248)**

P.L. 97-248, §292(b):

Amended the first sentence of Code Sec. 6673. **Effective** for any action or proceeding in the Tax Court commenced after 12-31-82 or pending in the United States Tax Court on the day which is 120 days after 7-18-84. Prior to amendment, the first sentence read as follows:

"Whenever it appears to the Tax Court that proceedings before it have been instituted by the taxpayer merely for delay, damages in an amount not in excess of $500 shall be awarded to the United States by the Tax Court in its decision."

P.L. 97-248, §292(d)(2)(A):

Amended the section heading of Code Sec. 6673 by striking out "Merely for Delay." and inserting "Primarily for Delay, Etc.". **Effective** for any action or proceeding in the Tax Court commenced after 12-31-82 or pending in the United States Tax Court on the day which is 120 days after 7-18-84.

• **1976, Tax Reform Act of 1976 (P.L. 94-455)**

P.L. 94-455, §1906(b)(13)(A):

Amended 1954 Code by substituting "Secretary" for "Secretary or his delegate" each place it appeared. **Effective** 2-1-77.

[Sec. 6674]
SEC. 6674. FRAUDULENT STATEMENT OR FAILURE TO FURNISH STATEMENT TO EMPLOYEE.

In addition to the criminal penalty provided by section 7204, any person required under the provisions of section 6051 or 6053(b) to furnish a statement to an employee who willfully furnishes a false or fraudulent statement, or who willfully fails to furnish a statement in the manner, at the time, and showing the information required under section 6051 or 6053(b), or regulations prescribed thereunder, shall for each such failure be subject to a penalty under this subchapter of $50, which shall be assessed and collected in the same manner as the tax on employers imposed by section 3111.

Amendments

• **1965, Social Security Amendments of 1965 (P.L. 89-97)**

P.L. 89-97, §313(e):

Amended Sec. 6674 by inserting "or 6053(b)" immediately after "6051" each place it appears. **Effective** with respect to tips received by employees after 1965.

ASSESSABLE PENALTIES

[Sec. 6675]

SEC. 6675. EXCESSIVE CLAIMS WITH RESPECT TO THE USE OF CERTAIN FUELS.

[Sec. 6675(a)]

(a) CIVIL PENALTY.—In addition to any criminal penalty provided by law, if a claim is made under section 6416(a)(4) (relating to certain sales of gasoline), section 6420 (relating to gasoline used on farms), 6421 (relating to gasoline used for certain nonhighway purposes or by local transit systems), or 6427 (relating to fuels not used for taxable purposes) for an excessive amount, unless it is shown that the claim for such excessive amount is due to reasonable cause, the person making such claim shall be liable to a penalty in an amount equal to whichever of the following is the greater:

(1) Two times the excessive amount; or

(2) $10.

Amendments

• **2005, Safe, Accountable, Flexible, Efficient Transportation Equity Act: A Legacy for Users (P.L. 109-59)**

P.L. 109-59, § 11163(d)(2):

Amended Code Sec. 6675(a) by inserting "section 6416(a)(4) (relating to certain sales of gasoline)," after "made under". **Effective** for sales after 12-31-2005.

• **1983, Surface Transportation Act of 1983 (P.L. 97-424)**

P.L. 97-424, § 515(b)(11)(A):

Amended Code Sec. 6675(a) by striking out "6424 (relating to lubricating oil used for certain nontaxable purposes),". **Effective** with respect to articles sold after 1-6-83.

P.L. 97-424, § 515(b)(11)(C):

Amended the heading of Code Sec. 6675 by striking out "OR LUBRICATING OIL" after "CERTAIN FUELS". **Effective** with respect to articles sold after 1-6-83.

• **1978, Energy Tax Act of 1978 (P.L. 95-618)**

P.L. 95-618, § 233(b)(2)(D):

Amended Code Sec. 6675(a) by changing "not used in highway motor vehicles" to "used for certain nontaxable purposes". **Effective** 12-1-78.

• **1970 (P.L. 91-258)**

P.L. 91-258, § 207(d)(8)(A), (B):

Amended Code Sec. 6675(a) by substituting "FUELS" for "GASOLINE" in the heading, by substituting "6424" for "or 6424", and by adding ", or 6427 (relating to fuels not used for taxable purposes)". **Effective** 7-1-70.

• **1965, Excise Tax Reduction Act of 1965 (P.L. 89-44)**

P.L. 89-44, § 202(c)(3)(A):

Amended Sec. 6675 by inserting "OR LUBRICATING OIL" in the heading, by inserting a comma in lieu of "or" in the second line of subsection (a), and by inserting ", or 6424 (relating to lubricating oil not used in highway motor vehicles)" after "transit systems)" in subsection (a). **Effective** 1-1-66.

• **1956 (P.L. 627, 84th Cong.)**

P.L. 627, 84th Cong., § 208(d)(2):

Amended Sec. 6675 by striking from the heading "FOR GASOLINE USED ON FARMS" and substituting "WITH RESPECT TO THE USE OF CERTAIN GASOLINE", and by inserting after "6420 (relating to gasoline used on farms)" in subsection (a) "or 6421 (relating to gasoline used for certain nonhighway purposes or by local transit systems)". **Effective** 7-1-56.

[Sec. 6675(b)]

(b) EXCESSIVE AMOUNT DEFINED.—For purposes of this section, the term "excessive amount" means in the case of any person the amount by which—

(1) the amount claimed under section 6416(a)(4), 6420, 6421, or 6427, as the case may be, for any period, exceeds

(2) the amount allowable under such section for such period.

Amendments

• **2005, Safe, Accountable, Flexible, Efficient Transportation Equity Act: A Legacy for Users (P.L. 109-59)**

P.L. 109-59, § 11163(d)(3):

Amended Code Sec. 6675(b)(1) by inserting "6416(a)(4)," after "under section". **Effective** for sales after 12-31-2005.

• **1983, Surface Transportation Act of 1983 (P.L. 97-424)**

P.L. 97-424, § 515(b)(11)(B):

Amended Code Sec. 6675(b)(1) by striking out "6424," before "or 6427". **Effective** with respect to articles sold after 1-6-83.

• **1970 (P.L. 91-258)**

P.L. 91-258, § 207(d)(8)(C):

Amended Code Sec. 6675(b) by substituting "6424, or 6427" for "or 6424" in paragraph (1). **Effective** 7-1-70.

• **1965, Excise Tax Reduction Act of 1965 (P.L. 89-44)**

P.L. 89-44, § 202(c)(3)(A):

Amended subsection (b)(1) by inserting "6420, 6421, or 6424," in lieu of "6420 or 6421,". **Effective** 1-1-66.

• **1956 (P.L. 627, 84th Cong.)**

P.L. 627, 84th Cong., § 208(d)(2):

Amended subsection (b) by inserting after "6420" the words "or 6421, as the case may be,". **Effective** 7-1-56.

[Sec. 6675(c)]

(c) ASSESSMENT AND COLLECTION OF PENALTY.—

For assessment and collection of penalty provided by subsection (a), see section 6206.

Amendments

• **1956 (P.L. 466, 84th Cong.)**

P.L. 466, 84th Cong., §§ 3 and 4(g):

Added Code Sec. 6675, and amended table of sections for subchapter B to reflect Sec. 6675.

[Sec. 6676]

SEC. 6676. ERRONEOUS CLAIM FOR REFUND OR CREDIT.

[Sec. 6676(a)]

(a) CIVIL PENALTY.—If a claim for refund or credit with respect to income tax is made for an excessive amount, unless it is shown that the claim for such excessive amount is due to reasonable cause, the person making such claim shall be liable for a penalty in an amount equal to 20 percent of the excessive amount.

Amendments

• **2015, Protecting Americans from Tax Hikes Act of 2015 (P.L. 114-113)**

P.L. 114-113, § 209(b), Div. Q:

Amended Code Sec. 6676(a) by striking "(other than a claim for a refund or credit relating to the earned income credit under section 32)" following "income tax". **Effective** for claims filed after 12-18-2015.

P.L. 114-113, § 209(c)(1), Div. Q:

Amended Code Sec. 6676(a) by striking "has a reasonable basis" and inserting "is due to reasonable cause". **Effective** for claims filed after 12-18-2015 [effective date changed by P.L. 115-141, § 101(k), Div. U.—CCH].

[Sec. 6676(b)]

(b) EXCESSIVE AMOUNT.—For purposes of this section, the term "excessive amount" means in the case of any person the amount by which the amount of the claim for refund or credit for any taxable year exceeds the amount of such claim allowable under this title for such taxable year.

ASSESSABLE PENALTIES

[Sec. 6676(c)]

(c) NONECONOMIC SUBSTANCE TRANSACTIONS TREATED AS LACKING REASONABLE CAUSE.—For purposes of this section, any excessive amount which is attributable to any transaction described in section 6662(b)(6) shall not be treated as due to reasonable cause.

Amendments

• **2018, Tax Technical Corrections Act of 2018 (P.L. 115-141)**

P.L. 115-141, §401(a)(305), Div. U:

Amended the heading of Code Sec. 6676(c) by striking "REASONABLE BASIS" and inserting "REASONABLE CAUSE". **Effective** 3-23-2018.

• **2015, Protecting Americans from Tax Hikes Act of 2015 (P.L. 114-113)**

P.L. 114-113, §209(c)(2), Div. Q:

Amended Code Sec. 6676(c) by striking "having a reasonable basis" and inserting "due to reasonable cause". **Effective** for claims filed after 12-18-2015 [effective date changed by P.L. 115-141, §101(k), Div. U—CCH].

• **2010, Health Care and Education Reconciliation Act of 2010 (P.L. 111-152)**

P.L. 111-152, §1409(d):

Amended Code Sec. 6676 by redesignating subsection (c) as subsection (d) and inserting after subsection (b) a new subsection (c). **Effective** for refunds and credits attributable to transactions entered into after 3-30-2010.

[Sec. 6676(d)]

(d) COORDINATION WITH OTHER PENALTIES.—This section shall not apply to any portion of the excessive amount of a claim for refund or credit which is subject to a penalty imposed under part II of subchapter A of chapter 68.

Amendments

• **2010, Health Care and Education Reconciliation Act of 2010 (P.L. 111-152)**

P.L. 111-152, §1409(d):

Amended Code Sec. 6676 by redesignating subsection (c) as subsection (d). **Effective** for refunds and credits attributable to transactions entered into after 3-30-2010.

• **2007, Small Business and Work Opportunity Tax Act of 2007 (P.L. 110-28)**

P.L. 110-28, §8247(a):

Amended part I of subchapter B of chapter 68 by inserting after Code Sec. 6675 a new Code Sec. 6676. **Effective** for any claim filed or submitted after 5-25-2007.

[Sec. 6676—Repealed]

Amendments

• **1989, Omnibus Budget Reconciliation Act of 1989 (P.L. 101-239)**

P.L. 101-239, §7711(b)(1):

Repealed Code Sec. 6676. **Effective** for returns and statements the due date for which (determined without regard to extensions) is after 12-31-89. Prior to repeal, Code Sec. 6676 read as follows:

SEC. 6676. FAILURE TO SUPPLY IDENTIFYING NUMBERS.

[Sec. 6676(a)]

(a) IN GENERAL.—If any person who is required by regulations prescribed under section 6109—

(1) to include his TIN in any return, statement, or other document,

(2) to furnish his TIN to another person, or

(3) except in the case of a return or statement required to be filed under section 6042, 6044, or 6049, to include in any return, statement, or other document made with respect to another person the TIN of such other person,

fails to comply with such requirement at the time prescribed by such regulations, such person shall, unless it is shown that such failure is due to reasonable cause and not to willful neglect, pay a penalty of $5 for each such failure described in paragraph (1) and $50 for each such failure described in paragraph (2) or (3), except that the total amount imposed on such person for all such failures during any calendar year shall not exceed $100,000.

Amendments

• **1988, Technical and Miscellaneous Revenue Act of 1988 (P.L. 100-647)**

P.L. 100-647, §1015(g)(1):

Amended Code Sec. 6676(a)(3) by striking out "6049, or 6050N" and inserting in lieu thereof "or 6049". **Effective** as if included in the provision of P.L. 99-514 to which it relates.

• **1986, Tax Reform Act of 1986 (P.L. 99-514)**

P.L. 99-514, §1501(b):

Amended Code Sec. 6676(a) by striking out "$50,000" and inserting in lieu thereof "$100,000". **Effective** for returns the due date for which (determined without regard to extensions) is after 12-31-86.

P.L. 99-514, §1523(b)(3):

Amended Code Sec. 6676 by striking out "or 6049" in subsection (a)(3) and inserting in lieu thereof "6049, or 6050N", by striking out "or 6049" in subsection (b)(1)(A) and inserting in lieu thereof "6049, or 6050N", and by striking out "AND DIVIDEND" in the heading for subsection (b) and inserting in lieu thereof ", DIVIDENDS, AND ROYALTIES". **Effective** with respect to payments made after 12-31-86.

[Sec. 6676(b)]

(b) PENALTIES INVOLVING FAILURES ON INTEREST AND DIVIDEND RETURNS.—

(1) IN GENERAL.—If any payor—

(A) is required to include in any return or statement required to be filed under section 6042, 6044, or 6049 with respect to any payee the TIN of such payee, and

(B) fails to include such number or includes an incorrect number,

then the payor shall pay a penalty of $50 for each such failure unless it is shown that the payor exercised due diligence in attempting to satisfy the requirement with respect to such TIN.

Amendments

• **1988, Technical and Miscellaneous Revenue Act of 1988 (P.L. 100-647)**

P.L. 100-647, §1015(g)(2)-(3):

Amended Code Sec. 6676 by striking out "6049, or 6050N" in subsection (b)(1)(A) and inserting in lieu thereof "or 6049", and by striking out ", Dividends, and Royalties" in the heading for subsection (b) and inserting in lieu thereof "and Dividend". **Effective** as if included in the provision of P.L. 99-514 to which it relates.

• **1986, Tax Reform Act of 1986 (P.L. 99-514)**

P.L. 99-514, §1523(b)(3):

Amended Code Sec. 6676 by striking out "or 6049" in subsection (b)(1)(A) and inserting in lieu thereof "6049, or 6050N," and striking out "AND DIVIDEND" in the heading for Subsection (b) and inserting in lieu thereof ", DIVIDENDS, AND ROYALTIES". **Effective** with respect to payments made after 12-31-86.

[Sec. 6676(c)]

(c) PENALTY FOR FAILURE TO SUPPLY IDENTIFYING NUMBER UNDER SECTION 215.—If any person who is required by regulations under section 215—

(1) to furnish his taxpayer identification number to another person, or

(2) to include on his return the taxpayer identification number of another person,

fails to comply with such requirement at the time prescribed by such regulations, such person shall, unless it is shown that such failure is due to reasonable cause and not to willful neglect, pay a penalty of $50 for each such failure.

Amendments

• **1984, Deficit Reduction Act of 1984 (P.L. 98-369)**

P.L. 98-369, §422(c):

Amended Code Sec. 6676 by redesignating subsection (c) as subsection (d) and inserting new subsection (c). **Effective** for payments made after 12-31-84.

[Sec. 6676(d)]

(d) PROCEDURES RELATING TO ASSESSMENT OF PENALTY.—

(1) SELF-ASSESSMENT OF PENALTY IMPOSED BY SUBSECTION (b).—Any penalty imposed under subsection (b) on any person—

(A) for purposes of this subtitle, shall be treated as an excise tax imposed by subtitle D, and

(B) shall be due and payable on April 1 of the calendar year following the calendar year for which the return or statement was made.

(2) DEFICIENCY PROCEDURES NOT TO APPLY.—Subchapter B of chapter 63 (relating to deficiency procedures for income, estate, gift, and certain excise taxes) shall not apply in respect of the assessment or collection of any penalty imposed by this section.

Amendments

• **1984, Deficit Reduction Act of 1984 (P.L. 98-369)**

P.L. 98-369, §422(c):

Amended Code Sec. 6676 by redesignating subsection (c) as subsection (d). **Effective** for payments made after 12-31-84.

[Sec. 6676(e)]

(e) PENALTY FOR FAILURE TO SUPPLY TIN OF DEPENDENT.—

(1) IN GENERAL.—If any person required under section 6109(e) to include the TIN of any dependent on his return fails to include such number on such return (or includes an incorrect number), such person shall, unless it is shown that such failure is due to reasonable cause and not willful neglect, pay a penalty of $5 for each such failure.

(2) SUBSECTION (a) NOT TO APPLY.—Subsection (a) shall not apply to any failure described in paragraph (1) of this subsection.

Amendments

• **1986, Tax Reform Act of 1986 (P.L. 99-514)**

P.L. 99-514, §1524(b):

Amended Code Sec. 6676 by adding at the end thereof new subsection (e). **Effective** for returns the due date for which (determined without regard to extensions) is after 12-31-87.

• **1983, Interest and Dividend Tax Compliance Act of 1983 (P.L. 98-67)**

P.L. 98-67, §105(a):

Added Code Sec. 6676. **Effective** with respect to payments made after 12-31-83. Prior to amendment, Code Sec. 6676 read as follows:

ASSESSABLE PENALTIES

[Sec. 6676(a)]

(a) CIVIL PENALTIES.—

(1) IN GENERAL.—If any person who is required by regulations prescribed under section 6109—

(A) to include his taxpayer identification number in any return, statement, or other document,

(B) to furnish his taxpayer identification number to another person, or

(C) to include in any return, statement, or other document made with respect to another person the taxpayer identification number of such other person,

fails to comply with such requirement at the time prescribed by such regulations, such person shall, unless it is shown that such failure is due to reasonable cause and not to willful neglect, pay a penalty of $5 for each such failure described in subparagraph (A) and $50 for each such failure described in subparagraph (B) or (C), except that the total amount imposed on such person for all such failures during any calendar year shall not exceed $50,000.

(2) TAXPAYER IDENTIFICATION NUMBER DEFINED.—The term "taxpayer identification number" means the identifying number assigned to a person under section 6109.

Amendments

• **1982, Tax Equity and Fiscal Responsibility Act of 1982 (P.L. 97-248)**

P.L. 97-248, § 316(a):

Amended Code Sec. 6676(a). **Effective** with respect to returns the due date for the filing of which (without regard to extensions) is after 12-31-82. Prior to amendment, Code Sec. 6676(a) read as follows:

(a) CIVIL PENALTY.—If any person who is required by regulations prescribed under section 6109—

(1) to include his identifying number in any return, statement, or other document,

(2) to furnish his identifying number to another person, or

(3) to include in any return, statement, or other document made with respect to another person the identifying number of such other person,

fails to comply with such requirement at the time prescribed by such regulations, such person shall pay a penalty of $5 for each such failure, unless it is shown that such failure is due to reasonable cause.

[Sec. 6676(b)]

(b) DEFICIENCY PROCEDURES NOT TO APPLY.—Subchapter B of chapter 63 (relating to deficiency procedures for income, estate, gift and certain excise taxes) shall not apply in respect of the assessment or collection of any penalty imposed by subsection (a).

Amendments

• **1974, Employee Retirement Income Security Act of 1974 (P.L. 93-406)**

P.L. 93-406, § 1016(a)(20):

Amended Code Sec. 6676(b) by changing "chapter 42" to "certain excise". For **effective** date, see amendment note for Code Sec. 410.

• **1969, Tax Reform Act of 1969 (P.L. 91-172)**

P.L. 91-172, § 101(j)(52):

Amended Code Sec. 6676(b) by substituting "gift, and chapter 42 taxes" for "and gift taxes". **Effective** 1-1-70.

• **1961 (P.L. 87-397)**

P.L. 87-397, § 1(b):

Added Code Sec. 6676.

[Sec. 6677]

SEC. 6677. FAILURE TO FILE INFORMATION WITH RESPECT TO CERTAIN FOREIGN TRUSTS.

[Sec. 6677(a)]

(a) CIVIL PENALTY.—In addition to any criminal penalty provided by law, if any notice or return required to be filed by section 6048—

(1) is not filed on or before the time provided in such section, or

(2) does not include all the information required pursuant to such section or includes incorrect information,

the person required to file such notice or return shall pay a penalty equal to the greater of $10,000 or 35 percent of the gross reportable amount. If any failure described in the preceding sentence continues for more than 90 days after the day on which the Secretary mails notice of such failure to the person required to pay such penalty, such person shall pay a penalty (in addition to the amount determined under the preceding sentence) of $10,000 for each 30-day period (or fraction thereof) during which such failure continues after the expiration of such 90-day period. At such time as the gross reportable amount with respect to any failure can be determined by the Secretary, any subsequent penalty imposed under this subsection with respect to such failure shall be reduced as necessary to assure that the aggregate amount of such penalties do not exceed the gross reportable amount (and to the extent that such aggregate amount already exceeds the gross reportable amount the Secretary shall refund such excess to the taxpayer).

Amendments

• **2010, Hiring Incentives to Restore Employment Act (P.L. 111-147)**

P.L. 111-147, § 535(a)(1)-(2):

Amended Code Sec. 6677(a) by inserting "the greater of $10,000 or" before "35 percent", and by striking the last sentence and inserting a new sentence. **Effective** for notices and returns required to be filed after 12-31-2009. Prior to being stricken, the last sentence of Code Sec. 6677(a) read as follows:

In no event shall the penalty under this subsection with respect to any failure exceed the gross reportable amount.

[Sec. 6677(b)]

(b) SPECIAL RULES FOR RETURNS UNDER SECTION 6048(b).—In the case of a return required under section 6048(b)—

(1) the United States person referred to in such section shall be liable for the penalty imposed by subsection (a), and

(2) subsection (a) shall be applied by substituting "5 percent" for "35 percent".

[Sec. 6677(c)]

(c) GROSS REPORTABLE AMOUNT.—For purposes of subsection (a), the term "gross reportable amount" means—

(1) the gross value of the property involved in the event (determined as of the date of the event) in the case of a failure relating to section 6048(a),

(2) the gross value of the portion of the trust's assets at the close of the year treated as owned by the United States person in the case of a failure relating to section 6048(b)(1), and

(3) the gross amount of the distributions in the case of a failure relating to section 6048(c).

[Sec. 6677(d)]

(d) REASONABLE CAUSE EXCEPTION.—No penalty shall be imposed by this section on any failure which is shown to be due to reasonable cause and not due to willful neglect. The fact that a foreign jurisdiction would impose a civil or criminal penalty on the taxpayer (or any other person) for disclosing the required information is not reasonable cause.

[Sec. 6677(e)]

(e) DEFICIENCY PROCEDURES NOT TO APPLY.—Subchapter B of chapter 63 (relating to deficiency procedures for income, estate, gift, and certain excise taxes) shall not apply in respect of the assessment or collection of any penalty imposed by subsection (a).

Amendments

• **1996, Small Business Job Protection Act of 1996 (P.L. 104-188)**

P.L. 104-188, § 1901(b):

Amended Code Sec. 6677. For the **effective** date, see Act Sec. 1901(d).

P.L. 104-188, § 1901(d), provides:

(d) EFFECTIVE DATES.—

(1) REPORTABLE EVENTS.—To the extent related to subsection (a) of section 6048 of the Internal Revenue Code of 1986, as amended by this section, the amendments made by this section shall apply to reportable events (as defined in such section 6048) occurring after the date of the enactment of this Act.

(2) GRANTOR TRUST REPORTING.—To the extent related to subsection (b) of such section 6048, the amendments made by this section shall apply to taxable years of United States persons beginning after December 31, 1995.

(3) REPORTING BY UNITED STATES BENEFICIARIES.—To the extent related to subsection (c) of such section 6048, the amendments made by this section shall apply to distributions received after the date of the enactment of this Act.

Prior to amendment, Code Sec. 6677 read as follows:

SEC. 6677. FAILURE TO FILE INFORMATION RETURNS WITH RESPECT TO CERTAIN FOREIGN TRUSTS.

ASSESSABLE PENALTIES

[Sec. 6677(a)]

(a) CIVIL PENALTY.—In addition to any criminal penalty provided by law, any person required to file a return under section 6048 who fails to file such return at the time provided in such section, or who files a return which does not show the information required pursuant to such section, shall pay a penalty equal to 5 percent of the amount transferred to a trust (or, in the case of a failure with respect to section 6048(c), equal to 5 percent of the value of the corpus of the trust at the close of the taxable year), but not more than $1,000, unless it is shown that such failure is due to reasonable cause.

Amendments

• **1976, Tax Reform Act of 1976 (P.L. 94-455)**

P.L. 94-455, §1013(d)(2):

Substituted "to a trust (or, in the case of a failure with respect to section 6048(c), equal to 5 percent of the value of the corpus of the trust at the close of the taxable year)" for "to a trust" in Code Sec. 6677(a). **Effective** for tax years ending after 12-31-75, but only in the case of—

(A) foreign trusts created after 5-21-74, and

(B) transfers of property to foreign trusts after 5-21-74.

• **1962, Revenue Act of 1962 (P.L. 87-834)**

P.L. 87-834, §7:

Added Code Sec. 6677(a). **Effective** 10-17-62.

[Sec. 6677(b)]

(b) DEFICIENCY PROCEDURES NOT TO APPLY.—Subchapter B of chapter 63 (relating to deficiency procedures for income, estate, gift, and certain excise taxes) shall not apply in respect of the assessment or collection of any penalty imposed by subsection (a).

Amendments

• **1974, Employee Retirement Income Security Act of 1974 (P.L. 93-406)**

P.L. 93-406, §1016(a)(21):

Amended Code Sec. 6677(b) by changing "chapter 42" to "certain excise". For **effective** date, see amendment note for Code Sec. 410.

• **1969, Tax Reform Act of 1969 (P.L. 91-172)**

P.L. 91-172, §101(j)(53):

Amended Code Sec. 6677(b) by substituting "gift, and chapter 42 taxes" for "and gift taxes". **Effective** 1-1-70.

• **1962, Revenue Act of 1962 (P.L. 87-834)**

P.L. 87-834, §7:

Added Code Sec. 6677(b). **Effective** 10-17-62.

[Sec. 6678—Repealed]

Amendments

• **1986, Tax Reform Act of 1986 (P.L. 99-514)**

P.L. 99-514, §1501(d)(2):

Repealed Code Sec. 6678. **Effective** for returns the due date for which (determined without regard to extensions) is after 12-31-86. Reproduced immediately below is the text of Code Sec. 6678 prior to repeal.

SEC. 6678. FAILURE TO FURNISH CERTAIN STATEMENTS.

[Sec. 6678(a)]

(a) IN GENERAL.—In the case of each failure—

(1) to furnish a statement under section 6041(d), 6041A(e), 6045(b), 6052(b), 6050H(d), 6050I(e), 6050J(e), 6050K(b), or 6050L(c), on the date prescribed therefor to a person with respect to whom a return has been made under section 6041(a), 6041A(a) or (b), 6045(a), 6052(a), 6050H(a), 6050I(a), 6050J(a), 6050K(a), or 6050L(a), respectively,

(2) to furnish a statement under section 6039(a) on the date prescribed therefor to a person with respect to whom such a statement is required, or

(3) to furnish a statement under—

(A) section 4997(a) (relating to statements with respect to windfall profit tax on crude oil),

(B) section 6050A(b) (relating to statements furnished by certain fishing boat operators),

(C) section 6050C (relating to information regarding windfall profit tax on crude oil),

(D) section 6051 (relating to information returns with respect to income tax withheld) if the statement is required to be furnished to the employee,

(E) subsection (b) or (c) of section 6053 (relating to statements furnished by employers with respect to tips),

(F) section 6031(b), 6034A, or 6037(b) (relating to statements furnished by certain pass-thru entities), or

(G) section 6045(d) (relating to statements required in the case of certain substitute payments),

on the date prescribed therefor to a person with respect to whom such a statement is required, unless it is shown that such failure is due to reasonable cause and not to willful neglect, there shall be paid (upon notice and demand by the Secretary and in the same manner as tax) by the person failing to so furnish the statement $50 for each such statement not so furnished, but the total amount imposed on the delinquent person for all such failures during any calendar year shall not exceed $50,000.

Amendments

• **1986, Tax Reform Act of 1986 (P.L. 99-514)**

P.L. 99-514, §1811(c)(1):

Amended Code Sec. 6678(a)(3) by striking out "or" at the end of subparagraph (E), by adding "or" at the end of subparagraph (F), and by inserting after subparagraph (F) new subparagraph (G). **Effective** as if included in the provision of P.L. 98-369 to which it relates.

• **1984, Deficit Reduction Act of 1984 (P.L. 98-369)**

P.L. 98-369, §145(b)(3):

Amended Code Sec. 6678(a)(1) by striking out "or 6052(b)" and inserting in lieu thereof "6052(b), or 6050H(d)", and by striking out "or 6052(a)" and inserting in lieu thereof "6052(a), or 6050H(a)". **Effective** for amounts received after 12-31-84. In the case of any obligation in existence on 12-31-84, no penalty shall be imposed under section 6676 of the Internal Revenue Code of 1954 by reason of the amendments made by Act Sec. 145 on any failure to supply a taxpayer identification number with respect to amounts received before 1-1-86 [**effective** date changed by P.L. 99-514, §1811].

P.L. 98-369, §146(b)(3):

Amended Code Sec. 6678(a)(1) by striking out "or 6050H(d)" and inserting in lieu thereof "6050H(d), or 6050I(e)", and by striking out "or 6050H(a)" and inserting in lieu thereof "6050H(a), or 6050I(a)". **Effective** for amounts received after 12-31-84. In the case of any obligation in existence on 12-31-84, no penalty shall be imposed under section 6676 of the Internal Revenue Code of 1954 by reason of the amendments made by Act Sec. 145 on any failure to supply a taxpayer identification number with respect to amounts received before 1-1-86 [**effective** date changed by P.L. 99-514, §1811].

P.L. 98-369, §148(b)(3):

Amended Code Sec. 6678 (a)(1) by striking out "or 6050I(e)" and inserting in lieu thereof "6050I(e), or 6050J(e)", and by striking out "or 6050I(a)" and inserting in lieu thereof "6050I(a), or 6050J(a)". **Effective** for acquisitions of property and abandonments of property after 12-31-84.

P.L. 98-369, §149(b)(2):

Amended Code Sec. 6678(a)(1) by striking out "or 6050J(e)" and inserting in lieu thereof "6050J(e), or 6050K(b)", and by striking out "or 6050J(a)" and inserting in lieu thereof "6050J(a), or 6050K(a)". **Effective** with respect to exchanges after 12-31-84.

P.L. 98-369, §155(b)(2):

Amended Code Sec. 6678 (a)(1) by striking out "or 6050K(b)" and inserting in lieu thereof "6050K(b), or 6050L(c)", and by striking out "or 6050K(a)" and inserting in lieu thereof "6050K(a), or 6050L(a)". **Effective** for contributions made after 12-31-84, in tax years ending after such date.

P.L. 98-369, §714(f):

Amended Code Sec. 6678(a)(3)(E) by striking out "section 6053(c)" [subsection (b) or (c) of section 6053] and inserting in lieu thereof "section 6053". **Effective** as if included in the provision of P.L. 97-248 to which it relates.

P.L. 98-369, §714(q)(3):

Amended Code Sec. 6678(a)(3) by striking out "or" at the end of subparagraph (D), by inserting "or" at the end of subparagraph (E), and by adding after subparagraph (E) new subparagraph (F). **Effective** for tax years beginning after 12-31-84.

• **1983, Interest and Dividend Tax Compliance Act of 1983 (P.L. 98-67)**

P.L. 98-67, §105(b)(2)(B)-(C):

Amended Code Sec. 6678(a)(1). **Effective** with respect to payments made after 12-31-83. Prior to amendment, Code Sec. 6678(a)(1) read as follows:

(1) to furnish a statement under section 6041(d), 6041A(e), 6042(c), 6044(e), 6045(b), 6049(c), or 6052(b), on the date prescribed therefor to a person with respect to whom a return has been made under section 6041(a), 6041(a) or (b), 6042(a)(1), 6044(a)(1), 6045(a), 6049(a), or 6052(a), respectively,

[Sec. 6678(b)]

(b) FAILURE TO FILE INTEREST AND DIVIDEND STATEMENTS.—

(1) IN GENERAL.—In the case of any person who fails to furnish a statement under section 6042(c), 6044(e), or 6049(c) on the date prescribed therefor to a person with respect to whom a return has been made under section 6042(a)(1), 6044(a)(1), or 6049(a), respectively, such person shall pay a penalty of $50 for each such failure unless it is shown that such person exercised due diligence in attempting to satisfy the requirement with respect to such statement.

(2) SELF-ASSESSMENT.—Any penalty imposed under paragraph (1) on any person—

(A) for purposes of this subtitle, shall be treated as an excise tax imposed by subtitle D, and

(B) shall be due and payable on April 1 of the calendar year following the calendar year for which such statement is required.

(3) DEFICIENCY PROCEDURES NOT TO APPLY.—Subchapter B of chapter 63 (relating to deficiency procedures for income, estate, gift, and certain excise taxes) shall not apply in respect of the assessment or collection of any penalty imposed by paragraph (1).

Amendments

• **1983, Interest and Dividend Tax Compliance Act of 1983 (P.L. 98-67)**

P.L. 98-67, §105(b)(2)(D):

Added Code Sec. 6678(b). **Effective** with respect to payments made after 12-31-83.

[Sec. 6678(c)]

(c) FAILURE TO NOTIFY PARTNERSHIP OF EXCHANGE OF PARTNERSHIP INTEREST.—In the case of any person who fails to furnish the notice required by section 6050K(c)(1) on the date prescribed therefor, unless it is shown that such failure is due to reasonable cause and not to willful neglect, such person shall pay a penalty of $50 for each such failure.

ASSESSABLE PENALTIES

Amendments

• **1984, Deficit Reduction Act of 1984 (P.L. 98-369)**

P.L. 98-369, §149(b)(3):

Added subsection (c). **Effective** with respect to exchanges after 12-31-84.

• **1983, Interest and Dividend Tax Compliance Act of 1983 (P.L. 98-67)**

P.L. 98-67, §105(b)(2)(A):

Added "(a) IN GENERAL.—" at the beginning of the section. **Effective** with respect to payments made after 12-31-83.

• **1983, Technical Corrections Act of 1982 (P.L. 97-448)**

P.L. 97-448, §201(i)(3):

Amended Code Sec. 6678(3) by redesignating subparagraphs (A) through (D) as subparagraphs (B) through (E), respectively, and by inserting before subparagraph (B) (as so redesignated) new subparagraph (A). **Effective** with respect to returns and statements the due dates for which (without regard to extensions) are after 1-12-83.

• **1982, Tax Equity and Fiscal Responsibility Act of 1982 (P.L. 97-248)**

P.L. 97-248, §309(b)(3):

Amended Code Sec. 6678(1) by striking out "6049(a)(1)" and inserting "6049(a)". **Effective** for amounts paid or treated as paid after 12-31-82.

P.L. 97-248, §311(a)(2):

Amended Code Sec. 6678(1) by inserting "6045(b)" after "6044(e)" and by inserting "6045(a)" after "6044(a)(1)". **Effective** 9-3-82.

P.L. 97-248, §312(b):

Amended Code Sec. 6678(1) by inserting "6041A(e)," after "6041(d)," and by inserting "6041A(a) or (b)," after "6041(a)". **Effective** for payments and sales made after 12-31-82.

P.L. 97-248, §314(b):

Amended Code Sec. 6678(3)(D) by striking out "section 6053(b)" and inserting "subsection (b) or (c) of section 6053". **Effective** for calendar years beginning after 12-31-82.

P.L. 97-248, §315(c):

Amended Code Sec. 6678 by striking out "$10" and inserting "$50" and by striking out "$25,000" and inserting "$50,000". **Effective** with respect to returns or statements the due date for the filing of which (without regard to extensions) is after 12-31-82.

• **1981, Economic Recovery Tax Act of 1981 (P.L. 97-34)**

P.L. 97-34, §723(a)(2):

Amended Code Sec. 6678 by striking out "or" at the end of paragraph (1), by inserting "or" at the end of paragraph (2), and by adding a paragraph (3). **Effective** for returns and statements required to be furnished after 12-31-81.

P.L. 97-34, §723(b)(2):

Amended Code Sec. 6678(1) by inserting "6041(d)" before "6042(c)" and by inserting "6041(a)" before "6042(a)(1)". **Effective** for returns and statements required to be furnished after 12-31-81.

• **1979 (P.L. 96-167)**

P.L. 96-167, §7:

Amended Code Sec. 6678. **Effective** for calendar years beginning after 1979. Prior to amendment, Code Sec. 6678 read as follows:

In the case of each failure to furnish a statement under section 6039(b), 6042(c), 6044(e), 6049(c), or 6052(b) on the date prescribed therefor to a person with respect to whom a return has been made under section 6039(a), 6042(a)(1), 6044(a)(1), 6049(a)(1), or 6052(a), respectively, unless it is shown that such failure is due to reasonable cause and not to willful neglect, there shall be paid (upon notice and demand by the Secretary and in the same manner as tax), by the person failing to so furnish the statement, $10 for each such statement not so furnished, but the total amount imposed on the delinquent person for all such failures during any calendar year shall not exceed $25,000.

• **1976, Tax Reform Act of 1976 (P.L. 94-455)**

P.L. 94-455, §1906(b)(13)(A):

Amended 1954 Code by substituting "Secretary" for "Secretary or his delegate" each place it appeared. **Effective** 2-1-77.

• **1964, Revenue Act of 1964 (P.L. 88-272)**

P.L. 88-272, §204(c)(2):

Amended Code Sec. 6678 to add references to "6052(b)" and "6052(a)".

P.L. 88-272, §221(b)(3):

Amended Code Sec. 6678 by inserting "6039(b)," before "6042(c)" and "6039(a)," before "6042(a)(1)". **Effective** for tax years ending after 12-31-63.

• **1962, Revenue Act of 1962 (P.L. 87-834)**

P.L. 87-834, §19(e):

Added Code Sec. 6678.

[Sec. 6679]

SEC. 6679. FAILURE TO FILE RETURNS, ETC., WITH RESPECT TO FOREIGN CORPORATIONS OR FOREIGN PARTNERSHIPS.

[Sec. 6679(a)]

(a) CIVIL PENALTY.—

(1) IN GENERAL.—In addition to any criminal penalty provided by law, any person required to file a return under section 6046 or 6046A who fails to file such return at the time provided in such section, or who files a return which does not show the information required pursuant to such section, shall pay a penalty of $10,000, unless it is shown that such failure is due to reasonable cause.

(2) INCREASE IN PENALTY WHERE FAILURE CONTINUES AFTER NOTIFICATION.—If any failure described in paragraph (1) continues for more than 90 days after the day on which the Secretary mails notice of such failure to the United States person, such person shall pay a penalty (in addition to the amount required under paragraph (1)) of $10,000 for each 30-day period (or fraction thereof) during which such failure continues after the expiration of such 90-day period. The increase in any penalty under this paragraph shall not exceed $50,000.

Amendments

• **2018, Tax Technical Corrections Act of 2018 (P.L. 115-141)**

P.L. 115-141, §401(a)(308), Div. U:

Amended Code Sec. 6679(a)(1) by striking "section 6046 and 6046A" and inserting "section 6046 or 6046A". **Effective** 3-23-2018.

• **2004, American Jobs Creation Act of 2004 (P.L. 108-357)**

P.L. 108-357, §413(c)(29)(A)-(B):

Amended Code Sec. 6679(a) by striking "6035, 6046, and [or] 6046A" in paragraph (1) and inserting "6046 and [or] 6046A", and by striking paragraph (3). **Effective** for tax years of foreign corporations beginning after 12-31-2004, and for tax years of United States shareholders with or within which such tax years of foreign corporations end. Prior to being stricken, Code Sec. 6679(a)(3) read as follows:

(3) REDUCED PENALTY FOR RETURNS RELATING TO FOREIGN PERSONAL HOLDING COMPANIES.—In the case of a return required under section 6035, paragraph (1) shall be applied by substituting "$1,000" for "$10,000", and paragraph (2) shall not apply.

• **1997, Taxpayer Relief Act of 1997 (P.L. 105-34)**

P.L. 105-34, §1143(b):

Amended Code Sec. 6679(a). **Effective** for transfers and changes after 8-5-97. Prior to amendment, Code Sec. 6679(a) read as follows:

(a) CIVIL PENALTY.—In addition to any criminal penalty provided by law, any person required to file a return under section 6035, 6046, or 6046A who fails to file such return at the time provided in such section, or who files a return which does not show the information required pursuant to such section, shall pay a penalty of $1,000, unless it is shown that such failure is due to reasonable cause.

• **1983, Technical Corrections Act of 1982 (P.L. 97-448)**

P.L. 97-448, §306(c)(2)(A):

Amended P.L. 97-248, §405(b) (see below) to read as follows:

"(b) PENALTY.—Subsection (a) of section 6679 (relating to failure to file returns as to organization or reorganization of foreign corporations and acquisition of their stock), as amended by section 340(b)(1), is amended by striking out `section 6035 or 6046' and inserting in lieu thereof `section 6035, 6046, or 6046A'." **Effective** as if included in the provision of P.L. 97-248 to which it relates.

P.L. 97-448, §306(c)(2)(B):

Amended P.L. 97-248, §405(c)(2) (see below) to read as follows:

"(2) The section heading of section 6679, as amended by section 340(b)(2), is amended to read as follows:

"SEC. 6679. FAILURE TO FILE RETURNS, ETC., WITH RESPECT TO FOREIGN CORPORATIONS OR FOREIGN PARTNERSHIPS.'"

Effective as if included in the provision of P.L. 97-248 to which it relates.

• **1982, Tax Equity and Fiscal Responsibility Act of 1982 (P.L. 97-248)**

P.L. 97-248, §340(b):

Amended Code Sec. 6679(a) by striking out "section 6046" and inserting "section 6035 or 6046" and by amending the section heading to read as "Failure To File Returns or Supply Information Under Section 6035 or 6046.". **Effective** for tax years of foreign corporations beginning after 9-3-82. Prior to amendment, the section heading read as follows:

"FAILURE TO FILE RETURNS AS TO ORGANIZATION OR REORGANIZATION OF FOREIGN CORPORATIONS AND AS TO ACQUISITIONS OF THEIR STOCK".

P.L. 97-248, §405(b):

Amended Code Sec. 6679(a) by striking out "section 6046" and inserting "section 6046 or 6046A". **Effective** for partnership tax years beginning after 9-3-82, and also to partnership tax years ending after that date if the partnership, each partner, and each indirect partner requests such application and if the Secretary or his delegate consents to such application.

P.L. 97-248, §405(c)(2):

Amended the section heading. For the **effective** date, see the amendment note for P.L. 97-248, §405(b). Prior to amendment, the section heading read as follows:

"Failure to File Returns as to Organization or Reorganization of Foreign Corporations and as to Acquisitions of Their Stock".

ASSESSABLE PENALTIES

[Sec. 6679(b)]

(b) DEFICIENCY PROCEDURES NOT TO APPLY.—Subchapter B of chapter 63 (relating to deficiency procedure for income, estate, gift, and certain excise taxes) shall not apply in respect of the assessment or collection of any penalty imposed by subsection (a).

Amendments

• **1974, Employee Retirement Income Security Act of 1974 (P.L. 93-406)**

P.L. 93-406, §1016(a)(22):

Amended Code Sec. 6679(b) by changing "chapter 42" to "certain excise". For the **effective** date, see the amendment note for Code Sec. 410.

• **1969, Tax Reform Act of 1969 (P.L. 91-172)**

P.L. 91-172, §101(j)(54):

Amended Code Sec. 6679(b) by substituting "gift, and chapter 42 taxes" for "and gift taxes". **Effective** 1-1-70.

• **1962, Revenue Act of 1962 (P.L. 87-834)**

P.L. 87-834, §20(c):

Added Code Sec. 6679. **Effective** 10-17-62.

[Sec. 6682]

SEC. 6682. FALSE INFORMATION WITH RESPECT TO WITHHOLDING.

[Sec. 6682(a)]

(a) CIVIL PENALTY.—In addition to any criminal penalty provided by law, if—

(1) any individual makes a statement under section 3402 or section 3406 which results in a decrease in the amounts deducted and withheld under chapter 24, and

(2) as of the time such statement was made, there was no reasonable basis for such statement,

such individual shall pay a penalty of $500 for such statement.

Amendments

• **1983, Interest and Dividend Tax Compliance Act of 1983 (P.L. 98-67)**

P.L. 98-67, §102(a):

Amended Code Sec. 6682(a)(1) by deleting "or section 3452(f)(1)(A)". **Effective** as of the close of 6-30-83.

P.L. 98-67, §107(a):

Amended Code Sec. 6682(a)(1) by adding "or section 3406". **Effective** 8-5-83.

• **1982, Tax Equity and Fiscal Responsibility Act of 1982 (P.L. 97-248)**

P.L. 97-248, §306(a):

Amended Code Sec. 6682(a)(1) by inserting "or section 3452(f)(1)(A)" after "section 3402". **Effective** for payments of interest, dividends, and patronage dividends paid or credited after 6-30-83.

[Sec. 6682(b)]

(b) EXCEPTION.—The Secretary may waive (in whole or in part) the penalty imposed under subsection (a) if the taxes imposed with respect to the individual under subtitle A for the taxable year are equal to or less than the sum of—

(1) the credits against such taxes allowed by part IV of subchapter A of chapter 1, and

(2) the payments of estimated tax which are considered payments on account of such taxes.

[Sec. 6682(c)]

(c) DEFICIENCY PROCEDURES NOT TO APPLY.—Subchapter B of chapter 63 (relating to deficiency procedures for income, estate, gift, and certain excise taxes) shall not apply in respect to the assessment or collection of any penalty imposed by subsection (a).

Amendments

• **1981, Economic Recovery Tax Act of 1981 (P.L. 97-34)**

P.L. 97-34, §721(a):

Amended Code Sec. 6682. **Effective** for acts and failures to act after 12-31-81. Prior to amendment, Code Sec. 6682 read as follows:

SEC. 6682. FALSE INFORMATION WITH RESPECT TO WITHHOLDING ALLOWANCES BASED ON ITEMIZED DEDUCTIONS.

(a) CIVIL PENALTY.—In addition to any criminal penalty provided by law, if any individual in claiming a withholding allowance under section 3402(f)(1)(F) states (1) as the amount of the wages (within the meaning of chapter 24) shown on his return for any taxable year an amount less than such wages actually shown, or (2) as the amount of the itemized deductions referred to in section 3402(m) shown on the return for any taxable year an amount greater than such deductions actually shown, he shall pay a penalty of $50 for such statement, unless (1) such statement did not result in a decrease in the amounts deducted and withheld under chapter 24, or (2) the taxes imposed with respect to the individual under subtitle A for the succeeding taxable year do not exceed the sum of (A) the credits against such taxes allowed by part IV of subchapter A of chapter 1, and (B) the payments of estimated tax which are considered payments on account of such taxes.

(b) DEFICIENCY PROCEDURES NOT TO APPLY.—Subchapter B of chapter 63 (relating to deficiency procedures for income, estate, gift, and certain excise taxes) shall not apply in respect to the assessment or collection of any penalty imposed by subsection (a).

• **1974, Employee Retirement Income Security Act of 1974 (P.L. 93-406)**

P.L. 93-406, §1016(a)(23):

Amended Code Sec. 6682(b) by changing "chapter 42" to "certain excise". For **effective** date, see amendment note for Code Sec. 410.

• **1969, Tax Reform Act of 1969 (P.L. 91-172)**

P.L. 91-172, §101(j)(55):

Amended Code Sec. 6682(b) by substituting "gift, and chapter 42 taxes" for "and gift taxes". **Effective** 1-1-70.

• **1966, Tax Adjustment Act of 1966 (P.L. 89-368)**

P.L. 89-368, §101(e):

Added Code Sec. 6682. **Effective** with respect to remuneration paid after 4-30-66.

[Sec. 6683—Repealed]

Amendments

• **2005, Gulf Opportunity Zone Act of 2005 (P.L. 109-135)**

P.L. 109-135, §403(n)(3)(A):

Repealed Code Sec. 6683. **Effective** as if included in the provision of the American Jobs Creation Act of 2004 (P.L. 108-357) to which it relates [**effective** for tax years of foreign corporations beginning after 12-31-2004, and for tax years of United States shareholders with or within which such tax years of foreign corporations end.—CCH]. Prior to repeal, Code Sec. 6683 read as follows:

SEC. 6683. FAILURE OF FOREIGN CORPORATION TO FILE RETURN OF PERSONAL HOLDING COMPANY TAX.

Any foreign corporation which—

(1) is a personal holding company for any taxable year, and

(2) fails to file or to cause to be filed with the Secretary a true and accurate return of the tax imposed by section 541,

shall, in addition to other penalties provided by law, pay a penalty equal to 10 percent of the taxes imposed by chapter 1 (including the tax imposed by section 541) on such foreign corporation for such taxable year. No penalty shall be imposed under this section on any failure which is shown to be due to reasonable cause and not willful neglect.

Amendments

• **1997, Taxpayer Relief Act of 1997 (P.L. 105-34)**

P.L. 105-34, §1281(c):

Amended Code Sec. 6683 by adding at the end a new sentence. **Effective** for tax years beginning after 8-5-97.

• **1976, Tax Reform Act of 1976 (P.L. 94-455)**

P.L. 94-455, §1906(b)(13)(A):

Amended 1954 Code by substituting "Secretary" for "Secretary or his delegate" each place it appeared. **Effective** 2-1-77.

• **1966, Foreign Investors Tax Act of 1966 (P.L. 89-809)**

P.L. 89-809, §104(h)(4)(A):

Added new Code Sec. 6683. **Effective** 1-1-67.

[Sec. 6684]

SEC. 6684. ASSESSABLE PENALTIES WITH RESPECT TO LIABILITY FOR TAX UNDER CHAPTER 42.

If any person becomes liable for tax under any section of chapter 42 (relating to private foundations and certain other tax-exempt organizations) by reason of any act or failure to act which is not due to reasonable cause and either—

ASSESSABLE PENALTIES

(1) such person has theretofore been liable for tax under such chapter, or

(2) such act or failure to act is both willful and flagrant,

then such person shall be liable for a penalty equal to the amount of such tax.

Amendments

• **1987, Revenue Act of 1987 (P.L. 100-203)**

P.L. 100-203, §10712(c)(4):

Amended Code Sec. 6684 by striking out "private foundations" and inserting in lieu thereof "private foundations and certain other tax-exempt organizations". **Effective** for tax years beginning after 12-22-87.

• **1969, Tax Reform Act of 1969 (P.L. 91-172)**

P.L. 91-172, §101(c):

Added Code Sec. 6684. **Effective** 1-1-70.

[Sec. 6685]

SEC. 6685. ASSESSABLE PENALTY WITH RESPECT TO PUBLIC INSPECTION REQUIREMENTS FOR CERTAIN TAX-EXEMPT ORGANIZATIONS.

In addition to the penalty imposed by section 7207 (relating to fraudulent returns, statements, or other documents), any person who is required to comply with the requirements of subsection (d) of section 6104 and who fails to so comply with respect to any return or application, if such failure is willful, shall pay a penalty of $5,000 with respect to each such return or application.

Amendments

• **1998, Tax and Trade Relief Extension Act of 1998 (P.L. 105-277)**

P.L. 105-277, §1004(b)(2)(D):

Amended Code Sec. 6685 by striking "or (e)" following "subsection (d)". **Effective**, generally, for requests made after the later of 12-31-98, or the 60th day after the Secretary of the Treasury first issues the regulations referred to in Code Sec. 6104(d)(4), as amended by Act Sec. 1004. For an exception, see Act Sec. 1004(b)(3)(B), below.

P.L. 105-277, §1004(b)(3)(B), provides:

(B) PUBLICATION OF ANNUAL RETURNS.—Section 6104(d) of such Code, as in effect before the amendments made by this subsection, shall not apply to any return the due date for which is after the date such amendments take effect under subparagraph (A).

• **1996, Taxpayer Bill of Rights 2 (P.L. 104-168)**

P.L. 104-168, §1313(b):

Amended Code Sec. 6685 by striking "$1,000" and inserting "$5,000". **Effective** for requests made on or after the 60th day after the Secretary of the Treasury first issues the regulations referred to [in] Code Sec. 6104(e)(3) of the Internal Revenue Code of 1986.

• **1987, Revenue Act of 1987 (P.L. 100-203)**

P.L. 100-203, §10704(b)(1):

Amended Code Sec. 6685. For the **effective** date, see Act Sec. 10704(d) below. Prior to amendment, Code Sec. 6685 read as follows:

SEC. 6685. ASSESSABLE PENALTIES WITH RESPECT TO PRIVATE FOUNDATION ANNUAL RETURNS.

In addition to the penalty imposed by section 7207 (relating to fraudulent returns, statements, or other documents), any person who is required to comply with the requirements of section 6104(d) (relating to private foundations' annual returns) and who fails to so comply with respect to any return, if such failure is willful, shall pay a penalty of $1,000 with respect to each such return.

P.L. 100-203, §10704(d), provides:

(d) EFFECTIVE DATE.—The amendments made by this section shall apply—

(1) to returns for years beginning after December 31, 1986, and

(2) on and after the date of the enactment of this Act in the case of applications submitted to the Internal Revenue Service—

(A) after July 15, 1987, or

(B) on or before July 15, 1987, if the organization has a copy of the application on July 15, 1987.

• **1980 (P.L. 96-603)**

P.L. 96-603, §1(d)(4):

Amended Code Sec. 6685. **Effective** for tax years beginning after 1980. Prior to amendment, Code Sec. 6685 provided:

SEC. 6685. ASSESSABLE PENALTIES WITH RESPECT TO PRIVATE FOUNDATION ANNUAL REPORTS.

In addition to the penalty imposed by section 7207 (relating to fraudulent returns, statements, or other documents), any person who is required to file the report and the notice required under section 6056 (relating to annual reports by private foundations) or to comply with the requirements of section 6104(d) (relating to public inspection of private foundations' annual reports) and who fails so to file or comply, if such failure is willful, shall pay a penalty of $1,000 with respect to each such report or notice.

• **1969, Tax Reform Act of 1969 (P.L. 91-172)**

P.L. 91-172, §101(e)(4):

Added Code Sec. 6685. **Effective** for tax years beginning after 12-31-69.

[Sec. 6686]

SEC. 6686. FAILURE TO FILE RETURNS OR SUPPLY INFORMATION BY DISC OR FORMER FSC.

In addition to the penalty imposed by section 7203 (relating to willful failure to file return, supply information, or pay tax) any person required to supply information or to file a return under section 6011(c) who fails to supply such information or file such return at the time prescribed by the Secretary, or who files a return which does not show the information required, shall pay a penalty of $100 for each failure to supply information (but the total amount imposed on the delinquent person for all such failures during any calendar year shall not exceed $25,000) or a penalty of $1,000 for each failure to file a return, unless it is shown that such failure is due to reasonable cause.

Amendments

• **2007, Tax Technical Corrections Act of 2007 (P.L. 110-172)**

P.L. 110-172, §11(g)(21):

Amended the heading of Code Sec. 6686 by inserting "FORMER" before "FSC". **Effective** 12-29-2007.

• **1984, Deficit Reduction Act of 1984 (P.L. 98-369)**

P.L. 98-369, §801(d)(15)(A):

Amended Code Sec. 6686 by striking out "section 6011(e)" and inserting in lieu thereof "section 6011(c)" and by changing the heading thereof. **Effective** for transactions after 12-31-84, in tax years ending after such date. Prior to amendment, the heading of Code Sec. 6686 read as follows:

SEC. 6686. FAILURE OF DISC TO FILE RETURNS.

• **1976, Tax Reform Act of 1976 (P.L. 94-455)**

P.L. 94-455, §1906(b)(13)(A):

Amended 1954 Code by substituting "Secretary" for "Secretary or his delegate" each place it appeared. **Effective** 2-1-77.

• **1971, Revenue Act of 1971 (P.L. 92-178)**

P.L. 92-178, §504(d):

Added Code Sec. 6686. **Effective** date is governed by the **effective** date for Code Sec. 992.

[Sec. 6687—Repealed]

Amendments

• **1989, Omnibus Budget Reconciliation Act of 1989 (P.L. 101-239)**

P.L. 101-239, §7711(b)(1):

Repealed Code Sec. 6687. **Effective** for returns and statements the due date for which (determined without regard to extensions) is after 12-31-89. Prior to repeal, Code Sec. 6687 read as follows:

SEC. 6687. FAILURE TO SUPPLY INFORMATION WITH RESPECT TO PLACE OF RESIDENCE.

(a) CIVIL PENALTY.—If any person fails to include on his return any information required under section 6017A with respect to his place of residence, he shall pay a penalty of $5 for each such failure, unless it is shown that such failure is due to reasonable cause.

(b) DEFICIENCY PROCEDURES NOT TO APPLY.—Subchapter B of chapter 63 (relating to deficiency procedures for income, estate, gift, and chapter 42 taxes) shall not apply in respect of the assessment or collection of any penalty imposed by subsection (a).

• **1972, State and Local Fiscal Assistance Act of 1972 (P.L. 92-512)**

P.L. 92-512, §144(b):

Added Code Sec. 6687. **Effective** 10-20-72.

[Sec. 6688]

SEC. 6688. ASSESSABLE PENALTIES WITH RESPECT TO INFORMATION REQUIRED TO BE FURNISHED UNDER SECTION 7654.

In addition to any criminal penalty provided by law, any person described in section 7654(a) who is required under section 937(c) or by regulations prescribed under section 7654 to furnish information and who fails to comply with such requirement at the time prescribed by such

ASSESSABLE PENALTIES

regulations, unless it is shown that such failure is due to reasonable cause and not to willful neglect, shall pay (upon notice and demand by the Secretary and in the same manner as tax) a penalty of $1,000 for each such failure.

Amendments

• **2004, American Jobs Creation Act of 2004 (P.L. 108-357)**

P.L. 108-357, § 908(b)(1)-(2):

Amended Code Sec. 6688 by inserting "under section 937(c) or" before "by regulations", and by striking "$100" and inserting "$1,000". **Effective** for tax years ending after 10-22-2004.

• **1976, Tax Reform Act of 1976 (P.L. 94-455)**

P.L. 94-455, § 1906(b)(13)(A):

Amended 1954 Code by substituting "Secretary" for "Secretary or his delegate" each place it appeared. **Effective** 2-1-77.

• **1974, Employee Retirement Income Security Act of 1974 (P.L. 93-406)**

P.L. 93-406, § 1016(b)(4):

Made technical correction to designate above Code Section as Code Sec. 6688.

• **1972 (P.L. 92-606)**

P.L. 92-606, § 1(c):

Added Code Section 6688 (as redesignated). **Effective** with respect to tax years beginning after 1972.

[Sec. 6689]

SEC. 6689. FAILURE TO FILE NOTICE OF REDETERMINATION OF FOREIGN TAX.

[Sec. 6689(a)]

(a) CIVIL PENALTY.—If the taxpayer fails to notify the Secretary (on or before the date prescribed by regulations for giving such notice) of foreign tax redetermination, unless it is shown that such failure is due to reasonable cause and not due to willful neglect, there shall be added to the deficiency attributable to such redetermination an amount (not in excess of 25 percent of the deficiency) determined as follows—

(1) 5 percent of the deficiency if the failure is for not more than 1 month, with

(2) an additional 5 percent of the deficiency for each month (or fraction thereof) during which the failure continues.

[Sec. 6689(b)]

(b) FOREIGN TAX REDETERMINATION DEFINED.—For purposes of this section, the term "foreign tax redetermination" means any redetermination for which a notice is required under subsection (c) of section 905 or paragraph (2) of section 404A(g).

Amendments

• **1980 (P.L. 96-603)**

P.L. 96-603, § 2(c)(2):

Added Code Sec. 6689. **Effective** with respect to employer contributions or accurals for tax years beginning after 1979. For a special rule, see Act Sec. 2(e)(2)-(4), below.

P.L. 96-603, § 2(e)(2)-(4) [as amended by P.L. 97-448, § 305(a)], provides:

(2) ELECTION TO APPLY AMENDMENTS RETROACTIVELY WITH RESPECT TO FOREIGN SUBSIDIARIES.—

(A) IN GENERAL.—The taxpayer may elect to have the amendments made by this section apply retroactively with respect to its foreign subsidiaries.

(B) SCOPE OF RETROACTIVE APPLICATION.—Any election made under this paragraph shall apply with respect to all foreign subsidiaries of the taxpayer for the taxpayer's open period.

(C) DISTRIBUTIONS BY FOREIGN SUBSIDIARY MUST BE OUT OF POST-1971 EARNINGS AND PROFITS.—The election under this paragraph shall apply to distributions made by a foreign subsidiary only if made out of accumulated profits (or earnings and profits) earned after December 31, 1970.

(D) REVOCATION ONLY WITH CONSENT.—An election under this paragraph may be revoked only with the consent of the Secretary of the Treasury or his delegate.

(E) OPEN PERIOD.—For purposes of this subsection, the term "open period" means, with respect to any taxpayer, all taxable years which begin before January 1, 1980, and which begin after December 31, 1971, and for which, on December 31, 1980, the making of a refund, or the assessment of a deficiency, was not barred by any law or rule of law.

(3) ALLOWANCE OF PRIOR DEDUCTIONS IN CASE OF CERTAIN FUNDED BRANCH PLANS.—

(A) IN GENERAL.—If—

(i) the taxpayer elects to have this paragraph apply, and

(ii) the taxpayer agrees to the assessment of all deficiencies (including interest thereon) arising from all erroneous deductions,

then an amount equal to $1/15$th of the aggregate of the prior deductions which would have been allowable if the amendments made by this section applied to taxable years beginning before January 1, 1980, shall be allowed as a deduction for the taxpayer's first taxable year beginning in 1980, and an equal amount shall be allowed for each of the succeeding 14 taxable years.

(B) PRIOR DEDUCTION.—For purposes of subparagraph (A), the term `prior deduction' means a deduction with respect to a qualified funded plan (within the meaning of section 404A(f)(1) of the Internal Revenue Code of 1954) of the taxpayer—

(i) which the taxpayer claimed for a taxable year (or could have claimed if the amendments made by this section applied to taxable years beginning before January 1, 1980) beginning before January 1, 1980,

(ii) which was not allowable, and

(iii) with respect to which, on December 1, 1980, the assessment of a deficiency was not barred by any law or rule of law.

(4) TIME AND MANNER FOR MAKING ELECTIONS.—

(A) TIME.—An election under paragraph (2) or (3) may be made only on or before the due date (including extensions) for filing the taxpayer's return of tax under chapter 1 of the Internal Revenue Code of 1954 for its first taxable year ending on or after December 31, 1980.

(B) MANNER.—An election under paragraph (2) may be made only by a statement attached to the taxpayer's return for its first taxable year ending on or after December 31, 1980. An election under paragraph (3) may be made only if the taxpayer, on or before the last day for making the election, files with the Secretary of the Treasury or his delegate such amended return and such other information as the Secretary of the Treasury or his delegate may require, and agrees to the assessment of a deficiency for any closed year falling within the open period, to the extent such deficiency is attributable to the operation of such election.

[Sec. 6690]

SEC. 6690. FRAUDULENT STATEMENT OR FAILURE TO FURNISH STATEMENT TO PLAN PARTICIPANT.

Any person required under section 6057(e) to furnish a statement to a participant who willfully furnishes a false or fraudulent statement, or who willfully fails to furnish a statement in the manner, at the time, and showing the information required under section 6057(e), or regulations prescribed thereunder, shall for each such act, or for each such failure, be subject to a penalty under this subchapter of $50, which shall be assessed and collected in the same manner as the tax on employers imposed by section 3111.

Amendments

• **1974, Employee Retirement Income Security Act of 1974 (P.L. 93-406)**

P.L. 93-406, § 1031(b)(2):

Added Code Sec. 6690. **Effective** 9-2-74.

[Sec. 6692]

SEC. 6692. FAILURE TO FILE ACTUARIAL REPORT.

The plan administrator (as defined in section 414(g)) of each defined benefit plan to which section 412 applies who fails to file the report required by section 6059 at the time and in the manner required by section 6059, shall pay a penalty of $1,000 for each such failure unless it is shown that such failure is due to reasonable cause.

Amendments

• **1974, Employee Retirement Income Security Act of 1974 (P.L. 93-406)**

P.L. 93-406, § 1033(b):

Added Code Sec. 6692. **Effective** 9-2-74.

ASSESSABLE PENALTIES

[Sec. 6693]

SEC. 6693. FAILURE TO PROVIDE REPORTS ON CERTAIN TAX-FAVORED ACCOUNTS OR ANNUITIES; PENALTIES RELATING TO DESIGNATED NONDEDUCTIBLE CONTRIBUTIONS.

[Sec. 6693(a)]

(a) REPORTS.—

(1) IN GENERAL.—If a person required to file a report under a provision referred to in paragraph (2) fails to file such report at the time and in the manner required by such provision, such person shall pay a penalty of $50 for each failure unless it is shown that such failure is due to reasonable cause.

(2) PROVISIONS.—The provisions referred to in this paragraph are—

(A) subsections (i) and (l) of section 408 (relating to individual retirement plans),

(B) section 220(h) (relating to Archer MSAs),

(C) section 223(h) (relating to health savings accounts),

(D) section 529(d) (relating to qualified tuition programs),

(E) section 529A(d) (relating to qualified ABLE programs), and

(F) section 530(h) (relating to Coverdell education savings accounts).

This subsection shall not apply to any report which is an information return described in section 6724(d)(1)(C)(i) or a payee statement described in section 6724(d)(2)(X).

Amendments

• **2014, Stephen Beck, Jr., Achieving a Better Life Experience Act of 2014 (P.L. 113-295)**

P.L. 113-295, §102(c), Division B:

Amended Code Sec. 6693(a)(2) by striking "and" at the end of subparagraph (D), by redesignating subparagraph (E) as subparagraph (F), and by inserting after subparagraph (D) a new subparagraph (E). **Effective** for tax years beginning after 12-31-2014.

• **2006, Pension Protection Act of 2006 (P.L. 109-280)**

P.L. 109-280, §1304(a), provides:

(a) PERMANENT EXTENSION OF MODIFICATIONS.—Section 901 of the Economic Growth and Tax Relief Reconciliation Act of 2001 [P.L. 107-16] (relating to sunset provisions) shall not apply to section 402 of such Act (relating to modifications to qualified tuition programs).

• **2003, Medicare Prescription Drug, Improvement, and Modernization Act of 2003 (P.L. 108-173)**

P.L. 108-173, §1201(g):

Amended Code Sec. 6693(a)(2) by redesignating subparagraphs (C) and (D) as subparagraphs (D) and (E), respectively, and by inserting after subparagraph (B) a new subparagraph (C). **Effective** for tax years beginning after 12-31-2003.

• **2001 (P.L. 107-22)**

P.L. 107-22, §1(b)(2)(C):

Amended Code Sec. 6693(a)(2)(D) by striking "education individual retirement" and inserting "Coverdell education savings". **Effective** 7-26-2001.

• **2001, Economic Growth and Tax Relief Reconciliation Act of 2001 (P.L. 107-16)**

P.L. 107-16, §402(a)(4)(A):

Amended Code Sec. 6693(a)(2)(C) by striking "qualified State tuition" and inserting "qualified tuition". **Effective** for tax years beginning after 12-31-2001.

P.L. 107-16, §901(a)-(b), provides [but see P.L. 109-280, §1304(a), above]:

SEC. 901. SUNSET OF PROVISIONS OF ACT.

(a) IN GENERAL.—All provisions of, and amendments made by, this Act shall not apply—

(1) to taxable, plan, or limitation years beginning after December 31, 2010, or

(2) in the case of title V, to estates of decedents dying, gifts made, or generation skipping transfers, after December 31, 2010.

(b) APPLICATION OF CERTAIN LAWS.—The Internal Revenue Code of 1986 and the Employee Retirement Income Security Act of 1974 shall be applied and administered to years, estates, gifts, and transfers described in subsection (a) as if the provisions and amendments described in subsection (a) had never been enacted.

• **2000, Community Renewal Tax Relief Act of 2000 (P.L. 106-554)**

P.L. 106-554, §202(b)(2)(E):

Amended Code Sec. 6693(a)(2)(B) by striking "medical savings accounts" and inserting "Archer MSAs". **Effective** 12-21-2000.

• **1998, Tax and Trade Relief Extension Act of 1998 (P.L. 105-277)**

P.L. 105-277, §4006(c)(4):

Amended Code Sec. 6693(a)(2)(C) and (D) by striking "Section" and inserting "section". **Effective** 10-21-98.

• **1997, Taxpayer Relief Act of 1997 (P.L. 105-34)**

P.L. 105-34, §211(e)(2)(B):

Amended Code Sec. 6693(a)(2) by striking "and" at the end of subparagraph (A), by striking the period at the end of subparagraph (B) and inserting ", and ", and by adding a new subparagraph (C). **Effective** 1-1-98.

P.L. 105-34, §211(e)(2)(C):

Amended Code Sec. 6693 by striking "INDIVIDUAL RETIREMENT" in the section heading and inserting "CERTAIN TAX-FAVORED". **Effective** 1-1-98.

P.L. 105-34, §213(c):

Amended Code Sec. 6693(a)(2) by striking "and" at the end of subparagraph (B), by striking the period at the end of subparagraph (C) and inserting ", and", and by adding a new subparagraph (D). **Effective** for tax years beginning after 12-31-97.

P.L. 105-34, §1602(a)(4):

Amended Code Sec. 6693(a) by adding at the end a new sentence. **Effective** as if included in the provision of P.L. 104-191 to which it relates [effective for tax years beginning after 12-31-96.—CCH].

• **1996, Health Insurance Portability and Accountability Act of 1996 (P.L. 104-191)**

P.L. 104-191, §301(g)(1):

Amended Code Sec. 6693(a). **Effective** for tax years beginning after 12-31-96. Prior to amendment, Code Sec. 6693(a) read as follows:

(a) The person required by subsection (i) or (l) of section 408 to file a report regarding an individual retirement account or individual retirement annuity at the time and in the manner required by such subsection shall pay a penalty of $50 for each failure unless it is shown that such failure is due to reasonable cause. This subsection shall not apply to any report which is an information return described in section 6724(d)(1)(C)(i) or a payee statement described in section 6724(d)(2)(W).

• **1996, Small Business Job Protection Act of 1996 (P.L. 104-188)**

P.L. 104-188, §1455(d)(3):

Amended Code Sec. 6693(a) by adding at the end a new sentence. **Effective** for returns, reports, and other statements the due date for which (determined without regard to extensions) is after 12-31-96.

[Sec. 6693(b)]

(b) PENALTIES RELATING TO NONDEDUCTIBLE CONTRIBUTIONS.—

(1) OVERSTATEMENT OF DESIGNATED NONDEDUCTIBLE CONTRIBUTIONS.—Any individual who—

(A) is required to furnish information under section 408(o)(4) as to the amount of designated nondeductible contributions made for any taxable year, and

(B) overstates the amount of such contributions made for such taxable year,

shall pay a penalty of $100 for each such overstatement unless it is shown that such overstatement is due to reasonable cause.

(2) FAILURE TO FILE FORM.—Any individual who fails to file a form required to be filed by the Secretary under section 408(o)(4) shall pay a penalty of $50 for each such failure unless it is shown that such failure is due to reasonable cause.

Amendments

• **1988, Technical and Miscellaneous Revenue Act of 1988 (P.L. 100-647)**

P.L. 100-647, §1011(b)(4)(A):

Amended Code Sec. 6693(b). **Effective** as if included in the provision of P.L. 99-514 to which it relates. Prior to amendment, Code Sec. 6693(b) read as follows:

(b) OVERSTATEMENT OF DESIGNATED NONDEDUCTIBLE CONTRIBUTIONS.—Any individual who—

(1) is required to furnish information under section 408(o)(4) as to the amount of designated nondeductible contributions made for any taxable year, and

(2) overstates the amount of such contributions made for such taxable year,

shall pay a penalty of $100 for each such overstatement unless it is shown that such overstatement is due to reasonable cause.

ASSESSABLE PENALTIES

P.L. 100-647, §1011(b)(4)(B)(i):

Amended Code Sec. 6693 by striking out "OVERSTATEMENT OF" and inserting in lieu thereof "PENALTIES RELATING TO" in the heading. **Effective** as if included in the provision of P.L. 99-514 to which it relates.

• **1986, Tax Reform Act of 1986 (P.L. 99-514)**

P.L. 99-514, §1102(d)(1):

Amended Code Sec. 6693 by redesignating subsection (b) as subsection (c) and by inserting after subsection (a) new subsection (b). **Effective** for contributions and distributions for tax years beginning after 12-31-86.

[Sec. 6693(c)]

(c) PENALTIES RELATING TO SIMPLE RETIREMENT ACCOUNTS.—

(1) EMPLOYER PENALTIES.—An employer who fails to provide 1 or more notices required by section 408(l)(2)(C) shall pay a penalty of $50 for each day on which such failures continue.

(2) TRUSTEE AND ISSUER PENALTIES.—A trustee or issuer who fails—

(A) to provide 1 or more statements required by the last sentence of section 408(i) shall pay a penalty of $50 for each day on which such failures continue, or

(B) to provide 1 or more summary descriptions required by section 408(l)(2)(B) shall pay a penalty of $50 for each day on which such failures continue.

(3) REASONABLE CAUSE EXCEPTION.—No penalty shall be imposed under this subsection with respect to any failure which the taxpayer shows was due to reasonable cause.

Amendments

• **1997, Taxpayer Relief Act of 1997 (P.L. 105-34)**

P.L. 105-34, §1601(d)(1)(C)(ii)(I)-(II):

Amended Code Sec. 6693(c)(2) by inserting "or issuer" after "trustee", and by inserting "AND ISSUER" after "TRUSTEE" in the heading. **Effective** as if included in the provision of P.L. 104-188 to which it relates [effective for tax years beginning after 12-31-96.—CCH].

• **1996, Small Business Job Protection Act of 1996 (P.L. 104-188)**

P.L. 104-188, §1421(b)(4)(B):

Amended Code Sec. 6693 by redesignating subsection (c) as subsection (d) and by inserting after subsection (b) a new subsection (c). **Effective** for tax years beginning after 12-31-96.

[Sec. 6693(d)]

(d) DEFICIENCY PROCEDURES NOT TO APPLY.—Subchapter B of chapter 63 (relating to deficiency procedures for income, estate, gift, and certain excise taxes) does not apply to the assessment or collection of any penalty imposed by this section.

Amendments

• **1996, Small Business Job Protection Act of 1996 (P.L. 104-188)**

P.L. 104-188, §1421(b)(4)(B):

Amended Code Sec. 6693 by redesignating subsection (c) as subsection (d). **Effective** for tax years beginning after 12-31-96.

• **1986, Tax Reform Act of 1986 (P.L. 99-514)**

P.L. 99-514, §1102(d)(1):

Amended Code Sec. 6693 by redesignating subsection (b) as subsection (c) and by inserting after subsection (a) new subsection (b). **Effective** for contributions and distributions for tax years beginning after 12-31-86.

P.L. 99-514, §1102(d)(2)(A):

Amended redesignated Code Sec. 6693(c) by striking out "subsection (a)" and inserting in lieu thereof "this section". **Effective** for contributions and distributions for tax years beginning after 12-31-86.

P.L. 99-514, §1102(d)(2)(B):

Amended Code Sec. 6693 by inserting "; OVERSTATEMENTS OF DESIGNATED NONDEDUCTIBLE CONTRIBUTIONS" after "ANNUITIES" in the heading. **Effective** for contributions and distributions for tax years beginning after 12-31-86.

• **1984, Deficit Reduction Act of 1984 (P.L. 98-369)**

P.L. 98-369, §147(b):

Amended Code Sec. 6693(a) by striking out "$10" and inserting in lieu thereof "$50". **Effective** for failures occurring after 7-18-84.

• **1980, Technical Corrections Act of 1979 (P.L. 96-222)**

P.L. 96-222, §101(a)(10)(H):

Amended Code Sec. 6693(a) by striking out the first "section 408(i)" and inserting "subsection (i) or (l) of section 408", and by striking out the second "section 408(i)" and inserting "such subsection". **Effective** with respect to failures occurring after 4-1-80.

• **1974, Employee Retirement Income Security Act of 1974 (P.L. 93-406)**

P.L. 93-406, §2002(f):

Added Code Sec. 6693. **Effective** 1-1-75.

[Sec. 6694]

SEC. 6694. UNDERSTATEMENT OF TAXPAYER'S LIABILITY BY TAX RETURN PREPARER.

[Sec. 6694(a)]

(a) UNDERSTATEMENT DUE TO UNREASONABLE POSITIONS.—

(1) IN GENERAL.—If a tax return preparer—

(A) prepares any return or claim of refund with respect to which any part of an understatement of liability is due to a position described in paragraph (2), and

(B) knew (or reasonably should have known) of the position,

such tax return preparer shall pay a penalty with respect to each such return or claim in an amount equal to the greater of $1,000 or 50 percent of the income derived (or to be derived) by the tax return preparer with respect to the return or claim.

(2) UNREASONABLE POSITION.—

(A) IN GENERAL.—Except as otherwise provided in this paragraph, a position is described in this paragraph unless there is or was substantial authority for the position.

(B) DISCLOSED POSITIONS.—If the position was disclosed as provided in section 6662(d)(2)(B)(ii)(I) and is not a position to which subparagraph (C) applies, the position is described in this paragraph unless there is a reasonable basis for the position.

(C) TAX SHELTERS AND REPORTABLE TRANSACTIONS.—If the position is with respect to a tax shelter (as defined in section 6662(d)(2)(C)(ii)) or a reportable transaction to which section 6662A applies, the position is described in this paragraph unless it is reasonable to believe that the position would more likely than not be sustained on its merits.

(3) REASONABLE CAUSE EXCEPTION.—No penalty shall be imposed under this subsection if it is shown that there is reasonable cause for the understatement and the tax return preparer acted in good faith.

Amendments

• **2008, Tax Extenders and Alternative Minimum Tax Relief Act of 2008 (P.L. 110-343)**

P.L. 110-343, Division C, §506(a):

Amended Code Sec. 6694(a). For the **effective** date, see Act Sec. 506(b), below. Prior to amendment, Code Sec. 6694(a) read as follows:

(a) UNDERSTATEMENT DUE TO UNREASONABLE POSITIONS.—

(1) IN GENERAL.—Any tax return preparer who prepares any return or claim for refund with respect to which any part of an understatement of liability is due to a position described in paragraph (2) shall pay a penalty with respect to each such return or claim in an amount equal to the greater of—

(A) $1,000, or

ASSESSABLE PENALTIES

(B) 50 percent of the income derived (or to be derived) by the tax return preparer with respect to the return or claim.

(2) UNREASONABLE POSITION.—A position is described in this paragraph if—

(A) the tax return preparer knew (or reasonably should have known) of the position,

(B) there was not a reasonable belief that the position would more likely than not be sustained on its merits, and

(C)(i) the position was not disclosed as provided in section 6662(d)(2)(B)(ii), or

(ii) there was no reasonable basis for the position.

(3) REASONABLE CAUSE EXCEPTION.—No penalty shall be imposed under this subsection if it is shown that there is reasonable cause for the understatement and the tax return preparer acted in good faith.

P.L. 110-343, Division C, § 506(b), provides:

(b) EFFECTIVE DATE.—The amendment made by this section shall apply—

(1) in the case of a position other than a position described in subparagraph (C) of section 6694(a)(2) of the Internal Revenue Code of 1986 (as amended by this section), to returns prepared after May 25, 2007, and

(2) in the case of a position described in such subparagraph (C), to returns prepared for taxable years ending after the date of the enactment of this Act [10-3-2008.—CCH].

• **2007, Small Business and Work Opportunity Tax Act of 2007 (P.L. 110-28)**

P.L. 110-28, § 8246(a)(2)(F)(i)(I):

Amended Code Sec. 6694 by striking "INCOME TAX RETURN PREPARER" in the heading and inserting "TAX RETURN PREPARER". **Effective** for returns prepared after 5-25-2007.

P.L. 110-28, § 8246(a)(2)(F)(i)(II):

Amended Code Sec. 6694 by striking "an income tax return preparer" each place it appears and inserting "a tax return preparer". **Effective** for returns prepared after 5-25-2007.

P.L. 110-28, § 8246(b):

Amended Code Sec. 6694(a). **Effective** for returns prepared after 5-25-2007. Prior to amendment, Code Sec. 6694(a) read as follows:

(a) UNDERSTATEMENTS DUE TO UNREALISTIC POSITIONS.—If—

(1) any part of any understatement of liability with respect to any return or claim for refund is due to a position for which there was not a realistic possibility of being sustained on its merits,

(2) any person who is a tax return preparer with respect to such return or claim knew (or reasonably should have known) of such position, and

(3) such position was not disclosed as provided in section 6662(d)(2)(B)(ii) or was frivolous,

such person shall pay a penalty of $250 with respect to such return or claim unless it is shown that there is reasonable cause for the understatement and such person acted in good faith.

• **1989, Omnibus Budget Reconciliation Act of 1989 (P.L. 101-239)**

P.L. 101-239, § 7732(a):

Amended Code Sec. 6694(a). **Effective** with respect to documents prepared after 12-31-89. Prior to amendment, Code Sec. 6694(a) read as follows:

(a) NEGLIGENT OR INTENTIONAL DISREGARD OF RULES AND REGULATIONS.—If any part of any understatement of liability with respect to any return or claim for refund is due to the negligent or intentional disregard of rules and regulations by any person who is an income tax return preparer with respect to such return or claim, such person shall pay a penalty of $100 with respect to such return or claim.

[Sec. 6694(b)]

(b) UNDERSTATEMENT DUE TO WILLFUL OR RECKLESS CONDUCT.—

(1) IN GENERAL.—Any tax return preparer who prepares any return or claim for refund with respect to which any part of an understatement of liability is due to a conduct described in paragraph (2) shall pay a penalty with respect to each such return or claim in an amount equal to the greater of—

(A) $5,000, or

(B) 75 percent of the income derived (or to be derived) by the tax return preparer with respect to the return or claim.

(2) WILLFUL OR RECKLESS CONDUCT.—Conduct described in this paragraph is conduct by the tax return preparer which is—

(A) a willful attempt in any manner to understate the liability for tax on the return or claim, or

(B) a reckless or intentional disregard of rules or regulations.

(3) REDUCTION IN PENALTY.—The amount of any penalty payable by any person by reason of this subsection for any return or claim for refund shall be reduced by the amount of the penalty paid by such person by reason of subsection (a).

Amendments

• **2015, Protecting Americans from Tax Hikes Act of 2015 (P.L. 114-113)**

P.L. 114-113, § 210(a), Div. Q:

Amended Code Sec. 6694(b)(1)(B) by striking "50 percent" and inserting "75 percent". **Effective** for returns prepared for tax years ending after 12-18-2015.

• **2007, Small Business and Work Opportunity Tax Act of 2007 (P.L. 110-28)**

P.L. 110-28, § 8246(a)(2)(F)(i)(II):

Amended Code Sec. 6694 by striking "an income tax return preparer" each place it appears and inserting "a tax return preparer". **Effective** for returns prepared after 5-25-2007.

P.L. 110-28, § 8246(b):

Amended Code Sec. 6694(b). **Effective** for returns prepared after 5-25-2007. Prior to amendment, Code Sec. 6694(b) read as follows:

(b) WILLFUL OR RECKLESS CONDUCT.—If any part of any understatement of liability with respect to any return or claim for refund is due—

(1) to a willful attempt in any manner to understate the liability for tax by a person who is a tax return preparer with respect to such return or claim, or

(2) to any reckless or intentional disregard of rules or regulations by any such person,

such person shall pay a penalty of $1,000 with respect to such return or claim. With respect to any return or claim, the amount of the penalty payable by any person by reason of this subsection shall be reduced by the amount of the penalty paid by such person by reason of subsection (a).

• **1989, Omnibus Budget Reconciliation Act of 1989 (P.L. 101-239)**

P.L. 101-239, § 7732(a):

Amended Code Sec. 6694(b). **Effective** with respect to documents prepared after 12-31-89. Prior to amendment, Code Sec. 6694(b) read as follows:

(b) WILLFUL UNDERSTATEMENT OF LIABILITY.—If any part of any understatement of liability with respect to any return or claim for refund is due to a willful attempt in any manner to understate the liability for a tax by a person who is an income tax return preparer with respect to such return or claim, such person shall pay a penalty of $500 with respect to such return or claim. With respect to any return or claim, the amount of the penalty payable by any person by reason of this subsection shall be reduced by the amount of the penalty paid by such person by reason of subsection (a).

[Sec. 6694(c)]

(c) EXTENSION OF PERIOD OF COLLECTION WHERE PREPARER PAYS 15 PERCENT OF PENALTY.—

(1) IN GENERAL.—If, within 30 days after the day on which notice and demand of any penalty under subsection (a) or (b) is made against any person who is a tax return preparer, such person pays an amount which is not less than 15 percent of the amount of such penalty and files a claim for refund of the amount so paid, no levy or proceeding in court for the collection of the remainder of such penalty shall be made, begun, or prosecuted until the final resolution of a proceeding begun as provided in paragraph (2). Notwithstanding the provisions of section 7421(a), the beginning of such proceeding or levy during the time such prohibition is in force may be enjoined by a proceeding in the proper court. Nothing in this paragraph shall be construed to prohibit any counterclaim for the remainder of such penalty in a proceeding begun as provided in paragraph (2).

(2) PREPARER MUST BRING SUIT IN DISTRICT COURT TO DETERMINE HIS LIABILITY FOR PENALTY.—If, within 30 days after the day on which his claim for refund of any partial payment of any penalty under subsection (a) or (b) is denied (or, if earlier, within 30 days after the expiration of 6 months after the day on which he filed the claim for refund), the tax return preparer fails to begin a proceeding in the appropriate United States district court for the determination of his liability for such penalty, paragraph (1) shall cease to apply with respect to such penalty, effective on the day following the close of the applicable 30-day period referred to in this paragraph.

(3) SUSPENSION OF RUNNING OF PERIOD OF LIMITATIONS ON COLLECTION.—The running of the period of limitations provided in section 6502 on the collection by levy or by a proceeding in court in respect of any penalty described in paragraph (1) shall be suspended for the period during which the Secretary is prohibited from collecting by levy or a proceeding in court.

ASSESSABLE PENALTIES

Amendments

• **2007, Small Business and Work Opportunity Tax Act of 2007 (P.L. 110-28)**

P.L. 110-28, §8246(a)(2)(F)(i)(II):
Amended Code Sec. 6694 by striking "an income tax return preparer" each place it appears and inserting "a tax return preparer". **Effective** for returns prepared after 5-25-2007.

P.L. 110-28, §8246(a)(2)(F)(i)(III):
Amended Code Sec. 6694(c)(2) by striking "the income tax return preparer" and inserting "the tax return preparer". **Effective** for returns prepared after 5-25-2007.

• **1989, Omnibus Budget Reconciliation Act of 1989 (P.L. 101-239)**

P.L. 101-239, §7737(a):
Amended Code Sec. 6694(c)(1) by adding at the end thereof a new sentence. **Effective** 12-19-89.

[Sec. 6694(d)]

(d) ABATEMENT OF PENALTY WHERE TAXPAYER LIABILITY NOT UNDERSTATED.—If at any time there is a final administrative determination or a final judicial decision that there was no understatement of liability in the case of any return or claim for refund with respect to which a penalty under subsection (a) or (b) has been assessed, such assessment shall be abated, and if any portion of such penalty has been paid the amount so paid shall be refunded to the person who made such payment as an overpayment of tax without regard to any period of limitations which, but for this subsection, would apply to the making of such refund.

[Sec. 6694(e)]

(e) UNDERSTATEMENT OF LIABILITY DEFINED.—For purposes of this section, the term "understatement of liability" means any understatement of the net amount payable with respect to any tax imposed by this title or any overstatement of the net amount creditable or refundable with respect to any such tax. Except as otherwise provided in subsection (d), the determination of whether or not there is an understatement of liability shall be made without regard to any administrative or judicial action involving the taxpayer.

Amendments

• **2007, Small Business and Work Opportunity Tax Act of 2007 (P.L. 110-28)**

P.L. 110-28, §8246(a)(2)(F)(i)(IV):
Amended Code Sec. 6694(e) by striking "subtitle A" and inserting "this title". **Effective** for returns prepared after 5-25-2007.

[Sec. 6694(f)]

(f) CROSS REFERENCE.—
For definition of tax return preparer, see section 7701(a)(36).

Amendments

• **2007, Small Business and Work Opportunity Tax Act of 2007 (P.L. 110-28)**

P.L. 110-28, §8246(a)(2)(F)(i)(V):
Amended Code Sec. 6694(f) by striking "income tax return preparer" and inserting "tax return preparer". **Effective** for returns prepared after 5-25-2007.

• **1976, Tax Reform Act of 1976 (P.L. 94-455)**

P.L. 94-455, §1203(b)(1):
Added Code Sec. 6694. **Effective** for documents prepared after 12-31-76.

[Sec. 6695]

SEC. 6695. OTHER ASSESSABLE PENALTIES WITH RESPECT TO THE PREPARATION OF TAX RETURNS FOR OTHER PERSONS.

[Sec. 6695(a)]

(a) FAILURE TO FURNISH COPY TO TAXPAYER.—Any person who is a tax return preparer with respect to any return or claim for refund who fails to comply with section 6107(a) with respect to such return or claim shall pay a penalty of $50 for such failure, unless it is shown that such failure is due to reasonable cause and not due to willful neglect. The maximum penalty imposed under this subsection on any person with respect to documents filed during any calendar year shall not exceed $25,000.

Amendments

• **2007, Small Business and Work Opportunity Tax Act of 2007 (P.L. 110-28)**

P.L. 110-28, §8246(a)(2)(G)(i)(I):
Amended Code Sec. 6695 by striking "INCOME" before "TAX RETURNS" in the heading. **Effective** for returns prepared after 5-25-2007.

P.L. 110-28, §8246(a)(2)(G)(i)(II):
Amended Code Sec. 6695 by striking "an income tax preparer" each place it appears and inserting "a tax return preparer". **Effective** for returns prepared after 5-25-2007.

• **1989, Omnibus Budget Reconciliation Act of 1989 (P.L. 101-239)**

P.L. 101-239, §7733(a)(1)-(2):
Amended Code Sec. 6695(a) by striking "$25" and inserting "$50", and by adding at the end thereof a new sentence. **Effective** for documents prepared after 12-31-89.

[Sec. 6695(b)]

(b) FAILURE TO SIGN RETURN.—Any person who is a tax return preparer with respect to any return or claim for refund, who is required by regulations prescribed by the Secretary to sign such return or claim, and who fails to comply with such regulations with respect to such return or claim shall pay a penalty of $50 for such failure, unless it is shown that such failure is due to reasonable cause and not due to willful neglect. The maximum penalty imposed under this subsection on any person with respect to documents filed during any calendar year shall not exceed $25,000.

Amendments

• **2007, Small Business and Work Opportunity Tax Act of 2007 (P.L. 110-28)**

P.L. 110-28, §8246(a)(2)(G)(i)(II):
Amended Code Sec. 6695 by striking "an income tax preparer" each place it appears and inserting "a tax return preparer". **Effective** for returns prepared after 5-25-2007.

• **1989, Omnibus Budget Reconciliation Act of 1989 (P.L. 101-239)**

P.L. 101-239, §7733(b)(1)-(2):
Amended Code Sec. 6695(b) by striking "$25" and inserting "$50", and by adding at the end thereof a new sentence. **Effective** for documents prepared after 12-31-89.

• **1985 (P.L. 99-44)**

P.L. 99-44, §1(b):
Repealed P.L. 98-369, §179(b)(2). **Effective** as if included in the amendment made by P.L. 98-369, §179(b)(2), and the Internal Revenue Code of 1954 shall be applied and administered as if such paragraph (and the amendment made by such paragraph) had not been enacted. Prior to repeal, Code Sec. 6695(b) to read as follows:

(b) FAILURE TO INFORM TAXPAYER OF CERTAIN RECORDKEEPING REQUIREMENTS OR TO SIGN RETURN.—Any person who is an income tax return preparer with respect to any return or claim for refund and who is required by regulations to sign such return or claim—

(1) shall advise the taxpayer of the substantiation requirements of section 274(d) and obtain written confirmation from the taxpayer that such requirements were met with respect to any deduction or credit claimed on such return or claim for refund, and

(2) shall sign such return or claim for refund.

Any person who fails to comply with the requirements of the preceding sentence with respect to any return or claim shall pay a penalty of $25 for such failure, unless it is shown that such failure is due to reasonable cause and not to willful neglect.

P.L. 99-44, §1(c), provides:

(c) REPEAL OF REGULATIONS.—Regulations issued before the date of the enactment of this Act to carry out the amendments made by paragraphs (1)(C), (2), and (3) of section 179(b) of the Tax Reform Act of 1984 shall have no force and effect.

ASSESSABLE PENALTIES

P.L. 99-44, § 5, provides:

Not later than October 1, 1985, the Secretary of the Treasury or his delegate shall prescribe regulations to carry out the provisions of this Act which shall fully reflect such provisions.

• **1984, Deficit Reduction Act of 1984 (P.L. 98-369)**

P.L. 98-369, § 179(b)(2):

Amended Code Sec. 6695(b). **Effective** for tax years beginning after 12-31-84. Prior to amendment, Code Sec. 6695(b) read as follows:

(b) Failure To Sign Return.—Any person who is an income tax return preparer with respect to any return or claim for refund, who is required by regulations prescribed by the Secretary to sign such return or claim, and who fails to comply with such regulations with respect to such return or claim shall pay a penalty of $25 for such failure, unless it is shown that such failure is due to reasonable cause and not due to willful neglect.

[Sec. 6695(c)]

(c) FAILURE TO FURNISH IDENTIFYING NUMBER.—Any person who is a tax return preparer with respect to any return or claim for refund and who fails to comply with section 6109(a)(4) with respect to such return or claim shall pay a penalty of $50 for such failure, unless it is shown that such failure is due to reasonable cause and not due to willful neglect. The maximum penalty imposed under this subsection on any person with respect to documents filed during any calendar year shall not exceed $25,000.

Amendments

• **2007, Small Business and Work Opportunity Tax Act of 2007 (P.L. 110-28)**

P.L. 110-28, § 8246(a)(2)(G)(i)(II):

Amended Code Sec. 6695 by striking "an income tax preparer" each place it appears and inserting "a tax return preparer". **Effective** for returns prepared after 5-25-2007.

• **1989, Omnibus Budget Reconciliation Act of 1989 (P.L. 101-239)**

P.L. 101-239, § 7733(c)(1)-(2):

Amended Code Sec. 6695(c) by striking "$25" and inserting "$50", and by adding at the end thereof a new sentence. **Effective** for documents prepared after 12-31-89.

[Sec. 6695(d)]

(d) FAILURE TO RETAIN COPY OR LIST.—Any person who is a tax return preparer with respect to any return or claim for refund who fails to comply with section 6107(b) with respect to such return or claim shall pay a penalty of $50 for each such failure, unless it is shown that such failure is due to reasonable cause and not due to willful neglect. The maximum penalty imposed under this subsection on any person with respect to any return period shall not exceed $25,000.

Amendments

• **2007, Small Business and Work Opportunity Tax Act of 2007 (P.L. 110-28)**

P.L. 110-28, § 8246(a)(2)(G)(i)(II):

Amended Code Sec. 6695 by striking "an income tax preparer" each place it appears and inserting "a tax return preparer". **Effective** for returns prepared after 5-25-2007.

[Sec. 6695(e)]

(e) FAILURE TO FILE CORRECT INFORMATION RETURNS.—Any person required to make a return under section 6060 who fails to comply with the requirements of such section shall pay a penalty of $50 for—

(1) each failure to file a return as required under such section, and

(2) each failure to set forth an item in the return as required under [such] section,

unless it is shown that such failure is due to reasonable cause and not due to willful neglect. The maximum penalty imposed under this subsection on any person with respect to any return period shall not exceed $25,000.

Amendments

• **1989, Omnibus Budget Reconciliation Act of 1989 (P.L. 101-239)**

P.L. 101-239, § 7733(d):

Amended Code Sec. 6695(e). **Effective** for documents prepared after 12-31-89. Prior to amendment, Code Sec. 6695(e) read as follows:

(e) FAILURE TO FILE CORRECT INFORMATION RETURN.—Any person required to make a return under section 6060 who fails to comply with the requirements of such section shall pay a penalty of—

(1) $100 for each failure to file a return as required under such section, and

(2) $5 for each failure to set forth an item in the return as required under such section,

unless it is shown that such failure is due to reasonable cause and not due to willful neglect. The maximum penalty imposed under this subsection on any person with respect to any return period shall not exceed $20,000.

[Sec. 6695(f)]

(f) NEGOTIATION OF CHECK.—Any person who is a tax return preparer who endorses or otherwise negotiates (directly or through an agent) any check made in respect of the taxes imposed by this title which is issued to a taxpayer (other than the tax return preparer) shall pay a penalty of $500 with respect to each such check. The preceding sentence shall not apply with respect to the deposit by a bank (within the meaning of section 581) of the full amount of the check in the taxpayer's account in such bank for the benefit of the taxpayer.

Amendments

• **2007, Small Business and Work Opportunity Tax Act of 2007 (P.L. 110-28)**

P.L. 110-28, § 8246(a)(2)(G)(i)(II):

Amended Code Sec. 6695 by striking "an income tax preparer" each place it appears and inserting "a tax return preparer". **Effective** for returns prepared after 5-25-2007.

P.L. 110-28, § 8246(a)(2)(G)(ii)(I)-(II):

Amended Code Sec. 6695(f) by striking "subtitle A" and inserting "this title", and by striking "the income tax return preparer" and inserting "the tax return preparer". **Effective** for returns prepared after 5-25-2007.

• **1978, Revenue Act of 1978 (P.L. 95-600)**

P.L. 95-600, § 701(cc)(1):

Amended Code Sec. 6695(f). **Effective** for documents prepared after 12-31-76.

• **1976, Tax Reform Act of 1976 (P.L. 94-455)**

P.L. 94-455, § 1203(f):

Added Code Sec. 6695. **Effective** for documents prepared after 12-31-76.

[Sec. 6695(g)]

(g) FAILURE TO BE DILIGENT IN DETERMINING ELIGIBILITY FOR CERTAIN TAX BENEFITS.—Any person who is a tax return preparer with respect to any return or claim for refund who fails to comply with due diligence requirements imposed by the Secretary by regulations with respect to determining—

(1) eligibility to file as a head of household (as defined in section 2(b)) on the return, or

(2) eligibility for, or the amount of, the credit allowable by section 24, 25A(a)(1), or 32,

shall pay a penalty of $500 for each such failure.

Sec. 6695(c)

ASSESSABLE PENALTIES

Amendments

• **2017, Tax Cuts and Jobs Act (P.L. 115-97)**

P.L. 115-97, §11001(b):

Amended Code Sec. 6695(g). **Effective** for tax years beginning after 12-31-2017. Prior to amendment, Code Sec. 6695(g) read as follows:

(g) FAILURE TO BE DILIGENT IN DETERMINING ELIGIBILITY FOR CHILD TAX CREDIT; AMERICAN OPPORTUNITY TAX CREDIT; AND EARNED INCOME CREDIT.—Any person who is a tax return preparer with respect to any return or claim for refund who fails to comply with due diligence requirements imposed by the Secretary by regulations with respect to determining eligibility for, or the amount of, the credit allowable by section 24, 25A(a)(1), or 32 shall pay a penalty of $500 for each such failure.

• **2015, Protecting Americans from Tax Hikes Act of 2015 (P.L. 114-113)**

P.L. 114-113, §207(a)(1)-(2), Div. Q:

Amended Code Sec. 6695(g) by striking "section 32" and inserting "section 24, 25A(a)(1), or 32", and in the heading by inserting "CHILD TAX CREDIT; AMERICAN OPPORTUNITY TAX CREDIT; AND" before "EARNED INCOME CREDIT". **Effective** for tax years beginning after 12-31-2015.

• **2011, United States–Korea Free Trade Agreement Implementation Act (P.L. 112-41)**

P.L. 112-41, §501(a):

Amended Code Sec. 6695(g) by striking "$100" and inserting "$500". **Effective** for documents prepared after 12-31-2011 [effective date changed by P.L. 115-141, §107(a), Div. U.—CCH].

• **2007, Small Business and Work Opportunity Tax Act of 2007 (P.L. 110-28)**

P.L. 110-28, §8246(a)(2)(G)(i)(II):

Amended Code Sec. 6695 by striking "an income tax preparer" each place it appears and inserting "a tax return preparer". **Effective** for returns prepared after 5-25-2007.

• **1997, Taxpayer Relief Act of 1997 (P.L. 105-34)**

P.L. 105-34, §1085(a)(2):

Amended Code Sec. 6695 by adding at the end a new subsection (g). **Effective** for tax years beginning after 12-31-96.

[Sec. 6695(h)]

(h) ADJUSTMENT FOR INFLATION.—

(1) IN GENERAL.—In the case of any failure relating to a return or claim for refund filed in a calendar year beginning after 2014, each of the dollar amounts under subsections (a), (b), (c), (d), (e), (f), and (g) shall be increased by an amount equal to such dollar amount multiplied by the cost-of-living adjustment determined under section 1(f)(3) for the calendar year determined by substituting "calendar year 2013" for "calendar year 2016" in subparagraph (A)(ii) thereof.

(2) ROUNDING.—If any amount adjusted under paragraph (1)—

(A) is not less than $5,000 and is not a multiple of $500, such amount shall be rounded to the next lowest multiple of $500, and

(B) is not described in subparagraph (A) and is not a multiple of $5, such amount shall be rounded to the next lowest multiple of $5.

Amendments

• **2018, Tax Technical Corrections Act of 2018 (P.L. 115-141)**

P.L. 115-141, §401(a)(299)(C), Div. U:

Amended Code Sec. 6695(h)(1) by inserting "an amount equal to" after "increased by" and by inserting "for the calendar year" after "section 1(f)(3)". **Effective** 3-23-2018.

P.L. 115-141, §401(a)(309), Div. U:

Amended Code Sec. 6695(h)(2) by striking "subparagraph (A)" and inserting "paragraph (1)". **Effective** 3-23-2018.

P.L. 115-141, §401(a)(310), Div. U:

Amended Code Sec. 6695(h)(2)(B) by striking "clause (i)" and inserting "subparagraph (A)". **Effective** 3-23-2018.

• **2017, Tax Cuts and Jobs Act (P.L. 115-97)**

P.L. 115-97, §11002(d)(1)(MM):

Amended Code Sec. 6695(h)(1) by striking "for 'calendar year 1992' in subparagraph (B)" and inserting "for 'calendar year 2016' in subparagraph (A)(ii)". **Effective** for tax years beginning after 12-31-2017.

• **2014, Stephen Beck, Jr., Achieving a Better Life Experience Act of 2014 (P.L. 113-295)**

P.L. 113-295, §208(c), Division B:

Amended Code Sec. 6695 by adding at the end a new subsection (h). **Effective** for returns or claims for refund filed after 12-31-2014 [effective date changed by P.L. 115-141, §105(a)(1)-(3), Div. U.—CCH].

[Sec. 6695A]

SEC. 6695A. SUBSTANTIAL AND GROSS VALUATION MISSTATEMENTS ATTRIBUTABLE TO INCORRECT APPRAISALS.

[Sec. 6695A(a)]

(a) IMPOSITION OF PENALTY.—If—

(1) a person prepares an appraisal of the value of property and such person knows, or reasonably should have known, that the appraisal would be used in connection with a return or a claim for refund, and

(2) the claimed value of the property on a return or claim for refund which is based on such appraisal results in a substantial valuation misstatement under chapter 1 (within the meaning of section 6662(e)), a substantial estate or gift tax valuation understatement (within the meaning of section 6662(g)), or a gross valuation misstatement (within the meaning of section 6662(h)), with respect to such property,

then such person shall pay a penalty in the amount determined under subsection (b).

Amendments

• **2007, Tax Technical Corrections Act of 2007 (P.L. 110-172)**

P.L. 110-172, §3(e)(1):

Amended Code Sec. 6695A(a)(2) by inserting "a substantial estate or gift tax valuation understatement (within the meaning of section 6662(g))," before "or a gross valuation misstatement". **Effective** as if included in the provision of the Pension Protection Act of 2006 (P.L. 109-280) to which it relates [effective generally for appraisals prepared with respect to returns or submission filed after 8-17-2006. For a special rule, see P.L. 109-432, §1219(e)(3), in the amendment notes for Code Sec. 6695A(c).—CCH].

P.L. 110-172, §11(a)(40):

Amended Code Sec. 6695A(a) by striking "then such person" [and all that follows] in paragraph (2) and inserting:

"then such person" [and all that follows].

Effective 12-29-2007.

[Sec. 6695A(b)]

(b) AMOUNT OF PENALTY.—The amount of the penalty imposed under subsection (a) on any person with respect to an appraisal shall be equal to the lesser of—

(1) the greater of—

(A) 10 percent of the amount of the underpayment (as defined in section 6664(a)) attributable to the misstatement described in subsection (a)(2), or

(B) $1,000, or

(2) 125 percent of the gross income received by the person described in subsection (a)(1) from the preparation of the appraisal.

[Sec. 6695A(c)]

(c) EXCEPTION.—No penalty shall be imposed under subsection (a) if the person establishes to the satisfaction of the Secretary that the value established in the appraisal was more likely than not the proper value.

Amendments

• **2006, Pension Protection Act of 2006 (P.L. 109-280)**

P.L. 109-280, §1219(b)(1):

Amended part I of subchapter B of chapter 68 by inserting after Code Sec. 6695 a new Code Sec. 6695A. **Effective** generally for appraisals prepared with respect to returns or submissions filed after 8-17-2006. For a special rule, see Act Sec. 1219(e)(3), below.

P.L. 109-280, §1219(e)(3), provides:

(3) SPECIAL RULE FOR CERTAIN EASEMENTS.—In the case of a contribution of a qualified real property interest which is a restriction with respect to the exterior of a building

ASSESSABLE PENALTIES

described in section 170(h)(4)(C)(ii) of the Internal Revenue Code of 1986, and an appraisal with respect to the contribution, the amendments made by subsections (a) and (b) shall apply to returns filed after July 25, 2006.

[Sec. 6696]

SEC. 6696. RULES APPLICABLE WITH RESPECT TO SECTIONS 6694, 6695, AND 6695A.

[Sec. 6696(a)]

(a) PENALTIES TO BE ADDITIONAL TO ANY OTHER PENALTIES.—The penalties provided by sections 6694, 6695, and 6695A shall be in addition to any other penalties provided by law.

Amendments

- **2018, Tax Technical Corrections Act of 2018 (P.L. 115-141)**

P.L. 115-141, §401(a)(311), Div. U:

Amended Code Sec. 6696(a) by striking "section 6694," and inserting "sections 6694,". **Effective** 3-23-2018.

- **2006, Pension Protection Act of 2006 (P.L. 109-280)**

P.L. 109-280, §1219(b)(2)(A):

Amended Code Sec. 6696 by striking "6694 and 6695" each place it appears in the text and heading thereof and inserting "6694, 6695, and 6695A". **Effective** generally for appraisals prepared with respect to returns or submissions filed after 8-17-2006. For a special rule, see Act Sec. 1219(e)(3), below.

P.L. 109-280, §1219(e)(3), provides:

(3) SPECIAL RULE FOR CERTAIN EASEMENTS.—In the case of a contribution of a qualified real property interest which is a restriction with respect to the exterior of a building described in section 170(h)(4)(C)(ii) of the Internal Revenue Code of 1986, and an appraisal with respect to the contribution, the amendments made by subsections (a) and (b) shall apply to returns filed after July 25, 2006.

[Sec. 6696(b)]

(b) DEFICIENCY PROCEDURES NOT TO APPLY.—Subchapter B of chapter 63 (relating to deficiency procedures for income, estate, gift, and certain excise taxes) shall not apply with respect to the assessment or collection of the penalties provided by sections 6694, 6695, and 6695A.

Amendments

- **2006, Pension Protection Act of 2006 (P.L. 109-280)**

P.L. 109-280, §1219(b)(2)(A):

Amended Code Sec. 6696 by striking "6694 and 6695" each place it appears in the text and inserting "6694, 6695, and 6695A". **Effective** generally for appraisals prepared with respect to returns or submissions filed after 8-17-2006. For a special rule, see Act Sec. 1219(e)(3) in the amendment notes for Code Sec. 6696(a).

[Sec. 6696(c)]

(c) PROCEDURE FOR CLAIMING REFUND.—Any claim for credit or refund of any penalty paid under section 6694, 6695, or 6695A shall be filed in accordance with regulations prescribed by the Secretary.

Amendments

- **2006, Pension Protection Act of 2006 (P.L. 109-280)**

P.L. 109-280, §1219(b)(2)(B):

Amended Code Sec. 6696 by striking "6694 or 6695" each place it appears in the text and inserting "6694, 6695, or 6695A". **Effective** generally for appraisals prepared with respect to returns or submissions filed after 8-17-2006. For a special rule, see Act Sec. 1219(e)(3) in the amendment notes for Code Sec. 6696(a).

[Sec. 6696(d)]

(d) PERIODS OF LIMITATION.—

(1) ASSESSMENT.—The amount of any penalty under section 6694(a), 6695, or 6695A shall be assessed within 3 years after the return or claim for refund with respect to which the penalty is assessed was filed, and no proceeding in court without assessment for the collection of such tax shall be begun after the expiration of such period. In the case of any penalty under section 6694(b), the penalty may be assessed, or a proceeding in court for the collection of the penalty may be begun without assessment, at any time.

(2) CLAIM FOR REFUND.—Except as provided in section 6694(d), any claim for refund of an overpayment of any penalty assessed under section 6694, 6695, or 6695A shall be filed within 3 years from the time the penalty was paid.

Amendments

- **2018, Tax Technical Corrections Act of 2018 (P.L. 115-141)**

P.L. 115-141, §401(a)(312), Div. U:

Amended Code Sec. 6696(d)(1) by striking "section 6695," and inserting "6695,". **Effective** 3-23-2018.

- **2007, Tax Technical Corrections Act of 2007 (P.L. 110-172)**

P.L. 110-172, §3(e)(2):

Amended Code Sec. 6696(d)(1) by striking "or under section 6695" and inserting ", section 6695, or 6695A". **Effective** as if included in the provision of the Pension Protection Act of 2006 (P.L. 109-280) to which it relates [effective generally for appraisals prepared with respect to returns or submission filed after 8-17-2006. For a special rule, see P.L. 109-280, §1219(e)(3), in the amendment notes for Code Sec. 6696(a).—CCH].

- **2006, Pension Protection Act of 2006 (P.L. 109-280)**

P.L. 109-280, §1219(b)(2)(B):

Amended Code Sec. 6696 by striking "6694 or 6695" each place it appears in the text and inserting "6694, 6695, or 6695A". **Effective** generally for appraisals prepared with respect to returns or submissions filed after 8-17-2006. For a special rule, see Act Sec. 1219(e)(3) in the amendment notes for Code Sec. 6696(a).

[Sec. 6696(e)]

(e) DEFINITIONS.—For purposes of sections 6694, 6695, and 6695A—

(1) RETURN.—The term "return" means any return of any tax imposed by this title, any administrative adjustment request under section 6227, and any partnership adjustment tracking report under section 6226(b)(4)(A).

(2) CLAIM FOR REFUND.—The term "claim for refund" means a claim for refund of, or credit against, any tax imposed by this title.

Amendments

- **2018, Tax Technical Corrections Act of 2018 (P.L. 115-141)**

P.L. 115-141, §206(n)(3), Div. U:

Amended Code Sec. 6696(e)(1) by inserting ", any administrative adjustment request under section 6227, and any partnership adjustment tracking report under section 6226(b)(4)(A)" before the period at the end. **Effective** as if included in section 1101 of the Bipartisan Budget Act of 2015 [effective generally for returns filed for partnership tax years beginning after 12-31-2017.—CCH].

- **2007, Small Business and Work Opportunity Tax Act of 2007 (P.L. 110-28)**

P.L. 110-28, §8246(a)(2)(H):

Amended Code Sec. 6696(e) by striking "subtitle A" each place it appears and inserting "this title". **Effective** for returns prepared after 5-25-2007.

- **2006, Pension Protection Act of 2006 (P.L. 109-280)**

P.L. 109-280, §1219(b)(2)(A):

Amended Code Sec. 6696 by striking "6694 and 6695" each place it appears in the text and heading thereof and inserting "6694, 6695, and 6695A". **Effective** generally for appraisals prepared with respect to returns or submissions filed after 8-17-2006. For a special rule, see Act Sec. 1219(e)(3) in the amendment notes for Code Sec. 6696(a).

- **1976, Tax Reform Act of 1976 (P.L. 94-455)**

P.L. 94-455, §1203(f):

Added Code Sec. 6696. **Effective** for documents prepared after 12-31-76.

ASSESSABLE PENALTIES

[Sec. 6697—Stricken]

Amendments

• 2010, Regulated Investment Company Modernization Act of 2010 (P.L. 111-325)

P.L. 111-325, §501(a):

Amended part I of subchapter B of chapter 68 by striking section 6697 (and by striking the item relating to such section in the table of sections of such part). **Effective** for tax years beginning after the date of the enactment of this Act. Prior to being stricken, Code Sec. 6697 read as follows:

SEC. 6697. ASSESSABLE PENALTIES WITH RESPECT TO LIABILITY FOR TAX OF REGULATED INVESTMENT COMPANIES.

[Sec. 6697(a)]

(a) CIVIL PENALTY.—In addition to any other penalty provided by law, any regulated investment company whose tax liability for any taxable year is deemed to be increased pursuant to section 860(c)(1)(A) shall pay a penalty in an amount equal to the amount of the interest (for which such company is liable) which is attributable solely to such increase.

Amendments

• 1986, Tax Reform Act of 1986 (P.L. 99-514)

P.L. 99-514, §667(a):

Amended the section heading and subsection (a) of Code Sec. 6697. **Effective** for tax years beginning after 12-31-86. Prior to amendment, the section heading and subsection (a) of Code Sec. 6697 read as follows:

SEC. 6697. ASSESSABLE PENALTIES WITH RESPECT TO LIABILITY FOR TAX OF QUALIFIED INVESTMENT ENTITIES.

(a) CIVIL PENALTY.—In addition to any other penalty provided by law, any qualified investment entity (as defined in section 860(b)) whose tax liability for any taxable year is deemed to be increased pursuant to section 860(c)(1)(A) (relating to interest and additions to tax determined with respect to the amount of the deduction for deficiency dividends allowed) shall pay a penalty in an amount equal to the amount of interest (for which such entity is liable) which is attributable solely to such increase.

• 1978, Revenue Act of 1978 (P.L. 95-600)

P.L. 95-600, §362(b):

Amended the heading of Code Sec. 6697 and Code Sec. 6697(a). **Effective** with respect to determinations after 11-6-78. Prior to amendment, the heading of Code Sec. 6697 and Code Sec. 6697(a) read as follows:

Sec. 6697. ASSESSABLE PENALTIES WITH RESPECT TO LIABILITY FOR TAX OF REAL ESTATE INVESTMENT TRUSTS.

(a) CIVIL PENALTY.—In addition to any other penalty provided by law, any real estate investment trust whose tax liability for any taxable year is deemed to be increased pursuant to section 859(b)(2)(A) (relating to interest and additions to tax determined with respect to the amount of the deduction for deficiency dividends allowed) shall pay a penalty in an amount equal to the amount of interest for which such trust is liable that is attributable solely to such increase.

[Sec. 6697(b)]

(b) 50-PERCENT LIMITATION.—The penalty payable under this section with respect to any determination shall not exceed one-half of the amount of the deduction allowed by section 860(a) for such taxable year.

Amendments

• 1978, Revenue Act of 1978 (P.L. 95-600)

P.L. 95-600, §362(b):

Amended Code Sec. 6697(b). **Effective** with respect to determinations after 11-6-78. Prior to amendment, Code Sec. 6697(b) read as follows:

"(b) 50-PERCENT LIMITATION.—The penalty payable under this section with respect to any determination shall not exceed one-half of the amount of the deduction allowed by section 859(a) for such taxable year."

[Sec. 6697(c)]

(c) DEFICIENCY PROCEDURES NOT TO APPLY.—Subchapter B of chapter 63 (relating to deficiency procedure for income, estate, gift, and certain excise taxes) shall not apply in respect of the assessment or collection of any penalty imposed by subsection (a).

Amendments

• 1976, Tax Reform Act of 1976 (P.L. 94-455)

P.L. 94-455, §1601(b)(1):

Added Code Sec. 6697. **Effective** date provided in Act Sec. 1608(a), below.

P.L. 94-455, §1608(a), provides:

(a) DEFICIENCY DIVIDEND PROCEDURES.—The amendments made by section 1601 shall apply with respect to determinations (as defined in section 859(c) of the Internal Revenue Code of 1954) occurring after the date of the enactment of this Act. If the amendments made by section 1601 apply to a taxable year ending on or before the date of enactment of this Act:

(1) the reference to section 857(b)(3)(A)(ii) in sections 857(b)(3)(C) and 859(b)(1)(B) of such Code, as amended, shall be considered to be a reference to section 857(b)(3)(A) of such Code, as in effect immediately before the enactment of this Act, and

(2) the reference to section 857(b)(2)(B) in section 859(a) of such Code, as amended, shall be considered to be a reference to section 857(b)(2)(C) of such Code, as in effect immediately before the enactment of this Act.

[Sec. 6698]

SEC. 6698. FAILURE TO FILE PARTNERSHIP RETURN.

[Sec. 6698(a)]

(a) GENERAL RULE.—In addition to the penalty imposed by section 7203 (relating to willful failure to file return, supply information, or pay tax), if any partnership required to file a return under section 6031, or a partnership adjustment tracking report under section 6226(b)(4)(A), for any taxable year—

(1) fails to file such return, or such report, at the time prescribed therefor (determined with regard to any extension of time for filing), or

(2) files a return or a report which fails to show the information required under section 6031 or 6226(b)(4)(A), respectively,

such partnership shall be liable for a penalty determined under subsection (b) for each month (or fraction thereof) during which such failure continues (but not to exceed 12 months), unless it is shown that such failure is due to reasonable cause.

Amendments

• 2018, Tax Technical Corrections Act of 2018 (P.L. 115-141)

P.L. 115-141, §206(n)(2)(A)-(C), Div. U:

Amended Code Sec. 6698(a) in the matter preceding paragraph (1) by inserting ", or a partnership adjustment tracking report under section 6226(b)(4)(A)," after "under section 6031", in paragraph (1) by inserting ", or such report," after "such return," and in paragraph (2) by inserting "or a report" after "a return", and by inserting "or 6226(b)(4)(A), respectively" before the comma at the end. **Effective** as if included in section 1101 of the Bipartisan Budget Act of 2015 [**effective** generally for returns filed for partnership tax years beginning after 12-31-2017.—CCH].

• 2007, Mortgage Forgiveness Debt Relief Act of 2007 (P.L. 110-142)

P.L. 110-142, §8(a):

Amended Code Sec. 6698(a) by striking "5 months" and inserting "12 months". **Effective** for returns required to be filed after 12-20-2007.

[Sec. 6698(b)]

(b) AMOUNT PER MONTH.—For purposes of subsection (a), the amount determined under this subsection for any month is the product of—

(1) $195, multiplied by

(2) the number of persons who were partners in the partnership during any part of the taxable year.

Amendments

• 2018, Tax Technical Corrections Act of 2018 (P.L. 115-141)

P.L. 115-141, §401(a)(313), Div. U:

Amended Code Sec. 6698(b)(2) by adding a period at the end. **Effective** 3-23-2018.

• 2009, Worker, Homeownership, and Business Assistance Act of 2009 (P.L. 111-92)

P.L. 111-92, §16(a):

Amended Code Sec. 6698(b)(1) by striking "$89" and inserting "$195". **Effective** for returns for tax years beginning after 12-31-2009.

• 2008, Worker, Retiree, and Employer Recovery Act of 2008 (P.L. 110-458)

P.L. 110-458, §127(a):

Amended Code Sec. 6698(b)(1) by striking "$85" and inserting "$89". **Effective** for returns required to be filed after 12-31-2008.

• 2007, Mortgage Forgiveness Debt Relief Act of 2007 (P.L. 110-142)

P.L. 110-142, §8(b):

Amended Code Sec. 6698(b)(1) by striking "$50" and inserting "$85". **Effective** for returns required to be filed after 12-20-2007.

ASSESSABLE PENALTIES

- **2007 (P.L. 110-141)**

P.L. 110-141, §2, provides:

SEC. 2. MODIFICATION OF PENALTY FOR FAILURE TO FILE PARTNERSHIP RETURNS.

For any return of a partnership required to be filed under section 6031 of the Internal Revenue Code of 1986 for a taxable year beginning in 2008, the dollar amount in effect under section 6698(b)(1) of such Code shall be increased by $1.

[Sec. 6698(c)]

(c) ASSESSMENT OF PENALTY.—The penalty imposed by subsection (a) shall be assessed against the partnership.

[Sec. 6698(d)]

(d) DEFICIENCY PROCEDURES NOT TO APPLY.— Subchapter B of chapter 63 (relating to deficiency procedures for income, estate, gift, and certain excise taxes) shall not apply in respect of the assessment or collection of any penalty imposed by subsection (a).

Amendments

- **1978, Revenue Act of 1978 (P.L. 95-600)**

P.L. 95-600, §211(a):

Added Code Sec. 6698. **Effective** with respect to returns for tax years beginning after 12-31-78.

[Sec. 6698(e)]

(e) ADJUSTMENT FOR INFLATION.—

(1) IN GENERAL.—In the case of any return required to be filed in a calendar year beginning after 2014, the $195 dollar amount under subsection (b)(1) shall be increased by an amount equal to such dollar amount multiplied by the cost-of-living adjustment determined under section 1(f)(3) for the calendar year determined by substituting "calendar year 2013" for "calendar year 2016" in subparagraph (A)(ii) thereof.

(2) ROUNDING.—If any amount adjusted under paragraph (1) is not a multiple of $5, such amount shall be rounded to the next lowest multiple of $5.

Amendments

- **2018, Tax Technical Corrections Act of 2018 (P.L. 115-141)**

P.L. 115-141, §401(a)(299)(D), Div. U:

Amended Code Sec. 6698(e)(1) by inserting "an amount equal to" after "increased by" and by inserting "for the calendar year" after "section 1(f)(3)". **Effective** 3-23-2018.

- **2017, Tax Cuts and Jobs Act (P.L. 115-97)**

P.L. 115-97, §11002(d)(1)(NN):

Amended Code Sec. 6698(e)(1) by striking "for 'calendar year 1992' in subparagraph (B)" and inserting "for 'calendar year 2016' in subparagraph (A)(ii)". **Effective** for tax years beginning after 12-31-2017.

- **2014, Stephen Beck, Jr., Achieving a Better Life Experience Act of 2014 (P.L. 113-295)**

P.L. 113-295, §208(d), Division B:

Amended Code Sec. 6698 by adding at the end a new subsection (e). **Effective** for returns required to be filed, and statements required to be furnished, after 12-31-2014 [effective date changed by P.L. 115-141, §105(a)(1)-(2), Div. U.—CCH].

[Sec. 6698A—Repealed]

Amendments

- **1980, Crude Oil Windfall Profit Tax Act of 1980 (P.L. 96-223)**

P.L. 96-223, §401(a):

Repealed Code Sec. 6698A(a)-(c), as added by P.L. 94-455, Act Sec. 2005(d)(2), and as redesignated by P.L. 95-600, Act Sec. 702(r)(1)(A), and P.L. 96-222. **Effective** with respect to decedents dying after 1976. However, see the amendment note for P.L. 96-223, Act Sec. 401(a), that follows Code Sec. 1014(d) for the text of Act Sec. 401(d) that authorizes the election of the carryover basis rules in the case of a decedent dying after 12-31-76 and before 11-7-78. Prior to repeal, Code Sec. 6698A read as follows:

SEC. 6698A. FAILURE TO FILE INFORMATION WITH RESPECT TO CARRYOVER BASIS PROPERTY.

[Sec. 6698A(a)]

(a) INFORMATION REQUIRED TO BE FURNISHED TO THE SECRETARY.—Any executor who fails to furnish information required under subsection (a) of section 6039A on the date prescribed therefor (determined with regard to any extension of time for filing), unless it is shown that such failure is due to reasonable cause and not to willful neglect, shall pay a penalty of $100 for each such failure, but the total amount imposed for all such failures shall not exceed $5,000.

Amendments

- **1978, Revenue Act of 1978 (P.L. 95-600)**

P.L. 95-600, §702(r)(1)(A):

Redesignated Code Sec. 6694(a) as Code Sec. 6698[A](a). **Effective** for estates of decedents dying after 12-31-76.

- **1976, Tax Reform Act of 1976 (P.L. 94-455)**

P.L. 94-455, §2005(d)(2), (f)(1):

Added Code Sec. 6694[A](a). **Effective** in respect of decedents dying after 12-31-79 (as amended by P.L. 95-600, Act Sec. 515(6)).

[Sec. 6698A(b)]

(b) INFORMATION REQUIRED TO BE FURNISHED TO BENEFICIARIES.—Any executor who fails to furnish in writing to each person described in subsection (b) of section 6039A the information required under such subsection, unless it is shown that such failure is due to reasonable cause and not to willful neglect, shall pay a penalty of $50 for each such failure, but the total amount imposed for all such failures shall not exceed $2,500.

Amendments

- **1978, Revenue Act of 1978 (P.L. 95-600)**

P.L. 95-600, §702(r)(1)(A):

Redesignated Code Sec. 6694(b) as Code Sec. 6698[A](b). **Effective** for estates of decedents dying after 12-31-76.

- **1976, Tax Reform Act of 1976 (P.L. 94-455)**

P.L. 94-455, §2005(d)(2), (f)(1):

Added Code Sec. 6694[A](b). **Effective** in respect of decedents dying after 12-31-79 (as amended by P.L. 95-600, Act Sec. 515(6)).

[Sec. 6698A(c)]

(c) DEFICIENCY PROCEDURES NOT TO APPLY.—Subchapter B of chapter 63 (relating to deficiency procedures for income, estate, gift, and certain excise taxes) shall not apply in respect of the assessment or collection of any penalty imposed by subsection (a).

Amendments

- **1980, Technical Corrections Act of 1979 (P.L. 96-222)**

P.L. 96-222, §107(a)(2)(D):

Redesignated Code Sec. 6698 as 6698A. **Effective** for estates of decedents dying after 12-31-76.

- **1978, Revenue Act of 1978 (P.L. 95-600)**

P.L. 95-600, §702(r)(1)(B):

Added Code Sec. 6698(c). **Effective** for estates of decedents dying after 12-31-76.

[Sec. 6699]

SEC. 6699. FAILURE TO FILE S CORPORATION RETURN.

[Sec. 6699(a)]

(a) GENERAL RULE.—In addition to the penalty imposed by section 7203 (relating to willful failure to file return, supply information, or pay tax), if any S corporation required to file a return under section 6037 for any taxable year—

(1) fails to file such return at the time prescribed therefor (determined with regard to any extension of time for filing), or

ASSESSABLE PENALTIES

(2) files a return which fails to show the information required under section 6037,

such S corporation shall be liable for a penalty determined under subsection (b) for each month (or fraction thereof) during which such failure continues (but not to exceed 12 months), unless it is shown that such failure is due to reasonable cause.

[Sec. 6699(b)]

(b) AMOUNT PER MONTH.—For purposes of subsection (a), the amount determined under this subsection for any month is the product of—

(1) $195, multiplied by

(2) the number of persons who were shareholders in the S corporation during any part of the taxable year.

Amendments

• **2009, Worker, Homeownership, and Business Assistance Act of 2009 (P.L. 111-92)**

P.L. 111-92, §16(a):

Amended Code Sec. 6699(b)(1) by striking "$89" and inserting "$195". **Effective** for returns for tax years beginning after 12-31-2009.

• **2008, Worker, Retiree, and Employer Recovery Act of 2008 (P.L. 110-458)**

P.L. 110-458, §128(a):

Amended Code Sec. 6699(b)(1) by striking "$85" and inserting "$89". **Effective** for returns required to be filed after 12-31-2008.

[Sec. 6699(c)]

(c) ASSESSMENT OF PENALTY.—The penalty imposed by subsection (a) shall be assessed against the S corporation.

[Sec. 6699(d)]

(d) DEFICIENCY PROCEDURES NOT TO APPLY.—Subchapter B of chapter 63 (relating to deficiency procedures for income, estate, gift, and certain excise taxes) shall not apply in respect of the assessment or collection of any penalty imposed by subsection (a).

Amendments

• **2007, Mortgage Forgiveness Debt Relief Act of 2007 (P.L. 110-142)**

P.L. 110-142, §9(a):

Amended part I of subchapter B of chapter 68 by adding at the end a new Code Sec. 6699. **Effective** for returns required to be filed after 12-20-2007.

[Sec. 6699(e)]

(e) ADJUSTMENT FOR INFLATION.—

(1) IN GENERAL.—In the case of any return required to be filed in a calendar year beginning after 2014, the $195 dollar amount under subsection (b)(1) shall be increased by an amount equal to such dollar amount multiplied by the cost-of-living adjustment determined under section 1(f)(3) for the calendar year determined by substituting "calendar year 2013" for "calendar year 2016" in subparagraph (A)(ii) thereof.

(2) ROUNDING.—If any amount adjusted under paragraph (1) is not a multiple of $5, such amount shall be rounded to the next lowest multiple of $5.

Amendments

• **2018, Tax Technical Corrections Act of 2018 (P.L. 115-141)**

P.L. 115-141, §401(a)(299)(E), Div. U:

Amended Code Sec. 6699(e)(1) by inserting "an amount equal to" after "increased by" and by inserting "for the calendar year" after "section 1(f)(3)". **Effective** 3-23-2018.

• **2017, Tax Cuts and Jobs Act (P.L. 115-97)**

P.L. 115-97, §11002(d)(1)(OO):

Amended Code Sec. 6699(e)(1) by striking "for 'calendar year 1992' in subparagraph (B)" and inserting "for 'calendar year 2016' in subparagraph (A)(ii)". **Effective** for tax years beginning after 12-31-2017.

• **2014, Stephen Beck, Jr., Achieving a Better Life Experience Act of 2014 (P.L. 113-295)**

P.L. 113-295, §208(e), Division B:

Amended Code Sec. 6699 by adding at the end a new subsection (e). **Effective** for returns required to be filed, and statements required to be furnished, after 12-31-2014 [**effective** date changed by P.L. 115-141, §105(a)(1)-(2), Div. U.—CCH].

[Sec. 6699—Repealed]

Amendments

• **1986, Tax Reform Act of 1986 (P.L. 99-514)**

P.L. 99-514, §1171(b)(7)(A):

Repealed Code Sec. 6699. **Effective** for compensation paid or accrued after 12-31-86, in tax years ending after such date.

P.L. 99-514, §1171(c)(2), provides:

(2) SECTIONS 404(i) AND 6699 TO CONTINUE TO APPLY TO PRE-1987 CREDITS.—The provisions of sections 404(i) and 6699 of the Internal Revenue Code of 1986 shall continue to apply with respect to credits under section 41 of such Code attributable to compensation paid or accrued before January 1, 1987 (or under section 38 of such Code with respect to qualified investment before January 1, 1983).

Reproduced immediately below is the text of Code Sec. 6699 prior to repeal by P.L. 99-514.

SEC. 6699. ASSESSABLE PENALTIES RELATING TO TAX CREDIT EMPLOYEE STOCK OWNERSHIP PLAN.

[Sec. 6699(a)]

(a) IN GENERAL.—If a taxpayer who has claimed an employee plan credit or a credit allowable under section 41 (relating to the employee stock ownership credit) for any taxable year—

(1) fails to satisfy any requirement provided by section 409 with respect to a qualified investment made before January 1, 1983,

(2) fails to make any contribution which is required under section 48(n) within the period required for making such contribution,

(3) fails to satisfy any requirement provided under section 409 with respect to a credit claimed under section 41 in taxable years ending after December 31, 1982, or

(4) fails to make any contribution which is required under section 41(c)(1)(B) within the period required for making such contribution,

the taxpayer shall pay a penalty in an amount equal to the amount involved in such failure.

• **1984, Deficit Reduction Act of 1984 (P.L. 98-369)**

P.L. 98-369, §491(e)(9):

Amended Code Sec. 6699(a)(1) and (3) by striking out "section 409A" and inserting in lieu thereof "section 409". **Effective** 1-1-84.

• **1981, Economic Recovery Tax Act of 1981 (P.L. 97-34)**

P.L. 97-34, §331(c)(3):

Amended Code Sec. 6699(a) by inserting "or a credit allowable under section 44G (relating to the employee stock ownership credit) after "employee plan credit", by striking out "section 409A, or" in paragraph (1) and inserting "section 409A with respect to a qualified investment made before January 1, 1983,", and by adding paragraphs (3) and (4). **Effective** for tax years ending after 12-31-82.

[Sec. 6699(b)]

(b) NO PENALTY WHERE THERE IS TIMELY CORRECTION OF FAILURE.—Subsection (a) shall not apply with respect to any failure if the employer corrects such failure (as determined by the Secretary) within 90 days after the Secretary notifies him of such failure.

[Sec. 6699(c)]

(c) AMOUNT INVOLVED DEFINED.—

(1) IN GENERAL.—For purposes of this section, the term "amount involved" means an amount determined by the Secretary.

(2) MAXIMUM AND MINIMUM AMOUNT.—

(A) The amount determined under paragraph (1) with respect to a failure described in paragraph (1) or (2) of subsection (a)—

(i) shall not exceed the amount of the employee plan credit claimed by the employer to which such failure relates, and

ASSESSABLE PENALTIES

(ii) shall not be less than the product of one-half of 1 percent of the amount referred to in clause (i), multiplied by the number of months (or parts thereof) during which such failure continues.

(B) The amount determined under paragraph (1) with respect to a failure described in paragraph (3) or (4) of subsection (a)—

(i) shall not exceed the amount of the credit claimed by the employer under section 41 to which such failure relates, and

(ii) shall not be less than the product of one-half of 1 percent of the amount referred to in clause (i), multiplied by the number of months (or parts thereof) during which such failure continues.

Amendments

• **1986, Tax Reform Act of 1986 (P.L. 99-514)**

P.L. 99-514, §1847(b)(9)(A)-(B):

Amended Code Sec. 6699 by striking out "section 44G" each place it appeared in subsections (a) and (c)(2)(B) and inserting in lieu thereof "section 41", and by striking out "section 44G(c)(1)(B)" in subsection (a)(4) and inserting in lieu thereof "section 41(c)(1)(B)". **Effective** as if included in the provision of P.L. 98-369 to which it relates.

• **1983, Technical Corrections Act of 1982 (P.L. 97-448)**

P.L. 97-448, §103(g)(2)(C):

Amended Code Sec. 6699(c)(2)(A)(ii) by striking out "subparagraph (A)" and inserting in lieu thereof "clause (i)". **Effective** as if included in the provision of P.L. 97-34 to which it relates.

P.L. 97-448, §103(g)(2)(D):

Amended Code Sec. 6699(c)(2)(B)(ii) by striking out "subparagraph (A)" and inserting in lieu thereof "clause (i)". **Effective** as if included in the provision of P.L. 97-34 to which it relates.

• **1981, Economic Recovery Tax Act of 1981 (P.L. 97-34)**

P.L. 97-34, §331(c)(4):

Amended Code Sec. 6699(c). **Effective** for tax years ending after 12-31-82.

• **1980, Technical Corrections Act of 1979 (P.L. 96-222)**

P.L. 96-222, §101(a)(7)(B):

Amended Act Sec. 141 of P.L. 95-600 by revising paragraph (g) which relates to the **effective** date for amendments concerning tax credit employee stock ownership plans. For the **effective** date, see the amendment note at P.L. 96-222, Act Sec. 101(a)(7)(B) following the text of Code Sec. 409A(n).

P.L. 96-222, §101(a)(7)(L)(iii)(VI) and (v)(IX):

Amended Code Sec. 6699(a) and 6699(c)(2)(A) by striking out "ESOP" and inserting "employee plan", and by striking out in the section heading of Code Sec. 6699 "ESOP" and inserting "Tax Credit Employee Stock Ownership Plan". **Effective** for tax years beginning after 12-31-78.

• **1978, Revenue Act of 1978 (P.L. 95-600)**

P.L. 95-600, §141(c)(1):

Added Code Sec. 6699. **Effective** with respect to qualified investment for tax years beginning after 12-31-78.

[Sec. 6700]

SEC. 6700. PROMOTING ABUSIVE TAX SHELTERS, ETC.

[Sec. 6700(a)]

(a) IMPOSITION OF PENALTY.—Any person who—

(1)(A) organizes (or assists in the organization of)—

(i) a partnership or other entity,

(ii) any investment plan or arrangement, or

(iii) any other plan or arrangement, or

(B) participates (directly or indirectly) in the sale of any interest in an entity or plan or arrangement referred to in subparagraph (A), and

(2) makes or furnishes or causes another person to make or furnish (in connection with such organization or sale)—

(A) a statement with respect to the allowability of any deduction or credit, the excludability of any income, or the securing of any other tax benefit by reason of holding an interest in the entity or participating in the plan or arrangement which the person knows or has reason to know is false or fraudulent as to any material matter, or

(B) a gross valuation overstatement as to any material matter,

shall pay, with respect to each activity described in paragraph (1), a penalty equal to $1,000 or, if the person establishes that it is lesser, 100 percent of the gross income derived (or to be derived) by such person from such activity. For purposes of the preceding sentence, activities described in paragraph (1)(A) with respect to each entity or arrangement shall be treated as a separate activity and participation in each sale described in paragraph (1)(B) shall be so treated. Notwithstanding the first sentence, if an activity with respect to which a penalty imposed under this subsection involves a statement described in paragraph (2)(A), the amount of the penalty shall be equal to 50 percent of the gross income derived (or to be derived) from such activity by the person on which the penalty is imposed.

Amendments

• **2018, Tax Technical Corrections Act of 2018 (P.L. 115-141)**

P.L. 115-141, §401(a)(314), Div. U:

Amended Code Sec. 6700(a) by striking "the $1,000" and inserting "$1,000". **Effective** 3-23-2018.

• **2004, American Jobs Creation Act of 2004 (P.L. 108-357)**

P.L. 108-357, §818(a):

Amended Code Sec. 6700(a) by adding at the end a new sentence. **Effective** for activities after 10-22-2004.

• **1989, Omnibus Budget Reconciliation Act of 1989 (P.L. 101-239)**

P.L. 101-239, §7734(a)(1)-(3):

Amended Code Sec. 6700(a) by inserting "(directly or indirectly)" after "participates" in paragraph (1)(B), by inserting "or causes another person to make or furnish" after "makes or furnishes" in paragraph (2), and by striking the flush left material following paragraph (2) and inserting new flush left material. **Effective** for activities after 12-31-89. Prior to amendment, the flush left material following Code Sec. 6700(a)(2) read as follows:

shall pay a penalty equal to the greater of $1,000 or 20 percent of the gross income derived or to be derived by such person from such activity.

[Sec. 6700(b)]

(b) RULES RELATING TO PENALTY FOR GROSS VALUATION OVERSTATEMENTS.—

(1) GROSS VALUATION OVERSTATEMENT DEFINED.—For purposes of this section, the term "gross valuation overstatement" means any statement as to the value of any property or services if—

(A) the value so stated exceeds 200 percent of the amount determined to be the correct valuation, and

(B) the value of such property or services is directly related to the amount of any deduction or credit allowable under chapter 1 to any participant.

(2) AUTHORITY TO WAIVE.—The Secretary may waive all or any part of the penalty provided by subsection (a) with respect to any gross valuation overstatement on a showing that there was a reasonable basis for the valuation and that such valuation was made in good faith.

[Sec. 6700(c)]

(c) PENALTY IN ADDITION TO OTHER PENALTIES.—The penalty imposed by this section shall be in addition to any other penalty provided by law.

Amendments

• **1984, Deficit Reduction Act of 1984 (P.L. 98-369)**

P.L. 98-369, §143(a):

Amended Code Sec. 6700(a) by striking out "10 percent" and inserting in lieu thereof "20 percent". **Effective** 7-19-84.

• **1982, Tax Equity and Fiscal Responsibility Act of 1982 (P.L. 97-248)**

P.L. 97-248, §320(a):

Added Code Sec. 6700. **Effective** 9-4-82.

ASSESSABLE PENALTIES

[Sec. 6701]
SEC. 6701. PENALTIES FOR AIDING AND ABETTING UNDERSTATEMENT OF TAX LIABILITY.

[Sec. 6701(a)]
(a) IMPOSITION OF PENALTY.—Any person—

(1) who aids or assists in, procures, or advises with respect to, the preparation or presentation of any portion of a return, affidavit, claim, or other document,

(2) who knows (or has reason to believe) that such portion will be used in connection with any material matter arising under the internal revenue laws, and

(3) who knows that such portion (if so used) would result in an understatement of the liability for tax of another person,

shall pay a penalty with respect to each such document in the amount determined under subsection (b).

Amendments

- **1989, Omnibus Budget Reconciliation Act of 1989 (P.L. 101-239)**

P.L. 101-239, §7735(a)(1)-(3):

Amended Code Sec. 6701(a) by striking "in connection with any matter arising under the internal revenue laws" after "document" in paragraph (1), by striking "who knows" in paragraph (2) and inserting "who knows (or has reason to believe)", and by striking "will result" in paragraph (3) and inserting "would result". **Effective** 12-31-89.

[Sec. 6701(b)]
(b) AMOUNT OF PENALTY.—

(1) IN GENERAL.—Except as provided in paragraph (2), the amount of the penalty imposed by subsection (a) shall be $1,000.

(2) CORPORATIONS.—If the return, affidavit, claim, or other document relates to the tax liability of a corporation, the amount of the penalty imposed by subsection (a) shall be $10,000.

(3) ONLY 1 PENALTY PER PERSON PER PERIOD.—If any person is subject to a penalty under subsection (a) with respect to any document relating to any taxpayer for any taxable period (or where there is no taxable period, any taxable event), such person shall not be subject to a penalty under subsection (a) with respect to any other document relating to such taxpayer for such taxable period (or event).

[Sec. 6701(c)]
(c) ACTIVITIES OF SUBORDINATES.—

(1) IN GENERAL.—For purposes of subsection (a), the term "procures" includes—

(A) ordering (or otherwise causing) a subordinate to do an act, and

(B) knowing of, and not attempting to prevent, participation by a subordinate in an act.

(2) SUBORDINATE.—For purposes of paragraph (1), the term "subordinate" means any other person (whether or not a director, officer, employee, or agent of the taxpayer involved) over whose activities the person has direction, supervision, or control.

[Sec. 6701(d)]
(d) TAXPAYER NOT REQUIRED TO HAVE KNOWLEDGE.—Subsection (a) shall apply whether or not the understatement is with the knowledge or consent of the persons authorized or required to present the return, affidavit, claim, or other document.

[Sec. 6701(e)]
(e) CERTAIN ACTIONS NOT TREATED AS AID OR ASSISTANCE.—For purposes of subsection (a)(1), a person furnishing typing, reproducing, or other mechanical assistance with respect to a document shall not be treated as having aided or assisted in the preparation of such document by reason of such assistance.

[Sec. 6701(f)]
(f) PENALTY IN ADDITION TO OTHER PENALTIES.—

(1) IN GENERAL.—Except as provided by paragraphs (2) and (3), the penalty imposed by this section shall be in addition to any other penalty provided by law.

(2) COORDINATION WITH RETURN PREPARER PENALTIES.—No penalty shall be assessed under subsection (a) or (b) of section 6694 on any person with respect to any document for which a penalty is assessed on such person under subsection (a).

(3) COORDINATION WITH SECTION 6700.—No penalty shall be assessed under section 6700 on any person with respect to any document for which a penalty is assessed on such person under subsection (a).

Amendments

- **1989, Omnibus Budget Reconciliation Act of 1989 (P.L. 101-239)**

P.L. 101-239, §7735(b)(1):

Amended Code Sec. 6701(f) by adding at the end thereof a new paragraph (3). **Effective** 12-31-89.

P.L. 101-239, §7735(b)(2):

Amended Code Sec. 6701(f)(1) by striking "paragraph (2)" and inserting "paragraphs (2) and (3)". **Effective** 12-31-89.

- **1982, Tax Equity and Fiscal Responsibility Act of 1982 (P.L. 97-248)**

P.L. 97-248, §324:

Added Code Sec. 6701. **Effective** 9-4-82. For provisions regarding burden of proof and prepayment forum, see Code Sec. 6703 as added by P.L. 97-248.

[Sec. 6702]
SEC. 6702. FRIVOLOUS TAX SUBMISSIONS.

[Sec. 6702(a)]
(a) CIVIL PENALTY FOR FRIVOLOUS TAX RETURNS.—A person shall pay a penalty of $5,000 if—

(1) such person files what purports to be a return of a tax imposed by this title but which—

(A) does not contain information on which the substantial correctness of the self-assessment may be judged, or

(B) contains information that on its face indicates that the self-assessment is substantially incorrect, and

(2) the conduct referred to in paragraph (1)—

(A) is based on a position which the Secretary has identified as frivolous under subsection (c), or

(B) reflects a desire to delay or impede the administration of Federal tax laws.

ASSESSABLE PENALTIES

[Sec. 6702(b)]

(b) CIVIL PENALTY FOR SPECIFIED FRIVOLOUS SUBMISSIONS.—

(1) IMPOSITION OF PENALTY.—Except as provided in paragraph (3), any person who submits a specified frivolous submission shall pay a penalty of $5,000.

(2) SPECIFIED FRIVOLOUS SUBMISSION.—For purposes of this section—

(A) SPECIFIED FRIVOLOUS SUBMISSION.—The term "specified frivolous submission" means a specified submission if any portion of such submission—

(i) is based on a position which the Secretary has identified as frivolous under subsection (c), or

(ii) reflects a desire to delay or impede the administration of Federal tax laws.

(B) SPECIFIED SUBMISSION.—The term "specified submission" means—

(i) a request for a hearing under—

(I) section 6320 (relating to notice and opportunity for hearing upon filing of notice of lien), or

(II) section 6330 (relating to notice and opportunity for hearing before levy), and

(ii) an application under—

(I) section 6159 (relating to agreements for payment of tax liability in installments),

(II) section 7122 (relating to compromises), or

(III) section 7811 (relating to taxpayer assistance orders).

(3) OPPORTUNITY TO WITHDRAW SUBMISSION.—If the Secretary provides a person with notice that a submission is a specified frivolous submission and such person withdraws such submission within 30 days after such notice, the penalty imposed under paragraph (1) shall not apply with respect to such submission.

[Sec. 6702(c)]

(c) LISTING OF FRIVOLOUS POSITIONS.—The Secretary shall prescribe (and periodically revise) a list of positions which the Secretary has identified as being frivolous for purposes of this subsection. The Secretary shall not include in such list any position that the Secretary determines meets the requirement of section 6662(d)(2)(B)(ii)(II).

[Sec. 6702(d)]

(d) REDUCTION OF PENALTY.—The Secretary may reduce the amount of any penalty imposed under this section if the Secretary determines that such reduction would promote compliance with and administration of the Federal tax laws.

[Sec. 6702(e)]

(e) PENALTIES IN ADDITION TO OTHER PENALTIES.—The penalties imposed by this section shall be in addition to any other penalty provided by law.

Amendments

• **2006, Tax Relief and Health Care Act of 2006 (P.L. 109-432)**

P.L. 109-432, Division A, §407(a):

Amended Code Sec. 6702. **Effective** for submissions made and issues raised after the date on which the Secretary first prescribes a list under Code Sec. 6702(c), as amended by Act Sec. 407(a). Prior to amendment, Code Sec. 6702 read as follows:

SEC. 6702. FRIVOLOUS INCOME TAX RETURN.

[Sec. 6702(a)]

(a) CIVIL PENALTY.—If—

(1) any individual files what purports to be a return of the tax imposed by subtitle A but which—

(A) does not contain information on which the substantial correctness of the self-assessment may be judged, or

(B) contains information that on its face indicates that the self-assessment is substantially incorrect; and

(2) the conduct referred to in paragraph (1) is due to—

(A) a position which is frivolous, or

(B) a desire (which appears on the purported return) to delay or impede the administration of Federal income tax laws,

then such individual shall pay a penalty of $500.

[Sec. 6702(b)]

(b) PENALTY IN ADDITION TO OTHER PENALTIES.—The penalty imposed by subsection (a) shall be in addition to any other penalty provided by law.

Amendments

• **1982, Tax Equity and Fiscal Responsibility Act of 1982 (P.L. 97-248)**

P.L. 97-248, §326(a):

Added Code Sec. 6702. **Effective** with respect to documents filed after 9-3-82.

[Sec. 6702(f)]

(f) PARTNERSHIP ADJUSTMENTS.—An administrative adjustment request under section 6227 and a partnership adjustment tracking report under section 6226(b)(4)(A) shall be treated as a return for purposes of this section.

Amendments

• **2018, Tax Technical Corrections Act of 2018 (P.L. 115-141)**

P.L. 115-141, §206(n)(4), Div. U:

Amended Code Sec. 6702 by adding at the end a new subsection (f). **Effective** as if included in section 1101 of the Bipartisan Budget Act of 2015 [**effective** generally for returns filed for partnership tax years beginning after 12-31-2017.—CCH]

[Sec. 6703]

SEC. 6703. RULES APPLICABLE TO PENALTIES UNDER SECTIONS 6700, 6701, AND 6702.

[Sec. 6703(a)]

(a) BURDEN OF PROOF.—In any proceeding involving the issue of whether or not any person is liable for a penalty under section 6700, 6701, or 6702, the burden of proof with respect to such issue shall be on the Secretary.

[Sec. 6703(b)]

(b) DEFICIENCY PROCEDURES NOT TO APPLY.—Subchapter B of chapter 63 (relating to deficiency procedures) shall not apply with respect to the assessment or collection of the penalties provided by sections 6700, 6701, and 6702.

[Sec. 6703(c)]

(c) EXTENSION OF PERIOD OF COLLECTION WHERE PERSON PAYS 15 PERCENT OF PENALTY.—

(1) IN GENERAL.—If, within 30 days after the day on which notice and demand of any penalty under section 6700 or 6701 is made against any person, such person pays an amount which is not less than 15 percent of the amount of such penalty and files a claim for refund of the amount so paid, no levy or proceeding in court for the collection of the remainder of such penalty shall be made, begun, or prosecuted until the final resolution of a proceeding begun as provided in paragraph (2). Notwithstanding the provisions of section 7421(a), the beginning of such

ASSESSABLE PENALTIES

proceeding or levy during the time such prohibition is in force may be enjoined by a proceeding in the proper court. Nothing in this paragraph shall be construed to prohibit any counterclaim for the remainder of such penalty in a proceeding begun as provided in paragraph (2).

(2) PERSON MUST BRING SUIT IN DISTRICT COURT TO DETERMINE HIS LIABILITY FOR PENALTY.—If, within 30 days after the day on which his claim for refund of any partial payment of any penalty under section 6700 or 6701 is denied (or, if earlier, within 30 days after the expiration of 6 months after the day on which he filed the claim for refund), the person fails to begin a proceeding in the appropriate United States district court for the determination of his liability for such penalty, paragraph (1) shall cease to apply with respect to such penalty, effective on the day following the close of the applicable 30-day period referred to in this paragraph.

(3) SUSPENSION OF RUNNING OF PERIOD OF LIMITATIONS ON COLLECTION.—The running of the period of limitations provided in section 6502 on the collection by levy or by a proceeding in court in respect of any penalty described in paragraph (1) shall be suspended for the period during which the Secretary is prohibited from collecting by levy or a proceeding in court.

Amendments

- **1989, Omnibus Budget Reconciliation Act of 1989 (P.L. 101-239)**

P.L. 101-239, §7736(a):
Amended Code Sec. 6703(c) by striking "section 6700, 6701, or 6702" each place it appears and inserting "section 6700 or 6701". **Effective** for returns filed after 12-31-89.

P.L. 101-239, §7737(a):
Amended Code Sec. 6703(c)(1) by adding at the end thereof a new sentence. **Effective** 12-19-89.

- **1982, Tax Equity and Fiscal Responsibility Act of 1982 (P.L. 97-248)**

P.L. 97-248, §322(a):
Added Code Sec. 6703. **Effective** 9-4-82.

[Sec. 6704]
SEC. 6704. FAILURE TO KEEP RECORDS NECESSARY TO MEET REPORTING REQUIREMENTS UNDER SECTION 6047(d).

[Sec. 6704(a)]

(a) LIABILITY FOR PENALTY.—Any person who—

(1) has a duty to report or may have a duty to report any information under section 6047(d), and

(2) fails to keep such records as may be required by regulations prescribed under section 6047(d) for the purpose of providing the necessary data base for either current reporting or future reporting,

shall pay a penalty for each calendar year for which there is any failure to keep such records.

Amendments

- **1986, Tax Reform Act of 1986 (P.L. 99-514)**

P.L. 99-514, §1848(e)(1)(A) and (B):
Amended Code Sec. 6704 by striking out "section 6047(e)" each place it appears in subsection (a) and inserting in lieu thereof "section 6047(d)", and by striking out "SECTION 6047(e)" in the section heading and inserting in lieu thereof "SECTION 6047(d)". **Effective** as if included in the provision of P.L. 98-369 to which it relates.

[Sec. 6704(b)]

(b) AMOUNT OF PENALTY.—

(1) IN GENERAL.—The penalty of any person for any calendar year shall be $50, multiplied by the number of individuals with respect to whom such failure occurs in such year.

(2) MAXIMUM AMOUNT.—The penalty under this section of any person for any calendar year shall not exceed $50,000.

[Sec. 6704(c)]

(c) EXCEPTIONS.—

(1) REASONABLE CAUSE.—No penalty shall be imposed by this section on any person for any failure which is shown to be due to reasonable cause and not to willful neglect.

(2) INABILITY TO CORRECT PREVIOUS FAILURE.—No penalty shall be imposed by this section on any failure by a person if such failure is attributable to a prior failure which has been penalized under this section and with respect to which the person has made all reasonable efforts to correct the failure.

(3) PRE-1983 FAILURES.—No penalty shall be imposed by this section on any person for any failure which is attributable to a failure occurring before January 1, 1983, if the person has made all reasonable efforts to correct such pre-1983 failure.

Amendments

- **1982, Tax Equity and Fiscal Responsibility Act of 1982 (P.L. 97-248)**

P.L. 97-248, §334(c)(1):
Added Code Sec. 6704. **Effective** 1-1-85.

[Sec. 6705]
SEC. 6705. FAILURE BY BROKER TO PROVIDE NOTICE TO PAYORS.

[Sec. 6705(a)]

(a) IN GENERAL.—Any person required under section 3406(d)(2)(B) to provide notice to any payor who willfully fails to provide such notice to such payor shall pay a penalty of $500 for each such failure.

[Sec. 6705(b)]

(b) PENALTY IN ADDITION TO OTHER PENALTIES.—Any penalty imposed by this section shall be in addition to any other penalty provided by law.

Amendments

- **1983, Interest and Dividend Tax Compliance Act of 1983 (P.L. 98-67)**

P.L. 98-67, §104(c)(1):
Added Code Sec. 6705. **Effective** with respect to payments made after 12-31-83.

[Sec. 6706]
SEC. 6706. ORIGINAL ISSUE DISCOUNT INFORMATION REQUIREMENTS.

[Sec. 6706(a)]

(a) FAILURE TO SHOW INFORMATION ON DEBT INSTRUMENT.—In the case of a failure to set forth on a debt instrument the information required to be set forth on such instrument under section 1275(c)(1), unless it is shown that such failure is due to reasonable cause and not to willful neglect, the issuer shall pay a penalty of $50 for each instrument with respect to which such a failure exists.

ASSESSABLE PENALTIES

[Sec. 6706(b)]

(b) FAILURE TO FURNISH INFORMATION TO SECRETARY.—Any issuer who fails to furnish information required under section 1275(c)(2) with respect to any issue of debt instruments on the date prescribed therefor (determined with regard to any extension of time for filing) shall pay a penalty equal to 1 percent of the aggregate issue price of such issue, unless it is shown that such failure is due to reasonable cause and not willful neglect. The amount of the penalty imposed under the preceding sentence with respect to any issue of debt instruments shall not exceed $50,000 for such issue.

[Sec. 6706(c)]

(c) DEFICIENCY PROCEDURES NOT TO APPLY.—Subchapter B of chapter 63 (relating to deficiency procedures for income, estate, gift, and certain excise taxes) shall not apply in respect of the assessment or collection of any penalty imposed by this section.

Amendments

• 1984, Deficit Reduction Act of 1984 (P.L. 98-369)

P.L. 98-369, § 41(c)(1):
Added Code Sec. 6706. Effective 8-17-84.

[Sec. 6707]

SEC. 6707. FAILURE TO FURNISH INFORMATION REGARDING REPORTABLE TRANSACTIONS.

[Sec. 6707(a)]

(a) IN GENERAL.—If a person who is required to file a return under section 6111(a) with respect to any reportable transaction—

(1) fails to file such return on or before the date prescribed therefor, or

(2) files false or incomplete information with the Secretary with respect to such transaction,

such person shall pay a penalty with respect to such return in the amount determined under subsection (b).

[Sec. 6707(b)]

(b) AMOUNT OF PENALTY.—

(1) IN GENERAL.—Except as provided in paragraph (2), the penalty imposed under subsection (a) with respect to any failure shall be $50,000.

(2) LISTED TRANSACTIONS.—The penalty imposed under subsection (a) with respect to any listed transaction shall be an amount equal to the greater of—

(A) $200,000, or

(B) 50 percent of the gross income derived by such person with respect to aid, assistance, or advice which is provided with respect to the listed transaction before the date the return is filed under section 6111.

Subparagraph (B) shall be applied by substituting "75 percent" for "50 percent" in the case of an intentional failure or act described in subsection (a).

[Sec. 6707(c)]

(c) RESCISSION AUTHORITY.—The provisions of section 6707A(d) (relating to authority of Commissioner to rescind penalty) shall apply to any penalty imposed under this section.

[Sec. 6707(d)]

(d) REPORTABLE AND LISTED TRANSACTIONS.—For purposes of this section, the terms "reportable transaction" and "listed transaction" have the respective meanings given to such terms by section 6707A(c).

Amendments

• 2004, American Jobs Creation Act of 2004 (P.L. 108-357)

P.L. 108-357, § 816(a):
Amended Code Sec. 6707. Effective for returns the due date for which is after 10-22-2004. Prior to amendment, Code Sec. 6707 read as follows:

SEC. 6707. FAILURE TO FURNISH INFORMATION REGARDING TAX SHELTERS.

[Sec. 6707(a)]

(a) FAILURE TO REGISTER TAX SHELTER.—

(1) IMPOSITION OF PENALTY.—If a person who is required to register a tax shelter under section 6111(a)—

(A) fails to register such tax shelter on or before the date described in section 6111(a)(1), or

(B) files false or incomplete information with the Secretary with respect to such registration,

such person shall pay a penalty with respect to such registration in the amount determined under paragraph (2) or (3), as the case may be. No penalty shall be imposed under the preceding sentence with respect to any failure which is due to reasonable cause.

(2) AMOUNT OF PENALTY.—Except as provided in paragraph (3), the penalty imposed under paragraph (1) with respect to any tax shelter shall be an amount equal to the greater of—

(A) 1 percent of the aggregate amount invested in such tax shelter, or

(B) $500.

(3) CONFIDENTIAL ARRANGEMENTS.—

(A) IN GENERAL.—In the case of a tax shelter (as defined in section 6111(d)), the penalty imposed under paragraph (1) shall be an amount equal to the greater of—

(i) 50 percent of the fees paid to all promoters of the tax shelter with respect to offerings made before the date such shelter is registered under section 6111, or

(ii) $10,000.

Clause (i) shall be applied by substituting "75 percent" for "50 percent" in the case of an intentional failure or act described in paragraph (1).

(B) SPECIAL RULE FOR PARTICIPANTS REQUIRED TO REGISTER SHELTER.—In the case of a person required to register such a tax shelter by reason of section 6111(d)(3)—

(i) such person shall be required to pay the penalty under paragraph (1) only if such person actually participated in such shelter,

(ii) the amount of such penalty shall be determined by taking into account under subparagraph (A)(i) only the fees paid by such person, and

(iii) such penalty shall be in addition to the penalty imposed on any other person for failing to register such shelter.

Amendments

• 1997, Taxpayer Relief Act of 1997 (P.L. 105-34)

P.L. 105-34, § 1028(b):
Amended Code Sec. 6707(a) by adding at the end a new paragraph (3). Effective for any tax shelter (as defined in Code Sec. 6111(d), as amended) interests in which are offered to potential participants after the Secretary of the Treasury prescribes guidance with respect to meeting requirements added by such amendments.

P.L. 105-34, § 1028(d)(1):
Amended Code Sec. 6707(a)(2) by striking "The penalty" and inserting "Except as provided in paragraph (3), the penalty". Effective for any tax shelter (as defined in Code Sec. 6111(d), as amended) interests in which are offered to potential participants after the Secretary of the Treasury prescribes guidance with respect to meeting requirements added by such amendments.

P.L. 105-34, § 1028(d)(2):
Amended Code Sec. 6707(a)(1)(A) [6707(a)(1)] by striking "paragraph (2)" and inserting "paragraph (2) or (3), as the case may be". Effective for any tax shelter (as defined in Code Sec. 6111(d), as amended) interests in which are offered to potential participants after the Secretary of the Treasury prescribes guidance with respect to meeting requirements added by such amendments.

• 1986, Tax Reform Act of 1986 (P.L. 99-514)

P.L. 99-514, § 1532(a):
Amended Code Sec. 6707(a)(2). Effective for failure with respect to tax shelters, interests in which are first offered for sale after 10-22-86. Prior to amendment, Code Sec. 6707(a)(2) read as follows:

(2) AMOUNT OF PENALTY.—The penalty imposed under paragraph (1) with respect to any tax shelter shall be an amount equal to the greater of—

(A) $500, or

(B) the lesser of (i) 1 percent of the aggregate amount invested in such tax shelter, or (ii) $10,000.

The $10,000 limitation in subparagraph (B) shall not apply where there is an intentional disregard of the requirements of section 6111(a).

ASSESSABLE PENALTIES

[Sec. 6707(b)]

(b) FAILURE TO FURNISH TAX SHELTER IDENTIFICATION NUMBER.—

(1) SELLERS, ETC.—Any person who fails to furnish the identification number of a tax shelter which such person is required to furnish under section 6111(b)(1) shall pay a penalty of $100 for each such failure.

(2) FAILURE TO INCLUDE NUMBER ON RETURN.—Any person who fails to include an identification number on a return on which such number is required to be included under section 6111(b)(2) shall pay a penalty of $250 for each such failure, unless such failure is due to reasonable cause.

Amendments

• **1986, Tax Reform Act of 1986 (P.L. 99-514)**

P.L. 99-514, §1533(a):
Amended Code Sec. 6707(b)(2) by striking out "$50" and inserting in lieu thereof "$250". **Effective** for returns filed after 10-22-86.

• **1984, Deficit Reduction Act of 1984 (P.L. 98-369)**

P.L. 98-369, §141(b):
Added Code Sec. 6707. **Effective** for any tax shelter (within the meaning of Code Sec. 6111) any interest in which is first sold to any investor after 8-31-84.

[Sec. 6707A]

SEC. 6707A. PENALTY FOR FAILURE TO INCLUDE REPORTABLE TRANSACTION INFORMATION WITH RETURN.

[Sec. 6707A(a)]

(a) IMPOSITION OF PENALTY.—Any person who fails to include on any return or statement any information with respect to a reportable transaction which is required under section 6011 to be included with such return or statement shall pay a penalty in the amount determined under subsection (b).

[Sec. 6707A(b)]

(b) AMOUNT OF PENALTY.—

(1) IN GENERAL.—Except as otherwise provided in this subsection, the amount of the penalty under subsection (a) with respect to any reportable transaction shall be 75 percent of the decrease in tax shown on the return as a result of such transaction (or which would have resulted from such transaction if such transaction were respected for Federal tax purposes).

(2) MAXIMUM PENALTY.—The amount of the penalty under subsection (a) with respect to any reportable transaction shall not exceed—

(A) in the case of a listed transaction, $200,000 ($100,000 in the case of a natural person), or

(B) in the case of any other reportable transaction, $50,000 ($10,000 in the case of a natural person).

(3) MINIMUM PENALTY.—The amount of the penalty under subsection (a) with respect to any transaction shall not be less than $10,000 ($5,000 in the case of a natural person).

Amendments

• **2010, Creating Small Business Jobs Act of 2010 (P.L. 111-240)**

P.L. 111-240, §2041(a):
Amended Code Sec. 6707A(b). **Effective** for penalties assessed after 12-31-2006. Prior to amendment, Code Sec. 6707A(b) read as follows:

(b) AMOUNT OF PENALTY.—

(1) IN GENERAL.—Except as provided in paragraph (2), the amount of the penalty under subsection (a) shall be—

(A) $10,000 in the case of a natural person, and

(B) $50,000 in any other case.

(2) LISTED TRANSACTION.—The amount of the penalty under subsection (a) with respect to a listed transaction shall be—

(A) $100,000 in the case of a natural person, and

(B) $200,000 in any other case.

[Sec. 6707A(c)]

(c) DEFINITIONS.—For purposes of this section:

(1) REPORTABLE TRANSACTION.—The term "reportable transaction" means any transaction with respect to which information is required to be included with a return or statement because, as determined under regulations prescribed under section 6011, such transaction is of a type which the Secretary determines as having a potential for tax avoidance or evasion.

(2) LISTED TRANSACTION.—The term "listed transaction" means a reportable transaction which is the same as, or substantially similar to, a transaction specifically identified by the Secretary as a tax avoidance transaction for purposes of section 6011.

[Sec. 6707A(d)]

(d) AUTHORITY TO RESCIND PENALTY.—

(1) IN GENERAL.—The Commissioner of Internal Revenue may rescind all or any portion of any penalty imposed by this section with respect to any violation if—

(A) the violation is with respect to a reportable transaction other than a listed transaction, and

(B) rescinding the penalty would promote compliance with the requirements of this title and effective tax administration.

(2) NO JUDICIAL APPEAL.—Notwithstanding any other provision of law, any determination under this subsection may not be reviewed in any judicial proceeding.

(3) RECORDS.—If a penalty is rescinded under paragraph (1), the Commissioner shall place in the file in the Office of the Commissioner the opinion of the Commissioner with respect to the determination, including—

(A) a statement of the facts and circumstances relating to the violation,

(B) the reasons for the rescission, and

(C) the amount of the penalty rescinded.

[Sec. 6707A(e)]

(e) PENALTY REPORTED TO SEC.—In the case of a person—

(1) which is required to file periodic reports under section 13 or 15(d) of the Securities Exchange Act of 1934 or is required to be consolidated with another person for purposes of such reports, and

(2) which—

(A) is required to pay a penalty under this section with respect to a listed transaction,

(B) is required to pay a penalty under section 6662A with respect to any reportable transaction at a rate prescribed under section 6662A(c), or

(C) is required to pay a penalty under section 6662(h) with respect to any reportable transaction and would (but for section 6662A(e)(2)(B)) have been subject to penalty under section 6662A at a rate prescribed under section 6662A(c),

the requirement to pay such penalty shall be disclosed in such reports filed by such person for such periods as the Secretary shall specify. Failure to make a disclosure in accordance with the preceding sentence shall be treated as a failure to which the penalty under subsection (b)(2) applies.

ASSESSABLE PENALTIES

Amendments
• **2007, Tax Technical Corrections Act of 2007 (P.L. 110-172)**

P.L. 110-172, §11(a)(41):

Amended Code Sec. 6707A(e)(2)(C) by striking "section 6662A(e)(2)(C)" and inserting "section 6662A(e)(2)(B)". **Effective** 12-29-2007.

[Sec. 6707A(f)]

(f) COORDINATION WITH OTHER PENALTIES.—The penalty imposed by this section shall be in addition to any other penalty imposed by this title.

Amendments
• **2004, American Jobs Creation Act of 2004 (P.L. 108-357)**

P.L. 108-357, §811(a):

Amended part I of subchapter B of chapter 68 by inserting after Code Sec. 6707 a new Code Sec. 6707A. **Effective** for returns and statements the due date for which is after 10-22-2004 and which were not filed before such date [effective date amended by P.L. 109-135, §403(w)].

[Sec. 6708]

SEC. 6708. FAILURE TO MAINTAIN LISTS OF ADVISEES WITH RESPECT TO REPORTABLE TRANSACTIONS.

[Sec. 6708(a)]

(a) IMPOSITION OF PENALTY.—

(1) IN GENERAL.—If any person who is required to maintain a list under section 6112(a) fails to make such list available upon written request to the Secretary in accordance with section 6112(b) within 20 business days after the date of such request, such person shall pay a penalty of $10,000 for each day of such failure after such 20th day.

(2) REASONABLE CAUSE EXCEPTION.—No penalty shall be imposed by paragraph (1) with respect to the failure on any day if such failure is due to reasonable cause.

Amendments
• **2004, American Jobs Creation Act of 2004 (P.L. 108-357)**

P.L. 108-357, §815(b)(5)(A):

Amended the heading for Code Sec. 6708. **Effective** for transactions with respect to which material aid, assistance, or advice referred to in Code Sec. 6111(b)(1)(A)(i) (as added by Act Sec. 815) is provided after 10-22-2004. Prior to amendment, the heading for Code Sec. 6708 read as follows:

SEC. 6708. FAILURE TO MAINTAIN LISTS OF INVESTORS IN POTENTIALLY ABUSIVE TAX SHELTERS.

P.L. 108-357, §817(a):

Amended Code Sec. 6708(a). **Effective** for requests made after 10-22-2004. Prior to amendment, Code Sec. 6708(a) read as follows:

(a) IN GENERAL.—Any person who fails to meet any requirement imposed by section 6112 shall pay a penalty of $50 for each person with respect to whom there is such a failure, unless it is shown that such failure is due to reasonable cause and not due to willful neglect. The maximum penalty imposed under this subsection for any calendar year shall not exceed $100,000.

• **1986, Tax Reform Act of 1986 (P.L. 99-514)**

P.L. 99-514, §1534(a):

Amended Code Sec. 6708(a) by striking out "$50,000" and inserting in lieu thereof "$100,000". **Effective** for failures occurring or continuing after 10-22-86.

[Sec. 6708(b)]

(b) PENALTY IN ADDITION TO OTHER PENALTIES.—The penalty imposed by this section shall be in addition to any other penalty provided by law.

Amendments
• **1984, Deficit Reduction Act of 1984 (P.L. 98-369)**

P.L. 98-369, §142(b):

Added Code Sec. 6708. **Effective** for any interest which is first sold to any investor after 8-31-84.

[Sec. 6709]

SEC. 6709. PENALTIES WITH RESPECT TO MORTGAGE CREDIT CERTIFICATES.

[Sec. 6709(a)]

(a) NEGLIGENCE.—If—

(1) any person makes a material misstatement in any verified written statement made under penalties of perjury with respect to the issuance of a mortgage credit certificate, and

(2) such misstatement is due to the negligence of such person,

such person shall pay a penalty of $1,000 for each mortgage credit certificate with respect to which such a misstatement was made.

[Sec. 6709(b)]

(b) FRAUD.—If a misstatement described in subsection (a)(1) is due to fraud on the part of the person making such misstatement, in addition to any criminal penalty, such person shall pay a penalty of $10,000 for each mortgage credit certificate with respect to which such a misstatement is made.

[Sec. 6709(c)]

(c) REPORTS.—Any person required by section 25(g) to file a report with the Secretary who fails to file the report with respect to any mortgage credit certificate at the time and in the manner required by the Secretary shall pay a penalty of $200 for such failure unless it is shown that such failure is due to reasonable cause and not to willful neglect. In the case of any report required under the second sentence of section 25(g), the aggregate amount of the penalty imposed by the preceding sentence shall not exceed $2,000.

[Sec. 6709(d)]

(d) MORTGAGE CREDIT CERTIFICATE.—The term "mortgage credit certificate" has the meaning given to such term by section 25(c).

Amendments
• **1986, Tax Reform Act of 1986 (P.L. 99-514)**

P.L. 99-514, §1862(d)(2):

Amended Code Sec. 6708 by redesignating the section 6708 which relates to penalties with respect to mortgage credit certificates as section 6709. **Effective** as if included in the provision of P.L. 98-369 to which it relates.

• **1984, Deficit Reduction Act of 1984 (P.L. 98-369)**

P.L. 98-369, §612(d)(1):

Added Code Sec. 6708 [6709]. **Effective** for interest paid or accrued after 12-31-84, on indebtedness incurred after 12-31-84.

ASSESSABLE PENALTIES

[Sec. 6710]
SEC. 6710. FAILURE TO DISCLOSE THAT CONTRIBUTIONS ARE NONDEDUCTIBLE.

[Sec. 6710(a)]

(a) IMPOSITION OF PENALTY.—If there is a failure to meet the requirement of section 6113 with respect to a fundraising solicitation by (or on behalf of) an organization to which section 6113 applies, such organization shall pay a penalty of $1,000 for each day on which such a failure occurred. The maximum penalty imposed under this subsection on failures by any organization during any calendar year shall not exceed $10,000.

[Sec. 6710(b)]

(b) REASONABLE CAUSE EXCEPTION.—No penalty shall be imposed under this section with respect to any failure if it is shown that such failure is due to reasonable cause.

[Sec. 6710(c)]

(c) $10,000 LIMITATION NOT TO APPLY WHERE INTENTIONAL DISREGARD.—If any failure to which subsection (a) applies is due to intentional disregard of the requirement of section 6113—

(1) the penalty under subsection (a) for the day on which such failure occurred shall be the greater of—

(A) $1,000, or

(B) 50 percent of the aggregate cost of the solicitations which occurred on such day and with respect to which there was such a failure,

(2) the $10,000 limitation of subsection (a) shall not apply to any penalty under subsection (a) for the day on which such failure occurred, and

(3) such penalty shall not be taken into account in applying such limitation to other penalties under subsection (a).

[Sec. 6710(d)]

(d) DAY ON WHICH FAILURE OCCURS.—For purposes of this section, any failure to meet the requirement of section 6113 with respect to a solicitation—

(1) by television or radio, shall be treated as occurring when the solicitation was telecast or broadcast,

(2) by mail, shall be treated as occurring when the solicitation was mailed,

(3) not by mail but in written or printed form, shall be treated as occurring when the solicitation was distributed, or

(4) by telephone, shall be treated as occurring when the solicitation was made.

Amendments

• **1987, Revenue Act of 1987 (P.L. 100-203)**

P.L. 100-203, §10701(b):

Amended subchapter B of chapter 68 by adding at the end thereof a new section 6710. **Effective** for solicitations after 1-31-88.

[Sec. 6711]
SEC. 6711. FAILURE BY TAX-EXEMPT ORGANIZATION TO DISCLOSE THAT CERTAIN INFORMATION OR SERVICE AVAILABLE FROM FEDERAL GOVERNMENT.

[Sec. 6711(a)]

(a) IMPOSITION OF PENALTY.—If—

(1) a tax-exempt organization offers to sell (or solicits money for) specific information or a routine service for any individual which could be readily obtained by such individual free of charge (or for a nominal charge) from an agency of the Federal Government,

(2) the tax-exempt organization, when making such offer or solicitation, fails to make an express statement (in a conspicuous and easily recognizable format) that the information or service can be so obtained, and

(3) such failure is due to intentional disregard of the requirements of this subsection,

such organization shall pay a penalty determined under subsection (b) for each day on which such a failure occurred.

[Sec. 6711(b)]

(b) AMOUNT OF PENALTY.—The penalty under subsection (a) for any day on which a failure referred to in such subsection occurred shall be the greater of—

(1) $1,000, or

(2) 50 percent of the aggregate cost of the offers and solicitations referred to in subsection (a)(1) which occurred on such day and with respect to which there was such a failure.

[Sec. 6711(c)]

(c) DEFINITIONS.—For purposes of this section—

(1) TAX-EXEMPT ORGANIZATION.—The term "tax-exempt organization" means any organization which—

(A) is described in subsection (c) or (d) of section 501 and exempt from taxation under section 501(a), or

(B) is a political organization (as defined in section 527(e)).

(2) DAY ON WHICH FAILURE OCCURS.—The day on which any failure referred to in subsection (a) occurs shall be determined under rules similar to the rules of section 6710(d).

Amendments

• **1987, Revenue Act of 1987 (P.L. 100-203)**

P.L. 100-203, §10705(a):

Amended part I of subchapter B of chapter 68 by adding section 6711. **Effective** for offers and solicitations after 1-31-88.

[Sec. 6712]
SEC. 6712. FAILURE TO DISCLOSE TREATY-BASED RETURN POSITIONS.

[Sec. 6712(a)]

(a) GENERAL RULE.—If a taxpayer fails to meet the requirements of section 6114, there is hereby imposed a penalty equal to $1000 ($10,000 in the case of a C corporation) on each such failure.

ASSESSABLE PENALTIES

[Sec. 6712(b)]

(b) AUTHORITY TO WAIVE.—The Secretary may waive all or any part of the penalty provided by this section on a showing by the taxpayer that there was reasonable cause for the failure and that the taxpayer acted in good faith.

[Sec. 6712(c)]

(c) PENALTY IN ADDITION TO OTHER PENALTIES.—The penalty imposed by this section shall be in addition to any other penalty imposed by law.

Amendments
- **1988, Technical and Miscellaneous Revenue Act of 1988 (P.L. 100-647)**

P.L. 100-647, §1012(aa)(5)(B):

Amended part I of subchapter B of chapter 68 by adding section 6712. **Effective** as if included in the provision of P.L. 99-514 to which it relates.

[Sec. 6713]

SEC. 6713. DISCLOSURE OR USE OF INFORMATION BY PREPARERS OF RETURNS.

[Sec. 6713(a)]

(a) IMPOSITION OF PENALTY.—If any person who is engaged in the business of preparing, or providing services in connection with the preparation of, returns of tax imposed by chapter 1, or any person who for compensation prepares any such return for any other person, and who—

(1) discloses any information furnished to him for, or in connection with, the preparation of any such return, or

(2) uses any such information for any purpose other than to prepare, or assist in preparing, any such return,

shall pay a penalty of $250 for each such disclosure or use, but the total amount imposed under this subsection on such a person for any calendar year shall not exceed $10,000.

[Sec. 6713(b)]

(b) ENHANCED PENALTY FOR IMPROPER USE OR DISCLOSURE RELATING TO IDENTITY THEFT.—

(1) IN GENERAL.—In the case of a disclosure or use described in subsection (a) that is made in connection with a crime relating to the misappropriation of another person's taxpayer identity (as defined in section 6103(b)(6)), whether or not such crime involves any tax filing, subsection (a) shall be applied—

(A) by substituting "$1,000" for "$250", and

(B) by substituting "$50,000" for "$10,000".

(2) SEPARATE APPLICATION OF TOTAL PENALTY LIMITATION.—The limitation on the total amount of the penalty under subsection (a) shall be applied separately with respect to disclosures or uses to which this subsection applies and to which it does not apply.

Amendments
- **2019, Taxpayer First Act (P.L. 116-25)**

P.L. 116-25, §2009(a)(1)-(2):

Amended Code Sec. 6713 by redesignating subsections (b) and (c) as subsections (c) and (d), respectively; and by inserting after subsection (a) a new subsection (b). **Effective** for disclosures or uses on or after 7-1-2019.

[Sec. 6713(c)]

(c) EXCEPTIONS.—The rules of section 7216(b) shall apply for purposes of this section.

Amendments
- **2019, Taxpayer First Act (P.L. 116-25)**

P.L. 116-25, §2009(a)(1):

Amended Code Sec. 6713 by redesignating subsections (b) and (c) as subsections (c) and (d), respectively. **Effective** for disclosures or uses on or after 7-1-2019.

[Sec. 6713(d)]

(d) DEFICIENCY PROCEDURES NOT TO APPLY.—Subchapter B of chapter 63 (relating to deficiency procedures for income, estate, gift, and certain excise taxes) shall not apply in respect of the assessment or collection of any penalty imposed by this section.

Amendments
- **2019, Taxpayer First Act (P.L. 116-25)**

P.L. 116-25, §2009(a)(1):

Amended Code Sec. 6713 by redesignating subsection (c) as subsection (d). **Effective** for disclosures or uses on or after 7-1-2019.

- **1989, Omnibus Budget Reconciliation Act of 1989 (P.L. 101-239)**

P.L. 101-239, §7816(v)(1):

Redesignated Code Sec. 6712 as Code Sec. 6713. **Effective** as if included in the provision of P.L. 100-647 to which it relates.

- **1988, Technical and Miscellaneous Revenue Act of 1988 (P.L. 100-647)**

P.L. 100-647, §6242(a):

Amended Part I of subchapter B of chapter 68 by adding Section 6712. **Effective** for disclosures or uses after 12-31-88.

[Sec. 6714]

SEC. 6714. FAILURE TO MEET DISCLOSURE REQUIREMENTS APPLICABLE TO QUID PRO QUO CONTRIBUTIONS.

[Sec. 6714(a)]

(a) IMPOSITION OF PENALTY.—If an organization fails to meet the disclosure requirement of section 6115 with respect to a quid pro quo contribution, such organization shall pay a penalty of $10 for each contribution in respect of which the organization fails to make the required disclosure, except that the total penalty imposed by this subsection with respect to a particular fundraising event or mailing shall not exceed $5,000.

[Sec. 6714(b)]

(b) REASONABLE CAUSE EXCEPTION.—No penalty shall be imposed under this section with respect to any failure if it is shown that such failure is due to reasonable cause.

Amendments
- **1993, Omnibus Budget Reconciliation Act of 1993 (P.L. 103-66)**

P.L. 103-66, §13173(b):

Amended part I of subchapter B of chapter 68 by inserting after Code Sec. 6713 a new Code Sec. 6714. **Effective** for quid pro quo contributions made on or after 1-1-94.

ASSESSABLE PENALTIES

[Sec. 6715]

SEC. 6715. DYED FUEL SOLD FOR USE OR USED IN TAXABLE USE, ETC.

[Sec. 6715(a)]

(a) IMPOSITION OF PENALTY.—If—

(1) any dyed fuel is sold or held for sale by any person for any use which such person knows or has reason to know is not a nontaxable use of such fuel,

(2) any dyed fuel is held for use or used by any person for a use other than a nontaxable use and such person knew, or had reason to know, that such fuel was so dyed,

(3) any person willfully alters, chemically or otherwise, or attempts to so alter, the strength or composition of any dye or marking done pursuant to section 4082 in any dyed fuel, or

(4) any person who has knowledge that a dyed fuel which has been altered as described in paragraph (3) sells or holds for sale such fuel for any use which the person knows or has reason to know is not a nontaxable use of such fuel,

then such person shall pay a penalty in addition to the tax (if any).

Amendments

- **2004, American Jobs Creation Act of 2004 (P.L. 108-357)**

P.L. 108-357, § 856(a):

Amended Code Sec. 6715(a) by striking "or" in paragraph (2), by inserting "or" at the end of paragraph (3), and by inserting after paragraph (3) a new paragraph (4). **Effective** 10-22-2004.

P.L. 108-357, § 856(b):

Amended Code Sec. 6715(a)(3) by striking "alters, or attempts to alter," and inserting "alters, chemically or otherwise, or attempts to so alter,". **Effective** 10-22-2004.

[Sec. 6715(b)]

(b) AMOUNT OF PENALTY.—

(1) IN GENERAL.—Except as provided in paragraph (2), the amount of the penalty under subsection (a) on each act shall be the greater of—
   (A) $1,000, or
   (B) $10 for each gallon of the dyed fuel involved.

(2) MULTIPLE VIOLATIONS.—In determining the penalty under subsection (a) on any person, paragraph (1) shall be applied by increasing the amount in paragraph (1)(A) by the product of such amount and the number of prior penalties (if any) imposed by this section on such person (or a related person or any predecessor of such person or related person).

[Sec. 6715(c)]

(c) DEFINITIONS.—For purposes of this section—

(1) DYED FUEL.—The term "dyed fuel" means any dyed diesel fuel or kerosene, whether or not the fuel was dyed pursuant to section 4082.

(2) NONTAXABLE USE.—The term "nontaxable use" has the meaning given such term by section 4082(b).

Amendments

- **1997, Taxpayer Relief Act of 1997 (P.L. 105-34)**

P.L. 105-34, § 1032(e)(11):

Amended Code Sec. 6715(c)(1) by inserting "or kerosene" after "diesel fuel". **Effective** 7-1-98.

[Sec. 6715(d)]

(d) JOINT AND SEVERAL LIABILITY OF CERTAIN OFFICERS AND EMPLOYEES.—If a penalty is imposed under this section on any business entity, each officer, employee, or agent of such entity who willfully participated in any act giving rise to such penalty shall be jointly and severally liable with such entity for such penalty.

Amendments

- **1996, Small Business Job Protection Act of 1996 (P.L. 104-188)**

P.L. 104-188, § 1703(n)(9)(A):

Redesignated Code Sec. 6714 as Code Sec. 6715. **Effective** as if included in the provision of P.L. 103-66 to which it relates.

P.L. 103-66, § 13242(b)(1):

Amended part I of subchapter B of chapter 68 by adding Code Sec. 6714. **Effective** 1-1-94.

[Sec. 6715(e)]

(e) NO ADMINISTRATIVE APPEAL FOR THIRD AND SUBSEQUENT VIOLATIONS.—In the case of any person who is found to be subject to the penalty under this section after a chemical analysis of such fuel and who has been penalized under this section at least twice after the date of the enactment of this subsection, no administrative appeal or review shall be allowed with respect to such finding except in the case of a claim regarding—

(1) fraud or mistake in the chemical analysis, or

(2) mathematical calculation of the amount of the penalty.

Amendments

- **2004, American Jobs Creation Act of 2004 (P.L. 108-357)**

P.L. 108-357, § 855(a):

Amended Code Sec. 6715 by inserting at the end a new subsection (e). **Effective** for penalties assessed after 10-22-2004.

[Sec. 6715A]

SEC. 6715A. TAMPERING WITH OR FAILING TO MAINTAIN SECURITY REQUIREMENTS FOR MECHANICAL DYE INJECTION SYSTEMS.

[Sec. 6715A(a)]

(a) IMPOSITION OF PENALTY—

(1) TAMPERING.—If any person tampers with a mechanical dye injection system used to indelibly dye fuel for purposes of section 4082, such person shall pay a penalty in addition to the tax (if any).

(2) FAILURE TO MAINTAIN SECURITY REQUIREMENTS.—If any operator of a mechanical dye injection system used to indelibly dye fuel for purposes of section 4082 fails to maintain the security standards for such system as established by the Secretary, then such operator shall pay a penalty in addition to the tax (if any).

[Sec. 6715A(b)]

(b) AMOUNT OF PENALTY.—The amount of the penalty under subsection (a) shall be—

ASSESSABLE PENALTIES

(1) for each violation described in paragraph (1), the greater of—

(A) $25,000, or

(B) $10 for each gallon of fuel involved, and

(2) for each—

(A) failure to maintain security standards described in paragraph (2), $1,000, and

(B) failure to correct a violation described in paragraph (2), $1,000 per day for each day after which such violation was discovered or such person should have reasonably known of such violation.

[Sec. 6715A(c)]

(c) JOINT AND SEVERAL LIABILITY.—

(1) IN GENERAL.—If a penalty is imposed under this section on any business entity, each officer, employee, or agent of such entity or other contracting party who willfully participated in any act giving rise to such penalty shall be jointly and severally liable with such entity for such penalty.

(2) AFFILIATED GROUPS.—If a business entity described in paragraph (1) is part of an affiliated group (as defined in section 1504(a)), the parent corporation of such entity shall be jointly and severally liable with such entity for the penalty imposed under this section.

Amendments

• 2004, American Jobs Creation Act of 2004 (P.L. 108-357)

P.L. 108-357, §854(b), provides:

(b) DYE INJECTOR SECURITY.—Not later than 180 days after the date of the enactment of this Act, the Secretary of the Treasury shall issue regulations regarding mechanical dye injection systems described in the amendment made by subsection (a), and such regulations shall include standards for making such systems tamper resistant.

P.L. 108-357, §854(c)(1):

Amended part I of subchapter B of chapter 68 by adding after Code Sec. 6715 a new Code Sec. 6715A. **Effective** on the 180th day after the date on which the Secretary issues the regulations described in subsection (b), above.

[Sec. 6716—Repealed]

Amendments

• 2013, American Taxpayer Relief Act of 2012 (P.L. 112-240)

P.L. 112-240, §101(a)(1)-(3), provides:

SEC. 101. PERMANENT EXTENSION AND MODIFICATION OF 2001 TAX RELIEF.

(a) PERMANENT EXTENSION.—

(1) IN GENERAL.—The Economic Growth and Tax Relief Reconciliation Act of 2001 is amended by striking title IX.

(2) CONFORMING AMENDMENT.—The Tax Relief, Unemployment Insurance Reauthorization, and Job Creation Act of 2010 is amended by striking section 304.

(3) EFFECTIVE DATE.—The amendments made by this subsection shall apply to taxable, plan, or limitation years beginning after December 31, 2012, and estates of decedents dying, gifts made, or generation skipping transfers after December 31, 2012.

• 2010, Tax Relief, Unemployment Insurance Reauthorization, and Job Creation Act of 2010 (P.L. 111-312)

P.L. 111-312, §301(a):

Amended Code Sec. 6716 to read as such provision would read if subtitle E of title V of the Economic Growth and Tax Relief Reconciliation Act of 2001 (P.L. 107-16) had never been enacted. [P.L. 107-16, §542(b)(4), added new Code Sec. 6716. Therefore, P.L. 111-312, §301(a), effectively repealed Code Sec. 6716.—CCH] **Effective** for estates of decedents dying, and transfers made, after 12-31-2009. For a special rule, see Act Sec. 301(c), below. Prior to amendment by P.L. 111-312, Code Sec. 6716 read as follows:

SEC. 6716. FAILURE TO FILE INFORMATION WITH RESPECT TO CERTAIN TRANSFERS AT DEATH AND GIFTS.

[Sec. 6716(a)]

(a) INFORMATION REQUIRED TO BE FURNISHED TO THE SECRETARY.—Any person required to furnish any information under section 6018 who fails to furnish such information on the date prescribed therefor (determined with regard to any extension of time for filing) shall pay a penalty of $10,000 ($500 in the case of information required to be furnished under section 6018(b)(2)) for each such failure.

[Sec. 6716(b)]

(b) INFORMATION REQUIRED TO BE FURNISHED TO BENEFICIARIES.—Any person required to furnish in writing to each person described in section 6018(e) or 6019(b) the information required under such section who fails to furnish such information shall pay a penalty of $50 for each such failure.

[Sec. 6716(c)]

(c) REASONABLE CAUSE EXCEPTION.—No penalty shall be imposed under subsection (a) or (b) with respect to any failure if it is shown that such failure is due to reasonable cause.

[Sec. 6716(d)]

(d) INTENTIONAL DISREGARD.—If any failure under subsection (a) or (b) is due to intentional disregard of the requirements under sections 6018 and 6019(b), the penalty under such subsection shall be 5 percent of the fair market value (as of the date of death or, in the case of section 6019(b), the date of the gift) of the property with respect to which the information is required.

[Sec. 6716(e)]

(e) DEFICIENCY PROCEDURES NOT TO APPLY.—Subchapter B of chapter 63 (relating to deficiency procedures for income, estate, gift, and certain excise taxes) shall not apply in respect of the assessment or collection of any penalty imposed by this section.

P.L. 111-312, §301(c), provides:

(c) SPECIAL ELECTION WITH RESPECT TO ESTATES OF DECEDENTS DYING IN 2010.—Notwithstanding subsection (a), in the case of an estate of a decedent dying after December 31, 2009, and before January 1, 2011, the executor (within the meaning of section 2203 of the Internal Revenue Code of 1986) may elect to apply such Code as though the amendments made by subsection (a) do not apply with respect to chapter 11 of such Code and with respect to property acquired or passing from such decedent (within the meaning of section 1014(b) of such Code). Such election shall be made at such time and in such manner as the Secretary of the Treasury or the Secretary's delegate shall provide. Such an election once made shall be revocable only with the consent of the Secretary of the Treasury or the Secretary's delegate. For purposes of section 2652(a)(1) of such Code, the determination of whether any property is subject to the tax imposed by such chapter 11 shall be made without regard to any election made under this subsection.

P.L. 111-312, §304, provides [but see P.L. 112-240, §101(a)(2)-(3), above]:

SEC. 304. APPLICATION OF EGTRRA SUNSET TO THIS TITLE.

Section 901 of the Economic Growth and Tax Relief Reconciliation Act of 2001 shall apply to the amendments made by this title.

• 2001, Economic Growth and Tax Relief Reconciliation Act of 2001 (P.L. 107-16)

P.L. 107-16, §542(b)(4):

Amended part I of subchapter B of chapter 68 by adding at the end a new Code Sec. 6716. **Effective** for estates of decedents dying after 12-31-2009.

P.L. 107-16, §901(a)-(b), as amended by P.L. 111-312, §101(a)(1), provides [but see P.L. 112-240, §101(a)(1) and (3), above]:

SEC. 901. SUNSET OF PROVISIONS OF ACT.

(a) IN GENERAL.—All provisions of, and amendments made by, this Act shall not apply—

(1) to taxable, plan, or limitation years beginning after December 31, 2012, or

(2) in the case of title V, to estates of decedents dying, gifts made, or generation skipping transfers, after December 31, 2012.

(b) APPLICATION OF CERTAIN LAWS.—The Internal Revenue Code of 1986 and the Employee Retirement Income Security Act of 1974 shall be applied and administered to years, estates, gifts, and transfers described in subsection (a) as if the provisions and amendments described in subsection (a) had never been enacted.

[Sec. 6717]

SEC. 6717. REFUSAL OF ENTRY.

[Sec. 6717(a)]

(a) IN GENERAL.—In addition to any other penalty provided by law, any person who refuses to admit entry or refuses to permit any other action by the Secretary authorized by section 4083(d)(1) shall pay a penalty of $1,000 for such refusal.

Sec. 6715A(b)(1)

ASSESSABLE PENALTIES

[Sec. 6717(b)]

(b) JOINT AND SEVERAL LIABILITY.—

(1) IN GENERAL.—If a penalty is imposed under this section on any business entity, each officer, employee, or agent of such entity or other contracting party who willfully participated in any act giving rise to such penalty shall be jointly and severally liable with such entity for such penalty.

(2) AFFILIATED GROUPS.—If a business entity described in paragraph (1) is part of an affiliated group (as defined in section 1504(a)), the parent corporation of such entity shall be jointly and severally liable with such entity for the penalty imposed under this section.

[Sec. 6717(c)]

(c) REASONABLE CAUSE EXCEPTION.—No penalty shall be imposed under this section with respect to any failure if it is shown that such failure is due to reasonable cause.

Amendments

• 2004, American Jobs Creation Act of 2004 (P.L. 108-357)

P.L. 108-357, §859(a):

Amended part I of subchapter B of chapter 68, as amended by this Act, by inserting after Code Sec. 6716 a new Code Sec. 6717. **Effective** 1-1-2005.

[Sec. 6718]

SEC. 6718. FAILURE TO DISPLAY TAX REGISTRATION ON VESSELS.

[Sec. 6718(a)]

(a) FAILURE TO DISPLAY REGISTRATION.—Every operator of a vessel who fails to display proof of registration pursuant to section 4101(a)(3) shall pay a penalty of $500 for each such failure. With respect to any vessel, only one penalty shall be imposed by this section during any calendar month.

Amendments

• 2004, American Jobs Creation Act of 2004 (P.L. 108-357)

P.L. 108-357, §862(b):

Amended Code Sec. 6718(a), as added by this Act, by striking "section 4101(a)(2)" and inserting "section 4101(a)(3)". **Effective** 1-1-2005.

[Sec. 6718(b)]

(b) MULTIPLE VIOLATIONS.—In determining the penalty under subsection (a) on any person, subsection (a) shall be applied by increasing the amount in subsection (a) by the product of such amount and the aggregate number of penalties (if any) imposed with respect to prior months by this section on such person (or a related person or any predecessor of such person or related person).

[Sec. 6718(c)]

(c) REASONABLE CAUSE EXCEPTION.—No penalty shall be imposed under this section with respect to any failure if it is shown that such failure is due to reasonable cause.

Amendments

• 2004, American Jobs Creation Act of 2004 (P.L. 108-357)

P.L. 108-357, §861(b)(1):

Amended part I of subchapter B of chapter 68, as amended by this Act, by inserting after Code Sec. 6717 a new Code Sec. 6718. **Effective** for penalties imposed after 12-31-2004.

[Sec. 6719]

SEC. 6719. FAILURE TO REGISTER OR REREGISTER.

[Sec. 6719(a)]

(a) FAILURE TO REGISTER OR REREGISTER.—Every person who is required to register or reregister under section 4101 and fails to do so shall pay a penalty in addition to the tax (if any).

[Sec. 6719(b)]

(b) AMOUNT OF PENALTY.—The amount of the penalty under subsection (a) shall be—

(1) $10,000 for each initial failure to register or reregister, and

(2) $1,000 for each day thereafter such person fails to register or reregister.

[Sec. 6719(c)]

(c) REASONABLE CAUSE EXCEPTION.—No penalty shall be imposed under this section with respect to any failure if it is shown that such failure is due to reasonable cause.

Amendments

• 2005, Safe, Accountable, Flexible, Efficient Transportation Equity Act: A Legacy for Users (P.L. 109-59)

P.L. 109-59, §11164(b)(1)(A)-(C):

Amended Code Sec. 6719 by inserting "or reregister" after "register" each place it appears, by inserting "OR REREGISTER" after "REGISTER" in the heading for subsection (a), and by inserting "OR REREGISTER" after "REGISTER" in the heading thereof. **Effective** for actions, or failures to act, after 8-10-2005.

• 2004, American Jobs Creation Act of 2004 (P.L. 108-357)

P.L. 108-357, §863(c)(1):

Amended part I of subchapter B of chapter 68, as amended by this Act, by inserting after Code Sec. 6718 a new Code Sec. 6719. **Effective** for penalties imposed after 12-31-2004.

[Sec. 6720]

SEC. 6720. FRAUDULENT ACKNOWLEDGMENTS WITH RESPECT TO DONATIONS OF MOTOR VEHICLES, BOATS, AND AIRPLANES.

Any donee organization required under section 170(f)(12)(A) to furnish a contemporaneous written acknowledgment to a donor which knowingly furnishes a false or fraudulent acknowledgment, or which knowingly fails to furnish such acknowledgment in the manner, at the time, and showing the information required under section 170(f)(12), or regulations prescribed thereunder, shall for each such act, or for each such failure, be subject to a penalty equal to—

(1) in the case of an acknowledgment with respect to a qualified vehicle to which section 170(f)(12)(A)(ii) applies, the greater of—

(A) the product of the highest rate of tax specified in section 1 and the sales price stated on the acknowledgment, or

ASSESSABLE PENALTIES

    (B) the gross proceeds from the sale of such vehicle, and
  (2) in the case of an acknowledgment with respect to any other qualified vehicle to which section 170(f)(12) applies, the greater of—
    (A) the product of the highest rate of tax specified in section 1 and the claimed value of the vehicle, or
    (B) $5,000.

Amendments

• **2004, American Jobs Creation Act of 2004 (P.L. 108-357)**

P.L. 108-357, § 884(b)(1):

Amended part I of subchapter B of chapter 68, as amended by this Act, by inserting after Code Sec. 6719 a new Code Sec. 6720. **Effective** for contributions made after 12-31-2004.

[Sec. 6720A]

SEC. 6720A. PENALTY WITH RESPECT TO CERTAIN ADULTERATED FUELS.

[Sec. 6720A(a)]

  (a) IN GENERAL.—Any person who knowingly transfers for resale, sells for resale, or holds out for resale any liquid for use in a diesel-powered highway vehicle or a diesel-powered train which does not meet applicable EPA regulations (as defined in section 45H(c)(3)), shall pay a penalty of $10,000 for each such transfer, sale, or holding out for resale, in addition to the tax on such liquid (if any).

[Sec. 6720A(b)]

  (b) PENALTY IN THE CASE OF RETAILERS.—Any person who knowingly holds out for sale (other than for resale) any liquid described in subsection (a), shall pay a penalty of $10,000 for each such holding out for sale, in addition to the tax on such liquid (if any).

Amendments

• **2005, Safe, Accountable, Flexible, Efficient Transportation Equity Act: A Legacy for Users (P.L. 109-59)**

P.L. 109-59, § 11167(a):

Amended part I of subchapter B of chapter 68 by adding at the end a new Code Sec. 6720A. **Effective** for any transfer, sale, or holding out for sale or resale occurring after 8-10-2005.

[Sec. 6720B]

SEC. 6720B. FRAUDULENT IDENTIFICATION OF EXEMPT USE PROPERTY.

In addition to any criminal penalty provided by law, any person who identifies applicable property (as defined in section 170(e)(7)(C)) as having a use which is related to a purpose or function constituting the basis for the donee's exemption under section 501 and who knows that such property is not intended for such a use shall pay a penalty of $10,000.

Amendments

• **2006, Pension Protection Act of 2006 (P.L. 109-280)**

P.L. 109-280, § 1215(c)(1):

Amended part I of subchapter B of chapter 68 by inserting after Code Sec. 6720A a new Code Sec. 6720B. **Effective** for identifications made after 8-17-2006.

[Sec. 6720C]

SEC. 6720C. PENALTY FOR FAILURE TO NOTIFY HEALTH PLAN OF CESSATION OF ELIGIBILITY FOR CONTINUATION COVERAGE PREMIUM ASSISTANCE.

[Sec. 6720C(a)]

  (a) IN GENERAL.—Except in the case of a failure described in subsection (b) or (c), any person required to notify a group health plan under section 9501(a)(2)(B) of the American Rescue Plan Act of 2021 who fails to make such a notification at such time and in such manner as the Secretary of Labor may require shall pay a penalty of $250 for each such failure.

[Sec. 6720C(b)]

  (b) INTENTIONAL FAILURE.—In the case of any such failure that is fraudulent, such person shall pay a penalty equal to the greater of—
    (1) $250, or
    (2) 110 percent of the premium assistance provided under section 9501(a)(1)(A) of the American Rescue Plan Act of 2021 after termination of eligibility under such section.

[Sec. 6720C(c)]

  (c) REASONABLE CAUSE EXCEPTION.—No penalty shall be imposed under this section with respect to any failure if it is shown that such failure is due to reasonable cause and not to willful neglect.

Amendments

• **2021, American Rescue Plan Act of 2021 (P.L. 117-2)**

P.L. 117-2, § 9501(b)(2)(A):

Amended part I of subchapter B of chapter 68 by adding at the end a new Code Sec. 6720C. **Effective** 3-11-2021.

[Sec. 6720C—Stricken]

Amendments

• **2018, Tax Technical Corrections Act of 2018 (P.L. 115-141)**

P.L. 115-141, § 401(d)(7)(B), Div. U:

Amended part I of subchapter B of chapter 68 by striking Code Sec. 6720C. **Effective** 3-23-2018. For a special rule, see Act Sec. 401(e), Div. U, below. Prior to being stricken, Code Sec. 6720C read as follows:

SEC. 6720C. PENALTY FOR FAILURE TO NOTIFY HEALTH PLAN OF CESSATION OF ELIGIBILITY FOR COBRA PREMIUM ASSISTANCE.

[Sec. 6720C(a)]

  (a) IN GENERAL.—Any person required to notify a group health plan under section 3001(a)(2)(C) of title III of division B of the American Recovery and Reinvestment Act of 2009 who fails to make such a notification at such time and in such manner as the Secretary of Labor may require shall pay a penalty of 110 percent of the premium reduction provided under such section after termination of eligibility under such subsection.

Amendments

• **2010, Temporary Extension Act of 2010 (P.L. 111-144)**

P.L. 111-144, § 3(b)(5)(D):

Amended Code Sec. 6720C(a) by striking "section 3002(a)(2)(C) of the Health Insurance Assistance for the Unemployed Act of 2009" and inserting "section 3001(a)(2)(C) of title III of division B of the American Recovery and Reinvestment Act of 2009". **Effective** as if included in the provision of section 3001 of division B of the American Recovery and Reinvestment Act of 2009 to which it relates [**effective** for failures occurring after 2-17-2009.—CCH].

ASSESSABLE PENALTIES

[Sec. 6720C(b)]

(b) REASONABLE CAUSE EXCEPTION.—No penalty shall be imposed under subsection (a) with respect to any failure if it is shown that such failure is due to reasonable cause and not to willful neglect.

Amendments

• **2009, American Recovery and Reinvestment Tax Act of 2009 (P.L. 111-5)**

P.L. 111-5, § 3001(a)(13)(A):

Amended part I of subchapter B of chapter 68 by adding at the end a new Code Sec. 6720C. **Effective** for failures occurring after 2-17-2009.

P.L. 115-141, § 401(e), Div. U, provides:

(e) GENERAL SAVINGS PROVISION WITH RESPECT TO DEADWOOD PROVISIONS.—If—

(1) any provision amended or repealed by the amendments made by subsection (b) or (d) applied to—

(A) any transaction occurring before the date of the enactment of this Act,

(B) any property acquired before such date of enactment, or

(C) any item of income, loss, deduction, or credit taken into account before such date of enactment, and

(2) the treatment of such transaction, property, or item under such provision would (without regard to the amendments or repeals made by such subsection) affect the liability for tax for periods ending after such date of enactment,

nothing in the amendments or repeals made by this section shall be construed to affect the treatment of such transaction, property, or item for purposes of determining liability for tax for periods ending after such date of enactment.

PART II—FAILURE TO COMPLY WITH CERTAIN INFORMATION REPORTING REQUIREMENTS

Sec. 6721.	Failure to file correct information returns.
Sec. 6722.	Failure to furnish correct payee statements.
Sec. 6723.	Failure to comply with other information reporting requirements.
Sec. 6724.	Waiver; definitions and special rules.
Sec. 6725.	Failure to report information under section 4101.

[Sec. 6721]

SEC. 6721. FAILURE TO FILE CORRECT INFORMATION RETURNS.

[Sec. 6721(a)]

(a) IMPOSITION OF PENALTY.—

(1) IN GENERAL.—In the case of a failure described in paragraph (2) by any person with respect to an information return, such person shall pay a penalty of $250 for each return with respect to which such a failure occurs, but the total amount imposed on such person for all such failures during any calendar year shall not exceed $3,000,000.

(2) FAILURES SUBJECT TO PENALTY.—For purposes of paragraph (1), the failures described in this paragraph are—

(A) any failure to file an information return with the Secretary on or before the required filing date, and

(B) any failure to include all of the information required to be shown on the return or the inclusion of incorrect information.

Amendments

• **2015, Trade Preferences Extension Act of 2015 (P.L. 114-27)**

P.L. 114-27, § 806(a)(1)-(2):

Amended Code Sec. 6721(a)(1) by striking "$100" and inserting "$250"; and by striking "$1,500,000" and inserting "$3,000,000". **Effective** with respect to returns and statements required to be filed after 12-31-2015.

• **2010, Creating Small Business Jobs Act of 2010 (P.L. 111-240)**

P.L. 111-240, § 2102(a)(1) (as amended by P.L. 113-295, § 207(a)(1), Division A):

Amended Code Sec. 6721(a)(1) by striking "$50" and inserting "$100". **Effective** with respect to information returns required to be filed, and payee statements required to be furnished, on or after 1-1-2011.

P.L. 111-240, § 2102(a)(2) (as amended by P.L. 113-295, § 207(a)(1), Division A):

Amended Code Sec. 6721(a)(1) by striking "$250,000" and inserting "$1,500,000". **Effective** with respect to information returns required to be filed, and payee statements required to be furnished, on or after 1-1-2011.

[Sec. 6721(b)]

(b) REDUCTION WHERE CORRECTION IN SPECIFIED PERIOD.—

(1) CORRECTION WITHIN 30 DAYS.—If any failure described in subsection (a)(2) is corrected on or before the day 30 days after the required filing date—

(A) the penalty imposed by subsection (a) shall be $50 in lieu of $250, and

(B) the total amount imposed on the person for all such failures during any calendar year which are so corrected shall not exceed $500,000.

(2) FAILURES CORRECTED ON OR BEFORE AUGUST 1.—If any failure described in subsection (a)(2) is corrected after the 30th day referred to in paragraph (1) but on or before August 1 of the calendar year in which the required filing date occurs—

(A) the penalty imposed by subsection (a) shall be $100 in lieu of $250, and

(B) the total amount imposed on the person for all such failures during the calendar year which are so corrected shall not exceed $1,500,000.

Amendments

• **2015, Trade Preferences Extension Act of 2015 (P.L. 114-27)**

P.L. 114-27, § 806(b)(1)(A)-(C):

Amended Code Sec. 6721(b)(1) by striking "$30" and inserting "$50"; by striking "$100" and inserting "$250"; and by striking "$250,000" and inserting "$500,000". **Effective** with respect to returns and statements required to be filed after 12-31-2015.

P.L. 114-27, § 806(b)(2)(A)-(C):

Amended Code Sec. 6721(b)(2) by striking "$60" and inserting "$100"; by striking "$100" (prior to amendment by Act Sec. 806(b)(2)(A)) and inserting "$250"; and by striking "$500,000" and inserting "$1,500,000". **Effective** with respect to returns and statements required to be filed after 12-31-2015.

• **2010, Creating Small Business Jobs Act of 2010 (P.L. 111-240)**

P.L. 111-240, § 2102(a)(1) (as amended by P.L. 113-295, § 207(a)(1), Division A):

Amended Code Sec. 6721(b)(1)(A) and (2)(A) by striking "$50" and inserting "$100". **Effective** with respect to information returns required to be filed, and payee statements required to be furnished, on or after 1-1-2011.

P.L. 111-240, § 2102(b)(1) (as amended by P.L. 113-295, § 207(a)(1), Division A):

Amended Code Sec. 6721(b)(1)(A) by striking "$15" and inserting "$30". **Effective** with respect to information returns required to be filed, and payee statements required to be furnished, on or after 1-1-2011.

P.L. 111-240, § 2102(b)(2) (as amended by P.L. 113-295, § 207(a)(1), Division A):

Amended Code Sec. 6721(b)(1)(B) by striking "$75,000" and inserting "$250,000". **Effective** with respect to information returns required to be filed, and payee statements required to be furnished, on or after 1-1-2011.

P.L. 111-240, § 2102(c)(1) (as amended by P.L. 113-295, § 207(a)(1), Division A):

Amended Code Sec. 6721(b)(2)(A) by striking "$30" and inserting "$60". **Effective** with respect to information returns required to be filed, and payee statements required to be furnished, on or after 1-1-2011.

P.L. 111-240, § 2102(c)(2) (as amended by P.L. 113-295, § 207(a)(1), Division A):

Amended Code Sec. 6721(b)(2)(B) by striking "$150,000" and inserting "$500,000". **Effective** with respect to information returns required to be filed, and payee statements required to be furnished, on or after 1-1-2011.

[Sec. 6721(c)]

(c) EXCEPTIONS FOR CERTAIN DE MINIMIS FAILURES.—

(1) EXCEPTION FOR DE MINIMIS FAILURE TO INCLUDE ALL REQUIRED INFORMATION.—If—

(A) an information return is filed with the Secretary,

ASSESSABLE PENALTIES

(B) there is a failure described in subsection (a)(2)(B) (determined after the application of section 6724(a)) with respect to such return, and

(C) such failure is corrected on or before August 1 of the calendar year in which the required filing date occurs,

for purposes of this section, such return shall be treated as having been filed with all of the correct required information.

(2) LIMITATION.—The number of information returns to which paragraph (1) applies for any calendar year shall not exceed the greater of—

(A) 10, or

(B) one-half of 1 percent of the total number of information returns required to be filed by the person during the calendar year.

(3) SAFE HARBOR FOR CERTAIN DE MINIMIS ERRORS.—

(A) IN GENERAL.—If, with respect to an information return filed with the Secretary—

(i) there are 1 or more failures described in subsection (a)(2)(B) relating to an incorrect dollar amount,

(ii) no single amount in error differs from the correct amount by more than $100, and

(iii) no single amount reported for tax withheld on the information return differs from the correct amount by more than $25,

then no correction shall be required and, for purposes of this section, such return shall be treated as having been filed with all of the correct required information.

(B) EXCEPTION.—Subparagraph (A) shall not apply with respect to any incorrect dollar amount to the extent that such error relates to an amount with respect to which an election is made under section 6722(c)(3)(B).

(C) REGULATORY AUTHORITY.—The Secretary may issue regulations to prevent the abuse of the safe harbor under this paragraph, including regulations providing that this paragraph shall not apply to the extent necessary to prevent any such abuse.

Amendments

- **2018, Tax Technical Corrections Act of 2018 (P.L. 115-141)**

P.L. 115-141, §101(f)(2), Div. U:

Amended Code Sec. 6721(c)(3)(A) by striking "any information return" and inserting "the information return". **Effective** as if included in the provision of the Protecting Americans from Tax Hikes Act of 2015 to which it relates [effective for returns required to be filed, and payee statements required to be furnished, after 12-31-2016.—CCH].

- **2015, Protecting Americans from Tax Hikes Act of 2015 (P.L. 114-113)**

P.L. 114-113, §202(a), Div. Q:

Amended Code Sec. 6721(c) by adding at the end a new paragraph (3). **Effective** for returns required to be filed, and payee statements required to be furnished, after 12-31-2016 [effective date changed by P.L. 115-141, §101(f)(3), Div. U.—CCH].

P.L. 114-113, §202(d)(1), Div. Q:

Amended Code Sec. 6721(c) by striking "EXCEPTION FOR DE MINIMIS FAILURES TO INCLUDE ALL REQUIRED INFORMATION" in the heading and inserting "EXCEPTIONS FOR CERTAIN DE MINIMIS FAILURES". **Effective** for returns required to be filed, and payee statements required to be furnished, after 12-31-2016 [effective date changed by P.L. 115-141, §101(f)(3), Div. U.—CCH].

P.L. 114-113, §202(d)(2), Div. Q:

Amended Code Sec. 6721(c)(1) by striking "IN GENERAL" in the heading and inserting "EXCEPTION FOR DE MINIMIS FAILURE TO INCLUDE ALL REQUIRED INFORMATION". **Effective** for returns required to be filed, and payee statements required to be furnished, after 12-31-2016 [effective date changed by P.L. 115-141, §101(f)(3), Div. U.—CCH].

[Sec. 6721(d)]

(d) LOWER LIMITATIONS FOR PERSONS WITH GROSS RECEIPTS OF NOT MORE THAN $5,000,000.—

(1) IN GENERAL.—If any person meets the gross receipts test of paragraph (2) with respect to any calendar year, with respect to failures during such calendar year—

(A) subsection (a)(1) shall be applied by substituting "$1,000,000" for "$3,000,000",

(B) subsection (b)(1)(B) shall be applied by substituting "$175,000" for "$500,000", and

(C) subsection (b)(2)(B) shall be applied by substituting "$500,000" for "$1,500,000".

(2) GROSS RECEIPTS TEST.—

(A) IN GENERAL.—A person meets the gross receipts test of this paragraph for any calendar year if the average annual gross receipts of such person for the most recent 3 taxable years ending before such calendar year do not exceed $5,000,000.

(B) CERTAIN RULES MADE APPLICABLE.—For purposes of subparagraph (A), the rules of paragraphs (2) and (3) of section 448(c) shall apply.

Amendments

- **2015, Trade Preferences Extension Act of 2015 (P.L. 114-27)**

P.L. 114-27, §806(c)(1)-(3):

Amended Code Sec. 6721(d)(1) in subparagraph (A) by striking "$500,000" and inserting "$1,000,000"; and by striking "$1,500,000" and inserting "$3,000,000"; in subparagraph (B) by striking "$75,000" and inserting "$175,000"; and by striking "$250,000" and inserting "$500,000"; and in subparagraph (C) by striking "$200,000" and inserting "$500,000"; and by striking "$500,000" (prior to amendment by Act Sec. 806(b)(3)(A)) and inserting "$1,500,000". **Effective** with respect to returns and statements required to be filed after 12-31-2015.

- **2010, Creating Small Business Jobs Act of 2010 (P.L. 111-240)**

P.L. 111-240, §2102(a)(2) (as amended by P.L. 113-295, §207(a)(1), Division A):

Amended Code Sec. 6721(d)(1)(A) by striking "$250,000" and inserting "$1,500,000". **Effective** with respect to information returns required to be filed, and payee statements required to be furnished, on or after 1-1-2011.

P.L. 111-240, §2102(b)(2) (as amended by P.L. 113-295, §207(a)(1), Division A):

Amended Code Sec. 6721(d)(1)(B) by striking "$75,000" and inserting "$250,000". **Effective** with respect to information returns required to be filed, and payee statements required to be furnished, on or after 1-1-2011.

P.L. 111-240, §2102(c)(2) (as amended by P.L. 113-295, §207(a)(1), Division A):

Amended Code Sec. 6721(d)(1)(C) by striking "$150,000" and inserting "$500,000". **Effective** with respect to information returns required to be filed, and payee statements required to be furnished, on or after 1-1-2011.

P.L. 111-240, §2102(d)(1)(A)-(C) (as amended by P.L. 113-295, §207(a)(1), Division A):

Amended Code Sec. 6721(d)(1) by striking "$100,000" in subparagraph (A) and inserting "$500,000", by striking "$25,000" in subparagraph (B) and inserting "$75,000", and by striking "$50,000" in subparagraph (C) and inserting "$200,000". **Effective** with respect to information returns required to be filed, and payee statements required to be furnished, on or after 1-1-2011.

P.L. 111-240, §2102(d)(2) (as amended by P.L. 113-295, §207(a)(1), Division A):

Amended Code Sec. 6721(d)(1) by striking "such taxable year" and inserting "such calendar year". **Effective** with respect to information returns required to be filed, and payee statements required to be furnished, on or after 1-1-2011.

[Sec. 6721(e)]

(e) PENALTY IN CASE OF INTENTIONAL DISREGARD.—If 1 or more failures described in subsection (a)(2) are due to intentional disregard of the filing requirement (or the correct information reporting requirement), then, with respect to each such failure—

(1) subsections (b), (c), and (d) shall not apply,

(2) the penalty imposed under subsection (a) shall be $500, or, if greater—

(A) in the case of a return other than a return required under section 6045(a), 6041A(b), 6050H, 6050I, 6050J, 6050K, or 6050L, 10 percent of the aggregate amount of the items required to be reported correctly,

(B) in the case of a return required to be filed by section 6045(a), 6050K, or 6050L, 5 percent of the aggregate amount of the items required to be reported correctly,

(C) in the case of a return required to be filed under section 6050I(a) with respect to any transaction (or related transactions), the greater of—

ASSESSABLE PENALTIES

(i) $25,000, or

(ii) the amount of cash (within the meaning of section 6050I(d)) received in such transaction (or related transactions) to the extent the amount of such cash does not exceed $100,000, or

(D) in the case of a return required to be filed under section 6050V, 10 percent of the value of the benefit of any contract with respect to which information is required to be included on the return, and

(3) in the case of any penalty determined under paragraph (2)—

(A) the $3,000,000 limitation under subsection (a) shall not apply, and

(B) such penalty shall not be taken into account in applying such limitation (or any similar limitation under subsection (b)) to penalties not determined under paragraph (2).

Amendments

- **2015, Trade Preferences Extension Act of 2015 (P.L. 114-27)**

P.L. 114-27, §806(d)(1)-(2):

Amended Code Sec. 6721(e) by striking "$250" in paragraph (2) and inserting "$500"; and by striking "$1,500,000" in paragraph (3)(A) and inserting "$3,000,000". **Effective** with respect to returns and statements required to be filed after 12-31-2015.

- **2010, Creating Small Business Jobs Act of 2010 (P.L. 111-240)**

P.L. 111-240, §2102(a)(2) (as amended by P.L. 113-295, §207(a)(1), Division A):

Amended Code Sec. 6721(e)(3)(A) by striking "$250,000" and inserting "$1,500,000". **Effective** with respect to information returns required to be filed, and payee statements required to be furnished, on or after 1-1-2011.

P.L. 111-240, §2102(e) (as amended by P.L. 113-295, §207(a)(1), Division A):

Amended Code Sec. 6721(e)(2) by striking "$100" and inserting "$250". **Effective** with respect to information returns required to be filed, and payee statements required to be furnished, on or after 1-1-2011.

- **2006, Pension Protection Act of 2006 (P.L. 109-280)**

P.L. 109-280, §1211(b)(2):

Amended Code Sec. 6721(e)(2) by striking "or" at the end of subparagraph (B), by striking "and" at the end of subparagraph (C) and inserting "or", and by adding at the end a new subparagraph (D). **Effective** for acquisitions of contracts after 8-17-2006.

- **1990, Omnibus Budget Reconciliation Act of 1990 (P.L. 101-508)**

P.L. 101-508, §11318(b)(1):

Amended Code Sec. 6721(e)(2)(A) by inserting "6050I," after "6050H,". **Effective** for amounts received after 11-5-90.

P.L. 101-508, §11318(b)(2):

Amended Code Sec. 6721(e)(2)(A) by striking "or" at the end. **Effective** for amounts received after 11-5-90.

P.L. 101-508, §11318(b)(3):

Amended Code Sec. 6721(e)(2)(B) by striking "and" and inserting "or". **Effective** for amounts received after 11-5-90.

P.L. 101-508, §11318(b)(4):

Amended Code Sec. 6721(e)(2) by inserting after subparagraph (B) a new subparagraph (C). **Effective** for amounts received after 11-5-90.

- **1989, Omnibus Budget Reconciliation Act of 1989 (P.L. 101-239)**

P.L. 101-239, §7711(a):

Amended Part II of subchapter B of chapter 68. **Effective** for returns and statements the due date for which (determined without regard to extensions) is after 12-31-89. Prior to amendment, Part II of subchapter B of chapter 68 read as follows:

PART II—FAILURE TO FILE CERTAIN INFORMATION RETURNS OR STATEMENTS

SEC. 6721. FAILURE TO FILE CERTAIN INFORMATION RETURNS.

[Sec. 6721(a)]

(a) GENERAL RULE.—In the case of each failure to file an information return with the Secretary on the date prescribed therefor (determined with regard to any extension of time for filing), the person failing to so file such return shall pay $50 for each such failure, but the total amount imposed on such person for all such failures during any calendar year shall not exceed $100,000.

[Sec. 6721(b)]

(b) PENALTY IN CASE OF INTENTIONAL DISREGARD.—If 1 or more failures to which subsection (a) applies are due to intentional disregard of the filing requirement, then, with respect to each such failure—

(1) the penalty imposed under subsection (a) shall be $100, or, if greater—

(A) in the case of a return other than a return required under section 6045(a), 6041A(b), 6050H, 6050J, 6050K, or 6050L, 10 percent of the aggregate amount of the items required to be reported (or, if greater, in the case of a return filed under Section 6050I, 10 percent of the taxable income derived from the transaction), or

(B) in the case of a return required to be filed by section 6045(a), 6050K, or 6050L, 5 percent of the aggregate amount of the items required to be reported, and

(2) in the case of any penalty determined under paragraph (1)—

(A) the $100,000 limitation under subsection (a) shall not apply, and

(B) such penalty shall not be taken into account in applying the $100,000 limitation to penalties not determined under paragraph (1).

Amendments

- **1988, Anti-Drug Abuse Act of 1988 (P.L. 100-690)**

P.L. 100-690, §7601 (a)(2)(A):

Amended Code Sec. 6721(b)(1)(A) by inserting "(or, if greater, in the case of a return filed under Section 6050I, 10 percent of the taxable income derived from the transaction)" after "reported". **Effective** for actions after 11-18-88.

- **1986, Tax Reform Act of 1986 (P.L. 99-514)**

P.L. 99-514, §1501(a):

Amended subchapter B of chapter 68 by adding new Code Sec. 6721. **Effective** for returns the due date for which (determined without regard to extensions) is after 12-31-86.

[Sec. 6722]

SEC. 6722. FAILURE TO FURNISH CERTAIN PAYEE STATEMENTS.

[Sec. 6722(a)]

(a) GENERAL RULE.—In the case of each failure to furnish a payee statement on the date prescribed therefor to the person to whom such statement is required to be furnished, the person failing to so furnish such statement shall pay $50 for each such failure, but the total amount imposed on such person for all such failures during any calendar year shall not exceed $100,000.

[Sec. 6722(b)]

(b) FAILURE TO NOTIFY PARTNERSHIP OF EXCHANGE OF PARTNERSHIP INTEREST.—In the case of any person who fails to furnish the notice required by section 6050K(c)(1) on the date prescribed therefor, such person shall pay a penalty of $50 for each such failure.

Amendments

- **1986, Tax Reform Act of 1986 (P.L. 99-514)**

P.L. 99-514, §1501(a):

Amended subchapter B of chapter 68 by adding new Code Sec. 6722. **Effective** for returns the due date for which (determined without regard to extensions) is after 12-31-86.

[Sec. 6723]

SEC. 6723. FAILURE TO INCLUDE CORRECT INFORMATION.

[Sec. 6723(a)]

(a) GENERAL RULE.—If—

(1) any person files an information return or furnishes a payee statement, and

(2) such person does not include all of the information required to be shown on such return or statement or includes incorrect information,

such person shall pay $5 for each return or statement with respect to which such failure occurs, but the total amount imposed on such person for all such failures during any calendar year shall not exceed $20,000.

[Sec. 6723(b)]

(b) PENALTY IN CASE OF INTENTIONAL DISREGARD.—If 1 or more failures to which subsection (a) applies are due to intentional disregard of the correct information reporting requirement, then, with respect to each such failure—

(1) the penalty imposed under subsection (a) shall be $100, or, if greater—

(A) in the case of a return other than a return required under section 6045(a), 6041A(b), 6050H, 6050J, 6050K, or 6050L, 10 percent of the aggregate amount of the items required to be reported correctly, or

(B) in the case of a return required to be filed by section 6045(a), 6050K, or 6050L, 5 percent of the aggregate amount of the items required to be reported correctly, and

(2) in the case of any penalty determined under paragraph (1)—

(A) the $20,000 limitation under subsection (a) shall not apply, and

(B) such penalty shall not be taken into account in applying the $20,000 limitation to penalties not determined under paragraph (1).

[Sec. 6723(c)]

(c) COORDINATION WITH SECTION 6676.—No penalty shall be imposed under subsection (a) or (b) with respect to any return or statement if a penalty is imposed under section 6676 (relating to failure to supply identifying number) with respect to such return or statement.

Amendments

- **1986, Tax Reform Act of 1986 (P.L. 99-514)**

P.L. 99-514, §1501(a):

Amended subchapter B of chapter 68 by adding new Code Sec. 6723. **Effective** for returns the due date for which (determined without regard to extensions) is after 12-31-86.

[Sec. 6724]

SEC. 6724. WAIVER; DEFINITIONS AND SPECIAL RULES.

[Sec. 6724(a)]

(a) REASONABLE CAUSE WAIVER.—No penalty shall be imposed under this part with respect to any failure if it is shown that such failure is due to reasonable cause and not to willful neglect.

[Sec. 6724(b)]

(b) PAYMENT OF PENALTY.—Any penalty imposed by this part shall be paid on notice and demand by the Secretary and in the same manner as tax.

[Sec. 6724(c)]

(c) SPECIAL RULES FOR FAILURE TO FILE INTEREST AND DIVIDEND RETURNS OR STATEMENTS.—

ASSESSABLE PENALTIES

(1) HIGHER STANDARDS FOR WAIVER.—In the case of any interest or dividend return or statement—

(A) subsection (a) shall not apply, but

(B) no penalty shall be imposed under this part if it is shown that the person otherwise liable for such penalty exercised due diligence in attempting to satisfy the requirement with respect to such return or statement.

(2) LIMITATIONS NOT TO APPLY.—In the case of any interest or dividend return or statement—

(A) the $100,000 limitations of sections 6721(a) and 6722(a) and the $20,000 limitation of section 6723(a) shall not apply (and any penalty imposed on any failure involving such a return or statement shall not be taken into account in applying such limitations to other penalties), and

(B) penalties imposed with respect to such returns or statements shall not be taken into account for purposes of applying such limitations with respect to other returns or statements.

(3) SELF ASSESSMENT.—Any penalty imposed under this part on any person with respect to an interest or dividend return or statement—

(A) shall be assessed and collected in the same manner as an excise tax imposed by subtitle D, and

(B) shall be due and payable on April 1 of the calendar year following the calendar year for which such return or statement is required.

(4) DEFICIENCY PROCEDURES NOT TO APPLY.—Subchapter B of chapter 63 (relating to deficiency procedures for income, estate, gift, and certain excise taxes) shall not apply in respect of the assessment or collection of any penalty imposed under this part with respect to an interest or dividend return or statement.

(5) INTEREST OR DIVIDEND RETURN OR STATEMENT.—For purposes of this subsection, the term "interest or dividend return or statement" means—

(A) any return required by section 6042(a)(1), 6044(a)(1), or 6049(a), and

(B) any statement required under section 6042(c), 6044(e), or 6049(c).

[Sec. 6724(d)]

(d) DEFINITIONS.—For purposes of this part—

(1) INFORMATION RETURN.—The term "information return" means—

(A) any statement of the amount of payments to another person required by—

(i) section 6041(a) or (b) (relating to certain information at source),

(ii) section 6042(a)(1) (relating to payments of dividends),

(iii) section 6044(a)(1) (relating to payments of patronage dividends),

(iv) section 6049(a) (relating to payments of interest),

(v) section 6050A(a) (relating to reporting requirements of certain fishing boat operators),

(vi) section 6050N(a) (relating to payments of royalties), or

(vii) section 6051(d) (relating to information returns with respect to income tax withheld), and

(B) any return required by—

(i) section 6041A(a) or (b) (relating to returns of direct sellers),

(ii) section 6045(a) or (d) (relating to returns of brokers),

(iii) section 6050H(a) (relating to mortgage interest received in trade or business from individuals),

(iv) section 6050I(a) (relating to cash received in trade or business),

(v) section 6050J(a) (relating to foreclosures and abandonments of security),

(vi) section 6050K(a) (relating to exchanges of certain partnership interests),

(vii) section 6050L(a) (relating to returns relating to certain dispositions of donated property),

(viii) section 6052(a) (relating to reporting payment of wages in the form of group-term life insurance),

(ix) section 6053(c)(1) (relating to reporting with respect to certain tips),

(x) section 1060(b) (relating to reporting requirements of transferors and transferees in certain asset acquisitions), or

(xi) subparagraph (A) or (C) of subsection (c)(4), or subsection (e), of section 4093 (relating to information reporting with respect to tax on diesel and aviation fuel).

(2) PAYEE STATEMENT.—The term "payee statement" means any statement required to be furnished under—

(A) section 6031(b) or (c), 6034A, or 6037(b) (relating to statements furnished by certain pass-thru entities),

(B) section 6039(a) (relating to information required in connection with certain options),

(C) section 6041(d) (relating to information at source),

(D) section 6041A(e) (relating to returns regarding payments of remuneration for services and direct sales),

(E) section 6042(c) (relating to returns regarding payments of dividends and corporate earnings and profits),

(F) section 6044(e) (relating to returns regarding payments of patronage dividends),

(G) section 6045(b) or (d) (relating to returns of brokers),

(H) section 6049(c) (relating to returns regarding payments of interest),

(I) section 6050A(b) (relating to reporting requirements of certain fishing boat operators),

(J) section 6050H(d) (relating to returns relating to mortgage interest received in trade or business from individuals),

(K) section 6050I(e) (relating to returns relating to cash received in trade or business),

(L) section 6050J(e) (relating to returns relating to foreclosures and abandonments of security),

(M) section 6050K(b) (relating to returns relating to exchanges of certain partnership interests),

(N) section 6050L(c) (relating to returns relating to certain dispositions of donated property),

(O) section 6050N(b) (relating to returns regarding payments of royalties),

(P) section 6051 (relating to receipts for employees),

(Q) section 6052(b) (relating to returns regarding payment of wages in the form of group-term life insurance),

(R) section 6053(b) or (c) (relating to reports of tips), or

(S) section 4093(c)(4)(B) (relating to certain purchasers of diesel and aviation fuels).

Amendments

• **1989, Omnibus Budget Reconciliation Act of 1989 (P.L. 101-239)**

P.L. 101-239, §7811(c)(3):

Amended Code Sec. 6724(d)(1)(B), prior to amendment by Act Sec. 7711(a), by striking clause (viii) and all that follows and inserting new clauses (viii)-(xi). **Effective** as if included in the provision of P.L. 100-647 to which it relates. Prior to amendment, Code Sec. 6724(d)(1)(B)(viii)-(xi) read as follows:

(viii) section 6052(a) (relating to reporting payment of wages in the form of group-term life insurance),

(ix) section 6053(c)(1) (relating to reporting with respect to certain tips),

(xi)[x] section 1060(b) (relating to reporting requirements of transferors and transferees in certain asset acquisitions), or

(xi) subparagraph (A) or (C) of subsection (c)(4), or subsection (d), of section 4093 (relating to information reporting with respect to tax on diesel and aviation fuels).

P.L. 101-239, §7813(a):

Amended Code Sec. 6724(d)(2), prior to amendment by Act Sec. 7711(a), by redesignating subparagraph (U) as subparagraph (S), by striking "or" at the end of subparagraph (Q), and by striking the period at the end of subparagraph (R) and inserting ", or ". **Effective** as if included in the provision of P.L. 100-647 to which it relates.

• **1988, Technical and Miscellaneous Revenue Act of 1988 (P.L. 100-647)**

P.L. 100-647, §1006(h)(3)(A):

Amended Code Sec. 6724(d)(1)(B) by striking out "or" at the end of clause (ix)[viii], by striking out the period at the end of clause (x)[ix] and inserting in lieu thereof ", or" and by adding at the end thereof new clause (xi)[x]. **Effective** as if included in the provision of P.L. 99-514 to which it relates.

P.L. 100-647, §1015(a):

Amended Code Sec. 6724(d)(2)(B) by striking out "6031(b)" and inserting in lieu thereof "6031(b) or (c)". **Effective** as if included in the provision of P.L. 99-514 to which it relates.

P.L. 100-647, §3001(b)(1):

Amended Code Sec. 6724(d)(1)(B) by striking out "or" and the end of clause (ix), by striking out the period at the end of clause (x) and inserting in lieu thereof ", or" and by adding at the end thereof a new clause (xi). **Effective** 1-1-89. For a special rule, see Act Sec. 3001(c)(2) below.

P.L. 100-647, §3001(b)(2):

Amended Code Sec. 6724(d)(2) by striking out "or" at the end of subparagraph (S) [Q], by striking out the period at the end of subparagraph (T) [R] and inserting in lieu thereof ", or" and by adding at the end thereof a new subparagraph (U) [S]. **Effective** 1-1-89. For a special rule, see Act Sec. 3001(c)(2) below.

P.L. 100-647, §3001(c)(2), provides:

(2) REFUNDS WITH INTEREST FOR PRE-EFFECTIVE DATE PURCHASES.—

(A) IN GENERAL.—In the case of fuel—

(i) which is purchased from a producer or importer during the period beginning on April 1, 1988, and ending on December 31, 1988,

(ii) which is used (before the claim under this subparagraph is filed) by any person in a nontaxable use (as defined in section 6427(l)(2) of the 1986 Code), and

(iii) with respect to which a claim is not permitted to be filed for any quarter under section 6427(i) of the 1986 Code,

the Secretary of the Treasury or the Secretary's delegate shall pay (with interest) to such person the amount of tax imposed on such fuel under section 4091 of the 1986 Code (to the extent not attributable to amounts described in section 6427(l)(3) of the 1986 Code) if claim therefor is filed not later than June 30, 1989. Not more than 1 claim may be filed under the preceding sentence and such claim shall not be taken into account under section 6427(f) of the 1986 Code. Any claim for refund filed under this paragraph shall be considered a claim for refund under section 6427(l) of the 1986 Code.

(B) INTEREST.—The amount of interest payable under subparagraph (A) shall be determined under section 6611 of the 1986 Code except that the date of the overpayment with respect to fuel purchased during any month shall be treated as being the 1st day of the succeeding month. No interest shall be paid under this paragraph with respect to fuel used by any agency of the United States.

(C) REGISTRATION PROCEDURES REQUIRED TO BE SPECIFIED.—Not later than the 30th day after the date of the enactment of this Act, the Secretary of the Treasury or the Secretary's delegate shall prescribe the procedures for complying with the requirements of section 4093(c)(3) of the 1986 Code (as added by this section).

• **1988, Omnibus Trade and Competitiveness Act of 1988 (P.L. 100-418)**

P.L. 100-418, §1941(b)(2)(M)(i)-(ii):

Amended Code Sec. 6724(d) by striking clause (i) in paragraph (1)(B) and redesignating clauses (ii)-(x) as clauses (i)-(ix), respectively, and by striking subparagraphs (A) and (K) of paragraph (2) and redesignating subparagraphs (B)-(J) and (L)-(T) as subparagraphs (A)-(R), respectively. **Effective** for crude oil removed from the premises on or after 8-23-88. Prior to amendment, Code Sec. 6724(d)(1)(B)(i), 6724(d)(2)(A) and (K) read as follows:

(i) section 4997(a) (relating to information with respect to windfall profit tax on crude oil),

* * *

Sec. 6721(e)(3)(B)

ASSESSABLE PENALTIES

(A) section 4997(a) (relating to records and information, regulations),

***

(K) section 6050C (relating to information regarding windfall profit tax on domestic crude oil),

[Sec. 6721(f)]

(f) ADJUSTMENT FOR INFLATION.—

(1) IN GENERAL.—In the case of any failure relating to a return required to be filed in a calendar year beginning after 2014, each of the dollar amounts under subsections (a), (b), (d) (other than paragraph (2)(A) thereof), and (e) shall be increased by an amount equal to such dollar amount multiplied by the cost-of-living adjustment determined under section 1(f)(3) for the calendar year determined by substituting "calendar year 2011" for "calendar year 2016" in subparagraph (A)(ii) thereof.

(2) ROUNDING.—If any amount adjusted under paragraph (1)—

(A) is not less than $75,000 and is not a multiple of $500, such amount shall be rounded to the next lowest multiple of $500, and

(B) is not described in subparagraph (A) and is not a multiple of $10, such amount shall be rounded to the next lowest multiple of $10.

Amendments

• 2018, Tax Technical Corrections Act of 2018 (P.L. 115-141)

P.L. 115-141, §401(a)(299)(F), Div. U:

Amended Code Sec. 6721(f)(1) by inserting "an amount equal to" after "increased by" and by inserting "for the calendar year" after "section 1(f)(3)". **Effective** 3-23-2018.

• 2017, Tax Cuts and Jobs Act (P.L. 115-97)

P.L. 115-97, §11002(d)(1)(PP):

Amended Code Sec. 6721(f)(1) by striking "for 'calendar year 1992' in subparagraph (B)" and inserting "for 'calendar year 2016' in subparagraph (A)(ii)". **Effective** for tax years beginning after 12-31-2017.

• 1986, Tax Reform Act of 1986 (P.L. 99-514)

P.L. 99-514, §1501(a):

Amended subchapter B of chapter 68 by adding new Code Sec. 6724. **Effective** for returns the due date for which (determined without regard to extensions) is after 12-31-86.

• 2014, Stephen Beck, Jr., Achieving a Better Life Experience Act of 2014 (P.L. 113-295)

P.L. 113-295, §208(f), Division B:

Amended Code Sec. 6721(f)(1) by striking "For each fifth calendar year beginning after 2012" and inserting "In the case of any failure relating to a return required to be filed in a calendar year beginning after 2014". **Effective** for returns required to be filed, and statements required to be furnished, after 12-31-2014 [effective date changed by P.L. 115-141, §105(a)(1)-(2), Div. U.—CCH].

• 2010, Creating Small Business Jobs Act of 2010 (P.L. 111-240)

P.L. 111-240, §2102(f) (as amended by P.L. 113-295, §207(a)(1), Division A):

Amended Code Sec. 6721(f) by adding at the end a new subsection (f). **Effective** with respect to information returns required to be filed, and payee statements required to be furnished, on or after 1-1-2011.

[Sec. 6722]

SEC. 6722. FAILURE TO FURNISH CORRECT PAYEE STATEMENTS.

[Sec. 6722(a)]

(a) IMPOSITION OF PENALTY.—

(1) GENERAL RULE.—In the case of each failure described in paragraph (2) by any person with respect to a payee statement, such person shall pay a penalty of $250 for each statement with respect to which such a failure occurs, but the total amount imposed on such person for all such failures during any calendar year shall not exceed $3,000,000.

(2) FAILURES SUBJECT TO PENALTY.—For purposes of paragraph (1), the failures described in this paragraph are—

(A) any failure to furnish a payee statement on or before the date prescribed therefor to the person to whom such statement is required to be furnished, and

(B) any failure to include all of the information required to be shown on a payee statement or the inclusion of incorrect information.

Amendments

• 2015, Trade Preferences Extension Act of 2015 (P.L. 114-27)

P.L. 114-27, §806(e)(1)(A)-(B):

Amended Code Sec. 6722(a)(1) by striking "$100" and inserting "$250"; and by striking "$1,500,000" and inserting "$3,000,000". **Effective** with respect to returns and statements required to be filed after 12-31-2015.

[Sec. 6722(b)]

(b) REDUCTION WHERE CORRECTION IN SPECIFIED PERIOD.—

(1) CORRECTION WITHIN 30 DAYS.—If any failure described in subsection (a)(2) is corrected on or before the day 30 days after the date prescribed for furnishing such statement—

(A) the penalty imposed by subsection (a) shall be $50 in lieu of $250, and

(B) the total amount imposed on the person for all such failures during any calendar year which are so corrected shall not exceed $500,000.

(2) FAILURES CORRECTED ON OR BEFORE AUGUST 1.—If any failure described in subsection (a)(2) is corrected after the 30th day referred to in paragraph (1) but on or before August 1 of the calendar year in which the date prescribed for furnishing such statement occurs—

(A) the penalty imposed by subsection (a) shall be $100 in lieu of $250, and

(B) the total amount imposed on the person for all such failures during the calendar year which are so corrected shall not exceed $1,500,000.

Amendments

• 2015, Trade Preferences Extension Act of 2015 (P.L. 114-27)

P.L. 114-27, §806(e)(2)(A)(i)-(iii):

Amended Code Sec. 6722(b)(1) by striking "$30" and inserting "$50"; by striking "$100" and inserting "$250"; and by striking "$250,000" and inserting "$500,000". **Effective** with respect to returns and statements required to be filed after 12-31-2015.

P.L. 114-27, §806(e)(2)(B)(i)-(iii):

Amended Code Sec. 6722(b)(2) by striking "$60" and inserting "$100"; by striking "$100" (prior to amendment by Act Sec. 806(e)(2)(B)(i)) and inserting "$250"; and by striking "$500,000" and inserting "$1,500,000". **Effective** with respect to returns and statements required to be filed after 12-31-2015.

• 2014, Tax Technical Corrections Act of 2014 (P.L. 113-295)

P.L. 113-295, §207(a)(2), Division A:

Amended Code Sec. 6722(b)(1) and (2) by striking "the required filing date" and inserting "the date prescribed for furnishing such statement". **Effective** as if included in the provision of the Creating Small Business Jobs Act of 2010 (P.L. 110-240) to which it relates [effective with respect to information returns required to be filed on or after 1-1-2011.—CCH.].

[Sec. 6722(c)]

(c) EXCEPTION FOR DE MINIMIS FAILURES.—

(1) IN GENERAL.—If—

(A) a payee statement is furnished to the person to whom such statement is required to be furnished,

ASSESSABLE PENALTIES

(B) there is a failure described in subsection (a)(2)(B) (determined after the application of section 6724(a)) with respect to such statement, and

(C) such failure is corrected on or before August 1 of the calendar year in which the date prescribed for furnishing such statement occurs,

for purposes of this section, such statement shall be treated as having been furnished with all of the correct required information.

(2) LIMITATION.—The number of payee statements to which paragraph (1) applies for any calendar year shall not exceed the greater of—

(A) 10, or

(B) one-half of 1 percent of the total number of payee statements required to be furnished by the person during the calendar year.

(3) SAFE HARBOR FOR CERTAIN DE MINIMIS ERRORS.—

(A) IN GENERAL.—If, with respect to any payee statement—

(i) there are 1 or more failures described in subsection (a)(2)(B) relating to an incorrect dollar amount,

(ii) no single amount in error differs from the correct amount by more than $100, and

(iii) no single amount reported for tax withheld on the payee statement differs from the correct amount by more than $25,

then no correction shall be required and, for purposes of this section, such statement shall be treated as having been furnished with all of the correct required information.

(B) EXCEPTION.—Subparagraph (A) shall not apply to any payee statement if the person to whom such statement is required to be furnished makes an election (at such time and in such manner as the Secretary may prescribe) that subparagraph (A) not apply with respect to such statement.

(C) REGULATORY AUTHORITY.—The Secretary may issue regulations to prevent the abuse of the safe harbor under this paragraph, including regulations providing that this paragraph shall not apply to the extent necessary to prevent any such abuse.

Amendments

- **2018, Tax Technical Corrections Act of 2018 (P.L. 115-141)**

P.L. 115-141, §101(f)(1)(A)-(B), Div. U:

Amended Code Sec. 6722(c)(3)(A) by striking "any information return" in clause (iii) and inserting "the payee statement", and by striking "filed" in the flush matter at the end and inserting "furnished". **Effective** as if included in the provision of the Protecting Americans from Tax Hikes Act of 2015 to which it relates [**effective** for returns required to be filed, and payee statements required to be furnished, after 12-31-2016.—CCH].

- **2015, Protecting Americans from Tax Hikes Act of 2015 (P.L. 114-113)**

P.L. 114-113, §202(b), Div. Q:

Amended Code Sec. 6722(c) by adding at the end a new paragraph (3). **Effective** for returns required to be filed, and payee statements required to be furnished, after 12-31-2016 [**effective** date changed by P.L. 115-141, §101(f)(3), Div. U.—CCH].

- **2014, Tax Technical Corrections Act of 2014 (P.L. 113-295)**

P.L. 113-295, §207(a)(2), Division A:

Amended Code Sec. 6722(c)(1)(C) by striking "the required filing date" and inserting "the date prescribed for furnishing such statement". **Effective** as if included in the provision of the Creating Small Business Jobs Act of 2010 to which it relates [**effective** with respect to information returns required to be filed on or after 1-1-2011.—CCH.].

P.L. 113-295, §207(a)(3), Division A:

Amended Code Sec. 6722(c)(2)(B) by striking "filed" and inserting "furnished". **Effective** as if included in the provision of the Creating Small Business Jobs Act of 2010 to which it relates [**effective** with respect to information returns required to be filed on or after 1-1-2011.—CCH.].

[Sec. 6722(d)]

(d) LOWER LIMITATIONS FOR PERSONS WITH GROSS RECEIPTS OF NOT MORE THAN $5,000,000.—

(1) IN GENERAL.—If any person meets the gross receipts test of paragraph (2) with respect to any calendar year, with respect to failures during such calendar year—

(A) subsection (a)(1) shall be applied by substituting "$1,000,000" for "$3,000,000",

(B) subsection (b)(1)(B) shall be applied by substituting "$175,000" for "$500,000", and

(C) subsection (b)(2)(B) shall be applied by substituting "$500,000" for "$1,500,000".

(2) GROSS RECEIPTS TEST.—A person meets the gross receipts test of this paragraph if such person meets the gross receipts test of section 6721(d)(2).

Amendments

- **2015, Trade Preferences Extension Act of 2015 (P.L. 114-27)**

P.L. 114-27, §806(e)(3)(A)-(C):

Amended Code Sec. 6722(d)(1) in subparagraph (A) by striking "$500,000" and inserting "$1,000,000"; and by striking "$1,500,000" and inserting "$3,000,000"; in subparagraph (B) by striking "$75,000" and inserting "$175,000"; and by striking "$250,000" and inserting "$500,000"; and in subparagraph (C) by striking "$200,000" and inserting "$500,000"; and by striking $500,000 (prior to amendment by Act Sec. 806(e)(3)(A) [806(e)(3)(C)(i)]) and inserting "$1,500,000". **Effective** with respect to returns and statements required to be filed after 12-31-2015.

[Sec. 6722(e)]

(e) PENALTY IN CASE OF INTENTIONAL DISREGARD.—If 1 or more failures to which subsection (a) applies are due to intentional disregard of the requirement to furnish a payee statement (or the correct information reporting requirement), then, with respect to each such failure—

(1) subsections (b), (c), and (d) shall not apply,

(2) the penalty imposed under subsection (a)(1) shall be $500, or, if greater—

(A) in the case of a payee statement other than a statement required under section 6045(b), 6041A(e) (in respect of a return required under section 6041A(b)), 6050H(d), 6050J(e), 6050K(b), or 6050L(c), 10 percent of the aggregate amount of the items required to be reported correctly, or

(B) in the case of a payee statement required under section 6045(b), 6050K(b), or 6050L(c), 5 percent of the aggregate amount of the items required to be reported correctly, and

(3) in the case of any penalty determined under paragraph (2)—

(A) the $3,000,000 limitation under subsection (a) shall not apply, and

(B) such penalty shall not be taken into account in applying such limitation to penalties not determined under paragraph (2).

Amendments

- **2015, Trade Preferences Extension Act of 2015 (P.L. 114-27)**

P.L. 114-27, §806(e)(4)(A)-(B):

Amended Code Sec. 6722(e) by striking "$250" in paragraph (2) and inserting "$500"; and by striking "$1,500,000" in paragraph (3)(A) and inserting "$3,000,000". **Effective** with respect to returns and statements required to be filed after 12-31-2015.

[Sec. 6722(f)]

(f) ADJUSTMENT FOR INFLATION.—

(1) IN GENERAL.—In the case of any failure relating to a statement required to be furnished in a calendar year beginning after 2014, each of the dollar amounts under subsections (a), (b), (d)(1), and (e) shall be increased by an amount equal to such dollar amount multiplied by the

ASSESSABLE PENALTIES

cost-of-living adjustment determined under section 1(f)(3) for the calendar year determined by substituting "calendar year 2011" for "calendar year 2016" in subparagraph (A)(ii) thereof.

(2) ROUNDING.—If any amount adjusted under paragraph (1)—

(A) is not less than $75,000 and is not a multiple of $500, such amount shall be rounded to the next lowest multiple of $500, and

(B) is not described in subparagraph (A) and is not a multiple of $10, such amount shall be rounded to the next lowest multiple of $10.

Amendments

• **2018, Tax Technical Corrections Act of 2018 (P.L. 115-141)**

P.L. 115-141, §401(a)(299)(G), Div. U:

Amended Code Sec. 6722(f)(1) by inserting "an amount equal to" after "increased by" and by inserting "for the calendar year" after "section 1(f)(3)". **Effective** 3-23-2018.

• **2017, Tax Cuts and Jobs Act (P.L. 115-97)**

P.L. 115-97, §11002(d)(1)(QQ):

Amended Code Sec. 6722(f)(1) by striking "for 'calendar year 1992' in subparagraph (B)" and inserting "for 'calendar year 2016' in subparagraph (A)(ii)". **Effective** for tax years beginning after 12-31-2017.

• **2014, Stephen Beck, Jr., Achieving a Better Life Experience Act of 2014 (P.L. 113-295)**

P.L. 113-295, §208(g), Division B:

Amended Code Sec. 6722(f)(1) by striking "For each fifth calendar year beginning after 2012" and inserting "In the case of any failure relating to a statement required to be furnished in a calendar year beginning after 2014". **Effective** for returns required to be filed, and statements required to be furnished, after 12-31-2014 [effective date changed by P.L. 115-141, §105(a)(1)-(2), Div. U.—CCH].

• **2010, Creating Small Business Jobs Act of 2010 (P.L. 111-240)**

P.L. 111-240, §2102(g) (as amended by P.L. 113-295, §207(a)(1), Division A):

Amended Code Sec. 6722. **Effective** with respect to information returns required to be filed, and payee statements required to be furnished, on or after 1-1-2011. Prior to amendment, Code Sec. 6722 read as follows:

SEC. 6722. FAILURE TO FURNISH CORRECT PAYEE STATEMENTS.

(a) GENERAL RULE.—In the case of each failure described in subsection (b) by any person with respect to a payee statement, such person shall pay a penalty of $50 for each statement with respect to which such a failure occurs, but the total amount imposed on such person for all such failures during any calendar year shall not exceed $100,000.

(b) FAILURES SUBJECT TO PENALTY.—For purposes of subsection (a), the failures described in this subsection are—

(1) any failure to furnish a payee statement on or before the date prescribed therefor to the person to whom such statement is required to be furnished, and

(2) any failure to include all of the information required to be shown on a payee statement or the inclusion of incorrect information.

(c) PENALTY IN CASE OF INTENTIONAL DISREGARD.—If 1 or more failures to which subsection (a) applies are due to intentional disregard of the requirement to furnish a payee statement (or the correct information reporting requirement), then, with respect to each failure—

(1) the penalty imposed under subsection (a) shall be $100, or, if greater—

(A) in the case of a payee statement other than a statement required under section 6045(b), 6041A(e) (in respect of a return required under section 6041A(b)), 6050H(d), 6050J(e), 6050K(b), or 6050L(c), 10 percent of the aggregate amount of the items required to be reported correctly, or

(B) in the case of a payee statement required under section 6045(b), 6050K(b), or 6050L(c), 5 percent of the aggregate amount of the items required to be reported correctly, and

(2) in the case of any penalty determined under paragraph (1)—

(A) the $100,000 limitation under subsection (a) shall not apply, and

(B) such penalty shall not be taken into account in applying such limitation to penalties not determined under paragraph (1).

• **1989, Omnibus Budget Reconciliation Act of 1989 (P.L. 101-239)**

P.L. 101-239, §7711(a):

Amended Code Sec. 6722. For text of Code Sec. 6722 prior to amendment, see the amendment notes following Code Sec. 6721. **Effective** for returns and statements the due date for which (determined without regard to extensions) is after 12-31-89.

[Sec. 6723]

SEC. 6723. FAILURE TO COMPLY WITH OTHER INFORMATION REPORTING REQUIREMENTS.

In the case of a failure by any person to comply with a specified information reporting requirement on or before the time prescribed therefor, such person shall pay a penalty of $50 for each such failure, but the total amount imposed on such person for all such failures during any calendar year shall not exceed $100,000.

Amendments

• **1989, Omnibus Budget Reconciliation Act of 1989 (P.L. 101-239)**

P.L. 101-239, §7711(a):

Amended Code Sec. 6723. For text of Code Sec. 6723 prior to amendment, see the amendment notes following Code Sec. 6721. **Effective** for returns and statements the due date for which (determined without regard to extensions) is after 12-31-89.

[Sec. 6724]

SEC. 6724. WAIVER; DEFINITIONS AND SPECIAL RULES.

[Sec. 6724(a)]

(a) REASONABLE CAUSE WAIVER.—No penalty shall be imposed under this part with respect to any failure if it is shown that such failure is due to reasonable cause and not to willful neglect.

[Sec. 6724(b)]

(b) PAYMENT OF PENALTY.—Any penalty imposed by this part shall be paid on notice and demand by the Secretary and in the same manner as tax.

[Sec. 6724(c)]

(c) SPECIAL RULE FOR FAILURE TO MEET MAGNETIC MEDIA REQUIREMENTS.—No penalty shall be imposed under section 6721 solely by reason of any failure to comply with the requirements of the regulations prescribed under section 6011(e)(2), except to the extent that such a failure occurs with respect to more than the applicable number (determined under section 6011(e)(5) with respect to the calendar year to which such returns relate) of information returns or with respect to a return described in section 6011(e)(4).

Amendments

• **2019, Taxpayer First Act (P.L. 116-25)**

P.L. 116-25, §2301(d):

Amended Code Sec. 6724(c) by striking "250 information returns (more than 100 information returns in the case of a partnership having more than 100 partners)" and inserting "the applicable number (determined under section 6011(e)(5) with respect to the calendar year to which such returns relate) of information returns". **Effective** 7-1-2019.

• **2010, Hiring Incentives to Restore Employment Act (P.L. 111-147)**

P.L. 111-147, §522(b):

Amended Code Sec. 6724(c) by inserting "or with respect to a return described in section 6011(e)(4)" before the end period. **Effective** for returns the due date for which (determined without regard to extensions) is after 3-18-2010.

• **1998, IRS Restructuring and Reform Act of 1998 (P.L. 105-206)**

P.L. 105-206, §6012(d):

Amended Code Sec. 6724(c) by inserting before the period "(more than 100 information returns in the case of a partnership having more than 100 partners)". **Effective** as if included in the provision of P.L. 105-34 to which it relates [effective for partnership tax years beginning after 12-31-97.—CCH].

ASSESSABLE PENALTIES

[Sec. 6724(d)]

(d) DEFINITIONS.—For purposes of this part—
   (1) INFORMATION RETURN.—The term "information return" means—
      (A) any statement of the amount of payments to another person required by—
         (i) section 6041(a) or (b) (relating to certain information at source),
         (ii) section 6042(a)(1) (relating to payments of dividends),
         (iii) section 6044(a)(1) (relating to payments of patronage dividends),
         (iv) section 6049(a) (relating to payments of interest),
         (v) section 6050A(a) (relating to reporting requirements of certain fishing boat operators),
         (vi) section 6050N(a) (relating to payments of royalties),
         (vii) section 6051(d) (relating to information returns with respect to income tax withheld),
         (viii) section 6050R (relating to returns relating to certain purchases of fish), or
         (ix) section 110(d) (relating to qualified lessee construction allowances for short-term leases),
      (B) any return required by—
         (i) section 6041A(a) or (b) (relating to returns of direct sellers),
         (ii) section 6043A(a) (relating to returns relating to taxable mergers and acquisitions),
         (iii) section 6045(a) or (d) (relating to returns of brokers),
         (iv) section 6045B(a) (relating to returns relating to actions affecting basis of specified securities),
         (v) section 6050H(a) or (h)(1)(relating to mortgage interest received in trade or business from individuals),
         (vi) section 6050I(a) or (g)(1) (relating to cash received in trade or business, etc.),
         (vii) section 6050J(a) (relating to foreclosures and abandonments of security),
         (viii) section 6050K(a) (relating to exchanges of certain partnership interests),
         (ix) section 6050L(a) (relating to returns relating to certain dispositions of donated property),
         (x) section 6050P (relating to returns relating to the cancellation of indebtedness by certain financial entities),
         (xi) section 6050Q (relating to certain long-term care benefits),
         (xii) section 6050S (relating to returns relating to payments for qualified tuition and related expenses),
         (xiii) section 6050T (relating to returns relating to credit for health insurance costs of eligible individuals),
         (xiv) section 6052(a) (relating to reporting payment of wages in the form of group-life insurance),
         (xv) section 6050V (relating to returns relating to applicable insurance contracts in which certain exempt organizations hold interests),
         (xvi) section 6053(c)(1) (relating to reporting with respect to certain tips),
         (xvii) subsection (b) or (e) of section 1060 (relating to reporting requirements of transferors and transferees in certain asset acquisitions),
         (xviii) section 4101(d) (relating to information reporting with respect to fuels taxes),
         (xix) subparagraph (C) of section 338(h)(10) (relating to information required to be furnished to the Secretary in case of elective recognition of gain or loss),
         (xx) section 264(f)(5)(A)(iv) (relating to reporting with respect to certain life insurance and annuity contracts),
         (xxi) section 6050U (relating to charges or payments for qualified long-term care insurance contracts under combined arrangements),
         (xxii) section 6039(a) (relating to returns required with respect to certain options),
         (xxiii) section 6050W (relating to returns to payments made in settlement of payment card transactions),
         (xxiv) section 6055 (relating to returns relating to information regarding health insurance coverage),
         (xxv) section 6056 (relating to returns relating to certain employers required to report on health insurance coverage),
         (xxvi) section 6050Y (relating to returns relating to certain life insurance contract transactions),

⇛ *Caution: Code Sec. 6724(d)(1)(B)(xxvii), below, as added by P.L. 117-58 and amended by P.L. 117-328, applies to distributions made after the date which is 3 years after December 29, 2022.*

         (xxvii) section 6045A(d) (relating to returns for certain digital assets), or

⇛ *Caution: Code Sec. 6724(d)(1)(B)(xxviii), below, as added by P.L. 117-328, applies to distributions made after the date which is 3 years after December 29, 2022.*

         (xxviii) section 6050Z (relating to reports relating to long-term care premium statements), and
      (C) any statement of the amount of payments to another person required to be made to the Secretary under—
         (i) section 408(i) (relating to reports with respect to individual retirement accounts or annuities), or
         (ii) section 6047(d) (relating to reports by employers, plan administrators, etc.), and
      (D) any statement required to be filed with the Secretary under section 6035.
Such term also includes any form, statement, or schedule required to be filed with the Secretary under chapter 4 or with respect to any amount from which tax was required to be deducted and withheld under chapter 3 (or from which tax would be required to be so deducted and withheld but for an exemption under this title or any treaty obligation of the United States).
   (2) PAYEE STATEMENT.—The term "payee statement" means any statement required to be furnished under—
      (A) section 6031(b) or (c), 6034A, or 6037(b) (relating to statements furnished by certain pass-thru entities),
      (B) section 6039(b)(relating to information required in connection with certain options),
      (C) section 6041(d) (relating to information at source),
      (D) section 6041A(e) (relating to returns regarding payments of remuneration for services and direct sales),
      (E) section 6042(c) (relating to returns regarding payments of dividends and corporate earnings and profits),
      (F) subsections (b) and (d) of section 6043A (relating to returns relating to taxable mergers and acquisitions),
      (G) section 6044(e) (relating to returns regarding payments of patronage dividends),
      (H) section 6045(b) or (d) (relating to returns of brokers),
      (I) section 6045A (relating to information required in connection with transfers of covered securities to brokers),

ASSESSABLE PENALTIES

(J) subsections (c) and (e) of section 6045B (relating to returns relating to actions affecting basis of specified securities),

(K) section 6049(c) (relating to returns regarding payments of interest),

(L) section 6050A(b) (relating to reporting requirements of certain fishing boat operators),

(M) section 6050H(d) or (h)(2) (relating to returns relating to mortgage interest received in trade or business from individuals),

(N) section 6050I(e) or paragraph (4) or (5) of section 6050I(g) (relating to cash received in trade or business, etc.),

(O) section 6050J(e) (relating to returns relating to foreclosures and abandonments of security),

(P) section 6050K(b) (relating to returns relating to exchanges of certain partnership interests),

(Q) section 6050L(c) (relating to returns relating to certain dispositions of donated property),

(R) section 6050N(b) (relating to returns regarding payments of royalties),

(S) section 6050P(d) (relating to returns relating to the cancellation of indebtedness by certain financial entities),

(T) section 6050Q(b) (relating to certain long-term care benefits),

(U) section 6050R(c) (relating to returns relating to certain purchases of fish),

(V) section 6051 (relating to receipts for employees),

(W) section 6052(b) (relating to returns regarding payment of wages in the form of group-term life insurance),

(X) section 6053(b) or (c) (relating to reports of tips),

(Y) section 6048(b)(1)(B) (relating to foreign trust reporting requirements),

(Z) section 408(i) (relating to reports with respect to individual retirement plans) to any person other than the Secretary with respect to the amount of payments made to such person,

(AA) section 6047(d) (relating to reports by plan administrators) to any person other than the Secretary with respect to the amount of payments made to such person,

(BB) section 6050S(d) (relating to returns relating to qualified tuition and related expenses),

(CC) section 264(f)(5)(A)(iv) (relating to reporting with respect to certain life insurance and annuity contracts),

(DD) section 6050T (relating to returns relating to credit for health insurance costs of eligible individuals),

(EE) section 6050U (relating to charges or payments for qualified long-term care insurance contracts under combined arrangements),

(FF) section 6050W(f) (relating to returns relating to payments made in settlement of payment card transactions),

(GG) section 6055(c) (relating to statements relating to information regarding health insurance coverage),

(HH) section 6056(c) (relating to statements relating to certain employers required to report on health insurance coverage),

⯈ *Caution: Code Sec. 6724(d)(2)(II)-(JJ), below, prior to amendment by P.L. 117-328, applies to distributions made on or before the date which is 3 years after December 29, 2022.*

(II) section 6035 (other than a statement described in paragraph (1)(D)), or

(JJ) section 6226(a)(2) (relating to statements relating to alternative to payment of imputed underpayment by partnership) or under any other provision of this title which provides for the application of rules similar to such section.

⯈ *Caution: Code Sec. 6724(d)(2)(II)-(JJ), below, as amended by P.L. 117-328, applies to distributions made after the date which is 3 years after December 29, 2022.*

(II) section 6035 (other than a statement described in paragraph (1)(D)),

(JJ) section 6226(a)(2) (relating to statements relating to alternative to payment of imputed underpayment by partnership) or under any other provision of this title which provides for the application of rules similar to such section,

⯈ *Caution: Code Sec. 6724(d)(2)(JJ), below, prior to redesignation as Code Sec. 6724(d)(2)(KK) and amendment by P.L. 117-328, applies to distributions made on or before the date which is 3 years after December 29, 2022.*

(JJ) subsection (a)(2), (b)(2), or (c)(2) of section 6050Y (relating to returns relating to certain life insurance contract transactions).

⯈ *Caution: Former Code Sec. 6724(d)(2)(JJ) was redesignated as Code Sec. 6724(d)(2)(KK), below, and amended by P.L. 117-328, applicable to distributions made after the date which is 3 years after December 29, 2022.*

(KK) subsection (a)(2), (b)(2), or (c)(2) of section 6050Y (relating to returns relating to certain life insurance contract transactions), or

⯈ *Caution: Code Sec. 6724(d)(2)(LL), below, as added by P.L. 117-328, applies to distributions made after the date which is 3 years after December 29, 2022.*

(LL) section 6050Z (relating to reports relating to long-term care premium statements).

Such term also includes any form, statement, or schedule required to be furnished to the recipient of any amount from which tax was required to be deducted and withheld under chapter 3 or 4 (or from which tax would be required to be so deducted and withheld but for an exemption under this title or any treaty obligation of the United States).

(3) SPECIFIED INFORMATION REPORTING REQUIREMENT.—The term "specified information reporting requirement" means—

(A) the notice required by section 6050K(c)(1) (relating to requirement that transferor notify partnership of exchange),

(B) any requirement contained in the regulations prescribed under section 6109 that a person—

(i) include his TIN on any return, statement, or other document (other than an information return or payee statement),

(ii) furnish his TIN to another person, or

(iii) include on any return, statement, or other document (other than an information return or payee statement) made with respect to another person the TIN of such person,

(C) any requirement under section 6109(h) that—

(i) a person include on his return the name, address, and TIN of another person, or

(ii) a person furnish his TIN to another person.

(4) REQUIRED FILING DATE.—The term "required filing date" means the date prescribed for filing an information return with the Secretary (determined with regard to any extension of time for filing).

Amendments

• **2022, SECURE 2.0 Act of 2022 (P.L. 117-328)**

P.L. 117-328, §334(d)(2)(A)-(B):

Amended Code Sec. 6724(d), in paragraph (1)(B), by adding "or" at the end of clause (xxvii) and by inserting after such clause a new clause (xxviii), and, in paragraph (2), by redesignating subparagraph (JJ), relating to section 6050Y, as subparagraph (KK) and moving such subparagraph to the position immediately after subparagraph (JJ), relating to section 6226(a)(2), by striking "or" at the end of subparagraph (II), by striking the period at the end of subparagraph (JJ), relating to section 6226(a)(2), and inserting a comma, by striking the period at the end of subparagraph (KK), as so redesignated, and inserting ", or", and by inserting after subparagraph (KK), as so redesignated, a new subparagraph (LL). **Effective** for distributions made after the date which is 3 years after 12-29-2022.

ASSESSABLE PENALTIES

• **2021, Infrastructure Investment and Jobs Act (P.L. 117-58)**

P.L. 117-58, § 80603(b)(2)(B), Div. H:

Amended Code Sec. 6724(d)(1)(B) by striking "or" at the end of clause (xxv), by striking "and" at the end of clause (xxvi), and by inserting after clause (xxvi) a new clause (xxvii). **Effective** for returns required to be filed, and statements required to be furnished, after 12-31-2023. For a special rule, see Act Sec. 80603(d)(1)-(2), Div. H, below.

P.L. 117-58, § 80603(d)(1)-(2), Div. H, provides:

(d) RULE OF CONSTRUCTION.—Nothing in this section or the amendments made by this section shall be construed to create any inference, for any period prior to the effective date of such amendments, with respect to—

(1) whether any person is a broker under section 6045(c)(1) of the Internal Revenue Code of 1986, or

(2) whether any digital asset is property which is a specified security under section 6045(g)(3)(B) of such Code.

• **2018, Tax Technical Corrections Act of 2018 (P.L. 115-141)**

P.L. 115-141, § 206(o), Div. U:

Amended Code Sec. 6724(d)(2) by striking "or" at the end of subparagraph (HH), by striking the period at the end of subparagraph (II) and inserting ", or", and by inserting after subparagraph (II) a new subparagraph (JJ)[(KK)]. [Note: The word "or" does not appear at the end of Code Sec. 6724(d)(2)(HH) and so cannot be stricken.—CCH] **Effective** as if included in section 1101 of the Bipartisan Budget Act of 2015 [effective generally for returns filed for partnership tax years beginning after 12-31-2017.—CCH].

P.L. 115-141, § 401(a)(315), Div. U:

Amended Code Sec. 6724(d)(1)(B)(xx) by striking "or" at the end. **Effective** 3-23-2018.

P.L. 115-141, § 401(a)(316), Div. U:

Amended Code Sec. 6724(d)(1)(B)(xxi) by striking "and" at the end. **Effective** 3-23-2018.

P.L. 115-141, § 401(a)(317), Div. U:

Amended Code Sec. 6724(d)(1) by striking "Such term also includes" and inserting "Such term also includes". **Effective** 3-23-2018.

P.L. 115-141, § 401(a)(318), Div. U:

Amended Code Sec. 6724(d)(2)(F) by striking the period at the end and inserting a comma. **Effective** 3-23-2018.

P.L. 115-141, § 401(a)(319), Div. U:

Amended Code Sec. 6724(d)(2)(M) by striking "(h)(2) relating" and inserting "(h)(2) (relating". **Effective** 3-23-2018.

P.L. 115-141, § 401(a)(320), Div. U:

Amended Code Sec. 6724(d)(2)(DD) by adding a comma at the end. **Effective** 3-23-2018.

• **2017, Tax Cuts and Jobs Act (P.L. 115-97)**

P.L. 115-97, § 11051(b)(2)(C):

Amended Code Sec. 6724(d)(3) by striking subparagraph (C) and by redesignating subparagraph (D) as subparagraph (C). For the **effective** date, see Act Sec. 11051(c), below. Prior to being stricken, Code Sec. 6724(d)(3)(C) read as follows:

(C) any requirement contained in the regulations prescribed under section 215 that a person—

(i) furnish his TIN to another person, or

(ii) include on his return the TIN of another person, and

P.L. 115-97, § 11051(c), provides:

(c) EFFECTIVE DATE.—The amendments made by this section shall apply to—

(1) any divorce or separation instrument (as defined in section 71(b)(2) of the Internal Revenue Code of 1986 as in effect before the date of the enactment of this Act) executed after December 31, 2018, and

(2) any divorce or separation instrument (as so defined) executed on or before such date and modified after such date if the modification expressly provides that the amendments made by this section apply to such modification.

P.L. 115-97, § 13520(c)(1)(A):

Amended Code Sec. 6724(d)(1)(B) by striking "or" at the end of clause (xxiv), by striking "and" at the end of clause (xxv) and inserting "or", and by inserting after such clause (xxv) a new clause (xxvi). [Note: The word "and" does not appear at the end of Code Sec. 6724(d)(1)(B)(xxv) and so cannot be stricken.—CCH.] For the **effective** date, see Act Sec. 13520(d), below.

P.L. 115-97, § 13520(c)(1)(B):

Amended Code Sec. 6724(d)(2) by striking "or" at the end of subparagraph (HH), by striking the period at the end of subparagraph (II) and inserting ", or", and by inserting after such subparagraph (II) a new subparagraph (JJ). For the **effective** date, see Act Sec. 13520(d), below.

P.L. 115-97, § 13520(d), provides:

(d) EFFECTIVE DATE.—The amendments made by this section shall apply to—

(1) reportable policy sales (as defined in section 6050Y(d)(2) of the Internal Revenue Code of 1986 (as added by subsection (a)) after December 31, 2017, and

(2) reportable death benefits (as defined in section 6050Y(d)(4) of such Code (as added by subsection (a)) paid after December 31, 2017.

• **2015, Surface Transportation and Veterans Health Care Choice Improvement Act of 2015 (P.L. 114-41)**

P.L. 114-41, § 2004(b)(2)(A):

Amended Code Sec. 6724(d)(1) by striking "and" at the end of subparagraph (B), by striking the period at the end of subparagraph (C) and inserting ", and", and by adding at the end a new subparagraph (D). **Effective** for property with respect to which an estate tax return is filed after 7-31-2015.

P.L. 114-41, § 2004(b)(2)(B):

Amended Code Sec. 6724(d)(2) by striking "or" at the end of subparagraph (GG), by striking the period at the end of subparagraph (HH) and inserting ", or", and by adding at the end a new subparagraph (II). **Effective** for property with respect to which an estate tax return is filed after 7-31-2015.

• **2014, Tax Technical Corrections Act of 2014 (P.L. 113-295)**

P.L. 113-295, § 220(x), Division A:

Amended Code Sec. 6724(d)(2)(FF) by striking "section 6050W(c)" and inserting "section 6050W(f)". **Effective** 12-19-2014.

• **2010, Patient Protection and Affordable Care Act (P.L. 111-148)**

P.L. 111-148, § 1502(b)(1):

Amended Code Sec. 6724(d)(1)(B) by striking "or" at the end of clause (xxii), by striking "and" at the end of clause (xxiii) and inserting "or", and by inserting after clause (xxiii) a new clause (xxiv). **Effective** for calendar years beginning after 2013.

P.L. 111-148, § 1502(b)(2):

Amended Code Sec. 6724(d)(2) by striking "or" at the end of subparagraph (EE), by striking the period at the end of subparagraph (FF) and inserting ", or" and by inserting after subparagraph (FF) a new subparagraph (GG). **Effective** for calendar years beginning after 2013.

P.L. 111-148, § 1514(b)(1):

Amended Code Sec. 6724(d)(1)(B), as amended by Act Sec. 1502(b)(1), by striking "or" at the end of clause (xxiii), by striking "and" at the end of clause (xxiv) and inserting "or", and by inserting after clause (xxiv) a new clause (xxv). **Effective** for periods beginning after 12-31-2013.

P.L. 111-148, § 1514(b)(2):

Amended Code Sec. 6724(d)(2), as amended by Act Sec. 1502(b)(2), by striking "or" at the end of subparagraph (FF), by striking the period at the end of subparagraph (GG) and inserting ", or" and by inserting after subparagraph (GG) a new subparagraph (HH). **Effective** for periods beginning after 12-31-2013.

P.L. 111-148, § 10108(j)(3)(E):

Amended Code Sec. 6724(d)(1)(B)(xxv), as added by Act Sec. 1514(b)(1), by striking "large" and inserting "certain". **Effective** for periods beginning after 12-31-2013.

P.L. 111-148, § 10108(j)(3)(F):

Amended Code Sec. 6724(d)(2)(HH), as added by Act Sec. 1514(b)(2), by striking "large" and inserting "certain". **Effective** for periods beginning after 12-31-2013.

• **2010, Hiring Incentives to Restore Employment Act (P.L. 111-147)**

P.L. 111-147, § 501(c)(6):

Amended Code Sec. 6724(d)(1) by inserting "under chapter 4 or" after "filed with the Secretary" in the last sentence thereof. **Effective** generally for payments made after 12-31-2012. For a special rule, see Act Sec. 501(d)(2), below.

P.L. 111-147, § 501(c)(7):

Amended [the last sentence of] Code Sec. 6724(d)(2) by inserting "or 4" after "chapter 3". **Effective** generally for payments made after 12-31-2012. For a special rule, see Act Sec. 501(d)(2), below.

P.L. 111-147, § 501(d)(2), provides:

(2) GRANDFATHERED TREATMENT OF OUTSTANDING OBLIGATIONS.—The amendments made by this section shall not require any amount to be deducted or withheld from any payment under any obligation outstanding on the date which is 2 years after the date of the enactment of this Act or from the gross proceeds from any disposition of such an obligation.

• **2008, Energy Improvement and Extension Act of 2008 (P.L. 110-343)**

P.L. 110-343, Division B, § 403(c)(2):

Amended Code Sec. 6724(d)(2), as amended by the Housing Assistance Tax Act of 2008 (P.L. 110-289), by redesignating subparagraphs (I) through (DD) as subparagraphs (J) through (EE), respectively, and by inserting after subparagraph (H) a new subparagraph (I). **Effective** 1-1-2011.

P.L. 110-343, Division B, § 403(d)(2)(A):

Amended Code Sec. 6724(d)(1)(B), as amended by the Housing Assistance Tax Act of 2008 (P.L. 110-289), by redesignating clause (iv) and each of the clauses which follow [clauses (v)-(xxii).—CCH] as clauses (v) through (xxiii), respectively, and by inserting after clause (iii) a new clause (iv). **Effective** 1-1-2011.

P.L. 110-343, Division B, § 403(d)(2)(B):

Amended Code Sec. 6724(d)(2), as amended by the Housing Assistance Tax Act of 2008 (P.L. 110-289) and by Act Sec. 403(c)(2), by redesignating subparagraphs (J) through (EE) as subparagraphs (K) through (FF), respectively, and by inserting after subparagraph (I) a new subparagraph (J). **Effective** 1-1-2011.

Sec. 6724(d)(4)

ASSESSABLE PENALTIES

• **2008, Housing Assistance Tax Act of 2008 (P.L. 110-289)**

P.L. 110-289, §3091(b)(1)(A)-(D):

Amended Code Sec. 6724(d)(1)(B) by striking "or" at the end of clause (xx), by redesignating the clause (xix) that follows clause (xx) as clause (xxi), by striking "and" at the end of clause (xxi), as redesignated by Act Sec. 3091(b)(1)(B), and inserting "or", and by adding at the end a new clause (xxii). **Effective** generally for returns for calendar years beginning after 12-31-2010. For a special rule, see Act Sec. 3091(e)(2)(B), below.

P.L. 110-289, §3091(b)(2):

Amended Code Sec. 6724(d)(2) by striking "or" at the end of subparagraph (BB), by striking the period at the end of the subparagraph (CC) and inserting ", or", and by inserting after subparagraph (CC) a new subparagraph (DD). **Effective** generally for returns for calendar years beginning after 12-31-2010. For a special rule, see Act Sec. 3091(e)(2)(B), below.

P.L. 110-289, §3091(e)(2)(B), provides:

(B) ELIGIBILITY FOR TIN MATCHING PROGRAM.—Solely for purposes of carrying out any TIN matching program established by the Secretary under section 3406(i) of the Internal Revenue Code of 1986—

(i) the amendments made [by] this section shall be treated as taking effect on the date of the enactment of this Act [7-30-2008.—CCH], and

(ii) each person responsible for setting the standards and mechanisms referred to in section 6050W(d)(2)(C) of such Code, as added by this section, for settling transactions involving payment cards shall be treated in the same manner as a payment settlement entity.

• **2007, Tax Technical Corrections Act of 2007 (P.L. 110-172)**

P.L. 110-172, §11(b)(2)(A):

Amended Code Sec. 6724(d)(1)(B)(iv) by inserting "or (h)(1)" after "section 6050H(a)". **Effective** as if included in the provision of the Tax Relief and Health Care Act of 2006 (P.L. 109-432) to which it relates [**effective** for amounts paid or accrued after 12-31-2006.—CCH].

P.L. 110-172, §11(b)(2)(B):

Amended Code Sec. 6724(d)(2)(K) by inserting "or (h)(2)" after "section 6050H(d)". **Effective** as if included in the provision of the Tax Relief and Health Care Act of 2006 (P.L. 109-432) to which it relates [**effective** for amounts paid or accrued after 12-31-2006.—CCH].

• **2006, Tax Relief and Health Care Act of 2006 (P.L. 109-432)**

P.L. 109-432, Division A, §403(c)(1):

Amended Code Sec. 6724(d)(1)(B) by striking "or" at the end of clause (xvii)[(xix)], by striking "and" at the end of clause (xviii)[(xx)] and inserting "or", and by adding at the end a new clause (xix)[(xxi)]. **Effective** for calendar years beginning after 12-20-2006.

P.L. 109-432, Division A, §403(c)(2):

Amended Code Sec. 6724(d)(2)(B) by striking "section 6039(a)" and inserting "section 6039(b)". **Effective** for calendar years beginning after 12-20-2006.

• **2006, Pension Protection Act of 2006 (P.L. 109-280)**

P.L. 109-280, §844(d)(2)(A):

Amended Code Sec. 6724(d)(1)(B) by striking "or" at the end of clause (xvii), by striking "and" at the end of clause (xviii) and inserting "or", and by adding at the end a new clause (xix). **Effective** for charges made after 12-31-2009.

P.L. 109-280, §844(d)(2)(B):

Amended Code Sec. 6724(d)(2) by striking "or" at the end of subparagraph (AA), by striking the period at the end of subparagraph (BB), and by inserting after subparagraph (BB) a new subparagraph (CC). **Effective** for charges made after 12-31-2009.

P.L. 109-280, §1211(b)(1):

Amended Code Sec. 6724(d)(1)(B), as amended by this Act, by redesignating clauses (xiv) through (xix) as clauses (xv) through (xx) and by inserting after clause (xiii) a new clause (xiv). **Effective** for acquisitions of contracts after 8-17-2006.

• **2004, American Jobs Creation Act of 2004 (P.L. 108-357)**

P.L. 108-357, §805(b)(1):

Amended Code Sec. 6724(d)(1)(B) by redesignating clauses (ii) through (xviii) as clauses (iii) through (xix), respectively, and by inserting after clause (i) a new clause (ii). **Effective** for acquisitions after 10-22-2004.

P.L. 108-357, §805(b)(2):

Amended Code Sec. 6724(d)(2) by redesignating subparagraphs (F) through (BB) as subparagraphs (G) through (CC), respectively, and by inserting after subparagraph (E) a new subparagraph (F). **Effective** for acquisitions after 10-22-2004.

P.L. 108-357, §853(d)(2)(L):

Amended Code Sec. 6724(d)(1)(B), as amended by Act Sec. 805(b)(1), by striking clause (xvi) and by redesignating the succeeding clauses accordingly. **Effective** for aviation-grade kerosene removed, entered, or sold after 12-31-2004. Prior to being stricken, Code Sec. 6724(d)(1)(b)(xvi), as redesignated by Act Sec. 805(b)(1), read as follows:

(xvi) subparagraph (A) or (C) of subsection (c)(4) of section 4093 (relating to information reporting with respect to tax on diesel and aviation fuels),

P.L. 108-357, §853(d)(2)(M):

Amended Code Sec. 6724(d)(2), as amended by Act Sec. 805(b)(2), by striking subparagraph (X) and by redesignating the succeeding subparagraphs accordingly. **Effective** for aviation-grade kerosene removed, entered, or sold after 12-31-2004. Prior to being stricken, Code Sec. 6724(d)(2)(X), as redesignated by Act Sec. 805(b)(2), read as follows:

(X) section 4093(c)(4)(B) (relating to certain purchasers of diesel and aviation fuels),

• **2002, Trade Act of 2002 (P.L. 107-210)**

P.L. 107-210, §202(c)(2)(A):

Amended Code Sec. 6724(d)(1)(B) by redesignating clauses (xi) through (xvii) as clauses (xii) through (xviii), respectively, and by inserting after clause (x) a new clause (xi). **Effective** 8-6-2002.

P.L. 107-210, §202(c)(2)(B):

Amended Code Sec. 6724(d)(2) by striking "or" at the end of subparagraph (Z), by striking the period at the end of subparagraph (AA) and inserting ", or", and by adding after subparagraph (AA) a new subparagraph (BB). **Effective** 8-6-2002.

• **2000, Community Renewal Tax Relief Act of 2000 (P.L. 106-554)**

P.L. 106-554, §319(23)(A):

Amended Code Sec. 6724(d)(1)(B) by striking clauses (xiv) through (xvii) and inserting new clauses (xiv) through (xvii). **Effective** 12-21-2000. Prior to amendment, Code Sec. 6724(d)(1)(B)(xiv)-(xvii) read as follows:

(xiv) subparagraph (A) or (C) of subsection (c)(4) of section 4093 (relating to information reporting with respect to tax on diesel and aviation fuels), or

(xv) section 4101(d) (relating to information reporting with respect to fuels taxes)[,]

(xvi) subparagraph (C) of section 338(h)(10) (relating to information required to be furnished to the Secretary in case of elective recognition of gain or loss); or

(xvii) section 264(f)(5)(A)(iv) (relating to reporting with respect to certain life insurance and annuity contracts).

• **1998, IRS Restructuring and Reform Act of 1998 (P.L. 105-206)**

P.L. 105-206, §6010(o)(4)(B):

Amended Code Sec. 6724(d)(1)(B) by striking "or" at the end of clause (xv), by striking the period at the end of clause (xvi) and inserting ", or", and by adding a new clause (xvii). **Effective** as if included in the provision of P.L. 105-34 to which it relates [**effective** for contracts issued after 6-8-97, in tax years ending after such date.—CCH].

P.L. 105-206, §6010(o)(4)(C) (as amended by P.L. 106-554, §319(23)(B)):

Amended Code Sec. 6724(d)(2) by striking "or" at the end of subparagraph (Y), by striking the period at the end of subparagraph (Z) and inserting "or", and by adding at the end a new subparagraph (AA). **Effective** as if included in the provision of P.L. 105-34 to which it relates [**effective** for contracts issued after 6-8-97, in tax years ending after such date.—CCH].

• **1997, Taxpayer Relief Act of 1997 (P.L. 105-34)**

P.L. 105-34, §201(c)(2)(A) (as amended by P.L. 105-206, §6004 (a)(3)):

Amended Code Sec. 6724(d)(1)(B) by redesignating clauses (x) through (xv) as clauses (xi) through (xvi), respectively, and by inserting after clause (ix) a new clause (x). **Effective** for expenses paid after 12-31-97 (in tax years ending after such date), for education furnished in academic periods beginning after such date.

P.L. 105-34, §201(c)(2)(B):

Amended Code Sec. 6724(d)(2) by striking "or" at the end of the next to last subparagraph, by striking the period at the end of the last subparagraph and inserting ", or", and by adding at the end a new subparagraph (Z). **Effective** for expenses paid after 12-31-97 (in tax years ending after such date), for education furnished in academic periods beginning after such date.

P.L. 105-34, §1213(b):

Amended Code Sec. 6724(d)(1)(A) by striking "or" at the end of clause (vii), by adding "or" at the end of clause (viii), and by adding at the end a new clause (ix). **Effective** for leases entered into after 8-5-97.

P.L. 105-34, §1602(d)(2)(A):

Amended Code Sec. 6724(d)(2) by striking so much as follows subparagraph (Q) and precedes the last sentence, and inserting new subparagraphs (R) through (Y). **Effective** as if included in the provision of P.L. 104-191 to which it relates [**effective** for benefits paid after 12-31-96.—CCH]. Prior to amendment, the material following Code Sec. 6724(d)(2)(Q) and preceding the last sentence read as follows:

(R) section 6051 (relating to receipts for employees),

(S) section 6050R(c) (relating to returns relating to certain purchases of fish),

(T) section 6052(b) (relating to returns regarding payment of wages in the form of group-term life insurance),

(U) section 6053(b) or (c) (relating to reports of tips),

(U)[(V)] section 4093(c)(4)(B) (relating to certain purchasers of diesel and aviation fuels),

(V)[(W)] section 6048(b)(1)(B) (relating to foreign trust reporting requirements),

(W)[(X)] section 408(i) (relating to reports with respect to individual retirement plans) to any person other than the Secretary with respect to the amount of payments made to such person, or

(X)[(Y)] section 6047(d) (relating to reports by plan administrators) to any person other than the Secretary with respect to the amount of payments made to such person.

• **1996, Health Insurance Portability and Accountability Act of 1996 (P.L. 104-191)**

P.L. 104-191, §323(b)(1):

Amended Code Sec. 6724(d)(1)(B) by redesignating clauses (ix) through (xiv) as clauses (x) through (xv), respectively, and by inserting after clause (viii) a new clause (ix). **Effective** for benefits paid after 12-31-96.

ASSESSABLE PENALTIES

P.L. 104-191, § 323(b)(2):

Amended Code Sec. 6724(d)(2) by redesignating subparagraphs (Q) through (T) as subparagraphs (R) through (U), respectively, and inserting after subparagraph (P) a new subparagraph (Q). **Effective** for benefits paid after 12-31-96.

• **1996, Small Business Job Protection Act of 1996 (P.L. 104-188)**

P.L. 104-188, § 1116(b)(2)(A):

Amended Code Sec. 6724(d)(1)(A) by striking "or" at the end of clause (vi), by striking "and" at the end of clause (vii) and inserting " or", and by adding at the end a new clause (viii). **Effective** for payments made after 12-31-97.

P.L. 104-188, § 1116(b)(2)(B):

Amended Code Sec. 6724(d)(2) by redesignating subparagraphs (R) through (U) as subparagraphs (S) through (V), respectively, and by inserting after subparagraph (Q) a new subparagraph (R). **Effective** for payments made after 12-31-97.

P.L. 104-188, § 1455(a)(1):

Amended Code Sec. 6724(d)(1) by striking "and" at the end of subparagraph (A), by striking the period at the end of subparagraph (B) and inserting ", and", and by inserting after subparagraph (B) a new subparagraph (C). **Effective** for returns, reports, and other statements the due date for which (determined without regard to extensions) is after 12-31-96.

P.L. 104-188, § 1455(a)(2):

Amended Code Sec. 6724(d)(2) by striking "or" at the end of subparagraph (U), by striking the period at the end of subparagraph (V) and inserting a comma, and by inserting after subparagraph (V) new subparagraphs (W) and (X). **Effective** for returns, reports, and other statements the due date for which (determined without regard to extensions) is after 12-31-96.

P.L. 104-188, § 1615(a)(2)(B):

Amended Code Sec. 6724(d)(3) by adding "and" at the end of subparagraph (C), striking subparagraph (D), and redesignating subparagraph (E) as subparagraph (D). **Effective**, generally, with respect to returns the due date for which (without regard to extensions) is on or after the 30th day after 8-20-96. For a special rule, see Act Sec. 1615(d)(2), below. Prior to amendment, Code Sec. 6724(d)(3)(D) read as follows:

(D) the requirement of section 6109(e) that a person include the TIN of any dependent on his return, and

P.L. 104-188, § 1615(d)(2), provides:

(2) SPECIAL RULE FOR 1995 AND 1996.—In the case of returns for taxable years beginning in 1995 or 1996, a taxpayer shall not be required by the amendments made by this section to provide a taxpayer identification number for a child who is born after October 31, 1995, in the case of a taxable year beginning in 1995 or November 30, 1996, in the case of a taxable year beginning in 1996.

P.L. 104-188, § 1702(c)(2)(A)-(B):

Amended Code Sec. 6724(d)(1)(B) by striking "or" at the end of clause (xii), and by striking the period at the end of clause (xiii) and inserting ", or". **Effective** as if included in the provision of P.L. 101-508 to which it relates.

P.L. 104-188, § 1704(j)(3):

Amended Code Sec. 6724(d)(3)(E) by striking "section 6109(f)" and inserting "section 6109(h)". **Effective** 8-20-96.

P.L. 104-188, § 1901(c)(1):

Amended Code Sec. 6724(d)(2) by striking "or" at the end of subparagraph (S), by striking the period at the end of subparagraph (T) and inserting ", or", and by inserting after subparagraph (T) a new subparagraph (U). For the **effective** date, see Act Sec. 1901(d), below.

P.L. 104-188, § 1901(d), provides:

(d) EFFECTIVE DATES.—

(1) REPORTABLE EVENTS.—To the extent related to subsection (a) of section 6048 of the Internal Revenue Code of 1986, as amended by this section, the amendments made by this section shall apply to reportable events (as defined in such section 6048) occurring after the date of the enactment of this Act.

(2) GRANTOR TRUST REPORTING.—To the extent related to subsection (b) of such section 6048, the amendments made by this section shall apply to taxable years of United States persons beginning after December 31, 1995.

(3) REPORTING BY UNITED STATES BENEFICIARIES.—To the extent related to subsection (c) of such section 6048, the amendments made by this section shall apply to distributions received after the date of the enactment of this Act.

• **1994, Violent Crime Control and Law Enforcement Act of 1994 (P.L. 103-322)**

P.L. 103-322, § 20415(b)(1):

Amended Code Sec. 6724(d)(1)(B)(iv). For the **effective** date, see Act Sec. 20415(c)-(d) below. Prior to amendment, Code Sec. 6724(d)(1)(B)(iv) read as follows:

(iv) section 6050I(a) (relating to cash received in trade or business),

P.L. 103-322, § 20415(b)(2):

Amended Code Sec. 6724(d)(2)(K). For the **effective** date, see Act Sec. 20415(c)-(d) below. Prior to amendment, Code Sec. 6724(d)(2)(K) read as follows:

(K) section 6050I(e) (relating to returns relating to cash received in trade or business),

P.L. 103-322, § 20415(c)-(d), provides:

(c) REGULATIONS.—The Secretary of the Treasury or the Secretary's delegate shall prescribe temporary regulations under the amendments made by this section within 90 days after the date of enactment of this Act.

(d) EFFECTIVE DATE.—The amendments made by this section shall take effect on the 60th day after the date on which the temporary regulations are prescribed under subsection (c).

• **1993, Omnibus Budget Reconciliation Act of 1993 (P.L. 103-66)**

P.L. 103-66, § 13252(b)(1):

Amended Code Sec. 6724(d)(1)(B)(viii)-(xiv) by inserting after clause (vii) a new clause (viii), and by redesignating the following clauses accordingly. **Effective** for discharges of indebtedness after 12-1-93. However, for exceptions, see Act Sec. 13252(d)(2) below.

P.L. 103-66, § 13252(b)(2):

Amended Code Sec. 6724(d)(2)(P)-(T) by redesignating subparagraphs (P) through (S) as subparagraphs (Q) through (T), respectively, and by inserting after subparagraph (O) new subparagraph (P). **Effective** for discharges of indebtedness after 12-1-93. However, for exceptions, see Act Sec. 13252(d)(2) below.

P.L. 103-66, § 13252(d)(2), provides:

(2) GOVERNMENTAL ENTITIES.—In the case of an entity referred to in section 6050P(c)(1)(B) of the Internal Revenue Code of 1986 (as added by this section), the amendments made by this section shall apply to discharges of indebtedness after the date of the enactment of this Act.

• **1992, Energy Policy Act of 1992 (P.L. 102-486)**

P.L. 102-486, § 1933(b):

Amended Code Sec. 6724(d)(3) by striking "and" at the end of subparagraph (C), by striking the period at the end of subparagraph (D) and inserting ", and", and by adding at the end thereof new subparagraph (E). **Effective** for tax years beginning after 12-31-91.

• **1990, Omnibus Budget Reconciliation Act of 1990 (P.L. 101-508)**

P.L. 101-508, § 11212(e)(1) (as amended by P.L. 104-188, § 1702(b)(1)):

Amended Code Sec. 6724(d)(1)(B) by striking "or" at the end of clause (x), by striking ", or subsection (e)," in clause (xi), by striking the period at the end of clause (xi) and inserting ", or", and by inserting after clause (xi) a new clause (xii). **Effective** 12-1-90.

P.L. 101-508, § 11323(b)(2):

Amended Code Sec. 6724(d)(1)(B)(x) by striking "section 1060(b)" and inserting "subsection (b) or (e) of section 1060". **Effective**, generally, for acquisitions after 10-9-90. For an exception, see Act Sec. 11323(d)(2), below.

P.L. 101-508, § 11323(c)(2):

Amended Code Sec. 6724(d)(1)(B) by striking "or" at the end of clause (x), by striking the period at the end of clause (xi) and inserting ", or", and by inserting after clause (xi) a new clause (xii). **Effective**, generally, for acquisitions after 10-9-90. For an exception, see Act Sec. 11323(d)(2), below.

P.L. 101-508, § 11323(d)(2), provides:

(2) BINDING CONTRACT EXCEPTION.—The amendments made by this section shall not apply to any acquisition pursuant to a written binding contract in effect on October 9, 1990, and at all times thereafter before such acquisition.

• **1989, Omnibus Budget Reconciliation Act of 1989 (P.L. 101-239)**

P.L. 101-239, § 7711(a):

Amended Code Sec. 6724. For text of Code Sec. 6724 prior to amendment, see the amendment notes following Code Sec. 6721. **Effective** for returns and statements the due date for which (determined without regard to extensions) is after 12-31-89.

[Sec. 6724(e)]

(e) SPECIAL RULE FOR CERTAIN PARTNERSHIP RETURNS.—If any partnership return under section 6031(a) is required under section 6011(e) to be filed on magnetic media or in other machine-readable form, for purposes of this part, each schedule required to be included with such return with respect to each partner shall be treated as a separate information return.

Amendments

• **1997, Taxpayer Relief Act of 1997 (P.L. 105-34)**

P.L. 105-34, § 1223(b):

Amended Code Sec. 6724 by adding at the end a new subsection (e). **Effective** for partnership tax years beginning after 12-31-97 [effective date changed by P.L. 105-206, § 6012(e)].

[Sec. 6724(f)]

(f) SPECIAL RULE FOR RETURNS OF EDUCATIONAL INSTITUTIONS RELATED TO HIGHER EDUCATION TUITION AND RELATED EXPENSES.—No penalty shall be imposed under section 6721 or 6722 solely by reason of failing to provide the TIN of an individual on a return or statement required by section

ASSESSABLE PENALTIES

6050S(a)(1) if the eligible educational institution required to make such return contemporaneously makes a true and accurate certification under penalty of perjury (and in such form and manner as may be prescribed by the Secretary) that it has complied with standards promulgated by the Secretary for obtaining such individual's TIN.

Amendments

- **2015, Trade Preferences Extension Act of 2015 (P.L. 114-27)**

P.L. 114-27, §805(a):

Amended Code Sec. 6724 by adding at the end a new subsection (f). **Effective** for returns required to be made, and statements required to be furnished, after 12-31-2015.

[Sec. 6724(g)]

(g) SPECIAL RULE FOR REPORTING CERTAIN ADDITIONAL TAXES.—No penalty shall be imposed under section 6721 or 6722 if—

(1) a person makes a return or report under section 6047(d) or 408(i) with respect to any distribution,

(2) such distribution is made following a rollover, transfer, or exchange described in section 72(t)(4)(C) or section 72(q)(3)(C),

(3) in making such return or report the person relies upon a certification provided by the taxpayer that the distributions satisfy the requirements of section 72(t)(4)(C)(iii) or section 72(q)(3)(B)(iii), as applicable, and

(4) such person does not have actual knowledge that the distributions do not satisfy such requirements.

Amendments

- **2022, SECURE 2.0 Act of 2022 (P.L. 117-328)**

P.L. 117-328, §323(c):

Amended Code Sec. 6724 by inserting at the end a new subsection (g). **Effective** for transfers, rollovers, and exchanges occurring after 12-31-2023. For a special rule, see Act Sec. 323(e)(3), below.

P.L. 117-328, §323(e)(3), provides:

(3) NO INFERENCE.—Nothing in the amendments made by this section shall be construed to create an inference with respect to the law in effect prior to the effective date of such amendments.

[Sec. 6725]

SEC. 6725. FAILURE TO REPORT INFORMATION UNDER SECTION 4101.

[Sec. 6725(a)]

(a) IN GENERAL.—In the case of each failure described in subsection (b) by any person with respect to a vessel or facility, such person shall pay a penalty of $10,000 in addition to the tax (if any).

[Sec. 6725(b)]

(b) FAILURES SUBJECT TO PENALTY.—For purposes of subsection (a), the failures described in this subsection are—

(1) any failure to make a report under section 4101(d) on or before the date prescribed therefor, and

(2) any failure to include all of the information required to be shown on such report or the inclusion of incorrect information.

[Sec. 6725(c)]

(c) REASONABLE CAUSE EXCEPTION.—No penalty shall be imposed under this section with respect to any failure if it is shown that such failure is due to reasonable cause.

Amendments

- **2004, American Jobs Creation Act of 2004 (P.L. 108-357)**

P.L. 108-357, §863(d)(1):

Amended part II of subchapter B of chapter 68 by adding at the end a new Code Sec. 6725. **Effective** for penalties imposed after 12-31-2004.

Subchapter C—Procedural Requirements

Sec. 6751.   Procedural requirements.

[Sec. 6751]

SEC. 6751. PROCEDURAL REQUIREMENTS.

[Sec. 6751(a)]

(a) COMPUTATION OF PENALTY INCLUDED IN NOTICE.—The Secretary shall include with each notice of penalty under this title information with respect to the name of the penalty, the section of this title under which the penalty is imposed, and a computation of the penalty.

[Sec. 6751(b)]

(b) APPROVAL OF ASSESSMENT.—

(1) IN GENERAL.—No penalty under this title shall be assessed unless the initial determination of such assessment is personally approved (in writing) by the immediate supervisor of the individual making such determination or such higher level official as the Secretary may designate.

(2) EXCEPTIONS.—Paragraph (1) shall not apply to—

(A) any addition to tax under section 6651, 6654, 6655, or 6662 (but only with respect to an addition to tax by reason of paragraph (9) or (10) of subsection (b) thereof); or

(B) any other penalty automatically calculated through electronic means.

Amendments

- **2022, SECURE 2.0 Act of 2022 (P.L. 117-328)**

P.L. 117-328, §605(a)(2)(D):

Amended Code Sec. 6751(b)(2)(A) by striking "subsection (b)(9)" and inserting "paragraph (9) or (10) of subsection (b)". **Effective** for contributions made after 12-29-2022. For a special rule, see Act Sec. 605(c)(2), below.

P.L. 117-328, §605(c)(2), provides:

(2) NO INFERENCE.—No inference is intended as to the appropriate treatment of contributions made in taxable years ending on or before the date specified in paragraph (1), or as to any contribution for which a deduction is not disallowed by reason of section 170(h)(7) of the Internal Revenue Code of 1986, as added by this section.

- **2020, Taxpayer Certainty and Disaster Tax Relief Act of 2020 (P.L. 116-260)**

P.L. 116-260, §212(b)(3), Div. EE:

Amended Code Sec. 6751(b)(2)(A) by striking "or 6655" and inserting "6655, or 6662 (but only with respect to an addition to tax by reason of subsection (b)(9) thereof)". **Effective** for tax years beginning after 12-31-2020.

[Sec. 6751(c)]

(c) PENALTIES.—For purposes of this section, the term "penalty" includes any addition to tax or any additional amount.

STAMPS—GENERAL PROVISIONS

Amendments

• **1998, IRS Restructuring and Reform Act of 1998 (P.L. 105-206)**

P.L. 105-206, §3306(a):

Amended chapter 68 by adding at the end a new subchapter C (Code Sec. 6751). **Effective** for notices issued, and penalties assessed, after 6-30-2001. In the case of any notice of penalty issued after 6-30-2001, and before 7-1-2003, the requirements of section 6751(a) of the Internal Revenue Code of 1986 shall be treated as met if such notice contains a telephone number at which the taxpayer can request a copy of the taxpayer's assessment and payment history with respect to such penalty [effective date changed by P.L. 106-554, §302(b)].

CHAPTER 69—GENERAL PROVISIONS RELATING TO STAMPS

Sec. 6801.	Authority for establishment, alteration, and distribution.
Sec. 6802.	Supply and distribution.
Sec. 6803.	Accounting and safeguarding.
Sec. 6804.	Attachment and cancellation.
Sec. 6805.	Redemption of stamps.
Sec. 6806.	Occupational tax stamps.
Sec. 6807.	Stamping, marking, and branding seized goods.
Sec. 6808.	Special provisions relating to stamps.

[Sec. 6801]

SEC. 6801. AUTHORITY FOR ESTABLISHMENT, ALTERATION, AND DISTRIBUTION.

[Sec. 6801(a)]

(a) ESTABLISHMENT AND ALTERATION.—The Secretary may establish, and from time to time alter, renew, replace, or change the form, style, character, material, and device of any stamp, mark, or label under any provision of the laws relating to internal revenue.

Amendments

• **1976, Tax Reform Act of 1976 (P.L. 94-455)**

P.L. 94-455, §1906(b)(13)(A):

Amended 1954 Code by substituting "Secretary" for "Secretary or his delegate" each place it appeared. **Effective** 2-1-77.

[Sec. 6801(b)]

(b) PREPARATION AND DISTRIBUTION OF REGULATIONS, FORMS, STAMPS AND DIES.—The Secretary shall prepare and distribute all the instructions, regulations, directions, forms, blanks, and stamps; and shall provide proper and sufficient adhesive stamps and other stamps or dies for expressing and denoting the several stamp taxes.

Amendments

• **1984, Deficit Reduction Act of 1984 (P.L. 98-369)**

P.L. 98-369, §454(c)(13):

Amended Code Sec. 6801(b) by striking out "several stamp taxes; except that stamps required by or prescribed pursuant to the provisions of section 5205 or section 5235 may be prepared and distributed by persons authorized by the Secretary, under such controls for the protection of the revenue as shall be deemed necessary." and inserting in lieu thereof "several stamp taxes." **Effective** 7-1-85.

• **1976 (P.L. 94-569)**

P.L. 94-569, §2:

Substituted a semicolon for a period after "taxes" and added the clause thereafter to Code Sec. 6801(b). **Effective** 10-20-76.

• **1976, Tax Reform Act of 1976 (P.L. 94-455)**

P.L. 94-455, §1906(b)(13)(A):

Amended 1954 Code by substituting "Secretary" for "Secretary or his delegate" each place it appeared. **Effective** 2-1-77.

[Sec. 6802]

SEC. 6802. SUPPLY AND DISTRIBUTION.

The Secretary shall furnish, without prepayment, to—

(1) POSTMASTER GENERAL.—The Postmaster General a suitable quantity of adhesive stamps, coupons, tickets, or such other devices as may be prescribed by the Secretary pursuant to section 6302(b) or this chapter, to be distributed to, and kept on sale by, the various postmasters in the United States in all post offices of the first and second classes, and such post offices of the third and fourth classes as—

(A) are located in county seats, or

(B) are certified by the Secretary to the Postmaster General as necessary;

(2) DESIGNATED DEPOSITARY OF THE UNITED STATES.—Any designated depositary of the United States a suitable quantity of adhesive stamps to be kept on sale by such designated depositary.

Amendments

• **1976, Tax Reform Act of 1976 (P.L. 94-455)**

P.L. 94-455, §1906(b)(13)(A):

Amended 1954 Code by substituting "Secretary" for "Secretary or his delegate" each place it appeared. **Effective** 2-1-77.

P.L. 94-455, §1906(a)(36):

Substituted a period for a semicolon at the end of Code Sec. 6802(2). **Effective** 2-1-77.

• **1965, Excise Tax Reduction Act of 1965 (P.L. 89-44)**

P.L. 89-44, §601(d):

Amended Sec. 6802 by deleting a parenthetical phrase: "(other than the stamps on playing cards)" following the words "adhesive stamps" in paragraph (1) and by deleting paragraph (3). **Effective** 6-22-65. Prior to deletion, paragraph (3) read as follows:

(3) STATE AGENTS.—Any person who is—

(A) duly appointed and acting as agent of any State for the sale of stock transfer stamps of such State, and

(B) designated by the Secretary or his delegate for the purpose,

a suitable quantity of such adhesive stamps as are required by section 4301, to be kept on sale by such person.

[Sec. 6803]

SEC. 6803. ACCOUNTING AND SAFEGUARDING.

[Sec. 6803(a)]

(a) BOND.—In cases coming within the provisions of paragraph (2) of section 6802, the Secretary may require a bond, with sufficient sureties, in a sum to be fixed by the Secretary, conditioned for the faithful return, whenever so required, of all quantities or amounts undisposed of and for the payment monthly for all quantities or amounts sold or not remaining on hand.

Amendments

• **1976, Tax Reform Act of 1976 (P.L. 94-455)**

P.L. 94-455, §1906(a)(37):

Added Code Sec. 6803(a).

• **1972 (P.L. 92-310)**

P.L. 92-310, §230(a):

Repealed Code Sec. 6803(a). **Effective** 6-6-72. Prior to repeal, Code Sec. 6803(a) read as follows:

STAMPS—GENERAL PROVISIONS

(a) THE POSTMASTER GENERAL.—

(1) BOND AND ACCOUNTING.—The Postmaster General may require each postmaster under paragraph (1) of section 6802 to furnish bond in such increased amount as he may from time to time determine, and each such postmaster shall deposit the receipts from the sale of such stamps, coupons, tickets, books, or other devices to the credit of, and render accounts to the Postmaster General at such times and in such form as the Postmaster General may by regulations prescribe.

(2) DEPOSIT OF RECEIPTS.—The Postmaster General shall at least once a month transfer to the Treasury as internal revenue collections, all receipts so deposited.

[Sec. 6803(b)]

(b) REGULATIONS.—The Secretary may from time to time make such regulations as he may find necessary to insure the safekeeping or prevent the illegal use of all adhesive stamps referred to in paragraph (2) of section 6802.

Amendments

• **1976, Tax Reform Act of 1976 (P.L. 94-455)**

P.L. 94-455, §1906(a)(37):

Amended Code Sec. 6803(b). Prior to amendment, Code Sec. 6803(b) read as follows:

(b) DEPOSITARIES AND STATE AGENTS.—

(1) BOND.—In cases coming within the provisions of paragraph (2) or (3) of section 6802, the Secretary or his delegate may require a bond, with sufficient sureties, in a sum to be fixed by the Secretary or his delegate, conditioned for the faithful return, whenever so required, of all quantities or amounts undisposed of and for the payment monthly for all quantities or amounts sold or not remaining on hand.

(2) REGULATIONS.—The Secretary or his delegate may from time to time make such regulations as he may find necessary to insure the safekeeping or prevent the illegal use of all adhesive stamps referred to in paragraphs (2) and (3) of section 6802.

[Sec. 6804]

SEC. 6804. ATTACHMENT AND CANCELLATION.

Except as otherwise expressly provided in this title, the stamps referred to in section 6801 shall be attached, protected, removed, canceled, obliterated, and destroyed, in such manner and by such instruments or other means as the Secretary may prescribe by rules or regulations.

Amendments

• **1976, Tax Reform Act of 1976 (P.L. 94-455)**

P.L. 94-455, §1906(b)(13)(A):

Amended 1954 Code by substituting "Secretary" for "Secretary or his delegate" each place it appeared. **Effective** 2-1-77.

[Sec. 6805]

SEC. 6805. REDEMPTION OF STAMPS.

[Sec. 6805(a)]

(a) AUTHORIZATION.—The Secretary, subject to regulations prescribed by him, may, upon receipt of satisfactory evidence of the facts, make allowance for or redeem such of the stamps, issued under authority of any internal revenue law, as may have been spoiled, destroyed, or rendered useless or unfit for the purpose intended, or for which the owner may have no use.

Amendments

• **1976, Tax Reform Act of 1976 (P.L. 94-455)**

P.L. 94-455, §1906(b)(13)(A):

Amended 1954 Code by substituting "Secretary" for "Secretary or his delegate" each place it appeared. **Effective** 2-1-77.

• **1958, Excise Tax Technical Changes Act of 1958 (P.L. 85-859)**

P.L. 85-859, §165(b):

Amended Sec. 6805(a) by striking out at the end thereof the phrase ", or which through mistake may have been improperly or unnecessarily used, or where the rates or duties represented thereby have been excessive in amount, paid in error, or in any manner wrongfully collected". **Effective** 1-1-59.

[Sec. 6805(b)]

(b) METHOD AND CONDITIONS OF ALLOWANCE.—Such allowance or redemption may be made, either by giving other stamps in lieu of the stamps so allowed for or redeemed, or by refunding the amount or value to the owner thereof, deducting therefrom, in case of repayment, the percentage, if any, allowed to the purchaser thereof; but no allowance or redemption shall be made in any case until the stamps so spoiled or rendered useless shall have been returned to the Secretary, or until satisfactory proof has been made showing the reason why the the same cannot be returned; or, if so required by the Secretary, when the person presenting the same cannot satisfactorily trace the history of said stamps from their issuance to the presentation of his claim as aforesaid.

Amendments

• **1976, Tax Reform Act of 1976 (P.L. 94-455)**

P.L. 94-455, §1906(b)(13)(A):

Amended 1954 Code by substituting "Secretary" for "Secretary or his delegate" each place it appeared. **Effective** 2-1-77.

[Sec. 6805(c)]

(c) TIME FOR FILING CLAIMS.—No claim for the redemption of, or allowance for, stamps shall be allowed under this section unless presented within 3 years after the purchase of such stamps from the Government.

Amendments

• **1958, Excise Tax Technical Changes Act of 1958 (P.L. 85-859)**

P.L. 85-859, §165(c):

Amended Sec. 6805(c) by adding the phrase "under this section" following "shall be allowed". **Effective** 1-1-59.

[Sec. 6805(d)]

(d) FINALITY OF DECISIONS.—The findings of fact in and the decision of the Secretary upon the merits of any claim presented under or authorized by this section shall, in the absence of fraud or mistake in mathematical calculation, be final and not subject to revision by any accounting officer.

Amendments

• **1976, Tax Reform Act of 1976 (P.L. 94-455)**

P.L. 94-455, §1906(b)(13)(A):

Amended 1954 Code by substituting "Secretary" for "Secretary or his delegate" each place it appeared. **Effective** 2-1-77.

[Sec. 6806]

SEC. 6806. OCCUPATIONAL TAX STAMPS.

Every person engaged in any business, avocation, or employment, who is thereby made liable to a special tax (other than a special tax under subchapter B of chapter 35, under subchapter B of chapter 36, or under subtitle E) shall place and keep conspicuously in his establishment or place of business all stamps denoting payment of such special tax.

JEOPARDY—TERMINATION OF TAXABLE YEAR

Amendments

• **1970 (P.L. 90-618)**

P.L. 90-618, §204:

Amended Code Sec. 6806. **Effective** 10-22-68. Prior to amendment, Code Sec. 6806 read as follows:

SEC. 6806. POSTING OCCUPATIONAL TAX STAMPS.

(a) GENERAL RULE.—Every person engaged in any business, avocation, or employment, who is thereby made liable to a special tax, shall place and keep conspicuously in his establishment or place of business all stamps denoting payment of said special tax.

(b) COIN-OPERATED GAMING DEVICES.—The Secretary or his delegate may by regulations require that stamps denoting the payment of the special tax imposed by section 4461 shall be posted on or in each device in such a manner that it will be visible to any person operating the device.

(c) OCCUPATIONAL WAGERING TAX.—Every person liable for special tax under section 4411 shall place and keep conspicuously in his principal place of business the stamp denoting the payment of such special tax; except that if he has no such place of business, he shall keep such stamp on his person, and exhibit it, upon request, to any officer or employee of the Treasury Department."

• **1965, Excise Tax Reduction Act of 1965 (P.L. 89-44)**

P.L. 89-44, §601(e):

Amended the heading in Code Sec. 6806(b) as reproduced in the amendment note for P.L. 90-618. **Effective** 6-22-65. Prior to amendment, the heading read:

"Coin-operated Amusement and Gaming Devices".

[Sec. 6807]

SEC. 6807. STAMPING, MARKING, AND BRANDING SEIZED GOODS.

If any article of manufacture or produce requiring brands, stamps, or marks of whatever kind to be placed thereon, is sold upon levy, forfeiture (except as provided in section 5688 with respect to distilled spirits), or other process provided by law, the same not having been branded, stamped, or marked, as required by law, the officer selling the same shall, upon sale thereof, fix or cause to be affixed the brands, stamps, or marks so required.

[Sec. 6808]

SEC. 6808. SPECIAL PROVISIONS RELATING TO STAMPS.

For special provisions on stamps relating to—

(1) Distilled spirits and fermented liquors, see chapter 51.

(2) Machine guns and short-barrelled firearms, see chapter 53.

(3) Tobacco, snuff, cigars and cigarettes, see chapter 52.

Amendments

• **1976, Tax Reform Act of 1976 (P.L. 94-455)**

P.L. 94-455, §1904(b)(5)(B):

Amended Code Sec. 6808 by striking out paragraph (4). **Effective** 2-1-77. Prior to amendment, Code Sec. 6808(4) read as follows:

"(4) Documents and other instruments, see chapter 34."

P.L. 94-455, §1904(b)(7)(A):

Amended Code Sec. 6808 by striking out paragraph (7). **Effective** 2-1-77. Prior to amendment, Code Sec. 6808(7) read as follows:

"(7) Oleomargarine, see subchapter F of chapter 38."

P.L. 94-455, §1904(b)(8)(B):

Amended Code Sec. 6808 by striking out paragraph (12). **Effective** 2-1-77. Prior to amendment, Code Sec. 6808(12) read as follows:

"(12) White phosphorous matches, see subchapter B of chapter 39."

P.L. 94-455, §1904(b)(9)(A):

Amended Code Sec. 6808 by striking out paragraph (10). **Effective** 2-1-77. Prior to amendment, Code Sec. 6808(10) read as follows:

"(10) Process, renovated, or adulterated butter, see subchapter C of chapter 39."

P.L. 94-455, §1952(n)(1):

Amended Code Sec. 6808 by striking out paragraph (2). **Effective** 2-1-77. Prior to amendment, Code Sec. 6808(2) read as follows:

"(2) Cotton futures, see subchapter D of chapter 39."; and redesignated former paragraphs (3), (6), and (11) as paragraphs (1), (2), and (3).

• **1974 (P.L. 93-490)**

P.L. 93-490, §3(b)(6):

Repealed paragraph (5) of Code Sec. 6808. **Effective** with respect to filled cheese manufactured, imported, or sold after 10-26-74. Prior to repeal, paragraph (5) read as follows:

"(5) Filled cheese, see subchapter C of chapter 39."

• **1970 (P.L. 91-513)**

P.L. 91-513, §1102(c):

Amended Code Sec. 6808 by deleting paragraph (8) which read as follows: "(8) Opium, opium for smoking, opiates and coca leaves, and marihuana, see subchapter A of chapter 39." **Effective** 5-1-71.

• **1965, Excise Tax Reduction Act of 1965 (P.L. 89-44)**

P.L. 89-44, §601(f):

Amended Sec. 6808 by striking out paragraphs: "(1) Capital stock, see chapter 34" and "(9) Playing cards, see subchapter A of chapter 36".

• **1963 (P.L. 88-36)**

P.L. 88-36, §201(d):

Amended Code Sec. 6808 by striking out paragraph (11) and by renumbering paragraphs (12) and (13) as paragraphs (11) and (12). Prior to amendment, paragraph (11) read as follows:

"(11) Silver bullion, subchapter F of chapter 39."

CHAPTER 70—JEOPARDY, RECEIVERSHIPS, ETC.

SUBCHAPTER A.	Jeopardy.
SUBCHAPTER B.	Receiverships, etc.

Subchapter A—Jeopardy

Part I.	Termination of taxable year.
Part II.	Jeopardy assessments.
Part III.	Special rules with respect to certain cash.

PART I—TERMINATION OF TAXABLE YEAR

Sec. 6851.	Termination assessments of income tax.
Sec. 6852.	Termination assessments in case of flagrant political expenditures of section 501(c)(3) organizations.

[Sec. 6851]

SEC. 6851. TERMINATION ASSESSMENTS OF INCOME TAX.

[Sec. 6851(a)]

(a) AUTHORITY FOR MAKING.—

(1) IN GENERAL.—If the Secretary finds that a taxpayer designs quickly to depart from the United States or to remove his property therefrom, or to conceal himself or his property therein, or to do any other act (including in the case of a corporation distributing all or a part of its assets in liquidation or otherwise) tending to prejudice or to render wholly or partially ineffectual proceedings to collect the income tax for the current or the immediately preceding taxable year unless such proceeding be brought without delay, the Secretary shall immediately make a determination of tax for the current taxable year or for the preceding taxable year, or both, as the case may be, and notwithstanding any other provision of law, such tax shall become immediately due and payable. The Secretary shall immediately assess the amount of the tax so determined (together with all interest, additional amounts, and additions to the tax provided by law) for the current taxable year or such

JEOPARDY—TERMINATION OF TAXABLE YEAR

preceding taxable year, or both, as the case may be, and shall cause notice of such determination and assessment to be given the taxpayer, together with a demand for immediate payment of such tax.

(2) COMPUTATION OF TAX.—In the case of a current taxable year, the Secretary shall determine the tax for the period beginning on the first day of such current taxable year and ending on the date of the determination under paragraph (1) as though such period were a taxable year of the taxpayer, and shall take into account any prior determination made under this subsection with respect to such current taxable year.

(3) TREATMENT OF AMOUNTS COLLECTED.—Any amounts collected as a result of any assessments under this subsection shall, to the extent thereof, be treated as a payment of tax for such taxable year.

(4) THIS SECTION INAPPLICABLE WHERE SECTION 6861 APPLIES.—This section shall not authorize any assessment of tax for the preceding taxable year which is made after the due date of the taxpayer's return for such taxable year (determined with regard to any extensions).

Amendments

• **1976, Tax Reform Act of 1976 (P.L. 94-455)**

P.L. 94-455, §1204(b)(1):

Amended Code Sec. 6851(a). For the **effective** date, see Act Sec. 1204(d), below. Prior to amendment, Code Sec. 6851(a) read as follows:

SEC. 6851. TERMINATION OF TAXABLE YEAR.

(a) INCOME TAX IN JEOPARDY.—

(1) IN GENERAL.—If the Secretary or his delegate finds that a taxpayer designs quickly to depart from the United States or to remove his property therefrom, or to conceal himself or his property therein, or to do any other act tending to prejudice or to render wholly or partly ineffectual proceedings to collect the income tax for the current or the preceding taxable year unless such proceedings be brought without delay, the Secretary or his delegate shall declare the taxable period for such taxpayer immediately terminated, and shall cause notice of such finding and declaration to be given the taxpayer, together with a demand for immediate payment of the tax for the taxable period so declared terminated and of the tax for the preceding taxable year or so much of such tax as is unpaid, whether or not the time otherwise allowed by law for filing return and paying the tax has expired; and such taxes shall thereupon become immediately due and payable. In any proceeding in court brought to enforce payment of taxes made due and payable by virtue of the provisions of this section, the finding of the Secretary or his delegate, made as herein provided, whether made after notice to the taxpayer or not, shall be for all purposes presumptive evidence of jeopardy.

(2) CORPORATION IN LIQUIDATION.—If the Secretary or his delegate finds that the collection of the income tax of a corporation for the current or the preceding taxable year will be jeopardized by the distribution of all or a portion of the assets of such corporation in the liquidation of the whole or any part of its capital stock, the Secretary or his delegate shall declare the taxable period for such taxpayer immediately terminated and shall cause notice of such finding and declaration to be given the taxpayer, together with a demand for immediate payment of the tax for the taxable period so declared terminated and of the tax for the preceding taxable year or so much of such tax as is unpaid, whether or not the time otherwise allowed by law for filing return and paying the tax has expired; and such taxes shall thereupon become immediately due and payable.

P.L. 94-455, §1204(d), as amended by P.L. 94-528, §2(a), provides:

(d) Effective Date.—The amendments made by this section apply with respect to action taken under section 6851, 6861, or 6862 of the Internal Revenue Code of 1954 where the notice and demand takes place after February 28, 1977.

[Sec. 6851(b)]

(b) NOTICE OF DEFICIENCY.—If an assessment of tax is made under the authority of subsection (a), the Secretary shall mail a notice under section 6212(a) for the taxpayer's full taxable year (determined without regard to any action taken under subsection (a)) with respect to which such assessment was made within 60 days after the later of (i) the due date of the taxpayer's return for such taxable year (determined with regard to any extensions), or (ii) the date such taxpayer files such return. Such deficiency may be in an amount greater or less than the amount assessed under subsection (a).

Amendments

• **1976, Tax Reform Act of 1976 (P.L. 94-455)**

P.L. 94-455, §1204(b)(1):

Amended Code Sec. 6851(b). For the **effective** date, see Act Sec. 1204(d), below. Prior to amendment, Code Sec. 6851(b) read as follows:

(b) REOPENING OF TAXABLE PERIOD.—Notwithstanding the termination of the taxable period of the taxpayer by the Secretary or his delegate, as provided in subsection (a), the Secretary or his delegate may reopen such taxable period each time the taxpayer is found by the Secretary or his delegate to have received income, within the current taxable year, since a termination of the period under subsection (a). A taxable period so terminated by the Secretary or his delegate may be reopenend by the taxpayer (other than a nonresident alien) if he files with the Secretary or his delegate a true and accurate return of the items of gross income and of the deductions and credits allowed under this title for such taxable period, together with such other information as the Secretary or his delegate may by regulations prescribe. If taxpayer is a nonresident alien the taxable period so terminated may be reopened by him if he files, or causes to be filed, with the Secretary or his delegate a true and accurate return of his total income derived from all sources within the United States, in the manner prescribed in this title.

P.L. 94-455, §1204(d), as amended by P.L. 94-528, §2(a), provides:

(d) Effective Date.—The amendments made by this section apply with respect to action taken under section 6851, 6861, or 6862 of the Internal Revenue Code of 1954 where the notice and demand takes place after February 28, 1977.

[Sec. 6851(c)]

(c) CITIZENS.—In the case of a citizen of the United States or of a possession of the United States about to depart from the United States, the Secretary may, at his discretion, waive any or all of the requirements placed on the taxpayer by this section.

Amendments

• **1976, Tax Reform Act of 1976 (P.L. 94-455)**

P.L. 94-455, §1906(b)(13)(A):

Amended 1954 Code by substituting "Secretary" for "Secretary or his delegate" each place it appeared. **Effective** 2-1-77.

[Sec. 6851(d)]

(d) DEPARTURE OF ALIEN.—Subject to such exceptions as may, by regulations, be prescribed by the Secretary—

(1) No alien shall depart from the United States unless he first procures from the Secretary a certificate that he has complied with all the obligations imposed upon him by the income tax laws.

(2) Payment of taxes shall not be enforced by any proceedings under the provisions of this section prior to the expiration of the time otherwise allowed for paying such taxes if, in the case of an alien about to depart from the United States, the Secretary determines that the collection of the tax will not be jeopardized by the departure of the alien.

Amendments

• **1976, Tax Reform Act of 1976 (P.L. 94-455)**

P.L. 94-455, §1906(b)(13)(A):

Amended 1954 Code by substituting "Secretary" for "Secretary or his delegate" each place it appeared. **Effective** 2-1-77.

• **1958, Technical Amendments Act of 1958 (P.L. 85-866)**

P.L. 85-866, §87:

Amended Code Sec. 6851(d). **Effective** 1-1-54. Prior to amendment, Code Sec. 6851(d) read as follows:

"(d) Departure of Alien.—No alien shall depart from the United States unless he first procures from the Secretary or his delegate a certificate that he has complied with all the obligations imposed upon him by the income tax laws.".

[Sec. 6851(e)]

(e) SECTIONS 6861(f) AND (g) TO APPLY.—The provisions of sections 6861(f) (relating to collection of unpaid amounts) and 6861(g) (relating to abatement if jeopardy does not exist) shall apply with respect to any assessment made under subsection (a).

Amendments

• **1976, Tax Reform Act of 1976 (P.L. 94-455)**

P.L. 94-455, §1204(b)(2):

Amended Code Sec. 6851(e). For the **effective** date, see Act Sec. 1204(d), below. Prior to amendment, Code Sec. 6851(e) read as follows:

(e) FURNISHING OF BOND WHERE TAXABLE YEAR IS CLOSED BY THE SECRETARY OR HIS DELEGATE.—Payment of taxes shall not be enforced by any proceedings under the provisions of this section prior to the expiration of the time otherwise allowed for paying such taxes if the taxpayer furnishes, under regulations prescribed by the Secretary or his delegate, a bond to insure the timely making of returns with respect to, and payment of, such taxes or any income or excess profits taxes for prior years.

JEOPARDY ASSESSMENTS

P.L. 94-455, §1204(d), as amended by P.L. 94-528, §2(a), provides:

(d) Effective Date.—The amendments made by this section apply with respect to action taken under section 6851, 6861, or 6862 of the Internal Revenue Code of 1954 where the notice and demand takes place after February 28, 1977.

[Sec. 6851(f)]

(f) CROSS REFERENCES.—
(1) For provisions permitting immediate levy in case of jeopardy, see section 6331(a).
(2) For provisions relating to the review of jeopardy, see section 7429.

Amendments

• **1976, Tax Reform Act of 1976 (P.L. 94-455)**

P.L. 94-455, §1204(b)(2):
Added Code Sec. 6851(f). For the **effective** date, see Act Sec. 1204(d), below.

P.L. 94-455, §1204(d), as amended by P.L. 94-528, §2(a), provides:

(d) Effective Date.—The amendments made by this section apply with respect to action taken under section 6851, 6861, or 6862 of the Internal Revenue Code of 1954 where the notice and demand takes place after February 28, 1977.

[Sec. 6852]

SEC. 6852. TERMINATION ASSESSMENTS IN CASE OF FLAGRANT POLITICAL EXPENDITURES OF SECTION 501(c)(3) ORGANIZATIONS.

[Sec. 6852(a)]

(a) AUTHORITY TO MAKE.—
(1) IN GENERAL.—If the Secretary finds that—
(A) a section 501(c)(3) organization has made political expenditures, and
(B) such expenditures constitute a flagrant violation of the prohibition against making political expenditures,

the Secretary shall immediately make a determination of any income tax payable by such organization for the current or immediate preceding taxable year, or both, and shall immediately make a determination of any tax payable under section 4955 by such organization or any manager thereof with respect to political expenditures during the current or preceding taxable year, or both. Notwithstanding any other provision of law, any such tax shall become immediately due and payable. The Secretary shall immediately assess the amount of tax so determined (together with all interest, additional amounts, and additions to the tax provided by law) for the current year or the preceding taxable year, or both, and shall cause notice of such determination and assessment to be given to the organization or any manager thereof, as the case may be, together with a demand for immediate payment of such tax.

(2) COMPUTATION OF TAX.—In the case of a current taxable year, the Secretary shall determine the taxes for the period beginning on the 1st day of such current taxable year and ending on the date of the determination under paragraph (1) as though such period were a taxable year of the organization, and shall take into account any prior determination made under this subsection with respect to such current taxable year.

(3) TREATMENT OF AMOUNTS COLLECTED.—Any amounts collected as a result of any assessments under this subsection shall, to the extent thereof, be treated as a payment of income tax for such taxable year, or tax under section 4955 with respect to the expenditure, as the case may be.

(4) SECTION INAPPLICABLE TO ASSESSMENTS AFTER DUE DATE.—This section shall not authorize any assessment of tax for the preceding taxable year which is made after the due date of the organization's return for such taxable year (determined with regard to any extensions).

[Sec. 6852(b)]

(b) DEFINITIONS AND SPECIAL RULES.—
(1) DEFINITIONS.—For purposes of this section, the terms "section 501(c)(3) organization", "political expenditure", and "organization manager" have the respective meanings given to such terms by section 4955.
(2) CERTAIN RULES MADE APPLICABLE.—The provisions of sections 6851(b), 6861(f), and 6861(g) shall apply with respect to any assessment made under subsection (a), except that determinations under section 6861(g) shall be made on the basis of whether the requirements of subsection (a)(1)(B) of this section are met in lieu of whether jeopardy exists.

Amendments

• **1987, Revenue Act of 1987 (P.L. 100-203)**

P.L. 100-203, §10713(b)(1):
Amended part I of subchapter A of chapter 70 by adding at the end thereof a new section 6852. **Effective** 12-22-87.

PART II—JEOPARDY ASSESSMENTS

Sec. 6861.	Jeopardy assessments of income, estate, gift, and certain excise taxes.
Sec. 6862.	Jeopardy assessment of taxes other than income, estate, gift, and certain excise taxes.
Sec. 6863.	Stay of collection of jeopardy assessments.
Sec. 6864.	Termination of extended period for payment in case of carryback.

[Sec. 6861]

SEC. 6861. JEOPARDY ASSESSMENTS OF INCOME, ESTATE, GIFT, AND CERTAIN EXCISE TAXES.

[Sec. 6861(a)]

(a) AUTHORITY FOR MAKING.—If the Secretary believes that the assessment or collection of a deficiency, as defined in section 6211, will be jeopardized by delay, he shall, notwithstanding the provisions of section 6213(a), immediately assess such deficiency (together with all interest, additional amounts, and additions to the tax provided for by law), and notice and demand shall be made by the Secretary for the payment thereof.

Amendments

• **1976, Tax Reform Act of 1976 (P.L. 94-455)**

P.L. 94-455, §1906(b)(13)(A):
Amended 1954 Code by substituting "Secretary" for "Secretary or his delegate" each place it appeared. **Effective** 2-1-77.

• **1974, Employee Retirement Income Security Act of 1974 (P.L. 93-406)**

P.L. 93-406, §1016(a)(24):
Amended the heading of Code Sec. 6861 by changing "and gift taxes" to "gift, and certain excise taxes". For **effective** date, see amendment note for Code Sec. 410.

[Sec. 6861(b)]

(b) DEFICIENCY LETTERS.—If the jeopardy assessment is made before any notice in respect of the tax to which the jeopardy assessment relates has been mailed under section 6212(a), then the Secretary shall mail a notice under such subsection within 60 days after the making of the assessment.

JEOPARDY ASSESSMENTS

Amendments

• **1976, Tax Reform Act of 1976 (P.L. 94-455)**

P.L. 94-455, § 1906(b)(13)(A):

Amended 1954 Code by substituting "Secretary" for "Secretary or his delegate" each place it appeared. **Effective** 2-1-77.

[Sec. 6861(c)]

(c) AMOUNT ASSESSABLE BEFORE DECISION OF TAX COURT.—The jeopardy assessment may be made in respect of a deficiency greater or less than that notice of which has been mailed to the taxpayer, despite the provisions of section 6212(c) prohibiting the determination of additional deficiencies, and whether or not the taxpayer has theretofore filed a petition with the Tax Court. The Secretary may, at any time before the decision of the Tax Court is rendered, abate such assessment, or any unpaid portion thereof, to the extent that he believes the assessment to be excessive in amount. The Secretary shall notify the Tax Court of the amount of such assessment, or abatement, if the petition is filed with the Tax Court before the making of the assessment or is subsequently filed, and the Tax Court shall have jurisdiction to redetermine the entire amount of the deficiency and of all amounts assessed at the same time in connection therewith.

Amendments

• **1976, Tax Reform Act of 1976 (P.L. 94-455)**

P.L. 94-455, § 1906(b)(13)(A):

Amended 1954 Code by substituting "Secretary" for "Secretary or his delegate" each place it appeared. **Effective** 2-1-77.

[Sec. 6861(d)]

(d) AMOUNT ASSESSABLE AFTER DECISION OF TAX COURT.—If the jeopardy assessment is made after the decision of the Tax Court is rendered, such assessment may be made only in respect of the deficiency determined by the Tax Court in its decision.

[Sec. 6861(e)]

(e) EXPIRATION OF RIGHT TO ASSESS.—A jeopardy assessment may not be made after the decision of the Tax Court has become final or after the taxpayer has filed a petition for review of the decision of the Tax Court.

[Sec. 6861(f)]

(f) COLLECTION OF UNPAID AMOUNTS.—When the petition has been filed with the Tax Court and when the amount which should have been assessed has been determined by a decision of the Tax Court which has become final, then any unpaid portion, the collection of which has been stayed by bond as provided in section 6863(b) shall be collected as part of the tax upon notice and demand from the Secretary, and any remaining portion of the assessment shall be abated. If the amount already collected exceeds the amount determined as the amount which should have been assessed, such excess shall be credited or refunded to the taxpayer as provided in section 6402, without the filing of claim therefor. If the amount determined as the amount which should have been assessed is greater than the amount actually assessed, then the difference shall be assessed and shall be collected as part of the tax upon notice and demand from the Secretary.

Amendments

• **1976, Tax Reform Act of 1976 (P.L. 94-455)**

P.L. 94-455, § 1906(b)(13)(A):

Amended 1954 Code by substituting "Secretary" for "Secretary or his delegate" each place it appeared. **Effective** 2-1-77.

[Sec. 6861(g)]

(g) ABATEMENT IF JEOPARDY DOES NOT EXIST.—The Secretary may abate the jeopardy assessment if he finds that jeopardy does not exist. Such abatement may not be made after a decision of the Tax Court in respect of the deficiency has been rendered, or, if no petition is filed with the Tax Court, after the expiration of the period for filing such petition. The period of limitation on the making of assessments and levy or a proceeding in court for collection, in respect of any deficiency, shall be determined as if the jeopardy assessment so abated had not been made, except that the running of such period shall in any event be suspended for the period from the date of such jeopardy assessment until the expiration of the 10th day after the day on which such jeopardy assessment is abated.

Amendments

• **1976, Tax Reform Act of 1976 (P.L. 94-455)**

P.L. 94-455, § 1906(b)(13)(A):

Amended 1954 Code by substituting "Secretary" for "Secretary or his delegate" each place it appeared. **Effective** 2-1-77.

[Sec. 6861(h)]

(h) CROSS REFERENCES.—

(1) For the effect of the furnishing of security for payment, see section 6863.

(2) For provision permitting immediate levy in case of jeopardy, see section 6331(a).

[Sec. 6862]

SEC. 6862. JEOPARDY ASSESSMENT OF TAXES OTHER THAN INCOME, ESTATE, GIFT, AND CERTAIN EXCISE TAXES.

[Sec. 6862(a)]

(a) IMMEDIATE ASSESSMENT.—If the Secretary believes that the collection of any tax (other than income tax, estate tax, gift tax, and the excise taxes imposed by chapters 41, 42, 43, and 44) under any provision of the internal revenue laws will be jeopardized by delay, he shall, whether or not the time otherwise prescribed by law for making return and paying such tax has expired, immediately assess such tax (together with all interest, additional amounts, and additions to the tax provided for by law). Such tax, additions to the tax, and interest shall thereupon become immediately due and payable, and immediate notice and demand shall be made by the Secretary for the payment thereof.

Amendments

• **1988, Omnibus Trade and Competitiveness Act of 1988 (P.L. 100-418)**

P.L. 100-418, § 1941(b)(2)(N):

Amended Code Sec. 6862(a) by striking "44, and 45" and inserting "and 44". **Effective** for crude oil removed from the premises on or after 8-23-88.

• **1980, Crude Oil Windfall Profit Tax Act of 1980 (P.L. 96-223)**

P.L. 96-223, § 101(f)(9):

Amended Code Sec. 6862(a) by striking out "certain excise taxes" and inserting "the excise taxes imposed by chapters 41, 42, 43, 44, and 45". For the **effective** date and transitional rules, see P.L. 96-223, Act Sec. 101(i), following Code Sec. 4986.

JEOPARDY ASSESSMENTS

- **1980, Technical Corrections Act of 1979 (P.L. 96-222)**

P.L. 96-222, §108(b)(1)(C):

Amended Code Sec. 6862(a) by changing "and certain excise taxes" to "the taxes imposed by chapters 41, 42, 43, and 44". **Effective** with respect to contributions, acts and expenditures made after 12-31-77.

- **1976, Tax Reform Act of 1976 (P.L. 94-455)**

P.L. 94-455, §1906(b)(13)(A):

Amended 1954 Code by substituting "Secretary" for "Secretary or his delegate" each place it appeared. **Effective** 2-1-77.

- **1974, Employee Retirement Income Security Act of 1974 (P.L. 93-406)**

P.L. 93-406, §1016(a)(25):

Amended Code Sec. 6862(a) and the heading. For **effective** date, see amendment note for Code Sec. 410. Prior to amendment, Code Sec. 6862(a) and the heading read as follows:

"**SEC. 6862. JEOPARDY ASSESSMENT OF TAXES OTHER THAN INCOME, ESTATE, AND GIFT TAXES.**

"(a) Immediate Assessment.—If the Secretary or his delegate believes that the collection of any tax (other than income tax, estate tax, and gift tax) under any provision of the internal revenue laws will be jeopardized by delay, he shall, whether or not the time otherwise prescribed by law for making return and paying such tax has expired, immediately assess such tax (together with all interest, additional amounts, and additions to the tax provided for by law). Such tax, additions to the tax, and interest shall thereupon become immediately due and payable, and immediate notice and demand shall be made by the Secretary or his delegate for the payment thereof."

[Sec. 6862(b)]

(b) IMMEDIATE LEVY.—

For provision permitting immediate levy in case of jeopardy, see section 6331(a).

[Sec. 6863]

SEC. 6863. STAY OF COLLECTION OF JEOPARDY ASSESSMENTS.

[Sec. 6863(a)]

(a) BOND TO STAY COLLECTION.—When an assessment has been made under section 6851, 6852, 6861, or 6862, the collection of the whole or any amount of such assessment may be stayed by filing with the Secretary, within such time as may be fixed by regulations prescribed by the Secretary, a bond in an amount equal to the amount as to which the stay is desired, conditioned upon the payment of the amount (together with interest thereon) the collection of which is stayed, at the time at which, but for the making of such assessment, such amount would be due. Upon the filing of the bond the collection of so much of the amount assessed as is covered by the bond shall be stayed. The taxpayer shall have the right to waive such stay at any time in respect of the whole or any part of the amount covered by the bond, and if as a result of such waiver any part of the amount covered by the bond is paid, then the bond shall, at the request of the taxpayer, be proportionately reduced. If any portion of such assessment is abated, the bond shall, at the request of the taxpayer, be proportionately reduced.

Amendments

- **2018, Tax Technical Corrections Act of 2018 (P.L. 115-141)**

P.L. 115-141, §401(a)(321), Div. U:

Amended Code Sec. 6863(a) by striking "6852,," and inserting "6852,". **Effective** 3-23-2018.

- **1987, Revenue Act of 1987 (P.L. 100-203)**

P.L. 100-203, §10713(b)(2)(E)(i)-(iii):

Amended Code Sec. 6863 by striking out "6851" in subsection (a) and inserting in lieu thereof "6851, 6852,", by striking out "6851 or 6861" in subsection (b)(3)(A) and inserting in lieu thereof "6851, 6852, or 6861", and by striking out "6851(a), or 6861(a)" and inserting in lieu thereof "6851(a), 6852(a), or [nor]6861(a)". **Effective** 12-22-87.

- **1976, Tax Reform Act of 1976 (P.L. 94-455)**

P.L. 94-455, §1204(c)(7):

Amended Code Sec. 6863(a) by substituting "6851, 6861," for "6861"; by substituting "an assessment" for "a jeopardy assessment" in the first sentence; and by substituting "such assessment" for "the jeopardy assessment" each time it appeared in Code Sec. 6863(a). **Effective** date as provided in Act Sec. 1204(d), below.

P.L. 94-455, §1204(d), as amended by P.L. 94-528, §2(a), provides:

(d) Effective Date.—The amendments made by this section apply with respect to action taken under section 6851, 6861, or 6862 of the Internal Revenue Code of 1954 where the notice and demand takes place after February 28, 1977.

- **1976, Tax Reform Act of 1976 (P.L. 94-455)**

P.L. 94-455, §1906(b)(13)(A):

Amended 1954 Code by substituting "Secretary" for "Secretary or his delegate" each place it appeared. **Effective** 2-1-77.

[Sec. 6863(b)]

(b) FURTHER CONDITIONS IN CASE OF INCOME, ESTATE, OR GIFT TAXES.—In the case of taxes subject to the jurisdiction of the Tax Court—

(1) PRIOR TO PETITION TO TAX COURT.—If the bond is given before the taxpayer has filed his petition under section 6213(a), the bond shall contain a further condition that if a petition is not filed within the period provided in such section, then the amount, the collection of which is stayed by the bond, will be paid on notice and demand at any time after the expiration of such period, together with interest thereon from the date of the jeopardy notice and demand to the date of notice and demand under this paragraph.

(2) EFFECT OF TAX COURT DECISION.—The bond shall be conditioned upon the payment of so much of such assessment (collection of which is stayed by the bond) as is not abated by a decision of the Tax Court which has become final. If the Tax Court determines that the amount assessed is greater than the amount which should have been assessed, then when the decision of the Tax Court is rendered the bond shall, at the request of the taxpayer, be proportionately reduced.

(3) STAY OF SALE OF SEIZED PROPERTY PENDING TAX COURT DECISION.—

(A) GENERAL RULE.—Where, notwithstanding the provisions of section 6213(a), an assessment has been made under section 6851, 6852, or 6861, the property seized for collection of the tax shall not be sold—

(i) before the expiration of the periods described in subsection (c)(1)(A) and (B),

(ii) before the issuance of the notice of deficiency described in section 6851(b) or 6861(b), and the expiration of the period provided in section 6213(a) for filing a petition with the Tax Court, and

(iii) if a petition is filed with the Tax Court (whether before or after making of such assessment), before the expiration of the period during which the assessment of the deficiency would be prohibited if neither sections 6851(a), 6852(a), nor 6861(a) were applicable.

Clauses (ii) and (iii) shall not apply in the case of a termination assessment under section 6851 if the taxpayer does not file a return for the taxable year by the due date (determined with regard to any extensions).

(B) EXCEPTIONS.—Such property may be sold if—

(i) the taxpayer consents to the sale,

(ii) the Secretary determines that the expenses of conservation and maintenance will greatly reduce the net proceeds, or

(iii) the property is of the type described in section 6336.

(C) REVIEW BY TAX COURT.—If, but for the application of subparagraph (B), a sale would be prohibited by subparagraph (A)(iii), then the Tax Court shall have jurisdiction to review the Secretary's determination under subparagraph (B) that the property may be sold. Such review may be commenced upon motion by either the Secretary or the taxpayer. An order of the Tax Court disposing of a motion under this paragraph shall be reviewable in the same manner as a decision of the Tax Court.

SPECIAL RULES WITH RESPECT TO CERTAIN CASH

Amendments

• **1989, Omnibus Budget Reconciliation Act of 1989 (P.L. 101-239)**

P.L. 101-239, §7822(d)(2):

Amended Act Sec. 10713(b)(2)(E) of P.L. 100-203, which amended Code Sec. 6863 by striking "6851(a) nor 6861(a)" in subsection (b)(3)(A)(iii) and inserting "6851(a), 6852(a), nor 6861(a)". **Effective** as if included in the provision of P.L. 100-203 to which it relates.

• **1988, Technical and Miscellaneous Revenue Act of 1988 (P.L. 100-647)**

P.L. 100-647, §6245(a):

Amended Code Sec. 6863(b)(3) by adding at the end thereof new subparagraph (C). **Effective** on the 90th day after 11-10-88.

• **1987, Revenue Act of 1987 (P.L. 100-203)**

P.L. 100-203, §10713(b)(2)(E)(i)-(iii):

Amended Code Sec. 6863 by striking out "6851" in subsection (a) and inserting in lieu thereof "6851, 6852,", by striking out "6851 or 6861" in subsection (b)(3)(A) and inserting in lieu thereof "6851, 6852, or 6861", and by striking out "6851(a), or 6861(a)" and inserting in lieu thereof "6851(a), 6852(a), or [nor]6861(a)". **Effective** 12-22-87.

• **1976, Tax Reform Act of 1976 (P.L. 94-455)**

P.L. 94-455, §1204(c)(8):

Amended Code Sec. 6863(b)(3)(A). For the **effective** date, see Act Sec. 1204(d), below. Prior to amendment, Code Sec. 6863(b)(3)(A) read as follows:

(A) GENERAL RULE.—Where, notwithstanding the provisions of section 6213(a), a jeopardy assessment has been made under section 6861 the property seized for the collection of the tax shall not be sold—

(i) if section 6861(b) is applicable, prior to the issuance of the notice of deficiency and the expiration of the time provided in section 6213(a) for filing petition with the Tax Court, and

(ii) if petition is filed with the Tax Court (whether before or after the making of such jeopardy assessment under section 6861), prior to the expiration of the period during which the assessment of the deficiency would be prohibited if section 6861(a) were not applicable.

P.L. 94-455, §1204(d), as amended by P.L. 94-528, §2(a), provides:

(d) Effective Date.—The amendments made by this section apply with respect to action taken under section 6851, 6861, or 6862 of the Internal Revenue Code of 1954 where the notice and demand takes place after February 28, 1977.

P.L. 94-455, §1906(b)(13)(A):

Amended 1954 Code by substituting "Secretary" for "Secretary or his delegate" each place it appeared. **Effective** 2-1-77.

P.L. 94-455, §1906(a)(38):

Amended Code Sec. 6863(b)(3) by striking out subparagraph (C). **Effective** 2-1-77. Prior to amendment, subparagraph (C) read as follows:

(C) APPLICABILITY.—Subparagraphs (A) and (B) shall be applicable only with respect to a jeopardy assessment made on or after January 1, 1955, and shall apply with respect to taxes imposed by this title and with respect to taxes imposed by the Internal Revenue Code of 1939.

[Sec. 6863(c)]

(c) STAY OF SALE OF SEIZED PROPERTY PENDING DISTRICT COURT DETERMINATION UNDER SECTION 7429.—

(1) GENERAL RULE.—Where a jeopardy assessment has been made under section 6862(a), the property seized for the collection of the tax shall not be sold—

(A) if a civil action is commenced in accordance with section 7429(b), on or before the day on which the district court judgment in such action becomes final, or

(B) if subparagraph (A) does not apply, before the day after the expiration of the period provided in section 7429(a) for requesting an administrative review, and if such review is requested, before the day after the expiration of the period provided in section 7429(b), for commencing an action in the district court.

(2) EXCEPTIONS.—With respect to any property described in paragraph (1), the exceptions provided by subsection (b)(3)(B) shall apply.

Amendments

• **1976, Tax Reform Act of 1976 (P.L. 94-455)**

P.L. 94-455, §1204(a)(9):

Added Code Sec. 6863(c). For the **effective** date, see Act Sec. 1204(d), below.

P.L. 94-455, §1204(d), as amended by P.L. 94-528, §2(a), provides:

(d) Effective Date.—The amendments made by this section apply with respect to action taken under section 6851, 6861, or 6862 of the Internal Revenue Code of 1954 where the notice and demand takes place after February 28, 1977.

[Sec. 6864]

SEC. 6864. TERMINATION OF EXTENDED PERIOD FOR PAYMENT IN CASE OF CARRYBACK.

For termination of extensions of time for payment of income tax granted to corporations expecting carrybacks in case of jeopardy, see section 6164(h).

PART III—SPECIAL RULES WITH RESPECT TO CERTAIN CASH

Sec. 6867.   Presumptions where owner of large amount of cash is not identified.

[Sec. 6867]

SEC. 6867. PRESUMPTIONS WHERE OWNER OF LARGE AMOUNT OF CASH IS NOT IDENTIFIED.

[Sec. 6867(a)]

(a) GENERAL RULE.—If the individual who is in physical possession of cash in excess of $10,000 does not claim such cash—

(1) as his, or

(2) as belonging to another person whose identity the Secretary can readily ascertain and who acknowledges ownership of such cash,

then, for purposes of sections 6851 and 6861, it shall be presumed that such cash represents gross income of a single individual for the taxable year in which the possession occurs, and that the collection of tax will be jeopardized by delay.

[Sec. 6867(b)]

(b) RULES FOR ASSESSING.—In the case of any assessment resulting from the application of subsection (a)—

(1) the entire amount of the cash shall be treated as taxable income for the taxable year in which the possession occurs,

(2) such income shall be treated as taxable at the highest rate of tax specified in section 1, and

(3) except as provided in subsection (c), the possessor of the cash shall be treated (solely with respect to such cash) as the taxpayer for purposes of chapters 63 and 64 and section 7429(a)(1).

Amendments

• **1988, Technical and Miscellaneous Revenue Act of 1988 (P.L. 100-647)**

P.L. 100-647, §1001(a)(1):

Amended Code Sec. 6867(b)(2) by striking out "at a 50-percent rate" and inserting in lieu thereof "at the highest rate of tax specified in section 1". **Effective** as if included in the provision of P.L. 99-514 to which it relates.

[Sec. 6867(c)]

(c) EFFECT OF LATER SUBSTITUTION OF TRUE OWNER.—If, after an assessment resulting from the application of subsection (a), such assessment is abated and replaced by an assessment against the owner of the cash, such later assessment shall be treated for purposes of all laws relating to lien, levy and collection as relating back to the date of the original assessment.

[Sec. 6867(d)]

(d) DEFINITIONS.—For purposes of this section—

(1) CASH.—The term "cash" includes any cash equivalent.

RECEIVERSHIPS, ETC.

(2) CASH EQUIVALENT.—The term "cash equivalent" means—
 (A) foreign currency,
 (B) any bearer obligation, and
 (C) any medium of exchange which—
  (i) is of a type which has been frequently used in illegal activities, and
  (ii) is specified as a cash equivalent for purposes of this part in regulations prescribed by the Secretary.
(3) VALUE OF CASH EQUIVALENT.—Any cash equivalent shall be taken into account—
 (A) in the case of a bearer obligation, at its face amount, and
 (B) in the case of any other cash equivalent, at its fair market value.

Amendments

• **1982, Tax Equity and Fiscal Responsibility Act of 1982 (P.L. 97-248)**

P.L. 97-248, §330(a):

Added Code Sec. 6867. **Effective** 9-4-82.

Subchapter B—Receiverships, Etc.

Sec. 6871. Claims for income, estate, gift, and certain excise taxes in receivership proceedings, etc.
Sec. 6872. Suspension of period on assessment.
Sec. 6873. Unpaid claims.

[Sec. 6871]

SEC. 6871. CLAIMS FOR INCOME, ESTATE, GIFT, AND CERTAIN EXCISE TAXES IN RECEIVERSHIP PROCEEDINGS, ETC.

[Sec. 6871(a)]

(a) IMMEDIATE ASSESSMENT IN RECEIVERSHIP PROCEEDINGS.—On the appointment of a receiver for the taxpayer in any receivership proceeding before any court of the United States or of any State or of the District of Columbia, any deficiency (together with all interest, additional amounts, and additions to the tax provided by law) determined by the Secretary in respect of a tax imposed by subtitle A or B or by chapter 41, 42, 43, or 44 on such taxpayer may, despite the restrictions imposed by section 6213(a) on assessments, be immediately assessed if such deficiency has not theretofore been assessed in accordance with law.

Amendments

• **1989, Omnibus Budget Reconciliation Act of 1989 (P.L. 101-239)**

P.L. 101-239, §7841(d)(2):

Amended Code Sec. 6871 by striking "44, or 45" each place it appears and inserting "or 44". **Effective** 12-19-89.

• **1980, Bankruptcy Tax Act of 1980 (P.L. 96-589)**

P.L. 96-589, §6(g)(1):

Amended Code Sec. 6871(a). **Effective** 10-1-79, but inapplicable to any proceeding under the Bankruptcy Act commenced before that date. See amendment note for P.L. 96-589 under Code Sec. 6871(c) for the text of Code Sec. 6871(a) prior to amendment.

• **1976, Tax Reform Act of 1976 (P.L. 94-455)**

P.L. 94-455, §1906(c)(1):

Amended Code Sec. 6871(a) by striking out "or Territory" after "any State." **Effective** 2-1-77.

P.L. 94-455, §1906(b)(13)(A):

Amended 1954 Code by substituting "Secretary" for "Secretary or his delegate" each place it appeared. **Effective** 2-1-77.

• **1958, Technical Amendments Act of 1958 (P.L. 85-866)**

P.L. 85-866, §88(a):

Amended Code Sec. 6871(a) by substituting the phrase "the filing or (where approval is required by the Bankruptcy Act) the approval of a petition of, or the approval of a petition against, any taxpayer" for the phrase "the approval of a petition of, or against, any taxpayer". **Effective** 1-1-54.

[Sec. 6871(b)]

(b) IMMEDIATE ASSESSMENT WITH RESPECT TO CERTAIN TITLE 11 CASES.—Any deficiency (together with all interest, additional amounts, and additions to the tax provided by law) determined by the Secretary in respect of a tax imposed by subtitle A or B or by chapter 41, 42, 43, or 44 on—

 (1) the debtor's estate in a case under title 11 of the United States Code, or
 (2) the debtor, but only if liability for such tax has become res judicata pursuant to a determination in a case under title 11 of the United States Code,

may, despite the restrictions imposed by section 6213(a) on assessments, be immediately assessed if such deficiency has not theretofore been assessed in accordance with law.

Amendments

• **1989, Omnibus Budget Reconciliation Act of 1989 (P.L. 101-239)**

P.L. 101-239, §7841(d)(2):

Amended Code Sec. 6871 by striking "44, or 45" each place it appears and inserting "or 44". **Effective** 12-19-89.

• **1980, Bankruptcy Tax Act of 1980 (P.L. 96-589)**

P.L. 96-589, §6(g)(1):

Amended Code Sec. 6871(b). **Effective** 10-1-79, but inapplicable to any proceeding under the Bankruptcy Act commenced before that date. See amendment note for P.L. 96-589 under Code Sec. 6871(c) for the text of Code Sec. 6871(b) prior to amendment.

• **1958, Technical Amendments Act of 1958 (P.L. 85-866)**

P.L. 85-866, §88(b):

Amended Code Sec. 6871(b) by substituting the phrase "the filing or (where approval is required by the Bankruptcy Act) the approval of a petition of, or the approval of a petition against, any taxpayer" for the phrase "approval of the petition". **Effective** 1-1-54.

[Sec. 6871(c)]

(c) CLAIM FILED DESPITE PENDENCY OF TAX COURT PROCEEDINGS.—In the case of a tax imposed by subtitle A or B or by chapter 41, 42, 43, or 44—

 (1) claims for the deficiency and for interest, additional amounts, and additions to the tax may be presented, for adjudication in accordance with law, to the court before which the receivership proceeding (or the case under title 11 of the United States Code) is pending, despite the pendency of proceedings for the redetermination of the deficiency pursuant to a petition to the Tax Court; but
 (2) in the case of a receivership proceeding, no petition for any such redetermination shall be filed with the Tax Court after the appointment of the receiver.

Amendments

• **1989, Omnibus Budget Reconciliation Act of 1989 (P.L. 101-239)**

P.L. 101-239, §7841(d)(2):

Amended Code Sec. 6871 by striking "44, or 45" each place it appears and inserting "or 44". **Effective** 12-19-89.

• **1980, Bankruptcy Tax Act of 1980 (P.L. 96-589)**

P.L. 96-589, §6(g)(1):

Amended Code Sec. 6871. **Effective** 10-1-79, but inapplicable to any proceeding under the Bankruptcy Act commenced before that date. Prior to amendment, Code Sec. 6871 provided:

Sec. 6867(d)(2)

TRANSFEREES AND FIDUCIARIES

"SEC. 6871. CLAIMS FOR INCOME, ESTATE, AND GIFT TAXES IN BANKRUPTCY AND RECEIVERSHIP PROCEEDINGS.

(a) IMMEDIATE ASSESSMENT.—Upon the adjudication of bankruptcy of any taxpayer in any liquidating proceeding, the filing or (where approval is required by the Bankruptcy Act) the approval of a petition of, or the approval of a petition against, any taxpayer in any other bankruptcy proceeding, or the appointment of a receiver for any taxpayer in any receivership proceeding before any court of the United States or of any State or of the District of Columbia, any deficiency (together with all interest, additional amounts, or additions to the tax provided by law) determined by the Secretary in respect of a tax imposed by subtitle A or B upon such taxpayer shall, despite the restrictions imposed by section 6213(a) upon assessments, be immediately assessed if such deficiency has not theretofore been assessed in accordance with law.

(b) CLAIM FILED DESPITE PENDENCY OF TAX COURT PROCEEDINGS.—In the case of a tax imposed by subtitle A or B claims for the deficiency and such interest, additional amounts, and additions to the tax may be presented, for adjudication in accordance with law, to the court before which the bankruptcy or receivership proceeding is pending, despite the pendency of proceedings for the redetermination of the deficiency in pursuance of a petition to the Tax Court; but no petition for any such redetermination shall be filed with the Tax Court after the adjudication of bankruptcy, the filing or (where approval is required by the Bankruptcy Act) the approval of a petition of, or the approval of a petition against, any taxpayer in any other bankruptcy proceeding, or the appointment of the receiver."

[Sec. 6872]

SEC. 6872. SUSPENSION OF PERIOD ON ASSESSMENT.

If the regulations issued pursuant to section 6036 require the giving of notice by any fiduciary in any case under title 11 of the United States Code, or by a receiver in any other court proceeding, to the Secretary of his qualification as such, the running of the period of limitations on the making of assessments shall be suspended for the period from the date of the institution of the proceeding to a date 30 days after the date upon which the notice from the receiver or other fiduciary is received by the Secretary; but the suspension under this sentence shall in no case be for a period in excess of 2 years.

Amendments

- **1980, Bankruptcy Tax Act of 1980 (P.L. 96-589)**

P.L. 96-589, §6(i)(12):

Amended Code Sec. 6872 by striking out "any proceeding under the Bankruptcy Act" and inserting in lieu thereof "any case under title 11 of the United States Code". **Effective** 10-1-79 but inapplicable to any proceeding under the Bankruptcy Act commenced before that date.

- **1976, Tax Reform Act of 1976 (P.L. 94-455)**

P.L. 94-455, §1906(b)(13)(A):

Amended 1954 Code by substituting "Secretary" for "Secretary or his delegate" each place it appeared. **Effective** 2-1-77.

[Sec. 6873]

SEC. 6873. UNPAID CLAIMS.

[Sec. 6873(a)]

(a) GENERAL RULE.—Any portion of a claim for taxes allowed in a receivership proceeding which is unpaid shall be paid by the taxpayer upon notice and demand from the Secretary after the termination of such proceeding.

Amendments

- **1980, Bankruptcy Tax Act of 1980 (P.L. 96-589)**

P.L. 96-589, §6(e)(2):

Amended Code Sec. 6873(a) by striking out "or any proceeding under the Bankruptcy Act" following "receivership proceeding". **Effective** 10-1-79, but inapplicable to any proceeding under the Bankruptcy Act commenced before that date.

- **1976, Tax Reform Act of 1976 (P.L. 94-455)**

P.L. 94-455, §1906(b)(13)(A):

Amended 1954 Code by substituting "Secretary" for "Secretary or his delegate" each place it appeared. **Effective** 2-1-77.

[Sec. 6873(b)]

(b) CROSS REFERENCES.—

(1) For suspension of running of period of limitations on collection, see section 6503(b).

(2) For extension of time for payment, see section 6161(c).

CHAPTER 71—TRANSFEREES AND FIDUCIARIES

Sec. 6901.	Transferred assets.
Sec. 6902.	Provisions of special application to transferees.
Sec. 6903.	Notice of fiduciary relationship.
Sec. 6904.	Prohibition of injunctions.
Sec. 6905.	Discharge of executor from personal liability for decedent's income and gift taxes.

[Sec. 6901]

SEC. 6901. TRANSFERRED ASSETS.

[Sec. 6901(a)]

(a) METHOD OF COLLECTION.—The amounts of the following liabilities shall, except as hereinafter in this section provided, be assessed, paid, and collected in the same manner and subject to the same provisions and limitations as in the case of the taxes with respect to which the liabilities were incurred:

(1) INCOME, ESTATE, AND GIFT TAXES.—

(A) TRANSFEREES.—The liability, at law or in equity, of a transferee of property—

(i) of a taxpayer in the case of a tax imposed by subtitle A (relating to income taxes),

(ii) of a decedent in the case of a tax imposed by chapter 11 (relating to estate taxes), or

(iii) of a donor in the case of a tax imposed by chapter 12 (relating to gift taxes),

in respect of the tax imposed by subtitle A or B.

(B) FIDUCIARIES.—The liability of a fiduciary under section 3713(b) of title 31, United States Code, in respect of the payment of any tax described in subparagraph (A) from the estate of the taxpayer, the decedent, or the donor, as the case may be.

(2) OTHER TAXES.—The liability, at law or in equity of a transferee of property of any person liable in respect of any tax imposed by this title (other than a tax imposed by subtitle A or B), but only if such liability arises on the liquidation of a partnership or corporation, or on a reorganization within the meaning of section 368(a).

Amendments

- **2018, Tax Technical Corrections Act of 2018 (P.L. 115-141)**

P.L. 115-141, §401(a)(322), Div. U:

Amended Code Sec. 6901(a)(1)(B) by striking "Code in" and inserting "Code, in". **Effective** 3-23-2018.

- **1982 (P.L. 97-258)**

P.L. 97-258, §3(f)(10):

Amended Code Sec. 6901(a)(1)(B) by striking out "section 3467 of the Revised Statutes (31 U.S.C. 192)" and substituting "section 3713(b) of title 31, United States Code". **Effective** 9-13-82.

TRANSFEREES AND FIDUCIARIES

[Sec. 6901(b)]

(b) LIABILITY.—Any liability referred to in subsection (a) may be either as to the amount of tax shown on a return or as to any deficiency or underpayment of any tax.

[Sec. 6901(c)]

(c) PERIOD OF LIMITATIONS.—The period of limitations for assessment of any such liability of a transferee or a fiduciary shall be as follows:

(1) INITIAL TRANSFEREE.—In the case of the liability of an initial transferee, within 1 year after the expiration of the period of limitation for assessment against the transferor;

(2) TRANSFEREE OF TRANSFEREE.—In the case of the liability of a transferee of a transferee, within 1 year after the expiration of the period of limitation for assessment against the preceding transferee, but not more than 3 years after the expiration of the period of limitation for assessment against the initial transferor;

except that if, before the expiration of the period of limitation for the assessment of the liability of the transferee, a court proceeding for the collection of the tax or liability in respect thereof has been begun against the initial transferor or the last preceding transferee, respectively, then the period of limitation for assessment of the liability of the transferee shall expire 1 year after the return of execution in the court proceeding.

(3) FIDUCIARY.—In the case of the liability of a fiduciary, not later than 1 year after the liability arises or not later than the expiration of the period for collection of the tax in respect of which such liability arises, whichever is the later.

[Sec. 6901(d)]

(d) EXTENSION BY AGREEMENT.—

(1) EXTENSION OF TIME FOR ASSESSMENT.—If before the expiration of the time prescribed in subsection (c) for the assessment of the liability, the Secretary and the transferee or fiduciary have both consented in writing to its assessment after such time, the liability may be assessed at any time prior to the expiration of the period agreed upon. The period so agreed upon may be extended by subsequent agreements in writing made before the expiration of the period previously agreed upon. For the purpose of determining the period of limitation on credit or refund to the transferee or fiduciary of overpayments of tax made by such transferee or fiduciary or overpayments of tax made by the transferor of which the transferee or fiduciary is legally entitled to credit or refund, such agreement and any extension thereof shall be deemed an agreement and extension thereof referred to in section 6511(c).

(2) EXTENSION OF TIME FOR CREDIT OR REFUND.—If the agreement is executed after the expiration of the period of limitation for assessment against the taxpayer with reference to whom the liability of such transferee or fiduciary arises, then in applying the limitations under section 6511(c) on the amount of the credit or refund, the periods specified in section 6511(b)(2) shall be increased by the period from the date of such expiration to the date of the agreement.

[Sec. 6901(e)]

(e) PERIOD FOR ASSESSMENT AGAINST TRANSFEROR.—For purposes of this section, if any person is deceased, or is a corporation which has terminated its existence, the period of limitation for assessment against such person shall be the period that would be in effect had death or termination of existence not occurred.

[Sec. 6901(f)]

(f) SUSPENSION OF RUNNING OF PERIOD OF LIMITATIONS.—The running of the period of limitations upon the assessment of the liability of a transferee or fiduciary shall, after the mailing to the transferee or fiduciary of the notice provided for in section 6212 (relating to income, estate, and gift taxes), be suspended for the period during which the Secretary is prohibited from making the assessment in respect of the liability of the transferee or fiduciary (and in any event, if a proceeding in respect of the liability is placed on the docket of the Tax Court, until the decision of the Tax Court becomes final), and for 60 days thereafter.

[Sec. 6901(g)]

(g) ADDRESS FOR NOTICE OF LIABILITY.—In the absence of notice to the Secretary under section 6903 of the existence of a fiduciary relationship, any notice of liability enforceable under this section required to be mailed to such person, shall, if mailed to the person subject to the liability at his last known address, be sufficient for purposes of this title, even if such person is deceased, or is under a legal disability, or, in the case of a corporation, has terminated its existence.

[Sec. 6901(h)]

(h) DEFINITION OF TRANSFEREE.—As used in this section, the term "transferee" includes donee, heir, legatee, devisee, and distributee, and with respect to estate taxes, also includes any person who, under section 6324(a)(2), is personally liable for any part of such tax.

[Sec. 6901(i)]

(i) EXTENSION OF TIME.—

For extensions of time by reason of armed service in a combat zone, see section 7508.

Amendments

• **1976, Tax Reform Act of 1976 (P.L. 94-455)**

P.L. 94-455, § 1906(b)(13)(A):

Amended Code Sec. 6901 by substituting "Secretary" for "Secretary or his delegate" each place it appeared. **Effective** 2-1-77.

[Sec. 6902]

SEC. 6902. PROVISIONS OF SPECIAL APPLICATION TO TRANSFEREES.

[Sec. 6902(a)]

(a) BURDEN OF PROOF.—In proceedings before the Tax Court the burden of proof shall be upon the Secretary to show that a petitioner is liable as a transferee of property of a taxpayer, but not to show that the taxpayer was liable for the tax.

Amendments

• **1976, Tax Reform Act of 1976 (P.L. 94-455)**

P.L. 94-455, § 1906(b)(13)(A):

Amended 1954 Code by substituting "Secretary" for "Secretary or his delegate" each place it appeared. **Effective** 2-1-77.

[Sec. 6902(b)]

(b) EVIDENCE.—Upon application to the Tax Court, a transferee of property of a taxpayer shall be entitled, under rules prescribed by the Tax Court, to a preliminary examination of books, papers, documents, correspondence, and other evidence of the taxpayer or a preceding transferee of the taxpayer's property, if the transferee making the application is a petitioner before the Tax Court for the redetermination of his liability in respect of the tax (including interest, additional amounts, and additions to the tax provided by law) imposed upon the taxpayer. Upon such application, the Tax Court may require by subpoena, ordered by the Tax Court or any division thereof and signed by a judge, the production of all such books, papers, documents, correspondence, and other evidence within the United States the production of which, in the opinion of the Tax Court or divisions thereof, is necessary to enable the transferee to ascertain the liability of the taxpayer or preceding transferee and will not result in undue hardship to the taxpayer or preceding transferee. Such examination shall be had at such time and place as may be designated in the subpoena.

[Sec. 6903]

SEC. 6903. NOTICE OF FIDUCIARY RELATIONSHIP.

[Sec. 6903(a)]

(a) RIGHTS AND OBLIGATIONS OF FIDUCIARY.—Upon notice to the Secretary that any person is acting for another person in a fiduciary capacity, such fiduciary shall assume the powers, rights, duties, and privileges of such other person in respect of a tax imposed by this title (except as otherwise specifically provided and except that the tax shall be collected from the estate of such other person), until notice is given that the fiduciary capacity has terminated.

Amendments

- **1976, Tax Reform Act of 1976 (P.L. 94-455)**

P.L. 94-455, § 1906(b)(13)(A):

Amended 1954 Code by substituting "Secretary" for "Secretary or his delegate" each place it appeared. **Effective** 2-1-77.

[Sec. 6903(b)]

(b) MANNER OF NOTICE.—Notice under this section shall be given in accordance with regulations prescribed by the Secretary.

Amendments

- **1976, Tax Reform Act of 1976 (P.L. 94-455)**

P.L. 94-455, § 1906(b)(13)(A):

Amended 1954 Code by substituting "Secretary" for "Secretary or his delegate" each place it appeared. **Effective** 2-1-77.

[Sec. 6904]

SEC. 6904. PROHIBITION OF INJUNCTIONS.

For prohibition of suits to restrain enforcement of liability of transferee, or fiduciary, see section 7421(b).

[Sec. 6905]

SEC. 6905. DISCHARGE OF EXECUTOR FROM PERSONAL LIABILITY FOR DECEDENT'S INCOME AND GIFT TAXES.

[Sec. 6905(a)]

(a) DISCHARGE OF LIABILITY.—In the case of liability of a decedent for taxes imposed by subtitle A or by chapter 12, if the executor makes written application (filed after the return with respect to such taxes is made and filed in such manner and such form as may be prescribed by regulations of the Secretary) for release from personal liability for such taxes, the Secretary may notify the executor of the amount of such taxes. The executor, upon payment of the amount of which he is notified, or 9 months after receipt of the application if no notification is made by the Secretary before such date, shall be discharged from personal liability for any deficiency in such tax thereafter found to be due and shall be entitled to a receipt or writing showing such discharge.

Amendments

- **1976, Tax Reform Act of 1976 (P.L. 94-455)**

P.L. 94-455, § 1906(b)(13)(A):

Amended 1954 Code by substituting "Secretary" for "Secretary or his delegate" each place it appeared. **Effective** 2-1-77.

- **1970, Excise, Estate, and Gift Tax Adjustment Act of 1970 (P.L. 91-614)**

P.L. 91-614, § 101(f):

Amended Code Sec. 6905(a) by substituting "9 months" for "1 year". **Effective** with respect to estates of decedents dying after 12-31-73.

[Sec. 6905(b)]

(b) DEFINITION OF EXECUTOR.—For purposes of this section, the term "executor" means the executor or administrator of the decedent appointed, qualified, and acting within the United States.

[Sec. 6905(c)]

(c) CROSS REFERENCE.—

For discharge of executor from personal liability for taxes imposed under chapter 11, see section 2204.

Amendments

- **1970, Excise, Estate, and Gift Tax Adjustment Act of 1970 (P.L. 91-614)**

P.L. 91-614, § 101(e)(1):

Added Code Sec. 6905. **Effective** with respect to decedents dying, or to gifts made, after 12-31-70.

CHAPTER 72—LICENSING AND REGISTRATION

SUBCHAPTER A.   Licensing.
SUBCHAPTER B.   Registration.

Subchapter A—Licensing

Sec. 7001.   Collection of foreign items.

[Sec. 7001]

SEC. 7001. COLLECTION OF FOREIGN ITEMS.

[Sec. 7001(a)]

(a) LICENSE.—All persons undertaking as a matter of business or for profit the collection of foreign payments of interest or dividends by means of coupons, checks, or bills of exchange shall obtain a license from the Secretary and shall be subject to such regulations enabling the Government to obtain the information required under subtitle A (relating to income taxes) as the Secretary shall prescribe.

LICENSING AND REGISTRATION

Amendments

- **1976, Tax Reform Act of 1976 (P.L. 94-455)**

P.L. 94-455, §1906(b)(13)(A):
Amended 1954 Code by substituting "Secretary" for "Secretary or his delegate" each place it appeared. **Effective** 2-1-77.

[Sec. 7001(b)]

(b) PENALTY FOR FAILURE TO OBTAIN LICENSE.—
For penalty for failure to obtain the license provided for in this section, see section 7231.

Subchapter B—Registration

Sec. 7011.   Registration—persons paying a special tax.
Sec. 7012.   Cross references.

[Sec. 7011]

SEC. 7011. REGISTRATION—PERSONS PAYING A SPECIAL TAX.

[Sec. 7011(a)]

(a) REQUIREMENT.—Every person engaged in any trade or business on which a special tax is imposed by law shall register with the Secretary his name or style, place of residence, trade or business, and the place where such trade or business is to be carried on. In case of a firm or company, the names of the several persons constituting the same, and the places of residence, shall be so registered.

Amendments

- **1976, Tax Reform Act of 1976 (P.L. 94-455)**

P.L. 94-455, §1906(b)(13)(A):
Amended 1954 Code by substituting "Secretary" for "Secretary or his delegate" each place it appeared. **Effective** 2-1-77.

[Sec. 7011(b)]

(b) REGISTRATION IN CASE OF DEATH OR CHANGE OF LOCATION.—Any person exempted under the provisions of section 4905 from the payment of a special tax, shall register with the Secretary in accordance with regulations prescribed by the Secretary.

Amendments

- **1976, Tax Reform Act of 1976 (P.L. 94-455)**

P.L. 94-455, §1906(b)(13)(A):
Amended 1954 Code by substituting "Secretary" for "Secretary or his delegate" each place it appeared. **Effective** 2-1-77.

[Sec. 7012]

SEC. 7012. CROSS REFERENCES.

(1) For provisions relating to registration in connection with firearms, see sections 5802, 5841, and 5861.

(2) For special rules with respect to registration by persons engaged in receiving wagers, see section 4412.

(3) For provisions relating to registration in relation to the taxes on gasoline and diesel fuel, see section 4101.

(4) For provisions relating to registration by dealers in distilled spirits, wines, and beer, see section 5124.

(5) For penalty for failure to register, see section 7272.

(6) For other penalties for failure to register with respect to wagering, see section 7262.

Amendments

- **2005, Safe, Accountable, Flexible, Efficient Transportation Equity Act: A Legacy for Users (P.L. 109-59)**

P.L. 109-59, §11125(b)(9):
Amended Code Sec. 7012 by redesignating paragraphs (4) and (5) as paragraphs (5) and (6), respectively, and by inserting after paragraph (3) a new paragraph (4). **Effective** 7-1-2008, but not applicable to taxes imposed for periods before such date.

- **1996, Small Business Job Protection Act of 1996 (P.L. 104-188)**

P.L. 104-188, §1702(b)(4)(A)-(B):
Amended Code Sec. 7012 by striking "production or importation of gasoline" in paragraph (3) and inserting "taxes on gasoline and diesel fuel", and by striking paragraph (4) and redesignating paragraphs (5) and (6) as paragraphs (4) and (5), respectively. **Effective** as if included in the provision of P.L. 101-508 to which it relates. Prior to amendment, Code Sec. 7012(4) read as follows:

(4) For provisions relating to registration in relation to the manufacture or production of lubricating oils, see section 4101.

- **1976, Tax Reform Act of 1976 (P.L. 94-455)**

P.L. 94-455, §1906(a)(39):
Amended Code Sec. 7012. **Effective** 2-1-77. Prior to amendment, Code Sec. 7012 read as follows:
SEC. 7012 CROSS REFERENCES.
(c) Firearms.—For provisions relating to registration in connection with firearms, see sections 5802, 5841, and 5854.
(f) For special rules with respect to registration by persons engaged in receiving wagers, see section 4412.
(g) For provisions relating to registration in relation to the production or importation of gasoline, see section 4101.
(h) For provisions relating to registration in relation to the manufacture or production of lubricating oils, see section 4101.

(i) Penalty.—
(1) For penalty for failure to register, see section 7272.
(2) For other penalties for failure to register with respect to wagering, see section 7262.

P.L. 94-455, §1904(b)(8)(C):
Amended Code Sec. 7012 by striking out subsection (e). **Effective** 2-1-77. Prior to amendment, Code Sec. 7012(e) read as follows:
(e) For provisions relating to registration in relation to the manufacture of white phosphorus matches, see section 4804(d).

- **1970 (P.L. 91-513)**

P.L. 91-513, §1102(d):
Repealed Secs. 7012(a) and (b). **Effective** 5-1-71. Prior to repeal, these sections read as follows:
"(a) Narcotic Drugs.—For provisions relating to registration in relation to narcotic drugs, see section 4722.
"(b) Marihuana.—For provisions relating to registration in relation to marihuana, see section 4753."

- **1965, Excise Tax Reduction Act of 1965 (P.L. 89-44)**

P.L. 89-44, §601(g):
Deleted Code Sec. 7012(d) which read: "(d) For provisions relating to registration in relation to the manufacture of playing cards, see section 4455."

- **1958, Tax Rate Extension Act of 1958 (P.L. 85-475)**

P.L. 85-475, §4(b), (c):
Amended Code Sec. 7012 by deleting former subsec. (i), and redesignating subsec. (j) as subsec. (i). Prior to deletion, subsec. (i) read:
"(i) For provisions relating to registration in relation to transportation of property for hire, see section 4273."

CHAPTER 73—BONDS

Sec. 7101.   Form of bonds.
Sec. 7102.   Single bond in lieu of multiple bonds.
Sec. 7103.   Cross references—other provisions for bonds.

[Sec. 7101]

SEC. 7101. FORM OF BONDS.

Whenever, pursuant to the provisions of this title (other than section 7485), or rules or regulations prescribed under authority of this title, a person is required to furnish a bond or security—

(1) GENERAL RULE.—Such bond or security shall be in such form and with such surety or sureties as may be prescribed by regulations issued by the Secretary.

(2) UNITED STATES BONDS AND NOTES IN LIEU OF SURETY BONDS.—The person required to furnish such bond or security may, in lieu thereof, deposit bonds or notes of the United States as provided in section 9303 of title 31, United States Code.

Amendments

- **1982 (P.L. 97-258)**

P.L. 97-258, §3(f)(11):
Amended Code Sec. 7101(2) by striking out "6 U.S.C. 15" and substituting "section 9303 of title 31, United States Code". **Effective** 9-13-82.

- **1976, Tax Reform Act of 1976 (P.L. 94-455)**

P.L. 94-455, §1906(b)(13)(A):
Amended 1954 Code by substituting "Secretary" for "Secretary or his delegate" each place it appeared. **Effective** 2-1-77.

- **1972 (P.L. 92-310)**

P.L. 92-310, §230(b):
Amended the first sentence of Code Sec. 7101 by substituting "section 7485" for "sections 7485 and 6803(a)(1)". **Effective** 6-6-72.

[Sec. 7102]

SEC. 7102. SINGLE BOND IN LIEU OF MULTIPLE BONDS.

In any case in which two or more bonds are required or authorized, the Secretary may provide for the acceptance of a single bond complying with the requirements for which the several bonds are required or authorized.

Amendments

- **1976, Tax Reform Act of 1976 (P.L. 94-455)**

P.L. 94-455, §1906(b)(13)(A):
Amended 1954 Code by substituting "Secretary" for "Secretary or his delegate" each place it appeared. **Effective** 2-1-77.

[Sec. 7103]

SEC. 7103. CROSS REFERENCES—OTHER PROVISIONS FOR BONDS.

[Sec. 7103(a)]

(a) EXTENSIONS OF TIME.—

(1) For bond where time to pay tax or deficiency has been extended, see section 6165.

(2) For bond to stay collection of a jeopardy assessment, see section 6863.

(3) For bond to stay assessment and collection prior to review of a Tax Court decision, see section 7485.

(4) For a bond to stay collection of a penalty assessed under section 6672, see section 6672(b).

(5) For bond in case of an election to postpone payment of estate tax where the value of a reversionary or remainder interest is included in the gross estate, see section 6165.

Amendments

- **1978 (P.L. 95-628)**

P.L. 95-628, §9(b)(2):
Added a new Code Sec. 7103(a)(4). **Effective** 11-10-78.

- **1976, Tax Reform Act of 1976 (P.L. 94-455)**

P.L. 94-455, §1204(c)(10):
Repealed Code Sec. 7103(a)(4). For **effective** date, see Act Sec. 1204(d), below. Prior to repeal, Sec. 7103(a)(4) read as follows:

(4) For furnishing of bond where taxable year is closed by the Secretary or his delegate, see section 6851(e).

P.L. 94-455, §1204(d), as amended by P.L. 94-528, §2(a), provides:

(d) Effective Date.—The amendments made by this section apply with respect to action taken under section 6851, 6861, or 6862 of the Internal Revenue Code of 1954 where the notice and demand takes place after February 28, 1977.

[Sec. 7103(b)]

(b) RELEASE OF LIEN OR SEIZED PROPERTY.—

(1) For the release of the lien provided for in section 6325 by furnishing the Secretary a bond, see section 6325(a)(2).

(2) For bond to obtain release of perishable goods which have been seized under forfeiture proceeding, see section 7324(3).

(3) For bond to release perishable goods under levy, see section 6336.

(4) For bond executed by claimant of seized goods valued at $100,000 or less, see section 7325(3).

Amendments

- **1986, Tax Reform Act of 1986 (P.L. 99-514)**

P.L. 99-514, §1566(c):
Amended Code Sec. 7103(b)(4) by striking out "$1,000" and inserting in lieu thereof "$100,000". **Effective** 10-22-86.

- **1976, Tax Reform Act of 1976 (P.L. 94-455)**

P.L. 94-455, §1906(b)(13)(A):
Amended 1954 Code by substituting "Secretary" for "Secretary or his delegate" each place it appeared. **Effective** 2-1-77.

[Sec. 7103(c)]

(c) MISCELLANEOUS.—

(1) For bond as a condition precedent to the allowance of the credit for accrued foreign taxes, see section 905(c).

(2) For bonds relating to alcohol and tobacco taxes, see generally subtitle E.

[Sec. 7103(d)—Repealed]

(d) BONDS REQUIRED WITH RESPECT TO CERTAIN PRODUCTS.

(1) For bond in case of articles taxable under subchapter B of chapter 37 processed for exportation without payment of the tax provided therein, see section 4513(c).

(2) For bond in case of oleomargarine removed from the place of manufacture for exportation to a foreign country, see section 4593(b).

Amendments

- **1976, Tax Reform Act of 1976 (P.L. 94-455)**

P.L. 94-455, §1906(a)(40):
Repealed Code Sec. 7103(d). **Effective** 2-1-77. Prior to repeal, Code Sec. 7103(d) read as follows:

CLOSING AGREEMENTS, COMPROMISES

(3) For requirement of bonds with respect to certain industries see—

(A) section 4596 relating to a manufacturer of oleomargarine;

(B) section 4814(c) relating to a manufacturer of process or renovated butter or adulterated butter;

(E) section 4804(c) relating to a manufacturer of white phosphorus matches.

• **1974 (P.L. 93-490)**

P.L. 93-490, §3(b)(7):

Repealed subparagraph (C) of paragraph (3) of Code Sec. 7103(d). **Effective** with respect to filled cheese manufactured, imported, or sold after 10-26-74.

Amendments

• **1972 (P.L. 92-310)**

P.L. 92-310, §230(c):

Repealed Code Sec. 7103(e). **Effective** 6-6-72. Prior to repeal, Code Sec. 7103(e) read as follows:

(e) PERSONNEL BONDS.

(1) For bonds of internal revenue personnel to insure faithful performance of duties, see section 7803(c).

• **1970 (P.L. 91-513)**

P.L. 91-513, §1102(e):

Repealed subparagraph (D) of Code Sec. 7103(d). **Effective** 5-1-71. Prior to repeal, subparagraph (D) read as follows:

"(D) section 4713 (b) relating to manufacturer of opium suitable for smoking purposes;". Effective on 5-1-71.

• **1965, Excise Tax Reduction Act of 1965 (P.L. 89-44)**

P.L. 89-44, §802(b)(3):

Amended Code Sec. 7103(d) by deleting a semicolon at the end of subparagraph (3)(E) and inserting a period in lieu thereof and by deleting subparagraph (3)(F). **Effective** 7-1-65. Prior to amendment, Code Sec. 7103(d)(3)(F) read as follows:

"(F) section 4101, relating to a producer or importer of gasoline or a manufacturer or producer of lubricating oils subject to tax under chapter 32."

[Sec. 7103(e)—Repealed]

(2) For jurisdiction of United States district courts, concurrently with the courts of the several States, in an action on the official bond of any internal revenue officer or employee, see section 7402(a).

(3) For bonds of postmasters to whom stamps have been furnished under section 6802(1), see section 6803(a)(1).

(4) For bonds in cases coming within the provisions of section 6802(2) or (3), relating to stamps furnished a designated depositary of the United States or State agent, see section 6803(b)(1).

CHAPTER 74—CLOSING AGREEMENTS AND COMPROMISES

Sec. 7121. Closing agreements.
Sec. 7122. Compromises.
Sec. 7123. Appeals dispute resolution procedures.
Sec. 7124. Cross references.

[Sec. 7121]

SEC. 7121. CLOSING AGREEMENTS.

[Sec. 7121(a)]

(a) AUTHORIZATION.—The Secretary is authorized to enter into an agreement in writing with any person relating to the liability of such person (or of the person or estate for whom he acts) in respect of any internal revenue tax for any taxable period.

Amendments

• **1976, Tax Reform Act of 1976 (P.L. 94-455)**

P.L. 94-455, §1906(b)(13)(A):

Amended 1954 Code by substituting "Secretary" for "Secretary or his delegate" each place it appeared. **Effective** 2-1-77.

[Sec. 7121(b)]

(b) FINALITY.—If such agreement is approved by the Secretary (within such time as may be stated in such agreement, or later agreed to) such agreement shall be final and conclusive, and, except upon a showing of fraud or malfeasance, or misrepresentation of a material fact—

(1) the case shall not be reopened as to the matters agreed upon or the agreement modified by any officer, employee, or agent of the United States, and

(2) in any suit, action, or proceeding, such agreement, or any determination, assessment, collection, payment, abatement, refund, or credit made in accordance therewith, shall not be annulled, modified, set aside, or disregarded.

Amendments

• **1976, Tax Reform Act of 1976 (P.L. 94-455)**

P.L. 94-455, §1906(b)(13)(A):

Amended 1954 Code by substituting "Secretary" for "Secretary or his delegate" each place it appeared. **Effective** 2-1-77.

[Sec. 7122]

SEC. 7122. COMPROMISES.

[Sec. 7122(a)]

(a) AUTHORIZATION.—The Secretary may compromise any civil or criminal case arising under the internal revenue laws prior to reference to the Department of Justice for prosecution or defense; and the Attorney General or his delegate may compromise any such case after reference to the Department of Justice for prosecution or defense.

Amendments

• **1976, Tax Reform Act of 1976 (P.L. 94-455)**

P.L. 94-455, §1906(b)(13)(A):

Amended 1954 Code by substituting "Secretary" for "Secretary or his delegate" each place it appeared. **Effective** 2-1-77.

[Sec. 7122(b)]

(b) RECORD.—Whenever a compromise is made by the Secretary in any case, there shall be placed on file in the office of the Secretary the opinion of the General Counsel for the Department of the Treasury or his delegate, with his reasons therefor, with a statement of—

(1) The amount of tax assessed,

(2) The amount of interest, additional amount, addition to the tax, or assessable penalty, imposed by law on the person against whom the tax is assessed, and

(3) The amount actually paid in accordance with the terms of the compromise.

Sec. 7103(e)—Repealed

CLOSING AGREEMENTS, COMPROMISES

Notwithstanding the foregoing provisions of this subsection, no such opinion shall be required with respect to the compromise of any civil case in which the unpaid amount of tax assessed (including any interest, additional amount, addition to the tax, or assessable penalty) is less than $50,000. However, such compromise shall be subject to continuing quality review by the Secretary.

Amendments

• **1996, Taxpayer Bill of Rights 2 (P.L. 104-168)**

P.L. 104-168, § 503(a):

Amended Code Sec. 7122(b) by striking "$500." and inserting "$50,000. However, such compromise shall be subject to continuing quality review by the Secretary.". **Effective** 7-30-96.

• **1976, Tax Reform Act of 1976 (P.L. 94-455)**

P.L. 94-455, § 1906(b)(13)(A):

Amended 1954 Code by substituting "Secretary" for "Secretary or his delegate" each place it appeared. **Effective** 2-1-77.

[Sec. 7122(c)]

(c) RULES FOR SUBMISSION OF OFFERS-IN-COMPROMISE.—

(1) PARTIAL PAYMENT REQUIRED WITH SUBMISSION.—

(A) LUMP-SUM OFFERS.—

(i) IN GENERAL.—The submission of any lump-sum offer-in-compromise shall be accompanied by the payment of 20 percent of the amount of such offer.

(ii) LUMP-SUM OFFER-IN-COMPROMISE.—For purposes of this section, the term "lump-sum offer-in-compromise" means any offer of payments made in 5 or fewer installments.

(B) PERIODIC PAYMENT OFFERS.—

(i) IN GENERAL.—The submission of any periodic payment offer-in-compromise shall be accompanied by the payment of the amount of the first proposed installment.

(ii) FAILURE TO MAKE INSTALLMENT DURING PENDENCY OF OFFER.—Any failure to make an installment (other than the first installment) due under such offer-in-compromise during the period such offer is being evaluated by the Secretary may be treated by the Secretary as a withdrawal of such offer-in-compromise.

(2) RULES OF APPLICATION.—

(A) USE OF PAYMENT.—The application of any payment made under this subsection to the assessed tax or other amounts imposed under this title with respect to such tax may be specified by the taxpayer.

(B) APPLICATION OF USER FEE.—In the case of any assessed tax or other amounts imposed under this title with respect to such tax which is the subject of an offer-in-compromise to which this subsection applies, such tax or other amounts shall be reduced by any user fee imposed under this title with respect to such offer-in-compromise.

(C) WAIVER AUTHORITY.—The Secretary may issue regulations waiving any payment required under paragraph (1) in a manner consistent with the practices established in accordance with the requirements under subsection (d)(3).

(3) EXCEPTION FOR LOW-INCOME TAXPAYERS.—Paragraph (1), and any user fee otherwise required in connection with the submission of an offer-in-compromise, shall not apply to any offer-in-compromise with respect to a taxpayer who is an individual with adjusted gross income, as determined for the most recent taxable year for which such information is available, which does not exceed 250 percent of the applicable poverty level (as determined by the Secretary).

Amendments

• **2019, Taxpayer First Act (P.L. 116-25)**

P.L. 116-25, § 1102(a):

Amended Code Sec. 7122(c) by adding at the end a new paragraph (3). **Effective** for offers-in-compromise submitted after 7-1-2019.

• **2006, Tax Increase Prevention and Reconciliation Act of 2005 (P.L. 109-222)**

P.L. 109-222, § 509(a):

Amended Code Sec. 7122 by redesignating subsections (c) and (d) as subsections (d) and (e), respectively, and by inserting after subsection (b) a new subsection (c). **Effective** for offers-in-compromise submitted on and after the date which is 60 days after 5-17-2006.

[Sec. 7122(d)]

(d) STANDARDS FOR EVALUATION OF OFFERS.—

(1) IN GENERAL.—The Secretary shall prescribe guidelines for officers and employees of the Internal Revenue Service to determine whether an offer-in-compromise is adequate and should be accepted to resolve a dispute.

(2) ALLOWANCES FOR BASIC LIVING EXPENSES.—

(A) IN GENERAL.—In prescribing guidelines under paragraph (1), the Secretary shall develop and publish schedules of national and local allowances designed to provide that taxpayers entering into a compromise have an adequate means to provide for basic living expenses.

(B) USE OF SCHEDULES.—The guidelines shall provide that officers and employees of the Internal Revenue Service shall determine, on the basis of the facts and circumstances of each taxpayer, whether the use of the schedules published under subparagraph (A) is appropriate and shall not use the schedules to the extent such use would result in the taxpayer not having adequate means to provide for basic living expenses.

(3) SPECIAL RULES RELATING TO TREATMENT OF OFFERS.—The guidelines under paragraph (1) shall provide that—

(A) an officer or employee of the Internal Revenue Service shall not reject an offer-in-compromise from a low-income taxpayer solely on the basis of the amount of the offer,

(B) in the case of an offer-in-compromise which relates only to issues of liability of the taxpayer—

(i) such offer shall not be rejected solely because the Secretary is unable to locate the taxpayer's return or return information for verification of such liability; and

(ii) the taxpayer shall not be required to provide a financial statement, and

(C) any offer-in-compromise which does not meet the requirements of subparagraph (A)(i) or (B)(i), as the case may be, of subsection (c)(1) may be returned to the taxpayer as unprocessable.

Amendments

• **2006, Tax Increase Prevention and Reconciliation Act of 2005 (P.L. 109-222)**

P.L. 109-222, § 509(a):

Amended Code Sec. 7122 by redesignating subsection (c) as subsection (d). **Effective** for offers-in-compromise submitted on and after the date which is 60 days after 5-17-2006.

P.L. 109-222, § 509(b)(1):

Amended Code Sec. 7122(d)(3), as redesignated by Act Sec. 509(a), by striking "; and" at the end of subparagraph (A) and inserting a comma, by striking the period at the end of subparagraph (B) and inserting ", and", and by adding at the end a new subparagraph (C). **Effective** for offers-in-compromise submitted on and after the date which is 60 days after 5-17-2006.

CLOSING AGREEMENTS, COMPROMISES

- **1998, IRS Restructuring and Reform Act of 1998 (P.L. 105-206)**

P.L. 105-206, § 3462(a):

Amended Code Sec. 7122 by adding at the end a new subsection (c). **Effective** for proposed offers-in-compromise and installment agreements submitted after 7-22-98.

[Sec. 7122(e)]

(e) ADMINISTRATIVE REVIEW.—The Secretary shall establish procedures—

(1) for an independent administrative review of any rejection of a proposed offer-in-compromise or installment agreement made by a taxpayer under this section or section 6159 before such rejection is communicated to the taxpayer; and

(2) which allow a taxpayer to appeal any rejection of such offer or agreement to the Internal Revenue Service Independent Office of Appeals.

Amendments

- **2019, Taxpayer First Act (P.L. 116-25)**

P.L. 116-25, § 1001(b)(1)(F):

Amended Code Sec. 7122(e)(2) by striking "Internal Revenue Service Office of Appeals" and inserting "Internal Revenue Service Independent Office of Appeals". **Effective** 7-1-2019.

- **2006, Tax Increase Prevention and Reconciliation Act of 2005 (P.L. 109-222)**

P.L. 109-222, § 509(a):

Amended Code Sec. 7122 by redesignating subsection (d) as subsection (e). **Effective** for offers-in-compromise submitted on and after the date which is 60 days after 5-17-2006.

- **1998, IRS Restructuring and Reform Act of 1998 (P.L. 105-206)**

P.L. 105-206, § 3462(c)(1):

Amended Code Sec. 7122, as amended by Act Sec. 3462(a), by adding at the end a new subsection (d). **Effective** for proposed offers-in-compromise and installment agreements submitted after 7-22-98.

P.L. 105-206, § 3462(d)(1)-(3), provides:

(d) PREPARATION OF STATEMENT RELATING TO OFFERS-IN-COMPROMISE.—The Secretary of the Treasury shall prepare a statement which sets forth in simple, non-technical terms the rights of a taxpayer and the obligations of the Internal Revenue Service relating to offers-in-compromise. Such statement shall—

(1) advise taxpayers who have entered into a compromise of the advantages of promptly notifying the Internal Revenue Service of any change of address or marital status;

(2) provide notice to taxpayers that in the case of a compromise terminated due to the actions of one spouse or former spouse, the Internal Revenue Service will, upon application, reinstate such compromise with the spouse or former spouse who remains in compliance with such compromise; and

(3) provide notice to the taxpayer that the taxpayer may appeal the rejection of an offer-in-compromise to the Internal Revenue Service Office of Appeals.

[Sec. 7122(f)]

(f) DEEMED ACCEPTANCE OF OFFER NOT REJECTED WITHIN CERTAIN PERIOD.—Any offer-in-compromise submitted under this section shall be deemed to be accepted by the Secretary if such offer is not rejected by the Secretary before the date which is 24 months after the date of the submission of such offer. For purposes of the preceding sentence, any period during which any tax liability which is the subject of such offer-in-compromise is in dispute in any judicial proceeding shall not be taken into account in determining the expiration of the 24-month period.

Amendments

- **2006, Tax Increase Prevention and Reconciliation Act of 2005 (P.L. 109-222)**

P.L. 109-222, § 509(b)(2):

Amended Code Sec. 7122, as amended by Act Sec. 509(a), by adding at the end a new subsection (f). **Effective** for offers-in-compromise submitted on and after the date which is 60 days after 5-17-2006.

[Sec. 7122(g)]

(g) FRIVOLOUS SUBMISSIONS, ETC.—Notwithstanding any other provision of this section, if the Secretary determines that any portion of an application for an offer-in-compromise or installment agreement submitted under this section or section 6159 meets the requirement of clause (i) or (ii) of section 6702(b)(2)(A), then the Secretary may treat such portion as if it were never submitted and such portion shall not be subject to any further administrative or judicial review.

Amendments

- **2014, Tax Technical Corrections Act of 2014 (P.L. 113-295)**

P.L. 113-295, § 220(y), Division A:

Amended Code Sec. 7122 by redesignating the second subsection (f) (relating to frivolous submissions, etc.) as subsection (g). **Effective** 12-19-2014.

- **2006, Tax Relief and Health Care Act of 2006 (P.L. 109-432)**

P.L. 109-432, Division A, § 407(d):

Amended Code Sec. 7122 by adding at the end a new subsection (f)[(g)]. **Effective** for submissions made and issues raised after the date on which the Secretary first prescribes a list under Code Sec. 6702(c), as amended by Act Sec. 407(a).

[Sec. 7123]

SEC. 7123. APPEALS DISPUTE RESOLUTION PROCEDURES.

[Sec. 7123(a)]

(a) EARLY REFERRAL TO APPEALS PROCEDURES.—The Secretary shall prescribe procedures by which any taxpayer may request early referral of 1 or more unresolved issues from the examination or collection division to the Internal Revenue Service Independent Office of Appeals.

Amendments

- **2019, Taxpayer First Act (P.L. 116-25)**

P.L. 116-25, § 1001(b)(1)(G):

Amended Code Sec. 7123(a) by striking "Internal Revenue Service Office of Appeals" and inserting "Internal Revenue Service Independent Office of Appeals". **Effective** 7-1-2019.

[Sec. 7123(b)]

(b) ALTERNATIVE DISPUTE RESOLUTION PROCEDURES.—

(1) MEDIATION.—The Secretary shall prescribe procedures under which a taxpayer or the Internal Revenue Service Independent Office of Appeals may request non-binding mediation on any issue unresolved at the conclusion of—

(A) appeals procedures; or

(B) unsuccessful attempts to enter into a closing agreement under section 7121 or a compromise under section 7122.

(2) ARBITRATION.—The Secretary shall establish a pilot program under which a taxpayer and the Internal Revenue Service Independent Office of Appeals may jointly request binding arbitration on any issue unresolved at the conclusion of—

(A) appeals procedures; or

(B) unsuccessful attempts to enter into a closing agreement under section 7121 or a compromise under section 7122.

Amendments

- **2019, Taxpayer First Act (P.L. 116-25)**

P.L. 116-25, §1001(b)(1)(G):

Amended Code Sec. 7123(b)(1)-(2) by striking "Internal Revenue Service Office of Appeals" and inserting "Internal Revenue Service Independent Office of Appeals". **Effective** 7-1-2019.

- **1998, IRS Restructuring and Reform Act of 1998 (P.L. 105-206)**

P.L. 105-206, §3465(a)(1):

Amended chapter 74 by redesignating Code Sec. 7123 as Code Sec. 7124 and by inserting after Code Sec. 7122 a new Code Sec. 7123. **Effective** 7-22-98.

P.L. 105-206, §3465(b)-(c), provides:

(b) APPEALS OFFICERS IN EACH STATE.—The Commissioner of Internal Revenue shall ensure that an appeals officer is regularly available within each State.

(c) APPEALS VIDEOCONFERENCING ALTERNATIVE FOR RURAL AREAS.—The Commissioner of Internal Revenue shall consider the use of the videoconferencing of appeals conferences between appeals officers and taxpayers seeking appeals in rural or remote areas.

[Sec. 7123(c)]

(c) ADMINISTRATIVE APPEAL RELATING TO ADVERSE DETERMINATION OF TAX-EXEMPT STATUS OF CERTAIN ORGANIZATIONS.—

(1) IN GENERAL.—The Secretary shall prescribe procedures under which an organization which claims to be described in section 501(c) may request an administrative appeal (including a conference relating to such appeal if requested by the organization) to the Internal Revenue Service Independent Office of Appeals of an adverse determination described in paragraph (2).

(2) ADVERSE DETERMINATIONS.—For purposes of paragraph (1), an adverse determination is described in this paragraph if such determination is adverse to an organization with respect to—

(A) the initial qualification or continuing qualification of the organization as exempt from tax under section 501(a) or as an organization described in section 170(c)(2),

(B) the initial classification or continuing classification of the organization as a private foundation under section 509(a), or

(C) the initial classification or continuing classification of the organization as a private operating foundation under section 4942(j)(3).

Amendments

- **2019, Taxpayer First Act (P.L. 116-25)**

P.L. 116-25, §1001(b)(1)(G):

Amended Code Sec. 7123(c)(1) by striking "Internal Revenue Service Office of Appeals" and inserting "Internal Revenue Service Independent Office of Appeals". **Effective** 7-1-2019.

- **2015, Protecting Americans from Tax Hikes Act of 2015 (P.L. 114-113)**

P.L. 114-113, §404(a), Div. Q:

Amended Code Sec. 7123 by adding at the end a new subsection (c). **Effective** for determinations made on or after 5-19-2014.

[Sec. 7124]

SEC. 7124. CROSS REFERENCES.

For criminal penalties for concealment of property, false statement, or falsifying and destroying records, in connection with any closing agreement, compromise, or offer of compromise, see section 7206.

Amendments

- **1998, IRS Restructuring and Reform Act of 1998 (P.L. 105-206)**

P.L. 105-206, §3465(a)(1):

Amended chapter 74 by redesignating Code Sec. 7123 as Code Sec. 7124. **Effective** 7-22-98.

- **1982 (P.L. 97-258)**

P.L. 97-258, §3(f)(12):

Amended Code Sec. 7123 by striking out "(a) CRIMINAL PENALTIES[.—]" in subsection (a), and by striking out subsection (b). **Effective** 9-13-82. Prior to being stricken, subsection (b) read as follows:

"(b) COMPROMISES AFTER JUDGMENT.—

For compromises after judgment, see R.S. 3469 (31 U.S.C. 194)."

CHAPTER 75—CRIMES, OTHER OFFENSES, AND FORFEITURES

SUBCHAPTER A.	Crimes.
SUBCHAPTER B.	Other offenses.
SUBCHAPTER C.	Forfeitures.
SUBCHAPTER D.	Miscellaneous penalty and forfeiture provisions.

Subchapter A—Crimes

Part I.	General provisions.
Part II.	Penalties applicable to certain taxes.

PART I—GENERAL PROVISIONS

Sec. 7201.	Attempt to evade or defeat tax.
Sec. 7202.	Willful failure to collect or pay over tax.
Sec. 7203.	Willful failure to file return, supply information, or pay tax.
Sec. 7204.	Fraudulent statement or failure to make statement to employees.
Sec. 7205.	Fraudulent withholding exemption certificate or failure to supply information.
Sec. 7206.	Fraud and false statements.
Sec. 7207.	Fraudulent returns, statements, or other documents.
Sec. 7208.	Offenses relating to stamps.
Sec. 7209.	Unauthorized use or sale of stamps.
Sec. 7210.	Failure to obey summons.
Sec. 7211.	False statements to purchasers or lessees relating to tax.
Sec. 7212.	Attempts to interfere with administration of internal revenue laws.
Sec. 7213.	Unauthorized disclosure of information.
Sec. 7213A.	Unauthorized inspection of returns or return information.
Sec. 7214.	Offenses by officers and employees of the United States.
Sec. 7215.	Offenses with respect to collected taxes.
Sec. 7216.	Disclosure or use of information by preparers of returns.
Sec. 7217.	Prohibition on executive branch influence over taxpayer audits and other investigations.

CRIMES

>>> *Caution: See 18 U.S.C. §3571, in the amendment notes, under which a larger fine may be imposed with respect to Code Sec. 7201.*

[Sec. 7201]

SEC. 7201. ATTEMPT TO EVADE OR DEFEAT TAX.

Any person who willfully attempts in any manner to evade or defeat any tax imposed by this title or the payment thereof shall, in addition to other penalties provided by law, be guilty of a felony and, upon conviction thereof, shall be fined not more than $100,000 ($500,000 in the case of a corporation), or imprisoned not more than 5 years, or both, together with the costs of prosecution.

Amendments

• **1987 (P.L. 100-185)**

P.L. 100-185, §6:

Amended 18 U.S.C. §3571, which provides as follows:

§3571. Sentence of fine.

(a) IN GENERAL.—A defendant who has been found guilty of an offense may be sentenced to pay a fine.

(b) FINES FOR INDIVIDUALS.—Except as provided in subsection (e) of this section, an individual who has been found guilty of an offense may be fined not more than the greatest of—

(1) the amount specified in the law setting forth the offense;

(2) the applicable amount under subsection (d) of this section;

(3) for a felony, not more than $250,000;

(4) for a misdemeanor resulting in death, not more than $250,000;

(5) for a Class A misdemeanor that does not result in death, not more than $100,000;

(6) for a Class B or C misdemeanor that does not result in death, not more than $5,000; or

(7) for an infraction, not more than $5,000.

(c) FINES FOR ORGANIZATIONS.—Except as provided in subsection (e) of this section, an organization that has been found guilty of an offense may be fined not more than the greatest of—

(1) the amount specified in the law setting forth the offense;

(2) the applicable amount under subsection (d) of this section;

(3) for a felony, not more than $500,000;

(4) for a misdemeanor resulting in death, not more than $500,000;

(5) for a Class A misdemeanor that does not result in death, not more than $200,000;

(6) for a Class B or C misdemeanor that does not result in death, not more than $10,000; and

(7) for an infraction, not more than $10,000.

(d) ALTERNATIVE FINE BASED ON GAIN OR LOSS.—If any person derives pecuniary gain from the offense, or if the offense results in pecuniary loss to a person other than the defendant, the defendant may be fined not more than the greater of twice the gross gain or twice the gross loss, unless imposition of a fine under this subsection would unduly complicate or prolong the sentencing process.

(e) SPECIAL RULE FOR LOWER FINE SPECIFIED IN SUBSTANTIVE PROVISION.—If a law setting forth an offense specifies no fine or a fine that is lower than the fine otherwise applicable under this section and such law, by specific reference, exempts the offense from the applicability of the fine otherwise applicable under this section, the defendant may not be fined more than the amount specified in the law setting forth the offense.

• **1982, Tax Equity and Fiscal Responsibility Act of 1982 (P.L. 97-248)**

P.L. 97-248, §329(a):

Amended Code Sec. 7201 by striking out "$10,000" and inserting "$100,000 ($500,000 in the case of a corporation)". **Effective** for offenses committed after 9-3-82.

>>> *Caution: See 18 U.S.C. §3571, in the amendment notes following Code Sec. 7201, under which a larger fine may be imposed with respect to Code Sec. 7202.*

[Sec. 7202]

SEC. 7202. WILLFUL FAILURE TO COLLECT OR PAY OVER TAX.

Any person required under this title to collect, account for, and pay over any tax imposed by this title who willfully fails to collect or truthfully account for and pay over such tax shall, in addition to other penalties provided by law, be guilty of a felony and, upon conviction thereof, shall be fined not more than $10,000, or imprisoned not more than 5 years, or both, together with the costs of prosecution.

[Sec. 7203]

SEC. 7203. WILLFUL FAILURE TO FILE RETURN, SUPPLY INFORMATION, OR PAY TAX.

Any person required under this title to pay any estimated tax or tax, or required by this title or by regulations made under authority thereof to make a return, keep any records, or supply any information, who willfully fails to pay such estimated tax or tax, make such return, keep such records, or supply such information, at the time or times required by law or regulations, shall, in addition to other penalties provided by law, be guilty of a misdemeanor and, upon conviction thereof, shall be fined not more than $25,000 ($100,000 in the case of a corporation), or imprisoned not more than 1 year, or both, together with the costs of prosecution. In the case of any person with respect to whom there is a failure to pay any estimated tax, this section shall not apply to such person with respect to such failure if there is no addition to tax under section 6654 or 6655 with respect to such failure. In the case of a willful violation of any provision of section 6050I, the first sentence of this section shall be applied by substituting "felony" for "misdemeanor" and "5 years" for "1 year".

Amendments

• **1990, Crime Control Act of 1990 (P.L. 101-647)**

P.L. 101-647, §3303(a):

Amended Code Sec. 7203 by striking "by substituting" and inserting "by substituting 'felony' for 'misdemeanor' and". **Effective** for actions, and failures to act, occurring after 11-29-90.

• **1988, Anti-Drug Abuse Act of 1988 (P.L. 100-690)**

P.L. 100-690, §7601(a)(2)(B):

Amended Code Sec. 7203 by adding at the end thereof a new sentence. **Effective** for actions after 11-18-88.

• **1984, Deficit Reduction Act of 1984 (P.L. 98-369)**

P.L. 98-369, §412(b)(9):

Amended Code Sec. 7203 by striking out "(other than a return required under the [sic] authority of section 6015)", following "to make a return". **Effective** with respect to tax years beginning after 12-31-84.

• **1982, Tax Equity and Fiscal Responsibility Act of 1982 (P.L. 97-248)**

P.L. 97-248, §327:

Amended Code Sec. 7203 by adding at the end a new sentence. **Effective** 9-3-82.

P.L. 97-248, §329(b):

Amended Code Sec. 7203 by striking out "$10,000" and inserting "$25,000 ($100,000 in the case of a corporation)". **Effective** for offenses committed after 9-3-82.

• **1968, Revenue and Expenditure Control Act of 1968 (P.L. 90-364)**

P.L. 90-364, §103(e)(5):

Amended Code Sec. 7203 by deleting "or section 6016" which formerly appeared after "section 6015" in the third line. **Effective** with respect to tax years beginning after 12-31-67.

[Sec. 7204]

SEC. 7204. FRAUDULENT STATEMENT OR FAILURE TO MAKE STATEMENT TO EMPLOYEES.

In lieu of any other penalty provided by law (except the penalty provided by section 6674) any person required under the provisions of section 6051 to furnish a statement who willfully furnishes a false or fraudulent statement or who willfully fails to furnish a statement in the manner, at the time, and showing the information required under section 6051, or regulations prescribed thereunder, shall, for each such offense, upon conviction thereof, be fined not more than $1,000, or imprisoned not more than 1 year, or both.

CRIMES

[Sec. 7205]
SEC. 7205. FRAUDULENT WITHHOLDING EXEMPTION CERTIFICATE OR FAILURE TO SUPPLY INFORMATION.

[Sec. 7205(a)]

(a) WITHHOLDING ON WAGES.—Any individual required to supply information to his employer under section 3402 who willfully supplies false or fraudulent information, or who willfully fails to supply information thereunder which would require an increase in the tax to be withheld under section 3402, shall, in addition to any other penalty provided by law, upon conviction thereof, be fined not more than $1,000, or imprisoned not more than 1 year, or both.

[Sec. 7205(b)]

(b) BACKUP WITHHOLDING ON INTEREST AND DIVIDENDS.—If any individual willfully makes a false certification under paragraph (1) or (2)(C) of section 3406(d), then such individual shall, in addition to any other penalty provided by law, upon conviction thereof, be fined not more than $1,000, or imprisoned not more than 1 year, or both.

Amendments

• **1989, Omnibus Budget Reconciliation Act of 1989 (P.L. 101-239)**

P.L. 101-239, §7711(b)(2):

Amended Code Sec. 7205(b). **Effective** for returns and statements the due date for which (determined without regard to extensions) is after 12-31-89. Prior to amendment, Code Sec. 7205(b) read as follows:

(b) BACKUP WITHHOLDING ON INTEREST AND DIVIDENDS.—If any individual willfully makes—

(1) any false certification or affirmation on any statement required by a payor in order to meet the due diligence requirements of section 6676(b), or

(2) a false certification under paragraph (1) or (2)(C) of section 3406(d),

then such individual shall, in addition to any other penalty provided by law, upon conviction thereof, be fined not more than $1,000, or imprisoned not more than 1 year, or both.

• **1984, Deficit Reduction Act of 1984 (P.L. 98-369)**

P.L. 98-369, §159(a)(1):

Amended Code Sec. 7205 by striking out "in lieu of" each place it appeared and inserting in lieu thereof "in addition to". **Effective** for actions and failures to act occurring after 7-18-84.

P.L. 98-369, §159(a)(2):

Amended Code Sec. 7205 by striking out "(except the penalty provided by section 6682)" each place it appeared. **Effective** for actions and failures to act occurring after 7-18-84.

• **1983, Interest and Dividend Tax Compliance Act of 1983 (P.L. 98-67)**

P.L. 98-67, §102(a):

Repealed the amendments to Code Sec. 7205 made by P.L. 97-248. **Effective** as of the close of 6-30-83. Code Sec. 7205, as amended by P.L. 97-248, which was to go into effect with respect to payments of interest, dividends, and patronage dividends paid or credited after 6-30-83, read as follows:

(a) WITHHOLDING ON WAGES.—Any individual required to supply information to his employer under section 3402 who willfully supplies false or fraudulent information, or who willfully fails to supply information thereunder which would require an increase in the tax to be withheld under section 3402, shall, in lieu of any other penalty provided by law (except the penalty provided by section 6682), upon conviction thereof, be fined not more than $1,000, or imprisoned not more than 1 year, or both.

(b) WITHHOLDING OF INTEREST AND DIVIDENDS.—Any person who—

(1) willfully files an exemption certificate with any payor under section 3452(f)(1)(A), which is known by him to be fraudulent or to be false as to any material matter, or

(2) is required to furnish notice under section 3452(f)(1)(B), and willfully fails to furnish such notice in the manner and at the time required pursuant to section 3452(f)(1)(B) or the regulations prescribed thereunder,

shall, in lieu of any penalty otherwise provided, upon conviction thereof, be fined not more than $500, or imprisoned not more than 1 year, or both.

P.L. 98-67, §107(b):

Amended Code Sec. 7205. **Effective** 10-5-83. Prior to amendment, Code Sec. 7205 read as follows:

Any individual required to supply information to his employer under section 3402 who willfully supplies false or fraudulent information, or who willfully fails to supply information thereunder which would require an increase in the tax to be withheld under section 3402, shall, in lieu of any other penalty provided by law (except the penalty provided by section 6682), upon conviction thereof, be fined not more than $1,000, or imprisoned not more than 1 year, or both.

• **1982, Tax Equity and Fiscal Responsibility Act of 1982 (P.L. 97-248)**

P.L. 97-248, §306(b):

Amended Code Sec. 7205 by striking out "Any individual" and inserting "(a) WITHHOLDING ON WAGES.—Any individual" and by adding a new subsection (b). **Effective** for payments of interest, dividends, and patronage dividends paid or credited after 6-30-83.

• **1981, Economic Recovery Tax Act of 1981 (P.L. 97-34)**

P.L. 97-34, §721(b):

Amended Code Sec. 7205 by striking out "$500" and inserting "$1,000". **Effective** for acts and failures to act after 12-31-81.

• **1966, Tax Adjustment Act of 1966 (P.L. 89-368)**

P.L. 89-368, §101(e):

Amended Code Sec. 7205 by substituting "3402" for "3402(f)" and by substituting "any other penalty provided by law (except the penalty provided by section 6682)" for "any penalty otherwise provided". **Effective** with respect to remuneration paid after 4-30-66.

➤➤➤ Caution: See 18 U.S.C. §3571, in the amendment notes following Code Sec. 7201, under which a larger fine may be imposed with respect to Code Sec. 7206.

[Sec. 7206]
SEC. 7206. FRAUD AND FALSE STATEMENTS.

Any person who—

(1) DECLARATION UNDER PENALTIES OF PERJURY.—Willfully makes and subscribes any return, statement, or other document, which contains or is verified by a written declaration that it is made under the penalties of perjury, and which he does not believe to be true and correct as to every material matter; or

(2) AID OR ASSISTANCE.—Willfully aids or assists in, or procures, counsels, or advises the preparation or presentation under, or in connection with any matter arising under, the internal revenue laws, of a return, affidavit, claim, or other document, which is fraudulent or is false as to any material matter, whether or not such falsity or fraud is with the knowledge or consent of the person authorized or required to present such return, affidavit, claim, or document; or

(3) FRAUDULENT BONDS, PERMITS, AND ENTRIES.—Simulates or falsely or fraudulently executes or signs any bond, permit, entry, or other document required by the provisions of the internal revenue laws, or by any regulation made in pursuance thereof, or procures the same to be falsely or fraudulently executed or advises, aids in, or connives at such execution thereof; or

(4) REMOVAL OR CONCEALMENT WITH INTENT TO DEFRAUD.—Removes, deposits, or conceals, or is concerned in removing, depositing, or concealing, any goods or commodities for or in respect whereof any tax is or shall be imposed, or any property upon which levy is authorized by section 6331, with intent to evade or defeat the assessment or collection of any tax imposed by this title; or

(5) COMPROMISES AND CLOSING AGREEMENTS.—In connection with any compromise under section 7122, or offer of such compromise, or in connection with any closing agreement under section 7121, or offer to enter into any such agreement, willfully—

(A) CONCEALMENT OF PROPERTY.—Conceals from any officer or employee of the United States any property belonging to the estate of a taxpayer or other person liable in respect of the tax, or

(B) WITHHOLDING, FALSIFYING, AND DESTROYING RECORDS.—Receives, withholds, destroys, mutilates, or falsifies any book, document, or record, or makes any false statement, relating to the estate or financial condition of the taxpayer or other person liable in respect of the tax;

shall be guilty of a felony and, upon conviction thereof, shall be fined not more than $100,000 ($500,000 in the case of a corporation) or imprisoned not more than 3 years, or both, together with the costs of prosecution.

CRIMES

Amendments

- **1982, Tax Equity and Fiscal Responsibility Act of 1982 (P.L. 97-248)**

P.L. 97-248, §329(c):

Amended Code Sec. 7206 by striking out "$5,000" and inserting "$100,000 ($500,000 in the case of a corporation)". **Effective** for offenses committed after 9-3-82.

[Sec. 7207]

SEC. 7207. FRAUDULENT RETURNS, STATEMENTS, OR OTHER DOCUMENTS.

Any person who willfully delivers or discloses to the Secretary any list, return, account, statement, or other document, known by him to be fraudulent or to be false as to any material matter, shall be fined not more than $10,000 ($50,000 in the case of a corporation), or imprisoned not more than 1 year, or both. Any person required pursuant to section 6047(b), section 6104(d), or subsection (i) or (j) of section 527 to furnish any information to the Secretary or any other person who willfully furnishes to the Secretary or such other person any information known by him to be fraudulent or to be false as to any material matter shall be fined not more than $10,000 ($50,000 in the case of a corporation), or imprisoned not more than 1 year, or both.

Amendments

- **2002 (P.L. 107-276)**

P.L. 107-276, §6(d):

Amended Code Sec. 7207 by striking "pursuant to subsection (b) of section 6047 or pursuant to subsection (d) of section 6104" and inserting "pursuant to section 6047(b), section 6104(d), or subsection (i) or (j) of section 527". **Effective** for reports and notices required to be filed on or after 11-2-2002.

- **1998, Tax and Trade Relief Extension Act of 1998 (P.L. 105-277)**

P.L. 105-277, §1004(b)(2)(E):

Amended Code Sec. 7207 by striking "or (e)" following "subsection (d)". **Effective**, generally, for requests made after the later of 12-31-98, or the 60th day after the Secretary of the Treasury first issues the regulations referred to in Code Sec. 6104(d)(4), as amended by Act Sec. 1004. For an exception, see Act Sec. 1004(b)(3)(B), below.

P.L. 105-277, §1004(b)(3)(B), provides:

(B) PUBLICATION OF ANNUAL RETURNS.—Section 6104(d) of such Code, as in effect before the amendments made by this subsection, shall not apply to any return the due date for which is after the date such amendments take effect under subparagraph (A).

- **1987, Revenue Act of 1987 (P.L. 100-203)**

P.L. 100-203, §10704(c):

Amended Code Sec. 7207 by striking out "subsection (d) of section 6104" and inserting in lieu thereof "subsection (d) or (e) of section 6104". For the **effective** date, see Act Sec. 10704(d), below.

P.L. 100-203, §10704(d), provides:

(d) EFFECTIVE DATE.—The amendments made by this section shall apply—

(1) to returns for years beginning after December 31, 1986, and

(2) on and after the date of the enactment of this Act in the case of applications submitted to the Internal Revenue Service—

(A) after July 15, 1987, or

(B) on or before July 15, 1987, if the organization has a copy of the application on July 15, 1987.

- **1984, Deficit Reduction Act of 1984 (P.L. 98-369)**

P.L. 98-369, §491(d)(51):

Amended Code Sec. 7207 by striking out "or (c)" following "subsection (b)". **Effective** for obligations issued after 12-31-83.

- **1982, Tax Equity and Fiscal Responsibility Act of 1982 (P.L. 97-248)**

P.L. 97-248, §329(d):

Amended Code Sec. 7207 by striking out "$1,000" each place it appeared and inserting "$10,000 ($50,000 in the case of a corporation)". **Effective** for offenses committed after 9-3-82.

- **1980 (P.L. 96-603)**

P.L. 96-603, §1(d)(5):

Amended Code Sec. 7207 by striking out "sections 6047(b) or (c), 6056, or 6104(d)" and inserting in lieu thereof "subsection (b) or (c) of section 6047 or pursuant to subsection (d) of section 6104". **Effective** for tax years beginning after 1980.

- **1976, Tax Reform Act of 1976 (P.L. 94-455)**

P.L. 94-455, §1906(b)(13)(A):

Amended 1954 Code by substituting "Secretary" for "Secretary or his delegate" each place it appeared. **Effective** 2-1-77.

- **1969, Tax Reform Act of 1969 (P.L. 91-172)**

P.L. 91-172, §101(e)(5):

Amended Code Sec. 7207 by inserting "sections 6047(b) or (c), 6056, or 6104(d)" in lieu of "section 6047(b) or (c)". **Effective** 1-1-70.

- **1962, Self-Employed Individuals Tax Retirement Act of 1962 (P.L. 87-792)**

P.L. 87-792, §7:

Amended Code Sec. 7207 by inserting after the period in line 4 a new sentence. **Effective** 1-1-63.

➤➤➤ **Caution:** See 18 U.S.C. §3571, in the amendment notes following Code Sec. 7201, under which a larger fine may be imposed with respect to Code Sec. 7208.

[Sec. 7208]

SEC. 7208. OFFENSES RELATING TO STAMPS.

Any person who—

(1) COUNTERFEITING.—With intent to defraud, alters, forges, makes, or counterfeits any stamp, coupon, ticket, book, or other device prescribed under authority of this title for the collection or payment of any tax imposed by this title, or sells, lends, or has in his possession any such altered, forged, or counterfeited stamp, coupon, ticket, book, or other device, or makes, uses, sells, or has in his possession any material in imitation of the material used in the manufacture of such stamp, coupon, ticket, book, or other device; or

(2) MUTILATION OR REMOVAL.—Fraudulently cuts, tears, or removes from any vellum, parchment, paper, instrument, writing, package, or article, upon which any tax is imposed by this title, any adhesive stamp or the impression of any stamp, die, plate, or other article provided, made, or used in pursuance of this title; or

(3) USE OF MUTILATED, INSUFFICIENT, OR COUNTERFEITED STAMPS.—Fraudulently uses, joins, fixes, or places to, with, or upon any vellum, parchment, paper, instrument, writing, package, or article, upon which any tax is imposed by this title,

(A) any adhesive stamp, or the impression of any stamp, die, plate, or other article, which has been cut, torn, or removed from any other vellum, parchment, paper, instrument, writing, package, or article, upon which any tax is imposed by this title; or

(B) any adhesive stamp or the impression of any stamp, die, plate, or other article of insufficient value; or

(C) any forged or counterfeited stamp, or the impression of any forged or counterfeited stamp, die, plate, or other article; or

(4) REUSE OF STAMPS.—

(A) PREPARATION FOR REUSE.—Willfully removes, or alters the cancellation or defacing marks of, or otherwise prepares, any adhesive stamp, with intent to use, or cause the same to be used, after it has already been used; or

(B) TRAFFICKING.—Knowingly or willfully buys, sells, offers for sale, or gives away, any such washed or restored stamp to any person for use, or knowingly uses the same; or

(C) POSSESSION.—Knowingly and without lawful excuse (the burden of proof of such excuse being on the accused has in possession any washed, restored, or altered stamp, which has been removed from any vellum, parchment, paper, instrument, writing, package, or article; or

(5) EMPTIED STAMPED PACKAGES.—Commits the offense described in section 7271 (relating to disposal and receipt of stamped packages) with intent to defraud the revenue, or to defraud any person;

shall be guilty of a felony and, upon conviction thereof, shall be fined not more that $10,000, or imprisoned not more than 5 years, or both.

[Sec. 7209]
SEC. 7209. UNAUTHORIZED USE OR SALE OF STAMPS.

Any person who buys, sells, offers for sale, uses, transfers, takes or gives in exchange, or pledges or gives in pledge, except as authorized in this title or in regulations made pursuant thereto, any stamp, coupon, ticket, book, or other device prescribed by the Secretary under this title for the collection or payment of any tax imposed by this title, shall, upon conviction thereof, be fined not more than $1,000, or imprisoned not more than 6 months, or both.

Amendments
- 1976, Tax Reform Act of 1976 (P.L. 94-455)

P.L. 94-455, §1906(b)(13)(A):

Amended 1954 Code by substituting "Secretary" for "Secretary or his delegate" each place it appeared. **Effective** 2-1-77.

[Sec. 7210]
SEC. 7210. FAILURE TO OBEY SUMMONS.

Any person who, being duly summoned to appear to testify, or to appear and produce books, accounts, records, memoranda, or other papers, as required under sections 6420(e)(2), 6421(g)(2), 6427(j)(2), 7602, 7603, and 7604(b), neglects to appear or to produce such books, accounts, records, memoranda, or other papers, shall, upon conviction thereof, be fined not more than $1,000, or imprisoned not more than 1 year, or both, together with costs of prosecution.

Amendments

- 1988, Technical and Miscellaneous Revenue Act of 1988 (P.L. 100-647)

P.L. 100-647, §1017(c)(9):

Amended Code Sec. 7210 by striking out "6421(f)(2)" and inserting in lieu thereof "6421(g)(2)" **Effective** as if included in the provision of P.L. 99-514 to which it relates.

- 1986, Tax Reform Act of 1986 (P.L. 99-514)

P.L. 99-514, §1703(e)(2)(G):

Amended Code Sec. 7210 by striking out "6427(i)(2)" and inserting in lieu thereof "6427(j)(2)". **Effective** for gasoline removed (as defined in section 4082 of the Internal Revenue Code of 1986, as amended) after 12-31-87.

- 1984, Deficit Reduction Act of 1984 (P.L. 98-369)

P.L. 98-369, §911(d)[c](2)(G):

Amended Code Sec. 7210 by striking out "6427(h)(2)" and inserting in lieu thereof "6427(i)(2)". **Effective** 8-1-84.

- 1983, Surface Transportation Act of 1983 (P.L. 97-424)

P.L. 97-424, §515(b)(12):

Amended Code Sec. 7210 by striking out "6424(d)(2)," before "6427(h)(2)". **Effective** 1-6-83.

- 1980, Crude Oil Windfall Profit Tax Act of 1980 (P.L. 96-223)

P.L. 96-223, §232(d)(4)(E):

Amended Code Sec. 7210 by substituting "6427(h)(2)" for "6427(g)(2)". **Effective** 1-1-79.

- 1978, Surface Transportation Assistance Act of 1978 (P.L. 95-599)

P.L. 95-599, §505(c)(5), (d):

Substituted "6427(g)(2)" for "6427(f)(2)" in Code Sec. 7210. **Effective** 1-1-79.

- 1976 (P.L. 94-530)

P.L. 94-530, §1(c)(6):

Substituted "6427(f)(2)" for "6427(e)(2)" in Code Sec. 7210. **Effective** 10-1-76.

- 1970 (P.L. 91-258)

P.L. 91-258, §207(d)(9):

Amended Code Sec. 7210 by adding "6427(e)(2)" in the third line. **Effective** 7-1-70.

- 1965, Excise Tax Reduction Act of 1965 (P.L. 89-44)

P.L. 89-44, §202(c)(4):

Amended Sec. 7210 by inserting "6424(d)(2)," after "6421(f)(2),". **Effective** 1-1-66.

- 1956 (P.L. 627, 84th Cong.)

P.L. 627, 84th Cong., 2nd Sess., §208(d)(3):

Amended Sec. 7210 by inserting after "sections 6420(e)(2)," the following: "6421(f)(2),". **Effective** 7-1-56.

- 1956 (P.L. 466, 84th Cong.)

P.L. 466, 84th Cong., 2nd Sess., §4(h):

Amended Code Sec. 7210 by striking out "sections 7602," and inserting in lieu thereof "sections 6420(e)(2), 7602,".

[Sec. 7211]
SEC. 7211. FALSE STATEMENTS TO PURCHASERS OR LESSEES RELATING TO TAX.

Whoever in connection with the sale or lease, or offer for sale or lease, of any article, or for the purpose of making such sale or lease, makes any statement, written or oral—

(1) intended or calculated to lead any person to believe that any part of the price at which such article is sold or leased, or offered for sale or lease, consists of a tax imposed under the authority of the United States, or

(2) ascribing a particular part of such price to a tax imposed under the authority of the United States,

knowing that such statement is false or that the tax is not so great as the portion of such price ascribed to such tax, shall be guilty of a misdemeanor and, upon conviction thereof, shall be punished by a fine of not more than $1,000, or by imprisonment for not more than 1 year, or both.

⋙→ *Caution: See 18 U.S.C. §3571, in the amendment notes following Code Sec. 7201, under which a larger fine may be imposed with respect to Code Sec. 7212.*

[Sec. 7212]
SEC. 7212. ATTEMPTS TO INTERFERE WITH ADMINISTRATION OF INTERNAL REVENUE LAWS.

[Sec. 7212(a)]

(a) CORRUPT OR FORCIBLE INTERFERENCE.—Whoever corruptly or by force or threats of force (including any threatening letter or communication) endeavors to intimidate or impede any officer or employee of the United States acting in an official capacity under this title, or in any other way corruptly or by force or threats of force (including any threatening letter or communication) obstructs or impedes, or endeavors to obstruct or impede, the due administration of this title, shall upon conviction thereof, be fined not more than $5,000, or imprisoned not more than 3 years, or both, except that if the offense is committed only by threats of force, the person convicted thereof shall be fined not more than $3,000, or imprisoned not more than 1 year, or both. The term "threats of force", as used in this subsection, means threats of bodily harm to the officer or employee of the United States or to a member of his family.

[Sec. 7212(b)]

(b) FORCIBLE RESCUE OF SEIZED PROPERTY.—Any person who forcibly rescues or causes to be rescued any property after it shall have been seized under this title, or shall attempt or endeavor so to do, shall, excepting in cases otherwise provided for, for every such offense, be fined not more than $500, or not more than double the value of the property so rescued, whichever is the greater, or be imprisoned not more than 2 years.

CRIMES

›››→ *Caution:* See 18 U.S.C. §3571, in the amendment notes following Code Sec. 7201, under which a larger fine may be imposed with respect to Code Sec. 7213.

[Sec. 7213]

SEC. 7213. UNAUTHORIZED DISCLOSURE OF INFORMATION.

[Sec. 7213(a)]

(a) RETURNS AND RETURN INFORMATION.—

(1) FEDERAL EMPLOYEES AND OTHER PERSONS.—It shall be unlawful for any officer or employee of the United States or any person described in section 6103(n) (or an officer or employee of any such person), or any former officer or employee, willfully to disclose to any person, except as authorized in this title, any return or return information (as defined in section 6103(b)). Any violation of this paragraph shall be a felony punishable upon conviction by a fine in any amount not exceeding $5,000, or imprisonment of not more than 5 years, or both, together with the costs of prosecution, and if such offense is committed by any officer or employee of the United States, he shall, in addition to any other punishment, be dismissed from office or discharged from employment upon conviction for such offense.

(2) STATE AND OTHER EMPLOYEES.—It shall be unlawful for any person (not described in paragraph (1)) willfully to disclose to any person, except as authorized in this title, any return or return information (as defined in section 6103(b)) acquired by him or another person under subsection (d), (i)(1)(C), (3)(B)(i), or (7)(A)(ii), (k)(10), (13), (14), or (15), (l)(6), (7), (8), (9), (10), (12), (15), (16), (19), (20), or (21) or (m)(2), (4), (5), (6), or (7) of section 6103 or under section 6104(c). Any violation of this paragraph shall be a felony punishable by a fine in any amount not exceeding $5,000, or imprisonment of not more than 5 years, or both, together with the costs of prosecution.

(3) OTHER PERSONS.—It shall be unlawful for any person to whom any return or return information (as defined in section 6103(b)) is disclosed in an manner unauthorized by this title thereafter willfully to print or publish in any manner not provided by law any such return or return information. Any violation of this paragraph shall be a felony punishable by a fine in any amount not exceeding $5,000, or imprisonment of not more than 5 years, or both, together with the costs of prosecution.

(4) SOLICITATION.—It shall be unlawful for any person willfully to offer any item of material value in exchange for any return or return information (as defined in section 6103(b)) and to receive as a result of such solicitation any such return or return information. Any violation of this paragraph shall be a felony punishable by a fine in any amount not exceeding $5,000, or imprisonment of not more than 5 years, or both, together with the costs of prosecution.

(5) SHAREHOLDERS.—It shall be unlawful for any person to whom a return or return information (as defined in section 6103(b)) is disclosed pursuant to the provisions of section 6103(e)(1)(D)(iii) willfully to disclose such return or return information in any manner not provided by law. Any violation of this paragraph shall be a felony punishable by a fine in any amount not to exceed $5,000, or imprisonment of not more than 5 years, or both, together with the costs of prosecution.

Amendments

• **2020, COVID-related Tax Relief Act of 2020 (P.L. 116-260)**

P.L. 116-260, §283(b)(2)(C), Div. N:

Amended Code Sec. 7213(a)(2) by striking "(k)(10), (13), or (14)" and inserting "(k)(10), (13), (14), or (15)". **Effective** for disclosures made on or after 12-27-2020.

• **2020, Consolidated Appropriations Act, 2021 (P.L. 116-260)**

P.L. 116-260, §102(b)(2)(C), Div. FF:

Amended Code Sec. 7213(a)(2) by striking "(k)(10), (13), or (14)" and inserting "(k)(10), (13), (14), or (15)". [Note: An identical amendment was made by P.L. 116-260, Act Sec. 283(b)(2)(C), Div. N. Therefore, this amendment cannot be made.—CCH] **Effective** for disclosures made on or after 12-27-2020.

• **2019, Taxpayer First Act (P.L. 116-25)**

P.L. 116-25, §1405(a)(2)(B):

Amended Code Sec. 7213(a)(2) by striking "(k)(10)" and inserting "(k)(10) or (13)". **Effective** for disclosures made after 7-1-2019.

P.L. 116-25, §2003(c)(2)(B):

Amended Code Sec. 7213(a)(2), as amended by this Act, by striking "or (13)" and inserting ", (13), or (14)". **Effective** 7-1-2019.

• **2016, Recovering Missing Children Act (P.L. 114-184)**

P.L. 114-184, §2(b)(2)(C):

Amended Code Sec. 7213(a)(2) by striking "(i)(3)(B)(i)" and inserting "(i)(1)(C), (3)(B)(i),". **Effective** for disclosures made after 6-30-2016.

• **2013, American Taxpayer Relief Act of 2012 (P.L. 112-240)**

P.L. 112-240, §209(b)(3):

Amended Code Sec. 7213(a)(2) by inserting "(k)(10)," before "(l)(6),". **Effective** 1-2-2013.

• **2010, Patient Protection and Affordable Care Act (P.L. 111-148)**

P.L. 111-148, §1414(d):

Amended Code Sec. 7213(a)(2) by striking "or (20)" and inserting "(20), or (21)". **Effective** 3-23-2010.

• **2006, Pension Protection Act of 2006 (P.L. 109-280)**

P.L. 109-280, §1224(b)(5):

Amended Code Sec. 7213(a)(2) by inserting "or under section 6104(c)" after "6103". **Effective** 8-17-2006 but shall not apply to requests made before such date.

• **2003, Medicare Prescription Drug, Improvement, and Modernization Act of 2003 (P.L. 108-173)**

P.L. 108-173, §105(e)(4):

Amended Code Sec. 7213(a)(2) by striking "or (16)" and inserting "(16), or (19)". **Effective** 12-8-2003.

P.L. 108-173, §811(c)(2)(C):

Amended Code Sec. 7213(a)(2), as amended by Act Sec. 105(e)(4), by striking "or (19)" and inserting "(19), or (20)". **Effective** 12-8-2003.

• **2002, Victims of Terrorism Tax Relief Act of 2001 (P.L. 107-134)**

P.L. 107-134, §201(c)(10):

Amended Code Sec. 7213(a)(2) by striking "(i)(3)(B)(i)," and inserting "(i)(3)(B)(i) or (7)(A)(ii),". **Effective** for disclosures made on or after 1-23-2002.

• **1997, Balanced Budget Act of 1997 (P.L. 105-33)**

P.L. 105-33, §11024(b)(8):

Amended Code Sec. 7213(a)(2) by striking "or (15)" and inserting "(15), or (16)". For the **effective** date, see Act Sec. 11721, below.

P.L. 105-33, §11721, provides:

Except as otherwise provided in this title, the provisions of this title shall take effect on the later of October 1, 1997, or the day the District of Columbia Financial Responsibility and Management Assistance Authority certifies that the financial plan and budget for the District government for fiscal year 1998 meet the requirements of section 201(c)(1) of the District of Columbia Financial Responsibility and Management Assistance Act of 1995, as amended by this title.

• **1997, Taxpayer Browsing Protection Act (P.L. 105-35)**

P.L. 105-35, §2(b):

Amended Code Sec. 7213(a)(2) by inserting "(5)," after "(m)(2), (4), ". **Effective** for violations occurring on and after 8-5-97.

• **1996, Taxpayer Bill of Rights 2 (P.L. 104-168)**

P.L. 104-168, §1206(b)(5):

Amended Code Sec. 7213(a)(2) by striking "or (12)" and inserting "(12), or (15)". **Effective** 7-30-96.

• **1990, Omnibus Budget Reconciliation Act of 1990 (P.L. 101-508)**

P.L. 101-508, §5111(b)(3):

Amended Code Sec. 7213(a)(2) by striking "(m)(2), (4), or (6)" and inserting "(m)(2), (4), (6), or (7)". **Effective** 11-5-90.

• **1989, Omnibus Budget Reconciliation Act of 1989 (P.L. 101-239)**

P.L. 101-239, §6202(a)(1)(C):

Amended Code Sec. 7213(a)(2) by striking "or (10)" and inserting "(10), or (12)". **Effective** 12-19-89.

• **1988, Technical and Miscellaneous Revenue Act of 1988 (P.L. 100-647)**

P.L. 100-647, §8008(c)(2)(B):

Amended Code Sec. 7213(a)(2) by striking "(m)(2) or (4)" and inserting "(m)(2), (4), or (6)". **Effective** 11-10-88.

• **1988, Family Support Act of 1988 (P.L. 100-485)**

P.L. 100-485, §701(b)(2)(C):

Amended Code Sec. 7213(a)(2) by striking "(9), (10), or (11)" and inserting "(9), or (10)". **Effective** 10-13-88. However, for a special rule, see Act Sec. 701(b)(3)(B), below.

P.L. 100-485, §701(b)(3)(B), provides:

(B) SPECIAL RULE.—Nothing in section 2653(c) of the Deficit Reduction Act of 1984 shall be construed to limit the application of paragraph (10) of section 6103(l) of the Internal Revenue Code of 1986 (as amended by this subsection).

- **1984, Child Support Enforcement Amendments of 1984 (P.L. 98-378)**

P.L. 98-378, §21(f)(5):

Amended Code Sec. 7213(a)(2) by striking out "or (10)" and inserting in lieu thereof "(10), or (11)". **Effective** with respect to refunds payable under Code Sec. 6402 after 12-31-85.

- **1984, Deficit Reduction Act of 1984 (P.L. 98-369)**

P.L. 98-369, §453(b)(4):

Amended Code Sec. 7213(a)(2) by striking out "or (8)" and inserting in lieu thereof "(8), or (9)". **Effective** on the first day of the first calendar month which begins more than 90 days after 7-18-84.

P.L. 98-369, §2653(b)(4):

Amended Code Sec. 7213(a)(2), as amended by Act Sec. 453(b)(4), by striking out "(l)(6), (7), (8), (9)" and inserting in lieu thereof "(l)(6), (7), (8), (9), or (10)". **Effective** with respect to refunds payable under Code Sec. 6402 after 12-31-85, and on or before 1-10-94 [effective date changed by P.L. 100-485].

- **1982, Debt Collection Act of 1982 (P.L. 97-365)**

P.L. 97-365, §8(c)(2):

Amended Code Sec. 7213(a)(2) by striking out "(m)(4)" and inserting in lieu thereof "(m)(2) or (4)". **Effective** 10-25-82.

- **1982, Tax Equity and Fiscal Responsibility Act of 1982 (P.L. 97-248)**

P.L. 97-248, §356(b)(2):

Amended Code Sec. 7213(a)(2) by striking out "(d)" and inserting "(d), (i)(3)(B)(i),". **Effective** 9-4-82.

- **1980 (P.L. 96-611)**

P.L. 96-611, §11(a)(4)(A):

Amended the first sentence of Code Sec. 7213(a)(2) by striking out "(l)(6) or (7)" and inserting in lieu thereof "(l)(6), (7), or (8)". **Effective** 12-5-80.

- **1980, Omnibus Reconciliation Act of 1980 (P.L. 96-499)**

P.L. 96-499, §302(b):

Amended Code Sec. 7213(a)(2) by striking out the first sentence and substituting the present first sentence in its place. Prior to amendment, the first sentence provided:

It shall be unlawful for any officer, employee, or agent, or former officer, employee, or agent, of any State (as defined in section 6103(b)(5)), any local child support enforcement agency, any educational institution, or any State food stamp agency (as defined in section 6103(l)(7)(C)) willfully to disclose to any person, except as authorized in this title, any return or return information (as defined in section 6103(b)) acquired by him or another person under subsection (d), (l)(6) or (7) [or 8], or (m)(4)(B) of section 6103.

Because of an enrollment error in P.L. 96-249 (see the following historical comment on P.L. 96-265), the amendment made by P.L. 96-499 does not reflect the amendments made to Code Sec. 6103(l). Thus, when Congress corrects the numbering of the provisions of Code Sec. 6103(l), it is expected that a conforming amendment will be made to Code Sec. 7123(a)(2).

- **1980, Social Security Disability Amendments of 1980 (P.L. 96-265)**

P.L. 96-265, §408(a)(2)(D):

Amended Code Sec. 7213(a)(2) by striking out "subsection (d), (l)(6), or (m)(4)(B)" and substituting "subsection (d), (l)(6) or (7), or (m)(4)(B)". **Effective** 6-9-80. These amendments duplicate prior amendments made to Code Sec. 7213(a)(2) by P.L. 96-249, which added an earlier Code Sec. 6103(l)(7). However, due to an error in the enrollment of P.L. 96-249, the new subsection (7) was added to Code Sec. 6103(i), instead of 6103(l), even though the changes made to Code Sec. 7213(a)(2) properly referred to Code Sec. 6103(l) as the section amended by P.L. 96-249. Thus, P.L. 96-265 added a second Code Sec. 6103(l)(7) because of this error. It is expected that technical corrections will be made, redesignating the subsection (7) added by P.L. 96-265 as subsection (8), and correcting the references contained in Code Sec. 7213(a)(2).

- **1980, Food Stamp Act Amendments of 1980 (P.L. 96-249)**

P.L. 96-249, §127(a)(2)(D)(i):

Amended Code Sec. 7213(a)(2) by striking out "or any educational institution" and inserting in lieu thereof "any educational institution, or any State food stamp agency (as defined in section 6103(l)(7)(C))". **Effective** 5-26-80.

P.L. 96-249, §127(a)(2)(D)(ii):

Amended Code Sec. 7213(a)(2) by striking out "subsection (d)(1), (6), or (m)(4)(B)" and inserting in lieu thereof "subsection (d), (l)(6) or (7), or (m)(4)(B)". **Effective** 5-26-80.

- **1978, Revenue Act of 1978 (P.L. 95-600)**

P.L. 95-600, §701(bb)(1)(C), (6)(A), (B), (C):

Amended Code Sec. 7213(a). **Effective** 1-1-77. Prior to amendment, Sec. 7213(a) read as follows:

(a) RETURNS AND RETURN INFORMATION.—

(1) FEDERAL EMPLOYEES AND OTHER PERSONS.—It shall be unlawful for any officer or employee of the United States or any person described in section 6103(n) (or an officer or employee of any such person), or any former officer or employee, to disclose to any person, except as authorized in this title, any return or return information (as defined in section 6103(b)). Any violation of this paragraph shall be a felony punishable upon conviction by a fine in any amount not exceeding $5,000, or imprisonment of not more than 5 years, or both, together with the costs of prosecution, and if such offense is committed by any officer or employee of the United States, he shall, in addition to any other punishment, be dismissed from office or discharged from employment upon conviction for such offense.

(2) STATE AND OTHER EMPLOYEES.—It shall be unlawful for any officer, employee, or agent, or former officer, employee, or agent, of any State (as defined in section 6103(b)(5)) or any local child support enforcement agency to disclose to any person, except as authorized in this title, any return or return information (as defined in section 6103(b)) acquired by him or another person under section 6103(d) or (1)(6). Any violation of this paragraph shall be a felony punishable by a fine in any amount not exceeding $5,000, or imprisonment of not more than 5 years, or both, together with the costs of prosecution.

(3) OTHER PERSONS.—It shall be unlawful for any person to whom any return or return information (as defined in section 6103(b)) is disclosed in a manner unauthorized by this title to thereafter print or publish in any manner not provided by law any such return or return information. Any violation of this paragraph shall be a felony punishable by a fine in any amount not exceeding $5,000, or imprisonment of not more than 5 years, or both, together with the costs of prosecution.

(4) SOLICITATION.—It shall be unlawful for any person to offer any item of material value in exchange for any return or return information (as defined in section 6103(b)) and to receive as a result of such solicitation any such return or return information. Any violation of this paragraph shall be a felony punishable by a fine in any amount not exceeding $5,000, or imprisonment of not more than 5 years, or both, together with the costs of prosecution.

(5) SHAREHOLDERS.—It shall be unlawful for any person to whom a return or return information (as defined in section 6103(b)) is disclosed pursuant to the provisions of section 6103(e)(1)(D)(iii) to disclose such return or return information in any manner not provided by law. Any violation of this paragraph shall be a felony punishable by a fine in any amount not to exceed $5,000, or imprisonment of not more than 5 years, or both, together with the costs of prosecution.

- **1976, Tax Reform Act of 1976 (P.L. 94-455)**

P.L. 94-455, §1202(d):

Amended Code Sec. 7213(a). **Effective** 1-1-77. Prior to amendment, Sec. 7213(a) read as follows:

(a) INCOME RETURNS.—

(1) FEDERAL EMPLOYEES AND OTHER PERSONS.—It shall be unlawful for any officer or employee of the United States to divulge or to make known in any manner whatever not provided by law to any person the amount or source of income, profits, losses, expenditures, or any particular thereof set forth or disclosed in any income return, or to permit any income return or copy thereof or any book containing any abstract or particulars thereof to be seen or examined by any person except as provided by law; and it shall be unlawful for any person to print or publish in any manner whatever not provided by law any income return, or any part thereof or source of income, profits, losses, or expenditures appearing in any income return; and any person committing an offense against the foregoing provision shall be guilty of a misdemeanor and, upon conviction thereof, shall be fined not more than $1,000, or imprisoned not more than 1 year, or both, together with the costs of prosecution; and if the offender be an officer or employee of the United States he shall be dismissed from office or discharged from employment.

(2) STATE EMPLOYEES.—Any officer, employee, or agent of any State or political subdivision, who divulges (except as authorized in section 6103(b), or when called upon to testify in any judicial or administrative proceeding to which the State or political subdivision, or such State or local official, body, or commission, as such, is a party), or who makes known to any person in any manner whatever not provided by law, any information acquired by him through an inspection permitted him or another under section 6103(b), or who permits any income return or copy thereof or any book containing any abstract or particulars thereof, or any other information, acquired by him through an inspection permitted him or another under section 6103(b), to be seen or examined by any person except as provided by law, shall be guilty of a misdemeanor and, upon conviction thereof, shall be fined not more than $1,000, or imprisoned not more than 1 year, or both, together with the costs of prosecution.

(3) SHAREHOLDERS.—Any shareholder who pursuant to the provisions of section 6103(c) is allowed to examine the return of any corporation, and who makes known in any manner whatever not provided by law the amount or source of income, profits, losses, expenditures, or any particular thereof, set forth or disclosed in any such return, shall be guilty of a misdemeanor and, upon conviction thereof, shall be fined not more than $1,000, or imprisoned not more than 1 year, or both, together with the costs of prosecution.

[Sec. 7213(b)]

(b) DISCLOSURE OF OPERATIONS OF MANUFACTURER OR PRODUCER.—Any officer or employee of the United States who divulges or makes known in any manner whatever not provided by law to any person the operations, style of work, or apparatus of any manufacturer or producer visited by him in the discharge of his official duties shall be guilty of a misdemeanor and, upon conviction thereof, shall be fined not more than $1,000, or imprisoned not more than 1 year, or both, together with the costs of prosecution; and the offender shall be dismissed from office or discharged from employment.

CRIMES

[Sec. 7213(c)—Repealed]

Amendments

• **1976, Tax Reform Act of 1976 (P.L. 94-455)**

P.L. 94-455, § 1202(d):

Repealed Code Sec. 7213(c). **Effective** 1-1-77. Prior to repeal, Code Sec. 7213(c) read as follows:

(c) OFFENSES RELATING TO REPRODUCTION OF DOCUMENTS.—Any person who uses any film or photoimpression, or reproduction therefrom, or who discloses any information contained in any such film, photoimpression, or reproduction, in violation of any provision of the regulations prescribed pursuant to section 7513(b), shall be fined not more than $1,000, or imprisoned not more than 1 year, or both.

• **1958, Technical Amendments Act of 1958 (P.L. 85-866)**

P.L. 85-866, § 90(c):

Redesignated 7213(c) as subsection 7213(d) and added a new subsection (c). **Effective** 1-1-54.

[Sec. 7213(c)]

(c) DISCLOSURES BY CERTAIN DELEGATES OF SECRETARY.—All provisions of law relating to the disclosure of information, and all provisions of law relating to penalties for unauthorized disclosure of information, which are applicable in respect of any function under this title when performed by an officer or employee of the Treasury Department are likewise applicable in respect of such function when performed by any person who is a "delegate" within the meaning of section 7701(a)(12)(B).

Amendments

• **1976, Tax Reform Act of 1976 (P.L. 94-455)**

P.L. 94-455, § 1202(d):

Redesignated Code Sec. 7213(d) as Code Sec. 7213(c). **Effective** 1-1-77.

• **1960, Social Security Amendments of 1960 (P.L. 86-778)**

P.L. 86-778, § 103(s):

Redesignated Code Sec. 7213(d) as Sec. 7213(e), and added a new subsection (d) to Code Sec. 7213. **Effective** 9-13-60.

[Sec. 7213(d)]

(d) DISCLOSURE OF SOFTWARE.—Any person who willfully divulges or makes known software (as defined in section 7612(d)(1)) to any person in violation of section 7612 shall be guilty of a felony and, upon conviction thereof, shall be fined not more than $5,000, or imprisoned not more than 5 years, or both, together with the costs of prosecution.

Amendments

• **1998, IRS Restructuring and Reform Act of 1998 (P.L. 105-206)**

P.L. 105-206, § 3413(b):

Amended Code Sec. 7213 by redesignating subsection (d) as subsection (e) and by inserting after subsection (c) a new subsection (d). **Effective**, generally, for summonses issued, and software acquired, after 7-22-98. For a special rule, see Act Sec. 3413(e)(2), below.

P.L. 105-206, § 3413(e)(2), provides:

(2) SOFTWARE PROTECTION.—In the case of any software acquired on or before such date of enactment, the requirements of section 7612(a)(2) of the Internal Revenue Code of 1986 (as added by such amendments) shall apply after the 90th day after such date. The preceding sentence shall not apply to the requirement under section 7612(c)(2)(G)(ii) of such Code (as so added).

[Sec. 7213(e)]

(e) CROSS REFERENCES.—

(1) PENALTIES FOR DISCLOSURE OF INFORMATION BY PREPARERS OF RETURNS.—For penalty for disclosure or use of information by preparers of returns, see section 7216.

(2) PENALTIES FOR DISCLOSURE OF CONFIDENTIAL INFORMATION.—For penalties for disclosure of confidential information by any officer or employee of the United States or any department or agency thereof, see 18 U. S. C. 1905.

(1) RETURNS OF FEDERAL UNEMPLOYMENT TAX.—

For special provisions applicable to returns of tax under chapter 23 (relating to Federal Unemployment Tax), see section 6106.

Amendments

• **1998, IRS Restructuring and Reform Act of 1998 (P.L. 105-206)**

P.L. 105-206, § 3413(b):

Redesignated Code Sec. 7213(d) as Sec. 7213(e). **Effective** for summonses issued, and software acquired, after 7-22-98. For a special rule, see Act Sec. 3413(e)(2) in the amendment notes following Code Sec. 7213(d).

• **1976, Tax Reform Act of 1976 (P.L. 94-455)**

P.L. 94-455, § 1202(d):

Redesignated Code Sec. 7213(e) as Sec. 7213(d). **Effective** 1-1-77.

P.L. 94-455, § 1202(h):

Amended Code Sec. 7213(d)(1). **Effective** 1-1-77. Prior to amendment, Sec. 7213(d)(1) read as follows:

• **1960, Social Security Amendments of 1960 (P.L. 86-778)**

P.L. 86-778, § 103(s):

Redesignated Code Sec. 7213(d) as Code Sec. 7213(e). **Effective** 9-13-60.

• **1958, Technical Amendments Act of 1958 (P.L. 85-866)**

P.L. 85-866, § 90(c):

Redesignated Code Sec. 7213(c) as Code Sec. 7213(d). **Effective** 1-1-54.

[Sec. 7213A]

SEC. 7213A. UNAUTHORIZED INSPECTION OF RETURNS OR RETURN INFORMATION.

[Sec. 7213A(a)]

(a) PROHIBITIONS.—

(1) FEDERAL EMPLOYEES AND OTHER PERSONS.—It shall be unlawful for—

(A) any officer or employee of the United States, or

(B) any person described in subsection (l)(18) or (n) of section 6103 or an officer or employee of any such person,

willfully to inspect, except as authorized in this title, any return or return information.

(2) STATE AND OTHER EMPLOYEES.—It shall be unlawful for any person (not described in paragraph (1)) willfully to inspect, except as authorized in this title, any return or return information acquired by such person or another person under a provision of section 6103 referred to in section 7213(a)(2) or under section 6104(c).

Amendments

• **2006, Pension Protection Act of 2006 (P.L. 109-280)**

P.L. 109-280, § 1224(b)(6):

Amended Code Sec. 7213A(a)(2) by inserting "or under section 6104(c)" after "7213(a)(2)". **Effective** 8-17-2006 but shall not apply to requests made before such date.

• **2002, Trade Act of 2002 (P.L. 107-210)**

P.L. 107-210, § 202(b)(3):

Amended Code Sec. 7213A(a)(1)(B) by striking "section 6103(n)" and inserting "subsection (l)(18) or (n) of section 6103". **Effective** 8-6-2002.

[Sec. 7213A(b)]

(b) PENALTY.—

(1) IN GENERAL.—Any violation of subsection (a) shall be punishable upon conviction by a fine in any amount not exceeding $1,000, or imprisonment of not more than 1 year, or both, together with the costs of prosecution.

(2) FEDERAL OFFICERS OR EMPLOYEES.—An officer or employee of the United States who is convicted of any violation of subsection (a) shall, in addition to any other punishment, be dismissed from office or discharged from employment.

[Sec. 7213A(c)]

(c) DEFINITIONS.—For purposes of this section, the terms "inspect", "return", and "return information" have the respective meanings given such terms by section 6103(b).

Amendments

● **1997, Taxpayer Browsing Protection Act (P.L. 105-35)**

P.L. 105-35, §2(a):

Amended part I of subchapter A of chapter 75 by adding Code Sec. 7213A. **Effective** for violations occurring on and after 8-5-97.

➤ *Caution: See 18 U.S.C. §3571, in the amendment notes following Code Sec. 7201, under which a larger fine may be imposed with respect to Code Sec. 7214.*

[Sec. 7214]

SEC. 7214. OFFENSES BY OFFICERS AND EMPLOYEES OF THE UNITED STATES.

[Sec. 7214(a)]

(a) UNLAWFUL ACTS OF REVENUE OFFICERS OR AGENTS.—Any officer or employee of the United States acting in connection with any revenue law of the United States—

(1) who is guilty of any extortion or willful oppression under color of law; or

(2) who knowingly demands other or greater sums than are authorized by law, or receives any fee, compensation, or reward, except as by law prescribed, for the performance of any duty; or

(3) who with intent to defeat the application of any provision of this title fails to perform any of the duties of his office or employment; or

(4) who conspires or colludes with any other person to defraud the United States; or

(5) who knowingly makes opportunity for any person to defraud the United States; or

(6) who does or omits to do any act with intent to enable any other person to defraud the United States; or

(7) who makes or signs any fraudulent entry in any book, or makes or signs any fraudulent certificate, return, or statement; or

(8) who, having knowledge or information of the violation of any revenue law by any person, or of fraud committed by any person against the United States under any revenue law, fails to report, in writing, such knowledge or information to the Secretary; or

(9) who demands, or accepts, or attempts to collect, directly or indirectly as payment or gift, or otherwise, any sum of money or other thing of value for the compromise, adjustment, or settlement of any charge or complaint for any violation or alleged violation of law, except as expressly authorized by law so to do;

shall be dismissed from office or discharged from employment and, upon conviction thereof, shall be fined not more than $10,000, or imprisoned not more than 5 years, or both. The court may in its discretion award out of the fine so imposed an amount, not in excess of one-half thereof, for the use of the informer, if any, who shall be ascertained by the judgment of the court. The court also shall render judgment against the said officer or employee for the amount of damages sustained in favor of the party injured, to be collected by execution.

Amendments

● **1976, Tax Reform Act of 1976 (P.L. 94-455)**

P.L. 94-455, §1906(b)(13)(A):

Amended 1954 Code by substituting "Secretary" for "Secretary or his delegate" each place it appeared. **Effective** 2-1-77.

[Sec. 7214(b)]

(b) INTEREST OF INTERNAL REVENUE OFFICER OR EMPLOYEE IN TOBACCO OR LIQUOR PRODUCTION.—Any internal revenue officer or employee interested, directly or indirectly, in the manufacture of tobacco, snuff, or cigarettes, or in the production, rectification, or redistillation of distilled spirits, shall be dismissed from office; and each such officer or employee so interested in any such manufacture or production, rectification, or redistillation or production of fermented liquors shall be fined not more than $5,000.

[Sec. 7214(c)]

(c) CROSS REFERENCE.—

For penalty on collecting or disbursing officers trading in public funds or debts or property, see 18 U. S. C. 1901.

Amendments

● **1958, Excise Tax Technical Changes Act of 1958 (P.L. 85-859)**

P.L. 85-859, §204(5):

Amended Sec. 7214(c) by changing the heading from "Cross References.—" to "Cross Reference.—"; by striking out paragraph (1) and by striking out "(2)" where it preceded "For penalty on collecting". **Effective** 1-1-59. Prior to amendment, paragraph (1) read as follows:

"(1) For penalty imposed for unlawfully removing or permitting to be removed distilled spirits from a bonded warehouse, see section 5632."

[Sec. 7215]

SEC. 7215. OFFENSES WITH RESPECT TO COLLECTED TAXES.

[Sec. 7215(a)]

(a) PENALTY.—Any person who fails to comply with any provision of section 7512(b) shall, in addition to any other penalties provided by law, be guilty of a misdemeanor, and, upon conviction thereof, shall be fined not more than $5,000, or imprisoned not more than one year, or both, together with the costs of prosecution.

[Sec. 7215(b)]

(b) EXCEPTIONS.—This section shall not apply—

(1) to any person, if such person shows that there was reasonable doubt as to (A) whether the law required collection of tax, or (B) who was required by law to collect tax, and

(2) to any person, if such person shows that the failure to comply with the provisions of section 7512(b) was due to circumstances beyond his control.

For purposes of paragraph (2), a lack of funds existing immediately after the payment of wages (whether or not created by the payment of such wages) shall not be considered to be circumstances beyond the control of a person.

CRIMES

Amendments

• **1983, Interest and Dividend Tax Compliance Act of 1983 (P.L. 98-67)**

P.L. 98-67, § 102(a):

Repealed the amendment made to Code Sec. 7215(b) by P.L. 97-248 (see below). **Effective** as of the close of 6-30-83, as though it had not been enacted. Prior to repeal, this sentence read as follows:

"For purposes of paragraph (2), a lack of funds existing immediately after the payment of wages or amounts subject to withholding under subchapter B of chapter 24 (whether or not created by the payment of such wages or amounts) shall not be considered to be circumstances beyond the control of a person."

• **1982, Tax Equity and Fiscal Responsibility Act of 1982 (P.L. 97-248)**

P.L. 97-248, § 307(a)(15):

Amended the last sentence of Code Sec. 7215(b) to read as shown under P.L. 98-67. **Effective** 7-1-83.

• **1958 (P.L. 85-321)**

P.L. 85-321, § 2:

Added Sec. 7215 to Chapter 75 of the Code. **Effective** 2-12-58.

[Sec. 7216]

SEC. 7216. DISCLOSURE OR USE OF INFORMATION BY PREPARERS OF RETURNS.

[Sec. 7216(a)]

(a) GENERAL RULE.—Any person who is engaged in the business of preparing, or providing services in connection with the preparation of, returns of the tax imposed by chapter 1, or any person who for compensation prepares any such return for any other person, and who knowingly or recklessly—

(1) discloses any information furnished to him for, or in connection with, the preparation of any such return, or

(2) uses any such information for any purpose other than to prepare, or assist in preparing, any such return, shall be guilty of a misdemeanor, and, upon conviction thereof,

shall be fined not more than $1,000 ($100,000 in the case of a disclosure or use to which section 6713(b) applies), or imprisoned not more than 1 year, or both, together with the costs of prosecution.

Amendments

• **2019, Taxpayer First Act (P.L. 116-25)**

P.L. 116-25, § 2009(b):

Amended Code Sec. 7216(a) by striking "$1,000" and inserting "$1,000 ($100,000 in the case of a disclosure or use to which section 6713(b) applies)". **Effective** for disclosures or uses on or after 7-1-2019.

• **1988, Technical and Miscellaneous Revenue Act of 1988 (P.L. 100-647)**

P.L. 100-647, § 6242(b):

Amended Code Sec. 7216(a) by striking out "and who—" and inserting in lieu thereof "and who knowingly or recklessly—". **Effective** for disclosures or uses after 12-31-88.

• **1984, Deficit Reduction Act of 1984 (P.L. 98-369)**

P.L. 98-369, § 412(b)(10):

Amended Code Sec. 7216(a) by striking out "or declarations or amended declarations of estimated tax under section 6015," following "chapter 1", and by striking out "return or declaration" each place it appeared and inserting in lieu thereof "return". **Effective** with respect to tax years beginning after 12-31-84.

[Sec. 7216(b)]

(b) EXCEPTIONS.—

(1) DISCLOSURE.—Subsection (a) shall not apply to a disclosure of information if such disclosure is made—

(A) pursuant to any other provision of this title, or

(B) pursuant to an order of a court.

(2) USE.—Subsection (a) shall not apply to the use of information in the preparation of, or in connection with the preparation of, State and local tax returns and declarations of estimated tax of the person to whom the information relates.

(3) REGULATIONS.—Subsection (a) shall not apply to a disclosure or use of information which is permitted by regulations prescribed by the Secretary under this section. Such regulations shall permit (subject to such conditions as such regulations shall provide) the disclosure or use of information for quality or peer reviews.

Amendments

• **1989, Omnibus Budget Reconciliation Act of 1989 (P.L. 101-239)**

P.L. 101-239, § 7739(a):

Amended Code Sec. 7216(b)(3) by adding at the end thereof a new sentence. **Effective** 12-19-89.

• **1976, Tax Reform Act of 1976 (P.L. 94-455)**

P.L. 94-455, § 1906(b)(13)(A):

Amended 1954 Code by substituting "Secretary" for "Secretary or his delegate" each place it appeared. **Effective** 2-1-77.

• **1971, Revenue Act of 1971 (P.L. 92-178)**

P.L. 92-178, § 316(a):

Added Code Sec. 7216. **Effective** 1-1-72.

[Sec. 7217]

SEC. 7217. PROHIBITION ON EXECUTIVE BRANCH INFLUENCE OVER TAXPAYER AUDITS AND OTHER INVESTIGATIONS.

[Sec. 7217(a)]

(a) PROHIBITION.—It shall be unlawful for any applicable person to request, directly or indirectly, any officer or employee of the Internal Revenue Service to conduct or terminate an audit or other investigation of any particular taxpayer with respect to the tax liability of such taxpayer.

[Sec. 7217(b)]

(b) REPORTING REQUIREMENT.—Any officer or employee of the Internal Revenue Service receiving any request prohibited by subsection (a) shall report the receipt of such request to the Treasury Inspector General for Tax Administration.

[Sec. 7217(c)]

(c) EXCEPTIONS.—Subsection (a) shall not apply to any written request made—

(1) to an applicable person by or on behalf of the taxpayer and forwarded by such applicable person to the Internal Revenue Service;

(2) by an applicable person for disclosure of return or return information under section 6103 if such request is made in accordance with the requirements of such section; or

(3) by the Secretary of the Treasury as a consequence of the implementation of a change in tax policy.

[Sec. 7217(d)]

(d) PENALTY.—Any person who willfully violates subsection (a) or fails to report under subsection (b) shall be punished upon conviction by a fine in any amount not exceeding $5,000, or imprisonment of not more than 5 years, or both, together with the costs of prosecution.

[Sec. 7217(e)]

(e) APPLICABLE PERSON.—For purposes of this section, the term "applicable person" means—

(1) the President, the Vice President, any employee of the executive office of the President, and any employee of the executive office of the Vice President; and

(2) any individual (other than the Attorney General of the United States) serving in a position specified in section 5312 of title 5, United States Code.

Amendments

• **1998, IRS Restructuring and Reform Act of 1998 (P.L. 105-206)**

P.L. 105-206, §1105(a):

Amended part I of subchapter A of chapter 75 by adding after Code Sec. 7216 a new Code Sec. 7217. **Effective** for requests made after 7-22-98.

[Sec. 7217—Repealed]

Amendments

• **1982, Tax Equity and Fiscal Responsibility Act of 1982 (P.L. 97-248)**

P.L. 97-248, §357(b)(1):

Repealed Code Sec. 7217. **Effective** for disclosures made after 9-3-82. Prior to amendment, Code Sec. 7217 read as follows:

SEC. 7217. CIVIL DAMAGES FOR UNAUTHORIZED DISCLOSURE OF RETURNS AND RETURN INFORMATION.

[Sec. 7217(a)]

(a) GENERAL RULE.—Whenever any person knowingly, or by reason of negligence, discloses a return or return information (as defined in section 6103(b)) with respect to a taxpayer in violation of the provisions of section 6103, such taxpayer may bring a civil action for damages against such person, and the district courts of the United States shall have jurisdiction of any action commenced under the provisions of this section.

[Sec. 7217(b)]

(b) NO LIABILITY FOR GOOD FAITH, BUT ERRONEOUS, INTERPRETATION.—No liability shall arise under this section with respect to any disclosure which results from a good faith, but erroneous, interpretation of section 6103.

Amendments

• **1978, Revenue Act of 1978 (P.L. 95-600)**

P.L. 95-600, §701(bb)(7)(B):

Added Code Sec. 7217(b). **Effective** with respect to disclosures made after 11-6-78.

[Sec. 7217(c)]

(c) DAMAGES.—In any suit brought under the provisions of subsection (a), upon a finding of liability on the part of the defendant, the defendant shall be liable to the plaintiff in an amount equal to the sum of—

(1) actual damages sustained by the plaintiff as a result of the unauthorized disclosure of the return or return information and, in the case of a willful disclosure or a disclosure which is the result of gross negligence, punitive damages, but in no case shall a plaintiff entitled to recovery receive less than the sum of $1,000 with respect to each instance of such unauthorized disclosure; and

(2) the costs of the action.

Amendments

• **1978, Revenue Act of 1978 (P.L. 95-600)**

P.L. 95-600, §701(bb)(7)(A):

Redesignated Code Sec. 7217(b) as Code Sec. 7217(c). **Effective** with respect to disclosures made after 11-6-78.

[Sec. 7217(d)]

(d) PERIOD FOR BRINGING ACTION.—An action to enforce any liability created under this section may be brought, without regard to the amount in controversy, within 2 years from the date on which the cause of action arises or at any time within 2 years after discovery by the plaintiff of the unauthorized disclosure.

Amendments

• **1978, Revenue Act of 1978 (P.L. 95-600)**

P.L. 95-600, §701(bb)(7)(A), (C):

Redesignated former Code Sec. 7217(c) as Code Sec. 7217(d) and amended, as so redesignated, by inserting "PERIOD FOR BRINGING ACTION.—".

• **1976, Tax Reform Act of 1976 (P.L. 94-455)**

P.L. 94-455, §1202(e):

Added Code Sec. 7217. **Effective** 1-1-77.

PART II—PENALTIES APPLICABLE TO CERTAIN TAXES

Sec. 7231.   Failure to obtain license for collection of foreign items.

Sec. 7232.   Failure to register or reregister under section 4101, false representations of registration status, etc.

[Sec. 7231]

SEC. 7231. FAILURE TO OBTAIN LICENSE FOR COLLECTION OF FOREIGN ITEMS.

Any person required by section 7001 (relating to collection of certain foreign items) to obtain a license who knowingly undertakes to collect the payments described in section 7001 without having obtained a license therefor, or without complying with regulations prescribed under section 7001, shall be guilty of a misdemeanor and, upon conviction thereof, shall be fined not more than $5,000, or imprisoned not more than 1 year, or both.

[Sec. 7232]

SEC. 7232. FAILURE TO REGISTER OR REREGISTER UNDER SECTION 4101, FALSE REPRESENTATIONS OF REGISTRATION STATUS, ETC.

Every person who fails to register or reregister as required by section 4101, or who in connection with any purchase of any taxable fuel (as defined in section 4083), or aviation fuel falsely represents himself to be registered as provided by section 4101, or who willfully makes any false statement in an application for registration or reregistration under section 4101, shall, upon conviction thereof, be fined not more than $10,000, or imprisoned not more than 5 years, or both, together with the costs of prosecution.

Amendments

• **2005, Safe, Accountable, Flexible, Efficient Transportation Equity Act: A Legacy for Users (P.L. 109-59)**

P.L. 109-59, §11164(b)(2)(A)-(C):

Amended Code Sec. 7232 by inserting "or reregister" after "register", by inserting "or reregistration" after "registration", and by inserting "OR REREGISTER" after "REGISTER" in the heading. **Effective** for actions, or failures to act, after 8-10-2005.

• **2004, American Jobs Creation Act of 2004 (P.L. 108-357)**

P.L. 108-357, §863(b):

Amended Code Sec. 7232 by striking "$5,000" and inserting "$10,000". **Effective** for penalties imposed after 12-31-2004.

• **1997, Taxpayer Relief Act of 1997 (P.L. 105-34)**

P.L. 105-34, §1032(e)(12)(A) (as amended by P.L. 105-206, §6010(h)(2)):

Amended Code Sec. 7232 by striking "gasoline, diesel fuel" and inserting "any taxable fuel (as defined in section 4083)". **Effective** 7-1-98.

P.L. 105-34, §1032(e)(12)(B):

Amended Code Sec. 7232 amended the heading. **Effective** 7-1-98. Prior to amendment, the section heading for Code Sec. 7232 read as follows:

SEC. 7232. FAILURE TO REGISTER, OR FALSE STATEMENT BY MANUFACTURER OR PRODUCER OF GASOLINE, DIESEL FUEL, OR AVIATION FUEL.

• **1996, Small Business Job Protection Act of 1996 (P.L. 104-188)**

P.L. 104-188, §1704(t)(20)(A)(i)-(ii):

Amended Code Sec. 7232 by striking "LUBRICATING OIL," after "GASOLINE," in the heading, and by striking "lubricating oil," after "gasoline," in the text. **Effective** 8-20-96.

• **1988, Technical and Miscellaneous Revenue Act of 1988 (P.L. 100-647)**

P.L. 100-647, §3001(b)(3)(A):

Amended Code Sec. 7232 by striking out "or lubricating oil" and inserting in lieu thereof ", lubricating oil, diesel fuel, or aviation fuel". **Effective**, generally, 1-1-89. For a special rule, see Act Sec. 3003(c)(2) below.

P.L. 100-647, §3001(b)(3)(B):

Amended Code Sec. 7232 by striking out "OR LUBRICATING OIL" and inserting in lieu thereof ", LUBRICATING OIL, DIESEL FUEL, OR AVIATION FUEL" in the heading. **Effective**, generally, 1-1-89. For a special rule, see Act Sec. 3003(c)(2) below.

P.L. 100-647, §3003(c)(2), provides:

(2) REFUNDS WITH INTEREST FOR PRE-EFFECTIVE DATE PURCHASES.—

(A) IN GENERAL.—In the case of fuel—

(i) which is purchased from a producer or importer during the period beginning on April 1, 1988, and ending on December 31, 1988,

Internal Revenue Code

OTHER OFFENSES

(ii) which is used (before the claim under this subparagraph is filed) by any person in a nontaxable use (as defined in section 6427(l)(2) of the 1986 Code), and

(iii) with respect to which a claim is not permitted to be filed for any quarter under section 6427(i) of the 1986 Code, the Secretary of the Treasury or the Secretary's delegate shall pay (with interest) to such person the amount of tax imposed on such fuel under section 4091 of the 1986 Code (to the extent not attributable to amounts described in section 6427(l)(3) of the 1986 Code) if claim therefor is filed not later than June 30, 1989. Not more than 1 claim may be filed under the preceding sentence and such claim shall not be taken into account under section 6427(i) of the 1986 Code. Any claim for refund filed under this paragraph shall be considered a claim for refund under section 6427(l) of the 1986 Code.

(B) INTEREST.—The amount of interest payable under subparagraph (A) shall be determined under section 6811 of the 1986 Code except that the date of the overpayment with respect to fuel purchased during any month shall be treated as being the 1st day of the succeeding month. No interest shall be paid under this paragraph with respect to fuel used by any agency of the United States.

(C) REGISTRATION PROCEDURES REQUIRED TO BE SPECIFIED:—Not later than the 30th day after the date of the enactment of this Act, the Secretary of the Treasury or the Secretary's delegate shall prescribe the procedures for complying with the requirements of section 4093(c)(3) of the 1986 Code (as added by this section).

Amendments

• **1990, Omnibus Budget Reconciliation Act of 1990 (P.L. 101-508)**

P.L. 101-508, §11801(c)(22)(D)(i):

Repealed Code Sec. 7240. **Effective** 11-5-90.

P.L. 101-508, §11821(b), provides:

(b) SAVINGS PROVISION.—If—

(1) any provision amended or repealed by this part applied to—

(A) any transaction occurring before the date of the enactment of this Act,

(B) any property acquired before such date of enactment, or

(C) any item of income, loss, deduction, or credit taken into account before such date of enactment, and

(2) the treatment of such transaction, property, or item under such provision would (without regard to the amendments made by this part) affect liability for tax for periods ending after such date of enactment,

nothing in the amendments made by this part shall be construed to affect the treatment of such transaction, property, or item for purposes of determining liability for tax for periods ending after such date of enactment.

[Sec. 7241—Repealed]

Amendments

• **1988, Omnibus Trade and Competitiveness Act of 1988 (P.L. 100-418)**

P.L. 100-418, §1941(b)(1):

Repealed Code Sec. 7241. **Effective** for crude oil removed from the premises on or after 8-23-88. Prior to amendment, Code Sec. 7241 read as follows:

SEC. 7241. WILLFUL FAILURE TO FURNISH CERTAIN INFORMATION REGARDING WINDFALL PROFIT TAX ON DOMESTIC CRUDE OIL.

Any person who is required under section 6050C (or regulations thereunder) to furnish any information or certification to any other person and who willfully fails to furnish such information or certification at the time or times required by law or regulations, shall, in addition to other penalties provided by law, be guilty of a misdemeanor and upon conviction thereof, shall be fined not more than $10,000, or imprisoned not more than 1 year, or both, together with the costs of prosecution.

• **1965, Excise Tax Reduction Act of 1965 (P.L. 89-44)**

P.L. 89-44, §802(b)(4):

Amended Code Sec. 7232. **Effective** 7-1-65. Prior to amendment, Code Sec. 7232 read as follows:

SEC. 7232. FAILURE TO REGISTER OR GIVE BOND, OR FALSE STATEMENT BY MANUFACTURER OR PRODUCER OF GASOLINE OR LUBRICATING OIL.

Every person who fails to register or give bond as required by section 4101, or who in connection with any purchase of gasoline or lubricating oil falsely represents himself to be registered and bonded as provided by section 4101, or who willfully makes any false statement in an application for registration under section 4101, shall, upon conviction thereof, be fined not more than $5,000, or imprisoned not more than 5 years, or both, together with the costs of prosecution.

[Sec. 7240—Repealed]

Prior to repeal, Code Sec. 7240 read as follows:

SEC. 7240. OFFICIALS INVESTING OR SPECULATING IN SUGAR.

Any person while acting in any official capacity in the administration of chapter 37, relating to manufactured sugar, who invests or speculates in sugar or liquid sugar, contracts relating thereto, or the stock or membership interests of any association or corporation engaged in the production or manufacture of sugar or liquid sugar, shall be dismissed from office or discharged from employment and shall be guilty of a felony and, upon conviction thereof, be fined not more than $10,000, or imprisoned not more than 2 years, or both.

• **1976, Tax Reform Act of 1976 (P.L. 94-455)**

P.L. 94-455, §1904(b)(6)(A):

Amended Code Sec. 7240 by striking out "subchapter A of" before "chapter 37". **Effective** 2-1-77.

• **1980, Crude Oil Windfall Profit Tax Act of 1980 (P.L. 96-223)**

P.L. 96-223, §101(e)(1):

Added Code Sec. 7241. For the **effective** date and transitional rules, see P.L. 96-223, Act Sec. 101(i), following Code Sec. 4986.

Subchapter B—Other Offenses

Sec. 7261.	Representation that retailers' excise tax is excluded from price of article.
Sec. 7262.	Violation of occupational tax laws relating to wagering—failure to pay special tax.
Sec. 7268.	Possession with intent to sell in fraud of law or to evade tax.
Sec. 7269.	Failure to produce records.
Sec. 7270.	Insurance policies.
Sec. 7271.	Penalties for offenses relating to stamps.
Sec. 7272.	Penalty for failure to register or reregister.
Sec. 7273.	Penalties for offenses relating to special taxes.
Sec. 7275.	Penalty for offenses relating to certain airline tickets and advertising.

[Sec. 7261]

SEC. 7261. REPRESENTATION THAT RETAILERS' EXCISE TAX IS EXCLUDED FROM PRICE OF ARTICLE.

Whoever, in connection with the sale or lease, or offer for sale or lease, of any article taxable under chapter 31, makes any statement, written or oral, in advertisement or otherwise, intended or calculated to lead any person to believe that the price of the article does not include the tax imposed by chapter 31, shall on conviction thereof be fined not more than $1,000.

[Sec. 7262]

SEC. 7262. VIOLATION OF OCCUPATIONAL TAX LAWS RELATING TO WAGERING—FAILURE TO PAY SPECIAL TAX.

Any person who does any act which makes him liable for special tax under subchapter B of chapter 35 without having paid such tax, shall, besides being liable to the payment of the tax, be fined not less than $1,000 and not more than $5,000.

[Sec. 7268]

SEC. 7268. POSSESSION WITH INTENT TO SELL IN FRAUD OF LAW OR TO EVADE TAX.

Every person who shall have in his custody or possession any goods, wares, merchandise, articles, or objects on which taxes are imposed by law, for the purpose of selling the same in fraud of the internal revenue laws, or with design to avoid payment of the taxes imposed thereon, shall be liable to a penalty of $500 or not less than double the amount of taxes fraudulently attempted to be evaded.

Sec. 7240—Repealed

OTHER OFFENSES

[Sec. 7269]

SEC. 7269. FAILURE TO PRODUCE RECORDS.

Whoever fails to comply with any duty imposed upon him by section 6018, 6036 (in the case of an executor), or 6075(a), or, having in his possession or control any record, file, or paper, containing or supposed to contain any information concerning the estate of the decedent, or, having in his possession or control any property comprised in the gross estate of the decedent, fails to exhibit the same upon request to the Secretary who desires to examine the same in the performance of his duties under chapter 11 (relating to estate taxes), shall be liable to a penalty of not exceeding $500, to be recovered, with costs of suit, in a civil action in the name of the United States.

Amendments

• **1976, Tax Reform Act of 1976 (P.L. 94-455)**

P.L. 94-455, §1906(b)(13)(A):

Amended 1954 Code by substituting "Secretary" for "Secretary or his delegate" each place it appeared. **Effective** 2-1-77.

[Sec. 7270]

SEC. 7270. INSURANCE POLICIES.

Any person who fails to comply with the requirements of section 4374 (relating to liability for tax on policies issued by foreign insurers), with intent to evade the tax shall, in addition to other penalties provided therefor, pay a fine of double the amount of the tax.

Amendments

• **1976, Tax Reform Act of 1976 (P.L. 94-455)**

P.L. 94-455, §1904(b)(5)(A):

Substituted "liability for tax on policies issued by foreign insurers" for "the affixing of stamps on insurance policies, etc." in Code Sec. 7270. **Effective** 2-1-77.

[Sec. 7271]

SEC. 7271. PENALTIES FOR OFFENSES RELATING TO STAMPS.

Any person who with respect to any tax payable by stamps—

(1) FAILURE TO ATTACH OR CANCEL STAMPS, ETC.—Fails to comply with rules or regulations prescribed pursuant to section 6804 (relating to attachment, cancellation, etc., of stamps), unless such failure is shown to be due to reasonable cause and not willful neglect; or

(2) INSTRUMENTS.—Makes, signs, issues, or accepts, or causes to be made, signed, issued, or accepted, any instrument, document, or paper of any kind or description whatsoever without the full amount of tax thereon being duly paid; or

(3) DISPOSAL AND RECEIPT OF STAMPED PACKAGES.—In the case of any container which is stamped, branded, or marked (whether or not under authority of law) in such manner as to show that the provisions of the internal revenue laws with respect to the contents or intended contents thereof have been complied with, and which is empty or contains any contents other than contents therein when the container was lawfully stamped, branded, or marked—

(A) Transfers or receives (whether by sale, gift, or otherwise) such container knowing it to be empty or to contain such other contents; or

(B) Stamps, brands, or marks such container, or otherwise produces such a stamped, branded, or marked container, knowing it to be empty or to contain such other contents;

shall be liable for each such offense to a penalty of $50.

Amendments

• **1976, Tax Reform Act of 1976 (P.L. 94-455)**

P.L. 94-455, §1906(a)(41):

Redesignated former Code Secs. 7271(3) and (4) as Secs. 7271(2) and (3) and struck out former Sec. 7271(2). **Effective** 2-1-77. Prior to amendment, Sec. 7271(2) read as follows:

(2) MANUFACTURE OR OFFER FOR SALE.—Manufactures or imports and sells, or offers for sale, or causes to be manufactured or imported and sold, or offered for sale, any playing cards, package, or other article without the full amount of tax being duly paid; or

[Sec. 7272]

SEC. 7272. PENALTY FOR FAILURE TO REGISTER OR REREGISTER.

[Sec. 7272(a)]

(a) IN GENERAL.—Any person (other than persons required to register under subtitle E, or persons engaging in a trade or business on which a special tax is imposed by such subtitle) who fails to register with the Secretary as required by this title or by regulations issued thereunder shall be liable to a penalty of $50 ($10,000 in the case of a failure to register or reregister under section 4101).

Amendments

• **2005, Safe, Accountable, Flexible, Efficient Transportation Equity Act: A Legacy for Users (P.L. 109-59)**

P.L. 109-59, §11164(b)(3)(A):

Amended Code Sec. 7272(a) by inserting "or reregister" after "failure to register". **Effective** for actions, or failures to act, after 8-10-2005.

P.L. 109-59, §11164(b)(3)(B):

Amended Code Sec. 7272 by inserting "OR REREGISTER" after "REGISTER" in the heading. **Effective** for actions, or failures to act, after 8-10-2005.

• **2004, American Jobs Creation Act of 2004 (P.L. 108-357)**

P.L. 108-357, §863(a):

Amended Code Sec. 7272(a) by inserting "($10,000 in the case of a failure to register under section 4101)" after "$50". **Effective** for penalties imposed after 12-31-2004.

• **1976, Tax Reform Act of 1976 (P.L. 94-455)**

P.L. 94-455, §1906(b)(13)(A):

Amended 1954 Code by substituting "Secretary" for "Secretary or his delegate" each place it appeared. **Effective** 2-1-77.

• **1958, Excise Tax Technical Changes Act of 1958 (P.L. 85-859)**

P.L. 85-859, §204(6):

Amended Code Sec. 7272(a) by inserting after the phrase "Any person" the following: "(other than persons required to register under subtitle E, or persons engaging in a trade or business on which a special tax is imposed by such subtitle)". **Effective** 9-3-58.

[Sec. 7272(b)]

(b) CROSS REFERENCES.—

For provisions relating to persons required by this title to register, see sections 4101, 4412, and 7011.

Amendments

• **1976, Tax Reform Act of 1976 (P.L. 94-455)**

P.L. 94-455, §1904(b)(8)(F):

Struck out "4804(d)," where the number appeared in Code Sec. 7272(b). **Effective** 2-1-77.

P.L. 94-455, §1906(a)(42):

Struck out "4722, 4753," where the numbers appeared in Code Sec. 7272(b). **Effective** 2-1-77.

OTHER OFFENSES

- **1965, Excise Tax Reduction Act of 1965 (P.L. 89-44)**

P.L. 89-44, §601(h):

Amended Sec. 7272(b) by deleting "4455," where it appeared between "4412," and "4722."

- **1958, Excise Tax Technical Changes Act of 1958 (P.L. 85-859)**

P.L. 85-859, §204(7):

Struck out "5802, 5841," where those numbers followed "4804(d)," in Sec. 7272(b). **Effective** 9-3-58.

- **1958, Tax Rate Extension Act of 1958 (P.L. 85-475)**

P.L. 85-475, §4(b):

Amended Sec. 7272(b) by deleting "4273," following "4101,". **Effective** as to amounts paid for transportation after 7-31-58.

[Sec. 7273]

SEC. 7273. PENALTIES FOR OFFENSES RELATING TO SPECIAL TAXES.

Any person who shall fail to place and keep stamps denoting the payment of the special tax as provided in section 6806 shall be liable to a penalty (not less than $10) equal to the special tax for which his business rendered him liable, unless such failure is shown to be due to reasonable cause. If such failure to comply with section 6806 is through willful neglect or refusal, then the penalty shall be double the amount above prescribed.

Amendments

- **1968, Gun Control Act of 1968 (P.L. 90-618)**

P.L. 90-618, §205:

Amended Code Sec. 7273. **Effective** 10-22-68. Prior to amendment, Code Sec. 7273 read as follows:

(a) GENERAL RULES.—Any person who shall fail to place and keep stamps denoting the payment of the special tax as provided in section 6806(a) or (b) (whichever is applicable) shall be liable to a penalty equal to the special tax for which his business rendered him liable (unless such failure is shown to be due to reasonable cause); but in no case shall said penalty be less than $10. Where the failure to comply with the provisions of section 6806(a) or (b) shall be through willful neglect or refusal, then the penalty shall be double the amount above prescribed. Nothing in this subsection shall in any way affect the liability of any person for exercising or carrying on any trade, business, or profession, or doing any act for the exercising, carrying on, or doing of which a special tax is imposed by law, without the payment thereof.

(b) FAILURE TO POST OR EXHIBIT SPECIAL WAGERING TAX STAMP.—Any person who, through negligence, fails to comply with section 6806(c) relating to the posting or exhibiting of the special wagering tax stamp, shall be liable to a penalty of $50. Any person who, through willful neglect or refusal, fails to comply with section 6806(c) shall be liable to a penalty of $100.

[Sec. 7275]

SEC. 7275. PENALTY FOR OFFENSES RELATING TO CERTAIN AIRLINE TICKETS AND ADVERTISING.

[Sec. 7275(a)]

(a) TICKETS.—In the case of transportation by air all of which is taxable transportation (as defined in section 4264), the ticket for such transportation shall show the total of—

(1) the amount paid for such transportation, and

(2) the taxes imposed by subsections (a) and (b) of section 4261.

Amendments

- **1982, Tax Equity and Fiscal Responsibility Act of 1982 (P.L. 97-248)**

P.L. 97-248, §281A(b)(1):

Amended Code Sec. 7275(a). **Effective** with respect to transportation beginning after 9-3-82. Prior to amendment, Code Sec. 7275 read as follows:

(a) TICKETS.—In the case of transportation by air all of which is taxable transportation (as defined in section 4262), the ticket for such transportation—

(1) shall show the total of (A) the amount paid for such transportation and (B) the taxes imposed by sections 4261(a) and (b), and

(2) if the ticket shows amounts paid with respect to any segment of such transportation, shall comply with paragraph (1) with respect to such segments as well as with respect to the sum of the segments.

[Sec. 7275(b)]

(b) ADVERTISING.—In the case of transportation by air all of which is taxable transportation (as defined in section 4262) or would be taxable transportation if section 4262 did not include subsection (b) thereof, any advertising made by or on behalf of any person furnishing such transportation (or offering to arrange such transportation) which states the cost of such transportation shall—

(1) state such cost as the total of (A) the amount to be paid for such transportation, and (B) the taxes imposed by sections 4261(a), (b), and (c), and

(2) if any such advertising states separately the amount to be paid for such transportation or the amount of such taxes, state such total at least as prominently as the more prominently stated of the amount to be paid for such transportation or the amount of such taxes and shall describe such taxes substantially as "user taxes to pay for airport construction and airway safety and operations."

Amendments

- **2018, Tax Technical Corrections Act of 2018 (P.L. 115-141)**

P.L. 115-141, §401(a)(323), Div. U:

Amended Code Sec. 7275(b)(2) by striking "taxes, shall" and inserting "taxes,". **Effective** 3-23-2018.

[Sec. 7275(c)]

(c) NON-TAX CHARGES.—

(1) IN GENERAL.—In the case of transportation by air for which disclosure on the ticket or advertising for such transportation of the amounts paid for passenger taxes is required by subsection (a)(2) or (b)(1)(B), if such amounts are separately disclosed, it shall be unlawful for the disclosure of such amounts to include any amounts not attributable to such taxes.

(2) INCLUSION IN TRANSPORTATION COST.—Nothing in this subsection shall prohibit the inclusion of amounts not attributable to the taxes imposed by subsection (a), (b), or (c) of section 4261 in the disclosure of the amount paid for transportation as required by subsection (a)(1) or (b)(1)(A), or in a separate disclosure of amounts not attributable to such taxes.

Amendments

- **2012, FAA Modernization and Reform Act of 2012 (P.L. 112-95)**

P.L. 112-95, §1104(a)(3):

Amended Code Sec. 7275 by redesignating subsection (c) as subsection (d) and by inserting after subsection (b) a new subsection (c). **Effective** for taxable transportation provided after 3-31-2012.

[Sec. 7275(d)]

(d) PENALTY.—Any person who violates any provision of subsection (a), (b), or (c) is, for each violation, guilty of a misdemeanor, and upon conviction thereof shall be fined not more than $100.

FORFEITURES

Amendments

- **2012, FAA Modernization and Reform Act of 2012 (P.L. 112-95)**

P.L. 112-95, §1104(a)(1)-(2):

Amended Code Sec. 7275 by redesignating subsection (c) as subsection (d), and by striking "subsection (a) or (b)" in subsection (d), as so redesignated, and inserting "subsection (a), (b), or (c)". **Effective** for taxable transportation provided after 3-31-2012.

- **1971 (P.L. 91-680)**

P.L. 91-680, §3:

Amended Code Secs. 7275(a) and (b). **Effective** for transportation beginning after 6-30-70. Prior to amendment, these sections read as follows:

"(a) Tickets.—In the case of transportation by air all of which is taxable transportation (as defined in section 4262), the ticket for such transportation—

"(1) shall show the total of (A) the amount paid for such transportation and (B) the taxes imposed by sections 4261(a) and (b), and

"(2) shall not show separately the amount paid for such transportation nor the amount of such taxes, and

"(3) if the ticket shows amounts paid with respect to any segment of such transportation, shall comply with paragraphs (1) and (2) with respect to such segments as well as with respect to the sum of the segments.

"(b) Advertising.—In the case of transportation by air all of which is taxable transportation (as defined in section 4262) or would be taxable transportation if section 4262 did not include subsection (b) thereof, any advertising made by or on behalf of any person furnishing such transportation (or offering to arrange such transportation) which states the cost of such transportation shall—

"(1) state such cost only as the total of (A) the amount to be paid for such transportation, and (B) the taxes imposed by sections 4261(a), (b), and (c), and

"(2) shall not state separately the amount to be paid for such transportation nor the amount of such taxes."

- **1970 (P.L. 91-258)**

P.L. 91-258, §203(c):

Added Code Sec. 7275. **Effective** for transportation beginning after 6-30-70.

- **1965, Excise Tax Reduction Act of 1965 (P.L. 89-44)**

P.L. 89-44, §601(i):

Repealed Sec. 7275. **Effective** Noon 12-31-65. Prior to repeal, Sec. 7275 read as follows:

"SEC. 7275. FAILURE TO PRINT CORRECT PRICE ON TICKETS.

"For penalty applicable to certain offenses relating to admissions taxes, see section 4234(b)."

Subchapter C—Forfeitures

| Part I. | Property subject to forfeiture. |
| Part II. | Provisions common to forfeitures. |

PART I—PROPERTY SUBJECT TO FORFEITURE

Sec. 7301.	Property subject to tax.
Sec. 7302.	Property used in violation of internal revenue laws.
Sec. 7303.	Other property subject to forfeiture.
Sec. 7304.	Penalty for fraudulently claiming drawback.

[Sec. 7301]

SEC. 7301. PROPERTY SUBJECT TO TAX.

[Sec. 7301(a)]

(a) TAXABLE ARTICLES.—Any property on which, or for or in respect whereof, any tax is imposed by this title which shall be found in the possession or custody or within the control of any person, for the purpose of being sold or removed by him in fraud of the internal revenue laws, or with design to avoid payment of such tax, or which is removed, deposited, or concealed, with intent to defraud the United States of such tax or any part thereof, may be seized, and shall be forfeited to the United States.

[Sec. 7301(b)]

(b) RAW MATERIALS.—All property found in the possession of any person intending to manufacture the same into property of a kind subject to tax for the purpose of selling such taxable property in fraud of the internal revenue laws, or with design to evade the payment of such tax, may also be seized, and shall be forfeited to the United States.

[Sec. 7301(c)]

(c) EQUIPMENT.—All property whatsoever, in the place or building, or any yard or enclosure, where the property described in subsection (a) or (b) is found, or which is intended to be used in the making of property described in subsection (a), with intent to defraud the United States of tax or any part thereof, on the property described in subsection (a) may also be seized, and shall be forfeited to the United States.

[Sec. 7301(d)]

(d) PACKAGES.—All property used as a container for, or which shall have contained, property described in subsection (a) or (b) may also be seized, and shall be forfeited to the United States.

[Sec. 7301(e)]

(e) CONVEYANCES.—Any property (including aircraft, vehicles, vessels, or draft animals) used to transport or for the deposit or concealment of property described in subsection (a) or (b), or any property used to transport or for the deposit or concealment of property which is intended to be used in the making or packaging of property described in subsection (a), may also be seized, and shall be forfeited to the United States.

Amendments

- **1958, Excise Tax Technical Changes Act of 1958 (P.L. 85-859)**

P.L. 85-859, §204(8):

Amended Code Sec. 7301(e). **Effective** 9-3-58. Prior to amendment, Code Sec. 7301(e) read as follows:

"(e) Conveyances.—Any property (including aircraft, vehicles, vessels, or draft animals) used to transport or for the deposit or concealment of property described in subsection (a) or (b) may also be seized, and shall be forfeited to the United States."

[Sec. 7302]

SEC. 7302. PROPERTY USED IN VIOLATION OF INTERNAL REVENUE LAWS.

It shall be unlawful to have or possess any property intended for use in violating the provisions of the internal revenue laws, or regulations prescribed under such laws, or which has been so used, and no property rights shall exist in any such property. A search warrant may issue as provided in chapter 205 of title 18 of the United States Code and the Federal Rules of Criminal Procedure for the seizure of such property. Nothing in this section shall in any manner limit or affect any criminal or forfeiture provision of the internal revenue laws, or of any other law. The seizure and forfeiture of any property under the provisions of this section and the disposition of such property subsequent to seizure and forfeiture, or the disposition of the proceeds from the sale of such property, shall be in accordance with existing laws or those hereafter in existence relating to seizures, forfeitures, and disposition of property or proceeds, for violation of the internal revenue laws.

[Sec. 7303]

SEC. 7303. OTHER PROPERTY SUBJECT TO FORFEITURE.

There may be seized and forfeited to the United States the following:

FORFEITURES

(1) COUNTERFEIT STAMPS.—Every stamp involved in the offense described in section 7208 (relating to counterfeit, reused, cancelled, etc., stamps), and the vellum, parchment, document, paper, package, or article upon which such stamp was placed or impressed in connection with such offense.

(2) FALSE STAMPING OF PACKAGES.—Any container involved in the offense described in section 7271 (relating to disposal of stamped packages), and of the contents of such container.

(3) FRAUDULENT BONDS, PERMITS, AND ENTRIES.—All property to which any false or fraudulent instrument involved in the offense described in section 7207 relates.

(4) PURCHASE OR RECEIPT OF ADULTERATED BUTTER.—All articles of adulterated butter (or the full value thereof) knowingly purchased or received by any person from any manufacturer or importer who has not paid the special tax provided in section 4821.

(5) PACKAGES OF OLEOMARGARINE.—All packages of oleomargarine subject to the tax under subchapter F of chapter 38 that shall be found without the stamps or marks provided for in that chapter.

Amendments

• **1976, Tax Reform Act of 1976 (P.L. 94-455)**

P.L. 94-455, § 1904(b)(8)(G):

Amended Code Sec. 7303 by striking out paragraph (6). **Effective** 2-1-77. Prior to amendment, Sec. 7303(6) read as follows:

(6) WHITE PHOSPHORUS MATCHES.—

(A) All packages of white phosphorus matches subject to tax under subchapter B of chapter 39 and found without the stamps required by subchapter B of chapter 39.

(B) All the white phosphorus matches owned by any manufacturer of white phosphorus matches, or any importer or exporter of matches, or in which he has any interest as owner if he shall omit, neglect, or refuse to do or cause to be done any of the things required by law in carrying on or conducting his business, or shall do anything prohibited by subchapter B of chapter 39, if there be no specific penalty or punishment imposed by any other provision of subchapter B of chapter 39 for the neglecting, omitting, or refusing to do, or for the doing or causing to be done, the thing required or prohibited.

P.L. 94-455, § 1904(b)(9)(D):

Redesignated Code Sec 7303, paragraphs (7) and (8) as paragraphs (2) and (3) and by striking out paragraphs (3), (4), and (5). **Effective** 2-1-77. Prior to amendment, Code Secs. 7303(3), 7303(4), and 7303(5) read as follows:

(3) OFFENSES BY MANUFACTURER OR IMPORTER OF OR WHOLESALE DEALER IN OLEOMARGARINE OR ADULTERATED BUTTER.—All oleomargarine or adulterated butter owned by any manufacturer or importer of or wholesale dealer in oleomargarine or adulterated butter, or in which he has any interest as owner, if he shall knowingly or willfully omit, neglect, or refuse to do, or cause to be done, any of the things required by law in the carrying on or conducting of his business, or if he shall do anything prohibited by subchapter F of chapter 38, of subchapter C of chapter 39.

• **1974 (P.L. 93-490)**

P.L. 93-490, § 3(b)(5):

Amended paragraphs (4) and (5) of Code Sec. 7303. **Effective** with respect to filled cheese manufactured, imported, or sold after 10-26-74. Prior to amendment, these paragraphs read as follows:

"(4) Purchase or receipt of filled cheese or adulterated butter.—All articles of filled cheese or adulterated butter (or the full value thereof) knowingly purchased or received by any person from any manufacturer or importer who has not paid the special tax provided in section 4821 or 4841.

"(5) Packages of oleomargarine or filled cheese.—All packages of oleomargarine or filled cheese subject to the tax under subchapter F of chapter 38, or part II of subchapter C of chapter 39, whichever is applicable, that shall be found without the stamps or marks provided for in the applicable subchapter or part thereof."

• **1958 (P.L. 85-881)**

P.L. 85-881, § [1](c):

Repealed paragraph (2) of Sec. 7303. **Effective** 9-2-58. Prior to repeal, paragraph (2) read as follows:

"(2) Oleomargarine and Filled Cheese.—Any oleomargarine, filled cheese, or adulterated butter, intended for human consumption which contains any ingredient adjudged, as provided in section 4817, 4818, or 4835, whichever is applicable, to be deleterious to the public health."

[Sec. 7304]

SEC. 7304. PENALTY FOR FRAUDULENTLY CLAIMING DRAWBACK.

Whenever any person fraudulently claims or seeks to obtain an allowance of drawback on goods, wares, or merchandise on which no internal tax shall have been paid, or fraudulently claims any greater allowance of drawback than the tax actually paid, he shall forfeit triple the amount wrongfully or fraudulently claimed or sought to be obtained, or the sum of $500, at the election of the Secretary.

Amendments

• **1976, Tax Reform Act of 1976 (P.L. 94-455)**

P.L. 94-455, § 1906(b)(13)(A):

Amended 1954 Code by substituting "Secretary" for "Secretary or his delegate" each place it appeared. **Effective** 2-1-77.

PART II—PROVISIONS COMMON TO FORFEITURES

Sec. 7321.	Authority to seize property subject to forfeiture.
Sec. 7322.	Delivery of seized personal property to United States marshal.
Sec. 7323.	Judicial action to enforce forfeiture.
Sec. 7324.	Special disposition of perishable goods.
Sec. 7325.	Personal property valued at $100,000 or less.
Sec. 7327.	Customs laws applicable.
Sec. 7328.	Cross references.

[Sec. 7321]

SEC. 7321. AUTHORITY TO SEIZE PROPERTY SUBJECT TO FORFEITURE.

Any property subject to forfeiture to the United States under any provision of this title may be seized by the Secretary.

Amendments

• **1976, Tax Reform Act of 1976 (P.L. 94-455)**

P.L. 94-455, § 1906(b)(13)(A):

Amended 1954 Code by substituting "Secretary" for "Secretary or his delegate" each place it appeared. **Effective** 2-1-77.

[Sec. 7322]

SEC. 7322. DELIVERY OF SEIZED PERSONAL PROPERTY TO UNITED STATES MARSHAL.

Any forfeitable property which may be seized under the provisions of this title may, at the option of the Secretary, be delivered to the United States marshal of the district, and remain in the care and custody and under the control of such marshal, pending disposal thereof as provided by law.

Amendments

• **1976, Tax Reform Act of 1976 (P.L. 94-455)**

P.L. 94-455, § 1906(b)(13)(A):

Amended 1954 Code by substituting "Secretary" for "Secretary or his delegate" each place it appeared. **Effective** 2-1-77.

FORFEITURES

[Sec. 7323]
SEC. 7323. JUDICIAL ACTION TO ENFORCE FORFEITURE.

[Sec. 7323(a)]
(a) NATURE AND VENUE.—The proceedings to enforce such forfeitures shall be in the nature of a proceeding in rem in the United States District Court for the district where such seizure is made.

[Sec. 7323(b)]
(b) SERVICE OF PROCESS WHEN PROPERTY HAS BEEN RETURNED UNDER BOND.—In case bond as provided in section 7324(3) shall have been executed and the property returned before seizure thereof by virtue of process in the proceedings in rem authorized in subsection (a) of this section, the marshal shall give notice of pendency of proceedings in court to the parties executing said bond, by personal service or publication, and in such manner and form as the court may direct, and the court shall thereupon have jurisdiction of said matter and parties in the same manner as if such property had been seized by virtue of process aforesaid.

[Sec. 7323(c)]
(c) COST OF SEIZURE TAXABLE.—The cost of seizure made before process issues shall be taxable by the court.

[Sec. 7324]
SEC. 7324. SPECIAL DISPOSITION OF PERISHABLE GOODS.

When any property which is seized under the provisions of section 7301 or section 7302 is liable to perish or become greatly reduced in price or value by keeping, or when it cannot be kept without great expense—

(1) APPLICATION FOR EXAMINATION.—The owner thereof, or the United States marshal of the district, may apply to the Secretary to examine it; and

(2) APPRAISAL.—If, in the opinion of the Secretary, it shall be necessary that such property should be sold to prevent such waste or expense, the Secretary shall appraise the same; and thereupon

(3) RETURN TO OWNER UNDER BOND.—The owner shall have such property returned to him upon giving bond in an amount equal to such appraised value to abide the final order, decree, or judgment of the court having cognizance of the case, and to pay the amount of said appraised value to the Secretary, the United States marshal, or otherwise, as may be ordered and directed by the court, which bond shall be filed by the Secretary with the United States attorney for the district in which the proceedings in rem authorized in section 7323 may be commenced.

(4) SALE IN ABSENCE OF BOND.—

(A) ORDER TO SELL.—If such owner shall neglect or refuse to give such bond, the Secretary shall issue to any Treasury officer or employee or to the United States marshal an order to sell the same.

(B) MANNER OF SALE.—Such Treasury officer or employee or the marshal shall as soon as practicable make public sale of such property in accordance with such regulations as may be prescribed by the Secretary.

(C) DISPOSITION OF PROCEEDS.—The proceeds of the sale, after deducting the reasonable costs of the seizure and sale, shall be paid to the court to abide its final order, decree, or judgment.

(5) FORM OF BOND AND SURETIES.—

For provisions relating to form and sureties on bonds, see section 7101.

Amendments

- **1976, Tax Reform Act of 1976 (P.L. 94-455)**

P.L. 94-455, §1906(b)(13)(A):

Amended 1954 Code by substituting "Secretary" for "Secretary or his delegate" each place it appeared. **Effective** 2-1-77.

- **1958, Technical Amendments Act of 1958 (P.L. 85-866)**

P.L. 85-866, §78:

Amended paragraph (3) of Sec. 7324 by striking out the word "district" where it appeared in the phrase "United States district attorney". **Effective** 1-1-54.

- **1958, Excise Tax Technical Changes Act of 1958 (P.L. 85-859)**

P.L. 85-859, §204(9):

Inserted, after "7301", in the first sentence of Sec. 7324, the phrase "or section 7302". **Effective** 9-3-58.

[Sec. 7325]
SEC. 7325. PERSONAL PROPERTY VALUED AT $100,000 OR LESS.

In all cases of seizure of any goods, wares, or merchandise as being subject to forfeiture under any provision of this title which, in the opinion of the Secretary, are of the appraised value of $100,000 or less, the Secretary shall, except in cases otherwise provided, proceed as follows:

(1) LIST AND APPRAISEMENT.—The Secretary shall cause a list containing a particular description of the goods, wares, or merchandise seized to be prepared in duplicate, and an appraisement thereof to be made by three sworn appraisers, to be selected by the Secretary who shall be respectable and disinterested citizens of the the United States residing within the internal revenue district wherein the seizure was made. Such list and appraisement shall be properly attested by the Secretary and such appraisers. Each appraiser shall be allowed for his services such compensation as the Secretary shall by regulations prescribe, to be paid in the manner similar to that provided for other necessary charges incurred in collecting internal revenue.

(2) NOTICE OF SEIZURE.—If such goods are found by such appraisers to be of the value of $100,000 or less, the Secretary shall publish a notice for 3 weeks, in some newspaper of the district where the seizure was made, describing the articles and stating the time, place, and cause of their seizure, and requiring any person claiming them to appear and make such claim within 30 days from the date of the first publication of such notice.

(3) EXECUTION OF BOND BY CLAIMANT.—Any person claiming the goods, wares, or merchandise so seized, within the time specified in the notice, may file with the Secretary a claim, stating his interest in the articles seized, and may execute a bond to the United States in the penal sum of $2,500, conditioned that, in case of condemnation of the articles so seized, the obligors shall pay all the costs and expenses of the proceedings to obtain such condemnation; and upon the delivery of such bond to the Secretary, he shall transmit the same, with the duplicate list or description of the goods seized, to the United States attorney for the district, and such attorney shall proceed thereon in the ordinary manner prescribed by law.

(4) SALE IN ABSENCE OF BOND.—If no claim is interposed and no bond is given within the time above specified, the Secretary shall give reasonable notice of the sale of the goods, wares, or merchandise by publication, and, at the time and place specified in the notice, shall, unless otherwise provided by law, sell the articles so seized at public auction, or upon competitive bids, in accordance with such regulations as may be prescribed by the Secretary.

MISCELLANEOUS PENALTY PROVISIONS

Amendments

- **1986, Tax Reform Act of 1986 (P.L. 99-514)**

P.L. 99-514, §1566(a):

Amended Code Sec. 7325 by striking out "$2,500" each place it appears (including the section heading) and inserting in lieu thereof "$100,000". **Effective** 10-22-86.

P.L. 99-514, §1566(b):

Amended Code Sec. 7325(3) by striking out "$250" and inserting in lieu thereof "$2,500". **Effective** 10-22-86.

- **1976, Tax Reform Act of 1976 (P.L. 94-455)**

P.L. 94-455, §1906(b)(13)(A):

Amended 1954 Code by substituting "Secretary" for "Secretary or his delegate" each place it appeared. **Effective** 2-1-77.

- **1958, Technical Amendments Act of 1958 (P.L. 85-866)**

P.L. 85-866, §78:

Amended Code Sec. 7325(3) by striking out the word "district" where it appeared in the phrase "United States district attorney". **Effective** 1-1-54.

Amendments

- **2018, Tax Technical Corrections Act of 2018 (P.L. 115-141)**

P.L. 115-141, §401(b)(50), Div. U:

Amended part II of subchapter C of chapter 75 by striking Code Sec. 7326. **Effective** 3-23-2018. For a special rule, see Act Sec. 401(e), Div. U, below. Prior to being stricken, Code Sec. 7326 read as follows:

SEC. 7326. DISPOSAL OF FORFEITED OR ABANDONED PROPERTY IN SPECIAL CASES.

[Sec. 7326(a)]

(a) COIN-OPERATED GAMING DEVICES.—Any coin-operated gaming device as defined in section 4462 upon which a tax is imposed by section 4461 and which has been forfeited under any provision of this title shall be destroyed, or otherwise disposed of, in such manner as may be prescribed by the Secretary.

Amendments

- **1965, Excise Tax Reduction Act of 1965 (P.L. 89-44)**

P.L. 89-44, §601(j):

Amended Code Sec. 7326 by substituting "4462" for "4462(a)(2)" in paragraph (a). **Effective** 6-22-65.

[Sec. 7326(b)]

(b) FIREARMS.—

For provisions relating to disposal of forfeited firearms, see section 5872(b).

Amendments

- **1976, Tax Reform Act of 1976 (P.L. 94-455)**

P.L. 94-455, §1906(a)(43):

Redesignated Code Sec. 7326(c) as Sec. 7326(b) and substituted "5872(b)" for "5862(b)" in Sec. 7326(b). **Effective** 2-1-77.

P.L. 94-455, §1906(b)(13)(A):

Amended 1954 Code by substituting "Secretary" for "Secretary or his delegate" each place it appeared. **Effective** 2-1-77.

- **1958, Excise Tax Technical Changes Act of 1958 (P.L. 85-859)**

P.L. 85-859, §204(10):

Struck out "$1,000" wherever it appeared in Code Sec. 7325 and substituted "$2,500". **Effective** 9-3-58.

P.L. 85-859, §204(12):

Amended paragraph (4) of Code Sec. 7325. **Effective** 9-3-58. Prior to amendment, paragraph (4) read as follows:

(4) SALE IN ABSENCE OF BOND.—If no claim is interposed and no bond is given within the time above specified, the Secretary or his delegate shall give reasonable notice of the sale of the goods, wares, or merchandise by publication, and, at the time and place specified in the notice, shall sell the articles so seized at public auction, or upon competitive bids, in accordance with such regulations as may be prescribed by the Secretary or his delegate.

[Sec. 7326—Stricken]

- **1970 (P.L. 91-513)**

P.L. 91-513, §1102(f):

Repealed Code Sec. 7326(b). **Effective** 5-1-71. Prior to repeal, Code Sec. 7326(b) read as follows:

(b) NARCOTIC DRUGS.—

For provisions relating to disposal of forfeited narcotic drugs, see sections 4714, 4733, and 4745(d).

- **1958, Excise Tax Technical Changes Act of 1958 (P.L. 85-859)**

P.L. 85-859, §204(13):

Amended Code Sec. 7326. **Effective** 9-3-58. Prior to amendment, Code Sec. 7326 read as follows:

SEC. 7326. DISPOSAL OF FORFEITED OR ABANDONED PROPERTY IN SPECIAL CASES.

(1) For provisions relating to disposal of forfeited narcotic drugs, see sections 4714, 4733, and 4745(d).

(2) For provisions relating to disposal of forfeited firearms, see section 5862(b).

P.L. 115-141, §401(e), Div. U, provides:

(e) GENERAL SAVINGS PROVISION WITH RESPECT TO DEADWOOD PROVISIONS.—If—

(1) any provision amended or repealed by the amendments made by subsection (b) or (d) applied to—

(A) any transaction occurring before the date of the enactment of this Act,

(B) any property acquired before such date of enactment, or

(C) any item of income, loss, deduction, or credit taken into account before such date of enactment, and

(2) the treatment of such transaction, property, or item under such provision would (without regard to the amendments or repeals made by such subsection) affect the liability for tax for periods ending after such date of enactment,

nothing in the amendments or repeals made by this section shall be construed to affect the treatment of such transaction, property, or item for purposes of determining liability for tax for periods ending after such date of enactment.

[Sec. 7327]

SEC. 7327. CUSTOMS LAWS APPLICABLE.

The provisions of law applicable to the remission or mitigation by the Secretary of forfeitures under the customs laws shall apply to forfeitures incurred or alleged to have been incurred under the internal revenue laws.

Amendments

- **1976, Tax Reform Act of 1976 (P.L. 94-455)**

P.L. 94-455, §1906(b)(13)(A):

Amended 1954 Code by substituting "Secretary" for "Secretary or his delegate" each place it appeared. **Effective** 2-1-77.

[Sec. 7328]

SEC. 7328. CROSS REFERENCES.

(1) For the issuance of certificates of probable cause relieving officers making seizures of responsibility for damages, see 28 U. S. C. 2465.

(2) For provisions relating to forfeitures generally in connection with alcohol taxes, see chapter 51.

(3) For provisions relating to forfeitures generally in connection with tobacco taxes, see chapter 52.

(4) For provisions relating to forfeitures generally in connection with taxes on certain firearms, see chapter 53.

Amendments

- **1976, Tax Reform Act of 1976 (P.L. 94-455)**

P.L. 94-455, §1904(b)(8)(H)(i):

Redesignated Code Sec. 7329 as Code Sec. 7328. **Effective** 2-1-77.

Subchapter D—Miscellaneous Penalty and Forfeiture Provisions

Sec. 7341.	Penalty for sales to evade tax.
Sec. 7342.	Penalty for refusal to permit entry or examination.
Sec. 7343.	Definition of term "person".
Sec. 7344.	Extended application of penalties relating to officers of the Treasury Department.
Sec. 7345.	Revocation or denial of passport in case of certain tax delinquencies.

Sec. 7326—Stricken

MISCELLANEOUS PENALTY PROVISIONS

[Sec. 7341]

SEC. 7341. PENALTY FOR SALES TO EVADE TAX.

[Sec. 7341(a)]

(a) NONENFORCEABILITY OF CONTRACT.—Whenever any person who is liable to pay any tax imposed by this title upon, for, or in respect of, any property sells or causes or allows the same to be sold before such tax is paid, with intent to avoid such tax, or in fraud of the internal revenue laws, any debt contracted in such sale, and any security given therefor, unless the same shall have been bona fide transferred to an innocent holder, shall be void, and the collection thereof shall not be enforced in any court.

[Sec. 7341(b)]

(b) FORFEITURE OF SUM PAID ON CONTRACT.—If such property has been paid for, in whole or in part, the sum so paid shall be deemed forfeited.

[Sec. 7341(c)]

(c) MOIETY.—Any person who shall sue for the sum so paid (in an action of debt) shall recover from the seller the amount so paid, one-half to his own use and the other half to the use of the United States.

[Sec. 7342]

SEC. 7342. PENALTY FOR REFUSAL TO PERMIT ENTRY OR EXAMINATION.

Any owner of any building or place, or person having the agency or superintendence of the same, who refuses to admit any officer or employee of the Treasury Department acting under the authority of section 7606 (relating to entry of premises for examination of taxable articles) or refuses to permit him to examine such article or articles, shall, for every such refusal, forfeit $500.

[Sec. 7343]

SEC. 7343. DEFINITION OF TERM "PERSON".

The term "person" as used in this chapter includes an officer or employee of a corporation, or a member or employee of a partnership, who as such officer, employee, or member is under a duty to perform the act in respect of which the violation occurs.

[Sec. 7344]

SEC. 7344. EXTENDED APPLICATION OF PENALTIES RELATING TO OFFICERS OF THE TREASURY DEPARTMENT.

All provisions of law imposing fines, penalties, or other punishment for offenses committed by an internal revenue officer or other officer of the Department of the Treasury, or under any agency or office thereof, shall apply to all persons whomsoever, employed, appointed, or acting under the authority of any internal revenue law, or any revenue provision of any law of the United States, when such persons are designated or acting as officers or employees in connection with such law, or are persons having the custody or disposition of any public money.

[Sec. 7345]

SEC. 7345. REVOCATION OR DENIAL OF PASSPORT IN CASE OF CERTAIN TAX DELINQUENCIES.

[Sec. 7345(a)]

(a) IN GENERAL.—If the Secretary receives certification by the Commissioner of Internal Revenue that an individual has a seriously delinquent tax debt, the Secretary shall transmit such certification to the Secretary of State for action with respect to denial, revocation, or limitation of a passport pursuant to section 32101 of the FAST Act.

[Sec. 7345(b)]

(b) SERIOUSLY DELINQUENT TAX DEBT.—

(1) IN GENERAL.—For purposes of this section, the term "seriously delinquent tax debt" means an unpaid, legally enforceable Federal tax liability of an individual—

(A) which has been assessed,

(B) which is greater than $50,000, and

(C) with respect to which—

(i) a notice of lien has been filed pursuant to section 6323 and the administrative rights under section 6320 with respect to such filing have been exhausted or have lapsed, or

(ii) a levy is made pursuant to section 6331.

(2) EXCEPTIONS.—Such term shall not include—

(A) a debt that is being paid in a timely manner pursuant to an agreement to which the individual is party under section 6159 or 7122, and

(B) a debt with respect to which collection is suspended with respect to the individual—

(i) because a due process hearing under section 6330 is requested or pending, or

(ii) because an election under subsection (b) or (c) of section 6015 is made or relief under subsection (f) of such section is requested.

[Sec. 7345(c)]

(c) REVERSAL OF CERTIFICATION.—

(1) IN GENERAL.—In the case of an individual with respect to whom the Commissioner makes a certification under subsection (a), the Commissioner shall notify the Secretary (and the Secretary shall subsequently notify the Secretary of State) if such certification is found to be erroneous or if the debt with respect to such certification is fully satisfied or ceases to be a seriously delinquent tax debt by reason of subsection (b)(2).

(2) TIMING OF NOTICE.—

(A) FULL SATISFACTION OF DEBT.—In the case of a debt that has been fully satisfied or has become legally unenforceable, such notification shall be made not later than the date required for issuing the certificate of release of lien with respect to such debt under section 6325(a).

(B) INNOCENT SPOUSE RELIEF.—In the case of an individual who makes an election under subsection (b) or (c) of section 6015, or requests relief under subsection (f) of such section, such notification shall be made not later than 30 days after any such election or request.

CIVIL ACTIONS BY U.S.

(C) INSTALLMENT AGREEMENT OR OFFER-IN-COMPROMISE.—In the case of an installment agreement under section 6159 or an offer-in-compromise under section 7122, such notification shall be made not later than 30 days after such agreement is entered into or such offer is accepted by the Secretary.

(D) ERRONEOUS CERTIFICATION.—In the case of a certification found to be erroneous, such notification shall be made as soon as practicable after such finding.

[Sec. 7345(d)]

(d) CONTEMPORANEOUS NOTICE TO INDIVIDUAL.—The Commissioner shall contemporaneously notify an individual of any certification under subsection (a), or any reversal of certification under subsection (c), with respect to such individual. Such notice shall include a description in simple and nontechnical terms of the right to bring a civil action under subsection (e).

[Sec. 7345(e)]

(e) JUDICIAL REVIEW OF CERTIFICATION.—

(1) IN GENERAL.—After the Commissioner notifies an individual under subsection (d), the taxpayer may bring a civil action against the United States in a district court of the United States, or against the Commissioner in the Tax Court, to determine whether the certification was erroneous or whether the Commissioner has failed to reverse the certification. For purposes of the preceding sentence, the court first acquiring jurisdiction over such an action shall have sole jurisdiction.

(2) DETERMINATION.—If the court determines that such certification was erroneous, then the court may order the Secretary to notify the Secretary of State that such certification was erroneous.

Amendments

- **2018, Tax Technical Corrections Act of 2018 (P.L. 115-141)**

P.L. 115-141, §103(a)(1)(A)-(B), Div. U:

Amended Code Sec. 7345(e)(1) by striking "or the Tax Court" and inserting ", or against the Commissioner in the Tax Court,", and by adding at the end: "For purposes of the preceding sentence, the court first acquiring jurisdiction over such an action shall have sole jurisdiction.". **Effective** as if included in section 32101 of the Fixing America's Surface Transportation Act [effective 12-4-2015.—CCH].

[Sec. 7345(f)]

(f) ADJUSTMENT FOR INFLATION.—In the case of a calendar year beginning after 2016, the dollar amount in subsection (b)(1)(B) shall be increased by an amount equal to—

(1) such dollar amount, multiplied by

(2) the cost-of-living adjustment determined under section 1(f)(3) for the calendar year, determined by substituting "calendar year 2015" for "calendar year 2016" in subparagraph (A)(ii) thereof.

If any amount as adjusted under the preceding sentence is not a multiple of $1,000, such amount shall be rounded to the nearest multiple of $1,000.

Amendments

- **2018, Tax Technical Corrections Act of 2018 (P.L. 115-141)**

P.L. 115-141, §103(a)(2), Div. U:

Amended Code Sec. 7345(f) by striking "subsection (a)" and inserting "subsection (b)(1)(B)". **Effective** as if included in section 32101 of the Fixing America's Surface Transportation Act [effective 12-4-2015.—CCH].

- **2017, Tax Cuts and Jobs Act (P.L. 115-97)**

P.L. 115-97, §11002(d)(1)(RR):

Amended Code Sec. 7345(f)(2) by striking "for 'calendar year 1992' in subparagraph (B)" and inserting "for 'calendar year 2016' in subparagraph (A)(ii)". **Effective** for tax years beginning after 12-31-2017.

[Sec. 7345(g)]

(g) DELEGATION OF CERTIFICATION.—A certification under subsection (a) or reversal of certification under subsection (c) may only be delegated by the Commissioner of Internal Revenue to the Deputy Commissioner for Services and Enforcement, or the Commissioner of an operating division, of the Internal Revenue Service.

Amendments

- **2015, Fixing America's Surface Transportation Act (P.L. 114-94)**

P.L. 114-94, §32101(a):

Amended subchapter D of chapter 75 by adding at the end a new Code Sec. 7345. **Effective** 12-4-2015.

CHAPTER 76—JUDICIAL PROCEEDINGS

SUBCHAPTER A.	Civil actions by the United States.
SUBCHAPTER B.	Proceedings by taxpayers and third parties.
SUBCHAPTER C.	The Tax Court.
SUBCHAPTER D.	Court review of Tax Court decisions.
SUBCHAPTER E.	Burden of proof.

Subchapter A—Civil Actions by the United States

Sec. 7401.	Authorization.
Sec. 7402.	Jurisdiction of district courts.
Sec. 7403.	Action to enforce lien or to subject property to payment of tax.
Sec. 7404.	Authority to bring civil action for estate taxes.
Sec. 7405.	Action for recovery of erroneous refunds.
Sec. 7406.	Disposition of judgments and moneys recovered.
Sec. 7407.	Action to enjoin tax return preparers.
Sec. 7408.	Actions to enjoin specified conduct related to tax shelters and reportable transactions.
Sec. 7409.	Action to enjoin flagrant political expenditures of section 501(c)(3) organizations.
Sec. 7410.	Cross references.

[Sec. 7401]

SEC. 7401. AUTHORIZATION.

No civil action for the collection or recovery of taxes, or of any fine, penalty, or forfeiture, shall be commenced unless the Secretary authorizes or sanctions the proceedings and the Attorney General or his delegate directs that the action be commenced.

CIVIL ACTIONS BY U.S.

Amendments

• **1976, Tax Reform Act of 1976 (P.L. 94-455)**

P.L. 94-455, § 1906(b)(13)(A):

Amended 1954 Code by substituting "Secretary" for "Secretary or his delegate" each place it appeared. **Effective** 2-1-77.

[Sec. 7402]
SEC. 7402. JURISDICTION OF DISTRICT COURTS.

[Sec. 7402(a)]

(a) To Issue Orders, Processes, and Judgments.—The district courts of the United States at the instance of the United States shall have such jurisdiction to make and issue in civil actions, writs and orders of injunction, and of *ne exeat republica,* orders appointing receivers, and such other orders and processes, and to render such judgments and decrees as may be necessary or appropriate for the enforcement of the internal revenue laws. The remedies hereby provided are in addition to and not exclusive of any and all other remedies of the United States in such courts or otherwise to enforce such laws.

[Sec. 7402(b)]

(b) To Enforce Summons.—If any person is summoned under the internal revenue laws to appear, to testify, or to produce books, papers, or other data, the district court of the United States for the district in which such person resides or may be found shall have jurisdiction by appropriate process to compel such attendance, testimony, or production of books, papers, or other data.

[Sec. 7402(c)]

(c) For Damages to United States Officers or Employees.—Any officer or employee of the United States acting under authority of this title, or any person acting under or by authority of any such officer or employee, receiving any injury to his person or property in the discharge of his duty shall be entitled to maintain an action for damages therefor, in the district court of the United States, in the district wherein the party doing the injury may reside or shall be found.

[Sec. 7402(d)—Repealed]

Amendments

• **1972 (P.L. 92-310)**

P.L. 92-310, § 230(d):

Repealed Code Sec. 7402(d). **Effective** 6-6-72. Prior to repeal, Code Sec. 7402(d) read as follows:

(d) Action on Bonds.—The United States district courts, concurrently with the courts of the several States, shall have jurisdiction of any action brought on the official bond of any internal revenue officer or employee required to give bond under regulations promulgated by authority of section 7803.

[Sec. 7402(e)]

(e) To Quiet Title.—The United States district courts shall have jurisdiction of any action brought by the United States to quiet title to property if the title claimed by the United States to such property was derived from enforcement of a lien under this title.

Amendments

• **1966, Federal Tax Lien Act of 1966 (P.L. 89-719)**

P.L. 89-719, § 107(a):

Redesignated Code Sec. 7402(e) as Code Sec. 7402(f) and added new Code Sec. 7402(e). **Effective**, generally, after 11-2-66. However, see the amendment note for Code Sec. 6323 for exceptions to this **effective** date.

[Sec. 7402(f)]

(f) General Jurisdiction.—

For general jurisdiction of the district courts of the United States in civil actions involving internal revenue, see section 1340 of Title 28 of the United States Code.

[Sec. 7403]
SEC. 7403. ACTION TO ENFORCE LIEN OR TO SUBJECT PROPERTY TO PAYMENT OF TAX.

[Sec. 7403(a)]

(a) Filing.—In any case where there has been a refusal or neglect to pay any tax, or to discharge any liability in respect thereof, whether or not levy has been made, the Attorney General or his delegate, at the request of the Secretary, may direct a civil action to be filed in a district court of the United States to enforce the lien of the United States under this title with respect to such tax or liability or to subject any property, of whatever nature, of the delinquent, or in which he has any right, title, or interest, to the payment of such tax or liability. For the purposes of the preceding sentence, any acceleration of payment under section 6166(g) shall be treated as a neglect to pay tax.

Amendments

• **1981, Economic Recovery Tax Act of 1981 (P.L. 97-34)**

P.L. 97-34, § 422(e)(8):

Amended Code Sec. 7403(a) by striking out "section 6166(g) or 6166A(h)" and inserting "section 6166(g)". **Effective** for estates of decedents dying after 12-31-81.

• **1976, Tax Reform Act of 1976 (P.L. 94-455)**

P.L. 94-455, § 1906(b)(13)(A):

Amended 1954 Code by substituting "Secretary" for "Secretary or his delegate" each place it appeared. **Effective** 2-1-77.

P.L. 94-455, § 2004(f)(2):

Added the last sentence to Code Sec. 7403(a). **Effective** for the estates of decedents dying after 12-31-76.

[Sec. 7403(b)]

(b) Parties.—All persons having liens upon or claiming any interest in the property involved in such action shall be made parties thereto.

[Sec. 7403(c)]

(c) Adjudication and Decree.—The court shall, after the parties have been duly notified of the action, proceed to adjudicate all matters involved therein and finally determine the merits of all claims to and liens upon the property, and, in all cases where a claim or interest of the United States therein is established, may decree a sale of such property, by the proper officer of the court, and a distribution of the proceeds of such sale according to the findings of the court in respect to the interests of the parties and of the United States. If the property is sold to satisfy a first lien held by the United States, the United States may bid at the sale such sum, not exceeding the amount of such lien with expenses of sale, as the Secretary directs.

CIVIL ACTIONS BY U.S.

Amendments

• **1976, Tax Reform Act of 1976 (P.L. 94-455)**

P.L. 94-455, § 1906(b)(13)(A):

Amended 1954 Code by substituting "Secretary" for "Secretary or his delegate" each place it appeared. **Effective** 2-1-77.

• **1966, Federal Tax Lien Act of 1966 (P.L. 89-719)**

P.L. 89-719, § 107(b):

Amended Code Sec. 7403(c) by adding the last sentence. **Effective**, generally, after 11-2-66. However, see the amendment note for Code Sec. 6323 for exceptions to this **effective** date.

[Sec. 7403(d)]

(d) RECEIVERSHIP.—In any such proceeding, at the instance of the United States, the court may appoint a receiver to enforce the lien, or, upon certification by the Secretary during the pendency of such proceedings that it is in the public interest, may appoint a receiver with all the powers of a receiver in equity.

Amendments

• **1976, Tax Reform Act of 1976 (P.L. 94-455)**

P.L. 94-455, § 1906(b)(13)(A):

Amended 1954 Code by substituting "Secretary" for "Secretary or his delegate" each place it appeared. **Effective** 2-1-77.

[Sec. 7404]

SEC. 7404. AUTHORITY TO BRING CIVIL ACTION FOR ESTATE TAXES.

If the estate tax imposed by chapter 11 is not paid on or before the due date thereof, the Secretary shall proceed to collect the tax under the provisions of general law; or appropriate proceedings in the name of the United States may be commenced in any court of the United States having jurisdiction to subject the property of the decedent to be sold under the judgment or decree of the court. From the proceeds of such sale the amount of the tax, together with the costs and expenses of every description to be allowed by the court, shall be first paid, and the balance shall be deposited according to the order of the court, to be paid under its direction to the person entitled thereto. This section insofar as it applies to the collection of a deficiency shall be subject to the provisions of sections 6213 and 6601.

Amendments

• **1976, Tax Reform Act of 1976 (P.L. 94-455)**

P.L. 94-455, § 1906(b)(13)(A):

Amended 1954 Code by substituting "Secretary" for "Secretary or his delegate" each place it appeared. **Effective** 2-1-77.

[Sec. 7405]

SEC. 7405. ACTION FOR RECOVERY OF ERRONEOUS REFUNDS.

[Sec. 7405(a)]

(a) REFUNDS AFTER LIMITATION PERIOD.—Any portion of a tax imposed by this title, refund of which is erroneously made, within the meaning of section 6514, may be recovered by civil action brought in the name of the United States.

[Sec. 7405(b)]

(b) REFUNDS OTHERWISE ERRONEOUS.—Any portion of a tax imposed by this title which has been erroneously refunded (if such refund would not be considered as erroneous under section 6514) may be recovered by civil action brought in the name of the United States.

[Sec. 7405(c)]

(c) INTEREST.—

For provision relating to interest on erroneous refunds, see section 6602.

[Sec. 7405(d)]

(d) PERIODS OF LIMITATION.—

For periods of limitations on actions under this section, see section 6532(b).

[Sec. 7406]

SEC. 7406. DISPOSITION OF JUDGMENTS AND MONEYS RECOVERED.

All judgments and moneys recovered or received for taxes, costs, forfeitures, and penalties shall be paid to the Secretary as collections of internal revenue taxes.

Amendments

• **1976, Tax Reform Act of 1976 (P.L. 94-455)**

P.L. 94-455, § 1906(b)(13)(A):

Amended 1954 Code by substituting "Secretary" for "Secretary or his delegate" each place it appeared. **Effective** 2-1-77.

[Sec. 7407]

SEC. 7407. ACTION TO ENJOIN TAX RETURN PREPARERS.

[Sec. 7407(a)]

(a) AUTHORITY TO SEEK INJUNCTION.—A civil action in the name of the United States to enjoin any person who is a tax return preparer from further engaging in any conduct described in subsection (b) or from further acting as a tax return preparer may be commenced at the request of the Secretary. Any action under this section shall be brought in the District Court of the United States for the district in which the tax return preparer resides or has his principal place of business or in which the taxpayer with respect to whose tax return the action is brought resides. The court may exercise its jurisdiction over such action (as provided in section 7402(a)) separate and apart from any other action brought by the United States against such tax return preparer or any taxpayer.

Amendments

• **2007, Small Business and Work Opportunity Tax Act of 2007 (P.L. 110-28)**

P.L. 110-28, § 8246(a)(2)(I)(i)(I):

Amended Code Sec. 7407 by striking "INCOME TAX RETURN PREPARERS" in the heading and inserting "TAX RETURN PREPARERS". **Effective** for returns prepared after 5-25-2007.

P.L. 110-28, § 8246(a)(2)(I)(i)(II):

Amended Code Sec. 7407 by striking "an income tax return preparer" each place it appears and inserting "a tax return preparer". **Effective** for returns prepared after 5-25-2007.

P.L. 110-28, §8246(a)(2)(I)(i)(III)-(IV):

Amended Code Sec. 7407(a) by striking "income tax preparer" both places it appears and inserting "tax return preparer", and by striking "income tax return" and inserting "tax return". **Effective** for returns prepared after 5-25-2007.

• **1989, Omnibus Budget Reconciliation Act of 1989 (P.L. 101-239)**

P.L. 101-239, §7738(b):

Amended Code Sec. 7407(a) by striking "Except as provided in subsection (c), a civil" and inserting "A civil". **Effective** for actions commenced after 12-31-89.

• **1976, Tax Reform Act of 1976 (P.L. 94-455)**

P.L. 94-455, §1203(g):

Added Code Sec. 7407(a). **Effective** for documents prepared after 12-31-76.

[Sec. 7407(b)]

(b) ADJUDICATION AND DECREES.—In any action under subsection (a), if the court finds—

(1) that a tax return preparer has—

(A) engaged in any conduct subject to penalty under section 6694 or 6695, or subject to any criminal penalty provided by this title,

(B) misrepresented his eligibility to practice before the Internal Revenue Service, or otherwise misrepresented his experience or education as a tax return preparer,

(C) guaranteed the payment of any tax refund or the allowance of any tax credit, or

(D) engaged in any other fraudulent or deceptive conduct which substantially interferes with the proper administration of the Internal Revenue laws, and

(2) that injunctive relief is appropriate to prevent the recurrence of such conduct,

the court may enjoin such person from further engaging in such conduct. If the court finds that a tax return preparer has continually or repeatedly engaged in any conduct described in subparagraphs (A) through (D) of this subsection and that an injunction prohibiting such conduct would not be sufficient to prevent such person's interference with the proper administration of this title, the court may enjoin such person from acting as a tax return preparer.

Amendments

• **2007, Small Business and Work Opportunity Tax Act of 2007 (P.L. 110-28)**

P.L. 110-28, §8246(a)(2)(I)(i)(II):

Amended Code Sec. 7407 by striking "an income tax return preparer" each place it appears and inserting "a tax return preparer". **Effective** for returns prepared after 5-25-2007.

• **1976, Tax Reform Act of 1976 (P.L. 94-455)**

P.L. 94-455, §1203(g):

Added Code Sec. 7407(b). **Effective** for documents prepared after 12-31-76.

[Sec. 7407(c)—Repealed]

Amendments

• **1989, Omnibus Budget Reconciliation Act of 1989 (P.L. 101-239)**

P.L. 101-239, §7738(a):

Repealed Code Sec. 7407(c). **Effective** for actions commenced after 12-31-89. Prior to repeal, Code Sec. 7407(c) read as follows:

(c) BOND TO STAY INJUNCTION.—No action to enjoin under subsection (b)(1)(A) shall be commenced or pursued with respect to any income tax return preparer who files and maintains, with the Secretary in the internal revenue district in which is located such preparer's legal residence or principal place of business, a bond in a sum of $50,000 as surety for the payment of penalties under sections 6694 and 6695.

• **1976, Tax Reform Act of 1976 (P.L. 94-455)**

P.L. 94-455, §1203(g):

Added Code Sec. 7407(c). **Effective** for documents prepared after 12-31-76.

[Sec. 7408]

SEC. 7408. ACTIONS TO ENJOIN SPECIFIED CONDUCT RELATED TO TAX SHELTERS AND REPORTABLE TRANSACTIONS.

[Sec. 7408(a)]

(a) AUTHORITY TO SEEK INJUNCTION.—A civil action in the name of the United States to enjoin any person from further engaging in specified conduct may be commenced at the request of the Secretary. Any action under this section shall be brought in the district court of the United States for the district in which such person resides, has his principal place of business, or has engaged in specified conduct. The court may exercise its jurisdiction over such action (as provided in section 7402(a)) separate and apart from any other action brought by the United States against such person.

Amendments

• **2004, American Jobs Creation Act of 2004 (P.L. 108-357)**

P.L. 108-357, §820(a):

Amended Code Sec. 7408 by redesignating subsection (c) as subsection (d) and by striking subsections (a) and (b) and inserting new subsections (a), (b), and (c). **Effective** 10-23-2004. Prior to being stricken, Code Sec. 7408(a) read as follows:

(a) AUTHORITY TO SEEK INJUNCTION.—A civil action in the name of the United States to enjoin any person from further engaging in conduct subject to penalty under section 6700 (relating to penalty for promoting abusive tax shelters, etc.) or section 6701 (relating to penalties for aiding and abetting understatement of tax liability) may be commenced at the request of the Secretary. Any action under this section shall be brought in the district court of the United States for the district in which such person resides, has his principal place of business, or has engaged in conduct subject to penalty under section 6700 or section 6701. The court may exercise its jurisdiction over such action (as provided in section 7402(a)) separate and apart from any other action brought by the United States against such person.

P.L. 108-357, §820(b)(1):

Amended the heading of Code Sec. 7408. **Effective** 10-23-2004. Prior to amendment, the heading of Code Sec. 7408 read as follows:

SEC. 7408. ACTION TO ENJOIN PROMOTERS OF ABUSIVE TAX SHELTERS, ETC.

[Sec. 7408(b)]

(b) ADJUDICATION AND DECREE.—In any action under subsection (a), if the court finds—

(1) that the person has engaged in any specified conduct, and

(2) that injunctive relief is appropriate to prevent recurrence of such conduct,

the court may enjoin such person from engaging in such conduct or in any other activity subject to penalty under this title.

Amendments

• **2004, American Jobs Creation Act of 2004 (P.L. 108-357)**

P.L. 108-357, §820(a):

Amended Code Sec. 7408 by redesignating subsection (c) as subsection (d) and by striking subsections (a) and (b) and inserting new subsections (a), (b), and (c). **Effective** 10-23-2004. Prior to being stricken, Code Sec. 7408(b) read as follows:

(b) ADJUDICATION AND DECREE.—In any action under subsection (a), if the court finds—

(1) that the person has engaged in any conduct subject to penalty under section 6700 (relating to penalty for promoting abusive tax shelters, etc.) or section 6701 (relating to penalties for aiding and abetting understatement of tax liability), and

(2) that injunctive relief is appropriate to prevent recurrence of such conduct,

the court may enjoin such person from engaging in such conduct or in any other activity subject to penalty under section 6700 or section 6701.

[Sec. 7408(c)]

(c) SPECIFIED CONDUCT.—For purposes of this section, the term "specified conduct" means any action, or failure to take action, which is—

(1) subject to penalty under section 6700, 6701, 6707, or 6708, or

CIVIL ACTIONS BY U.S.

(2) in violation of any requirement under regulations issued under section 330 of title 31, United States Code.

Amendments

• **2004, American Jobs Creation Act of 2004 (P.L. 108-357)**

P.L. 108-357, §820(a):

Amended Code Sec. 7408 by redesignating subsection (c) as subsection (d) and by striking subsections (a) and (b) and inserting new subsections (a), (b), and (c). **Effective** 10-23-2004.

[Sec. 7408(d)]

(d) CITIZENS AND RESIDENTS OUTSIDE THE UNITED STATES.—If any citizen or resident of the United States does not reside in, and does not have his principal place of business in, any United States judicial district, such citizen or resident shall be treated for purposes of this section as residing in the District of Columbia.

Amendments

• **2004, American Jobs Creation Act of 2004 (P.L. 108-357)**

P.L. 108-357, §820(a):

Amended Code Sec. 7408 by redesignating subsection (c) as subsection (d). **Effective** 10-23-2004.

• **1984, Deficit Reduction Act of 1984 (P.L. 98-369)**

P.L. 98-369, §143(b)(1):

Amended Code Sec. 7408(a) and (b) by inserting "or section 6701 (relating to penalties for aiding and abetting understatement of tax liability)" after "etc.)".

P.L. 98-369, §143(b)(2):

Amended Code Sec. 7408(a) by inserting "or section 6701" before the period at the end of the second sentence.

P.L. 98-369, §143(b)(3):

Amended Code Sec. 7408(b) by inserting "or section 6701" before the period.

• **1982, Tax Equity and Fiscal Responsibility Act of 1982 (P.L. 97-248)**

P.L. 97-248, §321(a):

Added Code Sec. 7408. **Effective** 9-4-82.

[Sec. 7409]

SEC. 7409. ACTION TO ENJOIN FLAGRANT POLITICAL EXPENDITURES OF SECTION 501(c)(3) ORGANIZATIONS.

[Sec. 7409(a)]

(a) AUTHORITY TO SEEK INJUNCTION.—

(1) IN GENERAL.—If the requirements of paragraph (2) are met, a civil action in the name of the United States may be commenced at the request of the Secretary to enjoin any section 501(c)(3) organization from further making political expenditures and for such other relief as may be appropriate to ensure that the assets of such organization are preserved for charitable or other purposes specified in section 501(c)(3). Any action under this section shall be brought in the district court of the United States for the district in which such organization has its principal place of business or for any district in which it has made political expenditures. The court may exercise its jurisdiction over such action (as provided in section 7402(a)) separate and apart from any other action brought by the United States against such organization.

(2) REQUIREMENTS.—An action may be brought under subsection (a) only if—

(A) the Internal Revenue Service has notified the organization of its intention to seek an injunction under this section if the making of political expenditures does not immediately cease, and

(B) the Commissioner of Internal Revenue has personally determined that—

(i) such organization has flagrantly participated in, or intervened in (including the publication or distribution of statements), any political campaign on behalf of (or in opposition to) any candidate for public office, and

(ii) injunctive relief is appropriate to prevent future political expenditures.

[Sec. 7409(b)]

(b) ADJUDICATION AND DECREE.—In any action under subsection (a), if the court finds on the basis of clear and convincing evidence that—

(1) such organization has flagrantly participated in, or intervened in (including the publication or distribution of statements), any political campaign on behalf of (or in opposition to) any candidate for public office, and

(2) injunctive relief is appropriate to prevent future political expenditures, the court may enjoin such organization from making political expenditures and may grant such other relief as may be appropriate to ensure that the assets of such organization are preserved for charitable or other purposes specified in section 501(c)(3).

[Sec. 7409(c)]

(c) DEFINITIONS.—For purposes of this section, the terms "section 501(c)(3) organization" and "political expenditures" have the respective meanings given to such terms by section 4955.

Amendments

• **1987, Revenue Act of 1987 (P.L. 100-203)**

P.L. 100-203, §10713(a)(1):

Amended subchapter A of chapter 76 by redesignating Code Sec. 7409 as Code Sec. 7410 and by inserting after Code Sec. 7408 a new Code Sec. 7409. **Effective** 12-22-87.

[Sec. 7410]

SEC. 7410. CROSS REFERENCES.

(1) For provisions for collecting taxes in general, see chapter 64.

(2) For venue in a civil action for the collection of any tax, see section 1396 of Title 28 of the United States Code.

(3) For venue of a proceeding for the recovery of any fine, penalty, or forfeiture, see section 1395 of Title 28 of the United States Code.

Amendments

• **1987, Revenue Act of 1987 (P.L. 100-203)**

P.L. 100-203, §10713(a)(1):

Amended subchapter A of chapter 76 by redesignating Code Sec. 7409 as Code Sec. 7410 and by inserting after Code Sec. 7408 a new Code Sec. 7409. **Effective** 12-22-87.

• **1982, Tax Equity and Fiscal Responsibility Act of 1982 (P.L. 97-248)**

P.L. 97-248, §321(a):

Redesignated Code Sec. 7408 as Code Sec. 7409.

• **1976, Tax Reform Act of 1976 (P.L. 94-455)**

P.L. 94-455, §1203(g):

Redesignated Code Sec. 7407 as Code Sec. 7408. **Effective** for documents prepared after 12-31-76.

Subchapter B—Proceedings by Taxpayers and Third Parties

Sec. 7421. Prohibition of suits to restrain assessment or collection.
Sec. 7422. Civil actions for refund.
Sec. 7423. Repayments to officers or employees.
Sec. 7424. Intervention.
Sec. 7425. Discharge of liens.
Sec. 7426. Civil actions by persons other than taxpayers.
Sec. 7427. Tax return preparers.
Sec. 7428. Declaratory judgments relating to status and classification of organizations under section 501(c)(3), etc.
Sec. 7429. Review of jeopardy levy or assessment procedures.
Sec. 7430. Awarding of costs and certain fees.
Sec. 7431. Civil damages for unauthorized inspection or disclosure of returns and return information.
Sec. 7432. Civil damages for failure to release lien.
Sec. 7433. Civil damages for certain unauthorized collection actions.
Sec. 7433A. Civil damages for certain unauthorized collection actions by persons performing services under qualified tax collection contracts.
Sec. 7434. Civil damages for fraudulent filing of information returns.
Sec. 7435. Civil damages for unauthorized enticement of information disclosure.
Sec. 7436. Proceedings for determination of employment status.
Sec. 7437. Cross references.

[Sec. 7421]
SEC. 7421. PROHIBITION OF SUITS TO RESTRAIN ASSESSMENT OR COLLECTION.

[Sec. 7421(a)]

(a) Tax.—Except as provided in sections 6015(e), 6212(a) and (c), 6213(a), 6232(c), 6330(e)(1), 6331(i), 6672(c), 6694(c), 7426(a) and (b)(1), 7429(b), and 7436, no suit for the purpose of restraining the assessment or collection of any tax shall be maintained in any court by any person, whether or not such person is the person against whom such tax was assessed.

Amendments

• **2015, Bipartisan Budget Act of 2015 (P.L. 114-74)**

P.L. 114-74, §1101(f)(10):

Amended Code Sec. 7421(a) by striking "6225(b), 6246(b)" and inserting "6232(c)". **Effective** generally for returns filed for partnership tax years beginning after 12-31-2017. For a special rule, see Act Sec. 1101(g)(4), below.

P.L. 114-74, §1101(g)(4), provides:

(4) Election.—A partnership may elect (at such time and in such form and manner as the Secretary of the Treasury may prescribe) for the amendments made by this section (other than the election under section 6221(b) of such Code (as added by this Act)) to apply to any return of the partnership filed for partnership taxable years beginning after the date of the enactment of this Act and before January 1, 2018.

• **2000, Community Renewal Tax Relief Act of 2000 (P.L. 106-554)**

P.L. 106-554, §313(b)(2)(B):

Amended Code Sec. 7421(a) by inserting "6330(e)(1)," after "6246(b),". **Effective** 12-21-2000.

P.L. 106-554, §319(24):

Amended Code Sec. 7421(a) by striking "6672(b)" and inserting "6672(c)". **Effective** 12-21-2000.

• **1998, Tax and Trade Relief Extension Act of 1998 (P.L. 105-277)**

P.L. 105-277, §4002(c)(1):

Amended Code Sec. 7421(a) by striking "6015(d)" and inserting "6015(e)". **Effective** as if included in the provision of P.L. 105-206 to which it relates [**effective**, generally, for any tax liability arising after 7-22-98, and any tax liability arising on or before 7-22-98, but remaining unpaid as of such date.—CCH].

P.L. 105-277, §4002(f):

Amended Code Sec. 7421(a) by inserting "6331(i)," after "6246(b),". **Effective** as if included in the provision of P.L. 105-206 to which it relates [**effective**, generally, for any tax liability arising after 7-22-98, and any tax liability arising on or before 7-22-98, but remaining unpaid as of such date.—CCH].

• **1998, IRS Restructuring and Reform Act of 1998 (P.L. 105-206)**

P.L. 105-206, §3201(e)(3):

Amended Code Sec. 7421(a) by inserting "6015(d)," after "sections". **Effective** for any liability for tax arising after 7-22-98, and any liability for tax arising on or before such date but remaining unpaid as of such date.

• **1981, Economic Recovery Tax Act of 1981 (P.L. 97-34)**

P.L. 105-34, §1222(b)(1):

Amended Code Sec. 7421(a) by inserting "6246(b)," after "6213(a),". **Effective** for partnership tax years beginning after 12-31-97 [effective date changed by P.L. 105-206, Act Sec. 6012(e)].

P.L. 105-34, §1239(e)(3):

Amended Code Sec. 7421(a), as amended by Act Sec. 1222, by inserting "6225(b)," after "6213(a),". **Effective** for partnership tax years ending after 8-5-97.

P.L. 105-34, §1454(b)(2):

Amended Code Sec. 7421(a) by striking "and 7429(b)" and inserting "7429(b), and 7436". **Effective** 8-5-97.

• **1978 (P.L. 95-628)**

P.L. 95-628, §9(b)(1):

Amended Code Sec. 7421(a) by inserting "6672(b), 6694(c)," after "6213(a),". **Effective** 11-10-78.

• **1976, Tax Reform Act of 1976 (P.L. 94-455)**

P.L. 94-455, §1204(c)(11):

Added "and 7429(b)" to Code Sec. 7421(a). For the **effective** date, see Act Sec. 1204(d), below.

P.L. 94-455, §1204(d), as amended by P.L. 94-528, §2(a), provides:

(d) Effective Date.—The amendments made by this section apply with respect to action taken under section 6851, 6861, or 6862 of the Internal Revenue Code of 1954 where the notice and demand takes place after February 28, 1977.

• **1966, Federal Tax Lien Act of 1966 (P.L. 89-719)**

P.L. 89-719, §110(c):

Amended Code Sec. 7421(a). **Effective**, generally, after 11-2-66. However, see the amendment note for Code Sec. 6323 for exceptions to this **effective** date. Prior to amendment, Code Sec. 7421(a) read as follows:

"(a) Tax.—Except as provided in sections 6212(a) and (c), and 6213(a), no suit for the purpose of restraining the assessment or collection of any tax shall be maintained in any court."

[Sec. 7421(b)]

(b) Liability of Transferee or Fiduciary.—No suit shall be maintained in any court for the purpose of restraining the assessment or collection (pursuant to the provisions of chapter 71) of—

(1) the amount of the liability, at law or in equity, of a transferee of property of a taxpayer in respect of any internal revenue tax, or

(2) the amount of the liability of a fiduciary under section 3713(b) of title 31, United States Code, in respect of any such tax.

Amendments

• **2018, Tax Technical Corrections Act of 2018 (P.L. 115-141)**

P.L. 115-141, §401(a)(324), Div. U:

Amended Code Sec. 7421(b)(2) by striking "Code in" and inserting "Code, in". **Effective** 3-23-2018.

• **1982 (P.L. 91-258)**

P.L. 97-258, §3(f)(13):

Amended Code Sec. 7421(b)(2) by striking out "section 3467 of the Revised Statutes (31 U.S.C. 192)" and substituting "section 3713(b) of title 31, United States Code". **Effective** 9-13-82.

PROCEEDINGS BY TAXPAYERS

[Sec. 7422]

SEC. 7422. CIVIL ACTIONS FOR REFUND.

[Sec. 7422(a)]

(a) NO SUIT PRIOR TO FILING CLAIM FOR REFUND.—No suit or proceeding shall be maintained in any court for the recovery of any internal revenue tax alleged to have been erroneously or illegally assessed or collected, or of any penalty claimed to have been collected without authority, or of any sum alleged to have been excessive or in any manner wrongfully collected, until a claim for refund or credit has been duly filed with the Secretary, according to the provisions of law in that regard, and the regulations of the Secretary established in pursuance thereof.

Amendments

• **1976, Tax Reform Act of 1976 (P.L. 94-455)**

P.L. 94-455, §1906(b)(13)(A):

Amended 1954 Code by substituting "Secretary" for "Secretary or his delegate" each place it appeared. **Effective** 2-1-77.

[Sec. 7422(b)]

(b) PROTEST OR DURESS.—Such suit or proceeding may be maintained whether or not such tax, penalty or sum has been paid under protest or duress.

[Sec. 7422(c)]

(c) SUITS AGAINST COLLECTION OFFICER A BAR.—A suit against any officer or employee of the United States (or former officer or employee) or his personal representative for the recovery of any internal revenue tax alleged to have been erroneously or illegally assessed or collected, or of any penalty claimed to have been collected without authority, or of any sum alleged to have been excessive or in any manner wrongfully collected shall be treated as if the United States had been a party to such suit in applying the doctrine of res judicata in all suits, in respect of any internal revenue tax, and in all proceedings in the Tax Court and on review of decisions of the Tax Court.

Amendments

• **1976, Tax Reform Act of 1976 (P.L. 94-455)**

P.L. 94-455, §1906(a)(44):

Amended Code Sec. 7422(c) by striking out "instituted after June 15, 1942," after "the doctrine of res judicata in all suits" and by striking out "where the petition to the Tax Court was filed after such date" from the end of the subsection. **Effective** 2-1-77.

[Sec. 7422(d)]

(d) CREDIT TREATED AS PAYMENT.—The credit of an overpayment of any tax in satisfaction of any tax liability shall, for the purpose of any suit for refund of such tax liability so satisfied, be deemed to be a payment in respect of such tax liability at the time such credit is allowed.

[Sec. 7422(e)]

(e) STAY OF PROCEEDINGS.—If the Secretary prior to the hearing of a suit brought by a taxpayer in a district court or the United States Court of Federal Claims for the recovery of any income tax, estate tax, gift tax, or tax imposed by chapter 41, 42, 43, or 44 (or any penalty relating to such taxes) mails to the taxpayer a notice that a deficiency has been determined in respect of the tax which is the subject matter of taxpayer's suit, the proceedings in taxpayer's suit shall be stayed during the period of time in which the taxpayer may file a petition with the Tax Court for a redetermination of the asserted deficiency, and for 60 days thereafter. If the taxpayer files a petition with the Tax Court, the district court or the United States Court of Federal Claims, as the case may be, shall lose jurisdiction of taxpayer's suit to whatever extent jurisdiction is acquired by the Tax Court of the subject matter of taxpayer's suit for refund. If the taxpayer does not file a petition with the Tax Court for a redetermination of the asserted deficiency, the United States may counterclaim in the taxpayer's suit, or intervene in the event of a suit as described in subsection (c) (relating to suits against officers or employees of the United States), within the period of the stay of proceedings notwithstanding that the time for such pleading may have otherwise expired. The taxpayer shall have the burden of proof with respect to the issues raised by such counterclaim or intervention of the United States except as to the issue of whether the taxpayer has been guilty of fraud with intent to evade tax. This subsection shall not apply to a suit by a taxpayer which, prior to the date of enactment of this title, is commenced, instituted, or pending in a district court or the United States Court of Federal Claims for the recovery of any income tax, estate tax, or gift tax (or any penalty relating to such taxes).

Amendments

• **2018, Tax Technical Corrections Act of 2018 (P.L. 115-141)**

P.L. 115-141, §401(a)(325)(A), Div. U:

Amended Code Sec. 7422(e) by striking "United States Claims Court" and inserting "United States Court of Federal Claims". [Note: Code Sec. 7422(e) does not contain the text "United States Claims Court". Therefore, this amendment cannot be made.—CCH] **Effective** 3-23-2018.

• **1992, Court of Federal Claims Technical and Procedural Improvements Act of 1992 (P.L. 102-572)**

P.L. 102-572, §902(b)(1):

Amended Code Sec. 7422(e) by striking "United States Claims Court" and inserting "United States Court of Federal Claims" each place it appears. **Effective** 10-29-92.

• **1988, Omnibus Trade and Competitiveness Act of 1988 (P.L. 100-418)**

P.L. 100-418, §1941(b)(2)(B)(x):

Amended Code Sec. 7422(e) by striking "44, or 45" each place it appears and inserting "or 44". **Effective** for crude oil removed from the premises on or after 8-23-88.

• **1982, Federal Courts Improvement Act of 1982 (P.L. 97-164)**

P.L. 97-164, §151:

Amended Code Sec. 7422(e) by striking out "Court of Claims" each place it appeared and inserting in lieu thereof "United States Claims Court". **Effective** 10-1-82. For an explanation of the effect of this change on pending cases, see the historical comment for P.L. 97-164, Act Sec. 403, following Code Sec. 6110(i).

• **1980, Crude Oil Windfall Profit Tax Act of 1980 (P.L. 96-223)**

P.L. 96-223, §101(f)(1)(J):

Amended Code Sec. 7422(e) by striking out "or 44" and inserting "44, or 45". For the **effective** date and transitional rules, see P.L. 96-223, Act Sec. 101(i), following Code Sec. 4986.

• **1976, Tax Reform Act of 1976 (P.L. 94-455)**

P.L. 94-455, §1307(d)(2)(F):

Substituted "chapter 41, 42," for "chapter 42" in Code Sec. 7422(e). **Effective** 10-4-76.

P.L. 94-455, §1605(b)(11):

Substituted "43, or 44" for "or 43" in Code Sec. 7422(e). **Effective** for tax years of real estate investment trusts beginning after 10-4-76.

P.L. 94-455, §1906(b)(13)(A):

Amended 1954 Code by substituting "Secretary" for "Secretary or his delegate" each place it appeared. **Effective** 2-1-77.

• **1974, Employee Retirement Income Security Act of 1974 (P.L. 93-406)**

P.L. 93-406, §1016(a)(26):

Amended Code Sec. 7422(e) by changing "chapter 42" to "chapter 42 or 43." For **effective** date, see amendment note for Code Sec. 410.

• **1969, Tax Reform Act of 1969 (P.L. 91-172)**

P.L. 91-172, §101(j)(56):

Amended the first sentence of Code Sec. 7422(e) by substituting "gift tax, or tax imposed by chapter 42" for "or gift tax". **Effective** 1-1-70.

[Sec. 7422(f)]

(f) LIMITATION ON RIGHT OF ACTION FOR REFUND.—

(1) GENERAL RULE.—A suit or proceeding referred to in subsection (a) may be maintained only against the United States and not against any officer or employee of the United States (or former officer or employee) or his personal representative. Such suit or proceeding may be

maintained against the United States notwithstanding the provisions of section 2502 of title 28 of the United States Code (relating to aliens' privilege to sue) and notwithstanding the provisions of section 1502 of such title 28 (relating to certain treaty cases).

(2) MISJOINDER AND CHANGE OF VENUE.—If a suit or proceeding brought in a United States district court against an officer or employee of the United States (or former officer or employee) or his personal representative is improperly brought solely by virtue of paragraph (1), the court shall order, upon such terms as are just, that the pleadings be amended to substitute the United States as a party for such officer or employee as of the time such action commenced, upon proper service of process on the United States. Such suit or proceeding shall upon request by the United States be transferred to the district or division where it should have been brought if such action initially had been brought against the United States.

Amendments

• **1971, Revenue Act of 1971 (P.L. 92-178)**

P.L. 92-178, §309(a):

Added "and notwithstanding the provisions of section 1502 of such title 28 (relating to certain treaty cases)" at the end of Code Sec. 7422(f)(1). **Effective** for suits or proceedings which are instituted after 1-30-67.

• **1966 (P.L. 89-713)**

P.L. 89-713, §3(a):

Redesignated Code Sec. 7422(f) as Code Sec. 7422(g) and added new Code Sec. 7422(f). **Effective** for suits brought against officers, employees, or personal representatives referred to therein which are instituted 90 days or more after 11-2-66.

[Sec. 7422(g)]

(g) SPECIAL RULES FOR CERTAIN EXCISE TAXES IMPOSED BY CHAPTER 42 OR 43.—

(1) RIGHT TO BRING ACTIONS.—

(A) IN GENERAL.—With respect to any taxable event, payment of the full amount of the first tier tax shall constitute sufficient payment in order to maintain an action under this section with respect to the second tier tax.

(B) DEFINITIONS.—For purposes of subparagraph (A), the terms "taxable event", "first tier tax", and "second tier tax" have the respective meanings given to such terms by section 4963.

(2) LIMITATION ON SUIT FOR REFUND.—No suit may be maintained under this section for the credit or refund of any tax imposed under section 4941, 4942, 4943, 4944, 4945, 4951, 4952, 4955, 4958, 4971, or 4975 with respect to any act (or failure to act) giving rise to liability for tax under such sections, unless no other suit has been maintained for credit or refund of, and no petition has been filed in the Tax Court with respect to a deficiency in, any other tax imposed by such sections with respect to such act (or failure to act).

(3) FINAL DETERMINATION OF ISSUES.—For purposes of this section, any suit for the credit or refund of any tax imposed under section 4941, 4942, 4943, 4944, 4945, 4951, 4952, 4955, 4958, 4971, or 4975 with respect to any act (or failure to act) giving rise to liability for tax under such sections, shall constitute a suit to determine all questions with respect to any other tax imposed with respect to such act (or failure to act) under such sections, and failure by the parties to such suit to bring any such question before the Court shall constitute a bar to such question.

Amendments

• **1996, Taxpayer Bill of Rights 2 (P.L. 104-168)**

P.L. 104-168, §1311(c)(4):

Amended Code Sec. 7422(g)(2) and (3) by inserting "4958," after "4955,". For the **effective** date of the above amendment, see Act Sec. 1311(d)(1)-(2), below.

P.L. 104-168, §1311(d)(1)-(2), provides:

(1) IN GENERAL.—The amendments made by this section (other than subsection (b)) shall apply to excess benefit transactions occurring on or after September 14, 1995.

(2) BINDING CONTRACTS.—The amendments referred to in paragraph (1) shall not apply to any benefit arising from a transaction pursuant to any written contract which was binding on September 13, 1995, and at all times thereafter before such transaction occurred.

• **1987, Revenue Act of 1987 (P.L. 100-203)**

P.L. 100-203, §10712:

Amended Code Sec. 7422(g)(2) and (3) by striking out "4952," and inserting in lieu thereof "4952, 4955,". **Effective** for tax years beginning after 12-22-87.

• **1986, Tax Reform Act of 1986 (P.L. 99-514)**

P.L. 99-514, §1899A(58):

Amended Code Sec. 7422(g)(1)(B) by striking out "section 4962" and inserting in lieu thereof "section 4963". **Effective** 10-22-86.

• **1980 (P.L. 96-596)**

P.L. 96-596, §2(c)(2):

Amended Code Sec. 7422(g)(1). **Effective** with respect to first-tier taxes as if included in the Internal Revenue Code of 1954 when such tax was first imposed. **Effective** for second-tier taxes assessed after 12-24-80 (except in cases where there is a court decision with regard to which res judicata applies on that date). Prior to amendment, Code Sec. 7422(g)(1) read:

(1) RIGHT TO BRING ACTIONS.—With respect to any act (or failure to act) giving rise to liability under section 4941, 4942, 4943, 4944, 4945, 4951, 4952, 4971, or 4975, payment of the full amount of tax imposed under section 4941(a) (relating to initial taxes on self-dealing), section 4942(a) (relating to initial tax on failure to distribute income), section 4943(a) (relating to initial tax on excess business holdings), section 4944(a) (relating to initial taxes on investments which jeopardize charitable purpose), section 4945(a) (relating to initial taxes on taxable expenditures), section 4951(a) (relating to initial taxes on self-dealing), 4952(a) (relating to initial taxes on taxable expenditures), 4971(a) (relating to initial tax on failure to meet minimum funding standard), or 4975(a) (relating to initial tax on prohibited transactions), section 4941(b) (relating to additional taxes on self-dealing), section 4942(b) (relating to additional tax on failure to distribute income), section 4943(b) (relating to additional tax on excess business holdings), section 4944(b) (relating to additional taxes on investments which jeopardize charitable purpose), section 4945(b) (relating to additional taxes on taxable expenditures), section 4951(b) (relating to additional taxes on self-dealing), 4952(b) (relating to additional taxes on taxable expenditures), section 4971(b) (relating to additional tax on failure to meet minimum funding standard), or section 4975(b) (relating to additional tax on prohibited transactions), shall constitute sufficient payment in order to maintain an action under this section with respect to such act (or failure to act).

• **1980, Technical Corrections Act of 1979 (P.L. 96-222)**

P.L. 96-222, §108(b)(1)(D), (E), (F):

Amended Code Sec. 7422(g) by changing "4944, 4945" each place it appeared to "4944, 4945, 4951, 4952,", by changing "section 4945(a) (relating to initial taxes on taxable expenditures)" to "section 4945(a) (relating to initial taxes on taxable expenditures), section 4951(a) (relating to initial taxes on self-dealing), 4952(a) (relating to initial taxes on taxable expenditures)", and by changing "section 4945(b) (relating to additional taxes on taxable expenditures)" to "section 4945(b) (relating to additional taxes on taxable expenditures), section 4951(b) (relating to additional taxes on self-dealing), section 4952(b) (relating to additional taxes on taxable expenditures)." **Effective** with respect to contributions, acts and expenditures made after 12-31-77.

• **1974, Employee Retirement Income Security Act of 1974 (P.L. 93-406)**

P.L. 93-406, §1016(a)(26):

Amended Code Sec. 7422(g). For **effective** date, see amendment note for Code Sec. 410. Prior to amendment, Code Sec. 7422(g) read as follows:

"(g) Special Rules for Certain Excise Taxes Imposed by Chapter 42.—

"(1) Right to bring actions.—With respect to any act (or failure to act) giving rise to liability under section 4941, 4942, 4943, 4944, or 4945, payment of the full amount of tax imposed under section 4941(a) (relating to initial taxes on self-dealing), section 4942(a) (relating to initial tax on failure to distribute income), section 4943(a) (relating to initial tax on excess business holdings), section 4944(a) (relating to initial taxes on investments which jeopardize charitable purpose), section 4945(a) (relating to initial taxes on taxable expenditures), section 4941(b) (relating to additional taxes on self-dealing), section 4942(b) (relating to additional tax on failure to distribute income), section 4943(b) (relating to additional tax on excess business holdings), section 4944(b) (relating to additional taxes on investments which jeopardize charitable purpose), or section 4945(b) (relating to additional taxes on taxable expenditures) shall constitute sufficent payment in order to maintain an action under this section with respect to such act (or failure to act).

"(2) Limitation on suit for refund.—No suit may be maintained under this section for the credit or refund of any tax imposed under section 4941, 4942, 4943, 4944, or 4945 with respect to any act (or failure to act) giving rise to liability for tax under such sections, unless no other suit has been maintained for credit or refund of, and no petition has been filed in the Tax Court with respect to a deficiency in, any other tax imposed by such sections with respect to such act (or failure to act).

"(3) Final determination of issues.—For purposes of this section, any suit for the credit or refund of any tax imposed under section 4941, 4942, 4943, 4944, or 4945 with respect to any act (or failure to act) giving rise to liability for tax under such sections, shall constitute a suit to determine all questions with respect to any other tax imposed with respect to such act (or failure to act) under such sections, and failure by the parties to such suit to bring any such question before the Court shall constitute a bar to such question."

• **1969, Tax Reform Act of 1969 (P.L. 91-172)**

P.L. 91-172, §101(i):

Added Code Sec. 7422(g). **Effective** 1-1-70.

PROCEEDINGS BY TAXPAYERS

Amendments

• **2015, Bipartisan Budget Act of 2015 (P.L. 114-74)**

P.L. 114-74, §1101(f)(11):

Amended Code Sec. 7422 by striking subsection (h). **Effective** generally for returns filed for partnership tax years beginning after 12-31-2017. For a special rule, see Act Sec. 1101(g)(4), below. Prior to being stricken, Code Sec. 7422(h) read as follows:

(h) SPECIAL RULE FOR ACTIONS WITH RESPECT TO PARTNERSHIP ITEMS.—No action may be brought for a refund attributable to partnership items (as defined in section 6231(a)(3)) except as provided in section 6228(b) or section 6230(c).

P.L. 114-74, §1101(g)(4), provides:

(4) ELECTION.—A partnership may elect (at such time and in such form and manner as the Secretary of the Treasury may prescribe) for the amendments made by this section (other than the election under section 6221(b) of such Code (as added by this Act)) to apply to any return of the partnership filed for partnership taxable years beginning after the date of the enactment of this Act and before January 1, 2018.

[Sec. 7422(i)]

(i) SPECIAL RULE FOR ACTIONS WITH RESPECT TO TAX SHELTER PROMOTER AND UNDERSTATEMENT PENALTIES.—No action or proceeding may be brought in the United States Court of Federal Claims for any refund or credit of a penalty imposed by section 6700 (relating to penalty for promoting abusive tax shelters, etc.) or section 6701 (relating to penalties for aiding and abetting understatement of tax liability).

Amendments

• **2018, Tax Technical Corrections Act of 2018 (P.L. 115-141)**

P.L. 115-141, §401(a)(325)(A), Div. U:

Amended Code Sec. 7422(i) by striking "United States Claims Court" and inserting "United States Court of Federal Claims". [Note: Code Sec. 7422(i) does not contain the text "United States Claims Court". Therefore, this amendment cannot be made.—CCH] **Effective** 3-23-2018.

[Sec. 7422(j)]

(j) SPECIAL RULE FOR ACTIONS WITH RESPECT TO ESTATES FOR WHICH AN ELECTION UNDER SECTION 6166 IS MADE.—

(1) IN GENERAL.—The district courts of the United States and the United States Court of Federal Claims shall not fail to have jurisdiction over any action brought by the representative of an estate to which this subsection applies to determine the correct amount of the estate tax liability of such estate (or for any refund with respect thereto) solely because the full amount of such liability has not been paid by reason of an election under section 6166 with respect to such estate.

(2) ESTATES TO WHICH SUBSECTION APPLIES.—This subsection shall apply to any estate if, as of the date the action is filed—

(A) no portion of the installments payable under section 6166 have been accelerated;

(B) all such installments the due date for which is on or before the date the action is filed have been paid;

(C) there is no case pending in the Tax Court with respect to the tax imposed by section 2001 on the estate and, if a notice of deficiency under section 6212 with respect to such tax has been issued, the time for filing a petition with the Tax Court with respect to such notice has expired; and

(D) no proceeding for declaratory judgment under section 7479 is pending.

(3) PROHIBITION ON COLLECTION OF DISALLOWED LIABILITY.—If the court redetermines under paragraph (1) the estate tax liability of an estate, no part of such liability which is disallowed by a decision of such court which has become final may be collected by the Secretary, and amounts paid in excess of the installments determined by the court as currently due and payable shall be refunded.

Amendments

• **1998, IRS Restructuring and Reform Act of 1998 (P.L. 105-206)**

P.L. 105-206, §3104(a):

Amended Code Sec. 7422 by redesignating subsection (j) as subsection (k) and by inserting after subsection (i) a new subsection (j). **Effective** for any claim for refund filed after 7-22-98.

[Sec. 7422(k)]

(k) CROSS REFERENCES.—

(1) For provisions relating generally to claims for refund or credit, see chapter 65 (relating to abatements, credit, and refund) and chapter 66 (relating to limitations).

(2) For duty of United States attorneys to defend suits, see section 507 of Title 28 of the United States Code.

(3) For jurisdiction of United States district courts, see section 1346 of Title 28 of the United States Code.

(4) For payment by the Treasury of judgments against internal revenue officers or employees, upon certificate of probable cause, see section 2006 of Title 28 of the United States Code.

Amendments

• **1998, IRS Restructuring and Reform Act of 1998 (P.L. 105-206)**

P.L. 105-206, §3104(a):

Amended Code Sec. 7422 by redesignating subsection (j) as subsection (k). **Effective** for any claim for refund filed after 7-22-98.

• **1984, Deficit Reduction Act of 1984 (P.L. 98-369)**

P.L. 98-369, §714(g)(1):

Redesignated subsection (i) of Code Sec. 7422 as subsection (j). **Effective** for any claim for refund or credit filed after 7-18-84.

• **1982, Tax Equity and Fiscal Responsibility Act of 1982 (P.L. 97-248)**

P.L. 97-248, §402(c)(11):

Redesignated Code Sec. 7422(h) as Code Sec. 7422(i). For **effective** date, see the amendment note for P.L. 97-248, Act Sec. 402(c)(11), following Code Sec. 7422(h) above.

Sec. 7422(h)—Stricken

[Sec. 7422(h)—Stricken]

• **1984, Deficit Reduction Act of 1984 (P.L. 98-369)**

P.L. 98-369, §714(p)(2)(H):

Amended Code Sec. 7422(h) by striking out "section 6131(a)(3)" and inserting in lieu thereof "section 6231(a)(3)". **Effective** as if included in the provision of P.L. 97-248 to which it relates.

• **1982, Tax Equity and Fiscal Responsibility Act of 1982 (P.L. 97-248)**

P.L. 97-248, §402(c)(11):

Added Code Sec. 7422(h). **Effective** for partnership tax years beginning after 9-3-82 and also to partnership tax years ending after that date if the partnership, each partner, and each indirect partner requests such application and the Secretary or his delegate consents to such application.

• **1992, Court of Federal Claims Technical and Procedural Improvements Act of 1992 (P.L. 102-572)**

P.L. 102-572, §902(b)(1):

Amended Code Sec. 7422(i) by striking "United States Claims Court" and inserting "United States Court of Federal Claims". **Effective** 10-29-92.

• **1984, Deficit Reduction Act of 1984 (P.L. 98-369)**

P.L. 98-369, §714(g)(1):

Redesignated subsection (i) of Code Sec. 7422 as subsection (j) and inserted new subsection (i). **Effective** for any claim for refund or credit filed after 7-18-84.

• **1969, Tax Reform Act of 1969 (P.L. 91-172)**

P.L. 91-172, §101(i):

Redesignated former Code Sec. 7422(g) as Code Sec. 7422(h). **Effective** 1-1-70.

• **1966 (P.L. 89-713)**

P.L. 89-713, §3(a):

Redesignated former Code Sec. 7422(f) as Code Sec. 7422(g). **Effective** as to suits brought against officers, employees, or personal representatives referred to therein which are instituted 90 days or more after 11-2-66.

• **1958, Technical Amendments Act of 1958 (P.L. 85-866)**

P.L. 85-866, §78:

Amended paragraph (2) by striking out the word "district" where it appeared in the phrase "United States district attorneys". **Effective** 1-1-54.

PROCEEDINGS BY TAXPAYERS

[Sec. 7423]

SEC. 7423. REPAYMENTS TO OFFICERS OR EMPLOYEES.

The Secretary, subject to regulations prescribed by the Secretary, is authorized to repay—

(1) COLLECTIONS RECOVERED.—To any officer or employee of the United States the full amount of such sums of money as may be recovered against him in any court, for any internal revenue taxes collected by him, with the cost and expense of suit; also

(2) DAMAGES AND COSTS.—All damages and costs recovered against any officer or employee of the United States in any suit brought against him by reason of anything done in the due performance of his official duty under this title.

Amendments

- **1976, Tax Reform Act of 1976 (P.L. 94-455)**

P.L. 94-455, § 1906(b)(13)(A):

Amended 1954 Code by substituting "Secretary" for "Secretary or his delegate" each place it appeared. **Effective** 2-1-77.

[Sec. 7424]

SEC. 7424. INTERVENTION.

If the United States is not a party to a civil action or suit, the United States may intervene in such action or suit to assert any lien arising under this title on the property which is the subject of such action or suit. The provisions of section 2410 of title 28 of the United States Code (except subsection (b)) and of section 1444 of title 28 of the United States Code shall apply in any case in which the United States intervenes as if the United States had originally been named a defendant in such action or suit. In any case in which the application of the United States to intervene is denied, the adjudication in such civil action or suit shall have no effect upon such lien.

Amendments

- **1966, Federal Tax Lien Act of 1966 (P.L. 89-719)**

P.L. 89-719, § 108:

Amended Code Sec. 7424. **Effective**, generally, after 11-2-66. However, see the amendment note for Code Sec. 6323 for exceptions to this **effective** date. Prior to amendment, Code Sec. 7424 read as follows:

SEC. 7424. CIVIL ACTION TO CLEAR TITLE TO PROPERTY.

(a) OBTAINING LEAVE TO FILE.—

(1) REQUEST FOR INSTITUTION OF PROCEEDINGS BY UNITED STATES.—Any person having a lien upon or any interest in the property referred to in section 7403, notice of which has been duly filed of record in the jurisdiction in which the property is located, prior to the filing of notice of the lien of the United States as provided in section 6323, or any person purchasing the property at a sale to satisfy such prior lien or interest, may make written request to the Secretary or his delegate to authorize the filing of a civil action as provided in section 7403.

(2) PETITION TO COURT.—If the Secretary or his delegate fails to authorize the filing of such civil action within 6 months after receipt of such written request, such person or purchaser may, after giving notice to the Secretary or his delegate, file a petition in the district court of the United States for the district in which the property is located, praying leave to file a civil action for a final determination of all claims to or liens upon the property in question.

(3) COURT ORDER.—After a full hearing in open court, the district court may in its discretion enter an order granting leave to file such civil action, in which the United States and all persons having liens upon or claiming any interest in the property shall be made parties.

(b) ADJUDICATION.—Upon the filing of such civil action, the district court shall proceed to adjudicate the matters involved therein, in the same manner as in the case of civil actions filed under section 7403. For the purpose of such adjudication, the assessment of the tax upon which the lien of the United States is based shall be conclusively presumed to be valid.

(c) COSTS.—All costs of the proceedings on the petition and the civil action shall be borne by the person filing the civil action.

[Sec. 7425]

SEC. 7425. DISCHARGE OF LIENS.

[Sec. 7425(a)]

(a) JUDICIAL PROCEEDINGS.—If the United States is not joined as a party, a judgment in any civil action or suit described in subsection (a) of section 2410 of title 28 of the United States Code, or a judicial sale pursuant to such a judgment, with respect to property on which the United States has or claims a lien under the provisions of this title—

(1) shall be made subject to and without disturbing the lien of the United States, if notice of such lien has been filed in the place provided by law for such filing at the time such action or suit is commenced, or

(2) shall have the same effect with respect to the discharge or divestment of such lien of the United States as may be provided with respect to such matters by the local law of the place where such property is situated, if no notice of such lien has been filed in the place provided by law for such filing at the time such action or suit is commenced or if the law makes no provision for such filing.

If a judicial sale of property pursuant to a judgment in any civil action or suit to which the United States is not a party discharges a lien of the United States arising under the provisions of this title, the United States may claim, with the same priority as its lien had against the property sold, the proceeds (exclusive of costs) of such sale at any time before the distribution of such proceeds is ordered.

[Sec. 7425(b)]

(b) OTHER SALES.—Notwithstanding subsection (a)[, a] sale of property on which the United States has or claims a lien, or a title derived from enforcement of a lien, under the provisions of this title, made pursuant to an instrument creating a lien on such property, pursuant to a confession of judgment on the obligation secured by such an instrument, or pursuant to a nonjudicial sale under a statutory lien on such property—

(1) shall, except as otherwise provided, be made subject to and without disturbing such lien or title, if notice of such lien was filed or such title recorded in the place provided by law for such filing or recording more than 30 days before such sale and the United States is not given notice of such sale in the manner prescribed in subsection (c)(1); or

(2) shall have the same effect with respect to the discharge or divestment of such lien or such title of the United States, as may be provided with respect to such matters by the local law of the place where such property is situated, if—

(A) notice of such lien or such title was not filed or recorded in the place provided by law for such filing more than 30 days before such sale,

(B) the law makes no provision for such filing, or

(C) notice of such sale is given in the manner prescribed in subsection (c)(1).

[Sec. 7425(c)]

(c) SPECIAL RULES.—

(1) NOTICE OF SALE.—Notice of a sale to which subsection (b) applies shall be given (in accordance with regulations prescribed by the Secretary) in writing, by registered or certified mail or by personal service, not less than 25 days prior to such sale, to the Secretary.

(2) CONSENT TO SALE.—Notwithstanding the notice requirement of subsection (b)(2)(C), a sale described in subsection (b) of property shall discharge or divest such property of the lien or title of the United States if the United States consents to the sale of such property free of such lien or title.

(3) SALE OF PERISHABLE GOODS.—Notwithstanding the notice requirement of subsection (b)(2)(C), a sale described in subsection (b) of property liable to perish or become greatly reduced in price or value by keeping, or which cannot be kept without great expense, shall

Internal Revenue Code   Sec. 7425(c)(3)

PROCEEDINGS BY TAXPAYERS

discharge or divest such property of the lien or title of the United States if notice of such sale is given (in accordance with regulations prescribed by the Secretary) in writing, by registered or certified mail or by personal service, to the Secretary before such sale. The proceeds (exclusive of costs) of such sale shall be held as a fund subject to the liens and claims of the United States, in the same manner and with the same priority as such liens and claims had with respect to the property sold, for not less than 30 days after the date of such sale.

(4) FORFEITURES OF LAND SALES CONTRACTS.—For purposes of subsection (b), a sale of property includes any forfeiture of a land sales contract.

Amendments

• **1986, Tax Reform Act of 1986 (P.L. 99-514)**

P.L. 99-514, §1572(a):

Amended Code Sec. 7425(c) by adding at the end thereof new paragraph (4). **Effective** for forfeitures after the 30th day after 10-22-86.

• **1976, Tax Reform Act of 1976 (P.L. 94-455)**

P.L. 94-455, §1906(b)(13)(A):

Amended 1954 Code by substituting "Secretary" for "Secretary or his delegate" each place it appeared. **Effective** 2-1-77.

[Sec. 7425(d)]

(d) REDEMPTION BY UNITED STATES.—

(1) RIGHT TO REDEEM.—In the case of a sale of real property to which subsection (b) applies to satisfy a lien prior to that of the United States, the Secretary may redeem such property within the period of 120 days from the date of such sale or the period allowable for redemption under local law, whichever is longer.

(2) AMOUNT TO BE PAID.—In any case in which the United States redeems real property pursuant to paragraph (1), the amount to be paid for such property shall be the amount prescribed by subsection (d) of section 2410 of title 28 of the United States Code.

(3) CERTIFICATE OF REDEMPTION.—

(A) IN GENERAL.—In any case in which real property is redeemed by the United States pursuant to this subsection, the Secretary shall apply to the officer designated by local law, if any, for the documents necessary to evidence the fact of redemption and to record title to such property in the name of the United States. If no such officer is designated by local law or if such officer fails to issue such documents, the Secretary shall execute a certificate of redemption therefor.

(B) FILING.—The Secretary shall, without delay, cause such documents or certificate to be duly recorded in the proper registry of deeds. If the State in which the real property redeemed by the United States is situated has not by law designated an office in which such certificate may be recorded, the Secretary shall file such certificate in the office of the clerk of the United States district court for the judicial district in which such property is situated.

(C) EFFECT.—A certificate of redemption executed by the Secretary shall constitute prima facie evidence of the regularity of such redemption and shall, when recorded, transfer to the United States all the rights, title, and interest in and to such property acquired by the person from whom the United States redeems such property by virtue of the sale of such property.

Amendments

• **1976, Tax Reform Act of 1976 (P.L. 94-455)**

P.L. 94-455, §1906(b)(13)(A):

Amended 1954 Code by substituting "Secretary" for "Secretary or his delegate" each place it appeared. **Effective** 2-1-77.

• **1966, Federal Tax Lien Act of 1966 (P.L. 89-719)**

P.L. 89-719, §109:

Redesignated former Code Sec. 7425 as Sec. 7427 and added new Code Sec. 7425. **Effective**, generally, after 11-2-66. However, see the amendment note for Code Sec. 6323 for exceptions to this **effective** date.

[Sec. 7426]

SEC. 7426. CIVIL ACTIONS BY PERSONS OTHER THAN TAXPAYERS.

[Sec. 7426(a)]

(a) ACTIONS PERMITTED.—

(1) WRONGFUL LEVY.—If a levy has been made on property or property has been sold pursuant to a levy, any person (other than the person against whom is assessed the tax out of which such levy arose) who claims an interest in or lien on such property and that such property was wrongfully levied upon may bring a civil action against the United States in a district court of the United States. Such action may be brought without regard to whether such property has been surrendered to or sold by the Secretary.

(2) SURPLUS PROCEEDS.—If property has been sold pursuant to a levy, any person (other than the person against whom is assessed the tax out of which such levy arose) who claims an interest in or lien on such property junior to that of the United States and to be legally entitled to the surplus proceeds of such sale may bring a civil action against the United States in a district court of the United States.

(3) SUBSTITUTED SALE PROCEEDS.—If property has been sold pursuant to an agreement described in section 6325(b)(3) (relating to substitution of proceeds of sale), any person who claims to be legally entitled to all or any part of the amount held as a fund pursuant to such agreement may bring a civil action against the United States in a district court of the United States.

(4) SUBSTITUTION OF VALUE.—If a certificate of discharge is issued to any person under section 6325(b)(4) with respect to any property, such person may, within 120 days after the day on which such certificate is issued, bring a civil action against the United States in a district court of the United States for a determination of whether the value of the interest of the United States (if any) in such property is less than the value determined by the Secretary. No other action may be brought by such person for such a determination.

Amendments

• **1998, IRS Restructuring and Reform Act of 1998 (P.L. 105-206)**

P.L. 105-206, §3106(b)(1):

Amended Code Sec. 7426(a) by adding at the end a new paragraph (4). **Effective** 7-22-98.

• **1976, Tax Reform Act of 1976 (P.L. 94-455)**

P.L. 94-455, §1906(b)(13)(A):

Amended 1954 Code by substituting "Secretary" for "Secretary or his delegate" each place it appeared. **Effective** 2-1-77.

[Sec. 7426(b)]

(b) ADJUDICATION.—The district court shall have jurisdiction to grant only such of the following forms of relief as may be appropriate in the circumstances:

(1) INJUNCTION.—If a levy or sale would irreparably injure rights in property which the court determines to be superior to rights of the United States in such property, the court may grant an injunction to prohibit the enforcement of such levy or to prohibit such sale.

(2) RECOVERY OF PROPERTY.—If the court determines that such property has been wrongfully levied upon, the court may—

(A) order the return of specific property if the United States is in possession of such property;

(B) grant a judgment for the amount of money levied upon; or

(C) if such property was sold, grant a judgment for an amount not exceeding the greater of—

(i) the amount received by the United States from the sale of such property, or

(ii) the fair market value of such property immediately before the levy.

PROCEEDINGS BY TAXPAYERS

For purposes of subparagraph (C), if the property was declared purchased by the United States at a sale pursuant to section 6335(e) (relating to manner and conditions of sale), the United States shall be treated as having received an amount equal to the minimum price determined pursuant to such section or (if larger) the amount received by the United States from the resale of such property.

(3) SURPLUS PROCEEDS.—If the court determines that the interest or lien of any party to an action under this section was transferred to the proceeds of a sale of such property, the court may grant a judgment in an amount equal to all or any part of the amount of the surplus proceeds of such sale.

(4) SUBSTITUTED SALE PROCEEDS.—If the court determines that a party has an interest in or lien on the amount held as a fund pursuant to an agreement described in section 6325(b)(3) (relating to substitution of proceeds of sale), the court may grant a judgment in an amount equal to all or any part of the amount of such fund.

(5) SUBSTITUTION OF VALUE.—If the court determines that the Secretary's determination of the value of the interest of the United States in the property for purposes of section 6325(b)(4) exceeds the actual value of such interest, the court shall grant a judgment ordering a refund of the amount deposited, and a release of the bond, to the extent that the aggregate of the amounts thereof exceeds such value determined by the court.

Amendments

• **1998, IRS Restructuring and Reform Act of 1998 (P.L. 105-206)**

P.L. 105-206, §3106(b)(2)(A):

Amended Code Sec. 7426(b) by adding at the end a new paragraph (5). **Effective** 7-22-98.

• **1982, Tax Equity and Fiscal Responsibility Act of 1982 (P.L. 97-248)**

P.L. 97-248, §350(a):

Amended Code Sec. 7426(b)(2)(C). **Effective** with respect to levies made after 12-31-82. Prior to amendment, Code Sec. 7426(b)(2)(C) read as follows:

"(C) grant a judgment for an amount not exceeding the amount received by the United States from the sale of such property."

[Sec. 7426(c)]

(c) VALIDITY OF ASSESSMENT.—For purposes of an adjudication under this section, the assessment of tax upon which the interest or lien of the United States is based shall be conclusively presumed to be valid.

[Sec. 7426(d)]

(d) LIMITATION ON RIGHTS OF ACTION.—No action may be maintained against any officer or employee of the United States (or former officer or employee) or his personal representative with respect to any acts for which an action could be maintained under this section.

[Sec. 7426(e)]

(e) SUBSTITUTION OF UNITED STATES AS PARTY.—If an action, which could be brought against the United States under this section, is improperly brought against any officer or employee of the United States (or former officer or employee) or his personal representative, the court shall order, upon such terms as are just, that the pleadings be amended to substitute the United States as a party for such officer or employee as of the time such action was commenced upon proper service of process on the United States.

[Sec. 7426(f)]

(f) PROVISION INAPPLICABLE.—The provisions of section 7422(a) (relating to prohibition of suit prior to filing claim for refund) shall not apply to actions under this section.

[Sec. 7426(g)]

(g) INTEREST.—Interest shall be allowed at the overpayment rate established under section 6621—

(1) in the case of a judgment pursuant to subsection (b)(2)(B), from the date the Secretary receives the money wrongfully levied upon to the date of payment of such judgment;

(2) in the case of a judgment pursuant to subsection (b)(2)(C), from the date of the sale of the property wrongfully levied upon to the date of payment of such judgment; and

(3) in the case of a judgment pursuant to subsection (b)(5) which orders a refund of any amount, from the date the Secretary received such amount to the date of payment of such judgment.

Amendments

• **1998, IRS Restructuring and Reform Act of 1998 (P.L. 105-206)**

P.L. 105-206, §3106(b)(2)(B):

Amended Code Sec. 7426(g) by striking "and" at the end of paragraph (1), by striking the period at the end of paragraph (2) and inserting "; and", and by adding at the end a new paragraph (3). **Effective** 7-22-98.

• **1986, Tax Reform Act of 1986 (P.L. 99-514)**

P.L. 99-514, §1511(c)(16):

Amended Code Sec. 7426(g) by striking out "an annual rate established under section 6621" and inserting in lieu thereof "the overpayment rate established under section 6621". **Effective** for purposes of determining interest for periods after 12-31-86.

• **1976, Tax Reform Act of 1976 (P.L. 94-455)**

P.L. 94-455, §1906(b)(13)(A):

Amended 1954 Code by substituting "Secretary" for "Secretary or his delegate" each place it appeared. **Effective** 2-1-77.

[Sec. 7426(h)]

(h) RECOVERY OF DAMAGES PERMITTED IN CERTAIN CASES.—

(1) IN GENERAL.—Notwithstanding subsection (b), if, in any action brought under this section, there is a finding that any officer or employee of the Internal Revenue Service recklessly or intentionally, or by reason of negligence, disregarded any provision of this title the defendant shall be liable to the plaintiff in an amount equal to the lesser of $1,000,000 ($100,000 in the case of negligence) or the sum of—

(A) actual, direct economic damages sustained by the plaintiff as a proximate result of the reckless or intentional or negligent disregard of any provision of this title by the officer or employee (reduced by any amount of such damages awarded under subsection (b)); and

(B) the costs of the action.

(2) REQUIREMENT THAT ADMINISTRATIVE REMEDIES BE EXHAUSTED; MITIGATION; PERIOD.—The rules of section 7433(d) shall apply for purposes of this subsection.

(3) PAYMENT AUTHORITY.—Claims pursuant to this section shall be payable out of funds appropriated under section 1304 of title 31, United States Code.

Amendments

• **1998, IRS Restructuring and Reform Act of 1998 (P.L. 105-206)**

P.L. 105-206, §3102(b):

Amended Code Sec. 7426 by redesignating subsection (h) as subsection (i) and by adding after subsection (g) a new subsection (h). **Effective** for actions of officers or employees of the Internal Revenue Service after 7-22-98.

PROCEEDINGS BY TAXPAYERS

[Sec. 7426(i)]

(i) CROSS REFERENCE.—

For period of limitation, see section 6532(c).

Amendments

• **1998, IRS Restructuring and Reform Act of 1998 (P.L. 105-206)**

P.L. 105-206, §3102(b):

Amended Code Sec. 7426 by redesignating subsection (h) as subsection (i). **Effective** for actions of officers or employees of the Internal Revenue Service after 7-22-98.

• **1976, Tax Reform Act of 1976 (P.L. 94-455)**

P.L. 94-455, §1906(b)(13)(A):

Amended 1954 Code by substituting "Secretary" for "Secretary or his delegate" each place it appeared. **Effective** 2-1-77.

• **1975 (P.L. 93-625)**

P.L. 93-625, §7(a)(2):

Amended Code Sec. 7426(g) by substituting "an annual rate established under section 6621" for "the rate of 6 percent per annum". For **effective** date, see the historical comment for P.L. 93-625 following the text of Code Sec. 6621.

• **1966, Federal Tax Lien Act of 1966 (P.L. 89-719)**

P.L. 89-719, §110(a):

Added Code Sec. 7426. **Effective**, generally, after 11-2-66. However, see the amendment note for Code Sec. 6323 for exceptions to this **effective** date.

[Sec. 7427]

SEC. 7427. TAX RETURN PREPARERS.

In any proceeding involving the issue of whether or not a tax return preparer has willfully attempted in any manner to understate the liability for tax (within the meaning of section 6694(b)), the burden of proof in respect of such issue shall be upon the Secretary.

Amendments

• **2007, Small Business and Work Opportunity Tax Act of 2007 (P.L. 110-28)**

P.L. 110-28, §8246(a)(2)(J)(i)(I)-(II):

Amended Code Sec. 7427 by striking "INCOME TAX RETURN PREPARERS" in the heading and inserting "TAX RETURN PREPARERS", and by striking "an income tax return preparer" and inserting "a tax return preparer". **Effective** for returns prepared after 5-25-2007.

• **1976, Tax Reform Act of 1976 (P.L. 94-455)**

P.L. 94-455, §1203(b):

Added Code Sec. 7427. **Effective** for documents prepared after 12-31-76.

[Sec. 7428]

SEC. 7428. DECLARATORY JUDGMENTS RELATING TO STATUS AND CLASSIFICATION OF ORGANIZATIONS UNDER SECTION 501(c)(3), ETC.

[Sec. 7428(a)]

(a) CREATION OF REMEDY.—In a case of actual controversy involving—

(1) a determination by the Secretary—

(A) with respect to the initial qualification or continuing qualification of an organization as an organization described in section 501(c)(3) which is exempt from tax under section 501(a) or as an organization described in section 170(c)(2),

(B) with respect to the initial classification or continuing classification of an organization as a private foundation (as defined in section 509(a)),

(C) with respect to the initial classification or continuing classification of an organization as a private operating foundation (as defined in section 4942(j)(3)),

(D) with respect to the initial classification or continuing classification of a cooperative as an organization described in section 521(b) which is exempt from tax under section 521(a), or

(E) with respect to the initial qualification or continuing qualification of an organization as an organization described in section 501(c) (other than paragraph (3)) or 501(d) and exempt from tax under section 501(a), or

(2) a failure by the Secretary to make a determination with respect to an issue referred to in paragraph (1),

upon the filing of an appropriate pleading, the United States Tax Court, the United States Court of Federal Claims, or the district court of the United States for the District of Columbia may make a declaration with respect to such initial qualification or continuing qualification or with respect to such initial classification or continuing classification. Any such declaration shall have the force and effect of a decision of the Tax Court or a final judgment or decree of the district court or the Court of Federal Claims, as the case may be, and shall be reviewable as such. For purposes of this section, a determination with respect to a continuing qualification or continuing classification includes any revocation of or other change in a qualification or classification.

Amendments

• **2018, Tax Technical Corrections Act of 2018 (P.L. 115-141)**

P.L. 115-141, §401(a)(325)(A), Div. U:

Amended Code Sec. 7428(a) by striking "United States Claims Court" and inserting "United States Court of Federal Claims". [Note: Code Sec. 7428(a) does not contain the text "United States Claims Court". Therefore, this amendment cannot be made.—CCH] **Effective** 3-23-2018.

P.L. 115-141, §401(a)(325)(B), Div. U:

Amended Code Sec. 7428(a) by striking "Claims Court" and inserting "Court of Federal Claims". [Note: Code Sec. 7428(a) does not contain the text "Claims Court". Therefore, this amendment cannot be made.—CCH] **Effective** 3-23-2018.

• **2015, Protecting Americans from Tax Hikes Act of 2015 (P.L. 114-113)**

P.L. 114-113, §406(a), Div. Q:

Amended Code Sec. 7428(a)(1) by striking "or" at the end of subparagraph (C) and by inserting after paragraph (D) a new subparagraph (E). [Note: Code Sec. 7428(a) does not contain the text "Claims Court". Therefore, this amendment cannot be made.—CCH] **Effective** for pleadings filed after 12-18-2015.

• **2004, American Jobs Creation Act of 2004 (P.L. 108-357)**

P.L. 108-357, §317(a):

Amended Code Sec. 7428(a)(1) by striking "or" at the end of subparagraph (B) and by adding at the end a new subparagraph (D). **Effective** for pleadings filed after 10-22-2004.

• **1992, Court of Federal Claims Technical and Procedural Improvements Act of 1992 (P.L. 102-572)**

P.L. 102-572, §902(b)(1)-(2):

Amended Code Sec. 7428(a) by striking "United States Claims Court" and inserting "United States Court of Federal Claims" and by striking "Claims Court" and inserting "Court of Federal Claims". **Effective** 10-29-92.

• **1982, Federal Courts Improvement Act of 1982 (P.L. 97-164)**

P.L. 97-164, §152:

Amended Code Sec. 7428(a)(2) by striking out "Court of Claims" each place it appeared and inserting in lieu thereof "Claims Court". For an explanation of the effect of this change on pending cases, see the historical comment for P.L. 97-164, Act Sec. 403, following Code Sec. 6110(i). **Effective** 10-1-82.

• **1978, Revenue Act of 1978 (P.L. 95-600)**

P.L. 95-600, §701(dd)(2):

Amended Code Sec. 7428(a) by adding the last sentence. **Effective** as if included in Code Sec. 7428 of the Internal Revenue Code of 1954 at the time such section was added to the Code.

[Sec. 7428(b)]

(b) LIMITATIONS.—

(1) PETITIONER.—A pleading may be filed under this section only by the organization the qualification or classification of which is at issue.

(2) EXHAUSTION OF ADMINISTRATIVE REMEDIES.—A declaratory judgment or decree under this section shall not be issued in any proceeding unless the Tax Court, the Court of Federal Claims, or the district court of the United States for the District of Columbia determines that the

PROCEEDINGS BY TAXPAYERS

organization involved has exhausted administrative remedies available to it within the Internal Revenue Service. An organization requesting the determination of an issue referred to in subsection (a)(1) shall be deemed to have exhausted its administrative remedies with respect to a failure by the Secretary to make a determination with respect to such issue at the expiration of 270 days after the date on which the request for such determination was made if the organization has taken, in a timely manner, all reasonable steps to secure such determination.

(3) TIME FOR BRINGING ACTION.—If the Secretary sends by certified or registered mail notice of his determination with respect to an issue referred to in subsection (a)(1) to the organization referred to in paragraph (1), no proceeding may be initiated under this section by such organization unless the pleading is filed before the 91st day after the date of such mailing.

(4) NONAPPLICATION FOR CERTAIN REVOCATIONS.—No action may be brought under this section with respect to any revocation of status described in section 6033(j)(1).

Amendments

• **2018, Tax Technical Corrections Act of 2018 (P.L. 115-141)**

P.L. 115-141, §401(a)(325)(B), Div. U:

Amended Code Sec. 7428(b) by striking "Claims Court" and inserting "Court of Federal Claims". [Note: Code Sec. 7428(b) does not contain the text "Claims Court". Therefore, this amendment cannot be made.—CCH] **Effective** 3-23-2018.

• **2006, Pension Protection Act of 2006 (P.L. 109-280)**

P.L. 109-280, §1223(c):

Amended Code Sec. 7428(b) by adding at the end a new paragraph (4). **Effective** for notices and returns with respect to annual periods beginning after 2006.

• **1992, Court of Federal Claims Technical and Procedural Improvements Act of 1992 (P.L. 102-572)**

P.L. 102-572, §902(b)(2):

Amended Code Sec. 7428(b)(2) by striking "Claims Court" and inserting "Court of Federal Claims". **Effective** 10-29-92.

• **1982, Federal Courts Improvement Act of 1982 (P.L. 97-164)**

P.L. 97-164, §152:

Amended Code Sec. 7428(b)(2) by striking out "Court of Claims" and inserting in lieu thereof "Claims Court". For an explanation of the effect of this change on pending cases, see the historical comment for P.L. 97-164, Act Sec. 403, following Code Sec. 6110(i). **Effective** 10-1-82.

[Sec. 7428(c)]

(c) VALIDATION OF CERTAIN CONTRIBUTIONS MADE DURING PENDENCY OF PROCEEDINGS.—

(1) IN GENERAL.—If—

(A) the issue referred to in subsection (a)(1) involves the revocation of a determination that the organization is described in section 170(c)(2),

(B) a proceeding under this section is initiated within the time provided by subsection (b)(3), and

(C) either—

(i) a decision of the Tax Court has become final (within the meaning of section 7481), or

(ii) a judgment of the district court of the United States for the District of Columbia has been entered, or

(iii) a judgment of the Court of Federal Claims has been entered,

and such decision or judgment, as the case may be, determines that the organization was not described in section 170(c)(2),

then, notwithstanding such decision or judgment, such organization shall be treated as having been described in section 170(c)(2) for purposes of section 170 for the period beginning on the date on which the notice of the revocation was published and ending on the date on which the court first determined in such proceeding that the organization was not described in section 170(c)(2).

(2) LIMITATION.—Paragraph (1) shall apply only—

(A) with respect to individuals, and only to the extent that the aggregate of the contributions made by any individual to or for the use of the organization during the period specified in paragraph (1) does not exceed $1,000 (for this purpose treating a husband and wife as one contributor), and

(B) with respect to organizations described in section 170(c)(2) which are exempt from tax under section 501(a) (for this purpose excluding any such organization with respect to which there is pending a proceeding to revoke the determination under section 170(c)(2)).

(3) EXCEPTION.—This subsection shall not apply to any individual who was responsible, in whole or in part, for the activities (or failures to act) on the part of the organization which were the basis for the revocation.

Amendments

• **2018, Tax Technical Corrections Act of 2018 (P.L. 115-141)**

P.L. 115-141, §401(a)(325)(B), Div. U:

Amended Code Sec. 7428(c)(1)(C)(iii) by striking "Claims Court" and inserting "Court of Federal Claims". [Note: Code Sec. 7428(c) does not contain the text "Claims Court". Therefore, this amendment cannot be made.—CCH] **Effective** 3-23-2018.

• **1992, Court of Federal Claims Technical and Procedural Improvements Act of 1992 (P.L. 102-572)**

P.L. 102-572, §902(b)(2):

Amended Code Sec. 7428(c)(1)(C)(iii) by striking "Claims Court" and inserting "Court of Federal Claims". **Effective** 10-29-92.

• **1982, Federal Courts Improvement Act of 1982 (P.L. 97-164)**

P.L. 97-164, §152:

Amended Code Sec. 7428(c)(1)(C)(iii) by striking out "Court of Claims" and inserting in lieu thereof "Claims Court". For an explanation of the effect of this change on pending cases, see the historical comment for P.L. 97-164, Act Sec. 403, following Code Sec. 6110(i). **Effective** 10-1-82.

• **1976, Tax Reform Act of 1976 (P.L. 94-455)**

P.L. 94-455, §1306(a):

Added Code Sec. 7428. For the **effective** date, see Act Sec. 1306(c), below.

P.L. 94-455, §1306(c), provides:

(c) EFFECTIVE DATE.—The amendments made by this section shall apply with respect to pleadings filed with the United States Tax Court, the district court of the United States for the District of Columbia, or the United States Court of Claims more than 6 months after the date of the enactment of this Act [October 4, 1976] but only with respect to determinations (or requests for determinations) made after January 1, 1976.

[Sec. 7428(d)]

(d) SUBPOENA POWER FOR DISTRICT COURT FOR DISTRICT OF COLUMBIA.—In any action brought under this section in the district court of the United States for the District of Columbia, a subpoena requiring the attendance of a witness at a trial or hearing may be served at any place in the United States.

Amendments

• **1984, Deficit Reduction Act of 1984 (P.L. 98-369)**

P.L. 98-369, §1033(b):

Amended Code Sec. 7428 by adding subsection (d) at the end thereof. **Effective** with respect to inquiries and examinations beginning after 12-31-84.

PROCEEDINGS BY TAXPAYERS

[Sec. 7429]

SEC. 7429. REVIEW OF JEOPARDY LEVY OR ASSESSMENT PROCEDURES.

[Sec. 7429(a)]

(a) ADMINISTRATIVE REVIEW.—

(1) ADMINISTRATIVE REVIEW.—

(A) PRIOR APPROVAL REQUIRED.—No assessment may be made under section 6851(a), 6852(a), 6861(a), or 6862, and no levy may be made under section 6331(a) less than 30 days after notice and demand for payment is made, unless the Chief Counsel for the Internal Revenue Service (or such Counsel's delegate) personally approves (in writing) such assessment or levy.

(B) INFORMATION TO TAXPAYER.—Within 5 days after the day on which such an assessment or levy is made, the Secretary shall provide the taxpayer with a written statement of the information upon which the Secretary relied in making such assessment or levy.

(2) REQUEST FOR REVIEW.—Within 30 days after the day on which the taxpayer is furnished the written statement described in paragraph (1), or within 30 days after the last day of the period within which such statement is required to be furnished, the taxpayer may request the Secretary to review the action taken.

(3) REDETERMINATION BY SECRETARY.—After a request for review is made under paragraph (2), the Secretary shall determine—

(A) whether or not—

(i) the making of the assessment under section 6851, 6861, or 6862, as the case may be, is reasonable under the circumstances, and

(ii) the amount so assessed or demanded as a result of the action taken under section 6851, 6861, or 6862 is appropriate under the circumstances, or

(B) whether or not the levy described in subsection (a)(1) is reasonable under the circumstances.

Amendments

• **1998, IRS Restructuring and Reform Act of 1998 (P.L. 105-206)**

P.L. 105-206, § 3434(a):

Amended Code Sec. 7429(a)(1). **Effective** for taxes assessed and levies made after 7-22-98. Prior to amendment, Code Sec. 7429(a)(1) read as follows:

(1) INFORMATION TO TAXPAYER.—Within 5 days after the day on which an assessment is made under section 6851(a), 6852(a), 6861(a), or 6862, or levy is made under section 6331(a) less than 30 days after notice and demand for payment is made under section 6331(a), the Secretary shall provide the taxpayer with a written statement of the information upon which the Secretary relies in making such assessment or levy.

• **1988, Technical and Miscellaneous Revenue Act of 1988 (P.L. 100-647)**

P.L. 100-647, § 6237(a)(1)-(2):

Amended Code Sec. 7429(a)(1) by inserting "or levy is made under section 6331(a) less than 30 days after notice and demand for payment is made under section 6331(a)," after "6862,", and by inserting "or levy" after "such assessment". **Effective** for jeopardy levies issued and assessments made on or after 7-1-89.

P.L. 100-647, § 6237(b):

Amended Code Sec. 7429(a)(3). **Effective** for jeopardy levies issued and assessments made on or after 7-1-89. Prior to amendment, Code Sec. 7429(a)(3) read as follows:

(3) REDETERMINATION BY SECRETARY.—After a request for review is made under paragraph (2), the Secretary shall determine whether or not—

(A) the making of the assessment under section 6851, 6852, 6861, or 6862, as the case may be, is reasonable under the circumstances, and

(B) the amount so assessed or demanded as a result of the action taken under section 6851, 6852, 6861, or 6862 is appropriate under the circumstances.

P.L. 100-647, § 6237(e)(3):

Amended Code Sec. 7429 by inserting "LEVY OR" after "JEOPARDY". **Effective** for jeopardy levies issued and assessments made on or after 7-1-89.

• **1987, Revenue Act of 1987 (P.L. 100-203)**

P.L. 100-203, § 10713(b)(2)(F)(i)-(ii):

Amended Code Sec. 7429 by striking out "6851(a)," each place it appears and inserting in lieu thereof "6851(a), 6852(a),", and by striking out "6851," each place it appears and inserting in lieu thereof "6851, 6852,". **Effective** 12-22-87.

[Sec. 7429(b)]

(b) JUDICIAL REVIEW.—

(1) PROCEEDINGS PERMITTED.—Within 90 days after the earlier of—

(A) the day the Secretary notifies the taxpayer of the Secretary's determination described in subsection (a)(3), or

(B) the 16th day after the request described in subsection (a)(2) was made,

the taxpayer may bring a civil action against the United States for a determination under this subsection in the court with jurisdiction determined under paragraph (2).

(2) JURISDICTION FOR DETERMINATION.—

(A) IN GENERAL.—Except as provided in subparagraph (B), the district courts of the United States shall have exclusive jurisdiction over any civil action for a determination under this subsection.

(B) TAX COURT.—If a petition for a redetermination of a deficiency under section 6213(a) has been timely filed with the Tax Court before the making of an assessment or levy that is subject to the review procedures of this section, and 1 or more of the taxes and taxable periods before the Tax Court because of such petition is also included in the written statement that is provided to the taxpayer under subsection (a), then the Tax Court also shall have jurisdiction over any civil action for a determination under this subsection with respect to all the taxes and taxable periods included in such written statement.

(3) DETERMINATION BY COURT.—Within 20 days after a proceeding is commenced under paragraph (1), the court shall determine—

(A) whether or not—

(i) the making of the assessment under section 6851, 6861, or 6862, as the case may be, is reasonable under the circumstances, and

(ii) the amount so assessed or demanded as a result of the action taken under section 6851, 6861, or 6862 is appropriate under the circumstances, or

(B) whether or not the levy described in subsection (a)(1) is reasonable under the circumstances.

If the court determines that proper service was not made on the United States or on the Secretary, as may be appropriate, within 5 days after the date of the commencement of the proceeding, then the running of the 20-day period set forth in the preceding sentence shall not begin before the day on which proper service was made on the United States or on the Secretary, as may be appropriate.

(4) ORDER OF COURT.—If the court determines that the making of such levy is unreasonable, that the making of such assessment is unreasonable, or that the amount assessed or demanded is inappropriate, then the court may order the Secretary to release such levy, to abate such assessment, to redetermine (in whole or in part) the amount assessed or demanded, or to take such other action as the court finds appropriate.

Amendments

• **1988, Technical and Miscellaneous Revenue Act of 1988 (P.L. 100-647)**

P.L. 100-647, § 6237(c):

Amended Code Sec. 7429(b). **Effective** for jeopardy levies issued or assessments made on or after 7-1-89. Prior to amendment, Code Sec. 7429(b) read as follows:

(b) JUDICIAL REVIEW.—

(1) ACTIONS PERMITTED.—Within 30 days after the earlier of—

(A) the day the Secretary notifies the taxpayer of his determination described in subsection (a)(3), or

(B) the 16th day after the request described in subsection (a)(2) was made, the taxpayer may bring a civil action against the United States in a district court of the United States for a determination under this subsection.

(2) DETERMINATION BY DISTRICT COURT.—Within 20 days after an action is commenced under paragraph (1), the district court shall determine whether or not—

(A) the making of the assessment under section 6851, 6852, 6861, or 6862, as the case may be, is reasonable under the circumstances, and

(B) the amount so assessed or demanded as a result of the action taken under section 6851, 6852, 6861, or 6862, is appropriate under the circumstances.

If the court determines that proper service was not made on the United States within 5 days after the date of the commencement of the action, the running of the 20-day period set forth in the preceding sentence shall not begin before the day on which proper service was made on the United States.

(3) ORDER OF DISTRICT COURT.—If the court determines that the making of such assessment is unreasonable or that the amount assessed or demanded is inappropriate, the court may order the Secretary to abate such assessment, to redetermine (in whole or in part) the amount assessed or demanded, or to take such other action as the court finds appropriate.

• **1987, Revenue Act of 1987 (P.L. 100-203)**

P.L. 100-203, §10713(b)(2)(F)(i)-(ii):

Amended Code Sec. 7429 by striking out "6851(a)," each place it appears and inserting in lieu thereof "6851(a), 6852(a),", and by striking out "6851," each place it appears and inserting in lieu thereof "6851, 6852,". **Effective** 12-22-87.

• **1984, Deficit Reduction Act of 1984 (P.L. 98-369)**

P.L. 98-369, §446(a):

Amended Code Sec. 7429(b)(2) by adding at the end thereof a new sentence. **Effective** for actions commenced after 7-18-84.

[Sec. 7429(c)]

(c) EXTENTION OF 20-DAY PERIOD WHERE TAXPAYER SO REQUESTS.—If the taxpayer requests an extension of the 20-day period set forth in subsection (b)(2) and establishes reasonable grounds why such extention should be granted, the court may grant an extension of not more than 40 additional days.

Amendments

• **1988, Technical and Miscellaneous Revenue Act of 1988 (P.L. 100-647)**

P.L. 100-647, §6237(e)(1):

Amended Code Sec. 7429(c) by striking out "district" before "court" each place it appears. **Effective** for jeopardy levies issued and assessments made on or after 7-1-89.

[Sec. 7429(d)]

(d) COMPUTATION OF DAYS.—For purposes of this section, Saturday, Sunday, or a legal holiday in the District of Columbia shall not be counted as the last day of any period.

[Sec. 7429(e)]

(e) VENUE.—

(1) DISTRICT COURT.—A civil action in a district court under subsection (b) shall be commenced only in the judicial district described in section 1402(a)(1) or (2) of title 28, United States Code.

(2) TRANSFER OF ACTIONS.—If a civil action is filed under subsection (b) with the Tax Court and such court finds that there is want of jurisdiction because of the jurisdiction provisions of subsection (b)(2), then the Tax Court shall, if such court determines it is in the interest of justice, transfer the civil action to the district court in which the action could have been brought at the time such action was filed. Any civil action so transferred shall proceed as if such action had been filed in the district court to which such action is transferred on the date on which such action was actually filed in the Tax Court from which such action is transferred.

Amendments

• **1988, Technical and Miscellaneous Revenue Act of 1988 (P.L. 100-647)**

P.L. 100-647, §6237(d):

Amended Code Sec. 7429(e). **Effective** for jeopardy levies issued and assessments made on or after 7-1-89. Prior to amendment, Code Sec. 7429(e) read as follows:

(e) VENUE.—A civil action under subsection (b) shall be commenced only in the judicial district described in section 1402(a)(1) or (2) of title 28, United States Code.

[Sec. 7429(f)]

(f) FINALITY OF DETERMINATION.—Any determination made by a court under this section shall be final and conclusive and shall not be reviewed by any other court.

Amendments

• **1988, Technical and Miscellaneous Revenue Act of 1988 (P.L. 100-647)**

P.L. 100-647, §6237(e)(1):

Amended Code Sec. 7429(f) by striking out "district" before "court" the first place "court" appears in the subsection. **Effective** for jeopardy levies issued and assessments made on or after 7-1-89.

[Sec. 7429(g)]

(g) BURDEN OF PROOF.—

(1) REASONABLENESS OF LEVY, TERMINATION, OR JEOPARDY ASSESSMENT.—In a proceeding under subsection (b) involving the issue of whether the making of a levy described in subsection (a)(1) or the making of an assessment under section 6851, 6852, 6861, or 6862 is reasonable under the circumstances, the burden of proof in respect to such issue shall be upon the Secretary.

(2) REASONABLENESS OF AMOUNT OF ASSESSMENT.—In a proceeding under subsection (b) involving the issue of whether an amount assessed or demanded as a result of action taken under section 6851, 6852, 6861, or 6862 is appropriate under the circumstances, the Secretary shall provide a written statement which contains any information with respect to which his determination of the amount assessed was based, but the burden of proof in respect of such issue shall be upon the taxpayer.

Amendments

• **1988, Technical and Miscellaneous Revenue Act of 1988 (P.L. 100-647)**

P.L. 100-647, §6237(e)(2)(A)-(C):

Amended Code Sec. 7429(g) by inserting "the making of a levy described in subsection (a)(1) or" after "whether" in paragraph (1); by striking out "TERMINATION" in the heading of paragraph (1) and inserting in lieu thereof "LEVY, TERMINATION,", and by striking out "an action" and inserting in lieu thereof "a proceeding" in paragraphs (1) and (2). **Effective** for jeopardy levies issued and assessments made on or after 7-1-89.

• **1987, Revenue Act of 1987 (P.L. 100-203)**

P.L. 100-203, §10713(b)(2)(F)(i)-(ii):

Amended Code Sec. 7429 by striking out "6851(a)," each place it appears and inserting in lieu thereof "6851(a), 6852(a),", and by striking out "6851," each place it appears and inserting in lieu thereof "6851, 6852,". **Effective** 12-22-87.

• **1976, Tax Reform Act of 1976 (P.L. 94-455)**

P.L. 94-455, §1204(a):

Added Code Sec. 7429. For the **effective** date, see Act Sec. 1204(d), below.

P.L. 94-455, §1204(d), as amended by P.L. 94-528, §2(a), provides:

(d) Effective Date.—The amendments made by this section shall apply with respect to action taken under section 6851, 6861, or 6862 of the Internal Revenue Code of 1954 where the notice and demand takes place after February 28, 1977.

PROCEEDINGS BY TAXPAYERS

[Sec. 7430]

SEC. 7430. AWARDING OF COSTS AND CERTAIN FEES.

[Sec. 7430(a)]

(a) IN GENERAL.—In any administrative or court proceeding which is brought by or against the United States in connection with the determination, collection, or refund of any tax, interest, or penalty under this title, the prevailing party may be awarded a judgment or a settlement for—

(1) reasonable administrative costs incurred in connection with such administrative proceeding within the Internal Revenue Service, and

(2) reasonable litigation costs incurred in connection with such court proceeding.

[Sec. 7430(b)]

(b) LIMITATIONS.—

(1) REQUIREMENT THAT ADMINISTRATIVE REMEDIES BE EXHAUSTED.—A judgment for reasonable litigation costs shall not be awarded under subsection (a) in any court proceeding unless the court determines that the prevailing party has exhausted the administrative remedies available to such party within the Internal Revenue Service. Any failure to agree to an extension of the time for the assessment of any tax shall not be taken into account for purposes of determining whether the prevailing party meets the requirements of the preceding sentence.

(2) ONLY COSTS ALLOCABLE TO THE UNITED STATES.—An award under subsection (a) shall be made only for reasonable litigation and administrative costs which are allocable to the United States and not to any other party.

(3) COSTS DENIED WHERE PARTY PREVAILING PROTRACTS PROCEEDINGS.—No award for reasonable litigation and administrative costs may be made under subsection (a) with respect to any portion of the administrative or court proceeding during which the prevailing party has unreasonably protracted such proceeding.

(4) PERIOD FOR APPLYING TO IRS FOR ADMINISTRATIVE COSTS.—An award may be made under subsection (a) by the Internal Revenue Service for reasonable administrative costs only if the prevailing party files an application with the Internal Revenue Service for such costs before the 91st day after the date on which the final decision of the Internal Revenue Service as to the determination of the tax, interest, or penalty is mailed to such party.

Amendments

• **1998, IRS Restructuring and Reform Act of 1998 (P.L. 105-206)**

P.L. 105-206, § 6012(h):

Amended Code Sec. 7430(b) by redesignating paragraph (5) as paragraph (4). **Effective** as if included in the provision of P.L. 105-34 to which it relates [effective for civil actions or proceedings commenced after 8-5-97.—CCH].

• **1997, Taxpayer Relief Act of 1997 (P.L. 105-34)**

P.L. 105-34, § 1285(b):

Amended Code Sec. 7430(b) by adding at the end a new paragraph (5)[(4)]. **Effective** for civil actions or proceedings commenced after 8-5-97.

• **1996, Taxpayer Bill of Rights 2 (P.L. 104-168)**

P.L. 104-168, § 703(a):

Amended Code Sec. 7430(b)(1) by adding at the end a new sentence. **Effective** in the case of proceedings commenced after 7-30-96.

P.L. 104-168, § 704(a):

Amended Code Sec. 7430(b) by striking paragraph (3) and by redesignating paragraph (4) as paragraph (3). **Effective** in the case of proceedings commenced after 7-30-96. Prior to amendment, Code Sec. 7430(b)(3) read as follows:

(3) EXCLUSION OF DECLARATORY JUDGMENT PROCEEDINGS.—

(A) IN GENERAL.—No award for reasonable litigation costs may be made under subsection (a) with respect to any declaratory judgment proceeding.

(B) EXCEPTION FOR SECTION 501(c)(3) DETERMINATION REVOCATION PROCEEDINGS.—Subparagraph (A) shall not apply to any proceeding which involves the revocation of a determination that the organization is described in section 501(c)(3).

[Sec. 7430(c)]

(c) DEFINITIONS.—For purposes of this section—

(1) REASONABLE LITIGATION COSTS.—The term "reasonable litigation costs" includes—

(A) reasonable court costs, and

(B) based upon prevailing market rates for the kind or quality of services furnished—

(i) the reasonable expenses of expert witnesses in connection with a court proceeding, except that no expert witness shall be compensated at a rate in excess of the highest rate of compensation for expert witnesses paid by the United States,

(ii) the reasonable cost of any study, analysis, engineering report, test, or project which is found by the court to be necessary for the preparation of the party's case, and

(iii) reasonable fees paid or incurred for the services of attorneys in connection with the court proceeding, except that such fees shall not be in excess of $125 per hour unless the court determines that an increase in the cost of living or a special factor, such as the limited availability of qualified attorneys for such proceeding, the difficulty of the issues presented in the case, or the local availability of tax expertise, justifies a higher rate.

In the case of any calendar year beginning after 1996, the dollar amount referred to in clause (iii) shall be increased by an amount equal to such dollar amount multiplied by the cost-of-living adjustment determined under section 1(f)(3) for such calendar year, by substituting "calendar year 1995" for "calendar year 2016" in subparagraph (A)(ii) thereof. If any dollar amount after being increased under the preceding sentence is not a multiple of $10, such dollar amount shall be rounded to the nearest multiple of $10.

(2) REASONABLE ADMINISTRATIVE COSTS.—The term "reasonable administrative costs" means—

(A) any administrative fees or similar charges imposed by the Internal Revenue Service, and

(B) expenses, costs, and fees described in paragraph (1)(B), except that any determination made by the court under clause (ii) or (iii) thereof shall be made by the Internal Revenue Service in cases where the determination under paragraph (4)(C) of the awarding of reasonable administrative costs is made by the Internal Revenue Service.

Such term shall only include costs incurred on or after whichever of the following is the earliest: (i) the date of the receipt by the taxpayer of the notice of the decision of the Internal Revenue Service Independent Office of Appeals; (ii) the date of the notice of deficiency; or (iii) the date on which the 1st letter of proposed deficiency which allows the taxpayer an opportunity for administrative review in the Internal Revenue Service Independent Office of Appeals is sent.

(3) ATTORNEYS' FEES.—

(A) IN GENERAL.—For purposes of paragraphs (1) and (2), fees for the services of an individual (whether or not an attorney) who is authorized to practice before the Tax Court or before the Internal Revenue Service shall be treated as fees for the services of an attorney.

(B) PRO BONO SERVICES.—The court may award reasonable attorneys' fees under subsection (a) in excess of the attorneys' fees paid or incurred if such fees are less than the reasonable attorneys' fees because an individual is representing the prevailing party for no fee or for a fee which (taking into account all the facts and circumstances) is no more than a nominal fee. This subparagraph shall apply only if such award is paid to such individual or such individual's employer.

(4) PREVAILING PARTY.—

(A) IN GENERAL.—The term "prevailing party" means any party in any proceeding to which subsection (a) applies (other than the United States or any creditor of the taxpayer involved)—

(i) which—

(I) has substantially prevailed with respect to the amount in controversy, or

(II) has substantially prevailed with respect to the most significant issue or set of issues presented, and

(ii) which meets the requirements of the 1st sentence of section 2412(d)(1)(B) of title 28, United States Code (as in effect on October 22, 1986) except to the extent differing procedures are established by rule of court and meets the requirements of section 2412(d)(2)(B) of such title 28 (as so in effect).

(B) EXCEPTION IF UNITED STATES ESTABLISHES THAT ITS POSITION WAS SUBSTANTIALLY JUSTIFIED.—

(i) GENERAL RULE.—A party shall not be treated as the prevailing party in a proceeding to which subsection (a) applies if the United States establishes that the position of the United States in the proceeding was substantially justified.

(ii) PRESUMPTION OF NO JUSTIFICATION IF INTERNAL REVENUE SERVICE DID NOT FOLLOW CERTAIN PUBLISHED GUIDANCE.—For purposes of clause (i), the position of the United States shall be presumed not to be substantially justified if the Internal Revenue Service did not follow its applicable published guidance in the administrative proceeding. Such presumption may be rebutted.

(iii) EFFECT OF LOSING ON SUBSTANTIALLY SIMILAR ISSUES.—In determining for purposes of clause (i) whether the position of the United States was substantially justified, the court shall take into account whether the United States has lost in courts of appeal for other circuits on substantially similar issues.

(iv) APPLICABLE PUBLISHED GUIDANCE.—For purposes of clause (ii), the term "applicable published guidance" means—

(I) regulations, revenue rulings, revenue procedures, information releases, notices, and announcements, and

(II) any of the following which are issued to the taxpayer: private letter rulings, technical advice memoranda, and determination letters.

(C) DETERMINATION AS TO PREVAILING PARTY.—Any determination under this paragraph as to whether a party is a prevailing party shall be made by agreement of the parties or—

(i) in the case where the final determination with respect to the tax, interest, or penalty is made at the administrative level, by the Internal Revenue Service, or

(ii) in the case where such final determination is made by a court, the court.

(D) SPECIAL RULES FOR APPLYING NET WORTH REQUIREMENT.—In applying the requirements of section 2412(d)(2)(B) of title 28, United States Code, for purposes of subparagraph (A)(ii) of this paragraph—

(i) the net worth limitation in clause (i) of such section shall apply to—

(I) an estate but shall be determined as of the date of the decedent's death, and

(II) a trust but shall be determined as of the last day of the taxable year involved in the proceeding, and

(ii) individuals filing a joint return shall be treated as separate individuals for purposes of clause (i) of such section.

(E) SPECIAL RULES WHERE JUDGMENT LESS THAN TAXPAYER'S OFFER.—

(i) IN GENERAL.—A party to a court proceeding meeting the requirements of subparagraph (A)(ii) shall be treated as the prevailing party if the liability of the taxpayer pursuant to the judgment in the proceeding (determined without regard to interest) is equal to or less than the liability of the taxpayer which would have been so determined if the United States had accepted a qualified offer of the party under subsection (g).

(ii) EXCEPTIONS.—This subparagraph shall not apply to—

(I) any judgment issued pursuant to a settlement; or

(II) any proceeding in which the amount of tax liability is not in issue, including any declaratory judgment proceeding, any proceeding to enforce or quash any summons issued pursuant to this title, and any action to restrain disclosure under section 6110(f).

(iii) SPECIAL RULES.—If this subparagraph applies to any court proceeding—

(I) the determination under clause (i) shall be made by reference to the last qualified offer made with respect to the tax liability at issue in the proceeding; and

(II) reasonable administrative and litigation costs shall only include costs incurred on and after the date of such offer.

(iv) COORDINATION.—This subparagraph shall not apply to a party which is a prevailing party under any other provision of this paragraph.

(5) ADMINISTRATIVE PROCEEDINGS.—The term "administrative proceeding" means any procedure or other action before the Internal Revenue Service.

(6) COURT PROCEEDINGS.—The term "court proceeding" means any civil action brought in a court of the United States (including the Tax Court and the United States Court of Federal Claims).

(7) POSITION OF UNITED STATES.—The term "position of the United States" means—

(A) the position taken by the United States in a judicial proceeding to which subsection (a) applies, and

(B) the position taken in an administrative proceeding to which subsection (a) applies as of the earlier of—

(i) the date of the receipt by the taxpayer of the notice of the decision of the Internal Revenue Service Independent Office of Appeals, or

(ii) the date of the notice of deficiency.

Amendments

• **2019, Taxpayer First Act (P.L. 116-25)**

P.L. 116-25, §1001(b)(1)(H):

Amended Code Sec. 7430(c)(7)(B)(i) by striking "Internal Revenue Service Office of Appeals" and inserting "Internal Revenue Service Independent Office of Appeals". **Effective** 7-1-2019.

P.L. 116-25, §1001(b)(2):

Amended Code Sec. 7430(c)(2) by striking "Internal Revenue Service Office of Appeals" each place it appears and inserting "Internal Revenue Service Independent Office of Appeals". **Effective** 7-1-2019.

• **2018, Tax Technical Corrections Act of 2018 (P.L. 115-141)**

P.L. 115-141, §401(a)(325)(A), Div. U:

Amended Code Sec. 7430(c)(6) by striking "United States Claims Court" and inserting "United States Court of Federal Claims". [Note: Code Sec. 7430(c)(6) does not contain the text "United States Claims Court". Therefore, this amendment cannot be made.—CCH] **Effective** 3-23-2018.

PROCEEDINGS BY TAXPAYERS

- **2017, Tax Cuts and Jobs Act (P.L. 115-97)**

P.L. 115-97, §11002(d)(1)(SS):

Amended Code Sec. 7430(c)(1) by striking "for 'calendar year 1992' in subparagraph (B)" and inserting "for 'calendar year 2016' in subparagraph (A)(ii)". **Effective** for tax years beginning after 12-31-2017.

- **2000, Community Renewal Tax Relief Act of 2000 (P.L. 106-554)**

P.L. 106-554, §319(25)(A)-(B):

Amended Code Sec. 7430(c)(3) by striking "ATTORNEYS" and inserting "ATTORNEYS'" in the paragraph heading, and by striking "attorneys fees" each place it appears in subparagraph (B) and inserting "attorneys' fees". **Effective** 12-21-2000.

- **1998, IRS Restructuring and Reform Act of 1998 (P.L. 105-206)**

P.L. 105-206, §3101(a)(1):

Amended Code Sec. 7430(c)(1)(B)(iii) by striking "$110" and inserting "$125". **Effective** for costs incurred more than 180 days after 7-22-98.

P.L. 105-206, §3101(a)(2):

Amended Code Sec. 7430(c)(1)(B)(iii) by inserting "the difficulty of the issues presented in the case, or the local availability of tax expertise," before "justifies a higher rate". **Effective** for costs incurred more than 180 days after 7-22-98.

P.L. 105-206, §3101(b):

Amended Code Sec. 7430(c)(2) by striking the last sentence and inserting a new flush sentence. **Effective** for costs incurred more than 180 days after 7-22-98. Prior to being stricken, the last sentence of Code Sec. 7430(c)(2) read as follows:

Such term shall only include costs incurred on or after the earlier of (i) the date of the receipt by the taxpayer of the notice of the decision of the Internal Revenue Service Office of Appeals, or (ii) the date of the notice of deficiency.

P.L. 105-206, §3101(c):

Amended Code Sec. 7430(c)(3). **Effective** for costs incurred and services performed more than 180 days after 7-22-98. Prior to amendment, Code Sec. 7430(c)(3) read as follows:

(3) ATTORNEY'S FEES.—For purposes of paragraphs (1) and (2), fees for the services of an individual (whether or not an attorney) who is authorized to practice before the Tax Court or before the Internal Revenue Service shall be treated as fees for the services of an attorney.

P.L. 105-206, §3101(d):

Amended Code Sec. 7430(c)(4)(B) by redesignating clause (iii) as clause (iv) and by inserting after clause (ii) a new clause (iii). **Effective** for costs incurred more than 180 days after 7-22-98.

P.L. 105-206, §3101(e)(1):

Amended Code Sec. 7430(c)(4) by adding at the end a new subparagraph (E). **Effective** for costs incurred more than 180 days after 7-22-98.

P.L. 105-206, §6014(e):

Amended Code Sec. 7430(c)(4)(D) by striking "subparagraph (A)(iii)" and inserting "subparagraph (A)(ii)". **Effective** for proceedings commenced after 8-5-97.

- **1997, Taxpayer Relief Act of 1997 (P.L. 105-34)**

P.L. 105-34, §1453(a):

Amended Code Sec. 7430(c)(4) by adding at the end a new subparagraph (D). **Effective** as if included in the provision of P.L. 105-34 to which it relates [effective for proceedings commenced after 8-5-97.—CCH].

- **1996, Taxpayer Bill of Rights 2 (P.L. 104-168)**

P.L. 104-168, §701(a):

Amended Code Sec. 7430(c)(4)(A) by striking clause (i) and by redesignating clauses (ii) and (iii) as clauses (i) and (ii), respectively. **Effective** in the case of proceedings commenced after 7-30-96. Prior to amendment, Code Sec. 7430(c)(4)(A)(i) read as follows:

(i) which establishes that the position of the United States in the proceeding was not substantially justified,

P.L. 104-168, §701(b):

Amended Code Sec. 7430(c)(4) by redesignating subparagraph (B) as subparagraph (C) and by inserting after subparagraph (A) a new subparagraph (B). **Effective** in the case of proceedings commenced after 7-30-96.

P.L. 104-168, §701(c)(1):

Amended Code Sec. 7430(c)(2)(B) by striking "paragraph (4)(B)" and inserting "paragraph (4)(C)". **Effective** in the case of proceedings commenced after 7-30-96.

P.L. 104-168, §701(c)(2):

Amended Code Sec. 7430(c)(4)(C), as redesignated by Act Sec. 701(b), by striking "subparagraph (A)" and inserting "this paragraph". **Effective** in the case of proceedings commenced after 7-30-96.

P.L. 104-168, §702(a)(1)-(3):

Amended Code Sec. 7430(c)(1) by striking "$75" in clause (iii) of subparagraph (B) and inserting "$110", by striking "an increase in the cost of living or" after "determines that" in clause (iii) of subparagraph (B), and by adding after clause (iii) two new sentences. **Effective** in the case of proceedings commenced after 7-30-96.

- **1992, Court of Federal Claims Technical and Procedural Improvements Act of 1992 (P.L. 102-572)**

P.L. 102-572, §902(b)(1):

Amended Code Sec. 7430(c) by striking "United States Claims Court" and inserting "United States Court of Federal Claims". **Effective** 10-29-92.

[Sec. 7430(d)]

(d) SPECIAL RULES FOR PAYMENT OF COSTS.—

(1) REASONABLE ADMINISTRATIVE COSTS.—An award for reasonable administrative costs shall be payable out of funds appropriated under section 1304 of title 31, United States Code.

(2) REASONABLE LITIGATION COSTS.—An award for reasonable litigation costs shall be payable in the case of the Tax Court in the same manner as such an award by a district court.

[Sec. 7430(e)]

(e) MULTIPLE ACTIONS.—For purposes of this section, in the case of—

(1) multiple actions which could have been joined or consolidated, or

(2) a case or cases involving a return or returns of the same taxpayer (including joint returns of married individuals) which could have been joined in a single court proceeding in the same court,

such actions or cases shall be treated as 1 court proceeding regardless of whether such joinder or consolidation actually occurs, unless the court in which such action is brought determines, in its discretion, that it would be inappropriate to treat such actions or cases as joined or consolidated.

[Sec. 7430(f)]

(f) RIGHT OF APPEAL.—

(1) COURT PROCEEDINGS.—An order granting or denying (in whole or in part) an award for reasonable litigation or administrative costs under subsection (a) in a court proceeding, may be incorporated as a part of the decision or judgment in the court proceeding and shall be subject to appeal in the same manner as the decision or judgment.

(2) ADMINISTRATIVE PROCEEDINGS.—A decision granting or denying (in whole or in part) an award for reasonable administrative costs under subsection (a) by the Internal Revenue Service shall be subject to the filing of a petition for review with the Tax Court under rules similar to the rules under section 7463 (without regard to the amount in dispute). If the Secretary sends by certified or registered mail a notice of such decision to the petitioner, no proceeding in the Tax Court may be initiated under this paragraph unless such petition is filed before the 91st day after the date of such mailing.

(3) APPEAL OF TAX COURT DECISION.—An order of the Tax Court disposing of a petition under paragraph (2) shall be reviewable in the same manner as a decision of the Tax Court, but only with respect to the matters determined in such order.

Amendments

- **1997, Taxpayer Relief Act of 1997 (P.L. 105-34)**

P.L. 105-34, §1285(a):

Amended Code Sec. 7430(f) by adding at the end a new paragraph (3). **Effective** for civil actions or proceedings commenced after 8-5-97.

P.L. 105-34, §1285(c)(1)-(2):

Amended Code Sec. 7430(f)(2) by striking "appeal to" and inserting "the filing of a petition for review with", and by adding at the end a new sentence. **Effective** for civil actions or proceedings commenced after 8-5-97.

- **1988, Technical and Miscellaneous Revenue Act of 1988 (P.L. 100-647)**

P.L. 100-647, §6239(a):

Amended Code Sec. 7430. **Effective** for proceedings commencing after 11-10-88. Prior to amendment, Code Sec. 7430 read as follows:

SEC. 7430. AWARDING OF COURT COSTS AND CERTAIN FEES.

[Sec. 7430(a)]

(a) IN GENERAL.—In the case of any civil proceeding which is—

(1) brought by or against the United States in connection with the determination, collection, or refund of any tax, interest, or penalty under this title, and

PROCEEDINGS BY TAXPAYERS

(2) brought in a court of the United States (including the Tax Court and the United States Claims Court),

the prevailing party may be awarded a judgment (payable in the case of the Tax Court in the same manner as such an award by a district court) for reasonable litigation costs incurred in such proceeding.

Amendments

• **1986, Tax Reform Act of 1986 (P.L. 99-514)**

P.L. 99-514, § 1551(f):

Amended Code Sec. 7430(a) by inserting "(payable in the case of the Tax Court in the same manner as such an award by a district court)" after "a judgment". **Effective** as if included in the amendments made by P.L. 97-248, Act Sec. 292.

[Sec. 7430(b)]

(b) LIMITATIONS.—

(1) REQUIREMENT THAT ADMINISTRATIVE REMEDIES BE EXHAUSTED.—A judgment for reasonable litigation costs shall not be awarded under subsection (a) unless the court determines that the prevailing party has exhausted the administrative remedies available to such party within the Internal Revenue Service.

(2) ONLY COSTS ALLOCABLE TO THE UNITED STATES.—An award under subsection (a) shall be made only for reasonable litigation costs which are allocable to the United States and not to any other party to the action or proceeding.

(3) EXCLUSION OF DECLARATORY JUDGMENT PROCEEDINGS.—

(A) IN GENERAL.—No award for reasonable litigation costs may be made under subsection (a) with respect to any declaratory judgment proceeding.

(B) EXCEPTION FOR SECTION 501(c)(3) DETERMINATION REVOCATION PROCEEDINGS.—Subparagraph (A) shall not apply to any proceeding which involves the revocation of a determination that the organization is described in section 501(c)(3).

(4) COST DENIED WHERE PARTY PREVAILING PROTRACTS PROCEEDINGS.—No award for reasonable litigation costs may be made under subsection (a) with respect to any portion of the civil proceeding during which the prevailing party has unreasonably protracted such proceeding.

Amendments

• **1986, Tax Reform Act of 1986 (P.L. 99-514)**

P.L. 99-514, § 1551(a):

Amended Code Sec. 7430(b) by striking out paragraph (1) and redesignating paragraphs (2), (3), and (4) as paragraphs (1), (2), and (3), respectively. **Effective** for amounts paid after 9-30-86, in civil actions or proceedings commenced after 12-31-85. For special rules, see Act Sec. 1551(h)(3) following Code Sec. 7430(c). Prior to amendment, Code Sec. 7430(b)(1) read as follows:

(1) MAXIMUM DOLLAR AMOUNT.—The amount of reasonable litigation costs which may be awarded under subsection (a) with respect to any prevailing party in any civil proceeding shall not exceed $25,000.

P.L. 99-514, § 1551(b):

Amended Code Sec. 7430(b) by adding at the end thereof new paragraph (4). **Effective** for amounts paid after 9-30-86, in civil actions or proceedings commenced after 12-31-85. For special rules, see Act Sec. 1551(h)(3) following Code Sec. 7430(c).

[Sec. 7430(c)]

(c) DEFINITIONS.—For purposes of this section—

(1) REASONABLE LITIGATION COSTS.—

(A) IN GENERAL.—The term "reasonable litigation costs" includes—

(i) reasonable court costs, and

(ii) based upon prevailing market rates for the kind or quality of services furnished—

(I) the reasonable expenses of expert witnesses in connection with the civil proceeding, except that no expert witness shall be compensated at a rate in excess of the highest rate of compensation for expert witnesses paid by the United States,

(II) the reasonable cost of any study, analysis, engineering report, test, or project which is found by the court to be necessary for the preparation of the party's case, and

(III) reasonable fees paid or incurred for the services of attorneys in connection with the civil proceeding, except that such fees shall not be in excess of $75 per hour unless the court determines that an increase in the cost of living or a special factor, such as the limited availability of qualified attorneys for such proceeding, justifies a higher rate.

(B) ATTORNEY'S FEES.—In the case of any proceeding in the Tax Court, fees for the services of an individual (whether or not an attorney) who is authorized to practice before the Tax Court shall be treated as fees for the services of an attorney.

(2) PREVAILING PARTY.—

(A) IN GENERAL.—The term "prevailing party" means any party to any proceeding described in subsection (a) (other than the United States or any creditor of the taxpayer involved) which—

(i) establishes that the position of the United States in the civil proceeding was not substantially justified,

(ii)(I) has substantially prevailed with respect to the amount in controversy, or

(II) has substantially prevailed with respect to the most significant issue or set of issues presented, and

(iii) meets the requirements of the 1st sentence of section 2412(d)(1)(B) of title 28, United States Code (as in effect on October 22, 1986) and meets the requirements of section 2412(d)(2)(B) of such title 28 (as so in effect).

(B) DETERMINATION AS TO PREVAILING PARTY.—Any determination under subparagraph (A) as to whether a party is a prevailing party shall be made—

(i) by the court, or

(ii) by agreement of the parties.

(3) CIVIL ACTIONS.—The term "civil proceeding" includes a civil action.

(4) POSITION OF UNITED STATES.—The term "position of the United States" includes—

(A) the position taken by the United States in the civil proceeding, and

(B) any administrative action or inaction by the District Counsel of the Internal Revenue Service (and all subsequent administrative action or inaction) upon which such proceeding is based.

Amendments

• **1988, Technical and Miscellaneous Revenue Act of 1988 (P.L. 100-647)**

P.L. 100-647, § 1015(i):

Amended Code Sec. 7430(c)(2)(A)(iii). **Effective** as if included in the provision of P.L. 99-514 to which it relates. Prior to amendment, Code Sec. 7430(c)(2)(A)(iii) read as follows:

(iii) meets the requirements of section 504(b)(1)(B) of title 5, United States Code (as in effect on the date of the enactment of the Tax Reform Act of 1986 and applied by taking into account the commencement of the proceeding described in subsection (a) in lieu of the initiation of the adjudication referred to in such section).

• **1986, Tax Reform Act of 1986 (P.L. 99-514)**

P.L. 99-514, § 1551(c):

Amended Code Sec. 7430(c)(1)(A). **Effective** for amounts paid after 9-30-86, in civil actions or proceedings commenced after 12-31-85. For special rules, see Act Sec. 1551(h)(3), below. Prior to amendment, Code Sec. 7430(c)(1)(A) read as follows:

(A) IN GENERAL.—the term "reasonable litigation costs" includes—

(i) reasonable court costs,

(ii) the reasonable expenses of expert witnesses in connection with the civil proceeding,

(iii) the reasonable cost of any study, analysis, engineering report, test, or project which is found by the court to be necessary for the preparation of the party's case, and

(iv) reasonable fees paid or incurred for the services of attorneys in connection with the civil proceeding.

P.L. 99-514, § 1151(d)(1), (2):

Amended Code Sec. 7430(c)(2) by striking out "was unreasonable" in clause (i), and inserting in lieu thereof "was not substantially justified", and by striking out "and" at the end of clause (i), by striking out the period at the end of clause (ii) and inserting in lieu thereof ", and", and by adding at the end thereof new clause (iii). **Effective** for amounts paid after 9-30-86, in civil actions or proceedings commenced after 12-31-85. For special rules, see Act Sec. 1551(h)(3), below.

P.L. 99-514, § 1551(e):

Amended Code Sec. 7430(c) by adding at the end thereof new paragraph (4). **Effective** for amounts paid after 9-30-86, in civil actions or proceedings commenced after 12-31-85.

P.L. 99-514, § 1551(h)(3), provides:

(3) APPLICABILITY OF AMENDMENTS TO CERTAIN PRIOR CASES.—The amendments made by this section shall apply to any case commenced after December 31, 1985, and finally disposed of before the date of the enactment of this Act, except that in any such case, the 30-day period referred to in section 2412(d)(1)(B) of title 28, United States Code, or Rule 231 of the Tax Court, as the case may be, shall be deemed to commence on the date of the enactment of this Act.

[Sec. 7430(d)]

(d) MULTIPLE ACTIONS.—For purposes of this section, in the case of—

(1) multiple actions which could have been joined or consolidated, or

(2) a case or cases involving a return or returns of the same taxpayer (including joint returns of married individuals) which could have been joined in a single proceeding in the same court,

such actions or cases shall be treated as one civil proceeding regardless of whether such joinder or consolidation actually occurs, unless the court in which such action is brought determines, in its discretion, that would be inappropriate to treat such actions or cases as joined or consolidated for purposes of this section.

[Sec. 7430(e)]

(e) RIGHT OF APPEAL.—An order granting or denying an award for reasonable litigation costs under subsection (a), in whole or in part, shall be incorporated as a part of the decision or judgment in the case and shall be subject to appeal in the same manner as the decision or judgment.

Amendments

• **1986, Tax Reform Act of 1986 (P.L. 99-514)**

P.L. 99-514, § 1551(g):

Amended Code Sec. 7430 by striking out subsection (f). **Effective** for amounts paid after 9-30-86, in civil actions or proceedings commenced after 12-31-85. See also Act Sec. 1551(h)(3) following Code Sec. 7430(c). Prior to deletion, Code Sec. 7430(f) read as follows:

(f) TERMINATION.—This section shall not apply to any proceeding commenced after December 31, 1985.

• **1984, Deficit Reduction Act of 1984 (P.L. 98-369)**

P.L. 98-369, § 714(c):

Amended Code Sec. 7430(a)(2) by striking out "including the Tax Court" and inserting in lieu thereof "including the Tax Court and the United States Claims Court". **Effective** as if included in the provision of P.L. 97-248 to which it relates.

• **1982, Tax Equity and Fiscal Responsibility Act of 1982 (P.L. 97-248)**

P.L. 97-248, § 292(a):

Redesignated Code Sec. 7430 as Code Sec. 7431 and added a new Code Sec. 7430. **Effective** for civil actions or proceedings commenced after 2-28-83, and ceases to apply to any proceeding commenced after 12-31-85.

PROCEEDINGS BY TAXPAYERS

[Sec. 7430(g)]

(g) QUALIFIED OFFER.—For purposes of subsection (c)(4)—

(1) IN GENERAL.—The term "qualified offer" means a written offer which—

(A) is made by the taxpayer to the United States during the qualified offer period;

(B) specifies the offered amount of the taxpayer's liability (determined without regard to interest);

(C) is designated at the time it is made as a qualified offer for purposes of this section; and

(D) remains open during the period beginning on the date it is made and ending on the earliest of the date the offer is rejected, the date the trial begins, or the 90th day after the date the offer is made.

(2) QUALIFIED OFFER PERIOD.—For purposes of this subsection, the term "qualified offer period" means the period—

(A) beginning on the date on which the 1st letter of proposed deficiency which allows the taxpayer an opportunity for administrative review in the Internal Revenue Service Independent Office of Appeals is sent, and

(B) ending on the date which is 30 days before the date the case is first set for trial.

Amendments

• **2019, Taxpayer First Act (P.L. 116-25)**

P.L. 116-25, § 1001(b)(1)(H):

Amended Code Sec. 7430(g)(2)(A) by striking "Internal Revenue Service Office of Appeals" and inserting "Internal Revenue Service Independent Office of Appeals". **Effective** 7-1-2019.

• **1998, IRS Restructuring and Reform Act of 1998 (P.L. 105-206)**

P.L. 105-206, § 3101(e)(2):

Amended Code Sec. 7430 by adding at the end a new subsection (g). **Effective** for costs incurred more than 180 days after 7-22-98.

[Sec. 7431]

SEC. 7431. CIVIL DAMAGES FOR UNAUTHORIZED INSPECTION OR DISCLOSURE OF RETURNS AND RETURN INFORMATION.

[Sec. 7431(a)]

(a) IN GENERAL.—

(1) INSPECTION OR DISCLOSURE BY EMPLOYEE OF UNITED STATES.—If any officer or employee of the United States knowingly, or by reason of negligence, inspects or discloses any return or return information with respect to a taxpayer in violation of any provision of section 6103, such taxpayer may bring a civil action for damages against the United States in a district court of the United States.

(2) INSPECTION OR DISCLOSURE BY A PERSON WHO IS NOT AN EMPLOYEE OF UNITED STATES.—If any person who is not an officer or employee of the United States knowingly, or by reason of negligence, inspects or discloses any return or return information with respect to a taxpayer in violation of any provision of section 6103 or in violation of section 6104(c), such taxpayer may bring a civil action for damages against such person in a district court of the United States.

Amendments

• **2006, Pension Protection Act of 2006 (P.L. 109-280)**

P.L. 109-280, § 1224(b)(7):

Amended Code Sec. 7431(a)(2) by inserting "or in violation of section 6104(c)" after "6103". **Effective** 8-17-2006 but shall not apply to requests made before such date.

• **1997, Taxpayer Browsing Protection Act (P.L. 105-35)**

P.L. 105-35, § 3(a)(1)-(2):

Amended Code Sec. 7431(a)(1) and (2) by striking "DISCLOSURE" in the heading and inserting "INSPECTION OR DISCLOSURE" and by striking "discloses" and inserting "inspects or discloses" in the text. **Effective** for inspections and disclosures occurring on and after 8-5-97.

P.L. 105-35, § 3(d)(4):

Amended the heading of Code Sec. 7431 by inserting "INSPECTION OR" before "DISCLOSURE". **Effective** for inspections and disclosures occurring on and after 8-5-97.

[Sec. 7431(b)]

(b) EXCEPTIONS.—No liability shall arise under this section with respect to any inspection or disclosure—

(1) which results from a good faith, but erroneous, interpretation of section 6103, or

(2) which is requested by the taxpayer.

Amendments

• **1997, Taxpayer Browsing Protection Act (P.L. 105-35)**

P.L. 105-35, § 3(c):

Amended Code Sec. 7431(b). **Effective** for inspections and disclosures occurring on and after 8-5-97. Prior to amendment, Code Sec. 7431(b) read as follows:

(b) NO LIABILITY FOR GOOD FAITH BUT ERRONEOUS INTERPRETATION.—No liability shall arise under this section with respect to any disclosure which results from a good faith, but erroneous, interpretation of section 6103.

[Sec. 7431(c)]

(c) DAMAGES.—In any action brought under subsection (a), upon a finding of liability on the part of the defendant, the defendant shall be liable to the plaintiff in an amount equal to the sum of—

(1) the greater of—

(A) $1,000 for each act of unauthorized inspection or disclosure of a return or return information with respect to which such defendant is found liable, or

(B) the sum of—

(i) the actual damages sustained by the plaintiff as a result of such unauthorized inspection or disclosure, plus

(ii) in the case of a willful inspection or disclosure or an inspection or disclosure which is the result of gross negligence, punitive damages, plus

(2) the costs of the action, plus

(3) in the case of a plaintiff which is described in section 7430(c)(4)(A)(ii), reasonable attorneys fees, except that if the defendant is the United States, reasonable attorneys fees may be awarded only if the plaintiff is the prevailing party (as determined under section 7430(c)(4)).

Amendments

• **1998, IRS Restructuring and Reform Act of 1998 (P.L. 105-206)**

P.L. 105-206, § 3101(f):

Amended Code Sec. 7431(c) by striking the period at the end of paragraph (2) and inserting ", plus", and by adding at the end a new paragraph (3). **Effective** for costs incurred more than 180 days after 7-22-98.

• **1997, Taxpayer Browsing Protection Act (P.L. 105-35)**

P.L. 105-35, § 3(d)(1):

Amended Code Sec. 7431(c)(1)(A) and (B)(i) by inserting "inspection or" before "disclosure". **Effective** for inspections and disclosures occurring on and after 8-5-97.

P.L. 105-35, § 3(d)(2):

Amended Code Sec. 7431(c)(1)(B)(ii) by striking "willful disclosure or a disclosure" and inserting "willful inspection or disclosure or an inspection or disclosure". **Effective** for inspections and disclosures occurring on and after 8-5-97.

PROCEEDINGS BY TAXPAYERS

[Sec. 7431(d)]

(d) PERIOD FOR BRINGING ACTION.—Notwithstanding any other provision of law, an action to enforce any liability created under this section may be brought, without regard to the amount in controversy, at any time within 2 years after the date of discovery by the plaintiff of the unauthorized inspection or disclosure.

Amendments

• **1997, Taxpayer Browsing Protection Act (P.L. 105-35)**

P.L. 105-35, §3(d)(1):

Amended Code Sec. 7431(d) by inserting "inspection or" before "disclosure". **Effective** for inspections and disclosures occurring on and after 8-5-97.

[Sec. 7431(e)]

(e) NOTIFICATION OF UNLAWFUL INSPECTION AND DISCLOSURE.—If any person is criminally charged by indictment or information with inspection or disclosure of a taxpayer's return or return information in violation of—

   (1) paragraph (1) or (2) of section 7213(a),

   (2) section 7213A(a), or

   (3) subparagraph (B) of section 1030(a)(2) of title 18, United States Code,

the Secretary shall notify such taxpayer as soon as practicable of such inspection or disclosure. The Secretary shall also notify such taxpayer if the Internal Revenue Service or a Federal or State agency (upon notice to the Secretary by such Federal or State agency) proposes an administrative determination as to disciplinary or adverse action against an employee arising from the employee's unauthorized inspection or disclosure of the taxpayer's return or return information. The notice described in this subsection shall include the date of the unauthorized inspection or disclosure and the rights of the taxpayer under such administrative determination.

Amendments

• **2019, Taxpayer First Act (P.L. 116-25)**

P.L. 116-25, §3002(a):

Amended Code Sec. 7431(e) by adding at the end two new sentences. **Effective** for determinations proposed after the date which is 180 days after 7-1-2019.

• **1997, Taxpayer Browsing Protection Act (P.L. 105-35)**

P.L. 105-35, §3(b):

Amended Code Sec. 7431 by redesignating subsections (e) and (f) as subsections (f) and (g), respectively, and by inserting after subsection (d) a new subsection (e). **Effective** for inspections and disclosures occurring on and after 8-5-97.

[Sec. 7431(f)]

(f) DEFINITIONS.—For purposes of this section, the terms "inspect", "inspection", "return", and "return information" have the respective meanings given such terms by section 6103(b).

Amendments

• **1997, Taxpayer Browsing Protection Act (P.L. 105-35)**

P.L. 105-35, §3(b):

Amended Code Sec. 7431 by redesignating subsection (e) as subsection (f). **Effective** for inspections and disclosures occurring on and after 8-5-97.

P.L. 105-35, §3(d)(3):

Amended Code Sec. 7431(f), as redesignated by Act Sec. 3(b). **Effective** for inspections and disclosures occurring on and after 8-5-97. Prior to amendment, Code Sec. 7431(f) read as follows:

(f) RETURN; RETURN INFORMATION.—For purposes of this section, the terms "return" and "return information" have the respective meanings given such terms in section 6103(b).

[Sec. 7431(g)]

(g) EXTENSION TO INFORMATION OBTAINED UNDER SECTION 3406.—For purposes of this section—

   (1) any information obtained under section 3406 (including information with respect to any payee certification failure under subsection (d) thereof) shall be treated as return information, and

   (2) any inspection or use of such information other than for purposes of meeting any requirement under section 3406 or (subject to the safeguards set forth in section 6103) for purposes permitted under section 6103 shall be treated as a violation of section 6103.

For purposes of subsection (b), the reference to section 6103 shall be treated as including a reference to section 3406.

Amendments

• **1997, Taxpayer Browsing Protection Act (P.L. 105-35)**

P.L. 105-35, §3(b):

Amended Code Sec. 7431 by redesignating subsection (f) as subsection (g). **Effective** for inspections and disclosures occurring on and after 8-5-97.

P.L. 105-35, §3(d)(6):

Amended Code Sec. 7431(g)(2), as redesignated by Act Sec. 3(b), by striking "any use" and inserting "any inspection or use". **Effective** for inspections and disclosures occurring on and after 8-5-97.

• **1983, Interest and Dividend Tax Compliance Act of 1983 (P.L. 98-67)**

P.L. 98-67, §104(b):

Added Code Sec. 7431(f).

• **1982, Tax Equity and Fiscal Responsibility Act of 1982 (P.L. 97-248)**

P.L. 97-248, §357(a):

Redesignated Code Sec. 7431 as Code Sec. 7432 and added a new Code Sec. 7431. **Effective** with respect to disclosures made after 9-3-82.

[Sec. 7431(h)]

(h) SPECIAL RULE FOR INFORMATION OBTAINED UNDER SECTION 6103(k)(9).—For purposes of this section, any reference to section 6103 shall be treated as including a reference to section 6311(e).

Amendments

• **1998, IRS Restructuring and Reform Act of 1998 (P.L. 105-206)**

P.L. 105-206, §6012(b)(3):

Amended Code Sec. 7431 by redesignating subsection (g) as subsection (h) and by striking "(8)" and inserting "(9)" in the heading. **Effective** as if included in the provision of P.L. 105-34 to which it relates [effective 5-5-98.—CCH].

• **1997, Taxpayer Relief Act of 1997 (P.L. 105-34)**

P.L. 105-34, §1205(c)(2):

Amended Code Sec. 7431 by adding at the end a new subsection (g). **Effective** on the day 9 months after 8-5-97.

[Sec. 7432]

SEC. 7432. CIVIL DAMAGES FOR FAILURE TO RELEASE LIEN.

[Sec. 7432(a)]

(a) IN GENERAL.—If any officer or employee of the Internal Revenue Service knowingly, or by reason of negligence, fails to release a lien under section 6325 on property of the taxpayer, such taxpayer may bring a civil action for damages against the United States in a district court of the United States.

[Sec. 7432(b)]

(b) DAMAGES.—In any action brought under subsection (a), upon a finding of liability on the part of the defendant, the defendant shall be liable to the plaintiff in an amount equal to the sum of—

   (1) actual, direct economic damages sustained by the plaintiff which, but for the actions of the defendant, would not have been sustained, plus

PROCEEDINGS BY TAXPAYERS

(2) the costs of the action.

[Sec. 7432(c)]

(c) PAYMENT AUTHORITY.—Claims pursuant to this section shall be payable out of funds appropriated under section 1304 of title 31, United States Code.

[Sec. 7432(d)]

(d) LIMITATIONS.—

(1) REQUIREMENT THAT ADMINISTRATIVE REMEDIES BE EXHAUSTED.—A judgment for damages shall not be awarded under subsection (b) unless the court determines that the plaintiff has exhausted the administrative remedies available to such plaintiff within the Internal Revenue Service.

(2) MITIGATION OF DAMAGES.—The amount of damages awarded under subsection (b)(1) shall be reduced by the amount of such damages which could have reasonably been mitigated by the plaintiff.

(3) PERIOD FOR BRINGING ACTION.—Notwithstanding any other provision of law, an action to enforce liability created under this section may be brought without regard to the amount in controversy and may be brought only within 2 years after the date the right of action accrues.

[Sec. 7432(e)]

(e) NOTICE OF FAILURE TO RELEASE LIEN.—The Secretary shall by regulation prescribe reasonable procedures for a taxpayer to notify the Secretary of the failure to release a lien under section 6325 on property of the taxpayer.

Amendments

• **1988, Technical and Miscellaneous Revenue Act of 1988 (P.L. 100-647)**

P.L. 100-647, § 6240(a):

Amended Subchapter B of chapter 76 by redesignating Code Sec. 7432 as Code Sec. 7433 and inserted after Code Sec. 7431 a new Code Sec. 7432. **Effective** for notices provided by the taxpayer of the failure to release a lien, and damages arising, after 12-31-88.

[Sec. 7433]

SEC. 7433. CIVIL DAMAGES FOR CERTAIN UNAUTHORIZED COLLECTION ACTIONS.

[Sec. 7433(a)]

(a) IN GENERAL.—If, in connection with any collection of Federal tax with respect to a taxpayer, any officer or employee of the Internal Revenue Service recklessly or intentionally, or by reason of negligence, disregards any provision of this title, or any regulation promulgated under this title, such taxpayer may bring a civil action for damages against the United States in a district court of the United States. Except as provided in section 7432, such civil action shall be the exclusive remedy for recovering damages resulting from such actions.

Amendments

• **1998, IRS Restructuring and Reform Act of 1998 (P.L. 105-206)**

P.L. 105-206, § 3102(a)(1)(A):

Amended Code Sec. 7433(a) by inserting ", or by reason of negligence," after "recklessly or intentionally". **Effective** for actions of officers or employees of the Internal Revenue Service after 7-22-98.

[Sec. 7433(b)]

(b) DAMAGES.—In any action brought under subsection (a) or petition filed under subsection (e), upon a finding of liability on the part of the defendant, the defendant shall be liable to the plaintiff in an amount equal to the lesser of $1,000,000 ($100,000, in the case of negligence) or the sum of—

(1) actual, direct economic damages sustained by the plaintiff as a proximate result of the reckless or intentional or negligent actions of the officer or employee, and

(2) the costs of the action.

Amendments

• **1998, IRS Restructuring and Reform Act of 1998 (P.L. 105-206)**

P.L. 105-206, § 3102(a)(1)(B)(i)-(ii):

Amended Code Sec. 7433(b), in the matter preceding paragraph (1), by inserting "($100,000, in the case of negligence)" after "$1,000,000", and in paragraph (1), by inserting "or negligent" after "reckless or intentional". **Effective** for actions of officers or employees of the Internal Revenue Service after 7-22-98.

P.L. 105-206, § 3102(c)(2):

Amended Code Sec. 7433(b) by inserting "or petition filed under subsection (e)" after "subsection (a)". **Effective** for actions of officers or employees of the Internal Revenue Service after 7-22-98.

• **1996, Taxpayer Bill of Rights 2 (P.L. 104-168)**

P.L. 104-168, § 801(a):

Amended Code Sec. 7433(b) by striking "$100,000" and inserting "$1,000,000". **Effective** for actions by officers or employees of the Internal Revenue Service after 7-30-96.

[Sec. 7433(c)]

(c) PAYMENT AUTHORITY.—Claims pursuant to this section shall be payable out of funds appropriated under section 1304 of title 31, United States Code.

[Sec. 7433(d)]

(d) LIMITATIONS.—

(1) REQUIREMENT THAT ADMINISTRATIVE REMEDIES BE EXHAUSTED.—A judgment for damages shall not be awarded under subsection (b) unless the court determines that the plaintiff has exhausted the administrative remedies available to such plaintiff within the Internal Revenue Service.

(2) MITIGATION OF DAMAGES.—The amount of damages awarded under subsection (b)(1) shall be reduced by the amount of such damages which could have reasonably been mitigated by the plaintiff.

(3) PERIOD FOR BRINGING ACTION.—Notwithstanding any other provision of law, an action to enforce liability created under this section may be brought without regard to the amount in controversy and may be brought only within 2 years after the date the right of action accrues.

Amendments

• **1998, IRS Restructuring and Reform Act of 1998 (P.L. 105-206)**

P.L. 105-206, § 3102(a)(2):

Amended Code Sec. 7433(d)(1). **Effective** for actions of officers or employees of the Internal Revenue Service after 7-22-98. Prior to amendment, Code Sec. 7433(d)(1) read as follows:

(1) AWARD FOR DAMAGES MAY BE REDUCED IF ADMINISTRATIVE REMEDIES NOT EXHAUSTED.—The amount of damages awarded under subsection (b) may be reduced if the court determines that the plaintiff has not exhausted the administrative remedies available to such plaintiff within the Internal Revenue Service.

PROCEEDINGS BY TAXPAYERS

• **1996, Taxpayer Bill of Rights 2 (P.L. 104-168)**

P.L. 104-168, §802(a):

Amended Code Sec. 7433(d)(1). **Effective** in the case of proceedings commenced after 7-30-96. Prior to amendment, Code Sec. 7433(d)(1) read as follows:

(1) REQUIREMENT THAT ADMINISTRATIVE REMEDIES BE EXHAUSTED.—A judgment for damages shall not be awarded under subsection (b) unless the court determines that the plaintiff has exhausted the administrative remedies available to such plaintiff within the Internal Revenue Service.

• **1988, Technical and Miscellaneous Revenue Act of 1988 (P.L. 100-647)**

P.L. 100-647, §6241(a):

Amended Subchapter B of chapter 76 by redesignating Code Sec. 7433 as Code Sec. 7434 and inserted after Code Sec. 7432 a new Code Sec. 7433. **Effective** for actions by officers or employees of the Internal Revenue Service after 11-10-88.

[Sec. 7433(e)]

(e) ACTIONS FOR VIOLATIONS OF CERTAIN BANKRUPTCY PROCEDURES.—

(1) IN GENERAL.—If, in connection with any collection of Federal tax with respect to a taxpayer, any officer or employee of the Internal Revenue Service willfully violates any provision of section 362 (relating to automatic stay) or 524 (relating to effect of discharge) of title 11, United States Code (or any successor provision), or any regulation promulgated under such provision, such taxpayer may petition the bankruptcy court to recover damages against the United States.

(2) REMEDY TO BE EXCLUSIVE.—

(A) IN GENERAL.—Except as provided in subparagraph (B), notwithstanding section 105 of such title 11, such petition shall be the exclusive remedy for recovering damages resulting from such actions.

(B) CERTAIN OTHER ACTIONS PERMITTED.—Subparagraph (A) shall not apply to an action under section 362(h) of such title 11 for a violation of a stay provided by section 362 of such title; except that—

(i) administrative and litigation costs in connection with such an action may only be awarded under section 7430; and

(ii) administrative costs may be awarded only if incurred on or after the date that the bankruptcy petition is filed.

Amendments

• **1998, IRS Restructuring and Reform Act of 1998 (P.L. 105-206)**

P.L. 105-206, §3102(c)(1):

Amended Code Sec. 7433 by adding at the end a new subsection (e). **Effective** for actions of officers or employees of the Internal Revenue Service after 7-22-98.

[Sec. 7433A]

SEC. 7433A. CIVIL DAMAGES FOR CERTAIN UNAUTHORIZED COLLECTION ACTIONS BY PERSONS PERFORMING SERVICES UNDER QUALIFIED TAX COLLECTION CONTRACTS.

[Sec. 7433A(a)]

(a) IN GENERAL.—Subject to the modifications provided by subsection (b), section 7433 shall apply to the acts and omissions of any person performing services under a qualified tax collection contract (as defined in section 6306(b)) to the same extent and in the same manner as if such person were an employee of the Internal Revenue Service.

[Sec. 7433A(b)]

(b) MODIFICATIONS.—For purposes of subsection (a):

(1) Any civil action brought under section 7433 by reason of this section shall be brought against the person who entered into the qualified tax collection contract with the Secretary and shall not be brought against the United States.

(2) Such person and not the United States shall be liable for any damages and costs determined in such civil action.

(3) Such civil action shall not be an exclusive remedy with respect to such person.

(4) Subsections (c), (d)(1), and (e) of section 7433 shall not apply.

Amendments

• **2004, American Jobs Creation Act of 2004 (P.L. 108-357)**

P.L. 108-357, §881(b)(1):

Amended subchapter B of chapter 76 by inserting after Code Sec. 7433 a new Code Sec. 7433A. **Effective** 10-22-2004.

[Sec. 7434]

SEC. 7434. CIVIL DAMAGES FOR FRAUDULENT FILING OF INFORMATION RETURNS.

[Sec. 7434(a)]

(a) IN GENERAL.—If any person willfully files a fraudulent information return with respect to payments purported to be made to any other person, such other person may bring a civil action for damages against the person so filing such return.

[Sec. 7434(b)]

(b) DAMAGES.—In any action brought under subsection (a), upon a finding of liability on the part of the defendant, the defendant shall be liable to the plaintiff in an amount equal to the greater of $5,000 or the sum of—

(1) any actual damages sustained by the plaintiff as a proximate result of the filing of the fraudulent information return (including any costs attributable to resolving deficiencies asserted as a result of such filing),

(2) the costs of the action, and

(3) in the court's discretion, reasonable attorneys' fees.

Amendments

• **1998, IRS Restructuring and Reform Act of 1998 (P.L. 105-206)**

P.L. 105-206, §6023(29):

Amended Code Sec. 7434(b)(3) by striking "attorneys fees" and inserting "attorneys' fees". **Effective** 7-22-98.

[Sec. 7434(c)]

(c) PERIOD FOR BRINGING ACTION.—Notwithstanding any other provision of law, an action to enforce the liability created under this section may be brought without regard to the amount in controversy and may be brought only within the later of—

(1) 6 years after the date of the filing of the fraudulent information return, or

(2) 1 year after the date such fraudulent information return would have been discovered by exercise of reasonable care.

PROCEEDINGS BY TAXPAYERS

[Sec. 7434(d)]

(d) COPY OF COMPLAINT FILED WITH IRS.—Any person bringing an action under subsection (a) shall provide a copy of the complaint to the Internal Revenue Service upon the filing of such complaint with the court.

[Sec. 7434(e)]

(e) FINDING OF COURT TO INCLUDE CORRECT AMOUNT OF PAYMENT.—The decision of the court awarding damages in an action brought under subsection (a) shall include a finding of the correct amount which should have been reported in the information return.

[Sec. 7434(f)]

(f) INFORMATION RETURN.—For purposes of this section, the term "information return" means any statement described in section 6724(d)(1)(A).

Amendments

• **1996, Taxpayer Bill of Rights 2 (P.L. 104-168)**

P.L. 104-168, § 601(a):

Amended subchapter B of Chapter 76 by redesignating Code Sec. 7434 as Code Sec. 7435 and by inserting after Code Sec. 7433 a new Code Sec. 7434. **Effective** for fraudulent information returns filed after 7-30-96.

[Sec. 7435]

SEC. 7435. CIVIL DAMAGES FOR UNAUTHORIZED ENTICEMENT OF INFORMATION DISCLOSURE.

[Sec. 7435(a)]

(a) IN GENERAL.—If any officer or employee of the United States intentionally compromises the determination or collection of any tax due from an attorney, certified public accountant, or enrolled agent representing a taxpayer in exchange for information conveyed by the taxpayer to the attorney, certified public accountant, or enrolled agent for purposes of obtaining advice concerning the taxpayer's tax liability, such taxpayer may bring a civil action for damages against the United States in a district court of the United States. Such civil action shall be the exclusive remedy for recovering damages resulting from such actions.

[Sec. 7435(b)]

(b) DAMAGES.—In any action brought under subsection (a), upon a finding of liability on the part of the defendant, the defendant shall be liable to the plaintiff in an amount equal to the lesser of $500,000 or the sum of—

(1) actual, direct economic damages sustained by the plaintiff as a proximate result of the information disclosure, and

(2) the costs of the action.

Damages shall not include the taxpayer's liability for any civil or criminal penalties, or other losses attributable to incarceration or the imposition of other criminal sanctions.

[Sec. 7435(c)]

(c) PAYMENT AUTHORITY.—Claims pursuant to this section shall be payable out of funds appropriated under section 1304 of title 31, United States Code.

[Sec. 7435(d)]

(d) PERIOD FOR BRINGING ACTION.—Notwithstanding any other provision of law, an action to enforce liability created under this section may be brought without regard to the amount in controversy and may be brought only within 2 years after the date the actions creating such liability would have been discovered by exercise of reasonable care.

[Sec. 7435(e)]

(e) MANDATORY STAY.—Upon a certification by the Commissioner or the Commissioner's delegate that there is an ongoing investigation or prosecution of the taxpayer, the district court before which an action under this section is pending shall stay all proceedings with respect to such action pending the conclusion of the investigation or prosecution.

[Sec. 7435(f)]

(f) CRIME-FRAUD EXCEPTION.—Subsection (a) shall not apply to information conveyed to an attorney, certified public accountant, or enrolled agent for the purpose of perpetrating a fraud or crime.

Amendments

• **1996, Taxpayer Bill of Rights 2 (P.L. 104-168)**

P.L. 104-168, § 601(a):

Amended subchapter B of Chapter 76 by redesignating Code Sec. 7434 as Code Sec. 7435. **Effective** for fraudulent information returns filed after 7-30-96.

P.L. 104-168, § 1203(a):

Amended subchapter B of chapter 76, as amended by Act Sec. 601(a), by redesignating Code Sec. 7435 as Code Sec. 7436 and by inserting after Code Sec. 7434 a new Code Sec. 7435. **Effective** for actions after 7-30-96.

[Sec. 7436]

SEC. 7436. PROCEEDINGS FOR DETERMINATION OF EMPLOYMENT STATUS.

[Sec. 7436(a)]

(a) CREATION OF REMEDY.—If, in connection with an audit of any person, there is an actual controversy involving a determination by the Secretary as part of an examination that—

(1) one or more individuals performing services for such person are employees of such person for purposes of subtitle C, or

(2) such person is not entitled to the treatment under subsection (a) of section 530 of the Revenue Act of 1978 with respect to such an individual,

upon the filing of an appropriate pleading, the Tax Court may determine whether such a determination by the Secretary is correct and the proper amount of employment tax under such determination. Any such redetermination by the Tax Court shall have the force and effect of a decision of the Tax Court and shall be reviewable as such.

Amendments

• **2000, Community Renewal Tax Relief Act of 2000 (P.L. 106-554)**

P.L. 106-554, § 314(f):

Amended Code Sec. 7436(a) by inserting before the period at the end of the first sentence "and the proper amount of employment tax under such determination".

Effective as if included in the provision of P.L. 105-34 to which it relates [effective 8-5-97.—CCH].

PROCEEDINGS BY TAXPAYERS

[Sec. 7436(b)]

(b) LIMITATIONS.—

(1) PETITIONER.—A pleading may be filed under this section only by the person for whom the services are performed.

(2) TIME FOR FILING ACTION.—If the Secretary sends by certified or registered mail notice to the petitioner of a determination by the Secretary described in subsection (a), no proceeding may be initiated under this section with respect to such determination unless the pleading is filed before the 91st day after the date of such mailing.

(3) NO ADVERSE INFERENCE FROM TREATMENT WHILE ACTION IS PENDING.—If, during the pendency of any proceeding brought under this section, the petitioner changes his treatment for employment tax purposes of any individual whose employment status as an employee is involved in such proceeding (or of any individual holding a substantially similar position) to treatment as an employee, such change shall not be taken into account in the Tax Court's determination under this section.

[Sec. 7436(c)]

(c) SMALL CASE PROCEDURES.—

(1) IN GENERAL.—At the option of the petitioner, concurred in by the Tax Court or a division thereof before the hearing of the case, proceedings under this section may (notwithstanding the provisions of section 7453) be conducted subject to the rules of evidence, practice, and procedure applicable under section 7463 if the amount of employment taxes placed in dispute is $50,000 or less for each calendar quarter involved.

(2) FINALITY OF DECISIONS.—A decision entered in any proceeding conducted under this subsection shall not be reviewed in any other court and shall not be treated as a precedent for any other case not involving the same petitioner and the same determinations.

(3) CERTAIN RULES TO APPLY.—Rules similar to the rules of the last sentence of subsection (a), and subsections (c), (d), and (e), of section 7463 shall apply to proceedings conducted under this subsection.

Amendments

• **1998, IRS Restructuring and Reform Act of 1998 (P.L. 105-206)**

P.L. 105-206, §3103(b)(1):

Amended Code Sec. 7436(c)(1) by striking "$10,000" and inserting "$50,000". **Effective** for proceedings commenced after 7-22-98.

[Sec. 7436(d)]

(d) SPECIAL RULES.—

(1) RESTRICTIONS ON ASSESSMENT AND COLLECTION PENDING ACTION, ETC.—The principles of subsections (a), (b), (c), (d), and (f) of section 6213, section 6214(a), section 6215, section 6503(a), section 6512, and section 7481 shall apply to proceedings brought under this section in the same manner as if the Secretary's determination described in subsection (a) were a notice of deficiency.

(2) AWARDING OF COSTS AND CERTAIN FEES.—Section 7430 shall apply to proceedings brought under this section.

[Sec. 7436(e)]

(e) EMPLOYMENT TAX.—The term "employment tax" means any tax imposed by subtitle C.

Amendments

• **1997, Taxpayer Relief Act of 1997 (P.L. 105-34)**

P.L. 105-34, §1454(a):

Amended subchapter B of chapter 76 by redesignating Code Sec. 7436 as Code Sec. 7437 and by inserting after Code Sec. 7435 a new Code Sec. 7436. **Effective** 8-5-97.

[Sec. 7437]

SEC. 7437. CROSS REFERENCES.

(1) For determination of amount of any tax, additions to tax, etc., in title 11 cases, see section 505 of title 11 of the United States Code.

(2) For exclusion of tax liability from discharge in cases under title 11 of the United States Code, see section 523 of such title 11.

(3) For recognition of tax liens in cases under title 11 of the United States Code, see sections 545 and 724 of such title 11.

(4) For collection of taxes in connection with plans for individuals with regular income in cases under title 11 of the United States Code, see section 1328 of such title 11.

(5) For provisions permitting the United States to be made party defendant in a proceeding in a State court for the foreclosure of a lien upon real estate where the United States may have claim upon the premises involved, see section 2410 of Title 28 of the United States Code.

(6) For priority of lien of the United States in case of insolvency, see section 3713(a) of title 31, United States Code.

(7) For interest on judgments for overpayments, see section 2411(a) of Title 28 of the United States Code.

(8) For review of a Tax Court decision, see section 7482.

(9) For statute prohibiting suits to replevy property taken under revenue laws, see section 2463 of Title 28 of the United States Code.

Amendments

• **1997, Taxpayer Relief Act of 1997 (P.L. 105-34)**

P.L. 105-34, §1454(a):

Amended subchapter B of chapter 76 by redesignating Code Sec. 7436 as Code Sec. 7437. **Effective** 8-5-97.

• **1996, Taxpayer Bill of Rights 2 (P.L. 104-168)**

P.L. 104-168, §1203(a):

Amended subchapter B of chapter 76, as amended by Act Sec. 601(a), by redesignating Code Sec. 7435 as Code Sec. 7436. **Effective** for actions after 7-30-96.

• **1988, Technical and Miscellaneous Revenue Act of 1988 (P.L. 100-647)**

P.L. 100-647, §6241(a):

Redesignated section 7433 as section 7434. **Effective** for actions by officers or employees of the Internal Revenue Service after 11-10-88.

• **1982 (P.L. 97-258)**

P.L. 97-258, §3(f)(14):

Amended Code Sec. 7430[2](6) by striking out "R.S. 3466 (31 U.S.C. 191)" and substituting "section 3713(a) of title 31, United States Code". Effective 9-13-82.

• **1982, Tax Equity and Fiscal Responsibility Act of 1982 (P.L. 97-248)**

P.L. 97-248, §292(a):

Redesignated Code Sec. 7430 as Code Sec. 7431. See, also, the amendment note for P.L. 97-248, Act Sec. 292(a), following Code Sec. 7430.

P.L. 97-248, §357(a):

Redesignated Code Sec. 7431 as Code Sec. 7432. See, also, the amendment note for P.L. 97-248, Act Sec. 292(a), following Code Sec. 7431.

• **1980, Bankruptcy Tax Act of 1980 (P.L. 96-589)**

P.L. 96-589, §6(d)(1), 6(i)(13):

Amended Code Sec. 7430 by striking out paragraphs (1), (2), and (3) and (4) and inserting in lieu thereof new paragraphs (1), (2), (3) and (4). **Effective** 10-1-79, but inapplicable to any proceeding under the Bankruptcy Act commenced before that date. Prior to amendment, Code Sec. 7430, paragraphs (1), (2), and (3) and (4) provided:

"(1) For exclusion of tax liability from discharge in bankruptcy, see section 17 of the Bankruptcy Act, as amended (11 U.S.C. 35).

(2) For limit on amount allowed in bankruptcy proceedings on debts owing to the United States, see section 57(j) of the Bankruptcy Act, as amended (11 U.S.C. 93).

JUDICIAL PROCEEDINGS—TAX COURT

(3) For recognition of tax liens in proceedings under the Bankruptcy Act, see section 67(b) and (c) of that act, as amended (11 U.S.C. 107).

(4) For collection of taxes in connection with wage earners' plans in bankruptcy courts, see section 680 of the Bankruptcy Act, as added June 22, 1938 (11 U.S.C. 1080)."

• **1976, Tax Reform Act of 1976 (P.L. 94-455)**

P.L. 94-455, §1203(b):

Redesignated former Code Sec. 7427 as Sec. 7428. **Effective** for documents prepared after 12-31-76.

P.L. 94-455, §1906(a)(45):

Amended former Code Sec. 7428 by striking out "52 Stat. 851;" from paragraph (1), "52 Stat. 867;" from paragraph (2), "52 Stat. 876-877;" from paragraph (3), and "52 Stat. 938;" from paragraph (4). **Effective** 2-1-77.

P.L. 94-455, §1306(a):

Redesignated former Code Sec. 7428 as 7430. For the **effective** date, see Act Sec. 1306(c), below.

P.L. 94-455, §1306(c), provides:

(c) EFFECTIVE DATE.—The amendments made by this section shall apply with respect to pleadings filed with the United States Tax Court, the district court of the United States for the District of Columbia, or the United States Court of Claims more than 6 months after the date of the enactment of this Act but only with respect to determination (or requests for determinations) made after January 1, 1976.

• **1966, Federal Tax Lien Act of 1966 (P.L. 89-719)**

P.L. 89-719, §109:

Redesignated Code Sec. 7425 as Code Sec. 7427. **Effective**, generally, after 11-2-66. However, see the amendment note for Code Sec. 6323 for exceptions to this **effective** date.

Subchapter C—The Tax Court

Part I.   Organization and jurisdiction.
Part II.   Procedure.
Part III.   Miscellaneous provisions.
Part IV.   Declaratory judgments.

PART I—ORGANIZATION AND JURISDICTION

Sec. 7441.   Status.
Sec. 7442.   Jurisdiction.
Sec. 7443.   Membership.
Sec. 7443A.   Special trial judges.
Sec. 7444.   Organization.
Sec. 7445.   Offices.
Sec. 7446.   Times and places of sessions.
Sec. 7447.   Retirement.
Sec. 7447A.   Retirement for special trial judges.
Sec. 7448.   Annuities to surviving spouses and dependent children of judges and special trial judges.

[Sec. 7441]

SEC. 7441. STATUS.

There is hereby established, under article I of the Constitution of the United States, a court of record to be known as the United States Tax Court. The members of the Tax Court shall be the chief judge and the judges of the Tax Court. The Tax Court is not an agency of, and shall be independent of, the executive branch of the Government.

Amendments

• **2015, Protecting Americans from Tax Hikes Act of 2015 (P.L. 114-113)**

P.L. 114-113, §441, Div. Q:

Amended Code Sec. 7441 by adding at the end a new sentence. **Effective** 12-18-2015.

• **1969, Tax Reform Act of 1969 (P.L. 91-172)**

P.L. 91-172, §951:

Amended Code Sec. 7441. **Effective** 12-30-69. Prior to amendment, Code Sec. 7441 read as follows:

The Board of Tax Appeals shall be continued as an independent agency in the Executive Branch of the Government, and shall be known as the Tax Court of the United States. The members thereof shall be known as the chief judge and the judges of the Tax Court.

P.L. 91-172, §961, provides:

The United States Tax Court established under the amendment made by section 951 [of P.L. 91-172] is a continuation of the Tax Court of the United States as it existed prior to the date of enactment of this Act [December 30, 1969], the judges of the Tax Court of the United States immediately prior to the date of enactment of this Act shall become the judges of the United States Tax Court upon the enactment of this Act, and no loss of rights or powers, interruption or jurisdiction, or prejudice to matters pending in the Tax Court of the United States before the date of enactment of this Act shall result from the enactment of this Act [P.L. 91-172].

[Sec. 7442]

SEC. 7442. JURISDICTION.

The Tax Court and its divisions shall have such jurisdiction as is conferred on them by this title, by chapters 1, 2, 3, and 4 of the Internal Revenue Code of 1939, by title II and title III of the Revenue Act of 1926 (44 Stat. 10-87), or by laws enacted subsequent to February 26, 1926.

[Sec. 7443]

SEC. 7443. MEMBERSHIP.

[Sec. 7443(a)]

(a) NUMBER.—The Tax Court shall be composed of 19 members.

Amendments

• **1980 (P.L. 96-439)**

P.L. 96-439, §1(a):

Amended Code Sec. 7443 by striking out "16" and substituting "19". **Effective** 2-1-81.

[Sec. 7443(b)]

(b) APPOINTMENT.—Judges of the Tax Court shall be appointed by the President, by and with the advice and consent of the Senate, solely on the grounds of fitness to perform the duties of the office.

Sec. 7441

JUDICIAL PROCEEDINGS—TAX COURT

Amendments

• **1980 (P.L. 96-439)**

P.L. 96-439, §1(b):

Amended Code Sec. 7443(b) by striking out the last sentence. **Effective** 2-1-81. Prior to being stricken, the last sentence of Code Sec. 7443(b) read as follows:

"No individual shall be a judge of the Tax Court unless he is appointed to that office before attaining the age of 65."

• **1969, Tax Reform Act of 1969 (P.L. 91-172)**

P.L. 91-172, §952(a):

Amended Code Sec. 7443(b) by adding the second sentence. **Effective** for judges appointed after 12-31-69.

[Sec. 7443(c)]

(c) SALARY.—

(1) Each judge shall receive salary at the same rate and in the same installments as judges of the district courts of the United States.

(2) For rate of salary and frequency of installment see section 135, title 28, United States Code, and section 5505, title 5, United States Code.

Amendments

• **1969, Tax Reform Act of 1969 (P.L. 91-172)**

P.L. 91-172, §953:

Amended Code Sec. 7443(c). **Effective** 12-30-69. Prior to amendment, subsection (c) read as follows:

(c) SALARY.—Each judge shall receive salary at the rate of $30,000 per annum, to be paid in monthly installments.

• **1964, Government Employees Salary Act of 1964 (P.L. 88-426)**

P.L. 88-426, §402(i):

Substituted "$30,000" for "$22,500" in Sec. 7443(c). **Effective** 7-1-64.

• **1955 (P.L. 9, 84th Con.)**

P.L. 9, 84th Cong., 1st Sess., §1(h):

Substituted "$22,500" for "$15,000" in Sec. 7443(c). **Effective** 3-1-55.

[Sec. 7443(d)]

(d) EXPENSES FOR TRAVEL AND SUBSISTENCE.—Judges of the Tax Court shall receive necessary traveling expenses, and expenses actually incurred for subsistence while traveling on duty and away from their designated stations, subject to the same limitations in amount as are now or may hereafter be applicable to the United States Court of International Trade.

Amendments

• **1980, Customs Courts Act of 1980 (P.L. 96-417)**

P.L. 96-417, §601(10):

Amended Code Sec. 7443(d) by striking out "Customs Court" and inserting in lieu thereof "Court of International Trade". **Effective** 11-1-80.

[Sec. 7443(e)]

(e) TERM OF OFFICE.—The term of office of any judge of the Tax Court shall expire 15 years after he takes office.

Amendments

• **1969, Tax Reform Act of 1969 (P.L. 91-172)**

P.L. 91-172, §952(b):

Amended Code Sec. 7443(e). **Effective** 12-30-69, except that—

(1) the term of office being served by a judge of the Tax Court on that date shall expire on the date it would have expired under the law in effect on the day preceding the date of enactment of this Act; and

(2) a judge of the Tax Court on the date of enactment of this Act may be reappointed in the same manner as a judge of the Tax Court hereafter appointed.

Prior to amendment by P.L. 91-172, Code Sec. 7443(e) read as follows:

(e) TERM OF OFFICE.—The terms of office of all judges of the Tax Court shall expire 12 years after the expiration of the terms for which their predecessors were appointed; but any judge appointed to fill a vacancy occurring prior to the expiration of the term for which his predecessor was appointed shall be appointed only for the unexpired term of his predecessor.

[Sec. 7443(f)]

(f) REMOVAL FROM OFFICE.—Judges of the Tax Court may be removed by the President, after notice and opportunity for public hearing, for inefficiency, neglect of duty, or malfeasance in office, but for no other cause.

[Sec. 7443(g)]

(g) DISBARMENT OF REMOVED JUDGES.—A judge of the Tax Court removed from office in accordance with subsection (f) shall not be permitted at any time to practice before the Tax Court.

[Sec. 7443A]

SEC. 7443A. SPECIAL TRIAL JUDGES.

[Sec. 7443A(a)]

(a) APPOINTMENT.—The chief judge may, from time to time, appoint special trial judges who shall proceed under such rules and regulations as may be promulgated by the Tax Court.

[Sec. 7443A(b)]

(b) PROCEEDINGS WHICH MAY BE ASSIGNED TO SPECIAL TRIAL JUDGES.—The chief judge may assign—

(1) any declaratory judgment proceeding,

(2) any proceeding under section 7463,

(3) any proceeding where neither the amount of the deficiency placed in dispute (within the meaning of section 7463) nor the amount of any claimed overpayment exceeds $50,000,

(4) any proceeding under section 6320 or 6330,

(5) any proceeding under section 7436(c),

(6) any proceeding under section 7623(b)(4), and

(7) any other proceeding which the chief judge may designate,

to be heard by the special trial judges of the court.

Amendments

• **2006, Tax Relief and Health Care Act of 2006 (P.L. 109-432)**

P.L. 109-432, Division A, §406(a)(2)(A):

Amended Code Sec. 7443A(b) by striking "and" at the end of paragraph (5), by redesignating paragraph (6) as paragraph (7), and by inserting after paragraph (5) a new paragraph (6). **Effective** for information provided on or after 12-20-2006.

• **2006, Pension Protection Act of 2006 (P.L. 109-280)**

P.L. 109-280, §857(a):

Amended Code Sec. 7443A(b) by striking "and" at the end of paragraph (4), by redesignating paragraph (5) as paragraph (6), and by inserting after paragraph (4) a new paragraph (5). **Effective** for any proceeding under Code Sec. 7436(c) with respect

JUDICIAL PROCEEDINGS—TAX COURT

to which a decision has not become final (as determined under Code Sec. 7481) before 8-17-2006.

• **1998, IRS Restructuring and Reform Act of 1998 (P.L. 105-206)**

P.L. 105-206, §3103(b)(1):

Amended Code Sec. 7443A(b)(3) by striking "$10,000" and inserting "$50,000". **Effective** for proceedings commencing after 7-22-98.

[Sec. 7443A(c)]

(c) AUTHORITY TO MAKE COURT DECISIONS.—The court may authorize a special trial judge to make the decision of the court with respect to any proceeding described in paragraph (1), (2), (3), (4), (5), or (6) of subsection (b), subject to such conditions and review as the court may provide.

Amendments

• **2006, Tax Relief and Health Care Act of 2006 (P.L. 109-432)**

P.L. 109-432, Division A, §406(a)(2)(B):

Amended Code Sec. 7443A(c) by striking "or (5)" and inserting "(5), or (6)". **Effective** for information provided on or after 12-20-2006.

• **2006, Pension Protection Act of 2006 (P.L. 109-280)**

P.L. 109-280, §857(b):

Amended Code Sec. 7443A(c) by striking "or 4" and inserting "(4), or (5)". **Effective** for any proceeding under Code Sec. 7436(c) with respect to which a decision has not become final (as determined under Code Sec. 7481) before 8-17-2006.

P.L. 105-206, §3401(c)(1) (as amended by P.L. 105-277, §4002(e)(1)):

Amended Code Sec. 7443A(b) by striking "and" at the end of paragraph (3), by redesignating paragraph (4) as paragraph (5), and by inserting after paragraph (3) a new paragraph (4). **Effective** for collection actions initiated after the date which is 180 days after 7-22-98.

• **1998, IRS Restructuring and Reform Act of 1998 (P.L. 105-206)**

P.L. 105-206, §3401(c)(2) (as amended by P.L. 105-277, §4002(e)(2)):

Amended Code Sec. 7443A(c) by striking "or (3)" and inserting "(3), or (4)". **Effective** for collection actions initiated after the date which is 180 days after 7-22-98.

[Sec. 7443A(d)]

(d) SALARY.—Each special trial judge shall receive salary—

(1) at a rate equal to 90 percent of the rate for judges of the Tax Court, and

(2) in the same installments as such judges.

[Sec. 7443A(e)]

(e) EXPENSES FOR TRAVEL AND SUBSISTENCE.—Subsection (d) of section 7443 shall apply to special trial judges subject to such rules and regulations as may be promulgated by the Tax Court.

Amendments

• **1986, Tax Reform Act of 1986 (P.L. 99-514)**

P.L. 99-514, §1556(a):

Amended Part I of subchapter C of chapter 76 by inserting after Code Sec. 7443 new Code Sec. 7443A. **Effective**, generally, 10-22-86. However, see Act Sec. 1556(c)(2) and (3), below.

P.L. 99-514, §1556(c)(2) and (3), provides:

(2) SALARY.—Subsection (d) of section 7443A of the Internal Revenue Code of 1954 (as added by this section) shall take effect on the 1st day of the 1st month beginning after the date of the enactment of this Act.

(3) NEW APPOINTMENTS NOT REQUIRED.—Nothing in the amendments made by this section shall be construed to require the reappointment of any individual serving as a special trial judge of the Tax Court on the day before the date of the enactment of this Act.

[Sec. 7443B—Repealed]

Amendments

• **2008, Worker, Retiree, and Employer Recovery Act of 2008 (P.L. 110-458)**

P.L. 110-458, §108(l):

Repealed Act Sec. 856 of the 2006 Act (P.L. 109-280) which added Code Sec. 7443B. Thus, Code Sec. 7443B is repealed. **Effective** as if included in the provision of the 2006 Act to which the amendment relates [**effective** 8-17-2006.—CCH]. Prior to repeal, Code Sec. 7443B read as follows:

SEC. 7443B. RECALL OF SPECIAL TRIAL JUDGES OF THE TAX COURT.

[Sec. 7443B(a)]

(a) RECALLING OF RETIRED SPECIAL TRIAL JUDGES.—Any individual who has retired pursuant to the applicable provisions of title 5, United States Code, upon reaching the age and service requirements established therein, may at or after retirement be called upon by the chief judge of the Tax Court to perform such judicial duties with the Tax Court as may be requested of such individual for any period or periods specified by the chief judge; except that in the case of any such individual—

(1) the aggregate of such periods in any 1 calendar year shall not (without such individual's consent) exceed 90 calendar days, and

(2) such individual shall be relieved of performing such duties during any period in which illness or disability precludes the performance of such duties.

Any act, or failure to act, by an individual performing judicial duties pursuant to this subsection shall have the same force and effect as if it were the act (or failure to act) of a special trial judge of the Tax Court.

[Sec. 7443B(b)]

(b) COMPENSATION.—For the year in which a period of recall occurs, the special trial judge shall receive, in addition to the annuity provided under the applicable provisions of title 5, United States Code, an amount equal to the difference between that annuity and the current salary of the office to which the special trial judge is recalled.

[Sec. 7443B(c)]

(c) RULEMAKING AUTHORITY.—The provisions of this section may be implemented under such rules as may be promulgated by the Tax Court.

Amendments

• **2006, Pension Protection Act of 2006 (P.L. 109-280)**

P.L. 109-280, §856(a):

Amended part I of subchapter C of chapter 76 by inserting after Code Sec. 7443A a new Code Sec. 7443B. **Effective** 8-17-2006.

[Sec. 7444]

SEC. 7444. ORGANIZATION.

[Sec. 7444(a)]

(a) SEAL.—The Tax Court shall have a seal which shall be judicially noticed.

[Sec. 7444(b)]

(b) DESIGNATION OF CHIEF JUDGE.—The Tax Court shall at least biennially designate a judge to act as chief judge.

[Sec. 7444(c)]

(c) DIVISIONS.—The chief judge may from time to time divide the Tax Court into divisions of one or more judges, assign the judges of the Tax Court thereto, and in case of a division of more than one judge, designate the chief thereof. If a division, as a result of a vacancy or the absence or inability of a judge assigned thereto to serve thereon, is composed of less than the number of judges designated for the division, the chief judge may assign other judges to the division or direct the division to proceed with the transaction of business without awaiting any additional assignment of judges thereto.

[Sec. 7444(d)]

(d) QUORUM.—A majority of the judges of the Tax Court or of any division thereof shall constitute a quorum for the transaction of the business of the Tax Court or of the division, respectively. A vacancy in the Tax Court or in any division thereof shall not impair the powers nor affect the duties of the Tax Court or division nor of the remaining judges of the Tax Court or division, respectively.

Sec. 7443A(c)

JUDICIAL PROCEEDINGS—TAX COURT

[Sec. 7445]

SEC. 7445. OFFICES.

The principal office of the Tax Court shall be in the District of Columbia, but the Tax Court or any of its divisions may sit at any place within the United States.

[Sec. 7446]

SEC. 7446. TIMES AND PLACES OF SESSIONS.

The times and places of the sessions of the Tax Court and of its divisions shall be prescribed by the chief judge with a view to securing reasonable opportunity to taxpayers to appear before the Tax Court or any of its divisions, with as little inconvenience and expense to taxpayers as is practicable.

[Sec. 7447]

SEC. 7447. RETIREMENT.

[Sec. 7447(a)]

(a) DEFINITIONS.—For purposes of this section—

(1) The term "Tax Court" means the United States Tax Court.

(2) The term "judge" means the chief judge or a judge of the Tax Court; but such term does not include any individual performing judicial duties pursuant to subsection (c).

(3) In any determination of length of service as judge there shall be included all periods (whether or not consecutive) during which an individual served as judge or as judge of the Tax Court of the United States, or as a member of the Board of Tax Appeals.

Amendments

• **1986, Tax Reform Act of 1986 (P.L. 99-514)**

P.L. 99-514, §1557(d)(1):

Amended Code Sec. 7447(a) by striking out paragraph (2) and by redesignating paragraphs (3) and (5) as paragraphs (2) and (3), respectively. **Effective** 10-22-86. However, for an exception see Act Sec. 1557(e)(2) following Code Sec. 7447(g). Prior to amendment, Code Sec. 7447(a)(2) read as follows:

(2) The term "Civil Service Commission" means the United States Civil Service Commission.

• **1969, Tax Reform Act of 1969 (P.L. 91-172)**

P.L. 91-172, §954(e)(1):

Repealed Code Sec. 7447(a)(4), but did not renumber (5). **Effective** 12-30-69. Prior to repeal, Sec. 7447(a)(4) read as follows:

(4) The term "Civil Service Retirement Act" means the Civil Service Retirement Act of May 29, 1930, as amended.

P.L. 91-172, §960(c):

Amended Code Sec. 7447(a)(1) by substituting the phrase "United States Tax Court" for the phrase "Tax Court of the United States". **Effective** 12-30-69.

P.L. 91-172, §960(d):

Amended Code Sec. 7447(a)(5) by substituting the phrase "or as judge of the Tax Court of the United States, or as a member of the Board of Tax Appeals." for the phrase "or as a member of the Board". **Effective** 12-30-69.

[Sec. 7447(b)]

(b) RETIREMENT.—

(1) Any judge shall retire upon attaining the age of 70.

(2) Any judge who meets the age and service requirements set forth in the following table may retire.

The judge has attained age:	And the years of service as a judge are at least:
65	15
66	14
67	13
68	12
69	11
70	10

(3) Any judge who is not reappointed following the expiration of the term of his office may retire upon the completion of such term, if (A) he has served as a judge of the Tax Court for 15 years or more and (B) not earlier than 9 months preceding the date of the expiration of the term of his office and not later than 6 months preceding such date, he advised the President in writing that he was willing to accept reappointment to the Tax Court.

(4) Any judge who becomes permanently disabled from performing his duties shall retire.

Section 8335(a) of title 5 of the United States Code (relating to automatic separation from the service) shall not apply in respect of judges. Any judge who retires shall be designated "senior judge".

Amendments

• **1986, Tax Reform Act of 1986 (P.L. 99-514)**

P.L. 99-514, §1557(a):

Amended Code Sec. 7447(b)(2). **Effective** 10-22-86. However, for an exception see Act Sec. 1557(e)(2) following Code Sec. 7447(g). Prior to amendment, Code Sec. 7447(b)(2) read as follows:

(2) Any judge who has attained the age of 65 may retire any time after serving as judge for 15 years or more.

• **1982, Miscellaneous Revenue Act of 1982 (P.L. 97-362)**

P.L. 97-362, §106(d):

Amended Code Sec. 7447(b) by adding at the end thereof "Any judge who retires shall be designated 'senior judge'." **Effective** with respect to petitions filed after 10-25-82.

• **1969, Tax Reform Act of 1969 (P.L. 91-172)**

P.L. 91-172, §954(a):

Amended Code Sec. 7447(b). **Effective** for—

(1) all judges of the Tax Court retiring on or after 12-30-69, and

(2) all individuals performing judicial duties pursuant to section 7447(c) or receiving retired pay pursuant to section 7447(d) on the day preceding 12-30-69.

Any individual who has served as a judge of the Tax Court for 18 years or more by the end of one year after December 30, 1969 may retire in accordance with the provisions of section 7447 of the Internal Revenue Code of 1954 as in effect on the day preceding December 30, 1969. Any individual who is a judge of the Tax Court on December 30, 1969, may retire under the provisions of section 7447 of such Code upon the completion of the term of his office, if he is not reappointed as a judge of the Tax Court and gives notice to the President within the time prescribed by section 7447(b) of such Code (or if his term expires within 6 months after December 30, 1969, gives notice to the President before the expiration of 3 months after December 30, 1969), and shall receive retired pay at a rate which bears the same ratio to the rate of the salary payable to a judge as the number of years he has served as a judge of the Tax Court bears to 15; except that the rate of such retired pay shall not exceed the rate of the salary of a judge of the Tax Court. For purposes of the preceding sentence the years of service as a judge of the Tax Court shall be determined in the manner set forth in section 7447(d) of such Code.

Prior to amendment by P.L. 91-172, Code Sec. 7447(b) read as follows:

(b) RETIREMENT.—

(1) Any judge who has served as judge for 18 years or more may retire at any time.

(2) Any judge who has served as judge for 10 years or more and has attained the age of 70 shall retire not later than the close of the third month beginning after whichever of the following months is the latest.

(A) the month in which he attained age 70;

JUDICIAL PROCEEDINGS—TAX COURT

(B) the month in which he completed 10 years of service as judge; or

(C) August 1953.

Section 2(a) of the Civil Service Retirement Act (relating to automatic separation from the service) shall not apply in respect of judges.

[Sec. 7447(c)]

(c) RECALLING OF RETIRED JUDGES.—At or after his retirement, any individual who has elected to receive retired pay under subsection (d) may be called upon by the chief judge of the Tax Court to perform such judicial duties with the Tax Court as may be requested of him for any period or periods specified by the chief judge; except that in the case of any such individual—

(1) the aggregate of such periods in any one calendar year shall not (without his consent) exceed 90 calendar days; and

(2) he shall be relieved of performing such duties during any period in which illness or disability precludes the performance of such duties.

Any act, or failure to act, by an individual performing judicial duties pursuant to this subsection shall have the same force and effect as if it were the act (or failure to act) of a judge of the Tax Court; but any such individual shall not be counted as a judge of the Tax Court for purposes of section 7443(a). Any individual who is performing judicial duties pursuant to this subsection shall be paid the same compensation (in lieu of retired pay) and allowances for travel and other expenses as a judge.

Amendments

• **1971 (P.L. 92-41)**

P.L. 92-41, §4(a):

Amended the first sentence of Code Sec. 7447(c) by substituting "At or after his retirement, any individual who has elected to receive" for "Any individual who is receiving". **Effective** as if included in the Internal Revenue Code of 1954 on the date of its enactment.

[Sec. 7447(d)]

(d) RETIRED PAY.—Any individual who—

(1) retires under paragraph (1), (2), or (3) of subsection (b) and elects under subsection (e) to receive retired pay under this subsection shall receive retired pay during any period at a rate which bears the same ratio to the rate of the salary payable to a judge during such period as the number of years he has served as judge bears to 10; except that the rate of such retired pay shall not be more than the rate of such salary for such period; or

(2) retires under paragraph (4) of subsection (b) and elects under subsection (e) to receive retired pay under this subsection shall receive retired pay during any period at a rate—

(A) equal to the rate of the salary payable to a judge during such period if before he retired he had served as a judge not less than 10 years; or

(B) one-half of the rate of the salary payable to a judge during such period if before he retired he had served as a judge less than 10 years.

Such retired pay shall begin to accrue on the day following the day on which his salary as judge ceases to accrue, and shall continue to accrue during the remainder of his life. Retired pay under this subsection shall be paid in the same manner as the salary of a judge. In computing the rate of the retired pay under paragraph (1) of this subsection for any individual who is entitled thereto, that portion of the aggregate number of years he has served as a judge which is a fractional part of 1 year shall be eliminated if it is less than 6 months, or shall be counted as a full year if it is 6 months or more. In computing the rate of the retired pay under paragraph (1) of this subsection for any individual who is entitled thereto, any period during which such individual performs services under subsection (c) on a substantially full-time basis shall be treated as a period during which he has served as a judge.

Amendments

• **1988, Technical and Miscellaneous Revenue Act of 1988 (P.L. 100-647)**

P.L. 100-647, §1015(k)(1):

Amended Code Sec. 7447(d) by adding at the end thereof a new sentence. **Effective** for purposes of determining the amount of retired pay for months beginning after 11-10-88, regardless of when the services under Code Sec. 7447(c) were performed.

• **1969, Tax Reform Act of 1969 (P.L. 91-172)**

P.L. 91-172, §954(b):

Amended Code Sec. 7447(d). **Effective** for judges retiring on or after 12-30-69 and to persons performing judicial duties or receiving retired pay on 12-29-69. However, see fuller statement of effective date under Code Sec. 7447(b). Prior to amendment, Code Sec. 7447(d) read as follows:

(d) RETIRED PAY.—Any individual who after August 7, 1953—

(1) ceases to be a judge by reason of paragraph (2) of subsection (b), or ceases to be a judge after having served as judge for 18 years or more; and

(2) elects under subsection (e) to receive retired pay under this subsection,

shall receive retired pay during any peirod at a rate which bears the same ratio to the rate of the salary payable to a judge during such period as the number of years he has served as judge bears to 24; except that the rate of such retired pay shall not be less than one-half of the rate of such salary for such period and not more than the rate of such salary for such period. Such retired pay shall begin to accrue on the day following the day on which his salary as judge ceases to accrue, and shall continue to accrue during the remainder of his life. Retired pay under this subsection shall be paid in the same manner as the salary of a judge. In computing the rate of the retired pay under this subsection for any individual who is entitled thereto, that portion of the aggregate number of years he has served as a judge which is a fractional part of 1 year shall be eliminated if it is less than 6 months, or shall be counted as a full year if it is 6 months or more.

• **1966 (P.L. 89-354)**

P.L. 89-354, §[1]:

Amended Code Sec. 7447(d) by substituting "during any period at a rate which bears the same ratio to the rate of the salary payable to a judge during such period" for "at a rate which bears the same ratio to the rate of the salary payable to him as judge at the time he ceases to be a judge" and by inserting "for such period" immediately after "the rate of such salary" each place it appears. **Effective** on or after the first day of the first calendar month which begins after 2-2-66.

[Sec. 7447(e)]

(e) ELECTION TO RECEIVE RETIRED PAY.—Any judge may elect to receive retired pay under subsection (d). Such an election—

(1) may be made only while an individual is a judge (except that in the case of an individual who fails to be reappointed as judge at the expiration of a term of office, it may be made at any time before the day after the day on which his successor takes office);

(2) once made, shall be irrevocable;

(3) in the case of any judge other than the chief judge, shall be made by filing notice thereof in writing with the chief judge; and

(4) in the case of the chief judge, shall be made by filing notice thereof in writing with the Office of Personnel Management.

The chief judge shall transmit to the Office of Personnel Management a copy of each notice filed with him under this subsection.

Amendments

• **1986, Tax Reform Act of 1986 (P.L. 99-514)**

P.L. 99-514, §1557(d)(2):

Amended Code Sec. 7447(e) by striking out "Civil Service Commission" each place it appears and inserting in lieu thereof "Office of Personnel Management". **Effective** 10-22-86. However, for an exception see Act Sec. 1557(e)(2) following Code Sec. 7447(g).

[Sec. 7447(f)]

(f) RETIRED PAY AFFECTED IN CERTAIN CASES.—In the case of an individual for whom an election to receive retired pay under subsection (d) is in effect—

(1) 1-YEAR FORFEITURE FOR FAILURE TO PERFORM JUDICIAL DUTIES.—If such individual during any calendar year fails to perform judicial duties required of him by subsection (c), such individual shall forfeit all rights to retired pay under subsection (d) for the 1-year period which begins on the 1st day on which he so fails to perform such duties.

(2) PERMANENT FORFEITURE OF RETIRED PAY WHERE CERTAIN NON-GOVERNMENT SERVICES PERFORMED.—If such individual performs (or supervises or directs the performance of) legal or accounting services in the field of Federal taxation for his client, his employer, or any of his employer's clients, such individual shall forfeit all rights to retired pay under subsection (d) for all periods beginning on or after the 1st day on which he engages in any such activity. The preceding sentence shall not apply to any civil office or employment under the Government of the United States.

(3) SUSPENSION OF RETIRED PAY DURING PERIOD OF COMPENSATED SERVICE.—If such individual accepts compensation for civil office or employment under the Government of the United States (other than the performance of judicial duties pursuant to subsection (c)), such individual shall forfeit all rights to retired pay under subsection (d) for the period for which such compensation is received.

(4) FORFEITURES OF RETIRED PAY UNDER PARAGRAPHS (1) AND (2) NOT TO APPLY WHERE INDIVIDUAL ELECTS TO FREEZE AMOUNT OF RETIRED PAY.—

(A) IN GENERAL.—If any individual makes an election under this paragraph—

(i) paragraphs (1) and (2) (and subsection (c)) shall not apply to such individual beginning on the date such election takes effect, and

(ii) the retired pay under subsection (d) payable to such individual for periods beginning on or after the date such election takes effect shall be equal to the retired pay to which such individual would be entitled without regard to this clause at the time of such election.

(B) ELECTION.—An election under this paragraph—

(i) may be made by an individual only if such individual meets the age and service requirements for retirement under paragraph (2) of subsection (b),

(ii) may be made only during the period during which the individual may make an election to receive retired pay or while the individual is receiving retired pay, and

(iii) shall be made in the same manner as the election to receive retired pay.

Such an election, once it takes effect, shall be irrevocable.

(C) WHEN ELECTION TAKES EFFECT.—Any election under this paragraph shall take effect on the 1st day of the 1st month following the month in which the election is made.

Amendments

• **1986, Tax Reform Act of 1986 (P.L. 99-514)**

P.L. 99-514, §1557(b):

Amended Code Sec. 7447(f). **Effective** 10-22-86. However, for an exception see Act Sec. 1557(e)(2) following Code Sec. 7447(g). Prior to amendment, Code Sec. 7447(f) read as follows:

(f) INDIVIDUALS RECEIVING RETIRED PAY TO BE AVAILABLE FOR RECALL.—Any individual who has elected to receive retired pay under subsection (d) who thereafter—

(1) accepts civil office or employment under the Government of the United States (other than the performance of judicial duties pursuant to subsection (c)); or

(2) performs (or supervises or directs the performance of) legal or accounting services in the field of Federal taxation or in the field of the renegotiation of Federal contracts for his client, his employer, or any of his employer's clients,

shall forfeit all rights to retired pay under subsection (d) for all periods beginning on or after the first day on which he accepts such office or employment or engages in any activity described in paragraph (2). Any individual who has elected to receive retired pay under subsection (d) who thereafter during any calendar year fails to perform judicial duties required of him by subsection (c) shall forfeit all rights to retired pay under subsection (d) for the 1-year period which begins on the first day on which he so fails to perform such duties.

[Sec. 7447(g)]

(g) COORDINATION WITH CIVIL SERVICE RETIREMENT.—

(1) GENERAL RULE.—Except as otherwise provided in this subsection, the provisions of the civil service retirement laws (including the provisions relating to the deduction and withholding of amounts from basic pay, salary, and compensation) shall apply in respect of service as a judge (together with other service as an officer or employee to whom such civil service retirement laws apply) as if this section had not been enacted.

(2) EFFECT OF ELECTING RETIRED PAY.—In the case of any individual who has filed an election to receive retired pay under subsection (d)—

(A) no annuity or other payment shall be payable to any person under the civil service retirement laws with respect to any service performed by such individual (whether performed before or after such election is filed and whether performed as judge or otherwise);

(B) no deduction for purposes of the Civil Service Retirement and Disability Fund shall be made from retired pay payable to him under subsection (d) or from any other salary, pay, or compensation payable to him, for any period beginning after the day on which such election is filed; and

(C) such individual shall be paid the lump-sum credit computed under sections 8331(8) and 8401(19) of title 5 of the United States Code upon making application therefor with the Office of Personnel Management.

Amendments

• **2022, SECURE 2.0 Act of 2022 (P.L. 117-328)**

P.L. 117-328, §701(c)(1)(A):

Amended Code Sec. 7447(g)(2)(C) by striking "section 8331(8)" and inserting "sections 8331(8) and 8401(19)". **Effective** 12-29-2022.

• **1986, Tax Reform Act of 1986 (P.L. 99-514)**

P.L. 99-514, §1557(d)(2):

Amended Code Sec. 7447(g)(2)(C) by striking out "Civil Service Commission" and inserting in lieu thereof "Office of Personnel Management". **Effective**, generally, 10-22-86. However, for an exception see Act Sec. 1557(e)(2), below.

P.L. 99-514, §1557(e)(2), provides:

(2) FORFEITURE OF RETIRED PAY.—The amendments made by this section shall not apply to any individual who, before the date of the enactment of this Act, forfeited his rights to retired pay under section 7447(d) of the Internal Revenue Code of 1954 by reason of the 1st sentence of section 7447(f) of such Code (as in effect on the day before such date).

• **1969, Tax Reform Act of 1969 (P.L. 91-172)**

P.L. 91-172, §954(c):

Amended Code Sec. 7447(g) by substituting new paragraph (2) for paragraphs (2)-(4). **Effective** 12-30-69. Prior to amendment by P.L. 91-172, Sec. 7447(g)(2)-(4) read as follows:

(2) EFFECT OF ELECTING RETIRED PAY.—In the case of any individual who has filed an election to receive retired pay under subsection (d) and who has not filed a waiver under paragraph (3) of this subsection—

(A) he shall not be entitled to any annuity under section 1, 2, 3A, 6, or 7 of the Civil Service Retirement Act for any period beginning on or after the day on which he files such election;

(B) no amount shall be returned to him under section 7(a) of such Act;

(C) subsections (b) and (c) of section 4 of such Act, and subsection (c) of section 12 of such Act, shall apply in respect of such individual as if he were retiring or had retired under section 1 of such Act on the date on which his retired pay under subsection (d) of this section began to accrue; except that—

(i) the amount of any annuity payable to a survivor of such individual under subsection (b) or (c) of such section 4 or under subsection (c) of such section 12 shall be based on a life annuity for such individual computed as provided in subsection (a) of such section 4, and

(ii) if such individual makes the election provided by subsection (b) or (c) of such section 4, his retired pay under subsection (d) of this section shall be reduced by the amount by which a life annuity computed as provided in subsection (a) of such section 4 would be reduced;

(D) in computing the aggregate amount of the annuity paid for purposes of section 12(g) of such Act, any retired pay which has accrued under subsection (d) of this section (including any such retired pay forfeited under subsection (f)) shall be included as if it were an annuity payable to him under such Act; and

(E) no deduction for purposes of the civil service retirement and disability fund shall be made from the retired pay payable to him under subsection (d) of this section, or from any other salary, pay, or compensation payable to him, for any period after the date on which such retired pay began to accrue.

(3) WAIVER OF CIVIL SERVICE BENEFITS.—

JUDICIAL PROCEEDINGS—TAX COURT

(A) Any individual who has elected to receive retired pay under subsection (d) of this section may, (at any time thereafter during the period prescribed by subsection (e)(1)) waive all benefits under the Civil Service Retirement Act. Such a waiver—

(i) once made, shall be irrevocable, and

(ii) shall be made in the same manner as is provided for an election by such individual under subsection (e). The chief judge shall transmit to the Civil Service Commission a copy of each notice of waiver filed with him under this paragraph.

(B) In the case of any individual who has made a waiver under this paragraph—

(i) no annuity shall be payable to any person under the Civil Service Retirement Act with respect to any service performed by such individual (whether performed before or after such waiver is filed and whether performed as judge or otherwise);

(ii) no deduction shall be made from any salary, pay, or compensation of such individual for purposes of the civil service retirement and disability fund for any period beginning after the day on which such waiver is filed;

(iii) except as provided in clause (iv), no refund shall be made under the Civil Service Retirement Act of any amount credited to the account of such individual or of any interest on any amount so credited;

(iv) additional sums voluntarily deposited by such individual under the second paragraph of section 10 of the Civil Service Retirement Act shall be promptly refunded, together with interest on such additional sums at 3 percent per annum (compounded on December 31 of each year) to the day of such filing; and

(v) subsections (e) and (g) of section 12 of the Civil Service Retirement Act shall not apply.

(4) EMPLOYEES' COMPENSATION.—

The fourth and sixth paragraphs of section 6 of the Civil Service Retirement Act shall apply in respect of retired pay accruing under subsection (d) of this section as if such retired pay were an annuity payable under such Act.

• **1969, Tax Reform Act of 1969 (P.L. 91-172)**

P.L. 91-172, § 954(e)(2):

Amended Code Sec. 7447(g)(1) by substituting the phrase "civil service retirement laws" for "Civil Service Retirement Act" and by substituting the phrase "such civil service retirement laws apply" for "such Act applies." **Effective** 12-30-69.

[Sec. 7447(h)]

(h) RETIREMENT FOR DISABILITY.—

(1) Any judge who becomes permanently disabled from performing his duties shall certify to the President his disability in writing. If the chief judge retires for disability, his retirement shall not take effect until concurred in by the President. If any other judge retires for disability, he shall furnish to the President a certificate of disability signed by the chief judge.

(2) Whenever any judge who becomes permanently disabled from performing his duties does not retire and the President finds that such judge is unable to discharge efficiently all the duties of his office by reason of permanent mental or physical disability and that the appointment of an additional judge is necessary for the efficient dispatch of business, the President shall declare such judge to be retired.

Amendments

• **1969, Tax Reform Act of 1969 (P.L. 91-172)**

P.L. 91-172, § 954(d):

Added Code Sec. 7447(h). **Effective** for judges retiring on or after 12-30-69, and to persons performing judicial duties or receiving retired pay on 12-29-69. However, see fuller statement of controlling effective dates under Code Sec. 7447(b).

[Sec. 7447(i)]

(i) REVOCATION OF ELECTION TO RECEIVE RETIRED PAY.—

(1) IN GENERAL.—Notwithstanding subsection (e)(2), an individual who has filed an election to receive retired pay under subsection (d) may revoke such election at any time before the first day on which retired pay (or compensation under subsection (c) in lieu of retired pay) would (but for such revocation) begin to accrue with respect to such individual.

(2) MANNER OF REVOKING.—Any revocation under this subsection shall be made by filing a notice thereof in writing with the Office of Personnel Management. The Office of Personnel Management shall transmit to the chief judge a copy of each notice filed under this subsection.

(3) EFFECT OF REVOCATION.—In the case of any revocation under this subsection—

(A) for purposes of this section, the individual shall be treated as not having filed an election to receive retired pay under subsection (d),

(B) for purposes of section 7448—

(i) the individual shall be treated as not having filed an election under section 7448(b), and

(ii) section 7448(g) shall not apply, and the amount credited to such individual's account (together with interest at 3 percent per annum, compounded on December 31 of each year to the date on which the revocation is filed) shall be returned to such individual,

(C) no credit shall be allowed for any service as a judge of the Tax Court unless with respect to such service either there has been deducted and withheld the amount required by the civil service retirement laws or there has been deposited in the Civil Service Retirement and Disability Fund an amount equal to the amount so required, with interest,

(D) the Tax Court shall deposit in the Civil Service Retirement and Disability Fund an amount equal to the additional amount it would have contributed to such Fund but for the election under subsection (e), and

(E) if subparagraph (D) is complied with, service on the Tax Court shall be treated as service with respect to which deductions and contributions had been made during the period of service.

Amendments

• **2022, SECURE 2.0 Act of 2022 (P.L. 117-328)**

P.L. 117-328, § 701(c)(1)(B):

Amended Code Sec. 7447(i)(2) by striking "Civil Service Commission" both places it appears and inserting "Office of Personnel Management". **Effective** 12-29-2022.

• **2014, Tax Technical Corrections Act of 2014 (P.L. 113-295)**

P.L. 113-295, § 221(a)(115), Division A:

Amended Code Sec. 7447(i)(3)(B)(ii) by striking "at 4 percent per annum to December 31, 1947, and 3 percent per annum thereafter", and inserting "at 3 percent per annum". **Effective** generally 12-19-2014. For a special rule, see Act Sec. 221(b)(2), Division A, below.

P.L. 113-295, § 221(b)(2), Division A, provides:

(2) SAVINGS PROVISION.—If—

(A) any provision amended or repealed by the amendments made by this section applied to—

(i) any transaction occurring before the date of the enactment of this Act,

(ii) any property acquired before such date of enactment, or

(iii) any item of income, loss, deduction, or credit taken into account before such date of enactment, and

(B) the treatment of such transaction, property, or item under such provision would (without regard to the amendments or repeals made by this section) affect the liability for tax for periods ending after date of enactment, nothing in the amendments or repeals made by this section shall be construed to affect the treatment of such transaction, property, or item for purposes of determining liability for tax for periods ending after such date of enactment.

• **1978 (P.L. 95-472)**

P.L. 95-472, § 1:

Added Code Sec. 7447(i). **Effective** as provided in Act Sec. 2, below.

P.L. 95-472, § 2, provides:

"(a) The amendment made by the first section of this Act shall apply with respect to revocations made after October 17, 1978.

(b) Any individual who elects to revoke under section 7447(i) of the Internal Revenue Code of 1954 within one year after October 17, 1978, shall be treated as having the requisite current service for purposes of redepositing funds in the Civil Service Retirement and Disability Fund and for purposes of reviving creditable service under subchapter III of chapter 83 of title 5 of the United States Code."

JUDICIAL PROCEEDINGS—TAX COURT

[Sec. 7447(j)]

(j) THRIFT SAVINGS PLAN.—

(1) ELECTION TO CONTRIBUTE.—

(A) IN GENERAL.—A judge of the Tax Court may elect to contribute to the Thrift Savings Fund established by section 8437 of title 5, United States Code.

(B) PERIOD OF ELECTION.—An election may be made under this paragraph only during a period provided under section 8432(b) of title 5, United States Code, for individuals subject to chapter 84 of such title.

(2) APPLICABILITY OF TITLE 5 PROVISIONS.—Except as otherwise provided in this subsection, the provisions of subchapters III and VII of chapter 84 of title 5, United States Code, shall apply with respect to a judge who makes an election under paragraph (1).

(3) SPECIAL RULES.—

(A) AMOUNT CONTRIBUTED.—The amount contributed by a judge to the Thrift Savings Fund in any pay period shall not exceed the maximum percentage of such judge's basic pay for such period as allowable under section 8440f of title 5, United States Code. Basic pay does not include any retired pay paid pursuant to this section.

(B) CONTRIBUTIONS FOR BENEFIT OF JUDGE.—No contributions under section 8432(c) of title 5, United States Code, shall be made for the benefit of a judge who has filed an election to receive retired pay under subsection (e).

(C) APPLICABILITY OF SECTION 8433(b) OF TITLE 5 WHETHER OR NOT JUDGE RETIRES.—Section 8433(b) of title 5, United States Code, applies with respect to a judge who makes an election under paragraph (1) and who either—

(i) retires under subsection (b), or

(ii) ceases to serve as a judge of the Tax Court but does not retire under subsection (b).

Retirement under subsection (b) is a separation from service for purposes of subchapters III and VII of chapter 84 of that title.

(D) APPLICABILITY OF SECTION 8351(b)(5) OF TITLE 5.—The provisions of section 8351(b)(5) of title 5, United States Code, shall apply with respect to a judge who makes an election under paragraph (1).

(E) EXCEPTION.—Notwithstanding subparagraph (C), if any judge retires under this section, or resigns without having met the age and service requirements set forth under subsection (b)(2), and such judge's nonforfeitable account balance is less than an amount that the Executive Director of the Federal Retirement Thrift Investment Board prescribes by regulation, the Executive Director shall pay the nonforfeitable account balance to the participant in a single payment.

(F) OFFSET.—In the case of a judge who receives a distribution from the Thrift Savings Plan and who later receives retired pay under subsection (d), the retired pay shall be offset by an amount equal to the amount of the distribution which represents the Government's contribution to the individual's Thrift Savings Account during years of service as a full-time judicial officer under the Federal Employees Retirement System, without regard to earnings attributable to such amount. Where such an offset would exceed 50 percent of the retired pay to be received in the first year, the offset may be divided equally over the first 2 years in which the individual receives the annuity.

Amendments

• 2022, SECURE 2.0 Act of 2022 (P.L. 117-328)

P.L. 117-328, § 701(a)(1):

Amended Code Sec. 7447(j)(3)(B). **Effective** for basic pay earned while serving as a judge of the United States Tax Court on or after 12-29-2022. Prior to amendment, Code Sec. 7447(j)(3)(B) read as follows:

(B) CONTRIBUTIONS FOR BENEFIT OF JUDGE.—No contributions may be made for the benefit of a judge under section 8432(c) of title 5, United States Code.

P.L. 117-328, § 701(a)(2):

Amended Code Sec. 7447(j)(3) by adding at the end a new subparagraph (F). **Effective** for basic pay earned while serving as a judge of the United States Tax Court on or after 12-29-2022.

• 2006, Pension Protection Act of 2006 (P.L. 109-280)

P.L. 109-280, § 853(a):

Amended Code Sec. 7447 by adding at the end a new subsection (j). **Effective** 8-17-2006, except that United States Tax Court judges may only begin to participate in the Thrift Savings Plan at the next open season beginning after such date.

[Sec. 7447(k)]

(k) TEACHING COMPENSATION OF RETIRED JUDGES.—For purposes of the limitation under section 501(a) of the Ethics in Government Act of 1978 (5 U.S.C. App.), any compensation for teaching approved under section 502(a)(5) of such Act shall not be treated as outside earned income when received by a judge of the United States Tax Court who has retired under subsection (b) for teaching performed during any calendar year for which such a judge has met the requirements of subsection (c), as certified by the chief judge, or has retired under subsection (b)(4).

Amendments

• 2022, SECURE 2.0 Act of 2022 (P.L. 117-328)

P.L. 117-328, § 701(d)(1):

Amended Code Sec. 7447 by adding at the end a new subsection (k). **Effective** for any individual serving as a retired judge of the United States Tax Court on or after 12-29-2022.

SEC. 7447A. RETIREMENT FOR SPECIAL TRIAL JUDGES.

[Sec. 7447A(a)]

(a) IN GENERAL.—

(1) RETIREMENT.—Any special trial judge appointed pursuant to section 7443A may retire from service as a special trial judge if the individual meets the age and service requirements set forth in the following table:

If the special trial judge has attained age:	And the years of service as a special trial judge are at least:
65	15
66	14
67	13
68	12
69	11
70	10

JUDICIAL PROCEEDINGS—TAX COURT

(2) LENGTH OF SERVICE.—In making any determination of length of service as a special trial judge there shall be included all periods (whether or not consecutive) during which an individual served as a special trial judge[.]

[Sec. 7447A(b)]

(b) RETIREMENT UPON DISABILITY.—Any special trial judge appointed pursuant to section 7443A who becomes permanently disabled from performing such individual's duties shall retire from service as a special trial judge.

[Sec. 7447A(c)]

(c) RECALLING OF RETIRED SPECIAL TRIAL JUDGES.—Any individual who has retired pursuant to subsection (a) may be called upon by the chief judge to perform such judicial duties with the Tax Court as may be requested of such individual for a period or periods specified by the chief judge, except that in the case of any such individual—

(1) the aggregate of such periods in any 1 calendar year shall not (without the consent of such individual) exceed 90 calendar days, and

(2) such individual shall be relieved of performing such duties during any period in which illness or disability precludes the performance of such duties.

Any act, or failure to act, by an individual performing judicial duties pursuant to this subsection shall have the same force and effect as if it were the act (or failure to act) of a special trial judge. Any individual who is performing judicial duties pursuant to this subsection shall be paid the same compensation (in lieu of retired pay) and allowances for travel and other expenses as a special trial judge.

[Sec. 7447A(d)]

(d) RETIRED PAY.—

(1) IN GENERAL.—Any individual who retires pursuant to subsection (a) and elects under subsection (e) to receive retired pay under this subsection shall receive retired pay during any period of retirement from service as a special trial judge at a rate which bears the same ratio to the rate of the salary payable to a special trial judge during such period as—

(A) the number of years such individual has served as special trial judge bears to,

(B) 15,

except that the rate of such retired pay shall not be more than the rate of such salary for such period.

(2) RETIREMENT UPON DISABILITY.—Any individual who retires pursuant to subsection (b) and elects under subsection (e) to receive retired pay under this subsection shall receive retired pay during any period of retirement from service as a special trial judge—

(A) at a rate equal to the rate of the salary payable to a special trial judge during such period, if the individual had at least 10 years of service as a special trial judge before retirement, and

(B) at a rate equal to $1/2$ the rate described in subparagraph (A), if the individual had fewer than 10 years of service as a special trial judge before retirement.

(3) BEGINNING DATE AND PAYMENT.—Retired pay under this subsection shall begin to accrue on the day following the date on which the individual's salary as a special trial judge ceases to accrue, and shall continue to accrue during the remainder of such individual's life. Retired pay under this subsection shall be paid in the same manner as the salary of a special trial judge.

(4) PARTIAL YEARS.—In computing the rate of the retired pay for an individual to whom paragraph (1) applies, any portion of the aggregate number of years such individual has served as a special trial judge which is a fractional part of 1 year shall be eliminated if it is less than 6 months, or shall be counted as a full year if it is 6 months or more.

(5) RECALLED SERVICE.—In computing the rate of the retired pay for an individual to whom paragraph (1) applies, any period during which such individual performs services under subsection (c) on a substantially full-time basis shall be treated as a period during which such individual has served as a special trial judge.

[Sec. 7447A(e)]

(e) ELECTION TO RECEIVE RETIRED PAY.—Any special trial judge may elect to receive retired pay under subsection (d). Such an election—

(1) may be made only while an individual is a special trial judge (except that in the case of an individual who fails to be reappointed as a special trial judge, such election may be made within 60 days after such individual leaves office as a special trial judge),

(2) once made, shall be irrevocable, and

(3) shall be made by filing notice thereof in writing with the chief judge.

The chief judge shall transmit to the Office of Personnel Management a copy of each notice filed with the chief judge under this subsection.

Amendments

- 2022, SECURE 2.0 Act of 2022 (P.L. 117-328)

P.L. 117-328, § 702(a):

Amended part I of subchapter C of chapter 76 by inserting after Code Sec. 7447 a new Code Sec. 7447A. For the **effective** date, see Act Sec. 702(d), below.

P.L. 117-328, § 702(d), provides:

d) EFFECTIVE DATE.—The amendments made by this section shall take effect on the date of the enactment of this Act [12-29-2022], except that section 7447A(e) of the Internal Revenue Code of 1986 (as added by this section) shall take effect on the date that is 180 days after such date of enactment [12-29-2022]. Special trial judges retiring on or after the date of the enactment of this Act [12-29-2022], and before the date that is 180 days after the date of such enactment, may file an election under such section not later than 60 days after such date.

[Sec. 7447A(f)]

(f) OTHER RULES MADE APPLICABLE.—The rules of subsections (f), (g), (h)(2), (i), and (j), and the first sentence of subsection (h)(1), of section 7447 shall apply to a special trial judge in the same manner as a judge of the Tax Court. For purposes of the preceding sentence, any reference to the President in such subsections shall be applied as if it were a reference to the chief judge.

Amendments

- 2022, SECURE 2.0 Act of 2022 (P.L. 117-328)

P.L. 117-328, § 702(a):

Amended part I of subchapter C of chapter 76 by inserting after Code Sec. 7447 a new Code Sec. 7447A. For the **effective** date, see Act Sec. 702(d), below.

P.L. 117-328, § 702(d), provides:

d) EFFECTIVE DATE.—The amendments made by this section shall take effect on the date of the enactment of this Act [12-29-2022], except that section 7447A(e) of the Internal Revenue Code of 1986 (as added by this section) shall take effect on the date that is 180 days after such date of enactment [12-29-2022]. Special trial judges retiring on or after the date of the enactment of this Act [12-29-2022], and before the date that is 180 days after the date of such enactment, may file an election under such section not later than 60 days after such date.

[Sec. 7448]

SEC. 7448. ANNUITIES TO SURVIVING SPOUSES AND DEPENDENT CHILDREN OF JUDGES AND SPECIAL TRIAL JUDGES.

[Sec. 7448(a)]

(a) DEFINITIONS.—For purposes of this section—

(1) The term "Tax Court" means the United States Tax Court.

(2) The term "judge" means the chief judge or a judge of the Tax Court, including any individual receiving retired pay (or compensation in lieu of retired pay) under section 7447 whether or not performing judicial duties pursuant to section 7447(c).

(3) The term "chief judge" means the chief judge of the Tax Court.

(4) The term "judge's salary" means the salary of a judge received under section 7443(c), retired pay received under section 7447(d), and compensation (in lieu of retired pay) received under section 7447(c).

(5) The term "special trial judge" means a judicial officer appointed pursuant to section 7443A, including any individual receiving an annuity under chapter 83 or 84 of title 5, United States Code.

(6) The term "special trial judge's salary" means the salary of a special trial judge received under section 7443A(d), any amount received as an annuity under chapter 83 or 84 of title 5, United States Code.

(7) The term "survivors annuity fund" means the Tax Court judges survivors annuity fund established by this section.

(8) The term "surviving spouse" means a surviving spouse of an individual, who either (A) shall have been married to such individual for at least 2 years immediately preceding his death or (B) is a parent of issue by such marriage, and who has not remarried.

(9) The term "dependent child" means an unmarried child, including a dependent stepchild or an adopted child, who is under the age of 18 years or who because of physical or mental disability is incapable of self-support.

(10) The terms "assassinated" and "assassination" mean the killing of a judge or special trial judge that is motivated by the performance by the judge or special trial judge of his or her official duties.

Amendments

• **2022, SECURE 2.0 Act of 2022 (P.L. 117-328)**

P.L. 117-328, § 701(b)(2):

Amended Code Sec. 7448(a) by adding at the end a new paragraph (10). **Effective** 12-29-2022.

• **2018, Tax Technical Corrections Act of 2018 (P.L. 115-141)**

P.L. 115-141, § 401(b)(51), Div. U:

Amended Code Sec. 7448(a)(5) by striking ", whether or not performing judicial duties under section 7443B" following "United States Code". **Effective** 3-23-2018. For a special rule, see Act Sec. 401(e), Div. U, below.

P.L. 115-141, § 401(b)(52), Div. U:

Amended Code Sec. 7448(a)(6) by striking ", and compensation received under section 7443B" following "United States Code". **Effective** 3-23-2018. For a special rule, see Act Sec. 401(e), Div. U, below.

P.L. 115-141, § 401(e), Div. U, provides:

(e) GENERAL SAVINGS PROVISION WITH RESPECT TO DEADWOOD PROVISIONS.—If—

(1) any provision amended or repealed by the amendments made by subsection (b) or (d) applied to—

(A) any transaction occurring before the date of the enactment of this Act,

(B) any property acquired before such date of enactment, or

(C) any item of income, loss, deduction, or credit taken into account before such date of enactment, and

(2) the treatment of such transaction, property, or item under such provision would (without regard to the amendments or repeals made by such subsection) affect the liability for tax for periods ending after such date of enactment,

nothing in the amendments or repeals made by this section shall be construed to affect the treatment of such transaction, property, or item for purposes of determining liability for tax for periods ending after such date of enactment.

• **2014, Tax Technical Corrections Act of 2014 (P.L. 113-295)**

P.L. 113-295, § 221(a)(116)(A)(i)-(ii), Division A:

Amended Code Sec. 7448(a)(2) by striking "or under section 1106 of the Internal Revenue Code of 1939" following "under section 7447", and by striking "or pursuant to section 1106(d) of the Internal Revenue Code of 1939" following "pursuant to section 7447(c)". **Effective** generally 12-19-2014. For a special rule, see Act Sec. 221(b)(2), Division A, below.

P.L. 113-295, § 221(b)(2), Division A, provides:

(2) SAVINGS PROVISION.—If—

(A) any provision amended or repealed by the amendments made by this section applied to—

(i) any transaction occurring before the date of the enactment of this Act,

(ii) any property acquired before such date of enactment, or

(iii) any item of income, loss, deduction, or credit taken into account before such date of enactment, and

(B) the treatment of such transaction, property, or item under such provision would (without regard to the amendments or repeals made by this section) affect the liability for tax for periods ending after date of enactment, nothing in the amendments or repeals made by this section shall be construed to affect the treatment of such transaction, property, or item for purposes of determining liability for tax for periods ending after such date of enactment.

• **2006, Pension Protection Act of 2006 (P.L. 109-280)**

P.L. 109-280, § 854(a):

Amended Code Sec. 7448(a), as amended by this Act, by redesignating paragraphs (5), (6), (7), and (8) [sic] as paragraphs (7), (8), (9), and (10) [sic], respectively, and by inserting after paragraph (4) new paragraphs (5) and (6). **Effective** 8-17-2006.

P.L. 109-280, § 854(c)(1):

Amended the heading of Code Sec. 7448 by inserting "AND SPECIAL TRIAL JUDGES" after "JUDGES". **Effective** 8-17-2006.

• **1976, Tax Reform Act of 1976 (P.L. 94-455)**

P.L. 94-455, § 1906(a)(46)(A):

Substituted "The term 'surviving spouse' means a surviving spouse of" for "The term 'widow' means a surviving wife of" and "a parent of issue" for "the mother of issue" in Code Sec. 7448(a)(6). **Effective** 2-1-77.

P.L. 94-455, § 1906(a)(46)(F):

Substituted "SURVIVING SPOUSES" for "WIDOWS" in the section heading for Code Sec. 7448. For earlier amendments to Code Sec. 7448(a), see the amendment note under Code Sec. 7448(t). **Effective** 2-1-77.

• **1969, Tax Reform Act of 1969 (P.L. 91-172)**

P.L. 91-172, § 960(c):

Amended Code Sec. 7448(a) by substituting the phrase "United States Tax Court" for the phrase "Tax Court of the United States". **Effective** 12-30-69.

[Sec. 7448(b)]

(b) ELECTION.—

(1) JUDGES.—Any judge may by written election filed while he is a judge (except that in the case of an individual who is not reappointed following expiration of his term of office, it may be made at any time before the day after the day on which his successor takes office) bring himself within the purview of this section. In the case of any judge other than the chief judge the election shall be filed with the chief judge; in the case of the chief judge the election shall be filed as prescribed by the Tax Court.

(2) SPECIAL TRIAL JUDGES.—Any special trial judge may by written election filed with the chief judge elect the application of this section. Such election shall be filed while such individual is a special trial judge.

Amendments

• **2022, SECURE 2.0 Act of 2022 (P.L. 117-328)**

P.L. 117-328, § 702(b)(2):

Amended Code Sec. 7448(b)(2). For the **effective** date, see Act Sec. 702(d), below. Prior to amendment, Code Sec. 7448(b)(2) read as follows:

(2) SPECIAL TRIAL JUDGES.—Any special trial judge may by written election filed with the chief judge bring himself or herself within the purview of this section. Such election shall be filed not later than the later of 6 months after—

(A) 6 months after the date of the enactment of this paragraph,

(B) the date the judge takes office, or

(C) the date the judge marries.

P.L. 117-328, § 702(d), provides:

(d) EFFECTIVE DATE.—The amendments made by this section shall take effect on the date of the enactment of this Act, except that section 7447A(e) of the Internal Revenue Code of 1986 (as added by this section) shall take effect on the date that is 180 days after such date of enactment. Special trial judges retiring on or after the date of the enactment of this Act, and before the date that is 180 days after the date of such enactment, may file an election under such section not later than 60 days after such date.

• **2006, Pension Protection Act of 2006 (P.L. 109-280)**

P.L. 109-280, § 854(b)(1)-(3):

Amended Code Sec. 7448(b) by striking the subsection heading and inserting "(b) ELECTION.—(1) JUDGES.—", by moving the text 2 ems to the right, and by adding at the end a new paragraph (2). **Effective** 8-17-2006. Prior to being stricken, the subsection heading for Code Sec. 7448(b) read as follows:

(b) ELECTION.—

• **1969, Tax Reform Act of 1969 (P.L. 91-172)**

P.L. 91-172, § 955(a):

Amended Code Sec. 7448(b). **Effective** 12-30-69. Prior to amendment by P.L. 91-172, subsection (b) read as follows:

JUDICIAL PROCEEDINGS—TAX COURT

(b) ELECTION.—Any judge may by written election filed with the chief judge within 6 months after the date on which he takes office after appointment or any reappointment, or within 6 months after the date upon which he first becomes eligible for retirement under section 7447(b), or within 6 months after the enactment of this section, bring himself within the purview of this section, except that, in the case of such an election by the chief judge, the election shall be filed as prescribed by the Tax Court subject to the preceding requirements as to the time of filing.

[Sec. 7448(c)]

(c) SURVIVORS ANNUITY FUND.—

(1) SALARY DEDUCTIONS.—There shall be deducted and withheld from the salary of each judge or special trial judge electing under subsection (b) a sum equal to 3.5 percent of such judge's or special trial judge's salary. The amounts so deducted and withheld from such judge's or special trial judge's salary, in accordance with such procedure as may be prescribed by the Comptroller General of the United States, be deposited in the Treasury of the United States to the credit of a fund to be known as the "Tax Court judicial officers survivors annuity fund" and said fund is appropriated for the payment of annuities, refunds, and allowances as provided by this section. Each judge or special trial judge electing under subsection (b) shall be deemed thereby to consent and agree to the deductions from his salary as provided in this subsection, and payment less such deductions shall be a full and complete discharge and acquittance of all claims and demands whatsoever for all judicial services rendered by such judge or special trial judge during the period covered by such payment, except the right to the benefits to which he or his survivors shall be entitled under the provisions of this section.

(2) APPROPRIATIONS WHERE UNFUNDED LIABILITY.—

(A) IN GENERAL.—Not later than the close of each fiscal year, there shall be deposited in the Treasury of the United States to the credit of the survivors annuity fund, in accordance with such procedures as may be prescribed by the Comptroller General of [the] United States, amounts required to reduce to zero the unfunded liability (if any) of such fund. Subject to appropriation Acts, such deposits shall be taken from sums available for such fiscal year for the payment of amounts described in subsection (a)(4) and section 7443A(d), and shall immediately become an integrated part of such fund.

(B) EXCEPTION.—The amount required by subparagraph (A) to be deposited in any fiscal year shall not exceed an amount equal to 11 percent of the aggregate amounts described in subsections (a)(4) and (a)(6) paid during such fiscal year.

(C) UNFUNDED LIABILITY DEFINED.—For purposes of subparagraph (A), the term "unfunded liability" means the amount estimated by the Secretary to be equal to the excess (as of the close of the fiscal year involved) of—

(i) the present value of all benefits payable from the survivors annuity fund (determined on an annual basis in accordance with section 9503 of title 31, United States Code), over

(ii) the sum of—

(I) the present values of future deductions under subsection (c) and future deposits under subsection (d), plus

(II) the balance in such fund as of the close of such fiscal year.

(D) AMOUNTS NOT CREDITED TO INDIVIDUAL ACCOUNTS.—Amounts appropriated pursuant to this paragraph shall not be credited to the account of any individual for purposes of subsection (g).

Amendments

- **2006, Pension Protection Act of 2006 (P.L. 109-280)**

P.L. 109-280, § 854(c)(3)(A)-(B):

Amended Code Sec. 7448(c)(1) by inserting "or special trial judge" after "judge" each place it appears other than in the phrase "chief judge", and by inserting "or special trial judge's" after "judge's" each place it appears. **Effective** 8-17-2006.

P.L. 109-280, § 854(c)(4)(A)-(B):

Amended Code Sec. 7448(c) by striking "Tax Court judges" and inserting "Tax Court judicial officers" in paragraph (1), by inserting "and section 7443A(d)" after "(a)(4)" in paragraph (2)(A), and by striking "subsection (a)(4)" and inserting "subsections (a)(4) and (a)(6)" in paragraph (2)(B). **Effective** 8-17-2006.

- **1986, Tax Reform Act of 1986 (P.L. 99-514)**

P.L. 99-514, § 1559(a)(1)(A):

Amended Code Sec. 7448(c) by striking out "3 percent" and inserting in lieu thereof "3.5 percent". **Effective** as provided in Act Sec. 1559(d) following Code Sec. 7448(g).

P.L. 99-514, § 1559(a)(2)(A)(i)-(iii):

Amended Code Sec. 7448(c) by striking out "(c) SALARY DEDUCTIONS.—There", by moving the text of such subsection 2 ems to the right, and by adding at the end thereof a new paragraph. **Effective** as provided in Act Sec. 1559(d) following Code Sec. 7448(g). Prior to amendment, Code Sec. 7448(c) read as follows:

(c) SALARY DEDUCTIONS.—There shall be deducted and withheld from the salary of each judge electing under subsection (b) a sum equal to 3 percent of such judge's salary. The amounts so deducted and withheld from such judge's salary shall, in accordance with such procedure as may be prescribed by the Comptroller General of the United States, be deposited in the Treasury and of the United States to the credit of a fund to be known as the "Tax Court judges survivors annuity fund" and said fund is appropriated for the payment of annuities, refunds, and allowances as provided by this section. Each judge electing under subsection (b) shall be deemed thereby to consent and agree to the deductions from his salary as provided in this subsection, and payment less such deductions shall be a full and complete discharge and acquittance of all claims and demands whatsoever for all judicial services rendered by such judge during the period covered by such payment, except the right to the benefits to which he or his survivors shall be entitled under the provisions of this section.

[Sec. 7448(d)]

(d) DEPOSITS IN SURVIVORS ANNUITY FUND.—Each judge or special trial judge electing under subsection (b) shall deposit, with interest at 3 percent per annum, compounded on December 31 of each year, to the credit of the survivors annuity fund, a sum equal to 3.5 percent of his judge's or special trial judge's salary and of his basic salary, pay, or compensation for service as a Senator, Representative, Delegate, or Resident Commissioner in Congress, and for any other civilian service within the purview of sections 8332 and 8411 of title 5 of the United States Code. Each such judge or special trial judge may elect to make such deposits in installments during the continuance of his service as a judge or special trial judge in such amount and under such conditions as may be determined in each instance by the chief judge. Notwithstanding the failure of a judge or special trial judge to make such deposit, credit shall be allowed for the service rendered, but the annuity of the surviving spouse of such judge or special trial judge shall be reduced by an amount equal to 10 percent of the amount of such deposit, computed as of the date of the death of such judge or special trial judge, unless such surviving spouse shall elect to eliminate such service entirely from credit under subsection (n), except that no deposit shall be required from a judge or special trial judge for any year with respect to which deductions from his salary were actually made under the civil service retirement laws and no deposit shall be required for any honorable service in the Army, Navy, Air Force, Marine Corps, or Coast Guard of the United States.

Amendments

- **2022, SECURE 2.0 Act of 2022 (P.L. 117-328)**

P.L. 117-328, § 701(c)(2)(A):

Amended Code Sec. 7448(d) by striking "section 8332" and inserting "sections 8332 and 8411". **Effective** 12-29-2022.

- **2018, Tax Technical Corrections Act of 2018 (P.L. 115-141)**

P.L. 115-141, § 401(b)(53), Div. U:

Amended Code Sec. 7448(d) by striking "at 4 percent per annum to December 31, 1947, and 3 percent per annum thereafter" and inserting "at 3 percent per annum". **Effective** 3-23-2018. For a special rule, see Act Sec. 401(e), Div. U, below.

P.L. 115-141, § 401(e), Div. U, provides:

(e) GENERAL SAVINGS PROVISION WITH RESPECT TO DEADWOOD PROVISIONS.—If—

(1) any provision amended or repealed by the amendments made by subsection (b) or (d) applied to—

(A) any transaction occurring before the date of the enactment of this Act,

(B) any property acquired before such date of enactment, or

(C) any item of income, loss, deduction, or credit taken into account before such date of enactment, and

(2) the treatment of such transaction, property, or item under such provision would (without regard to the amendments or repeals made by such subsection) affect the liability for tax for periods ending after such date of enactment,

nothing in the amendments or repeals made by this section shall be construed to affect the treatment of such transaction, property, or item for purposes of determining liability for tax for periods ending after such date of enactment.

- **2006, Pension Protection Act of 2006 (P.L. 109-280)**

P.L. 109-280, § 854(c)(3)(A)-(B):

Amended Code Sec. 7448(d) by inserting "or special trial judge" after "judge" each place it appears other than in the phrase "chief judge", and by inserting "or special trial judge's" after "judge's" each place it appears. **Effective** 8-17-2006.

JUDICIAL PROCEEDINGS—TAX COURT

• **1986, Tax Reform Act of 1986 (P.L. 99-514)**

P.L. 99-514, §1559(a)(1)(B):

Amended Code Sec. 7448(d) by striking out "3 percent" the second place it appears and inserting in lieu thereof "3.5 percent". **Effective** as provided in Act Sec. 1559(d) following Code Sec. 7448(g).

• **1976, Tax Reform Act of 1976 (P.L. 94-455)**

P.L. 94-455, §1906(a)(46)(E):

Substituted "surviving spouse" for "widow" in Code Sec. 7448(d). For earlier amendments to Code Sec. 7448(d), see the amendment note under Code Sec. 7448(t). **Effective** 2-1-77.

• **1969, Tax Reform Act of 1969 (P.L. 91-172)**

P.L. 91-172, §955(b)(1):

Amended Code Secs. 7448(d), (h), and (r) by substituting the phrase "civil service retirement laws" for the phrase "Civil Service Retirement Act" the last place it appeared in each subsection. **Effective** 12-30-69.

P.L. 91-172, §955(b)(2):

Amended Code Secs. 7448(d) and (n) by substituting the phrase "section 8332 of title 5 of the United States Code" for the phrase "section 3 of the Civil Service Retirement Act (5 U. S. C. 2253)". **Effective** 12-30-69.

[Sec. 7448(e)]

(e) INVESTMENT OF SURVIVORS ANNUITY FUND.—The Secretary of the Treasury shall invest from time to time, in interest-bearing securities of the United States or Federal farm loan bonds, such portions of the survivors annuity fund as in his judgment may not be immediately required for the payment of the annuities, refunds, and allowances as provided in this section. The income derived from such investments shall constitute a part of said fund for the purpose of paying annuities and of carrying out the provisions of subsections (g), (h), and (j).

[Sec. 7448(f)]

(f) CREDITING OF DEPOSITS.—The amount deposited by or deducted and withheld from the salary of each judge or special trial judge electing to bring himself within the purview of this section for credit to the survivors annuity fund shall be credited to an individual account of such judge or special trial judge.

Amendments

• **2006, Pension Protection Act of 2006 (P.L. 109-280)**

P.L. 109-280, §854(c)(3)(A)-(B):

Amended Code Sec. 7448(f) by inserting "or special trial judge" after "judge" each place it appears other than in the phrase "chief judge", and by inserting "or special trial judge's" after "judge's" each place it appears. **Effective** 8-17-2006.

[Sec. 7448(g)]

(g) TERMINATION.—If the service of any judge or special trial judge electing under subsection (b) terminates other than pursuant to the provisions of section 7447 or if any judge or special trial judge ceases to be married after making the election under subsection (b) and revokes (in a writing filed as provided in subsection (b)) such election, the amount credited to his individual account, together with interest at 3 percent per annum, compounded on December 31 of each year, to the date of his relinquishment of office, shall be returned to him. For the purpose of this section, the service of any judge or special trial judge electing under subsection (b) who is not reappointed following expiration of his term but who, at the time of such expiration, is eligible for and elects to receive retired pay under section 7447 shall be deemed to have terminated pursuant to said section.

Amendments

• **2014, Tax Technical Corrections Act of 2014 (P.L. 113-295)**

P.L. 113-295, §221(a)(116)(B), Division A:

Amended Code Sec. 7448(g) by striking "or other than pursuant to section 1106 of the Internal Revenue Code of 1939" following "provisions of section 7447". **Effective** generally 12-19-2014. For a special rule, see Act Sec. 221(b)(2), Division A, below.

P.L. 113-295, §221(a)(116)(C), Division A:

Amended Code Sec. 7448(g) by striking "at 4 percent per annum to December 31, 1947, and 3 percent per annum thereafter" and inserting "at 3 percent per annum". **Effective** generally 12-19-2014. For a special rule, see Act Sec. 221(b)(2), Division A, below.

P.L. 113-295, §221(b)(2), Division A, provides:

(2) SAVINGS PROVISION.—If—

(A) any provision amended or repealed by the amendments made by this section applied to—

(i) any transaction occurring before the date of the enactment of this Act,

(ii) any property acquired before such date of enactment, or

(iii) any item of income, loss, deduction, or credit taken into account before such date of enactment, and

(B) the treatment of such transaction, property, or item under such provision would (without regard to the amendments or repeals made by this section) affect the liability for tax for periods ending after date of enactment, nothing in the amendments or repeals made by this section shall be construed to affect the treatment of such transaction, property, or item for purposes of determining liability for tax for periods ending after such date of enactment.

• **2006, Pension Protection Act of 2006 (P.L. 109-280)**

P.L. 109-280, §854(c)(3)(A)-(B):

Amended Code Sec. 7448(g), by inserting "or special trial judge" after "judge" each place it appears other than in the phrase "chief judge", and by inserting "or special trial judge's" after "judge's" each place it appears. **Effective** 8-17-2006.

• **1986, Tax Reform Act of 1986 (P.L. 99-514)**

P.L. 99-514, §1559(c)(1):

Amended Code Sec. 7448(g) by inserting "or if any judge ceases to be married after making the election under subsection (b) and revokes (in a writing filed as provided in subsection (b)) such election" after "1939". **Effective** as provided in Act Sec. 1559(d), below.

P.L. 99-514, §1559(c)(2):

Amended Code Sec. 7448(g) by striking out "OF SERVICE" from the subsection heading. For the **effective** date, see Act Sec. 1559(d), below. Prior to amendment, the heading of Code Sec. 7448(g) read as follows:

(g) TERMINATION OF SERVICE.—

P.L. 99-514, §1559(d), provides:

(d) EFFECTIVE DATE.—

(1) SALARY DEDUCTIONS.—

(A) The amendment made by subsection (a)(1)(A) shall apply to amounts paid after November 1, 1986.

(B) The amendment made by subsection (a)(1)(B) shall apply to service after November 1, 1986.

(2) APPROPRIATIONS.—The amendments made by subsection (a)(2) shall apply to fiscal years beginning after 1986.

(3) COMPUTATION OF ANNUITIES.—The amendments made by subsection (b) shall apply to annuities the starting date of which is after November 1, 1986.

(4) OPPORTUNITY TO REVOKE SURVIVOR ANNUITY ELECTION.—

(A) IN GENERAL.—Any individual who before November 1, 1986, made an election under subsection (b) of section 7448 of the Internal Revenue Code of 1954 may revoke such election. Such a revocation shall constitute a complete withdrawal from the survivor annuity program provided for in such section and shall be filed as provided for elections under such subsection.

(B) EFFECT OF REVOCATION.—Any revocation under subparagraph (A) shall have the same effect as if there were a termination to which section 7448(g) of such Code applies on the date such revocation is filed.

(C) PERIOD REVOCATION PERMITTED.—Any revocation under subparagraph (A) may be made only during the 180-day period beginning on the date of the enactment of this Act.

(5) OPPORTUNITY TO ELECT SURVIVOR ANNUITY WHERE PRIOR REVOCATION.—Any individual who under paragraph (4) revoked an election under subsection (b) of section 7448 of such Code may thereafter make such an election only if such individual deposits to the credit of the survivors annuity fund under subsection (c) of such section the entire amount paid to such individual under paragraph (4), together with interest computed as provided in subsection (d) of such section.

[Sec. 7448(h)]

(h) ENTITLEMENT TO ANNUITY.—

(1) IN GENERAL.—

(A) ANNUITY TO SURVIVING SPOUSE.—If a judge or special trial judge described in paragraph (2) is survived by a surviving spouse but not by a dependent child, there shall be paid to such surviving spouse an annuity beginning with the day of the death of the judge or special trial judge or following the surviving spouse's attainment of age 50, whichever is the later, in an amount computed as provided in subsection (m).

JUDICIAL PROCEEDINGS—TAX COURT

(B) ANNUITY TO SURVIVING SPOUSE AND CHILD.—If a judge or special trial judge described in paragraph (2) is survived by a surviving spouse and dependent child or children, there shall be paid to such surviving spouse an annuity, beginning on the day of the death of the judge or special trial judge, in an amount computed as provided in subsection (m), and there shall also be paid to or on behalf of each such child an immediate annuity equal to the lesser of—

(i) 10 percent of the average annual salary of such judge or special trial judge (determined in accordance with subsection (m)), or

(ii) 20 percent of such average annual salary, divided by the number of such children.

(C) ANNUITY TO SURVIVING DEPENDENT CHILDREN.—If a judge or special trial judge described in paragraph (2) leaves no surviving spouse but leaves a surviving dependent child or children, there shall be paid to or on behalf of each such child an immediate annuity equal to the lesser of—

(i) 20 percent of the average annual salary of such judge or special trial judge (determined in accordance with subsection (m)), or

(ii) 40 percent of such average annual salary divided by the number of such children.

(2) COVERED JUDGES.—Paragraph (1) applies to any judge or special trial judge electing under subsection (b)—

(A) who dies while a judge or special trial judge after having rendered at least 18 months of civilian service computed as prescribed in subsection (n), for the last 18 months of which the salary deductions provided for by subsection (c)(1) or the deposits required by subsection (d) have actually been made or the salary deductions required by the civil service retirement laws have actually been made, or

(B) who dies by assassination after having rendered less than 18 months of civilian service computed as prescribed in subsection (n) if, for the period of such service, the salary deductions provided for by subsection (c)(1) or the deposits required by subsection (d) have actually been made.

(3) TERMINATION OF ANNUITY.—

(A) SURVIVING SPOUSE.—The annuity payable to a surviving spouse under this subsection shall be terminable upon such surviving spouse's death or such surviving spouse's remarriage before attaining age 55.

(B) SURVIVING CHILD.—Any annuity payable to a child under this subsection shall be terminable upon the earliest of—

(i) the child's attainment of age 18,

(ii) the child's marriage, or

(iii) the child's death,

except that if such child is incapable of self-support by reason of mental or physical disability the child's annuity shall be terminable only upon death, marriage, or recovery from such disability.

(C) DEPENDENT CHILD AFTER DEATH OF SURVIVING SPOUSE.—In case of the death of a surviving spouse of a judge or special trial judge leaving a dependent child or children of the judge or special trial judge surviving such spouse, the annuity of such child or children shall be recomputed and paid as provided in paragraph (1)(C).

(D) RECOMPUTATION WITH RESPECT TO OTHER DEPENDENT CHILDREN.—In any case in which the annuity of a dependent child is terminated under this subsection, the annuities of any remaining dependent child or children based upon the service of the same judge or special trial judge shall be recomputed and paid as though the child whose annuity was so terminated had not survived such judge.

(E) SPECIAL RULE FOR ASSASSINATED JUDGES.—In the case of a survivor of a judge or special trial judge described in paragraph (2)(B), there shall be deducted from the annuities otherwise payable under this section an amount equal to the amount of salary deductions that would have been made if such deductions had been made for 18 months prior to the death of the judge or special trial judge.

Amendments

- **2022, SECURE 2.0 Act of 2022 (P.L. 117-328)**

P.L. 117-328, § 701(b)(1):

Amended Code Sec. 7448(h). **Effective** 12-29-2022. Prior to amendment, Code Sec. 7448(h) read as follows:

(h) ENTITLEMENT TO ANNUITY.—In case any judge or special trial judge electing under subsection (b) shall die while a judge or special trial judge after having rendered at least 5 years of civilian service computed as prescribed in subsection (n), for the last 5 years of which the salary deductions provided for by subsection (c)(1) or the deposits required by subsection (d) have actually been made or the salary deductions required by the civil service retirement laws have actually been made—

(1) if such judge or special trial judge is survived by a surviving spouse but not by a dependent child, there shall be paid to such surviving spouse an annuity beginning with the day of the death of the judge or special trial judge or following the surviving spouse's attainment of the age of 50 years, whichever is the later, in an amount computed as provided in subsection (m); or

(2) if such judge or special trial judge is survived by a surviving spouse and a dependent child or children, there shall be paid to such surviving spouse an immediate annuity in an amount computed as provided in subsection (m), and there shall also be paid to or on behalf of each such child an immediate annuity equal to the lesser of—

(A) 10 percent of the average annual salary of such judge or special trial judge (determined in accordance with subsection (m)), or

(B) 20 percent of such average annual salary, divided by the number of such children; or

(3) if such judge or special trial judge leaves no surviving spouse but leaves a surviving dependent child or children, there shall be paid to or on behalf of each such child an immediate annuity equal to the lesser of—

(A) 20 percent of the average annual salary of such judge or special trial judge (determined in accordance with subsection (m)), or

(B) 40 percent of such average annual salary, divided by the number of such children.

The annuity payable to a surviving spouse under this subsection shall be terminable upon such surviving spouse's death or such surviving spouse's remarriage before attaining age 55. The annuity payable to a child under this subsection shall be terminable upon (A) his attaining the age of 18 years, (B) his marriage, or (C) his death, whichever first occurs, except that if such child is incapable of self-support by reason of mental or physical disability his annuity shall be terminable only upon death, marriage or recovery from such disability. In case of the death of a surviving spouse of a judge or special trial judge leaving a dependent child or children of the judge or special trial judge surviving such spouse, the annuity of such child or children shall be recomputed and paid as provided in paragraph (3) of this subsection. In any case in which the annuity of a dependent child is terminated under this subsection, the annuities of any remaining dependent child or children, based upon the service of the same judge or special trial judge, shall be recomputed and paid as though the child whose annuity was so terminated had not survived such judge or special trial judge.

- **2006, Pension Protection Act of 2006 (P.L. 109-280)**

P.L. 109-280, § 854(c)(3)(A)-(B):

Amended Code Sec. 7448(h) by inserting "or special trial judge" after "judge" each place it appears other than in the phrase "chief judge", and by inserting "or special trial judge's" after "judge's" each place it appears. **Effective** 8-17-2006.

- **1986, Tax Reform Act of 1986 (P.L. 99-514)**

P.L. 99-514, § 1559(a)(2)(B):

Amended Code Sec. 7448(h) by striking out "subsection (c)" and inserting in lieu thereof "subsection (c)(1)". **Effective** as provided in Act Sec. 1559(d) following Code Sec. 7448(g).

P.L. 99-514, § 1559(b)(1)(B):

Amended Code Sec. 7448(h) by striking out "or remarriage" and inserting in lieu thereof "or such surviving spouse's remarriage before attaining age 55". **Effective** as provided in Act Sec. 1559(d) following Code Sec. 7448(g).

P.L. 99-514, § 1559(b)(2)(A):

Amended Code Sec. 7448(h)(2) by striking out all that follows "equal to" and inserting in lieu thereof new text. **Effective** as provided in Act Sec. 1559(d) following Code Sec. 7448(g). Prior to amendment, Code Sec. 7448(h)(2) read as follows:

(2) if such judge is survived by a surviving spouse and a dependent child or children, there shall be paid to such surviving spouse an immediate annuity in an amount computed as provided in subsection (m), and there shall also be paid to or on behalf of each such child an immediate annuity equal to one-half the amount of the annuity of such surviving spouse, but not to exceed $4,644 per year divided by the number of such children or $1,548 per year, whichever is lesser; or

P.L. 99-514, § 1559(b)(2)(B):

Amended Code Sec. 7448(h)(3) by striking out all that follows "equal to" and inserting in lieu thereof new material. **Effective** as provided in Act Sec. 1559(d) following Code Sec. 7448(g). Prior to amendment, Code Sec. 7448(h)(3) read as follows:

(3) if such judge leaves no surviving spouse but leaves a surviving dependent child or children, there shall be paid to or on behalf of each such child an immediate annuity equal to the amount of the annuity to which such surviving spouse would have been entitled under paragraph (2) of this subsection had such spouse survived, but not to exceed $5,580 per year divided by the number of such children or $1,860 per year, whichever is lesser.

JUDICIAL PROCEEDINGS—TAX COURT

- **1984, Deficit Reduction Act of 1984 (P.L. 98-369)**

P.L. 98-369, §462(a):

Amended Code Sec. 7448(h) by striking out "$900 per year divided by the number of such children or $360 per year," in paragraph (2) and inserting in lieu thereof "$4,644 per year divided by the number of such children or $1,548 per year," and by striking out "$480 per year" in paragraph (3) and inserting in lieu thereof "$5,580 per year divided by the number of such children or $1,860 per year, whichever is lesser". **Effective** for annuities payable with respect to months beginning after 7-18-84.

- **1982, Miscellaneous Revenue Act of 1982 (P.L. 97-362)**

P.L. 97-362, §105(c), as amended by P.L. 97-448, §305(e), provides:

(c) CATCHUP FOR SURVIVORS ANNUITIES IN PAY STATUS ON DATE OF ENACTMENT.—If an annuity payable under section 7448(h) of the Internal Revenue Code of 1954 (relating to entitlement to annuity) to the surviving spouse of a judge of the United States Tax Court is being paid on the date of the enactment of this Act, [10-25-82] then the amount of that annuity shall be adjusted, as of the first day of the first month beginning more than 30 days after such date, to reflect the amount of the annuity which would have been payable if the amendment made by subsection (b) [see Code Sec. 7448(s)] applied with respect to increases in the salary of a judge under section 7443(c) of such Code taking effect after December 31, 1963.

- **1976, Tax Reform Act of 1976 (P.L. 94-455)**

P.L. 94-455, §1906(a)(46)(B):

Amended Code Sec. 7448(h) by making the following substitutions of terms: "surviving spouse" for "surviving widow or widower"; "such surviving spouse" for "such widow"; "a surviving spouse" for "a widow"; "surviving spouse's" for "widow's"; "surviving such spouse" for "surviving her". **Effective** 2-1-77.

P.L. 94-455, §1906(a)(46)(C):

Substituted "such spouse" for "she" in Code Sec. 7448(h). For earlier amendments to Code Sec. 7448(h), see the amendment note under Code Sec. 7448(t). **Effective** 2-1-77.

- **1969, Tax Reform Act of 1969 (P.L. 91-172)**

P.L. 91-172, §955(b)(1):

Amended Code Secs. 7448(d), (h), and (r) by substituting the phrase "civil service retirement laws" for the phrase "Civil Service Retirement Act" the last place it appeared in each subsection. **Effective** 12-30-69.

[Sec. 7448(i)]

(i) DETERMINATION BY CHIEF JUDGE.—

(1) DEPENDENCY AND DISABILITY.—Questions of dependency and disability arising under this section shall be determined by the chief judge subject to review only by the Tax Court, the decision of which shall be final and conclusive. The chief judge may order or direct at any time such medical or other examinations as he shall deem necessary to determine the facts relative to the nature and degree of disability of any dependent child who is an annuitant or applicant for annuity under this section, and may suspend or deny any such annuity for failure to submit to any examination so ordered or directed.

(2) ASSASSINATION.—The chief judge shall determine whether the killing of a judge or special trial judge was an assassination, subject to review only by the Tax Court. The head of any Federal agency that investigates the killing of a judge or special trial judge shall provide to the chief judge any information that would assist the chief judge in making such a determination.

- **2022, SECURE 2.0 Act of 2022 (P.L. 117-328)**

P.L. 117-328, §701(b)(3)(A)-(B):

Amended Code Sec. 7448(i) by striking "OF DEPENDENCY AND DISABILITY.—Questions" and inserting

"BY CHIEF JUDGE.—

(1) DEPENDENCY AND DISABILITY.—Questions", and by adding at the end a new paragraph (2). **Effective** 12-29-2022. Prior to amendment, Code Sec. 7448(i) read as follows:

(i) DETERMINATION OF DEPENDENCY AND DISABILITY.—Questions of dependency and disability arising under this section shall be determined by the chief judge subject to review only by the Tax Court, the decision of which shall be final and conclusive. The chief judge may order or direct at any time such medical or other examinations as he shall deem necessary to determine the facts relative to the nature and degree of disability of any dependent child who is an annuitant or applicant for annuity under this section, and may suspend or deny any such annuity for failure to submit to any examination so ordered or directed.

[Sec. 7448(j)]

(j) PAYMENTS IN CERTAIN CASES.—

(1) In any case in which—

(A) a judge or special trial judge electing under subsection (b) shall die while in office (whether in regular active service, retired from such service under section 7447, or receiving any annuity under chapter 83 or 84 of title 5, United States Code), before having rendered 5 years of civilian service computed as prescribed in subsection (n), or after having rendered 5 years of such civilian service but without a survivor or survivors entitled to annuity benefits provided by subsection (h), or

(B) the right of all persons entitled to annuity under subsection (h) based on the service of such judge or special trial judge shall terminate before a valid claim therefor shall have been established,

the total amount credited to the individual account of such judge or special trial judge, with interest at 3 percent per annum, compounded on December 31 of each year, to the date of the death of such judge or special trial judge, shall be paid, upon the establishment of a valid claim therefor, to the person or persons surviving at the date title to the payment arises, in the following order of precedence, and such payment shall be a bar to recovery by any other person:

(i) to the beneficiary or beneficiaries whom the judge or special trial judge may have designated by a writing filed prior to his death with the chief judge, except that in the case of the chief judge such designation shall be by a writing filed by him, prior to his death, as prescribed by the Tax Court;

(ii) if there be no such beneficiary, to the surviving spouse of such judge or special trial judge;

(iii) if none of the above, to the child or children of such judge or special trial judge and the descendants of any deceased children by representation;

(iv) if none of the above, to the parents of such judge or special trial judge or the survivor of them;

(v) if none of the above, to the duly appointed executor or administrator of the estate of such judge or special trial judge; and

(vi) if none of the above, to such other next of kin of such judge or special trial judge as may be determined by the chief judge to be entitled under the laws of the domicile of such judge or special trial judge at the time of his death.

Determination as to the surviving spouse, child, or parent of a judge or special trial judge for the purposes of this paragraph shall be made by the chief judge without regard to the definitions in paragraphs (8) and (9) of subsection (a).

(2) In any case in which the annuities of all persons entitled to annuity based upon the service of a judge or special trial judge shall terminate before the aggregate amount of annuity paid equals the total amount credited to the individual account of such judge or special trial judge, with interest at 3 percent per annum, compounded on December 31 of each year, to the date of the death of such judge or special trial judge, the difference shall be paid, upon establishment of a valid claim therefor, in the order of precedence prescribed in paragraph (1).

(3) Any accrued annuity remaining unpaid upon the termination (other than by death) of the annuity of any person based upon the service of a judge or special trial judge shall be paid to such person. Any accrued annuity remaining unpaid upon the death of any person receiving annuity based upon the service of a judge or special trial judge shall be paid, upon the establishment of a valid claim therefor, in the following order of precedence:

(A) to the duly appointed executor or administrator of the estate of such person;

(B) if there is no such executor or administrator payment may be made, after the expiration of thirty days from the date of the death of such person, to such individual or individuals as may appear in the judgment of the chief judge to be legally entitled thereto, and such payment shall be a bar to recovery by any other individual.

JUDICIAL PROCEEDINGS—TAX COURT

Amendments

• **2018, Tax Technical Corrections Act of 2018 (P.L. 115-141)**

P.L. 115-141, §401(a)(327), Div. U:

Amended Code Sec. 7448(j)(1)(A) by striking "Code,)," and inserting "Code),". **Effective** 3-23-2018.

• **2014, Tax Technical Corrections Act of 2014 (P.L. 113-295)**

P.L. 113-295, §221(a)(116)(C), Division A:

Amended Code Sec. 7448(j)(1) and (2) by striking "at 4 percent per annum to December 31, 1947, and 3 percent per annum thereafter" and inserting "at 3 percent per annum". **Effective** generally 12-19-2014. For a special rule, see Act Sec. 221(b)(2), Division A, below.

P.L. 113-295, §221(b)(2), Division A, provides:

(2) SAVINGS PROVISION.—If—

(A) any provision amended or repealed by the amendments made by this section applied to—

(i) any transaction occurring before the date of the enactment of this Act,

(ii) any property acquired before such date of enactment, or

(iii) any item of income, loss, deduction, or credit taken into account before such date of enactment, and

(B) the treatment of such transaction, property, or item under such provision would (without regard to the amendments or repeals made by this section) affect the liability for tax for periods ending after date of enactment, nothing in the amendments or repeals made by this section shall be construed to affect the treatment of such transaction, property, or item for purposes of determining liability for tax for periods ending after such date of enactment.

• **2006, Pension Protection Act of 2006 (P.L. 109-280)**

P.L. 109-280, §854(c)(3)(A)-(B):

Amended Code Sec. 7448(j) by inserting "or special trial judge" after "judge" each place it appears other than in the phrase "chief judge", and by inserting "or special trial judge's" after "judge's" each place it appears. **Effective** 8-17-2006.

P.L. 109-280, §854(c)(5)(A)-(B):

Amended Code Sec. 7448(j)(1) by striking "service or retired" and inserting "service, retired", and by inserting ", or receiving any annuity under chapter 83 or 84 of title 5, United States Code, [sic]" after "section 7447" in subparagraph (A), and by striking "subsections (a) (6) [sic] and (7)" and inserting "paragraphs (8) and (9) of subsection (a)" in the last sentence. **Effective** 8-17-2006.

• **1976, Tax Reform Act of 1976 (P.L. 94-455)**

P.L. 94-455, §1906(a)(46)(E):

Substituted "surviving spouse" for "widow" in Code Sec. 7448(j). **Effective** 2-1-77.

[Sec. 7448(k)]

(k) PAYMENTS TO PERSONS UNDER LEGAL DISABILITY.—Where any payment under this section is to be made to a minor, or to a person mentally incompetent or under other legal disability adjudged by a court of competent jurisdiction, such payment may be made to the person who is constituted guardian or other fiduciary by the law of the State of residence of such claimant or is otherwise legally vested with the care of the claimant or his estate. Where no guardian or other fiduciary of the person under legal disability has been appointed under the laws of the State of residence of the claimant, the chief judge shall determine the person who is otherwise legally vested with the care of the claimant or his estate.

[Sec. 7448(l)]

(l) METHOD OF PAYMENT OF ANNUITIES.—Annuities granted under the terms of this section shall accrue monthly and shall be due and payable in monthly installments on the first business day of the month following the month or other period for which the annuity shall have accrued. None of the moneys mentioned in this section shall be assignable, either in law or in equity, or subject to execution, levy, attachment, garnishment, or other legal process.

[Sec. 7448(m)]

(m) COMPUTATION OF ANNUITIES.—The annuity of the surviving spouse of a judge or special trial judge electing under subsection (b) shall be an amount equal to the sum of—

(1) the product of—

(A) 1.5 percent of the average annual salary (whether judge's or special trial judge's salary or compensation for other allowable service) received by such judge or special trial judge—

(i) for judicial service (including periods in which he received retired pay under section 7447(d), section 7447A(d), or any annuity under chapter 83 or 84 of title 5, United States Code) or for any other prior allowable service during the period of 3 consecutive years in which such judge or special trial judge received the largest such average annual salary, or

(ii) in the case of a judge or special trial judge who has served less than 3 years, during the total period of such service prior to such judge's or special trial judge's death, multiplied by the sum of, multiplied by

(B) the sum of—

(i) the judge's or special trial judge's years of such judicial service,

(ii) the judge's or special trial judge's years of prior allowable service as a Senator, Representative, Delegate, or Resident Commissioner in Congress,

(iii) the judge's or special trial judge's years of prior allowable service performed as a member of the Armed Forces of the United States, and

(iv) the judge's or special trial judge's years, not exceeding 15, of prior allowable service performed as a congressional employee (as defined in section 2107 of title 5 of the United States Code), plus

(2) three-fourths of 1 percent of such average annual salary multiplied by the judge's years of any other prior allowable service,

except that such annuity shall not exceed an amount equal to 50 percent of such average annual salary, nor be less than an amount equal to 25 percent of such average annual salary, and shall be further reduced in accordance with subsection (d) (if applicable). In determining the period of 3 consecutive years referred to in the preceding sentence, there may not be taken into account any period for which an election under section 7447(f)(4) is in effect.

Amendments

• **2022, SECURE 2.0 Act of 2022 (P.L. 117-328)**

P.L. 117-328, §701(b)(4):

Amended Code Sec. 7448(m). **Effective** 12-29-2022. Prior to amendment, Code Sec. 7448(m) read as follows:

(m) COMPUTATION OF ANNUITIES.—The annuity of the surviving spouse of a judge or special trial judge electing under subsection (b) shall be an amount equal to the sum of (1) 1.5 percent of the average annual salary (whether judge's or special trial judge's salary or compensation for other allowable service) received by such judge or special trial judge for judicial service (including periods in which he received retired pay under section 7447(d) or any annuity under chapter 83 or 84 of title 5, United States Code) or for any other prior allowable service during the period of 3 consecutive years in which he received the largest such average annual salary, multiplied by the sum of his years of such judicial service, his years of prior allowable service as a Senator, Representative, Delegate, or Resident Commissioner in Congress, his years of prior allowable service performed as a member of the Armed Forces of the United States, and his years, not exceeding 15, of prior allowable service performed as a congressional employee (as defined in section 2107 of title 5 of the United States Code), and (2) three-fourths of 1 percent of such average annual salary multiplied by his years of any other prior allowable service, except that such annuity shall not exceed an amount equal to 50 percent of such average annual salary, nor be less than an amount equal to 25 percent of such average annual salary, and shall be further reduced in accordance with subsection (d) (if applicable). In determining the period of 3 consecutive years referred to in the preceding sentence, there may not be taken into account any period for which an election under section 7447(f)(4) is in effect.

• **2018, Tax Technical Corrections Act of 2018 (P.L. 115-141)**

P.L. 115-141, §401(a)(328), Div. U:

Amended Code Sec. 7448(m) by striking "Code," and inserting "Code),". **Effective** 3-23-2018.

• **2006, Pension Protection Act of 2006 (P.L. 109-280)**

P.L. 109-280, §854(c)(3)(A)-(B):

Amended Code Sec. 7448(m) by inserting "or special trial judge" after "judge" each place it appears other than in the phrase "chief judge", and by inserting "or special trial judge's" after "judge's" each place it appears. **Effective** 8-17-2006.

P.L. 109-280, §854(c)(6):

Amended Code Sec. 7448(m)(1), as amended by this Act, by inserting "or any annuity under chapter 83 or 84 of title 5, United States Code" after "7447(d)". **Effective** 8-17-2006.

JUDICIAL PROCEEDINGS—TAX COURT

• **1986, Tax Reform Act of 1986 (P.L. 99-514)**

P.L. 99-514, §1557(c):

Amended Code Sec. 7448(m) by adding at the end thereof a new sentence. **Effective**, generally, on 10-22-86. However, for a special rule, see Act Sec. 1557(e)(2) following Code Sec. 7447(g).

P.L. 99-514, §1559(b)(1)(A)(i),(ii):

Amended Code Sec. 7448(m) by striking out "1¼ percent" and inserting in lieu thereof "1.5 percent" and by striking "but such annuity shall not" and all that follows down through the end thereof and inserting in lieu thereof "except that such annuity shall not exceed an amount equal to 50 percent of such averaging annual salary, nor be less than an amount equal to 25 percent of such average annual salary, and shall be further reduced in accordance with subsection (d) (if applicable)." **Effective** as provided in Act Sec. 1559(d) following Code Sec. 7448(g).

• **1982, Miscellaneous Revenue Act of 1982 (P.L. 97-362)**

P.L. 97-362, §105(a):

Amended Code Sec. 7448(m) (1) by striking out "5 consecutive years" and inserting in lieu thereof "3 consecutive years", and (2) by striking out "37½" and inserting in lieu thereof "40". **Effective** for annuities payable with respect to judges dying after 10-25-82.

• **1976, Tax Reform Act of 1976 (P.L. 94-455)**

P.L. 94-455, §1906(a)(46)(E):

Substituted "surviving spouse" for "widow" in Code Sec. 7448(m). For earlier amendments to Code Sec. 7448(m), see amendment note under Code Sec. 7448(t). **Effective** 2-1-77.

• **1971 (P.L. 92-41)**

P.L. 92-41, §4(b):

Amended Code Sec. 7448(m) by substituting "1¼ percent of the average annual salary (whether judge's salary or compensation for other allowable service) received by such judge for judicial service (including periods in which he received retired pay under section 7447(d)) or for any other prior allowable service during the period of 5 consecutive years in which he received the largest such average annual salary, multiplied by the sum of his years of such judicial service," in lieu of "1¼ percent of the average annual salary received by such judge for judicial service and any other prior allowable service during the last 5 years of such service prior to his death, or prior to his receiving retired pay under section 7447(d), whichever first occurs, multiplied by the sum of his years of judicial service,". **Effective** only for judges of the United States Tax Court dying on or after 7-1-71.

• **1969, Tax Reform Act of 1969 (P.L. 91-172)**

P.L. 91-172, §955(b)(3):

Amended Code Sec. 7448(m) by substituting the phrase "section 2107 of title 5 of the United States Code" for the phrase "section 1(c) of the Civil Service Retirement Act (5 U. S. C. 2251 (c))". **Effective** 12-30-69.

[Sec. 7448(n)]

(n) INCLUDIBLE SERVICE.—Subject to the provisions of subsection (d), the years of service of a judge or special trial judge which are allowable as the basis for calculating the amount of the annuity of his surviving spouse shall include his years of service as a member of the United States Board of Tax Appeals, as a judge or special trial judge of the Tax Court of the United States, and as a judge or special trial judge of the Tax Court, his years of service pursuant to any appointment under section 7443A, his years of service as a Senator, Representative, Delegate, or Resident Commissioner in Congress, his years of active service as a member of the Armed Forces of the United States not exceeding 5 years in the aggregate and not including any such service for which credit is allowed for the purposes of retirement or retired pay under any other provision of law, and his years of any other civilian service within the purview of sections 8332 and 8411 of title 5 of the United States Code.

Amendments

• **2022, SECURE 2.0 Act of 2022 (P.L. 117-328)**

P.L. 117-328, §701(c)(2)(B):

Amended Code Sec. 7448(n) by striking "section 8332" and inserting "sections 8332 and 8411". **Effective** 12-29-2022.

• **2006, Pension Protection Act of 2006 (P.L. 109-280)**

P.L. 109-280, §854(c)(3)(A)-(B):

Amended Code Sec. 7448(n) by inserting "or special trial judge" after "judge" each place it appears other than in the phrase "chief judge", and by inserting "or special trial judge's" after "judge's" each place it appears. **Effective** 8-17-2006.

P.L. 109-280, §854(c)(7):

Amended Code Sec. 7448(n) by inserting "his years of service pursuant to any appointment under section 7443A," after "of the Tax Court,". **Effective** 8-17-2006.

• **1976, Tax Reform Act of 1976 (P.L. 94-455)**

P.L. 94-455, §1906(a)(46)(E):

Substituted "surviving spouse" for "widow" in Code Sec. 7448(n). For earlier amendments to Code Sec. 7448(n), see amendment note under Code Sec. 7448(t). **Effective** 2-1-77.

• **1969, Tax Reform Act of 1969 (P.L. 91-172)**

P.L. 91-172, §955(b)(2):

Amended Code Secs. 7448(d) and (n) by substituting the phrase "section 8332 of title 5 of the United States Code" for the phrase "section 3 of the Civil Service Retirement Act (5 U. S. C. 2253)". **Effective** 12-30-69.

P.L. 91-172, §960(e):

Amended Code Sec. 7448(n) by inserting after the phrase "Tax Appeals" the phrase ", as a judge of the Tax Court of the United States,". **Effective** 12-30-69.

[Sec. 7448(o)]

(o) SIMULTANEOUS ENTITLEMENT.—Nothing contained in this section shall be construed to prevent a surviving spouse eligible therefor from simultaneously receiving an annuity under this section and any annuity to which such spouse would otherwise be entitled under any other law without regard to this section, but in computing such other annuity service used in the computation of such spouse's annuity under this section shall not be credited.

Amendments

• **1976, Tax Reform Act of 1976 (P.L. 94-455)**

P.L. 94-455, §1906(a)(46)(C):

Substituted "such spouse" for "she" in Code Sec. 7448(o). **Effective** 2-1-77.

P.L. 94-455, §1906(a)(46)(D):

Substituted "such spouse's" for "her" in Code Sec. 7448(o). **Effective** 2-1-77.

P.L. 94-455, §1906(a)(46)(E):

Substituted "surviving spouse" for "widow" in Code Sec. 7448(o). **Effective** 2-1-77.

[Sec. 7448(p)]

(p) ESTIMATES OF EXPENDITURES.—The chief judge shall submit to the President annual estimates of the expenditures and appropriations necessary for the maintenance and operation of the survivors annuity fund, and such supplemental and deficiency estimates as may be required from time to time for the same purposes, according to law. The chief judge shall cause periodic examinations of the survivors annuity fund to be made by an actuary, who may be an actuary employed by another department of the Government temporarily assigned for the purpose, and whose findings and recommendations shall be transmitted by the chief judge to the Tax Court.

Amendments

• **1984 (P.L. 98-216)**

P.L. 98-216, §3(c)(1):

Amended Code Sec. 7448(p) by striking out "Bureau of the Budget" and inserting in lieu thereof "President". **Effective** 2-14-84.

[Sec. 7448(q)]

(q) TRANSITIONAL PROVISION.—In the case of a judge who dies within 6 months after the date of enactment of this section after having rendered at least 5 years of civilian service computed as prescribed in subsection (n), but without having made an election as provided in subsection (b), an annuity shall be paid to his surviving spouse and surviving dependents as is provided in this section, as if such judge had elected on the day of his death to bring himself within the purview of this section but had not made the deposit provided for by subsection (d). An annuity shall be payable under this section computed upon the basis of the actual length of service as a judge and other allowable service of the judge and subject to the reduction required by subsection (d) even though no deposit has been made, as required by subsection (h) with respect to any of such service.

JUDICIAL PROCEEDINGS—TAX COURT

Amendments

• **1976, Tax Reform Act of 1976 (P.L. 94-455)**

P.L. 94-455, § 1906(a)(46)(E):

Substituted "surviving spouse" for "widow" in Code Sec. 7448(q). **Effective** 2-1-77.

[Sec. 7448(r)]

(r) WAIVER OF CIVIL SERVICE BENEFITS.—Any judge electing under subsection (b) shall, at the time of such election, waive all benefits under the civil service retirement laws. Such a waiver shall be made in the same manner and shall have the same force and effect as an election filed under section 7447(e).

Amendments

• **1969, Tax Reform Act of 1969 (P.L. 91-172)**

P.L. 91-172, § 955(b)(1):

Amended Code Secs. 7448(d), (h), and (r) by substituting the phrase "civil service retirement laws" for the phrase "Civil Service Retirement Act" the last place it appeared in each subsection. **Effective** 12-30-69.

P.L. 91-172, § 955(b)(4):

Amended Code Sec. 7448(r) by substituting the phrase "an election filed under section 7447(e)" for the phrase "a waiver filed under section 7447(g)(3)". **Effective** 12-30-69.

[Sec. 7448(s)]

(s) INCREASES IN SURVIVOR ANNUITIES.—Each time that an increase is made under section 8340(b) of title 5, United States Code, in annuities payable under subchapter III of chapter 83 of that title, each annuity payable from the survivors annuity fund under this section shall be increased at the same time by the same percentage by which annuities are increased under such section 8340(b).

Amendments

• **2006, Pension Protection Act of 2006 (P.L. 109-280)**

P.L. 109-280, § 851(a):

Amended Code Sec. 7448(s). **Effective** with respect to increases made under section 8340(b) of title 5, United States Code, in annuities payable under subchapter III of chapter 83 of that title, taking effect after 8-17-2006. Prior to amendment, Code Sec. 7448(s) read as follows:

(s) INCREASES ATTRIBUTABLE TO INCREASED PAY.—Whenever the salary of a judge under section 7443(c) is increased, each annuity payable from the survivors annuity fund which is based, in whole or in part, upon a deceased judge having rendered some portion of his or her final 18 months of service as a judge of the Tax Court, shall also be increased. The amount of the increase in such an annuity shall be determined by multiplying the amount of the annuity, on the date on which the increase in salary becomes effective, by 3 percent for each full 5 percent by which such salary has been increased.

• **1982, Miscellaneous Revenue Act of 1982 (P.L. 97-362)**

P.L. 97-362, § 105(b):

Added subsection (s). **Effective** with respect to increases in the salary of judges of the United States Tax Court taking effect after 10-25-82.

[Sec. 7448(t)]

(t) AUTHORIZATION OF APPROPRIATION.—Funds necessary to carry out the provisions of this section may be appropriated out of any money in the Treasury not otherwise appropriated.

Amendments

• **1982, Miscellaneous Revenue Act of 1982 (P.L. 97-362)**

P.L. 97-362, § 105(b):

Redesignated subsection (s) as (t). **Effective** with respect to increases in the salary of judges of the United States Tax Court taking effect after 10-25-82.

[Sec. 7448(u)]

(u) OTHER BENEFITS IN CASE OF ASSASSINATION.—In the case of a judge or special trial judge who is assassinated, an annuity shall be paid under this section notwithstanding a survivor's eligibility for or receipt of benefits under chapter 81 of title 5, United States Code, except that the annuity for which a surviving spouse is eligible under this section shall be reduced to the extent that the total benefits paid under this section and chapter 81 of that title for any year would exceed the current salary for that year of the office of the judge or special trial judge.

Amendments

• **2022, SECURE 2.0 Act of 2022 (P.L. 117-328)**

P.L. 117-328, § 701(b)(5):

Amended Code Sec. 7448 by adding at the end a new subsection (u). **Effective** 12-29-2022.

• **2006, Pension Protection Act of 2006 (P.L. 109-280)**

P.L. 109-280, § 854(c)(3)(A)-(B):

Amended Code Sec. 7448(u) by inserting "or special trial judge" after "judge" each place it appears other than in the phrase "chief judge", and by inserting "or special trial judge's" after "judge's" each place it appears [This amendment cannot be made, as Code Sec. 7448(u) does not exist.—CCH]. **Effective** 8-17-2006.

• **1961 (P.L. 87-370)**

P.L. 87-370, § 1:

Added Code Sec. 7448. **Effective** as provided therein.

PART II—PROCEDURE

Sec. 7451.	Petitions.
Sec. 7452.	Representation of parties.
Sec. 7453.	Rules of practice, procedure, and evidence.
Sec. 7454.	Burden of proof in fraud, foundation manager, and transferee cases.
Sec. 7455.	Service of process.
Sec. 7456.	Administration of oaths and procurement of testimony.
Sec. 7457.	Witness fees.
Sec. 7458.	Hearings.
Sec. 7459.	Reports and decisions.
Sec. 7460.	Provisions of special application to divisions.
Sec. 7461.	Publicity of proceedings.
Sec. 7462.	Publication of reports.
Sec. 7463.	Disputes involving $50,000 or less.
Sec. 7464.	Intervention by trustee of debtor's estate.
Sec. 7465.	Provisions of special application to transferees.
Sec. 7466.	Judicial conduct and disability procedures.

JUDICIAL PROCEEDINGS—TAX COURT

[Sec. 7451]

SEC. 7451. PETITIONS.

[Sec. 7451(a)]

(a) FEES.—The Tax Court is authorized to impose a fee in an amount not in excess of $60 to be fixed by the Tax Court for the filing of any petition.

[Sec. 7451(b)]

(b) TOLLING OF TIME IN CERTAIN CASES.—

(1) IN GENERAL.—Notwithstanding any other provision of this title, in any case (including by reason of a lapse in appropriations) in which a filing location is inaccessible or otherwise unavailable to the general public on the date a petition is due, the relevant time period for filing such petition shall be tolled for the number of days within the period of inaccessibility plus an additional 14 days.

(2) FILING LOCATION.—For purposes of this subsection, the term "filing location" means—

(A) the office of the clerk of the Tax Court, or

(B) any on-line portal made available by the Tax Court for electronic filing of petitions.

Amendments

• 2021, Infrastructure Investment and Jobs Act (P.L. 117-58)

P.L. 117-58, §80503(a)(1), Div. H:

Amended Code Sec. 7451 by striking "The Tax Court" and inserting "(a) FEES.—The Tax Court". **Effective** for petitions required to be timely filed (determined without regard to the amendments made by this section) after 11-15-2021.

P.L. 117-58, §80503(a)(2), Div. H:

Amended Code Sec. 7451 by adding at the end a new subsection (b). **Effective** for petitions required to be timely filed (determined without regard to the amendments made by this section) after 11-15-2021.

P.L. 117-58, §80503(b)(1), Div. H:

Amended the heading for Code Sec. 7451 by striking "FEE FOR FILING PETITION" and inserting "PETITIONS". **Effective** for petitions required to be timely filed (determined without regard to the amendments made by this section) after 11-15-2021.

• 2006, Pension Protection Act of 2006 (P.L. 109-280)

P.L. 109-280, §859(a):

Amended Code Sec. 7451 by striking all that follows "petition" and inserting a period. **Effective** 8-17-2006. Prior to being amended, the text of Code Sec. 7451 read as follows:

The Tax Court is authorized to impose a fee in an amount not in excess of $60 to be fixed by the Tax Court for the filing of any petition for the redetermination of a deficiency or for a declaratory judgment under part IV of this subchapter or under section 7428 or for judicial review under section 6226 or section 6228(a).

• 1982, Tax Equity and Fiscal Responsibility Act of 1982 (P.L. 97-248)

P.L. 97-248, §402(c)(12):

Amended Code Sec. 7451 by adding at the end "or for judicial review under section 6226 or section 6228(a)". **Effective** for partnership tax years beginning after 9-3-82, and also to partnership tax years ending after that date if the partnership, each partner, and each indirect partner requests such application and if the Secretary or his delegate consents to such application.

• 1981, Economic Recovery Tax Act of 1981 (P.L. 97-34)

P.L. 97-34, §751(a):

Amended Code Sec. 7451 by striking out "$10" and inserting "$60". **Effective** for petitions filed after 12-31-81.

• 1976, Tax Reform Act of 1976 (P.L. 94-455)

P.L. 94-455, §1306(b)(1):

Amended Code Sec. 7451 by adding "or under section 7428" at the end of the section. For the **effective** date, see Act Sec. 1306(c), below.

P.L. 94-455, §1306(c), provides:

(c) EFFECTIVE DATE.—The amendments made by this section shall apply with respect to pleadings filed with the United States Tax Court, the district court of the United States for the District of Columbia, or the United States Court of Claims more than 6 months after the date of the enactment of this Act [October 4, 1976] but only with respect to determinations (or requests for determinations) made after January 1, 1976.

• 1974, Employee Retirement Income Security Act of 1974 (P.L. 93-406)

P.L. 93-406, §1041(b)(1):

Amended Code Sec. 7451. **Effective** as to pleadings filed after 9-2-75. Prior to amendment, Code Sec. 7451 read as follows:

SEC. 7451. FEE FOR FILING PETITION.

The Tax Court is authorized to impose a fee in an amount not in excess of $10 to be fixed by the Tax Court for the filing of any petition for the redetermination of a deficiency.

[Sec. 7452]

SEC. 7452. REPRESENTATION OF PARTIES.

The Secretary shall be represented by the Chief Counsel for the Internal Revenue Service or his delegate in the same manner before the Tax Court as he has heretofore been represented in proceedings before such Court. The taxpayer shall continue to be represented in accordance with the rules of practice prescribed by the Court. No qualified person shall be denied admission to practice before the Tax Court because of his failure to be a member of any profession or calling.

Amendments

• 1976, Tax Reform Act of 1976 (P.L. 94-455)

P.L. 94-455, §1906(b)(13)(A):

Amended 1954 Code by substituting "Secretary" for "Secretary or his delegate" each place it appeared. **Effective** 2-1-77.

• 1959 (P.L. 86-368)

P.L. 86-368, §2(a):

Amended Code Sec. 7452 by striking out "Assistant General Counsel of the Treasury Department serving as Chief Counsel of the Internal Revenue Service, or the delegate of such Chief Counsel," and by substituting "Chief Counsel for the Internal Revenue Service or his delegate". **Effective** when the Chief Counsel for the Internal Revenue Service first appointed pursuant to Code Sec. 7801, as amended by P.L. 86-368, Act Sec. 1, qualifies and takes office.

[Sec. 7453]

SEC. 7453. RULES OF PRACTICE, PROCEDURE, AND EVIDENCE.

Except in the case of proceedings conducted under section 7436(c) or 7463, the proceedings of the Tax Court and its divisions shall be conducted in accordance with such rules of practice and procedure (other than rules of evidence) as the Tax Court may prescribe and in accordance with the Federal Rules of Evidence.

Amendments

• 2015, Protecting Americans from Tax Hikes Act of 2015 (P.L. 114-113)

P.L. 114-113, §425(a), Div. Q:

Amended Code Sec. 7453 by striking "the rules of evidence applicable in trials without a jury in the United States District Court of the District of Columbia" and inserting "the Federal Rules of Evidence". **Effective** for proceedings commenced after 12-18-2015 and, to the extent that it is just and practicable, to all proceedings pending on such date.

• 1997, Taxpayer Relief Act of 1997 (P.L. 105-34)

P.L. 105-34, §1454(b)(3):

Amended Code Sec. 7453 by striking "section 7463" and inserting "section 7436(c) or 7463". **Effective** 8-5-97.

• 1969, Tax Reform Act of 1969 (P.L. 91-172)

P.L. 91-172, §960(f):

Amended Code Sec. 7453 by adding the initial phrase "Except in the case of proceedings conducted under section 7463,". **Effective** 12-30-70.

JUDICIAL PROCEEDINGS—TAX COURT

[Sec. 7454]

SEC. 7454. BURDEN OF PROOF IN FRAUD, FOUNDATION MANAGER, AND TRANSFEREE CASES.

[Sec. 7454(a)]

(a) FRAUD.—In any proceeding involving the issue whether the petitioner has been guilty of fraud with intent to evade tax, the burden of proof in respect of such issue shall be upon the Secretary.

Amendments

• **1976, Tax Reform Act of 1976 (P.L. 94-455)**

P.L. 94-455, §1906(b)(13)(A):

Amended 1954 Code by substituting "Secretary" for "Secretary or his delegate" each place it appeared. **Effective** 2-1-77.

[Sec. 7454(b)]

(b) FOUNDATION MANAGERS.—In any proceeding involving the issue whether a foundation manager (as defined in section 4946(b)) has "knowingly" participated in an act of self-dealing (within the meaning of section 4941), participated in an investment which jeopardizes the carrying out of exempt purposes (within the meaning of section 4944), or agreed to the making of a taxable expenditure (within the meaning of section 4945), or whether the trustee of a trust described in section 501(c)(21) has "knowingly" participated in an act of self-dealing (within the meaning of section 4951) or agreed to the making of a taxable expenditure (within the meaning of section 4952), or whether an organization manager (as defined in section 4955(f)(2) has "knowingly" agreed to the making of a political expenditure (within the meaning of section 4955), or whether an organization manager (as defined in section 4912(d)(2)) has "knowingly" agreed to the making of disqualifying lobbying expenditures within the meaning of section 4912(b), or whether an organization manager (as defined in section 4958(f)(2)) has "knowingly" participated in an excess benefit transaction (as defined in section 4958(c)) the burden of proof in respect of such issue shall be upon the Secretary.

Amendments

• **2018, Tax Technical Corrections Act of 2018 (P.L. 115-141)**

P.L. 115-141, §401(a)(329), Div. U:

Amended Code Sec. 7454(b) by striking "4955,," and inserting "4955),". **Effective** 3-23-2018.

• **1996, Small Business Job Protection Act of 1996 (P.L. 104-188)**

P.L. 104-188, §1704(t)(43):

Amended Code Sec. 7454(b) by striking "section 4955(e)(2)" and inserting "section 4955(f)(2)". **Effective** 8-20-96.

• **1996, Taxpayer Bill of Rights 2 (P.L. 104-168)**

P.L. 104-168, §1311(c)(5):

Amended Code Sec. 7454(b) by inserting "or whether an organization manager (as defined in section 4958(f)(2)) has `knowingly' participated in an excess benefit transaction (as defined in section 4958(c))," after "section 4912(b),". For the **effective date**, see Act Sec. 1311(d)(1)-(2), below.

P.L. 104-168, §1311(d)(1)-(2), provides:

(d) EFFECTIVE DATES.—

(1) IN GENERAL.—The amendments made by this section (other than subsection (b)) shall apply to excess benefit transactions occurring on or after September 14, 1995.

(2) BINDING CONTRACTS.—The amendments referred to in paragraph (1) shall not apply to any benefit arising from a transaction pursuant to any written contract which was binding on September 13, 1995, and at all times thereafter before such transaction occurred.

• **1987, Revenue Act of 1987 (P.L. 100-203)**

P.L. 100-203, §10712(c)(6):

Amended Code Sec. 7454(b) by striking out "the burden of proof" and inserting in lieu thereof "or whether an organization manager (as defined in section 4955(e)(2)) has `knowingly' agreed to the making of a political expenditure (within the meaning of section 4955), the burden of proof". **Effective** for tax years beginning after 12-22-87.

P.L. 100-203, §10714(b):

Amended Code Sec. 7454(b) by striking out "the burden of proof" and inserting in lieu thereof " or whether an organization manager (as defined in section 4912(d)(2)) has `knowingly' agreed to the making of disqualifying lobbying expenditures within the meaning of section 4912(b), the burden of proof". **Effective** for tax years beginning after 12-22-87.

• **1980, Technical Corrections Act of 1979 (P.L. 96-222)**

P.L. 96-222, §108(b)(3)(B):

Amended Code Sec. 7454(b) by striking out "502(c)(21)" and inserting "501(c)(21)". **Effective** as if included in the provision of P.L. 95-227 to which it relates.

• **1978, Black Lung Benefits Revenue Act of 1977 (P.L. 95-227)**

P.L. 95-227, §4(d)(7):

Amended Code Sec. 7454(b). **Effective** with respect to contributions, acts and expenditures made after 12-31-77, in and for tax years beginning after such date. However, this effective date was contingent upon enactment of P.L. 95-239, which was enacted on 3-1-78. Prior to amendment, Code Sec. 7454(b) read as follows:

"(b) FOUNDATION MANAGERS.—In any proceedings involving the issue whether a foundation manager (as defined in section 4946(b)) has `knowingly, participated in an act of self-dealing (within the meaning of section 4941), participated in an investment which jeopardizes the carrying out of exempt purposes (within the meaning of section 4944), or agreed to the making of a taxable expenditure (within the meaning of section 4945), the burden of proof in respect of such issue shall be upon the Secretary."

• **1976, Tax Reform Act of 1976 (P.L. 94-455)**

P.L. 94-455, §1906(b)(13)(A):

Amended 1954 Code by substituting "Secretary" for "Secretary or his delegate" each place it appeared. **Effective** 2-1-77.

[Sec. 7454(c)]

(c) CROSS REFERENCE.—

For provisions relating to burden of proof as to transferee liability, see section 6902(a).

Amendments

• **1976, Tax Reform Act of 1976 (P.L. 94-455)**

P.L. 94-455, §1906(b)(13)(A):

Amended 1954 Code by substituting "Secretary" for "Secretary or his delegate" each place it appeared. **Effective** 2-1-77.

• **1969, Tax Reform Act of 1969 (P.L. 91-172)**

P.L. 91-172, §101(j)(57):

Amended Code Sec. 7454 by adding ", FOUNDATION MANAGER," in the title, by redesignating subsection (b) to be subsection (c), and by adding a new subsection (b). **Effective** 1-1-70.

[Sec. 7455]

SEC. 7455. SERVICE OF PROCESS.

The mailing by certified mail or registered mail of any pleading, decision, order, notice, or process in respect of proceedings before the Tax Court shall be held sufficient service of such pleading, decision, order, notice, or process.

Amendments

• **1958, Technical Amendments Act of 1958 (P.L. 85-866)**

P.L. 85-866, §89(b):

Amended Sec. 7455 by striking out "registered mail" and substituting "certified mail or registered mail". **Effective** only if the mailing occurs after 9-2-58.

[Sec. 7456]

SEC. 7456. ADMINISTRATION OF OATHS AND PROCUREMENT OF TESTIMONY.

[Sec. 7456(a)]

(a) IN GENERAL.—For the efficient administration of the functions vested in the Tax Court or any division thereof, any judge or special trial judge of the Tax Court, the clerk of the court or his deputies, as such, or any other employee of the Tax Court designated in writing for the purpose by the chief judge, may administer oaths, and any judge or special trial judge of the Tax Court may examine witnesses and require, by subpoena

JUDICIAL PROCEEDINGS—TAX COURT

ordered by the Tax Court or any division thereof and signed by the judge or special trial judge (or by the clerk of the Tax Court or by any other employee of the Tax Court when acting as deputy clerk)—

(1) the attendance and testimony of witnesses, and the production of all necessary returns, books, papers, documents, correspondence, and other evidence, from any place in the United States at any designated place of hearing, or

(2) the taking of a deposition before any designated individual competent to administer oaths under this title. In the case of a deposition the testimony shall be reduced to writing by the individual taking the deposition or under his direction and shall then be subscribed by the deponent.

Amendments

- **1984, Deficit Reduction Act of 1984 (P.L. 98-369)**

P.L. 98-369, §464(a):

Amended Code Sec. 7456(a) by striking out "commissioner" each place it appeared and inserting in lieu thereof "special trial judge". **Effective** 7-18-84.

- **1978, Revenue Act of 1978 (P.L. 95-600)**

P.L. 95-600, §502(c)(1), (2):

Amended Code Sec. 7456(a) by deleting "any judge of the Tax Court" each place it appeared and inserting in lieu thereof "any judge or commissioner of the Tax Court" and by deleting "by the judge" and inserting in lieu thereof "by the judge or commissioner". **Effective** 11-6-78.

[Sec. 7456(b)]

(b) PRODUCTION OF RECORDS IN THE CASE OF FOREIGN CORPORATIONS, FOREIGN TRUSTS OR ESTATES AND NONRESIDENT ALIEN INDIVIDUALS.—The Tax Court or any division thereof, upon motion and notice by the Secretary, and upon good cause shown therefor, shall order any foreign corporation, foreign trust or estate, or nonresident alien individual, who has filed a petition with the Tax Court, to produce, or, upon satisfactory proof to the Tax Court or any of its divisions, that the petitioner is unable to produce, to make available to the Secretary, and, in either case, to permit the inspection, copying, or photographing of such books, records, documents, memoranda, correspondence and other papers, wherever situated, as the Tax Court or any division thereof, may deem relevant to the proceedings and which are in the possession, custody or control of the petitioner, or of any person directly or indirectly under his control or having control over him or subject to the same common control. If the petitioner fails or refuses to comply with any of the provisions of such order, after reasonable time for compliance has been afforded to him, the Tax Court or any division thereof, upon motion, shall make an order striking out pleadings or parts thereof, or dismissing the proceeding or any part thereof, or rendering a judgment by default against the petitioner. For the purpose of this subsection, the term "foreign trust or estate" includes an estate or trust, any fiduciary of which is a foreign corporation or nonresident alien individual; and the term "control" is not limited to legal control.

Amendments

- **1976, Tax Reform Act of 1976 (P.L. 94-455)**

P.L. 94-455, §1906(b)(13)(A):

Amended 1954 Code by substituting "Secretary" for "Secretary or his delegate" each place it appeared. **Effective** 2-1-77.

[Sec. 7456(c)—Repealed]

Amendments

- **1986, Tax Reform Act of 1986 (P.L. 99-514)**

P.L. 99-514, §1556(b)(1):

Amended Code Sec. 7456 by striking out subsection (c) and redesignating subsection (e) as subsection (c). **Effective** 10-22-86. However, see Act Sec. 1556(c)(3), below. Prior to amendment, Code Sec. 7456(c) read as follows:

(c) SPECIAL TRIAL JUDGES.—The chief judge may from time to time appoint special trial judges who shall proceed under such rules and regulations as may be promulgated by the Tax Court. Each special trial judge shall receive pay at an annual rate determined under section 225 of the Federal Salary Act of 1967 (2 U.S.C. 351-361), as adjusted by section 461 of title 28, United States Code, and also necessary traveling expenses and per diem allowances, as provided in subchapter I of chapter 57 of title 5, United States Code, while traveling on official business and away from Washington, District of Columbia.

P.L. 99-514, §1556(c)(3), provides:

(3) NEW APPOINTMENTS NOT REQUIRED.—Nothing in the amendments made by this section shall be construed to require the reappointment of any individual serving as a special trial judge of the Tax Court on the day before the date of the enactment of this Act.

- **1984, Deficit Reduction Act of 1984 (P.L. 98-369)**

P.L. 98-369, §464(b):

Amended Code Sec. 7456(c) by striking out "COMMISSIONERS" in the heading and inserting in lieu thereof "SPECIAL TRIAL JUDGES"; by striking out "commissioners" and inserting in lieu thereof "special trial judges"; and by striking out "commissioner" and inserting in lieu thereof "special trial judge". **Effective** 7-18-84.

- **1982, Miscellaneous Revenue Act of 1982 (P.L. 97-362)**

P.L. 97-362, §106(c)(2):

Amended Code Sec. 7456(c) by striking out the last sentence. **Effective** 10-25-82. Prior to amendment, the last sentence read:

"The chief judge may assign proceedings under sections 6226, 6228(a), 7428, 7463, 7476, 7477, and 7478 to be heard by the commissioners of the court, and the court may authorize a commissioner to make the decision of the court with respect to such proceedings, subject to such conditions and review as the court may by rule provide."

- **1982, Tax Equity and Fiscal Responsibility Act of 1982 (P.L. 97-248)**

P.L. 97-248, §402(c)(13):

Amended Code Sec. 7456(c) by adding "6226, 6228(a)" before "7428". **Effective** for partnership tax years beginning after 9-3-82 and also to partnership tax years ending after that date if the partnership, each partner, and each indirect partner requests such application and if the Secretary or his delegate consents to such application.

- **1982, Federal Courts Improvement Act of 1982 (P.L. 97-164)**

P.L. 97-164, §153(a):

Amended the second sentence of Code Sec. 7456(c). **Effective** 10-1-82. Prior to amendment, the second sentence read:

"Each commissioner shall receive the same compensation and travel and subsistence allowances provided by law for commissioners of the United States Court of Claims."

P.L. 97-164, §153(b), provides:

(b) Notwithstanding the amendment made by subsection (a), until such time as a change in the salary rate of a commissioner of the United States Tax Court occurs in accordance with section 7456(c) of the Internal Revenue Code of 1954, the salary of such commissioner shall be equal to the salary of a commissioner of the Court of Claims immediately prior to the effective date of this Act.

- **1980, Technical Corrections Act of 1979 (P.L. 96-222)**

P.L. 96-222, §105(a)(1)(B):

Amended Code Sec. 7456(c) by changing "sections 7428" to "sections 7428, 7463". **Effective** 4-1-80.

- **1978, Revenue Act of 1978 (P.L. 95-600)**

P.L. 95-600, §336(b)(1):

Amended Code Sec. 7456(c) by adding the last sentence. **Effective** for requests for determinations made after 12-31-78.

- **1969, Tax Reform Act of 1969 (P.L. 91-172)**

P.L. 91-172, §958:

Amended Code Sec. 7456(c). **Effective** 12-30-69. Prior to amendment, subsection (c) read as follows:

(c) Commissioners.—The chief judge may from time to time by written order designate an attorney from the legal staff of the Tax Court to act as a commissioner in a particular case. The commissioner so designated shall proceed under such rules and regulations as may be promulgated by the Tax Court. The commissioner shall receive the same travel and subsistence allowances now or hereafter provided by law for commissioners of the United States Court of Claims.

[Sec. 7456(d)—Repealed]

(d) PROCEEDINGS WHICH MAY BE ASSIGNED TO SPECIAL TRIAL JUDGES.—The chief judge may assign—

(1) any declaratory judgment proceeding,

(2) any proceeding under section 7463,

Amendments

- **1986, Tax Reform Act of 1986 (P.L. 99-514)**

P.L. 99-514, §1556(b)(1):

Amended Code Sec. 7456 by striking out subsection (d). **Effective** 10-22-86. However, see Act Sec. 1556(c)(3) in the amendments for repealed Code Sec. 7456(c). Prior to amendment, Code Sec. 7456 (d) read as follows:

JUDICIAL PROCEEDINGS—TAX COURT

(3) any proceeding where neither the amount of the deficiency placed in dispute (within the meaning of section 7463) nor the amount of any claimed overpayment exceeds $10,000; and

(4) any other proceeding which the chief judge may designate,

to be heard by the special trial judges of the court, and the court may authorize a special trial judge to make the decision of the court with respect to any proceeding described in paragraph (1), (2), or (3), subject to such conditions and review as the court may provide.

- **1984, Deficit Reduction Act of 1984 (P.L. 98-369)**

P.L. 98-369, § 463(a):

Amended Code Sec. 7456(d). **Effective** as if enacted as part of P.L. 97-362. Prior to amendment, it read as follows:

(d) Proceedings Which May Be Assigned to Commissioners.—The chief judge may assign—

(1) any declaratory judgment proceeding,

(2) any proceeding under section 7463, and

(3) any other proceeding where neither the amount of the deficiency placed in dispute (within the meaning of section 7463) nor the amount of any claimed overpayment exceeds $5,000,

to be heard by the commissioners of the court, and the court may authorize a commissioner to make the decision of the court with respect to any such proceeding, subject to such conditions and review as the court may by rule provide.

P.L. 98-369, § 464(c):

Amended Code Sec. 7456(d) as amended by Act Sec. 463(a), by striking out "COMMISSIONERS" in the heading and inserting in lieu thereof "SPECIAL TRIAL JUDGES"; by striking out "commissioners" and inserting in lieu thereof "special trial judges"; and by striking out "commisssioner" and inserting in lieu thereof "special trial judge". **Effective** 7-18-84. Any reference in any law to a commissioner of the Tax Court shall be treated as a reference to a special trial judge of the Tax Court.

- **1982, Miscellaneous Revenue Act of 1982 (P.L. 97-362)**

P.L. 97-362, § 106(c)(1):

Added Code Sec. 7456(d). **Effective** 10-25-82.

[Sec. 7456(c)]

(c) INCIDENTAL POWERS.—The Tax Court and each division thereof shall have power to punish by fine or imprisonment, at its discretion, such contempt of its authority, and none other, as—

(1) misbehavior of any person in its presence or so near thereto as to obstruct the administration of justice;

(2) misbehavior of any of its officers in their official transactions; or

(3) disobedience or resistance to its lawful writ, process, order, rule, decree, or command.

It shall have such assistance in the carrying out of its lawful writ, process, order, rule, decree, or command as is available to a court of the United States. The United States marshal for any district in which the Tax Court is sitting shall, when requested by the chief judge of the Tax Court, attend any session of the Tax Court in such district and may otherwise provide, when requested by the chief judge of the Tax Court, for the security of the Tax Court, including the personal protection of Tax Court judges, court officers, witnesses, and other threatened persons in the interests of justice, where criminal intimidation impedes on the functioning of the judicial process or any other official proceeding. The United States Marshals Service retains final authority regarding security requirements for the Tax Court.

Amendments

- **2008, Court Security Improvement Act of 2007 (110-177)**

P.L. 110-177, § 102(ab):

Amended Code Sec. 7456(c) by striking the period at the end of the matter following paragraph (3) and inserting "and may otherwise provide, when requested by the chief judge of the Tax Court, for the security of the Tax Court, including the personal protection of Tax Court judges, court officers, witnesses, and other threatened persons in the interests of justice, where criminal intimidation impedes on the functioning of the judicial process or any other official proceeding. The United States Marshals Service retains final authority regarding security requirements for the Tax Court.". **Effective** 1-7-2008.

- **1986, Tax Reform Act of 1986 (P.L. 99-514)**

P.L. 99-514, § 1555(a):

Amended Code Sec. 7456(e) by adding at the end thereof a new sentence. **Effective** 10-22-86.

P.L. 99-514, § 1556(b)(1):

Amended Code Sec. 7456 by striking out subsections (c) and (d) and redesignating subsection (e) as subsection (c). **Effective** 10-22-86. However, see Act Sec. 1556(c)(3) in the amendments for repealed Code Sec. 7456(c).

- **1982, Miscellaneous Revenue Act of 1982 (P.L. 97-362)**

P.L. 97-362, § 106(c)(1):

Redesignated subsection (d) as (e). **Effective** 10-25-82.

- **1969, Tax Reform Act of 1969 (P.L. 91-172)**

P.L. 91-172, § 956:

Added Code Sec. 7456(d). **Effective** 12-30-69.

[Sec. 7457]

SEC. 7457. WITNESS FEES.

[Sec. 7457(a)]

(a) AMOUNT.—Any witness summoned or whose deposition is taken under section 7456 shall receive the same fees and mileage as witnesses in courts of the United States.

[Sec. 7457(b)]

(b) PAYMENT.—Such fees and mileage and the expenses of taking any such deposition shall be paid as follows:

(1) WITNESSES FOR SECRETARY.—In the case of witnesses for the Secretary, such payments shall be made by the Secretary out of any moneys appropriated for the collection of internal revenue taxes, and may be made in advance.

(2) OTHER WITNESSES.—In the case of any other witnesses, such payments shall be made, subject to rules prescribed by the Tax Court, by the party at whose instance the witness appears or the deposition is taken.

Amendments

- **1976, Tax Reform Act of 1976 (P.L. 94-455)**

P.L. 94-455, § 1906(b)(13)(A):

Amended 1954 Code by substituting "Secretary" for "Secretary or his delegate" each place it appeared. **Effective** 2-1-77.

[Sec. 7458]

SEC. 7458. HEARINGS.

Notice and opportunity to be heard upon any proceeding instituted before the Tax Court shall be given to the taxpayer and the Secretary. If an opportunity to be heard upon the proceeding is given before a division of the Tax Court, neither the taxpayer nor the Secretary shall be entitled to notice and opportunity to be heard before the Tax Court upon review, except upon a specific order of the chief judge. Hearings before the Tax Court and its divisions shall be open to the public, and the testimony, and, if the Tax Court so requires, the argument, shall be stenographically reported. The Tax Court is authorized to contract (by renewal of contract or otherwise) for the reporting of such hearings, and in such contract to fix the terms and conditions under which transcripts will be supplied by the contractor to the Tax Court and to other persons and agencies.

Amendments

- **1976, Tax Reform Act of 1976 (P.L. 94-455)**

P.L. 94-455, § 1906(b)(13)(A):

Amended 1954 Code by substituting "Secretary" for "Secretary or his delegate" each place it appeared. **Effective** 2-1-77.

P.L. 94-455, § 1906(b)(13)(L):

Amended Code Sec. 7458 by striking out "nor his delegate" after "Secretary". **Effective** 2-1-77.

JUDICIAL PROCEEDINGS—TAX COURT

[Sec. 7459]
SEC. 7459. REPORTS AND DECISIONS.

[Sec. 7459(a)]

(a) REQUIREMENT.—A report upon any proceeding instituted before the Tax Court and a decision thereon shall be made as quickly as practicable. The decision shall be made by a judge in accordance with the report of the Tax Court, and such decision so made shall, when entered, be the decision of the Tax Court.

[Sec. 7459(b)]

(b) INCLUSION OF FINDINGS OF FACT OR OPINIONS IN REPORT.—It shall be the duty of the Tax Court and of each division to include in its report upon any proceeding its findings of fact or opinion or memorandum opinion. The Tax Court shall report in writing all its findings of fact, opinions, and memorandum opinions. Subject to such conditions as the Tax Court may by rule provide, the requirements of this subsection and of section 7460 are met if findings of fact or opinion are stated orally and recorded in the transcript of the proceedings.

Amendments
- **1982, Miscellaneous Revenue Act of 1982 (P.L. 97-362)**

P.L. 97-362, § 106(b):

Amended Code Sec. 7459(b) by adding the last sentence. **Effective** 10-25-82.

[Sec. 7459(c)]

(c) DATE OF DECISION.—A decision of the Tax Court (except a decision dismissing a proceeding for lack of jurisdiction) shall be held to be rendered upon the date that an order specifying the amount of the deficiency is entered in the records of the Tax Court or, in the case of a declaratory judgment proceeding under part IV of this subchapter, or under section 7428 or in the case of an action brought under section 6234, the date of the court's order entering the decision. If the Tax Court dismisses a proceeding for reasons other than lack of jurisdiction and is unable from the record to determine the amount of the deficiency determined by the Secretary, or if the Tax Court dismisses a proceeding for lack of jurisdiction, an order to that effect shall be entered in the records of the Tax Court, and the decision of the Tax Court shall be held to be rendered upon the date of such entry.

Amendments
- **2015, Bipartisan Budget Act of 2015 (P.L. 114-74)**

P.L. 114-74, § 1101(f)(12):

Amended Code Sec. 7459(c) by striking "section 6226" and all that follows through "or 6252" and inserting "section 6234". **Effective** generally for returns filed for partnership tax years beginning after 12-31-2017. For a special rule, see Act Sec. 1101(g)(4), below. Prior to being stricken, "section 6226" and all that follows through "or 6252" read as follows:

section 6226, 6228(a), 6234(c)[,] 6247, or 6252

P.L. 114-74, § 1101(g)(4), provides:

(4) ELECTION.—A partnership may elect (at such time and in such form and manner as the Secretary of the Treasury may prescribe) for the amendments made by this section (other than the election under section 6221(b) of such Code (as added by this Act)) to apply to any return of the partnership filed for partnership taxable years beginning after the date of the enactment of this Act and before January 1, 2018.

- **1997, Taxpayer Relief Act of 1997 (P.L. 105-34)**

P.L. 105-34, § 1222(b)(2):

Amended Code Sec. 7459(c) by striking "or section 6228(a)" and inserting ", 6228(a), 6247, or 6252". **Effective** for partnership tax years beginning after 12-31-97 [**effective** date changed by P.L. 105-206, § 6012(e)].

P.L. 105-34, § 1239(e)(1):

Amended Code Sec. 7459(c) by striking "or section 6228(a)" [sic] and inserting ", 6228(a), or [sic]6234(c)[,]". **Effective** for partnership tax years ending after 8-5-97.

- **1982, Tax Equity and Fiscal Responsibility Act of 1982 (P.L. 97-248)**

P.L. 97-248, § 402(c)(14):

Amended Code Sec. 7459(c) by inserting after "or under section 7428" "or in the case of an action brought under section 6226 or section 6228(a)". **Effective** for partnership tax years beginning after 9-3-82 and also to partner tax years ending after that date if the partnership, each partner, and each indirect partner requests such application and if the Secretary or his delegate consents to such application.

- **1976, Tax Reform Act of 1976 (P.L. 94-455)**

P.L. 94-455, § 1906(b)(13)(A):

Amended 1954 Code by substituting "Secretary" for "Secretary or his delegate" each place it appeared. **Effective** 2-1-77.

P.L. 94-455, § 1306(b)(2):

Amended Code Sec. 7459(c) by inserting "or under section 7428" after "under part IV of this subchapter". For the **effective** date, see Act Sec. 1306(c), below.

P.L. 94-455, § 1306(c), provides:

(c) EFFECTIVE DATE.—The amendments made by this section shall apply with respect to pleadings filed with the United States Tax Court, the district court of the United States for the District of Columbia, or the United States Court of Claims more than 6 months after the date of the enactment of this Act [October 4, 1976] but only with respect to determinations (or requests for determinations) made after January 1, 1976.

- **1974, Employee Retirement Income Security Act of 1974 (P.L. 93-406)**

P.L. 93-406, § 1041(b)(2):

Amended Code Sec. 7459(c). **Effective** as to pleadings filed after 9-2-75. Prior to amendment, Code Sec. 7459(c) read as follows:

"(c) Date of Decision.—A decision of the Tax Court (except a decision dismissing a proceeding for lack of jurisdiction) shall be held to be rendered upon the date that an order specifying the amount of the deficiency is entered in the records of the Tax Court. If the Tax Court dismisses a proceeding for reasons other than lack of jurisdiction and is unable from the record to determine the amount of the deficiency determined by the Secretary or his delegate, or if the Tax Court dismisses a proceeding for lack of jurisdiction, an order to that effect shall be entered in the records of the Tax Court, and the decision of the Tax Court shall be held to be rendered upon the date of such entry."

[Sec. 7459(d)]

(d) EFFECT OF DECISION DISMISSING PETITION.—If a petition for a redetermination of a deficiency has been filed by the taxpayer, a decision of the Tax Court dismissing the proceeding shall be considered as its decision that the deficiency is the amount determined by the Secretary. An order specifying such amount shall be entered in the records of the Tax Court unless the Tax Court cannot determine such amount from the record in the proceeding, or unless the dismissal is for lack of jurisdiction.

Amendments
- **1976, Tax Reform Act of 1976 (P.L. 94-455)**

P.L. 94-455, § 1906(b)(13)(A):

Amended 1954 Code by substituting "Secretary" for "Secretary or his delegate" each place it appeared. **Effective** 2-1-77.

[Sec. 7459(e)]

(e) EFFECT OF DECISION THAT TAX IS BARRED BY LIMITATION.—If the assessment or collection of any tax is barred by any statute of limitations, the decision of the Tax Court to that effect shall be considered as its decision that there is no deficiency in respect of such tax.

[Sec. 7459(f)]

(f) FINDINGS OF FACT AS EVIDENCE.—The findings of the Board of Tax Appeals made in connection with any decision prior to February 26, 1926, shall, notwithstanding the enactment of the Revenue Act of 1926 (44 Stat. 9), continue to be prima facie evidence of the facts therein stated.

[Sec. 7459(g)]

(g) PENALTY.—

For penalty for taxpayer instituting proceedings before Tax Court merely for delay, see section 6673.

JUDICIAL PROCEEDINGS—TAX COURT

[Sec. 7460]
SEC. 7460. PROVISIONS OF SPECIAL APPLICATION TO DIVISIONS.

[Sec. 7460(a)]
(a) HEARINGS, DETERMINATIONS, AND REPORTS.—A division shall hear, and make a determination upon, any proceeding instituted before the Tax Court and any motion in connection therewith, assigned to such division by the chief judge, and shall make a report of any such determination which constitutes its final disposition of the proceeding.

[Sec. 7460(b)]
(b) EFFECT OF ACTION BY A DIVISION.—The report of the division shall become the report of the Tax Court within 30 days after such report by the division, unless within such period the chief judge has directed that such report shall be reviewed by the Tax Court. Any preliminary action by a division which does not form the basis for the entry of the final decision shall not be subject to review by the Tax Court except in accordance with such rules as the Tax Court may prescribe. The report of a division shall not be a part of the record in any case in which the chief judge directs that such report shall be reviewed by the Tax Court.

[Sec. 7461]
SEC. 7461. PUBLICITY OF PROCEEDINGS.

[Sec. 7461(a)]
(a) GENERAL RULE.—Except as provided in subsection (b), all reports of the Tax Court and all evidence received by the Tax Court and its divisions, including a transcript of the stenographic report of the hearings, shall be public records open to the inspection of the public.

[Sec. 7461(b)]
(b) EXCEPTIONS.—
(1) TRADE SECRETS OR OTHER CONFIDENTIAL INFORMATION.—The Tax Court may make any provision which is necessary to prevent the disclosure of trade secrets or other confidential information, including a provision that any document or information be placed under seal to be opened only as directed by the court.
(2) EVIDENCE, ETC.—After the decision of the Tax Court in any proceeding has become final, the Tax Court may, upon motion of the taxpayer or the Secretary, permit the withdrawal by the party entitled thereto of originals of books, documents, and records, and of models, diagrams, and other exhibits, introduced in evidence before the Tax Court or any division; or the Tax Court may, on its own motion, make such other disposition thereof as it deems advisable.

Amendments

• **1984, Deficit Reduction Act of 1984 (P.L. 98-369)**

P.L. 98-369, §465(a):

Amended Code Sec. 7461. **Effective** 7-18-84. Prior to amendment, it read as follows:
SEC. 7461. PUBLICITY OF PROCEEDINGS.
All reports of the Tax Court and all evidence received by the Tax Court and its divisions, including a transcript of the stenographic report of the hearings, shall be public records open to the inspection of the public; except that after the decision of the Tax Court in any proceeding has become final the Tax Court may, upon motion of the taxpayer or the Secretary, permit the withdrawal by the party entitled thereto of originals of books, documents, and records, and of models, diagrams, and other exhibits, introduced in evidence before the Tax Court or any division; or the Tax Court may, on its own motion, make such other disposition thereof as it deems advisable.

• **1976, Tax Reform Act of 1976 (P.L. 94-455)**

P.L. 94-455, §1906(b)(13)(A):

Amended 1954 Code by substituting "Secretary" for "Secretary or his delegate" each place it appeared. **Effective** 2-1-77.

[Sec. 7462]
SEC. 7462. PUBLICATION OF REPORTS.

The Tax Court shall provide for the publication of its reports at the Government Printing Office in such form and manner as may be best adapted for public information and use, and such authorized publication shall be competent evidence of the reports of the Tax Court therein contained in all courts of the United States and of the several States without any further proof or authentication thereof. Such reports shall be subject to sale in the same manner and upon the same terms as other public documents.

[Sec. 7463]
SEC. 7463. DISPUTES INVOLVING $50,000 OR LESS.

[Sec. 7463(a)]
(a) IN GENERAL.—In the case of any petition filed with the Tax Court for a redetermination of a deficiency where neither the amount of the deficiency placed in dispute, nor the amount of any claimed overpayment, exceeds—
(1) $50,000 for any one taxable year, in the case of the taxes imposed by subtitle A,
(2) $50,000, in the case of the tax imposed by chapter 11,
(3) $50,000 for any one calendar year, in the case of the tax imposed by chapter 12, or
(4) $50,000 for any 1 taxable period (or, if there is no taxable period, taxable event) in the case of any tax imposed by subtitle D which is described in section 6212(a) (relating to a notice of deficiency),
at the option of the taxpayer concurred in by the Tax Court or a division thereof before the hearing of the case, proceedings in the case shall be conducted under this section. Notwithstanding the provisions of section 7453, such proceedings shall be conducted in accordance with such rules of evidence, practice, and procedure as the Tax Court may prescribe. A decision, together with a brief summary of the reasons therefor, in any such case shall satisfy the requirements of sections 7459(b) and 7460.

Amendments

• **1998, IRS Restructuring and Reform Act of 1998 (P.L. 105-206)**

P.L. 105-206, §3103(a):

Amended Code Sec. 7463 by striking "$10,000" each place it appears (including the section heading) and inserting "$50,000". **Effective** for proceedings commenced after 7-22-98.

• **1984, Deficit Reduction Act of 1984 (P.L. 98-369)**

P.L. 98-369, §461(a)(1):

Amended Code Sec. 7463(a) by striking out "$5,000" each place it appeared and inserting in lieu thereof "$10,000". **Effective** 7-18-84.

P.L. 98-369, §461(a)(2)(A):

Amended Code Sec. 7463 by striking out "$5,000" in the heading and inserting in lieu thereof "$10,000". **Effective** 7-18-84.

• **1982, Miscellaneous Revenue Act of 1982 (P.L. 97-362)**

P.L. 97-362, §106(a):

Amended Code Sec. 7463(a) by striking out "or" at the end of paragraph (2), by adding "or" at the end of paragraph (3), and by inserting after paragraph (3) the new paragraph (4). **Effective** with respect to petitions filed after 10-25-82.

• **1978, Revenue Act of 1978 (P.L. 95-600)**

P.L. 95-600, §502(a)(1):

Amended Code Sec. 7463(a) by adding paragraphs (1), (2), and (3). **Effective** on the first day of the first calendar month beginning more than 180 days after 11-6-78. Prior to amendment, Code Sec. 7463(a)(1) and (2) read:
"(1) $1,500 for any one taxable year, in the case of the taxes imposed by subtitle A and chapter 12, or
"(2) $1,500, in the case of the tax imposed by chapter 11,".

JUDICIAL PROCEEDINGS—TAX COURT

[Sec. 7463(b)]

(b) FINALITY OF DECISIONS.—A decision entered in any case in which the proceedings are conducted under this section shall not be reviewed in any other court and shall not be treated as a precedent for any other case.

[Sec. 7463(c)]

(c) LIMITATION OF JURISDICTION.—In any case in which the proceedings are conducted under this section, notwithstanding the provisions of sections 6214(a) and 6512(b), no decision shall be entered redetermining the amount of a deficiency, or determining an overpayment, except with respect to amounts placed in dispute within the limits described in subsection (a) and with respect to amounts conceded by the parties.

[Sec. 7463(d)]

(d) DISCONTINUANCE OF PROCEEDINGS.—At any time before a decision entered in a case in which the proceedings are conducted under this section becomes final, the taxpayer or the Secretary may request that further proceedings under this section in such case be discontinued. The Tax Court, or the division thereof hearing such case, may, if it finds that (1) there are reasonable grounds for believing that the amount of the deficiency placed in dispute, or the amount of an overpayment, exceeds the applicable jurisdictional amount described in subsection (a), and (2) the amount of such excess is large enough to justify granting such request, discontinue further proceedings in such case under this section. Upon any such discontinuance, proceedings in such case shall be conducted in the same manner as cases to which the provisions of sections 6214(a) and 6512(b) apply.

Amendments

• **1976, Tax Reform Act of 1976 (P.L. 94-455)**

P.L. 94-455, §1906(b)(13)(A):

Amended 1954 Code by substituting "Secretary" for "Secretary or his delegate" each place it appeared. **Effective** 2-1-77.

[Sec. 7463(e)]

(e) AMOUNT OF DEFICIENCY IN DISPUTE.—For purposes of this section, the amount of any deficiency placed in dispute includes additions to the tax, additional amounts, and penalties imposed by chapter 68, to the extent that the procedures described in subchapter B of chapter 63 apply.

Amendments

• **1969, Tax Reform Act of 1969 (P.L. 91-172)**

P.L. 91-172, §957(a):

Added Code Sec. 7463. **Effective** 12-30-70.

[Sec. 7463(f)]

(f) ADDITIONAL CASES IN WHICH PROCEEDINGS MAY BE CONDUCTED UNDER THIS SECTION.—At the option of the taxpayer concurred in by the Tax Court or a division thereof before the hearing of the case, proceedings may be conducted under this section (in the same manner as a case described in subsection (a)) in the case of—

    (1) a petition to the Tax Court under section 6015(e) in which the amount of relief sought does not exceed $50,000,

    (2) an appeal under section 6330(d)(1)(A) to the Tax Court of a determination in which the unpaid tax does not exceed $50,000, and

    (3) a petition to the Tax Court under section 6404(h) in which the amount of the abatement sought does not exceed $50,000.

Amendments

• **2015, Protecting Americans from Tax Hikes Act of 2015 (P.L. 114-113)**

P.L. 114-113, §422(a)(1)-(3), Div. Q:

Amended Code Sec. 7463(f) by striking "and" at the end of paragraph (1), by striking the period at the end of paragraph (2) and inserting ", and", and by adding at the end a new paragraph (3). **Effective** for cases pending as of the day after the date of the enactment of this Act, and cases commenced after such date of enactment.

• **2000, Community Renewal Tax Relief Act of 2000 (P.L. 106-554)**

P.L. 106-554, §313(b)(1):

Amended Code Sec. 7463 by adding at the end a new subsection (f). **Effective** 12-21-2000.

• **1990, Omnibus Budget Reconciliation Act of 1990 (P.L. 101-508)**

P.L. 101-508, §11801(c)(21)(B):

Amended Code Sec. 7463 by striking subsection (f). **Effective** 11-5-90. Prior to being stricken, Code Sec. 7463(f) read as follows:

(f) QUALIFIED STATE INDIVIDUAL INCOME TAXES.—For purposes of this section, a deficiency placed in dispute or claimed overpayment with regard to a qualified State individual income tax to which subchapter E of chapter 64 applies, for a taxable year, shall be treated as a portion of a deficiency placed in dispute or claimed overpayment of the income tax for that taxable year.

P.L. 101-508, §11821(b), provides:

(b) SAVINGS PROVISION.—If—

(1) any provision amended or repealed by this part applied to—

(A) any transaction occurring before the date of the enactment of this Act,

(B) any property acquired before such date of enactment, or

(C) any item of income, loss, deduction, or credit taken into account before such date of enactment, and

(2) the treatment of such transaction, property, or item under such provision would (without regard to the amendments made by this part) affect liability for tax for periods ending after such date of enactment,

nothing in the amendments made by this part shall be construed to affect the treatment of such transaction, property, or item for purposes of determining liability for tax for periods ending after such date of enactment.

• **1972, State and Local Fiscal Assistance Act of 1972 (P.L. 92-512)**

P.L. 92-512, §203(b):

Amended Code Sec. 7463 by adding subsection (f), by substituting "$1,500" for "$1,000" in the heading of said section, and by making a similar substitution at the beginning of subparagraphs (1) and (2) of subsection (a). **Effective** 1-1-74, for the increase in the jurisdictional amount to $1,500 for the small tax case procedure. The **effective** date of Code Sec. 7463(f) is dependent upon the **effective** date for the federal collection of qualified state individual income taxes. See the amendment note for P.L. 92-512 under Code Sec. 6361.

[Sec. 7463(g)—Repealed]

Amendments

• **1980, Technical Corrections Act of 1979 (P.L. 96-222)**

P.L. 96-222, §105(a)(1)(A):

Repealed Code Sec. 7463(g). **Effective** 4-1-80. Prior to its repeal, Code Sec. 7463(g) read as follows:

"(g) COMMISSIONERS.—The chief judge of the Tax Court may assign proceedings conducted under this section to be heard by the Commissioners of the court, and the court may authorize a commissioner to make the decision of the court with respect to any such proceeding, subject to such conditions and review as the court may by rule provide."

• **1978, Revenue Act of 1978 (P.L. 95-600)**

P.L. 95-600, §502(b):

Added Code Sec. 7463(g). **Effective** 11-6-78.

[Sec. 7464]

SEC. 7464. INTERVENTION BY TRUSTEE OF DEBTOR'S ESTATE.

The trustee of the debtor's estate in any case under title 11 of the United States Code may intervene, on behalf of the debtor's estate, in any proceeding before the Tax Court to which the debtor is a party.

JUDICIAL PROCEEDINGS—TAX COURT

Amendments
• **1980, Bankruptcy Tax Act of 1980 (P.L. 96-589)**

P.L. 96-589, §6(c)(1):

Redesignated former Code Sec. 7464 as Code Sec. 7465 and inserted a new Code Sec. 7464. **Effective** 10-1-79, but inapplicable to any proceeding under the Bankruptcy Act commenced before that date.

[Sec. 7465]

SEC. 7465. PROVISIONS OF SPECIAL APPLICATION TO TRANSFEREES.

(1) For rules of burden of proof in transferee proceedings, see section 6902(a).

(2) For authority of Tax Court to prescribe rules by which a transferee of property of a taxpayer shall be entitled to examine books, records and other evidence, see section 6902(b).

Amendments
• **1980, Bankruptcy Tax Act of 1980 (P.L. 96-589)**

P.L. 96-589, §6(c)(1):

Redesignated former Code Sec. 7464 as Code Sec. 7465. **Effective** 10-1-79, but inapplicable to any proceeding commenced before that date.

• **1969, Tax Reform Act of 1969 (P.L. 91-172)**

P.L. 91-172, §957(a):

Redesignated prior Code Sec. 7463 as Code Sec. 7464. **Effective** 12-30-70.

[Sec. 7466]

SEC. 7466. JUDICIAL CONDUCT AND DISABILITY PROCEDURES.

[Sec. 7466(a)]

(a) IN GENERAL.—The Tax Court shall prescribe rules, consistent with the provisions of chapter 16 of title 28, United States Code, establishing procedures for the filing of complaints with respect to the conduct of any judge or special trial judge of the Tax Court and for the investigation and resolution of such complaints. In investigating and taking action with respect to any such complaint, the Tax Court shall have the powers granted to a judicial council under such chapter.

[Sec. 7466(b)]

(b) JUDICIAL COUNCIL.—The provisions of sections 354(b) through 360 of title 28, United States Code, regarding referral or certification to, and petition for review in the Judicial Conference of the United States, and action thereon, shall apply to the exercise by the Tax Court of the powers of a judicial council under subsection (a). The determination pursuant to section 354(b) or 355 of title 28, United States Code, shall be made based on the grounds for removal of a judge from office under section 7443(f), and certification and transmittal by the Conference of any complaint shall be made to the President for consideration under section 7443(f).

[Sec. 7466(c)]

(c) HEARINGS.—

(1) IN GENERAL.—In conducting hearings pursuant to subsection (a), the Tax Court may exercise the authority provided under section 1821 of title 28, United States Code, to pay the fees and allowances described in that section.

(2) REIMBURSEMENT FOR EXPENSES.—The Tax Court shall have the power provided under section 361 of such title 28 to award reimbursement for the reasonable expenses described in that section. Reimbursements under this paragraph shall be made out of any funds appropriated for purposes of the Tax Court.

Amendments
• **2015, Protecting Americans from Tax Hikes Act of 2015 (P.L. 114-113)**

P.L. 114-113, §431(a), Div. Q:

Amended part II of subchapter C of chapter 76 by adding at the end a new Code Sec. 7466. **Effective** for proceedings commenced after the date which is 180 days after 12-18-2015 and, to the extent that it is just and practicable, to all proceedings pending on such date.

PART III—MISCELLANEOUS PROVISIONS

Sec. 7470.	Administration.
Sec. 7470A.	Judicial conference.
Sec. 7471.	Employees.
Sec. 7472.	Expenditures.
Sec. 7473.	Disposition of fees.
Sec. 7474.	Fee for transcript of record.
Sec. 7475.	Practice fee.

[Sec. 7470]

SEC. 7470. ADMINISTRATION.

Notwithstanding any other provision of law, the Tax Court may exercise, for purposes of management, administration, and expenditure of funds of the Court, the authorities provided for such purposes by any provision of law (including any limitation with respect to such provision of law) applicable to a court of the United States (as that term is defined in section 451 of title 28, United States Code), except to the extent that such provision of law is inconsistent with a provision of this subchapter.

Amendments
• **2015, Protecting Americans from Tax Hikes Act of 2015 (P.L. 114-113)**

P.L. 114-113, §432(a), Div. Q:

Amended part III of subchapter C of chapter 76 by inserting before Code Sec. 7471 new Code Secs. 7470-7470A. **Effective** 12-18-2015.

[Sec. 7470A]

SEC. 7470A. JUDICIAL CONFERENCE.

[Sec. 7470A(a)]

(a) JUDICIAL CONFERENCE.—The chief judge may summon the judges and special trial judges of the Tax Court to an annual judicial conference, at such time and place as the chief judge shall designate, for the purpose of considering the business of the Tax Court and recommending means of improving the administration of justice within the jurisdiction of the Tax Court. The Tax Court shall provide by its rules for representation and active participation at such conferences by persons admitted to practice before the Tax Court and by other persons active in the legal profession.

[Sec. 7470A(b)]

(b) REGISTRATION FEE.—The Tax Court may impose a reasonable registration fee on persons (other than judges and special trial judges of the Tax Court) participating at judicial conferences convened pursuant to subsection (a). Amounts so received by the Tax Court shall be available to the Tax Court to defray the expenses of such conferences.

Amendments

• 2015, Protecting Americans from Tax Hikes Act of 2015 (P.L. 114-113)

P.L. 114-113, §432(a), Div. Q:

Amended part III of subchapter C of chapter 76 by inserting before Code Sec. 7471 new Code Secs. 7470-7470A. **Effective** 12-18-2015.

[Sec. 7471]

SEC. 7471. EMPLOYEES.

[Sec. 7471(a)]

(a) APPOINTMENT AND COMPENSATION.—

(1) CLERK.—The Tax Court may appoint a clerk without regard to the provisions of title 5, United States Code, governing appointments in the competitive service. The clerk shall serve at the pleasure of the Tax Court.

(2) JUDGE-APPOINTED EMPLOYEES.—

(A) IN GENERAL.—The judges and special trial judges of the Tax Court may appoint employees, in such numbers as the Tax Court may approve, without regard to the provisions of title 5, United States Code, governing appointments in the competitive service. Any such employee shall serve at the pleasure of the appointing judge.

(B) EXEMPTION FROM FEDERAL LEAVE PROVISIONS.—A law clerk appointed under this subsection shall be exempt from the provisions of subchapter I of chapter 63 of title 5, United States Code. Any unused sick leave or annual leave standing to the law clerk's credit as of the effective date of this subsection shall remain credited to the law clerk and shall be available to the law clerk upon separation from the Federal Government.

(3) OTHER EMPLOYEES.—The Tax Court may appoint necessary employees without regard to the provisions of title 5, United States Code, governing appointments in the competitive service. Such employees shall be subject to removal by the Tax Court.

(4) PAY.—The Tax Court may fix and adjust the compensation for the clerk and other employees of the Tax Court without regard to the provisions of chapter 51, subchapter III of chapter 53, or section 5373 of title 5, United States Code. To the maximum extent feasible, the Tax Court shall compensate employees at rates consistent with those for employees holding comparable positions in courts established under Article III of the Constitution of the United States.

(5) PROGRAMS.—The Tax Court may establish programs for employee evaluations, incentive awards, flexible work schedules, premium pay, and resolution of employee grievances.

(6) DISCRIMINATION PROHIBITED.—The Tax Court shall—

(A) prohibit discrimination on the basis of race, color, religion, age, sex, national origin, political affiliation, marital status, or handicapping condition; and

(B) promulgate procedures for resolving complaints of discrimination by employees and applicants for employment.

(7) EXPERTS AND CONSULTANTS.—The Tax Court may procure the services of experts and consultants under section 3109 of title 5, United States Code.

(8) RIGHTS TO CERTAIN APPEALS RESERVED.—Notwithstanding any other provision of law, an individual who is an employee of the Tax Court on the day before the effective date of this subsection and who, as of that day, was entitled to—

(A) appeal a reduction in grade or removal to the Merit Systems Protection Board under chapter 43 of title 5, United States Code,

(B) appeal an adverse action to the Merit Systems Protection Board under chapter 75 of title 5, United States Code,

(C) appeal a prohibited personnel practice described under section 2302(b) of title 5, United States Code, to the Merit Systems Protection Board under chapter 77 of that title,

(D) make an allegation of a prohibited personnel practice described under section 2302(b) of title 5, United States Code, with the Office of Special Counsel under chapter 12 of that title for action in accordance with that chapter, or

(E) file an appeal with the Equal Employment Opportunity Commission under part 1614 of title 29 of the Code of Federal Regulations,

shall continue to be entitled to file such appeal or make such an allegation so long as the individual remains an employee of the Tax Court.

(9) COMPETITIVE STATUS.—Notwithstanding any other provision of law, any employee of the Tax Court who has completed at least 1 year of continuous service under a non-temporary appointment with the Tax Court acquires a competitive status for appointment to any position in the competitive service for which the employee possesses the required qualifications.

(10) MERIT SYSTEM PRINCIPLES, PROHIBITED PERSONNEL PRACTICES, AND PREFERENCE ELIGIBLES.—Any personnel management system of the Tax Court shall—

(A) include the principles set forth in section 2301(b) of title 5, United States Code;

(B) prohibit personnel practices prohibited under section 2302(b) of title 5, United States Code; and

(C) in the case of any individual who would be a preference eligible in the executive branch, provide preference for that individual in a manner and to an extent consistent with preference accorded to preference eligibles in the executive branch.

Amendments

• 2011 (P.L. 111-366)

P.L. 111-366, §1(a):

Amended Code Sec. 7471(a). **Effective** on the date the United States Tax Court adopts a personnel management system after 1-4-2011. Prior to amendment, Code Sec. 7471(a) read as follows:

(a) APPOINTMENT AND COMPENSATION.—The Tax Court is authorized to appoint, in accordance with the provisions of title 5, United States Code, governing appointment in the competitive service, and to fix the basic pay of, in accordance with chapter 51 and subchapter III of chapter 53 of such title, such employees as may be necessary efficiently to execute the functions vested in the Tax Court.

• 1976, Tax Reform Act of 1976 (P.L. 94-455)

P.L. 94-455, §1906(a)(47)(A):

Amended Code Sec. 7471(a). **Effective** 2-1-77. Prior to amendment, Code Sec. 7471(a) read as follows:

(a) APPOINTMENT AND COMPENSATION.—The Tax Court is authorized in accordance with the civil service laws to appoint, and in accordance with the Classification Act of 1949 (63 Stat. 954; 5 U.S.C. chapter 21), as amended, to fix the compensation of, such employees as may be necessary efficiently to execute the functions vested in the Tax Court.

JUDICIAL PROCEEDINGS—TAX COURT

[Sec. 7471(b)]

(b) EXPENSES FOR TRAVEL AND SUBSISTENCE.—The employees of the Tax Court shall receive their necessary traveling expenses, and expenses for subsistence while traveling on duty and away from their designated stations, as provided in chapter 57 of title 5, United States Code.

Amendments

• **1976, Tax Reform Act of 1976 (P.L. 94-455)**

P.L. 94-455, §1906(a)(47)(B):

Substituted "as provided in chapter 57 of title 5, United States Code" for "as provided in the Travel Expense Act of 1949 (63 Stat. 166; 5 U.S.C. chapter 16)" in Code Sec. 7471(b). **Effective** 2-1-77.

[Sec. 7471(c)]

(c) SPECIAL TRIAL JUDGES.—

For compensation and travel and subsistence allowances of special trial judges of the Tax Court, see subsections (d) and (e) of section 7443A.

Amendments

• **1986, Tax Reform Act of 1986 (P.L. 99-514)**

P.L. 99-514, §1556(b)(2):

Amended Code Sec. 7471(c) by striking out "section 7456(c)" and inserting in lieu thereof "subsections (d) and (e) of section 7443A". **Effective** 10-22-86. However, see Act Sec. 1556(c)(3), below.

P.L. 99-514, §1556(c)(3), provides:

(3) NEW APPOINTMENTS NOT REQUIRED.—Nothing in the amendments made by this section shall be construed to require the reappointment of any individual serving as a special trial judge of the Tax Court on the day before the date of the enactment of this Act.

• **1984, Deficit Reduction Act of 1984 (P.L. 98-369)**

P.L. 98-369, §464(d):

Amended Code Sec. 7471(c) by striking out "COMMISSIONERS" in the heading and inserting in lieu thereof "SPECIAL TRIAL JUDGES", and by striking out "commissioners" and inserting in lieu thereof "special trial judges". **Effective** 7-18-84. Any reference to a commissioner of the Tax Court shall be treated as a reference to a special trial judge of the Tax Court.

• **1969, Tax Reform Act of 1969 (P.L. 91-172)**

P.L. 91-172, §960(g):

Amended Code Sec. 7471(c) by addition of the phrase "compensation and". **Effective** 12-30-69.

[Sec. 7472]

SEC. 7472. EXPENDITURES.

The Tax Court is authorized to make such expenditures (including expenditures for personal services and rent at the seat of Government and elsewhere, and for law books, books of reference, and periodicals), as may be necessary efficiently to execute the functions vested in the Tax Court. Notwithstanding any other provision of law, the Tax Court is authorized to pay on behalf of its judges, age 65 or over, any increase in the cost of Federal Employees' Group Life Insurance imposed after April 24, 1999, that is incurred after the date of the enactment of the Pension Protection Act of 2006, including any expenses generated by such payments, as authorized by the chief judge in a manner consistent with such payments authorized by the Judicial Conference of the United States pursuant to section 604(a)(5) of title 28, United States Code. Except as provided in section 7475, all expenditures of the Tax Court shall be allowed and paid, out of any moneys appropriated for purposes of the Tax Court, upon presentation of itemized vouchers therefor signed by the certifying officer designated by the chief judge.

Amendments

• **2009, Omnibus Appropriations Act, 2009 (P.L. 111-8)**

P.L. 111-8, §618:

Amended Code Sec. 7472 by inserting after the word "imposed" where it appears in the second sentence the following phrase "after April 24, 1999, that is incurred". **Effective** as if included in the amendment made by §852 of the Pension Protection Act of 2006 (P.L. 109-280) [effective 8-17-2006.—CCH].

• **2006, Pension Protection Act of 2006 (P.L. 109-280)**

P.L. 109-280, §852:

Amended Code Sec. 7472 by inserting after the first sentence a new sentence. **Effective** 8-17-2006.

• **1986, Tax Reform Act of 1986 (P.L. 99-514)**

P.L. 99-514, §1553(b)(1):

Amended Code Sec. 7472 by striking out "All" in the second sentence and inserting in lieu thereof "Except as provided in section 7475, all". **Effective** 1-1-87.

[Sec. 7473]

SEC. 7473. DISPOSITION OF FEES.

Except as provided in sections 7470A and 7475, all fees received by the Tax Court pursuant to this title shall be deposited into a special fund of the Treasury to be available to offset funds appropriated for the operation and maintenance of the Tax Court.

Amendments

• **2015, Protecting Americans from Tax Hikes Act of 2015 (P.L. 114-113)**

P.L. 114-113, §432(b), Div. Q:

Amended Code Sec. 7473. **Effective** 12-18-2015. Prior to amendment, Code Sec. 7473 read as follows:

SEC. 7473. DISPOSITION OF FEES.

Except as provided in section 7475, all fees received by the Tax Court shall be covered into the Treasury as miscellaneous receipts.

• **1986, Tax Reform Act of 1986 (P.L. 99-514)**

P.L. 99-514, §1553(b)(2):

Amended Code Sec. 7473 by striking out "All" and inserting in lieu thereof "Except as provided in section 7475, all". **Effective** 1-1-87.

[Sec. 7474]

SEC. 7474. FEE FOR TRANSCRIPT OF RECORD.

The Tax Court is authorized to fix a fee, not in excess of the fee fixed by law to be charged and collected therefor by the clerks of the district courts, for comparing, or for preparing and comparing, a transcript of the record, or for copying any record, entry, or other paper and the comparison and certification thereof.

[Sec. 7475]

SEC. 7475. PRACTICE FEE.

[Sec. 7475(a)]

(a) IN GENERAL.—The Tax Court is authorized to impose a periodic registration fee on practitioners admitted to practice before such Court. The frequency and amount of such fee shall be determined by the Tax Court, except that such amount may not exceed $30 per year.

[Sec. 7475(b)]

(b) USE OF FEES.—The fees described in subsection (a) shall be available to the Tax Court to employ independent counsel to pursue disciplinary matters and to provide services to pro se taxpayers.

JUDICIAL PROCEEDINGS—TAX COURT

Amendments

• **2006, Pension Protection Act of 2006 (P.L. 109-280)**

P.L. 109-280, §860(a):

Amended Code Sec. 7475(b) by inserting before the period at the end "and to provide services to pro se taxpayers". **Effective** 8-17-2006.

• **1986, Tax Reform Act of 1986 (P.L. 99-514)**

P.L. 99-514, §1553(a):

Amended part III of subchapter C of chapter 76 by adding at the end thereof new Code Sec. 7475. **Effective** 1-1-87.

PART IV—DECLARATORY JUDGMENTS

Sec. 7476. Declaratory judgments relating to qualification of certain retirement plans.
Sec. 7477. Declaratory judgments relating to value of certain gifts.
Sec. 7478. Declaratory judgments relating to status of certain governmental obligations.
Sec. 7479. Declaratory judgments relating to eligibility of estate with respect to installment payments under section 6166.

[Sec. 7476]

SEC. 7476. DECLARATORY JUDGMENTS RELATING TO QUALIFICATION OF CERTAIN RETIREMENT PLANS.

[Sec. 7476(a)]

(a) CREATION OF REMEDY.—In a case of actual controversy involving—

(1) a determination by the Secretary with respect to the initial qualification or continuing qualification of a retirement plan under subchapter D of chapter 1, or

(2) a failure by the Secretary to make a determination with respect to

(A) such initial qualification, or

(B) such continuing qualification if the controversy arises from a plan amendment or plan termination,

upon the filing of an appropriate pleading, the Tax Court may make a declaration with respect to such initial qualification or continuing qualification. Any such declaration shall have the force and effect of a decision of the Tax Court and shall be reviewable as such. For purposes of this section, a determination with respect to a continuing qualification includes any revocation of or other change in a qualification.

Amendments

• **1978, Revenue Act of 1978 (P.L. 95-600)**

P.L. 95-600, §701(dd)(1):

Amended Code Sec. 7476(a) by adding the last sentence. **Effective** as if included in Code Sec. 7476 of the Internal Revenue Code of 1954 at the time such section was added to the Code.

• **1976, Tax Reform Act of 1976 (P.L. 94-455)**

P.L. 94-455, §1042(d)(2)(C):

Amended the heading of Code Sec. 7476. For the **effective** date, see Act Sec. 1042(e), below.

P.L. 94-455, §1042(e), provides:

(1) The amendments made by this section (other than by subsection (d)) shall apply to transfers beginning after October 9, 1975, and to sales, exchanges, and distributions taking place after such date. The amendments made by subsection (d) shall apply with respect to pleadings filed with the Tax Court after the date of the enactment of this Act [October 4, 1976] but only with respect to transfers beginning after October 9, 1975.

• **1976, Tax Reform Act of 1976 (P.L. 94-455)**

P.L. 94-455, §1906(a)(48):

Amended Code Sec. 7476(a) by striking out "United States" before "Tax Court". **Effective** 2-1-77.

P.L. 94-455, §1906(b)(13)(A):

Amended 1954 Code by substituting "Secretary" for "Secretary or his delegate" each place it appeared. **Effective** 2-1-77.

[Sec. 7476(b)]

(b) LIMITATIONS.—

(1) PETITIONER.—A pleading may be filed under this section only by a petitioner who is the employer, the plan administrator, an employee who has qualified under regulations prescribed by the Secretary as an interested party for purposes of pursuing administrative remedies within the Internal Revenue Service, or the Pension Benefit Guaranty Corporation.

(2) NOTICE.—For purposes of this section, the filing of a pleading by any petitioner may be held by the Tax Court to be premature, unless the petitioner establishes to the satisfaction of the court that he has complied with the requirements prescribed by regulations of the Secretary with respect to notice to other interested parties of the filing of the request for a determination referred to in subsection (a).

(3) EXHAUSTION OF ADMINISTRATIVE REMEDIES.—The Tax Court shall not issue a declaratory judgment or decree under this section in any proceeding unless it determines that the petitioner has exhausted administrative remedies available to him within the Internal Revenue Service. A petitioner shall not be deemed to have exhausted his administrative remedies with respect to a failure by the Secretary to make a determination with respect to initial qualification or continuing qualification of a retirement plan before the expiration of 270 days after the request for such determination was made.

(4) PLAN PUT INTO EFFECT.—No proceeding may be maintained under this section unless the plan (and, in the case of a controversy involving the continuing qualification of the plan because of an amendment to the plan, the amendment) with respect to which a decision of the Tax Court is sought has been put into effect before the filing of the pleading. A plan or amendment shall not be treated as not being in effect merely because under the plan the funds contributed to the plan may be refunded if the plan (or the plan as so amended) is found to be not qualified.

(5) TIME FOR BRINGING ACTION.—If the Secretary sends by certified or registered mail notice of his determination with respect to the qualification of the plan to the persons referred to in paragraph (1) (or, in the case of employees referred to in paragraph (1), to any individual designated under regulations prescribed by the Secretary as a representative of such employee), no proceeding may be initiated under this section by any person unless the pleading is filed before the ninety-first day after the day after such notice is mailed to such person (or to his designated representative, in the case of an employee).

Amendments

• **1976, Tax Reform Act of 1976 (P.L. 94-455)**

P.L. 94-455, §1906(b)(13)(A):

Amended 1954 Code by substituting "Secretary" for "Secretary or his delegate" each place it appeared. **Effective** 2-1-77.

[Sec. 7476(c)]

(c) RETIREMENT PLAN.—For purposes of this section, the term "retirement plan" means—

(1) a pension, profit-sharing, or stock bonus plan described in section 401(a) or a trust which is part of such a plan, or

(2) an annuity plan described in section 403(a).

JUDICIAL PROCEEDINGS—TAX COURT

Amendments

• **1986, Tax Reform Act of 1986 (P.L. 99-514)**

P.L. 99-514, §1899A(59):

Amended Code Sec. 7476(c)(1) by striking out "plan,, or" and inserting in lieu thereof "plan, or". **Effective** 10-22-86.

• **1984, Deficit Reduction Act of 1984 (P.L. 98-369)**

P.L. 98-369, §491(d)(52):

Amended Code Sec. 7476(c) by striking out paragraph (3), by striking out ", or" at the end of paragraph (2) and inserting in lieu thereof a period, and by adding ", or" at the end of paragraph (1). **Effective** for obligations issued after 12-31-83. Prior to amendment, paragraph (3) read as follows:

(3) A bond purchase plan described in section 405(a).

• **1978, Revenue Act of 1978 (P.L. 95-600)**

P.L. 95-600, §336(b)(2)(A):

Struck out Code Sec. 7476(c), and redesignated Code Sec. 7476(d) as Code Sec. 7476(c). **Effective** for requests for determinations made after 12-31-78. Prior to striking, Code Sec. 7476(c) read:

"(c) COMMISSIONERS.—The chief judge of the Tax Court may assign proceedings under this section or section 7428 to be heard by the commissioners of the court, and the court may authorize a commissioner to make the decision of the court with respect to such proceeding, subject to such conditions and review as the court may by rule provide."

[Sec. 7476(d)]

(d) CROSS REFERENCE.—

For provisions concerning intervention by Pension Benefit Guaranty Corporation and Secretary of Labor in actions brought under this section and right of Pension Benefit Guaranty Corporation to bring action, see section 3001(c) of subtitle A of title III of the Employee Retirement Income Security Act of 1974.

Amendments

• **1978, Revenue Act of 1978 (P.L. 95-600)**

P.L. 95-600, §336(b)(2)(A):

Redesignated former Code Sec. 7476(e) as Code Sec. 7476(d). **Effective** for requests for determinations made after 12-31-78.

• **1974, Employee Retirement Income Security Act of 1974 (P.L. 93-406)**

P.L. 93-406, §1041(a):

Added Code Sec. 7476. **Effective** as to pleadings filed after 9-2-75.

[Sec. 7477]

SEC. 7477. DECLARATORY JUDGMENTS RELATING TO VALUE OF CERTAIN GIFTS.

[Sec. 7477(a)]

(a) CREATION OF REMEDY.—In a case of an actual controversy involving a determination by the Secretary of the value of any gift shown on the return of tax imposed by chapter 12 or disclosed on such return or in any statement attached to such return, upon the filing of an appropriate pleading, the Tax Court may make a declaration of the value of such gift. Any such declaration shall have the force and effect of a decision of the Tax Court and shall be reviewable as such.

[Sec. 7477(b)]

(b) LIMITATIONS.—

(1) PETITIONER.—A pleading may be filed under this section only by the donor.

(2) EXHAUSTION OF ADMINISTRATIVE REMEDIES.—The court shall not issue a declaratory judgment or decree under this section in any proceeding unless it determines that the petitioner has exhausted all available administrative remedies within the Internal Revenue Service.

(3) TIME FOR BRINGING ACTION.—If the Secretary sends by certified or registered mail notice of his determination as described in subsection (a) to the petitioner, no proceeding may be initiated under this section unless the pleading is filed before the 91st day after the date of such mailing.

Amendments

• **1997, Taxpayer Relief Act of 1997 (P.L. 105-34)**

P.L. 105-34, §506(c)(1):

Amended part IV of subchapter C of chapter 76 by inserting after Code Sec. 7476 a new Code Sec. 7477. **Effective** for gifts made after 8-5-97.

[Sec. 7477—Repealed]

Amendments

• **1984, Deficit Reduction Act of 1984 (P.L. 98-369)**

P.L. 98-369, §131(e)(1):

Repealed Code Sec. 7477. **Effective** for transfers or exchanges after 12-31-84, in tax years ending after such date. Special rules appear in Act Sec. 131(g)(2)(3) following Code Sec. 367(e). Prior to amendment, Code Sec. 7477 read as follows:

SEC. 7477. DECLARATORY JUDGMENTS RELATING TO TRANSFERS OF PROPERTY FROM THE UNITED STATES.

(a) CREATION OF REMEDY.—

(1) IN GENERAL.—In a case of actual controversy involving—

(A) a determination by the Secretary—

(i) that an exchange described in section 367(a)(1) is in pursuance of a plan having as one of its principal purposes the avoidance of Federal income taxes, or

(ii) of the terms and conditions pursuant to which an exchange described in section 367(a)(1) will be determined not to be in pursuance of a plan having as one of its principal purposes the avoidance of Federal income taxes, or

(B) a failure by the Secretary to make a determination as to whether an exchange described in section 367(a)(1) is in pursuance of a plan having as one of its principal purposes the avoidance of Federal income taxes,

upon the filing of an appropriate pleading, the Tax Court may make the appropriate declaration referred to in paragraph (2). Such declaration shall have the force and effect of a decision of the Tax Court and shall be reviewable as such.

(2) SCOPE OF DECLARATION.—The declaration referred to in paragraph (1) shall be—

(A) in the case of a determination referred to in subparagraph (A) of paragraph (1), whether or not such determination is reasonable, and, if it is not reasonable, a determination of the issue set forth in subparagraph (A)(ii) of paragraph (1), and

(B) in the case of a failure described in subparagraph (B) of paragraph (1), the determination of the issues set forth in subparagraph (A) of paragraph (1).

(b) LIMITATIONS.—

(1) PETITIONER.—A pleading may be filed under this section only by a petitioner who is a transferor or transferee of stock, securities, or property transferred in an exchange described in section 367(a)(1).

(2) EXHAUSTION OF ADMINISTRATIVE REMEDIES.—The Tax Court shall not issue a declaratory judgment or decree under this section in any proceeding unless it determines that the petitioner has exhausted administrative remedies available to him within the Internal Revenue Service. A petitioner shall not be deemed to have exhausted his administrative remedies with respect to a failure by the Secretary to make a determination with respect to whether or not an exchange described in section 367(a)(1) is in pursuance of a plan having as one of its principal purposes the avoidance of Federal income taxes before the expiration of 270 days after the request for such determination was made.

(3) EXCHANGE SHALL HAVE BEGUN.—No proceeding may be maintained under this section unless the exchange described in section 367(a)(1) with respect to which a decision of the Tax Court is sought has begun before the filing of the pleading.

(4) TIME FOR BRINGING ACTION.—If the Secretary sends by certified or registered mail to the petitioners referred to in paragraph (1) notice of his determination with respect to whether or not an exchange described in section 367(a)(1) is in pursuance of a plan having as one of its principal purposes the avoidance of Federal income taxes or with respect to the terms and conditions pursuant to which such an exchange will be determined not to be made in pursuance of such a plan, no proceeding may be initiated under this section by any petitioner unless the pleading is filed before the 91st day after the day after such notice is mailed to such petitioner.

• **1978, Revenue Act of 1978 (P.L. 95-600)**

P.L. 95-600, §336(b)(2)(B):

Amended Code Sec. 7477 by striking out subsection (c). **Effective** with respect to requests for determinations made after 12-31-78. Prior to deletion, Code Sec. 7477(c) read:

"(c) COMMISSIONERS.—The chief judge of the Tax Court may assign proceedings under this section to be heard by the commissioners of the court, and the court may authorize a commissioner to make the decision of the court with respect to such proceeding, subject to such conditions and review as the court may by rule provide."

• **1976, Tax Reform Act of 1976 (P.L. 94-455)**

P.L. 94-455, §1042(d)(1):

Added Code Sec. 7477.

JUDICIAL PROCEEDINGS—TAX COURT

P.L. 94-455, §1042(e)(1), provides:

(1) The amendments made by this section (other than by subsection (d)) shall apply to transfers beginning after October 9, 1975, and to sales, exchanges, and distributions taking place after such date. The amendments made by subsection (d) shall apply with respect to pleadings filed with the Tax Court after the date of the enactment of this Act [October 4, 1976] but only with respect to transfers beginning after October 9, 1975.

[Sec. 7478]

SEC. 7478. DECLARATORY JUDGMENTS RELATING TO STATUS OF CERTAIN GOVERNMENTAL OBLIGATIONS.

[Sec. 7478(a)]

(a) CREATION OF REMEDY.—In a case of actual controversy involving—

(1) a determination by the Secretary whether interest on prospective obligations will be excludable from gross income under section 103(a), or

(2) a failure by the Secretary to make a determination with respect to any matter referred to in paragraph (1),

upon the filing of an appropriate pleading, the Tax Court may make a declaration whether interest on such prospective obligations will be excludable from gross income under section 103(a). Any such declaration shall have the force and effect of a decision of the Tax Court and shall be reviewable as such.

Amendments

• **1988, Technical and Miscellaneous Revenue Act of 1988 (P.L. 100-647)**

P.L. 100-647, §1013(a)(42)(A)-(B):

Amended Code Sec. 7478(a) by striking out "whether prospective obligations are described in section 103(a)" in paragraph (1) and inserting in lieu thereof "whether interest on prospective obligations will be excludable from gross income under section 103(a)", and by striking out "whether such prospective obligations are described in section 103(a)" and inserting in lieu thereof "whether interest on such prospective obligations will be excludable from gross income under section 103(a)". **Effective** as if included in the provision of P.L. 99-514 to which it relates.

[Sec. 7478(b)]

(b) LIMITATIONS.—

(1) PETITIONER.—A pleading may be filed under this section only by the prospective issuer.

(2) EXHAUSTION OF ADMINISTRATIVE REMEDIES.—The court shall not issue a declaratory judgment or decree under this section in any proceeding unless it determines that the petitioner has exhausted all available administrative remedies within the Internal Revenue Service. A petitioner shall be deemed to have exhausted its administrative remedies with respect to a failure of the Secretary to make a determination with respect to an issue of obligations at the expiration of 180 days after the date on which the request for such determination was made if the petitioner has taken, in a timely manner, all reasonable steps to secure such determination.

(3) TIME FOR BRINGING ACTION.—If the Secretary sends by certified or registered mail notice of his determination as described in subsection (a)(1) to the petitioner, no proceeding may be initiated under this section unless the pleading is filed before the 91st day after the date of such mailing.

Amendments

• **1978, Revenue Act of 1978 (P.L. 95-600)**

P.L. 95-600, §336(a):

Added Code Sec. 7478. **Effective** with respect to requests for determinations made after 12-31-78.

SEC. 7479. DECLARATORY JUDGMENTS RELATING TO ELIGIBILITY OF ESTATE WITH RESPECT TO INSTALLMENT PAYMENTS UNDER SECTION 6166.

[Sec. 7479(a)]

(a) CREATION OF REMEDY.—In a case of actual controversy involving a determination by the Secretary of (or a failure by the Secretary to make a determination with respect to)—

(1) whether an election may be made under section 6166 (relating to extension of time for payment of estate tax where estate consists largely of interest in closely held business) with respect to an estate (or with respect to any property included therein), or

(2) whether the extension of time for payment of tax provided in section 6166(a) has ceased to apply with respect to an estate (or with respect to any property included therein),

upon the filing of an appropriate pleading, the Tax Court may make a declaration with respect to whether such election may be made or whether such extension has ceased to apply. Any such declaration shall have the force and effect of a decision of the Tax Court and shall be reviewable as such.

Amendments

• **1998, IRS Restructuring and Reform Act of 1998 (P.L. 105-206)**

P.L. 105-206, §6007(d):

Amended Code Sec. 7479(a)(1)-(2) by striking "an estate," and inserting "an estate (or with respect to any property included therein),". **Effective** as if included in the provision of P.L. 105-34 to which it relates [**effective** for estates of decedents dying after 8-5-97.—CCH].

[Sec. 7479(b)]

(b) LIMITATIONS.—

(1) PETITIONER.—A pleading may be filed under this section, with respect to any estate, only—

(A) by the executor of such estate, or

(B) by any person who has assumed an obligation to make payments under section 6166 with respect to such estate (but only if each other such person is joined as a party).

(2) EXHAUSTION OF ADMINISTRATIVE REMEDIES.—The court shall not issue a declaratory judgment or decree under this section in any proceeding unless it determines that the petitioner has exhausted all available administrative remedies within the Internal Revenue Service. A petitioner shall be deemed to have exhausted its administrative remedies with respect to a failure of the Secretary to make a determination at the expiration of 180 days after the date on which the request for such determination was made if the petitioner has taken, in a timely manner, all reasonable steps to secure such determination.

(3) TIME FOR BRINGING ACTION.—If the Secretary sends by certified or registered mail notice of his determination as described in subsection (a) to the petitioner, no proceeding may be initiated under this section unless the pleading is filed before the 91st day after the date of such mailing.

COURT REVIEW OF TAX COURT DECISIONS

Amendments

• **1997, Taxpayer Relief Act of 1997 (P.L. 105-34)**

P.L. 105-34, §505(a):

Amended part IV of subchapter C of chapter 76 by adding Code Sec. 7479. **Effective** for the estates of decedents dying after 8-5-97.

[Sec. 7479(c)]

(c) EXTENSION OF TIME TO FILE REFUND SUIT.—The 2-year period in section 6532(a)(1) for filing suit for refund after disallowance of a claim shall be suspended during the 90-day period after the mailing of the notice referred to in subsection (b)(3) and, if a pleading has been filed with the Tax Court under this section, until the decision of the Tax Court has become final.

Amendments

• **1998, IRS Restructuring and Reform Act of 1998 (P.L. 105-206)**

P.L. 105-206, §3104(b):

Amended Code Sec. 7479 by adding at the end a new subsection (c). **Effective** for any claim for refund filed after 7-22-98.

Subchapter D—Court Review of Tax Court Decisions

Sec. 7481.	Date when Tax Court decision becomes final.
Sec. 7482.	Courts of review.
Sec. 7483.	Notice of appeal.
Sec. 7484.	Change of incumbent in office.
Sec. 7485.	Bond to stay assessment and collection.
Sec. 7486.	Refund, credit, or abatement of amounts disallowed.
Sec. 7487.	Cross references.

[Sec. 7481]

SEC. 7481. DATE WHEN TAX COURT DECISION BECOMES FINAL.

[Sec. 7481(a)]

(a) REVIEWABLE DECISIONS.—Except as provided in subsections (b), (c), and (d), the decision of the Tax Court shall become final—

(1) TIMELY NOTICE OF APPEAL NOT FILED.—Upon the expiration of the time allowed for filing a notice of appeal, if no such notice has been duly filed within such time; or

(2) DECISION AFFIRMED OR APPEAL DISMISSED.—

(A) PETITION FOR CERTIORARI NOT FILED ON TIME.—Upon the expiration of the time allowed for filing a petition for certiorari, if the decision of the Tax Court has been affirmed or the appeal dismissed by the United States Court of Appeals and no petition for certiorari has been duly filed; or

(B) PETITION FOR CERTIORARI DENIED.—Upon the denial of a petition for certiorari, if the decision of the Tax Court has been affirmed or the appeal dismissed by the United States Court of Appeals; or

(C) AFTER MANDATE OF SUPREME COURT.—Upon the expiration of 30 days from the date of issuance of the mandate of the Supreme Court, if such Court directs that the decision of the Tax Court be affirmed or the appeal dismissed.

(3) DECISION MODIFIED OR REVERSED.—

(A) UPON MANDATE OF SUPREME COURT.—If the Supreme Court directs that the decision of the Tax Court be modified or reversed, the decision of the Tax Court rendered in accordance with the mandate of the Supreme Court shall become final upon the expiration of 30 days from the time it was rendered, unless within such 30 days either the Secretary or the taxpayer has instituted proceedings to have such decision corrected to accord with the mandate, in which event the decision of the Tax Court shall become final when so corrected.

(B) UPON MANDATE OF THE COURT OF APPEALS.—If the decision of the Tax Court is modified or reversed by the United States Court of Appeals, and if—

(i) the time allowed for filing a petition for certiorari has expired and no such petition has been duly filed, or

(ii) the petition for certiorari has been denied, or

(iii) the decision of the United States Court of Appeals has been affirmed by the Supreme Court, then the decision of the Tax Court rendered in accordance with the mandate of the United States Court of Appeals shall become final on the expiration of 30 days from the time such decision of the Tax Court was rendered, unless within such 30 days either the Secretary or the taxpayer has instituted proceedings to have such decision corrected so that it will accord with the mandate, in which event the decision of the Tax Court shall become final when so corrected.

(4) REHEARING.—If the Supreme Court orders a rehearing; or if the case is remanded by the United States Court of Appeals to the Tax Court for a rehearing, and if—

(A) the time allowed for filing a petition for certiorari has expired and no such petition has been duly filed, or

(B) the petition for certiorari has been denied, or

(C) the decision of the United States Court of Appeals has been affirmed by the Supreme Court,

then the decision of the Tax Court rendered upon such rehearing shall become final in the same manner as though no prior decision of the Tax Court has been rendered.

(5) DEFINITION OF "MANDATE".—As used in this section, the term "mandate", in case a mandate has been recalled prior to the expiration of 30 days from the date of issuance thereof, means the final mandate.

Amendments

• **1988, Technical and Miscellaneous Revenue Act of 1988 (P.L. 100-647)**

P.L. 100-647, §6246(b)(2):

Amended Code Sec. 7481(a) by striking out "subsection (b)" and inserting in lieu thereof "subsections (b) and (c)". **Effective** for assessments of deficiencies redetermined by the Tax Court made after 11-10-88.

P.L. 100-647, §6247(b)(2):

Amended Code Sec. 7481(a), as amended, by striking out "subsections (b) and (c)" and inserting in lieu thereof "subsections (b), (c), and (d)". **Effective** with respect to Tax Court cases for which the decision is not final on 11-10-88.

• **1976, Tax Reform Act of 1976 (P.L. 94-455)**

P.L. 94-455, §1906(b)(13)(A):

Amended 1954 Code by substituting "Secretary" for "Secretary or his delegate" each place it appeared. **Effective** 2-1-77.

COURT REVIEW OF TAX COURT DECISIONS

[Sec. 7481(b)]

(b) NONREVIEWABLE DECISIONS.—The decision of the Tax Court in a proceeding conducted under section 7436(c) or 7463 shall become final upon the expiration of 90 days after the decision is entered.

Amendments

- **1997, Taxpayer Relief Act of 1997 (P.L. 105-34)**

P.L. 105-34, §1454(b)(3):

Amended Code Sec. 7481(b) by striking "section 7463" and inserting "section 7436(c) or 7463". **Effective** 8-5-97.

- **1969, Tax Reform Act of 1969 (P.L. 91-172)**

P.L. 91-172, §960(h)(1):

Amended Code Sec. 7481 by inserting new subsection (a)(1), by substituting the word "appeal" for the phrase "petition for review" throughout (a)(2) and added new subsection (b). **Effective** 1-29-70. However, in the case of any decision of the Tax Court entered before January 29, 1970, the United States Courts of Appeal shall have jurisdiction to hear an appeal from such decision, if such appeal was filed within the time prescribed by Rule 13(a) of the Federal Rules of Appellate Procedure or by section 7483 of the Internal Revenue Code of 1954, as in effect at the time the decision of the Tax Court was entered. Prior to amendment by P.L. 91-172, paragraph (1) read as follows:

(1) Timely Petition for Review Not Filed.—Upon the expiration of the time allowed for filing a petition for review, if no such petition has been duly filed within such time; or

[Sec. 7481(c)]

(c) JURISDICTION OVER INTEREST DETERMINATIONS.—

(1) IN GENERAL.—Notwithstanding subsection (a), if, within 1 year after the date the decision of the Tax Court becomes final under subsection (a) in a case to which this subsection applies, the taxpayer files a motion in the Tax Court for a redetermination of the amount of interest involved, then the Tax Court may reopen the case solely to determine whether the taxpayer has made an overpayment of such interest or the Secretary has made an underpayment of such interest and the amount thereof.

(2) CASES TO WHICH THIS SUBSECTION APPLIES.—This subsection shall apply where—

(A)(i) an assessment has been made by the Secretary under section 6215 which includes interest as imposed by this title, and

(ii) the taxpayer has paid the entire amount of the deficiency plus interest claimed by the Secretary, and

(B) the Tax Court finds under section 6512(b) that the taxpayer has made an overpayment.

(3) SPECIAL RULES.—If the Tax Court determines under this subsection that the taxpayer has made an overpayment of interest or that the Secretary has made an underpayment of interest, then that determination shall be treated under section 6512(b)(1) as a determination of an overpayment of tax. An order of the Tax Court redetermining interest, when entered upon the records of the court, shall be reviewable in the same manner as a decision of the Tax Court.

Amendments

- **1997, Taxpayer Relief Act of 1997 (P.L. 105-34)**

P.L. 105-34, §1452(a):

Amended Code Sec. 7481(c). **Effective** 8-5-97. Prior to amendment, Code Sec. 7481(c) read as follows:

(c) JURISDICTION OVER INTEREST DETERMINATIONS.—Notwithstanding subsection (a), if—

(1) an assessment has been made by the Secretary under section 6215 which includes interest as imposed by this title,

(2) the taxpayer has paid the entire amount of the deficiency plus interest claimed by the Secretary, and

(3) within 1 year after the date the decision of the Tax Court becomes final under subsection (a), the taxpayer files a petition in the Tax Court for a determination that the amount of interest claimed by the Secretary exceeds the amount of interest imposed by this title,

then the Tax Court may reopen the case solely to determine whether the taxpayer has made an overpayment of such interest and the amount of any such overpayment. If the Tax Court determines under this subsection that the taxpayer has made an overpayment of interest, then that determination shall be treated under section 6512(b)(1) as a determination of an overpayment of tax. An order of the Tax Court redetermining the interest due, when entered upon the records of the court, shall be reviewable in the same manner as a decision of the Tax Court.

- **1988, Technical and Miscellaneous Revenue Act of 1988 (P.L. 100-647)**

P.L. 100-647, §6246(a):

Amended Code Sec. 7481 by adding at the end thereof new subsection (c). **Effective** for assessments of deficiencies redetermined by the Tax Court made after 11-10-88.

[Sec. 7481(d)]

(d) DECISIONS RELATING TO ESTATE TAX EXTENDED UNDER SECTION 6166.—If with respect to a decedent's estate subject to a decision of the Tax Court—

(1) the time for payment of an amount of tax imposed by chapter 11 is extended under section 6166, and

(2) there is treated as an administrative expense under section 2053 either—

(A) any amount of interest which a decedent's estate pays on any portion of the tax imposed by section 2001 on such estate for which the time of payment is extended under section 6166, or

(B) interest on any estate, succession, legacy, or inheritance tax imposed by a State on such estate during the period of the extension of time for payment under section 6166,

then, upon a motion by the petitioner in such case in which such time for payment of tax has been extended under section 6166, the Tax Court may reopen the case solely to modify the Court's decision to reflect such estate's entitlement to a deduction for such administration expenses under section 2053 and may hold further trial solely with respect to the claim for such deduction if, within the discretion of the Tax Court, such a hearing is deemed necessary. An order of the Tax Court disposing of a motion under this subsection shall be reviewable in the same manner as a decision of the Tax Court, but only with respect to the matters determined in such order.

Amendments

- **1988, Technical and Miscellaneous Revenue Act of 1988 (P.L. 100-647)**

P.L. 100-647, §6247(a):

Amended Code Sec. 7481, as amended, by adding at the end thereof new subsection (d). **Effective** with respect to Tax Court cases for which the decision is not final on 11-10-88.

[Sec. 7482]

SEC. 7482. COURTS OF REVIEW.

[Sec. 7482(a)]

(a) JURISDICTION.—

(1) IN GENERAL.—The United States Courts of Appeals (other than the United States Court of Appeals for the Federal Circuit) shall have exclusive jurisdiction to review the decisions of the Tax Court, except as provided in section 1254 of Title 28 of the United States Code, in the same manner and to the same extent as decisions of the district courts in civil actions tried without a jury; and the judgment of any such court shall be final, except that it shall be subject to review by the Supreme Court of the United States upon certiorari, in the manner provided in section 1254 of Title 28 of the United States Code.

COURT REVIEW OF TAX COURT DECISIONS

(2) INTERLOCUTORY ORDERS.—

(A) IN GENERAL.—When any judge of the Tax Court includes in an interlocutory order a statement that a controlling question of law is involved with respect to which there is a substantial ground for difference of opinion and that an immediate appeal from that order may materially advance the ultimate termination of the litigation, the United States Court of Appeals may, in its discretion, permit an appeal to be taken from such order, if application is made to it within 10 days after the entry of such order. Neither the application for nor the granting of an appeal under this paragraph shall stay proceedings in the Tax Court, unless a stay is ordered by a judge of the Tax Court or by the United States Court of Appeals which has jurisdiction of the appeal or a judge of that court.

(B) ORDER TREATED AS TAX COURT DECISION.—For purposes of subsections (b) and (c), an order described in this paragraph shall be treated as a decision of the Tax Court.

(C) VENUE FOR REVIEW OF SUBSEQUENT PROCEEDING.—If a United States Court of Appeals permits an appeal to be taken from an order described in subparagraph (A), except as provided in subsection (b)(2), any subsequent review of the decision of the Tax Court in the proceeding shall be made by such Court of Appeals.

(3) CERTAIN ORDERS ENTERED UNDER SECTION 6213(a).—An order of the Tax Court which is entered under authority of section 6213(a) and which resolves a proceeding to restrain assessment or collection shall be treated as a decision of the Tax Court for purposes of this section and shall be subject to the same review by the United States Court of Appeals as a similar order of a district court.

Amendments

• **1988, Technical and Miscellaneous Revenue Act of 1988 (P.L. 100-647)**

P.L. 100-647, §6243(b):

Amended Code Sec. 7482(a) by adding at the end thereof new paragraph (3). **Effective** for orders entered after 11-10-88.

• **1986, Tax Reform Act of 1986 (P.L. 99-514)**

P.L. 99-514, §1558(a):

Amended Code Sec. 7482(a) by adding at the end thereof new paragraph (2). **Effective** for any order of the Tax Court entered after 10-22-86.

P.L. 99-514, §1558(b):

Amended Code Sec. 7482(a) (as in effect before the amendment made by Act Sec. 1558(a)) by moving the text below the subsection heading and 2 ems to the right (so that the left margin of such text is aligned with the left margin of the paragraph (2) added by Act Sec. 1558(a)) and by inserting before such text "(1) In General.—". **Effective** for any order of the Tax Court entered after 10-22-86.

• **1982, Federal Courts Improvement Act of 1982 (P.L. 97-164)**

P.L. 97-164, §154:

Amended Code Sec. 7482(a) by inserting "(other than the United States Court of Appeals for the Federal Circuit)" after "United States Court of Appeals". For an explanation of the effect of this change on pending cases, see the historical comment for P.L. 97-164, Act Sec. 403, following Code Sec. 6110(i). **Effective** 10-1-82.

[Sec. 7482(b)]

(b) VENUE.—

(1) IN GENERAL.—Except as otherwise provided in paragraphs (2) and (3), such decisions may be reviewed by the United States court of appeals for the circuit in which is located—

(A) in the case of a petitioner seeking redetermination of tax liability other than a corporation, the legal residence of the petitioner,

(B) in the case of a corporation seeking redetermination of tax liability, the principal place of business or principal office or agency of the corporation, or, if it has no principal place of business or principal office or agency in any judicial circuit, then the office to which was made the return of the tax in respect of which the liability arises,

(C) in the case of a person seeking a declaratory decision under section 7476, the principal place of business, or principal office or agency of the employer,

(D) in the case of an organization seeking a declaratory decision under section 7428, the principal office or agency of the organization,

(E) in the case of a petition under section 6234, the principal place of business of the partnership,

(F) in the case of a petition under section 6015(e), the legal residence of the petitioner, or

(G) in the case of a petition under section 6320 or 6330—

(i) the legal residence of the petitioner if the petitioner is an individual, and

(ii) the principal place of business or principal office or agency if the petitioner is an entity other than an individual.

If for any reason no subparagraph of the preceding sentence applies, then such decisions may be reviewed by the Court of Appeals for the District of Columbia. For purposes of this paragraph, the legal residence, principal place of business, or principal office or agency referred to herein shall be determined as of the time the petition seeking redetermination of tax liability was filed with the Tax Court or as of the time the petition seeking a declaratory decision under section 7428 or 7476 or the petition under section 6234 was filed with the Tax Court.

(2) BY AGREEMENT.—Notwithstanding the provisions of paragraph (1), such decisions may be reviewed by any United States Court of Appeals which may be designated by the Secretary and the taxpayer by stipulation in writing.

(3) DECLARATORY JUDGMENT ACTIONS RELATING TO STATUS OF CERTAIN GOVERNMENTAL OBLIGATIONS.—In the case of any decision of the Tax Court in a proceeding under section 7478, such decision may only be reviewed by the Court of Appeals for the District of Columbia.

Amendments

• **2015, Protecting Americans from Tax Hikes Act of 2015 (P.L. 114-113)**

P.L. 114-113, §423(a)(1)-(3), Div. Q:

Amended Code Sec. 7482(b)(1) [as amended by P.L. 114-74] by striking "or" at the end of subparagraph (D), by striking the period at the end of subparagraph (E), and by inserting after subparagraph (E) new subparagraphs (F)-(G). **Effective** for petitions filed after 12-18-2015. For a special rule, see Act Sec. 423(b)(2), below.

P.L. 114-113, §423(b)(2), Div. Q, provides:

(2) EFFECT ON EXISTING PROCEEDINGS.—Nothing in this section shall be construed to create any inference with respect to the application of section 7482 of the Internal Revenue Code of 1986 with respect to court proceedings filed on or before the date of the enactment of this Act.

• **2015, Bipartisan Budget Act of 2015 (P.L. 114-74)**

P.L. 114-74, §1101(f)(13)(A)-(C):

Amended Code Sec. 7482(b)(1) by striking "section 6226, 6228[(a)], 6247, or 6252" and inserting "section 6234" in subparagraph (E), by striking subparagraph (F), by striking "or" at the end of subparagraph (E) and inserting a period, and by inserting "or" at the end of subparagraph (D), and by striking "section 6226, 6228(a), or 6234(c)" in the last sentence and inserting "section 6234". **Effective** generally for returns filed for partnership tax years beginning after 12-31-2017. For a special rule, see Act Sec. 1101(g)(4), below. Prior to being stricken, Code Sec. 7482(b)(1)(F) read as follows:

(F) in the case of a petition under section 6234(c)—

(i) the legal residence of the petitioner if the petitioner is not a corporation, and

(ii) the place or office applicable under subparagraph (B) if the petitioner is a corporation.

P.L. 114-74, §1101(g)(4), provides:

(4) ELECTION.—A partnership may elect (at such time and in such form and manner as the Secretary of the Treasury may prescribe) for the amendments made by this section (other than the election under section 6221(b) of such Code (as added by this Act)) to apply to any return of the partnership filed for partnership taxable years beginning after the date of the enactment of this Act and before January 1, 2018.

• **1997, Taxpayer Relief Act of 1997 (P.L. 105-34)**

P.L. 105-34, §1222(b)(3):

Amended Code Sec. 7482(b)(1)(E) by striking "or 6228(a)" and inserting ", 6228(a), 6247, or 6252". **Effective** for partnership tax years beginning after 12-31-97 [effective date changed by P.L. 105-206, §6012(e)].

P.L. 105-34, §1239(d)(1):

Amended Code Sec. 7482(b)(1) by striking "or" at the end of subparagraph (D), by striking the period at the end of subparagraph (E) and inserting ", or", and by inserting after subparagraph (E) a new subparagraph (F). **Effective** for partnership tax years ending after 8-5-97.

P.L. 105-34, §1239(d)(2):

Amended Code Sec. 7482(b)(1) by striking "or 6228(a)" in the last sentence and inserting ", 6228(a), or 6234(c)". **Effective** for partnership tax years ending after 8-5-97.

COURT REVIEW OF TAX COURT DECISIONS

• **1986, Tax Reform Act of 1986 (P.L. 99-514)**

P.L. 99-514, §1810(g)(2):

Amended Code Sec. 7482(b)(1) by striking out "section 7428, 7476 or 7477" and inserting in lieu thereof "section 7428 or 7476". **Effective** as if included in the provision of P.L. 98-369 to which it relates.

P.L. 99-514, §1899A(60):

Amended Code Sec. 7482(b)(1)(E) by striking out "partnership," and inserting in lieu thereof "partnership.". **Effective** 10-22-86.

• **1984, Deficit Reduction Act of 1984 (P.L. 98-369)**

P.L. 98-369, §131(e)(2)(A):

Amended Code Sec. 7482(b)(1) by striking out subparagraph (D) and by redesignating subparagraphs (E) and (F) as subparagraphs (D) and (E), respectively. **Effective** for transfers or exchanges after 12-31-84, in tax years ending after such date. Special rules appear in Act Sec. 131(g)(2) and (3) following Code Sec. 367. Prior to amendment, subparagraph (D) read as follows:

(D) in the case of a person seeking a declaratory judgment under section 7477, the legal residence of such person if such person is not a corporation, or the principal place of business or principal office or agency of such person if such person is a corporation,

• **1982, Tax Equity and Fiscal Responsibility Act of 1982 (P.L. 97-248)**

P.L. 97-248, §402(c)(15):

Amended Code Sec. 7482(b) by striking out "or" at the end of paragraph (D), by striking out the period at the end of subparagraph (E) and inserting ", or", by adding a new subparagraph (F), and by inserting ", or the petition under section 6226 or 6228(a)," after "or 7477". **Effective** for partnership tax years beginning after 9-3-82 and also to partnership tax years ending after that date if the partnership, each partner, and each indirect partner requests such application and the Secretary or his delegate consents to such application.

• **1978, Revenue Act of 1978 (P.L. 95-600)**

P.L. 95-600, §336(c)(1)(A), (B):

Amended Code Sec. 7482(b)(1) by striking out "provided in paragraph (2)" and inserting in lieu thereof "provided in paragraphs (2) and (3)", and added Code Sec. 7482(b)(3). **Effective** for requests for determinations made after 12-31-78.

• **1976, Tax Reform Act of 1976 (P.L. 94-455)**

P.L. 94-455, §1042(d)(2)(A):

Amended Code Sec. 7482(b)(1) by striking out "or" at the end of subparagraph (B), by substituting ", or" for the period at the end of subparagraph (C), and by adding a new subparagraph (D). For the **effective** date, see Act Sec. 1042(e)(1), below.

P.L. 94-455, §1042(e)(1), provides:

(1) The amendments made by this section (other than by subsection (d)) shall apply to transfers beginning after October 9, 1975, and to sales, exchanges, and distributions taking place after such date. The amendments made by subsection (d) shall apply with respect to pleadings filed with the Tax Court after the date of the enactment of this Act [October 4, 1976] but only with respect to transfers beginning after October 9, 1975.

P.L. 94-455, §1306(b)(4):

Amended Code Sec. 7482(b) by striking out "or" at the end of subparagraph (C), by substituting ", or" for the period at the end of subparagraph (D), and by adding Sec. 7482(b)(1)(E).

P.L. 94-455, §1306(b)(5):

Amended the last sentence of Code Sec. 7482(b)(1). Prior to amendment, the last sentence of Sec. 7482(b)(1) read as follows:

If for any reason subparagraph (A), (B) and (C) do not apply, then such decisions may be reviewed by the Court of Appeals for the District of Columbia. For purposes of this paragraph, the legal residence, principal place of business, or principal office or agency referred to herein shall be determined as of the time the petition seeking redetermination of tax liability was filed with the Tax Court or as of the time the petition seeking a declaratory decision under section 7476 was filed with the Tax Court.

P.L. 94-455, §1306(c), provides:

(c) EFFECTIVE DATE.—The amendments made by this section shall apply with respect to pleadings filed with the United States Tax Court, the district court of the United States for the District of Columbia, or the United States Court of Claims more than 6 months after the date of the enactment of this Act [October 4, 1976] but only with respect to determinations (or requests for determinations) made after January 1, 1976.

P.L. 94-455, §1906(b)(13)(A):

Amended 1954 Code by substituting "Secretary" for "Secretary or his delegate" each place it appeared. **Effective** 2-1-77.

• **1974, Employee Retirement Income Security Act of 1974 (P.L. 93-406)**

P.L. 93-406, §1041(b)(3):

Amended Code Sec. 7482(b)(1). **Effective** to pleadings filed after 9-2-75. Prior to amendment, Code Sec. 7482(b)(1) read as follows:

"(b) Venue.—

"(1) In general.—Except as otherwise provided in paragraph (2), such decisions may be reviewed by the United States court of appeals for the circuit in which is located—

"(A) in the case of a petitioner seeking redetermination of tax liability other than a corporation, the legal residence of the petitioner,

"(B) in the case of a corporation seeking redetermination of tax liability, the principal place of business or principal office or agency of the corporation, or, if it has no principal place of business or principal office or agency in any judicial circuit, then the office to which was made the return of the tax in respect of which the liability arises.

If for any reason neither subparagraph (A) nor (B) applies, then such decisions may be reviewed by the Court of Appeals for the District of Columbia. For purposes of this paragraph, the legal residence, principal place of business, or principal office or agency referred to herein shall be determined as of the time the petition seeking redetermination of tax liability was filed with the Tax Court."

• **1966 (P.L. 89-713)**

P.L. 89-713, §3(c):

Amended Code Sec. 7482(b)(1). **Effective** as to all decisions of the Tax Court entered after 11-2-66. Prior to amendment, Sec. 7482(b)(1) read as follows:

"(1) In general.—Except as provided in paragraph (2), such decisions may be reviewed by the United States Court of Appeals for the circuit in which is located the office to which was made the return of the tax in respect of which the liability arises, or, if no return was made, then by the United States Court of Appeals for the District of Columbia."

[Sec. 7482(c)]

(c) POWERS.—

(1) TO AFFIRM, MODIFY, OR REVERSE.—Upon such review, such courts shall have power to affirm or, if the decision of the Tax Court is not in accordance with law, to modify or to reverse the decision of the Tax Court, with or without remanding the case for a rehearing, as justice may require.

(2) TO MAKE RULES.—Rules for review of decisions of the Tax Court shall be those prescribed by the Supreme Court under section 2072 of title 28 of the United States Code.

(3) TO REQUIRE ADDITIONAL SECURITY.—Nothing in section 7483 shall be construed as relieving the petitioner from making or filing such undertakings as the court may require as a condition of or in connection with the review.

(4) TO IMPOSE PENALTIES.—The United States Court of Appeals and the Supreme Court shall have the power to require the taxpayer to pay to the United States a penalty in any case where the decision of the Tax Court is affirmed and it appears that the appeal was instituted or maintained primarily for delay or that the taxpayer's position in the appeal is frivolous or groundless.

Amendments

• **1989, Omnibus Budget Reconciliation Act of 1989 (P.L. 101-239)**

P.L. 101-239, §7731(b):

Amended Code Sec. 7482(c)(4). **Effective** for positions taken after 12-31-89, in proceedings which are pending on, or commenced after such date. Prior to amendment, Code Sec. 7482(c)(4) read as follows:

(4) TO IMPOSE DAMAGES.—The United States Court of Appeals and the Supreme Court shall have power to impose damages in any case where the decision of the Tax Court is affirmed and it appears that the notice of appeal was filed merely for delay.

• **1969, Tax Reform Act of 1969 (P.L. 91-172)**

P.L. 91-172, §960(h)(2):

Amended Code Sec. 7482(c)(2) by substituting the phrase "section 2072" for the phrase "section 2074" and by deleting the second sentence, which read as follows: "Until such rules become effective the rules adopted under authority of section 1141(c)(2) of the Internal Revenue Code of 1939 shall remain in effect." (See amendatory note under Code Sec. 7483, below.) Also amended Code Sec. 7482(c)(4) by substituting the phrase "notice of appeal" for the word "petition." **Effective** 1-29-70.

[Sec. 7483]

SEC. 7483. NOTICE OF APPEAL.

Review of a decision of the Tax Court shall be obtained by filing a notice of appeal with the clerk of the Tax Court within 90 days after the decision of the Tax Court is entered. If a timely notice of appeal is filed by one party, any other party may take an appeal by filing a notice of appeal within 120 days after the decision of the Tax Court is entered.

COURT REVIEW OF TAX COURT DECISIONS

Amendments
- **1969, Tax Reform Act of 1969 (P.L. 91-172)**

P.L. 91-172, § 959(a):

Amended Code Sec. 7483. **Effective** 1-29-70. However, in the case of any decision of the Tax Court entered before January 29, 1970, the United States Courts of Appeal shall have jurisdiction to hear an appeal from such decision, if such appeal was filed within the time prescribed by Rule 13(a) of the Federal Rules of Appellate Procedure or by section 7483 of the Internal Revenue Code of 1954, as in effect at the time the decision of the Tax Court was entered. Prior to amendment, Sec. 7483 read as follows:

SEC. 7483. PETITION FOR REVIEW.

The decision of the Tax Court may be reviewed by a United States Court of Appeals as provided in section 7482 if a petition for such review is filed by either the Secretary (or his delegate) or the taxpayer within 3 months after the decision is rendered. If, however, a petition for such review is so filed by one party to the proceeding, a petition for review of the decision of the Tax Court may be filed by any other party to the proceeding within 4 months after such decision is rendered.

[Sec. 7484]

SEC. 7484. CHANGE OF INCUMBENT IN OFFICE.

When the incumbent of the office of Secretary changes, no substitution of the name of his successor shall be required in proceedings pending before any appellate court reviewing the action of the Tax Court.

Amendments
- **1976, Tax Reform Act of 1976 (P.L. 94-455)**

P.L. 94-455, § 1906(b)(13)(A):

Amended 1954 Code by substituting "Secretary" for "Secretary or his delegate" each place it appeared. **Effective** 2-1-77.

[Sec. 7485]

SEC. 7485. BOND TO STAY ASSESSMENT AND COLLECTION.

[Sec. 7485(a)]

(a) UPON NOTICE OF APPEAL.—Notwithstanding any provision of law imposing restrictions on the assessment and collection of deficiencies, the review under section 7483 shall not operate as a stay of assessment or collection of any portion of the amount of the deficiency determined by the Tax Court unless a notice of appeal in respect of such portion is duly filed by the taxpayer, and then only if the taxpayer—

(1) on or before the time his notice of appeal is filed has filed with the Tax Court a bond in a sum fixed by the Tax Court not exceeding double the amount of the portion of the deficiency in respect of which the notice of appeal is filed, and with surety approved by the Tax Court, conditioned upon the payment of the deficiency as finally determined, together with any interest, additional amounts, or additions to the tax provided for by law, or

(2) has filed a jeopardy bond under the income or estate tax laws.

If as a result of a waiver of the restrictions on the assessment and collection of a deficiency any part of the amount determined by the Tax Court is paid after the filing of the appeal bond, such bond shall, at the request of the taxpayer, be proportionately reduced.

Amendments
- **1969, Tax Reform Act of 1969 (P.L. 91-172)**

P.L. 91-172, § 960(h)(3):

Amended Code Sec. 7485(a) by substituting the phrase "notice of appeal" for the phrase "petition for review" each time it appeared and substituting the phrase "appeal bond" for the phrase "review bond" in the last sentence. See discussion of effective date in the amendatory note following Code Sec. 7483. **Effective** 1-29-70.

[Sec. 7485(b)]

(b) BOND IN CASE OF APPEAL OF CERTAIN PARTNERSHIP-RELATED DECISIONS.—The condition of subsection (a) shall be satisfied if the partnership duly files notice of appeal from a decision under section 6234 and on or before the time the notice of appeal is filed with the Tax Court, a bond in an amount fixed by the Tax Court is filed, and with surety approved by the Tax Court, conditioned upon the payment of deficiencies attributable to the partnership-related items (as defined in section 6241) to which that decision relates as finally determined, together with any interest, penalties, additional amounts, or additions to the tax provided by law. Unless otherwise stipulated by the parties, the amount fixed by the Tax Court shall be based upon its estimate of the aggregate liability of the parties to the action.

Amendments
- **2018, Tax Technical Corrections Act of 2018 (P.L. 115-141)**

P.L. 115-141, § 201(c)(8), Div. U:

Amended Code Sec. 7485(b) by striking "partnership items" and inserting "partnership-related items (as defined in section 6241)". **Effective** as if included in section 1101 of the Bipartisan Budget Act of 2015 [effective generally for returns filed for partnership tax years beginning after 12-31-2017.—CCH].

P.L. 115-141, § 206(p)(8), Div. U:

Amended Code Sec. 7485(b) by striking "a partner" and inserting "the partnership". **Effective** as if included in section 1101 of the Bipartisan Budget Act of 2015 [effective generally for returns filed for partnership tax years beginning after 12-31-2017.—CCH].

- **2015, Bipartisan Budget Act of 2015 (P.L. 114-74)**

P.L. 114-74, § 1101(f)(14):

Amended Code Sec. 7485(b) by striking "section 6226, 6228(a), 6247, or 6252" and inserting "section 6234". **Effective** generally for returns filed for partnership tax years beginning after 12-31-2017. For a special rule, see Act Sec. 1101(g)(4), below.

P.L. 114-74, § 1101(g)(4), provides:

(4) ELECTION.—A partnership may elect (at such time and in such form and manner as the Secretary of the Treasury may prescribe) for the amendments made by this section (other than the election under section 6221(b) of such Code (as added by this Act)) to apply to any return of the partnership filed for partnership taxable years beginning after the date of the enactment of this Act and before January 1, 2018.

- **1997, Taxpayer Relief Act of 1997 (P.L. 105-34)**

P.L. 105-34, § 1222(b)(4)(A):

Amended Code Sec. 7485(b) by striking "or 6228(a)" and inserting ", 6228(a), 6247, or 6252". **Effective** for partnership tax years beginning after 12-31-97 [effective date changed by P.L. 105-206, § 6012(e)].

P.L. 105-34, § 1222(b)(4)(B):

Amended the heading of Code Sec. 7485(b). **Effective** for partnership tax years beginning after 12-31-97 [effective date changed by P.L. 105-206, § 6012(e)]. Prior to amendment, the heading for Code Sec. 7485(b) read as follows:

(b) BOND IN CASE OF APPEAL OF DECISION UNDER SECTION 6226 OR SECTION 6228(a).—

P.L. 105-34, § 1241(a)(1)-(2):

Amended Code Sec. 7485(b) by inserting "penalties," after "any interest,", and by striking "aggregate of such deficiencies" and inserting "aggregate liability of the parties to the action". **Effective** as if included in the amendments made by Act Sec. 402 of P.L. 97-248 [effective, generally, for partnership tax years beginning after 9-3-82.—CCH].

- **1982, Tax Equity and Fiscal Responsibility Act of 1982 (P.L. 97-248)**

P.L. 97-248, § 402(c)(16):

Redesignated subsection (b) as subsection (c) and added a new subsection (b). **Effective** for partnership tax years beginning after 9-3-82 and also to partnership tax years ending after that date if the partnership, each partner, and each indirect partner requests such application and if the Secretary or his delegate consents to such application.

[Sec. 7485(c)]

(c) CROSS REFERENCES.—

(1) For requirement of additional security notwithstanding this section, see section 7482(c)(3).

(2) For deposit of United States bonds or notes in lieu of sureties, see section 9303 of title 31, United States Code.

JUDICIAL PROCEEDINGS—BURDEN OF PROOF

Amendments

• **1982 (P.L. 97-258)**

P.L. 97-258, §3(f)(15):

Amended Code Sec. 7485(b)[c](2) by striking out "6 U.S.C. 15" and substituting "section 9303 of title 31, United States Code". **Effective** 9-13-82.

• **1982, Tax Equity and Fiscal Responsibility Act of 1982 (P.L. 97-248)**

P.L. 97-248, §402(c)(16):

Redesignated subsection (b) as subsection (c). For the **effective** date, see the amendment note for P.L. 97-248, Act Sec. 402(c)(16), following Code Sec. 7485(b).

[Sec. 7486]
SEC. 7486. REFUND, CREDIT, OR ABATEMENT OF AMOUNTS DISALLOWED.

In cases where assessment or collection has not been stayed by the filing of a bond, then if the amount of the deficiency determined by the Tax Court is disallowed in whole or in part by the court of review, the amount so disallowed shall be credited or refunded to the taxpayer, without the making of claim therefor, or, if collection has not been made, shall be abated.

[Sec. 7487]
SEC. 7487. CROSS REFERENCES.

(1) NONREVIEWABILITY.—For nonreviewability of Tax Court decisions in small claims cases, see section 7463(b).

(2) TRANSCRIPTS.—For authority of the Tax Court to fix fees for transcript of records, see section 7474.

Amendments

• **1969, Tax Reform Act of 1969 (P.L. 91-172)**

P.L. 91-172, §960(i)(1):

Amended Code Sec. 7487. **Effective** 12-30-70. Prior to amendment, Code Sec. 7487 read as follows:

"SEC. 7487. CROSS REFERENCE.

"For authority of the Tax Court to fix fees for transcripts of records, see section 7474."

Subchapter E—Burden of Proof

Sec. 7491.   Burden of proof.

[Sec. 7491]
SEC. 7491. BURDEN OF PROOF.

[Sec. 7491(a)]

(a) BURDEN SHIFTS WHERE TAXPAYER PRODUCES CREDIBLE EVIDENCE.—

(1) GENERAL RULE.—If, in any court proceeding, a taxpayer introduces credible evidence with respect to any factual issue relevant to ascertaining the liability of the taxpayer for any tax imposed by subtitle A or B, the Secretary shall have the burden of proof with respect to such issue.

(2) LIMITATIONS.—Paragraph (1) shall apply with respect to an issue only if—

(A) the taxpayer has complied with the requirements under this title to substantiate any item;

(B) the taxpayer has maintained all records required under this title and has cooperated with reasonable requests by the Secretary for witnesses, information, documents, meetings, and interviews; and

(C) in the case of a partnership, corporation, or trust, the taxpayer is described in section 7430(c)(4)(A)(ii).

Subparagraph (C) shall not apply to any qualified revocable trust (as defined in section 645(b)(1)) with respect to liability for tax for any taxable year ending after the date of the decedent's death and before the applicable date (as defined in section 645(b)(2)).

(3) COORDINATION.—Paragraph (1) shall not apply to any issue if any other provision of this title provides for a specific burden of proof with respect to such issue.

Amendments

• **1998, Tax and Trade Relief Extension Act of 1998 (P.L. 105-277)**

P.L. 105-277, §4002(b):

Amended Code Sec. 7491(a)(2) by adding at the end a new flush sentence. **Effective** as if included in the provision of P.L. 105-206 to which it relates [generally effective for court proceedings arising in connection with examinations commencing after 7-22-98.—CCH].

[Sec. 7491(b)]

(b) USE OF STATISTICAL INFORMATION ON UNRELATED TAXPAYERS.—In the case of an individual taxpayer, the Secretary shall have the burden of proof in any court proceeding with respect to any item of income which was reconstructed by the Secretary solely through the use of statistical information on unrelated taxpayers.

[Sec. 7491(c)]

(c) PENALTIES.—Notwithstanding any other provision of this title, the Secretary shall have the burden of production in any court proceeding with respect to the liability of any individual for any penalty, addition to tax, or additional amount imposed by this title.

Amendments

• **1998, IRS Restructuring and Reform Act of 1998 (P.L. 105-206)**

P.L. 105-206, §3001(a):

Amended Chapter 76 by adding at the end a new Code Sec. 7491. **Effective**, generally, for court proceedings arising in connection with examinations commencing after 7-22-98. For a special rule, see Act Sec. 3001(c)(2), below.

P.L. 105-206, §3001(c)(2), provides:

(2) TAXABLE PERIODS OR EVENTS AFTER DATE OF ENACTMENT.—In any case in which there is no examination, such amendments shall apply to court proceedings arising in connection with taxable periods or events beginning or occurring after such date of enactment.

CHAPTER 77—MISCELLANEOUS PROVISIONS

Sec. 7501.   Liability for taxes withheld or collected.
Sec. 7502.   Timely mailing treated as timely filing and paying.
Sec. 7503.   Time for performance of acts where last day falls on Saturday, Sunday, or legal holiday.
Sec. 7504.   Fractional parts of a dollar.
Sec. 7505.   Sale of personal property acquired by the United States.
Sec. 7506.   Administration of real estate acquired by the United States.
Sec. 7507.   Exemption of insolvent banks from tax.
Sec. 7508.   Time for performing certain acts postponed by reason of service in combat zone or contingency operation.
Sec. 7508A.   Authority to postpone certain deadlines by reason of Federally declared disaster, significant fire, or terrorist or military actions.

MISCELLANEOUS PROVISIONS

Sec. 7509.	Expenditures incurred by the United States Postal Service.
Sec. 7510.	Exemption from tax of domestic goods purchased for the United States.
Sec. 7512.	Separate accounting for certain collected taxes, etc.
Sec. 7513.	Reproduction of returns and other documents.
Sec. 7514.	Authority to prescribe or modify seals.
Sec. 7516.	Supplying training and training aids on request.
Sec. 7517.	Furnishing on request of statement explaining estate or gift evaluation.
Sec. 7518.	Tax incentives relating to merchant marine capital construction funds.
Sec. 7519.	Required payments for entities electing not to have required taxable year.
Sec. 7520.	Valuation tables.
Sec. 7521.	Procedures involving taxpayer interviews.
Sec. 7522.	Content of tax due, deficiency, and other notices.
Sec. 7523.	Graphic presentation of major categories of federal outlays and income.
Sec. 7524.	Annual notice of tax delinquency.
Sec. 7525.	Confidentiality privileges relating to taxpayer communications.
Sec. 7526.	Low-income taxpayer clinics.
Sec. 7526A.	Return preparation programs for applicable taxpayers.
Sec. 7527.	Advance payment of credit for health insurance costs of eligible individuals.
Sec. 7527A.	Advance payment of child tax credit.
Sec. 7528.	Internal Revenue Service user fees.
Sec. 7529.	Notification of suspected identity theft.
Sec. 7530.	Application of earned income tax credit to possessions of the United States.

[Sec. 7501]

SEC. 7501. LIABILITY FOR TAXES WITHHELD OR COLLECTED.

[Sec. 7501(a)]

(a) GENERAL RULE.—Whenever any person is required to collect or withhold any internal revenue tax from any other person and to pay over such tax to the United States, the amount of tax so collected or withheld shall be held to be a special fund in trust for the United States. The amount of such fund shall be assessed, collected, and paid in the same manner and subject to the same provisions and limitations (including penalties) as are applicable with respect to the taxes from which such fund arose.

[Sec. 7501(b)]

(b) PENALTIES.—
For penalties applicable to violations of this section, see sections 6672 and 7202.

[Sec. 7502]

SEC. 7502. TIMELY MAILING TREATED AS TIMELY FILING AND PAYING.

[Sec. 7502(a)]

(a) GENERAL RULE.—

(1) DATE OF DELIVERY.—If any return, claim, statement, or other document required to be filed, or any payment required to be made, within a prescribed period or on or before a prescribed date under authority of any provision of the internal revenue laws is, after such period or such date, delivered by United States mail to the agency, officer, or office with which such return, claim, statement, or other document is required to be filed, or to which such payment is required to be made, the date of the United States postmark stamped on the cover in which such return, claim, statement, or other document, or payment, is mailed shall be deemed to be the date of delivery or the date of payment, as the case may be.

(2) MAILING REQUIREMENTS.—This subsection shall apply only if—

(A) the postmark date falls within the prescribed period or on or before the prescribed date—

(i) for the filing (including any extension granted for such filing) of the return, claim, statement, or other document, or

(ii) for making the payment (including any extension granted for making such payment), and

(B) the return, claim, statement, or other document, or payment was, within the time prescribed in subparagraph (A), deposited in the mail in the United States in an envelope or other appropriate wrapper, postage prepaid, properly addressed to the agency, officer, or office with which the return, claim, statement, or other document is required to be filed, or to which such payment is required to be made.

[Sec. 7502(b)]

(b) POSTMARKS.—This section shall apply in the case of postmarks not made by the United States Postal Service only if and to the extent provided by regulations prescribed by the Secretary.

Amendments

- 1976, Tax Reform Act of 1976 (P.L. 94-455)

P.L. 94-455, §1906(b)(13)(A):
Amended 1954 Code by substituting "Secretary" for "Secretary or his delegate" each place it appeared. **Effective** 2-1-77.

P.L. 94-455, §1906(a)(49):
Substituted "United States Postal Service" for "United States Post Office" in Code Sec. 7502(b). **Effective** 2-1-77.

[Sec. 7502(c)]

(c) REGISTERED AND CERTIFIED MAILING; ELECTRONIC FILING.—

(1) REGISTERED MAIL.—For purposes of this section, if any return, claim, statement, or other document, or payment, is sent by United States registered mail—

(A) such registration shall be prima facie evidence that the return, claim, statement, or other document was delivered to the agency, officer, or office to which addressed; and

(B) the date of registration shall be deemed the postmark date.

MISCELLANEOUS PROVISIONS

(2) CERTIFIED MAIL; ELECTRONIC FILING.—The Secretary is authorized to provide by regulations the extent to which the provisions of paragraph (1) with respect to prima facie evidence of delivery and the postmark date shall apply to certified mail and electronic filing.

Amendments

• **1998, IRS Restructuring and Reform Act of 1998 (P.L. 105-206)**

P.L. 105-206, §2003(b):

Amended Code Sec. 7502(c). **Effective** 7-22-98. Prior to amendment, Code Sec. 7502(c) read as follows:

(c) REGISTERED AND CERTIFIED MAILING.—

(1) REGISTERED MAIL.—For purposes of this section, if any such return, claim, statement, or other document, or payment, is sent by United States registered mail—

(A) such registration shall be prima facie evidence that the return, claim, statement, or other document was delivered to the agency, officer, or office to which addressed, and

(B) the date of registration shall be deemed the postmark date.

(2) CERTIFIED MAIL.—The Secretary is authorized to provide by regulations the extent to which the provisions of paragraph (1) of this subsection with respect to prima facie evidence of delivery and the postmark date shall apply to certified mail.

• **1976, Tax Reform Act of 1976 (P.L. 94-455)**

P.L. 94-455, §1906(b)(13)(A):

Amended 1954 Code by substituting "Secretary" for "Secretary or his delegate" each place it appeared. **Effective** 2-1-77.

[Sec. 7502(d)]

(d) EXCEPTIONS.—This section shall not apply with respect to—

(1) the filing of a document in, or the making of a payment to, any court other than the Tax Court,

(2) currency or other medium of payment unless actually received and accounted for, or

(3) returns, claims, statements, or other documents, or payments, which are required under any provision of the internal revenue laws or the regulations thereunder to be delivered by any method other than by mailing.

[Sec. 7502(e)]

(e) MAILING OF DEPOSITS.—

(1) DATE OF DEPOSIT.—If any deposit required to be made (pursuant to regulations prescribed by the Secretary under section 6302(c)) on or before a prescribed date is, after such date, delivered by the United States mail to the bank, trust company, domestic building and loan association, or credit union authorized to receive such deposit, such deposit shall be deemed received by such bank, trust company, domestic building and loan association, or credit union on the date the deposit was mailed.

(2) MAILING REQUIREMENTS.—Paragraph (1) shall apply only if the person required to make the deposit establishes that—

(A) the date of mailing falls on or before the second day before the prescribed date for making the deposit (including any extension of time granted for making such deposit), and

(B) the deposit was, on or before such second day, mailed in the United States in an envelope or other appropriate wrapper, postage prepaid, properly addressed to the bank, trust company, domestic building and loan association, or credit union authorized to receive such deposit.

In applying subsection (c) for purposes of this subsection, the term "payment" includes "deposit", and the reference to the postmark date refers to the date of mailing.

(3) NO APPLICATION TO CERTAIN DEPOSITS.—Paragraph (1) shall not apply with respect to any deposit of $20,000 or more by any person who is required to deposit any tax more than once a month.

Amendments

• **1986, Tax Reform Act of 1986 (P.L. 99-514)**

P.L. 99-514, §1811(e):

Amended Code Sec. 7502(e)(3) by striking out "the tax" and inserting in lieu thereof "any tax". **Effective** as if included in the provision of P.L. 98-369 to which it relates.

• **1984, Deficit Reduction Act of 1984 (P.L. 98-369)**

P.L. 98-369, §157(a):

Added Code Sec. 7502(e)(3). **Effective** for deposits required to be made after 7-31-84.

• **1977 (P.L. 95-147)**

P.L. 95-147, §3(b):

Substituted ", trust company, domestic building and loan association, or credit union" for "or trust company" each place it appeared in Code Sec. 7502(e). **Effective** for amounts deposited after 10-28-77.

• **1976, Tax Reform Act of 1976 (P.L. 94-455)**

P.L. 94-455, §1906(b)(13)(A):

Amended 1954 Code by substituting "Secretary" for "Secretary or his delegate" each place it appeared. **Effective** 2-1-77.

• **1968, Revenue and Expenditure Control Act of 1968 (P.L. 90-364)**

P.L. 90-364, §106(a):

Amended Code Sec. 7502 by adding new subsection (e). **Effective** only for mailing occurring after 6-28-68.

• **1966 (P.L. 89-713)**

P.L. 89-713, §5(a):

Amended Code Sec. 7502. **Effective** only as to mailing occurring after 11-2-66. Prior to amendment, Code Sec. 7502 read as follows:

SEC. 7502. TIMELY MAILING TREATED AS TIMELY FILING.

(a) General Rule.—If any claim, statement, or other document (other than a return or other document required under authority of chapter 61), required to be filed within a prescribed period or on or before a prescribed date under authority of any provision of the internal revenue laws is, after such period or such date, delivered by United States mail to the agency, officer, or office with which such claim, statement, or other document is required to be filed, the date of the United States postmark stamped on the cover in which such claim, statement, or other document is mailed shall be deemed to be the date of delivery. This subsection shall apply only if the postmark date falls within the prescribed period or on or before the prescribed date for the filing of the claim, statement, or other document, determined with regard to any extension granted for such filing, and only if the claim, statement, or other document was, within the prescribed time, deposited in the mail in the United States in an envelope or other appropriate wrapper, postage prepaid, properly addressed to the agency, office, or officer with which the claim, statement, or other document is required to be filed.

(b) Stamp Machine.—This section shall apply in the case of postmarks not made by the United States Post Office only if and to the extent provided by regulations prescribed by the Secretary or his delegate.

(c) Registered and Certified Mail.—

(1) Registered mail.—If any such claim, statement, or other document is sent by United States registered mail, such registration shall be prima facie evidence that the claim, statement, or other document was delivered to the agency, office, or officer to which addressed, and the date of registration shall be deemed the postmark date.

(2) Certified mail.—The Secretary or his delegate is authorized to provide by regulations the extent to which the provisions of paragraph (1) of this subsection with respect to prima facie evidence of delivery and the postmark date shall apply to certified mail.

(d) Exception.—This section shall not apply with respect to the filing of a document in any court other than the Tax Court.

• **1958, Technical Amendments Act of 1958 (P.L. 85-866)**

P.L. 85-866, §89(a):

Amended Code Sec. 7502(c). **Effective** only where the mailing occurs after 9-2-58. Prior to amendment, Code Sec. 7502(c) read as follows:

(c) Registered Mail.—If any such claim, statement, or other document is sent by United States registered mail, such registration shall be prima facie evidence that the claim, statement, or other document was delivered to the agency, office, or officer to which addressed, and the date of registration shall be deemed the postmark date.

[Sec. 7502(f)]

(f) TREATMENT OF PRIVATE DELIVERY SERVICES.—

(1) IN GENERAL.—Any reference in this section to the United States mail shall be treated as including a reference to any designated delivery service, and any reference in this section to a postmark by the United States Postal Service shall be treated as including a reference to any date recorded or marked as described in paragraph (2)(C) by any designated delivery service.

MISCELLANEOUS PROVISIONS

(2) DESIGNATED DELIVERY SERVICE.—For purposes of this subsection, the term "designated delivery service" means any delivery service provided by a trade or business if such service is designated by the Secretary for purposes of this section. The Secretary may designate a delivery service under the preceding sentence only if the Secretary determines that such service—

(A) is available to the general public,

(B) is at least as timely and reliable on a regular basis as the United States mail,

(C) records electronically to its data base, kept in the regular course of its business, or marks on the cover in which any item referred to in this section is to be delivered, the date on which such item was given to such trade or business for delivery, and

(D) meets such other criteria as the Secretary may prescribe.

(3) EQUIVALENTS OF REGISTERED AND CERTIFIED MAIL.—The Secretary may provide a rule similar to the rule of paragraph (1) with respect to any service provided by a designated delivery service which is substantially equivalent to United States registered or certified mail.

Amendments

• **1996, Taxpayer Bill of Rights 2 (P.L. 104-168)**

P.L. 104-168, §1210:

Amended Code Sec. 7502 by adding at the end a new subsection (f). **Effective** 7-30-96.

[Sec. 7503]

SEC. 7503. TIME FOR PERFORMANCE OF ACTS WHERE LAST DAY FALLS ON SATURDAY, SUNDAY, OR LEGAL HOLIDAY.

When the last day prescribed under authority of the internal revenue laws for performing any act falls on Saturday, Sunday, or a legal holiday, the performance of such act shall be considered timely if it is performed on the next succeeding day which is not a Saturday, Sunday, or a legal holiday. For purposes of this section, the last day for the performance of any act shall be determined by including any authorized extension of time; the term "legal holiday" means a legal holiday in the District of Columbia; and in the case of any return, statement, or other document required to be filed, or any other act required under authority of the internal revenue laws to be performed, at any office of the Secretary, or at any other office of the United States or any agency thereof, located outside the District of Columbia but within an internal revenue district, the term "legal holiday" also means a Statewide legal holiday in the State where such office is located.

Amendments

• **1976, Tax Reform Act of 1976 (P.L. 94-455)**

P.L. 94-455, §1906(b)(13)(A):

Amended 1954 Code by substituting "Secretary" for "Secretary or his delegate" each place it appeared. **Effective** 2-1-77.

[Sec. 7504]

SEC. 7504. FRACTIONAL PARTS OF A DOLLAR.

The Secretary may by regulations provide that in the allowance of any amount as a credit or refund, or in the collection of any amount as a deficiency or underpayment, of any tax imposed by this title, a fractional part of a dollar shall be disregarded, unless it amounts to 50 cents or more, in which case it shall be increased to 1 dollar.

Amendments

• **1976, Tax Reform Act of 1976 (P.L. 94-455)**

P.L. 94-455, §1906(b)(13)(A):

Amended 1954 Code by substituting "Secretary" for "Secretary or his delegate" each place it appeared. **Effective** 2-1-77.

[Sec. 7505]

SEC. 7505. SALE OF PERSONAL PROPERTY ACQUIRED BY THE UNITED STATES.

[Sec. 7505(a)]

(a) SALE.—Any personal property acquired by the United States in payment of or as security for debts arising under the internal revenue laws may be sold by the Secretary in accordance with such regulations as may be prescribed by the Secretary.

Amendments

• **1976, Tax Reform Act of 1976 (P.L. 94-455)**

P.L. 94-455, §1906(b)(13)(A):

Amended 1954 Code by substituting "Secretary" for "Secretary or his delegate" each place it appeared. **Effective** 2-1-77.

• **1966, Federal Tax Lien Act of 1966 (P.L. 89-719)**

P.L. 89-719, §111(a):

Amended Code Sec. 7505(a). **Effective**, generally, after 11-2-66. However, see the amendment note for Code Sec. 6323 for exceptions to this **effective** date. Prior to amendment, Code Sec. 7505(a) read as follows:

"(a) Sale.—Any personal property purchased by the United States under the authority of section 6335(e) (relating to purchase for the account of the United States of property sold under levy) may be sold by the Secretary or his delegate in accordance with such regulations as may be prescribed by the Secretary or his delegate."

P.L. 89-719, §111(c):

Amended the heading of Code Sec. 7505 by substituting "ACQUIRED" for "PURCHASED". **Effective**, generally, after 11-2-66. However, see the amendment note for Code Sec. 6323 for exceptions to this **effective** date.

[Sec. 7505(b)]

(b) ACCOUNTING.—In case of the resale of such property, the proceeds of the sale shall be paid into the Treasury as internal revenue collections, and there shall be rendered a distinct account of all charges incurred in such sales.

[Sec. 7506]

SEC. 7506. ADMINISTRATION OF REAL ESTATE ACQUIRED BY THE UNITED STATES.

[Sec. 7506(a)]

(a) PERSON CHARGED WITH.—The Secretary shall have charge of all real estate which is or shall become the property of the United States by judgment of forfeiture under the internal revenue laws, or which has been or shall be assigned, set off, or conveyed by purchase or otherwise to the United States in payment of debts or penalties arising under the laws relating to internal revenue, or which has been or shall be vested in the United States by mortgage or other security for the payment of such debts, or which has been redeemed by the United States, and of all trusts created for the use of the United States in payment of such debts due them.

Amendments

• **1976, Tax Reform Act of 1976 (P.L. 94-455)**

P.L. 94-455, §1906(b)(13)(A):

Amended 1954 Code by substituting "Secretary" for "Secretary or his delegate" each place it appeared. **Effective** 2-1-77.

• **1966, Federal Tax Lien Act of 1966 (P.L. 89-719)**

P.L. 89-719, §111(b):

Amended Code Sec. 7506(a) by inserting "or which has been redeemed by the United States," immediately after "for the payment of such debts,". **Effective**, gener-

MISCELLANEOUS PROVISIONS

ally, after 11-2-66. However, see the amendment note for Code Sec. 6323 for exceptions to this **effective** date.

[Sec. 7506(b)]

(b) SALE.—The Secretary may, at public sale, and upon not less than 20 days' notice, sell and dispose of any real estate owned or held by the United States as aforesaid.

Amendments
• **1976, Tax Reform Act of 1976 (P.L. 94-455)**

P.L. 94-455, § 1906(b)(13)(A):

Amended 1954 Code by substituting "Secretary" for "Secretary or his delegate" each place it appeared. **Effective** 2-1-77.

[Sec. 7506(c)]

(c) LEASE.—Until such sale, the Secretary may lease such real estate owned as aforesaid on such terms and for such period as the Secretary shall deem proper.

Amendments
• **1976, Tax Reform Act of 1976 (P.L. 94-455)**

P.L. 94-455, § 1906(b)(13)(A):

Amended 1954 Code by substituting "Secretary" for "Secretary or his delegate" each place it appeared. **Effective** 2-1-77.

[Sec. 7506(d)]

(d) RELEASE TO DEBTOR.—In cases where real estate has or may become the property of the United States by conveyance or otherwise, in payment of or as security for a debt arising under the laws relating to internal revenue, and such debt shall have been paid, together with the interest thereon, at the rate of 1 percent per month, to the United States, within 2 years from the date of the acquisition of such real estate, it shall be lawful for the Secretary to release by deed or otherwise convey such real estate to the debtor from whom it was taken, or to his heirs or other legal representatives.

Amendments
• **1976, Tax Reform Act of 1976 (P.L. 94-455)**

P.L. 94-455, § 1906(b)(13)(A):

Amended 1954 Code by substituting "Secretary" for "Secretary or his delegate" each place it appeared. **Effective** 2-1-77.

[Sec. 7507]

SEC. 7507. EXEMPTION OF INSOLVENT BANKS FROM TAX.

[Sec. 7507(a)]

(a) ASSETS IN GENERAL.—Whenever and after any bank or trust company, a substantial portion of the business of which consists of receiving deposits and making loans and discounts, has ceased to do business by reason of insolvency or bankruptcy, no tax shall be assessed or collected, or paid into the Treasury of the United States, on account of such bank or trust company, which shall diminish the assets thereof necessary for the full payment of all its depositors; and such tax shall be abated from such national banks as are found by the Comptroller of the Currency to be insolvent; and the Secretary, when the facts shall appear to him, is authorized to remit so much of the said tax against any such insolvent banks and trust companies organized under State law as shall be found to affect the claims of their depositors.

Amendments
• **1976, Tax Reform Act of 1976 (P.L. 94-455)**

P.L. 94-455, § 1906(b)(13)(A):

Amended 1954 Code by substituting "Secretary" for "Secretary or his delegate" each place it appeared. **Effective** 2-1-77.

[Sec. 7507(b)]

(b) SEGREGATED ASSETS; EARNINGS.—Whenever any bank or trust company, a substantial portion of the business of which consists of receiving deposits and making loans and discounts, has been released or discharged from its liability to its depositors for any part of their claims against it, and such depositors have accepted, in lieu thereof, a lien upon subsequent earnings of such bank or trust company, or claims against assets segregated by such bank or trust company or against assets transferred from it to an individual or corporate trustee or agent, no tax shall be assessed or collected, or paid into the Treasury of the United States, on account of such bank or trust company, such individual or corporate trustee or such agent, which shall diminish the assets thereof which are available for the payment of such depositor claims and which are necessary for the full payment thereof. The term "agent", as used in this subsection, shall be deemed to include a corporation acting as a liquidating agent.

[Sec. 7507(c)]

(c) REFUND; REASSESSMENT; STATUTES OF LIMITATION.—

(1) Any such tax collected shall be deemed to be erroneously collected, and shall be refunded subject to all provisions and limitations of law, so far as applicable, relating to the refunding of taxes.

(2) Any tax, the assessment, collection, or payment of which is barred under subsection (a), or any such tax which has been abated or remitted shall be assessed or reassessed whenever it shall appear that payment of the tax will not diminish the assets as aforesaid.

(3) Any tax, the assessment, collection, or payment of which is barred under subsection (b), or any such tax which has been refunded shall be assessed or reassessed after full payment of such claims of depositors to the extent of the remaining assets segregated or transferred as described in subsection (b).

(4) The running of the statute of limitations on the making of assessment and collection shall be suspended during, and for 90 days beyond, the period for which, pursuant to this section, assessment or collection may not be made, and a tax may be reassessed as provided in paragraphs (2) and (3) of this subsection and collected, during the time within which, had there been no abatement, collection might have been made.

Amendments
• **1976, Tax Reform Act of 1976 (P.L. 94-455)**

P.L. 94-455, § 1906(a)(50):

Amended Code Sec. 7507(c) by striking out "after May 28, 1938," after "abated or remitted" in paragraph (2) and by striking out "after May 28, 1938," after "has been refunded" in paragraph (3). **Effective** 2-1-77.

MISCELLANEOUS PROVISIONS

[Sec. 7507(d)]

(d) EXCEPTION OF EMPLOYMENT TAXES.—This section shall not apply to any tax imposed by chapter 21 or chapter 23.

[Sec. 7508]

SEC. 7508. TIME FOR PERFORMING CERTAIN ACTS POSTPONED BY REASON OF SERVICE IN COMBAT ZONE OR CONTINGENCY OPERATION.

[Sec. 7508(a)]

(a) TIME TO BE DISREGARDED.—In the case of an individual serving in the Armed Forces of the United States, or serving in support of such Armed Forces, in an area designated by the President of the United States by Executive order as a "combat zone" for purposes of section 112, or when deployed outside the United States away from the individual's permanent duty station while participating in an operation designated by the Secretary of Defense as a contingency operation (as defined in section 101(a)(13) of title 10, United States Code) or which became such a contingency operation by operation of law, at any time during the period designated by the President by Executive order as the period of combatant activities in such zone for purposes of such section or at any time during the period of such contingency operation, or hospitalized as a result of injury received while serving in such an area or operation during such time, the period of service in such area or operation, plus the period of continuous qualified hospitalization attributable to such injury, and the next 180 days thereafter, shall be disregarded in determining, under the internal revenue laws, in respect of any tax liability (including any interest, penalty, additional amount, or addition to the tax) of such individual—

(1) Whether any of the following acts was performed within the time prescribed therefor:

(A) Filing any return of income, estate, gift, employment, or excise tax;

(B) Payment of any income, estate, gift, employment, or excise tax or any installment thereof or of any other liability to the United States in respect thereof;

(C) Filing a petition with the Tax Court, or filing a notice of appeal from a decision of the Tax Court;

(D) Allowance of a credit or refund of any tax;

(E) Filing a claim for credit or refund of any tax;

(F) Bringing suit upon any such claim for credit or refund;

(G) Assessment of any tax;

(H) Giving or making any notice or demand for the payment of any tax, or with respect to any liability to the United States in respect of any tax;

(I) Collection, by the Secretary, by levy or otherwise, of the amount of any liability in respect of any tax;

(J) Bringing suit by the United States, or any officer on its behalf, in respect of any liability in respect of any tax or in respect of any erroneous refund; and

(K) Any other act required or permitted under the internal revenue laws specified by the Secretary;

(2) The amount of any credit or refund; and

(3) Any certification of a seriously delinquent tax debt under section 7345.

Amendments

- **2021, Infrastructure Investment and Jobs Act (P.L. 117-58)**

P.L. 117-58, §80502(a)(1)-(2), Div. H:

Amended Code Sec. 7508(a)(1) by striking subparagraph (C) and inserting a new subparagraph (C), and by inserting "or in respect of any erroneous refund" after "any tax" in subparagraph (J). **Effective** for any period for performing an act which has not expired before 11-15-2021. Prior to being stricken, Code Sec. 7508(a)(1)(C) read as follows:

(C) Filing a petition with the Tax Court for redetermination of a deficiency, or for review of a decision rendered by the Tax Court;

- **2017, Tax Cuts and Jobs Act (P.L. 115-97)**

P.L. 115-97, §11026, provides:

For a special rule, see Act Sec. 11026 in the amendment notes for Code Sec. 112(c).

- **2015, Fixing America's Surface Transportation Act (P.L. 114-94)**

P.L. 114-94, §32101(d):

Amended Code Sec. 7508(a) by striking the period at the end of paragraph (2) and inserting "; and", and by adding at the end a new paragraph (3). **Effective** 12-4-2015.

- **2005, Katrina Emergency Tax Relief Act of 2005 (P.L. 109-73)**

P.L. 109-73, §403(a):

Amended Code Sec. 7508(a)(1)(A)-(B). **Effective** for any period for performing an act which has not expired before 8-25-2005. Prior to amendment, Code Sec. 7508(a)(1)(A)-(B) read as follows:

(A) Filing any return of income, estate, or gift tax (except income tax withheld at source and income tax imposed by subtitle C or any law superseded thereby);

(B) Payment of any income, estate, or gift tax (except income tax withheld at source and income tax imposed by subtitle C or any law superseded thereby) or any installment thereof or of any other liability to the United States in respect thereof;

P.L. 109-73, §403(b) [repealed by P.L. 109-135, §201(b)(4)(B)], provides:

(b) APPLICATION WITH RESPECT TO HURRICANE KATRINA.—In the case of any taxpayer determined by the Secretary of the Treasury to be affected by the Presidentially declared disaster relating to Hurricane Katrina, any relief provided by the Secretary of the Treasury under section 7508A of the Internal Revenue Code of 1986 shall be for a period ending not earlier than February 28, 2006, and shall be treated as applying to the filing of returns relating to, and the payment of, employment and excise taxes.

- **2003, Military Family Tax Relief Act of 2003 (P.L. 108-121)**

P.L. 108-121, §104(a)(1)-(4):

Amended Code Sec. 7508(a) by inserting ", or when deployed outside the United States away from the individual's permanent duty station while participating in an operation designated by the Secretary of Defense as a contingency operation (as defined in section 101(a)(13) of title 10, United States Code) or which became such a contingency operation by operation of law" after "section 112", by inserting in the first sentence "or at any time during the period of such contingency operation" after "for purposes of such section", by inserting "or operation" after "such an area", and by inserting "or operation" after "such area". **Effective** for any period for performing an act which has not expired before 11-11-2003.

P.L. 108-121, §104(b)(2):

Amended the heading for Code Sec. 7508 by inserting "**OR CONTINGENCY OPERATION**" after "**COMBAT ZONE**". **Effective** for any period for performing an act which has not expired before 11-11-2003.

- **2002, Victims of Terrorism Tax Relief Act of 2001 (P.L. 107-134)**

P.L. 107-134, §112(b):

Amended Code Sec. 7508(a)(1)(K) by striking "in regulations prescribed under this section" following "specified". **Effective** for disasters and terroristic or military actions occurring on or after 9-11-2001, with respect to any action of the Secretary of the Treasury, the Secretary of Labor, or the Pension Benefit Guaranty Corporation occurring on or after 10-23-2002.

- **1999 (P.L. 106-21)**

P.L. 106-21, §1(a)(8)-(d)(1), provides:

SECTION 1. AVAILABILITY OF CERTAIN TAX BENEFITS FOR SERVICES AS PART OF OPERATION ALLIED FORCE.

(a) GENERAL RULE.—For purposes of the following provisions of the Internal Revenue Code of 1986, a qualified hazardous duty area shall be treated in the same manner as if it were a combat zone (as determined under section 112 of such Code):

* * *

(8) Section 7508 (relating to time for performing certain acts postponed by reason of service in combat zone).

(b) QUALIFIED HAZARDOUS DUTY AREA.—For purposes of this section, the term "qualified hazardous duty area" means any area of the Federal Republic of Yugoslavia (Serbia/Montenegro), Albania, the Adriatic Sea, and the northern Ionian Sea (above the 39th parallel) during the period (which includes the date of the enactment of this Act) that any member of the Armed Forces of the United States is entitled to special pay under section 310 of title 37, United States Code (relating to special pay: duty subject to hostile fire or imminent danger) for services performed in such area.

(c) SPECIAL RULE FOR SECTION 7508.—Solely for purposes of applying section 7508 of the Internal Revenue Code of 1986, in the case of an individual who is performing services as part of Operation Allied Force outside the United States while deployed away from such individual's permanent duty station, the term "qualified hazardous duty area" includes, during the period for which the entitlement referred to in subsection (b) is in effect, any area in which such services are performed.

(d) EFFECTIVE DATES.—

(1) IN GENERAL.—Except as provided in paragraph (2), this section shall take effect on March 24, 1999.

- **1996 (P.L. 104-117)**

P.L. 104-117, §1(a)(8), (b) and (e)(1), provide:

SECTION 1. TREATMENT OF CERTAIN INDIVIDUALS PERFORMING SERVICES IN CERTAIN HAZARDOUS DUTY AREAS.

MISCELLANEOUS PROVISIONS

(a) GENERAL RULE.—For purposes of the following provisions of the Internal Revenue Code of 1986, a qualified hazardous duty area shall be treated in the same manner as if it were a combat zone (as determined under section 112 of such Code):

* * *

(8) Section 7508 (relating to time for performing certain acts postponed by reason of service in combat zone).

* * *

(b) QUALIFIED HAZARDOUS DUTY AREA.—For purposes of this section, the term "qualified hazardous duty area" means Bosnia and Herzegovina, Croatia, or Macedonia, if as of the date of the enactment of this section any member of the Armed Forces of the United States is entitled to special pay under section 310 of title 37, United States Code (relating to special pay; duty subject to hostile fire or imminent danger) for services performed in such country. Such term includes any such country only during the period such entitlement is in effect. Solely for purposes of applying section 7508 of the Internal Revenue Code of 1986, in the case of an individual who is performing services as part of Operation Joint Endeavor outside the United States while deployed away from such individual's permanent duty station, the term "qualified hazardous duty area" includes, during the period for which such entitlement is in effect, any area in which such services are performed.

* * *

(e) EFFECTIVE DATE.—

(1) IN GENERAL.—Except as provided in paragraph (2), the provisions of and amendments made by this section shall take effect on November 21, 1995.

• 1991 (P.L. 102-3)

P.L. 102-2, §1(b)(2):

Amended Code Sec. 7508(a)(2) by striking "(including interest)" after "credit or refund". **Effective** 8-2-90.

P.L. 102-2, §1(c)(1)(A):

Amended Code Sec. 7508(a) by striking "outside the United States" the first place it appears after "or hospitalized", and by striking "the period of continuous hospitalization outside the United States" and inserting "the period of continuous qualified hospitalization". **Effective** 8-2-90.

• 1976, Tax Reform Act of 1976 (P.L. 94-455)

P.L. 94-455, §1906(a)(51):

Substituted "SERVICE IN COMBAT ZONE" for "WAR" in the heading of Code Sec. 7508 and substituted "United States" for "States of the Union and the District of Columbia" in Sec. 7508(a). **Effective** 2-1-77.

P.L. 94-455, §1906(b)(13)(A):

Amended 1954 Code by substituting "Secretary" for "Secretary or his delegate" each place it appeared. **Effective** 2-1-77.

[Sec. 7508(b)]

(b) SPECIAL RULE FOR OVERPAYMENTS.—

(1) IN GENERAL.—Subsection (a) shall not apply for purposes of determining the amount of interest on any overpayment of tax.

(2) SPECIAL RULES.—If an individual is entitled to the benefits of subsection (a) with respect to any return and such return is timely filed (determined after the application of such subsection), subsections (b)(3) and (e) of section 6611 shall not apply.

Amendments

• 1991 (P.L. 102-2)

P.L. 102-2, §1(b)(1):

Amended Code Sec. 7508 by redesignating subsections (b), (c), and (d) as subsections (c), (d), and (e), respectively, and by inserting after subsection (a) new subsection (b). **Effective** 8-2-90.

[Sec. 7508(c)]

(c) APPLICATION TO SPOUSE.—The provisions of this section shall apply to the spouse of any individual entitled to the benefits of subsection (a). Except in the case of the combat zone designated for purposes of the Vietnam conflict, the preceding sentence shall not cause this section to apply for any spouse for any taxable year beginning more than 2 years after the date designated under section 112 as the date of termination of combatant activities in a combat zone.

Amendments

• 1991 (P.L. 102-2)

P.L. 102-2, §1(b)(1):

Redesignated Code Sec. 7508(b) as Code Sec. 7508(c). **Effective** 8-2-90.

• 1986, Tax Reform Act of 1986 (P.L. 99-514)

P.L. 99-514, §1708(a)(4):

Amended the last sentence of Code Sec. 7508(b). **Effective** for tax years beginning after 12-31-82. Prior to amendment, the last sentence of Code Sec. 7508(b) read as follows:

The preceding sentence shall not cause this section to apply to any spouse for any taxable year beginning—

(1) after December 31, 1982, in the case of service in the combat zone designated for purposes of the Vietnam conflict, or

(2) more than 2 years after the date designated under section 112 as the date of termination of combatant activities in that zone, in the case of any combat zone other than that referred to in paragraph (1).

• 1983, Technical Corrections Act of 1982 (P.L. 97-448)

P.L. 97-448, §307(d):

Amended Code Sec. 7508(b)(1) by striking out "January 2, 1978" and inserting in lieu thereof "December 31, 1982". **Effective** 1-12-83.

• 1976 (P.L. 94-569)

P.L. 94-569, §3(e):

Amended Code Sec. 7508(b). **Effective** 10-20-76. Prior to amendment, Sec. 7508(b) read as follows:

(b) APPLICATION TO SPOUSE.—The provisions of this section shall apply to the spouse of any individual entitled to the benefits of subsection (a). The preceding sentence shall not cause this section to apply to any spouse for any taxable year beginning more than 2 years after—

(1) the date of the enactment of this subsection [January 2, 1975], in the case of service in the combat zone designated for purposes of the Vietnam conflict, or

(2) the date designated under section 112 as the date of termination of combatant activities in that zone, in the case of any combat zone other than that referred to in paragraph (1).

• 1975 (P.L. 93-597)

P.L. 93-597, §5(a):

Added Code Sec. 7508(b). **Effective** with respect to tax years ending on or after 2-28-61.

[Sec. 7508(d)]

(d) MISSING STATUS.—The period of service in the area or contingency operation referred to in subsection (a) shall include the period during which an individual entitled to benefits under subsection (a) is in a missing status, within the meaning of section 6013(f)(3).

Amendments

• 2003, Military Family Tax Relief Act of 2003 (P.L. 108-121)

P.L. 108-121, §104(b)(1):

Amended Code Sec. 7508(d) by inserting "or contingency operation" after "area". **Effective** for any period for performing an act which has not expired before 11-11-2003.

• 1991 (P.L. 102-2)

P.L. 102-2, §1(b)(1):

Redesignated Code Sec. 7508(c) as Code Sec. 7508(d). **Effective** 8-2-90.

• 1975 (P.L. 93-597)

P.L. 93-597, §5(a):

Added Code Sec. 7508(c). **Effective** with respect to tax years ending on or after 2-28-61.

[Sec. 7508(e)]

(e) EXCEPTIONS.—

(1) TAX IN JEOPARDY; CASES UNDER TITLE 11 OF THE UNITED STATES CODE AND RECEIVERSHIPS; AND TRANSFERRED ASSETS.—Notwithstanding the provisions of subsection (a), any action or proceeding authorized by section 6851 (regardless of the taxable year for which the tax arose),

MISCELLANEOUS PROVISIONS

chapter 70, or 71, as well as any other action or proceeding authorized by law in connection therewith, may be taken, begun, or prosecuted. In any other case in which the Secretary determines that collection of the amount of any assessment would be jeopardized by delay, the provisions of subsection (a) shall not operate to stay collection of such amount by levy or otherwise as authorized by law. There shall be excluded from any amount assessed or collected pursuant to this paragraph the amount of interest, penalty, additional amount, and addition to the tax, if any, in respect of the period disregarded under subsection (a). In any case to which this paragraph relates, if the Secretary is required to give any notice to or make any demand upon any person, such requirement shall be deemed to be satisfied if the notice or demand is prepared and signed, in any case in which the address of such person last known to the Secretary is in an area for which United States post offices under instructions of the Postmaster General are not, by reason of the combatant activities, accepting mail for delivery at the time the notice or demand is signed. In such case the notice or demand shall be deemed to have been given or made upon the date it is signed.

(2) ACTION TAKEN BEFORE ASCERTAINMENT OF RIGHT TO BENEFITS.—The assessment or collection of any internal revenue tax or of any liability to the United States in respect of any internal revenue tax, or any action or proceeding by or on behalf of the United States in connection therewith, may be made, taken, begun, or prosecuted in accordance with law, without regard to the provisions of subsection (a), unless prior to such assessment, collection, action, or proceeding it is ascertained that the person concerned is entitled to the benefits of subsection (a).

(3) COLLECTION PERIOD AFTER ASSESSMENT NOT EXTENDED AS A RESULT OF HOSPITALIZATION.—With respect to any period of continuous qualified hospitalization described in subsection (a) and the next 180 days thereafter, subsection (a) shall not apply in the application of section 6502.

Amendments

- **2015, Protecting Americans from Tax Hikes Act of 2015 (P.L. 114-113)**

P.L. 114-113, §309(a), Div. Q:

Amended Code Sec. 7508(e) by adding at the end a new paragraph (3). **Effective** for taxes assessed before, on, or after 12-18-2015.

- **1991 (P.L. 102-2)**

P.L. 102-2, §1(b)(1):

Redesignated Code Sec. 7508(d) as Code Sec. 7508(e). **Effective** 8-2-90.

- **1980, Bankruptcy Tax Act of 1980 (P.L. 96-589)**

P.L. 96-589, §6(i)(14):

Amended the heading of Code Sec. 7508(d)(1) by striking out "BANKRUPTCY AND RECEIVERSHIPS" and inserting in lieu thereof "CASES UNDER TITLE 11 OF THE UNITED STATES CODE AND RECEIVERSHIPS". **Effective** 10-1-79, but inapplicable to any proceeding under the Bankruptcy Act commenced before that date.

- **1976, Tax Reform Act of 1976 (P.L. 94-455)**

P.L. 94-455, §1906(b)(13)(A):

Amended 1954 Code by substituting "Secretary" for "Secretary or his delegate" each place it appeared. **Effective** 2-1-77.

- **1975 (P.L. 93-597)**

P.L. 93-597, §5(a):

Redesignated former Code Sec. 7508(b) as Code Sec. 7508(d). **Effective** 1-2-75.

[Sec. 7508(f)]

(f) TREATMENT OF INDIVIDUALS PERFORMING DESERT SHIELD SERVICES.—

(1) IN GENERAL.—Any individual who performed Desert Shield services (and the spouse of such individual) shall be entitled to the benefits of this section in the same manner as if such services were services referred to in subsection (a).

(2) DESERT SHIELD SERVICES.—For purposes of this subsection, the term "Desert Shield services" means any services in the Armed Forces of the United States or in support of such Armed Forces if—

(A) such services are performed in the area designated by the President pursuant to this subparagraph as the "Persian Gulf Desert Shield area", and

(B) Such services are performed during the period beginning on August 2, 1990, and ending on the date on which any portion of the area referred to in subparagraph (A) is designated by the President as a combat zone pursuant to section 112.

Amendments

- **1991 (P.L. 102-2)**

P.L. 102-2, §1(a):

Amended Code Sec. 7508 by adding at the end thereof new subsection (f). **Effective** 8-2-90.

[Sec. 7508(g)]

(g) QUALIFIED HOSPITALIZATION.—For purposes of subsection (a), the term "qualified hospitalization" means—

(1) any hospitalization outside the United States, and

(2) any hospitalization inside the United States, except that not more than 5 years of hospitalization may be taken into account under this paragraph.

Paragraph (2) shall not apply for purposes of applying this section with respect to the spouse of an individual entitled to the benefits of subsection (a).

Amendments

- **1991 (P.L. 102-2)**

P.L. 102-2, §1(c)(2):

Amended Code Sec. 7508 by adding at the end thereof new subsection (g). **Effective** 8-2-90.

[Sec. 7508A]

SEC. 7508A. AUTHORITY TO POSTPONE CERTAIN DEADLINES BY REASON OF FEDERALLY DECLARED DISASTER, SIGNIFICANT FIRE, OR TERRORISTIC OR MILITARY ACTIONS.

[Sec. 7508A(a)]

(a) IN GENERAL.—In the case of a taxpayer determined by the Secretary to be affected by a federally declared disaster (as defined by section 165(i)(5)(A)), a significant fire, or a terroristic or military action (as defined in section 692(c)(2)), the Secretary may specify a period of up to 1 year that may be disregarded in determining, under the internal revenue laws, in respect of any tax liability of such taxpayer—

(1) whether any of the acts described in paragraph (1) of section 7508(a) were performed within the time prescribed therefor (determined without regard to extension under any other provision of this subtitle for periods after the date (determined by the Secretary) of such disaster, fire, or action),

(2) the amount of any interest, penalty, additional amount, or addition to the tax for periods after such date, and

(3) the amount of any credit or refund.

MISCELLANEOUS PROVISIONS

Amendments

• **2021, Infrastructure Investment and Jobs Act (P.L. 117-58)**

P.L. 117-58, §80504(a)(1), Div. H:

Amended Code Sec. 7508A(a) by inserting ", a significant fire," after "federally declared disaster (as defined in section 165(i)(5)(A))". **Effective** for fires for which assistance is provided after 11-15-2021.

P.L. 117-58, §80504(a)(2), Div. H:

Amended Code Sec. 7508A(a)(1) by inserting ", fire," after "disaster" each place it appears. **Effective** for fires for which assistance is provided after 11-15-2021.

P.L. 117-58, §80504(b)(1), Div. H:

Amended the heading for Code Sec. 7508A by striking "PRESIDENTIALLY DECLARED DISASTER" and inserting "FEDERALLY DECLARED DISASTER, SIGNIFICANT FIRE,". **Effective** for fires for which assistance is provided after 11-15-2021.

• **2018, Tax Technical Corrections Act of 2018 (P.L. 115-141)**

P.L. 115-141, §401(b)(10)(B), Div. U:

Amended Code Sec. 7508A(a) by striking "section 165(h)(3)(C)(i)" and inserting "section 165(i)(5)(A)". **Effective** 3-23-2018. For a special rule, see Act Sec. 401(e), Div. U, below.

P.L. 115-141, §401(e), Div. U, provides:

(e) GENERAL SAVINGS PROVISION WITH RESPECT TO DEADWOOD PROVISIONS.—If—

(1) any provision amended or repealed by the amendments made by subsection (b) or (d) applied to—

(A) any transaction occurring before the date of the enactment of this Act,

(B) any property acquired before such date of enactment, or

(C) any item of income, loss, deduction, or credit taken into account before such date of enactment, and

(2) the treatment of such transaction, property, or item under such provision would (without regard to the amendments or repeals made by such subsection) affect the liability for tax for periods ending after such date of enactment,

nothing in the amendments or repeals made by this section shall be construed to affect the treatment of such transaction, property, or item for purposes of determining liability for tax for periods ending after such date of enactment.

• **2008, Tax Extenders and Alternative Minimum Tax Relief Act of 2008 (P.L. 110-343)**

P.L. 110-343, Division C, §706(a)(2)(D)(vii):

Amended Code Sec. 7508A(a) by striking "Presidentially declared disaster (as defined in section 1033(h)(3))" and inserting "federally declared disaster (as defined by section 165(h)(3)(C)(i))". **Effective** for disasters declared in tax years beginning after 12-31-2007.

• **1997, Taxpayer Relief Act of 1997 (P.L. 105-34)**

P.L. 105-34, §911(a):

Amended chapter 77 by inserting after Code Sec. 7508 a new Code Sec. 7508A. **Effective** with respect to any period for performing an act that has not expired before 8-5-97.

[Sec. 7508A(b)]

(b) SPECIAL RULES REGARDING PENSIONS, ETC.—In the case of a pension or other employee benefit plan, or any sponsor, administrator, participant, beneficiary, or other person with respect to such plan, affected by a disaster, fire, or action described in subsection (a), the Secretary may specify a period of up to 1 year which may be disregarded in determining the date by which any action is required or permitted to be completed under this title. No plan shall be treated as failing to be operated in accordance with the terms of the plan solely as the result of disregarding any period by reason of the preceding sentence.

Amendments

• **2021, Infrastructure Investment and Jobs Act (P.L. 117-58)**

P.L. 117-58, §80504(a)(2), Div. H:

Amended Code Sec. 7508A(b) by inserting ", fire," after "disaster" each place it appears. **Effective** for fires for which assistance is provided after 11-15-2021.

[Sec. 7508A(c)]

(c) SPECIAL RULES FOR OVERPAYMENTS.—The rules of section 7508(b) shall apply for purposes of this section.

Amendments

• **2005, Katrina Emergency Tax Relief Act of 2005 (P.L. 109-73)**

P.L. 109-73, §403(b) [repealed by P.L. 109-135, §201(b)(4)(B)], provides:

(b) APPLICATION WITH RESPECT TO HURRICANE KATRINA.—In the case of any taxpayer determined by the Secretary of the Treasury to be affected by the Presidentially declared disaster relating to Hurricane Katrina, any relief provided by the Secretary of the Treasury under section 7508A of the Internal Revenue Code of 1986 shall be for a period ending not earlier than February 28, 2006, and shall be treated as applying to the filing of returns relating to, and the payment of, employment and excise taxes.

• **2002, Victims of Terrorism Tax Relief Act of 2001 (P.L. 107-134)**

P.L. 107-134, §112(a):

Amended Code Sec. 7508A. **Effective** for disasters and terroristic or military actions occurring on or after 9-11-2001, with respect to any action of the Secretary of the Treasury, the Secretary of Labor, or the Pension Benefit Guaranty Corporation occurring on or after 1-23-2002. Prior to amendment, Code Sec. 7508A read as follows:

SEC. 7508A. AUTHORITY TO POSTPONE CERTAIN TAX-RELATED DEADLINES BY REASON OF PRESIDENTIALLY DECLARED DISASTER.

(a) IN GENERAL.—In the case of a taxpayer determined by the Secretary to be affected by a Presidentially declared disaster (as defined by section 1033(h)(3)), the Secretary may prescribe regulations under which a period of up to 120 days may be disregarded in determining, under the internal revenue laws, in respect of any tax liability (including any penalty, additional amount, or addition to the tax) of such taxpayer—

(1) whether any of the acts described in paragraph (1) of section 7508(a) were performed within the time prescribed therefor, and

(2) the amount of any credit or refund.

(b) INTEREST ON OVERPAYMENTS AND UNDERPAYMENTS.—Subsection (a) shall not apply for the purpose of determining interest on any overpayment or underpayment.

• **2001, Economic Growth and Tax Relief Reconciliation Act of 2001 (P.L. 107-16)**

P.L. 107-16, §802(a):

Amended Code Sec. 7508A by striking "90 days" and inserting "120 days". **Effective** 6-7-2001.

P.L. 107-16, §901(a)-(b), as amended by P.L. 111-312, §101(a)(1), provides:

SEC. 901. SUNSET OF PROVISIONS OF ACT.

(a) IN GENERAL.—All provisions of, and amendments made by, this Act shall not apply—

(1) to taxable, plan, or limitation years beginning after December 31, 2012, or

(2) in the case of title V, to estates of decedents dying, gifts made, or generation skipping transfers, after December 31, 2012.

(b) APPLICATION OF CERTAIN LAWS.—The Internal Revenue Code of 1986 and the Employee Retirement Income Security Act of 1974 shall be applied and administered to years, estates, gifts, and transfers described in subsection (a) as if the provisions and amendments described in subsection (a) had never been enacted.

[Sec. 7508A(d)]

(d) MANDATORY 60-DAY EXTENSION.—

(1) IN GENERAL.—In the case of any qualified taxpayer, the period—

(A) beginning on the earliest incident date specified in the declaration to which the disaster area referred to in paragraph (2) relates, and

(B) ending on the date which is 60 days after the later of such earliest incident date described in subparagraph (A) or the date such declaration was issued,

shall be disregarded in determining, under the internal revenue laws, in respect of any tax liability of such qualified taxpayer, whether any of the acts described in subparagraphs (A) through (F) of section 7508(a)(1) were performed within the time prescribed therefor (determined without regard to extension under any other provision of this subtitle for periods after the date determined under subparagraph (B)).

(2) QUALIFIED TAXPAYER.—For purposes of this subsection, the term "qualified taxpayer" means—

(A) any individual whose principal residence (for purposes of section 1033(h)(4)) is located in a disaster area,

(B) any taxpayer if the taxpayer's principal place of business (other than the business of performing services as an employee) is located in a disaster area,

(C) any individual who is a relief worker affiliated with a recognized government or philanthropic organization and who is assisting in a disaster area,

MISCELLANEOUS PROVISIONS

(D) any taxpayer whose records necessary to meet a deadline for an act described in section 7508(a)(1) are maintained in a disaster area,

(E) any individual visiting a disaster area who was killed or injured as a result of the disaster, and

(F) solely with respect to a joint return, any spouse of an individual described in any preceding subparagraph of this paragraph.

(3) DISASTER AREA.—For purposes of this subsection, the term "disaster area" means an area in which a major disaster for which the President provides financial assistance under section 408 of the Robert T. Stafford Disaster Relief and Emergency Assistance Act (42 U.S.C. 5174) occurs.

(4) APPLICATION TO RULES REGARDING PENSIONS.—In the case of any person described in subsection (b), a rule similar to the rule of paragraph (1) shall apply for purposes of subsection (b) with respect to—

(A) making contributions to a qualified retirement plan (within the meaning of section 4974(c)) under section 219(f)(3), 404(a)(6), 404(h)(1)(B), or 404(m)(2),

(B) making distributions under section 408(d)(4),

(C) recharacterizing contributions under section 408A(d)(6), and

(D) making a rollover under section 402(c), 403(a)(4), 403(b)(8), or 408(d)(3).

(5) COORDINATION WITH PERIODS SPECIFIED BY THE SECRETARY.—Any period described in paragraph (1) with respect to any person (including by reason of the application of paragraph (4) shall be in addition to (or concurrent with, as the case may be) any period specified under subsection (a) or (b) with respect to such person.

(6) MULTIPLE DECLARATIONS.—For purposes of paragraph (1), in the case of multiple declarations relating to a disaster area which are issued within a 60-day period, a separate period shall be determined under such paragraph with respect to each such declaration.

Amendments

• 2021, Infrastructure Investment and Jobs Act (P.L. 117-58)

P.L. 117-58, §80501(a)(1)-(3), Div. H:

Amended Code Sec. 7508A(d)(1) by striking "the latest incident date so specified" in subparagraph (B) and inserting "the later of such earliest incident date described in subparagraph (A) or the date such declaration was issued", by striking "in the same manner as a period specified under subsection (a)" and inserting "in determining, under the internal revenue laws, in respect of any tax liability of such qualified taxpayer, whether any of the acts described in subparagraphs (A) through (F) of section 7508(a)(1) were performed within the time prescribed therefor (determined without regard to extension under any other provision of this subtitle for periods after the date determined under subparagraph (B))", by striking paragraph (3) and inserting a new paragraph (3), and by adding at the end a new paragraph (6). **Effective** for federally declared disasters declared after 11-15-2021. Prior to being stricken, Code Sec. 7508A(d)(3) reads as follows:

(3) DISASTER AREA.—For purposes of this subsection, the term "disaster area" has the meaning given such term under subparagraph (B) of section 165(i)(5) with respect to a Federally declared disaster (as defined in subparagraph (A) of such section).

• 2019, Taxpayer Certainty and Disaster Tax Relief Act of 2019 (P.L. 116-94)

P.L. 116-94, §205(a), Div. Q:

Amended Code Sec. 7508A by adding at the end a new subsection (d). **Effective** for federally declared disasters declared after 12-20-2019.

[Sec. 7508A(e)]

(e) SIGNIFICANT FIRE.—For purposes of this section, the term "significant fire" means any fire with respect to which assistance is provided under section 420 of the Robert T. Stafford Disaster Relief and Emergency Assistance Act.

Amendments

• 2021, Infrastructure Investment and Jobs Act (P.L. 117-58)

P.L. 117-58, §80504(a)(3), Div. H:

Amended Code Sec. 7508A by adding at the end a new subsection (e). **Effective** for fires for which assistance is provided after 11-15-2021.

[Sec. 7509]

SEC. 7509. EXPENDITURES INCURRED BY THE UNITED STATES POSTAL SERVICE.

The Postmaster General or his delegate shall at least once a month transfer to the Treasury of the United States a statement of the additional expenditures in the District of Columbia and elsewhere incurred by the United States Postal Service in performing the duties, if any, imposed upon such Service with respect to chapter 21, relating to the tax under the Federal Insurance Contributions Act, and the Secretary shall be authorized and directed to advance from time to time to the credit of the United States Postal Service, from appropriations made for the collection of the taxes imposed by chapter 21, such sums as may be required for such additional expenditures incurred by the United States Postal Service.

Amendments

• 1976, Tax Reform Act of 1976 (P.L. 94-455)

P.L. 94-455, §1906(b)(13)(A):

Amended 1954 Code by substituting "Secretary" for "Secretary or his delegate" each place it appeared. **Effective** 2-1-77.

P.L. 94-455, §1906(a)(52):

Amended Code Sec. 7509. **Effective** 2-1-77. Prior to amendment, Code Sec. 7509 read as follows:

SEC. 7509. EXPENDITURES INCURRED BY THE POST OFFICE DEPARTMENT.

The Postmaster General or his delegate shall at least once a month transfer to the Treasury of the United States, together with the receipts required to be deposited under section 6803(a), a statement of the additional expenditures in the District of Columbia and elsewhere incurred by the Post Office Department in performing the duties, if any, imposed upon such Department with respect to chapter 21, relating to the tax under the Federal Insurance Contributions Act, and the Secretary or his delegate shall be authorized and directed to advance from time to time to the credit of the Post Office Department, from appropriations made for the collection of the taxes imposed by chapter 21, such sums as may be required for such additional expenditures incurred by the Post Office Department.

[Sec. 7510]

SEC. 7510. EXEMPTION FROM TAX OF DOMESTIC GOODS PURCHASED FOR THE UNITED STATES.

The privilege existing by provision of law on December 1, 1873, or thereafter of purchasing supplies of goods imported from foreign countries for the use of the United States, duty free, shall be extended, under such regulations as the Secretary may prescribe, to all articles of domestic production which are subject to tax by the provisions of this title.

Amendments

• 1976, Tax Reform Act of 1976 (P.L. 94-455)

P.L. 94-455, §1906(b)(13)(A):

Amended 1954 Code by substituting "Secretary" for "Secretary or his delegate" each place it appeared. **Effective** 2-1-77.

[Sec. 7512]

SEC. 7512. SEPARATE ACCOUNTING FOR CERTAIN COLLECTED TAXES, ETC.

[Sec. 7512(a)]

(a) GENERAL RULE.—Whenever any person who is required to collect, account for, and pay over any tax imposed by subtitle C, or chapter 33—

(1) at the time and in the manner prescribed by law or regulations (A) fails to collect, truthfully account for, or pay over such tax, or (B) fails to make deposits, payments, or returns of such tax, and

(2) is notified, by notice delivered in hand to such person, of any such failure,

MISCELLANEOUS PROVISIONS

then all the requirements of subsection (b) shall be complied with. In the case of a corporation, partnership, or trust, notice delivered in hand to an officer, partner, or trustee, shall, for purposes of this section, be deemed to be notice delivered in hand to such corporation, partnership, or trust and to all officers, partners, trustees, and employees thereof.

Amendments

• **1988, Omnibus Trade and Competitiveness Act of 1988 (P.L. 100-418)**

P.L. 100-418, § 1941(b)(2)(O)(i):

Amended Code Sec. 7512(a) by striking ", by chapter 33, or by section 4986" and inserting "or chapter 33". **Effective** for crude oil removed from the premises on or after 8-23-88.

[Sec. 7512(b)]

(b) REQUIREMENTS.—Any person who is required to collect, account for, and pay over any tax imposed by subtitle C, or chapter 33, if notice has been delivered to such person in accordance with subsection (a), shall collect the taxes imposed by subtitle C, or chapter 33 which become collectible after delivery of such notice, shall (not later than the end of the second banking day after any amount of such taxes is collected) deposit such amount in a separate account in a bank (as defined in section 581), and shall keep the amount of such taxes in such account until payment over to the United States. Any such account shall be designated as a special fund in trust for the United States, payable to the United States by such person as trustee.

Amendments

• **1988, Omnibus Trade and Competitiveness Act of 1988 (P.L. 100-418)**

P.L. 100-418, § 1941(b)(2)(O)(i)-(ii):

Amended Code Sec. 7512(b) by striking ", by chapter 33, or by section 4986" and inserting "or chapter 33", and by striking ", chapter 33, or section 4986" and inserting "or chapter 33". **Effective** for crude oil removed from the premises on or after 8-23-88.

[Sec. 7512(c)]

(c) RELIEF FROM FURTHER COMPLIANCE WITH SUBSECTION (b).—Whenever the Secretary is satisfied, with respect to any notification made under subsection (a), that all requirements of law and regulations with respect to the taxes imposed by subtitle C, or chapter 33, as the case may be, will henceforth be complied with, he may cancel such notification. Such cancellation shall take effect at such time as is specified in the notice of such cancellation.

Amendments

• **1988, Omnibus Trade and Competitiveness Act of 1988 (P.L. 100-418)**

P.L. 100-418, § 1941(b)(2)(O)(ii):

Amended Code Sec. 7512(c) by striking ", by chapter 33, or section 4986" and inserting "or chapter 33". **Effective** for crude oil removed from the premises on or after 8-23-88.

• **1980, Crude Oil Windfall Profit Tax Act of 1980 (P.L. 96-223)**

P.L. 96-223, § 101(c)(3):

Amended Code Sec. 7512(a) and (b) by striking out "or by chapter 33" and inserting ", by chapter 33, or by section 4986", and by striking out in Code Sec. 7512 (b) and (c) "or chapter 33" and inserting ", chapter 33, or section 4986". For the **effective** date and transitional rules, see P.L. 96-223, Act Sec. 101(i), following Code Sec. 4986.

• **1976, Tax Reform Act of 1976 (P.L. 94-455)**

P.L. 94-455, § 1906(b)(13)(A):

Amended 1954 Code by substituting "Secretary" for "Secretary or his delegate" each place it appeared. **Effective** 2-1-77.

• **1958 (P.L. 85-321)**

P.L. 85-321, § [1]:

Added Code Sec. 7512 to Chapter 77 of the 1954 Code. Notification may be made under Sec. 7512(a)—

(1) in the case of taxes imposed by subtitle C, only with respect to pay periods beginning after 2-11-58; and

(2) in the case of taxes imposed by chapter 33, only with respect to taxes so imposed after 2-11-58.

[Sec. 7513]

SEC. 7513. REPRODUCTION OF RETURNS AND OTHER DOCUMENTS.

[Sec. 7513(a)]

(a) IN GENERAL.—The Secretary is authorized to have any Federal agency or any person process films or other photoimpressions of any return, document, or other matter, and make reproductions from films or photoimpressions of any return, document, or other matter.

[Sec. 7513(b)]

(b) REGULATIONS.—The Secretary shall prescribe regulations which shall provide such safeguards as in the opinion of the Secretary are necessary or appropriate to protect the film, photoimpressions, and reproductions made therefrom, against any unauthorized use, and to protect the information contained therein against any unauthorized disclosure.

Amendments

• **1976, Tax Reform Act of 1976 (P.L. 94-455)**

P.L. 94-455, § 1906(b)(13)(A):

Amended 1954 Code by substituting "Secretary" for "Secretary or his delegate" each place it appeared. **Effective** 2-1-77.

[Sec. 7513(c)—Repealed]

Amendments

• **1976, Tax Reform Act of 1976 (P.L. 94-455)**

P.L. 94-455, § 1202(f):

Repealed Code Sec. 7513(c). **Effective** 1-1-77. Prior to repeal, Code Sec. 7513(c) read as follows:

[Sec. 7513(c)]

(c) USE OF REPRODUCTIONS.—Any reproduction of any return, document, or other matter made in accordance with this section shall have the same legal status as the original; and any such reproduction shall, if properly authenticated, be admissible in evidence in any judicial or administrative proceeding, as if it were the original, whether or not the original is in existence.

(c) PENALTY.—

For penalty for violation of regulations for safeguarding against unauthorized use of any film or photoimpression, or reproduction made therefrom, and against unauthorized disclosure of information contained therein, see section 7213.

Amendments

• **1976, Tax Reform Act of 1976 (P.L. 94-455)**

P.L. 94-455, § 1202(f):

Redesignated Code Sec. 7513(d) as Code Sec. 7513(c). **Effective** 1-1-77.

• **1958, Technical Amendments Act of 1958 (P.L. 85-866)**

P.L. 85-866, § 90(a):

Added Code Sec. 7513. **Effective** 1-1-54.

MISCELLANEOUS PROVISIONS

[Sec. 7514]
SEC. 7514. AUTHORITY TO PRESCRIBE OR MODIFY SEALS.

The Secretary is authorized to prescribe or modify seals of office for the district directors of internal revenue and other officers or employees of the Treasury Department to whom any of the functions of the Secretary of the Treasury shall have been or may be delegated. Each seal so prescribed shall contain such device as the Secretary may select. Each seal shall remain in the custody of any officer or employee whom the Secretary may designate, and, in accordance with the regulations approved by the Secretary, may be affixed in lieu of the seal of the Treasury Department to any certificate or attestation (except for material to be published in the Federal Register) that may be required of such officer or employee. Judicial notice shall be taken of any seal prescribed in accordance with this authority, a facsimile of which has been published in the Federal Register together with the regulations prescribing such seal and the affixation thereof.

Amendments

- **1976, Tax Reform Act of 1976 (P.L. 94-455)**

P.L. 94-455, §1906(b)(13)(A):

Amended 1954 Code by substituting "Secretary" for "Secretary or his delegate" each place it appeared. **Effective** 2-1-77.

P.L. 94-455, §1906(b)(13)(M):

Substituted "functions of the Secretary of the Treasury" for "functions of the Secretary" in Code Sec. 7514. **Effective** 2-1-77.

- **1958, Technical Amendments Act of 1958 (P.L. 85-866)**

P.L. 85-866, §91(a):

Added Code Sec. 7514. **Effective** 1-1-54.

[Sec. 7515—Repealed]

Amendments

- **1976, Tax Reform Act of 1976 (P.L. 94-455)**

P.L. 94-455, §1202(h):

Repealed Code Sec. 7515. **Effective** 1-1-77. Prior to repeal, Code Sec. 7515 read as follows:

SEC. 7515. SPECIAL STATISTICAL STUDIES AND COMPILATIONS AND OTHER SERVICES ON REQUEST.

The Secretary or his delegate is authorized within his discretion, upon written request, to make special statistical studies and compilations involving data from any returns, declarations, statements, or other documents required by this title or by regulations or from any records established or maintained in connection with the administration and enforcement of this title, to engage in any such special study or compilation jointly with the party or parties requesting it, and to furnish transcripts of any such special study or compilation, upon the payment, by the party or parties making the request, of the cost of the work or services performed for such party or parties.

- **1962 (P.L. 87-870)**

P.L. 87-870, §(3)(a)(1):

Added Code Sec. 7515. **Effective** 10-24-62.

[Sec. 7516]
SEC. 7516. SUPPLYING TRAINING AND TRAINING AIDS ON REQUEST.

The Secretary is authorized within his discretion, upon written request, to admit employees and officials of any State, the Commonwealth of Puerto Rico, any possession of the United States, any political subdivision or instrumentality of any of the foregoing, the District of Columbia, or any foreign government to training courses conducted by the Internal Revenue Service, and to supply them with texts and other training aids. The Secretary may require payment from the party or parties making the request of a reasonable fee not to exceed the cost of the training and training aids supplied pursuant to such request.

Amendments

- **1976, Tax Reform Act of 1976 (P.L. 94-455)**

P.L. 94-455, §1906(b)(13)(A):

Amended 1954 Code by substituting "Secretary" for "Secretary or his delegate" each place it appeared. **Effective** 2-1-77.

- **1962 (P.L. 87-870)**

P.L. 87-870, §3(a)(1):

Added Code Sec. 7516. **Effective** 10-24-62.

[Sec. 7517]
SEC. 7517. FURNISHING ON REQUEST OF STATEMENT EXPLAINING ESTATE OR GIFT EVALUATION.

[Sec. 7517(a)]

(a) GENERAL RULE.—If the Secretary makes a determination or a proposed determination of the value of an item of property for purposes of the tax imposed under chapter 11, 12, or 13, he shall furnish, on the written request of the executor, donor, or the person required to make the return of the tax imposed by chapter 13 (as the case may be), to such executor, donor, or person a written statement containing the material required by subsection (b). Such statement shall be furnished not later than 45 days after the later of the date of such request or the date of such determination or proposed determination.

[Sec. 7517(b)]

(b) CONTENTS OF STATEMENT.—A statement required to be furnished under subsection (a) with respect to the value of an item of property shall—

(1) explain the basis on which the valuation was determined or proposed,

(2) set forth any computation used in arriving at such value, and

(3) contain a copy of any expert appraisal made by or for the Secretary.

[Sec. 7517(c)]

(c) EFFECT OF STATEMENT.—Except to the extent otherwise provided by law, the value determined or proposed by the Secretary with respect to which a statement is furnished under this section, and the method used in arriving at such value, shall not be binding on the Secretary.

Amendments

- **1976, Tax Reform Act of 1976 (P.L. 94-455)**

P.L. 94-455, §2008(a)(1):

Added Code Sec. 7517.

P.L. 94-455, §2008(d)(1), provides:

(1) The amendments made by subsection (a)—

(A) insofar as they relate to the tax imposed under chapter 11 of the Internal Revenue Code of 1954, shall apply to the estates of decedents dying after December 31, 1976, and

(B) insofar as they relate to the tax imposed under chapter 12 of such Code, shall apply to gifts made after December 31, 1976.

[Sec. 7518]
SEC. 7518. TAX INCENTIVES RELATING TO MERCHANT MARINE CAPITAL CONSTRUCTION FUNDS.

[Sec. 7518(a)]

(a) CEILING ON DEPOSITS.—

(1) IN GENERAL.—The amount deposited in a fund established under chapter 535 of title 46 of the United States Code (hereinafter in this section referred to as a "capital construction fund") shall not exceed for any taxable year the sum of:

(A) that portion of the taxable income of the owner or lessee for such year (computed as provided in chapter 1 but without regard to the carryback of any net operating loss or net capital loss and without regard to this section) which is attributable to the operation of the agreement vessels in the foreign or domestic commerce of the United States or in the fisheries of the United States,

(B) the amount allowable as a deduction under section 167 for such year with respect to the agreement vessels,

(C) if the transaction is not taken into account for purposes of subparagraph (A), the net proceeds (as defined in joint regulations) from—

(i) the sale or other disposition of any agreement vessel, or

(ii) insurance or indemnity attributable to any agreement vessel, and

(D) the receipts from the investment or reinvestment of amounts held in such fund.

(2) LIMITATIONS ON DEPOSITS BY LESSEES.—In the case of a lessee, the maximum amount which may be deposited with respect to an agreement vessel by reason of paragraph (1)(B) for any period shall be reduced by any amount which, under an agreement entered into under chapter 535 of title 46, United States Code, the owner is required or permitted to deposit for such period with respect to such vessel by reason of paragraph (1)(B).

(3) CERTAIN BARGES AND CONTAINERS INCLUDED.—For purposes of paragraph (1), the term "agreement vessel" includes barges and containers which are part of the complement of such vessel and which are provided for in the agreement.

Amendments

•2006 (P.L. 109-304)

P.L. 109-304, §17(e)(6)(A)-(B):

Amended Code Sec. 7518(a) by striking "section 607 of the Merchant Marine Act, 1936" and substituting "chapter 535 of title 46 of the United States Code" in paragraph (1); and by striking "section 607 of the Merchant Marine Act, 1936" and substituting "chapter 535 of title 46, United States Code" in paragraph (2). **Effective** 10-6-2006.

[Sec. 7518(b)]

(b) REQUIREMENTS AS TO INVESTMENTS.—

(1) IN GENERAL.—Amounts in any capital construction fund shall be kept in the depository or depositories specified in the agreement and shall be subject to such trustee and other fiduciary requirements as may be specified by the Secretary.

(2) LIMITATION ON FUND INVESTMENTS.—Amounts in any capital construction fund may be invested only in interest-bearing securities approved by the Secretary; except that, if such Secretary consents thereto, an agreed percentage (not in excess of 60 percent) of the assets of the fund may be invested in the stock of domestic corporations. Such stock must be currently fully listed and registered on an exchange registered with the Securities and Exchange Commission as a national securities exchange, and must be stock which would be acquired by prudent men of discretion and intelligence in such matters who are seeking a reasonable income and the preservation of their capital. If at any time the fair market value of the stock in the fund is more than the agreed percentage of the assets in the fund, any subsequent investment of amounts deposited in the fund, and any subsequent withdrawal from the fund, shall be made in such a way as to tend to restore the fund to a situation in which the fair market value of the stock does not exceed such agreed percentage.

(3) INVESTMENT IN CERTAIN PREFERRED STOCK PERMITTED.—For purposes of this subsection, if the common stock of a corporation meets the requirements of this subsection and if the preferred stock of such corporation would meet such requirements but for the fact that it cannot be listed and registered as required because it is nonvoting stock, such preferred stock shall be treated as meeting the requirements of this subsection.

[Sec. 7518(c)]

(c) NONTAXABILITY FOR DEPOSITS.—

(1) IN GENERAL.—For purposes of this title—

(A) taxable income (determined without regard to this section and chapter 535 of title 46, United States Code) for the taxable year shall be reduced by an amount equal to the amount deposited for the taxable year out of amounts referred to in subsection (a)(1)(A),

(B) gain from a transaction referred to in subsection (a)(1)(C) shall not be taken into account if an amount equal to the net proceeds (as defined in joint regulations) from such transaction is deposited in the fund,

(C) the earnings (including gains and losses) from the investment and reinvestment of amounts held in the fund shall not be taken into account,

(D) the earnings and profits (within the meaning of section 316) of any corporation shall be determined without regard to this section and chapter 535 of title 46, United States Code, and

(E) in applying the tax imposed by section 531 (relating to the accumulated earnings tax), amounts while held in the fund shall not be taken into account.

(2) ONLY QUALIFIED DEPOSITS ELIGIBLE FOR TREATMENT.—Paragraph (1) shall apply with respect to any amount only if such amount is deposited in the fund pursuant to the agreement and not later than the time provided in joint regulations.

Amendments

•2006 (P.L. 109-304)

P.L. 109-304, §17(e)(6)(B):

Amended Code Sec. 7518(c)(1) by striking "section 607 of the Merchant Marine Act, 1936" and substituting "chapter 535 of title 46, United States Code" in subparagraphs (A) and (D). **Effective** 10-6-2006.

[Sec. 7518(d)]

(d) ESTABLISHMENT OF ACCOUNTS.—For purposes of this section—

(1) IN GENERAL.—Within a capital construction fund 3 accounts shall be maintained:

(A) the capital account,

(B) the capital gain account, and

(C) the ordinary income account.

(2) CAPITAL ACCOUNT.—The capital account shall consist of—

(A) amounts referred to in subsection (a)(1)(B),

(B) amounts referred to in subsection (a)(1)(C) other than that portion thereof which represents gain not taken into account by reason of subsection (c)(1)(B),

(C) the percentage applicable under section 243(a)(1) of any dividend received by the fund with respect to which the person maintaining the fund would (but for subsection (c)(1)(C)) be allowed a deduction under section 243, and

(D) interest income exempt from taxation under section 103.

MISCELLANEOUS PROVISIONS

(3) CAPITAL GAIN ACCOUNT.—The capital gain account shall consist of—

(A) amounts representing capital gains on assets held for more than 6 months and referred to in subsection (a)(1)(C) or (a)(1)(D), reduced by

(B) amounts representing capital losses on assets held in the fund for more than 6 months.

(4) ORDINARY INCOME ACCOUNT.—The ordinary income account shall consist of—

(A) amounts referred to in subsection (a)(1)(A),

(B)(i) amounts representing capital gains on assets held for 6 months or less and referred to in subsection (a)(1)(C) or (a)(1)(D), reduced by

(ii) amounts representing capital losses on assets held in the fund for 6 months or less,

(C) interest (not including any tax-exempt interest referred to in paragraph (2)(D)) and other ordinary income (not including any dividend referred to in subparagraph (E)) received on assets held in the fund,

(D) ordinary income from a transaction described in subsection (a)(1)(C), and

(E) the portion of any dividend referred to in paragraph (2)(C) not taken into account under such paragraph.

(5) CAPITAL LOSSES ONLY ALLOWED TO OFFSET CERTAIN GAINS.—Except on termination of a capital construction fund, capital losses referred to in paragraph (3)(B) or in paragraph (4)(B)(ii) shall be allowed only as an offset to gains referred to in paragraph (3)(A) or (4)(B)(i), respectively.

[Sec. 7518(e)]

(e) PURPOSES OF QUALIFIED WITHDRAWALS.—

(1) IN GENERAL.—A qualified withdrawal from the fund is one made in accordance with the terms of the agreement but only if it is for:

(A) the acquisition, construction, or reconstruction of a qualified vessel,

(B) the acquisition, construction, or reconstruction of barges and containers which are part of the complement of a qualified vessel, or

(C) the payment of the principal on indebtedness incurred in connection with the acquisition, construction, or reconstruction of a qualified vessel or a barge or container which is part of the complement of a qualified vessel.

Except to the extent provided in regulations prescribed by the Secretary, subparagraph (B), and so much of subparagraph (C) as relates only to barges and containers, shall apply only with respect to barges and containers constructed in the United States.

(2) PENALTY FOR FAILING TO FULFILL ANY SUBSTANTIAL OBLIGATION.—Under joint regulations, if the Secretary determines that any substantial obligation under any agreement is not being fulfilled, he may, after notice and opportunity for hearing to the person maintaining the fund, treat the entire fund or any portion thereof as an amount withdrawn from the fund in a nonqualified withdrawal.

[Sec. 7518(f)]

(f) TAX TREATMENT OF QUALIFIED WITHDRAWALS.—

(1) ORDERING RULE.—Any qualified withdrawal from a fund shall be treated—

(A) first as made out of the capital account,

(B) second as made out of the capital gain account, and

(C) third as made out of the ordinary income account.

(2) ADJUSTMENT TO BASIS OF VESSEL, ETC., WHERE WITHDRAWAL FROM ORDINARY INCOME ACCOUNT.—If any portion of a qualified withdrawal for a vessel, barge, or container is made out of the ordinary income account, the basis of such vessel, barge, or container shall be reduced by an amount equal to such portion.

(3) ADJUSTMENT TO BASIS OF VESSEL, ETC., WHERE WITHDRAWAL FROM CAPITAL GAIN ACCOUNT.—If any portion of a qualified withdrawal for a vessel, barge, or container is made out of the capital gain account, the basis of such vessel, barge, or container shall be reduced by an amount equal to such portion.

(4) ADJUSTMENT TO BASIS OF VESSELS, ETC., WHERE WITHDRAWALS PAY PRINCIPAL ON DEBT.—If any portion of a qualified withdrawal to pay the principal on any indebtedness is made out of the ordinary income account or the capital gain account, then an amount equal to the aggregate reduction which would be required by paragraphs (2) and (3) if this were a qualified withdrawal for a purpose described in such paragraphs shall be applied, in the order provided in joint regulations, to reduce the basis of vessels, barges, and containers owned by the person maintaining the fund. Any amount of a withdrawal remaining after the application of the preceding sentence shall be treated as a nonqualified withdrawal.

(5) ORDINARY INCOME RECAPTURE OF BASIS REDUCTION.—If any property the basis of which was reduced under paragraph (2), (3), or (4) is disposed of, any gain realized on such disposition, to the extent it does not exceed the aggregate reduction in the basis of such property under such paragraphs, shall be treated as an amount referred to in subsection (g)(3)(A) which was withdrawn on the date of such disposition. Subject to such conditions and requirements as may be provided in joint regulations, the preceding sentence shall not apply to a disposition where there is a redeposit in an amount determined under joint regulations which will, insofar as practicable, restore the fund to the position it was in before the withdrawal.

[Sec. 7518(g)]

(g) TAX TREATMENT OF NONQUALIFIED WITHDRAWALS.—

(1) IN GENERAL.—Except as provided in subsection (h), any withdrawal from a capital construction fund which is not a qualified withdrawal shall be treated as a nonqualified withdrawal.

(2) ORDERING RULE.—Any nonqualified withdrawal from a fund shall be treated—

(A) first as made out of the ordinary income account,

(B) second as made out of the capital gain account, and

(C) third as made out of the capital account.

For purposes of this section, items withdrawn from any account shall be treated as withdrawn on a first-in-first-out basis; except that (i) any nonqualified withdrawal for research, development, and design expenses incident to new and advanced ship design, machinery and equipment, and (ii) any amount treated as a nonqualified withdrawal under the second sentence of subsection (f)(4), shall be treated as withdrawn on a last-in-first-out basis.

(3) OPERATING RULES.—For purposes of this title—

(A) any amount referred to in paragraph (2)(A) shall be included in income as an item of ordinary income for the taxable year in which the withdrawal is made,

(B) any amount referred to in paragraph (2)(B) shall be included in income for the taxable year in which the withdrawal is made as an item of gain realized during such year from the disposition of an asset held for more than 6 months, and

(C) for the period on or before the last date prescribed for payment of tax for the taxable year in which this withdrawal is made—

MISCELLANEOUS PROVISIONS

(i) no interest shall be payable under section 6601 and no addition to the tax shall be payable under section 6651,

(ii) interest on the amount of the additional tax attributable to any item referred to in subparagraph (A) or (B) shall be paid at the applicable rate (as defined in paragraph (4)) from the last date prescribed for payment of the tax for the taxable year for which such item was deposited in the fund, and

(iii) no interest shall be payable on amounts referred to in clauses (i) and (ii) of paragraph (2) or in the case of any nonqualified withdrawal arising from the application of the recapture provision of section 606(5) of the Merchant Marine Act, 1936 as in effect on December 31, 1969.

(4) INTEREST RATE.—For purposes of paragraph (3)(C)(ii), the applicable rate of interest for any nonqualified withdrawal shall be determined and published jointly by the Secretary of the Treasury or his delegate and the applicable Secretary and shall bear a relationship to 8 percent which the Secretaries determine under joint regulations to be comparable to the relationship which the money rates and investment yields for the calendar year immediately preceding the beginning of the taxable year bear to the money rates and investment yields for the calendar year 1970.

(5) AMOUNT NOT WITHDRAWN FROM FUND AFTER 25 YEARS FROM DEPOSIT TAXED AS NONQUALIFIED WITHDRAWAL.—

(A) IN GENERAL.—The applicable percentage of any amount which remains in a capital construction fund at the close of the 26th, 27th, 28th, 29th, or 30th taxable year following the taxable year for which such amount was deposited shall be treated as a nonqualified withdrawal in accordance with the following table:

If the amount remains in the fund at the close of the—	The applicable percentage is—
26th taxable year	20 percent
27th taxable year	40 percent
28th taxable year	60 percent
29th taxable year	80 percent
30th taxable year	100 percent

(B) EARNINGS TREATED AS DEPOSITS.—The earnings of any capital construction fund for any taxable year (other than net gains) shall be treated for purposes of this paragraph as an amount deposited for such taxable year.

(C) AMOUNTS COMMITTED TREATED AS WITHDRAWN.—For purposes of subparagraph (A), an amount shall not be treated as remaining in a capital construction fund at the close of any taxable year to the extent there is a binding contract at the close of such year for a qualified withdrawal of such amount with respect to an identified item for which such withdrawal may be made.

(D) AUTHORITY TO TREAT EXCESS FUNDS AS WITHDRAWN.—If the Secretary determines that the balance in any capital construction fund exceeds the amount which is appropriate to meet the vessel construction program objectives of the person who established such fund, the amount of such excess shall be treated as a nonqualified withdrawal under subparagraph (A) unless such person develops appropriate program objectives within 3 years to dissipate such excess.

(E) AMOUNTS IN FUND ON JANUARY 1, 1987.—For purposes of this paragraph, all amounts in a capital construction fund on January 1, 1987, shall be treated as deposited in such fund on such date.

(6) NONQUALIFIED WITHDRAWALS TAXED AT HIGHEST MARGINAL RATE.—

(A) IN GENERAL.—In the case of any taxable year for which there is a nonqualified withdrawal (including any amount so treated under paragraph (5)), the tax imposed by chapter 1 shall be determined—

(i) by excluding such withdrawal from gross income, and

(ii) by increasing the tax imposed by chapter 1 by the product of the amount of such withdrawal and the highest rate of tax specified in section 1 (section 11 in the case of a corporation).

In the case of a taxpayer other than a corporation, with respect to the portion of any nonqualified withdrawal made out of the capital gain account during a taxable year to which section 1(h) applies, the rate of tax taken into account under the preceding sentence shall not exceed 20 percent.

(B) TAX BENEFIT RULE.—If any portion of a nonqualified withdrawal is properly attributable to deposits (other than earnings on deposits) made by the taxpayer in any taxable year which did not reduce the taxpayer's liability for tax under chapter 1 for any taxable year preceding the taxable year in which such withdrawal occurs.—

(i) such portion shall not be taken into account under subparagraph (A), and

(ii) an amount equal to such portion shall be treated as allowed as a deduction under section 172 for the taxable year in which such withdrawal occurs.

(C) COORDINATION WITH DEDUCTION FOR NET OPERATING LOSSES.—Any nonqualified withdrawal excluded from gross income under subparagraph (A) shall be excluded in determining taxable income under section 172(b)(2).

Amendments

● **2017, Tax Cuts and Jobs Act (P.L. 115-97)**

P.L. 115-97, § 13001(b)(2)(Q):

Amended Code Sec. 7518(g)(6)(A) by striking "or 1201(a)" following "section 1(h)". **Effective** for tax years beginning after 12-31-2017.

P.L. 115-97, § 13001(b)(7)(A)-(B):

Amended Code Sec. 7518(g)(6)(A) by striking "With respect to the portion" and inserting "In the case of a taxpayer other than a corporation, with respect to the portion", and by striking "(34 percent in the case of a corporation)" following "not exceed 20 percent". **Effective** for tax years beginning after 12-31-2017.

● **2014, Tax Technical Corrections Act of 2014 (P.L. 113-295)**

P.L. 113-295, § 221(a)(117), Division A:

Amended Code Sec. 7518(g)(4) by striking "any nonqualified withdrawal" and all that follows through "'shall be determined" and inserting "any nonqualified withdrawal shall be determined". **Effective** generally 12-19-2014. For a special rule, see Act Sec. 221(b)(2), Division A, below. Prior to being stricken, "any nonqualified withdrawal" and all that follows through "shall be determined" read as follows:

any nonqualified withdrawal—

(A) made in a taxable year beginning in 1970 or 1971 is 8 percent, or

(B) made in a taxable year beginning after 1971, shall be determined

P.L. 113-295, § 221(b)(2), Division A, provides:

(2) SAVINGS PROVISION.—If—

(A) any provision amended or repealed by the amendments made by this section applied to—

(i) any transaction occurring before the date of the enactment of this Act,

(ii) any property acquired before such date of enactment, or

(iii) any item of income, loss, deduction, or credit taken into account before such date of enactment, and

(B) the treatment of such transaction, property, or item under such provision would (without regard to the amendments or repeals made by this section) affect the liability for tax for periods ending after date of enactment, nothing in the amendments or repeals made by this section shall be construed to affect the treatment of such transaction, property, or item for purposes of determining liability for tax for periods ending after such date of enactment.

● **2013, American Taxpayer Relief Act of 2012 (P.L. 112-240)**

P.L. 112-240, § 102(a), provides:

SEC. 102. PERMANENT EXTENSION AND MODIFICATION OF 2003 TAX RELIEF.

(a) PERMANENT EXTENSION.—The Jobs and Growth Tax Relief Reconciliation Act of 2003 is amended by striking section 303.

P.L. 112-240, § 102(c)(1)(D):

Amended the second sentence of Code Sec. 7518(g)(6)(A) by striking "15 percent" and inserting "20 percent". **Effective** for tax years beginning after 12-31-2012.

MISCELLANEOUS PROVISIONS

• **2006 (P.L. 109-304)**

P.L. 109-304, §17(e)(6)(C):

Amended Code Sec. 7518(g)(3)(C)(iii) by striking "Merchant Marine Act of 1936" and substituting "Merchant Marine Act, 1936". **Effective** 10-6-2006.

• **2003, Jobs and Growth Tax Relief Reconciliation Act of 2003 (P.L. 108-27)**

P.L. 108-27, §301(a)(2)(D):

Amended the second sentence of Code Sec. 7518(g)(6)(A) by striking "20 percent" and inserting "15 percent". **Effective** for tax years ending on or after 5-6-2003.

P.L. 108-27, §303, as amended by P.L. 109-222, §102, and P.L. 111-312, §102(a), provides [but see P.L. 112-240, §102(a), above]:

SEC. 303. SUNSET OF TITLE.

All provisions of, and amendments made by, this title shall not apply to taxable years beginning after December 31, 2012, and the Internal Revenue Code of 1986 shall be applied and administered to such years as if such provisions and amendments had never been enacted.

• **1997, Taxpayer Relief Act of 1997 (P.L. 105-34)**

P.L. 105-34, §311(c)(2):

Amended Code Sec. 7518(g)(6)(A) by striking "28 percent" in the second sentence and inserting "20 percent". **Effective** for tax years ending after 5-6-97.

• **1990, Omnibus Budget Reconciliation Act of 1990 (P.L. 101-508)**

P.L. 101-508, §11101(d)(7)(A):

Amended Code Sec. 7518(g)(6)(A) by striking "1(j)" and inserting "1(h)". **Effective** for tax years beginning after 12-31-90.

• **1988, Technical and Miscellaneous Revenue Act of 1988 (P.L. 100-647)**

P.L. 100-647, §1002(m)(1):

Amended Code Sec. 7518(g)(6)(A) by striking out "section 1(i)" and inserting in lieu thereof "section 1(j)". **Effective** as if included in the provision of P.L. 99-514 to which it relates.

P.L. 100-647, §1018(u)(23):

Amended Code Sec. 7518(g)(1) by striking out "not [a]qualified withdrawal" and inserting in lieu thereof "not a qualified withdrawal". **Effective** as if included in the provision of P.L. 99-514 to which it relates.

[Sec. 7518(h)]

(h) CERTAIN CORPORATE REORGANIZATIONS AND CHANGES IN PARTNERSHIPS.—Under joint regulations—

(1) a transfer of a fund from one person to another person in a transaction to which section 381 applies may be treated as if such transaction did not constitute a nonqualified withdrawal, and

(2) a similar rule shall be applied in the case of a continuation of a partnership.

[Sec. 7518(i)]

(i) DEFINITIONS.—For purposes of this section, any term defined in chapter 535 of title 46, United States Code, which is also used in this section (including the definition of "Secretary") shall have the meaning given such term by such chapter as in effect on the date of the enactment of this section.

Amendments

• **2018, Tax Technical Corrections Act of 2018 (P.L. 115-141)**

P.L. 115-141, §401(a)(352)(A)-(B), Div. U:

Amended Code Sec. 7518(i) by striking "section 607(k) of the Merchant Marine Act, 1936" and inserting "chapter 535 of title 46, United States Code,", and by striking "such section 607(k)" and inserting "such chapter". **Effective** 3-23-2018.

• **1986, Tax Reform Act of 1986 (P.L. 99-514)**

P.L. 99-514, §261(b):

Amended chapter 77 by adding at the end thereof new Code Sec. 7518. **Effective** for tax years beginning after 12-31-86.

[Sec. 7519]

SEC. 7519. REQUIRED PAYMENTS FOR ENTITIES ELECTING NOT TO HAVE REQUIRED TAXABLE YEAR.

[Sec. 7519(a)]

(a) GENERAL RULE.—This section applies to a partnership or S corporation for any taxable year, if—

(1) an election under section 444 is in effect for the taxable year, and

(2) the required payment determined under subsection (b) for such taxable year (or any preceding taxable year) exceeds $500.

[Sec. 7519(b)]

(b) REQUIRED PAYMENT.—For purposes of this section, the term "required payment" means, with respect to any applicable election year of a partnership or S corporation, an amount equal to—

(1) the excess of the product of—

(A) the applicable percentage of the adjusted highest section 1 rate, multiplied by

(B) the net base year income of the entity, over

(2) the net required payment balance.

For purposes of paragraph (1)(A), the term "adjusted highest section 1 rate" means the highest rate of tax in effect under section 1 as of the end of the base year plus 1 percentage point (or, in the case of applicable election years beginning in 1987, 36 percent).

Amendments

(2) the amount of the required payment for the preceding applicable election year.

• **1988, Technical and Miscellaneous Revenue Act of 1988 (P.L. 100-647)**

P.L. 100-647, §2004(e)(4)(A):

Amended Code Sec. 7519(b)(2). **Effective** as if included in the provision of P.L. 100-203 to which it relates. Prior to amendment, Code Sec. 7519(b)(2) read as follows:

[Sec. 7519(c)]

(c) REFUND OF PAYMENTS.—

(1) IN GENERAL.—If, for any applicable election year, the amount determined under subsection (b)(2) exceeds the amount determined under subsection (b)(1), the entity shall be entitled to a refund of such excess for such year.

(2) TERMINATION OF ELECTIONS, ETC.—If—

(A) an election under section 444 is terminated effective with respect to any year, or

(B) the entity is liquidated during any year, the entity shall be entitled to a refund of the net required payment balance.

(3) DATE ON WHICH REFUND PAYABLE.—Any refund under this subsection shall be payable on the later of—

(A) April 15 of the calendar year following—

(i) in the case of the year referred to in paragraph (1), the calendar year in which it begins,

(ii) in the case of the year referred to in paragraph (2), the calendar year in which it ends, or

(B) the day 90 days after the day on which claim therefor is filed with the Secretary.

Amendments

• **1990, Omnibus Budget Reconciliation Act of 1990 (P.L. 101-508)**

P.L. 101-508, §11704(a)(29):

Amended Code Sec. 7519(c)(3) by striking "payable on later of" and inserting "payable on the later of". **Effective** 11-5-90.

• **1988, Technical and Miscellaneous Revenue Act of 1988 (P.L. 100-647)**

P.L. 100-647, §2004(e)(5):

Amended Code Sec. 7519(c). **Effective** as if included in the provision of P.L. 100-203 to which it relates. Prior to amendment, Code Sec. 7519(c) read as follows:

MISCELLANEOUS PROVISIONS

(c) REFUND OF PAYMENTS.—If the amount determined under subsection (b)(2) exceeds the amount determined under subsection (b)(1), then the entity shall be entitled to a refund of such excess.

[Sec. 7519(d)]

(d) NET BASE YEAR INCOME.—For purposes of this section—

(1) IN GENERAL.—An entity's net base year income shall be equal to the sum of—

(A) the deferral ratio multiplied by the entity's net income for the base year, plus

(B) the excess (if any) of—

(i) the deferral ratio multiplied by the aggregate amount of applicable payments made by the entity during the base year, over

(ii) the aggregate amount of such applicable payments made during the deferral period of the base year.

For purposes of this paragraph, the term "deferral ratio" means the ratio which the number of months in the deferral period of the base year bears to the number of months in the partnership's or S corporation's taxable year.

(2) NET INCOME.—Net income is determined by taking into account the aggregate amount of the following items—

(A) PARTNERSHIPS.—In the case of a partnership, net income shall be the amount (not below zero) determined by taking into account the aggregate amount of the partnership's items described in section 702(a) (other than credits and tax-exempt income).

(B) S CORPORATIONS.—In the case of an S corporation, net income shall be the amount (not below zero) determined by taking into account the aggregate amount of the S corporation's items described in section 1366(a) (other than credits and tax-exempt income). If the S corporation was a C corporation for the base year, its taxable income for such year shall be treated as its net income for such year (and such corporation shall be treated as an S corporation for such taxable year for purposes of paragraph (3)).

(C) CERTAIN LIMITATIONS DISREGARDED.—For purposes of subparagraph (A) or (B), any limitation on the amount of any item described in either such paragraph which may be taken into account for purposes of computing the taxable income of a partner or shareholder shall be disregarded.

(3) APPLICABLE PAYMENTS.—

(A) IN GENERAL.—The term "applicable payment" means amounts paid by a partnership or S corporation which are includible in gross income of a partner or shareholder.

(B) EXCEPTIONS.—The term "applicable payment" shall not include any—

(i) gain from the sale or exchange of property between the partner or shareholder and the partnership or S corporation, and

(ii) dividend paid by the S corporation.

(4) APPLICABLE PERCENTAGE.—The applicable percentage is the percentage determined in accordance with the following table:

If the applicable election year of the partnership or S corporation begins during:	The applicable percentage is:
1987	25
1988	50
1989	75
1990 or thereafter	100

Notwithstanding the preceding provisions of this paragraph, the applicable percentage for any partnership or S corporation shall be 100 percent unless more than 50 percent of such entity's net income for the short taxable year which would have resulted if the entity had not made an election under section 444 would have been allocated to partners or shareholders who would have been entitled to the benefits of section 806(e)(2)(C) of the Tax Reform Act of 1986 with respect to such income.

(5) TREATMENT OF GUARANTEED PAYMENTS.—

(A) IN GENERAL.—Any guaranteed payment by a partnership shall not be treated as an applicable payment, and the amount of the net income of the partnership shall be determined by not taking such guaranteed payment into account.

(B) GUARANTEED PAYMENT.—For purposes of subparagraph (A), the term "guaranteed payment" means any payment referred to in section 707(c).

Amendments

- **1989, Omnibus Budget Reconciliation Act of 1989 (P.L. 101-239)**

P.L. 101-239, § 7821(b)(1)-(3):

Amended Code Sec. 7519(d)(4) by striking "for taxable years beginning after 1987," after "provisions of this paragraph", by striking "if more than 50 percent" and inserting "unless more than 50 percent", and by striking "who would not have been entitled" and inserting "who would have been entitled". **Effective** with respect to tax years beginning after 1988.

- **1988, Technical and Miscellaneous Revenue Act of 1988 (P.L. 100-647)**

P.L. 100-647, § 2004(e)(7):

Amended Code Sec. 7519(d)(2)(B) by inserting before the period at the end thereof "(and such corporation shall be treated as an S corporation for such taxable year for purposes of paragraph (3))". **Effective** as if included in the provision of P.L. 100-203 to which it relates.

P.L. 100-647, § 2004(e)(8):

Amended Code Sec. 7519(d) by adding at the end thereof a new paragraph (5). **Effective** as if included in the provision of P.L. 100-203 to which it relates.

P.L. 100-647, § 2004(e)(9):

Amended Code Sec. 7519(d)(4) by adding at the end thereof a new sentence. **Effective** as if included in the provision of P.L. 100-203 to which it relates.

P.L. 100-647, § 2004(e)(10):

Amended Code Sec. 7519(d)(2)(A) and (B) by striking out "(other than credits)" and inserting in lieu thereof "(other than credits and tax-exempt income)". **Effective** as if included in the provision of P.L. 100-203 to which it relates.

P.L. 100-647, § 2004(e)(14)(B):

Amended Code Sec. 7519(d)(3)(A) by striking out "or incurred" after "amounts paid". **Effective** as if included in the provision of P.L. 100-203 to which it relates.

[Sec. 7519(e)]

(e) OTHER DEFINITIONS AND SPECIAL RULES.—For purposes of this section—

(1) DEFERRAL PERIOD.—The term "deferral period" has the meaning given to such term by section 444(b)(4).

(2) YEARS.—

(A) BASE YEAR.—The term "base year" means, with respect to any applicable election year, the taxable year of the partnership or S corporation preceding such applicable election year.

(B) APPLICABLE ELECTION YEAR.—The term "applicable election year" means any taxable year of a partnership or S corporation with respect to which an election is in effect under section 444.

(3) REQUIREMENT OF REPORTING.—Each partnership or S corporation which makes an election under section 444 shall include on any required return or statement such information as the Secretary shall prescribe as is necessary to carry out the provisions of this section.

(4) NET REQUIRED PAYMENT BALANCE.—The term "net required payment balance" means the excess (if any) of—

MISCELLANEOUS PROVISIONS

(A) the aggregate of the required payments under this section for all preceding applicable election years, over

(B) the aggregate amount allowable as a refund to the entity under subsection (c) for all preceding applicable election years.

Amendments

• **1988, Technical and Miscellaneous Revenue Act of 1988 (P.L. 100-647)**

P.L. 100-647, § 2004(e)(4)(B):

Amended Code Sec. 7519(e) by adding at the end thereof a new paragraph (4). **Effective** as if included in the provision of P.L. 100-203 to which it relates.

[Sec. 7519(f)]

(f) ADMINISTRATIVE PROVISIONS.—

(1) IN GENERAL.—Except as otherwise provided in this subsection or in regulations prescribed by the Secretary, any payment required by this section shall be assessed and collected in the same manner as if it were a tax imposed by subtitle C.

(2) DUE DATE.—The amount of any payment required by this section shall be paid on or before April 15 of the calendar year following the calendar year in which the applicable election year begins (or such later date as may be prescribed by the Secretary).

(3) INTEREST.—For purposes of determining interest, any payment required by this section shall be treated as a tax; except that no interest shall be allowed with respect to any refund of a payment made under this section.

(4) PENALTIES.—

(A) IN GENERAL.—In the case of any failure by any person to pay on the date prescribed therefor any amount required by this section, there shall be imposed on such person a penalty of 10 percent of the underpayment. For purposes of the preceding sentence, the term "underpayment" means the excess of the amount of the payment required under this section over the amount (if any) of such payment paid on or before the date prescribed therefor. No penalty shall be imposed under this subparagraph on any failure which is shown to be due to reasonable cause and not willful neglect.

(B) NEGLIGENCE AND FRAUD PENALTIES MADE APPLICABLE.—For purposes of part II of subchapter A of chapter 68, any payment required by this section shall be treated as a tax.

(C) WILLFULL FAILURE.—If any partnership or S corporation willfully fails to comply with the requirements of this section, section 444 shall cease to apply with respect to such partnership or S corporation.

Amendments

• **1997, Taxpayer Relief Act of 1997 (P.L. 105-34)**

P.L. 105-34, § 1281(d):

Amended Code Sec. 7519(f)(4)(A) by adding at the end a new sentence. **Effective** for tax years beginning after 8-5-97.

• **1989, Omnibus Budget Reconciliation Act of 1989 (P.L. 101-239)**

P.L. 101-239, § 7721(c)(12):

Amended Code Sec. 7519(f)(4)(B) by striking "section 6653" and inserting "part II of subchapter A of chapter 68". **Effective** for returns the due date for which (determined without regard to extensions) is after 12-31-89.

[Sec. 7519(g)]

(g) REGULATIONS.—The Secretary shall prescribe such regulations as may be necessary or appropriate to carry out the provisions of this section and section 280H, including regulations providing for appropriate adjustments in the application of this section and sections 280H and 444 in cases where—

(1) 2 or more applicable election years begin in the same calendar year, or

(2) the base year is a taxable year of less than 12 months.

Amendments

• **1988, Technical and Miscellaneous Revenue Act of 1988 (P.L. 100-647)**

P.L. 100-647, § 2004(e)(6):

Amended Code Sec. 7519(g) by striking out "including regulations" and all that follows down through the period at the end thereof and inserting in lieu thereof new material. **Effective** as if included in the provision of P.L. 100-203 to which it relates. Prior to amendment, Code Sec. 7519(g) read as follows:

(g) REGULATIONS.—The Secretary shall prescribe such regulations as may be necessary or appropriate to carry out the provisions of this section and section 280H, including regulations for annualizing the income and applicable payments of an entity if the base year is a taxable year of less than 12 months.

• **1987, Revenue Act of 1987 (P.L. 100-203)**

P.L. 100-203, § 10206(b)(1):

Amended Chapter 77 by adding at the end thereof new section 7519. For the **effective** date, see Act Sec. 10206(d), below.

P.L. 100-203, § 10206(d), provides:

(d) EFFECTIVE DATES.—

(1) IN GENERAL.—Except as provided in this subsection, the amendments made by this section shall apply to taxable years beginning after December 31, 1986.

(2) REQUIRED PAYMENTS.—The amendments made by subsection (b) shall apply to applicable election years beginning after December 31, 1986.

(3) ELECTIONS.—Any election under section 444 of the Internal Revenue Code of 1986 (as added by subsection (a)) for an entity's 1st taxable year beginning after December 31, 1986, shall not be required to be made before the 90th day after the date of the enactment of this Act.

(4) SPECIAL RULE FOR EXISTING ENTITIES ELECTING S CORPORATION STATUS.—If a C corporation (within the meaning of section 1361(a)(2) of the Internal Revenue Code of 1986) with a taxable year other than the calendar year—

(A) made an election after September 18, 1986, and before January 1, 1988, under section 1362 of such Code to be treated as an S corporation, and

(B) elected to have the calendar year as the taxable year of the S corporation,

then section 444(b)(2)(B) of such Code shall be applied by taking into account the deferral period of the last taxable year of the C corporation rather than the deferral period of the taxable year being changed.

[Sec. 7520]

SEC. 7520. VALUATION TABLES.

[Sec. 7520(a)]

(a) GENERAL RULE.—For purposes of this title, the value of any annuity, any interest for life or a term of years, or any remainder or reversionary interest shall be determined—

(1) under tables prescribed by the Secretary, and

(2) by using an interest rate (rounded to the nearest $^2/_{10}$ths of 1 percent) equal to 120 percent of the Federal midterm rate in effect under section 1274(d)(1) for the month in which the valuation date falls.

If an income, estate, or gift tax charitable contribution is allowable for any part of the property transferred, the taxpayer may elect to use such Federal midterm rate for either of the 2 months preceding the month in which the valuation date falls for purposes of paragraph (2). In the case of transfers of more than 1 interest in the same property with respect to which the taxpayer may use the same rate under paragraph (2), the taxpayer shall use the same rate with respect to each such interest.

[Sec. 7520(b)]

(b) SECTION NOT TO APPLY FOR CERTAIN PURPOSES.—This section shall not apply for purposes of part I of subchapter D of chapter 1 or any other provision specified in regulations.

Sec. 7519(e)(4)(A)

MISCELLANEOUS PROVISIONS

[Sec. 7520(c)]

(c) TABLES.—

(1) IN GENERAL.—The tables prescribed by the Secretary for purposes of subsection (a) shall contain valuation factors for a series of interest rate categories.

(2) REVISION FOR RECENT MORTALITY CHARGES.—The Secretary shall revise the initial tables prescribed for purposes of subsection (a) to take into account the most recent mortality experience available as of the time of such revision. Such tables shall be revised not less frequently than once each 10 years to take into account the most recent mortality experience available as of the time of the revision.

Amendments

• 2014, Tax Technical Corrections Act of 2014 (P.L. 113-295)

P.L. 113-295, § 221(a)(118)(A), Division A:

Amended Code Sec. 7520(c) by striking paragraph (2) and redesignating paragraph (3) as paragraph (2). **Effective** generally 12-19-2014. For a special rule, see Act Sec. 221(b)(2), Division A, below. Prior to being stricken, Code Sec. 7520(c)(2) read as follows:

(2) INITIAL TABLE.—Not later than the day 3 months after the date of the enactment of this section, the Secretary shall prescribe initial tables for purposes of subsection (a). Such tables may be based on the same mortality experience as used for purposes of section 2031 on the date of the enactment of this section.

P.L. 113-295, § 221(a)(118)(B)(i)-(ii), Division A:

Amended Code Sec. 7520(c)(2) (as redesignated by Act Sec. 221(a)(118)(A), Division A) by striking "Not later than December 31, 1989, the" and inserting "The", and by striking "thereafter" following "10 years" in the last sentence thereof. **Effective** generally 12-19-2014. For a special rule, see Act Sec. 221(b)(2), Division A, below.

P.L. 113-295, § 221(b)(2), Division A, provides:

(2) SAVINGS PROVISION.—If—

(A) any provision amended or repealed by the amendments made by this section applied to—

(i) any transaction occurring before the date of the enactment of this Act,

(ii) any property acquired before such date of enactment, or

(iii) any item of income, loss, deduction, or credit taken into account before such date of enactment, and

(B) the treatment of such transaction, property, or item under such provision would (without regard to the amendments or repeals made by this section) affect the liability for tax for periods ending after date of enactment, nothing in the amendments or repeals made by this section shall be construed to affect the treatment of such transaction, property, or item for purposes of determining liability for tax for periods ending after such date of enactment.

[Sec. 7520(d)]

(d) VALUATION DATE.—For purposes of this section, the term "valuation date" means the date as of which the valuation is made.

[Sec. 7520(e)]

(e) TABLES TO INCLUDE FORMULAS.—For purposes of this section, the term "tables" includes formulas.

Amendments

• 1988, Technical and Miscellaneous Revenue Act of 1988 (P.L. 100-647)

P.L. 100-647, § 5031(a):

Amended Chapter 77 by adding at the end thereof a new section 7520. **Effective** in cases where the date the valuation is to be made occurs on or after the 1st day of the 6th calendar month beginning after 11-10-88.

[Sec. 7521]

SEC. 7521. PROCEDURES INVOLVING TAXPAYER INTERVIEWS.

[Sec. 7521(a)]

(a) RECORDING OF INTERVIEWS.—

(1) RECORDING BY TAXPAYER.—Any officer or employee of the Internal Revenue Service in connection with any in-person interview with any taxpayer relating to the determination or collection of any tax shall, upon advance request of such taxpayer, allow the taxpayer to make an audio recording of such interview at the taxpayer's own expense and with the taxpayer's own equipment.

(2) RECORDING BY IRS OFFICER OR EMPLOYEE.—An officer or employee of the Internal Revenue Service may record any interview described in paragraph (1) if such officer or employee—

(A) informs the taxpayer of such recording prior to the interview, and

(B) upon request of the taxpayer, provides the taxpayer with a transcript or copy of such recording but only if the taxpayer provides reimbursement for the cost of the transcription and reproduction of such transcript or copy.

[Sec. 7521(b)]

(b) SAFEGUARDS.—

(1) EXPLANATIONS OF PROCESSES.—An officer or employee of the Internal Revenue Service shall before or at an initial interview provide to the taxpayer—

(A) in the case of an in-person interview with the taxpayer relating to the determination of any tax, an explanation of the audit process and the taxpayer's rights under such process, or

(B) in the case of an in-person interview with the taxpayer relating to the collection of any tax, an explanation of the collection process and the taxpayer's rights under such process.

(2) RIGHT OF CONSULTATION.—If the taxpayer clearly states to an officer or employee of the Internal Revenue Service at any time during any interview (other than an interview initiated by an administrative summons issued under subchapter A of chapter 78) that the taxpayer wishes to consult with an attorney, certified public accountant, enrolled agent, enrolled actuary, or any other person permitted to represent the taxpayer before the Internal Revenue Service, such officer or employee shall suspend such interview regardless of whether the taxpayer may have answered one or more questions.

[Sec. 7521(c)]

(c) REPRESENTATIVES HOLDING POWER OF ATTORNEY.—Any attorney, certified public accountant, enrolled agent, enrolled actuary, or any other person permitted to represent the taxpayer before the Internal Revenue Service who is not disbarred or suspended from practice before the Internal Revenue Service and who has a written power of attorney executed by the taxpayer may be authorized by such taxpayer to represent the taxpayer in any interview described in subsection (a). An officer or employee of the Internal Revenue Service may not require a taxpayer to accompany the representative in the absence of an administrative summons issued to the taxpayer under subchapter A of chapter 78. Such an officer or employee, with the consent of the immediate supervisor of such officer or employee, may notify the taxpayer directly that such officer or employee believes such representative is responsible for unreasonable delay or hindrance of an Internal Revenue Service examination or investigation of the taxpayer.

[Sec. 7521(d)]

(d) SECTION NOT TO APPLY TO CERTAIN INVESTIGATIONS.—This section shall not apply to criminal investigations or investigations relating to the integrity of any officer or employee of the Internal Revenue Service.

MISCELLANEOUS PROVISIONS

Amendments

• **1998, IRS Restructuring and Reform Act of 1998 (P.L. 105-206)**

P.L. 105-206, § 3502, provides:

SEC. 3502. EXPLANATION OF TAXPAYERS' RIGHTS IN INTERVIEWS WITH THE INTERNAL REVENUE SERVICE.

The Secretary of the Treasury or the Secretary's delegate shall, as soon as practicable, but not later than 180 days after the date of the enactment of this Act, revise the statement required by section 6227 of the Omnibus Taxpayer Bill of Rights (Internal Revenue Service Publication No. 1) to more clearly inform taxpayers of their rights—

(1) to be represented at interviews with the Internal Revenue Service by any person authorized to practice before the Internal Revenue Service, and

(2) to suspend an interview pursuant to section 7521(b)(2) of the Internal Revenue Code of 1986.

• **1989, Omnibus Budget Reconciliation Act of 1989 (P.L. 101-239)**

P.L. 101-239, § 7816(u)(1):

Redesignated Code Sec. 7520 as Code Sec. 7521. **Effective** as if included in the provision of P.L. 100-647 to which it relates.

• **1988, Technical and Miscellaneous Revenue Act of 1988 (P.L. 100-647)**

P.L. 100-647, § 6228(a):

Added Code Sec. 7520. **Effective** for interviews conducted on or after the date which is 90 days after 11-10-88.

[Sec. 7522]

SEC. 7522. CONTENT OF TAX DUE, DEFICIENCY, AND OTHER NOTICES.

[Sec. 7522(a)]

(a) GENERAL RULE.—Any notice to which this section applies shall describe the basis for, and identify the amounts (if any) of, the tax due, interest, additional amounts, additions to the tax, and assessable penalties included in such notice. An inadequate description under the preceding sentence shall not invalidate such notice.

[Sec. 7522(b)]

(b) NOTICES TO WHICH SECTION APPLIES.—This section shall apply to—

(1) any tax due notice or deficiency notice described in section 6155, 6212, or 6303,

(2) any notice generated out of any information return matching program, and

(3) the 1st letter of proposed deficiency which allows the taxpayer an opportunity for administrative review in the Internal Revenue Service Independent Office of Appeals.

Amendments

• **2019, Taxpayer First Act (P.L. 116-25)**

P.L. 116-25, § 1001(b)(1)(I):

Amended Code Sec. 7522(b)(3) by striking "Internal Revenue Service Office of Appeals" and inserting "Internal Revenue Service Independent Office of Appeals". **Effective** 7-1-2019.

• **1990, Omnibus Budget Reconciliation Act of 1990 (P.L. 101-508)**

P.L. 101-508, § 11704(a)(30):

Redesignated Code Sec. 7521 as Code Sec. 7522. **Effective** on the date of enactment of this Act.

• **1988, Technical and Miscellaneous Revenue Act of 1988 (P.L. 100-647)**

P.L. 100-647, § 6233(a):

Added Code Sec. 7521. **Effective** for mailings made on or after 1-1-90.

P.L. 100-647, § 6233(d), provides:

(d) REPORT.—Not later than July 1, 1989, the Secretary of the Treasury or his delegate shall submit a report to the Committee on Ways and Means of the House of Representatives and the Committee on Finance of the Senate on the steps taken to carry out the amendments made by this section.

[Sec. 7523]

SEC. 7523. GRAPHIC PRESENTATION OF MAJOR CATEGORIES OF FEDERAL OUTLAYS AND INCOME.

[Sec. 7523(a)]

(a) GENERAL RULE.—In the case of any booklet of instructions for Form 1040, 1040A, or 1040EZ prepared by the Secretary for filing individual income tax returns for taxable years beginning in any calendar year, the Secretary shall include in a prominent place—

(1) a pie-shaped graph showing the relative sizes of the major outlay categories, and

(2) a pie-shaped graph showing the relative sizes of the major income categories.

[Sec. 7523(b)]

(b) DEFINITIONS AND SPECIAL RULES.—For purposes of subsection (a)—

(1) MAJOR OUTLAY CATEGORIES.—The term "major outlay categories" means the following:

(A) Defense, veterans, and foreign affairs.

(B) Social security, medicare, and other retirement.

(C) Physical, human, and community development.

(D) Social programs.

(E) Law enforcement and general government.

(F) Interest on the debt.

(2) MAJOR INCOME CATEGORIES.—The term "major income categories" means the following:

(A) Social security, medicare, and unemployment and other retirement taxes.

(B) Personal income taxes.

(C) Corporate income taxes.

(D) Borrowing to cover the deficit.

(E) Excise, customs, estate, gift, and miscellaneous taxes.

(3) REQUIRED FOOTNOTES.—The pie-shaped graph showing the major outlay categories shall include the following footnotes:

(A) A footnote to the category referred to in paragraph (1)(A) showing the percentage of the total outlays which is for defense, the percentage of total outlays which is for veterans, and the percentage of total outlays which is for foreign affairs.

(B) A footnote to the category referred to in paragraph (1)(C) showing that such category consists of agriculture, natural resources, environment, transportation, education, job training, economic development, space, energy, and general science.

(C) A footnote to the category referred to in paragraph (1)(D) showing the percentage of the total outlays which is for medicaid, supplemental nutrition assistance program benefits, and assistance under a State program funded under part A of title IV of the Social Security Act and the percentage of total outlays which is for public health, unemployment, assisted housing, and social services.

(4) DATA ON WHICH GRAPHS ARE BASED.—The graphs required under subsection (a) shall be based on data for the most recent fiscal year for which complete data is available as of the completion of the preparation of the instructions by the Secretary.

MISCELLANEOUS PROVISIONS

Amendments

• **2008, Food, Conservation, and Energy Act of 2008 (P.L. 110-246)**

P.L. 110-246, §4002(b)(1)(E):

Amended Code Sec. 7523(b)(3)(C) by striking "food stamps" and inserting "supplemental nutrition assistance program benefits". **Effective** 10-1-2008.

• **1996, Personal Responsibility and Work Opportunity Reconciliation Act of 1996 (P.L. 104-193)**

P.L. 104-193, §110(l)(8):

Amended Code Sec. 7523(b)(3)(C) by striking "aid to families with dependent children" and inserting "assistance under a State program funded under part A of title IV of the Social Security Act". **Effective** 7-1-97.

• **1990, Omnibus Budget Reconciliation Act of 1990 (P.L. 101-508)**

P.L. 101-508, §11622(a):

Amended chapter 77 by adding at the end thereof new Code Sec. 7523. **Effective** for instructions prepared for tax years beginning after 1990.

[Sec. 7524]

SEC. 7524. ANNUAL NOTICE OF TAX DELINQUENCY.

Not less often than annually, the Secretary shall send a written notice to each taxpayer who has a tax delinquent account of the amount of the tax delinquency as of the date of the notice.

Amendments

• **1996, Taxpayer Bill of Rights 2 (P.L. 104-168)**

P.L. 104-168, §1204(a):

Amended chapter 77 by adding at the end a new section 7524. **Effective** for calendar years after 1996.

[Sec. 7525]

SEC. 7525. CONFIDENTIALITY PRIVILEGES RELATING TO TAXPAYER COMMUNICATIONS.

[Sec. 7525(a)]

(a) UNIFORM APPLICATION TO TAXPAYER COMMUNICATIONS WITH FEDERALLY AUTHORIZED PRACTITIONERS.—

(1) GENERAL RULE.—With respect to tax advice, the same common law protections of confidentiality which apply to a communication between a taxpayer and an attorney shall also apply to a communication between a taxpayer and any federally authorized tax practitioner to the extent the communication would be considered a privileged communication if it were between a taxpayer and an attorney.

(2) LIMITATIONS.—Paragraph (1) may only be asserted in—

(A) any noncriminal tax matter before the Internal Revenue Service; and

(B) any noncriminal tax proceeding in Federal court brought by or against the United States.

(3) DEFINITIONS.—For purposes of this subsection—

(A) FEDERALLY AUTHORIZED TAX PRACTITIONER.—The term "federally authorized tax practitioner" means any individual who is authorized under Federal law to practice before the Internal Revenue Service if such practice is subject to Federal regulation under section 330 of title 31, United States Code.

(B) TAX ADVICE.—The term "tax advice" means advice given by an individual with respect to a matter which is within the scope of the individual's authority to practice described in subparagraph (A).

[Sec. 7525(b)]

(b) SECTION NOT TO APPLY TO COMMUNICATIONS REGARDING TAX SHELTERS.—The privilege under subsection (a) shall not apply to any written communication which is—

(1) between a federally authorized tax practitioner and—

(A) any person,

(B) any director, officer, employee, agent, or representative of the person, or

(C) any other person holding a capital or profits interest in the person, and

(2) in connection with the promotion of the direct or indirect participation of the person in any tax shelter (as defined in section 6662(d)(2)(C)(ii)).

Amendments

• **2004, American Jobs Creation Act of 2004 (P.L. 108-357)**

P.L. 108-357, §813(a):

Amended Code Sec. 7525(b). **Effective** for communications made on or after 10-22-2004. Prior to amendment, Code Sec. 7525(b) read as follows:

(b) SECTION NOT TO APPLY TO COMMUNICATIONS REGARDING CORPORATE TAX SHELTERS.—The privilege under subsection (a) shall not apply to any written communication between a federally authorized tax practitioner and a director, shareholder, officer, or employee, agent, or representative of a corporation in connection with the promotion of the direct or indirect participation of such corporation in any tax shelter (as defined in section 6662(d)(2)(C)(iii)).

• **1998, IRS Restructuring and Reform Act of 1998 (P.L. 105-206)**

P.L. 105-206, §3411(a):

Amended Chapter 77 by adding at the end a new Code Sec. 7525. **Effective** for communications made on or after 7-22-98.

P.L. 105-206, §3468, provides:

SEC. 3468. PROHIBITION ON REQUESTS TO TAXPAYERS TO GIVE UP RIGHTS TO BRING ACTIONS.

(a) PROHIBITION.—No officer or employee of the United States may request a taxpayer to waive the taxpayer's right to bring a civil action against the United States or any officer or employee of the United States for any action taken in connection with the internal revenue laws.

(b) EXCEPTIONS.—Subsection (a) shall not apply in any case where—

(1) a taxpayer waives the right described in subsection (a) knowingly and voluntarily; or

(2) the request by the officer or employee is made in person and the taxpayer's attorney or other federally authorized tax practitioner (within the meaning of section 7525(a)(3)(A) of the Internal Revenue Code of 1986) is present, or the request is made in writing to the taxpayer's attorney or other representative.

[Sec. 7526]

SEC. 7526. LOW-INCOME TAXPAYER CLINICS.

[Sec. 7526(a)]

(a) IN GENERAL.—The Secretary may, subject to the availability of appropriated funds, make grants to provide matching funds for the development, expansion, or continuation of qualified low income taxpayer clinics.

[Sec. 7526(b)]

(b) DEFINITIONS.—For purposes of this section—

(1) QUALIFIED LOW-INCOME TAXPAYER CLINIC.—

(A) IN GENERAL.—The term "qualified low-income taxpayer clinic" means a clinic that—

MISCELLANEOUS PROVISIONS

(i) does not charge more than a nominal fee for its services (except for reimbursement of actual costs incurred); and

(ii)(I) represents low-income taxpayers in controversies with the Internal Revenue Service; or

(II) operates programs to inform individuals for whom English is a second language about their rights and responsibilities under this title.

(B) REPRESENTATION OF LOW-INCOME TAXPAYERS.—A clinic meets the requirements of subparagraph (A)(ii)(I) if—

(i) at least 90 percent of the taxpayers represented by the clinic have incomes which do not exceed 250 percent of the poverty level, as determined in accordance with criteria established by the Director of the Office of Management and Budget; and

(ii) the amount in controversy for any taxable year generally does not exceed the amount specified in section 7463.

(2) CLINIC.—The term "clinic" includes—

(A) a clinical program at an accredited law, business, or accounting school in which students represent low-income taxpayers in controversies arising under this title; and

(B) an organization described in section 501(c) and exempt from tax under section 501(a) which satisfies the requirements of paragraph (1) through representation of taxpayers or referral of taxpayers to qualified representatives.

(3) QUALIFIED REPRESENTATIVE.—The term "qualified representative" means any individual (whether or not an attorney) who is authorized to practice before the Internal Revenue Service or the applicable court.

[Sec. 7526(c)]

(c) SPECIAL RULES AND LIMITATIONS.—

(1) AGGREGATE LIMITATION.—Unless otherwise provided by specific appropriation, the Secretary shall not allocate more than $6,000,000 per year (exclusive of costs of administering the program) to grants under this section.

(2) LIMITATION ON ANNUAL GRANTS TO A CLINIC.—The aggregate amount of grants which may be made under this section to a clinic for a year shall not exceed $100,000.

(3) MULTI-YEAR GRANTS.—Upon application of a qualified low-income taxpayer clinic, the Secretary is authorized to award a multi-year grant not to exceed 3 years.

(4) CRITERIA FOR AWARDS.—In determining whether to make a grant under this section, the Secretary shall consider—

(A) the numbers of taxpayers who will be served by the clinic, including the number of taxpayers in the geographical area for whom English is a second language;

(B) the existence of other low-income taxpayer clinics serving the same population;

(C) the quality of the program offered by the low-income taxpayer clinic, including the qualifications of its administrators and qualified representatives, and its record, if any, in providing service to low-income taxpayers; and

(D) alternative funding sources available to the clinic, including amounts received from other grants and contributions, and the endowment and resources of the institution sponsoring the clinic.

(5) REQUIREMENT OF MATCHING FUNDS.—A low-income taxpayer clinic must provide matching funds on a dollar-for-dollar basis for all grants provided under this section. Matching funds may include—

(A) the salary (including fringe benefits) of individuals performing services for the clinic; and

(B) the cost of equipment used in the clinic.

Indirect expenses, including general overhead of the institution sponsoring the clinic, shall not be counted as matching funds.

(6) PROVISION OF INFORMATION REGARDING QUALIFIED LOW-INCOME TAXPAYER CLINICS.—Notwithstanding any other provision of law, officers and employees of the Department of the Treasury may—

(A) advise taxpayers of the availability of, and eligibility requirements for receiving, advice and assistance from one or more specific qualified low-income taxpayer clinics receiving funding under this section, and

(B) provide information regarding the location of, and contact information for, such clinics.

Amendments

- **2019, Taxpayer First Act (P.L. 116-25)**

P.L. 116-25, §1402(a):

Amended Code Sec. 7526(c) by adding at the end a new paragraph (6). **Effective** 7-1-2019.

P.L. 116-25, §1403, provides:

SEC. 1403. NOTICE FROM IRS REGARDING CLOSURE OF TAXPAYER ASSISTANCE CENTERS.

Not later than 90 days before the date that a proposed closure of a Taxpayer Assistance Center would take effect, the Secretary of the Treasury (or the Secretary's delegate) shall—

(1) make publicly available (including by non-electronic means) a notice which—

(A) identifies the Taxpayer Assistance Center proposed for closure and the date of such proposed closure; and

(B) identifies the relevant alternative sources of taxpayer assistance which may be utilized by taxpayers affected by such proposed closure; and

(2) submit to Congress a written report that includes—

(A) the information included in the notice described in paragraph (1);

(B) the reasons for such proposed closure; and

(C) such other information as the Secretary may determine appropriate.

- **1998, IRS Restructuring and Reform Act of 1998 (P.L. 105-206)**

P.L. 105-206, §3601(a):

Amended chapter 77 by adding a new Code Sec. 7526. **Effective** 7-22-98.

[Sec. 7526A]

SEC. 7526A. RETURN PREPARATION PROGRAMS FOR APPLICABLE TAXPAYERS.

[Sec. 7526A(a)]

(a) ESTABLISHMENT OF VOLUNTEER INCOME TAX ASSISTANCE MATCHING GRANT PROGRAM.—The Secretary shall establish a Community Volunteer Income Tax Assistance Matching Grant Program under which the Secretary may, subject to the availability of appropriated funds, make grants to provide matching funds for the development, expansion, or continuation of qualified return preparation programs assisting applicable taxpayers and members of underserved populations.

[Sec. 7526A(b)]

(b) USE OF FUNDS.—

(1) IN GENERAL.—Qualified return preparation programs may use grants received under this section for—

(A) ordinary and necessary costs associated with program operation in accordance with cost principles under the applicable Office of Management and Budget circular, including—

(i) wages or salaries of persons coordinating the activities of the program,

(ii) developing training materials, conducting training, and performing quality reviews of the returns prepared under the program,

(iii) equipment purchases, and

(iv) vehicle-related expenses associated with remote or rural tax preparation services,

(B) outreach and educational activities described in subsection (c)(2)(B), and

(C) services related to financial education and capability, asset development, and the establishment of savings accounts in connection with tax return preparation.

(2) REQUIREMENT OF MATCHING FUNDS.—A qualified return preparation program must provide matching funds on a dollar-for-dollar basis for all grants provided under this section. Matching funds may include—

(A) the salary (including fringe benefits) of individuals performing services for the program,

(B) the cost of equipment used in the program, and

(C) other ordinary and necessary costs associated with the program.

Indirect expenses, including general overhead of any entity administering the program, shall not be counted as matching funds.

[Sec. 7526A(c)]

(c) APPLICATION.—

(1) IN GENERAL.—Each applicant for a grant under this section shall submit an application to the Secretary at such time, in such manner, and containing such information as the Secretary may reasonably require.

(2) PRIORITY.—In awarding grants under this section, the Secretary shall give priority to applications which demonstrate—

(A) assistance to applicable taxpayers, with emphasis on outreach to, and services for, such taxpayers,

(B) taxpayer outreach and educational activities relating to eligibility and availability of income supports available through this title, including the earned income tax credit, and

(C) specific outreach and focus on one or more underserved populations.

(3) AMOUNTS TAKEN INTO ACCOUNT.—In determining matching grants under this section, the Secretary shall only take into account amounts provided by the qualified return preparation program for expenses described in subsection (b).

[Sec. 7526A(d)]

(d) PROGRAM ADHERENCE.—

(1) IN GENERAL.—The Secretary shall establish procedures for, and shall conduct not less frequently than once every 5 calendar years during which a qualified return preparation program is operating under a grant under this section, periodic site visits—

(A) to ensure the program is carrying out the purposes of this section, and

(B) to determine whether the program meets such program adherence standards as the Secretary shall by regulation or other guidance prescribe.

(2) ADDITIONAL REQUIREMENTS FOR GRANT RECIPIENTS NOT MEETING PROGRAM ADHERENCE STANDARDS.—In the case of any qualified return preparation program which—

(A) is awarded a grant under this section, and

(B) is subsequently determined—

(i) not to meet the program adherence standards described in paragraph (1)(B), or

(ii) not to be otherwise carrying out the purposes of this section,

such program shall not be eligible for any additional grants under this section unless such program provides sufficient documentation of corrective measures established to address any such deficiencies determined.

[Sec. 7526A(e)]

(e) DEFINITIONS.—For purposes of this section—

(1) QUALIFIED RETURN PREPARATION PROGRAM.—The term "qualified return preparation program" means any program—

(A) which provides assistance to individuals, not less than 90 percent of whom are applicable taxpayers, in preparing and filing Federal income tax returns,

(B) which is administered by a qualified entity,

(C) in which all volunteers who assist in the preparation of Federal income tax returns meet the training requirements prescribed by the Secretary, and

(D) which uses a quality review process which reviews 100 percent of all returns.

(2) QUALIFIED ENTITY.—

(A) IN GENERAL.—The term "qualified entity" means any entity which—

(i) is an eligible organization,

(ii) is in compliance with Federal tax filing and payment requirements,

(iii) is not debarred or suspended from Federal contracts, grants, or cooperative agreements, and

(iv) agrees to provide documentation to substantiate any matching funds provided pursuant to the grant program under this section.

(B) ELIGIBLE ORGANIZATION.—The term "eligible organization" means—

(i) an institution of higher education which is described in section 102 (other than subsection (a)(1)(C) thereof) of the Higher Education Act of 1965 (20 U.S.C. 1002), as in effect on the date of the enactment of this section, and which has not been disqualified from participating in a program under title IV of such Act,

(ii) an organization described in section 501(c) and exempt from tax under section 501(a),

(iii) a local government agency, including—

(I) a county or municipal government agency, and

(II) an Indian tribe, as defined in section 4(13) of the Native American Housing Assistance and Self-Determination Act of 1996 (25 U.S.C. 4103(13)), including any tribally designated housing entity (as defined in section 4(22) of such Act (25 U.S.C. 4103(22))), tribal subsidiary, subdivision, or other wholly owned tribal entity,

(iv) a local, State, regional, or national coalition (with one lead organization which meets the eligibility requirements of clause (i), (ii), or (iii) acting as the applicant organization), or

(v) in the case of applicable taxpayers and members of underserved populations with respect to which no organizations described in the preceding clauses are available—

(I) a State government agency, or

MISCELLANEOUS PROVISIONS

(II) an office providing Cooperative Extension services (as established at the land-grant colleges and universities under the Smith-Lever Act of May 8, 1914).

(3) APPLICABLE TAXPAYERS.—The term "applicable taxpayer" means a taxpayer whose income for the taxable year does not exceed an amount equal to the completed phaseout amount under section 32(b) for a married couple filing a joint return with three or more qualifying children, as determined in a revenue procedure or other published guidance.

(4) UNDERSERVED POPULATION.—The term "underserved population" includes populations of persons with disabilities, persons with limited English proficiency, Native Americans, individuals living in rural areas, members of the Armed Forces and their spouses, and the elderly.

[Sec. 7526A(f)]

(f) SPECIAL RULES AND LIMITATIONS.—

(1) DURATION OF GRANTS.—Upon application of a qualified return preparation program, the Secretary is authorized to award a multi-year grant not to exceed 3 years.

(2) AGGREGATE LIMITATION.—Unless otherwise provided by specific appropriation, the Secretary shall not allocate more than $30 million per fiscal year (exclusive of costs of administering the program) to grants under this section.

[Sec. 7526A(g)]

(g) PROMOTION OF PROGRAMS.—

(1) IN GENERAL.—The Secretary shall promote tax preparation through qualified return preparation programs through the use of mass communications and other means.

(2) PROVISION OF INFORMATION REGARDING QUALIFIED RETURN PREPARATION PROGRAMS.—The Secretary may provide taxpayers information regarding qualified return preparation programs receiving grants under this section.

(3) REFERRALS TO LOW-INCOME TAXPAYER CLINICS.—Qualified return preparation programs receiving a grant under this section are encouraged, in appropriate cases, to—

(A) advise taxpayers of the availability of, and eligibility requirements for receiving, advice and assistance from qualified low-income taxpayer clinics receiving funding under section 7526, and

(B) provide information regarding the location of, and contact information for, such clinics.

Amendments

• 2019, Taxpayer First Act (P.L. 116-25)

P.L. 116-25, § 1401(a):

Amended chapter 77 by inserting after Code Sec. 7526 a new Code Sec. 7526A. **Effective** 7-1-2019.

[Sec. 7527]

SEC. 7527. ADVANCE PAYMENT OF CREDIT FOR HEALTH INSURANCE COSTS OF ELIGIBLE INDIVIDUALS.

[Sec. 7527(a)]

(a) GENERAL RULE.—Not later than the date that is 1 year after the date of the enactment of the Trade Adjustment Assistance Reauthorization Act of 2015, the Secretary shall establish a program for making payments on behalf of certified individuals to providers of qualified health insurance (as defined in section 35(e)) for such individuals.

Amendments

• 2015, Trade Adjustment Assistance Reauthorization Act of 2015 (P.L. 114-27)

P.L. 114-27, § 407(c)(1):

Amended Code Sec. 7527(a) by striking "August 1, 2003" and inserting "the date that is 1 year after the date of the enactment of the Trade Adjustment Assistance Reauthorization Act of 2015". **Effective** generally for coverage months in tax years beginning after 12-31-2013. For a transition rule, see Act Sec. 407(f)(3), below.

P.L. 114-27, § 407(f)(3), provides:

(3) TRANSITION RULE.—Notwithstanding section 35(g)(11)(B)(i) of the Internal Revenue Code of 1986 (as added by this title), an election to apply section 35 of such Code to an eligible coverage month (as defined in section 35(b) of such Code) (and not to claim the credit under section 36B of such Code with respect to such month) in a taxable year beginning after December 31, 2013, and before the date of the enactment of this Act—

(A) may be made at any time on or after such date of enactment and before the expiration of the 3-year period of limitation prescribed in section 6511(a) with respect to such taxable year; and

(B) may be made on an amended return.

[Sec. 7527(b)]

(b) LIMITATION ON ADVANCE PAYMENTS DURING ANY TAXABLE YEAR.—The Secretary may make payments under subsection (a) only to the extent that the total amount of such payments made on behalf of any individual during the taxable year does not exceed 72.5 percent of the amount paid by the taxpayer for coverage of the taxpayer and qualifying family members under qualified health insurance for eligible coverage months beginning in the taxable year.

Amendments

• 2011, Trade Adjustment Assistance Extension Act of 2011 (P.L. 112-40)

P.L. 112-40, § 241(b)(2)(A):

Amended Code Sec. 7527(b) by striking "65 percent (80 percent in the case of eligible coverage months beginning before February 13, 2011)" and inserting "72.5 percent". **Effective** for coverage months beginning after 2-12-2011.

• 2010, Omnibus Trade Act of 2010 (P.L. 111-344)

P.L. 111-344, § 111(b):

Amended Code Sec. 7527(b) by striking "January 1, 2011" and inserting "February 13, 2011". **Effective** for coverage months beginning after 12-31-2010.

• 2009, TAA Health Coverage Improvement Act of 2009 (P.L. 111-5)

P.L. 111-5, § 1899A(a)(2):

Amended Code Sec. 7527(b) by inserting "(80 percent in the case of eligible coverage months beginning before January 1, 2011)" after "65 percent". **Effective** for coverage months beginning on or after the first day of the first month beginning 60 days after 2-17-2009.

[Sec. 7527(c)]

(c) CERTIFIED INDIVIDUAL.—For purposes of this section, the term "certified individual" means any individual for whom a qualified health insurance costs credit eligibility certificate is in effect.

[Sec. 7527(d)]

(d) QUALIFIED HEALTH INSURANCE COSTS ELIGIBILITY CERTIFICATE.—

(1) IN GENERAL.—For purposes of this section, the term "qualified health insurance costs eligibility certificate" means any written statement that an individual is an eligible individual (as defined in section 35(c)) if such statement provides such information as the Secretary may require for purposes of this section and—

MISCELLANEOUS PROVISIONS

(A) in the case of an eligible TAA recipient (as defined in section 35(c)(2)) or an eligible alternative TAA recipient (as defined in section 35(c)(3)), is certified by the Secretary of Labor (or by any other person or entity designated by the Secretary), or

(B) in the case of an eligible PBGC pension recipient (as defined in section 35(c)(4)), is certified by the Pension Benefit Guaranty Corporation (or by any other person or entity designated by the Secretary).

(2) INCLUSION OF CERTAIN INFORMATION.—In the case of any statement described in paragraph (1), such statement shall not be treated as a qualified health insurance costs credit eligibility certificate unless such statement includes—

(A) the name, address, and telephone number of the State office or offices responsible for providing the individual with assistance with enrollment in qualified health insurance (as defined in section 35(e)),

(B) a list of the coverage options that are treated as qualified health insurance (as so defined) by the State in which the individual resides, and

(C) in the case of a TAA-eligible individual (as defined in section 4980B(f)(5)(C)(iv)(II)), a statement informing the individual that the individual has 63 days from the date that is 7 days after the date of the issuance of such certificate to enroll in such insurance without a lapse in creditable coverage (as defined in section 9801(c)).

Amendments

• **2011, Trade Adjustment Assistance Extension Act of 2011 (P.L. 112-40)**

P.L. 112-40, §241(b)(2)(B):

Amended Code Sec. 7527(d)(2) by striking "which is issued before February 13, 2011" following "statement described in paragraph (1)". **Effective** for certificates issued after the date which is 30 days after 10-21-2011.

• **2010, Omnibus Trade Act of 2010 (P.L. 111-344)**

P.L. 111-344, §118(a):

Amended Code Sec. 7527(d)(2) by striking "January 1, 2011" and inserting "February 13, 2011". **Effective** for certificates issued after 12-31-2010.

• **2009, TAA Health Coverage Improvement Act of 2009 (P.L. 111-5)**

P.L. 111-5, §1899H(a):

Amended Code Sec. 7527(d). **Effective** for certificates issued after the date that is 6 months after 2-17-2009. Prior to amendment, Code Sec. 7527(d) read as follows:

(d) QUALIFIED HEALTH INSURANCE COSTS CREDIT ELIGIBILITY CERTIFICATE.—For purposes of this section, the term "qualified health insurance costs credit eligibility certificate" means any written statement that an individual is an eligible individual (as defined in section 35(c)) if such statement provides such information as the Secretary may require for purposes of this section and—

(1) in the case of an eligible TAA recipient (as defined in section 35(c)(2)) or an eligible alternative TAA recipient (as defined in section 35(c)(3)), is certified by the Secretary of Labor (or by any other person or entity designated by the Secretary), or

(2) in the case of an eligible PBGC pension recipient (as defined in section 35(c)(4)), is certified by the Pension Benefit Guaranty Corporation (or by any other person or entity designated by the Secretary).

• **2002, Trade Act of 2002 (P.L. 107-210)**

P.L. 107-210, §202(a):

Amended chapter 77 by adding at the end a new Code Sec. 7527. **Effective** 8-6-2002.

[Sec. 7527(e)]

(e) PAYMENT FOR PREMIUMS DUE PRIOR TO COMMENCEMENT OF ADVANCE PAYMENTS.—

(1) IN GENERAL.—The program established under subsection (a) shall provide that the Secretary shall make 1 or more retroactive payments on behalf of a certified individual in an aggregate amount equal to 72.5 percent of the premiums for coverage of the taxpayer and qualifying family members under qualified health insurance for eligible coverage months (as defined in section 35(b)) occurring—

(A) after the date that is 1 year after the date of the enactment of the Trade Adjustment Assistance Reauthorization Act of 2015, and

(B) prior to the first month for which an advance payment is made on behalf of such individual under subsection (a).

(2) REDUCTION OF PAYMENT FOR AMOUNTS RECEIVED UNDER NATIONAL EMERGENCY GRANTS.—The amount of any payment determined under paragraph (1) shall be reduced by the amount of any payment made to the taxpayer for the purchase of qualified health insurance under a national emergency grant pursuant to section 173(f) of the Workforce Investment Act of 1998 (as in effect on the day before the date of enactment of the Workforce Innovation and Opportunity Act) for a taxable year including the eligible coverage months described in paragraph (1).

Amendments

• **2015, Trade Adjustment Assistance Reauthorization Act of 2015 (P.L. 114-27)**

P.L. 114-27, §407(c)(2):

Amended Code Sec. 7527(e)(1) by striking "occurring" and all that follows and inserting "occurring—"and new subparagraphs (A)-(B). **Effective** generally for coverage months in tax years beginning after 12-31-2013. For a transition rule, see Act Sec. 407(f)(3), below. Prior to being stricken, all that follows "occurring" in Code Sec. 7527(e)(1) read as follows:

prior to the first month for which an advance payment is made on behalf of such individual under subsection (a).

P.L. 114-27, §407(f)(3), provides:

(3) TRANSITION RULE.—Notwithstanding section 35(g)(11)(B)(i) of the Internal Revenue Code of 1986 (as added by this title), an election to apply section 35 of such Code to an eligible coverage month (as defined in section 35(b) of such Code) (and not to claim the credit under section 36B of such Code with respect to such month) in a taxable year beginning after December 31, 2013, and before the date of the enactment of this Act—

(A) may be made at any time on or after such date of enactment and before the expiration of the 3-year period of limitation prescribed in section 6511(a) with respect to such taxable year; and

(B) may be made on an amended return.

• **2014, Workforce Innovation and Opportunity Act (P.L. 113-128)**

P.L. 113-128, §512(r):

Amended Code Sec. 7527(e)(2) by inserting "(as in effect on the day before the date of enactment of the Workforce Innovation and Opportunity Act)" after "of 1998". **Effective** 7-22-2014.

• **2011, Trade Adjustment Assistance Extension Act of 2011 (P.L. 112-40)**

P.L. 112-40, §241(b)(2)(C):

Amended Code Sec. 7527(e)[(1)] by striking "80 percent" and inserting "72.5 percent". **Effective** for coverage months beginning after 2-12-2011.

P.L. 112-40, §241(b)(2)(D):

Amended Code Sec. 7527(e) by striking "In the case of eligible coverage months beginning before February 13, 2011—"before the text of paragraph (1). **Effective** for coverage months beginning after the date which is 30 days after 10-21-2011.

• **2010, Omnibus Trade Act of 2010 (P.L. 111-344)**

P.L. 111-344, §112(a):

Amended Code Sec. 7527(e) by striking "January 1, 2011" and inserting "February 13, 2011". **Effective** for coverage months beginning after 12-31-2010.

• **2009, TAA Health Coverage Improvement Act of 2009 (P.L. 111-5)**

P.L. 111-5, §1899B(a):

Amended Code Sec. 7527 by adding at the end a new subsection (e). **Effective** for coverage months beginning after 12-31-2008. For a transitional rule, see Act Sec. 1899B(c), below.

P.L. 111-5, §1899B(c), provides:

(c) TRANSITIONAL RULE.—The Secretary of the Treasury shall not be required to make any payments under section 7527(e) of the Internal Revenue Code of 1986, as added by this section, until after the date that is 6 months after the date of the enactment of this Act.

[Sec. 7527A]

SEC. 7527A. ADVANCE PAYMENT OF CHILD TAX CREDIT.

[Sec. 7527A(a)]

(a) IN GENERAL.—The Secretary shall establish a program for making periodic payments to taxpayers which, in the aggregate during any calendar year, equal the annual advance amount determined with respect to such taxpayer for such calendar year. Except as provided in subsection (b)(3)(B), the periodic payments made to any taxpayer for any calendar year shall be in equal amounts.

[Sec. 7527A(b)]

(b) ANNUAL ADVANCE AMOUNT.—For purposes of this section—

MISCELLANEOUS PROVISIONS

(1) IN GENERAL.—Except as otherwise provided in this subsection, the term "annual advance amount" means, with respect to any taxpayer for any calendar year, the amount (if any) which is estimated by the Secretary as being equal to 50 percent of the amount which would be treated as allowed under subpart C of part IV of subchapter A of chapter 1 by reason of section 24(i)(1) for the taxpayer's taxable year beginning in such calendar year if—

(A) the status of the taxpayer as a taxpayer described in section 24(i)(1) is determined with respect to the reference taxable year,

(B) the taxpayer's modified adjusted gross income for such taxable year is equal to the taxpayer's modified adjusted gross income for the reference taxable year,

(C) the only children of such taxpayer for such taxable year are qualifying children properly claimed on the taxpayer's return of tax for the reference taxable year, and

(D) the ages of such children (and the status of such children as qualifying children) are determined for such taxable year by taking into account the passage of time since the reference taxable year.

(2) REFERENCE TAXABLE YEAR.—Except as provided in paragraph (3)(A), the term "reference taxable year" means, with respect to any taxpayer for any calendar year, the taxpayer's taxable year beginning in the preceding calendar year or, in the case of taxpayer who did not file a return of tax for such taxable year, the taxpayer's taxable year beginning in the second preceding calendar year.

(3) MODIFICATIONS DURING CALENDAR YEAR.—

(A) IN GENERAL.—The Secretary may modify, during any calendar year, the annual advance amount with respect to any taxpayer for such calendar year to take into account—

(i) a return of tax filed by such taxpayer during such calendar year (and the taxable year to which such return relates may be taken into account as the reference taxable year), and

(ii) any other information provided by the taxpayer to the Secretary which allows the Secretary to determine payments under subsection (a) which, in the aggregate during any taxable year of the taxpayer, more closely total the Secretary's estimate of the amount treated as allowed under subpart C of part IV of subchapter A of chapter 1 by reason of section 24(i)(1) for such taxable year of such taxpayer.

(B) ADJUSTMENT TO REFLECT EXCESS OR DEFICIT IN PRIOR PAYMENTS.—In the case of any modification of the annual advance amount under subparagraph (A), the Secretary may adjust the amount of any periodic payment made after the date of such modification to properly take into account the amount by which any periodic payment made before such date was greater than or less than the amount that such payment would have been on the basis of the annual advance amount as so modified.

(4) DETERMINATION OF STATUS.—If information contained in the taxpayer's return of tax for the reference taxable year does not establish the status of the taxpayer as being described in section 24(i)(1), the Secretary shall, for purposes of paragraph (1)(A), determine such status based on information known to the Secretary.

(5) TREATMENT OF CERTAIN DEATHS.—A child shall not be taken into account in determining the annual advance amount under paragraph (1) if the death of such child is known to the Secretary as of the beginning of the calendar year for which the estimate under such paragraph is made.

[Sec. 7527A(c)]

(c) ON-LINE INFORMATION PORTAL.—The Secretary shall establish an on-line portal which allows taxpayers to—

(1) elect not to receive payments under this section, and

(2) provide information to the Secretary which would be relevant to a modification under subsection (b)(3)(B) of the annual advance amount, including information regarding—

(A) a change in the number of the taxpayer's qualifying children, including by reason of the birth of a child,

(B) a change in the taxpayer's marital status,

(C) a significant change in the taxpayer's income, and

(D) any other factor which the Secretary may provide.

[Sec. 7527A(d)]

(d) NOTICE OF PAYMENTS.—Not later than January 31 of the calendar year following any calendar year during which the Secretary makes one or more payments to any taxpayer under this section, the Secretary shall provide such taxpayer with a written notice which includes the taxpayer's taxpayer identity (as defined in section 6103(b)(6)), the aggregate amount of such payments made to such taxpayer during such calendar year, and such other information as the Secretary determines appropriate.

[Sec. 7527A(e)]

(e) ADMINISTRATIVE PROVISIONS.—

(1) APPLICATION OF ELECTRONIC FUNDS PAYMENT REQUIREMENT.—The payments made by the Secretary under subsection (a) shall be made by electronic funds transfer to the same extent and in the same manner as if such payments were Federal payments not made under this title.

(2) APPLICATION OF CERTAIN RULES.—Rules similar to the rules of subparagraphs (B) and (C) of section 6428A(f)(3) shall apply for purposes of this section.

(3) EXCEPTION FROM REDUCTION OR OFFSET.—Any payment made to any individual under this section shall not be—

(A) subject to reduction or offset pursuant to subsection (c), (d), (e), or (f) of section 6402 or any similar authority permitting offset, or

(B) reduced or offset by other assessed Federal taxes that would otherwise be subject to levy or collection.

(4) APPLICATION OF ADVANCE PAYMENTS IN THE POSSESSIONS OF THE UNITED STATES.—

(A) IN GENERAL.—The advance payment amount determined under this section shall be determined—

(i) by applying section 24(i)(1) without regard to the phrase "or is a bona fide resident of Puerto Rico (within the meaning of section 937(a))", and

(ii) without regard to section 24(k)(3)(C)(ii)(I).

(B) MIRROR CODE POSSESSIONS.—In the case of any possession of the United States with a mirror code tax system (as defined in section 24(k)), this section shall not be treated as part of the income tax laws of the United States for purposes of determining the income tax law of such possession unless such possession elects to have this section be so treated.

(C) ADMINISTRATIVE EXPENSES OF ADVANCE PAYMENTS.—

(i) MIRROR CODE POSSESSIONS.—In the case of any possession described in subparagraph (B) which makes the election described in such subparagraph, the amount otherwise paid by the Secretary to such possession under section 24(k)(1)(A) with respect to taxable years beginning in 2021 shall be increased by $300,000 if such possession has a plan, which has been approved by the Secretary, for making advance payments consistent with such election.

(ii) AMERICAN SAMOA.—The amount otherwise paid by the Secretary to American Samoa under subparagraph (A) of section 24(k)(3) with respect to taxable years beginning in 2021 shall be increased by $300,000 if the plan described in subparagraph (B) of such section includes a program, which has been approved by the Secretary, for making advance payments under rules similar to the rules of this section.

(iii) TIMING OF PAYMENT.—The Secretary may pay, upon the request of the possession of the United States to which the payment is to be made, the amount of the increase determined under clause (i) or (ii) immediately upon approval of the plan referred to in such clause, respectively.

[Sec. 7527A(f)]

(f) APPLICATION.—No payments shall be made under the program established under subsection (a) with respect to—

(1) any period before July 1, 2021, or

(2) any period after December 31, 2021.

[Sec. 7527A(g)]

(g) REGULATIONS.—The Secretary shall issue such regulations or other guidance as the Secretary determines necessary or appropriate to carry out the purposes of this section and subsections (i)(1) and (j) of section 24, including regulations or other guidance which provides for the application of such provisions where the filing status of the taxpayer for a taxable year is different from the status used for determining the annual advance amount.

Amendments

• **2021, American Rescue Plan Act of 2021 (P.L. 117-2)**

P.L. 117-2, § 9611(b)(1):

Amended chapter 77 by inserting after Code Sec. 7527 a new Code Sec. 7527A. **Effective** for tax years beginning after 12-31-2020. For a special rule, see Act Sec. 9611(c)(2), below.

P.L. 117-2, § 9611(c)(2), provides:

(2) ESTABLISHMENT OF ADVANCE PAYMENT PROGRAM.—The Secretary of the Treasury (or the Secretary's designee) shall establish the program described in section 7527A of the Internal Revenue Code of 1986 as soon as practicable after the date of the enactment of this Act, except that the Secretary shall ensure that the timing of the establishment of such program does not interfere with carrying out section 6428B(g) as rapidly as possible.

[Sec. 7528]

SEC. 7528. INTERNAL REVENUE SERVICE USER FEES.

[Sec. 7528(a)]

(a) GENERAL RULE.—The Secretary shall establish a program requiring the payment of user fees for—

(1) requests to the Internal Revenue Service for ruling letters, opinion letters, and determination letters, and

(2) other similar requests.

[Sec. 7528(b)]

(b) PROGRAM CRITERIA.—

(1) IN GENERAL.—The fees charged under the program required by subsection (a)—

(A) shall vary according to categories (or subcategories) established by the Secretary,

(B) shall be determined after taking into account the average time for (and difficulty of) complying with requests in each category (and subcategory), and

(C) shall be payable in advance.

(2) EXEMPTIONS, ETC.—

(A) IN GENERAL.—The Secretary shall provide for such exemptions (and reduced fees) under such program as the Secretary determines to be appropriate.

(B) EXEMPTION FOR CERTAIN REQUESTS REGARDING PENSION PLANS.—The Secretary shall not require payment of user fees under such program for requests for determination letters with respect to the qualified status of a pension benefit plan maintained solely by 1 or more eligible employers or any trust which is part of the plan. The preceding sentence shall not apply to any request—

(i) made after the later of—

(I) the fifth plan year the pension benefit plan is in existence, or

(II) the end of any remedial amendment period with respect to the plan beginning within the first 5 plan years, or

(ii) made by the sponsor of any prototype or similar plan which the sponsor intends to market to participating employers.

(C) DEFINITIONS AND SPECIAL RULES.—For purposes of subparagraph (B)—

(i) PENSION BENEFIT PLAN.—The term "pension benefit plan" means a pension, profit-sharing, stock bonus, annuity, or employee stock ownership plan.

(ii) ELIGIBLE EMPLOYER.—The term "eligible employer" means an eligible employer (as defined in section 408(p)(2)(C)(i)(I)) which has at least 1 employee who is not a highly compensated employee (as defined in section 414(q)) and is participating in the plan. The determination of whether an employer is an eligible employer under subparagraph (B) shall be made as of the date of the request described in such subparagraph.

(iii) DETERMINATION OF AVERAGE FEES CHARGED.—For purposes of any determination of average fees charged, any request to which subparagraph (B) applies shall not be taken into account.

(3) AVERAGE FEE REQUIREMENT.—The average fee charged under the program required by subsection (a) shall not be less than the amount determined under the following table:

Category	Average Fee
Employee plan ruling and opinion	$250
Exempt organization ruling	$350
Employee plan determination	$300
Exempt organization determination	$275
Chief counsel ruling	$200

(4) CERTIFIED PROFESSIONAL EMPLOYER ORGANIZATIONS.—The fee charged under the program in connection with the certification by the Secretary of a professional employer organization under section 7705 shall be an annual fee not to exceed $1,000 per year.

MISCELLANEOUS PROVISIONS

Amendments

• **2014, Stephen Beck, Jr., Achieving a Better Life Experience Act of 2014 (P.L. 113-295)**

P.L. 113-295, §206(f), Division B:

Amended Code Sec. 7528(b) by adding at the end a new paragraph (4). **Effective** for wages for services performed on or after January 1 of the first calendar year beginning more than 12 months after 12-19-2014. For a special rule, see P.L. 113-295, §206(h), Division B, below.

Amendments

• **2007, Small Business and Work Opportunity Tax Act of 2007 (P.L. 110-28)**

P.L. 110-28, §8244:

Amended Code Sec. 7528 by striking subsection (c). **Effective** 5-25-2007. Prior to being stricken, Code Sec. 7528(c) read as follows:

(c) TERMINATION.—No fee shall be imposed under this section with respect to requests made after September 30, 2014.

• **2004, American Jobs Creation Act of 2004 (P.L. 108-357)**

P.L. 108-357, §891(a):

Amended Code Sec. 7528(c) by striking "December 31, 2004" and inserting "September 30, 2014". **Effective** for requests after 10-22-2004.

SEC. 7529. NOTIFICATION OF SUSPECTED IDENTITY THEFT.

P.L. 113-295, §206(h), Division B, provides:

(h) NO INFERENCE.—Nothing contained in this section or the amendments made by this section shall be construed to create any inference with respect to the determination of who is an employee or employer—

(1) for Federal tax purposes (other than the purposes set forth in the amendments made by this section), or

(2) for purposes of any other provision of law.

[Sec. 7528(c)—Stricken]

• **2003 (P.L. 108-89)**

P.L. 108-89, §202(a):

Amended chapter 77 by adding at the end a new Code Sec. 7528. **Effective** for requests made after 10-1-2003.

P.L. 108-89, §202(c), provides:

(c) LIMITATIONS.—Notwithstanding any other provision of law, any fees collected pursuant to section 7528 of the Internal Revenue Code of 1986, as added by subsection (a), shall not be expended by the Internal Revenue Service unless provided by an appropriations Act.

[Sec. 7529]

[Sec. 7529(a)]

(a) IN GENERAL.—If the Secretary determines that there has been or may have been an unauthorized use of the identity of any individual, the Secretary shall, without jeopardizing an investigation relating to tax administration—

(1) as soon as practicable—

(A) notify the individual of such determination,

(B) provide instructions on how to file a report with law enforcement regarding the unauthorized use,

(C) identify any steps to be taken by the individual to permit law enforcement to access personal information of the individual during the investigation,

(D) provide information regarding actions the individual may take in order to protect the individual from harm relating to the unauthorized use, and

(E) offer identity protection measures to the individual, such as the use of an identity protection personal identification number, and

(2) at the time the information described in paragraph (1) is provided (or, if not available at such time, as soon as practicable thereafter), issue additional notifications to such individual (or such individual's designee) regarding—

(A) whether an investigation has been initiated in regards to such unauthorized use,

(B) whether the investigation substantiated an unauthorized use of the identity of the individual, and

(C) whether—

(i) any action has been taken against a person relating to such unauthorized use, or

(ii) any referral has been made for criminal prosecution of such person and, to the extent such information is available, whether such person has been criminally charged by indictment or information.

[Sec. 7529(b)]

(b) EMPLOYMENT-RELATED IDENTITY THEFT.—

(1) IN GENERAL.—For purposes of this section, the unauthorized use of the identity of an individual includes the unauthorized use of the identity of the individual to obtain employment.

(2) DETERMINATION OF EMPLOYMENT-RELATED IDENTITY THEFT.—For purposes of this section, in making a determination as to whether there has been or may have been an unauthorized use of the identity of an individual to obtain employment, the Secretary shall review any information—

(A) obtained from a statement described in section 6051 or an information return relating to compensation for services rendered other than as an employee, or

(B) provided to the Internal Revenue Service by the Social Security Administration regarding any statement described in section 6051,

which indicates that the social security account number provided on such statement or information return does not correspond with the name provided on such statement or information return or the name on the tax return reporting the income which is included on such statement or information return.

Amendments

• **2019, Taxpayer First Act (P.L. 116-25)**

P.L. 116-25, §2007(a):

Amended chapter 77 by adding at the end a new Code Sec. 7529. **Effective** for determinations made after the date that is 6 months after 7-1-2019. For a special rule, see Act Sec. 2007(b)(1) and (3), below.

P.L. 116-25, §2007(b)(1) and (3), provides:

(b) ADDITIONAL MEASURES.—

(1) EXAMINATION OF BOTH PAPER AND ELECTRONIC STATEMENTS AND RETURNS.—The Secretary of the Treasury (or the Secretary's delegate) shall examine the statements, information returns, and tax returns described in section 7529(b)(2) of the Internal Revenue Code of 1986 (as added by subsection (a)) for any evidence of employment-related identity theft, regardless of whether such statements or returns are submitted electronically or on paper.

***

(3) UNDERREPORTING OF INCOME.—The Secretary of the Treasury (or the Secretary's delegate) shall establish procedures to ensure that income reported in connection with the unauthorized use of a taxpayer's identity is not taken into account in determining any penalty for underreporting of income by the victim of identity theft.

Sec. 7528(c)—Stricken

MISCELLANEOUS PROVISIONS

[Sec. 7530]
SEC. 7530. APPLICATION OF EARNED INCOME TAX CREDIT TO POSSESSIONS OF THE UNITED STATES.

[Sec. 7530(a)]
(a) PUERTO RICO.—

(1) IN GENERAL.—With respect to calendar year 2021 and each calendar year thereafter, the Secretary shall, except as otherwise provided in this subsection, make payments to Puerto Rico equal to—

(A) the specified matching amount for such calendar year, plus

(B) in the case of calendar years 2021 through 2025, the lesser of—

(i) the expenditures made by Puerto Rico during such calendar year for education efforts with respect to individual taxpayers and tax return preparers relating to the earned income tax credit, or

(ii) $1,000,000.

(2) REQUIREMENT TO REFORM EARNED INCOME TAX CREDIT.—The Secretary shall not make any payments under paragraph (1) with respect to any calendar year unless Puerto Rico has in effect an earned income tax credit for taxable years beginning in or with such calendar year which (relative to the earned income tax credit which was in effect for taxable years beginning in or with calendar year 2019) increases the percentage of earned income which is allowed as a credit for each group of individuals with respect to which such percentage is separately stated or determined in a manner designed to substantially increase workforce participation.

(3) SPECIFIED MATCHING AMOUNT.—For purposes of this subsection—

(A) IN GENERAL.—The term "specified matching amount" means, with respect to any calendar year, the lesser of—

(i) the excess (if any) of—

(I) the cost to Puerto Rico of the earned income tax credit for taxable years beginning in or with such calendar year, over

(II) the base amount for such calendar year, or

(ii) the product of 3, multiplied by the base amount for such calendar year.

(B) BASE AMOUNT.—

(i) BASE AMOUNT FOR 2021.—In the case of calendar year 2021, the term "base amount" means the greater of—

(I) the cost to Puerto Rico of the earned income tax credit for taxable years beginning in or with calendar year 2019 (rounded to the nearest multiple of $1,000,000), or

(II) $200,000,000.

(ii) INFLATION ADJUSTMENT.—In the case of any calendar year after 2021, the term "base amount" means the dollar amount determined under clause (i) increased by an amount equal to—

(I) such dollar amount, multiplied by—

(II) the cost-of-living adjustment determined under section 1(f)(3) for such calendar year, determined by substituting "calendar year 2020" for "calendar year 2016" in subparagraph (A)(ii) thereof.

Any amount determined under this clause shall be rounded to the nearest multiple of $1,000,000.

(4) RULES RELATED TO PAYMENTS.—

(A) TIMING OF PAYMENTS.—The Secretary shall make payments under paragraph (1) for any calendar year—

(i) after receipt of such information as the Secretary may require to determine such payments, and

(ii) except as provided in clause (i), within a reasonable period of time before the due date for individual income tax returns (as determined under the laws of Puerto Rico) for taxable years which began on the first day of such calendar year.

(B) INFORMATION.—The Secretary may require the reporting of such information as the Secretary may require to carry out this subsection.

(C) DETERMINATION OF COST OF EARNED INCOME TAX CREDIT.—For purposes of this subsection, the cost to Puerto Rico of the earned income tax credit shall be determined by the Secretary on the basis of the laws of Puerto Rico and shall include reductions in revenues received by Puerto Rico by reason of such credit and refunds attributable to such credit, but shall not include any administrative costs with respect to such credit.

[Sec. 7530(b)]
(b) POSSESSIONS WITH MIRROR CODE TAX SYSTEMS.—

(1) IN GENERAL.—With respect to calendar year 2021 and each calendar year thereafter, the Secretary shall, except as otherwise provided in this subsection, make payments to the Virgin Islands, Guam, and the Commonwealth of the Northern Mariana Islands equal to—

(A) the cost to such possession of the earned income tax credit for taxable years beginning in or with such calendar year, plus

(B) in the case of calendar years 2021 through 2025, the lesser of—

(i) the expenditures made by such possession during such calendar year for education efforts with respect to individual taxpayers and tax return preparers relating to such earned income tax credit, or

(ii) $50,000.

(2) APPLICATION OF CERTAIN RULES.—Rules similar to the rules of subparagraphs (A), (B), and (C) of subsection (a)(4) shall apply for purposes of this subsection.

[Sec. 7530(c)]
(c) AMERICAN SAMOA.—

(1) IN GENERAL.—With respect to calendar year 2021 and each calendar year thereafter, the Secretary shall, except as otherwise provided in this subsection, make payments to American Samoa equal to—

(A) the lesser of—

(i) the cost to American Samoa of the earned income tax credit for taxable years beginning in or with such calendar year, or

(ii) $16,000,000, plus

(B) in the case of calendar years 2021 through 2025, the lesser of—

(i) the expenditures made by American Samoa during such calendar year for education efforts with respect to individual taxpayers and tax return preparers relating to such earned income tax credit, or

(ii) $50,000.

(2) REQUIREMENT TO ENACT AND MAINTAIN AN EARNED INCOME TAX CREDIT.—The Secretary shall not make any payments under paragraph (1) with respect to any calendar year unless American Samoa has in effect an earned income tax credit for taxable years beginning in or with such

ENFORCEMENT—EXAMINATION

calendar year which allows a refundable tax credit to individuals on the basis of the taxpayer's earned income which is designed to substantially increase workforce participation.

(3) INFLATION ADJUSTMENT.—In the case of any calendar year after 2021, the $16,000,000 amount in paragraph (1)(A)(ii) shall be increased by an amount equal to—

(A) such dollar amount, multiplied by—

(B) the cost-of-living adjustment determined under section 1(f)(3) for such calendar year, determined by substituting "calendar year 2020" for "calendar year 2016" in subparagraph (A)(ii) thereof.

Any increase determined under this clause shall be rounded to the nearest multiple of $100,000.

(4) APPLICATION OF CERTAIN RULES.—Rules similar to the rules of subparagraphs (A), (B), and (C) of subsection (a)(4) shall apply for purposes of this subsection.

[Sec. 7530(d)]

(d) TREATMENT OF PAYMENTS.—For purposes of section 1324 of title 31, United States Code, the payments under this section shall be treated in the same manner as a refund due from a credit provision referred to in subsection (b)(2) of such section.

Amendments

• 2021, American Rescue Plan Act of 2021 (P.L. 117-2)

P.L. 117-2, §9625(a):

Amended chapter 77 by adding at the end a new Code Sec. 7530. **Effective** 3-11-2021.

CHAPTER 78—DISCOVERY OF LIABILITY AND ENFORCEMENT OF TITLE

SUBCHAPTER A.	Examination and inspection.
SUBCHAPTER B	General powers and duties.
SUBCHAPTER D.	Possessions.

Subchapter A—Examination and Inspection

Sec. 7601.	Canvass of districts for taxable persons and objects.
Sec. 7602.	Examination of books and witnesses.
Sec. 7603.	Service of summons.
Sec. 7604.	Enforcement of summons.
Sec. 7605.	Time and place of examination.
Sec. 7606.	Entry of premises for examination of taxable objects.
Sec. 7608.	Authority of internal revenue enforcement officers.
Sec. 7609.	Special procedures for third-party summonses.
Sec. 7610.	Fees and costs for witnesses.
Sec. 7611.	Restrictions on church tax inquiries and examinations.
Sec. 7612.	Special procedures for summonses for computer software.
Sec. 7613.	Cross references.

[Sec. 7601]

SEC. 7601. CANVASS OF DISTRICTS FOR TAXABLE PERSONS AND OBJECTS.

[Sec. 7601(a)]

(a) GENERAL RULE.—The Secretary shall, to the extent he deems it practicable, cause officers or employees of the Treasury Department to proceed, from time to time, through each internal revenue district and inquire after and concerning all persons therein who may be liable to pay any internal revenue tax, and all persons owning or having the care and management of any objects with respect to which any tax is imposed.

Amendments

• 1976, Tax Reform Act of 1976 (P.L. 94-455)

P.L. 94-455, §1906(b)(13)(A):

Amended 1954 Code by substituting "Secretary" for "Secretary or his delegate" each place it appeared. **Effective** 2-1-77.

[Sec. 7601(b)]

(b) PENALTIES.—

For penalties applicable to forcible obstruction or hindrance of Treasury officers or employees in the performance of their duties, see section 7212.

[Sec. 7602]

SEC. 7602. EXAMINATION OF BOOKS AND WITNESSES.

[Sec. 7602(a)]

(a) AUTHORITY TO SUMMON, ETC.—For the purpose of ascertaining the correctness of any return, making a return where none has been made, determining the liability of any person for any internal revenue tax or the liability at law or in equity of any transferee or fiduciary of any person in respect of any internal revenue tax, or collecting any such liability, the Secretary is authorized—

(1) To examine any books, papers, records, or other data which may be relevant or material to such inquiry;

(2) To summon the person liable for tax or required to perform the act, or any officer or employee of such person, or any person having possession, custody, or care of books of account containing entries relating to the business of the person liable for tax or required to perform the act, or any other person the Secretary may deem proper, to appear before the Secretary at a time and place named in the summons and to produce such books, papers, records, or other data, and to give such testimony, under oath, as may be relevant or material to such inquiry; and

(3) To take such testimony of the person concerned, under oath, as may be relevant or material to such inquiry.

Sec. 7530(c)(3)

ENFORCEMENT—EXAMINATION

Amendments

• **1982, Tax Equity and Fiscal Responsibility Act of 1982 (P.L. 97-248)**

P.L. 97-248, §333(a):

Amended Code Sec. 7602 by striking out "For the purpose" and inserting "(a) Authority to Summon, Etc.—For the purpose". **Effective** 9-4-82.

• **1976, Tax Reform Act of 1976 (P.L. 94-455)**

P.L. 94-455, §1906(b)(13)(A):

Amended 1954 Code by substituting "Secretary" for "Secretary or his delegate" each place it appeared. **Effective** 2-1-77.

[Sec. 7602(b)]

(b) PURPOSE MAY INCLUDE INQUIRY INTO OFFENSE.—The purposes for which the Secretary may take any action described in paragraph (1), (2), or (3) of subsection (a) include the purpose of inquiring into any offense connected with the administration or enforcement of the internal revenue laws.

Amendments

• **1982, Tax Equity and Fiscal Responsibility Act of 1982 (P.L. 97-248)**

P.L. 97-248, §333(a):

Added Code Sec. 7602(b). **Effective** 9-4-82.

[Sec. 7602(c)]

(c) NOTICE OF CONTACT OF THIRD PARTIES.—

(1) GENERAL NOTICE.—An officer or employee of the Internal Revenue Service may not contact any person other than the taxpayer with respect to the determination or collection of the tax liability of such taxpayer unless such contact occurs during a period (not greater than 1 year) which is specified in a notice which—

(A) informs the taxpayer that contacts with persons other than the taxpayer are intended to be made during such period, and

(B) except as otherwise provided by the Secretary, is provided to the taxpayer not later than 45 days before the beginning of such period.

Nothing in the preceding sentence shall prevent the issuance of notices to the same taxpayer with respect to the same tax liability with periods specified therein that, in the aggregate, exceed 1 year. A notice shall not be issued under this paragraph unless there is an intent at the time such notice is issued to contact persons other than the taxpayer during the period specified in such notice. The preceding sentence shall not prevent the issuance of a notice if the requirement of such sentence is met on the basis of the assumption that the information sought to be obtained by such contact will not be obtained by other means before such contact.

(2) NOTICE OF SPECIFIC CONTACTS.—The Secretary shall periodically provide to a taxpayer a record of persons contacted during such period by the Secretary with respect to the determination or collection of the tax liability of such taxpayer. Such record shall also be provided upon request of the taxpayer.

(3) EXCEPTIONS.—This subsection shall not apply—

(A) to any contact which the taxpayer has authorized;

(B) if the Secretary determines for good cause shown that such notice would jeopardize collection of any tax or such notice may involve reprisal against any person; or

(C) with respect to any pending criminal investigation.

Amendments

• **2019, Taxpayer First Act (P.L. 116-25)**

P.L. 116-25, §1206(a):

Amended Code Sec. 7602(c)(1). **Effective** for notices provided, and contacts of persons made, after the date which is 45 days after 7-1-2019. Prior to amendment, Code Sec. 7602(c)(1) read as follows:

(1) GENERAL NOTICE.—An officer or employee of the Internal Revenue Service may not contact any person other than the taxpayer with respect to the determination or collection of the tax liability of such taxpayer without providing reasonable notice in advance to the taxpayer that contacts with persons other than the taxpayer may be made.

• **1998, IRS Restructuring and Reform Act of 1998 (P.L. 105-206)**

P.L. 105-206, §3417(a):

Amended Code Sec. 7602, as amended by Act Sec. 3412, by redesignating subsections (c) and (d) as subsections (d) and (e), respectively, and by inserting after subsection (b) a new subsection (c). **Effective** for contacts made after the 180th day after 7-22-98.

[Sec. 7602(d)]

(d) NO ADMINISTRATIVE SUMMONS WHEN THERE IS JUSTICE DEPARTMENT REFERRAL.—

(1) LIMITATION OF AUTHORITY.—No summons may be issued under this title, and the Secretary may not begin any action under section 7604 to enforce any summons, with respect to any person if a Justice Department referral is in effect with respect to such person.

(2) JUSTICE DEPARTMENT REFERRAL IN EFFECT.—For purposes of this subsection—

(A) IN GENERAL.—A Justice Department referral is in effect with respect to any person if—

(i) the Secretary has recommended to the Attorney General a grand jury investigation of, or the criminal prosecution of, such person for any offense connected with the administration or enforcement of the internal revenue laws, or

(ii) any request is made under section 6103(h)(3)(B) for the disclosure of any return or return information (within the meaning of section 6103(b)) relating to such person.

(B) TERMINATION.—A Justice Department referral shall cease to be in effect with respect to a person when—

(i) the Attorney General notifies the Secretary, in writing, that—

(I) he will not prosecute such person for any offense connected with the administration or enforcement of the internal revenue laws,

(II) he will not authorize a grand jury investigation of such person with respect to such an offense, or

(III) he will discontinue such a grand jury investigation,

(ii) a final disposition has been made of any criminal proceeding pertaining to the enforcement of the internal revenue laws which was instituted by the Attorney General against such person, or

(iii) the Attorney General notifies the Secretary, in writing, that he will not prosecute such person for any offense connected with the administration or enforcement of the internal revenue laws relating to the request described in subparagraph (A)(ii).

(3) TAXABLE YEARS, ETC., TREATED SEPARATELY.—For purposes of this subsection, each taxable period (or, if there is no taxable period, each taxable event) and each tax imposed by a separate chapter of this title shall be treated separately.

Amendments

• **1998, IRS Restructuring and Reform Act of 1998 (P.L. 105-206)**

P.L. 105-206, §3417(a):

Amended Code Sec. 7602, as amended by Act Sec. 3412, by redesignating subsection (c) as subsection (d). **Effective** for contacts made after the 180th day after 7-22-98.

• **1982, Tax Equity and Fiscal Responsibility Act of 1982 (P.L. 97-248)**

P.L. 97-248, §333(a):

Added Code Sec. 7602(c). **Effective** 9-4-82.

ENFORCEMENT—EXAMINATION

[Sec. 7602(e)]

(e) LIMITATION ON EXAMINATION ON UNREPORTED INCOME.—The Secretary shall not use financial status or economic reality examination techniques to determine the existence of unreported income of any taxpayer unless the Secretary has a reasonable indication that there is a likelihood of such unreported income.

Amendments

• **1998, IRS Restructuring and Reform Act of 1998 (P.L. 105-206)**

P.L. 105-206, §3412:

Amended Code Sec. 7602 by adding at the end a new subsection (d). **Effective** 7-22-98.

P.L. 105-206, §3417(a):

Amended Code Sec. 7602, as amended by Act Sec. 3412, by redesignating subsection (d) as subsection (e). **Effective** for contacts made after the 180th day after 7-22-98.

[Sec. 7602(f)]

(f) LIMITATION ON ACCESS OF PERSONS OTHER THAN INTERNAL REVENUE SERVICE OFFICERS AND EMPLOYEES.—The Secretary shall not, under the authority of section 6103(n), provide any books, papers, records, or other data obtained pursuant to this section to any person authorized under section 6103(n), except when such person requires such information for the sole purpose of providing expert evaluation and assistance to the Internal Revenue Service. No person other than an officer or employee of the Internal Revenue Service or the Office of Chief Counsel may, on behalf of the Secretary, question a witness under oath whose testimony was obtained pursuant to this section.

Amendments

• **2019, Taxpayer First Act (P.L. 116-25)**

P.L. 116-25, §1208(a):

Amended Code Sec. 7602 by adding at the end a new subsection (f). For the **effective** date, see Act Sec. 1208(b), below.

P.L. 116-25, §1208(b), provides:

(b) EFFECTIVE DATE.—The amendment made by this section—

(1) shall take effect on the date of the enactment of this Act; and

(2) shall not fail to apply to a contract in effect under section 6103(n) of the Internal Revenue Code of 1986 merely because such contract was in effect before the date of the enactment of this Act.

[Sec. 7603]

SEC. 7603. SERVICE OF SUMMONS.

[Sec. 7603(a)]

(a) IN GENERAL.—A summons issued under section 6420(e)(2), 6421(g)(2), 6427(j)(2), or 7602 shall be served by the Secretary, by an attested copy delivered in hand to the person to whom it is directed, or left at his last and usual place of abode; and the certificate of service signed by the person serving the summons shall be evidence of the facts it states on the hearing of an application for the enforcement of the summons. When the summons requires the production of books, papers, records, or other data, it shall be sufficient if such books, papers, records, or other data are described with reasonable certainty.

Amendments

• **1998, IRS Restructuring and Reform Act of 1998 (P.L. 105-206)**

P.L. 105-206, §3416(a):

Amended Code Sec. 7603 by striking "A summons issued" and inserting "(a) IN GENERAL.—A summons issued". **Effective** for summonses served after 7-22-98.

• **1988, Technical and Miscellaneous Revenue Act of 1988 (P.L. 100-647)**

P.L. 100-647, §1017(c)(9):

Amended Code Sec. 7603 by striking out "6421(f)(2)" and inserting in lieu thereof "6421(g)(2)". **Effective** as if included in the provision of P.L. 99-514 to which it relates.

• **1986, Tax Reform Act of 1986 (P.L. 99-514)**

P.L. 99-514, §1703(e)(2)(G):

Amended Code Sec. 7603 by striking out "6427(i)(2)" and inserting in lieu thereof "6427(j)(2)". **Effective** for gasoline removed (as defined in Code Sec. 4082, as amended) after 12-31-87.

• **1984, Deficit Reduction Act of 1984 (P.L. 98-369)**

P.L. 98-369, §911(d)[c](2)(G):

Amended Code Sec. 7603 by striking out "6427(h)(2)" and inserting in lieu thereof "6427(i)(2)". **Effective** 8-1-84.

• **1983, Surface Transportation Act of 1983 (P.L. 97-424)**

P.L. 97-424, §515(b)(12):

Amended Code Sec. 7603 by striking out "6424(d)(2)," before "6427(h)(2)". **Effective** 1-6-83.

• **1980, Crude Oil Windfall Profit Tax Act of 1980 (P.L. 96-223)**

P.L. 96-223, §232(d)(4)(E):

Amended Code Sec. 7603 by substituting "6427(h)(2)" for "6427(g)(2)". **Effective** 1-1-79.

• **1978, Surface Transportation Assistance Act of 1978 (P.L. 95-599)**

P.L. 95-599, §505(c)(5), (d):

Substituted "6427(g)(2)" for "6427(f)(2)" in Code Sec. 7603. **Effective** 1-1-79.

• **1976 (P.L. 94-530)**

P.L. 94-530, §1(c)(6):

Substituted "6427(f)(2)" for "6427(e)(2)" in Code Sec. 7603. **Effective** 10-1-76.

• **1976, Tax Reform Act of 1976 (P.L. 94-455)**

P.L. 94-455, §1906(b)(13)(A):

Amended 1954 Code by substituting "Secretary" for "Secretary or his delegate" each place it appeared. **Effective** 2-1-77.

• **1970 (P.L. 91-258)**

P.L. 91-258, §207(d)(9):

Amended Code Sec. 7603 by adding "6427(e)(2)" in the first line. **Effective** 7-1-70.

• **1965, Excise Tax Reduction Act of 1965 (P.L. 89-44)**

P.L. 89-44, §202(c)(4):

Amended Code Sec. 7603 by inserting "6424(d)(2)," after "6421(f)(2),". **Effective** 1-1-66.

• **1956 (P.L. 627, 84th Cong.)**

P.L. 627, 84th Cong., §208(d)(4):

Amended Code Sec. 7603 by inserting after "section 6420(e)(2)" the following: ", 6421(f)(2),". **Effective** 7-1-56.

• **1956 (P.L. 466, 84th Cong.)**

P.L. 466, 84th Cong., §4(i):

Amended Code Sec. 7603 by striking out the words "section 7602" in the first sentence and inserting in lieu thereof the words "section 6420(e)(2) or 7602".

[Sec. 7603(b)]

(b) SERVICE BY MAIL TO THIRD-PARTY RECORDKEEPERS.—

(1) IN GENERAL.—A summons referred to in subsection (a) for the production of books, papers, records, or other data by a third-party recordkeeper may also be served by certified or registered mail to the last known address of such recordkeeper.

(2) THIRD-PARTY RECORDKEEPER.—For purposes of paragraph (1), the term "third-party recordkeeper" means—

(A) any mutual savings bank, cooperative bank, domestic building and loan association, or other savings institution chartered and supervised as a savings and loan or similar association under Federal or State law, any bank (as defined in section 581), or any credit union (within the meaning of section 501(c)(14)(A)),

(B) any consumer reporting agency (as defined under section 603(f) of the Fair Credit Reporting Act (15 U.S.C. 1681a(f))),

(C) any person extending credit through the use of credit cards or similar devices,

(D) any broker (as defined in section 3(a)(4) of the Securities Exchange Act of 1934 (15 U.S.C. 78c(a)(4))),

(E) any attorney,

(F) any accountant,

ENFORCEMENT—EXAMINATION

(G) any barter exchange (as defined in section 6045(c)(3)),

(H) any regulated investment company (as defined in section 851) and any agent of such regulated investment company when acting as an agent thereof,

(I) any enrolled agent, and

(J) any owner or developer of a computer software source code (as defined in section 7612(d)(2)).

Subparagraph (J) shall apply only with respect to a summons requiring the production of the source code referred to in subparagraph (J) or the program and data described in section 7612(b)(1)(A)(ii) to which such source code relates.

Amendments

• **2000, Community Renewal Tax Relief Act of 2000 (P.L. 106-554)**

P.L. 106-554, § 319(26):

Amended Code Sec. 7603(b)(2) by striking the semicolon at the end of subparagraphs (A), (B), (C), (D), (E), (F), and (G) and inserting a comma. **Effective** 12-21-2000.

• **1998, IRS Restructuring and Reform Act of 1998 (P.L. 105-206)**

P.L. 105-206, § 3413(c):

Amended Code Sec. 7603(b)(2), as amended by Act Sec. 3416(a), by striking "and" at the end of subparagraph (H), by striking a period at the end of subparagraph (I) and inserting ", and", and by adding at the end a new subparagraph (J). **Effective**, generally, for summonses issued and software acquired after 7-22-98. For a special rule, see Act Sec. 3413(e)(2), below.

P.L. 105-206, § 3413(e)(2), provides:

(2) SOFTWARE PROTECTION.—In the case of any software acquired on or before such date of enactment, the requirements of section 7612(a)(2) of the Internal Revenue Code of 1986 (as added by such amendments) shall apply after the 90th day after such date. The preceding sentence shall not apply to the requirement under section 7612(c)(2)(G)(ii) of such Code (as so added).

P.L. 105-206, § 3416(a):

Amended Code Sec. 7603 by adding at the end a new subsection (b). **Effective** for summonses served after 7-22-98.

[Sec. 7604]
SEC. 7604. ENFORCEMENT OF SUMMONS.

[Sec. 7604(a)]

(a) JURISDICTION OF DISTRICT COURT.—If any person is summoned under the internal revenue laws to appear, to testify, or to produce books, papers, records, or other data, the United States district court for the district in which such person resides or is found shall have jurisdiction by appropriate process to compel such attendance, testimony, or production of books, papers, records, or other data.

[Sec. 7604(b)]

(b) ENFORCEMENT.—Whenever any person summoned under section 6420(e)(2), 6421(g)(2), 6427(j)(2), or 7602 neglects or refuses to obey such summons, or to produce books, papers, records, or other data, or to give testimony, as required, the Secretary may apply to the judge of the district court or to a United States commissioner for the district within which the person so summoned resides or is found for an attachment against him as for a contempt. It shall be the duty of the judge or commissioner to hear the application, and, if satisfactory proof is made, to issue an attachment, directed to some proper officer, for the arrest of such person, and upon his being brought before him to proceed to a hearing of the case; and upon such hearing the judge or the United States commissioner shall have power to make such order as he shall deem proper, not inconsistent with the law for the punishment of contempts, to enforce obedience to the requirements of the summons and to punish such person for his default or disobedience.

Amendments

• **1988, Technical and Miscellaneous Revenue Act of 1988 (P.L. 100-647)**

P.L. 100-647, § 1017(c)(9):

Amended Code Sec. 7604(b) by striking out "6421(f)(2)" and inserting in lieu thereof "6421(g)(2)". **Effective** as if included in the provision of P.L. 99-514 to which it relates.

• **1986, Tax Reform Act of 1986 (P.L. 99-514)**

P.L. 99-514, § 1703(e)(2)(G):

Amended Code Sec. 7604(b) and (c)(2) by striking out "6427(i)(2)" and inserting in lieu thereof "6427(j)(2)". **Effective** for gasoline removed (as defined in Code Sec. 4082, as amended) after 12-31-87.

• **1984, Deficit Reduction Act of 1984 (P.L. 98-369)**

P.L. 98-369, § 911(d)[c](2)(G):

Amended Code Sec. 7604(b) by striking out "6427(h)(2)" each place it appeared and inserting in lieu thereof "6427(i)(2)". **Effective** 8-1-84.

• **1983, Surface Transportation Act of 1983 (P.L. 97-424)**

P.L. 97-424, § 515(b)(12):

Amended Code Sec. 7604(b) by striking out "6424(d)(2)," before "6427(h)(2),". **Effective** 1-6-83.

• **1980, Crude Oil Windfall Profit Tax Act of 1980 (P.L. 96-223)**

P.L. 96-223, § 232(d)(4)(E):

Amended Code Sec. 7604(b) by substituting "6427(h)(2)" for "6427(g)(2)". **Effective** 1-1-79.

• **1978, Surface Transportation Assistance Act of 1978 (P.L. 95-599)**

P.L. 95-599, § 505(c)(5), (d):

Substituted "6427(g)(2)" for "6427(f)(2)" in Code Sec. 7604(b). **Effective** 1-1-79.

• **1976 (P.L. 94-530)**

P.L. 94-530, § 1(c)(6):

Substituted "6427(f)(2)" for "6427(e)(2)" in Code Sec. 7604(b). **Effective** 10-1-76.

• **1976, Tax Reform Act of 1976 (P.L. 94-455)**

P.L. 94-455, § 1906(b)(13)(A):

Amended 1954 Code by substituting "Secretary" for "Secretary or his delegate" each place it appeared. **Effective** 2-1-77.

• **1970 (P.L. 91-258)**

P.L. 91-258, § 207(d)(9):

Amended Code Sec. 7604(b) by adding "6427(e)(2)" in the second line. **Effective** 7-1-70.

• **1965, Excise Tax Reduction Act of 1965 (P.L. 89-44)**

P.L. 89-44, § 202(c)(4):

Amended Code Sec. 7604(b) by inserting "6424(d)(2)," after "6421(f)(2),". **Effective** 1-1-66.

• **1956 (P.L. 627, 84th Cong.)**

P.L. 627, 84th Cong., § 208(d)(4):

Amended Code Sec. 7604(b) by inserting after "section 6420(e)(2)" the following: ", 6421(f)(2),". **Effective** 7-1-56.

• **1956 (P.L. 466, 84th Cong.)**

P.L. 466, 84th Cong., § 4(i):

Amended Code Sec. 7604(b) by striking out the words "section 7602" in the first sentence and inserting in lieu thereof the words "section 6420(e)(2) or 7602".

[Sec. 7604(c)]

(c) CROSS REFERENCES.—

(1) AUTHORITY TO ISSUE ORDERS, PROCESSES, AND JUDGMENTS.—

For authority of district courts generally to enforce the provisions of this title, see section 7402.

(2) PENALTIES.—

For penalties applicable to violation of section 6420(e)(2), 6421(g)(2), 6427(j)(2), or 7602, see section 7210.

Amendments

• **1988, Technical and Miscellaneous Revenue Act of 1988 (P.L. 100-647)**

P.L. 100-647, § 1017(c)(9):

Amended Code Sec. 7604(c)(2) by striking out "6421(f)(2)" and inserting in lieu thereof "6421(g)(2)". **Effective** as if included in the provision of P.L. 99-514 to which it relates.

• **1986, Tax Reform Act of 1986 (P.L. 99-514)**

P.L. 99-514, § 1703(e)(2)(G):

Amended Code Sec. 7604(c)(2) by striking out "6427(i)(2)" and inserting in lieu thereof "6427(j)(2)". **Effective** for gasoline removed (as defined in Code Sec. 4082, as amended) after 12-31-87.

ENFORCEMENT—EXAMINATION

- **1984, Deficit Reduction Act of 1984 (P.L. 98-369)**

P.L. 98-369, §911(d)[c](2)(G):

Amended Code Sec. 7604(c)(2) by striking out "6427(h)(2)" and inserting in lieu thereof "6427(i)(2)". **Effective** 8-1-84.

- **1983, Surface Transportation Act of 1983 (P.L. 97-424)**

P.L. 97-424, §515(b)(12):

Amended Code Sec. 7604(c) by striking out "6424(d)(2)," before "6427(h)(2)". **Effective** 1-6-83.

- **1980, Crude Oil Windfall Profit Tax Act of 1980 (P.L. 96-223)**

P.L. 96-223, §232(d)(4)(E):

Amended Code Sec. 7604(c) by substituting "6427(h)(2)" for "6427(g)(2)". **Effective** 1-1-79.

- **1978, Surface Transportation Assistance Act of 1978 (P.L. 95-599)**

P.L. 95-599, §505(c)(6), (d):

Substituted "6427(g)(2)" for "6427(e)(2)" in Code Sec. 7604(c)(2). **Effective** 1-1-79.

- **1970 (P.L. 91-258)**

P.L. 91-258, §207(d)(9):

Amended Code Sec. 7604(c)(2) by adding "6427(e)(2)" therein. **Effective** 7-1-70.

- **1965, Excise Tax Reduction Act of 1965 (P.L. 89-44)**

P.L. 89-44, §202(c)(4):

Amended Code Sec. 7604(c)(2) by inserting "6424(d)(2)," after "6421(f)(2),". **Effective** 1-1-66.

- **1956 (P.L. 627, 84th Cong.)**

P.L. 627, 84th Cong., §208(d)(4):

Amended Code Sec. 7604(c)(2) by inserting after "section 6420(e)(2)" the following: ", 6421(f)(2),". **Effective** 7-1-56.

- **1956 (P.L. 466, 84th Cong.)**

P.L. 466, 84th Cong., §4(i):

Amended Code Sec. 7604(c)(2) by striking out the words "section 7602" and inserting in lieu thereof the words "section 6420(e)(2) or 7602".

[Sec. 7605]

SEC. 7605. TIME AND PLACE OF EXAMINATION.

[Sec. 7605(a)]

(a) TIME AND PLACE.—The time and place of examination pursuant to the provisions of section 6420(e)(2), 6421(g)(2), 6427(j)(2), or 7602 shall be such time and place as may be fixed by the Secretary and as are reasonable under the circumstances. In the case of a summons under authority of paragraph (2) of section 7602, or under the corresponding authority of section 6420(e)(2), 6421(g)(2), or 6427(j)(2), the date fixed for appearance before the Secretary shall not be less than 10 days from the date of the summons.

Amendments

- **1988, Technical and Miscellaneous Revenue Act of 1988 (P.L. 100-647)**

P.L. 100-647, §1017(c)(9):

Amended Code Sec. 7605(a) by striking out "6421(f)(2)" and inserting in lieu thereof "6421(g)(2)". **Effective** as if included in the provision of P.L. 99-514 to which it relates.

P.L. 100-647, §6228(b), provides:

(b) REGULATIONS WITH RESPECT TO TIME AND PLACE OF EXAMINATION.—The Secretary of the Treasury or the Secretary's delegate shall issue regulations to implement subsection (a) of section 7605 of the 1986 Code (relating to time and place of examination) within 1 year after the date of the enactment of this Act.

- **1986, Tax Reform Act of 1986 (P.L. 99-514)**

P.L. 99-514, §1703(e)(2)(G):

Amended Code Sec. 7605(a) by striking out "6427(i)(2)" and inserting in lieu thereof "6427(j)(2)". **Effective** for gasoline removed (as defined in Code Sec. 4082, as amended) after 12-31-87.

- **1984, Deficit Reduction Act of 1984 (P.L. 98-369)**

P.L. 98-369, §911(d)[c](2)(G):

Amended Code Sec. 7605(a) by striking out "6427(h)(2)" each place it appeared and inserting in lieu thereof "6427(i)(2)". **Effective** 8-1-84.

- **1983, Surface Transportation Act of 1983 (P.L. 97-424)**

P.L. 97-424, §515(b)(12):

Amended Code Sec. 7605(a) by striking out "6424(d)(2)," before "6427(h)(2)" each place it appeared. **Effective** 1-6-83.

- **1980, Crude Oil Windfall Profit Tax Act of 1980 (P.L. 96-223)**

P.L. 96-223, §232(d)(4)(E):

Amended Code Sec. 7605(a) by substituting "6427(h)(2)" for "6427(g)(2)". **Effective** 1-1-79.

- **1978, Surface Transportation Assistance Act of 1978 (P.L. 95-599)**

P.L. 95-599, §505(c)(5), (d):

Substituted "6427(g)(2)" for "6427(f)(2)" each place it appeared in Code Sec. 7605(a). **Effective** 1-1-79.

- **1976 (P.L. 94-530)**

P.L. 94-530, §1(c)(6):

Substituted "6427(f)(2)" for "6427(e)(2)" each place it appeared in Code Sec. 7605(a). **Effective** 10-1-76.

- **1976, Tax Reform Act of 1976 (P.L. 94-455)**

P.L. 94-455, §1906(b)(13)(A):

Amended 1954 Code by substituting "Secretary" for "Secretary or his delegate" each place it appeared. **Effective** 2-1-77.

- **1970 (P.L. 91-258)**

P.L. 91-258, §207(d)(9):

Amended Code Sec. 7605(a) by adding "6427(e)(2)" in the first sentence and by substituting "6424(d)(2), or 6427(e)(2)" for "or 6424(d)(2)" in the second sentence. **Effective** 7-1-70.

- **1965, Excise Tax Reduction Act of 1965 (P.L. 89-44)**

P.L. 89-44, §202(c)(4):

Amended Code Sec. 7605(a) by inserting "6424(d)(2)," after "6421(f)(2)," in the first sentence and by inserting "6420(e)(2), 6421(f)(2), or 6424(d)(2)," in lieu of "6420(e)(2) or 6421(f)(2)," in the second sentence. **Effective** 1-1-66.

- **1956 (P.L. 627, 84th Cong.)**

P.L. 627, 84th Cong., §208(d)(4):

Amended Code Sec. 7605(a) by inserting in the first sentence after "section 6420(e)(2)" the following: ", 6421(f)(2),". Amended the second sentence by inserting after "section 6420(e)(2)" the following: "or section 6421(f)(2)". **Effective** 7-1-56.

- **1956 (P.L. 466, 84th Cong.)**

P.L. 466, 84th Cong., §4(i):

Amended the first sentence of Code Sec. 7605(a) by striking out the words "section 7602" and inserting in lieu thereof the words "section 6420(e)(2) or 7602". Amended the second sentence of Code Sec. 7605(a) by adding after the words "section 7602" the words ", or under the corresponding authority of section 6420(e)(2),".

[Sec. 7605(b)]

(b) RESTRICTIONS ON EXAMINATION OF TAXPAYER.—No taxpayer shall be subjected to unnecessary examination or investigations, and only one inspection of a taxpayer's books of account shall be made for each taxable year unless the taxpayer requests otherwise or unless the Secretary, after investigation, notifies the taxpayer in writing that an additional inspection is necessary.

Amendments

- **1998, IRS Restructuring and Reform Act of 1998 (P.L. 105-206)**

P.L. 105-206, §3503, provides:

SEC. 3503. DISCLOSURE OF CRITERIA FOR EXAMINATION SELECTION.

(a) IN GENERAL.—The Secretary of the Treasury or the Secretary's delegate shall, as soon as practicable, but not later than 180 days after the date of the enactment of this Act, incorporate into the statement required by section 6227 of the Omnibus Taxpayer Bill of Rights (Internal Revenue Service Publication No. 1) a statement which sets forth in simple and nontechnical terms the criteria and procedures for selecting taxpayers for examination. Such statement shall not include any information the disclosure of which would be detrimental to law enforcement, but shall specify the general procedures used by the Internal Revenue Service, including whether taxpayers are selected for examination on the basis of information available in the media or on the basis of information provided to the Internal Revenue Service by informants.

(b) TRANSMISSION TO COMMITTEES OF CONGRESS.—The Secretary shall transmit drafts of the statement required under subsection (a) (or proposed revisions to any such statement) to the Committee on Ways and Means of the House of Representatives and the Committee on Finance of the Senate on the same day.

- **1976, Tax Reform Act of 1976 (P.L. 94-455)**

P.L. 94-455, §1906(b)(13)(A):

Amended 1954 Code by substituting "Secretary" for "Secretary or his delegate" each place it appeared. **Effective** 2-1-77.

ENFORCEMENT—EXAMINATION

[Sec. 7605(c)]

(c) Cross Reference.—

For provisions restricting church tax inquiries and examinations, see section 7611.

Amendments

• **1984, Deficit Reduction Act of 1984 (P.L. 98-369)**

P.L. 98-369, §1033(c)(1):

Amended Code Sec. 7605(c). **Effective** with respect to inquiries and examinations beginning after 12-31-84. Prior to amendment, Code Sec. 7605(c) read as follows:

(c) Restriction on Examination of Churches.—No examination of the books of account of a church or convention or association of churches shall be made to determine whether such organization may be engaged in the carrying on of an unrelated trade or business or may be otherwise engaged in activities which may be subject to tax under part III of subchapter F of chapter 1 of this title (sec. 511 and following, relating to taxation of business income of exempt organizations) unless the Secretary (such officer being no lower than a principal internal revenue officer for an internal revenue region) believes that such organization may be so engaged and so notifies the organization in advance of the examination. No examination of the religious activities of such an organization shall be made except to the extent necessary to determine whether such organization is a church or a convention or association of churches, and no examination of the books of account of such an organization shall be made other than to the extent necessary to determine the amount of tax imposed by this title.

• **1976, Tax Reform Act of 1976 (P.L. 94-455)**

P.L. 94-455, §1906(b)(13)(A):

Amended 1954 Code by substituting "Secretary" for "Secretary or his delegate" each place it appeared. **Effective** 2-1-77.

• **1969, Tax Reform Act of 1969 (P.L. 91-172)**

P.L. 91-172, §121(f):

Added subsection (c) to Code Sec. 7605. **Effective** 1-1-70.

[Sec. 7606]

SEC. 7606. ENTRY OF PREMISES FOR EXAMINATION OF TAXABLE OBJECTS.

[Sec. 7606(a)]

(a) Entry During Day.—The Secretary may enter, in the daytime, any building or place where any articles or objects subject to tax are made, produced, or kept, so far as it may be necessary for the purpose of examining said articles or objects.

[Sec. 7606(b)]

(b) Entry At Night.—When such premises are open at night, the Secretary may enter them while so open, in the performance of his official duties.

Amendments

• **1976, Tax Reform Act of 1976 (P.L. 94-455)**

P.L. 94-455, §1906(b)(13)(A):

Amended 1954 Code by substituting "Secretary" for "Secretary or his delegate" each place it appeared. **Effective** 2-1-77.

[Sec. 7606(c)]

(c) Penalties.—

For penalty for refusal to permit entry or examination, see section 7342.

[Sec. 7607—Repealed]

Amendments

• **1984 (P.L. 98-573)**

P.L. 98-573, §213(b)(1):

Repealed Code Sec. 7607. [Note: P.L. 98-473 had already repealed Code Sec. 7607.] **Effective** 10-15-84.

• **1984 (P.L. 98-473)**

P.L. 98-473, §320(b):

Repealed Code Sec. 7607. **Effective** 10-12-84. [Note: P.L. 98-573 also repealed Code Sec. 7607.] Prior to repeal, Code Sec. 7607 read as follows:

SEC. 7607. ADDITIONAL AUTHORITY FOR BUREAU OF CUSTOMS.

Officers of the customs (as defined in section 401(1) of the Tariff Act of 1930, as amended; 19 U.S.C., sec. 1401(1)), may—

(1) carry firearms, execute and serve search warrants and arrest warrants, and serve subpoenas and summonses issued under the authority of the United States, and

(2) make arrests without warrant for violations of any law of the United States relating to narcotic drugs (as defined in section 102(16) of the Controlled Substances Act) or marihuana (as defined in section 102(15) of the Controlled Substances Act) where the violation is committed in the presence of the person making the arrest or where such person has reasonable grounds to believe that the person to be arrested has committed or is committing such violation.

• **1970 (P.L. 91-513)**

P.L. 91-513, §1102(g)(1):

Amended Code Sec. 7607 by deleting "The Commissioner, Deputy Commissioner, Assistant to the Commissioner, and agents, of the Bureau of Narcotics of the Department of the Treasury, and officers" at the beginning of the section and substituting in lieu thereof the word "Officers". Paragraph (2) of Code Sec. 7607 was amended by substituting "narcotic drugs (as defined in section 102(16) of the Controlled Substances Act) or marihuana (as defined in section 102(15) of the Controlled Substances Act)" for "narcotic drugs (as defined in section 4731) or marihuana (as defined in section 4761)". **Effective** 5-1-71.

• **1956, Narcotic Control Act of 1956 (P.L. 728, 84th Cong.)**

P.L. 728, 84th Cong., 2d. Sess., §104:

Added Code Sec. 7607. **Effective** 7-19-56.

[Sec. 7608]

SEC. 7608. AUTHORITY OF INTERNAL REVENUE ENFORCEMENT OFFICERS.

[Sec. 7608(a)]

(a) Enforcement of Subtitle E and Other Laws Pertaining to Liquor, Tobacco, and Firearms.—Any investigator, agent, or other internal revenue officer by whatever term designated, whom the Secretary charges with the duty of enforcing any of the criminal, seizure, or forfeiture provisions of subtitle E or of any other law of the United States pertaining to the commodities subject to tax under such subtitle for the enforcement of which the Secretary is responsible, may—

(1) carry firearms;

(2) execute and serve search warrants and arrest warrants, and serve subpoenas and summonses issued under authority of the United States;

(3) in respect to the performance of such duty, make arrests without warrant for any offense against the United States committed in his presence, or for any felony cognizable under the laws of the United States if he has reasonable grounds to believe that the person to be arrested has committed, or is committing, such felony; and

(4) in respect to the performance of such duty, make seizures of property subject to forfeiture to the United States.

Amendments

• **1976, Tax Reform Act of 1976 (P.L. 94-455)**

P.L. 94-455, §1906(b)(13)(A):

Amended 1954 Code by substituting "Secretary" for "Secretary or his delegate" each place it appeared. **Effective** 2-1-77.

ENFORCEMENT—EXAMINATION

[Sec. 7608(b)]

(b) ENFORCEMENT OF LAWS RELATING TO INTERNAL REVENUE OTHER THAN SUBTITLE E.—

(1) Any criminal investigator of the Intelligence Division of the Internal Revenue Service whom the Secretary charges with the duty of enforcing any of the criminal provisions of the internal revenue laws, any other criminal provisions of law relating to internal revenue for the enforcement of which the Secretary is responsible, or any other law for which the Secretary has delegated investigatory authority to the Internal Revenue Service, is, in the performance of his duties, authorized to perform the functions described in paragraph (2).

(2) The functions authorized under this subsection to be performed by an officer referred to in paragraph (1) are—

(A) to execute and serve search warrants and arrest warrants, and serve subpoenas and summonses issued under authority of the United States;

(B) to make arrests without warrant for any offense against the United States relating to the internal revenue laws committed in his presence, or for any felony cognizable under such laws if he has reasonable grounds to believe that the person to be arrested has committed or is committing any such felony; and

(C) to make seizures of property subject to forfeiture under the internal revenue laws.

Amendments

• **1998, IRS Restructuring and Reform Act of 1998 (P.L. 105-206)**

P.L. 105-206, §1103(e)(4):

Amended Code Sec. 7608(b)(1) by striking "or of the Internal Security Division" after "of the Intelligence Division". **Effective** 7-22-98.

• **1988, Anti-Drug Abuse Act of 1988 (P.L. 100-690)**

P.L. 100-690, §7601(c)(1)(A)-(B) [amended by P.L. 104-168, §1205(a)]:

Amended Code Sec. 7608(b)(1) by striking out "or" before "any other" and inserting a comma, and by inserting ", or any other law for which the Secretary had delegated investigatory authority to the Internal Revenue Service," after "responsible". **Effective** 11-18-88.

• **1976, Tax Reform Act of 1976 (P.L. 94-455)**

P.L. 94-455, §1906(b)(13)(A):

Amended 1954 Code by substituting "Secretary" for "Secretary or his delegate" each place it appeared. **Effective** 2-1-77.

• **1962 (P.L. 87-863)**

P.L. 87-863, §6(a):

Amended Code Sec. 7608 by adding subsection (b), and deleting "Any" in line 1 and inserting the following: "(a) Enforcement of Subtitle E and Other Laws Pertaining to Liquor, Tobacco, and Firearms.—Any". **Effective** 10-24-62.

• **1958, Excise Tax Technical Changes Act of 1958 (P.L. 85-859)**

P.L. 85-859, §204(14):

Redesignated Code Sec. 7608 as Code Sec. 7609 and added new Code Sec. 7608. **Effective** 9-3-58.

[Sec. 7608(c)]

(c) RULES RELATING TO UNDERCOVER OPERATIONS.—

(1) CERTIFICATION REQUIRED FOR EXEMPTION OF UNDERCOVER OPERATIONS FROM CERTAIN LAWS.—With respect to any undercover investigative operation of the Internal Revenue Service (hereinafter in this subsection referred to as the "Service") which is necessary for the detection and prosecution of offenses under the internal revenue laws, any other criminal provisions of law relating to internal revenue, or any other law for which the Secretary has delegated investigatory authority to the Internal Revenue Service—

(A) sums authorized to be appropriated for the Service may be used—

(i) to purchase property, buildings, and other facilities, and to lease space, within the United States, the District of Columbia, and the territories and possessions of the United States without regard to—

(I) sections 1341 and 3324 of title 31, United States Code,

(II) sections 6301(a) and (b)(1)-(3) and 6306 of title 41, United States Code,

(III) chapter 45 of title 41, United States Code,

(IV) section 8141 of title 40, United States Code, and

(V) section 3901 of title 41, United States Code, and

(ii) to establish or to acquire proprietary corporations or business entities as part of the undercover operation, and to operate such corporations or business entities on a commercial basis, without regard to sections 9102 and 9103 of title 31, United States Code;

(B) sums authorized to be appropriated for the Service and the proceeds from the undercover operations may be deposited in banks or other financial institutions without regard to the provisions of section 648 of title 18, United States Code, and section 3302 of title 31, United States Code, and

(C) the proceeds from the undercover operation may be used to offset necessary and reasonable expenses incurred in such operation without regard to the provisions of section 3302 of title 31, United States Code.

This paragraph shall apply only upon the written certification of the Commissioner of Internal Revenue (or, if designated by the Commissioner, the Deputy Commissioner or an Assistant Commissioner of Internal Revenue) that any action authorized by subparagraph (A), (B), or (C) is necessary for the conduct of such undercover operation.

(2) LIQUIDATION OF CORPORATIONS AND BUSINESS ENTITIES.—If a corporation or business entity established or acquired as part of an undercover operation under subparagraph (B) of paragraph (1) with a net value over $50,000 is to be liquidated, sold, or otherwise disposed of, the Service, as much in advance as the Commissioner or his delegate determines is practicable, shall report the circumstances to the Secretary. The proceeds of the liquidation, sale, or other disposition, after obligations are met, shall be deposited in the Treasury of the United States as miscellaneous receipts.

(3) DEPOSIT OF PROCEEDS.—As soon as the proceeds from an undercover investigative operation with respect to which an action is authorized and carried out under subparagraphs (B) and (C) of paragraph (1) are no longer necessary for the conduct of such operation, such proceeds or the balance of such proceeds remaining at the time shall be deposited into the Treasury of the United States as miscellaneous receipts.

(4) AUDITS.—

(A) The Service shall conduct a detailed financial audit of each undercover investigative operation which is closed in each fiscal year; and

(i) submit the results of the audit in writing to the Secretary; and

(ii) not later than 180 days after such undercover operation is closed, submit a report to the Congress concerning such audit.

(B) The Service shall also submit a report annually to the Congress specifying as to its undercover investigative operations—

(i) the number, by programs, of undercover investigative operations pending as of the end of the 1-year period for which such report is submitted;

(ii) the number, by programs, of undercover investigative operations commenced in the 1-year period for which such report is submitted;

ENFORCEMENT—EXAMINATION

(iii) the number, by programs, of undercover investigative operations closed in the 1-year period for which such report is submitted, and

(iv) the following information with respect to each undercover investigative operation pending as of the end of the 1-year period for which such report is submitted or closed during such 1-year period—

(I) the date the operation began and the date of the certification referred to in the last sentence of paragraph (1),

(II) the total expenditures under the operation and the amount and use of the proceeds from the operation,

(III) a detailed description of the operation including the potential violation being investigated and whether the operation is being conducted under grand jury auspices, and

(IV) the results of the operation including the results of criminal proceedings.

(5) DEFINITIONS.—For purposes of paragraph (4)—

(A) CLOSED.—The term "closed" means the date on which the later of the following occurs;

(i) all criminal proceedings (other than appeals) are concluded, or

(ii) covert activities are concluded, whichever occurs later.

(B) EMPLOYEES.—The term "employees" has the meaning given such term by section 2105 of title 5, United States Code.

(C) UNDERCOVER INVESTIGATIVE OPERATION.—The term "undercover investigative operation" means any undercover investigative operation of the Service; except that, for purposes of subparagraphs (A) and (C) of paragraph (4), such term only includes an operation which is exempt from section 3302 or 9102 of title 31, United States Code.

Amendments

- **2011 (P.L. 111-350)**

P.L. 111-350, § 5(f)(1)-(3):

Amended Code Sec. 7608(c)(1) in subparagraph (A)(i)(II), by striking "sections 11(a) and 22" and substituting "sections 6301(a) and (b)(1)-(3) and 6306"; in subparagraph (A)(i)(III), by striking "section 255" and substituting "chapter 45"; and in subparagraph (A)(i)(V), by striking "section 254(a) and (c)" and substituting "section 3901". **Effective** 1-4-2011.

- **2008, Tax Extenders and Alternative Minimum Tax Relief Act of 2008 (P.L. 110-343)**

P.L. 110-343, Division C, § 401(a):

Amended Code Sec. 7608(c) by striking paragraph (6). **Effective** for operations conducted after 10-3-2008. Prior to being stricken, Code Sec. 7608(c)(6) read as follows:

(6) APPLICATION OF SECTION.—The provisions of this subsection—

(A) shall apply after November 17, 1988, and before January 1, 1990, and

(B) shall apply after the date of the enactment of this paragraph and before January 1, 2008.

All amounts expended pursuant to this subsection during the period described in subparagraph (B) shall be recovered to the extent possible, and deposited in the Treasury of the United States as miscellaneous receipts, before January 1, 2008.

- **2006, Tax Relief and Health Care Act of 2006 (P.L. 109-432)**

P.L. 109-432, Division A, § 121:

Amended Code Sec. 7608(c)(6) by striking "2007" both places it appears and inserting "2008". **Effective** 12-20-2006.

- **2005, Gulf Opportunity Zone Act of 2005 (P.L. 109-135)**

P.L. 109-135, § 304:

Amended Code Sec. 7608(c)(6) by striking "January 1, 2006" both places it appears and inserting "January 1, 2007". **Effective** 12-21-2005.

- **2003 (P.L. 108-178)**

P.L. 108-178, § 4(e):

Amended Code Sec. 7608(c)(1)(A)(i)(IV), as amended by section 3(f) of P.L. 107-217, by striking "title 40" and substituting "title 40, United States Code". **Effective** 8-21-2002.

- **2002 (P.L. 107-217)**

P.L. 107-217, § 3(f):

Amended Code Sec. 7608(c)(1)(A)(i)(IV) by striking "section 34 of title 40, United States Code" and substituting "section 8141 of title 40". **Effective** 8-21-2002.

- **2000, Community Renewal Tax Relief Act of 2000 (P.L. 106-554)**

P.L. 106-554, § 303:

Amended Code Sec. 7608(c)(6) and the last sentence of Code Sec. 7608 by striking "January 1, 2001" and inserting "January 1, 2006". **Effective** 12-21-2000.

- **1996, General Accounting Office Act of 1996 (P.L. 104-316)**

P.L. 104-316, § 113:

Amended Code Sec. 7608(c)(2) by striking "and the Comptroller General of the United States". **Effective** 10-19-96.

- **1996, Taxpayer Bill of Rights 2 (P.L. 104-168)**

P.L. 104-168, § 1205(b):

Amended Code Sec. 7608(c) by adding at the end a new paragraph (6). **Effective** 7-30-96.

P.L. 104-168, § 1205(c)(1)(A)-(C):

Amended Code Sec. 7608(c)(4)(B) by striking "preceding the period" following "1-year period" in clause (ii), by striking "and" at the end of clause (ii), and by striking clause (iii) and inserting new clauses (iii) and (iv). **Effective** 7-30-96. Prior to amendment, Code Sec. 7608(c)(4)(B)(iii) read as follows:

(iii) the number, by programs, of undercover investigative operations closed in the 1-year period preceding the period for which such report is submitted and, with respect to each such closed undercover operation, the results obtained and any civil claims made with respect thereto.

P.L. 104-168, § 1205(c)(2):

Amended Code Sec. 7608(c)(5)(C). **Effective** 7-30-96. Prior to amendment, Code Sec. 7608(c)(5)(C) read as follows:

(C) UNDERCOVER INVESTIGATIVE OPERATION.—The terms "undercover investigative operation" and "undercover operation" mean any undercover investigative operation of the Service—

(i) in which—

(I) the gross receipts (excluding interest earned) exceed $50,000; or

(II) expenditures, both recoverable and nonrecoverable (other than expenditures for salaries of employees), exceed $150,000; and

(ii) which is exempt from section 3302 or 9102 of title 31, United States Code.

Clauses (i) and (ii) shall not apply with respect to the report required under subparagraph (B) of paragraph (4).

- **1990, Omnibus Budget Reconciliation Act of 1990 (P.L. 101-508)**

P.L. 101-508, § 11704(a)(32):

Amended Code Sec. 7608(c)(1)(B) by striking the comma after "operations". **Effective** 11-5-90.

P.L. 101-508, § 11704(a)(33):

Amended Code Sec. 7608(c)(5)(C) by striking "interested" in clause (i)(I) and inserting "interest", and by striking "title 3" in clause (ii) and inserting "title 31". **Effective** 11-5-90.

- **1988, Anti-Drug Abuse Act of 1988 (P.L. 100-690)**

P.L. 100-690, § 7601(c)(2) [amended by P.L. 104-168, § 1205(a)]:

Amended Code Sec. 7608 by adding at the end thereof new subsection (c). **Effective** 11-18-88.

[Sec. 7609]

SEC. 7609. SPECIAL PROCEDURES FOR THIRD-PARTY SUMMONSES.

[Sec. 7609(a)]

(a) NOTICE.—

(1) IN GENERAL.—If any summons to which this section applies requires the giving of testimony on or relating to, the production of any portion of records made or kept on or relating to, or the production of any computer software source code (as defined in 7612(d)(2)) with respect to, any person (other than the person summoned) who is identified in the summons, then notice of the summons shall be given to any person so identified within 3 days of the day on which such service is made, but no later than the 23rd day before the day fixed in the summons as the day upon which such records are to be examined. Such notice shall be accompanied by a copy of the summons which has been served and shall contain an explanation of the right under subsection (b)(2) to bring a proceeding to quash the summons.

(2) SUFFICIENCY OF NOTICE.—Such notice shall be sufficient if, on or before such third day, such notice is served in the manner provided in section 7603 (relating to service of summons) upon the person entitled to notice, or is mailed by certified or registered mail to the last known address of such person, or, in the absence of a last known address, is left with the person summoned. If such notice is mailed, it shall be sufficient if mailed to the last known address of the person entitled to notice or, in the case of notice to the Secretary under section 6903 of the

ENFORCEMENT—EXAMINATION

existence of a fiduciary relationship, to the last known address of the fiduciary of such person, even if such person or fiduciary is then deceased, under a legal disability, or no longer in existence.

(3) NATURE OF SUMMONS.—Any summons to which this subsection applies (and any summons in aid of collection described in subsection (c)(2)(D)) shall identify the taxpayer to whom the summons relates or the other person to whom the records pertain and shall provide such other information as will enable the person summoned to locate the records required under the summons.

Amendments

• **1998, IRS Restructuring and Reform Act of 1998 (P.L. 105-206)**

P.L. 105-206, §3415(a):

Amended Code Sec. 7609(a)(1) by striking so much of such paragraph as precedes "notice of the summons" and inserting new material. **Effective** for summonses served after 7-22-98. Prior to amendment, Code Sec. 7609(a)(1) read as follows:

(1) IN GENERAL.—If—

(A) any summons described in subsection (c) is served on any person who is a third-party recordkeeper, and

(B) the summons requires the production of any portion of records made or kept of the business transactions or affairs of any person (other than the person summoned) who is identified in the description of the records contained in the summons,

then notice of the summons shall be given to any person so identified within 3 days of the day on which such service is made, but no later than the 23rd day before the day fixed in the summons as the day upon which such records are to be examined. Such notice shall be accompanied by a copy of the summons which has been served and shall contain an explanation of the right under subsection (b)(2) to bring a proceeding to quash the summons.

P.L. 105-206, §3415(c)(1):

Amended Code Sec. 7609(a) by striking paragraphs (3) and (4), by redesignating paragraph (5) as paragraph (3), and by striking in paragraph (3) (as so redesignated) "subsection (c)(2)(B)" and inserting "subsection (c)(2)(D)". **Effective** for summonses served after 7-22-98. Prior to being stricken, Code Sec. 7609(a)(3)-(4) read as follows:

(3) THIRD-PARTY RECORDKEEPER DEFINED.—For purposes of this subsection, the term "third-party recordkeeper" means—

(A) any mutual savings bank, cooperative bank, domestic building and loan association, or other savings institution chartered and supervised as a savings and loan or similar association under Federal or State law, any bank (as defined in section 581), or any credit union (within the meaning of section 501(c)(14)(A));

(B) any consumer reporting agency (as defined under section 603(d) of the Fair Credit Reporting Act (15 U.S.C. 1681a(f)));

(C) any person extending credit through the use of credit cards or similar devices;

(D) any broker (as defined in section 3(a)(4) of the Securities Exchange Act of 1934 (15 U.S.C. 78c(a)(4)));

(E) any attorney;

(F) any accountant;

(G) any barter exchange (as defined in section 6045(c)(3));

(H) any regulated investment company (as defined in section 851) and any agent of such regulated investment company when acting as an agent thereof; and

(I) any enrolled agent.

(4) EXCEPTIONS.—Paragraph (1) shall not apply to any summons—

(A) served on the person with respect to whose liability the summons is issued, or any officer or employee of such person,

(B) to determine whether or not records of the business transactions or affairs of an identified person have been made or kept, or

(C) described in subsection (f).

• **1996, Taxpayer Bill of Rights 2 (P.L. 104-168)**

P.L. 104-168, §1001(a):

Amended Code Sec. 7609(a)(3) by striking "and" at the end of subparagraph (G), by striking the period at the end of subparagraph (H) and inserting "; and", and by adding at the end a new subparagraph (I). **Effective** for summonses issued after 7-30-96.

• **1986, Tax Reform Act of 1986 (P.L. 99-514)**

P.L. 99-514, §656(a)(1)-(3):

Amended Code Sec. 7609(a)(3) by striking out "and" at the end of subparagraph (F); by striking out the period at the end of subparagraph (G) and inserting in lieu thereof "; and"; and by adding new subparagraph (H). **Effective** for summonses served after 10-22-86.

• **1982, Tax Equity and Fiscal Responsibility Act of 1982 (P.L. 97-248)**

P.L. 97-248, §311(b):

Amended Code Sec. 7609(a)(3) by striking out "and" at the end of subparagraph (E), by striking out the period at the end of subparagraph (F) and inserting "; and", and by adding new subparagraph (G). **Effective** for summonses served after 12-31-82.

P.L. 97-248, §331(d)(1):

Amended Code Sec. 7609(a)(1) by striking out "14th day" and inserting "23rd day" and by striking out the last sentence and inserting a new last sentence. **Effective** for summonses served after 12-31-82. Prior to amendment, the last sentence of Code Sec. 7609(a)(1) read as follows:

Such notice shall be accompanied by a copy of the summons which has been served and shall contain directions for staying compliance with the summons under subsection (b)(2).

[Sec. 7609(b)]

(b) RIGHT TO INTERVENE; RIGHT TO PROCEEDING TO QUASH.—

(1) INTERVENTION.—Notwithstanding any other law or rule of law, any person who is entitled to notice of a summons under subsection (a) shall have the right to intervene in any proceeding with respect to the enforcement of such summons under section 7604.

(2) PROCEEDING TO QUASH.—

(A) IN GENERAL.—Notwithstanding any other law or rule of law, any person who is entitled to notice of a summons under subsection (a) shall have the right to begin a proceeding to quash such summons not later than the 20th day after the day such notice is given in the manner provided in subsection (a)(2). In any such proceeding, the Secretary may seek to compel compliance with the summons.

(B) REQUIREMENT OF NOTICE TO PERSON SUMMONED AND TO SECRETARY.—If any person begins a proceeding under subparagraph (A) with respect to any summons, not later than the close of the 20-day period referred to in subparagraph (A) such person shall mail by registered or certified mail a copy of the petition to the person summoned and to such office as the Secretary may direct in the notice referred to in subsection (a)(1).

(C) INTERVENTION; ETC.—Notwithstanding any other law or rule of law, the person summoned shall have the right to intervene in any proceeding under subparagraph (A). Such person shall be bound by the decision in such proceeding (whether or not the person intervenes in such proceeding).

Amendments

• **1982, Tax Equity and Fiscal Responsibility Act of 1982 (P.L. 97-248)**

P.L. 97-248, §331(a):

Amended Code Sec. 7609(b)(2). **Effective** for summonses served after 12-31-82. Prior to amendment, Code Sec. 7609(b)(2) read as follows:

"(2) RIGHT TO STAY COMPLIANCE.—Notwithstanding any other law or rule of law, any person who is entitled to notice of a summons under subsection (a) shall have the right to stay compliance with the summons if, not later than the 14th day after the day such notice is given in the manner provided in subsection (a)(2)—

(A) notice in writing is given to the person summoned not to comply with the summons, and

(B) a copy of such notice not to comply with the summons is mailed by registered or certified mail to such person and to such office as the Secretary may direct in the notice referred to in subsection (a)(1)."

P.L. 97-248, §331(d)(2):

Amended the subsection heading of Code Sec. 7609(b). **Effective** for summonses served after 12-31-82. Prior to amendment, the subsection heading read as follows: "RIGHT TO INTERVENE; RIGHT TO STAY COMPLIANCE.—".

[Sec. 7609(c)]

(c) SUMMONS TO WHICH SECTION APPLIES.—

(1) IN GENERAL.—Except as provided in paragraph (2), this section shall apply to any summons issued under paragraph (2) of section 7602(a) or under section 6420(e)(2), 6421(g)(2), 6427(j)(2), or 7612.

(2) EXCEPTIONS.—This section shall not apply to any summons—

(A) served on the person with respect to whose liability the summons is issued, or any officer or employee of such person;

(B) issued to determine whether or not records of the business transactions or affairs of an identified person have been made or kept;

(C) issued solely to determine the identity of any person having a numbered account (or similar arrangement) with a bank or other institution described in section 7603(b)(2)(A);

(D) issued in aid of the collection of—

(i) an assessment made or judgment rendered against the person with respect to whose liability the summons is issued; or

ENFORCEMENT—EXAMINATION

(ii) the liability at law or in equity of any transferee or fiduciary of any person referred to in clause (i); or

(E)(i) issued by a criminal investigator of the Internal Revenue Service in connection with the investigation of an offense connected with the administration or enforcement of the internal revenue laws; and

(ii) served on any person who is not a third-party recordkeeper (as defined in section 7603(b)).

(3) JOHN DOE AND CERTAIN OTHER SUMMONSES.—Subsection (a) shall not apply to any summons described in subsection (f) or (g).

(4) RECORDS.—For purposes of this section, the term "records" includes books, papers, and other data.

Amendments

• **2005, Gulf Opportunity Zone Act of 2005 (P.L. 109-135)**

P.L. 109-135, §408(a)(1):

Amended Code Sec. 7609(c)(2) by inserting "or" at the end of subparagraph (D), by striking "; or" at the end of subparagraph (E) and inserting a period, and by striking subparagraph (F). **Effective** as if included in section 3415 of the Internal Revenue Service Restructuring and Reform Act of 1998 (P.L. 105-206) **[effective for summonses served after 7-22-98.—CCH]**. Prior to being stricken, Code Sec. 7609(c)(2)(F) read as follows:

(F) described in subsection (f) or (g).

P.L. 109-135, §408(a)(2):

Amended Code Sec. 7609(c) by redesignating paragraph (3) as paragraph (4) and by inserting after paragraph (2) a new paragraph (3). **Effective** as if included in section 3415 of the Internal Revenue Service Restructuring and Reform Act of 1998 (P.L. 105-206) **[effective for summonses served after 7-22-98.—CCH]**.

• **1998, IRS Restructuring and Reform Act of 1998 (P.L. 105-206)**

P.L. 105-206, §3415(c)(2):

Amended Code Sec. 7609(c). **Effective** for summonses served after 7-22-98. Prior to amendment, Code Sec. 7609(c) read as follows:

(c) SUMMONS TO WHICH SECTION APPLIES.—

(1) IN GENERAL.—Except as provided in paragraph (2), a summons is described in this subsection if it is issued under paragraph (2) of section 7602(a) or under section 6420(e)(2), 6421(g)(2), or 6427(j)(2) and requires the production of records.

(2) EXCEPTIONS.—A summons shall not be treated as described in this subsection if—

(A) it is solely to determine the identity of any person having a numbered account (or similar arrangement) with a bank or other institution described in subsection (a)(3)(A), or

(B) it is in aid of the collection of—

(i) the liability of any person against whom an assessment has been made or judgment rendered, or

(ii) the liability at law or in equity of any transferee or fiduciary of any person referred to in clause (i).

(3) RECORDS; CERTAIN RELATED TESTIMONY.—For purposes of this section—

(A) the term "records" includes books, papers, or other data, and

(B) a summons requiring the giving of testimony relating to records shall be treated as a summons requiring the production of such records.

• **1988, Technical and Miscellaneous Revenue Act of 1988 (P.L. 100-647)**

P.L. 100-647, §1017(c)(9):

Amended Code Sec. 7609(c)(1) by striking out "6421(f)(2)" and inserting in lieu thereof "6421(g)(2)". **Effective** as if included in the provision of P.L. 99-514 to which it relates.

• **1986, Tax Reform Act of 1986 (P.L. 99-514)**

P.L. 99-514, §1703(e)(2)(G):

Amended Code Sec. 7609(c)(1) by striking out "6427(i)(2)" and inserting in lieu thereof "6427(j)(2)". **Effective** for gasoline removed (as defined in Code Sec. 4082, as amended) after 12-31-87.

• **1984, Deficit Reduction Act of 1984 (P.L. 98-369)**

P.L. 98-369, §714(i):

Amended Code Sec. 7609(c)(1) by striking out "section 7602" and inserting in lieu thereof "section 7602(a)". **Effective** as if included in P.L. 97-248.

P.L. 98-369, §911(d)[c](2)(G):

Amended Code Sec. 7609(c)(1) by striking out "6427(h)(2)" and inserting in lieu thereof "6427(i)(2)". **Effective** 8-1-84.

• **1983, Surface Transportation Act of 1983 (P.L. 97-424)**

P.L. 97-424, §515(b)(12):

Amended Code Sec. 7609(c) by striking out "6424(d)(2)," before "or 6427(h)(2)". **Effective** 1-6-83.

• **1980, Crude Oil Windfall Profit Tax Act of 1980 (P.L. 96-223)**

P.L. 96-223, §232(d)(4)(E):

Amended Code Sec. 7609(c)(1) by substituting "6427(h)(2)" for "6427(g)(2)". **Effective** 1-1-79.

• **1978, Revenue Act of 1978 (P.L. 95-600)**

P.L. 95-600, §703(1)(4), (r):

Substituted "6427(f)(2)" for "6427(e)(2)" in Code Sec. 7609(c)(1). **Effective** 10-4-76.

• **1978, Surface Transportation Assistance Act of 1978 (P.L. 95-599)**

P.L. 95-599, §505(c)(6), (d):

Substituted "6427(g)(2)" for "6427(e)[f](2)" in Code Sec. 7609(c)(1). **Effective** 1-1-79.

[Sec. 7609(d)]

(d) RESTRICTION ON EXAMINATION OF RECORDS.—No examination of any records required to be produced under a summons as to which notice is required under subsection (a) may be made—

(1) before the close of the 23rd day after the day notice with respect to the summons is given in the manner provided in subsection (a)(2), or

(2) where a proceeding under subsection (b)(2)(A) was begun within the 20-day period referred to in such subsection and the requirements of subsection (b)(2)(B) have been met, except in accordance with an order of the court having jurisdiction of such proceeding or with the consent of the person beginning the proceeding to quash.

Amendments

• **1982, Tax Equity and Fiscal Responsibility Act of 1982 (P.L. 97-248)**

P.L. 97-248, §331(b):

Amended Code Sec. 7609(d). **Effective** for summonses served after 12-31-82. Prior to amendment, Code Sec. 7609(d) read as follows:

"(d) RESTRICTION ON EXAMINATION OF RECORDS.—No examination of any records required to be produced under a summons as to which notice is required under subsection (a) may be made—

(1) before the expiration of the 14-day period allowed for the notice not to comply under subsection (b)(2), or

(2) when the requirements of subsection (b)(2) have been met, except in accordance with an order issued by a court of competent jurisdiction authorizing examination of such records or with the consent of the person staying compliance."

[Sec. 7609(e)]

(e) SUSPENSION OF STATUTE OF LIMITATIONS.—

(1) SUBSECTION (b) ACTION.—If any person takes any action as provided in subsection (b) and such person is the person with respect to whose liability the summons is issued (or is the agent, nominee, or other person acting under the direction or control of such person), then the running of any period of limitations under section 6501 (relating to the assessment and collection of tax) or under section 6531 (relating to criminal prosecutions) with respect to such person shall be suspended for the period during which a proceeding, and appeals therein, with respect to the enforcement of such summons is pending.

(2) SUSPENSION AFTER 6 MONTHS OF SERVICE OF SUMMONS.—In the absence of the resolution of the summoned party's response to the summons, the running of any period of limitations under section 6501 or under section 6531 with respect to any person with respect to whose liability the summons is issued (other than a person taking action as provided in subsection (b)) shall be suspended for the period—

(A) beginning on the date which is 6 months after the service of such summons, and

(B) ending with the final resolution of such response.

Amendments

• **1998, IRS Restructuring and Reform Act of 1998 (P.L. 105-206)**

P.L. 105-206, §3415(c)(3):

Amended Code Sec. 7609(e)(2) by striking "third-party recordkeeper's" and all that follows through "subsection (f)" and inserting "summoned party's response to the summons". **Effective** for summonses served after 7-22-98. Prior to amendment, Code Sec. 7609(e)(2) read as follows:

(2) SUSPENSION AFTER 6 MONTHS OF SERVICE OF SUMMONS.—In the absence of the resolution of the third-party recordkeeper's response to the summons described in subsection (c), or the summoned party's response to a summons described in subsec-

ENFORCEMENT—EXAMINATION

tion (f), the running of any period of limitations under section 6501 or under section 6531 with respect to any person with respect to whose liability the summons is issued (other than a person taking action as provided in subsection (b)) shall be suspended for the period—

(A) beginning on the date which is 6 months after the service of such summons, and

(B) ending with the final resolution of such response.

• **1988, Technical and Miscellaneous Revenue Act of 1988 (P.L. 100-647)**

P.L. 100-647, §1014(l)(1)(A)-(B):

Amended Code Sec. 7609(e)(2) by inserting "or the summoned party's response to a summons described in subsection (f)," after "the summons described in subsection (c),", and by striking out "the summons is issued other" and inserting in lieu thereof "the summons is issued". **Effective** on the date of the enactment of this Act.

[Sec. 7609(f)]

(f) ADDITIONAL REQUIREMENT IN THE CASE OF A JOHN DOE SUMMONS.—Any summons described in subsection (c)(1) which does not identify the person with respect to whose liability the summons is issued may be served only after a court proceeding in which the Secretary establishes that—

(1) the summons relates to the investigation of a particular person or ascertainable group or class of persons,

(2) there is a reasonable basis for believing that such person or group or class of persons may fail or may have failed to comply with any provision of any internal revenue law, and

(3) the information sought to be obtained from the examination of the records or testimony (and the identity of the person or persons with respect to whose liability the summons is issued) is not readily available from other sources.

The Secretary shall not issue any summons described in the preceding sentence unless the information sought to be obtained is narrowly tailored to information that pertains to the failure (or potential failure) of the person or group or class of persons referred to in paragraph (2) to comply with one or more provisions of the internal revenue law which have been identified for purposes of such paragraph.

Amendments

• **2019, Taxpayer First Act (P.L. 116-25)**

P.L. 116-25, §1204(a):

Amended Code Sec. 7609(f) by adding at the end a flush sentence. **Effective** for summonses served after the date that is 45 days after 7-1-2019.

• **1986, Tax Reform Act of 1986 (P.L. 99-514)**

P.L. 99-514, §1561(a):

Amended Code Sec. 7609(e). **Effective** 10-22-86. Prior to amendment, Code Sec. 7609(e) read as follows:

(e) SUSPENSION OF STATUTE OF LIMITATIONS.—If any person takes any action as provided in subsection (b) and such person is the person with respect to whose liability the summons is issued (or is the agent, nominee, or other person acting under the direction or control of such person), then the running of any period of limitations under section 6501 (relating to the assessment and collection of tax) or under section 6531 (relating to criminal prosecutions) with respect to such person shall be suspended for the period during which a proceeding, and appeals therein, with respect to the enforcement of such summons is pending.

• **1998, IRS Restructuring and Reform Act of 1998 (P.L. 105-206)**

P.L. 105-206, §3415(c)(4)(A):

Amended Code Sec. 7609(f) by striking "described in subsection (c)" and inserting "described in subsection (c)(1)". **Effective** for summonses served after 7-22-98.

P.L. 105-206, §3415(c)(4)(B):

Amended Code Sec. 7609(f)(3) by inserting "or testimony" after "records". **Effective** for summonses served after 7-22-98.

[Sec. 7609(g)]

(g) SPECIAL EXCEPTION FOR CERTAIN SUMMONSES.—A summons is described in this subsection if, upon petition by the Secretary, the court determines, on the basis of the facts and circumstances alleged, that there is reasonable cause to believe the giving of notice may lead to attempts to conceal, destroy, or alter records relevant to the examination, to prevent the communication of information from other persons through intimidation, bribery, or collusion, or to flee to avoid prosecution, testifying, or production of records.

Amendments

• **1998, IRS Restructuring and Reform Act of 1998 (P.L. 105-206)**

P.L. 105-206, §3415(c)(5):

Amended Code Sec. 7609(g) by striking "In the case of any summons described in subsection (c), the provisions of subsections (a)(1) and (b) shall not apply if" and inserting "A summons is described in this subsection if". **Effective** for summonses served after 7-22-98.

[Sec. 7609(h)]

(h) JURISDICTION OF DISTRICT COURT; ETC.—

(1) JURISDICTION.—The United States district court for the district within which the person to be summoned resides or is found shall have jurisdiction to hear and determine any proceedings brought under subsection (b)(2), (f), or (g). An order denying the petition shall be deemed a final order which may be appealed.

(2) SPECIAL RULE FOR PROCEEDINGS UNDER SUBSECTIONS (f) AND (g).—The determinations required to be made under subsections (f) and (g) shall be made ex parte and shall be made solely on the petition and supporting affidavits.

Amendments

• **1984 (P.L. 98-620)**

P.L. 98-620, §402(28)(D):

Repealed Code Sec. 7609(h)(3). Not **effective** for cases pending on 11-8-84. Prior to repeal, Code Sec. 7609(h)(3) read as follows:

(3) PRIORITY.—Except as to cases the court considers of greater importance, a proceeding brought for the enforcement of any summons, or a proceeding under this section, and appeals, take precedence on the docket over all other cases and shall be assigned for hearing and decided at the earliest practicable date.

• **1982, Tax Equity and Fiscal Responsibility Act of 1982 (P.L. 97-248)**

P.L. 97-248, §331(c):

Amended Code Sec. 7609(h). **Effective** for summonses served after 12-31-82. Prior to amendment, Code Sec. 7609(h) read as follows:

"(h) JURISDICTION OF DISTRICT COURT.—

(1) The United States district court for the district within which the person to be summoned resides or is found shall have jurisdiction to hear and determine proceedings brought under subsections (f) or (g). The determinations required to be made under subsections (f) and (g) shall be made ex parte and shall be made solely upon the petition and supporting affidavits. An order denying the petition shall be deemed a final order which may be appealed.

(2) Except as to cases the court considers of greater importance, a proceeding brought for the enforcement of any summons, or a proceeding under this section, and appeals, take precedence on the docket over all cases and shall be assigned for hearing and decided at the earliest practicable date."

• **1976, Tax Reform Act of 1976 (P.L. 94-455)**

P.L. 94-455, §1205(a):

Added Code Sec. 7609. **Effective** with respect to any summons issued after 2-28-77.

[Sec. 7609(i)]

(i) DUTY OF SUMMONED PARTY.—

(1) RECORDKEEPER MUST ASSEMBLE RECORDS AND BE PREPARED TO PRODUCE RECORDS.—On receipt of a summons to which this section applies for the production of records, the summoned party shall proceed to assemble the records requested, or such portion thereof as the Secretary may prescribe, and shall be prepared to produce the records pursuant to the summons on the day on which the records are to be examined.

(2) SECRETARY MAY GIVE SUMMONED PARTY CERTIFICATE.—The Secretary may issue a certificate to the summoned party that the period prescribed for beginning a proceeding to quash a summons has expired and that no such proceeding began within such period, or that the taxpayer consents to the examination.

(3) PROTECTION FOR SUMMONED PARTY WHO DISCLOSES.—Any summoned party, or agent or employee thereof, making a disclosure of records or testimony pursuant to this section in good faith reliance on the certificate of the Secretary or an order of a court requiring production of records or the giving of such testimony shall not be liable to any customer or other person for such disclosure.

ENFORCEMENT—EXAMINATION

(4) NOTICE OF SUSPENSION OF STATUTE OF LIMITATIONS IN THE CASE OF A JOHN DOE SUMMONS.—In the case of a summons described in subsection (f) with respect to which any period of limitations has been suspended under subsection (e)(2), the summoned party shall provide notice of such suspension to any person described in subsection (f).

Amendments

• **1998, IRS Restructuring and Reform Act of 1998 (P.L. 105-206)**

P.L. 105-206, §3415(c)(6)(A):

Amended Code Sec. 7609(i) by striking "THIRD-PARTY RECORDKEEPER AND" after "DUTY OF" in the subsection heading. **Effective** for summonses served after 7-22-98.

P.L. 105-206, §3415(c)(6)(B):

Amended Code Sec. 7609(i)(1) by striking "described in subsection (c), the third-party recordkeeper" and inserting "to which this section applies for the production of records, the summoned party". **Effective** for summonses served after 7-22-98.

P.L. 105-206, §3415(c)(6)(C)(i)-(ii):

Amended Code Sec. 7609(i)(2) by striking "RECORDKEEPER" in the heading and inserting "SUMMONED PARTY", and by striking "the third-party recordkeeper" and inserting "the summoned party". **Effective** for summonses served after 7-22-98.

P.L. 105-206, §3415(c)(6)(D):

Amended Code Sec. 7609(i)(3). **Effective** for summonses served after 7-22-98. Prior to amendment, Code Sec. 7609(i)(3) read as follows:

(3) PROTECTION FOR RECORDKEEPER WHO DISCLOSES.—Any third-party recordkeeper, or agent or employee thereof, making a disclosure of records pursuant to this section in good-faith reliance on the certificate of the Secretary or an order of a court requiring production of records shall not be liable to any customer or other person for such disclosure.

• **1988, Technical and Miscellaneous Revenue Act of 1988 (P.L. 100-647)**

P.L. 100-647, §1015(l)(2)(A)-(B):

Amended Code Sec. 7609(i) by striking out "the third-party recordkeeper" in paragraph (4) and inserting in lieu thereof "the summoned party", and by inserting "AND SUMMONED PARTY" after "RECORDKEEPER" in the subsection heading. **Effective** on the date of the enactment of this Act.

• **1986, Tax Reform Act of 1986 (P.L. 99-514)**

P.L. 99-514, §1561(b):

Amended Code Sec. 7609(i) by adding at the end thereof new paragraph (4). **Effective** 10-22-86.

• **1982, Tax Equity and Fiscal Responsibility Act of 1982 (P.L. 97-248)**

P.L. 97-248, §332(a):

Added Code Sec. 7609(i). **Effective** for summonses served after 12-31-82.

[Sec. 7609(j)]

(j) USE OF SUMMONS NOT REQUIRED.—Nothing in this section shall be construed to limit the Secretary's ability to obtain information, other than by summons, through formal or informal procedures authorized by sections 7601 and 7602.

Amendments

• **1998, IRS Restructuring and Reform Act of 1998 (P.L. 105-206)**

P.L. 105-206, §3415(b):

Amended Code Sec. 7609 by adding at the end a new subsection (j). **Effective** for summonses served after 7-22-98.

[Sec. 7610]

SEC. 7610. FEES AND COSTS FOR WITNESSES.

[Sec. 7610(a)]

(a) IN GENERAL.—The Secretary shall by regulations establish the rates and conditions under which payment may be made of—

(1) fees and mileage to persons who are summoned to appear before the Secretary, and

(2) reimbursement for such costs that are reasonably necessary which have been directly incurred in searching for, reproducing, or transporting books, papers, records, or other data required to be produced by summons.

[Sec. 7610(b)]

(b) EXCEPTIONS.—No payment may be made under paragraph (2) of subsection (a) if—

(1) the person with respect to whose liability the summons is issued has a proprietary interest in the books, papers, records or other data required to be produced, or

(2) the person summoned is the person with respect to whose liability the summons is issued or an officer, employee, agent, accountant, or attorney of such person who, at the time the summons is served, is acting as such.

[Sec. 7610(c)]

(c) SUMMONS TO WHICH SECTION APPLIES.—This section applies with respect to any summons authorized under section 6420(e)(2), 6421(g)(2), 6427(j)(2), or 7602.

Amendments

• **1988, Technical and Miscellaneous Revenue Act of 1988 (P.L. 100-647)**

P.L. 100-647, §1017(c)(9):

Amended Code Sec. 7610(c) by striking out "6421(f)(2)" and inserting in lieu thereof "6421(g)(2)". **Effective** as if included in the provision of P.L. 99-514 to which it relates.

• **1986, Tax Reform Act of 1986 (P.L. 99-514)**

P.L. 99-514, §1703(e)(2)(G):

Amended Code Sec. 7610(c) by striking out "6427(i)(2)" and inserting in lieu thereof "6427(j)(2)". **Effective** for gasoline removed (as defined in Code Sec. 4082, as amended) after 12-31-87.

• **1984, Deficit Reduction Act of 1984 (P.L. 98-369)**

P.L. 98-369, §911(d)[c](2)(G):

Amended Code Sec. 7610(c) by striking out "6427(h)(2)" and inserting in lieu thereof "6427(i)(2)". **Effective** 8-1-84.

• **1983, Surface Transportation Act of 1983 (P.L. 97-424)**

P.L. 97-424, §515(b)(12):

Amended Code Sec. 7610(c) by striking out "6424(d)(2)," before "6427(h)(2)". **Effective** 1-6-83.

• **1980, Crude Oil Windfall Profit Tax Act of 1980 (P.L. 96-223)**

P.L. 96-223, §232(d)(4)(E):

Amended Code Sec. 7610(c) by substituting "6427(h)(2)" for "6427(g)(2)". **Effective** 1-1-79.

• **1978, Surface Transportation Assistance Act of 1978 (P.L. 95-599)**

P.L. 95-599, §505(c)(6), (d):

Substituted "6427(g)(2)" for "6427(e)(2)" in Code Sec. 7610(c). **Effective** 1-1-79.

• **1976, Tax Reform Act of 1976 (P.L. 94-455)**

P.L. 94-455, §1205(a):

Added Code Sec. 7610. **Effective** with respect to any summons issued after 2-28-77.

[Sec. 7611]

SEC. 7611. RESTRICTIONS ON CHURCH TAX INQUIRIES AND EXAMINATIONS.

[Sec. 7611(a)]

(a) RESTRICTIONS ON INQUIRIES.—

(1) IN GENERAL.—The Secretary may begin a church tax inquiry only if—

(A) the reasonable belief requirements of paragraph (2), and

(B) the notice requirements of paragraph (3), have been met.

(2) REASONABLE BELIEF REQUIREMENTS.—The requirements of this paragraph are met with respect to any church tax inquiry if an appropriate high-level Treasury official reasonably believes (on the basis of facts and circumstances recorded in writing) that the church—

(A) may not be exempt, by reason of its status as a church, from tax under section 501(a), or

ENFORCEMENT—EXAMINATION

(B) may be carrying on an unrelated trade or business (within the meaning of section 513) or otherwise engaged in activities subject to taxation under this title.

(3) INQUIRY NOTICE REQUIREMENTS.—

(A) IN GENERAL.—The requirements of this paragraph are met with respect to any church tax inquiry if, before beginning such inquiry, the Secretary provides written notice to the church of the beginning of such inquiry.

(B) CONTENTS OF INQUIRY NOTICE.—The notice required by this paragraph shall include—

(i) an explanation of—

(I) the concerns which gave rise to such inquiry, and

(II) the general subject matter of such inquiry, and

(ii) a general explanation of the applicable—

(I) administrative and constitutional provisions with respect to such inquiry (including the right to a conference with the Secretary before any examination of church records), and

(II) provisions of this title which authorize such inquiry or which may be otherwise involved in such inquiry.

Amendments

(B) the notice requirements of paragraph (3), have been met.

• **1986, Tax Reform Act of 1986 (P.L. 99-514)**

P.L. 99-514, § 1899(A)(62):

Amended Code Sec. 7611(a)(1) by striking out all that followed subparagraph (A) and inserting in lieu thereof subparagraph (B). **Effective** 10-22-86. Prior to amendment, all that followed subparagraph (A) of Code Sec. 7611(a)(1) read as follows:

[Sec. 7611(b)]

(b) RESTRICTIONS ON EXAMINATIONS.—

(1) IN GENERAL.—The Secretary may begin a church tax examination only if the requirements of paragraph (2) have been met and such examination may be made only—

(A) in the case of church records, to the extent necessary to determine the liability for, and the amount of, any tax imposed by this title, and

(B) in the case of religious activities, to the extent necessary to determine whether an organization claiming to be a church is a church for any period.

(2) NOTICE OF EXAMINATION; OPPORTUNITY FOR CONFERENCE.—The requirements of this paragraph are met with respect to any church tax examination if—

(A) at least 15 days before the beginning of such examination, the Secretary provides the notice described in paragraph (3) to both the church and the appropriate regional counsel of the Internal Revenue Service, and

(B) the church has a reasonable time to participate in a conference described in paragraph (3)(A)(iii), but only if the church requests such a conference before the beginning of the examination.

(3) CONTENTS OF EXAMINATION NOTICE, ET CETERA.—

(A) IN GENERAL.—The notice described in this paragraph is a written notice which includes—

(i) a copy of the church tax inquiry notice provided to the church under subsection (a),

(ii) a description of the church records and activities which the Secretary seeks to examine,

(iii) an offer to have a conference between the church and the Secretary in order to discuss, and attempt to resolve, concerns relating to such examination, and

(iv) a copy of all documents which were collected or prepared by the Internal Revenue Service for use in such examination and the disclosure of which is required by the Freedom of Information Act (5 U.S.C. 552).

(B) EARLIEST DAY EXAMINATION NOTICE MAY BE PROVIDED.—The examination notice described in subparagraph (A) shall not be provided to the church before the 15th day after the date on which the church tax inquiry notice was provided to the church under subsection (a).

(C) OPINION OF REGIONAL COUNSEL WITH RESPECT TO EXAMINATION.—Any regional counsel of the Internal Revenue Service who receives an examination notice under paragraph (1) may, within 15 days after such notice is provided, submit to the regional commissioner for the region an advisory objection to the examination.

(4) EXAMINATION OF RECORDS AND ACTIVITIES NOT SPECIFIED IN NOTICE.—Within the course of a church tax examination which (at the time the examination begins) meets the requirements of paragraphs (1) and (2), the Secretary may examine any church records or religious activities which were not specified in the examination notice to the extent such examination meets the requirement of subparagraph (A) or (B) of paragraph (1) (whichever applies).

[Sec. 7611(c)]

(c) LIMITATION ON PERIOD OF INQUIRIES AND EXAMINATIONS.—

(1) INQUIRIES AND EXAMINATIONS MUST BE COMPLETED WITHIN 2 YEARS.—

(A) IN GENERAL.—The Secretary shall complete any church tax status inquiry or examination (and make a final determination with respect thereto) not later than the date which is 2 years after the examination notice date.

(B) INQUIRIES NOT FOLLOWED BY EXAMINATIONS.—In the case of a church tax inquiry with respect to which there is no examination notice under subsection (b), the Secretary shall complete such inquiry (and make a final determination with respect thereto) not later than the date which is 90 days after the inquiry notice date.

(2) SUSPENSION OF 2-YEAR PERIOD.—The running of the 2-year period described in paragraph (1)(A) and the 90-day period in paragraph (1)(B) shall be suspended—

(A) for any period during which—

(i) a judicial proceeding brought by the church against the Secretary with respect to the church tax inquiry or examination is pending or being appealed,

(ii) a judicial proceeding brought by the Secretary against the church (or any official thereof) to compel compliance with any reasonable request of the Secretary in a church tax examination for examination of church records or religious activities is pending or being appealed, or

(iii) the Secretary is unable to take actions with respect to the church tax inquiry or examination by reason of an order issued in any judicial proceeding brought under section 7609,

(B) for any period in excess of 20 days (but not in excess of 6 months) in which the church or its agents fail to comply with any reasonable request of the Secretary for church records or other information, or

ENFORCEMENT—EXAMINATION

(C) for any period mutually agreed upon by the Secretary and the church.

[Sec. 7611(d)]

(d) LIMITATIONS ON REVOCATION OF TAX-EXEMPT STATUS, ETC.—

(1) IN GENERAL.—The Secretary may—

(A) determine that an organization is not a church which—

(i) is exempt from taxation by reason of section 501(a), or

(ii) is described in section 170(c), or

(B)(i) send a notice of deficiency of any tax involved in a church tax examination, or

(ii) in the case of any tax with respect to which subchapter B of chapter 63 (relating to deficiency procedures) does not apply, assess any underpayment of such tax involved in a church tax examination,

only if the appropriate regional counsel of the Internal Revenue Service determines in writing that there has been substantial compliance with the requirements of this section and approves in writing of such revocation, notice of deficiency, or assessment.

(2) LIMITATIONS ON PERIOD OF ASSESSMENT.—

(A) REVOCATION OF TAX-EXEMPT STATUS.—

(i) 3-YEAR STATUTE OF LIMITATIONS GENERALLY.—In the case of any church tax examination with respect to the revocation of tax-exempt status under section 501(a), any tax imposed by chapter 1 (other than section 511) may be assessed, or a proceeding in court for collection of such tax may be begun without assessment, only for the 3 most recent taxable years ending before the examination notice date.

(ii) 6-YEAR STATUTE OF LIMITATIONS WHERE TAX-EXEMPT STATUS REVOKED.—If an organization is not a church exempt from tax under section 501(a) for any of the 3 taxable years described in clause (i), clause (i) shall be applied by substituting "6 most recent taxable years" for "3 most recent taxable years".

(B) UNRELATED BUSINESS TAX.—In the case of any church tax examination with respect to the tax imposed by section 511 (relating to unrelated business income), such tax may be assessed, or a proceeding in court for the collection of such tax may be begun without assessment, only with respect to the 6 most recent taxable years ending before the examination notice date.

(C) EXCEPTION WHERE SHORTER STATUTE OF LIMITATIONS OTHERWISE APPLICABLE.—Subparagraphs (A) and (B) shall not be construed to increase the period otherwise applicable under subchapter A of chapter 66 (relating to limitations on assessment and collection).

[Sec. 7611(e)]

(e) INFORMATION NOT COLLECTED IN SUBSTANTIAL COMPLIANCE WITH PROCEDURES TO STAY SUMMONS PROCEEDING.—

(1) IN GENERAL.—If there has not been substantial compliance with—

(A) the notice requirements of subsection (a) or (b),

(B) the conference requirement described in subsection (b)(3)(A)(iii), or

(C) the approval requirement of subsection (d)(1) (if applicable),

with respect to any church tax inquiry or examination, any proceeding to compel compliance with any summons with respect to such inquiry or examination shall be stayed until the court finds that all practicable steps to correct the noncompliance have been taken. The period applicable under paragraph (1) or [of] subsection (c) shall not be suspended during the period of any stay under the preceding sentence.

(2) REMEDY TO BE EXCLUSIVE.—No suit may be maintained, and no defense may be raised in any proceeding (other than as provided in paragraph (1)), by reason of any noncompliance by the Secretary with the requirements of this section.

[Sec. 7611(f)]

(f) LIMITATIONS ON ADDITIONAL INQUIRIES AND EXAMINATIONS.—

(1) IN GENERAL.—If any church tax inquiry or examination with respect to any church is completed and does not result in—

(A) a revocation, notice of deficiency, or assessment described in subsection (d)(1), or

(B) a request by the Secretary for any significant change in the operational practices of the church (including the adequacy of accounting practices),

no other church tax inquiry or examination may begin with respect to such church during the applicable 5-year period unless such inquiry or examination is approved in writing by the Secretary or does not involve the same or similar issues involved in the preceding inquiry or examination. For purposes of the preceding sentence, an inquiry or examination shall be treated as completed not later than the expiration of the applicable period under paragraph (1) of subsection (c).

(2) APPLICABLE 5-YEAR PERIOD.—For purposes of paragraph (1), the term "applicable 5-year period" means the 5-year period beginning on the date the notice taken into account for purposes of subsection (c)(1) was provided. For purposes of the preceding sentence, the rules of subsection (c)(2) shall apply.

Amendments

• 1998, IRS Restructuring and Reform Act of 1998 (P.L. 105-206)

P.L. 105-206, §1102(e)(3):

Amended Code Sec. 7611(f)(1) by striking "Assistant Commissioner for Employee Plans and Exempt Organizations of the Internal Revenue Service" and inserting "Secretary". **Effective**, generally, 7-22-98. For a special rule, see Act Sec. 1102(f)(3)-(4), below.

P.L. 105-206, §1102(f)(3)-(4), provides:

(3) NATIONAL TAXPAYER ADVOCATE.—Notwithstanding section 7803(c)(1)(B)(iv) of such Code, as added by this section, in appointing the first National Taxpayer Advocate after the date of the enactment of this Act, the Secretary of the Treasury—

(A) shall not appoint any individual who was an officer or employee of the Internal Revenue Service at any time during the 2-year period ending on the date of appointment, and

(B) need not consult with the Internal Revenue Service Oversight Board if the Oversight Board has not been appointed.

(4) CURRENT OFFICERS.—

(A) In the case of an individual serving as Commissioner of Internal Revenue on the date of the enactment of this Act who was appointed to such position before such date, the 5-year term required by section 7803(a)(1) of such Code, as added by this section, shall begin as of the date of such appointment.

(B) Clauses (ii), (iii), and (iv) of section 7803(c)(1)(B) of such Code, as added by this section, shall not apply to the individual serving as Taxpayer Advocate on the date of the enactment of this Act.

[Sec. 7611(g)]

(g) TREATMENT OF FINAL REPORT OF REVENUE AGENT.—Any final report of an agent of the Internal Revenue Service shall be treated as a determination of the Secretary under paragraph (1) of section 7428(a), and any church receiving such a report shall be treated for purposes of sections 7428 and 7430 as having exhausted the administrative remedies available to it.

[Sec. 7611(h)]

(h) DEFINITIONS.—For purposes of this section—

ENFORCEMENT—EXAMINATION

(1) CHURCH.—The term "church" includes—
  (A) any organization claiming to be a church, and
  (B) any convention or association of churches.
(2) CHURCH TAX INQUIRY.—The term "church tax inquiry" means any inquiry to a church (other than an examination) to serve as a basis for determining whether a church—
  (A) is exempt from tax under section 501(a) by reason of its status as a church, or
  (B) is carrying on an unrelated trade or business (within the meaning of section 513) or otherwise engaged in activities which may be subject to taxation under this title.
(3) CHURCH TAX EXAMINATION.—The term "church tax examination" means any examination for purposes of making a determination described in paragraph (2) of—
  (A) church records at the request of the Internal Revenue Service, or
  (B) the religious activities of any church.
(4) CHURCH RECORDS.—
  (A) IN GENERAL.—The term "church records" means all corporate and financial records regularly kept by a church, including corporate minute books and lists of members and contributors.
  (B) EXCEPTION.—Such term shall not include records acquired—
    (i) pursuant to a summons to which section 7609 applies, or
    (ii) from any governmental agency.
(5) INQUIRY NOTICE DATE.—The term "inquiry notice date" means the date the notice with respect to a church tax inquiry is provided under subsection (a).
(6) EXAMINATION NOTICE DATE.—The term "examination notice date" means the date the notice with respect to a church tax examination is provided under subsection (b) to the church.
(7) APPROPRIATE HIGH-LEVEL TREASURY OFFICIAL.—The term ["]appropriate high-level Treasury official" means the Secretary of the Treasury or any delegate of the Secretary whose rank is no lower than that of a principal Internal Revenue officer for an internal revenue region.

Amendments

• **1996, Small Business Job Protection Act of 1996 (P.L. 104-188)**

P.L. 104-188, § 1704(t)(59):

Amended Code Sec. 7611(h)(7) by striking "approporiate" and inserting "appropriate". **Effective** 8-20-96.

[Sec. 7611(i)]

(i) SECTION NOT TO APPLY TO CRIMINAL INVESTIGATIONS, ETC.—This section shall not apply to—
  (1) any criminal investigation,
  (2) any inquiry or examination relating to the tax liability of any person other than a church,
  (3) any assessment under section 6851 (relating to termination assessments of income tax), section 6852 (relating to termination assessments in case of flagrant political expenditures of section 501(c)(3) organizations), or section 6861 (relating to jeopardy assessments of income taxes, etc.),
  (4) any willful attempt to defeat or evade any tax imposed by this title, or
  (5) any knowing failure to file a return of tax imposed by this title.

Amendments

• **1989, Omnibus Budget Reconciliation Act of 1989 (P.L. 101-239)**

P.L. 101-239, § 7822(d)(1):

Amended Act Sec. 10713(b)(2) of the Revenue Act of 1987 (P.L. 100-203) which amended Code Sec. 7611(i)(3). Code Sec. 7611(i)(3) is correctly amended by striking all that follows "income tax" and inserting ", section 6852 (relating to termination assessments in case of flagrant political expenditures of section 501(c)(3) organizations), or section 6861 (relating to jeopardy assessments of income taxes, etc.),". **Effective** as if included in the provision of P.L. 100-203 to which it relates.

• **1988, Technical and Miscellaneous Revenue Act of 1988 (P.L. 100-647)**

P.L. 100-647, § 1018(u)(49):

Amended Code Sec. 7611(i)(5) by striking out "the title" and inserting in lieu thereof "this title". **Effective** as if included in the provision of P.L. 99-514 to which it relates.

• **1987, Revenue Act of 1987 (P.L. 100-203)**

P.L. 100-203, § 10713(b)(2)(G):

Amended Code Sec. 7611(i)(3) by striking out "or section 6861" and inserting in lieu thereof "section 6852 (relating to termination assessments in case of political expenditures of section 501(c)(3)), or 6861". **Effective** 12-22-87.

• **1986, Tax Reform Act of 1986 (P.L. 99-514)**

P.L. 99-514, § 1899A(61)(A)-(C):

Amended Code Sec. 7611(i) by redesignating subparagraphs (A), (B), (C), (D), and (E) as paragraphs (1), (2), (3), (4), and (5), respectively, by striking out "etc.)," in paragraph (3) (as so redesignated) and inserting in lieu thereof "etc.)," and by striking out "the title" in paragraph (5) (as so redesignated) and inserting in lieu thereof "the title". **Effective** 10-22-86.

• **1984, Deficit Reduction Act of 1984 (P.L. 98-369)**

P.L. 98-369, § 1033(a):

Redesignated Code Sec. 7611 as Code Sec. 7612 and added Code Sec. 7611. **Effective** with respect to inquiries and examinations beginning after 12-31-84.

[Sec. 7612]

SEC. 7612. SPECIAL PROCEDURES FOR SUMMONSES FOR COMPUTER SOFTWARE.

[Sec. 7612(a)]

(a) GENERAL RULE.—For purposes of this title—
  (1) except as provided in subsection (b), no summons may be issued under this title, and the Secretary may not begin any action under section 7604 to enforce any summons to produce or analyze any tax-related computer software source code; and
  (2) any software and related materials which are provided to the Secretary under this title shall be subject to the safeguards under subsection (c).

[Sec. 7612(b)]

(b) CIRCUMSTANCES UNDER WHICH COMPUTER SOFTWARE SOURCE CODE MAY BE PROVIDED.—
  (1) IN GENERAL.—Subsection (a)(1) shall not apply to any portion, item, or component of tax-related computer software source code if—
    (A) the Secretary is unable to otherwise reasonably ascertain the correctness of any item on a return from—
      (i) the taxpayer's books, papers, records, or other data; or
      (ii) the computer software executable code (and any modifications thereof) to which such source code relates and any associated data which, when executed, produces the output to ascertain the correctness of the item;

(B) the Secretary identifies with reasonable specificity the portion, item, or component of such source code needed to verify the correctness of such item on the return; and

(C) the Secretary determines that the need for the portion, item, or component of such source code with respect to such item outweighs the risks of unauthorized disclosure of trade secrets.

(2) EXCEPTIONS.—Subsection (a)(1) shall not apply to—

(A) any inquiry into any offense connected with the administration or enforcement of the internal revenue laws;

(B) any tax-related computer software source code acquired or developed by the taxpayer or a related person primarily for internal use by the taxpayer or such person rather than for commercial distribution;

(C) any communications between the owner of the tax-related computer software source code and the taxpayer or related persons; or

(D) any tax-related computer software source code which is required to be provided or made available pursuant to any other provision of this title.

(3) COOPERATION REQUIRED.—For purposes of paragraph (1), the Secretary shall be treated as meeting the requirements of subparagraphs (A) and (B) of such paragraph if—

(A) the Secretary determines that it is not feasible to determine the correctness of an item without access to the computer software executable code and associated data described in paragraph (1)(A)(ii);

(B) the Secretary makes a formal request to the taxpayer for such code and data and to the owner of the computer software source code for such executable code; and

(C) such code and data is not provided within 180 days of such request.

(4) RIGHT TO CONTEST SUMMONS.—In any proceeding brought under section 7604 to enforce a summons issued under the authority of this subsection, the court shall, at the request of any party, hold a hearing to determine whether the applicable requirements of this subsection have been met.

[Sec. 7612(c)]

(c) SAFEGUARDS TO ENSURE PROTECTION OF TRADE SECRETS AND OTHER CONFIDENTIAL INFORMATION.—

(1) ENTRY OF PROTECTIVE ORDER.—In any court proceeding to enforce a summons for any portion of software, the court may receive evidence and issue any order necessary to prevent the disclosure of trade secrets or other confidential information with respect to such software, including requiring that any information be placed under seal to be opened only as directed by the court.

(2) PROTECTION OF SOFTWARE.—Notwithstanding any other provision of this section, and in addition to any protections ordered pursuant to paragraph (1), in the case of software that comes into the possession or control of the Secretary in the course of any examination with respect to any taxpayer—

(A) the software may be used only in connection with the examination of such taxpayer's return, any appeal by the taxpayer to the Internal Revenue Service Independent Office of Appeals, any judicial proceeding (and any appeals therefrom), and any inquiry into any offense connected with the administration or enforcement of the internal revenue laws;

(B) the Secretary shall provide, in advance, to the taxpayer and the owner of the software a written list of the names of all individuals who will analyze or otherwise have access to the software;

(C) the software shall be maintained in a secure area or place, and, in the case of computer software source code, shall not be removed from the owner's place of business unless the owner permits, or a court orders, such removal;

(D) the software may not be copied except as necessary to perform such analysis, and the Secretary shall number all copies made and certify in writing that no other copies have been (or will be) made;

(E) at the end of the period during which the software may be used under subparagraph (A)—

(i) the software and all copies thereof shall be returned to the person from whom they were obtained and any copies thereof made under subparagraph (D) on the hard drive of a machine or other mass storage device shall be permanently deleted; and

(ii) the Secretary shall obtain from any person who analyzes or otherwise had access to such software a written certification under penalty of perjury that all copies and related materials have been returned and that no copies were made of them;

(F) the software may not be decompiled or disassembled;

(G) the Secretary shall provide to the taxpayer and the owner of any interest in such software, as the case may be, a written agreement, between the Secretary and any person who is not an officer or employee of the United States and who will analyze or otherwise have access to such software, which provides that such person agrees not to—

(i) disclose such software to any person other than persons to whom such information could be disclosed for tax administration purposes under section 6103; or

(ii) participate for 2 years in the development of software which is intended for a similar purpose as the software examined; and

(H) the software shall be treated as return information for purposes of section 6103.

For purposes of subparagraph (C), the owner shall make available any necessary equipment or materials for analysis of computer software source code required to be conducted on the owner's premises. The owner of any interest in the software shall be considered a party to any agreement described in subparagraph (G).

Amendments

• 2019, Taxpayer First Act (P.L. 116-25)

P.L. 116-25, § 1001(b)(1)(J):

Amended Code Sec. 7612(c)(2)(A) by striking "Internal Revenue Service Office of Appeals" and inserting "Internal Revenue Service Independent Office of Appeals". Effective 7-1-2019.

[Sec. 7612(d)]

(d) DEFINITIONS.—For purposes of this section—

(1) SOFTWARE.—The term "software" includes computer software source code and computer software executable code.

(2) COMPUTER SOFTWARE SOURCE CODE.—The term "computer software source code" means—

(A) the code written by a programmer using a programming language which is comprehensible to appropriately trained persons and is not capable of directly being used to give instructions to a computer;

(B) related programmers' notes, design documents, memoranda, and similar documentation; and

(C) related customer communications.

(3) COMPUTER SOFTWARE EXECUTABLE CODE.—The term "computer software executable code" means—

ENFORCEMENT—GENERAL POWERS AND DUTIES

(A) any object code, machine code, or other code readable by a computer when loaded into its memory and used directly by such computer to execute instructions; and

(B) any related user manuals.

(4) OWNER.—The term "owner" shall, with respect to any software, include the developer of the software.

(5) RELATED PERSON.—A person shall be treated as related to another person if such persons are related persons under section 267 or 707(b).

(6) TAX-RELATED COMPUTER SOFTWARE SOURCE CODE.—The term "tax-related computer software source code" means the computer source code for any computer software program intended for accounting, tax return preparation or compliance, or tax planning.

Amendments

• **1998, IRS Restructuring and Reform Act of 1998 (P.L. 105-206)**

P.L. 105-206, § 3413(a):

Amended Subchapter A of chapter 78 by redesignating Code Sec. 7612 as Code Sec. 7613 and by inserting after Code Sec. 7611 a new Code Sec. 7612. **Effective**, generally, for summonses issued, and software acquired, after 7-22-98. For a special rule, see Act Sec. 3413(e)(2), below.

P.L. 105-206, § 3413(e)(2), provides:

(2) SOFTWARE PROTECTION.—In the case of any software acquired on or before such date of enactment, the requirements of section 7612(a)(2) of the Internal Revenue Code of 1986 (as added by such amendments) shall apply after the 90th day after such date. The preceding sentence shall not apply to the requirement under section 7612(c)(2)(G)(ii) of such Code (as so added).

[Sec. 7613]

SEC. 7613. CROSS REFERENCES.

[Sec. 7613(a)]

(a) INSPECTION OF BOOKS, PAPERS, RECORDS, OR OTHER DATA.—

For inspection of books, papers, records, or other data in the case of—

(1) Wagering, see section 4423.

(2) Alcohol, tobacco, and firearms taxes, see subtitle E.

[Sec. 7613(b)]

(b) SEARCH WARRANTS.—

For provisions relating to—

(1) Searches and seizures see Rule 41 of the Federal Rules of Criminal Procedure.

(2) Issuance of search warrants with respect to subtitle E, see section 5557.

(3) Search warrants with respect to property used in violation of the internal revenue laws, see section 7302.

Amendments

• **1998, IRS Restructuring and Reform Act of 1998 (P.L. 105-206)**

P.L. 105-206, § 3413(a):

Amended subchapter A of chapter 78 by redesignating Code Sec. 7612 as Code Sec. 7613. **Effective**, generally, for summonses issued, and software acquired, after 7-22-98.

• **1984, Deficit Reduction Act of 1984 (P.L. 98-369)**

P.L. 98-369, § 1033(a):

Redesignated Code Sec. 7611 as Code Sec. 7612. **Effective** with respect to inquiries and examinations beginning after 12-31-84.

• **1976, Tax Reform Act of 1976 (P.L. 94-455)**

P.L. 94-455, § 1205(a):

Redesignated Code Sec. 7609 as Code Sec. 7611. **Effective** with respect to any summons issued after 2-28-77.

P.L. 94-455, § 1904(b)(7)(D):

Amended Code Sec. 7611(a) by striking out former paragraph (1). **Effective** 2-1-77. Prior to amendment, Code Sec. 7611(a)(1) read as follows:

(1) Wholesale dealers in oleomargarine, see section 4595.

P.L. 94-455, § 1904(b)(9)(E):

Amended Code Sec. 7611(a) by striking out former paragraph (2) and by redesignating paragraphs (5) and (6) as paragraphs (1) and (2). **Effective** 2-1-77. Prior to amendment, Sec. 7611(a)(2) read as follows:

(2) Wholesale dealers in process or renovated butter or adulterated butter, see section 4815(b).

• **1970 (P.L. 91-513)**

P.L. 91-513, § 1102(h):

Repealed paragraphs (3) and (4) of Code Sec. 7609(a). **Effective** 5-1-71. Prior to repeal, these paragraphs read as follows:

(3) Opium, opiates, and coca leaves, see sections 4702(a), 4705, 4721, and 4773.

(4) Marihuana, see sections 4742, 4753(b), and 4773.

• **1958, Excise Tax Technical Changes Act of 1958 (P.L. 85-859)**

P.L. 85-859, § 204(14):

Redesignated Code Sec. 7608 as 7609. **Effective** 9-3-58.

P.L. 85-859, § 204(15):

Amended Code Sec. 7609 as redesignated by Act Sec. 204(14). **Effective** 9-3-58. Prior to amendment, old Code Sec. 7608 read as follows:

SEC. 7608. CROSS REFERENCES.

(a) INSPECTION OF BOOKS, PAPERS, RECORDS, OR OTHER DATA.—

For inspection of books, papers, records, or other data in the case of—

(1) Wholesale dealers in oleomargarine, see section 4597.

(2) Wholesale dealers in process or renovated butter or adulterated butter, see section 4815(b).

(3) Opium, opiates, and coca leaves, see sections 4702(a), 4705, 4721, and 4773.

(4) Marihuana, see sections 4742, 4753(b), and 4773.

(5) Wagering, see section 4423.

(b) SEARCH WARRANTS.—

For provisions relating to—

(1) Searches and seizures see Rule 41 of the Federal Rules of Criminal Procedure.

(2) Search warrants in connection with industrial alcohol, etc., see sections 5314 and 7302.

• **1956, Narcotic Control Act of 1956 (P.L. 728, 84th Cong.)**

P.L. 728, 84th Cong., 2d Sess., § 104:

Redesignated Code Sec. 7607 as 7608, and added a new Code Sec. 7607. **Effective** 7-19-56.

Subchapter B—General Powers and Duties

Sec. 7621.	Internal revenue districts.
Sec. 7622.	Authority to administer oaths and certify.
Sec. 7623.	Expenses of detection of underpayments and fraud, etc.
Sec. 7624.	Reimbursement to state and local law enforcement agencies.

[Sec. 7621]

SEC. 7621. INTERNAL REVENUE DISTRICTS.

[Sec. 7621(a)]

(a) ESTABLISHMENT AND ALTERATION.—The President shall establish convenient internal revenue districts for the purpose of administering the internal revenue laws. The President may from time to time alter such districts.

Sec. 7612(d)(3)(A)

ENFORCEMENT—GENERAL POWERS AND DUTIES

[Sec. 7621(b)]

(b) BOUNDARIES.—For the purpose mentioned in subsection (a), the President may subdivide any State or the District of Columbia, or may unite into one district two or more States.

Amendments

• **1976, Tax Reform Act of 1976 (P.L. 94-455)**

P.L. 94-455, § 1906(a)(53):

Amended Code Sec. 7621(b). **Effective** 2-1-77. Prior to amendment, Code Sec. 7621(b) read as follows:

(b) BOUNDARIES.—For the purpose mentioned in subsection (a), the President may subdivide any State, Territory, or the District of Columbia, or may unite into one District two or more States or a Territory and one or more States.

• **1959, Alaska Omnibus Bill (P.L. 86-70)**

P.L. 86-70, § 22(e):

Amended 1954 Code Sec. 7621(b). **Effective** 1-3-59. Prior to amendment, Code Sec. 7621(b) read as follows:

(b) BOUNDARIES.—For the purpose mentioned in subsection (a), the President may subdivide any State, Territory, or the District of Columbia, or may unite two or more States or Territories into one district.

[Sec. 7622]

SEC. 7622. AUTHORITY TO ADMINISTER OATHS AND CERTIFY.

[Sec. 7622(a)]

(a) INTERNAL REVENUE PERSONNEL.—Every officer or employee of the Treasury Department designated by the Secretary for that purpose is authorized to administer such oaths or affirmations and to certify to such papers as may be necessary under the internal revenue laws or regulations made thereunder.

Amendments

• **1976, Tax Reform Act of 1976 (P.L. 94-455)**

P.L. 94-455, § 1906(b)(13)(A):

Amended 1954 Code by substituting "Secretary" for "Secretary or his delegate" each place it appeared. **Effective** 2-1-77.

[Sec. 7622(b)]

(b) OTHERS.—Any oath or affirmation required or authorized under any internal revenue law or under any regulations made thereunder may be administered by any person authorized to administer oaths for general purposes by the law of the United States, or of any State or possession of the United States, or of the District of Columbia, wherein such oath or affirmation is administered. This subsection shall not be construed as an exclusive enumeration of the persons who may administer such oaths or affirmations.

Amendments

• **1976, Tax Reform Act of 1976 (P.L. 94-455)**

P.L. 94-455, § 1906(c)(2):

Amended Code Sec. 7622(b) by deleting ", Territory," from between "State" and "or possession". **Effective** 2-1-77.

[Sec. 7623]

SEC. 7623. EXPENSES OF DETECTION OF UNDERPAYMENTS AND FRAUD, ETC.

[Sec. 7623(a)]

(a) IN GENERAL.—The Secretary, under regulations prescribed by the Secretary, is authorized to pay such sums as he deems necessary for—

(1) detecting underpayments of tax, or

(2) detecting and bringing to trial and punishment persons guilty of violating the internal revenue laws or conniving at the same,

in cases where such expenses are not otherwise provided for by law. Any amount payable under the preceding sentence shall be paid from the proceeds of amounts collected by reason of the information provided, and any amount so collected shall be available for such payments.

Amendments

• **2006, Tax Relief and Health Care Act of 2006 (P.L. 109-432)**

P.L. 109-432, Division A, § 406(a)(1)(A)-(C):

Amended Code Sec. 7623 by striking "The Secretary" and inserting "(a) IN GENERAL.—The Secretary", by striking "and" at the end of paragraph (1) and inserting "or", and by striking "(other than interest)" following "paid from the proceeds of amounts". **Effective** for information provided on or after 12-20-2006.

• **1998, IRS Restructuring and Reform Act of 1998 (P.L. 105-206)**

P.L. 105-206, § 3804, provides:

SEC. 3804. STUDY OF PAYMENTS MADE FOR DETECTION OF UNDERPAYMENTS AND FRAUD.

Not later than 1 year after the date of the enactment of this Act, the Secretary of the Treasury shall conduct a study and report to Congress on the use of section 7623 of the Internal Revenue Code of 1986 including—

(1) an analysis of the present use of such section and the results of such use, and

(2) any legislative or administrative recommendations regarding the provisions of such section and its application.

• **1996, Taxpayer Bill of Rights 2 (P.L. 104-168)**

P.L. 104-168, § 1209(a):

Amended Code Sec. 7623. **Effective** on the date which is 6 months after 7-30-96. Prior to amendment, Code Sec. 7623 read as follows:

CODE SEC. 7623. EXPENSES OF DETECTION AND PUNISHMENT OF FRAUDS.

The Secretary, under regulations prescribed by the Secretary, is authorized to pay such sums, not exceeding in the aggregate the sum appropriated therefor, as he may deem necessary for detecting and bringing to trial and punishment persons guilty of violating the internal revenue laws, or conniving at the same, in cases where such expenses are not otherwise provided for by law.

P.L. 104-168, § 1209(d), provides:

(d) REPORT.—The Secretary of the Treasury or his delegate shall submit an annual report to the Committee on Ways and Means of the House of Representatives and the Committee on Finance of the Senate on the payments under section 7623 of the Internal Revenue Code of 1986 during the year and on the amounts collected for which such payments were made.

• **1976, Tax Reform Act of 1976 (P.L. 94-455)**

P.L. 94-455, § 1906(b)(13)(A):

Amended 1954 Code by substituting "Secretary" for "Secretary or his delegate" each place it appeared. **Effective** 2-1-77.

[Sec. 7623(b)]

(b) AWARDS TO WHISTLEBLOWERS.—

(1) IN GENERAL.—If the Secretary proceeds with any administrative or judicial action described in subsection (a) based on information brought to the Secretary's attention by an individual, such individual shall, subject to paragraph (2), receive as an award at least 15 percent but not more than 30 percent of the proceeds collected as a result of the action (including any related actions) or from any settlement in response to such action (determined without regard to whether such proceeds are available to the Secretary). The determination of the amount of such award by the Whistleblower Office shall depend upon the extent to which the individual substantially contributed to such action.

(2) AWARD IN CASE OF LESS SUBSTANTIAL CONTRIBUTION.—

(A) IN GENERAL.—In the event the action described in paragraph (1) is one which the Whistleblower Office determines to be based principally on disclosures of specific allegations (other than information provided by the individual described in paragraph (1)) resulting

ENFORCEMENT—GENERAL POWERS AND DUTIES

from a judicial or administrative hearing, from a governmental report, hearing, audit, or investigation, or from the news media, the Whistleblower Office may award such sums as it considers appropriate, but in no case more than 10 percent of the proceeds collected as a result of the action (including any related actions) or from any settlement in response to such action (determined without regard to whether such proceeds are available to the Secretary), taking into account the significance of the individual's information and the role of such individual and any legal representative of such individual in contributing to such action.

(B) NONAPPLICATION OF PARAGRAPH WHERE INDIVIDUAL IS ORIGINAL SOURCE OF INFORMATION.—Subparagraph (A) shall not apply if the information resulting in the initiation of the action described in paragraph (1) was originally provided by the individual described in paragraph (1).

(3) REDUCTION IN OR DENIAL OF AWARD.—If the Whistleblower Office determines that the claim for an award under paragraph (1) or (2) is brought by an individual who planned and initiated the actions that led to the underpayment of tax or actions described in subsection (a)(2), then the Whistleblower Office may appropriately reduce such award. If such individual is convicted of criminal conduct arising from the role described in the preceding sentence, the Whistleblower Office shall deny any award.

(4) APPEAL OF AWARD DETERMINATION.—Any determination regarding an award under paragraph (1), (2), or (3) may, within 30 days of such determination, be appealed to the Tax Court (and the Tax Court shall have jurisdiction with respect to such matter).

(5) APPLICATION OF THIS SUBSECTION.—This subsection shall apply with respect to any action—

(A) against any taxpayer, but in the case of any individual, only if such individual's gross income exceeds $200,000 for any taxable year subject to such action, and

(B) if the proceeds in dispute exceed $2,000,000.

(6) ADDITIONAL RULES.—

(A) NO CONTRACT NECESSARY.—No contract with the Internal Revenue Service is necessary for any individual to receive an award under this subsection.

(B) REPRESENTATION.—Any individual described in paragraph (1) or (2) may be represented by counsel.

(C) SUBMISSION OF INFORMATION.—No award may be made under this subsection based on information submitted to the Secretary unless such information is submitted under penalty of perjury.

Amendments

- **2018, Bipartisan Budget Act of 2018 (P.L. 115-123)**

P.L. 115-123, § 41108(a)(2), Div. D:

Amended Code Sec. 7623(b)(1) and (2)(A) by striking "collected proceeds (including penalties, interest, additions to tax, and additional amounts) resulting from the action" and inserting "proceeds collected as a result of the action". **Effective** for information provided before, on, or after 2-9-2018 with respect to which a final determination for an award has not been made before 2-9-2018.

P.L. 115-123, § 41108(b), Div. D:

Amended Code Sec. 7623(b)(1) and (2)(A) by inserting "(determined without regard to whether such proceeds are available to the Secretary)" after "in response to such action". **Effective** for information provided before, on, or after 2-9-2018 with respect to which a final determination for an award has not been made before 2-9-2018.

P.L. 115-123, § 41108(c), Div. D:

Amended Code Sec. 7623(b)(5)(B) by striking "tax, penalties, interest, additions to tax, and additional amounts" and inserting "proceeds". **Effective** for information provided before, on, or after 2-9-2018 with respect to which a final determination for an award has not been made before 2-9-2018.

- **2006, Tax Relief and Health Care Act of 2006 (P.L. 109-432)**

P.L. 109-432, Division A, § 406(a)(1)(A)-(D):

Amended Code Sec. 7623 by striking "The Secretary" and inserting "(a) IN GENERAL.—The Secretary", by striking "and" at the end of paragraph (1) and inserting "or", by striking "(other than interest)" following "paid from the proceeds of amounts", and by adding at the end a new subsection (b). **Effective** for information provided on or after 12-20-2006.

P.L. 109-432, Division A, § 406(b)-(d), provide:

(b) WHISTLEBLOWER OFFICE.—

(1) IN GENERAL.—Not later than the date which is 12 months after the date of the enactment of this Act, the Secretary of the Treasury shall issue guidance for the operation of a whistleblower program to be administered in the Internal Revenue Service by an office to be known as the "Whistleblower Office" which—

(A) shall at all times operate at the direction of the Commissioner of Internal Revenue and coordinate and consult with other divisions in the Internal Revenue Service as directed by the Commissioner of Internal Revenue,

(B) shall analyze information received from any individual described in section 7623(b) of the Internal Revenue Code of 1986 and either investigate the matter itself or assign it to the appropriate Internal Revenue Service office, and

(C) in its sole discretion, may ask for additional assistance from such individual or any legal representative of such individual.

(2) REQUEST FOR ASSISTANCE.—The guidance issued under paragraph (1) shall specify that any assistance requested under paragraph (1)(C) shall be under the direction and control of the Whistleblower Office or the office assigned to investigate the matter under paragraph (1)(A). No individual or legal representative whose assistance is so requested may by reason of such request represent himself or herself as an employee of the Federal Government.

(c) REPORT BY SECRETARY.—The Secretary of the Treasury shall each year conduct a study and report to Congress on the use of section 7623 of the Internal Revenue Code of 1986, including—

(1) an analysis of the use of such section during the preceding year and the results of such use, and

(2) any legislative or administrative recommendations regarding the provisions of such section and its application.

(d) EFFECTIVE DATE.—The amendments made by subsection (a) shall apply to information provided on or after the date of the enactment of this Act.

[Sec. 7623(c)]

(c) PROCEEDS.—For purposes of this section, the term "proceeds" includes—

(1) penalties, interest, additions to tax, and additional amounts provided under the internal revenue laws, and

(2) any proceeds arising from laws for which the Internal Revenue Service is authorized to administer, enforce, or investigate, including—

(A) criminal fines and civil forfeitures, and

(B) violations of reporting requirements.

Amendments

- **2018, Bipartisan Budget Act of 2018 (P.L. 115-123)**

P.L. 115-123, § 41108(a)(1), Div. D:

Amended Code Sec. 7623 by adding at the end a new subsection (c). **Effective** for information provided before, on, or after 2-9-2018 with respect to which a final determination for an award has not been made before 2-9-2018.

[Sec. 7623(d)]

(d) CIVIL ACTION TO PROTECT AGAINST RETALIATION CASES.—

(1) ANTI-RETALIATION WHISTLEBLOWER PROTECTION FOR EMPLOYEES.—No employer, or any officer, employee, contractor, subcontractor, or agent of such employer, may discharge, demote, suspend, threaten, harass, or in any other manner discriminate against an employee in the terms and conditions of employment (including through an act in the ordinary course of such employee's duties) in reprisal for any lawful act done by the employee—

(A) to provide information, cause information to be provided, or otherwise assist in an investigation regarding underpayment of tax or any conduct which the employee reasonably believes constitutes a violation of the internal revenue laws or any provision of Federal law relating to tax fraud, when the information or assistance is provided to the Internal Revenue Service, the Secretary of the Treasury, the Treasury Inspector General for Tax Administration, the Comptroller General of the United States, the Department of Justice, the United

ENFORCEMENT—GENERAL POWERS AND DUTIES

States Congress, a person with supervisory authority over the employee, or any other person working for the employer who has the authority to investigate, discover, or terminate misconduct, or

(B) to testify, participate in, or otherwise assist in any administrative or judicial action taken by the Internal Revenue Service relating to an alleged underpayment of tax or any violation of the internal revenue laws or any provision of Federal law relating to tax fraud.

(2) ENFORCEMENT ACTION.—

(A) IN GENERAL.—A person who alleges discharge or other reprisal by any person in violation of paragraph (1) may seek relief under paragraph (3) by—

(i) filing a complaint with the Secretary of Labor, or

(ii) if the Secretary of Labor has not issued a final decision within 180 days of the filing of the complaint and there is no showing that such delay is due to the bad faith of the claimant, bringing an action at law or equity for de novo review in the appropriate district court of the United States, which shall have jurisdiction over such an action without regard to the amount in controversy.

(B) PROCEDURE.—

(i) IN GENERAL.—An action under subparagraph (A)(i) shall be governed under the rules and procedures set forth in section 42121(b) of title 49, United States Code.

(ii) EXCEPTION.—Notification made under section 42121(b)(1) of title 49, United States Code, shall be made to the person named in the complaint and to the employer.

(iii) BURDENS OF PROOF.—An action brought under subparagraph (A)(ii) shall be governed by the legal burdens of proof set forth in section 42121(b) of title 49, United States Code, except that in applying such section—

(I) "behavior described in paragraph (1)" shall be substituted for "behavior described in paragraphs (1) through (4) of subsection (a)" each place it appears in paragraph (2)(B) thereof, and

(II) "a violation of paragraph (1)" shall be substituted for "a violation of subsection (a)" each place it appears.

(iv) STATUTE OF LIMITATIONS.—A complaint under subparagraph (A)(i) shall be filed not later than 180 days after the date on which the violation occurs.

(v) JURY TRIAL.—A party to an action brought under subparagraph (A)(ii) shall be entitled to trial by jury.

(3) REMEDIES.—

(A) IN GENERAL.—An employee prevailing in any action under paragraph (2)(A) shall be entitled to all relief necessary to make the employee whole.

(B) COMPENSATORY DAMAGES.—Relief for any action under subparagraph (A) shall include—

(i) reinstatement with the same seniority status that the employee would have had, but for the reprisal,

(ii) the sum of 200 percent of the amount of back pay and 100 percent of all lost benefits, with interest, and

(iii) compensation for any special damages sustained as a result of the reprisal, including litigation costs, expert witness fees, and reasonable attorney fees.

(4) RIGHTS RETAINED BY EMPLOYEE.—Nothing in this section shall be deemed to diminish the rights, privileges, or remedies of any employee under any Federal or State law, or under any collective bargaining agreement.

(5) NONENFORCEABILITY OF CERTAIN PROVISIONS WAIVING RIGHTS AND REMEDIES OR REQUIRING ARBITRATION OF DISPUTES.—

(A) WAIVER OF RIGHTS AND REMEDIES.—The rights and remedies provided for in this subsection may not be waived by any agreement, policy form, or condition of employment, including by a predispute arbitration agreement.

(B) PREDISPUTE ARBITRATION AGREEMENTS.—No predispute arbitration agreement shall be valid or enforceable, if the agreement requires arbitration of a dispute arising under this subsection.

Amendments

- 2019, Taxpayer First Act (P.L. 116-25)

P.L. 116-25, §1405(b):

Amended Code Sec. 7623 by adding at the end a new subsection (d). **Effective** 7-1-2019.

[Sec. 7624]

SEC. 7624. REIMBURSEMENT TO STATE AND LOCAL LAW ENFORCEMENT AGENCIES.

[Sec. 7624(a)]

(a) AUTHORIZATION OF REIMBURSEMENT.—Whenever a State or local law enforcement agency provides information to the Internal Revenue Service that substantially contributes to the recovery of Federal taxes imposed with respect to illegal drug-related activities (or money laundering in connection with such activities), such agency may be reimbursed by the Internal Revenue Service for costs incurred in the investigation (including but not limited to reasonable expenses, per diem, salary, and overtime) not to exceed 10 percent of the sum recovered.

[Sec. 7624(b)]

(b) RECORDS; 10 PERCENT LIMITATION.—The Internal Revenue Service shall maintain records of the receipt of information from a contributing agency and shall notify the agency when monies have been recovered as the result of such information. Following such notification, the agency shall submit a statement detailing the investigative costs it incurred. Where more than 1 State or local agency has given information that substantially contributes to the recovery of Federal taxes, the Internal Revenue Service shall equitably allocate investigative costs among such agencies not to exceed an aggregate amount of 10 percent of the taxes recovered.

[Sec. 7624(c)]

(c) NO REIMBURSEMENT WHERE DUPLICATIVE.—No State or local agency may receive reimbursement under this section if reimbursement has been received by such agency under a Federal or State forfeiture program or under State revenue laws.

Amendments

- 1988, Anti-Drug Abuse Act of 1988 (P.L. 100-690)

P.L. 100-690, §7602:

Amended subchapter B of chapter 78 by adding Code Section 7624. **Effective** for information first provided more than 90 days after 11-18-88.

ENFORCEMENT—POSSESSIONS

Subchapter C—Supervision of Operations of Certain Manufacturers—[Repealed]

[Sec. 7641—Repealed]

Amendments

• **1976, Tax Reform Act of 1976 (P.L. 94-455)**

P.L. 94-455, §1906(a)(54):

Repealed subchapter C of chapter 78. **Effective** 10-4-76. Prior to repeal, Code Sec. 7641 read as follows:

SEC. 7641. SUPERVISION OF OPERATIONS OF CERTAIN MANUFACTURERS.

Every manufacturer of oleomargarine, process or renovated butter or adulterated butter, or white phosphorus matches shall conduct his business under such surveillance of officers or employees of the Treasury Department as the Secretary or his delegate may by regulations require.

• **1974 (P.L. 93-490)**

P.L. 93-490, §3(b)(8):

Amended Code Sec. 7641 by deleting the words "filled cheese," before the word "oleomargarine". **Effective** with respect to filled cheese manufactured, imported, or sold after 10-26-74.

• **1970 (P.L. 91-513)**

P.L. 91-513, §1102(i):

Amended Code Sec. 7641 by deleting "opium suitable for smoking purposes," after "oleomargarine". **Effective** 5-1-71.

Subchapter D—Possessions

Sec. 7651.   Administration and collection of taxes in possessions.
Sec. 7652.   Shipments to the United States.
Sec. 7653.   Shipments from the United States.
Sec. 7654.   Coordination of United States and certain possession individual income taxes.
Sec. 7655.   Cross references.

[Sec. 7651]

SEC. 7651. ADMINISTRATION AND COLLECTION OF TAXES IN POSSESSIONS.

Except as otherwise provided in this subchapter, and except as otherwise provided in section 28(a) of the Revised Organic Act of the Virgin Islands and section 30 of the Organic Act of Guam (relating to the covering of the proceeds of certain taxes into the treasuries of the Virgin Islands and Guam, respectively)—

(1) APPLICABILITY OF ADMINISTRATIVE PROVISIONS.—All provisions of the laws of the United States applicable to the assessment and collection of any tax imposed by this title or of any other liability arising under this title (including penalties) shall, in respect of such tax or liability, extend to and be applicable in any possession of the United States in the same manner and to the same extent as if such possession were a State, and as if the term "United States" when used in a geographical sense included such possession.

(2) TAX IMPOSED IN POSSESSION.—In the case of any tax which is imposed by this title in any possession of the United States—

(A) INTERNAL REVENUE COLLECTIONS.—Such tax shall be collected under the direction of the Secretary, and shall be paid into the Treasury of the United States as internal revenue collections; and

(B) APPLICABLE LAWS.—All provisions of the laws of the United States applicable to the administration, collection, and enforcement of such tax (including penalties) shall, in respect of such tax, extend to and be applicable in such possession of the United States in the same manner and to the same extent as if such possession were a State, and as if the term "United States" when used in a geographical sense included such possession.

(3) OTHER LAWS RELATING TO POSSESSIONS.—This section shall apply notwithstanding any other provision of law relating to any possession of the United States.

(4) VIRGIN ISLANDS.—

(A) For purposes of this section, the reference in section 28(a) of the Revised Organic Act of the Virgin Islands to "any tax specified in section 3811 of the Internal Revenue Code" shall be deemed to refer to any tax imposed by chapter 2 or by chapter 21.

(B) For purposes of this title, section 28(a) of the Revised Organic Act of the Virgin Islands shall be effective as if such section 28(a) had been enacted before the enactment of this title and such section 28(a) shall have no effect on the amount of income tax liability required to be paid by any person to the United States.

Amendments

• **2007, Tax Technical Corrections Act of 2007 (P.L. 110-172)**

P.L. 110-172, §11(a)(34)(B):

Amended Code Sec. 7651 by striking paragraph (4) and by redesignating paragraph (5) as paragraph (4). **Effective** 12-29-2007. Prior to being stricken, Code Sec. 7651(4) read as follows:

(4) CANAL ZONE.—For purposes of this section, the term "possession of the United States" includes the Canal Zone.

• **1986, Tax Reform Act of 1986 (P.L. 99-514)**

P.L. 99-514, §1275(b):

Amended Code Sec. 7651(5)(B). For the **effective** date, see Act Sec. 1277(c)(2)(A)-(E), below. For special rules, see the full text of Act Sec. 1277 reproduced under the amendment notes for Code Sec. 48. Prior to amendment, Code Sec. 7651(5)(B) read as follows:

(B) For purposes of this title (other than section 881(b)(1)) or subpart C of part III of subchapter N of chapter 1), section 28(a) of the Revised Organic Act of the Virgin Islands shall be effective as if such section had been enacted subsequent to the enactment of this title.

P.L. 99-514, §1277(c)(2)(A)-(E), provides:

(2) SECTION 1275(b).—

(A) IN GENERAL.—The amendment made by section 1275(b) shall apply with respect to—

(i) any taxable year beginning after December 31, 1986, and

(ii) any pre-1987 open year.

(B) SPECIAL RULES.—In the case of any pre-1987 open year—

(i) the amendment made by section 1275(b) shall not apply to income from sources in the Virgin Islands or income effectively connected with the conduct of a trade or business in the Virgin Islands, and

(ii) the taxpayer shall be allowed a credit—

(I) against any additional tax imposed by subtitle A of the Internal Revenue Code of 1954 (by reason of the amendment made by section 1275(b)) on income not described in clause (i) and from sources in the United States,

(II) for any tax paid to the Virgin Islands before the date of the enactment of this Act and attributable to such income.

For purposes of clause (ii)(II), any tax paid before January 1, 1987, pursuant to a process in effect before August 16, 1986, shall be treated as paid before the date of the enactment of this Act.

(C) PRE-1987 OPEN YEAR.—For purposes of this paragraph, the term "pre-1987 open year" means any taxable year beginning before January 1, 1987, if on the date of the enactment of this Act the assessment of a deficiency of income tax for such taxable year is not barred by any law or rule of law.

(D) EXCEPTION.—In the case of any pre-1987 open year, the amendment made by section 1275(b) shall not apply to any domestic corporation if—

(i) during the fiscal year which ended May 31, 1986, such corporation was actively engaged directly or through a subsidiary in the conduct of a trade or business in the Virgin Islands and such trade or business consists of business related to marine activities, and

(ii) such corporation was incorporated on March 31, 1983, in Delaware.

(E) EXCEPTION FOR CERTAIN TRANSACTIONS.—

(i) IN GENERAL.—In the case of any pre-1987 open year, the amendment made by section 1275(b) shall not apply to any income derived from transactions described in clause (ii) by 1 or more corporations which were formed in Delaware on or about March 6, 1981, and which have owned 1 or more office buildings in St. Thomas, United States Virgin Islands, for at least 5 years before the date of the enactment of this Act.

(ii) DESCRIPTION OF TRANSACTIONS.—The transactions described in this clause are—

(I) the redemptions of limited partnership interests for cash and property described in an agreement (as amended) dated March 12, 1981,

(II) the subsequent disposition of the properties distributed in such redemptions, and

ENFORCEMENT—POSSESSIONS

(III) interest earned before January 1, 1987, on bank deposits of proceeds received from such redemptions to the extent such deposits are located in the United States Virgin Islands.

(iii) LIMITATION.—The aggregate reduction in tax by reason of this subparagraph shall not exceed $8,312,000. If the taxes which would be payable as the result of the application of the amendment made by section 1275(b) to pre-1987 open years exceeds the limitation of the preceding sentence, such excess shall be treated as attributable to income received in taxable years in reverse chronological order.

• **1984, Deficit Reduction Act of 1984 (P.L. 98-369)**

P.L. 98-369, § 130(c):

Amended Code Sec. 7651(5)(B) by inserting "(other than section 881(b)(1))" after "For purposes of this title". **Effective** for payments made after 3-1-84, in tax years ending after such date.

• **1984, Deficit Reduction Act of 1984 (P.L. 98-369)**

P.L. 98-369, § 801(d)(9):

Amended Code Sec. 7651(5)(B), as amended by this Act, by inserting "or subpart C of part III of subchapter N of chapter 1" after "881(b)(1)". **Effective** for transactions after 12-31-84, in tax years ending after such date.

• **1976, Tax Reform Act of 1976 (P.L. 94-455)**

P.L. 94-455, § 1906(b)(13)(A):

Amended 1954 Code by substituting "Secretary" for "Secretary or his delegate" each place it appeared. **Effective** 2-1-77.

• **1970 (P.L. 91-513)**

P.L. 91-513, § 1102(j):

Amended the first sentence of Code Sec. 7651 by deleting "and in sections 4705(b), 4735, and 4762 (relating to taxes on narcotic drugs and marihuana)" after the word "subchapter." **Effective** 5-1-71.

SEC. 7652. SHIPMENTS TO THE UNITED STATES.

[Sec. 7652(a)]

(a) PUERTO RICO.—

(1) RATE OF TAX.—Except as provided in section 5314, articles of merchandise of Puerto Rican manufacture coming into the United States and withdrawn for consumption or sale shall be subject to a tax equal to the internal revenue tax imposed in the United States upon the like articles of merchandise of domestic manufacture.

(2) PAYMENT OF TAX.—The Secretary shall by regulations prescribe the mode and time for payment and collection of the tax described in paragraph (1), including any discretionary method described in section 6302(b) and (c). Such regulations shall authorize the payment of such tax before shipment from Puerto Rico, and the provisions of section 7651(2)(B) shall be applicable to the payment and collection of such tax in Puerto Rico.

(3) DEPOSIT OF INTERNAL REVENUE COLLECTIONS.—All taxes collected under the internal revenue laws of the United States on articles produced in Puerto Rico and transported to the United States (less the estimated amount necessary for payment of refunds and drawbacks), or consumed in the island, shall be covered into the treasury of Puerto Rico.

Amendments

• **1976, Tax Reform Act of 1976 (P.L. 94-455)**

P.L. 94-455, § 1906(b)(13)(A):

Amended 1954 Code by substituting "Secretary" for "Secretary or his delegate" each place it appeared. **Effective** 2-1-77.

• **1965, Excise Tax Reduction Act of 1965 (P.L. 89-44)**

P.L. 89-44, § 808(b)(3):

Amended Code Sec. 7652(a)(3). Prior to amendment, Code Sec. 7652(a)(3) read as follows:

(3) Deposit of Internal Revenue Collections.—All taxes collected under the internal revenue laws of the United States on articles produced in Puerto Rico and transported to the United States, or consumed in the island, shall be covered into the treasury of Puerto Rico.

• **1958, Excise Tax Technical Changes Act of 1958 (P.L. 85-859)**

P.L. 85-859, § 204(17):

Amended Code Sec. 7652(a)(1) by striking out "5318" and substituting "5314". **Effective** 7-1-59.

[Sec. 7652(b)]

(b) VIRGIN ISLANDS.—

(1) TAXES IMPOSED IN THE UNITED STATES.—Except as provided in section 5314, there shall be imposed in the United States, upon articles coming into the United States from the Virgin Islands, a tax equal to the internal revenue tax imposed in the United States upon like articles of domestic manufacture.

(2) EXEMPTION FROM TAX IMPOSED IN THE VIRGIN ISLANDS.—Such articles shipped from such islands to the United States shall be exempt from the payment of any tax imposed by the internal revenue laws of such islands.

(3) DISPOSITION OF INTERNAL REVENUE COLLECTIONS.—The Secretary shall determine the amount of all taxes imposed by, and collected under the internal revenue laws of the United States on articles produced in the Virgin Islands and transported to the United States. The amount so determined less 1 percent and less the estimated amount of refunds or credits shall be subject to disposition as follows:

(A) The payment of an estimated amount shall be made to the government of the Virgin Islands before the commencement of each fiscal year as set forth in section 4(c)(2) of the Act entitled "An Act to authorize appropriations for certain insular areas of the United States, and for other purposes", approved August 18, 1978 (48 U.S.C. 1645), as in effect on the date of the enactment of the Trade and Development Act of 2000. The payment so made shall constitute a separate fund in the treasury of the Virgin Islands and may be expended as the legislature may determine.

(B) Any amounts remaining shall be deposited in the Treasury of the United States as miscellaneous receipts.

If at the end of any fiscal year the total of the Federal contribution made under subparagraph (A) with respect to the four calendar quarters immediately preceding the beginning of that fiscal year has not been obligated or expended for an approved purpose, the balance shall continue available for expenditure during any succeeding fiscal year, but only for emergency relief purposes and essential public projects. The aggregate amount of moneys available for expenditure for emergency relief purposes and essential public projects only shall not exceed the sum of $5,000,000 at the end of any fiscal year. Any unobligated or unexpended balance of the Federal contribution remaining at the end of a fiscal year which would cause the moneys available for emergency relief purposes and essential public projects only to exceed the sum of $5,000,000 shall thereupon be transferred and paid over to the Treasury of the United States as miscellaneous receipts.

Amendments

• **2000, Trade and Development Act of 2000 (P.L. 106-200)**

P.L. 106-200, § 602(b):

Amended so much of paragraph (3) of Code Sec. 7652(b) as preceded subparagraph (B). **Effective** with respect to transfers or payments made after 5-18-2000. Prior to amendment, so much of paragraph (3) as preceded subparagraph (B) read as follows:

(3) DISPOSITION OF INTERNAL REVENUE COLLECTIONS.—Beginning with the calendar quarter ending September 30, 1975, and quarterly thereafter, the Secretary shall determine the amount of all taxes imposed by, and collected during the quarter under, the internal revenue laws of the United States on articles produced in the Virgin Islands and transported to the United States. The amount so determined less 1 percent and less the estimated amount of refunds or credits shall be subject to disposition as follows:

(A) There shall be transferred and paid over, as soon as practical after the close of the quarter, to the government of the Virgin Islands from the amounts so determined a sum equal to the total amount of the revenue collected by the government of the Virgin Islands during the quarter, as certified by the Government Comptroller of the Virgin Islands. The moneys so transferred and paid over shall constitute a separate fund in the treasury of the Virgin Islands and may be expended as the legislature may determine.

ENFORCEMENT—POSSESSIONS

- **1983 (P.L. 98-213)**

P.L. 98-213, § 5(c):

Amended P.L. 94-455, § 1906(a)(55), in (B) by changing the language to be inserted to read "emergency relief purposes and essential public projects", and by adding new paragraph (D) to read as follows: `(D) by amending the second sentence in paragraph (A) by changing the colon after `determine' to a period and striking the remainder of the sentences.". **Effective** 12-8-83.

- **1976, Tax Reform Act of 1976 (P.L. 94-455)**

P.L. 94-455, § 1906(a)(55)(A):

Amended Code Sec. 7652(b)(3) by striking out subparagraph (B) and by redesignating former subparagraph (C) as subparagraph (B). **Effective** 2-1-77. Prior to amendment, subparagraph (B) read as follows:

(B) There shall also be transferred and paid over to the government of the Virgin Islands during each of the fiscal years ending June 30, 1955, and June 30, 1956, the sum of $1,000,000 or the balance of the internal revenue collections available under this paragraph (3) after payments are made under subparagraph (A), whichever amount is greater. The moneys so transferred and paid over shall be deposited in the separate fund established by subparagraph (A), but shall be obligated or expended for emergency purposes and essential public projects only, with the prior approval of the President or his designated representative.

P.L. 94-455, § 1906(a)(55)(B)-(C):

Amended Code Sec. 7652(b)(3) by striking out "approved emergency relief purposes and essential public projects as provided in subparagraph (B)" and inserting in lieu thereof "emergency relief purposes and essential public projects, with the prior approval of the President or his designated representative", and by striking out ", including payments under subparagraph (B),".

P.L. 94-455, § 1906(b)(13)(A):

Amended 1954 Code by substituting "Secretary" for "Secretary or his delegate" each place it appeared. **Effective** 2-1-77.

- **1976 (P.L. 94-202)**

P.L. 94-202, § 10:

Amended the first sentence of Code Sec. 7652(b)(3). **Effective** for all taxes imposed by, and collected after 6-30-75, under the internal revenue laws of the United States on articles produced in the Virgin Islands and transported to the United States. Prior to amendment the first sentence of Code Sec. 7652(b)(3) read as follows: "Beginning with the fiscal year ending June 30, 1954, and annually thereafter, the Secretary or his delegate shall determine the amount of all taxes imposed by, and collected during the fiscal year under, the internal revenue laws of the United States on articles produced in the Virgin Islands and transported to the United States."

Amended the first sentence of Code Sec. 7652(b)(3)(A). **Effective** for all taxes imposed and collected after 6-30-75, under the internal revenue laws of the United States on articles produced in the Virgin Islands and transported to the United States. Prior to amendment the first sentence of Code Sec. 7652(b)(3)(A) read as follows: "There shall be transferred and paid over to the government of the Virgin Islands from the amounts so determined a sum equal to the total amount of the revenue collected by the government of the Virgin Islands during the fiscal year, as certified by the Government Comptroller of the Virgin Islands."

Amended the first sentence immediately following Code Sec. 7652(b)(3)(C). Prior to amendment this sentence read as follows: "If at the end of any fiscal year the total of the Federal contribution made under subparagraph (a) at the beginning of that fiscal year has not been obligated or expended for an approved purpose, the balance shall continue available for expenditure during any succeeding fiscal year, but only for approved emergency relief purposes and essential public projects as provided in subparagraph (B)."

- **1958, Excise Tax Technical Changes Act of 1958 (P.L. 85-859)**

P.L. 85-859, § 204(18):

Amended Sec. 7652(b)(1) by striking out "5318" and substituting "5314". **Effective** 7-1-59.

[Sec. 7652(c)]

(c) ARTICLES CONTAINING DISTILLED SPIRITS.—For purposes of subsections (a)(3) and (b)(3), any article containing distilled spirits shall in no event be treated as produced in Puerto Rico or the Virgin Islands unless at least 92 percent of the alcoholic content in such article is attributable to rum.

Amendments

- **1984, Deficit Reduction Act of 1984 (P.L. 98-369)**

P.L. 98-369, § 2681(a):

Amended Code Sec. 7652 by redesignating subsection (c) as subsection (e) and by inserting after subsection (b) new subsection (c). **Effective** with respect to articles brought into the United States on or after 3-1-84, but not with respect to articles brought into the United States from Puerto Rico after 2-29-84, and before 1-1-85. Special rules appear below.

P.L. 98-369, § 2681(b)(2) and (3), provide:

(2) Exception for Puerto Rico for Periods Before January 1, 1985.—

(A) In General.—Subject to the limitations of subparagraphs (B) and (C), the amendments made by subsection (a) shall not apply with respect to articles containing distilled spirits brought into the United States from Puerto Rico after February 29, 1984, and before January 1, 1985.

(B) $130,000,000 Limitation.—In the case of such articles brought into the United States after February 29, 1984, and before July 1, 1984, the aggregate amount payable to Puerto Rico by reason of subparagraph (A) shall not exceed the excess of—

(i) $130,000,000, over

(ii) the aggregate amount payable to Puerto Rico under section 7652(a) of the Internal Revenue Code of 1954 with respect to such articles which were brought into the United States after June 30, 1983, and before March 1, 1984, and which would not meet the requirements of section 7652(c) of such Code.

(C) $75,000,000 Limitation.—The aggregate amount payable to Puerto Rico by reason of subparagraph (A) shall not exceed $75,000,000 in the case of articles—

(i) brought into the United States after June 30, 1984, and before January 1, 1985,

(ii) which would meet the requirements of section 7652(c) of such Code,

(iii) which have been redistilled in Puerto Rico, and

(iv) which do not contain distilled spirits derived from cane.

(3) Limitation on Incentive Payments to United States Distillers.—

(A) In General.—In the case of articles to which this paragraph applies, the aggregate amount of incentive payments paid to any United States distiller with respect to such articles shall not exceed the limitation described in subparagraph (C).

(B) Articles to which Paragraph Applies.—This paragraph shall apply to any article containing distilled spirits described in clauses (i) through (iv) of paragraph (2)(C).

(C) Limitation.—

(i) In General.—The limitation described in this subparagraph is $1,500,000.

(ii) Special Rule.—The limitation described in this subparagraph shall be zero with respect to any distiller who was not entitled to or receiving incentive payments as of March 1, 1984.

(D) Payments in Excess of Limitation.—If any United States distiller receives any incentive payment with respect to articles to which this paragraph applies in excess of the limitation described in subparagraph (C), such distiller shall pay to the United States the total amount of such incentive payments with respect to such articles in the same manner, and subject to the same penalties, as if such amount were tax due and payable under section 5001 of such Code on the date such payments were received.

(E) Incentive Payments.—

(i) In General.—For purposes of this paragraph, the term "incentive payment" means any payment made directly or indirectly by the Commonwealth of Puerto Rico to any United States distiller as an incentive to engage in redistillation operations.

(ii) Transportation Payments Excluded.—Such term shall not include any payment of a direct cost of transportation to or from Puerto Rico with respect to any article to which this paragraph applies.

[Sec. 7652(d)]

(d) ARTICLES OTHER THAN ARTICLES CONTAINING DISTILLED SPIRITS.—For purposes of subsections (a)(3) and (b)(3)—

(1) VALUE ADDED REQUIREMENT FOR PUERTO RICO.—Any article, other than an article containing distilled spirits, shall in no event be treated as produced in Puerto Rico unless the sum of—

(A) the cost or value of the materials produced in Puerto Rico, plus

(B) the direct costs of processing operations performed in Puerto Rico,

equals or exceeds 50 percent of the value of such article as of the time it is brought into the United States.

(2) PROHIBITION OF FEDERAL EXCISE TAX SUBSIDIES.—

(A) IN GENERAL.—No amount shall be transferred under subsection (a)(3) or (b)(3) in respect of taxes imposed on any article, other than an article containing distilled spirits, if the Secretary determines that a Federal excise tax subsidy was provided by Puerto Rico or the Virgin Islands (as the case may be) with respect to such article.

(B) FEDERAL EXCISE TAX SUBSIDY.—For purposes of this paragraph, the term "Federal excise tax subsidy" means any subsidy—

(i) of a kind different from, or

(ii) in an amount per value or volume of production greater than,

the subsidy which Puerto Rico or the Virgin Islands offers generally to industries producing articles not subject to Federal excise taxes.

(3) DIRECT COSTS OF PROCESSING OPERATIONS.—For purposes of this subsection, the term "direct cost of processing operations" has the same meaning as when used in section 213 of the Caribbean Basin Economic Recovery Act.

ENFORCEMENT—POSSESSIONS

Amendments

• **1984, Deficit Reduction Act of 1984 (P.L. 98-369)**

P.L. 98-369, § 2681(a):

Amended Code Sec. 7652 by redesignating subsection (c) as subsection (e) and by inserting after subsection (c) new subsection (d). **Effective** with respect to articles brought into the United States on or after 3-1-84, but not for articles brought into the United States from Puerto Rico after 2-29-84, and before 1-1-85. Special rules appear in the notes following Code Sec. 7652(c).

[Sec. 7652(e)]

(e) SHIPMENTS OF RUM TO THE UNITED STATES.—

(1) EXCISE TAXES ON RUM COVERED INTO TREASURIES OF PUERTO RICO AND VIRGIN ISLANDS.—All taxes collected under section 5001(a)(1) on rum imported into the United States (less the estimated amount necessary for payment of refunds and drawbacks) shall be covered into the treasuries of Puerto Rico and the Virgin Islands.

(2) SECRETARY PRESCRIBES FORMULA.—The Secretary shall, from time to time, prescribe by regulation a formula for the division of such tax collections between Puerto Rico and the Virgin Islands and the timing and methods for transferring such tax collections.

(3) RUM DEFINED.—For purposes of this subsection, the term "rum" means any article classified under item subheading 2208.40.00 of the Harmonized Tariff Schedule of the United States (19 U.S.C. 1202).

(4) COORDINATION WITH SUBSECTIONS (A) AND (B).—Paragraph (1) shall not apply with respect to any rum subject to tax under subsection (a) or (b).

Amendments

• **2020, Taxpayer Certainty and Disaster Tax Relief Act of 2020 (P.L. 116-260)**

P.L. 116-260, § 107(a)(2)(B), Div. EE:

Amended Code Sec. 7652(e) by striking paragraph (5). **Effective** for distilled spirits brought into the United States and removed after 12-31-2022. Prior to being stricken, Code Sec. 7652(e)(5) read as follows:

(5) DETERMINATION OF AMOUNT OF TAXES COLLECTED.—For purposes of this subsection, the amount of taxes collected under section 5001(a)(1) shall be determined without regard to section 5001(c).

• **2018, Bipartisan Budget Act of 2018 (P.L. 115-123)**

P.L. 115-123, § 41102(b)(1), Div. D:

Amended Code Sec. 7652(e) by adding at the end a new paragraph (5). **Effective** for distilled spirits brought into the United States after 12-31-2017.

• **1988, Omnibus Trade and Competitiveness Act of 1988 (P.L. 100-418)**

P.L. 100-418, § 1214(p)(1):

Amended Code Sec. 7652(e)(3) by striking "item 169.13 or 169.14 of the Tariff Schedules of the United States" and inserting "subheading 2208.40.00 of the Harmonized Tariff Schedule of the United States". **Effective** for crude oil removed from the premises on or after 8-23-88.

• **1984, Deficit Reduction Act of 1984 (P.L. 98-369)**

P.L. 98-369, § 2681(a):

Amended Code Sec. 7652 by redesignating subsection (c) as subsection (e). See the notes following Code Sec. 7652(c) for the **effective** date.

• **1983, Interest and Dividend Tax Compliance Act of 1983 (P.L. 98-67)**

P.L. 98-67, § 221(a):

Added Code Sec. 7652(c). **Effective** for articles imported into the United States after 6-30-83.

[Sec. 7652(f)]

(f) LIMITATION ON COVER OVER OF TAX ON DISTILLED SPIRITS.—For purposes of this section, with respect to taxes imposed under section 5001 or this section on distilled spirits, the amount covered into the treasuries of Puerto Rico and the Virgin Islands shall not exceed the lesser of the rate of—

(1) $10.50 ($13.25 in the case of distilled spirits brought into the United States after June 30, 1999, and before January 1, 2022), or

(2) the tax imposed under subsection (a)(1) of section 5001, determined as if subsection (c)(1) of such section did not apply, on each proof gallon.

Amendments

• **2018, Bipartisan Budget Act of 2018 (P.L. 115-123)**

P.L. 115-123, § 41102(a)(1), Div. D:

Amended Code Sec. 7652(f)(1) by striking "January 1, 2017" and inserting "January 1, 2022". **Effective** for distilled spirits brought into the United States after 12-31-2016.

• **2017, Tax Cuts and Jobs Act (P.L. 115-97)**

P.L. 115-97, § 13807(b):

Amended Code Sec. 7652(f)(2) by striking "section 5001(a)(1)" and inserting "subsection (a)(1) of section 5001, determined as if subsection (c)(1) of such section did not apply". **Effective** for distilled spirits removed after 12-31-2017.

P.L. 115-97, § 13809 (as added by P.L. 115-123, § 41111, Div. D), provides:

SEC. 13809. RULE OF CONSTRUCTION.

Nothing in this subpart, the amendments made by this subpart, or any regulation promulgated under this subpart or the amendments made by this subpart, shall be construed to preempt, supersede, or otherwise limit or restrict any State, local, or tribal law that prohibits or regulates the production or sale of distilled spirits, wine, or malt beverages.

• **2015, Protecting Americans from Tax Hikes Act of 2015 (P.L. 114-113)**

P.L. 114-113, § 172(a), Div. Q:

Amended Code Sec. 7652(f)(1) by striking "January 1, 2015" and inserting "January 1, 2017". **Effective** for distilled spirits brought into the United States after 12-31-2014.

• **2014, Tax Increase Prevention Act of 2014 (P.L. 113-295)**

P.L. 113-295, § 140(a), Division A:

Amended Code Sec. 7652(f)(1) by striking "January 1, 2014" and inserting "January 1, 2015". **Effective** for distilled spirits brought into the United States after 12-31-2013.

• **2013, American Taxpayer Relief Act of 2012 (P.L. 112-240)**

P.L. 112-240, § 329(a):

Amended Code Sec. 7652(f)(1) by striking "January 1, 2012" and inserting "January 1, 2014". **Effective** for distilled spirits brought into the United States after 12-31-2011.

• **2010, Tax Relief, Unemployment Insurance Reauthorization, and Job Creation Act of 2010 (P.L. 111-312)**

P.L. 111-312, § 755(a):

Amended Code Sec. 7652(f)(1) by striking "January 1, 2010" and inserting "January 1, 2012". **Effective** for distilled spirits brought into the United States after 12-31-2009.

• **2008, Tax Extenders and Alternative Minimum Tax Relief Act of 2008 (P.L. 110-343)**

P.L. 110-343, Division C, § 308(a):

Amended Code Sec. 7652(f)(1) by striking "January 1, 2008" and inserting "January 1, 2010". **Effective** for distilled spirits brought into the United States after 12-31-2007.

• **2006, Tax Relief and Health Care Act of 2006 (P.L. 109-432)**

P.L. 109-432, Division A, § 114(a):

Amended Code Sec. 7652(f)(1) by striking "2006" and inserting "2008". **Effective** for articles brought into the United States after 12-31-2005.

• **2004, Working Families Tax Relief Act of 2004 (P.L. 108-311)**

P.L. 108-311, § 305(a):

Amended Code Sec. 7652(f)(1) by striking "January 1, 2004" and inserting "January 1, 2006". **Effective** for articles brought into the United States after 12-31-2003.

• **2002, Job Creation and Worker Assistance Act of 2002 (P.L. 107-147)**

P.L. 107-147, § 609(a):

Amended Code Sec. 7652(f)(1) by striking "January 1, 2002" and inserting "January 1, 2004". **Effective** for articles brought into the United States after 12-31-2001.

• **1999, Tax Relief Extension Act of 1999 (P.L. 106-170)**

P.L. 106-170, § 512(a):

Amended Code Sec. 7652(f)(1). **Effective** 7-1-99. For special rules, see Act Sec. 512(b), below. Prior to amendment, Code Sec. 7652(f)(1) read as follows:

(1) $10.50 ($11.30 in the case of distilled spirits brought into the United States during the 5-year period beginning on October 1, 1993), or

P.L. 106-170, § 512(b), as amended by P.L. 106-200, § 602(a), provides:

(b) SPECIAL COVER OVER TRANSFER RULES.—Notwithstanding section 7652 of the Internal Revenue Code of 1986, the following rules shall apply with respect to any transfer before the first day of the month within which the date of the enactment of the Trade and Development Act of 2000 occurs, of amounts relating to the increase in the cover over of taxes by reason of the amendment made by subsection (a):

(1) INITIAL TRANSFER OF INCREMENTAL INCREASE IN COVER OVER.—The Secretary of the Treasury shall, within 15 days after the date of the enactment of this Act, transfer an amount equal to the lesser of—

(A) the amount of such increase otherwise required to be covered over after June 30, 1999, and before the date of the enactment of this Act; or

(B) $20,000,000.

ENFORCEMENT—POSSESSIONS

(2) SECOND TRANSFER OF INCREMENTAL INCREASE IN COVER OVER ATTRIBUTABLE TO PERIODS BEFORE RESUMPTION OF REGULAR PAYMENTS.—The Secretary of the Treasury shall transfer on the first payment date after the date of the enactment of the Trade and Development Act of 2000 an amount equal to the excess of—

(A) the amount of such increase otherwise required to be covered over after June 30, 1999, and before the first day of the month within which such date of enactment occurs, over

(B) the amount of the transfer described in paragraph (1).

• **1993, Omnibus Budget Reconciliation Act of 1993 (P.L. 103-66)**

P.L. 103-66, §13227(e):

Amended Code Sec. 7652(f)(1). **Effective** 10-1-93. Prior to amendment, Code Sec. 7652(f)(1) read as follows:

(1) $10.50, or

• **1984, Deficit Reduction Act of 1984 (P.L. 98-369)**

P.L. 98-369, §2682:

Amended Code Sec. 7652 by adding at the end thereof new subsection (f). **Effective** for articles containing distilled spirits brought into the United States after 9-30-85.

[Sec. 7652(g)]

(g) DRAWBACK FOR MEDICINAL ALCOHOL, ETC.—In the case of medicines, medicinal preparations, food products, flavors, flavoring extracts, or perfume containing distilled spirits, which are unfit for beverage purposes and which are brought into the United States from Puerto Rico or the Virgin Islands—

(1) subpart B of part II of subchapter A of chapter 51 shall be applied as if—

(A) the use and tax determination described in section 5111 had occurred in the United States by a United States person at the time the article is brought into the United States, and

(B) the rate of tax were the rate applicable under subsection (f) of this section, and

(2) no amount shall be covered into the treasuries of Puerto Rico or the Virgin Islands.

Amendments

• **2005, Safe, Accountable, Flexible, Efficient Transportation Equity Act: A Legacy for Users (P.L. 109-59)**

P.L. 109-59, §11125(b)(22)(A)-(B):

Amended Code Sec. 7652(g)(1) by striking "subpart F" and inserting "subpart B", and by striking "section 5131(a)" and inserting "section 5111". **Effective** 7-1-2008, but not applicable to taxes imposed for periods before such date.

• **1994, Uruguay Round Agreements Act (P.L. 103-465)**

P.L. 103-465, §136(b):

Amended Code Sec. 7652(g) by striking "or flavoring extracts" and inserting "flavoring extracts, or perfume". **Effective** 1-1-95.

• **1986, Tax Reform Act of 1986 (P.L. 99-514)**

P.L. 99-514, §1879(i)(1):

Amended Code Sec. 7652 by adding at the end thereof new subsection (g). **Effective** for articles brought into the United States after 10-22-86. However, for special rules, see Act Sec. 1879(i)(3)(A) and (B), below.

P.L. 99-514, §1879(i)(3)(A) and (B), provides:

(3)(A) Section 7652 of the Internal Revenue Code of 1954 (other than subsection (f) thereof) shall not prevent the payment to Puerto Rico or the Virgin Islands of amounts with respect to medicines, medicinal preparations, food products, flavors, or flavoring extracts containing distilled spirits, which are unfit for beverage purposes and which are brought into the United States from Puerto Rico or the Virgin Islands on or before the date of the enactment of this Act.

(B) With respect to articles brought into the United States after September 27, 1985, subparagraph (A) shall apply only if the Secretary of the Treasury or his delegate is satisfied that the amounts paid to Puerto Rico or the Virgin Islands under subparagraph (A) are being repaid to the proper persons who used the distilled spirits in such articles.

[Sec. 7652(h)]

(h) MANNER OF COVER OVER OF TAX MUST BE DERIVED FROM THIS TITLE.—No amount shall be covered into the treasury of Puerto Rico or the Virgin Islands with respect to taxes for which cover over is provided under this section unless made in the manner specified in this section without regard to—

(1) any provision of law which is not contained in this title or in a revenue Act; and

(2) whether such provision of law is a subsequently enacted provision or directly or indirectly seeks to waive the application of this subsection.

Amendments

• **2000, Trade and Development Act of 2000 (P.L. 106-200)**

P.L. 106-200, §602(c):

Amended Code Sec. 7652 by adding at the end new subsection (h). **Effective** with respect to transfers or payments made after 5-18-2000.

[Sec. 7652(i)]

(i) DETERMINATION OF TAXES COLLECTED.—For purposes of subsections (a)(3), (b)(3), and (e)(1), refunds under section 5001(c)(4) shall not be taken into account as a refund, and the amount of taxes imposed by and collected under section 5001(a)(1) shall be determined without regard to section 5001(c).

Amendments

• **2020, Taxpayer Certainty and Disaster Tax Relief Act of 2020 (P.L. 116-260)**

P.L. 116-260, §107(a)(2)(A), Div. EE:

Amended Code Sec. 7652 by adding at the end a new subsection (i). **Effective** for distilled spirits brought into the United States and removed after 12-31-2022. For a special rule, see Act Sec. 107(e)-(g), Div. EE, below.

P.L. 116-260, §107(e)-(g), Div. EE, provides:

(e) ADMINISTRATION OF REFUNDS.—The Secretary of the Treasury (or the Secretary's delegate within the Department of the Treasury) shall implement and administer sections 5001(c)(4), 5041(c)(7), and 5051(a)(6) of the Internal Revenue Code of 1986, as added by this Act, in coordination with the United States Customs and Border Protection of the Department of Homeland Security.

(f) REGULATIONS.—The Secretary of the Treasury (or the Secretary's delegate within the Department of the Treasury) shall prescribe such regulations as may be necessary or appropriate to carry out the purposes of this section, including regulations to require foreign producers to provide information necessary to enforce the volume limitations under sections 5001(c), 5041(c), and 5051(a) of such Code.

(g) REPORT.—Not later than 180 days after the date of the enactment of this Act, the Secretary of the Treasury (or the Secretary's delegate within the Department of the Treasury) shall, in coordination with the United States Customs and Border Protection of the Department of Homeland Security, prepare, submit to Congress, and make publicly available a report detailing the plans for implementing and administering sections 5001(c)(4), 5041(c)(7), and 5051(a)(6) of such Code, as added by this Act.

[Sec. 7653]

SEC. 7653. SHIPMENTS FROM THE UNITED STATES.

[Sec. 7653(a)]

(a) TAX IMPOSED.—

(1) PUERTO RICO.—All articles of merchandise of United States manufacture coming into Puerto Rico shall be entered at the port of entry upon payment of a tax equal in rate and amount to the internal revenue tax imposed in Puerto Rico upon the like articles of Puerto Rican manufacture.

ENFORCEMENT—POSSESSIONS

(2) VIRGIN ISLANDS.—There shall be imposed in the Virgin Islands upon articles imported from the United States a tax equal to the internal revenue tax imposed in such islands upon like articles there manufactured.

[Sec. 7653(b)]

(b) EXEMPTION FROM TAX IMPOSED IN THE UNITED STATES.—Articles, goods, wares, or merchandise going into Puerto Rico, the Virgin Islands, Guam, and American Samoa from the United States shall be exempted from the payment of any tax imposed by the internal revenue laws of the United States.

[Sec. 7653(c)]

(c) DRAWBACK OF TAX PAID IN THE UNITED STATES.—All provisions of law for the allowance of drawback of internal revenue tax on articles exported from the United States are, so far as applicable, extended to like articles upon which an internal revenue tax has been paid when shipped from the United States to Puerto Rico, the Virgin Islands, Guam, or American Samoa.

[Sec. 7653(d)]

(d) CROSS REFERENCE.—

For the disposition of the proceeds of all taxes collected under the internal revenue laws of the United States on articles produced in Guam and transported into the United States or its possessions, or consumed in Guam, see the Act of August 1, 1950 (48 U. S. C. 1421h).

Amendments

• 1976, Tax Reform Act of 1976 (P.L. 94-455)

P.L. 94-455, §1906(a)(56):

Amended Code Sec. 7653(d) by striking out "c. 512, 64 Stat. 392, section 30;" before "48 U.S.C. 1421h)." **Effective** 2-1-77.

• 1960, Hawaii Omnibus Act (P.L. 86-624)

P.L. 86-624, §18(h):

Amended Code Sec. 7653(d) by striking out ", its possessions or the Territory of Hawaii" and inserting in lieu thereof "or its possessions". **Effective** 8-21-59.

• 1959, Alaska Omnibus Bill (P.L. 86-70)

P.L. 86-70, §22(a):

Amended Code Sec. 7653(d) by striking out "its Territories or possessions" following "into the United States,", and by substituting "its possessions or the Territory of Hawaii,". **Effective** 1-3-59.

[Sec. 7654]

SEC. 7654. COORDINATION OF UNITED STATES AND CERTAIN POSSESSION INDIVIDUAL INCOME TAXES.

[Sec. 7654(a)]

(a) GENERAL RULE.—The net collection of taxes imposed by chapter 1 for each taxable year with respect to an individual to whom section 931 or 932(c) applies shall be covered into the Treasury of the specified possession of which such individual is a bona fide resident.

Amendments

• 1988, Technical and Miscellaneous Revenue Act of 1988 (P.L. 100-647)

P.L. 100-647, §1012(y):

Amended Code Sec. 7654(a) by striking out "an individual to which" and inserting in lieu thereof "an individual to whom". **Effective** as if included in the provision of P.L. 99-514 to which it relates.

[Sec. 7654(b)]

(b) DEFINITION AND SPECIAL RULE.—For purposes of this section—

(1) NET COLLECTION.—In determining net collections for a taxable year, an appropriate adjustment shall be made for credits allowed against the tax liability and refunds made of income taxes for the taxable year.

(2) SPECIFIED POSSESSION.—The term "specified possession" means Guam, American Samoa, the Northern Mariana Islands, and the Virgin Islands.

[Sec. 7654(c)]

(c) TRANSFERS.—The transfers of funds between the United States and any specified possession required by this section shall be made not less frequently than annually.

[Sec. 7654(d)]

(d) FEDERAL PERSONNEL.—In addition to the amount determined under subsection (a), the United States shall pay to each specified possession at such times and in such manner as determined by the Secretary—

(1) the amount of the taxes deducted and withheld by the United States under chapter 24 with respect to compensation paid to members of the Armed Forces who are stationed in such possession but who have no income tax liability to such possession with respect to such compensation by reason of the Servicemembers Civil Relief Act (50 U.S.C. 3901 et seq.), and

(2) the amount of the taxes deducted and withheld under chapter 24 with respect to amounts paid for services performed as an employee of the United States (or any agency thereof) in a specified possession with respect to an individual unless section 931 or 932(c) applies.

Amendments

• 2018, Tax Technical Corrections Act of 2018 (P.L. 115-141)

P.L. 115-141, §401(a)(330), Div. U:

Amended Code Sec. 7654(d)(1) by striking "50 App. U.S.C. 501 et seq." and inserting "50 U.S.C. 3901 et seq.". **Effective** 3-23-2018.

• 2003 (P.L. 108-189)

P.L. 108-189, §2(d):

Amended Code Sec. 7654(d)(1) by striking "Soldiers' and Sailors' Civil Relief Act" and inserting "Servicemembers Civil Relief Act". **Effective** 12-19-2003.

[Sec. 7654(e)]

(e) REGULATIONS.—The Secretary shall prescribe such regulations as may be necessary to carry out the provisions of this section and sections 931 and 932, including regulations prohibiting the rebate of taxes covered over which are allocable to United States source income and prescribing the information which the individuals to whom such sections may apply shall furnish to the Secretary.

Amendments

• 1986, Tax Reform Act of 1986 (P.L. 99-514)

P.L. 99-514, §1276(a):

Amended Code Sec. 7654. For the **effective** date as well as special rules, see Act Sec. 1277 reproduced in full text under the amendment notes for Code Sec. 48. Prior to amendment, Code Sec. 7654 read as follows:

SEC. 7654. COORDINATION OF UNITED STATES AND GUAM INDIVIDUAL INCOME TAXES

(a) GENERAL RULE.—The net collections of the income taxes imposed for each taxable year with respect to any individual to whom this subsection applies for such year shall be divided between the United States and Guam according to the following rules:

(1) net collections attributable to United States source income shall be covered into the Treasury of the United States;

(2) net collections attributable to Guam source income shall be covered into the treasury of Guam; and

DEFINITIONS

(3) all other net collections of such taxes shall be covered into the treasury of the jurisdiction (either the United States or Guam) with which such individual is required by section 935(b) to file his return for such year.

This subsection applies to an individual for a taxable year if section 935 applies to such individual for such year and if such individual has (or, in the case of a joint return, such individual and his spouse have) (A) adjusted gross income of $50,000 or more and (B) gross income of $5,000 or more derived from sources within the jurisdiction (either the United States or Guam) with which the individual is not required under section 935(b) to file his return for the year.

(b) DEFINITIONS AND SPECIAL RULES.—For purposes of this section—

(1) NET COLLECTIONS.—In determining net collections for a taxable year, appropriate adjustment shall be made for credits allowed against the tax liability for such year and refunds made of income taxes for such year.

(2) INCOME TAXES.—The term "income taxes" means—

(A) with respect to taxes imposed by the United States, the taxes imposed by chapter 1, and

(B) with respect to Guam, the Guam territorial income tax.

(3) SOURCE.—The determination of the source of income shall be based on the principles contained in part I of subchapter N of chapter 1 (section 861 and following).

(c) TRANSFERS.—The transfers of funds between the United States and Guam required by this section shall be made not less frequently than annually.

(d) MILITARY PERSONNEL IN GUAM.—In addition to any amount determined under subsection (a), the United States shall pay to Guam at such times and in such manner as determined by the Secretary the amount of the taxes deducted and withheld by the United States under chapter 24 with respect to compensation paid to members of the Armed Forces who are stationed in Guam but who have no income tax liability to Guam with respect to such compensation by reason of the Soldiers and Sailors Civil Relief Act (50 App. U.S.C., sec. 501 et seq.).

(e) REGULATIONS.—The Secretary shall prescribe such regulations as may be necessary to carry out the provisions of this section and section 935, including (but not limited to)—

(1) such regulations as are necessary to insure that the provisions of this title, as made applicable in Guam by section 31 of the Organic Act of Guam, apply in a manner which is consistent with this section and section 935, and

(2) regulations prescribing the information which the individuals to whom section 935 may apply, shall furnish to the Secretary.

• **1983, Interest and Dividend Tax Compliance Act of 1983 (P.L. 98-67)**

P.L. 98-67, §102(a):

Repealed the amendment made to Code Sec. 7654(d) by P.L. 97-248 (see below), as though it had not been enacted. **Effective** as of the close of 6-30-83.

• **1982, Tax Equity and Fiscal Responsibility Act of 1982 (P.L. 97-248)**

P.L. 97-248, §307(a)(16):

Amended Code Sec. 7654(d) by inserting "subchapter A of" before "chapter 24". **Effective** 7-1-83.

• **1976, Tax Reform Act of 1976 (P.L. 94-455)**

P.L. 94-455, §1906(b)(13)(A):

Amended 1954 Code by substituting "Secretary" for "Secretary or his delegate" each place it appeared. **Effective** 2-1-77.

• **1972 (P.L. 92-606)**

P.L. 92-606, §1(b):

Amended Code Sec. 7654. **Effective** with respect to tax years beginning after 12-31-72. Prior to amendment, Code Sec. 7654 read as follows:

SEC. 7654. PAYMENT TO GUAM AND AMERICAN SAMOA OF PROCEEDS OF TAX ON COCONUT AND PALM OIL.

All taxes collected under subchapter B of chapter 37 with respect to coconut oil wholly of the production of Guam or American Samoa, or produced from materials wholly of the growth or production of Guam or American Samoa, shall be held as separate funds and paid to the treasury of Guam or American Samoa, respectively. No part of the money from such funds shall be used, directly or indirectly, to pay a subsidy to the producers or processors of copra, coconut oil, or allied products, except that this sentence shall not be construed as prohibiting the use of such money, in accordance with regulations prescribed by the Secretary or his delegate, for the acquisition or construction of facilities for the better curing of copra or for bona fide loans to copra producers of Guam or American Samoa.

[Sec. 7655]

SEC. 7655. CROSS REFERENCES.

[Sec. 7655(a)]

(a) IMPOSITION OF TAX IN POSSESSIONS.—

For provisions imposing tax in possessions, see—

(1) Chapter 2, relating to self-employment tax;

(2) Chapter 21, relating to the tax under the Federal Insurance Contributions Act.

Amendments

• **1990, Omnibus Budget Reconciliation Act of 1990 (P.L. 101-508)**

P.L. 101-508, §11801(c)(22)(E)(i):

Amended Code Sec. 7655(a) by striking the semicolon at the end of paragraph (2) and inserting a period and by striking paragraph (3). **Effective** 11-5-90. Prior to repeal, Code Sec. 7655(a)(3) read as follows:

(3) Chapter 37, relating to tax on sugar.

• **1976, Tax Reform Act of 1976 (P.L. 94-455)**

P.L. 94-455, §1904(b)(6)(B):

Redesignated Code Sec. 7655(a)(5) as 7655(a)(3). **Effective** 2-1-77. Prior to amendment, former paragraph (5) read as follows:

(5) Subchapter A of chapter 37, relating to tax on sugar.

• **1970 (P.L. 91-513)**

P.L. 91-513, §1102(k):

Repealed paragraphs (3) and (4) of Code Sec. 7655(a). **Effective** 5-1-71. Prior to repeal, these paragraphs read as follows:

"(3) Parts I and III of subchapter A of chapter 39, relating to taxes in respect of narcotic drugs;

"(4) Parts II and III of subchapter A of chapter 39, relating to taxes in respect of marihuana;".

• **1958, Excise Tax Technical Changes Act of 1958 (P.L. 85-859)**

P.L. 85-859, §204(19):

Struck out paragraph (5) of Code Sec. 7655(a) and renumbered paragraph (6) as paragraph (5). **Effective** 1-1-59. Prior to amendment, old paragraph (5) read as follows:

(5) Chapter 51, relating to alcohol taxes;

[Sec. 7655(b)]

(b) OTHER PROVISIONS.—

For other provisions relating to possessions of the United States, see—

(1) Section 931, relating to income tax on residents of Guam, American Samoa, or the Northern Mariana Islands;

(2) Section 933, relating to income tax on residents of Puerto Rico.

Amendments

• **1990, Omnibus Budget Reconciliation Act of 1990 (P.L. 101-508)**

P.L. 101-508, §11801(c)(22)(E)(ii):

Amended Code Sec. 7655(b) by striking the semicolon at the end of paragraph (2) and inserting a period and by striking paragraph (3). **Effective** 11-5-90. Prior to repeal, Code Sec. 7655(b)(3) read as follows:

(3) Section 6418(b), relating to exportation of sugar to Puerto Rico.

• **1986, Tax Reform Act of 1986 (P.L. 99-514)**

P.L. 99-514, §1272(d)(11):

Amended Code Sec. 7655(b) by redesignating paragraphs (1) and (2) as paragraphs (2) and (3), respectively, and by inserting before paragraph (2), as so redesignated, new paragraph (1). For the **effective** date as well as special rules, see Act Sec. 1277 under the amendment notes for Code Sec. 48.

CHAPTER 79—DEFINITIONS

Sec. 7701.	Definitions.
Sec. 7702.	Life insurance contract defined.
Sec. 7702A.	Modified endowment contract defined.
Sec. 7702B.	Treatment of qualified long-term care insurance.
Sec. 7703.	Determination of marital status.
Sec. 7704.	Certain publicly traded partnerships treated as corporations.
Sec. 7705.	Certified professional employer organizations.

DEFINITIONS

[Sec. 7701]

SEC. 7701. DEFINITIONS.

[Sec. 7701(a)]

(a) When used in this title, where not otherwise distinctly expressed or manifestly incompatible with the intent thereof—

(1) PERSON.—The term "person" shall be construed to mean and include an individual, a trust, estate, partnership, association, company or corporation.

(2) PARTNERSHIP AND PARTNER.—The term "partnership" includes a syndicate, group, pool, joint venture, or other unincorporated organization, through or by means of which any business, financial operation, or venture is carried on, and which is not, within the meaning of this title, a trust or estate or a corporation; and the term "partner" includes a member in such a syndicate, group, pool, joint venture, or organization.

(3) CORPORATION.—The term "corporation" includes associations, joint-stock companies, and insurance companies.

(4) DOMESTIC.—The term "domestic" when applied to a corporation or partnership means created or organized in the United States or under the law of the United States or of any State unless, in the case of a partnership, the Secretary provides otherwise by regulations.

Amendments

• **1997, Taxpayer Relief Act of 1997 (P.L. 105-34)**

P.L. 105-34, §1151(a):

Amended Code Sec. 7701(a)(4) by inserting before the period "unless, in the case of a partnership, the Secretary provides otherwise by regulations". **Effective** 8-5-97. For a special rule, see Act Sec. 1151(b).

P.L. 105-34, §1151(b), provides:

(b) EFFECTIVE DATE.—Any regulations issued with respect to the amendment made by subsection (a) shall apply to partnerships created or organized after the date determined under section 7805(b) of the Internal Revenue Code of 1986 (without regard to paragraph (2) thereof) with respect to such regulations.

• **1976, Tax Reform Act of 1976 (P.L. 94-455)**

P.L. 94-455, §1906(c)(3):

Amended Code Sec. 7701(a)(4) by deleting "or Territory" after "State". **Effective** 2-1-77.

(5) FOREIGN.—The term "foreign" when applied to a corporation or partnership means a corporation or partnership which is not domestic.

(6) FIDUCIARY.—The term "fiduciary" means a guardian, trustee, executor, administrator, receiver, conservator, or any person acting in any fiduciary capacity for any person.

(7) STOCK.—The term "stock" includes shares in an association, joint-stock company, or insurance company.

(8) SHAREHOLDER.—The term "shareholder" includes a member in an association, joint-stock company, or insurance company.

(9) UNITED STATES.—The term "United States" when used in a geographical sense includes only the States and the District of Columbia.

Amendments

• **1960, Hawaii Omnibus Act (P.L. 86-624)**

P.L. 86-624, §18(i):

Amended 1954 Code Sec. 7701(a)(9) by striking out ", the Territory of Hawaii," immediately after the word "States". **Effective** 8-21-59.

• **1959, Alaska Omnibus Bill (P.L. 86-70)**

P.L. 86-70, §22(a):

Amended 1954 Code Sec. 7701(a)(9) by striking out "Territories of Alaska and", and by substituting "Territory of". **Effective** 1-3-59.

(10) STATE.—The term "State" shall be construed to include the District of Columbia, where such construction is necessary to carry out provisions of this title.

Amendments

• **1960, Hawaii Omnibus Act (P.L. 86-624)**

P.L. 86-624, §18(j):

Amended 1954 Code Sec. 7701(a)(10) by striking out "the Territory of Hawaii and" immediately after the word "include". **Effective** 8-21-59.

• **1959, Alaska Omnibus Bill (P.L. 86-70)**

P.L. 86-70, §22(a):

Amended 1954 Code Sec. 7701(a)(10) by striking out "Territories", and by substituting "Territory of Hawaii". **Effective** 1-3-59.

(11) SECRETARY OF THE TREASURY AND SECRETARY.—

(A) SECRETARY OF THE TREASURY.—The term "Secretary of the Treasury" means the Secretary of the Treasury, personally, and shall not include any delegate of his.

(B) SECRETARY.—The term "Secretary" means the Secretary of the Treasury or his delegate.

Amendments

• **1976, Tax Reform Act of 1976 (P.L. 94-455)**

P.L. 94-455, §1906(a)(57)(A):

Amended Code Sec. 7701(a)(11). **Effective** 2-1-77. Prior to amendment, Sec. 7701(a)(11) read as follows:

(11) SECRETARY.—The term "Secretary" means the Secretary of the Treasury.

(12) DELEGATE.—

(A) IN GENERAL.—The term "or his delegate"—

(i) when used with reference to the Secretary of the Treasury, means any officer, employee, or agency of the Treasury Department duly authorized by the Secretary of the Treasury directly, or indirectly by one or more redelegations of authority, to perform the function mentioned or described in the context; and

(ii) when used with reference to any other official of the United States, shall be similarly construed.

(B) PERFORMANCE OF CERTAIN FUNCTIONS IN GUAM OR AMERICAN SAMOA.—The term "delegate", in relation to the performance of functions in Guam or American Samoa with respect to the taxes imposed by chapters 1, 2 and 21, also includes any officer or employee of any other department or agency of the United States, or of any possession thereof, duly authorized by the Secretary (directly, or indirectly by one or more redelegations of authority) to perform such functions.

Amendments

• **1976, Tax Reform Act of 1976 (P.L. 94-455)**

P.L. 94-455, §1906(a)(57)(B):

Amended Code Sec. 7701(a)(12)(A). **Effective** 2-1-77. Prior to amendment, Sec. 7701(a)(12)(A) read as follows:

(12) DELEGATE.—

(A) IN GENERAL.—The term "Secretary or his delegate" means the Secretary of the Treasury, or any officer, employee, or agency of the Treasury Department duly authorized by the Secretary (directly, or indirectly by one or more redelegations of authority) to perform the function mentioned or described in the context, and the term "or his delegate" when used in connection with any other official of the United States shall be similarly construed.

• **1972 (P.L. 92-606)**

P.L. 92-606, §1(f)(4):

Amended Code Sec. 7701(a)(12)(B) by substituting "chapters 1, 2 and 21" for "chapters 1 and 21". **Effective** with respect to tax years beginning after 12-31-72.

DEFINITIONS

- **1960, Social Security Amendments of 1960 (P.L. 86-778)**

P.L. 86-778, §103(t):

Amended paragraph (12). Prior to amendment, it read as follows:

(12) DELEGATE.—The term "Secretary or his delegate" means the Secretary of the Treasury, or any officer, employee, or agency of the Treasury Department duly authorized by the Secretary (directly, or indirectly by one or more redelegations of authority) to perform the function mentioned or described in the context, and the term "or his delegate" when used in connection with any other official of the United States shall be similarly construed.

(13) COMMISSIONER.—The term "Commissioner" means the Commissioner of Internal Revenue.

(14) TAXPAYER.—The term "taxpayer" means any person subject to any internal revenue tax.

(15) MILITARY OR NAVAL FORCES AND ARMED FORCES OF THE UNITED STATES.—The term "military or naval forces of the United States" and the term "Armed Forces of the United States" each includes all regular and reserve components of the uniformed services which are subject to the jurisdiction of the Secretary of Defense, the Secretary of the Army, the Secretary of the Navy, or the Secretary of the Air Force, and each term also includes the Coast Guard. The members of such forces include commissioned officers and personnel below the grade of commissioned officers in such forces.

(16) WITHHOLDING AGENT.—The term "withholding agent" means any person required to deduct and withhold any tax under the provisions of section 1441, 1442, 1443, or 1461.

Amendments

- **1984, Deficit Reduction Act of 1984 (P.L. 98-369)**

P.L. 98-369, §474(r)(29)(K):

Amended Code Sec. 7701(a)(16) by striking out "1451,". **Effective** for tax years beginning after 12-31-83, and to carrybacks from such years but does not apply with respect to obligations issued before 1-1-84.

- **1983, Interest and Dividend Tax Compliance Act of 1983 (P.L. 98-67)**

P.L. 98-67, §102(a):

Repealed the amendment made to Code Sec. 7701(a)(16) by P.L. 97-248 as though it had not been enacted. **Effective** as of the close of 6-30-83.

- **1982, Tax Equity and Fiscal Responsibility Act of 1982 (P.L. 97-248)**

P.L. 97-248, §307(a)(17):

Amended Code Sec. 7701(a)(16) by striking out "or 1461" and inserting "1461 or 3451". **Effective** 7-1-83.

(17) HUSBAND AND WIFE.—As used in section 2516, if the husband and wife therein referred to are divorced, wherever appropriate to the meaning of such section, the term "wife" shall be read "former wife" and the term "husband" shall be read "former husband"; and, if the payments described in such section are made by or on behalf of the wife or former wife to the husband or former husband instead of vice versa, wherever appropriate to the meaning of such section, the term "husband" shall be read "wife" and the term "wife" shall be read "husband."

Amendments

- **2017, Tax Cuts and Jobs Act (P.L. 115-97)**

P.L. 115-97, §11051(b)(4)(A)-(B):

Amended Code Sec. 7701(a)(17) by striking "sections 682 and 2516" and inserting "section 2516", and by striking "such sections" each place it appears and inserting "such section". For the **effective** date, see Act Sec. 11051(c)(1)-(2), below.

P.L. 115-97, §11051(c)(1)-(2), provides:

(c) EFFECTIVE DATE.—The amendments made by this section shall apply to—

(1) any divorce or separation instrument (as defined in section 71(b)(2) of the Internal Revenue Code of 1986 as in effect before the date of the enactment of this Act) executed after December 31, 2018, and

(2) any divorce or separation instrument (as so defined) executed on or before such date and modified after such date if the modification expressly provides that the amendments made by this section apply to such modification.

- **2004, Working Families Tax Relief Act of 2004 (P.L. 108-311)**

P.L. 108-311, §207(24):

Amended Code Sec. 7701(a)(17) by striking "152(b)(4), 682," and inserting "682". **Effective** for tax years beginning after 12-31-2004.

- **1986, Tax Reform Act of 1986 (P.L. 99-514)**

P.L. 99-514, §1842(d):

Amended Code Sec. 7701(a)(17) by striking out "and 682" and inserting in lieu thereof ", 682, and 2516". **Effective** as if included in the provision of P.L. 98-369 to which it relates.

- **1984, Deficit Reduction Act of 1984 (P.L. 98-369)**

P.L. 98-369, 422(d)(3):

Amended Code Sec. 7701(a)(17) by striking out "71, 152(b)(4), 215, and 682" and inserting in lieu thereof "152(b)(4) and 682". **Effective** with respect to divorce or separation instruments (as defined in section 71(b)(2) of the Internal Revenue Code of 1954, as amended by this section) executed after 12-31-84. Also **effective** for any divorce or separation instrument (as so defined) executed before 1-1-85, but modified on or after such date if the modification expressly provides that the amendments made by this section shall apply to such modification.

(18) INTERNATIONAL ORGANIZATION.—The term "international organization" means a public international organization entitled to enjoy privileges, exemptions, and immunities as an international organization under the International Organizations Immunities Act (22 U. S. C. 288-288f).

(19) DOMESTIC BUILDING AND LOAN ASSOCIATION.—The term "domestic building and loan association" means a domestic building and loan association, a domestic savings and loan association, and a Federal savings and loan association—

(A) which is subject by law to supervision and examination by State or Federal authority having supervision over such associations;

(B) the business of which consists principally of acquiring the savings of the public and investing in loans; and

(C) at least 60 percent of the amount of the total assets of which (at the close of the taxable year) consists of—

(i) cash,

(ii) obligations of the United States or of a State or political subdivision thereof, and stock or obligations of a corporation which is an instrumentality of the United States or of a State or political subdivision thereof, but not including obligations the interest on which is excludable from gross income under section 103,

(iii) certificates of deposit in, or obligations of, a corporation organized under a State law which specifically authorizes such corporation to insure the deposits or share accounts of member associations,

(iv) loans secured by a deposit or share of a member,

(v) loans (including redeemable ground rents, as defined in section 1055) secured by an interest in real property which is (or, from the proceeds of the loan, will become) residential real property or real property used primarily for church purposes, loans made for the improvement of residential real property or real property used primarily for church purposes, provided that for purposes of this clause, residential real property shall include single or multifamily dwellings, facilities in residential developments dedicated to public use or property used on a nonprofit basis for residents, and mobile homes not used on a transient basis,

(vi) loans secured by an interest in real property located within an urban renewal area to be developed for predominantly residential use under an urban renewal plan approved by the Secretary of Housing and Urban Development under part A or part B of title I of the Housing Act of 1949, as amended, or located within any area covered by a program eligible for assistance under section 103 of the Demonstration Cities and Metropolitan Development Act of 1966, as amended, and loans made for the improvement of any such real property,

DEFINITIONS

(vii) loans secured by an interest in educational, health, or welfare institutions or facilities, including structures designed or used primarily for residential purposes for students, residents, and persons under care, employees, or members of the staff of such institutions or facilities,

(viii) property acquired through the liquidation of defaulted loans described in clause (v), (vi), or (vii),

(ix) loans made for the payment of expenses of college or university education or vocational training, in accordance with such regulations as may be prescribed by the Secretary,

(x) property used by the association in the conduct of the business described in subparagraph (B), and,

(xi) any regular or residual interest in a REMIC, but only in the proportion which the assets of such REMIC consist of property described in any of the preceding clauses of this subparagraph; except that if 95 percent or more of the assets of such REMIC are assets described in clauses (i) through (x), the entire interest in the REMIC shall qualify.

At the election of the taxpayer, the percentage specified in this subparagraph shall be applied on the basis of the average assets outstanding during the taxable year, in lieu of the close of the taxable year, computed under regulations prescribed by the Secretary. For purposes of clause (v), if a multifamily structure securing a loan is used in part for nonresidential purposes, the entire loan is deemed a residential real property loan if the planned residential use exceeds 80 percent of the property's planned use (determined as of the time the loan is made). For purposes of clause (v), loans made to finance the acquisition or development of land shall be deemed to be loans secured by an interest in residential real property if, under regulations prescribed by the Secretary, there is reasonable assurance that the property will become residential real property within a period of 3 years from the date of acquisition of such land; but this sentence shall not apply for any taxable year unless, within such 3-year period, such land becomes residential real property. For purposes of determining whether any interest in a REMIC qualifies under clause (xi), any regular interest in another REMIC held by such REMIC shall be treated as a loan described in a preceding clause under principles similar to the principles of clause (xi); except that, if such REMIC's are part of a tiered structure, they shall be treated as 1 REMIC for purposes of clause (xi).

Amendments

• **2018, Tax Technical Corrections Act of 2018 (P.L. 115-141)**

P.L. 115-141, §401(b)(54), Div. U:

Amended Code Sec. 7701(a)(19)(A) by striking "either (i)" and all that follows through "(ii)". **Effective** 3-23-2018. For a special rule, see Act Sec. 401(e), Div. U, below. Prior to amendment, Code Sec. 7701(a)(19)(A) read as follows:

(A) which either (i) is an insured institution within the meaning of section 401(a) of the National Housing Act (12 U. S. C. sec. 1724(a)), or (ii) is subject by law to supervision and examination by State or Federal authority having supervision over such associations;

P.L. 115-141, §401(e), Div. U, provides:

(e) GENERAL SAVINGS PROVISION WITH RESPECT TO DEADWOOD PROVISIONS.—If—

(1) any provision amended or repealed by the amendments made by subsection (b) or (d) applied to—

(A) any transaction occurring before the date of the enactment of this Act,

(B) any property acquired before such date of enactment, or

(C) any item of income, loss, deduction, or credit taken into account before such date of enactment, and

(2) the treatment of such transaction, property, or item under such provision would (without regard to the amendments or repeals made by such subsection) affect the liability for tax for periods ending after such date of enactment,

nothing in the amendments or repeals made by this section shall be construed to affect the treatment of such transaction, property, or item for purposes of determining liability for tax for periods ending after such date of enactment.

• **2004, American Jobs Creation Act of 2004 (P.L. 108-357)**

P.L. 108-357, §835(b)(10)(A)-(B):

Amended Code Sec. 7701(a)(19)(C)(xi) by striking "and any regular interest in a FASIT,", and by striking "or FASIT" each place it appears. For the **effective** date, see Act Sec. 835(c), below. Prior to amendment, Code Sec. 7701(a)(19)(C)(xi) read as follows:

(xi) any regular or residual interest in a REMIC, and any regular interest in a FASIT, but only in the proportion which the assets of such REMIC or FASIT consist of property described in any of the preceding clauses of this subparagraph; except that if 95 percent or more of the assets of such REMIC or FASIT are assets described in clauses (i) through (x), the entire interest in the REMIC or FASIT shall qualify.

P.L. 108-357, §835(c), provides:

(c) EFFECTIVE DATE.—

(1) IN GENERAL.—Except as provided in paragraph (2), the amendments made by this section shall take effect on January 1, 2005.

(2) EXCEPTION FOR EXISTING FASITS.—Paragraph (1) shall not apply to any FASIT in existence on the date of the enactment of this Act [10-22-2004.—CCH] to the extent that regular interests issued by the FASIT before such date continue to remain outstanding in accordance with the original terms of issuance.

• **1996, Small Business Job Protection Act of 1996 (P.L. 104-188)**

P.L. 104-188, §1621(b)(8):

Amended Code Sec. 7701(a)(19)(C)(xi). **Effective** 9-1-97. Prior to amendment, Code Sec. 7701(a)(19)(C)(xi) read as follows:

(xi) any regular or residual interest in a REMIC, but only in the proportion which the assets of such REMIC consist of property described in any of the preceding clauses of this subparagraph; except that if 95 percent or more of the assets of such REMIC are assets described in clauses (i) through (x), the entire interest in the REMIC shall qualify.

• **1988, Technical and Miscellaneous Revenue Act of 1988 (P.L. 100-647)**

P.L. 100-647, §1006(t)(12):

Amended Code Sec. 7701(a)(19)(C)(xi) by striking out "are loans described" and inserting in lieu thereof "are assets described". **Effective** as if included in the provision of P.L. 99-514 to which it relates.

P.L. 100-647, §1006(t)(25)(A):

Amended Code Sec. 7701(a)(19) by adding at the end thereof a new sentence. **Effective** as if included in the provision of P.L. 99-514 to which it relates.

• **1986, Tax Reform Act of 1986 (P.L. 99-514)**

P.L. 99-514, §671(b)(3):

Amended Code Sec. 7701(a)(19) by striking out "and" at the end of clause (ix), by striking out the period at the end of clause (x) and inserting in lieu thereof ", and", and by inserting after clause (x) the new clause (xi). **Effective** for tax years beginning after 12-31-86.

• **1976, Tax Reform Act of 1976 (P.L. 94-455)**

P.L. 94-455, §1906(b)(13)(A):

Amended 1954 Code by substituting "Secretary" for "Secretary or his delegate" each place it appeared. **Effective** 2-1-77.

• **1969, Tax Reform Act of 1969 (P.L. 91-172)**

P.L. 91-172, §432(c):

Amended Code Sec. 7701(a)(19). **Effective** for tax years beginning after 7-11-69. Prior to amendment, Code Sec. 7701(a)(19) read as follows:

(19) DOMESTIC BUILDING AND LOAN ASSOCIATION.—The term "domestic building and loan association" means a domestic building and loan association, a domestic savings and loan association, and a Federal savings and loan association—

(A) which either (i) is an insured institution within the meaning of section 401(a) of the National Housing Act (12 U. S. C., sec. 1724(a)), or (ii) is subject by law to supervision and examination by State or Federal authority having supervision over such associations;

(B) substantially all of the business of which consists of acquiring the savings of the public and investing in loans described in subparagraph (C);

(C) at least 90 percent of the amount of the total assets of which (as of the close of the taxable year) consists of (i) cash, (ii) obligations of the United States or of a State or political subdivision thereof, stock or obligations of a corporation which is an instrumentality of the United States or of a State or political subdivision thereof, and certificates of deposit in, or obligations of, a corporation organized under a State law which specifically authorizes such corporation to insure the deposits or share accounts of member associations, (iii) loans secured by an interest in real property and loans made for the improvement of real property, (iv) loans secured by a deposit or share of a member, (v) property acquired through the liquidation of defaulted loans described in clause (iii), and (vi) property used by the association in the conduct of the business described in subparagraph (B);

(D) of the assets of which taken into account under subparagraph (C) as assets constituting the 90 percent of total assets—

(i) at least 80 percent of the amount of such assets consists of assets described in clauses (i), (ii), (iv), and (vi) of such subparagraph and of loans secured by an interest in real property which is (or, from the proceeds of the loan, will become) residential real property or real property used primarily for church purposes, loans made for the improvement of residential real property or real property used primarily for church purposes, or property acquired through the liquidation of defaulted loans described in this clause; and

(ii) at least 60 percent of the amount of such assets consists of assets described in clauses (i), (ii), (iv), and (vi) of such subparagraph and of loans secured by an interest in real property which is (or, from the proceeds of the loan, will become) residential real property containing 4 or fewer family units or real property used primarily for church purposes, loans made for the improvement of residential real property containing 4 or fewer family units or real property used primarily for church purposes, or property acquired through the liquidation of defaulted loans described in this clause;

(E) not more than 18 percent of the amount of the total assets of which (as of the close of the taxable year) consists of assets other than those described in clause (i) of subparagraph (D), and not more than 36 percent of the amount of the total assets of which (as of the close of the taxable year) consists of assets other than those described in clause (ii) of subparagraph (D); and

DEFINITIONS

(F) except for property described in subparagraph (C), not more than 3 percent of the assets of which consists of stock of any corporation.

The term "domestic building and loan association" also includes any association which, for the taxable year, would satisfy the requirements of the first sentence of this paragraph if "41 percent" were substituted for "36 percent" in subparagraph (E). Except in the case of the taxpayer's first taxable year beginning after the date of the enactment of the Revenue Act of 1962, the second sentence of this paragraph shall not apply to an association for the taxable year unless such association (i) was a domestic building and loan association within the meaning of the first sentence of this paragraph for the first taxable year preceding the taxable year, or (ii) was a domestic building and loan association solely by reason of the second sentence of this paragraph for the first taxable year preceding the taxable year (but not for the second preceding taxable year). At the election of the taxpayer, the percentages specified in this paragraph shall be applied on the basis of the average assets outstanding during the taxable year, in lieu of the close of the taxable year, computed under regulations prescribed by the Secretary or his delegate.

• **1962, Revenue Act of 1962 (P.L. 87-834)**

P.L. 87-834, §6:

Amended Code Sec. 7701(a)(19). **Effective** for tax years beginning after 10-16-62. Prior to the amendment Sec. 7701(a)(19) read as follows:

"(19) Domestic building and loan association.—The term 'domestic building and loan association' means a domestic building and loan association, a domestic savings and loan association, and a Federal savings and loan association, substantially all the business of which is confined to making loans to members."

(20) EMPLOYEE.—For the purpose of applying the provisions of section 79 with respect to group-term life insurance purchased for employees, for the purpose of applying the provisions of sections 104, 105, and 106 with respect to accident and health insurance or accident and health plans, and for the purpose of applying the provisions of subtitle A with respect to contributions to or under a stock bonus, pension, profit-sharing, or annuity plan, and with respect to distributions under such a plan, or by a trust forming part of such a plan, and for purposes of applying section 125 with respect to cafeteria plans, the term "employee" shall include a full-time life insurance salesman who is considered an employee for the purpose of chapter 21.

Amendments

• **2014, Tax Technical Corrections Act of 2014 (P.L. 113-295)**

P.L. 113-295, §221(a)(119), Division A:

Amended Code Sec. 7701(a)(20) by striking "chapter 21" and all that follows and inserting "chapter 21.". **Effective** generally 12-19-2014. For a special rule, see Act Sec. 221(b)(2), Division A, below. Prior to being stricken, "chapter 21" and all that follows read as follows:

chapter 21, or in the case of services performed before January 1, 1951, who would be considered an employee if his services were performed during 1951.

P.L. 113-295, §221(b)(2), Division A, provides:

(2) SAVINGS PROVISION.—If—

(A) any provision amended or repealed by the amendments made by this section applied to—

(i) any transaction occurring before the date of the enactment of this Act,

(ii) any property acquired before such date of enactment, or

(iii) any item of income, loss, deduction, or credit taken into account before such date of enactment, and

(B) the treatment of such transaction, property, or item under such provision would (without regard to the amendments or repeals made by this section) affect the liability for tax for periods ending after date of enactment, nothing in the amendments or repeals made by this section shall be construed to affect the treatment of such transaction, property, or item for purposes of determining liability for tax for periods ending after such date of enactment.

• **1996, Small Business Job Protection Act of 1996 (P.L. 104-188)**

P.L. 104-188, §1402(b)(3):

Amended Code Sec. 7701(a)(20) by striking ", for the purpose of applying the provisions of section 101(b) with respect to employees' death benefits" after "accident and health plans". **Effective** with respect to decedents dying after 8-20-96.

• **1988, Technical and Miscellaneous Revenue Act of 1988 (P.L. 100-647)**

P.L. 100-647, §1011B(e)(1)-(2):

Amended Code Sec. 7701(a)(20) by striking out "106, and 125" and inserting in lieu thereof "and 106", and by inserting "and for purposes of applying section 125 with respect to cafeteria plans," before "the term". **Effective** as if included in the provision of P.L. 99-514 to which it relates.

• **1986, Tax Reform Act of 1986 (P.L. 99-514)**

P.L. 99-514, §1166(a):

Amended Code Sec. 7701(a)(20) by striking out "and 106" and inserting in lieu thereof "106, and 125". **Effective** for tax years beginning after 12-31-85.

• **1964, Revenue Act of 1964 (P.L. 88-272)**

P.L. 88-272, §204(a)(3):

Amended the beginning of paragraph (20) to read "For the purpose of applying the provisions of section 79 with respect to group-term life insurance purchased for employees, for the purpose of applying the provisions of section 104" in lieu of "For the purpose of applying the provisions of sections 104". **Effective** 1-1-64.

(21) LEVY.—The term "levy" includes the power of distraint and seizure by any means.

(22) ATTORNEY GENERAL.—The term "Attorney General" means the Attorney General of the United States.

(23) TAXABLE YEAR.—The term "taxable year" means the calendar year, or the fiscal year ending during such calendar year, upon the basis of which the taxable income is computed under subtitle A. "Taxable year" means, in the case of a return made for a fractional part of a year under the provisions of subtitle A or under regulations prescribed by the Secretary, the period for which such return is made.

Amendments

• **1976, Tax Reform Act of 1976 (P.L. 94-455)**

P.L. 94-455, §1906(b)(13)(A):

Amended 1954 Code by substituting "Secretary" for "Secretary or his delegate" each place it appeared. **Effective** 2-1-77.

(24) FISCAL YEAR.—The term "fiscal year" means an accounting period of 12 months ending on the last day of any month other than December.

(25) PAID OR INCURRED, PAID OR ACCRUED.—The terms "paid or incurred" and "paid or accrued" shall be construed according to the method of accounting upon the basis of which the taxable income is computed under subtitle A.

(26) TRADE OR BUSINESS.—The term "trade or business" includes the performance of the functions of a public office.

(27) TAX COURT.—The term "Tax Court" means the United States Tax Court.

Amendments

• **1969, Tax Reform Act of 1969 (P.L. 91-172)**

P.L. 91-172, §960(j):

Amended Code Sec. 7701(a)(27) by substituting the phrase "United States Tax Court" for the phrase "Tax Court of the United States." **Effective** 12-30-69.

(28) OTHER TERMS.—Any term used in this subtitle with respect to the application of, or in connection with, the provisions of any other subtitle of this title shall have the same meaning as in such provisions.

(29) INTERNAL REVENUE CODE.—The term "Internal Revenue Code of 1986" means this title, and the term "Internal Revenue Code of 1939" means the Internal Revenue Code enacted February 10, 1939, as amended.

Amendments

• **1988, Technical and Miscellaneous Revenue Act of 1988 (P.L. 100-647)**

P.L. 100-647, §1(c):

Amended Code Sec. 7701(a)(29) by striking out "of 1954" and inserting in lieu thereof "of 1986". **Effective** as if included in the provision of P.L. 99-514 to which it relates.

(30) UNITED STATES PERSON.—The term "United States person" means—

(A) a citizen or resident of the United States,

(B) a domestic partnership,

(C) a domestic corporation,

DEFINITIONS

(D) any estate (other than a foreign estate, within the meaning of paragraph (31)), and

(E) any trust if—

(i) a court within the United States is able to exercise primary supervision over the administration of the trust, and

(ii) one or more United States persons have the authority to control all substantial decisions of the trust.

Amendments

• **1997, Taxpayer Relief Act of 1997 (P.L. 105-34)**

P.L. 105-34, §1601(i)(3)(A):

Amended Code Sec. 7701(a)(30)(E)(ii) by striking "fiduciaries" and inserting "persons". **Effective** as if included in the provision of P.L. 104-188 to which it relates [generally **effective** for tax years beginning after 12-31-96.—CCH].

• **1996, Small Business Job Protection Act of 1996 (P.L. 104-188)**

P.L. 104-188, §1907(a)(1):

Amended Code Sec. 7701(a)(30) by striking "and" at the end of subparagraph (C) and by striking subparagraph (D) and by inserting new subparagraphs (D) and (E). **Effective** for tax years beginning after 12-31-96, or at the election of the trusteee of a trust, to tax years ending after the date of the enactment of this Act. Such an election, once made, is irrevocable. For an amendment to this **effective** date, see P.L. 105-34, §1161, below. Prior to amendment, Code Sec. 7701(a)(30)(D) read as follows:

(D) any estate or trust (other than a foreign estate or foreign trust, within the meaning of section 7701(a)(31)).

(31) FOREIGN ESTATE OR TRUST.—

(A) FOREIGN ESTATE.—The term "foreign estate" means an estate the income of which, from sources without the United States which is not effectively connected with the conduct of a trade or business within the United States, is not includible in gross income under subtitle A.

(B) FOREIGN TRUST.—The term "foreign trust" means any trust other than a trust described in subparagraph (E) of paragraph (30).

Amendments

• **1996, Small Business Job Protection Act of 1996 (P.L. 104-188)**

P.L. 104-188, §1907(a)(2):

Amended Code Sec. 7701(a)(31). **Effective** for tax years beginning after 12-31-96, or at the election of the trusteee of a trust, to tax years ending after the date of the enactment of this Act. Such an election, once made, is irrevocable. For an amendment to this **effective** date, see P.L. 105-34, §1161, below. Prior to amendment, Code Sec. 7701(a)(31) read as follows:

(31) FOREIGN ESTATE OR TRUST.—The terms "foreign estate" and "foreign trust" mean an estate or trust, as the case may be, the income of which, from sources without the United States which is not effectively connected with the conduct of a trade or business within the United States, is not includible in gross income under subtitle A.

• **1997, Taxpayer Relief Act of 1997 (P.L. 105-34)**

P.L. 105-34, §1161, provides:

ACT SEC. 1161. TRANSITION RULE FOR CERTAIN TRUSTS.

(a) IN GENERAL.—Paragraph (3) of section 1907(a) of the Small Business Job Protection Act of 1996 is amended by adding at the end the following flush sentence:

To the extent prescribed in regulations by the Secretary of the Treasury or his delegate, a trust which was in existence on August 20, 1996 (other than a trust treated as owned by the grantor under subpart E of part I of subchapter J of chapter 1 of the Internal Revenue Code of 1986), and which was treated as a United States person on the day before the date of the enactment of this Act may elect to continue to be treated as a United States person notwithstanding section 7701(a)(30)(E) of such Code.

• **1997, Taxpayer Relief Act of 1997 (P.L. 105-34)**

P.L. 105-34, §1161, provides:

ACT SEC. 1161. TRANSITION RULE FOR CERTAIN TRUSTS.

(a) IN GENERAL.—Paragraph (3) of section 1907(a) of the Small Business Job Protection Act of 1996 is amended by adding at the end the following flush sentence:

To the extent prescribed in regulations by the Secretary of the Treasury or his delegate, a trust which was in existence on August 20, 1996 (other than a trust treated as owned by the grantor under subpart E of part I of subchapter J of chapter 1 of the Internal Revenue Code of 1986), and which was treated as a United States person on the day before the date of the enactment of this Act may elect to continue to be treated as a United States person notwithstanding section 7701(a)(30)(E) of such Code.

(b) EFFECTIVE DATE.—The amendment made by subsection (a) shall take effect as if included in the amendments made by section 1907(a) of the Small Business Job Protection Act of 1996.

• **1962, Revenue Act of 1962 (P.L. 87-834)**

P.L. 87-834, §7:

Added paragraph (30) to Code Sec. 7701(a). **Effective** 10-17-62.

• **1966, Foreign Investors Tax Act of 1966 (P.L. 89-809)**

P.L. 89-809, §103(l)(1):

Amended Code Sec. 7701(a)(31) by substituting ", from sources without the United States which is not effectively connected with the conduct of a trade of business within the United States," for "from sources without the United States". **Effective** 1-1-67.

• **1962, Revenue Act of 1962 (P.L. 87-834)**

P.L. 87-834, §7:

Added paragraph (31) to Code Sec. 7701(a). **Effective** 10-17-62.

(32) COOPERATIVE BANK.—The term "cooperative bank" means an institution without capital stock organized and operated for mutual purposes and without profit, which—

(A) is subject by law to supervision and examination by State or Federal authority having supervision over such institutions, and

(B) meets the requirements of subparagraphs (B) and (C) of paragraph (19) of this subsection (relating to definition of domestic building and loan association).

In determining whether an institution meets the requirements referred to in subparagraph (B) of this paragraph, any reference to an association or to a domestic building and loan association contained in paragraph (19) shall be deemed to be a reference to such institution.

Amendments

• **2018, Tax Technical Corrections Act of 2018 (P.L. 115-141)**

P.L. 115-141, §401(b)(55), Div. U:

Amended Code Sec. 7701(a)(32)(A). **Effective** 3-23-2018. For a special rule, see Act Sec. 401(e), Div. U, below. Prior to amendment, Code Sec. 7701(a)(32)(A) read as follows:

(A) either—

(i) is an insured institution within the meaning of section 401(a) of the National Housing Act (12 U. S. C., sec. 1724(a)), or

(ii) is subject by law to supervision and examination by State or Federal authority having supervision over such institutions, and

P.L. 115-141, §401(e), Div. U, provides:

(e) GENERAL SAVINGS PROVISION WITH RESPECT TO DEADWOOD PROVISIONS.—If—

(1) any provision amended or repealed by the amendments made by subsection (b) or (d) applied to—

(A) any transaction occurring before the date of the enactment of this Act,

(B) any property acquired before such date of enactment, or

(C) any item of income, loss, deduction, or credit taken into account before such date of enactment, and

(2) the treatment of such transaction, property, or item under such provision would (without regard to the amendments or repeals made by such subsection) affect the liability for tax for periods ending after such date of enactment,

nothing in the amendments or repeals made by this section shall be construed to affect the treatment of such transaction, property, or item for purposes of determining liability for tax for periods ending after such date of enactment.

• **1969, Tax Reform Act of 1969 (P.L. 91-172)**

P.L. 91-172, §432(d):

Amended Code Sec. 7701(a)(32)(B) and deleted the third (last) sentence of Code Sec. 7701(a)(32). **Effective** for tax years beginning after 7-11-69. Prior to amendment, Code Sec. 7701(a)(32)(B) read as follows:

(32) Cooperative bank.—The term "cooperative bank" means an institution without capital stock organized and operated for mutual purposes and without profit, which—

(A) either—

(i) is an insured institution within the meaning of section 401(a) of the National Housing Act (12 U. S. C., sec. 1724(a)), or

(ii) is subject by law to supervision and examination by State or Federal authority having supervision over such institutions, and

(B) meets the requirements of subparagraphs (B), (C), (D), (E), and (F) of paragraph (19) of this subsection (relating to definition of domestic building and loan association) determined with the application of the second, third, and fourth sentences of paragraph (19).

In determining whether an institution meets the requirements referred to in subparagraph (B) of this paragraph, any reference to an association or to a domestic building and loan association contained in paragraph (19) shall be deemed to be a reference to such institution. In the case of an institution which, for the taxable year, is a cooperative bank within the meaning of the first sentence of this paragraph by reason of the application of the second and third sentences of paragraph (19) of this subsection, the deduction otherwise allowable under section 166(c) for a reasonable addition to the reserve for bad debts shall, under regulations prescribed by the

DEFINITIONS

Secretary or his delegate, be reduced in a manner consistent with the reductions provided by the table contained in section 593(b)(5).

• **1962 (P.L. 87-870)**

P.L. 87-870, § 5(a):

Added paragraph (32) to Code Sec. 7701(a). **Effective** 10-17-62.

> (33) REGULATED PUBLIC UTILITY.—The term "regulated public utility" means—
>
> (A) A corporation engaged in the furnishing or sale of—
>
> (i) electric energy, gas, water, or sewerage disposal services, or
>
> (ii) transportation (not included in subparagraph (C)) on an intrastate, suburban, municipal, or interurban electric railroad, on an intrastate, municipal, or suburban trackless trolley system, or on a municipal or suburban bus system, or
>
> (iii) transportation (not included in clause (ii)) by motor vehicle—
>
> if the rates for such furnishing or sale, as the case may be, have been established or approved by a State or political subdivision thereof, by an agency or instrumentality of the United States, by a public service or public utility commission or other similar body of the District of Columbia or of any State or political subdivision thereof, or by a foreign country or an agency or instrumentality or political subdivision thereof.
>
> (B) A corporation engaged as a common carrier in the furnishing or sale of transportation of gas by pipe line, if subject to the jurisdiction of the Federal Energy Regulatory Commission.
>
> (C) A corporation engaged as a common carrier (i) in the furnishing or sale of transportation by railroad, if subject to the jurisdiction of the Surface Transportation Board, or (ii) in the furnishing or sale of transportation of oil or other petroleum products (including shale oil) by pipe line, if subject to the jurisdiction of the Federal Energy Regulatory Commission or if the rates for such furnishing or sale are subject to the jurisdiction of a public service or public utility commission or other similar body of the District of Columbia or of any State.
>
> (D) A corporation engaged in the furnishing or sale of telephone or telegraph service, if the rates for such furnishing or sale meet the requirements of subparagraph (A).
>
> (E) A corporation engaged in the furnishing or sale of transportation as a common carrier by air, subject to the jurisdiction of the Secretary of Transportation.
>
> (F) A corporation engaged in the furnishing or sale of transportation by a water carrier subject to jurisdiction under subchapter II of chapter 135 of title 49.
>
> (G) A rail carrier subject to part A of subtitle IV of title 49, if (i) substantially all of its railroad properties have been leased to another such railroad corporation or corporations by an agreement or agreements entered into before January 1, 1954, (ii) each lease is for a term of more than 20 years, and (iii) at least 80 percent or more of its gross income (computed without regard to dividends and capital gains and losses) for the taxable year is derived from such leases and from sources described in subparagraphs (A) through (F), inclusive. For purposes of the preceding sentence, an agreement for lease of railroad properties entered into before January 1, 1954, shall be considered to be a lease including such term as the total number of years of such agreement may, unless sooner terminated, be renewed or continued under the terms of the agreement, and any such renewal or continuance under such agreement shall be considered part of the lease entered into before January 1, 1954.
>
> (H) A common parent corporation which is a common carrier by railroad subject to part A of subtitle IV of title 49 if at least 80 percent of its gross income (computed without regard to capital gains or losses) is derived directly or indirectly from sources described in subparagraphs (A) through (F), inclusive. For purposes of the preceding sentence, dividends and interest, and income from leases described in subparagraph (G), received from a regulated public utility shall be considered as derived from sources described in subparagraphs (A) through (F), inclusive, if the regulated public utility is a member of an affiliated group (as defined in section 1504) which includes the common parent corporation.

The term "regulated public utility" does not (except as provided in subparagraphs (G) and (H)) include a corporation described in subparagraphs (A) through (F), inclusive, unless 80 percent or more of its gross income (computed without regard to dividends and capital gains and losses) for the taxable year is derived from sources described in subparagraphs (A) through (F), inclusive. If the taxpayer establishes to the satisfaction of the Secretary that (i) its revenue from regulated rates described in subparagraph (A) or (D) and its revenue derived from unregulated rates are derived from the operation of a single interconnected and coordinated system or from the operation of more than one such system, and (ii) the unregulated rates have been and are substantially as favorable to users and consumers as are the regulated rates, then such revenue from such unregulated rates shall be considered, for purposes of the preceding sentence, as income derived from sources described in subparagraph (A) or (D).

Amendments

• **1996, Small Business Job Protection Act of 1996 (P.L. 104-188)**

P.L. 104-88, § 304(e)(1)-(6):

Amended Code Sec. 7701(a)(33) by striking "Federal Power Commission" and inserting in lieu thereof "Federal Energy Regulatory Commission" in subparagraph (B); by striking "Interstate Commerce Commission" and inserting in lieu thereof "Surface Transportation Board" in subparagraph (C)(i); by striking "Interstate Commerce Commission" and inserting in lieu thereof "Federal Energy Regulatory Commission" in subparagraph (C)(ii); by striking "common carrier" and all that follows through "1933" and inserting in lieu thereof "a water carrier subject to jurisdiction under subchapter II of chapter 135 of title 49" in subparagraph (F); by striking "railroad corporation subject to subchapter I of chapter 105" and inserting in lieu thereof "rail carrier subject to part A of subtitle IV" in subparagraph (G); and by striking "subchapter I of chapter 105" and inserting in lieu thereof "part A of subtitle IV" in subparagraph (H). **Effective** 1-1-96. Prior to amendment, Code Sec. 7701(a)(33)(F) read as follows:

> (F) A corporation engaged in the furnishing or sale of transportation by common carrier by water, subject to the jurisdiction of the Interstate Commerce Commission under subchapter III of chapter 105 of title 49, or subject to the jurisdiction of the Federal Maritime Board under the Intercoastal Shipping Act, 1933.

• **1984, Civil Aeronautics Board Sunset Act of 1984 (P.L. 98-443)**

P.L. 98-443, § 9(q):

Amended Code Sec. 7701(a)(33)(E) by striking out "Civil Aeronautics Board" and inserting in lieu thereof "Secretary of Transportation". **Effective** 1-1-85.

(34) [Repealed.]

• **1984 (P.L. 98-216)**

P.L. 98-216, § 3(c)(2):

Amended Code Sec. 7701(a)(33)(G) by striking out "part I of the Interstate Commerce Act" and inserting in lieu thereof "subchapter I of chapter 105 of title 49". **Effective** 2-14-84.

• **1983 (P.L. 97-449)**

P.L. 97-449, § 5(e):

Amended Code Sec. 7701(a)(33) by striking out in subparagraph (F) "part III of the Interstate Commerce Act" and substituting "subchapter III of chapter 105 of title 49"; and by striking out in subparagraph (H) "part I of the Interstate Commerce Act" and substituting "subchapter I of chapter 105 of title 49". **Effective** 1-12-83.

• **1976, Tax Reform Act of 1976 (P.L. 94-455)**

P.L. 94-455, § 1906(b)(13)(A):

Amended 1954 Code by substituting "Secretary" for "Secretary or his delegate" each place it appeared. **Effective** 2-1-77.

• **1964, Revenue Act of 1964 (P.L. 88-272)**

P.L. 88-272, § 234(b)(3):

Amended Code Sec. 7701(a) by adding paragraph (33). **Effective** with respect to tax years beginning after 12-31-63.

DEFINITIONS

Amendments

• **1984, Deficit Reduction Act of 1984 (P.L. 98-369)**

P.L. 98-369, §412(b)(11):

Amended Code Sec. 7701(a) by repealing paragraph (34). **Effective** with respect to tax years beginning after 12-31-84. Prior to amendment, it read as follows:

(34) Estimated Income Tax.—The term "estimated income tax" means—

(A) in the case of an individual, the estimate tax as defined in section 6015(d), or

(B) in the case of a corporation, the estimated tax as defined in section 6154(c).

• **1981, Economic Recovery Tax Act of 1981 (P.L. 97-34)**

P.L. 97-34, §725(c)(4):

Amended Code Sec. 7701(a)(34) by striking out "6015(c)" and inserting "6015(d)". **Effective** 1-1-81.

• **1968, Revenue and Expenditure Control Act of 1968 (P.L. 90-364)**

P.L. 90-364, §103(e)(6):

Amended Code Sec. 7701(a)(34) by substituting "section 6154(c)" for "section 6016(b)" in subparagraph (B). **Effective** with respect to tax years beginning after 12-31-67. However, the amendment is to be taken into account only as of 5-31-68.

• **1966, Tax Adjustment Act of 1966 (P.L. 89-368)**

P.L. 89-368, §102(c)(5):

Added Code Sec. 7701(a)(34). **Effective** 1-1-67.

(35) ENROLLED ACTUARY.—The term "enrolled actuary" means a person who is enrolled by the Joint Board for the Enrollment of Actuaries established under subtitle C of the title III of the Employee Retirement Income Security Act of 1974.

Amendments

• **1974, Employee Retirement Income Security Act of 1974 (P.L. 93-406)**

P.L. 93-406, §3043:

Amended Code Sec. 7701(a) by adding paragraph (35). **Effective** 9-2-74.

(36) TAX RETURN PREPARER.—

(A) IN GENERAL.—The term "tax return preparer" means any person who prepares for compensation, or who employs one or more persons to prepare for compensation, any return of tax imposed by this title or any claim for refund of tax imposed by this title. For purposes of the preceding sentence, the preparation of a substantial portion of a return or claim for refund shall be treated as if it were the preparation of such return or claim for refund.

(B) EXCEPTIONS.—A person shall not be a "tax return preparer" merely because such person—

(i) furnishes typing, reproducing, or other mechanical assistance,

(ii) prepares a return or claim for refund of the employer (or of an officer or employee of the employer) by whom he is regularly and continuously employed,

(iii) prepares as a fiduciary a return or claim for refund for any person, or

(iv) prepares a claim for refund for a taxpayer in response to any notice of deficiency issued to such taxpayer or in response to any waiver of restriction after the commencement of an audit of such taxpayer or another taxpayer if a determination in such audit of such other taxpayer directly or indirectly affects the tax liability of such taxpayer.

Amendments

• **2018, Tax Technical Corrections Act of 2018 (P.L. 115-141)**

P.L. 115-141, §401(a)(331), Div. U:

Amended Code Sec. 7701(a)(36)(B) by striking "an 'tax" and inserting "a 'tax". **Effective** 3-23-2018.

• **2007, Small Business and Work Opportunity Tax Act of 2007 (P.L. 110-28)**

P.L. 110-28, §8246(a)(1)(A)-(B):

Amended Code Sec. 7701(a)(36) by striking "income" each place it appears in the heading and the text, and in subparagraph (A), by striking "subtitle A" each place it appears and inserting "this title". **Effective** for returns prepared after 5-25-2007. Prior to amendment, Code Sec. 7701(a)(36) read as follows:

(36) INCOME TAX RETURN PREPARER.—

(A) IN GENERAL.—The term "income tax return preparer" means any person who prepares for compensation, or who employs one or more persons to prepare for compensation, any return of tax imposed by subtitle A or any claim for refund of tax imposed by subtitle A. For purposes of the preceding sentence, the preparation of a substantial portion of a return or claim for refund shall be treated as if it were the preparation of such return or claim for refund.

(B) EXCEPTIONS.—A person shall not be an "income tax return preparer" merely because such person—

(i) furnishes typing, reproducing, or other mechanical assistance,

(ii) prepares a return or claim for refund of the employer (or of an officer or employee of the employer) by whom he is regularly and continuously employed,

(iii) prepares as a fiduciary a return or claim for refund for any person, or

(iv) prepares a claim for refund for a taxpayer in response to any notice of deficiency issued to such taxpayer or in response to any waiver of restriction after the commencement of an audit of such taxpayer or another taxpayer if a determination in such audit of such other taxpayer directly or indirectly affects the tax liability of such taxpayer.

• **1978, Revenue Act of 1978 (P.L. 95-600)**

P.L. 95-600, §701(cc)(2):

Amended Code Sec. 7701(a)(36)(iii). **Effective** with respect to documents prepared after 12-31-76. Prior to amendment, Code Sec. 7701(b)(36)(iii) read:

"(iii) prepares a return or claim for refund for any trust or estate with respect to which he is a fiduciary, or"

• **1976, Tax Reform Act of 1976 (P.L. 94-455)**

P.L. 94-455, §1203(a):

Added Code Sec. 7701(a)(36). **Effective** for documents prepared after 12-31-76.

(37) INDIVIDUAL RETIREMENT PLAN.—The term "individual retirement plan" means—

(A) an individual retirement account described in section 408(a), and

(B) an individual retirement annuity described in section 408(b).

Amendments

• **1984, Deficit Reduction Act of 1984 (P.L. 98-369)**

P.L. 98-369, §491(d)(53):

Amended Code Sec. 7701(a)(37) by striking out subparagraph (C), by striking out ", and" at the end of subparagraph (B) and inserting in lieu thereof a period, and by adding "and" at the end of subparagraph (A). **Effective** for obligations issued after 12-31-83. Prior to amendment, subparagraph (C) read as follows:

(C) a retirement bond described in section 409.

• **1978, Revenue Act of 1978 (P.L. 95-600)**

P.L. 95-600, §157(k)(2):

Added Code Sec. 7701(a)(37). **Effective** for tax years beginning after 12-31-74.

(38) JOINT RETURN.—The term "joint return" means a single return made jointly under section 6013 by a husband and wife.

Amendments

• **1982, Tax Equity and Fiscal Responsibility Act of 1982 (P.L. 97-248)**

P.L. 97-248, §201(d)(10):

Added Code Sec. 7701(a)(38). **Effective** for tax years beginning after 12-31-82.

(39) PERSONS RESIDING OUTSIDE UNITED STATES.—If any citizen or resident of the United States does not reside in (and is not found in) any United States judicial district, such citizen or resident shall be treated as residing in the District of Columbia for purposes of any provision of this title relating to—

(A) jurisdiction of courts, or

(B) enforcement of summons.

DEFINITIONS

Amendments
• **1983, Technical Corrections Act of 1982 (P.L. 97-448)**

P.L. 97-448, §306(b)(3):

Redesignated Code Sec. 7701(a)(38) (as added by P.L. 97-248) as Code Sec. 7701(a)(39). **Effective** as if included in the provision of P.L 97-248 to which it relates.

(40) INDIAN TRIBAL GOVERNMENT.—

(A) In general.—The term "Indian tribal government" means the governing body of any tribe, band, community, village, or group of Indians, or (if applicable) Alaska Natives, which is determined by the Secretary, after consultation with the Secretary of the Interior, to exercise governmental functions.

(B) SPECIAL RULE FOR ALASKA NATIVES.—No determination under subparagraph (A) with respect to Alaska Natives shall grant or defer any status or powers other than those enumerated in section 7871. Nothing in the Indian Tribal Governmental Tax Status Act of 1982, or in the amendments made thereby, shall validate or invalidate any claim by Alaska Natives of sovereign authority over lands or people.

Amendments
• **1984 (P.L. 97-473)**

P.L. 97-473, §203:

Added Code Sec. 7701(a)(40). For the **effective** date, see the amendment note for P.L. 97-473, §204 following Code Sec. 7871.

(41) TIN.—The term "TIN" means the identifying number assigned to a person under section 6109.

Amendments
• **1983, Interest and Dividend Tax Compliance Act of 1983 (P.L. 98-67)**

P.L. 98-67, §104(d)(1):

Added Code Sec. 7701(a)(41). **Effective** with respect to payments made after 12-31-83.

(42) SUBSTITUTED BASIS PROPERTY.—The term "substituted basis property" means property which is—

(A) transferred basis property, or

(B) exchanged basis property.

(43) TRANSFERRED BASIS PROPERTY.—The term "transferred basis property" means property having a basis determined under any provision of subtitle A (or under any corresponding provision of prior income tax law) providing that the basis shall be determined in whole or in part by reference to the basis in the hands of the donor, grantor, or other transferor.

(44) EXCHANGED BASIS PROPERTY.—The term "exchanged basis property" means property having a basis determined under any provision of subtitle A (or under any corresponding provision of prior income tax law) providing that the basis shall be determined in whole or in part by reference to other property held at any time by the person for whom the basis is to be determined.

(45) NONRECOGNITION TRANSACTION.—The term "nonrecognition transaction" means any disposition of property in a transaction in which gain or loss is not recognized in whole or in part for purposes of subtitle A.

Amendments
• **1984, Deficit Reduction Act of 1984 (P.L. 98-369)**

P.L. 98-369, §43(a)(1):

Added Code Sec. 7701(a)(42)-(45). **Effective** for tax years ending after 7-18-84.

(46) DETERMINATION OF WHETHER THERE IS A COLLECTIVE BARGAINING AGREEMENT.—In determining whether there is a collective bargaining agreement between employee representatives and 1 or more employers, the term "employee representatives" shall not include any organization more than one-half of the members of which are employees who are owners, officers, or executives of the employer. An agreement shall not be treated as a collective bargaining agreement unless it is a bona fide agreement between bona fide employee representatives and 1 or more employers.

Amendments
• **1986, Tax Reform Act of 1986 (P.L. 99-514)**

P.L. 99-514, §1137:

Amended Code Sec. 7701(a)(46) by adding at the end thereof a new sentence. **Effective** 10-22-86.

(47) [Repealed].

Amendments
• **2013, American Taxpayer Relief Act of 2012 (P.L. 112-240)**

P.L. 112-240, §101(a)(1)-(3), provides:

SEC. 101. PERMANENT EXTENSION AND MODIFICATION OF 2001 TAX RELIEF.

(a) PERMANENT EXTENSION.—

(1) IN GENERAL.—The Economic Growth and Tax Relief Reconciliation Act of 2001 is amended by striking title IX.

(2) CONFORMING AMENDMENT.—The Tax Relief, Unemployment Insurance Reauthorization, and Job Creation Act of 2010 is amended by striking section 304.

(3) EFFECTIVE DATE.—The amendments made by this subsection shall apply to taxable, plan, or limitation years beginning after December 31, 2012, and estates of decedents dying, gifts made, or generation skipping transfers after December 31, 2012.

• **2010, Tax Relief, Unemployment Insurance Reauthorization, and Job Creation Act of 2010 (P.L. 111-312)**

P.L. 111-312, §301(a):

Amended Code Sec. 7701(a)(47) to read as such provision would read if subtitle E of title V of the Economic Growth and Tax Relief Reconciliation Act of 2001 (P.L. 107-16) had never been enacted. [P.L. 107-16, §542(e)(3), amended Code Sec. 7701 by adding a new paragraph (47). Therefore, P.L. 111-312, §301(a), effectively repealed Code Sec. 7701(a)(47).—CCH **Effective** for estates of decedents dying, and transfers made, after 12-31-2009. For a special rule, see Act Sec. 301(c), below. Prior to amendment by P.L. 111-312, Code Sec. 7701(a)(47) read as follows:

Amendments
• **1982, Tax Equity and Fiscal Responsibility Act of 1982 (P.L. 97-248)**

P.L. 97-248, §336(a):

Added Code Sec. 7701(a)(38)[(39)]. **Effective** 9-4-82.

Amendments
• **1984, Deficit Reduction Act of 1984 (P.L. 98-369)**

P.L. 98-369, §526(c)(1):

Added Code Sec. 7701(a)(46). **Effective** 4-1-84.

(47) EXECUTOR.—The term "executor" means the executor or administrator of the decedent, or, if there is no executor or administrator appointed, qualified, and acting within the United States, then any person in actual or constructive possession of any property of the decedent.

P.L. 111-312, §301(c), provides:

(c) SPECIAL ELECTION WITH RESPECT TO ESTATES OF DECEDENTS DYING IN 2010.—Notwithstanding subsection (a), in the case of an estate of a decedent dying after December 31, 2009, and before January 1, 2011, the executor (within the meaning of section 2203 of the Internal Revenue Code of 1986) may elect to apply such Code as though the amendments made by subsection (a) do not apply with respect to chapter 11 of such Code and with respect to property acquired or passing from such decedent (within the meaning of section 1014(b) of such Code). Such election shall be made at such time and in such manner as the Secretary of the Treasury or the Secretary's delegate shall provide. Such an election once made shall be revocable only with the consent of the Secretary of the Treasury or the Secretary's delegate. For purposes of section 2652(a)(1) of such Code, the determination of whether any property is subject to the tax imposed by such chapter 11 shall be made without regard to any election made under this subsection.

P.L. 111-312, §304, provides [but see P.L. 112-240, §101(a)(2)-(3), above]:

SEC. 304. APPLICATION OF EGTRRA SUNSET TO THIS TITLE.

Section 901 of the Economic Growth and Tax Relief Reconciliation Act of 2001 shall apply to the amendments made by this title.

DEFINITIONS

• **2001, Economic Growth and Tax Relief Reconciliation Act of 2001 (P.L. 107-16)**

P.L. 107-16, §542(e)(3):

Amended Code Sec. 7701(a) by adding at the end a new paragraph (47). **Effective** for estates of decedents dying after 12-31-2009.

P.L. 107-16, §901(a)-(b), as amended by P.L. 111-312, §101(a)(1), provides [but see P.L. 112-240, §101(a)(1) and (3), above]:

SEC. 901. SUNSET OF PROVISIONS OF ACT.

(a) IN GENERAL.—All provisions of, and amendments made by, this Act shall not apply—

(1) to taxable, plan, or limitation years beginning after December 31, 2012, or

(2) in the case of title V, to estates of decedents dying, gifts made, or generation skipping transfers, after December 31, 2012.

(b) APPLICATION OF CERTAIN LAWS.—The Internal Revenue Code of 1986 and the Employee Retirement Income Security Act of 1974 shall be applied and administered to years, estates, gifts, and transfers described in subsection (a) as if the provisions and amendments described in subsection (a) had never been enacted.

(48) OFF-HIGHWAY VEHICLES.—

(A) OFF-HIGHWAY TRANSPORTATION VEHICLES.—

(i) IN GENERAL.—A vehicle shall not be treated as a highway vehicle if such vehicle is specially designed for the primary function of transporting a particular type of load other than over the public highway and because of this special design such vehicle's capability to transport a load over the public highway is substantially limited or impaired.

(ii) DETERMINATION OF VEHICLE'S DESIGN.—For purposes of clause (i), a vehicle's design is determined solely on the basis of its physical characteristics.

(iii) DETERMINATION OF SUBSTANTIAL LIMITATION OR IMPAIRMENT.—For purposes of clause (i), in determining whether substantial limitation or impairment exists, account may be taken of factors such as the size of the vehicle, whether such vehicle is subject to the licensing, safety, and other requirements applicable to highway vehicles, and whether such vehicle can transport a load at a sustained speed of at least 25 miles per hour. It is immaterial that a vehicle can transport a greater load off the public highway than such vehicle is permitted to transport over the public highway.

(B) NONTRANSPORTATION TRAILERS AND SEMITRAILERS.—A trailer or semitrailer shall not be treated as a highway vehicle if it is specially designed to function only as an enclosed stationary shelter for the carrying on of an offhighway function at an off-highway site.

Amendments

• **2004, American Jobs Creation Act of 2004 (P.L. 108-357)**

P.L. 108-357, §852(a):

Amended Code Sec. 7701(a) by adding at the end a new paragraph (48). **Effective** 10-22-2004. For a special rule, see Act Sec. 852(c)(2), below.

P.L. 108-357, §852(c)(2), provides:

(2) FUEL TAXES.—With respect to taxes imposed under subchapter B of chapter 31 and part III of subchapter A of chapter 32, the amendment made by this section shall apply to taxable periods beginning after the date of the enactment of this Act [10-22-2004.—CCH].

(49) QUALIFIED BLOOD COLLECTOR ORGANIZATION.—The term "qualified blood collector organization" means an organization which is—

(A) described in section 501(c)(3) and exempt from tax under section 501(a),

(B) primarily engaged in the activity of the collection of human blood,

(C) registered with the Secretary for purposes of excise tax exemptions, and

(D) registered by the Food and Drug Administration to collect blood.

Amendments

• **2006, Pension Protection Act of 2006 (P.L. 109-280)**

P.L. 109-280, §1207(f):

Amended Code Sec. 7701(a) by inserting at the end a new paragraph (49). **Effective** 1-1-2007.

(50) TERMINATION OF UNITED STATES CITIZENSHIP.—

(A) IN GENERAL.—An individual shall not cease to be treated as a United States citizen before the date on which the individual's citizenship is treated as relinquished under section 877A(g)(4).

(B) DUAL CITIZENS.—Under regulations prescribed by the Secretary, subparagraph (A) shall not apply to an individual who became at birth a citizen of the United States and a citizen of another country.

Amendments

• **2008, Heroes Earnings Assistance and Relief Tax Act of 2008 (P.L. 110-245)**

P.L. 110-245, §301(c)(1):

Amended Code Sec. 7701(a) by adding at the end a new paragraph (50). **Effective** for any individual whose expatriation date (as so defined) is on or after 6-17-2008.

[Sec. 7701(b)]

(b) DEFINITION OF RESIDENT ALIEN AND NONRESIDENT ALIEN.—

(1) IN GENERAL.—For purposes of this title (other than subtitle B)—

(A) RESIDENT ALIEN.—An alien individual shall be treated as a resident of the United States with respect to any calendar year if (and only if) such individual meets the requirements of clause (i), (ii), or (iii):

(i) LAWFULLY ADMITTED FOR PERMANENT RESIDENCE.—Such individual is a lawful permanent resident of the United States at any time during such calendar year.

(ii) SUBSTANTIAL PRESENCE TEST.—Such individual meets the substantial presence test of paragraph (3).

(iii) FIRST YEAR ELECTION.—Such individual makes the election provided in paragraph (4).

(B) NONRESIDENT ALIEN.—An individual is a nonresident alien if such individual is neither a citizen of the United States nor a resident of the United States (within the meaning of subparagraph (A)).

(2) SPECIAL RULES FOR FIRST AND LAST YEAR OF RESIDENCY.—

(A) FIRST YEAR OF RESIDENCY.—

(i) IN GENERAL.—If an alien individual is a resident of the United States under paragraph (1)(A) with respect to any calendar year, but was not a resident of the United States at any time during the preceding calendar year, such alien individual shall be treated as a resident of the United States only for the portion of such calendar year which begins on the residency starting date.

(ii) RESIDENCY STARTING DATE FOR INDIVIDUALS LAWFULLY ADMITTED FOR PERMANENT RESIDENCE.—In the case of an individual who is a lawfully permanent resident of the United States at any time during the calendar year, but does not meet the substantial presence test of paragraph (3), the residency starting date shall be the first day in such calendar year on which he was present in the United States while a lawful permanent resident of the United States.

DEFINITIONS

　　　　(iii) RESIDENCY STARTING DATE FOR INDIVIDUALS MEETING SUBSTANTIAL PRESENCE TEST.—In the case of an individual who meets the substantial presence test of paragraph (3) with respect to any calendar year, the residency starting date shall be the first day during such calendar year on which the individual is present in the United States.

　　　　(iv) RESIDENCY STARTING DATE FOR INDIVIDUALS MAKING FIRST YEAR ELECTION.—In the case of an individual who makes the election provided by paragraph (4) with respect to any calendar year, the residency starting date shall be the 1st day during such calendar year on which the individual is treated as a resident of the United States under that paragraph.

　　(B) LAST YEAR OF RESIDENCY.—An alien individual shall not be treated as a resident of the United States during a portion of any calendar year if—

　　　　(i) such portion is after the last day in such calendar year on which the individual was present in the United States (or, in the case of an individual described in paragraph (1)(A)(i), the last day on which he was so described),

　　　　(ii) during such portion the individual has a closer connection to a foreign country than to the United States, and

　　　　(iii) the individual is not a resident of the United States at any time during the next calendar year.

　　(C) CERTAIN NOMINAL PRESENCE DISREGARDED.—

　　　　(i) IN GENERAL.—For purposes of subparagraphs (A)(iii) and (B), an individual shall not be treated as present in the United States during any period for which the individual establishes that he has a closer connection to a foreign country than to the United States.

　　　　(ii) NOT MORE THAN 10 DAYS DISREGARDED.—Clause (i) shall not apply to more than 10 days on which the individual is present in the United States.

(3) SUBSTANTIAL PRESENCE TEST.—

　　(A) IN GENERAL.—Except as otherwise provided in this paragraph, an individual meets the substantial presence test of this paragraph with respect to any calendar year (hereinafter in this subsection referred to as the "current year") if—

　　　　(i) such individual was present in the United States on at least 31 days during the calendar year, and

　　　　(ii) the sum of the number of days on which such individual was present in the United States during the current year and the 2 preceding calendar years (when multiplied by the applicable multiplier determined under the following table) equals or exceeds 183 days:

In the case of days in:	The applicable multiplier is:
Current year	1
1st preceding year	1/3
2nd preceding year	1/6

　　(B) EXCEPTION WHERE INDIVIDUAL IS PRESENT IN THE UNITED STATES DURING LESS THAN ONE-HALF OF CURRENT YEAR AND CLOSER CONNECTION TO FOREIGN COUNTRY IS ESTABLISHED.—An individual shall not be treated as meeting the substantial presence test of this paragraph with respect to any current year if—

　　　　(i) such individual is present in the United States on fewer than 183 days during the current year, and

　　　　(ii) it is established that for the current year such individual has a tax home (as defined in section 911(d)(3) without regard to the second sentence thereof) in a foreign country and has a closer connection to such foreign country than to the United States.

　　(C) SUBPARAGRAPH (B) NOT TO APPLY IN CERTAIN CASES.—Subparagraph (B) shall not apply to any individual with respect to any current year if at any time during such year—

　　　　(i) such individual had an application for adjustment of status pending, or

　　　　(ii) such individual took other steps to apply for status as a lawful permanent resident of the United States.

　　(D) EXCEPTION FOR EXEMPT INDIVIDUALS OR FOR CERTAIN MEDICAL CONDITIONS.—An individual shall not be treated as being present in the United States on any day if—

　　　　(i) such individual is an exempt individual for such day, or

　　　　(ii) such individual was unable to leave the United States on such day because of a medical condition which arose while such individual was present in the United States.

(4) FIRST-YEAR ELECTION.—

　　(A) An alien individual shall be deemed to meet the requirements of this subparagraph if such individual—

　　　　(i) is not a resident of the United States under clause (i) or (ii) of paragraph (1)(A) with respect to a calendar year (hereinafter referred to as the "election year"),

　　　　(ii) was not a resident of the United States under paragraph (1)(A) with respect to the calendar year immediately preceding the election year,

　　　　(iii) is a resident of the United States under clause (ii) of paragraph (1)(A) with respect to the calendar year immediately following the election year, and

　　　　(iv) is both—

　　　　　　(I) present in the United States for a period of at least 31 consecutive days in the election year, and

　　　　　　(II) present in the United States during the period beginning with the first day of such 31-day period and ending with the last day of the election year (hereinafter referred to as the "testing period") for a number of days equal to or exceeding 75 percent of the number of days in the testing period (provided that an individual shall be treated for purposes of this subclause as present in the United States for a number of days during the testing period not exceeding 5 days in the aggregate, notwithstanding his absence from the United States on such days).

　　(B) An alien individual who meets the requirements of subparagraph (A) shall, if he so elects, be treated as a resident of the United States with respect to the election year.

　　(C) An alien individual who makes the election provided by subparagraph (B) shall be treated as a resident of the United States for the portion of the election year which begins on the 1st day of the earliest testing period during such year with respect to which the individual meets the requirements of clause (iv) of subparagraph (A).

　　(D) The rules of subparagraph (D)(i) of paragraph (3) shall apply for purposes of determining an individual's presence in the United States under this paragraph.

　　(E) An election under subparagraph (B) shall be made on the individual's tax return for the election year, provided that such election may not be made before the individual has met the substantial presence test of paragraph (3) with respect to the calendar year immediately following the election year.

　　(F) An election once made under subparagraph (B) remains in effect for the election year, unless revoked with the consent of the Secretary.

(5) EXEMPT INDIVIDUAL DEFINED.—For purposes of this subsection—

DEFINITIONS

(A) IN GENERAL.—An individual is an exempt individual for any day if, for such day, such individual is—

(i) a foreign government-related individual,

(ii) a teacher or trainee,

(iii) a student, or

(iv) a professional athlete who is temporarily in the United States to compete in a sports event—

(I) which is organized for the primary purpose of benefiting an organization which is described in section 501(c)(3) and exempt from tax under section 501(a),

(II) all of the net proceeds of which are contributed to such organization, and,

(III) which utilizes volunteers for substantially all of the work performed in carrying out such event.

(B) FOREIGN GOVERNMENT-RELATED INDIVIDUAL.—The term "foreign government-related individual" means any individual temporarily present in the United States by reason of—

(i) diplomatic status, or a visa which the Secretary (after consultation with the Secretary of State) determines represents full-time diplomatic or consular status for purposes of this subsection,

(ii) being a full-time employee of an international organization, or

(iii) being a member of the immediate family of an individual described in clause (i) or (ii).

(C) TEACHER OR TRAINEE.—The term "teacher or trainee" means any individual—

(i) who is termporarily present in the United States under subparagraph (J) or (Q) of section 101(15) of the Immigration and Nationality Act (other than as a student), and

(ii) who substantially complies with the requirements for being so present.

(D) STUDENT.—The term "student" means any individual—

(i) who is temporarily present in the United States—

(I) under subparagraph (F) or (M) of section 101(15) of the Immigration and Nationality Act, or

(II) as a student under subparagraph (J) or (Q) of such section 101(15), and

(ii) who substantially complies with the requirements for being so present.

(E) SPECIAL RULES FOR TEACHERS, TRAINEES, AND STUDENTS.—

(i) LIMITATION ON TEACHERS AND TRAINEES.—An individual shall not be treated as an exempt individual by reason of clause (ii) of subparagraph (A) for the current year if, for any 2 calendar years during the preceding 6 calendar years, such person was an exempt person under clause (ii) or (iii) of subparagraph (A). In the case of an individual all of whose compensation is described in section 872(b)(3), the preceding sentence shall be applied by substituting "4 calendar years" for "2 calendar years".

(ii) LIMITATION ON STUDENTS.—For any calendar year after the 5th calendar year for which an individual was an exempt individual under clause (ii) or (iii) of subparagraph (A), such individual shall not be treated as an exempt individual by reason of clause (iii) of subparagraph (A), unless such individual establishes to the satisfaction of the Secretary that such individual does not intend to permanently reside in the United States and that such individual meets the requirements of subparagraph (D)(ii).

(6) LAWFUL PERMANENT RESIDENT.—For purposes of this subsection, an individual is a lawful permanent resident of the United States at any time if—

(A) such individual has the status of having been lawfully accorded the privilege of residing permanently in the United States as an immigrant in accordance with the immigration laws, and

(B) such status has not been revoked (and has not been administratively or judicially determined to have been abandoned).

An individual shall cease to be treated as a lawful permanent resident of the United States if such individual commences to be treated as a resident of a foreign country under the provisions of a tax treaty between the United States and the foreign country, does not waive the benefits of such treaty applicable to residents of the foreign country, and notifies the Secretary of the commencement of such treatment.

(7) PRESENCE IN THE UNITED STATES.—For purposes of this subsection—

(A) IN GENERAL.—Except as provided in subparagraph (B), (C), or (D) an individual shall be treated as present in the United States on any day if such individual is physically present in the United States at any time during such day.

(B) COMMUTERS FROM CANADA OR MEXICO.—If an individual regularly commutes to employment (or self-employment) in the United States from a place of residence in Canada or Mexico, such individual shall not be treated as present in the United States on any day during which he so commutes.

(C) TRANSIT BETWEEN 2 FOREIGN POINTS.—If an individual, who is in transit between 2 points outside the United States, is physically present in the United States for less than 24 hours, such individual shall not be treated as present in the United States on any day during such transit.

(D) CREW MEMBERS TEMPORARILY PRESENT.—An individual who is temporarily present in the United States on any day as a regular member of the crew of a foreign vessel engaged in transportation between the United States and a foreign country or a possession of the United States shall not be treated as present in the United States on such day unless such individual otherwise engages in any trade or business in the United States on such day.

(8) ANNUAL STATEMENTS.—The Secretary may prescribe regulations under which an individual who (but for subparagraph (B) or (D) of paragraph (3)) would meet the substantial presence test of paragraph (3) is required to submit an annual statement setting forth the basis on which such individual claims the benefits of subparagraph (B) or (D) of paragraph (3), as the case may be.

(9) TAXABLE YEAR.—

(A) IN GENERAL.—For purposes of this title, an alien individual who has not established a taxable year for any prior period shall be treated as having a taxable year which is the calendar year.

(B) FISCAL YEAR TAXPAYER.—If—

(i) an individual is treated under paragraph (1) as a resident of the United States for any calendar year, and

(ii) after the application of subparagraph (A), such individual has a taxable year other than a calendar year,

he shall be treated as a resident of the United States with respect to any portion of a taxable year which is within such calendar year.

(10) COORDINATION WITH SECTION 877.—If—

(A) an alien individual was treated as a resident of the United States during any period which includes at least 3 consecutive calendar years (hereinafter referred to as the "initial residency period"), and

(B) such individual ceases to be treated as a resident of the United States but subsequently becomes a resident of the United States before the close of the 3rd calendar year beginning after the close of the initial residency period,

DEFINITIONS

such individual shall be taxable for the period after the close of the initial residency period and before the day on which he subsequently became a resident of the United States in the manner provided in section 877(b). The preceding sentence shall apply only if the tax imposed pursuant to section 877(b) exceeds the tax which, without regard to this paragraph, is imposed pursuant to section 871.

(11) REGULATIONS.—The Secretary shall prescribe such regulations as may be necessary or appropriate to carry out the purposes of this subsection.

Amendments

• **2017, Tax Cuts and Jobs Act (P.L. 115-97)**

P.L. 115-97, §13304(a)(2)(F):

Amended Code Sec. 7701(b)(5)(A)(iv). **Effective** for amounts incurred or paid after 12-31-2017. Prior to amendment, Code Sec. 7701(b)(5)(A)(iv) read as follows:

(iv) a professional athlete who is temporarily in the United States to compete in a charitable sports event described in section 274(l)(1)(B).

• **2008, Heroes Earnings Assistance and Relief Tax Act of 2008 (P.L. 110-245)**

P.L. 110-245, §301(c)(2)(B):

Amended Code Sec. 7701(b)(6) by adding at the end a new flush sentence. **Effective** for any individual whose expatriation date (as so defined) is on or after 6-17-2008.

• **1997, Taxpayer Relief Act of 1997 (P.L. 105-34)**

P.L. 105-34, §1174(b)(1):

Amended Code Sec. 7701(b)(7) by adding at the end a new subparagraph (D). **Effective** for tax years beginning after 12-31-97.

P.L. 105-34, §1174(b)(2):

Amended Code Sec. 7701(b)(7)(A) by striking "or (C)" and inserting ", (C), or (D)". **Effective** for tax years beginning after 12-31-97.

• **1994, Social Security Independence and Program Improvements Act of 1994 (P.L. 103-296)**

P.L. 103-296, §320(a)(3):

Amended Code Sec. 7701(b)(5) by striking "subparagraph (J)" in subparagraphs (C)(i) and (D)(i)(II) and inserting "subparagraph (J) or (Q)". **Effective** with the calendar quarter following 8-15-94.

• **1988, Technical and Miscellaneous Revenue Act of 1988 (P.L. 100-647)**

P.L. 100-647, §1001(d)(2)(D):

Amended Code Sec. 7701(b)(5)(D)(i)(I) by striking out "subparagraph (F)" and inserting in lieu thereof "subparagraph (F) or (M)". **Effective** as if included in the provision of P.L. 99-514 to which it relates.

P.L. 100-647, §1018(g)(3):

Amended Code Sec. 7701(b)(5)(A)(iv) by striking out "section 274(k)(2)" and inserting in lieu thereof "section 274(l)(1)(B)". **Effective** as if included in the provision of P.L. 99-514 to which it relates.

• **1986, Tax Reform Act of 1986 (P.L. 99-514)**

P.L. 99-514, §1810(l)(1):

Amended Code Sec. 7701(b)(4)(E)(i) by adding at the end thereof a new sentence. **Effective** as if included in the provision of P.L. 98-369 to which it relates.

P.L. 99-514, §1810(l)(2)(A) and (B):

Amended Code Sec. 7701(b)(1)(A) by striking out "the requirements of clause (i) or (ii)" and inserting in lieu thereof "the requirements of clause (i), (ii), or (iii)", and by adding at the end thereof new clause (iii). **Effective** as if included in the provision of P.L. 98-369 to which it relates.

P.L. 99-514, §1810(l)(3):

Amended Code Sec. 7701(b)(2)(A) by adding at the end thereof new clause (iv). **Effective** as if included in the provision of P.L. 98-369 to which it relates.

P.L. 99-514, §1810(l)(4):

Amended Code Sec. 7701(b) by redesignating paragraphs (4), (5), (6), (7), (8), (9), and (10) as paragraphs (5), (6), (7), (8), (9), (10), and (11), respectively, and by inserting after paragraph (3) new paragraph (4). **Effective** as if included in the provision of P.L. 98-369 to which it relates.

P.L. 99-514, §1810(l)(5)(A):

Amended Code Sec. 7701(b)(4)(A) by striking out "or" at the end of clause (ii), by striking out the period at the end of clause (iii) and inserting ", or" and by adding after clause (iii) new clause (iv). **Effective** for periods after 10-22-86.

P.L. 99-514, §1899A(63):

Amended Code Sec. 7701(b)(4)(E)(i) by striking out "preceeding" and inserting in lieu thereof "preceding". **Effective** 10-22-86.

• **1984, Deficit Reduction Act of 1984 (P.L. 98-369)**

P.L. 98-369, §138(a):

Amended Code Sec. 7701 by redesignating subsections (b), (c), and (d) as subsections (c), (d), and (e), respectively, and by inserting after subsection (a) new subsection (b). **Effective** for tax years beginning after 12-31-84. A transitional rule appears below.

P.L. 98-369, §138(b)(2)-(3), provides:

(2) TRANSITIONAL RULE FOR APPLYING SUBSTANTIAL PRESENCE TEST.—

(A) If an alien individual was not a resident of the United States as of the close of calendar year 1984, the determination of whether such individual meets the substantial presence test of section 7701(b)(3) of the Internal Revenue Code of 1954 (as added by this section) shall be made by only taking into account presence after 1984.

(B) If an alien individual was a resident of the United States as of the close of calendar year 1984, but was not a resident of the United States as of the close of calendar year 1983, the determination of whether such individual meets such substantial presence test shall be made by only taking into account presence in the United States after 1983.

(3) TRANSITIONAL RULE FOR APPLYING LAWFUL RESIDENCE TEST.—In the case of any individual who—

(A) was a lawful permanent resident of the United States (within the meaning of section 7701(b)(5) of the Internal Revenue Code of 1954, as added by this section) throughout calendar year 1984, or

(B) was present in the United States at any time during 1984 while such individual was a lawful permanent resident of the United States (within the meaning of such section 7701(b)(5)), for purposes of section 7701(b)(2)(A) of such Code (as so added), such individual shall be treated as a resident of the United States during 1984.

[Sec. 7701(c)]

(c) INCLUDES AND INCLUDING.—The terms "includes" and "including" when used in a definition contained in this title shall not be deemed to exclude other things otherwise within the meaning of the term defined.

Amendments

• **1984, Deficit Reduction Act of 1984 (P.L. 98-369)**

P.L. 98-369, §138(a):

Amended Code Sec. 7701 by redesignating subsection (b) as subsection (c). **Effective** for tax years beginning after 12-31-84.

[Sec. 7701(d)]

(d) COMMONWEALTH OF PUERTO RICO.—Where not otherwise distinctly expressed or manifestly incompatible with the intent thereof, references in this title to possessions of the United States shall be treated as also referring to the Commonwealth of Puerto Rico.

Amendments

• **1984, Deficit Reduction Act of 1984 (P.L. 98-369)**

P.L. 98-369, §138(a):

Amended Code Sec. 7701 by redesignating subsection (c) as subsection (d). **Effective** for tax years beginning after 12-31-84.

[Sec. 7701(e)]

(e) TREATMENT OF CERTAIN CONTRACTS FOR PROVIDING SERVICES, ETC.—For purposes of chapter 1—

(1) IN GENERAL.—A contract which purports to be a service contract shall be treated as a lease of property if such contract is properly treated as a lease of property, taking into account all relevant factors including whether or not—

(A) the service recipient is in physical possession of the property,

(B) the service recipient controls the property,

(C) the service recipient has a significant economic or possessory interest in the property,

(D) the service provider does not bear any risk of substantially diminished receipts or substantially increased expenditures if there is nonperformance under the contract,

DEFINITIONS

(E) the service provider does not use the property concurrently to provide significant services to entities unrelated to the service recipient, and

(F) the total contract price does not substantially exceed the rental value of the property for the contract period.

(2) OTHER ARRANGEMENTS.—An arrangement (including a partnership or other pass-thru entity) which is not described in paragraph (1) shall be treated as a lease if such arrangement is properly treated as a lease, taking into account all relevant factors including factors similar to those set forth in paragraph (1).

(3) SPECIAL RULES FOR CONTRACTS OR ARRANGEMENTS INVOLVING SOLID WASTE DISPOSAL, ENERGY, AND CLEAN WATER FACILITIES.—

(A) IN GENERAL.—Notwithstanding paragraphs (1) and (2), and except as provided in paragraph (4), any contract or arrangement between a service provider and a service recipient—

(i) with respect to—

(I) the operation of a qualified solid waste disposal facility,

(II) the sale to the service recipient of electrical or thermal energy produced at a cogeneration or alternative energy facility,

(III) the operation of a water treatment works facility, or

(IV) the operation of a storage facility, and

(ii) which purports to be a service contract,

shall be treated as a service contract.

(B) QUALIFIED SOLID WASTE DISPOSAL FACILITY.—For purposes of subparagraph (A), the term "qualified solid waste disposal facility" means any facility if such facility provides solid waste disposal services for residents of part or all of 1 or more governmental units and substantially all of the solid waste processed at such facility is collected from the general public.

(C) COGENERATION FACILITY.—For purposes of subparagraph (A), the term "cogeneration facility" means a facility which uses the same energy source for the sequential generation of electrical or mechanical power in combination with steam, heat, or other forms of useful energy.

(D) ALTERNATIVE ENERGY FACILITY.—For purposes of subparagraph (A), the term "alternative energy facility" means a facility for producing electrical or thermal energy if the primary energy source for the facility is not oil, natural gas, coal, or nuclear power.

(E) WATER TREATMENT WORKS FACILITY.—For purposes of subparagraph (A), the term "water treatment works facility" means any treatment works within the meaning of section 212(2) of the Federal Water Pollution Control Act.

(F) STORAGE FACILITY.—For purposes of subparagraph (A), the term "storage facility" means a facility which uses energy storage technology within the meaning of section 48(c)(6).

(4) PARAGRAPH (3) NOT TO APPLY IN CERTAIN CASES.—

(A) IN GENERAL.—Paragraph (3) shall not apply to any qualified solid waste disposal facility, cogeneration facility, alternative energy facility, water treatment works facility, or storage facility used under a contract or arrangement if—

(i) the service recipient (or a related entity) operates such facility,

(ii) the service recipient (or a related entity) bears any significant financial burden if there is nonperformance under the contract or arrangement (other than for reasons beyond the control of the service provider),

(iii) the service recipient (or a related entity) receives any significant financial benefit if the operating costs of such facility are less than the standards of performance or operation under the contract or arrangement, or

(iv) the service recipient (or a related entity) has an option to purchase, or may be required to purchase, all or a part of such facility at a fixed and determinable price (other than for fair market value).

For purposes of this paragraph, the term "related entity" has the same meaning as when used in section 168(h).

(B) SPECIAL RULES FOR APPLICATION OF SUBPARAGRAPH (A) WITH RESPECT TO CERTAIN RIGHTS AND ALLOCATIONS UNDER THE CONTRACT.—For purposes of subparagraph (A), there shall not be taken into account—

(i) any right of a service recipient to inspect any facility, to exercise any sovereign power the service recipient may possess, or to act in the event of a breach of contract by the service provider, or

(ii) any allocation of any financial burden or benefits in the event of any change in any law.

(C) SPECIAL RULES FOR APPLICATION OF SUBPARAGRAPH (A) IN THE CASE OF CERTAIN EVENTS.—

(i) TEMPORARY SHUT-DOWNS, ETC.—For purposes of clause (ii) of subparagraph (A), there shall not be taken into account any temporary shut-down of the facility for repairs, maintenance, or capital improvements, or any financial burden caused by the bankruptcy or similar financial difficulty of the service provider.

(ii) REDUCED COSTS.—For purposes of clause (iii) of subparagraph (A), there shall not be taken into account any significant financial benefit merely because payments by the service recipient under the contract or arrangement are decreased by reason of increased production or efficiency or the recovery of energy or other products.

(5) EXCEPTION FOR CERTAIN LOW-INCOME HOUSING.—This subsection shall not apply to any property described in clause (i), (ii), (iii), or (iv) of section 1250(a)(1)(B) (relating to low-income housing) if—

(A) such property is operated by or for an organization described in paragraph (3) or (4) of section 501(c), and

(B) at least 80 percent of the units in such property are leased to low-income tenants (within the meaning of section 167(k)(3)(B)) (as in effect on the day before the date of the enactment of the Revenue Reconciliation Act of 1990).

(6) REGULATIONS.—The Secretary may prescribe such regulations as may be necessary or appropriate to carry out the provisions of this subsection.

Amendments

- **2022, Inflation Reduction Act of 2022 (P.L. 117-169)**

P.L. 117-169, §13102(n)(1)-(2):

Amended Code Sec. 7701(e) in paragraph (3)(A)(i) by striking "or" at the end of subclause (II), by striking "and" at the end of subclause (III) and inserting "or", and by adding at the end a new subclause (IV), and by adding at the end a new subparagraph (F); and in paragraph (4), by striking "or water treatment works facility" and inserting "water treatment works facility, or storage facility". **Effective** for property placed in service after 12-31-2022.

- **2018, Tax Technical Corrections Act of 2018 (P.L. 115-141)**

P.L. 115-141, §401(a)(332), Div. U:

Amended Code Sec. 7701(e)(5)(B) by striking "Reconciliation" and inserting "Reconciliation". **Effective** 3-23-2018.

- **1990, Omnibus Budget Reconciliation Act of 1990 (P.L. 101-508)**

P.L. 101-508, §11812(b)(13):

Amended Code Sec. 7701(e)(5)(B) by inserting before the period at the end thereof "(as in effect on the day before the date of the enactment of the Revenue Reconciliation Act of 1990)". **Effective** for property placed in service after the date of the enactment of this Act. However, for exceptions see Act Sec. 11812(c)(2)-(3) below.

P.L. 101-508, §11812(c)(2)-(3), provides:

(2) EXCEPTION.—The amendments made by this section shall not apply to any property to which section 168 of the Internal Revenue Code of 1986 does not apply by reason of subsection (f)(5) thereof.

(3) EXCEPTION FOR PREVIOUSLY GRANDFATHER EXPENDITURES.—The amendments made by this section shall not apply to rehabilitation expenditures described in section

DEFINITIONS

252(f)(5) of the Tax Reform Act of 1986 (as added by section 1002(l)(31) of the Technical and Miscellaneous Revenue Act of 1988).

• **1986, Tax Reform Act of 1986 (P.L. 99-514)**

P.L. 99-514, § 201(d)(14)(A):

Amended Code Sec. 7701(e)(4)(A) by striking out "section 168(j)" and inserting in lieu thereof "section 168(h)". For the **effective** date, see Act Sec. 203 under the amendment notes to Code Sec. 168.

P.L. 99-514, § 201(d)(14)(B):

Amended Code Sec. 7701(e)(5) by striking out "low-income housing (within the meaning of section 168(c)(2)(F))" and inserting in lieu thereof "property described in clause (i), (ii), (iii), or (iv) of section 1250(a)(1)(B) (relating to low income housing)". For the **effective** date, see Act Sec. 203 under the amendment notes to Code Sec. 168.

P.L. 99-514, § 1802(a)(9)(C):

Amended Code Sec. 7701(e)(4)(A) by adding at the end thereof a new sentence. **Effective** as if included in the provision of P.L. 98-369 to which it relates.

P.L. 99-514, § 1899A(64):

Amended Code Sec. 7701(e)(5) by striking out "section 168(C)(2)(F))" and inserting in lieu thereof "section 168(c)(2)(F))". **Effective** 10-22-86.

• **1984, Deficit Reduction Act of 1984 (P.L. 98-369)**

P.L. 98-369, § 31(e):

Amended Code Sec. 7701, as amended by this Act, by redesignating subsection (e) as subsection (f) and by inserting after subsection (d) new subsection (e). **Effective** for property placed in service by the taxpayer after 5-23-83, in tax years ending after such date, and to property placed in service by the taxpayer on or before 5-23-83, if the lease to the tax-exempt entity is entered into after 5-23-83. Special rules appear in Act Sec. 31(g) following Code Sec. 168.

[Sec. 7701(f)]

(f) USE OF RELATED PERSONS OR PASS-THRU ENTITIES.—The Secretary shall prescribe such regulations as may be necessary or appropriate to prevent the avoidance of those provisions of this title which deal with—

(1) the linking of borrowing to investment, or

(2) diminishing risks,

through the use of related persons, pass-thru entities, or other intermediaries.

Amendments

• **1984, Deficit Reduction Act of 1984 (P.L. 98-369)**

P.L. 98-369, § 53(c):

Amended Code Sec. 7701 by redesignating subsection (f) as (g) and by inserting after subsection (e) new subsection (f). For the **effective** date, see Act Sec. 53(e)(3), below.

P.L. 98-369, § 53(e)(3), as amended by P.L. 99-514, § 1804(b), provides:

(3) Related Person Provisions.—

(A) In General.—Except as otherwise provided in subparagraph (B), the amendment made by subsection (c) shall take effect on July 18, 1984.

(B) Special Rule for Purposes of Section 265(2).—The amendment made by subsection (c) insofar as it relates to section 265(2) of the Internal Revenue Code of 1954 shall apply to—

(i) term loans made after July 18, 1984, and

(ii) demand loans outstanding after July 18, 1984 (other than any loan outstanding on July 18, 1984, and repaid before September 18, 1984).

(C) Treatment of Renegotiations, Etc.—For purposes of this paragraph, any loan renegotiated, extended, or revised after July 18, 1984, shall be treated as a loan made after such date.

(D) Definition of Term and Demand Loans.—For purposes of this paragraph, the terms "demand loan" and "term loan" have the respective meanings given such terms by paragraphs (5) and (6) of section 7872(f) of the Internal Revenue Code of 1954, except that the second sentence of such paragraph (5) shall not apply.

[Sec. 7701(g)]

(g) CLARIFICATION OF FAIR MARKET VALUE IN THE CASE OF NONRECOURSE INDEBTEDNESS.—For purposes of subtitle A, in determining the amount of gain or loss (or deemed gain or loss) with respect to any property, the fair market value of such property shall be treated as being not less than the amount of any nonrecourse indebtedness to which such property is subject.

Amendments

• **1984, Deficit Reduction Act of 1984 (P.L. 98-369)**

P.L. 98-369, § 75(c):

Amended Code Sec. 7701, as amended by this Act, by redesignating subsection (g) as subsection (h) and by inserting after subsection (f) new subsection (g). **Effective** for distributions, sales, and exchanges made after 3-31-84, in tax years ending after such date.

[Sec. 7701(h)]

(h) MOTOR VEHICLE OPERATING LEASES.—

(1) IN GENERAL.—For purposes of this title, in the case of a qualified motor vehicle operating agreement which contains a terminal rental adjustment clause—

(A) such agreement shall be treated as a lease if (but for such terminal rental adjustment clause) such agreement would be treated as a lease under this title, and

(B) the lessee shall not be treated as the owner of the property subject to an agreement during any period such agreement is in effect.

(2) QUALIFIED MOTOR VEHICLE OPERATING AGREEMENT DEFINED.—For purposes of this subsection—

(A) IN GENERAL.—The term "qualified motor vehicle operating agreement" means any agreement with respect to a motor vehicle (including a trailer) which meets the requirements of subparagraphs (B), (C), and (D) of this paragraph.

(B) MINIMUM LIABILITY OF LESSOR.—An agreement meets the requirements of this subparagraph if under such agreement the sum of—

(i) the amount the lessor is personally liable to repay, and

(ii) the net fair market value of the lessor's interest in any property pledged as security for property subject to the agreement,

equals or exceeds all amounts borrowed to finance the acquisition of property subject to the agreement. There shall not be taken into account under clause (ii) any property pledged which is property subject to the agreement or property directly or indirectly financed by indebtedness secured by property subject to the agreement.

(C) CERTIFICATION BY LESSEE; NOTICE OF TAX OWNERSHIP.—An agreement meets the requirements of this subparagraph if such agreement contains a separate written statement separately signed by the lessee—

(i) under which the lessee certifies, under penalty of perjury, that it intends that more than 50 percent of the use of the property subject to such agreement is to be in a trade or business of the lessee, and

(ii) which clearly and legibly states that the lessee has been advised that it will not be treated as the owner of the property subject to the agreement for Federal income tax purposes.

(D) LESSOR MUST HAVE NO KNOWLEDGE THAT CERTIFICATION IS FALSE.—An agreement meets the requirements of this subparagraph if the lessor does not know that the certification described in subparagraph (C)(i) is false.

(3) TERMINAL RENTAL ADJUSTMENT CLAUSE DEFINED.—

(A) IN GENERAL.—For purposes of this subsection, the term "terminal rental adjustment clause" means a provision of an agreement which permits or requires the rental price to be adjusted upward or downward by reference to the amount realized by the lessor under the agreement upon sale or other disposition of such property.

(B) SPECIAL RULE FOR LESSEE DEALERS.—The term "terminal rental adjustment clause" also includes a provision of an agreement which requires a lessee who is a dealer in motor vehicles to purchase the motor vehicle for a predetermined price and then resell such vehicle where such provision achieves substantially the same results as a provision described in subparagraph (A).

DEFINITIONS

Amendments

• **1986, Tax Reform Act of 1986 (P.L. 99-514)**

P.L. 99-514, § 201(c):

Amended Code Sec. 7701 by redesignating subsection (h) as subsection (i) and by inserting after subsection (g) new subsection (h). For the **effective** date, see Act Sec. 203 under the amendment notes to Code Sec. 168.

[Sec. 7701(i)]

(i) TAXABLE MORTGAGE POOLS.—

  (1) TREATED AS SEPARATE CORPORATIONS.—A taxable mortgage pool shall be treated as a separate corporation which may not be treated as an includible corporation with any other corporation for purposes of section 1501.

  (2) TAXABLE MORTGAGE POOL DEFINED.—For purposes of this title—

    (A) IN GENERAL.—Except as otherwise provided in this paragraph, a taxable mortgage pool is any entity (other than a REMIC) if—

      (i) substantially all of the assets of such entity consists of debt obligations (or interests therein) and more than 50 percent of such debt obligations (or interests) consists of real estate mortgages (or interests therein),

      (ii) such entity is the obligor under debt obligations with 2 or more maturities, and

      (iii) under the terms of the debt obligations referred to in clause (ii) (or underlying arrangement), payments on such debt obligations bear a relationship to payments on the debt obligations (or interests) referred to in clause (i).

    (B) PORTION OF ENTITIES TREATED AS POOLS.—Any portion of an entity which meets the definition of subparagraph (A) shall be treated as a taxable mortgage pool.

    (C) EXCEPTION FOR DOMESTIC BUILDING AND LOAN.—Nothing in this subsection shall be construed to treat any domestic building and loan association (or portion thereof) as a taxable mortgage pool.

    (D) TREATMENT OF CERTAIN EQUITY INTERESTS.—To the extent provided in regulations, equity interest of varying classes which correspond to maturity classes of debt shall be treated as debt for purposes of this subsection.

  (3) TREATMENT OF CERTAIN REIT'S.—If—

    (A) a real estate investment trust is a taxable mortgage pool, or

    (B) a qualified REIT subsidiary (as defined in section 856(i)(2)) of a real estate investment trust is a taxable mortgage pool,

under regulations prescribed by the Secretary, adjustments similar to the adjustments provided in section 860E(d) shall apply to the shareholders of such real estate investment trust.

Amendments

• **2004, American Jobs Creation Act of 2004 (P.L. 108-357)**

P.L. 108-357, § 835(b)(11):

Amended Code Sec. 7701(i)(2)(A) by striking "or a FASIT" after "REMIC". For the **effective** date, see Act Sec. 835(c), below.

P.L. 108-357, § 835(c), provides:

(c) EFFECTIVE DATE.—

(1) IN GENERAL.—Except as provided in paragraph (2), the amendments made by this section shall take effect on January 1, 2005.

(2) EXCEPTION FOR EXISTING FASITS.—Paragraph (1) shall not apply to any FASIT in existence on the date of the enactment of this Act [10-22-2004.—CCH] to the extent that regular interests issued by the FASIT before such date continue to remain outstanding in accordance with the original terms of issuance.

• **1996, Small Business Job Protection Act of 1996 (P.L. 104-188)**

P.L. 104-188, § 1621(b)(9):

Amended Code Sec. 7701(i)(2)(A) by inserting "or a FASIT" after "a REMIC". **Effective** 9-1-97.

• **1986, Tax Reform Act of 1986 (P.L. 99-514)**

P.L. 99-514, § 673:

Amended Code Sec. 7701, as amended by Act Sec. 201(c), by redesignating subsection (i) as subsection (j) and by inserting after subsection (h) new subsection (i). For the **effective** date, see Act Sec. 675(c), below.

P.L. 99-514, § 675(c), provides:

(c) TREATMENT OF TAXABLE MORTGAGE POOLS.—

(1) IN GENERAL.—The amendment made by section 673 shall take effect on January 1, 1992.

(2) TREATMENT OF EXISTING ENTITIES.—The amendment made by section 673 shall not apply to any entity in existence on December 31, 1991. The preceding sentence shall cease to apply with respect to any entity as of the 1st day after December 31, 1991, on which there is a substantial transfer of cash or other property to such entity.

(3) SPECIAL RULE FOR COORDINATION WITH WASH-SALE RULES.—Notwithstanding paragraphs (1) and (2), for purposes of applying section 860F(d) of the Internal Revenue Code of 1986 (as added by this part), the amendment made by section 673 shall apply to taxable years beginning after December 31, 1986.

[Sec. 7701(j)]

(j) TAX TREATMENT OF FEDERAL THRIFT SAVINGS FUND.—

  (1) IN GENERAL.—For purposes of this title—

    (A) the Thrift Savings Fund shall be treated as a trust described in section 401(a) which is exempt from taxation under section 501(a);

    (B) any contribution to, or distribution from, the Thrift Savings Fund shall be treated in the same manner as contributions to or distributions from such a trust; and

    (C) subject to section 401(k)(4)(B) and any dollar limitation on the application of section 402(e)(3), contributions to the Thrift Savings Fund shall not be treated as distributed or made available to an employee or Member nor as a contribution made to the Fund by an employee or Member merely because the employee or Member has, under the provisions of subchapter III of chapter 84 of title 5, United States Code, and section 8351 of such title 5, an election whether the contribution will be made to the Thrift Savings Fund or received by the employee or Member in cash.

  (2) NONDISCRIMINATION REQUIREMENTS.—Notwithstanding any other provision of the law, the Thrift Savings Fund is not subject to the nondiscrimination requirements applicable to arrangements described in section 401(k) or to matching contributions (as described in section 401(m)), so long as it meets the requirements of this section.

  (3) COORDINATION WITH SOCIAL SECURITY ACT.—Paragraph (1) shall not be construed to provide that any amount of the employee's or Member's basic pay which is contributed to the Thrift Savings Fund shall not be included in the term "wages" for the purposes of section 209 of the Social Security Act or section 3121(a) of this title.

  (4) DEFINITIONS.—For purposes of this subsection, the terms "Member", "employee", and "Thrift Savings Fund" shall have the same respective meanings as when used in subchapter III of chapter 84 of title 5, United States Code.

  (5) COORDINATION WITH OTHER PROVISIONS OF LAW.—No provision of law not contained in this title shall apply for purposes of determining the treatment under this title of the Thrift Savings Fund or any contribution to, or distribution from, such Fund.

Amendments

• **1992, Unemployment Compensation Amendments of 1992 (P.L. 102-318)**

P.L. 102-318, § 521(b)(43):

Amended Code Sec. 7701(j)(1)(C) by striking "section 402(a)(8)" and inserting "section 402(e)(3)". **Effective** for distributions after 12-31-92.

• **1990, Omnibus Budget Reconciliation Act of 1990 (P.L. 101-508)**

P.L. 101-508, § 11704(a)(34):

Amended Code Sec. 7701(j)(1)(C) by striking so much of such subparagraph as precedes "contributions to the Thrift" and inserting the following: "(C) subject to section 401(k)(4)(B) and any dollar limitation on the application of section 402(a)(8),". **Effective** 11-5-90. Prior to amendment, subparagraph C read as follows:

DEFINITIONS

(C) subject to section 401(k)(4)(B), [and] any dollar limitation on the application of section 402(a)(8), contributions to the Thrift Savings Fund shall not be treated as distributed or made available to an employee or Member nor as a contribution made to the Fund by an employee or Member merely because the employee or Member has, under the provisions of subchapter III of chapter 84 of title 5, United States Code, and section 8351 of such title 5, an election whether the contribution will be made to the Thrift Savings Fund or received by the employee or Member in cash.

- **1988, Technical and Miscellaneous Revenue Act of 1988 (P.L. 100-647)**

P.L. 100-647, §1011A(m)(1):

Amended Code Sec. 7701(j)(1)(C) by inserting ", section 401(k)(4)(B)," after "paragraph (2) [subject to]". **Effective** as if included in the provision of P.L. 99-514 to which it relates.

- **1987, Continuing Appropriations, Fiscal Year 1988 (P.L. 100-202)**

P.L. 100-202, §624(a)(1)-(2):

Amended Code Sec. 7701(j) by deleting "the provisions of paragraph (2) and" following "subject to" in paragraph (1)(C) and by amending paragraph (2). **Effective** 12-22-87. Prior to amendment, Code Sec. 7701(j)(2) read as follows:

(2) NONDISCRIMINATION REQUIREMENTS.—Paragraph (1)(C) shall not apply to the Thrift Savings Fund unless the Fund meets the antidiscrimination requirements (other than any requirement relating to coverage) applicable to arrangements described in section 401(k) and to matching contributions. Rules similar to the rules of sections 401(k)(8) and 401(m)(8) (relating to no disqualification if excess contributions distributed) shall apply for purposes of the preceding sentence.

- **1986, Tax Reform Act of 1986 (P.L. 99-514)**

P.L. 99-514, §1147(a):

Amended Code Sec. 7701, as amended by Act Secs. 201(d) and 558(b), by redesignating subsection (j) as subsection (k) and by inserting after subsection (i) new subsection (j). **Effective** 10-22-86.

[Sec. 7701(k)]

(k) TREATMENT OF CERTAIN AMOUNTS PAID TO CHARITY.—In the case of any payment which, except for section 13143(b) of title 5, United States Code, might be made to any officer or employee of the Federal Government but which is made instead on behalf of such officer or employee to an organization described in section 170(c)—

(1) such payment shall not be treated as received by such officer or employee for all purposes of this title and for all purposes of any tax law of a State or political subdivision thereof, and

(2) no deduction shall be allowed under any provision of this title (or of any tax law of a State or political subdivision thereof) to such officer or employee by reason of having such payment made to such organization.

For purposes of this subsection, a Senator, a Representative in, or a Delegate or Resident Commissioner to, the Congress shall be treated as an officer or employee of the Federal Government.

Amendments

- **2022, (P.L. 117-286)**

2022 (P.L. 117-286), §4(c)(33):

Amended Code Sec. 7701(k) by striking "section 501(b) of the Ethics in Government Act of 1978," and inserting "section 13143(b) of title 5, United States Code," in the matter before paragraph (1). **Effective** 12-27-2022.

- **1991, Legislative Branch Appropriations Act (P.L. 102-90)**

P.L. 102-90, §314(e):

Amended the last sentence of Code Sec. 7701(k). **Effective** 1-1-92. Prior to amendment, the last sentence of Code Sec. 7701(k) read as follows:

For purposes of this subsection, a Representative in, or a Delegate or Resident Commissioner to, the Congress shall be treated as an officer or employee of the Federal Government and a Senator or officer (except the Vice President) or employee of the Senate shall not be treated as an officer or employee of the Federal Government.

- **1989, Ethics Reform Act (P.L. 101-194)**

P.L. 101-194, §602:

Amended Code Sec. 7701 by redesignating subsection (k) as subsection (l) and by inserting after subsection (j) a new subsection (k). For the **effective** date, see Act Sec. 603, below.

P.L. 101-194, §603, provides:

SEC. 603. EFFECTIVE DATE.

The amendments made by this title shall take effect on January 1, 1991. Such amendments shall cease to be effective if the provisions of section 703 are subsequently repealed, in which case the laws in effect before such amendments shall be deemed to be reenacted.

[Sec. 7701(l)]

(l) REGULATIONS RELATING TO CONDUIT ARRANGEMENTS.—The Secretary may prescribe regulations recharacterizing any multiple-party financing transaction as a transaction directly among any 2 or more of such parties where the Secretary determines that such recharacterization is appropriate to prevent avoidance of any tax imposed by this title.

Amendments

- **1993, Omnibus Budget Reconciliation Act of 1993 (P.L. 103-66)**

P.L. 103-66, §13238:

Amended Code Sec. 7701 by redesignating subsection (l) as subsection (m), and by inserting after subsection (k) new subsection (l). **Effective** 8-10-93.

[Sec. 7701(m)]

(m) DESIGNATION OF CONTRACT MARKETS.—Any designation by the Commodity Futures Trading Commission of a contract market which could not have been made under the law in effect on the day before the date of the enactment of the Commodity Futures Modernization Act of 2000 shall apply for purposes of this title except to the extent provided in regulations prescribed by the Secretary.

Amendments

- **2000, Community Renewal Tax Relief Act of 2000 (P.L. 106-554)**

P.L. 106-554, §401(i):

Amended Code Sec. 7701 by redesignating subsection (m) as subsection (n) and by inserting after subsection (l) a new subsection (m). **Effective** 12-21-2000.

[Sec. 7701(n)—Stricken]

Amendments

- **2008, Heroes Earnings Assistance and Relief Tax Act of 2008 (P.L. 110-245)**

P.L. 110-245, §301(c)(2)(C):

Amended Code Sec. 7701 by striking subsection (n) and by redesignating subsections (o) and (p) as subsections (n) and (o), respectively. **Effective** for any individual whose expatriation date (as so defined) is on or after 6-17-2008. Prior to being stricken, Code Sec. 7701(n) read as follows:

(n) SPECIAL RULES FOR DETERMINING WHEN AN INDIVIDUAL IS NO LONGER A UNITED STATES CITIZEN OR LONG-TERM RESIDENT.—For purposes of this chapter—

(1) UNITED STATES CITIZENS.—An individual who would (but for this paragraph) cease to be treated as a citizen of the United States shall continue to be treated as a citizen of the United States until such individual—

(A) gives notice of an expatriating act (with the requisite intent to relinquish citizenship) to the Secretary of State, and

(B) provides a statement in accordance with section 6039G (if such a statement is otherwise required).

(2) LONG-TERM RESIDENTS.—A long-term resident (as defined in section 877(e)(2)) who would (but for this paragraph) be described in section 877(e)(1) shall be treated as a lawful permanent resident of the United States and as not described in section 877(e)(1) until such individual—

(A) gives notice of termination of residency (with the requisite intent to terminate residency) to the Secretary of Homeland Security, and

(B) provides a statement in accordance with section 6039G (if such a statement is otherwise required).

- **2005, Gulf Opportunity Zone Act of 2005 (P.L. 109-135)**

P.L. 109-135, §403(v)(2):

Amended Code Sec. 7701(n). **Effective** as if included in the provision of the American Jobs Creation Act of 2004 (P.L. 108-357) to which it relates [**effective** for individuals who expatriate after 6-30-2004.—CCH]. Prior to amendment, Code Sec. 7701(n) read as follows:

(n) SPECIAL RULES FOR DETERMINING WHEN AN INDIVIDUAL IS NO LONGER A UNITED STATES CITIZEN OR LONG-TERM RESIDENT.—An individual who would (but for this subsection) cease to be treated as a citizen or resident of the United States shall continue to be treated as a citizen or resident of the United States, as the case may be, until such individual—

(1) gives notice of an expatriating act or termination of residency (with the requisite intent to relinquish citizenship or terminate residency) to the Secretary of State or the Secretary of Homeland Security, and

(2) provides a statement in accordance with section 6039G.

[Sec. 7701(n)]

(n) CONVENTION OR ASSOCIATION OF CHURCHES.—For purposes of this title, any organization which is otherwise a convention or association of churches shall not fail to so qualify merely because the membership of such organization includes individuals as well as churches or because individuals have voting rights in such organization.

Amendments

• 2008, Heroes Earnings Assistance and Relief Tax Act of 2008 (P.L. 110-245)

P.L. 110-245, §301(c)(2)(C):

Amended Code Sec. 7701 by redesignating subsection (o) as subsection (n). **Effective** for any individual whose expatriation date (as so defined) is on or after 6-17-2008.

• 2004, American Jobs Creation Act of 2004 (P.L. 108-357)

P.L. 108-357, §804(b):

Amended Code Sec. 7701 by redesignating subsection (n) as subsection (o) and by inserting after subsection (m) a new subsection (n). **Effective** for individuals who expatriate after 6-3-2004.

• 2006, Pension Protection Act of 2006 (P.L. 109-280)

P.L. 109-280, §1222:

Amended Code Sec. 7701 by redesignating subsection (o) as subsection (p) and by inserting after subsection (n) a new subsection (o). **Effective** 8-17-2006.

[Sec. 7701(o)]

(o) CLARIFICATION OF ECONOMIC SUBSTANCE DOCTRINE.—

(1) APPLICATION OF DOCTRINE.—In the case of any transaction to which the economic substance doctrine is relevant, such transaction shall be treated as having economic substance only if—

(A) the transaction changes in a meaningful way (apart from Federal income tax effects) the taxpayer's economic position, and

(B) the taxpayer has a substantial purpose (apart from Federal income tax effects) for entering into such transaction.

(2) SPECIAL RULE WHERE TAXPAYER RELIES ON PROFIT POTENTIAL.—

(A) IN GENERAL.—The potential for profit of a transaction shall be taken into account in determining whether the requirements of subparagraphs (A) and (B) of paragraph (1) are met with respect to the transaction only if the present value of the reasonably expected pre-tax profit from the transaction is substantial in relation to the present value of the expected net tax benefits that would be allowed if the transaction were respected.

(B) TREATMENT OF FEES AND FOREIGN TAXES.—Fees and other transaction expenses shall be taken into account as expenses in determining pre-tax profit under subparagraph (A). The Secretary shall issue regulations requiring foreign taxes to be treated as expenses in determining pre-tax profit in appropriate cases.

(3) STATE AND LOCAL TAX BENEFITS.—For purposes of paragraph (1), any State or local income tax effect which is related to a Federal income tax effect shall be treated in the same manner as a Federal income tax effect.

(4) FINANCIAL ACCOUNTING BENEFITS.—For purposes of paragraph (1)(B), achieving a financial accounting benefit shall not be taken into account as a purpose for entering into a transaction if the origin of such financial accounting benefit is a reduction of Federal income tax.

(5) DEFINITIONS AND SPECIAL RULES.—For purposes of this subsection—

(A) ECONOMIC SUBSTANCE DOCTRINE.—The term "economic substance doctrine" means the common law doctrine under which tax benefits under subtitle A with respect to a transaction are not allowable if the transaction does not have economic substance or lacks a business purpose.

(B) EXCEPTION FOR PERSONAL TRANSACTIONS OF INDIVIDUALS.—In the case of an individual, paragraph (1) shall apply only to transactions entered into in connection with a trade or business or an activity engaged in for the production of income.

(C) DETERMINATION OF APPLICATION OF DOCTRINE NOT AFFECTED.—The determination of whether the economic substance doctrine is relevant to a transaction shall be made in the same manner as if this subsection had never been enacted.

(D) TRANSACTION.—The term "transaction" includes a series of transactions.

Amendments

• 2010, Health Care and Education Reconciliation Act of 2010 (P.L. 111-152)

P.L. 111-152, §1409(a):

Amended Code Sec. 7701 by redesignating subsection (o) as subsection (p) and by inserting after subsection (n) a new subsection (o). **Effective** for transactions entered into after 3-30-2010.

[Sec. 7701(p)]

(p) CROSS REFERENCES.—

(1) OTHER DEFINITIONS.—

For other definitions, see the following sections of Title 1 of the United States Code:

(1) Singular as including plural, section 1.

(2) Plural as including singular, section 1.

(3) Masculine as including feminine, section 1.

(4) Officer, section 1.

(5) Oath as including affirmation, section 1.

(6) County as including parish, section 2.

(7) Vessel as including all means of water transportation, section 3.

(8) Vehicle as including all means of land transportation, section 4.

(9) Company or association as including successors and assigns, section 5.

(2) EFFECT OF CROSS REFERENCES.—

For effect of cross references in this title, see section 7806(a).

DEFINITIONS

Amendments

- **2010, Health Care and Education Reconciliation Act of 2010 (P.L. 111-152)**

P.L. 111-152, §1409(a):

Amended Code Sec. 7701 by redesignating subsection (o) as subsection (p). **Effective** for transactions entered into after 3-30-2010.

- **2008, Heroes Earnings Assistance and Relief Tax Act of 2008 (P.L. 110-245)**

P.L. 110-245, §301(c)(2)(C):

Amended Code Sec. 7701 by redesignating subsection (p) as subsection (o). **Effective** for any individual whose expatriation date (as so defined) is on or after 6-17-2008.

- **2006, Pension Protection Act of 2006 (P.L. 109-280)**

P.L. 109-280, §1222:

Amended Code Sec. 7701 by redesignating subsection (o) as subsection (p). **Effective** 8-17-2006.

- **2004, American Jobs Creation Act of 2004 (P.L. 108-357)**

P.L. 108-357, §804(b):

Amended Code Sec. 7701 by redesignating subsection (n) as subsection (o). **Effective** for individuals who expatriate after 6-3-2004.

- **2000, Community Renewal Tax Relief Act of 2000 (P.L. 106-554)**

P.L. 106-554, §401(i):

Amended Code Sec. 7701 by redesignating subsection (m) as subsection (n). **Effective** 12-21-2000.

- **1993, Omnibus Budget Reconciliation Act of 1993 (P.L. 103-66)**

P.L. 103-66, §13238:

Amended Code Sec. 7701 by redesignating subsection (l) as subsection (m). **Effective** 8-10-93.

- **1989, Ethics Reform Act (P.L. 101-194)**

P.L. 101-194, §602:

Amended Code Sec. 7701 by redesignating subsection (k) as subsection (l). For the **effective** date, see Act Sec. 603 in the amendment notes following Code Sec. 7701(k).

- **1986, Tax Reform Act of 1986 (P.L. 99-514)**

P.L. 99-514, §1147(a):

Amended Code Sec. 7701, as amended by Act Secs. 201(d) and 558(b), by redesignating subsection (j) as subsection (k). **Effective** 10-22-86.

[Sec. 7702]

SEC. 7702. LIFE INSURANCE CONTRACT DEFINED.

[Sec. 7702(a)]

(a) GENERAL RULE.—For purposes of this title, the term "life insurance contract" means any contract which is a life insurance contract under the applicable law, but only if such contract—

    (1) meets the cash value accumulation test of subsection (b), or

    (2)(A) meets the guideline premium requirements of subsection (c), and

        (B) falls within the cash value corridor of subsection (d).

[Sec. 7702(b)]

(b) CASH VALUE ACCUMULATION TEST FOR SUBSECTION (a)(1).—

    (1) IN GENERAL.—A contract meets the cash value accumulation test of this subsection if, by the terms of the contract, the cash surrender value of such contract may not at any time exceed the net single premium which would have to be paid at such time to fund future benefits under the contract.

    (2) RULES FOR APPLYING PARAGRAPH (1).—Determinations under paragraph (1) shall be made—

        (A) on the basis of interest at the greater of the applicable accumulation test minimum rate or the rate or rates guaranteed on issuance of the contract,

        (B) on the basis of the rules of subparagraph (B)(i) (and, in the case of qualified additional benefits, subparagraph (B)(ii)) of subsection (c)(3), and

        (C) by taking into account under subparagraphs (A) and (D) of subsection (e)(1) only current and future death benefits and qualified additional benefits.

    (3) APPLICABLE ACCUMULATION TEST MINIMUM RATE.—For purposes of paragraph (2)(A), the term "applicable accumulation test minimum rate" means the lesser of—

        (A) an annual effective rate of 4 percent, or

        (B) the insurance interest rate (as defined in subsection (f)(11)) in effect at the time the contract is issued.

Amendments

- **2020, Taxpayer Certainty and Disaster Tax Relief Act of 2020 (P.L. 116-260)**

P.L. 116-260, §205(a)(1), Div. EE:

Amended Code Sec. 7702(b)(2)(A) by striking "an annual effective rate of 4 percent" and inserting "the applicable accumulation test minimum rate". **Effective** for contracts issued after 12-31-2020.

P.L. 116-260, §205(a)(2), Div. EE:

Amended Code Sec. 7702(b) by adding at the end a new paragraph (3). **Effective** for contracts issued after 12-31-2020.

- **1986, Tax Reform Act of 1986 (P.L. 99-514)**

P.L. 99-514, §1825(a)(2):

Amended Code Sec. 7702(b)(2)(C) by striking out "subparagraphs (A) and (C)" and inserting in lieu thereof "subparagraphs (A) and (D)". **Effective** as if included in the provision of P.L. 98-369 to which it relates.

[Sec. 7702(c)]

(c) GUIDELINE PREMIUM REQUIREMENTS.—For purposes of this section—

    (1) IN GENERAL.—A contract meets the guideline premium requirements of this subsection if the sum of the premiums paid under such contract does not at any time exceed the guideline premium limitation as of such time.

    (2) GUIDELINE PREMIUM LIMITATION.—The term "guideline premium limitation" means, as of any date, the greater of—

        (A) the guideline single premium, or

        (B) the sum of the guideline level premiums to such date.

    (3) GUIDELINE SINGLE PREMIUM.—

        (A) IN GENERAL.—The term "guideline single premium" means the premium at issue with respect to future benefits under the contract.

        (B) BASIS ON WHICH DETERMINATION IS MADE.—The determination under subparagraph (A) shall be based on—

            (i) reasonable mortality charges which meet the requirements prescribed in regulations to be promulgated by the Secretary or that do not exceed the mortality charges specified in the prevailing commissioners' standard tables as defined in subsection (f)(10),

            (ii) any reasonable charges (other than mortality charges) which (on the basis of the company's experience, if any, with respect to similar contracts) are reasonably expected to be actually paid, and

DEFINITIONS

(iii) interest at the greater of the applicable guideline premium minimum rate or the rate or rates guaranteed on issuance of the contract.

(C) WHEN DETERMINATION MADE.—Except as provided in subsection (f)(7), the determination under subparagraph (A) shall be made as of the time the contract is issued.

(D) SPECIAL RULES FOR SUBPARAGRAPH (B)(ii).—

(i) CHARGES NOT SPECIFIED IN THE CONTRACT.—If any charge is not specified in the contract, the amount taken into account under subparagraph (B)(ii) for such charge shall be zero.

(ii) NEW COMPANIES, ETC.—If any company does not have adequate experience for purposes of the determination under subparagraph (B)(ii), to the extent provided in regulations, such determination shall be made on the basis of the industry-wide experience.

(E) APPLICABLE GUIDELINE PREMIUM MINIMUM RATE.—For purposes of subparagraph (B)(iii), the term "applicable guideline premium minimum rate" means the applicable accumulation test minimum rate (as defined in subsection (b)(3)) plus 2 percentage points.

(4) GUIDELINE LEVEL PREMIUM.—The term "guideline level premium" means the level annual amount, payable over a period not ending before the insured attains age 95, computed on the same basis as the guideline single premium, except that paragraph (3)(B)(iii) shall be applied by substituting "the applicable accumulation test minimum rate" for "the applicable guideline premium minimum rate".

Amendments

• **2020, Taxpayer Certainty and Disaster Tax Relief Act of 2020 (P.L. 116-260)**

P.L. 116-260, §205(b)(1), Div. EE:

Amended Code Sec. 7702(c)(3)(B)(iii) by striking "an annual effective rate of 6 percent" and inserting "the applicable guideline premium minimum rate". **Effective** for contracts issued after 12-31-2020.

P.L. 116-260, §205(b)(2), Div. EE:

Amended Code Sec. 7702(c)(3) by adding at the end a new subparagraph (E). **Effective** for contracts issued after 12-31-2020.

P.L. 116-260, §205(c)(1)-(2), Div. EE:

Amended Code Sec. 7702(c)(4) by striking "4 percent" and inserting "the applicable accumulation test minimum rate", and by striking "6 percent" and inserting "the applicable guideline premium minimum rate". **Effective** for contracts issued after 12-31-2020.

• **2017, Tax Cuts and Jobs Act (P.L. 115-97)**

P.L. 115-97, §13517(a)(4)(A):

Amended Code Sec. 7702(c)(3)(B) by striking clause (i) and inserting a new clause (i). **Effective** generally for tax years beginning after 12-31-2017. For a transition rule, see Act Sec. 13517(c)(2)-(3), below. Prior to being stricken, Code Sec. 7702(c)(3)(B)(i) read as follows:

(i) reasonable mortality charges which meet the requirements (if any) prescribed in regulations and which (except as provided in regulations) do not exceed the mortality charges specified in the prevailing commissioners' standard tables (as defined in section 807(d)(5)) as of the time the contract is issued,

P.L. 115-97, §13517(c)(2)-(3), provides:

(2) TRANSITION RULE.—For the first taxable year beginning after December 31, 2017, the reserve with respect to any contract (as determined under section 807(d) of the Internal Revenue Code of 1986) at the end of the preceding taxable year shall be determined as if the amendments made by this section had applied to such reserve in such preceding taxable year.

(3) TRANSITION RELIEF.—

(A) IN GENERAL.—If—

(i) the reserve determined under section 807(d) of the Internal Revenue Code of 1986 (determined after application of paragraph (2)) with respect to any contract as of the close of the year preceding the first taxable year beginning after December 31, 2017, differs from

(ii) the reserve which would have been determined with respect to such contract as of the close of such taxable year under such section determined without regard to paragraph (2),

then the difference between the amount of the reserve described in clause (i) and the amount of the reserve described in clause (ii) shall be taken into account under the method provided in subparagraph (B).

(B) METHOD.—The method provided in this subparagraph is as follows:

(i) If the amount determined under subparagraph (A)(i) exceeds the amount determined under subparagraph (A)(ii), 1/8 of such excess shall be taken into account, for each of the 8 succeeding taxable years, as a deduction under section 805(a)(2) or 832(c)(4) of such Code, as applicable.

(ii) If the amount determined under subparagraph (A)(ii) exceeds the amount determined under subparagraph (A)(i), 1/8 of such excess shall be included in gross income, for each of the 8 succeeding taxable years, under section 803(a)(2) or 832(b)(1)(C) of such Code, as applicable.

• **1988, Technical and Miscellaneous Revenue Act of 1988 (P.L. 100-647)**

P.L. 100-647, §5011(a):

Amended Code Sec. 7702(c)(3)(B) by striking out clauses (i) and (ii) and inserting in lieu thereof new clauses (i) and (ii). **Effective** for contracts entered into on or after 10-21-88. Prior to amendment, Code Sec. 7702(c)(3)(B)(i)-(ii) read as follows:

(i) the mortality charges specified in the contract (or, if none is specified, the mortality charges used in determining the statutory reserves for such contract),

(ii) any charges (not taken into account under clause (i)) specified in the contract (the amount of any charge not so specified shall be treated as zero), and

P.L. 100-647, §5011(b):

Amended Code Sec. 7702(c)(3) by adding at the end thereof a new subparagraph (D). **Effective** for contracts entered into on or after 10-21-88.

[Sec. 7702(d)]

(d) CASH VALUE CORRIDOR FOR PURPOSES OF SUBSECTION (a)(2)(B).—For purposes of this section—

(1) IN GENERAL.—A contract falls within the cash value corridor of this subsection if the death benefit under the contract at any time is not less than the applicable percentage of the cash surrender value.

(2) APPLICABLE PERCENTAGE.—

In the case of an insured with an attained age as of the beginning of the contract year of:		The applicable percentage shall decrease by a ratable portion for each full year:	
More than:	But not more than:	From:	To:
0	40	250	250
40	45	250	215
45	50	215	185
50	55	185	150
55	60	150	130
60	65	130	120
65	70	120	115
70	75	115	105
75	90	105	105
90	95	105	100

[Sec. 7702(e)]

(e) COMPUTATIONAL RULES.—

(1) IN GENERAL.—For purposes of this section (other than subsection (d))—

(A) the death benefit (and any qualified additional benefit) shall be deemed not to increase,

(B) the maturity date, including the date on which any benefit described in subparagraph (C) is payable, shall be deemed to be no earlier than the day on which the insured attains age 95, and no later than the day on which the insured attains age 100,

(C) the death benefits shall be deemed to be provided until the maturity date determined by taking into account subparagraph (B), and

DEFINITIONS

(D) the amount of any endowment benefit (or sum of endowment benefits, including any cash surrender value on the maturity date determined by taking into account subparagraph (B)) shall be deemed not to exceed the least amount payable as a death benefit at any time under the contract.

(2) LIMITED INCREASES IN DEATH BENEFIT PERMITTED.—Notwithstanding paragraph (1)(A)—

(A) for purposes of computing the guideline level premium, an increase in the death benefit which is provided in the contract may be taken into account but only to the extent necessary to prevent a decrease in the excess of the death benefit over the cash surrender value of the contract,

(B) for purposes of the cash value accumulation test, the increase described in subparagraph (A) may be taken into account if the contract will meet such test at all times assuming that the net level reserve (determined as if level annual premiums were paid for the contract over a period not ending before the insured attains age 95) is substituted for the net single premium,

(C) for purposes of the cash value accumulation test, the death benefit increases may be taken into account if the contract—

(i) has an initial death benefit of $5,000 or less and a maximum death benefit of $25,000 or less,

(ii) provides for a fixed predetermined annual increase not to exceed 10 percent of the initial death benefit or 8 percent of the death benefit at the end of the preceding year, and

(iii) was purchased to cover payment of burial expenses or in connection with prearranged funeral expenses.

For purposes of subparagraph (C), the initial death benefit of a contract shall be determined by treating all contracts issued to the same contract owner as 1 contract.

Amendments

- **1986, Tax Reform Act of 1986 (P.L. 99-514)**

P.L. 99-514, § 1825(a)(1)(A)-(D):

Amended Code Sec. 7702(e)(1) by striking out "shall be no earlier than" in subparagraph (B) and inserting in lieu thereof "shall be deemed to be no earlier than", by striking out "and" at the end of subparagraph (B), by redesignating subparagraph (C) as subparagraph (D) and inserting after subparagraph (B) new subparagraph (C), and by striking out "the maturity date described in subparagraph (B)" in subparagraph (D) (as so redesignated) and inserting in lieu thereof "the maturity date determined by taking into account subparagraph (B)". **Effective** as if included in the provision of P.L. 98-369 to which it relates.

P.L. 99-514, § 1825(a)(3):

Amended Code Sec. 7702(e)(1) by inserting "(other than subsection (d))" after "section". **Effective** as if included in the provision of P.L. 98-369 to which it relates.

P.L. 99-514, § 1825(a)(4)(A)-(C):

Amended Code Sec. 7702(e)(2) by striking out "and" at the end of subparagraph (A), by striking out the period at the end of subparagraph (B), and inserting in lieu thereof a comma and "and", and by adding at the end thereof new subparagraph (C). **Effective** with respect to contracts entered into after 10-22-86 [effective date changed by P.L. 100-647, § 1018(j)].

[Sec. 7702(f)]

(f) OTHER DEFINITIONS AND SPECIAL RULES.—For purposes of this section—

(1) PREMIUMS PAID.—

(A) IN GENERAL.—The term "premiums paid" means the premiums paid under the contract less amounts (other than amounts includible in gross income) to which section 72(e) applies and less any excess premiums with respect to which there is a distribution described in subparagraph (B) or (E) of paragraph (7) and any other amounts received with respect to the contract which are specified in regulations.

(B) TREATMENT OF CERTAIN PREMIUMS RETURNED TO POLICYHOLDER.—If, in order to comply with the requirements of subsection (a)(2)(A), any portion of any premium paid during any contract year is returned by the insurance company (with interest) within 60 days after the end of a contract year, the amount so returned (excluding interest) shall be deemed to reduce the sum of the premiums paid under the contract during such year.

(C) INTEREST RETURNED INCLUDIBLE IN GROSS INCOME.—Notwithstanding the provisions of section 72(e), the amount of any interest returned as provided in subparagraph (B) shall be includible in the gross income of the recipient.

(2) CASH VALUES.—

(A) CASH SURRENDER VALUE.—The cash surrender value of any contract shall be its cash value determined without regard to any surrender charge, policy loan, or reasonable termination dividends.

(B) NET SURRENDER VALUE.—The net surrender value of any contract shall be determined with regard to surrender charges but without regard to any policy loan.

(3) DEATH BENEFIT.—The term "death benefit" means the amount payable by reason of the death of the insured (determined without regard to any qualified additional benefits).

(4) FUTURE BENEFITS.—The term "future benefits" means death benefits and endowment benefits.

(5) QUALIFIED ADDITIONAL BENEFITS.—

(A) IN GENERAL.—The term "qualified additional benefits" means any—

(i) guaranteed insurability,

(ii) accidental death or disability benefit,

(iii) family term coverage,

(iv) disability waiver benefit, or

(v) other benefit prescribed under regulations.

(B) TREATMENT OF QUALIFIED ADDITIONAL BENEFITS.—For purposes of this section, qualified additional benefits shall not be treated as future benefits under the contract, but the charges for such benefits shall be treated as future benefits.

(C) TREATMENT OF OTHER ADDITIONAL BENEFITS.—In the case of any additional benefit which is not a qualified additional benefit—

(i) such benefit shall not be treated as a future benefit, and

(ii) any charge for such benefit which is not prefunded shall not be treated as a premium.

(6) PREMIUM PAYMENTS NOT DISQUALIFYING CONTRACT.—The payment of a premium which would result in the sum of the premiums paid exceeding the guideline premium limitation shall be disregarded for purposes of subsection (a)(2) if the amount of such premium does not exceed the amount necessary to prevent the termination of the contract on or before the end of the contract year (but only if the contract will have no cash surrender value at the end of such extension period).

(7) ADJUSTMENTS.—

(A) IN GENERAL.—If there is a change in the benefits under (or in other terms of) the contract which was not reflected in any previous determination or adjustment made under this section, there shall be proper adjustments in future determinations made under this section.

(B) RULE FOR CERTAIN CHANGES DURING FIRST 15 YEARS.—If—

(i) a change described in subparagraph (A) reduces benefits under the contract,

(ii) the change occurs during the 15-year period beginning on the issue date of the contract, and

(iii) a cash distribution is made to the policyholder as a result of such change,

section 72 (other than subsection (e)(5) thereof) shall apply to such cash distribution to the extent it does not exceed the recapture ceiling determined under subparagraph (C) or (D) (whichever applies).

(C) RECAPTURE CEILING WHERE CHANGE OCCURS DURING FIRST 5 YEARS.—If the change referred to in subparagraph (B)(ii) occurs during the 5-year period beginning on the issue date of the contract, the recapture ceiling is—

(i) in the case of a contract to which subsection (a)(1) applies, the excess of—

(I) the cash surrender value of the contract, immediately before the reduction, over

(II) the net single premium (determined under subsection (b)), immediately after the reduction, or

(ii) in the case of a contract to which subsection (a)(2) applies, the greater of—

(I) the excess of the aggregate premiums paid under the contract, immediately before the reduction, over the guideline premium limitation for the contract (determined under subsection (c)(2), taking into account the adjustment described in subparagraph (A)), or

(II) the excess of the cash surrender value of the contract, immediately before the reduction, over the cash value corridor of subsection (d) (determined immediately after the reduction).

(D) RECAPTURE CEILING WHERE CHANGE OCCURS AFTER 5TH YEAR AND BEFORE 16TH YEAR.—If the change referred to in subparagraph (B) occurs after the 5-year period referred to under subparagraph (C), the recapture ceiling is the excess of the cash surrender value of the contract, immediately before the reduction, over the cash value corridor of subsection (d) (determined immediately after the reduction and whether or not subsection (d) applies to the contract).

(E) TREATMENT OF CERTAIN DISTRIBUTIONS MADE IN ANTICIPATION OF BENEFIT REDUCTIONS.—Under regulations prescribed by the Secretary, subparagraph (B) shall apply also to any distribution made in anticipation of a reduction in benefits under the contract. For purposes of the preceding sentence, appropriate adjustments shall be made in the provisions of subparagraphs (C) and (D); and any distribution which reduces the cash surrender value of a contract and which is made within 2 years before a reduction in benefits under the contract shall be treated as made in anticipation of such reduction.

(8) CORRECTION OF ERRORS.—If the taxpayer establishes to the satisfaction of the Secretary that—

(A) the requirements described in subsection (a) for any contract year were not satisfied due to reasonable error, and

(B) reasonable steps are being taken to remedy the error,

the Secretary may waive the failure to satisfy such requirements.

(9) SPECIAL RULE FOR VARIABLE LIFE INSURANCE CONTRACTS.—In the case of any contract which is a variable contract (as defined in section 817), the determination of whether such contract meets the requirements of subsection (a) shall be made whenever the death benefits under such contract change but not less frequently than once during each 12-month period.

(10) PREVAILING COMMISSIONERS' STANDARD TABLES.—For purposes of subsection (c)(3)(B)(i), the term "prevailing commissioners' standard tables" means the most recent commissioners' standard tables prescribed by the National Association of Insurance Commissioners which are permitted to be used in computing reserves for that type of contract under the insurance laws of at least 26 States when the contract was issued. If the prevailing commissioners' standard tables as of the beginning of any calendar year (hereinafter in this paragraph referred to as the "year of change") are different from the prevailing commissioners' standard tables as of the beginning of the preceding calendar year, the issuer may use the prevailing commissioners' standard tables as of the beginning of the preceding calendar year with respect to any contract issued after the change and before the close of the 3-year period beginning on the first day of the year of change.

(11) INSURANCE INTEREST RATE.—For purposes of this section—

(A) IN GENERAL.—The term "insurance interest rate" means, with respect to any contract issued in any calendar year, the lesser of—

(i) the section 7702 valuation interest rate for such calendar year (or, if such calendar year is not an adjustment year, the most recent adjustment year), or

(ii) the section 7702 applicable Federal interest rate for such calendar year (or, if such calendar year is not an adjustment year, the most recent adjustment year).

(B) SECTION 7702 VALUATION INTEREST RATE.—The term "section 7702 valuation interest rate" means, with respect to any adjustment year, the prescribed U.S. valuation interest rate for life insurance with guaranteed durations of more than 20 years (as defined in the National Association of Insurance Commissioners' Standard Valuation Law) as effective in the calendar year immediately preceding such adjustment year.

(C) SECTION 7702 APPLICABLE FEDERAL INTEREST RATE.—The term "section 7702 applicable Federal interest rate" means, with respect to any adjustment year, the average (rounded to the nearest whole percentage point) of the applicable Federal mid-term rates (as defined in section 1274(d) but based on annual compounding) effective as of the beginning of each of the calendar months in the most recent 60-month period ending before the second calendar year prior to such adjustment year.

(D) ADJUSTMENT YEAR.—The term "adjustment year" means the calendar year following any calendar year that includes the effective date of a change in the prescribed U.S. valuation interest rate for life insurance with guaranteed durations of more than 20 years (as defined in the National Association of Insurance Commissioners' Standard Valuation Law).

(E) TRANSITION RULE.—Notwithstanding subparagraph (A), the insurance interest rate shall be 2 percent in the case of any contract which is issued during the period that—

(i) begins on January 1, 2021, and

(ii) ends immediately before the beginning of the first adjustment year that beings after December 31, 2021.

Amendments

• **2020, Taxpayer Certainty and Disaster Tax Relief Act of 2020 (P.L. 116-260)**

P.L. 116-260, §205(d), Div. EE:

Amended Code Sec. 7702(f) by adding at the end a new paragraph (11). **Effective** for contracts issued after 12-31-2020.

• **2017, Tax Cuts and Jobs Act (P.L. 115-97)**

P.L. 115-97, §13517(a)(4)(B):

Amended Code Sec. 7702(f) by adding at the end a new paragraph (10). **Effective** generally for tax years beginning after 12-31-2017. For a transition rule, see Act Sec. 13517(c)(2)-(3), below.

P.L. 115-97, §13517(c)(2)-(3), provides:

(2) TRANSITION RULE.—For the first taxable year beginning after December 31, 2017, the reserve with respect to any contract (as determined under section 807(d) of the Internal Revenue Code of 1986) at the end of the preceding taxable year shall be determined as if the amendments made by this section had applied to such reserve in such preceding taxable year.

(3) TRANSITION RELIEF.—

(A) IN GENERAL.—If—

(i) the reserve determined under section 807(d) of the Internal Revenue Code of 1986 (determined after application of paragraph (2)) with respect to any contract as of the close of the year preceding the first taxable year beginning after December 31, 2017, differs from

(ii) the reserve which would have been determined with respect to such contract as of the close of such taxable year under such section determined without regard to paragraph (2),

then the difference between the amount of the reserve described in clause (i) and the amount of the reserve described in clause (ii) shall be taken into account under the method provided in subparagraph (B).

(B) METHOD.—The method provided in this subparagraph is as follows:

DEFINITIONS

(i) If the amount determined under subparagraph (A)(i) exceeds the amount determined under subparagraph (A)(ii), 1/8 of such excess shall be taken into account, for each of the 8 succeeding taxable years, as a deduction under section 805(a)(2) or 832(c)(4) of such Code, as applicable.

(ii) If the amount determined under subparagraph (A)(ii) exceeds the amount determined under subparagraph (A)(i), 1/8 of such excess shall be included in gross income, for each of the 8 succeeding taxable years, under section 803(a)(2) or 832(b)(1)(C) of such Code, as applicable.

- **1986, Tax Reform Act of 1986 (P.L. 99-514)**

P.L. 99-514, § 1825(b)(1):

Amended Code Sec. 7702(f)(7). **Effective** as if included in the provision of P.L. 98-369 to which it relates. Prior to amendment, Code Sec. 7702(f)(7) read as follows:

(7) ADJUSTMENTS.—

(A) IN GENERAL.—In the event of a change in the future benefits or any qualified additional benefit (or in any other terms) under the contract which was not reflected in any previous determination made under this section, under regulations prescribed by the Secretary, there shall be proper adjustments in future determinations made under this section.

(B) CERTAIN CHANGES TREATED AS EXCHANGE.—In the case of any change which reduces the future benefits under the contract, such change shall be treated as an exchange of the contract for another contract.

P.L. 99-514, § 1825(b)(2):

Amended Code Sec. 7702(f)(1)(A) by striking out "less any other amounts received" and inserting in lieu thereof "less any excess premiums with respect to which there is a distribution described in subparagraph (B) or (E) of paragraph (7) and any other amounts received". **Effective** as if included in the provision of P.L. 98-369 to which it relates.

[Sec. 7702(g)]

(g) TREATMENT OF CONTRACTS WHICH DO NOT MEET SUBSECTION (a) TEST.—

(1) INCOME INCLUSION.—

(A) IN GENERAL.—If at any time any contract which is a life insurance contract under the applicable law does not meet the definition of life insurance contract under subsection (a), the income on the contract for any taxable year of the policyholder shall be treated as ordinary income received or accrued by the policyholder during such year.

(B) INCOME ON THE CONTRACT.—For purposes of this paragraph, the term "income on the contract" means, with respect to any taxable year of the policyholder, the excess of—

(i) the sum of—

(I) the increase in the net surrender value of the contract during the taxable year, and

(II) the cost of life insurance protection provided under the contract during the taxable year, over

(ii) the premiums paid (as defined in subsection (f)(1)) under the contract during the taxable year.

(C) CONTRACTS WHICH CEASE TO MEET DEFINITION.—If, during any taxable year of the policyholder, a contract which is a life insurance contract under the applicable law ceases to meet the definition of life insurance contract under subsection (a), the income on the contract for all prior taxable years shall be treated as received or accrued during the taxable year in which such cessation occurs.

(D) COST OF LIFE INSURANCE PROTECTION.—For purposes of this paragraph, the cost of life insurance protection provided under the contract shall be the lesser of—

(i) the cost of individual insurance on the life of the insured as determined on the basis of uniform premiums (computed on the basis of 5-year age brackets) prescribed by the Secretary by regulations, or

(ii) the mortality charge (if any) stated in the contract.

(2) TREATMENT OF AMOUNT PAID ON DEATH OF INSURED.—If any contract which is a life insurance contract under the applicable law does not meet the definition of life insurance contract under subsection (a), the excess of the amount paid by the reason of the death of the insured over the net surrender value of the contract shall be deemed to be paid under a life insurance contract for purposes of section 101 and subtitle B.

(3) CONTRACT CONTINUES TO BE TREATED AS INSURANCE CONTRACT.—If any contract which is a life insurance contract under the applicable law does not meet the definition of life insurance contract under subsection (a), such contract shall, notwithstanding such failure, be treated as an insurance contract for purposes of this title.

Amendments

- **1986, Tax Reform Act of 1986 (P.L. 99-514)**

P.L. 99-514, § 1825(c):

Amended Code Sec. 7702(g)(1)(B)(ii). **Effective** as if included in the provision of P.L. 98-369 to which it relates. Prior to amendment, Code Sec. 7702(g)(1)(B)(ii) read as follows:

(ii) the amount of premiums paid under the contract during the taxable year reduced by policyholder dividends received during such taxable year.

[Sec. 7702(h)]

(h) ENDOWMENT CONTRACTS RECEIVE SAME TREATMENT.—

(1) IN GENERAL.—References in subsections (a) and (g) to a life insurance contract shall be treated as including references to a contract which is an endowment contract under the applicable law.

(2) DEFINITION OF ENDOWMENT CONTRACT.—For purposes of this title (other than paragraph (1)), the term "endowment contract" means a contract which is an endowment contract under the applicable law and which meets the requirements of subsection (a).

[Sec. 7702(i)]

(i) TRANSITIONAL RULE FOR CERTAIN 20-PAY CONTRACTS.—

(1) IN GENERAL.—In the case of a qualified 20-pay contract, this section shall be applied by substituting "3 percent" for "4 percent" in subsection (b)(2).

(2) QUALIFIED 20-PAY CONTRACT.—For purposes of paragraph (1), the term "qualified 20-pay contract" means any contract which—

(A) requires at least 20 nondecreasing annual premium payments, and

(B) is issued pursuant to an existing plan of insurance.

(3) EXISTING PLAN OF INSURANCE.—For purposes of this subsection, the term "existing plan of insurance" means, with respect to any contract, any plan of insurance which was filed by the company issuing such contract in 1 or more States before September 28, 1983, and is on file in the appropriate State for such contract.

[Sec. 7702(j)]

(j) CERTAIN CHURCH SELF FUNDED DEATH BENEFIT PLANS TREATED AS LIFE INSURANCE.—

(1) IN GENERAL.—In determining whether any plan or arrangement described in paragraph (2) is a life insurance contract, the requirement of subsection (a) that the contract be a life insurance contract under applicable law shall not apply.

(2) DESCRIPTION.—For purposes of this subsection, a plan or arrangement is described in this paragraph if—

(A) such plan or arrangement provides for the payment of benefits by reason of the death of the individuals covered under such plan or arrangement, and

(B) such plan or arrangement is provided by a church for the benefit of its employees and their beneficiaries, directly or through an organization described in section 414(e)(3)(A) or an organization described in section 414(e)(3)(B)(ii).

(3) DEFINITIONS.—For purposes of this subsection—

(A) CHURCH.—The term "church" means a church or a convention or association of churches.

(B) EMPLOYEE.—The term "employee" includes an employee described in section 414(e)(3)(B).

Amendments

• **2004 (P.L. 108-476)**

P.L. 108-476, §1(a)(1) and (4) and (c), provides:

SECTION 1. CERTAIN ARRANGEMENTS MAINTAINED BY THE YMCA RETIREMENT FUND TREATED AS CHURCH PLANS.

(a) RETIREMENT PLANS.—

(1) IN GENERAL.—For purposes of sections 401(a) and 403(b) of the Internal Revenue Code of 1986, any retirement plan maintained by the YMCA Retirement Fund as of January 1, 2003, shall be treated as a church plan (within the meaning of section 414(e) of such Code) which is maintained by an organization described in section 414(e)(3)(A) of such Code.

* * *

(4) SELF-FUNDED DEATH BENEFIT PLAN.—For purposes of section 7702(j) of such Code, a retirement plan described in paragraph (1) shall be treated as an arrangement described in section 7702(j)(2).

* * *

(c) EFFECTIVE DATE.—This section shall apply to plan years beginning after December 31, 2003.

• **1988, Technical and Miscellaneous Revenue Act of 1988 (P.L. 100-647)**

P.L. 100-647, §6078(a):

Amended Code Sec. 7702 by inserting after subsection (i) new subsection (j). **Effective** as if included in the amendments made by section 221(a) of P.L. 98-369.

[Sec. 7702(k)]

(k) REGULATIONS.—The Secretary shall prescribe such regulations as may be necessary or appropriate to carry out the purposes of this section.

Amendments

• **1988, Technical and Miscellaneous Revenue Act of 1988 (P.L. 100-647)**

P.L. 100-647, §6078(a):

Amended Code Sec. 7702 by redesignating subsection (j) as subsection (k). **Effective** as if included in the amendments made by section 221(a) of P.L. 98-369.

• **1984, Deficit Reduction Act of 1984 (P.L. 98-369)**

P.L. 98-369, §221(a):

Added Code Sec. 7702. **Effective** for contracts issued after 12-31-84, in tax years ending after such date. Special rules appear below.

P.L. 98-369, §221(d)(2)-(5), as amended by P.L. 99-514, §1825(e):

(2) Special rule for certain contracts issued after June 30, 1984.—

(A) General rule.—Except as otherwise provided in this paragraph, the amendments made by this section shall apply also to any contract issued after June 30, 1984, which provides an increasing death benefit and has premium funding more rapid than 10-year level premium payments.

(B) Exception for certain contracts.—Subparagraph (A) shall not apply to any contract if—

(i) such contract (whether or not a flexible premium contract) would meet the requirements of section 101(f) of the Internal Revenue Code of 1954,

(ii) such contract is not a flexible premium life insurance contract (within the meaning of section 101(f) of such Code) and would meet the requirements of section 7702 of such Code determined by—

(I) substituting "3 percent" for "4 percent" in section 7702(b)(2) of such Code, and

(II) treating subparagraph (B) of section 7702(e)(1) of such Code as if it read as follows: "the maturity date shall be the latest maturity date permitted under the contract, but not less than 20 years after the date of issue or (if earlier) age 95", or

(iii) under such contract—

(I) the premiums (including any policy fees) will be adjusted from time-to-time to reflect the level amount necessary (but not less than zero) at the time of such adjustment to provide a level death benefit assuming interest crediting and an annual effective interest rate of not less than 3 percent, or

(II) at the option of the insured, in lieu of an adjustment under subclause (I) there will be a comparable adjustment in the amount of the death benefit.

(C) Certain contracts issued before October 1, 1984.—

(i) In general.—Subparagraph (A) shall be applied by substituting "September 30, 1984" for "June 30, 1984" thereof in the case of a contract—

(I) which would meet the requirements of section 7702 of such Code if "3 percent" were substituted for "4 percent" in section 7702(b)(2) of such Code, and the rate or rates guaranteed on issuance of the contract were determined without regard to any mortality charges and any initial excess interest guarantees, and

(II) the cash surrender value of which does not at any time exceed the net single premium which would have to be paid at such time to fund future benefits under the contract.

(ii) Definitions.—For purposes of clause (i)—

(I) In general.—Except as provided in subclause (II), terms used in clause (i) shall have the same meanings as when used in section 7702 of such Code.

(II) Net single premium.—The term "net single premium" shall be determined by substituting "3 percent" for "4 percent" in section 7702(b)(2) of such Code, by using the 1958 standard ordinary mortality and morbidity tables of the National Association of Insurance Commissioners, and by assuming a level death benefit.

(3) Transitional rule for certain existing plans of insurance.—A plan of insurance on file in 1 or more States before September 28, 1983, shall be treated for purposes of section 7702(i)(3) of such Code as a plan of insurance on file in 1 or more States before September 28, 1983, without regard to whether such plan of insurance is modified after September 28, 1983, to permit the crediting of excess interest or similar amounts annually and not monthly under contracts issued pursuant to such plan of insurance.

(4) Extension of flexible premium contract provisions.—The amendments made by subsection (b) shall take effect on January 1, 1984.

(5) Special rule for master contract.—For purposes of this subsection, in the case of a master contract, the date taken into account with respect to any insured shall be the first date on which such insured is covered under such contract.

[Sec. 7702A]

SEC. 7702A. MODIFIED ENDOWMENT CONTRACT DEFINED.

[Sec. 7702A(a)]

(a) GENERAL RULE.—For purposes of section 72, the term "modified endowment contract" means any contract meeting the requirements of section 7702—

(1) which—

(A) is entered into on or after June 21, 1988, and

(B) fails to meet the 7-pay test of subsection (b), or

(2) which is received in exchange for a contract described in paragraph (1) or this paragraph.

Amendments

• **2000, Community Renewal Tax Relief Act of 2000 (P.L. 106-554)**

P.L. 106-554, §318(a)(1):

Amended Code Sec. 7702A(a)(2) by inserting "or this paragraph" before the period. **Effective** as if included in the amendments made by section 5012 of P.L. 100-647 [**effective** for contracts entered into or materially changed on or after 6-21-88.—CCH].

[Sec. 7702A(b)]

(b) 7-PAY TEST.—For purposes of subsection (a), a contract fails to meet the 7-pay test of this subsection if the accumulated amount paid under the contract at any time during the 1st 7 contract years exceeds the sum of the net level premiums which would have been paid on or before such time if the contract provided for paid-up future benefits after the payment of 7 level annual premiums.

[Sec. 7702A(c)]

(c) COMPUTATIONAL RULES.—

(1) IN GENERAL.—Except as provided in this subsection, the determination under subsection (b) of the 7 level annual premiums shall be made—

(A) as of the time the contract is issued, and

(B) by applying the rules of section 7702(b)(2) and of section 7702(e) (other than paragraph (2)(C) thereof), except that the death benefit provided for the 1st contract year shall be deemed to be provided until the maturity date without regard to any scheduled reduction after the 1st 7 contract years.

DEFINITIONS

(2) REDUCTION IN BENEFITS DURING 1ST 7 YEARS.—

(A) IN GENERAL.—If there is a reduction in benefits under the contract within the 1st 7 contract years, this section shall be applied as if the contract had originally been issued at the reduced benefit level.

(B) REDUCTIONS ATTRIBUTABLE TO NONPAYMENT OF PREMIUMS.—Any reduction in benefits attributable to the nonpayment of premiums due under the contract shall not be taken into account under subparagraph (A) if the benefits are reinstated within 90 days after the reduction in such benefits.

(3) TREATMENT OF MATERIAL CHANGES.—

(A) IN GENERAL.—If there is a material change in the benefits under (or in other terms of) the contract which was not reflected in any previous determination under this section, for purposes of this section—

(i) such contract shall be treated as a new contract entered into on the day on which such material change takes effect, and

(ii) appropriate adjustments shall be made in determining whether such contract meets the 7-pay test of subsection (b) to take into account the cash surrender value under the contract.

(B) TREATMENT OF CERTAIN BENEFIT INCREASES.—For purposes of subparagraph (A), the term "material change" includes any increase in the death benefit under the contract or any increase in, or addition of, a qualified additional benefit under the contract. Such term shall not include—

(i) any increase which is attributable to the payment of premiums necessary to fund the lowest level of the death benefit and qualified additional benefits payable in the 1st 7 contract years (determined after taking into account death benefit increases described in subparagraph (A) or (B) of section 7702(e)(2)) or to crediting of interest or other earnings (including policyholder dividends) in respect of such premiums, and

(ii) to the extent provided in regulations, any cost-of-living increase based on an established broad-based index if such increase is funded ratably over the remaining period during which premiums are required to be paid under the contract.

(4) SPECIAL RULE FOR CONTRACTS WITH DEATH BENEFITS OF $10,000 OR LESS.—In the case of a contract—

(A) which provides an initial death benefit of $10,000 or less, and

(B) which requires at least 7 nondecreasing annual premium payments,

each of the 7 level annual premiums determined under subsection (b) (without regard to this paragraph) shall be increased by $75. For purposes of this paragraph, the contract involved and all contracts previously issued to the same policyholder by the same company shall be treated as one contract.

(5) REGULATORY AUTHORITY FOR CERTAIN COLLECTION EXPENSES.—The Secretary may by regulations prescribe rules for taking into account expenses solely attributable to the collection of premiums paid more frequently than annually.

(6) TREATMENT OF CERTAIN CONTRACTS WITH MORE THAN ONE INSURED.—If—

(A) a contract provides a death benefit which is payable only upon the death of 1 insured following (or occurring simultaneously with) the death of another insured, and

(B) there is a reduction in such death benefit below the lowest level of such death benefit provided under the contract during the 1st 7 contract years,

this section shall be applied as if the contract had originally been issued at the reduced benefit level.

Amendments

- **2002, Job Creation and Worker Assistance Act of 2002 (P.L. 107-147)**

P.L. 107-147, §416(f):

Provides that section 318(a)(2) of P.L. 106-554 is repealed, and Code Sec. 7702A(c)(3)(A)(ii) shall read and be applied as if this amendment had not been enacted. **Effective** 3-9-2002.

- **2000, Community Renewal Act of 2000 (P.L. 106-554)**

P.L. 106-554, §318(a)(2) (repealed by P.L. 107-47, §416(f)):

Amended Code Sec. 7702A(c)(3)(A)(ii) by striking "under the contract" and inserting "under the old contract". **Effective** as if included in the amendments made by section 5012 of P.L. 100-647 [effective for contracts entered into or materially changed on or after 6-21-88.—CCH].

- **1989, Omnibus Budget Reconciliation Act of 1989 (P.L. 101-239)**

P.L. 101-239, §7647(a):

Amended Code Sec. 7702A(c) by adding at the end thereof a new paragraph (6). **Effective** for contracts entered into on or after 9-14-89.

P.L. 101-239, §7815(a)(1):

Amended Code Sec. 7702A(c)(3)(B). **Effective** as if included in the provision of P.L. 100-647 to which it relates. Prior to amendment, Code Sec. 7702A(c)(3)(B) read as follows:

(B) TREATMENT OF CERTAIN INCREASES IN FUTURE BENEFITS.—For purposes of subparagraph (A), the term "material change" includes any increase in future benefits under the contract.

Such term shall not include—

(i) any increase which is attributable to the payment of premiums necessary to fund the lowest level of future benefits payable in the 1st 7 contract years (determined after taking into account death benefit increases described in subparagraph (A) or (B) of section 7702(e)(2)) or to crediting of interest or other earnings (including policyholder dividends) in respect of such premiums, and

(ii) to the extent provided in regulations, any cost-of-living increase based on an established broad-based index if such increase is funded ratably over the remaining life of the the [sic] contract.

P.L. 101-239, §7815(a)(4)(A)-(B):

Amended Code Sec. 7702A(c)(4) by striking "under $10,000" in the paragraph heading and inserting "of $10,000 or less", and by striking "the same insurer" and inserting "the same policyholder". **Effective** as if included in the provision of P.L. 100-647 to which it relates.

[Sec. 7702A(d)]

(d) DISTRIBUTIONS AFFECTED.—If a contract fails to meet the 7-pay test of subsection (b), such contract shall be treated as failing to meet such requirements only in the case of—

(1) distributions during the contract year in which the failure takes effect and during any subsequent contract year, and

(2) under regulations prescribed by the Secretary, distributions (not described in paragraph (1)) in anticipation of such failure.

For purposes of the preceding sentence, any distribution which is made within 2 years before the failure to meet the 7-pay test shall be treated as made in anticipation of such failure.

[Sec. 7702A(e)]

(e) DEFINITIONS.—For purposes of this section—

(1) AMOUNT PAID.—

(A) IN GENERAL.—The term "amount paid" means—

(i) the premiums paid under the contract, reduced by

(ii) amounts to which section 72(e) applies (determined without regard to paragraph (4)(A) thereof) but not including amounts includible in gross income.

(B) TREATMENT OF CERTAIN PREMIUMS RETURNED.—If, in order to comply with the requirements of subsection (b), any portion of any premium paid during any contract year is returned by the insurance company (with interest) within 60 days after the end of such contract year, the amount so returned (excluding interest) shall be deemed to reduce the sum of the premiums paid under the contract during such contract year.

DEFINITIONS

(C) INTEREST RETURNED INCLUDIBLE IN GROSS INCOME.—Notwithstanding the provisions of section 72(e), the amount of any interest returned as provided in subparagraph (B) shall be includible in the gross income of the recipient.

(2) CONTRACT YEAR.—The term "contract year" means the 12-month period beginning with the 1st month for which the contract is in effect, and each 12-month period beginning with the corresponding month in subsequent calendar years.

(3) OTHER TERMS.—Except as otherwise provided in this section, terms used in this section shall have the same meaning as when used in section 7702.

Amendments

• **1988, Technical and Miscellaneous Revenue Act of 1988 (P.L. 100-647)**

P.L. 100-647, §5012(c)(1):

Amended Chapter 79 by inserting after section 7702 a new section 7702A. **Effective**, generally, for contracts entered into on or after 6-21-88. See, also, Act Sec. 5012(e)(2)-(5), below.

P.L. 100-647, §5012(e)(2)-(5), as amended by P.L. 101-239, §7815(a)(2), provides:

(2) SPECIAL RULE WHERE DEATH BENEFIT INCREASES BY MORE THAN $150,000.—If the death benefit under the contract increases by more than $150,000 over the death benefit under the contract in effect on October 20, 1988, the rules of section 7702A(c)(3) of the 1986 Code (as added by this section) shall apply in determining whether such contract is issued on or after June 21, 1988. The preceding sentence shall not apply in the case of a contract which, as of June 21, 1988, required at least 7 level annual premium payments and under which the policyholder makes at least 7 level annual premium payments.

(3) CERTAIN OTHER MATERIAL CHANGES TAKEN INTO ACCOUNT.—A contract entered into before June 21, 1988, shall be treated as entered into after such date if—

(A) on or after June 21, 1988, the death benefit under the contract is increased (or a qualified additional benefit is increased or added) and before June 21, 1988, the owner of the contract did not have a unilateral right under the contract to obtain such increase or addition without providing additional evidence of insurability, or

(B) the contract is converted after June 20, 1988, from a term life insurance contract to a life insurance contract providing coverage other than term life insurance coverage without regard to any right of the owner of the contract to such conversion.

(4) CERTAIN EXCHANGES PERMITTED.—In the case of a modified endowment contract which—

(A) required at least 7 annual level premium payments,

(B) is entered into after June 20, 1988, and before the date of the enactment of this Act, and

(C) is exchanged within 3 months after such date of enactment for a life insurance contract which meets the requirements of section 7702A(b),

the contract which is received in exchange for such contract shall not be treated as a modified endowment contract if the taxpayer elects, notwithstanding section 1035 of the 1986 Code, to recognize gain on such exchange.

(5) SPECIAL RULE FOR ANNUITY CONTRACTS.—In the case of annuity contracts, the amendments made by subsection (d) shall apply to contracts entered into after October 21, 1988.

[Sec. 7702B]

SEC. 7702B. TREATMENT OF QUALIFIED LONG-TERM CARE INSURANCE.

[Sec. 7702B(a)]

(a) IN GENERAL.—For purposes of this title—

(1) a qualified long-term care insurance contract shall be treated as an accident and health insurance contract,

(2) amounts (other than policyholder dividends, as defined in section 808, or premium refunds) received under a qualified long-term care insurance contract shall be treated as amounts received for personal injuries and sickness and shall be treated as reimbursement for expenses actually incurred for medical care (as defined in section 213(d)),

(3) any plan of an employer providing coverage under a qualified long-term care insurance contract shall be treated as an accident and health plan with respect to such coverage,

(4) except as provided in subsection (e)(3), amounts paid for a qualified long-term care insurance contract providing the benefits described in subsection (b)(2)(A) shall be treated as payments made for insurance for purposes of section 213(d)(1)(D), and

(5) a qualified long-term care insurance contract shall be treated as a guaranteed renewable contract subject to the rules of section 816(e).

Amendments

• **2010, Patient Protection and Affordable Care Act (P.L. 111-148)**

P.L. 111-148, §8002 [repealed by P.L. 112-240, §642(b)(1)], provides:

SEC. 8002. ESTABLISHMENT OF NATIONAL VOLUNTARY INSURANCE PROGRAM FOR PURCHASING COMMUNITY LIVING ASSISTANCE SERVICES AND SUPPORT.

(a) ESTABLISHMENT OF CLASS PROGRAM.—

(1) IN GENERAL.—The Public Health Service Act (42 U.S.C. 201 et seq.), as amended by section 4302(a), is amended by adding at the end the following:

* * *

"SEC. 3210. TAX TREATMENT OF PROGRAM.

"The CLASS program shall be treated for purposes of the Internal Revenue Code of 1986 in the same manner as a qualified long-term care insurance contract for qualified long-term care services.".

[Sec. 7702B(b)]

(b) QUALIFIED LONG-TERM CARE INSURANCE CONTRACT.—For purposes of this title—

(1) IN GENERAL.—The term "qualified long-term care insurance contract" means any insurance contract if—

(A) the only insurance protection provided under such contract is coverage of qualified long-term care services,

(B) such contract does not pay or reimburse expenses incurred for services or items to the extent that such expenses are reimbursable under title XVIII of the Social Security Act or would be so reimbursable but for the application of a deductible or coinsurance amount,

(C) such contract is guaranteed renewable,

(D) such contract does not provide for a cash surrender value or other money that can be—

(i) paid, assigned, or pledged as collateral for a loan, or

(ii) borrowed,

other than as provided in subparagraph (E) or paragraph (2)(C),

(E) all refunds of premiums, and all policyholder dividends or similar amounts, under such contract are to be applied as a reduction in future premiums or to increase future benefits, and

(F) such contract meets the requirements of subsection (g).

(2) SPECIAL RULES.—

(A) PER DIEM, ETC. PAYMENTS PERMITTED.—A contract shall not fail to be described in subparagraph (A) or (B) of paragraph (1) by reason of payments being made on a per diem or other periodic basis without regard to the expenses incurred during the period to which the payments relate.

(B) SPECIAL RULES RELATING TO MEDICARE.—

(i) Paragraph (1)(B) shall not apply to expenses which are reimbursable under title XVIII of the Social Security Act only as a secondary payor.

(ii) No provision of law shall be construed or applied so as to prohibit the offering of a qualified long-term care insurance contract on the basis that the contract coordinates its benefits with those provided under such title.

(C) REFUNDS OF PREMIUMS.—Paragraph (1)(E) shall not apply to any refund on the death of the insured, or on a complete surrender or cancellation of the contract, which cannot exceed the aggregate premiums paid under the contract. Any refund on a complete surrender or cancellation of the contract shall be includible in gross income to the extent that any deduction or exclusion was allowable with respect to the premiums.

DEFINITIONS

[Sec. 7702B(c)]

(c) QUALIFIED LONG-TERM CARE SERVICES.—For purposes of this section—

(1) IN GENERAL.—The term "qualified long-term care services" means necessary diagnostic, preventive, therapeutic, curing, treating, mitigating, and rehabilitative services, and maintenance or personal care services, which—

(A) are required by a chronically ill individual, and

(B) are provided pursuant to a plan of care prescribed by a licensed health care practitioner.

(2) CHRONICALLY ILL INDIVIDUAL.—

(A) IN GENERAL.—The term "chronically ill individual" means any individual who has been certified by a licensed health care practitioner as—

(i) being unable to perform (without substantial assistance from another individual) at least 2 activities of daily living for a period of at least 90 days due to a loss of functional capacity,

(ii) having a level of disability similar (as determined under regulations prescribed by the Secretary in consultation with the Secretary of Health and Human Services) to the level of disability described in clause (i), or

(iii) requiring substantial supervision to protect such individual from threats to health and safety due to severe cognitive impairment.

Such term shall not include any individual otherwise meeting the requirements of the preceding sentence unless within the preceding 12-month period a licensed health care practitioner has certified that such individual meets such requirements.

(B) ACTIVITIES OF DAILY LIVING.—For purposes of subparagraph (A), each of the following is an activity of daily living:

(i) Eating.

(ii) Toileting.

(iii) Transferring.

(iv) Bathing.

(v) Dressing.

(vi) Continence.

A contract shall not be treated as a qualified long-term care insurance contract unless the determination of whether an individual is a chronically ill individual described in subparagraph (A)(i) takes into account at least 5 of such activities.

(3) MAINTENANCE OR PERSONAL CARE SERVICES.—The term "maintenance or personal care services" means any care the primary purpose of which is the provision of needed assistance with any of the disabilities as a result of which the individual is a chronically ill individual (including the protection from threats to health and safety due to severe cognitive impairment).

(4) LICENSED HEALTH CARE PRACTITIONER.—The term "licensed health care practitioner" means any physician (as defined in section 1861(r)(1) of the Social Security Act) and any registered professional nurse, licensed social worker, or other individual who meets such requirements as may be prescribed by the Secretary.

Amendments

• 1997, Taxpayer Relief Act of 1997 (P.L. 105-34)

P.L. 105-34, § 1602(b):

Amended Code Sec. 7702B(c)(2)(B) by inserting "described in subparagraph (A)(i)" after "chronically ill individual" in the last sentence. **Effective** as if included in the provision of P.L. 104-191 to which it relates [generally **effective** for contracts issued after 12-31-96.—CCH].

[Sec. 7702B(d)]

(d) AGGREGATE PAYMENTS IN EXCESS OF LIMITS.—

(1) IN GENERAL.—If the aggregate of—

(A) the periodic payments received for any period under all qualified long-term care insurance contracts which are treated as made for qualified long-term care services for an insured, and

(B) the periodic payments received for such period which are treated under section 101(g) as paid by reason of the death of such insured,

exceeds the per diem limitation for such period, such excess shall be includible in gross income without regard to section 72. A payment shall not be taken into account under subparagraph (B) if the insured is a terminally ill individual (as defined in section 101(g)) at the time the payment is received.

(2) PER DIEM LIMITATION.—For purposes of paragraph (1), the per diem limitation for any period is an amount equal to the excess (if any) of—

(A) the greater of—

(i) the dollar amount in effect for such period under paragraph (4), or

(ii) the costs incurred for qualified long-term care services provided for the insured for such period, over

(B) the aggregate payments received as reimbursements (through insurance or otherwise) for qualified long-term care services provided for the insured during such period.

(3) AGGREGATION RULES.—For purposes of this subsection—

(A) all persons receiving periodic payments described in paragraph (1) with respect to the same insured shall be treated as 1 person, and

(B) the per diem limitation determined under paragraph (2) shall be allocated first to the insured and any remaining limitation shall be allocated among the other such persons in such manner as the Secretary shall prescribe.

(4) DOLLAR AMOUNT.—The dollar amount in effect under this subsection shall be $175 per day (or the equivalent amount in the case of payments on another periodic basis).

(5) INFLATION ADJUSTMENT.—In the case of a calendar year after 1997, the dollar amount contained in paragraph (4) shall be increased at the same time and in the same manner as amounts are increased pursuant to section 213(d)(10).

(6) PERIODIC PAYMENTS.—For purposes of this subsection, the term "periodic payment" means any payment (whether on a periodic basis or otherwise) made without regard to the extent of the costs incurred by the payee for qualified long-term care services.

[Sec. 7702B(e)]

(e) TREATMENT OF COVERAGE PROVIDED AS PART OF A LIFE INSURANCE OR ANNUITY CONTRACT.—Except as otherwise provided in regulations prescribed by the Secretary, in the case of any long-term care insurance coverage (whether or not qualified) provided by a rider on or as part of a life insurance contract or an annuity contract—

DEFINITIONS

(1) IN GENERAL.—This title shall apply as if the portion of the contract providing such coverage is a separate contract.

(2) DENIAL OF DEDUCTION UNDER SECTION 213.—No deduction shall be allowed under section 213(a) for any payment made for coverage under a qualified long-term care insurance contract if such payment is made as a charge against the cash surrender value of a life insurance contract or the cash value of an annuity contract.

(3) PORTION DEFINED.—For purposes of this subsection, the term "portion" means only the terms and benefits under a life insurance contract or annuity contract that are in addition to the terms and benefits under the contract without regard to long-term care insurance coverage.

(4) ANNUITY CONTRACTS TO WHICH PARAGRAPH (1) DOES NOT APPLY.—For purposes of this subsection, none of the following shall be treated as an annuity contract:

(A) A trust described in section 401(a) which is exempt from tax under section 501(a).

(B) A contract—

(i) purchased by a trust described in subparagraph (A),

(ii) purchased as part of a plan described in section 403(a),

(iii) described in section 403(b),

(iv) provided for employees of a life insurance company under a plan described in section 818(a)(3), or

(v) from an individual retirement account or an individual retirement annuity.

(C) A contract purchased by an employer for the benefit of the employee (or the employee's spouse).

Any dividend described in section 404(k) which is received by a participant or beneficiary shall, for purposes of this paragraph, be treated as paid under a separate contract to which subparagraph (B)(i) applies.

Amendments

• **2006, Pension Protection Act of 2006 (P.L. 109-280)**

P.L. 109-280, §844(c):

Amended Code Sec. 7702B(e). **Effective** for contracts issued after 12-31-1996, but only with respect to tax years beginning after 12-31-2009. Prior to amendment, Code Sec. 7702B(e) read as follows:

(e) TREATMENT OF COVERAGE PROVIDED AS PART OF A LIFE INSURANCE CONTRACT.—Except as otherwise provided in regulations prescribed by the Secretary, in the case of any long-term care insurance coverage (whether or not qualified) provided by a rider on or as part of a life insurance contract—

(1) IN GENERAL.—This title shall apply as if the portion of the contract providing such coverage is a separate contract.

(2) APPLICATION OF SECTION 7702.—Section 7702(c)(2) (relating to the guideline premium limitation) shall be applied by increasing the guideline premium limitation with respect to a life insurance contract, as of any date—

(A) by the sum of any charges (but not premium payments) against the life insurance contract's cash surrender value (within the meaning of section 7702(f)(2)(A)) for such coverage made to that date under the contract, less

(B) any such charges the imposition of which reduces the premiums paid for the contract (within the meaning of section 7702(f)(1)).

(3) APPLICATION OF SECTION 213.—No deduction shall be allowed under section 213(a) for charges against the life insurance contract's cash surrender value described in paragraph (2), unless such charges are includible in income as a result of the application of section 72(e)(10) and the rider is a qualified long-term care insurance contract under subsection (b).

(4) PORTION DEFINED.—For purposes of this subsection, the term "portion" means only the terms and benefits under a life insurance contract that are in addition to the terms and benefits under the contract without regard to long-term care insurance coverage.

P.L. 109-280, §844(f):

Amended Code Sec. 7702B(e)(1), as in effect before amendment by Act Sec. 844(c), by striking "section" and inserting "title". **Effective** as if included in section 321(a) of the Health Insurance Portability and Accountability Act of 1996 [**effective** for contracts issued after 12-31-96.—CCH].

• **1998, IRS Restructuring and Reform Act of 1998 (P.L. 105-206)**

P.L. 105-206, §6023(28):

Amended the paragraph heading of paragraph (2) of Code Sec. 7702B(e) by inserting "SECTION" after "APPLICATION OF". **Effective** 7-22-98.

[Sec. 7702B(f)]

(f) TREATMENT OF CERTAIN STATE-MAINTAINED PLANS.—

(1) IN GENERAL.—If—

(A) an individual receives coverage for qualified long-term care services under a State long-term care plan, and

(B) the terms of such plan would satisfy the requirements of subsection (b) were such plan an insurance contract,

such plan shall be treated as a qualified long-term care insurance contract for purposes of this title.

(2) STATE LONG-TERM CARE PLAN.—For purposes of paragraph (1), the term "State long-term care plan" means any plan—

(A) which is established and maintained by a State or an instrumentality of a State,

(B) which provides coverage only for qualified long-term care services, and

(C) under which such coverage is provided only to—

(i) employees and former employees of a State (or any political subdivision or instrumentality of a State),

(ii) the spouses of such employees, and

(iii) individuals bearing a relationship to such employees or spouses which is described in any of subparagraphs (A) through (G) of section 152(d)(2).

Amendments

• **2004, Working Families Tax Relief Act of 2004 (P.L. 108-311)**

P.L. 108-311, §207(25):

Amended Code Sec. 7702B(f)(2)(C)(iii) by striking "paragraphs (1) through (8) of section 152(a)" and inserting "subparagraphs (A) through (G) of section 152(d)(2)". **Effective** for tax years beginning after 12-31-2004.

• **1996, Health Insurance Portability and Accountability Act of 1996 (P.L. 104-191)**

P.L. 104-191, §321(a):

Amended chapter 79 by inserting after Code Sec. 7702A a new Code Sec. 7702B. For the **effective** date and special rules, see Act Sec. 321(f)-(g), below.

P.L. 104-191, §321(f)-(g), provides:

(f) EFFECTIVE DATES.—

(1) GENERAL EFFECTIVE DATES.—

(A) IN GENERAL.—Except as provided in subparagraph (B), the amendments made by this section shall apply to contracts issued after December 31, 1996.

(B) RESERVE METHOD.—The amendment made by subsection (b) shall apply to contracts issued after December 31, 1997.

(2) CONTINUATION OF EXISTING POLICIES.—In the case of any contract issued before January 1, 1997, which met the long-term care insurance requirements of the State in which the contract was sitused at the time the contract was issued—

(A) such contract shall be treated for purposes of the Internal Revenue Code of 1986 as a qualified long-term care insurance contract (as defined in section 7702B(b) of such Code), and

(B) services provided under, or reimbursed by, such contract shall be treated for such purposes as qualified long-term care services (as defined in section 7702B(c) of such Code).

In the case of an individual who is covered on December 31, 1996, under a State long-term care plan (as defined in section 7702B(f)(2) of such Code), the terms of such plan on such date shall be treated for purposes of the preceding sentence as a contract issued on such date which met the long-term care insurance requirements of such State.

(3) EXCHANGES OF EXISTING POLICIES.—If, after the date of enactment of this Act and before January 1, 1998, a contract providing for long-term care insurance coverage is exchanged solely for a qualified long-term care insurance contract (as defined in section 7702B(b) of such Code), no gain or loss shall be recognized on the exchange. If, in addition to a qualified long-term care insurance contract, money or other property is received in the exchange, then any gain shall be recognized to the extent of the sum of the money and the fair market value of the other property received. For purposes of this paragraph, the cancellation of a contract providing for long-term care insurance coverage and reinvestment of the cancellation proceeds in a qualified long-term care insurance contract within 60 days thereafter shall be treated as an exchange.

(4) ISSUANCE OF CERTAIN RIDERS PERMITTED.—For purposes of applying sections 101(f), 7702, and 7702A of the Internal Revenue Code of 1986 to any contract—

DEFINITIONS

(A) the issuance of a rider which is treated as a qualified long-term care insurance contract under section 7702B, and

(B) the addition of any provision required to conform any other long-term care rider to be so treated,

shall not be treated as a modification or material change of such contract.

(5) APPLICATION OF PER DIEM LIMITATION TO EXISTING CONTRACTS.—The amount of per diem payments made under a contract issued on or before July 31, 1996, with respect to an insured which are excludable from gross income by reason of section 7702B of the Internal Revenue Code of 1986 (as added by this section) shall not be reduced under subsection (d)(2)(B) thereof by reason of reimbursements received under a contract issued on or before such date. The preceding sentence shall cease to apply as of the date (after July 31, 1996) such contract is exchanged or there is any contract modification which results in an increase in the amount of such per diem payments or the amount of such reimbursements.

(g) LONG-TERM CARE STUDY REQUEST.—The Chairman of the Committee on Ways and Means of the House of Representatives and the Chairman of the Committee on Finance of the Senate shall jointly request the National Association of Insurance Commissioners, in consultation with representatives of the insurance industry and consumer organizations, to formulate, develop, and conduct a study to determine the marketing and other effects of per diem limits on certain types of long-term care policies. If the National Association of Insurance Commissioners agrees to the study request, the National Association of Insurance Commissioners shall report the results of its study to such committees not later than 2 years after accepting the request.

[Sec. 7702B(g)]

(g) CONSUMER PROTECTION PROVISIONS.—

(1) IN GENERAL.—The requirements of this subsection are met with respect to any contract if the contract meets—

(A) the requirements of the model regulation and model Act described in paragraph (2),

(B) the disclosure requirement of paragraph (3), and

(C) the requirements relating to nonforfeitability under paragraph (4).

(2) REQUIREMENTS OF MODEL REGULATION AND ACT.—

(A) IN GENERAL.—The requirements of this paragraph are met with respect to any contract if such contract meets—

(i) MODEL REGULATION.—The following requirements of the model regulation:

(I) Section 7A (relating to guaranteed renewal or noncancellability), and the requirements of section 6B of the model Act relating to such section 7A.

(II) Section 7B (relating to prohibitions on limitations and exclusions).

(III) Section 7C (relating to extension of benefits).

(IV) Section 7D (relating to continuation or conversion of coverage).

(V) Section 7E (relating to discontinuance and replacement of policies).

(VI) Section 8 (relating to unintentional lapse).

(VII) Section 9 (relating to disclosure), other than section 9F thereof.

(VIII) Section 10 (relating to prohibitions against post-claims underwriting).

(IX) Section 11 (relating to minimum standards).

(X) Section 12 (relating to requirement to offer inflation protection), except that any requirement for a signature on a rejection of inflation protection shall permit the signature to be on an application or on a separate form.

(XI) Section 23 (relating to prohibition against preexisting conditions and probationary periods in replacement policies or certificates).

(ii) MODEL ACT.—The following requirements of the model Act:

(I) Section 6C (relating to preexisting conditions).

(II) Section 6D (relating to prior hospitalization).

(B) DEFINITIONS.—For purposes of this paragraph—

(i) MODEL PROVISIONS.—The terms "model regulation" and "model Act" mean the long-term care insurance model regulation, and the long-term care insurance model Act, respectively, promulgated by the National Association of Insurance Commissioners (as adopted as of January 1993).

(ii) COORDINATION.—Any provision of the model regulation or model Act listed under clause (i) or (ii) of subparagraph (A) shall be treated as including any other provision of such regulation or Act necessary to implement the provision.

(iii) DETERMINATION.—For purposes of this section and section 4980C, the determination of whether any requirement of a model regulation or the model Act has been met shall be made by the Secretary.

(3) DISCLOSURE REQUIREMENT.—The requirement of this paragraph is met with respect to any contract if such contract meets the requirements of section 4980C(d).

(4) NONFORFEITURE REQUIREMENTS.—

(A) IN GENERAL.—The requirements of this paragraph are met with respect to any level premium contract, if the issuer of such contract offers to the policyholder, including any group policyholder, a nonforfeiture provision meeting the requirements of subparagraph (B).

(B) REQUIREMENTS OF PROVISION.—The nonforfeiture provision required under subparagraph (A) shall meet the following requirements:

(i) The nonforfeiture provision shall be appropriately captioned.

(ii) The nonforfeiture provision shall provide for a benefit available in the event of a default in the payment of any premiums and the amount of the benefit may be adjusted subsequent to being initially granted only as necessary to reflect changes in claims, persistency, and interest as reflected in changes in rates for premium paying contracts approved by the appropriate State regulatory agency for the same contract form.

(iii) The nonforfeiture provision shall provide at least one of the following:

(I) Reduced paid-up insurance.

(II) Extended term insurance.

(III) Shortened benefit period.

(IV) Other similar offerings approved by the appropriate state regulatory agency.

(5) CROSS REFERENCE.—

For coordination of the requirements of this subsection with State requirements, see section 4980C(f).

Amendments

• **1997, Taxpayer Relief Act of 1997 (P.L. 105-34)**

P.L. 105-34, §1602(e):

Amended Code Sec. 7702B(g)(4)(B)(ii)-(iii) by striking "Secretary" and inserting "appropriate State regulatory agency". **Effective** as if included in the provision of P.L. 104-191 to which it relates [generally **effective** for contracts issued after 12-31-96.—CCH].

• **1996, Health Insurance Portability and Accountability Act of 1996 (P.L. 104-191)**

P.L. 104-191, §325:

Amended Code Sec. 7702B (as added by Act Sec. 321) by adding at the end a new subsection (g). **Effective** for contracts issued after 12-31-96. For a transitional rule, see Act Sec. 321(f), below.

P.L. 104-191, § 321(f), provides:

(f) EFFECTIVE DATES.—

(1) GENERAL EFFECTIVE DATES.—

(A) IN GENERAL.—Except as provided in subparagraph (B), the amendments made by this section shall apply to contracts issued after December 31, 1996.

(B) RESERVE METHOD.—The amendment made by subsection (b) shall apply to contracts issued after December 31, 1997.

(2) CONTINUATION OF EXISTING POLICIES.—In the case of any contract issued before January 1, 1997, which met the long-term care insurance requirements of the State in which the contract was sitused at the time the contract was issued—

(A) such contract shall be treated for purposes of the Internal Revenue Code of 1986 as a qualified long-term care insurance contract (as defined in section 7702B(b) of such Code), and

(B) services provided under, or reimbursed by, such contract shall be treated for such purposes as qualified long-term care services (as defined in section 7702B(c) of such Code).

In the case of an individual who is covered on December 31, 1996, under a State long-term care plan (as defined in section 7702B(f)(2) of such Code), the terms of such plan on such date shall be treated for purposes of the preceding sentence as a contract issued on such date which met the long-term care insurance requirements of such State.

(3) EXCHANGES OF EXISTING POLICIES.—If, after the date of enactment of this Act and before January 1, 1998, a contract providing for long-term care insurance coverage is exchanged solely for a qualified long-term care insurance contract (as defined in section 7702B(b) of such Code), no gain or loss shall be recognized on the exchange. If, in addition to a qualified long-term care insurance contract, money or other property is received in the exchange, then any gain shall be recognized to the extent of the sum of the money and the fair market value of the other property received. For purposes of this paragraph, the cancellation of a contract providing for long-term care insurance coverage and reinvestment of the cancellation proceeds in a qualified long-term care insurance contract within 60 days thereafter shall be treated as an exchange.

(4) ISSUANCE OF CERTAIN RIDERS PERMITTED.—For purposes of applying sections 101(f), 7702, and 7702A of the Internal Revenue Code of 1986 to any contract—

(A) the issuance of a rider which is treated as a qualified long-term care insurance contract under section 7702B, and

(B) the addition of any provision required to conform any other long-term care rider to be so treated,

shall not be treated as a modification or material change of such contract.

(5) APPLICATION OF PER DIEM LIMITATION TO EXISTING CONTRACTS.—The amount of per diem payments made under a contract issued on or before July 31, 1996, with respect to an insured which are excludable from gross income by reason of section 7702B of the Internal Revenue Code of 1986 (as added by this section) shall not be reduced under subsection (d)(2)(B) thereof by reason of reimbursements received under a contract issued on or before such date. The preceding sentence shall cease to apply as of the date (after July 31, 1996) such contract is exchanged or there is any contract modification which results in an increase in the amount of such per diem payments or the amount of such reimbursements.

[Sec. 7703]

SEC. 7703. DETERMINATION OF MARITAL STATUS.

[Sec. 7703(a)]

(a) GENERAL RULE.—For purposes of part V of subchapter B of chapter 1 and those provisions of this title which refer to this subsection—

(1) the determination of whether an individual is married shall be made as of the close of his taxable year; except that if his spouse dies during his taxable year such determination shall be made as of the time of such death; and

(2) an individual legally separated from his spouse under a decree of divorce or of separate maintenance shall not be considered as married.

[Sec. 7703(b)]

(b) CERTAIN MARRIED INDIVIDUALS LIVING APART.—For purposes of those provisions of this title which refer to this subsection, if—

(1) an individual who is married (within the meaning of subsection (a)) and who files a separate return maintains as his home a household which constitutes for more than one-half of the taxable year the principal place of abode of a child (within the meaning of section 152(f)(1)) with respect to whom such individual is entitled to a deduction for the taxable year under section 151 (or would be so entitled but for section 152(e)),

(2) such individual furnishes over one-half of the cost of maintaining such household during the taxable year, and

(3) during the last 6 months of the taxable year, such individual's spouse is not a member of such household,

such individual shall not be considered as married.

Amendments

• **2004, Working Families Tax Relief Act of 2004 (P.L. 108-311)**

P.L. 108-311, § 207(26)(A)-(B):

Amended Code Sec. 7703(b)(1) by striking "151(c)(3)" and inserting "152(f)(1)" and by striking "paragraph (2) or (4) of" after "entitled but for". **Effective** for tax years beginning after 12-31-2004.

• **1988, Technical and Miscellaneous Revenue Act of 1988 (P.L. 100-647)**

P.L. 100-647, § 1018(u)(41):

Amended Code Sec. 7703(b) by striking out "section 151(e)(3)" and inserting in lieu thereof "section 151(c)(3)". **Effective** as if included in the provision of P.L. 99-514 to which it relates.

• **1986, Tax Reform Act of 1986 (P.L. 99-514)**

P.L. 99-514, § 1301(j)(2)(A):

Added Code Sec. 7703. [P.L. 99-514, § 1301(j)(2) redesignated the substance of former Code Sec. 143 in new Code Sec. 7703.—CCH.]Text of former Code Sec. 143 reads as follows:

SEC. 143. DETERMINATION OF MARITAL STATUS.

[Sec. 143(a)]

(a) GENERAL RULE.—For purposes of part V—

(1) The determination of whether an individual is married shall be made as of the close of his taxable year; except that if his spouse dies during his taxable year such determination shall be made as of the time of such death; and

(2) An individual legally separated from his spouse under a decree of divorce or of separate maintenance shall not be considered as married.

Amendments

• **1977, Tax Reduction and Simplification Act of 1977 (P.L. 95-30)**

P.L. 95-30, § 101(d)(4):

Amended Code Sec. 143(a) by deleting "this part and" which formerly appeared in front of "part V". **Effective** for tax years beginning after 12-31-76.

• **1976, Tax Reform Act of 1976 (P.L. 94-455)**

P.L. 94-455, § 1901(a)(22):

Amended Code Sec. 143(a) substituted "this part and part V" for "this part". **Effective** for tax years beginning after 12-31-76.

[Sec. 143(b)]

(b) CERTAIN MARRIED INDIVIDUALS LIVING APART.—For purposes of those provisions of this title which refer to this subsection, if—

(1) an individual who is married (within the meaning of subsection (a)) and who files a separate return maintains as his home a household which constitutes for more than one-half of the taxable year the principal place of abode of a child (within the meaning of section 151(e)(3)) with respect to whom such individual is entitled to a deduction for the taxable year under section 151 (or would be so entitled but for paragraph (2) or (4) of section 152(e)),

(2) such individual furnishes over one-half of the cost of maintaining such household during the taxable year, and

(3) during the last 6 months of the taxable year, such individual's spouse is not a member of such household, such individual shall not be considered as married.

Amendments

• **1984, Deficit Reduction Act of 1984 (P.L. 98-369)**

P.L. 98-369, § 423(c)(1):

Amended Code Sec. 143(b). **Effective** for tax years beginning after 12-31-84. Prior to amendment, Code Sec. 143(b) read as follows:

(b) Certain Married Individuals Living Apart.—For purposes of part V, if—

(1) an individual who is married (within the meaning of subsection (a)) and who files a separate return maintains as his home a household which constitutes for more than one-half of the taxable year the principal place of abode of a dependent (A) who (within the meaning of section 152) is a son, stepson, daughter, or step-daughter of the individual, and (B) with respect to whom such individual is entitled to a deduction for the taxable year under section 151,

(2) such individual furnishes over half of the cost of maintaining such household during the taxable year, and

(3) during the entire taxable year such individual's spouse is not a member of such household, such individual shall not be considered as married.

• **1977, Tax Reduction and Simplification Act of 1977 (P.L. 95-30)**

P.L. 95-30, § 101(d)(4):

Amended Code Sec. 143(b) by deleting "this part and" which formerly appeared in front of "part V". **Effective** for tax years beginning after 12-31-76.

DEFINITIONS

- **1976, Tax Reform Act of 1976 (P.L. 94-455)**

P.L. 94-455, § 1901(a)(22):

Amended Code Sec. 143(b) by substituting "this part and part V" for "this part". **Effective** for tax years beginning after 12-31-76.

- **1969, Tax Reform Act of 1969 (P.L. 91-172)**

P.L. 91-172, § 802(b):

Amended Code Sec. 143 by substituting "(a) General Rule—For purposes of this part—" in place of "For purposes of this part—" and by adding Code Sec. 143(b). **Effective** for tax years beginning after 12-31-69.

[Sec. 7704]

SEC. 7704. CERTAIN PUBLICLY TRADED PARTNERSHIPS TREATED AS CORPORATIONS.

[Sec. 7704(a)]

(a) GENERAL RULE.—For purposes of this title, except as provided in subsection (c), a publicly traded partnership shall be treated as a corporation.

[Sec. 7704(b)]

(b) PUBLICLY TRADED PARTNERSHIP.—For purposes of this section, the term "publicly traded partnership" means any partnership if—

(1) interests in such partnership are traded on an established securities market, or

(2) interests in such partnership are readily tradable on a secondary market (or the substantial equivalent thereof).

[Sec. 7704(c)]

(c) EXCEPTION FOR PARTNERSHIPS WITH PASSIVE-TYPE INCOME.—

(1) IN GENERAL.—Subsection (a) shall not apply to any publicly traded partnership for any taxable year if such partnership met the gross income requirements of paragraph (2) for such taxable year and each preceding taxable year beginning after December 31, 1987, during which the partnership (or any predecessor) was in existence. For purposes of the preceding sentence, a partnership shall not be treated as being in existence during any period before the 1st taxable year in which such partnership (or a predecessor) was a publicly traded partnership.

(2) GROSS INCOME REQUIREMENTS.—A partnership meets the gross income requirements of this paragraph for any taxable year if 90 percent or more of the gross income of such partnership for such taxable year consists of qualifying income.

(3) EXCEPTION NOT TO APPLY TO CERTAIN PARTNERSHIPS WHICH COULD QUALIFY AS REGULATED INVESTMENT COMPANIES.—This subsection shall not apply to any partnership which would be described in section 851(a) if such partnership were a domestic corporation. To the extent provided in regulations, the preceding sentence shall not apply to any partnership a principal activity of which is the buying and selling of commodities (not described in section 1221(a)(1)), or options, futures, or forwards with respect to commodities.

Amendments

- **1999, Tax Relief Extension Act of 1999 (P.L. 106-170)**

P.L. 106-170, § 532(c)(2)(V):

Amended Code Sec. 7704(c)(3) by striking "section 1221(1)" and inserting "section 1221(a)(1)". **Effective** for any instrument held, acquired, or entered into, any transaction entered into, and supplies held or acquired on or after 12-17-99.

- **1988, Technical and Miscellaneous Revenue Act of 1988 (P.L. 100-647)**

P.L. 100-647, § 2004(f)(3):

Amended Code Sec. 7704(c)(1) by adding at the end thereof a new sentence. **Effective** as if included in the provision of P.L. 100-203 to which it relates.

[Sec. 7704(d)]

(d) QUALIFYING INCOME.—For purposes of this section—

(1) IN GENERAL.—Except as otherwise provided in this subsection, the term "qualifying income" means—

(A) interest,

(B) dividends,

(C) real property rents,

(D) gain from the sale or other disposition of real property (including property described in section 1221(a)(1)),

(E) income and gains derived from the exploration, development, mining or production, processing, refining, transportation (including pipelines transporting gas, oil, or products thereof), or the marketing of any mineral or natural resource (including fertilizer, geothermal energy, and timber), [or] industrial source carbon dioxide, or the transportation or storage of any fuel described in subsection (b), (c), (d), or (e) of section 6426, or any alcohol fuel defined in section 6426(b)(4)(A) or any biodiesel fuel as defined in section 40A(d)(1),

(F) any gain from the sale or disposition of a capital asset (or property described in section 1231(b)) held for the production of income described in any of the foregoing subparagraphs of this paragraph, and

(G) in the case of a partnership described in the second sentence of subsection (c)(3), income and gains from commodities (not described in section 1221(a)(1)) or futures, forwards, and options with respect to commodities.

For purposes of subparagraph (E), the term "mineral or natural resource" means any product of a character with respect to which a deduction for depletion is allowable under section 611; except that such term shall not include any product described in subparagraph (A) or (B) of section 613(b)(7).

(2) CERTAIN INTEREST NOT QUALIFIED.—Interest shall not be treated as qualifying income if—

(A) such interest is derived in the conduct of a financial or insurance business, or

(B) such interest would be excluded from the term "interest" under section 856(f).

(3) REAL PROPERTY RENT.—The term "real property rent" means amounts which would qualify as rent from real property under section 856(d) if—

(A) such section were applied without regard to paragraph (2)(C) thereof (relating to independent contractor requirements), and

(B) stock owned, directly or indirectly, by or for a partner would not be considered as owned under section 318(a)(3)(A) by the partnership unless 5 percent or more (by value) of the interests in such partnership are owned, directly or indirectly, by or for such partner.

(4) CERTAIN INCOME QUALIFYING UNDER REGULATED INVESTMENT COMPANY OR REAL ESTATE TRUST PROVISIONS.—The term "qualifying income" also includes any income which would qualify under section 851(b)(2)(A) or 856(c)(2).

(5) SPECIAL RULE FOR DETERMINING GROSS INCOME FROM CERTAIN REAL PROPERTY SALES.—In the case of the sale or other disposition of real property described in section 1221(a)(1), gross income shall not be reduced by inventory costs.

Amendments

- **2008, Energy Improvement and Extension Act of 2008 (P.L. 110-343)**

P.L. 110-343, Division B, § 116(a):

Amended Code Sec. 7704(d)(1)(E) by inserting "or industrial source carbon dioxide" after "timber". **Effective** 10-3-2008, in tax years ending after such date.

P.L. 110-343, Division B, § 208(a):

Amended Code Sec. 7704(d)(1)(E), as amended by this Act, by striking "or industrial source carbon dioxide" and inserting ", [or] industrial source carbon dioxide, or the transportation or storage of any fuel described in subsection (b), (c), (d), or (e) of section 6426, or any alcohol fuel defined in section 6426(b)(4)(A) or any biodiesel fuel

DEFINITIONS

as defined in section 40A(d)(1)" after "timber)". **Effective** 10-3-2008, in tax years ending after such date.

• **2004, American Jobs Creation Act of 2004 (P.L. 108-357)**

P.L. 108-357, § 331(e):

Amended Code Sec. 7704(d)(4) by striking "section 851(b)(2)" and inserting "section 851(b)(2)(A)". **Effective** for tax years beginning after 10-22-2004.

• **1999, Tax Relief Extension Act of 1999 (P.L. 106-170)**

P.L. 106-170, § 532(c)(2)(W):

Amended Code Sec. 7704(d)(1)(D) by striking "section 1221(1)" and inserting "section 1221(a)(1)". **Effective** for any instrument held, acquired, or entered into, any transaction entered into, and supplies held or acquired on or after 12-17-99.

P.L. 106-170, § 532(c)(2)(X):

Amended Code Sec. 7704(d)(1)(G) by striking "section 1221(1)" and inserting "section 1221(a)(1)". **Effective** for any instrument held, acquired, or entered into, any transaction entered into, and supplies held or acquired on or after 12-17-99.

P.L. 106-170, § 532(c)(2)(Y):

Amended Code Sec. 7704(d)(5) by striking "section 1221(1)" and inserting "section 1221(a)(1)". **Effective** for any instrument held, acquired, or entered into, any transaction entered into, and supplies held or acquired on or after 12-17-99.

• **1988, Technical and Miscellaneous Revenue Act of 1988 (P.L. 100-647)**

P.L. 100-647, § 2004(f)(4):

Amended Code Sec. 7704(d)(1) by adding at the end thereof a new sentence. **Effective** as if included in the provision of P.L. 100-203 to which it relates.

P.L. 100-647, § 2004(f)(5):

Amended Code Sec. 7704(d)(3). **Effective** as if included in the provision of P.L. 100-203 to which it relates. Prior to amendment, Code Sec. 7704(d)(3) read as follows:

(3) REAL PROPERTY RENT.—The term "real property rent" means amounts which would qualify as rent from real property under section 856(d) if such section were applied without regard to paragraph (2)(C) thereof (relating to independent contractor requirements).

[Sec. 7704(e)]

(e) INADVERTENT TERMINATIONS.—If—

(1) A partnership fails to meet the gross income requirements of subsection (c)(2),

(2) the Secretary determines that such failure was inadvertent,

(3) no later than a reasonable time after the discovery of such failure, steps are taken so that such partnership once more meets such gross income requirements, and

(4) such partnership agrees to make such adjustments (including adjustments with respect to the partners) or to pay such amounts as may be required by the Secretary with respect to such period,

then, notwithstanding such failure, such entity shall be treated as continuing to meet such gross income requirements for such period.

Amendments

• **1988, Technical and Miscellaneous Revenue Act of 1988 (P.L. 100-647)**

P.L. 100-647, § 2004(f)(1):

Amended Code Sec. 7704(e)(4) by striking out "as may be required" and inserting in lieu thereof "or to pay such amounts as may be required". **Effective** as if included in the provision of P.L. 100-203 to which it relates.

[Sec. 7704(f)]

(f) EFFECT OF BECOMING CORPORATION.—As of the 1st day that a partnership is treated as a corporation under this section, for purposes of this title, such partnership shall be treated as—

(1) transferring all of its assets (subject to its liabilities) to a newly formed corporation in exchange for the stock of the corporation, and

(2) distributing such stock to its partners in liquidation of their interests in the partnership.

Amendments

• **1987, Revenue Act of 1987 (P.L. 100-203)**

P.L. 100-203, § 10211(a):

Amended chapter 79 by adding at the end thereof new section 7704. For the **effective** date, see Act Sec. 10211(c), below.

P.L. 100-203, § 10211(c), as amended by P.L. 100-647, § 2004(f)(2), provides:

(c) Effective Date.—

(1) IN GENERAL.—The amendments made by this section shall apply—

(A) except as provided in subparagraph (B), to taxable years beginning after December 31, 1987, or

(B) in the case of an existing partnership, to taxable years beginning after December 31, 1997.

(2) EXISTING PARTNERSHIP.—For purposes of this subsection—

(A) IN GENERAL.—The term "existing partnership" means any partnership if—

(i) such partnership was a publicly traded partnership on December 17, 1987,

(ii) a registration statement indicating that such partnership was to be a publicly traded partnership was filed with the securities and exchange commission with respect to such partnership on or before such date, or

(iii) with respect to such partnership, an application was filed with a state regulatory commission on or before such date seeking permission to restructure a portion of a corporation as a publicly traded partnership.

(B) SPECIAL RULE WHERE SUBSTANTIAL NEW LINE OF BUSINESS ADDED AFTER DECEMBER 17, 1987.—A partnership which, but for this subparagraph, would be treated as an existing partnership shall cease to be treated as an existing partnership as of the 1st day after December 17, 1987, on which there has been an addition of a substantial new line of business with respect to such partnership.

(C) COORDINATION WITH PASSIVE-TYPE INCOME REQUIREMENTS.—In the case of an existing partnership, paragraph (1) of section 7704(c) of the Internal Revenue Code of 1986 (as added by this section) shall be applied by substituting for "December 31, 1987" the earlier of—

(i) December 31, 1997, or

(ii) the day (if any) as of which such partnership ceases to be treated as an existing partnership by reason of subparagraph (B)."

[Sec. 7704(g)]

(g) EXCEPTION FOR ELECTING 1987 PARTNERSHIPS.—

(1) IN GENERAL.—Subsection (a) shall not apply to an electing 1987 partnership.

(2) ELECTING 1987 PARTNERSHIP.—For purposes of this subsection, the term "electing 1987 partnership" means any publicly traded partnership if—

(A) such partnership is an existing partnership (as defined in section 10211(c)(2) of the Revenue Reconciliation Act of 1987),

(B) subsection (a) has not applied (and without regard to subsection (c)(1) would not have applied) to such partnership for all prior taxable years beginning after December 31, 1987, and before January 1, 1998, and

(C) such partnership elects the application of this subsection, and consents to the application of the tax imposed by paragraph (3), for its first taxable year beginning after December 31, 1997.

A partnership which, but for this sentence, would be treated as an electing 1987 partnership shall cease to be so treated (and the election under subparagraph (C) shall cease to be in effect) as of the 1st day after December 31, 1997, on which there has been an addition of a substantial new line of business with respect to such partnership.

(3) ADDITIONAL TAX ON ELECTING PARTNERSHIPS.—

(A) IMPOSITION OF TAX.—There is hereby imposed for each taxable year on the income of each electing 1987 partnership a tax equal to 3.5 percent of such partnership's gross income for the taxable year from the active conduct of trades and businesses by the partnership.

(B) ADJUSTMENTS IN THE CASE OF TIERED PARTNERSHIPS.—For purposes of this paragraph, in the case of a partnership which is a partner in another partnership, the gross income referred to in subparagraph (A) shall include the partnership's distributive share of the gross income of such other partnership from the active conduct of trades and businesses of such other partnership. A similar rule shall apply in the case of lower-tiered partnerships.

(C) TREATMENT OF TAX.—For purposes of this title, the tax imposed by this paragraph shall be treated as imposed by chapter 1 other than for purposes of determining the amount of any credit allowable under chapter 1 and shall be paid by the partnership. Section 6655

DEFINITIONS

shall be applied to such partnership with respect to such tax in the same manner as if the partnership were a corporation, such tax were imposed by section 11, and references in such section to taxable income were references to the gross income referred to in subparagraph (A).

(4) ELECTION.—An election and consent under this subsection shall apply to the taxable year for which made and all subsequent taxable years unless revoked by the partnership. Such revocation may be made without the consent of the Secretary, but, once so revoked, may not be reinstated.

Amendments

• **1998, IRS Restructuring and Reform Act of 1998 (P.L. 105-206)**

P.L. 105-206, § 6009(b)(1):

Amended Code Sec. 7704(g)(3)(C) by striking the period at the end and inserting "and shall be paid by the partnership. Section 6655 shall be applied to such partnership with respect to such tax in the same manner as if the partnership were a corporation, such tax were imposed by section 11, and references in such section to taxable income were references to the gross income referred to in subparagraph (A)." **Effective** for tax years beginning after 7-22-98.

• **1997, Taxpayer Relief Act of 1997 (P.L. 105-34)**

P.L. 105-34, § 964(a):

Amended Code Sec. 7704 by adding at the end thereof a new subsection (g). **Effective** for tax years beginning after 12-31-97.

[Sec. 7705]

SEC. 7705. CERTIFIED PROFESSIONAL EMPLOYER ORGANIZATIONS.

[Sec. 7705(a)]

(a) IN GENERAL.—For purposes of this title, the term "certified professional employer organization" means a person who applies to be treated as a certified professional employer organization for purposes of section 3511 and has been certified by the Secretary as meeting the requirements of subsection (b).

[Sec. 7705(b)]

(b) CERTIFICATION REQUIREMENTS.—A person meets the requirements of this subsection if such person—

(1) demonstrates that such person (and any owner, officer, and other persons as may be specified in regulations) meets such requirements as the Secretary shall establish, including requirements with respect to tax status, background, experience, business location, and annual financial audits,

(2) agrees that it will satisfy the bond and independent financial review requirements of subsection (c) on an ongoing basis,

(3) agrees that it will satisfy such reporting obligations as may be imposed by the Secretary,

(4) computes its taxable income using an accrual method of accounting unless the Secretary approves another method,

(5) agrees to verify on such periodic basis as the Secretary may prescribe that it continues to meet the requirements of this subsection, and

(6) agrees to notify the Secretary in writing within such time as the Secretary may prescribe of any change that materially affects the continuing accuracy of any agreement or information that was previously made or provided under this subsection.

[Sec. 7705(c)]

(c) BOND AND INDEPENDENT FINANCIAL REVIEW.—

(1) IN GENERAL.—An organization meets the requirements of this paragraph if such organization—

(A) meets the bond requirements of paragraph (2), and

(B) meets the independent financial review requirements of paragraph (3).

(2) BOND.—

(A) IN GENERAL.—A certified professional employer organization meets the requirements of this paragraph if the organization has posted a bond for the payment of taxes under subtitle C (in a form acceptable to the Secretary) that is in an amount at least equal to the amount specified in subparagraph (B).

(B) AMOUNT OF BOND.—For the period April 1 of any calendar year through March 31 of the following calendar year, the amount of the bond required is equal to the greater of—

(i) 5 percent of the organization's liability under section 3511 for taxes imposed by subtitle C during the preceding calendar year (but not to exceed $1,000,000), or

(ii) $50,000.

(3) INDEPENDENT FINANCIAL REVIEW REQUIREMENTS.—A certified professional employer organization meets the requirements of this paragraph if such organization—

(A) has, as of the most recent audit date, caused to be prepared and provided to the Secretary (in such manner as the Secretary may prescribe) an opinion of an independent certified public accountant as to whether the certified professional employer organization's financial statements are presented fairly in accordance with generally accepted accounting principles, and

(B) provides to the Secretary an assertion regarding Federal employment tax payments and an examination level attestation on such assertion from an independent certified public accountant not later than the last day of the second month beginning after the end of each calendar quarter.

Such assertion shall state that the organization has withheld and made deposits of all taxes imposed by chapters 21, 22, and 24 in accordance with regulations imposed by the Secretary for such calendar quarter and such examination level attestation shall state that such assertion is fairly stated, in all material respects.

(4) CONTROLLED GROUP RULES.—For purposes of the requirements of paragraphs (2) and (3), all certified professional employer organizations that are members of a controlled group within the meaning of sections 414(b) and (c) shall be treated as a single organization.

(5) FAILURE TO FILE ASSERTION AND ATTESTATION.—If the certified professional employer organization fails to file the assertion and attestation required by paragraph (3) with respect to any calendar quarter, then the requirements of paragraph (3) with respect to such failure shall be treated as not satisfied for the period beginning on the due date for such attestation.

(6) AUDIT DATE.—For purposes of paragraph (3)(A), the audit date shall be six months after the completion of the organization's fiscal year.

[Sec. 7705(d)]

(d) SUSPENSION AND REVOCATION AUTHORITY.—The Secretary may suspend or revoke a certification of any person under subsection (b) for purposes of section 3511 if the Secretary determines that such person is not satisfying the agreements or requirements of subsections (b) or (c), or fails to satisfy applicable accounting, reporting, payment, or deposit requirements.

[Sec. 7705(e)]

(e) WORK SITE EMPLOYEE.—For purposes of this title—

(1) IN GENERAL.—The term "work site employee" means, with respect to a certified professional employer organization, an individual who—

(A) performs services for a customer pursuant to a contract which is between such customer and the certified professional employer organization and which meets the requirements of paragraph (2), and

(B) performs services at a work site meeting the requirements of paragraph (3).

(2) SERVICE CONTRACT REQUIREMENTS.—A contract meets the requirements of this paragraph with respect to an individual performing services for a customer if such contract is in writing and provides that the certified professional employer organization shall—

(A) assume responsibility for payment of wages to such individual, without regard to the receipt or adequacy of payment from the customer for such services,

(B) assume responsibility for reporting, withholding, and paying any applicable taxes under subtitle C, with respect to such individual's wages, without regard to the receipt or adequacy of payment from the customer for such services,

(C) assume responsibility for any employee benefits which the service contract may require the certified professional employer organization to provide, without regard to the receipt or adequacy of payment from the customer for such benefits,

(D) assume responsibility for recruiting, hiring, and firing workers in addition to the customer's responsibility for recruiting, hiring, and firing workers,

(E) maintain employee records relating to such individual, and

(F) agree to be treated as a certified professional employer organization for purposes of section 3511 with respect to such individual.

(3) WORK SITE COVERAGE REQUIREMENT.—The requirements of this paragraph are met with respect to an individual if at least 85 percent of the individuals performing services for the customer at the work site where such individual performs services are subject to 1 or more contracts with the certified professional employer organization which meet the requirements of paragraph (2) (but not taking into account those individuals who are excluded employees within the meaning of section 414(q)(5)).

[Sec. 7705(f)]

(f) PUBLIC DISCLOSURE.—The Secretary shall make available to the public the name and address of—

(1) each person certified as a professional employer organization under subsection (a), and

(2) each person whose certification as a professional employer organization is suspended or revoked under subsection (d).

[Sec. 7705(g)]

(g) DETERMINATION OF EMPLOYMENT STATUS.—Except to the extent necessary for purposes of section 3511, nothing in this section shall be construed to affect the determination of who is an employee or employer for purposes of this title.

[Sec. 7705(h)]

(h) REGULATIONS.—The Secretary shall prescribe such regulations as may be necessary or appropriate to carry out the purposes of this section.

Amendments

• 2014, Stephen Beck, Jr., Achieving a Better Life Experience Act of 2014 (P.L. 113-295)

P.L. 113-295, §206(b), Division B:

Amended Chapter 79 by adding at the end a new Code Sec. 7705. **Effective generally for wages for services performed on or after January 1 of the first calendar year beginning more than 12 months after 12-19-2014.** For special rules, see Act Sec. 206(g)(2) and (h), Division B, below:

P.L. 113-295, §206(g)(2) and (h), Division B, provides:

(2) CERTIFICATION PROGRAM.—The Secretary of the Treasury shall establish the certification program described in section 7705(b) of the Internal Revenue Code of 1986, as added by subsection (b), not later than 6 months before the effective date determined under paragraph (1).

(h) NO INFERENCE.—Nothing contained in this section or the amendments made by this section shall be construed to create any inference with respect to the determination of who is an employee or employer—

(1) for Federal tax purposes (other than the purposes set forth in the amendments made by this section), or

(2) for purposes of any other provision of law.

CHAPTER 80—GENERAL RULES

SUBCHAPTER A.	Application of internal revenue laws.
SUBCHAPTER B.	Effective date and related provisions.
SUBCHAPTER C.	Provisions affecting more than one subtitle.

Subchapter A—Application of Internal Revenue Laws

Sec. 7801.	Authority of the Department of the Treasury.
Sec. 7802.	Internal Revenue Service Oversight Board.
Sec. 7803.	Commissioner of Internal Revenue; other officials.
Sec. 7804.	Other personnel.
Sec. 7805.	Rules and regulations.
Sec. 7806.	Construction of title.
Sec. 7807.	Rules in effect upon enactment of this title.
Sec. 7808.	Depositaries for collections.
Sec. 7809.	Deposit of collections.
Sec. 7810.	Revolving fund for redemption of real property.
Sec. 7811.	Taxpayer assistance orders.
Sec. 7812.	Streamlined critical pay authority for information technology positions.

[Sec. 7801]

SEC. 7801. AUTHORITY OF THE DEPARTMENT OF THE TREASURY.

[Sec. 7801(a)]

(a) POWERS AND DUTIES OF SECRETARY.—

(1) IN GENERAL.—Except as otherwise expressly provided by law, the administration and enforcement of this title shall be performed by or under the supervision of the Secretary of the Treasury.

APPLICATION OF LAWS

(2) ADMINISTRATION AND ENFORCEMENT OF CERTAIN PROVISIONS BY ATTORNEY GENERAL.—

(A) IN GENERAL.—The administration and enforcement of the following provisions of this title shall be performed by or under the supervision of the Attorney General; and the term "Secretary" or "Secretary of the Treasury" shall, when applied to those provisions, mean the Attorney General; and the term "internal revenue officer" shall, when applied to those provisions, mean any officer of the Bureau of Alcohol, Tobacco, Firearms, and Explosives so designated by the Attorney General:

(i) Chapter 53.

(ii) Chapters 61 through 80, to the extent such chapters relate to the enforcement and administration of the provisions referred to in clause (i).

(B) USE OF EXISTING RULINGS AND INTERPRETATIONS.—Nothing in the Homeland Security Act of 2002 alters or repeals the rulings and interpretations of the Bureau of Alcohol, Tobacco, and Firearms in effect on the effective date of such Act, which concerns the provisions of this title referred to in subparagraph (A). The Attorney General shall consult with the Secretary to achieve uniformity and consistency in administering provisions under chapter 53 of title 26, United States Code.

Amendments

• **2018, Tax Technical Corrections Act of 2018 (P.L. 115-141)**

P.L. 115-141, §401(a)(333)(A)-(B), Div. U:

Amended Code Sec. 7801(a)(2)(B) by striking "this Act" and inserting "the Homeland Security Act of 2002", and by striking "effective date of the Homeland Security Act of 2002" and inserting "effective date of such Act". **Effective** 3-23-2018.

• **2002, Homeland Security Act of 2002 (P.L. 107-296)**

P.L. 107-296, §1112(k)(1)-(2):

Amended Code Sec. 7801(a) by striking "SECRETARY.—Except" and inserting "SECRETARY.—(1) IN GENERAL.—Except" and by adding at the end a new paragraph (2). **Effective** 60 days after 11-25-2002.

• **1998 (P.L. 106-58)**

P.L. 106-58, §650, provides:

SEC. 650. ITEMIZED INCOME TAX RECEIPT.

(a) IN GENERAL.—Not later than April 15, 2000, the Secretary of the Treasury shall establish an interactive program on an Internet website where any taxpayer may generate an itemized receipt showing a proportionate allocation (in money terms) of the taxpayer's total tax payments among the major expenditure categories.

(b) INFORMATION NECESSARY TO GENERATE RECEIPT.—For purposes of generating an itemized receipt under subsection (a), the interactive program—

(1) shall only require the input of the taxpayer's total tax payments; and

(2) shall not require any identifying information relating to the taxpayer.

(c) TOTAL TAX PAYMENTS.—For purposes of this section, total tax payments of an individual for any taxable year are—

(1) the tax imposed by subtitle A of the Internal Revenue Code of 1986 for such taxable year (as shown on his return); and

(2) the tax imposed by section 3101 of such Code on wages received during such taxable year.

(d) CONTENT OF TAX RECEIPT.—

(1) MAJOR EXPENDITURE CATEGORIES.—For purposes of subsection (a), the major expenditure categories are:

(A) National defense.
(B) International affairs.
(C) Medicaid.
(D) Medicare.
(E) Means-tested entitlements.
(F) Domestic discretionary.
(G) Social Security.
(H) Interest payments.
(I) All other.

(2) OTHER ITEMS ON RECEIPT.—

(A) IN GENERAL.—In addition, the tax receipt shall include selected examples of more specific expenditure items, including the items listed in subparagraph (B), either at the budget function, subfunction, or program, project, or activity levels, along with any other information deemed appropriate by the Secretary of the Treasury and the Director of the Office of Management and Budget to enhance taxpayer understanding of the Federal budget.

(B) LISTED ITEMS.—The expenditure items listed in this subparagraph are as follows:

(i) Public schools funding programs.
(ii) Student loans and college aid.
(iii) Low-income housing programs.
(iv) Food stamp and welfare programs.
(v) Law enforcement, including the Federal Bureau of Investigation, law enforcement grants to the States, and other Federal law enforcement personnel.
(vi) Infrastructure, including roads, bridges, and mass transit.
(vii) Farm subsidies.
(viii) Congressional Member and staff salaries.
(ix) Health research programs.
(x) Aid to the disabled.
(xi) Veterans health care and pension programs.
(xii) Space programs.
(xiii) Environmental cleanup programs.
(xiv) United States embassies.
(xv) Military salaries.
(xvi) Foreign aid.
(xvii) Contributions to the North Atlantic Treaty Organization.
(xviii) Amtrak.
(xix) United States Postal Service.

(e) COST.—No charge shall be imposed to cover any cost associated with the production or distribution of the tax receipt.

(f) REGULATIONS.—The Secretary of the Treasury may prescribe such regulations as may be necessary to carry out this section.

• **1959 (P.L. 86-368)**

P.L. 86-368, §1:

Amended the heading of Code Sec. 7801 by inserting "THE" after "AUTHORITY OF". **Effective** 9-22-59.

[Sec. 7801(b)—Repealed]

Amendments

• **1982 (P.L. 97-258)**

P.L. 97-258, §5(b):

Repealed Code Sec. 7801(b). **Effective** 9-13-82. Prior to being repealed, Code Sec. 77801(b) read as follows:

(b) OFFICE OF GENERAL COUNSEL FOR THE DEPARTMENT.—

(1) GENERAL COUNSEL.—There shall be in the Department of the Treasury the office of General Counsel for the Department of the Treasury. The General Counsel shall be appointed by the President, by and with the advice and consent of the Senate. The General Counsel shall be the chief law officer of the Department and shall perform such duties as may be prescribed by the Secretary of the Treasury.

(2) ASSISTANT GENERAL COUNSELS.—The President is authorized to appoint, by and with the advice and consent of the Senate, an Assistant General Counsel who shall be the Chief Counsel for the Internal Revenue Service. The Chief Counsel shall be the chief law officer for the Internal Revenue Service and shall perform such duties as may be prescribed by the Secretary of the Treasury. The Secretary of the Treasury may appoint, without regard to the provisions of the civil service laws, and fix the duties of not to exceed five other assistant General Counsels.

(3) ATTORNEYS.—The Secretary of the Treasury may appoint and fix the duties of such other attorneys as he may deem necessary.

• **1976, Tax Reform Act of 1976 (P.L. 94-455)**

P.L. 94-455, §1906(b)(13)(B):

Substituted "Secretary of the Treasury" for "Secretary" each place it appeared in Code Sec. 7801(b). **Effective** 2-1-77.

• **1964, Government Employees Salary Act of 1964 (P.L. 88-426)**

P.L. 88-426, §305(39):

Deleted "and shall receive basic compensation at the annual rate of $19,000" from the first sentence of Sec. 7801(b)(2). **Effective** 7-1-64.

• **1959 (P.L. 86-368)**

P.L. 86-368, §1:

Amended Code Sec. 7801(b). **Effective** 9-22-59. Prior to amendment, Sec. 7801(b) read as follows:

"(b) General Counsel for the Department.—There shall be in the Department of the Treasury the office of General Counsel for the Department of the Treasury. The General Counsel shall be appointed by the President, by and with the advice and consent of the Senate. The General Counsel shall be the chief law officer of the Department and shall perform such duties as may be prescribed by the Secretary. The Secretary may appoint and fix the duties of an Assistant General Counsel who shall serve as Chief Counsel of the Internal Revenue Service and may appoint and fix the duties of not to exceed five other Assistant General Counsels. All Assistant General Counsels shall be appointed without regard to the provisions of the civil service laws. The Secretary may also appoint and fix the duties of such other attorneys as he may deem necessary."

[Sec. 7801(c)]

(c) FUNCTIONS OF DEPARTMENT OF JUSTICE UNAFFECTED.—Nothing in this section or section 301(f) of title 31 shall be considered to affect the duties, powers, or functions imposed upon, or vested in, the Department of Justice, or any officer thereof, by law existing on May 10, 1934.

APPLICATION OF LAWS

Amendments

• 1982 (P.L. 97-258)

P.L. 97-258, §2(f)(1):

Amended Code Sec. 7801(c) by inserting after "in this section" "or section 301(f) of title 31". **Effective** 9-13-82.

• 1959 (P.L. 86-368)

P.L. 86-368, §1:

Amended Code Sec. 7801(c) by inserting a comma preceding and following the phrase "or vested in". **Effective** 9-22-59.

[Sec. 7802]

SEC. 7802. INTERNAL REVENUE SERVICE OVERSIGHT BOARD.

[Sec. 7802(a)]

(a) ESTABLISHMENT.—There is established within the Department of the Treasury the Internal Revenue Service Oversight Board (hereafter in this subchapter referred to as the "Oversight Board").

[Sec. 7802(b)]

(b) MEMBERSHIP.—

(1) COMPOSITION.—The Oversight Board shall be composed of nine members, as follows:

(A) six members shall be individuals who are not otherwise Federal officers or employees and who are appointed by the President, by and with the advice and consent of the Senate.

(B) one member shall be the Secretary of the Treasury or, if the Secretary so designates, the Deputy Secretary of the Treasury.

(C) one member shall be the Commissioner of Internal Revenue.

(D) one member shall be an individual who is a full-time Federal employee or a representative of employees and who is appointed by the President, by and with the advice and consent of the Senate.

(2) QUALIFICATIONS AND TERMS.—

(A) QUALIFICATIONS.—Members of the Oversight Board described in paragraph (1)(A) shall be appointed without regard to political affiliation and solely on the basis of their professional experience and expertise in one or more of the following areas:

(i) Management of large service organizations.

(ii) Customer service.

(iii) Federal tax laws, including tax administration and compliance.

(iv) Information technology.

(v) Organization development.

(vi) The needs and concerns of taxpayers.

(vii) The needs and concerns of small businesses.

In the aggregate, the members of the Oversight Board described in paragraph (1)(A) should collectively bring to bear expertise in all of the areas described in the preceding sentence.

(B) TERMS.—Each member who is described in subparagraph (A) or (D) of paragraph (1) shall be appointed for a term of 5 years, except that of the members first appointed under paragraph (1)(A)—

(i) two members shall be appointed for a term of 3 years,

(ii) two members shall be appointed for a term of 4 years, and

(iii) two members shall be appointed for a term of 5 years.

(C) REAPPOINTMENT.—An individual who is described in subparagraph (A) or (D) of paragraph (1) may be appointed to no more than two 5-year terms on the Oversight Board.

(D) VACANCY.—Any vacancy on the Oversight Board shall be filled in the same manner as the original appointment. Any member appointed to fill a vacancy occurring before the expiration of the term for which the member's predecessor was appointed shall be appointed for the remainder of that term.

(3) ETHICAL CONSIDERATIONS.—

(A) FINANCIAL DISCLOSURE.—During the entire period that an individual appointed under subparagraph (A) or (D) of paragraph (1) is a member of the Oversight Board, such individual shall be treated as serving as an officer or employee referred to in section 13103(f) of title 5, United States Code, for purposes of subchapter I of chapter 131 of such title, except that section 13103(d) of such title shall apply without regard to the number of days of service in the position.

(B) RESTRICTIONS ON POST-EMPLOYMENT.—For purposes of section 207(c) of title 18, United States Code, an individual appointed under subparagraph (A) or (D) of paragraph (1) shall be treated as an employee referred to in section 207(c)(2)(A)(i) of such title during the entire period the individual is a member of the Board, except that subsections (c)(2)(B) and (f) of section 207 of such title shall not apply.

(C) MEMBERS WHO ARE SPECIAL GOVERNMENT EMPLOYEES.—If an individual appointed under subparagraph (A) or (D) of paragraph (1) is a special Government employee, the following additional rules apply for purposes of chapter 11 of title 18, United States Code:

(i) RESTRICTION ON REPRESENTATION.—In addition to any restriction under section 205(c) of title 18, United States Code, except as provided in subsections (d) through (i) of section 205 of such title, such individual (except in the proper discharge of official duties) shall not, with or without compensation, represent anyone to or before any officer or employee of—

(I) the Oversight Board or the Internal Revenue Service on any matter;

(II) the Department of the Treasury on any matter involving the internal revenue laws or involving the management or operations of the Internal Revenue Service; or

(III) the Department of Justice with respect to litigation involving a matter described in subclause (I) or (II).

(ii) COMPENSATION FOR SERVICES PROVIDED BY ANOTHER.—For purposes of section 203 of such title—

(I) such individual shall not be subject to the restrictions of subsection (a)(1) thereof for sharing in compensation earned by another for representations on matters covered by such section, and

(II) a person shall not be subject to the restrictions of subsection (a)(2) thereof for sharing such compensation with such individual.

(D) WAIVER.—The President may, only at the time the President nominates the member of the Oversight Board described in paragraph (1)(D), waive for the term of the member any appropriate provision of chapter 11 of title 18, United States Code, to the extent such waiver is necessary to allow such member to participate in the decisions of the Board while continuing to serve as a full-time Federal employee or a representative of employees. Any such waiver shall not be effective unless a written intent of waiver to exempt such member (and actual waiver language) is submitted to the Senate with the nomination of such member.

APPLICATION OF LAWS

(4) QUORUM.—Five members of the Oversight Board shall constitute a quorum. A majority of members present and voting shall be required for the Oversight Board to take action.

(5) REMOVAL.—

(A) IN GENERAL.—Any member of the Oversight Board appointed under subparagraph (A) or (D) of paragraph (1) may be removed at the will of the President.

(B) SECRETARY AND COMMISSIONER.— An individual described in subparagraph (B) or (C) of paragraph (1) shall be removed upon termination of service in the office described in such subparagraph.

(6) CLAIMS.—

(A) IN GENERAL.—Members of the Oversight Board who are described in subparagraph (A) or (D) of paragraph (1) shall have no personal liability under Federal law with respect to any claim arising out of or resulting from an act or omission by such member within the scope of service as a member.

(B) EFFECT ON OTHER LAW.—This paragraph shall not be construed—

(i) to affect any other immunities and protections that may be available to such member under applicable law with respect to such transactions;

(ii) to affect any other right or remedy against the United States under applicable law; or

(iii) to limit or alter in any way the immunities that are available under applicable law for Federal officers and employees.

Amendments

- **2022, (P.L. 117-286)**

2022 (P.L. 117-286), §4(c)(34):

Amended Code Sec. 7802(b)(3)(A) by striking "section 101(f) of the Ethics in Government Act of 1978 for purposes of title I of such Act, except that section 101(d) of such Act" and inserting "section 13103(f) of title 5, United States Code, for purposes of subchapter I of chapter 131 of such title, except that section 13103(d) of such title". **Effective** 12-27-2022.

- **2000, Community Renewal Tax Relief Act of 2000 (P.L. 106-554)**

P.L. 106-554, §319(27):

Amended Code Sec. 7802(b)(2)(B)(ii) by striking "; and" at the end and inserting ", and". **Effective** 12-21-2000.

[Sec. 7802(c)]

(c) GENERAL RESPONSIBILITIES.—

(1) OVERSIGHT.—

(A) IN GENERAL.—The Oversight Board shall oversee the Internal Revenue Service in its administration, management, conduct, direction, and supervision of the execution and application of the internal revenue laws or related statutes and tax conventions to which the United States is a party.

(B) MISSION OF IRS.—As part of its oversight functions described in subparagraph (A), the Oversight Board shall ensure that the organization and operation of the Internal Revenue Service allows it to carry out its mission.

(C) CONFIDENTIALITY.—The Oversight Board shall ensure that appropriate confidentiality is maintained in the exercise of its duties.

(2) EXCEPTIONS.—The Oversight Board shall have no responsibilities or authority with respect to—

(A) the development and formulation of Federal tax policy relating to existing or proposed internal revenue laws, related statutes, and tax conventions,

(B) specific law enforcement activities of the Internal Revenue Service, including specific compliance activities such as examinations, collection activities, and criminal investigations,

(C) specific procurement activities of the Internal Revenue Service, or

(D) except as provided in subsection (d)(3), specific personnel actions.

[Sec. 7802(d)]

(d) SPECIFIC RESPONSIBILITIES.—The Oversight Board shall have the following specific responsibilities:

(1) STRATEGIC PLANS.—To review and approve strategic plans of the Internal Revenue Service, including the establishment of—

(A) mission and objectives, and standards of performance relative to either, and

(B) annual and long-range strategic plans.

(2) OPERATIONAL PLANS.—To review the operational functions of the Internal Revenue Service, including—

(A) plans for modernization of the tax system,

(B) plans for outsourcing or managed competition, and

(C) plans for training and education.

(3) MANAGEMENT.—To—

(A) recommend to the President candidates for appointment as the Commissioner of Internal Revenue and recommend to the President the removal of the Commissioner;

(B) review the Commissioner's selection, evaluation, and compensation of Internal Revenue Service senior executives who have program management responsibility over significant functions of the Internal Revenue Service; and

(C) review and approve the Commissioner's plans for any major reorganization of the Internal Revenue Service.

(4) BUDGET.—To—

(A) review and approve the budget request of the Internal Revenue Service prepared by the Commissioner;

(B) submit such budget request to the Secretary of the Treasury; and

(C) ensure that the budget request supports the annual and long-range strategic plans.

(5) TAXPAYER PROTECTION.—To ensure the proper treatment of taxpayers by the employees of the Internal Revenue Service.

The Secretary shall submit the budget request referred to in paragraph (4)(B) for any fiscal year to the President who shall submit such request, without revision, to Congress together with the President's annual budget request for the Internal Revenue Service for such fiscal year.

[Sec. 7802(e)]

(e) BOARD PERSONNEL MATTERS.—

(1) COMPENSATION OF MEMBERS.—

(A) IN GENERAL.—Each member of the Oversight Board who—

(i) is described in subsection (b)(1)(A); or

(ii) is described in subsection (b)(1)(D) and is not otherwise a Federal officer or employee,

APPLICATION OF LAWS

shall be compensated at a rate of $30,000 per year. All other members shall serve without compensation for such service.

(B) CHAIRPERSON.—In lieu of the amount specified in subparagraph (A), the Chairperson of the Oversight Board shall be compensated at a rate of $50,000 per year.

(2) TRAVEL EXPENSES.—

(A) IN GENERAL.—The members of the Oversight Board shall be allowed travel expenses, including per diem in lieu of subsistence, at rates authorized for employees of agencies under subchapter I of chapter 57 of title 5, United States Code, to attend meetings of the Oversight Board and, with the advance approval of the Chairperson of the Oversight Board, while otherwise away from their homes or regular places of business for purposes of duties as a member of the Oversight Board.

(B) REPORT.—The Oversight Board shall include in its annual report under subsection (f)(3)(A) information with respect to the travel expenses allowed for members of the Oversight Board under this paragraph.

(3) STAFF.—

(A) IN GENERAL.—The Chairperson of the Oversight Board may appoint and terminate any personnel that may be necessary to enable the Board to perform its duties.

(B) DETAIL OF GOVERNMENT EMPLOYEES.—Upon request of the Chairperson of the Oversight Board, a Federal agency shall detail a Federal Government employee to the Oversight Board without reimbursement. Such detail shall be without interruption or loss of civil service status or privilege.

(4) PROCUREMENT OF TEMPORARY AND INTERMITTENT SERVICES.—The Chairperson of the Oversight Board may procure temporary and intermittent services under section 3109(b) of title 5, United States Code.

[Sec. 7802(f)]

(f) ADMINISTRATIVE MATTERS.—

(1) CHAIR.—

(A) TERM.—The members of the Oversight Board shall elect for a 2-year term a chairperson from among the members appointed under subsection (b)(1)(A).

(B) POWERS.—Except as otherwise provided by a majority vote of the Oversight Board, the powers of the Chairperson shall include—

(i) establishing committees;

(ii) setting meeting places and times;

(iii) establishing meeting agendas; and

(iv) developing rules for the conduct of business.

(2) MEETINGS.—The Oversight Board shall meet at least quarterly and at such other times as the Chairperson determines appropriate.

(3) REPORTS.—

(A) ANNUAL.—The Oversight Board shall each year report with respect to the conduct of its responsibilities under this title to the President, the Committees on Ways and Means, Government Reform and Oversight, and Appropriations of the House of Representatives and the Committees on Finance, Governmental Affairs, and Appropriations of the Senate.

(B) ADDITIONAL REPORT.—Upon a determination by the Oversight Board under subsection (c)(1)(B) that the organization and operation of the Internal Revenue Service are not allowing it to carry out its mission, the Oversight Board shall report such determination to the Committee on Ways and Means of the House of Representatives and the Committee on Finance of the Senate.

Amendments

• **1998, IRS Restructuring and Reform Act of 1998 (P.L. 105-206)**

P.L. 105-206, §1101(a):

Amended Code Sec. 7802. Effective 7-22-98.

P.L. 105-206, §1101(d)(2)-(3), provides:

(2) INITIAL NOMINATIONS TO INTERNAL REVENUE SERVICE OVERSIGHT BOARD.—The President shall submit the initial nominations under section 7802 of the Internal Revenue Code of 1986, as added by this section, to the Senate not later than 6 months after the date of the enactment of this Act.

(3) EFFECT ON ACTIONS PRIOR TO APPOINTMENT OF OVERSIGHT BOARD.—Nothing in this section shall be construed to invalidate the actions and authority of the Internal Revenue Service prior to the appointment of the members of the Internal Revenue Service Oversight Board.

Prior to amendment, Code Sec. 7802 read as follows:

SEC. 7802. COMMISSIONER OF INTERNAL REVENUE; ASSISTANT COMMISSIONERS; TAXPAYER ADVOCATE.

[Sec. 7802(a)]

(a) COMMISSIONER OF INTERNAL REVENUE.—There shall be in the Department of the Treasury a Commissioner of Internal Revenue, who shall be appointed by the President, by and with the advice and consent of the Senate. The Commissioner of Internal Revenue shall have such duties and powers as may be prescribed by the Secretary of the Treasury.

Amendments

• **1976, Tax Reform Act of 1976 (P.L. 94-455)**

P.L. 94-455, §1906(b)(13)(B):

Substituted "Secretary of the Treasury" for "Secretary" in Code Sec. 7802(a). Effective 2-1-77.

• **1974, Employee Retirement Income Security Act of 1974 (P.L. 93-406)**

P.L. 93-406, §1051(a):

Amended Code Sec. 7802(a). Effective 12-1-74. Prior to amendment Sec. 7802 read as follows:

SEC. 7802. COMMISSIONER OF INTERNAL REVENUE.

There shall be in the Department of the Treasury a Commissioner of Internal Revenue, who shall be appointed by the President, by and with the advice and consent of the Senate. The Commissioner of Internal Revenue shall have such duties and powers as may be prescribed by the Secretary.

[Sec. 7802(b)]

(b) ASSISTANT COMMISSIONER FOR EMPLOYEE PLANS AND EXEMPT ORGANIZATIONS.—

(1) ESTABLISHMENT OF OFFICE.—There is established within the Internal Revenue Service an office to be known as the "Office of Employee Plans and Exempt Organizations" to be under the supervision and direction of an Assistant Commissioner of Internal Revenue. As head of the Office, the Assistant Commissioner shall be responsible for carrying out such functions as the Secretary may prescribe with respect to organizations exempt from tax under section 501(a) and with respect to plans to which part I of subchapter D of chapter 1 applies (and with respect to organizations designed to be exempt under such section and plans designed to be plans to which such part applies).

(2) AUTHORIZATION OF APPROPRIATIONS.—There is authorized to be appropriated to the Department of the Treasury to carry out the functions of the Office an amount equal to the sum of—

(A) so much of the collections from taxes imposed under section 4940 (relating to excise tax based on investment income) as would have been collected if the rate of tax under such section was 2 percent during the second preceding fiscal year; and

(B) the greater of—

(i) an amount equal to the amount described in paragraph (A); or

(ii) $30,000,000.

Amendments

• **1982 (P.L. 97-258)**

P.L. 97-258, §2(f)(2):

Amended Code Sec. 7802(b) by inserting "(1) Establishment of Office.—" before "There" and by adding paragraph (2). Effective 9-13-82.

• **1976, Tax Reform Act of 1976 (P.L. 94-455)**

P.L. 94-455, §1906(b)(13)(A):

Amended 1954 Code by substituting "Secretary" for "Secretary or his delegate" each place it appeared. Effective 2-1-77.

• **1974, Employee Retirement Income Security Act of 1974 (P.L. 93-406)**

P.L. 93-406, §1051(a):

Added Code Sec. 7802(b). Effective 12-1-74.

[Sec. 7802(c)]

(c) ASSISTANT COMMISSIONER (TAXPAYER SERVICES).—There is established within the Internal Revenue Service an office to be known as the "Office for Taxpayer Services" to be under the supervision and direction of an Assistant Commissioner of the Internal Revenue. The Assistant Commissioner shall be responsible for taxpayer services such as telephone, walk-in, and taxpayer educational services, and the design and production of tax and informational forms.

APPLICATION OF LAWS

Amendments
• **1988, Technical and Miscellaneous Revenue Act of 1988 (P.L. 100-647)**

P.L. 100-647, § 6235(a):

Amended Code Sec. 7802 by adding at the end thereof new subsection (c). **Effective** on the date 180 days after 11-10-88.

[Sec. 7802(d)]

(d) OFFICE OF TAXPAYER ADVOCATE.—

(1) IN GENERAL.—There is established in the Internal Revenue Service an office to be known as the "Office of the Taxpayer Advocate". Such office shall be under the supervision and direction of an official to be known as the "Taxpayer Advocate" who shall be appointed by and report directly to the Commissioner of Internal Revenue. The Taxpayer Advocate shall be entitled to compensation at the same rate as the highest level official reporting directly to the Deputy Commissioner of the Internal Revenue Service.

(2) FUNCTIONS OF OFFICE.—

(A) IN GENERAL.—It shall be the function of the Office of Taxpayer Advocate to—

(i) assist taxpayers in resolving problems with the Internal Revenue Service,

(ii) identify areas in which taxpayers have problems in dealings with the Internal Revenue Service,

(iii) to the extent possible, propose changes in the administrative practices of the Internal Revenue Service to mitigate problems identified under clause (ii), and

(iv) identify potential legislative changes which may be appropriate to mitigate such problems.

(B) ANNUAL REPORTS.—

(i) OBJECTIVES.—Not later than June 30 of each calendar year after 1995, the Taxpayer Advocate shall report to the Committee on Ways and Means of the House of Representatives and the Committee on Finance of the Senate on the objectives of the Taxpayer Advocate for the fiscal year beginning in such calendar year. Any such report shall contain full and substantive analysis, in addition to statistical information.

(ii) ACTIVITIES.—Not later than December 31 of each calendar year after 1995, the Taxpayer Advocate shall report to the Committee on Ways and Means of the House of Representatives and the Committee on Finance of the Senate on the activities of the Taxpayer Advocate during the fiscal year ending during such calendar year. Any such report shall contain full and substantive analysis, in addition to statistical information, and shall—

(I) identify the initiatives the Taxpayer Advocate has taken on improving taxpayer services and Internal Revenue Service responsiveness,

(II) contain recommendations received from individuals with the authority to issue Taxpayer Assistance Orders under section 7811,

(III) contain a summary of at least 20 of the most serious problems encountered by taxpayers, including a description of the nature of such problems,

(IV) contain an inventory of the items described in subclauses (I), (II), and (III) for which action has been taken and the result of such action,

(V) contain an inventory of the items described in subclauses (I), (II), and (III) for which action remains to be completed and the period during which each item has remained on such inventory,

(VI) contain an inventory of the items described in subclauses (II) and (III) for which no action has been taken, the period during which each item has remained on such inventory, the reasons for the inaction, and identify any Internal Revenue Service official who is responsible for such inaction,

(VII) identify any Taxpayer Assistance Order which was not honored by the Internal Revenue Service in a timely manner, as specified under section 7811(b),

(VIII) contain recommendations for such administrative and legislative action as may be appropriate to resolve problems encountered by taxpayers,

(IX) describe the extent to which regional problem resolution officers participate in the selection and evaluation of local problem resolution officers, and

(X) include such other information as the Taxpayer Advocate may deem advisable.

(iii) REPORT TO BE SUBMITTED DIRECTLY.—Each report required under this subparagraph shall be provided directly to the Committees referred to in clauses (i) and (ii) without any prior review or comment from the Commissioner, the Secretary of the Treasury, any other officer or employee of the Department of the Treasury, or the Office of Management and Budget.

(3) RESPONSIBILITIES OF COMMISSIONER.—The Commissioner of Internal Revenue shall establish procedures requiring a formal response to all recommendations submitted to the Commissioner by the Taxpayer Advocate within 3 months after submission to the Commissioner.

Amendments
• **1996, Taxpayer Bill of Rights 2 (P.L. 104-168)**

P.L. 104-168, § 101(a):

Amended Code Sec. 7802 by adding at the end a new subsection (d). **Effective** 7-30-96.

P.L. 104-168, § 101(b)(2):

Amended the heading of Code Sec. 7802. **Effective** 7-30-96. Prior to amendment, the heading of Code Sec. 7802 read as follows:

SEC. 7802. COMMISSIONER OF INTERNAL REVENUE; ASSISTANT COMMISSIONER (EMPLOYEE PLANS AND EXEMPT ORGANIZATIONS).

[Sec. 7803]

SEC. 7803. COMMISSIONER OF INTERNAL REVENUE; OTHER OFFICIALS.

[Sec. 7803(a)]

(a) COMMISSIONER OF INTERNAL REVENUE.—

(1) APPOINTMENT.—

(A) IN GENERAL.—There shall be in the Department of the Treasury a Commissioner of Internal Revenue who shall be appointed by the President, by and with the advice and consent of the Senate. Such appointment shall be made from individuals who, among other qualifications, have a demonstrated ability in management.

(B) TERM.—The term of the Commissioner of Internal Revenue shall be a 5-year term, beginning with a term to commence on November 13, 1997. Each subsequent term shall begin on the day after the date on which the previous term expires.

(C) VACANCY.—Any individual appointed as Commissioner of Internal Revenue during a term as defined in subparagraph (B) shall be appointed for the remainder of that term.

(D) REMOVAL.—The Commissioner may be removed at the will of the President.

(E) REAPPOINTMENT.—The Commissioner may be appointed to serve more than one term.

(2) DUTIES.—The Commissioner shall have such duties and powers as the Secretary may prescribe, including the power to—

(A) administer, manage, conduct, direct, and supervise the execution and application of the internal revenue laws or related statutes and tax conventions to which the United States is a party; and

(B) recommend to the President a candidate for appointment as Chief Counsel for the Internal Revenue Service when a vacancy occurs, and recommend to the President the removal of such Chief Counsel.

If the Secretary determines not to delegate a power specified in subparagraph (A) or (B), such determination may not take effect until 30 days after the Secretary notifies the Committees on Ways and Means, Government Reform and Oversight, and Appropriations of the House of Representatives and the Committees on Finance, Governmental Affairs, and Appropriations of the Senate.

(3) EXECUTION OF DUTIES IN ACCORD WITH TAXPAYER RIGHTS.—In discharging his duties, the Commissioner shall ensure that employees of the Internal Revenue Service are familiar with and act in accord with taxpayer rights as afforded by other provisions of this title, including—

(A) the right to be informed,

(B) the right to quality service,

(C) the right to pay no more than the correct amount of tax,

(D) the right to challenge the position of the Internal Revenue Service and be heard,

(E) the right to appeal a decision of the Internal Revenue Service in an independent forum,

(F) the right to finality,

(G) the right to privacy,

(H) the right to confidentiality,

(I) the right to retain representation, and

(J) the right to a fair and just tax system.

(4) CONSULTATION WITH BOARD.—The Commissioner shall consult with the Oversight Board on all matters set forth in paragraphs (2) and (3) (other than paragraph (3)(A)) of section 7802(d).

APPLICATION OF LAWS

Amendments

• 2015, Protecting Americans from Tax Hikes Act of 2015 (P.L. 114-113)

P.L. 114-113, § 401(a), Div. Q:

Amended Code Sec. 7803(a) by redesignating paragraph (3) as paragraph (4) and by inserting after paragraph (2) a new paragraph (3). **Effective** 12-18-2015.

• 2007 (P.L. 110-176)

P.L. 110-176, § 1(a):

Amended Code Sec. 7803(a)(1). **Effective** as if included in the amendment made by section 1102(a) of the Internal Revenue Service Restructuring and Reform Act of 1998 (P.L. 105-206) [**effective** generally 7-22-98; for special rules, see P.L. 105-206, § 1102(f)(2)-(4), in the amendment notes for Code Sec. 7803(d).—CCH]. Prior to amendment, Code Sec. 7803(a)(1) read as follows:

(1) APPOINTMENT.—

(A) IN GENERAL.—There shall be in the Department of the Treasury a Commissioner of Internal Revenue who shall be appointed by the President, by and with the advice and consent of the Senate, to a 5-year term. Such appointment shall be made from individuals who, among other qualifications, have a demonstrated ability in management.

(B) VACANCY.—Any individual appointed to fill a vacancy in the position of Commissioner occurring before the expiration of the term for which such individual's predecessor was appointed shall be appointed only for the remainder of that term.

(C) REMOVAL.—The Commissioner may be removed at the will of the President.

(D) REAPPOINTMENT.—The Commissioner may be appointed to more than one 5-year term.

[Sec. 7803(b)]

(b) CHIEF COUNSEL FOR THE INTERNAL REVENUE SERVICE.—

(1) APPOINTMENT.—There shall be in the Department of the Treasury a Chief Counsel for the Internal Revenue Service who shall be appointed by the President, by and with the consent of the Senate.

(2) DUTIES.—The Chief Counsel shall be the chief law officer for the Internal Revenue Service and shall perform such duties as may be prescribed by the Secretary, including the duty—

(A) to be legal advisor to the Commissioner and the Commissioner's officers and employees;

(B) to furnish legal opinions for the preparation and review of rulings and memoranda of technical advice;

(C) to prepare, review, and assist in the preparation of proposed legislation, treaties, regulations, and Executive orders relating to laws which affect the Internal Revenue Service;

(D) to represent the Commissioner in cases before the Tax Court; and

(E) to determine which civil actions should be litigated under the laws relating to the Internal Revenue Service and prepare recommendations for the Department of Justice regarding the commencement of such actions.

If the Secretary determines not to delegate a power specified in subparagraph (A), (B), (C), (D), or (E), such determination may not take effect until 30 days after the Secretary notifies the Committees on Ways and Means, Government Reform and Oversight, and Appropriations of the House of Representatives and the Committees on Finance, Governmental Affairs, and Appropriations of the Senate.

(3) PERSONS TO WHOM CHIEF COUNSEL REPORTS.—The Chief Counsel shall report directly to the Commissioner of Internal Revenue, except that—

(A) the Chief Counsel shall report to both the Commissioner and the General Counsel for the Department of the Treasury with respect to—

(i) legal advice or interpretation of the tax law not relating solely to tax policy;

(ii) tax litigation; and

(B) the Chief Counsel shall report to the General Counsel with respect to legal advice or interpretation of the tax law relating solely to tax policy.

If there is any disagreement between the Commissioner and the General Counsel with respect to any matter jointly referred to them under subparagraph (A), such matter shall be submitted to the Secretary or Deputy Secretary for resolution.

(4) CHIEF COUNSEL PERSONNEL.—All personnel in the Office of Chief Counsel shall report to the Chief Counsel.

[Sec. 7803(c)]

(c) OFFICE OF THE TAXPAYER ADVOCATE.—

(1) ESTABLISHMENT.—

(A) IN GENERAL.—There is established in the Internal Revenue Service an office to be known as the "Office of the Taxpayer Advocate".

(B) NATIONAL TAXPAYER ADVOCATE.—

(i) IN GENERAL.—The Office of the Taxpayer Advocate shall be under the supervision and direction of an official to be known as the "National Taxpayer Advocate". The National Taxpayer Advocate shall report directly to the Commissioner of Internal Revenue and shall be entitled to compensation at the same rate as the highest rate of basic pay established for the Senior Executive Service under section 5382 of title 5, United States Code.

(ii) APPOINTMENT.—The National Taxpayer Advocate shall be appointed by the Secretary of the Treasury after consultation with the Commissioner of Internal Revenue and the Oversight Board and without regard to the provisions of title 5, United States Code, relating to appointments in the competitive service or the Senior Executive Service.

(iii) QUALIFICATIONS.—An individual appointed under clause (ii) shall have—

(I) a background in customer service as well as tax law; and

(II) experience in representing individual taxpayers.

(iv) RESTRICTION ON EMPLOYMENT.—An individual may be appointed as the National Taxpayer Advocate only if such individual was not an officer or employee of the Internal Revenue Service during the 2-year period ending with such appointment and such individual agrees not to accept any employment with the Internal Revenue Service for at least 5 years after ceasing to be the National Taxpayer Advocate. Service as an officer or employee of the Office of the Taxpayer Advocate shall not be taken into account in applying this clause.

(2) FUNCTIONS OF OFFICE.—

(A) IN GENERAL.—It shall be the function of the Office of the Taxpayer Advocate to—

(i) assist taxpayers in resolving problems with the Internal Revenue Service;

(ii) identify areas in which taxpayers have problems in dealings with the Internal Revenue Service;

(iii) to the extent possible, propose changes in the administrative practices of the Internal Revenue Service to mitigate problems identified under clause (ii); and

(iv) identify potential legislative changes which may be appropriate to mitigate such problems.

(B) ANNUAL REPORTS.—

(i) OBJECTIVES.—Not later than June 30 of each calendar year, the National Taxpayer Advocate shall report to the Committee on Ways and Means of the House of Representatives and the Committee on Finance of the Senate on the objectives of the Office of the

APPLICATION OF LAWS

Taxpayer Advocate for the fiscal year beginning in such calendar year. Any such report shall contain full and substantive analysis, in addition to statistical information.

(ii) ACTIVITIES.—Not later than December 31 of each calendar year, the National Taxpayer Advocate shall report to the Committee on Ways and Means of the House of Representatives and the Committee on Finance of the Senate on the activities of the Office of the Taxpayer Advocate during the fiscal year ending during such calendar year. Any such report shall contain full and substantive analysis, in addition to statistical information, and shall—

(I) identify the initiatives the Office of the Taxpayer Advocate has taken on improving taxpayer services and Internal Revenue Service responsiveness;

(II) contain recommendations received from individuals with the authority to issue Taxpayer Assistance Orders under section 7811;

(III) contain a summary of the 10 most serious problems encountered by taxpayers, including a description of the nature of such problems;

(IV) contain an inventory of the items described in subclauses (I), (II), and (III) for which action has been taken and the result of such action;

(V) contain an inventory of the items described in subclauses (I), (II), and (III) for which action remains to be completed and the period during which each item has remained on such inventory;

(VI) contain an inventory of the items described in subclauses (I), (II), and (III) for which no action has been taken, the period during which each item has remained on such inventory, the reasons for the inaction, and identify any Internal Revenue Service official who is responsible for such inaction;

(VII) identify any Taxpayer Assistance Order which was not honored by the Internal Revenue Service in a timely manner, as specified under section 7811(b);

(VIII) identify any Taxpayer Advocate Directive which was not honored by the Internal Revenue Service in a timely manner, as specified under paragraph (5);

(IX) contain recommendations for such administrative and legislative action as may be appropriate to resolve problems encountered by taxpayers;

(X) identify areas of the tax law that impose significant compliance burdens on taxpayers or the Internal Revenue Service, including specific recommendations for remedying these problems;

(XI) identify the 10 most litigated issues for each category of taxpayers, including recommendations for mitigating such disputes;

(XII) with respect to any statistical information included in such report, include a statement of whether such statistical information was reviewed or provided by the Secretary under section 6108(d) and, if so, whether the Secretary determined such information to be statistically valid and based on sound statistical methodology; and

(XIII) include such other information as the National Taxpayer Advocate may deem advisable.

(iii) REPORT TO BE SUBMITTED DIRECTLY.—Each report required under this subparagraph shall be provided directly to the committees described in clause (i) without any prior review or comment from the Commissioner, the Secretary of the Treasury, the Oversight Board, any other officer or employee of the Department of the Treasury, or the Office of Management and Budget. The preceding sentence shall not apply with respect to statistical information provided to the Secretary for review, or received from the Secretary, under section 6108(d).

(iv) COORDINATION WITH REPORT OF TREASURY INSPECTOR GENERAL FOR TAX ADMINISTRATION.—To the extent that information required to be reported under clause (ii) is also required to be reported under paragraph (1) or (2) of subsection (d) by the Treasury Inspector General for Tax Administration, the National Taxpayer Advocate shall not contain such information in the report submitted under such clause.

(C) OTHER RESPONSIBILITIES.—The National Taxpayer Advocate shall—

(i) monitor the coverage and geographic allocation of local offices of taxpayer advocates;

(ii) develop guidance to be distributed to all Internal Revenue Service officers and employees outlining the criteria for referral of taxpayer inquiries to local offices of taxpayer advocates;

(iii) ensure that the local telephone number for each local office of the taxpayer advocate is published and available to taxpayers served by the office; and

(iv) in conjunction with the Commissioner, develop career paths for local taxpayer advocates choosing to make a career in the Office of the Taxpayer Advocate.

(D) PERSONNEL ACTIONS.—

(i) IN GENERAL.—The National Taxpayer Advocate shall have the responsibility and authority to—

(I) appoint local taxpayer advocates and make available at least 1 such advocate for each State; and

(II) evaluate and take personnel actions (including dismissal) with respect to any employee of any local office of a taxpayer advocate described in subclause (I).

(ii) CONSULTATION.—The National Taxpayer Advocate may consult with the appropriate supervisory personnel of the Internal Revenue Service in carrying out the National Taxpayer Advocate's responsibilities under this subparagraph.

(E) COORDINATION WITH TREASURY INSPECTOR GENERAL FOR TAX ADMINISTRATION.—Before beginning any research or study, the National Taxpayer Advocate shall coordinate with the Treasury Inspector General for Tax Administration to ensure that the National Taxpayer Advocate does not duplicate any action that the Treasury Inspector General for Tax Administration has already undertaken or has a plan to undertake.

(3) RESPONSIBILITIES OF COMMISSIONER.— The Commissioner shall establish procedures requiring a formal response to all recommendations submitted to the Commissioner by the National Taxpayer Advocate within 3 months after submission to the Commissioner.

(4) OPERATION OF LOCAL OFFICES.—

(A) IN GENERAL.—Each local taxpayer advocate—

(i) shall report to the National Taxpayer Advocate or delegate thereof;

(ii) may consult with the appropriate supervisory personnel of the Internal Revenue Service regarding the daily operation of the local office of the taxpayer advocate;

(iii) shall, at the initial meeting with any taxpayer seeking the assistance of a local office of the taxpayer advocate, notify such taxpayer that the taxpayer advocate offices operate independently of any other Internal Revenue Service office and report directly to Congress through the National Taxpayer Advocate; and

APPLICATION OF LAWS

(iv) may, at the taxpayer advocate's discretion, not disclose to the Internal Revenue Service contact with, or information provided by, such taxpayer.

(B) MAINTENANCE OF INDEPENDENT COMMUNICATIONS.—Each local office of the taxpayer advocate shall maintain a separate phone, facsimile, and other electronic communication access, and a separate post office address.

(5) TAXPAYER ADVOCATE DIRECTIVES.—In the case of any Taxpayer Advocate Directive issued by the National Taxpayer Advocate pursuant to a delegation of authority from the Commissioner of Internal Revenue—

(A) the Commissioner or a Deputy Commissioner shall modify, rescind, or ensure compliance with such directive not later than 90 days after the issuance of such directive, and

(B) in the case of any directive which is modified or rescinded by a Deputy Commissioner, the National Taxpayer Advocate may (not later than 90 days after such modification or rescission) appeal to the Commissioner, and the Commissioner shall (not later than 90 days after such appeal is made) ensure compliance with such directive as issued by the National Taxpayer Advocate or provide the National Taxpayer Advocate with the reasons for any modification or rescission made or upheld by the Commissioner pursuant to such appeal.

Amendments

- 2019, Taxpayer First Act (P.L. 116-25)

P.L. 116-25, §1301(a)(1):

Amended Code Sec. 7803(c) by adding at the end a new paragraph (5). **Effective 7-1-2019.**

P.L. 116-25, §1301(a)(2):

Amended Code Sec. 7803(c)(2)(B)(ii) by redesignating subclauses (VIII) through (XI) as subclauses (IX) through (XII), respectively, and by inserting after subclause (VII) a new subclause (VIII). **Effective 7-1-2019.**

P.L. 116-25, §1301(b)(1):

Amended Code Sec. 7803(c)(2)(B)(ii)(III) by striking "at least 20 of the" and inserting "the 10". **Effective 7-1-2019.**

P.L. 116-25, §1301(b)(2):

Amended Code Sec. 7803(c)(2) by adding at the end a new subparagraph (E). **Effective 7-1-2019.**

P.L. 116-25, §1301(b)(3)(B):

Amended Code Sec. 7803(c)(2)(B)(ii), as amended by Act Sec. 1301(a), by striking "and" at the end subclause (XI), by redesignating subclause (XII) as subclause (XIII), and by inserting after subclause (XI) a new subclause (XII). **Effective 7-1-2019.**

P.L. 116-25, §1301(b)(3)(C):

Amended Code Sec. 7803(c)(2)(B)(iii) by adding at the end a new sentence. **Effective 7-1-2019.**

P.L. 116-25, §1301(c):

Amended Code Sec. 7803(c)(1)(B)(i) by striking ", or, if the Secretary of the Treasury so determines, at a rate fixed under section 9503 of such title" following "title 5, United States Code". **Effective** for compensation paid to individuals appointed as the National Taxpayer Advocate after 3-31-2019.

[Sec. 7803(d)]

(d) ADDITIONAL DUTIES OF THE TREASURY INSPECTOR GENERAL FOR TAX ADMINISTRATION.—

(1) ANNUAL REPORTING.—The Treasury Inspector General for Tax Administration shall include in one of the semiannual reports under section 405 of title 5, United States Code—

(A) an evaluation of the compliance of the Internal Revenue Service with—

(i) restrictions under section 1204 of the Internal Revenue Service Restructuring and Reform Act of 1998 on the use of enforcement statistics to evaluate Internal Revenue Service employees;

(ii) restrictions under section 7521 on directly contacting taxpayers who have indicated that they prefer their representatives be contacted;

(iii) required procedures under section 6320 upon the filing of a notice of a lien;

(iv) required procedures under subchapter D of chapter 64 for seizure of property for collection of taxes, including required procedures under section 6330 regarding levies; and

(v) restrictions under section 3707 of the Internal Revenue Service Restructuring and Reform Act of 1998 on designation of taxpayers;

(B) a review and a certification of whether or not the Secretary is complying with the requirements of section 6103(e)(8) to disclose information to an individual filing a joint return on collection activity involving the other individual filing the return;

(C) information regarding extensions of the statute of limitations for assessment and collection of tax under section 6501 and the provision of notice to taxpayers regarding requests for such extension;

(D) an evaluation of the adequacy and security of the technology of the Internal Revenue Service;

(E) any termination or mitigation under section 1203 of the Internal Revenue Service Restructuring and Reform Act of 1998;

(F) information regarding improper denial of requests for information from the Internal Revenue Service identified under paragraph (3)(A); and

(G) information regarding any administrative or civil actions with respect to violations of the fair debt collection provisions of section 6304, including—

(i) a summary of such actions initiated since the date of the last report, and

(ii) a summary of any judgments or awards granted as a result of such actions.

(2) SEMIANNUAL REPORTS.—

(A) IN GENERAL.—The Treasury Inspector General for Tax Administration shall include in each semiannual report under section 405 of title 5, United States Code—

(i) the number of taxpayer complaints during the reporting period;

(ii) the number of employee misconduct and taxpayer abuse allegations received by the Internal Revenue Service or the Inspector General during the period from taxpayers, Internal Revenue Service employees, and other sources;

(iii) a summary of the status of such complaints and allegations; and

(iv) a summary of the disposition of such complaints and allegations, including the outcome of any Department of Justice action and any monies paid as a settlement of such complaints and allegations.

(B) Clauses (iii) and (iv) of subparagraph (A) shall only apply to complaints and allegations of serious employee misconduct.

(3) OTHER RESPONSIBILITIES.—The Treasury Inspector General for Tax Administration shall—

(A) conduct periodic audits of a statistically valid sample of the total number of determinations made by the Internal Revenue Service to deny written requests to disclose information to taxpayers on the basis of section 6103 of this title or section 552(b)(7) of title 5, United States Code;

(B) establish and maintain a toll-free telephone number for taxpayers to use to confidentially register complaints of misconduct by Internal Revenue Service employees and incorporate the telephone number in the statement required by section 6227 of the Omnibus Taxpayer Bill of Rights (Internal Revenue Service Publication No. 1); and

(C) not later than December 31, 2010, submit a written report to Congress on the implementation of section 6103(k)(10).

APPLICATION OF LAWS

Amendments

- **2022, (P.L. 117-286)**

2022 (P.L. 117-286), §4(b)(46)(A)-(B):

Amended Code Sec. 7803(d) in paragraph (1) (matter before subparagraph (A)), by striking "section 5 of the Inspector General Act of 1978" and inserting "section 405 of title 5, United States Code", and in paragraph (2)(A) (matter before clause (i)), by striking "section 5 of the Inspector General Act of 1978" and inserting "section 405 of title 5, United States Code". **Effective** 12-27-2022.

- **2019, Taxpayer First Act (P.L. 116-25)**

P.L. 116-25, §1101, provides:

SEC. 1101. COMPREHENSIVE CUSTOMER SERVICE STRATEGY.

(a) IN GENERAL.—Not later than the date which is 1 year after the date of the enactment of this Act, the Secretary of the Treasury (or the Secretary's delegate) shall submit to Congress a written comprehensive customer service strategy for the Internal Revenue Service. Such strategy shall include—

(1) a plan to provide assistance to taxpayers that is secure, designed to meet reasonable taxpayer expectations, and adopts appropriate best practices of customer service provided in the private sector, including online services, telephone call back services, and training of employees providing customer services;

(2) a thorough assessment of the services that the Internal Revenue Service can co-locate with other Federal services or offer as self-service options;

(3) proposals to improve Internal Revenue Service customer service in the short term (the current and following fiscal year), medium term (approximately 3 to 5 fiscal years), and long term (approximately 10 fiscal years);

(4) a plan to update guidance and training materials for customer service employees of the Internal Revenue Service, including the Internal Revenue Manual, to reflect such strategy; and

(5) identified metrics and benchmarks for quantitatively measuring the progress of the Internal Revenue Service in implementing such strategy.

(b) UPDATED GUIDANCE AND TRAINING MATERIALS.—Not later than 2 years after the date of the enactment of this Act, the Secretary of the Treasury (or the Secretary's delegate) shall make available the updated guidance and training materials described in subsection (a)(4) (including the Internal Revenue Manual). Such updated guidance and training materials (including the Internal Revenue Manual) shall be written in a manner so as to be easily understood by customer service employees of the Internal Revenue Service and shall provide clear instructions.

P.L. 116-25, §1302, provides:

SEC. 1302. MODERNIZATION OF INTERNAL REVENUE SERVICE ORGANIZATIONAL STRUCTURE.

(a) IN GENERAL.—Not later than September 30, 2020, the Secretary of the Treasury (or the Secretary's delegate) shall submit to Congress a comprehensive written plan to redesign the organization of the Internal Revenue Service. Such plan shall—

(1) ensure the successful implementation of the priorities specified by Congress in this Act;

(2) prioritize taxpayer services to ensure that all taxpayers easily and readily receive the assistance that they need;

(3) streamline the structure of the agency including minimizing the duplication of services and responsibilities within the agency;

(4) best position the Internal Revenue Service to combat cybersecurity and other threats to the Internal Revenue Service; and

(5) address whether the Criminal Investigation Division of the Internal Revenue Service should report directly to the Commissioner of Internal Revenue.

(b) REPEAL OF RESTRICTION ON ORGANIZATIONAL STRUCTURE OF INTERNAL REVENUE SERVICE.—Paragraph (3) of section 1001(a) of the Internal Revenue Service Restructuring and Reform Act of 1998 shall cease to apply beginning 1 year after the date on which the plan described in subsection (a) is submitted to Congress.

P.L. 116-25, §1406, provides:

SEC. 1406. CUSTOMER SERVICE INFORMATION.

The Secretary of the Treasury (or the Secretary's delegate) shall provide helpful information to taxpayers placed on hold during a telephone call to any Internal Revenue Service help line, including the following:

(1) Information about common tax scams.

(2) Information on where and how to report tax scams.

(3) Additional advice on how taxpayers can protect themselves from identity theft and tax scams.

- **2008, Inmate Tax Fraud Prevention Act of 2008 (P.L. 110-428)**

P.L. 110-428, §2(c):

Amended Code Sec. 7803(d)(3) by striking "and" at the end of subparagraph (A), by striking the period at the end of subparagraph (B) and inserting "; and", and by adding at the end a new subparagraph (C). **Effective** for disclosures made after 12-31-2008.

- **1998, IRS Restructuring and Reform Act of 1998 (P.L. 105-206)**

P.L. 105-206, §1001, provides:

SEC. 1001. REORGANIZATION OF THE INTERNAL REVENUE SERVICE.

(a) IN GENERAL.—The Commissioner of Internal Revenue shall develop and implement a plan to reorganize the Internal Revenue Service. The plan shall—

(1) supersede any organization or reorganization of the Internal Revenue Service based on any statute or reorganization plan applicable on the effective date of this section;

(2) eliminate or substantially modify the existing organization of the Internal Revenue Service which is based on a national, regional, and district structure;

(3) establish organizational units serving particular groups of taxpayers with similar needs; [but see P.L. 116-25, §1302(b), above] and

(4) ensure an independent appeals function within the Internal Revenue Service, including the prohibition in the plan of ex parte communications between appeals officers and other Internal Revenue Service employees to the extent that such communications appear to compromise the independence of the appeals officers.

(b) SAVINGS PROVISIONS.—

(1) PRESERVATION OF SPECIFIC TAX RIGHTS AND REMEDIES.—Nothing in the plan developed and implemented under subsection (a) shall be considered to impair any right or remedy, including trial by jury, to recover any internal revenue tax alleged to have been erroneously or illegally assessed or collected, or any penalty claimed to have been collected without authority, or any sum alleged to have been excessive or in any manner wrongfully collected under the internal revenue laws. For the purpose of any action to recover any such tax, penalty, or sum, all statutes, rules, and regulations referring to the collector of internal revenue, the principal officer for the internal revenue district, or the Secretary, shall be deemed to refer to the officer whose act or acts referred to in the preceding sentence gave rise to such action. The venue of any such action shall be the same as under existing law.

(2) CONTINUING EFFECT OF LEGAL DOCUMENTS.—All orders, determinations, rules, regulations, permits, agreements, grants, contracts, certificates, licenses, registrations, privileges, and other administrative actions—

(A) which have been issued, made, granted, or allowed to become effective by the President, any Federal agency or official thereof, or by a court of competent jurisdiction, in the performance of any function transferred or affected by the reorganization of the Internal Revenue Service or any other administrative unit of the Department of the Treasury under this section, and

(B) which are in effect at the time this section takes effect, or were final before the effective date of this section and are to become effective on or after the effective date of this section,

shall continue in effect according to their terms until modified, terminated, superseded, set aside, or revoked in accordance with law by the President, the Secretary of the Treasury, the Commissioner of Internal Revenue, or other authorized official, a court of competent jurisdiction, or by operation of law.

(3) PROCEEDINGS NOT AFFECTED.—The provisions of this section shall not affect any proceedings, including notices of proposed rulemaking, or any application for any license, permit, certificate, or financial assistance pending before the Department of the Treasury (or any administrative unit of the Department, including the Internal Revenue Service) at the time this section takes effect, with respect to functions transferred or affected by the reorganization under this section but such proceedings and applications shall continue. Orders shall be issued in such proceedings, appeals shall be taken therefrom, and payments shall be made pursuant to such orders, as if this section had not been enacted, and orders issued in any such proceedings shall continue in effect until modified, terminated, superseded, or revoked by a duly authorized official, by a court of competent jurisdiction, or by operation of law. Nothing in this paragraph shall be deemed to prohibit the discontinuance or modification of any such proceeding under the same terms and conditions and to the same extent that such proceeding could have been discontinued or modified if this section had not been enacted.

(4) SUITS NOT AFFECTED.—The provisions of this section shall not affect suits commenced before the effective date of this section, and in all such suits, proceedings shall be had, appeals taken, and judgments rendered in the same manner and with the same effect as if this section had not been enacted.

(5) NONABATEMENT OF ACTIONS.—No suit, action, or other proceeding commenced by or against the Department of the Treasury (or any administrative unit of the Department, including the Internal Revenue Service), or by or against any individual in the official capacity of such individual as an officer of the Department of the Treasury, shall abate by reason of the enactment of this section.

(6) ADMINISTRATIVE ACTIONS RELATING TO PROMULGATION OF REGULATIONS.—Any administrative action relating to the preparation or promulgation of a regulation by the Department of the Treasury (or any administrative unit of the Department, including the Internal Revenue Service) relating to a function transferred or affected by the reorganization under this section may be continued by the Department of the Treasury through any appropriate administrative unit of the Department, including the Internal Revenue Service with the same effect as if this section had not been enacted.

(c) EFFECTIVE DATE.—This section shall take effect on the date of the enactment of this Act.

P.L. 105-206, §1102(a):

Amended Code Sec. 7803. **Effective**, generally, 7-22-98. For a special rule, see Act Sec. 1102(f)(2)-(4), below. The text prior to amendment follows the amendment notes for P.L. 105-206.

P.L. 105-206, §1102(f)(2)-(4), provides:

(2) CHIEF COUNSEL.—Section 7803(b)(3) of the Internal Revenue Code of 1986, as added by this section, shall take effect on the date that is 90 days after the date of the enactment of this Act.

(3) NATIONAL TAXPAYER ADVOCATE.—Notwithstanding section 7803(c)(1)(B)(iv) of such Code, as added by this section, in appointing the first National Taxpayer Advocate after the date of the enactment of this Act, the Secretary of the Treasury—

(A) shall not appoint any individual who was an officer or employee of the Internal Revenue Service at any time during the 2-year period ending on the date of appointment; and

(B) need not consult with the Internal Revenue Service Oversight Board if the Oversight Board has not been appointed.

(4) CURRENT OFFICERS.—

(A) In the case of an individual serving as Commissioner of Internal Revenue on the date of the enactment of this Act who was appointed to such position before such date, the 5-year term required by section 7803(a)(1) of such Code, as added by this section, shall begin as of the date of such appointment.

(B) Clauses (ii), (iii), and (iv) of section 7803(c)(1)(B) of such Code, as added by this section, shall not apply to the individual serving as Taxpayer Advocate on the date of the enactment of this Act.

APPLICATION OF LAWS

P.L. 105-206, § 3701, provides:
SEC. 3701. CATALOGING COMPLAINTS.

In collecting data for the report required under section 1211 of Taxpayer Bill of Rights 2 (Public Law 104-168), the Secretary of the Treasury or the Secretary's delegate shall, not later than January 1, 2000, maintain records of taxpayer complaints of misconduct by Internal Revenue Service employees on an individual employee basis.

P.L. 105-206, § 3705, provides:
SEC. 3705. INTERNAL REVENUE SERVICE EMPLOYEE CONTACTS.

(a) NOTICE.—The Secretary of the Treasury or the Secretary's delegate shall provide that—

(1) any manually generated correspondence received by a taxpayer from the Internal Revenue Service shall include in a prominent manner the name, telephone number, and unique identifying number of an Internal Revenue Service employee the taxpayer may contact with respect to the correspondence;

(2) any other correspondence or notice received by a taxpayer from the Internal Revenue Service shall include in a prominent manner a telephone number that the taxpayer may contact; and

(3) an Internal Revenue Service employee shall give a taxpayer during a telephone or personal contact the employee's name and unique identifying number.

(b) SINGLE CONTACT.—The Secretary of the Treasury or the Secretary's delegate shall develop a procedure under which, to the extent practicable and if advantageous to the taxpayer, one Internal Revenue Service employee shall be assigned to handle a taxpayer's matter until it is resolved.

(c) TELEPHONE HELPLINE IN SPANISH.—The Secretary of the Treasury or the Secretary's delegate shall provide, in appropriate circumstances, that taxpayer questions on telephone helplines of the Internal Revenue Service are answered in Spanish.

(d) OTHER TELEPHONE HELPLINE OPTIONS.—The Secretary of the Treasury or the Secretary's delegate shall provide, in appropriate circumstances, on telephone helplines of the Internal Revenue Service an option for any taxpayer to talk to an Internal Revenue Service employee during normal business hours. The person shall direct phone questions of the taxpayer to other Internal Revenue Service personnel who can provide assistance to the taxpayer.

(e) EFFECTIVE DATES.—

(1) IN GENERAL.—Except as otherwise provided in this subsection, this section shall take effect 60 days after the date of the enactment of this Act.

(2) SUBSECTION (c).—Subsection (c) shall take effect on January 1, 2000.

(3) SUBSECTION (d).—Subsection (d) shall take effect on January 1, 2000.

(4) UNIQUE IDENTIFYING NUMBER.—Any requirement under this section to provide a unique identifying number shall take effect 6 months after the date of the enactment of this Act.

P.L. 105-206, § 3706, provides:
SEC. 3706. USE OF PSEUDONYMS BY INTERNAL REVENUE SERVICE EMPLOYEES.

(a) IN GENERAL.—Any employee of the Internal Revenue Service may use a pseudonym only if—

(1) adequate justification for the use of a pseudonym is provided by the employee, including protection of personal safety; and

(2) such use is approved by the employee's supervisor before the pseudonym is used.

(b) EFFECTIVE DATE.—Subsection (a) shall apply to requests made after the date of the enactment of this Act.

P.L. 105-206, § 3709, provides:
SEC. 3709. LISTING OF LOCAL INTERNAL REVENUE SERVICE TELEPHONE NUMBERS AND ADDRESSES.

The Secretary of the Treasury or the Secretary's delegate shall, as soon as practicable, provide that the local telephone numbers and addresses of Internal Revenue Service offices located in any particular area be listed in a telephone book for that area.

Prior to amendment by P.L. 105-206, § 1102(a), Code Sec. 7803 read as follows:

SEC. 7803. OTHER PERSONNEL.

[Sec. 7803(a)]

(a) APPOINTMENT AND SUPERVISION.—The Secretary is authorized to employ such number of persons as the Secretary deems proper for the administration and enforcement of the internal revenue laws, and the Secretary shall issue all necessary directions, instructions, orders, and rules applicable to such persons.

Amendments

• **1976, Tax Reform Act of 1976 (P.L. 94-455)**

P.L. 94-455, § 1906(b)(13)(A):

Amended 1954 Code by substituting "Secretary" for "Secretary or his delegate" each place it appeared. **Effective** 2-1-77.

[Sec. 7803(b)]

(b) POSTS OF DUTY OF EMPLOYEES IN FIELD SERVICE OR TRAVELING.—

(1) DESIGNATION OF POST OF DUTY.—The Secretary shall determine and designate the posts of duty of all such persons engaged in field work or traveling on official business outside of the District of Columbia.

(2) DETAIL OF PERSONNEL FROM FIELD SERVICE.—The Secretary may order any such person engaged in field work to duty in the District of Columbia, for such periods as the Secretary may prescribe, and to any designated post of duty outside the District of Columbia upon the completion of such duty.

Amendments

• **1976, Tax Reform Act of 1976 (P.L. 94-455)**

P.L. 94-455, § 1906(b)(13)(A):

Amended 1954 Code by substituting "Secretary" for "Secretary or his delegate" each place it appeared. **Effective** 2-1-77.

[Sec. 7803(c)]

(c) DELINQUENT INTERNAL REVENUE OFFICERS AND EMPLOYEES.—If any officer or employee of the Treasury Department acting in connection with the internal revenue laws fails to account for and pay over any amount of money or property collected or received by him in connection with the internal revenue laws, the Secretary shall issue notice and demand to such officer or employee for payment of the amount which he failed to account for and pay over, and, upon failure to pay the amount demanded within the time specified in such notice, the amount so demanded shall be deemed imposed upon such officer or employee and assessed upon the date of such notice and demand, and the provisions of chapter 64 and all other provisions of law relating to the collection of assessed taxes shall be applicable in respect of such amount.

Amendments

• **1976, Tax Reform Act of 1976 (P.L. 94-455)**

P.L. 94-455, § 1906(a)(58):

Redesignated Code Sec. 7803(d) as Code Sec. 7803(c). Former Code Sec. 7803(c) had been repealed by P.L. 92-310 (see below).

P.L. 94-455, § 1906(b)(13)(A):

Amended 1954 Code by substituting "Secretary" for "Secretary or his delegate" each place it appeared. **Effective** 2-1-77.

• **1972 (P.L. 92-310)**

P.L. 92-310, § 230(e):

Repealed Code Sec. 7803(c). **Effective** 6-6-72. Prior to repeal, Code Sec. 7803(c) read as follows:

(c) BONDS OF EMPLOYEES.—Whenever the Secretary or his delegate deems it proper, he may require any such officer or employee to furnish such bond, or he may purchase such blanket or schedule bonds, as the Secretary or his delegate deems appropriate. The premium of any such bond or bonds may, in the discretion of the Secretary or his delegate, be paid from the appropriation for expenses of the Internal Revenue Service.

[Sec. 7803(e)]

(e) INDEPENDENT OFFICE OF APPEALS.—

(1) ESTABLISHMENT.—There is established in the Internal Revenue Service an office to be known as the "Internal Revenue Service Independent Office of Appeals".

(2) CHIEF OF APPEALS.—

(A) IN GENERAL.—The Internal Revenue Service Independent Office of Appeals shall be under the supervision and direction of an official to be known as the "Chief of Appeals". The Chief of Appeals shall report directly to the Commissioner of Internal Revenue and shall be entitled to compensation at the same rate as the highest rate of basic pay established for the Senior Executive Service under section 5382 of title 5, United States Code.

(B) APPOINTMENT.—The Chief of Appeals shall be appointed by the Commissioner of Internal Revenue without regard to the provisions of title 5, United States Code, relating to appointments in the competitive service or the Senior Executive Service.

(C) QUALIFICATIONS.—An individual appointed under subparagraph (B) shall have experience and expertise in—

(i) administration of, and compliance with, Federal tax laws,

(ii) a broad range of compliance cases, and

(iii) management of large service organizations.

(3) PURPOSES AND DUTIES OF OFFICE.—It shall be the function of the Internal Revenue Service Independent Office of Appeals to resolve Federal tax controversies without litigation on a basis which—

(A) is fair and impartial to both the Government and the taxpayer,

(B) promotes a consistent application and interpretation of, and voluntary compliance with, the Federal tax laws, and

(C) enhances public confidence in the integrity and efficiency of the Internal Revenue Service.

APPLICATION OF LAWS

(4) RIGHT OF APPEAL.—The resolution process described in paragraph (3) shall be generally available to all taxpayers.

(5) LIMITATION ON DESIGNATION OF CASES AS NOT ELIGIBLE FOR REFERRAL TO INDEPENDENT OFFICE OF APPEALS.—

(A) IN GENERAL.—If any taxpayer which is in receipt of a notice of deficiency authorized under section 6212 requests referral to the Internal Revenue Service Independent Office of Appeals and such request is denied, the Commissioner of Internal Revenue shall provide such taxpayer a written notice which—

(i) provides a detailed description of the facts involved, the basis for the decision to deny the request, and a detailed explanation of how the basis of such decision applies to such facts, and

(ii) describes the procedures prescribed under subparagraph (C) for protesting the decision to deny the request.

(B) REPORT TO CONGRESS.—The Commissioner of Internal Revenue shall submit a written report to Congress on an annual basis which includes the number of requests described in subparagraph (A) which were denied and the reasons (described by category) that such requests were denied.

(C) PROCEDURES FOR PROTESTING DENIAL OF REQUEST.—The Commissioner of Internal Revenue shall prescribe procedures for protesting to the Commissioner of Internal Revenue a denial of a request described in subparagraph (A).

(D) NOT APPLICABLE TO FRIVOLOUS POSITIONS.—This paragraph shall not apply to a request for referral to the Internal Revenue Service Independent Office of Appeals which is denied on the basis that the issue involved is a frivolous position (within the meaning of section 6702(c)).

(6) STAFF.—

(A) IN GENERAL.—All personnel in the Internal Revenue Service Independent Office of Appeals shall report to the Chief of Appeals.

(B) ACCESS TO STAFF OF OFFICE OF THE CHIEF COUNSEL.—The Chief of Appeals shall have authority to obtain legal assistance and advice from the staff of the Office of the Chief Counsel. The Chief Counsel shall ensure, to the extent practicable, that such assistance and advice is provided by staff of the Office of the Chief Counsel who were not involved in the case with respect to which such assistance and advice is sought and who are not involved in preparing such case for litigation.

(7) ACCESS TO CASE FILES.—

(A) IN GENERAL.—In any case in which a conference with the Internal Revenue Service Independent Office of Appeals has been scheduled upon request of a specified taxpayer, the Chief of Appeals shall ensure that such taxpayer is provided access to the nonprivileged portions of the case file on record regarding the disputed issues (other than documents provided by the taxpayer to the Internal Revenue Service) not later than 10 days before the date of such conference.

(B) TAXPAYER ELECTION TO EXPEDITE CONFERENCE.—If the taxpayer so elects, subparagraph (A) shall be applied by substituting "the date of such conference" for "10 days before the date of such conference".

(C) SPECIFIED TAXPAYER.—For purposes of this paragraph—

(i) IN GENERAL.—The term "specified taxpayer" means—

(I) in the case of any taxpayer who is a natural person, a taxpayer whose adjusted gross income does not exceed $400,000 for the taxable year to which the dispute relates, and

(II) in the case of any other taxpayer, a taxpayer whose gross receipts do not exceed $5 million for the taxable year to which the dispute relates.

(ii) AGGREGATION RULE.—Rules similar to the rules of section 448(c)(2) shall apply for purposes of clause (i)(II).

Amendments

• 2019, Taxpayer First Act (P.L. 116-25)

P.L. 116-25, § 1001(a):

Amended Code Sec. 7803 by adding at the end a new subsection (e). Generally effective 7-1-2019. For exception, see Act Sec. 1001(e)(2), below. For special rules, see Act Sec. 1001(c)-(d), below.

P.L. 116-25, § 1001(c)-(d), provides:

(c) OTHER REFERENCES.—Any reference in any provision of law, or regulation or other guidance, to the Internal Revenue Service Office of Appeals shall be treated as a reference to the Internal Revenue Service Independent Office of Appeals.

(d) SAVINGS PROVISIONS.—Rules similar to the rules of paragraphs (2) through (6) of section 1001(b) of the Internal Revenue Service Restructuring and Reform Act of 1998 shall apply for purposes of this section (and the amendments made by this section).

P.L. 116-25, § 1001(e)(2), provides:

(e) EFFECTIVE DATE.—

***

(2) ACCESS TO CASE FILES.—Section 7803(e)(7) of the Internal Revenue Code of 1986, as added by subsection (a), shall apply to conferences occurring after the date which is 1 year after the date of the enactment of this Act.

[Sec. 7803(f)]

(f) INTERNAL REVENUE SERVICE CHIEF INFORMATION OFFICER.—

(1) IN GENERAL.—There shall be in the Internal Revenue Service an Internal Revenue Service Chief Information Officer (hereafter referred to in this subsection as the "IRS CIO") who shall be appointed by the Commissioner of Internal Revenue.

(2) CENTRALIZED RESPONSIBILITY FOR INTERNAL REVENUE SERVICE INFORMATION TECHNOLOGY.—The Commissioner of Internal Revenue (and the Secretary) shall act through the IRS CIO with respect to all development, implementation, and maintenance of information technology for the Internal Revenue Service. Any reference in this subsection to the IRS CIO which directs the IRS CIO to take any action, or to assume any responsibility, shall be treated as a reference to the Commissioner of Internal Revenue acting through the IRS CIO.

(3) GENERAL DUTIES AND RESPONSIBILITIES.—The IRS CIO shall—

(A) be responsible for the development, implementation, and maintenance of information technology for the Internal Revenue Service,

(B) ensure that the information technology of the Internal Revenue Service is secure and integrated,

(C) maintain operational control of all information technology for the Internal Revenue Service,

(D) be the principal advocate for the information technology needs of the Internal Revenue Service, and

(E) consult with the Chief Procurement Officer of the Internal Revenue Service to ensure that the information technology acquired for the Internal Revenue Service is consistent with—

(i) the goals and requirements specified in subparagraphs (A) through (D), and

(ii) the strategic plan developed under paragraph (4).

(4) STRATEGIC PLAN.—

(A) IN GENERAL.—The IRS CIO shall develop and implement a multiyear strategic plan for the information technology needs of the Internal Revenue Service. Such plan shall—

(i) include performance measurements of such technology and of the implementation of such plan,

(ii) include a plan for an integrated enterprise architecture of the information technology of the Internal Revenue Service,

(iii) include and take into account the resources needed to accomplish such plan,

(iv) take into account planned major acquisitions of information technology by the Internal Revenue Service, and

APPLICATION OF LAWS

(v) align with the needs and strategic plan of the Internal Revenue Service.

(B) PLAN UPDATES.—The IRS CIO shall, not less frequently than annually, review and update the strategic plan under subparagraph (A) (including the plan for an integrated enterprise architecture described in subparagraph (A)(ii)) to take into account the development of new information technology and the needs of the Internal Revenue Service.

(5) SCOPE OF AUTHORITY.—

(A) INFORMATION TECHNOLOGY.—For purposes of this subsection, the term "information technology" has the meaning given such term by section 11101 of title 40, United States Code.

(B) INTERNAL REVENUE SERVICE.—Any reference in this subsection to the Internal Revenue Service includes a reference to all components of the Internal Revenue Service, including—

(i) the Office of the Taxpayer Advocate,

(ii) the Criminal Investigation Division of the Internal Revenue Service, and

(iii) except as otherwise provided by the Secretary with respect to information technology related to matters described in subsection (b)(3)(B), the Office of the Chief Counsel.

Amendments

• **2019, Taxpayer First Act (P.L. 116-25)**

P.L. 116-25, § 2101(a):

Amended Code Sec. 7803, as amended by Act Sec. 1001, by adding at the end a new subsection (f). **Effective** 7-1-2019.

P.L. 116-25, § 2101(b)-(c), provides:

(b) INDEPENDENT VERIFICATION AND VALIDATION OF THE CUSTOMER ACCOUNT DATA ENGINE 2 AND ENTERPRISE CASE MANAGEMENT SYSTEM.—

(1) IN GENERAL.—The Commissioner of Internal Revenue shall enter into a contract with an independent reviewer to verify and validate the implementation plans (including the performance milestones and cost estimates included in such plans) developed for the Customer Account Data Engine 2 and the Enterprise Case Management System.

(2) DEADLINE FOR COMPLETION.—Such contract shall require that such verification and validation be completed not later than the date which is 1 year after the date of the enactment of this Act.

(3) APPLICATION TO PHASES OF CADE 2.—

(A) IN GENERAL.—Paragraphs (1) and (2) shall not apply to phase 1 of the Customer Account Data Engine 2 and shall apply separately to each other phase.

(B) DEADLINE FOR COMPLETING PLANS.—Not later than 1 year after the date of the enactment of this Act, the Commissioner of Internal Revenue shall complete the development of plans for all phases of the Customer Account Data Engine 2.

(C) DEADLINE FOR COMPLETION OF VERIFICATION AND VALIDATION OF PLANS.—In the case of any phase after phase 2 of the Customer Account Data Engine 2, paragraph (2) shall be applied by substituting "the date on which the plan for such phase was completed" for "the date of the enactment of this Act".

(c) COORDINATION OF IRS CIO AND CHIEF PROCUREMENT OFFICER OF THE INTERNAL REVENUE SERVICE.—

(1) IN GENERAL.—The Chief Procurement Officer of the Internal Revenue Service shall—

(A) identify all significant IRS information technology acquisitions and provide written notification to the Internal Revenue Service Chief Information Officer (hereafter referred to in this subsection as the "IRS CIO") of each such acquisition in advance of such acquisition, and

(B) regularly consult with the IRS CIO regarding acquisitions of information technology for the Internal Revenue Service, including meeting with the IRS CIO regarding such acquisitions upon request.

(2) SIGNIFICANT IRS INFORMATION TECHNOLOGY ACQUISITIONS.—For purposes of this subsection, the term "significant IRS information technology acquisitions" means—

(A) any acquisition of information technology for the Internal Revenue Service in excess of $1 million; and

(B) such other acquisitions of information technology for the Internal Revenue Service (or categories of such acquisitions) as the IRS CIO, in consultation with the Chief Procurement Officer of the Internal Revenue Service, may identify.

(3) SCOPE.—Terms used in this subsection which are also used in section 7803(f) of the Internal Revenue Code of 1986 (as added by subsection (a)) shall have the same meaning as when used in such section.

[Sec. 7804]

SEC. 7804. OTHER PERSONNEL.

[Sec. 7804(a)]

(a) APPOINTMENT AND SUPERVISION.—Unless otherwise prescribed by the Secretary, the Commissioner of Internal Revenue is authorized to employ such number of persons as the Commissioner deems proper for the administration and enforcement of the internal revenue laws, and the Commissioner shall issue all necessary directions, instructions, orders, and rules applicable to such persons.

[Sec. 7804(b)]

(b) POSTS OF DUTY OF EMPLOYEES IN FIELD SERVICE OR TRAVELING.—Unless otherwise prescribed by the Secretary—

(1) DESIGNATION OF POST OF DUTY.—The Commissioner shall determine and designate the posts of duty of all such persons engaged in field work or traveling on official business outside of the District of Columbia.

(2) DETAIL OF PERSONNEL FROM FIELD SERVICE.—The Commissioner may order any such person engaged in field work to duty in the District of Columbia, for such periods as the Commissioner may prescribe, and to any designated post of duty outside the District of Columbia upon the completion of such duty.

[Sec. 7804(c)]

(c) DELINQUENT INTERNAL REVENUE OFFICERS AND EMPLOYEES.—If any officer or employee of the Treasury Department acting in connection with the internal revenue laws fails to account for and pay over any amount of money or property collected or received by him in connection with the internal revenue laws, the Secretary shall issue notice and demand to such officer or employee for payment of the amount which he failed to account for and pay over, and, upon failure to pay the amount demanded within the time specified in such notice, the amount so demanded shall be deemed imposed upon such officer or employee and assessed upon the date of such notice and demand, and the provisions of chapter 64 and all other provisions of law relating to the collection of assessed taxes shall be applicable in respect of such amount.

Amendments

• **1998, IRS Restructuring and Reform Act of 1998 (P.L. 105-206)**

P.L. 105-206, § 1104(a):

Amended Code Sec. 7804. **Effective** 7-22-98. Prior to amendment, Code Sec. 7804 read as follows:

SEC. 7804. EFFECT OF REORGANIZATION PLANS.

(a) APPLICATION.—The provisions of Reorganization Plan Numbered 26 of 1950 and Reorganization Plan Numbered 1 of 1952 shall be applicable to all functions vested by this title, or by any act amending this title (except as otherwise expressly provided in such amending act), in any officer, employee, or agency, of the Department of the Treasury.

(b) PRESERVATION OF EXISTING RIGHTS AND REMEDIES.—Nothing in Reorganization Plan Numbered 26 of 1950 or Reorganization Plan Numbered 1 of 1952 shall be considered to impair any right or remedy, including trial by jury, to recover any internal revenue tax alleged to have been erroneously or illegally assessed or collected, or any penalty claimed to have been collected without authority, or any sum alleged to have been excessive or in any manner wrongfully collected under the internal revenue laws. For the purpose of any action to recover any such tax, penalty, or sum, all statutes, rules, and regulations referring to the collector of internal revenue, the principal officer for the internal revenue district, or the Secretary, shall be deemed to refer to the officer whose act or acts referred to in the preceding sentence gave rise to such action. The venue of any such action shall be the same as under existing law.

• **1976, Tax Reform Act of 1976 (P.L. 94-455)**

P.L. 94-455, § 1906(b)(13)(A):

Amended 1954 Code by substituting "Secretary" for "Secretary or his delegate" each place it appeared. **Effective** 2-1-77.

[Sec. 7804(d)]

(d) PROHIBITION ON REHIRING EMPLOYEES INVOLUNTARILY SEPARATED.—The Commissioner may not hire any individual previously employed by the Commissioner who was removed for misconduct under this subchapter or chapter 43 or chapter 75 of title 5, United States Code, or whose employment was terminated under section 1203 of the Internal Revenue Service Restructuring and Reform Act of 1998 (26 U.S.C. 7804 note).

APPLICATION OF LAWS

Amendments
- **2019, Taxpayer First Act (P.L. 116-25)**

P.L. 116-25, §3001(a):
Amended Code Sec. 7804 by adding at the end a new subsection (d). **Effective** with respect to the hiring of employees after 7-1-2019.

[Sec. 7805]

SEC. 7805. RULES AND REGULATIONS.

[Sec. 7805(a)]

(a) AUTHORIZATION.—Except where such authority is expressly given by this title to any person other than an officer or employee of the Treasury Department, the Secretary shall prescribe all needful rules and regulations for the enforcement of this title, including all rules and regulations as may be necessary by reason of any alteration of law in relation to internal revenue.

Amendments
- **1976, Tax Reform Act of 1976 (P.L. 94-455)**

P.L. 94-455, §1906(b)(13)(A):
Amended 1954 Code by substituting "Secretary" for "Secretary or his delegate" each place it appeared. **Effective** 2-1-77.

[Sec. 7805(b)]

(b) RETROACTIVITY OF REGULATIONS.—

(1) IN GENERAL.—Except as otherwise provided in this subsection, no temporary, proposed, or final regulation relating to the internal revenue laws shall apply to any taxable period ending before the earliest of the following dates:

(A) The date on which such regulation is filed with the Federal Register.

(B) In the case of any final regulation, the date on which any proposed or temporary regulation to which such final regulation relates was filed with the Federal Register.

(C) The date on which any notice substantially describing the expected contents of any temporary, proposed, or final regulation is issued to the public.

(2) EXCEPTION FOR PROMPTLY ISSUED REGULATIONS.—Paragraph (1) shall not apply to regulations filed or issued within 18 months of the date of the enactment of the statutory provision to which the regulation relates.

(3) PREVENTION OF ABUSE.—The Secretary may provide that any regulation may take effect or apply retroactively to prevent abuse.

(4) CORRECTION OF PROCEDURAL DEFECTS.—The Secretary may provide that any regulation may apply retroactively to correct a procedural defect in the issuance of any prior regulation.

(5) INTERNAL REGULATIONS.—The limitation of paragraph (1) shall not apply to any regulation relating to internal Treasury Department policies, practices, or procedures.

(6) CONGRESSIONAL AUTHORIZATION.—The limitation of paragraph (1) may be superseded by a legislative grant from Congress authorizing the Secretary to prescribe the effective date with respect to any regulation.

(7) ELECTION TO APPLY RETROACTIVELY.—The Secretary may provide for any taxpayer to elect to apply any regulation before the dates specified in paragraph (1).

(8) APPLICATION TO RULINGS.—The Secretary may prescribe the extent, if any, to which any ruling (including any judicial decision or any administrative determination other than by regulation) relating to the internal revenue laws shall be applied without retroactive effect.

Amendments
- **1996, Taxpayer Bill of Rights 2 (P.L. 104-168)**

P.L. 104-168, §1101(a):
Amended Code Sec. 7805(b). **Effective** with respect to regulations which relate to statutory provisions enacted on or after 7-30-96. Prior to amendment, Code Sec. 7805(b) read as follows:

(b) RETROACTIVITY OF REGULATIONS OR RULINGS.—The Secretary may prescribe the extent, if any, to which any ruling or regulation, relating to the internal revenue laws, shall be applied without retroactive effect.

- **1976, Tax Reform Act of 1976 (P.L. 94-455)**

P.L. 94-455, §1906(b)(13)(A):
Amended 1954 Code by substituting "Secretary" for "Secretary or his delegate" each place it appeared. **Effective** 2-1-77.

[Sec. 7805(c)]

(c) PREPARATION AND DISTRIBUTION OF REGULATIONS, FORMS, STAMPS, AND OTHER MATTERS.—The Secretary shall prepare and distribute all the instructions, regulations, directions, forms, blanks, stamps, and other matters pertaining to the assessment and collection of internal revenue.

Amendments
- **1976, Tax Reform Act of 1976 (P.L. 94-455)**

P.L. 94-455, §1906(b)(13)(A):
Amended 1954 Code by substituting "Secretary" for "Secretary or his delegate" each place it appeared. **Effective** 2-1-77.

[Sec. 7805(d)]

(d) MANNER OF MAKING ELECTIONS PRESCRIBED BY SECRETARY.—Except to the extent otherwise provided by this title, any election under this title shall be made at such time and in such manner as the Secretary shall prescribe.

Amendments
- **1998, IRS Restructuring and Reform Act of 1998 (P.L. 105-206)**

P.L. 105-206, §3704:
Amended Code Sec. 7805(d) by striking "by regulations or forms" after "Secretary shall". **Effective** 7-22-98.

- **1984, Deficit Reduction Act of 1984 (P.L. 98-369)**

P.L. 98-369, §43(b):
Amended Code Sec. 7805 by adding at the end thereof new subsection (d). **Effective** for tax years ending after 7-18-84.

[Sec. 7805(e)]

(e) TEMPORARY REGULATIONS.—

(1) ISSUANCE.—Any temporary regulation issued by the Secretary shall also be issued as a proposed regulation.

(2) 3-YEAR DURATION.—Any temporary regulation shall expire within 3 years after the date of issuance of such regulation.

Sec. 7805

APPLICATION OF LAWS

Amendments

• **1988, Technical and Miscellaneous Revenue Act of 1988 (P.L. 100-647)**

P.L. 100-647, §6232(a):

Amended Code Sec. 7805 by adding at the end thereof new subsection (e). **Effective** for any regulation issued after 11-20-88.

[Sec. 7805(f)]

(f) REVIEW OF IMPACT OF REGULATIONS ON SMALL BUSINESS.—

(1) SUBMISSIONS TO SMALL BUSINESS ADMINISTRATION.—After publication of any proposed or temporary regulation by the Secretary, the Secretary shall submit such regulation to the Chief Counsel for Advocacy of the Small Business Administration for comment on the impact of such regulation on small business. Not later than the date 4 weeks after the date of such submission, the Chief Counsel for Advocacy shall submit comments on such regulation to the Secretary.

(2) CONSIDERATION OF COMMENTS.—In prescribing any final regulation which supersedes a proposed or temporary regulation which had been submitted under this subsection to the Chief Counsel for Advocacy of the Small Business Administration—

(A) the Secretary shall consider the comments of the Chief Counsel for Advocacy on such proposed or temporary regulation, and

(B) the Secretary shall discuss any response to such comments in the preamble of such final regulation.

(3) SUBMISSION OF CERTAIN FINAL REGULATIONS.—In the case of the promulgation by the Secretary of any final regulation (other than a temporary regulation) which does not supersede a proposed regulation, the requirements of paragraphs (1) and (2) shall apply; except that—

(A) the submission under paragraph (1) shall be made at least 4 weeks before the date of such promulgation, and

(B) the consideration (and discusssion) required under paragraph (2) shall be made in connection with the promulgation of such final regulation.

Amendments

• **1990, Omnibus Budget Reconciliation Act of 1990 (P.L. 101-508)**

P.L. 101-508, §11621(a):

Amended Code Sec. 7805(f). **Effective** for regulations issued after the date which is 30 days after 11-5-90. Prior to amendment, Code Sec. 7805(f) read as follows:

(f) IMPACT OF REGULATIONS ON SMALL BUSINESS REVIEWED.—After the publication of any proposed regulation by the Secretary and before the promulgation of any final regulation by the Secretary which does not supersede a proposed regulation, the Secretary shall submit such regulation to the Administrator of the Small Business Administration for comment on the impact of such regulation on small business. The Administrator shall have 4 weeks from the date of submission to respond.

• **1988, Technical and Miscellaneous Revenue Act of 1988 (P.L. 100-647)**

P.L. 100-647, §6232(a):

Amended Code Sec. 7805 by adding at the end thereof new subsection (f). **Effective** for any regulation issued after 11-20-88.

[Sec. 7806]

SEC. 7806. CONSTRUCTION OF TITLE.

[Sec. 7806(a)]

(a) CROSS REFERENCES.—The cross references in this title to other portions of the title, or other provisions of law, where the word "see" is used, are made only for convenience, and shall be given no legal effect.

[Sec. 7806(b)]

(b) ARRANGEMENT AND CLASSIFICATION.—No inference, implication, or presumption of legislative construction shall be drawn or made by reason of the location or grouping of any particular section or provision or portion of this title, nor shall any table of contents, table of cross references, or similar outline, analysis, or descriptive matter relating to the contents of this title be given any legal effect. The preceding sentence also applies to the sidenotes and ancillary tables contained in the various prints of this Act before its enactment into law.

[Sec. 7807]

SEC. 7807. RULES IN EFFECT UPON ENACTMENT OF THIS TITLE.

[Sec. 7807(a)]

(a) INTERIM PROVISION FOR ADMINISTRATION OF TITLE.—Until regulations are promulgated under any provision of this title which depends for its application upon the promulgation of regulations (or which is to be applied in such manner as may be prescribed by regulations) all instructions, rules or regulations which are in effect immediately prior to the enactment of this title shall, to the extent such instructions, rules, or regulations could be prescribed as regulations under authority of such provision, be applied as if promulgated as regulations under such provision.

[Sec. 7807(b)]

(b) PROVISIONS OF THIS TITLE CORRESPONDING TO PRIOR INTERNAL REVENUE LAWS.—

(1) REFERENCE TO LAW APPLICABLE TO PRIOR PERIOD.—Any provision of this title which refers to the application of any portion of this title to a prior period (or which depends upon the application to a prior period of any portion of this title) shall, when appropriate and consistent with the purpose of such provision, be deemed to refer to (or depend upon the application of) the corresponding provision of the Internal Revenue Code of 1939 or of such other internal revenue laws as were applicable to the prior period.

(2) ELECTIONS OR OTHER ACTS.—If an election or other act under the provisions of the Internal Revenue Code of 1939 would, if this title had not been enacted, be given effect for a period subsequent to the date of enactment of this title, and if corresponding provisions are contained in this title, such election or other act shall be given effect under the corresponding provisions of this title.

[Sec. 7808]

SEC. 7808. DEPOSITARIES FOR COLLECTIONS.

The Secretary is authorized to designate one or more depositaries in each State for the deposit and safe-keeping of the money collected by virtue of the internal revenue laws; and the receipt of the proper officer of such depositary to the proper officer or employee of the Treasury Department for the money deposited by him shall be a sufficient voucher for such Treasury officer or employee in the settlement of his accounts.

Amendments

• **1976, Tax Reform Act of 1976 (P.L. 94-455)**

P.L. 94-455, §1906(b)(13)(A):

Amended 1954 Code by substituting "Secretary" for "Secretary or his delegate" each place it appeared. **Effective** 2-1-77.

APPLICATION OF LAWS

[Sec. 7809]

SEC. 7809. DEPOSIT OF COLLECTIONS.

[Sec. 7809(a)]

(a) GENERAL RULE.—Except as provided in subsections (b) and (c) and in sections 6306, 7651, 7652, 7654, and 7810, the gross amount of all taxes and revenues received under the provisions of this title, and collections of whatever nature received or collected by authority of any internal revenue law, shall be paid daily into the Treasury of the United States under instructions of the Secretary as internal revenue collections, by the officer or employee receiving or collecting the same, without any abatement or deduction on account of salary, compensation, fees, costs, charges, expenses, or claims of any description. A certificate of such payment, stating the name of the depositor and the specific account on which the deposit was made, signed by the Treasurer of the United States, designated depositary, or proper officer of a deposit bank, shall be transmitted to the Secretary.

Amendments

• **2004, American Jobs Creation Act of 2004 (P.L. 108-357)**

P.L. 108-357, §881(a)(2)(A):

Amended Code Sec. 7809(a) by inserting "6306," before "7651". **Effective** 10-22-2004.

• **1976, Tax Reform Act of 1976 (P.L. 94-455)**

P.L. 94-455, §1906(a)(59):

Struck out "4735, 4762," before "7651". **Effective** for tax years beginning after 12-31-76.

P.L. 94-455, §1906(b)(13)(A):

Amended 1954 Code by substituting "Secretary" for "Secretary or his delegate" each place it appeared. **Effective** 2-1-77.

• **1966, Federal Tax Lien Act of 1966 (P.L. 89-719)**

P.L. 89-719, §112(b):

Amended Code Sec. 7809(a) by substituting "7654, and 7810," for "and 7654,". **Effective**, generally, after 11-2-66. However, see the amendment note for Code Sec. 6323 for exceptions to this **effective** date.

• **1962 (P.L. 87-870)**

P.L. 87-870, §3(b)(1):

Amended Code Sec. 7809(a) by substituting "subsections (b) and (c) and in" for "subsection (b),". **Effective** 10-24-62.

[Sec. 7809(b)]

(b) DEPOSIT FUNDS.—In accordance with instructions of the Secretary, there shall be deposited with the Treasurer of the United States in a deposit fund account—

(1) SUMS OFFERED IN COMPROMISE.—Sums offered in compromise under the provisions of section 7122;

(2) SUMS OFFERED FOR PURCHASE OF REAL ESTATE.—Sums offered for the purchase of real estate under the provisions of section 7506;

(3) SURPLUS PROCEEDS IN SALES UNDER LEVY.—Surplus proceeds in any sale under levy, after making allowance for the amount of the tax, interest, penalties, and additions thereto, and for costs and charges of the levy and sale; and

(4) SURPLUS PROCEEDS IN SALES OF REDEEMED PROPERTY.—Surplus proceeds in any sale under section 7506 of real property redeemed by the United States, after making allowance for the amount of the tax, interest, penalties, and additions thereto, and for the costs of sale.

Upon the acceptance of such offer in compromise or offer for the purchase of such real estate, the amount so accepted shall be withdrawn from such deposit fund account and deposited in the Treasury of the United States as internal revenue collections. Upon the rejection of any such offer, the Secretary shall refund to the maker of such offer the amount thereof.

Amendments

• **1976, Tax Reform Act of 1976 (P.L. 94-455)**

P.L. 94-455, §1906(b)(13)(A):

Amended 1954 Code by substituting "Secretary" for "Secretary or his delegate" each place it appeared. **Effective** 2-1-77.

• **1966, Federal Tax Lien Act of 1966 (P.L. 89-719)**

P.L. 89-719, §112(b):

Amended Code Sec. 7809(b) by striking out "and" at the end of paragraph (2), by substituting "; and" for the period at the end of paragraph (3), and by adding new paragraph (4). **Effective**, generally, after 11-2-66. However, see the amendment note for Code Sec. 6323 for exceptions to this **effective** date.

[Sec. 7809(c)]

(c) DEPOSIT OF CERTAIN RECEIPTS.—Moneys received in payment for—

(1) work or services performed pursuant to section 6103(p) (relating to furnishing of copies of returns or of return information), and section 6108(b) (relating to special statistical studies and compilations).

(2) work or services performed (including materials supplied) pursuant to section 7516 (relating to the supplying of training and training aids on request);

(3) other work or services performed for a State or a department or agency of the Federal Government (subject to all provisions of law and regulations governing disclosure of information) in supplying copies of, or data from, returns, statements, or other documents filed under authority of this title or records maintained in connection with the administration and enforcement of this title; and

(4) work or services performed (including materials supplied) pursuant to section 6110 (relating to public inspection of written determinations),

shall be deposited in a separate account which may be used to reimburse appropriations which bore all or part of the costs of such work or services, or to refund excess sums when necessary.

Amendments

• **2018, Tax Technical Corrections Act of 2018 (P.L. 115-141)**

P.L. 115-141, §401(a)(334), Div. U:

Amended Code Sec. 7809(c)(1) by striking "Work" and inserting "work". **Effective** 3-23-2018.

• **1976 (P.L. 94-528)**

P.L. 94-528, §2(d):

Struck out "and" at the end of paragraph (2), substituted a semicolon and "and" for the comma at the end of paragraph (3), and added a new paragraph (4) to Code Sec. 7809(c). **Effective** 10-4-76.

• **1976, Tax Reform Act of 1976 (P.L. 94-455)**

P.L. 94-455, §1202(h)(5):

Substituted "section 6103(p) (relating to furnishing of copies of returns or of return information), and section 6108(b) (relating to special statistical studies and compilations)" for "section 7515 (relating to special statistical studies and compilations for other services on request)" in Code Sec. 7809(c). **Effective** 1-1-77.

• **1962 (P.L. 87-870)**

P.L. 87-870, §3(b)(2):

Added Code Sec. 7809(c). **Effective** 10-24-62.

[Sec. 7809(d)]

(d) DEPOSIT OF FUNDS FOR LAW ENFORCEMENT AGENCY ACCOUNT.—

(1) IN GENERAL.—In the case of any amounts recovered as the result of information provided to the Internal Revenue Service by State and local law enforcement agencies which substantially contributed to such recovery, an amount equal to 10 percent of such amounts shall be deposited in a separate account which shall be used to make the reimbursements required under section 7624.

(2) DEPOSIT IN TREASURY AS INTERNAL REVENUE COLLECTIONS.—If any amounts remain in such account after payment of any qualified costs incurred under section 7624, such amounts shall be withdrawn from such account and deposited in the Treasury of the United States as internal revenue collections.

APPLICATION OF LAWS

Amendments

• **1988, Anti-Drug Abuse Act of 1988 (P.L. 100-690)**

P.L. 100-690, §7602(b):

Amended Code Sec. 7809 by adding at the end thereof new subsection (d). **Effective** for information first provided more than 90 days after 11-18-88.

P.L. 100-690, §7602(f), provides:

(f) AUTHORIZATION OF APPROPRIATIONS.—There is authorized to be appropriated from the account referred to in section 7809(d) of the Internal Revenue Code of 1986 such sums as may be necessary to make the payments authorized by section 7624 of such Code.

[Sec. 7810]

SEC. 7810. REVOLVING FUND FOR REDEMPTION OF REAL PROPERTY.

[Sec. 7810(a)]

(a) ESTABLISHMENT OF FUND.—There is established a revolving fund, under the control of the Secretary, which shall be available without fiscal year limitation for all expenses necessary for the redemption (by the Secretary) of real property as provided in section 7425(d) and section 2410 of title 28 of the United States Code. There are authorized to be appropriated from time to time such sums (not to exceed $10,000,000 in the aggregate) as may be necessary to carry out the purposes of this section.

Amendments

• **1984, Deficit Reduction Act of 1984 (P.L. 98-369)**

P.L. 98-369, §443:

Amended Code Sec. 7810(a) by striking out "$1,000,000" and inserting in lieu thereof "$10,000,000". **Effective** on the first day of the first calendar month which begins more than 90 days after 7-18-84.

[Sec. 7810(b)]

(b) REIMBURSEMENT OF FUND.—The fund shall be reimbursed from the proceeds of a subsequent sale of real property redeemed by the United States in an amount equal to the amount expended out of such fund for such redemption.

[Sec. 7810(c)]

(c) SYSTEM OF ACCOUNTS.—The Secretary shall maintain an adequate system of accounts for such fund and prepare annual reports on the basis of such accounts.

Amendments

• **1976, Tax Reform Act of 1976 (P.L. 94-455)**

P.L. 94-455, §1906(b)(13)(A):

Amended 1954 Code by substituting "Secretary" for "Secretary or his delegate" each place it appeared. **Effective** 2-1-77.

• **1966, Federal Tax Lien Act of 1966 (P.L. 89-719)**

P.L. 89-719, §112(a):

Added Code Sec. 7810. **Effective**, generally, after 11-2-66. However, see the amendment note for Code Sec. 6323 for exceptions to this **effective** date.

[Sec. 7811]

SEC. 7811. TAXPAYER ASSISTANCE ORDERS.

[Sec. 7811(a)]

(a) AUTHORITY TO ISSUE.—

(1) IN GENERAL.—Upon application filed by a taxpayer with the Office of the Taxpayer Advocate (in such form, manner, and at such time as the Secretary shall by regulations prescribe), the National Taxpayer Advocate may issue a Taxpayer Assistance Order if—

(A) the National Taxpayer Advocate determines the taxpayer is suffering or about to suffer a significant hardship as a result of the manner in which the internal revenue laws are being administered by the Secretary; or

(B) the taxpayer meets such other requirements as are set forth in regulations prescribed by the Secretary.

(2) DETERMINATION OF HARDSHIP.—For purposes of paragraph (1), a significant hardship shall include—

(A) an immediate threat of adverse action;

(B) a delay of more than 30 days in resolving taxpayer account problems;

(C) the incurring by the taxpayer of significant costs (including fees for professional representation) if relief is not granted; or

(D) irreparable injury to, or a long-term adverse impact on, the taxpayer if relief is not granted.

(3) STANDARD WHERE ADMINISTRATIVE GUIDANCE NOT FOLLOWED.—In cases where any Internal Revenue Service employee is not following applicable published administrative guidance (including the Internal Revenue Manual), the National Taxpayer Advocate shall construe the factors taken into account in determining whether to issue a Taxpayer Assistance Order in the manner most favorable to the taxpayer.

Amendments

• **2000, Community Renewal Tax Relief Act of 2000 (P.L. 106-554)**

P.L. 106-554, §319(28):

Amended Code Sec. 7811(a)(3) by striking "taxpayer assistance order" and inserting "Taxpayer Assistance Order". **Effective** 12-21-2000.

• **1998, IRS Restructuring and Reform Act of 1998 (P.L. 105-206)**

P.L. 105-206, §1102(c):

Amended Code Sec. 7811(a). **Effective** 7-22-98. Prior to amendment, Code Sec. 7811(a) read as follows:

(a) AUTHORITY TO ISSUE.—Upon application filed by a taxpayer with the Office of the Taxpayer Advocate (in such form, manner, and at such time as the Secretary shall by regulations prescribe), the Taxpayer Advocate may issue a Taxpayer Assistance Order if, in the determination of the Taxpayer Advocate, the taxpayer is suffering or about to suffer a significant hardship as a result of the manner in which the internal revenue laws are being administered by the Secretary.

• **1996, Taxpayer Bill of Rights 2 (P.L. 104-168)**

P.L. 104-168, §101(b)(1)(A)-(B):

Amended Code Sec. 7811 by striking "the Office of Ombudsman" in subsection (a) and inserting "the Office of the Taxpayer Advocate", and by striking "Ombudsman" each place it appears and inserting "Taxpayer Advocate". **Effective** 7-30-96.

[Sec. 7811(b)]

(b) TERMS OF A TAXPAYER ASSISTANCE ORDER.—The terms of a Taxpayer Assistance Order may require the Secretary within a specified time period—

(1) to release property of the taxpayer levied upon, or

(2) to cease any action, take any action as permitted by law, or refrain from taking any action, with respect to the taxpayer under—

(A) chapter 64 (relating to collection),

(B) subchapter B of chapter 70 (relating to bankruptcy and receiverships),

(C) chapter 78 (relating to discovery of liability and enforcement of title), or

(D) any other provision of law which is specifically described by the National Taxpayer Advocate in such order.

APPLICATION OF LAWS

Amendments

• **1998, IRS Restructuring and Reform Act of 1998 (P.L. 105-206)**

P.L. 105-206, § 1102(d)(1)(C):

Amended Code Sec. 7811(b)(2)(D) by striking "Taxpayer Advocate" and inserting "National Taxpayer Advocate". **Effective** 7-22-98.

• **1996, Taxpayer Bill of Rights 2 (P.L. 104-168)**

P.L. 104-168, § 102(a)(1)-(2):

Amended Code Sec. 7811(b) by inserting "within a specified time period" after "the Secretary", and by inserting "take any action as permitted by law," after "cease any action,". **Effective** 7-30-96.

[Sec. 7811(c)]

(c) AUTHORITY TO MODIFY OR RESCIND.—Any Taxpayer Assistance Order issued by the National Taxpayer Advocate under this section may be modified or rescinded—

(1) only by the National Taxpayer Advocate, the Commissioner of Internal Revenue, or the Deputy Commissioner of Internal Revenue, and

(2) only if a written explanation of the reasons for the modification or rescission is provided to the National Taxpayer Advocate.

Amendments

• **1998, IRS Restructuring and Reform Act of 1998 (P.L. 105-206)**

P.L. 105-206, § 1102(d)(1)(D):

Amended Code Sec. 7811(c) by striking "Taxpayer Advocate" each place it appears and inserting "National Taxpayer Advocate". **Effective** 7-22-98.

• **1996, Taxpayer Bill of Rights 2 (P.L. 104-168)**

P.L. 104-168, § 102(b):

Amended Code Sec. 7811(c). **Effective** 7-30-96. Prior to amendment, Code Sec. 7811(c) read as follows:

(c) AUTHORITY TO MODIFY OR RESCIND.—Any Taxpayer Assistance Order issued by the Ombudsman under this section may be modified or rescinded only by the Ombudsman, a district director, a service center director, a compliance center director, a regional director of appeals, or any superior of any such person.

[Sec. 7811(d)]

(d) SUSPENSION OF RUNNING OF PERIOD OF LIMITATION.—The running of any period of limitation with respect to any action described in subsection (b) shall be suspended for—

(1) the period beginning on the date of the taxpayer's application under subsection (a) and ending on the date of the National Taxpayer Advocate's decision with respect to such application, and

(2) any period specified by the National Taxpayer Advocate in a Taxpayer Assistance Order issued pursuant to such application.

Amendments

• **2000, Community Renewal Tax Relief Act of 2000 (P.L. 106-554)**

P.L. 106-554, § 319(29):

Amended Code Sec. 7811(d)(1) by striking "Ombudsman's" and inserting "National Taxpayer Advocate's". **Effective** 12-21-2000. [Note: This amendment was previously enacted by Act Sec. 1102(d)(2) of P.L. 105-206.—CCH].

• **1998, IRS Restructuring and Reform Act of 1998 (P.L. 105-206)**

P.L. 105-206, § 1102(d)(1)(E):

Amended Code Sec. 7811(d)(2) by striking "Taxpayer Advocate" and inserting "National Taxpayer Advocate". **Effective** 7-22-98.

P.L. 105-206, § 1102(d)(2):

Amended Code Sec. 7811(d)(1) by striking "Taxpayer Advocate's" and inserting "National Taxpayer Advocate's". **Effective** 7-22-98.

• **1996, Taxpayer Bill of Rights 2 (P.L. 104-168)**

P.L. 104-168, § 101(b)(1)(B):

Amended Code Sec. 7811 by striking "Ombudsman" each place it appears and inserting "Taxpayer Advocate". **Effective** 7-30-96.

[Sec. 7811(e)]

(e) INDEPENDENT ACTION OF NATIONAL TAXPAYER ADVOCATE.—Nothing in this section shall prevent the National Taxpayer Advocate from taking any action in the absence of an application under subsection (a).

Amendments

• **1998, IRS Restructuring and Reform Act of 1998 (P.L. 105-206)**

P.L. 105-206, § 1102(d)(1)(F):

Amended Code Sec. 7811(e) by striking "Taxpayer Advocate" and inserting "National Taxpayer Advocate". **Effective** 7-22-98.

P.L. 105-206, § 1102(d)(3):

Amended the heading of subsection (e) of Code Sec. 7811 by striking "TAXPAYER ADVOCATE" and inserting "NATIONAL TAXPAYER ADVOCATE". **E**ffective 7-22-98.

• **1996, Taxpayer Bill of Rights 2 (P.L. 104-168)**

P.L. 104-168, § 101(b)(1)(B):

Amended Code Sec. 7811(e) by striking "Ombudsman" each place it appears and inserting "Taxpayer Advocate". **Effective** 7-30-96.

[Sec. 7811(f)]

(f) NATIONAL TAXPAYER ADVOCATE.—For purposes of this section, the term "National Taxpayer Advocate" includes any designee of the National Taxpayer Advocate.

Amendments

• **1998, IRS Restructuring and Reform Act of 1998 (P.L. 105-206)**

P.L. 105-206, § 1102(d)(1)(G):

Amended Code Sec. 7811(f) by striking "Taxpayer Advocate" and inserting "National Taxpayer Advocate" each place it appears. **Effective** 7-22-98.

P.L. 105-206, § 1102(d)(3):

Amended the heading of subsection (f) of Code Sec. 7811 by striking "TAXPAYER ADVOCATE" and inserting "NATIONAL TAXPAYER ADVOCATE". **E**ffective 7-22-98.

• **1996, Taxpayer Bill of Rights 2 (P.L. 104-168)**

P.L. 104-168, § 101(b)(1)(B):

Amended Code Sec. 7811(f) by striking "Ombudsman" each place it appears and inserting "Taxpayer Advocate". **Effective** 7-30-96.

• **1988, Technical and Miscellaneous Revenue Act of 1988 (P.L. 100-647)**

P.L. 100-647, § 6230(a):

Amended Subchapter A of chapter 80 by adding a new Section 7811. **Effective** 1-1-89.

[Sec. 7811(g)]

(g) APPLICATION TO PERSONS PERFORMING SERVICES UNDER A QUALIFIED TAX COLLECTION CONTRACT.—Any order issued or action taken by the National Taxpayer Advocate pursuant to this section shall apply to persons performing services under a qualified tax collection contract (as defined in section 6306(b)) to the same extent and in the same manner as such order or action applies to the Secretary.

Amendments

• **2004, American Jobs Creation Act of 2004 (P.L. 108-357)**

P.L. 108-357, § 881(c):

Amended Code Sec. 7811 by adding at the end a new subsection (g). **Effective** 10-22-2004.

[Sec. 7812]

SEC. 7812. STREAMLINED CRITICAL PAY AUTHORITY FOR INFORMATION TECHNOLOGY POSITIONS.

In the case of any position which is critical to the functionality of the information technology operations of the Internal Revenue Service—

(1) section 9503 of title 5, United States Code, shall be applied—

EFFECTIVE DATE

(A) by substituting "during the period beginning on the date of the enactment of section 7812 of the Internal Revenue Code of 1986, and ending on September 30, 2025" for "Before September 30, 2013 in subsection (a)",

(B) without regard to subparagraph (B) of subsection (a)(1), and

(C) by substituting "the date of the enactment of the Taxpayer First Act" for "June 1, 1998" in subsection (a)(6),

(2) section 9504 of such title 5 shall be applied by substituting "During the period beginning on the date of the enactment of section 7812 of the Internal Revenue Code of 1986, and ending on September 30, 2025" for "Before September 30, 2013" each place it appears in subsections (a) and (b), and

(3) section 9505 of such title shall be applied—

(A) by substituting "During the period beginning on the date of the enactment of section 7812 of the Internal Revenue Code of 1986, and ending on September 30, 2025" for "Before September 30, 2013" in subsection (a), and

(B) by substituting "the information technology operations" for "significant functions" in subsection (a).

Amendments

• 2019, Taxpayer First Act (P.L. 116-25)

P.L. 116-25, §2103(a):

Amended subchapter A of chapter 80 by adding at the end a new Code Sec. 7812.
Effective 7-1-2019.

Subchapter B—Effective Date and Related Provisions

Sec. 7851.   Applicability of revenue laws.
Sec. 7852.   Other applicable rules.

[Sec. 7851]

SEC. 7851. APPLICABILITY OF REVENUE LAWS.

[Sec. 7851(a)]

(a) GENERAL RULES.—Except as otherwise provided in any section of this title—

(1) SUBTITLE A.—

(A) Chapters 1, 2, and 6 of this title shall apply only with respect to taxable years beginning after December 31, 1953, and ending after the date of enactment of this title, and with respect to such taxable years, chapters 1 (except sections 143 and 144) and 2, and section 3801, of the Internal Revenue Code of 1939 are hereby repealed.

(B) Chapter 3 of this title shall apply with respect to payments and transfers occurring after December 31, 1954, and as to such payments and transfers sections 143 and 144 and chapter 7 of the Internal Revenue Code of 1939 are hereby repealed.

(C) Any provision of subtitle A of this title the applicability of which is stated in terms of a specific date (occurring after December 31, 1953), or in terms of taxable years ending after a specific date (occurring after December 31, 1953), shall apply to taxable years ending after such specific date. Each such provision shall, in the case of a taxable year subject to the Internal Revenue Code of 1939, be deemed to be included in the Internal Revenue Code of 1939, but shall be applicable only to taxable years ending after such specific date. The provisions of the Internal Revenue Code of 1939 superseded by provisions of subtitle A of this title the applicability of which is stated in terms of a specific date (occurring after December 31, 1953) shall be deemed to be included in subtitle A of this title, but shall be applicable only to the period prior to the taking effect of the corresponding provision of subtitle A.

(D) Effective with respect to taxable years ending after March 31, 1954, and subject to tax under chapter 1 of the Internal Revenue Code of 1939—

(i) Sections 13(b)(3), 26(b)(2)(C), 26(h)(1)(C) (including the comma and the word "and" immediately preceding such section), 26(i)(3), 108(k), 207(a)(1)(C), 207(a)(3)(C), and the last sentence of section 362(b)(3) of such Code are hereby repealed; and

(ii) Sections 13(b)(2), 26(b)(2)(B), 26(h)(1)(B), 26(i)(2), 207(a)(1)(B), 207(a)(3)(B), 421(a)(1)(B), and the second sentence of section 362(b)(3) of such Code are hereby amended by striking out "and before April 1, 1954" (and any accompanying punctuation) wherever appearing therein.

(2) SUBTITLE B.—

(A) Chapter 11 of this title shall apply with respect to estates of decedents dying after the date of enactment of this title, and with respect to such estates chapter 3 of the Internal Revenue Code of 1939 is hereby repealed.

(B) Chapter 12 of this title shall apply with respect to the calendar year 1955 and all calendar years thereafter, and with respect to such years chapter 4 of the Internal Revenue Code of 1939 is hereby repealed.

(3) SUBTITLE C.—Subtitle C of this title shall apply only with respect to remuneration paid after December 31, 1954, except that chapter 22 of such subtitle shall apply only with respect to remuneration paid after December 31, 1954, which is for services performed after such date. Chapter 9 of the Internal Revenue Code of 1939 is hereby repealed with respect to remuneration paid after December 31, 1954, except that subchapter B of such chapter (and subchapter E of such chapter to the extent it relates to subchapter B) shall remain in force and effect with respect to remuneration paid after December 31, 1954, for services performed on or before such date.

(4) SUBTITLE D.—Subtitle D of this title shall take effect on January 1, 1955. Subtitles B and C of the Internal Revenue Code of 1939 (except chapters 7, 9, 15, 26, and 28, subchapter B of chapter 25, and parts VII and VIII of subchapter A of chapter 27 of such code) are hereby repealed effective January 1, 1955. Provisions having the same effect as section 6416(b)(2)(H), and so much of section 4082(c) as refers to special motor fuels, shall be considered to be included in the Internal Revenue Code of 1939 effective as of May 1, 1954. Section 2450(a) of the Internal Revenue Code of 1939 (as amended by the Excise Tax Reduction Act of 1954) applies to the period beginning on April 1, 1954, and ending on December 31, 1954.

(5) SUBTITLE E.—Subtitle E shall take effect on January 1, 1955, except that the provisions in section 5411 permitting the use of a brewery under regulations prescribed by the Secretary for the purpose of producing and bottling soft drinks, section 5554, and chapter 53 shall take effect on the day after the date of enactment of this title. Subchapter B of chapter 25, and part VIII of subchapter A of chapter 27, of the Internal Revenue Code of 1939 are hereby repealed effective on the day after the date of enactment of this title. Chapters 15 and 26, and part VII of subchapter A of chapter 27, of the Internal Revenue Code of 1939 are hereby repealed effective January 1, 1955.

(6) SUBTITLE F.—

(A) GENERAL RULE.—The provisions of subtitle F shall take effect on the day after the date of enactment of this title and shall be applicable with respect to any tax imposed by this title. The provisions of subtitle F shall apply with respect to any tax imposed by the Internal Revenue Code of 1939 only to the extent provided in subparagraphs (B) and (C) of this paragraph.

(B) ASSESSMENT, COLLECTION, AND REFUNDS.—Notwithstanding the provisions of subparagraph (A), and notwithstanding any contrary provision of subchapter A of chapter 63 (relating to assessment), chapter 64 (relating to collection), or chapter 65 (relating to abatements,

EFFECTIVE DATE

credits, and refunds) of this title, the provisions of part II of subchapter A of chapter 28 and chapters 35, 36, and 37 (except section 3777) of subtitle D of the Internal Revenue Code of 1939 shall remain in effect until January 1, 1955, and shall also be applicable to the taxes imposed by this title. On and after January 1, 1955, the provisions of subchapter A of chapter 63, chapter 64, and chapter 65 (except section 6405) of this title shall be applicable to all internal revenue taxes (whether imposed by this title or by the Internal Revenue Code of 1939), notwithstanding any contrary provision of part II of subchapter A of chapter 28, or of chapter 35, 36, or 37, of the Internal Revenue Code of 1939. The provisions of section 6405 (relating to reports of refunds and credits) shall be applicable with respect to refunds or credits allowed after the date of enactment of this title, and section 3777 of the Internal Revenue Code of 1939 is hereby repealed with respect to such refunds and credits.

(C) TAXES IMPOSED UNDER THE 1939 CODE.—After the date of enactment of this title, the following provisions of subtitle F shall apply to the taxes imposed by the Internal Revenue Code of 1939, notwithstanding any contrary provisions of such code:

(i) Chapter 73, relating to bonds.

(ii) Chapter 74, relating to closing agreements and compromises.

(iii) Chapter 75, relating to crimes and other offenses, but only insofar as it relates to offenses committed after the date of enactment of this title, and in the case of such offenses, section 6531, relating to periods of limitation on criminal prosecution, shall be applicable. The penalties (other than penalties which may be assessed) provided by the Internal Revenue Code of 1939 shall not apply to offenses, committed after the date of enactment of this title, to which chapter 75 of this title is applicable.

(iv) Chapter 76, relating to judicial proceedings.

(v) Chapter 77, relating to miscellaneous provisions, except that section 7502 shall apply only if the mailing occurs after the date of enactment of this title, and section 7503 shall apply only if the last date referred to therein occurs after the date of enactment of this title.

(vi) Chapter 78, relating to discovery of liability and enforcement of title.

(vii) Chapter 79, relating to definitions.

(viii) Chapter 80, relating to application of internal revenue laws, effective date, and related provisions.

(D) CHAPTER 28 AND SUBTITLE D OF 1939 CODE.—Except as otherwise provided in subparagraphs (B) and (C), the provisions of chapter 28 and of subtitle D of the Internal Revenue Code of 1939 shall remain in effect with respect to taxes imposed by the Internal Revenue Code of 1939.

(7) OTHER PROVISIONS.—If the effective date of any provision of the Internal Revenue Code of 1954 is not otherwise provided in this section or in any other section of this title, such provision shall take effect on the day after the date of enactment of this title. If the repeal of any provision of the Internal Revenue Code of 1939 is not otherwise provided by this section or by any other section of this title, such provision is hereby repealed effective on the day after the date of enactment of this title.

Amendments

- **2018, Tax Technical Corrections Act of 2018 (P.L. 115-141)**

P.L. 115-141, §401(a)(335), Div. U:

Amended Code Sec. 7851(a)(1)(A) by striking ", 4" following "1, 2". **Effective** 3-23-2018.

P.L. 115-141, §401(a)(336), Div. U:

Amended Code Sec. 7851(a)(1)(B) by striking "Chapters 3 and 5" and inserting "Chapter 3". **Effective** 3-23-2018.

- **1976, Tax Reform Act of 1976 (P.L. 94-455)**

P.L. 94-455, §1906(b)(13)(A):

Amended 1954 Code by substituting "Secretary" for "Secretary or his delegate" each place it appeared. **Effective** 2-1-77.

[Sec. 7851(b)]

(b) EFFECT OF REPEAL OF INTERNAL REVENUE CODE OF 1939.—

(1) EXISTING RIGHTS AND LIABILITIES.—The repeal of any provision of the Internal Revenue Code of 1939 shall not affect any act done or any right accruing or accrued, or any suit or proceeding had or commenced in any civil cause, before such repeal; but all rights and liabilities under such code shall continue, and may be enforced in the same manner, as if such repeal had not been made.

(2) EXISTING OFFICES.—The repeal of any provision of the Internal Revenue Code of 1939 shall not abolish, terminate, or otherwise change—

(A) any internal revenue district,

(B) any office, position, board, or committee, or

(C) the appointment or employment of any officer or employee,

existing immediately preceding the enactment of this title, the continuance of which is not manifestly inconsistent with any provision of this title, but the same shall continue unless and until changed by lawful authority.

(3) EXISTING DELEGATIONS OF AUTHORITY.—Any delegation of authority made pursuant to the provisions of Reorganization Plan Numbered 26 of 1950 or Reorganization Plan Numbered 1 of 1952, including any redelegation of authority made pursuant to any such delegation of authority, and in effect under the Internal Revenue Code of 1939 immediately preceding the enactment of this title shall, notwithstanding the repeal of such code, remain in effect for purposes of this title, unless distinctly inconsistent or manifestly incompatible with the provisions of this title. The preceding sentence shall not be construed as limiting in any manner the power to amend, modify, or revoke any such delegation or redelegation of authority.

[Sec. 7851(c)]

(c) CRIMES AND FORFEITURES.—All offenses committed, and all penalties or forfeitures incurred, under any provision of law hereby repealed, may be prosecuted and punished in the same manner and with the same effect as if this title had not been enacted.

[Sec. 7851(d)]

(d) PERIODS OF LIMITATION.—All periods of limitation, whether applicable to civil causes and proceedings, or to the prosecution of offenses, or for the recovery of penalties or forfeitures, hereby repealed shall not be affected thereby, but all suits, proceedings, or prosecutions, whether civil or criminal, for causes arising, or acts done or committed, prior to said repeal, may be commenced and prosecuted within the same time as if this title had not been enacted.

[Sec. 7851(e)]

(e) REFERENCE TO OTHER PROVISIONS.—For the purpose of applying the Internal Revenue Code of 1939 or the Internal Revenue Code of 1954 to any period, any reference in either such code to another provision of the Internal Revenue Code of 1939 or the Internal Revenue Code of 1954 which is not then applicable to such period shall be deemed a reference to the corresponding provision of the other code which is then applicable to such period.

INDIAN TRIBAL GOVERNMENTS

[Sec. 7852]
SEC. 7852. OTHER APPLICABLE RULES.

[Sec. 7852(a)]
(a) SEPARABILITY CLAUSE.—If any provision of this title, or the application thereof to any person or circumstances, is held invalid, the remainder of the title, and the application of such provision to other persons or circumstances, shall not be affected thereby.

[Sec. 7852(b)]
(b) REFERENCE IN OTHER LAWS TO INTERNAL REVENUE CODE OF 1939.—Any reference in any other law of the United States or in any Executive order to any provision of the Internal Revenue Code of 1939 shall, where not otherwise distinctly expressed or manifestly incompatible with the intent thereof, be deemed also to refer to the corresponding provision of this title.

[Sec. 7852(c)]
(c) ITEMS NOT TO BE TWICE INCLUDED IN INCOME OR DEDUCTED THEREFROM.—Except as otherwise distinctly expressed or manifestly intended, the same item (whether of income, deduction, credit, or otherwise) shall not be taken into account both in computing a tax under subtitle A of this title and a tax under chapter 1 or 2 of the Internal Revenue Code of 1939.

[Sec. 7852(d)]
(d) TREATY OBLIGATIONS.—

(1) IN GENERAL.—For purposes of determining the relationship between a provision of a treaty and any law of the United States affecting revenue, neither the treaty nor the law shall have preferential status by reason of its being a treaty or law.

(2) SAVINGS CLAUSE FOR 1954 TREATIES.—No provision of this title (as in effect without regard to any amendment thereto enacted after August 16, 1954) shall apply in any case where its application would be contrary to any treaty obligation of the United States in effect on August 16, 1954.

Amendments
- 1988, Technical and Miscellaneous Revenue Act of 1988 (P.L. 100-647)

P.L. 100-647, §1012(aa)(1)(A):
Amended Code Sec. 7852(d). **Effective** as if included in the provision of P.L. 99-514 to which it relates. Prior to amendment Code Sec. 7852(d) read as follows:

(d) TREATY OBLIGATIONS.—No provision of this title shall apply in any case where its application would be contrary to any treaty obligation of the United States in effect on the date of enactment of this title.

[Sec. 7852(e)]
(e) PRIVACY ACT OF 1974.—The provisions of subsections (d)(2), (3), and (4), and (g) of section 552a of title 5, United States Code, shall not be applied, directly or indirectly, to the determination of the existence or possible existence of liability (or the amount thereof) of any person for any tax, penalty, interest, fine, forfeiture, or other imposition or offense to which the provisions of this title apply.

Amendments
- 1976, Tax Reform Act of 1976 (P.L. 94-455)

P.L. 94-455, §1202(g):
Added Code Sec. 7852(e). **Effective** 1-1-77.

Subchapter C—Provisions Affecting More than One Subtitle

Sec. 7871. Indian tribal governments treated as States for certain purposes
Sec. 7872. Treatment of loans with below-market interest rates.
Sec. 7873. Federal tax treatment of income derived by Indians from exercise of fishing rights secured by treaty, etc.
Sec. 7874. Rules relating to expatriated entities and their foreign parents.

[Sec. 7871]
SEC. 7871. INDIAN TRIBAL GOVERNMENTS TREATED AS STATES FOR CERTAIN PURPOSES.

[Sec. 7871(a)]
(a) GENERAL RULE.—An Indian tribal government shall be treated as a State—

(1) for purposes of determining whether and in what amount any contribution or transfer to or for the use of such government (or a political subdivision thereof) is deductible under—

(A) section 170 (relating to income tax deduction for charitable, etc., contributions and gifts),

(B) sections 2055 and 2106(a)(2) (relating to estate tax deduction for transfers of public, charitable, and religious uses), or

(C) section 2522 (relating to gift tax deduction for charitable and similar gifts);

(2) subject to subsection (b), for purposes of any exemption from, credit or refund of, or payment with respect to, an excise tax imposed by—

(A) chapter 31 (relating to tax on special fuels),

(B) chapter 32 (relating to manufacturers excise taxes),

(C) subchapter B of chapter 33 (relating to communications excise tax), or

(D) subchapter D of chapter 36 (relating to tax on use of certain highway vehicles);

(3) for purposes of section 164 (relating to deduction for taxes);

(4) subject to subsection (c), for purposes of section 103 (relating to State and local bonds);

(5) for purposes of section 511(a)(2)(B) (relating to the taxation of colleges and universities which are agencies or instrumentalities of governments or their political subdivisions);

(6) for purposes of—

(A) section 105(e) (relating to accident and health plans),

(B) section 403(b)(1)(A)(ii) (relating to the taxation of contributions of certain employers for employee annuities), and

(C) section 454(b)(2) (relating to discount obligations); and

(7) for purposes of—

(A) chapter 41 (relating to tax on excess expenditures to influence legislation), and

(B) subchapter A of chapter 42 (relating to private foundations).

INDIAN TRIBAL GOVERNMENTS

Amendments

• **1993, Omnibus Budget Reconciliation Act of 1993 (P.L. 103-66)**

P.L. 103-66, §13222(d):

Amended Code Sec. 7871(a)(6) by striking subparagraph (B) and by redesignating subparagraphs (C) and (D) as subparagraphs (B) and (C), respectively. **Effective** for amounts paid or incurred after 12-31-93. Prior to amendment, Code Sec. 7871(a)(6)(B) read as follows:

(B) section 162(e) (relating to appearances, etc., with respect to legislation).

• **1986, Tax Reform Act of 1986 (P.L. 99-514)**

P.L. 99-514, §112(b)(4):

Amended Code Sec. 7871(a)(6) by striking out subparagraph (A) and by redesignating subparagraphs (B), (C), (D), (E), and (F) as subparagraphs (A), (B), (C), (D), and (E), respectively. **Effective** for tax years beginning after 12-31-86. Prior to amendment, Code Sec. 7871(a)(6)(A) read as follows:

(A) Section 24(c)(4) (defining State for purposes of credit for contribution to candidates for public offices),

P.L. 99-514, §123(b)(3):

Amended Code Sec. 7871(a)(6), as amended by Act Sec. 112(b)(4), by striking out subparagraph (B) and by redesignating subparagraphs (C), (D), and (E) as subparagraphs (B), (C), and (D), respectively. **Effective** for tax years beginning after 12-31-86. Prior to amendment, Code Sec. 7871(a)(6)(B) (as redesignated), read as follows:

(B) section 117(b)(2)(A) (relating to scholarships and fellowship grants), and

P.L. 99-514, §1301(j)(6):

Amended Code Sec. 7871(a)(4) by striking out "(relating to interest on certain governmental obligations)" and inserting in lieu thereof "(relating to State and local bonds)". **Effective** for bonds issued after 8-15-86. However, for transitional rules, see Act Secs. 1311-1318 under the amendment notes to Code Sec. 103.

P.L. 99-514, §1899A(65):

Amended Code Sec. 7871(a)(6)(F) (prior to amendment by Act Secs. 112(b)(4) and 123(b)(3)) by striking out the period at the end thereof and inserting in lieu thereof "; and". **Effective** 10-22-86.

• **1984, Deficit Reduction Act of 1984 (P.L. 98-369)**

P.L. 98-369, §474(r)(41):

Amended Code Sec. 7871(a)(6)(A) by striking out "section 41(c)(4)" and inserting in lieu thereof "section 24(c)(4)". **Effective** for tax years beginning after 12-31-83, and for carrybacks from such years.

P.L. 98-369, §1065(b):

Amended Code Sec. 7871(a)(6) by striking out subparagraphs (B) and (C) and inserting in lieu thereof subparagraphs (B)-(F). **Effective** for tax years beginning after 12-31-84. Prior to amendment, subparagraphs (B) and (C) read as follows:

(B) section 117(b)(2)(A) (relating to scholarships and fellowship grants), and

(C) section 403(b)(1)(A)(ii) (relating to the taxation of contributions certain employers for employee annuities); and

• **1983, Social Security Amendments of 1983 (P.L. 98-21)**

P.L. 98-21, §122(c)(6):

Amended Code Sec. 7871(a)(6). **Effective** for tax years beginning after 12-31-83. Prior to amendment, Code Sec. 7871(a)(6) read as follows:

(6) for purposes of—

(A) section 37(e)(9)(A) (relating to certain public retirement systems),

(B) section 41(c)(4) (defining State for purposes of credit for contribution to candidates for public offices),

(C) section 117(b)(2)(A) (relating to scholarships and fellowship grants), and

(D) section 403(b)(1)(A)(ii) (relating to the taxation of contributions of certain employers for employee annuities), and

[Sec. 7871(b)]

(b) ADDITIONAL REQUIREMENTS FOR EXCISE TAX EXEMPTIONS.—Paragraph (2) of subsection (a) shall apply with respect to any transaction only if, in addition to any other requirement of this title applicable to similar transactions involving a State or political subdivision thereof, the transaction involves the exercise of an essential governmental function of the Indian tribal government.

[Sec. 7871(c)]

(c) ADDITIONAL REQUIREMENTS FOR TAX-EXEMPT BONDS.—

(1) IN GENERAL.—Subsection (a) of section 103 shall apply to any obligation (not described in paragraph (3)) issued by an Indian tribal government (or subdivision thereof) only if such obligation is part of an issue substantially all of the proceeds of which are to be used in the exercise of any essential governmental function.

(2) NO EXEMPTION FOR PRIVATE ACTIVITY BONDS.—Except as provided in paragraph (3), subsection (a) of section 103 shall not apply to any private activity bond (as defined in section 141(a)) issued by an Indian tribal government (or subdivision thereof).

(3) EXCEPTION FOR CERTAIN PRIVATE ACTIVITY BONDS.—

(A) IN GENERAL.—In the case of an obligation to which this paragraph applies—

(i) paragraph (2) shall not apply,

(ii) such obligation shall be treated for purposes of this title as a qualified small issue bond, and

(iii) section 146 shall not apply.

(B) OBLIGATIONS TO WHICH PARAGRAPH APPLIES.—This paragraph shall apply to any obligation issued as part of an issue if—

(i) 95 percent or more of the net proceeds of the issue are to be used for the acquisition, construction, reconstruction, or improvement of property which is of a character subject to the allowance for depreciation and which is part of a manufacturing facility (as defined in section 144(a)(12)(C)),

(ii) such issue is issued by an Indian tribal government or a subdivision thereof,

(iii) 95 percent or more of the net proceeds of the issue are to be used to finance property which—

(I) is to be located on land which, throughout the 5-year period ending on the date of issuance of such issue, is part of the qualified Indian lands of the issuer, and

(II) is to be owned and operated by such issuer,

(iv) such obligation would not be a private activity bond without regard to subparagraph (C),

(v) it is reasonably expected (at the time of issuance of the issue) that the employment requirement of subparagraph (D)(i) will be met with respect to the facility to be financed by the net proceeds of the issue, and

(vi) no principal user of such facility will be a person (or group of persons) described in section 144(a)(6)(B).

For purposes of clause (iii), section 150(a)(5) shall apply.

(C) PRIVATE ACTIVITY BOND RULES TO APPLY.—An obligation to which this paragraph applies (other than an obligation described in paragraph (1)) shall be treated for purposes of this title as a private activity bond.

(D) EMPLOYMENT REQUIREMENTS.—

(i) IN GENERAL.—The employment requirements of this subparagraph are met with respect to a facility financed by the net proceeds of an issue if, as of the close of each calendar year in the testing period, the aggregate face amount of all outstanding tax-exempt private activity bonds issued to provide financing for the establishment which includes such facility is not more than 20 times greater than the aggregate wages (as defined by section 3121(a)) paid during the preceding calendar year to individuals (who are enrolled members of the Indian tribe of the issuer or the spouse of any such member) for services rendered at such establishment.

(ii) FAILURE TO MEET REQUIREMENTS.—

(I) IN GENERAL.—If, as of the close of any calendar year in the testing period, the requirements of this subparagraph are not met with respect to an establishment, section 103 shall cease to apply to interest received or accrued (on all private activity bonds issued to provide financing for the establishment) after the close of such calendar year.

(II) EXCEPTION.—Subclause (I) shall not apply if the requirements of this subparagraph would be met if the aggregate face amount of all tax-exempt private activity bonds issued to provide financing for the establishment and outstanding at the close of the 90th day after the close of the calendar year were substituted in clause (i) for such bonds outstanding at the close of such calendar year.

(iii) TESTING PERIOD.—For purposes of this subparagraph, the term "testing period" means, with respect to an issue, each calendar year which begins more than 2 years after the date of issuance of the issue (or, in the case of a refunding obligation, the date of issuance of the original issue).

(E) DEFINITIONS.—For purposes of this paragraph—

(i) QUALIFIED INDIAN LANDS.—The term ["]qualified Indian lands["] means land which is held in trust by the United States for the benefit of an Indian tribe.

(ii) INDIAN TRIBE.—The term "Indian tribe" means any Indian tribe, band, nation, or other organized group or community which is recognized as eligible for the special programs and services provided by the United States to Indians because of their status as Indians.

(iii) NET PROCEEDS.—The term "net proceeds" has the meaning given such term by section 150(a)(3).

Amendments

- **2018, Tax Technical Corrections Act of 2018 (P.L. 115-141)**

P.L. 115-141, §401(a)(337), Div. U:

Amended Code Sec. 7871(c)(3)(D)(ii)(II) by striking "calender" and inserting "calendar". **Effective** 3-23-2018.

- **1987, Revenue Act of 1987 (P.L. 100-203)**

P.L. 100-203, §10632(b)(1):

Amended Code Sec. 7871(c) by adding at the end thereof new paragraph (3). **Effective** for obligations issued after 10-13-87.

P.L. 100-203, §10632(b)(2):

Amended Code Sec. 7871(c)(2) by striking out "Subsection (a)" and inserting in lieu thereof "Except as provided in paragraph (3), subsection (a)". **Effective** for obligations issued after 10-13-87.

- **1986, Tax Reform Act of 1986 (P.L. 99-514)**

P.L. 99-514, §1301(j)(7):

Amended Code Sec. 7871(c)(2). **Effective** for bonds issued after 8-15-86. However, for transitional rules, see Act Secs. 1311-1318 under the amendment notes to Code Sec. 103. Prior to amendment, Code Sec. 7871(c)(2) read as follows:

(2) NO EXEMPTION FOR CERTAIN PRIVATE-ACTIVITY BONDS.—Subsection (a) of section 103 shall not apply to any of the following issued by an Indian tribal government (or subdivision thereof):

(A) An industrial development bond (as defined in section 103(b)(2)).

(B) An obligation described in section 103(l)(1)(A) (relating to scholarship bonds).

(C) A mortgage subsidy bond (as defined in paragraph (1) of section 103A(b) without regard to paragraph (2) thereof).

[Sec. 7871(d)]

(d) TREATMENT OF SUBDIVISIONS OF INDIAN TRIBAL GOVERNMENTS AS POLITICAL SUBDIVISIONS.—For the purposes specified in subsection (a), a subdivision of an Indian tribal government shall be treated as a political subdivision of a State if (and only if) the Secretary determines (after consultation with the Secretary of the Interior) that such subdivision has been delegated the right to exercise one or more of the substantial governmental functions of the Indian tribal government.

Amendments

- **1983 (P.L. 97-473)**

P.L. 97-473, §202(a) (as amended by P.L. 98-369, §1065(a)):

Added Code Sec. 7871. **Effective** dates provided in §204, below.

P.L. 97-473, §204, provides:

The amendments made by this title—

(1) insofar as they relate to chapter 1 of the Internal Revenue Code of 1954 (other than section 103 thereof), shall apply to taxable years beginning after December 31, 1982,

(2) insofar as they relate to section 103 of such Code, shall apply to obligations issued after December 31, 1982,

(3) insofar as they relate to chapter 11 of such Code, shall apply to estates of decedents dying after December 31, 1982,

(4) insofar as they relate to chapter 12 of such Code, shall apply to gifts made after December 31, 1982, and

(5) insofar as they relate to taxes imposed by subtitle D of such Code, shall take effect on January 1, 1983.

[Sec. 7871(e)]

(e) ESSENTIAL GOVERNMENTAL FUNCTION.—For purposes of this section, the term "essential governmental function' shall not include any function which is not customarily performed by State and local governments with general taxing powers.

Amendments

- **1987, Revenue Act of 1987 (P.L. 100-203)**

P.L. 100-203, §10632(a):

Amended Code Sec. 7871 by adding at the end thereof new subsection (e). **Effective** for obligations issued after 10-13-87.

[Sec. 7871(f)]

(f) TRIBAL ECONOMIC DEVELOPMENT BONDS.—

(1) ALLOCATION OF LIMITATION.—

(A) IN GENERAL.—The Secretary shall allocate the national tribal economic development bond limitation among the Indian tribal governments in such manner as the Secretary, in consultation with the Secretary of the Interior, determines appropriate.

(B) NATIONAL LIMITATION.—There is a national tribal economic development bond limitation of $2,000,000,000.

(2) BONDS TREATED AS EXEMPT FROM TAX.—In the case of a tribal economic development bond—

(A) notwithstanding subsection (c), such bond shall be treated for purposes of this title in the same manner as if such bond were issued by a State,

(B) the Indian tribal government issuing such bond and any instrumentality of such Indian tribal government shall be treated as a State for purposes of section 141, and

(C) section 146 shall not apply.

(3) TRIBAL ECONOMIC DEVELOPMENT BOND.—

(A) IN GENERAL.—For purposes of this section, the term "tribal economic development bond" means any bond issued by an Indian tribal government—

(i) the interest on which would be exempt from tax under section 103 if issued by a State or local government, and

(ii) which is designated by the Indian tribal government as a tribal economic development bond for purposes of this subsection.

(B) EXCEPTIONS.—Such term shall not include any bond issued as part of an issue if any portion of the proceeds of such issue are used to finance—

(i) any portion of a building in which class II or class III gaming (as defined in section 4 of the Indian Gaming Regulatory Act) is conducted or housed or any other property actually used in the conduct of such gaming, or

(ii) any facility located outside the Indian reservation (as defined in section 168(j)(6)).

(C) LIMITATION ON AMOUNT OF BONDS DESIGNATED.—The maximum aggregate face amount of bonds which may be designated by any Indian tribal government under subparagraph (A) shall not exceed the amount of national tribal economic development bond limitation allocated to such government under paragraph (1).

BELOW-MARKET INTEREST RATE LOANS

Amendments

• 2009, American Recovery and Reinvestment Tax Act of 2009 (P.L. 111-5)

P.L. 111-5, §1402(a):

Amended Code Sec. 7871 by adding at the end a new subsection (f). **Effective** for obligations issued after 2-17-2009.

P.L. 111-5, §1402(b), provides:

(b) STUDY.—The Secretary of the Treasury, or the Secretary's delegate, shall conduct a study of the effects of the amendment made by subsection (a). Not later than 1 year after the date of the enactment of this Act, the Secretary of the Treasury, or the Secretary's delegate, shall report to Congress on the results of the study conducted under this paragraph, including the Secretary's recommendations regarding such amendment.

[Sec. 7872]

SEC. 7872. TREATMENT OF LOANS WITH BELOW-MARKET INTEREST RATES.

[Sec. 7872(a)]

(a) TREATMENT OF GIFT LOANS AND DEMAND LOANS.—

(1) IN GENERAL.—For purposes of this title, in the case of any below-market loan to which this section applies and which is a gift loan or a demand loan, the forgone interest shall be treated as—

(A) transferred from the lender to the borrower, and

(B) retransferred by the borrower to the lender as interest.

(2) TIME WHEN TRANSFERS MADE.—Except as otherwise provided in regulations prescribed by the Secretary, any forgone interest attributable to periods during any calendar year shall be treated as transferred (and retransferred) under paragraph (1) on the last day of such calendar year.

Amendments

• 1996, Small Business Job Protection Act of 1996 (P.L. 104-188)

P.L. 104-188, §1704(t)(58)(A):

Amended Code Sec. 7872(a) by striking "foregone" each place it appears and inserting "forgone". **Effective** 8-20-96.

[Sec. 7872(b)]

(b) TREATMENT OF OTHER BELOW-MARKET LOANS.—

(1) IN GENERAL.—For purposes of this title, in the case of any below-market loan to which this section applies and to which subsection (a)(1) does not apply, the lender shall be treated as having transferred on the date the loan was made (or, if later, on the first day on which this section applies to such loan), and the borrower shall be treated as having received on such date, cash in an amount equal to the excess of—

(A) the amount loaned, over

(B) the present value of all payments which are required to be made under the terms of the loan.

(2) OBLIGATION TREATED AS HAVING ORIGINAL ISSUE DISCOUNT.—For purposes of this title—

(A) IN GENERAL.—Any below-market loan to which paragraph (1) applies shall be treated as having original issue discount in an amount equal to the excess described in paragraph (1).

(B) AMOUNT IN ADDITION TO OTHER ORIGINAL ISSUE DISCOUNT.—Any original issue discount which a loan is treated as having by reason of subparagraph (A) shall be in addition to any other original issue discount on such loan (determined without regard to subparagraph (A)).

[Sec. 7872(c)]

(c) BELOW-MARKET LOANS TO WHICH SECTION APPLIES.—

(1) IN GENERAL.—Except as otherwise provided in this subsection and subsection (g), this section shall apply to—

(A) GIFTS.—Any below-market loan which is a gift loan.

(B) COMPENSATION-RELATED LOANS.—Any below-market loan directly or indirectly between—

(i) an employer and an employee, or

(ii) an independent contractor and a person for whom such independent contractor provides services.

(C) CORPORATION-SHAREHOLDER LOANS.—Any below-market loan directly or indirectly between a corporation and any shareholder of such corporation.

(D) TAX AVOIDANCE LOANS.—Any below-market loan 1 of the principal purposes of the interest arrangements of which is the avoidance of any Federal tax.

(E) OTHER BELOW-MARKET LOANS.—To the extent provided in regulations, any below-market loan which is not described in subparagraph (A), (B), (C), or (F) if the interest arrangements of such loan have a significant effect on any Federal tax liability of the lender or the borrower.

(F) LOANS TO QUALIFIED CONTINUING CARE FACILITIES.—Any loan to any qualified continuing care facility pursuant to a continuing care contract.

(2) $10,000 DE MINIMIS EXCEPTION FOR GIFT LOANS BETWEEN INDIVIDUALS.—

(A) IN GENERAL.—In the case of any gift loan directly between individuals, this section shall not apply to any day on which the aggregate outstanding amount of loans between such individuals does not exceed $10,000.

(B) DE MINIMIS EXCEPTION NOT TO APPLY TO LOANS ATTRIBUTABLE TO ACQUISITION OF INCOME-PRODUCING ASSETS.—Subparagraph (A) shall not apply to any gift loan directly attributable to the purchase or carrying of income-producing assets.

(C) CROSS REFERENCE.—

For limitation on amount treated as interest where loans do not exceed $100,000, see subsection (d)(1).

(3) $10,000 DE MINIMIS EXCEPTION FOR COMPENSATION-RELATED AND CORPORATE-SHAREHOLDER LOANS.—

(A) IN GENERAL.—In the case of any loan described in subparagraph (B) or (C) of paragraph (1), this section shall not apply to any day on which the aggregate outstanding amount of loans between the borrower and lender does not exceed $10,000.

(B) EXCEPTION NOT TO APPLY WHERE 1 OF PRINCIPAL PURPOSES IS TAX AVOIDANCE.—Subparagraph (A) shall not apply to any loan the interest arrangements of which have as 1 of their principal purposes the avoidance of any Federal tax.

Amendments

• 1985 (P.L. 99-121)

P.L. 99-121, §201(b):

Amended Code Sec. 7872(c)(1) by adding at the end thereof new subparagraph (F). **Effective** with respect to loans made after 10-11-85.

P.L. 99-121, §201(c)(1):

Amended Code Sec. 7872(c)(1) by inserting "and subsection (g)" after "subsection". **Effective** with respect to loans made after 10-11-85.

BELOW-MARKET INTEREST RATE LOANS

P.L. 99-121, § 201(c)(2):
Amended Code Sec. 7872(c)(1)(E) by striking out "or (C)" and inserting in lieu thereof "(C), or (F)". **Effective** with respect to loans made after 10-11-85.

P.L. 99-121, § 204(a)(2), provides:
(2) SECTION 7872 NOT TO APPLY TO CERTAIN LOANS.—Section 7872 of the Internal Revenue Code of 1954 shall not apply to loans made on or before the date of the enactment of this Act to any qualified continuing care facility pursuant to a continuing care contract. For purposes of this paragraph, the terms "qualified continuing care facility" and "continuing care contract" have the meanings given such terms by section 7872(g) of such Code (as added by section 201).

[Sec. 7872(d)]

(d) SPECIAL RULES FOR GIFT LOANS.—

(1) LIMITATION ON INTEREST ACCRUAL FOR PURPOSES OF INCOME TAXES WHERE LOANS DO NOT EXCEED $100,000.—

(A) IN GENERAL.—For purposes of subtitle A, in the case of a gift loan directly between individuals, the amount treated as retransferred by the borrower to the lender as of the close of any year shall not exceed the borrower's net investment income for such year.

(B) LIMITATION NOT TO APPLY WHERE 1 OF PRINCIPAL PURPOSES IS TAX AVOIDANCE.—Subparagraph (A) shall not apply to any loan the interest arrangements of which have as 1 of their principal purposes the avoidance of any Federal tax.

(C) SPECIAL RULE WHERE MORE THAN 1 GIFT LOAN OUTSTANDING.—For purposes of subparagraph (A), in any case in which a borrower has outstanding more than 1 gift loan, the net investment income of such borrower shall be allocated among such loans in proportion to the respective amounts which would be treated as retransferred by the borrower without regard to this paragraph.

(D) LIMITATION NOT TO APPLY WHERE AGGREGATE AMOUNT OF LOANS EXCEED $100,000.—This paragraph shall not apply to any loan made by a lender to a borrower for any day on which the aggregate outstanding amount of loans between the borrower and lender exceeds $100,000.

(E) NET INVESTMENT INCOME.—For purposes of this paragraph—

(i) IN GENERAL.—The term "net investment income" has the meaning given such term by section 163(d)(4).

(ii) DE MINIMIS RULE.—If the net investment income of any borrower for any year does not exceed $1,000, the net investment income of such borrower for such year shall be treated as zero.

(iii) ADDITIONAL AMOUNTS TREATED AS INTEREST.—In determining the net investment income of a person for any year, any amount which would be included in the gross income of such person for such year by reason of section 1272 if such section applied to all deferred payment obligations shall be treated as interest received by such person for such year.

(iv) DEFERRED PAYMENT OBLIGATIONS.—The term "deferred payment obligation" includes any market discount bond, short-term obligation, United States savings bond, annuity, or similar obligation.

(2) SPECIAL RULE FOR GIFT TAX.—In the case of any gift loan which is a term loan, subsection (b)(1) (and not subsection (a)) shall apply for purposes of chapter 12.

Amendments

• **1988, Technical and Miscellaneous Revenue Act of 1988 (P.L. 100-647)**

P.L. 100-647, § 1005(c)(15):
Amended Code Sec. 7872(d)(1)(E)(i) by striking out "section 163(d)(3)" and inserting in lieu thereof "section 163(d)(4)". **Effective** as if included in the provision of P.L. 99-514 to which it relates. See, also, Act Sec. 1005(c)(13), below.

P.L. 100-647, § 1005(c)(13), provides:
(13) For purposes of applying the amendments made by this subsection and the amendments made by section 10102 of the Revenue Act of 1987, the provisions of this subsection shall be treated as having been enacted immediately before the enactment of the Revenue Act of 1987.

[Sec. 7872(e)]

(e) DEFINITIONS OF BELOW-MARKET LOAN AND FORGONE INTEREST.—For purposes of this section—

(1) BELOW-MARKET LOAN.—The term "below-market loan" means any loan if—

(A) in the case of a demand loan, interest is payable on the loan at a rate less than the applicable Federal rate, or

(B) in the case of a term loan, the amount loaned exceeds the present value of all payments due under the loan.

(2) FORGONE INTEREST.—The term "forgone interest" means, with respect to any period during which the loan is outstanding, the excess of—

(A) the amount of interest which would have been payable on the loan for the period if interest accrued on the loan at the applicable Federal rate and were payable annually on the day referred to in subsection (a)(2), over

(B) any interest payable on the loan properly allocable to such period.

Amendments

• **1996, Small Business Job Protection Act of 1996 (P.L. 104-188)**

P.L. 104-188, § 1704(t)(58)(A)-(B):
Amended Code Sec. 7872(e) by striking "foregone" each place it appears in paragraph (2) and inserting "forgone", and by striking "FOREGONE" in the subsection heading and the heading for paragraph (2) and inserting "FORGONE". **Effective** 8-20-96.

[Sec. 7872(f)]

(f) OTHER DEFINITIONS AND SPECIAL RULES.—For purposes of this section—

(1) PRESENT VALUE.—The present value of any payment shall be determined in the manner provided by regulations prescribed by the Secretary—

(A) as of the date of the loan, and

(B) by using a discount rate equal to the applicable Federal rate.

(2) APPLICABLE FEDERAL RATE.—

(A) TERM LOANS.—In the case of any term loan, the applicable Federal rate shall be the applicable Federal rate in effect under section 1274(d) (as of the day on which the loan was made), compounded semiannually.

(B) DEMAND LOANS.—In the case of a demand loan, the applicable Federal rate shall be the Federal short-term rate in effect under section 1274(d) for the period for which the amount of forgone interest is being determined, compounded semiannually.

(3) GIFT LOAN.—The term "gift loan" means any below-market loan where the forgoing of interest is in the nature of a gift.

(4) AMOUNT LOANED.—The term "amount loaned" means the amount received by the borrower.

(5) DEMAND LOAN.—The term "demand loan" means any loan which is payable in full at any time on the demand of the lender. Such term also includes (for purposes other than determining the applicable Federal rate under paragraph (2)) any loan if the benefits of the interest arrangements of such loan are not transferable and are conditioned on the future performance of substantial services by an individual. To the extent provided in regulations, such term also includes any loan with an indefinite maturity.

(6) TERM LOAN.—The term "term loan" means any loan which is not a demand loan.

(7) HUSBAND AND WIFE TREATED AS 1 PERSON.—A husband and wife shall be treated as 1 person.

BELOW-MARKET INTEREST RATE LOANS

(8) LOANS TO WHICH SECTION 483, 643(i), OR 1274 APPLIES.—This section shall not apply to any loan to which section 483, 643(i), or 1274 applies.

(9) NO WITHHOLDING.—No amount shall be withheld under chapter 24 with respect to—

(A) any amount treated as transferred or retransferred under subsection (a), and

(B) any amount treated as received under subsection (b).

(10) SPECIAL RULE FOR TERM LOANS.—If this section applies to any term loan on any day, this section shall continue to apply to such loan notwithstanding paragraphs (2) and (3) of subsection (c). In the case of a gift loan, the preceding sentence shall only apply for purposes of chapter 12.

(11) TIME FOR DETERMINING RATE APPLICABLE TO EMPLOYEE RELOCATION LOANS.—

(A) IN GENERAL.—In the case of any term loan made by an employer to an employee the proceeds of which are used by the employee to purchase a principal residence (within the meaning of section 121), the determination of the applicable Federal rate shall be made as of the date the written contract to purchase such residence was entered into.

(B) PARAGRAPH ONLY TO APPLY TO CASES TO WHICH SECTION 217 APPLIES.—Subparagraph (A) shall only apply to the purchase of a principal residence in connection with the commencement of work by an employee or a change in the principal place of work of an employee to which section 217 applies.

Amendments

• **2000, Community Renewal Tax Relief Act of 2000 (P.L. 106-554)**

P.L. 106-554, §319(30):

Amended Code Sec. 7872(f)(3) by striking "foregoing" and inserting "forgoing". **Effective** 12-21-2000.

• **1998, IRS Restructuring and Reform Act of 1998 (P.L. 105-206)**

P.L. 105-206, §6023(30):

Amended Code Sec. 7872(f)(2)(B) by striking "foregone" and inserting "forgone". **Effective** 7-22-98.

• **1997, Taxpayer Relief Act of 1997 (P.L. 105-34)**

P.L. 105-34, §312(d)(1):

Amended Code Sec. 7872(f)(11)(A) by striking "section 1034" and inserting "section 121". **Effective** for sales and exchanges after 5-6-97.

• **1996, Small Business Job Protection Act of 1996 (P.L. 104-188)**

P.L. 104-188, §1602(b)(7):

Amended Code Sec. 7872(f) by striking paragraph (12). For the **effective** date, see Act Sec. 1602(c), below. Prior to being stricken, Code Sec. 7872(f)(12) read as follows:

(12) SPECIAL RULE FOR CERTAIN EMPLOYER SECURITY LOANS.—This section shall not apply to any loan between a corporation (or any member of the controlled group of corporations which includes such corporation) and an employee stock ownership plan described in section 4975(e)(7) to the extent that the interest rate on such loan is equal to the interest rate paid on a related securities acquisition loan (as described in section 133(b)) to such corporation.

P.L. 104-188, §1602(c), provides:

(c) EFFECTIVE DATE.—

(1) IN GENERAL.—The amendments made by this section shall apply to loans made after the date of the enactment of this Act.

(2) REFINANCINGS.—The amendments made by this section shall not apply to loans made after the date of the enactment of this Act to refinance securities acquisition loans (determined without regard to section 133(b)(1)(B) of the Internal Revenue Code of 1986, as in effect on the day before the date of the enactment of this Act) made on or before such date or to refinance loans described in this paragraph if—

(A) the refinancing loans meet the requirements of section 133 of such Code (as so in effect),

(B) immediately after the refinancing the principal amount of the loan resulting from the refinancing does not exceed the principal amount of the refinanced loan (immediately before the refinancing), and

(C) the term of such refinancing loan does not extend beyond the last day of the term of the original securities acquisition loan.

For purposes of this paragraph, the term "securities acquisition loan" includes a loan from a corporation to an employee stock ownership plan described in section 133(b)(3) of such Code (as so in effect).

(3) EXCEPTION.—Any loan made pursuant to a binding written contract in effect before June 10, 1996, and at all times thereafter before such loan is made, shall be treated for purposes of paragraphs (1) and (2) as a loan made on or before the date of the enactment of this Act.

P.L. 104-188, §1906(c)(2):

Amended Code Sec. 7872(f)(8) by inserting ", 643(i)," before "or 1274" each place it appears. **Effective** for loans of cash or marketable securities made after 9-19-95.

• **1988, Technical and Miscellaneous Revenue Act of 1988 (P.L. 100-647)**

P.L. 100-647, §1018(u)(48):

Amended Code Sec. 7872(f) by redesignating paragraph (11) added by §1854 of P.L. 99-514 as paragraph (12). **Effective** as if included in the provision of P.L. 99-514 to which it relates.

• **1986, Tax Reform Act of 1986 (P.L. 99-514)**

P.L. 99-514, §1812(b)(2):

Amended Code Sec. 7872(f)(9). **Effective** as if included in the provision of P.L. 98-369 to which it relates. Prior to amendment, Code Sec. 7872(f)(9) read as follows:

(9) NO WITHHOLDING.—No amount shall be withheld under chapter 24 with respect to any amount treated as transferred or retransferred under subsection (a).

P.L. 99-514, §1812(b)(3):

Amended Code Sec. 7872(f)(5). **Effective** as if included in the provision of P.L. 98-369 to which it relates. Prior to amendment, Code Sec. 7872(f)(5) read as follows:

(5) DEMAND LOAN.—The term "demand loan" means any loan which is payable in full at any time on the demand of the lender. Such term also includes (for purposes other than determining the applicable Federal rate under paragraph (2)) any loan which is not transferable and the benefits of the interest arrangements of which is conditioned on the future performance of substantial services by an individual.

P.L. 99-514, §1812(b)(4):

Amended Code Sec. 7872(f)(2)(B) by inserting ", compounded semiannually" immediately before the period at the end thereof. **Effective** as if included in the provision of P.L. 98-369 to which it relates.

P.L. 99-514, §1854(c)(2)(B):

Amended Code Sec. 7872(f) by adding at the end thereof new paragraph (11). **Effective** as if included in the provision of P.L. 98-369 to which it relates.

• **1985 (P.L. 99-121)**

P.L. 99-121, §202:

Amended Code Sec. 7872(f) by adding at the end thereof new paragraph (11). **Effective** for contracts entered into after 6-30-85, in tax years ending after such date. For special rules, see Act Secs. 203 and 204(a)(2), following Code Sec. 7872(h).

[Sec. 7872(g)]

(g) EXCEPTION FOR CERTAIN LOANS TO QUALIFIED CONTINUING CARE FACILITIES.—

(1) IN GENERAL.—This section shall not apply for any calendar year to any below-market loan made by a lender to a qualified continuing care facility pursuant to a continuing care contract if the lender (or the lender's spouse) attains age 65 before the close of such year.

(2) $90,000 LIMIT.—Paragraph (1) shall apply only to the extent that the aggregate outstanding amount of any loan to which such paragraph applies (determined without regard to this paragraph), when added to the aggregate outstanding amount of all other previous loans between the lender (or the lender's spouse) and any qualified continuing care facility to which paragraph (1) applies, does not exceed $90,000.

(3) CONTINUING CARE CONTRACT.—For purposes of this section, the term "continuing care contract" means a written contract between an individual and a qualified continuing care facility under which—

(A) the individual or individual's spouse may use a qualified continuing care facility for their life or lives,

(B) the individual or individual's spouse—

(i) will first—

(I) reside in a separate, independent living unit with additional facilities outside such unit for the providing of meals and other personal care, and

(II) not require long-term nursing care, and

(ii) then will be provided long-term and skilled nursing care as the health of such individual or individual's spouse requires, and

BELOW-MARKET INTEREST RATE LOANS

(C) no additional substantial payment is required if such individual or individual's spouse requires increased personal care services or long-term and skilled nursing care.

(4) QUALIFIED CONTINUING CARE FACILITY.—

(A) IN GENERAL.—For purposes of this section, the term "qualified continuing care facility" means 1 or more facilities—

(i) which are designed to provide services under continuing care contracts, and

(ii) substantially all of the residents of which are covered by continuing care contracts.

(B) SUBSTANTIALLY ALL FACILITIES MUST BE OWNED OR OPERATED BY BORROWER.—A facility shall not be treated as a qualified continuing care facility unless substantially all facilities which are used to provide services which are required to be provided under a continuing care contract are owned or operated by the borrower.

(C) NURSING HOMES EXCLUDED.—The term "qualified continuing care facility" shall not include any facility which is of a type which is traditionally considered a nursing home.

(5) ADJUSTMENT OF LIMIT FOR INFLATION.—In the case of any loan made during any calendar year after 1986, the dollar amount in paragraph (2) shall be increased by an amount equal to—

(A) such amount, multiplied by

(B) the cost-of-living adjustment determined under section 1(f)(3) for the calendar year in which the taxable year begins, by substituting "calendar year 1985" for "calendar year 2016" in subparagraph (A)(ii) thereof.

Any increase under the preceding sentence shall be rounded to the nearest multiple of $100 (or, if such increase is a multiple of $50, such increase shall be increased to the nearest multiple of $100).

(6) SUSPENSION OF APPLICATION.—Paragraph (1) shall not apply for any calendar year to which subsection (h) applies.

Amendments

• **2017, Tax Cuts and Jobs Act (P.L. 115-97)**

P.L. 115-97, §11002(d)(14):

Amended Code Sec. 7872(g)(5). **Effective** for tax years beginning after 12-31-2017. Prior to amendment, Code Sec. 7872(g)(5) read as follows:

(5) ADJUSTMENT OF LIMIT FOR INFLATION.—

(A) IN GENERAL.—In the case of any loan made during any calendar year after 1986 to which paragraph (1) applies, the dollar amount in paragraph (2) shall be increased by the inflation adjustment for such calendar year. Any increase under the preceding sentence shall be rounded to the nearest multiple of $100 (or, if such increase is a multiple of $50, such increase shall be increased to the nearest multiple of $100).

(B) INFLATION ADJUSTMENT.—For purposes of subparagraph (A), the inflation adjustment for any calendar year is the percentage (if any) by which—

(i) the CPI for the preceding calendar year exceeds

(ii) the CPI for calendar year 1985.

For purposes of the preceding sentence, the CPI for any calendar year is the average of the Consumer Price Index as of the close of the 12-month period ending on September 30 of such calendar year.

• **2006, Tax Increase Prevention and Reconciliation Act of 2005 (P.L. 109-222)**

P.L. 109-222, §209(b)(1):

Amended Code Sec. 7872(g) by adding at the end a new paragraph (6). **Effective** for calendar years beginning after 12-31-2005, with respect to loans made before, on, or after such date.

• **1986, Tax Reform Act of 1986 (P.L. 99-514)**

P.L. 99-514, §1812(b)(5), as amended by P.L. 101-179, §307(a)(1)-(2), provides:

(5) CERTAIN ISRAEL BONDS NOT SUBJECT TO RULES RELATING TO BELOW-MARKET LOANS.—Section 7872 of the Internal Revenue Code of 1954 (relating to treatment of loans with below-market interest rates) shall not apply to any obligation issued by Israel or Poland if—

(A) the obligation is payable in United States dollars, and

(B) the obligation bears interest at an annual rate of not less than 4 percent.

• **1985 (P.L. 99-121)**

P.L. 99-121, §201(a):

Amended Code Sec. 7872 by redesignating subsection (g) as subsection (h) and by inserting after subsection (f) new subsection (g). **Effective** with respect to loans made after 10-11-85. For special rules, see the amendment notes following Code Sec. 7872(h).

[Sec. 7872(h)]

(h) EXCEPTION FOR LOANS TO QUALIFIED CONTINUING CARE FACILITIES.—

(1) IN GENERAL.—This section shall not apply for any calendar year to any below-market loan owed by a facility which on the last day of such year is a qualified continuing care facility, if such loan was made pursuant to a continuing care contract and if the lender (or the lender's spouse) attains age 62 before the close of such year.

(2) CONTINUING CARE CONTRACT.—For purposes of this section, the term "continuing care contract" means a written contract between an individual and a qualified continuing care facility under which—

(A) the individual or individual's spouse may use a qualified continuing care facility for their life or lives,

(B) the individual or individual's spouse will be provided with housing, as appropriate for the health of such individual or individual's spouse—

(i) in an independent living unit (which has additional available facilities outside such unit for the provision of meals and other personal care), and

(ii) in an assisted living facility or a nursing facility, as is available in the continuing care facility, and

(C) the individual or individual's spouse will be provided assisted living or nursing care as the health of such individual or individual's spouse requires, and as is available in the continuing care facility.

The Secretary shall issue guidance which limits such term to contracts which provide only facilities, care, and services described in this paragraph.

(3) QUALIFIED CONTINUING CARE FACILITY.—

(A) IN GENERAL.—For purposes of this section, the term "qualified continuing care facility" means 1 or more facilities—

(i) which are designed to provide services under continuing care contracts,

(ii) which include an independent living unit, plus an assisted living or nursing facility, or both, and

(iii) substantially all of the independent living unit residents of which are covered by continuing care contracts.

(B) NURSING HOMES EXCLUDED.—The term "qualified continuing care facility" shall not include any facility which is of a type which is traditionally considered a nursing home.

Amendments

• **2006, Tax Relief and Health Care Act of 2006 (P.L. 109-432)**

P.L. 109-432, Division A, §425(a):

Amended Code Sec. 7872(h) by striking paragraph (4). **Effective** as if included in section 209 of the Tax Increase Prevention and Reconciliation Act of 2005 (P.L. 109-222) [**effective** for calendar years beginning after 12-31-2005, with respect to loans made before, on, or after such date.—CCH]. Prior to being stricken, Code Sec. 7872(h)(4) read as follows:

(4) TERMINATION.—This subsection shall not apply to any calendar year after 2010.

• **2006, Tax Increase Prevention and Reconciliation Act of 2005 (P.L. 109-222)**

P.L. 109-222, §209(a):

Amended Code Sec. 7872 by redesignating subsection (h) as subsection (i) and inserting after subsection (g) a new subsection (h). **Effective** for calendar years beginning after 12-31-2005, with respect to loans made before, on, or after such date.

INDIAN FISHING RIGHTS SECURED BY TREATY

[Sec. 7872(i)]

(i) REGULATIONS.—

(1) IN GENERAL.—The Secretary shall prescribe such regulations as may be necessary or appropriate to carry out the purposes of this section, including—

(A) regulations providing that where, by reason of varying rates of interest, conditional interest payments, waivers of interest, disposition of the lender's or borrower's interest in the loan, or other circumstances, the provisions of this section do not carry out the purposes of this section, adjustments to the provisions of this section will be made to the extent necessary to carry out the purposes of this section,

(B) regulations for the purpose of assuring that the positions of the borrower and lender are consistent as to the application (or nonapplication) of this section, and

(C) regulations exempting from the application of this section any class of transactions the interest arrangements of which have no significant effect on any Federal tax liability of the lender or the borrower.

(2) ESTATE TAX COORDINATION.—Under regulations prescribed by the Secretary, any loan which is made with donative intent and which is a term loan shall be taken into account for purposes of chapter 11 in a manner consistent with the provisions of subsection (b).

Amendments

• 2006, Tax Increase Prevention and Reconciliation Act of 2005 (P.L. 109-222)

P.L. 109-222, § 209(a):

Amended Code Sec. 7872 by redesignating subsection (h) as subsection (i). **Effective** for calendar years beginning after 12-31-2005, with respect to loans made before, on, or after such date.

• 1986, Tax Reform Act of 1986 (P.L. 99-514)

P.L. 99-514, § 1812(b)(5), as amended by P.L. 101-179, § 307(a)(1)-(2), provides:

(5) CERTAIN ISRAEL BONDS NOT SUBJECT TO RULES RELATING TO BELOW-MARKET LOANS.—Section 7872 of the Internal Revenue Code of 1954 (relating to treatment of loans with below-market interest rates) shall not apply to any obligation issued by Israel or Poland if—

(A) the obligation is payable in United States dollars, and

(B) the obligation bears interest at an annual rate of not less than 4 percent.

• 1985 (P.L. 99-121)

P.L. 99-121, § 201(a):

Redesignated Code Sec. 7872(g) as Code Sec. 7872(h). **Effective** with respect to loans made after 10-11-85.

P.L. 99-121, § 203, provides:

SEC. 203. SECTION 7872 OF THE INTERNAL REVENUE CODE SHALL NOT APPLY TO NON-LOAN PAYMENTS TO CERTAIN RESIDENTIAL HOUSING FACILITIES FOR THE ELDERLY.

(a) GENERAL RULE.—For purposes of section 7872 of the Internal Revenue Code of 1954, payments made to a specified independent living facility for the elderly by a payor who is an individual at least 65 years old shall not be treated as loans provided—

(1) the independent living facility is designed and operated to meet some substantial combination of the health, physical, emotional, recreational, social, religious and similar needs of persons over the age of 65;

(2) in exchange for the payment, the payor obtains the right to occupy (or equivalent contractual right) independent living quarters located in the independent living facility;

(3) the amount of the payment is equal to the fair market value of the right to occupy the independent living quarters;

(4) upon leaving the independent living facility, the payor is entitled to receive a payment equal to at least 50 percent of the fair market value at that time of the right to occupy the independent living quarters, the timing of which payment may be contingent on the time when the independent living facility is able to locate a new occupant for such quarters; and

(5) the excess, if any, of the fair market value of the independent living quarters at the time the payor leaves such quarters (less a reasonable amount to cover costs) over the amount paid to the payor is used by an organization described in section 501(c)(3) of such Code to provide housing and related services for needy elderly persons.

(b) SPECIFIED INDEPENDENT LIVING FACILITY FOR THE ELDERLY.—

For purposes of this section—

(1) IN GENERAL.—The term "specified independent living facility for the elderly" means—

(A) the Our Lady of Life Apartments owned by a Missouri not-for-profit corporation with the same name,

(B) the Laclede Oaks Manor owned by the Lutheran Health Care Association of St. Louis, Missouri, and

(C) the Luther Center Northeast owned by the Lutheran Altenheim Society of Missouri.

(2) REQUIREMENTS.—A facility shall not be considered to be a specified independent living facility for the elderly—

(A) if it is located at any site other than the site which it occupied (or was in the process of occupying through construction) on the date of the enactment of this Act, or

(B) if its ownership is transferred after such date of enactment to a person other than an organization described in section 501(c)(3) of the Internal Revenue Code of 1954.

P.L. 99-121, § 204(a)(2), provides:

(2) SECTION 7872 NOT TO APPLY TO CERTAIN LOANS.—Section 7872 of the Internal Revenue Code of 1954 shall not apply to loans made on or before the date of the enactment of this Act to any qualified continuing care facility pursuant to a continuing care contract. For purposes of this paragraph, the terms "qualified continuing care facility" and "continuing care contract" have the meanings given such terms by section 7872(g) of such Code (as added by section 201).

P.L. 99-121, § 204(c), provides:

(c) SECTION 203.—The provisions of section 203 shall apply as if included in section 172(a) of the Tax Reform Act of 1984.

• 1984, Deficit Reduction Act of 1984 (P.L. 98-369)

P.L. 98-369, § 172(a):

Added Code Sec. 7872. **Effective** for term loans made after 6-6-84, and to demand loans outstanding after 6-6-84. However, see Act Sec. 172(c)(2)-(6), below, for exceptions and special rules.

P.L. 98-369, § 172(c)(2)-(6), provides:

(2) Exception for demand loans outstanding on June 6, 1984, and repaid within 60 days after date of enactment.—The amendments made by this section shall not apply to any demand loan which—

(A) was outstanding on June 6, 1984, and

(B) was repaid before the date 60 days after the date of the enactment of this Act.

(3) Exception for certain existing loans to continuing care facilities.—Nothing in this subsection shall be construed to apply the amendments made by this section to any loan made before June 6, 1984, to a continuing care facility by a resident of such facility which is contingent on continued residence at such facility.

(4) Applicable federal rate for periods before January 1, 1985.—For periods before January 1, 1985, the applicable Federal rate under paragraph (2) of section 7872(f) of the Internal Revenue Code of 1954, as added by this section, shall be 10 percent, compounded semiannually.

(5) Treatment of renegotiations, etc.—For purposes of this subsection, any loan renegotiated, extended, or revised after June 6, 1984, shall be treated as a loan made after such date.

(6) Definition of term and demand loans.—For purposes of this subsection, the terms "demand loan" and "term loan" have the respective meanings given such terms by paragraphs (5) and (6) of section 7872(f) of the Internal Revenue Code of 1954, as added by this section, but the second sentence of such paragraph (5) shall not apply.

[Sec. 7873]

SEC. 7873. FEDERAL TAX TREATMENT OF INCOME DERIVED BY INDIANS FROM EXERCISE OF FISHING RIGHTS SECURED BY TREATY, ETC.

[Sec. 7873(a)]

(a) IN GENERAL.—

(1) INCOME AND SELF-EMPLOYMENT TAXES.—No tax shall be imposed by subtitle A on income derived—

(A) by a member of an Indian tribe directly or through a qualified Indian entity, or

(B) by a qualified Indian entity,

from a fishing rights-related activity of such tribe.

(2) EMPLOYMENT TAXES.—No tax shall be imposed by subtitle C on remuneration paid for services performed in a fishing rights-related activity of an Indian tribe by a member of such tribe for another member of such tribe or for a qualified Indian entity.

EXPATRIATED ENTITIES AND THEIR FOREIGN PARENTS

[Sec. 7873(b)]

(b) DEFINITIONS.—For purposes of this section—

(1) FISHING RIGHTS-RELATED ACTIVITY.—The term "fishing rights-related activity" means, with respect to an Indian tribe, any activity directly related to harvesting, processing, or transporting fish harvested in the exercise of a recognized fishing right of such tribe or to selling such fish but only if substantially all of such harvesting was performed by members of such tribe.

(2) RECOGNIZED FISHING RIGHTS.—The term "recognized fishing rights" means, with respect to an Indian tribe, fishing rights secured as of March 17, 1988, by a treaty between such tribe and the United States or by an Executive order or an Act of Congress.

(3) QUALIFIED INDIAN ENTITY.—

(A) IN GENERAL.—The term "qualified Indian entity" means, with respect to an Indian tribe, any entity if—

(i) such entity is engaged in a fishing rights-related activity of such tribe,

(ii) all of the equity interests in the entity are owned by qualified Indian tribes, members of such tribes, or their spouses,

(iii) except as provided in regulations, in the case of an entity which engages to any extent in any substantial processing or transporting of fish, 90 percent or more of the annual gross receipts of the entity is derived from fishing rights-related activities of one or more qualified Indian tribes each of which owns at least 10 percent of the equity interests in the entity, and

(iv) substantially all of the management functions of the entity are performed by members of qualified Indian tribes.

For purposes of clause (iii), equity interests owned by a member (or the spouse of a member) of a qualified Indian tribe shall be treated as owned by the tribe.

(B) QUALIFIED INDIAN TRIBE.—For purposes of subparagraph (A), an Indian tribe is a qualified Indian tribe with respect to an entity if such entity is engaged in a fishing rights-related activity of such tribe.

[Sec. 7873(c)]

(c) SPECIAL RULES.—

(1) DISTRIBUTIONS FROM QUALIFIED INDIAN ENTITY.—For purposes of this section, any distribution with respect to an equity interest in a qualified Indian entity of an Indian tribe to a member of such tribe shall be treated as derived by such member from a fishing rights-related activity of such tribe to the extent such distribution is attributable to income derived by such entity from a fishing rights-related activity of such tribe.

(2) DE MINIMIS UNRELATED AMOUNTS MAY BE EXCLUDED.—If, but for this paragraph, all but a de minimis amount—

(A) derived by a qualified Indian tribal entity, or by an individual through such an entity, is entitled to the benefits of paragraph (1) of subsection (a), or

(B) paid to an individual for services is entitled to the benefits of paragraph (2) of subsection (a),

then the entire amount shall be entitled to the benefits of such paragraph.

Amendments

- **1988, Technical and Miscellaneous Revenue Act of 1988 (P.L. 100-647)**

P.L. 100-647, §3041(a):

Amended Subchapter C of chapter 80 by adding at the end thereof a new section 7873. **Effective** for all periods beginning before, on, or after 11-10-88.

P.L. 100-647, §3044(b), provides:

(b) NO INFERENCE CREATED.—Nothing in the amendments made by this subtitle shall create any inference as to the existence or non-existence or scope of any exemption from tax for income derived from fishing rights secured as of March 17, 1988, by any treaty, law, or Executive Order.

[Sec. 7874]

SEC. 7874. RULES RELATING TO EXPATRIATED ENTITIES AND THEIR FOREIGN PARENTS.

[Sec. 7874(a)]

(a) TAX ON INVERSION GAIN OF EXPATRIATED ENTITIES.—

(1) IN GENERAL.—The taxable income of an expatriated entity for any taxable year which includes any portion of the applicable period shall in no event be less than the inversion gain of the entity for the taxable year.

(2) EXPATRIATED ENTITY.—For purposes of this subsection—

(A) IN GENERAL.—The term "expatriated entity" means—

(i) the domestic corporation or partnership referred to in subparagraph (B)(i) with respect to which a foreign corporation is a surrogate foreign corporation, and

(ii) any United States person who is related (within the meaning of section 267(b) or 707(b)(1)) to a domestic corporation or partnership described in clause (i).

(B) SURROGATE FOREIGN CORPORATION.—A foreign corporation shall be treated as a surrogate foreign corporation if, pursuant to a plan (or a series of related transactions)—

(i) the entity completes after March 4, 2003, the direct or indirect acquisition of substantially all of the properties held directly or indirectly by a domestic corporation or substantially all of the properties constituting a trade or business of a domestic partnership,

(ii) after the acquisition at least 60 percent of the stock (by vote or value) of the entity is held—

(I) in the case of an acquisition with respect to a domestic corporation, by former shareholders of the domestic corporation by reason of holding stock in the domestic corporation, or

(II) in the case of an acquisition with respect to a domestic partnership, by former partners of the domestic partnership by reason of holding a capital or profits interest in the domestic partnership, and

(iii) after the acquisition the expanded affiliated group which includes the entity does not have substantial business activities in the foreign country in which, or under the law of which, the entity is created or organized, when compared to the total business activities of such expanded affiliated group.

An entity otherwise described in clause (i) with respect to any domestic corporation or partnership trade or business shall be treated as not so described if, on or before March 4, 2003, such entity acquired directly or indirectly more than half of the properties held directly or indirectly by such corporation or more than half of the properties constituting such partnership trade or business, as the case may be.

(3) COORDINATION WITH SUBSECTION (b).—A corporation which is treated as a domestic corporation under subsection (b) shall not be treated as a surrogate foreign corporation for purposes of paragraph (2)(A).

Amendments

- **2005, Gulf Opportunity Zone Act of 2005 (P.L. 109-135)**

P.L. 109-135, §403(u):

Amended Code Sec. 7874(a)(3). **Effective** as if included in the provision of the American Jobs Creation Act of 2004 (P.L. 108-357) to which it relates [effective for tax years ending after 3-4-2003.—CCH]. Prior to amendment, Code Sec. 7874(a)(3) read as follows:

(3) COORDINATION WITH SUBSECTION (b).—Paragraph (1) shall not apply to any entity which is treated as a domestic corporation under subsection (b).

EXPATRIATED ENTITIES AND THEIR FOREIGN PARENTS

[Sec. 7874(b)]

(b) INVERTED CORPORATIONS TREATED AS DOMESTIC CORPORATIONS.—Notwithstanding section 7701(a)(4), a foreign corporation shall be treated for purposes of this title as a domestic corporation if such corporation would be a surrogate foreign corporation if subsection (a)(2) were applied by substituting "80 percent" for "60 percent".

[Sec. 7874(c)]

(c) DEFINITIONS AND SPECIAL RULES.—

(1) EXPANDED AFFILIATED GROUP.—The term "expanded affiliated group" means an affiliated group as defined in section 1504(a) but without regard to section 1504(b)(3), except that section 1504(a) shall be applied by substituting "more than 50 percent" for "at least 80 percent" each place it appears.

(2) CERTAIN STOCK DISREGARDED.—There shall not be taken into account in determining ownership under subsection (a)(2)(B)(ii)—

(A) stock held by members of the expanded affiliated group which includes the foreign corporation, or

(B) stock of such foreign corporation which is sold in a public offering related to the acquisition described in subsection (a)(2)(B)(i).

(3) PLAN DEEMED IN CERTAIN CASES.—If a foreign corporation acquires directly or indirectly substantially all of the properties of a domestic corporation or partnership during the 4-year period beginning on the date which is 2 years before the ownership requirements of subsection (a)(2)(B)(ii) are met, such actions shall be treated as pursuant to a plan.

(4) CERTAIN TRANSFERS DISREGARDED.—The transfer of properties or liabilities (including by contribution or distribution) shall be disregarded if such transfers are part of a plan a principal purpose of which is to avoid the purposes of this section.

(5) SPECIAL RULE FOR RELATED PARTNERSHIPS.—For purposes of applying subsection (a)(2)(B)(ii) to the acquisition of a trade or business of a domestic partnership, except as provided in regulations, all partnerships which are under common control (within the meaning of section 482) shall be treated as 1 partnership.

(6) REGULATIONS.—The Secretary shall prescribe such regulations as may be appropriate to determine whether a corporation is a surrogate foreign corporation, including regulations—

(A) to treat warrants, options, contracts to acquire stock, convertible debt interests, and other similar interests as stock, and

(B) to treat stock as not stock.

[Sec. 7874(d)]

(d) OTHER DEFINITIONS.—For purposes of this section—

(1) APPLICABLE PERIOD.—The term "applicable period" means the period—

(A) beginning on the first date properties are acquired as part of the acquisition described in subsection (a)(2)(B)(i), and

(B) ending on the date which is 10 years after the last date properties are acquired as part of such acquisition.

(2) INVERSION GAIN.—The term "inversion gain" means the income or gain recognized by reason of the transfer during the applicable period of stock or other properties by an expatriated entity, and any income received or accrued during the applicable period by reason of a license of any property by an expatriated entity—

(A) as part of the acquisition described in subsection (a)(2)(B)(i), or

(B) after such acquisition if the transfer or license is to a foreign related person.

Subparagraph (B) shall not apply to property described in section 1221(a)(1) in the hands of the expatriated entity.

(3) FOREIGN RELATED PERSON.—The term "foreign related person" means, with respect to any expatriated entity, a foreign person which—

(A) is related (within the meaning of section 267(b) or 707(b)(1)) to such entity, or

(B) is under the same common control (within the meaning of section 482) as such entity.

[Sec. 7874(e)]

(e) SPECIAL RULES.—

(1) CREDITS NOT ALLOWED AGAINST TAX ON INVERSION GAIN.—Credits (other than the credit allowed by section 901) shall be allowed against the tax imposed by this chapter on an expatriated entity for any taxable year described in subsection (a) only to the extent such tax exceeds the product of—

(A) the amount of the inversion gain for the taxable year, and

(B) the highest rate of tax specified in section 11(b).

For purposes of determining the credit allowed by section 901, inversion gain shall be treated as from sources within the United States.

(2) SPECIAL RULES FOR PARTNERSHIPS.—In the case of an expatriated entity which is a partnership—

(A) subsection (a)(1) shall apply at the partner rather than the partnership level,

(B) the inversion gain of any partner for any taxable year shall be equal to the sum of—

(i) the partner's distributive share of inversion gain of the partnership for such taxable year, plus

(ii) gain recognized for the taxable year by the partner by reason of the transfer during the applicable period of any partnership interest of the partner in such partnership to the surrogate foreign corporation, and

(C) the highest rate of tax specified in the rate schedule applicable to the partner under this chapter shall be substituted for the rate of tax referred to in paragraph (1).

(3) COORDINATION WITH SECTION 172 AND MINIMUM TAX.—Rules similar to the rules of paragraphs (3) and (4) of section 860E(a) shall apply for purposes of subsection (a).

(4) STATUTE OF LIMITATIONS.—

(A) IN GENERAL.—The statutory period for the assessment of any deficiency attributable to the inversion gain of any taxpayer for any pre-inversion year shall not expire before the expiration of 3 years from the date the Secretary is notified by the taxpayer (in such manner as the Secretary may prescribe) of the acquisition described in subsection (a)(2)(B)(i) to which such gain relates and such deficiency may be assessed before the expiration of such 3-year period notwithstanding the provisions of any other law or rule of law which would otherwise prevent such assessment.

(B) PRE-INVERSION YEAR.—For purposes of subparagraph (A), the term "pre-inversion year" means any taxable year if—

(i) any portion of the applicable period is included in such taxable year, and

(ii) such year ends before the taxable year in which the acquisition described in subsection (a)(2)(B)(i) is completed.

EXPATRIATED ENTITIES AND THEIR FOREIGN PARENTS

Amendments

• **2017, Tax Cuts and Jobs Act (P.L. 115-97)**

P.L. 115-97, §13001(b)(1)(C):

Amended Code Sec. 7874(e)(1)(B) by striking "section 11(b)(1)" and inserting "section 11(b)". **Effective** for tax years beginning after 12-31-2017.

[Sec. 7874(f)]

(f) SPECIAL RULE FOR TREATIES.—Nothing in section 894 or 7852(d) or in any other provision of law shall be construed as permitting an exemption, by reason of any treaty obligation of the United States heretofore or hereafter entered into, from the provisions of this section.

[Sec. 7874(g)]

(g) REGULATIONS.—The Secretary shall provide such regulations as are necessary to carry out this section, including regulations providing for such adjustments to the application of this section as are necessary to prevent the avoidance of the purposes of this section, including the avoidance of such purposes through—

(1) the use of related persons, pass-through or other noncorporate entities, or other intermediaries, or

(2) transactions designed to have persons cease to be (or not become) members of expanded affiliated groups or related persons.

Amendments

• **2004, American Jobs Creation Act of 2004 (P.L. 108-357)**

P.L. 108-357, §801(a):

Amended subchapter C of chapter 80 by adding at the end a new Code Sec. 7874. **Effective** for tax years ending after 3-4-2003.

[The next page is 5201.]

Subtitle G—The Joint Committee on Taxation

CHAPTER 91.   Organization and membership of the Joint Committee.
CHAPTER 92.   Powers and duties of the Joint Committee.

CHAPTER 91—ORGANIZATION AND MEMBERSHIP OF THE JOINT COMMITTEE

Sec. 8001.   Authorization.
Sec. 8002.   Membership.
Sec. 8003.   Election of chairman and vice chairman.
Sec. 8004.   Appointment and compensation of staff.
Sec. 8005.   Payment of expenses.

[Sec. 8001]

SEC. 8001. AUTHORIZATION.

There shall be a joint congressional committee known as the Joint Committee on Taxation (hereinafter in this subtitle referred to as the "Joint Committee").

Amendments

• **1976, Tax Reform Act of 1976 (P.L. 94-455)**

P.L. 94-455, § 1907(a)(1):

Substituted "Joint Committee on Taxation" for "Joint Committee on Internal Revenue Taxation" in Code Sec. 8001. **Effective** 2-1-77.

[Sec. 8002]

SEC. 8002. MEMBERSHIP.

[Sec. 8002(a)]

(a) NUMBER AND SELECTION.—The Joint Committee shall be composed of 10 members as follows:

(1) FROM COMMITTEE ON FINANCE.—Five members who are members of the Committee on Finance of the Senate, three from the majority and two from the minority party, to be chosen by such Committee; and

(2) FROM COMMITTEE ON WAYS AND MEANS.—Five members who are members of the Committee on Ways and Means of the House of Representatives, three from the majority and two from the minority party, to be chosen by such Committee.

[Sec. 8002(b)]

(b) TENURE OF OFFICE.—

(1) GENERAL LIMITATION.—No person shall continue to serve as a member of the Joint Committee after he has ceased to be a member of the Committee by which he was chosen, except that—

(2) EXCEPTION.—The members chosen by the Committee on Ways and Means who have been reelected to the House of Representatives may continue to serve as members of the Joint Committee notwithstanding the expiration of the Congress.

[Sec. 8002(c)]

(c) VACANCIES.—A vacancy in the Joint Committee—

(1) EFFECT.—Shall not affect the power of the remaining members to execute the functions of the Joint Committee; and

(2) MANNER OF FILLING.—Shall be filled in the same manner as the original selection, except that—

(A) ADJOURNMENT OR RECESS OF CONGRESS.—In case of a vacancy during an adjournment or recess of Congress for a period of more than 2 weeks, the members of the Joint Committee who are members of the Committee entitled to fill such vacancy may designate a member of such Committee to serve until his successor is chosen by such Committee; and

(B) EXPIRATION OF CONGRESS.—In the case of a vacancy after the expiration of a Congress which would be filled by the Committee on Ways and Means, the members of such Committee who are continuing to serve as members of the Joint Committee may designate a person who, immediately prior to such expiration, was a member of such Committee and who is re-elected to the House of Representatives, to serve until his successor is chosen by such Committee.

[Sec. 8002(d)]

(d) ALLOWANCES.—The members shall serve without compensation in addition to that received for their services as members of Congress; but they shall be reimbursed for travel, subsistence, and other necessary expenses incurred by them in the performance of the duties vested in the Joint Committee, other than expenses in connection with meetings of the Joint Committee held in the District of Columbia during such times as the Congress is in session.

[Sec. 8003]

SEC. 8003. ELECTION OF CHAIRMAN AND VICE CHAIRMAN.

The Joint Committee shall elect a chairman and vice chairman from among its members.

[Sec. 8004]

SEC. 8004. APPOINTMENT AND COMPENSATION OF STAFF.

Except as otherwise provided by law, the Joint Committee shall have power to appoint and fix the compensation of the Chief of Staff of the Joint Committee and such experts and clerical, stenographic, and other assistants as it deems advisable.

Amendments

• **1976, Tax Reform Act of 1976 (P.L. 94-455)**

P.L. 94-455, § 1907(a)(2):

Substituted "compensation of the Chief of Staff of the Joint Committee" for "compensation of a clerk" in Code Sec. 8004. **Effective** 2-1-77.

[Sec. 8005]

SEC. 8005. PAYMENT OF EXPENSES.

The expenses of the Joint Committee shall be paid one-half from the contingent fund of the Senate and one-half from the contingent fund of the House of Representatives, upon vouchers signed by the chairman or the vice chairman.

JOINT COMMITTEE ON TAXATION

CHAPTER 92—POWERS AND DUTIES OF THE JOINT COMMITTEE

Sec. 8021.   Powers.
Sec. 8022.   Duties.
Sec. 8023.   Additional powers to obtain data.

[Sec. 8021]

SEC. 8021. POWERS.

[Sec. 8021(a)]

(a) TO OBTAIN DATA AND INSPECT INCOME RETURNS.—
For powers of the Joint Committee to obtain and inspect income returns, see section 6103(f).

Amendments

• **1988, Technical and Miscellaneous Revenue Act of 1988 (P.L. 100-647)**

P.L. 100-647, §1018(s)(1):

Amended Code Sec. 8021(a) by striking out "6103(d)" and inserting in lieu thereof "6103(f)". **Effective** as if included in the provision of P.L. 99-514 to which it relates.

[Sec. 8021(b)]

(b) RELATING TO HEARINGS AND SESSIONS.—The Joint Committee, or any subcommittee thereof, is authorized—

(1) TO HOLD.—To hold hearings and to sit and act at such places and times;

(2) TO REQUIRE ATTENDANCE OF WITNESSES AND PRODUCTION OF BOOKS.—To require by subpoena (to be issued under the signature of the chairman or vice chairman) or otherwise the attendance of such witnesses and the production of such books, papers, and documents;

(3) TO ADMINISTER OATHS.—To administer such oaths; and

(4) TO TAKE TESTIMONY.—To take such testimony;

as it deems advisable.

[Sec. 8021(c)]

(c) TO PROCURE PRINTING AND BINDING.—The Joint Committee, or any subcommittee thereof, is authorized to have such printing and binding done as it deems advisable.

[Sec. 8021(d)]

(d) TO MAKE EXPENDITURES.—The Joint Committee, or any subcommittee thereof, is authorized to make such expenditures as it deems advisable.

Amendments

• **1976, Tax Reform Act of 1976 (P.L. 94-455)**

P.L. 94-455, §1907(a)(3):

Amended Code Sec. 8021(d). **Effective** 2-1-77. Prior to amendment, Code Sec. 8021(d) read as follows:

(d) TO MAKE EXPENDITURES.

(1) GENERAL AUTHORITY.—The Joint Committee, or any subcommittee thereof, is authorized to make such expenditures as it deems advisable.

(2) LIMITATION.—The cost of stenographic services in reporting such hearings as the Joint Committee may hold shall not be in excess of 25 cents per 100 words.

[Sec. 8021(e)]

(e) INVESTIGATIONS.—The Joint Committee shall review all requests (other than requests by the chairman or ranking member of a committee or subcommittee) for investigations of the Internal Revenue Service by the Government Accountability Office, and approve such requests when appropriate, with a view towards eliminating overlapping investigations, ensuring that the Government Accountability Office has the capacity to handle the investigation, and ensuring that investigations focus on areas of primary importance to tax administration.

Amendments

• **2005, Gulf Opportunity Zone Act of 2005 (P.L. 109-135)**

P.L. 109-135, §412(rr)(5):

Amended Code Sec. 8021(e) by striking "General Accounting Office" each place it appears and inserting "Government Accountability Office". **Effective** 12-21-2005.

• **1998, IRS Restructuring and Reform Act of 1998 (P.L. 105-206)**

P.L. 105-206, §4001(a):

Amended Code Sec. 8021 by adding at the end a new subsection (e). **Effective** for requests made after 7-22-98.

[Sec. 8021(f)—Stricken]

Amendments

• **2018, Tax Technical Corrections Act of 2018 (P.L. 115-141)**

P.L. 115-141, §401(b)(56), Div. U:

Amended Code Sec. 8021 by striking subsection (f). **Effective** 3-23-2018. For a special rule, see Act Sec. 401(e), Div. U, below. Prior to being stricken, Code Sec. 8021(f) read as follows:

(f) RELATING TO JOINT REVIEWS.—

(1) IN GENERAL.—The Chief of Staff, and the staff of the Joint Committee, shall provide such assistance as is required for joint reviews described in paragraph (2).

(2) JOINT REVIEWS.—Before June 1 of each calendar year after 1998 and before 2005, there shall be a joint review of the strategic plans and budget for the Internal Revenue Service and such other matters as the Chairman of the Joint Committee deems appropriate. Such joint review shall be held at the call of the Chairman of the Joint Committee and shall include two members of the majority and one member of the minority from each of the Committees on Finance, Appropriations, and Governmental Affairs of the Senate, and the Committees on Ways and Means, Appropriations, and Government Reform and Oversight of the House of Representatives.

P.L. 115-141, §401(e), Div. U, provides:

(e) GENERAL SAVINGS PROVISION WITH RESPECT TO DEADWOOD PROVISIONS.—If—

(1) any provision amended or repealed by the amendments made by subsection (b) or (d) applied to—

(A) any transaction occurring before the date of the enactment of this Act,

(B) any property acquired before such date of enactment, or

(C) any item of income, loss, deduction, or credit taken into account before such date of enactment, and

(2) the treatment of such transaction, property, or item under such provision would (without regard to the amendments or repeals made by such subsection) affect the liability for tax for periods ending after such date of enactment,

nothing in the amendments or repeals made by this section shall be construed to affect the treatment of such transaction, property, or item for purposes of determining liability for tax for periods ending after such date of enactment.

• **2004, Working Families Tax Relief Act of 2004 (P.L. 108-311)**

P.L. 108-311, §321(a):

Amended Code Sec. 8021(f)(2) by striking "2004" and inserting "2005". **Effective** 10-4-2004.

P.L. 108-311, §321(c), provides:

(c) TIME FOR JOINT REVIEW.—The joint review required by section 8021(f)(2) of the Internal Revenue Code of 1986 to be made before June 1, 2004, shall be treated as timely if made before June 1, 2005.

• **1998, IRS Restructuring and Reform Act of 1998 (P.L. 105-206)**

P.L. 105-206, §4001(a):

Amended Code Sec. 8021 by adding at the end a new subsection (f). **Effective** 7-22-98.

JOINT COMMITTEE ON TAXATION

[Sec. 8022]

SEC. 8022. DUTIES.

It shall be the duty of the Joint Committee—

(1) INVESTIGATION.—

(A) OPERATION AND EFFECTS OF LAW.—To investigate the operation and effects of the Federal system of internal revenue taxes;

(B) ADMINISTRATION.—To investigate the administration of such taxes by the Internal Revenue Service or any executive department, establishment, or agency charged with their administration; and

(C) OTHER INVESTIGATIONS.—To make such other investigations in respect of such system of taxes as the Joint Committee may deem necessary.

(2) SIMPLIFICATION OF LAW.—

(A) INVESTIGATION OF METHODS.—To investigate measures and methods for the simplification of such taxes, particularly the income tax; and

(B) PUBLICATION OF PROPOSALS.—To publish, from time to time, for public examination and analysis, proposed measures and methods for the simplification of such taxes.

(3) REPORTS.—

(A) To report, from time to time, to the Committee on Finance and the Committee on Ways and Means, and, in its discretion, to the Senate or House of Representatives, or both, the results of its investigations, together with such recommendations as it may deem advisable.

(B) Subject to amounts specifically appropriated to carry out this subparagraph, to report, at least once each Congress, to the Committee on Finance and the Committee on Ways and Means on the overall state of the Federal tax system, together with recommendations with respect to possible simplification proposals and other matters relating to the administration of the Federal tax system as it may deem advisable.

(4) CROSS REFERENCE.—

For duties of the Joint Committee relating to refunds of income and estate taxes, see section 6405.

Amendments

• **2018, Tax Technical Corrections Act of 2018 (P.L. 115-141)**

P.L. 115-141, § 401(b)(57), Div. U:

Amended Code Sec. 8022(3) by striking subparagraph (C). **Effective** 3-23-2018. For a special rule, see Act Sec. 401(e), Div. U, below. Prior to being stricken, Code Sec. 8022(3)(C) read as follows:

(C) To report, for each calendar year after 1998 and before 2005, to the Committees on Finance, Appropriations, and Governmental Affairs of the Senate, and to the Committees on Ways and Means, Appropriations, and Government Reform and Oversight of the House of Representatives, with respect to the matters addressed in the joint review referred to in section 8021(f)(2).

P.L. 115-141, § 401(e), Div. U, provides:

(e) GENERAL SAVINGS PROVISION WITH RESPECT TO DEADWOOD PROVISIONS.—If—

(1) any provision amended or repealed by the amendments made by subsection (b) or (d) applied to—

(A) any transaction occurring before the date of the enactment of this Act,

(B) any property acquired before such date of enactment, or

(C) any item of income, loss, deduction, or credit taken into account before such date of enactment, and

(2) the treatment of such transaction, property, or item under such provision would (without regard to the amendments or repeals made by such subsection) affect the liability for tax for periods ending after such date of enactment,

nothing in the amendments or repeals made by this section shall be construed to affect the treatment of such transaction, property, or item for purposes of determining liability for tax for periods ending after such date of enactment.

• **2004, Working Families Tax Relief Act of 2004 (P.L. 108-311)**

P.L. 108-311, § 321(b)(1)-(2):

Amended Code Sec. 8022(3)(C) by striking "2004" and inserting "2005", and by striking "with respect to—"and all that follows and inserting "with respect to the matters addressed in the joint review referred to in section 8021(f)(2).". **Effective** 10-4-2004. Prior to amendment, Code Sec. 8022(3)(C) read as follows:

(C) To report, for each calendar year after 1998 and before 2004, to the Committees on Finance, Appropriations, and Governmental Affairs of the Senate, and to the Committees on Ways and Means, Appropriations, and Government Reform and Oversight of the House of Representatives, with respect to—

(i) strategic and business plans for the Internal Revenue Service;

(ii) progress of the Internal Revenue Service in meeting its objectives;

(iii) the budget for the Internal Revenue Service and whether it supports its objectives;

(iv) progress of the Internal Revenue Service in improving taxpayer service and compliance;

(v) progress of the Internal Revenue Service on technology modernization; and

(vi) the annual filing season.

• **1998, IRS Restructuring and Reform Act of 1998 (P.L. 105-206)**

P.L. 105-206, § 4002(a):

Amended Code Sec. 8022(3). **Effective** 7-22-98. Prior to amendment, Code Sec. 8022(3) read as follows:

(3) REPORTS.—To report, from time to time, to the Committee on Finance and the Committee on Ways and Means, and, in its discretion, to the Senate or the House of Representatives, or both, the results of its investigations, together with such recommendations as it may deem advisable.

• **1976, Tax Reform Act of 1976 (P.L. 94-455)**

P.L. 94-455, § 2133, provides:

SEC. 2133. TAX INCENTIVES STUDY.

(a) STUDY.—The Joint Committee on Taxation, in consultation with the Treasury, shall make a full and complete study and comparative analysis of the cost effectiveness of different kinds of tax incentives, including an analysis and study of the most effective way to use tax cuts in a period of business recession to provide a stimulus to the economy.

(b) REPORT.—The Joint Committee on Taxation shall submit to the Committee on Finance of the Senate and to the Committee on Ways and Means of the House of Representatives a final report of its study and investigation together with its recommendations, including recommendations for legislation, as it deems advisable.

(c) REPORTING DATE.—The final report called for in subsection (b) of this section shall be submitted no later than September 30, 1977. Effective on 10-4-76.

[Sec. 8023]

SEC. 8023. ADDITIONAL POWERS TO OBTAIN DATA.

[Sec. 8023(a)]

(a) SECURING OF DATA.—The Joint Committee or the Chief of Staff of the Joint Committee, upon approval of the Chairman or Vice Chairman, is authorized to secure directly from the Internal Revenue Service or the office of the Chief Counsel for the Internal Revenue Service, or directly from any executive department, board, bureau, agency, independent establishment, or instrumentality of the Government, information, suggestions, rulings, data, estimates, and statistics, for the purpose of making investigations, reports, and studies relating to internal revenue taxation. In the investigation by the Joint Committee on Taxation of the administration of the internal revenue taxes by the Internal Revenue Service, the Chief of Staff of the Joint Committee on Taxation is authorized to secure directly from the Internal Revenue Service such tax returns, or copies of tax returns, and other relevant information, as the Chief of Staff deems necessary for such investigation, and the Internal Revenue Service is authorized and directed to furnish such tax returns and information to the Chief of Staff together with a brief report, with respect to each return, as to any action taken or proposed to be taken by the Service as a result of any audit of the return.

Amendments

• **1976, Tax Reform Act of 1976 (P.L. 94-455)**

P.L. 94-455, § 1210(c):

Added the last sentence to Code Sec. 8023(a). **Effective** 1-1-77.

• **1959 (P.L. 86-368)**

P.L. 86-368, § 2(b):

Amended Code Sec. 8023(a) by striking out "(including the Assistant General Counsel of the Treasury Department serving as the Chief Counsel of the Internal

JOINT COMMITTEE ON TAXATION

Revenue Service)" and by substituting "or the office of the Chief Counsel for the Internal Revenue Service". **Effective** when the Chief Counsel for the Internal Revenue Service first appointed pursuant to Code Sec. 7801 (as amended by P.L. 86-368, § 1) qualifies and takes office.

[Sec. 8023(b)]

(b) FURNISHING OF DATA.—The Internal Revenue Service, the office of the Chief Counsel for the Internal Revenue Service, executive departments, boards, bureaus, agencies, independent establishments, and instrumentalities are authorized and directed to furnish such information, suggestions, rulings, data, estimates, and statistics directly to the Joint Committee or to the Chief of Staff of the Joint Committee, upon request made pursuant to this section.

Amendments

- **1959 (P.L. 86-368)**

P.L. 86-368, § 2(b):

Amended Code Sec. 8023(b) by striking out "(including the Assistant General Counsel of the Treasury Department serving as the Chief Counsel of the Internal Revenue Service)" and by substituting ", the office of the Chief Counsel for the Internal Revenue Service". **Effective** when the Chief Counsel for the Internal Revenue Service first appointed pursuant to Code Sec. 7801 (as amended by P.L. 86-368, § 1) qualifies and takes office.

[Sec. 8023(c)]

(c) APPLICATION OF SUBSECTIONS(a) AND(b).—Subsections (a) and (b) shall be applied in accordance with their provisions without regard to any reorganization plan becoming effective on, before, or after the date of the enactment of this subsection.

Amendments

- **1976, Tax Reform Act of 1976 (P.L. 94-455)**

P.L. 94-455, § 1907(a)(4):

Amended Code Sec. 8023(c). **Effective** 2-1-77. Prior to amendment, Code Sec. 8023(c) read as follows:

(c) Subsections (a) and (b) shall be applied in accordance with their provisions without regard to Reorganization Plan Numbered 26 of 1950 or to any other reorganization plan becoming effective on, before, or after February 28, 1951.

[The next page is 5301.]

Subtitle H—Financing of Presidential Election Campaigns

CHAPTER 95.   Presidential election campaign fund.
CHAPTER 96.   Presidential primary matching payment account.

CHAPTER 95—PRESIDENTIAL ELECTION CAMPAIGN FUND

Sec. 9001.   Short title.
Sec. 9002.   Definitions.
Sec. 9003.   Condition for eligibility for payments.
Sec. 9004.   Entitlement of eligible candidates to payments.
Sec. 9005.   Certification by Commission.
Sec. 9006.   Payments to eligible candidates.
Sec. 9007.   Examinations and audits; repayments.
Sec. 9008.   Payments for presidential nominating conventions.
Sec. 9009.   Reports to Congress; regulations.
Sec. 9010.   Participation by Commission in judicial proceedings.
Sec. 9011.   Judicial review.
Sec. 9012.   Criminal penalties.

[Sec. 9001]

SEC. 9001. SHORT TITLE.

This chapter may be cited as the "Presidential Election Campaign Fund Act".

Amendments

• 1971, Revenue Act of 1971 (P.L. 92-178)

P.L. 92-178, §801:

Added Code Sec. 9001. Effective 1-1-73.

[Sec. 9002]

SEC. 9002. DEFINITIONS.

For purposes of this chapter—

(1) The term "authorized committee" means, with respect to the candidates of a political party for President and Vice President of the United States, any political committee which is authorized in writing by such candidates to incur expenses to further the election of such candidates. Such authorization shall be addressed to the chairman of such political committee, and a copy of such authorization shall be filed by such candidates with the Commission. Any withdrawal of any authorization shall also be in writing and shall be addressed and filed in the same manner as the authorization.

(2) The term "candidate" means, with respect to any presidential election, an individual who (A) has been nominated for election to the office of President of the United States or the office of Vice President of the United States by a major party, or (B) has qualified to have his name on the election ballot (or to have the names of electors pledged to him on the election ballot) as the candidate of a political party for election to either such office in 10 or more States. For purposes of paragraphs (6) and (7) of this section and purposes of section 9004(a)(2), the term "candidate" means, with respect to any preceding presidential election, an individual who received popular votes for the office of President in such election. The term "candidate" shall not include any individual who has ceased actively to seek election to the office of President of the United States or to the office of Vice President of the United States, in more than one State.

(3) The term "Commission" means the Federal Election Commission established by section 306(a)(1) of the Federal Election Campaign Act of 1971.

(4) The term "eligible candidates" means the candidates of a political party for President and Vice President of the United States who have met all applicable conditions for eligibility to receive payments under this chapter set forth in section 9003.

(5) The term "fund" means the Presidential Election Campaign Fund established by section 9006(a).

(6) The term "major party" means, with respect to any presidential election, a political party whose candidate for the office of President in the preceding presidential election received, as the candidate of such party, 25 percent or more of the total number of popular votes received by all candidates for such office.

(7) The term "minor party" means with respect to any presidential election, a political party whose candidate for the office of President in the preceding presidential election received, as the candidate of such party, 5 percent or more but less than 25 percent of the total number of popular votes received by all candidates for such office.

(8) The term "new party" means, with respect to any presidential election, a political party which is neither a major party nor a minor party.

(9) The term "political committee" means any committee, association, or organization (whether or not incorporated) which accepts contributions or makes expenditures for the purpose of influencing, or attempting to influence, the nomination or election of one or more individuals to Federal, State, or local elective public office.

(10) The term "presidential election" means the election of presidential and vice-presidential electors.

(11) The term "qualified campaign expense" means an expense—

(A) incurred (i) by the candidate of a political party for the office of President to further his election to such office or to further the election of the candidate of such political party for the office of Vice President, or both (ii) by the candidate of a political party for the office of Vice President to further his election to such office or to further the election of the candidate of such political party for the office of President, or both, or (iii) by an authorized committee of the candidates of a political party for the offices of President and Vice President to further the election of either or both of such candidates to such offices,

(B) incurred within the expenditure report period (as defined in paragraph (12)), or incurred before the beginning of such period to the extent such expense is for property, services, or facilities used during such period, and

(C) neither the incurring nor payment of which constitutes a violation of any law of the United States or of the State in which such expense is incurred or paid.

An expense shall be considered as incurred by a candidate or an authorized committee if it is incurred by a person authorized by such candidate or such committee, as the case may be, to incur such expense on behalf of such candidate or such committee. If an authorized committee of the candidates of a political party for President and Vice President of the United States also incurs expenses to further the election of one or more other individuals to Federal, State, or local elective public office, expenses incurred by such committee which are not

PRESIDENTIAL ELECTION CAMPAIGNS

specifically to further the election of such other individual or individuals shall be considered as incurred to further the election of such candidates for President and Vice President in such proportion as the Commission prescribes by rules or regulations.

(12) The term "expenditure report period" with respect to any presidential election means—

(A) in the case of a major party, the period beginning with the first day of September before the election, or if earlier, with the date on which such major party at its national convention nominated its candidate for election to the office of President of the United States, and ending 30 days after the date of the presidential election; and

(B) in the case of a party which is not a major party, the same period as the expenditure report period of the major party which has the shortest expenditure report period for such presidential election under subparagraph (A).

Amendments

• **2007, Tax Technical Corrections Act of 2007 (P.L. 110-172)**

P.L. 110-172, §11(a)(42)(A):

Amended Code Sec. 9002(3) by striking "section 309(a)(1)" and inserting "section 306(a)(1)". **Effective** 12-29-2007.

• **1976, Federal Election Campaign Act Amendments of 1976 (P.L. 94-283)**

P.L. 94-283, §115(c)(1):

Amended Code Sec. 9002(3) by substituting "309(a)(1)" for "310(a)(1)." **Effective** 5-11-76.

P.L. 94-283, §306(a)(1):

Amended Code Sec. 9002 by adding the last sentence to paragraph (2).

• **1974, Federal Election Campaign Act Amendments of 1974 (P.L. 93-443)**

P.L. 93-443, §404(c)(1)-(3):

Amended paragraphs (1) and (11) of Code Sec. 9002 by substituting "Commission" for "Comptroller General" and substituted paragraph (3) for the following:

"(3) The term `Comptroller General' means the Comptroller General of the United States."

• **1971, Revenue Act of 1971 (P.L. 92-178)**

P.L. 92-178, §801:

Added Code Sec. 9002. **Effective** 1-1-73.

[Sec. 9003]

SEC. 9003. CONDITION FOR ELIGIBILITY FOR PAYMENTS.

[Sec. 9003(a)]

(a) IN GENERAL.—In order to be eligible to receive any payments under section 9006, the candidates of a political party in a presidential election shall, in writing—

(1) agree to obtain and furnish to the Commission such evidence as it may request of the qualified campaign expenses of such candidate,

(2) agree to keep and furnish to the Commission such records, books, and other information as it may request, and

(3) agree to an audit and examination by the Commission under section 9007 and to pay any amounts required to be paid under such section.

Amendments

• **1974, Federal Election Campaign Act Amendments of 1974 (P.L. 93-443)**

P.L. 93-443, §404(c)(4) and (5):

Amended Code Sec. 9003(a) by substituting "Commission" for "Comptroller General" and "it" for "he" throughout such section. **Effective** for tax years beginning after 12-31-74.

• **1971, Revenue Act of 1971 (P.L. 92-178)**

P.L. 92-178, §801:

Added Code Sec. 9003(a). **Effective** 1-1-73.

[Sec. 9003(b)]

(b) MAJOR PARTIES.—In order to be eligible to receive any payments under section 9006, the candidates of a major party in a presidential election shall certify to the Commission, under penalty of perjury, that—

(1) such candidates and their authorized committees will not incur qualified campaign expenses in excess of the aggregate payments to which they will be entitled under section 9004, and

(2) no contributions to defray qualified campaign expenses have been or will be accepted by such candidates or any of their authorized committees except to the extent necessary to make up any deficiency in payments received out of the fund on account of the application of section 9006(c), and no contributions to defray expenses which would be qualified campaign expenses but for subparagraph (C) of section 9002(11) have been or will be accepted by such candidates or any of their authorized committees.

Such certification shall be made within such time prior to the day of the presidential election as the Commission shall prescribe by rules or regulations.

Amendments

• **2018, Tax Technical Corrections Act of 2018 (P.L. 115-141)**

P.L. 115-141, §401(a)(338), Div. U:

Amended Code Sec. 9003(b)(2) by striking "section 9006(d)" and inserting "section 9006(c)". **Effective** 3-23-2018.

• **1974, Federal Election Campaign Act Amendments of 1974 (P.L. 93-443)**

P.L. 93-443, §404(c)(4) and (5):

Amended Code Sec. 9003(b) by substituting "Commission" for "Comptroller General" and "it" for "he" throughout such section. **Effective** for tax years beginning after 12-31-74.

• **1973 (P.L. 93-53)**

P.L. 93-53, §6(c):

Amended Code Sec. 9003(b)(2) by substituting "section 9006(d)" for "section 9006(c)". **Effective** 1-1-74.

• **1971, Revenue Act of 1971 (P.L. 92-178)**

P.L. 92-178, §801:

Added Code Sec. 9003(b). **Effective** 1-1-73.

[Sec. 9003(c)]

(c) MINOR AND NEW PARTIES.—In order to be eligible to receive any payments under section 9006, the candidates of a minor or new party in a presidential election shall certify to the Commission, under penalty of perjury, that—

(1) such candidates and their authorized committees will not incur qualified campaign expenses in excess of the aggregate payments to which the eligible candidates of a major party are entitled under section 9004, and

(2) such candidates and their authorized committees will accept and expend or retain contributions to defray qualified campaign expenses only to the extent that the qualified campaign expenses incurred by such candidates and their authorized committees certified to under paragraph (1) exceed the aggregate payments received by such candidates out of the fund pursuant to section 9006.

Such certification shall be made within such time prior to the day of the presidential election as the Commission shall prescribe by rules or regulations.

Sec. 9002(12)

PRESIDENTIAL ELECTION CAMPAIGNS

Amendments

• **1974, Federal Election Campaign Act Amendments of 1974 (P.L. 93-443)**

P.L. 93-443, §404(c)(4) and (5):

Amended Code Sec. 9003(c) by substituting "Commission" for "Comptroller General" and "it" for "he" throughout such section. **Effective** for tax years beginning after 12-31-74.

• **1971, Revenue Act of 1971 (P.L. 92-178)**

P.L. 92-178, §801:

Added Code Sec. 9003(c). **Effective** 1-1-73.

[Sec. 9003(d)]

(d) WITHDRAWAL BY CANDIDATE.—In any case in which an individual ceases to be a candidate as a result of the operation of the last sentence of section 9002(2), such individual—

(1) shall no longer be eligible to receive any payments under section 9006, except that such individual shall be eligible to receive payments under such section to defray qualified campaign expenses incurred while actively seeking election to the office of President of the United States or to the office of Vice President of the United States in more than one State; and

(2) shall pay to the Secretary, as soon as practicable after the date upon which such individual ceases to be a candidate, an amount equal to the amount of payments received by such individual under section 9006 which are not used to defray qualified campaign expenses.

Amendments

• **1976, Tax Reform Act of 1976 (P.L. 94-455)**

P.L. 94-455, §1906(b)(13)(A):

Amended 1954 Code by substituting "Secretary" for "Secretary or his delegate" each place it appeared. **Effective** 2-1-77.

• **1976, Federal Election Campaign Act Amendments of 1976 (P.L. 94-283)**

P.L. 94-283, §306(a)(2):

Added Code Sec. 9003(d). **Effective** 5-11-76.

[Sec. 9003(e)]

(e) CLOSED CAPTIONING REQUIREMENT.—No candidate for the office of President or Vice President may receive amounts from the Presidential Election Campaign Fund under this chapter or chapter 96 unless such candidate has certified that any television commercial prepared or distributed by the candidate will be prepared in a manner which ensures that the commercial contains or is accompanied by closed captioning of the oral content of the commercial to be broadcast in line 21 of the vertical blanking interval, or is capable of being viewed by deaf and hearing impaired individuals via any comparable successor technology to line 21 of the vertical blanking interval.

Amendments

• **1992, Treasury, Postal Service, and General Government Appropriations Act, 1993 (P.L. 102-393)**

P.L. 102-393, §534(a):

Amended Code Sec. 9003 by adding at the end thereof new subsection (e). **Effective** for amounts made available under chapter 95 or 96 of the Internal Revenue Code of 1986 more than thirty days after the date of the enactment of this Act.

[Sec. 9004]

SEC. 9004. ENTITLEMENT OF ELIGIBLE CANDIDATES TO PAYMENTS.

[Sec. 9004(a)]

(a) IN GENERAL.—Subject to the provisions of this chapter—

(1) The eligible candidates of each major party in a presidential election shall be entitled to equal payments under section 9006 in an amount which, in the aggregate, shall not exceed the expenditure limitations applicable to such candidates under section 315(b)(1)(B) of the Federal Election Campaign Act of 1971.

(2)(A) The eligible candidates of a minor party in a presidential election shall be entitled to payments under section 9006 equal in the aggregate to an amount which bears the same ratio to the amount allowed under paragraph (1) for a major party as the number of popular votes received by the candidate for President of the minor party, as such candidate, in the preceding presidential election bears to the average number of popular votes received by the candidates for President of the major parties in the preceding presidential election.

(B) If the candidate of one or more political parties (not including a major party) for the office of President was a candidate for such office in the preceding presidential election and received 5 percent or more but less than 25 percent of the total number of popular votes received by all candidates for such office, such candidate and his running mate for the office of Vice President, upon compliance with the provisions of section 9003(a) and (c), shall be treated as eligible candidates entitled to payments under section 9006 in an amount computed as provided in subparagraph (A) by taking into account all the popular votes received by such candidate for the office of President in the preceding presidential election. If eligible candidates of a minor party are entitled to payments under this subparagraph, such entitlement shall be reduced by the amount of the entitlement allowed under subparagraph (A).

(3) The eligible candidates of a minor party or a new party in a presidential election whose candidate for President in such election receives, as such candidate, 5 percent or more of the total number of popular votes cast for the office of President in such election shall be entitled to payments under section 9006 equal in the aggregate to an amount which bears the same ratio to the amount allowed under paragraph (1) for a major party as the number of popular votes received by such candidate in such election bears to the average number of popular votes received in such election by the candidates for President of the major parties. In the case of eligible candidates entitled to payments under paragraph (2), the amount allowable under this paragraph shall be limited to the amount, if any, by which the entitlement under the preceding sentence exceeds the amount of the entitlement under paragraph (2).

Amendments

• **2007, Tax Technical Corrections Act of 2007 (P.L. 110-172)**

P.L. 110-172, §11(a)(42)(B):

Amended Code Sec. 9004(a)(1) by striking "section 320(b)(1)(B)" and inserting "section 315(b)(1)(B)". **Effective** 12-29-2007.

• **1976, Federal Election Campaign Act Amendments of 1976 (P.L. 94-283)**

P.L. 94-283, §307(d):

Substituted "section 320(b)(1)(B) of the Federal Election Campaign Act of 1971" for "section 608(c)(1)(B) of title 18, United States Code" in Code Sec. 9004(a). **Effective** 5-11-76.

• **1974, Federal Election Campaign Act Amendments of 1974 (P.L. 93-443)**

P.L. 93-443, §404(a), (b):

Amended Code Sec. 9004(a) by substituting a new paragraph (1) and by substituting "allowed" for "computed" in paragraphs (2)(A) and (3). **Effective** for tax years beginning after 12-31-74. Prior to amendment, paragraph (1) of Code Sec. 9004(a) read as follows:

(1) The eligible candidates of a major party in a presidential election shall be entitled to payments under section 9006 equal in the aggregate to 15 cents multiplied by the total number of residents within the United States who have attained the age of 18, as determined by the Bureau of the Census, as of the first day of June of the year preceding the year of the presidential election.

[Sec. 9004(b)]

(b) LIMITATIONS.—The aggregate payments to which the eligible candidates of a political party shall be entitled under subsections (a)(2) and (3) with respect to a presidential election shall not exceed an amount equal to the lower of—

PRESIDENTIAL ELECTION CAMPAIGNS

(1) the amount of qualified campaign expenses incurred by such eligible candidates and their authorized committees, reduced by the amount of contributions to defray qualified campaign expenses received and expended or retained by such eligible candidates and such committees, or

(2) the aggregate payments to which the eligible candidates of a major party are entitled under subsection (a)(1), reduced by the amount of contributions described in paragraph (1) of this subsection.

[Sec. 9004(c)]

(c) RESTRICTIONS.—The eligible candidates of a political party shall be entitled to payments under subsection (a) only—

(1) to defray qualified campaign expenses incurred by such eligible candidates or their authorized committees, or

(2) to repay loans the proceeds of which were used to defray such qualified campaign expenses, or otherwise to restore funds (other than contributions to defray qualified campaign expenses received and expended by such candidates or such committees) used to defray such qualified campaign expenses.

Amendments

- 1971, Revenue Act of 1971 (P.L. 92-178)

P.L. 92-178, §801:
Added Code Sec. 9004. Effective 1-1-73.

[Sec. 9004(d)]

(d) EXPENDITURES FROM PERSONAL FUNDS.—In order to be eligible to receive any payment under section 9006, the candidate of a major, minor, or new party in an election for the office of President shall certify to the Commission, under penalty of perjury, that such candidate will not knowingly make expenditures from his personal funds, or the personal funds of his immediate family, in connection with his campaign for election to the office of President in excess of, in the aggregate, $50,000. For purposes of this subsection, expenditures from personal funds made by a candidate of a major, minor, or new party for the office of Vice President shall be considered to be expenditures by the candidate of such party for the office of President.

Amendments

- 1976, Federal Election Campaign Act Amendments of 1976 (P.L. 94-283)

P.L. 94-283, §301(a):
Added Code Sec. 9004(d). Effective 5-11-76.

P.L. 94-283, §301(b), provides:
For purposes of applying section 9004(d) of the Internal Revenue Code of 1954, as added by subsection (a), expenditures made by an individual after January 29, 1976, and before the date of the enactment [May 11, 1976] of this Act shall not be taken into account. Effective on 5-11-76.

[Sec. 9004(e)]

(e) DEFINITION OF IMMEDIATE FAMILY.—For purposes of subsection (d), the term "immediate family" means a candidate's spouse, and any child, parent, grandparent, brother, half-brother, sister, or half-sister of the candidate, and the spouses of such persons.

Amendments

- 1976, Federal Election Campaign Act Amendments of 1976 (P.L. 94-283)

P.L. 94-283, §301(a):
Added Code Sec. 9004(e). Effective 5-11-76.

[Sec. 9005]

SEC. 9005. CERTIFICATION BY COMMISSION.

[Sec. 9005(a)]

(a) INITIAL CERTIFICATIONS.—Not later than 10 days after the candidates of a political party for President and Vice President of the United States have met all applicable conditions for eligibility to receive payments under this chapter set forth in section 9003, the Commission shall certify to the Secretary of the Treasury for payment to such eligible candidates under section 9006 payment in full of amounts to which such candidates are entitled under section 9004.

Amendments

- 1976, Tax Reform Act of 1976 (P.L. 94-455)

P.L. 94-455, §1906(b)(13)(C):
Substituted "Secretary of the Treasury" for "Secretary" in Code Sec. 9005(a). Effective 2-1-77.

- 1974, Federal Election Campaign Act Amendments of 1974 (P.L. 93-443)

P.L. 93-443, §404(c)(6) and (7):
Substituted "Commission" for "Comptroller General" and "it" for "he" throughout the section. Effective for tax years beginning after 12-31-74.

P.L. 93-443, §405(a):
Amended Code Sec. 9005(a). Effective for tax years beginning after 12-31-74. Prior to amendment, Code Sec. 9005(a) read as follows:

(a) INITIAL CERTIFICATIONS.—On the basis of the evidence, books, records, and information furnished by the eligible candidates of a political party and prior to examination and audit under section 9007, the Comptroller General shall certify from time to time to the Secretary for payment to such candidates under section 9006 the payments to which such candidates are entitled under section 9004.

[Sec. 9005(b)]

(b) FINALITY OF CERTIFICATIONS AND DETERMINATIONS.—Initial certifications by the Commission under subsection (a), and all determinations made by it under this chapter, shall be final and conclusive, except to the extent that they are subject to examination and audit by the Commission under section 9007 and judicial review under section 9011.

Amendments

- 1974, Federal Election Campaign Act Amendments of 1974 (P.L. 93-443)

P.L. 93-443, §404(c)(6) and (7):
Substituted "Commission" for "Comptroller General" and "it" for "he" throughout Code Sec. 9005(b). Effective for tax years beginning after 12-31-74.

- 1971, Revenue Act of 1971 (P.L. 92-178)

P.L. 92-178, §801:
Added Code Sec. 9005. Effective 1-1-73.

[Sec. 9006]

SEC. 9006. PAYMENTS TO ELIGIBLE CANDIDATES.

[Sec. 9006(a)]

(a) ESTABLISHMENT OF CAMPAIGN FUND.—There is hereby established on the books of the Treasury of the United States a special fund to be known as the "Presidential Election Campaign Fund." The Secretary of the Treasury shall, from time to time, transfer to the fund an amount not in excess of the sum of the amounts designated (subsequent to the previous Presidential election) to the fund by individuals under section 6096. There

PRESIDENTIAL ELECTION CAMPAIGNS

is appropriated to the fund for each fiscal year, out of amounts in the general fund of the Treasury not otherwise appropriated, an amount equal to the amounts so designated during each fiscal year, which shall remain available to the fund without fiscal year limitation.

Amendments

• **1976, Tax Reform Act of 1976 (P.L. 94-455)**

P.L. 94-455, §1906(b)(13)(B):

Substituted "Secretary of the Treasury" for "Secretary" in Code Sec. 9006(a). **Effective** 2-1-77.

• **1974, Federal Election Campaign Act Amendments of 1974 (P.L. 93-443)**

P.L. 93-443, §§403(a), 404(c):

Amended Code Sec. 9006(a) by substituting "from time to time" for "as provided by appropriation acts" and by adding the last sentence. **Effective** for tax years beginning after 12-31-74.

• **1973 (P.L. 93-53)**

P.L. 93-53, §6(b):

Amended Code Sec. 9006(a). **Effective** for tax years beginning after 12-31-72. Any designation made under Code Sec. 6096 (as in effect for tax years beginning before 1-1-73) for the account of the candidates of any specified political party shall, for purposes of Code Sec. 9006(a) be treated solely as a designation to the Presidential Election Campaign Fund.

Prior to amendment, Code Sec. 9006(a) read as follows:

(a) Establishment of Campaign Fund.—There is hereby established on the books of the Treasury of the United States a special fund to be known as the "Presidential Election Campaign Fund". The Secretary shall maintain in the fund (1) a separate account for the candidates of each major party, each minor party, and each new party for which a specific designation is made under section 6096 for payment into an account in the fund and (2) a general account for which no specific designation is made. The Secretary shall, as provided by appropriation Acts, transfer to each account in the fund an amount not in excess of the sum of the amounts designated (subsequent to the previous presidential election) to such account by individuals under section 6096 for payment into such account of the fund.

[Sec. 9006(b)—Repealed]

(b) Transfer to the General Fund.—If, after a presidential election and after all eligible candidates have been paid the amount which they are entitled to receive under this chapter, there are moneys remaining in the fund, the Secretary shall transfer the moneys so remaining to the general fund of the Treasury.

Amendments

• **1976, Federal Election Campaign Act Amendments of 1976 (P.L. 94-283)**

P.L. 94-283, §302(a) and (b):

Repealed Code Sec. 9006(b). Prior to repeal, Code Sec. 9006(b) read as follows:

[Sec. 9006(b)]

(b) PAYMENTS FROM THE FUND.—Upon receipt of a certification from the Commission under section 9005 for payment to the eligible candidates of a political party, the Secretary of the Treasury shall pay to such candidates out of the fund the amount certified by the Commission. Amounts paid to any such candidates shall be under the control of such candidates.

Amendments

• **1976, Tax Reform Act of 1976 (P.L. 94-455)**

P.L. 94-455, §1906(b)(13)(B):

Substituted "Secretary of the Treasury" for "Secretary" in Code Sec. 9006(b). **Effective** 2-1-77.

• **1976, Federal Election Campaign Act Amendments of 1976 (P.L. 94-283)**

P.L. 94-283, §302(a) and (b):

Repealed Code Sec. 9006(b), and redesignated former Code Sec. 9006(c) as new Code Sec. 9006(b). **Effective** 5-11-76.

• **1973 (P.L. 93-53)**

P.L. 93-53, §6(b):

Amended Code Sec. 9006(c). **Effective** for tax years beginning after 12-31-72. Prior to amendment, Code Sec. 9006(c) read as follows:

(c) Payments from the Fund.—Upon receipt of a certification from the Comptroller General under section 9005 for payment to the eligible candidates of a political party, the Secretary shall pay to such candidates out of the specific account in the fund for such candidates the amount certified by the Comptroller General. Payments to eligible candidates from the account designated for them shall be limited to the amounts in such account at the time of payment. Amounts paid to any such candidates shall be under the control of such candidates.

[Sec. 9006(c)]

(c) INSUFFICIENT AMOUNTS IN FUND.—If at the time of a certification by the Commission under section 9005 for payment to the eligible candidates of a political party, the Secretary determines that the moneys in the fund are not, or may not be, sufficient to satisfy the full entitlements of the eligible candidates of all political parties, he shall withhold from such payment such amount as he determines to be necessary to assure that the eligible candidates of each political party will receive their pro rata share of their full entitlement. Amounts withheld by reason of the preceding sentence shall be paid when the Secretary determines that there are sufficient moneys in the fund to pay such amounts, or portions thereof, to all eligible candidates from whom amounts have been withheld, but, if there are not sufficient moneys in the fund to satisfy the full entitlement of the eligible candidates of all political parties, the amounts so withheld shall be paid in such manner that the eligible candidates of each political party receive their pro rata share of their full entitlement. In any case in which the Secretary determines that there are insufficient moneys in the fund to make payments under subsection (b), section 9008(i)(2), and section 9037(b), moneys shall not be made available from any other source for the purpose of making such payments.

Amendments

• **2014, Gabriella Miller Kids First Research Act (P.L. 113-94)**

P.L. 113-94, §2(b)(1):

Amended the third sentence of Code Sec. 9006(c) by striking "section 9008(b)(3)," and inserting "section 9008(i)(2),". **Effective** 4-3-2014.

• **2007, Tax Technical Corrections Act of 2007 (P.L. 110-172)**

P.L. 110-172, §11(a)(43):

Amended Code Sec. 9006(c) by striking "Comptroller General" each place it appears and inserting "Commission". **Effective** 12-29-2007.

• **1976, Tax Reform Act of 1976 (P.L. 94-455)**

P.L. 94-455, §1906(b)(13)(A):

Amended 1954 Code by substituting "Secretary" for "Secretary or his delegate" each place it appeared. **Effective** 2-1-77.

• **1976, Federal Election Campaign Act Amendments of 1976 (P.L. 94-283)**

P.L. 94-283, §302(a) and (b):

Redesignated Code Sec. 9006(c) as new Code Sec. 9006(b), redesignated Code Sec. 9006(d) as new Code Sec. 9006(c), and added the last sentence to new Code Sec. 9006(c). **Effective** 5-11-76.

• **1973 (P.L. 93-53)**

P.L. 93-53, §6(b):

Amended Code Sec. 9006(d). **Effective** for tax years beginning after 12-31-72. Prior to amendment, Code Sec. 9006(d) read as follows:

(d) Transfers from General Account to Separate Accounts.—

(1) If, on the 60th day prior to the presidential election, the moneys in any separate account in the fund are less than the aggregate entitlement under section 9004(a)(1) or (2) of the eligible candidates to which such account relates, 80 percent of the amount in the general account shall be transferred to the separate accounts (whether or not all the candidates to which such separate accounts relate are eligible candidates) in the ratio of the entitlement under section 9004(a)(1) or (2) of the candidates to which such accounts relate. No amount shall be transferred to any separate account under the preceding sentence which, when added to the moneys in that separate account prior to any payment out of that account during the calendar year, would be in excess of the aggregate entitlement under section 9004(a)(1) or (2) of the candidates to whom such account relates.

(2) If, at the close of the expenditure report period, the moneys in any separate account in the fund are not sufficient to satisfy any unpaid entitlement of the eligible candidates to which such account relates, the balance in the general account shall be transferred to the separate accounts in the following manner:

(A) For the separate account of the candidates of a major party, compute the percentage which the average number of popular votes received by the candidates for President of the major parties is of the total number of popular votes cast for the office of President in the election.

(B) For the separate account of the candidates of a minor or new party, compute the percentage which the popular votes received for President by the candidate to which such account relates is of the total number of popular votes cast for the office of President in the election.

(C) In the case of each separate account, multiply the applicable percentage obtained under paragraph (A) or (B) for such account by the amount of the money in the general account prior to any distribution made under paragraph (1), and transfer to such separate account an amount equal to the excess of the product of such multiplication over the amount of any distribution made under such paragraph to such account.

PRESIDENTIAL ELECTION CAMPAIGNS

- **1971, Revenue Act of 1971 (P.L. 92-178)**

P.L. 92-178, § 801:
Added Code Sec. 9006. **Effective** 1-1-73.

[Sec. 9007]

SEC. 9007. EXAMINATIONS AND AUDITS; REPAYMENTS.

[Sec. 9007(a)]

(a) EXAMINATIONS AND AUDITS.—After each presidential election, the Commission shall conduct a thorough examination and audit of the qualified campaign expenses of the candidates of each political party for President and Vice President.

Amendments

- **1974, Federal Election Campaign Act Amendments of 1974 (P.L. 93-443)**

P.L. 93-443, § 404(c):
Substituted "Commission" for "Comptroller General" and "it" for "he" in Code Sec. 9007(a). **Effective** for tax years beginning after 12-31-74.

[Sec. 9007(b)]

(b) REPAYMENTS.—

(1) If the Commission determines that any portion of the payments made to the eligible candidates of a political party under section 9006 was in excess of the aggregate payments to which candidates were entitled under section 9004, it shall so notify such candidates, and such candidates shall pay to the Secretary of the Treasury an amount equal to such portion.

(2) If the Commission determines that the eligible candidates of a political party and their authorized committees incurred qualified campaign expenses in excess of the aggregate payments to which the eligible candidates of a major party were entitled under section 9004, it shall notify such candidates of the amount of such excess and such candidates shall pay to the Secretary of the Treasury an amount equal to such amount.

(3) If the Commission determines that the eligible candidates of a major party or any authorized committee of such candidates accepted contributions (other than contributions to make up deficiencies in payments out of the fund on account of the application of section 9006(c)) to defray qualified campaign expenses (other than qualified campaign expenses with respect to which payment is required under paragraph (2)), it shall notify such candidates of the amount of the contributions so accepted, and such candidates shall pay to the Secretary of the Treasury an amount equal to such amount.

(4) If the Commission determines that any amount of any payment made to the eligible candidates of a political party under section 9006 was used for any purpose other than—

(A) to defray the qualified campaign expenses with respect to which such payment was made, or

(B) to repay loans the proceeds of which were used, or otherwise to restore funds (other than contributions to defray qualified campaign expenses which were received and expended) which were used, to defray such qualified campaign expenses,

it shall notify such candidates of the amount so used, and such candidates shall pay to the Secretary of the Treasury an amount equal to such amount.

(5) No payment shall be required from the eligible candidates of a political party under this subsection to the extent that such payment, when added to other payments required from such candidates under this subsection, exceeds the amount of payments received by such candidates under section 9006.

Amendments

- **1976, Tax Reform Act of 1976 (P.L. 94-455)**

P.L. 94-455, § 1906(b)(13)(C):
Substituted "Secretary of the Treasury" for "Secretary" in Code Sec. 9007(b). **Effective** 2-1-77.

- **1976, Federal Election Campaign Act Amendments of 1976 (P.L. 94-283)**

P.L. 94-283, § 307(e):
Substituted "section 9006(c)" for "section 9006(d)" in Code Sec. 9007(b)(3). **Effective** 5-11-76.

- **1974, Federal Election Campaign Act Amendments of 1974 (P.L. 93-443)**

P.L. 93-443, § 404(c):
Substituted "Commission" for "Comptroller General" and "it" for "he" wherever they appear. **Effective** for tax years beginning after 12-31-74.

- **1973 (P.L. 93-53)**

P.L. 93-53, § 6(c):
Amended Code Sec. 9007(b)(3) by substituting "section 9006(d) for "section 9006(c)". **Effective** 1-1-74.

[Sec. 9007(c)]

(c) NOTIFICATION.—No notification shall be made by the Commission under subsection (b) with respect to a presidential election more than 3 years after the day of such election.

Amendments

- **1974, Federal Election Campaign Act Amendments of 1974 (P.L. 93-443)**

P.L. 93-443, § 404(c):
Amended Code Sec. 9007(c) by substituting "Commission" for "Comptroller General" and "it" for "he" wherever they appear. **Effective** for tax years beginning after 12-31-74.

[Sec. 9007(d)]

(d) DEPOSIT OF REPAYMENTS.—All payments received by the Secretary of the Treasury under subsection (b) shall be deposited by him in the general fund of the Treasury.

Amendments

- **1976, Tax Reform Act of 1976 (P.L. 94-455)**

P.L. 94-455, § 1906(b)(13)(B):
Substituted "Secretary of the Treasury" for "Secretary" in Code Sec. 9007(d). **Effective** 2-1-77.

- **1974, Federal Election Campaign Act Amendments of 1974 (P.L. 93-443)**

P.L. 93-443, § 404(c):
Amended Code Sec. 9007(d) by substituting "Commission" for "Comptroller General" and "it" for "he" wherever they appear. **Effective** for tax years beginning after 12-31-74.

- **1971, Revenue Act of 1971 (P.L. 92-178)**

P.L. 92-178, § 801:
Added Code Sec. 9007. **Effective** 1-1-73.

PRESIDENTIAL ELECTION CAMPAIGNS

[Sec. 9008]
SEC. 9008. PAYMENTS FOR PRESIDENTIAL NOMINATING CONVENTIONS.

[Sec. 9008(a)]

(a) ESTABLISHMENT OF ACCOUNTS.—The Secretary shall maintain in the fund, in addition to any account which he maintains under section 9006(a), a separate account for the national committee of each major party and minor party. The Secretary shall deposit in each such account an amount equal to the amount which each such committee may receive under subsection (b). Such deposits shall be drawn from amounts designated by individuals under section 6096 and shall be made before any transfer is made to any account for any eligible candidate under section 9006(a).

Amendments

• **1974, Federal Election Campaign Act Amendments of 1974 (P.L. 93-443)**

P.L. 93-443, § 406(a):

Amended Code Sec. 9008(a). **Effective** for tax years beginning after 12-31-74. Prior to amendment, Code Sec. 9008(a) read as follows:

SEC. 9008. INFORMATION ON PROPOSED EXPENSES.

(a) Reports by Candidates.—The candidates of a political party for President and Vice President in a presidential election shall, from time to time as the Comptroller General may require, furnish to the Comptroller General a detailed statement, in such form as the Comptroller General may prescribe, of—

(1) the qualified campaign expenses incurred by them and their authorized committees prior to the date of such statement (whether or not evidence of such expenses has been furnished for purposes of section 9005), and

(2) the qualified campaign expenses which they and their authorized committees propose to incur on or after the date of such statement.

The Comptroller General shall require a statement under this subsection from such candidates of each political party at least once each week during the second, third, and fourth weeks preceding the day of the presidential election and at least twice during the week preceding such day.

[Sec. 9008(b)]

(b) ENTITLEMENT TO PAYMENTS FROM THE FUND.—

(1) MAJOR PARTIES.—Subject to the provisions of this section, the national committee of a major party shall be entitled to payments under paragraph (3), with respect to any presidential nominating convention, in amounts which, in the aggregate, shall not exceed $4,000,000.

(2) MINOR PARTIES.—Subject to the provisions of this section, the national committee of a minor party shall be entitled to payments under paragraph (3), with respect to any presidential nominating convention, in amounts which, in the aggregate, shall not exceed an amount which bears the same ratio to the amount the national committee of a major party is entitled to receive under paragraph (1) as the number of popular votes received by the candidate for President of the minor party, as such candidate, in the preceding presidential election bears to the average number of popular votes received by the candidates for President of the United States of the major parties in the preceding presidential election.

(3) PAYMENTS.—Upon receipt of certification from the Commission under subsection (g), the Secretary shall make payments from the appropriate account maintained under subsection (a) to the national committee of a major party or minor party which elects to receive its entitlement under this subsection. Such payments shall be available for use by such committee in accordance with the provisions of subsection (c).

(4) LIMITATION.—Payments to the national committee of a major party or minor party under this subsection from the account designated for such committee shall be limited to the amounts in such account at the time of payment.

(5) ADJUSTMENT OF ENTITLEMENTS.—The entitlements established by this subsection shall be adjusted in the same manner as expenditure limitations established by section 315(b) and section 315(d) of the Federal Election Campaign Act of 1971 are adjusted pursuant to the provisions of section 315(c) of such Act.

Amendments

• **1984 (P.L. 98-355)**

P.L. 98-355, § 1(a):

Amended Code Sec. 9008(b)(1) by striking out "$3,000,000 and inserting in lieu thereof "$4,000,000". **Effective** 1-1-84.

P.L. 98-355, § 1(b):

Amended Code Sec. 9008(b)(5) by striking out "section 320(b) and section 320(d)" and inserting in lieu thereof "section 315(b) and section 315(d)" and by striking out "section 320(c)" and inserting in lieu thereof "section 315(c)". **Effective** 1-1-84.

• **1980 (P.L. 96-187)**

P.L. 96-187, § 202:

Amended Code Sec. 9008(b)(1) by substituting "$3,000,000" for "$2,000,000". **Effective** 1-8-80.

• **1976, Federal Election Campaign Act Amendments of 1976 (P.L. 94-283)**

P.L. 94-283, § 307(a):

Substituted "section 320(b) and section 320(d) of the Federal Election Campaign Act of 1971 are adjusted pursuant to the provisions of section 320(c) of such Act" for "section 608(c) and section 608(f) of title 18, United States Code, are adjusted pursuant to the provisions of section 608(d) of such title" in Code Sec. 9008(b)(5). **Effective** 5-11-76.

• **1974, Federal Election Campaign Act Amendments of 1974 (P.L. 93-443)**

P.L. 93-443, § 406(a):

Amended Code Sec. 9008(b). **Effective** for tax years beginning after 12-31-74. Prior to amendment, Code Sec. 9008(b) read as follows:

(b) Publication.—The Comptroller General shall, as soon as possible after he receives each statement under subsection (a), prepare and publish a summary of such statement, together with any other data or information which he deems advisable, in the Federal Register. Such summary shall not include any information which identifies any individual who made a designation under section 6096.

• **1971, Revenue Act of 1971 (P.L. 92-178)**

P.L. 92-178, § 801:

Added Code Sec. 9008. **Effective** 1-1-73.

[Sec. 9008(c)]

(c) USE OF FUNDS.—No part of any payment made under subsection (b) shall be used to defray the expenses of any candidate or delegate who is participating in any presidential nominating convention. Such payments shall be used only—

(1) to defray expenses incurred with respect to a presidential nominating convention (including the payment of deposits) by or on behalf of the national committee receiving such payments; or

(2) to repay loans the proceeds of which were used to defray such expenses, or otherwise to restore funds (other than contributions to defray such expenses received by such committee) used to defray such expenses.

Amendments

• **1974, Federal Election Campaign Act Amendments of 1974 (P.L. 93-443)**

P.L. 93-443, § 406(a):

Added Code Sec. 9008(c). **Effective** for tax years beginning after 12-31-74.

[Sec. 9008(d)]

(d) LIMITATION OF EXPENDITURES.—

(1) MAJOR PARTIES.—Except as provided by paragraph (3), the national committee of a major party may not make expenditures with respect to a presidential nominating convention which, in the aggregate, exceed the amount of payments to which such committee is entitled under subsection (b)(1).

Internal Revenue Code   **Sec. 9008(d)(1)**

PRESIDENTIAL ELECTION CAMPAIGNS

(2) MINOR PARTIES.—Except as provided by paragraph (3), the national committee of a minor party may not make expenditures with respect to a presidential nominating convention which, in the aggregate, exceed the amount of the entitlement of the national committee of a major party under subsection (b)(1).

(3) EXCEPTION.—The Commission may authorize the national committee of a major party or minor party to make expenditures which, in the aggregate, exceed the limitation established by paragraph (1) or paragraph (2) of this subsection. Such authorization shall be based upon a determination by the Commission that, due to extraordinary and unforeseen circumstances, such expenditures are necessary to assure the effective operation of the presidential nominating convention by such committee.

(4) PROVISION OF LEGAL OR ACCOUNTING SERVICES.—For purposes of this section, the payment, by any person other than the national committee of a political party (unless the person paying for such services is a person other than the regular employer of the individual rendering such services) of compensation to any individual for legal or accounting services rendered to or on behalf of the national committee of a political party shall not be treated as an expenditure made by or on behalf of such committee with respect to its limitations on presidential nominating convention expenses.

Amendments

• **1976, Federal Election Campaign Act Amendments of 1976 (P.L. 94-283)**

P.L. 94-283, §303:
Added Code Sec. 9008(d)(4). **Effective** 5-11-76.

• **1974, Federal Election Campaign Act Amendments of 1974 (P.L. 93-443)**

P.L. 93-443, §406(a):
Added Code Sec. 9008(d). **Effective** for tax years beginning after 12-31-74.

[Sec. 9008(e)]

(e) AVAILABILITY OF PAYMENTS.—The national committee of a major party or minor party may receive payments under subsection (b)(3) beginning on July 1 of the calendar year immediately preceding the calendar year in which a presidential nominating convention of the political party involved is held.

Amendments

• **1974, Federal Election Campaign Act Amendments of 1974 (P.L. 93-443)**

P.L. 93-443, §406(a):
Added Code Sec. 9008(e). **Effective** for tax years beginning after 12-31-74.

[Sec. 9008(f)]

(f) TRANSFER TO THE FUND.—If, after the close of a presidential nominating convention and after the national committee of the political party involved has been paid the amount which it is entitled to receive under this section, there are moneys remaining in the account of such national committee, the Secretary shall transfer the moneys so remaining to the fund.

Amendments

• **1974, Federal Election Campaign Act Amendments of 1974 (P.L. 93-443)**

P.L. 93-443, §406(a):
Added Code Sec. 9008(f). **Effective** for tax years beginning after 12-31-74.

[Sec. 9008(g)]

(g) CERTIFICATION BY COMMISSION.—Any major party or minor party may file a statement with the Commission in such form and manner and at such times as it may require, designating the national committee of such party. Such statement shall include the information required by section 303(b) of the Federal Election Campaign Act of 1971, together with such additional information as the Commission may require. Upon receipt of a statement filed under the preceding sentences, the Commission promptly shall verify such statement according to such procedures and criteria as it may establish and shall certify to the Secretary for payment in full to any such committee of amounts to which such committee may be entitled under subsection (b). Such certifications shall be subject to an examination and audit which the Commission shall conduct no later than December 31 of the calendar year in which the presidential nominating convention involved is held.

Amendments

• **1974, Federal Election Campaign Act Amendments of 1974 (P.L. 93-443)**

P.L. 93-443, §406(a):
Added Code Sec. 9008(g). **Effective** for tax years beginning after 12-31-74.

[Sec. 9008(h)]

(h) REPAYMENTS.—The Commission shall have the same authority to require repayments from the national committee of a major party or a minor party as it has with respect to repayments from any eligible candidate under section 9007(b). The provisions of section 9007(c) and section 9007(d) shall apply with respect to any repayment required by the Commission under this subsection.

Amendments

• **1974, Federal Election Campaign Act Amendments of 1974 (P.L. 93-443)**

P.L. 93-443, §406(a):
Added Code Sec. 9008(h). **Effective** for tax years beginning after 12-31-74.

[Sec. 9008(i)]

(i) TERMINATION OF PAYMENTS FOR CONVENTIONS; USE OF AMOUNTS FOR PEDIATRIC RESEARCH INITIATIVE.—Effective on the date of the enactment of the Gabriella Miller Kids First Research Act—

(1) the entitlement of any major party or minor party to a payment under this section shall terminate; and

(2) all amounts in each account maintained for the national committee of a major party or minor party under this section shall be transferred to a fund in the Treasury to be known as the "10-Year Pediatric Research Initiative Fund", which shall be available only for the purpose provided in section 402A(a)(2) of the Public Health Service Act, and only to the extent and in such amounts as are provided in advance in appropriation Acts.

Amendments

• **2014, Gabriella Miller Kids First Research Act (P.L. 113-94)**

P.L. 113-94, §2(a):
Amended Code Sec. 9008 by adding at the end a new subsection (i). **Effective** 4-3-2014.

PRESIDENTIAL ELECTION CAMPAIGNS

[Sec. 9009]
SEC. 9009. REPORTS TO CONGRESS; REGULATIONS.

[Sec. 9009(a)]

(a) REPORTS.—The Commission shall, as soon as practicable after each presidential election, submit a full report to the Senate and House of Representatives setting forth—

(1) the qualified campaign expenses (shown in such detail as the Commission determines necessary) incurred by the candidates of each political party and their authorized committees;

(2) the amounts certified by it under section 9005 for payment to the eligible candidates of each political party; and

(3) the amount of payments, if any, required from such candidates under section 9007, and the reasons for each payment required.

Each report submitted pursuant to this section shall be printed as a Senate document.

Amendments

• **2014, Gabriella Miller Kids First Research Act (P.L. 113-94)**

P.L. 113-94, §2(c)(1)(A)-(C):

Amended Code Sec. 9009(a) by adding "and" at the end of paragraph (2); by striking the semicolon at the end of paragraph (3) and inserting a period; and by striking paragraphs (4), (5), and (6). **Effective** 4-3-2014. Prior to being stricken, Code Sec. 9009(a)(4)-(6) read as follows:

(4) the expenses incurred by the national committee of a major party or minor party with respect to a presidential nominating convention;

(5) the amounts certified by it under section 9008(g) for payment to each such committee; and

(6) the amount of payments, if any, required from such committees under section 9008(h), and the reasons for each such payment.

• **1974, Federal Election Campaign Act Amendments of 1974 (P.L. 93-443)**

P.L. 93-443, §§404(c), 406(b):

Amended Code Sec. 9009(a) by substituting "Commission" for "Comptroller General" and "it" for "he", and by adding paragraphs (4), (5) and (6). **Effective** for tax years beginning after 12-31-74.

[Sec. 9009(b)]

(b) REGULATIONS, ETC.—The Commission is authorized to prescribe such rules and regulations in accordance with the provisions of subsection (c), to conduct such examinations and audits (in addition to the examinations and audits required by section 9007(a)), to conduct such investigations, and to require the keeping and submission of such books, records, and information, as it deems necessary to carry out the functions and duties imposed on it by this chapter.

Amendments

• **1974, Federal Election Campaign Act Amendments of 1974 (P.L. 93-443)**

P.L. 93-443, §§404(c), 406(b):

Amended Code Sec. 9009(b) by substituting "Commission" for "Comptroller General" and "it" for "he". **Effective** for tax years beginning after 12-31-74.

[Sec. 9009(c)]

(c) REVIEW OF REGULATIONS.—

(1) The Commission, before prescribing any rule or regulation under subsection (b), shall transmit a statement with respect to such rule or regulation to the Senate and to the House of Representatives, in accordance with the provisions of this subsection. Such statement shall set forth the proposed rule or regulation and shall contain a detailed explanation and justification of such rule or regulation.

(2) If either such House does not, through appropriate action, disapprove the proposed rule or regulation set forth in such statement no later than 30 legislative days after receipt of such statement, then the Commission may prescribe such rule or regulation. Whenever a committee of the House of Representatives reports any resolution relating to any such rule or regulation, it is at any time thereafter in order (even though a previous motion to the same effect has been disagreed to) to move to proceed to the consideration of the resolution. The motion is highly privileged and is not debatable. An amendment to the motion is not in order, and it is not in order to move to reconsider the vote by which the motion is agreed to or disagreed to. The Commission may not prescribe any rule or regulation which is disapproved by either such House under this paragraph.

(3) For purposes of this subsection, the term "legislative days" does not include any calendar day on which both Houses of the Congress are not in session.

(4) For purposes of this subsection, the term "rule or regulation" means a provision or series of interrelated provisions stating a single separable rule of law.

Amendments

• **1976, Federal Election Campaign Act Amendments of 1976 (P.L. 94-283)**

P.L. 94-283, §304(a):

Amended Code Sec. 9009(c)(2) and added Code Sec. 9009(c)(4). **Effective** 5-11-76. Prior to amendment, Code Sec. 9009(c)(2) read as follows:

"(2) If either such House does not, through appropriate action, disapprove the proposed rule or regulation set forth in such statement no later than 30 legislative days after receipt of such statement, then the Commission may prescribe such rule or regulation. The Commission may not prescribe any rule or regulation which is disapproved by either such House under this paragraph."

• **1974, Federal Election Campaign Act Amendments of 1974 (P.L. 93-443)**

P.L. 93-443, §§404(c), 406(b):

Amended Code Sec. 9009(c) by substituting "Commission" for "Comptroller General" and "it" for "he" wherever they appear. **Effective** for tax years beginning after 12-31-74.

• **1971, Revenue Act of 1971 (P.L. 92-178)**

P.L. 92-178, §801:

Added Code Sec. 9009. **Effective** 1-1-73.

[Sec. 9010]
SEC. 9010. PARTICIPATION BY COMMISSION IN JUDICIAL PROCEEDINGS.

[Sec. 9010(a)]

(a) APPEARANCE BY COUNSEL.—The Commission is authorized to appear in and defend against any action filed under section 9011, either by attorneys employed in its office or by counsel whom it may appoint without regard to the provisions of title 5, United States Code, governing appointments in the competitive service, and whose compensation it may fix without regard to the provisions of chapter 51 and subchapter III of chapter 53 of such title.

Amendments

• **1974, Federal Election Campaign Act Amendments of 1974 (P.L. 93-443)**

P.L. 93-443, §404(c):

Amended Code Sec. 9010(a) by substituting "Commission" for "Comptroller General" and "it" for "he". **Effective** for tax years beginning after 1974.

PRESIDENTIAL ELECTION CAMPAIGNS

[Sec. 9010(b)]

(b) RECOVERY OF CERTAIN PAYMENTS.—The Commission is authorized through attorneys and counsel described in subsection (a) to appear in the district courts of the United States to seek recovery of any amounts determined to be payable to the Secretary of the Treasury as a result of examination and audit made pursuant to section 9007.

Amendments

• **1976, Tax Reform Act of 1976 (P.L. 94-455)**

P.L. 94-455, §1906(b)(13)(C):

Substituted "Secretary of the Treasury" for "Secretary" in Code Sec. 9010(b). **Effective** 2-1-77.

• **1974, Federal Election Campaign Act Amendments of 1974 (P.L. 93-443)**

P.L. 93-443, §404(c):

Amended Code Sec. 9010(b) by substituting "Commission" for "Comptroller General" and "it" for "he". **Effective** for tax years beginning after 1974.

[Sec. 9010(c)]

(c) DECLARATORY AND INJUNCTIVE RELIEF.—The Commission is authorized through attorneys and counsel described in subsection (a) to petition the courts of the United States for declaratory or injunctive relief concerning any civil matter covered by the provisions of this subtitle or section 6096. Upon application of the Commission, an action brought pursuant to this subsection shall be heard and determined by a court of three judges in accordance with the provisions of section 2284 of title 28, United States Code, and any appeal shall lie to the Supreme Court.

Amendments

• **1984 (P.L. 98-620)**

P.L. 98-620, §402(28)(E):

Amended Code Sec. 9010(c) by striking out the last sentence. Not **effective** for cases pending on 11-8-84. Prior to being stricken, the last sentence read as follows:

It shall be the duty of the judges designated to hear the case to assign the case for hearing at the earliest practicable date, to participate in the hearing and determination thereof, and to cause the case to be in every way expedited.

• **1974, Federal Election Campaign Act Amendments of 1974 (P.L. 93-443)**

P.L. 93-443, §404(c):

Substituted "Commission" for "Comptroller General" and "it" for "he" in Code Sec. 9010(c). **Effective** for tax years beginning after 12-31-74.

[Sec. 9010(d)]

(d) APPEAL.—The Commission is authorized on behalf of the United States to appeal from, and to petition the Supreme Court for certiorari to review, judgments or decrees entered with respect to actions in which it appears pursuant to the authority provided in this section.

Amendments

• **1974, Federal Election Campaign Act Amendments of 1974 (P.L. 93-443)**

P.L. 93-443, §404(c):

Amended Code Sec. 9010(d) by substituting "Commission" for "Comptroller General" and "it" for "he" wherever they appear. **Effective** for tax years beginning after 12-31-74.

• **1971, Revenue Act of 1971 (P.L. 92-178)**

P.L. 92-178, §801:

Added Code Sec. 9010. **Effective** 1-1-73.

[Sec. 9011]

SEC. 9011. JUDICIAL REVIEW.

[Sec. 9011(a)]

(a) REVIEW OF CERTIFICATION, DETERMINATION, OR OTHER ACTION BY THE COMMISSION.—Any certification, determination, or other action by the Commission made or taken pursuant to the provisions of this chapter shall be subject to review by the United States Court of Appeals for the District of Columbia upon petition filed in such Court by any interested person. Any petition filed pursuant to this section shall be filed within thirty days after the certification, determination, or other action by the Commission for which review is sought.

Amendments

• **1974, Federal Election Campaign Act Amendments of 1974 (P.L. 93-443)**

P.L. 93-443, §404(c):

Substituted "Commission" for "Comptroller General" in Code Sec. 9011(a). **Effective** for tax years beginning after 12-31-74.

[Sec. 9011(b)]

(b) SUITS TO IMPLEMENT CHAPTER.—

(1) The Commission, the national committee of any political party, and individuals eligible to vote for President are authorized to institute such actions, including actions for declaratory judgment or injunctive relief, as may be appropriate to implement or construe any provision of this chapter.

(2) The district courts of the United States shall have jurisdiction of proceedings instituted pursuant to this subsection and shall exercise the same without regard to whether a person asserting rights under provisions of this subsection shall have exhausted any administrative or other remedies that may be provided at law. Such proceedings shall be heard and determined by a court of three judges in accordance with the provisions of section 2284 of title 28, United States Code, and any appeal shall lie to the Supreme Court.

Amendments

• **2018, Tax Technical Corrections Act of 2018 (P.L. 115-141)**

P.L. 115-141, §401(a)(339), Div. U:

Amended Code Sec. 9011(b)(1) by striking "contrue" and inserting "construe". **Effective** 3-23-2018.

• **1984 (P.L. 98-620)**

P.L. 98-620, §402(28)(F):

Amended Code Sec. 9011(b)(2) by striking the last sentence. Not **effective** for cases pending on 11-8-84. Prior to being stricken, the last sentence read as follows: It shall be the duty of the judges designated to hear the case to assign the case for hearing at the earliest practicable date, to participate in the hearing and determination thereof, and to cause the case to be in every way expedited.

• **1974, Federal Election Campaign Act Amendments of 1974 (P.L. 93-443)**

P.L. 93-443, §404(c):

Amended Code Sec. 9011(b) by substituting "Commission" for "Comptroller General" wherever it appears. **Effective** for tax years beginning after 12-31-74.

• **1971, Revenue Act of 1971 (P.L. 92-178)**

P.L. 92-178, §801:

Added Code Sec. 9011. **Effective** 1-1-73.

PRESIDENTIAL ELECTION CAMPAIGNS

[Sec. 9012]

SEC. 9012. CRIMINAL PENALTIES.

[Sec. 9012(a)]

(a) EXCESS EXPENSES.—

(1) It shall be unlawful for an eligible candidate of a political party for President and Vice President in a presidential election or any of his authorized committees knowingly and willfully to incur qualified campaign expenses in excess of the aggregate payments to which the eligible candidates of a major party are entitled under section 9004 with respect to such election.

(2) Any person who violates paragraph (1) shall be fined not more than $5,000, or imprisoned not more than one year or both. In the case of a violation by an authorized committee, any officer or member of such committee who knowingly and willfully consents to such violation shall be fined not more than $5,000, or imprisoned not more than one year, or both.

Amendments

• **2014, Gabriella Miller Kids First Research Act (P.L. 113-94)**

P.L. 113-94, §2(c)(2)(A):

Amended Code Sec. 9012(a)(1) by striking the second sentence. **Effective** 4-3-2014. Prior to being stricken, the second sentence of Code Sec. 9012(a)(1) read as follows:

It shall be unlawful for the national committee of a major party or minor party knowingly and willfully to incur expenses with respect to a presidential nominating convention in excess of the expenditure limitation applicable with respect to such committee under section 9008(d), unless the incurring of such expenses is authorized by the Commission under section 9008(d)(3).

• **1974, Federal Election Campaign Act Amendments of 1974 (P.L. 93-443)**

P.L. 93-443, §§404(c), 406(b):

Amended Code Sec. 9012(a) by substituting "Commission" for "Comptroller General" and "it" for "he" and by adding the last sentence to paragraph (1). **Effective** for tax years beginning after 12-31-74.

[Sec. 9012(b)]

(b) CONTRIBUTIONS.—

(1) It shall be unlawful for an eligible candidate of a major party in a presidential election or any of his authorized committees knowingly and willfully to accept any contribution to defray qualified campaign expenses, except to the extent necessary to make up any deficiency in payments received out of the fund on account of the application of section 9006(c), or to defray expenses which would be qualified campaign expenses but for subparagraph (C) of section 9002(11).

(2) It shall be unlawful for an eligible candidate of a political party (other than a major party) in a presidential election or any of his authorized committees knowingly and willfully to accept and expend or retain contributions to defray qualified campaign expenses in an amount which exceeds the qualified campaign expenses incurred with respect to such election by such eligible candidate and his authorized committees.

(3) Any person who violates paragraph (1) or (2) shall be fined not more than $5,000, or imprisoned not more than one year, or both. In the case of a violation by an authorized committee, any officer or member of such committee who knowingly and willfully consents to such violation shall be fined not more than $5,000, or imprisoned not more than one year, or both.

Amendments

• **1976, Federal Election Campaign Act Amendments of 1976 (P.L. 94-283)**

P.L. 94-283, §307(f):

Amended Code Sec. 9012(b) by substituting "section 9006(c)" for "section 9006(d)". **Effective** 5-11-76.

• **1973 (P.L. 93-53)**

P.L. 93-53, §6(c):

Amended Code Sec. 9012(b)(1) by substituting "section 9006(d)" for "section 9006(c)". **Effective** 1-1-74.

[Sec. 9012(c)]

(c) UNLAWFUL USE OF PAYMENTS.—

(1) It shall be unlawful for any person who receives any payment under section 9006, or to whom any portion of any payment received under such section is transferred, knowingly and willfully to use, or authorize the use of, such payment or such portion for any purpose other than—

(A) to defray the qualified campaign expenses with respect to which such payment was made, or

(B) to repay loans the proceeds of which were used, or otherwise to restore funds (other than contributions to defray qualified campaign expenses which were received and expended) which were used, to defray such qualified campaign expenses.

(2) Any person who violates paragraph (1) shall be fined not more than $10,000, or imprisoned not more than five years, or both.

Amendments

• **2014, Gabriella Miller Kids First Research Act (P.L. 113-94)**

P.L. 113-94, §2(c)(2)(B):

Amended Code Sec. 9012(c) by striking paragraph (2) and redesignating paragraph (3) as paragraph (2). **Effective** 4-3-2014. Prior to being stricken, Code Sec. 9012(c)(2) read as follows:

(2) It shall be unlawful for the national committee of a major party or minor party which receives any payment under section 9008(b)(3) to use, or authorize the use of, such payment for any purpose other than a purpose authorized by section 9008(c).

• **1974, Federal Election Campaign Act Amendments of 1974 (P.L. 93-443)**

P.L. 93-443, §406(b):

Amended Code Sec. 9012(c) by redesignating paragraph (2) as paragraph (3) and by adding a new paragraph (2). **Effective** for tax years beginning after 12-31-74.

[Sec. 9012(d)]

(d) FALSE STATEMENTS, ETC.—

(1) It shall be unlawful for any person knowingly and willfully—

(A) to furnish any false, fictitious, or fraudulent evidence, books, or information to the Commission under this subtitle, or to include in any evidence, books, or information so furnished any misrepresentation of a material fact, or to falsify or conceal any evidence, books, or information relevant to a certification by the Commission or an examination and audit by the Commission under this chapter; or

(B) to fail to furnish to the Commission any records, books, or information requested by it for purposes of this chapter.

(2) Any person who violates paragraph (1) shall be fined not more than $10,000, or imprisoned not more than five years, or both.

[Sec. 9012(e)]

(e) KICKBACKS AND ILLEGAL PAYMENTS.—

(1) It shall be unlawful for any person knowingly and willfully to give or accept any kickback or any illegal payment in connection with any qualified campaign expense of eligible candidates or their authorized committees.

(2) Any person who violates paragraph (1) shall be fined not more than $10,000, or imprisoned not more than five years, or both.

PRESIDENTIAL ELECTION CAMPAIGNS

(3) In addition to the penalty provided by paragraph (2), any person who accepts any kickback or illegal payment in connection with any qualified campaign expenses of eligible candidates or their authorized committees, shall pay to the Secretary of the Treasury, for deposit in the general fund of the Treasury, an amount equal to 125 percent of the kickback or payment received.

Amendments

• **2014, Gabriella Miller Kids First Research Act (P.L. 113-94)**

P.L. 113-94, §2(c)(2)(C)-(D):

Amended Code Sec. 9012(e) by striking the second sentence in paragraph (1); and by striking ", or in connection with any expense incurred by the national committee of a major party or minor party with respect to a presidential nominating convention" following "or their authorized committees" in paragraph (3). **Effective** 4-3-2014. Prior to being stricken, the second sentence of Code Sec. 9012(e)(1) read as follows:

It shall be unlawful for the national committee of a major party or minor party knowingly and willfully to give or accept any kickback or any illegal payments in connection with any expense incurred by such committee with respect to a presidential nominating convention.

• **1976, Tax Reform Act of 1976 (P.L. 94-455)**

P.L. 94-455, §1906(b)(13)(C):

Substituted "Secretary of the Treasury" for "Secretary" in Code Sec. 9012(e). **Effective** 2-1-77.

• **1974, Federal Election Campaign Act Amendments of 1974 (P.L. 93-443)**

P.L. 93-443, §§404(c), 406(b):

Amended Code Sec. 9012(e) by substituting "Commission" for "Comptroller General" and "it" for "he" and by adding the last sentence to paragraph (1). **Effective** for tax years beginning after 12-31-74.

[Sec. 9012(f)]

(f) UNAUTHORIZED EXPENDITURES AND CONTRIBUTIONS.—

(1) Except as provided in paragraph (2), it shall be unlawful for any political committee which is not an authorized committee with respect to the eligible candidates of a political party for President and Vice President in a presidential election knowingly and willfully to incur expenditures to further the election of such candidates, which would constitute qualified campaign expenses if incurred by an authorized committee of such candidates, in an aggregate amount exceeding $1,000.

(2) This subsection shall not apply to (A) expenditures by a broadcaster regulated by the Federal Communications Commission, or by a periodical publication, in reporting the news or in taking editorial positions, or (B) expenditures by any organization described in section 501(c) which is exempt from tax under section 501(a) in communicating to its members the views of that organization.

(3) Any political committee which violates paragraph (1) shall be fined not more than $5,000, and any officer or member of such committee who knowingly and willfully consents to such violation and any other individual who knowingly and willfully violates paragraph (1) shall be fined not more more than $5,000, or imprisoned not more than one year, or both.

[Sec. 9012(g)]

(g) UNAUTHORIZED DISCLOSURE OF INFORMATION.—

(1) It shall be unlawful for any individual to disclose any information obtained under the provisions of this chapter except as may be required by law.

(2) Any person who violates paragraph (1) shall be fined not more than $5,000, or imprisoned not more than one year, or both.

Amendments

• **1971, Revenue Act of 1971 (P.L. 92-178)**

P.L. 92-178, §801:

Added Code Sec. 9012. **Effective** 1-1-73.

[Sec. 9013—Stricken]

Amendments

• **2018, Tax Technical Corrections Act of 2018 (P.L. 115-141)**

P.L. 115-141, §401(d)(8), Div. U:

Amended chapter 95 by striking Code Sec. 9013. **Effective** 3-23-2018. For a special rule, see Act 401(e), Div. U, below. Prior to being stricken, Code Sec. 9013 read as follows:

SEC. 9013. EFFECTIVE DATE OF CHAPTER.

The provisions of this chapter shall take effect on January 1, 1973.

Amendments

• **1971, Revenue Act of 1971 (P.L. 92-178)**

P.L. 92-178, §801:

Added Code Sec. 9013. **Effective** 1-1-73.

P.L. 115-141, §401(e), Div. U, provides:

(e) GENERAL SAVINGS PROVISION WITH RESPECT TO DEADWOOD PROVISIONS.—If—

(1) any provision amended or repealed by the amendments made by subsection (b) or (d) applied to—

(A) any transaction occurring before the date of the enactment of this Act,

(B) any property acquired before such date of enactment, or

(C) any item of income, loss, deduction, or credit taken into account before such date of enactment, and

(2) the treatment of such transaction, property, or item under such provision would (without regard to the amendments or repeals made by such subsection) affect the liability for tax for periods ending after such date of enactment,

nothing in the amendments or repeals made by this section shall be construed to affect the treatment of such transaction, property, or item for purposes of determining liability for tax for periods ending after such date of enactment.

CHAPTER 96—PRESIDENTIAL PRIMARY MATCHING PAYMENT ACCOUNT

Sec. 9031.	Short title.
Sec. 9032.	Definitions.
Sec. 9033.	Eligibility for payments.
Sec. 9034.	Entitlement of eligible candidates to payments.
Sec. 9035.	Qualified campaign expense limitations.
Sec. 9036.	Certification by Commission.
Sec. 9037.	Payments to eligible candidates.
Sec. 9038.	Examinations and audits; repayments.
Sec. 9039.	Reports to Congress; regulations.
Sec. 9040.	Participation by Commission in judicial proceedings.
Sec. 9041.	Judicial review.
Sec. 9042.	Criminal penalties.

[Sec. 9031]

SEC. 9031. SHORT TITLE.

This chapter may be cited as the "Presidential Primary Matching Payment Account Act."

PRESIDENTIAL ELECTION CAMPAIGNS

[Sec. 9032]
SEC. 9032. DEFINITIONS.

For purposes of this chapter—

(1) The term "authorized committee" means, with respect to the candidates of a political party for President and Vice President of the United States, any political committee which is authorized in writing by such candidates to incur expenses to further the election of such candidates. Such authorization shall be addressed to the chairman of such political committee, and a copy of such authorization shall be filed by such candidates with the Commission. Any withdrawal of any authorization shall also be in writing and shall be addressed and filed in the same manner as the authorization.

(2) The term "candidate" means an individual who seeks nomination for election to be President of the United States. For purposes of this paragraph, an individual shall be considered to seek nomination for election if he (A) takes the action necessary under the law of a State to qualify himself for nomination for election, (B) receives contributions or incurs qualified campaign expenses, or (C) gives his consent for any other person to receive contributions or to incur qualified campaign expenses on his behalf. The term "candidate" shall not include any individual who is not actively conducting campaigns in more than one State in connection with seeking nomination for election to be President of the United States.

(3) The term "Commission" means the Federal Election Commission established by section 306(a)(1) of the Federal Election Campaign Act of 1971.

(4) Except as provided by section 9034(a), the term "contribution"—

(A) means a gift, subscription, loan, advance, or deposit of money, or anything of value, the payment of which was made on or after the beginning of the calendar year immediately preceding the calendar year of the presidential election with respect to which such gift, subscription, loan, advance, or deposit of money, or anything of value, is made, for the purpose of influencing the results of a primary election,

(B) means a contract, promise, or agreement, whether or not legally enforceable, to make a contribution for any such purpose,

(C) means funds received by a political committee which are transferred to that committee from another committee, and

(D) means the payment by any person other than a candidate, or his authorized committee, of compensation for the personal services of another person which are rendered to the candidate or committee without charge, but

(E) does not include—

(i) except as provided in subparagraph (D), the value of personal services rendered to or for the benefit of a candidate by an individual who receives no compensation for rendering such service to or for the benefit of the candidate, or

(ii) payments under section 9037.

(5) The term "matching payment account" means the Presidential Primary Matching Payment Account established under section 9037(a).

(6) The term "matching payment period" means the period beginning with the beginning of the calendar year in which a general election for the office of President of the United States will be held and ending on the date on which the national convention of the party whose nomination a candidate seeks nominates its candidate for the office of President of the United States, or, in the case of a party which does not make such nomination by national convention, ending on the earlier of (A) the date such party nominates its candidate for the office of President of the United States, or (B) the last day of the last national convention held by a major party during such calendar year.

(7) The term "primary election" means an election, including a runoff election or a nominating convention or caucus held by a political party, for the selection of delegates to a national convention of a political party, or for the expression of a preference for the nomination of persons for election to the office of President of the United States.

(8) The term "political committee" means any individual, committee, association, or organization (whether or not incorporated) which accepts contributions or incurs qualified campaign expenses for the purpose of influencing, or attempting to influence, the nomination of any person for election to the office of President of the United States.

(9) The term "qualified campaign expense" means a purchase, payment, distribution, loan, advance, deposit, or gift of money or of anything of value—

(A) incurred by a candidate, or by his authorized committee, in connection with his campaign for nomination for election, and

(B) neither the incurring nor payment of which constitutes a violation of any law of the United States or of the State in which the expense is incurred or paid.

For purposes of this paragraph, an expense is incurred by a candidate or by an authorized committee if it is incurred by a person specifically authorized in writing by the candidate or committee, as the case may be, to incur such expense on behalf of the candidate or the committee.

(10) The term "State" means each State of the United States and the District of Columbia.

Amendments

• **2007, Tax Technical Corrections Act of 2007 (P.L. 110-172)**

P.L. 110-172, § 11(a)(42)(C):

Amended Code Sec. 9032(3) by striking "section 309(a)(1)" and inserting "section 306(a)(1)". **Effective** 12-29-2007.

• **1976, Federal Election Campaign Act Amendments of 1976 (P.L. 94-283)**

P.L. 94-283, § 115(c)(2):

Amended Code Sec. 9032(3) by substituting "309(a)(1)" for "310(a)(1)". **Effective** 5-11-76.

• **1974, Federal Election Campaign Act Amendments of 1974 (P.L. 93-443)**

P.L. 93-443, § 408(c):

Amended subtitle H by striking out chapter 96, containing Code Sec. 9021, and inserting new chapter 96. **Effective** for tax years beginning after 12-31-74.

[Sec. 9033]
SEC. 9033. ELIGIBILITY FOR PAYMENTS.

[Sec. 9033(a)]

(a) CONDITIONS.—To be eligible to receive payments under section 9037, a candidate shall, in writing—

(1) agree to obtain and furnish to the Commission any evidence it may request of qualified campaign expenses,

(2) agree to keep and furnish to the Commission any records, books, and other information it may request, and

(3) agree to an audit and examination by the Commission under section 9038 and to pay any amounts required to be paid under such section.

[Sec. 9033(b)]

(b) EXPENSE LIMITATION; DECLARATION OF INTENT; MINIMUM CONTRIBUTIONS.—To be eligible to receive payments under section 9037, a candidate shall certify to the Commission that—

PRESIDENTIAL ELECTION CAMPAIGNS

(1) the candidate and his authorized committees will not incur qualified campaign expenses in excess of the limitations on such expenses under section 9035,

(2) the candidate is seeking nomination by a political party for election to the office of President of the United States,

(3) the candidate has received matching contributions which, in the aggregate, exceed $5,000 in contributions from residents of each of at least 20 States, and

(4) the aggregate of contributions certified with respect to any person under paragraph (3) does not exceed $250.

Amendments

• **1976, Federal Election Campaign Act Amendments of 1976 (P.L. 94-283)**

P.L. 94-283, §305(c):

Amended Code Sec. 9033(b)(1) by substituting "limitations" for "limitation". Effective 5-11-76.

• **1974, Federal Election Campaign Act Amendments of 1974 (P.L. 93-443)**

P.L. 93-443, §408(c):

Amended subtitle H by striking out chapter 96, containing Code Sec. 9021, and inserting new chapter 96. Effective for tax years beginning after 12-31-74.

[Sec. 9033(c)]

(c) TERMINATION OF PAYMENTS.—

(1) GENERAL RULE.—Except as provided by paragraph (2), no payment shall be made to any individual under section 9037—

(A) if such individual ceases to be a candidate as a result of the operation of the last sentence of section 9032(2); or

(B) more than 30 days after the date of the second consecutive primary election in which such individual receives less than 10 percent of the number of votes cast for all candidates of the same party for the same office in such primary election, if such individual permitted or authorized the appearance of his name on the ballot, unless such individual certifies to the Commission that he will not be an active candidate in the primary involved.

(2) QUALIFIED CAMPAIGN EXPENSES; PAYMENTS TO SECRETARY.—Any candidate who is ineligible under paragraph (1) to receive any payments under section 9037 shall be eligible to continue to receive payments under section 9037 to defray qualified campaign expenses incurred before the date upon which such candidate becomes ineligible under paragraph (1).

(3) CALCULATION OF VOTING PERCENTAGE.—For purposes of paragraph (1)(B), if the primary elections involved are held in more than one State on the same date, a candidate shall be treated as receiving that percentage of the votes on such date which he received in the primary election conducted on such date in which he received the greatest percentage vote.

(4) REESTABLISHMENT OF ELIGIBILITY.—

(A) In any case in which an individual is ineligible to receive payments under section 9037 as a result of the operation of paragraph (1)(A), the Commission may subsequently determine that such individual is a candidate upon a finding that such individual is actively seeking election to the office of President of the United States in more than one State. The Commission shall make such determination without requiring such individual to reestablish his eligibility to receive payments under subsection (a).

(B) Notwithstanding the provisions of paragraph (1)(B), a candidate whose payments have been terminated under paragraph (1)(B) may again receive payments (including amounts he would have received but for paragraph (1)(B)) if he receives 20 percent or more of the total number of votes cast for candidates of the same party in a primary election held after the date on which the election was held which was the basis for terminating payments to him.

Amendments

• **1976, Federal Election Campaign Act Amendments of 1976 (P.L. 94-283)**

P.L. 94-283, §306(b)(2):

Added Code Sec. 9033(c). Effective 5-11-76.

[Sec. 9034]

SEC. 9034. ENTITLEMENT OF ELIGIBLE CANDIDATES TO PAYMENTS.

[Sec. 9034(a)]

(a) IN GENERAL.—Every candidate who is eligible to receive payments under section 9033 is entitled to payments under section 9037 in an amount equal to the amount of each contribution received by such candidate on or after the beginning of the calendar year immediately preceding the calendar year of the presidential election with respect to which such candidate is seeking nomination, or by his authorized committees, disregarding any amount of contributions from any person to the extent that the total of the amounts contributed by such person on or after the beginning of such preceding calendar year exceeds $250. For purposes of this subsection and section 9033(b), the term "contribution" means a gift of money made by a written instrument which identifies the person making the contribution by full name and mailing address, but does not include a subscription, loan, advance, or deposit of money, or anything of value or anything described in subparagraph (B), (C), or (D) of section 9032(4).

[Sec. 9034(b)]

(b) LIMITATIONS.—The total amount of payments to which a candidate is entitled under subsection (a) shall not exceed 50 percent of the expenditure limitation applicable under section 315(b)(1)(A) of the Federal Election Campaign Act of 1971.

Amendments

• **2007, Tax Technical Corrections Act of 2007 (P.L. 110-172)**

P.L. 110-172, §11(a)(42)(D):

Amended Code Sec. 9034(b) by striking "section 320(b)(1)(A)" and inserting "section 315(b)(1)(A)". Effective 12-29-2007.

• **1976, Federal Election Campaign Act Amendments of 1976 (P.L. 94-283)**

P.L. 94-283, §307(b):

Amended Code Sec. 9034(b) by substituting "section 320(b)(1)(A) of the Federal Election Campaign Act of 1971" for "section 608(c)(1)(A) of title 18, United States Code". Effective 5-11-76.

• **1974, Federal Election Campaign Act Amendments of 1974 (P.L. 93-443)**

P.L. 93-443, §408(c):

Amended subtitle H by striking out chapter 96, containing Code Sec. 9021, and inserting new chapter 96. Effective for tax years beginning after 12-31-74.

[Sec. 9035]

SEC. 9035. QUALIFIED CAMPAIGN EXPENSE LIMITATIONS.

[Sec. 9035(a)]

(a) EXPENDITURE LIMITATIONS.—No candidate shall knowingly incur qualified campaign expenses in excess of the expenditure limitation applicable under section 315(b)(1)(A) of the Federal Election Campaign Act of 1971, and no candidate shall knowingly make expenditures from his

PRESIDENTIAL ELECTION CAMPAIGNS

personal funds, or the personal funds of his immediate family, in connection with his campaign for nomination for election to the office of President in excess of, in the aggregate, $50,000.

Amendments

• **2014, Tax Technical Corrections Act of 2014 (P.L. 113-295)**

P.L. 113-295, §220(z), Division A:

Amended Code Sec. 9035(a) by striking "section 320(b)(1)(A)" and inserting "section 315(b)(1)(A)". **Effective** 12-19-2014.

[Sec. 9035(b)]

(b) DEFINITION OF IMMEDIATE FAMILY.—For purposes of this section, the term "immediate family" means a candidate's spouse, and any child, parent, grandparent, brother, half-brother, sister, or half-sister of the candidate, and the spouses of such persons.

Amendments

• **1976, Federal Election Campaign Act Amendments of 1976 (P.L. 94-283)**

P.L. 94-283, §§305(a), 307(c):

Amended Code Sec. 9035. **Effective** 5-11-76. Prior to amendment, this section read as follows:

SEC. 9035. QUALIFIED CAMPAIGN EXPENSE LIMITATION.

No candidate shall knowingly incur qualified campaign expenses in excess of the expenditure limitation applicable under section 608(c)(1)(A) of title 18, United States Code.

P.L. 94-283, §§305(d), provides:

(d) For purposes of applying section 9035(a) of the Internal Revenue Code, as amended by subsection (a), expenditures made by an individual after January 29, 1976, and before the date of the enactment [May 11, 1976] shall not be taken into account.

• **1974, Federal Election Campaign Act Amendments of 1974 (P.L. 93-443)**

P.L. 93-443, §408(c):

Amended subtitle H by striking out chapter 96, containing Code Sec. 9021, and inserting new chapter 96. **Effective** for tax years beginning after 12-31-74.

[Sec. 9036]

SEC. 9036. CERTIFICATION BY COMMISSION.

[Sec. 9036(a)]

(a) INITIAL CERTIFICATIONS.—Not later than 10 days after a candidate establishes his eligibility under section 9033 to receive payments under section 9037, the Commission shall certify to the Secretary for payment to such candidate under section 9037 payment in full of amounts to which such candidate is entitled under section 9034. The Commission shall make such additional certifications as may be necessary to permit candidates to receive payments for contributions under section 9037.

[Sec. 9036(b)]

(b) FINALITY OF DETERMINATIONS.—Initial certifications by the Commission under subsection (a), and all determinations made by it under this chapter, are final and conclusive, except to the extent that they are subject to examination and audit by the Commission under section 9038 and judicial review under section 9041.

Amendments

• **1974, Federal Election Campaign Act Amendments of 1974 (P.L. 93-443)**

P.L. 93-443, §408(c):

Amended subtitle H by striking out chapter 96, containing Code Sec. 9021, and inserting new chapter 96. **Effective** for tax years beginning after 12-31-74.

[Sec. 9037]

SEC. 9037. PAYMENTS TO ELIGIBLE CANDIDATES.

[Sec. 9037(a)]

(a) ESTABLISHMENT OF ACCOUNT.—The Secretary shall maintain in the Presidential Election Campaign Fund established by section 9006(a), in addition to any account which he maintains under such section, a separate account to be known as the Presidential Primary Matching Payment Account. The Secretary shall deposit into the matching payment account, for use by the candidate of any political party who is eligible to receive payments under section 9033, the amount available after the Secretary determines that amounts for payments under section 9006(e) and for payments under section 9008(i)(2) are available for such payments.

Amendments

• **2014, Gabriella Miller Kids First Research Act (P.L. 113-94)**

P.L. 113-94, §2(b)(2):

Amended the second sentence of Code Sec. 9037(a) by striking "section 9008(b)(3)" and inserting "section 9008(i)(2)". **Effective** 4-3-2014.

[Sec. 9037(b)]

(b) PAYMENTS FROM THE MATCHING PAYMENT ACCOUNT.—Upon receipt of a certification from the Commission under section 9036, but not before the beginning of the matching payment period, the Secretary shall promptly transfer the amount certified by the Commission from the matching payment account to the candidate. In making such transfers to candidates of the same political party, the Secretary shall seek to achieve an equitable distribution of funds available under subsection (a), and the Secretary shall take into account, in seeking to achieve an equitable distribution, the sequence in which such certifications are received.

Amendments

• **1976, Tax Reform Act of 1976 (P.L. 94-455)**

P.L. 94-455, §1906(b)(13)(A):

Amended 1954 Code by substituting "Secretary" for "Secretary or his delegate" each place it appeared. **Effective** 2-1-77.

• **1974, Federal Election Campaign Act Amendments of 1974 (P.L. 93-443)**

P.L. 93-443, §408(c):

Amended subtitle H by striking out chapter 96, containing Code Sec. 9021, and inserting new chapter 96. **Effective** for tax years beginning after 12-31-74.

[Sec. 9038]

SEC. 9038. EXAMINATIONS AND AUDITS; REPAYMENTS.

[Sec. 9038(a)]

(a) EXAMINATIONS AND AUDITS.—After each matching payment period, the Commission shall conduct a thorough examination and audit of the qualified campaign expenses of every candidate and his authorized committees who received payments under section 9037.

Internal Revenue Code

Sec. 9038(a)

PRESIDENTIAL ELECTION CAMPAIGNS

[Sec. 9038(b)]

(b) REPAYMENTS.—

(1) If the Commission determines that any portion of the payments made to a candidate from the matching payment account was in excess of the aggregate amount of payments to which such candidate was entitled under section 9034, it shall notify the candidate, and the candidate shall pay to the Secretary an amount equal to the amount of excess payments.

(2) If the Commission determines that any amount of any payment made to a candidate from the matching payment account was used for any purpose other than—

(A) to defray the qualified campaign expenses with respect to which such payment was made, or

(B) to repay loans the proceeds of which were used, or otherwise to restore funds (other than contributions to defray qualified campaign expenses which were received and expended) which were used, to defray qualified campaign expenses,

it shall notify such candidate of the amount so used, and the candidate shall pay to the Secretary an amount equal to such amount.

(3) Amounts received by a candidate from the matching payment account may be retained for the liquidation of all obligations to pay qualified campaign expenses incurred for a period not exceeding 6 months after the end of the matching payment period. After all obligations have been liquidated, that portion of any unexpended balance remaining in the candidate's accounts which bears the same ratio to the total unexpended balance as the total amount received from the matching payment account bears to the total of all deposits made into the candidate's accounts shall be promptly repaid to the matching payment account.

Amendments

• **1976, Tax Reform Act of 1976 (P.L. 94-455)**

P.L. 94-455, §1906(b)(13)(A):

Amended 1954 Code by substituting "Secretary" for "Secretary or his delegate" each place it appeared. **Effective** 2-1-77.

[Sec. 9038(c)]

(c) NOTIFICATION.—No notification shall be made by the Commission under subsection (b) with respect to a matching payment period more than 3 years after the end of such period.

[Sec. 9038(d)]

(d) DEPOSIT OF REPAYMENTS.—All payments received by the Secretary under subsection (b) shall be deposited by him in the matching payment account.

Amendments

• **1976, Tax Reform Act of 1976 (P.L. 94-455)**

P.L. 94-455, §1906(b)(13)(A):

Amended 1954 Code by substituting "Secretary" for "Secretary or his delegate" each place it appeared. **Effective** 2-1-77.

• **1974, Federal Election Campaign Act Amendments of 1974 (P.L. 93-443)**

P.L. 93-443, §408(c):

Amended subtitle H by striking out chapter 96, containing Code Sec. 9021, and inserting new chapter 96. **Effective** for tax years beginning after 12-31-74.

[Sec. 9039]

SEC. 9039. REPORTS TO CONGRESS; REGULATIONS.

[Sec. 9039(a)]

(a) REPORTS.—The Commission shall, as soon as practicable after each matching payment period, submit a full report to the Senate and House of Representatives setting forth—

(1) the qualified campaign expenses (shown in such detail as the Commission determines necessary) incurred by the candidates of each political party and their authorized committees,

(2) the amounts certified by it under section 9036 for payment to each eligible candidate, and

(3) the amount of payments, if any, required from candidates under section 9038, and the reasons for each payment required.

Each report submitted pursuant to this section shall be printed as a Senate document.

[Sec. 9039(b)]

(b) REGULATIONS, ETC.—The Commission is authorized to prescribe rules and regulations in accordance with the provisions of subsection (c), to conduct examinations and audits (in addition to the examinations and audits required by section 9038(a)), to conduct investigations, and to require the keeping and submission of any books, records, and information, which it determines to be necessary to carry out its responsibilities under this chapter.

[Sec. 9039(c)]

(c) REVIEW OF REGULATIONS.—

(1) The Commission, before prescribing any rule or regulation under subsection (b), shall transmit a statement with respect to such rule or regulation to the Senate and to the House of Representatives, in accordance with the provisions of this subsection. Such statement shall set forth the proposed rule or regulation and shall contain a detailed explanation and justification of such rule or regulation.

(2) If either such House does not, through appropriate action, disapprove the proposed rule or regulation set forth in such statement no later than 30 legislative days after receipt of such statement, then the Commission may prescribe such rule or regulation. Whenever a committee of the House of Representatives reports any resolution relating to any such rule or regulations, it is at any time thereafter in order (even though a previous motion to the same effect has been disagreed to) to move to proceed to the consideration of the resolution. The motion is highly privileged and is not debatable. An amendment to the motion is not in order, and it is not in order to move to reconsider the vote by which the motion is agreed to or disagreed to. The Commission may not prescribe any such rule or regulation which is disapproved by either such House under this paragraph.

(3) For purposes of this subsection, the term "legislative days" does not include any calendar day on which both Houses of the Congress are not in session.

(4) For purposes of this subsection, the term "rule or regulation" means a provision or series of interrelated provisions stating a single separable rule of law.

Amendments

• **1976, Federal Election Campaign Act Amendments of 1976 (P.L. 94-283)**

P.L. 94-283, §304(b):

Amended Code Sec. 9039(c) by adding the second, third and fourth sentences in paragraph (2) and by adding paragraph (4). **Effective** 5-11-76.

• **1974, Federal Election Campaign Act Amendments of 1974 (P.L. 93-443)**

P.L. 93-443, §408(c):

Amended subtitle H by striking out chapter 96, containing Code Sec. 9021, and inserting new chapter 96. **Effective** for tax years beginning after 12-31-74.

PRESIDENTIAL ELECTION CAMPAIGNS

[Sec. 9040]
SEC. 9040. PARTICIPATION BY COMMISSION IN JUDICIAL PROCEEDINGS.

[Sec. 9040(a)]

(a) APPEARANCE BY COUNSEL.—The Commission is authorized to appear in and defend against any action instituted under this section, either by attorneys employed in its office or by counsel whom it may appoint without regard to the provisions of title 5, United States Code, governing appointments in the competitive service, and whose compensation it may fix without regard to the provisions of chapter 51 and subchapter III of chapter 53 of such title.

[Sec. 9040(b)]

(b) RECOVERY OF CERTAIN PAYMENTS.—The Commission is authorized, through attorneys and counsel described in subsection (a), to institute actions in the district courts of the United States to seek recovery of any amounts determined to be payable to the Secretary as a result of an examination and audit made pursuant to section 9038.

Amendments
- 1976, Tax Reform Act of 1976 (P.L. 94-455)

P.L. 94-455, §1906(b)(13)(A):
Amended 1954 Code by substituting "Secretary" for "Secretary or his delegate" each place it appeared. **Effective** 2-1-77.

[Sec. 9040(c)]

(c) INJUNCTIVE RELIEF.—The Commission is authorized through attorneys and counsel described in subsection (a), to petition the courts of the United States for such injunctive relief as is appropriate to implement any provision of this chapter.

[Sec. 9040(d)]

(d) APPEAL.—The Commission is authorized on behalf of the United States to appeal from, and to petition the Supreme Court for certiorari to review, judgments or decrees entered with respect to actions in which it appears pursuant to the authority provided in this section.

Amendments
- 1974, Federal Election Campaign Act Amendments of 1974 (P.L. 93-443)

P.L. 93-443, §408(c):
Amended subtitle H by striking out chapter 96, containing Code Sec. 9021, and inserting new chapter 96. **Effective** for tax years beginning after 12-31-74.

[Sec. 9041]
SEC. 9041. JUDICIAL REVIEW.

[Sec. 9041(a)]

(a) REVIEW OF AGENCY ACTION BY THE COMMISSION.—Any Agency action by the Commission made under the provisions of this chapter shall be subject to review by the United States Court of Appeals for the District of Columbia Circuit upon petition filed in such court within 30 days after the agency action by the Commission for which review is sought.

[Sec. 9041(b)]

(b) REVIEW PROCEDURES.—The provisions of chapter 7 of title 5, United States Code, apply to judicial review of any agency action, as defined in section 551(13) of title 5, United States Code, by the Commission.

Amendments
- 1974, Federal Election Campaign Act Amendments of 1974 (P.L. 93-443)

P.L. 93-443, §408(c):
Amended subtitle H by striking out chapter 96, containing Code Sec. 9021, and inserting new chapter 96. **Effective** for tax years beginning after 12-31-74.

[Sec. 9042]
SEC. 9042. CRIMINAL PENALTIES.

[Sec. 9042(a)]

(a) EXCESS CAMPAIGN EXPENSES.—Any person who violates the provisions of section 9035 shall be fined not more than $25,000, or imprisoned not more than 5 years, or both. Any officer or member of any political committee who knowingly consents to any expenditure in violation of the provisions of section 9035 shall be fined not more than $25,000, or imprisoned not more than 5 years, or both.

[Sec. 9042(b)]

(b) UNLAWFUL USE OF PAYMENTS.—

(1) It is unlawful for any person who receives any payment under section 9037, or to whom any portion of any such payment is transferred, knowingly and willfully to use, or authorize the use of, such payment or such portion for any purpose other than—

(A) to defray qualified campaign expenses, or

(B) to repay loans the proceeds of which were used, or otherwise to restore funds (other than contributions to defray qualified campaign expenses which were received and expended) which were used, to defray qualified campaign expenses.

(2) Any person who violates the provisions of paragraph (1) shall be fined not more than $10,000, or imprisoned not more than 5 years, or both.

[Sec. 9042(c)]

(c) FALSE STATEMENTS, ETC.—

(1) It is unlawful for any person knowingly and willfully—

(A) to furnish any false, fictitious, or fraudulent evidence, books, or information to the Commission under this chapter, or to include in any evidence, books, or information so furnished any misrepresentation of a material fact, or to falsify or conceal any evidence, books, or information relevant to a certification by the Commission or an examination and audit by the Commission under this chapter, or

(B) to fail to furnish to the Commission any records, books, or information requested by it for purposes of this chapter.

PRESIDENTIAL ELECTION CAMPAIGNS

(2) Any person who violates the provisions of paragraph (1) shall be fined not more than $10,000, or imprisoned not more than 5 years, or both.

[Sec. 9042(d)]

(d) KICKBACKS AND ILLEGAL PAYMENTS.—

(1) It is unlawful for any person knowingly and willfully to give or accept any kickback or any illegal payment in connection with any qualified campaign expense of a candidate, or his authorized committees, who receives payments under section 9037.

(2) Any person who violates the provisions of paragraph (1) shall be fined not more than $10,000, or imprisoned not more than 5 years, or both.

(3) In addition to the penalty provided by paragraph (2), any person who accepts any kickback or illegal payment in connection with any qualified campaign expense of a candidate or his authorized committees shall pay to the Secretary for deposit in the matching payment account, an amount equal to 125 percent of the kickback or payment received.

Amendments

• **1974, Federal Election Campaign Act Amendments of 1974 (P.L. 93-443)**

P.L. 93-443, § 408(c):

Amended subtitle H by striking out chapter 96, containing Code Sec. 9021, and inserting new chapter 96. **Effective** for tax years beginning after 12-31-74. Prior to amendment, chapter 96 read as follows:

CHAPTER 96—PRESIDENTIAL ELECTION CAMPAIGN FUND ADVISORY BOARD

SEC. 9021. ESTABLISHMENT OF ADVISORY BOARD.

(a) Establishment of Board.—There is hereby established an advisory board to be known as the Presidential Election Campaign Fund Advisory Board (hereinafter in this section referred to as the "Board"). It shall be the duty and function of the Board to counsel and assist the Comptroller General of the United States in the performance of the duties and functions imposed on him under the Presidential Election Campaign Fund Act.

(b) Composition of Board.—The Board shall be composed of the following members:

(1) the majority leader and minority leader of the Senate and the Speaker and minority leader of the House of Representatives, who shall serve ex officio;

(2) two members representing each political party which is a major party (as defined in section 9002(6)), which members shall be appointed by the Comptroller General from recommendations submitted by such political party; and

(3) three members representing the general public, which members shall be selected by the members described in paragraphs (1) and (2).

The terms of the first members of the Board described in paragraphs (2) and (3) shall expire on the sixtieth day after the date of the first presidential election following January 1, 1973, and the terms of subsequent members described in paragraphs (2) and (3) shall begin on the sixty-first day after the date of a presidential election and expire on the sixtieth day following the date of the subsequent presidential election. The Board shall elect a Chairman from its members.

(c) Compensation.—Members of the Board (other than members described in subsection (b)(1)) shall receive compensation at the rate of $75 a day for each day they are engaged in performing duties and functions as such members, including traveltime, and, while away from their homes or regular places of business, shall be allowed travel expenses, including per diem in lieu of subsistence, as authorized by law for persons in the Government service employed intermittently.

(d) Status.—Service by an individual as a member of the Board shall not, for purposes of any other law of the United States be considered as service as an officer or employee of the United States.

• **1971, Revenue Act of 1971 (P.L. 92-178)**

P.L. 92-178, § 801:

Added Code Sec. 9021. **Effective** 12-10-71.

[The next page is 5401.]

Sec. 9042(c)(2)

Subtitle I—Trust Fund Code

[Sec. 9500]

SEC. 9500. SHORT TITLE.

This subtitle may be cited as the "Trust Fund Code of 1981".

Amendments

• **1981, Black Lung Benefits Revenue Act of 1981 (P.L. 97-119)**

P.L. 97-119, §103(a):

Added Code Sec. 9500 of new subtitle I. **Effective** 1-1-82.

CHAPTER 98—TRUST FUND CODE

Subchapter A.   Establishment of Trust Funds.
Subchapter B.   General provisions.

Subchapter A—Establishment of Trust Funds

Sec. 9501.   Black Lung Disability Trust Fund.
Sec. 9502.   Airport and Airway Trust Fund.
Sec. 9503.   Highway Trust Fund.
Sec. 9504.   Sport Fish Restoration and Boating Trust Fund.
Sec. 9505.   Harbor Maintenance Trust Fund.
Sec. 9506.   Inland Waterways Trust Fund.
Sec. 9507.   Hazardous Substance Superfund.
Sec. 9508.   Leaking Underground Storage Tank Trust Fund.
Sec. 9509.   Oil Spill Liability Trust Fund.
Sec. 9510.   Vaccine Injury Compensation Trust Fund.
Sec. 9511.   Patient-centered outcomes research trust fund.

[Sec. 9501]

SEC. 9501. BLACK LUNG DISABILITY TRUST FUND.

[Sec. 9501(a)]

(a) CREATION OF TRUST FUND.—

(1) IN GENERAL.—There is established in the Treasury of the United States a trust fund to be known as the "Black Lung Disability Trust Fund", consisting of such amounts as may be appropriated or credited to the Black Lung Disability Trust Fund.

(2) TRUSTEES.—The trustees of the Black Lung Disability Trust Fund shall be the Secretary of the Treasury, the Secretary of Labor, and the Secretary of Health and Human Services.

Amendments

• **1982, Tax Equity and Fiscal Responsibility Act of 1982 (P.L. 97-248)**

P.L. 97-248, §281(c)(2):

Amended the section heading. **Effective** 9-1-82. Prior to amendment, the section heading of Code Sec. 9501 read as follows: "ESTABLISHMENT OF BLACK LUNG DISABILITY TRUST FUND."

• **1981, Black Lung Benefits Revenue Act of 1981 (P.L. 97-119)**

P.L. 97-119, §103(a):

Added Code Sec. 9501(a) of new subtitle I. **Effective** 1-1-82.

P.L. 97-119, §103(d)(2), provides:

(2) Savings provisions.—The Black Lung Disability Trust Fund established by the amendments made by this section shall be treated for all purposes of law as the continuation of the Black Lung Disability Trust Fund established by section 3 of the Black Lung Benefits Revenue Act of 1977. Any reference in any law to the Black Lung Disability Trust Fund established by such section 3 shall be deemed to include a reference to the Black Lung Disability Trust Fund established by the amendments made by this section.

[Sec. 9501(b)]

(b) TRANSFER OF CERTAIN TAXES; OTHER RECEIPTS.—

(1) TRANSFER TO BLACK LUNG DISABILITY TRUST FUND OF AMOUNTS EQUIVALENT TO CERTAIN TAXES.—There are hereby appropriated to the Black Lung Disability Trust Fund amounts equivalent to the taxes received in the Treasury under section 4121 or subchapter B of chapter 42.

(2) CERTAIN REPAID AMOUNTS, ETC.—The following amounts shall be credited to the Black Lung Disability Trust Fund:

(A) Amounts repaid or recovered under subsection (b) of section 424 of the Black Lung Benefits Act (including interest thereon).

(B) Amounts paid as fines or penalties, or interest thereon, under section 423, 431, or 432 of the Black Lung Benefits Act.

(C) Amounts paid into the Black Lung Disability Trust Fund by a trust described in section 501(c)(21).

Amendments

• **1981, Black Lung Benefits Revenue Act of 1981 (P.L. 97-119)**

P.L. 97-119, §103(a):

Added Code Sec. 9501(b) of new subtitle I. **Effective** 1-1-82.

[Sec. 9501(c)]

(c) REPAYABLE ADVANCES.—

(1) AUTHORIZATION.—There are authorized to be appropriated to the Black Lung Disability Trust Fund, as repayable advances, such sums as may from time to time be necessary to make the expenditures described in subsection (d).

(2) REPAYMENT WITH INTEREST.—Repayable advances made to the Black Lung Disability Trust Fund shall be repaid, and interest on such advances shall be paid, to the general fund of the Treasury when the Secretary of the Treasury determines that moneys are available in the Black Lung Disability Trust Fund for such purposes.

(3) RATE OF INTEREST.—Interest on advances made pursuant to this subsection shall be at a rate determined by the Secretary of the Treasury (as of the close of the calendar month preceding the month in which the advance is made) to be equal to the current average market yield on outstanding marketable obligations of the United States with remaining periods to maturity comparable to the anticipated period during which the advance will be outstanding.

ESTABLISHMENT OF TRUST FUNDS

Amendments

• **2008, Energy Improvement and Extension Act of 2008 (P.L. 110-343)**

P.L. 110-343, Division B, §113(b) (as amended by P.L. 113-295, §210(b), Division A), provides:

(b) RESTRUCTURING OF TRUST FUND DEBT.—

(1) DEFINITIONS.—For purposes of this subsection—

(A) MARKET VALUE OF THE OUTSTANDING REPAYABLE ADVANCES, PLUS ACCRUED INTEREST.—The term "market value of the outstanding repayable advances, plus accrued interest" means the present value (determined by the Secretary of the Treasury as of the refinancing date and using the Treasury rate as the discount rate) of the stream of principal and interest payments derived assuming that each repayable advance that is outstanding on the refinancing date is due on the 30th anniversary of the end of the fiscal year in which the advance was made to the Trust Fund, and that all such principal and interest payments are made on September 30 of the applicable fiscal year.

(B) REFINANCING DATE.—The term "refinancing date" means the date occurring 2 days after the enactment of this Act.

(C) REPAYABLE ADVANCE.—The term "repayable advance" means an amount that has been appropriated to the Trust Fund in order to make benefit payments and other expenditures that are authorized under section 9501 of the Internal Revenue Code of 1986 and are required to be repaid when the Secretary of the Treasury determines that monies are available in the Trust Fund for such purpose.

(D) TREASURY RATE.—The term "Treasury rate" means a rate determined by the Secretary of the Treasury, taking into consideration current market yields on outstanding marketable obligations of the United States of comparable maturities.

(E) TREASURY 1-YEAR RATE.—The term "Treasury 1-year rate" means a rate determined by the Secretary of the Treasury, taking into consideration current market yields on outstanding marketable obligations of the United States with remaining periods to maturity of approximately 1 year, to have been in effect as of the close of business 1 business day prior to the date on which the Trust Fund issues obligations to the Secretary of the Treasury under paragraph (2)(B).

(F) TRUST FUND.—The term "Trust Fund" means the Black Lung Disability Trust Fund established under section 9501 of the Internal Revenue Code of 1986.

(2) REFINANCING OF OUTSTANDING PRINCIPAL OF REPAYABLE ADVANCES AND UNPAID INTEREST ON SUCH ADVANCES.—

(A) TRANSFER TO GENERAL FUND.—On the refinancing date, the Trust Fund shall repay the market value of the outstanding repayable advances, plus accrued interest, by transferring into the general fund of the Treasury the following sums:

(i) The proceeds from obligations that the Trust Fund shall issue to the Secretary of the Treasury in such amounts as the Secretaries of Labor and the Treasury shall determine and bearing interest at the Treasury rate, and that shall be in such forms and denominations and be subject to such other terms and conditions, including maturity, as the Secretary of the Treasury shall prescribe.

(ii) All, or that portion, of the appropriation made to the Trust Fund pursuant to paragraph (3) that is needed to cover the difference defined in that paragraph.

(B) REPAYMENT OF OBLIGATIONS.—In the event that the Trust Fund is unable to repay the obligations that it has issued to the Secretary of the Treasury under subparagraph (A)(i) and this subparagraph, or is unable to make benefit payments and other authorized expenditures, the Trust Fund shall issue obligations to the Secretary of the Treasury in such amounts as may be necessary to make such repayments, payments, and expenditures, with a maturity of 1 year, and bearing interest at the Treasury 1-year rate. These obligations shall be in such forms and denominations and be subject to such other terms and conditions as the Secretary of the Treasury shall prescribe.

(C) AUTHORITY TO ISSUE OBLIGATIONS.—The Trust Fund is authorized to issue obligations to the Secretary of the Treasury under subparagraphs (A)(i) and (B). The Secretary of the Treasury is authorized to purchase such obligations of the Trust Fund. For the purposes of making such purchases, the Secretary of the Treasury may use as a public debt transaction the proceeds from the sale of any securities issued under chapter 31 of title 31, United States Code, and the purposes for which securities may be issued under such chapter are extended to include any purchase of such Trust Fund obligations under this subparagraph.

(3) ONE-TIME APPROPRIATION.—There is hereby appropriated to the Trust Fund an amount sufficient to pay to the general fund of the Treasury the difference between—

(A) the market value of the outstanding repayable advances, plus accrued interest; and

(B) the proceeds from the obligations issued by the Trust Fund to the Secretary of the Treasury under paragraph (2)(A)(i).

(4) PREPAYMENT OF TRUST FUND OBLIGATIONS.—The Trust Fund is authorized to repay any obligation issued to the Secretary of the Treasury under subparagraphs (A)(i) and (B) of paragraph (2) prior to its maturity date by paying a prepayment price that would, if the obligation being prepaid (including all unpaid interest accrued thereon through the date of prepayment) were purchased by a third party and held to the maturity date of such obligation, produce a yield to the third-party purchaser for the period from the date of purchase to the maturity date of such obligation substantially equal to the Treasury yield on outstanding marketable obligations of the United States having a comparable maturity to this period.

• **1981, Black Lung Benefits Revenue Act of 1981 (P.L. 97-119)**

P.L. 97-119, §103(a):

Added Code Sec. 9501(c) of new subtitle I. **Effective** 12-1-82, except for Code Sec. 9501(c)(3), which is **effective** for advances made after 12-31-81.

[Sec. 9501(d)]

(d) EXPENDITURES FROM TRUST FUND.—Amounts in the Black Lung Disability Trust Fund shall be available, as provided by appropriation Acts, for—

(1) the payment of benefits under section 422 of the Black Lung Benefits Act in any case in which the Secretary of Labor determines that—

(A) the operator liable for the payment of such benefits—

(i) has not commenced payment of such benefits within 30 days after the date of an initial determination of eligibility by the Secretary of Labor, or

(ii) has not made a payment within 30 days after that payment is due,

except that, in the case of a claim filed on or after the date of the enactment of the Black Lung Benefits Revenue Act of 1981, amounts will be available under this subparagraph only for benefits accruing after the date of such initial determination, or

(B) there is no operator who is liable for the payment of such benefits,

(2) the payment of obligations incurred by the Secretary of Labor with respect to all claims of miners or their survivors in which the miner's last coal mine employment was before January 1, 1970,

(3) the repayment into the Treasury of the United States of an amount equal to the sum of the amounts expended by the Secretary of Labor for claims under part C of the Black Lung Benefits Act which were paid before April 1, 1978, except that the Black Lung Disability Trust Fund shall not be obligated to pay or reimburse any such amounts which are attributable to periods of eligibility before January 1, 1974,

(4) the repayment of, and the payment of interest on, repayable advances to the Black Lung Disability Trust Fund,

(5) the payment of all expenses of administration on or after March 1, 1978—

(A) incurred by the Department of Labor or the Department of Health and Human Services under part C of the Black Lung Benefits Act (other than under section 427(a) or 433), or

(B) incurred by the Department of the Treasury in administering subchapter B of chapter 32 and in carrying out its responsibilities with respect to the Black Lung Disability Trust Fund,

(6) the reimbursement of operators for amounts paid by such operators (other than as penalties or interest) before April 1, 1978, in satisfaction (in whole or in part) of claims of miners whose last employment in coal mines was terminated before January 1, 1970, and

(7) the reimbursement of operators and insurers for amounts paid by such operators and insurers (other than amounts paid as penalties, interest, or attorney fees) at any time in satisfaction (in whole or in part) of any claim denied (within the meaning of section 402(i) of the Black Lung Benefits Act) before March 1, 1978, and which is or has been approved in accordance with the provisions of section 435 of the Black Lung Benefits Act.

For purposes of the preceding sentence, any reference to section 402(i), 422, or 435 of the Black Lung Benefits Act shall be treated as a reference to such section as in effect immediately after the enactment of this section.

Amendments

• **1981, Black Lung Benefits Revenue Act of 1981 (P.L. 97-119)**

P.L. 97-119, §103(a):

Added Code Sec. 9501(d) of new subtitle I. **Effective** 1-1-82.

ESTABLISHMENT OF TRUST FUNDS

[Sec. 9502]

SEC. 9502. AIRPORT AND AIRWAY TRUST FUND.

[Sec. 9502(a)]

(a) CREATION OF TRUST FUND.—There is established in the Treasury of the United States a trust fund to be known as the "Airport and Airway Trust Fund", consisting of such amounts as may be appropriated, credited, or paid into the Airport and Airway Trust Fund as provided in this section, section 9503(c)(5), or section 9602(b).

Amendments

• **2010, Hiring Incentives to Restore Employment Act (P.L. 111-147)**

P.L. 111-147, § 444(b)(1):

Amended Code Sec. 9502(a) by striking "section 9503(c)(7)" and inserting "section 9503(c)(5)". **Effective** for transfers relating to amounts paid and credits allowed after 3-18-2010.

• **2005, Safe, Accountable, Flexible, Efficient Transportation Equity Act: A Legacy for Users (P.L. 109-59)**

P.L. 109-59, § 11161(c)(2)(A):

Amended Code Sec. 9502(a) by striking "appropriated or credited to the Airport and Airway Trust Fund as provided in this section or section 9602(b)" and inserting "appropriated, credited, or paid into the Airport and Airway Trust Fund as provided in this section, section 9503(c)(7), or section 9602(b)". **Effective** for fuels or liquids removed, entered, or sold after 9-30-2005.

[Sec. 9502(b)]

(b) TRANSFERS TO AIRPORT AND AIRWAY TRUST FUND.—There are hereby appropriated to the Airport and Airway Trust Fund amounts equivalent to—

(1) the taxes received in the Treasury under—

(A) section 4041(c) (relating to aviation fuels),

(B) section 4043 (relating to surtax on fuel used in aircraft part of a fractional ownership program),

(C) sections 4261 and 4271 (relating to transportation by air), and

(D) section 4081 with respect to aviation gasoline and kerosene to the extent attributable to the rate specified in section 4081(a)(2)(C), and

(2) the amounts determined by the Secretary of the Treasury to be equivalent to the amounts of civil penalties collected under section 47107(m) of title 49, United States Code.

There shall not be taken into account under paragraph (1) so much of the taxes imposed by section 4081 as are determined at the rate specified in section 4081(a)(2)(B).

Amendments

• **2014, Government Reports Elimination Act of 2014 (P.L. 113-188)**

P.L. 113-188, § 1501(b)(2)(D):

Amended Code Sec. 9502(b)(2) by striking "47107(n)" and inserting "47107(m)". **Effective** 11-26-2014.

• **2012, FAA Modernization and Reform Act of 2012 (P.L. 112-95)**

P.L. 112-95, § 1103(a)(3):

Amended Code Sec. 9502(b)(1) by redesignating subparagraphs (B) and (C) as subparagraphs (C) and (D), respectively, and by inserting after subparagraph (A) a new subparagraph (B). **Effective** for fuel used after 3-31-2012.

• **2005, Safe, Accountable, Flexible, Efficient Transportation Equity Act: A Legacy for Users (P.L. 109-59)**

P.L. 109-59, § 11161(c)(2)(B)(i)-(ii):

Amended Code Sec. 9502(b)(1) by striking "subsections (c) and (e) of section 4041" in subparagraph (A) and inserting "section 4041(c)", and by striking "and aviation-grade kerosene" in subparagraph (C) and inserting "and kerosene to the extent attributable to the rate specified in section 4081(a)(2)(C)". **Effective** for fuels or liquids removed, entered, or sold after 9-30-2005.

• **2004, American Jobs Creation Act of 2004 (P.L. 108-357)**

P.L. 108-357, § 853(d)(2)(N):

Amended Code Sec. 9502(b)(1) by adding "and" at the end of subparagraph (B) and by striking subparagraphs (C) and (D) and inserting a new subparagraph (C). **Effective** for aviation-grade kerosene removed, entered, or sold after 12-31-2004. Prior to being stricken, Code Sec. 9502(b)(1)(C)-(D) read as follows:

(C) section 4081 (relating to gasoline) with respect to aviation gasoline, and

(D) section 4091 (relating to aviation fuel), and

P.L. 108-357, § 853(d)(2)(O):

Amended the last sentence of Code Sec. 9502(b). **Effective** for aviation-grade kerosene removed, entered, or sold after 12-31-2004. Prior to amendment, the last sentence of Code Sec. 9502(b) read as follows:

There shall not be taken into account under paragraph (1) so much of the taxes imposed by sections 4081 and 4091 as are determined at the rates specified in section 4081(a)(2)(B) or 4091(b)(2).

• **1998, IRS Restructuring and Reform Act of 1998 (P.L. 105-206)**

P.L. 105-206, § 6010(g)(2):

Amended Code Sec. 9502(b) by moving the sentence added by Act Sec. 1031(d)(1)(C) of P.L. 105-34 at the end of paragraph (1) to the end of the subsection. **Effective** as if included in the provision of P.L. 105-34 to which it relates [**effective** for taxes received on and after 10-1-97.—CCH].

• **1997, Taxpayer Relief Act of 1997 (P.L. 105-34)**

P.L. 105-34, § 1031(d)(1)(A)-(C):

Amended Code Sec. 9502(b)(1) by striking "(to the extent that the rate of the tax on such gasoline exceeds 4.3 cents per gallon)" after "aviation gasoline" in subparagraph (C), by striking "to the extent attributable to the Airport and Airway Trust Fund financing rate" after "aviation fuel)" in subparagraph (D), and by adding at the end a new flush sentence. **Effective** with respect to taxes received in the Treasury on and after 10-1-97.

• **1997, Airport and Airway Trust Fund Tax Reinstatement Act of 1997 (P.L. 105-2)**

P.L. 105-2, § 2(c)(1):

Amended Code Sec. 9502(b). **Effective** 2-28-97. For a rule concerning the look-back safe harbor for deposits, see P.L. 105-2, § 2(f), below. Prior to amendment, Code Sec. 9502(b) read as follows:

(b) TRANSFER TO AIRPORT AND AIRWAY TRUST FUND OF AMOUNTS EQUIVALENT TO CERTAIN TAXES.—There is hereby appropriated to the Airport and Airway Trust Fund—

(1) amounts equivalent to the taxes received in the Treasury after August 31, 1982, and before January 1, 1997, under subsections (c) and (e) of section 4041 (taxes on aviation fuel) and under sections 4261 and 4271 (taxes on transportation by air);

(2) amounts determined by the Secretary of the Treasury to be equivalent to the taxes received in the Treasury after August 31, 1982, and before January 1, 1997, under section 4081 (to the extent of 15 cents per gallon), with respect to gasoline used in aircraft;

(3) amounts determined by the Secretary to be equivalent to the taxes received in the Treasury before January 1, 1997, under section 4091 (to the extent attributable to the Airport and Airway Trust Fund financing rate);

(4) amounts determined by the Secretary of the Treasury to be equivalent to the taxes received in the Treasury after August 31, 1982, and before January 1, 1997 under section 4071 with respect to tires of the types used on aircraft; and

(5) amounts determined by the Secretary of the Treasury to be equivalent to the amounts of civil penalties collected under section 47107(n) of title 49, United States Code.

P.L. 105-2, § 2(f), provides:

(f) APPLICATION OF LOOK-BACK SAFE HARBOR FOR DEPOSITS.—Nothing in the look-back safe harbor prescribed in Treasury Regulation section 40.6302(c)-1(c)(2) shall be construed to permit such safe harbor to be used with respect to any tax unless such tax was imposed throughout the look-back period.

• **1996, Federal Aviation Reauthorization Act of 1996 (P.L. 104-264)**

P.L. 104-264, § 806(1)-(3):

Amended Code Sec. 9502(b)(3)-(5) by striking "and" at the end of subsection (b)(3), by striking the period at the end of subsection (b)(4) and adding "; and" and by adding paragraph (5). **Effective** for fiscal years beginning after 9-30-96. For a special rule, see Act Sec. 3(b), below.

P.L. 104-264, § 3(b), provides:

(b) LIMITATION ON STATUTORY CONSTRUCTION.—Nothing in this Act or any amendment made by this Act shall be construed as affecting funds made available for a fiscal year ending before October 1, 1996.

• **1996, Small Business Job Protection Act of 1996 (P.L. 104-188)**

P.L. 104-188, § 1609(c)(1):

Amended Code Sec. 9502(b) by striking "January 1, 1996" each place it appears and inserting "January 1, 1997". **Effective** 8-27-96.

P.L. 104-188, § 1609(g)(4)(D):

Amended Code Sec. 9502(b)(2) by striking "14 cents" and inserting "15 cents". **Effective** 8-27-96.

P.L. 104-188, § 1703(n)(10):

Amended Code Sec. 9502(b)(2) by inserting "and before" after "1982,". **Effective** as if included in the provision of P.L. 103-66 to which it relates.

ESTABLISHMENT OF TRUST FUNDS

• **1993, Omnibus Budget Reconciliation Act of 1993 (P.L. 103-66)**

P.L. 103-66, § 13242(d)(33):

Amended Code Sec. 9502(b)(2) by striking "(to the extent attributable to the Highway Trust Fund financing rate and the deficit reduction rate)" and inserting "(to the extent of 14 cents per gallon)". **Effective** 1-1-94.

• **1990, Omnibus Budget Reconciliation Act of 1990 (P.L. 101-508)**

P.L. 101-508, § 11213(c)(2):

Amended Code Sec. 9502(b)(2) by inserting "and the deficit reduction rate" after "financing rate". **Effective** 11-5-90. However, see Act Sec. 11213(f) in the amendment notes following Code Sec. 4051(c).

P.L. 101-508, § 11213(d)(3):

Amended Code Sec. 9502(b) by striking "January 1, 1991" each place it appears and inserting "January 1, 1996". **Effective** 11-5-90. However, see Act Sec. 11213(f) in the amendment notes following Code Sec. 4051(c).

• **1989, Omnibus Budget Reconciliation Act of 1989 (P.L. 101-239)**

P.L. 101-239, § 7822(b)(5):

Amended Code Sec. 9502(b)(3) by striking ", and" and inserting "; and". **Effective** as if included in the provision of P.L. 100-203 to which it relates.

• **1987, Airport and Airway Revenue Act of 1987 (P.L. 100-223)**

P.L. 100-223, § 402(a)(3):

Amended Code Sec. 9502(b) by striking out "January 1, 1988" each place it appears and inserting in lieu thereof "January 1, 1991". **Effective** 12-30-87.

• **1987, Revenue Act of 1987 (P.L. 100-203)**

P.L. 100-203, § 10502(d)(12):

Amended Code Sec. 9502(b) by striking out "and" at the end of paragraph (2), by redesignating paragraph (3) as paragraph (4), and by inserting after paragraph (2) new paragraph (3). **Effective** for sales after 3-31-88.

• **1986, Superfund Amendments and Reauthorization Act of 1986 (P.L. 99-499)**

P.L. 99-499, § 521(b)(2)(A)-(B):

Amended Code Sec. 9502(b) by striking out "subsections (c) and (d) of section 4041" in paragraph (1) and inserting in lieu thereof "subsections (c) and (e) of section 4041", and by striking out "section 4081" in paragraph (2) and inserting in lieu thereof "section 4081 (to the extent attributable to the Highway Trust Fund financing rate)". **Effective** 1-1-87.

• **1984, Deficit Reduction Act of 1984 (P.L. 98-369)**

P.L. 98-369, § 735(c)(15):

Amended Code Sec. 9502(b)(3) by striking out "under paragraphs (2) and (3) of section 4071(a), with respect to tires and tubes of types used on aircraft" and inserting in lieu thereof "under section 4071 with respect to tires of the types used on aircraft". **Effective** as if included in the provision of the Highway Revenue Act of 1982 to which it relates.

[Sec. 9502(c)]

(c) APPROPRIATION OF ADDITIONAL SUMS.—There are hereby authorized to be appropriated to the Airport and Airway Trust Fund such additional sums as may be required to make the expenditures referred to in subsection (d) of this section.

[Sec. 9502(d)]

(d) EXPENDITURES FROM AIRPORT AND AIRWAY TRUST FUND.—

(1) AIRPORT AND AIRWAY PROGRAM.—Amounts in the Airport and Airway Trust Fund shall be available, as provided by appropriation Acts, for making expenditures before October 1, 2028, to meet those obligations of the United States—

(A) incurred under title I of the Airport and Airway Development Act of 1970 or of the Airport and Airway Development Act Amendments of 1976 or of the Aviation Safety and Noise Abatement Act of 1979 (as such Acts were in effect on the date of enactment of the Fiscal Year 1981 Airport Development Authorization Act) or under the Fiscal Year 1981 Airport Development Authorization Act or the provisions of the Airport and Airway Improvement Act of 1982 or the Airport and Airway Safety and Capacity Expansion Act of 1987 or the Federal Aviation Administration Research, Engineering, and Development Authorization Act of 1990 or the Aviation Safety and Capacity Expansion Act of 1990 or the Airport and Airway Safety, Capacity, Noise Improvement, and Intermodal Transportation Act of 1992 or the Airport Improvement Program Temporary Extension Act of 1994 or the Federal Aviation Administration Authorization Act of 1994 or the Federal Aviation Reauthorization Act of 1996 or the provisions of the Omnibus Consolidated and Emergency Supplemental Appropriations Act, 1999 providing for payments from the Airport and Airway Trust Fund or the Interim Federal Aviation Administration Authorization Act or section 6002 of the 1999 Emergency Supplemental Appropriations Act, Public Law 106-59, or the Wendell H. Ford Aviation Investment and Reform Act for the 21st Century or the Aviation and Transportation Security Act or the Vision 100—Century of Aviation Reauthorization Act or any joint resolution making continuing appropriations for the fiscal year 2008 or the Department of Transportation Appropriations Act, 2008 or the Airport and Airway Extension Act of 2008 or the Federal Aviation Administration Extension Act of 2008 or the Federal Aviation Administration Extension Act of 2008, Part II or the Federal Aviation Administration Extension Act of 2009 or any joint resolution making continuing appropriations for the fiscal year 2010 or the Fiscal Year 2010 Federal Aviation Administration Extension Act or the Fiscal Year 2010 Federal Aviation Administration Extension Act, Part II or the Federal Aviation Administration Extension Act of 2010 or the Airport and Airway Extension Act of 2010 or the Airport and Airway Extension Act of 2010, Part II or the Airline Safety and Federal Aviation Administration Extension Act of 2010 or the Airport and Airway Extension Act of 2010, Part III or the Airport and Airway Extension Act of 2010, Part IV or the Airport and Airway Extension Act of 2011 or the Airport and Airway Extension Act of 2011, Part II or the Airport and Airway Extension Act of 2011, Part III or the Airport and Airway Extension Act of 2011, Part IV or the Airport and Airway Extension Act of 2011, Part V or the Airport and Airway Extension Act of 2012 or the FAA Modernization and Reform Act of 2012 or the Airport and Airway Extension Act of 2015 or the Airport and Airway Extension Act of 2016 or the FAA Extension, Safety, and Security Act of 2016 or the Disaster Tax Relief and Airport and Airway Extension Act of 2017 or the Airport and Airway Extension Act of 2018 or the Airport and Airway Extension Act of 2018, Part II or the FAA Reauthorization Act of 2018 or title II of division B of the Continuing Appropriations Act, 2024 and Other Extensions Act or the Airport and Airway Extension Act of 2023, Part II or the Airport and Airway Extension Act of 2024 or the Airport and Airway Extension Act of 2024, Part II or the FAA Reauthorization Act of 2024;

(B) heretofore or hereafter incurred under part A of subtitle VII of title 49, United States Code, which are attributable to planning, research and development, construction, or operation and maintenance of—

(i) air traffic control,

(ii) air navigation,

(iii) communications, or

(iv) supporting services,

for the airway system; or

(C) for those portions of the administrative expenses of the Department of Transportation which are attributable to activities described in subparagraph (A) or (B).

Any reference in subparagraph (A) to an Act shall be treated as a reference to such Act and the corresponding provisions (if any) of title 49, United States Code, as such Act and provisions were in effect on the date of the enactment of the last Act referred to in subparagraph (A).

(2) TRANSFERS FROM AIRPORT AND AIRWAY TRUST FUND ON ACCOUNT OF CERTAIN REFUNDS.—The Secretary of the Treasury shall pay from time to time from the Airport and Airway Trust Fund into the general fund of the Treasury amounts equivalent to the amounts paid after August 31, 1982, in respect of fuel used in aircraft, under section 6420 (relating to amounts paid in respect of gasoline used on farms), 6421 (relating to amounts paid in respect of gasoline used for certain nonhighway purposes), or 6427 (relating to fuels not used for taxable purposes) (other than subsection (l)(4) thereof).

(3) TRANSFERS FROM THE AIRPORT AND AIRWAY TRUST FUND ON ACCOUNT OF CERTAIN SECTION 34 CREDITS.—The Secretary of the Treasury shall pay from time to time from the Airport and Airway Trust Fund into the general fund of the Treasury amounts equivalent to the credits allowed

ESTABLISHMENT OF TRUST FUNDS

under section 34 (other than payments made by reason of paragraph (4) of section 6427(l)) with respect to fuel used after August 31, 1982. Such amounts shall be transferred on the basis of estimates by the Secretary of the Treasury, and proper adjustments shall be made in amounts subsequently transferred to the extent prior estimates were in excess of or less than the credits allowed.

(4) TRANSFERS FOR REFUNDS AND CREDITS NOT TO EXCEED TRUST FUND REVENUES ATTRIBUTABLE TO FUEL USED.—The amounts payable from the Airport and Airway Trust Fund under paragraph (2) or (3) shall not exceed the amounts required to be appropriated to such Trust Fund with respect to fuel so used.

(5) TRANSFERS FROM AIRPORT AND AIRWAY TRUST FUND ON ACCOUNT OF REFUNDS OF TAXES ON TRANSPORTATION BY AIR.—The Secretary of the Treasury shall pay from time to time from the Airport and Airway Trust Fund into the general fund of the Treasury amounts equivalent to the amounts paid after December 31, 1995, under section 6402 (relating to authority to make credits or refunds) or section 6415 (relating to credits or refunds to persons who collected certain taxes) in respect of taxes under sections 4261 and 4271.

(6) TRANSFERS FROM THE AIRPORT AND AIRWAY TRUST FUND ON ACCOUNT OF CERTAIN AIRPORTS.—The Secretary of the Treasury may transfer from the Airport and Airway Trust Fund to the Secretary of Transportation or the Administrator of the Federal Aviation Administration an amount to make a payment to an airport affected by a diversion that is the subject of an administrative action under paragraph (3) or a civil action under paragraph (4) of section 47107(m) of title 49, United States Code.

Amendments

• **2024, FAA Reauthorization Act of 2024 (P.L. 118-63)**

P.L. 118-63, §1301(a)(1)-(2):

Amended Code Sec. 9502(d)(1) in the matter preceding subparagraph (A) by striking "May 11, 2024" and inserting "October 1, 2028"; and in subparagraph (A) by striking the semicolon at the end and inserting "or the FAA Reauthorization Act of 2024;". **Effective** 5-16-2024.

• **2024, Airport and Airway Extension Act of 2024, Part II (P.L. 118-60)**

P.L. 118-60, §201(a), provides:

SEC. 201. EXPENDITURE AUTHORITY FROM AIRPORT AND AIRWAY TRUST FUND.

(a) Sections 9502(d)(1) and 9502(e)(2) of the Internal Revenue Code of 1986 shall be applied by substituting "May 18, 2024" for "May 11, 2024".

P.L. 118-60, §201(b):

Amended Code Sec. 9502(d)(1)(A) by striking the semicolon at the end and inserting "or the Airport and Airway Extension Act of 2024, Part II;". **Effective** 5-10-2024.

• **2024, Airport and Airway Extension Act of 2024 (P.L. 118-41)**

P.L. 118-41, §201(a)(1)-(2):

Amended Code Sec. 9502(d)(1) in the matter preceding subparagraph (A) by striking "March 9, 2024" and inserting "May 11, 2024"; and in subparagraph (A) by striking the semicolon at the end and inserting "or the Airport and Airway Extension Act of 2024;". **Effective** 3-8-2024.

• **2023, Airport and Airway Extension Act of 2023, Part II (P.L. 118-34)**

P.L. 118-34, §201(a)(1)-(2):

Amended Code Sec. 9502(d)(1) in the matter preceding subparagraph (A) by striking "January 1, 2024" and inserting "March 9, 2024"; and in subparagraph (A) by striking the semicolon at the end and inserting "or the Airport and Airway Extension Act of 2023, Part II;". **Effective** 12-26-2023.

• **2023, Continuing Appropriations Act, 2024 and Other Extensions Act (P.L. 118-15)**

P.L. 118-15, §2211(a)(1)-(2):

Amended Code Sec. 9502(d)(1) in the matter preceding subparagraph (A) by striking "October 1, 2023" and inserting "January 1, 2024"; and in subparagraph (A) by striking the semicolon at the end and inserting "or title II of division B of the Continuing Appropriations Act, 2024 and Other Extensions Act;". **Effective** 9-30-2023.

• **2018, FAA Reauthorization Act of 2018 (P.L. 115-254)**

P.L. 115-254, §801(a)(1)-(2):

Amended Code Sec. 9502(d)(1) in the matter preceding subparagraph (A) by striking "October 1, 2018" and inserting "October 1, 2023"; and in subparagraph (A) by striking the semicolon at the end and inserting "or the FAA Reauthorization Act of 2018;". **Effective** 10-5-2018.

• **2018, Airport and Airway Extension Act of 2018, Part II (P.L. 115-250)**

P.L. 115-250, §4(a), provides:

(a) Sections 9502(d)(1) and 9502(e)(2) of the Internal Revenue Code of 1986 shall be applied by substituting "October 8, 2018" for "October 1, 2018".

P.L. 115-250, §4(b):

Amended Code Sec. 9502(d)(1)(A) by striking the semicolon at the end and inserting "or the Airport and Airway Extension Act of 2018, Part II;".

• **2018, Airport and Airway Extension Act of 2018 (P.L. 115-141)**

P.L. 115-141, §201(a)(1)-(2), Div. M:

Amended Code Sec. 9502(d)(1) in the matter preceding subparagraph (A) by striking "April 1, 2018" and inserting "October 1, 2018"; and in subparagraph (A) by striking the semicolon at the end and inserting "or the Airport and Airway Extension Act of 2018;". **Effective** 3-23-2018.

• **2018, Tax Technical Corrections Act of 2018 (P.L. 115-141)**

P.L. 115-141, §401(a)(340), Div. U:

Amended Code Sec. 9502(d)(2) by striking "farms," and inserting "farms)". **Effective** 3-23-2018.

• **2017, Disaster Tax Relief and Airport and Airway Extension Act of 2017 (P.L. 115-63)**

P.L. 115-63, §201(a)(1)-(2):

Amended Code Sec. 9502(d)(1) by striking "October 1, 2017" in the matter preceding subparagraph (A) and inserting "April 1, 2018"; and by striking the semicolon at the end of subparagraph (A) and inserting "or the Disaster Tax Relief and Airport and Airway Extension Act of 2017;". **Effective** 9-29-2017.

• **2016, FAA Extension, Safety, and Security Act of 2016 (P.L. 114-190)**

P.L. 114-190, §1201(a)(1)-(2):

Amended Code Sec. 9502(d)(1) by striking "July 16, 2016" in the matter preceding subparagraph (A) and inserting "October 1, 2017"; and by striking the semicolon at the end of subparagraph (A) and inserting "or the FAA Extension, Safety, and Security Act of 2016;". **Effective** 7-15-2016.

• **2016, Airport and Airway Extension Act of 2016 (P.L. 114-141)**

P.L. 114-141, §201(a)(1)-(2):

Amended Code Sec. 9502(d)(1) by striking "April 1, 2016" in the matter preceding subparagraph (A) and inserting "July 16, 2016"; and by striking the semicolon at the end of subparagraph (A) and inserting "or the Airport and Airway Extension Act of 2016;". **Effective** 3-30-2016.

• **2015, Airport and Airway Extension Act of 2015 (P.L. 114-55)**

P.L. 114-55, §201(a)(1)-(2):

Amended Code Sec. 9502(d)(1) by striking "October 1, 2015" in the matter preceding subparagraph (A) and inserting "April 1, 2016", and by striking the semicolon at the end of subparagraph (A) and inserting "or the Airport and Airway Extension Act of 2015;". **Effective** 9-30-2015.

• **2014, Government Reports Elimination Act of 2014 (P.L. 113-188)**

P.L. 113-188, §1501(b)(2)(D):

Amended Code Sec. 9502(d)(6) by striking "47107(n)" and inserting "47107(m)". **Effective** 11-26-2014.

• **2012, FAA Modernization and Reform Act of 2012 (P.L. 112-95)**

P.L. 112-95, §1102(a)(1)-(2):

Amended Code Sec. 9502(d)(1) by striking "February 18, 2012" in the matter preceding subparagraph (A) and inserting "October 1, 2015", and by striking the semicolon at the end of subparagraph (A) and inserting "or the FAA Modernization and Reform Act of 2012;". **Effective** 2-18-2012.

• **2012, Airport and Airway Extension Act of 2012 (P.L. 112-91)**

P.L. 112-91, §3(a)(1)-(2):

Amended Code Sec. 9502(d)(1) by striking "February 1, 2012" and inserting "February 18, 2012"; and by inserting "or the Airport and Airway Extension Act of 2012" before the semicolon at the end subparagraph (A). **Effective** 2-1-2012.

• **2011, Airport and Airway Extension Act of 2011, Part V (P.L. 112-30)**

P.L. 112-30, §203(a)(1)-(2):

Amended Code Sec. 9502(d)(1) by striking "September 17, 2011" and inserting "February 1, 2012"; and by inserting "or the Airport and Airway Extension Act of 2011, Part V" before the semicolon at the end of subparagraph (A). **Effective** 9-17-2011.

• **2011, Airport and Airway Extension Act of 2011, Part IV (P.L. 112-27)**

P.L. 112-27, §3(a)(1)-(2):

Amended Code Sec. 9502(d)(1) by striking "July 23, 2011" and inserting "September 17, 2011"; and by inserting "or the Airport and Airway Extension Act of 2011, Part IV" before the semicolon at the end of subparagraph (A). **Effective** 7-23-2011.

• **2011, Airport and Airway Extension Act of 2011, Part III (P.L. 112-21)**

P.L. 112-21, §3(a)(1)-(2):

Amended Code Sec. 9502(d)(1) by striking "July 1, 2011" and inserting "July 23, 2011"; and by inserting "or the Airport and Airway Extension Act of 2011, Part III" before the semicolon at the end of subparagraph (A). **Effective** 7-1-2011.

ESTABLISHMENT OF TRUST FUNDS

• **2011, Airport and Airway Extension Act of 2011, Part II (P.L. 112-16)**

P.L. 112-16, §3(a)(1)-(2):

Amended Code Sec. 9502(d)(1) by striking "June 1, 2011" and inserting "July 1, 2011"; and by inserting "or the Airport and Airway Extension Act of 2011, Part II" before the semicolon at the end of subparagraph (A). **Effective 6-1-2011.**

• **2011, Airport and Airway Extension Act of 2011 (P.L. 112-7)**

P.L. 112-7, §3(a)(1)-(2):

Amended Code Sec. 9502(d)(1) by striking "April 1, 2011" and inserting "June 1, 2011"; and by inserting "or the Airport and Airway Extension Act of 2011" before the semicolon at the end of subparagraph (A). **Effective 4-1-2011.**

• **2010, Airport and Airway Extension Act of 2010, Part IV (P.L. 111-329)**

P.L. 111-329, §3(a)(1)-(2):

Amended Code Sec. 9502(d)(1) by striking "January 1, 2011" and inserting "April 1, 2011", and by inserting "or the Airport and Airway Extension Act of 2010, Part IV" before the semicolon at the end of subparagraph (A). **Effective 1-1-2011.**

• **2010, Airport and Airway Extension Act of 2010, Part III (P.L. 111-249)**

P.L. 111-249, §3(a)(1)-(2):

Amended Code Sec. 9502(d)(1) by striking "October 1, 2010" and inserting "January 1, 2011"; and by inserting "or the Airport and Airway Extension Act of 2010, Part III" before the semicolon at the end of subparagraph (A). **Effective 10-1-2010.**

• **2010, Airline Safety and Federal Aviation Administration Extension Act of 2010 (P.L. 111-216)**

P.L. 111-216, §102(a)(1)-(2):

Amended Code Sec. 9502(d)(1) by striking "August 2, 2010" and inserting "October 1, 2010"; and by inserting "or the Airline Safety and Federal Aviation Administration Extension Act of 2010" before the semicolon at the end of subparagraph (A). **Effective 8-2-2010.**

• **2010, Airport and Airway Extension Act of 2010, Part II (P.L. 111-197)**

P.L. 111-197, §3(a)(1)-(2):

Amended Code Sec. 9502(d)(1) by striking "July 4, 2010" and inserting "August 2, 2010"; and by inserting "or the Airport and Airway Extension Act of 2010, Part II" before the semicolon at the end of subparagraph (A). **Effective 7-4-2010.**

• **2010, Airport and Airway Extension Act of 2010 (P.L. 111-161)**

P.L. 111-161, §3(a)(1)-(2):

Amended Code Sec. 9502(d)(1) by striking "May 1, 2010" and inserting "July 4, 2010"; and by inserting "or the Airport and Airway Extension Act of 2010" before the semicolon at the end of subparagraph (A). **Effective 5-1-2010.**

• **2010, Federal Aviation Administration Extension Act of 2010 (P.L. 111-153)**

P.L. 111-153, §3(a)(1)-(2):

Amended Code Sec. 9502(d)(1) by striking "April 1, 2010" and inserting "May 1, 2010"; and by inserting "or the Federal Aviation Administration Extension Act of 2010" before the semicolon at the end of subparagraph (A). **Effective 4-1-2010.**

• **2009, Fiscal Year 2010 Federal Aviation Administration Extension Act, Part II (P.L. 111-116)**

P.L. 111-116, §3(a)(1)-(2):

Amended Code Sec. 9502(d)(1) by striking "January 1, 2010" and inserting "April 1, 2010"; and by inserting "or the Fiscal Year 2010 Federal Aviation Administration Extension Act, Part II" before the semicolon at the end of subparagraph (A). **Effective 1-1-2010.**

• **2009, Fiscal Year 2010 Federal Aviation Administration Extension Act (P.L. 111-69)**

P.L. 111-69, §3(a)(1)-(2):

Amended Code Sec. 9502(d)(1) by striking "October 1, 2009" and inserting "January 1, 2010"; and by inserting "or the Fiscal Year 2010 Federal Aviation Administration Extension Act" before the semicolon at the end of subparagraph (A). **Effective 10-1-2009.**

• **2009, (P.L. 111-68)**

P.L. 111-68, §156(b), provides:

(b) Subsections (d)(1) and (e)(2) of section 9502 of such Code shall each be applied by substituting the date that is 1 day after the date specified in section 106(3) [October 31, 2009] of this joint resolution for "October 1, 2009".

P.L. 111-68, §156(c):

Amended Code Sec. 9502(d)(1)(A) by inserting "or any joint resolution making continuing appropriations for the fiscal year 2010" before the semicolon at the end. **Effective 10-1-2009.**

• **2009, Federal Aviation Administration Extension Act of 2009 (P.L. 111-12)**

P.L. 111-12, §3(a)(1)-(2):

Amended Code Sec. 9502(d)(1) by striking "April 1, 2009" and inserting "October 1, 2009", and by inserting "or the Federal Aviation Administration Extension Act of 2009" before the semicolon at the end of subparagraph (A). **Effective 4-1-2009.**

• **2008, Federal Aviation Administration Extension Act of 2008, Part II (P.L. 110-330)**

P.L. 110-330, §3(a)(1)-(2):

Amended Code Sec. 9502(d)(1) by striking "October 1, 2008" and inserting "April 1, 2009", and by inserting "or the Federal Aviation Administration Extension Act of 2008, Part II" before the semicolon at the end of subparagraph (A). **Effective 10-1-2008.**

• **2008, Federal Aviation Administration Extension Act of 2008 (P.L. 110-253)**

P.L. 110-253, §3(a)(1)-(2):

Amended Code Sec. 9502(d)(1) by striking "July 1, 2008" and inserting "October 1, 2008", and by inserting "or the Federal Aviation Administration Extension Act of 2008" before the semicolon at the end of subparagraph (A). **Effective 7-1-2008.**

• **2008, Airport and Airway Extension Act of 2008 (P.L. 110-190)**

P.L. 110-190, §3(a)(1)-(2):

Amended Code Sec. 9502(d)(1) by striking "March 1, 2008" and inserting "July 1, 2008", and by inserting "or the Airport and Airway Extension Act of 2008" before the semicolon at the end of subparagraph (A). **Effective 3-1-2008.**

• **2007, Department of Transportation Appropriations Act, 2008 (P.L. 110-161)**

P.L. 110-161, §116(c)(1)(A)-(B):

Amended Code Sec. 9502(d)(1) by striking "October 1, 2007" and inserting "March 1, 2008", and by inserting "or the Department of Transportation Appropriations Act, 2008" in subparagraph (A) before the semicolon at the end. **Effective 10-1-2007.**

• **2007 (P.L. 110-92)**

P.L. 110-92, §149(a), provides:

SEC. 149. (a) Sections 4081(d)(2)(B), 4261(j)(1)(A)(ii), 4271(d)(1)(A)(ii), 9502(d)(1), and 9502(f)(2) of the Internal Revenue Code of 1986 shall each be applied by substituting the date specified in section 106(3) of this joint resolution [November 16, 2007.—CCH] for "September 30, 2007" or "October 1, 2007", as the case may be.

P.L. 110-92, §149(b):

Amended Code Sec. 9502(d)(1)(A) by inserting "or any joint resolution making continuing appropriations for the fiscal year 2008" before the semicolon at the end. **Effective 9-29-2007.**

• **2006, Tax Relief and Health Care Act of 2006 (P.L. 109-432)**

P.L. 109-432, Division A, §420(b)(5)(A)-(B):

Amended Code Sec. 9502(d) by striking "and (l)(5)" following "subsection (l)(4)" in paragraph (2), and by striking "or (5)" following "paragraph (4)" in paragraph (3). **Effective** for kerosene sold after 9-30-2005. For special rules, see Act Sec. 420(c)(2) and (d), below.

P.L. 109-432, Division A, §420(c)(2) and (d), provide:

(c) EFFECTIVE DATE.—

* * *

(2) SPECIAL RULE FOR PENDING CLAIMS.—In the case of kerosene sold for use in aviation (other than kerosene to which section 6427(l)(4)(C)(ii) of the Internal Revenue Code of 1986 (as added by subsection (a)) applies or kerosene to which section 6427(l)(5) of such Code (as redesignated by subsection (b)) applies) after September 30, 2005, and before the date of the enactment of this Act, the ultimate purchaser shall be treated as having waived the right to payment under section 6427(l)(1) of such Code and as having assigned such right to the ultimate vendor if such ultimate vendor has met the requirements of subparagraph (A), (B), or (D) of section 6416(a)(1) of such Code.

(d) SPECIAL RULE FOR KEROSENE USED IN AVIATION ON A FARM FOR FARMING PURPOSES.—

(1) REFUNDS FOR PURCHASES AFTER DECEMBER 31, 2004, AND BEFORE OCTOBER 1, 2005.—The Secretary of the Treasury shall pay to the ultimate purchaser of any kerosene which is used in aviation on a farm for farming purposes and which was purchased after December 31, 2004, and before October 1, 2005, an amount equal to the aggregate amount of tax imposed on such fuel under section 4041 or 4081 of the Internal Revenue Code of 1986, as the case may be, reduced by any payment to the ultimate vendor under section 6427(l)(5)(C) of such Code (as in effect on the day before the date of the enactment of the Safe, Accountable, Flexible, Efficient Transportation Equity Act: a Legacy for Users).

(2) USE ON A FARM FOR FARMING PURPOSES.—For purposes of paragraph (1), kerosene shall be treated as used on a farm for farming purposes if such kerosene is used for farming purposes (within the meaning of section 6420(c)(3) of the Internal Revenue Code of 1986) in carrying on a trade or business on a farm situated in the United States. For purposes of the preceding sentence, rules similar to the rules of section 6420(c)(4) of such Code shall apply.

(3) TIME FOR FILING CLAIMS.—No claim shall be allowed under paragraph (1) unless the ultimate purchaser files such claim before the date that is 3 months after the date of the enactment of this Act.

(4) NO DOUBLE BENEFIT.—No amount shall be paid under paragraph (1) or section 6427(l) of the Internal Revenue Code of 1986 with respect to any kerosene described in paragraph (1) to the extent that such amount is in excess of the tax imposed on such kerosene under section 4041 or 4081 of such Code, as the case may be.

(5) APPLICABLE LAWS.—For purposes of this subsection, rules similar to the rules of section 6427(j) of the Internal Revenue Code of 1986 shall apply.

ESTABLISHMENT OF TRUST FUNDS

- **2005, Safe, Accountable, Flexible, Efficient Transportation Equity Act: A Legacy for Users (P.L. 109-59)**

P.L. 109-59, §11161(d)(1):

Amended Code Sec. 9502(d)(2) by inserting "(other than subsection (l)(4) and (l)(5) thereof)" after "or 6427 (relating to fuels not used for taxable purposes)". **Effective** for fuels or liquids removed, entered, or sold after 9-30-2005.

P.L. 109-59, §11161(d)(2):

Amended Code Sec. 9502(d)(3) by inserting "(other than payments made by reason of paragraph (4) or (5) of section 6427(l))" after "section 34". **Effective** for fuels or liquids removed, entered, or sold after 9-30-2005.

- **2003, Vision 100—Century of Aviation Reauthorization Act (P.L. 108-176)**

P.L. 108-176, §901(a)(1)-(2):

Amended Code Sec. 9502(d)(1) by striking "October 1, 2003" and inserting "October 1, 2007", and by inserting before the semicolon at the end of subparagraph (A) "or the Vision 100—Century of Aviation Reauthorization Act". **Effective** 12-12-2003.

- **2001, Aviation and Transportation Security Act (P.L. 107-71)**

P.L. 107-71, §123(b):

Amended Code Sec. 9502(d)(1)(A) by inserting "or the Aviation and Transportation Security Act" after "21st Century". **Effective** 11-19-2001.

- **2000, Wendell H. Ford Aviation Investment and Reform Act for the 21st Century (P.L. 106-181)**

P.L. 106-181, §1001(a)(1)-(2):

Amended Code Sec. 9502(d)(1) by striking "October 1, 1998" and inserting "October 1, 2003", and by inserting before the semicolon at the end of subparagraph (A) the following: "or the provisions of the Omnibus Consolidated and Emergency Supplemental Appropriations Act, 1999 providing for payments from the Airport and Airway Trust Fund or the Interim Federal Aviation Administration Authorization Act or section 6002 of the 1999 Emergency Supplemental Appropriations Act, Public Law 106-59, or the Wendell H. Ford Aviation Investment and Reform Act for the 21st Century". **Effective** 4-5-2000.

- **1997, Taxpayer Relief Act of 1997 (P.L. 105-34)**

P.L. 105-34, §1604(g)(5):

Amended Code Sec. 9502(d) by redesignating the paragraph added by Act Sec. 806 of the Federal Aviation Reauthorization Act of 1996 (P.L. 104-264) as paragraph (6). **Effective** 8-5-97.

- **1996, Federal Aviation Reauthorization Act of 1996 (P.L. 104-264)**

P.L. 104-264, §3(b), provides:

(b) LIMITATION ON STATUTORY CONSTRUCTION.—Nothing in this Act or any amendment made by this Act shall be construed as affecting funds made available for a fiscal year ending before October 1, 1996.

P.L. 104-264, §806(4):

Amended Code Sec. 9502(d) by adding paragraph (5)[(6)]. **Effective** for fiscal years beginning after 9-30-96. For a special rule, see Act Sec. 3(b), above.

P.L. 104-264, §1001(a):

Amended Code Sec. 9502(d)(1) by striking "October 1, 1996" and adding "October 1, 1998". **Effective** for fiscal years beginning after 9-30-96. For a special rule, see Act Sec. 3(b), above.

P.L. 104-264, §1001(b):

Amended Code Sec. 9502(d)(1)(A) by inserting before the semicolon at the end "or the Federal Aviation Reauthorization Act of 1996". **Effective** for fiscal years beginning after 9-30-96. For a special rule, see Act Sec. 3(b), above.

- **1996, Small Business Job Protection Act of 1996 (P.L. 104-188)**

P.L. 104-188, §1609(c)(3):

Amended Code Sec. 9502(d) by adding at the end a new paragraph (5). **Effective** 8-27-96.

- **1994, Federal Aviation Administration Authorization Act of 1994 (P.L. 103-305)**

P.L. 103-305, §401:

Amended Code Sec. 9502(d)(1) by striking "October 1, 1995" and inserting "October 1, 1996"; by inserting "or the Airport and Airway Safety, Capacity, Noise Improvement, and Intermodal Transportation Act of 1992" after "Capacity Expansion Act of 1990" in subparagraph (A); by striking "(as such Acts were in effect on the date of the enactment of the Airport Improvement Program Temporary Extension Act of 1994)" in subparagraph (A) and inserting "or the Federal Aviation Administration Authorization Act of 1994"; and by adding at the end a new flush sentence. **Effective** 8-23-94.

- **1994 (P.L. 103-272)**

P.L. 103-272, §5(g)(3):

Amended Code Sec. 9502(d)(1)(B) by striking "the Federal Aviation Act of 1958, as amended (49 U.S.C. 1301 et seq.)," and substituting "part A of subtitle VII of title 49, United States Code,". **Effective** 7-5-94.

- **1994, Airport Improvement Program Temporary Extension Act of 1994 (P.L. 103-260)**

P.L. 103-260, §108:

Amended Code Sec. 9502(d)(1)(A) by striking "(as such Acts were in effect on the date of the enactment of the Airport and Airway Safety, Capacity, Noise Improvement and Intermodal Transportation Act of 1992)" and inserting "or the Airport Improvement Program Temporary Extension Act of 1994 (as such Acts were in effect on the date of the enactment of the Airport Improvement Program Temporary Extension Act of 1994)". **Effective** 5-26-94.

- **1992, Airport and Airway Safety, Capacity, Noise Improvement, and Intermodal Transportation Act of 1992 (P.L. 102-581)**

P.L. 102-581, §501(1)-(2):

Amended Code Sec. 9502(d) by striking "October 1, 1992" and inserting "October 1, 1995", and by striking in subparagraph (A) "(as such Acts were in effect on the date of the enactment of the Aviation Safety and Capacity Expansion Act of 1990)" and inserting "(as such Acts were in effect on the date of the enactment of the Airport and Airway Safety, Capacity, Noise Improvement, and Intermodal Transportation Act of 1992)". **Effective** 10-31-92.

- **1990, Omnibus Budget Reconciliation Act of 1990 (P.L. 101-508)**

P.L. 101-508, §11211(b)(6)(G):

Amended Code Sec. 9502(d) by adding at the end thereof a new paragraph (4). **Effective** 12-1-90.

P.L. 101-508, §11213(d)(4):

Amended Code Sec. 9502(d)(1)(A) by striking "(as such Acts were in effect on the date of the enactment of the Airport and Airway Safety and Capacity Expansion Act of 1987)" and inserting "or the Federal Aviation Administration Research, Engineering, and Development Authorization Act of 1990 or the Aviation Safety and Capacity Expansion Act of 1990 (as such Acts were in effect on the date of the enactment of the Aviation Safety and Capacity Expansion Act of 1990)". **Effective** 11-5-90. However, see Act Sec. 11213(f) in the amendment notes following Code Sec. 4051(c).

- **1987, Airport and Airway Revenue Act of 1987 (P.L. 100-223)**

P.L. 100-223, §403(a):

Amended Code Sec. 9502(d)(1) by striking out "October 1, 1987" and inserting in lieu thereof "October 1, 1992". **Effective** 12-30-87.

P.L. 100-223, §403(b):

Amended Code Sec. 9502(d)(1)(A) by striking out "(as such Acts were in effect on the date of the enactment of the Surface Transportation Assistance Act of 1982)" and inserting in lieu thereof "or the Airport and Airway Safety and Capacity Expansion Act of 1987 (as such Acts were in effect on the date of the enactment of the Airport and Airway Safety and Capacity Expansion Act of 1987)". **Effective** 12-30-87.

- **1984, Deficit Reduction Act of 1984 (P.L. 98-369)**

P.L. 98-369, §474(r)(42):

Amended Code Sec. 9502(d)(3) by striking out "section 39" and inserting in lieu thereof "section 34", and by striking out "SECTION 39 CREDITS" in the heading and inserting in lieu thereof "SECTION 34 CREDITS". **Effective** for tax years beginning after 12-31-83, and for carrybacks from such years.

- **1983, Surface Transportation Act of 1983 (P.L. 97-424)**

P.L. 97-424, §426(e):

Amended Code Sec. 9502(d)(1)(A) by striking out the second time it appeared "the Airport and Airway Improvement Act of 1982" and inserting "the Surface Transportation Assistance Act of 1982". **Effective** 1-6-83.

- **1982, Tax Equity and Fiscal Responsibility Act of 1982 (P.L. 97-248)**

P.L. 97-248, §281(a):

Added Code Sec. 9502. **Effective** 9-1-82.

P.L. 97-248, §281(d)(2), provides:

(2) SAVINGS PROVISIONS.—The Airport and Airway Trust Fund established by the amendments made by this section shall be treated for all purposes of law as the continuation of the Airport and Airway Trust Fund established by section 208 of the Airport and Airway Revenue Act of 1970. Any reference in any law to the Airport and Airway Trust Fund established by such section 208 shall be deemed to include a reference to the Airport and Airway Trust Fund established by the amendments made by this section.

[Note: Section 208 of the Airport and Airway Revenue Act of 1970 was repealed by P.L. 97-248, §281(b).]

[Sec. 9502(e)]

(e) LIMITATION ON TRANSFERS TO TRUST FUND.—

(1) IN GENERAL.—Except as provided in paragraph (2), no amount may be appropriated or credited to the Airport and Airway Trust Fund on and after the date of any expenditure from the Airport and Airway Trust Fund which is not permitted by this section. The determination of whether an expenditure is so permitted shall be made without regard to—

(A) any provision of law which is not contained or referenced in this title or in a revenue Act; and

(B) whether such provision of law is a subsequently enacted provision or directly or indirectly seeks to waive the application of this subsection.

ESTABLISHMENT OF TRUST FUNDS

(2) EXCEPTION FOR PRIOR OBLIGATIONS.—Paragraph (1) shall not apply to any expenditure to liquidate any contract entered into (or for any amount otherwise obligated) before October 1, 2028, in accordance with the provisions of this section.

Amendments

• **2024, FAA Reauthorization Act of 2024 (P.L. 118-63)**

P.L. 118-63, §1301(b):

Amended Code Sec. 9502(e)(2) by striking "May 11, 2024" and inserting "October 1, 2028". **Effective** 5-16-2024.

• **2024, Airport and Airway Extension Act of 2024, Part II (P.L. 118-60)**

P.L. 118-60, §201(a), provides:

SEC. 201. EXPENDITURE AUTHORITY FROM AIRPORT AND AIRWAY TRUST FUND.

(a) Sections 9502(d)(1) and 9502(e)(2) of the Internal Revenue Code of 1986 shall be applied by substituting "May 18, 2024" for "May 11, 2024".

• **2024, Airport and Airway Extension Act of 2024 (P.L. 118-41)**

P.L. 118-41, §201(b):

Amended Code Sec. 9502(e)(2) by striking "March 9, 2024" and inserting "May 11, 2024". **Effective** 3-8-2024.

• **2023, Airport and Airway Extension Act of 2023, Part II (P.L. 118-34)**

P.L. 118-34, §201(b):

Amended Code Sec. 9502(e)(2) by striking "January 1, 2024" and inserting "March 9, 2024". **Effective** 12-26-2023.

• **2023, Continuing Appropriations Act, 2024 and Other Extensions Act (P.L. 118-15)**

P.L. 118-15, §2211(b):

Amended Code Sec. 9502(e)(2) by striking "October 1, 2023" and inserting "January 1, 2024". **Effective** 9-30-2023.

• **2018, FAA Reauthorization Act of 2018 (P.L. 115-254)**

P.L. 115-254, §801(b):

Amended Code Sec. 9502(e)(2) by striking "October 1, 2018" and inserting "October 1, 2023". **Effective** 10-5-2018.

• **2018, Airport and Airway Extension Act of 2018, Part II (P.L. 115-250)**

P.L. 115-250, §4(a), provides:

(a) Sections 9502(d)(1) and 9502(e)(2) of the Internal Revenue Code of 1986 shall be applied by substituting "October 8, 2018" for "October 1, 2018".

• **2018, Airport and Airway Extension Act of 2018 (P.L. 115-141)**

P.L. 115-141, §201(b), Div. M:

Amended Code Sec. 9502(e)(2) by striking "April 1, 2018" and inserting "October 1, 2018". **Effective** 3-23-2018.

• **2017, Disaster Tax Relief and Airport and Airway Extension Act of 2017 (P.L. 115-63)**

P.L. 115-63, §201(b):

Amended Code Sec. 9502(e)(2) by striking "October 1, 2017" and inserting "April 1, 2018". **Effective** 9-29-2017.

• **2016, FAA Extension, Safety, and Security Act of 2016 (P.L. 114-190)**

P.L. 114-190, §1201(b):

Amended Code Sec. 9502(e)(2) by striking "July 16, 2016" and inserting "October 1, 2017". **Effective** 7-15-2016.

• **2016, Airport and Airway Extension Act of 2016 (P.L. 114-141)**

P.L. 114-141, §201(b):

Amended Code Sec. 9502(e)(2) by striking "April 1, 2016" and inserting "July 16, 2016". **Effective** 3-30-2016.

• **2015, Airport and Airway Extension Act of 2015 (P.L. 114-55)**

P.L. 114-55, §201(b):

Amended Code Sec. 9502(e)(2) by striking "October 1, 2015" and inserting "April 1, 2016". **Effective** 9-30-2015.

• **2012, FAA Modernization and Reform Act of 2012 (P.L. 112-95)**

P.L. 112-95, §1102(b):

Amended Code Sec. 9502(e)(2) by striking "February 18, 2012" and inserting "October 1, 2015". **Effective** 2-18-2012.

• **2012, Airport and Airway Extension Act of 2012 (P.L. 112-91)**

P.L. 112-91, §3(b):

Amended Code Sec. 9502(e)(2) by striking "February 1, 2012" and inserting "February 18, 2012". **Effective** 2-1-2012.

• **2011, Airport and Airway Extension Act of 2011, Part V (P.L. 112-30)**

P.L. 112-30, §203(b):

Amended Code Sec. 9502(e)(2) by striking "September 17, 2011" and inserting "February 1, 2012". **Effective** 9-17-2011.

• **2011, Airport and Airway Extension Act of 2011, Part IV (P.L. 112-27)**

P.L. 112-27, §3(b):

Amended Code Sec. 9502(e)(2) by striking "July 23, 2011" and inserting "September 17, 2011". **Effective** 7-23-2011.

• **2011, Airport and Airway Extension Act of 2011, Part III (P.L. 112-21)**

P.L. 112-21, §3(b):

Amended Code Sec. 9502(e)(2) by striking "July 1, 2011" and inserting "July 23, 2011". **Effective** 7-1-2011.

• **2011, Airport and Airway Extension Act of 2011, Part II (P.L. 112-16)**

P.L. 112-16, §3(b):

Amended Code Sec. 9502(e)(2) by striking "June 1, 2011" and inserting "July 1, 2011". **Effective** 6-1-2011.

• **2011, Airport and Airway Extension Act of 2011 (P.L. 112-7)**

P.L. 112-7, §3(b):

Amended Code Sec. 9502(e)(2) by striking "April 1, 2011" and inserting "June 1, 2011". **Effective** 4-1-2011.

• **2010, Airport and Airway Extension Act of 2010, Part IV (P.L. 111-329)**

P.L. 111-329, §3(b):

Amended Code Sec. 9502(e)(2) by striking "January 1, 2011" and inserting "April 1, 2011". **Effective** 1-1-2011.

• **2010, Airport and Airway Extension Act of 2010, Part III (P.L. 111-249)**

P.L. 111-249, §3(b):

Amended Code Sec. 9502(e)(2) by striking "October 1, 2010" and inserting "January 1, 2011". **Effective** 10-1-2010.

• **2010, Airline Safety and Federal Aviation Administration Extension Act of 2010 (P.L. 111-216)**

P.L. 111-216, §102(b):

Amended Code Sec. 9502(e)(2) by striking "August 2, 2010" and inserting "October 1, 2010". **Effective** 8-2-2010.

• **2010, Airport and Airway Extension Act of 2010, Part II (P.L. 111-197)**

P.L. 111-197, §3(b):

Amended Code Sec. 9502(e)(2) by striking "July 4, 2010" and inserting "August 2, 2010". **Effective** 7-4-2010.

• **2010, Airport and Airway Extension Act of 2010 (P.L. 111-161)**

P.L. 111-161, §3(b):

Amended Code Sec. 9502(e)(2) by striking "May 1, 2010" and inserting "July 4, 2010". **Effective** 5-1-2010.

• **2010, Federal Aviation Administration Extension Act of 2010 (P.L. 111-153)**

P.L. 111-153, §3(b):

Amended Code Sec. 9502(e)(2) by striking "April 1, 2010" and inserting "May 1, 2010". **Effective** 4-1-2010.

• **2009, Fiscal Year 2010 Federal Aviation Administration Extension Act, Part II (P.L. 111-116)**

P.L. 111-116, §3(b):

Amended Code Sec. 9502(e)(2) by striking "January 1, 2010" and inserting "April 1, 2010". **Effective** 1-1-2010.

• **2009, Fiscal Year 2010 Federal Aviation Administration Extension Act (P.L. 111-69)**

P.L. 111-69, §3(b):

Amended Code Sec. 9502(e)(2) by striking "October 1, 2009" and inserting "January 1, 2010". **Effective** 10-1-2009.

• **2009, Fiscal Year 2010 Federal Aviation Administration Extension Act (P.L. 111-69)**

P.L. 111-69, §3(b):

Amended Code Sec. 9502(e)(2) by striking "January 1, 2010" and inserting "April 1, 2010". **Effective** 1-1-2010.

• **2009, (P.L. 111-68)**

P.L. 111-68, §156(b), provides:

(b) Subsections (d)(1) and (e)(2) of section 9502 of such Code shall each be applied by substituting the date that is 1 day after the date specified in section 106(3) [October 31, 2009] of this joint resolution for "October 1, 2009".

• **2009, Federal Aviation Administration Extension Act of 2009 (P.L. 111-12)**

P.L. 111-12, §3(b):

Amended Code Sec. 9502(e)(2) by striking "April 1, 2009" and inserting "October 1, 2009". **Effective** 4-1-2009.

• **2008, Federal Aviation Administration Extension Act of 2008, Part II (P.L. 110-330)**

P.L. 110-330, §3(b):

Amended Code Sec. 9502(e)(2) by striking the date specified in such paragraph [October 1, 2008.—CCH] and inserting "April 1, 2009". **Effective** 10-1-2008.

Sec. 9502(e)(2)

ESTABLISHMENT OF TRUST FUNDS

• **2008, Federal Aviation Administration Extension Act of 2008 (P.L. 110-253)**

P.L. 110-253, § 3(b):

Amended Code Sec. 9502(e)(2) by striking the date specified in such paragraph [July 1, 2008.—CCH] and inserting "October 1, 2008". **Effective** 7-1-2008.

• **2008, Airport and Airway Extension Act of 2008 (P.L. 110-190)**

P.L. 110-190, § 3(b):

Amended Code Sec. 9502(f)[(e)](2) by striking "March 1, 2008" and inserting "July 1, 2008". **Effective** 3-1-2008.

• **2007, Tax Technical Corrections Act of 2007 (P.L. 110-172)**

P.L. 110-172, § 11(f)(1):

Amended Code Sec. 9502 by redesignating subsection (f) as subsection (e). **Effective** as if included in the provision of the American Jobs Creation Act of 2004 (P.L. 108-357) to which it relates [effective for fuel sold or used after 12-31-2004.—CCH].

• **2007, Department of Transportation Appropriations Act, 2008 (P.L. 110-161)**

P.L. 110-161, § 116(c)(2):

Amended Code Sec. 9502(f)(2) by striking "October 1, 2007" and inserting "March 1, 2008". **Effective** 10-1-2007.

• **2007 (P.L. 110-92)**

P.L. 110-92, § 149(a), provides:

SEC. 149. (a) Sections 4081(d)(2)(B), 4261(j)(1)(A)(ii), 4271(d)(1)(A)(ii), 9502(d)(1), and 9502(f)(2) of the Internal Revenue Code of 1986 shall each be applied by substituting the date specified in section 106(3) of this joint resolution [November 16, 2007.—CCH] for "September 30, 2007" or "October 1, 2007", as the case may be.

• **2003, Vision 100—Century of Aviation Reauthorization Act (P.L. 108-176)**

P.L. 108-176, § 901(b):

Amended Code Sec. 9502(f)(2) by striking "October 1, 2003" and inserting "October 1, 2007". **Effective** 12-12-2003.

• **2000, Wendell H. Ford Aviation Investment and Reform Act for the 21st Century (P.L. 106-181)**

P.L. 106-181, § 1001(b):

Amended Code Sec. 9502 by adding at the end thereof new subsection (f). **Effective** 4-5-2000.

• **1997, Taxpayer Relief Act of 1997 (P.L. 105-34)**

P.L. 105-34, § 1031(d)(2):

Amended Code Sec. 9502 by striking subsection (f). **Effective** with respect to taxes received in the Treasury on and after 10-1-97. Prior to being stricken, Code Sec. 9502(f) read as follows:

(f) DEFINITION OF AIRPORT AND AIRWAY TRUST FUND FINANCING RATE.—For purposes of this section—

(1) IN GENERAL.—Except as otherwise provided in this subsection, the Airport and Airway Trust Fund financing rate is—

(A) in the case of fuel used in an aircraft in noncommercial aviation (as defined in section 4041(c)(2)), 17.5 cents per gallon, and

(B) in the case of fuel used in an aircraft other than in noncommercial aviation (as so defined), zero.

(2) ALCOHOL FUELS.—If the rate of tax on any fuel is determined under section 4091(c), the Airport and Airway Trust Fund financing rate is the excess (if any) of the rate of tax determined under section 4091(c) over 4.4 cents per gallon ($^{10}/_9$ of 4.4 cents per gallon in the case of a rate of tax determined under section 4091(c)(2)).

(3) TERMINATION.—Notwithstanding the preceding provisions of this subsection, the Airport and Airway Trust Fund financing rate shall be zero with respect to taxes imposed during any period that the rate of the tax imposed by section 4091(b)(1) is 4.3 cents per gallon.

• **1997, Airport and Airway Trust Fund Tax Reinstatement Act of 1997 (P.L. 105-2)**

P.L. 105-2, § 2(c)(2):

Amended Code Sec. 9502(f)(3). **Effective** 2-28-97. For a rule concerning the look-back safe harbor for deposits, see P.L. 105-2, § 2(f), below. Prior to amendment, Code Sec. 9502(f)(3) read as follows:

(3) TERMINATION.—Notwithstanding the preceding provisions of this subsection, the Airport and Airway Trust Fund financing rate shall be zero with respect to—

(A) taxes imposed after December 31, 1995, and before the date which is 7 calendar days after the date of the enactment of the Small Business Job Protection Act of 1996, and

(B) taxes imposed after December 31, 1996.

P.L. 105-2, § 2(f), provides:

(f) APPLICATION OF LOOK-BACK SAFE HARBOR FOR DEPOSITS.—Nothing in the look-back safe harbor prescribed in Treasury Regulation section 40.6302(c)-1(c)(2) shall be construed to permit such safe harbor to be used with respect to any tax unless such tax was imposed throughout the look-back period.

• **1996, Small Business Job Protection Act of 1996 (P.L. 104-188)**

P.L. 104-188, § 1609(c)(2):

Amended Code Sec. 9502(f)(3). **Effective** 8-27-96. Prior to amendment, Code Sec. 9502(f)(3) read as follows:

(3) TERMINATION.—Notwithstanding the preceding provisions of this subsection, the Airport and Airway Trust Fund financing rate is zero with respect to tax received after December 31, 1995.

P.L. 104-188, § 1609(g)(4)(C):

Amended Code Sec. 9502(f)(1)(A) by striking "section 4041(c)(4)" and inserting "section 4041(c)(2)". **Effective** 8-27-96.

• **1993, Omnibus Budget Reconciliation Act of 1993 (P.L. 103-66)**

P.L. 103-66, § 13242(d)(32):

Amended Code Sec. 9502 by adding at the end thereof new subsection (f). **Effective** 1-1-94.

[Sec. 9502(e)—Stricken]

Amendments

• **2007, Tax Technical Corrections Act of 2007 (P.L. 110-172)**

P.L. 110-172, § 11(f)(1):

Amended Code Sec. 9502 by striking subsection (e) and redesignating subsection (f) as subsection (e). **Effective** as if included in the provision of the American Jobs Creation Act of 2004 (P.L. 108-357) to which it relates [effective for fuel sold or used after 12-31-2004.—CCH]. Prior to being stricken, Code Sec. 9502(e) read as follows:

(e) CERTAIN TAXES ON ALCOHOL MIXTURES TO REMAIN IN GENERAL FUND.—For purposes of this section, the amounts which would (but for this subsection) be required to be appropriated under subparagraphs (A), (C), and (D) of subsection (b)(1) shall be reduced by—

(1) 0.6 cent per gallon in the case of taxes imposed on any mixture at least 10 percent of which is alcohol (as defined in section 4081(c)(3)) if any portion of such alcohol is ethanol, and

(2) 0.67 cent per gallon in the case of fuel used in producing a mixture described in paragraph (1).

• **1998, IRS Restructuring and Reform Act of 1998 (P.L. 105-206)**

P.L. 105-206, § 6023(31):

Amended Code Sec. 9502(e). **Effective** 7-22-98. Prior to amendment, Code Sec. 9502(e) read as follows:

(e) SPECIAL RULES FOR TRANSFERS INTO TRUST FUND.—

(1) INCREASES IN TAX REVENUES BEFORE 1993 TO REMAIN IN GENERAL FUND.—In the case of taxes imposed before January 1, 1993, the amounts required to be appropriated under paragraphs (1), (2), and (3) of subsection (b) shall be determined without regard to any increase in a rate of tax enacted by the Revenue Reconciliation Act of 1990.

(2) CERTAIN TAXES ON ALCOHOL MIXTURES TO REMAIN IN GENERAL FUND.—For purposes of this section, the amounts which would (but for this paragraph) be required to be appropriated under paragraphs (1), (2), and (3) of subsection (b) shall be reduced by—

(A) 0.6 cent per gallon in the case of taxes imposed on any mixture at least 10 percent of which is alcohol (as defined in section 4081(c)(3)) if any portion of such alcohol is ethanol, and

(B) 0.67 cent per gallon in the case of fuel used in producing a mixture described in subparagraph (A).

• **1992, Airport and Airway Safety, Capacity, Noise Improvement, and Intermodal Transportation Act of 1992 (P.L. 102-581)**

P.L. 102-581, § 502(a):

Amended Code Sec. 9502(e)(1). **Effective** as if included in § 11213 of P.L. 101-508 on 11-5-90. Prior to amendment Code Sec. 9502(e)(1) read as follows:

(1) INCREASES IN TAX REVENUES BEFORE 1993 TO REMAIN IN GENERAL FUND.—In the case of taxes imposed before January 1, 1993, the amounts which would (but for this paragraph) be required to be appropriated under paragraphs (1), (2), and (3) of subsection (b) shall be 3 cents per gallon less (3.5 cents per gallon less in the case of taxes imposed by section 4041(c)(1) and 4091) than the amounts which would (but for this sentence) be appropriated under such paragraphs.

• **1990, Omnibus Budget Reconciliation Act of 1990 (P.L. 101-508)**

P.L. 101-508, § 11213(c)(1):

Amended Code Sec. 9502 by adding at the end thereof a new subsection (e). **Effective** 11-5-90. However, see Act Sec. 11213(f) in the amendment notes following Code Sec. 4051(c).

[Sec. 9502(f)]

(f) ADDITIONAL TRANSFER TO TRUST FUND.—Out of money in the Treasury not otherwise appropriated, there is hereby appropriated $14,000,000,000 to the Airport and Airway Trust Fund.

Internal Revenue Code

Sec. 9502(f)

ESTABLISHMENT OF TRUST FUNDS

Amendments

• **2020, Continuing Appropriations Act, 2021 and Other Extensions Act (P.L. 116-159)**

P.L. 116-159, §1205:

Amended Code Sec. 9502 by adding at the end a new subsection (f). **Effective** 10-1-2020.

[Sec. 9503]

SEC. 9503. HIGHWAY TRUST FUND.

[Sec. 9503(a)]

(a) CREATION OF TRUST FUND.—There is established in the Treasury of the United States a trust fund to be known as the "Highway Trust Fund", consisting of such amounts as may be appropriated or credited to the Highway Trust Fund as provided in this section or section 9602(b).

[Sec. 9503(b)]

(b) TRANSFER TO HIGHWAY TRUST FUND OF AMOUNTS EQUIVALENT TO CERTAIN TAXES AND PENALTIES.—

(1) CERTAIN TAXES.—There are hereby appropriated to the Highway Trust Fund amounts equivalent to the taxes received in the Treasury before October 1, 2028, under the following provisions—

(A) section 4041 (relating to taxes on diesel fuels and special motor fuels),

(B) section 4051 (relating to retail tax on heavy trucks and trailers),

(C) section 4071 (relating to tax on tires),

(D) section 4081 (relating to tax on gasoline, diesel fuel, and kerosene), and

(E) section 4481 (relating to tax on use of certain vehicles).

For purposes of this paragraph, taxes received under sections 4041 and 4081 shall be determined without reduction for credits under section 6426 and taxes received under section 4081 shall be determined without regard to tax receipts attributable to the rate specified in section 4081(a)(2)(C).

(2) LIABILITIES INCURRED BEFORE OCTOBER 1, 2028.—There are hereby appropriated to the Highway Trust Fund amounts equivalent to the taxes which are received in the Treasury after September 30, 2028, and before July 1, 2029, and which are attributable to liability for tax incurred before October 1, 2028, under the provisions described in paragraph (1).

(3) [Stricken.]

(4) CERTAIN TAXES NOT TRANSFERRED TO HIGHWAY TRUST FUND.—For purposes of paragraphs (1) and (2), there shall not be taken into account the taxes imposed by—

(A) section 4041(d),

(B) section 4081 to the extent attributable to the rate specified in section 4081(a)(2)(B),

(C) section 4041 or 4081 to the extent attributable to fuel used in a train, or

(D) in the case of gasoline and special motor fuels used as described in paragraph (3)(D) or (4)(B) of subsection (c), section 4041 or 4081 with respect to so much of the rate of tax as exceeds—

(i) 11.5 cents per gallon with respect to taxes imposed before October 1, 2001,

(ii) 13 cents per gallon with respect to taxes imposed after September 30, 2001, and before October 1, 2003, and

(iii) 13.5 cents per gallon with respect to taxes imposed after September 30, 2003, and before October 1, 2005.

(5) CERTAIN PENALTIES.—

(A) IN GENERAL.—There are hereby appropriated to the Highway Trust Fund amounts equivalent to the penalties paid under sections 6715, 6715A, 6717, 6718, 6719, 6720A, 6725, 7232, and 7272 (but only with regard to penalties under such section related to failure to register under section 4101).

(B) PENALTIES RELATED TO MOTOR VEHICLE SAFETY.—

(i) IN GENERAL.—There are hereby appropriated to the Highway Trust Fund amounts equivalent to covered motor vehicle safety penalty collections.

(ii) COVERED MOTOR VEHICLE SAFETY PENALTY COLLECTIONS.—For purposes of this subparagraph, the term "covered motor vehicle safety penalty collections" means any amount collected in connection with a civil penalty under section 30165 of title 49, United States Code, reduced by any award authorized by the Secretary of Transportation to be paid to any person in connection with information provided by such person related to a violation of chapter 301 of such title which is a predicate to such civil penalty.

(6) LIMITATION ON TRANSFERS TO HIGHWAY TRUST FUND.—

(A) IN GENERAL.—Except as provided in subparagraph (B), no amount may be appropriated to the Highway Trust Fund on and after the date of any expenditure from the Highway Trust Fund which is not permitted by this section. The determination of whether an expenditure is so permitted shall be made without regard to—

(i) any provision of law which is not contained or referenced in this title or in a revenue Act, and

(ii) whether such provision of law is a subsequently enacted provision or directly or indirectly seeks to waive the application of this paragraph.

(B) EXCEPTION FOR PRIOR OBLIGATIONS.—Subparagraph (A) shall not apply to any expenditure to liquidate any contract entered into (or for any amount otherwise obligated) before October 1, 2026, in accordance with the provisions of this section.

Amendments

• **2021, Infrastructure Investment and Jobs Act (P.L. 117-58)**

P.L. 117-58, §80101(a)(1), Div. H:

Amended Code Sec. 9503(b)(6)(B) by striking "October 1, 2021" and inserting "October 1, 2026". **Effective** 11-15-2021.

P.L. 117-58, §80102(e)(1)(A)(i)-(iv), Div. H

Amended Code Sec. 9503(b) by striking "October 1, 2022" each place it appears and inserting "October 1, 2028" in paragraphs (1) and (2); by striking "October 1, 2022" and inserting "October 1, 2028" in the heading of paragraph (2); by striking "September 30, 2022" and inserting "September 30, 2028" in paragraph (2); and by striking "July 1, 2023" and inserting "July 1, 2029" in paragraph (2). **Effective** 10-1-2021.

• **2021, Further Surface Transportation Extension Act of 2021 (P.L. 117-52)**

P.L. 117-52, §4(a)(1):

Amended Code Sec. 9503(b)(6)(B) by striking "November 1, 2021" and inserting "December 4, 2021". **Effective** 10-31-2021. For a special rule, see Act Sec. 4(d)(1)-(3), below.

P.L. 117-52, §4(d)(1)-(3), provides:

(d) SPECIAL RULE FOR AMENDMENTS.—On the date of enactment of H.R. 3684 (117th Congress)—

ESTABLISHMENT OF TRUST FUNDS

(1) subsections (a), (b), and (c) of this section, the amendments made by such subsections, section 201 of the Surface Transportation Extension Act of 2021 (Public Law 117–44), and the amendments made by such section shall cease to be effective;

(2) the text of the laws amended by subsections (a), (b), and (c) of this section and section 201 of the Surface Transportation Extension Act of 2021 (Public Law 117–44) shall revert back so as to read as the text read on September 30, 2021; and

(3) the amendments made by H.R. 3684 (117th Congress) shall be executed as if this section and section 201 of the Surface Transportation Extension Act had not been enacted.

- **2021, Surface Transportation Extension Act of 2021 (P.L. 117-44)**

P.L. 117-44, §201(a)(1):

Amended Code Sec. 9503(b)(6)(B) by striking "October 1, 2021" and inserting "November 1, 2021". **Effective** 10-2-2021. For a special rule, see Act Sec. 201(d)(1)-(3), below.

P.L. 117-44, §201(d)(1)-(3), provides:

(d) SPECIAL RULE FOR EXECUTION OF AMENDMENTS.—On the date of enactment of H.R. 3684 (117th Congress)—

(1) this section and the amendments made by this section shall cease to be effective;

(2) the text of the laws amended by this section shall revert back so as to read as the text read on the day before the date of enactment of this section; and

(3) the amendments made by H.R. 3684 (117th Congress) shall be executed as if this section had not been enacted.

- **2020, Continuing Appropriations Act, 2021 and Other Extensions Act (P.L. 116-159)**

P.L. 116-159, §1201(1):

Amended Code Sec. 9503(b)(6)(B) by striking "October 1, 2020" and inserting "October 1, 2021". **Effective** 10-1-2020.

- **2015, Fixing America's Surface Transportation Act (P.L. 114-94)**

P.L. 114-94, §31101(a)(1):

Amended Code Sec. 9503(b)(6)(B) by striking "December 5, 2015" and inserting "October 1, 2020". **Effective** 12-4-2015.

P.L. 114-94, §31102(e)(1)(A)(i)-(iv):

Amended Code Sec. 9503(b) by striking "October 1, 2016" each place it appears in paragraphs (1)-(2) and inserting "October 1, 2022"; by striking "OCTOBER 1, 2016" in the heading of paragraph (2) and inserting "OCTOBER 1, 2022"; by striking "September 30, 2016" in paragraph (2) and inserting "September 30, 2022"; and by striking "July 1, 2017" in paragraph (2) and inserting "July 1, 2023". **Effective** 10-1-2016.

P.L. 114-94, §31202(a)(1)-(2):

Amended Code Sec. 9503(b)(5) by striking "There are hereby" and inserting

"(A) IN GENERAL.—There are hereby",

and by adding at the end a new paragraph (B). **Effective** for amounts collected after 12-4-2015.

- **2015, Surface Transportation Extension Act of 2015, Part II (P.L. 114-87)**

P.L. 114-87, §2001(a)(1):

Amended Code Sec. 9503(b)(6)(B) by striking "November 21, 2015" and inserting "December 5, 2015". **Effective** 11-20-2015.

- **2015, Surface Transportation Extension Act of 2015 (P.L. 114-73)**

P.L. 114-73, §2001(a)(1):

Amended Code Sec. 9503(b)(6)(B) by striking "October 30, 2015" and inserting "November 21, 2015". **Effective** 10-29-2015.

- **2015, Surface Transportation and Veterans Health Care Choice Improvement Act of 2015 (P.L. 114-41)**

P.L. 114-41, §2001(a)(1):

Amended Code Sec. 9503(b)(6)(B) by striking "August 1, 2015" and inserting "October 30, 2015". **Effective** 7-31-2015.

- **2015, Highway and Transportation Funding Act of 2015 (P.L. 114-21)**

P.L. 114-21, §2001(a)(1):

Amended Code Sec. 9503(b)(6)(B) by striking "June 1, 2015" and inserting "August 1, 2015". **Effective** 5-29-2015.

- **2014, Tax Technical Corrections Act of 2014 (P.L. 113-295)**

P.L. 113-295, §217(a), Division A:

Amended Code Sec. 9503(b)(1) by inserting "and taxes received under section 4081 shall be determined without regard to tax receipts attributable to the rate specified in section 4081(a)(2)(C)" before the period at the end. **Effective** as if included in the provision of the Safe, Accountable, Flexible, Efficient Transportation Equity Act of 2005: A Legacy for Users (P.L. 109-59) to which it relates [**effective** for fuels or liquids removed, entered, or sold after 9-30-2005.—CCH].

- **2014, Highway and Transportation Funding Act of 2014 (P.L. 113-159)**

P.L. 113-159, §2001(a)(1):

Amended Code Sec. 9503(b)(6)(B) by striking "October 1, 2014" and inserting "June 1, 2015". **Effective** 8-8-2014.

- **2012, Highway Investment, Job Creation, and Economic Growth Act of 2012 (P.L. 112-141)**

P.L. 112-141, §40101(a)(1):

Amended Code Sec. 9503(b)(6)(B) by striking "July 1, 2012" and inserting "October 1, 2014". **Effective** 7-1-2012.

P.L. 112-141, §40102(e)(1)(A)(i)-(iv):

Amended Code Sec. 9503(b) by striking "July 1, 2012" each place it appears in paragraphs (1) and (2) and inserting "October 1, 2016", by striking "JULY 1, 2012" in the heading of paragraph (2) and inserting "OCTOBER 1, 2016", by striking "June 30, 2012" in paragraph (2) and inserting "September 30, 2016", and by striking "April 1, 2013" in paragraph (2) and inserting "July 1, 2017". **Effective** 7-1-2012.

- **2012, Temporary Surface Transportation Extension Act of 2012 (P.L. 112-140)**

P.L. 112-140, §1(c), provides:

(c) SPECIAL RULE FOR EXECUTION OF AMENDMENTS IN MAP–21.—On the date of enactment of the MAP–21 [P.L. 112-141]—

(1) this Act and the amendments made by this Act shall cease to be effective;

(2) the text of the laws amended by this Act shall revert back so as to read as the text read on the day before the date of enactment of this Act; and

(3) the amendments made by the MAP–21 shall be executed as if this Act had not been enacted.

P.L. 112-140, §401(a)(1):

Amended Code Sec. 9503(b)(6)(B) by striking "July 1, 2012" and inserting "July 7, 2012". **Effective** 7-1-2012. For a special rule, see Act Sec. 1(c), above.

P.L. 112-140, §402(d)(1)(A)(i)-(iv):

Amended Code Sec. 9503(b) by striking "July 1, 2012" each place it appears in paragraphs (1) and (2) and inserting "July 7, 2012"; by striking "JULY 1, 2012" in the heading of paragraph (2) and inserting "JULY 7, 2012"; by striking "June 30, 2012" in paragraph (2) and inserting "July 6, 2012"; and by striking "April 1, 2013" in paragraph (2) and inserting "April 7, 2013". **Effective** 7-1-2012. For a special rule, see Act Sec. 1(c), above.

- **2012, Surface Transportation Extension Act of 2012 (P.L. 112-102)**

P.L. 112-102, §401(a)(1):

Amended Code Sec. 9503(b)(6)(B) by striking "April 1, 2012" and inserting "July 1, 2012". **Effective** 4-1-2012.

P.L. 112-102, §402(e)(1)(A)(i)-(iv):

Amended Code Sec. 9503(b) by striking "April 1, 2012" each place it appears in paragraphs (1) and (2) and inserting "July 1, 2012"; by striking "APRIL 1, 2012" in the heading of paragraph (2) and inserting "JULY 1, 2012"; by striking "March 31, 2012" in paragraph (2) and inserting "June 30, 2012"; and by striking "January 1, 2013" in paragraph (2) and inserting "April 1, 2013". **Effective** 4-1-2012.

- **2011, Surface Transportation Extension Act of 2011, Part II (P.L. 112-30)**

P.L. 112-30, §141(a)(1):

Amended Code Sec. 9503(b)(6)(B) by striking "October 1, 2011" and inserting "April 1, 2012". **Effective** 10-1-2011.

P.L. 112-30, §142(e)(1)(A)(i)-(iv):

Amended Code Sec. 9503(b) by striking "October 1, 2011" each place it appears in paragraphs (1) and (2) and inserting "April 1, 2012"; by striking "OCTOBER 1, 2011" in the heading of paragraph (2) and inserting "APRIL 1, 2012"; by striking "September 30, 2011" in paragraph (2) and inserting "March 31, 2012"; and by striking "July 1, 2012" in paragraph (2) and inserting "January 1, 2013". **Effective** 10-1-2011.

- **2011, Surface Transportation Extension Act of 2011 (P.L. 112-5)**

P.L. 112-5, §401(a)(1):

Amended Code Sec. 9503(b)(6)(B) by striking "March 5, 2011" and inserting "October 1, 2011". **Effective** 3-4-2011.

- **2010, Surface Transportation Extension Act of 2010, Part II (P.L. 111-322)**

P.L. 111-322, §2401(a)(1):

Amended Code Sec. 9503(b)(6)(B) by striking "December 31, 2010 (January 1, 2011, in the case of expenditures for administrative expenses)" and inserting "March 5, 2011". **Effective** 12-31-2010.

- **2010, Hiring Incentives to Restore Employment Act (P.L. 111-147)**

P.L. 111-147, §444(b)(2):

Amended Code Sec. 9503(b)(4)(D) by striking "paragraph (4)(D) or (5)(B)" and inserting "paragraph (3)(D) or (4)(B)". **Effective** for transfers relating to amounts paid and credits allowed after 3-18-2010.

P.L. 111-147, §445(a)(3):

Amended Code Sec. 9503(b)(6)(B) by striking "September 30, 2009 (October 1, 2009" and inserting "December 31, 2010 (January 1, 2011". **Effective** 9-30-2009.

- **2010, Temporary Extension Act of 2010 (P.L. 111-144)**

P.L. 111-144, §4, provides:

SEC. 4. EXTENSION OF SURFACE TRANSPORTATION PROGRAMS.

(a) IN GENERAL.—Except as provided in subsection (b), for purposes of the continued extension of surface transportation programs and related authority to make expenditures from the Highway Trust Fund and other trust funds under sections 157 through 162 of the Continuing Appropriations Resolution, 2010 (Public Law 111–68; 123 Stat. 2050), the date specified in section 106(3) of that resolution (Public Law 111–68; 123 Stat. 2045) shall be deemed to be March 28, 2010.

(b) EXCEPTION.—Subsection (a) shall not apply if an extension of the programs and authorities described in that subsection for a longer term than the extension contained in the Continuing Appropriations Resolution, 2010 (Public Law 111–68; 123 Stat. 2050), is enacted before the date of enactment of this Act.

ESTABLISHMENT OF TRUST FUNDS

• **2009, (P.L. 111-68)**

P.L. 111-68, §159(c)(1)-(2), provides:

(c) EXCEPTION TO LIMITATIONS ON TRANSFERS.—Subparagraph (B) of section 9503(b)(6) of such Code shall be applied—

(1) by substituting the date specified in section 106(3) [October 31, 2009] of this joint resolution for "September 30, 2009"; and

(2) by substituting the date that is 1 day after the date specified in section 106(3) [October 31, 2009] of this joint resolution for "October 1, 2009".

• **2005, Safe, Accountable, Flexible, Efficient Transportation Equity Act: A Legacy for Users (P.L. 109-59)**

P.L. 109-59, §11101(c)(1)(A)-(B):

Amended Code Sec. 9503(b)(1)-(2) by striking "2005" each place it appears and inserting "2011", and by striking "2006" and inserting "2012". **Effective** 8-10-2005.

P.L. 109-59, §11101(d)(1)(C):

Amended Code Sec. 9503(b)(6)(B) by striking "July 31, 2005" and inserting "September 30, 2009 (October 1, 2009, in the case of expenditures for administrative expenses)". **Effective** 8-10-2005.

P.L. 109-59, §11161(c)(2)(C):

Amended Code Sec. 9503(b) by striking paragraph (3). **Effective** for fuels or liquids removed, entered, or sold after 9-30-2005. Prior to being stricken, Code Sec. 9503(b)(3) read as follows:

(3) ADJUSTMENTS FOR AVIATION USES.—The amounts described in paragraph (1) and (2) with respect to any period shall (before the application of this subsection) be reduced by appropriate amounts to reflect any amounts transferred to the Airport and Airway Trust Fund under section 9502(b) with respect to such period.

P.L. 109-59, §11167(b):

Amended Code Sec. 9503(b)(5) by inserting "6720A," after "6719,". **Effective** for any transfer, sale, or holding out for sale or resale occurring after 8-10-2005.

• **2005, Surface Transportation Extension Act of 2005, Part VI (P.L. 109-42)**

P.L. 109-42, §7(a)(3):

Amended Code Sec. 9503(b)(6)(B) by adding at the end a new sentence. **Effective** 7-30-2005.

P.L. 109-42, §7(d)(1):

Amended Code Sec. 9503(b)(6)(B) by striking the last sentence. For the **effective date**, see Act Sec. 7(e)(2), below. Prior to being stricken, the last sentence of Code Sec. 9503(b)(6)(B) read as follows:

The preceding sentence shall be applied by substituting "August 15, 2005" for the date therein.

P.L. 109-42, §7(e)(2), provides:

(2) SUBSEQUENT REPEAL.—The amendments made by subsection (d) shall take effect on the date of the enactment of the Safe, Accountable, Flexible, Efficient Transportation Equity Act: A Legacy for Users and shall be executed immediately before the amendments made by such Act.

• **2005, Surface Transportation Extension Act of 2005, Part V (P.L. 109-40)**

P.L. 109-40, §9(a)(3):

Amended Code Sec. 9503(b)(6)(B) by striking "July 28, 2005" and inserting "July 31, 2005". **Effective** 7-28-2005.

• **2005, Surface Transportation Extension Act of 2005, Part IV (P.L. 109-37)**

P.L. 109-37, §9(a)(3):

Amended Code Sec. 9503(b)(6)(B) by striking "July 22, 2005" and inserting "July 28, 2005". **Effective** 7-22-2005.

• **2005, Surface Transportation Extension Act of 2005, Part III (P.L. 109-35)**

P.L. 109-35, §9(a)(3):

Amended Code Sec. 9503(b)(6)(B) by striking "July 20, 2005" and inserting "July 22, 2005". **Effective** 7-20-2005.

• **2005, Surface Transportation Extension Act of 2005, Part II (P.L. 109-20)**

P.L. 109-20, §9(a)(3):

Amended Code Sec. 9503(b)(6)(B) by striking "July 1, 2005" and inserting "July 20, 2005". **Effective** 7-1-2005.

• **2005, Surface Transportation Extension Act of 2005 (P.L. 109-14)**

P.L. 109-14, §9(a)(3):

Amended Code Sec. 9503(b)(6)(B) by striking "June 1, 2005" and inserting "July 1, 2005". **Effective** 5-31-2005.

• **2004, American Jobs Creation Act of 2004 (P.L. 108-357)**

P.L. 108-357, §301(c)(11):

Amended Code Sec. 9503(b)(1) by adding at the end a new flush sentence. **Effective** for fuel sold or used after 12-31-2004.

P.L. 108-357, §301(c)(12)(A)-(C):

Amended Code Sec. 9503(b)(4) by adding "or" at the end of subparagraph (C), by striking the comma at the end of subparagraph (D)(iii) and inserting a period, and by striking subparagraphs (E) and (F). **Effective** for fuel sold or used after 9-30-2004. Prior to being stricken, Code Sec. 9503(b)(4)(E) and (F) read as follows:

(E) in the case of fuels described in section 4041(b)(2)(A), 4041(k), or 4081(c), section 4041 or 4081 before October 1, 2003, and for the period beginning after September 30, 2004, and before October 1, 2005, with respect to a rate equal to 2.5 cents per gallon, or

(F) in the case of fuels described in section 4081(c)(2), such section before October 1, 2003, and for the period beginning after September 30, 2004, and before October 1, 2005, with respect to a rate equal to 2.8 cents per gallon.

P.L. 108-357, §868(a):

Amended Code Sec. 9503(b) by redesignating paragraph (5) as paragraph (6) and inserting after paragraph (4) a new paragraph (5). **Effective** for penalties assessed on or after 10-22-2004.

P.L. 108-357, §868(b)(1):

Amended the heading of Code Sec. 9503(b) by inserting "AND PENALTIES" after "TAXES". **Effective** for penalties assessed on or after 10-22-2004.

P.L. 108-357, §868(b)(2):

Amended the heading of Code Sec. 9503(b)(1) by striking "IN GENERAL" and inserting "CERTAIN TAXES". **Effective** for penalties assessed on or after 10-22-2004.

• **2004, Surface Transportation Extension Act of 2004, Part V (P.L. 108-310)**

P.L. 108-310, §13(a)(3):

Amended Code Sec. 9503(b)(5)(B) by striking "October 1, 2004" and inserting "June 1, 2005". **Effective** 9-30-2004.

P.L. 108-310, §13(c):

Amended Code Sec. 9503(b)(4)(E) and (F) by inserting "before October 1, 2003, and for the period beginning after September 30, 2004, and" before "before October 1, 2005". **Effective** for taxes imposed after 9-30-2003.

• **2004, Surface Transportation Extension Act of 2004, Part IV (P.L. 108-280)**

P.L. 108-280, §10(a)(3):

Amended Code Sec. 9503(b)(5)(B) by striking "August 1, 2004" and inserting "October 1, 2004". **Effective** 7-30-2004. For a special rule, see Act Sec. 10(a)(4), below.

P.L. 108-280, §10(a)(4) [stricken by P.L. 108-310, §13(a)(4)], provides:

(4) SPECIAL RULE FOR CORE HIGHWAY PROGRAMS.—

(A) IN GENERAL.—In the case of a core highway program, subsections (b)(5) and (c)(1) of section 9503 of such Code shall be applied by substituting "September 25, 2004" for "October 1, 2004".

(B) CORE HIGHWAY PROGRAM.—For purposes of subparagraph (A), the term "core highway program" means any program (other than any program carried out by the National Highway Traffic Safety Administration and any program carried out by the Federal Motor Carrier Administration) funded from the Highway Trust Fund (other than the Mass Transit Account).

• **2004, Surface Transportation Extension Act of 2004, Part III (P.L. 108-263)**

P.L. 108-263, §10(a)(3):

Amended Code Sec. 9503(b)(5)(B) by striking "July 1, 2004" and inserting "August 1, 2004". **Effective** 6-30-2004.

• **2004, Surface Transportation Extension Act of 2004, Part II (P.L. 108-224)**

P.L. 108-224, §10(a)(3):

Amended Code Sec. 9503(b)(5)(B) by striking "May 1, 2004" and inserting "July 1, 2004". **Effective** 4-30-2004.

• **2004, Surface Transportation Extension Act of 2004 (P.L. 108-202)**

P.L. 108-202, §12(a)(3):

Amended Code Sec. 9503(b)(5)(B) by striking "March 1, 2004" and inserting "May 1, 2004". **Effective** 2-29-2004.

• **2003, Surface Transportation Extension Act of 2003 (P.L. 108-88)**

P.L. 108-88, §12(a)(3):

Amended Code Sec. 9503(b)(5)(B) by striking "October 1, 2003" and inserting "March 1, 2004". **Effective** 9-30-2003.

• **2000, Community Renewal Tax Relief Act of 2000 (P.L. 106-554)**

P.L. 106-554, §318(e)(1):

Amended Code Sec. 9503(b) by striking paragraph (5) and redesignating paragraph (6) as paragraph (5). **Effective** with respect to taxes received in the Treasury after 12-21-2000. Prior to being stricken, Code Sec. 9503(b)(5) read as follows:

(5) GENERAL REVENUE DEPOSITS OF CERTAIN TAXES ON ALCOHOL MIXTURES.—For purposes of this section, the amounts which would (but for this paragraph) be required to be appropriated under subparagraphs (A) and (E) of paragraph (1) shall be reduced by—

(A) 0.6 cent per gallon in the case of taxes imposed on any mixture at least 10 percent of which is alcohol (as defined in section 4081(c)(3)) if any portion of such alcohol is ethanol, and

(B) 0.67 cent per gallon in the case of gasoline, diesel fuel, or kerosene used in producing a mixture described in subparagraph (A).

• **1998, Transportation Equity Act for the 21st Century (P.L. 105-178)**

P.L. 105-178, §9002(c)(1)(A)-(B):

Amended Code Sec. 9503(b) by striking "1999" each place it appears and inserting "2005", and by striking "2000" each place it appears and inserting "2006". **Effective** 6-9-98.

ESTABLISHMENT OF TRUST FUNDS

P.L. 105-178, §9002(f)(1):

Amended Code Sec. 9503(b)(1) by striking subparagraph (C), by striking "and tread rubber" in subparagraph (D), and by redesignating subparagraphs (D), (E), and (F) as subparagraphs (C), (D), and (E), respectively. **Effective** 6-9-98. Prior to being stricken, Code Sec. 9503(f)(1)(C) read as follows:

(C) section 4061 (relating to tax on trucks and truck parts),

P.L. 105-178, §9004(c):

Amended Code Sec. 9503(b) by adding at the end a new paragraph (6). **Effective** 6-9-98.

P.L. 105-178, §9005(a)(1):

Amended Code Sec. 9503(b)(4)(D), as amended by Act Sec. 9011(b)(2), by striking "exceeds 11.5 cents per gallon," and inserting new material following "rate of tax as". **Effective** 6-9-98.

P.L. 105-178, §9011(b)(2):

Amended Code Sec. 9503(b)(4)(D). **Effective** 6-9-98. Prior to amendment, Code Sec. 9503(b)(4)(D) read as follows:

(D) in the case of fuels used as described in paragraph (4)(D), (5)(B), or (6)(D) of subsection (c), section 4041 or 4081—

(i) with respect to so much of the rate of tax on gasoline or special motor fuels as exceeds 11.5 cents per gallon, and

(ii) with respect to so much of the rate of tax on diesel fuel or kerosene as exceeds 17.5 cents per gallon,

• **1997, Taxpayer Relief Act of 1997 (P.L. 105-34)**

P.L. 105-34, §901(a):

Amended Code Sec. 9503(b)(4). **Effective** for taxes received in the Treasury after 9-30-97. For a special rule, see Act Sec. 901(e), below. Prior to amendment, Code Sec. 9503(b)(4) read as follows:

(4) CERTAIN ADDITIONAL TAXES NOT TRANSFERRED TO HIGHWAY TRUST FUND.—For purposes of paragraphs (1) and (2)—

(A) there shall not be taken into account the taxes imposed by section 4041(d), and

(B) there shall be taken into account the taxes imposed by sections 4041 and 4081 only to the extent attributable to the Highway Trust Fund financing rate.

P.L. 105-34, §901(e), provides:

(e) DELAYED DEPOSITS OF HIGHWAY MOTOR FUEL TAX REVENUES.—Notwithstanding section 6302 of the Internal Revenue Code of 1986, in the case of deposits of taxes imposed by sections 4041 and 4081 (other than subsection (a)(2)(A)(ii)) of the Internal Revenue Code of 1986, the due date for any deposit which would (but for this subsection) be required to be made after July 31, 1998, and before October 1, 1998, shall be October 5, 1998.

P.L. 105-34, §1032(e)(13):

Amended Code Sec. 9503(b)(1)(E) by striking "and diesel fuel" and inserting ", diesel fuel, and kerosene". **Effective** 7-1-98.

P.L. 105-34, §1032(e)(14):

Amended Code Sec. 9503(b)(5)(B) by striking "or diesel fuel" and inserting ", diesel fuel, or kerosene". **Effective** 7-1-98.

• **1993, Omnibus Budget Reconciliation Act of 1993 (P.L. 103-66)**

P.L. 103-66, §13242(d)(34)(A)-(C):

Amended Code Sec. 9503(b)(1) by striking "gasoline," in subparagraph (E) and inserting "gasoline and diesel fuel), and", by striking subparagraph (F), and by redesignating subparagraph (G) as subparagraph (F). **Effective** 1-1-94. Prior to amendment, Code Sec. 9503(b)(1)(F) read as follows:

(F) section 4091 (relating to tax on diesel fuel), and

P.L. 103-66, §13242(d)(35)(A):

Amended Code Sec. 9503(b)(4)(B) by striking ",4081, and 4091" and inserting "and 4081" and by striking "rates under such sections" and inserting "rate". **Effective** 1-1-94.

P.L. 103-66, §13242(d)(35)(B):

Amended Code Sec. 9503(b)(4)(C), as amended by subchapter A of the Act, by striking "4091" and inserting "4081". [Amendment not made. Provision relating to Code Sec. 9503(b)(4)(C) dropped in Conference Agreement.] **Effective** 1-1-94.

P.L. 103-66, §13242(d)(36):

Amended Code Sec. 9503(b)(5) by striking ", (E) and (F)" and inserting "and (E)". **Effective** 1-1-94.

• **1991, Intermodal Surface Transportation Efficiency Act of 1991 (P.L. 102-240)**

P.L. 102-240, §8002(d)(1)(A)-(B):

Amended Code Sec. 9503(b) by striking "1995" each place it appears and inserting "1999", and by striking "1996" each place it appears and inserting "2000". **Effective** 12-18-91.

• **1990, Omnibus Budget Reconciliation Act of 1990 (P.L. 101-508)**

P.L. 101-508, §11211(a)(5)(D):

Amended Code Sec. 9503(b)(4)(B) by striking "4081" and inserting "4041, 4081". **Effective** for gasoline removed (as defined in section 4082 of the Internal Revenue Code of 1986) after 11-30-90.

P.L. 101-508, §11211(a)(5)(F):

Amended Code Sec. 9503(b) by adding at the end thereof a new paragraph (5). **Effective** for gasoline removed (as defined in section 4082 of the Internal Revenue Code of 1986) after 11-30-90.

P.L. 101-508, §11211(g)(1)(A)-(B):

Amended Code Sec. 9503(b) by striking "1993" each place it appears and inserting "1995", and by striking "1994" each place it appears and inserting "1996". **Effective** 11-5-90.

• **1989, Omnibus Budget Reconciliation Act of 1989 (P.L. 101-239)**

P.L. 101-239, §7822(b)(6):

Amended Code Sec. 9503(b)(4)(A) by striking "sections 4041(d)" and inserting "section 4041(d)". **Effective** as if included in the provision of P.L. 100-203 to which it relates.

• **1987, Revenue Act of 1987 (P.L. 100-203)**

P.L. 100-203, §10502(d)(13):

Amended Code Sec. 9503(b)(1) by striking out subparagraph (F) and inserting in lieu thereof new subparagraph (F). **Effective** for sales after 3-31-88. Prior to amendment, Code Sec. 9503(b)(1)(F) read as follows:

(F) Section 4091 (relating to tax on lubricating oil), and

P.L. 100-203, §10502(d)(14):

Amended Code Sec. 9503(b)(4). **Effective** for sales after 3-31-88. Prior to amendment, Code Sec. 9503(b)(4) read as follows:

(4) CERTAIN ADDITIONAL TAXES NOT TRANSFERRED TO HIGHWAY TRUST FUND.—For purposes of paragraphs (1) and (2), there shall not be taken into account the taxes imposed by section 4041(d) and so much of the taxes imposed by section 4081 as is attributable to the Leaking Underground Storage Tank Trust Fund financing rate.

• **1987, Surface Transportation and Uniform Relocation Assistance Act of 1987 (P.L. 100-17)**

P.L. 100-17, §503(a)(1)-(2):

Amended Code Sec. 9503(b) by striking out "1988" each place it appears and inserting in lieu thereof "1993", and by striking out "1989" each place it appears and inserting in lieu thereof "1994". **Effective** 4-2-87.

• **1986, Superfund Amendments and Reauthorization Act of 1986 (P.L. 99-499)**

P.L. 99-499, §521(b)(1)(A):

Amended Code Sec. 9503(b) by adding at the end thereof new paragraph (4). **Effective** 1-1-87.

[Sec. 9503(c)]

(c) EXPENDITURES FROM HIGHWAY TRUST FUND.—

(1) FEDERAL-AID HIGHWAY PROGRAM.—Except as provided in subsection (e), amounts in the Highway Trust Fund shall be available, as provided by appropriation Acts, for making expenditures before October 1, 2026, to meet those obligations of the United States heretofore or hereafter incurred which are authorized to be paid out of the Infrastructure Investment and Jobs Act or any other provision of law which was referred to in this paragraph before the date of the enactment of such Act (as such Act and provisions of law are in effect on the date of the enactment of such Act).

(2) FLOOR STOCKS REFUNDS.—The Secretary shall pay from time to time from the Highway Trust Fund into the general fund of the Treasury amounts equivalent to the floor stocks refunds made before July 1, 2029, under section 6412(a). The amounts payable from the Highway Trust Fund under the preceding sentence shall be determined by taking into account only the portion of the taxes which are deposited into the Highway Trust Fund.

(3) TRANSFERS FROM THE TRUST FUND FOR MOTORBOAT FUEL TAXES.—

(A) TRANSFER TO LAND AND WATER CONSERVATION FUND.—

(i) IN GENERAL.—The Secretary shall pay from time to time from the Highway Trust Fund into the land and water conservation fund provided for in chapter 2003 of title 54 amounts (as determined by the Secretary) equivalent to the motorboat fuel taxes received on or after October 1, 2005, and before October 1, 2028.

(ii) LIMITATION.—The aggregate amount transferred under this subparagraph during any fiscal year shall not exceed $1,000,000.

(B) EXCESS FUNDS TRANSFERRED TO SPORT FISH RESTORATION AND BOATING TRUST FUND.—Any amounts in the Highway Trust Fund—

ESTABLISHMENT OF TRUST FUNDS

(i) which are attributable to motorboat fuel taxes, and

(ii) which are not transferred from the Highway Trust Fund under subparagraph (A),

shall be transferred by the Secretary from the Highway Trust Fund into the Sport Fish Restoration and Boating Trust Fund.

(C) MOTORBOAT FUEL TAXES.—For purposes of this paragraph, the term "motorboat fuel taxes" means the taxes under section 4041(a)(2) with respect to special motor fuels used as fuel in motorboats and under section 4081 with respect to gasoline used as fuel in motorboats, but only to the extent such taxes are deposited into the Highway Trust Fund.

(D) DETERMINATION.—The amount of payments made under this paragraph after October 1, 1986 shall be determined by the Secretary in accordance with the methodology described in the Treasury Department's Report to Congress of June 1986 entitled "Gasoline Excise Tax Revenues Attributable to Fuel Used in Recreational Motorboats."

(4) TRANSFERS FROM THE TRUST FUND FOR SMALL-ENGINE FUEL TAXES.—

(A) IN GENERAL.—The Secretary shall pay from time to time from the Highway Trust Fund into the Sport Fish Restoration and Boating Trust Fund amounts (as determined by him) equivalent to the small-engine fuel taxes received on or after December 1, 1990, and before October 1, 2028.

(B) SMALL-ENGINE FUEL TAXES.—For purposes of this paragraph, the term "small-engine fuel taxes" means the taxes under section 4081 with respect to gasoline used as a fuel in the nonbusiness use of small-engine outdoor power equipment, but only to the extent such taxes are deposited into the Highway Trust Fund.

(5) TRANSFERS FROM THE TRUST FUND FOR CERTAIN AVIATION FUEL TAXES.—The Secretary shall pay at least monthly from the Highway Trust Fund into the Airport and Airway Trust Fund amounts (as determined by the Secretary) equivalent to the taxes received on or after October 1, 2005, under section 4081 with respect to so much of the rate of tax as does not exceed—

(A) 4.3 cents per gallon of kerosene subject to section 6427(l)(4)(A) with respect to which a payment has been made by the Secretary under section 6427(l), and

(B) 21.8 cents per gallon of kerosene subject to section 6427(l)(4)(B) with respect to which a payment has been made by the Secretary under section 6427(l).

Transfers under the preceding sentence shall be made on the basis of estimates by the Secretary, and proper adjustments shall be made in the amounts subsequently transferred to the extent prior estimates were in excess of or less than the amounts required to be transferred. Any amount allowed as a credit under section 34 by reason of paragraph (4) of section 6427(l) shall be treated for purposes of subparagraphs (A) and (B) as a payment made by the Secretary under such paragraph.

Amendments

- **2021, Infrastructure Investment and Jobs Act (P.L. 117-58)**

P.L. 117-58, §80101(a)(1), Div. H:

Amended Code Sec. 9503(c)(1) by striking "October 1, 2021" and inserting "October 1, 2026". **Effective** 11-15-2021.

P.L. 117-58, §80101(a)(2), Div. H:

Amended Code Sec. 9503(c)(1) by striking "Continuing Appropriations Act, 2021 and Other Extensions Act" and inserting "Infrastructure Investment and Jobs Act". **Effective** 11-15-2021.

P.L. 117-58, §80102(e)(1)(B), Div. H:

Amended Code Sec. 9503(c)(2) by striking "July 1, 2023" and inserting "July 1, 2029". **Effective** 10-1-2021.

P.L. 117-58, §80102(e)(2)(A), Div. H:

Amended Code Sec. 9503(c) by striking "October 1, 2022" and inserting "October 1, 2028" in paragraphs (3)(A)(i) and (4)(A). **Effective** 10-1-2021.

- **2021, Further Surface Transportation Extension Act of 2021 (P.L. 117-52)**

P.L. 117-52, §4(a)(1)-(2):

Amended Code Sec. 9503(c)(1) by striking "November 1, 2021" and inserting "December 4, 2021" and by striking "Surface Transportation Extension Act of 2021" each place it appears and inserting "Further Surface Transportation Extension Act of 2021". **Effective** 10-31-2021. For a special rule, see Act Sec. 4(d)(1)-(3), below.

P.L. 117-52, §4(d)(1)-(3), provides:

(d) SPECIAL RULE FOR AMENDMENTS.—On the date of enactment of H.R. 3684 (117th Congress)—

(1) subsections (a), (b), and (c) of this section, the amendments made by such subsections, section 201 of the Surface Transportation Extension Act of 2021 (Public Law 117-44), and the amendments made by such section shall cease to be effective;

(2) the text of the laws amended by subsections (a), (b), and (c) of this section and section 201 of the Surface Transportation Extension Act of 2021 (Public Law 117-44) shall revert back so as to read as the text read on September 30, 2021; and

(3) the amendments made by H.R. 3684 (117th Congress) shall be executed as if this section and section 201 of the Surface Transportation Extension Act had not been enacted.

- **2021, Surface Transportation Extension Act of 2021 (P.L. 117-44)**

P.L. 117-44, §201(a)(1)-(2):

Amended Code Sec. 9503(c)(1) by striking "October 1, 2021" and inserting "November 1, 2021", and by striking "Continuing Appropriations Act, 2021 and Other Extensions Act" and inserting "Surface Transportation Extension Act of 2021". **Effective** 10-2-2021. For a special rule, see Act Sec. 201(d)(1)-(3), below.

P.L. 117-44, §201(d)(1)-(3), provides:

(d) SPECIAL RULE FOR EXECUTION OF AMENDMENTS.—On the date of enactment of H.R. 3684 (117th Congress)—

(1) this section and the amendments made by this section shall cease to be effective;

(2) the text of the laws amended by this section shall revert back so as to read as the text read on the day before the date of enactment of this section; and

(3) the amendments made by H.R. 3684 (117th Congress) shall be executed as if this section had not been enacted.

- **2020, Continuing Appropriations Act, 2021 and Other Extensions Act (P.L. 116-159)**

P.L. 116-159, §1201(1)-(2):

Amended Code Sec. 9503(c)(1) by striking "October 1, 2020" and inserting "October 1, 2021" and by striking "FAST Act" and inserting "Continuing Appropriations Act, 2021 and Other Extensions Act". **Effective** 10-1-2020.

- **2018, Tax Technical Corrections Act of 2018 (P.L. 115-141)**

P.L. 115-141, §401(a)(341), Div. U:

Amended Code Sec. 9503(c)(5) by striking "and before October 1, 2011," following "October 1, 2005,". **Effective** 3-23-2018.

- **2015, Fixing America's Surface Transportation Act (P.L. 114-94)**

P.L. 114-94, §31101(a)(1)-(2):

Amended Code Sec. 9503(c)(1) by striking "December 5, 2015" and inserting "October 1, 2020", and by striking "Surface Transportation Extension Act of 2015, Part II" and inserting "FAST Act". **Effective** 12-4-2015.

P.L. 114-94, §31102(e)(1)(B):

Amended Code Sec. 9503(c)(2) by striking "July 1, 2017" and inserting "July 1, 2023". **Effective** 10-1-2016.

P.L. 114-94, §31102(e)(2)(A):

Amended Code Sec. 9503(c)(3)(A)(i) and (4)(A) by striking "October 1, 2016" and inserting "October 1, 2022". **Effective** 10-1-2016.

- **2015, Surface Transportation Extension Act of 2015, Part II (P.L. 114-87)**

P.L. 114-87, §2001(a)(1)-(2):

Amended Code Sec. 9503(c)(1) by striking "November 21, 2015" and inserting "December 5, 2015", and by striking "Surface Transportation Extension Act of 2015" and inserting "Surface Transportation Extension Act of 2015, Part II". **Effective** 11-20-2015.

- **2015, Surface Transportation Extension Act of 2015 (P.L. 114-73)**

P.L. 114-73, §2001(a)(1)-(2):

Amended Code Sec. 9503(c)(1) by striking "October 30, 2015" and inserting "November 21, 2015", and by striking "Surface Transportation and Veterans Health Care Choice Improvement Act of 2015" and inserting "Surface Transportation Extension Act of 2015". **Effective** 10-29-2015.

- **2015, Surface Transportation and Veterans Health Care Choice Improvement Act of 2015 (P.L. 114-41)**

P.L. 114-41, §2001(a)(1)-(2):

Amended Code Sec. 9503(c)(1) by striking "August 1, 2015" and inserting "October 30, 2015", and by striking "Highway and Transportation Funding Act of 2015" and inserting "Surface Transportation and Veterans Health Care Choice Improvement Act of 2015". **Effective** 7-31-2015.

- **2015, Highway and Transportation Funding Act of 2015 (P.L. 114-21)**

P.L. 114-21, §2001(a)(1)-(2):

Amended Code Sec. 9503(c)(1) by striking "June 1, 2015" and inserting "August 1, 2015", and by striking "Highway and Transportation Funding Act of 2014" and inserting "Highway and Transportation Funding Act of 2015". **Effective** 5-29-2015.

ESTABLISHMENT OF TRUST FUNDS

- **2014, (P.L. 113-287)**

P.L. 113-287, § 5(h):

Amended Code Sec. 9503(c)(3)(A)(i) by striking "title I of the Land and Water Conservation Fund Act of 1965" and substituting "chapter 2003 of title 54". **Effective** 12-19-2014.

- **2014, Highway and Transportation Funding Act of 2014 (P.L. 113-159)**

P.L. 113-159, § 2001(a)(1)-(2):

Amended Code Sec. 9503(c)(1) by striking "October 1, 2014" and inserting "June 1, 2015", and by striking "MAP-21" and inserting "Highway and Transportation Funding Act of 2014". **Effective** 8-8-2014.

- **2012, Highway Investment, Job Creation, and Economic Growth Act of 2012 (P.L. 112-141)**

P.L. 112-141, § 40101(a)(1)-(2):

Amended Code Sec. 9503(c)(1) by striking "July 1, 2012" and inserting "October 1, 2014", and by striking "Surface Transportation Extension Act of 2012" and inserting "MAP-21". **Effective** 7-1-2012.

P.L. 112-141, § 40102(e)(1)(B):

Amended Code Sec. 9503(c)(2) by striking "April 1, 2013" and inserting "July 1, 2017". **Effective** 7-1-2012.

P.L. 112-141, § 40102(e)(2)(A):

Amended Code Sec. 9503(c) by striking "July 1, 2012" and inserting "October 1, 2016" in paragraphs (3)(A)(i) and (4)(A). **Effective** 7-1-2012.

- **2012, Temporary Surface Transportation Extension Act of 2012 (P.L. 112-140)**

P.L. 112-140, § 1(c), provides:

(c) SPECIAL RULE FOR EXECUTION OF AMENDMENTS IN MAP–21.—On the date of enactment of the MAP–21 [P.L. 112-141]—

(1) this Act and the amendments made by this Act shall cease to be effective;

(2) the text of the laws amended by this Act shall revert back so as to read as the text read on the day before the date of enactment of this Act; and

(3) the amendments made by the MAP–21 shall be executed as if this Act had not been enacted.

P.L. 112-140, § 401(a)(1)-(2):

Amended Code Sec. 9503(c)(1) by striking "July 1, 2012" and inserting "July 7, 2012"; and by striking "Surface Transportation Extension Act of 2012" and inserting "Temporary Surface Transportation Extension Act of 2012". **Effective** 7-1-2012. For a special rule, see Act Sec. 1(c), above.

P.L. 112-140, § 402(d)(1)(B):

Amended Code Sec. 9503(c)(2) by striking "April 1, 2013" and inserting "April 7, 2013". **Effective** 7-1-2012. For a special rule, see Act Sec. 1(c), above.

P.L. 112-140, § 402(d)(2)(A):

Amended Code Sec. 9503(c) by striking "July 1, 2012" and inserting "July 7, 2012" in paragraphs (3)(A)(i) and (4)(A). **Effective** 7-1-2012. For a special rule, see Act Sec. 1(c), above.

- **2012, Surface Transportation Extension Act of 2012 (P.L. 112-102)**

P.L. 112-102, § 401(a)(1)-(2):

Amended Code Sec. 9503(c)(1) by striking "April 1, 2012" and inserting "July 1, 2012"; and by striking "Surface Transportation Extension Act of 2011, Part II" and inserting "Surface Transportation Extension Act of 2012". **Effective** 4-1-2012.

P.L. 112-102, § 402(e)(1)(B):

Amended Code Sec. 9503(c)(2) by striking "January 1, 2013" and inserting "April 1, 2013". **Effective** 4-1-2012.

P.L. 112-102, § 402(e)(2)(A):

Amended Code Sec. 9503(c)(3)(A)(i) and (4)(A) by striking "April 1, 2012" and inserting "July 1, 2012". **Effective** 4-1-2012.

- **2011, Surface Transportation Extension Act of 2011, Part II (P.L. 112-30)**

P.L. 112-30, § 141(a)(1)-(2):

Amended Code Sec. 9503(c)(1) by striking "October 1, 2011" and inserting "April 1, 2012"; and by striking "Surface Transportation Extension Act of 2011" and inserting "Surface Transportation Extension Act of 2011, Part II". **Effective** 10-1-2011.

P.L. 112-30, § 142(e)(1)(B):

Amended Code Sec. 9503(c)(2) by striking "July 1, 2012" and inserting "January 1, 2013". **Effective** 10-1-2011.

P.L. 112-30, § 142(e)(2)(A):

Amended Code Sec. 9503(c)(3(A)(i) and (4)(A) by striking "October 1, 2011" and inserting "April 1, 2012". **Effective** 10-1-2011.

- **2011, Surface Transportation Extension Act of 2011 (P.L. 112-5)**

P.L. 112-5, § 401(a)(1)-(2):

Amended Code Sec. 9503(c)(1) by striking "March 5, 2011" and inserting "October 1, 2011"; by striking "the Surface Transportation Extension Act of 2010, Part II" and inserting "the Surface Transportation Extension Act of 2011". **Effective** 3-4-2011.

- **2010, Surface Transportation Extension Act of 2010, Part II (P.L. 111-322)**

P.L. 111-322, § 2401(a)(1)-(2):

Amended Code Sec. 9503(c)(1) by striking "December 31, 2010 (January 1, 2011, in the case of expenditures for administrative expenses)" and inserting "March 5, 2011"; by striking "the Surface Transportation Extension Act of 2010" and inserting "the Surface Transportation Extension Act of 2010, Part II". **Effective** 12-31-2010.

- **2010, Hiring Incentives to Restore Employment Act (P.L. 111-147)**

P.L. 111-147, § 444(a):

Amended Code Sec. 9503(c) by striking paragraph (2) and by redesignating paragraphs (3), (4), (5), and (6) as paragraphs (2), (3), (4), and (5), respectively. **Effective** for transfers relating to amounts paid and credits allowed after 3-18-2010. Prior to being stricken, Code Sec. 9503(c)(2) read as follows:

(2) TRANSFERS FROM HIGHWAY TRUST FUND FOR CERTAIN REPAYMENTS AND CREDITS.—

(A) IN GENERAL.—The Secretary shall pay from time to time from the Highway Trust Fund into the general fund of the Treasury amounts equivalent to—

(i) the amounts paid before July 1, 2012, under—

(I) section 6420 (relating to amounts paid in respect of gasoline used on farms),

(II) section 6421 (relating to amounts paid in respect of gasoline used for certain nonhighway purposes or by local transit systems), and

(III) section 6427 (relating to fuels not used for taxable purposes), on the basis of claims filed for periods ending before October 1, 2011, and

(ii) the credits allowed under section 34 (relating to credit for certain uses of fuel) with respect to fuel used before October 1, 2011.

The amounts payable from the Highway Trust Fund under this subparagraph or paragraph (3) shall be determined by taking into account only the portion of the taxes which are deposited into the Highway Trust Fund. Clauses (i)(III) and (ii) shall not apply to claims under section 6427(e).

(B) TRANSFERS BASED ON ESTIMATES.—Transfers under subparagraph (A) shall be made on the basis of estimates by the Secretary, and proper adjustments shall be made in amounts subsequently transferred to the extent prior estimates were in excess or less than the amounts required to be transferred.

(C) EXCEPTION FOR USE IN AIRCRAFT AND MOTORBOATS.—This paragraph shall not apply to amounts estimated by the Secretary as attributable to use of gasoline and special fuels in motorboats or in aircraft.

P.L. 111-147, § 444(b)(3):

Amended Code Sec. 9503(c)(2), as redesignated by Act Sec. 444(a), by adding at the end a new sentence. **Effective** for transfers relating to amounts paid and credits allowed after 3-18-2010.

P.L. 111-147, § 445(a)(1)(A)-(B):

Amended Code Sec. 9503(c)(1) by striking "September 30, 2009 (October 1, 2009" and inserting "December 31, 2010 (January 1, 2011"; and by striking "under" and all that follows and inserting "under the Surface Transportation Extension Act of 2010 or any other provision of law which was referred to in this paragraph before the date of the enactment of such Act (as such Act and provisions of law are in effect on the date of the enactment of such Act).". **Effective** 9-30-2009. Prior to being stricken, all that followed "under" in Code Sec. 9503(c)(1) read as follows:

the first Continuing Appropriations Resolution for Fiscal Year 2010 enacted into law or any other provision of law which was referred to in this paragraph before the date of the enactment of such Continuing Appropriations Resolution (as such Resolution and provisions of law are in effect on the date of the enactment of the last amendment to such Resolution).

- **2010, Temporary Extension Act of 2010 (P.L. 111-144)**

P.L. 111-144, § 4, provides:

SEC. 4. EXTENSION OF SURFACE TRANSPORTATION PROGRAMS.

(a) IN GENERAL.—Except as provided in subsection (b), for purposes of the continued extension of surface transportation programs and related authority to make expenditures from the Highway Trust Fund and other trust funds under sections 157 through 162 of the Continuing Appropriations Resolution, 2010 (Public Law 111–68; 123 Stat. 2050), the date specified in section 106(3) of that resolution (Public Law 111–68; 123 Stat. 2045) shall be deemed to be March 28, 2010.

(b) EXCEPTION.—Subsection (a) shall not apply if an extension of the programs and authorities described in that subsection for a longer term than the extension contained in the Continuing Appropriations Resolution, 2010 (Public Law 111–68; 123 Stat. 2050), is enacted before the date of enactment of this Act.

- **2009, (P.L. 111-88)**

P.L. 111-88, § 103:

Amended Code Sec. 9503(c)(1) by inserting "the last amendment to" after "on the date of the enactment of". **Effective** 10-30-2009.

- **2009, (P.L. 111-68)**

P.L. 111-68, § 159(a)(1)(A)-(B), provides:

(a) EXTENSION OF AUTHORITY FOR EXPENDITURES FROM HIGHWAY TRUST FUND.—

(1) Paragraph (1) of section 9503(c) of the Internal Revenue Code of 1986 shall be applied—

(A) by substituting the date specified in section 106(3) [October 31, 2009] of this joint resolution for "September 30, 2009"; and

(B) by substituting the date that is 1 day after the date specified in section 106(3) [October 31, 2009] of this joint resolution for "October 1, 2009".

P.L. 111-68, § 159(a)(2):

Amended Code Sec. 9503(c)(1) by striking "under" and all that follows and inserting "under the first Continuing Appropriations Resolution for Fiscal Year 2010 enacted into law or any other provision of law which was referred to in this paragraph before the date of the enactment of such Continuing Appropriations Resolution (as such Resolution and provisions of law are in effect on the date of the enactment of such Resolution).". **Effective** 10-1-2009. Prior to being stricken, all the follows "under" in Code Sec. 9503(c)(1) read as follows:

the SAFETEA-LU Technical Corrections Act of 2008 or any other provision of law which was referred to in this paragraph before the date of the enactment of such Act

ESTABLISHMENT OF TRUST FUNDS

(as such Act and provisions of law are in effect on the date of the enactment of such Act).

• **2008, SAFETEA-LU Technical Corrections Act of 2008 (P.L. 110-244)**

P.L. 110-244, §121(c):

Amended Code Sec. 9503(c)(1) by striking "Safe, Accountable, Flexible, Efficient Transportation Equity Act: A Legacy for Users" and inserting "SAFETEA-LU Technical Corrections Act of 2008". **Effective** 6-6-2008.

• **2007, Tax Technical Corrections Act of 2007 (P.L. 110-172)**

P.L. 110-172, §11(a)(44):

Amended Code Sec. 9503(c) by redesignating paragraph (7) as paragraph (6). **Effective** 12-29-2007.

• **2006, Tax Relief and Health Care Act of 2006 (P.L. 109-432)**

P.L. 109-432, Division A, §420(b)(6)(A)-(B):

Amended Code Sec. 9503(c)(7)[(6)] by amending subparagraphs (A) and (B), and by striking "or (5)" following "paragraph (4)" in the matter following subparagraph (B). **Effective** for kerosene sold after 9-30-2005. For special rules, see Act Sec. 420(c)(2) and (d) in the amendment notes following Code Sec. 9502(d). Prior to amendment, Code Sec. 9503(c)(7)[(6)](A)-(B) read as follows:

(A) 4.3 cents per gallon of kerosene with respect to which a payment has been made by the Secretary under section 6427(l)(4), and

(B) 21.8 cents per gallon of kerosene with respect to which a payment has been made by the Secretary under section 6427(l)(5).

• **2005, Safe, Accountable, Flexible, Efficient Transportation Equity Act: A Legacy for Users (P.L. 109-59)**

P.L. 109-59, §11101(c)(1)(A)-(B):

Amended Code Sec. 9503(c)(2)-(3) by striking "2005" each place it appears and inserting "2011", and by striking "2006" each place it appears and inserting "2012". **Effective** 8-10-2005.

P.L. 109-59, §11101(c)(2)(A):

Amended Code Sec. 9503(c)(5)(A) by striking "2005" and inserting "2011". **Effective** 8-10-2005.

P.L. 109-59, §11101(d)(1)(A):

Amended Code Sec. 9503(c)(1). **Effective** 8-10-2005. Prior to amendment, Code Sec. 9503(c)(1) read as follows:

(1) FEDERAL-AID HIGHWAY PROGRAM.—Except as provided in subsection (e), amounts in the Highway Trust Fund shall be available, as provided by appropriation Acts, for making expenditures before August 15, 2005, to meet those obligations of the United States heretofore or hereafter incurred which are—

(A) authorized by law to be paid out of the Highway Trust Fund established by section 209 of the Highway Revenue Act of 1956,

(B) authorized to be paid out of the Highway Trust Fund under title I or II of the Surface Transportation Assistance Act of 1982,

(C) authorized to be paid out of the Highway Trust Fund under the Surface Transportation and Uniform Relocation Assistance Act of 1987,

(D) authorized to be paid out of the Highway Trust Fund under the Intermodal Surface Transportation Efficiency Act of 1991,

(E) authorized to be paid out of the Highway Trust Fund under the Transportation Equity Act for the 21st Century,

(F) authorized to be paid out of the Highway Trust Fund under the Surface Transportation Extension Act of 2003,

(G) authorized to be paid out of the Highway Trust Fund under the Surface Transportation Extension Act of 2004,

(H) authorized to be paid out of the Highway Trust Fund under the Surface Transportation Extension Act of 2004, Part II,

(I) authorized to be paid out of the Highway Trust Fund under the Surface Transportation Extension Act of 2004, Part III,

(J) authorized to be paid out of the Highway Trust Fund under the Surface Transportation Extension Act of 2004, Part IV,

(K) authorized to be paid out of the Highway Trust Fund under the Surface Transportation Extension Act of 2004, Part V,

(L) authorized to be paid out of the Highway Trust Fund under the Surface Transportation Extension Act of 2005,

(M) authorized to be paid out of the Highway Trust Fund under the Surface Transportation Extension Act of 2005, Part II,

(N) authorized to be paid out of the Highway Trust Fund under the Surface Transportation Extension Act of 2005, Part III,

(O) authorized to be paid out of the Highway Trust Fund under the Surface Transportation Extension Act of 2005, Part IV,

(P) authorized to be paid out of the Highway Trust Fund under the Surface Transportation Extension Act of 2005, Part V, or

(Q) authorized to be paid out of the Highway Trust Fund under the Surface Transportation Extension Act of 2005, Part VI.

In determining the authorizations under the Acts referred to in the preceding subparagraphs, such Acts shall be applied as in effect on the date of enactment of the Surface Transportation Extension Act of 2005, Part VI.

P.L. 109-59, §11115(a)(1)(A)-(C):

Amended Code Sec. 9503(c)(4) by striking so much of paragraph (4) as precedes subparagraph (D), by redesignating subparagraphs (D) and (E) as subparagraphs (C) and (D), respectively, and by inserting before subparagraph (C), as so redesignated, new subparagraphs (A) and (B). **Effective** 10-1-2005. Prior to amendment, Code Sec. 9503(c)(4) read as follows:

(4) TRANSFERS FROM THE TRUST FUND FOR MOTORBOAT FUEL TAXES.—

(A) TRANSFER TO BOAT SAFETY ACCOUNT.—

(i) IN GENERAL.—The Secretary shall pay from time to time from the Highway Trust Fund into the Boat Safety Account in the Aquatic Resources Trust Fund amounts (as determined by him) equivalent to the motorboat fuel taxes received on or after October 1, 1980, and before October 1, 2005.

(ii) LIMITATIONS.—

(I) LIMIT ON TRANSFERS DURING ANY FISCAL YEAR.—The aggregate amount transferred under this subparagraph during any fiscal year shall not exceed $60,000,000 for each of fiscal years 1989 and 1990 and $70,000,000 for each fiscal year thereafter.

(II) LIMIT ON AMOUNT IN FUND.—No amount shall be transferred under this subparagraph if the Secretary determines that such transfer would result in increasing the amount in the Boat Safety Account to a sum in excess of $60,000,000 for Fiscal Year 1987 only and $45,000,000 for each fiscal year thereafter.

In making the determination under subclause (II) for any fiscal year, the Secretary shall not take into account any amount appropriated from the Boat Safety Account in any preceding fiscal year but not distributed.

(B) $1,000,000 PER YEAR OF EXCESS TRANSFERRED TO LAND AND WATER CONSERVATION FUND.—

(i) IN GENERAL.—Any amount received in the Highway Trust Fund—

(I) which is attributable to motorboat fuel taxes, and

(II) which is not transferred from the Highway Trust Fund under subparagraph (A),

shall be transferred (subject to the limitation of clause (ii)) by the Secretary from the Highway Trust Fund into the land and water conservation fund provided for in title I of the Land and Water Conservation Fund Act of 1965.

(ii) LIMITATION.—The aggregate amount transferred under this subparagraph during any fiscal year shall not exceed $1,000,000.

(C) EXCESS FUNDS TRANSFERRED TO SPORT FISH RESTORATION ACCOUNT.—Any amount received in the Highway Trust Fund—

(i) which is attributable to motorboat fuel taxes, and

(ii) which is not transferred from the Highway Trust Fund under subparagraph (A) or (B),

shall be transferred by the Secretary from the Highway Trust Fund into the Sport Fish Restoration Account in the Aquatic Resources Trust Fund.

(D) MOTORBOAT FUEL TAXES.—For purposes of this paragraph, the term "motorboat fuel taxes" means the taxes under section 4041(a)(2) with respect to special motor fuels used as fuel in motorboats and under section 4081 with respect to gasoline used as fuel in motorboats, but only to the extent such taxes are deposited into the Highway Trust Fund.

(E) DETERMINATION.—The amount of payments made under this paragraph after October 1, 1986 shall be determined by the Secretary in accordance with the methodology described in the Treasury Department's Report to Congress of June 1986 entitled "Gasoline Excise Tax Revenues Attributable to Fuel Used in Recreational Motorboats."

P.L. 109-59, §11115(a)(2):

Amended Code Sec. 9503(c)(5)(A) by striking "Account in the Aquatic Resources" and inserting "and Boating". **Effective** 10-1-2005.

P.L. 109-59, §11161(c)(1):

Amended Code Sec. 9503(c) by adding at the end a new paragraph (7)[(6)]. **Effective** for fuels or liquids removed, entered, or sold after 9-30-2005.

• **2005, Surface Transportation Extension Act of 2005, Part VI (P.L. 109-42)**

P.L. 109-42, §9(a)(1)(A)-(E):

Amended Code Sec. 9503(c)(1) in the matter before subparagraph (A), by striking "July 31, 2005" and inserting "August 15, 2005", by striking "or" at the end of subparagraph (O), by striking the period at the end of subparagraph (P) and inserting ", or", by inserting after subparagraph (P) a new subparagraph (Q), and in the matter after subparagraph (Q), as added by Act Sec. 7(a)(1), by striking "Surface Transportation Extension Act of 2005, Part V" and inserting "Surface Transportation Extension Act of 2005, Part VI". **Effective** 7-30-2005.

• **2005, Surface Transportation Extension Act of 2005, Part V (P.L. 109-40)**

P.L. 109-40, §9(a)(1)(A)-(E):

Amended Code Sec. 9503(c)(1) in the matter before subparagraph (A), by striking "July 28, 2005" and inserting "July 31, 2005"; by striking "or" at the end of subparagraph (N); by striking the period at the end of subparagraph (O) and inserting ", or"; by inserting after subparagraph (O) a new subparagraph (P); and in the matter after subparagraph (P), as added by Act Sec. 9(a)(1), by striking "Surface Transportation Extension Act of 2005, Part IV" and inserting "Surface Transportation Extension Act of 2005, Part V". **Effective** 7-28-2005.

• **2005, Surface Transportation Extension Act of 2005, Part IV (P.L. 109-37)**

P.L. 109-37, §9(a)(1)(A)-(E):

Amended Code Sec. 9503(c)(1) in the matter before subparagraph (A), by striking "July 22, 2005" and inserting "July 28, 2005"; by striking "or" at the end of subparagraph (M); by striking the period at the end of subparagraph (N) and inserting ", or"; by inserting after subparagraph (N) a new subparagraph (O), and in the matter after subparagraph (O), as added by Act Sec. 9(a)(1), by striking "Surface Transportation Extension Act of 2005, Part III" and inserting "Surface Transportation Extension Act of 2005, Part IV". **Effective** 7-22-2005.

ESTABLISHMENT OF TRUST FUNDS

- **2005, Surface Transportation Extension Act of 2005, Part III (P.L. 109-35)**

P.L. 109-35, §9(a)(1)(A)-(E):

Amended Code Sec. 9503(c)(1) in the matter before subparagraph (A), by striking "July 20, 2005" and inserting "July 22, 2005"; by striking "or" at the end of subparagraph (L); by striking the period at the end of subparagraph (M) and inserting ", or"; by inserting after subparagraph (M) a new subparagraph (N); and in the matter after subparagraph (N), as added by Act Sec. 9(a)(1), by striking "Surface Transportation Extension Act of 2005, Part II" and inserting "Surface Transportation Extension Act of 2005, Part III". **Effective** 7-20-2005.

- **2005, Surface Transportation Extension Act of 2005, Part II (P.L. 109-20)**

P.L. 109-20, §9(a)(1)(A)-(E):

Amended Code Sec. 9503(c)(1) in the matter before subparagraph (A), by striking "July 1, 2005" and inserting "July 20, 2005", by striking "or" at the end of subparagraph (K), by striking the period at the end of subparagraph (L) and inserting ", or", by inserting after subparagraph (L) a new subparagraph (M), and in the matter after subparagraph (M), as added by Act Sec. 9(a)(1), by striking "Surface Transportation Extension Act of 2005" and inserting "Surface Transportation Extension Act of 2005, Part II". **Effective** 7-1-2005.

- **2005, Surface Transportation Extension Act of 2005 (P.L. 109-14)**

P.L. 109-14, §9(a)(1)(A)-(E):

Amended Code Sec. 9503(c)(1) in the matter before subparagraph (A), by striking "June 1, 2005" and inserting "July 1, 2005", by striking "or" at the end of subparagraph (J), by striking the period at the end of subparagraph (K) and inserting ", or", by inserting after subparagraph (K) a new subparagraph (L), and in the matter after subparagraph (L), as added by Act Sec. 9(a)(1), by striking "Surface Transportation Extension Act of 2004, Part V" and inserting "Surface Transportation Extension Act of 2005". **Effective** 5-31-2005.

- **2004, American Jobs Creation Act of 2004 (P.L. 108-357)**

P.L. 108-357, §301(c)(13):

Amended Code Sec. 9503(c)(2)(A) by adding at the end a new sentence. **Effective** for fuel sold or used after 12-31-2004.

- **2004, Surface Transportation Extension Act of 2004, Part V (P.L. 108-310)**

P.L. 108-310, §13(a)(1)(A)-(E):

Amended Code Sec. 9503(c)(1) in the matter before subparagraph (A), by striking "October 1, 2004" and inserting "June 1, 2005"; by striking "or" at the end of subparagraph (I); by striking the period at the end of subparagraph (J) and inserting ", or"; by inserting after subparagraph (J) a new subparagraph (K); and in the matter after subparagraph (K), as added by Act Sec. 13(a)(1), by striking "Surface Transportation Extension Act of 2004, Part IV" and inserting "Surface Transportation Extension Act of 2004, Part V". **Effective** 9-30-2004.

- **2004, Surface Transportation Extension Act of 2004, Part IV (P.L. 108-280)**

P.L. 108-280, §10(a)(1)(A)-(E):

Amended Code Sec. 9503(c)(1) in the matter before subparagraph (A), by striking "August 1, 2004" and inserting "October 1, 2004", by striking "or" at the end of subparagraph (H), by striking the period at the end of subparagraph (I) and inserting ", or", by inserting after subparagraph (I) a new subparagraph (J), and in the matter after subparagraph (J), as added by Act Sec. 10(a)(1), by striking "Surface Transportation Extension Act of 2004, Part III" and inserting "Surface Transportation Extension Act of 2004, Part IV". **Effective** 7-30-2004. For a special rule, see Act Sec. 10(a)(4), below.

P.L. 108-280, §10(a)(4) [stricken by P.L. 108-310, §13(a)(4)], provides:

(4) SPECIAL RULE FOR CORE HIGHWAY PROGRAMS.—

(A) IN GENERAL.—In the case of a core highway program, subsections (b)(5) and (c)(1) of section 9503 of such Code shall be applied by substituting "September 25, 2004" for "October 1, 2004".

(B) CORE HIGHWAY PROGRAM.—For purposes of subparagraph (A), the term "core highway program" means any program (other than any program carried out by the National Highway Traffic Safety Administration and any program carried out by the Federal Motor Carrier Administration) funded from the Highway Trust Fund (other than the Mass Transit Account).

- **2004, Surface Transportation Extension Act of 2004, Part III (P.L. 108-263)**

P.L. 108-263, §10(a)(1)(A)-(E):

Amended Code Sec. 9503(c)(1) in the matter before subparagraph (A), by striking "July 1, 2004" and inserting "August 1, 2004", by striking "or" at the end of subparagraph (G), by striking the period at the end of subparagraph (H) and inserting ", or", by inserting after subparagraph (H) a new subparagraph (I), and in the matter after subparagraph (I), as added by Act Sec. 10(a)(1), by striking "Surface Transportation Extension Act of 2004, Part II" and inserting "Surface Transportation Extension Act of 2004, Part III". **Effective** 6-30-2004.

- **2004, Surface Transportation Extension Act of 2004, Part II (P.L. 108-224)**

P.L. 108-224, §10(a)(1)(A)-(E):

Amended Code Sec. 9503(c)(1) in the matter before subparagraph (A), by striking "May 1, 2004" and inserting "July 1, 2004", by striking "or" at the end of subparagraph (F), by striking the period at the end of subparagraph (G) and inserting ", or", by inserting after subparagraph (G) a new subparagraph (H), and in the matter after subparagraph (H), as added by Act Sec. 10(a)(1), by striking "Surface Transportation Extension Act of 2004" and inserting "Surface Transportation Extension Act of 2004, Part II". **Effective** 4-30-2004.

- **2004, Surface Transportation Extension Act of 2004 (P.L. 108-202)**

P.L. 108-202, §12(a)(1)(A)-(E):

Amended Code Sec. 9503(c)(1) in the matter before subparagraph (A), by striking "March 1, 2004" and inserting "May 1, 2004", by striking "or" at the end of subparagraph (E), by striking the period at the end of subparagraph (F) and inserting ", or", by inserting after subparagraph (F) a new subparagraph (G), and in the matter after subparagraph (G), as added by Act Sec. 12(a)(1), by striking "Surface Transportation Extension Act of 2003" and inserting "Surface Transportation Extension Act of 2004". **Effective** 2-29-2004.

- **2003, Surface Transportation Extension Act of 2003 (P.L. 108-88)**

P.L. 108-88, §12(a)(1)(A)-(E):

Amended Code Sec. 9503(c)(1) in the matter before subparagraph (A), by striking "October 1, 2003" and inserting "March 1, 2004", by striking "or" at the end of subparagraph (D), by striking the period at the end of subparagraph (E) and inserting ", or", by inserting after subparagraph (E) a new subparagraph (F), and, in the matter after subparagraph (F), by striking "TEA 21 Restoration Act" and inserting "Surface Transportation Extension Act of 2003". **Effective** 9-30-2003.

- **1998, Transportation Equity Act for the 21st Century (P.L. 105-178)**

P.L. 105-178, §9002(c)(1)(A)-(B):

Amended Code Sec. 9503(c)(2)-(3) by striking "1999" each place it appears and inserting "2005", and by striking "2000" each place it appears and inserting "2006". **Effective** 6-9-98.

P.L. 105-178, §9002(c)(2)(A):

Amended Code Sec. 9503(c)(4)(A)(i) and (5)(A) by striking "1998" and inserting "2005". **Effective** 6-9-98.

P.L. 105-178, §9002(c)(3):

Amended the heading for Code Sec. 9503(c)(3). **Effective** 6-9-98. Prior to amendment, the heading read as follows:

(3) 1988 FLOOR STOCKS REFUNDS.—

P.L. 105-178, §9002(d)(1)(A):

Amended Code Sec. 9503(c)(1) by striking "1998" and inserting "2003". **Effective** 6-9-98.

P.L. 105-178, §9002(d)(1)(B)(i)-(ii):

Amended Code Sec. 9503(c)(1) by striking "or" at the end of subparagraph (C), by striking "1991." in subparagraph (D) and all that follows and inserting "1991, or", and by adding a new subparagraph (E) and flush sentence. **Effective** 6-9-98. Prior to amendment, the flush sentence at the end of Code Sec. 9503(c)(1) read as follows:

In determining the authorizations under the Acts referred to in the preceding subparagraphs, such Acts shall be applied as in effect on the date of the enactment of this sentence.

P.L. 105-178, §9002(f)(2):

Amended Code Sec. 9503(c)(2)(A)(i) by adding "and" at the end of subclause (II), by striking subclause (III), and by redesignating subclause (IV) as subclause (III). **Effective** 6-9-98. Prior to being stricken, Code Sec. 9503(c)(2)(A)(i)(III) read as follows:

(III) section 6424 (relating to amounts paid in respect of lubricating oil used for certain nontaxable purposes), and

P.L. 105-178, §9002(f)(3):

Amended Code Sec. 9503(c)(2)(A)(ii) by striking "gasoline, special fuels, and lubricating oil" each place it appears and inserting "fuel". **Effective** 6-9-98.

P.L. 105-178, §9002(f)(4) (as added by P.L. 105-206, §9015(a)):

Amended the last sentence of Code Sec. 9503(c)(1), as amended by subsection (d), by striking "the date of enactment of the Transportation Equity Act for the 21st Century" and inserting "the date of the enactment of the TEA 21 Restoration Act". **Effective** 6-9-98.

P.L. 105-178, §9004(b)(1):

Amended Code Sec. 9503(c) by striking paragraph (7). **Effective** as if included in the amendments made by P.L. 105-34, §901 [effective for taxes received in the Treasury after 9-30-97.—CCH]. Prior to being stricken, paragraph (7) read as follows:

(7) LIMITATION ON EXPENDITURES.—Notwithstanding any other provision of law, in calculating amounts under section 157(a) of title 23, United States Code, and sections 1013(c), 1015(a), and 1015(b) of the Intermodal Surface Transportation Efficiency Act of 1991 (Public Law 102-240; 105 Stat. 1914), deposits in the Highway Trust Fund resulting from the amendments made by the Taxpayer Relief Act of 1997 shall not be taken into account.

P.L. 105-178, §9005(a)(2):

Amended Code Sec. 9503(c)(4)(A)(ii) by adding at the end a new flush sentence. **Effective** 6-9-98.

P.L. 105-178, §9011(b)(1):

Amended Code Sec. 9503(c) by striking paragraph (6). **Effective** 6-9-98. Prior to being stricken, Code Sec. 9503(c)(6) read as follows:

(6) TRANSFERS FROM TRUST FUND OF CERTAIN RECREATIONAL FUEL TAXES, ETC.—

(A) IN GENERAL.—The Secretary shall pay from time to time from the Highway Trust Fund into the National Recreational Trails Trust Fund amounts (as determined by him) equivalent to 0.3 percent (as adjusted under subparagraph (C)) of the total Highway Trust Fund receipts for the period for which the payment is made.

(B) LIMITATION.—The amount paid into the National Recreational Trails Trust Fund under this paragraph during any fiscal year shall not exceed the amount obligated under section 1302 of the Intermodal Surface Transportation Efficiency Act of 1991 (as in effect on the date of the enactment of this paragraph) for such fiscal year to be expended from such Trust Fund.

ESTABLISHMENT OF TRUST FUNDS

(C) ADJUSTMENT OF PERCENTAGE.—

(i) FIRST YEAR.—Within 1 year after the date of the enactment of this paragraph, the Secretary shall adjust the percentage contained in subparagraph (A) so that it corresponds to the revenues received by the Highway Trust Fund from nonhighway recreational fuel taxes.

(ii) SUBSEQUENT YEARS.—Not more frequently than once every 3 years, the Secretary may increase or decrease the percentage established under clause (i) to reflect, in the Secretary's estimation, changes in the amount of revenues received in the Highway Trust Fund from nonhighway recreational fuel taxes.

(iii) AMOUNT OF ADJUSTMENT.—Any adjustment under clause (ii) shall be not more than 10 percent of the percentage in effect at the time the adjustment is made.

(iv) USE OF DATA.—In making the adjustments under clauses (i) and (ii), the Secretary shall take into account data on off-highway recreational vehicle registrations and use.

(D) NONHIGHWAY RECREATIONAL FUEL TAXES.—For purposes of this paragraph, the term "nonhighway recreational fuel taxes" means taxes under section 4041 and 4081 (to the extent deposited into the Highway Trust Fund) with respect to—

(i) fuel used in vehicles on recreational trails or back country terrain (including vehicles registered for highway use when used on recreational trails, trail access roads not eligible for funding under title 23, United States Code, or back country terrain), and

(ii) fuel used in campstoves and other non-engine uses in outdoor recreational equipment.

Such term shall not include small-engine fuel taxes (as defined by paragraph (5)) and taxes which are credited or refunded.

(E) TERMINATION.—No amount shall be paid under this paragraph after September 30, 1998.

• **1997, Surface Transportation Extension Act of 1997 (P.L. 105-130)**

P.L. 105-130, §9(a)(1)(A)-(D):

Amended Code Sec. 9503(c)(1), (c)(4)(A)[(i)], (c)(5)(A) and (c)(6)(E) by striking "1997" and inserting "1998" and by striking the last sentence in (c)(1)[(D)] and inserting a new flush sentence. **Effective** 10-1-97. Prior to being stricken, the last sentence in Code Sec. 9503(c)(1) read as follows:

In determining the authorizations under the Acts referred to in the preceding subparagraphs, such Acts shall be applied as in effect on the date of the enactment of the Intermodal Surface Transportation Efficiency Act of 1991.

• **1997, Taxpayer Relief Act of 1997 (P.L. 105-34)**

P.L. 105-34, §901(c):

Amended Code Sec. 9503(c) by adding a new paragraph (7). **Effective** for taxes received in the Treasury after 9-30-97.

P.L. 105-34, §901(d)(2):

Amended Code Sec. 9503(c)(2)(A) by striking "by taking into account only the Highway Trust Fund financing rate applicable to any fuel" in the last sentence and inserting "by taking into account only the portion of the taxes which are deposited into the Highway Trust Fund". **Effective** for taxes received in the Treasury after 9-30-97.

P.L. 105-34, §901(d)(3):

Amended Code Sec. 9503(c)(4)(D), (5)(B), and (6)(D) by striking "attributable to the Highway Trust Fund financing rate" and inserting "deposited into the Highway Trust Fund". **Effective** for taxes received in the Treasury after 9-30-97.

P.L. 105-34, §1601(f)(2)(A):

Amended Code Sec. 9503(c)(2)(A)(ii) by striking "(or with respect to qualified diesel-powered highway vehicles purchased before January 1, 1999)" before the period at the end of the sentence. **Effective** as if included in the provision of P.L. 104-188 to which it relates [**effective** for vehicles purchased after 8-20-96.—CCH].

• **1993, Omnibus Budget Reconciliation Act of 1993 (P.L. 103-66)**

P.L. 103-66, §13242(d)(37):

Amended Code Sec. 9503(c)(6)(D) by striking ", 4081, and 4091" and inserting "and 4081". **Effective** 1-1-94.

P.L. 103-66, §13242(d)(38):

Amended Code Sec. 9503(c)(4)(D) by striking "rates under such sections" and inserting "rate". **Effective** 1-1-94.

P.L. 103-66, §13242(d)(39):

Amended Code Sec. 9503(c)(5)(B) by striking "rate under such section" and inserting "rate". **Effective** 1-1-94.

• **1991, Intermodal Surface Transportation Efficiency Act of 1991 (P.L. 102-240)**

P.L. 102-240, §8002(e)(1):

Amended Code Sec. 9503(c)(1) by striking "1993" and inserting "1997". **Effective** 12-18-91.

P.L. 102-240, §8002(d)(1)(A)-(B):

Amended Code Sec. 9503(c)(2)-(3) by striking out "1995" each place it appears and inserting "1999", and by striking "1996" each place it appears and inserting "2000". **Effective** 12-18-91.

P.L. 102-240, §8002(d)(2)(A):

Amended Code Sec. 9503(c) by striking "1995" in paragraphs (4)(A)(i) and (5)(A) and inserting "1997". **Effective** 12-18-91.

P.L. 102-240, §8002(e)(2):

Amended Code Sec. 9503(c)(1) by striking subparagraph (D) and inserting new subparagraph (D). **Effective** 12-18-91. Prior to amendment, Code Sec. 9503(c)(1)(D) read as follows:

(D) hereafter authorized by a law which does not authorize the expenditure out of the Highway Trust Fund of any amount for a general purpose not covered by subparagraph (A), (B), or (C) as in effect on the date of the enactment of the Surface Transportation and Uniform Relocation Assistance Act of 1987.

P.L. 102-240, §8003(b):

Amended Code Sec. 9503(c) by adding at the end thereof new paragraph (6). **Effective** 12-18-91.

• **1990, Omnibus Budget Reconciliation Act of 1990 (P.L. 101-508)**

P.L. 101-508, §11211(a)(5)(E):

Amended Code Sec. 9503(c)(2)(A) by adding at the end thereof a new sentence. **Effective** for gasoline removed (as defined in section 4082 of the Internal Revenue Code of 1986) after 11-30-90.

P.L. 101-508, §11211(b)(6)(H):

Amended Code Sec. 9503(c)(4)(D) by striking "(to the extent attributable to the Highway Trust Fund financing rate)" and by inserting before the period ", but only to the extent such taxes are attributable to the Highway Trust Fund financing rates under such sections". **Effective** 12-1-90.

P.L. 101-508, §11211(g)(1)(A)-(B):

Amended Code Sec. 9503(c)(2)-(4) by striking "1993" each place it appears and inserting "1995", and by striking "1994" each place it appears and inserting "1996". **Effective** 11-5-90.

P.L. 101-508, §11211(i)(1):

Amended Code Sec. 9503(c) by adding at the end thereof a new paragraph (5). **Effective** 12-1-90.

• **1988, Coast Guard Authorization Act of 1988 (P.L. 100-448)**

P.L. 100-448, §6(a)(1)(A):

Amended Code Sec. 9503(c)(4)(A)(ii)(I)-(II) by striking out "for Fiscal Year 1987 only and $45,000,000 for each Fiscal Year thereafter" and inserting in lieu thereof "for each of fiscal years 1989 and 1990 and $70,000,000 for each fiscal year thereafter". **Effective** 10-1-88.

P.L. 100-448, §6(a)(1)(B):

Amended Code Sec. 9503(c)(4)(E) by striking out the second sentence. **Effective** 10-1-88. Prior to amendment, the second sentence read as follows:

Further, a portion of the payments made by the Secretary from Fiscal Year 1987 motorfuel excise tax receipts shall be used to increase the funding for boating safety programs during Fiscal Year 1987 only.

P.L. 100-448, §6(a)(3)(A)-(B):

Amended Code Sec. 9503(c)(4)(A)(ii)(I)-(II) by striking the quotation marks following "$60,000,000"; and by striking the semicolon before the period. **Effective** 10-1-88.

• **1987, Surface Transportation and Uniform Relocation Assistance Act of 1987 (P.L. 100-17)**

P.L. 100-17, §503(a)(1)-(2):

Amended Code Sec. 9503(c) by striking out "1988" each place it appears and inserting in lieu thereof "1993", and by striking out "1989" each place it appears and inserting in lieu thereof "1994". **Effective** 4-2-87.

P.L. 100-17, §503(b):

Amended Code Sec. 9503(c)(1) by striking out "or" at the end of subparagraph (B) and by striking out subparagraph (C) and inserting in lieu thereof new subparagraphs (C) and (D). **Effective** 4-2-87. Prior to amendment, Code Sec. 9503(c)(1)(C) read as follows:

(C) hereafter authorized by a law which does not authorize the expenditure out of the Highway Trust Fund of any amount for a general purpose not covered by subparagraph (A) or (B) as in effect on December 31, 1982.

• **1986, Coast Guard Authorization Act of 1986 (P.L. 99-640)**

P.L. 99-640, §7(a)(1)-(2):

Amended Code Sec. 9503(c)(4) by striking "45,000,000" each place it appears in subparagraph (A) and inserting in lieu thereof "60,000,000 for Fiscal Year 1987 only and $45,000,000 for each fiscal year thereafter;" and by adding at the end thereof new subparagraph (E). **Effective** 11-10-86.

• **1986, Superfund Amendments and Reauthorization Act of 1986 (P.L. 99-499)**

P.L. 99-499, §521(b)(1)(B):

Amended Code Sec. 9503(c)(4)(D) by striking out "section 4081" and inserting in lieu thereof "section 4081 (to the extent attributable to the Highway Trust Fund financing rate)". **Effective** 1-1-87.

• **1984, Deficit Reduction Act of 1984 (P.L. 98-369)**

P.L. 98-369, §474(r)(43):

Amended Code Sec. 9503(c)(2)(A)(ii) by striking out "section 39" and inserting in lieu thereof "section 34". **Effective** for tax years beginning after 12-31-83, and for carrybacks from such years.

P.L. 98-369, §911(d)[(c)](1)(B):

Amended Code Sec. 9503(c)(2)(A)(ii) by striking out "used before October 1, 1988" and inserting in lieu thereof "used before October 1, 1988 (or with respect to qualified diesel-powered highway vehicles purchased before January 1, 1988)". **Effective** 8-1-84.

P.L. 98-369, §1016(b)(1):

Amended Code Sec. 9503(c)(4)(A) by striking out "the National Recreational Boating Safety and Facilities Improvement Fund established by section 202 of the Recreational Boating Fund Act" in clause (i) and inserting in lieu thereof "the Boat Safety

Sec. 9503(c)(5)B)

ESTABLISHMENT OF TRUST FUNDS

Account in the Aquatic Resources Trust Fund"; by striking out "the amount in the National Recreational Boating Safety and Facilities Improvement Fund" in clause (ii) and inserting in lieu thereof "the amount in the Boat Safety Account", and by striking out "NATIONAL RECREATIONAL BOATING SAFETY AND FACILITIES IMPROVEMENT FUND" in the subparagraph heading and inserting in lieu thereof "BOAT SAFETY ACCOUNT". **Effective** 10-1-84. See, also, Act Sec. 1016(e)(2) in the amendment notes for Code Sec. 9504 for special rules.

P.L. 98-369, §1016(b)(2):

Amended Code Sec. 9503(c)(4) by redesignating paragraph (C) as paragraph (D) and by striking out paragraph (D) and inserting in lieu thereof new paragraphs (B)

and (C). **Effective** 10-1-84. See, also, Act Sec. 1016(e)(2) in the amendment notes for Code Sec. 9504 for special rules. Prior to amendment, paragraph (B) read as follows:

(B) EXCESS FUNDS TRANSFERRED TO LAND AND WATER CONSERVATION FUND.—Any amount received in the Highway Trust Fund which is attributable to motorboat fuel taxes and which is not transferred from the Highway Trust Fund under subparagraph (A) shall be transferred by the Secretary from the Highway Trust Fund into the land and water conservation fund provided for in title I of the Land and Water Conservation Fund Act of 1965.

[Sec. 9503(d)]

(d) ADJUSTMENTS OF APPORTIONMENTS.—

(1) ESTIMATES OF UNFUNDED HIGHWAY AUTHORIZATIONS AND NET HIGHWAY RECEIPTS.—The Secretary of the Treasury, not less frequently than once in each calendar quarter, after consultation with the Secretary of Transportation, shall estimate—

(A) the amount which would (but for this subsection) be the unfunded highway authorizations at the close of the next fiscal year, and

(B) the net highway receipts for the 48-month period beginning at the close of such fiscal year.

(2) PROCEDURE WHERE THERE IS EXCESS UNFUNDED HIGHWAY AUTHORIZATIONS.—If the Secretary of the Treasury determines for any fiscal year that the amount described in paragraph (1)(A) exceeds the amount described in paragraph (1)(B)—

(A) he shall so advise the Secretary of Transportation, and

(B) he shall further advise the Secretary of Transportation as to the amount of such excess.

(3) ADJUSTMENT OF APPORTIONMENTS WHERE UNFUNDED AUTHORIZATIONS EXCEED 4 YEARS' RECEIPTS.—

(A) DETERMINATION OF PERCENTAGE.—If, before any apportionment to the States is made, in the most recent estimate made by the Secretary of the Treasury there is an excess referred to in paragraph (2)(B), the Secretary of Transportation shall determine the percentage which—

(i) the excess referred to in paragraph (2)(B), is of

(ii) the amount authorized to be appropriated from the Trust Fund for the fiscal year for apportionment to the States.

If, but for this sentence, the most recent estimate would be one which was made on a date which will be more than 3 months before the date of the apportionment, the Secretary of the Treasury shall make a new estimate under paragraph (1) for the appropriate fiscal year.

(B) ADJUSTMENT OF APPORTIONMENTS.—If the Secretary of Transportation determines a percentage under subparagraph (A) for purposes of any apportionment, notwithstanding any other provision of law, the Secretary of Transportation shall apportion to the States (in lieu of the amount which, but for the provisions of this subsection, would be so apportioned) the amount obtained by reducing the amount authorized to be so apportioned by such percentage.

(4) APPORTIONMENT OF AMOUNTS PREVIOUSLY WITHHELD FROM APPORTIONMENT.—If, after funds have been withheld from apportionment under paragraph (3)(B), the Secretary of the Treasury determines that the amount described in paragraph (1)(A) does not exceed the amount described in paragraph (1)(B) or that the excess described in paragraph (1)(B) is less than the amount previously determined, he shall so advise the Secretary of Transportation. The Secretary of Transportation shall apportion to the States such portion of the funds so withheld from apportionment as the Secretary of the Treasury has advised him may be so apportioned without causing the amount described in paragraph (1)(A) to exceed the amount described in paragraph (1)(B). Any funds apportioned pursuant to the preceding sentence shall remain available for the period for which they would be available if such apportionment took effect with the fiscal year in which they are apportioned pursuant to the preceding sentence.

(5) DEFINITIONS.—For purposes of this subsection—

(A) UNFUNDED HIGHWAY AUTHORIZATIONS.—The term "unfunded highway authorizations" means, at any time, the excess (if any) of—

(i) the total potential unpaid commitments at such time as a result of the apportionment to the States of the amounts authorized to be appropriated from the Highway Trust Fund, over

(ii) the amount available in the Highway Trust Fund at such time to defray such commitments (after all other unpaid commitments at such time which are payable from the Highway Trust Fund have been defrayed).

(B) NET HIGHWAY RECEIPTS.—The term "net highway receipts" means, with respect to any period, the excess of—

(i) the receipts (including interest) of the Highway Trust Fund during such period, over

(ii) the amounts to be transferred during such period from such Fund under subsection (c) (other than paragraph (1) thereof).

(6) MEASUREMENT OF NET HIGHWAY RECEIPTS.—For purposes of making any estimate under paragraph (1) of net highway receipts for periods ending after the date specified in subsection (b)(1), the Secretary shall treat—

(A) each expiring provision of subsection (b) which is related to appropriations or transfers to the Highway Trust Fund to have been extended through the end of the 48-month period referred to in paragraph (1)(B), and

(B) with respect to each tax imposed under the sections referred to in subsection (b)(1), the rate of such tax during the 48-month period referred to in paragraph (1)(B) to be the same as the rate of such tax as in effect on the date of such estimate.

(7) REPORTS.—Any estimate under paragraph (1) and any determination under paragraph (2) shall be reported by the Secretary of the Treasury to the Committee on Ways and Means of the House of Representatives, the Committee on Finance of the Senate, the Committees on the Budget of both Houses, the Committee on Public Works and Transportation of the House of Representatives, and the Committee on Environment and Public Works of the Senate.

Amendments

• **2005, Safe, Accountable, Flexible, Efficient Transportation Equity Act: A Legacy for Users (P.L. 109-59)**

P.L. 109-59, §11102(a)(1)-(2):

Amended Code Sec. 9503(d) by striking "24-month" in paragraph (1)(B) and inserting "48-month", and by striking "2 YEARS'" in the heading for paragraph (3) and inserting "4 YEARS'". **Effective** 8-10-2005.

P.L. 109-59, §11102(b):

Amended Code Sec. 9503(d) by redesignating paragaph (6) as paragraph (7) and by inserting after paragraph (5) a new paragraph (6). **Effective** 8-10-2005.

• **2005, Surface Transportation Extension Act of 2005, Part VI (P.L. 109-42)**

P.L. 109-42, §7(c), provides:

(c) TEMPORARY RULE REGARDING ADJUSTMENTS.—During the period beginning on the date of the enactment of the Surface Transportation Extension Act of 2003

[9-30-2003.—CCH] and ending on August 14, 2005, for purposes of making any estimate under section 9503(d) of the Internal Revenue Code of 1986 of receipts of the Highway Trust Fund, the Secretary of the Treasury shall treat—

(1) each expiring provision of paragraphs (1) through (4) of section 9503(b) of such Code which is related to appropriations or transfers to such Fund to have been extended through the end of the 24-month period referred to in section 9503(d)(1)(B) of such Code, and

(2) with respect to each tax imposed under the sections referred to in section 9503(b)(1) of such Code, the rate of such tax during the 24-month period referred to in section 9503(d)(1)(B) of such Code to be the same as the rate of such tax as in effect on the date of the enactment of the Surface Transportation Extension Act of 2003.

• **2005, Surface Transportation Extension Act of 2005, Part V (P.L. 109-40)**

P.L. 109-40, §9(d), provides:

(d) TEMPORARY RULE REGARDING ADJUSTMENTS.—During the period beginning on the date of the enactment of the Surface Transportation Extension Act of 2003

ESTABLISHMENT OF TRUST FUNDS

[9-30-2003.—CCH] and ending on July 30, 2005, for purposes of making any estimate under section 9503(d) of the Internal Revenue Code of 1986 of receipts of the Highway Trust Fund, the Secretary of the Treasury shall treat—

(1) each expiring provision of paragraphs (1) through (4) of section 9503(b) of such Code which is related to appropriations or transfers to such Fund to have been extended through the end of the 24-month period referred to in section 9503(d)(1)(B) of such Code; and

(2) with respect to each tax imposed under the sections referred to in section 9503(b)(1) of such Code, the rate of such tax during the 24-month period referred to in section 9503(d)(1)(B) of such Code to be the same as the rate of such tax as in effect on the date of the enactment of the Surface Transportation Extension Act of 2003.

- **2005, Surface Transportation Extension Act of 2005, Part IV (P.L. 109-37)**

P.L. 109-37, §9(d), provides:

(d) TEMPORARY RULE REGARDING ADJUSTMENTS.—During the period beginning on the date of the enactment of the Surface Transportation Extension Act of 2003 [9-30-2003.—CCH] and ending on July 27, 2005, for purposes of making any estimate under section 9503(d) of the Internal Revenue Code of 1986 of receipts of the Highway Trust Fund, the Secretary of the Treasury shall treat—

(1) each expiring provision of paragraphs (1) through (4) of section 9503(b) of such Code which is related to appropriations or transfers to such Fund to have been extended through the end of the 24-month period referred to in section 9503(d)(1)(B) of such Code; and

(2) with respect to each tax imposed under the sections referred to in section 9503(b)(1) of such Code, the rate of such tax during the 24-month period referred to in section 9503(d)(1)(B) of such Code to be the same as the rate of such tax as in effect on the date of the enactment of the Surface Transportation Extension Act of 2003.

- **2005, Surface Transportation Extension Act of 2005, Part III (P.L. 109-35)**

P.L. 109-35, §9(d), provides:

(d) TEMPORARY RULE REGARDING ADJUSTMENTS.—During the period beginning on the date of the enactment of the Surface Transportation Extension Act of 2003 [9-30-2003.—CCH] and ending on July 21, 2005, for purposes of making any estimate under section 9503(d) of the Internal Revenue Code of 1986 of receipts of the Highway Trust Fund, the Secretary of the Treasury shall treat—

(1) each expiring provision of paragraphs (1) through (4) of section 9503(b) of such Code which is related to appropriations or transfers to such Fund to have been extended through the end of the 24-month period referred to in section 9503(d)(1)(B) of such Code; and

(2) with respect to each tax imposed under the sections referred to in section 9503(b)(1) of such Code, the rate of such tax during the 24-month period referred to in section 9503(d)(1)(B) of such Code to be the same as the rate of such tax as in effect on the date of the enactment of the Surface Transportation Extension Act of 2003.

- **2005, Surface Transportation Extension Act of 2005, Part II (P.L. 109-20)**

P.L. 109-20, §9(d), provides:

(d) TEMPORARY RULE REGARDING ADJUSTMENTS.—During the period beginning on the date of the enactment of the Surface Transportation Extension Act of 2003 [9-30-2003.—CCH] and ending on July 19, 2005, for purposes of making any estimate under section 9503(d) of the Internal Revenue Code of 1986 of receipts of the Highway Trust Fund, the Secretary of the Treasury shall treat—

(1) each expiring provision of paragraphs (1) through (4) of section 9503(b) of such Code which is related to appropriations or transfers to such Fund to have been extended through the end of the 24-month period referred to in section 9503(d)(1)(B) of such Code, and

(2) with respect to each tax imposed under the sections referred to in section 9503(b)(1) of such Code, the rate of such tax during the 24-month period referred to in section 9503(d)(1)(B) of such Code to be the same as the rate of such tax as in effect on the date of the enactment of the Surface Transportation Extension Act of 2003.

- **2005, Surface Transportation Extension Act of 2005 (P.L. 109-14)**

P.L. 109-14, §9(e), provides:

(e) TEMPORARY RULE REGARDING ADJUSTMENTS.—During the period beginning on the date of the enactment of the Surface Transportation Extension Act of 2003 [9-30-2003.—CCH] and ending on June 30, 2005, for purposes of making any estimate under section 9503(d) of the Internal Revenue Code of 1986 of receipts of the Highway Trust Fund, the Secretary of the Treasury shall treat—

(1) each expiring provision of paragraphs (1) through (4) of section 9503(b) of such Code which is related to appropriations or transfers to such Fund to have been extended through the end of the 24-month period referred to in section 9503(d)(1)(B) of such Code, and

(2) with respect to each tax imposed under the sections referred to in section 9503(b)(1) of such Code, the rate of such tax during the 24-month period referred to in section 9503(d)(1)(B) of such Code to be the same as the rate of such tax as in effect on the date of the enactment of the Surface Transportation Extension Act of 2003.

- **2004, Surface Transportation Extension Act of 2004, Part V (P.L. 108-310)**

P.L. 108-310, §13(e), provides:

(e) TEMPORARY RULE REGARDING ADJUSTMENTS.—During the period beginning on the date of the enactment of the Surface Transportation Extension Act of 2003 [9-30-2003.—CCH] and ending on May 31, 2005, for purposes of making any estimate under section 9503(d) of the Internal Revenue Code of 1986 of receipts of the Highway Trust Fund, the Secretary of the Treasury shall treat—

(1) each expiring provision of paragraphs (1) through (4) of section 9503(b) of such Code which is related to appropriations or transfers to such Fund to have been extended through the end of the 24-month period referred to in section 9503(d)(1)(B) of such Code; and

(2) with respect to each tax imposed under the sections referred to in section 9503(b)(1) of such Code, the rate of such tax during the 24-month period referred to in section 9503(d)(1)(B) of such Code to be the same as the rate of such tax as in effect on the date of the enactment of the Surface Transportation Extension Act of 2003.

P.L. 108-310, §13(f), provides:

(f) APPORTIONMENT OF HIGHWAY TRUST FUNDS FOR FISCAL YEAR 2004.—Section 9503(d)(3) of the Internal Revenue Code of 1986 shall not apply to any apportionment to the States of the amounts authorized to be appropriated from the Highway Trust Fund for the fiscal year ending September 30, 2004.

- **2004, Surface Transportation Extension Act of 2004, Part IV (P.L. 108-280)**

P.L. 108-280, §10(d), provides:

(d) TEMPORARY RULE REGARDING ADJUSTMENTS.—During the period beginning on the date of the enactment of the Surface Transportation Extension Act of 2003 [9-30-2003.—CCH] and ending on September 30, 2004, for purposes of making any estimate under section 9503(d) of the Internal Revenue Code of 1986 of receipts of the Highway Trust Fund, the Secretary of the Treasury shall treat—

(1) each expiring provision of paragraphs (1) through (4) of section 9503(b) of such Code which is related to appropriations or transfers to such Fund to have been extended through the end of the 24-month period referred to in section 9503(d)(1)(B) of such Code, and

(2) with respect to each tax imposed under the sections referred to in section 9503(b)(1) of such Code, the rate of such tax during the 24-month period referred to in section 9503(d)(1)(B) of such Code to be the same as the rate of such tax as in effect on the date of the enactment of the Surface Transportation Extension Act of 2003.

- **2004, Surface Transportation Extension Act of 2004, Part III (P.L. 108-263)**

P.L. 108-263, §10(d), provides:

(d) TEMPORARY RULE REGARDING ADJUSTMENTS.—During the period beginning on the date of the enactment of the Surface Transportation Extension Act of 2003 [9-30-2003.—CCH] and ending on July 31, 2004, for purposes of making any estimate under section 9503(d) of the Internal Revenue Code of 1986 of receipts of the Highway Trust Fund, the Secretary of the Treasury shall treat—

(1) each expiring provision of paragraphs (1) through (4) of section 9503(b) of such Code which is related to appropriations or transfers to such Fund to have been extended through the end of the 24-month period referred to in section 9503(d)(1)(B) of such Code, and

(2) with respect to each tax imposed under the sections referred to in section 9503(b)(1) of such Code, the rate of such tax during the 24-month period referred to in section 9503(d)(1)(B) of such Code to be the same as the rate of such tax as in effect on the date of the enactment of the Surface Transportation Extension Act of 2003.

- **2004, Surface Transportation Extension Act of 2004, Part II (P.L. 108-224)**

P.L. 108-224, §10(d), provides:

(d) TEMPORARY RULE REGARDING ADJUSTMENTS.—During the period beginning on the date of the enactment of the Surface Transportation Extension Act of 2003 [9-30-2003.—CCH] and ending on June 30, 2004, for purposes of making any estimate under section 9503(d) of the Internal Revenue Code of 1986 of receipts of the Highway Trust Fund, the Secretary of the Treasury shall treat—

(1) each expiring provision of paragraphs (1) through (4) of section 9503(b) of such Code which is related to appropriations or transfers to such Fund to have been extended through the end of the 24-month period referred to in section 9503(d)(1)(B) of such Code, and

(2) with respect to each tax imposed under the sections referred to in section 9503(b)(1) of such Code, the rate of such tax during the 24-month period referred to in section 9503(d)(1)(B) of such Code to be the same as the rate of such tax as in effect on the date of the enactment of the Surface Transportation Extension Act of 2003.

- **2004, Surface Transportation Extension Act of 2004 (P.L. 108-202)**

P.L. 108-202, §12(d), provides:

(d) TEMPORARY RULE REGARDING ADJUSTMENTS.—During the period beginning on the date of the enactment of the Surface Transportation Extension Act of 2003 [9-30-2003.—CCH] and ending on April 30, 2004, for purposes of making any estimate under section 9503(d) of the Internal Revenue Code of 1986 of receipts of the Highway Trust Fund, the Secretary of the Treasury shall treat—

(1) each expiring provision of paragraphs (1) through (4) of section 9503(b) of such Code which is related to appropriations or transfers to such Fund to have been extended through the end of the 24-month period referred to in section 9503(d)(1)(B) of such Code, and

(2) with respect to each tax imposed under the sections referred to in section 9503(b)(1) of such Code, the rate of such tax during the 24-month period referred to in section 9503(d)(1)(B) of such Code to be the same as the rate of such tax as in effect on the date of the enactment of the Surface Transportation Extension Act of 2003.

- **2003, Surface Transportation Extension Act of 2003 (P.L. 108-88)**

P.L. 108-88, §12(d), provides:

(d) TEMPORARY RULE REGARDING ADJUSTMENTS.—During the period beginning on the date of the enactment of this Act [9-30-2003.—CCH] and ending on February 29, 2004, for purposes of making any estimate under section 9503(d) of the Internal Revenue Code of 1986 of receipts of the Highway Trust Fund, the Secretary of the Treasury shall treat—

(1) each expiring provision of paragraphs (1) through (4) of section 9503(b) of such Code which is related to appropriations or transfers to such Fund to have been

extended through the end of the 24-month period referred to in section 9503(d)(1)(B) of such Code, and

(2) with respect to each tax imposed under the sections referred to in section 9503(b)(1) of such Code, the rate of such tax during the 24-month period referred to in section 9503(d)(1)(B) of such Code to be the same as the rate of such tax as in effect on the date of the enactment of this Act.

[Sec. 9503(e)]

(e) ESTABLISHMENT OF MASS TRANSIT ACCOUNT.—

(1) CREATION OF ACCOUNT.—There is established in the Highway Trust Fund a separate account to be known as the "Mass Transit Account" consisting of such amounts as may be transferred or credited to the Mass Transit Account as provided in this section or section 9602(b).

(2) TRANSFERS TO MASS TRANSIT ACCOUNT.—The Secretary of the Treasury shall transfer to the Mass Transit Account the mass transit portion of the amounts appropriated to the Highway Trust Fund under subsection (b) which are attributable to taxes under sections 4041 and 4081 imposed after March 31, 1983. For purposes of the preceding sentence, the term "mass transit portion" means, for any fuel with respect to which tax was imposed under section 4041 or 4081 and otherwise deposited into the Highway Trust Fund, the amount determined at the rate of—

(A) except as otherwise provided in this sentence, 2.86 cents per gallon,

(B) 1.43 cents per gallon in the case of any partially exempt methanol or ethanol fuel (as defined in section 4041(m)) none of the alcohol in which consists of ethanol,

(C) 1.86 cents per energy equivalent of a gallon of diesel (as defined in section 4041(a)(2)(D)) in the case of liquefied natural gas,

(D) 2.13 cents per energy equivalent of a gallon of gasoline (as defined in section 4041(a)(2)(C)) in the case of liquefied petroleum gas, and

(E) 9.71 cents per MCF (determined at standard temperature and pressure) in the case of compressed natural gas.

(3) EXPENDITURES FROM ACCOUNT.—Amounts in the Mass Transit Account shall be available, as provided by appropriation Acts, for making capital or capital related expenditures (including capital expenditures for new projects) before October 1, 2026, in accordance with the Infrastructure Investment and Jobs Act or any other provision of law which was referred to in this paragraph before the date of the enactment of such Act (as such Act and provisions of law are in effect on the date of the enactment of such Act).

(4) LIMITATION.—Rules similar to the rules of subsection (d) shall apply to the Mass Transit Account except that subsection (d)(1) shall be applied by substituting "12-month" for "24-month".

(5) PORTION OF CERTAIN TRANSFERS TO BE MADE FROM ACCOUNT.—

(A) IN GENERAL.—Transfers under paragraphs (2) and (3) of subsection (c) shall be borne by the Highway Account and the Mass Transit Account in proportion to the respective revenues transferred under this section to the Highway Account (after the application of paragraph (2)) and the Mass Transit Account.

(B) HIGHWAY ACCOUNT.—For purposes of subparagraph (A), the term "Highway Account" means the portion of the Highway Trust Fund which is not the Mass Transit Account.

Amendments

• **2021, Infrastructure Investment and Jobs Act (P.L. 117-58)**

P.L. 117-58, §80101(a)(1), Div. H:

Amended Code Sec. 9503(e)(3) by striking "October 1, 2021" and inserting "October 1, 2026". **Effective** 11-15-2021.

P.L. 117-58, §80101(a)(2), Div. H:

Amended Code Sec. 9503(e)(3) by striking "Continuing Appropriations Act, 2021 and Other Extensions Act" and inserting "Infrastructure Investment and Jobs Act". **Effective** 11-15-2021.

• **2021, Further Surface Transportation Extension Act of 2021 (P.L. 117-52)**

P.L. 117-52, §4(a)(1)-(2):

Amended Code Sec. 9503(e)(3) by striking "November 1, 2021" and inserting "December 4, 2021" and by striking "Surface Transportation Extension Act of 2021" each place it appears and inserting "Further Surface Transportation Extension Act of 2021". **Effective** 10-31-2021. For a special rule, see Act Sec. 4(d)(1)-(3), below.

P.L. 117-52, §4(d)(1)-(3), provides:

(d) SPECIAL RULE FOR AMENDMENTS.—On the date of enactment of H.R. 3684 (117th Congress)—

(1) subsections (a), (b), and (c) of this section, the amendments made by such subsections, section 201 of the Surface Transportation Extension Act of 2021 (Public Law 117-44), and the amendments made by such section shall cease to be effective;

(2) the text of the laws amended by subsections (a), (b), and (c) of this section and section 201 of the Surface Transportation Extension Act of 2021 (Public Law 117-44) shall revert back so as to read as the text read on September 30, 2021; and

(3) the amendments made by H.R. 3684 (117th Congress) shall be executed as if this section and section 201 of the Surface Transportation Extension Act had not been enacted.

• **2021, Surface Transportation Extension Act of 2021 (P.L. 117-44)**

P.L. 117-44, §201(a)(1)-(2):

Amended Code Sec. 9503(e)(3) by striking "October 1, 2021" and inserting "November 1, 2021", and by striking "Continuing Appropriations Act, 2021 and Other Extensions Act" and inserting "Surface Transportation Extension Act of 2021". **Effective** 10-2-2021. For a special rule, see Act Sec. 201(d)(1)-(3), below.

P.L. 117-44, §201(d)(1)-(3), provides:

(d) SPECIAL RULE FOR EXECUTION OF AMENDMENTS.—On the date of enactment of H.R. 3684 (117th Congress)—

(1) this section and the amendments made by this section shall cease to be effective;

(2) the text of the laws amended by this section shall revert back so as to read as the text read on the day before the date of enactment of this section; and

(3) the amendments made by H.R. 3684 (117th Congress) shall be executed as if this section had not been enacted.

• **2020, Continuing Appropriations Act, 2021 and Other Extensions Act (P.L. 116-159)**

P.L. 116-159, §1201(1):

Amended Code Sec. 9503(c)(1) by striking "October 1, 2020" and inserting "October 1, 2021" and by striking "FAST Act" and inserting "Continuing Appropriations Act, 2021 and Other Extensions Act". **Effective** 10-1-2020.

• **2019, Continuing Appropriations Act, 2020 (P.L. 116-59)**

P.L. 116-59, Div. A, §144, provides:

SEC. 144. Section 9503(e)(4) of the Internal Revenue Code of 1986 shall not apply during the period covered by this Act. [10-1-2019 through 11-21-2019.—CCH]

• **2018, Tax Technical Corrections Act of 2018 (P.L. 115-141)**

P.L. 115-141, §104(b)(1)-(2), Div. U:

Amended Code Sec. 9503(e)(2) by striking "per gallon" in subparagraph (C) and inserting "per energy equivalent of a gallon of diesel (as defined in section 4041(a)(2)(D))", and by striking "per gallon" in subparagraph (D) and inserting "per energy equivalent of a gallon of gasoline (as defined in section 4041(a)(2)(C))". **Effective** as if included in the provision of the Surface Transportation and Veterans Health Care Choice Improvement Act of 2015 to which it relates [**effective** for any sale or use of fuel after 12-31-2015.—CCH].

• **2015, Fixing America's Surface Transportation Act (P.L. 114-94)**

P.L. 114-94, §31101(a)(1)-(2):

Amended Code Sec. 9503(e)(3) by striking "December 5, 2015" and inserting "October 1, 2020", and by striking "Surface Transportation Extension Act of 2015, Part II" and inserting "FAST Act". **Effective** 12-4-2015.

• **2015, Surface Transportation Extension Act of 2015, Part II (P.L. 114-87)**

P.L. 114-87, §2001(a)(1)-(2):

Amended Code Sec. 9503(e)(3) by striking "November 21, 2015" and inserting "December 5, 2015", and by striking "Surface Transportation Extension Act of 2015" and inserting "Surface Transportation Extension Act of 2015, Part II". **Effective** 11-20-2015.

• **2015, Surface Transportation Extension Act of 2015 (P.L. 114-73)**

P.L. 114-73, §2001(a)(1)-(2):

Amended Code Sec. 9503(e)(3) by striking "October 30, 2015" and inserting "November 21, 2015", and by striking "Surface Transportation and Veterans Health Care Choice Improvement Act of 2015" and inserting "Surface Transportation Extension Act of 2015". **Effective** 10-29-2015.

ESTABLISHMENT OF TRUST FUNDS

- **2015, Surface Transportation and Veterans Health Care Choice Improvement Act of 2015 (P.L. 114-41)**

P.L. 114-41, § 2001(a)(1)-(2):

Amended Code Sec. 9503(e)(3) by striking "August 1, 2015" and inserting "October 30, 2015", and by striking "Highway and Transportation Funding Act of 2015" and inserting "Surface Transportation and Veterans Health Care Choice Improvement Act of 2015". **Effective** 7-31-2015.

- **2015, Highway and Transportation Funding Act of 2015 (P.L. 114-21)**

P.L. 114-21, § 2001(a)(1)-(2):

Amended Code Sec. 9503(e)(3) by striking "June 1, 2015" and inserting "August 1, 2015", and by striking "Highway and Transportation Funding Act of 2014" and inserting "Highway and Transportation Funding Act of 2015". **Effective** 5-29-2015.

- **2014, Highway and Transportation Funding Act of 2014 (P.L. 113-159)**

P.L. 113-159, § 2001(a)(1)-(2):

Amended Code Sec. 9503(e)(3) by striking "October 1, 2014" and inserting "June 1, 2015", and by striking "MAP-21" and inserting "Highway and Transportation Funding Act of 2014". **Effective** 8-8-2014.

- **2012, Highway Investment, Job Creation, and Economic Growth Act of 2012 (P.L. 112-141)**

P.L. 112-141, § 40101(a)(1)-(2):

Amended Code Sec. 9503(e)(3) by striking "July 1, 2012" and inserting "October 1, 2014", and by striking "Surface Transportation Extension Act of 2012" and inserting "MAP-21". **Effective** 7-1-2012.

- **2012, Temporary Surface Transportation Extension Act of 2012 (P.L. 112-140)**

P.L. 112-140, § 1(c), provides:

(c) SPECIAL RULE FOR EXECUTION OF AMENDMENTS IN MAP-21.—On the date of enactment of the MAP-21 [P.L. 112-141]—

(1) this Act and the amendments made by this Act shall cease to be effective;

(2) the text of the laws amended by this Act shall revert back so as to read as the text read on the day before the date of enactment of this Act; and

(3) the amendments made by the MAP-21 shall be executed as if this Act had not been enacted.

P.L. 112-140, § 401(a)(1)-(2):

Amended Code Sec. 9503(e)(3) by striking "July 1, 2012" and inserting "July 7, 2012"; and by striking "Surface Transportation Extension Act of 2012" and inserting "Temporary Surface Transportation Extension Act of 2012". **Effective** 7-1-2012. For a special rule, see Act Sec. 1(c), above.

- **2012, Surface Transportation Extension Act of 2012 (P.L. 112-102)**

P.L. 112-102, § 401(a)(1)-(2):

Amended Code Sec. 9503(e)(3) by striking "April 1, 2012" and inserting "July 1, 2012"; and by striking "Surface Transportation Extension Act of 2011, Part II" and inserting "Surface Transportation Extension Act of 2012". **Effective** 4-1-2012.

- **2011, Surface Transportation Extension Act of 2011, Part II (P.L. 112-30)**

P.L. 112-30, § 141(a)(1)-(2):

Amended Code Sec. 9503(e)(3) by striking "October 1, 2011" and inserting "April 1, 2012"; and by striking "Surface Transportation Extension Act of 2011" and inserting "Surface Transportation Extension Act of 2011, Part II". **Effective** 10-1-2011.

- **2011, Surface Transportation Extension Act of 2011 (P.L. 112-5)**

P.L. 112-5, § 401(a)(2)-(3):

Amended Code Sec. 9503(e)(3) by striking "the Surface Transportation Extension Act of 2010, Part II" and inserting "the Surface Transportation Extension Act of 2011"; and by striking "March 5, 2011" and inserting "October 1, 2011". **Effective** 3-4-2011.

- **2010, Surface Transportation Extension Act of 2010, Part II (P.L. 111-322)**

P.L. 111-322, § 2401(a)(2)-(3):

Amended Code Sec. 9503(e)(3) by striking "the Surface Transportation Extension Act of 2010" and inserting "the Surface Transportation Extension Act of 2010, Part II"; and by striking "January 1, 2011" and inserting "March 5, 2011". **Effective** 12-31-2010.

- **2010, Hiring Incentives to Restore Employment Act (P.L. 111-147)**

P.L. 111-147, § 442(b):

Amended Code Sec. 9503(e)(1) by striking "this subsection" and inserting "this section". **Effective** 3-18-2010.

P.L. 111-147, § 444(b)(4):

Amended Code Sec. 9503(e)(5)(A) by striking "(2), (3), and (4)" and inserting "(2) and (3)". **Effective** for transfers relating to amounts paid and credits allowed after 3-18-2010.

P.L. 111-147, § 445(a)(2)(A)-(B):

Amended Code Sec. 9503(e)(3) by striking "October 1, 2009" and inserting "January 1, 2011"; and by striking "in accordance with" and all that follows and inserting "in accordance with the Surface Transportation Extension Act of 2010 or any other provision of law which was referred to in this paragraph before the date of the enactment of such Act (as such Act and provisions of law are in effect on the date of the enactment of such Act).". **Effective** 9-30-2009. Prior to being stricken, all that followed "in accordance with" in Code Sec. 9503(e)(3) read as follows:

the first Continuing Appropriations Resolution for Fiscal Year 2010 enacted into law or any other provision of law which was referred to in this paragraph before the date of the enactment of such Continuing Appropriations Resolution (as such Resolution and provisions of law are in effect on the date of the enactment of the last amendment to such Resolution).

- **2010, Temporary Extension Act of 2010 (P.L. 111-144)**

P.L. 111-144, § 4, provides:

SEC. 4. EXTENSION OF SURFACE TRANSPORTATION PROGRAMS.

(a) IN GENERAL.—Except as provided in subsection (b), for purposes of the continued extension of surface transportation programs and related authority to make expenditures from the Highway Trust Fund and other trust funds under sections 157 through 162 of the Continuing Appropriations Resolution, 2010 (Public Law 111–68; 123 Stat. 2050), the date specified in section 106(3) of that resolution (Public Law 111–68; 123 Stat. 2045) shall be deemed to be March 28, 2010.

(b) EXCEPTION.—Subsection (a) shall not apply if an extension of the programs and authorities described in that subsection for a longer term than the extension contained in the Continuing Appropriations Resolution, 2010 (Public Law 111–68; 123 Stat. 2050), is enacted before the date of enactment of this Act.

- **2009, (P.L. 111-88)**

P.L. 111-88, § 103:

Amended Code Sec. 9503(e)(3) by inserting "the last amendment to" after "on the date of the enactment of". **Effective** 10-30-2009.

- **2009, (P.L. 111-68)**

P.L. 111-68, § 159(b)(1), provides:

(b) MASS TRANSIT ACCOUNT.—

(1) Paragraph (3) of section 9503(e) of such Code shall be applied by substituting the date that is 1 day after the date specified in section 106(3) [October 31, 2009] of this joint resolution for "October 1, 2009".

P.L. 111-68, § 159(b)(2):

Amended Code Sec. 9503(e)(3) by striking "in accordance with" and all that follows and inserting "in accordance with the first Continuing Appropriations Resolution for Fiscal Year 2010 enacted into law or any other provision of law which was referred to in this paragraph before the date of the enactment of such Continuing Appropriations Resolution (as such Resolution and provisions of law are in effect on the date of the enactment of such Resolution).". **Effective** 10-1-2009. Prior to being stricken, all the follows "in accordance with" in Code Sec. 9503(e)(3) read as follows:

the SAFETEA-LU Technical Corrections Act of 2008 or any other provision of law which was referred to in this paragraph before the date of the enactment of such Act (as such Act and provisions of law are in effect on the date of the enactment of such Act).

- **2005, Safe, Accountable, Flexible, Efficient Transportation Equity Act: A Legacy for Users (P.L. 109-59)**

P.L. 109-59, § 11101(d)(1)(B):

Amended Code Sec. 9503(e)(3). **Effective** 8-10-2005. Prior to amendment, Code Sec. 9503(e)(3) read as follows:

(3) EXPENDITURES FROM ACCOUNT.—Amounts in the Mass Transit Account shall be available, as provided by appropriation Acts, for making capital or capital-related expenditures before August 15, 2005 (including capital expenditures for new projects) in accordance with—

(A) section 5338(a)(1) or (b)(1) of title 49,

(B) the Intermodal Surface Transportation Efficiency Act of 1991,

(C) the Transportation Equity Act for the 21st Century,

(D) the Surface Transportation Extension Act of 2003,

(E) the Surface Transportation Extension Act of 2004,

(F) the Surface Transportation Extension Act of 2004, Part II,

(G) the Surface Transportation Extension Act of 2004, Part III,

(H) the Surface Transportation Extension Act of 2004, Part IV,

(I) the Surface Transportation Extension Act of 2004, Part V,

(J) the Surface Transportation Extension Act of 2005,

(K) the Surface Transportation Extension Act of 2005, Part II,

(L) the Surface Transportation Extension Act of 2005, Part III,

(M) the Surface Transportation Extension Act of 2005, Part IV,

(N) the Surface Transportation Extension Act of 2005, Part V, or

(O) the Surface Transportation Extension Act of 2005, Part VI,

as such section and Acts are in effect on the date of enactment of the Surface Transportation Extension Act of 2005, Part VI.

- **2005, Surface Transportation Extension Act of 2005, Part VI (P.L. 109-42)**

P.L. 109-42, § 7(a)(2)(A)-(E):

Amended Code Sec. 9503(e)(3) in the matter before subparagraph (A), by striking "July 31, 2005" and inserting "August 15, 2005", by striking "or" at the end of subparagraph (M), by inserting "or" at the end of subparagraph (N), by inserting after subparagraph (N) a new subparagraph (O), and in the matter after subparagraph (O), as added by Act Sec. 7(a)(2), by striking "Surface Transportation Extension Act of 2005, Part V" and inserting "Surface Transportation Extension Act of 2005, Part VI". **Effective** 7-30-2005.

Sec. 9503(e)(5)(B)

ESTABLISHMENT OF TRUST FUNDS

• **2005, Surface Transportation Extension Act of 2005, Part V (P.L. 109-40)**

P.L. 109-40, §9(a)(2)(A)-(E):

Amended Code Sec. 9503(e)(3) in the matter before subparagraph (A), by striking "July 28, 2005" and inserting "July 31, 2005"; by striking "or" at the end of subparagraph (L); by inserting "or" at the end of subparagraph (M); by inserting after subparagraph (M) a new subparagraph (N); and in the matter after subparagraph (N), as added by Act Sec. 9(a)(2), by striking "Surface Transportation Extension Act of 2005, Part IV" and inserting "Surface Transportation Extension Act of 2005, Part V". **Effective** 7-28-2005.

• **2005, Surface Transportation Extension Act of 2005, Part IV (P.L. 109-37)**

P.L. 109-37, §9(a)(2)(A)-(E):

Amended Code Sec. 9503(e)(3) in the matter before subparagraph (A), by striking "July 22, 2005" and inserting "July 28, 2005"; by striking "or" at the end of subparagraph (K); by inserting "or" at the end of subparagraph (L); by inserting after subparagraph (L) a new subparagraph (M); and in the matter after subparagraph (M), as added by Act Sec. 9(a)(2), by striking "Surface Transportation Extension Act of 2005, Part III" and inserting "Surface Transportation Extension Act of 2005, Part IV". **Effective** 7-22-2005.

• **2005, Surface Transportation Extension Act of 2005, Part III (P.L. 109-35)**

P.L. 109-35, §9(a)(2)(A)-(E):

Amended Code Sec. 9503(e)(3) in the matter before subparagraph (A), by striking "July 20, 2005" and inserting "July 22, 2005"; by striking "or" at the end of subparagraph (J); by inserting "or" at the end of subparagraph (K); by inserting after subparagraph (K) a new subparagraph (L); and in the matter after subparagraph (L), as added by Act Sec. 9(a)(2), by striking "Surface Transportation Extension Act of 2005, Part II" and inserting "Surface Transportation Extension Act of 2005, Part III". **Effective** 7-20-2005.

• **2005, Surface Transportation Extension Act of 2005, Part II (P.L. 109-20)**

P.L. 109-20, §9(a)(2)(A)-(E):

Amended Code Sec. 9503(e)(3) in the matter before subparagraph (A), by striking "July 1, 2005" and inserting "July 20, 2005", by striking "or" at the end of subparagraph (I), by inserting "or" at the end of subparagraph (J), by inserting after subparagraph (J) a new subparagraph (K), and in the matter after subparagraph (K), as added by Act Sec. 9(a)(2), by striking "Surface Transportation Extension Act of 2005" and inserting "Surface Transportation Extension Act of 2005, Part II". **Effective** 7-1-2005.

• **2005, Surface Transportation Extension Act of 2005 (P.L. 109-14)**

P.L. 109-14, §9(a)(2)(A)-(E):

Amended Code Sec. 9503(e)(3) in the matter before subparagraph (A), by striking "June 1, 2005" and inserting "July 1, 2005", by striking "or" at the end of subparagraph (H), by inserting "or" at the end of subparagraph (I), by inserting after subparagraph (I) a new subparagraph (J), and in the matter after subparagraph (J), as added by Act Sec. 9(a)(2), by striking "Surface Transportation Extension Act of 2004, Part V" and inserting "Surface Transportation Extension Act of 2005". **Effective** 5-31-2005.

• **2004, Surface Transportation Extension Act of 2004, Part V (P.L. 108-310)**

P.L. 108-310, §13(a)(2)(A)-(E):

Amended Code Sec. 9503(e)(3) in the matter before subparagraph (A), by striking "October 1, 2004" and inserting "June 1, 2005"; by striking "or" at the end of subparagraph (G); by inserting "or" at the end of subparagraph (H); by inserting after subparagraph (H) a new subparagraph (I); and in the matter after subparagraph (I), as added by Act Sec. 13(a)(2), by striking "Surface Transportation Extension Act of 2004, Part IV" and inserting "Surface Transportation Extension Act of 2004, Part V". **Effective** 9-30-2004.

• **2004, Surface Transportation Extension Act of 2004, Part IV (P.L. 108-280)**

P.L. 108-280, §10(a)(2)(A)-(E):

Amended Code Sec. 9503(e)(3) in the matter before subparagraph (A), by striking "August 1, 2004" and inserting "October 1, 2004", by striking "or" at the end of subparagraph (F), by inserting "or" at the end of subparagraph (G), by inserting after subparagraph (G) a new subparagraph (H), and in the matter after subparagraph (H), as added by Act Sec. 10(a)(2), by striking "Surface Transportation Extension Act of 2004, Part III" and inserting "Surface Transportation Extension Act of 2004, Part IV". **Effective** 7-30-2004.

• **2004, Surface Transportation Extension Act of 2004, Part III (P.L. 108-263)**

P.L. 108-263, §10(a)(2)(A)-(E):

Amended Code Sec. 9503(e)(3) in the matter before subparagraph (A), by striking "July 1, 2004" and inserting "August 1, 2004", by striking "or" at the end of subparagraph (E), by inserting ", or" at the end of subparagraph (F), by inserting after subparagraph (F) a new subparagraph (G), and in the matter after subparagraph (G), as added by Act Sec. 10(a)(2), by striking "Surface Transportation Extension Act of 2004, Part II" and inserting "Surface Transportation Extension Act of 2004, Part III". **Effective** 6-30-2004.

• **2004, Surface Transportation Extension Act of 2004, Part II (P.L. 108-224)**

P.L. 108-224, §10(a)(2)(A)-(E):

Amended Code Sec. 9503(e)(3) in the matter before subparagraph (A), by striking "May 1, 2004" and inserting "July 1, 2004", by striking "or" at the end of subparagraph (D), by inserting "or" at the end of subparagraph (E), by inserting after subparagraph (E) a new subparagraph (F), and in the matter after subparagraph (F), as added by Act Sec. 10(a)(2), by striking "Surface Transportation Extension Act of 2004" and inserting "Surface Transportation Extension Act of 2004, Part II". **Effective** 4-30-2004.

• **2004, Surface Transportation Extension Act of 2004 (P.L. 108-202)**

P.L. 108-202, §12(a)(2)(A)-(E):

Amended Code Sec. 9503(e)(3) in the matter before subparagraph (A), by striking "March 1, 2004" and inserting "May 1, 2004", by striking "or" at the end of subparagraph (C), by inserting "or" at the end of subparagraph (D), by inserting after subparagraph (D) a new subparagraph (E), and in the matter after subparagraph (E), as added by Act Sec. 12(a)(2), by striking "Surface Transportation Extension Act of 2003" and inserting "Surface Transportation Extension Act of 2004". **Effective** 2-29-2004.

• **2003, Surface Transportation Extension Act of 2003 (P.L. 108-88)**

P.L. 108-88, §12(a)(2)(A)-(E):

Amended Code Sec. 9503(e)(3) in the matter before subparagraph (A), by striking "October 1, 2003" and inserting "March 1, 2004", by striking "or" at the end of subparagraph (B), by inserting "or" after "Century," in subparagraph (C), by inserting after subparagraph (C) a new subparagraph (D), and, in the matter after subparagraph (D), by striking "TEA 21 Restoration Act" and inserting "Surface Transportation Extension Act of 2003". **Effective** 9-30-2003.

• **1998, Transportation Equity Act for the 21st Century (P.L. 105-178)**

P.L. 105-178, §9002(d)(2)(A):

Amended Code Sec. 9503(e)(3) by striking "1998" and inserting "2003". **Effective** 6-9-98.

P.L. 105-178, §9002(d)(2)(B)(i)-(iii):

Amended Code Sec. 9503(e)(3) by striking "or" at the end of subparagraph (A), by adding "or" at the end of subparagraph (B), and by striking all that follows subparagraph (B) and inserting a new subparagraph (C) and flush text. **Effective** 6-9-98. Prior to amendment, all that followed subparagraph (B) read as follows:

as section 5338(a)(1) or (b)(1) and the Intermodal Surface Transportation Efficiency Act of 1991 were in effect on December 18, 1991.

P.L. 105-178, §9002(e)(1):

Amended Code Sec. 9503(e)(2) by striking the last sentence and inserting new material. **Effective** as if included in the amendment made by P.L. 105-34, §901(b) [effective for taxes received in the Treasury after 9-30-97.—CCH]. Prior to amendment, the last sentence read as follows:

For purposes of the preceding sentence, the term "mass transit portion" means an amount determined at the rate of 2.85 cents for each gallon with respect to which tax was imposed under section 4041 or 4081.

P.L. 105-178, §9002(f)(5) (as added by P.L. 105-206, §9015(a)):

Amended Code Sec. 9503(e)(3), as amended by subsection (d), by striking "the date of enactment of the Transportation Equity Act for the 21st Century" and inserting "the date of the enactment of the TEA 21 Restoration Act". **Effective** 6-9-98.

P.L. 105-178, §9004(d):

Amended Code Sec. 9503(e)(4). **Effective** 6-9-98. Prior to amendment, Code Sec. 9503(e)(4) read as follows:

(4) LIMITATION.—Rules similar to the rules of subsection (d) shall apply to the Mass Transit Account except that subsection (d)(1) shall be applied by substituting "12-month" for "24-month".

• **1997, Surface Transportation Extension Act of 1997 (P.L. 105-130)**

P.L. 105-130, §9(a)(2)(A)-(B):

Amended Code Sec. 9503(e)(3) by striking "1997" and inserting "1998" and by striking all that follows "the enactment of" and inserting "the last sentence of subsection (c)(1)". [Note: This amendment cannot be reconciled with the amendment made to Code Sec. 9503(e)(3) by P.L. 105-102, §1.] **Effective** 10-1-97.

• **1997 (P.L. 105-102)**

P.L. 105-102, §1:

Amended Code Sec. 9503(e)(3) by striking "such Acts are in effect" and all that follows through the end of the paragraph and substituting "section 5338(a)(1) or (b)(1) and the Intermodal Surface Transportation Efficiency Act of 1991 were in effect on December 18, 1991". [Note: This amendment cannot be reconciled with the amendment made by P.L. 105-130, §9(a)(2)(B).] **Effective** 11-20-97. Prior to amendment, the flush text following Code Sec. 9503(e)(3) read as follows:

as such Acts are in effect on the date of the enactment of the Intermodal Surface Transportation Efficiency Act of 1991.

• **1997, Taxpayer Relief Act of 1997 (P.L. 105-34)**

P.L. 105-34, §901(b):

Amended Code Sec. 9503(e)(2) by striking "2 cents" and inserting "2.85 cents". **Effective** for taxes received in the Treasury after 9-30-97.

ESTABLISHMENT OF TRUST FUNDS

P.L. 105-34, §1601(f)(2)(B):

Amended Code Sec. 9503(e)(5)(A) by striking "; except that" and all that follows and inserting a period. **Effective** as if included in the provision of P.L. 104-188 to which it relates [**effective** for vehicles purchased after 8-20-96.—CCH]. Prior to amendment, Code Sec. 9503(e)(5)(A) read as follows:

(A) IN GENERAL.—Transfers under paragraphs (2), (3), and (4) of subsection (c) shall be borne by the Highway Account and the Mass Transit Account in proportion to the respective revenues transferred under this section to the Highway Account (after the application of paragraph (2)) and the Mass Transit Account; except that any such transfers to the extent attributable to section 6427(g) shall be borne only by the Highway Account.

• **1994 (P.L. 103-429)**

P.L. 103-429, §4:

Amended Code Sec. 9503(e)(3)(A) by striking "paragraph (1) or (3) of subsection (a), or paragraph (1) or (3) of subsection (b), of section 21 of the Federal Transit Act" and substituting "section 5338(a)(1) or (b)(1) of title 49". **Effective** 10-31-94.

• **1993, Omnibus Budget Reconciliation Act of 1993 (P.L. 103-66)**

P.L. 103-66, §13242(d)(40)(A)-(B):

Amended Code Sec. 9503(e)(2) by striking ", 4081, and 4091" and inserting "and 4081" and by striking ", 4081, or 4091" and inserting "or 4081". **Effective** 1-1-94.

P.L. 103-66, §13244(a):

Amended Code Sec. 9503(e)(2) by striking "1.5 cents" and inserting "2 cents". **Effective** for amounts attributable to taxes imposed on or after 10-1-95.

• **1991, Intermodal Surface Transportation Efficiency Act of 1991 (P.L. 102-240)**

P.L. 102-240, §8002(e)(1):

Amended Code Sec. 9503(e)(3) by striking "1993" and inserting "1997". **Effective** 12-18-91.

P.L. 102-240, §8002(f)(1)-(2):

Amended Code Sec. 9503(e)(3) by inserting "or capital-related" after "capital" the first place it appears and by striking "in accordance with section 21(a)(2) of the Urban Mass Transportation Act of 1964" and inserting "in accordance with —" and all that follows. **Effective** 12-18-91.

• **1990, Omnibus Budget Reconciliation Act of 1990 (P.L. 101-508)**

P.L. 101-508, §11211(h)(1):

Amended Code Sec. 9503(e)(2) by striking "1 cent" and inserting "1.5 cents". **Effective** for amounts attributable to taxes imposed on or after 12-1-90.

• **1987, Revenue Act of 1987 (P.L. 100-203)**

P.L. 100-203, §10502(d)(15):

Amended Code Sec. 9503(e)(2) by striking out "sections 4041 and 4081" and inserting in lieu thereof "sections 4041, 4081, and 4091", and by striking out "section 4041 or 4081" and inserting in lieu thereof "section 4041, 4081, or 4091". **Effective** for sales after 3-31-88.

• **1987, Surface Transportation and Uniform Relocation Assistance Act of 1987 (P.L. 100-17)**

P.L. 100-17, §503(a)(1)-(2):

Amended Code Sec. 9503(e) by striking out "1988" and inserting in lieu thereof "1993". **Effective** 4-2-87.

P.L. 100-17, §504:

Amended Code Sec. 9503(e) by adding at the end thereof new paragraph (5). **Effective** 4-2-87.

• **1984, Deficit Reduction Act of 1984 (P.L. 98-369)**

P.L. 98-369, §911(d)[c](1)(A), (B):

Amended Code Sec. 9503(e)(2). **Effective** 8-1-84. Prior to amendment, Code Sec. 9503(e)(2) read as follows:

(2) TRANSFERS TO MASS TRANSIT ACCOUNT.—The Secretary of the Treasury shall transfer to the Mass Transit Account one-ninth of the amounts appropriated to the Highway Trust Fund under subsection (b) which are attributable to taxes under sections 4041 and 4081 imposed after March 31, 1983.

• **1983, Surface Transportation Act of 1983 (P.L. 97-424)**

P.L. 97-424, §531(e):

Added Code Sec. 9503. **Effective** 1-1-83.

P.L. 97-424, §531(e)(2), provides:

(2) NEW HIGHWAY TRUST FUND TREATED AS CONTINUATION OF OLD.—The Highway Trust Fund established by the amendments made by this section shall be treated for all purposes of law as the continuation of the Highway Trust Fund established by section 209 of the Highway Revenue Act of 1956. Any reference in any law to the Highway Trust Fund established by such section 209 shall be deemed to include (wherever appropriate) a reference to the Highway Trust Fund established by the amendments made by this section.

[Sec. 9503(f)]

(f) DETERMINATION OF TRUST FUND BALANCES AFTER SEPTEMBER 30, 1998.—

(1) IN GENERAL.—For purposes of determining the balances of the Highway Trust Fund and the Mass Transit Account after September 30, 1998, the opening balance of the Highway Trust Fund (other than the Mass Transit Account) on October 1, 1998, shall be $8,000,000,000. The Secretary shall cancel obligations held by the Highway Trust Fund to reflect the reduction in the balance under this paragraph.

(2) RESTORATION OF FOREGONE INTEREST.—Out of money in the Treasury not otherwise appropriated, there is hereby appropriated—

(A) $14,700,000,000 to the Highway Account (as defined in subsection (e)(5)(B)) in the Highway Trust Fund; and

(B) $4,800,000,000 to the Mass Transit Account in the Highway Trust Fund.

(3) INCREASE IN FUND BALANCE.—There is hereby transferred to the Highway Account (as defined in subsection (e)(5)(B)) in the Highway Trust Fund amounts appropriated from the Leaking Underground Storage Tank Trust Fund under section 9508(c)(2).

(4) ADDITIONAL APPROPRIATIONS TO TRUST FUND.—Out of money in the Treasury not otherwise appropriated, there is hereby appropriated to—

(A) the Highway Account (as defined in subsection (e)(5)(B)) in the Highway Trust Fund—

(i) for fiscal year 2013, $6,200,000,000, and

(ii) for fiscal year 2014, $10,400,000,000, and

(B) the Mass Transit Account in the Highway Trust Fund, for fiscal year 2014, $2,200,000,000.

(5) ADDITIONAL SUMS.—Out of money in the Treasury not otherwise appropriated, there is hereby appropriated—

(A) $7,765,000,000 to the Highway Account (as defined in subsection (e)(5)(B)) in the Highway Trust Fund; and

(B) $2,000,000,000 to the Mass Transit Account in the Highway Trust Fund.

(6) ADDITIONAL INCREASE IN FUND BALANCE.—There is hereby transferred to the Highway Account (as defined in subsection (e)(5)(B)) in the Highway Trust Fund amounts appropriated from the Leaking Underground Storage Tank Trust Fund under section 9508(c)(3).

(7) ADDITIONAL SUMS.—Out of money in the Treasury not otherwise appropriated, there is hereby appropriated—

(A) $6,068,000,000 to the Highway Account (as defined in subsection (e)(5)(B)) in the Highway Trust Fund; and

(B) $2,000,000,000 to the Mass Transit Account in the Highway Trust Fund.

(8) FURTHER TRANSFERS TO TRUST FUND.—Out of money in the Treasury not otherwise appropriated, there is hereby appropriated—

(A) $51,900,000,000 to the Highway Account (as defined in subsection (e)(5)(B)) in the Highway Trust Fund; and

(B) $18,100,000,000 to the Mass Transit Account in the Highway Trust Fund.

(9) ADDITIONAL INCREASE IN FUND BALANCE.—There is hereby transferred to the Highway Account (as defined in subsection (e)(5)(B)) in the Highway Trust Fund amounts appropriated from the Leaking Underground Storage Tank Trust Fund under section 9508(c)(4).

(10) FURTHER TRANSFERS TO TRUST FUND.—Out of money in the Treasury not otherwise appropriated, there is hereby appropriated—

(A) $10,400,000,000 to the Highway Account (as defined in subsection (e)(5)(B)) in the Highway Trust Fund; and

(B) $3,200,000,000 to the Mass Transit Account in the Highway Trust Fund.

(11) FURTHER TRANSFERS TO TRUST FUND.—Out of money in the Treasury not otherwise appropriated, there is hereby appropriated—

(A) $90,000,000,000 to the Highway Account (as defined in subsection (e)(5)(B)) in the Highway Trust Fund; and

(B) $28,000,000,000 to the Mass Transit Account in the Highway Trust Fund.

ESTABLISHMENT OF TRUST FUNDS

(12) TREATMENT OF AMOUNTS.—Any amount appropriated or transferred under this subsection to the Highway Trust Fund shall remain available without fiscal year limitation.

Amendments

• **2021, Infrastructure Investment and Jobs Act (P.L. 117-58)**

P.L. 117-58, § 80103, Div. H:

Amended Code Sec. 9503(f) by redesignating paragraph (11) as paragraph (12) and inserting after paragraph (10) a new paragraph (11). **Effective** 11-15-2021.

• **2020, Continuing Appropriations Act, 2021 and Other Extensions Act (P.L. 116-159)**

P.L. 116-159, § 1204:

Amended Code Sec. 9503(f) by redesignating paragraph (10) as paragraph (11) and by inserting after paragraph (9) a new paragraph (10). **Effective** 10-1-2020.

• **2015, Fixing America's Surface Transportation Act (P.L. 114-94)**

P.L. 114-94, § 31201:

Amended Code Sec. 9503(f) by redesignating paragraph (8) as paragraph (10) and inserting after paragraph (7) new paragraphs (8)-(9). **Effective** 12-4-2015.

• **2015, Surface Transportation and Veterans Health Care Choice Improvement Act of 2015 (P.L. 114-41)**

P.L. 114-41, § 2002:

Amended Code Sec. 9503(f) by redesignating paragraph (7) as paragraph (8) and by inserting after paragraph (6) a new paragraph (7). **Effective** 7-31-2015.

• **2014, Highway and Transportation Funding Act of 2014 (P.L. 113-159)**

P.L. 113-159, § 2002(a):

Amended Code Sec. 9503(f) by redesignating paragraph (5) as paragraph (7) and inserting after paragraph (4) new paragraphs (5)-(6). **Effective** 8-8-2014.

• **2012, Highway Investment, Job Creation, and Economic Growth Act of 2012 (P.L. 112-141)**

P.L. 112-141, § 40201(b)(1):

Amended Code Sec. 9503(f) by inserting after paragraph (2) a new paragraph (3). **Effective** 7-6-2012.

P.L. 112-141, § 40201(b)(2)(A)-(B):

Amended Code Sec. 9503(f)(4) by inserting "or transferred" after "appropriated", and by striking "APPROPRIATED" before "AMOUNTS" in the heading thereof. **Effective** 7-6-2012.

P.L. 112-141, § 40251:

Amended Code Sec. 9503(f) by redesignating paragraph (4) as paragraph (5) and by inserting after paragraph (3) a new paragraph (4). **Effective** 7-6-2012.

• **2010, Hiring Incentives to Restore Employment Act (P.L. 111-147)**

P.L. 111-147, § 441(a):

Amended Code Sec. 9503(f)(1) by striking subparagraph (B). **Effective** 3-18-2010. Prior to being stricken, Code Sec. 9503(f)(1)(B) read as follows:

(B) notwithstanding section 9602(b), obligations held by such Fund after September 30, 1998, shall be obligations of the United States which are not interest-bearing.

P.L. 111-147, § 441(b)(1)-(2):

Amended Code Sec. 9503(f)(1), as amended by Act Sec. 441(1)[(a)], by striking ", and" at the end of subparagraph (A) and inserting a period; and by striking "1998" in the matter preceding subparagraph (A) and all that follows through "the opening balance" and inserting "1998, the opening balance". **Effective** 3-18-2010. Prior to amendment, Code Sec. 9503(f)(1) read as follows:

(1) IN GENERAL.—For purposes of determining the balances of the Highway Trust Fund and the Mass Transit Account after September 30, 1998—

(A) the opening balance of the Highway Trust Fund (other than the Mass Transit Account) on October 1, 1998, shall be $8,000,000,000, and

The Secretary shall cancel obligations held by the Highway Trust Fund to reflect the reduction in the balance under this paragraph.

P.L. 111-147, § 442(a):

Amended Code Sec. 9503(f)(2). **Effective** 3-18-2010. Prior to amendment, Code Sec. 9503(f)(2) read as follows:

(2) INCREASE IN FUND BALANCE.—Out of money in the Treasury not otherwise appropriated, there is hereby appropriated (without fiscal year limitation) to the Highway Trust Fund $7,000,000,000.

P.L. 111-147, § 443(a):

Amended Code Sec. 9503(f), as amended by this Act, by adding at the end a new paragraph (4)[(3)]. **Effective** 3-18-2010.

• **2009, (P.L. 111-46)**

P.L. 111-46, § 1:

Amended Code Sec. 9503(f) by striking paragraph (2) and adding at the end a new paragraph (2). **Effective** 8-7-2009. Prior to being stricken, Code Sec. 9503(f)(2) read as follows:

(2) RESTORATION OF FUND BALANCE.—Out of money in the Treasury not otherwise appropriated, there is hereby appropriated to the Highway Trust Fund $8,017,000,000.

• **2008 (P.L. 110-318)**

P.L. 110-318, § 1(a)(1)-(4):

Amended Code Sec. 9503(f) by redesignating paragraphs (1) and (2) as subparagraphs (A) and (B), respectively, and by moving such subparagraphs 2 ems to the right, by striking "For purposes" and inserting:

"(1) IN GENERAL.—For purposes",

by moving the flush sentence at the end of paragraph (1), as so amended, 2 ems to the right, and by adding at the end a new paragraph (2). **Effective** 9-15-2008.

P.L. 110-318, § 1(b):

Amended the last sentence of Code Sec. 9503(f)(1), as amended by Act Sec. 1(a), by striking "subsection" and inserting "paragraph". **Effective** 9-15-2008.

• **1998, Tax and Trade Relief Extension Act of 1998 (P.L. 105-277)**

P.L. 105-277, § 4006(b)(1):

Amended Code Sec. 9503(f)(2). **Effective** 10-1-98. Prior to amendment, Code Sec. 9503(f)(2) read as follows:

(2) no interest accruing after September 30, 1998, on any obligation held by such Fund shall be credited to such Fund.

• **1998, Transportation Equity Act for the 21st Century (P.L. 105-178)**

P.L. 105-178, § 9004(a)(1):

Amended Code Sec. 9503 by adding at the end a new subsection (f). **Effective** 10-1-98.

• **1997, Taxpayer Relief Act of 1997 (P.L. 105-34)**

P.L. 105-34, § 901(d)(1):

Amended Code Sec. 9503 by striking subsection (f). **Effective** for taxes received in the Treasury after 9-30-97. Prior to being stricken, Code Sec. 9503(f) read as follows:

(f) DEFINITION OF HIGHWAY TRUST FUND FINANCING RATE.—For purposes of this section—

(1) IN GENERAL.—Except as otherwise provided in this subsection, the Highway Trust Fund financing rate is—

(A) in the case of gasoline and special motor fuels, 11.5 cents per gallon (14 cents per gallon after September 30, 1995), and

(B) in the case of diesel fuel, 17.5 cents per gallon (20 cents per gallon after September 30, 1995).

(2) CERTAIN USES.—

(A) TRAINS.—In the case of fuel used in a train, the Highway Trust Fund financing rate is zero.

(B) CERTAIN BUSES.—In the case of diesel fuel used in a use described in section 6427(b)(1) (after the application of section 6427(b)(3)), the Highway Trust Fund financing rate is 3 cents per gallon.

(C) CERTAIN BOATS.—In the case of diesel fuel used in a boat described in clause (iv) of section 6421(e)(2)(B), the Highway Trust Fund financing rate is zero.

(D) COMPRESSED NATURAL GAS.—In the case of the tax imposed by section 4041(a)(3), the Highway Trust Fund financing rate is zero.

(E) CERTAIN OTHER NONHIGHWAY USES.—In the case of gasoline and special motor fuels used as described in paragraph (4)(D), (5)(B), or (6)(D) of subsection (c), the Highway Trust Fund financing rate is 11.5 cents per gallon; and, in the case of diesel fuel used as described in subsection (c)(6)(D), the Highway Trust Fund financing rate is 17.5 cents per gallon.

(3) ALCOHOL FUELS.—

(A) IN GENERAL.—If the rate of tax on any fuel is determined under section 4041(b)(2)(A), 4041(k), or 4081(c), the Highway Trust Fund financing rate is the excess (if any) of the rate so determined over—

(i) 6.8 cents per gallon after September 30, 1993, and before October 1, 1999,

(ii) 4.3 cents per gallon after September 30, 1999.

In the case of a rate of tax determined under section 4081(c), the preceding sentence shall be applied by increasing the rates specified in clauses (i) and (ii) by 0.1 cent.

(B) FUELS USED TO PRODUCE MIXTURES.—In the case of a rate of tax determined under section 4081(c)(2), subparagraph (A) shall be applied by substituting rates which are $^{10}/_9$ of the rates otherwise applicable under clauses (i) and (ii) of subparagraph (A).

(C) PARTIALLY EXEMPT METHANOL OR ETHANOL FUEL.—In the case of a rate of tax determined under section 4041(m), the Highway Trust Fund financing rate is the excess (if any) of the rate so determined over—

(i) 5.55 cents per gallon after September 30, 1993, and before October 1, 1995, and

(ii) 4.3 cents per gallon after September 30, 1995.

(4) TERMINATION.—Notwithstanding the preceding provisions of this subsection, the Highway Trust Fund financing rate is zero with respect to taxes received in the Treasury after June 30, 2000.

• **1993, Omnibus Budget Reconciliation Act of 1993 (P.L. 103-66)**

P.L. 103-66, § 13242(d)(41):

Amended Code Sec. 9503 by adding at the end thereof new subsection (f). **Effective** 1-1-94.

ESTABLISHMENT OF TRUST FUNDS

[Sec. 9504]

SEC. 9504. SPORT FISH RESTORATION AND BOATING TRUST FUND.

[Sec. 9504(a)]

(a) CREATION OF TRUST FUND.—There is hereby established in the Treasury of the United States a trust fund to be known as the "Sport Fish Restoration and Boating Trust Fund". Such Trust Fund shall consist of such amounts as may be appropriated, credited, or paid to it as provided in this section, section 9503(c)(3), section 9503(c)(4), or section 9602(b).

Amendments

• **2010, Hiring Incentives to Restore Employment Act (P.L. 111-147)**

P.L. 111-147, § 444(b)(5):

Amended Code Sec. 9504(a) by striking "section 9503(c)(4), section 9503(c)(5)" and inserting "section 9503(c)(3), section 9503(c)(4)". **Effective** for transfers relating to amounts paid and credits allowed after 3-18-2010.

• **2005, Safe, Accountable, Flexible, Efficient Transportation Equity Act: A Legacy for Users (P.L. 109-59)**

P.L. 109-59, § 11115(b)(1):

Amended Code Sec. 9504(a). **Effective** 10-1-2005. Prior to amendment, Code Sec. 9504(a) read as follows:

(a) CREATION OF TRUST FUND.—

(1) IN GENERAL.—There is hereby established in the Treasury of the United States a trust fund to be known as the "Aquatic Resources Trust Fund".

(2) ACCOUNTS IN TRUST FUND.—The Aquatic Resources Trust Fund shall consist of—

(A) a Sport Fish Restoration Account, and

(B) a Boat Safety Account.

Each such Account shall consist of such amounts as may be appropriated, credited, or paid to it as provided in this section, section 9503(c)(4), section 9503(c)(5) or section 9602(b).

P.L. 109-59, § 11115(b)(2)(D):

Amended Code Sec. 9504 by striking "AQUATIC RESOURCES" in the heading and inserting "SPORT FISH RESTORATION AND BOATING". **Effective** 10-1-2005.

• **1990, Omnibus Budget Reconciliation Act of 1990 (P.L. 101-508)**

P.L. 101-508, § 11211(i)(2):

Amended Code Sec. 9504(a)(2) by inserting "section 9503(c)(5)" after "section 9503(c)(4),". **Effective** 12-1-90.

[Sec. 9504(b)]

(b) SPORT FISH RESTORATION AND BOATING TRUST FUND.—

(1) TRANSFER OF CERTAIN TAXES TO TRUST FUND.—There is hereby appropriated to the Sport Fish Restoration and Boating Trust Fund amounts equivalent to the following amounts received in the Treasury on or after October 1, 1984—

(A) the taxes imposed by section 4161(a) (relating to sport fishing equipment), and

(B) the import duties imposed on fishing tackle under heading 9507 of the Harmonized Tariff Schedule of the United States (19 U.S.C. 1202) and on yachts and pleasure craft under chapter 89 of the Harmonized Tariff Schedule of the United States.

(2) EXPENDITURES FROM TRUST FUND.—Amounts in the Sport Fish Restoration and Boating Trust Fund shall be available, as provided by appropriation Acts, for making expenditures—

(A) to carry out the purposes of the Dingell-Johnson Sport Fish Restoration Act (as in effect on the date of the enactment of the Infrastructure Investment and Jobs Act),

(B) to carry out the purposes of section 7404(d) of the Transportation Equity Act for the 21st Century (as in effect on the date of the enactment of the Infrastructure Investment and Jobs Act), and

(C) to carry out the purposes of the Coastal Wetlands Planning Protection and Restoration Act (as in effect on the date of the enactment of the Infrastructure Investment and Jobs Act).

Amounts transferred to such account under section 9503(c)(4) may be used only for making expenditures described in subparagraph (C) of this paragraph.

Amendments

• **2021, Infrastructure Investment and Jobs Act (P.L. 117-58)**

P.L. 117-58, § 80101(b)(1), Div. H:

Amended Code Sec. 9504(b)(2) by striking "Continuing Appropriations Act, 2021 and Other Extensions Act" each place it appears and inserting "Infrastructure Investment and Jobs Act". **Effective** 11-15-2021.

• **2021, Further Surface Transportation Extension Act of 2021 (P.L. 117-52)**

P.L. 117-52, § 4(b)(1):

Amended Code Sec. 9504(b)(2) by striking "Surface Transportation Extension Act of 2021" each place it appears and inserting "Further Surface Transportation Extension Act of 2021". **Effective** 10-31-2021. For a special rule, see Act Sec. 4(d)(1)-(3), below.

P.L. 117-52, § 4(d)(1)-(3), provides:

(d) SPECIAL RULE FOR AMENDMENTS.—On the date of enactment of H.R. 3684 (117th Congress)—

(1) subsections (a), (b), and (c) of this section, the amendments made by such subsections, section 201 of the Surface Transportation Extension Act of 2021 (Public Law 117-44), and the amendments made by such section shall cease to be effective;

(2) the text of the laws amended by subsections (a), (b), and (c) of this section and section 201 of the Surface Transportation Extension Act of 2021 (Public Law 117-44) shall revert back so as to read as the text read on September 30, 2021; and

(3) the amendments made by H.R. 3684 (117th Congress) shall be executed as if this section and section 201 of the Surface Transportation Extension Act had not been enacted.

• **2021, Surface Transportation Extension Act of 2021 (P.L. 117-44)**

P.L. 117-44, § 201(b)(1):

Amended Code Sec. 9504(b)(2) by striking "Continuing Appropriations Act, 2021 and Other Extensions Act" each place it appears and inserting "Surface Transportation Extension Act of 2021". **Effective** 10-2-2021. For a special rule, see Act Sec. 201(d)(1)-(3), below.

P.L. 117-44, § 201(d)(1)-(3), provides:

(d) SPECIAL RULE FOR EXECUTION OF AMENDMENTS.—On the date of enactment of H.R. 3684 (117th Congress)—

(1) this section and the amendments made by this section shall cease to be effective;

(2) the text of the laws amended by this section shall revert back so as to read as the text read on the day before the date of enactment of this section; and

(3) the amendments made by H.R. 3684 (117th Congress) shall be executed as if this section had not been enacted.

• **2020, Continuing Appropriations Act, 2021 and Other Extensions Act (P.L. 116-159)**

P.L. 116-159, § 1202(1):

Amended Code Sec. 9504(b)(2) by striking "FAST Act" each place it appears and inserting "Continuing Appropriations Act, 2021 and Other Extensions Act". **Effective** 10-1-2020.

• **2015, Fixing America's Surface Transportation Act (P.L. 114-94)**

P.L. 114-94, § 31101(b)(1):

Amended Code Sec. 9504(b)(2) by striking "Surface Transportation Extension Act of 2015, Part II" each place it appears and inserting "FAST Act". **Effective** 12-4-2015.

• **2015, Surface Transportation Extension Act of 2015, Part II (P.L. 114-87)**

P.L. 114-87, § 2001(b)(1):

Amended Code Sec. 9504(b)(2) by striking "Surface Transportation Extension Act of 2015" each place it appears and inserting "Surface Transportation Extension Act of 2015, Part II". **Effective** 11-20-2015.

• **2015, Surface Transportation Extension Act of 2015 (P.L. 114-73)**

P.L. 114-73, § 2001(b)(1):

Amended Code Sec. 9504(b)(2) by striking "Surface Transportation and Veterans Health Care Choice Improvement Act of 20155" each place it appears and inserting "Surface Transportation Extension Act of 2015". **Effective** 10-29-2015.

• **2015, Surface Transportation and Veterans Health Care Choice Improvement Act of 2015 (P.L. 114-41)**

P.L. 114-41, § 2001(b)(1):

Amended Code Sec. 9504(b)(2) by striking "Highway and Transportation Funding Act of 2015" each place it appears and inserting "Surface Transportation and Veterans Health Care Choice Improvement Act of 2015". **Effective** 7-31-2015.

• **2015, Highway and Transportation Funding Act of 2015 (P.L. 114-21)**

P.L. 114-21, § 2001(b)(1):

Amended Code Sec. 9504(b)(2) by striking "Highway and Transportation Funding Act of 2014" each place it appears and inserting "Highway and Transportation Funding Act of 2015". **Effective** 5-29-2015.

ESTABLISHMENT OF TRUST FUNDS

• **2014, Highway and Transportation Funding Act of 2014 (P.L. 113-159)**

P.L. 113-159, § 2001(b)(1):

Amended Code Sec. 9504(b)(2) by striking "MAP-21" each place it appears and inserting "Highway and Transportation Funding Act of 2014". **Effective** 8-8-2014.

• **2012, Highway Investment, Job Creation, and Economic Growth Act of 2012 (P.L. 112-141)**

P.L. 112-141, § 40101(b)(1):

Amended Code Sec. 9504(b)(2) by striking "Surface Transportation Extension Act of 2012" each place it appears and inserting "MAP-21". **Effective** 7-1-2012.

• **2012, Temporary Surface Transportation Extension Act of 2012 (P.L. 112-140)**

P.L. 112-140, § 1(c), provides:

(c) SPECIAL RULE FOR EXECUTION OF AMENDMENTS IN MAP–21.—On the date of enactment of the MAP–21 [P.L. 112-141]—

(1) this Act and the amendments made by this Act shall cease to be effective;

(2) the text of the laws amended by this Act shall revert back so as to read as the text read on the day before the date of enactment of this Act; and

(3) the amendments made by the MAP–21 shall be executed as if this Act had not been enacted.

P.L. 112-140, § 401(b)(1):

Amended Code Sec. 9504(b)(2) by striking "Surface Transportation Extension Act of 2012" each place it appears and inserting "Temporary Surface Transportation Extension Act of 2012". **Effective** 7-1-2012. For a special rule, see Act Sec. 1(c), above.

• **2012, Surface Transportation Extension Act of 2012 (P.L. 112-102)**

P.L. 112-102, § 401(b)(1):

Amended Code Sec. 9504(b)(2) by striking "Surface Transportation Extension Act of 2011, Part II" each place it appears and inserting "Surface Transportation Extension Act of 2012". **Effective** 4-1-2012.

• **2011, Surface Transportation Extension Act of 2011, Part II (P.L. 112-30)**

P.L. 112-30, § 141(b)(1):

Amended Code Sec. 9504(b)(2) by striking "Surface Transportation Extension Act of 2011" each place it appears and inserting "Surface Transportation Extension Act of 2011, Part II". **Effective** 10-1-2011.

• **2011, Surface Transportation Extension Act of 2011 (P.L. 112-5)**

P.L. 112-5, § 401(b)(1):

Amended Code Sec. 9504(b)(2) by striking "Surface Transportation Extension Act of 2010, Part II" each place it appears and inserting "Surface Transportation Extension Act of 2011". **Effective** 3-4-2011.

• **2010, Surface Transportation Extension Act of 2010, Part II (P.L. 111-322)**

P.L. 111-322, § 2401(b)(1):

Amended Code Sec. 9504(b)(2) by striking "Surface Transportation Extension Act of 2010" and inserting "Surface Transportation Extension Act of 2010, Part II". **Effective** 12-31-2010.

• **2010, Hiring Incentives to Restore Employment Act (P.L. 111-147)**

P.L. 111-147, § 444(b)(6):

Amended Code Sec. 9504(b)(2) by striking "section 9503(c)(5)" and inserting "section 9503(c)(4)". **Effective** for transfers relating to amounts paid and credits allowed after 3-18-2010.

P.L. 111-147, § 445(b)(1)(A)-(C):

Amended Code Sec. 9504(b)(2) by striking "(as in effect" in subparagraph (A) and all that follows in such subparagraph and inserting "(as in effect on the date of the enactment of the Surface Transportation Extension Act of 2010),", by striking "(as in effect" in subparagraph (B) and all that follows in such subparagraph and inserting "(as in effect on the date of the enactment of the Surface Transportation Extension Act of 2010), and", and by striking "(as in effect" in subparagraph (C) and all that follows in such subparagraph and inserting "(as in effect on the date of the enactment of the Surface Transportation Extension Act of 2010).". **Effective** 9-30-2009. Prior to amendment, Code Sec. 9504(b)(2)(A)-(C) read as follows:

(2) EXPENDITURES FROM TRUST FUND.—Amounts in the Sport Fish Restoration and Boating Trust Fund shall be available, as provided by appropriation Acts, for making expenditures—

(A) to carry out the purposes of the Dingell-Johnson Sport Fish Restoration Act (as in effect on the date of the enactment of the last amendment to the first Continuing Appropriations Resolution for Fiscal Year 2010),

(B) to carry out the purposes of section 7404(d) of the Transportation Equity Act for the 21st Century (as in effect on the date of the enactment of the last amendment to the first Continuing Appropriations Resolution for Fiscal Year 2010), and

(C) to carry out the purposes of the Coastal Wetlands Planning Protection and Restoration Act (as in effect on the date of the enactment of the last amendment to the first Continuing Appropriations Resolution for Fiscal Year 2010).

Amounts transferred to such account under section 9503(c)(5) may be used only for making expenditures described in subparagraph (C) of this paragraph.

• **2009, (P.L. 111-88)**

P.L. 111-88, § 103:

Amended Code Sec. 9504(b)(2)(A)-(C) by inserting "the last amendment to" after "on the date of the enactment of". **Effective** 10-30-2009.

• **2009, (P.L. 111-68)**

P.L. 111-68, § 161(a)(1)-(3):

Amended Code Sec. 9504(b)(2) by striking "(as in effect" in subparagraph (A) and all that follows in such subparagraph and inserting "(as in effect on the date of the enactment of the first Continuing Appropriations Resolution for Fiscal Year 2010),"; by striking "(as in effect" in subparagraph (B) and all that follows in such subparagraph and inserting "(as in effect on the date of the enactment of the first Continuing Appropriations Resolution for Fiscal Year 2010), and"; and by striking "(as in effect" in subparagraph (C) and all that follows in such subparagraph and inserting "(as in effect on the date of the enactment of the first Continuing Appropriations Resolution for Fiscal Year 2010).". **Effective** 10-1-2009. Prior to amendment, Code Sec. 9504(b)(2) read as follows:

(2) EXPENDITURES FROM TRUST FUND.—Amounts in the Sport Fish Restoration and Boating Trust Fund shall be available, as provided by appropriation Acts, for making expenditures—

(A) to carry out the purposes of the Dingell-Johnson Sport Fish Restoration Act (as in effect on the date of the enactment of the Safe, Accountable, Flexible, Efficient Transportation Equity Act: A Legacy for Users),

(B) to carry out the purposes of section 7404(d) of the Transportation Equity Act for the 21st Century (as in effect on the date of the enactment of the Safe, Accountable, Flexible, Efficient Transportation Equity Act: A Legacy for Users), and

(C) to carry out the purposes of the Coastal Wetlands Planning Protection and Restoration Act (as in effect on the date of the enactment of the Safe, Accountable, Flexible, Efficient Transportation Equity Act: A Legacy for Users).

Amounts transferred to such account under section 9503(c)(5) may be used only for making expenditures described in subparagraph (C) of this paragraph.

• **2005, Safe, Accountable, Flexible, Efficient Transportation Equity Act: A Legacy for Users (P.L. 109-59)**

P.L. 109-59, § 11101(d)(2)(A):

Amended Code Sec. 9504(b)(2) by striking "Surface Transportation Extension Act of 2005, Part V" each place it appears and inserting "Safe, Accountable, Flexible, Efficient Transportation Equity Act: A Legacy for Users". **Effective** 8-10-2005.

P.L. 109-59, § 11115(b)(2)(A)(i)-(iii):

Amended Code Sec. 9504(b), as amended by Act Sec. 11101, by striking "ACCOUNT" in the heading and inserting "AND BOATING TRUST FUND", by striking "Account" both places it appears in paragraphs (1) and (2) and inserting "and Boating Trust Fund", and by striking "ACCOUNT" both places it appears in the headings for paragraphs (1) and (2) and inserting "TRUST FUND". **Effective** 10-1-2005.

P.L. 109-59, § 11151(c):

Amended Code Sec. 9504(b)(2) by striking in the last sentence "subparagraph (B)" and inserting "subparagraph (C)". **Effective** as if included in the provision of the Transportation Equity Act for the 21st Century to which it relates [effective 6-9-98.—CCH].

P.L. 109-59, § 11151(e)(1):

Amended Code Sec. 9504(b)(2)(A) by striking "the Act entitled 'An Act to provide that the United States shall aid the States in fish restoration and management projects, and for other purposes', approved August 9, 1950" and inserting "the Dingell-Johnson Sport Fish Restoration Act". **Effective** 8-10-2005.

• **2005, Surface Transportation Extension Act of 2005, Part VI (P.L. 109-42)**

P.L. 109-42, § 7(b)(1):

Amended Code Sec. 9504(b)(2) by adding at the end a new sentence. **Effective** 7-30-2005.

P.L. 109-42, § 7(d)(2):

Amended Code Sec. 9504(b)(2) by striking the last sentence. For the **effective** date, see Act Sec. 7(e)(2), below. Prior to being stricken, the last sentence of Code Sec. 9504(b)(2) read as follows:

Subparagraphs (A), (B), and (C) shall each be applied by substituting "Surface Transportation Extension Act of 2005, Part VI" for "Surface Transportation Extension Act of 2005, Part V".

P.L. 109-42, § 7(e)(2), provides:

(2) SUBSEQUENT REPEAL.—The amendments made by subsection (d) shall take effect on the date of the enactment of the Safe, Accountable, Flexible, Efficient Transportation Equity Act: A Legacy for Users and shall be executed immediately before the amendment made by such Act.

• **2005, Surface Transportation Extension Act of 2005, Part V (P.L. 109-40)**

P.L. 109-40, § 9(b)(1):

Amended Code Sec. 9504(b)(2) by striking "Surface Transportation Extension Act of 2005, Part IV" each place it appears and inserting "Surface Transportation Extension Act of 2005, Part V". **Effective** 7-28-2005.

• **2005, Surface Transportation Extension Act of 2005, Part IV (P.L. 109-37)**

P.L. 109-37, § 9(b)(1):

Amended Code Sec. 9504(b)(2) by striking "Surface Transportation Extension Act of 2005, Part III" each place it appears and inserting "Surface Transportation Extension Act of 2005, Part IV". **Effective** 7-22-2005.

ESTABLISHMENT OF TRUST FUNDS

• **2005, Surface Transportation Extension Act of 2005, Part III (P.L. 109-35)**

P.L. 109-35, § 9(b)(1):

Amended Code Sec. 9504(b)(2) by striking "Surface Transportation Extension Act of 2005, Part II" each place it appears and inserting "Surface Transportation Extension Act of 2005, Part III". **Effective** 7-20-2005.

• **2005, Surface Transportation Extension Act of 2005, Part II (P.L. 109-20)**

P.L. 109-20, § 9(b)(1):

Amended Code Sec. 9504(b)(2) by striking "Surface Transportation Extension Act of 2005" each place it appears and inserting "Surface Transportation Extension Act of 2005, Part II". **Effective** 7-1-2005.

• **2005, Surface Transportation Extension Act of 2005 (P.L. 109-14)**

P.L. 109-14, § 9(b)(1):

Amended Code Sec. 9504(b)(2) by striking "Surface Transportation Extension Act of 2004, Part V" each place it appears and inserting "Surface Transportation Extension Act of 2005". **Effective** 5-31-2005.

• **2004, Surface Transportation Extension Act of 2004, Part V (P.L. 108-310)**

P.L. 108-310, § 13(b)(1):

Amended Code Sec. 9504(b)(2) by striking "Surface Transportation Extension Act of 2004, Part IV" each place it appears and inserting "Surface Transportation Extension Act of 2004, Part V". **Effective** 9-30-2004.

• **2004, Surface Transportation Extension Act of 2004, Part IV (P.L. 108-280)**

P.L. 108-280, § 10(b)(1):

Amended Code Sec. 9504(b)(2) by striking "Surface Transportation Extension Act of 2004, Part III" each place it appears and inserting "Surface Transportation Extension Act of 2004, Part IV". **Effective** 7-30-2004.

• **2004, Surface Transportation Extension Act of 2004, Part III (P.L. 108-263)**

P.L. 108-263, § 10(b)(1):

Amended Code Sec. 9504(b)(2) by striking "Surface Transportation Extension Act of 2004, Part II" each place it appears and inserting "Surface Transportation Extension Act of 2004, Part III". **Effective** 6-30-2004.

• **2004, Surface Transportation Extension Act of 2004, Part II (P.L. 108-224)**

P.L. 108-224, § 10(b)(1):

Amended Code Sec. 9504(b)(2) by striking "Surface Transportation Extension Act of 2004" each place it appears and inserting "Surface Transportation Extension Act of 2004, Part II". **Effective** 4-30-2004.

• **2004, Surface Transportation Extension Act of 2004 (P.L. 108-202)**

P.L. 108-202, § 12(b)(1):

Amended Code Sec. 9504(b)(2) by striking "Surface Transportation Extension Act of 2003" each place it appears and inserting "Surface Transportation Extension Act of 2004". **Effective** 2-29-2004.

• **2003, Surface Transportation Extension Act of 2003 (P.L. 108-88)**

P.L. 108-88, § 12(b)(1)(A)-(B):

Amended Code Sec. 9504(b)(2) by striking "Wildlife and Sport Fish Restoration Programs Improvement Act of 2000" and inserting "Surface Transportation Extension Act of 2003" in subparagraph (A), and by striking "TEA 21 Restoration Act" and inserting "Surface Transportation Extension Act of 2003" in subparagraphs (B) and (C). **Effective** 9-30-2003.

• **2000, Wildlife and Sport Fish Restoration Programs Improvement Act of 2000 (P.L. 106-408)**

P.L. 106-408, § 126:

Amended Code Sec. 9504(b)(2)(A) by striking "(as in effect on the date of the enactment of the TEA 21 Restoration Act)" and inserting "(as in effect on the date of the enactment of the Wildlife and Sport Fish Restoration Programs Improvement Act of 2000)". **Effective** 11-1-2000.

• **1998, Transportation Equity Act for the 21st Century (P.L. 105-178)**

P.L. 105-178, § 9005(b)(1)-(3):

Amended Code Sec. 9504(b)(2) by striking "October 1, 1988)," and inserting "the date of the enactment of the Transportation Equity Act for the 21st Century)," in subparagraph (A), by striking "November 29, 1990" and inserting "the date of the enactment of the Transportation Equity Act for the 21st Century" in subparagraph (B), and by redesignating subparagraph (B) as subparagraph (C) and by inserting after subparagraph (A) a new subparagraph (B). **Effective** 6-9-98.

P.L. 105-178, § 9005(f)(1) (as added by P.L. 105-206, § 9015(b)):

Amended Code Sec. 9504(b)(2)(A), as amended by subsection (b)(1), by striking "the date of the enactment of the Transportation Equity Act for the 21st Century" and inserting "the date of the enactment of the TEA 21 Restoration Act". **Effective** 6-9-98.

P.L. 105-178, § 9005(f)(2) (as added by P.L. 105-206, § 9015(b)):

Amended Code Sec. 9504(b)(2)(B), as added by subsection (b)(3), by striking "such act" and inserting "the TEA 21 Restoration Act". **Effective** 6-9-98.

P.L. 105-178, § 9005(f)(3) (as added by P.L. 105-206, § 9015(b)):

Amended Code Sec. 9504(b)(2)(C), as amended by subsection (b)(2) and redesignated by subsection (b)(3), is amended by striking "the date of the enactment of the Transportation Equity Act for the 21st Century" and inserting "the date of the enactment of the TEA 21 Restoration Act". **Effective** 6-9-98.

• **1991, Intermodal Surface Transportation Efficiency Act of 1991 (P.L. 102-240)**

P.L. 102-240, § 8002(i):

Amended Code Sec. 9504(b)(2)(B). **Effective** 12-18-91. Prior to amendment, Code Sec. 9504(b)(2)(B) read as follows:

(B) to carry out the purposes of any law which is substantially identical to S. 3252 of the 101st Congress, as introduced.

• **1990, Omnibus Budget Reconciliation Act of 1990 (P.L. 101-508)**

P.L. 101-508, § 11211(i)(3):

Amended Code Sec. 9504(b)(2). **Effective** 12-1-90. Prior to amendment, Code Sec. 9504(b)(2) read as follows:

(2) EXPENDITURES FROM ACCOUNT.—Amounts in the Sport Fish Restoration Account shall be available, as provided by appropriation Acts, to carry out the purposes of the Act entitled "An Act to provide that the United States shall aid the States in fish restoration and management projects, and for other purposes", approved August 9, 1950 (as in effect on October 1, 1988).

• **1988, Coast Guard Authorization Act of 1988 (P.L. 100-448)**

P.L. 100-448, § 6(c)(3):

Amended Code Sec. 9504(b)(2) by striking "(as in effect on June 1, 1984)" and inserting "(as in effect on October 1, 1988)". **Effective** 10-1-88.

• **1988, Omnibus Trade and Competitiveness Act of 1988 (P.L. 100-418)**

P.L. 100-418, § 1214(p)(2)(A)-(B):

Amended Code Sec. 9504(b)(1)(B) by striking "subpart B of part 5 of schedule 7 of the Tariff Schedules of the United States" and inserting "heading 9507 of the Harmonized Tariff Schedule of the United States"; and by striking "subpart D of part 6 of schedule 6 of such Schedules" and inserting in lieu thereof "chapter 89 of the Harmonized Tariff Schedule of the United States". **Effective** for crude oil removed from the premises on or after 8-23-88.

[Sec. 9504(c)]

(c) EXPENDITURES FROM BOAT SAFETY ACCOUNT.—Amounts remaining in the Boat Safety Account on October 1, 2005, and amounts thereafter credited to the Account under section 9602(b), shall be available, without further appropriation, for making expenditures before October 1, 2010, to carry out the purposes of section 15 of the Dingell-Johnson Sport Fish Restoration Act (as in effect on the date of the enactment of the Safe, Accountable, Flexible, Efficient Transportation Equity Act: A Legacy for Users). For purposes of section 9602, the Boat Safety Account shall be treated as a Trust Fund established by this subchapter.

Amendments

• **2006 (P.L. 109-304)**

P.L. 109-304, § 16(c)(2):

Amended Code Sec. 9504(c) by striking "section 13106" and substituting "section 13107" [Note: This amendment cannot be made to the current version of Code Sec. 9504(c). However, it would have been able to be made to the version of Code Sec. 9504(c) prior to amendment by the Safe, Accountable, Flexible, Efficient Transportation Equity Act: A Legacy for Users (P.L. 109-59). See Act Sec. 18(a), below.—CCH]. **Effective** 10-6-2006.

P.L. 109-304, § 18(a), provides:

(a) CUTOFF DATE.—This Act replaces certain provisions enacted on or before April 30, 2005. If a law enacted after that date amends or repeals a provision replaced by this Act, that law is deemed to amend or repeal, as the case may be, the corresponding provision enacted by this Act. If a law enacted after that date is otherwise inconsistent with this Act, it supersedes this Act to the extent of the inconsistency.

• **2005, Sportfishing and Recreational Boating Safety Amendments Act of 2005 (P.L. 109-74)**

P.L. 109-74, § 301(a)(1)-(2):

Amended Code Sec. 9504(c) by striking "August 15, 2005" and inserting "October 1, 2005"; and by striking "Surface Transportation Extension Act of 2005, Part VI" and inserting "Sportfishing and Recreational Boating Safety Amendments Act of 2005". **Effective** 9-29-2005.

• **2005, Safe, Accountable, Flexible, Efficient Transportation Equity Act: A Legacy for Users (P.L. 109-59)**

P.L. 109-59, § 11115(c):

Amended Code Sec. 9504(c) [as amended by P.L. 109-74]. **Effective** 10-1-2005. Prior to amendment, Code Sec. 9504(c) read as follows:

(c) EXPENDITURES FROM BOAT SAFETY ACCOUNT.—Amounts in the Boat Safety Account shall be available, as provided by appropriation Acts, for making expenditures before

ESTABLISHMENT OF TRUST FUNDS

October 1, 2005, to carry out the purposes of section 13106 of title 46, United States Code (as in effect on the date of the enactment of the Sportfishing and Recreational Boating Safety Amendments Act of 2005).

• **2005, Surface Transportation Extension Act of 2005, Part VI (P.L. 109-42)**

P.L. 109-42, §7(b)(2)(A)-(B):

Amended Code Sec. 9504(c) by striking "July 31, 2005" and inserting "August 15, 2005", and by striking "Surface Transportation Extension Act of 2005, Part V" and inserting "Surface Transportation Extension Act of 2005, Part VI". **Effective** 7-30-2005.

• **2005, Surface Transportation Extension Act of 2005, Part V (P.L. 109-40)**

P.L. 109-40, §9(b)(2)(A)-(B):

Amended Code Sec. 9504(c) by striking "July 28, 2005" and inserting "July 31, 2005"; and by striking "Surface Transportation Extension Act of 2005, Part IV" and inserting "Surface Transportation Extension Act of 2005, Part V". **Effective** 7-28-2005.

• **2005, Surface Transportation Extension Act of 2005, Part IV (P.L. 109-37)**

P.L. 109-37, §9(b)(2)(A)-(B):

Amended Code Sec. 9504(c) by striking "July 22, 2005" and inserting "July 28, 2005"; and by striking "Surface Transportation Extension Act of 2005, Part III" and inserting "Surface Transportation Extension Act of 2005, Part IV". **Effective** 7-22-2005.

• **2005, Surface Transportation Extension Act of 2005, Part III (P.L. 109-35)**

P.L. 109-35, §9(b)(2)(A)-(B):

Amended Code Sec. 9504(c) by striking "July 20, 2005" and inserting "July 22, 2005"; and by striking "Surface Transportation Extension Act of 2005, Part II" and inserting "Surface Transportation Extension Act of 2005, Part III". **Effective** 7-20-2005.

• **2005, Surface Transportation Extension Act of 2005, Part II (P.L. 109-20)**

P.L. 109-20, §9(b)(2)(A)-(B):

Amended Code Sec. 9504(c) by striking "July 1, 2005" and inserting "July 20, 2005", and by striking "Surface Transportation Extension Act of 2005" and inserting "Surface Transportation Extension Act of 2005, Part II". **Effective** 7-1-2005.

• **2005, Surface Transportation Extension Act of 2005 (P.L. 109-14)**

P.L. 109-14, §9(b)(2)(A)-(B):

Amended Code Sec. 9504(c) by striking "June 1, 2005" and inserting "July 1, 2005", and by striking "Surface Transportation Extension Act of 2004, Part V" and inserting "Surface Transportation Extension Act of 2005". **Effective** 5-31-2005.

• **2004, Surface Transportation Extension Act of 2004, Part V (P.L. 108-310)**

P.L. 108-310, §13(b)(2)(A)-(B):

Amended Code Sec. 9504(c) by striking "October 1, 2004" and inserting "June 1, 2005"; and by striking "Surface Transportation Extension Act of 2004, Part IV" and inserting "Surface Transportation Extension Act of 2004, Part V". **Effective** 9-30-2004.

• **2004, Surface Transportation Extension Act of 2004, Part IV (P.L. 108-280)**

P.L. 108-280, §10(b)(2)(A)-(B):

Amended Code Sec. 9504(c) by striking "August 1, 2004" and inserting "October 1, 2004", and by striking "Surface Transportation Extension Act of 2004, Part III" and inserting "Surface Transportation Extension Act of 2004, Part IV". **Effective** 7-30-2004.

• **2004, Surface Transportation Extension Act of 2004, Part III (P.L. 108-263)**

P.L. 108-263, §10(b)(2)(A)-(B):

Amended Code Sec. 9504(c) by striking "July 1, 2004" and inserting "August 1, 2004", and by striking "Surface Transportation Extension Act of 2004, Part II" and inserting "Surface Transportation Extension Act of 2004, Part III". **Effective** 6-30-2004.

• **2004, Surface Transportation Extension Act of 2004, Part II (P.L. 108-224)**

P.L. 108-224, §10(b)(2)(A)-(B):

Amended Code Sec. 9504(c) by striking "May 1, 2004" and inserting "July 1, 2004", and by striking "Surface Transportation Extension Act of 2004" and inserting "Surface Transportation Extension Act of 2004, Part II". **Effective** 4-30-2004.

• **2004, Surface Transportation Extension Act of 2004 (P.L. 108-202)**

P.L. 108-202, §12(b)(2)(A)-(B):

Amended Code Sec. 9504(c) by striking "March 1, 2004" and inserting "May 1, 2004", and by striking "Surface Transportation Extension Act of 2003" and inserting "Surface Transportation Extension Act of 2004". **Effective** 2-29-2004.

• **2003, Surface Transportation Extension Act of 2003 (P.L. 108-88)**

P.L. 108-88, §12(b)(2)(A)-(B):

Amended Code Sec. 9504(c) by striking "October 1, 2003" and inserting "March 1, 2004", and by striking "TEA 21 Restoration Act" and inserting "Surface Transportation Extension Act of 2003". **Effective** 9-30-2003.

• **1998, Transportation Equity Act for the 21st Century (P.L. 105-178)**

P.L. 105-178, §9005(c)(1)-(2):

Amended Code Sec. 9504(c) by striking "1998" and inserting "2003", and by striking "October 1, 1988" and inserting "the date of the enactment of the Transportation Equity Act for the 21st Century". **Effective** 6-9-98.

P.L. 105-178, §9005(f)(4) (as added by P.L. 105-206, §9015(b)):

Amended Code Sec. 9504(c), as amended by subsection (c)(2), by striking "the date of enactment of the Transportation Equity Act for the 21st Century" and inserting "the date of the enactment of the TEA 21 Restoration Act". **Effective** 6-9-98.

• **1997, Surface Transportation Extension Act of 1997 (P.L. 105-130)**

P.L. 105-130, §9(b):

Amended Code Sec. 9504(c) by striking "April 1, 1998" and inserting "October 1, 1998". **Effective** 10-1-97.

• **1991, Intermodal Surface Transportation Efficiency Act of 1991 (P.L. 102-240)**

P.L. 102-240, §8002(d)(2)(C):

Amended Code Sec. 9504(c) by striking "1994" and inserting "1998". **Effective** 12-18-91.

• **1988, Coast Guard Authorization Act of 1988 (P.L. 100-448)**

P.L. 100-448, §6(a)(2)(A)-(B):

Amended Code Sec. 9504(c) by striking out "before April 1, 1989," and inserting in lieu thereof "before April 1, 1994,"; and by striking "(as in effect on June 1, 1984)" and inserting "(as in effect on October 1, 1988)". **Effective** 10-1-88.

[Sec. 9504(d)]

(d) LIMITATION ON TRANSFERS TO TRUST FUND.—

(1) IN GENERAL.—Except as provided in paragraph (2), no amount may be appropriated or paid to the Sport Fish Restoration and Boating Trust Fund on and after the date of any expenditure from such Trust Fund which is not permitted by this section. The determination of whether an expenditure is so permitted shall be made without regard to—

(A) any provision of law which is not contained or referenced in this title or in a revenue Act, and

(B) whether such provision of law is a subsequently enacted provision or directly or indirectly seeks to waive the application of this subsection.

(2) EXCEPTION FOR PRIOR OBLIGATIONS.—Paragraph (1) shall not apply to any expenditure to liquidate any contract entered into (or for any amount otherwise obligated) before October 1, 2026, in accordance with the provisions of this section.

Amendments

• **2021, Infrastructure Investment and Jobs Act (P.L. 117-58)**

P.L. 117-58, §80101(b)(2), Div. H:

Amended Code Sec. 9504(d)(2) by striking "October 1, 2021" and inserting "October 1, 2026". **Effective** 11-15-2021.

• **2021, Further Surface Transportation Extension Act of 2021 (P.L. 117-52)**

P.L. 117-52, §4(b)(2):

Amended Code Sec. 9504(d)(2) by striking "November 1, 2021" and inserting "December 4, 2021". **Effective** 10-31-2021. For a special rule, see Act Sec. 4(d)(1)-(3), below.

P.L. 117-52, §4(d)(1)-(3), provides:

(d) SPECIAL RULE FOR AMENDMENTS.—On the date of enactment of H.R. 3684 (117th Congress)—

(1) subsections (a), (b), and (c) of this section, the amendments made by such subsections, section 201 of the Surface Transportation Extension Act of 2021 (Public Law 117–44), and the amendments made by such section shall cease to be effective;

(2) the text of the laws amended by subsections (a), (b), and (c) of this section and section 201 of the Surface Transportation Extension Act of 2021 (Public Law 117–44) shall revert back so as to read as the text read on September 30, 2021; and

(3) the amendments made by H.R. 3684 (117th Congress) shall be executed as if this section and section 201 of the Surface Transportation Extension Act had not been enacted.

• **2021, Surface Transportation Extension Act of 2021 (P.L. 117-44)**

P.L. 117-44, §201(b)(2):

Amended Code Sec. 9504(d)(2) by striking "October 1, 2021" and inserting "November 1, 2021". **Effective** 10-2-2021. For a special rule, see Act Sec. 201(d)(1)-(3), below.

ESTABLISHMENT OF TRUST FUNDS

P.L. 117-44, §201(d)(1)-(3), provides:

(d) SPECIAL RULE FOR EXECUTION OF AMENDMENTS.—On the date of enactment of H.R. 3684 (117th Congress)—

(1) this section and the amendments made by this section shall cease to be effective;

(2) the text of the laws amended by this section shall revert back so as to read as the text read on the day before the date of enactment of this section; and

(3) the amendments made by H.R. 3684 (117th Congress) shall be executed as if this section had not been enacted.

• **2020, Continuing Appropriations Act, 2021 and Other Extensions Act (P.L. 116-159)**

P.L. 116-159, §1202(2):

Amended Code Sec. 9504(d)(2) by striking "October 1, 2020" and inserting "October 1, 2021". Effective 10-1-2020.

• **2015, Fixing America's Surface Transportation Act (P.L. 114-94)**

P.L. 114-94, §31101(b)(2):

Amended Code Sec. 9504(d)(2) by striking "December 5, 2015" and inserting "October 1, 2020". Effective 12-4-2015.

• **2015, Surface Transportation Extension Act of 2015, Part II (P.L. 114-87)**

P.L. 114-87, §2001(b)(2):

Amended Code Sec. 9504(d)(2) by striking "November 21, 2015" and inserting "December 5, 2015". Effective 11-20-2015.

• **2015, Surface Transportation Extension Act of 2015 (P.L. 114-73)**

P.L. 114-73, §2001(b)(2):

Amended Code Sec. 9504(d)(2) by striking "October 30, 2015" and inserting "November 21, 2015". Effective 10-29-2015.

• **2015, Surface Transportation and Veterans Health Care Choice Improvement Act of 2015 (P.L. 114-41)**

P.L. 114-41, §2001(b)(2):

Amended Code Sec. 9504(d)(2) by striking "August 1, 2015" and inserting "October 30, 2015". Effective 7-31-2015.

• **2015, Highway and Transportation Funding Act of 2015 (P.L. 114-21)**

P.L. 114-21, §2001(b)(2):

Amended Code Sec. 9504(d)(2) by striking "June 1, 2015" and inserting "August 1, 2015". Effective 5-29-2015.

• **2014, Highway and Transportation Funding Act of 2014 (P.L. 113-159)**

P.L. 113-159, §2001(b)(2):

Amended Code Sec. 9504(d)(2) by striking "October 1, 2014" and inserting "June 1, 2015". Effective 8-8-2014.

• **2012, Highway Investment, Job Creation, and Economic Growth Act of 2012 (P.L. 112-141)**

P.L. 112-141, §40101(b)(2):

Amended Code Sec. 9504(d)(2) by striking "July 1, 2012" and inserting "October 1, 2014". Effective 7-1-2012.

• **2012, Temporary Surface Transportation Extension Act of 2012 (P.L. 112-140)**

P.L. 112-140, §1(c), provides:

(c) SPECIAL RULE FOR EXECUTION OF AMENDMENTS IN MAP-21.—On the date of enactment of the MAP-21 [P.L. 112-141]—

(1) this Act and the amendments made by this Act shall cease to be effective;

(2) the text of the laws amended by this Act shall revert back so as to read as the text read on the day before the date of enactment of this Act; and

(3) the amendments made by the MAP-21 shall be executed as if this Act had not been enacted.

P.L. 112-140, §401(b)(2):

Amended Code Sec. 9504(d)(2) by striking "July 1, 2012" and inserting "July 7, 2012". Effective 7-1-2012. For a special rule, see Act Sec. 1(c), above.

• **2012, Surface Transportation Extension Act of 2012 (P.L. 112-102)**

P.L. 112-102, §401(b)(2):

Amended Code Sec. 9504(d)(2) by striking "April 1, 2012" and inserting "July 1, 2012". Effective 4-1-2012.

• **2011, Surface Transportation Extension Act of 2011, Part II (P.L. 112-30)**

P.L. 112-30, §141(b)(2):

Amended Code Sec. 9504(d)(2) by striking "October 1, 2011" and inserting "April 1, 2012". Effective 10-1-2011.

• **2011, Surface Transportation Extension Act of 2011 (P.L. 112-5)**

P.L. 112-5, §401(b)(2):

Amended Code Sec. 9504(d)(2) by striking "March 5, 2011" and inserting "October 1, 2011". Effective 3-4-2011.

Sec. 9504(d)(2)

• **2010, Surface Transportation Extension Act of 2010, Part II (P.L. 111-322)**

P.L. 111-322, §2401(b)(2):

Amended Code Sec. 9504(d)(2) by striking "January 1, 2011" and inserting "March 5, 2011". Effective 12-31-2010.

• **2010, Hiring Incentives to Restore Employment Act (P.L. 111-147)**

P.L. 111-147, §445(b)(2):

Amended Code Sec. 9504(d)(2) by striking "October 1, 2009" and inserting "January 1, 2011". Effective 9-30-2009.

• **2010, Temporary Extension Act of 2010 (P.L. 111-144)**

P.L. 111-144, §4, provides:

SEC. 4. EXTENSION OF SURFACE TRANSPORTATION PROGRAMS.

(a) IN GENERAL.—Except as provided in subsection (b), for purposes of the continued extension of surface transportation programs and related authority to make expenditures from the Highway Trust Fund and other trust funds under sections 157 through 162 of the Continuing Appropriations Resolution, 2010 (Public Law 111–68; 123 Stat. 2050), the date specified in section 106(3) of that resolution (Public Law 111–68; 123 Stat. 2045) shall be deemed to be March 28, 2010.

(b) EXCEPTION.—Subsection (a) shall not apply if an extension of the programs and authorities described in that subsection for a longer term than the extension contained in the Continuing Appropriations Resolution, 2010 (Public Law 111–68; 123 Stat. 2050), is enacted before the date of enactment of this Act.

• **2009, (P.L. 111-68)**

P.L. 111-68, §161(b), provides:

(b) Paragraph (2) of section 9504(d) of such Code shall be applied by substituting the date that is one day after the date specified in section 106(3) [October 31, 2009] of this joint resolution for "October 1, 2009".

• **2005, Safe, Accountable, Flexible, Efficient Transportation Equity Act: A Legacy for Users (P.L. 109-59)**

P.L. 109-59, §11101(d)(2)(B):

Amended Code Sec. 9504(d)(2) by striking "July 31, 2005" and inserting "October 1, 2009". Effective 8-10-2005.

P.L. 109-59, §11115(b)(2)(B)(i)-(iii):

Amended Code Sec. 9504(d), as amended by Act Sec. 11101, by striking "AQUATIC RESOURCES" before "TRUST FUND" in the heading, by striking "any Account in the Aquatic Resources" in paragraph (1) and inserting "the Sport Fish Restoration and Boating", and by striking "any such Account" in paragraph (1) and inserting "such Trust Fund". Effective 10-1-2005.

• **2005, Surface Transportation Extension Act of 2005, Part VI (P.L. 109-42)**

P.L. 109-42, §7(b)(3):

Amended Code Sec. 9504(d)(2) by adding at the end a new sentence. Effective 7-30-2005.

P.L. 109-42, §7(d)(3):

Amended Code Sec. 9504(d)(2) by striking the last sentence. For the **effective** date, see Act Sec. 7(e)(2), below. Prior to being stricken, the last sentence of Code Sec. 9504(d)(2) read as follows:

The preceding sentence shall be applied by substituting "August 15, 2005" for the date therein.

P.L. 109-42, §7(e)(2), provides:

(2) SUBSEQUENT REPEAL.—The amendments made by subsection (d) shall take effect on the date of the enactment of the Safe, Accountable, Flexible, Efficient Transportation Equity Act: A Legacy for Users and shall be executed immediately before the amendment made by such Act.

• **2005, Surface Transportation Extension Act of 2005, Part V (P.L. 109-40)**

P.L. 109-40, §9(b)(3):

Amended Code Sec. 9504(d)(2) by striking "July 28, 2005" and inserting "July 31, 2005". Effective 7-28-2005.

• **2005, Surface Transportation Extension Act of 2005, Part IV (P.L. 109-37)**

P.L. 109-37, §9(b)(3):

Amended Code Sec. 9504(d)(2) by striking "July 22, 2005" and inserting "July 28, 2005". Effective 7-22-2005.

• **2005, Surface Transportation Extension Act of 2005, Part III (P.L. 109-35)**

P.L. 109-35, §9(b)(3):

Amended Code Sec. 9504(d)(2) by striking "July 20, 2005" and inserting "July 22, 2005". Effective 7-20-2005.

ESTABLISHMENT OF TRUST FUNDS

• **2005, Surface Transportation Extension Act of 2005, Part II (P.L. 109-20)**

P.L. 109-20, §9(b)(3):

Amended Code Sec. 9504(d)(2) by striking "July 1, 2005" and inserting "July 20, 2005". **Effective** 7-1-2005.

• **2005, Surface Transportation Extension Act of 2005 (P.L. 109-14)**

P.L. 109-14, §9(b)(3):

Amended Code Sec. 9504(d)(2) by striking "June 1, 2005" and inserting "July 1, 2005". **Effective** 5-31-2005.

• **2004, Surface Transportation Extension Act of 2004, Part V (P.L. 108-310)**

P.L. 108-310, §13(b)(3):

Amended Code Sec. 9504(d)(2) by striking "October 1, 2004" and inserting "June 1, 2005". **Effective** 9-30-2004.

• **2004, Surface Transportation Extension Act of 2004, Part IV (P.L. 108-280)**

P.L. 108-280, §10(b)(3):

Amended Code Sec. 9504(d)(2) by striking "August 1, 2004" and inserting "October 1, 2004". **Effective** 7-30-2004.

• **2004, Surface Transportation Extension Act of 2004, Part III (P.L. 108-263)**

P.L. 108-263, §10(b)(3):

Amended Code Sec. 9504(d)(2) by striking "July 1, 2004" and inserting "August 1, 2004". **Effective** 6-30-2004.

• **2004, Surface Transportation Extension Act of 2004, Part II (P.L. 108-224)**

P.L. 108-224, §10(b)(3):

Amended Code Sec. 9504(d)(2) by striking "May 1, 2004" and inserting "July 1, 2004". **Effective** 4-30-2004.

• **2004, Surface Transportation Extension Act of 2004 (P.L. 108-202)**

P.L. 108-202, §12(b)(3):

Amended Code Sec. 9504(d)(2) by striking "March 1, 2004" and inserting "May 1, 2004". **Effective** 2-29-2004.

• **2003, Surface Transportation Extension Act of 2003 (P.L. 108-88)**

P.L. 108-88, §12(b)(3):

Amended Code Sec. 9504(d)(2) by striking "October 1, 2003" and inserting "March 1, 2004". **Effective** 9-30-2003.

• **1998, Transportation Equity Act for the 21st Century (P.L. 105-178)**

P.L. 105-178, §9005(d):

Amended Code Sec. 9504 by redesignating subsection (d) as subsection (e) and by inserting after subsection (c) a new subsection (d). **Effective** 6-9-98.

[Sec. 9504(e)]

(e) CROSS REFERENCE.—

For provision transferring motorboat fuels taxes to Sport Fish Restoration and Boating Trust Fund, see [section] 9503(c)(3).

Amendments

• **2010, Hiring Incentives to Restore Employment Act (P.L. 111-147)**

P.L. 111-147, §444(b)(7):

Amended Code Sec. 9504(e) by striking "section 9503(c)(4)" and inserting "[section] 9503(c)(3)". **Effective** for transfers relating to amounts paid and credits allowed after 3-18-2010.

• **2005, Safe, Accountable, Flexible, Efficient Transportation Equity Act: A Legacy for Users (P.L. 109-59)**

P.L. 109-59, §11115(b)(2)(C):

Amended Code Sec. 9504(e) by striking "Boat Safety Account and Sport Fish Restoration Account" and inserting "Sport Fish Restoration and Boating Trust Fund". **Effective** 10-1-2005.

• **1998, Transportation Equity Act for the 21st Century (P.L. 105-178)**

P.L. 105-178, §9005(d):

Amended Code Sec. 9504 by redesignating subsection (d) as subsection (e). **Effective** 6-9-98.

• **1984, Deficit Reduction Act of 1984 (P.L. 98-369)**

P.L. 98-369, §1016(a):

Added Code Sec. 9504. **Effective** 10-1-84. See Act Sec. 1016(e)(2), below, for special rules.

P.L. 98-369, §1016(e)(2), provides:

(2) Boat Safety Account Treated as Continuation of National Recreational Boating Safety and Facilities Improvement Fund.—The Boat Safety Account in the Aquatic Resources Trust Fund established by the amendments made by this section shall be treated for all purposes of law as the continuation of the National Recreational Boating Safety and Facilities Improvement Fund established by section 13107 of title 46, United States Code. Any reference in any law to the National Recreational Boating Safety and Facilities Improvement Fund established by such section shall be deemed to include (wherever appropriate) a reference to such Boat Safety Account.

[Sec. 9505]

SEC. 9505. HARBOR MAINTENANCE TRUST FUND.

[Sec. 9505(a)]

(a) CREATION OF TRUST FUND.—There is hereby established in the Treasury of the United States a trust fund to be known as the "Harbor Maintenance Trust Fund", consisting of such amounts as may be—

(1) appropriated to the Harbor Maintenance Trust Fund as provided in this section,

(2) transferred to the Harbor Maintenance Trust Fund by the Great Lakes St. Lawrence Seaway Development Corporation pursuant to section 13(a) of the Act of May 13, 1954, or

(3) credited to the Harbor Maintenance Trust Fund as provided in section 9602(b).

Amendments

• **2020, Water Resources Development Act of 2020 (P.L. 116-260)**

P.L. 116-260, §512(c)(3), Div. AA:

Amended Code Sec. 9505(a)(2) by striking "Saint Lawrence Seaway Development Corporation" and inserting "Great Lakes St. Lawrence Seaway Development Corporation". **Effective** 12-27-2020.

[Sec. 9505(b)]

(b) TRANSFER TO HARBOR MAINTENANCE TRUST FUND OF AMOUNTS EQUIVALENT TO CERTAIN TAXES.—There are hereby appropriated to the Harbor Maintenance Trust Fund amounts equivalent to the taxes received in the Treasury under section 4461 (relating to harbor maintenance tax).

[Sec. 9505(c)]

(c) EXPENDITURES FROM HARBOR MAINTENANCE TRUST FUND.—Amounts in the Harbor Maintenance Trust Fund shall be available, as provided by appropriation Acts, for making expenditures—

(1) to carry out section 210 of the Water Resources Development Act of 1986,

(2) for payments of rebates of tolls or charges pursuant to section 13(b) of the Act of May 13, 1954 (as in effect on April 1, 1987), and

(3) for the payment of all expenses of administration incurred by the Department of the Treasury, the Army Corps of Engineers, and the Department of Commerce related to the administration of subchapter A of chapter 36 (relating to harbor maintenance tax), but not in excess of $5,000,000 for any fiscal year.

ESTABLISHMENT OF TRUST FUNDS

Amendments

- **2014, Water Resources Reform and Development Act of 2014 (P.L. 113-121)**

P.L. 113-121, § 2102(c):

Amended Code Sec. 9505(c)(1) by striking "(as in effect on the date of the enactment of the Water Resources Development Act of 1996)" following "Water Resources Development Act of 1986". **Effective** 6-10-2014.

- **1996, Water Resources Development Act of 1996 (P.L. 104-303)**

P.L. 104-303, § 601:

Amended Code Sec. 9505(c)(1). **Effective** 10-12-96. Prior to amendment, Code Sec. 9505(c)(1) read as follows:

(1) to carry out section 210(a) of the Water Resources Development Act of 1986 (as in effect on the date of enactment of this section),

- **1993, North American Free Trade Agreement Implementation Act (P.L. 103-182)**

P.L. 103-182, § 683(a):

Amended Code Sec. 9505(c)(3). **Effective** for fiscal years beginning after 12-8-93. Prior to amendment, Code Sec. 9505(c)(3) read as follows:

(3) for the payment of all expenses of administration incurred—

(A) by the Department of the Treasury in administering subchapter A of chapter 36 (relating to harbor maintenance tax), but not in excess of $5,000,000 for any fiscal year, and

(B) for periods during which no fee applies under paragraph (9) or (10) of section 13031(a) of the Consolidated Omnibus Budget Reconciliation Act of 1985.

- **1986, Water Resources Development Act of 1986 (P.L. 99-662)**

P.L. 99-662, § 1403(a):

Amended subchapter A of chapter 98 by adding new Code Sec. 9505. **Effective** 4-1-87.

P.L. 99-662, § 1403(b), provides:

(b) AUTHORIZATION OF APPROPRIATIONS.—There are authorized to be appropriated to the Department of the Treasury (from the fees collected under paragraphs (9) and (10) of section 13031(a) of the Consolidated Omnibus Budget Reconciliation Act of 1985) such sums as may be necessary to pay all expenses of administration incurred by such Department in administering subchapter A of chapter 36 of the Internal Revenue Code of 1954 for periods to which such fees apply.

[Sec. 9506]

SEC. 9506. INLAND WATERWAYS TRUST FUND.

[Sec. 9506(a)]

(a) CREATION OF TRUST FUND.—There is hereby established in the Treasury of the United States a trust fund to be known as the "Inland Waterways Trust Fund", consisting of such amounts as may be appropriated or credited to such Trust Fund as provided in this section or section 9602(b).

[Sec. 9506(b)]

(b) TRANSFER TO TRUST FUND OF AMOUNTS EQUIVALENT TO CERTAIN TAXES.—There are hereby appropriated to the Inland Waterways Trust Fund amounts equivalent to the taxes received in the Treasury under section 4042 (relating to tax on fuel used in commercial transportation on inland waterways). The preceding sentence shall apply only to so much of such taxes as are attributable to the Inland Waterways Trust Fund financing rate under section 4042(b).

[Sec. 9506(c)]

(c) EXPENDITURES FROM TRUST FUND.—

(1) IN GENERAL.—Except as provided in paragraph (2), amounts in the Inland Waterways Trust Fund shall be available, as provided by appropriation Acts, for making construction and rehabilitation expenditures for navigation on the inland and coastal waterways of the United States described in section 206 of the Inland Waterways Revenue Act of 1978, as in effect on the date of the enactment of this section.

(2) EXCEPTION FOR CERTAIN PROJECTS.—Not more than ½ of the cost of any construction to which section 102(a) of the Water Resources Development Act of 1986 applies (as in effect on the date of the enactment of this section) may be paid from the Inland Waterways Trust Fund.

Amendments

- **1986, Water Resources Development Act of 1986 (P.L. 99-662)**

P.L. 99-662, § 1405(a):

Amended Subchapter A of chapter 98 by adding new Code Sec. 9506. For the **effective** date, see Act Sec. 1405(d), below.

P.L. 99-662, § 1405(d), provides:

(d) EFFECTIVE DATE.—

(1) IN GENERAL.—The amendments made by this section shall take effect on January 1, 1987.

(2) INLAND WATERWAYS TRUST FUND TREATED AS CONTINUATION OF OLD TRUST FUND.—The Inland Waterways Trust Fund established by the amendments made by this section shall be treated for all purposes of law as a continuation of the Inland Waterways Trust Fund established by section 203 of the Inland Waterways Revenue Act of 1978. Any reference in any law to the Inland Waterways Trust Fund established by such section 203 shall be deemed to include (wherever appropriate) a reference to the Inland Waterways Trust Fund established by this section.

- **1986, Superfund Amendments and Reauthorization Act of 1986 (P.L. 99-499)**

P.L. 99-499, § 521(b)(3):

Amended Code Sec. 9506(b)(1) by adding at the end thereof a new sentence. **Effective** 1-1-87.

[Sec. 9507]

SEC. 9507. HAZARDOUS SUBSTANCE SUPERFUND.

[Sec. 9507(a)]

(a) CREATION OF TRUST FUND.—There is established in the Treasury of the United States a trust fund to be known as the "Hazardous Substance Superfund" (hereinafter in this section referred to as the "Superfund"), consisting of such amounts as may be—

(1) appropriated to the Superfund as provided in this section,

(2) appropriated to the Superfund pursuant to section 517(b) of the Superfund Revenue Act of 1986, or

(3) credited to the Superfund as provided in section 9602(b).

[Sec. 9507(b)]

(b) TRANSFERS TO SUPERFUND.—There are hereby appropriated to the Superfund amounts equivalent to—

(1) the taxes received in the Treasury under section 4611, 4661, or 4671 (relating to environmental taxes),

(2) amounts recovered on behalf of the Superfund under the Comprehensive Environmental Response, Compensation, and Liability Act of 1980 (hereinafter in this section referred to as "CERCLA"),

(3) all moneys recovered or collected under section 311(b)(6)(B) of the Clean Water Act,

(4) penalties assessed under title I of CERCLA, and

(5) punitive damages under section 107(c)(3) of CERCLA.

In the case of the tax imposed by section 4611, paragraph (1) shall apply only to so much of such tax as is attributable to the Hazardous Substance Superfund financing rate under section 4611(c).

ESTABLISHMENT OF TRUST FUNDS

Amendments

• **2014, Tax Technical Corrections Act of 2014 (P.L. 113-295)**

P.L. 113-295, §221(a)(12)(L), Division A:

Amended Code Sec. 9507(b)(1) by striking "59A," following "section". **Effective** generally 12-19-2014. For a special rule, see Act Sec. 221(b)(2), Division A, below.

P.L. 113-295, §221(b)(2), Division A, provides:

(2) SAVINGS PROVISION.—If—

(A) any provision amended or repealed by the amendments made by this section applied to—

(i) any transaction occurring before the date of the enactment of this Act,

(ii) any property acquired before such date of enactment, or

(iii) any item of income, loss, deduction, or credit taken into account before such date of enactment, and

(B) the treatment of such transaction, property, or item under such provision would (without regard to the amendments or repeals made by this section) affect the liability for tax for periods ending after date of enactment, nothing in the amendments or repeals made by this section shall be construed to affect the treatment of such transaction, property, or item for purposes of determining liability for tax for periods ending after such date of enactment.

• **1989, Omnibus Budget Reconciliation Act of 1989 (P.L. 101-239)**

P.L. 101-239, §7505(d)(1), provides:

(d) OIL SPILL LIABILITY TRUST FUND TO BE OPERATING FUND.—

(1) IN GENERAL.—For purposes of sections 8032(d) and 8033(c) of the Omnibus Budget Reconciliation Act of 1986, the commencement date is January 1, 1990.

• **1986, Omnibus Budget Reconciliation Act of 1986 (P.L. 99-509)**

P.L. 99-509, §8032(c)(4):

Amended Code Sec. 9507(b) by adding at the end thereof a new sentence. For the **effective** date, see Act Sec. 8032(d), below.

P.L. 99-509, §8032(d), provides:

(d) EFFECTIVE DATE.—

(1) IN GENERAL.—Except as provided in paragraph (2), the amendments made by this section shall take effect on the commencement date (as defined in section 4611(f)(2) of the Internal Revenue Code of 1954, as added by this section).

(2) COORDINATION WITH SUPERFUND REAUTHORIZATION.—The amendments made by this section shall take effect only if the Superfund Amendments and Reauthorization Act of 1986 is enacted.

[Sec. 9507(c)]

(c) EXPENDITURES FROM SUPERFUND.—

(1) IN GENERAL.—Amounts in the Superfund shall be available, as provided in appropriation Acts, only for purposes of making expenditures—

(A) to carry out the purposes of—

(i) paragraphs (1), (2), (5), and (6) of section 111(a) of CERCLA as in effect on the date of the enactment of the Superfund Amendments and Reauthorization Act of 1986,

(ii) section 111(c) of CERCLA (as so in effect), other than paragraphs (1) and (2) thereof, and

(iii) section 111(m) of CERCLA (as so in effect), or

(B) hereafter authorized by a law which does not authorize the expenditure out of the Superfund for a general purpose not covered by subparagraph (A) (as so in effect).

(2) EXCEPTION FOR CERTAIN TRANSFERS, ETC., OF HAZARDOUS SUBSTANCES.—No amount in the Superfund or derived from the Superfund shall be available or used for the transfer or disposal of hazardous waste carried out pursuant to a cooperative agreement between the Administrator of the Environmental Protection Agency and a State if the following conditions apply—

(A) the transfer or disposal, if made on December 13, 1985, would not comply with a State or local requirement,

(B) the transfer is to a facility for which a final permit under section 3005(a) of the Solid Waste Disposal Act was issued after January 1, 1983, and before November 1, 1984, and

(C) the transfer is from a facility identified as the McColl Site in Fullerton, California.

[Sec. 9507(d)]

(d) AUTHORITY TO BORROW.—

(1) IN GENERAL.—There are authorized to be appropriated to the Superfund, as repayable advances, such sums as may be necessary to carry out the purposes of the Superfund.

(2) LIMITATION ON AGGREGATE ADVANCES.—The maximum aggregate amount of repayable advances to the Superfund which is outstanding at any one time shall not exceed an amount equal to the amount which the Secretary estimates will be equal to the sum of the amounts appropriated to the Superfund under subsection (b)(1) during the following 24 months.

(3) REPAYMENT OF ADVANCES.—

(A) IN GENERAL.—Advances made to the Superfund shall be repaid, and interest on such advances shall be paid, to the general fund of the Treasury when the Secretary determines that moneys are available for such purposes in the Superfund.

(B) FINAL REPAYMENT.—No advance shall be made to the Superfund after December 31, 2032, and all advances to such Fund shall be repaid on or before such date.

(C) RATE OF INTEREST.—Interest on advances made to the Superfund shall be at a rate determined by the Secretary of the Treasury (as of the close of the calendar month preceding the month in which the advance is made) to be equal to the current average market yield on outstanding marketable obligations of the United States with remaining periods to maturity comparable to the anticipated period during which the advance will be outstanding and shall be compounded annually.

Amendments

• **2022, Inflation Reduction Act of 2022 (P.L. 117-169)**

P.L. 117-169, §13601(b):

Amended Code Sec. 9507(d)(3)(B) by striking "December 31, 1995" and inserting "December 31, 2032". **Effective** 1-1-2023.

• **1990, Omnibus Budget Reconciliation Act of 1990 (P.L. 101-508)**

P.L. 101-508, §11231(c):

Amended Code Sec. 9507(d)(3)(B) by striking "December 31, 1991" and inserting "December 31, 1995". **Effective** 11-5-90.

[Sec. 9507(e)]

(e) LIABILITY OF UNITED STATES LIMITED TO AMOUNT IN TRUST FUND.—

(1) GENERAL RULE.—Any claim filed against the Superfund may be paid only out of the Superfund.

(2) COORDINATION WITH OTHER PROVISIONS.—Nothing in CERCLA or the Superfund Amendments and Reauthorization Act of 1986 (or in any amendment made by either of such Acts) shall authorize the payment by the United States Government of any amount with respect to any such claim out of any source other than the Superfund.

(3) ORDER IN WHICH UNPAID CLAIMS ARE TO BE PAID.—If at any time the Superfund has insufficient funds to pay all of the claims payable out of the Superfund at such time, such claims shall, to the extent permitted under paragraph (1), be paid in full in the order in which they were finally determined.

ESTABLISHMENT OF TRUST FUNDS

Amendments

• **1986, Superfund Amendments and Reauthorization Act of 1986 (P.L. 99-499)**

P.L. 99-499, § 517(a):

Amended subchapter A of chapter 98 of the Internal Revenue Code of 1986 by adding after Code Sec. 9506 new Code Sec. 9507. **Effective** 1-1-87. See also Act Sec. 517(e)(2), below.

P.L. 99-499, § 517(e)(2), provides:

(2) SUPERFUND TREATED AS CONTINUATION OF OLD TRUST FUND.—The Hazardous Substance Superfund established by the amendments made by this section shall be treated for all purposes of law as a continuation of the Hazardous Substance Response Trust Fund established by section 221 of the Hazardous Substance Response Revenue Act of 1980. Any reference in any law to the Hazardous Substance Response Trust Fund established by such section 221 shall be deemed to include (wherever appropriate) a reference to the Hazardous Substance Superfund established by the amendments made by this section.

[Sec. 9508]

SEC. 9508. LEAKING UNDERGROUND STORAGE TANK TRUST FUND.

[Sec. 9508(a)]

(a) CREATION OF TRUST FUND.—There is established in the Treasury of the United States a trust fund to be known as the "Leaking Underground Storage Tank Trust Fund", consisting of such amounts as may be appropriated or credited to such Trust Fund as provided in this section or section 9602(b).

[Sec. 9508(b)]

(b) TRANSFER TO TRUST FUND.—There are hereby appropriated to the Leaking Underground Storage Tank Trust Fund amounts equivalent to—

(1) taxes received in the Treasury under section 4041(d) (relating to additional taxes on motor fuels),

(2) taxes received in the Treasury under section 4081 (relating to tax on gasoline, diesel fuel, and kerosene) to the extent attributable to the Leaking Underground Storage Tax Trust Fund financing rate under such section,

(3) taxes received in the Treasury under section 4042 (relating to tax on fuel used in commercial transportation on inland waterways) to the extent attributable to the Leaking Underground Storage Tank Trust Fund financing rate under such section, and

(4) amounts received in the Treasury and collected under section 9003(h)(6) of the Solid Waste Disposal Act.

For purposes of this subsection, there shall not be taken into account the taxes imposed by sections 4041 and 4081 on diesel fuel sold for use or used as fuel in a diesel-powered boat.

Amendments

• **2004, American Jobs Creation Act of 2004 (P.L. 108-357)**

P.L. 108-357, § 853(d)(2)(P):

Amended Code Sec. 9508(b) by striking paragraph (3) and by redesignating paragraphs (4) and (5) as paragraphs (3) and (4), respectively. **Effective** for aviation-grade kerosene removed, entered, or sold after 12-31-2004. For special rules, see Act Sec. 853(f), below. Prior to being stricken, Code Sec. 9508(b)(3) read as follows:

(3) taxes received in the Treasury under section 4091 (relating to tax on aviation fuel) to the extent attributable to the Leaking Underground Storage Tank Trust Fund financing rate under such section,

P.L. 108-357, § 853(f), provides:

(f) FLOOR STOCKS TAX.—

(1) IN GENERAL.—There is hereby imposed on aviation-grade kerosene held on January 1, 2005, by any person a tax equal to—

(A) the tax which would have been imposed before such date on such kerosene had the amendments made by this section been in effect at all times before such date, reduced by

(B) the sum of—

(i) the tax imposed before such date on such kerosene under section 4091 of the Internal Revenue Code of 1986, as in effect on such date, and

(ii) in the case of kerosene held exclusively for such person's own use, the amount which such person would (but for this clause) reasonably expect (as of such date) to be paid as a refund under section 6427(l) of such Code with respect to such kerosene.

(2) EXCEPTION FOR FUEL HELD IN AIRCRAFT FUEL TANK.—Paragraph (1) shall not apply to kerosene held in the fuel tank of an aircraft on January 1, 2005.

(3) LIABILITY FOR TAX AND METHOD OF PAYMENT.—

(A) LIABILITY FOR TAX.—The person holding the kerosene on January 1, 2005, to which the tax imposed by paragraph (1) applies shall be liable for such tax.

(B) METHOD AND TIME FOR PAYMENT.—The tax imposed by paragraph (1) shall be paid at such time and in such manner as the Secretary of the Treasury (or the Secretary's delegate) shall prescribe, including the nonapplication of such tax on de minimis amounts of kerosene.

(4) TRANSFER OF FLOOR STOCK TAX REVENUES TO TRUST FUNDS.—For purposes of determining the amount transferred to any trust fund, the tax imposed by this subsection shall be treated as imposed by section 4081 of the Internal Revenue Code of 1986—

(A) in any case in which tax was not imposed by section 4091 of such Code, at the Leaking Underground Storage Tank Trust Fund financing rate under such section to the extent of 0.1 cents per gallon, and

(B) at the rate under section 4081(a)(2)(A)(iv) of such Code to the extent of the remainder.

(5) HELD BY A PERSON.—For purposes of this subsection, kerosene shall be considered as held by a person if title thereto has passed to such person (whether or not delivery to the person has been made).

(6) OTHER LAWS APPLICABLE.—All provisions of law, including penalties, applicable with respect to the tax imposed by section 4081 of such Code shall, insofar as applicable and not inconsistent with the provisions of this subsection, apply with respect to the floor stock tax imposed by paragraph (1) to the same extent as if such tax were imposed by such section.

• **1997, Taxpayer Relief Act of 1997 (P.L. 105-34)**

P.L. 105-34, § 1032(e)(13):

Amended Code Sec. 9508(b)(2) by striking "and diesel fuel" and inserting ", diesel fuel, and kerosene". **Effective** 7-1-98.

• **1993, Omnibus Budget Reconciliation Act of 1993 (P.L. 103-66)**

P.L. 103-66, § 13163(c):

Amended Code Sec. 9508(b) by adding at the end thereof a new sentence. **Effective** 1-1-94.

P.L. 103-66, § 13242(d)(42)(A)-(c):

Amended Code Sec. 9508(b) by inserting "and diesel fuel" after "gasoline" in paragraph (2), by striking "diesel fuel and" after "to tax on" in paragraph (3), and by striking "4091" [sic] in the last sentence, as added by Act Sec. 13163(c), and inserting "4081" [sic]. **Effective** 1-1-94.

• **1989, Omnibus Budget Reconciliation Act of 1989 (P.L. 101-239)**

P.L. 101-239, § 7822(b)(7):

Amended Code Sec. 9508(b)(3) by striking "Storage Trust Fund" and inserting "Storage Tank Trust Fund". **Effective** as if included in the provision of P.L. 100-203 to which it relates.

• **1987, Revenue Act of 1987 (P.L. 100-203)**

P.L. 100-203, § 10502(d)(16):

Amended Code Sec. 9508(b) by redesignating paragraphs (3) and (4) as paragraphs (4) and (5), respectively, and by inserting after paragraph (2) new paragraph (3). **Effective** for sales after 3-31-88.

[Sec. 9508(c)]

(c) EXPENDITURES.—

(1) IN GENERAL.—Except as provided in paragraphs (2), (3), and (4), amounts in the Leaking Underground Storage Tank Trust Fund shall be available, as provided in appropriation Acts, only for purposes of making expenditures to carry out sections 9003(h), 9003(i), 9003(j), 9004(f), 9005(c), 9010, 9011, 9012, and 9013 of the Solid Waste Disposal Act as in effect on the date of the enactment of Public Law 109-168.

(2) TRANSFER TO HIGHWAY TRUST FUND.—Out of amounts in the Leaking Underground Storage Tank Trust Fund there is hereby appropriated $2,400,000,000 to be transferred under section 9503(f)(3) to the Highway Account (as defined in section 9503(e)(5)(B)) in the Highway Trust Fund.

(3) ADDITIONAL TRANSFER TO HIGHWAY TRUST FUND.—Out of amounts in the Leaking Underground Storage Tank Trust Fund there is hereby appropriated $1,000,000,000 to be transferred under section 9503(f)(6) to the Highway Account (as defined in section 9503(e)(5)(B)) in the Highway Trust Fund.

(4) ADDITIONAL TRANSFER TO HIGHWAY TRUST FUND.—Out of amounts in the Leaking Underground Storage Tank Trust Fund there is hereby appropriated—

(A) on the date of the enactment of the FAST Act, $100,000,000,

ESTABLISHMENT OF TRUST FUNDS

(B) on October 1, 2016, $100,000,000, and

(C) on October 1, 2017, $100,000,000,

to be transferred under section 9503(f)(9) to the Highway Account (as defined in section 9503(e)(5)(B)) in the Highway Trust Fund.

Amendments

• **2018, Tax Technical Corrections Act of 2018 (P.L. 115-141)**

P.L. 115-141, §401(a)(342), Div. U:

Amended Code Sec. 9508(c)(1) by striking "the Public" and inserting "Public". **Effective** 3-23-2018.

• **2015, Fixing America's Surface Transportation Act (P.L. 114-94)**

P.L. 114-94, §31203(a):

Amended Code Sec. 9508(c) by adding at the end a new paragraph (4). **Effective** 12-4-2015.

P.L. 114-94, §31203(b):

Amended Code Sec. 9508(c)(1) by striking "paragraphs (2) and (3)" and inserting "paragraphs (2), (3), and (4)". **Effective** 12-4-2015.

• **2014, Highway and Transportation Funding Act of 2014 (P.L. 113-159)**

P.L. 113-159, §2002(b)(1):

Amended Code Sec. 9508(c) by adding at the end a new paragraph (3). **Effective** 8-8-2014.

P.L. 113-159, §2002(b)(2):

Amended Code Sec. 9508(c)(1) by striking "paragraph (2)" and inserting "paragraphs (2) and (3)". **Effective** 8-8-2014.

• **2012, Highway Investment, Job Creation, and Economic Growth Act of 2012 (P.L. 112-141)**

P.L. 112-141, §40201(a)(1)-(2):

Amended Code Sec. 9508(c) by striking "Amounts" and inserting "(1) IN GENERAL.—Except as provided in paragraph (2), amounts", and by adding at the end a new paragraph (2). **Effective** 7-6-2012.

• **2007, Tax Technical Corrections Act of 2007 (P.L. 110-172)**

P.L. 110-172, §11(a)(46), provides:

(46) The Internal Revenue Code of 1986 shall be applied and administered as if the amendments made by section 1(a) of Public Law 109-433 had never been enacted.

• **2006 (P.L. 109-433)**

P.L. 109-433, §1:

Amended Code Sec. 9508(c) by striking "section 9003(h)" and inserting "sections 9003(h), 9003(i), 9003(j), 9004(f), 9005(c), 9010, 9011, 9012, and 9013", and by striking "Superfund Amendments and Reauthorization Act of 1986" and inserting "Public Law 109-168". **Effective** 12-20-2006. [P.L. 109-432, §210(a)(1)-(2), made an identical amendment. Therefore, this amendment cannot be made. See also, P.L. 110-172, §11(a)(46), above.—CCH.]

• **2006, Tax Relief and Health Care Act of 2006 (P.L. 109-432)**

P.L. 109-432, Division A, §210(a)(1)-(2):

Amended Code Sec. 9508(c) by striking "section 9003(h)" and inserting "sections 9003(h), 9003(i), 9003(j), 9004(f), 9005(c), 9010, 9011, 9012, and 9013", and by striking "Superfund Amendments and Reauthorization Act of 1986" and inserting "Public Law 109-168". **Effective** 12-20-2006.

• **2005, Energy Tax Incentives Act of 2005 (P.L. 109-58)**

P.L. 109-58, §1362(c):

Amended Code Sec. 9508(c). **Effective** 10-1-2005. Prior to amendment, Code Sec. 9508(c) read as follows:

(c) EXPENDITURES.—

(1) IN GENERAL.—Except as provided in paragraph (2), amounts in the Leaking Underground Storage Tank Trust Fund shall be available, as provided in appropriation Acts, only for purposes of making expenditures to carry out section 9003(h) of the Solid Waste Disposal Act as in effect on the date of the enactment of the Superfund Amendments and Reauthorization Act of 1986.

(2) TRANSFERS FROM TRUST FUND FOR CERTAIN REPAYMENTS AND CREDITS.—

(A) IN GENERAL.—The Secretary shall pay from time to time from the Leaking Underground Storage Tank Trust Fund into the general fund of the Treasury amounts equivalent to—

(i) amounts paid under—

(I) section 6420 (relating to amounts paid in respect of gasoline used on farms),

(II) section 6421 (relating to amounts paid in respect of gasoline used for certain nonhighway purposes or by local transit systems), and

(III) section 6427 (relating to fuels not used for taxable purposes), and

(ii) credits allowed under section 34, with respect to the taxes imposed by section 4041(d) or by section 4081 (to the extent attributable to the Leaking Underground Storage Tank Trust Fund financing rate under such sections).

(B) TRANSFERS BASED ON ESTIMATES.—Transfers under subparagraph (A) shall be made on the basis of estimates by the Secretary, and proper adjustments shall be made in amounts subsequently transferred to the extent prior estimates were in excess of or less than the amounts required to be transferred.

• **2004, American Jobs Creation Act of 2004 (P.L. 108-357)**

P.L. 108-357, §853(d)(2)(Q):

Amended Code Sec. 9508(c)(2)(A) by striking "sections 4081 and 4091" and inserting "section 4081". **Effective** for aviation-grade kerosene removed, entered, or sold after 12-31-2004. For special rules, see Act Sec. 853(f), below.

P.L. 108-357, §853(f), provides:

(f) FLOOR STOCKS TAX.—

(1) IN GENERAL.—There is hereby imposed on aviation-grade kerosene held on January 1, 2005, by any person a tax equal to—

(A) the tax which would have been imposed before such date on such kerosene had the amendments made by this section been in effect at all times before such date, reduced by

(B) the sum of—

(i) the tax imposed before such date on such kerosene under section 4091 of the Internal Revenue Code of 1986, as in effect on such date, and

(ii) in the case of kerosene held exclusively for such person's own use, the amount which such person would (but for this clause) reasonably expect (as of such date) to be paid as a refund under section 6427(l) of such Code with respect to such kerosene.

(2) EXCEPTION FOR FUEL HELD IN AIRCRAFT FUEL TANK.—Paragraph (1) shall not apply to kerosene held in the fuel tank of an aircraft on January 1, 2005.

(3) LIABILITY FOR TAX AND METHOD OF PAYMENT.—

(A) LIABILITY FOR TAX.—The person holding the kerosene on January 1, 2005, to which the tax imposed by paragraph (1) applies shall be liable for such tax.

(B) METHOD AND TIME FOR PAYMENT.—The tax imposed by paragraph (1) shall be paid at such time and in such manner as the Secretary of the Treasury (or the Secretary's delegate) shall prescribe, including the nonapplication of such tax on de minimis amounts of kerosene.

(4) TRANSFER OF FLOOR STOCK TAX REVENUES TO TRUST FUNDS.—For purposes of determining the amount transferred to any trust fund, the tax imposed by this subsection shall be treated as imposed by section 4081 of the Internal Revenue Code of 1986—

(A) in any case in which tax was not imposed by section 4091 of such Code, at the Leaking Underground Storage Tank Trust Fund financing rate under such section to the extent of 0.1 cents per gallon, and

(B) at the rate under section 4081(a)(2)(A)(iv) of such Code to the extent of the remainder.

(5) HELD BY A PERSON.—For purposes of this subsection, kerosene shall be considered as held by a person if title thereto has passed to such person (whether or not delivery to the person has been made).

(6) OTHER LAWS APPLICABLE.—All provisions of law, including penalties, applicable with respect to the tax imposed by section 4081 of such Code shall, insofar as applicable and not inconsistent with the provisions of this subsection, apply with respect to the floor stock tax imposed by paragraph (1) to the same extent as if such tax were imposed by such section.

• **1989, Omnibus Budget Reconciliation Act of 1989 (P.L. 101-239)**

P.L. 101-239, §7822(b)(7):

Amended Code Sec. 9508(c)(2)(A) by striking "Storage Trust Fund" and inserting "Storage Tank Trust Fund". **Effective** as if included in the provision of P.L. 100-203 to which it relates.

• **1987, Revenue Act of 1987 (P.L. 100-203)**

P.L. 100-203, §10502(d)(17):

Amended Code Sec. 9508(c)(2)(A) by striking out clause (ii) and all that follows and inserting in lieu thereof new clause (ii). **Effective** for sales after 3-31-88. Prior to amendment, clause (ii) read as follows:

(ii) credits allowed under section 34, with respect to the taxes imposed by sections 4041(d) and 4081 (to the extent attributable to the Leaking Underground Storage Tank Trust Fund financing rate under section 4081).

[Sec. 9508(d)]

(d) LIABILITY OF THE UNITED STATES LIMITED TO AMOUNT IN TRUST FUND.—

(1) GENERAL RULE.—Any claim filed against the Leaking Underground Storage Tank Trust Fund may be paid only out of such Trust Fund.

(2) COORDINATION WITH OTHER PROVISIONS.—Nothing in the Comprehensive Environmental Response, Compensation, and Liability Act of 1980 or the Superfund Amendments and Reauthorization Act of 1986 (or in any amendment made by either of such Acts) shall authorize the payment by the United States Government of any amount with respect to any such claim out of any source other than the Leaking Underground Storage Tank Trust Fund.

(3) ORDER IN WHICH UNPAID CLAIMS ARE TO BE PAID.—If at any time the Leaking Underground Storage Tank Trust Fund has insufficient funds to pay all of the claims out of such Trust Fund at such time, such claims shall, to the extent permitted under paragraph (1), be paid in full in the order in which they were finally determined.

ESTABLISHMENT OF TRUST FUNDS

Amendments

• **1986, Superfund Amendments and Reauthorization Act of 1986 (P.L. 99-499)**

P.L. 99-499, §522(a):

Amended subchapter A of chapter 98 of the Internal Revenue Code of 1986 by adding after Code Sec. 9507 new Code Sec. 9508. **Effective** 1-1-87.

[Sec. 9508(e)]

(e) LIMITATION ON TRANSFERS TO LEAKING UNDERGROUND STORAGE TANK TRUST FUND.—

(1) IN GENERAL.—Except as provided in paragraph (2), no amount may be appropriated to the Leaking Underground Storage Tank Trust Fund on and after the date of any expenditure from the Leaking Underground Storage Tank Trust Fund which is not permitted by this section. The determination of whether an expenditure is so permitted shall be made without regard to—

(A) any provision of law which is not contained or referenced in this title or in a revenue Act, and

(B) whether such provision of law is a subsequently enacted provision or directly or indirectly seeks to waive the application of this paragraph.

(2) EXCEPTION FOR PRIOR OBLIGATIONS.—Paragraph (1) shall not apply to any expenditure to liquidate any contract entered into (or for any amount otherwise obligated) before October 1, 2026, in accordance with the provisions of this section.

Amendments

• **2021, Infrastructure Investment and Jobs Act (P.L. 117-58)**

P.L. 117-58, §80101(c), Div. H:

Amended Code Sec. 9508(e)(2) by striking "October 1, 2021" and inserting "October 1, 2026". **Effective** 11-15-2021.

• **2021, Further Surface Transportation Extension Act of 2021 (P.L. 117-52)**

P.L. 117-52, §4(c):

Amended Code Sec. 9508(e)(2) by striking "November 1, 2021" and inserting "December 4, 2021". **Effective** 10-31-2021. For a special rule, see Act Sec. 4(d)(1)-(3), below.

P.L. 117-52, §4(d)(1)-(3), provides:

(d) SPECIAL RULE FOR AMENDMENTS.—On the date of enactment of H.R. 3684 (117th Congress)—

(1) subsections (a), (b), and (c) of this section, the amendments made by such subsections, section 201 of the Surface Transportation Extension Act of 2021 (Public Law 117-44), and the amendments made by such section shall cease to be effective;

(2) the text of the laws amended by subsections (a), (b), and (c) of this section and section 201 of the Surface Transportation Extension Act of 2021 (Public Law 117-44) shall revert back so as to read as the text read on September 30, 2021; and

(3) the amendments made by H.R. 3684 (117th Congress) shall be executed as if this section and section 201 of the Surface Transportation Extension Act had not been enacted.

• **2021, Surface Transportation Extension Act of 2021 (P.L. 117-44)**

P.L. 117-44, §201(c):

Amended Code Sec. 9508(e)(2) by striking "October 1, 2021" and inserting "November 1, 2021". **Effective** 10-2-2021. For a special rule, see Act Sec. 201(d)(1)-(3), below.

P.L. 117-44, §201(d)(1)-(3), provides:

(d) SPECIAL RULE FOR EXECUTION OF AMENDMENTS.—On the date of enactment of H.R. 3684 (117th Congress)—

(1) this section and the amendments made by this section shall cease to be effective;

(2) the text of the laws amended by this section shall revert back so as to read as the text read on the day before the date of enactment of this section; and

(3) the amendments made by H.R. 3684 (117th Congress) shall be executed as if this section had not been enacted.

• **2020, Continuing Appropriations Act, 2021 and Other Extensions Act (P.L. 116-159)**

P.L. 116-159, §1203:

Amended Code Sec. 9508(e)(2) by striking "October 1, 2020" and inserting "October 1, 2021". **Effective** 10-1-2020.

• **2015, Fixing America's Surface Transportation Act (P.L. 114-94)**

P.L. 114-94, §31101(c):

Amended Code Sec. 9508(e)(2) by striking "December 5, 2015" and inserting "October 1, 2020". **Effective** 12-4-2015.

• **2015, Surface Transportation Extension Act of 2015, Part II (P.L. 114-87)**

P.L. 114-87, §2001(c):

Amended Code Sec. 9508(e)(2) by striking "November 21, 2015" and inserting "December 5, 2015". **Effective** 11-20-2015.

• **2015, Surface Transportation Extension Act of 2015 (P.L. 114-73)**

P.L. 114-73, §2001(c):

Amended Code Sec. 9508(e)(2) by striking "October 30, 2015" and inserting "November 21, 2015". **Effective** 10-29-2015.

• **2015, Surface Transportation and Veterans Health Care Choice Improvement Act of 2015 (P.L. 114-41)**

P.L. 114-41, §2001(c):

Amended Code Sec. 9508(e)(2) by striking "August 1, 2015" and inserting "October 30, 2015". **Effective** 7-31-2015.

• **2015, Highway and Transportation Funding Act of 2015 (P.L. 114-21)**

P.L. 114-21, §2001(c):

Amended Code Sec. 9508(e)(2) by striking "June 1, 2015" and inserting "August 1, 2015". **Effective** 5-29-2015.

• **2014, Highway and Transportation Funding Act of 2014 (P.L. 113-159)**

P.L. 113-159, §2001(c):

Amended Code Sec. 9508(e)(2) by striking "October 1, 2014" and inserting "June 1, 2015". **Effective** 8-8-2014.

• **2012, Highway Investment, Job Creation, and Economic Growth Act of 2012 (P.L. 112-141)**

P.L. 112-141, §40101(c):

Amended Code Sec. 9508(e)(2) by striking "July 1, 2012" and inserting "October 1, 2014". **Effective** 7-1-2012.

• **2012, Temporary Surface Transportation Extension Act of 2012 (P.L. 112-140)**

P.L. 112-140, §1(c), provides:

(c) SPECIAL RULE FOR EXECUTION OF AMENDMENTS IN MAP-21.—On the date of enactment of the MAP-21 [P.L. 112-141]—

(1) this Act and the amendments made by this Act shall cease to be effective;

(2) the text of the laws amended by this Act shall revert back so as to read as the text read on the day before the date of enactment of this Act; and

(3) the amendments made by the MAP-21 shall be executed as if this Act had not been enacted.

P.L. 112-140, §401(c):

Amended Code Sec. 9508(e)(2) by striking "July 1, 2012" and inserting "July 7, 2012". **Effective** 7-1-2012. For a special rule, see Act Sec. 1(c), above.

• **2012, Surface Transportation Extension Act of 2012 (P.L. 112-102)**

P.L. 112-102, §401(c):

Amended Code Sec. 9508(e)(2) by striking "April 1, 2012" and inserting "July 1, 2012". **Effective** 4-1-2012.

• **2011, Surface Transportation Extension Act of 2011, Part II (P.L. 112-30)**

P.L. 112-30, §141(c):

Amended Code Sec. 9508(e)(2) "October 1, 2011" and inserting "April 1, 2012". **Effective** 10-1-2011.

• **2005, Safe, Accountable, Flexible, Efficient Transportation Equity Act: A Legacy for Users (P.L. 109-59)**

P.L. 109-59, §11147(a):

Amended Code Sec. 9508 by adding at the end a new subsection (e). **Effective** 8-10-2005.

[Sec. 9509]

SEC. 9509. OIL SPILL LIABILITY TRUST FUND.

[Sec. 9509(a)]

(a) CREATION OF TRUST FUND.—There is established in the Treasury of the United States a trust fund to be known as the "Oil Spill Liability Trust Fund", consisting of such amounts as may be appropriated or credited to such Trust Fund as provided in this section or section 9602(b).

ESTABLISHMENT OF TRUST FUNDS

[Sec. 9509(b)]

(b) TRANSFERS TO TRUST FUND.—There are hereby appropriated to the Oil Spill Liability Trust Fund amounts equivalent to—

(1) taxes received in the Treasury under section 4611 (relating to environmental tax on petroleum) to the extent attributable to the Oil Spill Liability Trust Fund financing rate under section 4611(c),

(2) amounts recovered, under the Oil Pollution Act of 1990 for damages to natural resources which are required to be deposited in the Fund under section 1006(f) of such Act,

(3) amounts recovered by such Trust Fund under section 1015 of such Act,

(4) amounts required to be transferred by such Act from the revolving fund established under section 311(k) of the Federal Water Pollution Control Act,

(5) amounts required to be transferred by the Oil Pollution Act of 1990 from the Deepwater Port Liability Fund established under section 18(f) of the Deepwater Port Act of 1974,

(6) amounts required to be transferred by the Oil Pollution Act of 1990 from the Offshore Oil Pollution Compensation Fund established under section 302 of the Outer Continental Shelf Lands Act Amendments of 1978,

(7) amounts required to be transferred by the Oil Pollution Act of 1990 from the Trans-Alaska Pipeline Liability Fund established under section 204 of the Trans-Alaska Pipeline Authorization Act, and

(8) any penalty paid pursuant to section 311 of the Federal Water Pollution Control Act, section 309(c) of such Act (as a result of violations of such section 311), the Deepwater Port Act of 1974, or section 207 of the Trans-Alaska Pipeline Authorization Act.

Amendments

• **1990, Oil Pollution Act of 1990 (P.L. 101-380)**

P.L. 101-380, § 9001(a):

Amended Code Sec. 9509(b) by striking out all that follows paragraph (1) and inserting paragraphs (2)-(8). **Effective** 8-18-90. Prior to amendment, the material following paragraph (1) read as follows:

(2) amounts recovered, collected, or received under subtitle A of the Comprehensive Oil Pollution Liability and Compensation Act,

(3) amounts remaining (on January 1, 1990) in the Deepwater Port Liability Fund established by section 18(f) of the Deepwater Port Act of 1974,

(4) amounts remaining (on such date) in the Offshore Oil Pollution Compensation Fund established under section 302 of the Outer Continental Shelf Lands Act Amendments of 1978, and

(5) amounts credited to such trust fund under section 311(s) of the Federal Water Pollution Control Act.

• **1989, Omnibus Budget Reconciliation Act of 1989 (P.L. 101-239)**

P.L. 101-239, § 7505(d)(2)(B):

Amended Code Sec. 9509(b)(3) by striking "(on the 1st day the Oil Spill Liability Trust Fund financing rate under section 4611(c) applies)" and inserting "(on January 1, 1990)". **Effective** 12-19-89.

• **1988, Technical and Miscellaneous Revenue Act of 1988 (P.L. 100-647)**

P.L. 100-647, § 1018(u)(20), amended by P.L. 101-239, § 7811(m)(3):

Amended Code Sec. 9509(b)(3) by striking out "Deep Water" each place it appears and inserting in lieu thereof "Deepwater". **Effective** as if included in the provision of P.L. 99-514 to which it relates.

[Sec. 9509(c)]

(c) EXPENDITURES.—

(1) EXPENDITURE PURPOSES.—Amounts in the Oil Spill Liability Trust Fund shall be available, as provided in appropriation Acts or section 6002(b) of the Oil Pollution Act of 1990, only for purposes of making expenditures—

(A) for the payment of removal costs and other costs, expenses, claims, and damages referred to in section 1012 of such Act,

(B) to carry out sections 5 and 7 of the Intervention on the High Seas Act relating to oil pollution or the substantial threat of oil pollution,

(C) for the payment of liabilities incurred by the revolving fund established by section 311(k) of the Federal Water Pollution Control Act,

(D) to carry out subsections (b), (c), (d), (j), and (l) of section 311 of the Federal Water Pollution Control Act with respect to prevention, removal, and enforcement related to oil discharges (as defined in such section),

(E) for the payment of liabilities incurred by the Deepwater Port Liability Fund, and

(F) for the payment of liabilities incurred by the Offshore Oil Pollution Compensation Fund.

(2) LIMITATIONS ON EXPENDITURES.—

(A) $1,500,000,000 PER INCIDENT, ETC.—The maximum amount which may be paid from the Oil Spill Liability Trust Fund with respect to—

(i) any single incident shall not exceed $1,500,000,000, and

(ii) natural resource damage assessments and claims in connection with any single incident shall not exceed $750,000,000.

(B) $30,000,000 MINIMUM BALANCE.—Except in the case of payments of removal costs, a payment may be made from such Trust Fund only if the amount in such Trust Fund after such payment will not be less than $30,000,000.

Amendments

• **2022, Don Young Coast Guard Authorization Act of 2022 (P.L. 117-263)**

P.L. 117-263, § 11312(1)-(3):

Amended Code Sec. 9509(c)(2)(A) in clause (i) by striking "$1,000,000,000" and inserting "$1,500,000,000"; in clause (ii) by striking "$500,000,000" and inserting "$750,000,000"; and in the heading by striking "$1,000,000,000" and inserting "$1,500,000,000". **Effective** 12-23-2022.

• **1990, Oil Pollution Act of 1990 (P.L. 101-380)**

P.L. 101-380, § 9001(b):

Amended Code Sec. 9509(c)(1). **Effective** 8-18-90. Prior to amendment, paragraph (1) read as follows:

(1) GENERAL EXPENDITURE PURPOSES.—

(A) IN GENERAL.—Amounts in the Oil Spill Liability Trust Fund shall be available as provided in appropriation Acts, only for purposes of making expenditures for—

(i) the payment of removal costs described in the Comprehensive Oil Pollution Liability and Compensation Act,

(ii) the payment of claims under the Comprehensive Oil Pollution Liability and Compensation Act for damage which is not otherwise compensated,

(iii) carrying out subsection (c), (d), (i), and (l) of section 311 of the Federal Water Pollution Control Act with respect to any discharge of oil (as defined in such section),

(iv) carrying out section 5 of the Intervention on the High Seas Act relating to oil pollution or the substantial threat of oil pollution,

(v) the payment of all expenses of administration incurred by the Federal Government under the Comprehensive Oil Pollution Liability and Compensation Act, and

(vi) the payment of contributions to the International Fund under such Act.

(B) SPECIAL RULES.—

(i) PAYMENTS TO GOVERNMENTS ONLY FOR REMOVAL COSTS AND NATURAL RESOURCE DAMAGE ASSESSMENTS AND CLAIMS.—Except in the case of payments described in subparagraph (A)(v), amounts shall be available under subparagraph (A) for payments to any government only for—

(I) removal costs and natural resource damage assessments and claims, and

(II) administrative expenses related to such costs, assessments, or claims.

(ii) RESTRICTIONS ON CONTRIBUTIONS TO INTERNATIONAL FUND.—Under regulations prescribed by the Secretary, amounts shall be available under subparagraph (A) with respect to any contribution to the International Fund only in proportion to the portion of such fund used for a purpose for which amounts may be paid from the Oil Spill Liability Trust Fund.

P.L. 101-380, § 9001(c)(1)-(2):

Amended Code Sec. 9509(c)(2)(A) by striking out "$500,000,000" each place it appears and inserting "$1,000,000,000", and by striking "$250,000,000" and inserting "$500,000,000". **Effective** 8-18-90.

P.L. 101-380, § 9001(e)(2):

Amended Code Sec. 9509(c)(2)(B) by striking "described in paragraph (1)(A)(i)" and inserting "of removal costs". **Effective** 8-18-90.

ESTABLISHMENT OF TRUST FUNDS

• **1989, Omnibus Budget Reconciliation Act of 1989 (P.L. 101-239)**

P.L. 101-239, §7505(d)(2)(C):

Amended Code Sec. 9509(c)(1)[(A)] by striking out the last sentence. **Effective** 12-19-89. Prior to amendment, the last sentence of Code Sec. 9509(c)(1)[(A)] read as follows:

For purposes of this subparagraph, references to the Comprehensive Oil Pollution Liability and Compensation Act shall be treated as references to qualified authorizing legislation (as defined in section 4611).

[Sec. 9509(d)]

(d) AUTHORITY TO BORROW.—

(1) IN GENERAL.—There are authorized to be appropriated to the Oil Spill Liability Trust Fund, as repayable advances, such sums as may be necessary to carry out the purposes of such Trust Fund.

(2) LIMITATION ON AMOUNT OUTSTANDING.—The maximum aggregate amount of repayable advances to the Oil Spill Liability Trust Fund which is outstanding at any one time shall not exceed $1,000,000,000.

(3) REPAYMENT OF ADVANCES.—

(A) IN GENERAL.—Advances made to the Oil Spill Liability Trust Fund shall be repaid, and interest on such advances shall be paid, to the general fund of the Treasury when the Secretary determines that moneys are available for such purposes in such Fund.

(B) FINAL REPAYMENT.—No advance shall be made to the Oil Spill Liability Trust Fund after December 31, 1994, and all advances to such Fund shall be repaid on or before such date.

(C) RATE OF INTEREST.—Interest on advances made pursuant to this subsection shall be—

(i) at a rate determined by the Secretary of the Treasury (as of the close of the calendar month preceding the month in which the advance is made) to be equal to the current average market yield on outstanding marketable obligations of the United States with remaining periods to maturity comparable to the anticipated period during which the advance will be outstanding, and

(ii) compounded annually.

Amendments

• **1990, Oil Pollution Act of 1990 (P.L. 101-380)**

P.L. 101-380, §9001(d)(1):

Amended Code Sec. 9509(d)(2) by striking "$500,000,000" and inserting "$1,000,000,000". **Effective** 8-18-90.

P.L. 101-380, §9001(d)(2):

Amended Code Sec. 9509(d)(3)(B) by striking "December 31, 1991" and inserting "December 31, 1994". **Effective** 8-18-90.

[Sec. 9509(e)]

(e) LIABILITY OF THE UNITED STATES LIMITED TO AMOUNT IN TRUST FUND.—

(1) GENERAL RULE.—Any claim filed against the Oil Spill Liability Trust Fund may be paid only out of such Trust Fund.

(2) COORDINATION WITH OTHER PROVISIONS.—Nothing in the Oil Pollution Act of 1990 (or in any amendment made by such Act) shall authorize the payment by the United States Government of any amount with respect to any such claim out of any source other than the Oil Spill Liability Trust Fund.

(3) ORDER IN WHICH UNPAID CLAIMS ARE TO BE PAID.—If at any time the Oil Spill Liability Trust Fund has insufficient funds (or is unable by reason of subsection (c)(2)) to pay all of the claims out of such Trust Fund at such time, such claims shall, to the extent permitted under paragraph (1) and such subsection, be paid in full in the order in which they were finally determined.

Amendments

• **1990, Oil Pollution Act of 1990 (P.L. 101-380)**

P.L. 101-380, §9001(e)(1):

Amended Code Sec. 9509(e)(2) by striking "Comprehensive Oil Pollution Liability and Compensation Act" and inserting "Oil Pollution Act of 1990". **Effective** 8-18-90.

• **1989, Omnibus Budget Reconciliation Act of 1989 (P.L. 101-239)**

P.L. 101-239, §7505(d)(1), provides:

(d) OIL SPILL LIABILITY TRUST FUND TO BE OPERATING FUND.—

[Sec. 9509(f)]

(f) REFERENCES TO OIL POLLUTION ACT OF 1990.—Any reference in this section to the Oil Pollution Act of 1990 or any other Act referred to in a subparagraph of subsection (c)(1) shall be treated as a reference to such Act as in effect on the date of the enactment of this subsection.

Amendments

• **1990, Oil Pollution Act of 1990 (P.L. 101-380)**

P.L. 101-380, §9001(e)(3):

Amended Code Sec. 9509(f). **Effective** 8-18-90. Prior to amendment, Code Sec. 9095(f) read as follows:

(f) REFERENCES TO COMPREHENSIVE OIL POLLUTION LIABILITY AND COMPENSATION ACT.—For purposes of this section, references to the Comprehensive Oil Pollution Liability and Compensation Act shall be treated as references to any law enacted before December 31, 1990, which is substantially identical to subtitle E of title VI, or subtitle D of title VIII, of H.R. 5300 of the 99th Congress as passed by the House of Representatives.

(1) IN GENERAL.—For purposes of sections 8032(d) and 8033(c) of the Omnibus Budget Reconciliation Act of 1986, the commencement date is January 1, 1990.

• **1986, Omnibus Budget Reconciliation Act of 1986 (P.L. 99-509)**

P.L. 99-509, §8033(a):

Amended subchapter A of chapter 98 of the Internal Revenue Code of 1954 by adding new Code Sec. 9509. **Effective** on the commencement date (as defined in section 4611 of the Internal Revenue Code of 1954).

• **1989, Omnibus Budget Reconciliation Act of 1989 (P.L. 101-239)**

P.L. 101-239, §7505(d)(2)(A):

Amended Code Sec. 9509 by adding at the end thereof a new subsection (f). **Effective** 12-19-89.

[Sec. 9510]

SEC. 9510. VACCINE INJURY COMPENSATION TRUST FUND.

[Sec. 9510(a)]

(a) CREATION OF TRUST FUND.—There is established in the Treasury of the United States a trust fund to be known as the "Vaccine Injury Compensation Trust Fund", consisting of such amounts as may be apportioned or credited to such Trust Fund as provided in this section or section 9602(b).

Amendments

• **1988, Technical and Miscellaneous Revenue Act of 1988 (P.L. 100-647)**

P.L. 100-647, §2006(b)(1)-(2):

Amended Code Sec. 9510(a) by inserting "apportioned or" before "credited", and by inserting "this section or" before "section 9602(b)". **Effective** as if included in the amendments made by §9201 of P.L. 100-203.

[Sec. 9510(b)]

(b) TRANSFERS TO TRUST FUND.—

(1) IN GENERAL.—There are hereby appropriated to the Vaccine Injury Compensation Trust Fund amounts equivalent to the net revenues received in the Treasury from the tax imposed by section 4131 (relating to tax on certain vaccines).

ESTABLISHMENT OF TRUST FUNDS

(2) NET REVENUES.—For purposes of paragraph (1), the term "net revenues" means the amount estimated by the Secretary based on the excess of—

(A) the taxes received in the Treasury under section 4131 (relating to tax on certain vaccines), over

(B) the decrease in the tax imposed by chapter 1 resulting from the tax imposed by section 4131.

(3) LIMITATION ON TRANSFERS TO VACCINE INJURY COMPENSATION TRUST FUND.—No amount may be appropriated to the Vaccine Injury Compensation Trust Fund on and after the date of any expenditure from the Trust Fund which is not permitted by this section. The determination of whether an expenditure is so permitted shall be made without regard to—

(A) any provision of law which is not contained or referenced in this title or in a revenue Act, and

(B) whether such provision of law is a subsequently enacted provision or directly or indirectly seeks to waive the application of this paragraph.

Amendments

• **1999, Tax Relief Extension Act of 1999 (P.L. 106-170)**

P.L. 106-170, §523(b)(1):

Retroactively repealed section 1504 of the Vaccine Injury Compensation Program Modification Act (P.L. 105-277) so that it never took effect.

• **1998, Vaccine Injury Compensation Program Modification Act (P.L. 105-277)**

P.L. 105-277, Div. C, §1504(a)(2) (repealed by P.L. 106-170, §523(b)(1)):

Amended Code Sec. 9510(b) by adding at the end a new paragraph (3). **Effective** as if included in the provision of P.L. 105-34 to which it relates [effective 8-6-97.—CCH].

P.L. 105-277, Div. J, §4003(d)(2):

Amended Code Sec. 9510(b) by adding at the end a new paragraph (3). [Note: The amendments made by Div. C, Act Sec. 1504(a)(2), and Div. J, Act Sec. 4003(d)(2), of P.L. 105-277 are identical.—CCH.] **Effective** as if included in the provision of P.L. 105-34 to which it relates [effective 8-6-97.—CCH].

[Sec. 9510(c)]

(c) EXPENDITURES FROM TRUST FUND.—

(1) IN GENERAL.—Amounts in the Vaccine Injury Compensation Trust Fund shall be available, as provided in appropriation Acts, only for—

(A) the payment of compensation under subtitle 2 of title XXI of the Public Health Service Act (as in effect on October 18, 2000) for vaccine-related injury or death with respect to any vaccine—

(i) which is administered after September 30, 1988, and

(ii) which is a taxable vaccine (as defined in section 4132(a)(1)) at the time compensation is paid under such subtitle 2, or

(B) the payment of all expenses of administration (but not in excess of $9,500,000 for any fiscal year) incurred by the Federal Government in administering such subtitle.

(2) TRANSFERS FOR CERTAIN REPAYMENTS.—

(A) IN GENERAL.—The Secretary shall pay from time to time from the Vaccine Injury Compensation Trust Fund into the general fund of the Treasury amounts equivalent to amounts paid under section 4132(b) and section 6416 with respect to the taxes imposed by section 4131.

(B) TRANSFERS BASED ON ESTIMATES.—Transfers under subparagraph (A) shall be made on the basis of estimates by the Secretary, and proper adjustments shall be made in the amounts subsequently transferred to the extent prior estimates were in excess of or less than the amounts required to be transferred.

Amendments

• **2000, Community Renewal Tax Relief Act of 2000 (P.L. 106-554)**

P.L. 106-554, §318(f):

Amended Code Sec. 9510(c)(1)(A) by striking "December 31, 1999" and inserting "October 18, 2000". **Effective** 12-21-2000.

• **1999, Tax Relief Extension Act of 1999 (P.L. 106-170)**

P.L. 106-170, §523(b)(1):

Retroactively repealed section 1504 of P.L. 105-277 so that it never took effect.

P.L. 106-170, §523(b)(2):

Amended Code Sec. 9510(c)(1)(A) by striking "August 5, 1997" and inserting "December 31, 1999". **Effective** as if included in the provision of the Omnibus Consolidated and Emergency Supplemental Appropriations Act, 1999 to which it relates [effective 8-6-1997.—CCH].

• **1998, Vaccine Injury Compensation Program Modification Act (P.L. 105-277)**

P.L. 105-277, Div. C, §1504(a)(1) (repealed by P.L. 106-170, §523(b)(1)):

Amended Code Sec. 9510(c)(1). **Effective** as if included in the provision of P.L. 105-34 to which it relates [effective 8-6-97.—CCH]. Prior to amendment, Code Sec. 9510(c)(1) read as follows:

(1) IN GENERAL.—Amounts in the Vaccine Injury Compensation Trust Fund shall be available, as provided in appropriate Acts, only for the payment of compensation under subtitle 2 of title XXI of the Public Health Service Act (as in effect on the date of the enactment of this section) for vaccine-related injury or death with respect to vaccines administered after September 30, 1988, or for the payment of all expenses of administration (but not in excess of $6,000,000 for any fiscal year) incurred by the Federal Government in administering such subtitle.

• **1998, Tax and Trade Relief Extension Act of 1998 (P.L. 105-277)**

P.L. 105-277, §4003(d)(1):

Amended Code Sec. 9510(c)(1). **Effective** as if included in the provision of P.L. 105-34 to which it relates [effective 8-6-97.—CCH]. Prior to amendment, Code Sec. 9510(c)(1) read as follows:

(1) IN GENERAL.—Amounts in the Vaccine Injury Compensation Trust Fund shall be available, as provided in appropriate Acts, only for the payment of compensation under subtitle 2 of title XXI of the Public Health Service Act (as in effect on the date of the enactment of this section) for vaccine-related injury or death with respect to vaccines administered after September 30, 1988, or for the payment of all expenses of administration (but not in excess of $6,000,000 for any fiscal year) incurred by the Federal Government in administering such subtitle.

• **1993, Omnibus Budget Reconciliation Act of 1993 (P.L. 103-66)**

P.L. 103-66, §13421(b):

Amended Code Sec. 9510(c)(1) by striking "and before October 1, 1992," after "September 30, 1988,". **Effective** 8-10-93.

• **1989, Omnibus Budget Reconciliation Act of 1989 (P.L. 101-239)**

P.L. 101-239, §7841(g)(1):

Amended Code Sec. 9510(c)(1) by inserting ", or for the payment of all expenses of administration (but not in excess of $6,000,000 for any fiscal year) incurred by the Federal Government in administering such subtitle" before the period at the end thereof. **Effective** for fiscal years beginning after 9-30-89.

[Sec. 9510(d)]

(d) LIABILITY OF UNITED STATES LIMITED TO AMOUNT IN TRUST FUND.—

(1) GENERAL RULE.—Any claim filed against the Vaccine Injury Compensation Trust Fund may be paid only out of such Trust Fund.

(2) COORDINATION WITH OTHER PROVISIONS.—Nothing in the National Childhood Vaccine Injury Act of 1986 (or in any amendment made by such Act) shall authorize the payment by the United States Government of any amount with respect to any such claim out of any source other than the Vaccine Injury Compensation Trust Fund.

(3) ORDER IN WHICH UNPAID CLAIMS TO BE PAID.—If at any time the Vaccine Injury Compensation Trust Fund has insufficient funds to pay all of the claims out of such Trust Fund at such time, such claims shall, to the extent permitted under paragraph (1) be paid in full in the order in which they are finally determined.

ESTABLISHMENT OF TRUST FUNDS

Amendments

- **1987, Revenue Act of 1987 (P.L. 100-203)**

P.L. 100-203, §9202(a):

Amended subchapter A of chapter 98 by adding at the end thereof new Code Sec. 9510. **Effective** 1-1-88.

[Sec. 9511]

SEC. 9511. PATIENT-CENTERED OUTCOMES RESEARCH TRUST FUND.

[Sec. 9511(a)]

(a) CREATION OF TRUST FUND.—There is established in the Treasury of the United States a trust fund to be known as the "Patient-Centered Outcomes Research Trust Fund" (hereafter in this section referred to as the "PCORTF"), consisting of such amounts as may be appropriated or credited to such Trust Fund as provided in this section and section 9602(b).

[Sec. 9511(b)]

(b) TRANSFERS TO FUND.—

(1) APPROPRIATION.—There are hereby appropriated to the Trust Fund the following:

(A) For fiscal year 2010, $10,000,000.

(B) For fiscal year 2011, $50,000,000.

(C) For fiscal year 2012, $150,000,000.

(D) For fiscal year 2013—

(i) an amount equivalent to the net revenues received in the Treasury from the fees imposed under subchapter B of chapter 34 (relating to fees on health insurance and self-insured plans) for such fiscal year; and

(ii) $150,000,000.

(E) For each of fiscal years 2014, 2015, 2016, 2017, 2018, and 2019—

(i) an amount equivalent to the net revenues received in the Treasury from the fees imposed under subchapter B of chapter 34 (relating to fees on health insurance and self-insured plans) for such fiscal year; and

(ii) $150,000,000.

(F) For each of fiscal years 2020 through 2029—

(i) an amount equivalent to the net revenues received in the Treasury from the fees imposed under subchapter B of chapter 34 (relating to fees on health insurance and self-insured plans) for such fiscal year; and

(ii) the applicable amount (as defined in paragraph (4)) for the fiscal year.

The amounts appropriated under subparagraphs (A), (B), (C), (D)(ii), (E)(ii), and (F)(ii) shall be transferred from the general fund of the Treasury, from funds not otherwise appropriated.

(2) TRUST FUND TRANSFERS.—In addition to the amounts appropriated under paragraph (1), there shall be credited to the PCORTF the amounts transferred under section 1183 of the Social Security Act.

(3) LIMITATION ON TRANSFERS TO PCORTF.—No amount may be appropriated or transferred to the PCORTF on and after the date of any expenditure from the PCORTF which is not an expenditure permitted under this section. The determination of whether an expenditure is so permitted shall be made without regard to—

(A) any provision of law which is not contained or referenced in this chapter or in a revenue Act, and

(B) whether such provision of law is a subsequently enacted provision or directly or indirectly seeks to waive the application of this paragraph.

(4) APPLICABLE AMOUNT DEFINED.—In paragraph (1)(F)(ii), the term "applicable amount" means—

(A) for fiscal year 2020, $275,500,000;

(B) for fiscal year 2021, $285,000,000;

(C) for fiscal year 2022, $293,500,000;

(D) for fiscal year 2023, $311,500,000;

(E) for fiscal year 2024, $320,000,000;

(F) for fiscal year 2025, $338,000,000;

(G) for fiscal year 2026, $355,500,000;

(H) for fiscal year 2027, $363,500,000;

(I) for fiscal year 2028, $381,000,000; and

(J) for fiscal year 2029, $399,000,000.

Amendments

- **2019, Further Consolidated Appropriations Act, 2020 (P.L. 116-94)**

P.L. 116-94, §104(a)(1)(A)-(B), Div. N:

Amended Code Sec. 9511(b) in paragraph (1) by inserting after subparagraph (E) a new subparagraph (F); and by striking "and (E)(ii)" in the last sentence and inserting "(E)(ii), and (F)(ii)"; and by adding at the end a new paragraph (4). **Effective** 12-20-2019.

[Sec. 9511(c)]

(c) TRUSTEE.—The Secretary of the Treasury shall be a trustee of the PCORTF.

[Sec. 9511(d)]

(d) EXPENDITURES FROM FUND.—

(1) AMOUNTS AVAILABLE TO THE PATIENT-CENTERED OUTCOMES RESEARCH INSTITUTE.—Subject to paragraph (2), amounts in the PCORTF are available, without further appropriation, to the Patient-Centered Outcomes Research Institute established under section 1181(b) of the Social Security Act for carrying out part D of title XI of the Social Security Act (as in effect on the date of enactment of such Act).

(2) TRANSFER OF FUNDS.—

(A) IN GENERAL.—The trustee of the PCORTF shall provide for the transfer from the PCORTF of 20 percent of the amounts appropriated or credited to the PCORTF for each of fiscal years 2011 through 2029 to the Secretary of Health and Human Services to carry out section 937 of the Public Health Service Act.

(B) AVAILABILITY.—Amounts transferred under subparagraph (A) shall remain available until expended.

TRUST FUND—GENERAL PROVISIONS

(C) REQUIREMENTS.—Of the amounts transferred under subparagraph (A) with respect to a fiscal year, the Secretary of Health and Human Services shall distribute—

(i) 80 percent to the Office of Communication and Knowledge Transfer of the Agency for Healthcare Research and Quality (or any other relevant office designated by Agency for Healthcare Research and Quality) to carry out the activities described in section 937 of the Public Health Service Act; and

(ii) 20 percent to the Secretary to carry out the activities described in such section 937.

Amendments

• **2019, Further Consolidated Appropriations Act, 2020 (P.L. 116-94)**

P.L. 116-94, §104(a)(2), Div. N:

Amended Code Sec. 9511(d)(2)(A) by striking "2019" and inserting "2029". **Effective** 12-20-2019.

[Sec. 9511(e)]

(e) NET REVENUES.—For purposes of this section, the term "net revenues" means the amount estimated by the Secretary of the Treasury based on the excess of—

(1) the fees received in the Treasury under subchapter B of chapter 34, over

(2) the decrease in the tax imposed by chapter 1 resulting from the fees imposed by such subchapter.

[Sec. 9511(f)]

(f) TERMINATION.—No amounts shall be available for expenditure from the PCORTF after September 30, 2029, and any amounts in such Trust Fund after such date shall be transferred to the general fund of the Treasury.

Amendments

• **2019, Further Consolidated Appropriations Act, 2020 (P.L. 116-94)**

P.L. 116-94, §104(a)(3), Div. N:

Amended Code Sec. 9511(f) by striking "December 20, 2019" and inserting "September 30, 2029". **Effective** 12-20-2019.

• **2019, Further Continuing Appropriations Act, 2020, and Further Health Extenders Act of 2019 (P.L. 116-69)**

P.L. 116-69, Div. B, §1403:

Amended Code Sec. 9511(f) by striking "November 21" and inserting "December 20". **Effective** 11-21-2019.

• **2019, Continuing Appropriations Act, 2020, and Health Extenders Act of 2019 (P.L. 116-59)**

P.L. 116-59, Div. B, §1403:

Amended Code Sec. 9511(f) by striking "September 30" and inserting "November 21". **Effective** 9-27-2019.

• **2010, Patient Protection and Affordable Care Act (P.L. 111-148)**

P.L. 111-148, §6301(e)(1)(A):

Amended subchapter A of chapter 98 by adding at the end a new Code Sec. 9511. **Effective** 3-23-2010.

[Sec. 9511—Repealed]

Amendments

• **1998, Transportation Equity Act for the 21st Century (P.L. 105-178)**

P.L. 105-178, §9011(a):

Repealed Code Sec. 9511. **Effective** 6-9-98. Prior to repeal, Code Sec. 9511 read as follows:

SEC. 9511. NATIONAL RECREATIONAL TRAILS TRUST FUND.

(a) CREATION OF TRUST FUND.—There is established in the Treasury of the United States a trust fund to be known as the "National Recreational Trails Trust Fund", consisting of such amounts as may be credited or paid to such Trust Fund as provided in this section, section 9503(c)(6), or section 9602(b).

(b) CREDITING OF CERTAIN UNEXPENDED FUNDS.—There shall be credited to the National Recreational Trails Trust Fund amounts returned to such Trust Fund under section 1302(e)(8) of the Intermodal Surface Transportation Efficiency Act of 1991.

(c) EXPENDITURES FROM TRUST FUND.—Amounts in the National Recreational Trails Trust Fund shall be available, as provided in appropriation Acts, for making expenditures before October 1, 1998, to carry out the purposes of sections 1302 and 1303 of the Intermodal Surface Transportation Efficiency Act of 1991, as in effect on the date of the enactment of such Act.

• **1997, Surface Transportation Extension Act of 1997 (P.L. 105-130)**

P.L. 105-130, §9(c):

Amended Code Sec. 9511(c) by striking "1997" and inserting "1998". **Effective** 10-1-97.

• **1991, Intermodal Surface Transportation Efficiency Act of 1991 (P.L. 102-240)**

P.L. 102-240, §8003(a):

Added new Code Sec. 9511. **Effective** 12-18-91.

Subchapter B—General Provisions

Sec. 9601.   Transfer of amounts.
Sec. 9602.   Management of trust funds.

[Sec. 9601]

SEC. 9601. TRANSFER OF AMOUNTS.

The amounts appropriated by any section of subchapter A to any Trust Fund established by such subchapter shall be transferred at least monthly from the general fund of the Treasury to such Trust Fund on the basis of estimates made by the Secretary of the Treasury of the amounts referred to in such section. Proper adjustments shall be made in the amounts subsequently transferred to the extent prior estimates were in excess of or less than the amounts required to be transferred.

Amendments

• **2002, Trade Act of 2002 (P.L. 107-210)**

P.L. 107-210, §5201(a) and (d), provides:

SEC. 5201. FUND FOR WTO DISPUTE SETTLEMENTS.

(a) ESTABLISHMENT OF FUND.—There is established in the Treasury a fund for the payment of settlements under this section.

* * *

(d) MANAGEMENT OF FUND.—Sections 9601 and 9602(b) of the Internal Revenue Code of 1986 shall apply to the fund established under subsection (a) to the same extent as such provisions apply to trust funds established under subchapter A of chapter 98 of such Code.

• **1981, Black Lung Benefits Revenue Act of 1981 (P.L. 97-119)**

P.L. 97-119, §103(a):

Added Code Sec. 9601. **Effective** 1-1-82.

[Sec. 9602]

SEC. 9602. MANAGEMENT OF TRUST FUNDS.

[Sec. 9602(a)]

(a) REPORT.—It shall be the duty of the Secretary of the Treasury to hold each Trust Fund established by subchapter A, and (after consultation with any other trustees of the Trust Fund) to report to the Congress each year on the financial condition and the results of the operations of each such Trust Fund during the preceding fiscal year and on its expected condition and operations during the next 5 fiscal years. Such report shall be printed as a House document of the session of the Congress to which the report is made.

TRUST FUND—GENERAL PROVISIONS

[Sec. 9602(b)]

(b) INVESTMENT.—

(1) IN GENERAL.—It shall be the duty of the Secretary of the Treasury to invest such portion of any Trust Fund established by subchapter A as is not, in his judgment, required to meet current withdrawals. Such investments may be made only in interest-bearing obligations of the United States. For such purpose, such obligations may be acquired—

(A) on original issue at the issue price, or

(B) by purchase of outstanding obligations at the market price.

(2) SALE OF OBLIGATIONS.—Any obligation acquired by a Trust Fund established by subchapter A may be sold by the Secretary of the Treasury at the market price.

(3) INTEREST ON CERTAIN PROCEEDS.—The interest on, and the proceeds from the sale or redemption of, any obligations held in a Trust Fund established by subchapter A shall be credited to and form a part of the Trust Fund.

Amendments

- **1981, Black Lung Benefits Revenue Act of 1981 (P.L. 97-119)**

P.L. 97-119, § 103(a):

Added Code Sec. 9602. **Effective** 1-1-82.

[The next page is 5501.]

Subtitle J—Coal Industry Health Benefits

Chapter 99.   Coal Industry Health Benefits.

CHAPTER 99—COAL INDUSTRY HEALTH BENEFITS

Subchapter A.   Definitions of general applicability.
Subchapter B.   Combined benefit fund.
Subchapter C.   Health benefits of certain miners.
Subchapter D.   Other provisions.

Subchapter A—Definitions of General Applicability

Sec. 9701.   Definitions of general applicability.

[Sec. 9701]

SEC. 9701. DEFINITIONS OF GENERAL APPLICABILITY.

[Sec. 9701(a)]

(a) PLANS AND FUNDS.—For purposes of this chapter—

(1) UMWA BENEFIT PLAN.—

(A) IN GENERAL.—The term "UMWA Benefit Plan" means a plan—

(i) which is described in section 404(c), or a continuation thereof; and

(ii) which provides health benefits to retirees and beneficiaries of the industry which maintained the 1950 UMWA Pension Plan.

(B) 1950 UMWA BENEFIT PLAN.—The term "1950 UMWA Benefit Plan" means a UMWA Benefit Plan, participation in which is substantially limited to individuals who retired before 1976.

(C) 1974 UMWA BENEFIT PLAN.—The term "1974 UMWA Benefit Plan" means a UMWA Benefit Plan, prticipation in which is substantially limited to individuals who retired on or after January 1, 1976.

(2) 1950 UMWA PENSION PLAN.—The term "1950 UMWA Pension Plan" means a pension plan described in section 404(c) (or a continuation thereof), participation in which is substantially limited to individuals who retired before 1976.

(3) 1974 UMWA PENSION PLAN.—The term "1974 UMWA Pension Plan" means a pension plan described in section 404(c) (or a continuation thereof), participation in which is substantially limited to individuals who retired in 1976 and thereafter.

(4) 1992 UMWA BENEFIT PLAN.—The term "1992 UMWA Benefit Plan" means the plan referred to in section 9712.

(5) COMBINED FUND.—The term "Combined Fund" means the United Mine Workers of America Combined Benefit Fund established under section 9702.

Amendments

• **2018, Tax Technical Corrections Act of 2018 (P.L. 115-141)**

P.L. 115-141, §401(a)(343), Div. U:

Amended Code Sec. 9701(a)(4) by striking "section 9713A" and inserting "section 9712". **Effective** 3-23-2018.

[Sec. 9701(b)]

(b) AGREEMENTS.—For purposes of this section—

(1) COAL WAGE AGREEMENT.—The term "coal wage agreement" means—

(A) the National Bituminous Coal Wage Agreement, or

(B) any other agreement entered into between an employer in the coal industry and the United Mine Workers of America that required or requires one or both of the following:

(i) the provision of health benefits to retirees of such employer, eligibility for which is based on years of service credited under a plan established by the settlors and described in section 404(c) or a continuation of such plan; or

(ii) contributions to the 1950 UMWA Benefit Plan or the 1974 UMWA Benefit Plan, or any predecessor thereof.

(2) SETTLORS.—The term "settlors" means the United Mine Workers of America and the Bituminous Coal Operators' Association, Inc. (referred to in this chapter as the "BCOA").

(3) NATIONAL BITUMINOUS COAL WAGE AGREEMENT.—The term "National Bituminous Coal Wage Agreement" means a collective bargaining agreement negotiated by the BCOA and the United Mine Workers of America.

[Sec. 9701(c)]

(c) TERMS RELATING TO OPERATORS.—For purposes of this section—

(1) SIGNATORY OPERATOR.—The term "signatory operator" means a person which is or was a signatory to a coal wage agreement.

(2) RELATED PERSONS.—

(A) IN GENERAL.—A person shall be considered to be a related person to a signatory operator if that person is—

(i) a member of the controlled group of corporations (within the meaning of section 52(a)) which includes such signatory operator;

(ii) a trade or business which is under common control (as determined under section 52(b)) with such signatory operator; or

(iii) any other person who is identified as having a partnership interest or joint venture with a signatory operator in a business within the coal industry, but only if such business employed eligible beneficiaries, except that this clause shall not apply to a person whose only interest is as a limited partner.

A related person shall also include a successor in interest of any person described in clause (i), (ii), or (iii).

(B) TIME FOR DETERMINATION.—The relationships described in clauses (i), (ii), and (iii) of subparagraph (A) shall be determined as of July 20, 1992, except that if, on July 20, 1992, a signatory operator is no longer in business, the relationships shall be determined as of the time immediately before such operator ceased to be in business.

(3) 1988 AGREEMENT OPERATOR.—The term "1988 agreement operator" means—

(A) a signatory operator which was a signatory to the 1988 National Bituminous Coal Wage Agreement,

(B) an employer in the coal industry which was a signatory to an agreement containing pension and health care contribution and benefit provisions which are the same as those contained in the 1988 National Bituminous Coal Wage Agreement, or

COAL INDUSTRY HEALTH BENEFITS

(C) an employer from which contributions were actually received after 1987 and before July 20, 1992, by the 1950 UMWA Benefit Plan or the 1974 UMWA Benefit Plan in connection with employment in the coal industry during the period covered by the 1988 National Bituminous Coal Wage Agreement.

(4) LAST SIGNATORY OPERATOR.—The term "last signatory operator" means, with respect to a coal industry retiree, a signatory operator which was the most recent coal industry employer of such retiree.

(5) ASSIGNED OPERATOR.—The term "assigned operator" means, with respect to an eligible beneficiary defined in section 9703(f), the signatory operator to which liability under subchapter B with respect to the beneficiary is assigned under section 9706.

(6) OPERATORS OF DEPENDENT BENEFICIARIES.—For purposes of this chapter, the signatory operator, last signatory operator, or assigned operator of any eligible beneficiary under this chapter who is a coal industry retiree shall be considered to be the signatory operator, last signatory operator, or assigned operator with respect to any other individual who is an eligible beneficiary under this chapter by reason of a relationship to the retiree.

(7) BUSINESS.—For purposes of this chapter, a person shall be considered to be in business if such person conducts or derives revenue from any business activity, whether or not in the coal industry.

(8) SUCCESSOR IN INTEREST.—

(A) SAFE HARBOR.—The term "successor in interest" shall not include any person who—

(i) is an unrelated person to an eligible seller described in subparagraph (C); and

(ii) purchases for fair market value assets, or all of the stock, of a related person to such seller, in a bona fide, arm's-length sale.

(B) UNRELATED PERSON.—The term "unrelated person" means a purchaser who does not bear a relationship to the eligible seller described in section 267(b).

(C) ELIGIBLE SELLER.—For purposes of this paragraph, the term "eligible seller" means an assigned operator described in section 9704(j)(2) or a related person to such assigned operator.

Amendments

- 2006, Tax Relief and Health Care Act of 2006 (P.L. 109-432)

P.L. 109-432, Division C, § 211(d):

Amended Code Sec. 9701(c) by adding at the end a new paragraph (8). **Effective** for transactions after 12-20-2006.

[Sec. 9701(d)]

(d) ENACTMENT DATE.—For purposes of this chapter, the term "enactment date" means the date of the enactment of this chapter.

Amendments

- 1992, Energy Policy Act of 1992 (P.L. 102-486)

P.L. 102-486, § 19143:

Added Code Sec. 9701. **Effective** 10-24-92.

P.L. 102-486, § 19142, provides:

SEC. 19142. FINDINGS AND DECLARATION OF POLICY.

(a) FINDINGS.—The Congress finds that—

(1) the production, transportation, and use of coal substantially affects interstate and foreign commerce and the national public interest; and

(2) in order to secure the stability of interstate commerce, it is necessary to modify the current private health care benefit plan structure for retirees in the coal industry to identify persons most responsible for plan liabilities in order to stabilize plan funding and allow for the provision of health care benefits to such retirees.

(b) STATEMENT OF POLICY.—It is the policy of this subtitle—

(1) to remedy problems with the provision and funding of health care benefits with respect to the beneficiaries of multiemployer benefit plans that provide health care benefits to retirees in the coal industry;

(2) to allow for sufficient operating assets for such plans; and

(3) to provide for the continuation of a privately financed self-sufficient program for the delivery of health care benefits to the beneficiaries of such plans.

Subchapter B—Combined Benefit Fund

Part I.	Establishment and Benefits.
Part II.	Financing.
Part III.	Enforcement.
Part IV.	Other Provisions.

Part I—Establishment and Benefits

Sec. 9702.	Establishment of the United Mine Workers of America Combined Benefit Fund.
Sec. 9703.	Plan Benefits.

[Sec. 9702]

SEC. 9702. ESTABLISHMENT OF THE UNITED MINE WORKERS OF AMERICA COMBINED BENEFIT FUND.

[Sec. 9702(a)]

(a) ESTABLISHMENT.—

(1) IN GENERAL.—As soon as practicable (but not later than 60 days) after the enactment date, the persons described in subsection (b) shall designate the individuals to serve as trustees. Such trustees shall create a new private plan to be known as the United Mine Workers of America Combined Benefit Fund.

(2) MERGER OF RETIREE BENEFIT PLANS.—As of February 1, 1993, the settlors of the 1950 UMWA Benefit Plan and the 1974 UMWA Benefit Plan shall cause such plans to be merged into the Combined Fund, and such merger shall not be treated as an employer withdrawal for purposes of any 1988 coal wage agreement.

(3) TREATMENT OF PLAN.—The Combined Fund shall be—

(A) a plan described in section 302(c)(5) of the Labor Management Relations Act, 1947 (29 U.S.C. 186(c)(5)),

(B) an employee welfare benefit plan within the meaning of section 3(1) of the Employee Retirement Income Security Act of 1974 (29 U.S.C. 1002(1), and

(C) a multiemployer plan within the meaning of section 3(37) of such Act (29 U.S.C. 1002(37)).

(4) TAX TREATMENT.—For purposes of this title, the Combined Fund and any related trust shall be treated as an organization exempt from tax under section 501(a).

Sec. 9701(c)(3)(C)

COAL INDUSTRY HEALTH BENEFITS

[Sec. 9702(b)]

(b) BOARD OF TRUSTEES.—

(1) IN GENERAL.—For purposes of subsection (a), the board of trustees for the Combined Fund shall be appointed as follows:

(A) 2 individuals who represent employers in the coal mining industry shall be designated by the BCOA;

(B) 2 individuals designated by the United Mine Workers of America; and

(C) 3 individuals selected by the individuals appointed under subparagraphs (A) and (B).

(2) SUCCESSOR TRUSTEES.—Any successor trustee shall be appointed in the same manner as the trustee being succeeded. The plan establishing the Combined Fund shall provide for the removal of trustees.

(3) SPECIAL RULE.—If the BCOA ceases to exist, any trustee or successor under paragraph (1)(A) shall be designated by the 3 employers who were members of the BCOA on the enactment date and who have been assigned the greatest number of eligible beneficiaries under section 9706.

Amendments

• 2006, Tax Relief and Health Care Act of 2006 (P.L. 109-432)

P.L. 109-432, Division C, § 213(a):

Amended Code Sec. 9702(b). **Effective** on the date of the enactment of this Act. Prior to amendment, Code Sec. 9702(b) read as follows:

(b) BOARD OF TRUSTEES.—

(1) IN GENERAL.—For purposes of subsection (a), the board of trustees for the Combined Fund shall be appointed as follows:

(A) one individual who represents employers in the coal mining industry shall be designated by the BCOA;

(B) one individual shall be designated by the three employers, other than 1988 agreement operators, who have been assigned the greatest number of eligible beneficiaries under section 9706;

(C) two individuals designated by the United Mine Workers of America; and

(D) three persons selected by the persons appointed under subparagraphs (A), (B), and (C).

(2) SUCCESSOR TRUSTEES.—Any successor trustee shall be appointed in the same manner as the trustee being succeeded. The plan establishing the Combined Fund shall provide for the removal of trustees.

(3) SPECIAL RULES.—

(A) BCOA.—If the BCOA ceases to exist, any trustee or successor under paragraph (1)(A) shall be designated by the 3 employers who were members of the BCOA on the enactment date and who have been assigned the greatest number of eligible beneficiaries under section 9706.

(B) FORMER SIGNATORIES.—The initial trustee under paragraph (1)(B) shall be designated by the 3 employers, other than 1988 agreement operators, which the records of the 1950 UMWA Benefit Plan and 1974 UMWA Benefit Plan indicate have the greatest number of eligible beneficiaries as of the enactment date, and such trustee and any successor shall serve until November 1, 1993.

[Sec. 9702(c)]

(c) PLAN YEAR.—The first plan year of the Combined Fund shall begin February 1, 1993, and end September 30, 1993. Each succeeding plan year shall begin on October 1 of each calendar year.

Amendments

• 1992, Energy Policy Act of 1992 (P.L. 102-486)

P.L. 102-486, § 19143(a):

Added Code Sec. 9702. **Effective** 10-24-92.

[Sec. 9703]

SEC. 9703. PLAN BENEFITS.

[Sec. 9703(a)]

(a) IN GENERAL.—Each eligible beneficiary of the Combined Fund shall receive—

(1) health benefits described in subsection (b), and

(2) in the case of an eligible beneficiary described in subsection (f)(1), death benefits coverage described in subsection (c).

[Sec. 9703(b)]

(b) HEALTH BENEFITS.—

(1) IN GENERAL.—The trustees of the Combined Fund shall provide health care benefits to each eligible beneficiary by enrolling the beneficiary in a health care services plan which undertakes to provide such benefits on a prepaid risk basis. The trustees shall utilize all available plan resources to ensure that, consistent with paragraph (2), coverage under the managed care system shall to the maximum extent feasible be substantially the same as (and subject to the same limitations of) coverage provided under the 1950 UMWA Benefit Plan and the 1974 UMWA Benefit Plan as of January 1, 1992.

(2) PLAN PAYMENT RATES.—

(A) IN GENERAL.—The trustees of the Combined Fund shall negotiate payment rates with the health care services plans described in paragraph (1) for each plan year which are in amounts which—

(i) vary as necessary to ensure that beneficiaries in different geographic areas have access to a uniform level of health benefits; and

(ii) result in aggregate payments for such plan year from the Combined Fund which do not exceed the total premium payments required to be paid to the Combined Fund under section 9704(a) for the plan year, adjusted as provided in subparagraphs (B) and (C).

(B) REDUCTIONS.—The amount determined under subparagraph (A)(ii) for any plan year shall be reduced—

(i) by the aggregate death benefit premiums determined under section 9704(c) for the plan year, and

(ii) by the amount reserved for plan administration under subsection (d).

(C) INCREASES.—The amount determined under subparagraph (A)(ii) shall be increased—

(i) by any reduction in the total premium payments required to be paid under section 9704(a) by reason of transfers described in section 9705,

(ii) by any carryover to the plan year from any preceding plan year which—

(I) is derived from amounts described in section 9704(e)(3)(B)(i), and

(II) the trustees elect to use to pay benefits for the current plan year, and

(iii) any interest earned by the Combined Fund which the trustees elect to use to pay benefits for the current plan year.

(3) QUALIFIED PROVIDERS.—The trustees of the Combined Fund shall not enter into an agreement under paragraph (1) with any provider of services which is of a type which is required to be certified by the Secretary of Health and Human Services when providing services under title XVIII of the Social Security Act unless the provider is so certified.

(4) EFFECTIVE DATE.—Benefits shall be provided under paragraph (1) on and after February 1, 1993.

COAL INDUSTRY HEALTH BENEFITS

[Sec. 9703(c)]

(c) DEATH BENEFITS COVERAGE.—

(1) IN GENERAL.—The trustees of the Combined Fund shall provide death benefits coverage to each eligible beneficiary described in subsection (f)(1) which is identical to the benefits provided under the 1950 UMWA Pension Plan or 1974 UMWA Pension Plan, whichever is applicable, on July 20, 1992. Such coverage shall be provided on and after February 1, 1993.

(2) TERMINATION OF COVERAGE.—The 1950 UMWA Pension Plan and the 1974 UMWA Pension Plan shall each be amended to provide that death benefits coverage shall not be provided to eligible beneficiaries on and after February 1, 1993. This paragraph shall not prohibit such plans from subsequently providing death benefits not described in paragraph (1).

[Sec. 9703(d)]

(d) RESERVES FOR ADMINISTRATION.—The trustees of the Combined Fund may reserve for each plan year, for use in payment of the administrative costs of the Combined Fund, an amount not to exceed 5 percent of the premiums to be paid to the Combined Fund under section 9704(a) during the plan year.

[Sec. 9703(e)]

(e) LIMITATION ON ENROLLMENT.—The Combined Fund shall not enroll any individual who is not receiving benefits under the 1950 UMWA Benefit Plan or the 1974 UMWA Benefit Plan as of July 20, 1992.

[Sec. 9703(f)]

(f) ELIGIBLE BENEFICIARY.—For purposes of this subchapter, the term "eligible beneficiary" means an individual who—

(1) is a coal industry retiree who, on July 20, 1992, was eligible to receive, and receiving, benefits from the 1950 UMWA Benefit Plan or the 1974 UMWA Benefit Plan, or

(2) on such date was eligible to receive, and receiving, benefits in either such plan by reason of a relationship to such retiree.

Amendments

- 1992, Energy Policy Act of 1992 (P.L. 102-486)

P.L. 102-486, § 19143(a):
Added Code Sec. 9703. **Effective** 10-24-92.

Part II—Financing

Sec. 9704.	Liability of assigned operators.
Sec. 9705.	Transfers.
Sec. 9706.	Assignment of eligible beneficiaries.

[Sec. 9704]

SEC. 9704. LIABILITY OF ASSIGNED OPERATORS.

[Sec. 9704(a)]

(a) ANNUAL PREMIUMS.—Each assigned operator shall pay to the Combined Fund for each plan year beginning on or after February 1, 1993, an annual premium equal to the sum of the following three premiums—

(1) the health benefit premium determined under subsection (b) for such plan year, plus

(2) the death benefit premium determined under subsection (c) for such plan year, plus

(3) the unassigned beneficiaries premium determined under subsection (d) for such plan year.

Any related person with respect to an assigned operator shall be jointly and severally liable for any premium required to be paid by such operator.

[Sec. 9704(b)]

(b) HEALTH BENEFIT PREMIUM.—For purposes of this chapter—

(1) IN GENERAL.—The health benefit premium for any plan year for any assigned operator shall be an amount equal to the product of the per beneficiary premium for the plan year multiplied by the number of eligible beneficiaries assigned to such operator under section 9706.

(2) PER BENEFICIARY PREMIUM.—The Commissioner of Social Security shall calculate a per beneficiary premium for each plan year beginning on or after February 1, 1993, which is equal to the sum of—

(A) the amount determined by dividing—

(i) the aggregate amount of payments from the 1950 UMWA Benefit Plan and the 1974 UMWA Benefit Plan for health benefits (less reimbursements but including administrative costs) for the plan year beginning July 1, 1991, for all individuals covered under such plans for such plan year, by

(ii) the number of such individuals, plus

(B) the amount determined under subparagraph (A) multiplied by the percentage (if any) by which the medical component of the Consumer Price Index for the calendar year in which the plan year begins exceeds such component for 1992.

(3) ADJUSTMENTS FOR MEDICARE REDUCTIONS.—If, by reason of a reduction in benefits under title XVIII of the Social Security Act, the level of health benefits under the Combined Fund would be reduced, the trustees of the Combined Fund shall increase the per beneficiary premium for the plan year in which the reduction occurs and each subsequent plan year by the amount necessary to maintain the level of health benefits which would have been provided without such reduction.

Amendments

- 1994, Social Security Independence and Program Improvements Act of 1994 (P.L. 103-296)

P.L. 103-296, § 108(h)(9)(A):
Amended Code Sec. 9704(b)(2) by striking "Secretary of Health and Human Services" and inserting "Commissioner of Social Security". **Effective** 3-31-95.

[Sec. 9704(c)]

(c) DEATH BENEFIT PREMIUM.—The death benefit premium for any plan year for any assigned operator shall be equal to the applicable percentage of the amount, actuarially determined, which the Combined Fund will be required to pay during the plan year for death benefits coverage described in section 9703(c).

COAL INDUSTRY HEALTH BENEFITS

[Sec. 9704(d)]

(d) UNASSIGNED BENEFICIARIES PREMIUM.—

(1) PLAN YEARS ENDING ON OR BEFORE SEPTEMBER 30, 2006.—For plan years ending on or before September 30, 2006, the unassigned beneficiaries premium for any assigned operator shall be equal to the applicable percentage of the product of the per beneficiary premium for the plan year multiplied by the number of eligible beneficiaries who are not assigned under section 9706 to any person for such plan year.

(2) PLAN YEARS BEGINNING ON OR AFTER OCTOBER 1, 2006.—

(A) IN GENERAL.—For plan years beginning on or after October 1, 2006, subject to subparagraph (B), there shall be no unassigned beneficiaries premium, and benefit costs with respect to eligible beneficiaries who are not assigned under section 9706 to any person for any such plan year shall be paid from amounts transferred under section 9705(b).

(B) INADEQUATE TRANSFERS.—If, for any plan year beginning on or after October 1, 2006, the amounts transferred under section 9705(b) are less than the amounts required to be transferred to the Combined Fund under subsection (h)(2)(A) or (i) of section 402 of the Surface Mining Control and Reclamation Act of 1977 (30 U.S.C. 1232), then the unassigned beneficiaries premium for any assigned operator shall be equal to the operator's applicable percentage of the amount required to be so transferred which was not so transferred.

Amendments

• 2018, Tax Technical Corrections Act of 2018 (P.L. 115-141)

P.L. 115-141, §401(a)(344), Div. U:

Amended Code Sec. 9704(d)(2)(B) by striking "1232))," and inserting "1232),". **Effective** 3-23-2018.

• 2006, Tax Relief and Health Care Act of 2006 (P.L. 109-432)

P.L. 109-432, Division C, §212(a)(2)(A):

Amended Code Sec. 9704(d). **Effective** for plan years of the Combined Fund beginning after 9-30-2006. Prior to amendment, Code Sec. 9704(d) read as follows:

(d) UNASSIGNED BENEFICIARIES PREMIUM.—The unassigned beneficiaries premium for any plan year for any assigned operator shall be equal to the applicable percentage of the product of the per beneficiary premium for the plan year multiplied by the number of eligible beneficiaries who are not assigned under section 9706 to any person for such plan year.

[Sec. 9704(e)]

(e) PREMIUM ACCOUNTS; ADJUSTMENTS.—

(1) ACCOUNTS.—The trustees of the Combined Fund shall establish and maintain 3 separate accounts for each of the premiums described in subsections (b), (c), and (d). Such accounts shall be credited with the premiums received and amounts transferred under section 9705(b) and debited with expenditures allocable to such premiums.

(2) ALLOCATIONS.—

(A) ADMINISTRATIVE EXPENSES.—Administrative costs for any plan year shall be allocated to premium accounts under paragraph (1) on the basis of expenditures (other than administrative costs) from such accounts during the preceding plan year.

(B) INTEREST.—Interest shall be allocated to the account established for health benefit premiums.

(3) SHORTFALLS AND SURPLUSES.—

(A) IN GENERAL.—Except as provided in subparagraph (B), if, for any plan year, there is a shortfall or surplus in any premium account, the premium for the following plan year for each assigned operator shall be proportionately reduced or increased, whichever is applicable, by the amount of such shortfall or surplus. Amounts credited to an account from amounts transferred under section 9705(b) shall not be taken into account in determining whether there is a surplus in the account for purposes of this paragraph.

(B) EXCEPTION.—Subparagraph (A) shall not apply to any surplus in the health benefit premium account or the unassigned beneficiaries premium account which is attributable to—

(i) the excess of the premiums credited to such account for a plan year over the benefits (and administrative costs) debited to such account for the plan year, but such excess shall only be available for purposes of the carryover described in section 9703(b)(2)(C)(ii) (relating to carryovers of premiums not used to provide benefits), or

(ii) interest credited under paragraph (2)(B) for the plan year or any preceding plan year.

(C) NO AUTHORITY FOR INCREASED PAYMENTS.—Nothing in this paragraph shall be construed to allow expenditures for health care benefits for any plan year in excess of the limit under section 9703(b)(2).

Amendments

• 2006, Tax Relief and Health Care Act of 2006 (P.L. 109-432)

P.L. 109-432, Division C, §212(a)(2)(B)(i):

Amended Code Sec. 9704(e)(1) by inserting "and amounts transferred under section 9705(b)" after "premiums received". **Effective** for plan years of the Combined Fund beginning after 9-30-2006.

P.L. 109-432, Division C, §212(a)(2)(B)(ii):

Amended Code Sec. 9704(e)(3)(A) by adding at the end a new sentence. **Effective** for plan years of the Combined Fund beginning after 9-30-2006.

[Sec. 9704(f)]

(f) APPLICABLE PERCENTAGE.—For purposes of this section—

(1) IN GENERAL.—The term "applicable percentage" means, with respect to any assigned operator, the percentage determined by dividing the number of eligible beneficiaries assigned under section 9706 to such operator by the total number of eligible beneficiaries assigned under section 9706 to all such operators (determined on the basis of assignments as of October 1, 1993).

(2) ANNUAL ADJUSTMENTS.—In the case of any plan year beginning on or after October 1, 1994, the applicable percentage for any assigned operator shall be redetermined under paragraph (1) by making the following changes to the assignments as of October 1, 1993:

(A) Such assignments shall be modified to reflect any changes during the period beginning October 1, 1993, and ending on the last day of the preceding plan year pursuant to the appeals process under section 9706(f).

(B) The total number of assigned eligible beneficiaries shall be reduced by the eligible beneficiaries of assigned operators which (and all related persons with respect to which) had ceased business (within the meaning of section 9701(c)(6)) during the period described in subparagraph (A).

(C) In the case of plan years beginning on or after October 1, 2007, the total number of assigned eligible beneficiaries shall be reduced by the eligible beneficiaries whose assignments have been revoked under section 9706(h).

Amendments

• 2006, Tax Relief and Health Care Act of 2006 (P.L. 109-432)

P.L. 109-432, Division C, §212(a)(2)(C):

Amended Code Sec. 9704(f)(2) by adding at the end a new subparagraph (C). **Effective** for plan years of the Combined Fund beginning after 9-30-2006.

COAL INDUSTRY HEALTH BENEFITS

[Sec. 9704(g)]

(g) PAYMENT OF PREMIUMS.—

(1) IN GENERAL.—The annual premium under subsection (a) for any plan year shall be payable in 12 equal monthly installments, due on the twenty-fifth day of each calendar month in the plan year. In the case of the plan year beginning February 1, 1993, the annual premium under subsection (a) shall be added to such premium for the plan year beginning October 1, 1993.

(2) DEDUCTIBILITY.—Any premium required by this section shall be deductible without regard to any limitation on deductibility based on the prefunding of health benefits.

[Sec. 9704(h)]

(h) INFORMATION.—The trustees of the Combined Fund shall, not later than 60 days after the enactment date, furnish to the Commissioner of Social Security information as to the benefits and covered beneficiaries under the fund, and such other information as the Secretary may require to compute any premium under this section.

Amendments

• 1994, Social Security Independence and Program Improvements Act of 1994 (P.L. 103-296)

P.L. 103-296, § 108(h)(9)(A):

Amended Code Sec. 9704(h) by striking "Secretary of Health and Human Services" and inserting "Commissioner of Social Security". **Effective** 3-31-95.

[Sec. 9704(i)]

(i) TRANSITION RULES.—

(1) 1988 AGREEMENT OPERATORS.—

(A) 1ST YEAR COSTS.—During the plan year of the Combined Fund beginning February 1, 1993, the 1988 agreement operators shall make contributions to the Combined Fund in amounts necessary to pay benefits and administrative costs of the Combined Fund incurred during such year, reduced by the amount transferred to the Combined Fund under section 9705(a) on February 1, 1993.

(B) DEFICITS FROM MERGED PLANS.—During the period beginning February 1, 1993, and ending September 30, 1994, the 1988 agreement operators shall make contributions to the Combined Fund as are necessary to pay off the expenses accrued (and remaining unpaid) by the 1950 UMWA Benefit Plan and the 1974 UMWA Benefit Plan as of February 1, 1993, reduced by the assets of such plans as of such date.

(C) FAILURE.—If any 1988 agreement operator fails to meet any obligation under this paragraph, any contributions of such operator to the Combined Fund or any other plan described in section 404(c) shall not be deductible under this title until such time as the failure is corrected.

(D) PREMIUM REDUCTIONS.—

(i) 1ST YEAR PAYMENTS.—In the case of a 1988 agreement operator making contributions under subparagraph (A), the premium of such operator under subsection (a) shall be reduced by the amount paid under subparagraph (A) by such operator for the plan year beginning February 1, 1993.

(ii) DEFICIT PAYMENTS.—In the case [of] a 1988 agreement operator making contributions under subparagraph (B), the premium of such operator under subsection (a) shall be reduced by the amounts which are paid to the Combined Fund by reason of claims arising in connection with the 1950 UMWA Benefit Plan and the 1974 UMWA Benefit Plan as of February 1, 1993, including claims based on the "evergreen clause" found in the language of the 1950 UMWA Benefit Plan and the 1974 UMWA Benefit Plan, and which are allocated to such operator under subparagraph (E).

(iii) LIMITATION.—Clause (ii) shall not apply to the extent the amounts paid exceed the contributions.

(iv) PLAN YEARS.—Premiums under subsection (a) shall be reduced for the first plan year for which amounts described in clause (i) or (ii) are available and for any succeeding plan year until such amounts are exhausted.

(E) ALLOCATIONS OF CONTRIBUTIONS AND REFUNDS.—Contributions under subparagraphs (A) and (B), and premium reductions under subparagraph (D)(ii), shall be made ratably on the basis of aggregate contributions made by such operators under the applicable 1988 coal wage agreements as of January 31, 1993.

(2) 1ST PLAN YEAR.—In the case of the plan year of the Combined Fund beginning February 1, 1993—

(A) the premiums under subsections (a)(1) and (a)(3) shall be 67 percent of such premiums without regard to this paragraph, and

(B) the premiums under subsection (a) shall be paid as provided in subsection (g).

(3) STARTUP COSTS.—The 1950 UMWA Benefit Plan and the 1974 UMWA Benefit Plan shall pay the costs of the Combined Fund incurred before February 1, 1993. For purposes of this section, such costs shall be treated as administrative expenses incurred for the plan year beginning February 1, 1993.

Amendments

• 1992, Energy Policy Act of 1992 (P.L. 102-486)

P.L. 102-486, § 19143(a):

Added Code Sec. 9704. **Effective** 10-24-92.

[Sec. 9704(j)]

(j) PREPAYMENT OF PREMIUM LIABILITY.—

(1) IN GENERAL.—If—

(A) a payment meeting the requirements of paragraph (3) is made to the Combined Fund by or on behalf of—

(i) any assigned operator to which this subsection applies, or

(ii) any related person to any assigned operator described in clause (i), and

(B) the common parent of the controlled group of corporations described in paragraph (2)(B) is jointly and severally liable for any premium under this section which (but for this subsection) would be required to be paid by the assigned operator or related person,

then such common parent (and no other person) shall be liable for such premium.

(2) ASSIGNED OPERATORS TO WHICH SUBSECTION APPLIES.—

(A) IN GENERAL.—This subsection shall apply to any assigned operator if—

(i) the assigned operator (or a related person to the assigned operator)—

(I) made contributions to the 1950 UMWA Benefit Plan and the 1974 UMWA Benefit Plan for employment during the period covered by the 1988 agreement; and

(II) is not a 1988 agreement operator,

COAL INDUSTRY HEALTH BENEFITS

(ii) the assigned operator (and all related persons to the assigned operator) are not actively engaged in the production of coal as of July 1, 2005, and

(iii) the assigned operator was, as of July 20, 1992, a member of a controlled group of corporations described in subparagraph (B).

(B) CONTROLLED GROUP OF CORPORATIONS.—A controlled group of corporations is described in this subparagraph if the common parent of such group is a corporation the shares of which are publicly traded on a United States exchange.

(C) COORDINATION WITH REPEAL OF ASSIGNMENTS.—A person shall not fail to be treated as an assigned operator to which this subsection applies solely because the person ceases to be an assigned operator by reason of section 9706(h)(1) if the person otherwise meets the requirements of this subsection and is liable for the payment of premiums under section 9706(h)(3).

(D) CONTROLLED GROUP.—For purposes of this subsection, the term "controlled group of corporations" has the meaning given such term by section 52(a).

(3) REQUIREMENTS.—A payment meets the requirements of this paragraph if—

(A) the amount of the payment is not less than the present value of the total premium liability under this chapter with respect to the Combined Fund of the assigned operators or related persons described in paragraph (1) or their assignees, as determined by the operator's or related person's enrolled actuary (as defined in section 7701(a)(35)) using actuarial methods and assumptions each of which is reasonable and which are reasonable in the aggregate, as determined by such enrolled actuary;

(B) such enrolled actuary files with the Secretary of Labor a signed actuarial report containing—

(i) the date of the actuarial valuation applicable to the report; and

(ii) a statement by the enrolled actuary signing the report that, to the best of the actuary's knowledge, the report is complete and accurate and that in the actuary's opinion the actuarial assumptions used are in the aggregate reasonably related to the experience of the operator and to reasonable expectations; and

(C) 90 calendar days have elapsed after the report required by subparagraph (B) is filed with the Secretary of Labor, and the Secretary of Labor has not notified the assigned operator in writing that the requirements of this paragraph have not been satisfied.

(4) USE OF PREPAYMENT.—The Combined Fund shall—

(A) establish and maintain an account for each assigned operator or related person by, or on whose behalf, a payment described in paragraph (3) was made,

(B) credit such account with such payment (and any earnings thereon), and

(C) use all amounts in such account exclusively to pay premiums that would (but for this subsection) be required to be paid by the assigned operator.

Upon termination of the obligations for the premium liability of any assigned operator or related person for which such account is maintained, all funds remaining in such account (and earnings thereon) shall be refunded to such person as may be designated by the common parent described in paragraph (1)(B).

Amendments

• 2006, Tax Relief and Health Care Act of 2006 (P.L. 109-432)

P.L. 109-432, Division C, §211(a):

Amended Code Sec. 9704 by adding at the end a new subsection (j). **Effective** 12-20-2006.

[Sec. 9705]

SEC. 9705. TRANSFERS.

[Sec. 9705(a)]

(a) TRANSFER OF ASSETS FROM 1950 UMWA PENSION PLAN.—

(1) IN GENERAL.—From the funds reserved under paragraph (2), the board of trustees of the 1950 UMWA Pension Plan shall transfer to the Combined Fund—

(A) $70,000,000 on February 1, 1993,

(B) $70,000,000 on October 1, 1993, and

(C) $70,000,000 on October 1, 1994.

(2) RESERVATION.—Immediately upon the enactment date, the board of trustees of the 1950 UMWA Pension Plan shall segregate $210,000,000 from the general assets of the plan. Such funds shall be held in the plan until disbursed pursuant to paragraph (1). Any interest on such funds shall be deposited into the general assets of the 1950 UMWA Pension Plan.

(3) USE OF FUNDS.—Amounts transferred to the Combined Fund under paragraph (1) shall—

(A) in the case of the transfer on February 1, 1993, be used to proportionately reduce the premium of each assigned operator under section 9704(a) for the plan year of the Fund beginning February 1, 1993, and

(B) in the case of any other such transfer, be used to proportionately reduce the unassigned beneficiary premium under section 9704(a)(3) and the death benefit premium under section 9704(a)(2) of each assigned operator for the plan year in which transferred and for any subsequent plan year in which such funds remain available.

Such funds may not be used to pay any amounts required to be paid by the 1988 agreement operators under section 9704(i)(1)(B).

(4) TAX TREATMENT; VALIDITY OF TRANSFER.—

(A) NO DEDUCTION.—No deduction shall be allowed under this title with respect to any transfer pursuant to paragraph (1), but such transfer shall not adversely affect the deductibility (under applicable provisions of this title) of contributions previously made by employers, or amounts hereafter contributed by employers, to the 1950 UMWA Pension Plan, the 1950 UMWA Benefit Plan, the 1974 UMWA Pension Plan, the 1974 UMWA Benefit Plan, the 1992 UMWA Benefit Plan, or the Combined Fund.

(B) OTHER TAX PROVISIONS.—Any transfer pursuant to Paragraph (1)—

(i) shall not be treated as an employer reversion from a qualified plan for purposes of section 4980, and

(ii) shall not be includible in the gross income of any employer maintaining the 1950 UMWA Pension Plan.

(5) TREATMENT OF TRANSFER.—Any transfer pursuant to paragraph (1) shall not be deemed to violate, or to be prohibited by, any provision of law, or to cause the settlors, joint board of trustees, employers or any related person to incur or be subject to liability, taxes, fines, or penalties of any kind whatsoever.

COAL INDUSTRY HEALTH BENEFITS

[Sec. 9705(b)]

(b) TRANSFERS.—

(1) IN GENERAL.—The Combined Fund shall include any amount transferred to the Fund under subsections (h) and (i) of section 402 of the Surface Mining Control and Reclamation Act of 1977 (30 U.S.C. 1232).

(2) USE OF FUNDS.—Any amount transferred under paragraph (1) for any fiscal year shall be used to pay benefits and administrative costs of beneficiaries of the Combined Fund or for such other purposes as are specifically provided in the Act described in paragraph (1).

Amendments

• **2018, Tax Technical Corrections Act of 2018 (P.L. 115-141)**

P.L. 115-141, §401(a)(345), Div. U:

Amended Code Sec. 9705(b)(1) by striking "1232(h)" and inserting "1232". **Effective** 3-23-2018.

P.L. 115-141, §401(a)(346), Div. U:

Amended Code Sec. 9705(b)(2) by striking "Acts" and inserting "Act". **Effective** 3-23-2018.

• **2006, Tax Relief and Health Care Act of 2006 (P.L. 109-432)**

P.L. 109-432, Division C, §212(a)(1)(A)-(C):

Amended Code Sec. 9705(b) by striking "section 402(h)" and inserting "subsections (h) and (i) of section 402" in paragraph (1); by striking paragraph (2) and inserting a new paragraph (2); and by striking "FROM ABANDONED MINE RECLAMATION FUND" following "TRANSFERS" in the heading thereof. **Effective** for plan years of the Combined Fund beginning after 9-30-2006. Prior to being stricken, Code Sec. 9705(b)(2) read as follows:

(2) USE OF FUNDS.—Any amount transferred under paragraph (1) for any fiscal year shall be used to proportionately reduce the unassigned beneficiary premium under section 9704(a)(3) of each assigned operator for the plan year in which transferred.

• **1992, Energy Policy Act of 1992 (P.L. 102-486)**

P.L. 102-486, §19143(a):

Added Code Sec. 9705. **Effective** 10-24-92.

[Sec. 9706]

SEC. 9706. ASSIGNMENT OF ELIGIBLE BENEFICIARIES.

[Sec. 9706(a)]

(a) IN GENERAL.—For purposes of this chapter, the Commissioner of Social Security shall, before October 1, 1993, assign each coal industry retiree who is an eligible beneficiary to a signatory operator which (or any related person with respect to which) remains in business in the following order:

(1) First, to the signatory operator which—

(A) was a signatory to the 1978 coal wage agreement or any subsequent coal wage agreement, and

(B) was the most recent signatory operator to employ the coal industry retiree in the coal industry for at least 2 years.

(2) Second, if the retiree is not assigned under paragraph (1), to the signatory operator which—

(A) was a signatory to the 1978 coal wage agreement or any subsequent coal wage agreement, and

(B) was the most recent signatory operator to employ the coal industry retiree in the coal industry.

(3) Third, if the retiree is not assigned under paragraph (1) or (2), to the signatory operator which employed the coal industry retiree in the coal industry for a longer period of time than any other signatory operator prior to the effective date of the 1978 coal wage agreement.

Amendments

• **1994, Social Security Independence and Program Improvements Act of 1994 (P.L. 103-296)**

P.L. 103-296, §108(h)(9)(B)(i)-(ii):

Amended Code Sec. 9706 by striking "Secretary of Health and Human Services" each place it appears and inserting "Commissioner of Social Security" and by striking "Secretary" each place it appears and inserting "Commissioner". **Effective** 3-31-95.

[Sec. 9706(b)]

(b) RULES RELATING TO EMPLOYMENT AND REASSIGNMENT UPON PURCHASE.—For purposes of subsection (a)—

(1) AGGREGATION RULES.—

(A) RELATED PERSON.—Any employment of a coal industry retiree in the coal industry by a signatory operator shall be treated as employment by any related persons to such operator.

(B) CERTAIN EMPLOYMENT DISREGARDED.—Employment with—

(i) a person which is (and all related persons with respect to which are) no longer in business, or

(ii) a person during a period during which such person was not a signatory to a coal wage agreement,

shall not be taken into account.

(2) REASSIGNMENT UPON PURCHASE.—If a person becomes a successor of an assigned operator after the enactment date, the assigned operator may transfer the assignment of an eligible beneficiary under subsection (a) to such successor, and such successor shall be treated as the assigned operator with respect to such eligible beneficiary for purposes of this chapter. Notwithstanding the preceding sentence, the assigned operator transferring such assignment (and any related person) shall remain the guarantor of the benefits provided to the eligible beneficiary under this chapter. An assigned operator shall notify the trustees of the Combined Fund of any transfer described in this paragraph.

[Sec. 9706(c)]

(c) IDENTIFICATION OF ELIGIBLE BENEFICIARIES.—The 1950 UMWA Benefit Plan and the 1974 UMWA Benefit Plan shall, by the later of October 1, 1992, or the twentieth day after the enactment date, provide to the Commissioner of Social Security a list of the names and social security account numbers of each eligible beneficiary, including each deceased eligible beneficiary if any other individual is an eligible beneficiary by reason of a relationship to such deceased eligible beneficiary. In addition, the plans shall provide, where ascertainable from plan records, the names of all persons described in subsection (a) with respect to any eligible beneficiary or deceased eligible beneficiary.

Amendments

• **1994, Social Security Independence and Program Improvements Act of 1994 (P.L. 103-296)**

P.L. 103-296, §108(h)(9)(B)(i)-(ii):

Amended Code Sec. 9706 by striking "Secretary of Health and Human Services" each place it appears and inserting "Commissioner of Social Security" and by striking "Secretary" each place it appears and inserting "Commissioner". **Effective** 3-31-95.

COAL INDUSTRY HEALTH BENEFITS

[Sec. 9706(d)]

(d) COOPERATION BY OTHER AGENCIES AND PERSONS.—

(1) COOPERATION.—The head of any department, agency, or instrumentality of the United States shall cooperate fully and promptly with the Commissioner of Social Security in providing information which will enable the Commissioner to carry out his responsibilities under this section.

(2) PROVIDING OF INFORMATION.—

(A) IN GENERAL.—Notwithstanding any other provision of law, including section 6103, the head of any other agency, department, or instrumentality shall, upon receiving a written request from the Commissioner of Social Security in connection with this section, cause a search to be made of the files and records maintained by such agency, department, or instrumentality with a view to determining whether the information requested is contained in such files or records. The Commissioner shall be advised whether the search disclosed the information requested, and, if so, such information shall be promptly transmitted to the Commissioner, except that if the disclosure of any requested information would contravene national policy or security interests of the United States, or the confidentiality of census data, the information shall not be transmitted and the Secretary shall be so advised.

(B) LIMITATION.—Any information provided under subpart (A) shall be limited to information necessary for the Commissioner to carry out his duties under this section.

(3) TRUSTEES.—The trustees of the Combined Fund, the 1950 UMWA Benefit Plan, the 1974 UMWA Benefit Plan, the 1950 UMWA Pension Plan, and the 1974 UMWA Pension Plan shall fully and promptly cooperate with the Commissioner in furnishing, or assisting the Commissioner to obtain, any information the Commissioner needs to carry out the Commissioner's responsibilities under this section.

Amendments

• **1994, Social Security Independence and Program Improvements Act of 1994 (P.L. 103-296)**

P.L. 103-296, §108(h)(9)(B)(i)-(ii):

Amended Code Sec. 9706 by striking "Secretary of Health and Human Services" each place it appears and inserting "Commissioner of Social Security" and by striking "Secretary" each place it appears and inserting "Commissioner", and by striking "Secretary's" and inserting "Commissioner's". **Effective** 3-31-95.

[Sec. 9706(e)]

(e) NOTICE BY SECRETARY.—

(1) NOTICE TO FUND.—The Commissioner of Social Security shall advise the trustees of the Combined Fund of the name of each person identified under this section as an assigned operator, and the names and social security account numbers of eligible beneficiaries with respect to whom he is identified.

(2) OTHER NOTICE.—The Commissioner of Social Security shall notify each assigned operator of the names and social security account numbers of eligible beneficiaries who have been assigned to such person under this section and a brief summary of the facts related to the basis for such assignments.

Amendments

• **1994, Social Security Independence and Program Improvements Act of 1994 (P.L. 103-296)**

P.L. 103-296, §108(h)(9)(B)(i)-(ii):

Amended Code Sec. 9706 by striking "Secretary of Health and Human Services" each place it appears and inserting "Commissioner of Social Security" and by striking "Secretary" each place it appears and inserting "Commissioner". **Effective** 3-31-95.

[Sec. 9706(f)]

(f) RECONSIDERATION BY COMMISSIONER.—

(1) IN GENERAL.—Any assigned operator receiving a notice under subsection (e)(2) with respect to an eligible beneficiary may, within 30 days of receipt of such notice, request from the Commissioner of Social Security detailed information as to the work history of the beneficiary and the basis of the assignment.

(2) REVIEW.—An assigned operator may, within 30 days of receipt of the information under paragraph (1), request review of the assignment. The Commissioner of Social Security shall conduct such review if the Commissioner finds the operator provided evidence with the request constituting a prima facie case of error.

(3) RESULTS OF REVIEW.—

(A) ERROR.—If the Commissioner of Social Security determines under a review under paragraph (2) that an assignment was in error—

(i) the Commissioner shall notify the assigned operator and the trustees of the Combined Fund and the trustees shall reduce the premiums of the operator under section 9704 by (or if there are no such premiums, repay) all premiums paid under section 9704 with respect to the eligible beneficiary, and

(ii) the Commissioner shall review the beneficiary's record for reassignment under subsection (a).

(B) NO ERROR.—If the Commissioner of Social Security determines under a review conducted under paragraph (2) that no error occurred, the Commissioner shall notify the assigned operator.

(4) DETERMINATIONS.—Any determination by the Commissioner of Social Security under paragraph (2) or (3) shall be final.

(5) PAYMENT PENDING REVIEW.—An assigned operator shall pay the premiums under section 9704 pending review by the Commissioner of Social Security or by a court under this subsection.

(6) PRIVATE ACTIONS.—Nothing in this section shall preclude the right of any person to bring a separate civil action against another person for responsibility for assigned premiums, notwithstanding any prior decision by the Commissioner.

Amendments

• **1994, Social Security Independence and Program Improvements Act of 1994 (P.L. 103-296)**

P.L. 103-296, §108(h)(9)(B)(i)-(ii):

Amended Code Sec. 9706 by striking "Secretary of Health and Human Services" each place it appears and inserting "Commissioner of Social Security" and by striking "Secretary" each place it appears and inserting "Commissioner". **Effective** 3-31-95.

[Sec. 9706(g)]

(g) CONFIDENTIALITY OF INFORMATION.—Any person to which information is provided by the Commissioner of Social Security under this section shall not disclose such information except in any proceedings related to this section. Any civil or criminal penalty which is applicable to an unauthorized disclosure under section 6103 shall apply to any unauthorized disclosure under this section.

COAL INDUSTRY HEALTH BENEFITS

Amendments

• **1994, Social Security Independence and Program Improvements Act of 1994 (P.L. 103-296)**

P.L. 103-296, §108(h)(9)(B)(i)-(ii):

Amended Code Sec. 9706 by striking "Secretary of Health and Human Services" each place it appears and inserting "Commissioner of Social Security" and by striking "Secretary" each place it appears and inserting "Commissioner". **Effective** 3-31-95.

• **1992, Energy Policy Act of 1992 (P.L. 102-486)**

P.L. 102-486, §19143(a):

Added Code Sec. 9706. **Effective** 10-24-92.

[Sec. 9706(h)]

(h) ASSIGNMENTS AS OF OCTOBER 1, 2007.—

(1) IN GENERAL.—Subject to the premium obligation set forth in paragraph (3), the Commissioner of Social Security shall—

(A) revoke all assignments to persons other than 1988 agreement operators for purposes of assessing premiums for plan years beginning on and after October 1, 2007; and

(B) make no further assignments to persons other than 1988 agreement operators, except that no individual who becomes an unassigned beneficiary by reason of subparagraph (A) may be assigned to a 1988 agreement operator.

(2) REASSIGNMENT UPON PURCHASE.—This subsection shall not be construed to prohibit the reassignment under subsection (b)(2) of an eligible beneficiary.

(3) LIABILITY OF PERSONS DURING THREE FISCAL YEARS BEGINNING ON AND AFTER OCTOBER 1, 2007.—In the case of each of the fiscal years beginning on October 1, 2007, 2008, and 2009, each person other than a 1988 agreement operator shall pay to the Combined Fund the following percentage of the amount of annual premiums that such person would otherwise be required to pay under section 9704(a), determined on the basis of assignments in effect without regard to the revocation of assignments under paragraph (1)(A):

(A) For the fiscal year beginning on October 1, 2007, 55 percent.

(B) For the fiscal year beginning on October 1, 2008, 40 percent.

(C) For the fiscal year beginning on October 1, 2009, 15 percent.

Amendments

• **2006, Tax Relief and Health Care Act of 2006 (P.L. 109-432)**

P.L. 109-432, Division C, §212(a)(3):

Amended Code Sec. 9706 by adding at the end a new subsection (h). **Effective** for plan years of the Combined Fund beginning after 9-30-2006.

Part III—Enforcement

Sec. 9707.   Failure to pay premium.

[Sec. 9707]

SEC. 9707. FAILURE TO PAY PREMIUM.

[Sec. 9707(a)]

(a) FAILURES TO PAY.—

(1) PREMIUMS FOR ELIGIBLE BENEFICIARIES.—There is hereby imposed a penalty on the failure of any assigned operator to pay any premium required to be paid under section 9704 with respect to any eligible beneficiary.

(2) CONTRIBUTIONS REQUIRED UNDER THE MINING LAWS.—There is hereby imposed a penalty on the failure of any person to make a contribution required under section 402(h)(5)(B)(ii) of the Surface Mining Control and Reclamation Act of 1977 to a plan referred to in section 402(h)(2)(C) of such Act. For purposes of applying this section, each such required monthly contribution for the hours worked of any individual shall be treated as if it were a premium required to be paid under section 9704 with respect to an eligible beneficiary.

Amendments

• **2006, Tax Relief and Health Care Act of 2006 (P.L. 109-432)**

P.L. 109-432, Division C, §213(b)(1):

Amended Code Sec. 9707(a). **Effective** 12-20-2006. Prior to amendment, Code Sec. 9707(a) read as follows:

(a) GENERAL RULE.—There is hereby imposed a penalty on the failure of any assigned operator to pay any premium required to be paid under section 9704 with respect to any eligible beneficiary.

[Sec. 9707(b)]

(b) AMOUNT OF PENALTY.—The amount of the penalty imposed by subsection (a) on any failure with respect to any eligible beneficiary shall be $100 per day in the noncompliance period with respect to any such failure.

[Sec. 9707(c)]

(c) NONCOMPLIANCE PERIOD.—For purposes of this section, the term "noncompliance period" means, with respect to any failure to pay any premium or installment thereof, the period—

(1) beginning on the due date for such premium or installment, and

(2) ending on the date of payment of such premium or installment.

[Sec. 9707(d)]

(d) LIMITATIONS ON AMOUNT OF PENALTY.—

(1) IN GENERAL.—No penalty shall be imposed by subsection (a) on any failure during any period for which it is established to the satisfaction of the Secretary of the Treasury that none of the persons responsible for such failure knew, or exercising reasonable diligence would have known, that such failure existed.

(2) CORRECTIONS.—No penalty shall be imposed by subsection (a) on any failure if—

(A) such failure was due to reasonable cause and not to willful neglect, and

(B) such failure is corrected during the 30-day period beginning on the 1st date that any of the persons responsible for such failure knew, or exercising reasonable diligence would have known, that such failure existed.

(3) WAIVER.—In the case of a failure that is due to reasonable cause and not to willful neglect, the Secretary of the Treasury may waive all or part of the penalty imposed by subsection (a) for failures to the extent that the Secretary determines, in his sole discretion, that the payment of such penalty would be excessive relative to the failure involved.

COAL INDUSTRY HEALTH BENEFITS

Amendments

• **1996, Small Business Job Protection Act of 1996 (P.L. 104-188)**
P.L. 104-188, §1704(t)(65):
Amended Code Sec. 9707(d)(1) by striking "diligence," and inserting "diligence".
Effective 8-20-96.

[Sec. 9707(e)]

(e) LIABILITY FOR PENALTY.—The person failing to meet the requirements of section 9704 shall be liable for the penalty imposed by subsection (a).

[Sec. 9707(f)]

(f) TREATMENT.—For purposes of this title, the penalty imposed by this section shall be treated in the same manner as the tax imposed by section 4980B.

Amendments

• **1992, Energy Policy Act of 1992 (P.L. 102-486)**
P.L. 102-486, §19143(a):
Added Code Sec. 9707. **Effective** 10-24-92.

Part IV—Other Provisions

Sec. 9708.   Effect on pending claims or obligations.

[Sec. 9708]

SEC. 9708. EFFECT ON PENDING CLAIMS OR OBLIGATIONS.

All liability for contributions to the Combined Fund that arises on and after February 1, 1993, shall be determined exclusively under this chapter, including all liability for contributions to the 1950 UMWA Benefit Plan and the 1974 UMWA Benefit Plan for coal production on and after February 1, 1993. However, nothing in this chapter is intended to have any effect on any claims or obligations arising in connection with the 1950 UMWA Benefit Plan and the 1974 UMWA Benefit Plan as of February 1, 1993, including claims or obligations based on the "evergreen" clause found in the language of the 1950 UMWA Benefit Plan and the 1974 UMWA Benefit Plan. This chapter shall not be construed to affect any rights of subrogation of any 1988 agreement operator with respect to contributions due to the 1950 UMWA Benefit Plan or the 1974 UMWA Benefit Plan as of February 1, 1993.

Amendments

• **1992, Energy Policy Act of 1992 (P.L. 102-486)**
P.L. 102-486, §19143(a):
Added Code Sec. 9708. **Effective** 10-24-92.

Subchapter C—Health Benefits of Certain Miners

Part I.   Individual Employer Plans.
Part II.   1992 UMWA Benefit Plans.

Part I—Individual Employer Plans

Sec. 9711.   Continued Obligations of Individual Employer Plans.

[Sec. 9711]

SEC. 9711. CONTINUED OBLIGATIONS OF INDIVIDUAL EMPLOYER PLANS.

[Sec. 9711(a)]

(a) COVERAGE OF CURRENT RECIPIENTS.—The last signatory operator of any individual who, as of February 1, 1993, is receiving retiree health benefits from an individual employer plan maintained pursuant to a 1978 or subsequent coal wage agreement shall continue to provide health benefits coverage to such individual and the individual's eligible beneficiaries which is substantially the same as (and subject to all the limitations of) the coverage provided by such plan as of January 1, 1992. Such coverage shall continue to be provided for as long as the last signatory operator (and any related person) remains in business.

[Sec. 9711(b)]

(b) COVERAGE OF ELIGIBLE RECIPIENTS.—

(1) IN GENERAL.—The last signatory operator of any individual who, as of February 1, 1993, is not receiving retiree health benefits under the individual employer plan maintained by the last signatory operator pursuant to a 1978 or subsequent coal wage agreement, but has met the age and service requirements for eligibility to receive benefits under such plan as of such date, shall, at such time as such individual becomes eligible to receive benefits under such plan, provide health benefits coverage to such individual and the individual's eligible beneficiaries which is described in paragraph (2). This paragraph shall not apply to any individual who retired from the coal industry after September 30, 1994, or any eligible beneficiary of such individual.

(2) COVERAGE.—Subject to the provisions of subsection (d), health benefits coverage is described in this paragraph if it is substantially the same as (and subject to all the limitations of) the coverage provided by the individual employer plan as of January 1, 1992. Such coverage shall continue for as long as the last signatory operator (and any related person) remains in business.

[Sec. 9711(c)]

(c) JOINT AND SEVERAL LIABILITY OF RELATED PERSONS.—

(1) IN GENERAL.—Except as provided in paragraph (2), each related person of a last signatory operator to which subsection (a) or (b) applies shall be jointly and severally liable with the last signatory operator for the provision of health care coverage described in subsection (a) or (b).

(2) LIABILITY LIMITED IF SECURITY PROVIDED.—If—

(A) security meeting the requirements of paragraph (3) is provided by or on behalf of—

(i) any last signatory operator which is an assigned operator described in section 9704(j)(2), or

(ii) any related person to any last signatory operator described in clause (i), and

COAL INDUSTRY HEALTH BENEFITS

(B) the common parent of the controlled group of corporations described in section 9704(j)(2)(B) is jointly and severally liable for the provision of health care under this section which, but for this paragraph, would be required to be provided by the last signatory operator or related person,

then, as of the date the security is provided, such common parent (and no other person) shall be liable for the provision of health care under this section which the last signatory operator or related person would otherwise be required to provide. Security may be provided under this paragraph without regard to whether a payment was made under section 9704(j).

(3) SECURITY.—Security meets the requirements of this paragraph if—

(A) the security—

(i) is in the form of a bond, letter of credit, or cash escrow,

(ii) is provided to the trustees of the 1992 UMWA Benefit Plan solely for the purpose of paying premiums for beneficiaries who would be described in section 9712(b)(2)(B) if the requirements of this section were not met by the last signatory operator, and

(iii) is in an amount equal to 1 year of liability of the last signatory operator under this section, determined by using the average cost of such operator's liability during the prior 3 calendar years;

(B) the security is in addition to any other security required under any other provision of this title; and

(C) the security remains in place for 5 years.

(4) REFUNDS OF SECURITY.—The remaining amount of any security provided under this subsection (and earnings thereon) shall be refunded to the last signatory operator as of the earlier of—

(A) the termination of the obligations of the last signatory operator under this section, or

(B) the end of the 5-year period described in paragraph (3)(C).

Amendments

• **2018, Tax Technical Corrections Act of 2018 (P.L. 115-141)**

P.L. 115-141, § 401(a)(347), Div. U:

Amended Code Sec. 9711(c)(4)(B) by striking "paragraph (4)(C)" and inserting "paragraph (3)(C)". **Effective** 3-23-2018.

• **2006, Tax Relief and Health Care Act of 2006 (P.L. 109-432)**

P.L. 109-432, Division C, § 211(b):

Amended Code Sec. 9711(c). **Effective** 12-20-2006. Prior to amendment, Code Sec. 9711(c) read as follows:

(c) JOINT AND SEVERAL LIABILITY OF RELATED PERSONS.—Each related person of a last signatory operator to which subsection (a) or (b) applies shall be jointly and severally liable with the last signatory operator for the provision of health care coverage described in subsection (a) or (b).

[Sec. 9711(d)]

(d) MANAGED CARE AND COST CONTAINMENT.—The last signatory operator shall not be treated as failing to meet the requirements of subsection (a) or (b) if benefits are provided to eligible beneficiaries under managed care and cost containment rules and procedures described in section 9712(c) or agreed to by the last signatory operator and the United Mine Workers of America.

[Sec. 9711(e)]

(e) TREATMENT OF NONCOVERED EMPLOYEES.—The existence, level, and duration of benefits provided to former employees of a last signatory operator (and their eligible beneficiaries) who are not otherwise covered by this chapter and who are (or were) covered by a coal wage agreement shall only be determined by, and shall be subject to, collective bargaining, lawful unilateral action, or other applicable law.

[Sec. 9711(f)]

(f) ELIGIBLE BENEFICIARY.—For purposes of this section, the term "eligible beneficiary" means any individual who is eligible for health benefits under a plan described in subsection (a) or (b) by reason of the individual's relationship with the retiree described in such subsection (or to an individual who, based on service and employment history at the time of death, would have been so described but for such death).

[Sec. 9711(g)]

(g) RULES APPLICABLE TO THIS PART AND PART II.—For purposes of this part and part II—

(1) SUCCESSOR.—The term "last signatory operator" shall include a successor in interest of such operator.

(2) REASSIGNMENT UPON PURCHASE.—If a person becomes a successor of a last signatory operator after the enactment date, the last signatory operator may transfer any liability of such operator under this chapter with respect to an eligible beneficiary to such successor, and such successor shall be treated as the last signatory operator with respect to such eligible beneficiary for purposes of this chapter. Notwithstanding the preceding sentence, the last signatory operator transferring such assignment (and any related person) shall remain the guarantor of the benefits provided to the eligible beneficiary under this chapter. A last signatory operator shall notify the trustees of the 1992 UMWA Benefit Plan of any transfer described in this paragraph.

Amendments

• **1992, Energy Policy Act of 1992 (P.L. 102-486)**

P.L. 102-486, § 19143(a):

Added Code Sec. 9711. **Effective** 10-24-92.

Part II—1992 UMWA Benefit Plan

Sec. 9712.   Establishment and Coverage of 1992 UMWA Benefit Plan.

[Sec. 9712]

SEC. 9712. ESTABLISHMENT AND COVERAGE OF 1992 UMWA BENEFIT PLAN

[Sec. 9712(a)]

(a) CREATION OF PLAN.—

(1) IN GENERAL.—As soon as practicable after the enactment date, the settlors shall create a separate private plan which shall be known as the United Mine Workers of America 1992 Benefit Plan. For purposes of this title, the 1992 UMWA Benefit Plan shall be treated as an organization exempt from taxation under section 501(a). The settlors shall be responsible for designing the structure, administration and terms of the 1992 UMWA Benefit Plan, and for appointment and removal of the members of the board of trustees. The board of trustees shall initially consist of five members and shall thereafter be the number set by the settlors.

(2) TREATMENT OF PLAN.—The 1992 UMWA Benefit Plan shall be—

(A) a plan described in section 302(e)(5) of the Labor Management Relations Act, 1947 (29 U.S.C. 186(c)(5)),

(B) an employee welfare benefit plan within the meaning of section 3(1) of the Employee Retirement Income Security Act of 1974 (29 U.S.C. 1002(1)), and

(C) a multiemployer plan within the meaning of section 3(37) of such Act (29 U.S.C. 1002(37)).

COAL INDUSTRY HEALTH BENEFITS

(3) TRANSFERS UNDER OTHER FEDERAL STATUTES.—

(A) IN GENERAL.—The 1992 UMWA Benefit Plan shall include any amount transferred to the plan under subsections (h) and (i) of section 402 of the Surface Mining Control and Reclamation Act of 1977 (30 U.S.C. 1232).

(B) USE OF FUNDS.—Any amount transferred under subparagraph (A) for any fiscal year shall be used to provide the health benefits described in subsection (c) with respect to any beneficiary for whom no monthly per beneficiary premium is paid pursuant to paragraph (1)(A) or (3) of subsection (d).

(4) SPECIAL RULE FOR 1993 PLAN.—

(A) IN GENERAL.—The plan described in section 402(h)(2)(C) of the Surface Mining Control and Reclamation Act of 1977 (30 U.S.C. 1232(h)(2)(C)) shall include any amount transferred to the plan under subsections (h) and (i) of section 402 of the Surface Mining Control and Reclamation Act of 1977 (30 U.S.C. 1232).

(B) USE OF FUNDS.—Any amount transferred under subparagraph (A) for any fiscal year shall be used to provide the health benefits described in section 402(h)(2)(C)(i) of the Surface Mining Control and Reclamation Act of 1977 (30 U.S.C. 1232(h)(2)(C)(i)) to individuals described in section 402(h)(2)(C) of such Act (30 U.S.C. 1232(h)(2)(C)).

Amendments

- **2018, Tax Technical Corrections Act of 2018 (P.L. 115-141)**

P.L. 115-141, § 401(a)(348), Div. U:

Amended Code Sec. 9712(a)(4)(A) by inserting "section 402 of" after "subsections (h) and (i) of". Effective 3-23-2018.

- **2006, Tax Relief and Health Care Act of 2006 (P.L. 109-432)**

P.L. 109-432, Division C, § 212(b)(1):

Amended Code Sec. 9712(a) by adding at the end new paragraphs (3) and (4). Effective 12-20-2006.

[Sec. 9712(b)]

(b) COVERAGE REQUIREMENT.—

(1) IN GENERAL.—The 1992 UMWA Benefit Plan shall only provide health benefits coverage to any eligible beneficiary who is not eligible for benefits under the Combined Fund and shall not provide such coverage to any other individual.

(2) ELIGIBLE BENEFICIARY.—For purposes of this section, the term "eligible beneficiary" means an individual who—

(A) but for the enactment of this chapter, would be eligible to receive benefits from the 1950 UMWA Benefit Plan or the 1974 UMWA Benefit Plan, based upon age and service earned as of February 1, 1993; or

(B) with respect to whom coverage is required to be provided under section 9711, but who does not receive such coverage from the applicable last signatory operator or any related person,

and any individual who is eligible for benefits by reason of a relationship to an individual described in subparagraph (A) or (B). In no event shall the 1992 UMWA Benefit Plan provide health benefits coverage to any eligible beneficiary who is a coal industry retiree who retired from the coal industry after September 30, 1994, or any beneficiary of such individual.

[Sec. 9712(c)]

(c) HEALTH BENEFITS.—

(1) IN GENERAL.—The 1992 UMWA Benefit Plan shall provide health care benefits coverage to each eligible beneficiary which is substantially the same as (and subject to all the limitations of) coverage provided under the 1950 UMWA Benefit Plan and the 1974 UMWA Benefit Plan as of January 1, 1992.

(2) MANAGED CARE.—The 1992 UMWA Benefit Plan shall develop managed care and cost containment rules which shall be applicable to the payment of benefits under this subsection. Application of such rules shall not cause the plan to be treated as failing to meet the requirements of this subsection. Such rules shall preserve freedom of choice while reinforcing managed care network use by allowing a point of service decision as to whether a network medical provider will be used. Major elements of such rules may include, but are not limited to, elements described in paragraph (3).

(3) MAJOR ELEMENTS OF RULES.—Elements described in this paragraph are—

(A) implementing formulary for drugs and subjecting the prescription program to a rigorous review of appropriate use,

(B) obtaining a unit price discount in exchange for patient volume and preferred provider status with the amount of the potential discount varying by geographic region,

(C) limiting benefit payments to physicians to the allowable charge under title XVIII of the Social Security Act, while protecting beneficiaries from balance billing by providers,

(D) utilizing, in the claims payment function "appropriateness of service" protocols under title XVIII of the Social Security Act if more stringent,

(E) creating mandatory utilization review (UR) procedures, but placing the responsibility to follow such procedures on the physician or hospital, not the beneficiaries,

(F) selecting the most efficient physicians and state-of-the-art utilization management techniques, including ambulatory care techniques, for medical services delivered by the managed care network, and

(G) utilizing a managed care network provider system, as practiced in the health care industry, at the time medical services are needed (point-of-service) in order to receive maximum benefits available under this subsection.

(4) LAST SIGNATORY OPERATORS.—The board of trustees of the 1992 UMWA Benefit Plan shall permit any last signatory operator required to maintain an individual employer plan under section 9711 to utilize the managed care and cost containment rules and programs developed under this subsection if the operator elects to do so.

(5) STANDARDS OF QUALITY.—Any managed care system or cost containment adopted by the board of trustees of the 1992 UMWA Benefit Plan or by a last signatory operator may not be implemented unless it is approved by, and meets the standards of quality adopted by, a medical peer review panel, which has been established—

(A) by the settlors, or

(B) by the United Mine Workers of America and a last signatory operator or group of operators.

Standards of quality shall include accessibility to medical care, taking into account that accessibility requirements may differ depending on the nature of the medical need.

[Sec. 9712(d)]

(d) GUARANTEE OF BENEFITS.—

(1) IN GENERAL.—All 1988 last signatory operators shall be responsible for financing the benefits described in subsection (c) by meeting the following requirements in accordance with the contribution requirements established in the 1992 UMWA Benefit Plan:

(A) The payment of a monthly per beneficiary premium by each 1988 last signatory operator for each eligible beneficiary of such operator who is described in subsection (b)(2) and who is receiving benefits under the 1992 UMWA Benefit Plan.

COAL INDUSTRY HEALTH BENEFITS

(B) The provision of a security (in the form of a bond, letter of credit, or cash escrow) in an amount equal to a portion of the projected future cost to the 1992 UMWA Benefit Plan of providing health benefits for eligible and potentially eligible beneficiaries attributable to the 1988 last signatory operator.

(C) If the amounts transferred under subsection (a)(3) are less than the amounts required to be transferred to the 1992 UMWA Benefit Plan under subsections (h) and (i) of section 402 of the Surface Mining Control and Reclamation Act of 1977 (30 U.S.C. 1232), the payment of an additional backstop premium by each 1988 last signatory operator which is equal to such operator's share of the amounts required to be so transferred but which were not so transferred, determined on the basis of the number of eligible and potentially eligible beneficiaries attributable to the operator.

(2) ADJUSTMENTS.—The 1992 UMWA Benefit Plan shall provide for—

(A) annual adjustments of the per beneficiary premium to cover changes in the cost of providing benefits to eligible beneficiaries, and

(B) adjustments as necessary to the annual backstop premium to reflect changes in the cost of providing benefits to eligible beneficiaries for whom per beneficiary premiums are not paid.

(3) ADDITIONAL LIABILITY.—Any last signatory operator who is not a 1988 last signatory operator shall pay the monthly per beneficiary premium under paragraph (1)(A) for each eligible beneficiary described in such paragraph attributable to that operator.

(4) JOINT AND SEVERAL LIABILITY.—A 1988 last signatory operator or last signatory operator described in paragraph (3), and any related person to any such operator, shall be jointly and severally liable with such operator for any amount required to be paid by such operator under this section. The provisions of section 9711(c)(2) shall apply to any last signatory operator described in such section (without regard to whether security is provided under such section, a payment is made under section 9704(j), or both) and if security meeting the requirements of section 9711(c)(3) is provided, the common parent described in section 9711(c)(2)(B) shall be exclusively responsible for any liability for premiums under this section which, but for this sentence, would be required to be paid by the last signatory operator or any related person.

(5) DEDUCTIBILITY.—Any premium required by this section shall be deductible without regard to any limitation on deductibility based on the prefunding of health benefits.

(6) 1988 LAST SIGNATORY OPERATOR.—For purposes of this section, the term "1988 last signatory operator" means a last signatory operator which is a 1988 agreement operator.

Amendments

• **2006, Tax Relief and Health Care Act of 2006 (P.L. 109-432)**

P.L. 109-432, Division C, § 211(c):

Amended Code Sec. 9712(d)(4) by adding at the end a new sentence. **Effective** 12-20-2006.

P.L. 109-432, Division C, § 212(b)(2)(A):

Amended Code Sec. 9712(d)(1). **Effective** for fiscal years beginning on or after 10-1-2010. Prior to amendment, Code Sec. 9712(d)(1) read as follows:

(1) IN GENERAL.—All 1988 last signatory operators shall be responsible for financing the benefits described in subsection (c), in accordance with contribution requirements established in the 1992 UMWA Benefit Plan. Such contribution requirements, which shall be applied uniformly to each 1988 last signatory operator, on the basis of the number of eligible and potentially eligible beneficiaries attributable to each operator, shall include:

(A) the payment of an annual prefunding premium for all eligible and potentially eligible beneficiaries attributable to a 1988 last signatory operator,

(B) the payment of a monthly per beneficiary premium by each 1988 last signatory operator for each eligible beneficiary of such operator who is described in subsection (b)(2) and who is receiving benefits under the 1992 UMWA Benefit Plan, and

(C) the provision of security (in the form of a bond, letter of credit or cash escrow) in an amount equal to a portion of the projected future cost to the 1992 UMWA Benefit Plan of providing health benefits for eligible and potentially eligible beneficiaries attributable to the 1988 last signatory operator. If a 1988 last signatory operator is unable to provide the security required, the 1992 UMWA Benefit Plan shall require the operator to pay an annual prefunding premium that is greater than the premium otherwise applicable.

P.L. 109-432, Division C, § 212(b)(2)(B)(i)-(ii):

Amended Code Sec. 9712(d) by striking "prefunding" and inserting "backstop" in paragraph (2)(B), and by striking "paragraph (1)(B)" and inserting "paragraph (1)(A)" in paragraph (3). **Effective** for fiscal years beginning on or after 10-1-2010.

• **1992, Energy Policy Act of 1992 (P.L. 102-486)**

P.L. 102-486, § 19143(a):

Added Code Sec. 9712. **Effective** 10-24-92.

Subchapter D—Other Provisions

Sec. 9721. Civil enforcement.
Sec. 9722. Sham transactions.

[Sec. 9721]

SEC. 9721. CIVIL ENFORCEMENT.

The provisions of section 4301 of the Employee Retirement Income Security Act of 1974 shall apply, in the same manner as any claim arising out of an obligation to pay withdrawal liability under subtitle E of title IV of such Act, to any claim—

(1) arising out of an obligation to pay any amount required to be paid by this chapter; or

(2) arising out of an obligation to pay any amount required by section 402(h)(5)(B)(ii) of the Surface Mining Control and Reclamation Act of 1977 (30 U.S.C. 1232(h)(5)(B)(ii)).

Amendments

• **2006, Tax Relief and Health Care Act of 2006 (P.L. 109-432)**

P.L. 109-432, Division C, § 213(b)(2):

Amended Code Sec. 9721. **Effective** 12-20-2006. Prior to amendment, Code Sec. 9721 read as follows:

SEC. 9721. CIVIL ENFORCEMENT.

The provisions of section 4301 of the Employee Retirement Income Security Act of 1974 shall apply to any claim arising out of an obligation to pay any amount required to be paid by this chapter in the same manner as any claim arising out of an obligation to pay withdrawal liability under subtitle E of title IV of such Act. For purposes of the preceding sentence, a signatory operator and related persons shall be treated in the same manner as employers.

Amendments

• **1992, Energy Policy Act of 1992 (P.L. 102-486)**

P.L. 102-486, § 19143(a):

Added Code Sec. 9721. **Effective** 10-24-92.

[Sec. 9722]

SEC. 9722. SHAM TRANSACTIONS.

If a principal purpose of any transaction is to evade or avoid liability under this chapter, this chapter shall be applied (and such liability shall be imposed) without regard to such transaction.

Amendments

• **1992, Energy Policy Act of 1992 (P.L. 102-486)**

P.L. 102-486, § 19143(a):

Added Code Sec. 9722. **Effective** 10-24-92.

[The next page is 5601.]

Subtitle K—Group Health Plan Requirements

Chapter 100. Group health plan requirements.

CHAPTER 100—GROUP HEALTH PLAN REQUIREMENTS

Subchapter A. Requirements relating to portability, access, and renewability.
Subchapter B. Other requirements.
Subchapter C. General provisions.

Subchapter A—Requirements Relating to Portability, Access, and Renewability

Sec. 9801. Increased portability through limitation on preexisting condition exclusions.
Sec. 9802. Prohibiting discrimination against individual participants and beneficiaries based on health status.
Sec. 9803. Guaranteed renewability in multiemployer plans and certain multiple employer welfare arrangements.

[Sec. 9801]

SEC. 9801. INCREASED PORTABILITY THROUGH LIMITATION ON PREEXISTING CONDITION EXCLUSIONS.

[Sec. 9801(a)]

(a) LIMITATION ON PREEXISTING CONDITION EXCLUSION PERIOD; CREDITING FOR PERIODS OF PREVIOUS COVERAGE.—Subject to subsection (d), a group health plan may, with respect to a participant or beneficiary, impose a preexisting condition exclusion only if—

(1) such exclusion relates to a condition (whether physical or mental), regardless of the cause of the condition, for which medical advice, diagnosis, care, or treatment was recommended or received within the 6-month period ending on the enrollment date;

(2) such exclusion extends for a period of not more than 12 months (or 18 months in the case of a late enrollee) after the enrollment date; and

(3) the period of any such preexisting condition exclusion is reduced by the length of the aggregate of the periods of creditable coverage (if any) applicable to the participant or beneficiary as of the enrollment date.

[Sec. 9801(b)]

(b) DEFINITIONS.—For purposes of this section—

(1) PREEXISTING CONDITION EXCLUSION.—

(A) IN GENERAL.—The term "preexisting condition exclusion" means, with respect to coverage, a limitation or exclusion of benefits relating to a condition based on the fact that the condition was present before the date of enrollmentfor such coverage, whether or not any medical advice, diagnosis, care, or treatment was recommended or received before such date.

(B) TREATMENT OF GENETIC INFORMATION.—For purposes of this section, genetic information shall not be treated as a condition described in subsection (a)(1) in the absence of a diagnosis of the condition related to such information.

(2) ENROLLMENT DATE.—The term "enrollment date" means, with respect to an individual covered under a group health plan, the date of enrollment of the individual in the plan or, if earlier, the first day of the waiting period for such enrollment.

(3) LATE ENROLLEE.—The term "late enrollee" means, with respect to coverage under a group health plan, a participant or beneficiary who enrolls under the plan other than during—

(A) the first period in which the individual is eligible to enroll under the plan, or

(B) a special enrollment period under subsection (f).

(4) WAITING PERIOD.—The term "waiting period" means, with respect to a group health plan and an individual who is a potential participant or beneficiary in the plan, the period that must pass with respect to the individual before theindividual is eligible to be covered for benefits under the terms of the plan.

[Sec. 9801(c)]

(c) RULES RELATING TO CREDITING PREVIOUS COVERAGE.—

(1) CREDITABLE COVERAGE DEFINED.—For purposes of this part, the term "creditable coverage" means, with respect to an individual, coverage of the individual under any of the following:

(A) A group health plan.
(B) Health insurance coverage.
(C) Part A or part B of title XVIII of the Social Security Act.
(D) Title XIX of the Social Security Act, other than coverage consisting solely of benefits under section 1928.
(E) Chapter 55 of title 10, United States Code.
(F) A medical care program of the Indian Health Service or of a tribal organization.
(G) A State health benefits risk pool.
(H) A health plan offered under chapter 89 of title 5, United States Code.
(I) A public health plan (as defined in regulations).
(J) A health benefit plan under section 5(e) of the Peace Corps Act (22 U.S.C. 2504(e).

Such term does not include coverage consisting solely of coverage of excepted benefits (as defined in section 9832(c)).

(2) NOT COUNTING PERIODS BEFORE SIGNIFICANT BREAKS IN COVERAGE.—

(A) IN GENERAL.—A period of creditable coverage shall not be counted, with respect to enrollment of an individual under a group health plan, if, after such period and before the enrollment date, there was a 63-day period during all ofwhich the individual was not covered under any creditable coverage.

(B) WAITING PERIOD NOT TREATED AS A BREAK IN COVERAGE.—For purposes of subparagraph (A) and subsection (d)(4), any period that an individual is in a waiting period for any coverage under a group health plan or is in an affiliation period shall not be taken into account in determining the continuous period under subparagraph (A).

(C) AFFILIATION PERIOD.—

(i) IN GENERAL.—For purposes of this section, the term "affiliation period" means a period which, under the terms of the health insurance coverage offered by the health maintenance organization, must expire before the health insurance coverage becomes effective. During such an affiliation period, the organization is not required to provide health care services or benefits and no premium shall be charged to the participant or beneficiary.

(ii) BEGINNING.—Such period shall begin on the enrollment date.

GROUP HEALTH PLAN REQUIREMENTS

(iii) RUNS CONCURRENTLY WITH WAITING PERIODS.—Any such affiliation period shall run concurrently with any waiting period under the plan.

(D) TAA-ELIGIBLE INDIVIDUALS.—In the case of plan years beginning before January 1, 2014—

(i) TAA PRE-CERTIFICATION PERIOD RULE.—In the case of a TAA-eligible individual, the period beginning on the date the individual has a TAA-related loss of coverage and ending on the date which is 7 days after the date of the issuance by the Secretary (or by any person or entity designated by the Secretary) of a qualified health insurance costs credit eligibility certificate for such individual for purposes of section 7527 shall not be taken into account in determining the continuous period under subparagraph (A).

(ii) DEFINITIONS.—The terms "TAA-eligible individual" and "TAA-related loss of coverage" have the meanings given such terms in section 4980B(f)(5)(C)(iv).

(3) METHOD OF CREDITING COVERAGE.—

(A) STANDARD METHOD.—Except as otherwise provided under subparagraph (B), for purposes of applying subsection (a)(3), a group health plan shall count a period of creditable coverage without regard to the specific benefits for which coverage is offered during the period.

(B) ELECTION OF ALTERNATIVE METHOD.—A group health plan may elect to apply subsection (a)(3) based on coverage of any benefits within each of several classes or categories of benefits specified in regulations rather than as provided under subparagraph (A). Such election shall be made on a uniform basis for all participants and beneficiaries. Under such election a group health plan shall count a period of creditable coverage with respect to any class or category of benefits if any level of benefits is covered within such class or category.

(C) PLAN NOTICE.—In the case of an election with respect to a group health plan under subparagraph (B), the plan shall—

(i) prominently state in any disclosure statements concerning the plan, and state to each enrollee at the time of enrollment under the plan, that the plan has made such election, and

(ii) include in such statements a description of the effect of this election.

(4) ESTABLISHMENT OF PERIOD.—Periods of creditable coverage with respect to an individual shall be established through presentation of certifications described in subsection (e) or in such other manner as may be specified in regulations.

Amendments

• **2011, Trade Adjustment Assistance Extension Act of 2011 (P.L. 112-40)**

P.L. 112-40, §242(a)(1):

Amended Code Sec. 9801(c)(2)(D) by striking "February 13, 2011" and inserting "January 1, 2014". **Effective** generally for plan years beginning after 2-12-2011. For transitional rules, see Act Sec. 242(b)(2)(A)-(C), below.

P.L. 112-40, §242(b)(2)(A)-(C), provides:

(2) TRANSITIONAL RULES.—

(A) BENEFIT DETERMINATIONS.—Notwithstanding the amendments made by this section (and the provisions of law amended thereby), a plan shall not be required to modify benefit determinations for the period beginning on February 13, 2011, and ending 30 days after the date of the enactment of this Act, but a plan shall not fail to be qualified health insurance within the meaning of section 35(e) of the Internal Revenue Code of 1986 during this period merely due to such failure to modify benefit determinations.

(B) GUIDANCE CONCERNING PERIODS BEFORE 30 DAYS AFTER ENACTMENT.—Except as provided in subparagraph (A), the Secretary of the Treasury (or his designee), in consultation with the Secretary of Health and Human Services and the Secretary of Labor, may issue regulations or other guidance regarding the scope of the application of the amendments made by this section to periods before the date which is 30 days after the date of the enactment of this Act.

(C) SPECIAL RULE RELATING TO CERTAIN LOSS OF COVERAGE.—In the case of a TAA-related loss of coverage (as defined in section 4980B(f)(5)(C)(iv) of the Internal Revenue Code of 1986) that occurs during the period beginning on February 13, 2011, and ending 30 days after the date of the enactment of this Act, the 7-day period described in section 9801(c)(2)(D) of the Internal Revenue Code of 1986, section 701(c)(2)(C) of the Employee Retirement Income Security Act of 1974, and section 2701(c)(2)(C) of the Public Health Service Act shall be extended until 30 days after such date of enactment.

• **2010, Omnibus Trade Act of 2010 (P.L. 111-344)**

P.L. 111-344, §114(a):

Amended Code Sec. 9801(c)(2)(D) by striking "January 1, 2011" and inserting "February 13, 2011". **Effective** for plan years beginning after 12-31-2010.

• **2009, TAA Health Coverage Improvement Act of 2009 (P.L. 111-5)**

P.L. 111-5, §1899D(a):

Amended Code Sec. 9801(c)(2) by adding at the end a new subparagraph (D). **Effective** for plan years beginning after 2-17-2009.

• **1997, Taxpayer Relief Act of 1997 (P.L. 105-34)**

P.L. 105-34, §1531(b)(1)(A):

Amended Code Sec. 9801(c)(1) by striking "section 9805(c)" and inserting "section 9832(c)". **Effective** with respect to group health plans for plan years beginning on or after 1-1-98.

[Sec. 9801(d)]

(d) EXCEPTIONS.—

(1) EXCLUSION NOT APPLICABLE TO CERTAIN NEWBORNS.—Subject to paragraph (4), a group health plan may not impose any preexisting condition exclusion in the case of an individual who, as of the last day of the 30-day period beginning with the date of birth, is covered under creditable coverage.

(2) EXCLUSION NOT APPLICABLE TO CERTAIN ADOPTED CHILDREN.—Subject to paragraph (4), a group health plan may not impose any preexisting condition exclusion in the case of a child who is adopted or placed for adoption before attaining 18 years of age and who, as of the last day of the 30-day period beginning on the date of the adoption or placement for adoption, is covered under creditable coverage. The previous sentence shall not apply to coverage before the date of such adoption or placement for adoption.

(3) EXCLUSION NOT APPLICABLE TO PREGNANCY.—For purposes of this section, a group health plan may not impose any preexisting condition exclusion relating to pregnancy as a preexisting condition.

(4) LOSS IF BREAK IN COVERAGE.—Paragraphs (1) and (2) shall no longer apply to an individual after the end of the first 63-day period during all of which the individual was not covered under any creditable coverage.

[Sec. 9801(e)]

(e) CERTIFICATIONS AND DISCLOSURE OF COVERAGE.—

(1) REQUIREMENT FOR CERTIFICATION OF PERIOD OF CREDITABLE COVERAGE.—

(A) IN GENERAL.—A group health plan shall provide the certification described in subparagraph (B)—

(i) at the time an individual ceases to be covered under the plan or otherwise becomes covered under a COBRA continuation provision,

(ii) in the case of an individual becoming covered under such a provision, at the time the individual ceases to be covered under such provision, and

(iii) on the request on behalf of an individual made not later than 24 months after the date of cessation of the coverage described in clause (i) or (ii), whichever is later.

The certification under clause (i) may be provided, to the extent practicable, at a time consistent with notices required under any applicable COBRA continuation provision.

(B) CERTIFICATION.—The certification described in this subparagraph is a written certification of—

GROUP HEALTH PLAN REQUIREMENTS

(i) the period of creditable coverage of the individual under such plan and the coverage under such COBRA continuation provision, and

(ii) the waiting period (if any) (and affiliation period, if applicable) imposed with respect to the individual for any coverage under such plan.

(C) ISSUER COMPLIANCE.—To the extent that medical care under a group health plan consists of health insurance coverage offered in connection with the plan, the plan is deemed to have satisfied the certification requirement under this paragraph if the issuer provides for such certification in accordance with this paragraph.

(2) DISCLOSURE OF INFORMATION ON PREVIOUS BENEFITS.—

(A) IN GENERAL.—In the case of an election described in subsection (c)(3)(B) by a group health plan, if the plan enrolls an individual for coverage under the plan and the individual provides a certification of coverage of the individual under paragraph (1)—

(i) upon request of such plan, the entity which issued the certification provided by the individual shall promptly disclose to such requesting plan information on coverage of classes and categories of health benefits available under such entity's plan, and

(ii) such entity may charge the requesting plan or issuer for the reasonable cost of disclosing such information.

(3) REGULATIONS.—The Secretary shall establish rules to prevent an entity's failure to provide information under paragraph (1) or (2) with respect to previous coverage of an individual from adversely affecting any subsequent coverage of the individual under another group health plan or health insurance coverage.

[Sec. 9801(f)]

(f) SPECIAL ENROLLMENT PERIODS.—

(1) INDIVIDUALS LOSING OTHER COVERAGE.—A group health plan shall permit an employee who is eligible, but not enrolled, for coverage under the terms of the plan (or a dependent of such an employee if the dependent is eligible, but not enrolled, for coverage under such terms) to enroll for coverage under the terms of the plan if each of the following conditions is met:

(A) The employee or dependent was covered under a group health plan or had health insurance coverage at the time coverage was previously offered to the employee or individual.

(B) The employee stated in writing at such time that coverage under a group health plan or health insurance coverage was the reason for declining enrollment, but only if the plan sponsor (or the health insurance issuer offering healthinsurance coverage in connection with the plan) required such a statement at such time and provided the employee with notice of such requirement (and the consequences of such requirement) at such time.

(C) The employee's or dependent's coverage described in subparagraph (A)—

(i) was under a COBRA continuation provision and the coverage under such provision was exhausted; or

(ii) was not under such a provision and either the coverage was terminated as a result of loss of eligibility for the coverage (including as a result of legal separation, divorce, death, termination of employment, or reduction in the number of hours of employment) or employer contributions towards such coverage were terminated.

(D) Under the terms of the plan, the employee requests such enrollment not later than 30 days after the date of exhaustion of coverage described in subparagraph (C)(i) or termination of coverage or employer contribution described in subparagraph (C)(ii).

(2) FOR DEPENDENT BENEFICIARIES.—

(A) IN GENERAL.—If—

(i) a group health plan makes coverage available with respect to a dependent of an individual,

(ii) the individual is a participant under the plan (or has met any waiting period applicable to becoming a participant under the plan and is eligible to be enrolled under the plan but for a failure to enroll during a previous enrollment period), and

(iii) a person becomes such a dependent of the individual through marriage, birth, or adoption or placement for adoption,

the group health plan shall provide for a dependent special enrollment period described in subparagraph (B) during which the person (or, if not otherwise enrolled, the individual) may be enrolled under the plan as a dependent of the individual, and in the case of the birth or adoption of a child, the spouse of the individual may be enrolled as a dependent of the individual if such spouse is otherwise eligible for coverage.

(B) DEPENDENT SPECIAL ENROLLMENT PERIOD.—The dependent special enrollment period under this subparagraph shall be a period of not less than 30 days and shall begin on the later of—

(i) the date dependent coverage is made available, or

(ii) the date of the marriage, birth, or adoption or placement for adoption (as the case may be) described in subparagraph (A)(iii).

(C) NO WAITING PERIOD.—If an individual seeks coverage of a dependent during the first 30 days of such a dependent special enrollment period, the coverage of the dependent shall become effective—

(i) in the case of marriage, not later than the first day of the first month beginning after the date the completed request for enrollment is received;

(ii) in the case of a dependent's birth, as of the date of such birth; or

(iii) in the case of a dependent's adoption or placement for adoption, the date of such adoption or placement for adoption.

(3) SPECIAL RULES RELATING TO MEDICAID AND CHIP.—

(A) IN GENERAL.—A group health plan shall permit an employee who is eligible, but not enrolled, for coverage under the terms of the plan (or a dependent of such an employee if the dependent is eligible, but not enrolled, for coverage under such terms) to enroll for coverage under the terms of the plan if either of the following conditions is met:

(i) TERMINATION OF MEDICAID OR CHIP COVERAGE.—The employee or dependent is covered under a Medicaid plan under title XIX of the Social Security Act or under a State child health plan under title XXI of such Act and coverage of the employee or dependent under such a plan is terminated as a result of loss of eligibility for such coverage and the employee requests coverage under the group health plan not later than 60 days after the date of termination of such coverage.

(ii) ELIGIBILITY FOR EMPLOYMENT ASSISTANCE UNDER MEDICAID OR CHIP.—The employee or dependent becomes eligible for assistance, with respect to coverage under the group health plan under such Medicaid plan or State child health plan (including under any waiver or demonstration project conducted under or in relation to such a plan), if the employee requests coverage under the group health plan not later than 60 days after the date the employee or dependent is determined to be eligible for such assistance.

(B) EMPLOYEE OUTREACH AND DISCLOSURE.—

(i) OUTREACH TO EMPLOYEES REGARDING AVAILABILITY OF MEDICAID AND CHIP COVERAGE.—

(I) IN GENERAL.—Each employer that maintains a group health plan in a State that provides medical assistance under a State Medicaid plan under title XIX of the Social Security Act, or child health assistance under a State child health plan under title XXI of such Act, in the form of premium assistance for the purchase of coverage under a group health plan, shall provide to each

GROUP HEALTH PLAN REQUIREMENTS

employee a written notice informing the employee of potential opportunities then currently available in the State in which the employee resides for premium assistance under such plans for health coverage of the employee or the employee's dependents. For purposes of compliance with this clause, the employer may use any State-specific model notice developed in accordance with section 701(f)(3)(B)(i)(II) of the Employee Retirement Income Security Act of 1974 (29 U.S.C. 1181(f)(3)(B)(i)(II)).

(II) OPTION TO PROVIDE CONCURRENT WITH PROVISION OF PLAN MATERIALS TO EMPLOYEE.—An employer may provide the model notice applicable to the State in which an employee resides concurrent with the furnishing of materials notifying the employee of health plan eligibility, concurrent with materials provided to the employee in connection with an open season or election process conducted under the plan, or concurrent with the furnishing of the summary plan description as provided in section 104(b) of the Employee Retirement Income Security Act of 1974 (29 U.S.C. 1024).

(ii) DISCLOSURE ABOUT GROUP HEALTH PLAN BENEFITS TO STATES FOR MEDICAID AND CHIP ELIGIBLE INDIVIDUALS.—In the case of a participant or beneficiary of a group health plan who is covered under a Medicaid plan of a State under title XIX of the Social Security Act or under a State child health plan under title XXI of such Act, the plan administrator of the group health plan shall disclose to the State, upon request, information about the benefits available under the group health plan in sufficient specificity, as determined under regulations of the Secretary of Health and Human Services in consultation with the Secretary that require use of the model coverage coordination disclosure form developed under section 311(b)(1)(C) of the Children's Health Insurance Program Reauthorization Act of 2009, so as to permit the State to make a determination (under paragraph (2)(B), (3), or (10) of section 2105(c) of the Social Security Act or otherwise) concerning the cost-effectiveness of the State providing medical or child health assistance through premium assistance for the purchase of coverage under such group health plan and in order for the State to provide supplemental benefits required under paragraph (10)(E) of such section or other authority.

Amendments

- **2009, Children's Health Insurance Program Reauthorization Act of 2009 (P.L. 111-3)**

P.L. 111-3, §311(a):

Amended Code Sec. 9801(f) by adding at the end a new paragraph (3). For the **effective** date, see Act Sec. 3, below.

P.L. 111-3, §3, provides:

SEC. 3. GENERAL EFFECTIVE DATE; EXCEPTION FOR STATE LEGISLATION; CONTINGENT EFFECTIVE DATE; RELIANCE ON LAW.

(a) GENERAL EFFECTIVE DATE.—Unless otherwise provided in this Act, subject to subsections (b) through (d), this Act (and the amendments made by this Act) shall take effect on April 1, 2009, and shall apply to child health assistance and medical assistance provided on or after that date.

(b) EXCEPTION FOR STATE LEGISLATION.—In the case of a State plan under title XIX or State child health plan under XXI of the Social Security Act, which the Secretary of Health and Human Services determines requires State legislation in order for the respective plan to meet one or more additional requirements imposed by amendments made by this Act, the respective plan shall not be regarded as failing to comply with the requirements of such title solely on the basis of its failure to meet such an additional requirement before the first day of the first calendar quarter beginning after the close of the first regular session of the State legislature that begins after the date of enactment of this Act. For purposes of the previous sentence, in the case of a State that has a 2-year legislative session, each year of the session shall be considered to be a separate regular session of the State legislature.

(c) COORDINATION OF CHIP FUNDING FOR FISCAL YEAR 2009.—Notwithstanding any other provision of law, insofar as funds have been appropriated under section 2104(a)(11), 2104(k), or 2104(l) of the Social Security Act, as amended by section 201 of Public Law 110–173, to provide allotments to States under CHIP for fiscal year 2009—

(1) any amounts that are so appropriated that are not so allotted and obligated before April 1, 2009 are rescinded; and

(2) any amount provided for CHIP allotments to a State under this Act (and the amendments made by this Act) for such fiscal year shall be reduced by the amount of such appropriations so allotted and obligated before such date.

(d) RELIANCE ON LAW.—With respect to amendments made by this Act (other than title VII) that become effective as of a date—

(1) such amendments are effective as of such date whether or not regulations implementing such amendments have been issued; and

(2) Federal financial participation for medical assistance or child health assistance furnished under title XIX or XXI, respectively, of the Social Security Act on or after such date by a State in good faith reliance on such amendments before the date of promulgation of final regulations, if any, to carry out such amendments (or before the date of guidance, if any, regarding the implementation of such amendments) shall not be denied on the basis of the State's failure to comply with such regulations or guidance.

- **1996, Health Insurance Portability and Accountability Act of 1996 (P.L. 104-191)**

P.L. 104-191, §401(a):

Amended the Internal Revenue Code of 1986 by adding at the end Code Secs. 9801-9806. For the **effective** date, see Act Sec. 401(c), below.

P.L. 104-191, §401(c), provides:

(c) EFFECTIVE DATE.—

(1) IN GENERAL.—The amendments made by this section shall apply to plan years beginning after June 30, 1997.

(2) DETERMINATION OF CREDITABLE COVERAGE.—

(A) PERIOD OF COVERAGE.—

(i) IN GENERAL.—Subject to clause (ii), no period before July 1, 1996, shall be taken into account under chapter 100 of the Internal Revenue Code of 1986 (as added by this section) in determining creditable coverage.

(ii) SPECIAL RULE FOR CERTAIN PERIODS.—The Secretary of the Treasury, consistent with section 104, shall provide for a process whereby individuals who need to establish creditable coverage for periods before July 1, 1996, and who would have such coverage credited but for clause (i) may be given credit for creditable coverage for such periods through the presentation of documents or other means.

(B) CERTIFICATIONS, ETC.—

(i) IN GENERAL.—Subject to clauses (ii) and (iii), subsection (e) of section 9801 of the Internal Revenue Code of 1986 (as added by this section) shall apply to events occurring after June 30, 1996.

(ii) NO CERTIFICATION REQUIRED TO BE PROVIDED BEFORE JUNE 1, 1997.—In no case is a certification required to be provided under such subsection before June 1, 1997.

(iii) CERTIFICATION ONLY ON WRITTEN REQUEST FOR EVENTS OCCURRING BEFORE OCTOBER 1, 1996.—In the case of an event occurring after June 30, 1996, and before October 1, 1996, a certification is not required to be provided under such subsection unless an individual (with respect to whom the certification is otherwise required to be made) requests such certification in writing.

(C) TRANSITIONAL RULE.—In the case of an individual who seeks to establish creditable coverage for any period for which certification is not required because it relates to an event occurring before June 30, 1996—

(i) the individual may present other credible evidence of such coverage in order to establish the period of creditable coverage; and

(ii) a group health plan and a health insurance issuer shall not be subject to any penalty or enforcement action with respect to the plan's or issuer's crediting (or not crediting) such coverage if the plan or issuer has sought to comply in good faith with the applicable requirements under the amendments made by this section.

(3) SPECIAL RULE FOR COLLECTIVE BARGAINING AGREEMENTS.—Except as provided in paragraph (2), in the case of a group health plan maintained pursuant to 1 or more collective bargaining agreements between employee representatives and one or more employers ratified before the date of the enactment of this Act, the amendments made by this section shall not apply to plan years beginning before the later of—

(A) the date on which the last of the collective bargaining agreements relating to the plan terminates (determined without regard to any extension thereof agreed to after the date of the enactment of this Act), or

(B) July 1, 1997.

For purposes of subparagraph (A), any plan amendment made pursuant to a collective bargaining agreement relating to the plan which amends the plan solely to conform to any requirement added by this section shall not be treated as a termination of such collective bargaining agreement.

(4) TIMELY REGULATIONS.—The Secretary of the Treasury, consistent with section 104, shall first issue by not later than April 1, 1997, such regulations as may be necessary to carry out the amendments made by this section.

(5) LIMITATION ON ACTIONS.—No enforcement action shall be taken, pursuant to the amendments made by this section, against a group health plan or health insurance issuer with respect to a violation of a requirement imposed by such amendments before January 1, 1998, or, if later, the date of issuance of regulations referred to in paragraph (4), if the plan or issuer has sought to comply in good faith with such requirements.

[Sec. 9802]

SEC. 9802. PROHIBITING DISCRIMINATION AGAINST INDIVIDUAL PARTICIPANTS AND BENEFICIARIES BASED ON HEALTH STATUS.

[Sec. 9802(a)]

(a) IN ELIGIBILITY TO ENROLL.—

(1) IN GENERAL.—Subject to paragraph (2), a group health plan may not establish rules for eligibility (including continued eligibility) of any individual to enroll under the terms of the plan based on any of the following factors in relation to the individual or a dependent of the individual:

(A) Health status.

(B) Medical condition (including both physical and mental illnesses).
(C) Claims experience.
(D) Receipt of health care.
(E) Medical history.
(F) Genetic information.
(G) Evidence of insurability (including conditions arising out of acts of domestic violence).
(H) Disability.

(2) NO APPLICATION TO BENEFITS OR EXCLUSIONS.—To the extent consistent with section 9801, paragraph (1) shall not be construed—

(A) to require a group health plan to provide particular benefits (or benefits with respect to a specific procedure, treatment, or service) other than those provided under the terms of such plan; or

(B) to prevent such a plan from establishing limitations or restrictions on the amount, level, extent, or nature of the benefits or coverage for similarly situated individuals enrolled in the plan or coverage.

(3) CONSTRUCTION.—For purposes of paragraph (1), rules for eligibility to enroll under a plan include rules defining any applicable waiting periods for such enrollment.

[Sec. 9802(b)]

(b) IN PREMIUM CONTRIBUTIONS.—

(1) IN GENERAL.—A group health plan may not require any individual (as a condition of enrollment or continued enrollment under the plan) to pay a premium or contribution which is greater than such premium or contribution for a similarly situated individual enrolled in the plan on the basis of any factor described in subsection (a)(1) in relation to the individual or to an individual enrolled under the plan as a dependent of the individual.

(2) CONSTRUCTION.—Nothing in paragraph (1) shall be construed—

(A) to restrict the amount that an employer may be charged for coverage under a group health plan except as provided in paragraph (3); or

(B) to prevent a group health plan from establishing premium discounts or rebates or modifying otherwise applicable copayments or deductibles in return for adherence to programs of health promotion and disease prevention.

(3) NO GROUP-BASED DISCRIMINATION ON BASIS OF GENETIC INFORMATION.—

(A) IN GENERAL.—For purposes of this section, a group health plan may not adjust premium or contribution amounts for the group covered under such plan on the basis of genetic information.

(B) RULE OF CONSTRUCTION.—Nothing in subparagraph (A) or in paragraphs (1) and (2) of subsection (d) shall be construed to limit the ability of a group health plan to increase the premium for an employer based on the manifestation of a disease or disorder of an individual who is enrolled in the plan. In such case, the manifestation of a disease or disorder in one individual cannot also be used as genetic information about other group members and to further increase the premium for the employer.

Amendments

- **2008, Genetic Information Nondiscrimination Act of 2008 (P.L. 110-233)**

P.L. 110-233, §103(a)(1)-(2):

Amended Code Sec. 9802(b) by inserting "except as provided in paragraph (3)" before the semicolon in paragraph (2)(A); and by adding at the end a new paragraph (3). **Effective** with respect to group health plans for plan years beginning after the date that is 1 year after 5-21-2008.

P.L. 110-233, §103(f)(1), provides:

(1) REGULATIONS.—The Secretary of the Treasury shall issue final regulations or other guidance not later than 12 months after the date of the enactment of this Act to carry out the amendments made by this section.

P.L. 110-233, §209(a)(2)(B) and (c), provide:

(a) IN GENERAL.—Nothing in this title shall be construed to—

* * *

(2) ***

(B) provide for enforcement of, or penalties for violation of, any requirement or prohibition applicable to any employer, employment agency, labor organization, or joint labor-management committee subject to enforcement for a violation under—

(i) the amendments made by title I of this Act;

* * *

(c) RELATION TO AUTHORITIES UNDER TITLE I.—With respect to a group health plan, or a health insurance issuer offering group health insurance coverage in connection with a group health plan, this title does not prohibit any activity of such plan or issuer that is authorized for the plan or issuer under any provision of law referred to in clauses (i) through (iv) of subsection (a)(2)(B).

- **1996, Health Insurance Portability and Accountability Act of 1996 (P.L. 104-191)**

P.L. 104-191, §401(a):

Amended the Internal Revenue Code of 1986 by adding Code Sec. 9802. For the **effective** date, see Act Sec. 401(c), below.

P.L. 104-191, §401(c), provides:

(c) EFFECTIVE DATE.—

(1) IN GENERAL.—The amendments made by this section shall apply to plan years beginning after June 30, 1997.

(2) DETERMINATION OF CREDITABLE COVERAGE.—

(A) PERIOD OF COVERAGE.—

(i) IN GENERAL.—Subject to clause (ii), no period before July 1, 1996, shall be taken into account under chapter 100 of the Internal Revenue Code of 1986 (as added by this section) in determining creditable coverage.

(ii) SPECIAL RULE FOR CERTAIN PERIODS.—The Secretary of the Treasury, consistent with section 104, shall provide for a process whereby individuals who need to establish creditable coverage for periods before July 1, 1996, and who would have such coverage credited but for clause (i) may be given credit for creditable coverage for such periods through the presentation of documents or other means.

(B) CERTIFICATIONS, ETC.—

(i) IN GENERAL.—Subject to clauses (ii) and (iii), subsection (e) of section 9801 of the Internal Revenue Code of 1986 (as added by this section) shall apply to events occurring after June 30, 1996.

(ii) NO CERTIFICATION REQUIRED TO BE PROVIDED BEFORE JUNE 1, 1997.—In no case is a certification required to be provided under such subsection before June 1, 1997.

(iii) CERTIFICATION ONLY ON WRITTEN REQUEST FOR EVENTS OCCURRING BEFORE OCTOBER 1, 1996.—In the case of an event occurring after June 30, 1996, and before October 1, 1996, a certification is not required to be provided under such subsection unless an individual (with respect to whom the certification is otherwise required to be made) requests such certification in writing.

(C) TRANSITIONAL RULE.—In the case of an individual who seeks to establish creditable coverage for any period for which certification is not required because it relates to an event occurring before June 30, 1996—

(i) the individual may present other credible evidence of such coverage in order to establish the period of creditable coverage; and

(ii) a group health plan and a health insurance issuer shall not be subject to any penalty or enforcement action with respect to the plan's or issuer's crediting (or not crediting) such coverage if the plan or issuer has sought to comply in good faith with the applicable requirements under the amendments made by this section.

(3) SPECIAL RULE FOR COLLECTIVE BARGAINING AGREEMENTS.—Except as provided in paragraph (2), in the case of a group health plan maintained pursuant to 1 or more collective bargaining agreements between employee representatives and one or more employers ratified before the date of the enactment of this Act, the amendments made by this section shall not apply to plan years beginning before the later of—

(A) the date on which the last of the collective bargaining agreements relating to the plan terminates (determined without regard to any extension thereof agreed to after the date of the enactment of this Act), or

(B) July 1, 1997.

For purposes of subparagraph (A), any plan amendment made pursuant to a collective bargaining agreement relating to the plan which amends the plan solely to conform to any requirement added by this section shall not be treated as a termination of such collective bargaining agreement.

(4) TIMELY REGULATIONS.—The Secretary of the Treasury, consistent with section 104, shall first issue by not later than April 1, 1997, such regulations as may be necessary to carry out the amendments made by this section.

(5) LIMITATION ON ACTIONS.—No enforcement action shall be taken, pursuant to the amendments made by this section, against a group health plan or health insurance issuer with respect to a violation of a requirement imposed by such amendments before January 1, 1998, or, if later, the date of issuance of regulations referred to in paragraph (4), if the plan or issuer has sought to comply in good faith with such requirements.

GROUP HEALTH PLAN REQUIREMENTS

[Sec. 9802(c)]

(c) GENETIC TESTING.—

(1) LIMITATION ON REQUESTING OR REQUIRING GENETIC TESTING.—A group health plan may not request or require an individual or a family member of such individual to undergo a genetic test.

(2) RULE OF CONSTRUCTION.—Paragraph (1) shall not be construed to limit the authority of a health care professional who is providing health care services to an individual to request that such individual undergo a genetic test.

(3) RULE OF CONSTRUCTION REGARDING PAYMENT.—

(A) IN GENERAL.—Nothing in paragraph (1) shall be construed to preclude a group health plan from obtaining and using the results of a genetic test in making a determination regarding payment (as such term is defined for the purposes of applying the regulations promulgated by the Secretary of Health and Human Services under part C of title XI of the Social Security Act and section 264 of the Health Insurance Portability and Accountability Act of 1996, as may be revised from time to time) consistent with subsection (a).

(B) LIMITATION.—For purposes of subparagraph (A), a group health plan may request only the minimum amount of information necessary to accomplish the intended purpose.

(4) RESEARCH EXCEPTION.—Notwithstanding paragraph (1), a group health plan may request, but not require, that a participant or beneficiary undergo a genetic test if each of the following conditions is met:

(A) The request is made pursuant to research that complies with part 46 of title 45, Code of Federal Regulations, or equivalent Federal regulations, and any applicable State or local law or regulations for the protection of human subjects in research.

(B) The plan clearly indicates to each participant or beneficiary, or in the case of a minor child, to the legal guardian of such beneficiary, to whom the request is made that—

(i) compliance with the request is voluntary; and

(ii) non-compliance will have no effect on enrollment status or premium or contribution amounts.

(C) No genetic information collected or acquired under this paragraph shall be used for underwriting purposes.

(D) The plan notifies the Secretary in writing that the plan is conducting activities pursuant to the exception provided for under this paragraph, including a description of the activities conducted.

(E) The plan complies with such other conditions as the Secretary may by regulation require for activities conducted under this paragraph.

Amendments

- **2008, Genetic Information Nondiscrimination Act of 2008 (P.L. 110-233)**

P.L. 110-233, § 103(b):

Amended Code Sec. 9802 by redesignating subsection (c) as subsection (f) and by inserting after subsection (b) a new subsection (c). **Effective** with respect to group health plans for plan years beginning after the date that is 1 year after 5-21-2008. For a special rule, see Act Sec. 209(a)(2)(B) and (c) in the amendment notes for Code Sec. 9802(b).

P.L. 110-233, § 103(f)(1), provides:

(1) REGULATIONS.—The Secretary of the Treasury shall issue final regulations or other guidance not later than 12 months after the date of the enactment of this Act to carry out the amendments made by this section.

[Sec. 9802(d)]

(d) PROHIBITION ON COLLECTION OF GENETIC INFORMATION.—

(1) IN GENERAL.—A group health plan shall not request, require, or purchase genetic information for underwriting purposes (as defined in section 9832).

(2) PROHIBITION ON COLLECTION OF GENETIC INFORMATION PRIOR TO ENROLLMENT.—A group health plan shall not request, require, or purchase genetic information with respect to any individual prior to such individual's enrollment under the plan or in connection with such enrollment.

(3) INCIDENTAL COLLECTION.—If a group health plan obtains genetic information incidental to the requesting, requiring, or purchasing of other information concerning any individual, such request, requirement, or purchase shall not be considered a violation of paragraph (2) if such request, requirement, or purchase is not in violation of paragraph (1).

Amendments

- **2008, Genetic Information Nondiscrimination Act of 2008 (P.L. 110-233)**

P.L. 110-233, § 103(b):

Amended Code Sec. 9802 by inserting after subsection (c), as added by this Act, a new subsection (d). **Effective** with respect to group health plans for plan years beginning after the date that is 1 year after 5-21-2008. For a special rule, see Act Sec. 209(a)(2)(B) and (c) in the amendment notes for Code Sec. 9802(b).

P.L. 110-233, § 103(f)(1), provides:

(1) REGULATIONS.—The Secretary of the Treasury shall issue final regulations or other guidance not later than 12 months after the date of the enactment of this Act to carry out the amendments made by this section.

[Sec. 9802(e)]

(e) APPLICATION TO ALL PLANS.—The provisions of subsections (a)(1)(F), (b)(3), (c), and (d) and subsection (b)(1) and section 9801 with respect to genetic information, shall apply to group health plans without regard to section 9831(a)(2).

Amendments

- **2008, Genetic Information Nondiscrimination Act of 2008 (P.L. 110-233)**

P.L. 110-233, § 103(b):

Amended Code Sec. 9802 by inserting after subsection (d), as added by this Act, a new subsection (e). **Effective** with respect to group health plans for plan years beginning after the date that is 1 year after 5-21-2008. For a special rule, see Act Sec. 209(a)(2)(B) and (c) in the amendment notes for Code Sec. 9802(b).

P.L. 110-233, § 103(f)(1), provides:

(1) REGULATIONS.—The Secretary of the Treasury shall issue final regulations or other guidance not later than 12 months after the date of the enactment of this Act to carry out the amendments made by this section.

[Sec. 9802(f)]

(f) SPECIAL RULES FOR CHURCH PLANS.—A church plan (as defined in section 414(e)) shall not be treated as failing to meet the requirements of this section solely because such plan requires evidence of good health for coverage of—

(1) both any employee of an employer with 10 or less employees (determined without regard to section 414(e)(3)(C)) and any self-employed individual, or

(2) any individual who enrolls after the first 90 days of initial eligibility under the plan.

This subsection shall apply to a plan for any year only if the plan included the provisions described in the preceding sentence on July 15, 1997, and at all times thereafter before the beginning of such year.

- **2008, Genetic Information Nondiscrimination Act of 2008 (P.L. 110-233)**

P.L. 110-233, § 103(b):

Amended Code Sec. 9802 by redesignating subsection (c) as subsection (f). **Effective** with respect to group health plans for plan years beginning after the date that is 1 year after 5-21-2008. For a special rule, see Act Sec. 209(a)(2)(B) and (c) in the amendment notes for Code Sec. 9802(b).

P.L. 110-233, § 103(f)(1), provides:

(1) REGULATIONS.—The Secretary of the Treasury shall issue final regulations or other guidance not later than 12 months after the date of the enactment of this Act to carry out the amendments made by this section.

GROUP HEALTH PLAN REQUIREMENTS

- **1997, Taxpayer Relief Act of 1997 (P.L. 105-34)**

P.L. 105-34, § 1532(a):

Amended Code Sec. 9802 by adding at the end a new subsection (c). **Effective** as if included in the amendments made by Act Sec. 401(a) of P.L. 104-191 [generally **effective** for plan years beginning after 6-30-97.—CCH].

[Sec. 9802(g)]

(g) GENETIC INFORMATION OF A FETUS OR EMBRYO.—Any reference in this chapter to genetic information concerning an individual or family member of an individual shall—

(1) with respect to such an individual or family member of an individual who is a pregnant woman, include genetic information of any fetus carried by such pregnant woman; and

(2) with respect to an individual or family member utilizing an assisted reproductive technology, include genetic information of any embryo legally held by the individual or family member.

Amendments

- **2014, Tax Technical Corrections Act of 2014 (P.L. 113-295)**

P.L. 113-295, § 220(aa), Division A:

Amended Code Sec. 9802 by redesignating the second subsection (f) (relating to genetic information of a fetus or embryo) as subsection (g). **Effective** 12-19-2014.

- **2008, Genetic Information Nondiscrimination Act of 2008 (P.L. 110-233)**

P.L. 110-233, § 103(c):

Amended Code Sec. 9802, as amended by this Act, by adding at the end a new subsection (f)[(g)]. **Effective** with respect to group health plans for plan years beginning after the date that is 1 year after 5-21-2008. For a special rule, see Act Sec. 209(a)(2)(B) and (c) in the amendment notes for Code Sec. 9802(b).

P.L. 110-233, § 103(f)(1), provides:

(1) REGULATIONS.—The Secretary of the Treasury shall issue final regulations or other guidance not later than 12 months after the date of the enactment of this Act to carry out the amendments made by this section.

[Sec. 9803]

SEC. 9803. GUARANTEED RENEWABILITY IN MULTIEMPLOYER PLANS AND CERTAIN MULTIPLE EMPLOYER WELFARE ARRANGEMENTS.

[Sec. 9803(a)]

(a) IN GENERAL.—A group health plan which is a multiemployer plan (as defined in section 414(f)) or which is a multiple employer welfare arrangement may not deny an employer continued access to the same or different coverage under such plan, other than—

(1) for nonpayment of contributions;

(2) for fraud or other intentional misrepresentation of material fact by the employer;

(3) for noncompliance with material plan provisions;

(4) because the plan is ceasing to offer any coverage in a geographic area;

(5) in the case of a plan that offers benefits through a network plan, because there is no longer any individual enrolled through the employer who lives, resides, or works in the service area of the network plan and the plan applies this paragraph uniformly without regard to the claims experience of employers or a factor described in section 9802(a)(1) in relation to such individuals or their dependents; or

(6) for failure to meet the terms of an applicable collective bargaining agreement, to renew a collective bargaining or other agreement requiring or authorizing contributions to the plan, or to employ employees covered by such an agreement.

[Sec. 9803(b)]

(b) MULTIPLE EMPLOYER WELFARE ARRANGEMENT.—For purposes of subsection (a), the term "multiple employer welfare arrangement" has the meaning given such term by section 3(40) of the Employee Retirement Income Security Act of 1974, as in effect on the date of the enactment of this section.

Amendments

- **1996, Health Insurance Portability and Accountability Act of 1996 (P.L. 104-191)**

P.L. 104-191, § 401(a):

Amended the Internal Revenue Code of 1986 by adding Code Sec. 9803. For the **effective** date, see Act Sec. 401(c), below.

P.L. 104-191, § 401(c), provides:

(c) EFFECTIVE DATE.—

(1) IN GENERAL.—The amendments made by this section shall apply to plan years beginning after June 30, 1997.

(2) DETERMINATION OF CREDITABLE COVERAGE.—

(A) PERIOD OF COVERAGE.—

(i) IN GENERAL.—Subject to clause (ii), no period before July 1, 1996, shall be taken into account under chapter 100 of the Internal Revenue Code of 1986 (as added by this section) in determining creditable coverage.

(ii) SPECIAL RULE FOR CERTAIN PERIODS.—The Secretary of the Treasury, consistent with section 104, shall provide for a process whereby individuals who need to establish creditable coverage for periods before July 1, 1996, and who would have such coverage credited but for clause (i) may be given credit for creditable coverage for such periods through the presentation of documents or other means.

(B) CERTIFICATIONS, ETC.—

(i) IN GENERAL.—Subject to clauses (ii) and (iii), subsection (e) of section 9801 of the Internal Revenue Code of 1986 (as added by this section) shall apply to events occurring after June 30, 1996.

(ii) NO CERTIFICATION REQUIRED TO BE PROVIDED BEFORE JUNE 1, 1997.—In no case is a certification required to be provided under such subsection before June 1, 1997.

(iii) CERTIFICATION ONLY ON WRITTEN REQUEST FOR EVENTS OCCURRING BEFORE OCTOBER 1, 1996.—In the case of an event occurring after June 30, 1996, and before October 1, 1996, a certification is not required to be provided under such subsection unless an individual (with respect to whom the certification is otherwise required to be made) requests such certification in writing.

(C) TRANSITIONAL RULE.—In the case of an individual who seeks to establish creditable coverage for any period for which certification is not required because it relates to an event occurring before June 30, 1996—

(i) the individual may present other credible evidence of such coverage in order to establish the period of creditable coverage; and

(ii) a group health plan and a health insurance issuer shall not be subject to any penalty or enforcement action with respect to the plan's or issuer's crediting (or not crediting) such coverage if the plan or issuer has sought to comply in good faith with the applicable requirements under the amendments made by this section.

(3) SPECIAL RULE FOR COLLECTIVE BARGAINING AGREEMENTS.—Except as provided in paragraph (2), in the case of a group health plan maintained pursuant to 1 or more collective bargaining agreements between employee representatives and one or more employers ratified before the date of the enactment of this Act, the amendments made by this section shall not apply to plan years beginning before the later of—

(A) the date on which the last of the collective bargaining agreements relating to the plan terminates (determined without regard to any extension thereof agreed to after the date of the enactment of this Act), or

(B) July 1, 1997.

For purposes of subparagraph (A), any plan amendment made pursuant to a collective bargaining agreement relating to the plan which amends the plan solely to conform to any requirement added by this section shall not be treated as a termination of such collective bargaining agreement.

(4) TIMELY REGULATIONS.—The Secretary of the Treasury, consistent with section 104, shall first issue by not later than April 1, 1997, such regulations as may be necessary to carry out the amendments made by this section.

(5) LIMITATION ON ACTIONS.—No enforcement action shall be taken, pursuant to the amendments made by this section, against a group health plan or health insurance issuer with respect to a violation of a requirement imposed by such amendments before January 1, 1998, or, if later, the date of issuance of regulations referred to in paragraph (4), if the plan or issuer has sought to comply in good faith with such requirements.

GROUP HEALTH PLAN REQUIREMENTS

Subchapter B—Other Requirements

Sec. 9811.	Standards relating to benefits for mothers and newborns.
Sec. 9812.	Parity in the application of certain limits to mental health benefits.
Sec. 9813.	Coverage of dependent students on medically necessary leave of absence.
Sec. 9815.	Additional market reforms.
Sec. 9816.	Preventing surprise medical bills.
Sec. 9817.	Ending surprise air ambulance bills.
Sec. 9818.	Continuity of care.
Sec. 9819.	Maintenance of price comparison tool.
Sec. 9820.	Protecting patients and improving the accuracy of provider directory information.
Sec. 9822.	Other patient protections.
Sec. 9823.	Air ambulance report requirements.
Sec. 9824.	Increasing transparency by removing gag clauses on price and quality information.
Sec. 9825.	Reporting on pharmacy benefits and drug costs.

[Sec. 9811]

SEC. 9811. STANDARDS RELATING TO BENEFITS FOR MOTHERS AND NEWBORNS.

[Sec. 9811(a)]

(a) REQUIREMENTS FOR MINIMUM HOSPITAL STAY FOLLOWING BIRTH.—

(1) IN GENERAL.—A group health plan may not—

(A) except as provided in paragraph (2)—

(i) restrict benefits for any hospital length of stay in connection with childbirth for the mother or newborn child, following a normal vaginal delivery, to less than 48 hours, or

(ii) restrict benefits for any hospital length of stay in connection with childbirth for the mother or newborn child, following a caesarean section, to less than 96 hours; or

(B) require that a provider obtain authorization from the plan or the issuer for prescribing any length of stay required under subparagraph (A) (without regard to paragraph (2)).

(2) EXCEPTION.—Paragraph (1)(A) shall not apply in connection with any group health plan in any case in which the decision to discharge the mother or her newborn child prior to the expiration of the minimum length of stay otherwise required under paragraph (1)(A) is made by an attending provider in consultation with the mother.

[Sec. 9811(b)]

(b) PROHIBITIONS.—A group health plan may not—

(1) deny to the mother or her newborn child eligibility, or continued eligibility, to enroll or to renew coverage under the terms of the plan, solely for the purpose of avoiding the requirements of this section;

(2) provide monetary payments or rebates to mothers to encourage such mothers to accept less than the minimum protections available under this section;

(3) penalize or otherwise reduce or limit the reimbursement of an attending provider because such provider provided care to an individual participant or beneficiary in accordance with this section;

(4) provide incentives (monetary or otherwise) to an attending provider to induce such provider to provide care to an individual participant or beneficiary in a manner inconsistent with this section; or

(5) subject to subsection (c)(3), restrict benefits for any portion of a period within a hospital length of stay required under subsection (a) in a manner which is less favorable than the benefits provided for any preceding portion of such stay.

[Sec. 9811(c)]

(c) RULES OF CONSTRUCTION.—

(1) Nothing in this section shall be construed to require a mother who is a participant or beneficiary—

(A) to give birth in a hospital; or

(B) to stay in the hospital for a fixed period of time following the birth of her child.

(2) This section shall not apply with respect to any group health plan which does not provide benefits for hospital lengths of stay in connection with childbirth for a mother or her newborn child.

(3) Nothing in this section shall be construed as preventing a group health plan from imposing deductibles, coinsurance, or other cost-sharing in relation to benefits for hospital lengths of stay in connection with childbirth for a mother or newborn child under the plan, except that such coinsurance or other cost-sharing for any portion of a period within a hospital length of stay required under subsection (a) may not be greater than such coinsurance or cost-sharing for any preceding portion of such stay.

[Sec. 9811(d)]

(d) LEVEL AND TYPE OF REIMBURSEMENTS.—Nothing in this section shall be construed to prevent a group health plan from negotiating the level and type of reimbursement with a provider for care provided in accordance with this section.

[Sec. 9811(e)]

(e) PREEMPTION; EXCEPTION FOR HEALTH INSURANCE COVERAGE IN CERTAIN STATES.—The requirements of this section shall not apply with respect to health insurance coverage if there is a State law (including a decision, rule, regulation, or other State action having the effect of law) for a State that regulates such coverage that is described in any of the following paragraphs:

(1) Such State law requires such coverage to provide for at least a 48-hour hospital length of stay following a normal vaginal delivery and at least a 96-hour hospital length of stay following a caesarean section.

(2) Such State law requires such coverage to provide for maternity and pediatric care in accordance with guidelines established by the American College of Obstetricians and Gynecologists, the American Academy of Pediatrics, or other established professional medical associations.

(3) Such State law requires, in connection with such coverage for maternity care, that the hospital length of stay for such care is left to the decision of (or required to be made by) the attending provider in consultation with the mother.

GROUP HEALTH PLAN REQUIREMENTS

Amendments

• **1998, IRS Restructuring and Reform Act of 1998 (P.L. 105-206)**

P.L. 105-206, § 6015(e):

Amended Code Sec. 9811 by redesignating subsection (f), as added by Act Sec. 1531(a)(4) of P.L. 105-34, as subsection (e). **Effective** as if included in the provision of P.L. 105-34 to which it relates [effective for group health plans for plan years beginning on or after 1-1-98.—CCH].

• **1997, Taxpayer Relief Act of 1997 (P.L. 105-34)**

P.L. 105-34, § 1531(a)(4):

Amended subtitle K by inserting after Code Sec. 9803 a new subchapter B (Code Secs. 9811-9812). **Effective** with respect to group health plans for plan years beginning on or after 1-1-98.

[Sec. 9812]

SEC. 9812. PARITY IN MENTAL HEALTH AND SUBSTANCE USE DISORDER BENEFITS.

[Sec. 9812(a)]

(a) IN GENERAL.—

(1) AGGREGATE LIFETIME LIMITS.—In the case of a group health plan that provides both medical and surgical benefits and mental health and substance use disorder benefits—

(A) NO LIFETIME LIMIT.—If the plan does not include an aggregate lifetime limit on substantially all medical and surgical benefits, the plan may not impose any aggregate lifetime limit on mental health or substance use disorder benefits.

(B) LIFETIME LIMIT.—If the plan includes an aggregate lifetime limit on substantially all medical and surgical benefits (in this paragraph referred to as the "applicable lifetime limit"), the plan shall either—

(i) apply the applicable lifetime limit both to the medical and surgical benefits to which it otherwise would apply and to mental health and substance use disorder benefits and not distinguish in the application of such limit between such medical and surgical benefits and mental health and substance use disorder benefits; or

(ii) not include any aggregate lifetime limit on mental health or substance use disorder benefits that is less than the applicable lifetime limit.

(C) RULE IN CASE OF DIFFERENT LIMITS.—In the case of a plan that is not described in subparagraph (A) or (B) and that includes no or different aggregate lifetime limits on different categories of medical and surgical benefits, the Secretary shall establish rules under which subparagraph (B) is applied to such plan with respect to mental health and substance use disorder benefits by substituting for the applicable lifetime limit an average aggregate lifetime limit that is computed taking into account the weighted average of the aggregate lifetime limits applicable to such categories.

(2) ANNUAL LIMITS.—In the case of a group health plan that provides both medical and surgical benefits and mental health or substance use disorder benefits—

(A) NO ANNUAL LIMIT.—If the plan does not include an annual limit on substantially all medical and surgical benefits, the plan may not impose any annual limit on mental health or substance use disorder benefits.

(B) ANNUAL LIMIT.—If the plan includes an annual limit on substantially all medical and surgical benefits (in this paragraph referred to as the "applicable annual limit"), the plan shall either—

(i) apply the applicable annual limit both to medical and surgical benefits to which it otherwise would apply and to mental health and substance use disorder benefits and not distinguish in the application of such limit between such medical and surgical benefits and mental health and substance use disorder benefits; or

(ii) not include any annual limit on mental health or substance use disorder benefits that is less than the applicable annual limit.

(C) RULE IN CASE OF DIFFERENT LIMITS.—In the case of a plan that is not described in subparagraph (A) or (B) and that includes no or different annual limits on different categories of medical and surgical benefits, the Secretary shall establish rules under which subparagraph (B) is applied to such plan with respect to mental health and substance use disorder benefits by substituting for the applicable annual limit an average annual limit that is computed taking into account the weighted average of the annual limits applicable to such categories.

(3) FINANCIAL REQUIREMENTS AND TREATMENT LIMITATIONS.—

(A) IN GENERAL.—In the case of a group health plan that provides both medical and surgical benefits and mental health or substance use disorder benefits, such plan shall ensure that—

(i) the financial requirements applicable to such mental health or substance use disorder benefits are no more restrictive than the predominant financial requirements applied to substantially all medical and surgical benefits covered by the plan, and there are no separate cost sharing requirements that are applicable only with respect to mental health or substance use disorder benefits; and

(ii) the treatment limitations applicable to such mental health or substance use disorder benefits are no more restrictive than the predominant treatment limitations applied to substantially all medical and surgical benefits covered by the plan and there are no separate treatment limitations that are applicable only with respect to mental health or substance use disorder benefits.

(B) DEFINITIONS.—In this paragraph:

(i) FINANCIAL REQUIREMENT.—The term "financial requirement" includes deductibles, copayments, coinsurance, and out-of-pocket expenses, but excludes an aggregate lifetime limit and an annual limit subject to paragraphs (1) and (2).

(ii) PREDOMINANT.—A financial requirement or treatment limit is considered to be predominant if it is the most common or frequent of such type of limit or requirement.

(iii) TREATMENT LIMITATION.—The term "treatment limitation" includes limits on the frequency of treatment, number of visits, days of coverage, or other similar limits on the scope or duration of treatment.

(4) AVAILABILITY OF PLAN INFORMATION.—The criteria for medical necessity determinations made under the plan with respect to mental health or substance use disorder benefits shall be made available by the plan administrator in accordance with regulations to any current or potential participant, beneficiary, or contracting provider upon request. The reason for any denial under the plan of reimbursement or payment for services with respect to mental health or substance use disorder benefits in the case of any participant or beneficiary shall, on request or as otherwise required, be made available by the plan administrator to the participant or beneficiary in accordance with regulations.

(5) OUT-OF-NETWORK PROVIDERS.—In the case of a plan that provides both medical and surgical benefits and mental health or substance use disorder benefits, if the plan provides coverage for medical or surgical benefits provided by out-of-network providers, the plan shall provide coverage for mental health or substance use disorder benefits provided by out-of-network providers in a manner that is consistent with the requirements of this section.

(6) COMPLIANCE PROGRAM GUIDANCE DOCUMENT.—

(A) IN GENERAL.—The Secretary, the Secretary of Health and Human Services, and the Secretary of Labor, in consultation with the Inspector General of the Department of Health and Human Services, the Inspector General of the Department of Labor, and the Inspector General of the Department of the Treasury, shall issue a compliance program guidance document to help improve compliance with this section, section 2726 of the Public Health Service Act, and section 712 of the Employee Retirement Income Security Act of 1974, as

GROUP HEALTH PLAN REQUIREMENTS

applicable. In carrying out this paragraph, the Secretaries may take into consideration the 2016 publication of the Department of Health and Human Services and the Department of Labor, entitled "Warning Signs - Plan or Policy Non-Quantitative Treatment Limitations (NQTLs) that Require Additional Analysis to Determine Mental Health Parity Compliance".

(B) EXAMPLES ILLUSTRATING COMPLIANCE AND NONCOMPLIANCE.—

(i) IN GENERAL.—The compliance program guidance document required under this paragraph shall provide illustrative, de-identified examples (that do not disclose any protected health information or individually identifiable information) of previous findings of compliance and noncompliance with this section, section 2726 of the Public Health Service Act, or section 712 of the Employee Retirement Income Security Act of 1974, as applicable, based on investigations of violations of such sections, including—

(I) examples illustrating requirements for information disclosures and nonquantitative treatment limitations; and

(II) descriptions of the violations uncovered during the course of such investigations.

(ii) NONQUANTITATIVE TREATMENT LIMITATIONS.—To the extent that any example described in clause (i) involves a finding of compliance or noncompliance with regard to any requirement for nonquantitative treatment limitations, the example shall provide sufficient detail to fully explain such finding, including a full description of the criteria involved for approving medical and surgical benefits and the criteria involved for approving mental health and substance use disorder benefits.

(iii) ACCESS TO ADDITIONAL INFORMATION REGARDING COMPLIANCE.—In developing and issuing the compliance program guidance document required under this paragraph, the Secretaries specified in subparagraph (A)—

(I) shall enter into interagency agreements with the Inspector General of the Department of Health and Human Services, the Inspector General of the Department of Labor, and the Inspector General of the Department of the Treasury to share findings of compliance and noncompliance with this section, section 2726 of the Public Health Service Act, or section 712 of the Employee Retirement Income Security Act of 1974, as applicable; and

(II) shall seek to enter into an agreement with a State to share information on findings of compliance and noncompliance with this section, section 2726 of the Public Health Service Act, or section 712 of the Employee Retirement Income Security Act of 1974, as applicable.

(C) RECOMMENDATIONS.—The compliance program guidance document shall include recommendations to advance compliance with this section, section 2726 of the Public Health Service Act, or section 712 of the Employee Retirement Income Security Act of 1974, as applicable, and encourage the development and use of internal controls to monitor adherence to applicable statutes, regulations, and program requirements. Such internal controls may include illustrative examples of nonquantitative treatment limitations on mental health and substance use disorder benefits, which may fail to comply with this section, section 2726 of the Public Health Service Act, or section 712 of the Employee Retirement Income Security Act of 1974, as applicable, in relation to nonquantitative treatment limitations on medical and surgical benefits.

(D) UPDATING THE COMPLIANCE PROGRAM GUIDANCE DOCUMENT.—The Secretary, the Secretary of Health and Human Services, and the Secretary of Labor, in consultation with the Inspector General of the Department of Health and Human Services, the Inspector General of the Department of Labor, and the Inspector General of the Department of the Treasury, shall update the compliance program guidance document every 2 years to include illustrative, de-identified examples (that do not disclose any protected health information or individually identifiable information) of previous findings of compliance and noncompliance with this section, section 2726 of the Public Health Service Act, or section 712 of the Employee Retirement Income Security Act of 1974, as applicable.

(7) ADDITIONAL GUIDANCE.—

(A) IN GENERAL.—The Secretary, the Secretary of Health and Human Services, and the Secretary of Labor shall issue guidance to group health plans to assist such plans in satisfying the requirements of this section, section 2726 of the Public Health Service Act, or section 712 of the Employee Retirement Income Security Act of 1974, as applicable.

(B) DISCLOSURE.—

(i) GUIDANCE FOR PLANS.—The guidance issued under this paragraph shall include clarifying information and illustrative examples of methods that group health plans may use for disclosing information to ensure compliance with the requirements under this section, section 2726 of the Public Health Service Act, or section 712 of the Employee Retirement Income Security Act of 1974, as applicable, (and any regulations promulgated pursuant to such sections, as applicable).

(ii) DOCUMENTS FOR PARTICIPANTS, BENEFICIARIES, CONTRACTING PROVIDERS, OR AUTHORIZED REPRESENTATIVES.—The guidance issued under this paragraph shall include clarifying information and illustrative examples of methods that group health plans may use to provide any participant, beneficiary, contracting provider, or authorized representative, as applicable, with documents containing information that the health plans are required to disclose to participants, beneficiaries, contracting providers, or authorized representatives to ensure compliance with this section, section 2726 of the Public Health Service Act, or section 712 of the Employee Retirement Income Security Act of 1974, as applicable, compliance with any regulation issued pursuant to such respective section, or compliance with any other applicable law or regulation. Such guidance shall include information that is comparative in nature with respect to—

(I) nonquantitative treatment limitations for both medical and surgical benefits and mental health and substance use disorder benefits;

(II) the processes, strategies, evidentiary standards, and other factors used to apply the limitations described in subclause (I); and

(III) the application of the limitations described in subclause (I) to ensure that such limitations are applied in parity with respect to both medical and surgical benefits and mental health and substance use disorder benefits.

(C) NONQUANTITATIVE TREATMENT LIMITATIONS.—The guidance issued under this paragraph shall include clarifying information and illustrative examples of methods, processes, strategies, evidentiary standards, and other factors that group health plans may use regarding the development and application of nonquantitative treatment limitations to ensure compliance with this section, section 2726 of the Public Health Service Act, or section 712 of the Employee Retirement Income Security Act of 1974, as applicable, (and any regulations promulgated pursuant to such respective section), including—

(i) examples of methods of determining appropriate types of nonquantitative treatment limitations with respect to both medical and surgical benefits and mental health and substance use disorder benefits, including nonquantitative treatment limitations pertaining to—

(I) medical management standards based on medical necessity or appropriateness, or whether a treatment is experimental or investigative;

(II) limitations with respect to prescription drug formulary design; and

(III) use of fail-first or step therapy protocols;

(ii) examples of methods of determining—

(I) network admission standards (such as credentialing); and

GROUP HEALTH PLAN REQUIREMENTS

(II) factors used in provider reimbursement methodologies (such as service type, geographic market, demand for services, and provider supply, practice size, training, experience, and licensure) as such factors apply to network adequacy;

(iii) examples of sources of information that may serve as evidentiary standards for the purposes of making determinations regarding the development and application of nonquantitative treatment limitations;

(iv) examples of specific factors, and the evidentiary standards used to evaluate such factors, used by such plans in performing a nonquantitative treatment limitation analysis;

(v) examples of how specific evidentiary standards may be used to determine whether treatments are considered experimental or investigative;

(vi) examples of how specific evidentiary standards may be applied to each service category or classification of benefits;

(vii) examples of methods of reaching appropriate coverage determinations for new mental health or substance use disorder treatments, such as evidence-based early intervention programs for individuals with a serious mental illness and types of medical management techniques;

(viii) examples of methods of reaching appropriate coverage determinations for which there is an indirect relationship between the covered mental health or substance use disorder benefit and a traditional covered medical and surgical benefit, such as residential treatment or hospitalizations involving voluntary or involuntary commitment; and

(ix) additional illustrative examples of methods, processes, strategies, evidentiary standards, and other factors for which the Secretary determines that additional guidance is necessary to improve compliance with this section, section 2726 of the Public Health Service Act, or section 712 of the Employee Retirement Income Security Act of 1974, as applicable.

(D) PUBLIC COMMENT.—Prior to issuing any final guidance under this paragraph, the Secretary shall provide a public comment period of not less than 60 days during which any member of the public may provide comments on a draft of the guidance.

(8) COMPLIANCE REQUIREMENTS.—

(A) NONQUANTITATIVE TREATMENT LIMITATION (NQTL) REQUIREMENTS.—In the case of a group health plan that provides both medical and surgical benefits and mental health or substance use disorder benefits and that imposes nonquantitative treatment limitations (referred to in this section as "NQTLs") on mental health or substance use disorder benefits, such plan shall perform and document comparative analyses of the design and application of NQTLs and, beginning 45 days after the date of enactment of the Consolidated Appropriations Act, 2021, make available to the Secretary, upon request, the comparative analyses and the following information:

(i) The specific plan terms or other relevant terms regarding the NQTLs and a description of all mental health or substance use disorder and medical or surgical benefits to which each such term applies in each respective benefits classification.

(ii) The factors used to determine that the NQTLs will apply to mental health or substance use disorder benefits and medical or surgical benefits.

(iii) The evidentiary standards used for the factors identified in clause (ii), when applicable, provided that every factor shall be defined, and any other source or evidence relied upon to design and apply the NQTLs to mental health or substance use disorder benefits and medical or surgical benefits.

(iv) The comparative analyses demonstrating that the processes, strategies, evidentiary standards, and other factors used to apply the NQTLs to mental health or substance use disorder benefits, as written and in operation, are comparable to, and are applied no more stringently than, the processes, strategies, evidentiary standards, and other factors used to apply the NQTLs to medical or surgical benefits in the benefits classification.

(v) A disclosure of the specific findings and conclusions reached by the group health plan, including any results of the analyses described in this subparagraph that indicate that the plan is or is not in compliance with this section.

(B) SECRETARY REQUEST PROCESS.—

(i) SUBMISSION UPON REQUEST.—The Secretary shall request that a group health plan submit the comparative analyses described in subparagraph (A) for plans that involve potential violations of this section or complaints regarding noncompliance with this section that concern NQTLs and any other instances in which the Secretary determines appropriate. The Secretary shall request not fewer than 20 such analyses per year.

(ii) ADDITIONAL INFORMATION.—In instances in which the Secretary has concluded that the group health plan has not submitted sufficient information for the Secretary to review the comparative analyses described in subparagraph (A), as requested under clause (i), the Secretary shall specify to the plan the information the plan must submit to be responsive to the request under clause (i) for the Secretary to review the comparative analyses described in subparagraph (A) for compliance with this section. Nothing in this paragraph shall require the Secretary to conclude that a group health plan is in compliance with this section solely based upon the inspection of the comparative analyses described in subparagraph (A), as requested under clause (i).

(iii) REQUIRED ACTION.—

(I) IN GENERAL.—In instances in which the Secretary has reviewed the comparative analyses described in subparagraph (A), as requested under clause (i), and determined that the group health plan is not in compliance with this section, the plan—

(aa) shall specify to the Secretary the actions the plan will take to be in compliance with this section and provide to the Secretary additional comparative analyses described in subparagraph (A) that demonstrate compliance with this section not later than 45 days after the initial determination by the Secretary that the plan is not in compliance; and

(bb) following the 45-day corrective action period under item (aa), if the Secretary makes a final determination that the plan still is not in compliance with this section, not later than 7 days after such determination, shall notify all individuals enrolled in the plan that the plan has been determined to be not in compliance with this section.

(II) EXEMPTION FROM DISCLOSURE.—Documents or communications produced in connection with the Secretary's recommendations to a group health plan shall not be subject to disclosure pursuant to section 552 of title 5, United States Code.

(iv) REPORT.—Not later than 1 year after the date of enactment of this paragraph, and not later than October 1 of each year thereafter, the Secretary shall submit to Congress, and make publicly available, a report that contains—

(I) a summary of the comparative analyses requested under clause (i), including the identity of each group plan that is determined to be not in compliance after the final determination by the Secretary described in clause (iii)(I)(bb);

(II) the Secretary's conclusions as to whether each group health plan submitted sufficient information for the Secretary to review the comparative analyses requested under clause (i) for compliance with this section;

(III) for each group health plan that did submit sufficient information for the Secretary to review the comparative analyses requested under clause (i), the Secretary's conclusions as to whether and why the plan is in compliance with the disclosure requirements under this section;

(IV) the Secretary's specifications described in clause (ii) for each group health plan that the Secretary determined did not submit sufficient information for the Secretary to review the comparative analyses requested under clause (i) for compliance with this section; and

GROUP HEALTH PLAN REQUIREMENTS

(V) the Secretary's specifications described in clause (iii) of the actions each group health plan that the Secretary determined is not in compliance with this section must take to be in compliance with this section, including the reason why the Secretary determined the plan is not in compliance.

(C) COMPLIANCE PROGRAM GUIDANCE DOCUMENT UPDATE PROCESS.—

(i) IN GENERAL.—The Secretary shall include instances of noncompliance that the Secretary discovers upon reviewing the comparative analyses requested under subparagraph (B)(i) in the compliance program guidance document described in paragraph (6), as it is updated every 2 years, except that such instances shall not disclose any protected health information or individually identifiable information.

(ii) GUIDANCE AND REGULATIONS.—Not later than 18 months after the date of enactment of this paragraph, the Secretary shall finalize any draft or interim guidance and regulations relating to mental health parity under this section. Such draft guidance shall include guidance to clarify the process and timeline for current and potential participants and beneficiaries (and authorized representatives and health care providers of such participants and beneficiaries) with respect to plans to file complaints of such plans being in violation of this section, including guidance, by plan type, on the relevant State, regional, or national office with which such complaints should be filed.

(iii) STATE.—The Secretary shall share information on findings of compliance and noncompliance discovered upon reviewing the comparative analyses requested under subparagraph (B)(i) shall be shared with the State where the group health plan is located, in accordance with paragraph (6)(B)(iii)(II).

Amendments

- **2020, No Surprises Act (P.L. 116-260)**

P.L. 116-260, §203(a)(3), Div. BB:

Amended Code Sec. 9812(a) by adding at the end paragraphs (6)-(8). **Effective** 12-27-2020. For a special rule, see Act Sec. 203(b), Div. BB, below.

P.L. 116-260, §203(b), Div. BB, provides:

(b) GUIDANCE.—The Secretary of Health and Human Services, jointly with the Secretary of Labor and the Secretary of the Treasury, shall issue guidance to carry out the amendments made by paragraphs (1), (2), and (3) of subsection (a).

- **2018, Tax Technical Corrections Act of 2018 (P.L. 115-141)**

P.L. 115-141, §401(a)(349), Div. U:

Amended Code Sec. 9812(a)(3)(B)(i) by striking the comma at the end and inserting a period. **Effective** 3-23-2018.

- **2008, Paul Wellstone and Pete Domenici Mental Health Parity and Addiction Equity Act of 2008 (P.L. 110-343)**

P.L. 110-343, Division C, §512(c)(1):

Amended Code Sec. 9812(a) by adding at the end new paragraphs (3)-(5). For the **effective** date and special rules, see Act Sec. 512(d)-(f), below.

P.L. 110-343, Division C, §512(c)(6):

Amended Code Sec. 9812(a)(1)(B)(i), (1)(C), (2)(B)(i), and (2)(C) by striking "mental health benefits" and inserting "mental health and substance use disorder benefits" each place it appears. For the **effective** date and special rules, see Act Sec. 512(d)-(f), below.

P.L. 110-343, Division C, §512(c)(7):

Amended Code Sec. 9812 by striking "mental health benefits" and inserting "mental health or substance use disorder benefits" each place it appears (other than in any provision amended by Act Sec. 512(c)(6)). For the **effective** date and special rules, see Act Sec. 512(d)-(f), below.

P.L. 110-343, Division C, §512(d)-(f) [as amended by P.L. 110-460], provides:

(d) REGULATIONS.—Not later than 1 year after the date of enactment of this Act, the Secretaries of Labor, Health and Human Services, and the Treasury shall issue regulations to carry out the amendments made by subsections (a), (b), and (c), respectively.

(e) EFFECTIVE DATE.—

(1) IN GENERAL.—The amendments made by this section shall apply with respect to group health plans for plan years beginning after the date that is 1 year after the date of enactment of this Act, regardless of whether regulations have been issued to carry out such amendments by such effective date, except that the amendments made by subsections (a)(5), (b)(5), and (c)(5), relating to striking of certain sunset provisions, shall take effect on January 1, 2009.

(2) SPECIAL RULE FOR COLLECTIVE BARGAINING AGREEMENTS.—In the case of a group health plan maintained pursuant to one or more collective bargaining agreements between employee representatives and one or more employers ratified before the date of the enactment of this Act, the amendments made by this section shall not apply to plan years beginning before the later of—

(A) the date on which the last of the collective bargaining agreements relating to the plan terminates (determined without regard to any extension thereof agreed to after the date of the enactment of this Act), or

(B) January 1, 2010.

For purposes of subparagraph (A), any plan amendment made pursuant to a collective bargaining agreement relating to the plan which amends the plan solely to conform to any requirement added by this section shall not be treated as a termination of such collective bargaining agreement.

(f) ASSURING COORDINATION.—The Secretary of Health and Human Services, the Secretary of Labor, and the Secretary of the Treasury may ensure, through the execution or revision of an interagency memorandum of understanding among such Secretaries, that—

(1) regulations, rulings, and interpretations issued by such Secretaries relating to the same matter over which two or more such Secretaries have responsibility under this section (and the amendments made by this section) are administered so as to have the same effect at all times; and

(2) coordination of policies relating to enforcing the same requirements through such Secretaries in order to have a coordinated enforcement strategy that avoids duplication of enforcement efforts and assigns priorities in enforcement.

P.L. 110-343, Division C, §512(g)(3)(A):

Amended the heading of Code Sec. 9812. **Effective** 10-3-2008. Prior to amendment, the heading of Code Sec. 9812 read as follows:

PARITY IN THE APPLICATION OF CERTAIN LIMITS TO MENTAL HEALTH BENEFITS.

[Sec. 9812(b)]

(b) CONSTRUCTION.—Nothing in this section shall be construed—

(1) as requiring a group health plan to provide any mental health or substance use disorder benefits; or

(2) in the case of a group health plan that provides mental health or substance use disorder benefits, as affecting the terms and conditions of the plan relating to such benefits under the plan, except as provided in subsection (a).

Amendments

- **2008, Paul Wellstone and Pete Domenici Mental Health Parity and Addiction Equity Act of 2008 (P.L. 110-343)**

P.L. 110-343, Division C, §512(c)(2):

Amended Code Sec. 9812(b)(2). For the **effective** date and special rules, see Act Sec. 512(d)-(f) in the amendment notes for Code Sec. 9812(a). Prior to amendment, Code Sec. 9812(b)(2) read as follows:

(2) in the case of a group health plan that provides mental health benefits, as affecting the terms and conditions (including cost sharing, limits on numbers of visits or days of coverage, and requirements relating to medical necessity) relating to the amount, duration, or scope of mental health benefits under the plan, except as specifically provided in subsection (a) (in regard to parity in the imposition of aggregate lifetime limits and annual limits for mental health benefits).

P.L. 110-343, Division C, §512(c)(7):

Amended Code Sec. 9812 by striking "mental health benefits" and inserting "mental health or substance use disorder benefits" each place it appears (other than in any provision amended by Act Sec. 512(c)(6)). For the **effective** date and special rules, see Act Sec. 512(d)-(f) in the amendment notes for Code Sec. 9812(a).

[Sec. 9812(c)]

(c) EXEMPTIONS.—

(1) SMALL EMPLOYER EXEMPTION.—

(A) IN GENERAL.—This section shall not apply to any group health plan for any plan year of a small employer.

(B) SMALL EMPLOYER.—For purposes of subparagraph (A), the term "small employer" means, with respect to a calendar year and a plan year, an employer who employed an average of at least 2 (or 1 in the case of an employer residing in a State that permits small groups to include a single individual) but not more than 50 employees on business days during the preceding calendar year. For purposes of the preceding sentence, all persons treated as a single employer under subsection (b), (c), (m), or (o) of section 414 shall be treated as 1 employer and rules similar to rules of subparagraphs (B) and (C) of section 4980D(d)(2) shall apply.

Sec. 9812(a)(8)(B)(iv)(V)

GROUP HEALTH PLAN REQUIREMENTS

(2) COST EXEMPTION.—

(A) IN GENERAL.—With respect to a group health plan, if the application of this section to such plan results in an increase for the plan year involved of the actual total costs of coverage with respect to medical and surgical benefits and mental health and substance use disorder benefits under the plan (as determined and certified under subparagraph (C)) by an amount that exceeds the applicable percentage described in subparagraph (B) of the actual total plan costs, the provisions of this section shall not apply to such plan during the following plan year, and such exemption shall apply to the plan for 1 plan year. An employer may elect to continue to apply mental health and substance use disorder parity pursuant to this section with respect to the group health plan involved regardless of any increase in total costs.

(B) APPLICABLE PERCENTAGE.—With respect to a plan, the applicable percentage described in this subparagraph shall be—

(i) 2 percent in the case of the first plan year in which this section is applied; and

(ii) 1 percent in the case of each subsequent plan year.

(C) DETERMINATIONS BY ACTUARIES.—Determinations as to increases in actual costs under a plan for purposes of this section shall be made and certified by a qualified and licensed actuary who is a member in good standing of the American Academy of Actuaries. All such determinations shall be in a written report prepared by the actuary. The report, and all underlying documentation relied upon by the actuary, shall be maintained by the group health plan for a period of 6 years following the notification made under subparagraph (E).

(D) 6-MONTH DETERMINATIONS.—If a group health plan seeks an exemption under this paragraph, determinations under subparagraph (A) shall be made after such plan has complied with this section for the first 6 months of the plan year involved.

(E) NOTIFICATION.—

(i) IN GENERAL.—A group health plan that, based upon a certification described under subparagraph (C), qualifies for an exemption under this paragraph, and elects to implement the exemption, shall promptly notify the Secretary, the appropriate State agencies, and participants and beneficiaries in the plan of such election.

(ii) REQUIREMENT.—A notification to the Secretary under clause (i) shall include—

(I) a description of the number of covered lives under the plan involved at the time of the notification, and as applicable, at the time of any prior election of the cost-exemption under this paragraph by such plan;

(II) for both the plan year upon which a cost exemption is sought and the year prior, a description of the actual total costs of coverage with respect to medical and surgical benefits and mental health and substance use disorder benefits under the plan; and

(III) for both the plan year upon which a cost exemption is sought and the year prior, the actual total costs of coverage with respect to mental health and substance use disorder benefits under the plan.

(iii) CONFIDENTIALITY.—A notification to the Secretary under clause (i) shall be confidential. The Secretary shall make available, upon request and on not more than an annual basis, an anonymous itemization of such notifications, that includes—

(I) a breakdown of States by the size and type of employers submitting such notification; and

(II) a summary of the data received under clause (ii).

(F) AUDITS BY APPROPRIATE AGENCIES.—To determine compliance with this paragraph, the Secretary may audit the books and records of a group health plan relating to an exemption, including any actuarial reports prepared pursuant to subparagraph (C), during the 6 year period following the notification of such exemption under subparagraph (E). A State agency receiving a notification under subparagraph (E) may also conduct such an audit with respect to an exemption covered by such notification.

Amendments

• **2008, Paul Wellstone and Pete Domenici Mental Health Parity and Addiction Equity Act of 2008 (P.L. 110-343)**

P.L. 110-343, Division C, §512(c)(3)(A)-(B):

Amended Code Sec. 9812(c) by amending paragraph (1) and by striking paragraph (2) and inserting a new paragraph (2). For the **effective** date and special rules, see Act Sec. 512(d)-(f) in the amendment notes for Code Sec. 9812(a). Prior to amendment, Code Sec. 9812(c)(1) read as follows:

(1) SMALL EMPLOYER EXEMPTION.—This section shall not apply to any group health plan for any plan year of a small employer (as defined in section 4980D(d)(2)).

Prior to being stricken, Code Sec. 9812(c)(2) read as follows:

(2) INCREASED COST EXEMPTION.—This section shall not apply with respect to a group health plan if the application of this section to such plan results in an increase in the cost under the plan of at least 1 percent.

[Sec. 9812(d)]

(d) SEPARATE APPLICATION TO EACH OPTION OFFERED.—In the case of a group health plan that offers a participant or beneficiary two or more benefit package options under the plan, the requirements of this section shall be applied separately with respect to each such option.

[Sec. 9812(e)]

(e) DEFINITIONS.—For purposes of this section:

(1) AGGREGATE LIFETIME LIMIT.—The term "aggregate lifetime limit" means, with respect to benefits under a group health plan, a dollar limitation on the total amount that may be paid with respect to such benefits under the plan with respect to an individual or other coverage unit.

(2) ANNUAL LIMIT.—The term "annual limit" means, with respect to benefits under a group health plan, a dollar limitation on the total amount of benefits that may be paid with respect to such benefits in a 12-month period under the plan with respect to an individual or other coverage unit.

(3) MEDICAL OR SURGICAL BENEFITS.—The term "medical or surgical benefits" means benefits with respect to medical or surgical services, as defined under the terms of the plan, but does not include mental health or substance use disorder benefits.

(4) MENTAL HEALTH BENEFITS.—The term "mental health benefits" means benefits with respect to services for mental health conditions, as defined under the terms of the plan and in accordance with applicable Federal and State law.

(5) SUBSTANCE USE DISORDER BENEFITS.—The term "substance use disorder benefits" means benefits with respect to services for substance use disorders, as defined under the terms of the plan and in accordance with applicable Federal and State law.

Amendments

• **2008, Paul Wellstone and Pete Domenici Mental Health Parity and Addiction Equity Act of 2008 (P.L. 110-343)**

P.L. 110-343, Division C, §512(c)(4):

Amended Code Sec. 9812(e) by striking paragraph (4) and inserting new paragraphs (4)-(5). For the **effective** date and special rules, see Act Sec. 512(d)-(f) in the amendment notes for Code Sec. 9812(a). Prior to being stricken, Code Sec. 9812(e)(4) read as follows:

(4) MENTAL HEALTH BENEFITS.—The term "mental health benefits" means benefits with respect to mental health services, as defined under the terms of the plan, but does not include benefits with respect to treatment of substance abuse or chemical dependency.

P.L. 110-343, Division C, §512(c)(7):

Amended Code Sec. 9812 by striking "mental health benefits" and inserting "mental health or substance use disorder benefits" each place it appears (other than in any provision amended by Act Sec. 512(c)(6)). For the **effective** date and special rules, see Act Sec. 512(d)-(f) in the amendment notes for Code Sec. 9812(a).

GROUP HEALTH PLAN REQUIREMENTS

[Sec. 9812(f)—Stricken]

Amendments

- **2008, Paul Wellstone and Pete Domenici Mental Health Parity and Addiction Equity Act of 2008 (P.L. 110-343)**

P.L. 110-343, Division C, §512(c)(5):

Amended Sec. 9812 by striking subsection (f). **Effective** 1-1-2009. For special rules, see Act Sec. 512(d)-(f) in the amendment notes for Code Sec. 9812(a). Prior to being stricken, Code Sec. 9812(f) read as follows:

(f) APPLICATION OF SECTION.—This section shall not apply to benefits for services furnished—

(1) on or after September 30, 2001, and before January 10, 2002,

(2) on or after January 1, 2004, and before the date of the enactment of the Working Families Tax Relief Act of 2004,

(3) on or after January 1, 2008, and before the date of the enactment of the Heroes Earnings Assistance and Relief Tax Act of 2008, and

(4) after December 31, 2008.

- **2008, Heroes Earnings Assistance and Relief Tax Act of 2008 (P.L. 110-245)**

P.L. 110-245, §401(a)(1)-(2):

Amended Code Sec. 9812(f) by striking "and" at the end of paragraph (2), and by striking paragraph (3) and inserting new paragraphs (3) and (4). **Effective** 6-17-2008. Prior to being stricken, Code Sec. 9812(f)(3) read as follows:

(3) after December 31, 2007.

- **2006, Tax Relief and Health Care Act of 2006 (P.L. 109-432)**

P.L. 109-432, Division A, §115(a):

Amended Code Sec. 9812(f)(3) by striking "2006" and inserting "2007". **Effective** 12-20-2006.

- **2005 (P.L. 109-151)**

P.L. 109-151, §1(c):

Amended Code Sec. 9812(f)(3) by striking "December 31, 2005" and inserting "December 31, 2006". **Effective** 12-30-2005.

- **2004, Working Families Tax Relief Act of 2004 (P.L. 108-311)**

P.L. 108-311, §302(a)(1)-(2):

Amended Code Sec. 9812(f) by striking "and" at the end of paragraph (1), and by striking paragraph (2) and inserting new paragraphs (2) and (3). **Effective** 10-4-2004. Prior to being stricken, Code Sec. 9812(f)(2) read as follows:

(2) after December 31, 2003.

- **2002, Job Creation and Worker Assistance Act of 2002 (P.L. 107-147)**

P.L. 107-147, §610(a):

Amended Code Sec. 9812(f). **Effective** for plan years beginning after 12-31-2000. Prior to amendment, Code Sec. 9812(f) read as follows:

(f) SUNSET.—This section shall not apply to benefits for services furnished on or after December 31, 2002.

- **2001 (P.L. 107-116)**

P.L. 107-116, §701(c):

Amended Code Sec. 9812(f) by striking "September 30, 2001", and inserting "December 31, 2002". **Effective** 1-10-2002.

- **1997, Taxpayer Relief Act of 1997 (P.L. 105-34)**

P.L. 105-34, §1531(a)(4):

Amended subtitle K by inserting after Code Sec. 9811 a new Code Sec. 9812. **Effective** with respect to group health plans for plan years beginning on or after 1-1-98.

[Sec. 9813]

SEC. 9813. COVERAGE OF DEPENDENT STUDENTS ON MEDICALLY NECESSARY LEAVE OF ABSENCE.

[Sec. 9813(a)]

(a) MEDICALLY NECESSARY LEAVE OF ABSENCE.—In this section, the term "medically necessary leave of absence" means, with respect to a dependent child described in subsection (b)(2) in connection with a group health plan, a leave of absence of such child from a postsecondary educational institution (including an institution of higher education as defined in section 102 of the Higher Education Act of 1965), or any other change in enrollment of such child at such an institution, that—

(1) commences while such child is suffering from a serious illness or injury;

(2) is medically necessary; and

(3) causes such child to lose student status for purposes of coverage under the terms of the plan or coverage.

[Sec. 9813(b)]

(b) REQUIREMENT TO CONTINUE COVERAGE.—

(1) IN GENERAL.—In the case of a dependent child described in paragraph (2), a group health plan shall not terminate coverage of such child under such plan due to a medically necessary leave of absence before the date that is the earlier of—

(A) the date that is 1 year after the first day of the medically necessary leave of absence; or

(B) the date on which such coverage would otherwise terminate under the terms of the plan.

(2) DEPENDENT CHILD DESCRIBED.—A dependent child described in this paragraph is, with respect to a group health plan, a beneficiary under the plan who—

(A) is a dependent child, under the terms of the plan, of a participant or beneficiary under the plan; and

(B) was enrolled in the plan, on the basis of being a student at a postsecondary educational institution (as described in subsection (a)), immediately before the first day of the medically necessary leave of absence involved.

(3) CERTIFICATION BY PHYSICIAN.—Paragraph (1) shall apply to a group health plan only if the plan, or the issuer of health insurance coverage offered in connection with the plan, has received written certification by a treating physician of the dependent child which states that the child is suffering from a serious illness or injury and that the leave of absence (or other change of enrollment) described in subsection (a) is medically necessary.

[Sec. 9813(c)]

(c) NOTICE.—A group health plan shall include, with any notice regarding a requirement for certification of student status for coverage under the plan, a description of the terms of this section for continued coverage during medically necessary leaves of absence. Such description shall be in language which is understandable to the typical plan participant.

[Sec. 9813(d)]

(d) NO CHANGE IN BENEFITS.—A dependent child whose benefits are continued under this section shall be entitled to the same benefits as if (during the medically necessary leave of absence) the child continued to be a covered student at the institution of higher education and was not on a medically necessary leave of absence.

[Sec. 9813(e)]

(e) CONTINUED APPLICATION IN CASE OF CHANGED COVERAGE.—If—

(1) a dependent child of a participant or beneficiary is in a period of coverage under a group health plan, pursuant to a medically necessary leave of absence of the child described in subsection (b);

(2) the manner in which the participant or beneficiary is covered under the plan changes, whether through a change in health insurance coverage or health insurance issuer, a change between health insurance coverage and self-insured coverage, or otherwise; and

(3) the coverage as so changed continues to provide coverage of beneficiaries as dependent children, this section shall apply to coverage of the child under the changed coverage for the remainder of the period of the medically necessary leave of absence of the dependent child under the plan in the same manner as it would have applied if the changed coverage had been the previous coverage.

Sec. 9812(f)—Stricken

GROUP HEALTH PLAN REQUIREMENTS

Amendments

• **2008, Michelle's Law (P.L. 110-381)**

P.L. 110-381, § 2(c)(1):

Amended subchapter B of chapter 100 by inserting after Code Sec. 9812 a new Code Sec. 9813. **Effective** with respect to plan years beginning on or after the date that is one year after 10-9-2008 and to medically necessary leaves of absence beginning during such plan years.

[Sec. 9815]

SEC. 9815. ADDITIONAL MARKET REFORMS.

[Sec. 9815(a)]

(a) GENERAL RULE.—Except as provided in subsection (b)—

(1) the provisions of part A of title XXVII of the Public Health Service Act (as amended by the Patient Protection and Affordable Care Act) shall apply to group health plans, and health insurance issuers providing health insurance coverage in connection with group health plans, as if included in this subchapter; and

(2) to the extent that any provision of this subchapter conflicts with a provision of such part A with respect to group health plans, or health insurance issuers providing health insurance coverage in connection with group health plans, the provisions of such part A shall apply.

Amendments

• **2020, Coronavirus Aid, Relief, and Economic Security (CARES) Act (P.L. 116-136)**

P.L. 116-136, §§ 3202 and 3203, provide:

SEC. 3202. PRICING OF DIAGNOSTIC TESTING.

(a) REIMBURSEMENT RATES.—A group health plan or a health insurance issuer providing coverage of items and services described in section 6001(a) of division F of the Families First Coronavirus Response Act (Public Law 116–127) with respect to an enrollee shall reimburse the provider of the diagnostic testing as follows:

(1) If the health plan or issuer has a negotiated rate with such provider in effect before the public health emergency declared under section 319 of the Public Health Service Act (42 U.S.C. 247d), such negotiated rate shall apply throughout the period of such declaration.

(2) If the health plan or issuer does not have a negotiated rate with such provider, such plan or issuer shall reimburse the provider in an amount that equals the cash price for such service as listed by the provider on a public internet website, or such plan or issuer may negotiate a rate with such provider for less than such cash price.

(b) REQUIREMENT TO PUBLICIZE CASH PRICE FOR DIAGNOSTIC TESTING FOR COVID–19.—

(1) IN GENERAL.—During the emergency period declared under section 319 of the Public Health Service Act (42 U.S.C. 247d), each provider of a diagnostic test for COVID–19 shall make public the cash price for such test on a public internet website of such provider.

(2) CIVIL MONETARY PENALTIES.—The Secretary of Health and Human Services may impose a civil monetary penalty on any provider of a diagnostic test for COVID–19 that is not in compliance with paragraph (1) and has not completed a corrective action plan to comply with the requirements of such paragraph, in an amount not to exceed $300 per day that the violation is ongoing.

SEC. 3203. RAPID COVERAGE OF PREVENTIVE SERVICES AND VACCINES FOR CORONAVIRUS.

(a) IN GENERAL.—Notwithstanding 2713(b) of the Public Health Service Act (42 U.S.C. 300gg–13), the Secretary of Health and Human Services, the Secretary of Labor, and the Secretary of the Treasury shall require group health plans and health insurance issuers offering group or individual health insurance to cover (without cost-sharing) any qualifying coronavirus preventive service, pursuant to section 2713(a) of the Public Health Service Act (42 U.S.C. 300gg–13(a)) (including the regulations under sections 2590.715–2713 of title 29, Code of Federal Regulations, section 54.9815–2713 of title 26, Code of Federal Regulations, and section 147.130 of title 45, Code of Federal Regulations (or any successor regulations)). The requirement described in this subsection shall take effect with respect to a qualifying coronavirus preventive service on the specified date described in subsection (b)(2).

(b) DEFINITIONS.—For purposes of this section:

(1) QUALIFYING CORONAVIRUS PREVENTIVE SERVICE.—The term "qualifying coronavirus preventive service" means an item, service, or immunization that is intended to prevent or mitigate coronavirus disease 2019 and that is—

(A) an evidence-based item or service that has in effect a rating of "A" or "B" in the current recommendations of the United States Preventive Services Task Force; or

(B) an immunization that has in effect a recommendation from the Advisory Committee on Immunization Practices of the Centers for Disease Control and Prevention with respect to the individual involved.

(2) SPECIFIED DATE.—The term "specified date" means the date that is 15 business days after the date on which a recommendation is made relating to the qualifying coronavirus preventive service as described in such paragraph.

(3) ADDITIONAL TERMS.—In this section, the terms "group health plan", "health insurance issuer", "group health insurance coverage", and "individual health insurance coverage" have the meanings given such terms in section 2791 of the Public Health Service Act (42 U.S.C. 300gg–91), section 733 of the Employee Retirement Income Security Act of 1974 (29 U.S.C. 1191b), and section 9832 of the Internal Revenue Code, as applicable.

• **2020, Families First Coronavirus Response Act (P.L. 116-127)**

P.L. 116-127, § 6001 (as amended by P.L. 116-136, § 3201), provides:

(a) IN GENERAL.—A group health plan and a health insurance issuer offering group or individual health insurance coverage (including a grandfathered health plan (as defined in section 1251(e) of the Patient Protection and Affordable Care Act)) shall provide coverage, and shall not impose any cost sharing (including deductibles, copayments, and coinsurance) requirements or prior authorization or other medical management requirements, for the following items and services furnished during any portion of the emergency period defined in paragraph (1)(B) of section 1135(g) of the Social Security Act (42 U.S.C. 1320b–5(g)) beginning on or after the date of the enactment of this Act:

(1) An in vitro diagnostic test defined in section 809.3 of title 21, Code of Federal Regulations (or successor regulations) for the detection of SARS–CoV–2 or the diagnosis of the virus that causes COVID–19, and the administration of such a test, that—

(A) is approved, cleared, or authorized under section 510(k), 513, 515, or 564 of the Federal Food, Drug, and Cosmetic Act (21 U.S.C. 360(k), 360c, 360e, 360bbb–3);

(B) the developer has requested, or intends to request, emergency use authorization under section 564 of the Federal Food, Drug, and Cosmetic Act (21 U.S.C. 360bbb–3), unless and until the emergency use authorization request under such section 564 has been denied or the developer of such test does not submit a request under such section within a reasonable timeframe;

(C) is developed in and authorized by a State that has notified the Secretary of Health and Human Services of its intention to review tests intended to diagnose COVID–19; or

(D) other test that the Secretary determines appropriate in guidance.

(2) Items and services furnished to an individual during health care provider office visits (which term in this paragraph includes in-person visits and telehealth visits), urgent care center visits, and emergency room visits that result in an order for or administration of an in vitro diagnostic product described in paragraph (1), but only to the extent such items and services relate to the furnishing or administration of such product or to the evaluation of such individual for purposes of determining the need of such individual for such product.

(b) ENFORCEMENT.—The provisions of subsection (a) shall be applied by the Secretary of Health and Human Services, Secretary of Labor, and Secretary of the Treasury to group health plans and health insurance issuers offering group or individual health insurance coverage as if included in the provisions of part A of title XXVII of the Public Health Service Act, part 7 of the Employee Retirement Income Security Act of 1974, and subchapter B of chapter 100 of the Internal Revenue Code of 1986, as applicable.

(c) IMPLEMENTATION.—The Secretary of Health and Human Services, Secretary of Labor, and Secretary of the Treasury may implement the provisions of this section through sub-regulatory guidance, program instruction or otherwise.

(d) TERMS.—The terms "group health plan"; "health insurance issuer"; "group health insurance coverage", and "individual health insurance coverage" have the meanings given such terms in section 2791 of the Public Health Service Act (42 U.S.C. 300gg–91), section 733 of the Employee Retirement Income Security Act of 1974 (29 U.S.C. 1191b), and section 9832 of the Internal Revenue Code of 1986, as applicable.

[Sec. 9815(b)]

(b) EXCEPTION.—Notwithstanding subsection (a), the provisions of sections 2716 and 2718 of title XXVII of the Public Health Service Act (as amended by the Patient Protection and Affordable Care Act) shall not apply with respect to self-insured group health plans, and the provisions of this subchapter shall continue to apply to such plans as if such sections of the Public Health Service Act (as so amended) had not been enacted.

Amendments

• **2010, Patient Protection and Affordable Care Act (P.L. 111-148)**

P.L. 111-148, § 1563(f) (as redesignated by P.L. 111-148, § 10107(b)):

Amended subchapter B of chapter 100 by adding at the end a new Code Sec. 9815. **Effective** 3-23-2010.

GROUP HEALTH PLAN REQUIREMENTS

[Sec. 9816]

SEC. 9816. PREVENTING SURPRISE MEDICAL BILLS.

[Sec. 9816(a)]

(a) COVERAGE OF EMERGENCY SERVICES.—

(1) IN GENERAL.—If a group health plan provides or covers any benefits with respect to services in an emergency department of a hospital or with respect to emergency services in an independent freestanding emergency department (as defined in paragraph (3)(D)), the plan shall cover emergency services (as defined in paragraph (3)(C))—

(A) without the need for any prior authorization determination;

(B) whether the health care provider furnishing such services is a participating provider or a participating emergency facility, as applicable, with respect to such services;

(C) in a manner so that, if such services are provided to a participant or beneficiary by a nonparticipating provider or a nonparticipating emergency facility—

(i) such services will be provided without imposing any requirement under the plan for prior authorization of services or any limitation on coverage that is more restrictive than the requirements or limitations that apply to emergency services received from participating providers and participating emergency facilities with respect to such plan;

(ii) the cost-sharing requirement is not greater than the requirement that would apply if such services were provided by a participating provider or a participating emergency facility;

(iii) such cost-sharing requirement is calculated as if the total amount that would have been charged for such services by such participating provider or participating emergency facility were equal to the recognized amount (as defined in paragraph (3)(H)) for such services, plan, and year;

(iv) the group health plan—

(I) not later than 30 calendar days after the bill for such services is transmitted by such provider or facility, sends to the provider or facility, as applicable, an initial payment or notice of denial of payment; and

(II) pays a total plan payment directly to such provider or facility, respectively (in accordance, if applicable, with the timing requirement described in subsection (c)(6)) that is, with application of any initial payment under subclause (I), equal to the amount by which the out-of-network rate (as defined in paragraph (3)(K)) for such services exceeds the cost-sharing amount for such services (as determined in accordance with clauses (ii) and (iii)) and year; and

(iv) any cost-sharing payments made by the participant or beneficiary with respect to such emergency services so furnished shall be counted toward any in-network deductible or out-of-pocket maximums applied under the plan (and such in-network deductible and out-of-pocket maximums shall be applied) in the same manner as if such cost-sharing payments were made with respect to emergency services furnished by a participating provider or a participating emergency facility; and

(D) without regard to any other term or condition of such coverage (other than exclusion or coordination of benefits, or an affiliation or waiting period, permitted under section 2704 of the Public Health Service Act, including as incorporated pursuant to section 715 of the Employee Retirement Income Security Act of 1974 and section 9815 of this Act[sic], and other than applicable cost-sharing).

(2) AUDIT PROCESS AND REGULATIONS FOR QUALIFYING PAYMENT AMOUNTS.—

(A) AUDIT PROCESS.—

(i) IN GENERAL.—Not later than October 1, 2021, the Secretary, in consultation with the Secretary of Health and Human Services and the Secretary of Labor, shall establish through rulemaking a process, in accordance with clause (ii), under which group health plans are audited by the Secretary or applicable State authority to ensure that—

(I) such plans are in compliance with the requirement of applying a qualifying payment amount under this section; and

(II) such qualifying payment amount so applied satisfies the definition under paragraph (3)(E) with respect to the year involved, including with respect to a group health plan described in clause (ii) of such paragraph (3)(E).

(ii) AUDIT SAMPLES.—Under the process established pursuant to clause (i), the Secretary—

(I) shall conduct audits described in such clause, with respect to a year (beginning with 2022), of a sample with respect to such year of claims data from not more than 25 group health plans; and

(II) may audit any group health plan if the Secretary has received any complaint or other information about such plan or coverage, respectively, that involves the compliance of the plan with either of the requirements described in subclauses (I) and (II) of such clause.

(iii) REPORTS.—Beginning for 2022, the Secretary shall annually submit to Congress a report on the number of plans and issuers with respect to which audits were conducted during such year pursuant to this subparagraph.

(B) RULEMAKING.—Not later than July 1, 2021, the Secretary, in consultation with the Secretary of Labor and the Secretary of Health and Human Services, shall establish through rulemaking—

(i) the methodology the group health plan shall use to determine the qualifying payment amount, differentiating by large group market and small group market;

(ii) the information such plan or issuer, respectively, shall share with the nonparticipating provider or nonparticipating facility, as applicable, when making such a determination;

(iii) the geographic regions applied for purposes of this subparagraph, taking into account access to items and services in rural and underserved areas, including health professional shortage areas, as defined in section 332 of the Public Health Service Act; and

(iv) a process to receive complaints of violations of the requirements described in subclauses (I) and (II) of subparagraph (A)(i) by group health plans.

Such rulemaking shall take into account payments that are made by such plan that are not on a fee-for-service basis. Such methodology may account for relevant payment adjustments that take into account quality or facility type (including higher acuity settings and the case-mix of various facility types) that are otherwise taken into account for purposes of determining payment amounts with respect to participating facilities. In carrying out clause (iii), the Secretary shall consult with the National Association of Insurance Commissioners to establish the geographic regions under such clause and shall periodically update such regions, as appropriate, taking into account the findings of the report submitted under section 109(a) of the No Surprises Act.

(3) DEFINITIONS.—In this subchapter:

(A) EMERGENCY DEPARTMENT OF A HOSPITAL.—The term "emergency department of a hospital" includes a hospital outpatient department that provides emergency services (as defined in subparagraph (C)(i)).

(B) EMERGENCY MEDICAL CONDITION.—The term "emergency medical condition" means a medical condition manifesting itself by acute symptoms of sufficient severity (including severe pain) such that a prudent layperson, who possesses an average knowledge of health and medicine, could reasonably expect the absence of immediate medical attention to result in a condition described in clause (i), (ii), or (iii) of section 1867(e)(1)(A) of the Social Security Act.

(C) EMERGENCY SERVICES.—

(i) IN GENERAL.—The term "emergency services", with respect to an emergency medical condition, means—

(I) a medical screening examination (as required under section 1867 of the Social Security Act, or as would be required under such section if such section applied to an independent freestanding emergency department) that is within the capability of the emergency department of a hospital or of an independent freestanding emergency department, as applicable, including ancillary services routinely available to the emergency department to evaluate such emergency medical condition; and

(II) within the capabilities of the staff and facilities available at the hospital or the independent freestanding emergency department, as applicable, such further medical examination and treatment as are required under section 1867 of such Act, or as would be required under such section if such section applied to an independent freestanding emergency department, to stabilize the patient (regardless of the department of the hospital in which such further examination or treatment is furnished).

(ii) INCLUSION OF ADDITIONAL SERVICES.—

(I) IN GENERAL.—For purposes of this subsection and section 2799B–1 of the Public Health Service Act, in the case of a participant or beneficiary who is enrolled in a group health plan and who is furnished services described in clause (i) with respect to an emergency medical condition, the term "emergency services" shall include, unless each of the conditions described in subclause (II) are met, in addition to the items and services described in clause (i), items and services—

(aa) for which benefits are provided or covered under the plan; and

(bb) that are furnished by a nonparticipating provider or nonparticipating emergency facility (regardless of the department of the hospital in which such items or services are furnished) after the participant or beneficiary is stabilized and as part of outpatient observation or an inpatient or outpatient stay with respect to the visit in which the services described in clause (i) are furnished.

(II) CONDITIONS.—For purposes of subclause (I), the conditions described in this subclause, with respect to a participant or beneficiary who is stabilized and furnished additional items and services described in subclause (I) after such stabilization by a provider or facility described in subclause (I), are the following:

(aa) Such provider or facility determines such individual is able to travel using nonmedical transportation or nonemergency medical transportation.

(bb) Such provider furnishing such additional items and services satisfies the notice and consent criteria of section 2799B–2(d) with respect to such items and services.

(cc) Such individual is in a condition to receive (as determined in accordance with guidelines issued by the Secretary pursuant to rulemaking) the information described in section 2799B–2 and to provide informed consent under such section, in accordance with applicable State law.

(dd) Such other conditions, as specified by the Secretary, such as conditions relating to coordinating care transitions to participating providers and facilities.

(D) INDEPENDENT FREESTANDING EMERGENCY DEPARTMENT.—The term "independent freestanding emergency department" means a health care facility that—

(i) is geographically separate and distinct and licensed separately from a hospital under applicable State law; and

(ii) provides any of the emergency services (as defined in subparagraph (C)(i)).

(E) QUALIFYING PAYMENT AMOUNT.—

(i) IN GENERAL.—The term "qualifying payment amount" means, subject to clauses (ii) and (iii), with respect to a sponsor of a group health plan—

(I) for an item or service furnished during 2022, the median of the contracted rates recognized by the plan (determined with respect to all such plans of such sponsor that are offered within the same insurance market (specified in subclause (I), (II), or (III) of clause (iv)) as the plan) as the total maximum payment (including the cost-sharing amount imposed for such item or service and the amount to be paid by the plan) under such plans on January 31, 2019 for the same or a similar item or service that is provided by a provider in the same or similar specialty and provided in the geographic region in which the item or service is furnished, consistent with the methodology established by the Secretary under paragraph (2)(B), increased by the percentage increase in the consumer price index for all urban consumers (United States city average) over 2019, such percentage increase over 2020, and such percentage increase over 2021; and

(II) for an item or service furnished during 2023 or a subsequent year, the qualifying payment amount determined under this clause for such an item or service furnished in the previous year, increased by the percentage increase in the consumer price index for all urban consumers (United States city average) over such previous year.

(ii) NEW PLANS AND COVERAGE.—The term "qualifying payment amount" means, with respect to a sponsor of a group health plan in a geographic region in which such sponsor, respectively, did not offer any group health plan or health insurance coverage during 2019—

(I) for the first year in which such group health plan is offered in such region, a rate (determined in accordance with a methodology established by the Secretary) for items and services that are covered by such plan and furnished during such first year; and

(II) for each subsequent year such group health plan is offered in such region, the qualifying payment amount determined under this clause for such items and services furnished in the previous year, increased by the percentage increase in the consumer price index for all urban consumers (United States city average) over such previous year.

(iii) INSUFFICIENT INFORMATION; NEWLY COVERED ITEMS AND SERVICES.—In the case of a sponsor of a group health plan that does not have sufficient information to calculate the median of the contracted rates described in clause (i)(I) in 2019 (or, in the case of a newly covered item or service (as defined in clause (v)(III)), in the first coverage year (as defined in clause (v)(I)) for such item or service with respect to such plan) for an item or service (including with respect to provider type, or amount, of claims for items or services (as determined by the Secretary) provided in a particular geographic region (other than in a case with respect to which clause (ii) applies)) the term "qualifying payment amount"—

(I) for an item or service furnished during 2022 (or, in the case of a newly covered item or service, during the first coverage year for such item or service with respect to such plan), means such rate for such item or service determined by the sponsor through use of any database that is determined, in accordance with rulemaking described in paragraph (2)(B), to not have any conflicts of interest and to have sufficient information reflecting allowed amounts paid to a health care provider or facility for relevant services furnished in the applicable geographic region (such as a State all-payer claims database);

GROUP HEALTH PLAN REQUIREMENTS

(II) for an item or service furnished in a subsequent year (before the first sufficient information year (as defined in clause (v)(II)) for such item or service with respect to such plan), means the rate determined under subclause (I) or this subclause, as applicable, for such item or service for the year previous to such subsequent year, increased by the percentage increase in the consumer price index for all urban consumers (United States city average) over such previous year;

(III) for an item or service furnished in the first sufficient information year for such item or service with respect to such plan, has the meaning given the term qualifying payment amount in clause (i)(I), except that in applying such clause to such item or service, the reference to "furnished during 2022" shall be treated as a reference to furnished during such first sufficient information year, the reference to "on January 31, 2019" shall be treated as a reference to in such sufficient information year, and the increase described in such clause shall not be applied; and

(IV) for an item or service furnished in any year subsequent to the first sufficient information year for such item or service with respect to such plan, has the meaning given such term in clause (i)(II), except that in applying such clause to such item or service, the reference to "furnished during 2023 or a subsequent year" shall be treated as a reference to furnished during the year after such first sufficient information year or a subsequent year.

(iv) INSURANCE MARKET.—For purposes of clause (i)(I), a health insurance market specified in this clause is one of the following:

(I) The large group market (other than plans described in subclause (III)).

(II) The small group market (other than plans described in subclause (III)).

(III) In the case of a self-insured group health plan, other self-insured group health plans.

(v) DEFINITIONS.—For purposes of this subparagraph:

(I) FIRST COVERAGE YEAR.—The term "first coverage year" means, with respect to a group health plan and an item or service for which coverage is not offered in 2019 under such plan or coverage, the first year after 2019 for which coverage for such item or service is offered under such plan.

(II) FIRST SUFFICIENT INFORMATION YEAR.—The term "first sufficient information year" means, with respect to a group health plan—

(aa) in the case of an item or service for which the plan does not have sufficient information to calculate the median of the contracted rates described in clause (i)(I) in 2019, the first year subsequent to 2022 for which such sponsor has such sufficient information to calculate the median of such contracted rates in the year previous to such first subsequent year; and

(bb) in the case of a newly covered item or service, the first year subsequent to the first coverage year for such item or service with respect to such plan for which the sponsor has sufficient information to calculate the median of the contracted rates described in clause (i)(I) in the year previous to such first subsequent year.

(III) NEWLY COVERED ITEM OR SERVICE.—The term "newly covered item or service" means, with respect to a group health plan, an item or service for which coverage was not offered in 2019 under such plan or coverage, but is offered under such plan or coverage in a year after 2019.

(F) NONPARTICIPATING EMERGENCY FACILITY; PARTICIPATING EMERGENCY FACILITY.—

(i) NONPARTICIPATING EMERGENCY FACILITY.—The term "nonparticipating emergency facility" means, with respect to an item or service and a group health plan, an emergency department of a hospital, or an independent freestanding emergency department, that does not have a contractual relationship directly or indirectly with the plan for furnishing such item or service under the plan.

(ii) PARTICIPATING EMERGENCY FACILITY.—The term "participating emergency facility" means, with respect to an item or service and a group health plan, an emergency department of a hospital, or an independent freestanding emergency department, that has a contractual relationship directly or indirectly with the plan, with respect to the furnishing of such an item or service at such facility.

(G) NONPARTICIPATING PROVIDERS; PARTICIPATING PROVIDERS.—

(i) NONPARTICIPATING PROVIDER.—The term "nonparticipating provider" means, with respect to an item or service and a group health plan, a physician or other health care provider who is acting within the scope of practice of that provider's license or certification under applicable State law and who does not have a contractual relationship with the plan or issuer, respectively, for furnishing such item or service under the plan.

(ii) PARTICIPATING PROVIDER.—The term "participating provider" means, with respect to an item or service and a group health plan, a physician or other health care provider who is acting within the scope of practice of that provider's license or certification under applicable State law and who has a contractual relationship with the plan for furnishing such item or service under the plan.

(H) RECOGNIZED AMOUNT.—The term "recognized amount" means, with respect to an item or service furnished by a nonparticipating provider or nonparticipating emergency facility during a year and a group health plan—

(i) subject to clause (iii), in the case of such item or service furnished in a State that has in effect a specified State law with respect to such plan; such a nonparticipating provider or nonparticipating emergency facility; and such an item or service, the amount determined in accordance with such law;

(ii) subject to clause (iii), in the case of such item or service furnished in a State that does not have in effect a specified State law, with respect to such plan; such a nonparticipating provider or nonparticipating emergency facility; and such an item or service, the amount that is the qualifying payment amount (as defined in subparagraph (E)) for such year and determined in accordance with rulemaking described in paragraph (2)(B)) for such item or service; or

(iii) in the case of such item or service furnished in a State with an All-Payer Model Agreement under section 1115A of the Social Security Act, the amount that the State approves under such system for such item or service so furnished.

(I) SPECIFIED STATE LAW.—The term "specified State law" means, with respect to a State, an item or service furnished by a nonparticipating provider or nonparticipating emergency facility during a year and a group health plan, a State law that provides for a method for determining the total amount payable under such a plan (to the extent such State law applies to such plan, subject to section 514) in the case of a participant or beneficiary covered under such plan and receiving such item or service from such a nonparticipating provider or nonparticipating emergency facility.

(J) STABILIZE.—The term "to stabilize", with respect to an emergency medical condition (as defined in subparagraph (B)), has the meaning given in section 1867(e)(3) of the Social Security Act (42 U.S.C. 1395dd(e)(3)).

(K) OUT-OF-NETWORK RATE.—The term "out-of-network rate" means, with respect to an item or service furnished in a State during a year to a participant or beneficiary of a group health plan receiving such item or service from a nonparticipating provider or nonparticipating emergency facility—

(i) subject to clause (iii), in the case of such item or service furnished in a State that has in effect a specified State law with respect to such plan; such a nonparticipating provider or nonparticipating emergency facility; and such an item or service, the amount determined in accordance with such law;

(ii) subject to clause (iii), in the case such State does not have in effect such a law with respect to such item or service, plan, and provider or facility—

GROUP HEALTH PLAN REQUIREMENTS

(I) subject to subclause (II), if the provider or facility (as applicable) and such plan or coverage agree on an amount of payment (including if such agreed on amount is the initial payment sent by the plan under subsection (a)(1)(C)(iv)(I), subsection (b)(1)(C), or section 9817(a)(3)(A), as applicable, or is agreed on through open negotiations under subsection (c)(1)) with respect to such item or service, such agreed on amount; or

(II) if such provider or facility (as applicable) and such plan or coverage enter the independent dispute resolution process under subsection (c) and do not so agree before the date on which a certified IDR entity (as defined in paragraph (4) of such subsection) makes a determination with respect to such item or service under such subsection, the amount of such determination; or

(iii) in the case such State has an All-Payer Model Agreement under section 1115A of the Social Security Act, the amount that the State approves under such system for such item or service so furnished.

(L) COST-SHARING.—The term "cost-sharing" includes copayments, coinsurance, and deductibles.

[Sec. 9816(b)]

(b) COVERAGE OF NON-EMERGENCY SERVICES PERFORMED BY NONPARTICIPATING PROVIDERS AT CERTAIN PARTICIPATING FACILITIES.—

(1) IN GENERAL.—In the case of items or services (other than emergency services to which subsection (a) applies) for which any benefits are provided or covered by a group health plan furnished to a participant or beneficiary of such plan by a nonparticipating provider (as defined in subsection (a)(3)(G)(i)) (and who, with respect to such items and services, has not satisfied the notice and consent criteria of section 2799B–2(d) of the Public Health Service Act) with respect to a visit (as defined by the Secretary in accordance with paragraph (2)(B)) at a participating health care facility (as defined in paragraph (2)(A)), with respect to such plan, the plan—

(A) shall not impose on such participant or beneficiary a cost-sharing requirement for such items and services so furnished that is greater than the cost-sharing requirement that would apply under such plan had such items or services been furnished by a participating provider (as defined in subsection (a)(3)(G)(ii));

(B) shall calculate such cost-sharing requirement as if the total amount that would have been charged for such items and services by such participating provider were equal to the recognized amount (as defined in subsection (a)(3)(H)) for such items and services, plan, and year;

(C) not later than 30 calendar days after the bill for such items or services is transmitted by such provider, shall send to the provider an initial payment or notice of denial of payment;

(D) shall pay a total plan payment directly, in accordance, if applicable, with the timing requirement described in subsection (c)(6), to such provider furnishing such items and services to such participant or beneficiary that is, with application of any initial payment under subparagraph (C), equal to the amount by which the out-of-network rate (as defined in subsection (a)(3)(K)) for such items and services exceeds the cost-sharing amount imposed under the plan for such items and services (as determined in accordance with subparagraphs (A) and (B)) and year; and

(E) shall count toward any in-network deductible and in-network out-of-pocket maximums (as applicable) applied under the plan, any cost-sharing payments made by the participant or beneficiary (and such in-network deductible and out-of-pocket maximums shall be applied) with respect to such items and services so furnished in the same manner as if such cost-sharing payments were with respect to items and services furnished by a participating provider.

(2) DEFINITIONS.—In this section:

(A) PARTICIPATING HEALTH CARE FACILITY.—

(i) IN GENERAL.—The term "participating health care facility" means, with respect to an item or service and a group health plan, a health care facility described in clause (ii) that has a direct or indirect contractual relationship with the plan, with respect to the furnishing of such an item or service at the facility.

(ii) HEALTH CARE FACILITY DESCRIBED.—A health care facility described in this clause, with respect to a group health plan or health insurance coverage offered in the group or individual market, is each of the following:

(I) A hospital (as defined in 1861(e) of the Social Security Act).

(II) A hospital outpatient department.

(III) A critical access hospital (as defined in section 1861(mm)(1) of such Act).

(IV) An ambulatory surgical center described in section 1833(i)(1)(A) of such Act.

(V) Any other facility, specified by the Secretary, that provides items or services for which coverage is provided under the plan or coverage, respectively.

(B) VISIT.—The term "visit" shall, with respect to items and services furnished to an individual at a health care facility, include equipment and devices, telemedicine services, imaging services, laboratory services, preoperative and postoperative services, and such other items and services as the Secretary may specify, regardless of whether or not the provider furnishing such items or services is at the facility.

[Sec. 9816(c)]

(c) DETERMINATION OF OUT-OF-NETWORK RATES TO BE PAID BY HEALTH PLANS; INDEPENDENT DISPUTE RESOLUTION PROCESS.—

(1) DETERMINATION THROUGH OPEN NEGOTIATION.—

(A) IN GENERAL.—With respect to an item or service furnished in a year by a nonparticipating provider or a nonparticipating facility, with respect to a group health plan, in a State described in subsection (a)(3)(K)(ii) with respect to such plan and provider or facility, and for which a payment is required to be made by the plan pursuant to subsection (a)(1) or (b)(1), the provider or facility (as applicable) or plan may, during the 30-day period beginning on the day the provider or facility receives an initial payment or a notice of denial of payment from the plan regarding a claim for payment for such item or service, initiate open negotiations under this paragraph between such provider or facility and plan for purposes of determining, during the open negotiation period, an amount agreed on by such provider or facility, respectively, and such plan for payment (including any cost-sharing) for such item or service. For purposes of this subsection, the open negotiation period, with respect to an item or service, is the 30-day period beginning on the date of initiation of the negotiations with respect to such item or service.

(B) ACCESSING INDEPENDENT DISPUTE RESOLUTION PROCESS IN CASE OF FAILED NEGOTIATIONS.—In the case of open negotiations pursuant to subparagraph (A), with respect to an item or service, that do not result in a determination of an amount of payment for such item or service by the last day of the open negotiation period described in such subparagraph with respect to such item or service, the provider or facility (as applicable) or group health plan that was party to such negotiations may, during the 4-day period beginning on the day after such open negotiation period, initiate the independent dispute resolution process under paragraph (2) with respect to such item or service. The independent dispute resolution process shall be initiated by a party pursuant to the previous sentence by submission to the other party and to the Secretary of a notification (containing such information as specified by the Secretary) and for purposes of this subsection,

GROUP HEALTH PLAN REQUIREMENTS

the date of initiation of such process shall be the date of such submission or such other date specified by the Secretary pursuant to regulations that is not later than the date of receipt of such notification by both the other party and the Secretary.

(2) INDEPENDENT DISPUTE RESOLUTION PROCESS AVAILABLE IN CASE OF FAILED OPEN NEGOTIATIONS.—

(A) ESTABLISHMENT.—Not later than 1 year after the date of the enactment of this subsection, the Secretary, jointly with the Secretary of Health and Human Services and the Secretary of Labor, shall establish by regulation one independent dispute resolution process (referred to in this subsection as the "IDR process") under which, in the case of an item or service with respect to which a provider or facility (as applicable) or group health plan submits a notification under paragraph (1)(B) (in this subsection referred to as a "qualified IDR item or service"), a certified IDR entity under paragraph (4) determines, subject to subparagraph (B) and in accordance with the succeeding provisions of this subsection, the amount of payment under the plan for such item or service furnished by such provider or facility.

(B) AUTHORITY TO CONTINUE NEGOTIATIONS.—Under the independent dispute resolution process, in the case that the parties to a determination for a qualified IDR item or service agree on a payment amount for such item or service during such process but before the date on which the entity selected with respect to such determination under paragraph (4) makes such determination under paragraph (5), such amount shall be treated for purposes of subsection (a)(3)(K)(ii) as the amount agreed to by such parties for such item or service. In the case of an agreement described in the previous sentence, the independent dispute resolution process shall provide for a method to determine how to allocate between the parties to such determination the payment of the compensation of the entity selected with respect to such determination.

(C) CLARIFICATION.—A nonparticipating provider may not, with respect to an item or service furnished by such provider, submit a notification under paragraph (1)(B) if such provider is exempt from the requirement under subsection (a) of section 2799B–2 of the Public Health Service Act with respect to such item or service pursuant to subsection (b) of such section.

(3) TREATMENT OF BATCHING OF ITEMS AND SERVICES.—

(A) IN GENERAL.—Under the IDR process, the Secretary shall specify criteria under which multiple qualified IDR dispute items and services are permitted to be considered jointly as part of a single determination by an entity for purposes of encouraging the efficiency (including minimizing costs) of the IDR process. Such items and services may be so considered only if—

(i) such items and services to be included in such determination are furnished by the same provider or facility;

(ii) payment for such items and services is required to be made by the same group health plan or health insurance issuer;

(iii) such items and services are related to the treatment of a similar condition; and

(iv) such items and services were furnished during the 30 day period following the date on which the first item or service included with respect to such determination was furnished or an alternative period as determined by the Secretary, for use in limited situations, such as by the consent of the parties or in the case of low-volume items and services, to encourage procedural efficiency and minimize health plan and provider administrative costs.

(B) TREATMENT OF BUNDLED PAYMENTS.—In carrying out subparagraph (A), the Secretary shall provide that, in the case of items and services which are included by a provider or facility as part of a bundled payment, such items and services included in such bundled payment may be part of a single determination under this subsection.

(4) CERTIFICATION AND SELECTION OF IDR ENTITIES.—

(A) IN GENERAL.—The Secretary, jointly with the Secretary of Health and Human Services and the Secretary of Labor, shall establish a process to certify (including to recertify) entities under this paragraph. Such process shall ensure that an entity so certified—

(i) has (directly or through contracts or other arrangements) sufficient medical, legal, and other expertise and sufficient staffing to make determinations described in paragraph (5) on a timely basis;

(ii) is not—

(I) a group health plan, provider, or facility;

(II) an affiliate or a subsidiary of such a group health plan, provider, or facility; or

(III) an affiliate or subsidiary of a professional or trade association of such group health plans or of providers or facilities;

(iii) carries out the responsibilities of such an entity in accordance with this subsection;

(iv) meets appropriate indicators of fiscal integrity;

(v) maintains the confidentiality (in accordance with regulations promulgated by the Secretary) of individually identifiable health information obtained in the course of conducting such determinations;

(vi) does not under the IDR process carry out any determination with respect to which the entity would not pursuant to subclause (I), (II), or (III) of subparagraph (F)(i) be eligible for selection; and

(vii) meets such other requirements as determined appropriate by the Secretary.

(B) PERIOD OF CERTIFICATION.—Subject to subparagraph (C), each certification (including a recertification) of an entity under the process described in subparagraph (A) shall be for a 5-year period.

(C) REVOCATION.—A certification of an entity under this paragraph may be revoked under the process described in subparagraph (A) if the entity has a pattern or practice of noncompliance with any of the requirements described in such subparagraph.

(D) PETITION FOR DENIAL OR WITHDRAWAL.—The process described in subparagraph (A) shall ensure that an individual, provider, facility, or group health plan may petition for a denial of a certification or a revocation of a certification with respect to an entity under this paragraph for failure of meeting a requirement of this subsection.

(E) SUFFICIENT NUMBER OF ENTITIES.—The process described in subparagraph (A) shall ensure that a sufficient number of entities are certified under this paragraph to ensure the timely and efficient provision of determinations described in paragraph (5).

(F) SELECTION OF CERTIFIED IDR ENTITY.—The Secretary shall, with respect to the determination of the amount of payment under this subsection of an item or service, provide for a method—

(i) that allows for the group health plan and the nonparticipating provider or the nonparticipating emergency facility (as applicable) involved in a notification under paragraph (1)(B) to jointly select, not later than the last day of the 3-business day period following the date of the initiation of the process with respect to such item or service, for purposes of making such determination, an entity certified under this paragraph that—

(I) is not a party to such determination or an employee or agent of such a party;

(II) does not have a material familial, financial, or professional relationship with such a party; and

(III) does not otherwise have a conflict of interest with such a party (as determined by the Secretary); and

(ii) that requires, in the case such parties do not make such selection by such last day, the Secretary to, not later than 6 business days after such date of initiation—

(I) select such an entity that satisfies subclauses (I) through (III) of clause (i); and

(II) provide notification of such selection to the provider or facility (as applicable) and the plan or issuer (as applicable) party to such determination.

An entity selected pursuant to the previous sentence to make a determination described in such sentence shall be referred to in this subsection as the "certified IDR entity" with respect to such determination.

(5) PAYMENT DETERMINATION.—

(A) IN GENERAL.—Not later than 30 days after the date of selection of the certified IDR entity with respect to a determination for a qualified IDR item or service, the certified IDR entity shall—

(i) taking into account the considerations specified in subparagraph (C), select one of the offers submitted under subparagraph (B) to be the amount of payment for such item or service determined under this subsection for purposes of subsection (a)(1) or (b)(1), as applicable; and

(ii) notify the provider or facility and the group health plan party to such determination of the offer selected under clause (i).

(B) SUBMISSION OF OFFERS.—Not later than 10 days after the date of selection of the certifed IDR entity with respect to a determination for a qualified IDR item or service, the provider or facility and the group health plan party to such determination—

(i) shall each submit to the certified IDR entity with respect to such determination—

(I) an offer for a payment amount for such item or service furnished by such provider or facility; and

(II) such information as requested by the certified IDR entity relating to such offer; and

(ii) may each submit to the certified IDR entity with respect to such determination any information relating to such offer submitted by either party, including information relating to any circumstance described in subparagraph (C)(ii).

(C) CONSIDERATIONS IN DETERMINATION.—

(i) IN GENERAL.—In determining which offer is the payment to be applied pursuant to this paragraph, the certified IDR entity, with respect to the determination for a qualified IDR item or service shall consider—

(I) the qualifying payment amounts (as defined in subsection (a)(3)(E)) for the applicable year for items or services that are comparable to the qualified IDR item or service and that are furnished in the same geographic region (as defined by the Secretary for purposes of such subsection) as such qualified IDR item or service; and

(II) subject to subparagraph (D), information on any circumstance described in clause (ii), such information as requested in subparagraph (B)(i)(II), and any additional information provided in subparagraph (B)(ii).

(ii) ADDITIONAL CIRCUMSTANCES.—For purposes of clause (i)(II), the circumstances described in this clause are, with respect to a qualified IDR item or service of a nonparticipating provider, nonparticipating emergency facility, or group health plan, the following:

(I) The level of training, experience, and quality and outcomes measurements of the provider or facility that furnished such item or service (such as those endorsed by the consensus-based entity authorized in section 1890 of the Social Security Act).

(II) The market share held by the nonparticipating provider or facility or that of the plan or issuer in the geographic region in which the item or service was provided.

(III) The acuity of the individual receiving such item or service or the complexity of furnishing such item or service to such individual.

(IV) The teaching status, case mix, and scope of services of the nonparticipating facility that furnished such item or service.

(V) Demonstrations of good faith efforts (or lack of good faith efforts) made by the nonparticipating provider or nonparticipating facility or the plan or issuer to enter into network agreements and, if applicable, contracted rates between the provider or facility, as applicable, and the plan or issuer, as applicable, during the previous 4 plan years.

(D) PROHIBITION ON CONSIDERATION OF CERTAIN FACTORS.—In determining which offer is the payment to be applied with respect to qualified IDR items and services furnished by a provider or facility, the certified IDR entity with respect to a determination shall not consider usual and customary charges, the amount that would have been billed by such provider or facility with respect to such items and services had the provisions of section 2799B–1 of the Public Health Service Act or 2799B–2 of such Act (as applicable) not applied, or the payment or reimbursement rate for such items and services furnished by such provider or facility payable by a public payor, including under the Medicare program under title XVIII of the Social Security Act, under the Medicaid program under title XIX of such Act, under the Children's Health Insurance Program under title XXI of such Act, under the TRICARE program under chapter 55 of title 10, United States Code, or under chapter 17 of title 38, United States Code.

(E) EFFECTS OF DETERMINATION.—

(i) IN GENERAL.—A determination of a certified IDR entity under subparagraph (A)—

(I) shall be binding upon the parties involved, in the absence of a fraudulent claim or evidence of misrepresentation of facts presented to the IDR entity involved regarding such claim; and

(II) shall not be subject to judicial review, except in a case described in any of paragraphs (1) through (4) of section 10(a) of title 9, United States Code.

(ii) SUSPENSION OF CERTAIN SUBSEQUENT IDR REQUESTS.—In the case of a determination of a certified IDR entity under subparagraph (A), with respect to an initial notification submitted under paragraph (1)(B) with respect to qualified IDR items and services and the two parties involved with such notification, the party that submitted such notification may not submit during the 90-day period following such determination a subsequent notification under such paragraph involving the same other party to such notification with respect to such an item or service that was the subject of such initial notification.

(iii) SUBSEQUENT SUBMISSION OF REQUESTS PERMITTED.—In the case of a notification that pursuant to clause (ii) is not permitted to be submitted under paragraph (1)(B) during a 90-day period specified in such clause, if the end of the open negotiation period specified in paragraph (1)(A), that but for this clause would otherwise apply with respect to such notification, occurs during such 90-day period, such paragraph (1)(B) shall be applied as if the reference in such paragraph to the 4-day period beginning on the day after such open negotiation period were instead a reference to the 30-day period beginning on the day after the last day of such 90-day period.

(iv) REPORTS.—The Secretary, jointly with the Secretary of Labor and the Secretary of the Health and Human Services, shall examine the impact of the application of clause (ii) and whether the application of such clause delays payment determinations or impacts early, alternative resolution of claims (such as through open negotiations), and shall submit to Congress, not later than 2 years after the date of implementation of such clause an interim report (and not later than 4 years after such date of implementation, a final report) on whether any group health plans or health insurance issuers offering group or individual health insurance coverage or types of such plans or coverage have a pattern or practice of routine denial, low payment, or down-coding of claims, or otherwise abuse the 90-day period described in such clause, including recommendations on ways to discourage such a pattern or practice.

(F) COSTS OF INDEPENDENT DISPUTE RESOLUTION PROCESS.—In the case of a notification under paragraph (1)(B) submitted by a nonparticipating provider, nonparticipating emergency facility, or group health plan and submitted to a certified IDR entity—

(i) if such entity makes a determination with respect to such notification under subparagraph (A), the party whose offer is not chosen under such subparagraph shall be responsible for paying all fees charged by such entity; and

GROUP HEALTH PLAN REQUIREMENTS

(ii) if the parties reach a settlement with respect to such notification prior to such a determination, each party shall pay half of all fees charged by such entity, unless the parties otherwise agree.

(6) TIMING OF PAYMENT.—The total plan payment required pursuant to subsection (a)(1) or (b)(1), with respect to a qualified IDR item or service for which a determination is made under paragraph (5)(A) or with respect to an item or service for which a payment amount is determined under open negotiations under paragraph (1), shall be made directly to the nonparticipating provider or facility not later than 30 days after the date on which such determination is made.

(7) PUBLICATION OF INFORMATION RELATING TO THE IDR PROCESS.—

(A) PUBLICATION OF INFORMATION.—For each calendar quarter in 2022 and each calendar quarter in a subsequent year, the Secretary shall make available on the public website of the Department of the Treasury—

(i) the number of notifications submitted under paragraph (1)(B) during such calendar quarter;

(ii) the size of the provider practices and the size of the facilities submitting notifications under paragraph (1)(B) during such calendar quarter;

(iii) the number of such notifications with respect to which a determination was made under paragraph (5)(A);

(iv) the information described in subparagraph (B) with respect to each notification with respect to which such a determination was so made;

(v) the number of times the payment amount determined (or agreed to) under this subsection exceeds the qualifying payment amount, specified by items and services;

(vi) the amount of expenditures made by the Secretary during such calendar quarter to carry out the IDR process;

(vii) the total amount of fees paid under paragraph (8) during such calendar quarter; and

(viii) the total amount of compensation paid to certified IDR entities under paragraph (5)(F) during such calendar quarter.

(B) INFORMATION.—For purposes of subparagraph (A), the information described in this subparagraph is, with respect to a notification under paragraph (1)(B) by a nonparticipating provider, nonparticipating emergency facility, or group health plan—

(i) a description of each item and service included with respect to such notification;

(ii) the geography in which the items and services with respect to such notification were provided;

(iii) the amount of the offer submitted under paragraph (5)(B) by the group health plan and by the nonparticipating provider or nonparticipating emergency facility (as applicable) expressed as a percentage of the qualifying payment amount;

(iv) whether the offer selected by the certified IDR entity under paragraph (5) to be the payment applied was the offer submitted by such plan or by such provider or facility (as applicable) and the amount of such offer so selected expressed as a percentage of the qualifying payment amount;

(v) the category and practice specialty of each such provider or facility involved in furnishing such items and services;

(vi) the identity of the group health plan, provider, or facility, with respect to the notification;

(vii) the length of time in making each determination;

(viii) the compensation paid to the certified IDR entity with respect to the settlement or determination; and

(ix) any other information specified by the Secretary.

(C) IDR ENTITY REQUIREMENTS.—For 2022 and each subsequent year, an IDR entity, as a condition of certification as an IDR entity, shall submit to the Secretary such information as the Secretary determines necessary to carry out the provisions of this subsection.

(D) CLARIFICATION.—The Secretary shall ensure the public reporting under this paragraph does not contain information that would disclose privileged or confidential information of a group health plan or health insurance issuer offering group or individual health insurance coverage or of a provider or facility.

(8) ADMINISTRATIVE FEE.—

(A) IN GENERAL.—Each party to a determination under paragraph (5) to which an entity is selected under paragraph (3) in a year shall pay to the Secretary, at such time and in such manner as specified by the Secretary, a fee for participating in the IDR process with respect to such determination in an amount described in subparagraph (B) for such year.

(B) AMOUNT OF FEE.—The amount described in this subparagraph for a year is an amount established by the Secretary in a manner such that the total amount of fees paid under this paragraph for such year is estimated to be equal to the amount of expenditures estimated to be made by the Secretary for such year in carrying out the IDR process.

(9) WAIVER AUTHORITY.—The Secretary may modify any deadline or other timing requirement specified under this subsection (other than the establishment date for the IDR process under paragraph (2)(A) and other than under paragraph (6)) in cases of extenuating circumstances, as specified by the Secretary, or to ensure that all claims that occur during a 90-day period described in paragraph (5)(E)(ii), but with respect to which a notification is not permitted by reason of such paragraph to be submitted under paragraph (1)(B) during such period, are eligible for the IDR process.

Amendments

• **2020, No Surprises Act (P.L. 116-260)**

P.L. 116-260, § 103(c)(1)-(2), Div. BB:

Amended Code Sec. 9816, as added by Act Sec. 102, by redesignating subsection (c) as subsection (d); and by inserting after subsection (b) a new subsection (c). **Effective** 12-27-2020.

[Sec. 9816(d)]

(d) CERTAIN ACCESS FEES TO CERTAIN DATABASES.—In the case of a sponsor of a group health plan that, pursuant to subsection (a)(3)(E)(iii), uses a database described in such subsection to determine a rate to apply under such subsection for an item or service by reason of having insufficient information described in such subsection with respect to such item or service, such sponsor shall cover the cost for access to such database.

Amendments

• **2020, No Surprises Act (P.L. 116-260)**

P.L. 116-260, § 102(c)(1), Div. BB:

Amended subchapter B of chapter 100 by adding at the end a new Code Sec. 9816. **Effective** with respect to plan years beginning on or after 1-1-2022.

P.L. 116-260, § 103(c)(1), Div. BB:

Amended Code Sec. 9816, as added by Act Sec. 102, by redesignating subsection (c) as subsection (d). **Effective** 12-27-2020.

[Sec. 9816(e)]

(e) TRANSPARENCY REGARDING IN-NETWORK AND OUT-OF-NETWORK DEDUCTIBLES AND OUT-OF-POCKET LIMITATIONS.—A group health plan providing or covering any benefit with respect to items or services shall include, in clear writing, on any physical or electronic plan or insurance identification card issued to the participants or beneficiaries in the plan the following:

(1) Any deductible applicable to such plan.

Sec. 9816(c)(5)(F)(ii)

(2) Any out-of-pocket maximum limitation applicable to such plan.

(3) A telephone number and Internet website address through which such individual may seek consumer assistance information, such as information related to hospitals and urgent care facilities that have in effect a contractual relationship with such plan for furnishing items and services under such plan.

Amendments

• **2020, No Surprises Act (P.L. 116-260)**

P.L. 116-260, § 107(c), Div. BB:

Amended Code Sec. 9816, as added by Act Sec. 102(c) and amended by Act Sec. 103, by adding at the end a new subsection (e). **Effective** with respect to plan years beginning on or after 1-1-2022.

[Sec. 9816(f)]

(f) ADVANCED EXPLANATION OF BENEFITS.—

(1) IN GENERAL.—For plan years beginning on or after January 1, 2022, each group health plan shall, with respect to a notification submitted under section 2799B–6 of the Public Health Service Act by a health care provider or health care facility to the plan for a participant or beneficiary under such plan scheduled to receive an item or service from the provider or facility (or authorized representative of such participant or beneficiary), not later than 1 business day (or, in the case such item or service was so scheduled at least 10 business days before such item or service is to be furnished (or in the case of a request made to such plan or coverage by such participant or beneficiary), 3 business days) after the date on which the plan receives such notification (or such request), provide to the participant or beneficiary (through mail or electronic means, as requested by the participant or beneficiary) a notification (in clear and understandable language) including the following:

(A) Whether or not the provider or facility is a participating provider or a participating facility with respect to the plan with respect to the furnishing of such item or service and—

(i) in the case the provider or facility is a participating provider or facility with respect to the plan or coverage with respect to the furnishing of such item or service, the contracted rate under such plan for such item or service (based on the billing and diagnostic codes provided by such provider or facility); and

(ii) in the case the provider or facility is a nonparticipating provider or facility with respect to such plan, a description of how such individual may obtain information on providers and facilities that, with respect to such plan, are participating providers and facilities, if any.

(B) The good faith estimate included in the notification received from the provider or facility (if applicable) based on such codes.

(C) A good faith estimate of the amount the plan is responsible for paying for items and services included in the estimate described in subparagraph (B).

(D) A good faith estimate of the amount of any cost-sharing for which the participant or beneficiary would be responsible for such item or service (as of the date of such notification).

(E) A good faith estimate of the amount that the participant or beneficiary has incurred toward meeting the limit of the financial responsibility (including with respect to deductibles and out-of-pocket maximums) under the plan (as of the date of such notification).

(F) In the case such item or service is subject to a medical management technique (including concurrent review, prior authorization, and step-therapy or fail-first protocols) for coverage under the plan, a disclaimer that coverage for such item or service is subject to such medical management technique.

(G) A disclaimer that the information provided in the notification is only an estimate based on the items and services reasonably expected, at the time of scheduling (or requesting) the item or service, to be furnished and is subject to change.

(H) Any other information or disclaimer the plan determines appropriate that is consistent with information and disclaimers required under this section.

(2) AUTHORITY TO MODIFY TIMING REQUIREMENTS IN THE CASE OF SPECIFIED ITEMS AND SERVICES.—

(A) IN GENERAL.—In the case of a participant or beneficiary scheduled to receive an item or service that is a specified item or service (as defined in subparagraph (B)), the Secretary may modify any timing requirements relating to the provision of the notification described in paragraph (1) to such participant or beneficiary with respect to such item or service. Any modification made by the Secretary pursuant to the previous sentence may not result in the provision of such notification after such participant or beneficiary has been furnished such item or service.

(B) SPECIFIED ITEM OR SERVICE DEFINED.—For purposes of subparagraph (A), the term "specified item or service" means an item or service that has low utilization or significant variation in costs (such as when furnished as part of a complex treatment), as specified by the Secretary.

Amendments

• **2020, No Surprises Act (P.L. 116-260)**

P.L. 116-260, § 111(b), Div. BB:

Amended Code Sec. 9816, as added by Act Sec. 102 and further [sic] amended by the previous provisions of Division BB, Title I, by inserting after subsection (e) a new subsection (f). **Effective** 12-27-2020.

[Sec. 9817]

SEC. 9817. ENDING SURPRISE AIR AMBULANCE BILLS.

[Sec. 9817(a)]

(a) IN GENERAL.—In the case of a participant or beneficiary in a group health plan who receives air ambulance services from a nonparticipating provider (as defined in section 9816(a)(3)(G)) with respect to such plan, if such services would be covered if provided by a participating provider (as defined in such section) with respect to such plan—

(1) the cost-sharing requirement with respect to such services shall be the same requirement that would apply if such services were provided by such a participating provider, and any coinsurance or deductible shall be based on rates that would apply for such services if they were furnished by such a participating provider;

(2) such cost-sharing amounts shall be counted towards the in-network deductible and in-network out-of-pocket maximum amount under the plan for the plan year (and such in-network deductible shall be applied) with respect to such items and services so furnished in the same manner as if such cost-sharing payments were with respect to items and services furnished by a participating provider; and

(3) the group health plan shall—

(A) not later than 30 calendar days after the bill for such services is transmitted by such provider, send to the provider, an initial payment or notice of denial of payment; and

GROUP HEALTH PLAN REQUIREMENTS

(B) pay a total plan payment, in accordance with, if applicable, subsection (b)(6), directly to such provider furnishing such services to such participant, beneficiary, or enrollee that is, with application of any initial payment under subparagraph (A), equal to the amount by which the out-of-network rate (as defined in section 9816(a)(3)(K)) for such services and year involved exceeds the cost-sharing amount imposed under the plan for such services (as determined in accordance with paragraphs (1) and (2)).

[Sec. 9817(b)]

(b) DETERMINATION OF OUT-OF-NETWORK RATES TO BE PAID BY HEALTH PLANS; INDEPENDENT DISPUTE RESOLUTION PROCESS.—

(1) DETERMINATION THROUGH OPEN NEGOTIATION.—

(A) IN GENERAL.—With respect to air ambulance services furnished in a year by a nonparticipating provider, with respect to a group health plan, and for which a payment is required to be made by the plan pursuant to subsection (a)(3), the provider or plan may, during the 30-day period beginning on the day the provider receives a payment or a statement of denial of payment from the plan regarding a claim for payment for such service, initiate open negotiations under this paragraph between such provider and plan for purposes of determining, during the open negotiation period, an amount agreed on by such provider, and such plan for payment (including any cost-sharing) for such service. For purposes of this subsection, the open negotiation period, with respect to air ambulance services, is the 30-day period beginning on the date of initiation of the negotiations with respect to such services.

(B) ACCESSING INDEPENDENT DISPUTE RESOLUTION PROCESS IN CASE OF FAILED NEGOTIATIONS.—In the case of open negotiations pursuant to subparagraph (A), with respect to air ambulance services, that do not result in a determination of an amount of payment for such services by the last day of the open negotiation period described in such subparagraph with respect to such services, the provider or group health plan that was party to such negotiations may, during the 4-day period beginning on the day after such open negotiation period, initiate the independent dispute resolution process under paragraph (2) with respect to such services. The independent dispute resolution process shall be initiated by a party pursuant to the previous sentence by submission to the other party and to the Secretary of a notification (containing such information as specified by the Secretary) and for purposes of this subsection, the date of initiation of such process shall be the date of such submission or such other date specified by the Secretary pursuant to regulations that is not later than the date of receipt of such notification by both the other party and the Secretary.

(2) INDEPENDENT DISPUTE RESOLUTION PROCESS AVAILABLE IN CASE OF FAILED OPEN NEGOTIATIONS.—

(A) ESTABLISHMENT.—Not later than 1 year after the date of the enactment of this subsection, the Secretary, jointly with the Secretary of Health and Human Services and the Secretary of Labor, shall establish by regulation one independent dispute resolution process (referred to in this subsection as the "IDR process") under which, in the case of air ambulance services with respect to which a provider or group health plan submits a notification under paragraph (1)(B) (in this subsection referred to as a "qualified IDR air ambulance services"), a certified IDR entity under paragraph (4) determines, subject to subparagraph (B) and in accordance with the succeeding provisions of this subsection, the amount of payment under the plan for such services furnished by such provider.

(B) AUTHORITY TO CONTINUE NEGOTIATIONS.—Under the independent dispute resolution process, in the case that the parties to a determination for qualified IDR air ambulance services agree on a payment amount for such services during such process but before the date on which the entity selected with respect to such determination under paragraph (4) makes such determination under paragraph (5), such amount shall be treated for purposes of section 9816(a)(3)(K)(ii) as the amount agreed to by such parties for such services. In the case of an agreement described in the previous sentence, the independent dispute resolution process shall provide for a method to determine how to allocate between the parties to such determination the payment of the compensation of the entity selected with respect to such determination.

(C) CLARIFICATION.—A nonparticipating provider may not, with respect to an item or service furnished by such provider, submit a notification under paragraph (1)(B) if such provider is exempt from the requirement under subsection (a) of section 2799B–2 of the Public Health Service Act with respect to such item or service pursuant to subsection (b) of such section.

(3) TREATMENT OF BATCHING OF SERVICES.—The provisions of section 9816(c)(3) shall apply with respect to a notification submitted under this subsection with respect to air ambulance services in the same manner and to the same extent such provisions apply with respect to a notification submitted under section 9816(c) with respect to items and services described in such section.

(4) IDR ENTITIES.—

(A) ELIGIBILITY.—An IDR entity certified under this subsection is an IDR entity certified under section 9816(c)(4).

(B) SELECTION OF CERTIFIED IDR ENTITY.—The provisions of subparagraph (F) of section 9816(c)(4) shall apply with respect to selecting an IDR entity certified pursuant to subparagraph (A) with respect to the determination of the amount of payment under this subsection of air ambulance services in the same manner as such provisions apply with respect to selecting an IDR entity certified under such section with respect to the determination of the amount of payment under section 9816(c) of an item or service. An entity selected pursuant to the previous sentence to make a determination described in such sentence shall be referred to in this subsection as the "certified IDR entity" with respect to such determination.

(5) PAYMENT DETERMINATION.—

(A) IN GENERAL.—Not later than 30 days after the date of selection of the certified IDR entity with respect to a determination for qualified IDR ambulance services, the certified IDR entity shall—

(i) taking into account the considerations specified in subparagraph (C), select one of the offers submitted under subparagraph (B) to be the amount of payment for such services determined under this subsection for purposes of subsection (a)(3); and

(ii) notify the provider or facility and the group health plan party to such determination of the offer selected under clause (i).

(B) SUBMISSION OF OFFERS.—Not later than 10 days after the date of selection of the certified IDR entity with respect to a determination for qualified IDR air ambulance services, the provider and the group health plan party to such determination—

(i) shall each submit to the certified IDR entity with respect to such determination—

(I) an offer for a payment amount for such services furnished by such provider; and

(II) such information as requested by the certified IDR entity relating to such offer; and

(ii) may each submit to the certified IDR entity with respect to such determination any information relating to such offer submitted by either party, including information relating to any circumstance described in subparagraph (C)(ii).

(C) CONSIDERATIONS IN DETERMINATION.—

(i) IN GENERAL.—In determining which offer is the payment to be applied pursuant to this paragraph, the certified IDR entity, with respect to the determination for a qualified IDR air ambulance service shall consider—

(I) the qualifying payment amounts (as defined in section 9816(a)(3)(E)) for the applicable year for items or services that are comparable to the qualified IDR air ambulance service and that are furnished in the same geographic region (as defined by the Secretary for purposes of such subsection) as such qualified IDR air ambulance service; and

(II) subject to clause (iii), information on any circumstance described in clause (ii), such information as requested in subparagraph (B)(i)(II), and any additional information provided in subparagraph (B)(ii).

(ii) ADDITIONAL CIRCUMSTANCES.—For purposes of clause (i)(II), the circumstances described in this clause are, with respect to air ambulance services included in the notification submitted under paragraph (1)(B) of a nonparticipating provider, or group health plan the following:

(I) The quality and outcomes measurements of the provider that furnished such services.

(II) The acuity of the individual receiving such services or the complexity of furnishing such services to such individual.

(III) The training, experience, and quality of the medical personnel that furnished such services.

(IV) Ambulance vehicle type, including the clinical capability level of such vehicle.

(V) Population density of the pick up location (such as urban, suburban, rural, or frontier).

(VI) Demonstrations of good faith efforts (or lack of good faith efforts) made by the nonparticipating provider or nonparticipating facility or the plan to enter into network agreements and, if applicable, contracted rates between the provider and the plan during the previous 4 plan years.

(iii) PROHIBITION ON CONSIDERATION OF CERTAIN FACTORS.—In determining which offer is the payment amount to be applied with respect to qualified IDR air ambulance services furnished by a provider, the certified IDR entity with respect to such determination shall not consider usual and customary charges, the amount that would have been billed by such provider with respect to such services had the provisions of section 2799B–5 of the Public Health Service Act not applied, or the payment or reimbursement rate for such services furnished by such provider payable by a public payor, including under the Medicare program under title XVIII of the Social Security Act, under the Medicaid program under title XIX of such Act, under the Children's Health Insurance Program under title XXI of such Act, under the TRICARE program under chapter 55 of title 10, United States Code, or under chapter 17 of title 38, United States Code.

(D) EFFECTS OF DETERMINATION.—The provisions of section 9816(c)(5)(E)) shall apply with respect to a determination of a certified IDR entity under subparagraph (A), the notification submitted with respect to such determination, the services with respect to such notification, and the parties to such notification in the same manner as such provisions apply with respect to a determination of a certified IDR entity under section 9816(c)(5)(E), the notification submitted with respect to such determination, the items and services with respect to such notification, and the parties to such notification.

(E) COSTS OF INDEPENDENT DISPUTE RESOLUTION PROCESS.—The provisions of section 9816(c)(5)(F) shall apply to a notification made under this subsection, the parties to such notification, and a determination under subparagraph (A) in the same manner and to the same extent such provisions apply to a notification under section 9816(c), the parties to such notification and a determination made under section 9816(c)(5)(A).

(6) TIMING OF PAYMENT.—The total plan payment required pursuant to subsection (a)(3), with respect to qualified IDR air ambulance services for which a determination is made under paragraph (5)(A) or with respect to air ambulance services for which a payment amount is determined under open negotiations under paragraph (1), shall be made directly to the nonparticipating provider not later than 30 days after the date on which such determination is made.

(7) PUBLICATION OF INFORMATION RELATING TO THE IDR PROCESS.—

(A) IN GENERAL.—For each calendar quarter in 2022 and each calendar quarter in a subsequent year, the Secretary shall publish on the public website of the Department of the Treasury—

(i) the number of notifications submitted under the IDR process during such calendar quarter;

(ii) the number of such notifications with respect to which a final determination was made under paragraph (5)(A);

(iii) the information described in subparagraph (B) with respect to each notification with respect to which such a determination was so made.

(iv) the number of times the payment amount determined (or agreed to) under this subsection exceeds the qualifying payment amount;

(v) the amount of expenditures made by the Secretary during such calendar quarter to carry out the IDR process;

(vi) the total amount of fees paid under paragraph (8) during such calendar quarter; and

(vii) the total amount of compensation paid to certified IDR entities under paragraph (5)(E) during [sic] such calendar quarter.

(B) INFORMATION WITH RESPECT TO REQUESTS.—For purposes of subparagraph (A), the information described in this subparagraph is, with respect to a notification under the IDR process of a nonparticipating provider, or group health plan—

(i) a description of each air ambulance service included in such notification;

(ii) the geography in which the services included in such notification were provided;

(iii) the amount of the offer submitted under paragraph (2) by the group health plan and by the nonparticipating provider expressed as a percentage of the qualifying payment amount;

(iv) whether the offer selected by the certified IDR entity under paragraph (5) to be the payment applied was the offer submitted by such plan or issuer (as applicable) or by such provider and the amount of such offer so selected expressed as a percentage of the qualifying payment amount;

(v) ambulance vehicle type, including the clinical capability level of such vehicle;

(vi) the identity of the group health plan or health insurance issuer or air ambulance provider with respect to such notification;

(vii) the length of time in making each determination;

(viii) the compensation paid to the certified IDR entity with respect to the settlement or determination; and

(ix) any other information specified by the Secretary.

(C) IDR ENTITY REQUIREMENTS.—For 2022 and each subsequent year, an IDR entity, as a condition of certification as an IDR entity, shall submit to the Secretary such information as the Secretary determines necessary for the Secretary to carry out the provisions of this paragraph.

(D) CLARIFICATION.—The Secretary shall ensure the public reporting under this paragraph does not contain information that would disclose privileged or confidential information of a group health plan or health insurance issuer offering group or individual health insurance coverage or of a provider or facility.

(8) ADMINISTRATIVE FEE.—

(A) IN GENERAL.—Each party to a determination under paragraph (5) to which an entity is selected under paragraph (4) in a year shall pay to the Secretary, at such time and in such manner as specified by the Secretary, a fee for participating in the IDR process with respect to such determination in an amount described in subparagraph (B) for such year.

(B) AMOUNT OF FEE.—The amount described in this subparagraph for a year is an amount established by the Secretary in a manner such that the total amount of fees paid under this paragraph for such year is estimated to be equal to the amount of expenditures estimated to be made by the Secretary for such year in carrying out the IDR process.

GROUP HEALTH PLAN REQUIREMENTS

(9) WAIVER AUTHORITY.—The Secretary may modify any deadline or other timing requirement specified under this subsection (other than the establishment date for the IDR process under paragraph (2)(A) and other than under paragraph (6)) in cases of extenuating circumstances, as specified by the Secretary, or to ensure that all claims that occur during a 90-day period applied through paragraph (5)(D), but with respect to which a notification is not permitted by reason of such paragraph to be submitted under paragraph (1)(B) during such period, are eligible for the IDR process.

[Sec. 9817(c)]

(c) DEFINITIONS.—For purposes of this section:

(1) AIR AMBULANCE SERVICES.—The term "air ambulance service" means medical transport by helicopter or airplane for patients.

(2) QUALIFYING PAYMENT AMOUNT.—The term "qualifying payment amount" has the meaning given such term in section 9816(a)(3).

(3) NONPARTICIPATING PROVIDER.—The term "nonparticipating provider" has the meaning given such term in section 9816(a)(3).

Amendments

Sec. 9816 a new Code Sec. 9817. **Effective** with respect to plan years beginning on or after 1-1-2022.

• 2020, No Surprises Act (P.L. 116-260)

P.L. 116-260, §105(a)(3), Div. BB:

Amended subchapter B of chapter 100, as amended by Act Sec. 102(c) and further amended by the previous provisions of Division BB, Title I, by inserting after Code

[Sec. 9818]

SEC. 9818. CONTINUITY OF CARE.

[Sec. 9818(a)]

(a) ENSURING CONTINUITY OF CARE WITH RESPECT TO TERMINATIONS OF CERTAIN CONTRACTUAL RELATIONSHIPS RESULTING IN CHANGES IN PROVIDER NETWORK STATUS.—

(1) IN GENERAL.—In the case of an individual with benefits under a group health plan and with respect to a health care provider or facility that has a contractual relationship with such plan for furnishing items and services under such plan, if, while such individual is a continuing care patient (as defined in subsection (b)) with respect to such provider or facility—

(A) such contractual relationship is terminated (as defined in paragraph (b));

(B) benefits provided under such plan with respect to such provider or facility are terminated because of a change in the terms of the participation of such provider or facility in such plan; or

(C) a contract between such group health plan and a health insurance issuer offering health insurance coverage in connection with such plan is terminated, resulting in a loss of benefits provided under such plan with respect to such provider or facility;

the plan shall meet the requirements of paragraph (2) with respect to such individual.

(2) REQUIREMENTS.—The requirements of this paragraph are that the plan—

(A) notify each individual enrolled under such plan who is a continuing care patient with respect to a provider or facility at the time of a termination described in paragraph (1) affecting such provider on a timely basis of such termination and such individual's right to elect continued transitional care from such provider or facility under this section;

(B) provide such individual with an opportunity to notify the plan of the individual's need for transitional care; and

(C) permit the patient to elect to continue to have benefits provided under such plan, under the same terms and conditions as would have applied and with respect to such items and services as would have been covered under such plan had such termination not occurred, with respect to the course of treatment furnished by such provider or facility relating to such individual's status as a continuing care patient during the period beginning on the date on which the notice under subparagraph (A) is provided and ending on the earlier of—

(i) the 90-day period beginning on such date; or

(ii) the date on which such individual is no longer a continuing care patient with respect to such provider or facility.

[Sec. 9818(b)]

(b) DEFINITIONS.—In this section:

(1) CONTINUING CARE PATIENT.—The term "continuing care patient" means an individual who, with respect to a provider or facility—

(A) is undergoing a course of treatment for a serious and complex condition from the provider or facility;

(B) is undergoing a course of institutional or inpatient care from the provider or facility;

(C) is scheduled to undergo nonelective surgery from the provider or facility, including receipt of postoperative care from such provider or facility with respect to such a surgery;

(D) is pregnant and undergoing a course of treatment for the pregnancy from the provider or facility; or

(E) is or was determined to be terminally ill (as determined under section 1861(dd)(3)(A) of the Social Security Act) and is receiving treatment for such illness from such provider or facility.

(2) SERIOUS AND COMPLEX CONDITION.—The term "serious and complex condition" means, with respect to a participant or beneficiary under a group health plan—

(A) in the case of an acute illness, a condition that is serious enough to require specialized medical treatment to avoid the reasonable possibility of death or permanent harm; or

(B) in the case of a chronic illness or condition, a condition that—

(i) is life-threatening, degenerative, potentially disabling, or congenital; and

(ii) requires specialized medical care over a prolonged period of time.

(3) TERMINATED.—The term "terminated" includes, with respect to a contract, the expiration or nonrenewal of the contract, but does not include a termination of the contract for failure to meet applicable quality standards or for fraud.

Amendments

• 2020, No Surprises Act (P.L. 116-260)

P.L. 116-260, §113(b)(1), Div. BB:

Amended subchapter B of chapter 100, as amended by Act Secs. 102(c) and 105(a)(3), by inserting after Code Sec. 9817 a new Code Sec. 9818. **Effective** with respect to plan years beginning on or after 1-1-2022.

[Sec. 9819]

SEC. 9819. MAINTENANCE OF PRICE COMPARISON TOOL.

A group health plan shall offer price comparison guidance by telephone and make available on the Internet website of the plan or issuer a price comparison tool that (to the extent practicable) allows an individual enrolled under such plan, with respect to such plan year, such

GROUP HEALTH PLAN REQUIREMENTS

geographic region, and participating providers with respect to such plan or coverage, to compare the amount of cost-sharing that the individual would be responsible for paying under such plan with respect to the furnishing of a specific item or service by any such provider.

Amendments

- 2020, No Surprises Act (P.L. 116-260)

P.L. 116-260, §114(b)(1), Div. BB:

Amended subchapter B of chapter 100, as amended by Act Secs. 102, 105, and 113, by inserting after Code Sec. 9818 a new Code Sec. 9819. **Effective** with respect to plan years beginning on or after 1-1-2022.

[Sec. 9820]

SEC. 9820. PROTECTING PATIENTS AND IMPROVING THE ACCURACY OF PROVIDER DIRECTORY INFORMATION.

[Sec. 9820(a)]

(a) PROVIDER DIRECTORY INFORMATION REQUIREMENTS.—

(1) IN GENERAL.—For plan years beginning on or after January 1, 2022, each group health plan shall—

(A) establish the verification process described in paragraph (2);

(B) establish the response protocol described in paragraph (3);

(C) establish the database described in paragraph (4); and

(D) include in any directory (other than the database described in subparagraph (C)) containing provider directory information with respect to such plan the information described in paragraph (5).

(2) VERIFICATION PROCESS.—The verification process described in this paragraph is, with respect to a group health plan, a process—

(A) under which, not less frequently than once every 90 days, such plan verifies and updates the provider directory information included on the database described in paragraph (4) of such plan or issuer of each health care provider and health care facility included in such database;

(B) that establishes a procedure for the removal of such a provider or facility with respect to which such plan or issuer has been unable to verify such information during a period specified by the plan or issuer; and

(C) that provides for the update of such database within 2 business days of such plan or issuer receiving from such a provider or facility information pursuant to section 2799B–9 of the Public Health Service Act.

(3) RESPONSE PROTOCOL.—The response protocol described in this paragraph is, in the case of an individual enrolled under a group health plan who requests information through a telephone call or electronic, web-based, or Internet-based means on whether a health care provider or health care facility has a contractual relationship to furnish items and services under such plan, a protocol under which such plan or such issuer (as applicable), in the case such request is made through a telephone call—

(A) responds to such individual as soon as practicable and in no case later than 1 business day after such call is received, through a written electronic or print (as requested by such individual) communication; and

(B) retains such communication in such individual's file for at least 2 years following such response.

(4) DATABASE.—The database described in this paragraph is, with respect to a group health plan, a database on the public website of such plan or issuer that contains—

(A) a list of each health care provider and health care facility with which such plan or such issuer has a direct or indirect contractual relationship for furnishing items and services under such plan; and

(B) provider directory information with respect to each such provider and facility.

(5) INFORMATION.—The information described in this paragraph is, with respect to a print directory containing provider directory information with respect to a group health plan, a notification that such information contained in such directory was accurate as of the date of publication of such directory and that an individual enrolled under such plan should consult the database described in paragraph (4) with respect to such plan or contact such plan to obtain the most current provider directory information with respect to such plan.

(6) DEFINITION.—For purposes of this subsection, the term "provider directory information" includes, with respect to a group health plan, the name, address, specialty, telephone number, and digital contact information of each health care provider or health care facility with which such plan has a contractual relationship for furnishing items and services under such plan.

(7) RULE OF CONSTRUCTION.—Nothing in this section shall be construed to preempt any provision of State law relating to health care provider directories.

[Sec. 9820(b)]

(b) COST-SHARING FOR SERVICES PROVIDED BASED ON RELIANCE ON INCORRECT PROVIDER NETWORK INFORMATION.—

(1) IN GENERAL.—For plan years beginning on or after January 1, 2022, in the case of an item or service furnished to a participant or beneficiary of a group health plan by a nonparticipating provider or a nonparticipating facility, if such item or service would otherwise be covered under such plan if furnished by a participating provider or participating facility and if either of the criteria described in paragraph (2) applies with respect to such participant or beneficiary and item or service, the plan—

(A) shall not impose on such participant or beneficiary a cost-sharing amount for such item or service so furnished that is greater than the cost-sharing amount that would apply under such plan had such item or service been furnished by a participating provider; and

(B) shall apply the deductible or out-of-pocket maximum, if any, that would apply if such services were furnished by a participating provider or a participating facility.

(2) CRITERIA DESCRIBED.—For purposes of paragraph (1), the criteria described in this paragraph, with respect to an item or service furnished to a participant or beneficiary of a group health plan by a nonparticipating provider or a nonparticipating facility, are the following:

(A) The participant or beneficiary received through a database, provider directory, or response protocol described in subsection (a) information with respect to such item and service to be furnished and such information provided that the provider was a participating provider or facility was a participating facility, with respect to the plan for furnishing such item or service.

(B) The information was not provided, in accordance with subsection (a), to the participant or beneficiary and the participant or beneficiary requested through the response protocol described in subsection (a)(3) of the plan information on whether the provider was a participating provider or facility was a participating facility with respect to the plan for furnishing such item or service and was informed through such protocol that the provider was such a participating provider or facility was such a participating facility.

[Sec. 9820(c)]

(c) DISCLOSURE ON PATIENT PROTECTIONS AGAINST BALANCE BILLING.—For plan years beginning on or after January 1, 2022, each group health plan shall make publicly available, post on a public website of such plan or issuer, and include on each explanation of benefits for an item or service with respect to which the requirements under section 9816 applies—

GROUP HEALTH PLAN REQUIREMENTS

(1) information in plain language on—

(A) the requirements and prohibitions applied under sections 2799B–1 and 2799B–2 of the Public Health Service Act(relating [sic] to prohibitions on balance billing in certain circumstances);

(B) if provided for under applicable State law, any other requirements on providers and facilities regarding the amounts such providers and facilities may, with respect to an item or service, charge a participant or beneficiary of such plan with respect to which such a provider or facility does not have a contractual relationship for furnishing such item or service under the plan after receiving payment from the plan for such item or service and any applicable cost sharing payment from such participant or beneficiary; and

(C) the requirements applied under section 9816; and

(2) information on contacting appropriate State and Federal agencies in the case that an individual believes that such a provider or facility has violated any requirement described in paragraph (1) with respect to such individual.

Amendments

• 2020, No Surprises Act (P.L. 116-260)

P.L. 116-260, § 116(c), Div. BB:

Amended subchapter B of chapter 100, as amended by Act Secs. 102, 105, 113, and 114, by inserting after Code Sec. 9819 a new Code Sec. 9820. **Effective** 12-27-2020.

[Sec. 9822]

SEC. 9822. OTHER PATIENT PROTECTIONS.

[Sec. 9822(a)]

(a) CHOICE OF HEALTH CARE PROFESSIONAL.—If a group health plan requires or provides for designation by a participant or beneficiary of a participating primary care provider, then the plan shall permit each participant and beneficiary to designate any participating primary care provider who is available to accept such individual.

[Sec. 9822(b)]

(b) ACCESS TO PEDIATRIC CARE.—

(1) PEDIATRIC CARE.—In the case of a person who has a child who is a participant or beneficiary under a group health plan if the plan requires or provides for the designation of a participating primary care provider for the child, the plan shall permit such person to designate a physician (allopathic or osteopathic) who specializes in pediatrics as the child's primary care provider if such provider participates in the network of the plan.

(2) CONSTRUCTION.—Nothing in paragraph (1) shall be construed to waive any exclusions of coverage under the terms and conditions of the plan with respect to coverage of pediatric care.

[Sec. 9822(c)]

(c) PATIENT ACCESS TO OBSTETRICAL AND GYNECOLOGICAL CARE.—

(1) GENERAL RIGHTS.—

(A) DIRECT ACCESS.—A group health plan described in paragraph (2) may not require authorization or referral by the plan, issuer, or any person (including a primary care provider described in paragraph (2)(B)) in the case of a female participant or beneficiary who seeks coverage for obstetrical or gynecological care provided by a participating health care professional who specializes in obstetrics or gynecology. Such professional shall agree to otherwise adhere to such plan's policies and procedures, including procedures regarding referrals and obtaining prior authorization and providing services pursuant to a treatment plan (if any) approved by the plan.

(B) OBSTETRICAL AND GYNECOLOGICAL CARE.—A group health plan described in paragraph (2) shall treat the provision of obstetrical and gynecological care, and the ordering of related obstetrical and gynecological items and services, pursuant to the direct access described under subparagraph (A), by a participating health care professional who specializes in obstetrics or gynecology as the authorization of the primary care provider.

(2) APPLICATION OF PARAGRAPH.—A group health plan described in this paragraph is a group health plan that—

(A) provides coverage for obstetric or gynecologic care; and

(B) requires the designation by a participant or beneficiary of a participating primary care provider.

(3) CONSTRUCTION.—Nothing in paragraph (1) shall be construed to—

(A) waive any exclusions of coverage under the terms and conditions of the plan with respect to coverage of obstetrical or gynecological care; or

(B) preclude the group health plan involved from requiring that the obstetrical or gynecological provider notify the primary care health care professional or the plan or issuer of treatment decisions.

Amendments

• 2020, No Surprises Act (P.L. 116-260)

P.L. 116-260, § 102(c)(2), Div. BB:

Amended subchapter B of chapter 100, as amended by Act Sec. 102(c)(1), by adding at the end a new Code Sec. 9822. **Effective** with respect to plan years beginning on or after 1-1-2022.

[Sec. 9823]

SEC. 9823. AIR AMBULANCE REPORT REQUIREMENTS.

[Sec. 9823(a)]

(a) IN GENERAL.—Each group health plan shall submit to the Secretary, jointly with the Secretary of Labor and the Secretary of Health and Human Services—

(1) not later than the date that is 90 days after the last day of the first calendar year beginning on or after the date on which a final rule is promulgated pursuant to the rulemaking described in section 106(d) of the No Surprises Act, the information described in subsection (b) with respect to such plan year; and

(2) not later than the date that is 90 days after the last day of the calendar year immediately succeeding the plan year described in paragraph (1), such information with respect to such immediately succeeding plan year.

[Sec. 9823(b)]

(b) INFORMATION DESCRIBED.—For purposes of subsection (a), information described in this subsection, with respect to a group health plan is each of the following:

Sec. 9820(c)(1)

GROUP HEALTH PLAN REQUIREMENTS

(1) Claims data for air ambulance services furnished by providers of such services, disaggregated by each of the following factors:

(A) Whether such services were furnished on an emergent or nonemergent basis.

(B) Whether the provider of such services is part of a hospital-owned or sponsored program, municipality-sponsored program, hospital independent partnership (hybrid) program, independent program, or tribally operated program in Alaska.

(C) Whether the transport in which the services were furnished originated in a rural or urban area.

(D) The type of aircraft (such as rotor transport or fixed wing transport) used to furnish such services.

(E) Whether the provider of such services has a contract with the plan or issuer, as applicable, to furnish such services under the plan or coverage, respectively.

(2) Such other information regarding providers of air ambulance services as the Secretary may specify.

Amendments

• 2020, No Surprises Act (P.L. 116-260)

P.L. 116-260, § 106(b)(3)(A), Div. BB:

Amended subchapter B of chapter 100 by adding after Code Sec. 9822, as added by Act Sec. 102(c)(2)(A), a new Code Sec. 9823. **Effective** 12-27-2020. For a special rule, see Act Sec. 106(h), Div. BB, below.

P.L. 116-260, § 106(h), Div. BB:

(h) DEFINITIONS.—In this section, the terms "group health plan", "health insurance coverage", "individual health insurance coverage", "group health insurance coverage", and "health insurance issuer" have the meanings given such terms in section 2791 of the Public Health Service Act (42 U.S.C. 300gg–91).

[Sec. 9824]

SEC. 9824. INCREASING TRANSPARENCY BY REMOVING GAG CLAUSES ON PRICE AND QUALITY INFORMATION.

[Sec. 9824(a)]

(a) INCREASING PRICE AND QUALITY TRANSPARENCY FOR PLAN SPONSORS AND CONSUMERS.—

(1) IN GENERAL.—A group health plan may not enter into an agreement with a health care provider, network or association of providers, third-party administrator, or other service provider offering access to a network of providers that would directly or indirectly restrict a group health plan from—

(A) providing provider-specific cost or quality of care information or data, through a consumer engagement tool or any other means, to referring providers, the plan sponsor, participants or beneficiaries, or individuals eligible to become participants or beneficiaries of the plan;

(B) electronically accessing de-identified claims and encounter information or data for each participant or beneficiary in the plan, upon request and consistent with the privacy regulations promulgated pursuant to section 264(c) of the Health Insurance Portability and Accountability Act of 1996, the amendments made by the Genetic Information Nondiscrimination Act of 2008, and the Americans with Disabilities Act of 1990, including, on a per claim basis—

(i) financial information, such as the allowed amount, or any other claim-related financial obligations included in the provider contract;

(ii) provider information, including name and clinical designation;

(iii) service codes; or

(iv) any other data element included in claim or encounter transactions; or

(C) sharing information or data described in subparagraph (A) or (B), or directing that such data be shared, with a business associate as defined in section 160.103 of title 45, Code of Federal Regulations (or successor regulations), consistent with the privacy regulations promulgated pursuant to section 264(c) of the Health Insurance Portability and Accountability Act of 1996, the amendments made by the Genetic Information Nondiscrimination Act of 2008, and the Americans with Disabilities Act of 1990.

(2) CLARIFICATION REGARDING PUBLIC DISCLOSURE OF INFORMATION.—Nothing in paragraph (1)(A) prevents a health care provider, network or association of providers, or other service provider from placing reasonable restrictions on the public disclosure of the information described in such paragraph (1).

(3) ATTESTATION.—A group health plan shall annually submit to the Secretary an attestation that such plan is in compliance with the requirements of this subsection.

(4) RULES OF CONSTRUCTION.—Nothing in this section shall be construed to modify or eliminate existing privacy protections and standards under State and Federal law. Nothing in this subsection shall be construed to otherwise limit access by a group health plan or plan sponsor to data as permitted under the privacy regulations promulgated pursuant to section 264(c) of the Health Insurance Portability and Accountability Act of 1996, the amendments made by the Genetic Information Nondiscrimination Act of 2008, and the Americans with Disabilities Act of 1990.

Amendments

• 2020, No Surprises Act (P.L. 116-260)

P.L. 116-260, § 201(c), Div. BB:

Amended subchapter B of chapter 100, as amended by title I of Division BB, by adding at the end a new Code Sec. 9824. **Effective** 12-27-2020.

[Sec. 9825]

SEC. 9825. REPORTING ON PHARMACY BENEFITS AND DRUG COSTS.

[Sec. 9825(a)]

(a) IN GENERAL.—Not later than 1 year after the date of enactment of the Consolidated Appropriations Act, 2021, and not later than June 1 of each year thereafter, a group health plan shall submit to the Secretary, the Secretary of Health and Human Services, and the Secretary of Labor the following information with respect to the health plan in the previous plan year:

(1) The beginning and end dates of the plan year.

(2) The number of participants and beneficiaries.

(3) Each State in which the plan is offered.

(4) The 50 brand prescription drugs most frequently dispensed by pharmacies for claims paid by the plan, and the total number of paid claims for each such drug.

(5) The 50 most costly prescription drugs with respect to the plan by total annual spending, and the annual amount spent by the plan for each such drug.

(6) The 50 prescription drugs with the greatest increase in plan expenditures over the plan year preceding the plan year that is the subject of the report, and, for each such drug, the change in amounts expended by the plan in each such plan year.

(7) Total spending on health care services by such group health plan, broken down by—

(A) the type of costs, including—

Internal Revenue Code

GROUP HEALTH PLAN REQUIREMENTS

(i) hospital costs;
(ii) health care provider and clinical service costs, for primary care and specialty care separately;
(iii) costs for prescription drugs; and
(iv) other medical costs, including wellness services; and
(B) spending on prescription drugs by—
(i) the health plan; and
(ii) the participants and beneficiaries.
(8) The average monthly premium—
(A) paid by employers on behalf of participants and beneficiaries, as applicable; and
(B) paid by participants and beneficiaries.
(9) Any impact on premiums by rebates, fees, and any other remuneration paid by drug manufacturers to the plan or its administrators or service providers, with respect to prescription drugs prescribed to participants or beneficiaries in the plan, including—
(A) the amounts so paid for each therapeutic class of drugs; and
(B) the amounts so paid for each of the 25 drugs that yielded the highest amount of rebates and other remuneration under the plan from drug manufacturers during the plan year.
(10) Any reduction in premiums and out-of-pocket costs associated with rebates, fees, or other remuneration described in paragraph (9).

[Sec. 9825(b)]

(b) REPORT.—Not later than 18 months after the date on which the first report is required under subsection (a) and biannually thereafter, the Secretary, acting in coordination with the Inspector General of the Department of the Treasury, shall make available on the internet website of the Department of the Treasury a report on prescription drug reimbursements under group health plans, prescription drug pricing trends, and the role of prescription drug costs in contributing to premium increases or decreases under such plans, aggregated in such a way as no drug or plan specific information will be made public.

[Sec. 9825(c)]

(c) PRIVACY PROTECTIONS.—No confidential or trade secret information submitted to the Secretary under subsection (a) shall be included in the report under subsection (b).

Amendments

• 2020, No Surprises Act (P.L. 116-260)

P.L. 116-260, § 204(c), Div. BB:
Amended subchapter B of chapter 100, as amended by Act Sec. 201, by adding at the end a new Code Sec. 9825. **Effective** 12-27-2020.

Subchapter C—General Provisions

Sec. 9831.   General exceptions.
Sec. 9832.   Definitions.
Sec. 9833.   Regulations.
Sec. 9834.   Enforcement.

[Sec. 9831]

SEC. 9831. GENERAL EXCEPTIONS.

[Sec. 9831(a)]

(a) EXCEPTION FOR CERTAIN PLANS.—The requirements of this chapter shall not apply to—
(1) any governmental plan, and
(2) any group health plan for any plan year if, on the first day of such plan year, such plan has less than 2 participants who are current employees.

[Sec. 9831(b)]

(b) EXCEPTION FOR CERTAIN BENEFITS.—The requirements of this chapter shall not apply to any group health plan in relation to its provision of excepted benefits described in section 9832(c)(1).

Amendments

• 1997, Taxpayer Relief Act of 1997 (P.L. 105-34)

P.L. 105-34, § 1531(b)(1)(B):
Amended Code Sec. 9831(b) by striking "9805(c)(1)" and inserting "9832(c)(1)".
Effective with respect to group health plans for plan years beginning on or after 1-1-98.

[Sec. 9831(c)]

(c) EXCEPTION FOR CERTAIN BENEFITS IF CERTAIN CONDITIONS MET.—
(1) LIMITED, EXCEPTED BENEFITS.—The requirements of this chapter shall not apply to any group health plan in relation to its provision of excepted benefits described in section 9832(c)(2) if the benefits—
(A) are provided under a separate policy, certificate, or contract of insurance; or
(B) are otherwise not an integral part of the plan.
(2) NONCOORDINATED, EXCEPTED BENEFITS.—The requirements of this chapter shall not apply to any group health plan in relation to its provision of excepted benefits described in section 9832(c)(3) if all of the following conditions are met:
(A) The benefits are provided under a separate policy, certificate, or contract of insurance.
(B) There is no coordination between the provision of such benefits and any exclusion of benefits under any group health plan maintained by the same plan sponsor.
(C) Such benefits are paid with respect to an event without regard to whether benefits are provided with respect to such an event under any group health plan maintained by the same plan sponsor.
(3) SUPPLEMENTAL EXCEPTED BENEFITS.—The requirements of this chapter shall not apply to any group health plan in relation to its provision of excepted benefits described in section 9832(c)(4) if the benefits are provided under a separate policy, certificate, or contract of insurance.

GROUP HEALTH PLAN REQUIREMENTS

Amendments

• **1997, Taxpayer Relief Act of 1997 (P.L. 105-34)**

P.L. 105-34, §1531(a)(2):

Amended subtitle K by redesignating Code Secs. 9804, 9805, and 9806 as Code Secs. 9831, 9832, and 9833, respectively. **Effective** with respect to group health plans for plan years beginning on or after 1-1-98.

P.L. 105-34, §1531(b)(1)(C):

Amended Code Sec. 9831(c)(1) by striking "9805(c)(2)" and inserting "9832(c)(2)". **Effective** with respect to group health plans for plan years beginning on or after 1-1-98.

P.L. 105-34, §1531(b)(1)(D):

Amended Code Sec. 9831(c)(2) by striking "9805(c)(3)" and inserting "9832(c)(3)". **Effective** with respect to group health plans for plan years beginning on or after 1-1-98.

P.L. 105-34, §1531(b)(1)(E):

Amended Code Sec. 9831(c)(3) by striking "9805(c)(4)" and inserting "9832(c)(4)". **Effective** with respect to group health plans for plan years beginning on or after 1-1-98.

• **1996, Health Insurance Portability and Accountability Act of 1996 (P.L. 104-191)**

P.L. 104-191, §401(a):

Amended the Internal Revenue Code of 1986 by adding Code Sec. 9804. For the **effective** date, see Act Sec. 401(c), below.

P.L. 104-191, §401(c), provides:

(c) EFFECTIVE DATE.—

(1) IN GENERAL.—The amendments made by this section shall apply to plan years beginning after June 30, 1997.

(2) DETERMINATION OF CREDITABLE COVERAGE.—

(A) PERIOD OF COVERAGE.—

(i) IN GENERAL.—Subject to clause (ii), no period before July 1, 1996, shall be taken into account under chapter 100 of the Internal Revenue Code of 1986 (as added by this section) in determining creditable coverage.

(ii) SPECIAL RULE FOR CERTAIN PERIODS.—The Secretary of the Treasury, consistent with section 104, shall provide for a process whereby individuals who need to establish creditable coverage for periods before July 1, 1996, and who would have such coverage credited but for clause (i) may be given credit for creditable coverage for such periods through the presentation of documents or other means.

(B) CERTIFICATIONS, ETC.—

(i) IN GENERAL.—Subject to clauses (ii) and (iii), subsection (e) of section 9801 of the Internal Revenue Code of 1986 (as added by this section) shall apply to events occurring after June 30, 1996.

(ii) NO CERTIFICATION REQUIRED TO BE PROVIDED BEFORE JUNE 1, 1997.—In no case is a certification required to be provided under such subsection before June 1, 1997.

(iii) CERTIFICATION ONLY ON WRITTEN REQUEST FOR EVENTS OCCURRING BEFORE OCTOBER 1, 1996.—In the case of an event occurring after June 30, 1996, and before October 1, 1996, a certification is not required to be provided under such subsection unless an individual (with respect to whom the certification is otherwise required to be made) requests such certification in writing.

(C) TRANSITIONAL RULE.—In the case of an individual who seeks to establish creditable coverage for any period for which certification is not required because it relates to an event occurring before June 30, 1996—

(i) the individual may present other credible evidence of such coverage in order to establish the period of creditable coverage; and

(ii) a group health plan and a health insurance issuer shall not be subject to any penalty or enforcement action with respect to the plan's or issuer's crediting (or not crediting) such coverage if the plan or issuer has sought to comply in good faith with the applicable requirements under the amendments made by this section.

(3) SPECIAL RULE FOR COLLECTIVE BARGAINING AGREEMENTS.—Except as provided in paragraph (2), in the case of a group health plan maintained pursuant to 1 or more collective bargaining agreements between employee representatives and one or more employers ratified before the date of the enactment of this Act, the amendments made by this section shall not apply to plan years beginning before the later of—

(A) the date on which the last of the collective bargaining agreements relating to the plan terminates (determined without regard to any extension thereof agreed to after the date of the enactment of this Act), or

(B) July 1, 1997.

For purposes of subparagraph (A), any plan amendment made pursuant to a collective bargaining agreement relating to the plan which amends the plan solely to conform to any requirement added by this section shall not be treated as a termination of such collective bargaining agreement.

(4) TIMELY REGULATIONS.—The Secretary of the Treasury, consistent with section 104, shall first issue by not later than April 1, 1997, such regulations as may be necessary to carry out the amendments made by this section.

(5) LIMITATION ON ACTIONS.—No enforcement action shall be taken, pursuant to the amendments made by this section, against a group health plan or health insurance issuer with respect to a violation of a requirement imposed by such amendments before January 1, 1998, or, if later, the date of issuance of regulations referred to in paragraph (4), if the plan or issuer has sought to comply in good faith with such requirements.

[Sec. 9831(d)]

(d) EXCEPTION FOR QUALIFIED SMALL EMPLOYER HEALTH REIMBURSEMENT ARRANGEMENTS.—

(1) IN GENERAL.—For purposes of this title (and notwithstanding any other provision of this title), the term "group health plan" shall not include any qualified small employer health reimbursement arrangement.

(2) QUALIFIED SMALL EMPLOYER HEALTH REIMBURSEMENT ARRANGEMENT.—For purposes of this subsection—

(A) IN GENERAL.—The term "qualified small employer health reimbursement arrangement" means an arrangement which—

(i) is described in subparagraph (B), and

(ii) is provided on the same terms to all eligible employees of the eligible employer.

(B) ARRANGEMENT DESCRIBED.—An arrangement is described in this subparagraph if—

(i) such arrangement is funded solely by an eligible employer and no salary reduction contributions may be made under such arrangement,

(ii) such arrangement provides, after the employee provides proof of coverage, for the payment of, or reimbursement of, an eligible employee for expenses for medical care (as defined in section 213(d)) incurred by the eligible employee or the eligible employee's family members (as determined under the terms of the arrangement), and

(iii) the amount of payments and reimbursements described in clause (ii) for any year do not exceed $4,950 ($10,000 in the case of an arrangement that also provides for payments or reimbursements for family members of the employee).

(C) CERTAIN VARIATION PERMITTED.—For purposes of subparagraph (A)(ii), an arrangement shall not fail to be treated as provided on the same terms to each eligible employee merely because the employee's permitted benefit under such arrangement varies in accordance with the variation in the price of an insurance policy in the relevant individual health insurance market based on—

(i) the age of the eligible employee (and, in the case of an arrangement which covers medical expenses of the eligible employee's family members, the age of such family members), or

(ii) the number of family members of the eligible employee the medical expenses of which are covered under such arrangement.

The variation permitted under the preceding sentence shall be determined by reference to the same insurance policy with respect to all eligible employees.

(D) RULES RELATING TO MAXIMUM DOLLAR LIMITATION.—

(i) AMOUNT PRORATED IN CERTAIN CASES.—In the case of an individual who is not covered by an arrangement for the entire year, the limitation under subparagraph (B)(iii) for such year shall be an amount which bears the same ratio to the amount which would (but for this clause) be in effect for such individual for such year under subparagraph (B)(iii) as the number of months for which such individual is covered by the arrangement for such year bears to 12.

(ii) INFLATION ADJUSTMENT.—In the case of any year beginning after 2016, each of the dollar amounts in subparagraph (B)(iii) shall be increased by an amount equal to—

(I) such dollar amount, multiplied by

(II) the cost-of-living adjustment determined under section 1(f)(3) for the calendar year in which the taxable year begins, determined by substituting "calendar year 2015" for "calendar year 2016" in subparagraph (A)(ii) thereof.

If any dollar amount increased under the preceding sentence is not a multiple of $50, such dollar amount shall be rounded to the next lowest multiple of $50.

(3) OTHER DEFINITIONS.—For purposes of this subsection—

GROUP HEALTH PLAN REQUIREMENTS

(A) ELIGIBLE EMPLOYEE.—The term "eligible employee" means any employee of an eligible employer, except that the terms of the arrangement may exclude from consideration employees described in any clause of section 105(h)(3)(B) (applied by substituting "90 days" for "3 years" in clause (i) thereof).

(B) ELIGIBLE EMPLOYER.—The term "eligible employer" means an employer that—

(i) is not an applicable large employer as defined in section 4980H(c)(2), and

(ii) does not offer a group health plan to any of its employees.

(C) PERMITTED BENEFIT.—The term "permitted benefit" means, with respect to any eligible employee, the maximum dollar amount of payments and reimbursements which may be made under the terms of the qualified small employer health reimbursement arrangement for the year with respect to such employee.

(4) NOTICE.—

(A) IN GENERAL.—An employer funding a qualified small employer health reimbursement arrangement for any year shall, not later than 90 days before the beginning of such year (or, in the case of an employee who is not eligible to participate in the arrangement as of the beginning of such year, the date on which such employee is first so eligible), provide a written notice to each eligible employee which includes the information described in subparagraph (B).

(B) CONTENTS OF NOTICE.—The notice required under subparagraph (A) shall include each of the following:

(i) A statement of the amount which would be such eligible employee's permitted benefit under the arrangement for the year.

(ii) A statement that the eligible employee should provide the information described in clause (i) to any health insurance exchange to which the employee applies for advance payment of the premium assistance tax credit.

(iii) A statement that if the employee is not covered under minimum essential coverage for any month the employee may be subject to tax under section 5000A for such month and reimbursements under the arrangement may be includible in gross income.

Amendments

• **2019, Further Consolidated Appropriations Act, 2020 (P.L. 116-94)**

P.L. 116-94, §503(b)(2), Div. N:

Amended Code Sec. 9831(d)(1) by striking "except as provided in section 4980I(f)(4)" before "and notwithstanding any other provision". **Effective** for tax years beginning after 12-31-2019.

• **2017, Tax Cuts and Jobs Act (P.L. 115-97)**

P.L. 115-97, §11002(d)(1)(TT):

Amended Code Sec. 9831(d)(2)(D)(ii)(II) by striking "for 'calendar year 1992' in subparagraph (B)" and inserting "for 'calendar year 2016' in subparagraph (A)(ii)". **Effective** for tax years beginning after 12-31-2017.

• **2016, 21st Century Cures Act (P.L. 114-255)**

P.L. 114-255, §18001(a)(1):

Amended Code Sec. 9831 by adding at the end a new subsection (d). **Effective** for years beginning after 12-31-2016. For a special rule, see Act Sec. 18001(a)(7)(B), below.

P.L. 114-255, §18001(a)(7)(B), provides:

(B) TRANSITION RELIEF.—The relief under Treasury Notice 2015-17 shall be treated as applying to any plan year beginning on or before December 31, 2016.

[Sec. 9832]

SEC. 9832. DEFINITIONS.

[Sec. 9832(a)]

(a) GROUP HEALTH PLAN.—For purposes of this chapter, the term "group health plan" has the meaning given to such term by section 5000(b)(1).

[Sec. 9832(b)]

(b) DEFINITIONS RELATING TO HEALTH INSURANCE.—For purposes of this chapter—

(1) HEALTH INSURANCE COVERAGE.—

(A) IN GENERAL.—Except as provided in subparagraph (B), the term "health insurance coverage" means benefits consisting of medical care (provided directly, through insurance or reimbursement, or otherwise) under any hospital or medical service policy or certificate, hospital or medical service plan contract, or health maintenance organization contract offered by a health insurance issuer.

(B) NO APPLICATION TO CERTAIN EXCEPTED BENEFITS.—In applying subparagraph (A), excepted benefits described in subsection (c)(1) shall not be treated as benefits consisting of medical care.

(2) HEALTH INSURANCE ISSUER.—The term "health insurance issuer" means an insurance company, insurance service, or insurance organization (including a health maintenance organization, as defined in paragraph (3)) which is licensed to engage in the business of insurance in a State and which is subject to State law which regulates insurance (within the meaning of section 514(b)(2) of the Employee Retirement Income Security Act of 1974, as in effect on the date of the enactment of this section). Such term does not include a group health plan.

(3) HEALTH MAINTENANCE ORGANIZATION.—The term "health maintenance organization" means—

(A) a Federally qualified health maintenance organization (as defined in section 1301(a) of the Public Health Service Act (42 U.S.C. 300e(a))),

(B) an organization recognized under State law as a health maintenance organization, or

(C) a similar organization regulated under State law for solvency in the same manner and to the same extent as such a health maintenance organization.

[Sec. 9832(c)]

(c) EXCEPTED BENEFITS.—For purposes of this chapter, the term "excepted benefits" means benefits under one or more (or any combination thereof) of the following:

(1) BENEFITS NOT SUBJECT TO REQUIREMENTS.—

(A) Coverage only for accident, or disability income insurance, or any combination thereof.

(B) Coverage issued as a supplement to liability insurance.

(C) Liability insurance, including general liability insurance and automobile liability insurance.

(D) Workers' compensation or similar insurance.

(E) Automobile medical payment insurance.

(F) Credit-only insurance.

(G) Coverage for on-site medical clinics.

(H) Other similar insurance coverage, specified in regulations, under which benefits for medical care are secondary or incidental to other insurance benefits.

(2) BENEFITS NOT SUBJECT TO REQUIREMENTS IF OFFERED SEPARATELY.—

(A) Limited scope dental or vision benefits.

GROUP HEALTH PLAN REQUIREMENTS

(B) Benefits for long-term care, nursing home care, home health care, community-based care, or any combination thereof.

(C) Such other similar, limited benefits as are specified in regulations.

(3) BENEFITS NOT SUBJECT TO REQUIREMENTS IF OFFERED AS INDEPENDENT, NONCOORDINATED BENEFITS.—

(A) Coverage only for a specified disease or illness.

(B) Hospital indemnity or other fixed indemnity insurance.

(4) BENEFITS NOT SUBJECT TO REQUIREMENTS IF OFFERED AS SEPARATE INSURANCE POLICY.—Medicare supplemental health insurance (as defined under section 1882(g)(1) of the Social Security Act), coverage supplemental to the coverage provided under chapter 55 of title 10, United States Code, and similar supplemental coverage provided to coverage under a group health plan.

[Sec. 9832(d)]

(d) OTHER DEFINITIONS.—For purposes of this chapter—

(1) COBRA CONTINUATION PROVISION.—The term "COBRA continuation provision" means any of the following:

(A) Section 4980B, other than subsection (f)(1) thereof insofar as it relates to pediatric vaccines.

(B) Part 6 of subtitle B of title I of the Employee Retirement Income Security Act of 1974 (29 U.S.C. 1161 et seq.), other than section 609 of such Act.

(C) Title XXII of the Public Health Service Act.

(2) GOVERNMENTAL PLAN.—The term "governmental plan" has the meaning given such term by section 414(d).

(3) MEDICAL CARE.—The term "medical care" has the meaning given such term by section 213(d) determined without regard to—

(A) paragraph (1)(C) thereof, and

(B) so much of paragraph (1)(D) thereof as relates to qualified long-term care insurance.

(4) NETWORK PLAN.—The term "network plan" means health insurance coverage of a health insurance issuer under which the financing and delivery of medical care are provided, in whole or in part, through a defined set of providers under contract with the issuer.

(5) PLACED FOR ADOPTION DEFINED.—The term "placement", or being "placed", for adoption, in connection with any placement for adoption of a child with any person, means the assumption and retention by such person of a legal obligation for total or partial support of such child in anticipation of adoption of such child. The child's placement with such person terminates upon the termination of such legal obligation.

(6) FAMILY MEMBER.—The term "family member" means, with respect to any individual—

(A) a dependent (as such term is used for purposes of section 9801(f)(2)) of such individual, and

(B) any other individual who is a first-degree, second-degree, third-degree, or fourth-degree relative of such individual or of an individual described in subparagraph (A).

(7) GENETIC INFORMATION.—

(A) IN GENERAL.—The term "genetic information" means, with respect to any individual, information about—

(i) such individual's genetic tests,

(ii) the genetic tests of family members of such individual, and

(iii) the manifestation of a disease or disorder in family members of such individual.

(B) INCLUSION OF GENETIC SERVICES AND PARTICIPATION IN GENETIC RESEARCH.—Such term includes, with respect to any individual, any request for, or receipt of, genetic services, or participation in clinical research which includes genetic services, by such individual or any family member of such individual.

(C) EXCLUSIONS.—The term "genetic information" shall not include information about the sex or age of any individual.

(8) GENETIC TEST.—

(A) IN GENERAL.—The term "genetic test" means an analysis of human DNA, RNA, chromosomes, proteins, or metabolites, that detects genotypes, mutations, or chromosomal changes.

(B) EXCEPTIONS.—The term "genetic test" does not mean—

(i) an analysis of proteins or metabolites that does not detect genotypes, mutations, or chromosomal changes, or

(ii) an analysis of proteins or metabolites that is directly related to a manifested disease, disorder, or pathological condition that could reasonably be detected by a health care professional with appropriate training and expertise in the field of medicine involved.

(9) GENETIC SERVICES.—The term "genetic services" means—

(A) a genetic test;

(B) genetic counseling (including obtaining, interpreting, or assessing genetic information); or

(C) genetic education.

(10) UNDERWRITING PURPOSES.—The term "underwriting purposes" means, with respect to any group health plan, or health insurance coverage offered in connection with a group health plan—

(A) rules for, or determination of, eligibility (including enrollment and continued eligibility) for benefits under the plan or coverage;

(B) the computation of premium or contribution amounts under the plan or coverage;

(C) the application of any pre-existing condition exclusion under the plan or coverage; and

(D) other activities related to the creation, renewal, or replacement of a contract of health insurance or health benefits.

Amendments

• **2008, Genetic Information Nondiscrimination Act of 2008 (P.L. 110-233)**

P.L. 110-233, § 103(d):

Amended Code Sec. 9832(d) by adding at the end new paragraphs (6)-(10). **Effective** with respect to group health plans for plan years beginning after the date that is 1 year after 5-21-2008. For a special rule, see Act Sec. 209(a)(2)(B) and (c) in the amendment notes for Code Sec. 9802(b).

P.L. 110-233, § 103(f)(1), provides:

(1) REGULATIONS.—The Secretary of the Treasury shall issue final regulations or other guidance not later than 12 months after the date of the enactment of this Act to carry out the amendments made by this section.

• **1997, Taxpayer Relief Act of 1997 (P.L. 105-34)**

P.L. 105-34, § 1531(a)(2):

Redesignated Code Sec. 9805 as Code Sec. 9832. **Effective** with respect to group health plans for plan years beginning on or after 1-1-98.

• **1996, Health Insurance Portability and Accountability Act of 1996 (P.L. 104-191)**

P.L. 104-191, § 401(a):

Amended the Internal Revenue Code of 1986 by adding Code Sec. 9805. For the **effective** date, see Act Sec. 401(c), below.

P.L. 104-191, § 401(c), provides:

(c) EFFECTIVE DATE.—

(1) IN GENERAL.—The amendments made by this section shall apply to plan years beginning after June 30, 1997.

(2) DETERMINATION OF CREDITABLE COVERAGE.—

(A) PERIOD OF COVERAGE.—

(i) IN GENERAL.—Subject to clause (ii), no period before July 1, 1996, shall be taken into account under chapter 100 of the Internal Revenue Code of 1986 (as added by this section) in determining creditable coverage.

(ii) SPECIAL RULE FOR CERTAIN PERIODS.—The Secretary of the Treasury, consistent with section 104, shall provide for a process whereby individuals who need to establish

GROUP HEALTH PLAN REQUIREMENTS

creditable coverage for periods before July 1, 1996, and who would have such coverage credited but for clause (i) may be given credit for creditable coverage for such periods through the presentation of documents or other means.

(B) CERTIFICATIONS, ETC.—

(i) IN GENERAL.—Subject to clauses (ii) and (iii), subsection (e) of section 9801 of the Internal Revenue Code of 1986 (as added by this section) shall apply to events occurring after June 30, 1996.

(ii) NO CERTIFICATION REQUIRED TO BE PROVIDED BEFORE JUNE 1, 1997.—In no case is a certification required to be provided under such subsection before June 1, 1997.

(iii) CERTIFICATION ONLY ON WRITTEN REQUEST FOR EVENTS OCCURRING BEFORE OCTOBER 1, 1996.—In the case of an event occurring after June 30, 1996, and before October 1, 1996, a certification is not required to be provided under such subsection unless an individual (with respect to whom the certification is otherwise required to be made) requests such certification in writing.

(C) TRANSITIONAL RULE.—In the case of an individual who seeks to establish creditable coverage for any period for which certification is not required because it relates to an event occurring before June 30, 1996—

(i) the individual may present other credible evidence of such coverage in order to establish the period of creditable coverage; and

(ii) a group health plan and a health insurance issuer shall not be subject to any penalty or enforcement action with respect to the plan's or issuer's crediting (or not crediting) such coverage if the plan or issuer has sought to comply in good faith with the applicable requirements under the amendments made by this section.

(3) SPECIAL RULE FOR COLLECTIVE BARGAINING AGREEMENTS.—Except as provided in paragraph (2), in the case of a group health plan maintained pursuant to 1 or more collective bargaining agreements between employee representatives and one or more employers ratified before the date of the enactment of this Act, the amendments made by this section shall not apply to plan years beginning before the later of—

(A) the date on which the last of the collective bargaining agreements relating to the plan terminates (determined without regard to any extension thereof agreed to after the date of the enactment of this Act), or

(B) July 1, 1997.

For purposes of subparagraph (A), any plan amendment made pursuant to a collective bargaining agreement relating to the plan which amends the plan solely to conform to any requirement added by this section shall not be treated as a termination of such collective bargaining agreement.

(4) TIMELY REGULATIONS.—The Secretary of the Treasury, consistent with section 104, shall first issue by not later than April 1, 1997, such regulations as may be necessary to carry out the amendments made by this section.

(5) LIMITATION ON ACTIONS.—No enforcement action shall be taken, pursuant to the amendments made by this section, against a group health plan or health insurance issuer with respect to a violation of a requirement imposed by such amendments before January 1, 1998, or, if later, the date of issuance of regulations referred to in paragraph (4), if the plan or issuer has sought to comply in good faith with such requirements.

[Sec. 9833]

SEC. 9833. REGULATIONS.

The Secretary, consistent with section 104 of the Health Care Portability and Accountability Act of 1996, may promulgate such regulations as may be necessary or appropriate to carry out the provisions of this chapter. The Secretary may promulgate any interim final rules as the Secretary determines are appropriate to carry out this chapter.

Amendments

- **1997, Taxpayer Relief Act of 1997 (P.L. 105-34)**

P.L. 105-34, §1531(a)(2):

Redesignated Code Sec. 9806 as Code Sec. 9833. **Effective** with respect to group health plans for plan years beginning on or after 1-1-98.

- **1996, Health Insurance Portability and Accountability Act of 1996 (P.L. 104-191)**

P.L. 104-191, §401(a):

Amended the Internal Revenue Code of 1986 by adding Code Sec. 9806. For the **effective** date, see Act Sec. 401(c), below.

P.L. 104-191, §401(c), provides:

(c) EFFECTIVE DATE.—

(1) IN GENERAL.—The amendments made by this section shall apply to plan years beginning after June 30, 1997.

(2) DETERMINATION OF CREDITABLE COVERAGE.—

(A) PERIOD OF COVERAGE.—

(i) IN GENERAL.—Subject to clause (ii), no period before July 1, 1996, shall be taken into account under chapter 100 of the Internal Revenue Code of 1986 (as added by this section) in determining creditable coverage.

(ii) SPECIAL RULE FOR CERTAIN PERIODS.—The Secretary of the Treasury, consistent with section 104, shall provide for a process whereby individuals who need to establish creditable coverage for periods before July 1, 1996, and who would have such coverage credited but for clause (i) may be given credit for creditable coverage for such periods through the presentation of documents or other means.

(B) CERTIFICATIONS, ETC.—

(i) IN GENERAL.—Subject to clauses (ii) and (iii), subsection (e) of section 9801 of the Internal Revenue Code of 1986 (as added by this section) shall apply to events occurring after June 30, 1996.

(ii) NO CERTIFICATION REQUIRED TO BE PROVIDED BEFORE JUNE 1, 1997.—In no case is a certification required to be provided under such subsection before June 1, 1997.

(iii) CERTIFICATION ONLY ON WRITTEN REQUEST FOR EVENTS OCCURRING BEFORE OCTOBER 1, 1996.—In the case of an event occurring after June 30, 1996, and before October 1, 1996, a certification is not required to be provided under such subsection unless an individual (with respect to whom the certification is otherwise required to be made) requests such certification in writing.

(C) TRANSITIONAL RULE.—In the case of an individual who seeks to establish creditable coverage for any period for which certification is not required because it relates to an event occurring before June 30, 1996—

(i) the individual may present other credible evidence of such coverage in order to establish the period of creditable coverage; and

(ii) a group health plan and a health insurance issuer shall not be subject to any penalty or enforcement action with respect to the plan's or issuer's crediting (or not crediting) such coverage if the plan or issuer has sought to comply in good faith with the applicable requirements under the amendments made by this section.

(3) SPECIAL RULE FOR COLLECTIVE BARGAINING AGREEMENTS.—Except as provided in paragraph (2), in the case of a group health plan maintained pursuant to 1 or more collective bargaining agreements between employee representatives and one or more employers ratified before the date of the enactment of this Act, the amendments made by this section shall not apply to plan years beginning before the later of—

(A) the date on which the last of the collective bargaining agreements relating to the plan terminates (determined without regard to any extension thereof agreed to after the date of the enactment of this Act), or

(B) July 1, 1997.

For purposes of subparagraph (A), any plan amendment made pursuant to a collective bargaining agreement relating to the plan which amends the plan solely to conform to any requirement added by this section shall not be treated as a termination of such collective bargaining agreement.

(4) TIMELY REGULATIONS.—The Secretary of the Treasury, consistent with section 104, shall first issue by not later than April 1, 1997, such regulations as may be necessary to carry out the amendments made by this section.

(5) LIMITATION ON ACTIONS.—No enforcement action shall be taken, pursuant to the amendments made by this section, against a group health plan or health insurance issuer with respect to a violation of a requirement imposed by such amendments before January 1, 1998, or, if later, the date of issuance of regulations referred to in paragraph (4), if the plan or issuer has sought to comply in good faith with such requirements.

[Sec. 9834]

SEC. 9834. ENFORCEMENT.

For the imposition of tax on any failure of a group health plan to meet the requirements of this chapter, see section 4980D.

Amendments

- **2008, Genetic Information Nondiscrimination Act of 2008 (P.L. 110-233)**

P.L. 110-233, §103(e)(1):

Amended subchapter C of chapter 100 by adding at the end a new Code Sec. 9834. **Effective** with respect to group health plans for plan years beginning after the date that is 1 year after 5-21-2008. For a special rule, see Act Sec. 209(a)(2)(B) and (c) in the amendment notes for Code Sec. 9802(b).

P.L. 110-233, §103(f)(1), provides:

(f) REGULATIONS AND EFFECTIVE DATE.—

(1) REGULATIONS.—The Secretary of the Treasury shall issue final regulations or other guidance not later than 12 months after the date of the enactment of this Act to carry out the amendments made by this section.

[End of Code.]

[The next page is 5701.]

TOPICAL INDEX

References are to Code Section numbers.

A

Abandonment of family by parent, tax relief
. collection on obligations 6305
Abatement of tax 6404
. Armed Forces members 692
. assessments attributable to error by IRS . . . . .
. . . . 6404(e)
. assessments attributable to
. . mathematical error by IRS . . . . . . 6404(d)
. astronauts 692
. deficiency found by Tax Court
. . disallowed 7486
. erroneous written advice by IRS . . . . . 6404(f)
. excessive, late, or erroneous
. . assessments . . . . 6404(a)
. failure to provide notice of liability . . . . . 6404(g)
. insolvent banks 7507
. jeopardy assessments . . . . . 6861(c); 6861(g)
. private foundations . . . . 507(g)
. prohibition against filing claim . . . . 6404(b)
. review of denial of request for
. . abatement . . . . 6404(h)
. small tax balances . . . . 6404(c)
. victims of certain terrorist attacks 692
. wines lost or destroyed . . . . 5370(a)
ABC transactions 636
Accelerated cost recovery system
. allowance of deduction . . . . 168(a)
. alternative system . . . . 168(g)
. applicable convention . . . . 168(d)
. applicable depreciation method . . . . 168(b)
. applicable recovery period . . . . 168(c)
. churning transactions . . . . 168(f)(5)
. classification of property . . . . 168(e)
. definitions and special rules . . . . 168(i)
. election to be excluded from . . . . 168(f)(1)
. fifteen-year property . . . . 168(e)(3)(E)
. films and videotape . . . . 168(f)(3)
. five-year property . . . . 168(e)(3)(B)
. imported property . . . . 168(g)
. Indian reservation property . . . . 168(j)
. leasehold improvements . . . . 168(i)(8)
. property used predominantly outside
. . U.S. . . . . 168(g)
. qualified improvement property . . . . 168(e)(6)
. rent-to-own property . . . . 168(i)(14)
. residential v. nonresidential property . . 168(e)(2)
. seven-year property . . . . 168(e)(3)(C)
. special depreciation allowance
. . certain property acquired after
. . . December 31, 2007, and before January 1,
. . . 2013 . . . . 168(k)
. tax-exempt bond financed property . . 168(g)(5)
. tax-exempt use property . . . . . . 168(g); 168(h)
. ten-year property . . . . 168(e)(3)(D)
. three-year property . . . . 168(e)(3)(A)
. twenty-year property . . . . 168(e)(3)(F)
Accelerated death benefits . . . . 101(g)
. qualified riders treated as life insurance . . . . .
. . . . 818(g)
Accelerated depreciation
. property placed in service before 1987
. . tax preference item . . . . 57(a)(6)
Accident and health plans—see Health and
. accident plans
Accounting for collected taxes 7512
Accounting methods—see also Accounting
. periods . . . . 446—483
. books and records—see Books and records
. carryover by acquiring corporation . . . 381(c)(4)
. cash method
. . limitation on use 448
. change in . . . . 446(e)
. . adjustments required by 481
. . different businesses . . . . 446(d)
. . election of method . . . . 446(c)
. . excise taxes collected 7512
. farming corporations 447
. hybrid methods . . . . 446(c)
. installment method 453
. . election out of . . . . 453(d)

Accounting methods—continued
. installment method—continued
. . gain or loss on disposition of
. . . obligations 453B
. . nondealers, special rules 453A
. . inventories 471; 472
. . long-term contracts 460
. . membership dues income 456
. . nonaccrual experience method . . . . 448(d)(5)
. . records—see Books and records
. . securities dealers
. . . mark-to-market method 475
. . subscriptions, prepaid 455
. . sugar cane farming, corporations in . . . 447(e)
. . withheld taxes 7512
. . year deductions allowed 461
. . . economic performance rule . . . . . . 461(h)
. . . rental agreements, deferred payments . . 467
. . year income taxable 451
Accounting periods—see also Accounting
. methods . . . . 441—444
. annual accounting period . . . . 441(c)
. change 442
. insurance companies 843
. real estate investment trusts 859
. books not kept . . . . 441(g)
. calendar year . . . . 441(d)
. change of 442; 443
. . personal holding company tax
. . . computation not affected 546
. 52-53 week year . . . . 441(f)
. fiscal year . . . . 441(e)
. partners and partnerships 706
. real estate investment trusts 859
. short period, returns 443
. taxable year defined . . . . 441(b)
Accounting records—see Books and records
Accrual basis of accounting
. charitable contributions . . . . 170(a)(2)
. contributions of employer to retirement
. . plan . . . . 404(a)(7)
. death during year
. . year deductions taken . . . . 461(b)
. . year income taxable . . . . 451(d)
. foreign tax credit 905
. magazines, paperbacks and recordings
. . returned 458
. real property taxes . . . . 461(c)
. . limitation on acceleration . . . . 461(d)
. settlement funds, designated 468B
. utility services . . . . 451(h)
Accumulated earnings credit . . . . 535(c)
Accumulated earnings tax . . . . 531—537
. accumulated taxable income 535
. income distributed to U.S.-owned
. . foreign corporation . . . . 535(d)
. burden of proof 534
. dividends paid deduction . . . . 563(a)
. evidence of purpose to avoid income tax . . 533
. imposition of tax 531
. income not placed on annual basis 536
. liability for tax 532
. rate of tax 531
. reasonable needs of the business,
. . accumulations of surplus to meet 537
Accumulated taxable income 535
Accumulation trusts . . . . 665—668
. distribution . . . . 904(f)(4)
Accuracy-related penalty 6662
. gross valuation misstatements, increase
. . in penalty . . . . 6662(h)
. substantial estate or gift tax valuation
. . understatement . . . . 6662(g)
. substantial overstatement of pension
. . liabilities . . . . 6662(f)
. substantial understatement of tax . . . . 6662(d)
. substantial valuation misstatement . . . . 6662(e)
. tax shelters, corporations . . . . . 6662(d)(2)(C)
**Achieving a Better Life Experience
(ABLE) program** 529A
. excess contributions . . . . 4973(h)

Acquiring corporations
. assets of target corporations . . . . 338(e)
. carryovers . . . . 381—384
. stock purchases as asset acquisitions . . 338(a)
**Acquisition indebtedness, debt-
financed property** . . . . 514(c)
Acquisitions made to evade or avoid tax . . 269
Activities not engaged in for profit 183
**Acts, time for performing, last day on
Saturday, Sunday, or holiday** 7503
Actuaries and actuarial reports
. enrollment of actuaries . . . . 7701(a)(35)
. periodic report, requirement of 6059
. . failure to file, penalty 6692
Additional recovery rebate credit 6428A
Additions to tax . . . . 6651—6658
. bad checks tendered in payment of tax . . 6657
. bankruptcy proceedings 6658
. estimated tax, large corporations . . 6655(d)(2);
. . 6655(g)(2)
. failure to
. . file information returns 6652
. . file tax returns . . . . 6651(a)
. . make deposit of taxes 6656
. . pay estimated tax, corporations 6655
. . pay estimated tax, individuals 6654
. . pay stamp tax 6653
. . pay tax . . . . 6651(a)
. interest on . . . . 6601(e)(2)
. notice of charges 6631
Addresses, deficiency notice . . . . 6212(b)
Adjudication, bankruptcy . . . . 6871(b)
Adjusted basis
. adjustments required by law 1016
. annuity contracts 1021
. controlled foreign corporation's stock 961
. depletion deduction 612
. depreciation deduction . . . . 167(c)
. distributions by corporations having loan
. . from United States . . . . 312(i)
. gain or loss, for determination of 1011
. investment credit property . . . . 50(c)
. mines or mineral deposits . . . . 616(c)
. partner's interest 705
. Section 1245 property . . . . 1245(c)
Adjusted gross income
. charitable contributions limited . . . . 170(b)(1)(H)
. defined 62
. itemized deductions limited 68
Administration and procedure . . . . 6001—7874
Administration expenses of estates . . . 642(g);
. 2053
Administrative appeal of liens 6326
**Administrative review of decisions,
prohibition of** 6406
Administrators—see Executors and
. administrators
Adoption
. assistance programs 137
. . exclusions from gross income . . . . . . 137(a)
. child's status as dependent . . . . . 152(f)(1)(B)
. distributions from retirement plans . . 72(t)(2)(H)
. expenses
. . credit against tax 23
. . exclusion from income 137
Advance payment
. credit for health insurance costs of
. . eligible individuals 7527
Advanced energy project credit 48C
Advanced nuclear power facilities
. investment credit 48D
. production credit 45X
Advanced nuclear power facilities
. credit for production 45J
Adverse party defined . . . . 672(a)
**Advertising activities, unrelated trade or
business** . . . . 513(c)

5702

Topical Index
References are to Code Section numbers.

Advertising expenditures
. foreign broadcasts directed to U.S. .... 162(j)
. local charges
.. exclusion from selling price .... 4216(e)
.. political convention program 276

Affidavits, fraudulent .... 7206(2)

Affiliated corporations
. consolidated returns .... 1501—1505
. corporate acquisition indebtedness,
  deductibility of .... 279(g)
. dividends paid deduction .... 562(d)
. dividends received deduction 243
. earnings and profits 1552
. intragroup transactions
.. basis of stock .... 358(g)
. retirement plans, service group ... 414(m)(5)
. service group, employees of ...... 414(m)

Affiliated group defined .... 1504(a)

Agencies
. targeted jobs, individuals designated for ......
  .... 51(d)(12)

Agents
. acts to be performed, employment taxes . 3504
. fiduciaries and receivers filing returns . 6012(b)

Agricultural chemicals security credit ... 45O
. denial of double benefit .... 280C(f)

Agricultural labor
. defined .... 3121(g); 3306(k)
. Federal Insurance Contributions Act
  taxes .... 3121(b)(1)
. Federal Unemployment Tax Act taxes . 3306(k)
. withholding of income tax on wages ......
  .... 3401(a)(2)

Agricultural or horticultural cooperatives
. qualified business income deduction . 199A(g)

Agricultural organizations
. dues, unrelated business income .... 512(d)
. exempt status .... 501(c)(5)

**Aiding and abetting understatement of
liability, penalty** 6701

Air ambulance services
. group health plans
.. out-of-network providers 9817
.. report requirements 9823

Air Force personnel—see Armed Forces of the U.S.

Aircraft
. donations
.. fraudulent acknowledgments 6720
. emergency medical fixed wing aircraft
.. exemption from aviation excise tax . 4041(l)
. foreign aircraft earnings exemption . 872(b)(2);
  883(a)(2)
. fractional ownership program
.. excise tax on fuel 4043
.. income from leased aircraft 861
. supplies, exemption from manufacturers
  excise tax .... 4221(a)(3)

Airline tickets, deposit of taxes .... 6302(e)

Airport and airways use tax
. advertising violations, penalties 7275
. air ambulances providing emergency
  medical transportation .... 4261(g)
. helicopter use .... 4041(l); 4261(e); 4261(f)
. refund or credit, fuel for nontaxable
  purposes .... 6427(a)
. seaplanes .... 4261(i)
. special rules .... 4261(e)
. taxable transportation .... 4261(b); 4262
. ticket printing requirements, penalty for
  violation .... 7275(a)
. trust fund 9502
.. management 9602

Alaska
. empowerment zones
.. special eligibility for certain areas .. 1392(d)
. harbor maintenance excise tax
  exemption .... 4462(b)

Alaska Native Settlement Trusts
. election 646
. information statement 6039H
. payments and transfers 139G; 247

Alcohol fuel mixture credit .... 6426(b)

Alcohol, fuel use of .... 40; 87; 4041(m)

Alcohol, fuel use of—continued
. information reporting 4104

Alcohol taxes .... 5001—5690
. beer imported in bulk 5418
. denaturation .... 5241—5244
. income tax credit 5011
. industrial use of distilled spirits .. 5271—5275
. refunds 6423
. wine and flavor content, tax refund 5010
. wine imported in bulk 5364
. withdrawals 5313

Aliens
. departure from U.S. .... 6851(d)
. nonresident—see Nonresident aliens
. reciprocal penalty tax for discriminatory
  tax by foreign country 891; 896

Alimony and separate maintenance
. deduction of payments 215
.. adjusted gross income computation ......
  .... 62(a)(10)
. inclusion in gross income of amounts
  received .... 61(a)(8); 71
. individual retirement account, transfer ......
  .... 408(d)(6)
. trust income paying 682

Allocation
. basis for gain or loss .... 358(b)
. income and deductions, related
  taxpayers 482
. personal service corporations 269A
. principal and interest, deferred payment
  sales 483
. travel expenses .... 274(c)

Alternate valuation
. generation-skipping transfer tax ... 667(b)(6)

Alternative fuel credit .... 6426(d)

Alternative fuel mixture credit .... 6426(e)

**Alternative fuel vehicle refueling
property credit** 30C

Alternative minimum tax .... 55—59
. adjustment in exclusion for computing . 443(d)
. alternative minimum taxable income . 55(b)(2)
. adjustments in computing 56
.. losses, denial of 58
. definitions and special rules 59
. exemption amount .... 55(d)
.. tax years 2018–2025 .... 55(d)(4)
. foreign tax credit .... 59(a)
. imposition of 55
. inflation adjustment ...... 55(d)(3) ; 55(d)(4)(B)
. noncorporate taxpayers .... 55(b)(1)
. special rules .... 6166(b)(2)(D); 6166(b)(7)
. tax preferences, items of 57
. tentative minimum tax .... 55(b)

Alternative motor vehicle credit 30B

Alternative taxes
. mutual savings bank conducting life
  insurance business 594

American opportunity credit 25A

American Samoa
. alien residents of, tax on 876
. child tax credit .... 24(k)(3)
. coordination of individual income tax
  with U.S. 7654
. earned income credit .... 7530(c)
. foreign corporations .... 881(b)
. governmental employees
.. return and payment of tax ...... 3125(c)
. income from sources within 931
. self-employment tax for residents .. 1402(a)(9)

Amortization
. bond discount or premium 171
.. carryover by acquiring corporation . 381(c)(9)
. experimental expenditures .... 174(b)
. goodwill and certain other intangibles ... 197
. insurance companies, policy acquisition
  costs of 848
. leases, acquisition costs 178
. pollution control facilities 169
. research expenditures .... 174(b)

Amounts at risk
. deductions of expenses in case of
  certain activities 465

Annual accounting period .... 441(c)

Annual notice of tax delinquency 7524

**Annualized excludable disability
amount** .... 139C(c)

Annualizing income .... 443(b)
. accumulated earnings tax computation .. 536
. avoidance of penalty for underpayment
  of estimated tax ...... 6654(d)(2); 6655(e)
. personal holding companies 546

Annuities and annuity contracts
. accumulated deductible employee
  contributions, tax treatment ...... 72(o)
. adjusted basis of annuity contract 1021
. amounts received as annuities, inclusion
  in gross income .... 61(a)(9); 72
. church employees .... 403(b)(9)
. contracts not held by natural persons ... 72(u)
. deductibility of amounts paid for 264
. definition of annuity contract ..... 1035(b)(2)
. determination of survivor ..... 401(a)(13)(D)
. disability annuities under Foreign
  Service Act, exemption of amounts received
  .... 104(a)(4)
. distributions
.. cash withdrawals prior to starting date . 72(e)
.. premature, penalty .... 72(q)
.. unemployed persons and health
   insurance premiums .... 72(t)(2)(D)
. dividends on .... 72(e)(1)
. early distributions from qualified
  retirement plans .... 72(t)
. estate tax, gross estate valuation 2039
. excess contributions, excise tax 4973
. exchange of contracts, gain or loss
  recognition 1035
. foreign income .... 871(f)
. foreign insurer issuing, excise tax 4371
. gross estate valuation 2039
. gross income .... 61(a)(9)
. individual retirement accounts—see Individual
  retirement accounts
. joint and survivor annuities, amounts
  received by surviving annuitant ... 691(d)
. loans .... 72(p)
. long-term care insurance rider
.. information reporting 6050U
. sale of, adjusted basis 1021
. servicemen, family benefits ...... 72(n); 122
. simplified method of taxing annuity
  payments .... 72(d)
. starting date .... 72(c)(4)
. Tax Court judges
.. dependents 7448
. teachers .... 403(b)
. valuation tables 7520
. withholding .... 3402(o); 3405

Annuity trusts 664

Anorthosite, percentage depletion .... 613(b)

Anti-conversion rules, capital gains ... 1258

Anti-cruelty societies
. bequests to 2055
.. nonresident aliens .... 2106(a)(2)(A)
. contributions to .... 170(c)
. exempt organizations .... 501(c)(3)
. gift tax deduction 2522
. trusts created for .... 642(c)

Antimony, percentage depletion .... 613(b)

Antitrust law violations
. recoveries of damages 186
. treble damage payments .... 162(g)

Apostolic associations, exemption .... 501(d)

Appeals from Tax Court decisions . 7481—7487

Applicable corporation .... 59(k)

Applicable credits, elective payment of . 6417

Appraisals
. charitable deduction property ..... 170(f)(11)
. penalties
.. valuation misstatement 6695A

Appreciated financial positions
. constructive sales treatment .... 1259(c)
. regulations .... 1259(f)
. special rules .... 1259(e)

Appreciated property
. charitable contributions .. 170(b)(1)(C); 170(e)

ADV

Topical Index
References are to Code Section numbers.

Appreciated property—continued
- distribution by corporation
  - recognition of gain or loss .... 311(b)
- distributions of
  - earnings and profits, effect on ..... 312(b)

Arbitrage bonds 148

Arbitrage operations in securities ...... 1233(f)

Archer medical savings accounts (MSAs) 220
- adjusted gross income computation .. 62(a)(16)
- defined .... 220(d)(1)
- distributions
  - tax treatment .... 220(f)
  - use for menstrual care products .. 220(d)(2)(A)
- employer contributions .... 106(b)
  - failure to make 4980E
- excise tax on excess contributions 4973
- Medicare Advantage MSAs
  - defined .... 138(a)
  - distributions .... 138(c)
  - penalties .... 138(c)(2)
- tax advantages 138

Architectural and transportation barrier removal expenses 190

Armed Forces of the U.S.
- annuities .... 72(n); 122
- benefits as income 134
- combat zone compensation
  - exclusion from gross income .. 112; 3401(a)(1)
  - inclusion in gross income for purposes of contributions to IRA ...... 219(f)(7)
- communication tax exemption .... 4253(d)
- death of member
  - abatement of tax 692
  - estate tax 2201
- definition .... 7701(a)(15)
- earned income credit, eligibility of overseas personnel .... 32(c)(4)
- expenses of reserve members
  - trade and business deduction .... 62(a)
- fringe benefits
  - qualified military base realignment and closure .... 132(a)(8); 132(n)
- moving expenses
  - deductibility .... 217(g)
- residence sold by member, nonrecognition of gain .... 121(d)
- withholding of tax on compensation . 3401(a)(1)
- receipts .... 6051(b)

Artistic work of invention, capital asset status .... 1221(a)(3); 1231(b)(1)(C)

Artworks and copyrights, charitable contributions .... 2055(e)(4)

Assessable penalties .... 6671—6725

Assessment of tax .... 6201—6216
- authority 6201
- bankruptcy and receivership .... 6871—6873
- bond to stay pending review of Tax Court decision 7485
- criminal restitution treated as tax .. 6201(a)(4)
- employment taxes 6205
- interest on deficiencies 6621
- jeopardy assessments .... 534(d); 6861—6864
- limitations period .... 6501—6504
- method of assessment 6203
- prohibition of suits to restrain 7421
- reasonable verification of returns ... 6201(d)
- regulations establishing mode or time of assessment 6202
- restrictions on
  - Armed Forces members dying 692
  - exceptions .... 6213(b)
  - insolvent banks 7507
  - petition to Tax Court 6213
  - victims of certain terrorist attacks dying .. 692
- suits by taxpayers to restrain 7421
- supplemental 6204
- suspension of running of period of limitation 6503
- time limitation .... 6501—6504

Assessments against local benefits .. 164(c)(1)

Asset acquisitions
- basis, allocation of 1060
- stock purchases treated as .... 338(a)

Association, corporate status ...... 7701(a)(3)

Assumption of liability—see Liabilities assumed

Astronauts
- death in the line of duty
  - abatement of tax ..... 692(d)(5); 2201(b)(3)

At-risk limitation on losses
- active closely held C corporations .... 465(c)(7)
- extension of rules .... 465(c)(3)
- geothermal deposits .... 465(e)(1)
- recapture of at-risk losses .... 465(e)
- safe harbor leases .... 168(f)

At-risk rules, investment credit 49

Attorneys' fees
- payments to
  - returns required .... 6045(f)
- reimbursement by government of taxpayer's costs 7430

Audit standards, selection of returns
- protection from disclosure .... 6103(b)(2)

Automatic contribution errors
- correction of .... 414(cc)

Automatic enrolment
- requirements for 414A

Automobiles
- alternative motor vehicle credit 30B
- lien for taxes, validity .... 6323(b)
- luxury
  - depreciation, limitation .... 280F(a)
- plug-in electric drive motor vehicle credit .. 30D

Aviation use tax—see Airport and airways use tax

Avoidance of tax—see Evasion or avoidance of tax

Awards
- employer-provided, deduction of cost .. 274(b)
- inclusion in gross income 74
- scholarships 117

Away from home expenses .... 162(a)(2); 162(h); 162(p); 274(c)

B

Backup withholding 3406
- false certification, penalty .... 7205(b)

Bad checks in payment of tax 6657

Bad debts
- banks 582
- deduction .... 166(b)
- insurance companies other than life or mutual .... 832(c)
- political parties, amounts owed by ... 271
- qualified business indebtedness, discharge .... 108(c)
- reserves 593
- mutual savings institutions, additions to reserves 593

Bail
- cash bail of more than $10,000, information returns .... 6050I(g)

Bail-out, preferred stock 306

Bail and sagger clay deposits, percentage depletion .... 613(b)

Bankruptcy and receivership ..... 6871—6873
- assessment of tax .... 6871—6873
- failure to pay tax .... 6658(a)
- individuals, rules for .... 1398(a)
- notice of qualification as receiver ... 6036
- payment of tax, extensions of time .. 6161(c)
- retirement plans
  - prohibition on benefits increase ... 401(a)(33)
- tax entity .... 1398(a); 1399
- trustee, Tax Court 7464

Banks .... 581—597
- bad debts
  - reserves 585
  - worthless securities 582
- building and loan associations .... 591—593
- common trust 584
- cooperative banks .... 591—593
- credit card transactions
  - reporting requirements 6050W
- defined 581
- exclusion from definition of personal holding company .... 542(c)(2)
- FDIC premiums, deduction limitation .. 162(r)

Banks—continued
- Federal National Mortgage Association stock purchases, expenses incurred .. 162(d)
- foreign central banks, interest from obligations of the U.S. 895
- information returns with respect to common trust funds 6032
- insolvent, exemption from tax 7507
- losses on securities 582
- mutual savings banks—see Mutual savings institutions
- reserves for losses on loans 585
- S corporations
  - change from bad debt reserve method of accounting .... 1361(g)
  - restricted bank director stock . 1361(f); 1368(f)
  - securities held by, gain on .... 582(c)
- tax preferences 291

Bargain sales to charitable organizations .... 1011(b)

Barite, percentage depletion .... 613(b)

Base erosion
- U.S. source income, minimum tax amount 59A

Basis .... 1011—1023
- adjusted—see Adjusted basis
- allocation of .... 358(b)
- annuity contract 1021
- asset acquisitions 1060
- assumption of liability .... 362(d)
- bequests .... 1014(b)
- appreciated property acquired in transfer from estate or trust 1040
- cost 1012
- Federal National Mortgage Association stock 1054
- gift property 1015
- inherited property 1014
- installment obligations .... 453B(b)
- inventory value 1013
- involuntary conversion, property acquired through .... 1033(b)
- leased property
  - lessee, improvements by 1019
- limitation on
  - assumption of liability .... 362(d)
- related persons, property imported from 1059A
- liquidation distributions 334
- subsidiary .... 334(b)
- March 1, 1913, property acquired before . 1053
- 1932 Act establishing .... 1052(a)
- 1934 Act establishing .... 1052(b)
- 1939 Code establishing .... 1052(c)
- nontaxable distributions 307
- paid-in surplus, property acquired as .. 362
- partners and partnerships
  - allocation rules 755
  - contributed property 723
  - distributee partner's interest 733
  - distributions of property other than money 732
  - interest of partner 705; 722
  - optional 743; 754
  - transfer of partnership interest 742
  - undistributed partnership property, adjustment to basis 734
- property acquired by issuance of stock or as paid-in surplus .... 362(a)
- property acquired from decedent 1014
- appreciated property within one year of death .... 1014(e)
- estate and income tax purposes, consistency of treatment ...... 1014(f)
- reporting requirement 6035
- property distributions .... 301(d)
- property received in liquidations 334
- recomputed, Section 1245 property .. 1245(a)(2)
- reduction of basis
  - discharge of indebtedness 1017
  - nontaxed portion of extraordinary dividends 1059
- reorganizations
  - basis to corporations 362
  - basis to distributees 358

Topical Index
References are to Code Section numbers.

Basis—continued
- Section 1245 property, adjustment to basis . . . . 1245(c)
- stock and stock rights 307
- substituted basis . . . . 1016(b)
- transfers in trust 1015
- wash sales . . . . 1091(d)

Bauxite, percentage depletion . . . . 613(b)

Beer, tax on . . . . 5051—5056
- foreign producers
  - information returns 6038E
- imported in bulk 5418
- reduced rate disallowed
  - smuggled or illegally produced beer . . . 5067
- removals for use of foreign embassies, etc. . . . . 5053(g)
- violation of provisions relating to, penalty, seizure, and forfeiture . . 5671—5675

Below-market loan defined . . . . 7872(e)(1)

Benefit overpayments
- rules applicable to . . . . 414(aa)

Beneficiaries of estates and trusts
- complex trusts 662
- defined . . . . 643(c)
- depreciation . . . . 167(d)
- income, trusts distributing current income only 652
- information statement from fiduciary . . 6034A
- nonresident aliens 875
- real estate investment trusts 857
- retirement plan 402
- returns . . . . 6034A(c)
- simple trusts 652

Benevolent life insurance associations, exemption . . . . 501(c)(12)

Bentonite, percentage depletion . . . . . 613(b)

Bequests
- basis for gain or loss . . . . 1014(b)
- charitable 2055
- exempt income 102
- surviving spouse recipient, estate tax . . 2056

Beryllium, percentage depletion . . . . . 613(b)

Bicycle commuters
- transportation fringe benefits . . . . 132(f)(1)(D)

Biodiesel fuels
- income tax credit 40A
- excise tax credit 6426

Biomass, defined . . . . 45K(c)(3)

Bismuth, percentage depletion . . . . . . 613(b)

Black lung benefit trusts
- allowance of deduction . . . . 192(a)
- contributions 192
- excess contributions, special taxes . . . 4953
- exempt status . . . . 501(c)(21)
- fund for 9501
- management 9602
- self-dealing, special taxes 4951
- taxable expenditures, taxes imposed . . 4952
- transfer to fund 9601

Blind persons
- standard deduction . . . . 63(f)

Blocked foreign income, controlled foreign corporation . . . . 964(b)

Board and lodging . . . . 119; 162(a)

Board of Tax Appeals—see Tax Court

Boards of trade, exemption . . . . 501(c)(6)

Boats
- donations
  - fraudulent acknowledgments 6720
- excise taxes
  - alternative fuels . . . . 4041(a)(2)

Bona fide resident of a foreign country defined . . . . 911(d)(5)

Bond discount 6049

Bond for payment of tax
- extensions of time granted 6165
- false and fraudulent, criminal penalties . 7206(3)
- posting by taxpayer . . . . 7101—7103
- stay of collection of assessment 6863

Bonds
- amortizable bond premium 171
- arbitrage bonds 148

Bonds—continued
- convertible, repurchased by issuer 249
- defined . . . . 150; 171(d)
- enterprise zone facility bonds
  - modifications . . . . 1394(b)(2)
- government bonds
  - arbitrage rebate exception . . . . 148(f)(4)(D)
- hedge bonds . . . . 149(g)
- high-yield nonpurpose investments
  - repeal of debt service-based limitation . . . . 148(c)(2)(B)
- in lieu of personal property . . . . 2032A(e)(11)
- losses
  - nonregistered form . . . . 165(j)
- market discount—see Market discount bonds
- mortgage subsidy financing
  - disaster areas . . . . 143(k)(11)
- municipal bond defined . . . . 75(b)
- nonregistered
  - issuer, excise tax 4701
- premiums
  - amortizable 171
  - dealers in tax-exempt securities 75
- qualified 501(c) bonds
  - termination of limitation . . . . 145(b)(5)
- registered form requirement . . . . 163(f)
- unregistered, capital gains treatment denied 1287
- registration 149
- repeal of expired provisions . . . 148(c)(2)(B)
- retirement of
  - exempt income 108
- Section 501(c)(3) . . . . 145(b)(5)
- state and local bonds
  - rebate from earnings under construction bond rules . . 148(f)(4)(C)(xvi)
  - repeal of $100,000 limitation on unspent proceeds . . . . 148(f)(4)(B)(ii)
- stripped 1286
- tax credit bonds
  - mutual funds, election to pass through to shareholders 853A
- tribal economic development bonds . . 7871(f)

Bonus depreciation . . . . 168(k)
- qualified reuse and recycling property . 168(m)

Books and records
- controlled foreign corporations . . . . . 964(c)
- Domestic International Sales Corporations . . . . 6011(d)
- examination of 7602; 7605
- failure to keep
  - accounting period . . . . 441(g)
- failure to produce 7269
- summons 7210
- falsified, criminal penalties . . . . . . 7206(5)(B)
- firearms manufacturers, importers, and dealers 5843
- foreign corporations engaged in U.S. business 6038C
- liquor taxes 5555
  - bonded wine cellar proprietor 5367
  - breweries 5415
  - distilleries 5207
  - retail dealers 5122
  - wholesale dealers 5121
- notice requiring 6001
- petroleum products manufacturers . . . 4102
- regulations requiring 6001
- summons 7602
- tobacco materials manufacturers and dealers 5741
- wagering transactions 4403

Boot received in nontaxable exchange . . 356

Bows and arrows, excise tax . . . . 4161(b)

Branch profits tax
- foreign corporations 884

Breweries . . . . 5401—5418
- establishment . . . . 5401—5403
- operation of . . . . 5411—5418

Bribes . . . . 162(c)
- foreign government officials, to . . . 162(c)(1)

Brokers
- information returns 6045
- basis reporting . . . . 6045(g)
- broker-to-broker transactions 6045A

Brokers—continued
- information returns—continued
  - exception for certain sales or exchanges . . . . 6045(e)(5)
  - options . . . . 6045(h)
- notice to payors
  - failure to furnish, penalty 6705

Brother as dependent . . . . 152(f)(4)

Building and loan associations—see Mutual savings institutions

Building improvement costs . . . . 263(a)

Burden of proof
- accumulated earnings tax 534
- assumption of liability in connection with certain exchanges . . . . 357(b)(2)
- court proceedings 7491
- foundation managers . . . . 7454(b)
- fraud
  - proceedings before Tax Court . . . . 7454(a)
- issues . . . . 7422(e)
- tax return preparers, proceedings involving 7427
- transferee 7454

Buses
- excise tax . . . . 6421(b)
- nontaxable uses . . . . 6427(b)
- highway motor vehicle use tax . . . 4481—4484

Business energy credit . . . . 48(a)

Business expenses . . . . 162—176
- accelerated cost recovery system 168
- amortizable bond premium 171
- bad debts 166
- charitable contributions 170
- circulation expenditures 173
- compensation exceeding $1 million . . 162(m)
- compensation paid . . . . 162(a)
- conservation expenditures, soil and water 175
- creation or organization of 195
- depreciation 167
- election to expense certain depreciable assets 179
- installment method of accounting . . . 453(i)
- employee achievement awards . . . . . 274(j)
- employer liability trust, contributions to . 194A
- entertainment—see Entertainment expenses
- environmental remediation costs 198
- experimental expenditures 174
- Federal National Mortgage Association stock purchases . . . . 162(d)
- fertilizer costs of farmers 180
- fines and penalties
  - prohibition of deduction, modification . 6050X
- foreign advertising broadcast to U.S. . 162(j)
- gifts—see Gifts
- health care costs of self-employed individuals . . . . 162(l)
- illegal payments, foreign government officials . . . . 952(a)
- illegal transactions 280E
- interest paid 163
- lobbying . . . . 162(e)
- losses 165
- members of reserve component of Armed Forces or Foreign Service . . 162(p)
- net operation loss deduction 172
- related taxpayers, transactions between . 267
- rent paid . . . . 162(a)
- research expenditures 174
- rural mail carriers . . . . 162(o)
- soil conservation expenditures 175
- state legislators' travel expenses away from home . . . . 162(h)
- stock redemption or reacquisition expenses . . . . 162(k)
- substantiation . . . . 274(d)
- taxes paid 164
- traveling—see Traveling expenses
- unpaid within 2½ months after close of taxable year, disallowance . . . . 267(a)(2)
- water conservation expenditures 175

Business gifts, deduction of cost . . . . 274(b)

Business income of tax-exempts . . 511—515

Business leagues, exemption . . . . . 501(c)(6)

Topical Index
References are to Code Section numbers.

Business leases, unrelated income 514
Business needs, corporation 537
Business outside U.S., foreign
  corporations 881
Business use of home
. deductibility of expenses in connection
  with 280A

C

Cadmium, percentage depletion . . . . . 613(b)
Cafeteria plans 125
. defined . . . . 125(d)
. health flexible spending arrangements
. . contributions limited . . . . 125(i)
. . unused benefits, individuals called to
    active duty . . . . 125(h)
. highly compensated participants and
    key employees . . . . 125(b)
. qualified benefits defined . . . . 125(f)
. simple cafeteria plans
. . small employers . . . . 125(j)
Calcium carbonates, percentage
  depletion . . . . 613(b)
Calendar quarter, defined, gift tax . . . . 2502(b)
Calendar year
. change of accounting period to or from . . 442
. defined . . . . 441(d)
Campaign fund contributions . . . . . 6096; 9001—
  9012
. Presidential primary matching payment
    account . . . . 9031—9042
Cancellation of debt—see Discharge of
  indebtedness
Cancellation of lease or distributor's
  agreement, capital gain 1241
Canvass of districts for taxable persons
  and objects 7601
Capital assets
. defined 1221
. holding period 1223
Capital contributions, exclusion from
  gross income 118
Capital expenditures 263
. commodity futures transactions
. . carrying charges, deduction of . . . . . 263(g)
. insurance companies, policy acquisition
    costs of 848
. inventory, costs 263A
Capital gains and losses . . . . 1202—1298
. allowance of deduction for losses . . . 165(f)
. anti-conversion rules 1258
. cancellation of debt 1234A
. cancellation of lease, payment for . . . 1241
. capital asset defined 1221
. capital gain net income defined . . . . 1222(9)
. capital gains rate, maximum . . . . 1(h)
. carryback and carryover of capital loss . . 1212
. . acquiring corporation . . . . 381(c)(3)
. . regulated investment companies . 1212(a)(3)
. casualty losses . . . . 1231(a)
. coal disposal . . . . 631(c)
. constructive ownership transactions . . 1260
. croplands or wetlands, disposition of . . 1257
. dealers in securities 1236
. determination of . . . . 1221—1223
. dividend income . . . . 1(h)(11)
. employees' annuities 403
. foreign service gains
. . limitation computation . . . . 904(b)(3)(C)
. franchises 1253
. holding period 1223
. homeowners' associations, tax on 528
. individuals
. . holding periods for long-term capital
     assets . . . . 1(h)
. . long-term capital gains rates . . . . . . 1(h);
    55(b)(1)(A); 55(b)(3); 57(a)(7)
. involuntary conversions . . . . 1231(a)
. lease cancellation payment 1241
. life insurance companies . . . . 818(b)
. limitation on capital losses 1211
. long-term capital gains
. . defined . . . . 1222(3)
. . revised holding periods and tax rates . . 1(h)

Capital gains and losses—continued
. long-term capital loss defined . . . . . 1222(4)
. net capital gain defined . . . . 1222(11)
. net capital loss defined . . . . 1222(10)
. net capital loss, limitation
. . corporate acquisitions . . . . 383(b)
. net long-term capital gain defined . . . 1222(7)
. net long-term capital loss defined . . . 1222(8)
. net short-term capital gain defined . . . 1222(5)
. net short-term capital loss defined . . . 1222(6)
. oil or gas property, disposition of interest
  in 1254
. options 1234
. partnerships
. . carried interest, holding period
    extended 1061
. patents 1235
. principal residence, gain from sale of . . 121
. property used in trade or business . . . 1231
. real estate subdivided for sale 1237
. reduction in rates for individuals . . . . 1(h)(1)
. regulated investment companies . . . . 852(b)
. . capital loss carryover . . . . 1212(a)(3)
. related taxpayers, transactions between . 1239
. securities dealers 1236
. short sales . . . . 1233; 1233(h)
. short-term capital gain defined . . . . . 1222(1)
. short-term capital loss defined . . . . . 1222(2)
. small business stock
. . rollover of gain 1045
. subdivided lots 1237
. timber 631
. trade or business property sold or
  exchanged 1231
. trademarks and trade names 1253
. unregistered obligations, sale or
  disposition 1287
Carbon oxide sequestration credit 45Q
Caribbean basin
. conventions, deductibility of expenses
  . . . . 274(h)(6)
Carrier
. defined . . . . 3231(g)
Carrybacks and carryovers
. capital loss 1212
. . adjustments required by change in
    method of accounting . . . . 481(b)(3)(A)
. . assessment and collection, limitations
  . . . . 6501(h)
. . refunds and credits, limitations . . . 6511(d)(2)
. charitable contributions of individuals . . 170(d)
. contributions
. . charitable . . . . 170(b)
. . retirement plans . . . . 404(d)
. corporate acquisitions 381; 382
. dividend carryover, personal holding
  companies . . . . 564(b)
. expected carrybacks, extension of time
    for payment of tax 6164
. foreign tax credits unused . . . . 904(c)
. . deficiency resulting, assessment . . . 6501(i)
. limitation on carryovers 382
. net operating loss—see Net operating loss
  carrybacks and carryovers
. unused tax credits 39
Carrying charges, deductibility
. commodity futures transactions . . . . . 263(g)
. election to charge to capital account
  exercised 266
. installment sales . . . . 163(b)
Carved-out production payments . . . . . 636(a)
Cash method of accounting . . . . 446(c)
. limitation on use of 448
Cash receipts of more than $10,000,
  information returns 6050I
. reporting requirements for criminal court
    clerks . . . . 6050I(g)
Cash received in trade or business
. information returns 6050I
Casual laborers, exemption from
  withholding . . . . 3401(a)(4)
Casual sales of personal property,
  installment method of accounting . . . 453(b)
Casualty losses . . . . 165(c)(3)
. estate tax deduction 2054

Casualty losses—continued
. nonbusiness losses . . . . 165(h)
. personal property, netting . . . . 1231(a)
. reimbursement for increased living
  expenses 123
Cellulosic biofuel producer credit—see Second
  generation biofuel producer credit
Cemetery companies, exemption . . 501(c)(13)
Cent, fractional part disregarded 6313
Certified mail, use of . . . . 7502(c)
Chambers of commerce, exemption . . 501(c)(6)
Charitable contributions 170
. accrual-basis corporations . . . . 170(a)(2)
. appraisals . . . . 170(f)(11)(E)
. appreciated property . . . . 170(b)(1)(C); 170(e)
. . allocation of basis . . . . 170(e)(2)
. . stock in S corporation . . . . 170(e)
. bargain sales to charitable organizations
  . . . . 1011(b)
. . capital gains property . . . 170(b)(1)(C); 170(e)
. . ordinary income property . . . . 170(e)
. carryover of excess contributions . . . . 170(d)
. . acquiring corporation . . . . 381(c)(19)
. clothing and household items . . . . . 170(f)(16)
. conservation contribution . 170(b)(1)(E); 170(h)
. corporations
. . deduction limit . . . . 170(b)(2)
. . research use property . . . . 170(e)(4)
. deduction for nonitemizers . . . . 170(p)
. deductions denied . . . . 170(f)
. dispositions of donated property,
  information returns 6050L
. donor advised funds
. . nondeductible donations . . . . 170(f)(18);
    2055(e)(5); 2522(c)(5)
. . research use property . . . . 170(e)(4)
. estate and gift tax deductions . . . .
  . . . . 2055(e); 2522(c)
. . nonresident aliens . . . . 2106(a)(2)
. estates . . . . 642(c)
. federal employees, on behalf of . . . . . 7701(k)
. gift tax deduction in computing 2522
. gifts of partial interests . . . . 170(f)(3)
. lobbying activities, nondeductible . . . 170(f)(9)
. maximum deduction for individuals . . . 170(b)
. medical research gifts . . . . 170(b)(1)(A)(iii)
. nonitemizers, deduction . . . . 170(p)
. nonresident aliens . . . . 873(b)(2)
. percentage limit increased . . . . . 170(b)(1)(G)
. pool arrangements . . . . . 170(f)(2); 642(c)(3);
    642(c)(5)
. private organizations as donees . . . . 170(f)(1)
. property placed in trust . . . . 170(f)(2)
. quid pro quo contributions 6115; 6714
. recapture
. . nonexempt purpose . . . . 170(e)(7)
. remainder interests in trusts . . . . . . 170(f)(2)
. section 1245 property . . . . 170(e)
. standard mileage rate . . . . 170(i)
. students maintained in the home . . . . 170(g)
. travel expenses . . . . 170(j)
. trusts . . . . 642(c); 681
. $250 or more, substantiation . . . . . . 170(f)(8)
Charitable hospitals
. exempt status
. . requirements . . . . 501(r)
. . tax on failure to meet requirements . . 4959
. information returns . . . . 6033(b)(15)
Charitable organizations—see also Exempt
  organizations
. exemption . . . . 501(c)(3)
. lobbying expenditures, tax on excess . . . 4911
Charitable remainder trusts 664
. qualified gratuitous transfers . . . . 664(g)
Charitable risk pools . . . . 501(n)
Charitable split-interest trusts
. reformation
. . estate and gift taxes . . . 2055(e)(3); 2522(c)(4)
Check-off system, political campaign
  contributions . . . . 6096; 9001—9012
Checks
. payment of tax by 6311
. . bad checks, penalties 6657

Topical Index
References are to Code Section numbers.

Chemicals
. tax on manufacturer, importer or producer .... 4661(b)

Child and dependent care credit 21
. possessions of the United States ... 21(h)
. special rules for 2021 .... 21(g)

Child care facilities
. nonprofit, exemption from tax ...... 501(k)

Child support enforcement, disclosures of information .... 6103(l)(6)

Child tax credit 24
. advance payment .... 24(j); 7527A
. allowance of credit .... 24(a)
. fraudulent claims prevention ...... 24(g)
. identification requirements .... 24(e)
. possessions of the United States ... 24(k)
. qualifying child defined .... 24(c)
. refundable portion .... 24(d)
. special rules for 2021 .... 24(i)

Children
. adoption expenses 23
. . child with special needs, definition of .... 23(d)(3)
. . alternative minimum tax .... 59(j)
. birth or adoption
. . distributions from retirement plans .... 72(t)(2)(H)
. . child tax credit 24
. . earnings of, inclusion in gross income 73
. missing or exploited child investigation
. . disclosure of return information .... 6103(i)(1)(C)
. payments for support of v. alimony ... 71(c)
. qualifying child defined .... 24(c)
. unearned income of .... 1(g)
. . alternative minimum tax .... 59(j)

China clay, percentage depletion .... 613(b)

Christian Science practitioners, self-employment tax .... 1402(e)

Christmas trees, inclusion in term timber .... 631(a)

Chromite, percentage depletion ...... 613(b)

Church employees
. social security coverage .... 1402(a)(14)

Church plans
. self-employed ministers
. . exclusions .... 414(e)(5)(A)

Churches, restriction on examination of .... 7605(c)

Churches, restrictions on inquiries and examinations of 7611

Cigars and cigarette taxes ...... 5701—5763

Circulation expenditures 173

Circumstances of adjustment 1312

Citizens
. definition .... 3121(e)
. departure from U.S., termination assessment of income tax ...... 6851(c)
. estate tax .... 2001—2056
. expatriation to avoid tax 877
. foreign income 911
. foreign tax credit .... 901—908
. individuals losing citizenship, information returns 6039G
. nonresident alien married to, community income of 879

Civic leagues
. exemption .... 501(c)(4)
. private inurement prohibition .... 501(c)(4)(B)

Civil actions by U.S. .... 7401—7410

Civil service employees, Federal Insurance Contributions Act taxes ... 3122

Civil suit, District Court 7402

Claim-of-right
. refund procedure .... 1341; 6411(d)

Claims
. abatement .... 6404(b)
. deficiency dividends deduction ... 547(e)
. refund—see Refunds and credits: claim for refund
. unpaid, bankruptcy and receivership ... 6873

Court of Federal Claims, United States . 6110(j); 7422(e); 7428

Classes, accelerated cost recovery system .... 168(e)

Clay, percentage depletion .... 613(b)

Clean electricity
. investment credit 48E
. production credit 45Y

Clean fuel production credit 45Z

Clean hydrogen production credit 45V

Clergy
. parsonage rental value furnished, exclusion from gross income 107
. self-employed
. . church contributions to retirement accounts .... 404(a)(10)
. . church plans .... 414(e)(5)
. . social security coverage .... 1402(e)

Clifford rule .... 671—679

Closely held business, estate interest in
. extension of time for estate tax payment .. 6166

Closing agreements 7121
. penalties for false statements .... 7206(5)

Closing of taxable year
. partners and partnerships .... 706(c)

Club dues
. denial of deduction .... 274(a)(3)

Clubs, social, exemption .... 501(c)(7)

Coal
. disposal of, deductibility of expenses ... 272
. excise tax 4121
. expenses of mining 272
. percentage depletion for mines ... 613(b)
. qualifying advanced coal project credit ... 48A
. . recapture of credit .... 48A(i)
. royalties .... 631(c)

Coal industry health benefits .... 9701—9722
. enforcement provisions 9721
. individual employer plans 9711
. 1992 UMWA Benefit Plan 9712
. sham transactions 9722
. United Mine Workers of America Combined Benefit Fund ..... 9702—9708

Coast Guard personnel—see Armed Forces of the U.S.

Cobalt, percentage depletion .... 613(b)

COBRA continuation coverage
. PBGC recipients
. . extension .... 4980B(f)(2)(B)(i)(V)
. premium assistance 6432
. . cessation of eligibility, penalty for failure to notify 6720C
. . coordination with health coverage tax credit .... 35(g)(9)
. . exclusion from gross income 139I
. TAA-eligible individuals
. . extension .... 4980B(f)(2)(B)(i)(VI)

Collectibles, investment in by individual retirement accounts .... 408(n)

Collection—see also Withholding of tax at source; Withholding of income tax on wages ... 6301—6344
. airline tickets .... 6302(e)
. appeals dispute resolution 7123
. authority 6301
. bond to stay pending review of Tax Court decision 7485
. communication services .... 6302(e)
. delinquent tax debts
. . passport restrictions 7345
. deposit of collections 7809
. depositaries for, designation of .. 7808
. distilled spirits 5007
. electronic fund transfer system ... 6302(h)
. employment taxes 3501
. excise taxes 4291
. failure to make, penalties 7202
. fair collection practices 6304
. levy
. . right to hearing prior to levy ... 6330
. limitations period .... 6501—6504
. liquor taxes 5061

Collection—continued
. method of 6302
. notice and demand 6303
. ozone depleting chemicals ...... 6302(f)
. possessions of the United States .. 7651
. private debt collectors 6306
. . civil damages for unauthorized collection actions 7433A
. . special compliance personnel program funding 6307
. regulations establishing mode or time of collection 6302
. seizure of property for ..... 6330—6344
. special compliance personnel program .. 6307
. stay of collection of jeopardy assessments 6863
. suits by taxpayers to restrain 7421
. suspension of running of period of limitations 6503
. unauthorized actions by IRS personnel, damages 7433
. withholding on wages 3402

Collection of foreign items, licensing ... 7001
. failure to obtain license, penalties .. 7231

Collective bargaining agreement determination .... 7701(a)(46)

Collectively bargained retirement plans ... 413
. multiple employer plans
. . pooled plan providers .... 413(c)

College club domestic employees, exemption from withholding ... 3401(a)(3)

Columbium, percentage depletion ... 613(b)

Combat zone compensation
. exclusion from gross income ... 112; 3401(a)(1)
. inclusion in gross income
. . contributions to individual retirement accounts .... 219(f)(7)

Combat zone service, time for performing acts postponed by 7508

Commissioner of Internal Revenue
. duties and powers .... 7803(a)
. Office of Taxpayer Advocate ..... 7803(c)

Commodities dealers
. anti-conversion rules .... 1258(d)(5)
. mark-to-market accounting method ... 475(e); 475(f)
. self-employment tax .... 1402(i)

Commodity Credit Corporation
. loans
. . inclusion in income 77
. . information reporting 6039J
. . property pledged to .... 1016(a)(8)

Commodity futures transactions ... 1233
. carrying charges, deduction of .. 263(g)
. hedging transactions .... 1233(g)
. regulated futures contracts marked to market
. . definition .... 1256(b)
. . hedging transactions, inapplication of rules .... 1256(e)
. . mixed straddles, elections ..... 1256(d)
. . special rules .... 1256(f)
. . tax treatment, general rule .... 1256(a)
. . terminations .... 1256(c)
. straddles, recognition of gain or loss ... 1092

Common carriers
. communication tax exemption ..... 4253(f)

Common trust funds 584
. regulated investment companies, status as .... 851(a)(2)
. returns 6032
. transfers to regulated investment companies .... 584(h)

Communications satellite system, foreign corporation operating ... 883(b)

Communications tax .... 4251—4254
. deposit of tax .... 6302(e)

Community chests, funds and foundations, exemption .... 501(c)(3)

Community income
. nonresident aliens 879

Topical Index
References are to Code Section numbers.

Community income—continued
. U.S. resident or citizen married to
  nonresident alien 879
Community newspaper plans
. minimum funding rules . . . . 430(m)
Community property
. basis after death of spouse . . . . . . 1014(b)(6)
. individual retirement accounts . . . . 408(g)
. self-employment income . . . . 1402(a)(5)
. small business corporation stock . . . 1371(c)
. special use valuation, estate tax relief . . . . . .
  . . . . 2032A(e)(10)
. spouses living apart . . . . 66(a)
Compensation from services
. gross income . . . . 61(a)(1)
Compensation paid . . . . 162(a)
. deduction, employment credits affecting . . . . .
  . . . . 280C(a)
. deferred compensation plans . . . . 401—421
. information returns . . . . 6041(a)
. social security coverage for employees
  of foreign subsidiary 176
Compensation received
. children 73
. deferred compensation plans . . . . 401—421
. foreign government employees, exempt
  income 893
. injuries, amounts received for . . . . 104—106
. international organization employees,
  exemption 893
. levy, exemption from . . . . 6334(d)
. sick pay . . . . 104—106
Complex trusts . . . . 661—663
Compromise of taxes 7122
. penalties for false statements . . . . . 7206(5)
Computation of tax
. changes in rates during year 15
. rounding-off to dollar amounts 6102
Computation of taxable income . . . . 61—291
. employment taxes 3502
Computer software, depreciation . . . 167(f)
Condemnation of property, gain or loss . 1033; 1231(a)
Confidentiality
. privileged communication
. . extension to authorized practitioners . . 7525
. treaties and tax convention information . 6105
**Conflict-of-interest requirements, sale
  of property to comply with** 1043
Congress
. disclosure of returns to committees . . . 6103(f)
. members of
. . charitable contributions on behalf of . 7701(k)
. . expenses of 162
Congressional Budget Office
. disclosure of return information to
  officers and employees . . . . 6103(j)(6)
**Consent dividends, dividends paid
  deduction** 565
Consent stock defined . . . . 565(f)
**Consent to use or disclosure of
  information by persons preparing returns** . .
  7216
**Conservation, charitable contribution of
  real property for** . . . . 170(h)
Conservation expenditures 175
. recapture . . . . 1252(a)
**Conservation subsidies provided by
  public utilities** 136
Consolidated returns . . . . 1501—1563
Consolidation of corporations—see
  Reorganizations
Constructive ownership of stock
. corporate distributions and adjustments . 318
. losses nondeductible . . . . 267(c)
. personal holding company status
  determination . . . . 544(a)
**Constructive ownership transactions,
  gains** 1260
**Constructive payment, withheld taxes
  considered as paid** 3123

Constructive sale price defined . . . . 4216(b)
**Consumer cooperatives, information
  returns** . . . . 6044(c)
**Consumer Operated and Oriented Plan (CO-OP)
  program**
. grants and loans
. . exempt status for health insurance
    issuer recipients . . . . 501(c)(29)
**Contested liability, accrual-basis
  taxpayer's deduction or credit** . . . . 461(f)
**Contingency operation service, time for
  performing acts postponed by** 7508
Continental shelf areas 638
Continuity-of-care requirements
. group health plans 9818
Contributions
. accident and health plans, employer's
  contributions 106
. capital—see Contributions to capital
. charitable—see Charitable contributions
. nondeductibility, statement of 6113
. . failure to provide, penalty 6710
. political parties, bad debts . . . . . . 271(b)(2)
. retirement plan 404
. . catchup contributions . . . . 414(v)
. . elective deferrals as Roth
    contributions 402A
. . minimum vesting standards . . . . . . 411(a)
. . unfunded deferred benefits . . . . . . 404(b)
. . welfare benefit plans 419
. state unemployment funds, credits
  against federal unemployment tax . . 3306(g)
Contributions to capital
. exclusion from gross income 118
. partnerships . . . . 721—724
. . liabilities increased, treatment as
    contribution of money . . . . 752(a)
. water and sewerage disposal utilities . . 118(c)
**Contributions to political candidates and
  organizations**
. appreciated property 84
. check-off system . . . . . . 6096; 9001—9012
. indirect contributions 276
Control defined, reorganizations . . . 368(c)
Controlled corporations
. accumulated earnings credit limit . . . 1561
. acquisition to evade or avoid tax . . . 269
. allocation of income and deductions
  among 482
. brother-sister controlled groups . . . 1563(a)(2); 1563(c)(2)(B)
. component members . . . . 1563(b)
. definition of controlled group . . . . .
  . . . . 851(c)(3); 1563(a)
. distribution
. . additional consideration received . . 356(b)
. . special rules . . . . 355(e)(4)
. . stock or obligations 355
. . voting rights . . . . 2036(b)
Controlled foreign corporations (CFCs) . 951—965
. accounts of United States shareholders . . .
  . . . . 964(c)
. blocked foreign income . . . . 964(b)
. definition . . . . 957(a)
. dividends received deduction 965
. earnings and profits . . . . 964(a)
. earnings invested in United States
  property 956
. earnings previously taxed, exclusion
  from gross income 959
. export trade corporation status . . . . 971(a)(3)
. foreign tax credit for domestic
  corporation shareholder 960
. individual shareholders, election to be
  taxed at corporate rates 962
. insurance income . . . . 953; 957(b)
. records of United States shareholders . 964(c)
. related person factoring income . . . . 864(d)
. stock ownership rules 958
. Subpart F income . . . . 952(a)
. taxable year 898
. United States person defined . . . . . 957(c)

Controlled foreign corporations (CFCs)—continued
. U.S. shareholders
. . global intangible low-tax income . . 951A
. . inclusions in gross income . . . . . 951(a)
**Controls defined, regulated investment
  companies** . . . . 851(c)(2)
**Convenience of employer, exclusion of
  value of meals or lodging furnished for** . 119
Conventions
. cruise ships, costs incurred
. . deductibility of . . . . 274(h)(2)
. . reporting requirements . . . . 274(h)(5)
. foreign, expenses incurred . . . . . . 274(h)(1)
. . Caribbean basin countries . . . . . . 274(h)(6)
. unrelated trade or business . . . . . . 513(d)
Conversion transactions 1258
. commodities dealers . . . . 1258(d)(5)
. defined . . . . 1258(c)
. options dealers . . . . 1258(d)(5)
. straddles . . . . 1258(d)(1)
**Convertible securities, personal holding
  companies** . . . . 544(b)
**Cooperative and small employer charity (CSEC)
  plans**
. defined . . . . 414(y)
. election out of CSEC status . . . . . . 414(y)(3)
. minimum funding rules 433
Cooperative banks—see Mutual savings
  institutions
**Cooperative hospital service
  organizations** . . . . 501(e)
Cooperative housing corporations
. stock held by governmental units . . . 216(b)(4)
. stock held in, treatment as residential
  property of tenant-stockholder
. . sales proceeds of 65-year-olds . . . 121(d)
**Cooperative service organizations of
  educational organizations** . . . . . . 501(f)
**Cooperative telephone companies,
  exemption** . . . . 501(c)(12)
Cooperatives
. collective investment cooperatives of
  educational organizations, exempt status . .
  . . . . 501(f)
. distributions, nonpatronage, deduction
  for . . . . 1382(c)
. gross income . . . . 1382(a)
. information returns 6044
. nonqualified written notices of allocation
  redeemed, computation of tax 1383
. patronage dividends—see Patronage dividends
. returns, due dates . . . . 6072(d)
**Copyrighted artworks, estate and gift
  tax** . . . . 2055(e)(4); 2522(c)(3)
Copyrights
. royalties, personal holding company
  income . . . . 543(a)(4)
. sales to foreign corporations, nature of
  gain 1249
Corporate acquisition indebtedness
. affiliated group . . . . 279(g)
. defined . . . . 279(b)
. foreign corporations . . . . 279(f)
. interest paid or incurred, deductibility of . 279
Corporate acquisitions
. credits, excess, limitations on 383
Corporate alternative minimum tax
. foreign tax credit . . . . 59(l)
Corporate stock, repurchase of 4501
. covered corporation . . . . 4501(b)
. exceptions . . . . 4501(e)
. foreign corporations, acquisition of stock
  of . . . . 4501(d)
. general rule . . . . 4501(a)
. regulations and guidance . . . . 4501(f)
. repurchase, defined . . . . 4501(c)
Corporations
. accumulated earnings tax . . . . 531—537
. . accumulated taxable income 535
. . burden of proof 534

Topical Index
References are to Code Section numbers.

Corporations—continued
- accumulated earnings tax—continued
  - evidence of purpose to avoid income tax ... 533
  - income not placed on annual basis ... 536
  - liability for tax ... 532
  - rate of tax ... 531
  - reasonable needs of the business, accumulations of surplus to meet ... 537
- affiliated—see Affiliated corporations
- avoidance of tax on stockholders ... 531—565
- business deductions ... 162
- capital gains and losses—see Capital gains and losses
- capital restructuring, information returns ... 6043(c)
- charitable contributions ... 170(a)
  - deduction limit ... 170(b)(2)
  - food inventory ... 170(e)(3)(C)
  - research use property ... 170(e)(4)
- compensation exceeding $1 million ... 162(m)
- controlled groups, accumulated earnings tax ... 1561
- debt-financed acquisitions—see Debt-financed acquisitions
- deductions ... 161—199A
  - disallowance of certain ... 163(l)
- definition ... 7701(a)(3)
- dissolution
  - information returns ... 6043
- distributions—see Distributions by corporations and Dividends
- estimated tax—see Estimated tax, corporations
- export trade corporations ... 970—971
- fiscal-year basis, proration of tax ... 15
- foreign ownership, information returns ... 6038A
- foreign tax credit ... 901(b)(1)
- golden parachute payments ... 280G
  - excise tax imposed ... 4999
- interests in, treatment as stock or indebtedness ... 385
- minimum tax for tax preferences ... 55—59
  - reduction in ... 291
- multiple—see Controlled corporations
- net capital losses, carryback ... 1212(a)
- normal tax ... 11(b)
- organization of
  - expenditures incurred ... 248
  - transfer to corporation controlled by transferor ... 351
- partnership and trust interests, transfers of ... 386
- personal service corporations ... 269A
- publicly traded partnerships treated as ... 7704
- rate of tax on ... 11(b)
  - change during year ... 15
  - exceptions ... 11(c)
- reasonable accumulations ... 537
- recapitalization, information returns ... 6043(c)
- related, stock redemption through use of ... 304
- reorganization of—see Reorganizations
- returns
  - consolidated returns ... 1501—1505
  - extensions of time ... 6081(b)
  - foreign shareholders ... 6039C(a)
  - information ... 6041—6046
  - place for filing ... 6091(b)(2)
  - requirement of ... 6012(a)(2)
  - signatures ... 6062
  - time for filing ... 6072(a)
- S corporations—see S corporations
- small business—see Small business corporations
- successor, carryovers ... 381
- sugar cane farming
  - accounting methods ... 447(e)
- tax shelters, substantial understatement penalty ... 6662(d)(2)(C)

Correction of errors ... 1311
Corundum, percentage depletion ... 613(b)
Cosmetic surgery, medical expenses ... 213(d)(9)
Cost, basis of property ... 1012
Cost depletion, basis for ... 612
Cost-of-living adjustments
- retirement plans ... 401(a)(17)(B); 415(d)

Cost-of-living allowances, foreign service employees ... 912(2)

Court actions—see Suits by taxpayers and Suits by United States
Courts of Appeal
- delay proceedings ... 6673(b)
- Federal Circuit ... 7482(a)
- frivolous appeal to, damages ... 6673(b)
- jurisdiction ... 7482(a)
- petition for review of Tax Court decision ... 7483

Coverdell education savings accounts ... 530
- excess contributions to ... 4973(e)

Credit unions
- exemption ... 501(c)(14)

Credits, transfer of ... 6418
Credits against tax—see also Refunds and credits
- additional recovery rebate credit ... 6428A
- adoption expenses ... 23
- advanced manufacturing investment credit ... 48D
  - production credit ... 45X
- advanced nuclear power facility production credit ... 45J
- agricultural chemicals security credit ... 45O
- alcohol fuels credit ... 40; 87
  - alcohol credit ... 40(b)(2)
  - alcohol mixture credit ... 40(b)(1)
  - second generation biofuel producer credit ... 40(b)(6)
  - small ethanol producer credit ... 40(b)(4)
- alternative fuel vehicle refueling property credit ... 30C
- alternative fuels credit ... 6426
- alternative motor vehicle credit ... 30B
- American opportunity credit ... 25A
- biodiesel fuels credit ... 40A; 87
  - biodiesel credit ... 40A(b)(2)
  - biodiesel mixture credit ... 40A(b)(1)
  - small agri-biodiesel producer credit ... 40A(b)(4)
- carbon oxide sequestration credit ... 45Q
- cellulosic biofuel producer credit—see second generation biofuel producer credit
- child care credit ... 21
  - employer-provided ... 45F
- child tax credit ... 24
- clean electricity
  - investment credit ... 48E
  - production credit ... 45Y
- clean fuel production credit ... 45Z
- clean hydrogen production credit ... 45V
- contributions to state unemployment funds ... 3302; 3303
- corporate acquisitions, limitation on ... 383
- dependent care credit ... 21
- disabled individuals, expenditure to provide access to ... 44
- disabled persons, permanently and totally ... 22
- distilled spirits ... 5011
- earned income credit ... 32
  - identification requirements for qualifying child ... 32(c)(3)(D)(i)
  - nonresident aliens, eligibility ... 32(c)(1)(D)
  - overseas military personnel, eligibility ... 32(c)(4)
  - prisoners, eligibility ... 32(c)(2)(B)(iv)
- education credits
  - American opportunity credit ... 25A
  - lifetime learning credit ... 25A
- elderly or disabled persons ... 22
- electricity production, renewable resources ... 45
- employer-provided child care credit ... 45F
- employer social security taxes paid with respect to tip income ... 45B
- employment-related expenses ... 21
- empowerment zone, employment credit ... 1396
- energy investment credit ... 48
- enhanced oil recovery credit ... 43
- estate tax ... 2010; 2012—2016; 2102
- estates and trusts ... 642(a)
- first-time homebuyer credit ... 36
- foreign taxes paid—see Foreign tax credit
- fuel cell motor vehicle credit ... 30B(b)
- fuel production, nonconventional source ... 45K
- gasoline tax, nonhighway use ... 34
- general business credit—see General business credit
- gift tax ... 2505

Credits against tax—continued
- health coverage tax credit ... 35
  - advance payment of credit ... 7527
- health insurance coverage
  - premium assistance refundable credit ... 36B
  - small employers, credit for employee expenses ... 45R
- household and dependent care services expenses ... 21
- Indian employment credit ... 45A
- investment credit—see Investment credit
- lifetime learning credit ... 25A
- limitation based on tax liability ... 26
- low-income housing credit ... 42
- low sulfur diesel fuel production credit ... 45H
- military differential wage payments, employer credit ... 45P
- mine rescue team training credit ... 45N
- minimum tax liability, prior year ... 53
- mortgage interest ... 25
- new energy efficient homes credit ... 45L
- new markets tax credit ... 45D
- nonrefundable credits
  - adoption expenses ... 23
- nonresident aliens ... 874
- oil and gas production
  - marginal wells ... 45I
- orphan drug credit ... 45C
- partners ... 702
- payroll credit
  - paid family leave ... 3132; 3133
  - paid sick leave ... 3131; 3133
- plug-in electric drive motor vehicle credit ... 30D
- premium assistance refundable credit ... 36B
- previously-owned clean vehicles credit ... 25E
- prior year minimum tax liability ... 53
- qualified commercial clean vehicle credit ... 45W
- railroad track maintenance credit ... 45G
- recovery rebate credit, 2020 ... 6428
- recovery rebate credit, 2021 ... 6428B
- refundable credits
  - additional recovery rebate credit ... 6428A
  - American opportunity credit, partially refundable ... 25A(i)
  - child tax credit, partially refundable ... 24(d)
  - earned income credit ... 32
  - employee retention credit ... 3134
  - first-time homebuyer credit ... 36
  - gasoline tax, nonhighway use ... 34
  - health insurance costs of eligible individuals ... 35
  - health insurance premium assistance credit ... 36B
  - overpayment of tax ... 37
  - recovery rebate credit, 2020 ... 6428
  - recovery rebate credit, 2021 ... 6428B
  - tax withheld at source, nonresident aliens and foreign corporations ... 33
  - tax withheld on wages ... 31
- renewable diesel fuels credit ... 40A
- renewable electricity production credit ... 45
- research credit ... 41
- residential clean energy credit ... 25D
- residential energy property credit ... 25C
- retirement plan contributions ... 25B
- second generation biofuel producer credit ... 40(b)(6)
- small employer automatic enrollment credit ... 45T
- small employer pension plan startup costs ... 45E
- social security tax, special refunds ... 31(b)
- targeted jobs tax credit—see Work opportunity credit
- tax credit bonds
  - mutual funds, election to pass through to shareholders ... 853A
- tax withheld on nonresident aliens and foreign partnerships ... 33
- tax withheld on wages ... 31
- unused, carryback and carryforward ... 39
- work opportunity credit ... 51—52
- zero-emission nuclear power production credit ... 45U

Criminal penalties ... 7201—7232
- failure to pay tax ... 7215
- firearms tax violations ... 5871

Topical Index
References are to Code Section numbers.

Criminal penalties—continued
. gasoline and other fuel taxes, failure to register or false statement 7232
. tobacco tax violations 5762
. withheld taxes not deposited in account for the United States 7215

Criminal prosecutions, limitations period 6531

Crop-financing organizations, exemption . . . . 501(c)(16)

Crop insurance proceeds . . . . 451(f)

Cruelty prevention organizations, exemption . . . . 501(c)(3)

Curtesy interest, valuation of gross estate 2034

Custodial accounts
. individual retirement accounts . . . . 408(h)
. regulated investment company stock . . . . 403(b)(7)(A)

Cutting of timber, treatment as sale or exchange . . . . 631(a)

D

Damages
. administrative remedies not exhausted . 7433(d)
. collection actions by IRS personnel, unauthorized 7433
. exemption from tax . . . . 104(a)(2)
. failure to release lien 7432
. fraudulent filing of information returns by third party 7434
. frivolous appeals 6673
. recovery 186
. treble damage payments . . . . 162(g)
. unauthorized disclosure of returns and return information 7217
. unauthorized enticement of information disclosure 7435
. wrongly incarcerated individuals, payments to 139F

Dealers
. commodities and options
. . self-employment tax . . . . 1402(i)
. installment method of accounting
. . dealer dispositions, defined . . . . 453(l)
. . nondealers of real property, special rules 453A
. securities
. . capital gains and losses 1236
. . short sales . . . . 1233(e)(4)
. . tax-exempt securities, adjustment for bond premium 75

Death benefits of employees 101
. life insurance, flexible premium
. . proceeds . . . . 101(f)

Death taxes
. credit against estate tax 2014; 2015
. public safety officers . . . . 101(h)
. redemption of stock to pay 303

Debt-financed acquisitions
. bonds and other evidences of indebtedness . . . . 279(b)
. corporate acquisition indebtedness . . . 279(b)
. corporate interests, treatment as stock or indebtedness 385
. limitation on deduction of bond premium on repurchase 249

Debt-financed income, unrelated 514

Debt-financed property
. acquisition indebtedness . . . . 514(c)
. defined . . . . 514(b)

Debt instruments
. defined . . . . 1275(a)(1)
. issued for property
. . determination of issue price 1274
. . special rules where stated principal amount does not exceed $2,800,000 . . . . 1274A
. retirement, sale, or exchange
. . original issue discount rules 1271
. short-term . . . . 1281—1283
. . acquisition discount, inclusion in current income 1281

Debt instruments—continued
. short-term—continued
. . deferral of interest deduction allocable to 1282

Debtors
. taxable year, bankruptcy . . . . 1398(e)

Decedents
. basis of property acquired from 1014
. . appreciated property within one year of death . . . . 1014(e)
. credits against tax . . . . 691(b)
. . accrual basis . . . . 461(b)
. deductions
. . accrual basis . . . . 461(b)
. . allowance of . . . . 691(b)
. . estate tax paid . . . . 691(c)
. income in respect of 691; 692
. . partner dying, payments to successor in interest 736
. . partner receiving 753
. installment obligations transmitted at death . . . . 453B(c)
. medical expenses paid after death . . . 213(c)

Declaratory judgment suits 7428; 7476

Declaratory judgments
. estates
. . installment payments under Sec. 6166 . 7479
. gifts
. . valuation . . . . 2001(f); 7477
. partnerships
. . oversheltered returns (pre-2018) 6234

Deductions . . . . 151—249
. adjusted gross income computation 62
. allocation among related taxpayers 482
. allowance of 161; 211; 241
. charitable contributions—see Charitable contributions
. depletion . . . . 611—614
. depreciation—see Depreciation
. development expenditures, mines or mineral property 616
. dividends paid—see Dividends paid deduction
. dividends received by corporations . . . . 243—246A
. energy efficient commercial buildings . . 179D
. foreign corporations . . . . 882(c)
. gift tax . . . . 2522—2524
. individuals—see Personal deductions
. interest—see Interest paid
. itemized—see Itemized deductions
. limitation
. . allocable to property used by government 470
. marital deduction, estate tax 2056
. mining . . . . 611—617
. . development expenditures 616
. . exploration expenditures 617
. moving expenses—see Moving expenses: deduction
. natural resources . . . . 611—617
. nondeductible items . . . . 261—280H
. personal exemptions—see Personal exemptions
. self-employment tax, post-1989 . . . . . 164(f)
. refineries
. . election to expense 179C
. . taxes paid 164
. tenant-stockholders of cooperatives
. . payments to corporation . . . . 216(d)
. tertiary injectants 193

Deferred compensation . . . . 401—436
. employment tax . . . . 3121(v)
. foreign plans . . . . 404A(a)
. independent contractors . . . . 404(d)
. information requirements for plans providing . . . . 6058; 6652(e)
. nonqualified deferred compensation plans
. . inclusion in gross income 409A
. state, local and exempt organization plans 457
. unemployment tax . . . . 3306(r)

Deferred payment sales, allocation of payments to interest 483

Deficiencies . . . . 6211—6216

Deficiencies—continued
. annual notice 7524
. assessment against partners . . . . 6511(g)
. assessment of, restrictions . . . . 6213(a)
. waiver . . . . 6213(d)
. defined 6211
. extension of time for payment . . . . . . 6161(b)
. . bond requirement 6165
. found by Tax Court
. . assessment 6215
. . disallowed on review by Courts of Appeals, refunds and credits 7486
. interest on 6601
. . abatement 6404
. notices of 6212
. . partnership level 6221
. petition to Tax Court 6213
. restrictions applicable to 6213
. suspension of filing period for excise taxes . . . . 6213(e)
. Tax Court jurisdiction 6214

Deficiency dividends deduction
. personal holding companies 547
. real estate investment trusts 859

Defined benefit plans
. amendments
. . limitations on underfunded plans . . . 436
. . minimum funding waiver period . 412(c)(7)(A)
. . retroactive treatment . . . . 412(d)(2)
. benefit limitations
. . single-employer plans 436
. cooperative plans
. . minimum funding rules 433
. excess pension assets, transfers to employee health accounts 420
. funding requirements . . . . 412(l)
. . election for certain plans . . . . 412(l)(12)
. . minimum contribution . . . . 412(a)(2)
. . multiemployer plans 430
. governmental plans
. . purchase of permissive service credit . . . . 415(n)
. limitations, contributions and benefits . . 415(b)
. liquidity shortfall . . . . 401(a)(32)
. . excise tax . . . . 4971(f)
. normal retirement age defined . . . . . . 411(f)
. single-employer
. . minimum funding standards 430
. top-heavy 416
. underfunded plans
. . accrual of benefits frozen 436
. . amendment limitations 436

Defined contribution plans
. church employees
. . contributions by employer . . . . 403(b)(9)
. . coordination with social security . . . 401(l)
. lifetime income investment, portability . . . . 401(a)(38)
. limitations, contributions and benefits . . 415(c)
. top-heavy 416

Definitions 7701
. adverse party . . . . 672(a)
. affiliated group . . . . 1504(a)
. agricultural labor . . . . 3306(k)
. American vessel . . . . 3121(f); 3306(m)
. annuity contract . . . . 1035(b)(2)
. average account benefits ratio . . . . . 3241(c)
. balance . . . . 3303(c)(6)
. bank 581
. below-market loan . . . . 7872(e)(1)
. bona fide resident of foreign country . 911(d)(5)
. business holdings . . . . 4943(c); 4943(d)
. capital asset 1221
. capital gain dividend . . . . . 854(a); 857(b)(3)(B)
. capital gain net income . . . . 1222(9)
. carrier . . . . 3231(g)
. certified professional employer organization 7705
. charitable contribution . . . . 170(c)
. collective bargaining agreement determination . . . . 7701(a)(46)
. Commissioner . . . . 7701(a)(13)
. common trust fund . . . . 584(a)
. company . . . . 3231(f)
. compensation . . . . 3231(e); 3306(h)
. complete liquidation . . . . 346(a)

Topical Index

References are to Code Section numbers.

Definitions—continued
- computation date . . . . 3303(c)(7)
- consent stock . . . . 565(f)(1)
- constructive sale price . . . . 4216(b)
- contributions . . . . 3306(g)
- control . . . . 368(c)
- controlled group of corporations . . . . . 1563(a)
- cooperative bank . . . . 7701(a)(32)
- cooperative housing corporation . . . . . 216(b)
- corporation . . . . 7701(a)(3)
- cost of securities sold . . . . 75(b)
- debt instruments . . . . 1275(a)(1)
- deficiency 6211
- deficiency dividends . . . . 547(d)
- delegate . . . . 7701(a)(12)
- dependent 152
- determination . . . . 1313(a)
- distilled spirits 5002
- dividend . . . . 316; 6042(b)
- dividends paid deduction 561
- domestic building and loan association . . . . 7701(a)(19)
- donor advised fund . . . . 4966(d)(2)
- electing large partnerships 775; 6255
- employee . . . . . . 3231(b); 3306(i); 3401(c); 7701(a)(20)
- employee representative . . . . 3231(c)
- employer . . . . . . 3231(a); 3306(a); 3401(d)
- employment . . . . 3121(b); 3306(c)
- endowment contract . . . . 1035(b)(1)
- enrolled actuary . . . . 7701(a)(35)
- exchanged basis property . . . . 7701(a)(44)
- executor 2203; 7701
- exemption amount . . . . 151(d)
- factoring discount . . . . 5891(c)(4)
- fiduciary . . . . 7701(a)(6)
- fiscal year . . . . 7701(a)(24)
- foreign corporation . . . . . . 901(d); 7701(a)(5)
- foreign currency contracts . . . . 1256(g)
- foreign earned income . . . . 911(b)
- foreign estate . . . . 7701(a)(31)
- foreign insurer or reinsurer . . . . 4372(a)
- foreign partnership . . . . 7701(a)(5)
- foreign trust . . . . 7701(a)(31)
- forgone interest . . . . 7872(e)(2)
- foundation manager . . . . 4946(b)
- general power of appointment . . . . 2041(b)(1); 2514(c)
- generation-skipping transfers 2611
- grass roots expenditures 4911
- gross estate 2031; 2103
- guaranteed employment account . . . 3303(c)(4)
- head of household . . . . 2(b)(1)
- holder . . . . 1235(b)
- holding period, gain from disposition of depreciable real property . . . . . . 1250(e)
- husband and wife . . . . 7701(a)(17)
- includible corporation . . . . 1504(b)
- Indian tribal governments . . . . . . 7701(a)(40)
- influencing legislation 4911
- installment method . . . . 453(c)
- interest . . . . 6049(b)
- international organization . . . . . . 7701(a)(18)
- investment in the contract . . . . 72(c)
- key employee . . . . 416(i)(1)(A)
- levy . . . . 7701(a)(21)
- life insurance company 816
- life insurance company taxable income . . . . 801(b)
- life insurance contract . . . . . 1035(b)(3); 7702
- life insurance deductions 804
- life insurance gross income 803
- liquidation of a partner's interest . . . . . 761(d)
- lobbying expenditures 4911
- long-term capital gain . . . . 1222(3)
- long-term capital loss . . . . 1222(4)
- lottery . . . . 4421(2)
- manufacturers of stills 5102
- material advisor . . . . 6111(b)(1)
- mathematical or clerical errors . . . . . . 6213(g)
- military or naval forces of the United States . . . . 7701(a)(15)
- modified endowment contract 7702A
- motor vehicle operating agreements . . . 7701(h)
- municipal bond . . . . 75(b)
- net capital gain . . . . 1222(11)
- net capital loss . . . . 1222(10)
- net earnings from self-employment . . . 1402(a)
- net long-term capital gain . . . . 1222(7)

Definitions—continued
- net long-term capital loss . . . . 1222(8)
- net operating loss . . . . 172(c)
- net short-term capital gain . . . . 1222(5)
- net short-term capital loss . . . . 1222(6)
- nonadverse party . . . . 672(b)
- nonresident alien . . . . 7701(b)
- operating foundation . . . . 4942(j)(3)
- ordinary income 64
- ordinary loss 65
- organizational expenditures . . . . 248(b)
- overpayment . . . . 6401(a)
- paid or accrued . . . . 7701(a)(25)
- paid or incurred . . . . 7701(a)(25)
- parent corporation . . . . 424(e)
- partial liquidation . . . . 302(e)
- partially pooled account . . . . 3303(c)(3)
- partner . . . . 761(b); 7701(a)(2)
- partnership . . . . 761(a); 7701(a)(2)
- partnership agreement . . . . 761(c)
- party to a reorganization . . . . 368(b)
- pay period . . . . 3121(c); 3306(d)
- payroll period . . . . 3401(b)
- pension plan contracts . . . . 818(a)
- person . . . . 7343; 7701(a)(1)
- personal holding company 542
- . income 543
- personal service corporations 269A
- political party . . . . 271(b); 276(b)
- pooled fund . . . . 3303(c)(2)
- possessions corporations . . . . 367(d)(2)
- preceding calendar period . . . . 2502(b)
- preferred dividends . . . . 565(f)(2)
- private communication service . . . . . 4252(d)
- prohibited transactions . . . . . 503(b); 4975(c)
- property
- . depletion 614
- . estate tax purposes . . . . 2013(e)
- . used in the trade or business . . . . . 1231(b)
- qualified appraisal . . . . 170(f)(11)(E)
- qualified appraiser . . . . 170(f)(11)(E)
- qualified disaster . . . . 139(c)
- qualified disaster relief payment . . . . . 139(b)
- qualified joint venture . . . . 761(f)
- qualified state or local political organization . . . . 527(e)
- real estate investment trust 856
- reduced rate . . . . 3303(c)(8)
- regulated futures contracts . . . . 1256(a)
- regulated investment company 851
- regulated public utility . . . . 7701(a)(33)
- related or subordinate party . . . . 672(c)
- related taxpayer . . . . 1313(c)
- reorganization 368
- reportable transaction . . . . 6707A(c)(1)
- reserve account . . . . 3303(c)(1)
- resident alien . . . . 7701(b)
- roll-your-own tobacco . . . . 5702(p)
- rubber . . . . 4072(b)
- S corporation . . . . 1361(a)
- Sec. 179 property . . . . 179(d)(1)
- Sec. 306 stock . . . . 306(c)
- Sec. 1245 property . . . . 1245(a)(3)
- Sec. 1250 property . . . . 1250(c)
- secretary . . . . 7701(a)(11)
- securities . . . . 1236(c)
- self-employment income . . . . 1402(b)
- service . . . . 3231(d)
- shareholder . . . . 7701(a)(8)
- short-term capital gain . . . . 1222(1)
- short-term capital loss . . . . 1222(2)
- short-time compensation program . . . 3306(v)
- small business corporation . . . . 1361(b)
- sponsoring organization . . . . 4966(d)(1)
- sport fishing equipment . . . . 4162(a)
- state . . . . 3306(j); 7701(a)(10)
- state agency . . . . 3306(e)
- stock or securities . . . . 7701(a)(7)
- stock purchase plans . . . . 423(b)
- straddles . . . . 1092(c)
- structured settlement . . . . 5891(c)(1)
- . factoring transaction . . . . 5891(c)(3)
- . payment rights . . . . 5891(c)(2)
- subsidiary corporation . . . . 424(f)
- substituted basis property . . . . . . 7701(a)(42)
- surviving spouse . . . . 2(a)
- tax return preparer . . . . 7701(a)(36)
- taxable chemical 4662

Definitions—continued
- taxable estate 2051
- . nonresident aliens . . . . 2106(a)
- taxable gifts 2503
- taxable income 63
- taxable mortgage pools . . . . 7701(i)
- taxable year . . . . 7701(a)(23)
- taxpayer . . . . 1313(b)
- telephone service . . . . 4252(a); 4252(b)
- teletypewriter exchange service . . . . . 4252(c)
- tires of the type used on highway vehicles . . . . 4072(a)
- tract . . . . 1237(c)
- trade or business . . . . . 1402(c); 7701(a)(26)
- transferred basis property . . . . . . 7701(a)(43)
- transportation fringe . . . . 132(f)
- transportation, taxable 4262; 4272
- undistributed net income . . . . 665(a)
- undistributed personal holding company income 545
- unemployment fund . . . . 3306(f)
- United States person . . . . 957(c)
- United States property . . . . 956(c)
- unrealized receivables . . . . 751(c)
- wager . . . . 4421(1)
- wages . . . . 3121(a); 3306(b); 3401(a)
- welfare benefit fund . . . . 419(e)
- withholding agent . . . . 7701(a)(16)

Demand for payment of tax 6155; 6303

Demolition of historic structures
- deductibility of expenses of 280B

Denaturation of alcohol . . . . . 5241—5244

Dental expenses 213

Dependent care assistance programs . . . 129
- earned income limitation . . . . 129(b)
- exclusion from income, employer-provided services . . . . 129(a)
- payments to related individuals . . . . 129(c)
- requirements . . . . 129(d)

Dependents
- credit for expenses in caring for 21
- definition 152
- divorced parents . . . . 152(e)
- earnings 73
- exemption . . . . 151(c)
- expenses for care, credit against tax . . . 21
- foster children . . . . 152(f)(1)(C)
- health insurance coverage
- benefits extended to children under age 27 . . . 105(b); 162(l); 401(h); 501(c)(9)
- married . . . . 152(b)(2)
- medical expenses . . . . 213(a)
- missing children . . . . 152(f)(6)
- personal exemption for . . . . 151(c)
- . disallowed . . . . 151(d)(2)
- qualifying child . . . . 152(c)
- qualifying relative . . . . 152(d)
- taxpayer identification numbers . . . . . 151(e)

Depletion . . . . 611—617
- allowance of deduction 611
- basis for cost depletion 612
- estates and trusts . . . . 642(e)
- operating mineral interests rules . . . . 614(b)
- percentage depletion 613
- property defined 614
- tax preference item, alternative minimum tax . . . . 57(a)(1)

Deposit of taxes 7809
- additions to tax and penalty for failure to make . . . . 6656(a)
- electronic fund transfer system . . . . 6302(h)
- timely mailing as timely deposit . . . . 7502(e)
- . large depositors . . . . 7502(e)(3)

Depositaries for collection of taxes
- designation of 7808
- electronic fund transfer system . . . . 6302(h)
- payment to . . . . 6302(c)

Depreciable property, gain from disposition—
see also Sec. 1245 property
- real estate disposition 1250
- . adjustments to basis . . . . 1250(h)
- . gain, applicable percentage in determining . . . . 1250(a)(2)
- . holding period defined . . . . 1250(e)
- . leasehold improvements, additional depreciation . . . . 1250(b)(4)

Depreciable property, gain from disposition—continued
  real estate disposition—continued
    qualified low-income housing . . . . . 1250(g)
    Section 1250 property defined . . . . . 1250(c)
    substantially improved property . . . . 1250(f)
    straight-line adjustments, computation of . . . . 1250(b)(5)

Depreciation—see also Accelerated cost recovery system 167
  automobiles, luxury . . . . 280F(a)
  biofuel ethanol plant property
    additional depreciation allowance . . . . 168(l)
  bonus depreciation . . . . 168(k)
  computer software . . . . 167(f)
  earnings and profits, effect on . . . . . . 312(k)
  estates and trusts . . . . 642(e)
  expense deduction v. 179
  income forecast method . . . . 167(g)
    limitation on use . . . . 167(g)(6)
    participations and residuals . . . . . . 167(g)(7)
  methods of computing, carryover by acquiring corporation . . . . 381(c)(6)
  mortgage servicing rights . . . . 167(f)
  property used for personal purposes . . 280F(b)
  public utility property . . . . 168(f)(2)
  real estate—see Real estate depreciation
  reuse and recycling property
    additional depreciation allowance . . . 168(m)
  Section 197 intangibles, properties excluded from . . . . 167(f)
  tenant-stockholders of cooperative . . . 216(c)
  term interests . . . . 167(e)

Designated drugs
  during noncompliance periods 5000D

Designee of taxpayer
  disclosure of returns to . . . . 6103(c)

Development expenditures 616
  oil and gas wells, intangible expenses . . 263(c)

Diesel fuel, low sulfur
  credit for production 45H
  denial of double benefit . . . . 280C(d)

Diesel fuel, special fuels tax 4041
  exception to dyeing requirements . . . 4082(c)
  gasoline tax, exemption from 4082

Disabled individuals
  Achieving a Better Life Experience (ABLE) program 529A
  credit against tax 22
    amount of . . . . 22(c)
    limitations . . . . 22(d)
  credit for expenditures to provide access to 44
  dependent
    age requirements . . . . 152(c)(3)(B)
  permanently and totally
    credit against tax 22
    refunds and credits
      suspension of limitations period . . 6511(h)

Disability-related first responder retirement payments 139C

Disaster areas
  state and local bonds
    mortgage subsidy financing . . . . 143(k)(11)
  underpayment of tax, interest abatement . . . . 7508A(a)

Disaster losses . . . . 165(h); 165(i)
  principal residence, involuntary conversion . . . . 1033(h)
  renters, involuntary conversions . . . 1033(h)
  residence demolished or relocated by order . . . . 165(k)

Disaster payments . . . . 451(f)

Disaster relief payments 139

DISC—see Domestic International Sales Corporations

Discharge of indebtedness
  basis adjustment 1017
  deferral
    reacquisition of business debt . . . . 108(i)
  exempt income 108
  gain or loss treatment 1234A
  income from . . . . 61(a)(12)
  information returns 6050P

Discharge of indebtedness—continued
  student loans . . . . 108(f)
    discharges in 2021-2025 . . . . . . 108(f)(5)

Disclaimers
  gift tax 2518

Disclosure of returns and information . . 6103
  child support enforcement . . . . . . 6103(l)(6)
  collection activities with respect to joint returns . . . . 6103(e)(8)
  contractors . . . . 6103(p)(9)
  cybersecurity . . . . 6103(k)(14)
  Department of Health and Human Services
    Medicare supplier or provider of services . . . . 6103(l)(22)
    program participation eligibility determinations . . . . 6103(l)(21)
  disclosure for other than tax purposes . . 6103(l)
  Food and Nutrition Act of 2008 . . . 6103(l)(7)
  identity theft tax refund fraud prevention . . . . 6103(k)(14)
  missing or exploited child investigation . . . . 6103(i)(1)(C)
  non-IRS employees . . . . 7602(f)
  preparers of returns . . . . 6713(b); 7216
  prisoners . . . . 6103(k)(10)
  procedure and recordkeeping . . . . 6103(p)
  Social Security Administration
    Part D premium subsidy for high-income beneficiaries . . . . . 6103(l)(20)
  unauthorized enticement of information disclosure, damages 7435
  unauthorized, penalties for 7431
  wagering tax information 4424
  whistleblowers . . . . 6103(k)(13)

Discounted obligations 454

Discrimination suit costs
  adjusted gross income . . . . . . 62(a)(19)[(20)]

Dissolution of corporation, information returns 6043

Distilled spirits . . . . 5001—5011
  foreign producers
    information returns 6038E
  general provisions relating to . . . 5291—5314
  industrial use . . . . 5271—5275
  nonbeverage domestic drawback claimants . . . . 5111—5114
  reduced tax rate disallowed
    smuggled or illegally produced spirits . 5067
  signs 5180
  stills
    manufacturers of, notice requirements . 5101
    premises prohibited for distilling . . . 5178

Distilleries . . . . 5171—5182
  bonded premises . . . . 5211—5216
  denaturation . . . . 5241—5244
  establishment 5171
  general provisions relating to . . . 5201—5207
  operation . . . . 5201—5244
  production . . . . 5221—5223
  storage . . . . 5231—5236

Distraint 6331

Distributions by corporations . . . . 301—385
  additional consideration received 356
  basis to distributees 358
    property distributions . . . . 301(d)
  controlled corporation's stock and securities 355
    additional consideration received . . 356(b)
  earnings and profits, effect on 312
  gain or loss to corporation 311
    appreciated property distributed . . . 311(b)
  liquidation—see Liquidations
  property 301
    earnings and profits, effect on 312
  redemption of stock . . . . 302—304
  reorganizations—see Reorganizations
  special rules . . . . 401(a)(13)(C)
  stock and stock rights 305

Distributions by foreign trusts—see Foreign trusts: distributions by

Distributions by partnerships . . . . 731—737
  basis of distributed property other than money 732
  basis of distributee partner's interest . . 733

Distributions by partnerships—continued
  extent of recognition of gain or loss . . . 731
  liabilities decreased, treatment as distribution to partner . . . . 752(b)
  marketable securities . . . . 731(c)
  sales and exchanges, distributions treated as . . . . 751(b)
  share of partner 704

Distributions by retirement plans
  lump-sum—see also Lump-sum distributions, retirement plans . . . . 402(e)(4)
  rollovers—see also Rollovers . . . . . 402(c)

Distributions by trusts . . . . 665—668
  accumulation distribution allocated to preceding years 666
  accumulation distribution defined . . . 665(b)
  amounts deemed distributed in preceding years . . . . 667(a)
  preceding taxable year defined . . . . 665(e)
  taxes imposed on the trust . . . . 665(d)
  total taxes deemed distributed . . . . 666(b)
  undistributed net income defined . . . 665(a)

Distributorship agreements, cancellation payments 1241

District Courts
  jurisdiction 7402
    Railroad Retirement Tax Act provisions, authority to order compliance with 3232

District of Columbia employees, returns and payment of tax . . . . 3125(d)

District of Columbia Retirement Protection Act
  disclosure of return information . . . 6103(l)(16)

Dividend carryover, personal holding companies 564

Dividend income, corporations
  basis in stock reduced by nontaxed portion of extraordinary dividends . . . 1059
  dividends received deduction . . . . 243—246

Dividend income, individuals . . . . . 61(a)(7)
  capital gains treatment . . . . 1(h)(11)

Dividends
  backup withholding 3406
  building and loan associations, deduction . . . . 591(a)
  cooperative banks, deduction . . . . . 591(a)
  corporation recipient—see Dividend income, corporations
  deduction for—see Dividends paid deduction; Dividends received deduction
  deficiency, deduction for
    personal holding companies 547
  defined 316
  in kind—see Dividends in kind
  individual recipient—see Dividend income, individuals
  information returns 6042
  liquidation distributions—see Liquidations: dividends
  mutual savings banks, deduction 591
  paid, deduction—see also Dividends paid deduction . . . . 561—565
  patronage dividends
    information returns 6044
  preferential dividends, dividends paid deduction . . . . 562(c)
  property—see Dividends in kind
  real estate investment trusts, payment after close of year 858
  received, deduction—see also Dividends received deduction . . . . 243—246
  received from real estate investment trusts . . . . 857(c)
  regulated investment companies . . . 854; 855
    limitations applicable to dividends received 854
    payment after close of year 855
  stock—see Stock dividends and rights
  substitute dividends
    U.S.-source dividends treatment . . 871(m)
  taxed as capital gain . . . . 1(h)(11)
  withholding of tax at source
    nonresident aliens and foreign corporations . . . . 1441(b); 1442

Topical Index
References are to Code Section numbers.

Dividends in kind 301
. gain or loss to corporation 311
Dividends paid deduction . . . . . . 561—565
. accumulated earnings tax . . . . 563(a)
. affiliated corporations . . . . 562(d)
. consent dividends 565
. definition 561
. eligible dividends 562
. . payment on last day of year . . . . . . 563(c)
. liquidation distributions . . . . 562(b)
. payment of dividends after close of
    taxable year 563
. personal holding companies
. . computation of personal holding
      company tax . . . . 563(b)
. . dividend carryover 564
. preferential dividends . . . . 562(c)
. real estate investment trusts . . . . . . 562(e)
Dividends received deduction . . . . 243—246
. debt-financed portfolio stock 246A
. participation exemption deduction . . 245A
. temporary
. . controlled foreign corporation 965
Divorce
. alimony and separate maintenance—see
    Alimony and separate maintenance
. divorce distributions from retirement
    plans . . . . . . 72(m)(10); 402(e)(1); 414(p)
. transfers between spouses incident to . . 1041
Documents
. stamp taxes—see Stamp taxes
. timely mailing as timely filing 7502
Dollar amount computations . . 3402(b)(4); 6102; 7504
Domestic crude oil
. environmental tax . . . . 4611(a)
. . credit against tax . . . . . . 4612(c); 4612(d)
. . rate of tax . . . . 4611(c)
. Trans-Alaska Pipeline Fund payments,
    credit against tax . . . . 4612(e)
Domestic defined . . . . 7701(a)(4)
Domestic International Sales Corporations—
    see also Foreign Sales Corporations
    . . . . 991—997
. actual distributions
. . adjustments to basis of shareholder's
      stock . . . . 996(e)
. . disqualification . . . . 995(b)(2)
. . dividends received deduction . . . . . 246(d)
. . earnings and profits . . . . 996(f)
. . failure to qualify . . . . 995(b)(2)
. . foreign shareholders . . . . 996(g)
. . order of absorption . . . . 996(a)
. . order of application . . . . 996(c)
. . property 997
. . qualification requirements,
      distributions to meet . . . . 992(c)
. . revocation of election . . . . 995(b)(2)
. affiliated corporations, consolidated
    returns . . . . 1504(b)
. assets, transfers of . . . . 995(e)
. books and records . . . . 6011(d)
. conditions for qualification . . . . 992(c)
. consolidated returns . . . . 1504(b)
. constructive distributions . . . . 995(b)
. . adjustments to basis of shareholder's
      stock . . . . 996(e)
. . disqualification . . . . 995(b)(2)
. . dividends received deduction . . . . . 246(d)
. . 50% rule . . . . 995(b)(1)(D)
. . foreign investment attributable to
      producer's loans . . . . 995(b)(1)(G); 995(d)
. . foreign tax credit . . . . 904(f)
. . interest on producer's loans . . . . . . 993(d)
. . qualification requirements,
      distributions to meet . . . . 992(c)
. . revocation of election . . . . 995(b)(2)
. . sales or exchanges, gain from . . 995(b)(1)(B)
. deferred income
. . tax preference items 291
. disqualification, constructive dividends
    . . . . 995(b)(2)
. dividends received deduction . . . . . . 246(d)
. earnings and profits
. . actual distributions . . . . 996(f)
. . measure of tax . . . . 995(a)
. . ordering rules for losses . . . . 996(b)

Domestic International Sales Corporations—
continued
. election . . . . 992(b)
. 50% rule, constructive distributions
    . . . . 995(b)(1)(D)
. foreign investment attributable to
    producer's loans, constructive distributions
    . . . . 995(b)(1)(G); 995(d)
. foreign shareholders, distributions to . 996(g)
. foreign tax credit for distributions . . . 901(d)
. information requirements . . . 6011(d); 6072(b)
. . failure to meet, penalties 6686
. intercompany pricing, measure of tax . . 994
. interest on DISC-related deferred tax
    liability . . . . 995(f)
. interest on producer's loans,
    constructive distributions . . . . 993(d);
    995(b)(1)(A)
. measure of tax
. . earnings and profits . . . . 995(a)
. . intercompany pricing 994
. . taxable income 994
. minimum capital requirement . . . . . 992(a)(1)(C)
. non-DISC treated as DISC . . . . 992(a)(2)
. nonqualifying corporations . . . . 992(d)
. one class of stock requirement . . . . . 992(a)
. order of absorption, actual distributions
    . . . . 996(a)
. order of application, actual distributions
    . . . . 996(c)
. personal holding companies . . . . . . 992(e)
. pricing rules 994
. property distributions 997
. qualified export assets . . . . . . 993(b); 993(c)
. qualified export receipts . . . . 993(a)
. qualifying corporations . . . . 992(a)
. . statute of limitations . . . . 6501(g)(3)
. returns . . . . 6011(d); 6072(b)
. revocation of election, constructive
    distributions . . . . 995(b)(2)
. sales or exchanges, gain as constructive
    distributions . . . . . 995(b)(1)(B); 995(b)(1)(C)
. shareholder, tax on 991
. stock transfers . . . . 995(c)
. . death as reason . . . . 1014(d)
. . redemptions, adjustments . . . . 996(d)
. . sales . . . . 996(d)
. taxable income, measure of tax 994
Domestic servants, withholding . . . 3401(a)(3)
Donor advised funds . . . . 4966—4967
. excise taxes
. . excess benefit transactions . . . . . . 4958(c)(2)
. . excess business holdings . . . . 4943(e)
. . prohibited benefits 4967
. . taxable distributions 4966
. . nondeductible contributions . . . 170(f)(18);
    2055(e)(5); 2522(c)(5)
. sponsoring organizations
. . reporting requirements . . . . 6033(k)
Dower interest, valuation of gross estate
    2034
Drawbacks
. exportation of liquor 5062
. fraudulently claimed, forfeiture 7304
. tobacco tax 5706
**Drilling and development costs, oil and
gas wells** . . . . 263(c)
. tertiary injectants 193
Drought, livestock sold because of . . 1033(e)
Drugs
. deductibility of cost . . . . 213(b)
. designated drugs during noncompliance
    periods 5000D
**Dual consolidated loss, consolidated
returns** . . . . 1503(c)
Due dates
. returns . . . . 6071—6075
. Saturday, Sunday, or holiday 7503
. timely mailing as timely filing 7502
Dues
. entertainment expenses . . . . 274(a)(2)
. lobbying organizations, limitation on
    deduction . . . . 162(e)
. membership organizations
. . prepaid 456

Dyed fuel penalties 6715
. exceptions . . . . 4082(c)

E

Earned income credit 32
. childless individuals . . . . 32(n)
. credit and phaseout percentages . . . 32(b)
. credits against tax
. . denial for recklessness or fraud . . . 32(k)
. earned income defined . . . . 911(d)(2)
. fraudulent claims prevention . . . . . . 32(m)
. identification requirements for qualifying
    child . . . . 32(c)(3)(D)(i)
. improperly claimed . . . . 32(k)
. nonresident aliens, eligibility . . . . 32(c)(1)(D)
. overseas military personnel, eligibility . . 32(c)(4)
. possessions of the United States . . . 7530
. prisoners, eligibility . . . . 32(c)(2)(B)(iv)
. supplemental child credit . . . . 32(m)
Earnings and profits
. accumulated earnings tax . . . . . . 531—537
. affiliated corporations 1552
. basis adjustment, investment tax credit
    . . . . 312(k)
. carryover by acquiring corporation . . 381(c)(2)
. depreciation affecting . . . . 312(k)
. . exception for recovery and section 179
      property . . . . 312(k)(3)
. distributions by corporations affecting . 312
. information returns as to 6042
. interest paid
. . unregistered obligations . . . . 312(m)
. property distributions affecting 312
. real estate investment trusts . . . . . . 857(d)
. regulated investment companies . . . 852(c)
Economic substance doctrine
. codified . . . . 7701(o)
. underpayments of tax
. . accuracy-related penalty . . 6662(b)(6); 6662(i)
Education individual retirement accounts—see
    Coverdell education savings accounts
Educational expenses
. American opportunity credit 25A
. exclusion for employees 127
. interest on education loans 221
. Lifetime learning credit 25A
. qualified higher education expenses . . 72(t)(7)
. qualified state tuition programs . . 135(c)(2)(C);
    529
. . computer and internet access
      expenses . . . . 529(e)(3)(A)(iii)
Educational institutions
. collective investment cooperatives of
    educational organizations, exempt status
    . . . . 501(f)
. excise taxes, exemption
. . manufacturers . . . . 4221(a)(5)
. failure to provide taxpayer identification
    number
. . waiver of penalty . . . . 6724(f)
. income tax, exemption . . . . 501(c)(3)
. lodging furnished to employee . . . . . 119(d)
. . academic health center . . . . 119(d)(4)(B)
. returns 6050S
Effective dates 7851
Elderly persons
. architectural and transportation barrier
    removal for, expenses of 190
. credit against tax 22
. . amount of . . . . 22(c)
. . limitations . . . . 22(d)
. standard deduction . . . . 63(f)
Electing large partnerships . . 771—777; 6240—
6242; 6245—6248
. adjustment proceedings . . . . . 774; 6246—6247;
    6251—6252
. adjustments to partnership items . . 6245—6248
. . limitations period 6248
. alternative minimum tax adjustments
    and preferences 772
. capital gains and losses at partnership
    level 772
. computations 773
. defined 775
. disqualified holders under REMIC rules . . 774
. oil and gas properties 776

Topical Index
References are to Code Section numbers.

Electing large partnerships—continued
. passive loss limitation activities 772
. percentage depletion 776
. reporting requirements
.. due date 6252
.. request for administrative adjustment ... 6251
.. separately stated items 772
Electioneering, prohibition against 4945
Elections—see particular type
Electricity production credit, renewable resources 45
Electronic filing
. exempt organizations .... 6033(n)
.. unrelated business income .... 6011(h)
. financial institutions
.. withholding on foreign transfers .... 6011(e)(4)
Electronic fund transfer system, payment of tax .... 6302(h)
Employee retention credit
. employers affected by COVID-19 3134
Employee stock options .... 421—424
. stock purchase plans 423
.. modification, extension, renewal of option .... 424(h)
.. requirements of plan .... 423(b)
.. returns 6039
Employee stock ownership credit—see Tax credit employee stock ownership plans
Employee stock ownership plans (ESOPs)—see also Tax credit employee stock ownership plans
. definition .... 4975(e)(7)
. dividends paid, deduction .... 404(k)
. information returns .... 6047(e)
Employees
. accident and health plan benefits .. 104—106
. annuities—see Employees' annuities
. business deductions, floor 67
. definition .. 1402(d); 3121(d); 3231(b); 3306(i); 3401(c); 7701(a)(20)
. disability benefits .... 104—106
. expenses, adjusted gross income computation .... 62(a)(2)
. federal—see Federal officers and employees
. gifts and awards .... 274(b)
. gifts, gross income .... 102(c)
. health accounts, transfers of excess pension assets to 420
. incentive stock options 422
. independent contractor
.. real estate agents .... 3508(a)
. leased employee
.. pension plans .... 414(n)
. meals and lodging furnished for convenience of employer 119
. option to purchase stock received by 421
. sick benefits .... 104—106
. sick pay, third-party paid .... 6051(f)
. stock options 421
. withholding of tax on wages—see Withholding of income tax on wages
Employees' annuities 403; 404
. beneficiaries, taxability .... 403(a)
. contributions by employees
.. deductibility .... 404(a)(2)
. divorce distributions .... 72(m)(10)
. eligible rollover distributions ...... 403(a)(4)
. direct trustee-to-trustee transfers .... 403(a)(5)
. exempt organization's purchase of ... 403(b)
. investment valuation
.. divorce distributions .... 72(m)(10)
.. employee consideration, computation of .... 72(m)(2)
.. transfers for consideration .... 72(g)
. rollovers—see also Rollovers .... 72(o)(4)
Employees' beneficiary associations, exemption .... 501(c)(9)
. nondiscrimination requirements 505
Employees' benefits
. affiliated service groups .... 414(m)
. educational assistance plans 127
. group term life insurance
.. nondiscrimination .... 79(d)
Employees' trusts—see Retirement plans
Employer contributions to long-term care benefits .... 106(c)

Employer contributions to Archer MSAs ... 106(b)
. excise tax for failure to make 4980E
Employer liability trusts, contributions to 194A
Employer-provided child care credit 45F
Employers
. achievement awards to employees, deductible .... 274(j)
. defined .... 3231(a); 3306(a); 3401(d)
. employment tax liability .... 3509(a)
. foreign deferred compensation plans ... 404A(a)
. health insurance coverage
.. cost reported on Form W-2 .... 6051(a)(14); 6051(g)
. large employers
.. minimum essential coverage, penalty 4980H
.. minimum essential coverage, reporting requirements 6056
. military differential wage payments, credit 45P
. small employers
.. automatic enrollment credit 45T
.. health insurance tax credit 45R
.. pension plan startup costs 45E
.. simple cafeteria plans .... 125(j)
. withholding of income tax on wages—see Withholding of income tax on wages
Employment credits
. empowerment zones 1396
. wages paid, effect .... 280C(a)
Employment defined ...... 3121(b); 3306(c)
Employment-related expenses
. credit against tax 21
. defined .... 21(b)(2)
. limitations .... 21(c); 21(d)
Employment status
. proceedings for determination of 7436
Employment taxes
. deferred compensation .... 3121(v)
. employer liability .... 3509(a)
. federal government employees ..... 3121(u)
. FICA—see Social security taxes (FICA)
. FICA and FUTA wage bases
.. motion picture payroll services 3512
. FUTA—see Unemployment Tax Act (FUTA) taxes
. governmental employers, returns 3126
. professional employer organizations, certification 3511
. Railroad Retirement Act taxes—see Railroad Retirement Act taxes
. salary reduction arrangements ...... 3121(v)
. self-employment—see Self-employment tax
. social security—see Social security taxes (FICA)
. unemployment—see Unemployment Tax Act (FUTA) taxes
. withholding—see Social security taxes (FICA); Withholding of income tax on wages
Empowerment zones .... 1391—1397F
. bonds .... 1394(f)
. definitions and special rules 1393
. designation procedures 1391
. eligibility
.. Alaska .... 1392(d)
.. Hawaii .... 1392(d)
. eligibility criteria 1392
. employment credit 1396
. enterprise zone business, defined 1397C
. enterprise zone facility .... 1394(b)
. Indian reservations, exclusion of .... 1393(a)(4)
. private activity bonds 1394
. qualified zone property, defined 1397D
. rollover of investments, nonrecognition of gain 1397B
Endowment insurance
. definition of endowment contract ..... 1035(b)(1)
. income .... 61(a)(10); 72
. interest paid to purchase 264
Energy conservation subsidies, exclusion from gross income 136
Energy efficient commercial building property deduction 179D

Energy grants and financing, returns by administrators of programs 6050D
Energy incentives
. advanced coal project credit 48A
. advanced energy project credit 48C
. alternative fuel vehicle refueling property credit 30C
. alternative fuels credit 6426
. alternative motor vehicle credit 30B
. biodiesel fuels credit 40A; 6426
. carbon oxide sequestration credit 45Q
. clean electricity investment credit 48E
. clean electricity production credit 45Y
. clean fuel production credit 45Z
. clean hydrogen production credit 45V
. energy efficient commercial building property deduction 179D
. energy investment credit 48
. fuel cell motor vehicle credit .... 30B(b)
. gasification project credit 48B
. new energy efficient homes credit 45L
. plug-in electric drive motor vehicle credit .. 30D
. qualified commercial clean vehicle credit . 45W
. renewable electricity production credit ... 45
. residential clean energy credit 25D
. residential energy property credit 25C
. second generation biofuel production credit .... 40(b)(6)
. zero-emission nuclear power production credit 45U
Energy investment credit 48
Enhanced oil recovery credit 43
Enterprise communities ...... 1391—1397D
. definitions and special rules 1393
. designation procedures 1391
. eligibility criteria 1392
. employment credit 1396
. enterprise zone business, defined 1397C
. enterprise zone facility .... 1394(b)
. Indian reservations, exclusion of .... 1393(a)(4)
. private activity bonds 1394
. qualified zone property, defined 1397D
Enterprise zones—see also Empowerment zones
. carryover by acquiring corporation . 381(c)(26)
. enterprise zone business, defined 1397C
. enterprise zone facility .... 1394(b)
. private activity bonds 1394
Entertainment expenses 274
. business meals .... 274(k)
. 50 percent of expenses allowed .... 274(n)
. compensation, expenses treated as .. 274(e)(2)
. convention expenses .... 274(h)
. customers, entertainment sold to ... 274(e)(8)
. facility maintenance
.. personal or Sec. 1231 asset .... 274(g)
. food and beverages for employees on employer's premises .... 274(e)(1)
. foreign conventions .... 274(h)(1)
. individuals subject to federal hours of service .... 274(n)(3)
. recreational expenses for employees . 274(e)(4)
. reimbursed expenses .... 274(e)(3)
. substantiation requirement .... 274(d)
. taxes and interest paid, deductibility .... 274(f)
. travel .... 274(m)
Entry of premises for examination of taxable objects 7606
. penalty for refusal to permit 7342
Environmental remediation costs
. expensing of 198
Erosion, expenditures to prevent 175
Errors, correction of 1311
Escheat
. overpayments of tax 6408
ESOP—see Employee stock ownership plans (ESOPs)
Estate tax .... 2001—2209
. abatement claims .... 6404(b)
. annuities
.. survivor annuities .... 401(a)(13)(D)
. Armed Forces member, combat zone-related death 2201
. astronaut, death in line of duty 2201
. beneficiaries of life insurance policies, liability of 2206

Topical Index
References are to Code Section numbers.

Estate tax—continued
. casualty losses . . . . 642(g); 2054
. charitable contribution of copyrighted
　artworks . . . . 2055(e)(4)
. charitable contributions deduction . . . 2055(e)
. . nonresident aliens . . . . 2106(a)(2)
. charitable use, transfers for 2055
. collection
. . civil action 7404
. . credits against tax . . . 2010; 2012—2016; 2102
. . unified credit 2010
. deductibility . . . . 691(c)
. deductions in computing 2053
. deficiency notice . . . . 6212(b)(3)
. executor
. . defined 2203
. . liability for payment . . . . 2002; 2204(d)
. expatriation to avoid tax 2107
. extension of time for payment . . . 6161(a)(2);
　6163; 6166; 6601(j)
. fiduciary
. . discharge from personal liability 2204
. generation-skipping transfers . . . 2601—2663
. gross estate, valuation . . . . 2031—2045
. . alternate valuation 2032
. . annuities 2039
. . curtesy interest 2034
. . defined 2031
. . dower interest 2034
. . farm property 2032A
. . gifts made within 3 years of death 2035
. . joint interests 2040
. . life insurance proceeds 2042
. . powers of appointment exercised by
　　decedent 2041
. . prior interests 2045
. . property for which marital deduction
　　was previously allowed 2044
. . property in which decedent had an
　　interest 2033
. . real property 2032A
. . recovery in case of marital deduction
　　property 2207A
. . retained life estate, transfers with 2036
. . revocable transfers 2038
. . timber . . . . 2032A(e)(13)
. . trade or business property 2032A
. . transfers for insufficient consideration . 2043
. . transfers taking effect at death 2037
. jeopardy assessments 6861
. lien for tax . . . . 6324(a); 6324A; 6324B
. marital deduction, coordination . . . . . 2001(e)
. payment
. . extension of time . . . 6161(a)(2); 6161(b)(2);
　　6163
. . reimbursement out of estate 2205
. possessions' residents considered as
　U.S. citizens . . . . 2501(b)
. possessions' residents considered
　nonresidents not citizens of U.S. 2209
. pre-1967 provisions, application 2108
. public use, transfers for 2055
. qualified domestic trust 2056A
. rate of tax 2001
. redemption of stock to pay 303
. religious use, transfers for 2055
. returns 6018
. . due date . . . . 6075(a)
. . place for filing . . . . 6091(b)(3)
. right of recovery where decedent
　retained interest 2207B
. special use valuation, involuntary
　conversions . . . . 121(d)(8)
. split-interest transfers
. . election . . . . 2056(b)(7)
. . special rule for charitable remainder
　　trusts . . . . 2056(b)(8)
. state death taxes
. . deduction 2058
. statement explaining valuation for,
　furnishing of 7517
. stock transferred with retained voting
　rights, exclusion . . . . 2036(b)
. tax on prior transfers, credit against tax . 2013
. taxable estate . . . . 2051—2058
. taxes due, deduction from gross estate . 2053
. unified credit against 2010
. . applicable credit amount . . . . 2010(c)
. victims of certain terrorist attacks 2201

Estates and trusts—see also Trusts . . 641—683
. accumulation trusts . . . . 665—668
. administration expenses . . . 642(g); 2053(a)
. amortization deduction . . . . 642(f)
. bankruptcy . . . . 1398(e)
. charitable contributions . . . . 642(c)
. charitable remainder trusts 664
. computation of tax . . . . 641(b)
. credits against tax . . . . 642(a)
. deductions allowable 642
. depletion deduction . . . . 642(e)
. depreciation deduction . . . . 642(e)
. disallowance of double deductions . . . 642(g)
. distributable net income defined . . . . 643(a)
. escheat, overpayments of tax 6408
. estimated tax—see Estimated tax, estates and
　trusts
. excess deductions on termination
　available to beneficiaries . . . . 642(h)
. excess distributions by trusts—see Distributions
　by trusts
. fiduciary
. . information statement to beneficiary . . 6034A
. foreign
. . recognition of gain on transfers to 684
. foreign tax credit . . . . 642(a); 901(b)(5)
. imposition of tax 641
. income from interest in . . . . 61(a)(15)
. interests in corporations or partnerships
　transferred, valuation 2701
. interests in trusts transferred, valuation . 2702
. itemized deductions, floor on
　miscellaneous . . . . 67(e)
. lapsing rights and restrictions, treatment
　of 2704
. loans from foreign trusts . . . . 643(i)
. multiple trusts, treatment of . . . . 643(f)
. net operating loss deduction . . . . . . 642(d)
. nonexempt trusts, curbs 4947
. personal exemptions, deduction for . . 642(b)
. qualified domestic trust 2056A
. rates of tax . . . . 1(e)
. return requirements . . 6012(a)(3)—6012(a)(5);
　6018
. revocable trusts 645
. rights and restrictions disregarded . . . 2703
. rights and restrictions lapsing 2704
. tax preferences . . . . 59(c)
. tax years of 644
. trust income for benefit of spouse or
　grantor 677
. unit investment trusts . . . . 851(f)
. unused loss carryovers available to
　beneficiaries on termination . . . . . . 642(h)

Estimated tax, corporations
. adjustment of overpayment 6425
. assessment . . . . 6201(b)
. credits against estimated tax . . . . . . 6402(b)
. failure to pay 6655
. large corporations . . . 6655(d)(2); 6655(g)(2)
. payment
. . considered on account of income tax . 6315

Estimated tax, estates and trusts
. failure to pay . . . . 6654(l)
. payments treated as paid by beneficiary
　. . . . . 643(g)
. quarterly payments 6654

Estimated tax, individuals
. assessment . . . . 6201(b)
. credits against estimated tax . . . . . . 6402(b)
. failure to pay 6654
. limitation on use of preceding year's tax . . . .
　. . . . . 6654(d)(1)(C)(i)
. payment
. . considered on account of income tax . 6315
. penalty, exception . . . . 6654(e)
. waiver of penalty . . . . 6654(d)

ETC—see Export trade corporations

Ethanol, credit for small producers of—see also
　Alcohol, fuel use of . . . . 40(b)(4)

Evasion or avoidance of tax
. acquisitions made for purpose of 269
. corporations used to avoid income tax
　on shareholders . . . . 531—565
. insurance companies, reinsurance . . . 845
. liability assumed for purpose of . . . . 357(b)

Evasion or avoidance of tax—continued
. limitations on assessment and collection . . . .
　. . . . . 6501(c)(2)
. notice . . . . 6672(b)
. penalties 7201
. possession with intent to sell for
　purposes of 7268
. sales for purpose of 7341

Examination of books and witnesses . . 7602;
　7605

**Examination of premises, penalty for
　refusal to permit** 7342

**Excess benefits transactions, exempt
　organizations** 4958
. rules for supporting organizations . . 4958(c)(3)

**Excess business holdings, private
　foundations** 4943
. additional tax . . . . 4943(b)
. donor advised funds, application of tax . 4943(e)
. initial tax . . . . 4943(a)
. philanthropic business holdings
　exception . . . . 4943(g)
. supporting organizations, application of
　tax . . . . 4943(f)

Excess itemized deductions, definition . . 63(c)

**Excess pension assets, transfers to
　employee health accounts** 420

**Excessive withholding, refunds and
　credits** 6414

Exchanges of property
. annuities 1035
. assumption of liability 357
. basis to distributees 358
. election to treat transfers as 1057
. endowment contracts 1035
. farm property, valuation of gross estate
　. . . . . 2032A(i)
. gain or loss 1001
. insurance policies, nonrecognition of
　gain or loss 1035
. investment property 1031
. involuntary conversions 1033
. nontaxable . . . . 1031—1045
. productive use or investment property . 1031
. related persons . . . . 1031(f)
. reorganization—see Reorganizations
. securities transferred under certain
　agreements 1058
. stock for property 1032
. stock for stock of same corporation . . 1036
. tax-free . . . . 1031—1045
. U.S. obligations 1037

Excise taxes
. airways use tax—see Airport and airways use
　tax
. alcohol fuel credit, coordination with . . 40(c)
. alternative fuels . . . . 4041(a)
. Archer MSAs
. . excess contributions 4973
. . failure by employer to make
　　contributions 4980E
. bows and arrows . . . . 4161(b)
. buses . . . . 4221(e)(3); 6421(b)
. cash or deferred arrangement
. . excess contributions 4979
. charitable hospitals
. . failure to meet requirements 4959
. chemicals . . . . 4661(b)
. . definitions and special rules 4662
. coal 4121
. collection, accounting 7512
. communications . . . . 4251—4254
. contributions to employer plans,
　nondeductible 4972
. donor advised funds
. . excess benefit transactions . . . . . 4958(c)(2)
. . excess business holdings . . . . . . 4943(e)
. . prohibited benefits 4967
. . taxable distributions 4966
. employee stock ownership plans and
　worker-owned cooperatives
. . dispositions of securities by 4978
. . excess benefit transactions 4958
. . excess business holdings 4943
. . excess contributions to health savings
　　accounts . . . . 4973(g)

EST

Topical Index
References are to Code Section numbers.

Excise taxes—continued
- exempt organizations
  - excess executive compensation 4960
  - failure to pay
    - criminal penalties 7215
    - separate accounting 7512
  - first tier tax abatement 4962
  - floor stocks refunds 6412
  - foundations—see private foundations
- fractional ownership aircraft progam
  - surtax on fuel 4043
- fringe benefits, excess 4977
- fuel taxes
  - alcohol fuel mixture credit ..... 6426(b)
  - alternative fuel credit ..... 6426(d)
  - alternative fuel mixture credit ..... 6426(e)
  - biodiesel mixture credit ..... 6426(c)
  - diesel fuels 4083
  - information reporting 4104
- fuels containing alcohol ..... 4041(k); 4041(m); 4081(c)
- gas guzzlers 4064
- golden parachute payments, excess 4999
- greenmail 5881
- group health plans, failure to meet requirements 4980D
- harbor maintenance tax ..... 4461—4462
- highway motor vehicle use tax ..... 4481—4484
- imported substances ..... 4671—4672
- individual retirement accounts, excess contributions 4973
- inland waterways use tax 4042
- jeopardy assessment 6862
- kerosene ..... 4081(a)(2)(A)(iii); 4082(d); 4083(a); 4101(e)
- liquidity shortfall, retirement plans ..... 4971(f)
- manufacturers taxes—see Manufacturers excise taxes
- meter-dose inhalers, chemicals used in ..... 4682(g)
- minimum standards for funding retirement plans, failure to meet 4971
- occupational taxes
  - tobacco manufacturers and exporters ..... 5731—5734
  - wagering ..... 4411—4414
- overpayment
  - refunds and credits 6415; 6416
- ozone-depleting chemicals ..... 4681; 4682; 6302(f)
- political expenditures of exempt organizations 4955
- prepaid telephone cards ..... 4251(d)
- private colleges and universities
  - investment income 4968
- private foundations
  - excess business holdings 4943
  - investment income 4940
  - second tier tax abatement 4961
- prohibited tax shelter transactions
  - tax-exempt entities 4965
- prohibited transactions of retirement plans 4975
- real estate investment trusts 4981
- recreational motorboats ..... 4041(a)(2)
- regulated investment companies, undistributed income 4982
- retirement plans
  - accumulations in 4974
- reversions of assets from qualified plan 4980
- securities, qualified, prohibited allocation 4979A
- services—see particular tax
- ship voyages for passengers, persons providing 4471; 4472
- special fuels
  - nontaxable uses 6427
- suspension of filing period ..... 6213(e)
- tanning salon services 5000B
- tires 4071
- transportation of persons by air ..... 4261—4263
- transportation of property by air 4271; 4272
- trucks and trailers
  - definitions 4052
  - exemptions 4053
  - imposition of tax 4051
- vaccines 4131; 4132
- wagering ..... 4401—4424
  - refunds and credits 6419

Excise taxes—continued
- welfare benefit plans
  - disqualified 4976

Exclusions from gross income—see Exempt income

Executors and administrators
- definition of executor 2203
- discharge from personal liability 2204
- decedent's taxes 6905
- estate tax, liability for payment 2002
- farm and real property, transfers 1040
- liability for tax ..... 6901—6904
- notice of qualification as executor 6036

Exempt facility bonds 142
- qualified broadband projects ..... 142(n)
- qualified carbon dioxide capture facilities ..... 142(o)

Exempt income ..... 101—139I
- accident and health plans 105; 106
- adoption assistance programs ..... 137(b)(1)
- adoption expenses 137
- armed forces members
  - combat zone compensation 112
- capital contributions 118
- citizens of United States residing in foreign country 911; 912
- clergymen, rental value of parsonage 107
- COBRA premium assistance 139I
- combat zone compensation exclusion for members of armed forces 112
- contributions to capital of corporation 118
- cost of living allowances ..... 912(2)
- cost-sharing payments 126
- death benefits 101
- dependent care assistance program payments 129
- disaster relief payments 139
- discharge of indebtedness, income from ..... 108; 108(a); 1017(a)
  - reduction of basis 1017
- distributions of stock under public utility dividend reinvestment plans ..... 305(f)
- energy conservation subsidies 136
- expenses related to ..... 265(a)(1)
- foreign central banks of issue 861; 895
- foreign corporations 883
  - employees of 893
- foreign governments 892
- foster care payments 131
- fringe benefits 132
- gain from sale of principal residence 121
- gifts 102
- hospitals ..... 501(o)
- improvements made by lessee 109
- Indian general welfare benefits 139E
- Indian health care benefits 139D
- inheritances 102
- injuries or sickness, amounts received for ..... 104—106
- interest
  - received in action to recover property seized by IRS 139H
  - related to ..... 265(a)(2)
- international organizations 892
  - employees of 893
- lessor
  - improvements made by lessee 109
- life insurance proceeds 101
- lodging furnished for convenience of employer 119
- meals furnished for convenience of employer 119
- ministers, rental value of parsonages 107
- municipalities 115
- Peace Corps members ..... 912(3)
- periodic personal injury payments 130
- political subdivisions 115
- recoveries, tax benefit items 111
- residence sale proceeds, 55-year-olds 121
  - election, time for making ..... 121(c)
  - new residence sold or condemned, basis ..... 121(d)
  - partial use of residence for business ..... 121(d)
  - special rules ..... 121(d)
- scholarships 117
- shipowners' protection and indemnity associations 526
- sick pay ..... 104—106

Exempt income—continued
- small business stock, exclusion of gain from 1202
- states 115
- stock or rights distributed to shareholders ..... 305(a)
- stripped preferred stock ..... 305(e)
- survivor's benefits
  - slain police officers ..... 101(h)
- unemployment compensation
  - exclusion for 2020 ..... 85(c)
- volunteer emergency medical responders, benefits 139B
- volunteer firefighters, benefits 139B

Exempt-interest dividends
- regulated investment companies ..... 852(b)

Exempt organizations ..... 501—530
- amateur sports organizations ..... 501(j)
- application for exemption, public inspection ..... 6104(a)
- bargain sales to ..... 1011(b)
- black lung benefit trusts ..... 501(c)(21)
- business income, taxation of ..... 511—515
- charitable hospitals
  - eligibility requirements ..... 501(r)
- charitable risk pools ..... 501(n)
- child care centers ..... 501(k)
- commercial-type insurance, provision of ..... 501(m)
- deferred compensation plans 457
- employees, net earnings from self-employment ..... 1402(e)
- employer liability trusts ..... 501(c)(22)
- excess executive compensation
  - excise tax 4960
- excess benefits transactions excise tax 4958
- exclusion from definition of personal holding company ..... 542(c)(1)
- farmers' cooperatives—see also Farmers' cooperatives 521
- feeder organizations 502
- FICA tax exemption, waiver of ..... 3121(k)
- foreign tax-exempts, withholding on income 1443
  - payment of withheld tax 1461
- health care coverage on a not-for-profit basis ..... 501(c)(26)
- homeowners associations 528
- information or service available from federal government
  - failure to disclose, penalty 6711
- information returns 6033
- inspection of annual returns ..... 6104(e)
- list of ..... 501(c)
- lobbying expenditures, excise tax on disqualifying 4912
- new organizations, notification of IRS ..... 508(a); 508(b)
- nonprofit health insurance issuers ..... 501(c)(29)
- political expenditures of
  - excise tax on 4955
  - injunctions against 7409
  - termination assessments 6852
- political organizations 527
- private foundations—see Private foundations
- prohibited transactions engaged in, denial of exemption 503
- property used by, investment credit ..... 50(b)(3)
- reporting requirements
  - failure to file return or notice ..... 6033(j)
  - interests in insurance contracts 6050V
  - supporting organizations ..... 6033(l)
- requirements for exemption 503
- returns ..... 6033; 6501(g)(2)
  - electronic filing requirement ..... 6033(n)
- S corporation shareholders ..... 1361(c)(6)
- scholarship funding corporations ..... 150(d)(3)
- shipowners' protection and indemniy associations 526
- supporting organizations ..... 509(f)
  - excess benefit transactions ..... 4958(c)(3)
  - excess business holdings ..... 4943(f)
- terrorist organizations
  - suspension of tax-exempt status ..... 501(p)
- types ..... 501(c)(14)
- unrelated business income—see Unrelated business income
- veterans' organizations ..... 501(c)(19); 501(c)(23)

Topical Index
References are to Code Section numbers.

Exempt organizations—continued
. voluntary board members, exemption from withholding penalty .... 6672(e)

Exempt securities—see Securities: exempt

Exemption from tax
. common trust funds .... 584(b)
. communications tax 4253; 4293
. domestic goods purchased for United States 7510
. educational organizations
.. manufacturers tax .... 4221(a)(5)
. excise taxes, United States government . 4293
. farmers, special fuels tax .... 4041(f)
. firearms taxes 4182; 5852; 5853
. highway motor vehicle use tax 4483
. insolvent banks 7507
. manufacturers excise tax
.. aircraft supplies .... 4221(a)(3)
.. educational organizations ..... 4221(a)(5)
.. exports .... 4221(a)(2)
.. Indian-produced articles 4225
.. sales or resales to manufacturers . 4221(a)(1)
.. states and municipalities ...... 4221(a)(4)
.. vessel supplies .... 4221(a)(3)
.. shipments to U.S. possessions .... 7653(b)
. tobacco taxes 5704
. transportation of persons by air 4293
. wagering tax 4402

Exemptions
. dependents—see Dependents
. estate tax 2201
. personal—see Personal exemptions
. withholding .... 3402(f)

Expatriated entities 7874
. stock compensation of insiders 4985

Expatriation
. avoidance of tax 877
. estate tax 2107
. information returns 6039G
. mark-to-market tax imposed 877A

Expenses
. business—see Business expenses
. export promotion .... 971(d)
. nonbusiness—see Personal deductions

Experimental expenditures 174

Exploration
. deduction and recapture 617

Export promotion expenses defined .... 971(d)

Export shipments, exemption ...... 4221(a)(2)

Export trade assets
. defined .... 971(c)

Export trade corporations .... 970—971
. controlled foreign corporations ..... 971(a)(3)
. definition .... 971(a)

Export trade income
. defined .... 971(b)

Expropriation losses
. recoveries 80; 1351

Extensions of time
. estate tax payment .... 6166; 6601(j)
. filing returns 6081
. payment of tax—see Payment of tax: extension of time

F

Family and medical leave
. general business credit
.. employer credit for wages paid 45S

Family members
. expenses 262
. losses of .... 267(b)
. partnerships composed of .... 704(e)
. personal residence rented to .... 280A(d)
. treated as one shareholder of S corporation .... 1361(c)(1)

Farm property
. valuation of gross estate 2032A

Farmers and farming
. agricultural labor defined ... 3121(g); 3306(k)
. conservation expenditures 175
. contaminated livestock, involuntary conversion .... 1033(f)
. cooperatives—see Farmers cooperatives

Farmers and farming—continued
. corporations, accounting methods for ... 447
. crop insurance proceeds .... 451(f)
. crop, unharvested, sold with land 268
. disaster payments .... 451(f)
. discharge of indebtedness .... 108(g)
. estate tax
.. real estate, special use valuation ... 121(d)(8)
. estimated tax, failure to pay .... 6654(i)
. fertilizer costs, expensing of 180
. gain from disposition of farm land 1252
. gasoline tax refunds 6420
.. credit against tax 34
.. excessive amounts refunded, assessment and collection 6206
.. excessive claims, penalties 6675
. illegal federal irrigation subsidies 90
. income-averaging election 1301
. land clearing expenses
.. recapture 1252
. livestock—see Livestock
. losses
.. minimum tax .... 58(a)
. soil conservation expenditures 175
. special fuels tax, exemption .... 4041(f)
. unharvested crop sold with land 268
. water conservation expenditures 175

Farmers' cooperatives .... 1381—1383
. crop-financing organizations ..... 501(c)(16)
. dividends received from, dividends received deduction .... 246(a)
. exemption 521
. information returns 6044
. patronage dividends—see Patronage dividends
. per-unit retain allocations .... 1382(b)(3)

Farming syndicates
. deductions of expenses, limitations on ... 464
. defined .... 461(k)

Federal Bureau of Prisons
. requirement to provide prisoner information 6116

FASIT—see Financial asset securitization investment trust

Federal Communications Commission
. ordered exchanges, Sec. 1245 property .... 1245(b)(5)

Federal government employees
. charitable contributions on behalf of .. 7701(k)
. Social Security tax .... 3121(u)

Federal Insurance Contributions Act—see Social security taxes (FICA)

Federal National Mortgage Association
. basis of 1054
. cost of purchasing .... 162(d)

Federal officers and employees
. death in military action .... 692(c)
. disclosure of returns to ..... 6103(h); 6103(i)
. offenses of, penalties 7214
. unauthorized disclosure of information by, penalties 7213

Federal outlays and income, graphic presentation of major categories of .. 7523

Federal procurement payment
. foreign recipient, taxation 5000C

Federal Unemployment Tax Act—see Unemployment Tax Act (FUTA)

Federally declared disasters
. authority to postpone certain deadlines 7508A
. automatic extension of filing deadlines .... 7508A(d)
. establishment of amount of loss ... 165(i)(3)
. involuntary conversions .... 1033(h)

Feeder organizations .... 502; 511—515
. business lease rents and deductions ... 514
. foreign tax credit 515
. unrelated trade or business defined 513

Fees
. clubs, entertainment expenses ... 274(a)(2)
. Tax Court 7451

Feldspar, percentage depletion ...... 613(b)

Fertilizer costs, farmers' deduction 180

Fiduciaries .... 6901—6905

Fiduciaries—continued
. defined .... 7701(a)(6)
. information statement to beneficiaries of estates and trusts 6034A
. return requirements .... 6012(b)
. signing of returns by 6062

52-53 week year, accounting period .... 441(f)

55-year-olds and over, sales proceeds from residential property
. exclusion from gross income 121
.. election, time for making .... 121(c)
.. new residence sold or condemned, basis .... 121(d)(8)
.. partial use of residence for business .... 121(d)(5)
.. special rules .... 121(d)

Filing of returns
. place 6091
. time .... 6071—6072; 6075

Film and television productions
. expensing election 181

Finance companies, exception from definition of personal holding company .... 542(c)(6)

Financial entities
. discharge of indebtedness, information returns 6050P

Financial institutions
. credit card transactions
.. reporting requirements 6050W
. exempt income .... 265(b)
. FDIC premiums, deduction limitation ... 162(r)
. foreign
.. dividend equivalents, fixed or determinable annual or periodical income .... 871(m)
.. withholding, rules expanded 1471
. foreign transfers
.. withholding, electronic filing of returns .... 6011(e)(4)
. insolvent, deposits in
.. losses .... 165(l)

Fines, deductibility .... 162(f)
. reporting requirement 6050X

Fire losses
. deduction from gross income ...... 165(c)(3)
. estate tax, deductibility 2054

Firearms
. registration 5841
. taxes .... 4181; 4182; 5801—5872
. transfers 5812

FIRPTA (Foreign Investment in Real Property Tax Act of 1980) ... 861(a)(5); 897; 6039C

First 65 days rule, distributions by trusts .... 663(b)

First-time homebuyer credit 36
. exception, long-time resident ...... 36(c)(6)
. recapture of credit .... 36(f)

FISC .... 993(e)

Fiscal year accounting period .... 441(e)
. change to or from 442

Fish, resale of 6050R

Fishermen
. estimated tax, failure to pay .... 6654(i)
. FUTA exclusion .... 3306(c)(18)

Fishing boat operators
. FICA tax .... 3121(b)(20)
. information returns 6050A

Fishing business
. defined .... 1301(b)(4)
. income averaging 1301

Fishing equipment, excise tax .. 4161(a); 4162

Fishing rights of Indians, treaty-secured
. income derived from exercise of 7873

501(c)(3) bonds
. interest on 145

Flake graphite, percentage depletion .. 613(b)

Flexible spending arrangements (FSAs)
. long-term care benefits .... 106(c)
. rollover to health savings accounts ... 106(e)

5716 EXE

Topical Index
References are to Code Section numbers.

Floor stocks refunds 6412
Fluorspar deposits, percentage
  depletion . . . . 613(b)
Food stamps, disclosures of return
  information . . . . 6103(l)(7)
Foreclosure property, real estate investment
  trusts
. defined . . . . 856(e)
. income . . . . 857(b)(4)
Foreclosures and abandonments of security
. information returns 6050J
Foreign affiliates of domestic employers
. pension plan coverage for employees . . . 406
. social security coverage for employees . . 406; 3121(l)
Foreign areas allowances . . . . 912(1)
Foreign base company income 954
. banking or financing income . . . . 954(h)
. exclusions . . . . 954(b)
. export trade . . . . 970(a)
. insurance business income . . . . 954(i)
. sales income . . . . 954(d)
. services income . . . . 954(e)
Foreign capital gains and losses,
  limitation computations . . . . . 904(b)(3)(C)
Foreign central banks, interest from
  obligations of the U.S. 895
Foreign conventions
. entertainment expense deduction
.. Caribbean basin countries . . . . . . 274(h)(6)
.. substantiation . . . . 274(h)(1)
Foreign corporations . . . . 881—891; 898
. accumulated earnings tax . . . . 535(d)
. acquiring stock
.. target affiliate . . . . 338(h)
. base erosion minimum tax amount . . . 59A
. branch profits tax 884
. consent dividends . . . . 565(e)
. controlled—see Controlled foreign corporations (CFCs)
. corporate acquisition indebtedness,
  deductibility of . . . . 279(f)
. credits . . . . 33; 882(c)(3)
. definition . . . . 901(d); 7701(a)(5)
. dividends received from
.. corporate deduction . . . . 243(e); 245
.. domestic corporation recipient . . 861(a)(2)(B)
.. gross-up 78
. domestic corporation, treatment as . . . . 897(i)
. earnings and profits
.. determination of . . . . 986(a)
. exempt income 883
. export trade corporations . . . . 970—971
. failure to file returns 6679
. foreign ownership, information returns . 6038A
. foreign tax credit . . . . 901(b)(4); 906
. formation of, information returns 6046
. Guam and Mariana Islands corporations . . . . 881(b)
. imposition of tax on
.. nonresident foreign corporations . . . 881
.. resident foreign corporations 882
. information returns 6038; 6046
. engaged in U.S. business 6038C
. insurance business carried on, method
  of taxing 842
. intangibles, transfer of . . . . 367(d)
. interest received, portfolio debt
  investments . . . . 881(c)
. nonresident alien owned, taxable
  income . . . . 545(b)
. nonresident foreign corporations
.. dividends of regulated investment
   companies . . . . 881(e)
. original issue discount . . . . 881(a)(3)
. participation exemption deduction . . 91; 245A
. real property in U.S. owned by
.. sale or exchange . . . . 861(a)(5); 897; 1445; 6039C
. reciprocal penalty tax for discriminatory
  tax by foreign country 891; 896
. reorganizations 367
.. information returns 6046
. returns, due dates . . . . 6072(c)
. similar credit requirement, alien
  residents . . . . 901(c)

Foreign corporations—continued
. stapled stock 269B
. stock sold or exchanged, gain 1248
. stock transfers . . . . 304(b)(5)
. taxable year 898
. transportation income, tax on 887
. unrelated business income . . . . . 512(b)(17)
. Virgin Islands and American Samoa
  corporations . . . . 881(b)
. withholding of tax on—see Withholding of tax at source
Foreign countries
. credit for taxes—see Foreign tax credit
. discriminatory taxes, reprisal 891; 896
. taxes imposed by, credit . . 27; 642(a); 702; 841; 874; 882(c)(3); 901—908
Foreign currency
. contracts . . . . 1256(g)
. payment of tax in 6316
. transactions . . . . 985—989; 988(e)
. real estate investment trusts . . . . . 856(n)
Foreign death taxes
. deduction from value of gross estate . . 2053(d)
Foreign deferred compensation plans . . . . 404A(a)
Foreign embassies
. distilled spirits for use of 5066
Foreign estate defined . . . . . . 7701(a)(31)
Foreign expropriation losses
. defined . . . . 1351(b)
. capital loss . . . . 1212(a)
Foreign financial assets
. assets exceeding $50,000
.. reporting requirements 6038D
. information reporting
.. statute of limitations period extended
   . . . . 6501(c)(8)
. omission of income
.. statute of limitations period extended . . . . 6501(e)(1)(A)
. undisclosed assets
.. underpayment of tax penalty . . . . 6662(j)
Foreign gifts 6039F
Foreign governments
. bribe payments to officials and
  employees . . . . 162(c)(1)
. discriminatory taxes imposed, reciprocal
  penalty tax 891
. exempt income 892
.. compensation of foreign government
   employees 893
. expropriation of property, loss deduction
.. recoveries 80; 1351; 6167
. improper payments to officials of . . . 162(c)
Foreign income . . . . 901—937
. deduction v. exclusion . . . . 6011(d)
. election to exclude from gross income . 911(e)
. moving expense deduction . . . 217(h); 217(i)
Foreign insurance policies
. failure to pay tax, penalty 7270
Foreign items
. collection of, information returns . . . 6041(b)
. licensing for collection of 7001
.. failure to obtain license, penalties . . 7231
. tax preferences 59
Foreign loss, overall, recapture . . . 904(f)
Foreign officials, improper payments to . . . . 162(c)
Foreign oil and gas
. income 907
. loss
.. defined . . . . 907(c)(2)
.. recapture . . . . 907(c)(2)
. taxes . . . . 907(b)
Foreign organizations
. exemption . . . . 512(a)
. private foundations, taxes on 4948
Foreign parents
. expatriated entities 7874
Foreign partnership
. definition . . . . 7701(a)(5)
. information returns 6038
. interests 6046A

Foreign personal holding companies
. controlled foreign corporations, income . . . . 954(c)
. information returns 6046
. reorganizations, information returns . . 6046
Foreign persons or entities
. investment credit for property used by . . . . 50(b)(4)
. tax on federal procurement payment . . 5000C
Foreign private foundations
. dividend equivalents
.. fixed or determinable annual or
   periodical income . . . . 871(m)
Foreign Sales Corporations
. information requirements
.. failure to meet, penalties 6686
Foreign service allowances 912
Foreign shareholders
. domestic corporation . . . . 6039C(a)
Foreign sources, information returns
  from 982
Foreign students and exchange visitors
. compensation . . . . 872(b)(3)
. rates of tax . . . . 871(c)
. scholarships . . . . 1441(b)
. withholding exemptions . . . . 3402(f)(6)
Foreign tax credit . . . . 27; 901—909
. adjustments on payment of accrued
  taxes . . . . 905(c)
. allowance of credit . . . . 901(a)
. alternative minimum tax . . . . 59(e)(3)
. amount allowed . . . . 901(b)
. corporate . . . . 59(l)
. carryover by acquiring corporation,
  special limitations . . . . 383(c)
. controlled foreign corporations 960
.. stock sale . . . . 964(e)
. corporations treated as foreign . . . . 901(d)
. death taxes paid to foreign country 2014; 2016
. decedent's estate . . . . 691(b)
. deconsolidation, avoidance of limitations
  by . . . . 904(i)
. denial of credit . . . . 901(j); 901(m)
. determination of . . . . 986(a)
. dividends from noncontrolled section
  902 corporations
.. look-thru rule . . . . 904(d)
. domestic loss
.. recharacterization . . . . 904(g)
. estates and trusts . . . . 642(a)
. feeder organizations 515
. foreign mineral income . . . . 901(e)
. insurance companies 841
. international boycott, reduction for
  participation in 908
. limitations on credit 904
. matching rule, taxes and income . . . 909
. minimum holding period for certain taxes
  . . . . 901(k)
. nonresident aliens . . . . 874(c)
. oil and gas income, foreign . . . . . . 907(a)
. oil and gas properties
.. carryback or carryover of disallowed
   credits . . . . 907(f)
. oil and gas purchases and sales . . . 901(f); 907
. overall limitation . . . . 904(a); 904(b)
.. certain income, separate application of
   provision . . . . 904(d)
. per-country limitation . . . . 904(a)
. possessions corporation . . . . 901(g)
. proof of credits . . . . 905(b)
. reduction of
.. penalty . . . . 6038(c)
. regulated investment company
  shareholders 853
. source rules
.. U.S.-owned foreign corporations . . 904(h)
. subsidies, taxes used to provide . . . 901(i)
. taxes in lieu of income, war profits, and
  excess profits taxes 903
. year in which credit taken . . . . . . 905(a)
Foreign taxes
. credit for—see Foreign tax credit
. discriminatory, reciprocal penalty . . 891; 896
. oil and gas properties . . . . 907(b)

Foreign taxes—continued
. redetermination, failure to notify . . . . . 6689(a)
Foreign trusts . . . . 904(f)(4)
. accumulation distributions
. . interest charge on 668
. creation of or transfers to, information
. . returns 6048
. . failure to file returns 6677
. definition . . . . 7701(a)(31)
. distributions by
. . distributable net income . . . . 643(a)(6)
. . distributions through nominees . . . 643(i)
. . loans from . . . . 643(i)
. reporting requirements
. . owners . . . . 6048(b)(1)
. . penalty 6677
. situs . . . . 404(a)(4)
. . taxability of proceeds . . . . 402(d)
. tax paid by beneficiary . . . . 667(d)
. transfers of property to, gain recognition . . 684
. trust property
. . uncompensated use treated as
. . . distribution . . . . 679(c)(6)
. U.S. beneficiaries 679
. . presumptive treatment . . . . 679(d)
Forfeitures . . . . 7301—7328
. firearms tax violations 5872
. liquor tax violations . . . . 5601—5690
. tobacco tax violations 5763
**Foster care payments, exclusion from
gross income** 131
Foster child as dependent . . . . 152(f)(1)(C)
Foundations—see Private foundations
Fractional parts of a cent disregarded . . 6313
Fractional parts of a dollar disregarded . . 7504
Fractional parts of a year, returns 443
Franchises
. capital gains and losses 1253
Fraternal societies
. contributions to . . . . 170(c)
. exemption from tax . . . . 501(c)(8)
. lodge system organizations, exempt
. . status . . . . 501(c)(10)
. gifts to 2522
. transfers to, estate tax 2055
**Fraternities, college, domestic
employees, exemption from withholding** . . .
. . . . 3401(a)(3)
Fraud
. criminal prosecutions, statute of
. . limitations 6531
. damages for fraudulent returns filed by
. . third party 7434
. deficiency dividends deduction
. . disallowed because of . . . . 547(g)
. detection of, informer's rewards 7623
. . anti-retaliation protection for
. . . whistleblower employees . . . . . 7623(d)
. . whistleblower reward program . . . 7623(b)
. innocent spouse rule . . . . 6013(e)
. penalties for . . . . 6674; 7201—7207
Fringe benefits
. excess
. . excise tax, employer 4977
. . gross income, exclusion 132
. . plans, information returns 6039D
Frivolous tax submissions 6702
Fuel cell motor vehicle credit . . . . . . 30B(b)
**Fuel production credit, nonconventional
source** 45K
Fuels for nontaxable uses
. off-highway business use . . . . 4041(b)
Fuels tax
. credits
. . information reporting 4104
. . two-party exchanges 4105
Funding standards, retirement plans—see
Retirement plans: funding standards, minimum
Fundraising solicitations
. contributions, statement of
. . nondeductibility 6113
. . failure to provide, penalty 6710
Funeral expenses, estate tax 2053

FOR

Topical Index
References are to Code Section numbers.

Funeral trusts 685

G

Gain or loss
. amount, determination of 1001
. appreciated property distributed by
. . corporation . . . . 311(b)
. basis, adjusted 1011
. built-in gains
. . loss corporations 384
. capital—see Capital gains and losses
. coal sold 631
. computation 1001
. condemnation of property . . . . 1231(a)
. contributions to capital of partnership . . . 721
. exchanges—see Exchanges of property
. installment obligations disposed of . . 453B
. installment sales . . . . 1001(d)
. insurance policies exchanged 1035
. involuntary conversions . . . . . . 1033; 1231(a)
. liquidations . . . . 331—346
. . shareholder . . . . 331(a)
. money received in exchange for stock . . 1032
. natural resources sold 631
. partnerships
. . capital contribution of partner to 721
. . disposition of contributed property . . 724
. . disposition of distributed property . . 735
. . distributions of 731
. . interest transferred 741
. . precontribution gain on contributed
. . . property 737
. property received in exchange for stock . . 1032
. real property, U.S. 897
. recognition . . . . 1001(c)
. regulated futures contracts marked to
. . market 1234A; 1256
. sale of property to comply with conflict-
. . of-interest requirements 1043
. sales of stock to employee stock
. . ownership plans 1042
. securities futures contracts 1234B
. stock disposed of
. . controlled corporations . . . . 355(e)
. . preferred stock bail-out 306
. . treasury stock 1032
. straddles 1092; 1234A
. term interests sold . . . . 1001(e)
. timber sold 631
. transfers of property between spouses
. . or incident to divorce 1041
Gallonage taxes
. distilled spirits, wines and beer . . . 5001—5068
Gambling
. excise tax . . . . 4401—4405
. Indian casino profits, withholding on . . 3402(r)
. losses . . . . 165(d)
. winnings
. . nonresident aliens . . . . 871(j)
. . withholding tax . . . . 3402(q)
Gas guzzler tax . . . . 1016(d); 4064; 4217(e)
Gas property
. depletion . . . . 611; 613(b)
**Gas royalties, personal holding
company income** . . . . 543(a)(3)
Gasoline taxes
. definitions 4083
. diesel fuel, exemption for 4082
. farmers' refunds 6420
. credit against tax 34
. excessive amounts refunded,
. . assessment and collection 6206
. gasoline mixture . . . . 4081(c)
. manufacturers excise tax . . . . . . 4081—4083
. . alcohol mixture . . . . 4081(c)
. refunds and credits 6420
. . credit against tax 34
. . excessive amounts refunded,
. . . assessment and collection 6206
. . excessive claims, penalties 6675
. registration and bond of taxpayers . . . 4101
. failure to register or false statement,
. . penalty 7232
. state
. . deductibility . . . . 164(b)(4)
. willful failure to pay, persons liable . . . 4103

General business credit 38
. family medical leave payments
. . employer credit for wages paid 45S
. ordering rules . . . . 38(d)
. special rules . . . . 38(c)
. New York Liberty Zone . . . . 38(c)(3)
. unused business credits
. . deduction for 196
General sales taxes, state and local
. deductibility
. . in lieu of state and local income taxes . . .
. . . . 164(b)
Generation-skipping transfers . . . 2601—2663
. administration 2661
. alternate valuation . . . . 667(b)(6)
. amount of tax
. . exemption . . . . 2631—2632
. . inclusion ratio 2642
. . inflation adjustment . . . . 2631(c)
. . taxable amount in case of direct skip . . 2623
. . taxable amount in case of taxable
. . . distribution 2621
. . taxable amount in case of taxable
. . . termination 2622
. assignment of generation 2651
. basis adjustment . . . . 2654(a)
. deceased parent . . . . 2651(e)
. definitions, miscellaneous 2652
. disclaimers . . . . 2654(c)
. generation assignment . . . . 2651(e)
. gift tax 2515
. imposition of tax 2601
. . definition of generation-skipping
. . . transfer 2611
. . direct skip 2612
. . liability for 2603
. . multiple skips 2653
. . skip person and non-skip person . . . 2613
. . taxable terminations and distributions . . 2612
. . transfer affected 2601
. income in respect of decedent
. . estate tax deduction . . . . 691(c)(3)
. rate of tax 2641
. regulations, authority to promulgate . . 2663
. return requirements 2662
. trustees, limitation of personal liability . . 2654(d)
. valuation 2624
Geopressurized gas equipment . . 613A(b)(3)(C)
Geothermal deposits
. at-risk limitation for losses in developing . . .
. . . . 465(e)(1)
. depletion . . . . 613(e)
. intangible drilling costs . . . . 57(a)(2)
Gift tax . . . . 2501—2524
. abatement claims . . . . 6404(b)
. annual exclusion . . . . 2503(b)
. bankruptcy and receivership . . 6161(c); 6871—6873
. basis of property, inclusion . . . . 1015(d)
. charitable contributions deduction,
. . disallowance . . . . 2522(c)
. . easements in real property . . . . . . 2522(d)
. charitable gifts of copyrighted artwork . . .
. . . . 2522(c)(3)
. credit against 2505
. credit against estate tax 2012
. deductions in computing . . . . . 2522—2524
. deficiencies . . . . 6211—6216
. disclaimers 2518
. generation-skipping transfers, treatment
. . of 2515
. husband and wife
. . charitable remainder trusts, special
. . . rule . . . . 2523(g)
. . election, life estate for donee-spouse . . 2523(f)
. imposition of tax 2501
. jeopardy assessment 6861
. lien for tax . . . . 6324(b)
. marital deduction
. . right of recovery of property 2207A
. possessions' residents considered
. . nonresidents not citizens of U.S. . . . 2501(c)
. possessions' residents considered U.S.
. . citizens 2208
. powers of appointment 2514
. property settlement agreements 2516
. rate of tax 2502

Gift tax—continued
. returns 6019
. . due date . . . . 6075(b)
. split-interest transfers
. . election . . . . 2523(f)
. . special rule for remainder charitable
trusts . . . . 2523(g)
. statement explaining valuation for,
furnishing of 7517
. transfers . . . . 2035; 2511—2519

Gifts
. . . . 170
. basis for gain or loss 1015
. business gifts, deduction of cost . . . . 274(b)
. . substantiation of expenditures . . . . 274(d)
. exempt income 102
. large gifts from foreign persons 6039F
. Section 1245 property . . . . 1245(b)(1)
. Section 1250 property . . . . 1250(d)(1)
. taxable gifts defined . . . . 2503(a)
. valuation of 2512

Golden parachute payments 280G
. excise tax imposed 4999
. limitations
. . Troubled Assets Relief Program . . . 280G(e)

Goodwill
. amortization 197

Government depositaries, payment of
tax to . . . . 5703(c); 6302(c)
. electronic fund transfer system . . . . . 6302(h)
. failure to make 6656; 7215; 7512

Government obligations, interest on . . . . 103; 141—150

Governmental employer, return and
payment of tax by 3404

Governmental excess benefit
arrangements . . . 415(m); 457(e)(14); 457(g)

Governmental unit, investment credit
for property used by . . . . 50(b)(4)

Granite, percentage depletion . . . . 613(b)

Grantor trusts . . . . 671—679
. administrative powers 675
. foreign person as grantor . . . . 672(f)
. income for benefit of grantor 677
. power to control beneficial enjoyment in
grantor 674
. reversionary interests 673
. revocable trusts 676

Graphic presentation of major
categories of federal outlays and income . . .
. . . . 7523

Graphite, percentage depletion . . . . . . 613(b)

Grass roots expenditures . . . . 501(h)
. definition 4911

Greenmail, excise tax on 5881

Gross estate . . . . 2031—2046
. defined 2103

Gross income
. adjusted gross income 62
. alimony payments received 71
. annuities, amounts received as 72
. . railroad retirement benefits, tier 2 . . 72(r)
. awards 74
. Commodity Credit loans 77
. controlled taxpayers, allocation among . . . 482
. dealers in tax-exempt securities 75
. deferred compensation
. . nonqualified deferred compensation
plans 409A
. defined . . . . 61(a)
. exclusions—see Exempt income
. fringe benefits 132
. indebtedness, discharge of . . . . 108(a)
. military benefits 134
. nonresident aliens 872
. prizes 74
. property transferred in connection with
performance of service 83
. railroad retirement benefits, tier 1 86
. railroad retirement benefits, tier 2 . . . . 72(r)
. railroad unemployment insurance act,
sick pay . . . . 105(i)
. reimbursed moving expenses 82

Gross income—continued
. scholarships . . . . 117(a)
. social security and tier 1 railroad
retirement benefits 86
. tuition reduction . . . . 117(d)
. unemployment compensation 85

Gross income requirement, personal
holding companies . . . . 542(a)(1)

Gross-up of dividends, foreign tax credit
purposes 78

Ground rents
. mortgage interest . . . . 163(c); 1055

Group health plans . . . . 9801—9834
. air ambulance claims
. . reports 9823
. air ambulance services
. . out-of-network providers 9817
. continuation coverage
. . failure to satisfy requirements, excise
tax imposed 4980B
. continuity-of-care requirements 9818
. cost-sharing
. . price comparison tool 9819
. . provider directory information 9820
. definitions 9832
. dependent students
. . medical leave, continuation of
coverage 9813
. discrimination based on genetic
information prohibited 9802
. discrimination based on health status
prohibited 9802
. emergency services, coverage
. . out-of-network providers 9816
. enrollment period
. . Medicaid or CHIP coverage, change in
eligibility . . . . 9801(f)(3)
. failure to meet requirements, excise tax . . . .
. . . . 4980D
. maternity stay mandates 9811
. mental health benefit parity 9812
. . substance use disorders 9812
. new market reforms 9815
. nonconforming, contributions to
imposition of tax 5000
. out-of-network providers
. . air ambulance services 9817
. . emergency services, coverage 9816
. patient protections
. . access to care 9822
. . portability . . . . 9801—9803
. . preexisting condition exclusion limitation . . 9801
. price and quality information
. . gag clauses, prohibition 9824
. . price comparison tool 9819
. . provider directory information 9820
. renewability in multiemployer plans . . 9803
. report requirements
. . air ambulance services 9823
. . drug costs 9825
. . pharmacy benefits 9825
. requirements, exceptions 9831
. . qualified small employer health
reimbursement arrangements . . . 9831(d)

Group legal service organizations, exempt
status
. nondiscrimination requirements 505

Group-term life insurance 79
. cost determination, uniform premium
table method . . . . 79(c)
. deduction of tax from wages . . . 3102(d); 3202(d)
. employee taxed on part of employer's
cost 79
. employees exempted from provisions . . 79
. former employees . . . . 79(e)
. information returns 6052
. nondiscrimination . . . . 79(d)
. retirement plans, exemption 79
. returns regarding payment of wages in
the form of 6052

Guam
. coordination of individual income tax . . . 7654
. . penalties for failure to furnish
information 6688
. foreign corporations, exception . . . . . 881(b)

Guam—continued
. governmental employees, return and
payment of tax . . . . 3125(b)
. income from sources within 931
. residents of, self-employment tax . . 1402(a)(9)
. residents of, tax on 876

H

Halon 1211
. excise tax on imported, recycled
. . repeal of exemption . . . . 4682(d)(1)

Handicapped persons
. architectural and transportation barrier
removal, expenses of 190

Harbor maintenance
. Alaska, Hawaii, and possessions . . . 4462(b)
. excise tax . . . . 4461—4462
. . nonapplicability to exports . . . . . . 4462(d)
. trust fund 9505
. management 9602

Hawaii
. empowerment zones
. . special eligibility . . . . 1392(d)
. harbor maintenance excise tax
exemption . . . . 4462(b)

Hazardous substances
. trust fund 9507
. . management 9602

Head of household
. defined . . . . 2(b)(1)
. rate of tax . . . . 1(b)
. status, determination . . . . . . 2(b)(2); 2(b)(3)

Health accounts, transfers of excess
pension assets to employee 420

Health and accident plans
. benefits received 105
. dependent students
. . medical leave, continuation of
coverage 9813
. employer contributions 106
. group health plans—see Group health plans
. Indian tribal governments
. . benefits excluded from gross income . . 139D
. mental health parity requirements 9812
. new market reforms 9815
. reporting requirements
. . employer-sponsored coverage cost . . . . . .
. . . . 6051(a)(14)
. . minimum essential coverage, large
employers 6056

Health care coverage—see Group health plans

Health care coverage providers on a
not-for-profit basis, exemption . . 501(c)(26)

Health care professionals
. student loans
. . repayment assistance, exclusion from
gross income . . . . 108(f)(4)

Health flexible spending arrangements
. contributions limited . . . . 125(i)
. distributions
. . use for menstrual care products . . . . 106(f)
. unused benefits, individuals called to
active duty . . . . 125(h)

Health insurance
. employer-sponsored plans
. . cost reported on Form W-2 . . . 6051(a)(14)
. . minimum essential coverage, large
employers 6056
. group health plans—see also Group health
plans
. . new market reforms 9815
. health coverage tax credit 35
. . advance payment 7527
. . election . . . . 35(g)(11)
. . eligible individual defined . . . . 35(c)
. . qualified health insurance . . . . 35(e)
. . returns 6050T
. minimum essential coverage
. . reporting requirements 6055; 6056

Health insurance benefits . . . . 104(a)(3); 105(a)
. coal industry . . . . 9701—9722

Topical Index
References are to Code Section numbers.

Health insurance providers
. excessive employee remuneration,
. . deduction limitation . . . . 162(m)(6)
. reporting requirements
. . minimum essential coverage 6055

Health reimbursement arrangements (HRAs)
. distributions
. . use for menstrual care products . . . 106(f)
. rollover to health savings accounts . . . 106(e)

Health savings accounts (HSAs) 223
. adjusted gross income . . . . 62(a)(19)
. contributions by employer . . . . 106(d)
. . annual limit . . . . 223(b)(2)
. . part-year coverage limit . . . . 223(b)(8)
. defined . . . . 223(d)(1)
. distributions . . . . 223(f)
. . use for menstrual care products . 223(d)(2)(A)
. . use for nonqualified medical
. . . expenses, additional tax . . . . . 223(f)(4)
. eligibility
. . veterans disability benefits . . . . 223(c)(1)(C)
. failure of employer to make comparable
. . contributions 4980G
. rollovers
. . flexible spending arrangements . . . . 106(e)
. . health reimbursement arrangements . 106(e)
. . IRAs . . . . 408(d)(9)

Hedge bonds . . . . 149(g)

Heir, included as transferee . . . . 6901(h)

**Higher education expenses, U.S.
savings bonds for** 135

Highways
. motor vehicle use tax . . . . 4481—4484
. trust fund for 9503
. . taxes transferred to . . . . 9503(b)(4)

Historic structures
. demolition expenses, deductibility of . . . 280B

Hobby losses 183

Holding period 1223
. involuntarily converted property 1223

Holiday as last day for performing acts . 7503

Home office expenses 280A

Homeowners' associations
. defined . . . . 528(c)
. return requirements . . . . 6012(a)(7)
. tax on 528

Hope credit for higher education—see American opportunity credit

Horticultural organizations
. dues, unrelated business income . . . . 512(d)
. exemption . . . . 501(c)(5)

Hospital insurance
. rates of tax . . . . 3101(b)
. self-employment tax . . . . 1401(b)

**Hospital service organizations,
cooperative** . . . . 501(e)

**Household and dependent care services
expenses**
. credit against tax 21
. dollar limit on amount creditable . . . . . 21(c)
. earned income limitation . . . . 21(d)
. taxpayer identification numbers . . . . . 21(e)

Humane societies—see Anti-cruelty societies

Husband and wife
. alimony—see Alimony and separate
. . maintenance
. community property, separate return . . . 66(a)
. defined . . . . 7701(a)(17)
. different taxable years . . . . 6013(a)(2)
. estate tax
. . marital deduction 2056
. gifts to spouse
. . deduction in computing gift tax 2523
. . dispositions, life estates 2519
. . election, life estate for donee-spouse . 2523(f)
. . special rule, charitable remainder
. . . trusts . . . . 2523(g)
. gifts to third party, gift tax 2513
. innocent spouse relief
. . partner's spouse . . . . 6230(a)(3)
. joint returns 6013
. . disclosure of collection activities on
. . . spouse . . . . 6103(e)(8)
. . marital status determination . . . 105(d)(5)

Husband and wife—continued
. joint returns—continued
. . self-employment tax 6017
. . personal exemptions . . . . 151(b)
. . retirement accounts, deductibility of
. . . contributions to . . . . 219(c)
. . separate household, joint returns,
. . . special rules . . . . 105(d)(5)
. . 65 and over
. . . residence sale proceeds . . . . 121(d)
. transfers of property between spouses
. . or incident to divorce
. . nonrecognition of gain 1041

Hybrid entities or transactions
. related party payments 267A

I

Identifying numbers for taxpayers 6109

Identity theft
. notification 7529
. refund fraud . . . . 6103(k)(13)
. return preparer
. . enhanced penalty . . . . 6713(b)

Illegal payments . . . . 162(c)
. business expenses 280E
. foreign government officials, payments
. . to . . . . 952(a)

Illness, compensation for 104

Ilmenite, percentage depletion . . . . . . 613(b)

Imported property
. alternative depreciation . . . . 168(g)

Improper accumulation of surplus—see
Accumulated earnings tax

Improvements
. capital expenditures 263
. lessee making 109
. . adjusted basis 1019
. . exclusion from gross income of lessor . . 109

**Imputed interest, deferred payment
sales** 483

Incentive stock options 422
. carryover of unused limit . . . . 422(c)(4)
. definition . . . . 422(b)
. disabled persons, special rule . . . . . 422(c)(6)
. dispositions where amount realized is
. . less than value of exercise . . . . . 422(c)(2)
. exercise when price is less than value of
. . stock . . . . 422(c)(1)
. fair market value . . . . 422(c)(7)
. $100,000 per year limitation . . . . . . 422(d)
. tax preference item . . . . 57(a)(3)
. ten-percent shareholder . . . . 422(c)(5)
. transfers by insolvent individuals . . . 422(c)(3)

Income
. adjusted gross income—see Adjusted gross
. . income
. allocation among related taxpayers 482
. annualizing . . . . 443(b)
. common trust funds 584
. decedents 691; 692
. estates and trusts . . . . 643(b)
. exempt—see Exempt income
. expenses for production of 212
. foreign personal holding companies—see
. . Foreign personal holding companies
. foreign, tax-exempt, withholding on . . . 1443
. . payment of withheld tax 1461
. ordinary v. capital gains
. . anti-conversion rules 1258
. . partners 702
. possessions of the United States,
. . income from sources within 931
. . production of, expenses 212
. . Puerto Rican sources 933
. sources outside United States . 862; 901—989
. sources partly within and partly without
. . United States 863
. . international communications income
. . . . 863(e)
. . space and ocean activities . . . . . . 863(d)
. . transportation income . . . . 863(c)
. sources within the United States 861
. sources without the United States 862

Income averaging
. farmers and fishermen 1301

Income forecast method of depreciation . . .
. . . . 167(g)

Income in respect of a decedent . . 61(a)(14)
. generation-skipping transfer
. . estate tax deduction . . . . 691(c)(3)

Indebtedness
. assumed—see Liabilities assumed
. bad debts—see Bad debts
. business, qualified . . . . 108(c)
. discharge of, exclusion from gross
. . income . . . . 108; 1017(b)
. . reduction of basis 1017
. interest on—see Interest paid; Interest received

**Independent contractors, deferred
compensation plans** . . . . 404(d)

Independent Office of Appeals . . . . . 7803(e)

Indexing of taxes
. income tax brackets . . . . 1(f)
. personal exemption . . . . 151(d)

Indian employment credit 45A

Indian reservations
. empowerment zones, exclusion from . . .
. . . . 1393(a)(4)
. property, accelerated cost recovery
. . system . . . . 168(j)

Indian tribal governments
. general welfare benefits
. . exclusion from gross income 139E
. health care benefits
. . exclusion from gross income 139D

Indians
. articles produced by, exemption from
. . manufacturers excise tax 4225
. casino profits, withholding on . . . . . 3402(r)
. fishing rights secured by treaty, income . 7873
. tribal governments treated as states . . . 7871
. . excise tax exemptions . . . . 7871(b)
. . general rule . . . . 7871(a)
. . subdivisions of tribal government . . 7871(d)
. . tax-exempt bonds . . . . 7871(c)
. . tribal economic development bonds . . 7871(f)

Individual retirement accounts 408
. active participants, pension plans
. . limitation on deduction . . . . 219(g)
. annuity defined . . . . 408(b)
. backloaded (Roth) IRAs 408A
. borrowings, effect on annuity contract . . .
. . . . 408(e)(3)
. community property laws, effect . . . . 408(g)
. contributions to, deductibility 219
. . adjusted gross income computation . . .
. . . . 62(a)(7)
. . combat zone compensation, inclusion
. . . in gross income . . . . 219(f)(7)
. . correction of excess contribution . . 219(f)(6);
. . . . 408(d)(5)
. . extension of time for making . . . 408(d)(5)
. . time for making . . . . 219(f)(3)
. . correction of excess contribution . . 219(f)(6);
. . . . 408(d)(5)
. custodial accounts . . . . 408(h)
. deemed IRAs . . . . 408(q)
. definitions . . . . 219(e); 7701(a)(37)
. distributions by, tax treatment . . . . . 408(d)
. . first-time homebuyers . . . . 72(t)(8)
. divorce, transfer of account . . . . . 408(d)(6)
. divorced individuals . . . . 219(b)(4)
. endowment contract purchased by . . 408(e)(5)
. excess contributions, excise tax 4973
. exempt status . . . . 408(e)(1)
. loss of, prohibited transactions . . . . 408(e)(2)
. increased deduction . . . . 4973(b)(2)
. inherited accounts . . . 219(d)(4); 408(d)(3)(C)
. investment in collectibles . . . . 408(m)
. Kay Bailey Hutchison Spousal IRA . . . 219(c)
. limitations
. . amounts contributed under
. . . endowment contract . . . . 219(d)(3)
. . individuals aged 70½ . . . . 219(d)(1)
. . recontributed amounts . . . . 219(d)(2)
. married persons' contributions,
. . deductibility . . . . 219(c)
. nondeductible contributions
. . special rules and definitions . . . . . 408(o)
. pledge of account as security, effect . 408(e)(4)
. qualifying accounts . . . . 408(c)

HEA

Individual retirement accounts—continued
. reports . . . . 408(i)
. . failure to furnish, penalty 6693
. returns . . . . 6058(d); 6058(e)
. rollovers—see also Rollovers
. . health savings accounts, rollovers to . . . . 408(d)(9)
. . . inherited accounts . . . . 408(d)(3)(C)
. . . partial . . . . 408(d)(3)(D)
. . Roth IRAs 408A
. . excess contributions to . . . . 4973(f)
. simplified employee pensions
. . . definition . . . . 408(k)
. . . maximum limitation . . . . 408(j)

Individuals
. activities not engaged in for profit 183
. bankrupt, rules for . . . . 1398(a)
. charitable contributions 170
. credits—see Credits against tax
. deductions . . . . 161—224
. estimated tax—see Estimated tax, individuals
. fiscal-year basis, proration of tax 15
. foreign tax credit . . . . 901(b)(1)
. gross income, inclusions in . . . . 71—90
. head-of-household rates . . . . 1(b)
. minimum tax for tax preferences 5559
. moving expenses—see Moving expenses
. personal exemptions 151
. . exemption amount defined . . . . 151(d)
. rates of tax . . . . 1—3
. . change during year 15
. . head of household . . . . 1(b)
. . indexing income tax brackets . . . . 1(f)
. . phaseout of marriage penalty . . . . 1(f)
. . rate reductions after 2000 . . . . 1(i)
. retirement accounts—see Individual retirement accounts
. returns . . . . 6012(a)(1)
. . place for filing . . . . 6091(b)(1)
. . time for filing . . . . 6072(a)
. tax preferences
. . 10-year writeoff . . . . 59(e)
. tax tables 3
. taxable income less than $20,000 3
. unmarried, rates of tax . . . . 1(c)

Information returns . . . . 6031—6053
. address and phone number of
     information contact . . . . 6041(d)
. alcohol fuels tax credit 4104
. banks maintaining common trust funds . . 6032
. biodiesel tax credit 4104
. brokers 6045
. . broker-to-broker transactions 6045A
. . exceptions for sales or exchanges of
     certain principal residences 6045
. . carryover basis property acquired from
     decedent 6039A
. cash receipts of more than $10,000 . . . . 6050I
. cash received in trade or business 6050I
. charitable deduction property,
     dispositions of 6050L
. charitable hospitals . . . . 6033(b)(15)
. citizenship, individuals losing 6039G
. Commodity Credit Corporation 6039J
. compensation for services . . . . 6041A(a)
. corporations
. . foreign ownership 6038A
. deferred compensation plans . . . 6058; 6652(e)
. discharge of indebtedness 6050P
. disclosure . . . . 7217(b)
. dissolution of corporation 6043
. dividend payments 6042
. employee stock ownership plans . . . . . 6047(e)
. energy grants and financing 6050D
. estates and trusts, beneficiaries 6034A
. exempt organizations 6033
. failure to file 6652
. failure to file correct 6721
. failure to keep records for 6704
. federal executive agencies, persons
     receiving contracts from 6050M
. fish, resale of 6050R
. fishing boat operators 6050A
. foreclosures and abandonments of
     security 6050J
. foreign corporations 6038
. . engaged in U.S. business 6038C
. foreign partnership interests 6046A

Information returns—continued
. foreign persons holding United States
     property interests 6039C
. foreign sources, request for 982
. foreign trusts, creation of or transfers to . 6048
. fraudulent returns filed by third party,
     damages 7434
. fringe benefit plans 6039D
. group-term life insurance 6052
. health insurance costs of eligible
     individuals
. . credit 6050T
. health insurance coverage 6055; 6056
. individual retirement accounts . . . . . . 408(i)
. information contact, address and phone
     number of . . . . 6041(d)
. insurance contracts
. . interest in, acquisition 6050V
. interest payments 6049
. life insurance contracts
. . employer-owned 6039I
. liquidation of corporation 6043
. long-term care benefits 6050Q
. long-term care insurance riders on
     annuity and life insurance contracts . 6050U
. mortgage insurance premiums . . . . . 6050H(h)
. mortgage interest received in trade or
     business from individuals 6050H
. nonprofit health insurance issuers . . . 6033(m)
. partnership 6031
. partnership interests exchanged 6050K
. patronage dividends 6044
. payments of $600 or more . . . . 6041(a)
. political organizations . . . . 6033(g)
. qualified small employer health
     reimbursement arrangements
. . failure to provide written notice . . . 6652(o)
. railroad retirement benefits 6050G
. real estate transactions . . . . 6045(e)
. reasonable verification of returns . . . . 6201(d)
. resident status 6039E
. retirement plans 6047; 6057
. fraudulent statement or failure to
     furnish statement to plan participant,
     penalty 6690
. royalties, payments of 6050N
. S corporations 6037
. securities issuers
. . basis, organizational actions affecting 6045B
. sick pay, third-party paid 6051
. social security benefits 6050F
. state and local tax refunds 6050E
. statements to payees . . . . 6042(c)
. stock options 6039
. tax return preparers 6060
. $10 or more in dividends, payments of . . . . 6042(a)(1)(A)
. tip income . . . . 6053(c)
. transfers to foreign persons 6038B
. trusts claiming charitable deductions . . . 6034
. unauthorized 7213A
. unemployment compensation 6050B
. withholding of income tax on wages,
     receipts for employees 6051

Information technology
. positions
. . critical pay authority 7812
Information, unauthorized disclosure . . . 7213
Informers, rewards for . . . . 7214(a); 7623
Inheritance
. basis to recipient 1014
. exempt 102
. life or terminable interest acquired by . . 273
Inheritance tax—see Estate tax
Injunctions
. political expenditures of exempt
     organizations 7409
Injuries or sickness, compensation for . . 104—106; 130
Inland waterways
. trust fund for 9506
Inland waterways use tax 4042
Innocent spouse relief 6015
. fraud cases . . . . 6013(e)

Innocent spouse relief—continued
. partner's spouse
. . special rules . . . . . . 6230(a)(3); 6230(c)(5)
Insolvent banks, exemption from tax . . . 7507
**Inspection of books and records,
     wagering tax enforcement** 4423
Inspection of returns 6103
. exempt organizations 6104
. petroleum products tax 4102
. private foundations' annual reports . . . 6104(d)
Inspection of written determinations . . . 6110
Installment method of accounting 453
. carryover by acquiring corporation . . . 381(c)(8)
. definitions and special rules . . . . . . 453(f)
. election out of . . . . 453(d)
. nondealers of real property, special
     rules 453A
. shareholders in Sec. 337 liquidations . . 453(h)
Installment obligations
. basis of . . . . 453B(b)
. canceled or unenforceable . . . . 453B(f)
. gain or loss on disposition 453B
. life insurance companies, transfers to
     controlled companies . . . . 453B(e)
. liquidation distributions . . . . 453B(d)
. S corporations . . . . 453B(h)
. S corporations, liquidating distributions
     of . . . . 453B(h)
. sale by manufacturer . . . . 4216(c)
. transmission at death . . . . 453B(c)
Installment payment of tax
. agreements for 6159
. application, frivolous submission . . . . 7122(g)
. fees . . . . 6159(f)
. notice of change in agreement . . . . . 6159(b)(5)
. overpayment credited against unpaid
     installments 6403
Installment sales
. dealer dispositions . . . . 453(l)
. imputed interest 483
. related parties . . . . 483(f)
. installment method of accounting 453
. election out of . . . . 453(d)
. interest charge not separately stated,
     deduction . . . . 163(b)
. revolving credit plans . . . . 453(j)
. sale of depreciable property to spouse
     or 80-percent owned entity . . . . 453(g)
. Sec. 179 property . . . . 453(i)
. second dispositions by related persons . . . . 453(e)
. selling price not readily ascertainable . . 453(j)
Instrumentalities of the United States
. exemption . . . . 501(c)(1)
. Federal Insurance Contributions Act
     taxes 3112
Insurance
. deductibility of amounts paid for 264
. foreign insurer issuing policy, excise tax
     on . . . . 4371—4374
. long-term care premium statements,
     reports relating to 6050Z
. policies exchanged, nonrecognition of
     gain or loss 1035
. premiums, interest on loans to pay 264
. pro rata interest disallowance . . . . . . 264(f)
. proceeds received . . . . 101; 104—106
Insurance companies . . . . 801—848
. accounting periods 843
. Blue Cross, Blue Shield organizations . . . 833
. companies other than life insurance
     tax on 831
. consolidated return . . . . 1503(b); 1504(c)
. defined . . . . 816(a); 831(c)
. discounted unpaid losses 846
. exempt status . . . . 501(c)(15)
. foreign tax credit 841
. interinsurers . . . . 832(f)
. lease guaranty insurance written,
     special deduction . . . . 832(e)(6)
. life insurance companies—see also Life
     insurance companies . . . . 801—818
. long-term care contracts, issuer
     requirements 4980C
. marine, mutual 831; 832

Topical Index
References are to Code Section numbers.

Insurance companies—continued
. mortgage guaranty insurance written,
. . special deduction . . . . 832(e)
. mutual
. . reciprocal, election by 835
. policy acquisition costs, capitalization of . . 848
. reinsurance agreements, tax avoidance
. . or evasion 845
. small companies, alternative tax . . . . 831(b)
. state and local obligation insurance
. . written, special deduction . . . . . . 832(e)(6)
. successor, carryovers by . . . . 381(c)(22)
. taxable income 832
. taxable investment income 834

**Insurance contracts, amounts received
for living expenses** 123

Intangible assets (Sec. 197 intangibles)
. amortization 197

Intangible drilling and development costs
. oil and gas wells . . . . 263(c)
. . incurrence outside the United States . . 263(i)
. . tax preference item . . . . 57(a)(2)
. . writeoff . . . . 59(e)
. . straight line recovery, tax preferences . 57(b)

Interest forgone, defined . . . . 7872(e)(2)

Interest on deficiencies 6601
. abatement 6404
. notice of charges 6631
. rate, determination 6621
. suspension 6603

Interest on overpayments 6611

Interest paid
. cooperative housing tenant stockholders . . 216
. corporations
. . disqualified debt instruments . . . . . . 163(l)
. debt-financed acquisitions—see Debt-financed
. . acquisitions
. deduction 163
. . registered obligations . . . . 163(f)
. deferred payment 483
. education loans 221
. financial institutions 265
. information returns 6049
. . reporting of credit on clean renewable
. . . energy bonds . . . . 6049(d)(8)
. insurance purchased with borrowed
. . funds 264
. investment indebtedness, limitation . . . 163(d)
. loans to pay insurance premiums 264
. loans with below-market interest rates . . 7872
. mortgage 25
. mortgage insurance premiums . . . 163(h)(3)(E)
. original issue discount . . . . 163(e)
. . high yield obligations . . . . . 163(e)(5); 163(i)
. overpayments, IRS paid 6611
. personal interest . . . . 163(h)
. prepaid, method of accounting . . . . . . 461(g)
. pro rata interest disallowance . . . . . . 264(f)
. related person, limitation . . . . 163(j)
. related taxpayers, transactions between . . 267
. section 6166 interest . . . . 163(k)

Interest received . . . . 61(a)(4)
. allocation, rules for . . . . 864(e)
. backup withholding 3406
. deposits, frozen . . . . 451(i)
. governmental obligations, exemption . . . 103;
. . 141—150
. municipal obligations—see State and local
. . obligations: interest on
. portfolio debt investments
. . foreign corporations . . . . 881(c)
. . nonresident aliens . . . . 871(h)
. U.S. savings bonds, higher education
. . tuition and fees 135

Internal Revenue Districts 7621

Internal Revenue Laws
. application of . . . . 7801—7809
. attempts to interfere with administration
. . of 7212
. construction of 7806
. effective dates of provisions 7851
. enforcement . . . . 7601—7655
. forfeiture of property used in violation of . 7302

Internal Revenue Service
. appeals dispute resolution 7123

Internal Revenue Service—continued
. audit standards, selection of returns
. . executive branch influence prohibited . 7217
. . protection from disclosure . . . . . . 6103(b)(2)
. authority of personnel to administer
. . oaths 7622
. Chief Counsel . . . . 7803(b)
. Chief Information Officer . . . . 7803(f)
. Chief of Appeals . . . . 7803(e)(2)
. Commissioner of Internal Revenue
. . appointment and supervision of
. . . personnel 7804
. . duties and powers . . . . 7803(a)
. districts 7621
. employees removed for misconduct
. . prohibition on rehiring . . . . 7804(d)
. enforcement of revenue laws 7601; 7655
. Independent Office of Appeals . . . . . . 7803(e)
. interest paid by 6621; 6622
. oaths, authority of personnel to
. . administer 7622
. offenses by officers and employees of,
. . penalties 7214
. Office of Taxpayer Advocate . . . . 7803(c)
. . statistical support . . . . 6108(d)
. . Taxpayer Advocate Directive . . . . . 7803(c)(5)
. Oversight Board
. . membership and responsibilities 7802
. personnel
. . appointment and supervision by
. . . Commissioner 7804
. private debt collectors 6306
. . outstanding inactive tax receivables . 6306(c)
. . special compliance personnel program
. . . funding 6307
. rulings 7805
. taxpayer interviews, procedures 7522
. unauthorized collection actions,
. . damages 7433
. unauthorized inspection of returns or
. . return information 7213A
. undercover operations . . . . 7608(c)
. user fees 7528

International air travel, head tax . . . . 4261(c)

International boycotts
. determination as to particular operations . . .
. . . . 999(d)
. factor . . . . 999(c)
. foreign tax credit reduction for
. . participation in 908
. participation in or cooperation . . . . . . 999(b)
. . related persons . . . . 999(e)
. reports by taxpayers . . . . 999(a)
. . failure to make . . . . 999(f)

International organizations
. compensation of employees, exempt
. . income 893
. former federal employees, employment
. . taxes . . . . 3121(y)

Inventories 471; 472; 473
. amounts included in 263A
. appreciation of, partnerships . . . . . . 751(d)
. basis of property included in 1013
. carryover by acquiring corporation . . . 381(c)(5)
. costs, limitation on
. . related persons, property imported
. . . from 1059A
. LIFO 472
. . election by small businesses to use
. . . single pool 474
. . qualified liquidations 473
. . small businesses 474
. . use of government-provided indexes . . 472(f)
. partnerships, gain or loss on sale . . 735(a)(2);
. . 751
. shrinkage of . . . . 471(b)
. tobacco articles, manufactured and
. . imported 5721
. wine premises 5369

Investment companies . . . . 851—855
. exchanges between . . . . 368(a)(2)(F)
. taxable income . . . . 852(b)

Investment credit . . . . 46—50
. advanced coal project credit 48A
. advanced energy project credit 48C
. advanced manufacturing investment
. . credit 48D

Investment credit—continued
. amount of credit 46
. at-risk rules 49
. automobiles, luxury . . . . 280F(a)
. basis adjustment . . . . 50(c)
. . earnings and profit . . . . 312(k)
. carryback and carryover of unused
. . credit
. . deficiency attributable to carryback . . . . .
. . . . 6601(d)(2)
. . interest on tax, effect of carryback on
. . . computation . . . . 6601(d)(2)
. . refund or credit attributable to . . . 6511(d)(4)
. clean electricity investment credit 48E
. energy credit 48
. gasification project credit 48B
. property not eligible . . . . 50(b)
. property used for personal purposes . . 280F(b)
. recapture . . . . 50(a)
. rehabilitation credit 47

Investment expenses 212

Investment in the contract defined . . . . 72(c)

Investment income
. Medicare tax 1411
. estimated tax, failure to pay . . . . . . 6654(a)

Investment indebtedness, interest paid
. . . . 163(d)

Investment property, exchange of 1031

Investment tax credit—see Investment credit

Investment trusts, real estate . . . . 856—860

Involuntary conversions 1033
. basis . . . . 1033(b)
. capital gains and losses 1231
. carryovers by acquiring corporations . . . . .
. . . . 381(c)(13)
. holding period of involuntarily converted
. . property 1223
. livestock contaminated . . . . 1033(f)
. principal residence, disaster areas . . 1033(h)
. renters, disaster areas . . . . 1033(h)
. replacement of property by related
. . person . . . . 1033(i)
. replacement of property within 2-year
. . period . . . . 1033(a)(2)(B)
. residence, exclusion of proceeds for
. . 65-year-olds . . . . 121(d)
. Sec. 1245 property . . . . 1245(b)(4)
. Sec. 1250 property . . . . 1250(d)(4)
. special use valuation, estate tax relief . . .
. . . . 121(d)(8)

IRA plus accounts—see Roth IRAs

Iron ore
. disposal of, deductibility of expenses . . 272
. expenses of mining 272

Iron ore royalties
. royalties, capital gains treatment 631

Irrigation subsidies, illegal federal 90

Itemized deductions
. additional individual . . . . 211—224
. capital costs
. . EPA sulfur regulations compliance . . . 179B
. corporations, special deductions . . . 241—249
. defined . . . . 63(d)
. dental expenses 213
. . threshold amount . . . . 213(a)
. floor on 67
. health savings accounts 223
. individuals and corporations . . . . . 161—199A
. medical expenses 213
. . threshold amount . . . . 213(a)
. overall limitation on 68

J

Jeopardy
. assessment of tax . . . . 6861—6864
. notice . . . . 6331(a); 6331(d)
. . review of procedures 7429
. election to itemize . . . . 63(g)
. levy
. . review of procedures 7429
. presumption of 6867

Jobs tax credit—see Work opportunity credit
Joint and survivor annuities . . . . 691(d)
Joint Committee on Taxation . . . . 8001—8023
Joint fiduciaries, returns . . . . 6012(b)(5)
Joint interests, estate tax 2040
Joint returns 6013
. deficiency notice . . . . 6212(b)(2)
. disclosure of collection activities on
    spouse . . . . 6103(e)(8)
. rate of tax . . . . 1(a)
. relief from joint and several liability 6015
. separate returns before, time deemed
    filed . . . . 6013(b)(3)(A)
. special rules
. . husband and wife living apart . . . 105(d)(5)
Joint tenancy
. estate tax
. . valuation of property held as 2040
**Judgment lien creditors, validity of lien
   for taxes against** 6323
Jurisdiction
. Courts of Appeals . . . . 7482(a)
. District Courts 7402
. Railroad Retirement Tax Act
    provisions, authority to order compliance
    with 3232
. Tax Court 6214; 7442
Jury duty pay remitted to employer
. adjusted gross income . . . . 62(a)(13)
**Justices and judges, retired, service performed
   by**
. FICA tax . . . . 3121(i)

K

Kerosene
. dyeing requirements . . . . 4082(d)
. excise tax
. . registration as terminal facility . . . . . 4101(e)
. . taxed as diesel fuel . . . . . . 4081(a)(2)(A)(iii)
. . nontaxable use . . . . 6427(l)
Key employees
. group term life insurance . . . . 79(d)
. retirement plans
. . top-heavy 416
Kickbacks to foreign officials . . . . 162(c)
Kyanite, percentage depletion . . . . 613(b)

L

Labor organizations, exemption . . . . 501(c)(5)
Land clearing expenses of farmers
. recapture 1252
Large employers
. health insurance coverage
. . minimum essential coverage, penalty . . . .
    . . . . 4980H
. . reporting requirements 6056
Large gifts from foreign persons 6039F
Last-in, first-out inventories—see LIFO
   inventories
Laterite, percentage depletion . . . . 613(b)
Lead, percentage depletion . . . . 613(b)
Leaking underground storage tanks . . . . .
. . . . 4081(d)(3)
. trust funds for . . . . 4041(d); 9508
. limitations on transfer to . . . . 9508(e)
Leases and leaseholds
. amortization costs, acquisition 178
. business leases, unrelated business
    taxable income 514
. cancellation payments 1241
. exclusions
. . lessee construction allowances 110
. improvements
. . accelerated cost recovery system . . 168(i)(8)
. . rent-to-own property . . . . 168(i)(14)
. service contracts v. . . . . 7701(e)
. treatment as sale excise taxes 4217
**Legislation, expenditures in promoting
   or combating** . . . . 162(e)
. tax on excess 4911
Lepidolite, percentage depletion . . . . . 613(b)

Lessor and lessee
. false statements to lessees 7211
. improvements made by lessee
. . basis of property to lessor 1019
. . exclusion from gross income of lessor . . 109
Letters, capital asset status . . . . 1221(a)(3)
Levy . . . . 6331—6344
. application of proceeds of 6342
. authority to release 6343
. exemptions from 6334
. hearing on
. . frivolous requests . . . . 6330(g)
. . notice of right prior to levy 6330
. inflation adjustment of exemption
    amount . . . . 6334(f)
. notice of levy . . . . 6331(a)
. production of books 6333
. property exempt from 6334
. redemption of property after sale 6337
. retirement plans, improper levy . . . . . 6343(f)
. sale of seized property 6335; 6336
. statute of limitations 6502; 6503
. surrender of property subject to levy . . . 6332
Liabilities assumed
. corporate acquisitions (carryovers) . 381(c)(16)
. corporate distributions and adjustments . . . .
    . . . . 301(b)(2); 312(c); 357; 358(d)
. incorporation of a business . . . . 357(c)(3)
. partner's contribution to capital 752
Liability for tax
. business in more than one location,
    occupational tax 4903
. change of location, occupational tax . . . 4905
. closing agreements in connection with . . 7121
. . penalties for false statements . . . . . 7206(5)
. common trust funds . . . . 584(c)
. compromises 7122
. . penalties for false statements . . . . . 7206(5)
. court proceedings
. . burden of proof 7491
. credit limitation based on 26
. death, occupational tax in case of 4905
. different business of same ownership
    and location 4903
. distilled spirits 5005
. estate tax, recipient of property over
    which decedent had power of appointment
    2207
. generation-skipping transfer tax 2603
. gift tax 2501
. . husband and wife . . . . 2513(d)
. joint returns
. . relief from joint and several liability . . . 6015
. partners, occupational taxes 4902
. political organizations 527
. . notices and reports . . . . 527(i)—527(k)
. Railroad Retirement Tax Act taxes . . . 3202(b)
. third-party contact, advance notice of . . 7602(c)
. tobacco taxes 5703
. . occupational taxes 5733
. understatements by tax return preparers . 6694
. wagering tax . . . . 4401(c)
. wages paid or provided for by third
    parties . . . . 3121(a); 3505
. withheld taxes 7501
Licensing, collection of foreign items . . . 7001
. failure to obtain license, penalties . . . 7001(b);
    7231
Lien for taxes . . . . 6320—6326
. administrative appeal of 6326
. automobile . . . . 6323(b)
. discharge of liens 7425
. distilled spirits 5004
. failure to release, damages 7432
. notice of lien . . . . 6331(a)
. right to hearing 6320
. suits by United States to enforce 7403
. withdrawal of notice . . . . 6323(j)
Life estate, sale . . . . 1001(e)
Life insurance
. accelerated death benefits . . . . 101(g)
. . riders treated as insurance contracts . 818(g)
. beneficiaries' liability for estate tax 2206
. contracts defined 7702
. definition of life insurance contract . . 1035(b)(3)

Life insurance—continued
. employer-owned
. . returns and records 6039I
. flexible premium contract . . . . 101(f)
. gross estate valuation, life insurance
    proceeds 2042
. income from life insurance contracts . 61(a)(10)
. interest paid on indebtedness to
    purchase 264
. long-term care insurance rider
. . information reporting 6050U
. modified endowment contract, defined . . 7702A
. modified guaranteed contracts 817A
. policies exchanged 1035
. proceeds received
. . amounts received as annuity 72
. . exempt income 101
. . flexible premium . . . . 101(f)
. self-employed individuals
. . retirement plans . . . . 404(e)
Life insurance companies . . . . 801—818
. accounting provisions 811
. benevolent associations, exemption . . . . . .
    . . . . 501(c)(12)
. deductions, general 805
. defined 816
. definitions and special rules 818
. exclusion from definition of personal
    holding company . . . . 542(c)(3)
. installment obligations transferred to
    controlled company . . . . 453B(e)
. modified guaranteed contracts 817A
. mutual
. . contiguous country branches 814
. . mutual savings bank conducting life
    insurance business 594
. net investment income
. . company's share and shareholders'
    share of, defined 812
. net operating loss carrybacks and
    carryovers
. . losses arising in 2018, 2019, and 2020 . . . .
    . . . . 172(b)(1)(D)(iii)
. policyholder dividends deduction 808
. reportable sales of life insurance
    contracts
. . reporting requirements 6050Y
. reserves 807
. variable contracts, treatment of 817
Life tenants
. adjusted gross income, special
    deductions . . . . 62(a)(5)
. depletion deduction . . . . 611(b)(2)
. depreciation deduction . . . . 167(d)
Lifetime learning credit
. education expenses 25A
. . payee statement requirement . . . . 25A(g)(8)
LIFO inventories 472
. election by small businesses to use
    single pool 474
. use of government indexes in pricing
    inventory . . . . 472(f)
Like-kind exchanges
. Sec. 1245 property . . . . 1245(b)(4)
. Sec. 1250 property . . . . 1250(d)(4)
Limitations period—see Statute of limitations
Liquidations
. basis of property received 334
. complete, definition . . . . 346(a)
. distributing corporation, effects on . . 336—338
. dividends
. . basis 334
. . dividends paid deduction . . . . 562(b)
. . information returns 6043
. . installment obligations . . . . 453B(d)
. gain or loss to shareholders 331
. information returns 6043
. partial liquidation
. . definition . . . . 302(e)
. . noncorporate shareholder . . . . 302(b)(4)
. recipients of distributions, effects on . . . . .
    . . . . 331—334
. subsidiaries 332; 337
. . basis of property received 334

Topical Index
References are to Code Section numbers.

Liquidity shortfall, defined benefit plans
. . . . 401(a)(32)
. excise tax . . . . 4971(f)
Liquor taxes . . . . 5001—5690
. determination of tax 5006
. gallonage taxes . . . . 5001—5068
. . beer . . . . 5051—5056
. . distilled spirits . . . . 5001—5011
. general provisions relating to . . . . 5551—5562
. losses caused by disaster 5064
. territorial extent of law 5065
Literary organizations
. bequests to 2055
. . nonresident aliens . . . . 2106(a)(2)(A)
. gifts to 2522
. tax exempt . . . . 501(c)(3)
Literary property, sale . . . . 1221(a)(3)
Lithium, percentage depletion . . . . . . 613(b)
Livestock
. contaminated, involuntary conversion . 1033(f)
. drought, sales on account of, income
     derived from . . . . 451(g)
. holding period . . . . 1231(b)(3)
. involuntary conversion . . . . 1033(d); 1033(e)
. property used in trade or business . 1231(b)(3)
. recapture of depreciation . . . . 1245(a)(2)
Living expenses 262
. amounts received under insurance
     contracts for 123
**Loan companies, exception from
     definition of personal holding company**
. . . . 542(c)(6)
Loans
. annuities, distributions from . . 72(e)(4)(A); 72(p)
. below-market, defined . . . . 7872(e)(1)
. below-market interest rates 7872
. Commodity Credit Corporation, income . . 77
. insurance premiums paid with proceeds,
     interest deduction . . . . 264(a)(3)
. insured by United States, distribution of
     proceeds by corporation . . . . 312(i)
. low-interest 7872
Lobbying
. expenses incurred . . . . 162(e)
. . defined . . . . 501(h)
. . exempt organizations, excise tax 4912
. . public charities, denial of exemption to
     . . . . 501(h); 504
. . tax on excess 4911
. prohibition against . . . . 4945(d); 4945(e)
**Local advertising charges, exclusion
     from selling price** . . . . 4216(e)
Local benefits, taxes assessed against . .
. . . . 164(c)(1)
**Local government exemption, excise
     taxes** . . . . 4221(a)(4)
**Lodge system, fraternal societies
     operating under** . . . . 170(c); 501(c)(8)
Lodging . . . . 119; 162(a)
. investment credit for property used to
     furnish . . . . 50(b)(2)
Long-term capital gain defined . . . . . 1222(3)
Long-term capital loss defined . . . . . 1222(4)
Long-term care benefits
. contributions by employer . . . . 106(c)
. eligible long-term care premiums . . 213(d)(10)
. information returns 6050Q; 6050U
. insurance contracts 7702B
. issuer requirements 4980C
. premiums for self-employed individuals . .
. . . . 162(l)(2)(C)
Long-term care insurance
. riders on annuity and life insurance
     contracts 6050U
. long-term care premium statements,
     reports relating to 6050Z
Long-term contracts 460
. look-back method not applicable . . . 460(b)(6)
Loss corporations
. built-in gains of acquired company,
     offset against 384
Losses 165
. bad debts—see Bad debts

Losses—continued
. capital—see Capital gains and losses
. expropriation by foreign government
. . recoveries 80; 1351
. gross estate, deduction from 2054
. insolvent financial institutions, deposits
     in . . . . 165(l)
. nonregistered obligations . . . . 165(j)
. nonresident aliens . . . . 873(b)
. partners, limitation on allowance . . . . 704(d)
. principal residence, disaster areas . . . 1033(h)
. related taxpayers, transactions between . . 267
. renters, disaster areas . . . . 1033(h)
. securities dealers . . . . 1236(b)
. small business investment companies . . 1242;
     1243
. wash sales 1091
Low-income community development
. credit against tax 45D
. qualified opportunity zones . . 1400Z-1 ; 1400Z-2
Low-income housing credit 42
Low-income housing projects
. depreciation of expenditures to
     rehabilitate
. . recapture of additional depreciation . . . .
     . . . . 1250(a)(2)(B)
. solar and wind facilities . . . . 48(e)
Low-income taxpayer clinics
. information, provision of . . . . 7526(c)(6)
. matching grants 7526
Low-interest loans 7872
Lump-sum distributions, retirement plans
. aggregation of plan and trust
     distributions . . . . 402(e)(4)(D)(ii)
. cost-of-living arrangement transfers . . .
     . . . . 402(e)(4)(D)(vi)
. defined . . . . 402(e)(4)(D)(i)
. divorce distributions . . . . 402(e)(4)(D)(v);
     402(e)(4)(D)(vii)
. exclusions from income
. . net unrealized appreciation of
     employer securities . . 402(e)(4)(B); 402(j)
. nonresident aliens, tax imposed . . . . . 871(b)
. tax imposed . . . . 402(e)(4)
. . nonresident aliens . . . . 871(b)
. withholding of tax at source . . . . . . 3405(b)

M

Magazines
. circulation expenditures 173
. publishers, prepaid subscription income . . 455
Magnetic media requirement for returns . .
. . . . 6011(e)
Manufacturers excise taxes . . . . 4064—4227
. constructive sale price . . . . 4216(b)
. exemptions
. . exports . . . . 4221(a)(2)
. . firearms 4182
. . Indian-produced articles 4225
. . State and local government . . . . 4221(a)(4)
. . supplies for vessels and airplanes . . . .
     . . . . 4221(a)(3)
. . tires with internal wire fastening 4073
. export sales . . . . 4221(a)(2)
. firearms 4181; 4182
. gasoline . . . . 4081—4083
. . alcohol mixture . . . . 4081(c)
. Indian-produced articles, exemption . . . 4225
. lease considered as sale 4217
. petroleum products . . . . 4081—4105
. price defined 4216
. purchasing manufacturer as
     manufacturer 4223
. recreational equipment . . . . 4161—4182
. . time for payment of tax . . . . 6302(d)
. registration 4222
. repairs not treated as manufacture . . . 4052(f)
. sales by other than manufacturer or
     importer 4219
. sales or resales to manufacturers,
     exemption . . . . 4221(a)(1)
. sporting goods 4161
. State and municipality exemption . . 4221(a)(4)
. tires . . . . 4071—4073
. use by manufacturer or importer
     considered sale 4218

Manufacturers excise taxes—continued
. vessel supplies exempt . . . . 4221(a)(3)
**March 1, 1913, basis of property
     acquired before** 1053
Marines—see Armed Forces of the U.S.
Marital deduction
. coordination . . . . 2001(e)
. estate tax 2056
Marital status
. determination of 7703
Mark-to-market method
. passive foreign investment companies
     (PFICs) 1296
. securities dealers 475
Market discount on bonds . . . . . 1276—1278
. accrued market discount
. . deferral of interest deduction allocable
     to 1277
. . disposition gain representing, ordinary
     income treatment 1276
. definitions and special rules 1278
Marriage penalty elimination . . . . . . 1(f)(8)
Maternity care standards 9811
Mathematical errors in returns . . . 6201(a)(3);
     6213(b)
Meals and lodging . . . . 119; 162(a)
. business meals, entertainment
     expenses . . . . 274(e)(1)
**Mechanics' lienors, validity of lien for
     taxes against** 6323
Medical care defined . . . . 213(d)
Medical expenses 213
Medical referral payments . . . . 162(c)
Medical reimbursement plans . . . . . 105(h)
Medical research gifts . . . . . 170(b)(1)(A)(iii)
Medical savings accounts—see Archer medical
     savings accounts (MSAs)
Medicare Advantage MSAs 138
. distributions
. . qualified medical expenses . . . . . . 138(c)
. eligible individuals . . . . 220(b)(7)
. national limit of participants . . . . . . 138(f)
. penalties . . . . 138(c)(2)
. trustees
. . reports to disclose fair market value of
     assets . . . . 138(e)
Medicare tax
. additional tax on high-income taxpayers . .
     . . . . 1401(b)(2); 3101(b)(2); 3102(f)
. . estimated tax, failure to pay . . . . . . 6654(m)
. investment income 1411
. . estimated tax, failure to pay . . . . . . 6654(a)
Medicine, deductibility limited . . . . . 213(b)
Membership organizations
. deductibility of cost of furnishing goods
     and services 277
. prepaid dues income 456
Memorandums, capital asset status . 1221(a)(3)
Mental health benefits
. parity requirements 9812
. substance use disorders 9812
Merchant Marine capital construction funds
. tax incentives 7518
Merger—see Reorganizations
**Meter-dose inhalers, excise tax on
     chemicals used in** . . . . 4682(g)
Mica, percentage depletion . . . . 613(b)
Military—see Armed Forces of the U.S.
Military spouse retirement plan eligibility credit
. for small employers 45AA
Mineral production payments 636
Mineral properties
. disposition of, capital gain or loss 1254
Mine rescue team training credit 45N
. denial of double benefit . . . . 280C(e)
Mines and mining
. depletion . . . . 611—614

Topical Index
References are to Code Section numbers.

Mines and mining—continued
. election to aggregate mineral interests . . . . . 614(b)(4); 614(c)
. exploration expenditures
.. acquiring corporation's right to deduct . . . . . 381(c)(10)
.. unlimited deduction for domestic mining 617
. safety equipment
.. election to expense 179E

Minimum essential coverage
. individuals without insurance, penalty . 5000A
. large employers, penalty 4980H
. reporting requirements 6055; 6056

Minimum funding standards 412
. community newspaper plans . . . . . 430(m)
. cooperative and small employer charity (CSEC) plans 433
. multiemployer plans 431
.. endangered or critical status 432
. single-employer defined benefit pension plans 430

Minimum tax—see Alternative minimum tax

Minimum tax credit
. prior year liability, credit for 53
. carryovers in corporate acquisitions . . . . . 381(c)(25)

Mining and solid waste reclamation and closing costs
. taxable year 468

Mining exploration expenditures 617
. acquiring corporation's right to deduct . . . . . 381(c)(10)

Ministers of the gospel—see Clergy

Minor children
. unearned income of . . . . . 1(g)
. alternative minimum tax . . . . . 59(j)

Mitigation of effect of limitations and other provisions . . . . . 1311—1314
. amount of adjustment 1314
. circumstances of adjustment 1312
. correction of errors 1311
. method of adjustment 1314
. self-employment tax and Federal Insurance Contributions Act tax 6521

Modified guaranteed contracts, life insurance companies 817A

Money order, use in payment of tax 6311

Mortgage credit certificates . . . . . 25(c)
. information requirements
.. failure to meet, penalties 6709
.. misstatements, penalties 6709

Mortgage guaranty insurance, special deductions for insurance companies writing . . . . . 832(e)

Mortgage revenue bonds
. disaster areas . . . . . 143(k)(11)
. interest on 143

Mortgages
. estate tax deduction 2053
. insurance premiums treated as interest . . . . . 163(h)(3)(E)
. interest paid, credit 25
. interest received in trade or business from individuals
.. information returns 6050H
. points, taxable year of deduction . . . 461(g)(2)
. servicing rights, depreciation . . . . . 167(f)

Motion picture films
. amounts at risk, deductions of expenses in connection with 465

Motor vehicle operating agreements
. definition . . . . . 7701(h)

Motor vehicles
. alternative motor vehicle credit 30B
. donations
.. fraudulent acknowledgments 6720
. highway use tax . . . . . 4481—4484

Moving expenses
. adjusted gross income . . . . . 62(a)(15)
. Armed Forces of U.S., members of . . 217(g)
. deduction . . . . . 217(a)
.. mileage limitation . . . . . 217(c)(1)

Moving expenses—continued
. deduction—continued
.. qualified expenses . . . . . 217(b)
.. self-employed individuals . . . . . 217(f)
.. work test . . . . . 217(c)(2)
.. defined . . . . . 217(b)
.. foreign earned income, deduction . . 217(h); 217(i)
. reimbursement, inclusion in gross income 82

Multiemployer health care plans, guaranteed renewability 9803

Multiemployer plans
. funding
.. critical status . . . . . 432; 4971(g)
.. endangered status . . . . . 432; 4971(g)
.. minimum funding standards 431

Multiple corporations—see Controlled corporations

Multiple employers, withholding of tax on wages . . . . . 3402(f)(7)

Multiple support agreements . . . . 152(d)(3); 152(e)(5)

Multiple trusts . . . . . 643(f); 665—668

Municipalities
. income received by, exclusion from gross income 115
. obligations of—see State and local obligations

Mutual deposit guarantee funds, exempt status . . . . . 501(c)(14)

Mutual ditch and irrigation companies, exemption . . . . . 501(c)(12)

Mutual funds—see Regulated investment companies

Mutual savings institutions . . . . . 591—597
. deductions
.. dividends paid on deposits . . . . . 591(a)
. domestic building and loan association defined . . . . . 7701(a)(19)
. exemption of organizations providing funds for, and insurance of, shares or deposits in . . . . . 501(c)(14)(C)
. federal financial assistance, transactions in which provided 597
. interest deduction 265
. life insurance business conducted by, alternative tax 594
. reserves 593
. securities held by, gain on . . . . . 582(c)
. stock associations, conversion to . . . 591(b)
. tax preferences 291

Mutual telephone companies, exemption . . . . . 501(c)(12)

N

National banks—see Banks

Native Americans
. articles produced by, exemption from manufacturers excise tax 4225
. casino profits, withholding on . . . . . 3402(r)
. fishing rights secured by treaty, income . 7873
. Indian employment credit 45A
. Indian reservation property
.. accelerated cost recovery system . . . 168(j)
.. tribal governments treated as states . . 7871
.. excise tax exemptions . . . . . 7871(b)
.. general rule . . . . . 7871(a)
.. subdivisions of tribal government . . 7871(d)
.. tax-exempt bonds . . . . . 7871(c)

Natural resources . . . . . 611—638
. continental shelf areas 638
. mineral production payments 636

Nephelite syenite, percentage depletion . . . . . 613(b)

Net capital gain defined . . . . . 1222(11)

Net capital loss
. corporate acquisitions, limitations . . . 383(a)
. definitions . . . . . 1222(10)

Net earnings from self-employment defined . . . . . 1402(a)

Net long-term capital gain defined . . . 1222(7)

Net long-term capital loss defined . . . 1222(8)

Net operating loss carrybacks and carryovers . . . . . 172(b)
. acquiring corporation . . . . . 381(c)(1); 382
. computations, law applicable . . . . . 172(e)
. estates and trusts . . . . . 642(h)
. farming losses . . . . . 172(b)(1)(B)
. insurance companies . . . . . 172(b)(1)(C)
. losses arising in 2018, 2019, and 2020 . . . . . 172(b)(1)(D)

Net operating loss deduction 172
. common trust funds . . . . . 584(g)
. defined . . . . . 172(c)
. estates and trusts . . . . . 642(h)

Net short-term capital gain defined . . 1222(5)

Net short-term capital loss defined . . 1222(6)

Netting of casualty losses . . . . . 1231(a)

New energy efficient homes credit 45L

New markets tax credit 45D

News services
. communications tax exemption . . . . . 4253(b)

Newsletter fund contributions . . . . . 527(g)

Newspapers
. circulation expenditures 173
. prepaid income from subscriptions . . . 455

Nickel, percentage depletion . . . . . 613(b)

Nonbusiness debts . . . . . 166(d)

Nonbusiness expenses—see Personal deductions

Nondeductibles . . . . . 261—280H
. contributions, required statement . . . 6113
. failure to provide, penalty 6710

Nondiscrimination requirements
. health care insurance 9802

Nonqualified annuities, property transferred in connection with performance of service . . . . . 403(c)

Nonrecourse financing, defined . . 49(a)(1)(D)(iii)

Nonresident aliens . . . . . 871—879 ; 887
. charitable contributions . . . . . 873(b)(2)
. community income treatment 879
. consent dividends . . . . . 565(e)
. credits 33
. deductions 873; 874
. defined . . . . . 7701(b)
. dividends of regulated investment companies
.. exemption . . . . . 871(k)
. earned income credit, eligibility . . . 32(c)(1)(D)
. election to treat as resident of U.S. . . 6013(g)
. employed by United States, pensions . . . . . 402(e)(2)
. estate tax . . . . . 2101—2108
. estimated tax, failure to pay . . . . . 6654(j)
. FICA tax . . . . . 3121(b)(19)
. foreign tax credit . . . . . 901(b)(4); 906
. FUTA tax . . . . . 3306(c)(19)
. gambling winnings . . . . . 871(j)
. gift tax, deductions in computing . . . 2522(b)
. gross income 872
. imposition of tax on 871
. interest received, portfolio debt investments . . . . . 871(h)
. losses . . . . . 873(b)
. original issue discount . . . . . 871(g)
. partnerships 875
. personal exemption . . . . . 873(b)(3)
. property within the United States . . . 2104
. property without the United States . . 2105
. real property in U.S. owned by
.. sale or exchange . . . 861(a)(5); 897; 1445; 6039C
. return requirements . . . . . 6013(h)
.. due date . . . . . 6072(c)
. Social Security benefits, taxation of . . 871(a)(3)
. tax credit for the elderly . . . . . 22(f)
. tax on, scope
.. certain interest and dividends . . . . . 871(i)
. transfer of property to, recognition of gain 684
. transportation income, tax on 887
. U.S. resident or citizen married to, community income of 879

Topical Index
References are to Code Section numbers.

Nonresident aliens—continued
. withholding of tax on—see also
. . Withholding of tax at source . . . . 1441; 3401(a)(6)
. . overwithheld tax, refunds and credits . . 1464
. . payment of withheld tax 1461
. . recipient of income paying tax, recollection from withholding agent . 1463

Nonresident citizens
. exclusions
. . definitions . . . . 911(d)
. . election . . . . 911(e)
. . foreign earned income . . . . 911(b)
. . housing cost amount . . . . 911(c)
. . residence requirement . . . . 911(d)(5)
. . special rules . . . . 911(d)
. . waiver of period of stay in foreign country . . . . 911(d)(4)

Nontaxable exchanges . . . . 1031—1045

Northern Mariana Islands, U.S. income tax
. coordination of individual income tax . . . 7654
. foreign corporations . . . . 881(b)
. income from sources within 931
. residents of, tax on 876

Notes
. sale of
. . bank's losses . . . . 582(c)

Notice
. change in installment agreement for payment of tax . . . . 6159(b)(5)
. deficiencies 6212; 7521
. delinquencies 7524
. levy on wages . . . . 6331(a)
. notice and demand for payment of tax . 6155; 6303; 7521
. pension plans
. . benefit accruals reduced 4980F
. withdrawal of lien . . . . 6323(j)

Nuclear power plants
. decommissioning costs 88
. reserve fund payment deduction 468A

O

Oaths
. authority to administer 7622

Obligations
. installment—see Installment obligations
. registered form requirement . . . . 163(f)
. . unregistered, capital gains treatment denied 1287
. short-term, issued on discount basis . . 454(b)
. state obligations—see State and local obligations
. U.S. obligations—see United States obligations

Obsolescence . . . . 167(a)

Occupational taxes
. business in more than one location, liability in case of 4903
. change of location, liability in case of . . . 4905
. death, liability in case of 4905
. different business of same ownership and location, liability in case of 4904
. federal agencies or 4907
. firearms importers, manufacturers, and dealers 5801
. payment 4901
. state law application 4906
. tobacco manufacturers and exporters . 5731—5734
. wagers, acceptance of . . . . 4411—4414

Offers-in-compromise 7122
. application, frivolous submission . . . 7122(g)
. rules for submission . . . . 7122(c)

Office of Taxpayer Advocate . . . . 7803(c)

Officers of the United States government—see Federal officers and employees

Oil and gas properties
. capital gains and losses 1254
. carryback and carryover of disallowed credits . . . . 907(f)
. depletion . . . . 611—614
. development expenditures 616
. enhanced oil recovery credit 43

Oil and gas properties—continued
. extraction taxes . . . . 907(c)(5)
. foreign, credit against tax for income from 907
. foreign taxes paid . . . . 907(b)
. marginal well production credit 45I
. percentage depletion
. . limitations 613A
. . producers, nonconventional sources . . 45K
. purchase or sale, foreign, foreign tax credit . . . . 901(f); 907
. tax preferences
. . 10-year writeoff . . . . 59(e)

Oil, domestic, environmental tax . . . . 4611(b)

Oil royalties, personal holding company income . . . . 543(a)(3)

Oil shale, treatment processes . . . 613(c)(4)(H)

Oil spills
. trust fund for 9509

Olivine, percentage depletion . . . . 613(b)

Ombudsman
. taxpayer assistance orders 7811

Operating mineral interests rules for percentage depletion computation . . 614(b)

Options
. brokers, information reporting . . . . . . 6045(h)
. dealers . . . . 1236(e)
. . anti-conversion rules . . . . 1258(d)(5)
. . self-employment tax . . . . 1402(i)
. employees' stock options 421
. sale or exchange of 1234

Ordinary income
. defined 64

Ordinary loss
. defined 65

Organization fees
. partners and partnerships 709

Organizational expenditures 248

Original issue discount . . . . 1271—1275
. debt instruments—retirement, sale, or exchange 1271
. determination of amount 1273
. determination of issue price
. . debt instruments issued for property . 1274
. foreign corporations . . . . 881(a)(3)
. inclusion in income, current 1272
. information requirements
. . failure to meet, penalties 6706
. interest paid . . . . 163(e)
. high yield obligations . . . . 163(e)(5); 163(i)
. nonresident aliens . . . . 871(g)
. tax-exempt obligations 1288

Orphan drug credit 45C
. denial of double benefit . . . . 280C(b)

Outdoor advertising displays
. real property replacement upon conversion of . . . . 1033(f)

Overall limitation on foreign tax credit . 904(a); 904(b)

Overlapping pay periods . . . . 3402(g)

Overpayments of—see Refunds and credits

Overseas allowances 912

Oversheltered returns
. partnerships
. . declaratory judgments (pre-2018) 6234

Ownership of stock, rules in determining personal holding company status 544

Ozone-depleting chemicals, excise tax . 4681; 4682; 6302(f)

P

Paid-in surplus, basis of property acquired as . . . . 362(a)

Paid or accrued, defined . . . . 7701(a)(25)

Paid or incurred, defined . . . . 7701(a)(25)

Parent, defined . . . . 73(c)

Parsonage rental value 107

Partners and partnerships . . . . 701—777
. adjustments (post-2017) 6225
. . administrative adjustment requests . . . 6227

Partners and partnerships—continued
. adjustments (post-2017)—continued
. . imputed underpayments (post-2017) . . 6225
. . judicial review (post-2017) 6234
. . judicial review (pre-2018) 6226
. . limitations period 6235
. . notice (post-2017) 6231
. . administrative proceedings (pre-2018) . 6223; 6230
. . notice (post-2017) 6231
. . notice (pre-2018) 6223
. . partnership representative (post-2017) . 6223
. . participation in 6224
. adoption of taxable year . . . . 706(b)
. assessment of deficiencies against . . 6511(g); 6232
. bond to stay 7485
. interest and penalties (post-2017) 6233
. limitations period 6229
. restrictions (pre-2018) 6225
. bankruptcy . . . . 1398(b)(2)
. basis
. . allocation rules 755
. . contributed property . . . . 723; 737(c)
. . partnership property 743; 754
. . transferee partner's interest 742
. closing of taxable year . . . . 706(c)
. computation of taxable income 703
. continuation of partnership 708
. contributed property
. . gain or loss on disposition of 724
. . precontribution gain 737
. contributions to capital . . . . 721—723
. credits of partner 702
. death of partner
. . payments to successor in interest 736
. definitions (post-2017) 6241
. definitions (pre-2018) 761; 6231
. distributions by partnership . . . . . 731—737
. . basis of distributed property other than money 732
. . basis of distributee partner's interest . . 733
. . extent of recognition of gain or loss . . . 731
. . marketable securities . . . . 731(c)
. . Sec. 1245 property distributed to partner . . . . 1245(b)(6)
. distributive shares 704
. electing 1987 partnerships . . . . 7704(g)
. electing large partnership—see Electing large partnerships
. failure to file timely or complete returns, penalties 6698
. family partnerships . . . . 704(e)
. foreign partners' share of effectively connected income
. . withholding at source 1446
. foreign partnership interests 6046A
. foreign tax credit . . . . 901(b)(5)
. gross income, distribution of share of . 61(a)(13)
. income of partner 702
. information returns 6031
. . nominee reporting . . . . 6031(c)
. . signatures 6063
. interests exchanged
. . information returns 6050K
. inventory items sold . . . . 735(a)(2); 751
. investment partnerships
. . carried interest holding period 1061
. liabilities increased, treatment as contribution of money . . . . 752(a)
. liability for tax . . . . 701—709
. occupational tax liability of partners . . . 4902
. organization fees 709
. partner's tax treatment 6222
. partnership items 6221
. . tax treatment 6221
. partnership representative, designation (post-2017) 6223
. pension trusts for employees . . . . 414(c)
. publicly traded 7704
. qualified business income deduction . . . 199A
. refund, civil action 7422
. retiring partner, payments made to 736
. returns 6031
. . due dates . . . . 6072(b)
. . electronic filing requirement . . . . . 6011(e)(5)

Topical Index

References are to Code Section numbers.

Partners and partnerships—continued
. returns—continued
.. extension for entities determined not to be partnerships (pre-2018) 6233
. spouse of partner
.. innocent spouse relief .... 6230(a)(3)
. syndication fees 709
. taxable income, computation ... 703
. taxable years .... 444; 706(b); 7519
. termination of partnership ..... 708(b)
. transactions between 707
. transfers of interests in partnership . 741—743
.. corporations 386
. unrealized receivables sold .... 735(a)(1); 751
. unrelated trade or business ..... 512(c)
. year in which partnership income is includible .... 706(a)

Party to a reorganization, defined .... 368(b)

Pass-through entities
. itemized deductions, floor on miscellaneous .... 67(c)
. qualified business income deduction ... 199A

Passive activities
. losses
.. minimum tax .... 58(b)
. losses and credits 469

Passive foreign investment companies (PFICs) .... 1291—1298
. election of mark-to-market for stock 1296
. information reporting
.. election .... 1295(b)
.. shareholder returns .... 1298(f)
.. statute of limitations period suspended . ... 6501(c)(8)

Passport restrictions
. delinquent tax debts 7345

Patents
. sale or exchange of 1235
.. foreign corporation purchaser, nature of gain 1249

Patient-Centered Outcomes Research Trust Fund 9511
. funding .... 4375—4377

Patronage dividends .... 1381—1388
. amount paid or received, determination of .... 1388(e)
. backup withholding 3406
. cooperatives, netting of gains and losses by .... 1388(j)
. definition .... 1388(a)
. dividends-received deduction ..... 246(a)
. gross income of patron, amounts includible .... 1385(a)
. information returns 6044
. nonqualified per-unit retain certificate . 1388(i)
. nonqualified written notice of allocation .... 1388(d)
. payment period .... 1382(d)
. per-unit retain allocation ...... 1388(f)
. per-unit retain certificate ...... 1388(g)
. pooling arrangements, products marketed under .... 1382(e)
. qualified per-unit retain certificate .... 1388(h)
. qualified written notice of allocation . 1388(c)
. taxable income computation, distributee cooperative .... 1382(b)
. written notice of allocation defined ... 1388(b)

Pay period, defined .... 3121(c); 3306(d)
Payee statements, failure to file correct . 6722
Payment of tax
. checks 6311
.. bad 6657
. commercially acceptable means, by ... 6311
. consolidated returns 1503
. demand for payment 6155
. depositaries for government ..... 6302(c)
. due dates—see Due dates
. electronic fund transfer system .... 6302(h)
. employment taxes 3501
. estate tax
.. accelerated payment .... 6166(g)(1)
.. executor's liability 2002
.. failure to make payment of principal and interest .... 6166(g)(3)

Payment of tax—continued
. estimated tax
.. payment considered on account of income tax 6315
.. extension of time .... 6161—6167
.. bond requirement 6165
.. carrybacks expected by corporation .. 6164
.. interest 6601
. failure to pay
.. additions to tax and penalty 6651
. foreign currency 6316
. fractional parts of a cent disregarded ... 6313
. installment payments
.. agreement 6159
. interest rate
.. notice of interest charges 6631
. limitation on use of preceding year's tax .... 6654(d)(1)(C)(i)
. notice and demand 6155
. occupational taxes 4901
. place for making payment 6151
. receipt for taxes 6314
. time for making payment 6151
. tobacco taxes .... 5703(b)
.. occupational taxes 5732
. when payment deemed made 6513
. withheld tax on nonresident aliens, foreign partnerships, and foreign corporations 1461
. withheld tax on wages .... 6302(c)

Payroll period
. defined .... 3401(b)
. overlapping .... 3402(g)

Peace Corps, allowances for volunteers and volunteer members
. exempt status .... 912(3)
. FICA tax .... 3121(i); 3121(p); 3122
. withholding of tax on wages .... 3401(a)(13)
.. receipts for employees .... 6051(a)

Pecuniary bequests, special use valuation, estate tax relief .... 2032A(e)(9)

Penalties
. accuracy-related penalty 6662
.. understatements with respect to reportable transactions 6662A
.. valuation misstatement 6695A
. adulterated fuels 6720A
. airline ticket and advertising offenses ... 7275
. annuities, premature distributions ... 72(q)
. appraisers 6695A
. assessable .... 6671—6725
. bad checks in payment of tax 6657
. brokers, failure to provide notice to payors 6705
. charitable contributions, disclosure requirements 6115; 6714
. claim for credit or refund
.. erroneous 6676
. COBRA premium assistance
.. cessation of eligibility, failure to notify 6720C
. computation
.. notice to taxpayer 6751
. credit
.. erroneous claim 6676
. criminal—see Criminal penalties
. delay proceedings in Tax Court and other courts 6673
. deposit of taxes
.. exception for first-time depositors of payroll taxes .... 6656(c)
.. failure to make .... 6656(a)
. disclosure of return information, unauthorized 7431
. dyed fuels 6715
. estimated tax
.. additional Medicare tax on high- income taxpayers, failure to pay .. 6654(m)
. evasion of tax 6672; 7201
. exempt organizations providing information or services available from federal government
.. sale or solicitation without disclosure statement 6711

Penalties—continued
. exempt use property
.. fraudulent identification 6720B
. failure to disclose reportable transactions 6707A
. failure to disclose treaty-based return positions 6712
. failure to file correct discharge of indebtedness 6050P
. failure to file returns 6651; 6652; 6698; 6699
. failure to pay stamp tax 6653
. failure to pay tax ... 6651; 6653—6655; 7202; 7203
.. substitute returns .... 6651(g)
. failure to produce records 7269
. firearms taxes violations 5861
. foreign financial assets
.. failure to furnish information ... 6038D(d)
.. undisclosed assets, underpayment of tax .... 6662(j)
. foreign tax redetermination, notification of .... 6689(a)
. foreign trusts
.. failure to file or report information .. 6677(a)
. fraud 6663
. frivolous return 6702
. fuels tax
.. failure to register 6719
.. failure to report information 6725
. Guam–U.S. tax coordination, failure to furnish information 6688
. health insurance coverage
.. individuals without insurance 5000A
.. minimum essential coverage 4980H
. individual retirement accounts
.. failure to furnish reports 6693
. information, correct, failure to include . 6723
. information returns
.. failure to file 6652
.. failure to file correct 6721
.. foreign corporate shareholders ... 6038(b)
. liquor tax violations .... 5601—5690
. mechanical dye injection systems
.. failure to maintain security 6715A
. notice
.. computation of penalty 6751
. partners, failure to file timely or complete returns 6698
. payee statements
.. failure to file correct 6722
. preparers of returns
.. improper disclosure or use of information by 6713
.. understatement of taxpayer's liability . 6694
. private foundation provision violations ... 6684; 6685
. qualified retirement plans, premature distributions .... 72(t)
. reasonable cause exception
.. reportable transaction understatements .... 6664(d)
.. underpayments .... 6664(c)
. reasonable cause waiver .... 6724(a)
. refund
.. erroneous claim 6676
. refusal of entry 6717
. reportable transactions
.. failure to disclose information ... 6707A
.. failure to file information returns .. 6707
.. failure to maintain lists of advisees .. 6708
. retirement plans
.. failure to notify distributees ..... 6652(h)
. rollover distributions
.. failure to provide written explanation . 6652(j)
. simple retirement accounts
.. failure to furnish reports .... 6693(c)
. suspension
.. failure to provide notice of liability .. 6404(g)
. tax registration
.. failure to display on vessels 6718
. tax shelters
.. abusive 6700
.. corporations, substantial underpayment penalty ... 6662(d)(2)(C)
. tobacco tax violations 5761

Topical Index
References are to Code Section numbers.

Penalties—continued
- underpayment of tax
  - transactions lacking economic substance . . . . . . 6662(b)(6); 6662(i)
- waiver 6724
- withholding certificate, false 6682

Penny elimination on returns 6102

Pension plans—see Retirement plans
- simplified employee pensions—see Simplified employee pensions

Pensions
- gross income . . . . 61(a)(11)
- individuals—see Individual retirement accounts
- nonresident alien employees of the United States . . . . 402(e)(2)
- withholding of tax at source 3405

Percentage depletion 613
- carryover by acquiring corporation . . 381(c)(18)
- geothermal deposits . . . . 613(e)
- oil and gas wells
  - denial of deduction . . . . . . 613(d); 613A(b)
  - operating mineral interests rules . . . . 614(b)
  - rates . . . . 613(b)
- reduction, corporate minimum tax 291
- tax preference item . . . . 57(a)(1)
- treatment processes in the case of oil shale . . . . 613(c)(4)(H)

Percentage method of withholding . . 3402(b)

Performing artists
- adjusted gross income . . . . 62(a)(2)(B); 62(b)

Periodicals, circulation expenditures 173

Permissive service credits
- purchase of . . . . 415(n)

Personal deductions 262
- alimony paid 215
- amortizable bond premium 171
- bad debts 166
- charitable contributions 170
- cooperative housing, tenant-stockholders 216
- dental expenses 213
- gifts 170
- income-producing expenses 212
- interest paid 163
- interest paid to cooperative housing corporation 216
- losses 165
- medical expenses 213
- production of income, expenses for 212
- taxes paid 164
- taxes paid to cooperative housing corporation 216

Personal exemptions . . . . 151—153
- estates . . . . 642(b)
- indexing of . . . . 151(d)
- nonresident aliens . . . . 873(b)(3)
- short-period returns . . . . 443(c)
- taxpayer identification number required . . . . 151(e)
- trusts . . . . 642(b)

Personal expenses—see Personal deductions

Personal holding companies . . . . . 541—547
- annualization of income 546
- corporations filing consolidated returns . . 542(b)
- deduction for deficiency dividends 547
- deficiency dividends, deduction 547
  - carryover by acquiring corporation . . . . 381(c)(17)
- defined 542
- dividend carryover, acquiring corporation . . . . 381(c)(14)
- dividends paid deduction, dividends paid after close of taxable year 563
- Domestic International Sales Corporation status . . . . 992(d)
- finance companies, exception from definition . . . . 542(c)(6)
- foreign—see Foreign personal holding companies
- imposition of tax on 541
- liquidating distributions, denial of dividends-paid deduction . . . . . . 562(b)
- personal holding company income 543
- 60% of adjusted ordinary gross income requirement . . . . 542(a)(1)

Personal holding companies—continued
- special rules . . . . 542(d)
- stock ownership 544
- undistributed personal holding company income 545

Personal interest
- disallowance of deduction for . . . . . . 163(h)

Personal property, installment sales 453
- dealers
  - installment method of accounting for . . 453A

Personal service corporations
- allocation of income and deductions . . . 269A
- defined 269A
- graduated rates . . . . 11(b)
- taxable year . . . . 280H; 441(i); 444

Petroleum products
- environmental tax . . . . 4611(a)
- manufacturers excise tax . . . . . . 4081—4102

Petroleum storage facilities, treatment as Sec. 1245 property . . . . 1245(a)(3)(E)

PFICs—see Passive foreign investment companies (PFICs)

Phosphate rock, percentage depletion . . 613(b)

Piggyback trailers, retail sales tax . . . . 4051(d)

Place for filing returns 6091

Platinum, percentage depletion . . . . . 613(b)

Political activities
- public charities, denial of exemption to . . . 504

Political candidates and organizations, contributions to
- appreciated property transferred to 84
- debts owed by political parties 271
- indirect contributions 276
- liability of organization for tax 527
- presidential campaigns . . . . 6096; 9001—9012
- primary matching payment account . . 9031—9042
- return requirement for organizations . . . . 6012(a)(6)

Political expenditures of exempt organizations
- excise tax on 4955
- injunctions against 7409
- termination assessments 6852

Political subdivisions
- income received by, exclusion from gross income 115

Pollution control facilities
- amortization 169

Portability of health care insurance . . 9801—9803

Possessions corporations
- foreign tax credit . . . . 901(g)

Possessions corporations, Domestic International Sales Corporation status
- definitions . . . . 367(d)(2)
- intangibles, transfer of . . . . 367(d)
- shipments from the United States 7653
- shipments to the United States 7652

Possessions of the United States
- child and dependent care credit . . . . . . 21(h)
- child tax credit . . . . 24(k)
- collection of tax in 7651
- earned income credit 7530
- harbor maintenance excise tax exemption . . . . 4462(b)
- resident, defined 937
- source rules 937

Postmarks, timely mailing as timely filing 7502

Powers of appointment
- estate tax 2041
- gift tax 2514

Preexisting condition exclusion limitation, health care plans 9801

Preference items 57

Preferential dividends, dividends paid deduction . . . . 562(c)

Preferred dividends, defined . . . . . 565(f)(2)

Premature withdrawal penalties, adjusted gross income . . . . 62(a)(9)

Premium assistance refundable credit . . . 36B
- denial of double benefit . . . . 280C(g)
- individuals receiving unemployment compensation 36B

Prepaid income
- dues 456
- subscriptions 455

Prepaid interest
- method of accounting . . . . 461(g)

Prepaid telephone cards, excise taxes . 4251(d)

Preparers of returns—see Tax return preparers

Prescription drug plans
- federal subsidies 139A

President and his appointees
- disclosure of returns to . . . . 6103(g)

Presidential campaign fund
- contributions 6096
- matching payment account . . . . 9031—9042

Price, defined 4216

Principal residence
- cancellation of debt, income exclusion . . . . 108(a)(1)(E); 108(h)
- exclusion of gain from sale 121
  - nonqualified use . . . . 121(b)(5)
- first-time homebuyers
  - credit against tax 36
- members of uniformed services, Foreign Service, and intelligence community . . . . 121(d)(9)
- involuntary conversion of property, disaster areas . . . . 1033(h)
- residential energy property credit 25C

Prisoners
- disclosure of information by prison administrators 6116
- disclosure of return information . . 6103(k)(10)
- earned income credit, eligibility . 32(c)(2)(B)(iv)

Private activity bonds
- empowerment zones 1394
- exempt facility bonds 142
- general rules . . . . 141—147
- miscellaneous requirements 147
- mortgage revenue bonds 143
- qualified bonds 141
- volume cap 146

Private foundations . . . . 4940—4948
- adjusted net income . . . . 4942(f)
- annual reports
  - failure to file, penalties . . . . . . 6652(c)(1)
  - public inspection . . . . 6104(d)
- business stock ownership, 20% limit . . 4943(c)
- care facilities for the elderly . . . . . 4942(j)(5)
- charter requirements . . . . 508(e)
- continuation of status . . . . 509(b)
- declaratory judgment suits 7428
- deficiencies of prior years, correction . . . . 4942(h)(2)
- definition . . . . 509(a)
- disqualified person defined . . . . . 4946(a)(1)
- distributions
  - supporting organizations . . . . . . 4942(g)(4)
- distributions exceeding income for five years, relief . . . . 4942(i)
- electioneering, prohibition against . . . 4945(d)
- excess business holdings, special taxes . . 4943
- excise tax based on investment income . . 4940
- failure to distribute income, special taxes . . . . 4942(a); 4942(b)
- first tier, excise tax abatement 4962
- foreign organizations, taxes on 4948
- gifts or bequests to, denial of deduction for . . . . 508(d)
- government officials, dealings with . . . . 4941(d)(1)(F)
- gross investment income defined . . . . . 509(e)
- information reports
  - public inspection . . . . 6104(d)
- information returns 6033
  - failure to file, penalties . . . . . . 6652(c)(1)
- investment income 4940
- investments jeopardizing charitable purposes, special taxes 4944
- lobbying, prohibition against . 4945(d); 4945(e)

Topical Index
References are to Code Section numbers.

Private foundations—continued
. minimum investment return . . . . 4942(e)
. nonexempt trusts 4947
. penalties 6684; 6685
. presumption in absence of IRS
. . notification . . . . 508(b)
. qualifying distributions
. . defined . . . . 4942(g)
. . treatment . . . . 4942(h)
. refunds and credits, statute of limitations
. . . . 6511(f)
. second tier, excise tax abatement 4961
. self-dealers, special taxes 4941
. set-asides . . . . 4942(g)(2)
. state officials, information to . . . . . . 6104(c)
. support defined . . . . 509(d)
. supporting organizations, requirements . 509(f)
. tax on . . . . 507(c)
. taxable expenditures, special taxes . . . 4945
. termination of status . . . . . 507; 6501(c)(6)
Private inurement prohibition, exempt organizations . . . . 501(c)(4)(B)
Private mail delivery services, timely mailing as timely filing . . . . 7502(f)
Prizes, income 74
. cash option . . . . 451(j)
. Olympic and Paralympic medals, exclusion . . . . 74(d)
Product liability losses
. accumulated earnings tax . . . . 537(b)(4)
Product samples stored in home . . . 280A(c)(2)
Production payments 636
Professional employer organizations
. certification 7705
. employment taxes 3511
Profit-sharing distributions—see Distributions by retirement plans
Prohibited transactions
. denial of exempt status to organizations engaging in 503
. extension of grace period . . . . 856(e)(3)
. foreign organizations as private foundations . . . . 4948(c)
. pension plans, excise tax 4975
. real estate investment trusts . . . . . . 857(b)(6)
. . exclusion of certain sales . . . . . 857(b)(6)(C); 857(b)(6)(D)
. . sales not meeting requirements . . 857(b)(6)(F)
. . special rules . . . . 857(b)(6)(E)
Property
. accelerated cost recovery system
. . classes . . . . 168(e)
. . definitions . . . . 168(e)
. dividends paid in 301
. gain or loss to corporation 311
. farm and real, transfers of 1040
. predominantly used in business
. . depreciation, limitation . . . . 280F(b)
Property settlement agreements 2516
Property transferred in connection with performance of service 83
Proprietorships—see Sole proprietorship
Public safety officers
. death benefits . . . . 104(a)(6)
Public school teachers and employees, annuities . . . . 403(b)
Public utilities
. depreciation of property . . . . 168(f)(2)
. distributions of stock and stock rights
. . exclusion from gross income of recipient . . . . 305(f)
. energy conservation subsidies provided to customers 136
Publishers
. circulation expenditures 173
. prepaid subscription income 455
Puerto Rico
. child tax credit . . . . 24(k)(2)
. earned income credit . . . . 7530(a)
. income from sources within 933
. residents of, tax on 876
. foreign tax credit . . . . . . 901(b)(2); 901(b)(3)

Q

Qualification of retirement plan 401
. custodial accounts and contracts . . . . 401(f)
Qualified domestic trust 2056A
Qualified business income deduction . . 199A
Qualified commercial clean vehicle credit 45W
Qualified first responder
. retirement payments . . . . 139C(b)
. service . . . . 139C(d)
Qualified low-income residential building project . . . . 48(e)
Qualified improvement property . . . . 168(e)(6)
Qualified mortgage bond
. interest on 143
Qualified nonpersonal use vehicle defined . . . . 274(i)
Qualified opportunity zones
. designation 1400Z-1
. reinvestment, deferral of gain 1400Z-2
Qualified retirement savings contributions . . . . 6433(d)
Qualified small employer health reimbursement arrangements
. exclusion from gross income
. . minimum essential coverage requirement . . . . 106(g)
. exemption from group health plan requirements . . . . 9831(d)
. notice requirement
. . penalty . . . . 6652(o)
. premium tax credit . . . . 36B(c)(4)
Qualified tuition programs 529
. contributions to . . . . 135(c)(2)(C)
. distributions
. . education loan repayments . . . . . 529(c)(9)
. . registered apprenticeship programs
. . . . 529(c)(8)
. . higher education expenses
. . . computer and internet access expenses . . . . 529(e)(3)(A)(iii)
Quartz crystals, percentage depletion . 613(b)
Quid pro quo **contributions**
. charitable contributions, disclosure requirements 6115; 6714

R

Railroad retirement benefits, tier 1
. information returns 6050F
. liability for tax 86
Railroad retirement benefits, tier 2
. liability for tax . . . . 72(r)
Railroad Retirement Tax Act taxes . 3201—3241
. acts to be performed by agents 3504
. collection 3501
. compensation determined 3212
. deduction of tax from compensation . . 3202
. determination of tier 2 tax rate 3241
. district court jurisdiction in ordering compliance with provisions of 3232
. erroneous payments, credits against tax . 3503
. payment 3501
. rates 3201; 3221
. refunds and credits 6413
. taxable income computation, nondeductibility 3502
Railroad track maintenance credit 45G
Railroad unemployment repayment tax . 3321
Railroads
. high-speed intercity
. . exempt facility bonds . . . . . 142(c); 142(i)
. . reorganizations . . . . 354(c)
. rolling stock
. . improvements, repair treatment . . . 263(d)
. . rentals, sources of income . . . . . . 861(a)
. . ties, expenditures for, deductibility of . 263(f)
. track maintenance credit 45G
Rates of tax
. alternative minimum tax 55
. change during year 15
. joint return after death of either spouse
. . . . 6013(d)

Rates of tax—continued
. charitable organizations taxable at corporation rates . . . . 511(a)
. chemicals . . . . 4661(b)
. cigarettes . . . . 5701(b)
. cigars . . . . 5701(a)
. corporations . . . . 11(a)
. . accumulated earnings tax 531
. . charitable organizations taxable at corporation rates . . . . 511(a)
. distilled spirits 5001
. employment taxes
. . Federal Insurance Contributions Act . 3101; 3111
. . Federal Unemployment Tax Act taxes . 3301
. . Railroad Retirement Tax Act . . . 3201; 3211; 3221
. . self-employment 1401
. estate tax 2001
. estates . . . . 1(e); 1(j)
. excise taxes—see particular tax under this heading
. firearms
. . making of firearms . . . . 5821(a)
. . occupational tax 5801
. . transfer tax . . . . 5811(a)
. gift tax 2502
. head of household . . . . 1(b); 1(j)
. husband and wife . . . . 1(a); 1(d); 1(j)
. indexing income tax brackets . . . . 1(f)
. individuals . . . . 1—3
. . reductions, post-2000 . . . . 1(i)
. . tax years 2018–2025 . . . . 1(j)
. personal holding company tax 541
. self-employment income 1401
. smokeless tobacco . . . . 5701(e)
. tobacco
. . occupational tax 5731
. trusts . . . . 1(e); 1(j)
Reacquisitions of real property, gain . . . 1038
Real estate
. acquired by United States, administration 7506
. charitable contribution
. . conservation purpose . . . . 170(h)
. depreciation—see Real estate depreciation
. effectively connected with U.S. trade or business, disposition . . . . 897(a)
. foreign corporation owning U.S.
. . sale or exchange . . . . 861(a)(5); 897; 1445; 6039C
. gain from disposition of depreciable property 1250
. . adjustments to basis . . . . 1250(h)
. . exceptions . . . . 1250(d)
. . holding period defined . . . . 1250(d)
. . leasehold improvements, additional depreciation . . . . 1250(b)(4)
. . qualified low-income housing . . . . 1250(g)
. . Section 1250 property defined . . . 1250(c)
. installment sale, year income reported . 453(b)
. investment trusts—see Real estate investment trusts (REITs)
. nonresident alien owning U.S.
. . sale or exchange . . . . 861(a)(5); 897; 1445; 6039C
. repossessions, gain 1038
. revolving fund for redemption 7810
. subdivision and sale 1237
. taxes . . . . 164(a)(1)
. . accrual . . . . 461(c); 461(d)
. . apportionment between buyer and seller . . . . 164(d)
. . deduction 164
. tract, defined . . . . 1237(c)
. valuation of gross estate 2032A
Real estate agents
. independent contractor . . . . 3508(a)
Real estate boards, exemption . . . . . 501(c)(6)
Real estate depreciation
. rehabilitation property
. . recapture of additional depreciation . 1250(a)

Topical Index
References are to Code Section numbers.

Real estate investment trusts (REITS) .. 856—860
. capital gains
.. treatment of undistributed ...... 857(b)(D)
. deficiency dividends 860
.. acquiring corporation .... 381(c)(23)
. definition 856
.. general .... 856(a)
.. interest .... 856(f)
.. limitations .... 856(c)
. determination of ownership .... 857(f)
. distributions .... 355(h)
. dividends and interest
.. individual's exclusion .... 857(c)
. dividends paid deduction .... 562(e)
. excess noncash income .... 857(e)
. excise tax 4981
. foreclosures
.. income from .... 857(b)(4)
.. special rules .... 856(e)
. foreign currency transactions ...... 856(n)
. impermissible tenant service income . 856(d)(7)
. income defined .... 857(b)
. net operating loss carrybacks and carryovers
.. losses arising in 2018, 2019, and 2020 ..... 172(b)(1)(D)(ii)
. prohibited transactions ...... 857(b)(6)(C)—(F)
. rents, real property .... 856(c)
. status, determination .... 856(b)
. taxable subsidiary .... 856(l)

Real estate mortgage investment conduits (REMICs) .... 860A—860G

Real estate reporting person, defined .... 6045(e)(2)

Real property
. applicable convention, ACRS ...... 168(d)
. foreign
.. special rules .... 1031(h)
.. transfer by executor of estate
... recognition of gain 1040

Reasonable accumulations by corporations 537

Reasonable verification of returns .... 6201(d)

Recapture
. at-risk losses .... 465(e)
. depreciation
.. livestock sales .... 1245(a)(2)
.. rehabilitation housing .... 1250(a)
. distributions made to Federal Savings and Loan Insurance Corporation . 593(e)(1)
. first-time homebuyer credit .... 36(f)
. foreign losses .... 904(f)
. gain
.. disposition of Sec. 126 property 1255
.. investment credit .... 50(a)

Receipt, payment of tax .... 6311—6317

Receivership—see Bankruptcy and receivership

Reclamation laws, basis of property sold pursuant to .... 1033(c)

Recognition of gain or loss .... 1001(c)

Recomputed basis, Sec. 1245 property .... 1245(a)(2)

Recordkeeping, charged tips ...... 6041(e)

Records—see Books and records

Recoveries
. accelerated cost recovery system
.. general asset accounts .... 168(i)(4)
. damages, antitrust violations 186
. exclusion from gross income 111
. right of recovery in case of marital deduction property 2207A

Recovery rebate credit 6428; 6428B

Recreational equipment, manufacturers excise tax .... 4161—4182
. time for payment of tax .... 6302(d)

Recreational expenses .... 274(e)(4)

Redeemable ground rents ..... 163(c); 1055

Redemption of nonqualified written notices of allocation, cooperatives . 1385(c)

Redemption of property seized for nonpayment of taxes 6337

Redemption of stock, distributions by corporations in .... 302—304
. partial liquidation
.. noncorporate shareholder .... 302(b)(4)
. related taxpayers 304

Redevelopment bonds
. interest on 144

Reduction of basis, discharge of indebtedness 1017

Refineries
. election to expense 179C

Reforestation expenditures 194
. adjusted gross income computation . 62(a)(11)
. trusts and estates, treatment ...... 194(c)(4)

Refunds and credits—see also Credits against tax .... 6401—6430
. administrative procedure .... 6411(d)
. alcohol taxes 6423
. authority to make 6402
. claim for refund
.. erroneous 6676
.. period of limitation on filing claim .. 6511(a)
.. timely mailing as timely filing 7502
. date of allowance of 6407
. debts owed Federal Agencies, collection of .... 6402(d)
. diesel fuel
.. nontaxable use .... 6427(l)
. disregarded for government assistance eligibility 6409
. distilled spirits 5008
. electronic funds transfer, misdirected . 6402(n)
. employment taxes 3503; 6413
. erroneous refunds, civil action by United States to recover 7405
. escheat, overpayments of tax 6408
. excessive tax withheld 6414
. excise taxes overpaid 6415; 6416
. expiration of limitation period 6514
. floor stocks refunds 6412
. fractional parts of dollar disregarded ... 7504
. fuel production, nonconventional source
.. excessive claims, penalties 6675
.. farmers 6420
.. local transit systems' use of gasoline .. 6421
.. nonhighway use of gasoline 6421
. interest on erroneous refund 6602
. interest on overpayments 6611
. investment tax credit—see Investment credit
. kerosene
.. nontaxable use .... 6427(l)
. limitations on .... 6511—6515
.. petition to Tax Court filed 6512
. offsets
.. past-due state income tax obligations .... 6402(e)
.. offset of past-due support against overpayments .... 6402(c)
.. unemployment compensation debts . 6402(f)
.. overpayments of Social Security .... 6402(g)
. overwithheld taxes on nonresident aliens, foreign partnerships, and foreign corporations 1464
. prohibition of administrative review of decisions of Secretary 6406
. reports of 6405
. suits for—see Suits by taxpayers
. tentative carryback adjustments 6411
. tobacco taxes 5705; 6423
. wagering tax 6419

Regional filing of returns .... 6091(b)

Registration 7011; 7012
. gasoline and other fuel taxes
.. failure to register or false statement, penalty 7232
. gasoline tax 4101
. lubricating oil tax 4101
.. failure to register or false statement, penalty 7232
. manufacturers excise taxes 4222
. occupational tax on wagers 4412
. penalty for failure to register 7272

Regulated futures contracts marked to market 1256

Regulated investment companies .. 851—855; 860

Regulated investment companies—continued
. asset test .... 851(b)(3)
. de minimis asset test failures ...... 851(d)
. capital loss carryovers .... 1212(a)(3)
. custodial accounts for stock ..... 403(b)(7)(A)
. deficiency dividends 860
. definition 851
. qualified publicly traded partnership .. 851(h)
. distributions
.. return of capital, allocation requirements .... 316(b)(4)
.. stock redemption .... 302(b)(5)
. dividends .... 881(e); 1441(c)(12)
.. capital gain dividend, defined ... 852(b)(3)(C)
.. exempt-interest dividends ... 852(b)(5); 852(g)
.. exemptions, nonresident aliens ..... 871(k)
.. dividends and interest, limitations to 854
. earnings and profits, capital loss treatment .... 852(c)
. exempt-interest dividends
.. pass-through distributions .... 852(g)
. foreign tax credits
.. pass-through distributions .... 852(g)
. gross income test .... 851(b)(2)
.. failure to satisfy .... 851(i)
. late-year losses, deferral .... 852(b)(8)
. load charges, treatment of .... 852(f)
. passive activity rule .... 469(k)(4)
. return of capital, allocation requirements .... 316(b)(4)
. stock
.. estate tax treatment .... 2105(d)
. tax credit bonds
.. election to pass through credits to shareholders 853A
. tax-exempt income, interest and expenses relating to .... 265(a)(3)
. transfers from common trust funds .. 584(h)
. undistributed income, excise tax 4982
. unit investment trusts, redemptions by . 852(d)

Regulations of Treasury Department ... 7805
. retroactivity of regulations .... 7805(b)
. small business, impact on .... 7805(f)

Rehabilitation expenditures
. credit against tax 47

Reimbursed expenses
. employer's deduction .... 274(e)(4)
. moving expenses, inclusion in income 82

REITs—see Real estate investment trusts (REITs)

Related taxpayers
. allocation of income and deductions among 482
. definition .... 1313(c)
. installment sales
.. rate of imputed interest, special rule .. 483(f)
.. second dispositions by related persons .... 453(e)
. interest paid, limitation .... 163(j)
. redemption of stock 304
. replacement of involuntarily converted property .... 1033(i)
. transactions between
.. capital gains and losses 1239
.. controlled groups .... 267(f)
.. deductions disallowed .... 267(a)
.. exchanges of property held for productive use or investment .... 1031(f)
.. pass-through entities .... 267(e)

Religious orders
. FICA tax coverage, election of ..... 3121(r)

Religious organizations
. bequests to .... 2055(a)(2)
.. nonresident aliens .... 2106(a)(2)(A)
. contributions to .... 170(b)
. employees
.. annuities for .... 403(b)(9)
.. plans .... 415(c)(7)
.. exemption .... 501(d)
. self-employment tax for members ... 1402(e)
. trusts for .... 642(c)

Remainder interests
. credit for death taxes 2015
. extension of time for payment of estate tax on 6163

REMICs—see Real estate mortgage investment conduits (REMICs)

Renewable electricity production credit . . . 45
. solar and wind facilities placed in low-income communities . . . . 48(e)

Renewable energy bonds
. nonrefundable credit to holders
. . reporting . . . . 6049(d)(8)

Rent
. deduction . . . . 162(a)
. family members . . . . 280A(d)
. income . . . . 61(a)(5)
. information return . . . . 6041(a)
. real property . . . . 856(d)

Renters
. involuntary conversion of property,
. . disaster areas . . . . 1033(h)

Reorganizations . . . . 351—368
. assumption of liability 357
. basis to corporations 362
. basis to distributees 358
. carryovers 381; 382
. control defined . . . . 368(a)(2)(H); 368(c)
. definition 368
. effects on corporations that are parties
. . to 361
. effects on transferor corporation 362
. exchanges of stock and securities 354
. foreign corporations 367
. information returns 6046
. liabilities assumed 357
. merger . . . . 368(a)
. nonrecognition of gain or loss to
. . corporations 361
. party to a reorganization defined . . . . . . 368(b)
. railroads . . . . 354(c)
. stock and securities exchanged in 354
. additional consideration received 356
. stock-for-stock . . . . 368(a)(1)

Replacement property
. involuntary conversions, two-year
. . provision . . . . 1033(a)(2)(B)

Reportable transactions
. accuracy-related penalty on
. . understatements 6662A
. . reasonable cause exception . . . . 6664(d)
. material advisors 6112
. penalties
. . failure to disclose information 6707A
. . failure to file information returns 6707
. . failure to maintain lists of advisees 6708

Repossessions of real property, gain . . . 1038

**Reproduction of returns and other
documents** 7513

Request for prompt assessment . . . . . 6501(d)

Research credit
. adjustments for certain acquisitions . . . . 41(f)(3)
. alternative simplified credit election . . . 41(c)(4)
. base amount . . . . 41(c)
. carrybacks and carryovers of unused
. . credit
. . . amount allowable . . . . 41(a)
. . . refund or credit attributable to . . 6511(d)(4)(C)
. . tentative carryback and refund
. . . adjustments 6411
. denial of double benefit . . . . 280C(c)
. expenditures 41; 174
. general rule . . . . 41(a)
. pass-through of credit, special rule . . . . . 41(g)
. qualified expenditures . . . . 41(b)
. qualified organizations, basic research . . . 41(e)
. qualified research, definition . . . . 41(d)
. qualified small businesses . . . . 41(h)
. sources of income, allocation . . . . 864(g)
. special rules . . . . 41(f)

**Research use property, charitable
contribution** . . . . 170(e)(4)

Reserves
. bad debts 593
. life insurance companies 807

Resident alien
. defined . . . . 7701(b)

Residential property
. business use of, deductibility of
. . expenses in connection with 280A

Residential property—continued
. new energy efficient homes credit 45L
. principal residence
. . exclusion of gain on sale 121
. . residential clean energy credit 25D
. . residential energy property credit 25C

Restricted stock plans . . . . 83(a)—83(i)

**Retail commission salesmen,
withholding of tax on noncash payments to** . . . . 3402(j)

Retail sales tax, deduction for . . . . . . 164(b)(4)

Retailers' excise taxes
. penalties 7261

Retirement plans . . . . 401—404
. accrued benefit requirements . . . . 411(b)
. . allocation between employer and
. . . employee contributions . . . . 411(c)
. . termination or discontinuance of
. . . contributions . . . . 411(d)
. actuaries and actuarial reports—see Actuaries
. . and actuarial reports
. administrator of plan . . . . 414(g)
. affiliated service groups . . . . 414(m)(5)
. aggregation of plans . . . . 415(g)
. assignment of benefits under domestic
. . relations order . . . . 401(a)(13); 414(p)
. assignment or alienation
. . fiduciary breach . . . . 401(a)(13)(C)
. bankruptcy of plan sponsor
. . prohibition on benefits increase . . 401(a)(33)
. beneficiaries, taxability of 402
. benefits or contributions
. . permitted disparities . . . . 401(l)
. . reduced benefit accruals, notice 4980F
. benefits received, limitations on . . . 404(j); 415
. break in service . . . . 410(a)(5); 411(a)(6)
. cafeteria plans 125
. cash arrangements . . . . 401(k); 402(e)(3)
. church plans . . . . 414(e); 415(c)(7)
. contributions by employer . . . . 403(b)(9)
. . election . . . . 410(d)
. . self-employed ministers . . . . 414(e)(5)
. collectively bargained plans 413
. combining of plans . . . . 415(f)
. compensation, defined . . . . 414(s)
. compensation limit . . . . 401(a)(17)
. . cost-of-living adjustment . . . 401(a)(17)(B)
. consolidation of plans . . . . 414(l)
. contributions to plans
. . acquiring corporation . . . . 381(c)(11)
. . carryover of unused deductions . . . . . 404(d)
. . catchup contributions . . . . 414(v)
. . credit against tax 25B
. . dividends paid on ESOP securities,
. . . deduction . . . . 404(k)
. . elective deferrals treated as Roth
. . . contributions 402A
. . employee contribution v. employer
. . . contribution . . . . 414(h)
. . employer's deduction 404
. . limitations on . . . . 404(j); 404(l); 415
. . negotiated plans . . . . 404(c)
. . nondiscrimination test . . . . 401(m)
. . welfare benefit plans 419
. controlled corporate group plans . . . . . 414(b)
. controlled group rules, application of . . 414(t)
. cooperative and small employer charity
. . (CSEC) plans
. . defined . . . . 414(y)
. . minimum funding rules 433
. cost of living adjustments
. . . . 401(a)(17)(B); 415(d)
. death benefits . . . . 401(a)(9)(B)
. deferred arrangements . . . . 401(k); 402(e)(3)
. defined benefit plan . . . . 401(j); 414(j)
. . limitation for benefits . . . . 415(b)
. . special rules . . . . 415(k)
. defined contribution plan . . . . 401(j); 414(i)
. . limitation for contributions . . . . 415(c)
. . special rules . . . . 415(k)
. distributions . . . . 401(a)(9); 402
. . birth or adoption . . . . 72(t)(2)(H)
. . first-time homebuyers . . . . 72(t)(8)
. . foreign situs trusts, taxability . . . . . . 402(d)
. . lump-sum—see Lump-sum distributions,
. . . retirement plans
. . rollovers—see Rollovers

Retirement plans—continued
. distributions—continued
. . unemployed persons using funds for
. . . health insurance premiums . . . . 72(t)(2)(D)
. . withholding at source . . . . 3405(a)
. divorce distributions . . . . . 72(m)(10); 402(e)(1);
. . . . 402(e)(4)(D)(vii)
. employee contributions, deductibility . . . . 72(o)
. excess pension assets, transfers to
. . employee health accounts 420
. exclusions from income
. . net unrealized appreciation of
. . . employer securities . . . . 402(e)(4)
. 50% control . . . . 415(h)
. first-time homebuyers . . . . 72(t)(8)
. foreign affiliates of domestic employers . . . 406
. foreign situs trusts, taxability . . . . 402(d)
. funding standards, minimum . . 412; 430—433
. . account requirement . . . . 412(b)
. . alternative standard . . . . 412(g)
. . amortization periods, extension . . . . . 412(e)
. . community newspaper plans . . . . 430(m)
. . contributions, liability . . . . 412(b)
. . cooperative and small employer
. . . charity (CSEC) plans 433
. . defined benefit plans . . . . 412(l); 430
. . eligible multiemployer plan . . . 412(b)(7)(F)
. . excepted plans . . . . 412(h)
. . failure to meet, excise tax 4971
. . insurance contract plans . . . . 412(i)
. . lien, imposition of . . . . 412(n)
. . minimum required contributions . . . . . 430(b)
. . multiemployer plans 431
. . quarterly payments . . . . 412(m)
. . replacement interest rate . . . . 412(b)(5)(B);
. . . . 412(l)(7)(C)
. . single-employer defined benefit plans . . 430
. . special rules . . . . 412(c)
. . variances . . . . 412(c); 412(d)
. . waivers and extensions, requirements
. . . relating to . . . . 412(f)
. governmental plan . . . . 414(d)
. excess benefit arrangements . . . . . . 415(m);
. . . . 457(e)(14); 457(g)
. hardship distributions . . . . 401(k)(14)
. highly compensated employee . . . . . . 414(q)
. individual retirement accounts—see Individual
. . retirement accounts
. information requirements 6057
. . fraudulent statement or failure to
. . . furnish statement to plan participant,
. . . penalty 6690
. information to be filed 6047
. joint and survivor annuities . . . . 401(a)(11); 417
. limitations on contributions and benefits . . 415
. liquidity shortfall . . . . 401(a)(32)
. . excise tax . . . . 4971(f)
. loans as distributions . . . . 72(p)
. lump-sum distributions—see Lump-sum
. . distributions, retirement plans
. medical expenses for retired employees . . . .
. . . . 401(h)
. merger of plans . . . . 414(l)
. minimum coverage requirements . . . . . 410(b)
. minimum funding standards—see funding
. . standards, minimum, under this heading
. minimum participation standards 410
. minimum vesting standards 411
. missing participants, assignment of
. . benefits upon plan termination . . . 401(a)(34)
. multiemployer plan . . . . 414(f); 418E
. participation standards 410
. partnerships, employees of . . . . 414(c)
. pension-linked emergency savings
. . accounts . . . . 402A(e)
. penalties
. . failure to notify distributees . . . . 6652(h)
. . prohibited transactions, excise tax 4975
. . proprietorships, employees of . . . . . . 414(c)
. qualification 401
. records not available for past periods . . . 415(i)
. registration, annual 6057
. reports 6047
. retirement plans, accumulation in
. . excise tax 4974
. retirement plans, early distributions from
. . additional tax . . . . 72(t)
. retroactive changes in plan . . . . 401(b)

Topical Index
References are to Code Section numbers.

Retirement plans—continued
- rollovers—see Rollovers
- security requirement . . . . 401(a)(29)
- separate line of business, special rules . . . 414(r)
- service for predecessor employer . . . . 414(a)
- simple retirement accounts . . . . 404(m)
- small employer
  - military spouse retirement plan eligibility credit 45AA
  - pension plan startup costs 45E
- union negotiated pension plans . . . . . . 401(i)
- vesting standards 411
  - top-heavy plans 416
- veterans' reemployment rights . . . . . 414(u)
- withholding of tax at source 3405
- year defined . . . . 415(j)

Retirement savings contributions credit . . . 25B

Retroactivity of regulations . . . . 7805(b)

Returns . . . . 6011—6110
- amended
  - statute of limitations . . . . . . 6501(c)(7)
- brokers . . . . 6045(a)
- computation of tax by Internal Revenue Service 6014
- consolidated returns . . . . 1501—1505
- cooperatives, time for filing . . . . . . 6072(d)
- corporation
  - domestic, foreign shareholders . . . 6039C(a)
- disclosure of 6103
  - disclosure for other than tax purposes . . . . 6103(l)
  - procedure and recordkeeping . . . . . 6103(p)
- Domestic International Sales Corporations . . . . 6011(d); 6072(b)
- due dates . . . . 6071—6075
- energy grants and financing 6050D
- estate tax 6018
- execution by Secretary . . . . 6020(b)
- exempt organizations
  - electronic filing requirement . . . . . 6033(n)
- extensions of time for filing . . . . . 6081; 7508A(d)
- failure to file
  - additions to tax 6651; 6652
  - fraud penalty 7203
  - limitations on assessment and collection . . . . 6501(c)(3)
  - partnership 6698
  - S corporation 6699
- substitute returns . . . . 6651(g)
- untimely and incomplete partnership returns, penalties 6698
- untimely and incomplete S corporation returns, penalty 6699
- filing requirements . . . . 6012(a)
- for purposes of the District of Columbia Retirement Protection Act of 1997 . . . . 6103(l)(16)
- fraudulent
  - filed by third party, damages 7434
  - penalties 7207
- frivolous 6702
- general stock ownership corporations . . . 6039B
- generation-skipping transfer tax . . . . . 2621(c)
- gift tax 6019
- government employer, withheld taxes . . . 3404
- health insurance costs of eligible individuals, credit 6050T
- higher education tuition 6050S
- husband and wife—see Joint returns
- individual retirement accounts . . . . 6058(d); 6058(e)
- information returns—see Information returns
- inspection—see Inspection of returns
- international boycotts . . . . 999(a)
  - failure to report . . . . 999(f)
- joint returns 6013
  - relief from joint and several liability . . . 6015
- joint returns after separate returns, time deemed filed . . . . 6013(b)(3)(A)
- liquor taxes 5555
- magnetic media requirement . . . . . . 6011(e)
- mathematical errors in . . . 6201(a)(3); 6213(b)
- mergers and acquisitions 6043A
- occupational taxes
  - tobacco . . . . 5732(c)
- oversheltered returns (pre-2018) 6234
- partnership
  - failure to file timely, penalties 6698

Returns—continued
- partnership—continued
  - non-partnership entities (pre-2018) . . 6233(a)
  - penny elimination 6102
  - period covered by 6101
  - persons required to make 6012
  - place for filing . . . . 6091(b)
  - political organizations . . . 6012(a)(6); 6033(g)
  - prepared by Secretary . . . . 6020(a)
  - preparers—see Tax return preparers
  - real property in U.S., substantial investor . . . . 6039C(b)
  - reasonable verification of returns . . . 6201(d)
  - regional filing . . . . 6091(b)
  - requirement of 6011; 6012
  - rounding-off to dollar amounts 6102
- S corporation
  - failure to file timely, penalty 6699
  - self-employment tax 6017
- short-period—see Short-period returns
- signatures on . . . . 6061—6064
- time for filing . . . . 6071—6075
  - extension 6081
- timely mailing as timely filing 7502
  - private mail delivery services . . . . 7502(f)
- treaty-based return positions, disclosure . 6114
  - failure to disclose, penalty 6712
- unauthorized inspection of 7213A
- unemployment compensation 6050B
- unrelated business income
  - electronic filing requirement . . . . . 6011(h)
- verification 6065
- when deemed filed 6513

Reversionary interest
- credit for death taxes on 2015
- defined . . . . 2037(b)
- estate tax
  - proceeds of life insurance . . . . . . 2042(2)
  - transfers taking effect at death . . . 2037(b)
- extension of time for payment of estate tax on 6163
- grantor treated as owner 673

Revocable trusts 676

Revolving fund for redemption of property 7810

Rewards for informers . . . . . 7214(a); 7623

Right of contribution where more than one person is liable, failure to withhold . . . . 6672(d)

Rollovers
- defined benefit plan limitations . . 415(b)(2)(A)—415(b)(2)(B)
- defined contribution plan limitations . . 415(c)(2)
- direct transfers . . . . 401(a)(31); 402(e)(6)
- disputed property sales . . . . 402(c)(6)
- divorce distributions . . . . 402(e)(1)
- eligible rollover distributions . . . . . . 402(c)
  - statement of rollover eligibility . . . . 402(f)
- employees' annuities—see also Employees' annuities . . . . 403(a)(4); 403(b)(8)
- empowerment zone investments, nonrecognition of gain 1397B
- exclusions from income . . . . 402(c)(1)
  - maximum rollover amount . . . . . . 402(c)(2)
- frozen deposits . . . . 402(c)(7)
- individual retirement accounts—see also Individual retirement accounts . . . 408(d)(3)
- simple retirement accounts . . . . . 408(d)(3)(G)
- small business stock 1045
- statement of rollover eligibility . . . . . 402(f)
  - penalties, failure to provide written explanation . . . . 6652(i)
- surviving spouse distributions . . . . 402(c)(9)
- tax imposed . . . . 402(e)(4)
- transfers . . . . 401(a)(31); 402(e)(6)
  - frozen deposits . . . . 402(c)(7)
  - rollover contributions . . . . 402(c)(5)
  - timing of . . . . 402(c)(3)
- trustee-to-trustee transfers . . . 401(a)(31); 402(e)(6)
- withholding of tax at source . . . . . . 3405(c)

Roth IRAs
- contributions to, deductibility . . . . . 408A(c)
- distribution rules . . . . 408A(d)
- elective deferrals as contributions 402A
- excess contributions . . . . 4973(f)
- income limitations . . . . 408A(c)(3)

Rounding-off to dollar amounts . . 6102; 7504

Royalties
- adjusted gross income . . . . 62(a)(4)
- coal . . . . 631(c)
- income . . . . 61(a)(6)
- information returns 6050N
- iron ore 631
- patents, treatment in case of sale or exchange 1235
- personal holding company income . . . 543(a)(1)

Rubber defined . . . . 4072(b)

Rulings of Internal Revenue Service . . . 7805

S

S corporations . . . . 1361—1379
- activities not engaged in for profit 183
- at-risk limitation on losses . . . . 465(e)
- basis of stock 1367
- built-in gains tax 1374
- consistency of shareholder returns . . . 6037(c)
- coordination with subchapter C 1371
- definition 1361
- definitions and special rule 1377
- depletion . . . . 613A(c)(11)
- distributions 1368
  - restricted bank director stock . . . . 1368(f)
- elections 1362
  - effect on corporation 1363
  - inadvertent invalid elections or terminations . . . . 1362(f)
  - late elections treated as timely . . . 1362(b)(5)
- exempt organizations as shareholders . . . . 1361(c)(6)
- failure to file timely or complete returns, penalty 6699
- foreign income 1373
- fringe benefits 1372
- information returns 6037
- passive investment income 1375
- qualified business income deduction . . . 199A
- related taxpayers 267
- repayment of loans for qualifying employer securities . . . . 4975(f)(7)
- restricted bank director stock . . . 1361(f); 1368(f)
- returns 6037
  - due dates . . . . 6072(b)
  - failure to file timely or complete, penalty 6699
- revocation of election 1362
- shareholders . . . . 1361(c)
  - consistency of returns . . . . 6037(c)
  - family members treated as one shareholder . . . . 1361(c)(1)
  - pass-thru of items 1366
  - small business trusts . . . 641(c); 1361(e)
- stock held by exempt organization, unrelated business income . . . . . 512(e)
- subsidiaries . . . . 1361(b)(3)
- taxable year 444; 1378; 7519
- termination of election 1362

Salaries—see Compensation paid; Compensation received

Sales of property
- apportionment of taxes between buyer and seller in year of sale . . . . . . 164(d)
- casual sales, accounting 453
- conflict-of-interest requirements, compliance with 1043
- crop, unharvested, sold with land 268
- depreciable property 1245
- farmland, gain 1252
- foreign corporation stock, character of gain 1248
- installment sales 453
- inventory property . . . . 861(a)(6)
- livestock sales on account of drought . . . 451(g)
- losses, adjusted gross income computation . . . . 62(a)(3)
- natural resources 631
- patents and copyrights, foreign corporation purchaser 1249
- property seized for nonpayment of taxes—see also Seizure of property; sale of seized property 6335

Topical Index
References are to Code Section numbers.

Sales of property—continued
. real estate
.. subdivision and sale 1237
.. short sales 1233
. source of income .... 861(a)(5)
. timber 631
. wash sales 1091
Sales taxes, deductibility .. 164(b)(4); 164(b)(5)
Salespersons
. non-cash remuneration, withholding .. 3402(j)
Saturday as last day for performing acts . 7503
Saver's credit 25B
Saver's credit 25B
. applicable percentage .... 6433(b)
. applicable retirement savings vehicle .. 6433(e)
. eligible individual .... 6433(c)
. generally .... 6433(a)
. inflation adjustments .... 6433(h)
. other definitions and special rules ... 6433(f)
. qualified retirement savings
    contributions .... 6433(d)
.. secretary of information relating to
    contributions, provision by ..... 6433(g)
Savings and loan associations—see Mutual savings institutions
Savings bonds—see United States obligations
Scholarship funding corporations ... 150(d)(3)
Scholarships, exempt income 117
Scientific organizations, exemption .. 501(c)(3)
Seals, authority to prescribe or modify .. 7514
**Sec. 126 property, disposition,
    recapture of gain** 1255
Sec. 179 deduction 179
. computer software .... 179(d)(1)(A)(ii)
. election .... 179(c)
. limitations .... 179(b)
. qualified real property .... 179(e)
Sec. 197 intangibles
. amortization 197
. depreciation of certain property
    excluded from Section 197 ..... 167(f)
Sec. 306 stock 306
. attribution rules .... 306(c)
. controlled corporation, transfer .. 306(c)
. sold or exchanged .... 306(a)
Sec. 501(c)(4) organizations
. notification requirement 506
Sec. 1245 property
. basis, adjustments to .... 1245(c)
. death, transfer at .... 1245(b)(2)
. defined .... 1245(a)(3)
. FCC ordered exchanges .... 1245(b)(5)
. gain from disposition, nature of .. 1245(a)(1)
. gifts .... 1245(b)(1)
. involuntary conversions .... 1245(b)(4)
. like-kind exchanges .... 1245(b)(4)
. partnership distribution to partner .. 1245(b)(6)
. percentage depletion computation,
    effect of Section 1245 gains .... 613(a)
. petroleum storage facilities ... 1245(a)(3)(F)
. recomputed basis .... 1245(a)(2)
. SEC ordered exchanges .... 1245(b)(5)
. single-purpose structures ...... 1245(a)(3)(D)
. tax-free exchanges .... 1245(b)(3)
**Sec. 1248 stock, losses from sale or
    exchange** .... 751(e)
Sec. 1250 property
. capital gain
.. reduction, corporate minimum tax 291
. death, transfer at .... 1250(d)(2)
. defined .... 1250(c)
. gifts .... 1250(d)(1)
. involuntary conversions .... 1250(d)(4)
. like-kind exchanges .... 1250(d)(4)
. tax-free exchanges .... 1250(d)(3)
Sec. 6166 interest .... 163(k)
. installment payments of 7479
**Second generation biofuel producer
    credit** .... 40(b)(6)
. black liquor excluded .... 40(b)(6)(E)(iii)
Secretary defined .... 7701(a)(11)

Secretary of the Treasury
. assessment authority 6201
. criminal restitution .... 6201(a)(4)
. collection authority 6301
. prohibition of administrative review of
    decisions of 6406
Securities
. allocations of
.. statute of limitations .... 4979A(d)
. arbitrage operations in .... 1233(f)
. controlled corporation's, distribution of . 355
.. additional consideration received ... 356(b)
. corporate distributions .... 312(d)
. dealers
.. capital gains and losses 1236
.. mark-to-market method 475
.. short sales .... 1233(e)(4)
.. tax-exempt securities, adjustment for
    bond premium 75
. defined .... 1236(c)
. dispositions of, employee stock
    ownership plans and worker-owned
    cooperatives
.. excise taxes 4978
. exchange in reorganization 354
. exempt
.. dealers in 75
.. interest relating to .... 265(a)(2)
. futures contracts 1234B
. issuers, information reporting
.. basis, organizational actions affecting .. 6045B
. partnership distributions of marketable
    securities .... 731(c)
. transfer to brokers
.. information reporting 6045A
. wash sales 1091
. worthless, deduction for .... 165(g); 582
Securities and Exchange Commission
. certifying as to investment companies
    furnishing capital to development
    corporations .... 851(e)
. exchanges or distributions in obedience
    to orders of
.. Section 1245 property .... 1245(b)(5)
**Security interest holders, validity of lien
    for taxes against** 6323
Seizure of property .... 6331—6344
. forfeiture, property subject to .. 7301—7328
. levy and distraint 6331
. liquor tax violations .... 5601—5690
. property exempt from levy 6334
. redemption of property 6337
. sale of seized property 6335; 6336
.. certificate of sale 6338; 6339
.. deed of real property 6338; 6339
.. expense of levy and sale 6341
.. records of sale 6340
. structuring transaction 139H
. surrender of property subject to levy .. 6332
Self-dealing by private foundations ... 4941
**Self-employed individuals, health care
    costs** .... 162(l)
Self-employed individuals, retirement benefits
. bond purchase plans
.. contributions to .... 62(a)(6)
.. information requirements .... 6047(c); 7207
. clergy .... 404(a)(10)
.. church plans .... 414(e)(5)
. contributions to plans ..... 404(a)(8); 404(e)
. employer liability payments ...... 404(g)
. information to be filed 6047
. life insurance, contributions for .. 404(e)
. lump-sum distribution, retirement plan .. 402(g)
. owner-employees
.. benefits .... 401(a)(10)
.. qualification of plans .. 401(a); 401(c)—401(d)
Self-employment assistance programs
. Unemployment Tax Act (FUTA) taxes .. 3306(t)
Self-employment income defined .... 1402(b)
Self-employment tax .... 1401—1403
. deduction, post-1989 .... 164(f)
. hospital insurance .... 1401(b)
.. additional tax on high-income
    taxpayers .... 1401(b)(2)

Self-employment tax—continued
. members of certain religious faiths,
    exemption .... 1402(g)
. returns 6017
Selling price, exclusions from
. local advertising charges .... 4216(e)
Separability clause .... 7852(a)
Separate maintenance—see Alimony and
    separate maintenance
Separate returns
. rates of tax .... 1(d)
Service contracts v. leases of property . 7701(e)
Servicemen and -women—see Armed Forces of
    the U.S.
Services, excise tax on—see particular tax
Services of child 73
**Services, property transferred in
    connection with performance of** .. 83(a)—83(i)
Sexual harassment
. settlement payments subject to
    nondisclosure agreement
.. deduction prohibited .... 162(q)
Shareholders
. controlled foreign corporations
.. inclusions for U.S. shareholders,
    special rules .... 956(b)
. defined .... 7701(a)(8)
. elections of
.. medium of dividend payment ..... 305(b)(1)
. liquidations .... 331(a)
. regulated investment companies,
    foreign tax credit 853
. regulated investment companies,
    taxation of 852
. taxes paid by corporation .... 164(e)
**Shipowners' protection and indemnity
    associations** 526
Shipping activities, international
. alternative tax 1352
.. election 1354
.. revocation 1354
.. termination 1354
. credits, allocation 1358
. deductions, allocation 1358
. definitions 1355
. depreciation 1357
. election to determine corporate tax using
    per ton rate .... 1352—1359
. income, allocation 1358
. interest 1357
. items not subject to regular tax .. 1357
. notional shipping income 1353
. qualifying 1356
. qualifying vessels, disposition .. 1359
. special rules 1355
Ships
. foreign, earnings exempt income to
    foreign corporation .... 883(a)(1)
. leased, income from 861
. passenger voyages, excise tax imposed . 4471; 4472
Short-period returns .... 443(b)(3)
Short sales 1233
Short-term capital gain defined .... 1222(1)
Short-term capital loss defined .... 1222(2)
Short-term obligations .... 1281—1283
. acquisition discount
.. inclusion in current income 1281
. deferral of interest deduction allocable to
    deferral of interest deduction allocable to .. 1282
Short-time compensation program .. 3306(v)
Sick pay .... 104—106
. employees, third-party paid ...... 6051(f)
Signatures on returns .... 6061—6064
Simple retirement accounts .... 408(p)

Internal Revenue Code — SIM — 5733

Simple retirement accounts—continued
. failure to furnish reports . . . . 6693(c)
. investment in collectibles . . . . 408(m)(3)
. reports . . . . 408(l)(2)
. rollovers . . . . 408(d)(3)(G)

Simple trusts 651; 652

Simplified employee pensions
. definition . . . . 408(k)
. distributions, special rules . . . . 402(h)
. employer's deductions for contributions . . . . 404(h)
. maximum deduction for employer contributions . . . . 404(h)
. reports . . . . 408(l)

Simplified method of taxing annuity payments . . . . 72(d)

Single persons, tax rate . . . . 1(c)

Single-premium insurance contracts, deductibility of amounts paid for . . . . 264(b)

Single purpose agricultural or horticultural structure . . . . 168(i)(13); 1245(a)(3)(D)

Sister as dependent . . . . 152(f)(4)

Sitting placement services, employer status 3506

65 and over
. tax credit 22

Small business corporations—see also S corporations
. definition . . . . 1244(c)(3)
. investment companies, losses 1242; 1243
. LIFO inventories
.. election to use single pool 474
. losses on small business stock 1244
. rollover of gain 1045
. small business stock . 1033(f); 1202; 1244(c)(3)
.. active business requirement . . . . 1202(e)
.. exclusion of gain from 1202
.. partial exclusion . . . . 1202(a)
.. qualified small business . . . . 1202(d)
.. qualified small business stock . . . . . 1202(c)
.. tax preference item, exclusion of gain . . . . 57(a)(7)

Small business trusts . . . . . . 641(c); 1361(e)

Small employers
. automatic enrollment credit 45T
. health insurance coverage tax credit . . . 45R
.. denial of double benefit . . . . 280C(h)
. military spouse retirement plan eligibility credit 45AA
. pension plan startup costs 45E
. simple cafeteria plans . . . . 125(j)

Small issue bonds
. interest on 144

Social clubs
. deductibility of cost of furnishing goods and services to members 277
. exemption . . . . 501(c)(7)

Social security benefits
. information returns 6050F
. liability for tax 86
. lump sum received . . . . 86(e)
. nonresident aliens, taxation of . . . . . 871(a)(3)
. overpayments offset against tax refund . . . . 6402(g)

Social security coverage
. foreign affiliates of domestic employers, employees of 406

Social security taxes (FICA) . . . . . 3101—3127
. acts to be performed by agents 3504
. adjustment of tax . . . . 6205(a)
. civil servants 3122
. collection 3501
. concurrent employment by two or more employers . . . . 3121(s)
. deposits . . . . 6302(g)
. employee defined . . . . 3121(d)
. employees of churches and church-controlled organizations . . . . . . 1402(a)(14)
.. exemption election . . . . 3121(w)
. employees of foreign subsidiary, deduction for payments in behalf of . . . 176

Social security taxes (FICA)—continued
. employers and employees both members of religious faiths opposed to 3127
. employment defined . . . . 3121(b)
. erroneous payments, credits against tax . . 3503
. included and excluded service defined . 3121(c)
. overwithheld tax, credit against income tax . . . . 31(b); 6414
. payment 3501
. rate of tax
.. employee's tax 3101
.. employer's tax 3111
. refunds and credits . . . . 31(b); 6413
. self-employment tax . . . . 1401(a)
. taxable income computation, nondeductibility 3502
. tip income, employer credit for 45B
. underpayments . . . . 6205(b)
. wages defined 3121
. withholding of tax from wages 3102

Social welfare organizations
. private inurement prohibition . . . . 501(c)(4)(B)
. exemption . . . . 501(c)(4)

Sodium chloride, percentage depletion . . . . 613(b)

Soil conservation expenditures 175
. recapture . . . . 1252(a)

Solar and wind facilities
. low-income communities . . . . 48(e)

Sole proprietorship
. pension trusts for employees . . . . 414(c)

Solicitations for funds
. contributions, statement of nondeductibility 6113
. failure to provide, penalty 6710

Sound recordings
. ACRS depreciation . . . . 168(f)(4)

Sources of income . . . . 861—865
. interest . . . . 864(e)
. partly within and partly without U.S. . . . 863(b)
. personal property, sales of 865
. railroad rolling stock . . . . 861(d)
. research and experimental expenditures, allocation . . . . 864(g)
. within United States 861
. without United States 862

Special fuels, excise tax . . . . 4041—4043

Special use valuation of real estate, estate tax relief
. basis increase where recapture . . . . . . 1016(c)
. exchange of qualified real property . . 2032A(i)
. failure to use for qualified use . . . . . 2032A(c)(7)
. family member defined . . . . 2032A(e)(2)
. farms, method of valuation . . . . . 2032A(e)(7)(B)
. involuntary conversions . . . . 121(d)(8)
. liens . . . . 6325(d)(3)
. qualified real
.. surviving spouse, special rules . 2032A(b)(5)
. qualified real property
.. decedents who are retired or disabled, special rules . . . . 2032A(b)(4)
.. replacement property . . . . 2032A(e)(14)
.. use by family member . . . . 2032A(b)(1)
. timber
.. recapture upon disposition . . . 2032A(c)(2)(E)
.. valuation . . . . 2032A(e)(13)
. transfers
.. farms 1040

Spin-offs, split-offs, split-ups 355

Split-interest transfers to spouse and charity, estate and gift tax . . . . . 2056(b)(7); 2056(b)(8); 2523(f); 2523(g)

Splitting of income . . . . 1(a)

Spodumene, percentage depletion . . . . 613(b)

Sponsoring organizations
. donor advised funds . . . . 170(f)(18); 2055(e)(5); 2522(c)(5); 4966
.. reporting requirements . . . . . 508(f); 6033(k)

Sport Fish Restoration and Boating Trust Fund 9504

Sporting goods, manufacturers excise tax 4161

Spouse—see Husband and wife

Stamp taxes
. assessment . . . . 6201(a)(2)
. cancellation of stamps, penalty 7271
. failure to pay, penalty 6653

Stamps
. criminal penalties for offenses relating to . 7208
. general provisions relating to . . . . 6801—6808
. unauthorized use or sale of 7209
. violations of provisions relating to, forfeitures . . . . 7303(1)

Standard deduction
. additional standard deduction
.. blind and aged . . . . 63(c)(3); 63(f)
. amount of . . . . 63(c)
. basic . . . . 63(c)(2)
.. limitation for certain dependents . . . 63(c)(5)
. income from sources outside United States . . . . 862(b)
. income from sources within United States . . . . 861(b)
. ineligibility of certain individuals . . . . 63(c)(6)
. inflation adjustment . . . . 63(c)(4)
. withholding exemption . . . . 3402(f)(1)(E)

Stapled stock 269B

Start-up expenditures, business organized or acquired 195

State and local obligations—see also United States obligations
. arbitrage bonds 148
. declaratory judgments, Tax Court . . . . . 7478; 7482(b)(3)
. interest on
.. exclusion from gross income . . 103; 141—150
.. municipal bond defined . . . . 75(b)
.. private activity bonds 147
.. short-term obligations issued on discount basis . . . . 454(b)

State and local taxes
. past-due state income tax obligations
.. reduction of federal refund . . . . 6402(e)
. refunds
.. information returns 6050E

State death taxes
. deduction from value of gross estate . . . 2058

State government employees, return and payment of tax . . . . 3125(a)

State legislators' travel expenses, deductibility of . . . . 162(h)

State or local government deferred compensation plans 457

State tax officials
. disclosure of returns to . . . . 6103(d)

Statements, false and fraudulent . 7206; 7211

Statements to payees of dividends and interest . . . . 6042(c); 6044(e); 6049(c)

States
. contributions to State unemployment funds, credits against tax 3302; 3303
. defined . . . . 3121(e)(1); 7701(a)(10)
. escheat, overpayments of tax 6408
. gasoline taxes, deductibility . . . . 164(b)(4)
. income received by, exclusion from gross income 115
. manufacturers excise tax exemption . . . . 4221(a)(4)
. obligations of—see State and local obligations
. sales taxes, deductibility . . . . 164(b)(4)
. sickness and disability fund benefits, exemption . . . . 105(e)(2)

Statistical publications and studies 6108

Statute of limitations
. assessment and collection of tax . 6501—6504
. foreign tax credit carrybacks . . . . 6501(i)
. claim for refund 6511
. collection of tax . . . . 6501—6504
. credit or refund after expiration of 6514
. foreign financial assets
.. omission of income . . . . 6501(e)(1)(A)

Statute of limitations—continued
. levy and distraint 6502; 6503
. mitigation of effect ..... 1311—1314; 6521
.. amount of adjustment 1314
.. correction of errors 1311
.. method of adjustment 1314
. passive foreign investment companies
.. information reporting .... 6501(c)(8)
.. penalties .... 6696(d)
. refunds or credits .... 6511—6515
. suspension of running 6503

Statutory merger or consolidation as reorganization .... 368(a)

Stills
. manufacturers of, notice requirements ... 5101
. premises prohibited for distilling 5178

Stock
. arbitrage operations in .... 1233(f)
. consent stock .... 565(f)(1)
. constructive ownership 318
. controlled corporation's, distribution of .. 355
.. additional consideration received .... 356(b)
.. recognition of gain .... 355(e)
. corporate shareholder
.. basis reduction, nontaxed portion of
    extraordinary dividends 1059
. dividends paid in—see Stock dividends and
    rights
. exchange of, gain or loss recognition
.. property received for stock 1032
.. reorganization 354
.. stock for stock of same corporation ... 1036
. Federal National Mortgage Association,
    basis in hands of holder 1054
. gain or loss on sale by corporation 1032
. intragroup transactions .... 358(g)
. March 1, 1913 value 1053
. nonqualified preferred
.. treatment of .... 351(g)
. options of employees 421
. ownership rule
.. affiliated corporations ... 1504(a); 1563(e)
.. controlled foreign corporations 958
.. corporate distributions and
    adjustments 318
.. employee stock options .... 424(d)
.. multiple surtax exemptions .... 1563(e)
.. nondeductible losses .... 267(c)
.. personal holding companies .. 542(a)(2); 544
. preferred
.. bail-out 306
. property acquired by issuance of, basis ... 362
. redemption of .... 302—304
.. defined .... 317(b)
. sales of, to employee stock ownership
    plans
.. nonrecognition of gain 1042
. Sec. 306 stock 306
. stapled 269B
. transfers by foreign corporations .... 304(b)(5)
. wash sales 1091

Stock associations, conversion to mutual savings banks .... 591(b)

Stock bonus plans—see Retirement plans

Stock distributions
. excess, passive foreign investment
    companies 1291

Stock dividends and rights
. basis 307
. distributions of, exclusion from gross
    income of recipient 305
. earnings and profits, effect on .... 312(d)
. taxes paid by corporation .... 164(e)

Stock options
. bargain element, tax preference item .. 57(a)(3)
. employees .... 421—424
. incentive stock options 422
. straddles, recognition of gain or loss
    .... 1092(c)(4)

Stock purchase plans 423

Stock redemptions
. costs of, business expense status .... 162(k)

Stone, percentage depletion .... 613(b)

Storm losses, deductibility .... 165(c)(3)
. estate tax 2054

Straddles, recognition of gain or loss 1092
. anti-conversion rules .... 1258(d)(1)
. mixed straddle regulations .... 1092(b)
. mixed straddles, elections .... 1256(d)
. stock transactions .... 1092(c)(4)

Stripped bonds 1286

Stripped preferred stock .... 305(e)

Structured settlement factoring transactions 5891
. exception for certain approved
    transactions .... 5891(b)
. imposition of tax .... 5891(a)

Students
. dependent, defined .... 152(f)(2)
. group health plans
.. medical leave, continuation of
    coverage 9813
. loan bonds
.. interest on 144
. loans
.. income from discharge of
    indebtedness .... 108(f)
.. maintenance in the home .... 170(g)
. scholarship awards, exemption 117

Subchapter S corporations—see S corporations

Subpart F income 952
. export trade corporations 970
. income includible for annualized
    estimated tax payment .... 6654(d)(2)(D)
.. corporations .... 6655(e)(4)

Subscriptions, prepaid income from ... 455

Subsidiaries
. definition of subsidiary corporation .... 424(f)
. domestic subsidiary doing business
    outside U.S.
.. pension plan coverage for employees .. 407
. employee stock options granted by .. 421(a)(2)
. foreign subsidiary of domestic parent
.. consolidated returns .... 1504(d)
.. social security coverage for
    employees 176
. group losses offsetting income of
    subsidiary paying preferred dividends
    .... 1503(f)
. liquidation of 332; 337
.. basis of property received 334
. real estate investment trust subsidiary,
    taxable .... 856(l)
. S corporations .... 1361(b)(3)

Substituted basis .... 1016(b)

Substituted basis property defined
    .... 7701(a)(42)
. exchanged basis property .... 7701(a)(44)
. transferred basis property ...... 7701(a)(43)

Successor corporations, carryovers by ... 381; 382

Suits by taxpayers .... 7421—7430
. civil actions for refund 7422
. exhaustion of administrative remedies . 7430(b)
. reasonable litigation costs .... 7430(c)
. reimbursement of costs by 7430
. restraining assessment or collection of
    tax 7421
. statute of limitations .... 6532(a)
. third party suits 7426
. U.S. position substantially justified
    .... 7430(c)(4)(B)

Suits by United States .... 7401—7409
. reimbursement of taxpayer's costs by
    government 7430
. statute of limitations
.. criminal prosecutions 6531
.. recovery of erroneous refunds ..... 6532(b)

Sulphur deposits, percentage depletion
    .... 613(b)

Summons
. books and witnesses 7602
. computer software
.. limited access to source code 7612
. corporation
.. period of limitations, suspension of
    running of .... 6503(j)
. enforcement of .... 7402(b); 7604
. issuance .... 7602(a)

Summons—continued
. penalty for failure to obey 7210
. service 7603
. third-party, special procedures for 7609

Sunday as last day for performing acts ... 7503

Supplemental child credit .... 32(m)

Supplemental unemployment benefit payments, withholding ...... 3402(o)(1)(A)

Supplemental unemployment benefit trusts, exempt status .... 501(c)(17)

Supporting organizations ... 509(a)(3); 509(f)
. excess benefit transactions .... 4958(c)(3)
. excess business holdings .... 4943(f)
. private foundation distributions .... 4942(g)(4)
. reporting requirements .... 6033(l)

Supreme Court of the U.S.
. delay proceedings .... 6673(b)
. frivolous appeal to, damages .... 6673(b)
. review of decisions by
.. courts of appeals decisions .... 7482(a)
.. Tax Court decisions .... 7482(c)(2)

Surplus, improper accumulations ... 531—537

Surviving spouse—see Widows and widowers

Sustainable aviation fuel credit .... 40B; 6426(k)

T

Tables
. computation of tax for individuals 3

Talc, percentage depletion .... 613(b)

Tanning salons
. excise tax on tanning services 5000B

Targeted jobs tax credit—see Work opportunity credit

Tax benefit items
. recovery
.. acquiring corporation .... 381(c)(12)

Tax benefit rule 111

Tax check-off system, political campaign contributions .. 6096; 9001—9012

Tax Court .... 7441—7479
. administration 7470
. appeals from decisions of 7483
. bond on appeal from 7485
. burden of proof 7454
. date decision becomes final 7481
. declaratory judgments
.. gifts, valuation of .... 2001(f)
. deficiencies disallowed by 6215
. delay proceedings 6673
. employees 7471
. employment status
.. proceedings for determination of 7436
. expenditures authorized 7472
. fees
.. disposition of 7473
.. filing petitions .... 7451(a)
.. transcript of 7474
.. witness 7457
. frivolous appeal to, damages 6673
. hearings 7458
. judges
.. annual conference 7470A
.. annuities for dependents 7448
.. complaints, procedures for filing 7466
.. retirement 7447; 7447A
.. salary .... 7443(c)
.. survivors, annuities 7448
.. term of office .... 7443(e)
. jurisdiction 7442
. membership 7443
. notice of appeal 7483
. oaths, administration of 7456
. offices, location 7445
. organization 7444
. overpayment of tax determined by,
    refunds and credits .... 6512(b)
. partnerships
.. oversheltered returns (pre-2018) 6234
. petitions 7451
.. filing fee .... 7451(a)
.. tolling of time .... 7451(b)
. place of sessions 7446
. practice fee, authority to impose 7475

Topical Index
References are to Code Section numbers.

Tax Court—continued
. procedure . . . . 7451—7465
. publicity of proceedings 7461
. reports 7459
. . publication of 7462
. representation of parties 7452
. retirement of judges 7447
. review of decisions of . . . . . . 7481—7487
. rules 7453
. service of process 7455
. special trial judges . . . . 7456(c)
. . appointment of 7443A
. . proceedings assigned to . . . . . . 7456(d)
. . retirement for 7447A
. status 7441
. tax disputes involving $50,000 or less . . 7463
. testimony before, procurement of 7456
. time of sessions 7446
. transcript of record fee 7474
. witness fees 7457

Tax credit employee stock ownership plans 409
. qualified gratuitous transfers to . . . . . 664(g)

Tax-exempt bond financed property
. alternative depreciation . . . . 168(g)
. empowerment zones 1394

Tax-exempt income—see Exempt income

Tax-exempt interest
. tax preference item . . . . 57(a)(5)

Tax-exempt obligations
. original issue discount 1288

Tax-exempt organizations—see Exempt organizations

Tax-exempt use property
. alternative depreciation . . . . . . 168(g); 168(h)

Tax-free dividends, effect of depreciation on earnings and profits . . . . 312(k)

Tax-free exchanges . . . . 1031—1045
. investment property 1031
. involuntary conversions 1033
. Section 1245 property . . . . 1245(b)(3)
. Section 1250 property . . . . 1250(d)(3)
. stock for property 1032

Tax practitioners
. privileged communications 7525

Tax preferences, minimum tax 57
. losses disallowed 58

Tax rates
. corporations . . . . 11(b)
. individuals . . . . 1(j)
. . long-term capital gains rates . . . 1(h); 55(b)(3)
. long-term capital gains
. . revised holding periods and tax rates . . . 1(h)
. ten percent rate bracket . . . . 1(i)

Tax return preparers
. action to enjoin 7407
. burden of proof in action involving 7427
. copy of return to taxpayer and copy retained by 6107
. defined . . . . 7701(a)(36)
. disclosure or use of information 7216
. . identity theft . . . . 6713(b)
. . penalty for improper 6713
. information returns 6060
. penalties 6694; 6695
. understatement of taxpayer's liability
. . unreasonable position . . . . 6694(a)
. . willful or reckless conduct . . . . 6694(b)
. volunteer income tax assistance program 7526A

Tax shelters
. abusive, penalties for 6700; 7408
. corporations, substantial understatement penalty . . . . 6662(d)(2)(C)
. deductions, special rules . . . . 461(i)
. passive activities
. . losses and credits 469
. prohibited transactions
. . excise tax 4965

Taxable estate . . . . 2051—2058
. nonresident aliens 2106

Taxable gifts 2503; 2504

Taxable income
. computation . . . . 281—291
. . common trust fund participants . . . . 584(c)
. . cooperatives 1382
. . partnership 703
. . period for 441
. deductions, allowance of 211; 241
. defined 63

Taxable mortgage pools
. definition . . . . 7701(i)

Taxable year
. change in 442
. controlled foreign corporations . . . . 898(c)(1)
. defined . . . . 441(b); 7701(a)(23)
. foreign corporations 898
. foreign personal holding companies . . 898(c)(2)
. partner and partnership 706; 7519
. partnership 444
. personal service corporation . 280H; 441(i); 444
. rate change during 15
. S corporation 444; 7519

Taxes
. accrual of real property taxes . . . . . . 461(c)
. cooperative housing tenant stockholders . . 216
. deductibility 164; 275
. Railroad Retirement Tax Act taxes, deduction from compensation 3202

Taxpayer assistance
. low-income taxpayer clinics
. . matching grants 7526
. volunteer income tax assistance program
. . matching grants 7526A

Taxpayer assistance orders 7811

Taxpayer identification number
. dependents claimed as an exemption . 6109(e)
. disclosure of . . . . 6103(m)
. earned income credit, identification requirement for qualifying child . . . . 32(c)(3)(D)(i)
. exemption requirements . . . . 151(e)
. household and dependent care services . 21(e)
. supplying of 6109

Taxpayer interviews, procedures 7522

Taxpayer rights
. collection activities
. . appeals dispute resolution 7123
. . fair debt collection practices 6304
. court proceedings
. . burden of proof 7491
. examination activities
. . executive branch influence on audits prohibited 7217
. levy
. . right to hearing prior to levy 6330
. privileged communication
. . extension to authorized practitioners . . 7525

Teachers
. deductions for adjusted gross income
. . out-of-pocket classroom expenses . . . . 62(a)(2)(D)

Teachers' annuities . . . . 403(b)

Teachers' retirement fund associations, exemption . . . . 501(c)(11)

Telephone companies, mutual, exemption . . . . 501(c)(12)

Telephone service, communications tax . . . . 4251—4254

Teletypewriter exchange service, communications tax . . . . . . 4251—4254

Tenant-stockholders in cooperatives, depreciation deduction . . . . 216(c)

Tentative carry-back adjustments 6411
. assessment period . . . . 6501(k)

Term interests
. depreciation . . . . 167(e)
. sold, gain or loss . . . . 1001(e)

Terminable interests, shrinkage in value . 273

Terminal railroad corporations 281

Termination assessments of income tax . 6851
. political expenditures of exempt organizations 6852

Terrorist attacks
. victims
. . abatement of tax 692
. . estate tax 2201

Terroristic or military action
. authority to postpone certain deadlines 7508A
. death of military or civilian employees of U.S. 692(c)

Tertiary injectants, oil production 193

Testing for public safety, exemption of organizations engaged in . . . . . . 501(c)(3)

Theatrical productions
. expensing election 181

Theft losses
. deduction from gross income . . . . . 165(e)
. gross estate's value reduced by 2054

Thenardite, percentage depletion . . . . 613(b)

Third parties
. advance notice of contact . . . . . . 7602(c)

Thorium, percentage depletion . . . . . 613(b)

Thrift Savings Funds, Federal
. tax treatment of . . . . 7701(j)

Throwback rule, excess distributions by trusts . . . . 665—668

Throwback rule, trusts 666

Tier 2 tax rate determination 3241

Timber
. capital gains and losses 631
. depletion 611
. valuation in gross estate . . . . . 2032A(e)(13)

Timely mailing as timely filing 7502

Tin, percentage depletion . . . . 613(b)

Tips
. charged, employer's reporting requirements . . . . 6041(e)
. employer credit for FICA payments . . . 45B
. information returns 6053
. special rules . . . . 3202(c)
. withholding . . . . 3402(k)

Tires and tubes
. heavy truck tires
. . credit for tire tax . . . . 4051(d)
. manufacturers excise tax . . . . . . 4071—4073
. use by manufacturer or importer considered sale . . . . 4218(b)

Titanium, percentage depletion . . . . . 613(b)

Title-holding companies, exemption . . 501(c)(2)

Tobacco taxes . . . . 5701—5763
. fines for violations of provisions . . 5761—5763
. forfeitures 5763
. occupational taxes . . . . 5731—5734
. operations by manufacturers and importers of articles . . . . 5721—5723
. penalties for violations . . . . . . 5761—5763
. qualification requirements for manufacturers of articles and dealers in tobacco materials . . . . 5711—5713
. records of manufacturers and importers of articles and dealers in tobacco materials 5741
. refunds 6423
. restrictions on importation of tobacco . . 5754
. roll-your-own tobacco . . . . 5702(p)

Trade Adjustment Assistance program
. group health plans
. . COBRA continuation coverage . . . . 4980B(f)(2)(B)(i)(VI)
. . pre-certification rule . . . . . . 9801(c)(2)(D)
. health coverage tax credit 35

Trade, boards of, exemption . . . . . . 501(c)(6)

Trade or business
. defined . . . . 1402(c); 7701(a)(26)
. expenses—see Business expenses
. gross income from . . . . 61(a)(2)
. information returns
. . remuneration for services . . . . . . 6041A(a)
. profits paid to exempt organizations . . . 502
. property used in 1231
. self-employment tax . . . . 1402(c)
. within the U.S. defined . . . . 864(b)

Topical Index
References are to Code Section numbers.

Trade or business property
. valuation of gross estate 2032A
Trade shows
. unrelated trade or business . . . . 513(d)
Trademark and trade name expenditures
. capital gains and losses 1253
Training, authority to admit to 7516
Trans-Alaska Pipeline Liability Fund
. unused payments, credit against tax . . 4612(e)
Transferees . . . . 6901—6904
. burden of proof 7454
. partnership basis to . . . . 732(d)
Transfers
. between spouses or incident to divorce
. . nonrecognition of gain 1041
. common trust fund to regulated
    investment company . . . . 584(h)
. estate tax 2055
. firearms 5812
. foreign persons, to
. . information returns 6038B
. gift tax . . . . 2511—2519
. . educational and medical expenses . 2503(e)
. intangibles, possessions corporations . 367(d)
. possessions corporations, by
    intangibles . . . . 367(d)
. right to receive income in respect of
    decedent . . . . 691(a)(2)
. special use valuation
. . farms 1040
Transportation by air
. availability for hire . . . . 4282(b)
. international transportation facilities . . 4261(c)
. members of affiliated group . . . . 4282(c)
. persons . . . . 4261—4263; 4281; 4282
. property 4271; 4272; 4281; 4282
Transportation fringe benefits . . . . 132(f)
Trash containers, excise tax . . . . 4053(6)
Traveling expenses . . . . 162(a)(2)
. foreign travel, repeal of allocation
    requirement . . . . 274(c)
. state legislators . . . . 162(h)
. substantiation 274
Treasury bonds—see United States obligations
Treasury Department
. authority 7801
Treasury stock, sale or exchange 1032
Treaties
. confidentiality of information 6105
. disclosure of return positions based on . 6114
. . failure to disclose, penalty 6712
. income affected by 894
. obligations v. Code provisions . . . . . . 7852(d)
**Treble damage payments under
    antitrust laws** . . . . 162(g)
Trona, percentage depletion . . . . 613(b)
Troubled Assets Relief Program
. executive compensation limitations . 162(m)(5)
. . golden parachute payments . . . . . 280G(e)
. ownership changes
. . net operating losses and net
    unrealized built-in losses . . . . . . 382(n)
Trucks and trailers
. excise tax on heavy trucks
. . definitions 4052
. . exemptions 4053
. . imposition of tax 4051
. highway motor vehicle use tax . . . 4481—4484
Trust companies, taxation as bank . . . 581
Trust funds
. airport and airway 9502
. black lung disability 9501
. harbor maintenance 9505
. hazardous substance superfund 9507
. highway 9503
. inland waterways 9506
. leaking underground storage tank . . 4041; 9508
. management 9602
. oil spill liability 9509
. patient-centered outcomes research . . 9511
. sport fish restoration and boating 9504
. transfer of amounts appropriated 9601

Trust funds—continued
. United Mine Workers of America
    Combined Benefit Fund . . . . . 9702—9708
. vaccine injury compensation 9510
Trusts—see also Estates and trusts . . 641—685
. accumulation distributions
    . . . . 665—668; 904(f)(4)
. . defined . . . . 665(b)
. . retention of character of amounts
    distributed . . . . 667(e)
. Alaska Native Settlement Trusts . . 646; 6039H
. alimony 682
. alternative minimum tax 55
. amortization deduction . . . . 642(f)
. amounts deemed distributed in
    preceding years . . . . 667(a)
. basis of property acquired by transfers
    in trust 1015
. beneficiaries—see Beneficiaries of estates and
    trusts
. charitable trusts . . . . 511(b)
. Clifford rule . . . . 671—679
. complex trusts . . . . 661—663
. contributions deduction, limitation 681
. credits against tax . . . . 642(a)
. deductions
. . complex trusts . . . . 661(a)
. . depletion . . . . 642(e)
. . depreciation . . . . 642(e)
. . simple trusts . . . . 651(a)
. . trusts distributing current income only . . 651
. distributions by—see also Distributions by trusts
. . first sixty-five days rule . . . . 663(b)
. employees' trusts—see Retirement plans
. excess deductions on termination
    available to beneficiaries . . . . 642(h)
. exchange fund, use as 683
. foreign
. . creation of or transfers to, information
    returns 6048
. . distributions by—see also Foreign trusts:
    distributions by . . . . 901(b)(5)
. funeral 685
. grantor trusts . . . . 671—679
. . power to control beneficial enjoyment
    in grantor 674
. . revocable 676
. grantors and others treated as
    substantial owners . . . . 671—679
. imposition of tax 641
. income for benefit of grantor 677
. information returns where charitable
    deductions claimed 6034
. interests transferred, valuation 2702
. loans from foreign trusts . . . . 643(i)
. multiple trusts
. . amounts deemed distributed in
    preceding years, tax on . . . . 667(c)
. net operating loss carrybacks and
    carryovers . . . . 642(h)
. net operating loss deduction . . . . 642(d)
. pension trusts—see Retirement plans
. person other than grantor treated as
    substantial owner 678
. personal exemptions, deduction for . . . 642(b)
. power to control beneficial enjoyment in
    grantor 674
. profit-sharing—see Retirement plans
. prohibited transactions 503
. property transferred at less than fair
    market value to
. . tax imposed on gain 644
. rates of tax . . . . 1(e)
. real estate investment trusts . . . . 856—860
. refunds of excess distributions 667
. revocable 676
. . certain treated as part of estate 645
. separate shares treated as separate
    trusts . . . . 663(c)
. simple trusts 651; 652
. small business trusts . . . . 641(c)
. tax preferences . . . . 59(c)
. taxable years of 644
. taxes imposed on the trust defined . . . 665(d)
. throwback rule 666
. transfers by
. . recognition of gain 684
. . special use valuation election . . . . 1040(b)

Trusts—continued
. transfers of interests by corporations 386
. undistributed net income defined . . . . 665(a)
. unused net operating loss carryovers
    and carrybacks available to beneficiaries . .
    . . . . 642(h)
Tungsten, percentage depletion . . . . . 613(b)

U

UMWA Benefit Plan (1992)—see also United
Mine Workers of America Combined Benefit
Fund
. establishment and coverage of 9712
**Unauthorized enticement of information
    disclosures, damages** 7435
**Undercover operations of Internal
    Revenue Service** . . . . 7608(c)
Underpayment of tax—see Deficiencies
Understatement of liability
. aiding and abetting, penalty 6701
. tax return preparer, penalty 6694
Undistributed net income defined . . . . 665(a)
**Undistributed personal holding
    company income** 545
Unemployment compensation benefits
. erroneous payment due to fraud
. . refund offset . . . . 6402(f)
. information returns 6050B
. liability for tax 85
. repayment of supplemental payments . . . . .
    . . . . 62(a)(12)
Unemployment Tax Act (FUTA) taxes . . 3301—
    3311
. acts to be performed by agents 3504
. collection 3501
. concurrent employment by two or more
    employers . . . . 3306(p)
. credits against tax 3302; 3303
. deductions as constructive payments . . . 3307
. deferred compensation . . . . 3306(r)
. exclusions
. . fishermen . . . . 3306(c)(1)
. . students . . . . 3306(q)
. governmental entities
. . state law coverage 3309
. . instrumentalities of the U.S. 3308
. judicial review 3310
. nonprofit organizations
. . state law coverage 3309
. payment 3501
. . quarterly basis 6157; 6317
. . time period basis 6157
. rate of tax 3301
. salary reduction arrangements . . . . . . 3306(r)
. seamen on U.S. vessels . . . . 3305(g)
. self-employment assistance programs . 3306(t)
. short-time compensation program . . . 3306(v)
. State laws
. . applicability of 3305
. . approval of 3304
. successor employers, credits against
    tax . . . . 3302(e)
. taxable income computation,
    nondeductibility 3502
. tips . . . . 3306(s)
Unenrolled participants
. eliminating unnecessary plan
    requirements related to . . . . 414(bb)
Unharvested crop sold with land 268
Unified credit
. applicable credit amount . . . . 2010(c)
Union-negotiated pension plans . . . . . 401(i)
Unit investment trusts . . . . 851(f)
. redemptions by . . . . 852(d)
**United Mine Workers of America Combined
Benefit Fund**
. annual premiums paid by assigned
    operators 9704
. . failure to pay premium penalty 9707
. assignment of eligible beneficiaries . . . 9706
. claims or obligations connected with
    other UMWA benefit plans 9708
. eligible beneficiaries 9706

Topical Index
References are to Code Section numbers.

United Mine Workers of America Combined Benefit Fund—continued
. establishment of 9702
. health and death benefits 9703
. transfer of 1950 UMWA Pension Plan assets to 9705

United States
. administration of real property acquired by 7506
. excise tax exemption 4293
. instrumentalities of
. . Federal Insurance Contributions Act taxes 3112
. obligations of—see United States obligations
. sale of personal property purchased by . . . 7505

United States nationals . . . 152(b)(3); 873(b)(3)

United States obligations
. exchanges, gain on 1037
. higher education tuition and fees, exempt interest 135
. matured savings bonds retained . . . . 454(c)
. short-term obligations issued on discount basis . . . . 454(b)

United States person defined . . . . . . 957(c); 7701(a)(30)

United States Postal Service, expenditures incurred by 7509

United States property
. controlled foreign corporations
. . corporation ceases to be controlled foreign corporation . . . . 956(b)(3)
. . defined . . . . 956(d)
. . inclusions for U.S. shareholders, special rules . . . . 956(b)

United States real property
. controlled foreign corporations
. . corporation ceases to be controlled foreign corporation . . . . 956(b)(3)
. . inclusions for U.S. shareholders, special rules . . . . 956(b)
. . defined . . . . 956(d)
. disposition 897
. withholding of tax at source 1445
. interests held by foreign persons, information returns 6039C

United States Tax Court—see Tax Court

Unitrusts 664

Unmarried individuals, rates of tax . . . . 1(c)

Unrealized receivables, gain or loss on sale . . . . 735(a)(1); 751

Unrelated business income . . . . . . 501(b); 512
. advertising activities . . . . 513(c)
. agricultural or horticultural organization dues . . . . 512(d)
. churches
. . restriction on examination of . 7605(c); 7611
. foreign corporations . . . . 512(b)(17)
. $1,000 deduction . . . . 512(b)(12)
. returns
. . electronic filing requirement . . . . . 6011(h)
. S corporation stock . . . . 512(e)

Unrelated debt-financed income 514

Unrelated trade or business 513
. defined 513
. low-cost articles, distribution of . . . . . 513(h)
. partnerships . . . . 512(c)
. telephone or electric company, pole rentals . . . . 513(g)
. trade shows . . . . 513(d)
. treatment of sponsorship payments . . 513(i)

Uranium
. percentage depletion . . . . 613(b)

Use tax, highway motor vehicles . . 4481—4484

User fees
. Internal Revenue Service 7528

V

Vacation homes
. rental of, deductibility of expenses in connection with 280A

Vaccines
. excise tax 4131; 4132
. . vaccine injury compensation trust fund . . 9510

Valuation of gifts 2512

Valuation tables
. annuities, etc. 7520

Vehicles
. plug-in electric drive motor vehicle credit . . . 30D
. previously-owned clean vehicles credit . . 25E

Verification of returns 6065

Vermiculite, percentage depletion . . . 613(b)

Vessel supplies, exemption from manufacturers excise tax . . . . 4221(a)(3)

Veterans
. contributions or gifts to organizations of 170(c); 2522
. exempt organizations . . 501(c)(19); 501(c)(23)
. health savings accounts
. . eligibility . . . . 223(c)(1)(C)
. reemployment rights . . . . 414(u)
. unemployed veterans
. . work opportunity credit . . . . 51(d)(14)

Veterans' mortgage bonds
. interest on 143

Viatical settlements . . . . 101(g)

Vinegar plants . . . . 5501—5505

Virgin Islands
. coordination of individual income tax . . . 7654
. foreign corporations, exception . . . . . 881(b)
. imports and exports, taxes on . . . . . 7652(b); 7653(a)(2)
. income taxes, coordination with U.S. . . . 932
. reduction of tax liability to, limitations . . . 934
. withholding of tax on income sourced within Virgin Islands 1444

Voluntary employee beneficiary associations, exempt status . . . . . . 501(c)(9)
. nondiscrimination requirements 505

Voluntary withholding . . . . 3402(p)

Volunteer firefighters and emergency medical responders
. benefits, exclusion from gross income . . 139B

Volunteer income tax assistance program
. matching grants 7526A

W

Wage bracket withholding . . . . 3402(c)

Wage earners' returns . . . . 6014; 6151(b)

Wagering losses . . . . 165(d)

Wagering taxes . . . . 4401—4424
. disclosure of wagering tax information . . 4424
. excise tax on wagers
. . refunds and credits 6419
. lottery defined . . . . 4421(2)
. occupational tax
. . failure to post stamps, penalties 7273
. . penalties for violations 7262
. . rate of tax 4411
. . registration 4412
. rate of tax . . . . 4401(a)
. record requirements 4403
. territorial extent 4404
. wager defined . . . . 4421(1)

Wages
. defined
. . FICA . . . . 3121(a)
. . FUTA . . . . 3306(b)
. . self-employment tax . . . . 1402(d)
. . withholding of tax on wages . . . . . 3401(a)

Waivers
. family attribution rules . . . . 302(c)

Wash sales 1091

Water and sewerage disposal utilities
. contributions to capital . . . . 118(c)

Water conservation expenditures 175
. recapture . . . . 1252(a)

Welfare benefit plans 419
. disqualified benefits, excise tax 4976
. qualified asset account, limitation . . . 419A

Welfare organizations, exemption . . . 501(c)(4)

Whaling
. native Alaskan subsistence whaling
. . expenses paid by whaling captains . . 170(n)

Whistleblower reward program . . . . . 7623(b)

Whistleblower reward program—continued
. attorney fees . . . . 62(a)(21)

Whistleblowers
. disclosure of return information . . . . 6103(k)(13)
. retaliation, protection against . . . . . . 7623(d)

Widows and widowers
. bequests to surviving spouse, estate tax . . 2056
. death benefits, exempt income . . . . 101(d)(3)
. definition of surviving spouse . . . . 2(a)
. joint returns . . . . 1(a); 2(a)
. residence sale proceeds, exclusion for 65-year-olds 121
. rollover distributions . . . . 402(c)(9)

Wines
. bonded and tax-paid premises . . . 5351—5392
. cellar treatment and classification . . 5381—5388
. classification of . . . . 5381—5388
. foreign producers
. . information returns 6038E
. imported in bulk 5364
. penalties for violation of provisions relating to . . . . 5661—5663
. tax on . . . . 5041—5045
. . credit disallowed 5067

Withdrawal of notice of lien for taxes . . 6323(j)

Withholding agent, defined . . . . . . 7701(a)(16)

Withholding of income tax on wages . . 3401—3404
. accounting for withheld taxes 7512
. additional withholding . . . . 3402(i)
. agents, acts to be performed by 3504
. allowances based on itemized deductions . . . . 3402(m)
. alternative methods of computing amounts to be withheld . . . . 3402(h)
. annuities . . . . 3402(o)
. average wages . . . . 3402(h)
. collection . . . . 3501; 6205(b)
. credit for tax withheld . . . . 31(a)
. definitions 3401
. employee defined . . . . 3401(c)
. employees incurring no income tax liability . . . . 3402(n)
. employer defined . . . . 3401(d); 3402
. employer's liability 3403
. statements for employees . 6051; 6674; 7204
. excessive taxes withheld, refunds and credits 6414
. exemption certificates . . . . 3402(f)(2)
. . fraudulent, penalties 7205
. . tax liability absent . . . . 3402(n)
. extension of withholding to payments other than wages . . . . 3402(o)
. failure to pay over taxes
. . criminal penalties 7215
. . separate accounting 7512
. . fraudulent statement, penalties 7204
. governmental employer 3404
. included and excluded wages . . . . . . 3401(a)
. Indian casino profits . . . . 3402(r)
. itemized deductions, withholding allowances based on . . . . 3402(m)
. liability for tax 3403; 3504; 7501
. multiple employers . . . . 3402(f)(7)
. noncash remuneration to retail commission salesmen . . . . 3402(j)
. notice of failure to pay . . . . 6672(b)
. overlapping pay periods . . . . 3402(g)
. payment 3404; 3501
. . depositaries . . . . 6302(c); 6656
. . deposits . . . . 6302(g)
. . . exception to penalty for first-time depositors . . . . 6656(c)
. . penalties 6674; 7204
. percentage method . . . . 3402(b)
. period of less than one week . . . 3402(b)(4)
. rate tables . . . . 3402(c)
. receipts for employees . . 6051; 6674; 7204
. refunds and credits . . . . 31(a); 6414
. reimbursed expenses as wages . . . . 274(e)(4)
. right of contribution where more than one person liable . . . . 6672(d)
. statements for employees 6051
. . fraudulent, penalties 7204
. supplemental unemployment benefits . . . 3402(o)(1)(A)

Topical Index
References are to Code Section numbers.

Withholding of income tax on wages—continued
. tables, wage bracket withholding .... 3402(c)
. tax paid by recipient .... 3402(d)
. third-party liability .... 3121(a)
. tips .... 3402(k)
. underwithholding, waiver of addition to
  tax 6654
. voluntary .... 3402(p)
. voluntary board members of exempt
  organizations .... 6672(e)
. wage bracket tables .... 3402(c)
. withheld taxes considered as
  constructively paid 3123

Withholding of tax at source—see also
Withholding of income tax on wages . 1441—1464
. accounting for withheld taxes 7512
. annuities 3405
. backup withholding—see Backup withholding
. credit to recipient of income 1462
. credits against income tax 31; 33
. foreign corporations ...... 1441(b); 1442
. . dispositions of U.S. property interests . 1445
. foreign entities
. . expansion of withholding rules 1472
. foreign financial institutions
. . expansion of withholding rules 1471
. foreign persons
. . REMICs .... 860G(b)
. foreign transfers
. . financial institutions, electronic filing of
    returns .... 6011(e)(4)
. gambling winnings .... 3402(q)
. liability for withheld tax 7501
. lump-sum distributions, retirement plans .....
    .... 3405(b)
. nonresident aliens
. . dispositions of U.S. property interests . 1445

Withholding of tax at source—continued
. overwithheld tax, refunds and credits ... 1464
. partnerships
. . foreign partners' share of effectively
    connected income 1446
. payment 1461
. pensions 3405
. recipient paying tax, re-collection from
    withholding agent 1463
. responsible person
. . plan administrator .... 3405(d)
. rollover distributions .... 3405(c)
. Virgin Islands, income sourced within ... 1444
. withheld amount not deductible ..... 3502(b)
. withholding allowances
. . false information 6682
. withholding certificate, fraudulent 7205

Witnesses, examination of ...... 7602—7605
. failure to testify 7210
. fees and costs for 7610

Woodlands
. gross estate
. . special valuation .... 2032A(e)(13)

Work opportunity credit .... 51—52
. carrybacks
. . tentative carryback adjustment
    assessment period .... 6501(k)
. designated community residents .... 51(d)(5)
. designated local agency .... 51(d)(12)
. election to have targeted jobs credit not
    apply .... 51(j)
. qualified SSI recipient .... 51(d)(9)
. rules for computing .... 51—52
. . agricultural labor, special rules ..... 51(h)
. . amount, determination of .... 51(a)
. . certification of .... 51(d)(13)

Work opportunity credit—continued
. rules for computing—continued
. . coordination with payroll tax
    forgiveness .... 51(c)(5)
. . eligibility of individuals .... 51(i)
. . employees performing services for
    other persons .... 51(k)
. . qualified wages defined .... 51(b)
. . railway labor, special rules .... 51(h)
. . second year wages of long-term family
    assistance recipients .... 51(e)
. . successor employers, treatment of ... 51(k)
. . targeted groups, members of ..... 51(d)
. . termination .... 51(c)(4)
. . wages defined .... 51(c)
. special rules 52

Workers' compensation
. employment tax .... 3121(a)(2)(B)

Written determinations, inspection of ... 6110

Y

Year
. change of, accounting .... 442; 481(a)
. deductions allowed 461
. . disaster losses .... 165(i)
. . economic performance rule ...... 461(h)
. . points paid to acquire mortgages .. 461(g)(2)
. . rental agreements, deferred payments .. 467
. income reported .... 451—456

Z

**Zero-emission nuclear power
production credit** 45U

Public Laws Amending the Internal Revenue Code

Public Law No.	Popular Name	Enactment Date
517, 83rd Cong.	Revised Organic Act of the Virgin Islands	7-22-54
703, 83rd Cong.	Atomic Energy Act of 1954	8-30-54
729, 83rd Cong.		8-31-54
746, 83rd Cong.		8-31-54
761, 83rd Cong.	Social Security Amendments of 1954	9-1-54
767, 83rd Cong.		9-1-54
1, 84th Cong.		1-20-55
9, 84th Cong.		3-2-55
18, 84th Cong.	Tax Rate Extension Act of 1955	3-30-55
74, 84th Cong.		6-15-55
299, 84th Cong.		8-9-55
306, 84th Cong.		8-9-55
317, 84th Cong.		8-9-55
321, 84th Cong.		8-9-55
333, 84th Cong.		8-9-55
354, 84th Cong.		8-11-55
355, 84th Cong.		8-11-55
366, 84th Cong.		8-11-55
367, 84th Cong.		8-11-55
379, 84th Cong.		8-12-55
384, 84th Cong.		8-12-55
385, 84th Cong.		8-12-55
396, 84th Cong.		1-28-56
398, 84th Cong.		1-28-56
400, 84th Cong.		1-28-56
414, 84th Cong.		2-20-56
429, 84th Cong.	Life Insurance Company Tax Act for 1955	3-13-56
458, 84th Cong.	Tax Rate Extension Act of 1956	3-29-56
466, 84th Cong.		4-2-56
495, 84th Cong.		4-27-56
511, 84th Cong.	Bank Holding Company Act of 1956	5-9-56
545, 84th Cong.		5-29-56
627, 84th Cong.	Federal-Aid Highway Act of 1956	6-29-56
628, 84th Cong.		6-29-56
629, 84th Cong.		6-29-56
700, 84th Cong.		7-11-56
726, 84th Cong.	Mutual Security Act of 1956	7-18-56
728, 84th Cong.	Narcotic Control Act of 1956	7-18-56
784, 84th Cong.		7-24-56
796, 84th Cong.		7-25-56
880, 84th Cong.	Social Security Amendments of 1956	8-1-56
881, 84th Cong.	Servicemen's and Veterans' Survivor Benefits Act	8-1-56
896, 84th Cong.		8-1-56
1010, 84th Cong.		8-6-56
1011, 84th Cong.		8-6-56
1015, 84th Cong.		8-7-56
1022, 84th Cong.		8-7-56
85-12	Tax Rate Extension Act of 1957	3-29-57
85-56	Veterans' Benefits Act of 1957	6-17-57
85-74		6-29-57
85-165		8-26-57
85-235		8-30-57
85-239		8-30-57
85-320		2-11-58
85-321		2-11-58
85-323		2-11-58
85-345		3-17-58
85-367		4-7-58
85-380		4-16-58
85-475	Tax Rate Extension Act of 1958	6-30-58
85-517		7-11-58
85-840	Social Security Amendments of 1958	8-28-58
85-859	Excise Tax Technical Changes Act of 1958	9-2-58
85-866	Technical Amendments Act of 1958	9-2-58
85-866	Small Business Tax Revision Act of 1958	9-2-58
85-881		9-2-58
86-28		5-19-59
86-69	Life Insurance Company Income Tax Act of 1959	6-25-59
86-70	Alaska Omnibus Bill	6-25-59
86-75	Tax Rate Extension Act of 1959	6-30-59

5742 PUBLIC LAWS AMENDING THE INTERNAL REVENUE CODE

Public Law No.	Popular Name	Enactment Date
86-141		8-7-59
86-168	Farm Credit Act of 1959	8-18-59
86-175		8-21-59
86-280		9-16-59
86-319		9-21-59
86-342	Federal-Aid Highway Act of 1959	9-21-59
86-344		9-21-59
86-346		9-22-59
86-368		9-22-59
86-376		9-23-59
86-413		4-8-60
86-416		4-8-60
86-418		4-8-60
86-422		4-8-60
86-428		4-22-60
86-429	Narcotics Manufacturing Act of 1960	4-22-60
86-435		4-22-60
86-437		4-22-60
86-440		4-22-60
86-459	Dealer Reserve Income Adjustment Act of 1960	5-13-60
86-470		5-14-60
86-478		6-1-60
86-496		6-8-60
86-564	Public Debt and Tax Rate Extension Act of 1960	6-30-60
86-592		7-6-60
86-594		7-6-60
86-624	Hawaii Omnibus Act	7-12-60
86-667		7-14-60
86-707	Overseas Differentials and Allowances Act	9-6-60
86-723	Foreign Service Act Amendments of 1960	9-8-60
86-778	Social Security Amendments of 1960	9-13-60
86-779		9-14-60
86-780		9-14-60
86-781		9-14-60
87-6	Temporary Extended Unemployment Compensation Act of 1961	3-24-61
87-15		3-31-61
87-29		5-4-61
87-59		6-27-61
87-61	Federal-Aid Highway Act of 1961	6-29-61
87-64	Social Security Amendments of 1961	6-30-61
87-72	Tax Rate Extension Act of 1961	6-30-61
87-109		7-26-61
87-256	Mutual Educational and Cultural Exchange Act of 1961	9-21-61
87-293	Peace Corps Act	9-22-61
87-321		9-26-61
87-370		10-4-61
87-397		10-5-61
87-403		2-2-62
87-426		3-31-62
87-456	Tariff Classification Act of 1962	5-24-62
87-508	Tax Rate Extension Act of 1962	6-28-62
87-535	Sugar Act Amendments of 1962	7-13-62
87-682		9-25-62
87-710		9-27-62
87-722		9-28-62
87-768		10-9-62
87-770		10-9-62
87-790		10-10-62
87-792	Self-Employed Individuals Tax Retirement Act of 1962	10-10-62
87-794	Trade Expansion Act of 1962	10-11-62
87-834	Revenue Act of 1962	10-16-62
87-858		10-23-62
87-863		10-23-62
87-870		10-23-62
87-876		10-24-62
88-4		4-2-63
88-9		4-10-63
88-31		5-29-63
88-36		6-4-63
88-52	Tax Rate Extension Act of 1963	6-29-63
88-133		10-5-63
88-173		11-7-63
88-272	Revenue Act of 1964	2-26-64
88-342		6-30-64

PUBLIC LAWS AMENDING THE INTERNAL REVENUE CODE

Public Law No.	Popular Name	Enactment Date
88-348	Excise Tax Rate Extension Act of 1964	6-30-64
88-380		7-17-64
88-426	Government Employees Salary Act of 1964	8-14-64
88-484		8-22-64
88-539		8-31-64
88-554		8-31-64
88-563	Interest Equalization Tax Act	9-2-64
88-570		9-2-64
88-571		9-2-64
88-650		10-13-64
88-653		10-13-64
89-44	Excise Tax Reduction Act of 1965	6-21-65
89-97	Social Security Amendments of 1965	7-30-65
89-212		9-29-65
89-243	Interest Equalization Tax Extension Act of 1965	10-9-65
89-331	Sugar Act Amendments of 1965	11-8-65
89-352		2-2-66
89-354		2-2-66
89-365		3-8-66
89-368	Tax Adjustment Act of 1966	3-15-66
89-384		4-8-66
89-389		4-14-66
89-493		7-5-66
89-523		8-1-66
89-570		9-12-66
89-621		10-4-66
89-699		10-30-66
87-700		10-30-66
89-713		11-2-66
89-719	Federal Tax Lien Act of 1966	11-2-66
89-721		11-2-66
89-722		11-2-66
89-739		11-2-66
89-793		11-8-66
89-800		11-8-66
89-809	Foreign Investors Tax Act of 1966	11-13-66
90-26		6-13-67
90-59	Interest Equalization Tax Extension Act of 1967	7-31-67
90-73		8-29-67
90-78		8-31-67
90-225		12-27-67
90-240		1-2-68
90-248	Social Security Amendments of 1967	1-2-68
90-285		4-12-68
90-346		6-18-68
90-364	Revenue and Expenditure Control Act of 1968	6-28-68
90-607		10-21-68
90-615		10-21-68
90-618	Gun Control Act of 1968	10-22-68
90-619		10-22-68
90-621		10-22-68
90-622		10-22-68
90-624		10-22-68
90-630		10-22-68
90-634	Renegotiation Amendments Act of 1968	10-24-68
91-36		6-30-69
91-50		8-2-69
91-53		8-7-69
91-65		8-25-69
91-128	Interest Equalization Tax Extension Act of 1969	11-26-69
91-172	Tax Reform Act of 1969	12-30-69
91-215		3-17-70
91-258	Airport and Airway Revenue Act of 1970	5-21-70
91-373	Employment Security Amendments of 1970	8-10-70
91-420		9-25-70
91-513		10-27-70
91-518	Rail Passenger Service Act of 1970	10-30-70
91-605	Federal-Aid Highway Act of 1970	12-31-70
91-606	Disaster Relief Act of 1970	12-31-70
91-614	Excise, Estate, and Gift Tax Adjustment Act of 1970	12-31-70
91-618		12-31-70
91-659		1-8-71
91-673		1-12-71
91-676		1-12-71

Internal Revenue Code

Public Law No.	Popular Name	Enactment Date
91-677		1-12-71
91-678		1-12-71
91-679		1-12-71
91-680		1-12-71
91-681		1-12-71
91-683		1-12-71
91-684		1-12-71
91-686		1-12-71
91-687		1-12-71
91-688		1-12-71
91-691		1-12-71
91-693		1-12-71
92-5		3-17-71
92-9	Interest Equalization Tax Extension Act of 1971	4-1-71
92-41		7-1-71
92-138	Sugar Act Amendments of 1971	10-14-71
92-178	Revenue Act of 1971	12-10-71
92-279		4-26-72
92-310		6-6-72
92-329		6-30-72
92-336		7-1-72
92-418		8-29-72
92-512	State and Local Fiscal Assistance Act of 1972	10-20-72
92-558		10-25-72
92-580		10-27-72
92-603	Social Security Amendments of 1972	10-30-72
92-606		10-31-72
93-17	Interest Equalization Tax Extension Act of 1973	4-10-73
93-53		7-1-73
93-66		7-9-73
93-69		7-10-73
93-233		12-31-73
93-288	Disaster Relief Act of 1974	5-22-74
93-310		6-8-74
93-368		8-7-74
93-406	Employee Retirement Income Security Act of 1974	9-2-74
93-443	Federal Election Campaign Act Amendments of 1974	10-15-74
93-445		10-16-74
93-480		10-26-74
93-482		10-26-74
93-483		10-26-74
93-490		10-26-74
93-499		10-29-74
93-597		1-2-75
93-625		1-3-75
94-12	Tax Reduction Act of 1975	3-29-75
94-45	Emergency Compensation and Special Unemployment Assistance Extension Act of 1975	6-30-75
94-81		8-9-75
94-92		8-9-75
94-93		8-9-75
94-164	Revenue Adjustment Act of 1975	12-23-75
94-202		1-2-76
94-253		3-31-76
94-267		4-15-76
94-273	Fiscal Year Adjustment Act	4-21-76
94-280		5-5-76
94-283	Federal Election Campaign Act Amendments of 1976	5-11-76
94-331		6-30-76
94-396		9-3-76
94-401		9-7-76
94-414		9-17-76
94-452	Bank Holding Company Tax Act of 1976	10-2-76
94-455	Tax Reform Act of 1976	10-4-76
94-514		10-15-76
94-528		10-17-76
94-529		10-17-76
94-530		10-17-76
94-547		10-18-76
94-553	Copyrights Act	10-19-76
94-563		10-19-76
94-566	Unemployment Compensation Amendments of 1976	10-20-76
94-568		10-20-76
94-569		10-20-76
95-19	Emergency Unemployment Compensation Act of 1977	4-12-77

PUBLIC LAWS AMENDING THE INTERNAL REVENUE CODE 5745

Public Law No.	Popular Name	Enactment Date
95-30	Tax Reduction and Simplification Act of 1977	5-23-77
95-147		10-28-77
95-171		11-12-77
95-172		11-12-77
95-176		11-14-77
95-210		12-13-77
95-216		12-20-77
95-227	Black Lung Benefits Revenue Act of 1977	2-10-78
95-339	New York City Loan Guarantee Act of 1978	8-8-78
95-345		8-15-78
95-423		10-6-78
95-427		10-7-78
95-458		10-14-78
95-472		10-17-78
95-473		10-17-78
95-479	Veterans' Disability Compensation and Survivors' Benefits Act of 1978	10-18-78
95-488		10-20-78
95-502	Inland Waterways Revenue Act of 1978	10-21-78
95-599	Surface Transportation Assistance Act of 1978	11-6-78
95-600	Revenue Act of 1978	11-6-78
95-615	Tax Treatment Extension Act of 1978	11-8-78
95-618	Energy Tax Act of 1978	11-9-78
95-628		11-10-78
96-39	Trade Agreements Act of 1979	7-26-79
96-72	Export Administration Act of 1979	9-29-79
96-84		10-10-79
96-167		12-29-79
96-178		1-2-80
96-187	Federal Election Campaign Act Amendments of 1979	1-8-80
96-222	Technical Corrections Act of 1979	4-1-80
96-223	Crude Oil Windfall Profit Tax Act of 1980	4-2-80
96-249	Food Stamp Act Amendments of 1980	5-26-80
96-265	Social Security Disability Amendments of 1980	6-9-80
96-272	Adoption Assistance and Child Welfare Act of 1980	6-17-80
96-283	Deep Seabed Hard Mineral Resources Act	6-28-80
96-298		7-1-80
96-364	Multiemployer Pension Plan Amendments Act of 1980	9-26-80
96-417	Customs Courts Act of 1980	10-10-80
96-439		10-13-80
96-451	Recreational Boating Safety and Facilities Improvement Act of 1980	10-14-80
96-454	Household Goods Transportation Act of 1980	10-15-80
96-465	Foreign Service Act of 1980	10-17-80
96-471	Installment Sales Revision Act of 1980	10-19-80
96-499	Omnibus Reconciliation Act of 1980	12-5-80
96-510	Comprehensive Environmental Response, Compensation, and Liability Act of 1980	12-11-80
96-541		12-17-80
96-589	Bankruptcy Tax Act of 1980	12-24-80
96-595		12-24-80
96-596		12-24-80
96-598		12-24-80
96-601		12-24-80
96-603		12-28-80
96-605	Miscellaneous Revenue Act of 1980	12-28-80
96-608		12-28-80
96-613		12-28-80
97-34	Economic Recovery Tax Act of 1981	8-13-81
97-35	Omnibus Budget Reconciliation Act of 1981	8-13-81
97-51		10-1-81
97-119	Black Lung Benefits Revenue Act of 1981	12-29-81
97-123		12-29-81
97-164	Federal Courts Improvement Act of 1982	4-2-82
97-216	Urgent Supplemental Appropriations Act, 1982	7-18-82
97-248	Tax Equity and Fiscal Responsibility Act of 1982	9-3-82
97-258		9-13-82
97-261	Bus Regulatory Reform Act of 1982	9-20-82
97-354	Subchapter S Revision Act of 1982	10-19-82
97-362	Miscellaneous Revenue Act of 1982	10-25-82
97-365	Debt Collection Act of 1982	10-25-82
97-414	Orphan Drug Act	1-4-83
97-424	Surface Transportation Assistance Act of 1982	1-6-83
97-448	Technical Corrections Act of 1982	1-12-83
97-449		1-12-83
97-452		1-12-83
97-455		1-12-83

Internal Revenue Code

PUBLIC LAWS AMENDING THE INTERNAL REVENUE CODE

Public Law No.	Popular Name	Enactment Date
97-473		1-14-83
98-21	Social Security Amendments of 1983	4-20-83
98-67	Interest and Dividend Tax Compliance Act of 1983	8-5-83
98-76	Railroad Retirement Solvency Act of 1983	8-12-83
98-135	Federal Supplemental Compensation Amendments of 1983	10-24-83
98-213		12-8-83
98-216		2-14-84
98-259		4-10-84
98-355		7-11-84
98-369	Deficit Reduction Act of 1984	7-18-84
98-378	Child Support Enforcement Amendments of 1984	8-16-84
98-397	Retirement Equity Act of 1984	8-23-84
98-443	Civil Aeronautics Board Sunset Act of 1984	10-4-84
98-473		10-12-84
98-573		10-30-84
98-611		10-31-84
98-612		10-31-84
98-620		11-8-84
99-44		5-24-85
99-92		8-16-85
99-121		10-11-85
99-221	Cherokee Leasing Act	12-26-85
99-234	Federal Civilian Employee and Contractor Travel Expenses Act of 1985	1-2-86
99-272	Consolidated Omnibus Budget Reconciliation Act of 1985	4-7-86
99-308	Firearms Owner's Protection Act	5-19-86
99-335		6-6-86
99-386	Congressional Reports Elimination Act of 1986	8-22-86
99-499	Superfund Amendments and Reauthorization Act of 1986	10-17-86
99-509	Omnibus Budget Reconciliation Act of 1986	10-21-86
99-514	Tax Reform Act of 1986	10-22-86
99-595		10-31-86
99-640	Coast Guard Authorization Act of 1986	11-10-86
99-662	Water Resources Development Act of 1986	11-17-86
100-17	Surface Transportation and Uniform Relocation Assistance Act of 1987	4-2-87
100-202	Continuing Appropriations, Fiscal Year 1988	12-22-87
100-203	Revenue Act of 1987	12-22-87
100-223	Airport and Airway Revenue Act of 1987	12-30-87
100-360	Medicare Catastrophic Coverage Act of 1988	7-1-88
100-418	Omnibus Trade and Competitiveness Act of 1988	8-23-88
100-448	Coast Guard Authorization Act of 1988	9-28-88
100-485	Family Support Act of 1988	10-13-88
100-647	Technical and Miscellaneous Revenue Act of 1988	11-10-88
100-690	Anti-Drug Abuse Act of 1988	11-18-88
100-707	Disaster Relief and Emergency Assistance Amendments of 1988	11-23-88
101-73	Financial Institutions Reform, Recovery, and Enforcement Act of 1989	8-9-89
101-140		11-8-89
101-194	Ethics Reform Act of 1989	11-30-89
101-221	Steel Trade Liberalization Program Implementation Act	12-12-89
101-234	Medicare Catastrophic Coverage Repeal Act of 1989	12-13-89
101-239	Omnibus Budget Reconciliation Act of 1989	12-19-89
101-280		5-4-90
101-380	Oil Pollution Act of 1990	8-18-90
101-382	Customs and Trade Act of 1990	8-20-90
101-508	Omnibus Budget Reconciliation Act of 1990	11-5-90
101-624	Food, Agriculture, Conservation, and Trade Act of 1990	11-28-90
101-647	Crime Control Act of 1990	11-29-90
101-649	Immigration Act of 1990	11-29-90
102-2		1-30-91
102-90	Legislative Branch Appropriations Act	8-14-91
102-164	Emergency Unemployment Compensation Act of 1991	11-15-91
102-227	Tax Extension Act of 1991	12-11-91
102-240	Intermodal Surface Transportation Efficiency Act of 1991	12-18-91
102-244		2-7-92
102-318	Unemployment Compensation Amendments of 1992	7-3-92
102-393	Treasury, Postal Service, and General Government Appropriations Act, 1993	10-6-92
102-486	Energy Policy Act of 1992	10-24-92
102-568	Veterans' Benefits Act of 1992	10-29-92
102-572	Court of Federal Claims Technical and Procedural Improvements Act of 1992	10-29-92
102-581	Airport and Airway Safety, Capacity, Noise Improvement, and Intermodal Transportation Act of 1992	10-31-92
103-66	Omnibus Budget Reconciliation Act of 1993	8-10-93
103-149	South African Democratic Transition Support Act of 1993	11-22-93

PUBLIC LAWS AMENDING THE INTERNAL REVENUE CODE

Public Law No.	Popular Name	Enactment Date
103-178	Intelligence Authorization Act for Fiscal Year 1994	12-3-93
103-182	North American Free Trade Agreement Implementation Act	12-8-93
103-260	Airport Improvement Program Temporary Extension Act of 1994	5-26-94
103-272		7-5-94
103-296	Social Security Independence and Program Improvements Act of 1994	8-15-94
103-305	Federal Aviation Administration Authorization Act of 1994	8-23-94
103-322	Violent Crime Control and Law Enforcement Act of 1994	9-13-94
103-337	National Defense Authorizations Act for Fiscal Year 1995	10-5-94
103-387	Social Security Domestic Employment Reform Act of 1994	10-22-94
103-429		10-31-94
103-465	Uruguay Round Agreements Act	12-8-94
104-7	Self-Employed Health Insurance Act	4-11-95
104-88	ICC Termination Act of 1995	12-29-95
104-117		3-20-96
104-134	Debt Collection Improvement Act of 1996	4-26-96
104-168	Taxpayer Bill of Rights 2	7-30-96
104-188	Small Business Job Protection Act of 1996	8-20-96
104-191	Health Insurance Portability and Accountability Act of 1996	8-21-96
104-193	Personal Responsibility and Work Opportunity Reconciliation Act of 1996	8-22-96
104-201	National Defense Authorization Act for Fiscal Year 1997	9-23-96
104-208	Deposit Insurance Funds Act of 1996	9-30-96
104-264	Federal Aviation Reauthorization Act of 1996	10-9-96
104-303	Water Resources Development Act of 1996	10-12-96
104-316	General Accounting Office Act of 1996	10-19-96
105-2	Airport and Airway Trust Fund Tax Reinstatement Act of 1997	2-28-97
105-33	Balanced Budget Act of 1997	8-5-97
105-34	Taxpayer Relief Act of 1997	8-5-97
105-35	Taxpayer Browsing Protection Act	8-5-97
105-61	Treasury and General Government Appropriations Act, 1998	10-10-97
105-65	Departments of Veterans Affairs and Housing and Urban Development, and Independent Agencies Appropriations Act, 1998	10-27-97
105-78	Departments of Labor, Health and Human Services and Education, and Related Agencies Appropriations Act, 1998	11-13-97
105-102		11-20-97
105-115	Food and Drug Administration (FDA) Modernization Act of 1997	11-21-97
105-130	Surface Transportation Extension Act of 1997	12-1-97
105-178	Transportation Equity Act for the 21st Century	6-9-98
105-206	Internal Revenue Service Restructuring and Reform Act of 1998	7-22-98
105-261		10-17-98
105-277	Tax and Trade Relief Extension Act of 1998	10-21-98
105-277	Vaccine Injury Compensation Program Modification Act	10-21-98
105-306	Noncitizen Benefit Clarification and Other Technical Amendments Act of 1998	10-28-98
106-21		4-19-99
106-36	Miscellaneous Trade and Technical Corrections Act of 1999	6-25-99
106-78	Agriculture, Rural Development, Food and Drug Administration, and Related Agencies Appropriations Act, 2000	10-22-99
106-170	Tax Relief Extension Act of 1999	12-17-99
106-181	Wendell H. Ford Aviation Investment and Reform Act for the 21st Century	4-5-2000
106-200	Trade and Development Act of 2000	5-18-2000
106-230		7-1-2000
106-408	Wildlife and Sport Fish Restoration Programs Improvement Act of 2000	11-1-2000
106-476	Imported Cigarette Compliance Act of 2000	11-9-2000
106-519	FSC Repeal and Extraterritorial Income Exclusion Act of 2000	11-15-2000
106-554	Community Renewal Tax Relief Act of 2000	12-21-2000
106-573	Installment Tax Correction Act of 2000	12-28-2000
107-15	Fallen Hero Survivor Benefit Fairness Act of 2001	6-5-2001
107-16	Economic Growth and Tax Relief Reconciliation Act of 2001	6-7-2001
107-22		7-26-2001
107-71	Aviation and Transportation Security Act	11-19-2001
107-90	Railroad Retirement and Survivors' Improvement Act of 2001	12-21-2001
107-110	No Child Left Behind Act of 2001	1-8-2002
107-116	Departments of Labor, Health and Human Services, and Education, and Related Agencies Appropriations Act, 2002	1-10-2002
107-131		1-16-2002
107-134	Victims of Terrorism Tax Relief Act of 2001	1-23-2002
107-147	Job Creation and Worker Assistance Act of 2002	3-9-2002
107-181	Clergy Housing Allowance Clarification Act of 2002	5-20-2002
107-210	Trade Act of 2002	8-6-2002
107-217		8-21-2002
107-276		11-2-2002
107-296	Homeland Security Act of 2002	11-25-2002

Internal Revenue Code

PUBLIC LAWS AMENDING THE INTERNAL REVENUE CODE

Public Law No.	Popular Name	Enactment Date
107-330	Veterans Benefits Act of 2002	12-6-2002
108-27	Jobs and Growth Tax Relief Reconciliation Act of 2003	5-28-2003
108-88	Surface Transportation Extension Act of 2003	9-30-2003
108-89		10-1-2003
108-121	Military Family Tax Relief Act of 2003	11-11-2003
108-173	Medicare Prescription Drug, Improvement, and Modernization Act of 2003	12-8-2003
108-176	Vision 100—Century of Aviation Reauthorization Act	12-12-2003
108-178		12-15-2003
108-189		12-19-2003
108-202	Surface Transportation Extension Act of 2004	2-29-2004
108-203	Social Security Protection Act of 2004	3-2-2004
108-218	Pension Funding Equity Act of 2004	4-10-2004
108-224	Surface Transportation Extension Act of 2004, Part II	4-30-2004
108-263	Surface Transportation Extension Act of 2004, Part III	6-30-2004
108-280	Surface Transportation Extension Act of 2004, Part IV	7-30-2004
108-310	Surface Transportation Extension Act of 2004, Part V	9-30-2004
108-311	Working Families Tax Relief Act of 2004	10-4-2004
108-357	American Jobs Creation Act of 2004	10-22-2004
108-375	Ronald W. Reagan National Defense Authorization Act for Fiscal Year 2005	10-28-2004
108-429	Miscellaneous Trade and Technical Corrections Act of 2004	12-3-2004
108-493		12-23-2004
109-6		3-31-2005
109-7		4-15-2005
109-14	Surface Transportation Extension Act of 2005	5-31-2005
109-20	Surface Transportation Extension Act of 2005, Part II	7-1-2005
109-35	Surface Transportation Extension Act of 2005, Part III	7-20-2005
109-37	Surface Transportation Extension Act of 2005, Part IV	7-22-2005
109-40	Surface Transportation Extension Act of 2005, Part V	7-28-2005
109-42	Surface Transportation Extension Act of 2005, Part VI	7-30-2005
109-58	Energy Tax Incentives Act of 2005	8-8-2005
109-59	Safe, Accountable, Flexible, Efficient Transportation Equity Act: A Legacy for Users	8-10-2005
109-73	Katrina Emergency Tax Relief Act of 2005	9-23-2005
109-74	Sportfishing and Recreational Boating Safety Amendments Act of 2005	9-29-2005
109-135	Gulf Opportunity Zone Act of 2005	12-21-2005
109-151		12-30-2005
109-171	Deficit Reduction Act of 2005	2-8-2006
109-222	Tax Increase Prevention and Reconciliation Act of 2005	5-17-2006
109-227	Heroes Earned Retirement Opportunities Act	5-29-2006
109-241	Coast Guard and Maritime Transportation Act of 2006	7-11-2006
109-280	Pension Protection Act of 2006	8-17-2006
109-304		10-6-2006
109-432	Tax Relief and Health Care Act of 2006	12-20-2006
109-433		12-20-2006
110-28	U.S. Troop Readiness, Veterans' Care, Katrina Recovery, and Iraq Accountability Appropriations Act, 2007	5-25-2007
110-28	Small Business and Work Opportunity Tax Act of 2007	5-25-2007
110-92		9-29-2007
110-140	Energy Independence and Security Act of 2007	12-19-2007
110-142	Mortgage Forgiveness Debt Relief Act of 2007	12-20-2007
110-161	Department of Transportation Appropriations Act, 2008	12-26-2007
110-166	Tax Increase Prevention Act of 2007	12-26-2007
110-172	Tax Technical Corrections Act of 2007	12-29-2007
110-176		1-4-2008
110-177	Court Security Improvement Act of 2007	1-7-2008
110-185	Economic Stimulus Act of 2008	2-13-2008
110-190	Airport and Airway Extension Act of 2008	2-28-2008
110-233	Genetic Information Nondiscrimination Act of 2008	5-21-2008
110-244	SAFETEA-LU Technical Corrections Act of 2008	6-6-2008
110-245	Heroes Earnings Assistance and Relief Tax Act of 2008	6-17-2008
110-246	Food, Conservation, and Energy Act of 2008	5-22-2008
110-246	Heartland, Habitat, Harvest, and Horticulture Act of 2008	5-22-2008
110-253	Federal Aviation Administration Extension Act of 2008	6-30-2008
110-289	Housing Assistance Tax Act of 2008	7-30-2008
110-289	Federal Housing Finance Regulatory Reform Act of 2008	7-30-2008
110-317	Hubbard Act	8-29-2008
110-318		9-15-2008
110-328	SSI Extension for Elderly and Disabled Refugees Act	9-30-2008
110-330	Federal Aviation Administration Extension Act of 2008, Part II	9-30-2008
110-343	Emergency Economic Stabilization Act of 2008	10-3-2008
110-343	Energy Improvement and Extension Act of 2008	10-3-2008
110-343	Tax Extenders and Alternative Minimum Tax Relief Act of 2008	10-3-2008
110-343	Paul Wellstone and Pete Domenici Mental Health Parity and Addiction Equity Act of 2008	10-3-2008
110-343	Heartland Disaster Tax Relief Act of 2008	10-3-2008
110-351	Fostering Connections to Success and Increasing Adoptions Act of 2008	10-7-2008

PUBLIC LAWS AMENDING THE INTERNAL REVENUE CODE 5749

Public Law No.	Popular Name	Enactment Date
110-381	Michelle's Law	10-9-2008
110-428	Inmate Tax Fraud Prevention Act of 2008	10-15-2008
110-458	Worker, Retiree, and Employer Recovery Act of 2008	12-23-2008
111-3	Children's Health Insurance Program Reauthorization Act of 2009	2-4-2009
111-5	American Recovery and Reinvestment Tax Act of 2009	2-17-2009
111-8	Omnibus Appropriations Act, 2009	3-11-2009
111-12	Federal Aviation Administration Extension Act of 2009	3-30-2009
111-46		8-7-2009
111-68		10-1-2009
111-69	Fiscal Year 2010 Federal Aviation Administration Extension Act	10-1-2009
111-88		10-30-2009
111-92	Worker, Homeownership, and Business Assistance Act of 2009	11-6-2009
111-116	Fiscal Year 2010 Federal Aviation Administration Extension Act, Part II	12-16-2009
111-144	Temporary Extension Act of 2010	3-2-2010
111-147	Hiring Incentives to Restore Employment Act	3-18-2010
111-148	Patient Protection and Affordable Care Act	3-23-2010
111-152	Health Care and Education Reconciliation Act of 2010	3-30-2010
111-153	Federal Aviation Administration Extension Act of 2010	3-31-2010
111-159	TRICARE Affirmation Act	4-26-2010
111-161	Airport and Airway Extension Act of 2010	4-30-2010
111-173		5-27-2010
111-192	Preservation of Access to Care for Medicare Beneficiaries and Pension Relief Act of 2010	6-25-2010
111-197	Airport and Airway Extension Act of 2010, Part II	7-2-2010
111-198	Homebuyer Assistance and Improvement Act of 2010	7-2-2010
111-203	Dodd-Frank Wall Street Reform and Consumer Protection Act	7-21-2010
111-216	Airline Safety and Federal Aviation Administration Extension Act of 2010	8-1-2010
111-226		8-10-2010
111-237	Firearms Excise Tax Improvement Act of 2010	8-16-2010
111-240	Creating Small Business Jobs Act of 2010	9-27-2010
111-249	Airport and Airway Extension Act of 2010, Part III	9-30-2010
111-291	Claims Resolution Act of 2010	12-8-2010
111-309	Medicare and Medicaid Extenders Act of 2010	12-15-2010
111-312	Tax Relief, Unemployment Insurance Reauthorization, and Job Creation Act of 2010	12-17-2010
111-322	Continuing Appropriations and Surface Transportation Extensions Act, 2011	12-22-2010
111-325	Regulated Investment Company Modernization Act of 2010	12-22-2010
111-329	Airport and Airway Extension Act of 2010, Part IV	12-22-2010
111-344	Omnibus Trade Act of 2010	12-29-2010
111-347	James Zadroga 9/11 Health and Compensation Act of 2010	1-2-2011
111-350		1-4-2011
111-366		1-4-2011
112-5	Surface Transportation Extension Act of 2011	3-4-2011
112-7	Airport and Airway Extension Act of 2011	3-31-2011
112-9	Comprehensive 1099 Taxpayer Protection and Repayment of Exchange Subsidy Overpayments Act of 2011	4-14-2011
112-10	Department of Defense and Full-Year Continuing Appropriations Act, 2011	4-15-2011
112-16	Airport and Airway Extension Act of 2011, Part II	5-31-2011
112-21	Airport and Airway Extension Act of 2011, Part III	6-29-2011
112-27	Airport and Airway Extension Act of 2011, Part IV	8-5-2011
112-30	Surface and Air Transportation Programs Extension Act of 2011	9-16-2011
112-40	Trade Adjustment Assistance Extension Act of 2011	10-21-2011
112-41	United States-Korea Free Trade Agreement Implementation Act	10-21-2011
112-56	VOW to Hire Heroes Act of 2011	11-21-2011
112-91	Airport and Airway Extension Act of 2012	1-31-2012
112-95	FAA Modernization and Reform Act of 2012	2-14-2012
112-96	Middle Class Tax Relief and Job Creation Act of 2012	2-22-2012
112-102	Surface Transportation Extension Act of 2012	3-30-2012
112-140	Temporary Surface Transportation Extension Act of 2012	6-29-2012
112-141	Highway Investment, Job Creation, and Economic Growth Act of 2012	7-6-2012
112-141	Moving Ahead for Progress in the 21st Century Act (MAP-21)	7-6-2012
112-239	National Defense Authorization Act for Fiscal Year 2013	1-2-2013
112-240	American Taxpayer Relief Act of 2012	1-2-2013
113-15		6-25-2013
113-22		7-25-2013
113-94	Gabriella Miller Kids First Research Act	4-3-2014
113-97	Cooperative and Small Employer Charity Pension Flexibility Act	4-7-2014
113-121	Water Resources Reform and Development Act of 2014	6-10-2014
113-128	Workforce Innovation and Opportunity Act	7-22-2014
113-159	Highway and Transportation Funding Act of 2014	8-8-2014
113-168	Tribal General Welfare Exclusion Act of 2014	9-26-2014
113-188	Government Reports Elimination Act of 2014	11-26-2014
113-235	Consolidated and Further Continuing Appropriations Act, 2015	12-16-2014
113-287		12-19-2014
113-295	Tax Increase Prevention Act of 2014	12-19-2014
113-295	Tax Technical Corrections Act of 2014	12-19-2014

Internal Revenue Code

PUBLIC LAWS AMENDING THE INTERNAL REVENUE CODE

Public Law No.	Popular Name	Enactment Date
113-295	Stephen Beck, Jr., Achieving a Better Life Experience Act of 2014	12-19-2014
114-10	Medicare Access and CHIP Reauthorization Act of 2015	4-16-2015
114-14	Don't Tax Our Fallen Public Safety Heroes Act	5-22-2015
114-21	Highway and Transportation Funding Act of 2015	5-29-2015
114-26	Defending Public Safety Employees' Retirement Act	6-29-2015
114-27	Trade Preferences Extension Act of 2015	6-29-2015
114-27	Trade Adjustment Assistance Reauthorization Act of 2015	6-29-2015
114-41	Surface Transportation and Veterans Health Care Choice Improvement Act of 2015	7-31-2015
114-55	Airport and Airway Extension Act of 2015	9-30-2015
114-73	Surface Transportation Extension Act of 2015	10-29-2015
114-74	Bipartisan Budget Act of 2015	11-2-2015
114-87	Surface Transportation Extension Act of 2015, Part II	11-20-2015
114-92	National Defense Authorization Act for Fiscal Year 2016	11-25-2015
114-94	Fixing America's Surface Transportation Act	12-4-2015
114-95	Every Student Succeeds Act	12-10-2015
114-113	Consolidated Appropriations Act, 2016	12-18-2015
114-125	Trade Facilitation and Trade Enforcement Act of 2015	2-24-2016
114-141	Airport and Airway Extension Act of 2016	3-30-2016
114-184	Recovering Missing Children Act	6-30-2016
114-190	FAA Extension, Safety, and Security Act of 2016	7-15-2016
114-239	United States Appreciation for Olympians and Paralympians Act of 2016	10-7-2016
114-255	21st Century Cures Act	12-13-2016
114-328	National Defense Authorization Act for Fiscal Year 2017	12-23-2016
115-63	Disaster Tax Relief and Airport and Airway Extension Act of 2017	9-29-2017
115-97		12-22-2017
115-120		1-22-2018
115-123	Bipartisan Budget Act of 2018	2-9-2018
115-141	Consolidated Appropriations Act, 2018	3-23-2018
115-232	John S. McCain National Defense Authorization Act for Fiscal Year 2019	8-13-2018
115-243	Tribal Social Security Fairness Act of 2018	9-20-2018
115-250	Airport and Airway Extension Act of 2018, Part II	9-29-2018
115-254	FAA Reauthorization Act of 2018	10-5-2018
115-271	Substance Use-Disorder Prevention that Promotes Opioid Recovery and Treatment (SUPPORT) for Patients and Communities Act of 2018	10-24-2018
116-25	Taxpayer First Act	7-1-2019
116-59	Continuing Appropriations Act, 2020, and Health Extenders Act of 2019	10-1-2019
116-69	Further Continuing Appropriations Act, 2020, and Further Health Extenders Act of 2019	11-21-2019
116-91	Fostering Undergraduate Talent by Unlocking Resources for Education Act	12-19-2019
116-92	National Defense Authorization Act for Fiscal Year 2020	12-20-2019
116-94	Further Consolidated Appropriations Act, 2020	12-20-2019
116-136	Coronavirus Aid, Relief, and Economic Security Act	3-27-2020
116-159	Continuing Appropriations Act, 2021 and Other Extensions Act	10-1-2020
116-260	Consolidated Appropriations Act, 2021	12-27-2020
117-2	American Rescue Plan Act of 2021	3-11-2021
117-44	Surface Transportation Extension Act of 2021	10-2-2021
117-52	Further Surface Transportation Extension Act of 2021	10-31-2021
117-58	Infrastructure Investment and Jobs Act	11-15-2021
117-103	Consolidated Appropriations Act, 2022	3-15-2022
117-167	CHIPS Act of 2022	8-9-2022
117-169		8-16-2022
117-263	Don Young Coast Guard Authorization Act of 2022	12-23-2022
117-286		12-27-2022
117-328	Consolidated Appropriations Act, 2023	12-29-2022
117-328	SECURE 2.0 Act of 2022	12-29-2022
118-15	Continuing Appropriations Act, 2024 and Other Extensions Act	9-30-2023
118-34	Airport and Airway Extension Act of 2023, Part II	12-26-2023
118-41	Airport and Airway Extension Act of 2024	3-8-2024
118-60	Airport and Airway Extension Act of 2024, Part II	5-10-2024
118-63	FAA Reauthorization Act of 2024	5-16-2024